Dictionary

Houghton Mifflin Company • BOSTON

All correspondence and inquiries should be directed to
Reference Division, Houghton Mifflin Company.
One Beacon Street, Boston, MA 02108

Library of Congress Cataloging in Publication Data
Main entry under title:

Students' dictionary.

Summary: Defines more than 100,000 entries and includes such features as usage notes, synonyms, photographs and drawings, a manual of style for writers, biographical and geographical entries, and tables of information.
1. English language—Dictionaries. [1. English language—Dictionaries] I. Houghton Mifflin Company.
PE1625.S84 1981 423 81-4199
ISBN 0-395-28684-0 AACR2

CONTENTS

STAFF

Editor in Chief
Fernando de Mello Vianna

Director of Editorial Operations
Margery S. Berube

Project Editor
Pamela DeVinne

Supervising Editor
Anne D. Steinhardt

Associate Editor
Mark Boyer

Etymologies
Marion Severynse

Synonyms and Usage Notes
Anne H. Soukhanov

**Biographical and
Geographic Section**
Kaethe Ellis

Supplementary Editing
Dolores R. Harris

Art Director
Geoffrey Hodgkinson

Picture and Research Editor
Carole D. La Mond

Picture Researcher
Sarah A. O'Reilly

Contributing Editors
Walter M. Havighurst
Eden Force Eskin
Paul Laccavole
Andrea Denson Wechsler
James E. Shea *Science*

**Manuscript Coding
and Composition**
Brenda Bregoli
Joanne Nichols
John Frederick Eppling
Donna L. Muise

Proofreading
Kathleen Gerard
Sally Hehir
Deborah A. Karacozian
Mary L. Mahoney
Jane Manilych
Trudy Nelson
Deborah Posner

Cover Design
Geoffrey Hodgkinson

PREFACE

This Dictionary, the latest member of the American Heritage Dictionary family, is an entirely new work and reflects the basic lexicographic approach of *The American Heritage Dictionary.*

The editors have endeavored to preserve Houghton Mifflin's traditional concern for precision and clarity in language and to provide sensible usage guidance. Such guidance has become one of the most distinctive and essential tools of the American Heritage Dictionary family, enabling users to achieve grace and precision in language. This Dictionary not only offers basic information on words, such as their spelling and pronunciation, but it also offers information about where a word has come from, what its various shades of meaning are today, and what its social status is.

The Dictionary contains more than 100,000 entries; its word list, ranging from the language of Milton and Shakespeare to the idiom of the present day, is that of the educated adult or of the college-bound student.

The Dictionary's fresh approach to design is obvious at a glance. The most recent advances in computer typesetting and graphic design have been utilized, and the Dictionary is pleasing to browse in and attractive to consult. The innovative modular design has enabled the editors to include more than 1,500 illustrations, both line drawings and photographs. The pictures have been chosen with a view to complementing the subjects they illustrate.

In the preparation of a work of this scope the contribution of many minds and hands is of the utmost importance. Our thanks go to all the people who toiled diligently and long at the myriad tasks involved in editing and creating this Dictionary.

PICTURE CREDITS

The following list of credits includes the names of organizations and individuals who helped secure illustrations for the dictionary. The editors wish to thank all of them — as well as others not specifically mentioned — for their assistance. We are grateful to Laurel L. Cook for her pen-and-ink drawings of plants and to William J. Stenstrom and the students of the Medical College of Georgia who supplied the anatomy illustrations. George Miksch Sutton supplied the pen-and-ink drawings of birds. The credits are arranged alphabetically by entry word, which is printed in boldface type. In those cases where two or more illustrations are credited to the same entry word, dashes are used to separate them sequentially from left to right. The abbreviations SDZ, MFA, MMA, LC, ES and EPA stand for respectively, the Zoological Society of San Diego, the Museum of Fine Arts, Boston, the Metropolitan Museum of Art, the Library of Congress, Evelyn M. Shafer, and Editorial Photocolor Archives.

aardvark Photo Researchers; **abbey** British Tourist Authority, **Aberdeen Angus** Photo Researchers; **aborigine** Australian News and Information Bureau; **abstract** MFA; **abstractionism** Ken Robert Buck, Picture Cube; **accordion** M. Hohner, Inc.; **Achilles** MFA; **acorn** Photo Researchers; **acrobat** Ringling Brothers and Barnum & Bailey Circus; **acropolis** Greek National Tourist Office; **acupuncture** Betsy Cole, Picture Cube; **addax** SDZ; **adder** SDZ; **admiral butterfly** Photo Researchers; **adrenal gland** D. Conway; **advertisement** Gary Goodman, Picture Cube — WEEI-FM; **adz** Frank Siteman; **Aegisthus** MFA; **afghan** Frank Siteman; **Afghan hound** ES; **agate** Photo Researchers; **agouti** SDZ; **aileron** Frank Siteman; **aircraft carrier** USN; **Airedale** ES; **airplane** Boeing Photo; **airport** Frank Siteman; **albatross** Photo Researchers; **alfalfa** USDA; **alligator** SDZ; **alpaca** SDZ; **alpenhorn** Bettmann Archive; **altar** George Robinson; **altarpiece** Picture Archive; **althorn** American Music Conference; **amaryllis** Burpee Seeds; **Amazon** MFA; **ambulance** Allen J. Smith; **Amish** Pennsylvania Dutch Visitors Bureau; **amoeba** Photo Researchers; **amphitheater** Photo Researchers; **amulet** MFA; **amusement park** Frank Siteman; **anaconda** SDZ; **andiron** MFA; **aneurysm** A. McKinney; **angelfish** Photo Researchers; **anopheles** USDA; **anteater** SDZ; **antelope** Photo Researchers; **anther** Photo Researchers; **antique** MFA; **aorta** A. McKinney; **aoudad** SDZ; **ape** SDZ; **aphid** USDA; **Aphrodite** MFA; **apiary** USDA; **Apollo** MMA; **appendix** J. Martini; **apple** Irene Shwachman, Picture Cube; **apron** MFA; **aqueduct** French Government Tourist Office; **arch** Convention and Visitors Bureau, St. Louis — French Government Tourist Office; **archery** Frank Siteman; **Argus** MFA; **ark** Picture Archive; **armadillo** Interior: Sport Fisheries and Wildlife; **armoire** MFA; **armor** MFA; **arrowhead** Frank Siteman; **artichoke** Photo Researchers; **asparagus** Photo Researchers; **ass** SDZ; **astronaut** NASA; **Athena** MMA; **Atlas** Rockefeller Center, Inc.; **atomic bomb** The Burton Holmes Collection; **auction** Sotheby Parke Bernet; **auger** Frank Siteman; **auk** Photo Researchers; **aureole** Isabella Stewart Gardner Museum; **autograph** Charles Hamilton, Autographs; **aviator** NASA; **aviatrix** LC; **avocet** SDZ; **awl** Stanley Tools; **ax** Frank Siteman; **axolotl** SDZ; **aye-aye** Photo Researchers.

babirusa SDZ; **baboon** SDZ; **backhand** Ira Kirschenbaum, Stock, Boston; **backpack** George Bellerose, Stock, Boston; **Bactrian camel** SDZ; **badger** Interior: Sport Fisheries & Wildlife; **balalaika** Bettmann Archive; **balance** Frank Siteman; **bald eagle** Interior: Sport Fisheries & Wildlife; **baobab** Richard Wood, Picture Cube; **Barbary ape** SDZ; **barbed wire** Interior: Sport Fisheries & Wildlife; **barnacle** Allen D. Moore; **barometer** Frank Siteman; **bartizan** EPA; **bascule bridge** British Tourist Authority; **basenji** ES; **basilisk** SDZ; **basset hound** ES; **bassoon** Ron Schick; **bathyscaphe** USN; **bay window** Frank Siteman; **beagle** ES; **beaker** Frank Siteman; **bear** SDZ; **bearskin** British Tourist Authority; **beaver** SDZ; **beetle** SDZ; **bell¹** Philadelphia Convention and Visitors Bureau; **bell buoy** U.S. Coast Guard; **beret** USN; **berth** Japan Air Lines; **Bessemer converter** American Iron and Steel Institute; **billiards** Frank Siteman; **billy goat** SDZ; **binnacle** Mystic Seaport; **binoculars** Frank Siteman; **bison** SDZ; **bit²** Frank Siteman; **bleachers** Jeff Dunn; **blimp** Goodyear; **bloodhound** ES; **bloomers** Bettmann Archive; **bobcat** Interior: Sport Fisheries & Wildlife; **boll weevil** USDA; **bonnet** National Gallery of Art, Index of American Design; **bonsai** Frank Siteman; **borzoi** ES; **bowie knife** Bettmann Archive; **bow-**

sprit Mystic Seaport; **boxer²** ES; **Braille** John Urban; **brain** W. Carter; **breakwater** Jeff Dunn; **breastplate** Ellis Herwig, Stock, Boston; **bridge** Greg Brull, The Stockmarket; **bridle** Margaret Thompson, Picture Cube; **brig¹** Mystic Seaport; **brocade** MFA; **bronchus** W. Carter; **buggy** Ellis Herwig, Stock, Boston; **bugle** Bettmann Archive; **bulldog** ES; **bull mastiff** ES; **bull terrier** ES; **buoy** U.S. Coast Guard; **bust** MFA; **butterfly** USDA; **Byzantine** Frank Siteman.

cable car Albuquerque Convention and Visitors Bureau; **calash** Shelburne Museum; **calculator** Hewlett-Packard Co.; **caliper** Frank Siteman; **cameo** MFA; **camshaft** Frank Siteman; **Canada goose** Frank Siteman; **candelabrum** Frank Siteman; **candlesticks** MFA; **canopy** MFA; **cantilever** Walter Silver; **capital²** Carol Palmer; **Capitol** LC; **carapace** Pghoto Researchers; **carbine** Frank Siteman; **cardinal** Grant Heilman; **carpus** W. Carter; **caryatid** K. Anderson, Picture Cube; **cask** Frank Siteman; **caster** MFA; **catafalque** Kennedy Library; **caterpillar** Frank Siteman; **cathedral** EPA; **cecropia moth** Grant Heilman; **cell** Grant Heilman; **cello** Ron Schick; **cenotaph** Allen D. Moore; **centaur** MMA; **Cerberus** MFA; **cerebellum** J. Martini; **cerebral cortex** A. McKinney; **chafing dish** MFA; **chalice** MFA; **chameleon** Grant Heilman; **chandelier** Frank Siteman; **chariot** MMA; **charm** MFA; **chase²** Frank Siteman; **cheetah** SDZ; **cherub** EPA; **chevron** Jeff Dunn; **chignon** Carol Palmer; **chihuahua** ES; **chimney sweep** Paula Gross, Picture Cube; **chimpanzee** SDZ; **chin** Ron Schick; **chisel** Frank Siteman; **chopsticks** Allen J. Smith; **chow** ES; **chromosome** Grant Heilman; **chuck²** Frank Siteman; **civet** SDZ; **claw hammer** Stanley Tools; **cloisonné** EPA; **cloister** MMA; **Clydesdale** Anheuser-Busch, Inc.; **cockade** Frank Siteman; **cog** Frank Siteman; **collie** ES; **colon²** A. Piette; **colonial** John Hopf, Newport County Chamber of Commerce; **compass** Allen J. Smith; **compote** Jeff Dunn; **compound eye** Photo Researchers; **concertina** Allen D. Moore; **conch** Frank Siteman; **condor** SDZ; **conger** Photo Researchers; **conservatory** Frank Siteman; **control tower** Allen J. Smith; **convertible** General Motors; **coot** SDZ; **coping saw** Frank Siteman; **copperhead** Grant Heilman; **Corinthian** Allen D. Moore; **cornice** Allen D. Moore; **coupe** Bettmann Archive; **covered wagon** Bettmann Archive; **crampon** Allen D. Moore; **crane** SDZ; **crest** Allen D. Moore; **crocodile** SDZ; **crown** British Tourist Authority; **cruet** Anchor Hocking Corp.; **cubism** EPA; **cueball** Ed Hof, Picture Cube; **cutter** Mystic Seaport.

Dalmatian ES; **dam¹** Frank Siteman; **dashiki** Margaret Thompson, Picture Cube; **decoy** L.L. Bean Co.; **Demeter** MMA; **demijohn** Jeff Dunn; **dewlap** Grant Heilman; **dhow** Mystic Seaport; **diamondback** SDZ; **Diana** EPA; **dingo** SDZ; **discus** Barbara Alper, Stock, Boston; **Doberman pinscher** ES; **dolphin** Jeff Rotman, New England Aquarium; **doublet** MFA; **drawbridge** Elizabeth Hamlin, Stock, Boston; **duck¹** Allen J. Smith; **dugout** Boston Red Sox; **dulcimer** Ken Robert Buck, Picture Cube.

ear W. Carter; **echidna** SDZ; **egret** SDZ; **eider** SDZ; **embryo** Grant Heilman; **endocrine** A. McKinney; **epaulet** LC; **Eskimo** Alaska Historical Library; **esophagus** R. Partch; **ewer** MFA; **expressionism** MFA; **eye** S. Collins; **eyestalk** Photo Researchers.

fanlight Jeff Dunn; **fantail** Photo Researchers; **fawn** Grant Heilman; **feeler** Jeff Dunn; **felucca** The Burton Holmes Collection; **femur** A.

Piette; **fencing** Jeff Dunn; **ferret** Interior: Sport Fisheries & Wildlife; **ferrule** Allen D. Moore; **fibula** A. Piette; **fichu** Bettmann Archive; **fiddle** Frank Siteman; **figurehead** Jeff Albertson, Stock, Boston; **fireboat** Boston Fire Dept.; **fjord** The Burton Holmes Collection; **flea** Photo Researchers; **fleur-de-lis** Jeff Dunn; **flicker²** Photo Researchers; **flute** Ron Schick; **flying buttress** Carol Palmer; **font** MFA; **football** Baltimore Colts; **forehand** Jeff Dunn; **foreshorten** EPA; **fox** Interior: Sport Fisheries & Wildlife; **fox terrier** ES; **fret³** Allen D. Moore; **frieze¹** Ed Hof, Picture Cube; **futurism** EPA.

gaiter Allen D. Moore; **gallbladder** S. Collins; **gannet** SDZ; **gargoyle** Frank Siteman; **gazelle** SDZ; **gear** Frank Siteman, Picture Cube; **gecko** Grant Heilman; **gerbil** Carol Palmer; **German shepherd** ES; **gibbon** SDZ; **Gila monster** SDZ; **glockenspiel** Carol Palmer; **gnu** SDZ; **goldfinch** Grant Heilman; **gondola** Andrew Brilliant; **goose** Carol Palmer; **gorilla** SDZ; **goshawk** Grant Heilman; **grandfather clock** MFA; **grand piano** Steinway & Sons; **Great Dane** ES; **great horned owl** Grant Heilman; **grizzly bear** SDZ; **guitar** Allen D. Moore.

habit Allen J. Smith — Frank Siteman; **halter** Frank Siteman; **hammer** Stanley Tools; **harness** Margaret Thompson, Picture Cube; **harp** Andrew Brilliant; **heart** J. Martini; **Hercules** MFA; **hieroglyphic** MFA; **holster** Frank Siteman; **honeycomb** Grant Heilman; **honeysuckle** Grant Heilman; **hookah** Frank Siteman; **hoop skirt** Bettmann Archive; **hornet** Grant Heilman; **horse** Frank Siteman; **howdah** Frank Siteman; **howitzer** USN; **humerus** A. Piette; **hummingbird** Grant Heilman; **hurdy-gurdy** MFA; **hydra** Grant Heilman.

ibex SDZ; **icebreaker** U.S. Coast Guard; **igloo** Alaska Historical Library; **illuminate** Empire State Building Co.; **illusion** Isabella Stewart Gardner Museum; **inauguration** UPI; **incubator** Harry Wilks, Stock, Boston; **infantry** U.S. Signal Corps; **ingot** American Iron and Steel Institute; **inkstand** MFA; **instrument** Beech Aircraft Corp.; **interlock** Allen D. Moore; **interurban** Harry Wilks, Stock, Boston.

jabot Frank Siteman, Picture Cube; **jellyfish** Grant Heilman; **jigsaw** Jeff Dunn; **jinriksha** The Burton Holmes Collection; **jodhpurs** Andrew Brilliant; **Joshua tree** Frank Siteman; **judo** Frank Siteman; **junk²** Mystic Seaport; **Jupiter** NASA.

kangaroo SDZ; **karate** Bobbi Carrey, Picture Cube; **kayak** Great Canadian; **kepi** Frank Siteman; **kettledrum** Andrew Brilliant; **kidney** A. Piette; **kimono** Allen J. Smith; **kinkajou** SDZ; **koala** SDZ.

larynx J. Martini; **lei** Hawaii Tourist Authority; **Lhasa apso** ES; **light meter** Allen D. Moore; **light pen** Allen D. Moore; **lion** Grant Heilman; **liver¹** W. Carter; **lobster** Photo Researchers; **locust¹** USDA; **lorgnette** Bettmann Archive; **lung** S. Collins; **lute** MFA; **lyre** MFA.

Magen David Peter Vandermark; **magnetic field** Grant Heilman; **mallard** Frank Siteman; **mandolin** MFA; **mansard** Jeff Dunn; **maraca** Frank Siteman; **marquetry** Peter Vandermark; **Mars** MFA; **mastiff** ES; **mastoid** R. Partch; **maxilla** S. Collins; **meerschaum** Frank Siteman; **merganser** Interior: Sport Fisheries & Wildlife; **metacarpus** W. Carter; **microfilm** Frank Siteman; **micrometer** Peter Vandermark; **microscope** Fred Bodin, Stock, Boston; **milestone** Walter Silver; **mink** USDA; **missile** U.S. Army; **Möbius strip** Peter Vandermark; **monarch butterfly** Jeff Dunn; **mongoose** SDZ; **monocle** Nicholas Sapieha, Stock, Boston; **moose** SDZ; **mortar** Jeff Dunn; **mosquito** Grant Heilman; **mummy** MFA; **musk ox** SDZ; **muskrat** USDA; **mute** Peter Vandermark; **muzzle** ES.

nave Allen D. Moore; **neoclassicism** EPA; **newel** Allen D. Moore; **Newfoundland** ES; **niche** Allen D. Moore; **Nike** MMA.

obi Allen J. Smith; **oboe** Ron Schick; **ocelot** SDZ; **octopus** Grant Heilman; **okapi** SDZ; **omnibus** Shelburne Museum; **opossum** SDZ; **optic nerve** S. Collins; **organ** Aeolian-Skinner Organ Co.; **otter** New England Aquarium; **ovum** W. Carter; **owl** USDA; **oxbow** Peter Vandermark.

paddock Allen D. Moore; **pagoda** The Burton Holmes Collection; **palanquin** The Burton Holmes Collection; **pancreas** A. McKinney; **panda** National Zoological Park; **panther** SDZ; **parapet** Carol Palmer; **parietal** A. McKinney; **parrot** Peter Southwick, Stock, Boston; **pawl** Allen D. Moore; **peacock** Grant Heilman; **pectoral** A. Piette; **pedestal** Allen J. Smith; **pelvis** R. Partch; **pendulum** Allen D. Moore; **penguin** Bill Wasserman, New England Aquarium; **peregrine falcon** Allen D. Moore; **phalanx** W. Carter; **pheasant** Grant Heilman; **piano** Steinway & Sons; **pig** USDA; **pilaster** Allen D. Moore; **pince-nez** LC; **pincers** Photo Researchers; **pitchpipe** Jeff Dunn; **plane²** Frank Siteman; **plinth** Allen D. Moore; **plow** Allen D. Moore; **plume** Bettmann Archive; **polar bear** SDZ; **poncho** Antonio Mendoza, Picture Cube; **poodle** ES; **porcupine** SDZ; **Portuguese man-of-war** Grant Heilman; **prairie dog** SDZ; **pre-Columbian** MFA; **pressure suit** NASA; **prickly pear** Frank Siteman; **priedieu** MFA; **primitive** MFA; **pronghorn** Interior: Sport Fisheries & Wildlife; **protozoan** Grant Heilman; **protractor** Jeff Dunn; **puffin** Walter S. Frost, Picture Cube; **pug** ES; **pulley** D. Carpenter, Picture Cube; **pulmonary artery** J.

Martini; **pump** Christopher Morrow, Stock, Boston; **pumpkin** Frank Siteman; **punt¹** Mystic Seaport; **pyramid** Frank Siteman.

quarter-deck Mystic Seaport; **quarter horse** Grant Heilman; **quartz** Peter Vandermark; **quatrefoil** Allen D. Moore; **queen** Lou Jones; **quiver²** George X. Bellerose, Stock, Boston; **Quonset hut** Allen D. Moore.

rabbit USDA; **raccoon** SDZ; **radar** U.S. Army; **radius** J. Martini; **rat** Grant Heilman; **rattlesnake** Grant Heilman; **reamer** Allen D. Moore; **reaper** International Harvester; **recorder** Ron Schick; **reel¹** Allen J. Smith; **relic** MFA; **relief** MFA; **resistor** Frank Siteman; **respirator** Walter Silver; **retort²** Peter Vandermark; **revetment** Allen D. Moore; **rhesus monkey** Grant Heilman; **rhinoceros** Grant Heilman; **ripsaw** Peter Vandermark; **roller coaster** Magic Mt.; **roost** Carol Palmer; **rooster** USDA; **Rorschach test** Jeff Dunn; **rose window** Frank Siteman; **roughrider** LC; **roundhouse** Union Pacific Railroad; **rubbing** courtesy of Nancy Woolley, Walter Silver; **ruff** LC; **running board** William Litant, Museum of Transportation, Boston.

sabot Bettmann Archive; **sacrum** S. Collins; **saguaro** Grant Heilman; **Saint Bernard** ES; **samovar** Murry Belsky; **sampan** Rick Smolan, Stock, Boston; **sarcophagus** MMA; **sari** Frank Siteman, Picture Cube; **saxophone** Ron Schick; **scallop** Frank Siteman; **scapula** J. Martini; **schnauzer** ES; **scorpion** Grant Heilman; **screech owl** Grant Heilman; **scythe** Frank Siteman; **sea anemone** Grant Heilman; **sea horse** Grant Heilman; **sea lion** Grant Heilman; **sea urchin** Grant Heilman; **sedan** Walter Silver; **senate** K. Jewell; **shagbark** Grant Heilman; **shamrock** Grant Heilman; **shark** Grant Heilman; **sheep** USDA; **shell** Frank Siteman; **shorthorn** USDA; **side wheel** Mystic Seaport; **silhouette** Allen D. Moore; **skimmer** Grant Heilman; **skink** Grant Heilman; **sledgehammer** Stanley Tools; **sleigh** Massachusetts Historical Society; **sloop** Mystic Seaport; **slot machine** Frank Siteman; **sluice** Idaho Power Company; **small intestine** R. Partch; **snail** Grant Heilman; **snake** Grant Heilman; **snowshoe** L.L. Bean; **soccer** Chris Stafford, Harvard University; **spanker** Mystic Seaport; **sparrow hawk** Grant Heilman; **spats** Allen D. Moore; **spear** Australian Information Service; **sphenoid bone** A. McKinney; **sphinx** Frank Siteman; **sphygmomanometer** Allen D. Moore; **spider** Grant Heilman; **spine** W. Carter; **spinnaker** Mystic Seaport; **spinning wheel** Donald F. Eaton, Sturbridge Village; **spiral** Allen D. Moore; **spleen** J. Martini; **spoke** Peter Vandermark; **spoonbill** Grant Heilman; **sporran** Allen D. Moore; **springer spaniel** ES; **sprit** Mystic Seaport; **sprocket** Peter Vandermark; **square rig** LC; **squid** Grant Heilman; **squirrel** Allen D. Moore; **stained glass** Peter Vandermark; **stalactite** Grant Heilman; **steamship** Frank Siteman; **steeplechase** Allen D. Moore; **stern-wheeler** Mystic Seaport; **stethoscope** Armed Forces Institute of Pathology; **stirrup** Allen J. Smith; **stomach** R. Partch; **stovepipe** LC; **strop** Peter Vandermark; **submarine** US Navy; **subway** Allen D. Moore; **suffragette** LC; **sulky** Shelburne Museum; **sunburst** Peter Vandermark; **surrey** Shelburne Museum; **suspension bridge** Grant Heilman; **swastika** Frank Siteman; **symphony orchestra** courtesy of Chicago Symphony Orchestra.

tabernacle Allen D. Moore; **tambourine** Walter Silver; **tam-o'-shanter** Allen D. Moore; **tankard** MFA; **tarot** Walter Silver; **tartan** Allen D. Moore; **team** Anheuser-Busch; **telescope** U.S. Naval Observatory; **temple** The Burton Holmes Collection; **ten-gallon hat** Allen D. Moore; **tentacle** Mary Price, New England Aquarium; **tepee** LC; **thatch** Frank Siteman; **thermometer** Walter Silver; **Thetis** MFA; **tide** G. Blouin, NFB Phototeque; **tiller²** Mystic Seaport; **tintype** Allen D. Moore; **tippet** MFA; **toad** Frank Siteman; **tomahawk** Museum of the American Indian; **top hat** Frank Siteman; **topiary** Allen D. Moore; **torii** The Burton Holmes Collection; **tracery** Walter Silver; **tractor** International Harvester; **transit** Frank Siteman; **trapeze** Frank Siteman; **treadmill** Walter Silver; **trefoil** Allen D. Moore; **triangle** Ron Schick; **tricorn** Frank Siteman; **tricycle** Allen D. Moore; **tripod** Allen D. Moore; **triptych** MMA; **Triton** MFA; **trombone** Ron Schick; **trumpet** Ron Schick; **tuba** Ron Schick; **tuning fork** Kitching Scientific; **tureen** MFA; **turtle** Grant Heilman.

ukulele Jeff Dunn; **ulna** J. Martini; **unicorn** Allen D. Moore; **unicycle** Frank Siteman; **upholstery** Allen D. Moore; **urn** MFA.

valance Jeff Dunn; **valve** Jeff Dunn; **vase** Waterford Glass, Inc.; **vat** Allen D. Moore; **vibraphone** Jeff Dunn; **viola¹** Ron Schick; **violin** New England Conservatory; **virginal** MFA; **visor** LC – EPA; **volcano** UPI; **volute** Jeff Dunn; **voting machine** Jeff Dunn; **vulture** Grant Heilman.

wader Allen D. Moore; **wallaby** SDZ; **war bonnet** Montana Chamber of Commerce; **waterfall** Yosemite; **water spaniel** ES; **water wheel** Grant Heilman; **wattle** Margaret Thompson, Picture Cube; **weasel** USDA; **weld** Jon Chase; **Welsh corgi** ES; **whaleboat** Mystic Seaport; **whelk** Grant Heilman; **wherry** Mystic Seaport; **whippet** ES; **wickiup** Museum of the American Indian; **wigwam** Museum of the American Indian; **windlass** Mystic Seaport; **wolf** SDZ; **wolverine** SDZ; **worm gear** Jeff Dunn; **wrestling** Allen D. Moore.

yarmulke Walter Silver; **zebra** SDZ; **zeppelin** Bettmann Archive; **zither** Jeff Dunn.

HOW TO USE YOUR DICTIONARY

WHAT IS A DICTIONARY?

In a word, a dictionary is a wordbook. It is an alphabetically arranged list of the most common words in a language. But a dictionary is really much more than an alphabetical index of words. For example,

THE DICTIONARY

- shows you how to spell, syllabicate, and pronounce words;
- indicates parts of speech;
- shows plurals, inflected forms, and variant spellings;
- indicates when expressions are slang, informal, archaic, or nonstandard;
- defines single words, compounds, and idioms;
- supplements and clarifies definitions with illustrative examples;
- provides word origins (etymologies);
- lists and discusses synonyms;
- gives detailed guidance concerning English usage;
- provides interesting, attractive pictorial illustrations;
- lists biographical and geographic names.

As you can see, your Dictionary does the work of at least a dozen specialized reference books. And if you read these explanatory notes carefully, you'll be able to get the most from this book.

FINDING THE WORD YOU LOOK UP

Quarters of the alphabet. If you examine your Dictionary, you'll see that it consists of four roughly equal parts, divided as follows:

1st quarter	2nd quarter
A B C D	**E F G H I J K L**
3rd quarter	4th quarter
M N O P Q R	**S T U V W X Y Z**

The first quarter contains all words beginning with the letters *A* through *D*; the second quarter, all words beginning with *E* through *L*; the third quarter, all words beginning with *M* through *R*; and the fourth quarter, all words beginning with *S* through *Z*. Thus if you were

looking up the words *whiplash, xylophone,* and *Y-chromosome,* you would look for them in the last quarter and not in the first three quarters of the book.

Exercises

1. In which quarter of the Dictionary will you find

president	**intense**
advent	**unusual**

2. Turn to the entries above; see how fast you can locate them by using the quarters of the A–Z list.

Guide words. Boldface guide words appear at the top of each page. They indicate the alphabetical spread of terms entered and defined on each page. The guide word on the left represents the first boldface main entry on the page, and the guide word on the right represents the last boldface main entry on the page. The guide words are an aid to finding the word being looked up. Example:

teller / tempo   952

Exercises

1. Turn to page 555. What are the guide words on this page?

2. What is the first main entry on page 555? The last main entry?

THE ENTRIES

The words and phrases that you look up in this Dictionary are called *entries, entry words,* or *main entries.* Entry words are set in boldface type a little to the left of the rest of the column. Main entries containing definitions for more than one part of speech are called *combined entries.*

Here is a typical main entry:

u·su·rer (yōō′zhər-ər) *n.* A person who lends money at an exorbitant or unlawful rate of interest. [Middle English, from Norman French, from Medieval Latin *ūsūrārius,* from Latin *ūsūra,* interest, usury.]

And here is a combined entry in which the main-entry head word functions as more than one part of speech:

ken·nel[1] (kĕn′əl) *n.* **1.** A shelter for a dog. **2.** An establishment where dogs are bred, trained, or boarded. —*v.* **-neled** or **-nelled, -nel·ing** or **-nel·ling.** To keep or place in or as if in a kennel. —*intr.v.* To shelter in or as if in a kennel. [Middle English *kenel*, ult. from Latin *canis*, dog.]

Such entries and their components are discussed in detail in these explanatory notes.

Alphabetical entry order. All entries are listed in alphabetical order, as shown in this typical sequence:

as·tute	a·sym·met·ric	at
a·sun·der	a·sym·me·try	At
a·sy·lum	as·ymp·tote	at·a·vism

Compounds that are written open (**air base**), hyphenated (**air-condition**), and solid (**aircraft**) are alphabetized as if they were solid. Compounds containing like particles (**House of Commons, house of correction**, and **House of Lords**) are alphabetized according to their differing final elements (**Commons, correction**, and **Lords**).

If a compound contains a numeral, that numeral is ignored in alphabetization. Thus *carbon 14* appears right after *carbon* in this sequence: **car·bon, carbon 14, car·bo·na·ceous, car·bo·na·do, car·bon·ate.**

Exercises

1. Using your Dictionary, arrange these entries in alphabetical order:

highborn	highball
high	higher-up
High-Church	highbred
highfalutin	highboy
high-class	highbrow

2. Which entry comes first in your Dictionary—**strontium 90** or **strontium**?

3. Using your Dictionary, arrange these entries in alphabetical order:

–ide	I'd
idea	ideal
id	–id

Centered dots: syllable division. An entry is divided into syllables by means of boldface centered dots: **aard·vark; am·nes·ty; jig·ger**[1]**; jig·ger**[2]**.**

Hyphenated compounds retain their hyphens in boldface: **all-pur·pose; an·te-bel·lum.**

Exercise

Using your Dictionary, divide these words into syllables. Use centered dots to show the syllable divisions:

sabra	justify
spacecraft	quebracho
labor	justification

Superscript numerals: homographs. Words that are spelled alike but that have different ori-gins are called *homographs.* Homographs are signaled by superscript (raised) numerals immediately after the main-entry words:

junk[1] . . . *n.* **1.** Scrap materials . . . . [From earlier *junk*, old, worn-out pieces of nautical rope or cable, from Middle English *jonke.*]
junk[2] . . . *n.* A Chinese flat-bottomed ship with a high poop . . . . [Ult. from Malay *jong*, sea-going ship.]

Although **junk**[1] and **junk**[2] are both nouns, they have different origins, as shown in the bracketed etymologies. Hence they are considered homographs.

Exercises

1. Why are **ball**[1] and **ball**[2] listed as homographs?

2. How many homographs can you find for the word **dock**?

3. How many homographs can you find for the word **bit**?

4. How many homographs can you find for the prefix **a-**? Why are they listed as homographs?

PRONUNCIATION

Pronunciation is given for all main entries and for other forms as needed. It is indicated in parentheses following the form to which it applies.

The set of symbols used is designed to enable the reader to reproduce a satisfactory pronunciation with no more than a quick reference to the key. All pronunciations given are acceptable in all circumstances. When more than one is given, the first is assumed to be the most common, but the difference in frequency may be insignificant.

Americans do not all speak alike; nevertheless they can understand one another, at least on the level of speech sounds. For most words a single set of symbols can represent the pronunciation found in each regional variety of American English, provided the symbols are planned for the purpose stated above: to enable the reader to reproduce a satisfactory pronunciation. When a single pronunciation is offered in this Dictionary, the reader will supply those features of his own regional speech that are called forth by his reading of the key. Apart from regional variations in pronunciation, there are variations among social groups. The pronunciations recorded in this Dictionary are exclusively those of educated speech. In every community educated speech is accepted and understood by everyone, including those who do not themselves use it.

Pronunciation Key. A shorter form of this key appears at the bottom of each page.

Explanatory Notes

ə: This nonalphabetical symbol is called a *schwa.* The symbol is used in the Dictionary to represent a reduced vowel, that is, a vowel that receives the weakest level of stress (which is unmarked) within a word and that therefore nearly always has a different quality than it would if it were stressed, as in **telegraph** (tĕl′ĭ-grăf′) and **telegraphy** (tə-lĕg′rə-fē). Vowels are never reduced to a single exact vowel; the schwa sound varies, sometimes according to the "full" vowel it is representing and often according to the sounds surrounding it.

â: These symbols represent vowels that have
î been altered by a following *r*. In some re-
û gional varieties of American English the words **Mary, merry,** and **marry** are pronounced alike: (mĕr′ē). However, in many individual American speech patterns the three words are distinguished. It is this pattern that the Dictionary represents: **Mary** (mâr′ē), **merry** (mĕr′ē), **marry** (măr′ē). Some words are heard in all three pronunciations, indistinctly grading one into another. For these words the Dictionary represents only (â): **care** (kâr), **dairy** (dâr′ē).

In words such as **hear, beer,** and **dear** the vowel could be represented by (ē) were it not for the effect of the following *r*, which makes it approach (ĭ) in sound. In this Dictionary a special symbol, (î), is used for this combination, as in **beer** (bîr).

The symbol (û) is used to represent the sound of the vowel in such words as **her** and **fur**: (hûr), (fûr).

ô: There are regional differences in the dis-
ō tinctions among various pronunciations of the syllable *-or-*. In pairs such as **for, four; horse, hoarse;** and **morning, mourning** the vowel varies between (ô) and (ō). In this Dictionary these vowels are represented as follows: **for** (fôr), **four** (fôr, fōr); **horse** (hôrs), **hoarse** (hôrs, hōrs). Other words for which both forms are shown include those such as **more** (môr, mōr) and **glory** (glôr′ē, glōr′ē).

Another group of words with variation in the pronunciation of the *-or-* syllable includes words such as **forest** and **horrid**, in which the pronunciation of *o* before *r* varies between (ô) and (ŏ). In these words the (ôr) pronunciation is given first: **forest** (fôr′ĭst, fŏr′-).

Syllabic Consonants. Two consonants are often represented as complete syllables. These are *l* and *n* (called *syllabics*) when they occur after stressed syllables ending in or followed by *d* or *t* in such words as **cradle** (krād′l), **rattle** (răt′l), **redden** (rĕd′n), and **cotton** (kŏt′n). Both syllabic *l* and syllabic *n* also occur following *-rt-* and *-rd-* in such words as **myrtle** (mûr′tl), **hurdle** (hûr′dl), **certain** (sûr′tn), and **ardent** (är′dnt). Syllabic *n* is not shown following *-nd-* or *-nt-*, as in **abandon** (ə-băn′dən) and **mountain** (moun′tən); but syllabic *l* is shown in that position: **candle** (kăn′dl), **mantle** (măn′tl).

Stress. In this Dictionary stress, the relative degree of loudness with which the syllables of a word (or phrase) are spoken, is indicated in three different ways. An unmarked syllable has the weakest stress in the word. The strongest, or *primary*, stress is marked with a bold mark (′). An intermediate level of stress, here called *secondary*, is marked with a similar but lighter mark (′).

Words of one syllable show no stress mark, since there is no other stress level to which the syllable is compared.

Exercise

Following are some words with their pronunciations. Use your Dictionary to help you mark the primary and secondary stresses; then draw a line under the syllable with the primary stress.

   be·gin (bĭ gĭn)   **coun·ter·feit** (koun tər fĭt)

Syllabication. The pronunciations are syllabicated for clarity. Syllabication of the pronunciation does not necessarily match the syllabication of the entry word being pronounced. The former follows strict, though not obvious, phonological rules; the latter represents the established practice of printers and editors.

Exercise

Look up the following words in your Dictionary. Write down how many syllables each has.

thought ____   mariner ____   pentameter ____

garnet ____   marked ____   athlete ____

The Schwa. In a word the schwa sound may be spelled by any vowel—*a, e, i, o, u,* or even *y*. It may also be spelled by a combination of vowels.

Exercise

Look up the pronunciations of the following words. Rewrite the words below on the lines. Then underline the vowels in the words that are pronounced ə.

motivate _____

parent _____

anemia _____

parakeet _____

fountain _____

inaugurate _____

vinyl _____

PRONUNCIATION KEY

ă	pat	m	am, man, mum	v	cave, valve, vine
ā	aid, fey, pay	n	no, sudden	w	with
â	air, care, wear	ng	thing	y	yes
ä	father	ŏ	horrible, pot	yōo	abuse, use
b	bib	ō	go, hoarse, row, toe	z	rose, size, xylophone, zebra
ch	church	ô	alter, caught, for, paw	zh	garage, pleasure, vision
d	deed	oi	boy, noise, oil		
ĕ	pet, pleasure	ou	cow, out	ə	about, silent, pencil, lemon, circus
ē	be, bee, easy, leisure	ŏŏ	took		
f	fast, fife, off, phase, rough	ōō	boot, fruit	ər	butter
g	gag	p	pop		

FOREIGN

œ	*French* feu
ü	*French* tu
ᴋʜ	*Scottish* loch
ɴ	*French* bon

h	hat	r	roar
hw	which	s	miss, sauce, see
ĭ	pit	sh	dish, ship
ī	by, guy, pie	t	tight
î	dear, deer, fierce, mere	th	path, thin
j	judge	*th*	bathe, this
k	cat, kick, pique	ŭ	cut, rough
l	lid, needle	û	circle, firm, heard, term, turn, urge, word

STRESS

Primary stress ′
bi·ol′o·gy

Secondary stress ′
bi′o·log′i·cal

VOWEL SOUNDS AND DIACRITICAL MARKS

The Macron. When a vowel has a macron (⁻), it is pronounced as in the name of that vowel: ā as in *cane,* ē as in *bee,* ī as in *bite,* ō as in *hope.* It is also used for the ōō sound in *food.*

Exercises

1. Which of these words have the ā (long a) sound? Check them.

__ pane	__ feign	__ rein	__ suede
__ pan	__ rain	__ height	__ reign
__ fade	__ ran	__ weight	__ pay
__ they	__ that	__ straight	__ key

2. Which of these words have the ē (long e) sound? Check them.

__ beet	__ people	__ conceit	__ they
__ bet	__ aegis	__ feint	__ peace
__ beat	__ sieve	__ pie	__ piece
__ seize	__ aerial	__ key	

3. Which of these words have the ī (long i) sound? Check them.

__ pie	__ may	__ height	__ sight
__ pin	__ my	__ weight	__ buy
__ pine	__ ail	__ weird	__ sylph
__ piece	__ aisle	__ ski	__ sky

4. Which of these words have the ō (long o) sound? Check them.

___ show	___ should	___ broad	___ toe
___ shop	___ shoulder	___ beau	___ amoeba
___ foam	___ brooch	___ thought	___ oh
___ sew	___ broach	___ though	

5. Which of these words have the ōō (long oo) sound? Check them.

___ boot	___ soup	___ though	___ fruit
___ book	___ soul	___ blood	___ sleuth
___ no	___ now	___ shoe	___ blue
___ new	___ do	___ quit	

The Breve. When a vowel has a breve (˘), it is pronounced with the "short" sound: ă as in *can*, ĕ as in *bet*, ĭ as in *bit*, ŏ as in *hop*, ŭ as in *cut*. It is also used to show the ŏŏ sound in book.

Exercises

Circle the word that answers each question below.

1. Which is an article of clothing?

hāt   hăt   hŏt

2. Which is for drinking?

kŭp   kōōp   kŏp

3. Which do you read?

bōōk   bŭk   băk

4. Which is part of your body?

hēd   hăd   hĕd

5. Which is the opposite of push?

pŏl   pōōl   pŏŏl

6. Which would you use in baseball?

mĭt   mīt   mŭt

7. Which is a cooking utensil?

pōōt   pŏt   pŭt

The Circumflex. Vowel sounds with a circumflex are the â in *fare* or *fair*, the î in *pier* or *weird*, the ô in *for*, and the û in *fur*. The ô is also that of the vowel sound in *saw* and *talk*.

Exercise

Below is a list of words. Some have the sounds of circumflex vowels. List the words with that vowel sound next to the circumflex vowels below. Some words do not belong on the list.

pair	peer	purr	pearl
par	poor	pure	pare
pear	pore	pour	parry
pier	paw	per	

â _____

î _____

ô _____

û _____

The Dieresis. When the vowel *a* has a dieresis (¨), it is pronounced with the ä sound in *father*.

Exercise

Which of these words have the ä sound?

___ fall	___ sarcastic	___ naive
___ cataract	___ pare	___ park
___ ark	___ far	___ tab

Other Vowel Sounds. Two vowel sounds are written with two letters each. The two letters represent one sound. They are:

ou for the sound in *how* or *shout*

oi for the sound in *toy* or *coin*

Exercises

1. Which of these words have the *ou* sound? Check them.

___ loud	___ know	___ should	___ shown
___ now	___ spout	___ brown	___ soup

2. Which of these words have the *oi* sound? Check them.

___ point	___ joy	___ loin
___ Freudian	___ coincide	___ lion

Consonants. Pronunciations are given just for the sounds you hear. Silent letters are not given in pronunciations.

The letter *g* is used in pronunciations for the sound of *g* as in *goat* or *girl*. The letter *j* is used for the sound of *g* as in *giant* and *gem*.

The letter *f* is used for the sound of *f*, as in *fit*, the sound of *ph*, as in *alphabet*, and the sound of *gh*, as in *tough*.

Only three consonants in English are not used in the pronunciation system. They are *c*, *q*, and *x*.

Exercises

1. What is the first sound in each of these words?

civil	___	maybe	___
choir	___	photograph	___
gone	___	knit	___
ginger	___	lark	___
cold	___	ghost	___

2. What is the last sound in each of these words?

photograph	___	enough	___
name	___	television	___
numb	___	say	___
condemn	___	fill	___
cause	___		

Consonant sounds can be shown either as single letters or as combinations of letters.

Some consonants are shown by means of a combination of letters that you use in spelling. Two of these are th and *th*. The th combination stands for the sound you hear at the beginning of *think* and *thumb* and at the end of *bath* and *both*. The *th* combination stands for the sound you hear at the beginning of *this* and *then* and in the middle of *mother* and *weather*.

Exercise

After each word below write a 1 if the letters th in that word have the sound that th stands for. Write a 2 if the sound is the one that *th* stands for.

throw	_____	thank	_____
death	_____	myth	_____
breathe	_____	brother	_____
bother	_____	growth	_____
healthy	_____	bathe	_____

Another combination of consonants that you will see is *hw*. If you pronounce *which* and *witch* differently, you are using the sound that *hw* stands for when you say *which* and the sound that *w* alone stands for when you say *witch*.

Exercise

After each word below write the symbol that would be used in your Dictionary for the beginning sound. Use *hw, w,* or *h.*

whether	_____	whine	_____
whose	_____	wind	_____
whip	_____	whom	_____
wisp	_____	while	_____
weather	_____	whirl	_____
where	_____	whiskers	_____

Still another combination of consonants used in your Dictionary is *zh*. This combination stands for the sound you hear in the middle of *treasure* and *vision*. It never comes at the beginning of a word and seldom comes at the end.

Exercise

Say each word below to yourself. If you hear the sound that *zh* stands for, put a check mark after the word.

treasure	_____	mission	_____
measure	_____	decision	_____
division	_____	fissure	_____
session	_____	future	_____

Foreign Sounds. Some sounds are used in English only in words from other languages that are still foreign in their pronunciations. The sounds are:

œ ü KH N

In many instances English sounds replace these as the words become part of our language.

SOUND-SPELLING CORRESPONDENCES

The following table is designed to aid the user in locating in the Dictionary words whose pronunciation is known but whose spelling presents difficulties. Such difficulties are caused by the fact that so many speech sounds can be spelled in more than one way, since the standard alphabet has twenty-six characters to represent the forty or more sounds used in the English language. If you are unable to find a word when you look it up, check this table and try another combination of letters that represent the same sound.

Sound	Spelling	In These Sample Words
a (as in p**a**t)	ai	pl**ai**d
	al	c**al**f, h**al**f, s**al**ve
	au	l**au**gh
a (as in m**a**ne)	ai	**ai**de, **ai**grette, m**ai**ze, p**ai**n, pl**ai**n, refr**ai**n, st**ai**n
	ao	g**ao**l
	au	g**au**ge
	ay	cl**ay**, d**ay**, p**ay**ment, pl**ay**er, s**ay**ing, tr**ay**
	e	bouqu**e**t, consomm**e**, fort**e**, sach**e**t, sued**e**
	ea	br**ea**k, gr**ea**t
	ei	chow m**ei**n, r**ei**ndeer, s**ei**ne, v**ei**l, v**ei**n
	eig	d**eig**n, f**eig**n, r**eig**n
	eigh	**eigh**t, n**eigh**bor, sl**eigh**, w**eigh**
	ey	f**ey**, ob**ey**, pr**ey**, th**ey**

Sound	Spelling	In These Sample Words
a (as in c**a**re)	ae	**ae**rate, **ae**rial, **ae**robatics, **ae**ronautics, **ae**rosol
	ai	**ai**r, b**ai**rn, f**ai**r, h**ai**rdresser, l**ai**r, p**ai**r
	ay	pr**ay**er
	e	**e**re, th**e**re, wh**e**re
	ea	b**ea**r, p**ea**r, t**ea**r, w**ea**r
	ei	**Ei**re, h**ei**r, th**ei**r
a (as in f**a**ther)	ah	**ah**, m**ah**jong, sh**ah**
	al	b**al**m, c**al**m, p**al**m, ps**al**m
	e	s**e**rgeant
	ea	h**ea**rken, h**ea**rt, h**ea**rten, h**ea**rth, h**ea**rthstone
b (as in **b**ib)	bb	blu**bb**er, ca**bb**age, e**bb**, ro**bb**er
	bh	**bh**ang
	pb	cu**pb**oard, ras**pb**erry

Sound	Spelling	In These Sample Words
ch (as in **church**)	c	**c**ello
	cz	**Cz**ech
	tch	ba**tch**, ca**tch**, la**tch**, pa**tch**, sti**tch**
	ti	bes**ti**al, ques**ti**on, sugges**ti**on
	tu	den**tu**re, na**tu**ralism, na**tu**re, pas**tu**re
d (as in **deed**)	ed	mail**ed**, ring**ed**, wing**ed**
	dd	bla**dd**er, gla**dd**en, la**dd**er, sa**dd**le
	dh	**dh**ow
e (as in p**e**t)	a	**a**ny, m**a**ny
	ae	**ae**sthetic
	ai	ag**ai**n, s**ai**d
	ay	s**ay**s
	ea	cl**ea**nse, l**ea**den, m**ea**sure, m**ea**surement, thr**ea**d
	ei	h**ei**fer, S**ei**ne
	eo	l**eo**pard
	ie	fr**ie**nd
	oe	**Oe**dipus
	u	b**u**rial
e (as in b**e**)	ae	C**ae**sar, encyclop**ae**dia, p**ae**an
	ay	qu**ay**
	ea	b**ea**ch, **ea**ch, l**ea**p, r**ea**ch, r**ea**p, s**ea**board
	ee	b**ee**t, cr**ee**p, m**ee**k
	ei	conc**ei**t, dec**ei**t, rec**ei**ve, rec**ei**pt
	eo	p**eo**ple
	ey	cov**ey**, k**ey**, monk**ey**
	i	min**i**skirt, p**i**ano, solar**i**um, sympos**i**um
	ie	bel**ie**ve, f**ie**nd, s**ie**ge
	oe	am**oe**ba, ph**oe**nix
	y	comed**y**, qualit**y**, tracheotom**y**
f (as in **fife**)	ff	sti**ff**, sni**ff**le, whi**ff**
	gh	enou**gh**, rou**gh**, trou**gh**
	lf	ca**lf**, ha**lf**
	ph	al**ph**abet, gra**ph**, **ph**oto, s**ph**incter
g (as in **gag**)	gg	bra**gg**ed, dru**gg**ed, slu**gg**ish
	gh	**gh**astly, **gh**erkin, **gh**etto, **gh**ost
	gu	**gu**errilla, **gu**ess, **gu**est
	gue	analo**gue**, catalo**gue**, epilo**gue**
h (as in **h**at)	wh	**wh**o, **wh**ose
	g	**G**ila monster
	j	**J**erez
i (as in p**i**t)	a	certific**a**te, clim**a**te, vill**a**ge
	e	**e**nough, r**e**buff, r**e**cite
	ee	b**ee**n
	ia	carr**ia**ge, marr**ia**ge
	ie	s**ie**ve
	o	w**o**men
	u	b**u**sy
	ui	b**ui**lt
	y	c**y**st, d**y**spepsia, n**y**mph, s**y**mbol
i (as in p**ie**)	ai	**ai**sle
	ay	**ay**e, b**ay**ou
	ei	**ei**derdown, h**ei**ght, s**ei**smograph, st**ei**n
	ey	**ey**e
	ie	d**ie**, l**ie**, t**ie**
	igh	r**igh**t, s**igh**, th**igh**
	is	**is**land

Sound	Spelling	In These Sample Words
	uy	b**uy**
	y	l**y**re, m**y**opia, sk**y**
	ye	r**ye**
i (as in p**i**er)	e	c**e**real, h**e**re, s**e**ries
	ea	cl**ea**r, **ea**r, sm**ea**r
	ee	b**ee**r, st**ee**r, v**ee**r
	ei	w**ei**rd
j (as in **j**ar)	d	deci**d**uous, gra**d**uate, indivi**d**ual
	dg	ju**dg**ment, lo**dg**ing, tru**dg**ing
	di	sol**di**er
	dj	a**dj**ective
	g	a**g**itate, an**g**ina, **g**em, re**g**ister
	ge	diver**ge**, mer**ge**r, ven**ge**ance
	gg	exa**gg**erate
k (as in **k**ick)	c	**c**all, e**c**stasy, e**c**zema
	cc	a**cc**ount, su**cc**otash, su**cc**ulent
	cch	sa**cch**arin
	ch	al**ch**emy, **ch**aos, s**ch**edule, s**ch**ool
	ck	a**ck**nowledge, cra**ck**, kna**ck**, pa**ck**age
	cqu	la**cqu**er
	cu	bis**cu**it, cir**cu**it
	lk	ba**lk**, ta**lk**, wa**lk**
	qu	**qu**ay
	que	pla**que**, tor**que**
kw (as in **qu**ick)	ch	**ch**oir
	cqu	a**cqu**aint, a**cqu**ire, a**cqu**it
l (as in **l**id)	ll	**ll**ama, ta**ll**
	lh	**Lh**asa
m (as in **m**um)	chm	dra**chm**
	gm	paradi**gm**, phle**gm**
	lm	ba**lm**, ca**lm**, psa**lm**
	mb	du**mb**, plu**mb**
	mm	ha**mm**er, ma**mm**oth, mu**mm**y
	mn	autu**mn**, hy**mn**, sole**mn**
n (as in **n**o)	gn	ali**gn**, **gn**at, **gn**arled
	kn	**kn**ee, **kn**ife, **kn**ow
	mn	**mn**emonic
	nn	ca**nn**y, i**nn**, ba**nn**er
	pn	**pn**eumonia
ng (as in thi**ng**)	n	a**n**chor, co**n**gress, i**n**k, u**n**cle
	ngue	to**ngue**
o (as in p**o**t)	a	w**a**ffle, w**a**tch, w**a**ter, wh**a**t
	ho	**ho**nest
	ou	tr**ou**gh
o (as in n**o**)	au	h**au**tboy, m**au**ve
	eau	b**eau**, bur**eau**, trouss**eau**
	eo	y**eo**man
	ew	s**ew**
	oa	cr**oa**k, f**oa**m, m**oa**n, r**oa**ch
	oe	f**oe**, J**oe**
	oh	**oh**, **oh**m
	oo	br**oo**ch
	ou	b**ou**lder, sh**ou**lder
	ough	bor**ough**, d**ough**, thor**ough**
	ow	cr**ow**, l**ow**
	owe	**owe**, Marl**owe**

Sound	Spelling	In These Sample Words
o (as in **paw** or f**o**r)	a	**all**, w**a**ter
	al	b**al**k, t**al**k, w**al**k
	ah	Ut**ah**
	ar	w**ar**m
	as	Arkans**as**
	au	c**au**ght, c**au**liflower, d**au**ghter, g**au**nt
	aw	**aw**e, **aw**ful, **aw**ning, br**aw**l
	oa	br**oa**d, **oa**r
	ough	b**ough**t, br**ough**t, th**ough**t, wr**ough**t
oi (as in n**oi**se)	oy	b**oy**, cl**oy**, r**oy**al
ou (as in **ou**t)	au	sauerkr**au**t
	aue	s**aue**rbraten
	hou	**hou**r
	ough	b**ough**
	ow	f**ow**l, sc**ow**l, s**ow**
oo (as in t**oo**k)	o	w**o**man, w**o**lf
	ou	c**ou**ld, sh**ou**ld, w**ou**ld
	u	b**u**sh, c**u**shion, f**u**ll
oo (as in b**oo**t)	eu	l**eu**kemia, man**eu**ver, rh**eu**matic
	ew	dr**ew**, shr**ew**, fl**ew**
	ieu	l**ieu**, l**ieu**tenant
	o	d**o**, m**o**ve, tw**o**
	oe	can**oe**
	ou	gr**ou**p, s**ou**p, tr**ou**pe
	ough	thr**ough**
	u	pr**u**dent, r**u**de
	ue	ag**ue**, bl**ue**, fl**ue**
	ui	br**ui**se, fr**ui**t, j**ui**ce
p (as in **p**o**p**)	pp	ha**pp**y, sna**pp**er, stri**pp**er
r (as in **r**oa**r**)	rh	**rh**apsody, **rh**eumatism, **rh**ythm
	rr	che**rr**y, ma**rr**iage, po**rr**idge
	rrh	ci**rrh**osis
	wr	**wr**ing, **wr**inkle, **wr**ite
s (as in **s**ay)	c	**c**ellar, **c**ent, **c**yst
	ce	ma**ce**, practi**ce**, sau**ce**
	ps	**ps**alm, **ps**eudonym, **ps**ychology
	sc	ab**sc**ess, adole**sc**ent, fa**sc**inate, **sc**ene
	sch	**sch**ism
	ss	la**ss**, pa**ss**, sa**ss**afras
	sth	i**sth**mus
sh (as in **sh**ip)	ce	o**ce**anic
	ch	**ch**ancre, **ch**andelier, mar**ch**ioness
	ci	defi**ci**ent, musi**ci**an, spe**ci**al
	psh	**psh**aw
	s	**s**ugar, **s**ure
	sc	con**sc**ience
	sch	**sch**ist, **sch**ottische
	se	nau**se**ous
	si	pen**si**on
	ss	mi**ss**ion, ti**ss**ue
	ti	elec**ti**on, na**ti**on, vibra**ti**on
t (as in **t**ie)	ed	bump**ed**, crash**ed**, stopp**ed**
	ght	bou**ght**, cau**ght**, wrou**ght**
	pt	**pt**armigan, **pt**erodactyl
	th	**Th**omas
	tt	be**tt**er, le**tt**uce, si**tt**er
	tw	**tw**o

Sound	Spelling	In These Sample Words
th (as in **th**ink)	phth	**phth**isis
u (as in c**u**t)	o	inc**o**me, s**o**me, s**o**n
	oe	d**oe**s
	oo	bl**oo**d, fl**oo**d
	ou	c**ou**ple, d**ou**blet, tr**ou**ble
yoo (as in **u**se)	eau	b**eau**tiful
	eu	**eu**genic, **eu**phoria, f**eu**d
	eue	q**ueue**
	ew	f**ew**, p**ew**, p**ew**ter
	ieu	ad**ieu**
	iew	v**iew**
	u	p**u**berty, p**u**ce
	ue	c**ue**, p**ue**rile
	you	**you**
	yu	**yu**le
u (as in f**u**r)	ear	**ear**n, l**ear**n, y**ear**n
	er	c**er**tain, f**er**n, h**er**d, t**er**m
	eur	restaurat**eur**
	ir	b**ir**d, f**ir**st, th**ir**ty
	or	w**or**d, w**or**k
	our	j**our**nal, j**our**ney, sc**our**ge
	yr	m**yr**tle
	yrrh	m**yrrh**
v (as in **v**al**v**e)	f	o**f**
	ph	Ste**ph**en
w (as in **w**ith)	o	**o**ne
	ou	**Ou**agadougou
	u	g**u**anine, g**u**ano, g**u**ava
y (as in **y**es)	i	min**i**on, on**i**on, opin**i**on
	j	halleru**j**ah
z (as in **z**ebra)	cz	**cz**ar
	s	her**s**, ri**s**e, your**s**
	ss	de**ss**ert, hu**ss**ar
	x	**x**erography, **x**ylophone
	zz	bu**zz**, fu**zz**
zh (as in barra**ge**)	ge	gara**ge**, mira**ge**
	s	plea**s**ure, vi**s**ion

Note: The letter *x* spells six sounds in English: ks, as in bo**x**, e**x**it; gz, as in e**x**act, e**x**ist; sh, as in an**x**ious; gzh, as in lu**x**urious, lu**x**ury; ksh (a variant of gzh), also as in lu**x**urious, lu**x**ury; and z, as in an**x**iety, **X**erox.

A, e, i, o, or **u**

These vowels are often represented in phonetic transcriptions by a symbol called the schwa (ə). The schwa is used to represent the indeterminate vowel sound in many unstressed syllables. It receives the weakest level of stress within a word and thus varies in sound from word to word. The **a** in **a**bout, the **e** in it**e**m, the **i** in edi**-**ble, the **o** in gall**o**p, and the **u** in circ**u**s are all pronounced with the schwa sound. Here are some frequently misspelled words that contain syllables with the schwa sound:

abs**e**nce defin**i**te exagg**e**rate hum**oro**us priv**-** il**e**ge correspond**e**nce desp**e**rate grammar prej**u**dice sep**a**rate

Part-of-speech labels. The following abbreviated italicized part-of-speech labels tag the grammatical functions of the entries:

n.	= noun
adj.	= adjective
adv.	= adverb
pron.	= pronoun
conj.	= conjunction
prep.	= preposition
v.	= verb
tr.v.	= transitive verb
intr.v.	= intransitive verb
interj.	= interjection

Each entry carries a part-of-speech label, with the exception of open compounds (such as **saber-toothed tiger, song thrush,** and **whole note**). Here is an example of a part-of-speech label at a main entry: **saber** (sā′bər) *n.*

Many words can function as more than one part of speech. For instance, the word *so* can be an adverb, an adjective, a conjunction, and an interjection. In such cases the different parts of speech are all labeled within a combined entry:

so¹ . . . *adv.* **1.** In the condition or manner expressed or indicated; thus . . . —*adj.* True; factual . . . —*conj.* With the result or consequence that . . . —*interj.* A word used to express surprise or comprehension . . . .

Notice that run-in part-of-speech labels are introduced by dashes.

Sometimes it is possible to define multiple parts of speech by means of a single sense. In cases like this, combined part-of-speech labels are used:

a·ground (ə-ground′) *adv. & adj.* Stranded in shallow water or on a reef or shoal . . . .

Exercises

1. Why does the entry **whole milk** appear without a part-of-speech label?

2. How many parts of speech are labeled at the entry **well**¹? **Well**²? List them.

3. What part of speech is **get**?

4. What is the part-of-speech label at **abroad**? Why is it written as it is?

Capitalization of entries. Entries that are always capitalized are entered accordingly: **Sabbath; House of Commons.**

Capitalized entries having noncapitalized senses repeat the main-entry word in lower-case boldface type at those senses:

Star Chamber. 1. A former English court . . . **2. star chamber.** Any court . . . .

Common-noun main entries having capitalized senses repeat the main-entry in boldface initial capitals at those senses:

sab·bat·i·cal . . . *adj.* . . . . **1. Sabbatical.** Pertaining to . . . the Sabbath. **2.** Pertaining to a sabbatical year.

Trademarks are entered in capital letters:

Da·cron (dā′krŏn′, dăk′rŏn′) *n.* A trademark for a synthetic polyester textile fiber or fabric that resists stretching and wrinkling. —*modifier: a Dacron shirt.*

Exercises

1. Using your Dictionary, identify these words either as common nouns or as proper nouns: *easter, fiddler crab, gascon, gasconade.*

2. Identify the sense(s) in which you would capitalize these words:

Word	Sense Number(s)
galaxy	
cabala	
grace	
black	
dame	

3. Identify the sense(s) in which you would not capitalize these words:

Word	Sense Number(s)
Babel	
Bolshevik	
Deity	
Puritan	

Variant spellings of main entries. This Dictionary recognizes two types of spelling variants: primary variants and secondary variants. Primary variants are set in boldface type and are linked to main-entry head words by the word "or." Both spellings are equally correct: **ax** or **axe.**

Secondary variants, also set in boldface type, appear after the part-of-speech labels and are introduced by the word "Also." These secondary variants are not as commonly used as the head-word form, but they are entirely acceptable. Example:

fa·çade (fə-säd′) *n.* Also **fa·cade.**

Variants are entered separately at their own alphabetical places when their spellings place them alphabetically at a distance from their head words with other entries intervening. Thus at the head word **ameba** we see

a·me·ba (ə-mē′bə) *n., pl.* **-bas.** Var. of **a·moe·ba.**

And at **amoeba,** we find

a·moe·ba (ə-mē′bə) *n., pl.* **-bas.** Also **ameba.**

Notice that the variant entry carries a pronunciation, part-of-speech label, plural label and plural form, and the abbreviation "Var.," indicating that it is a variant of the head word set in boldface type.

British variants are also given at their own alphabetical places according to the same criteria:

col·our (kŭl'ər) *n. & v. Brit.* Var. of **color**.

Exercises

1. In the middle column list the variant spellings for the words given in the left column. Are they primary or secondary variants?

Entry   Variant Spelling(s)   Type of Variant

hijack

cabala

endoblast

adz

vespertine

2. Look up each of the variant spellings in the above list. Are they entered at their own alphabetical places? If so, why? If not, why?

Inflected forms: verbs. The majority of English verbs form their past tense and past participle by adding the suffix *-ed* to the present tense, and form their present participle by adding the suffix *-ing* to the present tense. Such verbs are considered *regular* and are not inflected in this Dictionary:

scratch (skrăch) *tr.v.*
gnaw (nô) *tr.v.*

At the entry for an irregular verb the irregular past tense, past participle, and present participle appear in boldface type immediately after the part-of-speech label. Other irregular inflected forms (such as the present tense, third person singular) may be shown if a major stem change occurs.

Irregularities in inflection include stem changes, the doubling of consonants or the dropping of vowels, inflections having variant spellings, inflections resulting in changed pronunciations, and any forms that might cause uncertainty. Here are some examples of irregularly inflected forms shown either in full form or in clipped form in this Dictionary:

ban ... *tr.v.* **banned, ban·ning.**
break ... *v.* **broke** ... or *archaic* **brake** ..., **bro·ken** ..., **break·ing.**
gas ... *v.* **gassed, gas·sing.**
hur·ry ... *v.* **-ried, -ry·ing.**
put ... **put, put·ting.**

Irregular inflected forms appearing at an alphabetical distance from their head words are separately entered at their own alphabetical places:

swol·len ... *v.* A past participle of **swell**.

Inflected forms: adjectives and adverbs. If an adjective or adverb can form the comparative and superlative degree by the addition of *-er* and *-est*, these inflected forms appear in either clipped or full form:

sharp ... *adj.* **-er, -est.**
good ... *adj.* **bet·ter** ..., **best.**
well² ... *adv.* **bet·ter** ..., **best.**
cheer·y ... *adj.* **-i·er, -i·est.**

Plurals. Regular noun plurals (i.e., those formed by adding *-s* or *-es* to unaltered base words) are not shown. Irregular plurals (i.e., those involving spelling changes, stem changes, and variant forms, and those that are identical in form with the base words) are shown in boldface type after the part-of-speech label. They are signaled by the italic abbreviation *pl.* Irregular plurals may be shown in clipped or full form. Examples:

cher·ry ... *n., pl.* **-ries.**
ha·lo ... *n., pl.* **-los** or **-loes.**
don·key ... *n., pl.* **-keys.**
deer ... *n., pl.* **deer.**
attorney general *pl.* **attorneys general.**

Sometimes a plural applies only to a particular sense of an entry. Such restricted plurals are shown in boldface type at the appropriate sense:

Mad·am ... *n.* **1.** *pl.* **Mes·dames** (mā-dăm'). A title of courtesy used alone as a form of address.... **2.** ......

ground¹ ... *n.* **1.** ..... **2.** ..... **3.** Often **grounds.** An area of land set aside for a particular purpose: *burial grounds.* **4. grounds.** The land surrounding or forming part of a house or other building: *The embassy has beautiful grounds.*

The boldface plural *Mesdames* in sense **1.** of the first example indicates that only this plural can be used for sense **1.** Sense **2.**, carrying no label, is formed in the regular way, as *madams.* In sense **3.** of the second example the plural indicates that one often uses this term in the plural, but not always — hence the qualifier "Often." In sense **4.** of the second example, however, one always uses the word in the plural. Hence *grounds* is stipulated without a qualifying adverb.

Sometimes a plural form is more widely used than the singular. Such terms are entered and defined as main entries and are labeled *pl.n.* Example:

al·gae ... *pl.n.* The less frequently used sing. is **al·ga.** ... Any of various primitive, chiefly aquatic, one-celled or multicellular plants. ......

Some nouns are plural in form but may govern a singular or plural verb. Parenthetic italic notes at such terms indicate the correct usage:

a·cous·tics ... *n.* **1.** *(used with a sing. verb).* The scientific study of sound, esp. of its generation, transmission, and perception. **2.** *(used with a pl. verb).* The total effect of sound produced in an enclosed space: *The acoustics of the new concert hall are poor.*

An irregular plural is also entered at its own alphabetical place if a sufficient number of entries intervenes between it and its head word:

ap·pen·di·ces . . . *n.* A plural of **appendix.**
. . . .
ap·pen·dix . . . *n., pl.* **-dix·es** or **-di·ces** . . . . . .

Exercises

1. Using your Dictionary, write the inflected forms of each of these irregular verbs:

do[1]	wake[1]
wag[1]	shine
dream	wring
prove	get
ride	lead[1]
lend	tear[1]

2. Look up the following entry words. Write down the grammatical information given after each entry:

bit[4]	lit
took	swum
caught	lain
ate	dug[2]
laid	bitten

3. Give the irregular plurals of these nouns. If plural forms vary according to some individual senses, say so.

tooth	index
sheep	banjo
goose	ferry
father-in-law	syllabus
antenna	vertebra
cactus	diagnosis
curriculum	sergeant at arms

4. List the comparative and superlative degrees of these irregular adjectives:

good	little
hot	many

Labels. Entries and senses requiring orientation labels are clearly tagged. This Dictionary employs temporal labels (such as *Archaic*), usage labels (*Informal, Slang, Nonstandard,* and *Poet.*), dialect labels (such as *Regional*), language labels (such as *French*), field labels (such as *Law*), and status labels (such as *Rare*). Labels appearing in italics before the definitions apply to all senses of a word. Labels that appear within numbered and/or lettered senses and subsenses apply only to the senses and subsenses in which they appear. Examples:

hip[2] . . . Also **hep.** . . . *Slang.* Aware of the most recent developments and trends.

wow . . . *interj.* A word used to express wonder, amazement, excitement, enthusiasm, etc. —*n. Informal.* An outstanding success. —*tr.v. Informal.* To be or have a great success with: *wowed the audience.*

In the second example notice that the *Informal* label applies to both the noun and the verb in the combined entry. Here is an example in which the label applies to both lettered subsenses:

jaw . . . *n.* **6.** *Slang.* **a.** Back talk. **b.** Chatter.

When a label appears first in a combined entry, it governs the entire entry:

slug[3] (slŭg). *Slang.* —*tr.v.* **slugged, slug·ging.** To strike heavily, esp. with the fist. —See Syns at **hit.** —*n.* A hard, heavy blow, as with the fist. [Perh. from SLUG (bullet).]

Thus the *Slang* label at **slug**[3] applies to the noun and the verb.

Temporal labels. The *Archaic* label indicates that an entry or a sense is no longer used widely in modern English. See **wrought.**

Usage labels. Usage labels indicate various levels of usage and style that may or may not be appropriate in all settings. *Informal* generally applies to words that are used in spoken English or in ordinary writing but that might not be considered appropriate in very formal compositions. See **guru** *n.* **2.** *Slang* includes witty, colorful, often facetious expressions that are considered inappropriate to a formal situation. See **croak** —*intr.v.* **4.** The label *Nonstandard* means "not standard." It warns you that you may be criticized for using a particular expression on any level. See **alright.** The label *Poet.* means "poetic." It restricts the use of a term chiefly to verse. See **o'er.**

Dialect labels. The labels *Regional* and *Chiefly Regional* indicate that a term is peculiar to a particular geographical region. See **wrangle** *n.* **2.**

Language labels. Language labels (such as *French*) indicate that a particular term, though used in English, may not yet be fully naturalized. See **au revoir.** Labels such as *Brit.* and *Scot.* indicate that a word or a sense is used chiefly in the British Commonwealth. See the two labels at **bonnet** *n.* **2.** and **5.**

Field labels. Field labels (such as *Math.* and *Law*) indicate that a word or a sense is used primarily but not invariably in a particular field of study or profession. See **set**[2] *n.* **7.** and **principal** *n.* **5.**

Status labels. The status label *Rare* indicates that a term is rarely used in modern English. There are very few *Rare* terms entered in this book.

Exercise

What orientation labels (e.g., language, usage, status) do these entries carry?

Entry	Label
ad infinitum	
aloha	
gyp	
durst	
rip-off	
boot[1]	
dukes	
throw the book at	
(see **book**)	
forte[2]	

Sense division. When an entry has more than one sense, these are introduced by boldface sequential sense numbers. When a numbered sense contains closely related subsenses, these are signaled by boldface letters. Example:

sis·ter . . . *n.* **1. a.** A girl or woman having the same mother and father as another person. **b.** A girl or woman having one parent in common with another; half sister. **2.** A woman or girl who shares a common ancestry, allegiance, character, or purpose with another or others. . . . . .

Order of definitions. Definitions are not arranged historically or by frequency of use. Rather, they are ordered *analytically*—i.e., according to central meaning clusters from which related subsenses and additional separate senses may evolve. Example:

make . . . *v.* . . . —*tr.v.* **1. a.** To bring into existence by or as if by shaping, fashioning, or constructing: *make a ladder from scrap lumber.* **b.** To cause to appear or occur; bring about: *make trouble.* **2. a.** To cause to be or become: *The cold air and unaccustomed exercise made him ravenously hungry.* **b.** To appoint to a position or office: *made her treasurer.* **c.** To cause to perform or experience an action: *Heat makes a gas expand.* **d.** To compel: *make him obey.*

As you can see, the central, physical sense of *make* (i.e., to construct or build) is given first in sense **1.a.** followed by the figurative (nonphysical) sense (i.e., to bring about) in sense **1.b.** In sense **2.a.** the central sense is that of causing a result, followed in **2.b., 2.c.,** and **2.d.** by closely related subsenses. It is felt that the use of a meaningful, logical sense order presents the definitions as coherent units rather than as a string of seemingly disconnected, unrelated senses.

Scientific definitions. Your Dictionary contains a representative selection of definitions of scientific terms. A few words must be said about them.

Many definitions of plants and animals contain examples of a specialized system of nomenclature. This system of Latin names is used internationally to identify, as unambiguously as possible, each known organism as well as to place it within a hierarchy of related organisms.

The names shown are widely accepted by taxonomists and are in general accordance with taxonomic designations. In some instances, especially in the field of botany, there have been considerable changes and difference of opinion regarding certain taxa in recent years. Names chosen here reflect an effort to select the most acceptable and authoritative designations.

The taxonomic designations in this Dictionary take several forms. The categories in order higher than genus, such as family or class, are identified by category and are capitalized:

grasshopper . . . *n.* **1.** Any of numerous insects of the families Locustidae (or Acrididae) and Tettigonidae. . . . . .

Designations of genus and other lower taxa appear as one-, two-, or three-word phrases in italics with only the genus name capitalized. The two-word phrase, or binomial, describes an organism's genus and species:

radish . . . *n.* **1.** Any of various plants of the genus *Raphanus,* esp. *R. sativus,* with a thickened, edible root. . . . . .

Three-word phrases, or trinomials, describe an organism's subspecies or variety in addition:

Brussels sprouts . . . *n.* . . . **1.** A variety of cabbage, *Brassica oleracea gemmifera,* that has a stout stem. . . . . .

Most taxonomic designations are not entered in the A–Z list as entries, because they occur mainly in scientific literature.

Illustrative examples. Thousands of illustrative examples—many of them attributed quotations—follow the definitions. These italic examples show the defined entries in action. They are especially helpful in illustrating figurative senses, transitive and intransitive verbs, and shades of meaning. Examples:

stretch . . . —*intr.v.* **1.** . . . **2.** To extend or reach over a given distance or area in a given direction: *"On both sides of us stretched the wet plain"* (Ernest Hemingway). **3.** To lie down at full length: *We stretched out on the beach.* **4.** To extend over a given period of time: *"This story stretches over a whole generation"* (William Golding).

un·der·sea . . . *adj.* Of, done, existing, or created for use beneath the surface of the sea: *undersea life; undersea exploration.*

Notice that the illustrations in **stretch 2.** and **4.** are quotations. The authors' names appear in parentheses after the quotations. Notice also that this Dictionary contains full-sentence illustrative examples (see **stretch 3.**) and phrasal illustrations (see the example **undersea**).

Alternate terms and cross-references. An alternate term is a word or expression that is synonymous with a main-entry head word but that differs markedly from it in spelling or form. For example, the words *kneecap* and *patella* are synonyms. *Patella* is the technical term, while *kneecap* is the nontechnical term. Such terms are defined like this:

knee·cap . . . *n.* The patella.

The entry **kneecap** is a cross-reference entry to **patella**, where the full definition is given.

pa·tel·la . . . *n.* . . . A flat, triangular bone located at the front of the knee joint; the kneecap.

Since the preferred term is the technical one, the full definition appears there and the nontechnical term *kneecap* is cross-referred to it.

Other alternate terms are introduced at the ends of main-entry definitions by the phrase "Also called." For instance, at the entry **propeller** we see

pro·pel·ler . . . *n.* Also **pro·pel·lor.** A device for propelling aircraft or boats, esp. one with radiating blades mounted on a revolving power-driven shaft. Also called **screw** and **screw propeller.**

The boldface terms **screw** and **screw propeller** are alternate terms of **propeller.** They are also entered at their own alphabetical places as cross-references to the main-entry **propeller.**

Phrasal verbs. Phrasal verbs are alphabetically run in and defined as subentries of their main-entry base words. They are introduced by the italic bold subhead *—phrasal verbs*, and they follow the last main-entry verb definition. For example, at the main entry **go¹** *v.*, you will find many phrasal verbs, among them *go about, go away, go for, go on,* and *go out.* Look at the entry below:

go¹ . . . *v.* . . . . **5.** To take part to the extent of: *go fifty-fifty on a deal.* —See Syns at **die.** *—phrasal verbs.* **go about. 1.** To busy oneself with: *go about one's business.* **2.** To change direction in a sailing vessel; to tack. **go along.** To be in agreement; cooperate: *He went along with the majority.* . . . .

No part-of-speech labels are included at phrasal verb entries.

Exercises

1. Turn to the main entry **come.** How many phrasal verbs can you find there? List them.

2. Where can the following phrasal verbs be found? List the main entries at which they appear in the right column.

phrasal verb	**main entry**
push around	
make out	
face off	
buy up	

Idioms. Idioms are introduced by the boldface italic subhead *—idioms* and are run in alphabetically and defined within main entries. The idioms, like the phrasal verbs, are set in boldface type. At the main entry **go¹**, for instance, these idioms appear:

go¹ . . . *v.* (intransitive and transitive senses) . . . . *—phrasal verbs.* . . . . —*n., pl.* **goes.** *Informal.* . . . . . . (definitions of the noun subentry) . . . . . —*adj. Informal.* (definition of the adjective subentry) . . . . . *—idioms.* **from the word go.** *Informal.* From the very beginning or from the bottom of the heart: *They're staunch Republicans from the word go.* **go far.** To succeed; prosper greatly: *Speak softly and carry a big stick; you will go far.* **go (someone) one better.** To surpass or outdo. **go together.** To be sweethearts. **on the go.** *Informal.* Perpetually busy. **to go.** To be taken out, as restaurant food and drink: *We want coffee and sandwiches to go.*

Notice that many of the idioms carry illustrative examples.

Exercise

List the main entries at which these idioms are found:

Idiom	**Main Entry**
arm in arm	
at ease	
face to face	
no good	

Modifiers. Nouns that can be used attributively, i.e., as adjectival modifiers, are often introduced by the boldface italic subhead *—modifier*. Modifiers are not defined because they undergo no meaning changes. Example:

ghet·to . . . . *n., pl.* . . . **1.** A section or quarter in a European city. . . . **2.** A slum section of an American city. . . . *—modifier: ghetto children.*

In combined entries modifiers appear after the last noun definition:

gas . . . *n., pl.* . . . **1.** . . . . **2.** . . . . (all noun definitions given) . . . . *—modifier: a gas tank in a car; a gas burner.* —*v.* **gassed, gas·sing.** —*tr.v.*

Exercise

Write examples in which these nouns can be used as adjectival modifiers of other nouns.

backwoods	nomination
book	outline
name	windjammer

Etymologies. Like a person or a nation, every word has a past—an origin and a history of development. These word histories—called etymologies—are enclosed in square brackets and placed after the definitions but before any undefined run-on subentries, synonym studies, or Usage notes.

Look at the etymology for *bleak:*

bleak . . . *adj.* . . . **1.** Exposed to the elements; unsheltered; barren: *bleak moors.* **2.** Cold and cutting; harsh: *a bleak winter wind.* **3.** Dreary and somber: *a bleak prognosis.* —See Syns at **gloomy.** [Middle English *bleike,* pale, from Old Norse *bleikr,* shining, white.] —**bleak′ly** *adv.* —**bleak′ness** *n.*

Notice that the words "bleike" and "bleikr," from which the modern English word *bleak* came, are set in italics. The meanings of these words ("pale, shining, and white," respectively) are set off by commas and are called glosses.

If a language, a word form, or a gloss does not change from one stage of the word's development to the next, it is not repeated. In the example at **bleak,** though, changes have occurred in all three, so the form, meaning, and language are given for every stage.

Some entries do not have etymologies. These include obvious derivatives of other words already having etymologies; for example, *transaction,* a derivative of *transact,* does not have an etymology because the full etymology is at *transact.* Other words without etymologies are compounds made up of two or more English words that are also entered separately in the Dictionary with their own etymologies. Two examples are *backbone* (see the etymologies at *back* and at *bone*) and *brown bread* (see the etymologies at *brown* and at *bread*). Still other words without etymologies are trademarks.

Some compounds show etymologies for only one of their elements. Example:

brown Betty . . . A baked pudding. . . . [*Betty,* pet form of *Elizabeth.*]

The etymology for the word *brown* is given at the entry **brown,** but *Betty* is not separately entered with its own etymology. Therefore the etymology for *Betty* is shown here.

Some words are made up of parts of words entered elsewhere in this Dictionary. These words are called blends. The etymology at *transceiver,* which is formed from the *trans-* segment of the word *transmitter* and the *-ceiver* segment of the word *receiver,* is written like this:

transceiver
n. . . . .
[TRANS(MITTER) + (RE)CEIVER.]

Etymologies having words written in small-capital letters indicate that you should go to the etymologies of those words for further information.

Some English words come from personal names. They are called eponyms. For example:

mar·ti·net . . . . *n.* A rigid disciplinarian. [After Jean Martinet, 17th-cent. French general.]

The surname *Martinet,* from which our Eng-

lish word *martinet* comes, is in italics in the etymology. A short gloss ("17th-cent. French general") tells you something about the person.

This Dictionary shows only those etymologies that are reasonably certain and generally accepted. Any doubt as to a word's origin is indicated by the abbreviations *prob.* (probably), *poss.* (possibly), and *perh.* (perhaps). Sometimes the exact ancestral form of a modern English word is unknown, but if the language group from which the entry word is borrowed is certain, that language group is shown:

skulk . . . . . . [Middle English *skulken,* of Scandinavian orig.]

If the origin of a word is completely unknown, or if it is uncertain or disputed, the etymology tells you so:

posh . . . *adj. Informal.* Smart and fashionable; exclusive. [Orig. unknown.]

Exercises

1. What is the origin of *bag*?

2. From what languages do *bistro* and *dacha* come?

3. From what name does *begonia* come?

4. What kind of word is *skyjack*? From what words is it formed?

5. What is the etymology for the word *widgeon*?

Undefined run-on entries. Words that are essentially self-explanatory—i.e., those whose meanings can be readily derived from their main-entry definitions—are often run on undefined in boldface type at the very ends of main entries. Examples:

ghast·ly . . . *adj.* . . . **1.** Terrifying; dreadful. . . . **2.** Having a deathlike pallor. . . . **3.** Extremely unpleasant. . . . —*adv.* Dreadfully. . . . [Etymology. . . .] —**ghast′li·ness** *n.*

ge·o·mor·phol·o·gy . . . *n.* The geological study of . . . land forms. —**ge′o·mor′pho·log′ic** (-môr′fə-lŏj′ĭk) or **ge′o·mor′pho·log′i·cal** *adj.* —**ge′o·mor′pho·log′i·cal·ly** *adv.*

Notice that stress and sometimes pronunciations are shown in undefined run-ons. Notice also that variants, such as **geomorphologic** and **geomorphological,** are separated by the word "or." Italic part-of-speech labels are given for all undefined run-ons.

Exercises

1. For each of these main-entry head words list the undefined run-on entries found there. Mark syllables and stress when possible:

fabulous	**habitable**
oaf	**kaleidoscope**

2. Some of the italic words in the following sentences are main entries and some are run-on entries. Label the main entries *ME* and the run-ons *RO:*

___ **a.** He wrote *dramaturgical* works.

___ **b.** Is that an *erasable* marker?

___ **c.** That movie was a real *shocker.*

___ **d.** A water *filtration* plant was built here.

___ **e.** The land is still *reclaimable.*

___ **f.** I bought a *geographical* dictionary.

SPECIAL FEATURES

SYNONYM STUDIES

What is a synonym? A synonym is a word that has the same or nearly the same meaning as another word or a group of other words. For instance, *brave* is a synonym of *courageous.*
Why are people interested in synonyms? A person may have in mind one word (for instance, *brave*), but he or she may want a more colorful word (such as *valiant*), a less colorful word (such as *unafraid*), or perhaps a less formal word (such as *gutsy*) that can be used to express the same meaning as *brave.* The synonym studies in your Dictionary are intended to help you use the English language with accuracy, color, variety, and precision.
Components of the synonym studies. Your Dictionary contains hundreds of synonym studies in which you will find

• synonyms alphabetically listed in boldface;

• part-of-speech labels for all synonym lists;

• *Core meanings* defining the sense(s) or meaning(s) that all the listed synonyms share;

• illustrative examples showing the synonyms in typical usage contexts;

• in some cases, extended discussion of synonyms with additional illustrative examples.

Here is a typical synonym study—this one found at the main entry **brave:**

> **Syns: brave,** audacious, bold, courageous, dauntless, fearless, gallant, gutsy *(Informal),* heroic, intrepid, mettlesome, plucky, stouthearted, unafraid, undaunted, valiant, valorous *adj. Core meaning:* Having or showing courage (*a brave soldier; a brave rescue*).

Synonym studies begin on a separate line after main entries and are signaled by the indented italic boldface heading *Syns.*
   Notice that the word *brave* heads the list in the example. Since *brave* is the main-entry head word, it comes first in the synonym list. All terms requiring labels are tagged (see **gutsy**). Notice that the two parenthetic phrases illustrate *brave* and its synonyms in typical contexts. You can substitute any of the other synonyms in that list for *brave* in the illustrative examples.
   This Dictionary contains both relatively short synonym studies and relatively long ones in which the synonyms are discussed in greater detail. Look at **calm:**

> **Syns: calm,** peaceful, placid, serene, tranquil *adj. Core meaning:* Free of movement, noise, or disturbing emotion (*spent a calm night asleep*). While CALM is the most general term implying freedom from agitation, PEACEFUL and TRANQUIL stress undisturbed serenity (*peaceful times; a tranquil lifestyle*). PLACID suggests not being easily shaken physically or emotionally (*a placid lake; a placid disposition*). SERENE suggests a lofty, almost spiritual calm (*a serene smile*).

Here the meaning shared by all the synonyms is supplemented by additional discussion enabling you to discriminate between the various shades of meaning for each synonym.
   A few synonym studies combine simple lists of synonyms and core meanings with extended discussion in separate numbered senses. For instance, at **gather,** sense **1.** carries a rather short synonym list, but sense **2.** includes detailed discrimination of the synonyms in that list, plus added examples.
   Synonym studies having more than one list contain boldface sense numbers; for instance, at **same** we see

> **Syns: 1. same,** identical, selfsame, very *adj. Core meaning:* Being one and not another or others (*the same seat I had yesterday*). **2. same,** equal, equivalent, identical *adj. Core meaning:* Agreeing exactly in value, quantity, or effect (*the same words that the President used*).

Locating synonym studies by cross-references. Cross-references direct you to full synonym studies. For instance, if you have in mind the noun *win* but you seek another word for it, you will turn to the main entry **win** in this Dictionary. At the end of the noun definition of **win** you will find this cross-reference:

—See Syns at **victory.**

You will then turn to the main entry **victory.** At the end of that entry you will find a full synonym study.
   Some synonym studies contain cross-references to other studies. For example, at the end of the synonym study at **general** you will find this cross-reference:

—See also Syns at **public.**

Exercises

1. Where will you find full synonym studies for these words?

assist   ungainly   incorrect

2. Match the words in the left column with their synonyms in the right column:

a. bulk	labyrinthine
b. cheerful	premier
c. complex	mass
d. forbid	decree
e. judge	happy
f. labor	proscribe
g. name	toil
h. primary	moniker

USAGE NOTES

Your Dictionary contains hundreds of Usage notes—some short and others quite long—that offer detailed, illustrated guidance with regard to problems of grammar, syntax, diction, and writing style. These notes are based on the opinions of a large panel of experts—the Usage Panel of the *American Heritage Dictionary*—and on numerous citations showing the actual use of words in print by a broad group of writers over a long period of time.

The Usage notes are not prescriptions telling you that you *must* speak or write in one way and in one way only. Rather, they reflect standard American English as it is written and spoken by educated users today. In short, the Usage notes are designed to help you express yourself fluently, clearly, and concisely in formal and informal settings—and in such a way as to avoid criticism.

In many of the notes several ways of expressing the same idea are given, and various levels of usage (formal, informal, and nonstandard) are discussed and illustrated. Whenever necessary, the differences in British and American English are pointed out.

A typical Usage note. A usage note is located at the very end of the main entry to which it refers. If a main entry has a synonym study as well as a Usage note, the Usage note comes last. Usage notes are indented and are signaled by the italic boldface heading *Usage* followed in boldface type by the word or words under discussion. Look at the usage guidance provided at the entry **compose**:

> ***Usage:* compose, comprise.** *Compose* means to make up the constituent parts of something, and therefore to constitute or form it: *Five boroughs compose New York City. New York City is composed of five boroughs. Comprise* means to consist of or be made up of: *New York City comprises five boroughs.* Remember: the whole comprises the parts; the parts do not comprise the whole, nor is the whole comprised of its parts. See also Usage note at **include**.

Notice that italic illustrative examples illustrate the points being made in the note.

Some Usage notes discuss multiple topics. Separate topics are signaled by sequential boldface numerals:

> ***Usage:* 1. but.** The word *but* can be a conjunction meaning with the exception of: *No one* (subject) *but*

(conjunction) *I* (nominative) *heard it.* In this situation, the pronoun following *but* agrees in case with the word that precedes *but.* The word *but* can also function as a preposition meaning except for: *No one* (subject) *heard it but* (preposition) *me* (object). When *but* and the word following it occur at the end of a sentence, *but* is gen. construed as a preposition with its object being in the objective case. **2. but that, but what.** The expressions *but that* and *but what* occur in sentences that begin with negatives and follow words like *doubt, know,* and *question: I don't doubt but that it will fail. I don't know but what I'll go.* Usage studies indicate that these expressions occur on all levels and are standard American idiom. Nevertheless, they are a bit wordy, so we recommend that you avoid them in formal compositions. The sentences can be recast to read: *I don't doubt that it will fail. I might go.* See also Usage note at **cannot**.

In the last example grammatical, syntactical, and style problems are discussed. Notice that alternative wordings are given when troublesome locutions are exemplified (see **but 2**).

Cross-references to Usage notes. As you can see in the Usage notes **compose** and **but**, cross-references direct you to more information at other related Usage notes.

The terms *may* and *might* are discussed in the Usage note at the entry **may**. If you turn to the entry **might**, you will find a cross-reference to this note at the end of the verb definitions:

—See Usage note at **may**.

Troublesome usage problems. Difficult usage problems abound in English. Ask any person who speaks English as a second language whether he or she finds our language logical and easy to master. The answer will be a resounding "No!"

Some of the areas treated by the Usage notes in your Dictionary include grammar and syntax (see the Usage notes at **bring 2.** and **sneak**, which discuss inflection; the note at **between 4.**, where the problem of case is detailed; the note at **double negative**, where negation patterns are treated; and the notes at **everybody, data,** and **media**, where subject-verb agreement is explained).

Diction and style problems are also comprehensively discussed. For instance, many notes discuss and discriminate confused and misused terms such as **compose/comprise** (see the note at **compose**), nonstandard locutions (see the note at **alright**), and often controversial style questions (see the note at **split infinitive**).

The changing language. Some of the Usage notes may surprise you, because they do not reflect many of the ultraconservative opinions of yesteryear's grammarians. For example, if you look up the note at **unique**, you will see that in some cases this adjective—once considered absolute (incapable of comparison or qualification)—can indeed be qualified and compared. And if you look up the Usage note at **shall/will**, you'll find that they are virtually interchangeable today.

Remember that language and its usage are

not inscribed in stone. They are in a constant state of change. These changes reflect what is actually being written and said by writers and speakers. The Usage notes in this Dictionary take such changes into account.

ALPHABET LETTER HISTORIES

Another special feature of your Dictionary is the inclusion of alphabet letter histories appearing on the first page of each alphabetical sequence of entry words.

For example, turn to the beginning of the letter *A* and you will see an illustrated history of that letter, tracing its ancestry 3,000 years.

BIOGRAPHICAL ENTRIES

All biographical entries in this Dictionary are included in a special section in the back. This separate listing contains information about people—both living and dead—who have helped shape the world of today. In it you can discover when and where people lived, why they are famous, and how to spell and pronounce their names.

All entries are listed in alphabetical order, according to the rules used for the general vocabulary. Identically spelled names of persons are combined, and the individual subentries arranged in chronological order.

Exercises

1. What was Catherine II called? When did she live?
2. What nationality was Henry Hudson? What area did he explore?
3. What political office did Sir John A. Macdonald hold? What years did he hold it?
4. What was the Duke of Wellington's real name?

5. How is Margaret Mead identified?
6. What prize did Lawrence Klein win? What year did he win it?

GEOGRAPHIC ENTRIES

All geographic entries are also entered in a special section in the back of your Dictionary. In this section, you will find cities, countries, states of the United States, provinces of Canada, historical places, and such topographical features as rivers and oceans, mountains and deserts, peninsulas and continents. The entries will tell you how to spell and pronounce these places and features, where they are located, how many people live there, and why they are historically important.

Population totals for all cities and countries reflect the latest figures available; all population counts for the United States are based on the 1980 Census.

Many geographic entries can generate other words. These you will find in boldface type immediately following the definition. These runons will show you how to spell and pronounce adjectives and nouns relating to the main entry.

Exercises

1. What is the population of Pierre, South Dakota? How is the name of the city pronounced?
2. What was Babylonia? Where was it located?
3. What is the former name of Zimbabwe?
4. What famous event in history took place near Hastings, England? What year did it occur?
5. What is the population of Los Angeles?
6. What is the capital of Ontario?
7. What adjective and noun are related to the entry for Vienna?

ABBREVIATIONS USED IN THE ENTRIES

approx.	approximately
cent.	century
dim.	diminutive
esp.	especially
gen.	generally
obs.	obsolete
orig.	originally; origin
perh.	perhaps
poss.	possibly
prob.	probably
specif.	specifically
ult.	ultimately
U.S.	United States (adj.)
usu.	usually
var.	variant

FIELD LABELS USED IN THE ENTRIES

(Abbreviated or Spelled Out)

Accounting	
Acoustics	
Aerospace	
Alg.	Algebra
Anat.	Anatomy
Anthropol.	Anthropology
Archaeol.	Archaeology
Archaic	
Archit.	Architecture
Astrol.	Astrology
Astron.	Astronomy
Astrophysics	
Aviation	
Ballet	
Biochem.	Biochemistry
Biol.	Biology
Bot.	Botany
Brit.	British
Cards	
Celtic Myth.	Celtic Mythology
Chem.	Chemistry
Chiropractics	
Comm.	Commerce
Computers	
Dentistry	
Eccles.	Ecclesiastical; Ecclesiastics
Ecol.	Ecology
Econ.	Economics
Egypt. Myth.	Egyptian Mythology
Elect.	Electricity
Electronics	
Engineering	
Finance	
Genetics	
Geol.	Geology
Geom.	Geometry
Gk. Myth.	Greek Mythology
Golf	
Gov.	Government
Gram.	Grammar

Heraldry	
Hinduism	
Homeopathy	
Hort.	Horticulture
Insurance	
Islam	
Judaism	
Law	
Libr. Service	Library Service
Ling.	Linguistics
Logic	
Mar. Law.	Marine Law or Maritime Law
Math.	Mathematics
Med.	Medicine
Metallurgy	
Meteorol.	Meteorology
Microbiol.	Microbiology
Mil.	Military
Mineral.	Mineralogy
Mormon Ch.	Mormon Church
Mus.	Music
Myth.	Mythology
Naut.	Nautical
Norse Myth.	Norse Mythology
Optics	
Paleontol.	Paleontology
Pathol.	Pathology
Pharm.	Pharmacology or Pharmacy
Philos.	Philosophy
Phonet.	Phonetics
Physics	
Physiol.	Physiology
Poet.	Poetic
Poker	
Printing	
Pros.	Prosody
Psychiat.	Psychiatry
Psychoanal.	Psychoanalysis
Psychol.	Psychology
Radio & TV.	Radio and Television
Rhet.	Rhetoric
Rom. Cath. Ch.	Roman Catholic Church
Rom. Myth.	Roman Mythology
Sci. Fic	Science Fiction
Statistics	
Tennis	
Theol.	Theology
Trig.	Trigonometry
Vet. Med.	Veterinary Medicine
WWI.	World War I
WWII.	World War II
Zool.	Zoology

ABBREVIATIONS USED IN ETYMOLOGIES

abbr.	abbreviation
adj.	adjective; adjectival
adv.	adverb; adverbial
cent.	century
comp.	comparative
conj.	conjunction
dial.	dialectal
dim.	diminutive

ety.	etymology
fem.	feminine
freq.	frequentative
fut.	future
gerund.	gerundive
imit.	imitative
imper.	imperative
masc.	masculine
n.	noun
naut.	nautical
neut.	neuter
obs.	obsolete
orig.	origin
part.	participle; participial
past part.	past participle
perh.	perhaps
pl.	plural
poss.	possibly
pres. part.	present participle
prob.	probably
p. t.	past tense
sing.	singular
superl.	superlative
transl.	translation
ult.	ultimately
usu.	usually
var.	variant

ABBREVIATIONS USED IN BIOGRAPHICAL and GEOGRAPHIC ENTRIES

c.	circa
Cap.	capital
dim.	diminutive
E	east
esp.	especially
ft	foot; feet
gen.	generally
km	kilometer(s)
m	meter(s)
mi	mile(s)
N	north
NE	northeast
NW	northwest
obs.	obsolete
orig.	originally; origin
perh.	perhaps
Pop.	population
poss.	possibly
prob.	probably
S	south
SE	southeast
SW	southwest
specif.	specifically
sq km	square kilometer(s)
sq mi	square mile(s)
ult.	ultimately
U.S.	United States (adj.)
usu.	usually
var.	variant
W	west

| Phoenician | Greek | Roman | Medieval | Modern |

Phoenician – About 3,000 years ago the Phoenicians and other Semitic peoples began to use graphic signs to represent individual speech sounds instead of syllables or whole words. They used this symbol to represent a consonant, the glottal stop, and gave it the name 'aleph, the Phoenician word for "ox," which begins with a glottal stop (represented in modern transliteration by ').

Greek – The Greeks did not have a glottal stop sound in their language, so when they borrowed and adapted the Phoenician alphabet they used 'aleph to represent the sound of the vowel "a," a sound it still represents. The Greeks altered the shape of the letter and changed its name to alpha to conform to the phonetic rules of their language.

Roman – The Romans borrowed the alphabet from the Greeks via the Etruscans and adapted it for carving Latin in stone. This monumental script, as it is called, became the basis for modern printed capital letters.

Medieval – By medieval times – around 1,200 years ago – the Roman monumental capitals had become adapted to being relatively quickly written on paper, parchment, or vellum. The cursive minuscule alphabet became the basis of modern printed lower-case letters.

Modern – Since the invention of printing about 500 years ago many modifications have been made in the shapes and styles of the letter A, but its basic form has remained unchanged.

---

a or **A** (ā) *n., pl.* **a's** or **A's. 1.** The first letter of the English alphabet. **2. A** The best or highest grade, as in school. **3. A** *Mus.* The sixth tone in the scale of C major.

a (ə; ā *when stressed*) *indefinite article.* Also before a vowel **an** (ən; ăn *when stressed*). **1.** —Used as a determiner before a noun to make it stand for any individual in the class named by the word: *a dog; an apple. She was a Stanhope before her marriage.* It functions in the same way with plural forms modified by *few, good many,* or *great many: a few cats; a good many apples; a great many rules.* It is also placed before number collectives like *dozen, hundred,* etc.: *a dozen eggs; a hundred dollars.* **2.** —Used as an equivalent of other determiners: **a.** One: *I didn't say a word.* **b.** Any; each: *A mad dog must be destroyed.* **c.** One like another: *He is a Churchill in eloquence and leadership.* **d.** A certain: *A Mr. Whipple wishes to speak to you.* **e.** The same: *Birds of a feather flock together. Chopin composed many pieces of a type.* **3.** —Used to mean: **a.** A particular example of a (named class): *Champagne is a very fine wine.* **b.** Some kind of: *Copper is a metal.* **c.** A certain amount of; some: *He heard a faint crying in the nursery.* **d.** A work by: *At the museum yesterday they sold a Cézanne.* **4.** —Used in combination with certain determiners such as *what, quite, rather, such,* and *many* as an intensifying unit: *What a fine party. I've never seen such a lovely room. She is quite an athlete. He is rather a smart fellow. Many a man will spring to the defense of his country.* **5.** —Used as a preposition meaning "in each" or "per": *once a month; two dollars a gallon.* [Middle English, from Old English *ān,* one.]

   Usage: a, an. 1. Use *a* before a word or abbreviation beginning with a consonant sound: *a B.A. degree; a closet; a human being; a one; a usage glossary; a U.S. congressman.* Use *an* before a word or abbreviation beginning with a vowel sound: *an A.B. degree; an isometric exercise; an F.C.C. regulation; an hour; an honorary degree; an apricot; an heir.* Both *a* and *an* are possible before words with *h* in an unaccented first syllable: *heroic, hilarious, historic, historical, historian, hotel,* and *hypothesis,* for example. In this case, *a* is more frequently used in writing while *an* is the more usual choice in speech. When numbers are used in a sentence, treat them as written-out words and make your choice of *a* or *an* according to the rules above: *a 40-hour week* (*a* before *forty*), *an 8-hour day* (*an* before *eight*). **2.** *A* and *an* should be omitted from these common constructions because their inclusion is redundant: *no such (a) thing; took half (a) day.*

a-¹. A prefix meaning without, not, or opposite to: **amoral, aseptic.** [Greek *a-, an-,* not.]

a-². A prefix meaning: **1.** On or in the direction of or toward: **aboard. 2.** In the act of or on the way to: **a-singing, a-going.** [Middle English, from Old English, *an,* in, at, on.]

a-³. A prefix meaning: **1.** Up, out, or away: **awake. 2.** Intensified action: **abide.** [Middle English, from Old English *ā-,* out, up.]

a-⁴. A prefix meaning of or from: **anew, afresh.** [Middle English *a-, o-,* reduced form of OF.]

aard·vark (ärd'värk') *n.* A burrowing mammal, *Orycteropus afer,* of southern Africa, that has a stocky, hairy body, large ears, a long, tubular snout, and powerful digging claws. [Obs. Afrikaans : Dutch *aarde,* earth + *vark,* pig.]

aardvark

ab-. A prefix meaning away from, from: **abnormal.** [Latin, from *ab,* away from.]

ab·a·ca (ăb'ə-kä') *n.* A Philippine plant, *Musa textilis,* related to the banana. Its leafstalks are the source of Manila hemp. [Spanish *abacá,* from Tagalog *abaká.*]

a·back (ə-băk') *adv.* —**taken aback.** Surprised or stopped by something startling or disagreeable.

ab·a·cus (ăb'ə-kəs) *n.* **1.** A manual counting and computing device consisting of a frame holding parallel rods strung with movable beads. **2.** A slab on the top of a column. [Latin *abacus,* from Greek *abax,* slab, orig. a drawing board covered with dust, from Hebrew *'ābhāq,* dust.]

a·baft (ə-băft') *adv.* Toward the stern: *It was fast sailing with the wind abaft.* —*prep.* Toward the stern from. [Middle English *o(n) baft* : on, at + *baft,* behind, from Old English *beæftan.*]

ab·a·lo·ne (ăb'ə-lō'nē) *n.* Any of the various large, edible saltwater gastropods of the genus *Haliotis,* having an ear-shaped shell with a row of holes and a brightly colored iridescent lining. [American Spanish *abulón.*]

| ă pat | ā pay | â care | ä father | ĕ pet | ē be | hw which | ĭ pit | ī tie | î pier | ŏ pot | ō toe | ô paw, for | oi noise |
| ōō took | ōō boot | ou out | th thin | th this | ŭ cut | | û urge | zh vision | ə about, item, edible, gallop, circus |

a·ban·don (ə-băn′dən) *tr.v.* **1.** To leave and stop looking after; desert: *abandon one's family.* **2.** To cease to use or occupy and leave behind: *abandon ship; abandon a farm and move to the city.* **3.** To give up; cease work on: *abandon a project.* **4.** To give up completely: *abandon all hope.* **5.** To yield (oneself) to an impulse or emotion: *abandon themselves to despair.* —*n.* Relaxed or reckless carelessness: *The soldier rode with the skillful abandon of a cowboy.* [Middle English *abandounen,* from Old French *abandoner,* from *a bandon,* "in one's power."] —**a·ban′don·er** *n.* —**a·ban′don·ment** *n.*

   Syns: 1. abandon, desert, forsake, leave, quit, throw over *v.* *Core meaning:* To give up without intending to return or claim again (*abandoned his family*). **2. abandon, desist, discontinue, give up, lay off** (*Slang*), **quit, renounce, stop** *v.* *Core meaning:* To cease trying to accomplish or continue (*abandoned her studies*).

a·ban·doned (ə-băn′dənd) *adj.* **1.** Deserted or given up; derelict: *an abandoned house.* **2.** Recklessly unrestrained: *an abandoned life of luxury.*

a·base (ə-bās′) *tr.v.* **a·based, a·bas·ing.** To lower in rank, prestige, or esteem; to humble; humiliate. [Middle English *abassen,* from Old French *abaissier* : Late Latin *ad-,* to + *bassus,* low.] —**a·base′ment** *n.*

a·bash (ə-băsh′) *tr.v.* To make ashamed or uneasy; disconcert. [Middle English *abaisen,* to gape with surprise, from Old French *e(s)bahir.*] —**a·bash′ment** *n.*

a·bate (ə-bāt′) *v.* **a·bat·ed, a·bat·ing.** —*tr.v.* To reduce in amount, degree, or intensity; lessen: *The racehorse did not abate his speed.* —*intr.v.* To subside: *The storm abated.* —See Syns at **decrease.** [Middle English *abaten,* from Old French *abattre,* to beat down : Latin *ad-,* at, to + *battuere,* to beat.] —**a·bat′a·ble** *adj.* —**a·bate′ment** *n.* —**a·bat′er** *n.*

ab·at·toir (ăb′ə-twär′) *n.* A slaughterhouse. [French, from *abattre,* to beat down, abate.]

ab·ba·cy (ăb′ə-sē) *n., pl.* **-cies.** The office, term, or jurisdiction of an abbot.

ab·bé (ăb′ā′, ă-bā′) *n. French.* A title orig. given to the superior of an abbey, now applied to any ecclesiastic.

ab·bess (ăb′ĭs) *n.* A nun who is the head of a convent.

ab·bey (ăb′ē) *n., pl.* **-beys. 1.** A monastery or convent. **2.** A church that once belonged to a monastery.

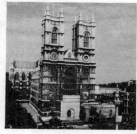

abbey   Aberdeen Angus

ab·bot (ăb′ət) *n.* The superior of a monastery. [Middle English *abbod,* from Old French, from Latin *abbās,* from Greek, from Aramaic *abba,* father.]

ab·bre·vi·ate (ə-brē′vē-āt′) *tr.v.* **-at·ed, -at·ing.** To shorten (a word or phrase) by leaving out some of the letters. [Middle English *abbreviaten,* from Late Latin *abbreviāre* : Latin *ad-,* toward + *brevis,* short.] —**ab·bre′vi·a·tor** *n.*

ab·bre·vi·a·tion (ə-brē′vē-ā′shən) *n.* **1.** The act or product of abbreviating. **2.** A shortened form of a word or phrase; for example, *Mass.* for *Massachusetts.*

ABC (ā′bē-sē′) *n., pl.* **ABC's. 1.** Often **ABC's.** The alphabet. **2. ABC's.** The rudiments of reading and writing. **3.** The basic facts of a subject: *the ABC of chemistry.*

ab·di·cate (ăb′dĭ-kāt′) *v.* **-cat·ed, -cat·ing.** —*tr.v.* To relinquish (power or responsibility) formally: *abdicate the throne.* —*intr.v.* To relinquish formally high office or responsibility: *Queen Juliana abdicated in 1980.* [Latin *abdicāre,* to disclaim : *ab-,* away from + *dicāre,* to proclaim.] —**ab′di·ca′tion** *n.* —**ab′di·ca′tor** *n.*

ab·do·men (ăb′də-mən, ăb-dō′mən) *n.* **1.** The part of the body in human beings and other mammals that lies between the thorax and the pelvis and encloses the digestive organs; belly. **2.** In arthropods, the major part of the body behind the thorax. [Latin *abdōmen,* belly.] —**ab·dom′i·nal** (-dŏm′ə-nəl) *adj.* —**ab·dom′i·nal·ly** *adv.*

ab·duct (ăb-dŭkt′) *tr.v.* **1.** To carry off by force; kidnap. **2.** *Anat.* **a.** To draw (a part of the body) away from a position near or parallel to the median line of the body. **b.** To separate (similar parts). [From Latin *abdūcere* : *ab-,* away + *dūcere,* to lead.] —**ab·duc′tion** *n.* —**ab·duc′tor** *n.*

a·beam (ə-bēm′) *adv.* At right angles to the keel of a ship.

a·bed (ə-běd′) *adv.* In bed: *He lay abed.*

Ab·er·deen An·gus (ăb′ər-dēn′ ăng′gəs). Any of a breed of black, hornless beef cattle that originated in Aberdeen and Angus counties, Scotland.

ab·er·rant (ă-bĕr′ənt, ə-bĕr′-) *adj.* **1.** Deviating from the proper or expected course. **2.** Deviating from what is normal; untrue to type; atypical.

ab·er·ra·tion (ăb′ə-rā′shən) *n.* **1.** A deviation from the normal, proper, or expected course. **2.** An unsound mental state; a mental lapse. **3.** *Optics.* A defect of focus, as blurring or distortion, in an image. **4.** An apparent change in the position of a celestial object as the motion of the earth changes the position of the observer and the distance that the light from the object must travel to reach the observer. [Latin *aberrātiō,* diversion, from *aberrāre,* to go astray : *ab-,* from + *errāre,* to stray.]

a·bet (ə-bĕt′) *tr.v.* **a·bet·ted, a·bet·ting.** To encourage or help, esp. in doing something wrong. [Middle English *abetten,* from Old French *abeter,* to entice.] —**a·bet′ment** *n.* —**a·bet′tor** or **a·bet′ter** *n.*

a·bey·ance (ə-bā′əns) *n.* **1.** The condition of being temporarily set aside; suspension: *hold a matter in abeyance until a later date.* **2.** *Law.* A condition of undetermined ownership, as of an estate without a legal heir. [From Old French *abeance,* desire, from *abaer,* to yearn for.]

ab·hor (ăb-hôr′) *tr.v.* **a·bhorred, -hor·ring.** To regard with horror or loathing; detest: *abhor violence in all forms.* —See Syns at **despise.** [Middle English *abhorren,* from Latin *abhorrēre,* to shrink from : *ab-,* from + *horrēre,* to shudder.] —**ab·hor′rer** *n.*

ab·hor·rent (ăb-hôr′ənt, -hŏr′-) *adj.* **1.** Horrible; hateful; repellent. **2.** Feeling repugnance or loathing. **3.** In opposition. —**ab·hor′rence** *n.* —**ab·hor′rent·ly** *adv.*

a·bide (ə-bīd′) *v.* **a·bode** (ə-bōd′) or **a·bid·ed, a·bid·ing.** —*tr.v.* **1.** To wait patiently for; await. **2.** To put up with; tolerate: *abide the pain.* —*intr.v* **1.** To remain in one place or state; to stay. **2.** To continue; endure. **3.** To reside or dwell. —*phrasal verb.* **abide by.** To conform to; comply with: *abide by an agreement.* [Middle English *abiden,* Old English *ābīdan* : A-³ + *bīdan,* to remain, await.] —**a·bid′ance** *n.* —**a·bid′er** *n.*

a·bid·ing (ə-bī′dĭng) *adj.* Long-lasting; enduring: *abiding love; abiding faith.* —**a·bid′ing·ly** *adv.*

a·bil·i·ty (ə-bĭl′ĭ-tē) *n., pl.* **-ties. 1.** The power to do something: *the ability to speak.* **2.** A natural or acquired skill or talent: *a person of great musical ability.* [Middle English *abilite,* from Old French *habilite,* from Latin *habilis,* able.]

   Syns: 1. ability, capability, competence, faculty, might *n.* *Core meaning:* Physical or mental power to perform (*had the ability to learn math*). **2. ability, command, craft, expertise, knack, know-how** (*Informal*), **mastery, skill** *n.* *Core meaning:* Natural or acquired facility in an activity (*has fine technical ability*).

-ability or **-ibility.** A suffix meaning capable of or causing: *availability.* [Middle English *-abilite, -ibilite,* from Old French from Latin *-abilitas, -ibilitas.*]

ab·ject (ăb′jĕkt′, ăb-jĕkt′) *adj.* **1.** Lacking all self-respect; servile: *an abject coward; abject surrender.* **2.** Of the most miserable kind; wretched: *abject poverty.* [Middle English, from Latin *abjicere,* to cast away : *ab-,* away from + *jacere,* to throw.] —**ab′ject′ly** *adv.* —**ab·jec′tion** *n.*

ab·jure (ăb-jŏŏr′) *tr.v.* **-jured, -jur·ing. 1.** To recant solemnly; repudiate: *abjure one's beliefs.* **2.** To renounce under oath; forswear. [Middle English *abjuren,* from Old French *abjurer,* from Latin *abjūrāre* : *ab-,* away + *jūrāre,* to swear.] —**ab′ju·ra′tion** *n.* —**ab·jur′er** *n.*

ab·la·tion (ă-blā′shən) *n.* **1.** *Med.* Surgical excision or amputation of any part of the body. **2.** *Aerospace.* The removal of the heat shield of a spacecraft or missile by melting or vaporization caused by atmospheric friction. [Latin *ablātiō*, from *ablātus*, removed.]

ab·la·tive (ăb′lə-tĭv) *adj.* Designating a grammatical case indicating separation, direction away from, and sometimes manner or agency, found in some Indo-European languages. —*n.* **1.** The ablative case. **2.** A word in the ablative case. [Middle English, from Old French *ablatif*, from Latin *ablātīvus*, from *ablātus*, removed, past part. of *auferre*, to carry away.]

a·blaze (ə-blāz′) *adj.* **1.** On fire; in flames; blazing: *The tent was ablaze.* **2.** Radiant with bright color.

a·ble (ā′bəl) *adj.* **a·bler**, **a·blest**. **1.** Having the skill, power, or resources to do something: *She is able to drive.* **2.** Capable; talented; skillful: *He is an extremely able worker.* [Middle English, from Old French, from Latin *habilis*, manageable, from *habēre*, to hold, handle.] —**a′bly** *adv.*

–able or **–ible.** A suffix used to form adjectives meaning: **1.** Susceptible, capable, or worthy of (the action of a verb or implied verb): **debatable, collapsible. 2.** Inclined to (the nature of a noun or implied noun): **knowledgeable, fashionable.** [Middle English, from Old French, from Latin *-ābilis, -ībilis*.]

a·ble-bod·ied (ā′bəl-bŏd′ēd) *adj.* Strong and healthy.

able-bodied seaman. A merchant seaman certified for all seaman's duties. Also called **able seaman.**

a·bloom (ə-bloom′) *adj.* In bloom; flowering.

ab·lu·tion (ə-bloo′shən) *n.* A washing or cleansing of the body, esp. as part of a religious ceremony. [Middle English, from Latin *ablūtiō*, from *abluere*, to wash away : *ab-*, away from + *luere*, to wash.]

ab·ne·gate (ăb′nĭ-gāt′) *tr.v.* **-gat·ed, -gat·ing.** To deny to oneself; renounce. [Latin *abnegāre*, to refuse : *ab-*, away from + *negāre*, to deny.] —**ab′ne·ga′tion** *n.*

ab·nor·mal (ăb-nôr′məl) *adj.* Not normal; irregular; deviant.

ab·nor·mal·i·ty (ăb′nôr-măl′ĭ-tē) *n., pl.* **-ties. 1.** The condition of not being normal. **2.** Something that is not normal.

a·board (ə-bôrd′, ə-bōrd′) *adv.* On, onto, or inside a ship, train, airplane, etc.: *All aboard!* —*prep.* On board of; onto; in: *life aboard ship.*

a·bode (ə-bōd′) *v.* A past tense and past participle of **abide.** —*n.* A dwelling place; home. [Middle English *abood*, from Old English *abād*.]

a·bol·ish (ə-bŏl′ĭsh) *tr.v.* To do away with; put an end to: *We must abolish sexism.* [Middle English *abolysshen*, from Old French *abolire*, from Latin *abolēre*, to destroy.] —**a·bol′ish·a·ble** *adj.* —**a·bol′ish·er** *n.* —**a·bol′ish·ment** *n.*

ab·o·li·tion (ăb′ə-lĭsh′ən) *n.* **1.** An act of abolishing or the condition of being abolished. **2.** The prohibition of slavery in the United States. —**ab′o·li′tion·ar′y** *adj.*

ab·o·li·tion·ism (ăb′ə-lĭsh′ə-nĭz′əm) *n.* Advocacy of the abolition of slavery. —**ab′o·li′tion·ist** *n.*

ab·o·ma·sum (ăb′ō-mā′səm) *n., pl.* **-sa** (-sə). The fourth division of the stomach in ruminant animals, such as camels or cows, in which true digestion takes place. [AB- + OMASUM.] —**ab′o·ma′sal** *adj.*

A-bomb (ā′bŏm′) *n.* Another name for an **atomic bomb.**

a·bom·i·na·ble (ə-bŏm′ə-nə-bəl) *adj.* **1.** Outrageously bad; loathsome: *an abominable crime.* **2.** Thoroughly unpleasant: *abominable weather.* —See Syns at **unspeakable.** —**a·bom′i·na·bly** *adv.*

abominable snowman. A large, hairy manlike or apelike creature that supposedly lives on the snow-covered heights of the Himalayas. Also called **yeti.**

a·bom·i·nate (ə-bŏm′ə-nāt′) *tr.v.* **-nat·ed, -nat·ing.** To regard as outrageously bad; detest; abhor. —See Syns at **hate.** [From Latin *abōminārī*, "to shun as a bad omen" : *ab-*, away from + *ōmen*, omen.] —**a·bom′i·na′tor** *n.*

a·bom·i·na·tion (ə-bŏm′ə-nā′shən) *n.* **1.** A repugnance for someone or something; loathing. **2.** Something that produces great dislike or repugnance.

a·bo·rig·i·nal (ăb′ə-rĭj′ə-nəl) *adj.* **1.** Native; indigenous: *aboriginal peoples.* **2.** Of or pertaining to an aborigine or aborigines: *aboriginal customs.* —*n.* An aborigine. —**ab′o·rig′i·nal·ly** *adv.*

a·bo·rig·i·ne (ăb′ə-rĭj′ə-nē) *n.* Any member of a group of people who are the first known to have lived in a given region. [Latin *Aborīginēs*, pre-Roman tribes, reshaped by

aborigine

folk ety. as if from *ab orīgine*, "from the beginning."]

a·born·ing (ə-bôr′nĭng, -bōr′-) *adv.* While coming into being or getting under way: *The revolution died aborning.*

a·bort (ə-bôrt′) *intr.v.* **1.** To terminate pregnancy prematurely. **2.** To cease growth before full development. **3.** To terminate an operation or procedure before completion: *The missile launching aborted at 10 a.m.* —*tr.v.* **1.** To cause to terminate pregnancy prematurely. **2.** To conclude prematurely: *The pilot aborted the landing.* [Latin *abortus*, past part. of *aborīrī*, to miscarry : *ab-*, off, away + *orīrī*, to be born.]

a·bor·tion (ə-bôr′shən) *n.* **1.** Induced termination of pregnancy before the embryo or fetus is capable of survival. **2.** Any fatally premature expulsion of an embryo or fetus from the uterus; miscarriage. **3. a.** Any abnormal failure to grow or develop. **b.** The result of such a failure.

a·bor·tive (ə-bôr′tĭv) *adj.* Failing to accomplish an intended objective; fruitless: *an abortive revolution.* —**a·bor′tive·ly** *adv.* —**a·bor′tive·ness** *n.*

a·bound (ə-bound′) *intr.v.* **1.** To be great in number or amount: *Wildlife abounds in the area.* **2.** To be fully supplied; teem: *The area abounds with plants.* [Middle English *abounden*, from Old French *abonder*, from Latin *abundāre*, to overflow : *ab-*, from + *unda*, wave.]

a·bout (ə-bout′) *prep.* **1.** Concerning: *stories about animals.* **2.** In the nature of: *something odd about his accent.* **3.** In connection with or in reference to: *what Indian rituals really were about.* **4.** In the matter of: *careful about handling broken glass.* **5.** Over or for: *crazy about cowboys.* **6. a.** On the point of. Followed by the infinitive with *to*: *about to go.* **b.** *Informal.* Anywhere near intending: *I'm not about to do anything he asks.* **7.** Near in time: *about noon.* Also used adverbially: *about ready to start.* **8.** All around: *Look about you for a good campsite.* Also used adverbially: *looking about for a hiding place.* **9.** Around in: *a bear prowling about the woods.* **10.** In the possession of: *He has his wits about him.* —*adv.* **1.** Approximately; roughly: *about two days.* **2.** To and fro: *Great waves tossed the ship about.* **3.** Around so as to face in the reverse direction: *Instantly the shark whipped about.* [Middle English *about*, from Old English *abūtan, onbūtan* : *on*, at + *būtan*, outside of.]

a·bout-face (ə-bout′fās′, ə-bout′fās′) *n.* **1.** The act of pivoting the body to face in the opposite direction from the original, esp. in military marching drills. **2.** A total change of attitude or standpoint: *The candidate did an about-face.* —*intr.v.* **-faced, -fac·ing.** To reverse direction.

a·bove (ə-bŭv′) *adv.* **1.** In or to a higher place or position. **2.** In an earlier part of a text: *figures quoted above.* —*prep.* **1.** Over or higher than: *seagulls hovering just above the waves.* **2.** Upstream or uphill from: *The road is snowed in above this point.* **3.** Superior to in rank or quality: *The President is above all military officers.* **4.** In excess of; over: *Last week's spending was above normal.* —*adj.* Appearing or stated earlier: *the above figures.* —**idioms. above all.** First of all; most important. [Middle English *aboven*, from Old English *abufan* : *a-*, on + *bufan*, above.]

a·bove·board (ə-bŭv′bôrd′, -bōrd′) *adv. & adj.* Without deceit or trickery; open. [Orig. "above the gambling table, not changing cards under the table."]

ab·ra·ca·dab·ra (ăb′rə-kə-dăb′rə) *n.* **1.** A word once held to possess magical powers to ward off disease or disaster.

ă pat	ā pay	â care	ä father	ĕ pet	ē be	hw which
ŏŏ took	ōō boot	ou out	th thin	*th* this	ŭ cut	
ĭ pit	ī tie	î pier	ŏ pot	ō toe	ô paw, for	oi noise
û urge	zh vision	ə about, item, edible, gallop, circus				

2. Jargon; gibberish. [Late Latin, from Late Greek *abrasadabra*, a magic word used by an ancient religious sect.]

a·brade (ə-brād′) *tr.v.* **a·brad·ed, a·brad·ing.** To rub off or wear away by friction; erode. [Latin *abrādere*, to scrape off : *ab-*, off + *rādere*, to scrape.]

a·bra·sion (ə-brā′zhən) *n.* **1.** The process of wearing down or rubbing away by means of friction. **2.** A scraped or worn area: *a skin abrasion.*

a·bra·sive (ə-brā′sĭv, -sĭv) *adj.* **1.** Causing abrasion. **2.** Causing friction or resentment in people: *an abrasive personality.* —*n.* A substance that abrades.

a·breast (ə-brĕst′) *adv. & adj.* **1.** Standing or advancing side by side: *They lined up four abreast.* **2.** Up to date with: *keeping abreast of the latest fashions.*

a·bridge (ə-brĭj′) *tr.v.* **a·bridged, a·bridg·ing. 1.** To reduce the length of; condense: *abridge a novel.* **2.** To limit; curtail: *"The right of citizens of the United States to vote shall not be denied or abridged . . . on account of sex."* (U.S. Constitution, 19th Amendment). [Middle English *abregen*, from Old French *abregier*, from Late Latin *abbreviāre*, to abbreviate.] —**a·bridg′er** *n.*

a·bridg·ment (ə-brĭj′mənt) *n.* Also **a·bridge·ment. 1.** The act of abridging or the condition of being abridged. **2.** An abridged version or condensation of a book, article, etc.

a·broad (ə-brôd′) *adv. & adj.* **1.** In or to foreign places: *going abroad.* **2.** Broadly or widely: *scattering seeds abroad.* **3.** Outdoors and about: *people abroad in spite of the downpour.* **4.** In circulation: *a nasty rumor abroad.*

ab·ro·gate (ăb′rə-gāt′) *tr.v.* **-gat·ed, -gat·ing.** To abolish by authority: *abrogate a treaty.* [From Latin *abrogāre* : *ab-*, away + *rogāre*, to ask, propose.] —**ab′ro·ga′tion** *n.*

a·brupt (ə-brŭpt′) *adj.* **1.** Unexpectedly sudden: *an abrupt turn.* **2.** Curt; brusque: *an abrupt reply.* **3.** Touching on one subject after another with sudden transitions: *abrupt, nervous speech.* **4.** Very steep: *an abrupt cliff.* [Latin *abruptus,* past part. of *abrumpere,* to break off : *ab-,* off + *rumpere,* to break.] —**a·brupt′ly** *adv.* —**a·brupt′ness** *n.*

ab·scess (ăb′sĕs′) *n.* A collection of pus in any part of the body, caused by infection and surrounded by an inflamed area. —*intr.v.* To form an abscess. [Latin *abscēssus,* departure, from *abscēdere,* to go away : *abs-, ab-,* away from + *cēdere,* to go.]

ab·scis·sa (ăb-sĭs′ə) *n., pl.* **-sas** or **-scis·sae** (-sĭs′ē). The coordinate representing the distance of a point from the *y*-axis in a plane Cartesian coordinate system, measured along a line parallel to the *x*-axis. [New Latin *(linea) abscissa,* "cut-off (line)," from Latin *abscindere,* to cut off : *abs-, ab-,* away + *caedere,* to cut.]

ab·scond (ăb-skŏnd′) *intr.v.* To leave quickly and secretly and hide oneself, esp. to avoid arrest: *The cashier had absconded with the money.* [Latin *abscondere* : *abs-, ab-,* away + *condere,* to hide.]

ab·sence (ăb′səns) *n.* **1.** The state of being away: *took over in his absence.* **2.** The time during which one is away: *an absence of four days.* **3.** Lack: *an absence of curiosity.*

ab·sent (ăb′sənt) *adj.* **1.** Missing or not present. **2.** Not existent; lacking. **3.** Absorbed in thought: *an absent look on his face.* —*tr.v.* (ăb-sĕnt′). To keep (oneself) away: *He absented himself from work.* [Middle English, from Old French, from Latin *absēns,* pres. part. of *abesse,* to be away : *ab-,* away from + *esse,* to be.] —**ab′sent·ly** *adv.*

ab·sen·tee (ăb′sən-tē′) *n.* A person who is absent, as from work.

ab·sen·tee·ism (ăb′sən-tē′ĭz′əm) *n.* Habitual failure to appear, esp. for work or other regular duty.

ab·sent-mind·ed (ăb′sənt-mīn′dĭd) *adj.* Lost in thought; preoccupied. —**ab′sent-mind′ed·ly** *adv.* —**ab′sent-mind′ed·ness** *n.*

ab·sinthe (ăb′sĭnth) *n.* Also **ab·sinth.** A strong green alcoholic liqueur flavored with wormwood. [French, from Latin *absinthium,* wormwood, from Greek *apsinthion.*]

ab·so·lute (ăb′sə-loot′) *adj.* **1.** Perfect in quality or nature; complete. **2.** Not mixed; pure; unadulterated: *absolute alcohol.* **3. a.** Not limited by restrictions or exceptions; unconditional: *He has my absolute confidence.* **b.** Unqualified in extent or degree; total: *absolute silence.* **4.** Not limited by constitutional provisions or other restraints: *absolute monarchy; absolute freedom.* **5.** Unrelated to and independent of anything else: *The judge*

evaluated the absolute merits of the case. **6.** Not to be doubted or questioned; positive; certain: *absolute proof.* **7.** *Gram.* **a.** Denoting a construction in a sentence that is syntactically independent of the main clause. For example, in *Their ship having sailed, we went home, Their ship having sailed* is an absolute phrase. **b.** Pertaining to a transitive verb when its object is implied but not stated. For example, *inspires* in *We have a teacher who inspires.* **c.** Pertaining to an adjective or pronoun that stands alone, the noun it modifies being implied but not stated; for example, *Theirs* and *best* in *Theirs were the best.* **8.** *Physics.* **a.** Pertaining to measurements or units of measurement derived from fundamental relationships of space, mass, and time. **b.** Pertaining to absolute temperature. —*n.* Something that is absolute. [Middle English *absolut,* from Latin *absolvere,* , to free from : *ab-,* away from + *solvere,* to loose.] —**ab′so·lute′ness** *n.*

Syns: absolute, despotic, dictatorial, totalitarian, tyrannical *adj.* **Core meaning:** Having supreme, unlimited power and control (*an absolute ruler*).

ab·so·lute·ly (ăb′sə-loot′lē, ăb′sə-loot′lē) *adv.* **1.** Completely; perfectly: *absolutely essential; absolutely certain; stand absolutely still.* **2.** Without reservation or qualification; positively: *do absolutely nothing; get absolutely nowhere; absolutely refuse to answer.*

absolute pitch. 1. The precise pitch of a tone, as established by its rate of vibration measured on a standard scale. **2.** The ability to identify the pitch of any tone heard or to reproduce a tone without reference to another previously sounded. Also called **perfect pitch.**

absolute temperature. Temperature measured or calculated with absolute zero as the reference.

absolute value. 1. The numerical value or magnitude of a real number without regard to its sign. **2.** The positive square root of the sum of the squares of the real and imaginary parts of a complex number.

absolute zero. The temperature at which a substance contains no thermal energy, equal to $-273.15°C$ or $-459.67°F$.

ab·so·lu·tion (ăb′sə-loo′shən) *n.* **1.** The formal release from sin, esp. as given by a priest as part of the sacrament of penance. **2.** Forgiveness.

ab·so·lut·ism (ăb′sə-loo′tĭz′əm) *n.* A form of government in which all power is vested in the monarch; despotism. —**ab′so·lut′ist** *n. & adj.* —**ab′so·lut·is′tic** *adj.*

ab·solve (ăb-zŏlv′, -sŏlv′) *tr.v.* **-solved, -solv·ing. 1.** To clear of blame or guilt. **2.** To relieve of a requirement or obligation. **3.** To give absolution to. —See Syns at **vindicate.** [Middle English *absolven,* from Latin *absolvere,* to free from : *ab-,* away from + *solvere,* to loose, free.] —**ab·solv′a·ble** *adj.* —**ab·solv′er** *n.*

ab·sorb (ăb-sôrb′, -zôrb′) *tr.v.* **1.** To take in; soak up: *A sponge absorbs moisture.* **2.** To take in and assimilate: *Plants absorb energy from the sun.* **3.** To take in or receive (sound or other flow of energy) with little or none of it being transmitted or reflected: *Thick rugs absorb sound.* **4.** To occupy completely; take up entirely: *The work absorbs all of my time.* [Old French *absorber,* from Latin *absorbēre,* from *ab-,* away from + *sorbēre,* to suck.] —**ab·sorb′a·bil′i·ty** *n.* —**ab·sorb′a·ble** *adj.* —**ab·sorb′er** *n.*

ab·sorbed (ăb-sôrbd′, -zôrbd′) *adj.* **1.** Engrossed: *an absorbed audience.* **2.** Sucked up or in. **3.** Assimilated. —**ab·sorb′ed·ly** (-sôr′bĭd-lē, -zôr′-) *adv.*

ab·sorb·ent (ăb-sôr′bənt, -zôr′-) *adj.* Capable of absorbing something: *absorbent cotton.* —*n.* A substance having this capability. —**ab·sorb′en·cy** *n.*

ab·sorb·ing (ăb-sôr′bĭng, -zôr′-) *adj.* Holding one's interest or attention; engrossing: *an absorbing novel.*

ab·sorp·tion (ăb-sôrp′shən, -zôrp′-) *n.* **1.** The act or process of absorbing. **2.** A state of mental concentration. —**ab·sorp′tive** *adj.*

ab·stain (ăb-stān′) *intr.v.* To keep from doing something voluntarily: *abstain from drinking; abstain from voting.* [Middle English *absteinen,* from Old French *abstenir,* from Latin *abstinēre* : *abs-, ab-,* away from + *tenēre,* to hold.] —**ab·stain′er** *n.*

ab·ste·mi·ous (ăb-stē′mē-əs) *adj.* Sparing, esp. in the use of alcohol or food. [Latin *abstēmius* : *ab-,* away from + *tēmētum,* wine.] —**ab·ste′mi·ous·ly** *adv.* —**ab·ste′mi·ous·ness** *n.*

ă pat	ā pay	â care	ä father	ĕ pet	ē be	hw which	ĭ pit	ī tie	î pier	ŏ pot	ō toe	ô paw, for	oi noise
oo took	oo boot	ou out	th thin	th this	ŭ cut		û urge	zh vision	ə about, item, edible, gallop, circus				

ab·sten·tion (ăb-stĕn′shən) *n.* **1.** The practice of abstaining. **2.** An act of abstaining, esp. the withholding of a vote at an election: *one vote for, two against, and four abstentions.*

ab·sti·nence (ăb′stə-nəns) *n.* **1.** Abstention, esp. from alcoholic beverages. **2.** Abstention from specified foods on certain holy days. **—ab′sti·nent** *adj.*

ab·stract (ăb′străkt′, ăb-străkt′) *adj.* **1.** Considered apart from concrete existence: *A two-dimensional plane is an abstract concept.* **2.** Theoretical rather than practical: *an abstract approach to the problem.* **3.** Difficult to understand: *Your explanation is too abstract for me.* **4.** Expressing a general quality or property thought of separately from the person or thing possessing it: *abstract words like "truth" and "justice."* **5.** In art, concerned with designs or shapes that do not represent any recognizable person or thing: *an abstract painting; an abstract sculpture.* **—n.** (ăb′străkt′). **1.** A statement giving the important points of a text; summary: *an abstract of a speech.* **2.** The concentrated essence of a larger whole. **3.** Something abstract, as a term. **—tr.v.** (ăb-străkt′). **1.** To take away; remove: *processes to abstract metal from ore.* **2.** To remove without permission; filch. **3.** To think of (a quality or attribute) without reference to a particular example or object; consider theoretically. **4.** To summarize: *It was not easy to abstract his article.* **—idiom. in the abstract.** Apart from actual substance or experience: *He tends to formulate his theories in the abstract.* [Middle English, from Latin *abstractus,* drawn away, past part. of *abstrahere,* to remove : *ab-,* away from + *trahere,* to pull.] **—ab·stract′er** *n.*

abstractionism

ab·stract·ed (ăb-străk′tĭd) *adj.* Absent-minded. **—ab·stract′ed·ly** *adv.* **—ab·stract′ed·ness** *n.*

ab·strac·tion (ăb-străk′shən) *n.* **1.** The act or process of removing or separating: *the abstraction of metal from ore.* **2.** An abstract idea: *abstractions difficult to understand.* **3.** Preoccupation; absent-mindedness.

ab·strac·tion·ism (ăb-străk′shə-nĭz′əm) *n.* A style in modern art that is primarily concerned with designs and shapes that do not represent any recognizable person or thing. **—ab·strac′tion·ist** *n. & adj.*

ab·struse (ăb-strōōs′) *adj.* Difficult to understand: *abstruse ideas.* [From Latin *abstrūdere,* to hide : *ab-,* away + *trūdere,* to push.] **—ab·struse′ly** *adv.* **—ab·struse′ness** *n.*

ab·surd (ăb-sûrd′, -zûrd′) *adj.* Contrary to common sense. —See Syns at **foolish.** [French *absurde,* from Latin *absurdus.*] **—ab·surd′ness** *n.* **—ab·surd′ly** *adv.*

ab·surd·i·ty (ăb-sûr′dĭ-tē, -zûr′-) *n., pl.* **-ties. 1.** The condition or quality of being absurd; foolishness. **2.** An absurd action, thing, or idea.

a·bun·dance (ə-bŭn′dəns) *n.* **1.** A great amount or quantity: *an abundance of water.* **2.** Affluence; wealth.

a·bun·dant (ə-bŭn′dənt) *adj.* **1.** In plentiful supply; ample: *abundant rainfall.* **2.** Rich; abounding: *a forest abundant in oak trees.* [Middle English *abundaunt,* from Old French *abundant,* from Latin *abundāns,* pres. part. of *abundāre,* to abound.] **—a·bun′dant·ly** *adv.*

a·buse (ə-byōōz′) *tr.v.* **a·bused, a·bus·ing. 1.** To use wrongly or improperly; to misuse. **2.** To hurt or injure by maltreatment. **3.** To attack with coarse or insulting words; revile. **—n.** (ə-byōōs′). **1.** Misuse: *the abuse of power.* **2.** A corrupt practice or custom: *governmental abuses.* **3.** Maltreatment: *His old truck has taken much abuse.* **4.** Insult-

ing or coarse language. [Middle English *abusen,* from Old French *abuser,* from *abus,* improper use, from Latin *abūtī* to make (improper) use of : *ab-,* away + *ūtī,* to use.] **—a·bus′er** *n.*

Syns: abuse, maltreat, mistreat, misuse *v.* *Core meaning:* To treat or use wrongly. ABUSE, MALTREAT, and MISTREAT all express actions harmful to others (*a child abused by her parents; a man who maltreated his dog; mistreated her daughter*), but ABUSE can also imply doing harm to oneself (*abused my eyes by reading in poor light*). MISUSE is gen. applied to improper use due to ignorance or oversight (*misused our energy resources*).

a·bu·sive (ə-byōō′sĭv) *adj.* **1.** Of, pertaining to, or characterized by abuse: *an abusive dictator.* **2.** Wrongly or incorrectly used or treated: *abusive use of a machine.* **3.** Insulting; reviling: *abusive remarks.* **—a·bu′sive·ly** *adv.* **—a·bu′sive·ness** *n.*

a·but (ə-bŭt′) *v.* **a·but·ted, a·but·ting. —intr.v.** To touch at one end or side of something; lie adjacent: *My house abuts on his property.* **—tr.v.** To border upon. [Middle English *abutten,* from Old French *abuter,* to buttress : *a,* to + *buter,* to strike, finish.] **—a·but′ter** *n.*

a·but·ment (ə-bŭt′mənt) *n.* **1.** The act of abutting. **2. a.** Something that abuts. **b.** That on which something abuts. **c.** The point of contact of two abutting objects or parts; junction. **3.** *Engineering.* **a.** A structure that supports the end of a bridge. **b.** A structure that anchors the cables of a suspension bridge.

a·bysm (ə-bĭz′əm) *n.* An abyss. [Middle English *abisme,* from Old French, from Late Latin *abyssus.*]

a·bys·mal (ə-bĭz′məl) *adj.* **1.** Immeasurably great; profound: *abysmal ignorance.* **2.** Of or resembling an abyss. **—a·bys′mal·ly** *adv.*

a·byss (ə-bĭs′) *n.* **1. a.** The primeval chaos. **b.** The bottomless pit; hell. **2.** An unfathomable chasm or any immeasurably profound abyss or void: *the vast abysses of space and time.* [Late Latin *abyssus,* from Greek *abussos,* bottomless : *a-,* not + *bussos,* bottom.]

Ac The symbol for the element actinium.

a·ca·cia (ə-kā′shə) *n.* **1.** Any of various chiefly tropical trees of the genus *Acacia,* with feathery leaves and tight clusters of small yellow or white flowers. Some species yield gums that have a wide variety of uses. **2.** Any of several related trees, such as the locust. **3. Gum arabic.** [Latin, from Greek *akakia,* prob. from Egyptian.]

ac·a·deme (ăk′ə-dēm′) *n.* **1.** Often **Academe.** The world of scholarship and higher education; the scholastic life or environment. **2.** A scholar, teacher, or pedant. [From Greek *Akadēmia,* academy.]

ac·a·dem·ic (ăk′ə-dĕm′ĭk) *adj.* **1.** Of or pertaining to a school or college: *an academic degree.* **2.** Liberal or classical rather than technical or vocational: *academic studies.* **3.** Formalistic; conventional. **4.** Theoretical; speculative: *"I took an academic interest in the thought of stealing the car"* (John Knowles). **—ac′a·dem′i·cal·ly** *adv.*

academic freedom. Liberty to pursue and teach relevant knowledge and to discuss it freely without interference.

ac·a·de·mi·cian (ăk′ə-də-mĭsh′ən, ə-kăd′ə-) *n.* A member of an academy or society of learned men, artists, etc.

a·cad·e·my (ə-kăd′ə-mē) *n., pl.* **-mies. 1.** A school for special instruction. **2.** A secondary or college-preparatory school, esp. a private one. **3.** An association of scholars. **4. Academy.** A specified society of scholars or artists. **5. Academy. a.** Platonism. **b.** The disciples of Plato. [Latin *Acadēmia,* from Greek *Akadēmia,* the Platonic school of philosophy, from *Akadēmia,* place in Athens where Plato taught.]

a·can·thus (ə-kăn′thəs) *n.* **1.** Any of various plants of the genus *Acanthus,* native to the Mediterranean region, with large, segmented, thistlelike leaves. **2.** Decoration in the form of such leaves, used esp. on capitals of Corinthian columns. [Greek *akanthos,* thorn plant, from *akantha,* thorn.]

a cap·pel·la (ä′ kə-pĕl′ə). *Mus.* Without instrumental accompaniment. [Italian, "in the manner of the chapel."]

ac·cede (ăk-sēd′) *intr.v.* **-ced·ed, -ced·ing. 1.** To give one's assent; to consent; agree: *I acceded to her request.* **2.** To come into an office or dignity: *He acceded to the presidency.* [Middle English *acceden,* from Latin *accēdere,* to

---

ă pat　　ā pay　　â care　　ä father　　ĕ pet　　ē be　　hw which

ōō took　　ōō boot　　ou out　　th thin　　th this　　ŭ cut

ĭ pit　　ī tie　　î pier　　ŏ pot　　ō toe　　ô paw, for　　oi noise

û urge　　zh vision　　ə about, item, edible, gallop, circus

go near, agree : *ad-*, to + *cēdere*, to go.] —**ac·ced′ence** *n.*

ac·cel·er·an·do (ä-chĕl′ə-rän′dō, äk-sĕl′ə-). *Mus.* —*adj.* Gradually becoming faster. —*adv.* So as to become faster. —*n., pl.* **-dos.** A gradual speeding up. [Italian, "accelerating."]

ac·cel·er·ate (äk-sĕl′ə-rāt′) *v.* **-at·ed, -at·ing.** —*tr.v.* **1.** To increase the speed of; quicken. **2.** To cause to happen sooner than expected; hasten: *measures to accelerate tax reform.* **3.** *Physics.* To cause a change of velocity. —*intr.v.* To move or act faster. —See Syns at **expedite.** [From Latin *accelerāre* : *ad-* (intensive) + *celer*, swift.] —**ac·cel′er·a′tive** *adj.*

ac·cel·er·a·tion (äk-sĕl′ə-rā′shən) *n.* **1.** The act or process of accelerating; an increase in speed. **2.** *Physics.* Symbol **a** The rate at which velocity changes per unit of time.

acceleration of gravity. Symbol **g** The acceleration of freely falling bodies under the influence of terrestrial gravity, equal to 980.665 cm/sec² or approximately 32 ft/sec² at sea level.

ac·cel·er·a·tor (äk-sĕl′ə-rā′tər) *n.* **1.** Someone or something that accelerates. **2.** A mechanical device, esp. the gas pedal of an automobile, for increasing the speed of a machine. **3.** *Chem.* A substance that increases the speed of a chemical reaction. **4.** *Physics.* Any device, such as a cyclotron, that accelerates charged subatomic particles or nuclei to energies useful for research. Also called **particle accelerator** and **atom smasher.**

ac·cel·er·om·e·ter (äk-sĕl′ə-rŏm′ĭ-tər) *n.* An instrument that measures and indicates acceleration.

ac·cent (äk′sĕnt) *n.* **1.** Vocal stress or emphasis given to a particular syllable, word, or phrase. **2.** A style of speech or pronunciation that is typical of a certain region or country: *a southern accent. She speaks with a French accent.* **3.** An **accent mark. 4.** Rhythmically significant stress in a line of verse. **5. a.** Special stress given to a musical note within a phrase. **b.** A mark representing this stress. **6.** *Math.* **a.** A mark, or one of several marks, used as a superscript to distinguish among variables represented by the same symbol. **b.** A mark used as a superscript to indicate the first derivative of a variable. **7.** A mark or one of several marks used as a superscript to indicate a unit, such as feet (′) and inches (″) in linear measurement. **8.** A distinctive feature or quality. —*tr.v.* **1.** To stress in speech or music: *accent the first syllable of a word; accent every third note.* **2.** To mark with a printed accent. **3.** To give prominence to; call attention to; accentuate. [Middle English, from Old French, from Latin *accentus*, accentuation, orig. "song added to (speech)" : *ad-*, to + *canere*, to sing.]

accent mark. 1. A mark used to indicate which syllable or syllables of a word are stressed in pronunciation. **2.** In certain foreign languages, and in English words borrowed from such languages, a mark placed over a letter to indicate a certain feature of pronunciation. For example, in the word *exposé* the final *e* is pronounced ā.

ac·cen·tu·al (äk-sĕn′chōō-əl) *adj.* Of or pertaining to accent. —**ac·cen′tu·al·ly** *adv.*

ac·cen·tu·ate (äk-sĕn′chōō-āt′) *tr.v.* **-at·ed, -at·ing. 1.** To mark or pronounce with a stress or accent. **2.** To give prominence to; emphasize. —**ac·cen′tu·a′tion** *n.*

ac·cept (äk-sĕpt′) *tr.v.* **1.** To receive (something offered) gladly: *accept an award.* **2.** To receive with favor into a place or group: *They've begun to accept him at school.* **3.** To regard as true; believe in: *to accept a theory.* **4.** To bear up under patiently or resignedly: *accept one's fate.* **5. a.** To answer affirmatively: *accept an invitation.* **b.** To take up; assume: *accept an office.* **6.** *Comm.* To consent to pay, as by a signed agreement. —*intr.v.* To receive something willingly. —See Syns at **believe.** [Middle English *accepten*, from Old French *accepter*, from Latin *accipere*, to receive : *ad-*, to + *capere*, to take.]

Usage: **accept, except.** Of these verbs, only *accept* means to receive or admit, to regard as right or true, or to bear up under. *Except*, often misused in the preceding senses, means to leave out, exclude, or excuse.

ac·cept·a·ble (äk-sĕp′tə-bəl) *adj.* Satisfactory; adequate: *an acceptable person for the job; acceptable working conditions.* —**ac·cept′a·bil′i·ty** or **ac·cept′a·ble·ness** *n.* —**ac·cept′a·bly** *adv.*

ac·cep·tance (äk-sĕp′təns) *n.* **1.** The act or process of tak-

ing something offered: *the acceptance of a bribe.* **2.** The condition of being accepted or acceptable: *Many prejudiced people feel insecure about their acceptance by others.* **3.** Favorable reception; approval. **4.** Belief in something; agreement; assent. **5.** *Comm.* **a.** A formal indication by a debtor of willingness to pay a draft or bill of exchange. **b.** An endorsed draft or bill of exchange.

ac·cep·ta·tion (äk′sĕp-tā′shən) *n.* The usual meaning, as of a word or expression.

ac·cep·tor (äk-sĕp′tər) *n.* Also **ac·cept·er.** A person who signs a draft or bill of exchange.

ac·cess (äk′sĕs) *n.* **1.** A means of approaching or nearing; passage: *gain access through the basement.* **2.** The right to enter or make use of: *have access to secret files.* **3.** The condition or quality of being easy to approach or enter: *a city with easy access to the sea.* **4.** A sudden outburst; a fit: *an access of rage.* [Middle English, from Old French *acces*, arrival, from Latin *accēdere*, to arrive : *ad-*, to + *cēdere*, to come.]

ac·ces·sa·ry (äk-sĕs′ə-rē) *n. & adj.* Var. of **accessory.**

ac·ces·si·ble (äk-sĕs′ə-bəl) *adj.* **1.** Easily approached or entered: *The lake is accessible from the highway.* **2.** Easily obtained: *documents accessible to all staff members.* **3.** Open to: *accessible to flattery.* —See Syns at **convenient.** —**ac·ces′si·bil′i·ty** *n.* —**ac·ces′si·bly** *adv.*

ac·ces·sion (äk-sĕsh′ən) *n.* **1.** The attainment of rank or dignity. **2. a.** An increase by means of something added: *an accession of property.* **b.** An addition. **3.** Agreement; assent: *accession to a proposal.* —**ac·ces′sion·al** *adj.*

ac·ces·so·ry (äk-sĕs′ə-rē) *n., pl.* **-ries.** Also **ac·ces·sa·ry. 1.** Something supplementary; an adjunct. **2. a.** Someone who incites, aids, or abets a lawbreaker in the commission of a crime, but is not present at the time of the crime, called an **accessory before the fact. b.** Someone who aids a criminal after the commission of a crime, but was not present at the time of the crime, called an **accessory after the fact.** —*adj.* **1.** Having a subordinate function. **2.** Serving to aid or abet a lawbreaker, either before or after the commission of the crime, without being present at the time the crime was committed. [Middle English *accessorie*, from Medieval Latin *accessōrius*, from Latin *accessus*, access.]

ac·ci·dence (äk′sĭ-dəns, -dĕns′) *n.* The section of grammar that deals with the inflections of words.

ac·ci·dent (äk′sĭ-dənt, -dĕnt′) *n.* **1.** An unexpected and undesirable event; a mishap: *a traffic accident.* **2.** Anything that occurs unexpectedly: *meet by accident.* **3.** Any circumstance or attribute that is not essential to the nature of something. **4.** Fortune; chance: *rich by accident of birth.* **5.** *Geol.* An irregular or unusual natural formation or occurrence. [Middle English, from Old French, from Latin *accidere*, to fall upon, happen : *ad-*, to + *cadere*, to fall.]

ac·ci·den·tal (äk′sĭ-dĕn′tl) *adj.* **1.** Occurring unexpectedly and unintentionally; by chance: *an accidental meeting.* **2.** Part of, but not essential; supplementary; incidental. —*n.* **1.** A factor or attribute that is not essential. **2.** *Mus.* A sharp, flat, or natural that is not in the key signature. —**ac′ci·den′tal·ly** *adv.*

Syns: **accidental, casual, chance, fluky, fortuitous, inadvertent** *adj.* Core meaning: Occurring unexpectedly (*an accidental meeting*).

ac·claim (ə-klām′) *tr.v.* To salute or hail; applaud: *a novel acclaimed by all.* —*n.* Enthusiastic applause, praise, or approval. —See Syns at **praise.** [Latin *acclāmāre*, to shout at : *ad-*, to + *clāmāre*, to shout.] —**ac·claim′er** *n.*

ac·cla·ma·tion (äk′lə-mā′shən) *n.* **1.** A shout or salute of enthusiastic approval, acceptance, or welcome. **2.** An oral vote, esp. a vote of approval taken without formal ballot: *a motion approved by acclamation.* —**ac·clam′a·to′ry** (ə-klăm′ə-tôr′ē, -tōr′ē) *adj.*

ac·cli·mate (ə-klī′mĭt, ăk′lə-māt′) *v.* **-mat·ed, -mat·ing.** —*tr.v.* To accustom (something or someone) to a new environment or situation; adapt. —*intr.v.* To become accustomed to a new environment. [French *acclimater* : *ac-*, to, from Latin *ad-* + *climat*, climate.] —**ac′cli·ma′tion** *n.*

ac·cli·ma·tize (ə-klī′mə-tīz′) *v.* **-tized, -tiz·ing.** —*tr.v.* To acclimate (someone or something). —*intr.v.* To acclimate. —**ac·cli′ma·ti·za′tion** *n.*

ac·cliv·i·ty (ə-klĭv′ĭ-tē) *n., pl.* **-ties.** An upward slope. [Latin *acclīvitās*, from *acclīvis*, uphill : *ad-*, to + *clīvus*, slope.]

ă pat	ā pay	â care	ä father	ĕ pet	ē be	hw which	ĭ pit	ī tie	î pier	ŏ pot	ō toe	ô paw, for	oi noise
ōō took	ōō boot	ou out	th thin	th this	ŭ cut		û urge	zh vision	ə about, item, edible, gallop, circus				

ac·co·lade (ăk'ə-lād', ăk'ə-lād') n. **1.** An embrace of greeting or salutation. **2.** Praise; approval. **3.** A ceremonial tap on the shoulder with the flat of a sword, given when knighthood is granted. [French, from Provençal *acolar,* to embrace : Latin *ad-,* to + *collum,* neck.]

ac·com·mo·date (ə-kŏm'ə-dāt') v. **-dat·ed, -dat·ing.** —*tr.v.* **1.** To do a favor or service for; oblige: *I shall try to accommodate you in this matter.* **2.** To provide for; supply with. **3.** To contain comfortably or have space for: *an airport built to accommodate the largest planes.* **4.** To make suitable; adapt; adjust: *He accommodates himself well to new surroundings.* **5.** To settle; reconcile. —*intr.v.* To become adjusted to, as the eye to focusing on objects at a distance. [From Latin *accommodāre,* to make fit : *ad-,* to + *commodus,* fit, "conforming with the (right) measure."]

ac·com·mo·dat·ing (ə-kŏm'ə-dā'tĭng) adj. Helpful and obliging. —**ac·com'mo·dat'ing·ly** adv.

ac·com·mo·da·tion (ə-kŏm'ə-dā'shən) n. **1.** The act of accommodating or the condition of being accommodated. **2.** Anything that meets a need; a convenience. **3. accommodations. a.** Room and board; lodgings. **b.** A seat, compartment, or room on a public vehicle. **4.** Reconciliation or settlement of opposing views; compromise. **5.** *Physiol.* Adaptation or adjustment by an organism, organ, or part, as by the eye in focusing on objects at different distances.

ac·com·pa·ni·ment (ə-kŭm'pə-nə-mənt, ə-kŭmp'nə-) n. **1.** Anything that supplements something else. **2.** Music played along as support or embellishment.

ac·com·pa·nist (ə-kŭm'pə-nĭst, ə-kŭmp'nĭst) n. A musician who performs an accompaniment.

ac·com·pa·ny (ə-kŭm'pə-nē, ə-kŭmp'nē) v. **-nied, -ny·ing.** —*tr.v.* **1.** To go along with: *He accompanied his sister home.* **2.** To supplement; add to: *The teacher accompanied the lesson with slides.* **3.** To occur or happen with: *Thunder accompanies lightning.* **4.** To perform an accompaniment to. —*intr.v.* To play a musical accompaniment. [Middle English *accompanien,* from Old French *accompagner* : *ac-,* to, from Latin *ad-* + *compan(g),* companion.]

ac·com·plice (ə-kŏm'plĭs) n. One who aids or abets a lawbreaker in a criminal act but is not necessarily present at the time of the crime. [Middle English, from *a complice,* an associate, from Old French *complice,* from Latin *complex,* closely connected.]

ac·com·plish (ə-kŏm'plĭsh) tr.v. To succeed in doing; reach the end of; achieve; complete; finish: *accomplish an assignment.* [Middle English *accomplissen,* from Old French *accomplir,* to complete : Latin *ad-,* to + *complēre,* "to fill up."] —**ac·com'plish·er** n.

   Syns: accomplish, achieve, attain, reach, realize, score *v.* Core meaning: To succeed in doing (*accomplished her objective and won the race*).

ac·com·plished (ə-kŏm'plĭsht) adj. **1.** Completed; finished; done: *an accomplished task.* **2.** Skilled; expert: *an accomplished dancer.* **3.** Sophisticated; polished: *an accomplished hostess.*

ac·com·plish·ment (ə-kŏm'plĭsh-mənt) n. **1.** The act of accomplishing or of being accomplished; completion. **2.** Something completed successfully; an achievement. **3.** Social poise.

ac·cord (ə-kôrd') tr.v. **1.** To make conform or agree; bring into harmony. **2.** To bestow upon; grant: *I accord you my blessing.* —*intr.v.* To be in agreement, unity, or harmony: *His ideas accord with mine.* —*n.* **1.** Agreement; harmony: *His ideas are in accord with mine.* **2.** A settlement or compromise of conflicting opinions, esp. one between nations. —**idiom. of (one's) own accord.** By oneself or itself; without assistance or outside influence: *She made this decision of her own accord.* [Middle English *acorden,* from Old French *acorder* : Latin *ad-,* to + *cor,* heart.]

ac·cor·dance (ə-kôr'dns) n. —**in accordance with.** In agreement with: *act in accordance with the rules.*

ac·cor·dant (ə-kôr'dnt) adj. In agreement or harmony; corresponding; consonant. —**ac·cord'ant·ly** adv.

ac·cord·ing·ly (ə-kôr'dĭng-lē) adv. **1.** In keeping with what is known, stated, or expected: *Learn the rules and act accordingly.* **2.** Consequently; therefore.

according to. 1. As stated or indicated by; on the authority of: *according to historians; according to statistics.* **2.** In keeping with; in agreement with: *Proceed according*

to instructions. **3.** As determined by: *a list arranged according to the first letter of each word.*

ac·cor·di·on (ə-kôr'dē-ən) n. A portable musical instrument with a small keyboard and free metal reeds that sound when air is forced past them by pleated bellows that are operated by the player. —*adj.* Having folds or bends like the bellows of an accordion: *accordion pleats.* [German *Akkordion,* from *Akkord,* agreement, harmony, from Old French *acorder,* to accord.] —**ac·cor'di·on·ist** n.

accordion

ac·cost (ə-kôst', ə-kŏst') tr.v. To approach and speak to first. [Old French *accoster,* to come alongside : Latin *ad-,* near + *costa,* side, rib.]

ac·count (ə-kount') n. **1.** A written or spoken description of events; a narrative: *an exciting account of his adventures.* **2.** A set of reasons; explanation: *Give an account for your strange behavior.* **3.** Often **accounts.** A record or written statement, esp. of business dealings or money received or spent. **4.** A business arrangement, as with a bank or store, in which money is kept, exchanged, or owed: *a savings account; a charge account.* **5.** Importance; standing; worth: *a man of little account.* —*tr.v.* To consider or esteem; regard. —*phrasal verb.* **account for. 1.** To give the reason for; explain: *We cannot account for these strange happenings.* **2.** To take into consideration; note: *Account for all the facts in giving your answer.* **3.** To be responsible for: *Carelessness accounts for many accidents.* —*idioms.* **call to account.** To demand an explanation from. **give an account of (oneself).** To behave (well or poorly). **on account of** or **on (someone's) account.** Because of: *Don't worry on her account.* **on no account.** Under no circumstances; never. **take account of** or **take into account.** To take note of; consider: *In solving a problem, take everything into account.* **turn to good account.** To make good use of: *turn one's losses to good account.* [Middle English, from Old French *acont,* from *acompter,* reckon : *ac-,* to + *compter,* to count.]

ac·count·a·ble (ə-koun'tə-bəl) adj. **1.** Obliged to answer for one's actions; responsible: *Congressmen are accountable to the voters.* **2.** Capable of being explained. —**ac·count'a·bil'i·ty** or **ac·count'a·ble·ness** n. —**ac·count'a·bly** adv.

ac·count·an·cy (ə-koun'tən-sē) n. The profession of being an accountant.

ac·count·ant (ə-koun'tənt) n. A person who keeps, audits, and inspects the financial records of individuals or business concerns and prepares financial and tax reports.

ac·count·ing (ə-koun'tĭng) n. The bookkeeping methods involved in making a financial record of business transactions and in the preparation of statements concerning the operations of a business.

ac·cou·ter (ə-koo'tər) tr.v. Also Brit. **ac·cou·tre, -tred, -tring.** To outfit and equip, esp. for a particular purpose: *The explorers were accoutered for outdoor living.* [French *accoutrer,* from Old French *acoustrer* : Latin *ad-,* to + *consuere,* to sew together.]

ac·cou·ter·ments (ə-koo'tər-mənts, -trə-) pl.n. Also Brit. **ac·cou·tre·ments. 1.** Articles of clothing or equipment; trappings. **2.** A soldier's equipment apart from his clothing and weapons.

ac·cou·tre (ə-koo'tər) v. **-tred, -tring.** Brit. Var. of **accouter.**

ac·cou·tre·ments (ə-koo'tər-mənts, -trə-) pl.n. Brit. Var. of **accouterments.**

ac·cred·it (ə-krĕd'ĭt) tr.v. **1.** To ascribe or attribute to; credit with. **2. a.** To supply with credentials or authority; authorize: *The college has been accredited by the state.* **b.** To send or appoint as an ambassador to a foreign government. **3.** To believe. [French *accréditer,* from (mettre)*

à *crédit*, "(to put) to credit."] —**ac·cred′i·ta′tion** *n.*

ac·cre·tion (ə-krē′shən) *n.* **1.** Any growth or increase in size by gradual external addition. **2.** The product of this process. **3.** Something added that produces such an increase. [From Latin *accrētus*, past part. of *accrescĕre*, to accrue.] —**ac·cre′tion·ar′y** or **ac·cre′tive** *adj.*

ac·cru·al (ə-krōō′əl) *n.* **1.** The act or process of accruing; increase. **2.** Something that increases or accrues.

ac·crue (ə-krōō′) *intr.v.* **-crued, -cru·ing. 1.** To come as a gain, addition, or increment: *benefits that accrue from scientific research.* **2.** To increase or accumulate: *Interest accrues in a savings account.* [Middle English *acrewen*, prob. from Old French *accrue*, growth, from *accreistre*, to increase : Latin *ad-*, in addition + *crēscere*, to grow.]

ac·cul·tur·a·tion (ə-kŭl′chə-rā′shən) *n.* The process of altering a society, esp. the modification of a primitive culture by contact with an advanced culture.

ac·cu·mu·late (ə-kyōō′myə-lāt′) *v.* **-lat·ed, -lat·ing.** —*tr.v.* To amass or gather; collect: *accumulate wealth; accumulate knowledge.* —*intr.v.* To grow or increase; mount up: *snow accumulating on the road.* —See Syns at **gather.** [From Latin *accumulāre* : *ad-*, to + *cumulus*, a heap.]

ac·cu·mu·la·tion (ə-kyōō′myə-lā′shən) *n.* **1.** The act or process of amassing or gathering: *the accumulation of knowledge.* **2.** A mass of something accumulated: *an accumulation of rubbish.*

ac·cu·mu·la·tor (ə-kyōō′myə-lā′tər) *n.* **1.** Someone or something that accumulates. **2.** *Brit.* An automobile storage battery.

ac·cu·ra·cy (ăk′yər-ə-sē) *n.* The condition or quality of being accurate; exactness; correctness.

ac·cu·rate (ăk′yər-ĭt) *adj.* **1.** Having no errors; correct. **2.** Conforming to or deviating only slightly from a standard: *an accurate timepiece.* [From Latin *accūrāre*, to attend to carefully : *ad-*, to + *cūra*, care.] —**ac′cu·rate·ly** *adv.* —**ac′cu·rate·ness** *n.*

Syns: accurate, correct, exact, faithful, precise, right, true, veracious *adj. Core meaning:* Conforming to fact (*gave an accurate description of the robber*).

ac·curs·ed (ə-kûr′sĭd, ə-kûrst′) *adj.* Also **ac·curst** (ə-kûrst′). **1.** Under a curse; damned. **2.** Hateful or very unfortunate. —**ac·curs′ed·ly** *adv.*

ac·cu·sa·tion (ăk′yōō-zā′shən) *n.* **1.** The act of accusing or condition of being accused. **2.** *Law.* A formal charge that a person is guilty of some punishable offense.

ac·cu·sa·tive (ə-kyōō′zə-tĭv) *adj.* Of or pertaining to the grammatical case of a noun, pronoun, adjective, or participle that is the direct object of a verb or the object of certain prepositions. —*n.* **1.** The accusative case. **2.** A word in the accusative case. [Middle English, from Latin *(casus) accūsātīvus*, "(case) indicating accusation."]

ac·cu·sa·to·ri·al (ə-kyōō′zə-tôr′ē-əl, -tôr′-) *adj.* Also **ac·cu·sa·to·ry** (ə-kyōō′zə-tôr′ē, -tôr′ē). Containing accusation.

ac·cuse (ə-kyōōz′) *tr.v.* **-cused, -cus·ing. 1.** To charge with a shortcoming or error. **2.** *Law.* To bring a formal charge against (someone) for a punishable offense: *He was accused of the crime.* [Middle English *acusen*, from Old French *acuser*, from Latin *accūsāre*, : *ad-*, to + *causa*, cause.] —**ac·cus′er** *n.* —**ac·cus′ing·ly** *adv.*

ac·cused (ə-kyōōzd′) *n.* **the accused.** *Law.* The defendant or defendants in a criminal case.

ac·cus·tom (ə-kŭs′təm) *tr.v.* To familiarize, as by constant practice, use, or habit. [Middle English *accustomen*, from Old French *aco(u)stumer* : *a-*, to + *costume*, custom.]

ac·cus·tomed (ə-kŭs′təmd) *adj.* Usual, characteristic, or habitual: *his accustomed morning walk.* —**idiom. accustomed to.** Used to; in the habit of: *accustomed to doing what he wants.*

ace (ās) *n.* **1. a.** A single pip or spot on a playing card, die, or domino. **b.** A playing card, die, or domino having one spot or pip. **2.** In racket games: **a.** A serve that one's opponent fails to return. **b.** A point scored by the failure of one's opponent to return a serve. **3.** A military aircraft pilot who has destroyed five or more enemy aircraft. **4.** *Informal.* A person who is an expert in his field. **5.** *Physics.* A unit of matter, a **quark.** —*tr.v.* **aced, ac·ing.** *Slang.* **1.** To get the better of (someone): *aced him right out of the running.* **2.** To receive a grade of A on (a test or examination): *He aced his term paper.* —**idioms. within an ace of.**

On the verge of; very near to: *within an ace of calling for help.* **ace in the hole. 1.** A hidden advantage. **2.** *Golf.* A hole in one. [Middle English *aas*, from Old French *as*, from Latin *ās*, unit.]

-aceous. A suffix meaning: **1.** Of or pertaining to: *sebaceous.* **2.** Resembling or of the nature of: *farinaceous.* **3.** Belonging to a taxonomic category, esp. a botanical family: *orchidaceous.* [From Latin *-āceus*, "of a specific kind or group."]

a·cer·bi·ty (ə-sûr′bĭ-tē) *n., pl.* **-ties. 1.** Sourness of taste. **2.** Acrimony; harshness; irritability.

acet-. Var. of **aceto-.**

ac·e·tab·u·lum (ăs′ĭ-tăb′yə-ləm) *n., pl.* **-la** (-lə). The cup-shaped cavity in the hipbone into which the head of the thighbone fits. [Latin *acētābulum*, vinegar cup, from *acētum*, vinegar.]

ac·et·al·de·hyde (ăs′ĭt-ăl′də-hīd′) *n.* A colorless, flammable liquid, C_2H_4O, used to manufacture acetic acid, perfumes, and drugs. Also called **aldehyde.** [ACET(O)- + ALDEHYDE.]

ac·et·a·min·o·phen (ăs′ĭt-ə-mĭn′ə-fən) *n.* A crystalline compound, $C_8H_9NO_2$, used to relieve pain and fever. [ACET(O)- + AMIN(O)- + PHEN(OL).]

ac·et·an·i·lide (ăs′ĭt-ăn′ə-līd′) *n.* Also **ac·et·an·i·lid** (-lĭd). A white crystalline compound, $C_6H_5NH(COCH_3)$, used medicinally to relieve pain and reduce fever. [ACET(O)- + ANIL(INE) + -IDE.]

ac·e·tate (ăs′ĭ-tāt′) *n.* **1.** A salt or ester of acetic acid. **2.** Cellulose acetate or any of various products, such as a fabric, derived from it. [ACET(O)- + -ATE.]

a·ce·tic (ə-sē′tĭk, ə-sĕt′ĭk) *adj.* Of, pertaining to, or containing acetic acid or vinegar. [From Latin *acetum*, vinegar.]

acetic acid. A clear, colorless organic acid, CH_3COOH, with a distinctive pungent odor. It is found in vinegar and used in the manufacture of rubber, plastics, and drugs.

aceto- or **acet-.** A prefix meaning the presence of acetic acid or the acetyl radical: *acetate.* [From Latin *acetum*, vinegar.]

ac·e·tone (ăs′ĭ-tōn′) *n.* A colorless, volatile, extremely flammable liquid, CH_3COCH_3, widely used as an organic solvent.

ac·e·tyl (ăs′ĭ-tĭl, ə-sēt′l) *n.* The acetic acid radical CH_3CO.

a·ce·tyl·cho·line (ə-sēt′l-kō′lēn′) *n.* A white crystalline compound, $C_7H_{17}NO_3$, that transmits nerve impulses across intercellular gaps. [ACETYL + *choline*, one of the B vitamins.]

a·cet·y·lene (ə-sēt′l-ēn′, -ĭn) *n.* A colorless, highly flammable or explosive gas, C_2H_2, used for metal welding and cutting and as an illuminant.

a·ce·tyl·sal·i·cyl·ic acid (ə-sēt′l-săl′ĭ-sĭl′ĭk). A common drug, aspirin. [ACETYL + SALICYLIC ACID.]

A·chae·an (ə-kē′ən) *n.* Also **A·cha·ian** (ə-kī′ən, ə-kā′-). **1.** A member of one of the four principal tribes of ancient Greece believed to have created the Mycenaean civilization. **2.** A Greek, esp. of the Mycenaean era.

ache (āk) *intr.v.* **ached, ach·ing. 1.** To suffer a dull, sustained pain. **2.** *Informal.* To yearn painfully: *I ache to see her again.* —*n.* A dull, steady pain. [Middle English *aken*, from Old English *ācan*.]

a·chene (ā-kēn′) *n.* Also **a·kene.** A small, dry, thin-walled fruit, such as that of the buttercup and dandelion, that does not split open when ripe. [New Latin *achenium*, "one that does not yawn or split open" : *a-*, not + Greek *khainein*, to yawn.]

Ach·e·ron (ăk′ə-rŏn′) *n.* *Gk. Myth.* **1.** The river of the lower world over which Charon ferried the souls of the dead to Hades. **2.** Hades.

a·chieve (ə-chēv′) *v.* **a·chieved, a·chiev·ing.** —*tr.v.* **1.** To carry out with success; accomplish: *achieved his goal.* **2.** To attain or get; reach: *She achieved the presidency of the company.* —*intr.v.* To accomplish something successfully. —See Syns at **accomplish.** [Middle English *acheven*, from Old French *achever*, from *a chef*, "to a head" : Latin *ad-* + *caput*, head.] —**a·chiev′a·ble** *adj.* —**a·chiev′er** *n.*

a·chieve·ment (ə-chēv′mənt) *n.* **1.** The act of accomplishing something. **2.** Something that has been accomplished successfully, esp. by means of skill or perseverance.

achievement test. A test for the measurement and comparison of skills in various fields of study.

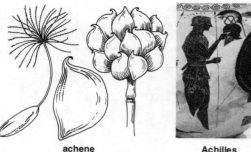

achene   Achilles

acorn

A·chil·les (ə-kǐl′ēz) *n. Gk. Myth.* The hero of Homer's *Iliad*, son of Peleus and Thetis.

Achilles' heel. A small but mortal weakness. [From the myth that Achilles was vulnerable only in the heel.]

Achilles' tendon. The large tendon running from the heel bone to the calf muscle of the leg.

ach·ro·mat·ic (ăk′rə-măt′ĭk) *adj.* **1. a.** Of or designating a color, such as black, white, or neutral gray, that has no hue. **b.** Colorless. **2.** *Optics.* Refracting white light without breaking it into the colors of the spectrum. [From Greek *akhrōmatos*, colorless : *a-*, without + *khrōma*, color.] **—ach′ro·mat′i·cal·ly** *adv.*

ac·id (ăs′ĭd) *n.* **1.** *Chem.* Any of a large class of substances, the aqueous solutions of which are capable of turning litmus indicators red, of reacting with and dissolving certain metals to form salts, of reacting with bases or alkalis to form salts, or that have a sour taste. **2.** A substance having a sour taste. **3.** *Slang.* A drug, **LSD.** *—adj.* **1.** *Chem.* **a.** Of or pertaining to an acid. **b.** Having a high concentration of acid. **2.** Having a sour taste. **3.** Biting; ill-tempered; sharp; caustic: *an acid wit.* [Latin *acidus*, sharp, sour, from *acēre*, to be sour.] **—ac′id·ly** *adv.* **—ac′id·ness** *n.*

a·cid·ic (ə-sĭd′ĭk) *adj.* **1.** Acid. **2.** Tending to form an acid.

a·cid·i·fy (ə-sĭd′ə-fī′) *v.* **-fied, -fy·ing.** *—tr.v.* To make acid. *—intr.v.* To become acid. **—a·cid′i·fi′a·ble** *adj.* **—a·cid′i·fi·ca′tion** *n.* **—a·cid′i·fi′er** *n.*

a·cid·i·ty (ə-sĭd′ĭ-tē) *n.* **1.** The condition or quality of being acid. **2.** *Med.* **Hyperacidity.**

ac·i·do·sis (ăs′ĭ-dō′sĭs) *n.* A condition of pathologically high acidity of the blood. **—ac′i·dot′ic** (ăs′ĭ-dŏt′ĭk) *adj.*

acid test. A decisive, critical test of worth or quality.

a·cid·u·late (ə-sĭj′ŏō-lāt′) *v.* **-lat·ed, -lat·ing.** *—tr.v.* To make slightly acid. *—intr.v.* To become slightly acid. **—a·cid′u·la′tion** *n.*

a·cid·u·lous (ə-sĭj′ə-ləs, ə-sĭd′yə-) *adj.* Sour in feeling or manner; biting; caustic.

ac·knowl·edge (ăk-nŏl′ĭj) *tr.v.* **-edged, -edg·ing. 1. a.** To confess or admit the existence or truth of. **b.** To recognize as being valid or having force or power: *She was acknowledged an expert in her field.* **2. a.** To express recognition of: *He acknowledged our presence.* **b.** To express thanks or gratitude for: *acknowledge her help.* **3.** To report the receipt of: *acknowledge a letter.* **4.** *Law.* To accept or certify as legally binding: *acknowledge a deed.* [Middle English, blend of *acknowen*, to acknowledge, from Old English *oncnāwan* + KNOWLEDGE.] **—ac·knowl′edge·a·ble** *adj.*

Syns: **acknowledge, admit, allow, concede, confess, grant, own up** *v. Core meaning:* To recognize, often reluctantly, the reality or truth of (*finally acknowledged the error*).

ac·knowl·edg·ment (ăk-nŏl′ĭj-mənt) *n.* Also **ac·knowl·edge·ment. 1.** The act of admitting to something. **2.** Recognition of someone's or something's existence, validity, authority, or right. **3.** An answer or response in return for something done. **4.** An expression or token of appreciation or thanks. **5.** *Law.* A formal declaration made to authoritative witnesses to ensure legal validity.

ac·me (ăk′mē) *n.* The highest point; peak: *the acme of perfection.* [Greek *akmē*, summit.]

ac·ne (ăk′nē) *n.* An inflammatory disease of the oil glands, characterized by pimples, esp. on the face. [New Latin, from Greek *akmē*, eruption on the face, point, acme.]

ac·o·lyte (ăk′ə-līt′) *n.* **1.** A person who assists a priest in the

celebration of Mass. **2.** An attendant or follower. [Middle English *acolite*, from Old French, from Medieval Latin *acolytus*, from Greek *akolouthos*, follower, following : *a-*, together + *keleuthos*, path.]

ac·o·nite (ăk′ə-nīt′) *n.* **1.** Any plant of the genus *Aconitum.* **2.** The dried, poisonous root of a species of monkshood, *A. napellus*, used in medicine to relieve pain or fever. [Latin *aconītum*, from Greek *akoniton.*]

a·corn (ā′kôrn′, ā′kərn) *n.* The fruit of the oak tree, consisting of a thick-walled nut usu. set in a woody, cuplike base. [Middle English, from Old English *æcern.*]

acorn squash. A type of squash shaped somewhat like an acorn and having a longitudinally ridged rind.

a·cous·tic (ə-kōō′stĭk) or **a·cous·ti·cal** (-stĭ-kəl) *adj.* **1.** Of or pertaining to sound, the sense of hearing, or the science of sound. **2.** Designed to aid in hearing. [Greek *akoustikos*, from *akouein*, to hear.] **—a·cous′ti·cal·ly** *adv.*

a·cous·tics (ə-kōō′stĭks) *n.* **1.** (*used with a sing. verb*). The scientific study of sound, esp. of its generation, transmission, and perception. **2.** (*used with a pl. verb*). The total effect of sound produced in an enclosed space: *The acoustics of the new concert hall are poor.*

ac·quaint (ə-kwānt′) *tr.v.* To make familiar or informed: *acquaint oneself with the facts.* [Middle English *aqueynten*, from Old French *acointer*, Latin *accognōscere*, to know perfectly : *ad-* (intensive) + *cognōscere*, to know.]

ac·quain·tance (ə-kwān′təns) *n.* **1.** Knowledge or information about someone or something. **2.** Knowledge of a person acquired by a relationship less intimate than friendship. **3.** A person or persons whom one knows. **—ac·quain′tance·ship′** *n.*

ac·quaint·ed (ə-kwān′tĭd) *adj.* **1.** Known to each other. **2.** Informed; familiar.

ac·qui·esce (ăk′wē-ĕs′) *intr.v.* **-esced, -esc·ing.** To consent or comply without protest; to assent. [Latin *acquiēscere*, to agree tacitly : *ad-*, at, to + *quiēs*, rest.] **—ac′qui·es′cence** (ăk′wē-ĕs′əns) *n.* **—ac′qui·es′cent** *adj.*

ac·quire (ə-kwīr′) *tr.v.* **-quired, -quir·ing. 1.** To gain possession of. **2.** To get by one's own efforts. [Middle English *acqueren*, from Old French *acquerre*, from Latin *acquīrere*, to add to, get : *ad-*, in addition to + *quaerere*, to seek, obtain.] **—ac·quir′a·ble** *adj.*

ac·quire·ment (ə-kwīr′mənt) *n.* **1.** The act of acquiring. **2.** An attainment, as a skill or social accomplishment.

ac·qui·si·tion (ăk′wĭ-zĭsh′ən) *n.* **1.** The act of acquiring. **2.** Something acquired, esp. as an addition to an established category or group.

ac·quis·i·tive (ə-kwĭz′ĭ-tĭv) *adj.* **1.** Eager to acquire possessions; grasping. **2.** Tending to acquire and retain ideas or information: *an acquisitive mind.* **—ac·quis′i·tive·ly** *adv.* **—ac·quis′i·tive·ness** *n.*

ac·quit (ə-kwĭt′) *tr.v.* **-quit·ted, -quit·ting. 1.** To free or clear from a charge or accusation. **2.** To release or discharge from duty or obligation. **3.** To repay (an obligation). **4. acquit (oneself).** To conduct oneself; behave: *The warriors acquitted themselves bravely.* **—**See Syns at **vindicate.** [Middle English *acquiten*, from Old French *aquiter* : Latin *ad-*, to + *quiēs*, quiet.]

ac·quit·tal (ə-kwĭt′l) *n.* The judgment of a jury or judge that a person is not guilty of a crime as charged.

a·cre (ā′kər) *n.* A unit of area used in land measurement and equal to 4,840 sq. yd. or 43,560 sq. ft. [Middle English, from Old English *æcer*, field, acre.]

ă pat   ā pay   â care   ä father   ĕ pet   ē be   hw which   ĭ pit   ī tie   î pier   ŏ pot   ō toe   ô paw, for   oi noise
ōō took   ōō boot   ou out   th thin   th this   ŭ cut   û urge   zh vision   ə about, item, edible, gallop, circus

acrobat

Acropolis

a·cre·age (ā'kər-Ĭj) *n.* Land area as measured or expressed in acres.

a·cre-foot (ā'kər-fŏŏt') *n.* The volume of water (43,560 cu. ft.) that will cover an area of one acre to a depth of one foot.

ac·rid (ăk'rĭd) *adj.* **1.** Harsh or bitter to the sense of taste or smell. **2.** Sharp or biting in language or tone. [From Latin *ācer* sharp, bitter.] **—a·crid'i·ty** (ə-krĭd'Ĭ-tē) or **ac'rid·ness** *n.* **—ac'rid·ly** *adv.*

ac·ri·mo·ni·ous (ăk'rə-mō'nē-əs) *adj.* Bitter in language, manner, etc.; rancorous: *acrimonious bickering.* **—ac'ri·mo'ni·ous·ly** *adv.* **—ac'ri·mo'ni·ous·ness** *n.*

ac·ri·mo·ny (ăk'rə-mō'nē) *n.* Bitterness or ill-natured animosity, esp. in speech or manner. [Latin *ācrimōnia,* sharpness, from *ācer,* bitter.]

acro-. A prefix meaning: **1.** A height or summit: **acrophobia. 2.** An extremity of the body or an outer end: **acromegaly.** [From Greek *akros,* topmost, extreme.]

ac·ro·bat (ăk'rə-băt') *n.* A person skilled in feats of agility and balance. [French *acrobate,* from Greek *akrobatēs,* from *akrobatein,* to walk on tiptoe : *akros,* topmost + *bainein,* to walk.] **—ac'ro·bat'ic** *adj.* **—ac'ro·bat'i·cal·ly** *adv.*

ac·ro·bat·ics (ăk'rə-băt'Ĭks) *pl.n.* **1.** The actions of an acrobat. **2.** A display of spectacular agility: *vocal acrobatics.*

ac·ro·meg·a·ly (ăk'rō-měg'ə-lē) *n.* A disease marked by the enlargement of the bones of the hands, feet, and face, resulting from chronic overactivity of the pituitary gland. [ACRO- + Greek *megas,* big.] **—ac'ro·me·gal'ic** (-mə-găl'Ĭk) *adj.*

ac·ro·nym (ăk'rə-nĭm') *n.* A word formed from the initial letters of a name, as *WAC* for Women's Army Corps. [ACR(O)- + -ONYM.]

ac·ro·pho·bi·a (ăk'rə-fō'bē-ə) *n.* Abnormally intense fear of being in high places.

a·crop·o·lis (ə-krŏp'ə-lĭs) *n.* **1.** The fortified height or citadel of an ancient Greek city. **2. Acropolis.** The citadel of Athens, on which the Parthenon was built. [Greek *akropolis : akros,* topmost + *polis,* city.]

a·cross (ə-krôs', ə-krŏs') *prep.* **1. a.** To or from the other side of: *driving across the continent.* **b.** On the other side of: *a hill across the valley.* **2.** At right angles to the direction indicated by "along": **a.** Crosswise over: *A frog leaped across our path.* **b.** Crosswise upon: *lay one board across another.* **—adv. 1. a.** From one side to the other: *He called across to us.* **b.** In breadth: *A tornado may be only 100 feet across.* **2.** Over: *I want to get my point across.* [Middle English *acros,* on *croice,* from Old French *a croix,* "in the form of a cross."]

a·cross-the-board (ə-krôs'thə-bôrd', -bōrd', ə-krŏs'-) *adj.* **1.** Designating a racing wager whereby equal amounts are bet on the same contestant to win, place, or show. **2.** Including all categories: *an across-the-board wage increase.*

a·cros·tic (ə-krô'stĭk, ə-krŏs'tĭk) *n.* A poem or series of lines in which certain letters, usu. the first in each line, form a name, motto, or message read in sequence. [French *acrostiche,* from Old French, from Greek *akrostikhis : akros,* extreme + *stikhos,* line of verse.]

a·cryl·ic (ə-krĭl'Ĭk) *adj.* Of any synthetic fiber or resin derived from acrylic acid or its derivatives. **—n. 1.** A paint in which the vehicle is acrylic resin. **2. Acrylic resin. 3. Acrylic fiber.** [From ACR(ID) + -YL + -IC.]

acrylic acid. An easily polymerized, colorless, corrosive liquid, H_2C:CHCOOH, used in emulsion paints, adhesives, plastics, etc.

acrylic fiber. Any of numerous synthetic fibers polymerized from acrylonitrile. Also called **acrylic.**

acrylic resin. Any of numerous thermoplastic or thermosetting polymers or copolymers of acrylic acid, methacrylic acid, esters of these acids, or acrylonitrile, used to produce synthetic rubbers, exceptionally clear, lightweight plastics resistant to weather and corrosion, and other resin forms and lubricants. Also called **acrylic.**

ac·ry·lo·ni·trile (ăk'rə-lō-nī'trəl) *n.* A colorless, liquid organic compound, H_2C:CHCN, used in the manufacture of acrylic rubber and fibers. [ACRYL(IC RESIN) + NITRILE.]

act (ăkt) *tr.v.* **1.** To play the part of; perform on stage: *He acted Hamlet to great acclaim.* **2.** To pose as or behave like: *act the outraged parent.* **3.** To behave as suitable for: *act your age.* **—intr.v. 1.** To perform an action; do something: *She acted quickly in the crisis.* **2.** To perform in a dramatic role or roles. **3.** To behave or comport oneself: *act like a lady.* **4.** To pretend or put on a false show: *She acted as if nothing was bothering her.* **5.** To appear or seem to be: *The dog acts friendly.* **6.** To operate or function in a specific way: *His mind acts quickly.* **7.** To serve or function as a substitute: *act as chairperson. A coin can act as a screwdriver.* **—phrasal verbs. act on** (or **upon**). To do something as a result of: *He acted on my advice.* **act out.** Perform in or as if in a play; dramatize: *act out a story.* **act up.** To behave in an unusual or undesirable way; misbehave: *Our old jalopy is acting up again.* **—n. 1.** A kind of movement or behavior; action: *such acts as running, writing, or breathing.* **2.** A thing done; a deed: *an act of bravery; unlawful acts.* **3.** The process of doing something: *caught in the act of stealing.* **4. a.** A performance for an audience, often forming part of a longer show: *a magician's act.* **b.** One of the main divisions of a play or other dramatic work: *an opera in five acts.* **5.** An insincere pretense; false show: *His boasting is just an act.* **6.** A law, esp. one enacted by a legislative body: *an act of Congress.* [Middle English *acte,* from Latin *actus* (past part. *actus*), to drive, to do.] **—act'a·bil'i·ty** *n.* **—act'a·ble** *adj.*

ACTH A protein hormone synthesized by or extracted from mammalian pituitaries for use in stimulating secretion of cortisone and other adrenal cortex hormones. Also called **corticotropin.** [From A(DRENO)C(ORTICO)T(ROPIC) H(ORMONE).]

ac·tin (ăk'tĭn) *n.* A protein, active with myosin in muscular contraction. [From Latin *actus,* an·act + -IN.]

act·ing (ăk'tĭng) *adj.* Temporarily assuming the duties or authority of another: *the acting principal.* **—n.** The occupation or performance of an actor.

ac·tin·ic (ăk-tĭn'Ĭk) *adj.* Of or pertaining to actinism.

actinic ray. Any form of radiation, such as ultraviolet rays or x-rays, that can cause chemical changes in an object that it strikes.

ac·ti·nide (ăk'tə-nīd') *n.* Any of a series of chemically similar, mostly synthetic, radioactive elements with atomic numbers ranging from 89 (actinium) through 103 (lawrencium). [From Greek *aktis,* ray + -IDE.]

ac·ti·nism (ăk'tə-nĭz'əm) *n.* The intrinsic property in radiation that produces photochemical activity.

ac·tin·i·um (ăk-tĭn′ē-əm) *n. Symbol* **Ac** A radioactive element found in uranium ores and used, in equilibrium with its decay products, as a source of alpha rays. Its longest-lived isotope is Ac 227 with a half-life of 21.7 years. Atomic number 89; melting point 1,050°C; boiling point (estimated) 3,200°C; specific gravity (calculated) 10.07; valence 3. [Greek *aktis,* ray + -IUM.]

ac·ti·no·my·cete (ăk′tə-nō-mī′sēt′) *n.* Any of numerous gen. filamentous and often pathogenic microorganisms of the order Actinomycetales, resembling both bacteria and fungi. [Greek *aktis,* ray + -MYCETE.]

ac·ti·no·zo·an (ăk′tə-nō-zō′ən) *n.* Anthozoan. [From New Latin *actinozoa,* "the radiated life-forms."]

ac·tion (ăk′shən) *n.* **1. a.** A thing done; deed: *take responsibility for one's actions. Actions speak louder than words.* **b.** Often **actions.** Behavior; conduct: *a small child's amusing actions.* **2.** The activity, process, or fact of doing something: *Verbs show action.* **3.** Motion; movement: *the constant action of a pendulum.* **4.** Energetic or effective activity: *firemen springing into action.* **5.** The activities or events of a play, story, etc.: *The action of "Macbeth" takes place in Scotland.* **6.** Any physical change, as in position, size, mass, energy, velocity, etc., that an object or system undergoes: *the action of a sail in the wind.* **7. a.** The way in which something works or exerts its influence, often within a larger system: *the action of the liver in digestion.* **b.** The effect of this: *the corrosive action of acid on metal.* **8.** The operating parts of a mechanism: *the action of a piano.* **9.** Battle; combat: *Send the fresh troops into action.* **10.** A lawsuit. —*modifier: Verbs are action words. Make quick action sketches.* —*idiom.* **take action.** To do something as a result of something else that has taken place: *The colonists took action against the tax laws.*

ac·tion·a·ble (ăk′shə-nə-bəl) *adj.* Giving just cause for legal action. —**ac′tion·a·bly** *adv.*

ac·ti·vate (ăk′tə-vāt′) *tr.v.* **-vat·ed, -vat·ing. 1.** To set in motion; make active: *activate the procedure.* **2.** To create or organize (a military unit, post, etc). **3.** To purify (sewage) by aeration. **4.** *Chem.* To start or accelerate a reaction in, as by heating. **5.** *Physics.* To make (a substance) radioactive. —**ac′ti·va′tion** *n.* —**ac′ti·va′tor** *n.*

ac·tive (ăk′tĭv) *adj.* **1.** Moving or tending to move about; engaged in physical action: *Athletes are more active than office workers.* **2.** Performing or capable of performing an action or process; functioning; working: *active cells in living plants and animals; an active volcano.* **3.** Taking part or requiring participation in activities: *an active member of the club; soldiers in active service.* **4.** Full of energy; busy: *an active mind.* **5.** Causing action or change; effective: *active efforts for improvement.* **6.** *Gram.* Showing or expressing action: *an active verb.* **7.** Tending to form chemical compounds easily: *an active element.* **8.** *Mus.* Suggesting that something follows: *active tones.* See Syns at **vigorous.** —*n. Gram.* The active voice. [Middle English, from Old French *actif,* from Latin *actīvus,* from *actus,* act.] —**ac′tive·ly** *adv.* —**ac′tive·ness** *n.*

active voice. A form of a transitive verb or phrasal verb that shows that the subject of the sentence is performing or causing the action expressed by the verb. In the sentence *John bought the book, bought* is in the active voice.

ac·tiv·ist (ăk′tə-vĭst) *n.* A person who believes in or takes part in direct effective action to bring about changes in government, social conditions, etc. —*modifier: an activist point of view.* —**ac′tiv·ism** *n.*

ac·tiv·i·ty (ăk-tĭv′ĭ-tē) *n., pl.* **ac·tiv·i·ties. 1.** The condition or process of being active; action. **2.** A particular kind of action or behavior: *the nesting activities of birds.* **3.** A planned or organized thing to do, as in a school subject or social group. **4.** Energetic movement or action; busyness: *The department store was a scene of great activity.*

act of God. *Law.* An unforeseeable or inevitable occurrence, as a tornado, caused by nature and not by man.

ac·tor (ăk′tər) *n.* **1.** A performer, esp. a person who acts a part in a play, motion picture, or other dramatic performance. **2.** Someone who takes part; participant.

ac·tress (ăk′trĭs) *n.* A female theatrical performer.

Acts (ăkts) *n.* See table at **Bible.**

ac·tu·al (ăk′chōō-əl) *adj.* **1. a.** Existing in fact or reality; existent: *He distrusted our actual intentions.* **b.** Existing

at the present moment; present; current: *Inflation is one of the worst actual conditions.* **2.** Corresponding to all human facts: *An actual tornado destroyed the town.* **3.** Based on fact: *an actual account of what happened.* [Middle English *actuel,* from Old French, from Late Latin *actuālis,* "pertaining to acts," from Latin *actus,* an act.]

ac·tu·al·i·ty (ăk′chōō-ăl′ĭ-tē) *n., pl.* **-ties. 1.** The condition or fact of being actual; reality. **2.** Something that is actual.

ac·tu·al·ize (ăk′chōō-ə-līz′) *tr.v.* **-ized, -iz·ing.** To realize in action: *actualized our goals.* —**ac′tu·al·i·za′tion** *n.*

ac·tu·al·ly (ăk′chōō-ə-lē) *adv.* In fact; really.

ac·tu·ar·y (ăk′chōō-ĕr′ē) *n., pl.* **-ies.** One who computes insurance risks and premiums. [Latin *actuārius,* secretary of accounts, from *actus,* public employment, act.]

ac·tu·ate (ăk′chōō-āt′) *tr.v.* **-at·ed, -at·ing. 1.** To put into action or motion: *a lever that actuates the emergency brake.* **2.** To cause to act. [From Medieval Latin *actuāre,* from Latin *actus,* an act.] —**ac′tu·a′tion** *n.*

a·cu·i·ty (ə-kyōō′ĭ-tē) *n.* Keenness; acuteness: *visual acuity; acuity of mind.* [Middle English *acuitie,* from Medieval Latin *acuitās,* from Latin *acuere,* to sharpen, from *acus,* needle.]

a·cu·men (ə-kyōō′mən, ăk′yə-) *n.* Quickness and accuracy of judgment: *business acumen.* [Latin *acūmen,* sharpness, from *acuere,* to sharpen.]

ac·u·punc·ture (ăk′yōō-pŭngk′chər) *n.* A traditional Chinese therapeutic technique whereby the body is punctured with fine needles. [Latin *acus,* needle + PUNCTURE.]

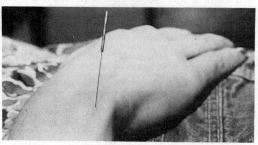

acupuncture

a·cute (ə-kyōōt′) *adj.* **1.** Keenly perceptive; discerning; shrewd: *an acute sense of smell.* **2.** Reacting readily to impressions; sensitive. **3.** Of great importance or consequence; crucial: *an acute need for funds.* **4.** Extremely severe or sharp; intense: *acute pain.* **5.** *Med.* Reaching a crisis rapidly: *acute appendicitis.* **6.** *Geom.* Designating angles that are less than 90 degrees. —See Syns at **critical** and **sharp.** [From Latin *acuere,* to sharpen, from *acus,* needle.] —**a·cute′ly** *adv.* —**a·cute′ness** *n.*

acute accent. A mark used over a vowel to indicate sound quality or length. For example, the French word "été" (summer) has two acute accents.

ad (ăd) *n.* An advertisement.

ad-. A prefix meaning motion toward: *adsorb.* [Latin, from *ad,* to, toward, at.]

ad·age (ăd′ĭj) *n.* A short proverb; a saying. [French, from Old French, from Latin *adagium,* proverb.]

a·da·gio (ə-dä′jō, -jē-ō′) *adv. Mus.* Slowly. Used as a direction. —*adj. Mus.* Slow in tempo; slower than andante. —*n., pl.* **-gios. 1.** *Mus.* A composition or movement played in this tempo. **2.** *Ballet.* The slow section of a pas de deux. [Italian, "at ease."]

ad·a·mant (ăd′ə-mənt, -mănt′) *n.* A legendary stone believed to be impenetrable. —*adj.* Firm in purpose or opinion; unyielding: *an adamant decision.* [Middle English, diamond, magnet, from Old French *adamaunt,* from Latin *adamās,* from Greek *adamas,* hard metal, diamond.] —**ad′a·mant·ly** *adv.*

ad·a·man·tine (ăd′ə-măn′tēn′, -tĭn, -tīn′) *adj.* **1.** Having the hardness or luster of a diamond. **2.** Unyielding; inflexible.

Ad·am's apple (ăd′əmz). The projection of the largest laryngeal cartilage at the front of the throat, most noticeable in men.

a·dapt (ə-dăpt′) *tr.v.* **1.** To adjust to a specified use or pur-

---

pose. **2.** To make fit for a particular environment, condition, etc., as through a process of natural development: *Gills and fins adapt a fish for living in water.* —*intr.v.* To become adapted: *Camels have adapted to desert conditions.* [Latin *adaptāre,* to fit to : *ad-,* to + *aptāre,* to fit, from *aptus,* apt.]

a·dapt·a·ble (ə-dăp′tə-bəl) *adj.* Capable of adapting or of being adapted. —**a·dapt′a·bil′i·ty** *n.*

ad·ap·ta·tion (ăd′ăp-tā′shən) *n.* **1. a.** The condition of being adapted. **b.** The act or process of adapting. **2.** Something produced or changed by being adapted: *That play is an adaptation of a novel.* **3.** An alteration or adjustment, often hereditary, by which a species or individual improves its condition in relationship to its environment. **4.** The responsive alteration of a sense organ to repeated stimuli. **5.** Change in behavior of an individual or group in adjustment to new or modified cultural surroundings. —**ad′ap·ta′tion·al** *adj.* —**ad′ap·ta′tion·al·ly** *adv.*

a·dapt·er (ə-dăp′tər) *n.* **1.** Someone or something that adapts. **2.** A device used to connect different parts of one or more pieces of apparatus.

a·dap·tive (ə-dăp′tĭv) *adj.* **1.** Of or pertaining to adaptation. **2.** Tending to adapt: *man's adaptive nature.* —**a·dap′tive·ness** *n.*

add (ăd) *tr.v.* **1.** To join or unite so as to increase in size, quantity, or scope. **2.** To combine (figures) to form a sum. **3.** To say or write further. —*intr.v.* **1.** To create or constitute an addition: *He adds to his savings each week.* **2.** To find a sum in arithmetic. —*phrasal verbs.* **add up. 1.** To come to a correct or desired total: *His figures don't add up.* **2.** To be reasonable, plausible, or consistent; make sense. **add up to.** To mean; indicate: *Those warning signs add up to trouble.* [Middle English *adden,* from Latin *addere* : *ad-,* to + *dere,* to put, from *dare,* to do.]

ad·dax (ăd′ăks′) *n.* An antelope, *Addax nasomaculatus,* of northern Africa, with long, spirally twisted horns. [Latin *addāx.*]

addax

ad·dend (ăd′ĕnd′, ə-dĕnd′) *n.* Any of a set of numbers to be added. [Short for ADDENDUM.]

ad·den·dum (ə-dĕn′dəm) *n., pl.* **-da** (-də). Something added or to be added, esp. a supplement to a book. [Latin, from *addere,* to add.]

ad·der (ăd′ər) *n.* **1.** Any of various poisonous Old World snakes of the family Viperidae, esp. the common viper, *Vipera berus,* of Eurasia. **2.** Any of several nonpoisonous snakes popularly believed to be harmful, such as the hognose snake, or puff adder, of North America. [Middle English *addre,* from Old English *nædre,* snake.]

adder

ad·der's-tongue (ăd′ərz-tŭng′) *n.* **1.** Any of several ferns of the genus *Ophioglossum;* esp. *O. vulgatum,* of the Northern Hemisphere, that has a single sterile, leaflike frond and a spore-bearing stalk. **2.** Any of various plants of the genus *Erythronium,* such as the dogtooth violet.

ad·dict (ə-dĭkt′) *tr.v.* To devote or give (oneself) habitually or compulsively. —*n.* (ăd′ĭkt). **1.** Someone who is addicted to a harmful substance, esp. to narcotics. **2.** A devoted fan: *a science-fiction addict.* [Latin *addictus,* one awarded to another as a slave, past part. of *addicere,* to award to : *ad-,* to + *dicere,* to say, pronounce, adjudge.] —**ad·dic′tion** *n.* —**ad·dic′tive** *adj.*

Ad·di·son's disease (ăd′ĭ-sənz). A usu. fatal disease caused by failure of the adrenal cortex to function and marked by a bronzelike skin color, anemia, and prostration. [Discovered by Thomas *Addison* (1793–1860), English physician.]

ad·di·tion (ə-dĭsh′ən) *n.* **1.** The act or process of adding: *the addition of seasoning to food.* **2.** Something added: *an addition to the family.* **3.** The process of computing with sets of numbers so as to find their sum. —*modifier: an addition problem.* —*idioms.* **in addition.** Besides; also; as well as. **in addition to.** Over and above; besides.

ad·di·tion·al (ə-dĭsh′ə-nəl) *adj.* Added; extra: *additional information.* —**ad·di′tion·al·ly** *adv.*

ad·di·tive (ăd′ĭ-tĭv) *adj.* Marked, produced by, or involving addition. —*n.* A substance added in small amounts to something else to improve or strengthen it.

additive identity element. Zero.

additive inverse. Either one of a pair of numbers, as *a* and −*a,* whose sum is zero (0).

ad·dle (ăd′l) *v.* **-dled, -dling.** —*tr.v.* To muddle; confuse. —*intr.v.* **1.** To become rotten; spoil. **2.** To become confused. —See Syns at **confuse.** [From Middle English *adel,* rotten, putrid, from Old English *adela,* filth, urine.]

ad·dress (ə-drĕs′) *n.* **1.** (*also* ăd′rĕs′). **a.** The place where someone lives, works, or receives mail or where a business is located: *your home address.* **b.** A direction on a piece of mail, giving the name and location of the receiver or sender: *a return address.* **2.** A formal speech: *the President's inaugural address.* **3.** Spoken or written communication. A **form of address** is a title or set of words used when speaking or writing formally to someone, such as an official. **4.** A way of speaking or behaving: *a man of blunt address.* **5.** *Computers.* A set of digits used in information storage or retrieval that are assigned to a specific memory location. —*modifier: an address book.* —*tr.v.* **1.** To speak to: *The man addressed him respectfully.* **2.** To give a speech to: *The mayor will address our club.* **3.** To refer to directly; call; greet: *Address the judge as "Your Honor."* **4.** To put a direction on (a piece of mail) to show where it should go: *address an envelope.* **5.** To direct to a particular person, group, or place: *She addressed her remarks to the newcomers.* —*phrasal verb.* **address (oneself) to. 1.** To speak to. **2.** To direct (one's) efforts or attention toward: *You must address yourself to your homework.* [Middle English *addressen,* from Old French *adresser,* : Latin *ad-,* to + *dīrectus,* direct.]

ad·dress·ee (ăd′rĕs-ē′, ə-drĕs′ē′) *n.* The person to whom something is addressed.

ad·duce (ə-dōōs′, ə-dyōōs′, ă-) *tr.v.* **-duced, -duc·ing.** To cite as an example or means of proof in an argument; bring forward for consideration. [Latin *addūcere,* to bring to : *ad-,* toward + *dūcere,* to lead.]

ad·duct (ə-dŭkt′, ă-) *tr.v. Physiol.* To pull or draw toward the main axis, as muscles. [Back-formation from ADDUCTOR.] —**ad·duc′tive** *adj.*

ad·duc·tor (ə-dŭk′tər, ă-) *n.* A muscle that adducts. [Latin *adductor,* "a bringer toward," from *addūcere,* adduce.]

–ade. A suffix meaning a sweetened drink of: *lemonade.*

ad·e·nine (ăd′n-ēn′, -ĭn) *n.* A purine derivative, $C_5H_5N_5$, that is a constituent of nucleic acid in the pancreas, spleen, and other organs. [From Greek *adēn,* gland + -INE.]

ad·e·noid (ăd′n-oid′) *adj.* Also **ad·e·noi·dal** (ăd′n-oid′l). **1.** Glandlike; glandular. **2.** Of or pertaining to the adenoids. —*pl.n.* **adenoids.** Lymphoid tissue growths in the nose above the throat that when swollen may obstruct nasal breathing and make speech difficult. [Greek *adēn,* gland + -OID.]

ad·e·noi·dal (ăd'n-oid'l) adj. 1. Var. of **adenoid**. 2. Having a nasal tone. 3. Mouth-breathing or gaping.

a·den·o·sine (ə-dĕn'ə-sēn') n. An organic compound, $C_{10}H_{13}N_5O_4$, that is a structural component of nucleic acids. [Blend of ADENINE and RIBOSE.]

adenosine di·phos·phate (dī-fŏs'fāt'). ADP.

adenosine tri·phos·phate (trī-fŏs'fāt'). ATP.

a·dept (ə-dĕpt') adj. Skillful and effective; proficient: *an adept performance.* —n. (ăd'ĕpt'). An initiate; an expert. [Latin *adeptus*, "having attained (knowledge)," past part. of *adipīscī*, to attain : toward + *apīscī*, to reach for.] —**a·dept'ly** adv. —**a·dept'ness** n.

ad·e·quate (ăd'ĭ-kwĭt) adj. 1. Able to satisfy a requirement; suitable. 2. Barely satisfactory; mediocre. [From Latin *adaequāre*, to make equal to : ad-, toward + *aequus*, equal.] —**ad'e·qua·cy** (-kwə-sē), or **ad'e·quate·ness** n. —**ad'e·quate·ly** adv.

ad·here (ăd-hîr') intr.v. **-hered, -her·ing.** 1. To stick or hold fast. 2. To be devoted or loyal to; give continuing support: *adhere to one's beliefs.* 3. To follow closely; observe: *adhere to a plan.* [Latin *adhaerēre*, to stick to : ad, toward + *haerēre*, to stick.]

ad·her·ence (ăd-hîr'əns) n. 1. The process or condition of adhering. 2. Faithful attachment; devotion.

ad·her·ent (ăd-hîr'ənt) adj. 1. Sticking or holding fast. 2. *Bot.* Growing or fused together. —n. A supporter, as of a cause or individual; an advocate: *an adherent of women's liberation.* —**ad·her'ent·ly** adv.

ad·he·sion (ăd-hē'zhən) n. 1. The act or condition of adhering. 2. Attachment or devotion; loyalty. 3. A condition in which body tissues that are normally separate are joined together: *an adhesion of the intestinal walls.* 4. The physical attraction or joining of two substances, esp. the macroscopically observable attraction of dissimilar substances.

ad·he·sive (ăd-hē'sĭv) adj. 1. Tending to adhere; sticky. 2. Gummed so as to adhere. —n. An adhesive substance, such as paste. —**ad·he'sive·ly** adv. —**ad·he'sive·ness** n.

adhesive tape. A tape lined on one side with an adhesive, often used to hold bandages in place.

ad hoc (ăd hŏk'). For a specific purpose, case, or situation: *an ad hoc committee.* [Latin, "toward this."]

ad·i·a·bat·ic (ăd'ē-ə-băt'ĭk, ā'dī-ə-) adj. Occurring without gain or loss of heat: *the adiabatic passage of sound through air.* [Greek *adiabatos*, "impassable (to heat)" : a-, not + *diabatos*, passable, *diabainein*, to go through.] —**ad'i·a·bat'i·cal·ly** adv.

a·dieu (ə-dōō', ə-dyōō') interj. Good-by; farewell. —n., pl. **a·dieus** or **a·dieux** (ə-dōōz', ə-dyōōz'). A farewell. [Middle English, from Old French, from *a dieu*, "(I commend you) to God" : Latin *ad*, to + *deus*, god.]

ad in·fi·ni·tum (ăd ĭn'fə-nī'təm). *Abbr.* **ad inf.** *Latin.* To infinity; without end; limitless.

a·di·os (ä'dē-ōs', ăd'ē-) interj. Good-by; farewell. [Spanish *adios*, transl. of French *adieu*, adieu.]

ad·i·pose (ăd'ə-pōs') adj. Of or related to animal fat; fatty. —n. The fat found in adipose tissue. [From Latin *adeps*, fat.] —**ad'i·pose'ness** or **ad'i·pos'i·ty** (-pŏs'ĭ-tē) n.

adipose tissue. Connective tissue in the body that contains stored cellular fat.

ad·ja·cent (ə-jā'sənt) adj. Next to; adjoining. [Middle English, from Latin *adjacēns*, pres. part. of *adjacēre*, to lie near : ad-, near to + *jacēre*, to lie.] —**ad·ja'cen·cy** (ə-jā'sən-sē) n. —**ad·ja'cent·ly** adv.

adjacent angle. Either of two angles having a common

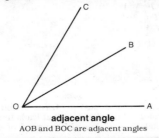

adjacent angle
AOB and BOC are adjacent angles

side and a common vertex and lying on opposite sides of the common side.

ad·jec·ti·val (ăj'ĭk-tī'vəl) adj. Of, pertaining to, or functioning as an adjective. —**ad'jec·ti'val·ly** adv.

ad·jec·tive (ăj'ĭk-tĭv) n. 1. *Gram.* A word used to describe a noun or to limit its meaning. For example, in the sentence *The young boy is very tall, young* and *tall* are adjectives. Most adjectives can be modified by words such as "very," "highly," and "extremely" and can be compared either by the addition of the *-er* and *-est* endings or by the placement of the words "more" and "most" in front of them; for example, *the young boy, the youngest boy; the more intelligent girl, the most intelligent girl.* 2. *Ling.* Any of a form class distinguished in English morphologically by one of several suffixes, such as *-able, -ous, -er,* and *-est.* 3. A dependent or subordinate. —adj. 1. Pertaining to or acting as an adjective; adjectival. 2. Dependent; subordinate. [Middle English, from Old French *adjectif,* from Latin *adjectīvus,* attributive, from *adjicere,* to throw to, add : ad-, to + *jacere,* to throw.]

ad·join (ə-join') tr.v. To be next to: *The bath adjoins the bedroom.* —intr.v. To be contiguous: *The rooms adjoin.* [Middle English *adjoinen,* from Old French *ajoindre,* from Latin *adjungere,* to join to.]

ad·journ (ə-jûrn') tr.v. To suspend until a later stated time. —intr.v. 1. To suspend proceedings to another time: *a motion to adjourn.* 2. *Informal.* To move from one place to another: *adjourned to the living room.* [Middle English *ajournen,* from Old French *ajourner,* "to put off to an appointed day" : Latin *ad-* + Late Latin *diurnum,* day, from Latin *diurnus,* daily, from *diēs,* day.] —**ad·journ'ment** n.

ad·judge (ə-jŭj') tr.v. **-judged, -judg·ing.** 1. To determine, rule, or declare by law: *The murderer was adjudged insane.* 2. To award (costs, damages, etc.) by law. 3. To regard, consider, or deem. [Middle English *ajugen,* from Old French *ajuger,* from Latin *adjūdicāre,* to adjudicate.]

ad·ju·di·cate (ə-jōō'dĭ-kāt') tr.v. **-cat·ed, -cat·ing.** To hear and settle (a case) by judicial procedure. [From Latin *adjūdicāre,* to award to (judicially) : ad-, to + *jūdicāre,* to be a judge, from *jūdex,* a judge.] —**ad·ju'di·ca'tion** n. —**ad·ju'di·ca'tive** adj. —**ad·ju'di·ca'tor** n.

ad·junct (ăj'ŭngkt') n. 1. Something attached to another thing but in a subordinate position: *The card shop is an adjunct of the bookstore.* 2. A person associated with another in a subordinate or auxiliary capacity. 3. A word or words added in order to clarify, qualify, or modify other words. [Latin *adjunctum,* from *adjungere,* to adjoin.]

ad·jure (ə-jōōr') tr.v. **-jured, -jur·ing.** 1. To command or enjoin solemnly, as under oath. 2. To appeal to earnestly. [Middle English *adjuren,* from Latin *adjūrāre,* to swear to : ad-, to + *jūrāre,* to swear.] —**ad·jur'er** or **ad·ju'ror** n.

ad·just (ə-jŭst') tr.v. 1. To change so as to match or fit; make correspond. 2. To bring into proper relationship; correct: *adjust the color on the television.* 3. To adapt or conform, as to new conditions. 4. To make accurate by regulation; adapt: *adjust prices for inflation.* 5. *Insurance.* To decide how much is to be paid (on a claim). —intr.v. To adapt oneself: *adjust to a new work schedule.* [From Old French *ajoster* : Latin *ad-,* near to + *juxtā,* close by, near.] —**ad·just'a·ble** adj. —**ad·just'er** or **ad·jus'tor** n.

ad·just·ment (ə-jŭst'mənt) n. 1. a. The act of adjusting: *adjustment to new surroundings.* b. The condition of being adjusted: *machinery in proper adjustment.* 2. A means for adjusting: *the adjustments on a camera.* 3. The settlement of a debt or claim. 4. Modification; correction: *an adjustment on a bill.*

ad·ju·tant (ăj'ə-tənt) n. 1. *Mil.* A staff officer who helps a commanding officer with administrative affairs. 2. An assistant. 3. A stork, the **marabou.** [Latin *adjūtāns,* pres. part. of *adjūtāre,* to assist, aid.] —**ad'ju·tan·cy** n.

adjutant general pl. **adjutants general.** The chief administrative officer, a major general, of the U.S. Army.

ad lib (ăd lĭb'). In an unrestrained manner; spontaneously.

ad-lib (ăd-lĭb'). *Informal.* —v. **-libbed, -lib·bing.** —tr.v. To improvise and deliver extemporaneously. —intr.v. To improvise a speech, lines, etc.; extemporize. —n. Words, music, or actions ad-libbed. —**modifier:** *an ad-lib remark.* [From Latin *ad libitum,* "at (one's) pleasure."]

ad·min·is·ter (ăd-mĭn'ĭ-stər) tr.v. 1. To have charge of; di-

---

rect; manage. **2. a.** To give or apply in a formal way: *administer the last rites.* **b.** To apply as a remedy: *administer a sedative.* **3.** To mete out; dispense: *administer justice.* **4.** To manage or dispose of (trusts and estates) under a will or an official appointment. **5.** To give (an oath, the sacraments, etc.) formally or officially. —*intr.v.* To manage as an administrator. [Middle English *administren*, from Old French *administrer*, from Latin *administrāre*, to be an aid to : *ad-*, to + *ministrāre*, to serve, from *minister*, servant.]

ad·min·is·trate (ăd-mĭn′ĭ-strāt′) *tr.v.* **-trat·ed, -trat·ing.** To administer.

ad·min·is·tra·tion (ăd-mĭn′ĭ-strā′shən) *n.* **1.** The act of administering. **2.** The activity and affairs of a government. **3.** Often **the Administration.** The persons collectively who make up the executive branch of a government. **4.** The management of any institution, public or private: *the school administration.* **5.** The term of office of an executive officer or body. **6.** *Law.* The management and disposal of a trust or estate. **7.** The dispensing, applying, or tendering of something, such as an oath, or medicine.

ad·min·is·tra·tive (ăd-mĭn′ĭ-strā′tĭv, -strə-) *adj.* Of, for, or relating to government or management: *an administrative officer.* —**ad·min′is·tra′tive·ly** *adv.*

ad·min·is·tra·tor (ăd-mĭn′ĭ-strā′tər) *n.* **1.** A person who administers, esp. business or public affairs; an executive. **2.** A person whom a court appoints to administer an estate.

ad·mi·ra·ble (ăd′mər-ə-bəl) *adj.* Deserving admiration; excellent. —**ad′mi·ra·ble·ness** *n.* —**ad′mir·a·bly** *adv.*

ad·mi·ral (ăd′mər-əl) *n.* **1.** The commander in chief of a navy or fleet. **2.** A naval officer, **Admiral of the Fleet.** **3.** In the U.S. Navy, U.S. Coast Guard, and Royal Canadian Navy: **a.** An officer of the next-to-the-highest rank. **b.** Any of several high-ranking naval officers including **rear admiral** and **vice admiral.** **4.** The ship carrying an admiral; flagship. **5.** Any of various brightly colored butterflies of the genera *Limentitis* and *Vanessa.* [Middle English, from Medieval Latin *a(d)mīrālis*, from Old French *amiral*, from Arabic *'amīr-al-* : *'amīr*, commander + *al*, the.]

admiral butterfly

Admiral of the Fleet. The highest rank in the U.S. Navy and Royal Canadian Navy, equivalent to General of the Army or Field Marshal. Also called **Admiral,** and **Fleet Admiral.**

ad·mi·ral·ty (ăd′mər-əl-tē) *n., pl.* **-ties. 1. a.** A court that has jurisdiction over all maritime cases. **b.** Maritime law. **2. Admiralty.** The department of the British government (Board of Admiralty) that has control over naval affairs.

ad·mi·ra·tion (ăd′mə-rā′shən) *n.* **1.** A feeling of pleasure, wonder, and approval. **2.** An object of wonder; marvel. —See Syns at **favor.**

ad·mire (ăd-mīr′) *v.* **-mired, -mir·ing.** —*tr.v.* **1.** To regard with wonder, pleasure, and approval. **2.** To have a high opinion of; esteem; respect. **3.** *Archaic.* To marvel or wonder at. —*intr.v.* To feel admiration. [Latin *admīrārī*, to wonder at : *ad-*, to, at + *mīrārī*, to wonder, from *mīrus*, wonderful.] —**ad·mir′er** *n.* —**ad·mir′ing·ly** *adv.*

ad·mis·si·ble (ăd-mĭs′ə-bəl) *adj.* **1.** Capable of being accepted: *admissible evidence.* **2.** Worthy of admission. —**ad·mis′si·bil′i·ty** or **ad·mis′si·ble·ness** *n.*

ad·mis·sion (ăd-mĭsh′ən) *n.* **1.** The act of admitting or the condition of being allowed to enter. **2.** The right to enter; access: *application for admission.* **3.** An entrance fee.

4. The act or process of acceptance and entry into a position or situation: *admission to the bar.* **5.** A confession or acknowledgment. —*modifier: an admission fee.* —See Usage note at **admittance.** —**ad·mis′sive** (-mĭs′ĭv) *adj.*

ad·mit (ăd-mĭt′) *v.* **-mit·ted, -mit·ting.** —*tr.v.* **1.** To permit to enter. **2.** To serve as a means of entrance: *This ticket admits the whole group.* **3.** To permit to join or exercise certain rights, functions, or privileges: *Great Britain was admitted to the Common Market.* **4.** To have room for; accommodate. **5.** To afford opportunity for; allow; permit. **6.** To acknowledge; confess: *admit the truth.* **7.** To grant or accept as true or valid, as for the sake of argument; concede. —*intr.v.* **1.** To afford possibility; allow: *That problem admits of no solution.* **2.** To allow entrance; afford access: *This door admits to the main hall.* —See Syns at **acknowledge.** [Middle English *admitten*, from Latin *admittere*, to send in to : *ad-*, to + *mittere*, to send.]

ad·mit·tance (ăd-mĭt′ns) *n.* **1.** The act of admitting or entering. **2.** Permission or right to enter.

Usage: **admittance, admission.** Use *admittance* for physical entry to a specific place: *no admittance to the jury room.* Use *admission* for figurative entry (*admission of evidence*) or, when physical entry is involved, in the sense of right of participation: *admission to a society; the price of admission to a theater.*

ad·mit·ted·ly (ăd-mĭt′ĭd-lē) *adv.* By general admission: *They were, admittedly, nervous.*

ad·mix (ăd-mĭks′) *tr.v.* To mix or blend. —*intr.v.* To be or become mixed or blended.

ad·mix·ture (ăd-mĭks′chər) *n.* **1. a.** The act of mixing. **b.** The state of being mixed. **2.** A combination, mixture, or blend. **3.** Anything added in mixing.

ad·mon·ish (ăd-mŏn′ĭsh) *tr.v.* **1.** To reprove mildly: *He admonished me for sulking.* **2.** To advise, warn, urge, or caution: *She admonished us to be careful.* [Middle English *admonissen*, from Old French *admonester*, from Latin *admonēre*, to bring to mind : *ad-*, to + *monēre*, to remind, advise.] —**ad·mon′ish·ing·ly** *adv.* —**ad·mon′ish·ment** *n.*

Syns: **admonish, rebuke, reprimand, reproach, reprove** *v.* *Core meaning:* To address someone disapprovingly because of a fault or misdeed. While ADMONISH refers to mild, warning criticism (*admonished me to drive slowly*), REPROVE and REPROACH imply somewhat stronger disapproval (*reproved the mischievous child*). REBUKE refers to sharp criticism (*rebuked the insolent child*) and REPRIMAND indicates the severest, often formal criticism of another (*a congressman reprimanded by his peers for taking bribes*).

ad·mo·ni·tion (ăd′mə-nĭsh′ən) *n.* **1.** Mild criticism. **2.** Cautionary advice or warning. [From Latin *admonitiō*, from *admonēre*, to admonish.]

ad·mon·i·to·ry (ăd-mŏn′ĭ-tôr′ē, -tōr′ē) *adj.* Urging caution: *an admonitory remark.*

ad nau·se·am (ăd nô′zē-əm). *Latin.* To the point of nausea; to a disgusting or ridiculous degree.

a·do (ə-dōō′) *n.* Bustle; fuss; trouble: *without further ado.* [Middle English, from *at do*, "to do."]

a·do·be (ə-dō′bē) *n.* **1. a.** Sun-dried, unburned brick of clay and straw. **b.** One such brick. **2.** Clay or soil from which such bricks are made. **3.** A structure built with such bricks. —*modifier: an adobe house.* [Spanish *adobe*, from Arabic *aṭṭōba*, *al-ṭōba*, "the brick."]

adobe

ad·o·les·cence (ăd′l-ĕs′əns) *n.* **1.** The period of physical and psychological development that leads from childhood to adulthood. **2.** Any transitional period of development between youth and maturity: *the adolescence of a nation.*

ad·o·les·cent (ăd′l-ĕs′ənt) *n.* A boy or girl, esp. a teen-ager, in the stage of development between childhood and adulthood. —*adj.* Of or going through adolescence. —See Syns at **young.** [Middle English, from Old French, from Latin *adolescēre,* to grow up : *ad-,* toward + *alēscere,* to grow, from *alere,* to nourish.]

A·don·is (ə-dŏn′ĭs, ə-dō′nĭs) *n.* **1.** *Gk. Myth.* A youth loved by Aphrodite for his striking beauty. **2. adonis.** Any young man of great physical beauty.

a·dopt (ə-dŏpt′) *tr.v.* **1.** To take into one's family through legal means and raise as one's own child. **2.** To accept and use or follow as one's own: *adopt a new technique.* **3.** To vote to accept: *adopt a resolution.* **4.** To choose as a required textbook in a course. [Latin *adoptāre,* to choose for oneself : *ad-,* to + *optāre,* to choose, desire.] —**a·dopt′a·ble** *adj.* —**a·dopt′er** *n.* —**a·dop′tion** *n.*

a·dop·tive (ə-dŏp′tĭv) *adj.* **1.** Tending to adopt. **2.** Acquired or related by adoption: *adoptive parents.* —**a·dop′tive·ly** *adv.*

a·dor·a·ble (ə-dôr′ə-bəl, ə-dōr′-) *adj.* **1.** *Informal.* Delightful; lovable; charming. **2.** Worthy of worship or adoration. —**a·dor′a·bil′i·ty** or **a·dor′a·ble·ness** *n.* —**a·dor′a·bly** *adv.*

a·dore (ə-dôr′, ə-dōr′) *tr.v.* **a·dored, a·dor·ing. 1.** To worship as divine. **2.** To love deeply; idolize. **3.** *Informal.* To like very much: *They adore skiing.* —See Syns at **love.** [Middle English *adoren,* from Old French *adorer,* from Latin *adōrāre,* to pray to : *ad-,* to + *ōrāre,* to speak, pray.] —**ad′o·ra′tion** *n.* —**a·dor′er** *n.* —**a·dor′ing·ly** *adv.*

a·dorn (ə-dôrn′) *tr.v.* To decorate with or as with ornaments. [Middle English *adornen,* from Old French *adorner,* from Latin *adornāre* : *ad-,* to + *ornāre,* to furnish, deck.]

a·dorn·ment (ə-dôrn′mənt) *n.* **1.** The act of adorning; decoration: *jewelry worn for personal adornment.* **2.** Something that adorns or beautifies; an ornament.

ADP. An adenosine derivative formed in cells that is reversibly converted to ATP for the storage of energy. Also called **adenosine diphosphate.**

a·dre·nal (ə-drē′nəl) *adj.* **1.** At, near, or on the kidneys. **2.** Of or pertaining to the adrenal glands or their secretions. —*n.* An adrenal gland. [AD- + RENAL.]

adrenal gland. Either of two small dissimilarly shaped endocrine glands, one located above each kidney, consisting of the cortex that secretes steroid hormones and the medulla that secretes epinephrine. Also called **suprarenal gland.**

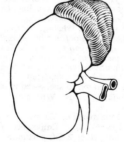

adrenal gland

A·dren·a·lin (ə-drĕn′ə-lĭn). A trademark for a preparation of adrenaline.

a·dren·a·line (ə-drĕn′ə-lĭn) *n.* A secretion of the adrenal glands, **epinephrine.**

a·drift (ə-drĭft′) *adv. & adj.* **1.** Drifting or floating freely; without anchor. **2.** Without direction or purpose.

a·droit (ə-droit′) *adj.* **1.** Dexterous; deft. **2.** Skillful and adept under pressing conditions: *an adroit answer.* [French, from *a droit,* "rightly" : Latin *ad-,* to + *dīrectus,* direct.] —**a·droit′ly** *adv.* —**a·droit′ness** *n.*

ad·sorb (ăd-sôrb′, -zôrb′) *tr.v.* To take up by adsorption. [AD- + Latin *sorbēre,* to drink in, suck.]

ad·sorp·tion (ăd-sôrp′shən, -zôrp′-) *n.* The assimilation of a gas, vapor, or dissolved matter by the surface of a solid or liquid. —**ad·sorp′tive** *adj.*

ad·u·late (ăj′ōō-lāt′) *tr.v.* **-lat·ed, -lat·ing.** To praise excessively. [Back-formation from ADULATION.] —**ad′u·la′tor** *n.* —**ad′u·la·to′ry** *adj.*

ad·u·la·tion (ăj′ōō-lā′shən) *n.* **1.** Excessive praise or flattery. **2.** Uncritical admiration; hero worship: *the boy's adulation of the athlete.* [Middle English *adulacioun,* from Old French *adulation,* from Latin *adulātiō,* from *adulārī,* to flatter.]

a·dult (ə-dŭlt′, ăd′ŭlt′) *n.* **1.** A person who has attained maturity or legal age. **2.** A fully grown, mature organism, such as an insect that has completed its final stage of metamorphosis. —**modifier:** *an adult adviser.* —*adj.* **1.** Fully developed and mature. **2.** Pertaining to, befitting, or intended for mature persons: *adult education.* —See Syns at **mature.** [Latin *adultus,* past part. of *adolescēre,* to grow up : *ad-,* to + *alēscere,* to grow, from *alere,* to nourish.] —**a·dult′hood** *n.*

a·dul·ter·ant (ə-dŭl′tər-ənt) *n.* A substance that adulterates. —*adj.* Adulterating.

a·dul·ter·ate (ə-dŭl′tə-rāt′) *tr.v.* **-at·ed, -at·ing.** To make impure or inferior by adding unnecessary, improper, or otherwise undesirable ingredients. [Latin *adulterāre,* to pollute, commit adultery.] —**a·dul′ter·a′tion** *n.*

a·dul·ter·er (ə-dŭl′tər-ər) *n.* A man who commits adultery.

a·dul·ter·ess (ə-dŭl′tər-ĭs, ə-dŭl′trĭs) *n.* A woman who commits adultery.

a·dul·ter·ous (ə-dŭl′tər-əs, -trəs) *adj.* Pertaining to, inclined to, or marked by adultery: *an adulterous relationship; an adulterous spouse.* —**a·dul′ter·ous·ly** *adv.*

a·dul·ter·y (ə-dŭl′tə-rē, -trē) *n., pl.* **-ries.** Voluntary sexual intercourse between a married person and a partner other than the lawful husband or wife. [Middle English *adulterie,* from Old French *avoutrie,* from Latin *adulterium,* from *adulter,* adulterer, from *adulterāre,* to adulterate.]

ad·um·brate (ăd′əm-brāt′, ə-dŭm′-) *tr.v.* **-brat·ed, -brat·ing. 1.** To give a sketchy outline of. **2.** To foreshadow. **3.** To disclose partially. [From Latin *adumbrāre,* overshadow : *ad-,* to + *umbra,* shadow.] —**ad′um·bra′tion** *n.* —**ad·um′bra·tive** (-brə-tĭv) *adj.*

ad va·lo·rem (ăd′ və-lôr′əm, -lōr′-). In proportion to the value: *ad valorem duties on new goods.* [Latin.]

ad·vance (ăd-văns′) *v.* **-vanced, -vanc·ing.** —*tr.v.* **1.** To move or bring forward in position. **2.** To put forward; propose; suggest. **3.** To aid the progress of; to further: *advance the cause of civil rights.* **4.** To raise in rank; promote. **5.** To cause to occur sooner. **6.** To raise in amount or rate; to increase. **7.** To pay (money or interest) before legally due. **8.** To supply or lend. —*intr.v.* **1.** To go or move forward or onward. **2.** To make progress; improve. **3.** To rise in rank, position, or value. —See Syns at **lend.** —**phrasal verb. advance on** (or **upon**). To move against, as when attacking. —*n.* **1.** The act or process of moving or going forward; progress. **2.** Improvement; progress. **3.** An increase of price or value. **4. advances.** Personal approaches made to secure acquaintance, favor, etc.; overtures. **5. a.** The furnishing of funds or goods on credit. **b.** The funds or goods so furnished; a loan. **6.** Payment of money before legally or normally due. —*adj.* **1.** Made or given ahead of time; prior: *advance warning.* **2.** Going before; in front; forward: *an advance man for the convention.* —**idiom. in advance. 1.** Ahead of time: *Make arrangements in advance.* **2.** In front: *He stood a little distance in advance.* [Middle English *advancen,* from Old French *avancier,* from Latin *abante,* from before : *ab-,* away from + *ante,* before.] —**ad·vanc′er** *n.*

Syns: 1. advance, proceed, progress *v.* *Core meaning:* To move forward. ADVANCE is most often limited to concrete instances of forward motion (*advanced a step or two*) but it can also refer to nonphysical movement (*advanced the deadline by one month*). PROCEED stresses continuing motion (*proceeding to the city via freeway*). PROGRESS suggests steady improvement or development (*found that her music studies were progressing well*). **2. advance, further, promote** *v.* *Core meaning:* To cause to move forward or upward, as toward a goal (*medical research that advanced our knowledge of life itself*). PROMOTE and FURTHER stress active support and encouragement (*a campaign to promote a new product; furthering one's career by attending night school*).

ă pat	ā pay	â care	ä father	ĕ pet	ē be	hw which	ĭ pit	ī tie	î pier	ŏ pot	ō toe	ô paw, for	oi noise
ōō took	ōō boot	ou out	th thin	th this	ŭ cut		û urge	zh vision	ə about, item, edible, gallop, circus

ad·vanced (ăd-vănst′) *adj.* **1.** Highly developed or complex: *an advanced civilization.* **2.** At a higher level than others: *an advanced student; advanced courses.* **3.** Ahead of the times; progressive: *advanced ideas.* **4. a.** Far along in course: *illness in its advanced stages.* **b.** Very old: *a man of advanced age.*

ad·vance·ment (ăd-văns′mənt) *n.* **1.** The act of advancing. **2.** A forward step; an improvement: *new advancements in word processing.* **3.** Development; progress: *the advancement of knowledge.* **4.** A getting ahead; promotion: *opportunity for advancement.*

ad·van·tage (ăd-văn′tĭj) *n.* **1.** A favorable factor or circumstance. **2.** Benefit or profit; gain. **3.** A favorable position; superiority. **4.** *Tennis.* The first point scored after deuce, or the resulting score. **—idioms. take advantage of. 1.** To put to good use; avail oneself of. **2.** To profit selfishly by; exploit. **to advantage.** To good effect; profitably; favorably. [Middle English *avantage,* from Old French, from *avant,* before, from Latin *abante,* from before : *ab-,* away from + *ante,* before.]

ad·van·ta·geous (ăd′văn-tā′jəs, ăd′vən-) *adj.* Affording benefit or gain; profitable; useful. **—ad′van·ta′geous·ly** *adv.* **—ad′van·ta′geous·ness** *n.*

ad·vent (ăd′vĕnt′) *n.* **1.** The coming or arrival, esp. of something awaited or momentous: *the advent of summer.* **2. Advent. a.** The birth of Christ. **b.** The **Second Advent. c.** The period including four Sundays before Christmas. [Middle English, from Latin *advenīre,* to come to : *ad,* to + *venīre,* to come.]

Ad·vent·ist (ăd′vĕn′tĭst) *n.* A member of a Christian denomination that believes Christ's second coming and the end of the world are near at hand. **—Ad′vent·ism** *n.*

ad·ven·ti·tious (ăd′vĕn-tĭsh′əs) *adj.* **1.** Acquired by chance; not inherent; accidental. **2.** *Biol.* Appearing in an unusual place or in an irregular manner: *adventitious shoots.* [Latin *adventīcius,* arriving (from outside), from *adventus,* arrival.] **—ad′ven·ti′tious·ly** *adv.* **—ad′ven·ti′tious·ness** *n.*

ad·ven·ture (ăd-vĕn′chər) *n.* **1.** An undertaking of a hazardous nature; a risky enterprise. **2.** An unusual experience marked by excitement or suspense. **3.** Participation in such experiences. **4.** A financial speculation or business venture. **—modifier:** *an adventure story.* **—v.** **-tured, -turing.** **—tr.v.** To venture; risk; dare. **—intr.v.** To take risks; engage in hazardous activities. [Middle English *aventure,* from Old French, from Latin *adventūrus,* from *advenīre,* to arrive : *ad-,* to + *venīre,* to come.]

ad·ven·tur·er (ăd-vĕn′chər-ər) *n.* **1.** A person who seeks or has adventures. **2.** A soldier of fortune. **3.** A heavy speculator in business or trade. **4.** A person who seeks wealth and position by unscrupulous means.

ad·ven·tur·ess (ăd-vĕn′chər-ĭs) *n.* A woman who seeks social and financial advancement by dubious means.

ad·ven·tur·ous (ăd-vĕn′chər-əs) *adj.* **1.** Also **ad·ven·ture·some** (-səm). Inclined to undertake new and daring enterprises; bold. **2.** Hazardous; risky; reckless. **—ad·ven′tur·ous·ly** *adv.* **—ad·ven′tur·ous·ness** *n.*

ad·verb (ăd′vûrb′) *n. Gram.* A word used to modify a verb, an adjective, or another adverb. For example, in the sentences *Bob left early, Ann is very pretty,* and *The dog ran very fast,* the words *early, very,* and *fast* are adverbs. Adverbs usu. answer questions beginning with "when," "where," and "how" and modify other words with respect to time, place, manner, or degree: *Bob left early* (time), *She went upstairs* (place), *Dick reads well* (manner), *Ann is very pretty* (degree). Many adverbs can be compared: *Dick reads well, but Joe reads better.* [Middle English, from Old French *adverbe,* from Latin *adverbium : ad-,* additional + *verbum,* word.]

ad·ver·bi·al (ăd-vûr′bē-əl) *adj.* **1.** Used as an adverb: *an adverbial phrase.* **2.** Of or pertaining to an adverb: *an adverbial form.* **—ad·ver′bi·al·ly** *adv.*

ad·ver·sar·y (ăd′vər-sĕr′ē) *n., pl.* **-ies.** An opponent; enemy. —See Syns at **opponent.**

ad·ver·sa·tive (ăd-vûr′sə-tĭv) *adj.* Expressing antithesis or opposition: *an adversative conjunction.* **—n.** An adversative word, as *however* or *but.*

ad·verse (ăd-vûrs′, ăd′vûrs′) *adj.* **1.** Antagonistic in design or effect; hostile; opposed: *adverse criticism.* **2.** Contrary to one's interests or welfare; unfavorable; unpropitious:

adverse circumstances. **3.** In an opposite or opposing direction or position: *adverse currents.* —See Syns at **unfavorable.** —See Usage note at **averse.** [Middle English, from Old French *advers,* from Latin *advertere,* to turn toward (with hostility) : *ad-,* toward + *vertere,* to turn.] **—ad·verse′ly** *adv.* **—ad·verse′ness** *n.*

ad·ver·si·ty (ăd-vûr′sĭ-tē) *n., pl.* **-ties. 1.** Great hardship or affliction; misfortune. **2.** A calamitous event.

ad·vert (ăd-vûrt′) *intr.v.* To call attention; refer: *advert to a problem.* [Middle English *adverten,* from Old French *advertir,* from Latin *advertere,* to turn toward : *ad-,* to + *vertere,* to turn.]

ad·ver·tise (ăd′vər-tīz′) *v.* **-tised, -tising.** **—tr.v. 1.** To make public announcement of, esp. to proclaim the advantages of (a product or business) so as to increase sales. **2.** To make known; call attention to: *She advertised her disappointment.* **—intr.v. 1.** To call the attention of the public to a product or business. **2.** To inquire in a public notice, as in a newspaper: *advertise for an apartment.* [Middle English *advertisen,* from Old French *advertir,* advert.] **—ad′ver·tis′er** *n.*

ad·ver·tise·ment (ăd′vər-tīz′mənt, ăd-vûr′tĭs-mənt, -tĭz-) *n.* A public notice, as in a newspaper or on the radio, designed to attract attention or patronage. Also called **ad.**

advertisement

ad·ver·tis·ing (ăd′vər-tī′zĭng) *n.* **1.** The act of attracting public attention to a product or business. **2.** The business of preparing and distributing advertisements. **3.** Advertisements collectively.

ad·vice (ăd-vīs′) *n.* Opinion about how to solve a problem; counsel; guidance. [Middle English *advise,* from Old French *advis,* opinion, from Latin *advīsum : ad,* to + *vīsum,* view, appearance, past. part. of *vidēre,* to see.]

ad·vis·a·ble (ăd-vī′zə-bəl) *adj.* Worthy of being recommended or suggested; prudent; sensible; expedient. **—ad·vis·a·bil′i·ty** *n.* **—ad·vis′a·bly** *adv.*

ad·vise (ăd-vīz′) *v.* **-vised, -vising.** **—tr.v. 1.** To offer advice to; to counsel: *The doctor advised rest.* **2.** To recommend; suggest: *I advise you to take the bus.* **3.** To inform; notify: *advise a person of a decision.* **—intr.v. 1.** To consult; take counsel: *advise with one's associates.* **2.** To offer advice. [Middle English *advisen,* from Old French *adviser :* Latin *ad-,* to, at + *videre,* to see.] **—ad·vi′ser** or **ad·vis′or** *n.*

ad·vis·ed·ly (ăd-vī′zĭd-lē) *adv.* With careful consideration; deliberately.

ad·vise·ment (ăd-vīz′mənt) *n.* Careful consideration.

ad·vi·so·ry (ăd-vī′zə-rē) *adj.* **1.** Empowered to advise: *a student advisory committee.* **2.** Of, pertaining to, or containing advice: *an advisory memorandum.*

ad·vo·ca·cy (ăd′və-kə-sē) *n.* Active support, as of a cause, idea, or policy.

ad·vo·cate (ăd′və-kāt′) *tr.v.* **-cated, -cating.** To speak in favor of; recommend or support. **—n.** (ăd′və-kĭt, -kāt′). **1.** A person who argues for a cause; supporter or defender: *an advocate of gun control.* **2.** A person who pleads in another's behalf: *The candidate's advocates campaigned throughout the state.* **3.** *Brit.* A courtroom lawyer. [From Middle English *advocat,* a lawyer, from Old French, from Latin *advocātus,* "one summoned (to give evidence)," from *advocāre,* to call to : *ad,* to + *vocāre,* to call.] **—ad′vo·ca′tor** *n.*

adz or **adze** (ădz) *n.* An axlike tool with a curved blade at right angles to the handle, used for dressing wood. [Middle English *adse,* from Old English *adesa.*]

ae·dile (ē′dīl′) *n.* In ancient Rome, a magistrate who had

adz

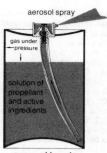

Aegisthus   aerosol bomb

charge of public works, police, and the grain supply. [Latin *aedīlis,* from *aedēs,* house.]

ae·gis (ē'jĭs) *n.* Also **e·gis. 1.** *Gk. Myth.* The shield of Zeus, lent by him to Athena. **2.** Protection. **3.** Sponsorship; patronage. [Latin, from Greek *aigis.*]

Ae·gis·thus (ĭ-jĭs'thəs) *n. Gk. Myth.* The lover of Clytemnestra, who aided her in killing her husband Agamemnon and was killed in revenge by Orestes.

Ae·ne·as (ĭ-nē'əs) *n. Gk. Myth.* The Trojan hero of the *Aeneid,* son of Anchises and Aphrodite, who wandered the world for seven years.

Ae·ne·id (ĭ-nē'ĭd) *n.* The Latin epic poem by Virgil, relating the adventures of Aeneas after the destruction of Troy.

Ae·o·li·an (ē-ō'lē-ən) *adj.* **1.** Of or pertaining to Aeolis, a region of Asia Minor, or its people. **2.** Of or pertaining to Aeolus, god of the winds.

Aeolian harp. A musical instrument consisting of an open box over which strings are stretched that sound when wind passes over them. Also called **wind harp.**

Ae·o·lus (ē'ə-ləs) *n. Gk. Myth.* **1.** The god of the winds. **2.** A king of Thessaly and ancestor of the Aeolians.

aer-. Var. of **aero-.**

aer·ate (âr'āt') *tr.v.* **-at·ed, -at·ing. 1.** To supply or charge (liquid) with a gas, esp. carbon dioxide. **2.** To expose to the circulation of air. **3.** To supply (blood) with oxygen. **—aer·a'tion** *n.* **—aer'a·tor** *n.*

aer·i·al (âr'ē-əl, ā-îr'ē-əl) *adj.* **1.** Of, in, or caused by the air. **2.** Reaching high into the air; lofty. **3.** Suggestive of air, as in lightness; airy. **4.** Unsubstantial; imaginary. **5.** Of, for, or by aircraft: *aerial surveillance.* **6.** *Bot.* Borne in the air rather than underground or underwater: *aerial roots.* *—n.* (âr'ē-əl). *Electronics.* An antenna. [From Latin *āerius,* from Greek *āērios,* from *aēr,* air.]

aer·i·al·ist (âr'ē-ə-lĭst) *n.* An acrobat who performs on a tightrope, trapeze, or similar apparatus.

aer·ie (âr'ē, ăr'ē, îr'ē) *n., pl.* **-ies.** Also **aer·y** or **eyr·ie** or **eyr·y. 1.** The nest of an eagle or other predatory bird, built on a high place. **2.** A house or stronghold built on a height. [Medieval Latin *aeria,* from Old French *aire,* from Latin *ārea,* open field, threshing floor, bird's nest.]

aero– or **aer-.** A prefix meaning: **1.** Air, gas, or the atmosphere: **aerate. 2.** Aircraft: **aeronautics.** [Middle English, from Old French, from Latin, from Greek, from *aēr,* air.]

aer·o·bat·ics (âr'ə-băt'ĭks) *n.* (*used with a sing. or pl. verb*). The performance of stunts, such as rolls and loops, with an airplane. [AERO-+ (ACRO)BATICS.]

aer·o·bic (â-rō'bĭk) *adj.* **1.** Requiring or living in the presence of molecular or free oxygen. **2.** Of, pertaining to, or caused by aerobic organisms. [AERO- + Greek *bios,* life.]

aer·o·drome (âr'ə-drōm') *n. Brit.* Var. of **airdrome.**

aer·o·dy·nam·ics (âr'ō-dī-năm'ĭks) *n.* (*used with a sing. verb*). The science that deals with the motion of gases, and esp. with the atmospheric forces exerted on moving objects. **—aer'o·dy·nam'ic** *adj.*

aer·o·me·chan·ics (âr'ō-mə-kăn'ĭks) *n.* (*used with a sing. verb*). The sciences of aerodynamics and aerostatics. **—aer'o·me·chan'i·cal** *adj.*

aer·o·naut (âr'ə-nôt') *n.* A pilot or navigator of a balloon or lighter-than-air craft. [AERO- + Greek *nautēs,* sailor.]

aer·o·nau·tic (âr'ə-nô'tĭk) or **aer·o·nau·ti·cal** (-tĭ-kəl) *adj.* Of or pertaining to aeronautics or aircraft. **—aer'o·nau'ti·cal·ly** *adv.*

aer·o·nau·tics (âr'ə-nô'tĭks) *n.* (*used with a sing. verb*). **1.** The design and practice of aircraft. **2.** The theory and practice of aircraft navigation.

aer·o·pause (âr'ə-pôz') *n.* The region of the atmosphere above which aircraft cannot fly.

aer·o·plane (âr'ə-plān') *n. Brit.* Var. of **airplane.**

aer·o·sol (âr'ə-sôl', -sŏl', -sōl') *n.* **1.** A gaseous suspension of fine solid or liquid particles. **2. a.** A substance, such as a detergent, insecticide, or paint, that is packaged under pressure with a gaseous propellant for release as an aerosol. **b.** An aerosol bomb. [AERO- + SOL(UTION).]

aerosol bomb. A *usu.* hand-held container or dispenser from which an aerosol is released.

aer·o·space (âr'ə-spās') *n.* **1.** The region consisting of the earth's atmosphere and outer space. **2.** The science and technology of flight both in the earth's atmosphere and in outer space. **—modifier:** *the aerospace industry.*

aer·y (âr'ē, ăr'ē, îr'ē) *n., pl.* **-ies.** Var. of **aerie.**

Aes·cu·la·pi·us (ĕs'kyoō-lā'pē-əs) *n. Rom. Myth.* The god of medicine and healing.

Ae·so·pi·an (ē-sō'pē-ən) *adj.* **1.** Of or in the manner of Aesop's animal fables. **2.** Disguised in allegorical suggestions so as to elude political censorship: *a speech filled with Aesopian allusions.*

aes·thete or **es·thete** (ĕs'thēt') *n.* **1.** A person who develops a superior appreciation of the beautiful, esp. in art. **2.** A person whose pursuit and admiration of beauty and art are thought to be affected and excessive. [Back-formation from AESTHETIC.]

aes·thet·ic or **es·thet·ic** (ĕs-thĕt'ĭk) *adj.* **1.** Of aesthetics. **2. a.** Of or pertaining to the sense of the beautiful: *the aesthetic faculties.* **b.** Artistic: *an aesthetic success.* **3.** Having a love of beauty. [From Greek *aisthētikos,* pertaining to sense perception, from *aisthenasthai,* to perceive.] **—aes·thet'i·cal·ly** *adv.*

aes·thet·i·cism or **es·thet·i·cism** (ĕs-thĕt'ĭ-sĭz'əm) *n.* **1.** The devotion to or pursuit of the beautiful; the cult of beauty and good taste. **2. a.** The belief that beauty is the basic principle from which all other principles are derived. **b.** The doctrine in which art and artists are held to have no obligations other than that of striving for beauty.

aes·thet·ics or **es·thet·ics** (ĕs-thĕt'ĭks) *n.* (*used with a sing. verb*). **1.** The branch of philosophy that deals with the theories and forms of beauty and of the fine arts. **2.** The theories and descriptions of the psychological responses to beauty and artistic experiences.

aes·ti·vate (ĕs'tə-vāt') *intr.v.* **-vat·ed, -vat·ing.** Also **es·ti·vate.** *Zool.* To pass the summer or periods of drought in a state of dormancy. [From Latin *aestīvāre,* from *aestās,* summer.] **—aes'ti·va'tion** *n.*

ae·ther (ē'thər) *n.* **1. Aether.** *Gk. Myth. & Poet.* The clear upper air breathed by the Olympians. **2.** Var. of **ether.**

a·far (ə-fär') *adv.* Far away; far off.

a·feard (ə-fîrd') *adj.* Also **a·feared.** *Archaic.* Afraid. [Middle English *afered,* from Old English *āfǣred,* past part. of *āfǣran,* to frighten : *ā-,* (intensive) + *fǣr,* fear.]

af·fa·ble (ăf'ə-bəl) *adj.* **1.** Easy to speak to; approachable; amiable. **2.** Mild; gentle; benign: *an affable greeting.* — See Syns at **amiable.** [Old French, from Latin *affābilis,* from *affārī,* to speak to : *ad-,* to + *fārī,* to speak.] **—af'fa·bil'i·ty** *n.* **—af'fa·bly** *adv.*

af·fair (ə-fâr') *n.* **1.** Anything done or to be done; concern;

business. **2. affairs.** Transactions or matters of professional or business interests or public concern: *world affairs; a man of affairs.* **3.** Any object or contrivance: *Our first car was a ramshackle affair.* **4.** Often **affairs.** A private matter; personal concern: *Don't pry into my affairs.* **5.** A matter causing scandal and controversy: *the Dreyfus affair.* **6.** A love affair, esp. a brief one. **7.** A social gathering; party. [Middle English *afere,* from Old French *afaire,* from *a faire,* "to do" : Latin *ad-,* to + *facere,* to do.]

af·fect¹ (ə-fĕkt′) *tr.v.* **1.** To have an influence on; bring about a change in: *Geography affects people's way of living.* **2.** To touch or move the emotions of: *She was not affected by his death.* **3.** To attack or infect: *Anthrax affects cattle and sheep.* —*n.* (ăf′ĕkt′). *Psychol.* A feeling or emotion as distinguished from cognition, thought, or action. —See Usage note at **effect.** [Latin *afficere* (past part. *affectus*), to do something to, exert influence on : *ad-,* to + *facere,* to do.]

af·fect² (ə-fĕkt′) *tr.v.* **1.** To simulate or imitate in order to make some desired impression; pretend; feign: *He affected an English accent.* **2.** To display a preference for; like; prefer: *He affects three-piece suits.* [Middle English *affecter,* from Latin *affectāre,* to strive after, freq. of *afficere,* to affect.] —**af·fect′ed·ly** *adv.* —**af·fect′ed·ness** *n.*

af·fec·ta·tion (ăf′ĕk-tā′shən) *n.* **1.** A show, pretense, or display: *an affectation of wonder.* **2.** Any artificial behavior adopted to impress others. [Latin *affectātiō,* from *affectāre,* to strive after, affect.]

af·fec·tion (ə-fĕk′shən) *n.* **1.** A warm or tender feeling toward another; fondness. **2.** A disease or diseased condition. **3.** Mental disposition or tendency. [Middle English *affecioun,* from Old French *affection,* from Latin *affectiō,* disposition, from *afficere,* to affect.]

af·fec·tion·ate (ə-fĕk′shə-nĭt) *adj.* Having or showing fond feelings or affection. —**af·fec′tion·ate·ly** *adv.*

af·fec·tive (ə-fĕk′tĭv) *adj. Psychol.* Pertaining to or resulting from emotions rather than from thought. **2.** Pertaining to or arousing affection or emotion; emotional.

af·fer·ent (ăf′ər-ənt) *adj.* Directed or leading to a central organ or part of an organism: *afferent nerves.* [Latin *afferēns,* pres. part. of *afferre,* to bring toward : *ad-,* toward + *ferre,* to bring.]

af·fi·ance (ə-fī′əns) *tr.v.* **-anced, -anc·ing.** To pledge or promise marriage; betroth. [From Old French *affiancer,* to trust, from *affier,* to trust to, from Medieval Latin *affīdāre* : Latin *ad-,* to + *fīdere,* to trust.]

af·fi·da·vit (ăf′ĭ-dā′vĭt) *n. Law.* A written declaration made under oath before a notary public or other authorized officer. [Medieval Latin *affīdāvit,* "he has pledged," from *affīdāre,* to trust to : Latin *ad-,* to + *fīdere,* to trust.]

af·fil·i·ate (ə-fĭl′ē-āt′) *v.* **-at·ed, -at·ing.** —*tr.v.* **1.** To adopt or accept as an associate. **2.** To associate (oneself) as a subordinate, subsidiary, or member with: *The local was affiliated with the national union.* —*intr.v.* To associate or join with an organization, group, etc.: *We decided to affiliate.* —*n.* (ə-fĭl′ē-ĭt, -āt′). A person or organization associated with another in a subordinate relationship. [From Medieval Latin *affīliāre,* to adopt as a son" : Latin *ad-,* to + *fīlius,* son.] —**af·fil′i·a′tion** *n.*

af·fin·i·ty (ə-fĭn′ĭ-tē) *n., pl.* **-ties. 1.** A natural personal attraction; liking. **2.** Relationship by marriage. **3.** An inherent similarity between things; relationship. **4.** A relationship or resemblance between biological species that implies a common origin. **5.** A chemical attraction or force that causes the atoms of certain elements to combine with atoms of another element and remain in the combined state. [Middle English *affinite,* from Old French *afinite,* from Latin *affinitās,* from *affinis,* neighboring : *ad-,* to + *finis,* border.]

af·firm (ə-fûrm′) *tr.v.* **1.** To declare positively or firmly; maintain to be true. **2.** To ratify or confirm. —*intr.v. Law.* To declare solemnly and formally, but not under oath. — See Syns at **assert.** [Middle English *affermen,* from Old French *afermer,* from Latin *affirmāre,* : *ad-,* to + *firmus,* firm.] —**af·firm′a·ble** *adj.* —**af·firm′ant** *adj. & n.* —**af′firm′a·tion** *n.*

af·firm·a·tive (ə-fûr′mə-tĭv) *adj.* **1.** Giving assent; responding as with the word *yes.* **2.** Asserting that something is true as represented; confirming: *an affirmative response.*

—*n.* **1.** A word or phrase signifying assent. **2.** The side in a debate that upholds a proposition. —**af·firm′a·tive·ly** *adv.*

affirmative action. Action taken to provide equal opportunity, as in hiring, for members of previously disadvantaged groups, such as women and minorities, often with specific goals and timetables.

af·fix (ə-fĭks′) *tr.v.* **1.** To secure (an object) to another; attach: *affix a label to a package.* **2.** To place at the end; append: *affix a postscript.* —*n.* (ăf′ĭks′). **1.** Something that is attached, joined, or added. **2.** A word element, such as a prefix or suffix, that is always attached to a base, stem, or root. —See Syns at **attach.** [Medieval Latin *affīxāre,* to fix to.]

af·fla·tus (ə-flā′təs) *n.* An inspiration, as of an artist. [Latin *afflātus,* inspiration, past part. of *afflāre,* to breathe on : *ad-,* toward + *flāre,* to blow.]

af·flict (ə-flĭkt′) *tr.v.* To inflict pain or suffering upon; distress. [Middle English *afflicten,* from Latin *affligere,* to dash against : *ad-,* to + *flīgere,* to strike.]

af·flic·tion (ə-flĭk′shən) *n.* **1.** A condition of pain or distress. **2.** A cause of pain or suffering.

af·flu·ence (ăf′lōō-əns) *n.* **1.** Wealth; riches. **2.** A plentiful supply; abundance. **3.** A flowing toward.

af·flu·ent (ăf′lōō-ənt) *adj.* **1.** Rich; wealthy; opulent: *an affluent society.* **2.** Copious; abundant. **3.** Flowing freely. —See Syns at **rich.** —*n.* A tributary stream or river. [Middle English, from Old French, from Latin *affluēns,* pres. part. of *affluere,* to flow to : *ad-,* toward + *fluere,* to flow.] —**af′flu·ent·ly** *adv.*

af·ford (ə-fôrd′, ə-fōrd′) *tr.v.* **1.** To have the financial means for. **2.** To be able to spare or give up: *I can afford one hour for lunch.* **3.** To be able to do without harming oneself: *He can afford to be tolerant.* **4.** To provide: *Swimming affords good exercise.* [Middle English *aforthen,* from Old English *geforthian,* to further, achieve, from *forth,* forward.] —**af·ford′a·ble** *adj.*

af·fray (ə-frā′) *n.* A noisy quarrel or brawl. [Middle English, from Old French *effray,* from *affreer,* to startle.]

af·fri·cate (ăf′rĭ-kĭt) *n. Phonet.* A sound when a stop is followed by a fricative; for example, the *j* sound in *judge.* Also called **affricative.** [Latin (*vox*) *affricāta,* "rubbed" (sound) : *ad-,* to + *fricāre,* to rub.]

af·fright (ə-frīt′) *Archaic.* —*tr.v.* To frighten; terrify. —*n.* Sudden terror; fear.

af·front (ə-frŭnt′) *tr.v.* **1.** To insult intentionally. **2.** To meet face to face defiantly; confront. —See Syns at **insult.** —*n.* An intentional offense, slight, or insult. [Middle English *affronten,* to meet, from Old French *afronter* : Latin *ad-,* to + *frōns,* forehead.]

Af·ghan (ăf′găn′, -gən) *n.* **1.** A native of Afghanistan. **2.** An Iranian language, **Pashto. 3. afghan.** A coverlet knitted or crocheted in colorful geometric designs. —*adj.* Of or pertaining to Afghanistan, its people, or their language.

afghan   Afghan hound

Afghan hound. A large, slender dog of an ancient breed, with long, thick hair, a pointed muzzle, and drooping ears.

a·fi·ci·o·na·do (ə-fĭsh′ə-nä′dō, ə-fē′sē-ə-, ə-fĭs′ē-ə-) *n., pl.* **-dos.** An enthusiastic admirer or follower; devotee. [Spanish, from *aficionar,* to incite affection, from *aficion,* affection, from Latin *affectiō.*]

a·field (ə-fēld′) *adv.* **1.** Off the desired track; astray. **2.** Away from one's home. **3.** To or on a field.

a·fire (ə-fīr′) *adj. & adv.* **1.** On fire; burning. **2.** Intensely interested and involved.

a·flame (ə-flām') *adj. & adv.* **1.** On fire; flaming. **2.** Keenly excited.

a·float (ə-flōt') *adj.* **1.** Floating. **2.** On board ship; at sea. **3.** In circulation: *Rumors of war are afloat.* **4.** Awash; flooded. **5.** Free or out of difficulty: *We couldn't keep the store afloat.* **—a·float'** *adv.*

a·flut·ter (ə-flŭt'ər) *adj.* In a flutter; nervous and excited.

a·foot (ə-fŏot') *adj.* **1.** Walking; on foot. **2.** In the process of happening; astir: *Plans are afoot.* **—a·foot'** *adv.*

a·fore (ə-fôr', ə-fōr') *adv. & prep.* Archaic. Before. [Middle English *afor(e)n*, from Old English *onforan*: *on*, at + *for*, fore.]

a·fore·men·tioned (ə-fôr'měn'shənd, ə-fōr'-) *adj.* Mentioned previously or before.

a·fore·said (ə-fôr'sěd', ə-fōr'-) *adj.* Spoken of earlier.

a·fore·thought (ə-fôr'thôt', ə-fōr'-) *adj.* Planned beforehand; premeditated: *malice aforethought.*

a for·ti·o·ri (ä' fôr'shē-ôr'ē, ä' fôr'shē-ōr'ī). *Latin.* For a stronger reason; all the more. Said of a conclusion arrived at with greater logical necessity than another.

a·foul (ə-foul') *adv.* In a snarl or entanglement. **—idiom.** **run** (or **fall**) **afoul of.** To have trouble with: *She ran afoul of the law.* **—a·foul'** *adj.*

a·fraid (ə-frād') *adj.* **1.** Filled with fear; frightened. **2.** Reluctant; averse: *not afraid to work.* **3.** Filled with regret: *I'm afraid you're wrong.* [Middle English *affraied*, past part. of *affraien*, to frighten, from Old French *affreer*, to startle.]

a·fresh (ə-frĕsh') *adv.* Once more; again; anew.

Af·ri·can (ăf'rĭ-kən) *adj.* Of or pertaining to Africa or any of its peoples or languages. *—n.* **1.** A person born or living in Africa. **2.** A member of one of the indigenous peoples of Africa.

African violet. Any of several plants of the genus *Saintpaulia*, native to tropical Africa and widely cultivated as house plants, esp. *S. ionantha*, having violet, white, or pink flowers.

Af·ri·kaans (ăf'rĭ-käns', -känz') *n.* A language developed from 17th-cent. Dutch that is now one of the official languages of the Republic of South Africa.

Af·ri·kan·er (ăf'rĭ-kä'nər) *n.* A descendant of the Dutch settlers of South Africa.

Af·ro (ăf'rō) *n., pl.* **-ros.** A full, rounded hair style in which dense frizzy hair is worn naturally. *—adj.* **1.** Of or pertaining to an Afro. **2.** African in style.

Af·ro-A·mer·i·can (ăf'rō-ə-měr'ĭ-kən) *adj.* Of or pertaining to Americans of African and esp. of black ancestry. **—Af'ro-A·mer'i·can** *n.*

aft (ăft) *adv. & adj.* At, in, toward, or near a ship's stern. [Prob. short for ABAFT.]

af·ter (ăf'tər) *prep.* **1.** In a place or order following: *The caboose comes after the freight cars.* **2. a.** In pursuit of: *running after the fire engine.* **b.** Out to get: *They're after me.* **3.** About; concerning: *I asked after you.* **4.** At a later time than: *after the war.* **5.** Past the hour of: *five minutes after three.* **6.** With the same name as: *named after her mother.* *—conj.* As soon as or following the time that: *We can eat after we get home.* *—adv.* **1.** Afterward: *forever after.* **2.** Behind: *And Jill came tumbling after.* *—adj.* **1.** Later: *in after years.* **2.** Nearer a ship's stern: *the after quarter.* [Middle English, from Old English *æfter.*]

after all. Nevertheless: *We'll win the game after all.*

af·ter·birth (ăf'tər-bûrth') *n.* The placenta and fetal membranes expelled from the uterus after childbirth.

af·ter·burn·er (ăf'tər-bûr'nər) *n.* A device for increasing the thrust of a jet engine by burning additional fuel with the uncombined oxygen in the hot exhaust gases.

af·ter·deck (ăf'tər-děk') *n.* The part of a ship's deck past amidships toward the stern.

af·ter·ef·fect (ăf'tər-ĭ-fěkt') *n.* An effect or secondary effect following some delay, esp. a delayed physiological or psychological response to a stimulus.

af·ter·glow (ăf'tər-glō') *n.* **1.** The light remaining after removal of a source of illumination: **a.** The atmospheric glow after sunset. **b.** The glow of an incandescent metal as it cools. **2.** The comfortable feeling following a pleasant experience.

af·ter·im·age (ăf'tər-ĭm'ĭj) *n.* A visual image that continues to be seen after exposure to an external stimulus ceases.

af·ter·life (ăf'tər-līf') *n.* Life or existence after death.

af·ter·math (ăf'tər-măth') *n.* A consequence or result, esp. of a disaster or misfortune. [AFTER + obs. *math*, mowing, from Old English *mæth.*]

af·ter·noon (ăf'tər-nōōn') *n.* The part of the day from noon until sunset. **—modifier:** *an afternoon nap.*

af·ter·taste (ăf'tər-tāst') *n.* **1.** A taste that remains in the mouth after the substance that caused it is no longer there. **2.** A feeling that remains after an event or experience.

af·ter·thought (ăf'tər-thôt') *n.* An idea or explanation that occurs to one after an event or decision.

af·ter·ward (ăf'tər-wərd) *adv.* Also **af·ter·wards** (-wərdz). In or at a later time; subsequently.

Usage: **afterward, afterwards.** Both words are acceptable, but *afterward* occurs most often in written American usage.

Ag The symbol for the element silver [Latin *argentum*].

a·gain (ə-gĕn') *adv.* **1.** Once more; anew. **2.** To a previous place or position: *He left home, but went back again.* **3.** Furthermore: *Let me say it again.* **4.** On the other hand: *He might go, and then again he might not.* **—idioms.** **again and again.** Repeatedly; frequently. **as much again.** Twice as much. [Middle English, from Old English *ongeagn*, in return, toward, against.]

a·gainst (ə-gĕnst') *prep.* **1.** In a direction or course opposite to: *sailing against the wind.* **2.** So as to come into contact with: *waves dashing against the shore.* **3.** In hostile opposition or resistance to: *struggling against change.* **4.** Contrary to: *against my better judgment.* **5.** In contrast to: *dark colors against a light background.* **6.** As a defense or safeguard from: *wearing gloves against the chill.* **7.** To the account or debt of: [Middle English, from *again*, against, again.]

Ag·a·mem·non (ăg'ə-měm'nŏn') *n. Gk. Myth.* The king of Mycenae, leader of the Greeks against Troy.

a·gape (ə-gāp', ə-găp') *adj.* With the mouth wide open, as in wonder, amazement, etc.

a·gar (ä'gär', ä'gär) *n.* Also **a·gar-a·gar** (ä'gär-ä'gär, ä'gär-ä'-). A gelatinous material prepared from certain saltwater algae and used as a base for bacterial culture media and for thickening certain foods. [Malay, "jelly, gelatin."]

ag·a·ric (ăg'ə-rĭk, ə-găr'ĭk) *n.* Any fungus of the family Agaricacae, esp. the common cultivated mushroom. [Latin *agaricum*, from Greek *agarikon*, after *Agaria*, an ancient city.]

ag·ate (ăg'ĭt) *n.* **1.** A hard, fine-grained variety of chalcedony with bands of color. **2.** A marble made of this or a glass imitation of it. **3.** A printer's type size. [Old French, from Latin *achātēs*, from Greek *akhātēs.*]

agate

a·ga·ve (ə-gä'vē, ə-gā'-) *n.* Any of numerous fleshy-leaved tropical American plants of the genus *Agave*, which includes the century plant. Some species yield valuable fibers. [New Latin, "noble (plant)" (prob. so named from its height), from Greek *agauos*, noble.]

age (āj) *n.* **1.** The period of time during which someone or something exists. **2.** A lifetime. **3.** That time in life when a person assumes certain civil and personal rights and responsibilities: *he's under age.* **4.** Any period of life denoted as differing from other periods; a stage: *the age of adolescence.* **5.** The latter portion of life: *old age.* **6.** Often **Age.** Any period in history or geology designated by distinctive characteristics: *the age of enlightenment.* **7.** Informal. An extended period of time: *They left ages ago.* *—v.* **aged,** **ag·ing.** *—tr.v.* To cause to grow older or more mature.

—*intr.v.* **1.** To become old. **2.** To show characteristics associated with old age. [Middle English, from Old French, from Latin *aetās.*]

-age. A suffix that forms nouns and means: **1.** Collectively: **leafage. 2.** Relation to or connection with: **parentage. 3.** Action or process: **cleavage. 4.** Condition or position: **vagabondage, marriage. 5.** Charge or fee: **postage, cartage. 6.** Residence or place: **vicarage, orphanage.** [Middle English, from Old French, from Late Latin *-āticum.*]

a·ged (ā′jĭd) *adj.* **1.** Old; on in years. **2.** Of or characteristic of old age. **3.** (ājd). Of the age of. **4.** Having developed a certain quality as a result of aging; mature: *an aged cheese.* —See Syns at **old.** —*n.* **the aged.** Very old people. —**a′ged·ness** *n.*

age·ing (ā′jĭng) *n. Brit.* Var. of **aging.**

age·ism (ā′jĭz′əm) *n.* Discrimination based on age, esp. discrimination against middle-aged and elderly people. —**age′ist** *n.*

age·less (āj′lĭs) *adj.* **1.** Seeming never to grow old. **2.** Existing forever. —**age′less·ly** *adv.* —**age′less·ness** *n.*

age-long (āj′lông′, -lŏng′) *adj.* Lasting or continuing for a long time: *the age-long evolution of mammals.*

a·gen·cy (ā′jən-sē) *n., pl.* **-cies. 1.** The action, power, or mode of operation by which something is done; a means. **2.** A business or service authorized to act for others: *an employment agency.* **3.** A governmental department of administration or regulation. [Latin *agentia,* from *agēns,* acting, agent.]

a·gen·da (ə-jěn′də) *pl.n.* The less frequently used sing. is **a·gen·dum** (ə-jěn′dəm). *(used with a sing. verb).* A list of things to be done, esp. the program for a meeting. [Latin, pl. of *agendum,* from *agere,* to do.]

Usage: **Agenda,** though historically a plural noun, has been construed by many to be singular and has consequently developed its own plural: *agendas.*

a·gent (ā′jənt) *n.* **1.** Someone or something that acts or has the power or authority to act. **2.** Someone or something that acts for or as the representative of another: *an insurance agent.* **3.** A means or mode by which something is done or caused; an instrument: *a disease-causing agent.* **4.** A force or substance that causes some changes: *a chemical agent.* **5.** A representative of a government or administrative department of a government: *an FBI agent.* [Middle English, from Latin *agēns,* pres. part. of *agere,* to act, drive, do.]

a·gent pro·vo·ca·teur (ä-zhän′ prô-vô-kä-tûr′) *pl.* **a·gents pro·vo·ca·teurs** (ä-zhän′ prô-vô-kä-tûr′). *French.* A person who infiltrates an organization in order to incite its members to commit acts for which they will incur punishment.

age-old (āj′ōld′) *adj.* Very old; ancient: *age-old rocks.*

ag·er·a·tum (ăj′ə-rā′təm) *n.* **1.** Any of various plants of the genus *Ageratum;* esp. *A. houstonianum,* a commonly cultivated species with clusters of usu. violet-blue flowers. **2.** Any of several other plants having similar flower clusters. [From Latin *agēraton,* from Greek *agēratos,* ageless : *a-,* not + *gēras,* old age.]

ag·glom·er·ate (ə-glŏm′ə-rāt′) *v.* **-at·ed, -at·ing.** —*tr.v.* To make or form into a rounded mass. —*intr.v.* To take the shape of a rounded mass. —*adj.* (ə-glŏm′ər-ĭt). Gathered into a rounded mass. —*n.* (ə-glŏm′ər-ĭt). **1.** A jumbled mass of things clustered together. **2.** A volcanic rock consisting of rounded and angular fragments fused together. [From Latin *agglomerāre* : *ad-,* to + *glomus,* ball.] —**ag·glom′er·a′tive** *adj.*

ag·glom·er·a·tion (ə-glŏm′ə-rā′shən) *n.* **1.** The process or act of agglomerating. **2.** A confused or jumbled mass; agglomerate.

ag·glu·ti·nant (ə-glōōt′n-ənt) *n.* A substance that makes things stick together. —*adj.* Causing agglutination.

ag·glu·ti·nate (ə-glōōt′n-āt′) *v.* **-nat·ed, -nat·ing.** —*tr.v.* **1.** To join together by causing adhesion, as with glue. **2.** *Ling.* To form (words) by combining words or words and word elements. **3.** *Physiol.* To cause (red blood cells or microorganisms) to clump together. —*intr.v.* **1.** To join together into a group or mass. **2.** *Ling.* To form words by agglutination. **3.** To undergo agglutination. [From Latin *agglūtināre* : *ad-,* to + *glūten,* glue.]

ag·glu·ti·na·tion (ə-glōōt′n-ā′shən) *n.* **1.** The process of ag-

glutinating; adhesion of distinct parts. **2.** A mass formed in this manner. **3.** *Ling.* The formation of words from smaller words or word parts that retain their original forms and meanings with little change.

ag·glu·ti·na·tive (ə-glōōt′n-ā′tĭv) *adj.* **1.** Tending toward, concerning, or characteristic of agglutination. **2.** *Ling.* Designating words formed by agglutination.

ag·gran·dize (ə-grăn′dīz′, ăg′rən-dīz′) *tr.v.* **-dized, -diz·ing. 1.** To make greater in power, influence, etc. **2.** To make (something) seem greater; exaggerate. [From French *aggrandir,* : Latin *ad-,* to + *grandis,* grand.] —**ag·gran′dize·ment** *n.* —**ag·gran′diz·er** *n.*

ag·gra·vate (ăg′rə-vāt′) *tr.v.* **-vat·ed, -vat·ing. 1.** To make worse or more troublesome: *aggravate an injury.* **2.** To annoy; provoke; irritate. —See Syns at **annoy.** [From Latin *aggravāre,* to make heavier : *ad-,* in addition to + *gravāre,* to burden, from *gravis,* heavy.] —**ag′gra·vat′ing·ly** *adv.*

ag·gra·va·tion (ăg′rə-vā′shən) *n.* **1.** The act or process of aggravating. **2.** The condition of being aggravated. **3.** A thing that irritates or makes worse. **4.** Exasperation; annoyance; irritation.

ag·gre·gate (ăg′rə-gĭt′, -gāt′) *adj.* Gathered together into a mass or sum so as to constitute a whole; total: *The aggregate work force at our plant numbers 2,500.* —*n.* (ăg′rə-gĭt). Any total or whole considered with reference to its constituent parts; an assemblage or group of distinct particulars massed together: *An empire is the aggregate of many states.* —*tr.v.* (ăg′rə-gāt′) **-gat·ed, -gat·ing. 1.** To gather into a mass, sum, or whole. **2.** To total up to; amount to. [Middle English *aggregat,* from Latin *aggregāre,* to add to (the flock) : *ad-,* to + *gregāre,* to herd, from *grex,* flock.] —**ag′gre·gate·ly** *adv.* —**ag′gre·ga′tion** *n.* —**ag′gre·ga′tive** *adj.*

ag·gres·sion (ə-grěsh′ən) *n.* **1.** The action of a country in launching an unprovoked attack on another. **2.** The habit or practice of launching attacks. **3.** Hostile action or behavior. [Latin *aggressiō,* from *aggredī,* to attack, approach : *ad-,* toward + *gradī,* to go.]

ag·gres·sive (ə-grěs′ĭv) *adj.* **1.** Quick to attack or act in a hostile fashion. **2.** Assertive; bold: *an aggressive salesman.* —**ag·gres′sive·ly** *adv.* —**ag·gres′sive·ness** *n.*

ag·gres·sor (ə-grěs′ər) *n.* A person or country that attacks another without cause or justification.

ag·grieve (ə-grēv′) *tr.v.* **-grieved, -griev·ing. 1.** To distress or afflict; trouble. **2.** To injure or treat unjustly; wrong. [Middle English *agreven,* from Old French *agrever,* from Latin *aggravāre,* to make heavier, aggravate.]

a·ghast (ə-găst′) *adj.* Shocked, as by something horrible; terrified. [Middle English *agast,* past part. of *agasten,* to frighten : *a-* (intensive) + Old English *gāst,* ghost.]

ag·ile (ăj′əl, ăj′īl′) *adj.* **1.** Able to move in a quick and easy fashion; nimble. **2.** Mentally alert: *an agile mind.* [Middle English, from Old French, from Latin *agilis,* easily moved, nimble, from *agere,* to drive.] —**ag′ile·ly** *adv.*

a·gil·i·ty (ə-jĭl′ĭ-tē) *n.* The condition or quality of being agile; nimbleness; briskness.

ag·ing (ā′jĭng) *n.* Also *Brit.* **age·ing. 1.** The process of becoming old or mature. **2.** Any artificial process for imparting the characteristics and properties of age.

ag·i·tate (ăj′ĭ-tāt′) *v.* **-tat·ed, -tat·ing.** —*tr.v.* **1.** To move or shake with violence: *a storm agitating the ocean.* **2.** To upset, disturb, or excite: *Grief agitated the widow.* —*intr.v.* To stir up public interest in a cause: *agitating for passage of a new law.* [Latin *agitāre,* freq. of *agere,* to do, drive.] —**ag′i·tat′ed·ly** *adv.*

ag·i·ta·tion (ăj′ĭ-tā′shən) *n.* **1.** The act of agitating. **2.** The condition of being agitated; disturbance; commotion. **3.** Extreme emotional disturbance or excitement. **4.** Energetic action or discussion to arouse public interest on a matter of controversy, such as a political or social issue.

ag·i·ta·tor (ăj′ĭ-tā′tər) *n.* **1.** A person who agitates, esp. one who engages in political agitation. **2.** A mechanism that stirs or shakes, as in a washing machine.

A·glai·a (ə-glā′ə, ə-glī′ə) *n. Gk. Myth.* One of the three Graces.

a·gleam (ə-glēm′) *adj. & adv.* Brightly shining.

a·glim·mer (ə-glĭm′ər) *adj. & adv.* Lighting up faintly; glimmering.

a·glit·ter (ə-glĭt′ər) *adj. & adv.* Glittering; sparkling.

ă pat　ā pay　â care　ä father　ě pet　ē be　hw which
ŏŏ took　ōō boot　ou out　th thin　*th* this　ŭ cut

ĭ pit　ī tie　î pier　ŏ pot　ō toe　ô paw, for　oi noise
û urge　zh vision　ə about, item, edible, gallop, circus

a·glow (ə-glō') *adj. & adv.* In a glow; glowing: *the faces of the spectators aglow with delight.*

Ag·ni (ŭg'nē) *n.* *Hinduism.* The Vedic god of fire and guardian of man.

ag·nos·tic (ăg-nŏs'tĭk) *n.* Someone who believes that there can be no proof of the existence of God but does not deny the possibility that God exists. —*adj.* Of or pertaining to agnostics or their doctrines. [A- (not) + GNOSTIC.] —**ag·nos'ti·cal·ly** *adv.* —**ag·nos'ti·cism** *n.*

Ag·nus De·i (ăg'nəs dē'ī', än'yŏŏs dā'ē, äg'nōŏs'). **1.** The Lamb of God, an emblem of Christ, derived from the Bible. **2.** A symbolic representation of Christ as a lamb. **3. a.** A liturgical prayer to Christ. **b.** The musical accompaniment for such a prayer. [Latin.]

a·go (ə-gō') *adj.* Gone by; past: *two years ago.* —*adv.* In the past: *They lived there long ago.* [Middle English, past part. of *agon*, to go away, be past, from Old English *āgān* : *ā-* (intensive) + *gān*, to go.]

Usage: Use *ago* alone or followed by *that* or *when*, not *since: saw them a week ago; was a week ago that (or when) I saw her last.*

a·gog (ə-gŏg') *adv. & adj.* In a state of keen anticipation; highly excited. [Middle English, from Old French *en gogues*, "in merriments," from *gogue*, merriment.]

a·gon·ic line (ā-gŏn'ĭk, ə-gŏn'-). An imaginary line connecting points on the earth's surface where the magnetic declination is zero. [From Greek *agonos*, having no angle.]

ag·o·nize (ăg'ə-nīz') *v.* **-nized, -niz·ing.** —*intr.v.* **1.** To make a great effort; struggle: *agonize over a decision.* **2.** To be in agony. —*tr.v.* To cause great pain or anguish to: *His death agonized me.* —**ag'o·niz'ing·ly** *adv.*

ag·o·ny (ăg'ə-nē) *n., pl.* **-nies.** **1.** Intense physical or mental pain; anguish; suffering. **2.** The convulsive movements of the body that sometimes precede death and resemble a struggle for life. **3.** A sudden emotion of a particular sort: *an agony of doubt.* **4.** A violent or intense struggle. [Middle English *agonie*, from Old French, from Late Latin *agōnia*, from Greek *agōn*, contest, from *agein*, to drive.]

ag·o·ra (ăg'ə-rə) *n., pl.* **-rae** (-rē', -rī') or **-ras.** A marketplace in ancient Greece, customarily used as a place of assembly. [Greek *agora*, from *ageirein*, to assemble.]

ag·o·ra·pho·bi·a (ăg'ə-rə-fō'bē-ə) *n.* Abnormal fear of open spaces. [AGORA + -PHOBIA.] —**ag'o·ra·pho'bic** (-fō'bĭk, -fŏb'ĭk) *adj.*

a·gou·ti (ə-gōō'tē) *n., pl.* **-tis** or **-ties.** Also **a·gou·ty** *pl.* **-ties.** Any of several burrowing rodents of the genus *Dasyprocta*, of tropical America, with grizzled fur. [French, from Spanish *agutí*, from Guarani *acutí*.]

agouti

a·grar·i·an (ə-grâr'ē-ən) *adj.* **1.** Relating to or concerning the land and its ownership or cultivation. **2.** Pertaining to agricultural or rural matters. —*n.* A person who favors equitable distribution of land. [From Latin *agrārius*, from *ager*, land, field.]

a·grar·i·an·ism (ə-grâr'ē-ə-nĭz'əm) *n.* A movement for equitable distribution of land and for agrarian reform.

a·gree (ə-grē') *v.* **a·greed, a·gree·ing.** —*intr.v.* **1.** To grant consent; accede: *He agreed to accompany us.* **2.** To come into or be in accord: *The copy agrees with the original.* **3.** To be of one opinion: *"Didst thou not agree with me for a penny?"* (Matthew 20:13). **4.** To come to an understanding or to terms: *Is it possible to agree on such great problems?* **5.** To be suitable; appropriate: *Spicy food does not agree with him.* **6.** *Gram.* To correspond in gender, number, case, or person. —*tr.v.* To grant or concede: *He agreed that we should go.* [Middle English *agreen*, from

Old French *agreer* : Latin *ad-*, to + *grātus*, pleasing, beloved, agreeable.]

Syns: **agree, coincide, conform, correspond. v.** *Core meaning:* To be mutually compatible. AGREE can mean freedom from conflict and the arriving at a settlement (*agreed to a cease-fire; agreed on the choice of a wedding present*). AGREE, COINCIDE, and CORRESPOND can stress exact agreement in space, time, or thought (*angles that agree; satellite orbits coinciding with each other; opinions that correspond*). CONFORM emphasizes a close resemblance, esp. to a desired standard (*behavior conforming to the rules*).

a·gree·a·ble (ə-grē'ə-bəl) *adj.* **1.** Pleasing; pleasant: *an agreeable sight.* **2.** Willing to agree or consent: *He was agreeable to the suggestion.* **3.** In accord; suitable: *We find this plan agreeable to our purposes.* —See Syns at **amiable.** —**a·gree'a·ble·ness** *n.* —**a·gree'a·bly** *adv.*

a·greed (ə-grēd') *adj.* Determined by common consent: *the agreed meeting place; the agreed price.*

a·gree·ment (ə-grē'mənt) *n.* **1.** Harmony of opinion; accord: *in complete agreement.* **2.** An arrangement or understanding between parties regarding a method of action; covenant; treaty. **3.** *Gram.* Correspondence between words in gender, number, case, or person.

ag·ri·busi·ness (ăg'rə-bĭz'nĭs) *n.* Farming engaged in as big business, including the production, processing, and distribution of farm products and the manufacture of farm machinery, equipment, and supplies. [AGRI(CULTURE) + BUSINESS.]

ag·ri·cul·tur·al·ist (ăg'rĭ-kŭl'chər-ə-lĭst) *n.* Var. of **agriculturist.**

ag·ri·cul·ture (ăg'rĭ-kŭl'chər) *n.* The science, art, and business of cultivating the soil, producing crops, and raising livestock. [Latin *agricultūra* : *ager*, land + *cultūra*, cultivation, culture.] —**ag'ri·cul'tur·al** *adj.* —**ag'ri·cul'tur·al·ly** *adv.*

ag·ri·cul·tur·ist (ăg'rĭ-kŭl'chər-ĭst) *n.* Also **ag·ri·cul·tur·al·ist** (-chər-ə-lĭst). **1.** An expert in agricultural science. **2.** A farmer.

a·gron·o·my (ə-grŏn'ə-mē) *n.* Also **ag·ro·nom·ics** (ăg'rə-nŏm'ĭks). The application of the various soil and plant sciences to soil management and the raising of crops; scientific agriculture. [French *agronomie* : Greek *agros*, open field + *nomos*, law.] —**ag'ro·nom'ic** (ăg'rə-nŏm'ĭk) or **ag'ro·nom'i·cal** *adj.* —**a·gron'o·mist** *n.*

a·ground (ə-ground') *adv. & adj.* Stranded in shallow water or on a reef or shoal: *The ship ran aground.*

a·gue (ā'gyōō) *n.* **1.** A fever, like that of malaria, in which there are periods of chill, fever, and sweating. **2.** A chill or fit of shivering. [Middle English, from Old French *aguē*, from Medieval Latin *(fēbris) acūta*, "sharp (fever)," from *acuere*, to sharpen, from *acus*, needle.]

ah (ä) *interj.* A word used to express various emotions, such as surprise, delight, satisfaction, pain, or dislike.

a·ha (ä-hä') *interj.* A word used to express satisfaction, triumph, or pleasure.

a·head (ə-hĕd') *adv.* **1.** At or to the front: *The Republicans moved ahead in the polls.* **2.** In advance: *To get tickets you have to phone ahead.* **3.** Forward or onward. —**idioms. ahead of. 1.** In front of: *the road ahead of us.* **2.** Before or in advance of: *He arrived ahead of us. His ideas are ahead of their time.* **be ahead.** *Informal.* To be gaining or winning. **get ahead.** To near or attain success.

a·hem (ə-hĕm') *interj.* A word used to attract attention or to express doubt or warning.

a·hoy (ə-hoi') *interj.* A word used to hail a ship or to attract a person's attention.

Ah·ri·man (ä'rĭ-mən) *n.* *Zoroastrianism.* The spirit of evil, understood by some as the arch rival of Ormazd.

A·hu·ra Maz·da (ä'hŏŏ-rə măz'də, măz'-). *Zoroastrianism.* Ormazd.

aid (ād) *intr.v.* To help; assist. —*tr.v.* To give help or assistance to. —See Syns at **help.** —*n.* **1.** The act or result of helping; assistance; cooperation. **2.** Something or someone that helps or is helpful; helper: *visual aids used in teaching; a hearing aid; a secretary who is a real aid to our office.* [Middle English *aiden*, from Old French *aider*, from Latin *adjūtāre*, freq. of *adjuvāre*, to give aid to, help : *ad*, to + *juvāre*, to help.] —**aid'er** *n.*

ă pat   ā pay   â care   ä father   ĕ pet   ē be   hw which
ōō took   ōō boot   ou out   th thin   th this   ŭ cut
ĭ pit   ī tie   î pier   ŏ pot   ō toe   ô paw, for   oi noise
û urge   zh vision   ə about, item, edible, gallop, circus

aide (ād) *n.* **1.** An aide-de-camp. **2.** An assistant; helper: *a nurse's aide.* [French, from *aider*, to help, aid.]

aide-de-camp (ād'də-kămp') *n., pl.* **aides-de-camp.** A naval or military officer acting as confidential assistant to a general or an admiral. [French, "camp assistant."]

ai·grette or **ai·gret** (ā-grĕt', ā'grĕt') *n.* **1.** A tuft of upright plumes or feathers, esp. the tail feathers of an egret. **2.** An ornament, as a spray of gems, resembling such a tuft. [French *aigrette*, egret.]

ail (āl) *intr.v.* To feel ill or have pain; be unwell. —*tr.v.* To cause pain; make ill or uneasy; trouble: *What's ailing him?* [Middle English *eilen*, from Old English *eglan*.]

ai·lan·thus (ā-lăn'thəs) *n.* A deciduous tree, *Ailanthus altissima*, native to China, used esp. as a shade tree. It has compound leaves and clusters of greenish flowers with an unpleasant odor. Also called **tree of heaven.** [From Amboinese *ai lanto*, "tree (of) heaven."]

ai·ler·on (ā'lə-rŏn') *n.* Either of two movable flaps on the wings of an airplane that can be used to control the plane's rolling and banking movements. [French, dim. of *aile*, wing, from Old French, from Latin *āla.*]

aileron

ail·ing (ā'lĭng) *adj.* In ill health; sickly; unwell.

ail·ment (āl'mənt) *n.* A physical or mental disorder, esp. a mild illness.

aim (ām) *tr.v.* To direct (a weapon, remark, blow, etc.) at someone or something. —*intr.v.* **1.** To direct a weapon: *The gunner aimed carefully.* **2.** To determine a course: *aim at better education.* **3.** To propose or intend; try: *We aim to solve the problem.* —*n.* **1.** The act of aiming or pointing. **2.** The sighting or line of fire of something aimed. **3.** Purpose; intention; plan: *His aim was to write a best-selling novel.* [Middle English *aimen*, from Old French *aesmer*, to guess at : Latin *ad-*, to + *aestimāre*, to estimate.]

aim·less (ām'lĭs) *adj.* Without direction or purpose. —**aim'less·ly** *adv.* —**aim'less·ness** *n.*

ain't (ānt). *Nonstandard.* Contraction of am not. Also extended to mean *are not, is not, has not,* and *have not.*

Usage: **ain't.** This contraction of *am not* developed at about the time of the settlement of America. It has never been accepted in formal English. It is appropriate only to deliberately informal usage, chiefly to record uneducated speech, or as a device for providing humor, shock, or other special effect. Like all such devices, this one leaves the writer open to the risk of having his or her intention misunderstood. The interrogative form *ain't I?* has the virtue of agreement between pronoun and verb (unlike *ain't* used with other pronouns such as *it, he,* or *they,* or with nouns); but even this form has only slightly more acceptance than the others.

Ai·nu (ī'nōō) *n., pl.* **Ainu** or **-nus.** **1.** A member of an aboriginal Caucasian people inhabiting the northernmost islands of Japan. **2.** The language of the Ainu people.

air (âr) *n.* **1.** A colorless, odorless, tasteless gaseous mixture surrounding the earth and consisting mainly of nitrogen and oxygen with lesser amounts of argon, carbon dioxide, neon, helium, and other gases; the atmosphere. **2.** The space above the earth; sky; firmament. **3.** An atmospheric movement; breeze; wind. **4.** Utterance; publicity; circulation: *give air to one's grievances.* **5.** A peculiar or characteristic impression; aura: *The room had an air of loneliness. He has an air of gentility.* **6. airs.** Affectation;

haughty pose: *She gives herself aristocratic airs.* **7.** *Mus.* A melody or tune. —*modifier: air travel; air power.* —*tr.v.* **1.** To expose so that air can dry, cool, or freshen; ventilate. **2.** To give public utterance to; circulate. —*idioms.* **clear the air.** To dispel tension or misunderstanding through frank and open discussion. **in the air.** Abroad; prevalent. **on** (or **off**) **the air.** Radio & TV. Being (or not being) broadcast. **take the air.** To go outdoors for fresh air; take a short walk or ride. **up in the air.** Not decided; uncertain; in suspense. **walk on air.** To feel elated or extremely happy. [Old French, from Latin *āēr*, from Greek *āēr.*]

air base. A base for military aircraft.

air bladder. An air-filled, saclike structure in many fishes that functions to maintain buoyancy or in some species as an aid in respiration or hearing. Also called **swim bladder.**

air·borne (âr'bôrn', -bōrn') *adj.* **1.** Carried by or through the air: *airborne pollen.* **2.** Transported in aircraft: *airborne troops.* **3.** Flying; in flight.

air brake. A brake operated by compressed air.

air·brush (âr'brŭsh') *n.* Also **air brush.** An atomizer that uses compressed air to spray paint or other liquids.

air chamber. An enclosure filled with air for a special purpose, esp. one in a hydraulic system in which air compresses and expands to regulate the flow of a fluid.

air-con·di·tion (âr'kən-dĭsh'ən) *tr.v.* To provide with or ventilate by air conditioning.

air conditioner. Any apparatus for controlling, esp. lowering, the temperature and humidity of an enclosure.

air conditioning. A system of air conditioners or the condition produced by it.

air-cool (âr'kōōl') *tr.v.* To cool by a flow of air.

air corridor. An air route established by international agreement.

air·craft (âr'krăft') *n., pl.* **aircraft.** Any machine or device, including airplanes, helicopters, gliders, and dirigibles, capable of atmospheric flight.

aircraft carrier. A large naval ship designed to serve as a seagoing base, having a long flat deck on which aircraft can take off and land.

aircraft carrier

air·drome (âr'drōm') *n.* Also *Brit.* **aer·o·drome** (âr'ə-drōm'). An airport.

air·drop (âr'drŏp') *n.* A delivery, as of supplies or troops, by parachute from aircraft in flight. —*v.* **-dropped, -dropping.** —*tr.v.* To drop from an aircraft. —*intr.v.* To drop, as supplies or troops, from an aircraft.

Aire·dale (âr'dāl') *n.* A large terrier with rather long legs and a wiry tan coat marked with black. [From *Airedale*, a valley in Yorkshire, England.]

Airedale

ă pat   ā pay   â care   ä father   ĕ pet   ē be   hw which   ĭ pit   ī tie   î pier   ŏ pot   ō toe   ô paw, for   oi noise
ōō took   ōō boot   ou out   th thin   *th* this   ŭ cut   û urge   zh vision   ə about, item, edible, gallop, circus

air·field (âr'fēld') *n.* A place, usu. with paved runways, where aircraft can take off and land.

air·foil (âr'foil') *n.* An aircraft part or surface, such as a wing, propeller blade, or rudder, designed to control stability, direction, lift, thrust, or propulsion.

air force. **1.** The aviation branch of a country's armed forces, such as the U.S. Air Force. **2.** A unit of the U.S. Air Force larger than an air division and smaller than an air command.

air gun. A gun discharged by compressed air.

air hole. **1.** A hole or opening through which gas or air may pass. **2.** An opening in the frozen surface of a body of water. **3.** *Aviation.* An air pocket.

air·ing (âr'ĭng) *n.* **1.** Exposure to the air for drying, cooling, freshening, etc. **2.** Public expression or discussion. **3.** Exercise out of doors: *I took my dog for an airing.*

air lane. A regular route of travel for aircraft; an airway.

air·less (âr'lĭs) *adj.* **1.** Without air. **2.** Lacking fresh air; stuffy. **3.** Without a breeze or wind; still.

air·lift (âr'lĭft') *n.* A system of transporting troops or supplies by air when surface routes are blocked. —*tr.v.* To transport by air, as when ground routes are blocked.

air·line (âr'līn') *n.* **1.** A system providing scheduled transport of passengers and freight by air. **2.** An air route. **3.** The shortest distance between two geographical points; a direct line. —*modifier: an airline pilot.*

air·lin·er (âr'lī'nər) *n.* An airplane adapted for carrying passengers and operated by an airline.

air lock. **1.** An airtight chamber, usu. located between two regions of unequal pressure, in which air pressure can be regulated. **2.** A bubble or pocket of air or vapor, as in a pipe, that stops the normal flow of fluid through the conducting part.

air·mail (âr'māl') *tr.v.* To send (a letter, package, etc.) by air mail. —*adj.* Of, relating to, or for use with airmail: *an airmail stamp; an airmail letter.*

air mail. **1.** The system of conveying mail by aircraft. **2.** Mail conveyed by aircraft.

air·man (âr'mən) *n.* **1.** An enlisted man or woman in the U.S. Air Force. **2.** An aviator.

airman basic. An enlisted person of the lowest rank in the U.S. Air Force.

air mass. A large body of air with only small horizontal variations of temperature, pressure, and moisture.

air·plane (âr'plān') *n.* Also *Brit.* **aer·o·plane** (âr'ə-plān'). Any of various winged vehicles capable of flight, gen. heavier than air and propelled by jet engines or propellers. [French *aéroplane*, from Late Greek *aeroplanos*, wandering in the air : *aēr*, air + *planasthai*, to wander.]

airplane

air plant. *Bot.* An epiphyte.

air pocket. A downward air current that causes an aircraft to lose altitude abruptly. Also called **air hole.**

air police. Military police of an air force.

air·port (âr'pôrt', -pōrt') *n.* A facility that provides space

airport

for aircraft to take off and land, usu. equipped with a control tower, hangars, and accommodations for passengers and cargo.

air pump. A pump for compressing, removing, or forcing a flow of air.

air raid. An attack by hostile military aircraft, esp. when armed with bombs.

air rifle. A low-powered rifle, such as a BB gun, that uses manually compressed air to fire small pellets.

air sac. An air-filled space in the body, esp. an alveolus of a lung or one of the spaces in a bird's body, that connects the lungs and bone cavities.

air shaft. A passage that allows fresh air to enter a tunnel, mine, or other enclosed space; an airway.

air·ship (âr'shĭp') *n.* A self-propelled lighter-than-air craft with directional control surfaces; dirigible.

air·sick (âr'sĭk') *adj.* Suffering from airsickness.

air·sick·ness (âr'sĭk'nĭs) *n.* Nausea and discomfort experienced when riding in an aircraft, as a result of nervousness, motions, or changes in pressure.

air·space (âr'spās') *n.* The portion of the atmosphere above a particular land area, esp. above a nation.

air speed. The speed of an aircraft relative to the air.

air·strip (âr'strĭp') *n.* A cleared area serving as an airfield, esp. temporarily or in an emergency.

air·tight (âr'tīt') *adj.* **1.** Not permitting the entry or passage of air or gas. **2.** Having no weak points; sound: *an airtight excuse.*

air-to-air missile (âr'tə-âr'). A missile, usu. guided, designed to be fired from aircraft at aircraft.

air-to-sur·face missile (âr'tə-sûr'fĭs). A missile, usu. guided, designed to be fired from aircraft at targets on the ground. Also called **air-to-ground missile.**

air·waves (âr'wāvz') *pl.n.* The medium used for the transmission of radio and television signals.

air·way (âr'wā') *n.* **1.** A passageway or shaft through which air circulates, as in ventilating a mine. **2.** A designated route of passage for an aircraft; an air lane.

air·wor·thy (âr'wûr'thē) *adj.* Prepared and in fit condition to fly: *an airworthy airplane.* —**air'wor'thi·ness** *n.*

air·y (âr'ē) *adj.* **-i·er, -i·est.** **1.** Of or like the air. **2.** High in the air; lofty; towering: *an airy mountain peak.* **3.** Open to the air; breezy: *airy rooms.* **4.** Performed in the air; aerial. **5.** Resembling air; immaterial: *an airy apparition.* **6.** Unreal or impractical: *airy schemes.* **7.** Light as air; delicate: *an airy veil.* **8.** Light-hearted or gay: *an airy mood; an airy melody.* —**air'i·ly** *adv.* —**air'i·ness** *n.*

aisle (īl) *n.* **1.** A part of a church divided laterally from the nave by a row of pillars or columns. **2.** A passageway between rows of seats, as in a theater or auditorium. **3.** Any passageway, as between counters in a department store or rows of trees in an orchard. [Middle English *eile*, from Old French *aile*, wing of a building, from Latin *āla*, wing.]

a·jar¹ (ə-jär') *adv. & adj.* Partially opened: *Leave the door ajar.* [Middle English *on char*, "in the act of turning" : *on,* in + *char*, a turn, from Old English *cierr.*]

a·jar² (ə-jär') *adv. & adj.* Not harmonious; jarring: *ajar with the times. Her nerves ajar and all on edge, she was in no state to perform.* [A- (on) + JAR (discord).]

A·jax (ā'jăks') *n. Gk. Myth.* **1.** A warrior of great strength and bravery who fought against Troy. **2.** A warrior of small stature and arrogant character who fought against Troy, one of the swiftest of the Greeks.

a·kene (ā-kēn') *n. Bot.* Var. of **achene.**

a·kim·bo (ə-kĭm'bō) *adj. & adv.* With the hands on the hips and the elbows bowed outward. [Middle English *in kenebowe,* "in keen bow," in a sharp curve.]

a·kin (ə-kĭn') *adj.* **1.** Of the same kin; related by blood. **2.** Having a similar quality or character; analogous. **3.** *Ling.* Cognate. [A- (of) + KIN.]

Ak·ka·di·an (ə-kā'dē-ən) *n.* **1.** A native or inhabitant of Akkad, a region of ancient Mesopotamia. **2.** The Semitic language of the Akkadians. —*adj.* Of, pertaining to, or relating to the Akkadians or their language.

Al The symbol for the element aluminum.

-al¹. A suffix that forms adjectives from nouns: **adjectival; postal.**

-al². A suffix that forms nouns from verbs: **denial; arrival.**

ă pat	ā pay	â care	ä father	ĕ pet	ē be	hw which	ĭ pit	ī tie	î pier	ŏ pot	ō toe	ô paw, for	oi noise
ŏŏ took	ōō boot	ou out	th thin	*th* this	ŭ cut		û urge	zh vision	ə about, item, edible, gallop, circus

a·la (ā′lə) *n., pl.* **a·lae** (ā′lē′). A winglike structure or part, such as an ear lobe or the membranous border of some seeds. [Latin *āla*, wing.]

à la (ä′lä, ä′lə, ăl′ə). Also **a la.** In the style or manner of: *a satire à la Mark Twain.* [French *à la (mode de).*]

al·a·bas·ter (ăl′ə-băs′tər) *n.* **1.** A dense, translucent, white or tinted fine-grained gypsum. **2.** A variety of hard calcite, translucent and sometimes banded. [Middle English *alabastre*, from Old French, from Latin *alabaster*, from Greek *alabastros*, from Egyptian *'a-la-Baste*, "vessel of (the goddess) Baste."]

à la carte (ä′ lä kärt′, ä′lə, ăl′ə). With a separate price for each item on the menu. [French, "by the menu."]

a·lack (ə-lăk′) *interj.* Also **a·lack·a·day** (ə-lăk′ə-dā′). *Archaic.* A word used to express sorrow or regret. [Middle English *alacke*, "ah, (what) loss!"]

a·lac·ri·ty (ə-lăk′rĭ-tē) *n.* **1.** Cheerful willingness; eagerness: *accepted the invitation with alacrity.* **2.** Speed or quickness; celerity: *The job was done with alacrity.* [Latin *alacritās*, from *alacer*, lively, eager.] **—a·lac′ri·tous** *adj.*

a·lae (ā′lē′) *n. Biol.* The plural of **ala.**

à la king (ä′ lä kĭng′, ä′lə, ăl′ə). Cooked in a cream sauce with green pepper or pimiento and mushrooms.

à la mode (ä′ lä mōd′, ä′lə, ăl′ə). **1.** According to or in style or fashion. **2. a.** Served with ice cream. **b.** Braised with vegetables and served in a rich, brown sauce. [French, "in the fashion."]

a·larm (ə-lärm′) *n.* **1.** A sudden fear caused by an apprehension of danger; fright. **2.** A warning of danger: *Sound the alarm.* **3.** A device that warns of danger by means of a sound or signal: *a fire alarm.* **4.** The sounding mechanism of an alarm clock. **5.** A call to arms. **—modifier:** *an alarm system.* **—tr.v.** **1.** To frighten by a sudden revelation of danger. **2.** To warn of or indicate approaching or existing danger. **—See Syns at frighten.** [Middle English *alarme*, from Old French, from Old Italian *allarme*, from *all'arme*, "to arms."]

alarm clock. A clock that can be set to sound a bell or buzzer at any desired hour.

a·larm·ing (ə-lär′mĭng) *adj.* Causing great fear or anxiety; frightening. **—a·larm′ing·ly** *adv.*

a·larm·ist (ə-lär′mĭst) *n.* A person who needlessly alarms others by spreading false or exaggerated rumors of impending danger or catastrophe.

a·lar·um (ə-lär′əm, ə-lăr′-) *n. Archaic.* An alarm, esp. a call to arms. [Middle English *alarom*.]

a·la·ry (ā′lə-rē) *adj.* **1.** Of or pertaining to wings. **2.** Resembling a wing; wing-shaped. [Latin *ālārius*, from *āla*, wing.]

a·las (ə-lăs′) *interj.* A word expressing sorrow, grief, or regret. [Middle English, from Old French : *a*, ah + *las*, wretched, from Latin *lassus*, weary.]

A·las·kan malamute (ə-lăs′kən). A dog, the **malamute.**

a·late (ā′lāt′) *adj.* Also **a·lat·ed** (ā′lā′tĭd). *Biol.* Having thin, winglike extensions or parts. [Latin *ālātus*, from *āla*, wing.]

alb (ălb) *n.* A long, white linen robe with tapered sleeves worn by a priest at Mass. [Middle English, from Old English, from Medieval Latin *alba*, white, from Latin *albus*.]

al·ba·core (ăl′bə-kôr′, -kōr′) *n., pl.* **albacore** or **-cores.** A large marine fish, *Thunnus alalunga*, of warm seas, having edible flesh that is a major source of canned tuna. [Portuguese *albacor*, from Arabic *al-bakrah* : *al*, the + *bakr*, young camel.]

Al·ba·ni·an (ăl-bā′nē-ən, -bān′yən, ôl-) *adj.* Of or pertaining to Albania, its inhabitants, or their language. **—n.** **1.** A native or inhabitant of Albania. **2.** The Indo-European language of Albania.

al·ba·tross (ăl′bə-trôs′, -trŏs′) *n., pl.* **albatross** or **-tross·es.** **1.** Any of various large, web-footed birds of the family Diomedeidae, chiefly of the oceans of the Southern Hemisphere, with a hooked beak and very long wings. **2.** A handicap or constant burden. [From Portuguese *alcatraz*, pelican, from Arabic *al-ghattās*, white-tailed sea eagle.]

al·be·do (ăl-bē′dō) *n., pl.* **-dos.** The fraction of the light or other electromagnetic radiation that is reflected from a surface, as of a planet, that it strikes. [Late Latin *albēdō*, whiteness, from Latin *albus*, white.]

al·be·it (ôl-bē′ĭt, ăl-) *conj.* Although; even though; notwith-

standing. [Middle English *al be it*, "let it be entirely (that)."]

Al·bi·gen·ses (ăl′bə-jĕn′sēz′) *pl.n.* A denomination of a religious sect in France in the 12th and 13th cent. that was exterminated by the Inquisition for heresy. [Medieval Latin, inhabitants of *Albiga*, Albi, town in southern France (where the sect was dominant).] **—Al′bi·gen′si·an** (-sē-ən, -shən) *adj.*

al·bi·nism (ăl′bə-nĭz′əm) *n.* **1.** Absence of normal pigmentation in a person, animal, or plant. **2.** The condition of being an albino.

al·bi·no (ăl-bī′nō) *n., pl.* **-nos.** An organism lacking normal pigmentation, as a person who has abnormally pale skin, very light hair, and lacks normal eye coloring, or an animal that has white hair or fur and red eyes. [Portuguese, from *albo*, white, from Latin *albus*.]

Al·bi·on (ăl′bē-ən) *n.* A literary name for Britain.

al·bite (ăl′bīt′) *n.* A widely distributed white feldspar, $NaAlSi_3O_8$, containing sodium. [Swedish *albit*, from Latin *albus*, white.]

al·bum (ăl′bəm) *n.* **1.** A book or binder with blank pages for the insertion and preservation of stamps, photographs, etc. **2. a.** A set of two or more phonograph records sold or stored together under one binding. **b.** The holder for such records. **c.** One 12-inch long-playing record in a slip case. **3.** A printed collection of musical compositions, pictures, or literary selections, or a recording of different musical pieces: *an album of fight songs; a photography album of French castles.* [Latin, blank tablet, from *albus*, white.]

al·bu·men (ăl-byōō′mən) *n.* A nutritive substance, such as the white of an egg that surrounds a developing embryo. [Latin *albūmen*, from *albus*, white.]

al·bu·min (ăl-byōō′mən) *n.* Any of several simple, water-soluble proteins that are coagulated by heat and are found in egg white, blood serum, milk, and various animal and plant tissues. [ALBUM(EN) + -IN.]

al·bu·min·ous (ăl-byōō′mə-nəs) *adj.* Of, like, or pertaining to albumin or albumen.

al·bur·num (ăl-bûr′nəm) *n. Bot.* Sapwood. [Latin, from *albus*, white.]

al·caz·ar (ăl-căz′ər, ăl′kə-zär′) *n.* A Spanish palace or fortress, orig. one built by the Moors. [Spanish *alcázar*, from Arabic *al-qasr* : *al*, the + *qasr*, castle, from Latin *castra*, fort, pl. of *castrum*, camp.]

Al·ces·tis (ăl-sĕs′tĭs) *n. Gk. Myth.* The wife of a king of Thessaly. She agreed to die in place of her husband, and was rescued from Hades by Hercules.

al·che·mist (ăl′kə-mĭst) *n.* A practitioner of alchemy.

al·che·my (ăl′kə-mē) *n.* **1.** A medieval chemical philosophy that had as its aims the conversion of base metals into gold and the search for and development of a potion that would give eternal youth. **2.** Any seemingly magical power or process of changing something common into something better: *"that alchemy . . . by which women can concoct a subtle poison from ordinary trifles"* (Nathaniel Hawthorne). [Middle English *alkamie*, from Old French *alquemie*, from Medieval Latin *alchymia*, from Arabic *al-kīmiyā'*, "the art of transmutation."] **—al·chem′i·cal** (-kĕm′ĭ-kəl) or **al·chem′ic** *adj.* **—al·chem′i·cal·ly** *adv.*

Alc·me·ne (ălk-mē′nē) *n. Gk. Myth.* The mother of Hercules by Zeus.

al·co·hol (ăl′kə-hôl′) *n.* **1.** A colorless volatile flammable liquid, C_2H_5OH, synthesized or obtained by fermentation of sugars and starches, and widely used, either pure or

albatross

denatured, as a solvent, in drugs, cleaning solutions, explosives, and intoxicating beverages. Also called **ethanol**, **ethyl alcohol**, and **grain alcohol**. **2.** An intoxicating liquor containing alcohol. **3.** Any of a series of hydroxyl compounds, with the general formula $C_nH_{2n+1}OH$, including ethanol and methyl alcohol (wood alcohol). [New Latin *alcohol (vini)*, spirit (of wine), from Medieval Latin *alcohol*, fine powder used to tint the eyelids, from Arabic *al-kohl*, kohl.]

al·co·hol·ic (ăl′kə-hô′lĭk, -hŏl′ĭk) *adj.* **1.** Of, containing, or resulting from alcohol, esp. ethanol. **2.** Suffering from alcoholism. —*n.* A person who drinks alcoholic liquors habitually and to excess or one who suffers from alcoholism.

al·co·hol·ism (ăl′kə-hô-lĭz′əm) *n.* **1.** Excessive drinking of or addiction to alcoholic beverages. **2.** A chronic pathological condition, chiefly of the nervous and digestive systems, caused by this.

Al·co·ran (ăl′kô-răn′, -rän′) *n.* Also **Al·ko·ran**. The sacred book of the Moslems, the Koran.

al·cove (ăl′kōv′) *n.* **1.** A small recessed or partly enclosed area connected to or forming part of a room. **2.** A similar structure in a garden. [French *alcôve*, from Spanish *alcoba*, from Arabic *al-qubbah*, "the vault."]

Al·deb·a·ran (ăl-dĕb′ə-rən) *n.* A brilliant red double star in the constellation Taurus, one of the brightest stars in the sky, 68 light-years from Earth.

al·de·hyde (ăl′də-hīd′) *n.* **1.** Any of a class of highly reactive organic chemical compounds characterized by the common group CHO, and used in the manufacture of resins, dyes, and organic acids. **2.** Acetaldehyde. [German *Aldehyd*, from New Latin *al(cohol) dehyd(rogenatum)*, "dehydrogenized alcohol."]

al·der (ôl′dər) *n.* Any of various deciduous shrubs or trees of the genus *Alnus*, that grow in cool, moist places and have reddish wood used in cabinet work. [Middle English, from Old English *aler, alor*.]

al·der·man (ôl′dər-mən) *n.* **1.** In many town and city governments in the United States, a member of the legislative body, usu. representing a specific ward or district. **2.** In England and Ireland, a member of the higher branch of the municipal or borough council. **3.** In Anglo-Saxon England, a lord or (later) the chief officer of a shire. [Middle English *alderman*, guild official, from Old English *(e)aldormann*, viceroy : *ealdor*, chief, elder + *mann*, man.]

Al·der·ney (ôl′dər-nē) *n., pl.* **-neys**. One of a breed of small dairy cattle orig. raised in the Channel Islands.

al·dol·ase (ăl′də-lās′, -lāz′) *n.* An enzyme that catalyzes the breakdown of a fructose ester into triose sugars. [ALD(EHYDE) + -OL + -ASE.]

al·dos·ter·one (ăl-dŏs′tə-rōn′, ăl′dō-stə-rōn′) *n.* A steroid hormone secreted by the adrenal cortex that serves as a regulator of the salt and water balance in the body. [*Aldo-*, aldehyde + STER(OL) + -ONE.]

al·drin (ôl′drən, ăl′-) *n.* An insecticide that is primarily a derivative of napthelene. [After Kurt *Alder* (1902–58), German chemist.]

ale (āl) *n.* A fermented, bitter alcoholic beverage that contains malt and hops and is similar to but heavier than beer and is brewed by rapid fermentation. [Middle English, from Old English *ealu*.]

a·le·a·to·ry (ā′lē-ə-tôr′ē, -tōr′ē) *adj.* Dependent upon chance, luck, or contingency. [Latin *āleātōrius*, from *āleātor*, gambler, from *ālea*, dice.]

a·lee (ə-lē′) *adv.* Away from the wind.

ale·house (āl′hous′) *n.* A place where ale is sold.

a·lem·bic (ə-lĕm′bĭk) *n.* **1.** An apparatus formerly used for distilling. **2.** Something that purifies, alters, or transforms by a process comparable to distillation. [Middle English, from Old French *alambic*, from Medieval Latin *alambicum*, from Arabic *al-anbīq* : *al*, the + *anbīg*, still, from Greek *ambix*, cup.]

a·lert (ə-lûrt′) *adj.* **1.** Vigilantly attentive; watchful: *alert to danger*. **2.** Mentally quick; perceptive; intelligent: *an alert student*. —See Syns at **clever**. —*n.* **1.** A warning signal of attack or danger, esp. a siren warning of an air raid. **2.** The period of time during which such a warning is in effect. —*tr.v.* **1.** To notify of approaching danger or action; warn: *alerted the town to the attack*. **2.** To make aware of; inform: *alert the public to the need for pollution control*.

—*idiom.* **on the alert.** Watchful and prepared; on guard. [French *alerte*, from Italian *all'erta*, "on the watch."] —**a·lert'ly** *adv.* —**a·lert'ness** *n.*

    Syns: **alert, observant, open-eyed, vigilant, wakeful, wary, watchful, wide-awake** *adj.* Core meaning: Vigilantly attentive (*alert to danger*). See also Syns at **clever**.

A·leut (ə-lōōt′, ăl′ē-ōōt′) *n., pl.* **Aleut** or **A·leuts**. **1.** Also **A·leu·tian** (ə-lōō′shən). An Eskimo native of the Aleutian Islands. **2.** A group of related languages spoken in the Aleutian Islands.

A·leu·tian (ə-lōō′shən) *adj.* Of or pertaining to the Aleuts, their culture, or their language. —*n.* Var. of **Aleut**.

ale·wife (āl′wīf′) *n.* A fish, *Alosa pseudoharengus*, of North American Atlantic waters, closely related to the herrings. [Prob. from French *alose*, a shad.]

Al·ex·an·dri·an (ăl′ĭg-zăn′drē-ən) *adj.* **1.** Of or pertaining to Alexander the Great. **2.** Of or pertaining to Alexandria, Egypt. **3.** Of, characteristic of, or designating a learned school of Hellenistic literature, science, and philosophy located at Alexandria in the last three cent. B.C.

al·ex·an·drine (ăl′ĭg-zăn′drĭn) *n.* Also **Al·ex·an·drine**. *Pros.* A line of English verse composed in iambic hexameter, usu. with a caesura after the third foot, such as Alexander Pope's example: *"That like a wounded snake drags its slow length along."* [French *alexandrin*, from Old French, from *Alexandre*, title of a romance about Alexander the Great, written in this meter.]

a·lex·i·a (ə-lĕk′sē-ə) *n.* A disorder characterized by loss of the ability to read, caused by brain lesions. Also called **word blindness**. [A- (without) + Greek *lexis*, speech.]

al·fal·fa (ăl-făl′fə) *n.* A plant, *Medicago sativa*, that has cloverlike leaves and clusters of small purple flowers, widely grown as feed for cattle and other livestock, and used as a commercial source of chlorophyll and as a cover crop. [Spanish, from Arabic *al-faṣfaṣah*.]

alfalfa
A plant

alfalfa
A cover crop

al·fres·co (ăl-frĕs′kō) *adv.* Also **al fresco**. In the fresh air; outdoors: *lunch alfresco*. —*adj.* Taking place outdoors; outdoor: *an alfresco party*. [Italian, "in the fresh (air)."]

al·gae (ăl′jē) *pl.n.* The less frequently used sing. is **al·ga** (ăl′gə). Any of various primitive, chiefly aquatic, one-celled or multicellular plants that lack true stems, roots, and leaves but usu. contain chlorophyll. Included among the algae are kelps and other seaweeds, and the diatoms. [Latin *algae*, pl. of *alga*, seaweed.] —**al′gal** (ăl′gəl) *adj.*

al·ge·bra (ăl′jə-brə) *n.* A branch of mathematics in which symbols, such as letters of the alphabet, are used to represent numbers or a specified set of numbers, and in which the relationship between the symbols is expressed and worked out by general operations that hold for all the numbers in the set. [Medieval Latin, from Arabic *al-jebr*, *al-jabr*, "the (science of) reuniting" (referring to solving algebraic equations).] —**al′ge·bra′ist** (-brā′ĭst) *n.*

al·ge·bra·ic (ăl′jə-brā′ĭk) *adj.* Of, or used in algebra.

al·gin (ăl′jən) *n.* A gelatinous substance obtained from brown algae, esp. the giant kelp, and used as a thickener and emulsifier. [ALG(A) + -IN.]

AL·GOL or **Al·gol** (ăl′gŏl′, -gôl′) *n.* A language for programming a computer, used esp. for scientific problems. [ALGO(RITHMIC) + L(ANGUAGE).]

Al·gol (ăl′gŏl′, -gôl′) *n.* A double eclipsing variable star in the constellation Perseus.

Al·gon·kin (ăl-gŏng′kĭn) *n.* Var. of **Algonquin.**

Al·gon·qui·an (ăl-gŏng′kwē-ən, -kē-ən) *n., pl.* **Algonquian** or **-ans.** **1.** A principal family of about 50 North American Indian languages spoken in an area from the Atlantic seaboard west to the Rocky Mountains, and from Labrador south to North Carolina and Tennessee, and used by such tribes as the Ojibwa, Delaware, Cree, Fox, Blackfoot, Illinois, Shawnee, and Arapaho. **2.** A member of a tribe using a language of this family. —*adj.* Of or constituting this language family.

Al·gon·quin (ăl-gŏng′kwĭn, -kĭn) *n., pl.* **Algonquin** or **-quins.** Also **Al·gon·kin** (-kĭn). **1.** Any of several North American Indian tribes of southeastern Canada. **2.** The Algonquian language of these tribes. **3.** Any Indian of these tribes.

al·go·rithm (ăl′gə-rĭth′əm) *n.* A mathematical rule or procedure for solving a problem: *an algorithm for division.* [Var. of *algorism,* from Medieval Latin *algorismus,* after Mohammed ibn-Musa *al-Khwarizmi* (780–850?), Arab mathematician.]

a·li·as (ā′lē-əs, āl′yəs) *n., pl.* **-as·es.** An assumed name. —*adv.* Otherwise named: *Johnson, alias Rogers.* [Latin *aliās,* otherwise, from *alius,* other.]

al·i·bi (ăl′ə-bī′) *n., pl.* **-bis.** **1.** *Law.* A form of defense whereby a defendant attempts to prove that he was elsewhere when the crime in question was committed. **2.** *Informal.* An excuse. —*intr.v.* **-bied, -bi·ing.** *Informal.* To make an excuse or excuses for oneself or another. [Latin *alibī,* elsewhere : *alius,* other + *ubī,* where.]

a·li·en (ā′lē-ən, āl′yən) *adj.* **1.** Of, belonging to, or characteristic of another country, society, or people; foreign. **2.** Not natural or characteristic; strange; unfamiliar: *alien traditions of an extinct tribe.* **3.** Being inconsistent or opposed; contradictory; adverse: *Lying is alien to his nature.* —See Syns at **foreign.** —*n.* **1.** A foreign-born person living in one country while still a citizen of another; foreigner. **2.** A member of another family, people, region, etc. **3.** A person who is excluded from some group; an outsider. **4.** *Sci. Fic.* A living creature or being from anywhere other than Earth. [Middle English, from Old French, from Latin *aliēnus,* from *alius,* other.]

al·ien·a·ble (ăl′yə-nə-bəl, ā′lē-ə-) *adj. Law.* Capable of being transferred to the ownership of another. —**al′ien·a·bil′i·ty** *n.*

al·ien·ate (ăl′yə-nāt′, ā′lē-ə-) *tr.v.* **-at·ed, -at·ing. 1.** To cause (someone previously friendly or affectionate) to become unfriendly or indifferent; estrange: *alienated his friends.* **2.** To cause to be withdrawn or indifferent; turn away: *The government scandals alienated many young people from politics.* **3.** *Law.* To transfer (property) to the ownership of another. —See Syns at **estrange.** —**al′ien·a′tor** *n.*

al·ien·a·tion (ăl′yə-nā′shən, ā′lē-ə-) *n.* **1.** The condition of being an outsider; a state of isolation. **2.** *Psychol.* A state of estrangement between the self and the objective world or between different parts of the personality. **3.** The act of alienating; estrangement; disaffection: *"In the decades after 1795 there was a profound alienation between classes in Britain"* (E.P. Thompson). **4.** *Law.* The act of transferring property, or title to it, to another.

al·ien·ist (ăl′yə-nĭst, ā′lē-ə-) *n. Law.* A psychiatrist, esp. one accepted by a court as an expert. [French *aliéniste,* from *aliéné,* insane, from Latin *aliēnāre,* to alienate.]

a·light¹ (ə-līt′) *intr.v.* **a·light·ed** or **a·lit** (ə-lĭt′), **a·light·ing. 1.** To come down and settle, as after flight: *a bird alighting on a branch.* **2.** To get off; dismount: *alight from a train.* [Middle English *alighten,* from Old English *ālīhtan* : *ā-* (intensive) + *līhtan,* to dismount, lighten.]

a·light² (ə-līt′) *adj.* **1.** Lighted; glowing; lit up: *Her eyes were alight with joy.* **2.** On fire; burning. [Middle English *alight,* from Old English *ālīht,* past part. of *ālīhtan,* to light up : *a-,* up + *līhtan,* to light, from *līht,* light.] —**a·light′** *adv.*

a·lign (ə-līn′) *tr.v.* **1.** To bring into or arrange in a straight line: *aligned the row of chairs.* **2.** To ally (oneself) with one side of an argument, cause, nation, etc.: *Chinese foreign policy is no longer aligned with the Soviet Union's.* **3.** To adjust (a device, mechanism, or its parts) to produce a proper relationship or condition: *align the car's wheels.* —*intr.v.* To fall into line. [French *aligner,* from Old French : *a-,* to + *ligne,* line.] —**a·lign′er** *n.*

a·lign·ment (ə-līn′mənt) *n.* **1.** Arrangement or position in a

straight line. **2.** The act of aligning or the condition of being aligned. **3.** The policy of allying with a certain bloc. **4.** The process of aligning a device or mechanism or the condition of being aligned.

a·like (ə-līk′) *adj.* Having a very close resemblance to another; like: *She and her mother are very much alike.* —See Syns at **like.** —*adv.* In the same way or manner; to the same degree; similarly: *They dress and walk alike.* [Middle English *ilik,* from Old English *gelīc* : *ge-* (collective prefix) + *līc,* form.] —**a·like′ness** *n.*

al·i·ment (ăl′ə-mənt) *n.* **1.** Food; nourishment. **2.** Something that supports or sustains: *"Liberty is to faction what air is to fire, an aliment without which it instantly expires"* (James Madison). [Middle English, from Latin *alimentum,* from *alere,* to nourish.] —**al′i·men′tal** (-mĕn′tl) *adj.*

al·i·men·ta·ry (ăl′ə-mĕn′tə-rē, -trē) *adj.* **1.** Of or pertaining to food or nutrition. **2.** Providing nourishment.

alimentary canal. The mucous-membrane-lined tube of the digestive system that extends from the mouth to the anus and includes the pharynx, esophagus, stomach, and intestines.

al·i·men·ta·tion (ăl′ə-mĕn-tā′shən) *n.* **1.** The act or process of giving or receiving nourishment. **2.** Support; sustenance.

al·i·mo·ny (ăl′ə-mō′nē) *n., pl.* **-nies.** *Law.* An allowance for support made under court order and usu. given by a man to his former wife after a divorce or legal separation. [Latin *alimōnia,* nutriment, support, from *alere,* to nourish.]

al·i·phat·ic (ăl′ə-făt′ĭk) *adj.* Of, pertaining to, or designating organic chemical compounds in which the carbon atoms are linked in open chains rather than rings. [From Greek *aleiphar,* oil, from *aleiphein,* to anoint.]

al·i·quot (ăl′ĭ-kwŏt′, -kwət) *adj.* Of, pertaining to, or designating a number that divides exactly into another number. For example, 3 is an aliquot part of 9. [French *(partie) aliquote,* aliquot (part), from Latin *aliquot,* some, several : *alius,* some, other + *quot,* how many.]

a·lit (ə-lĭt′) *v.* A past tense and past participle of **alight.**

a·live (ə-līv′) *adj.* **1.** Having life; living. **2.** In existence or operation; active: *Keep your hopes alive.* **3.** Full of life; animated; lively: *The party didn't come alive until midnight.* —**idioms. alive to.** Aware of; sensitive to: *alive to the moods of others.* **alive with.** Swarming with: *The pool was alive with fish.* [Middle English, from Old English *on līfe* : *on,* in + *līf,* life.] —**a·live′ness** *n.*

Syns: **alive, live, living** *adj.* Core meaning: Having life or existence (*the best soccer player alive; a real live lizard. The living relatives inherited the money.*).

a·liz·a·rin (ə-lĭz′ə-rĭn) *n.* Also **a·liz·a·rine** (-rĭn, -rēn′). An orange-red crystalline compound, $C_{14}H_8O_4$, used in dyes. [French *alizarine,* from *alizari,* madder (a plant), from Spanish, from Arabic *al-'aṣārah,* the juice pressed out.]

al·ka·li (ăl′kə-lī′) *n., pl.* **-lis** or **-lies. 1.** Any of a group of compounds, such as sodium hydroxide or potassium hydroxide, that have strong water-soluble bases and are formed from a related alkali metal. **2.** Any of a group of salts, such as sodium carbonate, formed from a related alkali metal. **3.** Any of various basic, soluble mineral salts found in natural water and arid soils. [Middle English *alcaly,* from Medieval Latin *alcali,* from Arabic *al qalīy,* the ashes, from *qalay,* to fry.]

alkali metal. Any of a group of soft, white, low-density, low-melting, highly reactive metallic elements, including lithium, sodium, potassium, rubidium and cesium.

al·ka·line (ăl′kə-lĭn, -līn′) *adj.* **1.** Of, pertaining to, or containing an alkali. **2.** Capable of neutralizing an acid; basic. —**al′ka·lin′i·ty** (-lĭn′ĭ-tē) *n.*

alkaline earth. 1. An oxide of an alkaline-earth metal. **2.** An alkaline-earth metal. —**al′ka·line-earth′** *adj.*

alkaline-earth metal. Any of a group of basic metallic elements, esp. calcium, strontium, and barium, but gen. including beryllium, magnesium, and radium.

al·ka·lize (ăl′kə-līz′) *v.* **-lized, -liz·ing.** Also **al·ka·lin·ize** (-lĭ-nīz′), **-ized, iz·ing.** —*tr.v.* To make alkaline. —*intr.v.* To become an alkali. —**al′ka·li·za′tion** *n.*

al·ka·loid (ăl′kə-loid′) *n.* Any of a class of colorless, bitter, organic compounds that contain nitrogen, are derived from seed plants, and include nicotine, quinine, and morphine. [ALKAL(I) + -OID.] —**al'ka·loi'dal** (-loid'l) *adj.*

al·kane series (ăl'kān'). *Chem.* The **paraffin series.** [ALK(YL) + -ANE.]

Al·ko·ran (ăl'kô-răn', -rän') *n.* Var. of **Alcoran.**

al·kyd resin (ăl'kĭd). *Chem.* A widely used durable synthetic resin derived from glycerol and phthalic anhydride, used in paints. Also called **alkyd.** [Blend of *alkyl,* from *alc(ohol)* + *-yl* and ACID.]

al·kyl (ăl'kəl) *n.* A monovalent radical, such as ethyl or propyl, having the general formula $C_nH_{2n} + 1$. [ALC(OHOL) + -YL.]

all (ôl) *adj.* **1.** The total extent or number of: *All five boys are good students. He has lived all his life in Paris.* **2.** Constituting the whole of: *He spent all day in court.* **3.** The utmost possible: *in all truth.* **4.** Every: *all manner of men.* **5.** Any: *proven beyond all doubt.* **6.** Nothing but; only: *all skin and bones.* —See Syns at **whole.** —*pron.* Each and every one: *All aboard the ship were drowned.* —*n.* Everything one has: *He gave all.* —*adv.* **1.** Wholly; entirely: *She's all wrong.* **2.** Each; apiece: *a score of five all.* **3.** Exclusively: *The cake is all for him.* —*Note: All* is often used with certain function words to form prepositional and adverbial groups. Some of the most frequent groups are: **above all.** Before everything else; most of all: *truth above all.* **after all.** Nevertheless: *The girls decided to go shopping after all.* **all but.** Very nearly: *She all but fainted.* **all in all.** Everything being taken into account: *All in all he's a good athlete.* **all the same.** Nevertheless: *She's a nice person, all the same.* —*idioms.* **all in.** *Informal.* Tired or exhausted. **all of.** Not less than: *It's all of ten miles to town.* **all out.** With every effort possible: *The team went all out to win.* **all over. 1.** Finished. **2.** Everywhere. **3.** *Informal.* Thoroughly or typically: *That's me all over.* [Middle English *al(le),* from Old English *all, eall.*]

Usage: **all. 1.** When the pronoun *all* means *everything, the whole,* it takes a singular verb: *All is not lost.* When *all* means *each one of a group,* it takes a plural verb: *All are now accounted for.* When a noun follows the expression *all but one,* it is singular and so is a verb after the noun: *All but one ship is accounted for. All of* invariably precedes a noun, but *all* is sufficient: *all (of) the buildings.* **2.** The adverb *all* can be used with *that* in negative and interrogative sentences implying comparison: *She's not all that bright. Is she all that bright?*

all-. Var. of **allo-.**

a·la bre·ve (ä'lə brĕv'ā). *Mus.* A direction indicating that the half note is the unit of time. [Italian, "according to the breve."]

Al·lah (ăl'ə, ä'lə) *n.* The supreme being in Islam.

all-A·mer·i·can (ôl'ə-mĕr'ĭ-kən) *adj.* **1.** Representing the whole of the United States or chosen as the best in the United States. **2.** *Sports.* Chosen as the best amateur in the United States at a particular position or event. —*n.* An all-American athlete.

al·lan·to·is (ə-lăn'tō-ĭs) *n., pl.* **al·lan·to·i·des** (ăl'ən-tō'ĭ-dēz'). A membranous sac that develops from the hindgut of the embryos of mammals, birds, and reptiles. It takes part in the formation of the umbilical cord and placenta in mammals. [From Greek *allantoeidēs,* sausage-shaped.]

all-a·round (ôl'ə-round') *adj.* Var. of **all-round.** —See Usage note at **all-round.**

al·lay (ə-lā') *tr.v.* **1.** To lessen or relieve; reduce the intensity of: *The pill allayed the pain.* **2.** To calm or pacify; set to rest: *allay one's fears.* [Middle English *alaien,* from Old English *ālecgan,* to lay aside.]

all clear. 1. A signal, usu. by siren, that an air raid or air-raid drill is over. **2.** A term signifying the absence of immediate obstacles or impending danger.

al·le·ga·tion (ăl'ĭ-gā'shən) *n.* **1.** Something alleged; an assertion. **2.** The act of alleging. **3.** A statement offered without proof, as an excuse or plea; mere assertion. **4.** *Law.* An assertion made by a person that must be proved with evidence.

al·lege (ə-lĕj') *tr.v.* **-leged, -leg·ing. 1.** To declare or assert to be true, usu. without offering proof. **2.** To cite as a plea or excuse: *He refused to contribute, alleging his poverty.* [Middle English *alleg(g)en,* perh. from Old French *alleguer,* from Latin *allēgāre,* to send on a mission, dispatch, cite : *ad-,* toward + *lēgāre,* to charge.] —**al·leg'er** *n.*

al·leged (ə-lĕjd', ə-lĕj'ĭd) *adj.* Asserted to be as described but not so proved; supposed: *the alleged murderer.* —**al·leg'ed·ly** (ə-lĕj'ĭd-lē) *adv.*

al·le·giance (ə-lē'jəns) *n.* **1.** Obligation of obedience or loyalty to one's country, government, or ruler. **2.** Loyalty or devotion to a cause, person, etc. **3.** The obligations of a vassal to his overlord. [Middle English *allegeaunce,* from Old French *ligeance,* from *li(e)ge,* liege.]

al·le·gor·i·cal (ăl'ĭ-gôr'ĭ-kəl, -gŏr'-) or **al·le·gor·ic** (-gôr'ĭk, -gŏr'-) *adj.* Of, pertaining to, or containing allegory. —**al'·le·gor'i·cal·ly** *adv.*

al·le·go·rize (ăl'ĭ-gə-rīz', -gə-rīz') *v.* **-rized, -riz·ing.** —*tr.v.* **1.** To express as, or in the form of, an allegory. **2.** To interpret or treat as an allegory. —*intr.v.* To use or make allegory. —**al'le·go'ri·za'tion** *n.*

al·le·go·ry (ăl'ĭ-gôr'ē, -gōr'ē) *n., pl.* **-ries. 1.** A literary, dramatic, or pictorial device in which each literal character, object, and event represent symbols illustrating an idea or moral or religious principle. **2.** An instance of such representation. [Middle English *allegorie,* from Old French, from Latin *allēgoria,* from Greek, from *allēgorein,* to speak figuratively : *allos,* other + *agoreuein,* to speak, from *agora,* an assembly.] —**al'le·go'rist** *n.*

al·le·gret·to (ăl'ĭ-grĕt'ō). *Mus.* —*adv.* In quick tempo; slower than allegro but faster than andante. Used as a direction. —*n., pl.* **-tos.** A movement or passage in this tempo. [Italian, dim. of *allegro,* lively.] —**al'le·gret'to** *adj.*

al·le·gro (ə-lĕg'rō, ə-lā'grō). *Mus.* —*adv.* In rapid tempo; faster than allegretto but slower than presto. Used as a direction. —*n., pl.* **-gros.** A movement or passage in this tempo. [Italian, "lively," from Latin *alacer.*] —**al·le'gro** *adj.*

al·lele (ə-lēl') *n.* Any of a group of genes that occur as alternative forms at a given site. [Ult. from Greek *allēlōn,* reciprocally, from *allos,* other.] —**al·le'lic** *adj.*

al·le·lu·ia (ăl'ə-lōō'yə) *interj.* Hallelujah.

al·le·mande (ăl'ə-mănd', -mänd', ăl'ə-mănd', -mänd') *n.* **1. a.** A stately 16th-cent. dance in $^2/_2$ time. **b.** A musical composition written to accompany or as if to accompany this dance, often used as the first movement of a suite. **2.** A lively late 18th-cent. dance in $^3/_4$ time, similar to a waltz. [French, German, from Latin *Alemannus.*]

al·ler·gen (ăl'ər-jən) *n.* A substance that causes an allergy. [ALLER(GY) + -GEN.] —**al'ler·gen'ic** (-jĕn'ĭk) *adj.*

al·ler·gic (ə-lûr'jĭk) *adj.* **1.** Of, concerning, or resulting from allergy. **2.** Having an allergy. **3.** *Informal.* Having a dislike; averse: *allergic to work.*

al·ler·gist (ăl'ər-jĭst) *n.* A physician who specializes in the treatment of allergies.

al·ler·gy (ăl'ər-jē) *n., pl.* **-gies. 1.** Hypersensitive bodily reaction to environmental factors or substances, such as pollens, foods, dust, or microorganisms, in amounts that do not affect most people. **2.** *Informal.* A strong dislike. —*modifier: an allergy attack.* [German *Allergie* : Greek *alles,* other + *ergon,* work, effect.]

al·le·vi·ate (ə-lē'vē-āt') *tr.v.* **-at·ed, -at·ing.** To make more bearable; relieve; lessen: *alleviate pain.* [Late Latin *alleviāre,* to lighten : Latin *ad-,* toward + *levis,* light.] —**al·le'·vi·a'tion** *n.* —**al·le'vi·a'tive** *adj.* —**al·le'vi·a'tor** *n.*

al·ley[1] (ăl'ē) *n., pl.* **-leys. 1.** A narrow street or passageway between or behind buildings. **2.** A path between flowerbeds or trees in a garden or park. **3.** A **bowling alley.** —*idiom.* **up (one's) alley.** Compatible with one's interests or qualifications. [Middle English *aley,* from Old French *alee,* from *aler,* to go, from Latin *ambulāre,* to walk.]

al·ley[2] (ăl'ē) *n., pl.* **-leys.** A large playing marble, often used as the shooter. [Short for ALABASTER.]

alley cat. 1. A homeless cat; a stray cat. **2.** A domestic cat with no known ancestry.

al·ley·way (ăl'ē-wā') *n.* A narrow passage between buildings.

All Fools' Day. April Fools' Day.

all fours. All four limbs of an animal or person: *A baby crawls on all fours.*

all hail. *Archaic.* All health. Used as a greeting.

All·hal·low·mas (ôl-hăl'ō-məs) or **All·hal·lows** (ôl-hăl'ōz). *n.* **All Saints' Day.**

al·li·ance (ə-lī'əns) *n.* **1. a.** A formal pact of union or confederation between nations in a common interest or cause, such as defense or trade benefits. **b.** The nations so conjoined. **2.** Any union, relationship, or connection by kinship, marriage, common interest, etc.

al·lied (ə-līd′, ăl′īd′) *adj.* **1.** Joined; united; confederated. **2.** Of a similar nature; related: *allied sciences of biophysics and biochemistry.* **3.** Allied. Of or pertaining to the Allies.

Al·lies (ăl′īz′, ə-līz′) *pl.n.* **1.** *WWI.* The nations allied against the Central Powers of Europe. They were Russia, France, Great Britain, and later many others, including the United States. **2.** *WWII.* The nations, primarily Great Britain, Russia, and the United States, allied against the Axis.

al·li·ga·tor (ăl′ĭ-gā′tər) *n.* **1.** Either of two large, amphibious reptiles, *Alligator mississipiensis,* of the southeastern United States, or *A. sinensis,* of China, having sharp teeth and powerful jaws, and differing from crocodiles in having a broader, shorter snout. **2.** Leather made from the hide of an alligator. **3.** A tool with strong, adjustable jaws, often toothed. [Earlier *alagarto,* from Spanish *el lagarto* : Latin *ille,* that + *lacertus,* lizard.]

alligator

alligator pear. The avocado tree or its fruit. [From the belief that the trees grow in places infested by alligators.]

all-im·por·tant (ôl′ĭm-pôr′tnt) *adj.* Very important; vital.

al·lit·er·ate (ə-lĭt′ə-rāt′) *v.* **-at·ed, -at·ing.** —*intr.v.* **1.** To use alliteration. **2.** To contain alliteration. —*tr.v.* To form or arrange with alliteration.

al·lit·er·a·tion (ə-lĭt′ə-rā′shən) *n.* The repetition of the same initial consonant sound in two or more words in a line of speech or writing for poetic or emphatic effect, as in "When to the sessions of sweet silent thought" (Shakespeare). [From AD-, to + Latin *littera,* letter.]

al·lit·er·a·tive (ə-lĭt′ə-rā′tĭv, -ər-ə-tĭv) *adj.* Of or characterized by alliteration. —**al·lit′er·a′tive·ly** *adv.*

allo- or **all-.** A prefix meaning divergence, opposition, or difference: **allotrope.** [Greek, from *allos,* other.]

al·lo·cate (ăl′ə-kāt′) *tr.v.* **-cat·ed, -cat·ing.** **1.** To designate for a special purpose; set apart: *allocate funds for research.* **2.** To distribute according to plan; allot: *allocate a room for each group.* [From Medieval Latin *allocāre,* to place to : Latin *ad-,* toward + *locāre,* to place, from *locus,* place.] —**al′lo·ca′tion** *n.*

al·lo·morph (ăl′ə-môrf′) *n. Ling.* Any of the variant forms of a morpheme. For example, the phonetic *s* of *cats, z* of *dogs,* and *iz* of *horses* are allomorphs of the plural morpheme *s.* [ALLO- + -MORPH.] —**al′lo·mor′phic** *adj.*

al·lop·a·thy (ə-lŏp′ə-thē) *n.* Therapy or treatment of disease with remedies that produce effects that differ from those of the disease treated. [ALLO- + -PATHY.] —**al′lo·path′ic** (ăl′ə-păth′ĭk) *adj.*

al·lo·phone (ăl′ə-fōn′) *n. Ling.* Any of the variant forms of a phoneme. For example, the aspirated *p* of *pit* and the unaspirated *p* of *spit* are allophones of the phoneme p. [ALLO- + PHONE.] —**al′lo·phon′ic** (-fŏn′ĭk) *adj.*

al·lot (ə-lŏt′) *tr.v.* **-lot·ted, -lot·ting.** **1.** To distribute or parcel out by lot; apportion: *allot tracts of land.* **2.** To assign a portion for a particular purpose; allocate: *allot three weeks to a project.* [Middle English *alotten,* from Old French *aloter* : *a-,* to + *lot,* a portion, lot.] —**al·lot′ter** *n.*

al·lot·ment (ə-lŏt′mənt) *n.* **1.** The act of allotting. **2.** Something allotted.

al·lo·trope (ăl′ə-trōp′) *n.* Any of the different forms in which certain elements, such as sulfur, can appear under

the same conditions. Graphite and diamonds are allotropes of carbon. [Back-formation from ALLOTROPY.]

al·lot·ro·py (ə-lŏt′rə-pē) *n.* The existence, esp. in the solid state, of two or more crystalline or molecular structural forms of an element. [ALLO- + -TROPY.] —**al′lo·trop′ic** (ăl′ə-trŏp′ĭk) or **al′lo·trop′i·cal** (-trŏp′ĭ-kəl) *adj.*

all-out (ôl′out′) *adj.* **1.** Using all one's resources: *an all-out effort.* **2.** Complete. —See Syns at **utter.**

all-o·ver (ôl′ō′vər) *adj.* Covering an entire surface: *an all-over pattern.*

al·low (ə-lou′) *tr.v.* **-lowed, -low·ing.** **1.** To let do or happen; permit: *Please allow me to finish.* **2.** To let have; permit to have: *allow oneself five dollars a day.* **3.** To make provision for: *allow time for discussion.* **4.** To permit the presence of; let in: *No pets allowed.* **5.** To provide; allot: *allow funds in case of emergency.* **6.** To admit; concede; grant: *I allow that some mistakes have been made.* **7.** To allow as a discount or in exchange: *He allowed me $20 on my old typewriter.* —See Syns at **acknowledge** and **permit.** —*phrasal verbs.* **allow for.** To make an allowance or provision for: *Allow for bad weather.* **allow of.** To permit: *a treatise allowing of several interpretations.* [Middle English *allowen,* from Old French *allouer,* to permit, approve, a blend of Medieval Latin *allocāre,* to allocate, and Latin *allaudāre,* to give praise to.] —**al·low′a·ble** *adj.* —**al·low′a·bly** *adv.*

al·low·ance (ə-lou′əns) *n.* **1.** The act of allowing. **2.** An amount of money, food, etc. given at regular intervals for a specific purpose: *a travel allowance.* **3.** A price reduction given in exchange for used merchandise; a discount: *an allowance of $500 on the old car.* —*idiom.* **make allowance** (or **allowances**) **for.** To take into account; allow for: *make allowance for his inexperience.*

al·loy (ăl′oi′, ə-loi′) *n.* **1.** *Metallurgy.* **a.** A solid metal in which the atoms of a metallic element and those of one or more other elements, metallic or nonmetallic, are intermingled. For example, pewter is an alloy of copper, antimony, and lead. **b.** A less valuable metal mixed with a more valuable one, often to give an added quality such as durability or malleability. **2.** Anything added that lowers value or purity. —*tr.v.* (ə-loi′, ăl′oi′). **1.** *Metallurgy.* **a.** To combine (metals or other substances) to form an alloy. **b.** To lower purity or value of (a metal) by mixing with a cheaper metal. **2.** To lessen the value or quality of; mar. [Old French *aloi,* from *aloier, aleier,* to alloy, from Latin *alligāre,* to bind to, ally.]

all-pur·pose (ôl′pûr′pəs) *adj.* Useful in many ways: *an all-purpose glue.*

all right. Also *nonstandard* **al·right** (ôl′rīt′). **1.** Satisfactory; average: *Her work is all right, but could be better.* **2.** Correct: *These figures are perfectly all right.* **3.** Not sick or injured; safe: *Are you all right?* **4.** Very well; yes: *All right, I'll go.* **5.** Without a doubt: *That's him all right!*
   Usage: **all right, alright.** Although the variant *alright* has been widely used since at least the 1890s, we nevertheless recommend that you use *all right.*

all-right (ôl′rīt′) *adj. Slang.* **1.** Dependable; honorable: *an all-right fellow.* **2.** Good; excellent: *an all-right movie.*

all-round (ôl′round′) *adj.* Also **all-a-round** (ôl′ə-round′). **1.** Comprehensive in extent or depth: *all-round education.* **2.** Able to do many or all things well; versatile: *an all-round athlete.*
   Usage: **all-round, all-around.** The form *all-round* is preferable. Both forms are hyphenated, and each is used only as an adjective before a noun: *all-round capability; an all-round student leader.* These should not be confused with *all round* (or *all around*), written without hyphens and used adverbially (*a plan better all round*) and prepositionally (*went all round the town*).

All Saints' Day. November 1, a Christian festival in honor of all saints. Also called **Allhallowmas** and **Allhallows.**

All Souls' Day. November 2, observed by the Roman Catholic Church as a day of prayer for souls in purgatory.

all·spice (ôl′spīs′) *n.* **1.** A tropical American tree, *Pimenta officinalis,* having small white flowers and aromatic berries. **2.** The dried berries of this tree, used whole or ground as a spice.

all-star (ôl′stär′) *adj.* Made up wholly of star performers: *a play with an all-star cast.*

all-time (ôl'tīm') *adj.* Unsurpassed until now; of all time: *set an all-time attendance record.*

all told. In all; with everything considered; altogether: *It was a good party all told.*

al·lude (ə-lōōd') *intr.v.* **-lud·ed, -lud·ing.** To make an indirect reference to; mention casually or in passing: *The President alluded to the war without mentioning it by name.* [Latin *allūdere,* to play with : *ad-,* to + *lūdere,* to play, from *lūdus,* game.]
   Usage: Allude and **elude** resemble each other in sound and appearance but not in meaning. To *allude* is to make an indirect reference to something. To *elude* is to avoid, evade, or escape someone or something.

al·lure (ə-lōōr') *v.* **-lured, -lur·ing.** —*tr.v.* To entice with something desirable; tempt. —*intr.v.* To tempt or fascinate. —See Syns at **attract.** —*n.* The power of attracting; fascination: *the allure of the sea.* [Middle English *aluren,* from Old French *aleurrer : a-,* to + *leurrer,* to lure, from *loirre, leurre,* lure.]

al·lure·ment (ə-lōōr'mənt) *n.* **1.** The act of alluring. **2.** Fascination; attractiveness. **3.** Something that allures.

al·lu·sion (ə-lōō'zhən) *n.* A passing or casual reference to something; indirect mention: *an allusion to the scandal.* [Late Latin *allūsiō,* a playing with, from Latin *allūdere* (past part. *allūsus*), to play with.]
   Usage: allusion, illusion. These unrelated nouns are confused esp. because they sound alike. An *allusion* is an indirect mention or reference. An *illusion* is an erroneous perception or impression. See also **delusion.**

al·lu·sive (ə-lōō'sĭv) *adj.* Containing or making allusions; suggestive. —**al·lu'sive·ly** *adv.*

al·lu·vi·a (ə-lōō'vē-ə) *n.* A plural of **alluvium.**

al·lu·vi·al (ə-lōō'vē-əl) *adj.* Of, pertaining to, or composed of alluvium.

al·lu·vi·um (ə-lōō'vē-əm) *n., pl.* **-vi·ums** or **-vi·a** (-vē-ə). Any sediment, such as mud, sand, or gravel, carried and deposited by flowing water, as in a river bed, flood plain, or delta. [Latin, from *alluvius,* alluvial, from *alluere,* to wash against : *ad-,* to + *lavere,* to wash.]

al·ly (ə-lī', ăl'ī') *v.* **-lied, -ly·ing.** —*tr.v.* **1.** To unite or connect in a formal relationship or bond for a specific purpose, as by treaty or other agreement: *The United States allies itself with Great Britain.* **2.** To unite or connect in a personal relationship, as by marriage, friendship, common interest, etc. —*intr.v.* To enter into an alliance. —*n.* (ăl'ī', ə-lī'), *pl.* **-lies. 1.** A person or country that is united with another for a common purpose. **2.** A friend or close associate. —See Syns at **partner.** [Middle English *allien,* from Old French *alier,* from Latin *alligāre,* to bind to : *ad-,* to + *ligāre,* to bind.]

al·ma ma·ter or **Al·ma Ma·ter** (ăl'mə mä'tər, äl'mə). **1.** The school, college, or university a person attended. **2.** Its song or anthem. [Latin, "fostering mother."]

al·ma·nac (ôl'mə-năk', ăl'-) *n.* **1.** An annual publication in calendar form that includes data, weather forecasts, astronomical and often other information. **2.** An annual publication composed of various lists, charts, and tables of useful information in many different fields. [Middle English *almenak,* from Medieval Latin *almanachus.*]

al·might·y (ôl-mī'tē) *adj.* **1.** All-powerful; omnipotent: *almighty God.* **2.** *Informal.* Great: *an almighty din.* —*n.* **—the Almighty.** God. [Middle English *almighty,* from Old English *ealmihtig : eall,* all + *mihtig,* mighty.]

al·mond (ä'mənd, ăm'ənd) *n.* **1.** A small tree, *Prunus amygdalus,* having pink flowers and fruit containing an edible nut. **2.** The nut of this tree, with a soft, yellowish-tan shell. —*modifier: almond extract.* [Middle English *almande,* from Old French, from Late Latin *amandula,* from Latin *amygdala,* from Greek *amugdalē.*]

al·mo·ner (ăl'mə-nər, ä'mə-) *n.* A person who distributes alms, as for a church or royal family.

al·most (ôl'mōst', ôl-mōst') *adv.* Slightly short of; nearly: *almost done but not quite.* [Middle English, from Old English *(e)almǣst,* completely, for the most part : *eall,* all + *mǣst,* most.]

alms (ämz) *pl.n.* Money or goods given to the poor in charity. [Middle English *almes,* from Old English *ælmesse,* from Late Latin *eleēmosyna,* from Greek *eleēmosunē,* pity, from *eleos.*]

al·ni·co (ăl'nĭ-kō') *n., pl.* **-cos.** Any of several alloys of aluminum, cobalt, copper, iron, nickel, and often other metals, used in making strong permanent magnets.

al·oe (ăl'ō) *n.* **1.** Any of various plants of the genus *Aloe,* mostly native to southern Africa, with fleshy, spiny-toothed leaves and red or yellow flowers. **2.** aloes (*used with a sing. verb*). A bitter laxative drug made from the leaves of certain aloe plants. [Middle English, from Old English *aluwe,* from Latin *aloē,* from Greek.]

a·loft (ə-lôft', ə-lŏft') *adv.* **1.** In or into a place high above the ground. **2.** *Naut.* At or toward the upper rigging of a ship. [Middle English, from Old Norse *ā lopt : ā,* on, in + *lopt,* air, sky.]

a·lo·ha (ä-lō'hä') *interj.* A word used to express greeting or farewell. [Hawaiian.]

a·lone (ə-lōn') *adj.* **1.** Without the company of anyone or anything else: *She lives alone.* **2.** Only; solely: *God alone knows.* **3.** With nothing else added: *New York City alone has over eight million people.* —*adv.* Without aid or help: *I can do it alone.* —*idioms.* **leave alone.** To leave in peace; not bother or interrupt. **let alone. 1.** To leave alone. **2.** Not to speak of: *I can't even do arithmetic, let alone algebra.* **let well enough alone.** To be satisfied with things as they are and not try to change them. **stand alone.** To be without equal. [Middle English, from *al one : al,* all + *one,* one.]
   Syns: alone, lonely, lonesome, solitary *adj.* Core meaning: Apart from all others. ALONE, LONE, and SOLITARY all stress singleness (*was alone on the beach; a lone pine on a hill; solitary confinement*). LONELY and LONESOME describe a sense of isolation felt as a result of a lack of companionship (*the lonely existence of a bereaved widow; was lonesome for her old friends*).

a·long (ə-lông', ə-lŏng') *adv.* **1.** In a line with something or following the length or path of it: *trees growing along by the river.* Also used prepositionally: *a parade moving along the main street.* **2.** Forward: *moving along.* **3.** In association; together: *one thing along with another.* **4.** As company; as a companion: *Bring your parents along.* **5.** Somewhat advanced: *The evening was well along.* **6.** Approaching: *along about midnight.* —*idioms.* **all along.** Always or all the time: *I was right all along.* **get along. 1.** To go onward. **2.** To manage successfully or survive: *I'll get along somehow.* **3.** To be compatible; agree. [Middle English, from Old English *andlang,* "extending opposite" : *and-,* against + *lang,* extending, long.]

a·long·shore (ə-lông'shôr', -shōr', ə-lŏng'-) *adv.* Along, near, or by the shore.

a·long·side (ə-lông'sīd', ə-lŏng'-) *adv.* Along, near, at, or to the side: *The bus pulled up alongside.* —*prep.* By the side of: *The truck was parked alongside the garage.*

a·loof (ə-lōōf') *adj.* Distant, esp. in one's relations with other people; indifferent; reserved: *His aloof manner alienated many people.* —*adv.* At a distance, but within view; apart: *We stood aloof from the crowd.* [From earlier *aloufe!* "(steer the ship) up into the wind!" : *a-,* to + *loufe,* side of a ship, from Old French *lof.*] —**a·loof'ly** *adv.* —**a·loof'ness** *n.*

a·loud (ə-loud') *adv.* **1.** In a loud tone. **2.** With the voice; orally: *Read this passage aloud.*

alp (ălp) *n.* A high mountain, esp. one of the Alps. [Back-formation from *Alps,* a mountain system in Europe.]

almond

alpaca

alpenhorn

altar

altarpiece

al·pac·a (ăl-păk′ə) n. **1.** A domesticated South American mammal, *Lama pacos*, related to the llama, and having fine, long wool. **2. a.** The silky wool of this animal. **b.** Cloth made from this wool. **3.** A glossy cotton or rayon and wool fabric, usu. black. —*modifier:* an alpaca suit. [Spanish, from Aymara *allpaca.*]

al·pen·horn (ăl′pən-hôrn′) n. A curved wooden horn, sometimes as long as 6 meters, or 20 feet, used by herdsmen in the Alps to call cows to pasture.

al·pen·stock (ăl′pən-stŏk′) n. A long staff with an iron point, used by mountain climbers. [German *Alpenstock* : *Alpen*, Alps + *Stock*, a staff, from Old High German *stoc.*]

al·pha (ăl′fə) n. **1.** The first letter in the Greek alphabet, written A. **2.** The first of anything; beginning. **3.** *Astron.* The brightest or main star in a constellation. [Greek.]

alpha and omega. The first and the last: *"I am Alpha and Omega, the beginning and the ending, saith the Lord"* (Revelation 1:8).

al·pha·bet (ăl′fə-bĕt′, -bĭt) n. **1.** The letters of a given language, arranged in the order fixed by custom. **2.** Any system of characters or symbols representing sounds or things. [Latin *alphabētum*, from Greek *alphabētos* : *alpha*, alpha + *beta*, beta.]

al·pha·bet·i·cal (ăl′fə-bĕt′ĭ-kəl) or **al·pha·bet·ic** (-bĕt′ĭk) adj. **1.** Arranged in the customary order of the letters of a language. **2.** Of, pertaining to, or expressed by an alphabet. —**al′pha·bet′i·cal·ly** adv.

al·pha·bet·ize (ăl′fə-bĭ-tīz′) tr.v. **-ized, -iz·ing. 1.** To arrange in alphabetical order. **2.** To express by or supply with an alphabet. —**al′pha·bet′i·za′tion** (ăl′fə-bĕt′ĭ-zā′shən) n. —**al′pha·bet·iz′er** n.

Alpha Cen·tau·ri (sĕn-tôr′ē). A double star in Centaurus, the brightest in the constellation, 4.4 light-years from Earth.

al·pha·nu·mer·ic (ăl′fə-nōō-mĕr′ĭk, -nyōō-) adj. Consisting of both alphabetic and numerical symbols. [ALPHA(BET) + NUMERIC(AL).]

alpha particle. *Symbol α* *Physics.* A positively charged composite particle, indistinguishable from a helium atom nucleus, consisting of two protons and two neutrons. It is given off by certain radioactive substances.

alpha ray. A stream of alpha particles.

al·pine (ăl′pīn′, -pĭn) adj. **1.** Of or pertaining to high mountains. **2. Alpine.** Of, pertaining to, or characteristic of the Alps or their inhabitants. **3.** *Biol.* Living or growing on mountains above the timberline.

al·read·y (ôl-rĕd′ē) adv. By this (or a specified) time; before; previously: *I have already finished the job.* [Middle English *al redy* : *al*, all + *redy*, ready.]

Usage: **already, all ready.** *All ready* expresses complete readiness; *already* expresses time adverbially: *He was all ready, but the plane had already departed.*

al·right (ôl-rīt′) adv. Nonstandard. All right. —See Usage note at **all right.**

al·so (ôl′sō) adv. Besides; in addition; too. —*conj.* And in addition: *She studied math, also music and drama.* [Middle English, from Old English *(e)alswā*, even so, altogether thus : *(e)al-*, all + *swā*, so.]

al·so-ran (ôl′sō-răn′) n. Informal. One that is defeated in a race, election, or other competition; a loser.

Al·ta·ic (ăl-tā′ĭk) n. A language family of Europe and Asia, including Turkic, Tungus, Mongolian, and possibly Korean. —*adj.* **1.** Of or pertaining to the Altai Mountains or their inhabitants. **2.** Of or pertaining to the Altaic languages.

Al·ta·ir (ăl-tīr′, ăl-târ′) n. A very bright, double, variable star in the constellation Aquila, approximately 15.7 light-years from Earth.

al·tar (ôl′tər) n. **1.** Any elevated structure upon which sacrifices may be offered or before which other religious ceremonies may be enacted. **2.** In Christian churches, a table upon which the Eucharist is celebrated. [Middle English *alter*, from Old English *altar*, from Latin *altāre*, "material for burning sacrificial offerings."]

altar boy. An attendant to a clergyman in the performance of a liturgical service.

al·tar·piece (ôl′tər-pēs′) n. A painting or carving placed above and behind an altar.

al·ter (ôl′tər) tr.v. **1.** To change or make different; modify. **2.** To adjust (a garment) for a better fit. **3.** *Informal.* To castrate or spay (an animal). —*intr.v.* To change or become different. —See Syns at **change.** [Middle English *alteren*, from Old French *alterer*, from Medieval Latin *alterāre*, from Latin *alter*, other.] —**al′ter·a·ble** adj. —**al′ter·a·bly** adv.

al·ter·a·tion (ôl′tə-rā′shən) n. **1.** The act of altering. **2.** The condition resulting from altering; a modification; change.

al·ter·a·tive (ôl′tə-rā′tĭv) adj. **1.** Tending to alter or produce alteration. **2.** Tending to restore normal health. —*n.* An alterative medication or treatment.

al·ter·cate (ôl′tər-kāt′) intr.v. **-cat·ed, -cat·ing.** To argue or dispute vehemently. [Latin *altercārī*, to have differences with another, from *alter*, another.]

al·ter·ca·tion (ôl′tər-kā′shən) n. A noisy, angry quarrel.

al·ter e·go (ôl′tər ē′gō). **1.** Another side of oneself. **2.** An intimate friend; constant companion. [Latin, "other I."]

al·ter·nate (ôl′tər-nāt′, ăl′-) v. **-nat·ed, -nat·ing.** —*intr.v.* **1.** To occur in successive turns: *The rainy season alternates with the dry season.* **2.** To pass back and forth from one state, action, or place to a second indefinitely: *alternate between optimism and pessimism.* —*tr.v.* **1.** To do or execute by turns: *They alternated walking and running.* **2.** To cause to follow in turns; interchange regularly: *She alternated the red, yellow, and purple flowers.* —*adj.* (ôl′tər-nĭt, ăl′-). **1.** Happening or following in turns: *alternate periods of rain and drought.* **2.** Designating or pertaining to every other one of a series: *alternate lines.* **3.** In place of another; substitute: *an alternate plan.* **4.** *Bot.* Growing at alternating intervals on either side of a stem, as leaves. —*n.* (ôl′tər-nĭt, ăl′-). A person acting in the place of another; a substitute. —See Usage note at **alternative.** [From Latin *alternāre*, from *alternus*, by turns, interchangeable, from *alter*, other.] —**al′ter·nate·ly** adv.

alternate angle. An angle on one side of a transversal that

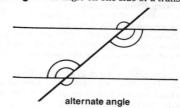

alternate angle

cuts two lines, having one of the intersected lines as a side.

al·ter·nat·ing cur·rent. An electric current that reverses direction in a circuit at regular intervals.

al·ter·na·tion (ôl′tər-nā′shən, ăl′-) n. Regular and successive change from one thing to another and back again.

al·ter·na·tive (ôl-tûr′nə-tĭv, ăl-) n. 1. One of two or more possibilities from which to choose: *Raising taxes may be unpopular, but the alternatives are even worse.* 2. A choice between two or more possibilities: *The alternative is between increased taxes or a budget deficit.* 3. A remaining choice or additional option: *You leave me no alternative.* —adj. Allowing or necessitating a choice between two or more possibilities: *I can suggest two alternative plans.* —See Syns at **choice.** —al·ter′na·tive·ly adv.

Usage: **alternative, alternate.** As a noun or an adjective *alternative* carries the meaning of one or the other: *annihilation, the alternative to surrender.* Or it can be used acceptably for more than two courses or choices: *four alternative game plans.* On the other hand, *alternate* carries the meaning of one coming after the other: *alternate periods of prosperity and recession; worked on alternate weekends.*

al·ter·na·tor (ôl′tər-nā′tər, ăl′-) n. An electric generator that produces alternating current.

al·the·a (ăl-thē′ə) n. Also **al·thae·a.** 1. A shrub, the **rose of Sharon.** 2. Any plant of the genus *Althaea*, which includes the hollyhock. [Latin, marsh mallows, from Greek *althaia*, "healer," from *althein*, to heal.]

al·tho (ôl-thō′) conj. Var. of **although.** —See Usage note at **although.**

alt·horn (ălt′hôrn′) n. Also **alto horn.** A brass wind instrument that sometimes replaces the French horn.

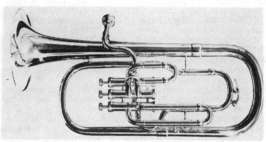

althorn

al·though (ôl-thō′) conj. Also **al·tho.** Regardless of the fact that; even though. [Middle English : ALL + THOUGH.]

Usage: **although, tho, though.** The words *although* and *though* are interchangeable: *Although* (or *though*) *she was tired, she went to work. Although* usu. occurs first in its clause, but *though* can occur in final position or after a word describing the subject: *We didn't respond, though. We are wiser though poorer.* Do not use the variant *tho* in formal prose.

al·tim·e·ter (ăl-tĭm′ĭ-tər) n. An instrument, esp. an aneroid barometer used in aircraft, that measures and indicates the height at which an object is located. [Latin *altus*, high + -METER.] —al·tim′e·try (-trē) n.

al·ti·tude (ăl′tĭ-tōōd′, -tyōōd′) n. 1. Geog. The height of a thing measured in relation to a reference level, esp. above sea level or the earth's surface. Also called **elevation.** 2. Often **altitudes.** A high location or area. 3. Astron. The angular height of a celestial object above the horizon. 4. Geom. The perpendicular distance from the base of a geometric figure to the opposite vertex, parallel side, or parallel surface. [Middle English, from Latin *altitūdō*, from *altus*, high.] —al·ti·tu′di·nal adj.

al·to (ăl′tō) n., pl. **-tos.** Mus. 1. A low singing voice of a woman or boy or, sometimes, a high singing voice of a man, lower than a soprano and higher than a tenor. 2. The range between soprano and tenor. 3. A singer whose voice lies within this range. 4. An instrument that sounds within this range. 5. A vocal or instrumental part written for such a voice or instrument. —*modifier:* an alto flute. [Italian, "high," from Latin *altus*, high.]

al·to·cu·mu·lus (ăl′tō-kyōō′myə-ləs) n. A rounded, fleecy white or gray cloud formation, found typically at a height of 4 kilometers, or 2½ miles.

al·to·geth·er (ôl′tə-gĕth′ər, ôl′tə-gĕth′ər) adv. 1. Entirely; completely; utterly: *The noise faded away altogether.* 2. With all included or counted; in all: *Altogether 100 people were there.* 3. On the whole; with everything considered: *Altogether, I'm sorry it happened.* —**idiom. in the altogether.** In the nude. [Middle English *al togeder* : ALL + TOGETHER.]

alto horn. Var. of **althorn.**

al·to·stra·tus (ăl′tō-strā′təs, -străt′əs) n. A cloud formation that extends in bluish or gray sheets or layers, found typically at a height of 5½ kilometers, or about 3½ miles.

al·tru·ism (ăl′trōō-ĭz′əm) n. Unselfish concern for the welfare of others; selflessness. [French *altruisme*, from *altrui-*, var. of *autrui*, other, from Old French *autre*, from Latin *alter*.] —al′tru·ist n. —al′tru·is′tic adj. —al′tru·is′ti·cal·ly adv.

al·um (ăl′əm) n. Any of various double sulfates of a trivalent metal such as aluminum, chromium, or iron, and a univalent metal such as potassium or sodium, esp. aluminum potassium sulfate, $AlK(SO_4)_2 \cdot 12H_2O$, used medicinally as topical astringents and styptics. [Middle English, from Old French, from Latin *alūmen*.]

a·lu·mi·na (ə-lōō′mə-nə) n. Any of several forms of aluminum oxide, Al_2O_3, that occur naturally as corundum, in bauxite, and with various impurities as ruby, sapphire, and emery. [From Latin *alūmen* alum.]

al·u·min·i·um (ăl′yə-mĭn′ē-əm) n. Brit. Var. of **aluminum.**

a·lu·mi·nous (ə-lōō′mə-nəs) adj. Of, pertaining to, or containing aluminum or alum.

a·lu·mi·num (ə-lōō′mə-nəm) n. Also Brit. **a·lu·min·i·um** (ăl′yə-mĭn′ē-əm). Symbol **Al** A silvery-white, ductile metallic element, the most abundant in the earth's crust, but found only in combination, chiefly in bauxite. It is used to form many hard, light, corrosion-resistant alloys. Atomic number 13, atomic weight 26.98, melting point 660.2°C, boiling point 2,467°C, specific gravity 2.69, valence 3. [New Latin, earlier *alumium*, from ALUMINA + -IUM.]

aluminum oxide. Chem. Alumina.

a·lum·na (ə-lŭm′nə) n., pl. **-nae** (-nē′). A female graduate of a school, college, or university. —See Usage note at **alumnus.** [Latin, fem. of ALUMNUS.]

a·lum·nus (ə-lŭm′nəs) n., pl. **-ni** (-nī′). A male graduate of a school, college, or university. [Latin *alumnus*, a pupil, foster son, from *alere*, to nourish.]

Usage: **alumnus, alumna.** *Alumnus* is the masculine form for a graduate or former student; the plural is *alumni*. The feminine terms are *alumna* and *alumnae*. The plural *alumni* is often used to denote all graduates or former students of co-educational schools.

al·ve·o·lar (ăl-vē′ə-lər) adj. 1. Anat. **a.** Pertaining to the jaw section that contains the tooth sockets. **b.** Pertaining to the alveoli of the lungs. 2. Phonet. Formed with the tip of the tongue touching or near the upper alveoli of the jaw, as English *t, d,* and *s.* —n. Phonet. An alveolar sound.

al·ve·o·lus (ăl-vē′ə-ləs) n., pl. **-li** (-lī′). 1. A small cavity or pit, as a honeycomb cell. 2. A tooth socket in the jawbone. 3. An air sac of the lungs. [Latin, small cavity.]

al·ways (ôl′wāz, -wēz, -wĭz) adv. 1. On every occasion: *He always leaves at six o'clock.* 2. Continuously; forever: *They will be friends always.* [Middle English *alwayes*, adv. genitive of *alwei*, from Old English *ealne weg*, "(along) all the way" : *eall*, all + *weg*, way.]

a·lys·sum (ə-lĭs′əm) n. 1. Any of various plants of the genus *Alyssum*, with dense clusters of yellow or white flowers. 2. **Sweet alyssum.** [From Greek *alusson*, a plant believed to cure rabies : *a-*, not + *lussa*, rabies, madness.]

am (ăm; unstressed əm). First person singular present tense of **be.**

Am The symbol for the element americium.

a·mal·gam (ə-măl′gəm) n. 1. Any of various alloys of mercury with another metal or metals. 2. Any combination or mixture of diverse elements: *The show is an amalgam of comedy, music, and satire.* [Middle English *amalgame*, from Old French, from Medieval Latin *amalgama*.]

a·mal·ga·mate (ə-măl′gə-māt′) v. **-mat·ed, -mat·ing.** —tr.v. 1. To mix so as to make a whole; combine: *amalgamate three companies.* 2. To mix (a metal) with mercury.

ă pat   ā pay   â care   ä father   ĕ pet   ē be   hw which   ĭ pit   ī tie   î pier   ŏ pot   ō toe   ô paw, for   oi noise
ōō took   ōō boot   ou out   th thin   th this   ŭ cut   û urge   zh vision   ə about, item, edible, gallop, circus

—intr.v. **1.** To combine, unite, or consolidate. **2.** To unite mercury with another metal.

a·mal·ga·ma·tion (ə-măl′gə-mā′shən) *n.* **1.** The act of amalgamating. **2.** A consolidation, as of several corporations. **3.** *Chem.* The dissolving of a metal in mercury to form an alloy.

am·a·ni·ta (ăm′ə-nī′tə, -nē′tə) *n.* Any of various mushrooms of the genus *Amanita,* most of which are poisonous. [From Greek *amanitai,* mushrooms.]

am·an·u·en·sis (ə-măn′yōō-ĕn′sĭs) *n., pl.* **-ses** (-sēz′). One employed to take dictation or to copy manuscript; secretary. [Latin *āmanuensis,* from *(servus) ā manū,* "(slave) at hand(writing)," from *ab-,* by + *manus,* hand.]

am·a·ranth (ăm′ə-rănth′) *n.* **1.** Any of various, often weedy, plants of the genus *Amaranthus,* with clusters of small greenish or purplish flowers. **2.** *Poet.* An imaginary flower that never fades. [New Latin *amaranthus,* var. (influenced by *-anthus,* flower) of Latin *amarantus,* from Greek *amarantos,* unfading, from *a-,* not + *marainein,* to wither.] **am·a·ran·thine** (ăm′ə-rǎn′thǐn, -thǐn′) *adj.* **1.** Of or resembling the amaranth. **2.** Eternally beautiful.

am·a·ryl·lis (ăm′ə-rǐl′ǐs) *n.* **1.** A bulbous, tropical plant, *Amaryllis belladonna,* with large, lilylike flowers. **2.** Any of several related or similar plants. [After *Amaryllis,* a shepherdess in classical poetry.]

amaryllis

Amazon

a·mass (ə-măs′) *tr.v.* To gather up; collect; accumulate, esp. for oneself: *amass wealth.* —See Syns at **gather.** [Old French *amasser* : *a-,* to + *masser,* to gather together, from *masse,* a mass.] **—a·mass′er** *n.* **—a·mass′ment** *n.*

am·a·teur (ăm′ə-chŏŏr′, -ə-tər, -ə-tyŏŏr′) *n.* **1.** A person who engages in any art, science, study, or athletic activity as a pastime rather than as a profession. **2.** An athlete who has never competed for money. **3.** A person who does something poorly or without professional skill. *—modifier: an amateur boxer; an amateur performance.* [French, from Latin *amātōr,* a lover, from *amāre,* to love.] **—am′a·teur′ism** *n.*

Syns: amateur, dilettante, nonprofessional *n.* *Core meaning:* A person lacking professional skill and ease in a given activity. AMATEUR and NONPROFESSIONAL additionally refer to one who engages in an activity for enjoyment rather than money *(golfers who are amateurs; boxers who are nonprofessionals),* whereas DILETTANTE refers to one whose interest in an activity is merely superficial *(As a painter he is a dilettante.).*

am·a·teur·ish (ăm′ə-chŏŏr′ĭsh, -tûr′ĭsh, -tyŏŏr′ĭsh) *adj.* Characteristic of an amateur; not professional; unskillful. **—am′a·teur′ish·ly** *adv.* **—am′a·teur′ish·ness** *n.*

am·a·to·ry (ăm′ə-tôr′ē, -tōr′ē) *adj.* Of, pertaining to, or expressive of love, esp. sexual love. [Latin *amātōrius,* from *amātōr,* a lover, from *amāre,* to love.]

a·maze (ə-māz′) *tr.v.* **a·mazed, a·maz·ing.** To fill with surprise or wonder; astonish. **1.** *n. Archaic.* Amazement. [Middle English *amasen,* from Old English *āmasian,* to bewilder.] **—a·maz′ed·ly** (ə-mā′zĭd-lē) **—a·maz′ing·ly** *adv.*

a·maze·ment (ə-māz′mənt) *n.* A state of extreme surprise or wonder; astonishment.

a·maz·ing (ə-mā′zĭng) *adj.* Causing amazement; surprising; wonderful. —See Syns at **fabulous.** **—a·maz′ing·ly** *adv.*

Am·a·zon (ăm′ə-zŏn′, -zən) *n.* **1.** *Gk. Myth.* A member of a nation of female warriors. **2.** Often **amazon.** Any tall, vig-

orous, aggressive woman. **—Am′a·zo′ni·an** (ăm′ə-zō′nē-ən) *adj.*

am·bas·sa·dor (ăm-băs′ə-dər) *n.* **1.** A diplomatic official of the highest rank appointed as representative in residence by one government to another. **2. a. ambassador-at-large.** An ambassador not assigned to a particular country. **b. ambassador extraordinary.** An ambassador assigned to a specific mission. **c. ambassador plenipotentiary.** An ambassador empowered to negotiate treaties. **3.** A diplomatic official heading his country's permanent mission to certain international organizations, such as the United Nations. **4.** Any messenger or representative. [Middle English *ambassadour,* from Old French *ambassadeur,* from Medieval Latin *ambactia,* mission, from Latin *ambactus,* vassal.] **—am·bas′sa·do′ri·al** (-dôr′ē-əl, -dōr′-) *adj.* **—am·bas′sa·dor·ship′** *n.*

am·ber (ăm′bər) *n.* **1.** A hard, translucent, yellow or brownish-yellow fossil resin, used for making jewelry and other ornamental objects. **2.** A brownish yellow. *—modifier: an amber necklace.* *—adj.* Brownish yellow. [Middle English *ambre,* from Old French, from Medieval Latin *ambra, ambar,* from Arabic *'anbar.*]

am·ber·gris (ăm′bər-grĭs, -grēs′) *n.* A waxy, grayish substance formed in the intestines of sperm whales and found floating at sea or washed ashore. It is used in perfumes. [Middle English *ambregris,* from Old French *ambre gris,* "amber gray."]

ambi-. A prefix meaning both: **ambidextrous.** [Latin, round, on both sides.]

am·bi·ance (ăm′bē-əns) *n.* Also **am·bi·ence.** The special or distinct atmosphere of an environment or setting. [French, from *ambiant,* surrounding.]

am·bi·dex·trous (ăm′bĭ-děk′strəs) *adj.* **1.** Capable of using both hands with equal facility. **2.** Unusually dexterous or skillful; adroit. [Late Latin *ambidexter,* an ambidextrous person, from AMBI- + *dexter,* right-handed.] **—am′bi·dex·ter′i·ty** (ăm′bĭ-děk-stěr′ĭ-tē) *n.* **—am′bi·dex′trous·ly** *adv.*

am·bi·ence (ăm′bē-əns) *n.* Var. of **ambiance.**

am·bi·ent (ăm′bē-ənt) *adj.* Surrounding; encircling; encompassing. [Latin *ambiēns,* pres. part. of *ambīre,* to go around, from *ambi-,* around + *īre,* to go.]

am·bi·gu·i·ty (ăm′bĭ-gyōō′ĭ-tē) *n., pl.* **-ties.** **1.** The condition of being ambiguous. **2.** Something ambiguous: *There were numerous ambiguities in his statement.*

am·big·u·ous (ăm-bĭg′yōō-əs) *adj.* **1.** Having two or more possible meanings or interpretations; vague: *an ambiguous statement by the governor.* **2.** Doubtful or uncertain: *the country's ambiguous economic future.* [Latin *ambiguus,* uncertain, from *ambigere,* to wander about : *ambi-,* around + *agere,* to drive, lead.] **—am·big′u·ous·ly** *adv.* **—am·big′u·ous·ness** *n.*

am·bi·tion (ăm-bĭsh′ən) *n.* **1.** A strong desire to achieve something, such as fame or fortune. **2.** The object desired: *Her ambition is to have her own business.* [Middle English *ambicioun,* from Old French *ambition,* from Latin *ambitiō,* a going around (for votes), from *ambīre,* to go around.]

am·bi·tious (ăm-bĭsh′əs) *adj.* **1.** Full of or motivated by ambition: *an ambitious politician.* **2.** Greatly desirous; eager: *ambitious to learn medicine.* **3.** Requiring much effort: *an ambitious plan.* **—am·bi′tious·ly** *adv.*

am·biv·a·lence (ăm-bĭv′ə-ləns) *n.* The simultaneous existence of two conflicting feelings, such as love and hate, about a person, object, or idea. [German *Ambivalenz* (coined by Freud), from AMBI- + VALENCE.] **—am·biv′a·lent** *adj.* **—am·biv′a·lent·ly** *adv.*

am·ble (ăm′bəl) *intr.v.* **-bled, -bling. 1.** To move along smoothly by lifting first both legs on one side and then both on the other: *The horses ambled from the corral.* **2.** To walk slowly or leisurely. *—n.* **1.** An ambling gait, esp. of a horse. **2.** An unhurried or leisurely pace. [Middle English *amblen,* from Old French *ambler,* from Latin *ambulāre,* to walk.] **—am′bler** *n.*

Am·boi·nese (ăm′boi-nēz′, -nēs′) *n.* The language of Amboina, an island in the Moluccas, Indonesia.

am·bro·sia (ăm-brō′zhə) *n.* **1.** *Gk. & Rom. Myth.* The food of the gods, thought to impart immortality. **2.** Anything with a very delicious flavor or fragrance. [Latin, from Greek, from *ambrotos,* immortal : *a-,* not + *brotos,* mortal.] **—am·bro′sial** *adj.*

ă pat   ā pay   â care   ä father   ĕ pet   ē be   hw which
ŏŏ took   ōō boot   ou out   th thin   th this   ŭ cut
ĭ pit   ī tie   î pier   ŏ pot   ō toe   ô paw, for   oi noise
û urge   zh vision   ə about, item, edible, gallop, circus

am·bu·lance (ăm′byə-ləns) *n.* A vehicle specially equipped to transport the sick or wounded. [French, from (*hôpital*) *ambulant*, itinerant (hospital), from Latin *ambulāns*, pres. part. of *ambulāre*, to ambulate.]

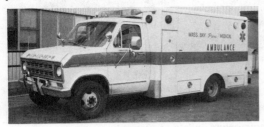

ambulance

am·bu·lant (ăm′byə-lənt) *adj.* Moving or walking about.

am·bu·late (ăm′byə-lāt′) *intr.v.* **-lat·ed, -lat·ing.** To move about; walk. [Latin *ambulāre*, to walk.]

am·bu·la·to·ry (ăm′byə-lə-tôr′ē, -tōr′ē) *adj.* **1.** Of, pertaining to, or for walking. **2.** Capable of walking; not bedridden: *an ambulatory patient.* **3.** Moving about; not stationary. —*n., pl.* **-ries.** A covered place for walking, as in a cloister.

am·bus·cade (ăm′bə-skād′, ăm′bə-skād′) *n.* An ambush. —*tr.v.* **-cad·ed, -cad·ing.** To ambush. [Old French *embuscade*, from Old Italian *imboscare*, to ambush.] —**am′bus·cad′er** *n.*

am·bush (ăm′bŏosh) *n.* **1.** The act of lying in wait to attack by surprise. **2. a.** A surprise attack made from a concealed position. **b.** The concealed position. **3.** Any hidden peril or trap. —*tr.v.* To attack from a concealed position. [From Middle English *embushen*, to ambush, from Old French *embuschier*.] —**am′bush′er** *n.*

a·me·ba (ə-mē′bə) *n.* Var. of **amoeba.**

a·me·bic (ə-mē′bĭk) *adj.* Var. of **amoebic.**

amebic dysentery. A disease of human beings, caused by a parasitic ameba. Its symptoms are diarrhea, abdominal cramps, and fever.

a·me·lio·rate (ə-mēl′yə-rāt′) *v.* **-rat·ed, -rat·ing.** —*tr.v.* To make better; improve: *ameliorate a tense situation.* —*intr.v.* To become better. [French *améliorer*, from Old French *ameilliorer*, from Latin *ad-*, to + *melior*, better.] —**a·me′lio·ra·ble** (-rə-bəl) *adj.* —**a·me′lio·ra′tion** *n.* —**a·me′lio·ra′tive** *adj.* —**a·me′lio·ra′tor** *n.*

a·men (ä-měn′, ā-) *interj.* So be it. A word used at the end of a prayer or to express approval. [Middle English, from Old English, from Late Latin *āmēn*, from Greek *amēn*, from Hebrew *āmēn*, certainly, verily.]

A·men (ä′mən) *n.* Also **A·mon.** *Egypt. Myth.* The god of life and reproduction, represented as a man with a ram's head.

a·me·na·ble (ə-mē′nə-bəl, ə-měn′ə-) *adj.* **1.** Willing to yield or cooperate; agreeable: *I'm amenable to your suggestion.* **2.** Responsible to authority; accountable: *We are all amenable to the law.* [From French *amener*, to lead, bring, from Old French, from Latin *ad-*, to + *mināre*, to drive (cattle), from *minārī*, "to shout at," from *minae*, threats.] —**a·me′na·bil′i·ty** or **a·me′na·ble·ness** *n.* —**a·me′na·bly** *adv.*

a·mend (ə-měnd′) *tr.v.* **1.** To correct or rectify, esp. errors in a text or piece of writing. **2.** To alter (a law, motion, etc.) formally by adding, deleting, or rephrasing. **3.** To improve; to better: *amend a situation.* —*intr.v.* To better one's conduct; to reform. —See Syns at **correct.** [Middle English *amenden*, from Old French *amender*, from Latin *ēmendāre*, to free from faults, from *ex-*, out of + *mendum*, defect.] —**a·mend′a·ble** *adj.*

a·men·da·to·ry (ə-měn′də-tôr′ē, -tōr′ē) *adj.* Serving or tending to amend; corrective.

a·mend·ment (ə-měnd′mənt) *n.* **1.** A change for the better; improvement: *signs of repentance and amendment.* **2.** A correction. **3. a.** A revision or change, as in a law. **b.** A formal statement of such a change.

a·mends (ə-měndz′) *pl.n.* Reparation or payment made as satisfaction for insult or injury. —*idiom.* **make amends.** To make up (to someone) for insult or injury.

a·men·i·ty (ə-měn′ĭ-tē, ə-mē′nĭ-) *n., pl.* **-ties. 1.** Pleasant-ness; agreeableness. **2.** Anything that provides or increases comfort; a convenience: *The neighborhood has many recreational amenities.* **3. amenities.** Social courtesies; manners. [Middle English *amenite*, from Old French, from Latin *amoenitās*, from *amoenus*, pleasant, delightful.]

a·merce (ə-mûrs′) *tr.v.* **a·merced, a·merc·ing. 1.** To punish by a fine imposed arbitrarily at the discretion of the court. **2.** To punish. [Middle English *amercien*, from Norman French *amercier*, from *a merci*, at the mercy of]

A·mer·i·can (ə-měr′ĭ-kən) *adj.* **1.** Of, pertaining to, or characteristic of the United States, its people, culture, institutions, history, or language. **2.** Of, in, or pertaining to North America or South America, or the Western Hemisphere. —*n.* A native or inhabitant of the United States or the Americas.

A·mer·i·ca·na (ə-měr′ĭ-kä′nə, -kăn′ə, -kā′nə) *pl.n.* A collection of books, papers, objects, etc., relating to American history, folklore, etc.

American Beauty. A type of rose with red flowers.

American cheese. A smooth, mild cheddar cheese, white to yellow in color.

American eagle. The **bald eagle,** esp. as it appears on the Great Seal of the United States.

American English. The English language as used in the United States.

American Indian. A member of any of the aboriginal peoples of North America (except the Eskimos), South America, and the West Indies.

A·mer·i·can·ism (ə-měr′ĭ-kə-nĭz′əm) *n.* **1.** A custom, trait, or tradition originating in the United States. **2.** A word, phrase, or usage characteristic of American English.

Usage: One kind of **Americanism** consists of words or expressions used only in American English, and not in British or any other variety of English, as *Chicano, hero sandwich, get to first base.* The other kind are words that originated in American English and that spread to other branches of English, as *muskrat, gooey, typewriter.*

A·mer·i·can·ize (ə-měr′ĭ-kə-nīz′) —*tr.v.* **-ized, -iz·ing.** —*tr.v.* To make American in culture, manners, customs, or speech. —*intr.v.* To become American in spirit, methods, or characteristics. —**A·mer′i·can·i·za′tion** *n.*

American plan. A system of hotel management in which a guest pays a fixed daily rate for room, meals, and service.

American Spanish. Spanish as used in the Western Hemisphere.

a·mer·i·ci·um (ăm′ə-rĭsh′ē-əm) *n. Symbol* **Am** A white metallic element, produced from plutonium, having isotopes with mass numbers from 237 to 246 and half-lives from 25 minutes to 7,950 years. Its longest-lived isotopes, Am 241 and Am 243, are alpha-ray emitters used as radiation sources in research. Atomic number 95, specific gravity 11.7, valences 3, 4, 5, 6. [From *America.*]

Am·er·ind (ăm′ə-rīnd′) *n.* An American Indian or an Eskimo. [AMER(ICAN) + IND(IAN).] —**Am′er·in′di·an** *adj. & n.*

am·e·thyst (ăm′ə-thĭst) *n.* **1.** A purple or violet form of transparent quartz used as a gemstone. **2.** A purple or violet color. —*adj.* Purple; violet. [Middle English *ametist*, from Old French *ametiste*, from Latin *amethystus*, from Greek *amethustos*, "anti-intoxicant" (amethyst was thought to be a remedy for intoxication) : *a-*, not + *methuskein*, to intoxicate, from *methu*, wine.]

Am·har·ic (ăm-hăr′ĭk, äm-hä′rĭk) *n.* A southern Semitic language that is the official language of Ethiopia.

a·mi·a·ble (ā′mē-ə-bəl) *adj.* **1.** Having a pleasant disposition; good-natured; friendly: *an amiable couple.* **2.** Pleasant; agreeable; congenial: *an amiable gathering; an amiable setting.* [Middle English, from Old French, from Late Latin *amīcābilis*, amicable.] —**a′mi·a·bil′i·ty** or **a′mi·a·ble·ness** *n.* —**a′mi·a·bly** *adv.*

Syns: amiable, affable, agreeable, complaisant, cordial, easy, easygoing, genial, good-natured, *adj. Core meaning:* Pleasant and friendly (*an amiable companion; an amiable conversation*). See also Syns at **friendly.**

am·i·ca·ble (ăm′ĭ-kə-bəl) *adj.* Characterized by or showing friendliness; peaceable: *an amicable discussion.* —See Syns at **friendly.** [Middle English, from Late Latin *amīcābilis*, from Latin *amīcus*, friend.] —**am′i·ca·bil′i·ty** or **am′i·ca·ble·ness** *n.* —**am′i·ca·bly** *adv.*

ă pat ā pay â care ä father ĕ pet ē be hw which   ĭ pit ī tie î pier ŏ pot ō toe ô paw, for oi noise
ŏŏ took ōō boot ou out th thin *th* this ŭ cut   û urge zh vision ə about, item, edible, gallop, circus

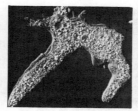

Amish

amoeba

am·ice (ăm′ĭs) *n.* A liturgical vestment that consists of an oblong piece of white linen worn around the neck and shoulders and partly under the alb. [Middle English *amyse*, prob. from Old French *amis*, pl. of *amit*, from Latin *amictus*, "(a garment) thrown around one," from *amicīre*, to throw around : *ambi-*, around + *jacere*, to throw.]

a·mid (ə-mĭd′) *prep.* Also **a·midst** (ə-mĭdst′). Surrounded by; in the middle of; among. [Middle English *amidde*, from Old English *onmiddan* : ON + *midd(e)*, middle.]

am·ide (ăm′īd, -ĭd) *n.* **1.** An organic compound, such as acetamide, containing the CONH₂ group. **2.** A compound with a metal replacing hydrogen in ammonia, such as sodium amide, NaNH₂. [AM(MONIA) + -IDE.] —**a·mid′ic** (ə-mĭd′ĭk) *adj.*

a·mid·ships (ə-mĭd′shĭps) *adv.* Also **a·mid·ship** (-shĭp′). Midway between the bow and the stern of a ship.

a·midst (ə-mĭdst′) *prep.* Var. of **amid**.

a·mine (ə-mēn′, ăm′ĭn) *n.* Any of a group of organic compounds of nitrogen that may be considered ammonia derivatives in which one or more hydrogen atoms has been replaced by a hydrocarbon radical. [AM(MONIUM) + -INE.]

a·mi·no acid (ə-mē′nō, ăm′ə-nō) Any of a class of organic compounds that contain the groups NH₂ and COOH and that are essential components of proteins. [From AMINE.]

A·mish (ä′mĭsh, ăm′ĭsh) *pl.n.* Mennonites of a sect that settled primarily in southeastern Pennsylvania in the late 17th cent. [German *amisch*, after Jacob Amman, Swiss Mennonite bishop.] —**A′mish** *adj.*

a·miss (ə-mĭs′) *adj.* Out of proper order; wrong; faulty: *What is amiss? I can find nothing amiss.* —*adv.* In an improper or defective way. —*idiom.* **take amiss.** To misunderstand; feel offended by: *Don't take what she says amiss.* [Middle English *a mis*, from A- (on, at) + *mis*, a mistake, from *missen*, to miss.]

a·mi·to·sis (ā′mĭ-tō′sĭs, ăm′ə-) *n.* Simple cell division in which the nucleus divides without the formation of chromosomes. [New Latin, from A- (not) + MITOSIS.] —**a′mi·tot′ic** (ā′mĭ-tŏt′ĭk, ăm′ə-) *adj.*

am·i·ty (ăm′ĭ-tē) *n.*, *pl.* **-ties.** Peaceful relations, as between nations; friendship. [Middle English *amite*, from Old French *amitie*, from Medieval Latin *amīcitās*, from Latin *amīcus*, friend.]

am·me·ter (ăm′mē′tər) *n.* An instrument that measures electric current in amperes. [AM(PERE) + -METER.]

am·mo (ăm′ō) *n.* Ammunition.

am·mo·nia (ə-mōn′yə, ə-mō′nē-ə) *n.* **1.** A colorless, pungent gas, NH₃, used to manufacture fertilizers and a wide variety of nitrogen-containing organic and inorganic chemicals. **2. Ammonium hydroxide.** [From Latin *(sal) ammōniācus*, "(salt) of Amen," from Greek *Ammōn*, Amen (orig. obtained near the temple of Amen, in Libya).]

am·mon·ite (ăm′ə-nīt′) *n.* The coiled, flat fossil shell of any of various extinct mollusks of the Mesozoic age. [New Latin *Ammonītēs*, from Latin *(cornus) Ammōnis*, "(horn) of Amen" (because it resembles the horns of Amen).]

Am·mon·ite (ăm′ə-nīt′) *n.* A member of a Semitic people living east of the Jordan River, mentioned frequently in the Old Testament.

am·mo·ni·um (ə-mō′nē-əm) *n.* The chemical ion, NH₄⁺, whose compounds act like alkali metals in chemical reactions. [New Latin, from AMMON(IA) + -IUM.]

ammonium chloride. A white crystalline compound, NH₄Cl, used in dry cells, as a soldering flux, and as an expectorant. Also called **sal ammoniac**.

ammonium hydroxide. An alkali solution, NH₄OH, formed by dissolving ammonia gas in water, and used as a household cleanser and to manufacture a wide variety of products. Also called **ammonia**.

ammonium nitrate. A colorless crystalline salt, NH₄NO₃, used in fertilizers, explosives, and solid rocket propellants.

ammonium sulfate. A brownish-gray to white crystalline salt, (NH₄)₂SO₄, used in fertilizers and water purification.

am·mu·ni·tion (ăm′yə-nĭsh′ən) *n.* **1. a.** The projectiles, along with their fuses and primers, that can be fired from guns or otherwise propelled. **b.** Any kind of explosive material, such as rockets, grenades, etc. **2.** Any means of offense or defense: *The accident at the power plant gave new ammunition to the opponents of nuclear power.* [Old French, from *l'amunition*, the munition.]

am·ne·sia (ăm-nē′zhə) *n.* Partial or total loss of memory, esp. when caused by shock, psychological disturbance, brain injury, or illness. [From Greek *amnēsia*, from *a-*, not + *mnasthai*, to remember.] —**am·ne′si·ac′** (-zē-ăk′, -zhē-ăk′) or **am·ne′sic** (-zĭk, -sĭk) *n. & adj.*

am·nes·ty (ăm′nĭ-stē) *n.*, *pl.* **-ties.** A governmental pardon, esp. for political offenses. —*tr.v.* **-tied, -ty·ing.** To grant amnesty to. [Greek *amnēstia*, "forgetfulness," from *amnēstos*, forgotten, from *a-*, not + *mnasthai*, to remember.]

am·ni·o·cen·te·sis (ăm′nē-ō-sĕn-tē′sĭs) *n.*, *pl.* **-ses** (-sēz′). The surgical withdrawal of a sample of amniotic fluid from a pregnant female, esp. for use in the determination of sex or genetic disorder in the fetus. [AMNIO(N) + Greek *kentesis*, a pricking.]

am·ni·on (ăm′nē-ən, -ŏn′) *n.*, *pl.* **-ons** or **-ni·a** (-nē-ə). A thin, tough, membranous sac that contains a watery fluid in which the embryo of a mammal, bird, or reptile floats. [New Latin, from Greek, sacrificial plate to hold a victim's blood, sac.] —**am′ni·ot′ic** (-ŏt′ĭk) or **am′ni·on′ic** (-ŏn′ĭk) *adj.*

a·moe·ba (ə-mē′bə) *n.*, *pl.* **-bas** or **-bae** (-bē). Also **a·me·ba.** Any of various protozoans of the class Sarcodina, found in water and soil and as internal parasites, characteristically having an indefinite, changeable form. [From Greek *amoibē*, change.]

a·moe·bic (ə-mē′bĭk) *adj.* Also **a·me·bic. 1.** Of, like, or pertaining to an amoeba. **2.** Caused by an amoeba or amoebas.

a·mok (ə-mŭk′, ə-mŏk′) *adv.* Var. of **amuck**.

A·mon (ä′mən) *n. Egypt. Myth.* Var. of **Amen**.

a·mong (ə-mŭng′) *prep.* Also **a·mongst** (ə-mŭngst′). **1.** In or through the midst of. **2.** In the company of: *among friends.* **3.** With portions to each of: *The soda was shared out among them.* **4.** Between one another: *fighting among themselves.* —See Usage note at **between**. [Middle English *among*, from Old English *on gemang*, from ON + *gemang*, a crowd.]

a·mon·til·la·do (ə-mŏn′tə-lä′dō) *n.*, *pl.* **-dos.** A pale dry sherry. [Spanish *(vino) amontillado*, "(wine) made in Montilla," a Spanish town.]

a·mor·al (ā-môr′əl, ā-mŏr′əl) *adj.* **1.** Not admitting of moral distinctions or judgments; neither moral nor immoral. **2.** Lacking moral judgment; not caring about right and wrong. [A- (not) + MORAL.] —**a′mo·ral′i·ty** (ā′mô-răl′ĭ-tē), *n.* —**a·mor′al·ly** *adv.*

am·o·rous (ăm′ər-əs) *adj.* **1.** Inclined to love; tending to fall in love easily. **2.** Produced by or showing love: *an amorous glance.* **3.** Of or associated with love: *an amorous poem.* [Middle English, from Old French, from Medieval Latin *amōrōsus*, from Latin *amor*, love.] —**am′or·ous·ly** *adv.* —**am′or·ous·ness** *n.*

a·mor·phous (ə-môr′fəs) *adj.* **1.** Without definite form; shapeless: *an amorphous mass of wax.* **2.** Of no particular type or character; unorganized: *a confusing, amorphous painting with elements of too many different styles.* **3.** General or vague; unclear: *amorphous ideas.* **4.** *Chem.* Lacking distinct crystalline structure: *Glass is an amorphous substance.* [Greek *amorphos* : *a-*, without + *morphē*, shape.] **—a·mor'phous·ly** *adv.* **—a·mor'phous·ness** *n.*

am·or·ti·za·tion (ăm'ər-tĭ-zā'shən, ə-môr'-) *n.* **1.** The act or process of amortizing. **2.** The money set aside for this purpose.

am·or·tize (ăm'ər-tīz', ə-môr'tīz') *tr.v.* **-tized, -tiz·ing. 1.** To liquidate (a debt) by installment payments, usu. paid at regular intervals. **2.** *Accounting.* To write off (expenditures) by prorating over a certain period. [Middle English *amortisen*, from Old French *amortir*, from Latin *ad-*, to + *mors*, death.]

a·mount (ə-mount') *n.* **1.** The total of two or more quantities; aggregate. **2.** A number; sum: *The amount still due is fifty dollars.* **3.** A principal plus its interest, as in a loan. **4.** Quantity: *She has a great amount of talent.* —*intr.v.* **1.** To add up in number or quantity: *The total purchase amounts to ten dollars.* **2.** To be equal in value, effect, or meaning: *Disobeying orders amounts to treason.* [Middle English *amounten*, to rise, from Old French *amonter*, from *amont*, upward, "to the mountain" : Latin *ad-*, to + *mōns*, mountain.]

a·mour (ə-mōōr') *n.* A love affair, esp. an illicit one. [Middle English, from Old French, from Latin *amor*, love.]

am·per·age (ăm'pər-ĭj, ăm'pîr'ĭj) *n.* The strength of an electric current as measured or expressed in amperes.

am·pere (ăm'pîr') *n.* The standard unit for measuring the strength of an electric current, equal to a flow of one Coulomb per second. [After André Marie *Ampère* (1775–1836), French mathematician and physicist.]

am·per·sand (ăm'pər-sănd') *n.* The character or sign (&) representing *and*. [Contraction of "*and per se and*," "& (the sign) by itself (equals) *and*."]

am·phet·a·mine (ăm-fĕt'ə-mēn', -mĭn) *n.* A colorless volatile liquid, $C_9H_{13}N$, used as a drug to counter depression, as a central nervous system stimulant, and to reduce the appetite. [A(LPHA) M(ETHYL) PH(ENYL) ET(HYL) AMINE.]

am·phib·i·an (ăm-fĭb'ē-ən) *n.* **1.** Any of various cold-blooded vertebrates of the class Amphibia, such as a frog, toad, or salamander, that hatch from eggs laid in the water and breathe by means of gills and later develop into an adult form that has air-breathing lungs. **2.** Any amphibious organism. **3.** An aircraft that can take off and land either on land or on water. **4.** A vehicle that can move over land and on water. —*adj.* **1.** Of or pertaining to an amphibian, esp. one of the Amphibia. **2.** Built as an amphibian. [From New Latin *Amphibia*, pl. of *amphibium*, an amphibian, from Greek *amphibion*, neut. of *amphibios*, amphibious.]

am·phib·i·ous (ăm-fĭb'ē-əs) *adj.* **1.** Capable of living both on land and in water. **2.** Capable of operating on both land and water: *amphibious vehicles.* **3.** Launched from the sea with navy, land, and air forces against an enemy on land: *an amphibious invasion.* [Greek *amphibios*, "living a double life" : *amphi-*, both + *bios*, life.] **—am·phib'i·ous·ly** *adv.* **—am·phib'i·ous·ness** *n.*

am·phi·bole (ăm'fə-bōl') *n.* Any of a large group of rock-forming minerals that contain various combinations of sodium, calcium, magnesium, iron, and aluminum. [French, from Late Latin *amphibolus*, ambiguous (from its many varieties), from Greek *amphibolos*, doubtful, from *amphi-*, around + *ballein*, to throw around; doubt : *amphi-*, around + *ballein*, to throw.] **—am·phi·bol'ic** (-bŏl'ĭk) *adj.*

am·phi·the·a·ter (ăm'fə-thē'ə-tər) *n.* Also **am·phi·the·a·tre. 1.** An oval or round structure having tiers of seats that rise gradually outward from an open space or arena at the center. **2.** Any arena where contests are held. **3.** A level area surrounded by upward sloping ground. **4.** An upper, sloping gallery in a theater. [Latin *amphitheatrum*, from Greek *amphitheatron*, from *amphi-*, around + THEATER.]

Am·phi·tri·te (ăm'fĭ-trī'tē) *n.* *Gk. Myth.* The wife of Poseidon, goddess of the sea, and one of the Nereids.

am·pho·ra (ăm'fər-ə) *n.*, *pl.* **-rae** (-fə-rē') or **-ras.** A two-handled jar with a narrow neck, used by the ancient Greeks and Romans to carry wine or oil. [Latin *amphora*,

from Greek *amphoreus*, from *amphi-*, around + *pherein*, to bear.]

am·pho·ter·ic (ăm'fə-tĕr'ĭk) *adj.* *Chem.* Capable of reacting either as an acid or a base. [From Greek *amphoteros*, either of two, from *amphō*, both.]

am·ple (ăm'pəl) *adj.* **1.** Of large or great size, amount, extent, or capacity: *an ample living room.* **2. a.** Large in degree or kind: *an ample reward.* **b.** More than enough; abundant: *ample evidence; ample food for everyone.* **3.** Sufficient for a particular need; adequate: *ample provisions for a week.*—See Syns at **broad.** [Middle English, from Old French, from Latin *amplus.*] **—am'ple·ness** *n.* **—am'ply** (-plē) *adv.*

am·pli·fi·ca·tion (ăm'plə-fĭ-kā'shən) *n.* **1.** The act or result of amplifying. **2.** An addition to or expansion of any statement or idea. **3.** A statement with such an addition. **4.** *Physics.* **a.** The process of increasing the magnitude of a variable quantity, esp. of a voltage or current, without altering any other quality. **b.** The result of such a process.

am·pli·fi·er (ăm'plə-fī'ər) *n.* **1.** A person or thing that amplifies, enlarges, or extends. **2.** *Physics.* Any of various devices or electronic circuits that produce amplification, esp. a component in a sound-reproduction system.

am·pli·fy (ăm'plə-fī') *v.* **-fied, -fy·ing.** —*tr.v.* **1.** To make larger or more powerful; extend; increase: *He bought that company to amplify his business interests.* **2.** To add to, as by illustrations; develop; expand: *He amplified his point by citing additional details.* **3.** *Physics.* To produce amplification of. —*intr.v.* To write or discourse at length; expatiate: *Let me amplify so you'll understand completely.* [Middle English *amplifien*, from Old French *amplifier*, from Latin *amplificāre* : *amplus*, ample + *facere*, to make.]

am·pli·tude (ăm'plĭ-tōōd', -tyōōd') *n.* **1.** Greatness of size; magnitude; extent. **2.** Abundance; fullness. **3.** Breadth or range, as of mind. **4.** *Physics.* The maximum value taken on by a quantity whose value changes. —See Syns at **bulk.** [Latin *amplitūdō*, from *amplus*, ample.]

amplitude modulation. A system of radio transmission in which the amplitude of the carrier wave is adjusted so that it is proportional to the measure of the sound or other information that is to be transmitted.

am·poule or **am·pule** (ăm'pōōl', -pyōōl') *n.* Also **am·pul.** A small, sealed glass vial that holds one dose of medicine, used as a container for a hypodermic injection. [French, from Old French, from Latin *ampulla*, ampulla.]

am·pul·la (ăm-pōōl'ə, -pŭl'ə) *n.*, *pl.* **-pul·lae** (-pōōl'ē, -pŭl'ē). **1.** A nearly round bottle with two handles used by the ancient Romans for wine, oil, or perfume. **2.** A container used in the church for wine, water, or holy oil. [Latin, dim. of *amp(h)ora*, amphora.]

am·pu·tate (ăm'pyōō-tāt') *tr.v.* **-tat·ed, -tat·ing.** To cut off (a part of the body), esp. by surgery. [Latin *amputāre*, to cut around : AM(BI)- + *putāre*, to cut.] **—am'pu·ta'tion** *n.* **—am'pu·ta'tor** *n.*

am·pu·tee (ăm'pyōō-tē') *n.* A person who has had one or more limbs removed by amputation.

Am·trak (ăm'trăk') *n.* A public corporation chartered by the Federal government and authorized to operate rail passenger services between major cities of the United States. [AM(ERICAN) + TRA(C)K.]

a·muck (ə-mŭk') *adv.* Also **a·mok** (ə-mŭk', ə-mŏk'). **1.** In a frenzy to do violence or kill: *The mob ran amuck, firing*

amphitheater

amulet

amusement park

anaconda

rifles and hurling missiles. **2.** In a jumbled or faulty manner; all over: *When Father carves a turkey, potatoes fly amuck. Plans went amuck.* [Malay *amok,* furious attack.]

am·u·let (ăm′yə-lĭt) *n.* An object worn, esp. around the neck, to protect against evil or injury; a charm. [Latin *amulētum.*]

a·muse (ə-myōōz′) *tr.v.* **a·mused, a·mus·ing. 1.** To keep pleasantly entertained, occupied, or pleased; divert: *He amused me with adventure stories.* **2.** To cause to laugh or smile by giving pleasure. **—a·mused′** *adj.: an amused smile.* **—a·mus′ing** *adj.: an amusing movie.* [Old French *amuser,* "to cause to idle away time" : *a,* to + *muser,* to idle.] **—a·mus′a·ble** *adj.* **—a·mus′ed·ly** (ə-myōō′zĭd-lē) *adv.* **—a·mus′er** *n.*

Syns: amuse, divert, entertain *v. Core meaning:* To provide pleasure to (*The variety show amused us*).

a·muse·ment (ə-myōōz′mənt) *n.* **1.** The state of being amused, entertained, or pleased. **2.** Something that amuses.

amusement park. A commercial park that has stands for refreshments and offers various forms of entertainment.

am·yl (ăm′əl) *n.* The univalent organic radical C_5H_{11}, occurring in several isomeric forms in many organic compounds. [Latin *amylum,* starch, from Greek *amulos,* "not ground in a mill" : *a-,* not + *mulē,* mill.]

amyl-. Var. of the prefix **amylo-.**

amyl alcohol. Any of eight colorless, sharp-smelling isomers, $C_5H_{11}OH$, one of which is the principal constituent of fusel oil.

am·y·lase (ăm′ə-lās′, -lāz′) *n.* Any of various enzymes that convert starch to sugar. [AMYL(O)- + -ASE.]

amylo- or **amyl-.** A prefix meaning starch: **amylase.** [From Latin *amylum,* starch. See **amyl.**]

am·y·lop·sin (ăm′ə-lŏp′sĭn) *n.* The starch-digesting amylase produced by the pancreas. [AMYLO- + (TRY)PSIN.]

an¹ (ən; ăn *when stressed*) *indefinite article.* A form of *a* used before words beginning with a vowel or with an unpronounced *h: an elephant; an hour.* —See Usage note at **a.** [Middle English *an,* from Old English *ān,* one.]

an² (ən; ăn *when stressed*) *conj.* Also **an′.** *Archaic.* And if; if: *"An I may hide my face, let me play Thisby too"* (Shakespeare). [Middle English *an,* Old English *an,* short for AND.]

an-. A prefix meaning not or without: **anaerobe.** [Greek *an-,* not, without, lacking.]

-an. A suffix meaning: **1.** Pertaining to, belonging to, or resembling: **Mexican. 2.** Believing in or adhering to: **Mohammedan.** [Latin *-ānus,* adj. suffix.]

ana-. A prefix meaning: **1.** Upward progression: **anabolism. 2.** Renewal or intensification: **anaphylaxis.** [Greek, from *ana,* up, throughout, according to.]

-ana or **-iana.** A suffix meaning a collection of material pertaining to a notable place or person: **Americana.** [New Latin, from Latin *-āna,* "the things pertaining to," neut. pl. of *ānus,* -AN.]

An·a·bap·tist (ăn′ə-băp′tĭst) *n.* A member of one of the radical movements of the Reformation that insisted that only adult baptism was valid and held that true Christians should not bear arms, use force, or hold government office. [New Latin *anabaptista,* from Late Greek *anabaptizein,* to baptize again : Greek *ana-,* again + *baptizein,* to baptize.] **—An′a·bap′tism** *n.*

a·nab·o·lism (ə-năb′ə-lĭz′əm) *n.* The metabolic process by which simple substances, such as food, are changed into the complex materials of living tissue. [ANA- + (META)BO-LISM.] **—an′a·bol′ic** (ăn′ə-bŏl′ĭk) *adj.*

a·nach·ro·nism (ə-năk′rə-nĭz′əm) *n.* **1.** The representation of something as existing or happening at other than its proper or historical time: *The play had the anachronism of George Washington receiving a telegraph message.* **2.** Anything out of its proper time: *Cavalry is an anachronism in modern warfare.* [French *anachronisme,* from Greek *anakhronismos* : *ana-,* backward + *khronizein,* to belong to a particular time, from *khronos, time.*] **—a·nach′ro·nis′tic** or **a·nach′ro·nous** (-nəs) *adj.* **—a·nach′ro·nis′ti·cal·ly** *adv.*

an·a·co·lu·thon (ăn′ə-kə-lōō′thŏn′) *n., pl.* **-thons** or **-tha** (-thə). An abrupt change within a sentence from one grammatical construction to another, sometimes used for rhetorical effect; for example, *I warned him that if he continues to drink, what will become of him?* [Late Latin, from Greek *anakolouthon,* inconsistent : *an-,* not + *akolouthos,* following : *a-,* together + *keleuthos,* path.]

an·a·con·da (ăn′ə-kŏn′də) *n.* **1.** A large, nonpoisonous snake, *Eunectes murinus,* of tropical South America, that crushes its prey in its coils. **2.** Any of several similar snakes. [Var. of Singhalese *henakandayā.*]

a·nad·ro·mous (ə-năd′rə-məs) *adj.* Migrating up rivers from the sea to breed in fresh water, as salmon. [Greek *anadromos,* a running up : *ana-,* up + *dromos,* a running.]

a·nae·mi·a (ə-nē′mē-ə) *n.* Var. of **anemia.**

a·nae·mic (ə-nē′mĭk) *adj.* Var. of **anemic.**

an·aer·obe (ăn′ə-rōb′, ăn-âr′ōb′) *n.* An anaerobic microorganism. [AN- + AEROBE.]

an·aer·o·bic (ăn′ə-rō′bĭk, ăn-â-) *adj.* **1.** Capable of living or growing in an environment lacking free oxygen. **2.** Of or produced by anaerobes.

an·aes·the·sia (ăn′ĭs-thē′zhə) *n.* Var. of **anesthesia.**

an·aes·the·si·ol·o·gy (ăn′ĭs-thē′zē-ŏl′ə-jē) *n.* Var. of **anesthesiology.**

an·aes·thet·ic (ăn′ĭs-thĕt′ĭk) *adj. & n.* Var. of **anesthetic.**

an·aes·the·tist (ə-nĕs′thĭ-tĭst) *n.* Var. of **anesthetist.**

an·aes·the·tize (ə-nĕs′thĭ-tīz′) *tr.v.* **-tized, -tiz·ing.** Var. of **anesthetize.**

an·a·gram (ăn′ə-grăm′) *n.* **1.** A word or phrase formed by reordering the letters of another word or phrase. For example, *mean* is an anagram of *amen.* **2. anagrams.** A game in which players form words from a collection of randomly picked letters. [French *anagramme,* from New Latin *anagramma,* from ANA- + -GRAM.]

a·nal (ā′nəl) *adj.* Of, pertaining to, or near the anus.

an·al·ge·si·a (ăn′əl-jē′zē-ə, -zhə) *n.* Inability to feel pain while remaining conscious, a condition usu. produced by a drug or drugs. [From Greek *analgēsia* : AN- + Greek *algēsia,* sense of pain, from *algos,* pain.]

an·al·ge·sic (ăn′əl-jē′zĭk, -sĭk) *n.* A drug that reduces or eliminates pain. **—adj.** Of or causing analgesia.

an·a·log (ăn′ə-lôg′, -lŏg′) *n.* Var. of **analogue.**

analog computer. Also **analogue computer.** A computer in which numerical data are represented by analogous measurable quantities such as lengths, electric currents, or voltages.

an·a·log·i·cal (ăn′ə-lŏj′ĭ-kəl) *adj.* Of, composed of, or based upon an analogy. **—an′a·log′i·cal·ly** *adv.*

a·nal·o·gous (ə-năl′ə-gəs) *adj.* **1.** Alike in certain ways: *Their situations are analogous because both men lost their jobs and have families to support.* **2.** *Biol.* Similar in function but not in origin or structure, as the gills of a fish and the lungs of a mammal. —See Syns at **like.** [Latin *analogus,* from Greek *analogos,* proportionate, resembling : *ana-,* according to + *logos,* proportion, word.]

an·a·logue (ăn′ə-lôg′, -lŏg′) *n.* Also **an·a·log.** **1.** Something that is analogous **2.** *Biol.* An analogous organ.

analogue computer. Var. of **analog computer.**

a·nal·o·gy (ə-năl′ə-jē) *n., pl.* **-gies.** **1.** A similarity in some ways, esp. in function or position, between things otherwise unlike; resemblance: *an analogy between the body and a machine.* **2.** Any comparison based on similarity or correspondence; a parallel: *I think his analogy between the breakdowns of the Roman Empire and the British Empire is false.* **3.** *Logic.* A form of inference based on the assumption that if two things are known to be alike in some respects, then they must be alike in other respects: *Mosaic Law became a large collection of cases from which judges could draw analogies.* **4.** *Biol.* Similarity in function but with differences in structure and origin. [Latin *analogia,* from Greek, from *analogos,* analogous.]

an·a·lyse (ăn′ə-līz′) *tr.v.* **-lysed, -lys·ing.** *Brit.* Var. of **ana·lyze.**

a·nal·y·sis (ə-năl′ĭ-sĭs) *n., pl.* **-ses** (-sēz′). **1.** *Chem.* **a.** Separation of a substance into its constituent elements to determine either their nature **(qualitative analysis)** or their proportions **(quantitative analysis). b.** A statement or report, esp. written, of the findings of such an operation. **2.** The breaking up of any whole, such as an idea, condition, event, etc., into its parts in order to study them individually so as to determine their nature, significance, or function. **3. Psychoanalysis.** [New Latin, from Greek *analusis,* a releasing, from *analuein,* to undo : *ana-,* back + *luein,* to loosen.]

an·a·lyst (ăn′ə-lĭst) *n.* **1.** A person who analyzes: *a systems analyst; a news analyst.* **2.** A licensed practitioner of psychoanalysis.

an·a·lyt·ic (ăn′ə-lĭt′ĭk) or **an·a·lyt·i·cal** (-ĭ-kəl) *adj.* **1.** Of or pertaining to analysis. **2.** Dividing into elemental parts or basic principles. **3.** Reasoning from a perception of the parts and interrelations of a subject; using analysis. —**an′·a·lyt′i·cal·ly** *adv.*

analytic geometry. The study of geometric structures and properties principally by algebraic operations on variables of a coordinate system.

an·a·lyze (ăn′ə-līz′) *tr.v.* **-lyzed, -lyz·ing.** Also *Brit.* **an·a·lyse, -lysed, -lys·ing. 1.** To examine in detail: *analyze the causes of inflation.* **2.** To make a chemical analysis of. **3.** To psychoanalyze. [French *analyser,* from *analyse,* analysis, from New Latin ANALYSIS.] —**an′a·lyz′er** *n.*

an·a·pest (ăn′ə-pĕst′) *n.* Also **an·a·paest. 1.** A metrical foot composed of two short syllables followed by one long one. **2.** A line of verse in this meter: " *'Twas the night before Christmas and all through the house"* (Clement Moore). [Latin *anapaestus,* from Greek *anapaistos,* "struck back" (an anapest being a dactyl reversed) : *ana-,* back + *paiein,* to strike.] —**an′a·pes′tic** *adj.*

an·a·phase (ăn′ə-fāz′) *n. Biol.* The stage of mitosis and meiosis in which the chromosomes move toward the poles of the nuclear spindle. [ANA- ("progressive") + PHASE.]

an·a·phy·lax·is (ăn′ə-fə-lăk′sĭs) *n.* Hypersensitivity to a foreign substance, esp. in animals, induced by a preliminary injection of the substance. [New Latin from ANA- + (PRO)PHYLAXIS.] —**an′a·phy·lac′tic** (-lăk′tĭk) *adj.*

an·ar·chic (ăn-är′kĭk) or **an·ar·chi·cal** (-kəl). *adj.* **1.** Of, like, or promoting anarchy. **2.** Lacking order or control; lawless. —**an·ar′chi·cal·ly** *adv.*

an·ar·chism (ăn′ər-kĭz′əm) *n.* **1.** The theory that all forms of government are oppressive and should be abolished. **2.** Active resistance and terrorism against the state or any established order. —**an′ar·chist** *n.* —**an′ar·chis′tic** *adj.*

an·ar·chy (ăn′ər-kē) *n., pl.* **-chies. 1.** Absence of any form of governmental authority or law. **2.** Political disorder and confusion. **3.** Absence of any cohering principle, as a common standard or purpose; disorder and confusion. [Greek *anarkhia,* from *anarkhos,* without a ruler : AN- + *arkhos,* ruler.]

an·as·tig·mat·ic (ăn-ăs′tĭg-măt′ĭk) *adj.* **1.** Capable of forming an accurate image of a point; not astigmatic: *an anastigmatic lens.* **2.** Pertaining to a compound lens in which the separate components compensate for the astigmatism of each. [AN- + ASTIGMATIC.]

a·nas·to·mo·sis (ə-năs′tə-mō′sĭs) *n., pl.* **-ses** (-sēz′). The union or connection of branches, as of rivers, veins of leaves, or blood vessels. [From Greek *anastomōsis,* opening, from *anastomoun,* to furnish with a mouth, from *ana-,* up + *stoma,* a mouth.]

a·nath·e·ma (ə-năth′ə-mə) *n., pl.* **-mas. 1.** A formal ecclesiastical ban, curse, or excommunication. **2.** A vehement denunciation; curse: *"the sound of a witch's anathemas in some unknown tongue"* (Nathaniel Hawthorne). **3.** Someone or something intensely disliked: *His name is an anathema to me.* [Late Latin, a curse, a person cursed, an offering, from Greek *anathēma,* votive offering, from *anatithenai,* to dedicate : *ana-,* up + *tithenai,* to put.]

a·nath·e·ma·tize (ə-năth′ə-mə-tīz′) *tr.v.* **-tized, -tiz·ing.** To proclaim an anathema against; denounce or curse.

an·a·tom·i·cal (ăn′ə-tŏm′ĭ-kəl) or **an·a·tom·ic** (-tŏm′ĭk). *adj.* **1.** Of or pertaining to anatomy or dissection. **2.** Structural as opposed to functional: *an anatomical abnormality.* —**an′a·tom′i·cal·ly** *adv.*

a·nat·o·mist (ə-năt′ə-mĭst) *n.* An expert in anatomy.

a·nat·o·mize (ə-năt′ə-mīz′) *tr.v.* **-mized, -miz·ing. 1.** To dissect (an animal or plant) in order to study the structure. **2.** To analyze in great detail.

a·nat·o·my (ə-năt′ə-mē) *n., pl.* **-mies. 1.** The structure of a plant or animal or of any of its parts. **2.** The scientific study of the shape and structure of organisms and their parts. **3.** The dissection of a plant or animal to disclose and study the various parts, their positions, structure, and interrelation. **4.** A skeleton or anatomical model. **5.** Any detailed examination or analysis: *the anatomy of a presidential campaign.* **6.** The human body. —**modifier:** *an anatomy lesson.* [Middle English *anatomie,* from Old French, from Latin *anatomia,* from Greek *anatemnein,* to dissect : *ana-,* up + *temnein,* to cut.]

-ance or **-ancy.** A suffix indicating an action, quality, or condition: **riddance, compliancy.** [Middle English, from Old French, from Latin *-antia,* abstract noun suffix of *-ant-,* stem of *-āns,* pres. part. ending, -ANT.]

an·ces·tor (ăn′sĕs′tər) *n.* **1.** Any person from whom one is descended, esp. of a generation earlier than a grandparent; a forefather. **2.** *Biol.* The organism or stock from which later kinds have evolved. **3.** A forerunner or predecessor; prototype: *The harpsichord is an ancestor of the piano.* [Middle English *ancestre,* from Old French, from Latin *antecessor,* from *antecēdere,* to go before : *ante-,* before + *cēdere,* to go.]

Syns: ancestor, antecedent, forebear, forefather, progenitor *n.* Core meaning: A person from whom one is descended (*My ancestors were Puritan farmers*).

an·ces·tral (ăn-sĕs′trəl) *adj.* **1.** Of ancestors: *ancestral spirits.* **2.** Coming from ancestors: *ancestral wealth.* **3.** Being an ancestor: *the ancestral Indo-European language, from which English and Greek are descended.* —**an·ces′tral·ly** *adv.*

an·ces·tress (ăn′sĕs′trĭs) *n.* A female ancestor.

an·ces·try (ăn′sĕs′trē) *n., pl.* **-tries. 1.** Ancestral descent or lineage: *Their family is of Macedonian ancestry.* **2.** Ancestors taken as a group.

An·chi·ses (ăn-kī′sēz′) *n. Gk. & Rom. Myth.* The father of Aeneas, rescued by his son from fallen Troy.

an·chor (ăng′kər) *n.* **1.** A heavy object of iron or steel attached to a vessel by a cable and cast overboard to keep the vessel in place, either by its weight or by its flukes gripping the bottom. **2.** Anything used to provide a rigid point of support, as for securing a rope or cable. **3.** Something that gives a person security or stability: *Faith is his anchor.* **4.** *Radio & TV.* An anchorman or anchorwoman. —*tr.v.* **1.** To hold fast by or as if by an anchor: *anchor the tent with spikes.* **2.** *Radio & TV.* To narrate or coordinate (a newscast in which several correspondents give reports). —*intr.v.* To drop anchor; lie at anchor, as a ship. —*idiom.* **at anchor.** Anchored; held fast. [Middle English *anker,* from Old English *ancer, ancor,* from Latin *anc(h)ora,* from Greek *ankura.*]

ă pat ā pay â care ä father ĕ pet ē be hw which ĭ pit ī tie î pier ŏ pot ō toe ô paw, for oi noise
ōō took ōō boot ou out th thin th this ŭ cut û urge zh vision ə about, item, edible, gallop, circus

an·chor·age (ăng′kər-ĭj) *n.* **1.** A place for anchoring ships. **2.** A fee charged for anchoring. **3. a.** The act of anchoring. **b.** The condition of being at anchor. **4.** Something that holds firmly or that can be relied on.

an·cho·rite (ăng′kə-rīt′) *n.* Also **an·cho·ret** (-rĕt′). A person who is in seclusion for religious reasons; hermit; recluse. [Middle English, from Medieval Latin *anchorīta*; from Late Greek *anakhōrētēs*, from *anakhōrein*, to withdraw : Greek *ana-*, back + *khōrein*, to make room.] —**an′cho·rit′ic** (-rĭt′ĭk) *adj.*

an·chor·man (ăng′kər-măn′) *n.* **1.** *Sports.* The runner who performs the last stage of a relay race. **2.** *Radio & TV.* A person who anchors a newscast.

an·chor·wom·an (ăng′kər-wŏŏm′ən) *n.* *Radio & TV.* A woman who narrates a newscast in which several correspondents give reports.

an·cho·vy (ăn′chō-vē, ăn-chō′vē) *n., pl.* **-vies.** Any of various small, herringlike saltwater fishes of the family Engraulidae. Several species are widely used as food fish, usu. salted and canned. —*modifier:* anchovy paste. [Spanish *anchova, anchoa,* perh. from Basque *anchu.*]

an·cien ré·gime (ăN-syăN′ rā-zhēm′). **1.** The political and social system existing in France before the Revolution of 1789. **2.** Any former socio-political system. [French, "old regime."]

an·cient (ān′shənt) *adj.* **1.** Very old; aged. **2.** Of or occurring in times long past, esp. prior to the fall of Rome (A.D. 476). —See Syns at **early** and **old.** —*n.* **1.** A very old person. **2.** A person who lived in ancient times. **3. the ancients.** The peoples of the classical nations of antiquity, esp. the Greek and Roman authors. [Middle English *ancien,* from Old French, from Vulgar Latin *anteānus,* "going before," from Latin *ante,* before.] —**an′cient·ly** *adv.* —**an′cient·ness** *n.*

an·cil·lar·y (ăn′sə-lĕr′ē) *adj.* **1.** Of secondary importance; subordinate: *the main company and its ancillary factories.* **2.** Helping; auxiliary; supplementary. [Latin *ancillāris,* servile, from *ancilla,* maidservant, fem. dim. of *anculus,* servant.]

-ancy. Var. of the suffix **-ance.**

and (ənd, ən; ănd *when stressed*) *conj.* **1.** Together with or along with; as well as: *trials and tribulations; a long and happy life.* **2.** Added to; plus: *Two and two make four.* **3.** As a result: *Seek, and ye shall find.* **4.** To. Used between finite verbs in the infinitive or imperative: *Try and find it.* **5.** *Archaic.* Then. Used to begin a sentence: *And he said unto her . . .* **6.** *Archaic.* If: *and it please you.* [Middle English *and,* from Old English *and, ond.*]
Usage: **and etc.** Make this just *etc.* The word *and* is part of **et cetera** (abbreviated **etc.**), which means *and other unspecified things of the same class.*

an·dan·te (än-dän′tā, ăn-dăn′tē). *Mus.* —*adv.* Moderately slowly; faster than adagio, but more slowly than allegretto. Used as a direction: *performed andante.* —*adj.* Moderately slow: *an andante movement.* —*n.* An andante movement or passage. [Italian, "walking," pres. part. of *andare,* to walk, from Latin *ambulāre,* to walk.]

an·dan·ti·no (än-dän-tē′nō, ăn-dăn-tē′nō). *Mus.* —*adv.* Slightly faster than andante in tempo. Used as a direction. —*adj.* Slightly faster than andante: *an andantino section.* —*n., pl.* **-nos.** An andantino movement or passage. [Italian, dim. of ANDANTE.]

and·i·ron (ănd′ī′ərn) *n.* One of a pair of metal supports for

andiron

holding up logs in a fireplace. [Middle English *aundiren,* var. of Old French *andier, firedog.*]

and/or. Used to indicate that either *and* or *or* may be used to connect words, phrases, or clauses.
Usage: **and/or.** Unless there is a real need to set forth three distinct and exclusive possibilities in the sense of *one or the other or both,* the expression *and/or* can usu. be replaced by *and* or *or* used singly, with no loss of meaning.

andro-. A prefix meaning: **1.** The male sex or masculine: **androgen. 2.** *Bot.* Stamen or anther: **androecium.** [Greek, from *anēr,* man.]

an·droe·ci·um (ăn-drē′shē-əm, -shəm) *n., pl.* **-ci·a** (-shē-ə, -shə). The stamens of a flower. [From ANDR(O)- + Greek *oikion,* residence, dim. of *oikos,* house.]

an·dro·gen (ăn′drə-jən) *n.* Any of the hormones that develop and maintain masculine physical characteristics. —**an′dro·gen′ic** (-jĕn′ĭk) *adj.*

an·drog·y·nous (ăn-drŏj′ə-nəs) *adj.* **1.** Having female and male characteristics in one; hermaphroditic. **2.** *Bot.* Composed of flowers with stamens and flowers with pistils in one cluster. [Latin *androgynus,* from Greek *androgunos* : ANDRO- + -GYNOUS.] —**an·drog′y·ny** (-ə-nē) *n.*

an·droid (ăn′droid′) *n.* *Sci. Fict.* An artificially created man. [Late Greek *androeidēs,* manlike : ANDR(O)- + -OID.]

An·drom·a·che (ăn-drŏm′ə-kē) *n.* *Gk. Myth.* The faithful wife of Hector, who was captured by the Greeks at the fall of Troy after her husband was slain.

An·drom·e·da (ăn-drŏm′ĭ-də) *n.* **1.** *Gk. Myth.* The wife of Perseus, who had rescued her from a sea monster. **2.** A constellation in the Northern Hemisphere near Lacerta and Perseus.

-andry. A suffix meaning number of husbands: **monandry.** [From Greek *anēr,* man.]

-ane. *Chem.* A suffix meaning a saturated hydrocarbon: **hexane, propane.** [Var. of -ENE, -INE, or -ONE.]

an·ec·dote (ăn′ĭk-dōt′) *n.* A short account of some interesting or humorous incident. [French, from Greek *anekdota,* "things unpublished," from *anekdotos,* unpublished, from AN- + *ekdidonai,* to give out : *ek-,* out + *didonai,* to give.] —**an′ec·do′tal** *adj.*

a·ne·mi·a (ə-nē′mē-ə) *n.* Also **a·nae·mi·a.** A pathological condition in which the blood, because of a lack of hemoglobin, too few red blood cells, or poorly formed red blood cells, cannot carry enough oxygen to the body tissues. [From Greek *anaimia* : *an-,* without + *haima,* blood.]

a·ne·mic (ə-nē′mĭk) *adj.* Also **a·nae·mic. 1.** Of, relating to, or suffering from anemia. **2.** Lacking vitality; listless: *an anemic effort.*

an·e·mom·e·ter (ăn′ə-mŏm′ĭ-tər) *n.* An instrument for measuring the speed of wind. [Greek *anemos,* wind + -METER.] —**an′e·mo·met′ric** (-mō-mĕt′rĭk), *adj.*

a·nem·o·ne (ə-nĕm′ə-nē) *n.* **1.** Any of various plants of the genus *Anemone,* with white, purple, or red flowers. **2.** A saltwater invertebrate, the **sea anemone.** [Latin *anemōnē,* from Greek *anemos,* wind.]

a·nent (ə-nĕnt′) *prep.* Regarding; concerning; about. [Middle English *anent, onevent,* from Old English *onemn, on efen,* alongside, together : ON + *efen,* even.]

an·er·oid barometer (ăn′ə-roid′). A barometer that measures atmospheric pressure by means of the changes in shape of an elastic disk that covers a chamber in which there is a partial vacuum. [From French *anéroïde,* from A- (not) + Greek *nēron,* water.]

an·es·the·sia (ăn′ĭs-thē′zhə) *n.* Also **an·aes·the·sia. 1.** Total or partial loss of physical sensation produced by disease or an anesthetic. **2.** A condition of unconsciousness produced by an anesthetic (**general anesthesia**) or of the loss of sensibility to pain in a specific area (**local anesthesia**). [From Greek *anaisthēsia,* lack of sensation : AN- + *aisthēsis,* feeling, from *aisthanesthai,* to feel.]

an·es·the·si·ol·o·gy (ăn′ĭs-thē′zē-ŏl′ə-jē) *n.* Also **an·aes·the·si·ol·o·gy.** The medical study of anesthetics, their effects, and their use. [ANESTHESI(A) + -LOGY.] —**an′es·the·si·ol′o·gist** *n.*

an·es·thet·ic (ăn′ĭs-thĕt′ĭk) *adj.* Also **an·aes·thet·ic.** Of, resembling, or causing anesthesia. —*n.* Any agent that causes unconsciousness or insensitivity to pain.

an·es·the·tist (ə-nĕs′thĭ-tĭst) *n.* Also **an·aes·the·tist.** A physician trained to administer anesthetics.

ă pat	ā pay	â care	ä father	ĕ pet	ē be	hw which	ĭ pit	ī tie	î pier	ŏ pot	ō toe	ô paw, for	oi noise
ŏŏ took	ōō boot	ou out	th thin	*th* this	ŭ cut		û urge	zh vision	ə about, item, edible, gallop, circus				

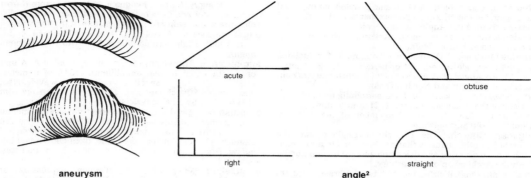

acute

obtuse

right

straight

aneurysm   angle²

an·es·the·tize (ə-nĕs′thĭ-tīz′) *tr.v.* **-tized, -tiz·ing.** Also **an·aes·the·tize.** To induce anesthesia in, esp. by means of a drug. **—an·es′the·ti·za′tion** *n.*

an·eu·rysm (ăn′yə-rĭz′əm) *n.* Also **an·eu·rism.** A blood-filled sac formed by the dilation of the wall of a blood vessel, due to injury or disease. [Greek *aneurusma,* from *aneurunein,* to dilate : *ana-,* "throughout" + *eurunein,* to dilate, widen, from *eurus,* wide.]

a·new (ə-nōō′, ə-nyōō′) *adv.* **1.** Once more; again. **2.** In a new and different way, form, or manner. [Middle English *anewe, of newe,* from Old English *of nīwe:* OF + *nīwe,* new.]

an·gel (ān′jəl) *n.* **1.** *Theol.* An immortal, spiritual being attendant upon God. In medieval angelology, there are nine orders of angels: seraphim, cherubim, thrones, dominations or dominions, virtues, powers, principalities, archangels, and angels. **2.** The conventional representation of such a being in the image of a human figure with a halo and wings. **3.** A familiar spirit: *the bright angel of his genius; the dark angel of his disease.* **4. a.** A kind and lovable person. **b.** A person manifesting goodness, purity, and selflessness. **5.** *Informal.* A financial backer of an enterprise, esp. a dramatic production. [Middle English, from Old French *angele,* from Late Latin *angelus,* from Greek *angelos,* messenger.]

an·gel·fish (ān′jəl-fĭsh′) *n., pl.* **angelfish** or **-fish·es. 1.** Any of several brightly colored fishes of the family Chaetodontidae, of warm seas, with a flattened body. **2.** A tropical, freshwater fish, *Pterophyllum scalare,* with a flattened, usu. striped body.

angelfish

an·gel·ic (ăn-jĕl′ĭk) or **an·gel·i·cal** (-ĭ-kəl). *adj.* **1.** Of or like angels: *angelic hosts.* **2.** *Informal.* **a.** Pure and lovely. **b.** Kind and lovable. **—an·gel′i·cal·ly** *adv.*

an·gel·i·ca (ăn-jĕl′ĭ-kə) *n.* **1.** Any of various plants of the genus *Angelica,* of the parsley family, esp. *A. archangelica,* that is used in medicine and as a flavoring. **2.** The candied stem of this plant, used in baking. [From Medieval Latin *(herba) angelica,* "angelic (herb)."]

An·ge·lus (ăn′jə-ləs) *n.* Also **an·ge·lus.** *Rom. Cath. Ch.* **1.** A devotional prayer at morning, noon, and night to commemorate the Annunciation. **2.** A bell rung as a call to recite this prayer. [Medieval Latin, *"Angelus (Domini),"* "The Angel (of the Lord)" (the beginning of the liturgy commemorating the Incarnation).]

an·ger (ăng′gər) *n.* A feeling of great displeasure or hostility toward someone or something caused by a sense of injury or wrong; rage; wrath. *—tr.v.* To make angry; enrage or provoke. *—intr.v.* To become angry: *She angers too quickly.* [Middle English, from Old Norse *angr,* grief.]

An·ge·vin (ăn′jə-vĭn) *adj.* **1.** Of or pertaining to the province of Anjou, France. **2.** Of or pertaining to the Plantagenet kings of England. *—n.* **1.** A native or inhabitant of Anjou. **2.** A member of the Plantagenet family or line.

an·gi·na (ăn-jī′nə) *n.* **1.** Any disease of the throat or chest, such as croup or diphtheria, in which painful, choking spasms occur. **2. Angina pectoris.** [Latin, quinsy, from Greek *ankhonē,* a strangling.]

angina pec·to·ris (pĕk′tə-rĭs). A condition marked by severe spasmodic pain in the chest, caused by an insufficient supply of blood to the heart muscle, usu. due to coronary disease. Also called **angina.** [New Latin, "angina of the chest."]

an·gi·o·sperm (ăn′jē-ə-spûrm′) *n.* Any plant of the class Angiospermae, characterized by having seeds enclosed in an ovary; a flowering plant. [Greek *angeion,* vessel + SPERM.]

an·gle¹ (ăng′gəl) *intr.v.* **-gled, -gling. 1.** To fish with a hook and line. **2.** To try to get something by using schemes or tricks: *She angled for the promotion at work.* *—n.* A devious method; scheme. [Middle English *anglen,* from *angel,* a fishhook, from Old English *angul, ongul.*]

an·gle² (ăng′gəl) *n.* **1.** *Geom.* **a.** The figure formed by two lines diverging from a common point. **b.** The figure formed by two planes diverging from a common line. **c.** The space between such lines or surfaces. **d.** The distance of difference between these lines or planes, measured in degrees. **2.** A sharp or projecting corner, as of a building. **3.** The place, position, or direction from which an object is presented to view; point of view: *It's a handsome building from any angle.* **4.** A particular part or phase, as of a problem; aspect: *Examine the situation from another angle.* **—modifier:** *an angle bracket.* *—v.* **-gled, -gling.** *—tr.v.* **1.** To move or turn at an angle: *angling the camera for a closer view.* **2.** To hit (a ball, puck, etc.) at an angle: *angle a golf shot.* **3.** *Informal.* To impart a biased aspect or point of view to (a story or anecdote). *—intr.v.* To continue along or turn at angles or by angles: *The path angled through the woods.* [Middle English, from Old French, from Latin *angulus,* angle, corner.]

angle iron. A length of steel or iron bent at a right angle along its long dimension, used as a structural support.

angle of incidence. The angle formed by the path of a body or of radiation striking a surface and a line drawn perpendicular to the surface at the point of impact.

angle of reflection. The acute angle formed by the path of a reflected body or reflected radiation with a perpendicular to the surface at the point of reflection.

an·gler (ăng′glər) *n.* **1.** A person who fishes with a hook and lines. **2.** A scheming person. **3.** An **anglerfish.**

an·gler·fish (ăng′glər-fĭsh′) *n., pl.* **anglerfish** or **-fish·es.** Any of various saltwater fishes of the order Lophiiformes (or Pediculati), with a long dorsal fin ray that is suspended over the mouth and that serves as a lure to attract prey. Also called **angler.**

å pat	ā pay	â care	ä father	ĕ pet	ē be	hw which	ĭ pit	ī tie	î pier	ŏ pot	ō toe	ô paw, for	oi noise
ōō took	ōō boot	ou out	th thin	*th* this	ŭ cut		û urge	zh vision	ə about, item, edible, gallop, circus				

An·gles (ăng′gəlz) *pl. n.* A Germanic people who migrated to England in the 5th cent. and together with the Jutes and Saxons formed the Anglo-Saxon peoples.

an·gle·worm (ăng′gəl-wûrm′) *n.* A worm, such as an earthworm, used as bait in fishing.

An·gli·a (ăng′glē-ə). The medieval Latin name for England.

An·gli·an (ăng′glē-ən) *adj.* Of or pertaining to the Angles. —*n.* 1. An Angle. 2. A group of Old English dialects consisting of Mercian and Northumbrian.

An·gli·can (ăng′glĭ-kən) *adj.* 1. Of, pertaining to, or characteristic of the Anglican Church. 2. Of or pertaining to England or the English. —*n.* A member of the Anglican Church. —**An′gli·can·ism** *n.*

Anglican Church. The Church of England and the churches in other nations that are in complete agreement with it as to doctrine and discipline and are in communion with the Archbishop of Canterbury.

An·gli·cism (ăng′glĭ-sĭz′əm) *n.* 1. A word, phrase, or idiom peculiar to the English language, esp. as spoken in England; Briticism. 2. A typically English quality, custom, etc.

An·gli·cize (ăng′glĭ-sīz′) *v.* **-cized, -ciz·ing.** —*tr.v.* To make or adapt to English in form, pronunciation, idiom, style, or character. For example, *chaps* has been Anglicized from the Spanish *chaparejos.* —*intr.v.* To become English in form or character. —**An′gli·ci·za′tion** *n.*

an·gling (ăng′glĭng) *n.* The act or sport of fishing with a hook and line.

Anglo-. A prefix meaning English or England: **Anglophile.**

An·glo-A·mer·i·can (ăng′glō-ə-mĕr′ĭ-kən) *adj.* 1. Of, relating to, or between England and America, esp. the United States. 2. Of or relating to Anglo-Americans. —*n.* An American, esp. a U.S. resident, whose ancestry and culture are English.

An·glo-French (ăng′glō-frĕnch′) *adj.* English and French. —*n.* French as used in England.

An·glo-In·di·an (ăng′glō-ĭn′dē-ən) *n.* A person of English and Indian descent. —**An′glo-In′di·an** *adj.*

An·glo-Nor·man (ăng′glō-nôr′mən) *adj.* Of or pertaining to the Normans who settled in England after 1066, their descendants, or their language. —*n.* 1. A Norman settler in England after 1066. 2. Norman French as used in England.

An·glo·phile (ăng′glə-fīl′) *n.* An admirer of England and English things. [ANGLO- + -PHILE.] —**An′glo·phil′i·a** (-fĭl′ē-ə) *n.*

An·glo·phobe (ăng′glə-fōb′) *n.* A person who has an aversion to or fear of England or English things. [ANGLO- + -PHOBE.] —**An′glo·pho′bi·a** (-fō′bē-ə) *n.*

An·glo·phone (ăng′glə-fōn′) *adj.* English-speaking. —*n.* An English-speaking person, esp. in Canada.

An·glo-Sax·on (ăng′glō-săk′sən) *n.* 1. A member of one of the Germanic peoples who settled in Britain in the 5th and 6th cent. 2. Any of the descendants of these peoples who were dominant until the Norman Conquest of 1066. 3. Old English. 4. Any person of English ancestry. —*adj.* Of or characteristic of Anglo-Saxons, their descendants, their language, or culture; English.

An·go·ra (ăng-gôr′ə, -gōr′ə) *n.* 1. Often **angora. a.** The long, silky hair of the Angora goat. **b.** The fine, light hair of the Angora rabbit. 2. Often **angora.** A yarn or fabric made from the hair of an Angora goat or rabbit. 3. An **Angora cat.** 4. An **Angora goat.** 5. An **Angora rabbit.** —*modifier:* *an angora sweater.* [From *Angora,* the former name for Ankara.]

Angora cat. A long-haired domestic cat. Also called **Angora.**

Angora goat. Any of a breed of domestic goats having long, silky hair. Also called **Angora.**

Angora rabbit. One of a breed of domestic rabbits having long, soft, usu. white hair. Also called **Angora.**

an·gos·tu·ra bark (ăng′gə-stoor′ə, -styoor′ə). The bitter, aromatic bark of either of two Brazilian trees, used as a tonic. Also called **angostura.** [From *Angostura,* former name of Ciudad Bolívar.]

an·gry (ăng′grē) *adj.* **-gri·er, -gri·est.** 1. Feeling or showing anger: *an angry customer.* 2. Resulting from anger: *an angry silence.* 3. Having a menacing aspect; seeming to threaten: *angry clouds.* 4. Inflamed: *an angry cut.* —**an′gri·ly** (-grə-lē) *adv.* —**an′gri·ness** *n.*

Syns: *angry, furious, indignant, irate, mad, sore (Informal), wrathful adj. Core meaning:* Feeling or showing displeasure and hostility (*an angry customer; an angry look*).

angst (ängkst) *n.* A feeling of anxiety. [German *Angst,* from Middle High German *angest,* from Old High German *angust.*]

ang·strom or **Ång·ström** (ăng′strəm) *n. Symbol* **A** A unit of length equal to one ten-billionth (10⁻¹⁰) of a meter, used esp. to specify radiation wavelengths. Also called **angstrom unit.** [After A. J. *Ångström* (1814–1874), Swedish physicist.]

an·guish (ăng′gwĭsh) *n.* An agonizing physical or mental pain; torment; torture. —See Syns at **distress.** —*tr.v.* To cause to suffer or feel anguish. —*intr.v.* To suffer or feel anguish. [Middle English *anguisshe,* from Old French *anguisse,* from Latin *angustia,* narrowness, from *angustus,* narrow.]

an·guished (ăng′gwĭsht) *adj.* Feeling, expressing, or caused by anguish: "*On thy cold forehead starts the anguished dew*" (Samuel Taylor Coleridge).

an·gu·lar (ăng′gyə-lər) *adj.* 1. Of, having, forming, or consisting of an angle or angles. 2. Measured in terms of an angle. 3. Bony and lean; gaunt: *a nervous, angular lady.* 4. Sharp-cornered: *bulky or angular packages.* 5. Lacking grace or smoothness; awkward: *an angular gait; angular melodies.* —**an·gu·lar′i·ty** (-lăr′ĭ-tē) or **an′gu·lar·ness** *n.* —**an′gu·lar·ly** *adv.*

an·hy·dride (ăn-hī′drīd) *n.* A chemical compound formed from another, such as an acid, by the removal of water. [ANHYDR(OUS) + -IDE.]

an·hy·drite (ăn-hī′drīt) *n.* A white to grayish granular mineral of anhydrous calcium sulfate, $CaSO_4$, that occurs in gypsum deposits. [ANHYDR(OUS) + -ITE.]

an·hy·drous (ăn-hī′drəs) *adj.* Without water, esp. of crystallization. [Greek *anudros,* waterless : AN- + *hudōr,* water.]

an·i·line (ăn′ə-lĭn) *n.* Also **an·i·lin.** A colorless, oily, poisonous benzene derivative, $C_6H_5NH_2$, used in rubber, dyes, resins, pharmaceuticals, varnishes, and rocket fuels. [German *Anilin,* from *anil,* indigo.]

an·i·ma (ăn′ə-mə) *n.* The soul. [Latin, fem. of *animus.*]

an·i·mad·ver·sion (ăn′ə-măd-vûr′zhən, -shən) *n.* 1. Hostile criticism. 2. A hostile or critical remark.

an·i·mad·vert (ăn′ə-măd-vûrt′) *intr.v.* To remark or comment critically, usu. with strong disapproval or censure: *He felt impelled to animadvert on the wickedness of governments.* [Latin *animadvertere,* to direct the mind to : *animus,* mind + *advertere,* to turn to : *ad-,* to + *vertere,* to turn.]

an·i·mal (ăn′ə-məl) *n.* 1. Any organism of the kingdom Animalia, distinguished from plants by certain typical characteristics, such as being able to move from place to place, by growing to a definite, limited size and shape, and by eating food rather than manufacturing it by photosynthesis. 2. a. Any such living being other than a human being. b. A mammal as distinguished from a bird, reptile, fish, insect, etc. 3. A person whose behavior suggests an animal; a brutish person. —*adj.* 1. Of, relating to, or characteristic of animals. 2. Relating to the sensual or physical nature of man rather than to the mind or soul: *animal vitality; a person's crude animal tastes.* [Latin, from *animalis,* living, from *animus,* breath, soul.]

an·i·mal·cule (ăn′ə-măl′kyool) *n.* Also **an·i·mal·cu·lum** (-kyə-ləm) *pl.* **-la** (-lə). A microscopic or minute organism usu. thought of as an animal, as an amoeba or paramecium. [New Latin *animalculum,* dim. of ANIMAL.] —**an′i·mal′cu·lar** (-kyə-lər) *adj.*

animal husbandry. The care and breeding of domestic animals such as cattle, hogs, sheep, and horses.

an·i·mal·ism (ăn′ə-mə-lĭz′əm) *n.* 1. A condition of enjoying sound health and the wholesome satisfaction of physical drives. 2. The doctrine that man is purely animal with no spiritual nature. —**an′i·mal·ist** *n.* —**an′i·mal·is′tic** *adj.*

an·i·mal·i·ty (ăn′ə-măl′ĭ-tē) *n.* 1. The characteristics or nature of an animal. 2. The animal as distinct from the spiritual nature of man.

animal spirits. Vigorous buoyancy of good health.

an·i·mate (ăn′ə-māt′) *tr.v.* **-mat·ed, -mat·ing.** 1. To give life to; fill with life. 2. To impart zest or zest to; enliven:

"The party was animated by all kinds of men and women" (René Dubos). **3.** To fill with spirit, courage, or resolution; inspire; encourage: *The noblest patriotism animated her.* **4.** To make, design, or produce (a cartoon) so as to create the illusion of motion. —*adj.* (ăn′ə-mĭt). **1.** Possessing life; living. **2.** Of or relating to animal life as distinct from plant life. **3.** Belonging to the class of nouns that stand for living things: *The word "dog" is animate, the word "car" inanimate.* [Latin *animāre,* to fill with breath, from *anima,* breath, soul.]

an·i·mat·ed (ăn′ə-mā′tĭd) *adj.* **1.** Filled with life, activity, vigor, or spirit; lively; spirited; vivacious: *an animated discussion.* **2.** Made or designed so as to seem alive and moving: *an animated doll; animated puppets.* —**an′i·mat′ed·ly** *adv.*

animated cartoon. A motion picture consisting of a photographed series of drawings.

an·i·mat·er (ăn′ə-mā′tər) *n.* Var. of **animator.**

an·i·ma·tion (ăn′ə-mā′shən) *n.* **1.** The act, process, or result of animating. **2.** The condition or quality of being alive; liveliness; spirit; vitality. **3. a.** The art and process of preparing animated cartoons. **b.** An animated cartoon.

a·ni·ma·to (ä′nə-mä′tō, än′ə-). *Mus.* —*adj.* Animated; lively. —*adv.* In an animated or lively manner. [Italian.]

an·i·ma·tor (ăn′ə-mā′tər) *n.* Also **an·i·mat·er.** **1.** Someone or something that animates. **2.** An artist or technician who prepares or produces animated cartoons.

an·i·mism (ăn′ə-mĭz′əm) *n.* Any of various beliefs among primitive tribes whereby natural phenomena and animate and inanimate things have souls. [German *Animismus,* from Latin *anima,* breath, soul. See **animal.**] —**an′i·mist** *n.* —**an′i·mis′tic** *adj.*

an·i·mos·i·ty (ăn′ə-mŏs′ĭ-tē) *n., pl.* **-ties.** Bitter hostility or open enmity; active hatred. [Middle English *animosite,* from Old French, from Late Latin *animōsitās,* vehemence, spirit, from Latin *animōsus,* bold, spirited, from *animus,* soul, mind.]

an·i·mus (ăn′ə-məs) *n.* **1.** An intention or purpose; a motive behind an action. **2.** A feeling of animosity; bitter hostility or hatred. [Latin, mind, soul.]

an·i·on (ăn′ī′ən) *n.* A negatively charged ion that migrates to an anode, as in electrolysis. [Greek, "that which goes up" (i.e., toward the anode), neut. pres. part. of *anienai,* to go up : *an(a)-,* up + *ienai,* to go.] —**an′i·on′ic** (-ŏn′ĭk) *adj.*

an·ise (ăn′ĭs) *n.* **1.** A plant, *Pimpinella anisum,* of the Mediterranean region, with clusters of yellowish-white flowers and licorice-flavored seeds. **2. Aniseed.** [Middle English *anis,* from Old French, from Latin *anīsum,* from Greek *anison.*]

an·i·seed (ăn′ī-sēd′) *n.* The licorice-flavored seed of the anise plant, used for flavoring. Also called **anise.** [Middle English *anis seed,* from ANISE + SEED.]

ankh (ăngk) *n.* A cross shaped like a T with a loop at the top. [Egyptian.]

an·kle (ăng′kəl) *n.* **1.** The joint between the foot and the leg. **2.** The slender section of the leg above this joint. [Middle English *ankel,* of Old Norse orig.]

an·kle·bone (ăng′kəl-bōn′) *n. Anat.* Another name for the **talus.**

an·klet (ăng′klĭt) *n.* **1.** A bracelet or chain worn around the ankle. **2.** A short sock that reaches just above the ankle.

an·ky·lo·sis (ăng′kə-lō′sĭs) *n.* **1.** *Anat.* The consolidation of bones or their parts forming a single unit. **2.** *Pathol.* The stiffening of a joint as the result of abnormal bone fusion. [New Latin, from Greek *ankulōsis,* stiffening of the joints, from *ankuloun,* to bend, from *ankulos,* bent, curved, crooked.] —**an′ky·lot′ic** (-lŏt′ĭk) *adj.*

an·nal·ist (ăn′ə-lĭst) *n.* A person who writes annals; a chronicler. —**an′nal·is′tic** *adj.*

an·nals (ăn′əlz) *pl.n.* **1.** A record of events written in the order of their occurrence, year by year. **2.** Any descriptive account or record; a history. **3.** A periodical journal compiling the records and reports of a particular learned field. [Latin *librī annālēs,* "yearly (books)," from *annālis,* yearly, from *annus,* year.]

an·neal (ə-nēl′) *tr.v.* **1.** To subject (glass or metal) to a process of heating and slow cooling in order to toughen and reduce brittleness. **2.** To temper. [Middle English *anelen,*

from Old English *onǣlan* : ON + *ǣlan,* to set fire to, from *āl,* fire.]

an·ne·lid (ăn′ə-lĭd) *adj.* Of or belonging to the phylum Annelida, which includes the earthworms, leeches, and other worms having cylindrical segmented bodies. —*n.* An annelid worm. [New Latin *Annelida,* from French *annélide* : *annelés,* ringed, from Old French *annel,* ring, from Latin *annellus,* dim. of *ānulus,* small ring + -IDE.]

an·nex (ə-nĕks′) *tr.v.* **1.** To add or join to, esp. to a larger or more significant thing. **2.** To incorporate (territory) into an existing country or state. —*n.* (ăn′ĕks). **1.** A building added on to a larger one or an auxiliary building situated near a main one: *the library annex.* **2.** An addition to a record or document; an appendix or addendum. [Middle English *annexen,* from Old French *annexer,* from Latin *annectere* : *ad-,* to + *nectere,* to tie.]

an·nex·a·tion (ăn′ĭk-sā′shən) *n.* **1.** The act or process of annexing. **2.** Something that has been annexed.

an·ni·hi·late (ə-nī′ə-lāt′) *tr.v.* **-lat·ed, -lat·ing.** **1.** To destroy completely; wipe out. **2.** *Informal.* To overwhelm completely. [Late Latin *annihilāre* : Latin *ad-,* to + *nihil,* nothing.] —**an·ni′hi·la·ble** (-lə-bəl) *adj.* —**an·ni′hi·la′tion** *n.* —**an·ni′hi·la′tor** *n.*

an·ni·ver·sa·ry (ăn′ə-vûr′sə-rē) *n., pl.* **-ries.** **1.** The annual recurrence of the date of an event that took place in some preceding year: *a wedding anniversary.* **2.** A commemorative celebration on this date. —*modifier: an anniversary party.* [Middle English *anniversarie,* from Medieval Latin *anniversāria,* from Latin *anniversārius,* "returning yearly" : *annus,* year + *versus,* past part. of *vertere,* to turn.]

an·no Dom·i·ni (ăn′ō dŏm′ə-nī′, dŏm′ə-nē). *Abbr.* **A.D.** *Latin.* In the year of the Lord. A phrase, almost always abbreviated to A.D., used to indicate dates since the birth of Christ.

an·no·tate (ăn′ō-tāt′) *tr.v.* **-tat·ed, -tat·ing.** To furnish (a literary work) with critical commentary or explanatory notes; to gloss. [Latin *annotāre,* to note down : *ad-,* to + *notāre,* to mark, from *nota,* a mark, note.] —**an′no·ta′tive** *adj.* —**an′no·ta′tor** *n.*

an·no·ta·tion (ăn′ō-tā′shən) *n.* **1.** The act or process of annotating. **2.** An explanatory note; commentary.

an·nounce (ə-nouns′) *tr.v.* **-nounced, -nounc·ing.** **1.** To declare or proclaim officially or formally. **2.** To proclaim the presence or arrival of: *announce a caller.* **3.** To serve as an announcer of: *announced hockey games on television.* [Middle English *announcen,* from Old French *annoncer,* from Latin *annuntiāre* : *ad-,* to + *nuntiāre,* to announce, from *nuntius,* messenger.]

an·nounce·ment (ə-nouns′mənt) *n.* **1.** The act of announcing. **2.** An official statement. **3.** A printed or published statement or notice.

an·nounc·er (ə-noun′sər) *n.* **1.** Someone who announces. **2.** A radio or television performer who provides program continuity and delivers commercial and other announcements.

an·noy (ə-noi′) *tr.v.* To bother or irritate. —*intr.v.* To behave in an annoying manner. [Middle English *anoien,* from Old French *anoier, enuier,* from Late Latin *inodiāre,* to make odious : Latin *in,* in + *odium,* hatred.] —**an·noy′er** *n.* —**an·noy′ing·ly** *adv.*

Syns: annoy, aggravate, *(Informal),* **bother, bug** *(Slang),* disturb, chafe, exasperate, fret, gall, get, irk, irritate, nettle, peeve, provoke, ruffle, vex *v. Core meaning:* To trouble (another) by causing mental discomfort (*Their constant bickering annoys me.*).

an·noy·ance (ə-noi′əns) *n.* **1.** Something that annoys; a nuisance. **2.** The act of annoying. **3.** Vexation; irritation.

an·nu·al (ăn′yōō-əl) *adj.* **1.** Occurring or done every year; yearly: *an annual examination.* **2.** Of or pertaining to a year; determined by a year's time: *an annual income; the annual turnover of merchandise.* **3.** *Bot.* Living and growing for only one year or season. —*n.* **1.** A periodical published yearly; yearbook. **2.** *Bot.* A plant that lives and grows for only one year or season, during which the life cycle is completed. [Middle English *annuel,* from Old French, from Late Latin *annuālis,* from Latin *annus,* year.] —**an′nu·al·ly** *adv.*

annual ring. One of the layers of wood, esp. in a tree trunk, that indicates a year's growth.

an·nu·i·tant (ə-nōō′ĭ-tənt, ə-nyōō′-) *n.* A person who re-

ă pat	ā pay	â care	ä father	ĕ pet	ē be	hw which
I pit	ī tie	î pier	ŏ pot	ō toe	ô paw, for	oi noise
ōō took	ōō boot	ou out	th thin	th this	ŭ cut	
û urge	zh vision	ə about, item, edible, gallop, circus				

ceives or is qualified to receive an annuity.

an·nu·i·ty (ə-nōō'ĭ-tē, ə-nyōō'-) *n., pl.* **-ties. 1.** An amount of money paid at regular intervals. **2.** An investment on which a person receives fixed payments for a lifetime or a certain number of years. [Middle English *annuite*, from Old French, from Medieval Latin *annuitās*, yearly payment, from Latin *annuus*, yearly, from *annus*, year.]

an·nul (ə-nŭl') *tr.v.* **-nulled, -nul·ling.** To make or declare void or invalid, as a marriage or a law; nullify; cancel. [Middle English *annullen*, from Old French *annuller*, from Late Latin *annullāre* : Latin *ad-*, to + *nullus*, none, null.]

an·nu·lar (ăn'yə-lər) *adj.* Shaped or formed like a ring. [Old French *annulaire*, from Latin *annulāris*, from *annulus*, ring.]

annular eclipse. A solar eclipse in which the moon blocks all but a bright ring around the edge of the sun.

an·nu·li (ăn'yə-lī') *n.* A plural of **annulus.**

an·nul·ment (ə-nŭl'mənt) *n.* **1.** The act of annulling. **2.** A legal declaration that a marriage was never valid.

an·nu·lus (ăn'yə-ləs) *n., pl.* **-lus·es** or **-li** (-lī'). A ringlike part, structure, or marking. [Latin *annulus*, ring.]

an·nun·ci·ate (ə-nŭn'sē-āt') *tr.v.* **-at·ed, -at·ing.** To announce; proclaim. [Latin *annuntiāre*, to ANNOUNCE.]

an·nun·ci·a·tion (ə-nŭn'sē-ā'shən) *n.* **1.** The act of announcing. **2.** An announcement; proclamation. **3. Annunciation. a.** The angel Gabriel's announcement to Mary that she was to become the mother of Jesus. **b.** The festival, on Mar. 25, in celebration of this event.

an·ode (ăn'ōd') *n.* **1.** Any positively charged electrode, as of an electrolytic cell, storage battery, or electron tube, toward which current flows. **2.** The negatively charged terminal of a primary cell or of a storage battery that is supplying current. [Greek *anodos*, a way up : *ana-*, up + *hodos*, road, way.]

an·o·dyne (ăn'ə-dīn') *n.* **1.** A medicine that relieves pain. **2.** Anything that soothes or comforts. [Latin *anōdynus*, from Greek *anōdunos*, free from pain, from AN- + *odunē*, pain.]

a·noint (ə-noint') *tr.v.* **1.** To apply oil, ointment, or a similar substance to. **2.** To put oil on as a sign of sanctification or consecration in a religious ceremony: *"My head with oil thou dost anoint"* (Psalms 23:5). [Middle English *anointen*, from Old French *enoindre*, from Latin *inunguere* : *in-*, upon + *unguere*, to smear, anoint.] **—a·noint'er** *n.* **—a·noint'ment** *n.*

anointing of the sick. *Rom. Cath. Ch.* The sacrament of anointing a critically ill person, praying for recovery, and asking for the absolution of sins.

a·nom·a·lous (ə-nŏm'ə-ləs) *adj.* Differing from what is normal; abnormal. [Late Latin *anōmalos*, from Greek, uneven : AN- + *homalos*, even, from *homos*, same.] **—a·nom'a·lous·ly** *adv.* **—a·nom'a·lous·ness** *n.*

a·nom·a·ly (ə-nŏm'ə-lē) *n., pl.* **-lies. 1.** Deviation or departure from what is normal or common; abnormality. **2.** Something that is unusual, irregular, or abnormal.

a·non (ə-nŏn') *adv.* **1.** At another time; again. **2.** *Archaic.* In a short time; soon: *"Of this discourse we more will hear anon"* (Shakespeare). **—idiom. ever (or now) and anon.** Time after time; now and then. [Middle English *anon, onon*, from Old English *on ān*, "into one," at once : *on*, in, ON + *ān*, one.]

a·non·y·mous (ə-nŏn'ə-məs) *adj.* **1.** Nameless or unnamed: *a panel of medical experts and anonymous young addicts.* **2.** Having an unknown or withheld authorship or agency: *an anonymous letter; an anonymous poem.* [Late Latin *anōnymus*, from Greek *anōnumos*, nameless, from AN- + *onoma*, name.] **—an'o·nym'i·ty** (ăn'ə-nĭm'ĭ-tē) *n.* **—a·non'y·mous·ly** *adv.*

a·noph·e·les (ə-nŏf'ə-lēz') *n.* Any of various mosquitoes of the genus *Anopheles*, many of which transmit malaria to man. [From Greek *anōphelēs*, useless, hurtful, from AN- + *ophelos*, advantage.]

an·o·rex·i·a (ăn'ə-rĕk'sē-ə) *n.* Loss of appetite, esp. as a result of disease. [Greek : *an-* (not) + *oregein*, to desire.]

an·oth·er (ə-nŭth'ər) *adj.* **1.** Different: *another way of doing things.* **2.** Changed: *He's been another person since he got that job.* **3. a.** Some other and later: *We'll discuss this at another time.* **b.** Some other and former: *She belongs to another era.* **4.** Additional; one more: *having another cup*

of coffee. **5.** New: *He thinks he's another Babe Ruth.* **—pron. 1.** An additional or different one. **2.** Something or someone different from or in contrast to the first one named: *A baby is one thing to baby-sit, a six-year-old another.* **3.** One of a group of things: *one thing and another.* [Middle English *an other.*]

an·ox·i·a (ăn-ŏk'sē-ə, ə-nŏk'-) *n.* **1.** Absence of oxygen. **2.** *Pathol.* A deficiency of oxygen. [AN- + OX(Y)- + -IA.]

an·swer (ăn'sər) *n.* **1.** A spoken or written reply, as to a question, statement, request, or letter. **2. a.** A solution or result, as to a problem. **b.** The correct response or solution. **3.** An act in response or retaliation. **4.** *Law.* The defense or answer to charges filed against a defendant. **—intr.v. 1.** To respond in words or action. **2.** To be liable or accountable: *You will have to answer for this waste.* **3.** To serve the purpose; suffice; do: *"Often I do use three words where one would answer"* (Mark Twain). **4.** To correspond; match: *a car answering to the description.* **—tr.v. 1.** To reply to: *She answered him curtly.* **2.** To respond correctly to. **3.** To correspond to: *a person answering this description.* **4.** To be responsible for; meet; discharge (a claim, debt, etc.). **—phrasal verb. answer back.** To reply defiantly; talk back. [Middle English *answer(e)*, from Old English *andswaru.*]

Syns: answer, rejoin, reply, respond, retort, return *v.* **Core meaning:** To speak or act in response to (*answering a question; answering a letter*).

an·swer·a·ble (ăn'sər-ə-bəl) *adj.* **1.** Responsible; accountable; liable: *You are answerable for him.* **2.** Able to be answered: *questions not wholly answerable.*

ant (ănt) *n.* Any of various insects of the family Formicidae, characteristically having wings only in the males and fertile females, and living in colonies that have a complex social organization. [Middle English *ante, amete*, from Old English *æmette.*]

ant-. Var. of the prefix **anti-.**

-ant. A suffix meaning performing, promoting, or causing an action: **deodorant.** [Middle English, from Old French, from Latin *-ans*, pres. part. ending of first conjugation verbs.]

ant·ac·id (ănt-ăs'ĭd) *adj.* Capable of neutralizing an acid; basic. **—n.** An antacid substance, esp. a medicinal remedy to neutralize excess stomach acid. [ANT(I)- + ACID.]

an·tag·o·nism (ăn-tăg'ə-nĭz'əm) *n.* **1.** Unfriendly feeling; hostility. **2.** Mutual resistance; opposition. **3.** The condition of being an opposing principle or force.

an·tag·o·nist (ăn-tăg'ə-nĭst) *n.* **1.** One who opposes and actively competes with another; an adversary. **2.** *Anat.* A muscle that opposes another muscle. **3.** *Pharm.* A drug that counteracts another drug. **—See Syns at opponent.**

an·tag·o·nis·tic (ăn-tăg'ə-nĭs'tĭk) *adj.* Having a feeling of antagonism. **—an·tag'o·nis'ti·cal·ly** *adv.*

an·tag·o·nize (ăn-tăg'ə-nīz') *tr.v.* **-nized, -niz·ing. 1.** To incur the dislike of. **2.** To counteract. [Greek *antagōnizesthai*, to struggle against : *anti-*, against + *agōnizesthai*, to struggle, from *agōn*, contest.]

Ant·arc·tic (ănt-ärk'tĭk, -är'tĭk) *adj.* Of or pertaining to the regions surrounding the South Pole.

Antarctic Circle. The parallel of latitude 66 degrees 33 minutes south, forming the boundary between the South Temperate Zone and the South Frigid Zone.

An·tar·es (ăn-târ'ēz') *n.* The brightest star in the southern sky, about 424 light-years from Earth in the constellation Scorpius.

an·te (ăn'tē) *n.* **1.** *Poker.* The stake that each player must put into the pool before receiving a hand or before receiv-

anopheles

anteater   antelope   anther

ing new cards. **2.** *Slang.* The amount to be paid as one's share. *—v.* **-ted** or **-teed, -te·ing.** *—tr.v.* **1.** *Poker.* To put (one's stake) into the pool. **2.** *Slang.* To pay (one's share). *—intr.v.* To put in one's stake: *Who didn't ante?* [From Latin *ante,* before.]

ante-. A prefix meaning: **1.** In front of: *anteroom.* **2.** Earlier than or before: *antenatal.* [Latin, from *ante,* before.]

ant·eat·er (ănt'ē'tər) *n.* **1.** Any of several tropical American mammals of the family Myrmecophagidae that lack teeth and feed on ants and termites; esp., *Myrmecophaga tridactyla,* which has a long, narrow snout, a long, sticky tongue, and a long, shaggy-haired tail. **2.** Any of several other animals that feed on ants, such as the echidna and the pangolin.

an·te·bel·lum (ăn'tē-bĕl'əm) *adj.* Belonging to the period prior to the U.S. Civil War: *an ante-bellum mansion.* [Latin *ante bellum,* "before the war."]

an·te·ce·dent (ăn'tĭ-sēd'nt) *adj.* Going before; preceding; prior. *—n.* **1.** Something or someone that precedes. **2.** Any event prior to another. **3. antecedents.** A person's ancestors, ancestry, or past life. **4.** The word, phrase, or clause that a relative pronoun refers to. **5.** *Math.* The first term of a ratio. —See Syns at **ancestor.** **—an'te·ce'dence** *n.* **—an'te·ce'dent·ly** *adv.*

an·te·cham·ber (ăn'tē-chām'bər) *n.* An anteroom.

an·te·date (ăn'tĭ-dāt') *tr.v.* **-dat·ed, -dat·ing.** **1.** To be of an earlier date than; precede in time. **2.** To give a date earlier than the actual date; date back.

an·te·di·lu·vi·an (ăn'tĭ-də-lōō'vē-ən) *adj.* **1.** Occurring or belonging to the era before the Biblical Flood. **2.** Antiquated; primitive. *—n.* **1.** Something or someone that lived or existed before the Flood. **2.** A very old person. [From ANTE- + Latin *dīluvium,* flood.]

an·te·lope (ăn'tə-lōp') *n., pl.* **antelope** or **-lopes.** **1.** Any of various long-horned, cud-chewing animals of the family Bovidae of Africa and Asia. **2.** An animal that resembles a true antelope, esp. the pronghorn of western North America. **3.** Leather made from the hide of an antelope. [Middle English, from Old French *antelop,* a fabulous Oriental beast, from Medieval Latin *anthalopus,* from Late Greek *antholops.*]

an·te me·rid·i·em (ăn'tē mə-rĭd'ē-əm). *Abbr.* **A.M., a.m., A.M.** Before noon. Used chiefly in the abbreviated form to specify the hour; for example, 10:30 A.M. [Latin, from ANTE- + *merīdiēs,* midday, noon (see **meridian**).]

an·ten·na (ăn-tĕn'ə) *n.* **1.** *pl.* **-ten·nae** (-tĕn'ē). One of the pair of sensory organs on the head of an insect, myriapod, or crustacean. **2.** *pl.* **-nas.** A metallic apparatus for sending and receiving radio waves; an aerial. [Medieval Latin, from Latin, sail yard.]

an·te·pe·nult (ăn'tē-pē'nŭlt', -pĭ-nŭlt') *n.* The third syllable from the end in a word. For example, *te* is the antepenult of the word *antepenult.* [Late Latin *antepaenultima,* fem. of *antepaenultimus,* antepenultimate.]

an·te·pe·nul·ti·mate (ăn'tē-pə-nŭl'tə-mĭt) *adj.* Second from the last; third from the end. *—n.* An antepenult. [Late Latin *antepaenultimus* : ANTE- + *paenultimus,* next to last.]

an·te·ri·or (ăn-tîr'ē-ər) *adj.* **1.** Placed in front; located forward. **2.** Prior in time; earlier. **3. a.** Located near the head in lower animals. **b.** Located on or near the front of the body in higher animals. **c.** Located on or near the front of an organ or on the ventral surface of the body in human

beings. [Latin, comparative of *ante,* before.] **—an·te'ri·or·ly** *adv.*

an·te·room (ăn'tē-rōōm', -rōōm') *n.* A waiting room.

an·them (ăn'thəm) *n.* **1.** A song of praise or loyalty: *a national anthem.* **2.** A choral composition, usu. of moderate length, with a sacred text. [Middle English *antem, antefn,* from Old English *antefn,* from Medieval Latin *antiphōna,* from Late Greek *antiphōnos,* singing in response, from Greek *anti-,* opposite + *phōnē,* voice.]

an·ther (ăn'thər) *n.* The pollen-bearing part at the upper end of a stamen of a flower. [Ult. from Greek *anthos,* flower.]

an·ther·id·i·um (ăn'thə-rĭd'ē-əm) *n., pl.* **-i·a** (-ē-ə). An organ that produces male sex cells in the algae, fungi, mosses, and ferns. [New Latin, from *anthera,* ANTHER + -IDIUM.]

ant·hill (ănt'hĭl') *n.* A mound of earth or sand formed by ants or termites in digging or building a nest.

antho-. A prefix meaning a flower: *anthozoan.* [Greek *anthos,* blossom, flower.]

an·thol·o·gize (ăn-thŏl'ə-jīz') *tr.v.* **-gized, -giz·ing.** To compile or include in an anthology.

an·thol·o·gy (ăn-thŏl'ə-jē) *n., pl.* **-gies.** A collection of literary pieces, such as poems, stories, or plays, usu. by various authors. [New Latin *anthologia,* from Medieval Greek, from Greek, "flower gathering," a collection, from ANTHO- + -LOGY.] **—an'tho·log'i·cal** (ăn'thə-lŏj'ĭ-kəl) *adj.* **—an·thol'o·gist** *n.*

an·tho·zo·an (ăn'thə-zō'ən) *n.* Any of various saltwater organisms of the class Anthozoa that grow singly or in colonies and include the corals and sea anemones. Also called **actinozoan.** [New Latin *Anthozoa,* "flowerlike organisms," from ANTHO- + Greek *zōion,* animal.] **—an'tho·zo'an** or **an'tho·zo'ic** (-zō'ĭk) *adj.*

an·thra·cene (ăn'thrə-sēn') *n.* A crystalline hydrocarbon, $C_6H_4(CH_2)C_6H_4$, extracted from coal tar and used in the manufacture of dyes and organic chemicals. [Greek *anthrax,* charcoal, coal, anthrax + -ENE.]

an·thra·cite (ăn'thrə-sīt') *n.* A hard coal with a high carbon content and little volatile matter that burns with a clean flame. Also called **hard coal.** [Greek *anthrakitēs,* a kind of coal, from *anthrax,* coal.] **—an'thra·cit'ic** (-sĭt'ĭk) *adj.*

an·thrax (ăn'thrăks') *n.* An infectious, usu. fatal disease of warm-blooded animals, esp. of cattle and sheep, caused by *Bacillus anthracis.* It is transmissible to man, capable of affecting various organs, and characterized by malignant ulcers. [Latin, virulent ulcer, from Greek, coal, carbuncle, pustule.]

anthropo-. A prefix meaning man or human: *anthropogenesis.* [From Greek *anthrōpos,* man.]

an·thro·po·cen·tric (ăn'thrə-pō-sĕn'trĭk) *adj.* **1.** Regarding man as the central fact of the universe. **2.** Interpreting reality exclusively in terms of human values and experience.

an·thro·poid (ăn'thrə-poid') *adj.* **1.** Resembling a human being. Said of the apes of the family Pongidae, which includes gorillas, chimpanzees, orang-utans, and gibbons. **2.** Resembling or characteristic of an ape; apelike. *—n.* Any member of the family Pongidae. [ANTHROP(O)- + -OID.] **—an'thro·poi'dal** *adj.*

an·thro·pol·o·gy (ăn'thrə-pŏl'ə-jē) *n.* The science of the origins and the physical, social, and cultural development and behavior of human beings. [ANTHROPO- + -LOGY.] **—an'thro·po·log'ic** (-pə-lŏj'ĭk) or **an'thro·po·log'i·cal** *adj.* **—an'-**

ă pat   ā pay   â care   ä father   ĕ pet   ē be   hw which
ŏŏ took   ōō boot   ou out   th thin   *th* this   ŭ cut
ĭ pit   ī tie   î pier   ŏ pot   ō toe   ô paw, for   oi noise
û urge   zh vision   ə about, item, edible, gallop, circus

thro·po·log'i·cal·ly *adv.* —an'thro·pol'o·gist *n.*

an·thro·po·mor·phism (ăn'thrə-pə-môr'fĭz'əm) *n.* The attribution of human motivation, characteristics, or behavior to inanimate objects, animals, or natural phenomena. —an'thro·po·mor'phic *adj.*

an·thro·po·mor·phous (ăn'thrə-pə-môr'fəs) *adj.* Having or suggesting human form and appearance. [Greek *anthropomorphos,* from ANTHROPO- + -MORPHOUS.]

an·thro·poph·a·gi (ăn'thrə-pŏf'ə-jī) *pl.n. Sing.* **-gus** (-gəs). Eaters of human flesh; cannibals. [From Latin *anthrophophagus,* from Greek *anthrōpophagos,* man-eating, from ANTHROPO- + *phagein,* to eat.] —an'thro·po·phag'ic (-pə-făj'ĭk) or —an'thro·poph'a·gous (-pŏf'ə-gəs) *adj.* —an'thro·poph'a·gy (-jē) *n.*

an·ti (ăn'tī', -tē) *n., pl.* **-tis.** *Informal.* A person who is opposed to a group, policy, proposal, or practice.

anti- or **ant-.** A prefix meaning: **1.** Opposition to, effectiveness against, or counteraction: **antacid, antibody.** **2.** Situation opposite to: **antigravity.** **3.** Reciprocal correspondence to: **antilogarithm.** **4.** Converse operation to: **anticyclone.** *Note:* When *anti-* is followed by a capital letter or the letter *i,* it appears with a hyphen: *anti-American; anti-intellectual.* [Greek, from *anti,* opposite, against.]

an·ti·air·craft (ăn'tē-âr'krăft', -tī-) *adj.* Used against aircraft attack: *antiaircraft weapons.*

an·ti·bal·lis·tic missile (ăn'tē-bə-lĭs'tĭk, -tī-). A defensive missile designed to intercept and destroy a ballistic missile in flight.

an·ti·bi·o·sis (ăn'tē-bī-ō'sĭs, -tī-) *n.* An association between two or more organisms that is injurious to one of them. [New Latin, from ANTI- + Greek *biōsis,* way of life.]

an·ti·bi·ot·ic (ăn'tē-bī-ŏt'ĭk, -tī-) *n.* Any of various substances, such as penicillin and streptomycin, produced by certain fungi, bacteria, and other organisms, that are effective in inhibiting the growth of or destroying microorganisms and are widely used in the prevention and treatment of diseases. —*adj.* **1.** Of, using, or acting as an antibiotic or antibiotics. **2.** Of or pertaining to antibiosis. [New Latin *antibioticus,* from ANTI- + Greek *biōtikos,* of life, from *bios,* mode of life.]

an·ti·bod·y (ăn'tī-bŏd'ē) *n.* Any of various proteins in the blood that are generated in reaction to foreign proteins or carbohydrates, neutralize them, and thus produce immunity against certain microorganisms or their toxins. [ANTI- + BODY.]

an·tic (ăn'tĭk) *n.* **1.** Often **antics.** An odd or extravagant act or gesture; a caper; prank. **2.** *Archaic.* A clown. —*adj.* Odd; ludicrous; fantastic. [Italian *antico,* "ancient," "grotesque," from Latin *antīquus.*]

An·ti·christ (ăn'tī-krīst') *n.* **1.** In early Christian prophecy, a great enemy who would set himself up against Christ at the end of the world. **2. antichrist.** Any enemy of Christ.

an·tic·i·pate (ăn-tĭs'ə-pāt') *tr.v.* **-pat·ed, -pat·ing. 1.** To foresee, expect, or consider in advance: *We hadn't anticipated so many guests.* **2.** To act upon before an expected time: *anticipate a rise in prices.* **3.** To project as part of the future: *In his book he anticipates a utopia ruled by an elite.* **4.** To deal with in advance: *I try to anticipate trouble.* [Latin *anticipāre,* to take before, from ANTE- + *capere,* to take.] —an·tic'i·pa'tor *n.* —an·tic'·i·pa·to'ry (-pə-tôr'ē, -tôr'ē) *adj.*

an·tic·i·pa·tion (ăn-tĭs'ə-pā'shən) *n.* **1.** Expectation, esp. happy or eager expectation. **2.** Something anticipated. **3.** Foreknowledge or apprehension.

an·ti·cler·i·cal (ăn'tē-klĕr'ĭ-kəl, -tī-) *adj.* Opposed to the church's influence in political affairs. —an'ti·cler'i·cal·ism *n.*

an·ti·cli·mac·tic (ăn'tē-klī-măk'tĭk) *adj.* Of or accompanied by an anticlimax. —an'ti·cli·mac'ti·cal·ly *adv.*

an·ti·cli·max (ăn'tē-klī'măks') *n.* **1.** A decline viewed in disappointing contrast with a previous rise: *the anticlimax of a brilliant career.* **2.** Something trivial or commonplace coming at the end of a series of significant events: *The business of nominating a vice-presidential candidate is often an anticlimax.*

an·ti·cline (ăn'tī-klīn') *n. Geol.* A formation in which several strata of rock are folded so that they slope down on both sides of a crest. [ANTI- + Greek *klinein,* to lean.]

an·ti·co·ag·u·lant (ăn'tē-kō-ăg'yə-lənt, -tī-) *n.* Any sub-

stance that suppresses or counteracts coagulation, esp. of the blood. —*adj.* Acting as an anticoagulant.

an·ti·cy·clone (ăn'tī-sī'klōn') *n.* An extensive system of winds that spiral outward around a region of high barometric pressure, circling clockwise in the Northern Hemisphere and counterclockwise in the Southern Hemisphere. —an'ti·cy·clon'ic (-sī-klŏn'ĭk) *adj.*

an·ti·dote (ăn'tī-dōt') *n.* **1.** A remedy or other agent that counteracts the effects of a poison. **2.** Anything that relieves or counteracts something injurious. [Latin *antidotum,* from Greek *antidoton,* from *antididonai,* to give as a remedy against : ANTI- + *didonai,* to give.] —an'ti·dot'al (ăn'tī-dōt'l) *adj.*

an·ti·fed·er·al·ist (ăn'tē-fĕd'ər-ə-lĭst, -fĕd'rə-lĭst, -tī-) *n.* **1.** Someone opposed to federalism. **2. Antifederalist.** A person who was opposed to the ratification of the U.S. Constitution. —an'ti·fed'er·al·ism *n.*

an·ti·freeze (ăn'tī-frēz') *n.* A liquid, such as ethylene glycol mixed with another liquid, such as water, to lower its freezing point.

an·ti·gen (ăn'tī-jən) *n.* Also **an·ti·gene** (-jēn'). Any substance that, when introduced into the body, stimulates the production of an antibody. [ANTI- + -GEN.] —an'ti·gen'ic (-jĕn'ĭk) *adj.* —an'ti·gen'i·cal·ly *adv.*

An·tig·o·ne (ăn-tĭg'ə-nē') *n. Gk. Myth.* The daughter of Oedipus, who performed funeral rites over her brother's body in defiance of her uncle Creon.

an·ti·he·ro (ăn'tē-hîr'ō, -tī-) *n.* The protagonist in certain forms of modern fiction and drama characterized by a lack of traditional heroic qualities.

an·ti·his·ta·mine (ăn'tē-hĭs'tə-mēn', -mĭn) *n.* Any of various drugs used to relieve symptoms of allergies or colds by interfering with the action of histamine. —an'ti·his'ta·min'ic (-mĭn'ĭk) *adj.*

an·ti·knock (ăn'tē-nŏk', -tī-) *n.* A substance, such as tetraethyl lead, added to gasoline to reduce engine knock.

an·ti·log (ăn'tī-lôg', -lŏg') *n.* A shortened form of **antilogarithm,** gen. used in writing mathematical expressions.

an·ti·log·a·rithm (ăn'tī-lô'gə-rĭth'əm, -lŏg'ə-) *n.* The number for which a given logarithm stands; for example, where log x equals y, the x is the antilogarithm of y. Also called **antilog.**

an·ti·ma·cas·sar (ăn'tī-mə-kăs'ər) *n.* A small cover for the backs or arms of chairs and sofas to keep them unsoiled. [ANTI- + *macassar,* oil from *Makassar,* a city in Indonesia.]

an·ti·mat·ter (ăn'tē-măt'ər) *n.* A form of matter in which every atomic particle is replaced by its corresponding antiparticle.

an·ti·mo·ny (ăn'tə-mō'nē) *n. Symbol* **Sb** A metallic element having four allotropic forms, the most common of which is a hard, extremely brittle, lustrous, silver-white, crystalline material. It is used in a wide variety of alloys, esp. with lead in battery plates, and in the manufacture of flameproofing compounds, paints, and ceramic products. Atomic number 51, atomic weight 121.75, melting point 630.5°C, boiling point 1,380°C, specific gravity 6.691, valences 3, 5. [Middle English, from Medieval Latin *antimonium.*]

an·ti·neu·tri·no (ăn'tē-nōō-trē'nō, -nyōō-, -tī-) *n., pl.* **-nos.** *Physics.* The antiparticle corresponding to the neutrino.

an·ti·neu·tron (ăn'tē-nōō'trŏn', -nyōō'-, -tī-) *n. Symbol* **n̄** *Physics.* The antiparticle corresponding to the neutron.

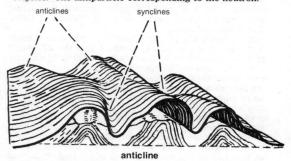

anticline

an·ti·node (ăn′tĭ-nōd′) *n. Physics.* The region or point of maximum amplitude between adjacent nodes.

an·ti·ox·i·dant (ăn′tē-ŏk′sĭ-dənt, -tī-) *n.* A chemical compound or substance that inhibits oxidation.

an·ti·par·ti·cle (ăn′tē-pär′tĭ-kəl, -tī-) *n.* A subatomic particle, such as a positron, antiproton, or antineutron, having the same mass, average lifetime, spin, magnitude of magnetic moment, and magnitude of electric charge as the particle to which it corresponds, but having the opposite sign of electric charge, opposite intrinsic parity, and opposite direction of magnetic moment.

an·ti·pas·to (ăn′tĭ-pä′stō, -päs′tō) *n., pl.* **-tos** or **-ti** (-tē). An Italian appetizer consisting of smoked meats, fish, olives, hot peppers, cheese, etc., served with oil and vinegar. [Italian, from ANTE- (before) + *pasto*, food, from Latin *pascere* (past part. *pastus*), to feed.]

an·ti·pa·thet·ic (ăn-tĭp′ə-thĕt′ĭk) or **an·tip·a·thet·i·cal** (-ĭ-kəl). *adj.* **1.** Having a feeling of aversion or opposition: *antipathetic to new ideas.* **2.** Causing a feeling of antipathy. **—an·tip′a·thet′i·cal·ly** *adv.*

an·tip·a·thy (ăn-tĭp′ə-thē) *n., pl.* **-thies. 1.** A strong feeling of aversion or opposition. **2.** The object of such aversion. [Latin *antipathia*, from Greek *antipatheia*, from *antipáthēs*, of opposite feelings, from ANTI- (opposite) + *pathos*, feeling.]

an·ti·per·son·nel (ăn′tē-pûr′sə-nĕl′, -tī-) *adj.* Used against military or civilian population.

an·ti·per·spi·rant (ăn′tē-pûr′spər-ənt) *n.* A preparation applied to the skin to reduce or prevent excessive perspiration.

an·ti·phon (ăn′tə-fŏn′) *n.* **1.** A devotional composition sung responsively as part of a liturgy. **2.** A short liturgical text chanted responsively before a psalm or canticle. [Late Latin *antiphona*, from Greek *antiphōna*, sung responses, ANTHEM.]

an·tiph·o·ny (ăn-tĭf′ə-nē) *n., pl.* **-nies.** An arrangement in which the performers of a musical composition are divided into two or more groups that play, or sing, alternately. **—an·tiph′o·nal** (-nəl) *adj.*

an·tip·o·dal (ăn-tĭp′ə-dəl) *adj.* **1.** Of, pertaining to, or situated on the opposite side or opposite sides of the earth. **2.** Exactly opposite; diametrically opposed.

an·ti·pode (ăn′tĭ-pōd′) *n.* A direct or diametrical opposite. [Back-formation from ANTIPODES.]

an·tip·o·des (ăn-tĭp′ə-dēz′) *pl.n.* **1.** Any two places or regions that are on opposite sides of the earth. **2.** (*sometimes used with a sing. verb*). Something that is the exact opposite of another. [Middle English, from Latin, from Greek, from *antipous*, with the feet opposite : ANTI- + *pous*, foot.]

an·ti·pope (ăn′tĭ-pōp′) *n.* A person claiming to be pope in opposition to the one chosen by church law.

an·ti·pro·ton (ăn′tē-prō′tŏn′, -tī-) *n. Physics.* The antiparticle corresponding to the proton.

an·ti·py·ret·ic (ăn′tē-pī-rĕt′ĭk, -tī-) *adj.* Reducing or tending to reduce fever. **—n.** A medication that reduces fever. [ANTI- + Greek *puretos*, fever, from *pur*, fire.]

an·ti·quar·i·an (ăn′tĭ-kwâr′ē-ən) *adj.* **1.** Of or pertaining to antiquaries or the study of antiquities. **2.** Dealing in or having to do with old rare books. **—n.** An antiquary.

an·ti·quar·y (ăn′tĭ-kwĕr′ē) *n., pl.* **-ies.** A student or collector of antiquities.

an·ti·quate (ăn′tĭ-kwāt′) *tr.v.* **-quat·ed, -quat·ing.** To make obsolete or old-fashioned.

an·ti·quat·ed (ăn′tĭ-kwā′tĭd) *adj.* **1.** So old as to be no longer useful or suitable; outmoded; obsolete: *antiquated laws; antiquated elegance.* **2.** Very old; aged.

an·tique (ăn-tēk′) *adj.* **1.** Of or belonging to ancient times, esp. those of ancient Greece or Rome. **2.** Belonging to, made in, or typical of an earlier period. **3.** Archaic or former: *Music in the antique sense included the study of mathematics.* **4.** Very old; aged: *an antique woman.* **—See** Syns at **old. —n.** An object having special value because of its age, esp. a work of art or handicraft that is over 100 years old. **—tr.v.** **-tiqued, -tiqu·ing.** To give the appearance of an antique to. [French, from Latin *antīquus*, ancient.] **—an·tique′ly** *adv.* **—an·tique′ness** *n.*

Usage: The use of *old* before **antique** is redundant and should be avoided: *the antique chest,* not *the old antique chest.*

an·tiq·ui·ty (ăn-tĭk′wĭ-tē) *n., pl.* **-ties. 1.** Often **Antiquity.** Ancient times, esp. the times preceding the Middle Ages. **2.** The quality of being old or ancient: *a carving of great antiquity.* **3. antiquities.** Relics and monuments dating from a time long past.

an·ti·scor·bu·tic (ăn′tē-skôr-byōō′tĭk, -tī-) *adj.* Curing or preventing scurvy. **—n.** An antiscorbutic food or drug. [ANTI- + Latin *scorbūtus*, scurvy.]

an·ti·Sem·i·tism (ăn′tē-sĕm′ĭ-tĭz′əm, -tī-) *n.* Prejudice, discrimination, or hostility against Jews. **—an′ti-Sem′ite′** (-sĕm′īt′) *n.* **—an′ti-Se·mit′ic** (-sə-mĭt′ĭk) *adj.*

an·ti·sep·sis (ăn′tĭ-sĕp′sĭs) *n.* The destruction of microorganisms that cause disease, fermentation, or rot. [ANTI- + SEPSIS.]

an·ti·sep·tic (ăn′tĭ-sĕp′tĭk) *adj.* **1.** Of, pertaining to, or designating antisepsis. **2.** Capable of producing antisepsis. **3.** Thoroughly clean. **4.** Devoid of enlivening or enriching qualities; austere; drab. **—n.** An antiseptic substance or agent. **—See** Syns at **clean.** [ANTI- + SEPTIC.] **—an′ti·sep′ti·cal·ly** *adv.*

an·ti·se·rum (ăn′tĭ-sîr′əm) *n., pl.* **-rums** or **-ra** (-rə). Human or animal serum containing antibodies for at least one antigen.

an·ti·so·cial (ăn′tē-sō′shəl, -tī-) *adj.* **1.** Avoiding the company of others; not sociable. **2.** Opposed to or interfering with society: *drugs that cause crime or aggressive antisocial behavior.*

an·ti·spas·mod·ic (ăn′tē-spăz-mŏd′ĭk, -tī-) *adj.* Easing or preventing spasms. **—n.** An antispasmodic drug.

an·ti·tank (ăn′tē-tăngk′, -tī-) *adj.* Used against enemy tanks or other armored vehicles.

an·tith·e·sis (ăn-tĭth′ĭ-sĭs) *n., pl.* **-ses** (-sēz′). **1.** Direct contrast; opposition: *Between our good intentions and our vices there is always antithesis.* **2.** The direct or exact opposite: *Vice is the antithesis of virtue.* **3.** *Rhet.* The juxtaposition or placing side by side of sharply contrasting ideas in balanced or parallel words, phrases, or grammatical structures; for example, *"Millions for defense but not a cent for tribute"* (Robert Goodloe Harper). [Late Latin, from Greek, opposition, from *antitithenai*, to oppose : ANTI- + *tithenai*, to set, place.] **—an′ti·thet′i·cal** (ăn′tĭ-thĕt′ĭ-kəl) or **an′ti·thet′ic** (-thĕt′-ĭk). **—an′ti·thet′i·cal·ly** *adv.*

an·ti·tox·ic (ăn′tĭ-tŏk′sĭk) *adj.* **1.** Counteracting a toxin or poison. **2.** Of or pertaining to an antitoxin.

an·ti·tox·in (ăn′tĭ-tŏk′sĭn) *n.* **1.** An antibody formed in response to, and capable of neutralizing, a biological poison. **2.** An animal serum containing such antibodies.

an·ti·trades (ăn′tĭ-trādz′) *pl.n.* The westerly winds above the trade winds of the tropics, which become the westerly winds of the middle latitudes.

an·ti·trust (ăn′tē-trŭst′, -tī-) *adj.* Opposing or regulating trusts, cartels, or similar business monopolies: *an antitrust suit; antitrust laws*

ant·ler (ănt′lər) *n.* One of a pair of hard, bony, deciduous growths, usu. elongated and branched, that characteristically grow on the heads of male deer and related animals. [Middle English *aunteler*, from Old French *antoillier*, from ANTE- + Latin *oculus*, eye.]

ant lion. **1.** Any insect of the family Myrmeleontidae, of which the adults resemble dragon flies. **2.** The larva of such an insect that digs holes to trap ants and other insects for food. Also called **doodlebug.**

antique

an·to·nym (ăn'tə-nĭm') *n.* A word having a sense opposite to a sense of another word. For example, *light* is an antonym of *dark.* [ANT(I)- + -ONYM.] —**an·ton'y·mous** (ăn-tŏn'ə-məs) *adj.*

A·nu·bis (ə-nōō'bĭs, ə-nyōō'-) *n. Egypt. Myth.* A jackal-headed god who conducted the dead to judgment.

a·nus (ā'nəs) *n.* The excretory opening of the alimentary canal. [Latin *ānus.*]

an·vil (ăn'vĭl) *n.* **1.** A heavy block of iron or steel with a smooth, flat top on which metals are shaped by hammering. **2.** *Anat.* A bone in the middle ear, the **incus.** [Middle English *anvil(t), anvelt,* from Old English *anfealt, anfilt.*]

anx·i·e·ty (ăng-zī'ĭ-tē) *n., pl.* **-ties. 1.** A state of uneasiness and distress about the future; apprehension; worry. **2.** Eagerness or earnestness, often marked by uneasiness: *her anxiety to do well.* **3.** *Psychiatry.* Intense fear or dread that lacks a specific cause or threat. [Latin *anxietās,* from *anxius,* anxious.]
Syns: **anxiety, care, concern, disquietude, worry** *n. Core meaning:* A troubled state of mind (*parental anxiety*).

anx·ious (ăngk'shəs, ăng'shəs) *adj.* **1.** Having a feeling of uneasiness; worried: *anxious about his child.* **2.** Marked by uneasiness or worry: *anxious times.* **3.** Eagerly earnest or desirous: *anxious to begin.* [Latin *anxius,* from *angere,* to torment, choke.] —**anx'ious·ly** *adv.* —**anx'ious·ness** *n.*
Usage: **anxious, eager.** These terms overlap to some extent when *anxious* has the sense of eagerly or earnestly desirous. In such instances, however, *anxious* should be used only when anxiety is present in some degree; otherwise, *eager* is usually a much better choice: *anxious to hear that you arrived safely; anxious to see the new quarters* (where there is ground for concern); *eager to see your new apartment, your new car.*

an·y (ĕn'ē) *adj.* **1.** One or some, no matter which, out of three or more: *Take any book you want.* **2.** Every: *Any kid in my gang would do the same.* **3.** Some: *Is there any soda?* **4.** Much: *He doesn't need any strength to chop kindling.* —*pron.* Any person or thing or any persons or things; anybody or anything. —*adv.* At all: *He doesn't feel any better.* [Middle English *any, eny,* from Old English *ænig.*]
Usage: **1.** The pronoun **any** takes a singular verb when it means one, and a plural verb when it means some: *Any of these gifts* (any one of them) *is fine. Are any* (some; more than one) *of them within our budget?* **2.** *Any* is followed by *other(s)* in comparisons of like entities: *She is a better doctor than any other. These houses are more expensive than any others on the block.* **3.** *Any* (adjective) can be used with a singular or a plural noun: *Ask any student. Any students late for school must have excuses.* **4.** *Any* (adverb) when standing alone is chiefly appropriate to informal usage in interrogative and negative contexts, as: *Did the pills help any? At least it didn't hurt any.*

an·y·bod·y (ĕn'ē-bŏd'ē, -bŭd'ē) *pron.* Any person; anyone. —*n.* A person of some consequence: *everybody who is anybody.* —See Usage note at **anyone.**

an·y·how (ĕn'ē-hou') *adv.* **1.** In any case; at any rate; anyway: *It was raining, but I walked home anyhow.* **2.** Just the same; nevertheless; anyway: *You may know these words, but study them anyhow.* **3.** Carelessly; neglectfully. —See Usage note **2** at **anyway.**

an·y·more (ĕn'ē-môr', -mōr') *adv.* At the present; from now on. Used only in negative and interrogative constructions: *We mustn't talk anymore.*
Usage: **anymore, any more.** *Anymore* is an adverb of time, used in negative and interrogative constructions: *He doesn't go anymore* (at present)*. Will they be away anymore* (from now on)*?* The two-word form *any* (adjective) + *more* (noun) is used in referring to a given thing, specified or understood: *The lamps were reasonable, but we don't need any more.*

an·y·one (ĕn'ē-wŭn', -wən) *pron.* Any person; anybody.
Usage: **1. anyone, any one.** *Anyone*—equivalent to *anybody*—refers to any person whatsoever: *Anyone could foresee what might happen.* In contrast, *any* (adjective) + *one* (noun) refers to any person or thing of a specified group: *Select any one of the three candidates.* **2. anyone, anybody.** These indefinite pronouns are used with singular verbs: *Anyone* (or *anybody*) *who is late must have a rea-*

son. Accompanying pronouns and pronominal adjectives within such constructions are usu. singular in formal writing: *Anyone* (or *anybody*) *is free to vote as he* (or *she* or *he or she* or *he/she*) *chooses.*

an·y·place (ĕn'ē-plās') *adv.* To, in, or at any place; anywhere: *I can go anyplace I like.*
Usage: **anyplace, any place, anywhere.** *Anyplace* is an adverb equivalent to *anywhere.* In formal writing *anywhere* occurs more often. In contrast, *any* (adjective) + *place* (noun) is the only possible choice in an example such as: *free to take any place that is not occupied.*

an·y·thing (ĕn'ē-thĭng') *pron.* Any object, occurrence, or matter whatever. —*idiom.* **anything but.** By no means; not at all: *This job is anything but easy.*

an·y·time (ĕn'ē-tīm') *adv.* **1.** At any time: *Call me anytime you want to.* **2.** At any time whatsoever: *It was as tricky a job of roping as they'd ever see anytime.*

an·y·way (ĕn'ē-wā') *adv.* **1.** In any case; at any rate; anyhow: *Both girls would wear, or anyway carry, white gloves.* **2.** Just the same; nevertheless; anyhow: *The ball was slippery, but Henry caught it anyway.*
Usage: **1. anyway, any way.** These are interchangeable only in the sense of *in any manner whatever: Handle it anyway* (or *in any way*) *you choose.* When the sense is *at any rate* or *anyhow,* only *anyway* is possible: *The cost was high but we proceeded anyway.* When the sense is *any course or direction,* only *any* (adjective) + *way* (noun) is possible: *Try any way that feels right. Any way they turned, danger was present.* **Anyways,** for **anyway,** is not acceptable. **2. Anyway** and **anyhow** are used exactly alike when they mean *in any case* or *at any rate: Anyway* (or *anyhow*)*, we won't forget you.*

an·y·ways (ĕn'ē-wāz') *adv. Nonstandard.* Anyway. —See Usage note **1** at **anyway.**

an·y·where (ĕn'ē-hwâr', -wâr') *adv.* **1.** To, in, or at any place: *They travel anywhere they want to.* **2.** To any extent or degree; at all: *Before my hand was anywhere near him, he was gone.* —*idioms.* **anywhere from.** Any quantity, degree, time, etc., between specified bounds: *Brushing eliminates anywhere from 45 to 90 per cent of cavities.* **get anywhere.** To succeed.
Usage: **Anywhere** is the only acceptable form. *Anywheres* is characteristic of uneducated speech. See also **anyplace.**

an·y·wheres (ĕn'ē-hwârz', -wârz') *adv. Nonstandard.* Anywhere. —See Usage note at **anywhere.**

an·y·wise (ĕn'ē-wīz') *adv.* In any way or manner.

A-O·K (ā'ō-kā') *adj., adv., & interj.* Also **A-O·kay.** *Informal.* Perfect; excellent.

A-one (ā'wŭn') *adj.* Also **A-1.** *Informal.* First-class; excellent.

a·or·ta (ā-ôr'tə) *n., pl.* **-tas** or **-tae** (-tē'). The main trunk of the systemic arteries, starting at the left ventricle of the heart and branching to carry blood to all the organs of the body except the lungs. [New Latin, from Greek *aortē,* aorta, from *aeirein,* to raise up.] —**a·or'tal** or **a·or'tic** *adj.*

aorta   aoudad

a·ou·dad (ä'ōō-dăd') *n.* A wild sheep, *Ammotragus lervia,* of northern Africa, with long, curved horns and a beardlike growth of hair on the neck and chest. Also called **Barbary sheep.** [French, from Berber *audad.*]

a·pace (ə-pās') *adv.* At a rapid pace; swiftly: *Inflation grew apace.* [Middle English *apas, apace,* step by step, from

Old French *a pas* : *a,* to + *pas,* step, pace.]

A·pach·e (ə-păch′ē) *n., pl.* **Apache** or **-es. 1.** An Athapascan-speaking tribe of North American Indians inhabiting the southwestern United States and northern Mexico. **2.** A member of this tribe. **3.** Any of the languages of this tribe.

ap·a·nage (ăp′ə-nĭj) *n.* Var. of **appanage.**

a·part (ə-pärt′) *adv.* **1.** At a distance in time or position from each other: *two trees about ten feet apart.* Also used adjectively: *They were seldom apart in the daytime.* **2.** To either side or in opposite directions from each other: *The negatively charged foil strips swing apart.* **3. a.** In or into separate pieces: *A fault is a place where rock has broken and moved apart.* **b.** To pieces: *falling apart.* **—idiom. apart from.** With the exception of; other than; aside from: *Apart from her temper, she's all right.* [Middle English, from Old French *a part,* to the side : *a,* to + PART.]

a·part·heid (ə-pärt′hīt′, -hāt′) *n.* An official policy of the Republic of South Africa enforcing racial segregation and maintaining white supremacy. [Afrikaans, "apartness," from *apart,* separate, from French *à part,* from Old French *a part* : APART + -heid, -hood.]

a·part·ment (ə-pärt′mənt) *n.* **1.** A room or suite of rooms used by one household in a building occupied by more than one household. **2.** A room. [French *appartement,* from Italian *appartemento,* from *appartare,* to separate, from *a parte,* apart, from Latin *ad,* to + *pars,* PART.]

ap·a·thet·ic (ăp′ə-thĕt′ĭk) *adj.* Feeling or showing little or no emotion; uninterested; indifferent: *apathetic about the election.* [Blend of APATHY and PATHETIC.]

ap·a·thy (ăp′ə-thē) *n.* Lack of feeling or interest in things gen. found exciting, interesting, or moving; indifference. —See Syns at **disinterest.** [Greek *apatheia,* from *apathēs,* without feeling : A- (without) + *pathos,* feeling.]

ape (āp) *n.* **1.** Any of various large, tailless Old World primates of the family Pongidae, including the chimpanzee, gorilla, gibbon, and orang-utan. **2.** Any monkey. **3.** A mimic or imitator. **4.** *Informal.* A clumsy, ill-bred, coarse person. —*tr.v.* **aped, ap·ing.** To imitate the actions of; to mimic. [Middle English *ape,* from Old English *apa.*] —**ape′like′** *adj.*

ape

a·pe·ri·ent (ə-pîr′ē-ənt) *adj.* Mildly purgative; laxative. —*n.* A mild laxative. [Latin *aperiēns,* pres. part. of *aperīre,* to uncover, open.]

a·pé·ri·tif (ä-pĕr′ĭ-tēf′) *n.* A drink, usu. of a fortified wine, taken to stimulate the appetite before a meal. [French,

from Old French *aperitif,* from Medieval Latin *aperitīvus,* from Latin *aperīre,* to open.]

ap·er·ture (ăp′ər-chər) *n.* **1.** A hole, gap, slit, or other opening: *an aperture in the wall.* **2.** *Optics.* An opening or entrance through which light or other electromagnetic radiation can pass into a camera, telescope, or other instrument. [Latin *apertūra,* from *aperīre* (past part. *apertus*), to open.]

a·pex (ā′pĕks) *n., pl.* **a·pex·es** or **a·pi·ces** (ā′pĭ-sēz′, ăp′ĭ-). **1.** The peak or highest point of something: *the apex of her career.* **2.** The highest point of a geometric figure; a vertex. [Latin, point, summit, top.]

a·pha·sia (ə-fā′zhə) *n.* Partial or total loss of the ability to express and understand ideas, gen. resulting from brain damage. [From Greek, from A- (without) + -*phasia,* speech, from *phanai,* to say.] —**a·pha′si·ac′** (-zē-ăk′) *n.* —**a·pha′sic** (-zĭk, -sĭk) *adj. & n.*

a·phe·li·on (ə-fē′lē-ən, ə-fēl′yən) *n., pl.* **-li·a** (-lē-ə). The point in the orbit of a planet or other celestial body farthest from the sun. [New Latin, var. of *aphelium* : Greek *ap(o)-,* away from + *hélios,* sun.]

a·phid (ā′fĭd, ăf′ĭd) *n.* Any of various small, soft-bodied insects of the family Aphididae that suck sap from plants. [From APHIS.]

a·phis (ā′fĭs, ăf′ĭs) *n., pl.* **a·phi·des** (ā′fĭ-dēz′, ăf′ĭ-). An aphid, esp. one of the genus *Aphis.* [Orig. unknown.]

aph·o·rism (ăf′ə-rĭz′əm) *n.* **1.** A brief statement of a principle. **2.** A tersely phrased statement of a truth or opinion; maxim; an adage. For example, "The only way to have a friend is to be one" is an aphorism. [Old French *aphorisme,* from Greek *aphorismos,* a delimitation, from *aphorizein,* to mark off by boundaries : *ap(o)-,* off, away from + *horos,* boundary.] —**aph′o·ris′tic** (ăf′ə-rĭs′tĭk) *adj.* —**aph′o·ris′ti·cal·ly** *adv.*

aph·ro·dis·i·ac (ăf′rə-dĭz′ē-ăk′) *adj.* Stimulating or intensifying sexuality. —*n.* An aphrodisiac drug or food.

Aph·ro·di·te (ăf′rə-dī′tē) *n. Gk. Myth.* The goddess of love and beauty, identified with the Roman Venus.

a·pi·ar·y (ā′pē-ĕr′ē) *n., pl.* **-ies.** A place where bees and beehives are kept for their honey. [Latin *apiārium,* beehive, from *apis,* bee.] —**a′pi·ar′i·an** (ā′pē-âr′ē-ən) *adj. & n.* —**a′pi·a·rist** (ā′pē-ə-rĭst) *n.*

ap·i·cal (ăp′ĭ-kəl, ā′pĭ-) *adj.* Of, pertaining to, located at, or constituting the apex.

a·pi·ces (ā′pĭ-sēz′, ăp′ĭ-) *n.* A plural of **apex.**

a·pi·cul·ture (ā′pĭ-kŭl′chər) *n.* The raising of bees. [Latin *apis,* bee + CULTURE.] —**a′pi·cul′tur·al** *adj.* —**a′pi·cul′tur·ist** *n.*

a·piece (ə-pēs′) *adv.* To or for each one; each: *Give them an apple apiece.*

ap·ish (ā′pĭsh) *adj.* **1.** Slavishly imitative. **2.** Silly; foolish. **3.** Like an ape. —**ap′ish·ly** *adv.* —**ap′ish·ness** *n.*

a·plomb (ə-plŏm′, ə-plŭm′) *n.* Self-confidence; poise; assurance. —See Syns at **confidence.** [French, uprightness, from Old French *a plomb,* perpendicularly : *a,* to + *plomb,* lead weight, from Latin *plumbum,* lead.]

A·poc·a·lypse (ə-pŏk′ə-lĭps′) *n.* **1.** The last book of the New Testament, Revelation. See Table at **Bible. 2. apocalypse.** A prophetic disclosure; revelation. [Middle English *Apocalipse,* from Late Latin *Apocalypsis,* from Greek *apokalupsis,* revelation, from *apokaluptein,* to uncover : *apo-,* reversal + *kaluptein,* to cover.]

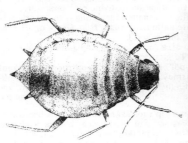

aphid

Aphrodite

apiary

| ă pat | ā pay | â care | ä father | ĕ pet | ē be | hw which | ĭ pit | ī tie | î pier | ŏ pot | ō toe | ô paw, for | oi noise |
| ŏŏ took | ŏŏ boot | ou out | th thin | *th* this | ŭ cut | û urge | zh vision | ə about, item, edible, gallop, circus | | | | | |

a·poc·a·lyp·tic (ə-pŏk′ə-lĭp′tĭk) or **a·poc·a·lyp·ti·cal** (-tĭ-kəl) *adj.* Of or pertaining to a prophetic disclosure or revelation. —**a·poc′a·lyp′ti·cal·ly** *adv.*

a·poc·o·pe (ə-pŏk′ə-pē) *n.* A cutting off or omitting of the last sound or syllable of a word; for example, *goin'* for *going.* [Latin *apocopē,* from Greek *apokopē,* from *apokoptein,* to cut off : *apo-,* off + *koptein,* to cut.]

A·poc·ry·pha (ə-pŏk′rə-fə) *pl.n. (used with a sing. verb).* **1.** The 14 Biblical books not included in the Old Testament by Protestants as being of doubtful authorship and authority. Eleven of these books are accepted by the Roman Catholic Church. See Table at **Bible. 2. apocrypha.** Any writings of questionable authorship or authenticity. [Middle English *Apocripha,* from Medieval Latin *(scripta) apocrypha,* hidden (writings), from Late Latin *apocryphus,* from Greek *apokruphos,* from *apokruptein,* to hide away : *apo-,* away + *kruptein,* to hide.]

a·poc·ry·phal (ə-pŏk′rə-fəl) *adj.* **1.** Of doubtful authorship or authenticity. **2.** False; counterfeit.

ap·o·gee (ăp′ə-jē) *n.* **1.** The point in the orbit of a natural or artificial satellite of the earth at which the satellite is farthest from the earth. **2.** The farthest or highest point; apex. [French *apogée,* from New Latin *apogaeum,* from Greek *apogaios,* "away from the earth" : *apo-,* away from + *gaia, gē,* earth.]

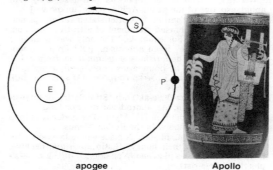

apogee   **Apollo**

A·pol·lo (ə-pŏl′ō) *n.* **1.** *Gk. Myth.* The god of the sun, prophecy, music, medicine, and poetry. **2. apollo.** Any young man of great physical beauty.

Ap·ol·lo·ni·an (ăp′ə-lō′nē-ən) *adj.* **1.** Of or pertaining to Apollo or his cult. **2. apollonian.** Of a theoretical or rational nature; clearly defined and well-ordered.

A·pol·lyon (ə-pŏl′yən) *n.* In the Bible, the devil; Satan.

a·pol·o·get·ic (ə-pŏl′ə-jĕt′ĭk) *adj.* **1.** Expressing or making an apology. **2.** Explaining or defending in speech or writing. —*n.* A formal defense or apology. —**a·pol′o·get′i·cal·ly** *adv.*

a·pol·o·get·ics (ə-pŏl′ə-jĕt′ĭks) *n. (used with a sing. verb).* The branch of theology that deals with the defense and proof of Christianity.

ap·o·lo·gi·a (ăp′ə-lō′jē-ə, -jə) *n.* A formal defense or justification. [Late Latin, APOLOGY.]

a·pol·o·gist (ə-pŏl′ə-jĭst) *n.* A person who argues in defense or justification of another person or cause.

a·pol·o·gize (ə-pŏl′ə-jīz′) *intr.v.* **-gized, -giz·ing. 1.** To make an apology; say one is sorry. **2.** To make a formal defense or justification in speech or writing. —**a·pol′o·giz′er** *n.*

a·pol·o·gy (ə-pŏl′ə-jē) *n., pl.* **-gies. 1.** A statement expressing regret for an offense or fault. **2.** A formal justification or defense, as of an idea, cause, etc.: *an apology for gun control.* **3.** An inferior substitute: *a poor apology for a leader.* [Old French *apologie,* from Late Latin *apologia,* from Greek *apologiā,* speech in defense : *apo-,* defense + *logos,* discourse, speech.]

ap·o·phthegm (ăp′ə-thĕm′) *n.* Var. of **apothegm.**

ap·o·plec·tic (ăp′ə-plĕk′tĭk) *adj.* **1.** Of, resembling, or causing apoplexy. **2.** Having or showing symptoms of apoplexy. —**ap′o·plec′ti·cal·ly** *adv.*

ap·o·plex·y (ăp′ə-plĕk′sē) *n.* A condition in which a blood vessel in the brain breaks or becomes blocked and causes tissue damage that may result in loss of muscular control, paralysis, unconsciousness, and, often, death. [Middle English *apoplexie,* from Old French, from Late Latin *apoplēxia,* from Greek, from *apoplēssein,* to cripple by a stroke : *apo-* (intensive) + *plēssein,* to strike.]

a·pos·ta·sy (ə-pŏs′tə-sē) *n., pl.* **-sies.** An abandonment of one's religious faith, political party, creed, etc. [Middle English *apostasie,* from Late Latin *apostasia,* from Greek, desertion, from *apostanai,* to rebel : *apo-,* away from + *stanai,* to stand.]

a·pos·tate (ə-pŏs′tāt′, -tĭt) *n.* A person who forsakes his faith or principles. —*adj.* Guilty of apostasy.

a·pos·ta·tize (ə-pŏs′tə-tīz′) *intr.v.* **-tized, -tiz·ing.** To give up or abandon one's faith or political party.

a pos·te·ri·o·ri (ä′pŏs-tîr′ē-ôr′ē, -ōr′ē, -ôr′ī, -ōr′ī, ä′). Denoting reasoning from facts or particulars to general principles or from effects to causes; inductive; empirical. [Latin, "from the subsequent."]

a·pos·tle (ə-pŏs′əl) *n.* **1.** Often **Apostle.** One of the twelve disciples chosen by Christ to preach his gospel. **2.** A missionary of the early Christian Church: *Saint Patrick, the apostle of Ireland.* **3.** One of the 12 members of the Mormon administrative council. **4.** A person who leads or advocates a cause or movement: *an apostle of conservation.* [Middle English *apostel, apostle,* from Old English *apostol,* from Late Latin *apostolus,* from Greek *apostolos,* messenger, envoy, from *apostellein,* to send away from : *apo-,* away from + *stellein,* to place.]

A·pos·tles' Creed (ə-pŏs′əlz). A Christian creed thought to have been written by the Twelve Apostles. It begins, "I believe in God the Father Almighty."

ap·os·tol·ic (ăp′ə-stŏl′ĭk) *adj.* **1.** Of or pertaining to the Apostles or the times when they lived. **2.** Of or pertaining to the faith, teaching, or practice of the Apostles. **3.** Of or pertaining to the pope as successor of Saint Peter.

a·pos·tro·phe¹ (ə-pŏs′trə-fē) *n.* A mark (') used to indicate the omission of a letter or letters from a word *(aren't),* the possessive case *(Tom's hat),* and certain plurals, esp. those of numbers and letters. [French, from Late Latin *apostrophus,* from Greek *(prosōidia) apostrophos,* "(accent of) turning away," from *apostrephein,* to turn away : *apo-,* away + *strephein,* to turn.]

a·pos·tro·phe² (ə-pŏs′trə-fē) *n.* A digression in discourse, esp. a turning away from an audience to address an absent or imaginary person. [Latin *apostrophē,* from Greek *apostrephein,* to turn away.] —**ap′os·troph′ic** (ăp′ə-strŏf′ĭk) *adj.*

a·pos·tro·phize (ə-pŏs′trə-fīz′) *v.* **-phized, -phiz·ing.** —*tr.v.* To address by apostrophe. —*intr.v.* To speak in apostrophe.

a·poth·e·car·ies' measure (ə-pŏth′ĭ-kĕr′ēz). A system of liquid volume measure used in pharmacy.

apothecaries' weight. A system of weights used in pharmacy and based on an ounce equal to 480 grains and a pound equal to 12 ounces.

a·poth·e·car·y (ə-pŏth′ĭ-kĕr′ē) *n., pl.* **-ries.** A person who is trained in the preparation of drugs and medicines; druggist; pharmacist. [Middle English *apotecarie,* from Medieval Latin *apothecārius,* from Latin *apothēca,* storehouse, from Greek *apothēkē* : *apo-,* away + *tithenai,* to put.]

ap·o·thegm (ăp′ə-thĕm′) *n.* Also **ap·o·phthegm.** A terse and witty instructive saying; maxim; proverb. [Greek *apophthegma,* a pointed saying : *apo-,* away from + *phthengesthai,* to speak.]

a·poth·e·o·sis (ə-pŏth′ē-ō′sĭs, ăp′ə-thē′ə-sĭs) *n., pl.* **-ses** (-sēz′). **1.** Glorification to divine rank or stature; deification. **2.** A glorified or exalted ideal: *She is the apotheosis of fitness.* [Late Latin *apotheōsis,* from Greek *apotheōsis: apo-, change + theos,* god.]

a·poth·e·o·size (ə-pŏth′-ə-sīz′, ăp′ə-thē′ə-sīz′) *tr.v.* **sized, -siz·ing.** To glorify; exalt.

ap·pall (ə-pôl′) *tr.v.* To fill with horror and amazement; to shock; dismay: *The poor living conditions appalled me.* [Middle English *ap(p)allen,* from Old French *apalir,* to grow pale : *a-,* to + *palir,* to grow pale.] —**ap·pall′ing·ly** *adv.*

ap·pa·loo·sa (ăp′ə-loo′sə) *n.* A horse of a breed developed in northwestern North America, having a characteristically spotted rump. [Perh. after the *Palouse* Indians.]

ap·pa·nage (ăp′ə-nĭj) *n.* Also **ap·a·nage. 1.** Land or some other source of revenue given by a king for the maintenance of a member of the ruling family. **2.** A prequisite. **3.** A natural accompaniment or adjunct. [French *apanage*, from Old French, from *apaner*, to make provisions for, from Medieval Latin *appānāre* : Latin *ad-*, to + *pānis*, bread.]

ap·pa·ra·tus (ăp'ə-rā'təs, -răt'əs) *n., pl.* **apparatus** or **-tus·es. 1.** The means by which a specified function or task is performed: *a complex apparatus for space explorers.* **2.** Equipment, esp. laboratory equipment: *a lab with a wealth of apparatus.* **3.** A device or mechanism formed by a group of parts working together, as in a machine. **4.** *Physiol.* A group of organs having a collective function: *the respiratory apparatus.* **5.** A system: *a growing economic apparatus.* [Latin *apparātus*, past part. of *apparāre*, to prepare : *ad-*, to + *parāre*, to make ready.]

ap·par·el (ə-păr'əl) *n.* **1.** Clothing, esp. outer garments: *nobles in rich apparel.* **2.** Anything that covers or adorns: *trees with their apparel of foliage.* —*tr.v.* **-eled** or **-elled, -el·ing** or **-el·ling. 1.** To dress or clothe. **2.** To adorn; embellish. [Middle English *appareil*, from Old French *apareil*, preparation, furnishings, from *apareillier*, to prepare, from Latin *apparāre* : *ad-*, toward + *parāre*, to make ready.]

ap·par·ent (ə-păr'ənt, ə-pâr'-) *adj.* **1.** Readily seen, perceived, or understood; plain or obvious: *for no apparent reason.* **2.** Appearing as such but not necessarily so: *an apparent advantage.* [Middle English, from Old French *aparent*, pres. part. of *aparoir*, appear.] —**ap·par'ent·ly** *adv.* —**ap·par'ent·ness** *n.*

ap·pa·ri·tion (ăp'ə-rĭsh'ən) *n.* **1.** A ghostly figure; specter. **2.** A sudden or unusual sight. **3.** An appearance. [Middle English *apparicioun*, from Old French *apparition*, from Late Latin *appāritiō*, appearance, from Latin *appārēre*, APPEAR.] —**ap'pa·ri'tion·al** *adj.*

ap·peal (ə-pēl') *n.* **1.** An urgent or earnest request: *an appeal for help.* **2.** A resort or application to some higher authority, as for sanction or a decision: *an appeal to reason.* **3.** The power of attracting or of arousing interest: *The countryside has appeal for tourists.* **4.** *Law.* **a.** The transfer or request for transfer of a case from a lower to a higher court for a new hearing. **b.** A case so transferred. —*intr.v.* **1.** To make an urgent or earnest request: *I appeal to you for help.* **2.** To have recourse, as for sanction or decision; to resort. **3.** To be attractive or interesting: *That dress appeals to her.* **4.** *Law.* To make or apply for an appeal. —*tr.v. Law.* To transfer or apply to transfer (a case) to a higher court for rehearing. —See Syns at **attract.** [Middle English *appelen, apelen,* from Old French *apeler,* from Latin *appellāre,* to apply, to entreat, address.] —**ap·peal'a·ble** *adj.* —**ap·peal'er** *n.*

ap·pear (ə-pîr') *intr.v.* **1.** To come into view; become visible: *A boat appeared on the horizon.* **2.** To come into existence. **3.** To seem or look: *The coat appears to be blue.* **4.** To seem likely: *It appears that they will be late.* **5.** To come before the public: *She has appeared in two plays.* **6.** *Law.* To present oneself formally before a court as defendant, plaintiff, or counsel. [Middle English *apperen, aperen,* from Old French *aparoir,* from Latin *appārēre* : *ad-*, to + *pārēre,* to show.]

Syns: appear, look, seem *v. Core meaning:* To have the appearance of (*He appeared happy but he really wasn't.*).

ap·pear·ance (ə-pîr'əns) *n.* **1.** The act of appearing; a coming into sight: *the sudden appearance of clouds.* **2.** The act of coming into public view: *a rare live appearance.* **3.** The outward aspect of someone or something: *a good appearance.* **4.** A pretense or semblance; false show: *keeping up an appearance of diligence.* **5. appearances.** Outward indications; circumstances: *They are very cheerful, to all appearances, despite their poverty.* —*idioms.* **keep up appearances.** To keep up the outward indications of what is normal, proper, etc. **put in an appearance.** To appear briefly; attend.

ap·pease (ə-pēz') *tr.v.* **-peased, -peas·ing. 1.** To calm or pacify, esp. by giving what is demanded; placate; soothe. **2.** To satisfy or relieve: *A glass of iced tea appeased his thirst.* [Middle English *appesen, apesen,* from Old French *apaisier,* from Latin *ad-*, to + *pāx,* peace.] —**ap·peas'a·ble** *adj.* —**ap·peas'a·bly** *adv.* —**ap·peas'er** *n.*

ap·pease·ment (ə-pēz'mənt) *n.* **1.** The act of appeasing or the condition of being appeased. **2.** The policy of granting concessions to a threatening nation in an attempt to maintain peace.

ap·pel·lant (ə-pĕl'ənt) *adj.* Appellate. —*n.* Someone who appeals a court decision.

ap·pel·late (ə-pĕl'ĭt) *adj.* Having the power to hear appeals and to reverse previous court decisions: *an appellate court.* [Latin *appellātus,* past part. of *appellāre,* APPEAL.]

ap·pel·la·tion (ăp'ə-lā'shən) *n.* **1.** A name or title: *He is known by the appellation "Big Bill."* **2.** *Archaic.* The act of naming. —See Syns at **name.** [Middle English *appellacioun,* from Latin *apellātiō,* from *appellāre,* to appeal.]

ap·pel·la·tive (ə-pĕl'ə-tĭv) *adj.* Of or relating to the assignment of names. —*n.* A name or descriptive epithet. [Middle English, from Late Latin *appellātīvus,* from *appellāre,* to call by name, APPEAL.]

ap·pend (ə-pĕnd') *tr.v.* To add as a supplement; attach: *The committee appended a list of errors to the report.* [Latin *appendere* : *ad-*, to + *pendere,* to hang.]

ap·pend·age (ə-pĕn'dĭj) *n.* **1.** Something appended or attached. **2.** *Biol.* Any part or organ that is joined to an axis or trunk, as a finger or a branch of a tree.

ap·pen·dec·to·my (ăp'ən-dĕk'tə-mē) *n., pl.* **-mies.** The surgical removal of the vermiform appendix. [APPEND(IX) + -ECTOMY.]

ap·pen·di·ces (ə-pĕn'dĭ-sēz') *n.* A plural of **appendix.**

ap·pen·di·ci·tis (ə-pĕn'dĭ-sī'tĭs) *n.* Inflammation of the appendix. [New Latin, from APPENDIX + -ITIS.]

ap·pen·dix (ə-pĕn'dĭks) *n., pl.* **-dix·es** or **-di·ces** (-dĭ-sēz'). **1.** A collection of supplementary material at the end of a book. **2.** *Anat.* A slender, closed tube attached to the large intestine near the point at which it joins the small intestine; the vermiform appendix. [Latin, appendage, from *appendere,* append.]

appendix   apple

ap·per·ceive (ăp'ər-sēv') *tr.v.* **-ceived, -ceiv·ing.** *Psychol.* To understand in terms of past perceptions or experience. [Middle English *apperceiven,* from Old French *aperceivre* : *a-,* to + *perceivre,* perceive.]

ap·per·cep·tion (ăp'ər-sĕp'shən) *n. Psychol.* **1.** Conscious perception with full awareness. **2.** The process of understanding by which newly observed qualities of an object are related to past experience. —**ap'per·cep'tive** *adj.*

ap·per·tain (ăp'ər-tān') *intr.v.* To belong as a function or part; have relation: *the problems that appertain to social and economic reform.* [Middle English *apperteinen,* from Old French *apartenir,* from Latin *ad-,* to + *pertinēre,* pertain.]

ap·pe·tite (ăp'ĭ-tīt') *n.* **1.** A desire for food or drink. **2.** A strong desire for something: *an appetite for education.* [Middle English *apetit,* from Old French, from Latin *appetītus,* from *ad-,* toward + *petere,* to seek.]

ap·pe·tiz·er (ăp'ĭ-tī'zər) *n.* A food or drink served before a meal to stimulate the appetite.

ap·pe·tiz·ing (ăp'ĭ-tī'zĭng) *adj.* Stimulating or appealing to the appetite: *an appetizing meal.*

ap·plaud (ə-plôd') *intr.v.* To express approval by clapping the hands. —*tr.v.* **1.** To express praise or approval of by clapping the hands, cheering, etc.: *applaud the actors.* **2.** To express approval publicly. —See Syns at **praise. ap·plaud'er** *n.*

ap·plause (ə-plôz') *n.* **1.** Praise or approval expressed by the clapping of hands. **2.** Public approval. [Medieval Latin *applausus,* from Latin, past part. of *applaudere,* APPLAUD.]

ap·ple (ăp'əl) *n.* **1.** A tree, *Pyrus malus,* of temperate regions, having fragrant pink or white flowers and edible fruit. **2.** The firm, rounded, often red-skinned fruit of this tree or any of its varieties. *—modifier: an apple pie.* *—idiom.* **apple of (one's) eye.** Something or someone very much liked or loved. [Middle English *appel,* from Old English *æppel.*]

ap·ple·jack (ăp′əl-jăk′) *n.* Brandy distilled from hard cider.

ap·ple·sauce (ăp′əl-sôs′) *n.* **1.** Apples stewed to a pulp, sweetened, and sometimes spiced. **2.** *Slang.* Foolishness; nonsense.

ap·pli·ance (ə-plī′əns) *n.* A device or instrument, esp. one operated by electricity or gas and designed for household use. *—modifier: an appliance dealer.* [From APPLY.]

ap·pli·ca·ble (ăp′lĭ-kə-bəl, ə-plĭk′ə-) *adj.* Capable of being applied; appropriate. **—ap′pli·ca·bil′i·ty** *n.* **—ap′pli·ca·bly** *adv.*

ap·pli·cant (ăp′lĭ-kənt) *n.* A person who applies for something: *an applicant for a job.* [Latin *applicāns,* pres. part. of *applicāre,* APPLY.]

ap·pli·ca·tion (ăp′lĭ-kā′shən) *n.* **1.** The act of applying. **2.** Something that is applied, such as a medicine or a cosmetic. **3.** A method of applying or using; a specific use: *the application of science to industry.* **4.** The capacity of being usable; relevance: *Geometry has practical applications.* **5.** Careful work and attention; diligence. **6. a.** A request, as for a job or admittance to a school. **b.** The form or document upon which such a request is made.

ap·pli·ca·tor (ăp′lĭ-kā′tər) *n.* An instrument for applying something, such as medicine or glue.

ap·plied (ə-plīd′) *adj.* Put into practice; used: *applied physics.*

ap·pli·qué (ăp′lĭ-kā′) *n.* A decoration, design, or trimming made by sewing or attaching pieces of one material to the surface of another. *—adj.* Of or like this kind of decoration. *—tr.v.* **-quéd, -qué·ing.** To decorate with appliqué work. [French, past part. of *appliquer,* to put on, apply, from Latin *applicāre,* APPLY.]

ap·ply (ə-plī′) *v.* **-plied, -ply·ing.** *—tr.v.* **1.** To bring into contact with something; put on, upon, or to: *apply glue sparingly to the edges.* **2.** To put to or adapt for a special use: *The government applied all its money to the war debt.* **3.** To use (a special word or phrase) in referring to a particular person or thing: *"Underground Railroad" was the name applied to the system used to aid in the escape of fugitive slaves.* **4.** To devote (oneself or one's efforts) to something: *He applied himself to his books.* *—intr.v.* **1.** To be pertinent or relevant; concern: *This rule does not apply to you.* **2.** To request employment, acceptance, or admission: *She applied to college.* [Middle English *aplien,* from Old French *aplier,* from Latin *applicāre,* to join to : *ad-,* to + *plicāre,* to fold together.]

ap·pog·gia·tu·ra (ə-pŏj′ə-tŏŏr′ə) *n. Mus.* An embellishing note, usu. one step above or below the note it precedes, indicated by a small note or special sign. [Italian, from *appoggiare,* to lean on : Latin *ad-,* to + *podium,* balcony, from Greek *podion,* dim. of *pous,* foot.]

ap·point (ə-point′) *tr.v.* **1.** To select or designate for an office, position, or duty. **2.** To decide on or set by authority: *We appointed three o'clock for the meeting.* **3.** To furnish; equip: *The mansion was comfortably appointed.* [Middle English *apointen,* from Old French *apointier,* to arrange, from *(rendre) à point,* "(to bring) to a point" : *a-,* to + *point,* point.]

ap·point·ee (ə-poin′tē′, ăp′oin-) *n.* A person who is appointed to an office or position.

ap·point·ive (ə-poin′tĭv) *adj.* Pertaining to or filled by appointment: *an appointive office.*

ap·point·ment (ə-point′mənt) *n.* **1.** The act of appointing to an office or position. **2.** The office or position to which a person has been appointed. **3.** An arrangement to do something or meet someone at a particular time and place. **4. appointments.** Furnishings, fittings, or equipment: *table appointments; room appointments.* *—modifier: an appointment book.*

ap·por·tion (ə-pôr′shən, ə-pōr′-) *tr.v.* To divide and assign according to some plan or proportion; allot. [Old French *apportionner : a-,* to + *portionner,* to divide into portions.]

ap·por·tion·ment (ə-pôr′shən-mənt, ə-pōr′-) *n.* **1.** The act of apportioning or the condition of being apportioned: *the ap-*

portionment of direct taxes on the basis of state population. **2. a.** The proportional distribution of the number of members of the U.S. House of Representatives on the basis of the population of each state. **b.** A similar distribution in other U.S. legislative bodies, as of a state.

ap·pose (ə-pōz′) *tr.v.* **-posed, -pos·ing.** To arrange (things) near to each other or side by side. [Back-formation from APPOSITION (by analogy with COMPOSE, COMPOSITION).]

ap·po·site (ăp′ə-zĭt) *adj.* Appropriate or pertinent. [Latin *appositus,* "situated near," past part. of *appōnere,* to place near to.] **—ap′po·site·ly** *adv.*

ap·po·si·tion (ăp′ə-zĭsh′ən) *n.* **1.** The act of placing side by side or next to each other. **2. a.** *Gram.* A construction in which a noun or noun phrase is placed with another noun as a further explanation or description. For example, in the sentence *Helen, the sister of Allen, is very pretty, Helen* and *the sister of Allen* are in apposition. **b.** The relationship between such nouns or noun phrases. **3.** *Biol.* The growth of successive layers of a cell wall. [Middle English *apposicioun,* from Medieval Latin *appositiō,* from Latin *appōnere,* to place near to : *ad-,* near to + *pōnere,* to put.] **—ap′po·si′tion·al** *adj.* **—ap′po·si′tion·al·ly** *adv.*

ap·pos·i·tive (ə-pŏz′ĭ-tĭv) *adj.* In or concerning apposition: *an appositive phrase.* *—n.* A noun or phrase that is placed in apposition with another noun. In the sentence *Helen, the sister of Allen, is very pretty,* the appositive is *the sister of Allen.* **—ap·pos′i·tive·ly** *adv.*

ap·prais·al (ə-prā′zəl) *n.* **1.** The act of appraising or the condition of being appraised: *an appraisal of the judicial system.* **2.** An expert or official valuation of something, as for taxation.

ap·praise (ə-prāz′) *tr.v.* **-praised, -prais·ing. 1.** To evaluate, esp. in an official capacity. **2.** To estimate the quality, amount, size, and other features of; to judge: *appraised him as a valuable worker.* [Middle English *appreisen,* partly from *preise,* value, praise, partly from Old French *aprisier,* from Late Latin *appretiāre,* to set a value on : Latin *ad-,* to + *pretium,* price.] **—ap·praise′ment** *n.* **—ap·prais′er** *n.*

ap·pre·ci·a·ble (ə-prē′shə-bəl) *adj.* Capable of being noticed, estimated, or measured; noticeable. —See Syns at **perceptible. —ap·pre′cia·bly** *adv.*

ap·pre·ci·ate (ə-prē′shē-āt′) *v.* **-at·ed, -at·ing.** *—tr.v.* **1.** To recognize the quality, worth, significance, importance, etc., of; value highly: *He appreciated the freedoms he had.* **2.** To be aware of the artistic values of; enjoy and understand critically or emotionally: *He appreciates literature and music.* **3.** To raise in value or price: *Speculation appreciated the gold market.* *—intr.v.* To go up in value or price: *Gold appreciated yesterday for a new record.* [Late Latin *appretiāre,* APPRAISE.] **—ap·pre′ci·a·tor** *n.*

Syns: appreciate, cherish, esteem, prize, respect, treasure, value *v.* **Core meaning:** To recognize the worth, importance, or value of (*a person who appreciated classical music*).

ap·pre·ci·a·tion (ə-prē′shē-ā′shən) *n.* **1.** The recognition of the worth, quality, importance, etc., of people and things. **2.** Gratefulness; gratitude: *They expressed their appreciation with a gift.* **3.** Awareness of artistic values. **4.** A rise in value or price.

ap·pre·ci·a·tive (ə-prē′shə-tĭv, -shē-ā′tĭv) *adj.* Capable of or showing appreciation. **—ap·pre′cia·tive·ly** *adv.*

ap·pre·hend (ăp′rĭ-hĕnd′) *tr.v.* **1.** To take into custody; arrest. **2.** To grasp mentally; understand: *apprehend the theories of Einstein.* **3.** To look forward to fearfully; anticipate with anxiety. —See Syns at **arrest.** [Middle English *apprehenden,* from Latin *apprehendere,* to seize : *ad-,* to + *prehendere,* to seize.]

ap·pre·hen·sion (ăp′rĭ-hĕn′shən) *n.* **1.** Fear or dread of what may happen; anxiety. **2.** The act of seizing or capturing; arrest. **3.** The ability to apprehend or understand; understanding.

ap·pre·hen·sive (ăp′rĭ-hĕn′sĭv) *adj.* Fearful; uneasy: *apprehensive about the future.* **—ap′pre·hen′sive·ly** *adv.*

ap·pren·tice (ə-prĕn′tĭs) *n.* **1.** A person who works for another without pay in return for instruction in a craft or trade. **2.** A person who is learning a trade, usu. a member of a labor union. **3.** Any beginner. *—modifier: an apprentice carpenter.* *—tr.v.* **-ticed, -tic·ing.** To place or take on as an apprentice. [Middle English *aprentis*, from Old French, from *aprendre*, to learn, from Latin *appre(he)ndere*, APPREHEND.] **—ap·pren′tice·ship**′ (ə-prĕn′tĭs-shĭp′) *n.*

ap·prise¹ (ə-prīz′) *tr.v.* **-prised, -pris·ing.** Also chiefly *Brit.* **ap·prize.** To cause to know; give notice to; inform: *He apprised her of the principal's message.* [From French *apprendre* (past part. *appris*), to cause to learn, inform, from Old French *aprendre*, to learn, from Latin *appre(he)ndere*, APPREHEND.]

ap·prise² (ə-prīz′) *tr.v.* **-prised, -pris·ing.** *Brit.* Var. of **apprize** (appraise).

ap·prize¹ (ə-prīz′) *tr.v.* **-prized, -priz·ing.** Also *Brit.* **ap·prise.** To appraise.

ap·prize² (ə-prīz′) *tr.v.* **-prized, -priz·ing.** *Brit.* Var. of **apprise** (inform).

ap·proach (ə-prōch′) *intr.v.* To come near or nearer in place, time, or size: *As spring approached, our work neared completion.* **—tr.v. 1.** To come or go near or nearer to. **2.** To come close to in appearance, quality, condition, or other characteristics; to approximate: *What approaches the joy of singing?* **3.** To make a proposal to; make overtures to: *approach the president for a job.* **4.** To begin to deal with or work on: *approach a task.* **—n. 1.** The act of coming or drawing near: *the approach of winter; the approach of the stranger.* **2.** A way or means of reaching someone or a destination; an access: *the approach to the bridge.* **3.** The method used in dealing with or accomplishing something: *a logical approach to the problem.* **4.** Often **approaches.** An advance or overture made by one person to another. **5.** *Golf.* The stroke with which the player tries to get the ball onto the putting green. **6. approaches.** *Mil.* Trenches or bulwarks for the protection of troops besieging a fortified position. [Middle English *aprochen*, from Old French *aprochier*, from Late Latin *appropiāre* : Latin *ad-*, to + *propius*, nearer, from *prope*, near.]

ap·proach·a·ble (ə-prō′chə-bəl) *adj.* **1.** Capable of being approached or reached; accessible. **2.** Easily approached; friendly: *an approachable person.* **—ap·proach′a·bil′i·ty** *n.*

ap·pro·ba·tion (ăp′rə-bā′shən) *n.* **1.** Praise; commendation: *not a murmur of approbation or blame.* **2.** Official approval: *a bill that received the approbation of all branches of the government.* [From Latin *approbāre*, APPROVE.]

ap·pro·pri·ate (ə-prō′prē-ĭt) *adj.* Suitable for a particular person, condition, occasion, or place; proper; fitting: *appropriate clothes; an appropriate blend of music and text.* —See Syns at **convenient. —tr.v.** (ə-prō′prē-āt′) **-at·ed, -at·ing. 1.** To set apart for a specific use: *appropriate money for education.* **2.** To take possession of or make use of exclusively for oneself, often without permission. [Middle English *appropriaten*, from Late Latin *appropriāre*, to make one's own : Latin *ad-*, to + *propius*, own.] **—ap·pro′pri·ate·ly** *adv.* **—ap·pro′pri·ate·ness** *n.* **—ap·pro′pri·a′tor** *n.*

ap·pro·pri·a·tion (ə-prō′prē-ā′shən) *n.* **1.** The act of appropriating to oneself or to a specific use or purpose. **2.** Public funds set aside for a specific purpose.

ap·prov·al (ə-prōō′vəl) *n.* **1.** An official approbation; a sanction. **2.** Favorable regard: *The voters expressed their approval by voting for her.* **—idiom. on approval.** For examination or trial without the obligation to buy.

ap·prove (ə-prōōv′) *v.* **-proved, -prov·ing. —tr.v. 1.** To think of or regard favorably; consider right or good: *She approved my choice of food for the picnic.* **2.** To confirm or consent to officially; sanction; ratify: *The Senate approved the treaty.* **—intr.v.** To voice or demonstrate approval: *The Puritans did not approve of card playing on Sunday.* [Middle English *approven*, from Old French *aprover*, from Latin *approbāre*, to make good : *ad-*, to + *probus*, good.]

ap·prox·i·mate (ə-prŏk′sə-mĭt) *adj.* **1.** Almost exact or accurate: *the approximate height of a building.* **2.** Very similar; closely resembling. **—v.** (ə-prŏk′sə-māt′) **-mat·ed, -mat·ing. —tr.v. 1.** To come close to; be nearly the same as. **2.** To cause to approach; bring near. **—intr.v.** To come near or close in degree, nature, quality, etc. [Late Latin *approximāre*, to come near to : Latin *ad-*, to + *proximus*, nearest.] **—ap·prox′i·mate·ly** *adv.*

ap·prox·i·ma·tion (ə-prŏk′sə-mā′shən) *n.* The act, process, or result of approximating: *decimal approximations of square roots.*

ap·pur·te·nance (ə-pûrt′n-əns) *n.* **1.** Something added to another, more important thing; an appendage; accessory. **2. appurtenances.** Any equipment, such as clothing, tools, or instruments, used for a specific purpose or task; gear. **3.** *Law.* A right, privilege, or property that belongs with a principal property and goes along with it in case of passage of title, conveyance, or inheritance. [Middle English *appurtenaunce, apurtenaunce*, from Old French *apertenance*, from Late Latin *appertinēre*, APPERTAIN.] **—ap·pur′te·nant** *adj.*

ap·ri·cot (ăp′rĭ-kŏt′, ā′prĭ-) *n.* **1.** A tree, *Prunus armeniaca*, native to western Asia and Africa, widely cultivated for its edible fruit. **2.** The juicy, yellow-orange peachlike fruit of this tree. **3.** A yellowish orange. **—modifier:** *an apricot tart.* **—adj.** Yellowish orange. [Orig. uncertain.]

A·pril (ā′prəl) *n.* The fourth month of the year according to the Gregorian calendar. April has 30 days. **—modifier:** *April showers.* [Middle English, from Latin *aprīlis*, perh. "month of Venus," from Etruscan *apru*, from Greek *Aphrō*, short form of *Aphroditē*, Aphrodite.]

April fool. The victim of a trick played on April Fools' Day.

April Fools' Day. Apr. 1, a traditional day for playing practical jokes. Also called **All Fools' Day.**

a pri·o·ri (ä′ prē-ôr′ē, -ōr′ē, ā′ prī-ôr′ī, -ōr′ī). **1.** Proceeding from a known or assumed cause to a necessarily related effect; deductive. **2.** Based on a hypothesis or theory rather than on experiment or experience. **3.** Made before or without examination. [Latin, "from the previous (causes or hypotheses)."]

a·pron (ā′prən) *n.* **1.** A garment, usu. fastened in the back, worn over all or part of the front of the body to protect clothing. **2.** Anything resembling an apron in appearance or function, as a protective shield for a machine. **3.** The paved strip in front of an airport hangar. **4.** The part of a stage in a theater extending in front of the curtain. **—tr.v.** To cover, protect, or provide with an apron. **—idiom. tied to (someone's) apron strings.** Dominated by or dependent on someone. [Middle English *(an) apron*, orig. *(a) napron*, from Old French *naperon*, dim. of *nape*, tablecloth, from Latin *mappa*, napkin.]

apron

ap·ro·pos (ăp′rə-pō′) *adj.* Relevant or fitting: *He said nonfiction was more apropos for our time than fiction.* **—adv.** By the way; incidentally: *Apropos, where were you last night?* **—prep.** Concerning; regarding: *Apropos our date, I can make it.* **—idiom. apropos of.** With reference to: *a funny story apropos of politics.* [French *à propos*, "to the purpose."]

apse (ăps) *n.* A semicircular or polygonal, usu. domed, projection of a building, esp. the end where the altar is located.

apt (ăpt) *adj.* **1.** Exactly suitable; appropriate: *an apt reply.* **2.** Likely: *Where are barnacles most apt to be found?* **3.** Having a tendency; inclined: *I would be apt to accept his statement.* **4.** Quick to learn: *an apt student.* [Middle English, from Latin *aptus*, past part. of *apere*, to fasten.] **—apt′ly** *adv.* **—apt′ness** *n.*

ap·ter·yx (ăp′tə-rĭks) *n.* A bird, the **kiwi.** [New Latin, from A- (without) + Greek *pterux*, wing, from *pteron*, feather, wing.]

ă pat ā pay â care ä father ĕ pet ē be hw which ĭ pit ī tie î pier ŏ pot ō toe ô paw, for oi noise
ōō took ōō boot ou out th thin th this ŭ cut û urge zh vision ə about, item, edible, gallop, circus

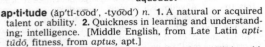

aqueduct

Arabian

ap·ti·tude (ăp'tĭ-tōōd', -tyōōd') *n.* **1.** A natural or acquired talent or ability. **2.** Quickness in learning and understanding; intelligence. [Middle English, from Late Latin *aptitūdō*, fitness, from *aptus*, apt.]

aqua for·tis (fôr'tĭs). Also **aq·ua·for·tis.** *Chem.* **Nitric acid.** [New Latin, "strong water."]

Aq·ua·lung (ăk'wə-lŭng', ä'kwə-) *n.* A trademark for a **scuba**, an underwater breathing apparatus.

aq·ua·ma·rine (ăk'wə-mə-rēn', ä'kwə-) *n.* **1.** A transparent blue-green variety of beryl, used as a gemstone. **2.** A light greenish blue. —*adj.* Light greenish blue. [New Latin *aqua marīna*, from Latin, sea water, from AQUA + *marīnus*, of the sea, marine.]

aq·ua·naut (ăk'wə-nôt', ä'kwə-) *n.* A person trained to work or assist in scientific research conducted in underwater installations, esp. those deep in the sea. [AQUA + Greek *nautēs*, sailor, from *naus*, ship.]

aqua re·gi·a (rē'jē-ə). A corrosive, fuming, volatile mixture of hydrochloric and nitric acids, used for testing metals and dissolving platinum and gold. Also called **nitrohydrochloric acid.** [New Latin, "royal water" (because it dissolves gold).]

a·quar·i·um (ə-kwâr'ē-əm) *n., pl.* **-ums** or **-i·a** (-ē-ə). **1.** A tank, bowl, or other water-filled enclosure in which fish or other aquatic animals and, often, plants are kept. **2.** A place where such animals and plants are displayed to the public. [From Latin *aquārius*, of water, from *aqua*, water.]

A·quar·i·us (ə-kwâr'ē-əs) *n.* **1.** A constellation in the equatorial region of the Southern Hemisphere near Pisces and Aquila. **2.** The 11th sign of the **zodiac.** [Middle English, from Latin, from AQUA + -ARY.]

a·quat·ic (ə-kwăt'ĭk, ə-kwŏt'-) *adj.* **1.** Of or in water: *an aquatic environment.* **2.** Living or growing in or on the water: *aquatic mammals.* **3.** Taking place in or on the water: *aquatic sports.* —*n.* **1.** An aquatic organism. **2. aquatics.** Sports performed in or on the water. [Old French *aquatique*, from Latin *aquāticus*, from *aqua*, water.]

aq·ua·tint (ăk'wə-tĭnt', ä'kwə-) *n.* **1.** A process of etching capable of producing several tones by varying the etching time of different areas of a copper plate so that the resulting print resembles the flat tints of an ink or wash drawing. **2.** An etching made in this way. —*tr.v.* To etch in aquatint. [French *aquatinte*, from Italian *acqua tinta*, "tinted water," water color, hence aquatint etching (which imitates water color).]

aqua vi·tae (vī'tē). **1.** Alcohol. **2.** Whiskey, brandy, or other strong liquor. [Middle English *aquavite*, from Medieval Latin *aqua vītae*, "water of life."]

aq·ue·duct (ăk'wĭ-dŭkt') *n.* **1.** A large pipe or channel made to carry water from a distant source. **2.** A bridgelike structure designed to carry such a pipe or channel over a river or low ground. **3.** *Anat.* A channel or passage in the body for carrying fluids. [Latin *aquae ductus*, from AQUA + DUCT.]

a·que·ous (ā'kwē-əs, ăk'wē-) *adj.* **1.** Pertaining to, similar to, containing, or dissolved in water; watery. **2.** *Geol.* Formed from matter deposited by water, as certain sedimentary rocks. [Medieval Latin *aqueus*, from Latin *aqua*, water.]

aqueous humor. A clear, lymphlike fluid that fills the space between the cornea and the lens of the eye.

Aq·ui·la (ăk'wə-lə) *n.* A constellation in the Northern

Hemisphere and the Milky Way near Aquarius and Serpens Cauda.

aq·ui·line (ăk'wə-līn', -lĭn) *adj.* **1.** Of or similar to an eagle. **2.** Curved or hooked like an eagle's beak: *an aquiline nose.* [Latin *aquilīnus*, from *aquila*, eagle.]

ar (âr, är) *n.* Var. of **are** (surface measure).

-ar. A suffix used to form adjectives meaning like, pertaining to, or of the nature of: **titular, polar.** [Middle English *ar, -er*, from Old French *-er*, from Latin *-āris*, alteration of *-ālis*, -AL.]

Ar The symbol for the element argon.

Ar·ab (ăr'əb) *n.* **1.** A native or inhabitant of Arabia. **2.** A member of a Semitic people of the Middle East and North Africa. **3.** Any of a nomadic people living in North African and Near Eastern desert regions; Bedouin. **4.** Any of a breed of swift, intelligent, graceful horses native to Arabia. —*adj.* Arabian.

ar·a·besque (ăr'ə-běsk') *n.* **1.** An ornamental design of interwoven flowers, leaves, or geometric forms. **2.** *Ballet.* A position in which the dancer stands on one leg with the other leg extended straight back. —*adj.* In the fashion of or formed as an arabesque. [French, from Italian *arabesco*, "made or done in the Arabic fashion."]

A·ra·bi·an (ə-rā'bē-ən) *adj.* Of or concerning Arabia or the Arabs; Arab. —*n.* **1.** A native or inhabitant of Arabia. **2.** A horse of a breed native to Arabia; Arab.

Ar·a·bic (ăr'ə-bĭk) *adj.* Of or pertaining to Arabia, the Arabs, their language, or their culture. —*n.* The Semitic language of the Arabs, now spoken in Arabia, Jordan, Syria, Iraq, Israel, Egypt, and parts of northern Africa.

Arabic numerals. The numerical symbols 1, 2, 3, 4, 5, 6, 7, 8, 9, and 0.

ar·a·ble (ăr'ə-bəl) *adj.* Fit for cultivation: *arable land.* [Middle English, from Old French, from Latin *arābilis*, from *arāre*, to plow.]

Ar·a·by (ăr'ə-bē) *n.* A literary name for Arabia.

a·rach·nid (ə-răk'nĭd) *n.* Any of various arthropods of the class Arachnida, such as a spider, scorpion, or tick, having four pairs of legs and a body divided into two segments. [From Greek *arakhnē*, spider.] —**a·rach'ni·dan** (-nə-dən) *adj. & n.*

a·rach·noid (ə-răk'noid') *adj.* **1.** Resembling a spider's web. **2.** Of or relating to the arachnids. **3.** Covered with or consisting of thin, soft, entangled hairs like those of a cobweb. —*n.* **1.** An arachnid. **2.** *Anat.* A delicate membrane of the spinal cord and brain, lying between the pia mater and dura mater.

a·rag·o·nite (ə-răg'ə-nīt', ăr'ə-gə-) *n.* An orthorhombic mineral form of crystalline calcium carbonate, dimorphous with calcite. [First found in *Aragon*, a region of northeastern Spain.]

Ar·a·ma·ic (ăr'ə-mā'ĭk) *n.* A Semitic language used in southwestern Asia after about 300 B.C. —**Ar·a·ma'ic** *adj.*

Ar·au·ca·ni·an (ăr'ô-kä'nē-ən) *n.* Also **A·rau·can** (ə-rô'kən). **1.** A South American Indian language family spoken in Chile and the western pampas of Argentina. **2.** An Indian of this linguistic stock. —**Ar'au·ca'ni·an** *adj.*

Ar·a·wa·kan (ăr'ə-wä'kən) *n., pl.* **Arawakan** or **-kans.** **1.** A South American Indian language family spoken in a wide area comprising the Amazon basin in Brazil, Venezuela, Colombia, the Guianas, Peru, Bolivia, and Paraguay. **2.** An Indian or an Indian people of this linguistic stock. —**Ar'a·wa'kan** *adj.*

ar·bi·ter (är′bĭ-tər) *n.* **1.** A person chosen or appointed to judge or decide a disputed issue; an arbitrator. **2.** Something or someone having the power to ordain or judge at will: *living in a world where science is the final arbiter; the arbiter of the fashion world.* [Middle English *arbitre*, from Old French, from Latin *arbiter*, judge.]

ar·bit·ra·ment (är-bĭt′rə-mənt) *n.* **1.** The act of arbitrating. **2.** The judgment or award of an arbiter.

ar·bi·trar·y (är′bĭ-trĕr′ē) *adj.* **1.** Based on whim or impulse, not on reason or law: *arbitrary trade regulations imposed by the authorities.* **2.** Using or based on absolute or dictatorial powers: *an arbitrary government; an arbitrary decree.* **3.** Not limited by law; absolute; despotic. [Middle English, from Latin *arbitrārius*, from *arbiter*, arbiter.] —**ar′bi·trar′i·ly** (-trâr′ə-lē) *adv.* —**ar′bi·trar′i·ness** *n.*

ar·bi·trate (är′bĭ-trāt′) *v.* **-trat·ed, -trat·ing.** —*tr.v.* **1.** To judge or decide as or in the manner of an arbitrator: *arbitrate the navigation rights.* **2.** To submit to settlement by arbitration: *agreed to arbitrate their quarrels.* —*intr.v.* **1.** To serve as an arbitrator. **2.** To submit a dispute to arbitration. —See Syns at **judge.**

ar·bi·tra·tion (är′bĭ-trā′shən) *n.* The process by which the parties to a dispute submit their differences to an impartial person or group for judgment or settlement.

ar·bi·tra·tor (är′bĭ-trā′tər) *n.* A person chosen to settle a dispute or controversy.

ar·bor¹ (är′bər) *n.* Also *Brit.* **ar·bour.** A shady garden shelter or bower, often made of rustic work or latticework on which vines, roses, etc., are grown. [Middle English *erber, herber,* garden, shady bower, from Old French *erbier, herbier,* herbage, plot of grass, from *herbe,* herb.]

ar·bor² (är′bər) *n.* **1.** An axis or shaft supporting a rotating part on a lathe. **2.** A bar for supporting cutting tools. **3.** A spindle of a wheel, as in watches and clocks. [Latin, tree.]

ar·bo·re·al (är-bôr′ē-əl, -bōr′-) *adj.* **1.** Pertaining to or like a tree. **2.** Living in trees: *arboreal animals.*

ar·bo·res·cent (är′bə-rĕs′ənt) *adj.* Having the form or characteristics of a tree; treelike. [Latin *arborēscere,* to grow to be a tree, from *arbor,* tree.] —**ar′bo·res′cence** *n.*

ar·bo·re·tum (är′bə-rē′təm) *n., pl.* **-tums** or **-ta** (-tə). A place for the scientific study and public exhibition of rare trees. [From Latin *arborētum,* a place grown with trees, from *arbor,* tree.]

ar·bor·vi·tae (är′bər-vī′tē) *n.* Also **ar·bor vi·tae.** Any of several evergreen shrubs and trees of the genus *Thuja,* with small, scalelike leaves, often planted in gardens. Also called **tree of life.** [New Latin, "tree of life."]

ar·bour (är′bər) *n. Brit.* Var. of **arbor** (bower).

ar·bu·tus (är-byoo′təs) *n.* **1.** Any of several broad-leaved evergreen trees of the genus *Arbutus,* with clusters of white or pinkish flowers. **2.** The **trailing arbutus.** [From Latin *arbūtus,* strawberry tree.]

arc (ärk) *n.* **1.** Anything shaped like a bow, curve, or arch. **2.** *Geom.* A segment of a curve. **3.** A bright discharge or streak produced when an electric current jumps across the gap between two electrodes separated by a gas. —*intr.v.* **arced** (ärkt) or **arcked, arc·ing** (är′kĭng) or **arck·ing.** To move in or form an arc. [Middle English *ark,* from Old English *arc,* from Latin *arcus,* bow, arc.]

ar·cade (är-kād′) *n.* **1.** *Archit.* **a.** A series of arches supported by columns, piers, or pillars. **b.** An arched, roofed building or part of a building. **2.** A roofed passageway or lane, esp. one with shops on either side. —*tr.v.* **-cad·ed, -cad·ing.** To provide with or form into an arcade or arcades. [French, from Italian *arcata,* from *arco,* arch, from Latin *arcus.*]

Ar·ca·di·a (är-kā′dē-ə) *n.* **1.** A region in ancient Greece regarded as an ideal of rural simplicity and contentment and often used as a literary setting. **2.** Often **arcadia.** Any similar region. —**Ar·ca′di·an** *adj. & n.*

ar·cane (är-kān′) *adj.* Known or understood only by a few; esoteric. [Latin *arcānus,* closed, secret, from *arca,* chest.]

ar·ca·num (är-kā′nəm) *n., pl.* **-na** (-nə) or **-nums.** **1.** A profound secret; mystery. **2.** The reputed great secret of nature that alchemists sought to find. **3.** An elixir. [Latin *arcānum,* a mystery, secret, from *arcānus,* ARCANE.]

arch¹ (ärch) *n.* **1.** *Archit.* **a.** A curved structure that spans an open space and supports a roadway, ceiling, or similar load. The downward thrust of the load over the open space

arch
A curved structure

arch
A monument

is transferred to the sides. **b.** A monument built in this form. **2.** Something curved like an arch: *the arch of the rainbow.* **3.** *Anat.* Any of various arch-shaped structures of the body, esp. in the foot. —*modifier: an arch bridge.* —*tr.v.* **1.** To supply with an arch. **2.** To cause to form an arch or similar curve: *arch one's eyebrows. The cat arched his back.* **3.** To span: *A rude bridge arched the flood.* —*intr.v.* To form an arch or archlike curve: *The bridge arched across the river.* [Middle English *arche,* from Old French, from Latin *arcus.*]

arch² (ärch) *adj.* **1.** Chief; principal: *the arch thief.* **2.** Mischievous: *an arch glance.* [From ARCH-.] —**arch′ly** *adv.* —**arch′ness** *n.*

arch-. A prefix meaning: **1.** Highest rank or chief status: **archduke. 2.** Ultimate of a kind: **archfiend.** [Middle English, from Old English *ærce-,* and Old French *arch(e)-,* both from Latin *arch(i)-,* from Greek *arkh(i)-,* from *arkhos,* chief, ruler, from *arkhein,* to begin, rule.]

-arch. A suffix meaning a ruler or leader: **matriarch.** [Middle English *-arche,* from Old French, from Late Latin *-archa,* from Latin *-archēs,* from Greek *-arkhēs,* from *arkhos,* ruler.]

archaeo- or **archeo-.** A prefix meaning ancient times or an early condition: **archaeopteryx.** [From Greek *arkhaios,* ancient, from *arkhē,* beginning, from *arkhein,* to begin.]

ar·chae·ol·o·gy or **ar·che·ol·o·gy** (är′kē-ŏl′ə-jē) *n.* **1.** The recovery by scientific methods of material evidence that remains from man's life and culture in past ages, such as graves, buildings, tools, and pottery. **2.** The detailed study of this evidence. [French *archéologie,* from Late Latin *archaeologia,* from Greek *arkhaiologia,* from *arkhaios* + -LOGY.] —**ar′chae·o·log′i·cal** (är′kē-ə-lŏj′ĭ-kəl) or **ar′chae·o·log′ic** *adj.* —**ar′chae·ol′o·gist** *n.*

ar·chae·op·ter·yx (är′kē-ŏp′tə-rĭks) *n.* An extinct primitive bird of the genus *Archaeopteryx,* of the Jurassic period, having lizardlike characteristics and representing a transitional form between reptiles and birds. [New Latin, "ancient bird," from ARCHAEO- + Greek *pterux,* bird, wing.]

Ar·chae·o·zo·ic (är′kē-ə-zō′ĭk) *adj. & n.* Var. of **Archeozoic.**

ar·cha·ic (är-kā′ĭk) *adj.* **1.** Of a very early, often primitive, period: *archaic sculpture; archaic fish.* **2.** No longer current; antiquated: *archaic laws.* **3.** In language, designating a term that was once common and continues to have a limited general use, but is now used only when it is intended to suggest an earlier style. [French *archaïque,* from Greek *arkhaikos,* from *arkhaios,* ancient, from *arkhē,* beginning, from *arkhein,* to begin.] —**ar·cha′i·cal·ly** *adv.*

ar·cha·ism (är′kē-ĭz′əm, -kā-) *n.* **1.** An archaic word, phrase, idiom, or expression. **2.** An archaic style, quality, or usage. —**ar′cha·ist** *n.* —**ar′cha·is′tic** *adj.*

arch·an·gel (ärk′ān′jəl) *n. Theol.* **1.** A celestial being next in rank above an angel. **2. archangels.** The eighth of the nine orders of angels.

arch·bish·op (ärch·bĭsh′əp) *n.* A bishop of the highest rank. —**arch·bish′op·ric** (ärch·bĭsh′ə-prĭk′) *n.*

arch·dea·con (ärch·dē′kən) *n.* A church official, chiefly of the Anglican Church, in charge of temporal and other affairs in a diocese. —**arch·dea′con·ate** (-kə-nĭt) *n.* —**arch·dea′con·ry** (-kən-rē) *n.* —**arch·dea′con·ship′** (-kən-shĭp′) *n.*

arch·di·o·cese (ärch·dī′ə-sĭs, -sēs′, -sēz′) *n.* The area under an archbishop's jurisdiction. —**arch′di·oc′e·san** (-ŏs′ĭ-sən) *adj.*

ă pat　　ā pay　　â care　　ä father　　ĕ pet　　ē be　　hw which　　ĭ pit　　ī tie　　î pier　　ŏ pot　　ō toe　　ô paw, for　　oi noise
oo took　　oo boot　　ou out　　th thin　　th this　　ŭ cut　　û urge　　zh vision　　ə about, item, edible, gallop, circus

arch·du·cal (ärch-d $\overline{oo}$ ′kəl, -dy $\overline{oo}$ ′-) *adj.* Of or pertaining to an archduke.

arch·duch·ess (ärch-dŭch′ĭs) *n.* **1.** The wife or widow of an archduke. **2.** A former royal princess of Austria.

arch·duke (ärch-d $\overline{oo}$ k′, -dy $\overline{oo}$ k′) *n.* A royal prince of Austria.

ar·che·go·ni·um (är′kĭ-gō′nē-əm) *n., pl.* **-ni·a** (-nē-ə). The multicellular female sex organ of mosses and related plants that produces a single egg. [From Greek *arkhegonos*, "of ancient descent," original.] —**ar′che·go′ni·al** *adj.*

arch·en·e·my (ärch-ĕn′ə-mē) *n., pl.* **-mies. 1.** A chief or principal enemy. **2. Archenemy.** The devil; Satan.

ar·chen·ter·on (är-kĕn′tə-rŏn′, -rən) *n.* The embryonic digestive tract, essentially a cavity in the gastrula. [From ARCH- + Greek *enteron*, intestine.] —**ar′chen·ter′ic** (är′-kĕn-tĕr′ĭk) *adj.*

archeo-. Var. of the prefix **archaeo-.**

ar·che·ol·o·gy (är′kē-ŏl′ə-jē) *n.* Var. of **archaeology.**

Ar·che·o·zo·ic (är′kē-ə-zō′ĭk). Also **Ar·chae·o·zo·ic.** —*adj.* Of, belonging to, or designating the earlier of two gen. arbitrary divisions of the Precambrian era. —*n.* The Archeozoic era. [ARCHEO- + -ZOIC.]

arch·er (är′chər) *n.* A person who shoots with a bow and arrow. [Middle English, from Old French *archier, archer,* ult. from Latin *arcus,* arch, bow.]

arch·er·y (är′chə-rē) *n.* **1.** The art, sport, or skill of shooting with a bow and arrows. **2.** A troop or body of archers.

archery

ar·che·type (är′kĭ-tīp′) *n.* An original model or type after which other similar things are patterned; a prototype. [Latin *archetypum,* from Greek *arkhetupos,* exemplary : ARCH- + *tupos,* mold, model.] —**ar′che·typ′al** (-tī′pəl) or **ar′che·typ′ic** (-tīp′ĭk) or **ar′che·typ′i·cal** *adj.* —**ar′che·typ′i·cal·ly** *adv.*

arch·fiend (ärch-fēnd′) *n.* **1.** A chief or foremost fiend. **2. the Archfiend.** The devil; Satan.

ar·chi·e·pis·co·pal (är′kē-ĭ-pĭs′kə-pəl) *adj.* Of or pertaining to an archbishop or an archbishopric. —**ar′chi·e·pis′co·pal·ly** *adv.*

ar·chi·pel·a·go (är′kə-pĕl′ə-gō′) *n., pl.* **-goes** or **-gos. 1.** A large group of islands. **2.** A sea in which there is a large group of islands. [Italian *Arcipelago,* "the chief sea," from ARCH- + Greek *pelagos,* sea.] —**ar′chi·pe·lag′ic** (-pə-lăj′ĭk) *adj.*

ar·chi·tect (är′kĭ-tĕkt′) *n.* **1.** A person who designs and supervises the construction of buildings or other large structures. **2.** Any planner or deviser: *"Chief architect and plotter of these woes"* (Shakespeare). [Old French *architecte,* from Latin *architectus, architectōn,* from Greek *arkhitektōn,* master builder : ARCH- + *tektōn,* carpenter, craftsman.]

ar·chi·tec·ton·ic (är′kĭ-tĕk-tŏn′ĭk) or **ar·chi·tec·ton·i·cal** (-ĭ-kəl). *adj.* **1.** Of or pertaining to architecture or design. **2.** Having qualities like architecture; designed and structured. —**ar′chi·tec·ton′i·cal·ly** *adv.*

ar·chi·tec·ton·ics (är′kĭ-tĕk-tŏn′ĭks) *n. (used with a sing. verb).* **1.** The science of architecture. **2.** Structural design, as in a musical work.

ar·chi·tec·ture (är′kĭ-tĕk′chər) *n.* **1.** The art and science of designing and erecting buildings. **2.** A structure or structures in general. **3.** A style and method of design and construction: *Byzantine architecture.* —**ar′chi·tec′tur·al** *adj.* —**ar′chi·tec′tur·al·ly** *adv.*

ar·chi·trave (är′kĭ-trāv′) *n. Archit.* **1.** The lowermost part of an entablature that rests directly on top of a column in classical architecture. Also called **epistyle. 2.** The molding around a door or window. [Old French, from Old Italian, "chief beam" : ARCH- + *trave,* beam, from Latin *trabs.*]

ar·chives (är′kīvz′) *pl.n.* **1.** An organized body of records pertaining to an organization or institution. **2.** A place where such records are kept. [French, orig. sing. *archive,* from Late Latin *archīum, archīvum,* from Greek *arkheion,* public office, from *arkhē,* beginning, hence first place, from *arkhein,* to begin.]

ar·chi·vist (är′kə-vĭst, -kī′-) *n.* A person who is in charge of archives; a custodian of archives.

arch·way (ärch′wā′) *n.* **1.** A passageway under an arch. **2.** An arch that covers or encloses an entrance or passageway.

-archy. A suffix meaning rule or government: **oligarchy.** [Middle English *-archie,* from Old French, from Latin *-archia,* from Greek *-arkhia,* from *-arkhēs,* -ARCH.]

arc lamp. An electric lamp in which light is produced by an electric arc that crosses between electrodes separated by a gas. Also called **arc light.**

arc·tic (ärk′tĭk, är′tĭk) *adj.* **1.** Extremely cold; frigid. **2. Arctic.** Of the region lying north of the Arctic Circle. —See Syns at **frigid.** [Middle English *artik,* from Medieval Latin *articus,* from Latin *arcticus,* from Greek *arktikos,* from *arktos,* bear, Ursa Major.]

Arctic Circle. The parallel of latitude 66 degrees 33 minutes north; the boundary between the North Temperate and North Frigid zones.

Arc·tu·rus (ärk-t $\overline{oo}$ r′əs, -ty $\overline{oo}$ r′-) *n.* The brightest star in the constellation Boötes.

-ard or **-art.** A suffix meaning a person who does something to excess: **drunkard, braggart.** [Middle English, from Old French *-ard, -art.*]

ar·dent (är′dnt) *adj.* Expressing or characterized by warmth of passion, emotion, desire, etc.; passionate: *an ardent lover.* [Middle English *ardaunt,* from Old French *ardant,* from Latin *ardēre,* to burn.] —**ar′den·cy** (är′dn-sē) or **ar′dent·ness** *n.* —**ar′dent·ly** *adv.*

ar·dor (är′dər) *n.* Also *Brit.* **ar·dour.** Intensity of emotion, passion, desire, etc.: *a lover's ardor; religious ardor.* —See Syns at **passion.** [Middle English *ardour,* from Old French, from Latin *ardor,* from *ardēre,* to burn.]

ar·du·ous (är′j $\overline{oo}$ -əs) *adj.* **1.** Demanding great care, effort, or labor; strenuous: *"the arduous work of preparing a Dictionary of the English Language"* (Thomas Babington Macaulay). **2.** Testing severely the powers of endurance; full of hardships: *a long, arduous, and exhausting war.* **3.** Hard to climb or surmount; steep: *an arduous path; an arduous assignment.* —See Syns at **burdensome.** [Latin *arduus.*] —**ar′du·ous·ly** *adv.* —**ar′du·ous·ness** *n.*

are[1] (är). **1.** Second person singular present tense of **be. 2.** First, second, and third person plural present tense of **be.**

are[2] (âr, är) *n.* Also **ar** (är). *Abbr.* **a, a.** A metric unit of area equal to 100 square meters. [French, from Latin *ārea,* AREA.]

ar·e·a (âr′ē-ə) *n.* **1.** A section or region, as of land: *a farming area; the New York area.* **2.** A surface, esp. a part of the earth's surface: *a landing area; mountainous areas.* **3.** A distinct part or section, as of a building, set aside for a specific function: *an area for business and an area for exercise.* **4.** The range or scope of anything: *the area of finance.* **5.** The measure of a planar region or of the surface of a solid. [Latin *ārea,* open field.] —**ar′e·al** *adj.*

Area Code. Often **area code.** A three-digit number assigned to a telephone area, as in the United States and Canada, used when placing a call from one such area to another.

ar·e·a·way (âr′ē-ə-wā′) *n.* **1.** A small sunken area allowing access to basement doors or light and air to basement windows. **2.** A passageway between buildings.

a·re·na (ə-rē′nə) *n.* **1.** The area in the center of an ancient Roman amphitheater where contests and other spectacles were held. **2.** A modern auditorium for sports events. **3.** A sphere or field of conflict, interest, or activity: *the political arena.* [Latin *(h)arēna,* sand, arena covered with sand.]

arena theater. A theater in which the stage is at the center of the auditorium, surrounded by seats, and without a proscenium. Also called **theater-in-the-round.**

aren't (ärnt, är′ənt). **1.** Are not: *They aren't there.* **2.** Am not. Used in questions: *I'm properly dressed for school, aren't I?*

Usage: Aren't standing for *am not* (in the phrase *aren't I*) is orig. a British variant of *ain't*. Unlike *ain't*, it is now acceptable esp. when used in speech or informal writing.

a·re·o·la (ə-rē′ə-lə) *n., pl.* **-lae** (-lē′) or **-las.** Also **ar·e·ole** (âr′ē-ōl′). **1.** *Biol.* A small space or interstice, such as an area bounded by small veins in a leaf or an insect's wing. **2.** *Anat.* A small, dark-colored area around a center portion, as around a nipple or part of the iris of the eye. [From Latin *āreola*, dim. of *ārea*, open place, AREA.] —**a·re′o·lar** *adj.*

Ar·es (âr′ēz′) *n. Gk. Myth.* The god of war, identified with the Roman god Mars.

ar·gent (är′jənt) *n. Archaic & Poet.* Silver or anything resembling it. —*adj. Poet.* Of silver. [Middle English, from Old French, from Latin *argentum*.]

Ar·go (är′gō′) *n. Gk. Myth.* The ship in which Jason sailed in search of the Golden Fleece.

ar·gon (är′gŏn′) *n. Symbol* **Ar** A colorless, odorless, inert gaseous element constituting approximately one per cent of the earth's atmosphere, from which it is commercially obtained by fractionation for use in electric lamps, fluorescent tubes, radio vacuum tubes, and as an inert gas shield in arc welding. Atomic number 18, atomic weight 39.94, melting point –189.4°C, boiling point –185.9°C. [Greek, neut. of *argos*, inert, "not working" : *a-*, without + *ergon*, work.]

Ar·go·naut (är′gə-nôt′) *n.* **1.** *Gk. Myth.* Any of the men who sailed with Jason on the *Argo* in search of the Golden Fleece. **3.** *argonaut.* A saltwater mollusk, the **paper nautilus.**

ar·go·sy (är′gə-sē) *n., pl.* **-sies. 1.** A large merchant ship. **2.** A fleet of such ships. [Earlier *argose*, from Italian *ragusea*, vessel of *Ragusa*, formerly Dubrovnik, Yugoslavia.]

ar·got (är′gō, -gət) *n.* A specialized vocabulary or set of idioms used by a particular class or group, esp. the jargon of the underworld. [French.]

ar·gue (är′gyōō) *v.* **-gued, -gu·ing.** —*tr.v.* **1.** To put forth reasons for or against (an opinion, a proposal, etc.); debate: *The lawyer argued his case.* **2.** To prove or attempt to prove by reasoning; maintain in argument; contend. **3.** To give evidence of; indicate: *"Similarities cannot always be used to argue descent"* (Isaac Asimov). **4.** To persuade or influence, as by presenting reasons: *He argued me into going.* —*intr.v.* **1.** To put forth reasons for or against an opinion, procedure, proposal, etc.: *The senator argued in favor of the bill.* **2.** To engage in a quarrel; to dispute: *argued with his friends.* [Middle English *arguen*, from Old French *arguer*, to blame, argue against, from Latin *arguere*, to assert, prove.] —**ar′gu·a·ble** *adj.* —**ar′gu·a·bly** *adv.* —**ar′gu·er** *n.*

Syns: argue, bicker, contend, dispute, fight, hassle (Slang), quarrel, quibble, squabble, tiff, wrangle *v. Core meaning:* To engage in a verbal exchange expressing conflict of opinions (*The children argue constantly over toys.*).

ar·gu·ment (är′gyə-mənt) *n.* **1.** A discussion of differing points of view; a debate. **2.** A quarrel or dispute. **3. a.** A course of reasoning aimed at demonstrating the truth or falsehood of something. **b.** A fact or statement offered as proof or evidence. **4.** A summary or short statement of the plot or subject of a literary work.

ar·gu·men·ta·tion (är′gyə-měn-tā′shən) *n.* **1.** The presentation and elaboration of an argument. **2.** Deductive reasoning in debate. **3.** A debate.

ar·gu·men·ta·tive (är′gyə-měn′tə-tĭv) *adj.* **1.** Given to arguing; disputatious. **2.** Of or characterized by argument: *an argumentative discourse.* —**ar′gu·men′ta·tive·ly** *adv.* —**ar′gu·men′ta·tive·ness** *n.*

Ar·gus (är′gəs) *n. Gk. Myth.* A giant with a hundred eyes who was slain by Hermes.

Ar·gus-eyed (är′gəs-īd′) *adj.* Extremely observant; vigilant.

ar·gyle or **ar·gyll** (är′gīl′) *n.* Also **Ar·gyle** or **Ar·gyll. 1.** A knitting pattern of varicolored, diamond-shaped areas on a solid color background. **2.** A sock knit in such a pattern. —*modifier:* *argyle mittens.* [Orig. the pattern on the tartan of the Scottish clan Campbell of *Argyle* or *Argyll*.]

a·ri·a (är′ē-ə) *n. Mus.* **1.** An air; melody. **2.** A solo vocal piece with instrumental accompaniment, as in an opera or oratorio. [Italian, melody, "(atmospheric) air," from Latin *āēr*, air.]

Ar·i·ad·ne (ăr′ē-ăd′nē) *n. Gk. Myth.* The daughter of King Minos who gave Theseus the thread with which to find his way out of the Minotaur's labyrinth.

Ar·i·an[1] (ăr′ē-ən, âr′-) *adj.* Pertaining to Arianism. —*n.* A believer in Arianism.

Ar·i·an[2] (ăr′ē-ən, âr′-) *n. & adj.* Var. of **Aryan.**

-arian. A suffix meaning: **1.** Sect: **Unitarian. 2.** A belief: **vegetarian.** [Latin *-ārius*, -ARY + -AN.]

Ar·i·an·ism (ăr′ē-ə-nĭz′əm, âr′-) *n. Theol.* The doctrines of Arius, a Greek Christian theologian condemned as a heretic, who denied that Jesus was of the same substance as God and held instead that he was only the highest of created beings.

ar·id (ăr′ĭd) *adj.* **1.** Lacking moisture or rainfall; parched; dry: *an arid climate.* **2.** Lacking interest or feeling; lifeless; dull: *a long, arid story.* [French *aride*, from Latin *āridus*, from *ārēre*, to be dry or parched.] —**a·rid′i·ty** (ə-rĭd′ĭ-tē) or **ar′id·ness** *n.*

Ar·ies (âr′ēz′, âr′ē-ēz′) *n.* **1.** A constellation in the Northern Hemisphere. **2.** The first sign of the **zodiac.**

a·right (ə-rīt′) *adv.* In the right or proper way; properly; correctly. [Middle English *aright*, from Old English *ariht, on riht* : A- (on) + *riht*, right (noun).]

ar·il (ăr′əl) *n.* An outer covering of some seeds that is often fleshy or brightly colored, as in the bittersweet or nutmeg. [From Medieval Latin *arillus*, grape seed.]

a·rise (ə-rīz′) *intr.v.* **a·rose** (ə-rōz′), **a·ris·en** (ə-rĭz′ən), **a·ris·ing. 1.** To get up, as from sitting or sleeping. **2.** To move upward; ascend: *A mist arose from the lake.* **3.** To come into being; originate: *Myths arose as an attempt to explain natural occurrences.* **4.** To result or proceed: *The situation arose from some temporary defect.* —See Syns at **begin.** [Middle English *arisen*, from Old English *ārīsan.*]

a·ris·toc·ra·cy (ăr′ĭ-stŏk′rə-sē) *n., pl.* **-cies. 1.** A social class based on inherited wealth, status, and sometimes titles. **2.** A government controlled by such a class. **3.** Any group or class considered to be superior: *the aristocracy of Wall Street bankers.* [Old French *aristocratie*, from Late Latin *aristocratia*, from Greek *aristokratia*, "rule by the best" : *aristos*, best + -CRACY.]

a·ris·to·crat (ə-rĭs′tə-krăt′, ăr′ĭs-) *n.* **1.** A member of the nobility or aristocracy. **2.** A person having the tastes, manners, and other characteristics of an upper class. **3.** A person who favors government by the aristocracy. —**a·ris′to·crat′ic** or **a·ris′to·crat′i·cal** *adj.* —**a·ris′to·crat′i·cal·ly** *adv.*

Ar·is·to·te·li·an (ăr′ĭs-tə-tē′lē-ən, -tēl′yən) *adj.* Of or pertaining to Aristotle or his philosophy, in which knowledge is based on experience and observation rather than on abstract theory or ideals. —*n.* A follower of Aristotle or his teachings. —**Ar′is·to·te′li·an·ism** *n.*

Aristotelian logic. Aristotle's deductive method of logic, esp. the theory of the syllogism.

a·rith·me·tic (ə-rĭth′mə-tĭk) *n.* **1.** The study of the properties of and relations between numbers on which the operations of addition, subtraction, multiplication, division, raising to powers, and extracting roots are performed, and also the study of the properties of the operations themselves. **2.** Computation using these operations: *Bookkeeping can require a lot of arithmetic.* —*adj.* **ar·ith·met·ic** (ăr′ĭth-mĕt′ĭk) or **ar·ith·met·i·cal** (-ĭ-kəl). Of or pertaining to

Argus

ark

armadillo

armoire

armor

arithmetic: *arithmetic procedures; arithmetic computations.* [Middle English *arithmet(r)ik*, from Old French *ar(i)smetique*, from Latin *arithmética*, from Greek *arithmētikē (tekhnē)*, "(the art) of counting," from *arithmein*, to count, from *arithmos*, number.] —**ar′ith·met′i·cal·ly** *adv.*

a·rith·me·ti·cian (ə-rĭth′mə-tĭsh′ən) *n.* An expert in arithmetic.

ar·ith·met·ic mean (ăr′ĭth-mĕt′ĭk). The number obtained by adding all the members of a set and dividing the result by the number of members in the set. If the set A contains just 4, 18, 2, and 8, then the arithmetic mean of A is (4 + 18 + 2 + 8) ÷ 4 = 8. Also called **average** and **mean**.

arithmetic progression. A sequence of numbers such as 1, 3, 5, 7, 9 or 3, 7, 11, 15 in which the difference between any successive pair of numbers is the same.

-arium. A suffix indicating a place or housing for: **terrarium.** [Latin, from the neuter of *-ārius*, -ARY.]

ark (ärk) *n.* **1.** In the Old Testament, the ship built by Noah for survival during the Flood. **2. Ark.** The chest containing the Ten Commandments on stone tablets, carried by the Hebrews during their wanderings. Also called **Ark of the Covenant. 3. Holy Ark.** A cabinet in a synagogue in which the scrolls of the Torah are kept. **4.** Any large, commodious boat or vehicle. [Middle English *ark*, from Old English *arc, aerc, earc*, from Latin *arca*, chest, box, coffer.]

arm[1] (ärm) *n.* **1. a.** Either of the upper limbs of the human body that connects the hand and wrist to the shoulder. **b.** The similar forelimb of an animal, as of an ape or a bear. **2.** A part that branches or seems to branch from a main body as an arm: *an arm of the sea; the arm of a starfish.* **3.** A part designed to cover or support the human arm: *the arm of a dress; the arm of a chair.* **4.** An administrative or functional branch, as of an organization. **5.** Authority or effect that extends or seems to extend from a main source: *the arm of the law.* —**idioms. arm in arm.** With the arm of one person linked in the arm of another. **at arm's length.** At a distance; not on friendly or intimate terms: *He keeps his fellow workers at arm's length.* **twist (someone's) arm.** To force or press (someone) to do as one wishes. **with open arms.** In a very friendly manner. [Middle English *arm*, from Old English *arm, earm*.]

arm[2] (ärm) *n.* **1. arms.** Weapons, esp. those used in warfare or defense. **2.** A weapon. Used mainly in combination with another word: *a firearm such as a pistol or rifle.* **3.** A branch of a military force, such as the infantry, cavalry, or air corps. —*intr.v.* **1.** To supply or equip oneself with weapons or other means of defense. **2.** To prepare oneself for or as if for warfare. —*tr.v.* **1.** To equip with weapons. **2.** To prepare for war; fortify. **3.** To provide with anything that strengthens, increases efficiency, etc. **4.** To prepare (a bomb, for example) for detonation, as by releasing a safety device. —**armed** *adj.: an armed police escort.* —**idiom. up in arms.** Aroused and ready to fight. [Back-formation from ARMS (pl.).] —**arm′er** *n.*

ar·ma·da (är-mä′də, -mā′-) *n.* A fleet of warships. [Spanish, from Medieval Latin *armāta*, army, fleet, from Latin *armāre*, to arm, from *arma*, arms.]

ar·ma·dil·lo (är′mə-dĭl′ō) *n., pl.* **-los.** Any of several omnivorous, burrowing mammals of the family Dasypodidae, of southern North America and Central America, with a covering of jointed, armorlike, bony plates. [Spanish, from *armado*, armed.]

Ar·ma·ged·don (är′mə-gĕd′n) *n.* **1.** The scene of a final bat-

tle between the forces of good and evil, prophesied in the Bible to occur at the end of the world. **2.** Any decisive conflict.

ar·ma·ment (är′mə-mənt) *n.* **1.** The weapons and supplies of war with which a military unit is equipped. **2.** Often **armaments.** All the military forces and war equipment of a country. **3.** A military force equipped for war. **4.** The process of arming for war. [From Latin *armāmenta*, implements, from *arma*, arms.]

ar·ma·ture (är′mə-chŏŏr, -chər) *n.* **1.** *Elect.* **a.** The rotating part of a motor or generator consisting essentially of copper wire wound around an iron core. **b.** The moving part of an electromagnetic device such as a relay, buzzer, or loudspeaker. **c.** A piece of soft iron connecting the poles of a magnet. **2.** *Biol.* The protective covering or structure of an animal or plant. **3.** Any protective covering; armor. **4.** A framework serving as a supporting core for clay sculpture. [Latin *armātūra*, equipment, from *armāre*, to arm.]

arm·chair (ärm′châr′) *n.* A chair with supports on the sides for the arms or elbows. —*adj.* Remote from the field of action; not involved: *an armchair quarterback.*

armed forces (ärmd). The military forces of a country.

Ar·me·ni·an (är-mē′nē-ən, -mēn′yən) *n.* **1.** A native or inhabitant of Armenia. **2.** The Indo-European language of the Armenians. —*adj.* Of Armenia, the Armenians, their culture, or their language.

arm·ful (ärm′fŏŏl′) *n., pl.* **-fuls.** As much as one or both arms can hold.

arm·hole (ärm′hōl′) *n.* An opening for the arm in a garment or the place where a sleeve is attached.

ar·mi·stice (är′mĭ-stĭs) *n.* A temporary suspension of hostilities between warring countries by agreement; a truce. [French, from New Latin *armistitium*, from Latin *arma*, ARMS + *-stitium*, "stoppage."]

Armistice Day. Nov. 11, **Veterans' Day.**

arm·let (ärm′lĭt) *n.* **1.** A band worn around the upper arm for ornament or identification. **2.** A small arm, as of the sea.

ar·moire (ärm-wär′, är′mər) *n.* A large ornate movable cabinet or wardrobe. [Old French, var. of *armaire*, from Latin *armārium*, closet, from *arma*, ARMS.]

ar·mor (är′mər) *n.* Also *Brit.* **ar·mour. 1.** A defensive covering, such as chain mail, formerly worn in warfare to protect the body against weapons. **2.** Any tough protective covering, such as the bony scales or plates covering certain animals. **3.** Anything that provides protection; a safeguard: *the armor of truth.* **4.** A protective metal covering as used on tanks, battleships, etc. **5.** The armored vehicles of an army. —*tr.v.* To cover with armor: *armor a warship.* [Middle English *armure*, from Old French, from Latin *armātūra*, equipment, from *armāre*, to arm.]

ar·mored (är′mərd) *adj.* **1.** Covered with or having armor: *armored vehicles.* **2.** Equipped with armored vehicles, as an army division.

ar·mor·er (är′mər-ər) *n.* **1.** A person who makes or repairs armor. **2.** A manufacturer of weapons, esp. firearms. **3.** *Mil.* An enlisted man in charge of maintenance and repair of the small arms of his unit.

ar·mo·ri·al (är-môr′ē-əl, -mōr′-) *adj.* Of or pertaining to heraldry or coats of arms. —*n.* A book or treatise on heraldry.

ar·mor·y (är′mə-rē) *n., pl.* **-ies. 1.** A storehouse for military weapons; an arsenal. **2.** A building that serves as head-quarters and often as a training center for military reserve personnel. **3.** An arms factory.

ar·mour (är′mər) *n. & v. Brit.* Var. of **armor.**

arm·pit (ärm′pĭt′) *n.* The hollow under the arm at the shoulder.

arm·rest (ärm′rĕst′) *n.* A support for the arm, as on the inner surface of the door of a vehicle.

arms (ärmz) *pl.n.* **1.** Weapons. **2.** Warfare. **3.** Heraldic bearings. **4.** Insignia, as of a state, official, family, or organization. [Middle English *armes,* from Old French, from Latin *arma,* weapons, tools.]

ar·my (är′mē) *n., pl.* **-mies. 1.** A large body of people organized and trained for warfare on land. **2.** Often **Army.** The entire military land forces of a country. **3.** Often **Army.** The largest tactical and administrative unit in a country's army: *The general commanded the Fifth Army.* **4.** Any large group of people organized for a specific cause. **5.** A large multitude, as of people or animals: *an army of shoppers.* **—modifier:** *an army officer.* [Middle English *armee,* from Old French, from Medieval Latin *armāta,* army, fleet, armada.]

army ant. Any of various chiefly tropical New World voracious ants of the subfamily Dorylinae that form large colonies and move from place to place. Also called **legionary ant.**

ar·ni·ca (är′nĭ-kə) *n.* **1.** Any of various plants of the genus *Arnica,* with bright-yellow, rayed flowers. **2.** A tincture of the dried flower heads of *A. montana,* used for sprains and bruises. [New Latin *Arnica* (orig. unknown).]

a·ro·ma (ə-rō′mə) *n.* A pleasant odor, characteristic of a particular plant, spice, or food: *the aroma of freshly ground coffee.* [Latin *arōma,* from Greek, aromatic herb or spice.]

ar·o·mat·ic (ăr′ə-măt′ĭk) *adj.* **1.** Having an aroma; fragrant, sweet-smelling, or spicy: *aromatic mint leaves.* **2.** *Chem.* Of, pertaining to, or containing the six-carbon ring characteristic of the benzene series and related organic groups. **—n.** An aromatic plant or substance. **—ar′o·mat′i·cal·ly** *adv.*

a·rose (ə-rōz′) *v.* Past tense of **arise.**

a·round (ə-round′) *prep.* **1.** Near in time to; close to: *around the year 1450.* **2.** All about; all over in: *The reporter looked around the room.* Also used adverbially: *Come up to the shop and I'll take you around.* **3.** In a circle surrounding: *Soon they were whirling around the tree trunk.* Also used adverbially: *The workmen gathered around to get paid off.* **4.** In a group or groups surrounding: *the Indian tribes around the Great Lakes.* **5.** Round about so as to enclose: *Vines had grown up around the lower branches.* **6.** On or to the farther side of: *just around the corner.* Also used adverbially: *After a month off Cape Horn, they finally got around.* **—adv.** About so as to face in the reverse direction: *The horses were turned around double-quick.* **—adj.** Available: *I'll be around when you need me.* **—idioms. get around.** *Informal.* To have wide knowledge of worldly matters. **get around to.** *Informal.* To find time or occasion to give one's attention to. [Middle English : A- (on) + ROUND (n.).]

a·rouse (ə-rouz′) *v.* **a·roused, a·rous·ing. —tr.v. 1.** To awaken from or as if from sleep. **2.** To stir up; stimulate; excite: *arouse strikers to violence.* **—intr.v.** To wake up; awaken. **—See** Syns at **provoke.** [A- (intensive) + ROUSE.] **—a·rous′al** *n.* **—a·rous′er** *n.*

ar·peg·gi·o (är-pĕj′ē-ō′, -pĕj′ō) *n., pl.* **-os. 1.** The playing or singing of a chord in rapid succession rather than all at once. **2.** A chord played or sung in this manner. [Italian, "chord played as on a harp," from *arpeggiare,* to play the harp, from *arpa,* harp.]

ar·que·bus (är′kə-bəs, -kwə-) *n.* Var. of **harquebus.**

ar·raign (ə-rān′) *tr.v.* **1.** *Law.* To summon before a court to answer to an indictment. **2.** To accuse; denounce: *"Johnson arraigned the modern politics of this country as entirely devoid of all principle"* (James Boswell). [Middle English *arreinen,* from Old French *araisnier* : Latin *ad-,* to + *ratiō,* reason, from *rērī,* to think, reckon.] **—ar·raign′ment** *n.*

ar·range (ə-rānj′) *v.* **-ranged, -rang·ing. —tr.v. 1.** To put into a specific order or relation; dispose: *Arrange these*

words alphabetically. **2.** To plan for: *arrange a picnic.* **3.** To agree about; settle: *"It has been arranged for him by his family to marry a girl of his own class"* (Edmund Wilson). **4.** To reset (music) for other instruments or voices or for another style of performance. **—intr.v. 1.** To come to an agreement: *We arranged with Ellen to babysit.* **2.** To make preparations; to plan: *arrange for milk to be delivered.* [Middle English *arengen,* from Old French *arangier* : *a-,* to + *rengier,* to put in a line, from *renc, reng,* line, row.] **—ar·rang′er** *n.*

ar·range·ment (ə-rānj′mənt) *n.* **1.** The act or process of arranging: *Arrangement of flowers is an intricate art.* **2.** The condition, manner, or result of being arranged: *an alphabetical arrangement of words.* **3.** A collection or set of things that have been arranged: *a flower arrangement.* **4. arrangements.** Plans or preparations: *make arrangements for a vacation.* **5.** An agreement; settlement; disposition. **6. a.** A version of a musical composition that differs from the original in style, difficulty, or use of performers: *a jazz arrangement of a Bach fugue.* **b.** A composition so arranged.

ar·rant (ăr′ənt) *adj.* Thoroughgoing; out-and-out. **—See** Syns at **utter.** [Var. of ERRANT.] **—ar′rant·ly** *adv.*

ar·ray (ə-rā′) *tr.v.* **1.** To arrange or draw up, as troops in battle order. **2.** To dress up in fine clothes; adorn: *She was splendidly arrayed in red velvet.* **—n. 1.** An orderly arrangement, esp. of troops ready for battle. **2.** An impressive display or collection: *a formidable array of talent; "a heathenish array of monstrous clubs and spears"* (Herman Melville). **3.** Splendid attire; finery: *a princess clad in fine array.* **4.** *Math.* **a.** A rectangular arrangement of quantities in rows and columns, as in a matrix. **b.** Numerical data linearly ordered by magnitude. [Middle English *arayen, arrayen,* from Old French *areer, arayer.*]

ar·rear·age (ə-rîr′ĭj) *n.* **1.** The condition of being in arrears. **2.** An amount owed in payment.

ar·rears (ə-rîrz′) *pl.n.* **1.** Unpaid or overdue debts: *You have arrears of $23.00.* **2.** The condition of being behind in fulfilling obligations or payments: *in arrears.* [Middle English *ar(r)ere,* behind, from Old French *arriere, arrere,* from Late Latin *ad retrō,* backward : *ad-,* toward + *retrō,* backward.]

ar·rest (ə-rĕst′) *tr.v.* **1.** To prevent the motion, progress, growth, or spread of; stop or check: *arrest floodwaters with sandbags.* **2.** To seize and hold under authority of the law. **3.** To attract and hold briefly; engage: *The first chapter arrested the reader's attention.* **—n. 1.** The act of arresting or the condition of being arrested. **2.** A device for arresting motion, esp. of a moving part. **—idiom. under arrest.** Held in legal custody. [Middle English *aresten,* from Old French *arester* : Latin *ad-,* to + *restāre,* to stay behind, rest.] **—ar·rest′er** or **ar·res′tor** *n.*

   Syns: **arrest, apprehend, bust** (*Informal*), **collar** (*Informal*), **detain, nab** (*Slang*), **pick up, pinch** (*Slang*), **run in, seize** *v.* Core meaning: To take into custody as a prisoner (*was arrested for grand auto theft*).

ar·rest·ing (ə-rĕs′tĭng) *adj.* Capturing and holding the attention; striking: *an arresting display of courage.* **—ar·rest′ing·ly** *adv.*

ar·ri·val (ə-rī′vəl) *n.* **1.** The act of arriving: *the arrival of the general at the airport.* **2.** Someone or something that arrives or has arrived: *many new arrivals at the hotel.*

ar·rive (ə-rīv′) *intr.v.* **-rived, -riv·ing. 1.** To reach a destination; come to a particular place: *The train arrived on time.* **2.** To reach a goal or objective: *They arrived at an understanding.* **3.** To come finally or after a delay: *The day of crisis has arrived.* **4.** To achieve success or recognition: *a young singer who has truly arrived.* [Middle English *ariven,* from Old French *ariver.*]

ar·ro·gance (ăr′ə-gəns) *n.* The quality or condition of being arrogant; insolent pride; haughtiness.

ar·ro·gant (ăr′ə-gənt) *adj.* Excessively and unpleasantly self-important, as in disregarding all other opinions but one's own; haughty; conceited: *arrogant boasts.* [Middle English, from Latin *arrogāns,* pres. part. of *arrogāre,* ARROGATE.] **—ar′ro·gant·ly** *adv.*

   Syns: **arrogant, disdainful, haughty, insolent, lordly, overbearing, presumptuous, proud, supercilious, superior** *adj.* Core meaning: Overly convinced of one's own superiority and importance (*an arrogant person who looked down on others*).

ar·ro·gate (ăr′ə-gāt′) *tr.v.* **-gat·ed, -gat·ing. 1.** To take, claim, or assume without right: *The governor arrogated the powers of the legislature.* **2.** To attribute to another without reason: *arrogate ulterior motives to a rival.* [Latin *arrogāre*, to claim for oneself : *ad-*, to + *rogāre*, to ask.] **—ar′ro·ga′tion** *n.* **—ar′ro·ga′tive** *adj.* **—ar′ro·ga′tor** *n.*

ar·row (ăr′ō) *n.* **1.** A straight, thin shaft that is shot from a bow and usu. made of light wood, with a pointed head at one end and feathers to steady its flight at the other. **2.** Anything similar in shape, as a sign or mark used to indicate direction. [Middle English *arewe, arwe,* from Old English *arwe, earh.*]

ar·row·head (ăr′ō-hĕd′) *n.* **1.** The pointed, removable striking tip of an arrow. **2.** Something shaped like an arrowhead, such as a mark indicating a limit on a drawing. **3.** Any aquatic or marsh plant of the genus *Sagittaria,* with arrowhead-shaped leaves and white flowers.

ar·row·root (ăr′ō-rōōt′, -rŏŏt′) *n.* **1.** A tropical American plant, *Maranta arundinacea,* with roots that yield an edible starch. **2.** The starch from this plant and from certain plants of the genera *Manihot, Curcuma,* and *Tacca.* [The root was used by the American Indians to absorb poison from arrow wounds.]

arrow worm. Any of various small, slender saltwater worms of the phylum Chaetognatha, with prehensile bristles on each side of the mouth.

ar·roy·o (ə-roi′ō) *n., pl.* **-os.** Southwestern U.S. **1.** A deep gully cut by an intermittent stream; a dry gulch. **2.** A small stream or creek. [Spanish, ult. from Latin *arrugia,* mineshaft.]

ar·se·nal (ăr′sə-nəl) *n.* **1.** A building or place for the storage, manufacture, or repair of arms and ammunition. **2.** A source of supply for arms and other munitions: *"We must be the great arsenal of democracy"* (F.D. Roosevelt). **3.** A stock of weapons. [Italian *arsenale, arzanale,* orig., naval dockyard, from Arabic *dār-aṣ-ṣinā′ah.*]

ar·se·nate (ăr′sə-nĭt, -nāt′) *n.* A salt or ester of arsenic acid.

ar·se·nic (ăr′sə-nĭk) *n.* **1.** *Symbol* **As** A highly poisonous metallic element that has three allotropic forms, yellow, black, or gray, of which the brittle, crystalline gray is the most common. Arsenic and its compounds are used in insecticides, weed killers, solid-state doping agents, and various alloys. Atomic number 33, atomic weight 74.922, valence 3 or 5. Gray arsenic melts at 817°C (at 28 atm pressure), sublimes at 613°C, and has a specific gravity of 5.73. **2. Arsenic trioxide. —***adj.* **ar·sen·ic** (ăr-sĕn′ĭk). Of or containing arsenic, esp. with valence 5. [Middle English, from Old French, from Latin *arsenicum,* from Greek *arsenikon, arrhenikon,* yellow substances, alteration of Syriac *zarnīkā.*]

ar·sen·i·cal (ăr-sĕn′ĭ-kəl) *adj.* Of or containing arsenic. **—***n.* A drug or preparation containing arsenic.

ar·son (ăr′sən) *n.* The crime of intentionally setting fire to buildings or other property. [Norman French, from Old French, from Medieval Latin *arsiō,* act of burning, from Latin *ardēre,* to burn.] **—ar′son·ist** *n.*

art¹ (ärt) *n.* **1.** The work of man in imitating, changing, or counteracting nature: *The beauty of this park owes more to art than to nature.* **2. a.** Painting, sculpture, poetry, music, or other activities that involve the creation of what is considered beautiful: *the fine arts; a work of art.* **b.** The study of these activities: *I took art in school.* **c.** A work or works resulting from these activities, as a painting or a piece of sculpture: *His art is unusual in both color and form.* **3.** A practical skill; craft; knack: *the art of sewing; the baker's art.* **4.** The body of knowledge of a particular field: *the art of medicine; the industrial arts.* **5. arts.** The liberal arts; the humanities: *college of arts and sciences.* **6. a. arts.** Artful devices; stratagems; tricks. **b.** Artfulness; contrivance; cunning. **—***modifier:* *art forms; an art dealer.* [Middle English, from Old French, from Latin *ars.*]

art² (ərt; ärt *when stressed*). *Archaic.* A form of the present tense of **be,** used with *thou.*

-art. Var. of the suffix **-ard.**

Ar·te·mis (ăr′tə-mĭs) *n. Gk. Myth.* The goddess of the hunt and the moon, identified with the Roman goddess Diana.

ar·te·ri·al (är-tîr′ē-əl) *adj.* **1.** Of, resembling, or occurring in an artery or arteries. **2.** Of or designating the blood in the arteries that has absorbed oxygen in the lungs and is bright red; not venous. **3.** Of or designating a route of transportation carrying a main flow with many branches: *an arterial highway.* **—***n.* A through road or street. **—ar·te′ri·al·ly** *adv.*

ar·te·ri·o·scle·ro·sis (är-tîr′ē-ō-sklə-rō′sĭs) *n.* A chronic disease in which thickening and hardening of arterial walls interferes with blood circulation. [New Latin, from Latin *artēria,* ARTERY + SCLEROSIS.] **—ar·te′ri·o·scle·rot′ic** (-rŏt′ĭk) *adj.*

ar·ter·y (är′tə-rē) *n., pl.* **-ies. 1.** *Anat.* Any of a branching system of muscular tubes that carry blood away from the heart. **2.** A major transportation route from which other routes branch. [Middle English *arterie,* from Latin *artēria,* from Greek.]

ar·te·sian well (är-tē′zhən). A deep well that passes through hard, impermeable rock and reaches water that is under enough pressure to rise to the surface without being pumped. [French *(puit) artésien,* (well) of Artois, a region of France, where such wells were first drilled.]

art·ful (ärt′fəl) *adj.* **1.** Exhibiting art or skill: *an artful cook.* **2.** Skillful, esp. in finding the means to an end; clever; ingenious: *artful reasoning.* **3.** Deceitful or tricky; cunning; crafty: *the Artful Dodger in Dickens' "Oliver Twist."* **4.** Not genuine; artificial. **—art′ful·ly** *adv.* **—art′ful·ness** *n.*

ar·thrit·ic (är-thrĭt′ĭk) *adj.* Afflicted with arthritis. **—***n.* A person who suffers from arthritis.

ar·thri·tis (är-thrī′tĭs) *n.* Inflammation and stiffness of a joint or joints in the body. [Latin, from Greek, from *arthron,* joint + -ITIS.]

ar·thro·pod (är′thrə-pŏd′) *n.* Any of numerous invertebrates of the phylum Arthropoda, which includes the insects, crustaceans, arachnids, and myriapods, that have a horny, segmented external covering and jointed limbs. [From Greek *arthron,* joint + -POD.] **—ar·throp′o·dous** (är-thrŏp′ə-dəs) or **ar·throp′o·dal** (-dəl) *adj.*

Ar·thur (är′thər) *n.* A legendary king of ancient Britain in the 6th cent. A.D. who gathered his knights at the Round Table.

Ar·thu·ri·an (är-thŏŏr′ē-ən) *adj.* Of or pertaining to King Arthur and his knights of the Round Table: *Arthurian legends.*

ar·ti·choke (är′tĭ-chōk′) *n.* **1.** A thistlelike plant, *Cynara scolymus,* that has a large flower head with numerous

arrowhead

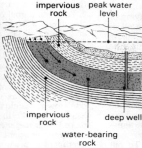

impervious rock   peak water level

impervious rock

deep well

water-bearing rock

artesian well

artichoke

fleshy, scalelike bracts. **2.** The unopened flower head of this plant, cooked and eaten as a vegetable. **3.** The **Jerusalem artichoke.** [Italian *arciciocco*, alteration of *arcicioffo*, from Old Spanish *alcarchofa*, from Arabic *al-kharshūf*.]

ar·ti·cle (är′tĭ-kəl) *n.* **1.** An individual thing in a class; an item: *an article of clothing.* **2.** A particular section or item of a series in a written document such as a contract, constitution, or treaty. **3.** A nonfictional piece of writing that forms an independent part of a publication; a report or essay: *an article on migrant workers.* **4.** *Gram.* Any of a class of words that function as determiners and are used to introduce nouns and to specify their application. In English the articles are *a, an,* and *some* (indefinite articles) and *the* (definite article). —*tr.v.* **-cled, -cling.** To bind by articles set forth in a contract: *article an apprentice for seven years.* [Middle English, from Old French, from Latin *articulus,* dim. of *artus,* joint.]

ar·tic·u·lar (är-tĭk′yə-lər) *adj.* Of, pertaining to, or occurring in a joint or joints: *articular pain.* [Middle English *articuler,* from Latin *articulāris,* from *articulus,* small joint, ARTICLE.]

ar·tic·u·late (är-tĭk′yə-lĭt) *adj.* **1.** Endowed with the power of speech. **2.** Spoken in or divided into clear and distinct words or syllables. **3.** Capable of, speaking in, or characterized by clear, expressive language: *The senator is the most articulate candidate.* **4.** *Biol.* Having joints or segments. —*v.* (är-tĭk′yə-lāt′) **-lat·ed, -lat·ing.** —*tr.v.* **1.** To utter (a speech sound or sounds) by moving the necessary organs of speech. **2.** To pronounce distinctly and carefully; enunciate: *articulate one's consonants.* **3.** To express verbally; give words to: *She was unable to articulate her fears.* **4.** *Anat.* To unite by forming a joint or joints; join together in such a way as to permit movement: *The elbow articulates the arm.* —*intr.v.* **1.** To utter a speech sound or sounds. **2.** To speak clearly and distinctly: *He articulates well.* **3.** To form a joint; be jointed: *The hand and arm articulate at the wrist.* [Latin *articulāre,* to divide into joints, from *articulus,* small joint, ARTICLE.] —**ar·tic′u·late·ly** *adv.* —**ar·tic′u·late·ness** *n.*

ar·tic·u·la·tion (är-tĭk′yə-lā′shən) *n.* **1.** The act or process of speaking clearly; enunciation. **2. a.** The movements of speech organs employed in producing a particular speech sound. **b.** Any speech sound, esp. a consonant. **3. a.** The act of jointing together or the condition of being jointed together. **b.** The method or manner of jointing. **4.** *Zool.* A joint between bones or between movable parts of an outside shell. **5.** *Bot.* **a.** A joint between two separable parts, as a leaf and a stem. **b.** A node or a space on a stem between two nodes. —**ar·tic′u·la·tive** (-lə-tĭv, -lā′tĭv) or **ar·tic′·u·la·to·ry** (-lə-tôr′ē, -tōr′ē) *adj.*

ar·tic·u·la·tor (är-tĭk′yə-lā′tər) *n.* **1.** A person or thing that articulates. **2.** A movable organ, such as the tongue, lips, or glottis, that is used in producing speech sounds.

ar·ti·fact (är′tə-făkt′) *n.* An object produced by human workmanship, esp. a tool or ornament of archaeological interest. [Latin *arte,* by skill, ART + *factum,* something made, from *facere,* to do, make.]

ar·ti·fice (är′tə-fĭs) *n.* **1.** A crafty device or stratagem; ruse. **2.** Mean deception; trickery. **3.** Ingenuity; cleverness; skill. [French, from Old French, craftsmanship, from Latin *artificium,* from *artifex,* craftsman : *ars,* ART + *-fex,* -maker.]

ar·tif·i·cer (är-tĭf′ĭ-sər) *n.* **1.** A skilled worker; craftsman. **2.** A person adept at designing and constructing; an inventor.

ar·ti·fi·cial (är′tə-fĭsh′əl) *adj.* **1.** Made by man rather than occurring in nature: *an artificial sweetener.* **2.** Made in imitation of something natural: *artificial flowers.* **3.** Not genuine or natural; affected; feigned; pretended: *an artificial smile; an artificial display of affection.* [Middle English, from Old French, from Latin *artificiālis,* from *artificium,* ARTIFICE.] —**ar′ti·fi′ci·al′i·ty** (är′tə-fĭsh′ē-ăl′ĭ-tē) *n.* —**ar′ti·fi′cial·ly** *adv.*

Syns: artificial, manmade, ersatz, synthetic *adj.* Core meaning: Made by human beings, not by nature (*an artificial lake; artifical furs*).

artificial respiration. Any of various methods used to restore normal breathing in an asphyxiated but living person, usu. by rhythmic forcing of air into and out of the lungs.

ar·til·ler·y (är-tĭl′ə-rē) *n.* **1.** Large-caliber firing weapons, such as howitzers, cannons, and missile launchers on mounts, that are too heavy to carry and are served by crews. **2.** Troops armed with such weapons. **3.** The branch of an armed force that specializes in the use of large, mounted guns. **4.** The science of the use of guns; gunnery. [Middle English *artil(le)rie,* from Old French *artillerie,* from *atillier,* to fortify, arm, from Latin *aptāre,* to fit, adapt, from *aptus,* fitting, apt.]

ar·ti·san (är′tĭ-zən, -sən) *n.* A person manually skilled in making a particular product; craftsman. [Old French, from Italian *artigiano,* from Latin *artītus,* skilled in arts, from *ars,* art.]

art·ist (är′tĭst) *n.* **1.** A person who practices any of the fine arts, esp. painting, sculpture, or music. **2.** A person whose work shows skill: *an artist on the basketball court.*

ar·tis·tic (är-tĭs′tĭk) *adj.* **1.** Of art or artists: *acclaimed by the artistic community.* **2.** Appreciative of or sensitive to art or beauty: *an artistic temperament.* **3.** Showing skill and good taste: *an artistic design.* —**ar·tis′ti·cal·ly** *adv.*

art·ist·ry (är′tĭ-strē) *n.* Artistic ability, quality, or workmanship.

art·less (ärt′lĭs) *adj.* **1.** Without cunning or deceit; ingenuous; naive: *The artless child was always being tricked by his sister.* **2.** Free of artificiality; natural; simple: *an artless perfection.* **3.** Lacking art or skill; crude: *an ugly, artless sculpture.* **4.** Uncultured; ignorant. —**art′less·ly** *adv.* —**art′less·ness** *n.*

art·y (är′tē) *adj.* **-i·er, -i·est.** *Informal.* Pretentious or affected in trying to appear artistic. —**art′i·ness** *n.*

ar·um (âr′əm, ăr′-) *n.* **1.** Any of various plants of the genus *Arum,* with arrow-shaped leaves and small flowers on a spadex that is surrounded by or enclosed within a spathe. **2.** Any of several similar or related plants, such as the **calla lily.** [From Latin *arum,* cuckoopint, from Greek *aron.*]

-ary A suffix meaning of, engaged in, or connected with: **parliamentary, reactionary.** [Middle English *-arie,* from Old French, from Latin *-ārius,* n. and adj. suffix.]

Ar·y·an (âr′ē-ən, ăr′-) *n.* Also **Ar·i·an. 1.** A member of the prehistoric people that spoke Indo-European. **2.** Indo-European or a language descended from it, esp. Indo-Iranian. **3.** In Nazi ideology, a Caucasian gentile, esp. of Nordic type. —*adj.* Of or pertaining to Aryans or their culture or language.

as (ăz; əz *when unstressed*) *adv.* **1.** Equally: *You'll have to go a long way to find someone as nice.* **2.** For instance: *large carnivores, as tigers.* —*Note: As* is used with certain words to form the following adverbial groups: **as good as.** Practically: *When he got home he was as good as dead.* **as much as.** Virtually: *She was as much as admitted having lied.* **as well.** Also; too: *People were there from out of town as well.* **as yet.** So far; up until now: *I haven't heard from him as yet.* —*conj.* **1.** To the same degree or quantity that; equally with: *sweet as sugar.* **2.** In the same way that: *When in Rome, do as the Romans do.* **3.** At the same time that; while: *She winked as our eyes met.* **4.** Since; because: *He stayed home, as he was ill.* **5.** Though: *Nice as it is, I don't want it.* **6.** *Informal.* That: *I don't know as I can.* —*Note: As* is used with certain words to form the following conjunctional groups: **as far as.** To the extent that: *She is home as far as I know.* **as if** (or **though**). In the same way that it would be if: *She acted as if she wanted to leave.* **as long as.** Since: *As long as you're writing them, please say hello for me.* **as soon as.** Immediately after: *We'll get to work as soon as we're told what to do.* —*pron.* **1.** That; who; which. Preceded by *same* or *such* as antecedent: *I got the same grade as you.* Used in some dialects (and formerly in standard English) with a noun or pronoun as antecedent: *Those as want to can come with me.* **2.** A fact that: *Roses are red, as we all know.* —*Note: As* is used with *much* to form a pronominal group: **as much.** All that; the same: *I might have guessed as much.* —*prep.* **1.** The same as; like: *He stared as a man possessed.* **2.** In the role or function of: *acting as a peacemaker.* —*Note: As* is used with certain words to form the following prepositional groups: **as for.** With regard to; concerning: *As for me, I'll stay.* **as of.** At or on (a specified time or date): *This assignment is due as of Monday.* **as to. 1.** Concerning; about: *different views as to the best way to start.* **2.** According to;

ă pat   ā pay   â care   ä father   ĕ pet   ē be   hw which
ŏŏ took   ōō boot   ou out   th thin   *th* this   ŭ cut
ĭ pit   ī tie   î pier   ŏ pot   ō toe   ô paw, for   oi noise
û urge   zh vision   ə about, item, edible, gallop, circus

by: *The stones were classified as to hardness.* **as well as.** Besides: *a brilliant student as well as a good athlete.* **—idioms. as is.** *Informal.* Just the way it is, without changes. **as it were.** In a manner of speaking: *He was a Robin Hood, as it were, until the cops caught up with him.* [Middle English *as, alse, alswa* (adv. and conj.), from Old English *alswā, ealswā, aelswā,* just as, likewise, ALSO.]

　　Usage: 1. When **as** is a conjunction meaning in the same way that, it is followed by a noun or pronoun in the subjective case: *Do as I do. You like her as much as I* [like her]. If a verb (as *do*) or a clearly understood but unexpressed verb (as *like*) occurs after *as,* use the subjective case. On the other hand, when *as* functions as a preposition meaning the same as, it is followed by a noun or pronoun in the objective case: *You need her as much as* [you need] *me.* **2.** When the conjunction *as* is used as the equivalent of *since* or *because,* ambiguity can result because *as* can be misconstrued as a reference to time and not cause: *She did not hear the bell as she was in the locker room.* Use of *since* or *because* would have made the intended meaning clearer. **3. as. . .as, so. . .as.** In positive constructions *as. . .as* is used: *He is as strong as an ox.* In negative constructions, either *as. . .as* or *so. . .as* may be used: *not as* (or *so*) *bright as their parents.* See also Usage note at **consider.**

As The symbol for the element arsenic.

as·a·fet·i·da (ăs′ə-fĕt′ĭ-də) *n.* Also **as·a·foet·i·da.** A yellowbrown, bitter, bad-smelling substance obtained from the roots of several plants of the genus *Ferula,* formerly used in medicine. [Middle English *asa-fetida,* from Medieval Latin *asafoetida : asa,* gum, from Persian *azā* + Latin *foetidus,* smelly, fetid.]

as·bes·tos (ăs-bĕs′təs, ăz-) *n.* Also **as·bes·tus.** Any of several fibrous minerals that are resistant to heat, flames, and chemical change, used for fireproofing, electrical insulation, building materials, brake linings, and chemical filters. **—modifier:** *asbestos material.* [Latin, an incombustible fiber, from Greek *asbestos,* inextinguishable : *a-,* not + *sbennunai,* to extinguish.]

as·cend (ə-sĕnd′) *intr.v.* **1.** To go or move upward; rise: *The balloon ascended rapidly.* **2.** To slope upward: *The road ascended near the village.* **—tr.v. 1.** To move upward upon or along; climb: *The climbers ascended the mountain.* **2.** To come to occupy: *The queen ascended the throne ten years ago.* **—See Syns at rise.** [Middle English *ascenden,* from Latin *ascendere : ad-,* toward + *scandere,* to climb.] **—as·cend′a·ble** or **as·cend′i·ble** *adj.*

as·cen·dan·cy (ə-sĕn′dən-sē) *n.* Also **as·cen·den·cy** or **as·cen·dance** (-dəns) or **as·cen·dence.** The condition of being in the ascendant; domination.

as·cen·dant (ə-sĕn′dənt). Also **as·cen·dent.** **—adj. 1.** Moving upward; ascending; rising. **2.** Coming into or achieving a position of power or influence; dominant: *Communism may be ascendant in Latin America.* **—n. 1.** The position or condition of being dominant or in power: *The senator reached the ascendant in his state's Republican Party.* **2.** *Astrol.* The sign of the zodiac that rises in the east at the time of a particular event, as a person's birth. **—idiom: in the ascendant.** Rising in power or influence.

as·cen·dence (ə-sĕn′dəns) or **as·cen·den·cy** (-dən-sē) *n.* Vars. of **ascendancy.**

as·cen·dent (ə-sĕn′dənt) *adj.* Var. of **ascendant.**

as·cend·ing (ə-sĕn′dĭng) *adj.* Going, growing, or moving upward: *in ascending order of importance; a tree with ascending branches.* **—as·cend′ing·ly** *adv.*

as·cen·sion (ə-sĕn′shən) *n.* **1.** The act or process of ascending; ascent: *her ascension to power.* **2.** *Astron.* The rising of a star above the horizon. **3. the Ascension.** *Theol.* The ascent of Christ into heaven, celebrated on Ascension Day, the 40th day after Easter. **—as·cen′sion·al** *adj.*

as·cent (ə-sĕnt′) *n.* **1.** The act or process of ascending. **2.** An advancement, esp. in status, rank, etc.: *a quick ascent from clerk to store manager.* **3.** An upward slope or incline: *the steep ascent to the fortress.*

as·cer·tain (ăs′ər-tān′) *tr.v.* To discover through examination or experimentation; find out: *ascertain the cause of the illness.* [Middle English *ascertainen,* from Old French *acertainer : a-,* to + *certain,* certain.] **—as′cer·tain′a·ble** *adj.* **—as′cer·tain′ment** *n.*

as·cet·ic (ə-sĕt′ĭk) *n.* A person who renounces comforts and pleasures in order to lead a life of rigid self-denial, esp. as an act of religious devotion. **—adj.** Characteristic of an ascetic; self-denying; austere. [Greek *askētikos,* from *askētēs,* hermit, "one who practices an art," from *askein,* to work.] **—as·cet′i·cal·ly** *adv.*

as·cet·i·cism (ə-sĕt′ĭ-sĭz′əm) *n.* **1.** Ascetic practice or discipline. **2.** A religious doctrine that the ascetic life releases the soul from bondage to the body and permits union with the divine.

as·cid·i·an (ə-sĭd′ē-ən) *n.* Any of various saclike saltwater animals of the class Ascidiacea, having a tough outer covering and including the sea squirts. **—adj.** Of or belonging to the Ascidiacea. [From Greek *askidion,* little wineskin, from *askos,* wineskin.]

as·cid·i·um (ə-sĭd′ē-əm) *n.,* pl. **-i·a** (-ē-ə). *Bot.* A sac-shaped or bottle-shaped part or organ, such as the leaf of a pitcher plant. [From Greek *askidion,* little wineskin, from *askos,* wineskin.]

as·co·my·cete (ăs′kō-mī′sēt′, -mī-sēt′) *n.* Any of numerous fungi, including yeasts and mildews, that produce spores in a saclike structure. [From Greek *ascos,* bag, bladder + -MYCETE.] **—as′co·my·ce′tous** *adj.*

a·scor·bic acid (ə-skôr′bĭk) *n.* A white, crystalline, water-soluble vitamin, $C_6H_8O_6$, found in citrus fruits, tomatoes, potatoes, and leafy green vegetables. It is used to prevent scurvy. Also called **vitamin C.** [A- (not) + SCORB(UT)IC.]

as·cot (ăs′kət, -kŏt′) *n.* A wide necktie or scarf tied so that the ends are laid flat, one on top of the other. [After *Ascot,* England, site of a famous horse race.]

as·cribe (ə-skrīb′) *tr.v.* **-cribed, -crib·ing. 1.** To attribute to a specific cause, source, or origin: *The bad harvest was ascribed to lack of rain.* **2.** To assign as an attribute: *ascribe envy to his rival.* [Middle English *ascriben,* from Latin *ascrībere,* to add to in writing : *ad-,* in addition + *scrībere,* to write.] **—as·crib′a·ble** *adj.*

as·crip·tion (ə-skrĭp′shən) *n.* The act of ascribing: *the ascription of victory to teamwork.*

-ase. A suffix meaning an enzyme: *amylase.* [From (DIA-ST)ASE.]

a·sep·sis (ā-sĕp′sĭs, ə-) *n.* The condition of being aseptic. [A- (without) + SEPSIS.]

a·sep·tic (ə-sĕp′tĭk, ā-) *adj.* **1.** Free from disease-causing microorganisms: *aseptic surgical instruments.* **2.** Lacking animation or emotion: *an aseptic smile.* [A- (not) + SEP-TIC.]

a·sex·u·al (ā-sĕk′shoo-əl) *adj.* **1.** Having no evident sex or sex organs; sexless: *an asexual organism.* **2.** Pertaining to or characterizing reproduction not involving sex organs or the union of sex cells. [A- (not) + SEXUAL.] **—a·sex′u·al′i·ty** (ā-sĕk′shoo-ăl′ĭ-tē) *n.* **—a·sex′u·al·ly** *adv.*

As·gard (ăs′gärd′, äz′-) *n. Norse Myth.* The abode of the gods and slain heroes of war.

ash¹ (ăsh) *n.* **1.** The grayish-white to black, soft solid material that remains after something has been burned completely. **2.** *Geol.* Pulverized particles of matter ejected by volcanic eruption. **3. ashes.** Human remains, esp. after cremation. [Middle English *asshe,* from Old English *asce, æsce.*]

ash² (ăsh) *n.* **1.** Any of various trees of the genus *Fraxinus,* with compound leaves, clusters of small greenish flowers, and winged seeds. **2.** The hard, durable wood of any of these trees.

a·shamed (ə-shāmd′) *adj.* **1.** Feeling shame or guilt: *I was ashamed of his behavior.* **2.** Reluctant through fear of shame: *We were ashamed to admit our mistake.* [Middle English, from Old English *āscamod,* past part. of *āscamian,* to feel shame.] **—a·sham′ed·ly** (ə-shā′mĭd-lē) *adv.*

ash·en (ăsh′ən) *adj.* Resembling ashes in color; pale; pallid: *an ashen complexion.*

Ash·ke·na·zi (ăsh′kə-nä′zē, -năz′ē) *n.,* pl. **-na·zim** (-nä′zĭm, -năz′ĭm). A member or descendant of the Jewish community that settled in central or eastern Europe during and after the Middle Ages. **—Ash′ke·na′zic** *adj.*

ash·lar (ăsh′lər) *n.* Also **ash·ler. 1.** A squared block of building stone. **2.** Masonry made of such stones. **3.** A thin rectangle of stone for facing walls. [Middle English *asheler,* from Old French *aisselier,* beam, from Latin *axilla,* dim. of *axis,* board.]

ă pat	ā pay	â care	ä father	ĕ pet	ē be	hw which	ĭ pit	ī tie	î pier	ŏ pot	ō toe	ô paw, for	oi noise
oo took	oo boot	ou out	th thin	th this	ŭ cut		û urge	zh vision	ə about, item, edible, gallop, circus				

a·shore (ə-shôr′, ə-shōr′) *adv.* **1.** Toward or on the shore: *steer the boat ashore.* **2.** On land: *liberty ashore for all hands.*

ash·tray (ăsh′trā′) *n.* A receptacle for tobacco ashes.

A·shur (ä′shŏŏr′) *n. Assyrian Myth.* The principal deity and god of war.

Ash Wednesday. The first day of Lent and the seventh Wednesday before Easter.

ash·y (ăsh′ē) *adj.* **-i·er, -i·est. 1.** Of, resembling, or covered with ashes. **2.** Having the color of ashes.

A·sian (ā′zhən, ā′shən) *adj.* Of or pertaining to Asia or its people. —*n.* A native or inhabitant of Asia. —See Usage note at **Asiatic.**

A·si·at·ic (ā′zhē-ăt′ĭk, -shē-, -zē-) *adj.* Asian. —*n.* An Asian.

> **Usage: Asiatic, Asian.** *Asiatic* is interchangeable with *Asian* in referring to places, animals, etc.: *the Asiatic part of Turkey; the Asiatic python.* However, *Asian* is the preferred term in referring to the people of Asia (*Afro-Asian politics*) because in this sense *Asiatic* is sometimes taken to be offensive.

Asiatic cholera. A disease, a form of **cholera.**

a·side (ə-sīd′) *adv.* **1.** To one side: *step aside; draw the curtain aside..* **2.** Apart: *a day set aside for rejoicing.* **3.** In reserve: *money put aside for Christmas presents.* **4.** Out of one's thoughts or mind: *put one's fears aside.* —*n.* **1.** A line spoken by a character in a play that the other actors on stage are not supposed to hear. **2.** A departure from the main subject; digression.

aside from. Apart from; except for: *Aside from a miracle, nothing can save our team from losing.*

as·i·nine (ăs′ə-nīn′) *adj.* Like an ass; stupid or silly. [Latin *asininus,* from *asinus,* ass.] —**as′i·nine′ly** *adv.*

as·i·nin·i·ty (ăs′ə-nĭn′ĭ-tē) *n., pl.* **-ties. 1.** The quality of being asinine; stupidity. **2.** An asinine action or remark: *a speech full of asininities.*

ask (ăsk, äsk) *tr.v.* **1.** To put a question to. **2.** To seek information about; inquire about: *ask directions.* **3.** To request of or for; solicit: *May I ask a favor of you?* **4.** To expect or demand: *ask too much of a child.* **5.** To invite: *We asked her to the picnic.* —*intr.v.* **1.** To inquire: *Ask at the desk. We asked about his mother.* **2.** To make a request: *asked for withdrawal of the troops.* —*phrasal verb.* **ask for.** To provoke; incite: *ask for trouble.* [Middle English *asken, axen,* from Old English *āscian, ācsian.*] —**ask′er** *n.*

a·skance (ə-skăns′) *adv.* **1.** With a sidelong or oblique glance; sidewise. **2.** With disapproval, suspicion, or distrust. [Earlier *a scanche,* obliquely, from Middle English *ascaunce, ascaunces,* "as if to say," "so to speak": AS + *quances,* as if, from Old French *quanses,* from Medieval Latin *quam si,* alteration of Latin *quasi,* as if, quasi.]

a·skew (ə-skyŏŏ′) *adv. & adj.* Out of line; crooked; awry: *a picture hanging askew. The rug is askew.* [A- (on) + SKEW.]

a·slant (ə-slănt′) *adj.* Slanting. —*adv.* At a slant. —*prep.* Slanting over or across.

a·sleep (ə-slēp′) *adj.* **1.** Sleeping. **2.** Inactive; dormant: *a sleeping volcano.* **3.** Numb: *My leg is asleep.* **4.** Dead. —*adv.* Into a condition of sleep: *fall asleep.*

asp (ăsp) *n.* Any of several venomous snakes of Africa and Asia Minor, such as the small cobra *Naja haje* or the horned viper *Cerastes cornutus.* [Middle English *aspis,* from Latin, from Greek *aspis.*]

as·par·a·gus (ə-spăr′ə-gəs) *n.* **1.** Any of several plants of the genus *Asparagus,* native to Eurasia, that have small scales or needlelike branchlets rather than true leaves. **2.** The succulent young shoots of this plant, cooked and eaten as a vegetable. [Latin, from Greek *asparagos.*]

as·pect (ăs′pĕkt) *n.* **1.** A particular facial expression or appearance; air: *a weary soldier of grim aspect.* **2.** Appearance to the eye: *the wild aspect of the jungle.* **3.** The way in which an idea, problem, situation, etc., is viewed by the mind; an element or facet: *all aspects of the case.* **4.** A position facing or commanding a given direction; exposure: *a southern aspect.* **5.** A side or surface facing in a particular direction: *the ventral aspect of the body.* **6.** *Astrol.* The position of the stars or planets in relation to one another or to the subject, thought to influence human affairs. [Middle English, from Latin *aspectus,* a view, past

part. of *aspicere,* look at : *ad-,* to + *specere,* to look.]

as·pen (ăs′pən) *n.* Any of several trees of the genus *Populus,* with leaves that are attached by flattened leafstalks so that they flutter readily in the wind. [Middle English *aspe,* from Old English *æspe.*]

as·per·i·ty (ă-spĕr′ĭ-tē) *n.* **1.** Roughness or harshness, as of surface, weather, or sound. **2.** Ill temper; irritability: *a note of asperity in her voice.* [Latin *asperitās,* from *asper,* rough.]

as·perse (ə-spûrs′, ă-) *tr.v.* **-persed, -pers·ing.** To spread false charges or insinuations against; to slander. [Latin *aspergere,* to sprinkle on, spatter : *ad-,* to + *spargere,* to strew, scatter.] —**as·per′sive** *adj.*

as·per·sion (ə-spûr′zhən, -shən) *n.* A damaging or slanderous report or remark: *I resented her casting aspersions on my motives.*

as·phalt (ăs′fôlt) *n.* **1.** A brownish-black mixture of bitumens obtained from natural deposits or as a petroleum byproduct, used in paving, roofing, and waterproofing. **2.** A mixture of asphalt and gravel or sand, used for paving or roofing. —*tr.v.* To pave or coat with asphalt. —*modifier:* *asphalt highways.* [Middle English, from Late Latin *asphaltus,* from Greek *asphaltos,* pitch, asphalt, prob. "binding agent (used by stone masons)" : *a-,* not + *sphallein,* to cause to fall.] —**as·phal′tic** (ăs-fôl′tĭk) *adj.*

as·pho·del (ăs′fə-dĕl′) *n.* Any of several Mediterranean plants of the genera *Asphodeline* and *Asphodelus* that have clusters of white or yellow flowers. [Latin *asphodelus,* from Greek *asphodelos.*]

as·phyx·i·a (ăs-fĭk′sē-ə, -fĭk′sə) *n.* Lack of oxygen or increased carbon dioxide in the blood, causing unconsciousness or death. [From Greek *asphuxia,* stopping of the pulse : *a-,* not + *sphuxis,* heartbeat, pulsation.]

as·phyx·i·ate (ăs-fĭk′sē-āt′) *v.* **-at·ed, -at·ing.** —*tr.v.* To cause asphyxia in; smother. —*intr.v.* To undergo asphyxia; suffocate. —**as·phyx′i·a′tion** *n.* —**as·phyx′i·a′tor** *n.*

as·pic (ăs′pĭk) *n.* **1.** A cold dish of meat, fish, vegetables, or fruit combined and set in a gelatin mold. **2.** A jelly made from chilled meat or fish juices and gelatin, and served as a garnish. [French, a snake, from the different colors of the jelly, as compared with those of the snake, from Latin *aspis,* ASP.]

as·pi·dis·tra (ăs′pĭ-dĭs′trə) *n.* Any of several Asian plants of the genus *Aspidistra;* esp. *A. lurida,* that has long, evergreen leaves and is widely cultivated as a house plant. [From Greek *aspis,* shield.]

as·pi·rant (ăs′pər-ənt, ə-spīr′-) *n.* A person who aspires, esp. after advancement, honors, or a high position. —*adj.* Aspiring.

as·pi·rate (ăs′pə-rāt′) *tr.v.* **-rat·ed, -rat·ing. 1.** *Phonet.* **a.** To pronounce (a vowel or word) with the release of breath associated with English *h,* as in *Hartford.* **b.** To follow (a consonant) with a clearly audible puff of breath. For example, the English *p, t,* and *k* are aspirated before vowels, as in the words *pail, top,* and *kind.* **2.** *Med.* To remove (liquids or gases), as from a body cavity, by means of an aspirator. —*n.* (ăs′pər-ĭt) *Phonet.* **1.** The speech sound represented by the English *h.* **2.** The puff of breath following the pronunciation of certain consonants. **3.** Any speech sound followed by a puff of breath. —*adj.* (ăs′pər-ĭt) *Phonet.* Aspirated, as a speech sound. [Latin *aspīrāre,*

asparagus
The plant

asparagus
The shoot

to breathe upon : *ad-*, to + *spīrāre*, to breathe.]

as·pi·ra·tion (ăs′pə-rā′shən) *n.* **1. a.** A strong desire for high achievement. **b.** An object of such desire; goal. **2.** *Phonet.* **a.** The pronunciation of a consonant with an aspirate. **b.** An aspirate. **3.** *Med.* Removal of liquids or gases with an aspirator.

as·pi·ra·tor (ăs′pə-rā′tər) *n.* **1.** Any device that removes liquids or gases from a body cavity by suction. **2.** A suction pump used to create a partial vacuum.

as·pire (ə-spīr′) *intr.v.* **-pired, -pir·ing.** **1.** To have a great ambition; desire strongly: *aspire to be an actress; aspire to great knowledge.* **2.** *Archaic.* To rise upward; soar: *"On what wings dare he aspire?"* (William Blake). [Middle English *aspiren,* from Old French *aspirer,* from Latin *aspīrāre,* to breathe upon, favor, desire, ASPIRATE.] **—as·pir′er** *n.* **—as·pir′ing·ly** *adv.*

as·pi·rin (ăs′pə-rĭn, -prĭn) *n.* **1.** A white crystalline compound of acetylsalicylic acid, C₉H₈O₄, commonly used as a drug to relieve pain and reduce fever. **2.** A tablet of aspirin. [AC(ETYL) + *spir(aeic acid),* old name for salicylic acid, from SPIRAEA + -IN.]

ass (ăs) *n., pl.* **ass·es** (ăs′ĭz). **1.** Any of several hoofed mammals of the genus *Equus,* resembling and closely related to the horses and zebras, esp. the domesticated donkey. **2.** A vain, self-important, silly, or stupid person. [Middle English *asse,* from Old English *assa,* from Old Irish *asan,* from Latin *asinus.*]

ass

as·sail (ə-sāl′) *tr.v.* **1.** To attack with violent blows; assault. **2.** To attack verbally, as with argument, ridicule, or censure: *The speaker assailed his critics in a bitter statement.* —See Syns at **attack.** [Middle English *asailen,* from Old French *asaillir,* from Latin *assilīre,* to jump on : *ad-,* to + *salīre,* to leap.] **—as·sail′a·ble** *adj.* **—as·sail′er** *n.*

as·sail·ant (ə-sā′lənt) *n.* A person who assails; an attacker.

as·sas·sin (ə-săs′ĭn) *n.* A murderer, esp. one who carries out a plot to kill a public official or other prominent person. [French, from Medieval Latin *assassīnus,* from Arabic *ḥashshāshīn,* pl. of *ḥashshāsh,* "hashish addict," from *ḥashīsh,* hashish.]

as·sas·si·nate (ə-săs′ə-nāt′) *tr.v.* **-nat·ed, -nat·ing.** **1.** To murder (a prominent person). **2.** To destroy or injure maliciously: *assassinate a person's character.* **—as·sas′si·na′-tion** *n.*

as·sault (ə-sôlt′) *n.* **1.** A violent attack, either physical or verbal. **2.** An attack upon a fortified area or place. **3.** *Law.* An unlawful attempt or threat to injure another physically. **4.** Rape. —*tr.v.* To attack or assail violently. —*intr.v.* To make an assault. —See Syns at **attack.** [Middle English *assaut,* from Old French, from Latin *assultus,* past part. of *assilīre,* ASSAIL.] **—as·sault′er** *n.*

assault and battery. *Law.* The threat to use force upon another and the carrying out of the threat.

as·say (ăs′ā′, ă-sā′) *n.* **1. a.** The chemical analysis of a substance, esp. of an ore or drug. **b.** A substance to be so analyzed. **c.** The result of such an analysis. **2.** Any analysis or examination. —*tr.v.* (ă-sā′, ăs′ā′). **1.** To subject to chemical analysis; analyze. **2.** To examine by trial or experiment; put to a test: *assay one's ability.* **3.** To evaluate; assess. **4.** To attempt; try: *assay an escape.* —*intr.v.* To be shown by analysis as having a certain proportion, usu. of a precious metal. [Middle English, from Old French *assai, essai,* trial, essay.] **—as·say′a·ble** *adj.* **—as·say′er** *n.*

as·sem·blage (ə-sĕm′blĭj) *n.* **1.** The act of assembling or the condition of being assembled. **2.** A collection of persons or things. **3.** A fitting together of parts, as of a machine. **4.** A sculpture consisting of an arrangement of miscellaneous objects, such as scraps of metal, cloth, and string.

as·sem·ble (ə-sĕm′bəl) *v.* **-bled, -bling.** —*tr.v.* **1.** To bring or gather together into a group or whole. **2.** To fit or join together the parts of. —*intr.v.* To gather together; congregate. —See Syns at **gather.** [Middle English *assemblen,* from Old French *assembler,* from Latin *ad-,* to + *simul,* together, at the same time.] **—as·sem′bler** *n.*

as·sem·bly (ə-sĕm′blē) *n., pl.* **-blies.** **1.** The act of assembling or the condition of being assembled. **2.** A group of persons gathered together for a common purpose. **3. Assembly.** In certain U.S. states, the lower house of the legislature. **4. a.** The putting together of manufactured parts to make a completed product, esp. a machine. **b.** A set of parts so assembled: *the steering assembly of a truck.* **5.** The signal calling troops to form ranks.

assembly line. A line of factory workers and equipment on which the product being assembled passes consecutively from operation to operation, gen. on some kind of conveyor, until completed.

as·sent (ə-sĕnt′) *intr.v.* To express agreement; concur: *assent to his plan.* —*n.* **1.** Agreement, as to a proposal; compliance. **2.** Acquiescence; consent: *We need the client's assent before proceeding.* [Middle English *assenten,* from Old French *assenter,* from Latin *assentīre,* "to join in feeling," agree with : *ad-,* toward + *sentīre,* to feel, think.] **—as·sent′er** or **as·sen′tor** *n.*

as·sert (ə-sûrt′) *tr.v.* **1.** To state positively; affirm: *She still asserts that her story is true.* **2.** To insist upon recognition of; defend or maintain: *assert one's independence.* —*idiom.* **assert oneself.** To express oneself forcefully or boldly. [Latin *asserere,* "to join to oneself," maintain, claim : *ad-,* to + *serere,* to join.] **—as·sert′a·ble** or **as·sert′-i·ble** *adj.*

Syns: assert, affirm, declare, hold, maintain *v.* Core meaning: To put into words positively and with conviction (*asserted his innocence*).

as·ser·tion (ə-sûr′shən) *n.* **1.** The act of asserting or declaring. **2.** A positive declaration: *His assertion has yet to be proved.*

as·ser·tive (ə-sûr′tĭv) *adj.* Inclined to bold assertion; positive; confident: *an assertive salesman.* **—as·ser′tive·ly** *adv.* **—as·ser′tive·ness** *n.*

as·sess (ə-sĕs′) *tr.v.* **1.** To estimate the value of (property) for taxation. **2.** To set or determine the amount of (a tax, fine, or other payment). **3.** To charge (a person) with a tax, fine, or other special payment. **4.** To analyze and determine the significance, importance, etc., of; estimate; evaluate; appraise: *How do you assess your chances of winning?* [Middle English *assessen,* from Old French *assesser,* from Latin *assidēre,* "to sit beside," be an assistant judge : *ad-,* near to + *sedēre,* to sit.] **—as·sess′a·ble** *adj.*

as·sess·ment (ə-sĕs′mənt) *n.* **1.** The act of assessing. **2.** An amount assessed: *The assessment on the car is $100.*

as·ses·sor (ə-sĕs′ər) *n.* An official who makes assessments, as for taxation.

as·set (ăs′ĕt′) *n.* **1.** A valuable item that is owned. **2.** A useful or valuable quality or thing: *An agreeable personality is a great asset.* **3. assets.** The entries on a balance sheet showing all of a person's or business' properties. Assets include cash, inventory, claims against others that may be applied directly or indirectly to cover liabilities, and intangibles, such as a trademark or good will. [Norman French *asetz,* from Old French *asez,* "enough (to satisfy creditors)," from Latin *ad* + *satis,* sufficient.]

as·sev·er·ate (ə-sĕv′ə-rāt′) *tr.v.* **-at·ed, -at·ing.** To declare seriously or positively; affirm. [Latin *assevērāre* : *ad-,* to + *sevērus,* earnest.] **—as·sev′er·a′tion** *n.*

as·si·du·i·ty (ăs′ĭ-dōō′ĭ-tē, -dyōō′-) *n., pl.* **-ties.** **1.** Close and constant application; diligence. **2. assiduities.** Constant personal attentions; solicitude: *grateful for her assiduities when I was ill.*

as·sid·u·ous (ə-sĭj′ōō-əs) *adj.* Constant and careful in application or attention; diligent: *an assiduous worker.* [Latin *assiduus,* from *assidēre,* to sit beside, attend to : *ad-,* near to + *sedēre*, to sit.] —**as·sid'u·ous·ly** *adv.* —**as·sid'u·ous·ness** *n.*

as·sign (ə-sīn') *tr.v.* **1.** To set apart for a particular purpose; designate: *assign a day for the examination.* **2.** To select for a duty or office; appoint. **3.** To give out as a task; allot: *assign lessons.* **4.** To ascribe; attribute: *assign that building to the classical period.* **5.** *Law.* To transfer (property, rights, or interests) to another. **6.** *Mil.* To place (a unit or personnel) integrally into a particular organization. —*n. Law.* An assignee. [Middle English *assignen,* from Old French *assigner,* from Latin *assignāre,* to mark out : *ad-,* to + *signāre,* to mark, from *signum,* sign.] —**as·sign'a·bil'i·ty** *n.* —**as·sign'a·ble** *adj.* —**as·sign'er** *n.*

as·sig·na·tion (ăs'ĭg-nā'shən) *n.* **1.** The act of assigning. **2.** Something assigned; assignment. **3.** An appointment for a secret meeting between lovers; tryst.

as·sign·ee (ə-sī'nē', ăs'ī-nē') *n.* **1.** *Law.* A person to whom an assignment is made. **2.** A person appointed to act for another; deputy; agent.

as·sign·ment (ə-sīn'mənt) *n.* **1.** The act of assigning. **2.** Something assigned, as a task. **3.** A position or post of duty to which one is assigned: *an assignment with the embassy in Paris.* **4.** *Law.* **a.** The transfer of a claim, right, interest, or property. **b.** The document or deed by which this transfer is made.

as·sim·i·late (ə-sĭm'ə-lāt') *v.* **-lat·ed, -lat·ing.** —*tr.v.* **1.** To take in, digest, and transform (food) into living tissue. **2.** To absorb and incorporate (knowledge). **3.** To take or absorb (an immigrant or culturally distinct group) into the prevailing culture or social traditions. **4.** *Ling.* To alter (a sound) by assimilation. —*intr.v.* To become assimilated. [Middle English *assimilaten,* from Latin *assimilāre,* to make similar to : *ad-,* to + *similis,* similar.]

as·sim·i·la·tion (ə-sĭm'ə-lā'shən) *n.* **1. a.** The act or process of assimilating. **b.** The condition or process of being assimilated. **2.** The process by which nourishment is changed into living tissue; constructive metabolism. **3.** *Ling.* The process by which a sound is changed to make it resemble a neighboring sound. For example, the prefix *in-* in *intolerable* becomes *im-* in *impossible* by assimilation. **4.** The process whereby a minority or immigrant group gradually adopts the characteristics of another culture.

as·sim·i·la·tive (ə-sĭm'ə-lā'tĭv) *adj.* Also **as·sim·i·la·to·ry** (-lə-tôr'ē, -tōr'ē). Marked by or causing assimilation.

as·sist (ə-sĭst') *tr.v.* **1.** To aid; to help. **2.** To work with as an assistant: *The nurses assisted the doctor.* —*intr.v.* **1.** To give aid or support. **2.** To be present; participate; attend: *assist at the reception.* —See Syns at **help.** —*n.* **1.** An act of giving aid; help. **2. a.** *Baseball.* A fielding and throwing of the ball that enables a teammate to put out a runner. **b.** A pass of the ball or puck to the teammate scoring a goal, as in basketball or ice hockey. [Middle English *assisten,* from Old French *assister,* from Latin *assistere,* to stand beside : *ad-,* near to + *sistere,* to stand.]

as·sis·tance (ə-sĭs'təns) *n.* **1.** The act of assisting. **2.** Aid; help: *qualifying for financial assistance.*

as·sis·tant (ə-sĭs'tənt) *n.* Someone who assists; a helper; an aide. —*adj.* **1.** Holding an auxiliary position; subordinate: *an assistant coach.* **2.** Giving aid; helping.

as·size (ə-sīz') *n.* **1.** *Eng. Hist.* A session of a legislative body or one of its decrees. **2. assizes. a.** One of the periodic court sessions held in each of the counties of England and Wales for the trial of civil or criminal cases. **b.** The time or place of such sessions. [Middle English *assise,* from Old French, from *asseior,* to seat, from Latin *assidēre,* to sit beside.]

as·so·ci·ate (ə-sō'shē-āt', -sē-) *v.* **-at·ed, -at·ing.** —*tr.v.* **1.** To bring (a person) into a relationship: *We associated ourselves with the campaign.* **2.** To connect or join together; combine; link: *Crime is often associated with poverty.* **3.** To connect in the mind or imagination: *"I always somehow associate Chatterton with autumn"* (John Keats). —*intr.v.* **1.** To join in or form a league, union, or association. **2.** To combine or unite. **3.** To keep company: *She associates with older girls.* —*n.* (ə-sō'shē-ĭt, -āt', -sē-). **1.** A person united with another or others in some action, enterprise, or business; partner; colleague. **2.** A companion; comrade. **3.** Anything that accompanies or is associ-

ated with another. **4.** A member of an institution or society who is granted only partial status or privileges: *The new lawyer was hired as an associate.* —See Syns at **partner.** —*adj.* (ə-sō'shē-ĭt, -āt', -sē-). **1.** Joined with another or others and having equal or nearly equal status: *an associate editor.* **2.** Having partial status or privileges: *an associate member of the club.* [Middle English *associaten,* from Latin *associāre,* to join to : *ad-,* to + *sociāre,* to join, from *socius,* companion.]

as·so·ci·a·tion (ə-sō'sē-ā'shən, -shē-) *n.* **1.** The act of associating. **2.** The state of being associated. **3.** An organized body of people who have some common interest, activity, or purpose; a society: *a trade association.* **4.** An idea or train of ideas triggered by another idea or stimulus: *What associations does the word "geography" bring to your mind?* —**as·so'ci·a'tion·al** *adj.*

as·so·ci·a·tive (ə-sō'shē-ā'tĭv, -sē-, -shə-tĭv) *adj.* **1.** Of, characterized by, resulting from, or causing association: *associative feelings.* **2.** *Math.* Independent of the grouping of elements. Said of mathematical operations: *If a + (b + c) = (a + b) + c,* the operation indicated by + is associative.

as·so·nance (ăs'ə-nəns) *n.* *Pros.* A partial rhyme in which the accented vowel sounds correspond but the consonants differ, as in *brave* and *vain.* [French, from Latin *assonāre,* to sound in response to : *ad-,* to + *sonāre,* to sound.] —**as'so·nant** *adj. & n.*

as·sort (ə-sôrt') —*tr.v.* To separate into groups; classify. —*intr.v.* To fall into a class; match. [Old French *assorter* : Latin *ad-,* to + *sors,* chance, fortune, lot.] —**as·sort'er** *n.*

as·sort·ed (ə-sôr'tĭd) *adj.* **1.** Consisting of a number of different kinds; various: *a box of assorted chocolates.* **2.** Placed in classes; classified: *The coat comes in assorted sizes.* **3.** Suited or matched.

as·sort·ment (ə-sôrt'mənt) *n.* **1.** The act of assorting; separation into classes. **2.** A collection of various things; a variety.

as·suage (ə-swāj') *tr.v.* **-suaged, -suag·ing. 1.** To make less burdensome or painful; to ease: *"Assuage the anguish of your bereavement"* (Abraham Lincoln). **2.** To satisfy, as thirst; appease. **3.** To pacify or calm: *My apology did not assuage his anger.* [Middle English *aswagen,* from Old French *assouagier* : Latin *ad-,* to + *suāvis,* sweet.] —**as·suage'ment** *n.*

as·sume (ə-soōm') *tr.v.* **-sumed, -sum·ing. 1.** To put or take on (a role, appearance, etc.); to don. **2.** To take upon oneself; undertake: *assuming the responsibility.* **3.** To invest oneself with: *assume the presidency.* **4.** To take for oneself or as one's right or privilege: *The nation assumes authority to set offshore fishing limits.* **5.** To take on; adopt: *The spreading virus has assumed a new form.* **6.** To feign; pretend: *assume an air of indifference.* **7.** To take for granted; suppose: *We assumed he knew we were leaving.* [Middle English *assumen,* from Latin *assumere,* to adopt : *ad-,* to + *sūmere,* to take.] —**as·sum'a·ble** *adj.* —**as·sum'a·bly** *adv.* —**as·sum'er** *n.*

as·sumed (ə-soōmd') *adj.* **1.** Pretended; adopted; fictitious: *an assumed name.* **2.** Taken for granted: *an assumed fact.* —**as·sum'ed·ly** (-mĭd-lē) *adv.*

as·sum·ing (ə-soō'mĭng) *adj.* Presumptuous; pretentious; arrogant: *an assuming manner.*

as·sump·tion (ə-sŭmp'shən) *n.* **1.** The act of assuming: *The assumption of office.* **2.** A statement, fact, or idea accepted as true without proof; supposition: *false assumptions about what she is really like.* **3. the Assumption. a.** *Theol.* The bodily taking up of the Virgin Mary into heaven after her death. **b.** A church feast on Aug. 15 celebrating this event. —**as·sump'tive** *adj.*

as·sur·ance (ə-shoōr'əns) *n.* **1.** The act of assuring or the condition of being assured. **2.** A statement or indication that inspires confidence; guarantee: *He gave us his assurance he would pay.* **3. a.** Freedom from doubt; certainty: *Our doubts were relieved with assurance.* **b.** Self-confidence: *playing with complete assurance.* **4.** Boldness; audacity. —See Syns at **confidence.**

as·sure (ə-shoōr') *tr.v.* **-sured, -sur·ing. 1.** To inform confidently, with a view to removing doubt: *I assured her I'd be home on time.* **2.** To cause to feel sure; convince: *The bright sun assured us it would be a lovely day.* **3.** To give confidence to; reassure: *assure a frightened child.* **4.** To

| ă pat | ā pay | â care | ä father | ĕ pet | ē be | hw which | ĭ pit | ī tie | î pier | ŏ pot | ō toe | ô paw, for | oi noise |
| oō took | oō boot | ou out | th thin | th this | ŭ cut | û urge | zh vision | ə about, item, edible, gallop, circus |

make certain; ensure: *The results from Texas assured his election.* [Middle English *assuren,* from Old French *assurer,* from Medieval Latin *assēcūrāre,* to make sure : Latin *ad-,* to + *sēcūrus,* secure.] **—as·sur'a·ble** *adj.* **—as·sur'er** *n.*

as·sured (ə-shoŏrd') *adj.* **1.** Undoubted; guaranteed: *an assured success.* **2.** Confident; bold: *an assured manner.* **—as·sur'ed·ly** (ə-shoŏr-ĭd-lē) *adv.* **—as·sur'ed·ness** *n.*

As·syr·i·an (ə-sîr'ē-ən) *adj.* Of or pertaining to Assyria, its people, language, or culture. *—n.* **1.** A native or inhabitant of Assyria. **2.** The Semitic language of Assyria.

As·tar·te (ə-stär'tē) *n. Phoenician Myth.* The goddess of love and fertility.

as·ta·tine (ăs'tə-tēn', -tĭn) *n. Symbol* **At** A highly unstable radioactive element that resembles iodine in solution and accumulates in the thyroid gland. Its longest lived isotope is At 210, having a half-life of 8.3 hours, and it is used in medicine as a radioactive tracer. Atomic number 85, valences prob. 1, 3, 5, or 7. [From Greek *astatos,* unstable : *a-,* not + *statos,* standing.]

as·ter (ăs'tər) *n.* **1.** Any of various plants of the genus *Aster,* with rayed, daisylike flowers that range in color from white to purplish or pink. **2.** *Biol.* A star-shaped structure in the cytoplasm of the cell and associated with the centrosome during mitosis and meiosis. [From Latin *astēr,* star, from Greek.]

aster   astronaut

as·ter·isk (ăs'tə-rĭsk') *n.* A star-shaped figure (*) used in printing to indicate an omission or a reference to a footnote. *—tr.v.* To mark with an asterisk. [Late Latin *asteriscus,* from Greek *asteriskos,* from *astēr,* star.]

as·ter·ism (ăs'tə-rĭz'əm) *n. Mineral.* A six-rayed starlike figure produced in some crystal structures by reflected or transmitted light. [Greek *asterismos,* from *asterizein,* to arrange in constellations, from *astēr,* star.]

a·stern (ə-stûrn') *adv.* **1.** Behind a ship. **2.** At or toward the rear of a ship. **—a·stern'** *adj.*

as·ter·oid (ăs'tə-roid') *n.* **1.** Any of numerous small objects that orbit the sun, chiefly in the region between Mars and Jupiter. Also called **planetoid.** **2.** A starfish. *—adj.* Also **as·ter·oi·dal** (ăs'tə-roid'l). Star-shaped. [Greek *asteroeidēs,* like a star : *astēr,* star + *-OID.*]

asth·ma (ăz'mə, ăs'-) *n.* A chronic respiratory disease, often arising from allergies, and accompanied by difficulty in breathing, tightness of the chest, and coughing. [Middle English *asma,* from Medieval Latin, from Greek *asthma.*]

asth·mat·ic (ăz-măt'ĭk, ăs-) *adj.* Of or having asthma: *an asthmatic child.* *—n.* A person with asthma. **—asth·mat'i·cal·ly** *adv.*

a·stig·ma·tism (ə-stĭg'mə-tĭz'əm) *n.* **1.** A refractive defect of a lens, esp. of the lens of the eye that prevents focusing of sharp, distinct images. **2.** Faulty vision caused by such defects in the lens of the eye. [A- (without) + Greek *stigma,* spot, mark, from *stizein,* to tattoo.] **—as'tig·mat'ic** (ăs'tĭg-măt'ĭk) *adj.*

a·stir (ə-stûr') *adj.* **1.** Moving about; in excited motion. **2.** Out of bed; awake. [Scottish *asteer* : A- (on) + *steer,* var. of STIR (n.).]

as·ton·ish (ə-stŏn'ĭsh) *tr.v.* To fill with wonder or surprise; amaze. —See Syns at **fabulous.** [Prob. extension of obs. *astony,* Middle English *astonen,* from Old French *estoner* : Latin *ex-,* out of + *tonāre,* to thunder.] **—as·ton'ish·ing·ly** *adv.*

as·ton·ish·ment (ə-stŏn'ĭsh-mənt) *n.* **1.** Great surprise or amazement. **2.** A cause of amazement; a marvel.

as·tound (ə-stound') *tr.v.* To strike with sudden wonder; surprise; amaze. [Orig. the past part. of obs. *astone,* to amaze, from Middle English *astonen,* ASTONISH.]

astr-. Var. of the prefix **-astro.**

as·tra·chan (ăs'trə-kăn', -kən) *n.* Var. of **astrakhan.**

a·strad·dle (ə-străd'l) *prep.* Astride; astride of: *astraddle a horse.*

as·trag·a·lus (ə-străg'ə-ləs) *n., pl.* -**li** (-lī'). A bone, the **talus.** [From Greek *astragalos,* vertebra, the ball of the ankle joint.]

as·tra·khan (ăs'trə-kăn', -kən) *n.* Also **as·tra·chan.** **1.** The curly fur made from the skins of young lambs of the region of Astrakhan in the U.S.S.R. **2.** A wool fabric with a curly pile, made to resemble this fur.

as·tral (ăs'trəl) *adj.* **1.** Of, pertaining to, emanating from, or resembling the stars. **2.** *Biol.* Pertaining to or shaped like an aster; star-shaped. [Late Latin *astrālis,* from Latin *astrum,* star, from Greek *astron.*]

a·stray (ə-strā') *adv.* **1.** Away from the correct path or direction. **2.** Toward evil or wrong ways: *led astray by greed and laziness.* [Middle English *astray, astraie,* from Old French *estraier,* to stray.]

a·stride (ə-strīd') *prep.* **1.** With a leg on each side of: *He jumped astride the horse.* Also used adverbially: *riding astride.* **2.** On both sides of or spanning: *a safe position astride the bridge.*

astride of. Astride: *He stood astride of the fallen log.*

as·trin·gent (ə-strĭn'jənt) *adj.* **1.** Tending to draw together or tighten living tissue. **2.** Harsh; severe: *an astringent comment.* *—n.* An astringent substance or drug, such as alum. [Latin *astringere,* to bind together : *ad-,* to + *stringere,* to bind.] **—as·trin'gen·cy** (-jən-sē) *n.* **—as·trin'gent·ly** *adv.*

astro- or **astr-.** A prefix meaning outer space: **astronautics.** [Middle English, from Old French, from Latin, from Greek *astron,* star.]

as·tro·labe (ăs'trə-lāb') *n.* A medieval instrument used to determine the altitude of the sun or other celestial bodies, replaced by the sextant. [Middle English, from Old French, from Medieval Latin *astrolabium,* from Greek *(organon) astrolabon,* "(instrument) for taking the stars" : *astron,* star + *lambanein,* to take.]

as·trol·o·gy (ə-strŏl'ə-jē) *n.* The study of the positions and aspects of heavenly bodies in the belief that they have an influence on the course of human affairs. [Middle English *astrologie,* from Old French, from Latin *astrologia,* from Greek, from *astrologos,* astronomer, (later) astrologer : *astron,* star + *-LOGY.*] **—as·trol'o·ger** *n.* **—as·tro·log'ic** (ăs'trə-lŏj'ĭk) or **as·tro·log'i·cal** *adj.* **—as·tro·log'i·cal·ly** *adv.*

as·tro·naut (ăs'trə-nôt') *n.* A person trained to serve in the crew of a spacecraft. [ASTRO- + Greek *nautēs,* sailor, from *naus,* ship.]

as·tro·nau·tics (ăs'trə-nô'tĭks) *n. (used with sing. verb).* The science and technology of space flight and the design, construction, and operation of spacecraft. [ASTRO- + Latin *nauticus,* nautical.] **—as'tro·nau'tic** or **as'tro·nau'ti·cal** *adj.* **—as'tro·nau'ti·cal·ly** *adv.*

as·tron·o·mer (ə-strŏn'ə-mər) *n.* A scientist specializing in astronomy. [Middle English, from Late Latin *astronomus,* from Greek *astronomos,* "star-arranger" : *astron,* star + *nemein,* to arrange.]

as·tro·nom·i·cal (ăs'trə-nŏm'ĭ-kəl) or **as·tro·nom·ic** (-nŏm'ĭk) *adj.* **1.** Of or pertaining to astronomy. **2.** Inconceivably large; immense: *The national budget is astronomical.* **—as'tro·nom'i·cal·ly** *adv.*

astronomical unit. A unit of distance equal to the average distance between the earth and the sun, about 150 kilometers or 93 million miles.

as·tron·o·my (ə-strŏn'ə-mē) *n.* The scientific study of the universe beyond the earth, esp. the observation, calculation, and interpretation of the positions, dimensions, distribution, motion, composition, and evolution of celestial bodies and phenomena.

as·tro·phys·ics (ăs'trō-fĭz'ĭks) *n. (used with a sing. verb).* The science that studies the physical and chemical nature of celestial bodies and the phenomena that occur in outer space. **—as′tro·phys′i·cal** *adj.* **—as′tro·phys′i·cist** (-fĭz′ĭ-sĭst) *n.*

as·tute (ə-stoōt′, ə-styoōt′) *adj.* Keen in judgment; shrewd; crafty: *an astute diplomat; an astute appraisal.* —See Syns at **shrewd.** [Latin *astūtus,* from *astus,* craft.] **—as·tute′ly** *adv.* **—as·tute′ness** *n.*

a·sun·der (ə-sŭn′dər) *adv.* **1.** Into separate parts or groups: *The bridge fell asunder.* **2.** Apart in position or direction: *a town torn asunder by scandal.* [Middle English *asonder,* from Old English *onsundran : on,* on + *sunder,* apart, separate.]

a·sy·lum (ə-sī′ləm) *n.* **1.** An institution for the care of the mentally ill or the aged. **2.** A place offering protection or safety; refuge. **3.** A temple or church affording sanctuary against arrest for criminals or debtors. **4.** Protection and immunity from extradition granted by a government to a political fugitive from another country. [Middle English *asilum,* from Latin *asylum,* from Greek *asulon,* sanctuary, from *asulos,* inviolable : *a-,* without + *sulon,* right of seizure.]

a·sym·met·ric (ā′sĭ-mĕt′rĭk) or **a·sym·met·ri·cal** (-rĭ-kəl) *adj.* Not symmetrical. **—a′sym·met′ri·cal·ly** *adv.*

a·sym·me·try (ā-sĭm′ĭ-trē) *n.* Lack of symmetry or balance.

as·ymp·tote (ăs′ĭm-tōt′, -ĭmp-) *n.* A straight line that is approached but never met by a moving point on a curve as the point moves an infinite distance from the origin. [New Latin *asymptōta,* from Greek *asumptōtos,* not falling together : *a-,* not + *sumpiptein,* to fall together : *sun-,* together + *piptein,* to fall.] **—as′ymp·tot′ic** (-tŏt′ĭk) or **as′ymp·tot′i·cal** *adj.*

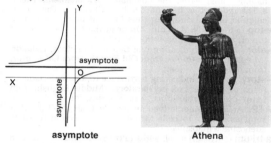

asymptote

at (ăt; ət *when unstressed*) *prep.* **1.** —Used to indicate position, location, or state: *at home; at rest.* **2.** —Used to indicate a direction or goal: *look at us.* **3.** —Used to indicate location in time: *at noon.* **4.** —Used to indicate manner, means, or cause: *getting there at top speed.* **5.** —Used informally as an intensive with *where: trying to figure out where things are really at.* **—Note:** *At* is used with certain words to form the following adverbial groups: **at all.** In any way whatsoever: *no good at all.* **at once. 1.** At one time; simultaneously: *everything happening at once.* **2.** Immediately: *Leave the room at once.* **at one.** In harmony: *feeling at one with the world.* [Middle English *at, atte,* from Old English *æt.*]

Usage: The word **at** is a preposition requiring an object. The adverb *where* meaning at which place cannot be used as the object of *at* in these sentences following *he* (in the first) or *is* (in the second): *Where is he now? This is where he is.*

At The symbol for the element astatine.

at·a·vism (ăt′ə-vĭz′əm) *n.* **1.** The reappearance of a characteristic in an organism after several generations of absence caused by a recessive gene or complementary genes. **2.** An individual or part displaying atavism. [French *atavisme,* from Latin *atavus,* ancestor : *atta,* father + *avus,* grandfather.] **—at′a·vist** *n.* **—at′a·vis′tic** *adj.* **—at′a·vis′ti·cal·ly** *adv.*

a·tax·i·a (ə-tăk′sē-ə) *n.* Loss or lack of muscular coordination. [Greek, from *ataktos,* disorderly : *a-,* not + *tattein,* to arrange.]

a·tax·ic (ə-tăk′sĭk) *adj.* Of or pertaining to ataxia. **—n.** An individual exhibiting symptoms of ataxia.

ate (āt) *v.* Past tense of **eat.**

-ate[1]. A suffix indicating: **1. a.** Possessing: **affectionate. b.** Shaped like: **lyrate. c.** Having the general characteris-

tics of: **Latinate. 2. a.** A substance derived from: **stearate. b.** *Chem.* The salt or ester of an acid: **nitrate. 3.** Verbs with an unrestricted spread of meanings, such as to make in a specified way, to apply, to operate upon: **pollinate.** [Middle English *-at,* from Old French, from Latin *-ātus,* ending of the past part. of verbs in *-āre.*]

-ate[2]. A suffix indicating rank or office: **rabbinate.** [Latin *-ātus.*]

at·el·ier (ăt′l-yā′) *n.* A workshop or studio, esp. an artist's studio. [French, from Old French *astelier,* woodpile, hence carpenter's shop, from *astele,* splinter, chip, from Late Latin *astella,* var. of Latin *astula,* dim. of *assis,* board, plank.]

Ath·a·pas·can (ăth′ə-păs′kən) *n.* Also **Ath·a·bas·can** (-băs′kən). **1.** A linguistic stock of North American Indians, including languages of Alaska and northwestern Canada, the coast of Oregon and California, and the Navaho and Apache languages of the southwestern United States. **2.** A member of an Athapascan-speaking tribe. **—Ath′a·pas′can** *adj.*

a·the·ism (ā′thē-ĭz′əm) *n.* Disbelief in or denial of the existence of God. [Old French *atheisme,* from Greek *atheos,* godless, from *a-,* without + *theos,* god.]

a·the·ist (ā′thē-ĭst) *n.* A person who denies the existence of God. **—a′the·is′tic** *adj.*

A·the·na (ə-thē′nə). Also **A·the·ne** (-nē) *n. Gk. Myth.* The goddess of wisdom and the arts, identified with the Roman goddess Minerva. Also called **Pallas Athena.**

ath·e·nae·um (ăth′ə-nē′əm) *n.* Also **ath·e·ne·um. 1.** An institution, such as a literary club or scientific academy, for the promotion of learning. **2.** A library, reading room, or similar place. [Late Latin *Athēnaeum,* a Roman school of art, after Greek *Athēnaion,* the temple of Athena at Athens.]

A·the·ne (ə-thē′nē) *n. Gk. Myth.* Var. of **Athena.**

ath·er·o·scle·ro·sis (ăth′ə-rō-sklə-rō′sĭs) *n.* An arteriosclerosis in which fatty deposits form on inner arterial walls. [Latin *athērōma,* a tumor filled with gruel-like pus, from Greek + SCLEROSIS.]

a·thirst (ə-thûrst′) *adj.* **1.** Strongly desirous; eager: *athirst for freedom.* **2.** *Archaic.* Thirsty.

ath·lete (ăth′lēt′) *n.* **1.** A person who takes part in competitive sports. **2.** A person who possesses the natural aptitudes for physical exercises and sports, as strength, agility, and endurance. [Middle English, from Latin *athlēta,* from Greek *athlētēs,* from *athlein,* to contend for an award, from *athlon,* award, prize.]

ath·lete's foot (ăth′lēts′). A contagious skin infection caused by parasitic fungi usu. affecting the feet and causing itching, blisters, cracking, and scaling.

ath·let·ic (ăth-lĕt′ĭk) *adj.* **1.** Of, pertaining to, or for athletics or athletes: *athletic ability; an athletic club.* **2.** Physically strong; muscular. **—ath·let′i·cal·ly** *adv.*

ath·let·ics (ăth-lĕt′ĭks) *n. (used with a pl. verb).* Athletic activities; sports.

at-home (ət-hōm′) *n.* An informal reception.

athletic supporter. An elastic support for the male genitals, worn during sports or other strenuous activity. Also called **jock strap.**

a·thwart (ə-thwôrt′) *adv.* **1.** From side to side; crosswise; transversely. **2.** So as to thwart or obstruct; perversely. **—prep. 1.** From one side to the other of; across. **2.** Contrary to; against. **3.** *Naut.* Across the course, line, or length of.

a·tilt (ə-tĭlt′) *adj. & adv.* In a tilted position; inclined upward.

-ation. A suffix indicating: **1.** Action or process of: **negotiation. 2.** State, condition, or quality of: **moderation. 3.** Result or product of: **civilization.** [Middle English *-acioun,* from Old French *-ation,* from Latin *-ātiō,* abstract noun suffix, from *-ātus,* -ATE.]

-ative. A suffix indicating relation, nature, or tendency: **formative.** [Middle English, from Old French *-atif,* from Latin *-ātīvus,* from *-ātus,* -ATE.]

At·lan·tic (ăt-lăn′tĭk) *adj.* Of, in, near, on, or pertaining to the Atlantic Ocean.

Atlantic Standard Time. Standard time as reckoned in the region between the meridians at 52.5° and 67.5° west of Greenwich, England. The eastern edge of Canada is in this region.

Athena

| ă pat | ā pay | â care | ä father | ĕ pet | ē be | hw which | ĭ pit | ī tie | î pier | ŏ pot | ō toe | ô paw, for | oi noise |
| oō took | ōō boot | ou out | th thin | *th* this | ŭ cut | | û urge | zh vision | ə about, item, edible, gallop, circus |

At·lan·tis (ăt-lăn′tĭs) *n.* A legendary island in the Atlantic Ocean west of Gibraltar, said by Plato to have sunk beneath the sea during an earthquake.

At·las (ăt′ləs) *n.* **1.** *Gk. Myth.* A Titan condemned to support the heavens upon his shoulders. **2. atlas.** Any person supporting a great burden. **3. atlas.** A book or bound collection of maps. **4. atlas.** Any volume of tables, charts, etc., that illustrates a particular subject: *an anatomical atlas.*

Atlas

at·mos·phere (ăt′mə-sfîr′) *n.* **1.** The gaseous mass or envelope surrounding the earth and is held by the body's gravitational field. **2.** The atmosphere or climate in a specific place: *a stuffy atmosphere.* **3.** *Abbr.* **atm** *Physics.* A unit of pressure equal to 1.01325×10^5 newtons per square meter. **4.** Environment or surroundings regarded as having a psychological, physical, or other influence: *the quiet atmosphere of a hospital. He grew up in an atmosphere of austerity.* **5.** The predominant tone or mood of a work of art: *the atmosphere of a story.* **6.** *Informal.* A quality or effect considered to be exotic or romantic: *We love the atmosphere of that little restaurant.* [New Latin *atmosphaera* : *atmos*, vapor + -SPHERE.]

at·mos·pher·ic (ăt′mə-sfĕr′ĭk, -sfîr′ĭk) or **at·mos·pher·i·cal** (-ĭ-kəl) *adj.* **1.** Of, pertaining to, or existing in the atmosphere: *atmospheric flight.* **2.** Produced by, dependent on, or coming from the atmosphere: *atmospheric pressure.* —**at′mos·pher′i·cal·ly** *adv.*

at·mos·pher·ics (ăt′mə-sfĕr′ĭks, -sfîr′ĭks) *n.* (used with a sing. verb). **1.** Electromagnetic radiation produced by natural phenomena such as lightning. **2.** Radio interference produced by such radiation.

at·oll (ăt′ôl′, -ŏl′, ā′tôl′, ā′tŏl′) *n.* A coral island or a string of coral islands forming a ring that encloses a lagoon wholly or in part. [Malayalam *atoḷu*, "reef," native name for the Maldive Islands.]

at·om (ăt′əm) *n.* **1.** Anything considered the smallest irreducible particle of any substance or element. **2.** *Physics & Chem.* **a.** A unit of matter, the smallest unit of an element, consisting of a dense, positively charged nucleus surrounded by a system of electrons equal in number to the number of nuclear protons, and characteristically remaining undivided in chemical reactions except for limited removal, transfer, or exchange of certain electrons. **b.** This unit regarded as a source of nuclear energy. **3.** A tiny amount; bit or jot: *She hasn't an atom of talent.* [Middle English *attome*, from Latin *atomus*, from Greek *atomos*, indivisible : *a-*, not + *temnein*, to cut.]

atom bomb. Another name for an **atomic bomb.**

a·tom·ic (ə-tŏm′ĭk) *adj.* **1.** Of or relating to an atom or atoms. **2.** Of or employing nuclear energy; nuclear: *an atomic submarine.* **3.** Very small; infinitesimal. —**a·tom′i·cal·ly** *adv.*

atomic bomb. **1.** An explosive weapon of great destructive power derived from the rapid release of energy in the fission of heavy atomic nuclei, as of uranium 235. **2.** Any bomb deriving its destructive power from the release of nuclear energy. Also called **atom bomb** and **A-bomb.**

atomic energy. **1.** The energy released from an atomic nucleus in fission or fusion. **2.** This energy regarded as a source of practical power.

atomic mass. The mass of an atomic system or constitu-

ent, usu. expressed in atomic mass units.

atomic mass unit. *Abbr.* **amu** A unit of mass equal to $1/12$ the mass of the carbon isotope with mass number 12, approx. 1.6604×10^{-24} gram.

atomic number. *Symbol* **Z** The number of protons in an atomic nucleus.

atomic theory. The physical theory of the structure, properties, and behavior of the atom.

atomic weight. *Abbr.* **at wt** The average weight of an atom of an element, usu. expressed in relation to the isotope of carbon taken to have a standard weight of 12.

at·om·ize (ăt′ə-mīz′) *tr.v.* **-ized, -iz·ing.** **1.** To reduce or separate into atoms. **2. a.** To break up (a liquid) into a fine mist or spray. **b.** To spray (a liquid) in this form. **3.** To subject to bombardment with atomic weapons. —**at′om·i·za′tion** *n.*

at·om·iz·er (ăt′ə-mī′zər) *n.* A device for producing a fine spray, esp. of perfume or medicine.

atom smasher. *Physics.* Another name for **accelerator.**

a·ton·al (ā-tō′nəl) *adj. Mus.* Having no apparent key or tonality. —**a·to·nal′i·ty** (ā′tō-năl′ĭ-tē) *n.* —**a·ton′al·ly** *adv.*

a·tone (ə-tōn′) *v.* **a·toned, a·ton·ing.** —*intr.v.* To make amends, as for a sin or fault: *atone for tardiness by staying late.* —*tr.v. Archaic.* To expiate. [Middle English *atonen*, to be reconciled, from *at one*, of one mind, in accord, from AT + ONE.]

a·tone·ment (ə-tōn′mənt) *n.* **1.** Amends or reparation made for an injury or wrong; expiation; recompense. **2.** In the Hebrew Scriptures, man's reconciliation with God after having transgressed the covenant. **3. Atonement.** *Theol.* **a.** The redemptive life and death of Christ. **b.** The reconciliation of God and man thus brought about by Christ.

a·top (ə-tŏp′) *adv. Archaic.* On or at the top. —*prep.* On top of: *a restaurant atop the mountain.*

-ator. A suffix indicating one that acts or does: **radiator.** [Middle English *-atour*, from Old French, from Latin *-ātor*, from *ātus*, -ATE + -OR.]

-atory. A suffix indicating pertinence to, characteristic of, result of, or effect of: **perspiratory.** [Middle English, from Latin *-ātōrius*, from *-ātus*, -ATE + -*ōrius*, -ORY.]

ATP. An adenosine-derived nucleotide, $C_{10}H_{16}N_5O_{13}P_3$, that supplies energy to cells through its conversion to ADP; adenosine triphosphate.

a·tri·um (ā′trē-əm) *n., pl.* **a·tri·a** (ā′trē-ə) or **-ums.** **1.** An open central court, esp. in an ancient Roman house. **2.** A cavity or chamber of the body, esp. one of the chambers of the heart that receive blood from the veins. Also called **auricle.** [Latin *ātrium.*]

a·tro·cious (ə-trō′shəs) *adj.* **1.** Extremely evil or cruel; monstrous: *an atrocious crime.* **2.** Exceptionally bad; abominable: *atrocious furniture; atrocious behavior.* — See Syns at **outrageous.** [From Latin *ātrōx*, "dark-looking," horrible.] —**a·tro′cious·ly** *adv.* —**a·tro′cious·ness** *n.*

a·troc·i·ty (ə-trŏs′ĭ-tē) *n., pl.* **-ties.** **1.** Atrocious condition, quality, or behavior; monstrousness; vileness. **2.** An atrocious action, situation, or object; an outrage.

at·ro·phy (ăt′rə-fē) *n., pl.* **-phies.** **1.** *Pathol.* The emaciation or wasting away of tissues, organs, or the entire body. **2.** Any wasting away or diminution: *atrophy of one's unused talents.* —*v.* **-phied, -phy·ing.** —*tr.v.* To cause to wither; affect with atrophy: *a disease that atrophied her arm.* —*intr.v.* To waste away; wither: *The muscle atrophied from disuse.* [Late Latin *atrophia*, from Greek,

atomic bomb

from *atrophos,* ill-nourished : *a-,* without + *trophē,* nourishment.] **—a·tro′phic** (ā-trŏ′fĭk) *adj.*

at·ro·pine (ăt′rə-pēn′, -pĭn) *n.* Also **at·ro·pin** (-pĭn). A poisonous, bitter, crystalline alkaloid, $C_{17}H_{23}NO_3$, obtained from belladonna and related plants. It is used to dilate the pupil of the eye and as an anesthetic and antispasmodic. [German *Atropin,* from New Latin *Atropa,* genus of belladonna, from Greek *atropos,* unchangeable, inflexible : *a-,* not + *trepein,* to turn.]

at·tach (ə-tăch′) *tr.v.* **1.** To fasten on or affix to; connect or join: *attach the wires.* **2.** To connect as an adjunct or associated part. **3.** To affix or add something at the end, as a signature; append. **4.** To think of as belonging to; ascribe or assign: *I attach no significance to the threat.* **5.** To bind by personal ties of affection or loyalty: *He's very attached to his mother.* **6.** *Mil.* To assign (personnel) to a unit on a temporary basis. **7.** *Law.* To seize (persons or property) by legal writ. *—intr.v.* **1.** To fasten; affix: *The wires attach here.* **2.** To go with; fasten itself: *the present stigma that attaches to their political views.* [Middle English *attachen,* from Old French *attacher, estachier,* to fasten (with a stake), from *estache,* stake.] **—at·tach′a·ble** *adj.* **—at·tach′er** *n.*
   Syns: attach, affix, clip, connect, couple, fasten, fix, secure *v.* *Core meaning:* To join one thing to another (*the hinges to which the door is attached*).

at·ta·ché (ăt′ə-shā′, ă-tă′shā′) *n.* A person assigned to the staff of an embassy or a diplomatic mission to serve in a particular capacity: *cultural attaché.* [French, "one attached (to a diplomatic mission).'']

attaché case. A briefcase resembling a small suitcase, with hinges and flat sides.

at·tach·ment (ə-tăch′mənt) *n.* **1.** The act of attaching or the condition of being attached. **2.** Something that attaches one thing to another; a tie, band, or fastening. **3.** A bond of affection or loyalty; fond regard: *a strong attachment to a friend.* **4.** A supplementary part; an accessory: *a food processor with attachments.* **5.** *Law.* **a.** The legal seizure of a person or property. **b.** The writ ordering such a seizure.

at·tack (ə-tăk′) *tr.v.* **1.** To set upon with violent force; begin hostilities against or a conflict with. **2.** To criticize strongly or in a hostile manner. **3.** To start work on with purpose and vigor: *attack a problem.* **4.** To affect harmfully; afflict: *Flu attacked thousands of people.* *—intr.v.* To make an attack; launch an assault: *The troops attacked at dawn.* *—n.* **1.** The act of attacking; an assault. **2.** Occurrence or onset of a disease. **3.** The initial movement in any task or undertaking: *an attack on a messy room.* **4.** *Mus.* The manner in which a tone, phrase, or passage is begun: *a hard, cutting attack.* [French *attaquer,* from Old French, from Old Italian *attaccare.*] **—at·tack′er** *n.*
   Syns: attack, assail, assault, beset, fall on (or **upon**), **strike** *v.* *Core meaning:* To set upon with violent force (*The terrorists attacked the train without warning.*).

at·tain (ə-tān′) *tr.v.* **1.** To gain, accomplish, or achieve by mental or physical effort. **2.** To arrive at, as in time. *—intr.v.* To succeed in gaining or reaching; arrive at: *He attained to the highest office in the land. —See Syns at* **accomplish.** [Middle English *atteignen,* from Old French *ataindre,* to reach to, from Latin *attingere : ad-,* to + *tangere,* to touch.] **—at·tain′a·bil′i·ty** or **at·tain′a·ble·ness** *n.* **—at·tain′a·ble** *adj.*

at·tain·der (ə-tān′dər) *n.* **1.** The loss of all civil rights legally by a person who has been sentenced for a serious crime, such as murder or treason. **2.** *Archaic.* Dishonor. [Middle English *attendre,* conviction, from Norman French, "corruption of blood (of a criminal),'' from Old French *ataindre,* to stain, affect, ATTAIN.]

at·tain·ment (ə-tān′mənt) *n.* **1.** The act of attaining. **2.** Often **attainments.** Something that is attained or acquired, as a skill or ability: *a man well-known for his scientific attainments.*

at·taint (ə-tānt′) *tr.v.* **1.** *Law.* To condemn by a sentence of attainder. **2.** *Archaic.* To disgrace or dishonor. *—n.* **1.** Attainder. **2.** *Archaic.* A disgrace or dishonor. [Middle English *attaynten,* from Old French *ataint,* past part. of *ataindre,* to convict, affect, ATTAIN.]

at·tar (ăt′ər) *n.* A fragrant essential oil obtained from the petals of flowers, esp. certain species of roses, used in

making perfume. [Persian *'aṭir,* perfumed, from *'iṭr,* perfume, of Arabic orig.]

at·tempt (ə-tĕmpt′) *tr.v.* To make an effort to do; to try: *Don't attempt to climb that mountain alone.* *—n.* **1.** An effort or try. **2.** An attack; an assault: *an attempt on the dictator's life.* [Middle English *attempten,* from Old French *attempter,* from Latin *attemptāre : ad-,* to + *temptāre,* to tempt.] **—at·tempt′a·ble** *adj.*

at·tend (ə-tĕnd′) *tr.v.* **1.** To be present at; go to: *attend class.* **2.** To accompany as a circumstance or follow as a result: *Bad luck attended his trip.* **3.** To accompany as an attendant or servant; wait upon. **4.** To take care or charge of: *The nurse attended the invalid.* **5.** To listen to; heed. *—intr.v.* **1.** To be present. **2.** To pay attention. **3.** To remain ready to serve; wait: *We attend upon your wishes.* *—phrasal verb.* **attend to.** To apply or direct oneself: *Please attend to the matter at once.* [Middle English *attenden,* from Old French *atendre,* from Latin *attendere,* to stretch toward : *ad-,* toward + *tendere,* to stretch.]

at·ten·dance (ə-tĕn′dəns) *n.* **1.** The act or practice of being present: *His attendance at school is perfect.* **2.** The persons or number of persons who are present: *an attendance of 50,000 at the football game.*

at·ten·dant (ə-tĕn′dənt) *n.* **1.** A person who attends or waits upon another. **2.** A person who is present, as at a class. **3.** An accompanying thing or circumstance; a consequence. *—adj.* Accompanying or consequent: *attendant circumstances.* **—at·tend′ant·ly** *adv.*

at·ten·tion (ə-tĕn′shən) *n.* **1.** Concentration of the mental powers upon someone or something; a close or careful observing or listening: *Pay attention to the footnotes.* **2.** The ability or power to concentrate mentally. **3.** Observant consideration; notice: *Your suggestion has come to our attention.* **4.** Consideration or courtesy: *attention to others' feelings.* **5. attentions.** Acts of courtesy, consideration, or gallantry indicating romantic interest. **6.** *Mil.* **a.** The posture assumed by a soldier, with the body erect, eyes to the front, arms at the sides, and heels together. **b.** A command to assume this position. [Middle English *attencioun,* from Latin *attentiō,* from *attendere,* ATTEND.]

at·ten·tive (ə-tĕn′tĭv) *adj.* **1.** Paying attention; observant; listening: *attentive during class.* **2.** Courteous or devoted; considerate; thoughtful: *an attentive husband.* **—at·ten′tive·ly** *adv.* **—at·ten′tive·ness** *n.*

at·ten·u·ate (ə-tĕn′yōō-āt′) *v.* **-at·ed, -at·ing.** *—tr.v.* **1.** To make slender, fine, or small: *attenuate strands of pure gold.* **2.** To reduce in strength, force, value, or amount; weaken. **3.** To lessen in density; dilute or rarefy (a liquid or gas). *—intr.v.* To become thin, weak, or fine. *—adj.* (ə-tĕn′yōō-ĭt). **1.** Thinned; diluted; weakened. **2.** *Bot.* Gradually tapering to a point; slender and pointed. [Latin *attenuāre : ad-,* to + *tenuis,* thin.] **—at·ten′u·a·ble** (-ə-bəl) *adj.* **—at·ten′u·a′tion** *n.*

at·test (ə-tĕst′) *tr.v.* **1.** To affirm to be correct, true, or genuine, esp. by affixing one's signature as witness: *attest a will.* **2.** To supply evidence or proof of: *The vast palaces attested the wealth of the empire.* **3.** To put under oath. *—intr.v.* To bear witness; give testimony: *I attest to his good faith.* [Middle English *attester,* from Old French, from Latin *attestārī : ad-,* to + *testis,* witness.] **—at·test′ant** *n.* **—at·test′er** *n.* **—at′tes·ta′tion** (ăt′ĕs-tā′shən, ăt′ə-stā′-) *n.*

at·tic (ăt′ĭk) *n.* **1.** A story, room, or space directly below the roof of a house. **2.** *Archit.* A low wall or story above the cornice of a classical façade. [From *Attic story,* orig. a small top story having square columns in the Attic style.]

At·tic (ăt′ĭk) *adj.* **1.** Of, pertaining to, or characteristic of ancient Athens or the Athenians. **2.** Often **attic.** Characterized by classical purity and simplicity. *—n.* The Ancient Greek dialect of Athens, in which the bulk of Classical Greek literature is written.

at·tire (ə-tīr′) *tr.v.* **-tired, -tir·ing.** To dress, esp. in elaborate or formal garments; clothe; garb: *The emperor was attired in ceremonial robes. —See Syns at* **dress.** *—n.* **1.** Clothing, costume, or apparel: *white tennis attire.* **2.** *Heraldry.* The antlers of a deer. [Middle English *attiren,* from Old French *atirier,* to arrange into ranks, put in order : *a-,* to + *tire,* order, rank.]

at·ti·tude (ăt′ĭ-tōōd′, -tyōōd′) *n.* **1.** A position of the body or manner of carrying oneself, indicative of a mood or condi-

---

tion: *"Men . . . sprawled alone or in heaps, in the careless attitudes of death"* (John Reed). **2.** A state of mind or feeling with regard to a person, subject, etc.: *What is your attitude toward his paintings?* **3.** The orientation of an aircraft's axes relative to some reference line or plane, such as the horizon. **4.** The orientation of a spacecraft relative to its direction of motion. [French, from Italian *attitudine*, from Late Latin *aptitūdō*, fitness, from Latin *aptus*, apt.]

at·tor·ney (ə-tûr′nē) *n., pl.* **-neys.** A person legally appointed or empowered to act for another, esp. an attorney at law. [Middle English *attourney*, from Old French *atorner*, to appoint : *a-*, to + *torner*, to turn.]

attorney at law. A lawyer.

attorney general, *pl.* **attorneys general.** The chief law officer and legal counsel of the government of a state or the United States.

at·tract (ə-trăkt′) *tr.v.* **1.** To draw or direct to oneself or itself by some quality or action: *Sugar attracts insects. A magnet attracts nails. Their beaches attract many tourists.* **2.** To evoke interest or admiration in; to allure: *As a girl she attracted dozens of suitors.* —*intr.v.* To possess or use the power of attraction; be magnetic or alluring. [Middle English *attracten*, from Latin *attrahere* : *ad-*, toward + *trahere*, to draw.] —**at·tract′a·ble** *adj.*

Syns: attract, allure, appeal, draw, lure, magnetize, pull, take *v. Core meaning:* To direct or impel (another) to oneself by some quality or action (*A new star who attracted the fans' attention. A handsome face attracts all eyes.*).

at·trac·tion (ə-trăk′shən) *n.* **1.** The act or power of attracting: *the attraction of a magnet.* **2.** The quality of attracting; allure; charm. **3.** A feature, characteristic, or factor that attracts: *Money was not the least of her attractions.* **4.** A public spectacle or entertainment.

at·trac·tive (ə-trăk′tĭv) *adj.* **1.** Capable of attracting: *the attractive force of magnetism.* **2.** Pleasing to the eye or mind; appealing: *an attractive girl; an attractive offer.* —See Syns at **beautiful.** —**at·trac′tive·ly** *adv.* —**at·trac′tive·ness** *n.*

at·trib·ute (ə-trĭb′yoot) *tr.v.* **-ut·ed, -ut·ing.** To regard or consider as belonging to or resulting from someone or something; ascribe: *attribute air pollution to the exhaust of cars and buses.* —*n.* (ăt′rə-byoot′). **1.** A quality or characteristic belonging to a person or thing; a distinctive feature: *"Travel has lost the attributes of privilege and fashion"* (John Cheever). **2.** An object associated with and serving to identify a character, personage, or office: *A lightning bolt is the attribute of Zeus. His attributes are honesty and intelligence.* **3.** *Gram.* An adjective or a phrase used as an adjective. In the phrase "first-class hotel," "first-class" is the attribute of "hotel." [Latin *attribuere* : *ad-*, to + *tribuere*, to allot, from *tribus*, tribe.] —**at·trib′ut·a·ble** *adj.* —**at·trib′ut·er** *n.*

at·tri·bu·tion (ăt′rə-byoo′shən) *n.* **1.** The act of attributing. **2.** Something that is ascribed; an attribute.

at·trib·u·tive (ə-trĭb′yə-tĭv) *n. Gram.* A word or word group, such as an adjective or the equivalent of an adjective, that is placed adjacent to the noun it modifies without a linking verb. In the phrases *the pale girl* and *John's hands, pale* and *John's* are attributives. —*adj.* **1.** *Gram.* Of or functioning as an attributive. **2.** Of or having the nature of an attribution or attribute. **3.** Of an attributed origin: *an attributive Rubens.* —**at·trib′u·tive·ly** *adv.* —**at·trib′u·tive·ness** *n.*

at·tri·tion (ə-trĭsh′ən) *n.* **1.** A wearing away or rubbing down by friction. **2.** A gradual diminution in number or strength due to constant stress: *a war of attrition.* **3.** A gradual, natural reduction in membership or personnel, as through retirement, resignation, or death. [Middle English *attricioun*, from Medieval Latin *attrītiō*, from Latin, a rubbing against, from *atterere*, to rub against : *ad-*, toward, against + *terere*, to rub.] —**at·tri′tion·al** *adj.*

at·tune (ə-toon′, ə-tyoon′) *tr.v.* **-tuned, -tun·ing. 1.** To tune. **2.** To bring into harmony; adjust: *a person attuned to the times.* [AD- (to) + TUNE.]

a·twit·ter (ə-twĭt′ər) *adj.* In a state of nervous excitement.

a·typ·i·cal (ā-tĭp′ĭ-kəl) or **a·typ·ic** (ā-tĭp′ĭk). *adj.* Not typical; varying from the type; abnormal: *atypical behavior; atypical petals.* —**a·typ′i·cal·ly** *adv.*

Au The symbol for the element gold. [Latin *aurum*.]

au·burn (ô′bərn) *n.* A reddish brown. —*adj.* Reddish brown: *auburn hair.* [Middle English *aborne*, blond, from Old French *auborne, alborne*, from Medieval Latin *alburnus*, whitish, from Latin *albus*, white.]

au cou·rant (ō′ koo-rän′). Informed on current affairs; up-to-date. [French, "in the current."]

auc·tion (ôk′shən) *n.* **1.** A public sale in which property or goods are sold to the highest bidder. **2.** *Cards.* The bidding in the game of bridge. —*modifier:* *an auction block; auction rooms.* —*tr.v.* To sell at or by an auction: *auction a house; auction off a diamond ring.* [Latin *auctiō*, (a sale by) increase (of bids), from *augēre*, to increase.]

auction

auction bridge. A variety of the game of bridge in which tricks made in excess of the contract are scored toward game.

auc·tion·eer (ôk′shə-nîr′) *n.* A person who conducts an auction. —*tr.v.* To auction.

auc·to·ri·al (ôk-tôr′ē-əl, -tōr′-) *adj.* Of or pertaining to an author. [From Latin *auctor*, author.]

au·da·cious (ô-dā′shəs) *adj.* **1.** Fearlessly daring; bold: *an audacious explorer.* **2.** Lacking restraint or circumspection; arrogantly insolent; impudent: *audacious behavior.* —See Syns at **brave** and **impudent.** [Old French *audacieux*, from *audace*, boldness, from Latin *audācia*, from *audāx*, bold, from *audēre*, to dare, from *avidus*, avid.] —**au·da′cious·ly** *adv.* —**au·da′cious·ness** *n.*

au·dac·i·ty (ô-dăs′ĭ-tē) *n., pl.* **-ties. 1.** Courage and resolution; boldness; daring: *The audacity of a few navigators led to the discovery of the New World.* **2.** Unrestrained impudence; presumption; insolence. **3.** An instance of boldness or presumption.

au·di·ble (ô′də-bəl) *adj.* Capable of being heard: *an audible whisper.* [Late Latin *audībilis*, from *audīre*, to hear.] —**au·di·bil′i·ty** *n.* —**au′di·bly** *adv.*

au·di·ence (ô′dē-əns) *n.* **1.** A gathering of spectators or listeners, as at a play, movie, concert, etc. **2.** The readers, hearers, or viewers reached by a book, radio broadcast, or television program. **3.** A formal hearing or conference: *an audience with the pope.* **4.** An opportunity to be heard or to express one's views. **5.** The act of hearing or attending. [Middle English, from Old French, from Latin *audientia*, from *audīre*, to hear.]

au·di·o (ô′dē-ō′) *adj.* **1.** Of or pertaining to sound or hearing. **2.** Of or pertaining to the reproduction or broadcasting of sound. —*n.* **1.** The audio part of television equipment. **2.** Audio broadcasting or reception. **3.** Audible sound. [From AUDIO-.]

audio-. A prefix meaning sound or hearing: **audiometer.** [From Latin *audīre*, to hear.]

audio frequency. A range of frequencies, usu. from 15 cycles per second to 20,000 cycles per second. Only sound waves that lie in this range are audible to the normal human ear.

au·di·om·e·ter (ô′dē-ŏm′ĭ-tər) *n.* An instrument for measuring hearing for tones of normally audible frequencies. [AUDIO- + -METER.] —**au′di·o·met′ric** (-ō-mĕt′rĭk) *adj.* —**au′di·om′e·try** *n.*

au·di·o·vis·u·al (ô′dē-ō-vĭzh′oo-əl) *adj.* **1.** Both audible and visible. **2.** Of or pertaining to educational materials that make use of electrical devices to present information in both audible and visible form, as filmstrips or recordings. **au·di·o·vis·u·als** (ô′dē-ō-vĭzh′oo-əlz) *n.* (used with a pl.

verb). Educational materials that present information in audible and visible form.

au·dit (ô′dĭt) *n.* **1.** An official examination of records or accounts to check their accuracy. **2.** An adjustment of accounts. **3.** An examined and verified account. —*tr.v.* **1.** To examine, verify, or correct (financial records or accounts). **2.** To attend (a college course) without receiving academic credit. —*intr.v.* To examine accounts. [Middle English, from Latin *audītus,* a hearing, from *audīre,* to hear.]

au·di·tion (ô-dĭsh′ən) *n.* **1.** The act or sense of hearing. **2.** A presentation of something heard; a hearing: *"Many a dizzy venture at the Opera House had owed its audition to her"* (Ronald Firbank). **3.** A test or trial performance, as of an actor, musician, or other performer applying for employment. —*tr.v.* To give (someone) an audition. —*intr.v.* To perform or be tested in an audition: *He auditioned for a part in the play.* [Latin *audītiō,* from *audīre,* to hear.]

au·di·tor (ô′dĭ-tər) *n.* **1.** A hearer or listener: *the auditors of a concert.* **2.** A person who examines financial records or accounts in order to check their accuracy. **3.** A person who audits courses.

au·di·to·ri·um (ô′dĭ-tôr′ē-əm, -tōr′-) *n., pl.* **-ums** or **-to·ri·a** (-tôr′ē-ə, -tōr′-). **1.** A room to accommodate the audience in a school, theater, or other building. **2.** A large building for public meetings or artistic performances. [Latin *audītōrium,* from *audīre,* to hear.]

au·di·to·ry (ô′dĭ-tôr′ē, -tōr′ē) *adj.* Of or pertaining to the sense, the organs, or the experience of hearing. [Late Latin *audītōrius,* from Latin *audīre,* to hear.]

auf Wie·der·seh·en (ouf vē′dər-zā′ən). *German.* Until we see one another again; farewell.

Au·ge·an (ô-jē′ən) *adj.* Exceedingly filthy from long neglect. [From *Augeas,* legendary king, who left his stable uncleaned for thirty years.]

au·ger (ô′gər) *n.* **1.** A tool, larger than a gimlet, for boring holes in wood. **2.** A large tool for boring into the earth. [Middle English *an auger,* orig. *a nauger,* from Old English *nafogār,* "tool for piercing wheel hubs."]

auger

aught[1] (ôt). Also **ought.** —*pron.* **1.** All: *For aught we know he may have changed his name.* **2.** *Archaic.* Anything at all; any least part. —*adv. Archaic.* At all; in any respect. [Middle English *aught,* from Old English *āuht, āwiht,* anything.]

aught[2] (ôt) *n.* Also **ought. 1.** A cipher; the symbol 0; zero. **2.** *Archaic.* Nothing. [From *an aught,* orig. *a* NAUGHT (zero).]

aug·ment (ôg-mĕnt′) *tr.v.* To make larger, as in size, extent, or quantity; enlarge; increase: *The library has been augmented by 5,000 new books.* —*intr.v.* To become greater; enlarge. —See Syns at **increase.** [Middle English *augmenten,* from Old French *augmenter,* from Late Latin *augmentāre,* from Latin *augēre,* to increase.] —**aug·ment′·a·ble** *adj.* —**aug′men·ta′tion** *n.* —**aug·ment′er** *n.*

aug·men·ta·tive (ôg-mĕn′tə-tĭv) *adj.* Also **aug·men·tive** (-mĕn′tĭv). **1.** Having the tendency or ability to augment. **2.** *Gram.* Producing an increase in the size or intensity of the meaning of the original word, as the word *up* in the phrase *eat up.* —*n. Gram.* An augmentative word or suffix.

au gra·tin (ō grät′n, grăt′n). Covered with bread crumbs and often grated cheese and browned in an oven. [French, "with the crust (of bread crumbs)."]

au·gur (ô′gər) *n.* **1.** A religious official of ancient Rome who foretold events by observing and interpreting signs and omens. **2.** A seer or prophet; soothsayer. —*tr.v.* **1.** To predict or prognosticate, as from signs or omens. **2.** To serve as an omen of; betoken: *Early returns augured victory for him.* —*intr.v.* To conjecture or foretell from signs or omens. —*idiom.* **augur well** (or **ill**). To indicate or prom-

ise a favorable or unfavorable outcome: *A cloudless sky augurs well for the picnic.* [Latin, a senior priest of divination.]

au·gu·ry (ô′gyə-rē) *n., pl.* **-ries. 1.** The art, ability, or practice of auguring; divination. **2.** The rite performed by an augur. **3.** A sign or omen; an indication.

au·gust (ô-gŭst′) *adj.* **1.** Inspiring awe or reverence; majestic. **2.** Venerable for reasons of age or high rank. [Latin *augustus,* venerable, magnificent.] —**au·gust′ly** *adv.* —**au·gust′ness** *n.*

Au·gust (ô′gəst) *n.* The eighth month of the year, after July and before September. August has 31 days. —*modifier: an August heat wave; an August vacation.* [Middle English, from Old English, from Latin *(mensis) Augustus,* (month) of Augustus (Caesar).]

Au·gus·tan (ô-gŭs′tən) *adj.* **1.** Pertaining to or characteristic of Augustus Caesar, his times, and the golden age of Latin literature that flowered during his reign. **2.** Pertaining to or characteristic of the classical tastes and principles that mark the literary style popular during the reign of Queen Anne in England. —*n.* An artist or writer of an Augustan age.

auk (ôk) *n.* Any of several sea birds of the family Alcidae, of northern regions, with a chunky body and short wings, such as the razor-billed auk. [Norwegian *alk,* from Old Norse *ālka.*]

auk

auld (ōld) *adj. Scot.* Old.

auld lang syne (ōld′ lăng zīn′, sīn′). The good old days long past. [Scottish, "old long since."]

aunt (ănt, änt) *n.* **1.** The sister of one's father or mother. **2.** The wife of one's uncle. [Middle English *aunte,* from Old French *ante,* from Latin *amita,* paternal aunt.]

au·ra (ôr′ə) *n.* **1.** An invisible breath or emanation. **2.** A distinctive air or quality that characterizes a person or thing: *a man with an aura of nobility and mystery.* [Middle English, from Latin, breeze, from Greek.]

au·ral (ôr′əl) *adj.* Of, pertaining to, or received through the ear or sense of hearing: *aural stimulation.* [From Latin *auris,* ear.]

au·re·ate (ôr′ē-ĭt) *adj.* **1.** Of a golden color; gilded. **2.** Speaking or writing in a florid and pompous style. [Middle English *aureat,* from Medieval Latin *aureātus,* from Latin *aureus,* from *aurum,* gold.]

au·re·ole (ôr′ē-ōl′) *n.* Also **au·re·o·la** (ô-rē′ə-lə). **1.** A circle of light or radiance surrounding the head or body of a representation of a sacred figure; a halo. **2.** A glow that surrounds a luminous celestial object, such as the sun or moon, esp. when observed through fog or haze. [Middle

aureole

ă pat	ā pay	â care	ä father	ĕ pet	ē be	hw which	ĭ pit	ī tie	î pier	ŏ pot	ō toe	ô paw, for	oi noise
ōō took	ōō boot	ou out	th thin	*th* this	ŭ cut		û urge	zh vision	ə about, item, edible, gallop, circus				

English *aureole,* from Old French *auriole,* from Medieval Latin *aureola,* golden, from Latin *aurum,* gold.]

au re·voir (ō' rə-vwár'). *French.* Until we meet again; good-by.

au·ri·cle (ôr'ĭ-kəl) *n.* **1. a.** *Anat.* The external part of the ear, the **pinna. b.** An **atrium,** a chamber of the heart. **2.** *Biol.* Any earlike part, process, or appendage, esp. at the base of an organ. [Latin *auricula,* dim. of *auris,* ear.]

au·ric·u·lar (ô-rĭk'yə-lər) *adj.* **1.** Of or pertaining to the sense or organs of hearing. **2.** Perceived by or spoken into the ear: *an auricular confession.* **3.** Having the shape of an ear. **4.** Of or pertaining to an atrium of the heart. —**au·ric'-u·lar·ly** *adv.*

au·rif·er·ous (ô-rĭf'ər-əs) *adj.* Containing gold; gold-bearing: *auriferous rocks and gravels.* [Latin *aurifer,* from *aurum,* gold.]

au·rochs (ou'rŏks', ôr'ŏks') *n., pl.* **aurochs.** An extinct horned animal of the Old World, believed to be the ancestor of domestic cattle. [German, from Old High German *ūrohso* : *ūro,* bison + *ohso,* ox.]

Au·ro·ra (ô-rôr'ə, ô-rōr'ə, ə-) *n.* **1.** *Rom. Myth.* The goddess of the dawn, identified with the Greek goddess Eos. **2. aurora.** A brilliant display of streaming lights, visible in the night sky chiefly in the polar regions and sometimes in temperate zones, thought to result from electrically charged particles, esp. those from the sun, entering the earth's magnetic field. **3. aurora.** *Poet.* The dawn.

aurora aus·tra·lis (ô-strā'lĭs). The aurora of the Southern Hemisphere; the southern lights. [New Latin, from AURORA + AUSTRAL.]

aurora bo·re·al·is (bôr'ē-ăl'ĭs, bōr'-). The aurora of the Northern Hemisphere; the northern lights. [New Latin, from AURORA + BOREAL.]

au·rous (ôr'əs) *adj.* Of or pertaining to gold, esp. with valence 1. [Late Latin *aurōsus,* from Latin *aurum,* gold.]

aus·cul·tate (ô'skəl-tāt') *v.* **-tat·ed, -tat·ing.** —*tr.v.* To examine (a person) by auscultation. —*intr.v.* To examine by auscultation. —**aus'cul·ta'tive** *adj.* —**aus'cul·ta'tor** *n.*

aus·cul·ta·tion (ô'skəl-tā'shən) *n.* **1.** The act of listening. **2.** *Med.* Diagnostic monitoring of the sounds made by internal organs or any internal bodily part. [Latin *auscultātiō,* from *auscultāre,* to listen to.]

aus·pice (ô'spĭs) *n., pl.* **aus·pic·es** (ô'spĭ-sēz', -sĭz). **1.** Often **auspices.** Protection or support; patronage: *The contest was run under the auspices of our organization.* **2. a.** A portent or omen, esp. when observed in the actions of birds. **b.** Divination from the actions of birds. [Latin *auspicium,* bird divination, from *auspex,* a bird augur : *avis,* bird + *specere,* to look.]

aus·pi·cious (ô-spĭsh'əs) *adj.* **1.** Attended by favorable circumstances; propitious: *an auspicious beginning for the business venture.* **2.** Marked by success; fortunate; prosperous: *The bazaar was an auspicious event for the building fund.* —See Syns at **favorable.** —**aus·pi'cious·ly** *adv.* —**aus·pi'cious·ness** *n.*

aus·tere (ô-stîr') *adj.* **1.** Severe or stern in disposition or appearance; somber; grave: *"An austere man that never laughed or smiled"* (Alan Paton). **2.** Severely simple, as in living habits; ascetic. **3.** Without adornment or ornamentation; simple; bare: *austere living quarters.* **4.** Harsh or barren: *an austere land to live in.* **5.** *Archaic.* Bitter or sour to the taste; astringent. [Middle English, from Old French, from Latin *austērus,* from Greek *austēros,* harsh, rough.] —**aus·tere'ly** *adv.* —**aus·tere'ness** *n.*

aus·ter·i·ty (ô-stĕr'ĭ-tē) *n., pl.* **-ties. 1.** The condition of being austere. **2.** Severely simple living conditions, esp. as an economic policy: *wartime austerity.* **3.** Often **austerities.** An ascetic habit or practice: *the austerities of hermits.* —*modifier: austerity measures.*

aus·tral (ô'strəl) *adj.* Of, pertaining to, or coming from the south: *austral winds.* [Middle English, from Latin *austrālis,* from *auster,* south.]

Aus·tra·lian (ô-strāl'yən) *n.* **1.** A native or citizen of Australia. **2.** An aborigine of Australia. **3.** Any of the languages of the Australian aborigines. —*adj.* Of or pertaining to Australia or its inhabitants and their languages or cultures.

Aus·tra·loid (ô'strə-loid') *adj.* Of or relating to an ethnic group including the Australian aborigines.

aus·tra·lo·pith·e·cine (ô-strā'lō-pĭth'ĭ-sīn') *n.* Any of several extinct manlike primates of the genera *Australopithecus* and *Paranthropus* or *Zinjanthropus,* known chiefly from Pleistocene fossil remains found in southern and eastern Africa. —*adj.* Of, pertaining to, or characteristic of the australopithecines. [From New Latin *Australopithecus,* "southern ape," from AUSTRAL + *pithēcus,* ape, from Greek *pithēkos.*]

au·then·tic (ô-thĕn'tĭk) *adj.* **1.** Worthy of trust, reliance, or belief; true; credible: *authentic records.* **2.** Not counterfeit or copied; having an undisputed origin; genuine: *an authentic Gutenberg Bible.* **3.** *Law.* Executed with due process of law: *an authentic deed.* [Middle English *autentik,* from Old French *autentique,* from Late Latin *authenticus,* from Greek *authentikos,* from *authentēs,* author.] —**au·then'ti·cal·ly** *adv.*

au·then·ti·cate (ô-thĕn'tĭ-kāt') *tr.v.* **-cat·ed, -cat·ing. 1.** To establish as being true; prove: *authenticate a story.* **2.** To establish (a painting, antique, etc.) as being genuine. **3.** To invest with legal validity, as a deed. —**au·then'ti·cat'ed** *adj.: an authenticated painting.* —**au·then'ti·ca'tion** *n.* —**au·then'ti·ca'tor** *n.*

au·then·tic·i·ty (ô'thĕn-tĭs'ĭ-tē) *n.* The condition or quality of being authentic or genuine.

au·thor (ô'thər) *n.* **1. a.** The original writer of a literary work. **b.** A person who practices writing as a profession. **c.** An author's works collectively. **2.** The beginner, originator, or creator of anything: *the author of an idea.* —*tr.v.* To be the author of; write: *He has authored several books.* [Middle English *autour,* from Old French *autor,* from Latin *auctor,* from *augēre* (past part. *auctus*), to create, increase.]

au·thor·i·tar·i·an (ə-thôr'ĭ-târ'ē-ən, ə-thŏr'-, ô-) *adj.* Characterized by or favoring absolute obedience to authority, as opposed to individual freedom. —*n.* A person who believes in authoritarian policies. —**au·thor'i·tar'i·an·ism** *n.*

au·thor·i·ta·tive (ə-thôr'ĭ-tā'tĭv, ə-thŏr'-, ô-) *adj.* **1.** Having or arising from proper authority; official: *the general's authoritative manner.* **2.** Having or showing expert knowledge: *authoritative sources.* —**au·thor'i·ta'tive·ly** *adv.* —**au·thor'i·ta'tive·ness** *n.*

au·thor·i·ty (ə-thôr'ĭ-tē, ə-thŏr'-, ô-) *n., pl.* **-ties. 1. a.** The right and power to command, enforce laws, determine, etc.: *The principal had the authority to close the school.* **b.** A person, group, or organization that has this right and power: *school authorities; the Transit Authority.* **2.** Power delegated to others; authorization: *You have my authority to decide.* **3.** An accepted source of expert information or advice, as a book or person: *an authority on history.* **4.** An expert in a given field: *a well-known plant authority.* **5.** Power to influence or to affect resulting from knowledge or experience: *write with authority.* —See Syns at **power.** [Middle English *autorite,* from Old French *auctorite,* from Latin *auctōritās,* from *auctor,* AUTHOR.]

au·thor·i·za·tion (ô'thər-ĭ-zā'shən) *n.* **1.** The act of authorizing. **2.** Permission or right granted by someone with authority.

au·thor·ize (ô'thə-rīz') *tr.v.* **-ized, -iz·ing. 1.** To grant authority or power to: *The President authorized him to form a commission.* **2.** To approve or give permission for: *authorize a highway project.* **3.** To be sufficient grounds for; justify: *a rule authorized by custom.* —See Syns at **permit.** —**au'thor·iz'er** *n.*

au·thor·ship (ô'thər-shĭp') *n.* **1.** The profession or occupation of writing. **2.** A source or origin, as of a book or idea: *a treatise of unknown authorship.*

au·tism (ô'tĭz'əm) *n.* **1.** Abnormal subjectivity; acceptance of fantasy rather than reality. **2.** A form of childhood schizophrenia characterized by acting out and withdrawal; infantile autism. [New Latin *autismus,* from AUT(O)- + -ISM.] —**au·tis'tic** (ô-tĭs'tĭk) *adj.*

aut- Var. of the prefix **auto-.**

au·to (ô'tō) *n., pl.* **-tos.** *Informal.* An automobile.

auto- or **aut-** A prefix meaning: **1.** Acting or directed from within: *autism.* **2.** Self; same: *autobiography.* [Greek, from *autos,* self.]

au·to·bi·o·graph·i·cal (ô'tō-bī'ə-grăf'ĭ-kəl) or **au·to·bi·o·graph·ic** (-grăf'ĭk) *adj.* Of or based on a person's own life. —**au'to·bi·o·graph'i·cal·ly** *adv.*

ă pat	ā pay	â care	ä father	ĕ pet	ē be	hw which	ĭ pit	ī tie	î pier	ŏ pot	ō toe	ô paw, for	oi noise
ōō took	ōō boot	ou out	th thin	th this	ŭ cut		û urge	zh vision	ə about, item, edible, gallop, circus

Thomas Hood

Gertrude Stein

Emily Dickinson

Thomas Jefferson

Napoleon

autograph

au·to·bi·og·ra·phy (ô′tō-bī-ŏg′rə-fē, -bē-) *n., pl.* **-phies.** The story of a person's life written by that person; memoirs. [AUTO- + BIOGRAPHY.]

au·to·clave (ô′tō-klāv′) *n.* A pressurized, steam-heated container used for sterilization. [French, "self-locking," from AUTO- + Latin *clāvis*, key.]

au·toc·ra·cy (ô-tŏk′rə-sē) *n., pl.* **-cies.** 1. Government by a single person having unlimited power; despotism. 2. A country or state having this form of government.

au·to·crat (ô′tə-krăt′) *n.* 1. A ruler with absolute or unrestricted power; despot. 2. Any arrogant and domineering person. [French *autocrate*, from Greek *autokratēs*, ruling by oneself : AUTO- + -CRAT.] **—au′to·crat′ic** or **au′to·crat′i·cal** *adj.* **—au′to·crat′i·cal·ly** *adv.*

au·to·da·fé (ou′tō-də-fā′, ô′tō-) *n., pl.* **au·tos·da·fé** (ou′tōz-, ô′tōz-). 1. The public announcement of the sentences imposed on persons tried by the Inquisition. 2. The public execution of these sentences by the secular authorities, esp. the burning of heretics at the stake. [Portuguese, "act of the faith".]

au·to·graph (ô′tə-grăf′) *n.* 1. A signature or handwriting, usu. of a famous person, that is saved by an admirer or collector. 2. A manuscript in the author's own handwriting. **—modifier:** *an autograph collection.* **—tr.v.** To write one's name or signature on; to sign. **—au′to·graph′ic** or **au′to·graph′i·cal** *adj.* **—au′to·graph′i·cal·ly** *adv.*

au·to·mate (ô′tə-māt′) *v.* **-mat·ed, -mat·ing.** **—tr.v.** 1. To enable (a process, factory, or machine) to operate with little or no human supervision; convert to automation. 2. To control or operate by automation. **—intr.v.** To convert to or make use of automation: *Costs forced the factory to automate.*

au·to·mat·ic (ô′tə-măt′ĭk) *adj.* 1. Capable of operating correctly without the control of a human being; self-operating or self-regulating: *an automatic elevator; an automatic process.* 2. Done or produced by the body without conscious control or awareness: *The heartbeat is automatic.* 3. Capable of firing continuously until out of ammunition: *an automatic rifle.* **—n.** A device or machine, esp. a firearm that is wholly or partially automatic. [Greek *automatos*, acting by itself, spontaneous, acting of one's own will, from AUTO- + *-matos*, willing.] **—au′to·mat′i·cal·ly** *adv.*

au·to·ma·tion (ô′tə-mā′shən) *n.* 1. The automatic operation or control of a process, machine, equipment, or system. 2. The mechanical and electronic techniques and equipment used to achieve such operation or control. 3. The condition of being automatically controlled or operated. [From AUTOMATIC.] **—au′to·ma′tive** *adj.*

au·tom·a·ton (ô-tŏm′ə-tən, -tŏn′) *n.* 1. An automatic machine, esp. a robot. 2. Someone or something that behaves in an automatic or mechanical fashion. [Latin, self-operating machine, from Greek *automaton*, from *automatos*, AUTOMATIC.]

au·to·mo·bile (ô′tə-mō-bēl′, -mō′bēl′, ô′tə-mō-bēl′) *n.* A self-propelled land vehicle, as a four-wheeled passenger vehicle, powered by an internal-combustion engine. **—modifier:** *an automobile engine; an automobile accident.* [French, from AUTO- + MOBILE.] **—au′to·mo·bil′ist** *n.*

au·to·mo·tive (ô′tə-mō′tĭv) *adj.* 1. Self-moving; self-propelling. 2. Of or pertaining to automobiles, trucks, buses, or other land vehicles that are self-propelled.

au·to·nom·ic (ô′tə-nŏm′ĭk) *adj.* 1. *Physiol.* Of or pertaining to the autonomic nervous system. 2. Resulting from internal causes; self-generated. **—au′to·nom′i·cal·ly** *adv.*

autonomic nervous system. The division of the vertebrate nervous system that regulates involuntary action, as of the intestines, heart, and glands.

au·ton·o·mous (ô-tŏn′ə-məs) *adj.* 1. **a.** Independent. **b.** Self-contained. 2. **a.** Independent of the laws of another state or government; self-governing. **b.** Of an autonomy. [Greek *autonomos*, self-ruling, from AUTO- + *nomos*, law.] **—au·ton′o·mous·ly** *adv.*

au·ton·o·my (ô-tŏn′ə-mē) *n., pl.* **-mies.** 1. Self-government or the right of self-government; self-determination; independence. 2. A self-governing state, community, or group. **—See Syns at freedom.**

au·top·sy (ô′tŏp′sē, ô′tăp-) *n., pl.* **-sies.** The examination of a dead body to determine the cause of death; post-mortem. [New Latin *autopsia*, from Greek, a seeing for oneself : AUT(O)- + *opsis*, sight.]

au·to·some (ô′tə-sōm′) *n.* Any chromosome that is not a sex chromosome. [AUTO- + (CHROMO)SOME.] **—au′to·so′mal** (-sō′məl) *adj.*

au·to·sug·ges·tion (ô′tō-səg-jĕs′chən) *n. Psychol.* The process by which a person induces self-acceptance of an opinion, belief, or plan of action.

au·tot·o·my (ô-tŏt′ə-mē) *n. Zool.* The spontaneous casting off of a body part, as the tail of certain lizards, for self-protection. [AUTO- + -TOMY.] **—au′to·tom′ic** (ô′tə-tŏm′ĭk) *adj.*

au·tumn (ô′təm) *n.* The season of the year between summer and winter, lasting from the autumnal equinox in late Sept. to the winter solstice in late Dec. **—modifier:** *autumn colors.* [Middle English *autumpne*, from Old French *autompne*, from Latin *autumnus*.] **—au·tum′nal** (ô-tŭm′nəl) *adj.*

autumnal equinox. The equinox that occurs on about Sept. 22 or 23 when the sun crosses the celestial equator going north to south, marking the beginning of autumn In the Northern Hemisphere.

aux·il·ia·ry (ôg-zĭl′yə-rē, -zĭl′ə-) *adj.* 1. Giving assistance or support; aiding; helping: *Conflict is auxiliary to drama.* 2. Held in or used as a reserve; subsidiary; supplementary; additional: *an auxiliary gas tank; auxiliary troops.* 3. *Naut.* Equipped with a motor to supplement the sails. **—n., pl.** **-ries.** 1. Someone or something that assists or helps; an assistant. 2. A group or organization that assists or is supplementary to a larger one: *a women's auxiliary.* 3. **auxiliaries.** Foreign troops serving a country in war. 4. An auxiliary verb. [Latin *auxiliārius*, from *auxilium*, help.]

auxiliary verb. A verb that comes first in a verb phrase and helps form the tense, mood, or voice of the main verb. *Have, may, can, must,* and *will* are some auxiliary verbs. Also called **auxiliary.**

a·vail (ə-vāl′) *tr.v.* To be of use or advantage to; help: *Nothing can avail him now.* **—intr.v.** To be of use, value, or advantage. **—n.** Use, benefit, or advantage: *His efforts were to no avail.* **—idiom. avail (oneself) of.** To make use of. [Middle English *availen* : A- (intensive) + *vailen*, to avail, from Old French *valoir*, to be worth, from Latin *valēre*.] **—a·vail′ing·ly** *adv.*

a·vail·a·ble (ə-vā′lə-bəl) *adj.* 1. Capable of being obtained: *Tickets are available at the box office.* 2. Capable of being reached; at hand and ready to serve: *All available volunteers were pressed into service.* **—a·vail′a·bil′i·ty** or **a·vail′a·ble·ness** *n.* **—a·vail′a·bly** *adv.*

av·a·lanche (ăv′ə-lănch′) *n.* 1. A fall or slide of a large mass

aviator   aviatrix   avocado   avocet

of snow, rock, or other material down a mountainside. **2.** Something resembling such an overwhelming fall or slide: *an avalanche of Christmas packages.* [French, from Swiss French *avalantse.*]

Av·a·lon (ăv′ə-lŏn′) *n.* Also **Av·al·lon.** *Celtic Myth.* An island paradise in the western seas where King Arthur and other heroes went at death.

a·vant-garde (ä′vänt-gärd′) *n.* A group, as of writers and artists, who are the leaders in inventing and applying unconventional styles and new techniques in a given field. —*adj.* Of or exhibiting new or advanced ideas, as in the arts; ultramodern: *an avant-garde magazine.* [French, vanguard, "advance guard."]

av·a·rice (ăv′ər-ĭs) *n.* An extreme desire to amass wealth; greed; cupidity. [Middle English, from Old French, from Latin *avāritia,* from *avārus,* greedy, from *avēre,* to desire.]

av·a·ri·cious (ăv′ə-rĭsh′əs) *adj.* Immoderately fond of accumulating riches; greedy for wealth. —**av′a·ri′cious·ly** *adv.* —**av′a·ri′cious·ness** *n.*

a·vast (ə-văst′) *interj.* Hold on! Stop! Used as a command aboard ship. [Shortened from Dutch *houd vast,* "hold fast," from *houden,* to hold + *vast,* fast.]

av·a·tar (ăv′ə-tär′) *n.* **1. a.** The embodiment of some known model or category. **b.** An entity regarded as an extreme manifestation of its kind; exemplar; archetype: *an avatar of stupidity.* **2.** *Hindu Myth.* The descent to earth of a deity in human or animal form. Used esp. as a generic term for the incarnations of Vishnu. [Sanskrit *avatāra,* descent, from *avatarati,* he descends : *ava,* down + *tarati,* he crosses.]

a·vaunt (ə-vônt′, ə-vänt′) *interj.* Archaic. Be gone! Go away! [Middle English, from Old French *avant,* forward, from Latin *abante* : *ab-,* from + *ante,* before.]

a·venge (ə-vĕnj′) *tr.v.* **a·venged, a·veng·ing. 1.** To take revenge or exact satisfaction for (a wrong, injury, etc.): *avenge a murder.* **2.** To take vengeance on behalf of: *avenge one's sister.* [Middle English *avengen* : *a-,* to + *vengen,* to revenge, from Old French *vengier,* from Latin *vindicāre,* from *vindex,* protector, avenger.] —**a·veng′er** *n.* —**a·veng′ing·ly** *adv.*

Usage: **avenge, revenge.** *Avenge* is only a verb; *revenge* is both noun and verb, though more common as a noun.

av·e·nue (ăv′ə-nōō′, -nyōō′) *n.* **1.** A wide street or thoroughfare. **2.** A path or lane lined with trees. **3.** A means of reaching or achieving something: *We must seek new avenues of trade.* [French, from Old French, *avenir,* to approach, arrive, from Latin *advenīre,* to come to : *ad-,* to + *venīre,* to come.]

a·ver (ə-vûr′) *tr.v.* **a·verred, a·ver·ring. 1.** To state positively and firmly; assert; affirm: *The defendant continued to aver his innocence.* **2.** *Law.* To assert formally as a fact; justify or prove (a plea). [Middle English *averren,* from Old French *averer,* from Medieval Latin *advērāre,* to assert as true : Latin *ad-,* to + *vērus,* true.] —**a·ver′ment** *n.*

av·er·age (ăv′ər-ĭj, ăv′rĭj) *n.* **1.** *Math.* **a.** A number that typifies a set of numbers of which it is a function. **b.** The **arithmetic mean. 2. a.** A relative proportion or degree indicating position or achievement: *a class average.* **b.** A representative type. —*adj.* **1.** Of, pertaining to, or constituting a mathematical average: *an average population density of 155 persons per square mile.* **2.** Normal or ordinary: *an average American.* **3.** Not exceptional; undistinguished: *He is just an average student.* —See Syns at

ordinary. —*v.* **-aged, -ag·ing.** —*tr.v.* **1.** To compute the average of (a set of numbers). **2.** To accomplish or obtain an average of: *average three hours' work a day.* **3.** To distribute proportionately. —*intr.v.* **1.** To be or amount to an average. **2.** To buy or sell more goods or shares to obtain more than an average price. —*idiom.* **on the average.** As a mean rate, amount, etc. [Earlier *averie,* financial loss on damaged shipping (shared among investors), from Old French *avarie,* from Old Italian *avaria,* from Arabic *'awārīyah,* damaged goods, from *'awar,* fault, blemish.]

a·verse (ə-vûrs′) *adj.* **1.** Opposed; reluctant: *Cats are averse to getting themselves wet.* **2.** *Bot.* Turned away from the central stem or axis. [Latin *āversus,* past part. of *āvertere,* AVERT.] —**a·verse′ly** *adv.* —**a·verse′ness** *n.*

Usage: **averse, adverse.** Although both words express opposition, *averse* indicates opposition on the subject's part (*A perfectionist averse to overlooking errors*) and *adverse* indicates opposition contrary to the subject's interest or will (*a court decision adverse to our client's welfare*). Both words can be used with *to.*

a·ver·sion (ə-vûr′zhən, -shən) *n.* **1.** Intense dislike: *He has an aversion to hard work.* **2.** A feeling of extreme repugnance.

a·vert (ə-vûrt′) *tr.v.* **1.** To turn away or aside: *avert one's eyes.* **2.** To keep from happening; prevent: *avert disaster.* [Middle English *averten,* from Old French *āvertir,* from Latin *āvertere* : *ab-,* away from + *vertere,* to turn.] —**a·vert′i·ble** or **a·vert′a·ble** *adj.*

A·ves·ta (ə-věs′tə) *n.* The sacred writings of the ancient Persians.

a·vi·an (ā′vē-ən) *adj.* Of, pertaining to, or characteristic of birds. [From Latin *avis,* bird.]

a·vi·ar·y (ā′vē-ĕr′ē) *n., pl.* **-ies.** A large cage or enclosure specially built to hold live birds, as in a zoo. [Latin *aviārium,* from *avis,* bird.]

a·vi·a·tion (ā′vē-ā′shən, ăv′ē-) *n.* **1.** The operation of aircraft. **2.** The design and production of aircraft. **3.** Military aircraft. —*modifier: an aviation cadet; an aviation show.* [French, from Latin *avis,* bird.]

a·vi·a·tor (ā′vē-ā′tər, ăv′ē-) *n.* A person who flies an aircraft; a pilot. [French *aviateur,* from *aviation,* AVIATION.]

a·vi·a·trix (ā′vē-ā′trĭks, ăv′ē-) *n.* A female aviator.

av·id (ăv′ĭd) *adj.* **1. a.** Eager: *avid for adventure.* **b.** Greedy: *avid for power.* **2.** Enthusiastic; ardent: *an avid reader; an avid sportsman.* [French *avide,* from Latin *avidus,* from *avēre,* to long for.] —**av′id·ly** *adv.*

av·o·ca·do (ăv′ə-kä′dō, ä′və-) *n., pl.* **-dos. 1.** A tropical American tree, *Persea americana,* cultivated for its edible fruit. **2.** The oval or pear-shaped fruit of this tree, with leathery green or blackish skin, a large seed, and bland, greenish-yellow pulp. —*modifier: an avocado salad.* Also called **alligator pear.** [Spanish *aguacate,* from Nahuatl *ahuacatl,* "testicle" (from the shape of the fruit).]

av·o·ca·tion (ăv′ə-kä′shən) *n.* **1.** An activity engaged in, usu. for enjoyment, in addition to one's regular work or profession; hobby. **2.** *Archaic.* A person's regular work or profession. [Latin *āvocātiō,* a calling away, diversion, from *āvocāre,* to call away : *ab-,* away + *vocāre,* to call.]

av·o·cet (ăv′ə-sĕt′) *n.* Any of several long-legged shore birds of the genus *Recurvirostra,* with a long, slender, upturned beak. [French *avocette,* from Italian *avocetta.*]

A·vo·ga·dro's law (ä′və-gä′drōz, ăv′ə-). The principle that equal volumes of different gases under identical conditions of pressure and temperature contain the same number of molecules. Also called **Avogadro's hypothesis, principle,** or **rule.** [After Amedeo *Avogadro* (1776–1856), Italian physicist.]

a·void (ə-void') *tr.v.* **1.** To keep away from; stay clear of; shun: *avoid crowds; avoid rich foods.* **2.** To evade; dodge: *quick enough to avoid the blow.* **3.** To keep from happening; prevent: *a clumsy attempt to avoid getting wet.* **4.** To refrain from: *avoided taking sides in the cold war.* **5.** *Law.* To annul or make void; invalidate. [Middle English *avoiden,* from Norman French *avoider,* from Old French *esvuidier,* "to empty out" : *es-,* out + *vuidier,* to empty, from Latin *vocāre,* to be empty.] —**a·void'a·ble** *adj.* —**a·void'a·bly** *adv.* —**a·void'ance** *n.* —**a·void'er** *n.*

Syns: avoid, bypass, dodge, duck, elude, escape, eschew, evade, get around, shun *v. Core meaning:* To keep away from (*avoid noisy neighbors*).

av·oir·du·pois weight (ăv'ər-də-poiz'). A system of weights and measures, used in most English-speaking countries, based on one pound containing 16 ounces or 7,000 grains and equal to 453.59 grams. [Middle English *avoir de pois,* "commodities sold by weight," from Old French *aver de peis,* "goods of weight."]

a·vouch (ə-vouch') *tr.v.* **1.** To take responsibility for; vouch for; to guarantee. **2.** To assert positively; affirm. **3.** To acknowledge one's responsibility for; confess; avow. [Middle English *avouchen,* from Old French *avochier,* from Latin *advocāre,* to call on (as adviser) : *ad-,* to + *vocāre,* to call.]

a·vow (ə-vou') *tr.v.* To acknowledge openly; admit freely; confess: *avow one's guilt.* [Middle English *avowen,* from Old French *avouer,* from Latin *advocāre,* to call on. See **avouch.**]

a·vow·al (ə-vou'əl) *n.* An open admission or acknowledgment.

a·vowed (ə-voud') *adj.* Openly acknowledged: *an avowed rebel.* —**a·vow·ed·ly** (ə-vou'ĭd-lē) *adv.*

a·vun·cu·lar (ə-vŭng'kyə-lər) *adj.* Of, pertaining to, or resembling an uncle, esp. a benevolent one. [From Latin *avunculus,* maternal uncle.]

aw (ô) *interj.* A word used to express doubt, disgust, etc.

a·wait (ə-wāt') *tr.v.* **1.** To wait for: *He awaited news of his loved ones.* **2.** To be in store for: *No one knows what awaits her in life.* —*intr.v.* To wait. [Middle English *awaiten,* from Old North French *awaitier,* watch for, wait on.]

a·wake (ə-wāk') *v.* **a·woke** (ə-wōk'), **a·waked, a·wak·ing.** —*tr.v.* **1.** To rouse from sleep; waken: *The alarm clock awoke me at seven.* **2.** To stir the interest of; excite. **3.** To produce or stir up (memories, thoughts, etc.): *Her beauty awoke a feeling of love in him.* —*intr.v.* **1.** To wake up: *He awoke at dawn.* **2.** To become alert: *He awoke to the fact that he was being followed.* **3.** To become aware of: *They awoke to reality.* —*adj.* **1.** Not asleep: *He was awake all night.* **2.** Alert; vigilant; watchful. [Middle English *awaken,* from Old English *awacan* : *a-* (intensive) + *wacan, wacian,* to wake.]

Usage: **awake, awaken, wake, waken.** Though alike in meaning, these verbs are somewhat differentiated in usage. Each can be employed transitively and intransitively, but *awake* is principally intransitive (*awoke early*) and *waken* is more often transitive (*awaked wakening them*). In the passive voice, *awaken* and *waken* are the more common: *They were awakened* (or *wakened*) *by the sound of gunfire.* In figurative usage (as opposed to the physical act of rousing), *awake* and *awaken* are the more common: *awoke to the peril; when their fears were awakened.* Only *wake* is used with *up: woke up at seven.* In American usage, the most common past participle of *wake* is *waked* (*after she had waked him*), but in Britain *woke* or *woken* are acceptable. Likewise, in American usage, the most common past participle of *awake* is *awaked* (*had awaked during the storm*) but in Britain *awoke* is acceptable.

a·wak·en (ə-wā'kən) *tr.v.* To cause to wake up. —*intr.v.* To wake up; awake. —See Usage note at **awake.** [Middle English *awak(e)nen,* from Old English *āwæcnan, āwæcnian* : *A-* (on) + *wæcnian,* to waken.]

a·ward (ə-wôrd') *tr.v.* **1.** To grant as merited or due. **2.** To

declare as legally due: *awarded damages to the plaintiff.* **3.** To bestow for performance or quality: *award a prize.* —*n.* **1.** A decision, as one made by a judge or arbitrator. **2.** Something awarded, as a medal or a sum of money. [Middle English *awarden,* from Norman French *awarder,* var. of Old North French *eswarder,* to judge after careful observation, from *es-,* out + *warder,* to observe, judge.]

a·ware (ə-wâr') *adj.* Being mindful or conscious of; knowing; cognizant: *aware of their limitations.* [Middle English *awar, iwar,* from Old English *gewær.*] —**a·ware'ness** *n.*

Syns: aware, cognizant, conversant, hip (*Slang*), knowing, mindful *adj. Core meaning:* Being conscious and understanding of (*We are well aware of their dishonesty*).

a·wash (ə-wŏsh', ə-wôsh') *adj.* **1.** Level with or washed by waves. **2.** Flooded. **3.** Floating on water or waves. —*a·wash'* *adv.*

a·way (ə-wā') *adv.* **1.** At or to a distance: *a house two miles away.* **2.** In or to a different place or direction: *Don't look away now.* **3.** From one's presence or possession: *Take these things away. Her old bicycle was given away by the janitor.* **4.** Out of existence: *fading away.* **5.** Continuously: *working away.* **6.** Immediately: *Fire away!* —*adj.* **1.** Absent: *He's away from home.* **2.** At a distance: *He's miles away.* **3.** Played on the opposing team's home grounds: *home games and away games.* **4.** *Baseball.* Out: *The count is three and two with two away in the ninth.* —*idiom.* **do** (or **make**) **away with.** **1.** To get rid of: *doing away with outmoded laws.* **2.** To murder. [Middle English *away, on way,* from Old English *aweg, oweg, onweg,* "on the way (from)."]

awe (ô) *n.* A feeling of wonder, fear, and respect inspired by something mighty or majestic: *gazing in awe at the mountains.* —*tr.v.* **awed, aw·ing.** To fill with awe: *The size of the plane awed everyone.* [Middle English *awe, age,* from Old Norse *agi.*]

a·weigh (ə-wā') *adj.* Hanging just clear of the bottom, as the anchor of a ship at the moment of sailing. [A- (on) + WEIGH.]

awe·some (ô'səm) *adj.* **1.** Inspiring awe. **2.** Characterized by awe. —**awe'some·ly** *adv.* —**awe'some·ness** *n.*

awe·struck (ô'strŭk') *adj.* Also **awe-strick·en** (ô'strĭk'ən). Full of or exhibiting awe.

aw·ful (ô'fəl) *adj.* **1.** Inspiring awe or fear; fearsome: *the awful stillness before the tornado.* **2.** *Informal.* Very bad or unpleasant; horrible: *awful weather; an awful book.* **3.** *Informal.* Great; considerable: *an awful lot of homework.* [Middle English *awful, aweful,* from AWE + -FUL.] —**aw'ful·ness** *n.*

aw·ful·ly (ô'fə-lē, ô'flē) *adv.* **1.** In a manner that inspires awe; terribly. **2.** *Informal.* Very: *He did seem awfully confused.* **3.** *Informal.* Very badly: *She behaved awfully.* **4.** *Informal.* Very much. Used as an intensive: *Thanks awfully.*

a·while (ə-hwīl', ə-wīl') *adv.* For a short time: *We waited awhile.*

awk·ward (ôk'wərd) *adj.* **1.** Not moving gracefully; clumsy: *an awkward dancer.* **2.** Unnatural or clumsy, as in speech, behavior, etc.: *Jill became shy and awkward whenever Bob was around.* **3.** Causing embarrassment; trying: *an awkward silence.* **4.** Difficult to handle or manage; cumbersome: *an awkward bundle to carry.* [Middle English *awkeward,* "in the wrong direction," awry : *awke,* backhanded, perverse, wrong, from Old Norse *ōfugr,* turned backward + -WARD.] —**awk'ward·ly** *adv.* —**awk'ward·ness** *n.*

Syns: awkward, gawky, graceless, inept, lumpish, ungainly *adj. Core meaning:* Lacking physical grace (*an awkward dancer*). See also Syns at **unfortunate.**

awl (ôl) *n.* A pointed tool for making holes, as in wood or leather. [Middle English *aule, al,* from Old English *eal, al.*]

awl

awn (ôn) *n.* A slender terminal bristle, such as those found at the tips of the spikelets in many grasses. [Middle English *awne, agene,* from Old Norse *ōgn.*]

awn·ing (ô'nĭng) *n.* A rooflike structure, often of canvas, set up over a window, door, etc., as a shelter from weather.

a·woke (ə-wōk') *v.* Past tense of **awake.**

a·wry (ə-rī') *adv.* **1.** Turned to one side or out of shape; askew. **2.** Wrong; amiss: *Our plans went awry.* —*adj.* To one side; crooked: *His tie is awry.* [Middle English *awrie, on wry,* : ON + *wry,* twisted, from *wrien,* to twist, from Old English *wrīgian,* to turn.]

ax or **axe** (ăks) *n., pl.* **ax·es** (ăk'sĭz). **1.** A chopping tool with a head that has a sharp blade mounted on a long handle. **2.** Any similar tool or weapon, as a battle-ax. —*tr.v.* **axed, ax·ing.** To work on with an ax. —*idioms.* **get the ax.** *Informal.* To be fired from one's job. **have an ax to grind.** To pursue a selfish or subjective aim. [Middle English *axe,* from Old English *æx.*]

ax

ax·es *n.* **1.** (ăk'sēz'). Plural of **axis. 2.** (ăk'sĭz). Plural of **ax.**

ax·i·al (ăk'sē-əl) *adj.* Of, on, around, or forming an axis.

ax·il (ăk'sĭl) *n.* The angle between the upper surface of a leafstalk, flower stalk, or branch and the stem or axis from which it arises. [Latin *axilla,* AXILLA.]

ax·il·la (ăk-sĭl'ə) *n., pl.* **ax·il·lae** (ăk-sĭl'ē). The armpit or an analogous part. [Latin *axilla,* armpit.]

ax·il·lar·y (ăk'sə-lĕr'ē) *adj.* **1.** *Anat.* Of, relating to, or near the axilla. **2.** *Bot.* Of, pertaining to, or located in an axil.

ax·i·om (ăk'sē-əm) *n.* **1.** A self-evident or universally recognized truth; maxim. **2.** An established rule, principle, or law. **3.** *Math. & Logic.* A statement that is assumed to be true without proof. [Latin *axiōma,* from Greek, "that which is thought fitting or worthy," from *axioun,* to think worthy, from *axios,* worthy.]

ax·i·o·mat·ic (ăk'sē-ə-măt'ĭk) or **ax·i·o·mat·i·cal** (-ĭ-kəl) *adj.* Of, pertaining to, or resembling an axiom; self-evident. —**ax'i·o·mat'i·cal·ly** *adv.*

ax·is (ăk'sĭs) *n., pl.* **ax·es** (ăk'sēz'). **1.** A straight line around which an object or geometric figure rotates or can be imagined to rotate: *The axis of the earth passes through both of its poles.* **2.** A line, ray, or line segment with respect to which a figure or object is symmetrical. **3.** A reference line from which or along which distances or angles are measured in a system of coordinates: *the x-axis.* **4.** *Anat.* **a.** The second cervical vertebra on which the head turns. **b.** Any of various central structures, as the spinal column or standard abstract lines, used as a positional referent. **5.** *Bot.* The main stem or central part about which organs or plant parts such as branches are arranged. **6. the Axis.** The alliance of Germany, Italy, Japan, and other nations that opposed the Allies in World War II. [Latin, hub, axis, axle.]

ax·le (ăk'səl) *n.* **1.** A supporting shaft or spindle on which one or more wheels revolve. **2.** An axletree. [Middle English *axil, axel,* from Old Norse *öxull.*]

ax·le·tree (ăk'səl-trē') *n.* A crossbar or rod that supports a vehicle, and has a spindle at each end on which a wheel turns.

ax·o·lotl (ăk'sə-lŏt'l) *n.* Any of several western North American and Mexican salamanders of the genus *Ambystoma* that, unlike most amphibians, often retain and continue to breathe with external gills and become sexually mature without undergoing metamorphosis. [Nahuatl, from *atl,* water + *xolotl,* servant, spirit.]

ax·on (ăk'sŏn) *n.* Also **ax·one** (ăk'sōn'). The core of a nerve fiber that usu. conducts impulses away from the body of a nerve cell. Also called **neuraxon.** [From Greek *axōn,* axis.]

ay[1] (ī) *interj. Archaic.* Alas; ah. Used to express surprise or distress.

ay[2] (ī) *n. & adv.* **1.** Var. of **aye** (affirmative). **2.** Var. of **aye** (always).

aye[1] (ī). Also **ay.** —*n.* **1.** An affirmative vote or voter. **2. the ayes.** Those who vote "yes": *The ayes have it; the motion is carried.* —*adv.* Yes; yea. [Earlier *ay, ei,* orig. *I,* prob. the same word as the pron. *I,* used as an affirmative answer.]

aye[2] (ā) *adv.* Also **ay.** *Poet.* Always; ever. [Middle English *ay, ei,* from Old Norse *ei.*]

aye-aye (ī'ī') *n.* A lemur, *Daubentonia madagascariensis,* of Madagascar, with large ears, a long, bushy tail, and rodentlike teeth. [French, from Malagasay *aiay,* prob. imit. of its cry.]

Ay·ma·ra (ī'mä-rä') *n., pl.* **Aymara** or **-ras. 1.** An Indian people of Boliva and Peru. **2. a.** A member of this people. **b.** The language.

a·zal·ea (ə-zāl'yə) *n.* Any of a group of deciduous or evergreen shrubs, part of the genus *Rhododendron,* of the North Temperate Zone, many of which are cultivated for their showy, variously colored flowers. [New Latin, "the dry plant" (growing in dry soil), from Greek *azaleos,* dry.]

az·i·muth (ăz'ə-məth) *n. Abbr.* **az. 1.** The horizontal angular distance from a fixed reference direction to a position, object, or object referent, as to a great circle intersecting a celestial body, usu. measured clockwise in degrees along the horizon from a point due south. **2.** *Mil.* The lateral deviation of a projectile or bomb. [Middle English, from Old French *azimut,* from Arabic *as-sumūt,* pl. of *as-samt,* "the way," compass bearing, from Latin *semita,* path.]

Az·tec (ăz'tĕk') *n.* **1.** A member of an Indian people of Central Mexico noted for their advanced civilization before Hernando Cortés invaded Mexico in 1519. **2.** Their language, **Nahuatl.** —*adj.* Also **Az·tec·an** (ăz'tĕk'ən). Of the Aztecs, their language, culture, or empire.

az·ure (ăzh'ər) *n.* A light to medium blue, like that of the sky. —*adj.* Light to medium blue. [Middle English, from Old French *azur,* from Old Spanish *azul, azur,* from Arabic *allāzaward,* lapis lazuli.]

az·u·rite (ăzh'ə-rīt') *n.* A blue vitreous mineral of basic copper carbonate, $2CuCO_3 \cdot Cu(OH)_2$, used as a copper ore and as a gemstone. [French, from AZURE + -ITE.]

axolotl

aye-aye

Bb

Phoenician – *About 3,000 years ago the Phoenicians and other Semitic peoples began to use graphic signs to represent individual speech sounds instead of syllables or whole words. They used this symbol to represent the sound of the consonant "b" and gave it the name bēth, the Phoenician word for "house."*

Greek – *The Greeks borrowed the Phoenician alphabet with some modifications. They changed the shape and orientation of bēth and altered the name to beta to conform to the phonetic rules of their language. They used beta to represent the sound of the letter "b," as bēth did in Phoenician.*

Roman – *The Romans borrowed the alphabet from the Greeks via the Etruscans and adapted it for carving Latin in stone. This monumental script, as it is called, became the basis for modern printed capital letters.*

Medieval – *By medieval times – around 1,200 years ago – the Roman monumental capitals had become adapted to being relatively quickly written on paper, parchment, or vellum. The upper loop of B was eliminated to reduce the number of pen strokes. The cursive minuscule alphabet became the basis of modern printed lower-case letters.*

Modern – *Since the invention of printing about 500 years ago many modifications have been made in the shapes and styles of the letter B, but its basic form has remained unchanged.*

---

b or **B** (bē) *n., pl.* **b's** or **B's.** **1.** The second letter of the English alphabet. **2.** Any of the speech sounds represented by this letter. **3. B** The second-highest grade, as in school. **4. B** *Mus.* The seventh tone in the scale of C major.

B The symbol for the element boron.

Ba The symbol for the element barium.

baa (bă, bä) *intr.v.* **baaed, baa·ing.** To make a bleating sound, as a sheep does. —*n.* The bleat of a sheep.

Ba·al (bā'əl) *n., pl.* **-al·im** (-ə-lĭm). **1.** Any of various local fertility and nature gods of the ancient Semitic peoples, considered to be false idols by the Hebrews. **2.** Often **baal.** Any false god or idol.

Bab·bitt (băb'ĭt) *n.* A member of the American middle class whose attachment to its business and social ideals is such as to make of him a model of narrow-mindedness and self-satisfaction. [After George F. *Babbitt*, main character in Sinclair Lewis' novel *Babbitt* (1922).]

Babbitt metal. Any of several soft alloys of tin, copper, and antimony used to provide lubrication of moving mechanical parts. Also called **babbitt.** [After Isaac *Babbitt* (1799–1862), American inventor.]

bab·ble (băb'əl) *v.* **-bled, -bling.** —*intr.v.* **1.** To utter indistinct or meaningless words or sounds: *babbling like a baby.* **2.** To talk foolishly or idly; to chatter. **3.** To make a continuous low, murmuring sound, as flowing water. —*tr.v.* **1.** To utter in a rapid, indistinct voice. **2.** To blurt out impulsively; to blab. —*n.* **1.** Indistinct or meaningless words or sounds: *a babble of voices.* **2.** Idle or foolish talk; chatter. **3.** A continuous low murmuring sound. [Middle English *babelen.*] —**bab'bler** *n.*

babe (bāb) *n.* **1.** A baby; an infant. **2.** *Slang.* An innocent or naive person. [Middle English *babe.*]

Ba·bel (bā'bəl, băb'əl) *n.* **1.** In the Old Testament, the site of a tower that was being built to reach the heavens. God halted its construction by suddenly causing everyone to speak diferent languages. **2. babel.** A confusion of sounds, voices, or languages.

ba·bies'-breath (bā'bēz-brĕth') *n.* Var. of **baby's-breath.**

bab·i·ru·sa (băb'ə-roō'sə, bä'bə-) *n.* Also **bab·i·rus·sa, bab·i·rous·sa.** A wild pig, *Babyrousa babyrussa,* of the East Indies, with long, upward-curving tusks in the male. [Malay *bābīrūsa* : *bābī,* hog + *rūsa,* deer.]

Bab·ism (bä'bĭz'əm) *n.* The beliefs and practices of a 19th-cent. Persian religious sect, in which polygamy, concubinage, slavery, and the use of alcohol or drugs were forbidden.

ba·boon (bă-boōn') *n.* Any of several chiefly African monkeys of the genus *Chaeropithecus* (or *Papio*) and related genera, with an elongated, doglike muzzle. [Middle English *baboyne,* from Old French *babuin.*]

baboon

ba·bush·ka (bə-boōsh'kə) *n.* A woman's head scarf, folded triangularly and worn tied under the chin. [Russian, grandmother, dim. of *baba,* old woman.]

ba·by (bā'bē) *n., pl.* **-bies. 1.** A very young boy or girl; an infant. **2.** The youngest member of a family or group. **3.** A very young animal. **4.** A young person who acts like a baby. **5.** *Slang.* An object of personal concern or interest: *The project was his baby.* —*modifier: a baby bird; my baby sister; baby talk; a baby carriage.* —*tr.v.* **-bied, -by·**

babirusa

---

ing. To treat oversolicitously; coddle. [Middle English *ba-bie.*]

Syns: baby, cater to, coddle, indulge, mollycoddle, pamper, spoil *v.* Core meaning: To treat with excessive indulgence (*needlessly babied their child*).

ba·by·hood (bā′bē-hŏod′) *n.* The condition or time of being a baby.

ba·by·ish (bā′bē-ĭsh) *adj.* **1.** Like a baby; childlike. **2.** Childish; immature. —**ba′by·ish·ly** *adv.* —**ba′by·ish·ness** *n.*

Bab·y·lon (băb′ə-lən, -lŏn′) *n.* Any city or place of great luxury and corruption.

ba·by′s-breath (bā′bēz-brĕth′) *n.* Also **ba·bies′-breath.** **1.** Any plant of the genus *Gypsophila*, esp., *G. paniculatum*, with numerous small white flowers in branching clusters. **2.** Any of several other plants with small, pleasantly scented flowers.

ba·by·sit (bā′bē-sĭt′) *intr.v.* **-sat** (-sǎt′), **-sit·ting.** To care for children when the parents are not at home.

baby sitter. A person hired to baby-sit. Also called **sitter.**

bac·ca·lau·re·ate (băk′ə-lôr′ē-ĭt) *n.* **1.** The academic degree of Bachelor conferred upon graduates of most U.S. colleges and universities. **2.** An address delivered to a graduating class at commencement. [Medieval Latin *baccalaureātus, baccalārius,* bachelor.]

bac·ca·rat (bä′kə-rä′, băk′ə-) *n.* Also **bac·ca·ra.** A gambling game in which the winner is the player holding two or three cards totaling closest to nine. [French *baccara.*]

Bac·chae (băk′ē) *pl.n.* The priestesses and female wor-

bachelor's-button

shipers of Bacchus. [Latin, from Greek *Bakkhai,* pl. of *Bakkhē,* priest of Bacchus.]

bac·cha·nal (băk′ə-nǎl′, bä′kə-näl′, băk′ə-nəl) *n.* **1.** A participant in the Bacchanalia. **2.** Often **bacchanals.** The Bacchanalia. **3.** Any drunken or riotous celebration. **4.** A reveler. —*adj.* Of, pertaining to, or typical of the worship of Bacchus. —**bac′cha·na′lian** (-nǎl′yən, -nǎ′lē-ən) *adj.*

Bac·cha·na·lia (băk′ə-nǎl′yə, -nǎ′lē-ə) *n., pl.* **Bacchanalia.** **1.** The ancient Roman festival in honor of Bacchus. **2.** **bacchanalia.** A riotous or drunken festivity.

bac·chant (bə-kănt′, -känt′, băk′ənt) *n., pl.* **-chants** or **bacchan·tes** (bə-kăn′tēz′, -kän′-, -kănts′, -känts′). **1.** A priest or worshiper of Bacchus. **2.** A boisterous reveler.

bac·chante (bə-kăn′tē, -kän′-, bə-kănt′, -känt′) *n.* A priestess or female worshiper of Bacchus.

Bac·chic (băk′ĭk) *adj.* **1.** Of or pertaining to Bacchus. **2. bacchic.** Drunken and carousing; bacchanalian.

Bac·chus (băk′əs) *n. Rom. Myth.* The god of grape-growing and of wine, often identified with the Greek god Dionysus.

bach·e·lor (băch′ə-lər, băch′lər) *n.* **1.** An unmarried man. **2.** In feudal times, a young knight in the service of another knight. Also called **bachelor-at-arms. 3. Bachelor. a.** A college or university degree signifying completion of undergraduate studies and graduation. **b.** The title of a person with this degree: *Bachelor of Arts; Bachelor of Science.* [Middle English *bacheler,* from Old French, squire, from Medieval Latin *baccalārius.*] —**bach′e·lor·hood′** *n.*

bach·e·lor′s-but·ton (băch′ə-lərz-bŭt′n, băch′lərz-) *n.* **1.** The cornflower. **2.** The common European daisy. **3.** Any of several other plants having buttonlike flowers or flower heads.

bac·il·lar·y (băs′ə-lĕr′ē, bə-sĭl′ə-rē) *adj.* Also **ba·cil·lar** (bə-

sĭl′ər, băs′ə-lər). **1.** Rod-shaped. **2.** Of, pertaining to, or caused by bacilli.

ba·cil·lus (bə-sĭl′əs) *n., pl.* **-cil·li** (-sĭl′ī). **1.** Any of various rod-shaped bacteria of the genus *Bacillus.* **2.** Any of various bacteria, esp. a rod-shaped bacterium. —See Usage note at **germ.** [Late Latin, from Latin *baculum,* rod, stick.]

back (băk) *n.* **1. a.** In human beings and other vertebrates, the region of the body that is closest to the spine; the region from the base of the neck to the pelvis. **b.** The analogous dorsal region in other animals, such as insects. **2.** The spine; backbone. **3.** The rear or reverse side of something, as of a coin, door, or sheet of paper. **4.** A part that supports or strengthens from the rear: *the back of a chair.* **5.** Football. Any of the players in a team's backfield. —*adv.* **1.** To or toward the rear: *Move back, please.* **2.** To or toward a former place, time, or condition: *They went back to their old home.* **3.** In a delayed condition: *The rains set the construction job back many days.* **4.** In reserve or concealment: *He held part of the money back.* **5.** In return: *If he hits you, hit him back.* —Note: Back, sometimes preceded by *in,* is often used with *of* to form the prepositional group **back (or in back) of.** Behind: *a tool shed back of the barn.* —*adj.* **1.** At the back or rear: *the back porch.* **2.** Remote or off the main roads: *back country.* **3.** Overdue: *back rent.* —*tr.v.* **1.** To cause to move backward or in a reverse direction: *The police backed the crowd into a corner.* **2.** To furnish or strengthen with a back or backing. **3.** To provide support, assistance, or encouragement for: *She backed her friend's decision.* **4.** To give evidence in support of; substantiate: *backing up an argument with facts.* **5.** To bet on. **6.** To form the back or background of. —*intr.v.* **1.** To move backward: *She backed toward the door.* **2.** To shift to a counterclockwise direction: *During the night the wind backed around to the northeast.* —*phrasal verbs.* **back down.** To withdraw from a stand that one has taken. **back off.** To retreat or retire, as from an untenable or dangerous position. **back out.** To retire or withdraw from something. **back up. 1.** To move in a reverse direction. **2.** To retreat. **3.** To rise and flow backward: *Gas was backing up and leaking into the room.* **4.** To assist, esp. as an auxiliary: *Scouts backed up municipal lifeguards in the emergency.* —*idioms.* **back and fill.** To maneuver a sailing vessel in a narrow channel by adjusting the sails so as to let the wind in and out of them in alternation. **behind (one's) back.** When one is not present. **break the back of.** To destroy: *The army broke the back of the resistance.* **go back on. 1.** To fail to keep (a promise or commitment). **2.** To betray or desert (a person). [Middle English *bak,* from Old English *bæc.*]

back·ache (băk′āk′) *n.* A pain or discomfort in the region of the spine or back.

back·bite (băk′bīt′) *v.* **-bit** (-bĭt′), **-bit·ten** (-bĭt′n) or *informal* **-bit, -bit·ing.** —*tr.v.* To slander the character or reputation of (an absent person). —*intr.v.* To speak spitefully or slanderously of a person behind his back. —**back′bit′er** *n.*

back·board (băk′bôrd′, -bōrd′) *n.* **1.** A board placed under or behind something to provide firmness or support. **2.** *Basketball.* The elevated, vertical board from which the basket projects.

back·bone (băk′bōn′) *n.* **1.** The vertebrate spine or spinal column. **2.** Anything that resembles a backbone in appearance or position, such as the keel of a ship. **3.** A principal support; mainstay: *Agriculture is the backbone of the economy.* **4.** Strength of character; fortitude; determination.

back·break·ing (băk′brā′kĭng) *adj.* Requiring great physical exertion; exhausting. —See Syns at **burdensome.**

back·door (băk′dôr′, -dōr′) *adj.* Done or formed secretly or in an underhanded manner; clandestine.

back·drop (băk′drŏp′) *n.* **1.** A curtain, often painted to show a scene in the background, hung at the back of a stage **2.** The setting, as of a historical event.

back·er (băk′ər) *n.* Someone who supports or gives aid to a person, group, or enterprise.

back·field (băk′fēld′) *n. Football.* **1.** The players stationed behind the line of scrimmage. **2.** The area occupied by these players.

back·fire (băk′fīr′) *n.* **1.** A controlled fire started in the path of an oncoming uncontrolled fire in order to deprive it of fuel and so extinguish it. **2.** An explosion of prematurely ignited fuel or of unburned exhaust gases in an internal-combustion engine. —*intr.v.* **-fired, -fir·ing. 1.** To start or use a backfire. **2.** To explode in or make the sound of a backfire. **3.** To produce an unexpected and undesired result: *His plan backfired.*

back·for·ma·tion (băk′fôr-mā′shən) *n. Ling.* **1.** A new word created by removing from an existing word what is mistakenly thought to be an affix, as *laze* from *lazy* or *edit* from *editor.* **2.** The process of forming words in this way.

back·gam·mon (băk′găm′ən) *n.* A game for two persons, played on a specially marked board with pieces whose moves are determined by throws of dice.

back·ground (băk′ground′) *n.* **1. a.** The part of a picture, scene, view, etc., that appears as if in the distance. **b.** The general scene or surface upon which designs, figures, etc., are seen or represented: *a white background covered with blue stars.* **2.** An inconspicuous position: *a presidential adviser who stays in the background.* **3.** Soft music played to accompany the dialogue or action in a play, motion picture, etc. Also called **background music. 4.** The circumstances or events surrounding or leading up to something: *filling her in on the background of the case.* **5.** A person's experience, training, and education: *a perfect background for the job.* **6.** A person's national, racial, or family origin: *people of different backgrounds.* —*modifier:* *background noise; background color.*

back·hand (băk′hănd′) *n.* **1.** *Sports.* A stroke or motion, as of a racket, made with the back of the hand facing outward and the arm moving forward. **2.** Handwriting characterized by letters that slant to the left. —*modifier:* *a backhand stroke.* —*adj.* Backhanded. —*adv.* With a backhand stroke or motion. —*tr.v.* To perform or catch backhand.

backhand   backpack

back·hand·ed (băk′hăn′dĭd) *adj.* **1.** Made with the motion or direction of a backhand: *a backhanded stroke in tennis; a backhanded slap.* **2.** Slanting toward the left: *backhanded penmanship.* **3.** Containing a disguised insult or rebuke: *a backhanded compliment.* —**back′hand′ed·ly** *adv.* —**back′hand′ed·ness** *n.*

back·ing (băk′ĭng) *n.* **1.** Material that forms, supports, or strengthens the back of something. **2. a.** Support or aid: *financial backing.* **b.** Approval or endorsement: *official backing from the mayor.* **3.** Persons who provide aid or support.

back·lash (băk′lăsh′) *n.* **1.** A sudden or violent backward whipping motion. **2.** Hostile reaction on the part of one social group to the demands made by another.

back·log (băk′lôg′, -lŏg′) *n.* **1.** A large log placed at the back of a fire to support other logs and maintain heat. **2.** A reserve supply or source. **3.** An accumulation, esp. of unfinished work or unfilled orders. —*v.* **-logged, -log·ging.** —*tr.v.* To acquire as a backlog. —*intr.v.* To become a backlog.

back number. 1. An out-of-date periodical or newspaper. **2.** *Informal.* An old-fashioned person or thing.

back·pack (băk′păk′) *n.* **1.** A knapsack, often mounted on a lightweight frame, that is worn on the back to carry camping supplies. **2.** Any piece of equipment made to be used while being carried on the back. —*intr.v.* To hike while carrying supplies in a backpack. —*tr.v.* To carry in a backpack. —**back′pack′er** *n.*

back·rest (băk′rĕst′) *n.* A support or rest for the back.

back seat. 1. A seat in the back, esp. of a vehicle or an auditorium. **2.** *Informal.* A subordinate position.

back-seat driver (băk′sēt′). *Informal.* **1.** A passenger in a car who constantly advises, corrects, or nags the driver. **2.** Any person who persists in giving unsolicited advice.

back·side (băk′sīd′) *n.* **1.** The back or rear part of something. **2.** *Informal.* The buttocks; rump.

back·slide (băk′slīd′) *intr.v.* **-slid** (-slĭd′), **-slid** or **-slid·den** (-slĭd′n),**-slid·ing.** To lapse into sin, improper habits, etc.; to relapse. —**back′slid′er** *n.*

back·spin (băk′spĭn′) *n.* A spin that tends to slow, stop, or reverse the motion of an object, esp. of a ball.

back·stage (băk′stāj′) *adv.* **1.** In or toward the dressing rooms behind the performing area in a theater. **2.** In or toward a place closed to public view; privately: *backstage at the museum.* —*modifier:* *a backstage orchestra; backstage political maneuverings.*

back·stay (băk′stā′) *n.* **1.** A rope or shroud extending from the top of the mast aft to the ship's side or stern to help support the mast. **2.** A support at or for the back of something.

back·stop (băk′stŏp′) *n.* **1.** A screen or fence in back of the playing area, as in tennis or baseball, used to stop a ball's movement. **2.** *Baseball.* The catcher.

back·stroke (băk′strōk′) *n.* A swimming stroke executed with the swimmer on his back, using a flutter kick, and moving the arms alternately upward and backward.

back talk. An insolent or disrespectful retort.

back·track (băk′trăk′) *intr.v.* **1.** To return over the route by which one has come. **2.** To reverse one's position or policy; to retreat.

back·up (băk′ŭp′) *n.* **1.** A reserve, as of provisions. **2.** A person standing by and ready to serve as a substitute. **3.** Support or backing. **4.** An overflow caused by clogged plumbing. —*modifier:* *a back-up pilot.*

back·ward (băk′wərd) *adv.* Also **back·wards** (-wərdz). **1.** In a direction opposite to forward: *He jumped backward to get out of the way.* **2.** Rear end first: *With its hind legs a toad can dig its way into the ground backward.* **3.** In reverse order or direction: *Palindromes are words or sentences that are the same when read backward or forward.* **4.** To a worse condition: *The country is drifting steadily backward.* **5.** Into the past: *Japan's industrial era extends backward only a little over a hundred years.* —*adj.* **1. a.** Behind others, as in economic or social progress: *backward peoples; backward areas.* **b.** Unprogressive; reactionary: *lapsing into the old, backward ways.* **2.** Directed or moving toward the rear: *a backward glance.* —See Syns at **depressed.** —*idiom.* **bend over backward.** To do one's utmost. —**back′ward·ly** *adv.* —**back′ward·ness** *n.*

   Usage: backward, backwards. Only *backward* is an adjective: *a backward step; backward nations.* The adverb may be spelled *backward* or *backwards*, and the two forms can be used in these examples: *stepped backward; a mirror facing backwards.*

back·wash (băk′wŏsh′, -wôsh′) *n.* **1.** Water moved backward, as by the action of oars or a motor. **2.** A backward flow of air, as from the propeller of an aircraft. **3.** The result of some event; aftermath.

back·wa·ter (băk′wô′tər, -wŏt′ər) *n.* **1.** Water held or pushed back by or as if by a dam or current, esp. a body of stagnant water thus formed. **2.** A place or situation regarded as stagnant or backward: *a cultural backwater.* —*modifier:* *a backwater town.*

back·woods (băk′woodz′, -woodz′) *pl.n.* Heavily wooded, uncultivated, thinly settled areas. —*modifier:* *a backwoods region.*

back·woods·man (băk′woodz′mən, -woodz′-) *n.* A person who lives or was brought up in the backwoods.

back yard. Also **back·yard** (băk′yärd′). A yard at the rear of a house.

ba·con (bā′kən) *n.* The salted and smoked meat from the back and sides of a pig. —*idiom.* **bring home the bacon.** *Informal.* **1.** To make a living. **2.** To succeed. [Middle English, from Old French.]

bac·te·ri·a (băk-tîr′ē-ə) *pl.n. Sing.* **-te·ri·um** (-tîr′ē-əm). Any of numerous one-celled organisms of the class Schizo-

---

Bactrian camel

badger

cetes, occurring in a wide variety of forms, existing either as free-living organisms or as parasites, and having a wide range of biochemical, often disease-causing, properties. — See Usage note at **germ.** [Greek *baktērion*, dim. of *baktron*, rod.]

bac·te·ri·al (băk-tîr′ē-əl) *adj.* Of or caused by bacteria. —**bac·te′ri·al·ly** *adv.*

bac·te·ri·cide (băk-tîr′ĭ-sīd′) *n.* A substance that destroys bacteria. —**bac·te′ri·ci′dal** (-tîr′ĭ-sīd′l) *adj.*

bac·te·ri·ol·o·gist (băk-tîr′ē-ŏl′ə-jĭst) *n.* A person who specializes in bacteriology.

bac·te·ri·ol·o·gy (băk-tîr′ē-ŏl′ə-jē) *n.* The study of bacteria, esp. in relation to medicine and agriculture. —**bac·te′ri·o·log′ic** (-ə-lŏj′ĭk) or **bac·te′ri·o·log′i·cal** *adj.* —**bac·te′ri·o·log′i·cal·ly** *adv.*

bac·te·ri·o·phage (băk-tîr′ē-ə-fāj′) *n.* A submicroscopic, usu. viral, organism that destroys bacteria.

bac·te·ri·um (băk-tîr′ē-əm) *n.* Singular of **bacteria.**

Bac·tri·an camel (băk′trē-ən). A two-humped camel, *Camelus bactrianus*, native to central and southwestern Asia. [From *Bactria,* an ancient country in southwestern Asia.]

bad¹ (băd) *adj.* **worse** (wûrs), **worst** (wûrst). **1.** Not good; inferior; poor: *a bad book.* **2.** Unfavorable: *bad luck; bad weather.* **3.** Disagreeable; unpleasant: *a bad odor; be in a bad mood.* **4.** Upsetting; disturbing: *bad news; a bad dream.* **5.** Faulty; incorrect; improper: *bad grammar; bad judgment; bad manners.* **6.** Not working properly; defective: *The car's brakes are bad.* **7.** Disobedient; naughty: *a bad boy.* **8.** Harmful in effect; detrimental: *Candy is bad for your teeth.* **9.** In poor health; ill; diseased: *I feel bad today. He has a bad knee.* **10.** Severe; violent; intense: *a bad cold; a bad snowstorm.* **11.** Sorry; regretful: *I feel very bad about what happened.* **12.** Rotten; spoiled: *a bad apple.* —*n.* Something bad: *You must learn to accept the bad with the good.* —*adv. Informal.* Badly. —*idioms.* **be in bad.** *Informal.* To be in trouble or disfavor. **not half (or so) bad.** Reasonably good. **too bad.** Regrettable; unfortunate. [Middle English *badde.*] —**bad′ness** *n.*

bad² (băd) *v. Archaic.* A past tense of **bid.**

bad blood. Bitterness between two or more persons.

bade (băd, bād) *v.* A past tense of **bid.**

badge (băj) *n.* **1.** A device or emblem worn as an insignia of rank, office, or membership in an organization, or as an award or honor. **2.** Any characteristic mark or sign: *He wore his diamond ring as a badge of success.* [Middle English *bag(g)e,* from Norman French *bage.*]

badg·er (băj′ər) *n.* **1.** Any of several carnivorous, burrowing animals of the family Mustelidae, such as *Meles meles,* of Eurasia, or *Taxidea taxus,* of North America, with short legs, long claws on the front feet, and a grizzled coat. **2.** The fur of a badger. —*tr.v.* To trouble or harry persistently with many questions, protests, or entreaties; pester. [Poss. from BADGE (from the white mark on its forehead).]

bad·i·nage (băd′ə-näzh′) *n.* Light, playful banter; flippant repartee. [French, from *badin,* fool, joker.]

bad·lands (băd′lăndz′) *pl.n.* Often **Badlands.** An area of barren land characterized by eroded ridges, peaks, and mesas.

bad·ly (băd′lē) *adv.* **1.** In a bad manner. **2.** Very much; greatly.

bad·min·ton (băd′mĭn′tən) *n.* A game played by volleying a shuttlecock back and forth over a high, narrow net by means of a light, long-handled racket. [After *Badminton,* the country seat of the dukes of Beaufort in Gloucestershire, England, where the game supposedly was first played.]

baf·fle (băf′əl) *tr.v.* **-fled, -fling. 1.** To cause uncertainty in; puzzle; perplex: *Contradictory evidence baffled the jury.* **2.** To foil, thwart, or frustrate: *"secret writing which shall baffle investigation"* (Edgar Allan Poe). **3.** To provide with or enclose with a structure that stops or regulates the movement of a gas, sound, or liquid: *baffle a loudspeaker.* —*n.* A structure or enclosure designed to stop or regulate the movement of a gas, sound, or liquid. [Orig. unknown.] —**baf′fle·ment** *n.* —**baf′fler** *n.*

bag (băg) *n.* **1.** A container in the form of a sack or pouch, made from a flexible material, such as paper, cloth, plastic, or leather. **2.** A woman's handbag; purse. **3.** A suitcase, satchel, or other piece of hand luggage. **4.** An organic sac or pouch, such as the udder of a cow. **5.** Something resembling a bag or pouch. **6.** The amount held in a bag; bagful. **7.** *Brit.* A unit of dry measure equal to three bushels. **8.** The amount of game killed or permitted to be killed in a single day or hunting expedition. **9.** *Baseball.* A base. **10.** *Informal.* A collection of persons or things: *His friends were a mixed bag.* **11.** *Slang.* An area of classification, interest, or skill: *Cooking is not my bag.* —*v.* **bagged, bagging.** —*tr.v.* **1.** To put into a bag. **2.** To cause to bulge like a bag. **3.** To capture or kill, as game. **4.** *Informal.* To gain possession of; capture: *He bagged the blue ribbon.* —*intr.v.* **1.** To hang or bulge loosely. **2.** To swell out. —*idioms.* **bag and baggage.** *Informal.* **1.** With all one's belongings. **2.** Entirely; completely. **holding the bag.** *Informal.* Having full responsibility or blame thrust upon one. **in the bag.** *Slang.* Assured of successful outcome. [Middle English *bagge,* from Old Norse *baggi.*]

ba·gasse (bə-găs′) *n.* The dry pulp remaining from a plant, as sugar cane, after the juice has been extracted. [French, from Spanish *bagazo,* dregs, from *baga,* husk, from Latin *bāca,* berry.]

bag·a·telle (băg′ə-tĕl′) *n.* **1.** An unimportant or insignificant thing; a trifle. **2.** A game played on an oblong table with a cue and balls. [French, from Italian *bagatella,* from Latin *bāca,* berry.]

ba·gel (bā′gəl) *n.* A ring-shaped roll with a tough, chewy texture, made from plain yeast dough that is dropped briefly into nearly boiling water and then baked. [Yiddish *beygel,* from Middle High German *bouc,* ring, from Old High German *boug.*]

bag·gage (băg′ĭj) *n.* **1.** The trunks, bags, parcels, and suitcases in which one carries one's belongings while traveling; luggage. **2.** The movable equipment and supplies of an army. [Middle English *bagage,* from Old French, from *bague,* bundle, pack.]

bag·ging (băg′ĭng) *n.* Material used for making bags.

bag·gy (băg′ē) *adj.* **-gi·er, -gi·est.** Bulging or hanging loosely. —**bag′gi·ly** *adv.* —**bag′gi·ness** *n.*

bag·pipe (băg′pīp′) *n.* Often **bagpipes.** A musical instrument with a flexible bag inflated either by a tube with valves or by bellows, a double-reed melody pipe, and from one to four drone pipes. —**bag′pip′er** *n.*

ba·guette (bă-gĕt′) *n.* Also **ba·guet.** **1.** A gem cut into the form of a narrow rectangle. **2.** The form of such a gem. [French, from Italian *bacchetta,* dim. of *bacchio,* rod, from Latin *baculum,* stick, staff.]

ă pat　ā pay　â care　ä father　ĕ pet　ē be　hw which　ĭ pit　ī tie　î pier　ŏ pot　ō toe　ô paw, for　oi noise
ōō took　ōō boot　ou out　th thin　th this　ŭ cut　û urge　zh vision　ə about, item, edible, gallop, circus

bah (bä, bă) *interj.* A word used to express contempt or disgust.

Ba·ha·i (bə-hä′ē, -hī′) *adj.* Of, pertaining to, or designating a religion founded in 1863 by Bahaullah, and emphasizing the spiritual unity of all mankind. —*n.* A teacher of or believer in the Bahai faith. —**Ba·ha′ism** *n.* —**Ba·ha′ist** *adj.* & *n.*

bail¹ (bāl) *n.* **1.** Security, usu. a sum of money, exchanged for the release of an arrested person as a guarantee of his appearance for trial. **2.** The release so obtained. **3.** The person who provides the security for such a release. —*tr.v.* **1.** To secure the release of (a person) by providing bail. **2.** To release (a person) for whom bail has been paid. —*phrasal verb.* **bail out. 1.** *Informal.* To extricate (another) from a difficult situation. **2.** To parachute from an airplane in distress. —*idiom.* **go bail for.** To supply bail for; act as security for. [Middle English *baile*, custody, from Old French *bail*, from *baillier*, to take charge of, from Latin *bājulus*, carrier.]

bail² (bāl) —*tr.v.* **1.** To remove (water) from a boat by repeatedly filling a container and emptying it over the side. **2.** To empty (a boat) of water by this means: *bail out the canoe.* —*intr.v.* **1.** To empty a boat of water by scooping or dipping: *bail with a coffee can.* **2.** *Slang.* To abandon a project or enterprise. [Middle English *baille*, bucket, from Old French, prob. from Latin *bājulus*, carrier.] —**bail′er** *n.*

bail³ (bāl) *n.* **1.** The arched, hooplike handle of a pail, kettle, etc. **2.** An arch or hoop, such as those used to support the top of a covered wagon. [Middle English *baile*, handle.]

bail⁴ (bāl) *n. Cricket.* One of the two crossbars that form the top of a wicket. [Poss. from Old French *bail*, crossbeam.]

bail·ee (bā-lē′) *n.* A person to whom property is bailed.

bail·iff (bā′lĭf) *n.* **1.** A court attendant entrusted with a variety of duties, such as the custody of prisoners under arraignment, the protection of jurors, and the maintenance of order in a courtroom during a trial. **2.** An official who assists a British sheriff and who has the power to execute writs, processes, and arrests. **3.** *Brit.* An overseer of an estate; steward. [Middle English *baillif*, from Old French, from Latin *bājulus*, carrier.]

bail·i·wick (bā′lə-wĭk′) *n.* **1.** The office or district of a bailiff. **2.** A person's specific area of interest, skill, or authority. [Middle English *bailliwik* : *bailli*, bailiff + *wik*, dwelling.]

bail·out (bāl′out′) *n.* **1.** The act of leaving a plane by parachute, esp. during an emergency. **2.** The act of extricating a person or thing from a difficult situation.

bails·man (bālz′mən) *n. Law.* One who provides bail or security for another.

bairn (bârn) *n. Scot.* A child. [Middle English *barn*, from Old English *bearn*.]

bait (bāt) *n.* **1.** Food or other lure placed on a hook or in a trap and used in the taking of fish, birds, or other animals. **2.** Anything used to lure or entice. **3.** *Brit.* A stop for food or rest during a trip. —*tr.v.* **1.** To put bait on: *bait a fishhook.* **2.** To lure or entice, esp. by trickery or strategy. **3.** To set dogs upon (a chained animal) for sport. **4.** To torment with repeated verbal attacks, insults, or ridicule. **5.** To tease. [Middle English, partly from Old Norse *beita*, to hunt with dogs, and partly from Old Norse *beita* (a separate word), food, fish bait.] —**bait′er** *n.*

    Usage: baited, bated. The words *baited* and *bated* are often confused. *Baited* (meaning hooked, lured, or tormented) should not be used in the expression *with bated breath* where the proper term *bated* means restrained or held in check.

baize (bāz) *n.* A thick cotton or woolen cloth that looks like felt, used chiefly as a cover for billiard tables. [French *baie* (pl. *baies*), from *bai*, bay (prob. from its orig. green color).]

bake (bāk) *v.* **baked, bak·ing.** —*tr.v.* **1.** To cook (bread, pastry, or other food) with continuous, even, dry heat, esp. in an oven. **2.** To harden or dry by heating in or as if in an oven: *bake clay pottery.* —*intr.v.* **1.** To cook food by baking: *She bakes frequently.* **2.** To become cooked by baking: *The muffins baked quickly.* **3.** To become hard or dry by exposure to steady, dry heat: *The ground baked in the hot sun.* —*n.* **1.** The act or process of baking. **2.** The

balalaika

balance

amount baked. [Middle English *baken*, from Old English *bacan.*]

Ba·ke·lite (bā′kə-līt′) *n.* A trademark for any of a group of thermosetting plastics having high chemical and electrical resistance and used in a variety of manufactured articles.

bak·er (bā′kər) *n.* **1.** A person who bakes and sells bread, cakes, etc. **2.** A portable oven.

baker's dozen. A group of 13; one dozen plus one. [From the former custom among bakers of adding an extra roll to every dozen against the possibility that 12 rolls might weigh light.]

bak·er·y (bā′kə-rē) *n., pl.* **-ries.** A place where products such as bread, cake, and pastries are baked or sold.

bak·ing (bā′kĭng) *n.* **1.** The act or process of baking. **2.** The amount baked at one time.

baking powder. Any of various powdered mixtures of baking soda, starch, and an acidic compound such as cream of tartar, used as leavening.

baking soda. Sodium bicarbonate.

bal·a·lai·ka (băl′ə-lī′kə) *n.* A musical instrument with a triangular body and three strings. [Russian.]

bal·ance (băl′əns) *n.* **1.** A device in which the weight of an object is measured by putting it at one end of a rod that swings on a pivot at its center and adding known weights to the other side until the rod is level and motionless. **2.** A condition in which all forces or influences are canceled by equal and opposite forces or influences: *Man has upset the balance in nature by killing off certain species.* **3.** A condition in which an equation represents a correct statement in mathematics or chemistry. **4.** *Accounting.* **a.** An equality between the debit and credit sides of an account. **b.** A difference between two such sides: *There is a balance due of $50.00.* **5.** *Informal.* Something left over; a remainder: *The balance of the evidence goes against him.* **6.** A satisfying proportion or arrangement achieved between parts or elements; harmony: *a balance of color in the room.* **7.** A condition of bodily stability, as when standing erect: *lose one's balance.* **8.** Emotional stability; sanity: *He seemed off balance after his long illness.* **9.** An action or influence that results in even, suitable, or fair distribution, as of power among branches of a government: *the U.S. system of checks and balances.* **10.** A balance wheel. —*v.* **-anced, -anc·ing.** —*tr.v.* **1.** To weigh or poise in or as if in a balance: *balance the weights on both sides of the scale.* **2.** To compare as if weighing in the mind: *balance the good and bad points of taking a vacation.* **3.** To bring into or maintain in a state of equilibrium: *balance a book on her head.* **4.** To act as an equalizing weight or force to; to offset; to counterbalance. **5.** *Accounting.* **a.** To compute the difference between the debits and credits of (an account). **b.** To reconcile or equalize the sums of the debits and credits of (an account). **c.** To settle (an account) by paying what is owed. **6.** To bring into or keep in equal or satisfying proportion or harmony: *The new couch balances the room perfectly.* **7.** To bring (a mathematical or chemical equation) into the correct balance. —*intr.v.* **1.** To be in or come into equilibrium. **2.** To be equal or equivalent. **3.** To sway or waver as if losing or regaining equilibrium. —*idioms.* **in the balance.** With the result or outcome still uncertain. **strike a balance.** To reach a condition between extremes. [Middle English, from Old French, from Late Latin *(lībra) bilanx*, (a balance) having two scales : Latin *bi-*, two + *lanx*, scale.]

balance of payments. A systematic recording of a nation's total payments to foreign countries, including the price of imports and the outflow of capital and gold, and its total receipts from abroad, including the price of exports and the inflow of capital and gold.

balance of power. A distribution of power between nations, whereby no one nation is able to dominate or conquer the others.

balance of trade. The difference in value between the total exports and imports of a nation.

balance sheet. A statement of the assets and liabilities of a business or individual at a specified date.

balance wheel. A wheel that regulates rate of movement in machine parts, as in a watch; a balance.

bal·brig·gan (băl-brĭg′ən) *n.* A knitted cotton material used for underwear, hose, etc. [After *Balbriggan,* Irish seaport where it was first manufactured.]

bal·co·ny (băl′kə-nē) *n., pl.* **-nies.** **1.** A platform that projects from the wall of a building and is surrounded by a railing, balustrade, or parapet. **2.** An upper section of seats in a theater or auditorium. [Italian *balcone,* from Old Italian, scaffold.]

bald (bôld) *adj.* **-er, -est. 1.** Lacking hair on the head. **2.** Lacking natural or usual covering: *a bald spot on the lawn.* **3.** Having white feathers or markings on the head: *a bald eagle.* **4.** Plain; undisguised; blunt: *a bald statement.* —See Syns at **bare.** [Middle English *ballede.*] —**bald′ly** *adv.* —**bald′ness** *n.*

bal·da·chin (bôl′də-kĭn, băl′-) *n.* Also **bal·da·chi·no** (băl′də-kē′nō). A canopy of fabric placed over an altar, throne, or dais. [Italian *baldacchino,* from Old Italian, from *Baldacco,* Baghdad, famous in the Middle Ages for its brocades.]

bald eagle. A North American eagle, *Haliaeetus leucocephalus,* with a dark body and wings and a white head and tail. Also called **American eagle.**

bald eagle

bal·der·dash (bôl′dər-dăsh′) *n.* Words without sense; nonsense. [Orig. unknown.]

bald·head·ed (bôld′hĕd′ĭd) *adj.* Having a bald head.

bald·pate (bôld′pāt′) *n.* **1.** A baldheaded person. **2.** A duck, the widgeon.

bal·dric (bôl′drĭk) *n.* A usu. ornamented belt, worn across the chest to support a sword or bugle. [Middle English *baud(e)rik,* from Old French *baldrei.*]

Bal·dwin (bôl′dwĭn) *n.* A red-skinned American variety of apple. [After Loammi *Baldwin* (1740–1807), American engineer and soldier.]

bale¹ (bāl) *n.* A large bound package of raw or finished material: *a bale of hay.* —*tr.v.* **baled, bal·ing.** To wrap in bales. [Middle English, prob. from Old French.] —**bal′er** *n.*

bale² (bāl) *n. Poet.* **1.** Evil influence. **2.** Sorrow; anguish. [Middle English *bale,* from Old English *balu, bealu.*]

ba·leen (bə-lēn′) *n.* Whalebone. [Middle English *balene,* whale, baleen, from Old French *baleine,* from Latin *ballaena,* whale.]

bale·ful (bāl′fəl) *adj.* **1.** Harmful or malignant in intent or effect. **2.** Portending evil; dire. —**bale′ful·ly** *adv.* —**bale′ful·ness** *n.*

Usage: **baleful, baneful.** Both adjectives describe what is harmful but *baleful* applies esp. to what menaces, exerts an evil influence, or foreshadows evil: *baleful warnings; a baleful look. Baneful* is more often used to mean directly destructive: *baneful treatment; a baneful influence.*

balk (bôk). Also **baulk.** —*intr.v.* **1.** To stop short and refuse to go on: *All the horses took the jump but his balked.* **2.** To refuse obstinately or abruptly; shrink: *He balked at the very idea of compromise.* **3.** *Baseball.* To make an illegal motion before pitching, the penalty for which is that all runners automatically advance a base. —*tr.v.* To put obstacles in the way of; check or thwart: *The police balked their escape plans.* —*n.* **1.** A hindrance, check, or defeat. **2.** A blunder or failure. **3.** *Baseball.* The act of balking. **4. a.** An unplowed strip of land. **b.** A ridge between furrows. **5.** A wooden beam or rafter. [Middle English *balken,* to plow up in ridges, from Old English *balc,* ridge, from Old Norse *balkr,* partition.] —**balk′er** *n.*

balk·y (bô′kē) *adj.* **-i·er, -i·est.** Tending to balk; stubborn; obstinate: *a balky horse.* —See Syns at **contrary.**

ball¹ (bôl) *n.* **1. a.** A spherical or almost spherical body. **b.** Any spherical entity: *a ball of flame.* **2. a.** Any of various rounded movable objects used in sports and games. **b.** A game, esp. baseball, played with such an object. **3.** *Sports.* A ball moving, thrown, hit, or kicked in a particular manner: *a low ball.* **4.** *Baseball.* A pitched ball not swung at by the batter that does not pass through the strike zone. **5. a.** A solid projectile of spherical or pointed shape, as that shot from a cannon. **b.** Projectiles of this kind. **6.** A rounded part or protuberance, esp. of the body: *the ball of the foot.* —*tr.v.* To form into a ball. —*intr.v.* To become formed into a ball. —*idioms.* **ball up.** *Slang.* To confuse or bungle. **carry the ball.** *Informal.* To carry the burden of, or take the initiative in (a project). **have something on the ball.** *Slang.* To have ability or acumen. **on the ball.** *Slang.* Alert, competent, or efficient. **play ball. 1.** To begin or resume a ball game or other activity. **2.** *Informal.* To cooperate. [Middle English *bal,* from Old Norse *böllr.*]

ball² (bôl) *n.* A formal gathering for social dancing. —*idiom.* **have a ball.** *Slang.* To have a very enjoyable time. [French *bal,* from Old French, from *baller,* to dance, from Late Latin *ballāre,* from Greek *ballizein.*]

bal·lad (băl′əd) *n.* **1.** A narrative poem, often of folk origin and intended to be sung, consisting of simple stanzas and usu. having a recurrent refrain. **2.** The music for such a poem. **3.** A popular song of a romantic or sentimental nature. [Middle English *balade,* from Old French *ballade,* from Provençal *balada,* piece for dancing, Late Latin *ballāre,* to dance.]

bal·lade (bə-läd′, bă-) *n.* **1.** *Pros.* A verse form usu. consisting of three stanzas of eight or ten lines each, with the same concluding line in each stanza, and an envoy, or brief final stanza, ending with the same last line as that of the preceding stanzas. **2.** A musical composition, usu. for the piano, having the romantic or dramatic quality of a ballad. [Early form of BALLAD.]

ball and chain. A heavy iron ball fastened by a chain to a prisoner's leg.

ball-and-sock·et joint (bôl′ən-sŏk′ĭt). A joint consisting of a spherical knob or knoblike part fitted into a socket so that some degree of motion is possible in nearly any direction, often occurring between bones.

bal·last (băl′əst) *n.* **1.** Any heavy material carried in a vehicle mainly to provide weight for stability. **2.** Coarse gravel or crushed rock laid to form a foundation for roads or railroad tracks. **3.** Something that gives stability, esp. to character. —*tr.v.* To provide, fill in, or steady with ballast. [Perh. from Old Swedish *barlast,* "bare load" (cargo carried only for its weight).]

ball bearing. 1. A bearing, as for a turning shaft, in which the moving and stationary parts are held apart by a number of small, hard balls that turn between them and reduce friction. **2.** A small, hard ball used in such a bearing.

bal·le·ri·na (băl′ə-rē′nə) *n.* A female ballet dancer. [Italian, from *ballare,* to dance, from Late Latin *ballāre.*]

bal·let (bă-lā′, băl′ā′) *n.* **1.** An artistic dance form characterized by grace and precision of movement and an elaborate formal technique. **2.** A theatrical presentation of group or solo dancing, conveying a story, theme, or atmosphere. **3.** A musical composition written or used for ballet. **4.** A company or group that performs ballet. [French, from

Italian *balletto*, dim. of *ballo*, a dance, a ball.]

bal·lis·ta (bə-lĭs′tə) *n., pl.* **-tae** (-tē′). A military device used in ancient and medieval warfare to hurl heavy projectiles. [Latin, from Greek *ballein*, to throw.]

bal·lis·tic (bə-lĭs′tĭk) *adj.* **1.** Of or pertaining to ballistics. **2.** Of or pertaining to projectiles, their motion, or their effects. [From **BALLISTA**.] —**bal·lis′ti·cal·ly** *adv.*

ballistic missile. A projectile that assumes a free-falling path after a controlled, self-powered ascent.

bal·lis·tics (bə-lĭs′tĭks) *n. (used with a sing. verb).* **1. a.** The study of the dynamics of projectiles. **b.** The study of the flight characteristics of projectiles. **2. a.** The study of the functioning of firearms. **b.** The study of the firing, flight, and effect of ammunition. —**bal′lis·ti′cian** (băl′ĭ-stĭsh′ən) *n.*

ball lightning. A phenomenon associated with thunderstorms that is usu. thought to consist of a moving, luminous sphere of ionized gas.

bal·loon (bə-lōōn′) *n.* **1.** A spherical, flexible, nonporous bag inflated with a gas lighter than air, such as helium, that causes it to rise and float in the atmosphere, esp. such a bag with sufficient capacity to lift a suspended gondola. **2.** Any of variously shaped, brightly colored, inflatable rubber bags used as toys. **3.** A rounded or irregularly shaped outline containing the words a character in a cartoon is represented as saying. —*intr.v.* **1.** To ascend or ride in a balloon. **2.** To expand or swell out like a balloon. —*tr.v.* To cause to expand by or as if by inflating. [French *ballon*, from Italian *pallone*, from *palla*, ball, from Middle High German *balle*.] —**bal·loon′ist** *n.*

bal·lot (băl′ət) *n.* **1.** A written or printed paper or ticket used to cast or register a vote. **2.** The act, process, or method of voting, esp. by the use of secret ballots or voting machines. **3.** A list of candidates running for office in an election; a ticket. **4.** The total of all votes cast in an election. **5.** The right to vote; franchise. —*intr.v.* To cast a ballot; to vote. [Italian *ballotta*, small ball or pebble used for voting, from dial. *balla*, ball, from Middle High German *balle*.]

ball park. A park or stadium in which ball games are played. —*idiom.* **in the ball park.** *Informal.* Within the proper range; approximately right.

ball-point pen (bôl′point′). A pen with a small ball bearing that serves as its writing point.

ball·room (bôl′rōōm′, -rōōm′) *n.* A large room for dancing. —*modifier: a ballroom dress.*

bal·ly·hoo (băl′ē-hōō′) *Informal.* —*n.* **1.** Sensational or clamorous advertising. **2.** Noisy shouting or uproar. —*tr.v.* To advertise in a loud or sensational manner. [Orig. unknown.]

balm (bäm) *n.* **1.** An aromatic, oily resin obtained from various tropical trees and shrubs and used as a soothing ointment. **2.** Any of several plants with a pleasant, spicy odor, esp. *Melissa officinalis*, the lemon balm. **3.** Something that soothes, heals, or comforts. [Middle English *basme*, from Old French, from Latin *balsamum*, balsam.]

balm of Gilead. **1.** An aromatic evergreen tree of the genus *Commiphora*, esp. *C. opobalsamum*, of Africa and Asia Minor. **2.** A fragrant resin obtained from this tree. **3.** A fragrant resin obtained from the balsam fir.

balm·y (bä′mē) *adj.* **-i·er, -i·est.** **1.** Having the quality or fragrance of balm. **2.** Mild and pleasant: *balmy climates.* **3.** *Slang.* Eccentric; crazy. [Sense 3, var. of **BARMY**.] —**balm′i·ly** *adv.* —**balm′i·ness** *n.*

ba·lo·ney (bə-lō′nē) *n.* Also **bo·lo·ney.** **1.** *pl.* **-neys.** *Informal.* Var. of **bologna.** **2.** *Slang.* Nonsense.

bal·sa (bôl′sə) *n.* **1.** A tree, *Ochroma lagopus*, of tropical America, with wood that is unusually light in weight. **2.** The wood of this tree used for rafts, model airplanes, etc. [Spanish.]

bal·sam (bôl′səm) *n.* **1.** An oily or gummy oleoresin obtained from various trees and shrubs and used as a base for cough syrups, other medications, and perfumes. **2.** Any similar substance, esp. a fragrant ointment used as medication. **3.** Any of various trees yielding an aromatic, resinous substance, esp. the balsam fir. **4.** Any of several plants of the genus *Impatiens*, esp. *I. balsamina*, cultivated for its double flowers of various colors. [Latin *balsamum*, from Greek *balsamon*, from Hebrew *bāsām*, spice.]

balsam fir. An evergreen tree, *Abies balsamea*, of north-

eastern North America, that has small needles and cones.

Bal·tic (bôl′tĭk) *adj.* **1.** Of or pertaining to the Baltic Sea, or to the Baltic States and their inhabitants or cultures. **2.** Of the Baltic peoples or their languages. —*n.* A group of Indo-European languages including Lithuanian and Latvian.

Bal·ti·more oriole (bôl′tə-môr′, -mōr′). An American songbird, *Icterus galbula*, the male of which has bright-orange, black, and white plumage. [After George Calvert *Baltimore* (1580?–1632), 1st Baron, English colonist, the colors of whose coat of arms are the same as those of the male bird.]

bal·us·ter (băl′ə-stər) *n.* One of the posts that supports a handrail or banister. [French *baluster*, from Italian *balaustra*, flower of the pomegranate (from its shape), from Latin *balaustium*, from Greek *balaustion*.]

bal·us·trade (băl′ə-strād′) *n.* **1.** A handrail and the row of posts that support it, as on a balcony. **2.** A massive stone banister. [French, from Italian *balaustrata*, from *balaustra*, baluster.]

bam·bi·no (băm-bē′nō, bäm-) *n., pl.* **-nos** or **-ni** (-nē). **1.** A child; baby. **2.** A representation of the infant Jesus. [Italian, dim. of *bambo*, child, fool.]

bam·boo (băm-bōō′) *n., pl.* **-boos.** **1.** Any of various mostly tropical grasses of the genus *Bambusa*, with hollow, jointed stems. **2.** The strong woody stems of these plants, used in construction, crafts, for window blinds, fishing poles, etc. [Prob. from Malay *bambū*.]

bam·boo·zle (băm-bōō′zəl) *tr.v.* **-zled, -zling.** *Informal.* To deceive by elaborate trickery; hoodwink. [Prob. a var. of *bumbazzle*, from *bombace*, padding, bombast.]

ban (băn) *tr.v.* **banned, ban·ning.** **1.** To prohibit (something), esp. by law, decree, etc.; forbid. **2.** *Archaic.* To heap curses upon. —See Syns at **forbid.** —*n.* **1.** An excommunication or condemnation by church officials. **2.** A prohibition imposed by law or official decree. **3.** Censure through public opinion. **4.** A curse or imprecation. [Middle English *bannen*, to summon, banish, curse, partly from Old English *bannan*, to proclaim, and partly from Old Norse *banna*, to prohibit, curse.]

ba·nal (bə-näl′, -năl′, bā′nəl) *adj.* Lacking originality, esp. meaningless and dull; trite. [French, commonplace, from Old French, shared, from *ban*, summons to military service.] —**ba·nal′i·ty** (bə-năl′ĭ-tē, bā-) *n.* —**ba·nal′ly** *adv.*

ba·nan·a (bə-năn′ə) *n.* **1.** Any of several treelike tropical or subtropical plants of the genus *Musa*, esp. *M. sapientum*, a widely cultivated species with long, broad leaves and hanging clusters of edible fruit. **2.** The crescent-shaped fruit of any of these plants, with white, pulpy flesh and thick, easily removed yellow or reddish skin. —*modifier: banana peel.* [Portuguese and Spanish, from a native West African name.]

band[1] (bănd) *n.* **1. a.** A thin strip of metal, cloth, or other flexible material used to bind, support, or hold things together. **b.** A stripe, mark, or area suggestive of such a strip: *the band of colors forming the rainbow.* **2. bands.** The two strips hanging from the front of a collar as part of the dress of certain clergymen, scholars, and lawyers. **3.** A range or interval, esp. of radio wavelengths: *the shortwave band.* —*tr.v.* **1.** To tie, bind, or encircle with a band. **2.** To mark or identify (an animal) with a band. [Middle English, from Old French *bande*, bond, tie, link.]

band[2] (bănd) *n.* **1.** A group of people or animals acting together. **2.** A group of musicians who play together: *a lively dance band; a marching band.* —*tr.v.* To assemble or unite in a group: *band everyone by the fireplace.* —*intr.v.* To form a group; unite: *band together for warmth and protection.* [Old French *bande*, a troop, from Italian *banda*.]

band[3] (bănd) *n.* **1.** A physical restraint; a manacle or fetter. **2.** A moral or legal restraint; a bond: *the band of slavery.* [Middle English, from Old Norse.]

ban·dage (băn′dĭj) *n.* A strip of cloth or other material used to bind, cover, or protect a wound or other injury. —*tr.v.* **-daged, -dag·ing.** To apply a bandage to. [French, from *bande*, band, strip.]

Band-Aid (bănd′ād′) *n.* **1.** A trademark for an adhesive bandage with a gauze pad in the center. **2.** Any superficial or temporary remedy or solution.

ban·dan·na or **ban·dan·a** (băn-dăn′ə) *n.* A large handker-

---

ă pat	ā pay	â care	ä father	ĕ pet	ē be	hw which	ĭ pit	ī tie	î pier	ŏ pot	ō toe	ô paw, for	oi noise
ōō took	ōō boot	ou out	th thin	*th* this	ŭ cut		û urge	zh vision	ə about, item, edible, gallop, circus				

chief, usu. patterned and brightly colored. [Prob. from Portuguese *bandana,* from Hindi *bāndhnū,* a dyeing process in which the cloth is tied, from *bāndhnā,* to tie, from Sanskrit *bandhnáti.*]

band·box (bănd′bŏks′) *n.* A lightweight, rounded box, orig. designed to hold clean collars but now used for any small articles of apparel.

ban·deau (băn-dō′) *n., pl.* **-deaux** (-dōz′) or **-deaus.** A narrow band for the hair. [French, from Old French *bandel,* dim. of *bande,* band, strip.]

ban·de·role or **ban·de·rol** (băn′də-rōl′) *n.* A narrow forked flag or streamer attached to a staff or lance or flown from a masthead. [French, from Italian *bandiera,* banner.]

ban·di·coot (băn′dĭ-kōōt′) *n.* Any of several ratlike marsupials of the family Peramelidae, of Australia and adjacent islands, with a long, tapering snout and long hind legs.

ban·dit (băn′dĭt) *n.* A robber, often one who is a member of a gang of outlaws. [Italian *bandito,* from *bandire,* to band together.] —**ban′dit·ry** *n.*

band·mas·ter (bănd′măs′tər) *n.* The conductor of a musical band.

ban·do·leer or **ban·do·lier** (băn′də-lîr′) *n.* A military belt that has small pockets or loops for carrying cartridges and is worn over the shoulder and across the chest. [French *bandoulière,* from Spanish *bandolera,* from *banda,* sash.]

band saw. A power saw that consists mainly of a toothed metal band driven around a pair of wheels.

band shell. A bandstand with a concave, almost hemispheric wall at the rear.

bands·man (băndz′mən) *n.* A musician who plays an instrument in a band.

band·stand (bănd′stănd′) *n.* A platform for a band or orchestra, often roofed when outdoors.

band·wag·on (bănd′wăg′ən) *n.* **1.** An elaborately decorated wagon used to transport musicians in a parade. **2.** *Informal.* A cause or party that attracts increasing numbers of followers. —**idiom. get, climb,** or **jump on the bandwagon.** To join or shift support to a popular cause or successful trend.

ban·dy (băn′dē) *tr.v.* **-died, -dy·ing. 1.** To toss, throw, or strike back and forth: *bandy a ball.* **2.** To give and take (words or blows); to exchange. **3.** To discuss in a casual or frivolous manner: *bandy gossip.* —*adj.* Bent or curved outward; bowed: *bandy legs.* [Perh. from Old French *bander,* to bandy at tennis, oppose oneself against.]

ban·dy-leg·ged (băn′dē-lĕg′ĭd) *adj.* Bowlegged.

bane (bān) *n.* **1.** *Poet.* Fatal injury or ruin. **2.** A cause of death, destruction, or ruin. [Middle English, from Old English *bana,* slayer, cause of death, ruin.]

bane·ber·ry (băn′bĕr′ē) *n* Any plant of the genus *Actaea,* with clusters of white flowers and poisonous red or white berries.

baneberry

bane·ful (bān′fəl) *adj.* Full of venom or harm; destructive; pernicious: *baneful criticism.* —See Usage note at **baleful.**

bang¹ (băng) *n.* **1.** The sudden loud noise of an explosion: *the bang of guns.* **2.** A sudden loud impact or thump: *a bang on the head.* **3.** *Informal.* A sudden burst of action. **4.** *Slang.* A sense of excitement; a thrill. —*tr.v.* **1.** To strike heavily and repeatedly; hit noisily: *banging the table with his fist.* **2.** To close suddenly and loudly; to slam. **3.** To handle noisily or violently: *bang the dishes in the sink.* —*intr.v.* **1.** To make a sudden loud noise, as an ex-

plosion. **2.** To crash noisily against or into something: *The boat banged into the dock.* —*adv.* Exactly; precisely: *The arrow hit bang on the target.* [Prob. of Scandinavian orig.]

bang² (băng) *n.* Often **bangs.** Hair cut straight across the forehead. —*tr.v.* To cut (hair) straight across. [Perh. from Old Norse *banga,* to cut off.]

ban·gle (băng′gəl) *n.* A hooplike bracelet or anklet, esp. one with no clasp. [Hindi *bangrī,* glass bracelet.]

bang-up (băng′ŭp′) *adj. Slang.* Very good or successful; excellent: *a bang-up job; a bang-up party.*

ban·ian (băn′yən) *n.* Var. of **banyan.**

ban·ish (băn′ĭsh) *tr.v.* **1.** To force to leave a country or place by official decree; exile. **2.** To drive away; cast out. [Middle English *banishen,* from Old French *banir.*] —**ban′ish·ment** *n.*

ban·is·ter (băn′ĭ-stər) *n.* Also **ban·nis·ter.** The handrail supported by posts along a staircase. [Var. of BALUSTER.]

ban·jo (băn′jō) *n., pl.* **-jos** or **-joes.** A musical instrument, prob. invented in the United States, somewhat like a guitar but having a smaller, circular body with stretched vellum on one side, and four or sometimes five strings. [Dial. var. of *bandore,* an ancient instrument, from Portugese *bandurra,* from Late Latin *pandūra,* a lute.] —**ban′jo·ist** *n.*

bank¹ (băngk) *n.* **1.** Ground, often sloping, along the edge of a river, creek, pond, etc. **2.** A hillside or slope. **3.** Earth or other material piled into a sloping mass or surface: *a bank of earth.* **4.** A dense mass: *a snow bank.* **5.** Often **banks.** An elevated area of the ocean floor over which the water is relatively shallow. **6.** The sideways tilt of an aircraft in making a turn. —*tr.v.* **1.** To border or protect with a ridge or embankment. **2.** To pile up; amass: *bank earth along a wall.* **3.** To cover (a fire) with ashes, fresh fuel, etc., to insure continued slow burning. **4.** To construct with a slope rising to the outside edge. **5.** To tilt (an aircraft) sideways in flight. —*intr.v.* **1.** To take the form of or rise in a bank or banks. **2.** To tilt an aircraft sideways when turning. [Middle English *banke,* prob. of Scandinavian orig.]

bank² (băngk) *n.* **1.** A place or organization in which money is kept for saving or business purposes or is invested, supplied for loans, or exchanged. **2.** A small container in which money is saved: *a piggy bank.* **3.** A supply of or storage place for something useful or necessary: *a blood bank; the memory bank of a computer.* **4.** Any place of safekeeping or storage. **5. a.** The funds held by a dealer or banker in some gambling games. **b.** The reserve pieces, cards, chips, or play money in some games from which the players may draw, as in poker or dominoes. —*modifier:* *bank robbers; a bank account.* —*tr.v.* To deposit (money) in a bank. —*intr.v.* **1.** To transact business with a bank. **2.** To operate a bank. **3.** To hold the bank in some gambling games. —*phrasal verb.* **bank on.** To have confidence in; rely on; count on. [French *banque,* from Italian *banca,* bench, moneychanger's table, from Old High German *banc.*]

bank³ (băngk) *n.* **1.** A set of similar or matched things arranged in a row: *a bank of elevators.* **2.** A row of keys on a keyboard. —*tr.v.* To arrange or set up in a row. [Middle English, from Old French *banc.*]

bank·book (băngk′bŏŏk′) *n.* A booklet in which a bank enters the amounts deposited in or taken out of an account. Also called **passbook.**

bank·er (băng′kər) *n.* **1.** A person who owns or is an executive of a bank. **2.** The player in charge of the bank in some gambling games.

bank·ing (băng′kĭng) *n.* The business of a bank or the occupation of a banker.

bank note. A note issued by an authorized bank representing its promise to pay a specific sum to the bearer on demand and acceptable as money.

bank·roll (băngk′rōl′) *n.* **1.** A roll of paper money. **2.** *Informal.* A person's ready cash. —*tr.v.* To underwrite the cost of, as a show, business venture, etc.

bank·rupt (băngk′rŭpt′, -rəpt) *adj.* **1.** Legally declared unable to pay one's debts because of lack of money and in turn having one's remaining property administered by or divided among one's creditors. **2.** Completely without money; financially ruined. **3.** Lacking in some resource or quality: *bankrupt in manners.* —*tr.v.* To cause to become

bankrupt. —*n.* A person who is bankrupt. [French *banqueroute,* from Italian *banca rotta,* "broken counter."]

bank·rupt·cy (băngk′rŭpt′sē, -rəp-sē) *n., pl.* **-cies.** The condition of being legally bankrupt; financial ruin.

ban·ner (băn′ər) *n.* **1.** A flag or similar piece of material, often bearing a motto or legend. **2.** The flag of a nation, state, army, or sovereign. **3.** A headline spanning the width of a newspaper page. —*adj.* Unusually good; outstanding: *a banner year for our company.* [Middle English *banere,* from Old French *baniere,* from Late Latin *bandum,* standard.]

ban·ner·et (băn′ər-ĭt, -ə-rĕt′) *n.* Also **ban·ner·ette** (băn′ə-rĕt′). A small banner.

ban·nis·ter (băn′ĭ-stər) *n.* Var. of **banister.**

ban·nock (băn′ək) *n. Scot. & Brit.* A griddlecake, usu. unleavened, made of oatmeal, barley, or wheat flour. [Middle English *bannok,* from Old English *bannuc.*]

banns (bănz) *pl.n.* Also **bans.** A spoken or published announcement in a church of an intended marriage. [Middle English *banes,* pl. of *bane, ban,* proclamation, partly from Old English *gebann* and partly from Old French *ban.*]

ban·quet (băng′kwĭt) *n.* **1.** An elaborate and sumptuous repast. **2.** A ceremonial dinner honoring a particular guest or occasion. —*tr.v.* To entertain at a banquet. —*intr.v.* To partake of a banquet; to feast. [Old French, dim. of *banc,* bench.] —**ban′quet·er** *n.*

ban·quette (băng-kĕt′) *n.* **1.** A long upholstered bench, either placed against or built into a wall. **2.** *Mil.* A platform lining a trench or parapet wall where soldiers may stand when firing. [French, from Provençal *banqueta,* dim. of *banca,* bench.]

bans (bănz) *pl. n.* Var. of **banns.**

ban·shee (băn′shē) *n.* Also **ban·shie.** In Gaelic folklore, a female spirit believed to presage a death in the family by wailing outside the house. [Irish Gaelic *bean sidhe,* "woman of the fairies."]

ban·tam (băn′təm) *n.* **1.** Any of various breeds of miniature chickens. **2.** A small person who is always ready to fight. —*adj.* **1.** Diminutive; small. **2.** Spirited or aggressive. — See Syns at **little.** [From the belief that the fowl were native to *Bantam,* a town in Java.]

ban·tam·weight (băn′təm-wāt′) *n.* A boxer in the lowest weight class, approximately 51 to 54 kilograms or 112 to 118 pounds.

ban·ter (băn′tər) *n.* Good-humored, playful teasing or conversation. —*tr.v.* To tease or joke in a playful manner. —*intr.v.* To exchange mildly teasing remarks. [Orig. unknown.] —**ban′ter·er** *n.* —**ban′ter·ing·ly** *adv.*

Ban·tu (băn′tōō) *n., pl.* **Bantu** or **-tus.** **1.** A member of a group of Negroid peoples of central and southern Africa. **2.** A group of related languages spoken by the Bantu. —**Ban′tu** *adj.*

ban·yan (băn′yən) *n.* Also **ban·ian.** A tree, *Ficus benghalensis,* of tropical India and the East Indies, with large, oval leaves and spreading branches from which many aerial roots grow downward and develop into additional trunks. [From *banian,* a Hindu merchant (after one such tree beneath which *banians* traded).]

ban·zai (bän-zī′) *n.* A Japanese battle cry, patriotic cheer, or greeting. [Japanese, "(may you live) ten thousand years."]

ba·o·bab (bā′ō-băb′, bä′-) *n.* A tree, *Adansonia digitata,* of tropical Africa, with a trunk up to 9 meters, or about 30 feet, in diameter and large hard-shelled, hanging fruit called monkey bread. [Prob. a native Central African name.]

bap·tism (băp′tĭz′əm) *n.* **1.** The solemn ceremony, in which, as a result of the use of water, a person is cleansed of sin and admitted to membership in a Christian church. **2.** A first experience: *a soldier's baptism under fire.* [Middle English *bapteme,* from Old French, from Late Latin *baptisma,* from Greek *baptizein,* to baptize.]

bap·tis·mal (băp-tĭz′məl) *adj.* **1.** Of or pertaining to baptism: *a baptismal ceremony.* **2.** Given at baptism: *a child's baptismal name.* —**bap·tis′mal·ly** *adv.*

Bap·tist (băp′tĭst) *n.* **1.** A member of a Protestant church group that believes in baptism only for people old enough to understand the meaning. Baptists are usually baptized by placing the whole body in water. **2. the Baptist.** A name given to Saint John the Baptist, who baptized Christ. —*modifier: a Baptist minister.*

bap·tis·ter·y (băp′tĭ-strē) *n., pl.* **-ies.** Also **bap·tis·try** *pl.* **-tries. 1.** A part of a church, or a separate building, in which baptism is performed. **2.** A font used for baptism. **3.** A tank for baptizing by total immersion used in certain Baptist churches.

bap·tize (băp-tīz′, băp′tīz′) *tr.v.* **-tized, -tiz·ing. 1.** To dip or immerse in water or to sprinkle water on (a person) during a baptismal ceremony. **2. a.** To cleanse or purify. **b.** To initiate. **3.** To give a first or Christian name to. [Middle English *baptizen,* from Old French *baptiser,* from Late Latin *baptizāre,* from Greek *baptizein,* from *baptein,* to dip.] —**bap·tiz′er** *n.*

bar (bär) *n.* **1.** A narrow, straight piece of metal or other material, often used to close an opening or as part of a machine or other device. **2.** A solid, oblong piece of a substance: *a bar of soap.* **3.** A stripe, band, or similar narrow marking. **4.** *Heraldry.* A pair of horizontal parallel lines drawn across a shield. **5.** Something that prevents entry or progress; a barrier; obstacle. **6.** A ridge of sand, gravel, etc., on a shore or stream bed, formed by the action of tides or currents. **7. a.** A high counter at which drinks, esp. alcoholic drinks, and sometimes food are served. **b.** A place having such a counter. **8. a.** The railing in a courtroom in front of which the judges, lawyers, and defendants sit. **b.** The occupation of a lawyer; the legal profession. **9.** *Mus.* **a.** Often **bar line.** Any of the vertical lines drawn across a staff to divide it into measures. **b.** A measure of music. —*tr.v.* **barred, bar·ring. 1.** To close or fasten with a bar or bars: *bar the gate.* **2.** To close off; obstruct: *Fallen branches barred the way.* **3.** To keep out; exclude: *Hunters are barred from wildlife sanctuaries.* **4.** To forbid; prohibit: *wrestling with no holds barred.* **5.** To mark with stripes or narrow bands. —*prep.* **bar none.** With no exceptions. [Middle English *barre,* from Old French.]

barb (bärb) *n.* **1.** A sharp point projecting in reverse direction to the main point of a weapon or tool, as on an arrow, fishhook, or spear. **2.** A cutting or biting remark. **3.** *Bot.* A hooked bristle or hairlike projection. **4.** One of the many parallel filaments projecting from the main shaft of a feather. —*tr.v.* To provide or furnish with a barb or barbs. [Middle English *barbe,* beard, from Old French, from Latin *barba.*]

bar·bar·i·an (bär-bâr′ē-ən) *n.* **1.** A member of a people considered by those of another nation or group to be primitive, uncivilized, or savage. **2.** A crude, uncivilized, or brutal person. —*adj.* Of, characteristic, or resembling a barbarian; savage. [French *barbarien,* from Latin *barbaria,* foreign country, from *barbarus,* barbarous.] —**bar·bar′i·an·ism** *n.*

Syns: *barbarian, barbaric, barbarous adj.* All three adjectives can mean uncivilized and are interchangeable in this example: *barbarian tribes.* But BARBARIAN and BARBARIC also mean lacking refinement: *barbaric (or barbarian) eating habits.* BARBARIC and BARBAROUS can also describe what is violently savage and cruel: *a barbarous (or barbaric) murder.*

bar·bar·ic (bär-băr′ĭk) *adj.* **1.** Of or typical of a barbarian or barbarians; regarded as crude or uncivilized. **2.** Brutal; savage; cruel. —See Syns at **barbarian.**

bar·ba·rism (bär′bə-rĭz′əm) *n.* **1.** Existence in a crude, un-

baobab

civilized state: *mankind's progress from barbarism toward civilization.* **2.** A brutal or cruel condition, act, or custom. **3.** A word or expression regarded as being incorrect and showing lack of education or refinement.

bar·bar·i·ty (bär-băr′ĭ-tē) *n., pl.* **-ties. 1.** Cruel or brutal behavior. **2.** A barbarous act. **3.** Crudeness.

bar·ba·rize (bär′bə-rīz′) *v.* **-ized, -iz·ing.** *—tr.v.* To make barbarous. *—intr.v.* To become barbarous.

bar·ba·rous (bär′bər-əs) *adj.* **1.** Wild; primitive; uncivilized. **2.** Brutal; savage; cruel. **3.** Uncultured or unrefined, esp. in the use of words. —See Syns at **barbarian** and **cruel.** [Latin *barbarus*, from Greek *barbaros*, non-Greek, foreign, rude.] **—bar′ba·rous·ly** *adv.* **—bar′ba·rous·ness** *n.*

Bar·ba·ry ape (bär′bə-rē). A tailless monkey, *Macaca sylvana*, of Gibraltar and northern Africa.

Barbary ape   barbed wire

bar·be·cue (bär′bĭ-kyōō′) *n.* **1.** A grill, pit, or fireplace for roasting meat, often outdoors. **2.** A whole animal carcass or section thereof roasted or broiled over an open fire or on a spit, often basted with a spicy sauce. **3.** A social gathering, usu. held outdoors, at which food is cooked in this way. *—tr.v.* **-cued, -cu·ing.** To roast, broil, or grill (meat) over hot coals or an open fire, often basting it with a spicy sauce. [American Spanish *barbacoa*, from Haitian Creole, framework of sticks set on posts, from Taino.]

barbed (bärbd) *adj.* **1.** Having sharp, hooked parts; armed with a barb or barbs: *the barbed head of a harpoon.* **2.** Sharp; cutting; stinging: *barbed criticism.*

barbed wire. Twisted strands of fence wire with barbs at regular intervals.

bar·bel (bär′bəl) *n.* **1.** One of the slender, whiskerlike sensory organs on the head of certain fishes, such as catfish. **2.** Any of several Old World freshwater fish of the genus *Barbus.* [Middle English, from Old French, from Late Latin *barbellus*, from Latin *barba*, beard.]

bar·bell (bär′běl′) *n.* A bar with adjustable weights at each end, lifted for sport or exercise.

bar·ber (bär′bər) *n.* A person whose work is cutting hair and shaving or trimming beards. *—tr.v.* **1.** To cut the hair of. **2.** To shave or trim the beard of. [Middle English *barbour*, from Old French *barbeor*, from Latin *barba*, beard.]

bar·ber·ry (bär′běr′ē) *n., pl.* **-ries.** Any of various shrubs of the genus *Berberis*, with small leaves, clusters of yellow flowers, and small orange or red berries. [Middle English *barbere*, from Old French *berberis*, from Arabic *barbārīs*.]

bar·bi·can (bär′bĭ-kən) *n.* A tower or other fortification at a gate or drawbridge at the approach to a medieval castle or town. [Middle English, from Old French *barbacane*, from Medieval Latin *barbacana*.]

bar·bi·tal (bär′bĭ-tôl′) *n.* A white crystalline compound, $C_8H_{12}N_2O_3$, used as a sedative. [BARBIT(URIC ACID) + (VERON)AL.]

bar·bi·tu·rate (bär-bĭch′ər-ĭt, -ə-rāt′, bär′bĭ-tōōr′ĭt, -āt′, -tyōōr′ĭt, -āt′) *n.* Any of a group of barbituric acid derivatives used as sedatives or sleep-producing drugs. [BARBITUR(IC ACID) + -ATE.]

bar·bi·tu·ric acid (bär′bĭ-tōōr′ĭk, -tyōōr′-). An organic acid, $C_4H_4N_2O_3$, used in the manufacture of barbiturates and some plastics. [Perh. ult. from the name *Barbara* + URIC + ACID.]

bar·ca·role (bär′kə-rōl′) *n.* Also **bar·ca·rolle. 1.** A Venetian gondolier's song. **2.** A musical composition imitating this.

[French, from Italian *barcaruola*, from *barcaruolo*, gondolier, from *barca*, barge.]

bard (bärd) *n.* **1.** One of an ancient Celtic order of singing poets who composed and recited verses on the legends and history of their tribes. **2.** Any poet, esp. an exalted national poet. [Middle English, from Gaelic and Irish *bárd* and Welsh *bardd*.] **—bard′ic** *adj.*

bare[1] (bâr) *adj.* **bar·er, bar·est. 1.** Without the usual or appropriate covering or clothing; naked: *a bare head.* **2.** Exposed to view; undisguised: *He laid bare the secret agreements between the unions.* **3.** Lacking the usual furnishings, equipment, or decoration: *walls bare of pictures.* **4.** Without addition or qualification; simple; plain: *the bare facts.* **5.** Just sufficient; mere: *the bare necessities of life.* *—tr.v.* **bared, bar·ing.** To make bare; strip of covering; reveal. [Middle English *bare*, from Old English *bær*.] **—bare′ness** *n.*

Syns: bare, bald, naked, nude *adj.* Core meaning: Without the usual covering. BARE, BALD, NAKED, and NUDE can apply to persons and things (*a bare arm, bare fields; a bald head, bald wintery hills; naked feet, naked tree branches; a nude cherub, a nude statue*). BARE, BALD, and sometimes NAKED also describe what is blunt or without qualification (*the bare facts; the bald truth; a naked lie*). See also Syns at **empty.**

bare[2] (bâr) *v. Archaic.* Past tense of **bear.** [Middle English, from Old English *bær*.]

bare·back (bâr′băk′) *adv.* On a horse, pony, etc., with no saddle: *riding bareback. —adj.: a bareback rider.*

bare·faced (bâr′fāst′) *adj.* **1.** Having no covering over the face. **2.** Presumptuous and shameless; bold; brazen: *a barefaced lie.* **—bare′fac′ed·ly** (-fā′sĭd-lē, -fāst′lē) *adv.* **—bare′fac′ed·ness** *n.*

bare·foot (bâr′fōōt′) *adj.* Also **bare·foot·ed** (-fōōt′ĭd). Without shoes or other covering on the feet: *a barefoot boy.* *—adv.: running barefoot over the grass.*

bare·hand·ed (bâr′hăn′dĭd) *adv.* With the hands alone; without a glove, tool, weapon, etc.: *fighters boxing barehanded. —adj.: a barehanded catch.*

bare·head·ed (bâr′hěd′ĭd) *adj.* With the head uncovered. *—adv.: walking bareheaded in the rain.*

bare·ly (bâr′lē) *adv.* By a very little; almost not; hardly; just: *We could barely see the shore in the dark.*

bar·gain (bär′gĭn) *n.* **1.** An agreement or contract, esp. one involving the sale and purchase of goods or services. **2.** The terms or conditions of such an agreement: *He couldn't meet his part of the bargain.* **3.** The property acquired or services rendered as a result of such an agreement. **4.** Something offered or acquired at a price advantageous to the buyer. *—intr.v.* **1.** To negotiate the terms of a sale, exchange, or other agreement. **2.** To arrive at an agreement. *—tr.v.* To exchange; to trade: *He bargained his watch for a meal.* *—phrasal verb.* **bargain for.** To expect; count on: *giving us more trouble than we had bargained for.* *—idioms.* **into (or in) the bargain.** Over and above what is expected. **strike a bargain.** To agree on the terms of a purchase or joint undertaking. [Middle English *bargaynen*, from Old French *bargaignier*, to haggle in the market.] **—bar′gain·er** *n.*

barge (bärj) *n.* **1.** A long, large boat, usu. flat-bottomed, used for transporting freight on rivers, canals, and coastal waters. **2.** A large pleasure boat used for parties, pageants, or formal ceremonies. **3.** *Naval.* A power boat reserved for the use of a flag officer. *—v.* **barged, barg·ing.** *—tr.v.* To carry by barge. *—intr.v. Informal.* **1.** To move about clumsily: *The rhinoceros barged through the brush.* **2.** To enter rudely and abruptly; intrude: *He barged into the meeting.* [Middle English, from Old French.]

bar·ite (bâr′īt′, băr′-) *n.* A colorless crystalline mineral of barium sulfate that is the chief source of barium. [Greek *barutēs*, weight, from *barus*, heavy.]

bar·i·tone (bär′ĭ-tōn′) *n.* Also **bar·y·tone. 1.** A moderately low singing voice of a man, higher than a bass and lower than a tenor. **2.** A man having such a voice. **3.** A part written for a voice having such a range. **4.** A brass wind instrument with a similar range. *—modifier: a powerful baritone voice; a baritone solo.* [Italian *baritono*, from Greek *barutonos*, deep sounding: *barus*, heavy + *tonos*, tone.]

bar·i·um (bâr′ē-əm, băr′-) *n. Symbol* **Ba** One of the elements, a soft, silvery-white, alkaline-earth metal, used to deoxidize copper, in various alloys, and in rat poison. Atomic number 56, atomic weight 137.34, melting point 725°C, boiling point 1,140°C, specific gravity 3.50, valence 2. [From earlier *beryta,* barite.] **—bar'ic** (băr'ĭk) *adj.*

barium sulfate. A fine white powder, BaSO₄, used as a pigment, as a filler for textiles, rubbers, and plastics, and in taking x-ray photographs of the digestive tract.

bark¹ (bärk) *n.* **1.** The short, gruff sound made by a dog and certain other animals. **2.** A sound similar to this, such as a gunshot or cough. *—intr.v.* **1.** To make or utter a bark. **2.** *Informal.* To cough. **3.** To speak sharply; to snap: *He barked at his assistant. —tr.v.* To utter in a loud, harsh voice: *He barked his commands. —idiom.* **bark up the wrong tree.** *Informal.* To wastefully misdirect one's energies. [From Middle English *berken,* to bark, from Old English *beorcan.*]

bark² (bärk) *n.* **1.** The outer covering of the woody stems, branches, roots, and main trunks of trees and other woody plants. **2.** A specific kind of bark used for a special purpose, as in tanning or medicine. *—tr.v.* **1.** To remove bark from (a tree or log). **2.** To rub off the skin of; to bruise: *He barked his shins on the rocks.* [Middle English *barke,* from Old Norse *börkr.*]

bark³ (bärk) *n.* Also **barque.** **1.** A sailing ship with from three to five masts, all of them square-rigged except the after mast, which is fore-and-aft rigged. **2.** *Poet.* Any boat, esp. a small sailing vessel. [Middle English *barke,* prob. ult. from Greek *baris,* Egyptian barge.]

bar·keep·er (bär'kē'pər) *n.* Also **bar·keep** (bär'kēp'). **1.** A person who owns or runs a bar for the sale of alcoholic beverages. **2.** A bartender.

bar·ken·tine (bär'kən-tēn') *n.* Also **bar·quen·tine.** A sailing ship with from three to five masts of which only the foremast is square-rigged, the other masts being fore-and-aft rigged. [Prob. blend of BARK (boat) and BRIGANTINE.]

bark·er (bär'kər) *n.* **1.** Someone or something that makes a barking sound. **2.** *Informal.* An employee who stands at the entrance to a show and solicits customers with loud, colorful sales talk.

bar·ley (bär'lē) *n.* **1.** A cereal grass, *Hordeum vulgare,* bearing bearded flower spikes with edible seeds. **2.** The grain of this plant, used as food and in making beer, ale, and whiskey. *—modifier: barley soup.* [Middle English *barrlig,* orig. "of barley," from Old English *bærlic,* from *bære,* barley.]

bar·ley·corn (bär'lē-kôrn') *n.* The grain of barley.

barm (bärm) *n.* The yeasty foam that rises to the surface of fermenting malt liquors. [Middle English *berme,* from Old English *beorma.*]

bar·maid (bär'mād') *n.* A woman who serves drinks at a bar; bartender.

bar·man (bär'mən) *n.* A man who serves drinks at a bar; bartender.

bar mitz·vah (bär mĭts'və). Also **bar miz·vah.** *Judaism.* **1.** A thirteen-year-old Jewish male, considered an adult and thenceforth responsible for his moral and religious duties. **2.** The ceremony consecrating and celebrating this status. [Hebrew *bar mitzvāh,* "son of command."]

barm·y (bär'mē) *adj.* **-i·er, -i·est.** **1.** Full of barm; frothy; foamy. **2.** *Brit. Slang.* Out of one's mind; crazy.

barn (bärn) *n.* A large farm building used for storing farm products and for sheltering cattle and other livestock. *—modifier: the barn door.* [Middle English *bern,* from Old English *bern, berern,* from *bære,* barley + *ern,* place, house.]

bar·na·cle (bär'nə-kəl) *n.* Any of various saltwater crustaceans of the order Cirripedia that in the adult stage form a hard shell and remain attached to a submerged surface, thus fouling ship bottoms. [Middle English *bernak,* a species of goose, from Medieval Latin *bernaca, berneca,* (from the belief that the geese were produced from the shellfish).] **—bar'na·cled** *adj.*

barn·storm (bärn'stôrm') *intr.v.* **1.** To travel about the countryside presenting plays, lecturing, or making political speeches. **2.** To tour county fairs and carnivals as a stunt flyer. **—barn'storm'er** *n.*

barn swallow. A widely distributed bird, *Hirundo rustica,* with a deeply forked tail, that often builds its nest on the

barnacle   barometer

rafters of barns.

barn·yard (bärn'yärd') *n.* The yard or area of ground surrounding a barn, often enclosed by a fence.

bar·o·graph (băr'ə-grăf') *n.* A recording barometer. [Greek *baros,* weight + -GRAPH.]

ba·rom·e·ter (bə-rŏm'ĭ-tər) *n.* **1.** An instrument for measuring atmospheric pressure, used in weather forecasting and in determining elevation. **2.** Anything that gives notice of fluctuations; an indicator: *Interest rates are a major economic barometer.* [Greek *baros,* weight + -METER.]

bar·o·met·ric (băr'ə-mĕt'rĭk) or **bar·o·met·ri·cal** (-rĭ-kəl) *adj.* Of or measured by a barometer. **—bar'o·met'ri·cal·ly** *adv.*

bar·on (băr'ən) *n.* **1.** A feudal tenant holding his rights and title directly from the king or another feudal superior. **2. a.** A member of the lowest rank of nobility in Great Britain, certain European countries, and Japan. **b.** The rank or title of such a nobleman. **3.** A businessman of great wealth and influence; magnate: *a railroad baron.* [Middle English, from Old French *ber,* from Medieval Latin *barō,* man, warrior.]

bar·on·age (băr'ə-nĭj) *n.* **1.** The rank, title, or dignity of a baron. **2.** All of the peers of a kingdom.

bar·on·ess (băr'ə-nĭs) *n.* **1.** The wife or widow of a baron. **2.** A woman holding a barony in her own right.

bar·on·et (băr'ə-nĭt, băr'ə-nĕt') *n.* **1.** A British hereditary title of honor, ranking next below a baron, held by commoners. **2.** The bearer of such a title.

bar·on·et·age (băr'ə-nĭt-ĭj, -nĕt-) *n.* **1.** The rank or dignity of a baronet. **2.** Baronets in general.

ba·ro·ni·al (bə-rō'nē-əl) *adj.* **1.** Of or pertaining to a baron or barony. **2.** Suitable for a baron; stately. **—See Syns at grand.**

bar·o·ny (băr'ə-nē) *n., pl.* **-nies.** The rank or domain of a baron.

ba·roque (bə-rōk') *adj.* **1.** Often **Baroque.** Of or in a style of art and architecture developed in Europe from about 1550 to 1700, with extremely elaborate and ornate forms. **2.** Often **Baroque.** Of or in a style of musical composition that flourished in Europe from about 1600 to 1750, notable for strictness of form and elaborateness of ornamentation. **3.** Irregular in shape: *a baroque pearl.* **4.** Elaborate and fantastic; outlandish: *a strange, baroque novel. —n.* The baroque style or period in art, architecture, and music. [French, from Italian *barocco,* after Federigo Barocci (1528–1612), Italian painter.]

ba·rouche (bə-rōōsh') *n.* A four-wheeled, horse-drawn carriage with a folding top, two double seats inside facing one another, and a driver's seat outside. [German *Barutsche,* from Italian *baroccio,* from Latin *birotus,* two-wheeled.]

barque (bärk) *n.* Var. of **bark** (ship).

bar·quen·tine (bär'kən-tēn') *n.* Var. of **barkentine.**

bar·racks (băr'əks) *n.* (used with a sing. or pl. verb). **1.** A building or group of buildings used to house soldiers. **2.** Any large building used for temporary quarters. [From French *baraque,* from Italian *baracca,* soldier's tent, from Spanish *barraca,* mud hut.]

bar·ra·cu·da (băr'ə-kōō'də) *n., pl.* **barracuda** or **-das.** Any of various voracious, mostly tropical, saltwater fishes of the genus *Sphyraena,* with a long, narrow body and fanglike teeth. [Spanish.]

bar·rage (bə-räzh') *n.* **1.** A rapid, concentrated discharge of missiles or artillery fire. **2.** An overwhelming, concentrated attack or outpouring: *a barrage of questions; a barrage of fists.* —*tr.v.* **-raged, -rag·ing.** To direct a barrage at: *barrage the speaker with questions.* [French, from *(tir de) barrage,* barrier (fire), from *barrer,* to bar.]

bar·ra·try (băr′ə-trē) *n., pl.* **-tries. 1.** *Law.* The offense of exciting or stirring up quarrels or groundless lawsuits. **2.** An unlawful breach of duty on the part of a ship's master or crew, resulting in injury to the ship's owner. **3.** The sale or purchase of positions in the church or state. [Middle English *barratrie,* the purchase of church offices, from Old French *baraterie,* deception, from *barater,* to cheat, to barter.]

bar·rel (băr′əl) *n.* **1.** A large wooden container with round, flat ends of equal size and sides that bulge out slightly. **2. a.** A barrel with something in it: *a barrel of oil.* **b.** The amount held by a barrel: *peel a barrel of potatoes.* **3.** Any of various measures of volume or capacity ranging from about 117 to 159 liters, or 31 to 42 gallons, esp. a quantity of petroleum equal to about 119 liters, or 31.5 gallons. **4. a.** The long tube of a gun. **b.** A cylindrical machine part. **5.** *Informal.* A great amount: *a barrel of fun.* —*v.* **-reled** or **-relled, -rel·ing** or **-rel·ling.** —*tr.v.* To put or pack in a barrel or barrels. —*intr.v. Slang.* To move at breakneck speed: *He barreled along the highway.* [Middle English *barel,* from Old French *baril.*]

barrel organ. A portable musical instrument similar to a small organ, in which the airflow to the pipes is controlled by valves that are operated by turning a barrel with a hand crank.

bar·ren (băr′ən) *adj.* **1. a.** Not producing offspring; childless or fruitless. **b.** Incapable of producing offspring; infertile; sterile. **2.** Lacking vegetation, esp. useful vegetation; unproductive. **3.** Unproductive of results or gains; unprofitable: *barren efforts.* **4.** Without something specified; devoid; lacking: *writing barren of insight: a life barren of pleasure.* —*n.* Often **barrens.** A tract of unproductive land. [Middle English *barein(e),* from Old French *baraigne.*] —**bar′ren·ly** *adv.* —**bar′ren·ness** *n.*

bar·rette (bə-rĕt′, bä-) *n.* A bar-shaped or oval clip used to hold the hair in place. [French, dim. of *barre,* bar.]

bar·ri·cade (băr′ĭ-kād′, băr′ĭ-kād′) *n.* **1.** An often hastily built wall-like structure set up to close off a passageway, to keep back attackers or crowds, etc. **2.** Anything acting to obstruct passage; a barrier. —*tr.v.* **-cad·ed, -cad·ing.** To close off, block, or protect with a barricade. [French, from Old French, from *barrique,* barrel (from the fact that the earliest barricades were made of earth-filled barrels).]

bar·ri·er (băr′ē-ər) *n.* **1.** A fence, wall, or other structure built to hold back or obstruct movement or passage. **2.** A boundary or limit: *the sound barrier.* **3.** Anything that hinders or restricts: *Insufficient technology is a barrier to industrial growth.* **4.** Anything that separates or holds apart: *a language barrier.* [Middle English *barrere,* from Old French *barriere,* prob. from *barre,* bar.]

barrier reef. A long narrow ridge of coral or rock near and parallel to a coastline.

bar·ring (băr′ĭng) *prep.* **1.** Apart from the possibility of; excepting: *Barring strong headwinds, the plane will arrive on schedule.* **2.** Except for: *This is their first public appearance, barring a preview in Boston.*

bar·ri·o (bä′rē-ō′) *n., pl.* **-os. 1.** A chiefly Spanish-speaking community or neighborhood in a U.S. city. **2.** An enclave, ward, or district in a Latin-American country or in the Philippines. [Spanish, from Arabic *barr,* open area.]

bar·ris·ter (băr′ĭ-stər) *n. Brit.* A lawyer who argues cases in a law court.

bar·room (băr′rōōm′, -rōōm′) *n.* A room or building in which alcoholic beverages are sold at a counter or bar.

bar·row¹ (băr′ō) *n.* **1.** A wheelbarrow. **2.** A traylike form with handles at each end, used for carrying loads. [Middle English *bar(o)we,* from Old English *bearwe,* basket, wheelbarrow.]

bar·row² (băr′ō) *n. Archaeol.* A large mound of earth or stones placed over a burial site in ancient times. [Middle English *borewe,* from Old English *beorg.*]

bar sinister. *Heraldry.* A bend.

bar·tend·er (băr′tĕn′dər) *n.* A person who mixes and serves alcoholic drinks at a bar.

bar·ter (bär′tər) *intr.v.* To trade goods or services without using money. —*tr.v.* To exchange (goods or services) without using money. —*n.* **1.** The act or practice of bartering. **2.** Something that is bartered. [Middle English *barteren,* prob. from Old French *barater,* to barter, cheat.] —**bar′ter·er** *n.*

bar·ti·zan (bär′tĭ-zən, bär′tĭ-zăn′) *n.* A small, overhanging turret on a wall or tower. [Scottish *bartisane,* var. of *bratticing,* timberwork.]

bascule bridge   bartizan

Bart·lett (bärt′lĭt) *n.* A widely grown English variety of pear having large, juicy, yellow fruit. [After Enoch *Bartlett* (1779–1860), American merchant.]

bar·y·on (băr′ē-ŏn′) *n.* Any of a family of subatomic particles that are gen. more massive than the proton. [Greek *barus,* heavy + -ON.]

bar·y·tone (băr′ĭ-tōn′) *n.* Var. of **baritone.**

ba·sal (bā′səl, -zəl) *adj.* **1.** Pertaining to, located at, or forming a base. **2.** Of primary importance; basic; fundamental. —**ba′sal·ly** *adv.*

basal metabolism. The least amount of energy required to maintain vital functions in an organism when at complete rest.

ba·salt (bə-sôlt′, bā′sôlt′) *n.* A hard, dense, dark rock formed by volcanic action. [From Latin *basaltēs, basanītēs (lapis),* touchstone, from Greek *basanītēs,* from Egyptian *bakhan.*] —**ba·sal′tic** *adj.*

bascule bridge. A counterbalanced drawbridge that can be raised to permit the passage of ships beneath it. [From French *bascule,* seesaw.]

base¹ (bās) *n.* **1.** The lowest or bottom part: *the base of the cliff.* **2.** A part or layer on which something rests; a support; foundation: *Soft ground makes a poor base for buildings.* **3.** The chief ingredient or element of something; basis: *a paint with an oil base.* **4.** A starting point or central place; headquarters: *The explorers established a base at the foot of the mountain.* **5.** A center of supplies or operations for a military or naval force. **6.** *Sports.* A starting point, safety area, or goal, esp. in baseball, one of the four corners of the infield that must be touched by a runner to score a run. **7.** *Geom.* **a.** The side or face that is considered to be the bottom of a geometric figure. **b.** The measure of such a face or side. **8.** *Math.* **a.** In a system of numeration, the factor by which a number is multiplied when its numeral is shifted one place to the left. For example, if ten is the base, 42 is ten times as great as 4.2. **b.** The number to which an exponent or logarithm is applied. For example, if $6^2 = 6 \times 6 = 36$, six is the base. **c.** The number to which the per cent is applied in a percentage problem. For example, if 40 is the base, 20 per cent of 40 is 8. **9.** *Ling.* A word or word part to which other parts may be added. For example, in *filled, refill,* and *filling, fill* is the base. **10.** *Chem.* Any of a large class of substances, typically the hydroxides of metals, that when dissolved in water are capable of reacting with an acid to form a salt, are capable of turning blue litmus red, and have a characteristic slippery feel and bitter taste. **11.** *Electronics.* The terminal of a transistor that acts somewhat like the grid of a vacuum tube. —*tr. v.* **based, bas·ing. 1.** To support; to found: *base an opinion on facts.* **2.** To use or have as a starting point or base: *The composer based this song on an old folk melody.* [Middle English, from Old French, from Latin *basis,* pedestal, base, from Greek.]

base² (bās) *adj.* **bas·er, bas·est. 1.** Morally bad or wrong; mean; contemptible: *base instincts; a base act.* **2.** Lowly; menial: *forced into base slavery.* **3.** Inferior in quality or value: *base metals.* **4.** Greatly depreciated in value; debased: *base currency.* **5.** *Archaic.* Of low birth, rank, or position. [Middle English *bas,* low, inferior, from Old French, from Late Latin *bassus,* fat, low.] —**base′ly** *adv.* —**base′ness** *n.*

base·ball (bās′bôl′) *n.* **1.** A game played with a usu. wooden bat and hard ball by two opposing teams of nine players. Each team plays alternately in the field and at bat, the players at bat having to run a course of four bases laid out in a diamond pattern in order to score. **2.** The ball used in this game. —*modifier: baseball players.*

base·board (bās′bôrd′, -bōrd′) *n.* A molding along the lower edge of an interior wall, where it meets the floor.

base·born (bās′bôrn′) *adj.* **1.** Of humble birth. **2.** Born of unwed parents; illegitimate.

base·burn·er (bās′bûr′nər) *n.* A stove or furnace that automatically replenishes consumed fuel from above.

base hit. *Baseball.* A hit by which the batter reaches base safely, without an error or force play being made.

base·less (bās′lĭs) *adj.* Having no basis or foundation in fact; unfounded.

base line. 1. A line serving as a base for measurement or comparison. **2.** *Baseball.* A path between successive bases, bounded by imaginary lines within which a base runner must stay. **3.** A line bounding each back end of a court in tennis and other court games.

base·man (bās′mən) *n. Baseball.* A player assigned to first, second, or third base.

base·ment (bās′mənt) *n.* **1.** The substructure or foundation of a building. **2.** The lowest story of a building, often below ground level. [Prob. BASE (bottom) + -MENT.]

ba·sen·ji (bə-sĕn′jē) *n., pl.* **-jis.** A small dog of a breed orig. from Africa, having a short, smooth coat, and not uttering the barking sound characteristic of most dogs. [From Bantu.]

basenji

base on balls. *Baseball.* A walk.

base path. *Baseball.* The area between the bases on the field that is used by the base runner.

base runner. *Baseball.* A member of the team at bat who has safely reached or is trying to reach a base.

ba·ses¹ (bā′sēz′) *n.* Plural of **basis.**

bas·es² (bā′sĭz) *n.* Plural of **base.**

bash (băsh) *tr.v. Informal.* To strike with a heavy and crushing blow. —See Syns at **hit.** —*n.* **1.** *Informal.* A heavy, crushing blow. **2.** *Slang.* A party. [Orig. unknown.]

bash·ful (băsh′fəl) *adj.* Timid and embarrassed with other people; shy. [Middle English *baschen,* to abash, short for *abashen* + -FUL.] —**bash′ful·ly** *adv.* —**bash′ful·ness** *n.*

ba·sic (bā′sĭk) *adj.* **1.** Forming a foundation or basis; fundamental; essential. **2.** First and necessary before doing or undertaking something else: *basic training.* **3.** *Chem.* **a.** Producing an excess of hydroxyl ions in solution. **b.** Of, producing, or resulting from a base. —*n.* Often **basics.** Something basic or fundamental. —**ba′si·cal·ly** *adv.*

BA·SIC or **Ba·sic** (bā′sĭk) *n.* A language for programming a computer. [B(EGINNERS') A(LL-PURPOSE) S(YMBOLIC) I(N-STRUCTION) C(ODE).]

bas·il (băz′əl, bā′zəl) *n.* **1.** An herb, *Ocimum basilicum,* na-

tive to the Old World with spikes of small white flowers and aromatic leaves used as seasoning. Also called **sweet basil. 2.** The dried leaves of this herb. [Middle English *basile,* from Old French, from Medieval Latin *basilicum,* from Greek *basilikon,* royal, from *basileus,* king.]

bas·i·lar (băs′ə-lər) *adj.* Also **bas·i·lar·y** (-lĕr′ē). Of or located at or near the base, esp. the base of the skull.

ba·sil·i·ca (bə-sĭl′ĭ-kə) *n.* **1.** A type of ancient Roman building having two rows of columns dividing the interior into a nave and two side aisles, and an arched, semicircular part at one end, used as a court or place of assembly. **2.** A building of this type used as a Christian church. [Latin, from Greek *basilikē (stoa),* "royal (court)," from *basiieus,* king.]

bas·i·lisk (băs′ə-lĭsk′, băz′-) *n.* **1.** A legendary serpent or dragon said to have the power of killing by its breath and glance. **2.** Any of various tropical American lizards of the genus *Basiliscus,* with an erectile crest at the back of the head. [Middle English, from Latin *basiliscus,* from Greek *basiliskos,* dim. of *basileus,* king.]

basilisk

ba·sin (bā′sən) *n.* **1.** A round, open, shallow container often used for holding water to wash in. **2. a.** A basin with something in it: *a basin of water.* **b.** The amount that a basin holds. **3.** A natural or manmade hollow or enclosed place filled with water. **4.** The entire region from which a river and its tributaries collect water. [Middle English *ba(s)cin,* from Old French *bacin.*]

ba·sis (bā′sĭs) *n., pl.* **-ses** (-sēz′). **1.** Something that serves as a foundation; a supporting element: *the basis of a decision.* **2.** The main part or basic ingredient. **3.** A standard by which something is rated or compared. [Latin, pedestal, foot, base, from Greek.]

bask (băsk) *intr.v.* **1.** To expose oneself pleasantly to warmth: *bask by the fire.* **2.** To thrive in the presence of a pleasant or advantageous influence or atmosphere: *basking in the limelight.* [Middle English *basken.*]

bas·ket (băs′kĭt) *n.* **1.** A container made of interwoven twigs, strips of wood, rushes, etc. **2. a.** A basket with something in it: *a basket of flowers.* **b.** The amount that a basket holds: *eat a basket of peaches.* **3.** *Basketball.* **a.** A metal hoop with an open-ended net suspended from it, placed at a height of ten feet above the court. **b.** A goal scored by throwing the ball through this loop. [Middle English, from Norman French.]

bas·ket·ball (băs′kĭt-bôl′) *n.* **1.** A game played between two teams of five players each, the object being to throw the ball through an elevated basket on the opponent's side of the rectangular court. **2.** The large, round, inflated ball used in this game. —*modifier:* a *basketball game.*

bas·ket·ry (băs′kĭ-trē) *n.* **1.** The craft or process of making baskets. **2.** Baskets collectively.

basket weave. A textile weave in which double threads are interlaced to produce a checkered pattern similar to that of a woven basket.

bas mitz·vah (bäs mĭts′və). Var. of **bat mitzvah.**

basque (băsk) *n.* A woman's close-fitting bodice. [French, var. of earlier *baste,* from Provençal *basta.*]

Basque (băsk) *n.* **1.** One of a people of unknown origin inhabiting the western Pyrenees in France and Spain. **2.** The language of the Basques, unrelated to any other language.

bas-re·lief (bä′rĭ-lēf′) *n. Sculpture.* Low relief. [French, from Italian *bassorilievo : basso,* low, from Late Latin *bassus,* low + *rilievo,* relief.]

bass¹ (băs) *n., pl.* **bass** or **bass·es. 1.** Any of several North American freshwater fishes of the family Centrarchidae, related to but larger than the sunfishes. **2.** Any of various saltwater fishes of the family Serranidae, such as the sea bass and the striped bass. [Middle English, var. of *barse*, from Old English *bærs*.]

bass² (bās) *n.* **1.** The lowest range of musical tones. **2.** The lowest man's singing voice. **3.** A man having such a voice. **4.** A part written in the range of this voice. **5.** An instrument, esp. a double bass, having about the same range as this voice. —*modifier: a bass voice; a bass aria.* [Middle English *bas*, low, base.]

bass³ (bās) *n.* A fibrous plant product, bast. [Var. of BAST.]

bass clef (bās). A musical symbol that indicates that the note written on the fourth line from the bottom of the staff is the F below middle C.

bas·set (băs′ĭt) *n.* A basset hound. [French, Old French, from *basset*, short and low, from *bas*, low, base.]

basset hound. A short-haired dog of a breed originating in France, with a long body, short, crooked forelegs, and long, drooping ears. Also called **basset**.

basset hound

bass horn (bās). *Mus.* A tuba.

bas·si·net (băs′ə-nĕt′, băs′ə-nĕt′) *n.* An oblong basket resting on legs, used as a crib for an infant. [French, small basin, from Old French *bacinet*, dim. of *bacin*, basin.]

bas·so (băs′ō, bä′sō) *n., pl.* **-sos** or **-si** (-sē) A bass singer, esp. an operatic bass. [Italian, from Late Latin *bassus*, fat, short, low.]

bas·soon (bə-sōōn′, bă-) *n.* A low-pitched woodwind instrument having a long wooden body connected to a double reed by a bent metal tube. [French *basson*, from Italian *bassone*, from *basso*, basso.] —**bas·soon′ist** *n.*

bassoon

bass viol (bās). *Mus.* **1.** A double bass. **2.** A viola da gamba.

bass·wood (băs′wŏŏd′) *n.* **1.** Any of several linden trees of eastern North America, esp. *Tilia americana*, with clusters of fragrant yellowish flowers. **2.** The soft, light-colored wood of any of these trees.

bast (băst) *n.* **1.** *Bot.* The fibrous or somewhat woody outer layer of the stems of certain plants, such as flax and hemp. **2.** Fibrous material obtained from such plants or from certain trees used to make cordage and textiles. Also called **bass**. [Middle English *baste*, from Old English *bæst*.]

bas·tard (băs′tərd) *n.* **1.** An illegitimate child. **2.** *Slang.* A mean person. —*modifier: the Duke's bastard son.* —*adj.* Of mixed or uncertain origin, and considered inferior: *a bastard language.* [Middle English, from Old French.] —**bas′tard·y** *n.*

baste¹ (bāst) *tr.v.* **bast·ed, bast·ing.** To sew loosely with large running stitches so as to hold together temporarily. [Middle English *basten*, from Old French *bastir*, to build, prepare, baste.]

baste² (bāst) *tr.v.* **bast·ed, bast·ing.** To pour pan drippings or other liquid over (meat) while roasting.

baste³ (bāst) *tr.v.* **bast·ed, bast·ing.** **1.** To beat vigorously; thrash. **2.** To berate. [Orig. unknown.]

bas·ti·na·do (băs′tə-nā′dō, -nä′-) *n., pl.* **-does. 1.** A beating with a stick or cudgel, esp. on the soles of the feet. **2.** A stick or cudgel. —*v.* **-doed, -do·ing.** To subject to a beating; thrash. [Spanish *bastonada*, from *baston*, stick, from Late Latin *bastum*.]

bas·tion (băs′chən, -tē-ən) *n.* **1.** A projecting part of a rampart or other fortification. **2.** Any well-defended position; a stronghold. [French, from earlier *bastillon*, from Old French *bastille*, bastille.]

bat¹ (băt) *n.* **1.** A stout wooden stick or club; cudgel. **2.** A blow, as with a stick. **3. a.** *Baseball.* A rounded usu. wooden club, tapering at the handle, used to strike the ball. **b.** *Cricket.* A wooden club of similar function, having a broad, flat-surfaced hitting end and a distinct, narrow handle. **4.** *Slang.* A binge; spree. —*v.* **bat·ted, bat·ting.** —*tr.v.* **1.** To hit with, or as if with, a club or bat. **2.** *Baseball.* To have (a certain percentage) as a batting average. —*intr.v. Baseball.* To be the hitting team or hitter: *Our team batted first.* —*idioms.* **at bat.** Having a turn as a hitter in baseball. **go to bat for.** To support or defend. **right off the bat.** Without hesitation; immediately. [Middle English *bat*, from Old English *batt*, cudgel, club.]

bat² (băt) *n.* Any of various nocturnal flying mammals of the order Chiroptera, with a mouselike body and membranous wings that extend from the forelimbs to the hind legs and tail. —*idiom.* **have bats in (one's) belfry.** *Slang.* To have foolish or crazy ideas. [Var. of Middle English *bakke*, of Scandinavian orig.]

bat³ (băt) *tr.v.* **bat·ted, bat·ting.** To move with a flapping or fluttering motion; to blink: *to bat one's eyelashes.* —*idiom.* **bat an eye.** To show some sign of surprise or emotion. [Prob. from Middle English *baten*, from Old French *battre*, to beat, batter.]

bat·boy (băt′boi′) *n.* A boy who takes care of a baseball team's bats and equipment.

batch (băch) *n.* **1.** An amount prepared or produced at one time: *a batch of cookies.* **2.** A group of persons or things: *a batch of tourists.* [Middle English *bacche*, from Old English *bacan*, to bake.]

bate (bāt) *tr.v.* **bat·ed, bat·ing.** **1.** To lessen the force of; hold in check; restrain. **2.** To take away; subtract. [Middle English *baten*, short for *abaten*, to abate.]

ba·teau (bă-tō′) *n., pl.* **-teaux** (-tōz′). A light, flat-bottomed boat with flaring sides, used esp. in Louisiana and Canada. [Canadian French, from French, from Old French *batel*, from Old English *bāt*, boat.]

bat·ed (bā′tĭd) *adj.* —**with bated breath.** With one's breath held in, as in excitement or awe. —See Usage note at **bait.**

bath (băth, bäth) *n., pl.* **baths** (băthz, băthz, băths, bäths). **1. a.** The act of washing or soaking the body in water. **b.** The water used for a bath. **2.** A soaking in or exposure to a liquid or something similar to a liquid: *a steam bath; a sun bath.* **3.** A bathtub or bathroom: *a house with 2½ baths.* **4. baths. a.** A building equipped for bathing: *the ruins of Roman public baths.* **b.** A spa. **5.** A liquid, or a liquid and its container, in which an object is dipped or soaked in order to process it in some way: *a bath of dye.* —*modifier: a bath towel; bath oil.* [Middle English *bath*, from Old English *bath*.]

bathe (bāth) *v.* **bathed, bath·ing.** —*intr.v.* **1.** To take a bath; wash oneself. **2.** To go into the water for swimming or recreation. —*tr.v.* **1.** To give a bath to: *bathe the baby.* **2.** To soak in a liquid for soothing or healing purposes: *bathed her swollen legs.* **3.** To make wet; moisten: *Tears bathed her cheeks.* **4.** To seem to wash or pour over; flood; suffuse: *Moonlight bathed the porch.* [Middle English *bathen*, from Old English *bathian*.] —**bath′er** *n.*

ba·thet·ic (bə-thĕt′ĭk) *adj.* Characterized by bathos. [Prob. a blend of BATHOS and PATHETIC.]

bath·house (băth′hous′, bäth′-) *n.* **1.** A building equipped for bathing. **2.** A building, as at a beach, used by swimmers for changing clothes.

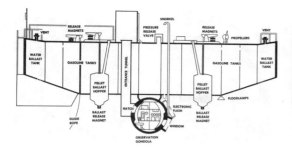

bathyscaphe
Model drawing

bathyscaphe
The vessel

bath·o·lith (băth′ə-lĭth′) *n.* A mass of igneous rock that has flowed into surrounding strata at great depths. [From Greek *bathus*, deep + -LITH.]

ba·thos (bā′thŏs′) *n.* **1. a.** A sudden and incongruous change from a lofty or serious style to one that is very commonplace. **b.** An anticlimax. **2. a.** Insincere or grossly sentimental pathos. **b.** Extreme triteness or dullness. [Greek, depth, from *bathus*, deep.]

bath·room (băth′rōōm′, -rŏŏm′, bäth′-) *n.* A room equipped for taking a bath or shower and usu. also containing a sink and toilet.

bath·tub (băth′tŭb′, bäth′-) *n.* A tub to bathe in, esp. one permanently installed in a bathroom.

bath·y·scaphe (băth′ĭ-skăf′) *n.* Also **bath·y·scaph.** A free-diving, self-contained deep-sea research vessel, consisting essentially of a large flotation hull filled with gasoline, with a manned observation capsule fixed to its underside, and able to move freely over the ocean bottom. [Greek *bathus*, deep + *skaphē*, basin, light boat.]

bath·y·sphere (băth′ĭ-sfîr′) *n.* A reinforced, spherical deep-diving chamber, manned, and lowered by cable deep into the ocean to make underwater observations. [Greek *bathus*, deep + -SPHERE.]

ba·tik (bə-tēk′, băt′ĭk) *n.* **1.** A method of dyeing print into a fabric in which parts of the cloth, not intended to be dyed, are covered with removable wax. **2.** The print that is dyed into cloth. **3.** The cloth so dyed. —*modifier: a batik scarf.* [Malay, from Javanese, "painted."]

ba·tiste (bə-tēst′, bă-) *n.* A fine, thin, light fabric usu. of cotton or linen, used esp. for clothing. [French.]

bat mitz·vah (bät mĭts′və). Also **bas mitz·vah** (bäs), Jewish religious ceremony for girls, similar to the more commonly held bar mitzvah for boys. [Hebrew *bat mitzvāh*, "daughter of commandment."]

ba·ton (bə-tŏn′, băt′n) *n.* **1.** A thin, tapered stick often used by the conductor in leading a band, chorus, or orchestra. **2.** A stick or staff such as that passed in a relay race or carried as a symbol of office. **3.** The hollow metal rod with heavy rubber tips twirled by a drum major or majorette. [French *bâton*, from Old French *baton*, from Late Latin *bastum*, stick.]

ba·tra·chi·an (bə-trā′kē-ən) *adj.* Of or pertaining to frogs and toads. —*n.* A frog or toad. [From Greek *batrakhos*, frog.]

bats (băts) *adj. Slang.* Crazy; eccentric; insane.

bats·man (băts′mən) *n. Baseball & Cricket.* A batter.

bat·tal·ion (bə-tăl′yən) *n.* **1.** A tactical military unit, typically consisting of a headquarters company and four infantry companies or a headquarters battery and four artillery batteries. **2.** A large group of people: *a battalion of firefighters.* [Old French *bataillon*, from Old Italian *battaglione*, from *battaglia*, troop.]

bat·ten¹ (băt′n) *n.* **1.** A narrow strip of wood, used for flooring. **2.** One of several flexible strips of wood placed in pockets at the outer edge of a sail to keep it flat. —*tr.v.* **1.** To furnish with battens: *batten a sail.* **2.** —**batten down.** To fasten or make secure with or as if with battens: *batten down the hatches.* [From French *bâton*, baton.]

bat·ten² (băt′n) *intr.v.* **1.** To become fat. **2.** To thrive and prosper, esp. at another's expense. [Ult. from Old Norse *batna*, to improve.]

bat·ter¹ (băt′ər) —*tr.v.* **1.** To hit heavily and repeatedly with violent blows: *The boxer battered his opponent.* **2.** To damage by heavy wear. —*intr.v.* To pound repeatedly with heavy blows: *Waves battered against the pier.* [Middle English *bateren*, from Old French *bat(t)re*, to beat, from Latin *battuere*.]

bat·ter² (băt′ər) *n. Baseball & Cricket.* The player at bat.

bat·ter³ (băt′ər) *n.* A thick, beaten mixture, as of flour, milk, and eggs, used in cooking. [Middle English *bater*, prob. from *bàteren*, to batter.]

bat·ter·ing-ram (băt′ər-ĭng-răm′) *n.* Also **battering ram.** **1.** A heavy wooden beam with an iron head used in warfare in ancient times to batter down walls and gates. **2.** Any device resembling this.

battering-ram

bat·ter·y (băt′ə-rē) *n., pl.* **-ies.** **1. a.** A number of electric cells connected together to supply current or voltage. **b.** A small dry cell designed to power a portable electric device. **2. a.** A group or set of large guns, as of artillery. **b.** A place where such guns are set up. **c.** A unit of soldiers in the artillery. **3.** A group of things or people used or doing something together: *a battery of reporters; a battery of tests.* **4.** *Baseball.* The combination of a team's pitcher and catcher. **5.** *Law.* An unlawful beating of another person. [French *batterie*, from *battre*, to beat, from Old French *bat(t)re*, to batter.]

bat·ting (băt′ĭng) *n.* Cotton or wool fiber wadded into rolls or sheets, used to stuff mattresses, line quilts, etc. [From the beating of raw cotton or wool to clean it.]

batting average. The ratio of the number of a baseball player's hits to the number of times at bat.

bat·tle (băt′l) *n.* **1.** A large-scale combat between two armed forces. **2.** Any intense competition or hard struggle: *a political battle; a battle of wits.* —*v.* **-tled, -tling.** —*intr.v.* To engage in or as if in battle: *The troops battled bravely.* —*tr.v.* To fight against: *battled the storm for hours.* [Middle English *bataille*, from Old French, from Late Latin *battuālia*, fighting and fencing exercises, from Latin *battuere*, to batter.] —**bat′tler** *n.*

bat·tle-ax or **bat·tle-axe** (băt′l-ăks′) *n., pl.* **-ax·es.** **1.** A heavy broad-headed ax, formerly used as a weapon in ancient and medieval times. **2.** *Slang.* A quarrelsome, overbearing woman.

battle cry. **1.** A shout uttered by troops in battle. **2.** A slogan used by the supporters of a cause.

bat·tle·dore (băt′l-dôr′, -dōr′) *n.* A wooden paddle used in an early form of the game of badminton to strike the shuttlecock. [Middle English *batildore*.]

bat·tle·field (băt′l-fēld′) *n.* **1.** A field or area where a battle

battleship

bay window

is fought. **2.** Any area of conflict: *the battlefield of the war against poverty.* Also called **battleground.**

bat·tle·front (băt'l-frŭnt') *n.* The area where opponents meet or clash in battle: *a contest fought on political and military battlefronts.*

bat·tle·ground (băt'l-ground') *n.* A battlefield.

bat·tle·ment (băt'l-mənt) *n.* Often **battlements.** A parapet built on top of a wall, with indentations for defense or decoration. —**bat'tle·ment'ed** (-mĕn'tĭd) *adj.*

battle royal *pl.* **battles royal. 1.** A battle or confused fight in which many people participate. **2.** A bitter, intense quarrel.

bat·tle·ship (băt'l-shĭp') *n.* Any of a class of the largest modern warships, carrying the greatest number of guns and batteries and clad with the heaviest armor.

bat·ty (băt'ē) *adj.* **-ti·er, -ti·est.** *Slang.* Crazy; insane. —See Syns at **insane.**

bau·ble (bô'bəl) *n.* **1.** A small, showy ornament or trinket of little value. **2.** *Archaic.* A court jester's baton. [Middle English *babel, babulle,* from Old French *babel, baubel,* plaything.]

baulk (bôk) *v. & n.* Var. of **balk.**

baux·ite (bôk'sīt') *n.* The principal ore of aluminum, 30 to 75 per cent Al_2O_3·nH_2O, with ferric oxide and silica as impurities. [French, after Les *Baux,* southern France.]

baw·bee (bô-bē', bô'bē) *n.* *Scot.* A halfpenny.

bawd (bôd) *n.* **1.** A woman who keeps a brothel; a madam. **2.** A prostitute. [Middle English *bawde,* prob. from Old French *baude,* lively, bold, from Old High German *bald.*]

bawd·ry (bô'drē) *n.* Obscene or coarse language dealing with sex. [Middle English *bawdery,* from *bawde,* bawd.]

bawd·y (bô'dē) *adj.* **-i·er, -i·est.** Coarsely and humorously indecent: *bawdy jokes.* —**bawd'i·ly** *adv.* —**bawd'i·ness** *n.*

bawl (bôl) —*intr.v.* **1.** To cry or sob loudly; to howl. **2.** To cry out loudly and vehemently; to shout; to bellow. —*tr.v.* To utter in a loud, vehement voice. —*phrasal verb.* **bawl out.** *Informal.* To find fault with loudly or harshly. —See Syns at **scold.** —*n.* A loud, bellowing cry; a wail: *the bawl of a stray calf.* [Middle English *baulen.*] —**bawl'er** *n.*

bay¹ (bā) *n.* A body of water partly enclosed by land, but having a wide outlet to the sea. [Middle English *baye,* from Old French *baie,* from Old Spanish *bahia.*]

bay² (bā) *n.* **1.** *Archit.* A part of a room or building that projects beyond the main outside wall and is often surrounded by windows on three sides. **2.** Any similar alcove or compartment: *a bay for fodder in the barn.* **3.** A bomb bay. **4.** A room or compartment that is used as a hospital on a ship: *a sick bay.* [Middle English, from Old French *baee,* an opening, from *baer,* to gape.]

bay³ (bā) *adj.* Reddish brown. —*n.* **1.** A reddish brown. **2.** An animal, esp. a horse, of this color. [Middle English, from Old French *bai,* from Latin *badius.*]

bay⁴ (bā) *n.* A deep, prolonged barking, esp. of hounds closing in on prey. —*intr.v.* To utter a deep, prolonged bark or howl. —*tr.v.* **1.** To pursue or challenge with barking: "I had rather be a dog, and bay the moon" (Shakespeare). **2.** To express by barking. —*idiom.* **at (or to) bay. 1.** In or into a position of or like that of an animal cornered by and facing its pursuers. **2.** At a distance so as to ward off threatening danger: *keep trouble at bay.* [Middle English *baien,* short for *abaien,* from Old French *abayer.*]

bay⁵ (bā) *n.* **1.** A laurel, *Laurus nobilis,* native to the Medi-

terranean area, with stiff, glossy, aromatic leaves. **2.** Any of several similar trees or shrubs. [Middle English *baye,* laurel berry, from Old French *baie,* from Latin *bāca,* berry.]

bay·ber·ry (bā'bĕr'ē) *n.* **1.** Any of several aromatic shrubs or small trees of the genus *Myrica,* esp. *M. pensylvanica,* of eastern North America, bearing gray, waxy, pleasant-smelling berries used in making candles. **2.** A tropical American tree, *Pimenta acris,* yielding an oil used in making bay rum. **3.** The fruit of any of these trees or shrubs.

bay leaf. The dried, aromatic leaf of the bay, *Laurus nobilis,* used as seasoning in cooking.

bay·o·net (bā'ə-nĭt, -nĕt', bā'ə-nĕt') *n.* A knife adapted to fit the muzzle end of a rifle and used in close combat. —*tr.v.* **-net·ed** or **-net·ted, -net·ing** or **-net·ting.** To stab or prod with a bayonet. [French *baïonnette,* after *Bayonne,* France.]

bay·ou (bī'ōō, bī'ō) *n., pl.* **-ous.** *Southern U.S.* A marshy, sluggish body of water connected with a lake, river, etc.. [Louisiana French, from Choctaw *bayuk.*]

bay rum. A fragrant lotion obtained by distilling the leaves of the bayberry tree, *Pimenta acris,* with rum, and now also synthesized from alcohol, water, and various oils.

bay window. 1. A large window or group of windows projecting from the outer wall of a building and forming an alcove in the room within. **2.** *Slang.* A protruding belly; paunch.

ba·zaar (bə-zär') *n.* Also **ba·zar. 1.** An Oriental market, usu. consisting of a street lined with shops and stalls. **2.** A shop or part of a store for the sale of miscellaneous articles. **3.** A fair or sale at which miscellaneous articles are sold, usu. for charitable purposes: *a church bazaar.* [Earlier *bazarro, bazar,* prob. from Italian *bazarro,* from Turkish, from Persian *bāzār.*]

ba·zoo·ka (bə-zōō'kə) *n.* A portable tube-shaped weapon that fires antitank rockets. [After the *bazooka,* a crude wind instrument, invented and named by American comedian Bob Burns (1896–1956).]

BB (bē'bē') *n.* A size of lead shot that measures about .46 cm, or 0.18 in., in diameter. [Perh. from the letter *b.*]

be (bē) *intr.v.*

The eight standard forms of the verb *be* are:

	I	*he/she/it*	*we/you/they*
Present Tense	**am**	**is**	**are**
Past Tense	**was**	**was**	**were**
Present Participle	**being**		
Past Participle	**been**		

---

1. To exist: *I think, therefore I am.* Often used with *there: There once was a poor woodcutter.* **2.** To occupy a position. Often used with a specifying prepositional phrase: *The groceries are on the table.* "Oh, to be in England, Now that April's there" (Robert Browning). **3.** To take place; occur: *Where is the show?* **4.** To come or go. Used mainly in the perfect tense: *Have you ever been to town?* **5.** *Archaic.* To belong; befall. Used in the subjunctive, and now only in a few set phrases: *Peace be unto you.* **6.** —Used as a copula in such senses as: **a.** To equal in identity or meaning: *That book is mine.* **b.** To signify or stand for: *A is excellent; C is passing.* **c.** To belong to a specified class or group: *Man is a primate.* **d.** To have or show a specified quality or characteristic: *She is lovely. All men are mortal.* **7.** —Used as an auxiliary verb in certain constructions, as: **a.** With the past participle of a class of verbs to form the passive voice: *Elections are held once a year.* **b.** With the present participle of a verb to express a continuing action: *We are working to improve housing conditions.* **c.** With the past participle of certain verbs of motion to form the perfect tense: *"Where be those roses gone which sweetened so our eyes?"* (Sir Philip Sidney). **d.** With *to* and the infinitive of another verb to indicate: (1) duty or necessity: *I am to inform you that the package has arrived.* (2) supposition: *How am I to know the answer?* (3) the future: *They are to be married Monday.* **—idiom. let be.** *Informal.* To let (someone) alone: *Go away and let me be.* [Middle English *be(e)n,* from Old English *bēon.*]

    Usage: be. In regional dialects in England and America, there are many variants such as *I been, you was,* and *he be.* These variants are not acceptable in formal, standard English.

be-. A prefix meaning: **1.** A complete or profuse covering or affecting: **becloud, besmear. 2.** A thorough or excessive degree: **bewilder. 3.** An action that causes a condition to exist: **beset, befriend.** [Middle English *be-,* from Old English *be-, bi-.*]

Be The symbol for the element beryllium.

beach (bēch) *n.* The shore of a body of water, esp. when sandy or pebbly. **—modifier:** *a beach towel.* **—tr.v. 1.** To haul or drive (a boat) ashore. **2.** To go ashore. [Earlier *bayche, baich.*]

beach·comb·er (bēch′kō′mər) *n.* **1.** Someone who lives on what he can find or beg on the seashore. **2.** A long wave rolling in toward a beach.

beach·head (bēch′hĕd′) *n.* **1.** A position on an enemy shoreline captured by advance troops of an invading force. **2.** A first achievement that opens the way for further development.

bea·con (bē′kən) *n.* **1.** A signal fire, esp. one used to warn of an enemy's approach. **2.** A lighthouse or other signaling or guiding device on a coast. **3.** A radio transmitter that emits a characteristic signal as a warning or guide. **4.** Anything that warns or guides. **—tr.v.** To provide a beacon for. **—intr.v.** To serve as a beacon. [Middle English *beken,* sign, standard, from Old English *bēacen.*]

bead (bēd) *n.* **1.** A small, often round, piece of glass, metal, wood, etc., with a hole in it through which a string can be drawn. **2. beads.** A necklace of beads on a string. **3. beads.** A rosary. **4.** Any small, round object: *a bead of sweat.* **5.** A small knob of metal located at the muzzle of a rifle or pistol and used in taking aim. **6.** *Archit.* Beadwork. **—tr.v.** To decorate with beads or beading: *bead a dress.* **—intr.v.** To collect into beads: *Dew beaded on the window.* **—idioms. count (or say or tell) one's beads.** To pray with a rosary. **draw a bead on.** To take careful aim at. [Middle English *bede, bead,* prayer, prayer bead, from Old English *gebed,* prayer.]

bead·ing (bē′dĭng) *n.* **1.** Beads or material used for beads. **2.** Ornamentation with beads. **3.** *Archit.* A narrow, half-rounded molding. **4.** A narrow piece of openwork lace through which ribbon may be run.

bea·dle (bēd′l) *n.* **1.** In the Church of England, a minor parish official whose duties include keeping order and ushering during services. **2.** *Judaism.* A shammes. [Middle English *bedele,* herald, beadle, from Old English *bydel.*]

bead·work (bēd′wûrk′) *n.* **1.** Decorative work in beads. **2.** *Archit.* A strip of molding shaped like a string of beads.

bead·y (bē′dē) *adj.* **-i·er, -i·est. 1.** Small, round, and shiny, often with greed, suspicion, etc.: *beady eyes.* **2.** Decorated or covered with beads.

bea·gle (bē′gəl) *n.* A small hound with a smooth coat, drooping ears, and short legs, often used as a hunting dog. [Middle English *begle.*]

beak (bēk) *n.* **1.** The horny, projecting structure forming the mandibles of a bird; a bill. **2.** A part or organ resembling this, as in some turtles, insects, or fish. **3.** Any hard,

beagle   beaker

cone-shaped, or pointed structure or part. **4.** *Informal.* A person's nose. [Middle English *bec,* from Old French, from Latin *beccus.*]

beak·er (bē′kər) *n.* **1. a.** A large drinking cup with a wide mouth. **b.** The contents of such a cup. **2.** A laboratory container consisting of an open glass cylinder with a pouring lip. [Middle English *beker,* from Old Norse *bikarr.*]

beam (bēm) *n.* **1.** A long, rigid piece of wood or metal used to support or reinforce a structure or a part of a structure. **2.** *Naut.* The widest part of a ship. **3.** The bar from which the weights are hung in a balance. **4.** A group of particles or waves traveling close together in parallel paths. **5.** Light projected into space, as by a flashlight or searchlight. **6.** A radio beam. **7.** A faint indication; a glimpse; gleam: *a beam of hope.* **—tr.v.** To emit or transmit (radiant energy or a radio signal) in a beam. **—intr.v. 1.** To send off light; shine: *the sun beaming in the sky.* **2.** To smile broadly: *His face beamed with delight.* **—idiom. on the beam. 1.** Following the radio beam, as an aircraft. **2.** *Informal.* On the right track. [Middle English *beme,* from Old English *bēam,* tree, beam.]

bean (bēn) *n.* **1.** Any of several plants of the genus *Phaseolus,* with compound leaves, white or yellow flowers, and seed-bearing pods, esp. the lima bean and string bean. **2.** The edible seed or pod of any of these plants. **3.** Any of several related plants bearing similar pods and seeds, such as the broad bean. **4.** Any of various other seeds or pods resembling beans, such as the coffee bean or the vanilla bean. **5.** *Slang.* The head. **—modifier:** *a bean plant; bean soup.* **—tr.v.** *Slang.* To hit on the head. **—idiom. spill the beans.** To tell something that was meant to be kept secret. [Middle English *ben(e),* from Old English *bēan.*]

bean·bag (bēn′băg′) *n.* A small bag filled with dried beans and used for throwing in games.

bean ball. A baseball pitch aimed at the batter's head.

bean curd. A soft, cheeselike food made from puréed soybeans, used in Oriental cooking.

bean·ie (bē′nē) *n.* A small brimless cap.

bean·pole (bēn′pōl′) *n.* **1.** A pole around which a bean vine twines as it grows. **2.** *Slang.* A tall, thin person.

bean sprout. A young, tender shoot of certain beans, such as the soybean, used in Oriental cooking.

bean·stalk (bēn′stôk′) *n.* The stem of a bean plant.

bear¹ (bâr) *v.* **bore** (bôr, bōr) or *archaic* **bare** (bâr), **borne** (bôrn) or **born, bear·ing. —tr.v. 1.** To support; hold up: *The raft can bear the weight of five men.* **2.** To carry on one's person: *the right to bear arms.* **3.** To have or carry in the mind: *bear a grudge.* **4.** To transmit; relate: *bearing glad tidings.* **5.** To have as a visible characteristic: *bearing a scar on his right arm.* **6.** To carry (oneself) in a specified way: *She bore herself with grace and dignity.* **7.** To be accountable for; assume: *bear the responsibility.* **8.** To have a tolerance for; endure: *"better fitted than others to bear the diseases of the country"* (Darwin). **9.** To stand up under; permit: *The case will bear investigation.* **10.** To give birth to. **11.** To produce; yield. **12.** To offer; render: *bearing witness.* **13.** To move by steady pressure; to push: *boats borne by the tide.* **—intr.v. 1.** To yield a product; produce: *That apple tree bears well.* **2.** To press or weigh on: *guilt bore heavily upon them.* **3.** To proceed in a specified direction: *Bear right at the fork in the road.* **—phrasal verbs. bear down. 1.** To press or weigh on: *Financial pressure bore down on him.* **2.** To exert oneself: *I bore down* *and got the job done on time.* **bear down on. 1.** To exert pressure on: *bear down on the lever.* **2.** To make a strong effort toward: *He told us to bear down on the job or we'd be fired.* **3.** To move rapidly: *The train bore down on the track to arrive on time.* **bear on** (or **upon**). To apply or relate to: *That example does not bear on our problem.* **bear out.** To prove right; support; confirm: *The test results bear out his claim.* **bear up.** To find strength to resist; endure: *You must bear up in times of crisis.* **bear with.** To be patient or tolerant with: *Bear with me for a minute.* **bring to bear.** To exert pressure; influence: *brought his experience to bear in the negotiations.* —*idiom.* **bear in mind.** To be careful or vigilant. [Middle English *beren,* from Old English *beran.*]

Usage: **bear.** The past participle forms of this verb are *born* and *borne. Born* is used only when referring to the offspring of mammals, and only in the passive voice: *The child was born on August 1. Borne,* when indicating the act of birth, is used only of the mother, but it can be used either in the active voice or in the passive voice: *She has borne three children. Three children were borne by her, one of whom was born blind.* When the verb *bear* means anything other than to bring forth young, the only correct past participle is *borne: They had borne the heavy load well. You have borne up under stress. She had borne a scar since childhood. The soil has borne abundant crops.*

bear² (bâr) *n.* **1.** Any of various large usu. omnivorous mammals of the family Ursidae that have a shaggy coat and a short tail, and walk with the entire lower surface of the foot touching the ground. **2.** Any of various animals resembling a bear, such as the koala. **3. a.** A person who is awkward, clumsy, or ill-mannered. **b.** One who shows endurance: *a bear for hard work.* **4.** An investor, esp. one in the stock market, who sells shares in the expectation that prices will fall. —*modifier:* *bear meat; a bear market.* [Middle English *bere,* from Old English *bera.*]

bear²

bearskin

bear·a·ble (bâr'ə-bəl) *adj.* Capable of being borne; endurable; tolerable. —**bear'a·bly** *adv.*

bear·ber·ry (bâr'bĕr'ē) *n., pl.* **-ries.** A trailing evergreen shrub, *Arctostaphylos uva-ursi,* of northern regions, with white or pink flowers and red berries.

beard (bîrd) *n.* **1. a.** The hair on the chin, cheeks, and throat of a man. **b.** This hair allowed to grow and cover the skin. **2.** Any similar hairlike growth such as that on or near the face of certain mammals. **3.** A tuft or group of bristles on certain plants. —*tr.v.* **1.** To furnish with a beard. **2.** To confront or defy boldly. [Middle English *berd,* from Old English *beard.*]

bear·er (bâr'ər) *n.* **1.** Someone or something that carries or supports. **2.** A porter. **3.** A person who presents for payment a check, money order, or other redeemable note. **4.** Any fruit-bearing plant or tree.

bear·ing (bâr'ĭng) *n.* **1.** The manner in which a person carries or conducts himself; deportment: *the poise and bearing of a champion.* **2.** *Machinery.* Any part or device that supports, guides, and reduces the friction of motion between fixed and moving machine parts. **3.** Any structural part that bears weight or acts as a support. **4. a.** The act or period of producing fruit or offspring. **b.** The quantity produced; the yield or crop. **5.** Direction, esp. angular direction measured using geographical or celestial reference lines. **6.** Often **bearings.** The awareness of one's position or

situation in relation to one's surroundings: *We lost our bearings in the mountains.* **7.** Relevance, relationship, or connection: *facts that have no bearing on our situation.* **8.** *Heraldry.* Any figure on a coat of arms.

bear·ish (bâr'ĭsh) *adj.* **1.** Like a bear; clumsy, boorish, or surly. **2.** Causing, expecting, or characterized by falling stock-market prices. —**bear'ish·ly** *adv.* —**bear'ish·ness** *n.*

bear·skin (bâr'skĭn') *n.* **1.** The skin of a bear. **2.** A tall military headdress made of black fur.

beast (bēst) *n.* **1.** Any animal except a human being; esp., any large, four-footed animal. **2.** The qualities of an animal; animal nature. **3.** A brutal or vile person. [Middle English *beste,* from Old French, from Latin *bēstia.*]

beast·ly (bēst'lē) *adj.* **-li·er, -li·est. 1.** Of or like a beast; savage. **2.** Disagreeable; nasty: *What beastly behavior!* —*adv. Brit. Informal.* Very. —**beast'li·ness** *n.*

beast of burden. An animal, such as a donkey, used for transporting loads.

beat (bēt) *v.* **beat, beat·en** (bēt'n) or **beat, beat·ing.** —*tr.v.* **1.** To strike or hit repeatedly: *beat the rug with a stick.* **2.** To punish by hitting or whipping; flog. **3.** To pound or strike against repeatedly: *waves beating the shore.* **4.** To shape, flatten or break by repeated blows: *He beat the glowing metal into a dagger.* **5.** To mix or stir rapidly with an instrument to a frothy consistency: *beat two eggs in a bowl.* **6.** To hunt through in order to locate; scour: *We beat the countryside for the rustlers.* **7.** To flap as wings. **8.** To sound (a signal), as on a drum: *beat out a warning.* **9.** To mark or count (time or rhythm) with the hands or with a baton. **10.** To defeat or subdue, as in a contest or battle. **11.** *Informal.* To excel or surpass: *Nothing beats a home-cooked meal.* **12.** *Informal.* To avoid or counter the effects of; circumvent: *beat the traffic.* **13.** *Slang.* To perplex or baffle: *It beats me.* —*intr.v.* **1.** To inflict repeated blows: *hail beating on the roof.* **2.** To throb or pulsate rhythmically: *My heart was beating a mile a minute.* **3.** To emit sound when struck: *The gong beat thunderously.* **4.** To sound a signal, as on a drum. **5.** To permit rapid whipping to a froth: *Heavy cream beats well.* **6.** To hunt through woods or underbrush in search of game. **7.** *Naut.* To progress against the wind by tacking. —See Syns at **defeat.** —*phrasal verbs.* **beat back.** To force to retreat or withdraw: *beat back the invasion; beat back inflation.* **beat off.** To drive away: *beat off the wild deer.* **beat up.** *Informal.* To give a thorough beating to; thrash. —*n.* **1.** A stroke or blow, esp. one that produces a sound or acts as a signal. **2.** A sequential pulsation or throb. **3.** *Mus.* **a.** A regular and rhythmical unit of time. **b.** The gesture given by a conductor or the symbol representing this unit of time. **4.** The measured and rhythmical sound or pattern of verse; meter. **5.** The area regularly covered by a policeman, sentry, or newspaper reporter. **6.** *Physics.* The recurrent pulsation heard when sound waves of nearly equal frequency are combined. **7.** *Journalism. Slang.* The reporting of a news item obtained ahead of one's competitors; a scoop. **8.** A beatnik. —*adj. Informal.* Worn-out; fatigued. —*idioms.* **beat a retreat.** To flee or withdraw. **beat about (or around) the bush.** To approach a subject in a roundabout manner; hedge. **beat it.** *Slang.* To get going; go away. **beat (one's) brains out.** *Informal.* To try energetically. [Middle English *beten,* from Old English *bēatan.*]

beat·en (bēt'n) *v.* A past participle of **beat.** —*adj.* **1.** Made thin or formed by hammering: *beaten tin.* **2.** Worn by many footsteps; much traveled: *a beaten path.* **3. a.** Tired and worn-out. **b.** Vanquished or defeated: *a beaten man.* —*idiom.* **off the beaten track** (or **path**). Not well-known; unusual.

beat·er (bē'tər) *n.* **1.** Someone or something that beats, esp. an instrument for beating: *a carpet beater.* **2.** A person who drives wild game from under cover for a hunter.

be·a·tif·ic (bē'ə-tĭf'ĭk) *adj.* Showing or producing extreme joy or bliss: *a beatific smile.* [Late Latin *beātificus* : Latin *beātus,* blessed, from *beāre,* to make happy + *facere,* to do.] —**be·a'tif'i·cal·ly** *adv.*

be·at·i·fi·ca·tion (bē-ăt'ə-fĭ-kā'shən) *n.* **1.** The act of beatifying. **2.** The state of being beatified. **3.** *Rom. Cath. Ch.* An act of the pope declaring that a deceased person is beatified, a step prior to canonization.

be·at·i·fy (bē-ăt'ə-fī') *tr.v.* **-fied, -fy·ing. 1.** To make blissfully happy. **2.** *Rom. Cath. Ch.* To proclaim (a deceased person) to be one of the blessed and thus worthy of public religious honor. [Late Latin *beātificāre*, from *beātificus*, beatific.]

beat·ing (bē'tĭng) *n.* **1.** Punishment by whipping, flogging, or thrashing. **2.** A defeat or loss. **3.** A throbbing or pulsation, as of the heart.

be·at·i·tude (bē-ăt'ĭ-tōōd', -tyōōd') *n.* **1.** Supreme blessedness or happiness. **2. the Beatitudes.** The nine declarations of blessedness made by Jesus in the Sermon on the Mount. Matthew 5:3–11. [Latin *beātitūdo*, from *beātus*, blessed.]

beat·nik (bēt'nĭk) *n.* A person who acts and dresses with exaggerated disregard for what is thought proper; a beat.

beau (bō) *n., pl.* **beaus** or **beaux** (bōz). **1.** The sweetheart of a woman or girl. **2.** A dandy. [French, fine, handsome, from Latin *bellus.*]

Beau Brum·mell (brŭm'əl). A dandy; fop. [After George Bryan ("*Beau*") Brummell (1778–1840), British dandy.]

Beau·fort scale (bō'fərt). A scale of wind velocities, using code numbers ranging from 0 (calm) to 17 (hurricane). [After Sir Francis *Beaufort* (1774–1857), British admiral.]

beau geste (bō zhĕst'), *pl.* **beaux gestes** (bō zhĕst') or **beau gestes** (bō zhĕst'). **1.** A gracious gesture. **2.** A gesture that appears noble but is in fact meaningless, empty, or social. [French, "beautiful gesture."]

beau i·de·al (bō' ĭ-dē'əl), *pl.* **beau i·de·als. 1.** The concept of perfect beauty. **2.** An ideal type or model (of something). [French *beau idéal*, "ideal beauty."]

beau monde (bō mŏnd'; *French* bō mÔND'), *pl.* **beaux mondes** (bō mÔND') or **beau mondes** (bō mŏndz'). Fashionable society. [French, "beautiful world."]

beau·te·ous (byōō'tē-əs, -tyəs) *adj.* Beautiful, esp. to the sight. —**beau'te·ous·ly** *adv.* —**beau'te·ous·ness** *n.* —See Syns at **beautiful.**

beau·ti·cian (byōō-tĭsh'ən) *n.* One skilled in hairdressing or cosmetic treatments. [BEAUT(Y) + -ICIAN.]

beau·ti·ful (byōō'tə-fəl) *adj.* Having beauty in any of its forms; pleasing to the senses or the mind. —*n.* **the beautiful.** Beauty, as an aesthetic or philosophical principle. —**beau'ti·ful·ly** *adv.* —**beau'ti·ful·ness** *n.*

>**Syns: beautiful, attractive, beauteous, comely, fair², good-looking, gorgeous, handsome, lovely, pretty, ravishing** *adj.* Core meaning: Having qualities that please the senses or the mind (*a beautiful face*).

beau·ti·fy (byōō'tə-fī') *v.* **-fied, -fy·ing.** —*tr.v.* To make beautiful or more beautiful. —*intr.v.* To become beautiful. [BEAUT(Y) + -FY.] —**beau'ti·fi·ca'tion** *n.* —**beau'ti·fi'er** *n.*

beau·ty (byōō'tē) *n., pl.* **-ties. 1.** A quality or combination of qualities that please the senses or mind, usu. associated with harmony of form or color, excellence of craftsmanship, truthfulness, originality, or other, often unspecifiable property. **2.** A person or thing that is beautiful: *She is a beauty. The antique car is a beauty.* **3.** The feature that is most effective, gratifying, or telling: *The beauty of the venture is that we stand to lose nothing.* [Middle English *beau(l)te*, from Old French *bealte, beaute*, from Latin *bellus*, pretty, handsome, fine.]

beauty parlor. An establishment providing women with hair treatment, manicures, facials, and the like. Also called **beauty salon** and **beauty shop.**

beaux (bō) *n.* A plural of **beau.**

beaux-arts (bō-zär') *pl.n. French.* The fine arts.

bea·ver¹ (bē'vər) *n.* **1.** A large, aquatic rodent of the genus

beaver¹

Castor, with thick brown fur, webbed hind feet, a paddlelike, hairless tail, and chisellike front teeth adapted for gnawing bark and felling trees used to build dams. **2.** The fur of a beaver. **3.** A top hat, orig. made of the beaver's underfur. —**modifier:** *a beaver dam; beaver skins.* [Middle English *bever*, from Old English *be(o)for*.]

bea·ver² (bē'vər) *n.* A movable piece usu. attached to a helmet, to protect the mouth and chin. [Middle English *baviere*, from Old French, from *baver*, to slaver.]

be·calm (bĭ-käm') *tr.v.* **1.** To render (a ship) motionless for lack of wind. **2.** To make calm or still; soothe.

be·came (bĭ-kām') *v.* The past tense of **become.**

be·cause (bĭ-kôz', -kŭz') *conj.* For the reason that; since. —**because of.** By reason of; on account of. —See Usage note at **reason.** [Middle English *bi cause.*]

be·chance (bĭ-chăns') *v.* **-chanced, -chanc·ing.** *Archaic.* —*intr.v.* To happen. —*tr.v.* To befall.

beck (bĕk) *n. Archaic.* A beckoning gesture. —**idiom. at one's beck and call.** Willingly obedient; at one's service. [Middle English, from *becken*, to beckon.]

beck·on (bĕk'ən) *tr.v.* **1.** To signal or summon (another), as by nodding or waving. **2.** To attract or entice: "*a lovely, sunny country that seemed to beckon them on to the Emerald City*" (L. Frank Baum). —*intr.v.* **1.** To make a summoning or signaling gesture: *She beckoned with a nod.* **2.** To have a strong attraction; be enticing: *Adventure beckons.* [Middle English *becken*, from Old English *bēcnan*.]

be·cloud (bĭ-kloud') *tr.v.* To darken or obscure with or as if with clouds.

be·come (bĭ-kŭm') *v.* **-came** (-kām'), **-come, -com·ing.** —*intr.v.* To grow or come to be: *The territory became a state.* —*tr.v.* **1.** To be appropriate or suitable to: "*it would not become me . . . to interfere with parties*" (Swift). **2.** To look good with; suit: *The uniform becomes him.* —*phrasal verb.* **become of.** To be the fate or subsequent condition of: *What will become of her?* [Middle English *becomen*, from Old English *becuman*.]

be·com·ing (bĭ-kŭm'ĭng) *adj.* **1.** Appropriate; suitable. **2.** Pleasing or attractive. —**be·com'ing·ly** *adv.*

bed (bĕd) *n.* **1.** A piece of furniture for reclining and sleeping, usu. consisting of a frame and a mattress resting on springs. **2.** Any place used for sleeping. **3.** A place where one may sleep for a night; lodging. **4.** A small plot of planted land: *flower beds.* **5.** The bottom of a body of water. **6. a.** A supporting or underlying part; foundation: *railroad tracks on a bed of gravel.* **b.** A layer of food surmounted by another kind of food: *lobster on a bed of rice.* **7.** *Geol.* A deposit, as of ore. —**modifier:** *bed sheets; a bed lamp.* —*v.* **bed·ded, bed·ding.** —*tr.v.* **1.** To furnish with a bed or sleeping place. **2.** To put to bed. **3.** To spread litter for: *He bedded down the sheep under a lean-to.* **4.** To plant in a prepared bed of soil. **5.** To lay flat or arrange in layers. —*intr.v.* **1.** To go to bed. **2.** To form layers or strata. [Middle English *bed(e)*, from Old English *bed(d)*.]

be·daub (bĭ-dôb') *tr.v.* To smear; soil.

be·daz·zle (bĭ-dăz'əl) *tr.v.* **-zled, -zl·ing. 1.** To dazzle so completely as to confuse or blind. **2.** To enchant.

bed·bug (bĕd'bŭg') *n.* A wingless, bloodsucking insect, *Cimex lectularius*, that has a flat, reddish body and a disagreeable odor and often infests human dwellings.

bed·cham·ber (bĕd'chām'bər) *n.* A bedroom.

bed·clothes (bĕd'klōz', -klōthz') *pl.n.* Coverings, such as sheets and blankets, used on a bed.

bed·ding (bĕd'ĭng) *n.* **1.** Bedclothes. **2.** Straw or similar material for animals to sleep on. **3.** Something that forms a foundation or bottom layer. **4.** *Geol.* Stratification of rocks into beds.

be·deck (bĭ-dĕk') *tr.v.* To adorn in a showy fashion.

be·dev·il (bĭ-dĕv'əl) *tr.v.* **-iled** or **-illed, -il·ing** or **-il·ling. 1.** To torment or plague; harass. **2.** To worry, annoy, or frustrate. **3.** To bewitch. —**be·dev'il·ment** *n.*

be·dew (bĭ-dōō', -dyōō') *tr.v.* To wet with or as if with dew.

bed·fast (bĕd'făst') *adj.* Bedridden.

bed·fel·low (bĕd'fĕl'ō) *n.* **1.** A person with whom one shares a bed. **2.** An associate, collaborator, or ally.

be·dight (bĭ-dīt') *tr.v.* **-dight** or **-dight·ed, -dight·ing.** *Archaic.* To dress or adorn. [Middle English *bedighten*.]

be·dim (bĭ-dĭm′) *tr.v.* **-dimmed, -dim·ming.** To make dim.

be·di·zen (bĭ-dī′zən, -dĭz′ən) *tr.v.* Rare. To dress or ornament vulgarly or tastelessly. [BE + *dizen,* to dress.]

bed·lam (bĕd′ləm) *n.* **1.** Any place or situation of noisy uproar and confusion. **2.** *Archaic.* A lunatic asylum; madhouse. [Middle English *Bedlem,* Hospital of St. Mary of Bethlehem, London, an insane asylum.]

bed·lam·ite (bĕd′lə-mīt′) *n.* A madman; lunatic.

Bed·ou·in (bĕd′ōō-ĭn, bĕd′wĭn) *n.* An Arab of any of the nomadic tribes of the deserts of North Africa, Arabia, and Syria. [Middle English *Bedoin,* from Old French *beduin,* from Arabic *badāwī,* from *badw,* desert.]

bed·pan (bĕd′păn′) *n.* A receptacle used as a toilet by a bedridden person.

bed·post (bĕd′pōst′) *n.* Any of the four vertical posts at the corners of some beds.

bed·rid·den (bĕd′rĭd′n) *adj.* Also **bed·rid** (-rĭd′). Confined to bed by illness or infirmity. [Middle English *bedreden,* from Old English *bedrida,* one who is bedridden.]

bed·rock (bĕd′rŏk′) *n.* **1.** The solid rock that underlies all loose materials on the earth's surface. **2.** The lowest or bottom level. **3.** Fundamental principles.

bed·roll (bĕd′rōl′) *n.* Portable outdoor bedding.

bed·room (bĕd′rōōm′, -rŏŏm′) *n.* A room for sleeping.

bed·side manner (bĕd′sīd′). The attitude and conduct of a doctor in the presence of a patient.

bed·sore (bĕd′sôr′, -sōr′) *n.* An ulcer or sore caused by pressure, occurring during long confinement to bed.

bed·spread (bĕd′sprĕd′) *n.* A usu. decorative bed covering.

bed·spring (bĕd′sprĭng′) *n.* The springs supporting the mattress of a bed.

bed·stead (bĕd′stĕd′) *n.* The frame supporting a bed.

bed·straw (bĕd′strô′) *n.* Any of various plants of the genus *Galium,* with whorled leaves, small white or yellow flowers, and prickly burrs. [From its former use as a mattress stuffing.]

bed·time (bĕd′tīm′) *n.* The time when one goes to bed.

bee (bē) *n.* **1.** Any of various winged, hairy-bodied, usu. stinging insects of the order Hymenoptera, including many solitary species as well as those that live in colonies, such as the honeybee of the family Apidae, and characterized by specialized structures for sucking nectar and gathering pollen from flowers. **2.** A gathering where people combine work, competition, and amusement: *a quilting bee.* **—idiom. a bee in (one's) bonnet:** An idea that fills most of one's thoughts. [Middle English *bee,* from Old English *bēo.*]

bee·bread (bē′brĕd′) *n.* A mixture of pollen and nectar, fed by bees to their larvae.

beech (bēch) *n.* **1.** Any hardwood tree of the genus *Fagus* of the Northern Hemisphere, characterized by smooth, light-colored bark and edible nuts. **2.** The wood of any of these trees. [Middle English *beche,* from Old English *bēce.*]

beech·nut (bēch′nŭt′) *n.* The small, edible nut of the beech tree.

beef (bēf) *n., pl.* **beeves** (bēvz). **1.** A full-grown steer, bull, ox, or cow, esp. one intended for use as meat. **2.** The flesh of a slaughtered steer, bull, ox, or cow. **3.** *Informal.* Human muscle; brawn. **4.** *pl.* **beefs.** *Slang.* A complaint. **—modifier:** *beef stew.* **—intr.v.** *Slang.* To complain. **—phrasal verb. beef up.** *Slang.* To reinforce; build up. [Middle English *boef,* beef, ox, from Old French *boef,* from Latin *bōs,* ox.]

beef cattle. Cattle raised for use as meat.

beef·eat·er (bēf′ē′tər) *n.* A yeoman of the royal guard in England or a warder of the Tower of London.

beef tea. Broth made from beef extract or by boiling pieces of lean beef, often used as a restorative.

beef·y (bē′fē) *adj.* **-i·er, -i·est.** Muscular in build; heavy; brawny: *a beefy wrestler.* **—beef′i·ness** *n.*

bee·hive (bē′hīv′) *n.* **1.** A hive, either natural or man-made, for bees. **2.** Any place teeming with activity.

bee·keep·er (bē′kē′pər) *n.* A person who keeps bees.

bee·line (bē′līn′) *n.* A fast, straight course. [From the belief that a pollen-laden bee flies straight back to its hive.]

Be·el·ze·bub (bē-ĕl′zə-bŭb′) *n.* **1.** The Devil. **2.** In Milton's

Paradise Lost, the chief of the fallen angels, next to Satan in power.

been (bĭn) *v.* The past participle of **be.** [Middle English *ben.*]

beer (bĭr) *n.* **1.** A fermented alcoholic beverage brewed from malt and flavored with hops. **2.** Any of various drinks made from extracts of roots and plants. [Middle English *ber(e),* from Old English *bēor.*]

beest·ings (bē′stĭngz) *n. (used with a sing. or pl. verb).* The first milk given by a cow or other mammal after parturition. [Middle English *bestynge,* from Old English *bēost,* beestings.]

bees·wax (bēz′wăks′) *n.* **1.** The yellowish wax secreted by the honeybee for making honeycombs. **2.** Commercial wax obtained from this, used in making candles, crayons, and polishes.

beet (bēt) *n.* **1.** Any of several widely cultivated plants of the genus *Beta,* esp. *B. vulgaris,* with leaves sometimes eaten as greens and a thickened, fleshy root. **2.** The bulbous root of this plant, eaten as a vegetable. [Middle English *bete,* from Old English *bēte,* from Latin *bēta.*]

bee·tle[1] (bēt′l) *n.* **1.** Any of numerous insects of the order Coleoptera, with biting mouth parts and front wings modified to form horny wing covers that overlie the membranous rear wings when at rest. **2.** Any insect resembling a beetle. [Middle English *bityl,* from Old English *bitela.*]

beetle[1]

bee·tle[2] (bēt′l) *adj.* Jutting; overhanging: *beetle brows.* **—intr.v.** **-tled, -tling.** To overhang. [Middle English *bitel-(brouwed),* (having) protruding (eyebrows).]

bee·tle[3] (bēt′l) *n.* **1.** A heavy mallet with a large wooden head. **2.** A small wooden household mallet. **—tr.v.** **-tled, -tling.** To pound with a beetle. [Middle English *betel,* from Old English *bietel.*]

bee·tle-browed (bēt′l-broud′) *adj.* Having large, overhanging brows.

beeves (bēvz) *n.* A plural of **beef.**

be·fall (bĭ-fôl′) *v.* **-fell** (-fĕl′), **-fall·en** (-fôl′ən), **-fall·ing.** **—intr.v.** To come to pass; happen. **—tr.v.** To happen to: *Great harm befell them.* [Middle English *befallen,* from Old English *befeallan,* to fall, belong.]

be·fit (bĭ-fĭt′) *tr.v.* **-fit·ted, -fit·ting.** To be suitable to or appropriate for: *His fate befits his actions.*

be·fog (bĭ-fôg′, -fŏg′) *tr.v.* **-fogged, -fog·ging.** To cover with or as if with fog; obscure or confuse.

be·fool (bĭ-fōōl′) *tr.v.* To make a fool of; to hoodwink.

be·fore (bĭ-fôr′, -fōr′) *adv.* **1.** Earlier; previously: *I told you about her before.* **2.** *Archaic.* In front; ahead: "With the cross of Jesus going on before" (Sabine Baring-Gould). **—prep.** **1.** Ahead of; earlier than: *He got there before me.* **2.** Prior to: *the old days before the war.* **3.** In front of: *Eat what's set before you.* **4. a.** Under the consideration of: *the case now before the court.* **b.** In the presence of: *He was brought before the judge.* **5.** In preference to or in higher esteem than: *I'd take the Rolling Stones before Bob Dylan any day.* **—conj.** **1.** In advance of the time when: *before he went.* **2.** Sooner than: *He would die before he would give in.* [Middle English *before(n),* from Old English *beforan.*]

be·fore·hand (bĭ-fôr′hănd′, -fōr′-) *adv.* In advance; early: *He arrived beforehand.* **—be·fore′hand′** *adj.*

be·foul (bĭ-foul′) *tr.v.* **1.** To make dirty; to soil. **2.** To speak badly of: *She befouled his reputation.*

---

be·friend (bĭ-frĕnd′) *tr.v.* To act as a friend to; to aid; to assist: *befriend someone in need.*

be·fud·dle (bĭ-fŭd′l) *tr.v.* **-dled, -dling. 1.** To confuse; perplex. **2.** To stupefy with or as if with alcoholic drink —See Syns at **confuse.**

beg (bĕg) *v.* **begged, beg·ging.** —*tr.v.* **1.** To ask for as charity: *He begged coins.* **2.** To ask earnestly for; entreat: *I beg your tolerance.* —*intr.v.* **1.** To solicit alms. **2.** To make a humble or urgent plea: *beg for tolerance.* —*phrasal verb.* **beg off** (or **out**). To ask to be released or excused from (a penalty or obligation). —*idioms.* **beg the question. 1.** To assume the conclusion to one's argument to be true. **2.** To equivocate or dodge the issue. **go begging.** To go or remain unused or unanswered: *Her pleas for help went begging.* [Middle English *beggen.*]

be·gan (bĭ-găn′) *v.* The past tense of **begin.** [Middle English, from Old English.]

be·get (bĭ-gĕt′) *tr.v.* **-got** (-gŏt′) or *archaic* **-gat** (-găt′), **-got·ten** (-gŏt′n) or **-got, -get·ting. 1.** To father; to sire. **2.** To cause to exist: *Knowledge begets wisdom.* [Middle English *begeten,* to acquire, procreate, from Old English *begietan.*] —**be·get′ter** *n.*

beg·gar (bĕg′ər) *n.* **1.** A person who begs, esp. one who begs alms for a living. **2.** Someone who has no money; a pauper. **3.** A rascal; rogue. —*tr.v.* **1.** To impoverish; make a beggar of. **2.** To exhaust the resources of: *Her beauty beggars all description.*

beg·gar·ly (bĕg′ər-lē) *adj.* **1.** Of or pertaining to a beggar; very poor: *a beggarly pension.* **2.** Mean; contemptible: *a beggarly king.* —**beg′gar·li·ness** *n.*

beg·gar's-lice (bĕg′ərz-līs′) *pl.n.* **1.** (*used with a sing. or pl. verb*). Any of several plants with small, prickly fruit that cling to clothing or the fur of animals. **2.** The seeds of such a plant.

beg·gar-ticks (bĕg′ər-tĭks′) *pl.n.* **1.** (*used with a sing. or pl. verb*). Any of several plants with prickly seeds that cling to clothing or the fur of animals. **2.** The seeds of any of these plants.

beg·gar·y (bĕg′ə-rē) *n.* **1.** Extreme poverty; penury. **2.** Beggars in general.

be·gin (bĭ-gĭn′) *v.* **-gan** (-găn′), **-gun** (-gŭn′), **-gin·ning.** —*intr.v.* **1.** To start to do something; commence: *I'll begin after lunch.* **2.** To come into being: *when life began.* **3.** To do or be in the least degree: *That suggestion only begins to answer our problem.* —*tr.v.* **1.** To start to do; commence: *Begin the show.* **2.** To cause to come into being; originate; start: *begin the business.* [Middle English *beginnen,* from Old English *beginnan.*]

> **Syns: begin, arise, commence, originate, start** *v.* Core meaning: To come into existence (*an uprising that began with labor strikes*).

be·gin·ner (bĭ-gĭn′ər) *n.* **1.** Someone who begins something. **2.** Someone who is just starting to learn or do something; a novice.

be·gin·ning (bĭ-gĭn′ĭng) *n.* **1.** The act or process of beginning; a start; commencement. **2.** The time when something begins or is begun: *"In the beginning God created the heaven and the earth"* (Genesis 1:1). **3.** The place where something begins or is begun: *at the beginning of the road.* **4.** The source or origin of something; a cause: *"The fear of the Lord is the beginning of wisdom"* (Psalms 111:10). **5.** The first part: *the beginning of the play.* Often **beginnings.** The early or rudimentary phase: *the beginnings of history.*

be·gird (bĭ-gûrd′) *tr.v.* **-girt** (-gûrt′) or **-gird·ed, -girt, -gird·ing.** To gird or encircle; surround.

be·gone (bĭ-gôn′, -gŏn′) *interj.* Used as an order of dismissal. [Middle English.]

be·go·nia (bĭ-gōn′yə) *n.* Any of various plants of the genus *Begonia,* mostly native to the tropics but widely cultivated, with leaves that are often brightly colored or veined and irregular, waxy flowers of various colors. [After Michel Bégon (1638–1710), governor of Santo Domingo.]

be·got (bĭ-gŏt′) *v.* The past tense and a past participle of **beget.**

be·got·ten (bĭ-gŏt′n) *v.* A past participle of **beget.**

be·grime (bĭ-grīm′) *tr.v.* **-grimed, -grim·ing.** To smear or soil with dirt or grime.

be·grudge (bĭ-grŭj′) *tr.v.* **-grudged, -grudg·ing. 1.** To envy (someone) the possession or enjoyment of. **2.** To give with reluctance: *begrudge her a loan.*

be·guile (bĭ-gīl′) *tr.v.* **-guiled, -guil·ing. 1.** To deceive by cunning; delude. **2.** To amuse or charm; delight. **3.** To pass (time) pleasantly. [BE- + GUILE (verb).] —**be·guile′ment** *n.* —**be·guil′er** *n.*

be·guine (bĭ-gēn′) *n.* **1.** A ballroom dance based on a native dance of Martinique and St. Lucia. **2.** The music for this dance. [From French *béguin,* hood, flirtation.]

be·gun (bĭ-gŭn′) *v.* The past participle of **begin.**

be·half (bĭ-hăf′) *n.* Interest; benefit. —*idioms.* **in behalf of.** In the interest of; for the benefit of: *The farmers were acting in behalf of their neighbors.* **on behalf of.** On the part of: *I'll thank you now, on behalf of Mrs. Jones.* [Middle English *(on min) behalfe,* "on my side."]

> *Usage:* **in behalf of, on behalf of.** *In behalf of* means in the interest of another or for the benefit of another, whereas *on behalf of* means on the part of another or as the agent of another. If you speak *in behalf of* another, you may be acting independently and without the knowledge of the other person. But if you speak *on behalf of* another, you are presumably the other person's agent or representative. The illustrations shown with the definitions of these two idioms exemplify the differences in meaning.

be·have (bĭ-hāv′) *v.* **-haved, -hav·ing.** —*intr.v.* **1.** To act, react, or function in a particular way: *The car behaves well at high speeds.* **2. a.** To conduct oneself in a specified way: *He behaved badly.* **b.** To conduct oneself in a proper way: *Try to behave.* —*tr.v.* To conduct (oneself) properly: *Behave yourself.* [Middle English *behaven* : *be-,* thoroughly + *haven,* to have.]

be·hav·ior (bĭ-hāv′yər) *n.* Also *Brit.* **be·hav·iour. 1.** The manner in which one behaves; deportment; demeanor. **2.** The actions or reactions of persons or things under specified circumstances: *studying the behavior of matter at extremely low temperatures.* —**be·hav′ior·al** *adj.*

be·hav·ior·ism (bĭ-hāv′yə-rĭz′əm) *n.* The psychological school that believes that objectively observable behavior, rather than mental conditions, constitutes the essential scientific basis of psychological data and investigation. —**be·hav′ior·ist** *n.* —**be·hav′ior·is′tic** *adj.*

be·hav·iour (bĭ-hāv′yər) *n.* Brit. var. of **behavior.**

be·head (bĭ-hĕd′) *tr.v.* To separate the head from; decapitate.

be·he·moth (bĭ-hē′məth, bē′ə-məth) *n.* **1.** In the Old Testament, a huge animal, possibly the hippopotamus. **2.** Something enormous in size: *a behemoth of a football player.* [Hebrew *bəhēmōth,* "great beast" from *bəhēmāh,* beast.]

be·hest (bĭ-hĕst′) *n.* An order or authoritative command; a request: *We came at his behest.* [Middle English, from Old English *behæs,* vow.]

be·hind (bĭ-hīnd′) *prep.* **1.** At the back or in the rear of: *the shed behind the barn.* Often used with a reflexive object: *He glanced quickly behind him.* Also used adverbially: *He sneaked up on us from behind.* **2.** On the farther side of or on the other side of (something intervening): *a wall safe behind the painting.* **3.** Underlying; in the background of: *Behind his every action was greed.* **4.** In support of: *most of the electorate was behind him.* **5. a.** Following: *A security car drove close behind the President's car.* **b.** In pursuit of: *heard the sound of horses' hoofs behind him.*

begonia

6. After (a set time); later than: *behind schedule.* —*adv.* **1.** In the place or situation that is left: *sent good-bys for the friends who stayed behind.* **2.** Falling back or backward. Often used adjectivally: *always behind in his work.* —*n. Informal.* The buttocks or backside. [Middle English *bihinden,* from Old English *bihindan.*]

be·hind·hand (bĭ-hīnd′hănd′) *adv.* Behind time; late or slow. —**be·hind′hand′** *adj.*

be·hold (bĭ-hōld′) *tr.v.* **-held** (-hĕld′), **-hold·ing.** To gaze at; look upon. —*interj.* Used to express amazement. [Middle English *beholden,* from Old English *behealdan,* to possess, hold, observe.]

be·hold·en (bĭ-hōl′dən) *adj.* Obliged; indebted. [Middle English *beholden,* from Old English *behealden,* past part. of *behealdan,* to behold.]

be·hoof (bĭ-hōōf′) *n.* Benefit; advantage; use. [Middle English *behove,* from Old English *behōf.*]

be·hoove (bĭ-hōōv′) *tr.v.* **-hooved, -hoov·ing.** To be necessary or proper for: *"It behooved him now to be a man and learn to live without her"* (Louis Auchincloss). [Middle English *behoven,* from Old English *behōfian,* to require, be fitting.]

beige (bāzh) *n.* A light grayish or yellowish brown. —*adj.* Light grayish or yellowish brown. [French, from Old French *bege.*]

be·ing (bē′ĭng) *n.* **1.** The state of existing; existence: *come into being.* **2.** Someone or something that is alive, esp. a person. **3.** One's basic or essential nature: *Such conflict strikes at our very being.* **4.** *Philos.* That which can be conceived as existing. **5. the Supreme Being.** God. —*conj. Informal.* Since; because: *Being as we're friends, I'll tell you.*

Usage: **being as, being as how.** As variants of *since,* *because,* or *inasmuch as,* these expressions occur primarily in regional speech. Avoid using them in formal compositions except when you are intentionally reproducing speech as dialogue: *We proceeded leisurely, since* (not *being as* or *being how*) *the bus was not yet due.* The expression *seeing as how* is used in approximately the same sense, and it too is inappropriate outside dialogue.

bel (bĕl) *n.* The logarithm to the base 10 of the ratio of two levels of power, used to measure voltage or sound intensity. One bel equals ten decibels. [After Alexander Graham Bell (1847–1922), American inventor.]

be·la·bor (bĭ-lā′bər) *tr.v.* **1.** To beat or attack with blows. **2.** To assail verbally. **3.** To go over repeatedly; harp upon: *belabor a point.*

be·lat·ed (bĭ-lā′tĭd) *adj.* Tardy; late: *a belated birthday card.* —See Syns at **late.** [BE- + obs. *lated,* from *late.*] —**be·lat′ed·ly** *adv.* —**be·lat′ed·ness** *n.*

be·lay (bĭ-lā′) *tr.v. Naut.* To secure or make fast (a rope) by winding on a cleat or pin. —*intr.v.* **1.** To be made secure. **2.** *Rare.* To stop. Used chiefly in the imperative: *Belay there!* [Middle English *beleggen,* to beset, surround, from Old English *belecgan,* to cover.]

belaying pin. *Naut.* A removable pin, fitted in a hole in the rail of a boat, and used for securing running gear.

bel can·to (bĕl kăn′tō, kän′-). A style of operatic singing characterized by brilliant vocal technique. [Italian, "beautiful singing."]

belch (bĕlch) *intr.v.* **1.** To expel gas noisily from the stomach through the mouth. **2.** To expel the contents violently; erupt: *The volcano belched with a roar.* **3.** To gush forth: *smoke belched from the chimney.* —*tr.v.* **1.** To expel (gas) noisily from the stomach through the mouth. **2.** To eject violently from within: *The volcano belched hot lava.* —*n.* A belching; an eructation. [Middle English *belchen.*]

bel·dam (bĕl′dəm) *n.* Also **bel·dame.** An old woman, esp. one who is loathsome or ugly. [Middle English, grandmother : Old French *belle,* beautiful + *dame,* mother, dam.]

be·lea·guer (bĭ-lē′gər) *tr.v.* **1.** To besiege by surrounding with troops: *beleaguer a town.* **2.** To harass; plague; beset: *beleaguered by problems.* [Dutch *belegeren:* be-, around + *leger,* camp, from Middle Dutch.]

bel·fry (bĕl′frē) *n., pl.* **-fries. 1.** A bell tower, esp. one attached to a building. **2.** The part of a tower or steeple in which bells are hung. [Middle English *berfrey,* portable siege tower, bell tower, from Old French *berfrei.*]

Be·li·al (bē′lē-əl, bēl′yəl) *n.* **1.** A personification of the Devil alluded to in the New Testament. **2.** In Milton's *Paradise Lost,* one of the fallen angels.

be·lie (bĭ-lī′) *tr.v.* **-lied, -ly·ing. 1.** To misrepresent or picture falsely; disguise: *His rough words belied his gentle nature.* **2.** To show to be false: *Their laughter belied their grief.* **3.** To disappoint or leave unfulfilled: *The results belied their hopes.* —See Syns at **disprove.** [Middle English *belien,* from Old English *beléogan.*]

be·lief (bĭ-lēf′) *n.* **1.** The act or condition of placing trust or confidence in a person or thing; faith. **2.** Mental acceptance of the truth or actuality of something: *our belief in the democratic process.* **3.** Something believed or accepted as true, esp. a particular tenet or a body of tenets: *religious beliefs.* [Middle English *beleve,* from Old English *bileafe.*]

Syns: **belief, conviction, feeling, idea, mind, notion, opinion, sentiment, view** *n. Core meaning:* Something believed or accepted as true (*a belief in life after death*).

be·lieve (bĭ-lēv′) *v.* **-lieved, -liev·ing.** —*tr.v.* **1.** To accept as true or real. **2.** To have confidence in; trust: *believe what she says.* **3.** To expect or suppose; think: *I believe he'll come.* —*intr.v.* **1.** To have faith, esp. religious faith. **2.** To have faith or confidence; to trust: *I believe in his ability.* **3.** To have confidence in the truth, value, or existence of something: *believe in free will.* —*idiom.* **make believe.** To pretend. [Middle English *bileven, beleven,* from Old English *beléfan.*] —**be·liev′a·ble** *adj.* —**be·liev′er** *n.*

Syns: **1. believe, accept, buy** (Slang), **swallow** (Slang) *v. Core meaning:* To regard as true or real (*believed the story*). **2. believe, consider, deem, figure** (Informal), **hold, think** *v. Core meaning:* To have an opinion (*believes that jogging is healthful*).

be·lit·tle (bĭ-lĭt′l) *tr.v.* **-tled, -tling.** To speak of as small or unimportant; deprecate; disparage: *He belittled my opinion.* —**be·lit′tle·ment** *n.* —**be·lit′tler** *n.*

bell¹ (bĕl) *n.* **1.** A hollow metal instrument, usu. cup-shaped with a flared opening that rings when struck. **2.** Something shaped like a bell, as the flared mouth of some musical wind instruments. **3.** *Naut.* **a.** A stroke on a bell to mark the hour. **b.** The time indicated by the striking of a bell, divided into half hours. —*tr.v.* To shape or cause to flare like a bell. —*idiom.* **bell the cat.** To perform a daring action. [Middle English *belle,* from Old English *belle.*]

bell¹   bell buoy

bell² (bĕl) *n.* The baying cry of certain animals, as a beagle on the hunt. —*intr.v.* To bellow; bay. [Middle English *bellen,* to bay, from Old English *bellan.*]

bel·la·don·na (bĕl′ə-dŏn′ə) *n.* **1.** A poisonous Eurasian plant, *Atropa belladonna,* with purplish-red flowers and small black poisonous berries. Also called **deadly nightshade. 2.** A drug derived from this plant used to treat asthma, colic, and hyperacidity. [Italian, "fair lady."]

bell-bot·tom (bĕl′bŏt′əm) *adj.* Having legs that flare out at the bottom: *bell-bottom trousers.*

bell-bot·toms (bĕl′bŏt′əmz) *pl.n.* Bell-bottom trousers.

bell-boy (bĕl′boi′) *n.* A boy or man employed by a hotel to carry luggage, run errands, etc.; bellhop.

bell buoy. A buoy fitted with a warning bell.

belle (bĕl) *n.* An attractive and much-admired girl or woman, esp. the most attractive at a given place: *the belle of the ball.* [French, "beautiful," from Latin *bellus,* handsome, pretty.]

Bel·ler·o·phon (bə-lĕr′ə-fŏn′) n. Gk. Myth. The Corinthian hero who slew the Chimera.

belles-let·tres (bĕl-lĕt′rə) pl. n. (used with a sing. verb). Literature regarded for its artistic value rather than for its didactic or informative content. [French, "fine letters," literature.]

bell·flow·er (bĕl′flou′ər) n. Any of various plants of the genus Campanula, with blue, bell-shaped flowers.

bell glass. A belljar.

bell·hop (bĕl′hŏp′) n. A bellboy.

bel·li·cose (bĕl′ĭ-kōs′) adj. Warlike or quarrelsome in manner or temperament: a bellicose nation; a bellicose personality. [Middle English, from Latin bellicōsus, from bellum, war.] —**bel′li·cos′i·ty** (-kŏs′ĭ-tē) n.

bel·lig·er·ence (bə-lĭj′ər-əns) n. A warlike or hostile attitude, nature, or inclination.

bel·lig·er·en·cy (bə-lĭj′ər-ən-sē) n. The condition of being at war or engaged in a warlike conflict. —See Syns at **conflict.**

bel·lig·er·ent (bə-lĭj′ər-ənt) adj. 1. Inclined to or willing to fight; hostile: a belligerent person. 2. Of, pertaining to, or engaged in warfare: the belligerent powers. —n. A person or nation engaged in war. [Latin belligerāns, pres. part. of belligerāre, to wage war, from belliger, waging war : bellum, war + gerere, to bear, carry.] —**bel·lig′er·ent·ly** adv.

bell jar. A bell-shaped glass vessel with an open base used to protect objects or to establish a controlled environment in scientific experiments; bell glass.

bell·man (bĕl′mən) n. A town crier.

bel·low (bĕl′ō) intr.v. 1. To emit a loud, hollow roar, as a bull. 2. To shout in a deep voice. —tr.v. To utter in a loud and powerful voice: fans bellowing encouragement. —n. 1. The roar of a bull, elephant, or other large animal. 2. A very loud utterance; a shout. [Middle English belwen.]

bel·lows (bĕl′ōz, -əz) n. (used with a sing. or pl. verb). 1. An apparatus for producing a strong current of air, as for sounding a pipe organ or increasing the draft to a fire, consisting of a flexible, valved air chamber that is contracted and expanded by pumping to force the air through a nozzle. 2. Something resembling a bellows, such as the pleated windbag of an accordion. [Middle English belwes, belows.]

bell·weth·er (bĕl′wĕth′ər) n. 1. A male sheep that wears a bell and leads a flock of sheep. 2. Someone or something that leads or initiates: a new automobile that is a bellwether of future designs.

bel·ly (bĕl′ē) n., pl. -lies. 1. The abdomen (in mammals). 2. The underside of the body of certain vertebrates. 3. a. The stomach. b. The appetite for food. 4. Any part that bulges or protrudes: the belly of a sail. 5. The deep, hollow interior of something: a ship's belly. 6. The bulging part of a muscle. —v. -lied, -ly·ing. —intr.v. To swell out; to bulge: "Mud-colored clouds bellied downwards from the sky" (Thomas Hardy). —tr.v. To cause to bulge. [Middle English bely, from Old English bel(i)g, bag, purse, bellows.]

bel·ly·ache (bĕl′ē-āk′) n. An ache or pain in the stomach or abdomen. —intr.v. -ached, -ach·ing. Slang. To grumble or complain, esp. in a whining manner.

bel·ly·band (bĕl′ē-bănd′) n. A band passed around the belly of an animal to secure something, as a saddle.

bel·ly·but·ton (bĕl′ē-bŭt′n) n. Informal. The navel.

belly flop. A playful or faulty dive in which the front of the body hits flat against the surface.

bel·ly·ful (bĕl′ē-fŏŏl′) n. Informal. An excessive amount: I've had a bellyful of trouble today.

belly laugh. A deep, jovial laugh.

be·long (bĭ-lông′, -lŏng′) intr.v. 1. To have a proper or suitable place: Those clothes belong in the closet. 2. **belong to.** a. To be the property or concern of: "The earth belongs to the living" (Thomas Jefferson). b. To be a member of an organization: belong to a fraternity. 3. To be part of or in natural association with something: That belongs with the other gifts. [Middle English belongen : be-, thoroughly + longen, to suit, from Old English langian, to yearn for.]

be·long·ing (bĭ-lông′ĭng, -lŏng′-) n. 1. **belongings.** Personal possessions; effects. 2. Close and secure relationship: a sense of belonging.

be·lov·ed (bĭ-lŭv′ĭd, -lŭvd′) adj. Dearly loved. —n. Someone or something that is loved.

be·low (bĭ-lō′) adv. 1. Following or farther down on a page: footnotes listed below. 2. In or to a lower place or level: pausing on the bridge to admire the rapids below. Also used prepositionally: We stood at the window and watched the people in the street below us. 3. On or to a lower floor or deck: The trunks were stowed in a compartment below. 4. Further down, as along a slope or valley: From below, the thousands of toiling men looked like ants at work. Also used prepositionally: an old mine a hundred feet down the hill below our hut. 5. On earth: all creatures here below. —prep. 1. Underneath; under; beneath: Below the earth there was a race of wicked gnomes. 2. Lower than, as on a graduated scale: We use negative numbers to show temperatures below zero. Also used adverbially: temperatures of zero and below. [Middle English bilooghe : bi, + loogh, low.]

belt (bĕlt) n. 1. A band of leather, cloth, or other flexible material, worn around the waist to support clothing, secure tools or weapons, or serve as decoration. 2. Anything that resembles a belt by encircling or surrounding: a belt of outbuildings. 3. An encircling route or highway. 4. A continuous band or chain for transferring motion or power or conveying materials from one wheel or shaft to another, such as a fan belt or conveyor belt. 5. A band of tough material beneath the tread of a tire, used for reinforcement. 6. A geographical region that is distinctive in some specific way: the Sun Belt. 7. Informal. A powerful blow; a punch. 8. Slang. A strong emotional reaction. 9. Slang. A drink of hard liquor. —tr.v. 1. To attach with or as if with a belt. 2. To strike with a belt. 3. Informal. To strike forcefully. 4. Slang. To sing in a loud and forceful manner: belt a song. —See Syns at **hit.** —**idioms. below the belt.** 1. Boxing. Below the waistline, where a blow is foul. 2. Not according to rule; unfair. **tighten (one's) belt.** To become thrifty and frugal. **under (one's) belt.** To have gained knowledge or experience of by doing (something) for the first time. [Middle English belt, from Old English belt, ult. from Latin balteus.]

belt·ing (bĕl′tĭng) n. 1. Belts in general. 2. The material used to make belts.

be·lu·ga (bə-lōō′gə) n. 1. The **white whale.** 2. A sturgeon, Huso huso, of the Black and Caspian seas, whose roe is used for caviar. [Russian byeluga, sturgeon, and byelukha, white whale.]

be·moan (bĭ-mōn′) tr.v. 1. To lament; mourn over. 2. To express pity or grief for.

be·muse (bĭ-myōōz′) tr.v. -mused, -mus·ing. To confuse or stupefy.

bench (bĕnch) n. 1. A long seat, with or without a back. 2. a. The seat for judges in a courtroom. b. The office or position of a judge. c. The judge or judges composing a court. 3. A strong worktable, as one used in carpentry. 4. A platform on which animals, esp. dogs, are exhibited. 5. Sports. a. The place where the players on a team sit while they are not participating in the game. b. The reserve players on a team. 9. A level expanse of land along a shore or coast; shelf. —tr.v. 1. To seat on a bench. 2. To show (dogs) in a bench show. 3. Sports. To keep out or remove (a player) from a game. [Middle English bench, from Old English benc.]

bench mark. A surveyor's mark made on some stationary object, used as a reference point, as in tidal observations and surveys.

bench warrant. Law. A warrant issued by a judge or court, ordering the apprehension of an offender.

bend¹ (bĕnd) v. bent (bĕnt), bend·ing. —tr.v. 1. a. To cause to assume a curved or angular shape. b. To force to assume a different shape or direction: A telescope lens bends light. 2. To cause to swerve from a straight line; deflect. 3. To influence coercively; subdue: bend them to our will. 4. —bent on. To decide; to resolve: bent on leaving. 5. To apply (the mind) closely; concentrate: Bend your mind to your studies. 6. Naut. To fasten: bend a mainsail onto the boom. —intr.v. 1. a. To turn or be altered from straightness or from an initial shape or position: Wire bends easily. b. To assume a curved, crooked, or angular form or direction: The saplings bent in the wind. 2. To take a new

---

direction; to swerve: *The road bends left.* **3.** To incline the body; to stoop. **4.** To bow in submission; yield. —*n.* **1.** The act of bending. **2.** The condition of being bent. **3.** Something bent; a curve; crook. **4.** *Naut.* **a. bends.** The thick planks in a ship's side; the wales. **b.** A knot that joins a rope to a rope or another object. **5. the bends. Caisson disease.** —*idiom.* **bend over backward.** To make a strong effort. [Middle English *benden,* from Old English *bendan.*]

bend² (běnd) *n. Heraldry.* A diagonal band on an escutcheon. [Middle English *bend,* from Old English *bend,* ribbon, band.]

bend·er (běn′dər) *n.* **1.** Someone or something that bends. **2.** *Slang.* A drinking spree.

be·neath (bĭ-nēth′) *prep.* **1. a.** Directly underneath: *a cat sleeping beneath the stove.* Also used adverbially: *The diagram is explained in the legend printed beneath.* **b.** Underneath in relation to something that screens or shelters: *figs and olives planted beneath the date trees.* Also used adverbially: *The branches parted, and a patch of sunlight reached the mossy ground beneath.* **c.** Underneath or on the other side of an intervening surface: *Water is found stored in rock and soil beneath the ground.* Also used adverbially: *Certain delineations enable us to see the body structures beneath.* **2.** At a level lower than or further down from: *a spring just beneath the summit.* Also used adverbially: *Hikers looked down into the plain beneath.* **3.** Far below or unworthy of: *beneath contempt.* [Middle English *beneithe(n),* from Old English *binithan : bi,* by + *nithan, neothan,* from below.]

ben·e·dic·tion (běn′ĭ-dĭk′shən) *n.* **1.** A blessing. **2.** An invocation of divine blessing, usu. at the end of a service. **3.** The condition of blessedness. [Middle English *benediccioun,* from Old French *benediction,* from Latin *benedictiō,* from *benedīcere,* to bless, speak well of : *bene,* well + *dīcere,* to say.]

ben·e·fac·tion (běn′ə-făk′shən, běn′ə-făk-) *n.* **1.** The act of conferring help or a benefit. **2.** A charitable gift or deed. [Late Latin *benefactiō,* from *beneficere,* to do well : Latin *bene,* well + *facere,* to do.]

ben·e·fac·tor (běn′ə-făk′tər) *n.* A person who gives financial or other aid.

ben·e·fac·tress (běn′ə-făk′trĭs) *n.* A female benefactor.

ben·e·fice (běn′ə-fĭs) *n.* A church office, as a rectory, endowed with property and revenue-producing assets.

be·nef·i·cence (bə-něf′ĭ-səns) *n.* **1.** The quality of charity or kindness. **2.** A charitable act or gift. [Old French, from Latin *beneficentia,* from *beneficus,* beneficent, generous : *bene,* well + *facere,* to do.]

be·nef·i·cent (bə-něf′ĭ-sənt) *adj.* **1.** Of performing acts of kindness or charity. **2.** Producing benefit; beneficial: *a beneficent gesture.* —**be·nef′i·cent·ly** *adv.*

ben·e·fi·cial (běn′ə-fĭsh′əl) *adj.* Promoting a favorable result; enhancing well-being; advantageous: *The warm weather is beneficial to his health.* [From obs. *benefice,* benefit.] —**ben·e·fi′cial·ly** *adv.*

ben·e·fi·ci·ar·y (běn′ə-fĭsh′ē-ĕr′ē, -fĭsh′ə-rē) *n., pl.* **-ies.** **1.** Someone who receives a benefit: *The rich will be the beneficiaries of a tax cut.* **2.** *Law.* The recipient of funds, property, or other benefits from an insurance policy, will, or other settlement.

ben·e·fit (běn′ə-fĭt) *n.* **1.** Anything that promotes or enhances well-being; advantage. **2.** *Archaic.* A kindly deed. **3.** Payments made in accordance with a wage agreement, insurance contract, or public assistance program: *unemployment benefits.* **4.** A public entertainment or social event held to raise funds for a person or cause. —*tr.v.* To be helpful or useful to: *a program to benefit the disabled.* —*intr.v.* To improve or gain advantage; to profit: *benefit from his example.* [Middle English *benfet,* from Norman French, from Latin *benefactum : bene,* well + *facere,* to do.]

be·nev·o·lence (bə-něv′ə-ləns) *n.* **1.** An inclination to do kind or charitable acts; good will. **2.** A kindly act.

be·nev·o·lent (bə-něv′ə-lənt) *adj.* **1.** Desiring or inclined to do good; kindly. **2.** Of or concerned with charity: *a benevolent fund.* [Middle English, from Latin *benevolēns : bene,* well + *velle,* to wish.] —**be·nev′o·lent·ly** *adv.*

be·night·ed (bĭ-nī′tĭd) *adj.* **1.** Overtaken by darkness or night. **2.** In moral or intellectual darkness; unenlightened;

ignorant. [BE- + NIGHT.] —**be·night′ed·ly** *adv.*

be·nign (bĭ-nīn′) *adj.* **1.** Of a kind disposition: *a benign person.* **2.** Showing gentleness; kindly: *a benign embrace.* **3.** Tending to promote well-being; beneficial: *a benign climate.* **4.** *Pathol.* Not malignant: *a benign tumor.* —See Syns at **kind.** [Middle English *benigne,* from Old French, from Latin *benignus,* "well-born."] —**be·nign′ly** *adv.*

be·nig·nant (bĭ-nĭg′nənt) *adj.* **1.** Favorable; beneficial: *the benignant effect of relaxation.* **2.** Kind and gracious: *a benignant ruler.* —**be·nig′nan·cy** (-nən-sē) *n.* —**be·nig′nant·ly** *adv.*

ben·i·son (běn′ĭ-zən, -sən) *n.* A blessing or benediction. [Middle English *benes(u)n,* from Old French *beneisson,* from Latin *benedictiō,* benediction.]

bent¹ (běnt) *v.* The past tense and past participle of **bend.** —*adj.* **1.** Not straight; crooked. **2.** On a fixed course of action; determined: *"I perceived he was bent on refusing my mediation"* (Emily Brontë). —*n.* An individual tendency, disposition, or inclination: *a natural bent for science.*

bent² (běnt) *n.* **1.** Any of several grasses of the genus *Agrostis,* some species of which are used in lawn mixtures and for hay. Also called **bent grass.** **2.** *Archaic.* A moor; heath. [Middle English *bent,* grassy plain.]

ben·thos (běn′thŏs) *n.* **1.** The bottom of the sea or of a lake. **2.** The organisms living on sea or lake bottoms. [Greek, depth of the sea.]

be·numb (bĭ-nŭm′) *tr.v.* **1.** To make numb, esp. by cold. **2.** To make inactive; stupefy.

Ben·ze·drine (běn′zĭ-drēn′) *n.* A trademark for a brand of amphetamine.

ben·zene (běn′zēn′, běn-zēn′) *n.* Also **ben·zine.** A colorless, flammable liquid, C_6H_6, derived from petroleum and used in chemical products including detergents, insecticides, and motor fuels. Also called **benzol.** [BENZ(OIN) + -ENE.]

benzene ring. The molecular structure in benzene and its substitutional derivatives, distinguished by six carbon atoms linked in a hexagonal ring with alternating single and double bonds.

ben·zine (běn′zēn′, běn-zēn′) or **ben·zin** (běn′zĭn′) *n.* **1.** A mixture of hydrocarbons, ligroin. **2.** Var. of **benezene.** [BENZ(OIN) + -INE.]

ben·zo·ate (běn′zō-āt′, -ĭt) *n.* A salt or ester of benzoic acid. [BENZ(OIN) + -ATE.]

benzoate of soda. *Chem.* **Sodium benzoate.**

ben·zo·ic acid (běn-zō′ĭk). A white crystalline acid, C_6H_5COOH, used in perfumes, germicides, and to season tobacco. [BENZO(IN) + -IC + ACID.]

ben·zo·in (běn′zō-ĭn, -zoin′) *n.* **1.** Any of several resins containing benzoic acid, obtained from trees of the genus *Styrax,* and used in ointments, perfumes, and medicine. **2.** Any of various aromatic shrubs and trees of the genus *Lindera,* which includes the spicebush. [Earlier *benjoin,* from French, from New Latin *benzoe,* from Arabic *lubān jāwī,* "frankincense of Java."]

ben·zol (běn′zôl′, -zōl′) *n.* Another name for **benzene.** [BENZ(OIN) + -OL.]

Be·o·wulf (bā′ə-wŏŏlf′) *n.* The hero of an anonymous Old English epic poem.

be·queath (bĭ-kwēth′, -kwēth′) *tr.v.* **1.** *Law.* To leave or give (property) to a person by will. **2.** To pass on or hand down: *He bequeathed his vision and ideals to his followers.* [Middle English *bequethen,* from Old English *becwethan,* to say, bequeath : *be-,* about, over + *cwethan,* to say, speak.] —**be·queath′al** (bĭ-kwē′thəl, -thəl) *n.*

be·quest (bĭ-kwěst′) *n.* **1.** The act of bequeathing. **2.** That which is bequeathed; legacy.

be·rate (bĭ-rāt′) *tr.v.* **-rat·ed, -rat·ing.** To scold harshly. [BE- + RATE (verb).]

Ber·ber (bûr′bər) *n.* **1.** A member of one of several Moslem tribes of North Africa. **2.** The Hamitic languages of these tribes.

ber·ceuse (běr-sœz′) *n., pl.* **-ceuses** (-sœz′). **1.** A lullaby. **2.** A musical composition with a soothing accompaniment. [French, from *bercer,* to rock.]

be·reave (bĭ-rēv′) *tr.v.* **-reaved** or **-reft** (-rěft′), **-reav·ing. 1.** To deprive of, esp. life or hope. **2.** To leave desolate, esp. by death. [Middle English *bireven,* from Old English *berēafian.*] —**be·reave′ment** *n.*

ă pat ā pay â care ä father ĕ pet ē be hw which ĭ pit ī tie î pier ŏ pot ō toe ô paw, for oi noise
ōŏ took ōō boot ou out th thin *th* this ŭ cut û urge zh vision ə about, item, edible, gallop, circus

Usage: bereaved, bereft. *Bereaved* is most commonly used in connection with the loss of a loved one: *She was bereaved at her mother's death. Bereft* is used in connection with the loss of hope, faith, etc.: *a man bereft of purpose.*

be·ret (bə-rā′, bĕr′ā′) *n.* A round, visorless cloth cap, orig. worn by male Basques. [French *béret,* from Late Latin *birrus,* hooded cape.]

beret

berth

berg (bûrg) *n.* An iceberg.

ber·ga·mot (bûr′gə-mŏt′) *n.* **1.** A small, spiny tree, *Citrus aurantium bergamia,* bearing sour, pear-shaped fruit, the rind of which yields an aromatic oil. **2.** The oil itself, used in perfumery. **3.** Any of several aromatic mint plants of the genus *Monarda.* [French *bergamote,* from Italian *bergamotta.*]

ber·i·ber·i (bĕr′ē-bĕr′ē) *n.* A disease of the peripheral nervous system caused by a lack of thiamine and characterized by partial paralysis, emaciation, and anemia. [Singhalese, from *beri,* weakness.]

ber·ke·li·um (bər-kē′lē-əm, bûrk′lē-əm) *n. Symbol* **Bk** A synthetic element having 9 isotopes with mass numbers from 243 to 250 and half-lives from 3 hours to 1,380 years. Atomic number 97, valences 3, 4. [After *Berkeley,* California.]

ber·lin (bər-lĭn′) *n.* **1.** A light wool used in making clothing. Also called **Berlin wool. 2.** A four-wheeled covered carriage. [After *Berlin,* Germany.]

Ber·mu·da onion (bər-myōō′də). A large, mild-flavored, yellow-skinned variety of onion.

Bermuda shorts. Shorts that end slightly above the knees.

Ber·noul·li's law (bər-nōō′lēz). Also **Bernoulli's principle.** *Physics.* The law that states that a fluid in motion exerts less pressure on a surface that is parallel to the direction of flow than does a stationary fluid. The pressure is inversely proportional to the velocity. [After Daniel *Bernoulli* (1700–82), Swiss mathematician.]

ber·ry (bĕr′ē) *n., pl.* **-ries. 1.** Any of various usu. fleshy, edible fruits, such as the strawberry, blackberry, or raspberry. **2.** A fleshy fruit, such as the grape or tomato, developed from a single ovary and having few or many seeds. **3.** Any of various seeds or dried kernels, such as that of the coffee plant. —*intr.v.* **-ried, -ry·ing. 1.** To gather berries. **2.** To bear berries. [Middle English *berye,* from Old English *beri(g)e.*]

ber·serk (bər-sûrk′, -zûrk′) *adj.* In or into a frenetic or violent frenzy; crazed. —**ber·serk′** *adv.*

ber·serk·er (bər-sûr′kər, -zûr′-) *n. Norse Myth.* A fierce warrior who fought in battle with frenzied violence and fury. [Old Norse *berserkr,* "bear's skin" : *bjǫrn,* a bear + *serkr,* shirt.]

berth (bûrth) *n.* **1.** A built-in bed or bunk on a ship or train. **2.** *Naut.* A space at a wharf for a ship to dock. **3.** *Naut.* Enough space for a ship to maneuver. **4.** A position of employment, esp. on a ship. —*tr.v.* **1.** To bring (a ship) to a berth. **2.** To provide with a berth. —*intr.v.* To come to a berth; dock. —*idiom.* **give a wide berth to.** To stay at a substantial distance from; avoid. [Prob. from BEAR (to go in a certain direction).]

ber·tha (bûr′thə) *n.* A wide, deep collar that covers the shoulders of a dress. [French *berthe,* after Queen *Bertha* (d. 783), mother of Charlemagne.]

Ber·til·lon system (bûr′tl-ŏn′; *Fr.* bĕr-tē-yôn′). A former system for identifying persons by means of a record of various body measurements, coloring, and markings. [After Alphonse *Bertillon* (1853–1914), French criminologist.]

ber·yl (bĕr′əl) *n.* A hard mineral, essentially a silicate of aluminum and beryllium, $Be_3Al_2Si_6O_{18}$, occurring in various colors. It is the chief source of beryllium and is used as a gem. [Middle English, from Old French, from Latin *bēryllus,* from Greek *bērullos.*]

be·ryl·li·um (bə-rĭl′ē-əm) *n. Symbol* **Be** A high-melting, lightweight, corrosion-resistant, rigid, steel-gray metallic element used as an aerospace structural material, as a moderator and reflector in nuclear reactors, and in copper alloys. Atomic number 4, atomic weight 9.0122, melting point 1,278°C, boiling point 2,970°C, specific gravity 1.848 valence 2. [From BERYL.]

be·seech (bĭ-sēch′) *tr.v.* **-sought** (-sôt′) or **-seeched, -seech·ing. 1.** To address an earnest or urgent request to; implore: *I beseech your patience.* **2.** To ask earnestly; beg for: *beseech forgiveness.* [Middle English *besechen,* to seek thoroughly.]

be·seem (bĭ-sēm′) *tr.v. Archaic.* To be appropriate for.

be·set (bĭ-sĕt′) *tr.v.* **-set, -set·ting. 1.** To trouble persistently; harass: "*. . .beset by a ghostly band of doubts*" (Sherwood Anderson). **2. a.** To attack from all sides. **b.** To surround; hem in. **3.** To stud, as with jewels: *a tiara beset with rubies.* —See Syns at **attack.**

be·set·ting (bĭ-sĕt′ĭng) *adj.* Constantly troubling or attacking.

be·shrew (bĭ-shrōō′) *tr.v. Archaic.* To call evil upon; to curse. [Middle English *beshrewen,* to curse : *be-,* thoroughly + *shrewen,* to curse, from *shrewe,* a shrew.]

be·side (bĭ-sīd′) *prep.* **1.** At the side of: *She sat down beside her boyfriend.* **2.** In comparison with: *He is quite short beside his brother.* **3.** Apart from; wide of: *His remark was entirely beside the point.* —*idiom.* **beside (oneself).** Out of one's wits with excitement, anger, etc. [Middle English *biside,* from Old English *be sīdan,* "by the side."]

Usage: beside, besides. *Beside* is a preposition in modern English: *a hut beside the road; a small contribution beside yours. Besides* can be a preposition and an adverb. In these examples, *besides* is a preposition: *contributed a great deal besides that; had few friends besides us.* And in these examples *besides* is an adverb: *I was tired; besides, I had done my share. She cleaned her room but did ver y little besides.*

be·sides (bĭ-sīdz′) *adv.* **1.** In addition: *Every warrior was mounted and had a spare horse besides.* **2.** Moreover; furthermore: *was tired of chatting, and besides it was getting late.* —*prep.* **1.** In addition to: *The Congress of Vienna did other things besides remaking Europe.* **2.** Other than; except for: *nothing to eat besides leftovers.* —See Usage note at **beside.**

be·siege (bĭ-sēj′) *tr.v.* **-sieged, -sieg·ing. 1.** To surround and blockade in order to capture; lay siege to. **2.** To crowd around; hem in: *Protesters besieged the President's car.* **3.** To harass or importune, as with requests. —**be·sieg′er** *n.*

be·smear (bĭ-smîr′) *tr.v.* To smear over.

be·smirch (bĭ-smûrch′) *tr.v.* **1.** To soil. **2.** To harm the purity or luster of; to tarnish; to dishonor.

be·som (bē′zəm) *n.* A bundle of twigs attached to a handle, used as a broom. [Middle English *besem,* from Old English *bes(e)ma.*]

be·sot (bĭ-sŏt′) *tr.v.* **-sot·ted, -sot·ting.** To muddle or stupefy, esp. with liquor. [BE- + SOT.]

be·sought (bĭ-sôt′) *v.* A past tense and past participle of **beseech.**

be·spake (bĭ-spāk′) *v. Archaic.* Past tense of **bespeak.**

be·spat·ter (bĭ-spăt′ər) *tr.v.* **1.** To spatter or soil thoroughly, as with mud. **2.** To slander; defame.

be·speak (bĭ-spēk′) *tr.v.* **-spoke** (-spōk′) or *archaic* **-spake** (-spāk′), **-spo·ken** (-spō′kən) or **-spoke, -speak·ing. 1.** To be or give a sign of; indicate: *a worried look that bespoke her concern.* **2.** *Archaic.* To speak to; address. **3.** To engage or claim in advance; to reserve. **4.** To foretell; portend: *economic troubles that bespeak a future recession.*

be·spec·ta·cled (bĭ-spĕk′tə-kəld) *adj.* Wearing eyeglasses.

be·spoke (bĭ-spōk′) *v.* The past tense and a past participle of **bespeak.** —*adj. Brit.* Also **be·spo·ken** (bĭ-spō′kən).

| ă pat | ā pay | â care | ä father | ĕ pet | ē be | hw which | ĭ pit | ī tie | î pier | ŏ pot | ō toe | ô paw, for | oi noise |
| ōō took | ōō boot | ou out | *th* thin | *th* this | ŭ cut | | û urge | zh vision | ə about, item, edible, gallop, circus |

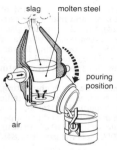

Bessemer converter
Model drawing

Bessemer converter
The container

betel palm

Made-to-order; custom-made.

be·spo·ken (bĭ-spō′kən) *v.* A past participle of **bespeak.** —*adj.* *Brit.* Var. of **bespoke.**

be·spread (bĭ-sprĕd′) *tr.v.* To cover or spread over, usu. thickly: *a sky bespread with clouds.*

be·sprin·kle (bĭ-sprĭng′kəl) *tr.v.* **-kled, -kling.** To sprinkle over: *egg salad besprinkled with parsley.*

Bes·se·mer converter (bĕs′ə-mər). A large pear-shaped container in which molten iron is converted to steel by the Bessemer process. [After Sir Henry *Bessemer* (1813–98), British inventor.]

Bessemer process. A method for making steel by blasting compressed air through molten iron and burning out excess carbon and other impurities.

best (bĕst) *adj.* Superlative of **good.** **1.** —Used to indicate the highest degree of excellence, quality, achievement, etc.: *the best craftsmen.* **2.** —Used to indicate the highest degree of appropriateness or suitability: *the best place to dig a well.* **3.** —Used to indicate the highest social standing or respectability: *frequented by the best people.* **4.** —Used to indicate the largest portion of something specified: *the best part of a journey.* **5.** —Used to indicate the highest degree of closeness: *his best friend.* —*adv.* Superlative of **well.** **1.** In the most excellent way; most properly or successfully: *Which of the two pictures best fits your description?* **2.** Most: *What does he like to eat best?* —*n.* Someone or something that is best, as: **1.** The best person or persons: *It happens to be the best of us.* **2.** One's best effort or appearance: *do your best.* **3.** One's best wishes or regards: *Give them my best.* —*tr.v.* To get the better of; to defeat: *besting their rivals in every game.* —See Syns at **defeat.** —*idioms.* **as best (one) can.** As well as one can. **at best. 1.** Interpreted most favorably; at most: *His remark was at best a well-meaning blunder.* **2.** Under the most favorable conditions: *This car does 120 at best.* **for the best.** For the ultimate good. **get the best of.** To defeat or outwit. **had best.** Should; ought to: *You had best get out of here.* **make the best of it.** To do as well as possible under unfavorable conditions. [Middle English *best,* from Old English *bet(e)st.*]

>   *Usage:* **best, better.** *Best* is the adverbial and adjectival superlative form of *good* and *well. Better* is the adverbial and adjectival comparative form of *good* and *well.* While *better* is used to indicate superiority of one over another when only two are present (*This house is better than that one. She dances better than Sue.*), it is also used in incomplete or understood comparisons in which the unstated element is clearly implied: *wanted a better life for her children. Best* is used to indicate preeminence in a group of three or more (*the best house in town; dances best of all*). *Best* can also be used to refer to a number of persons or things considered foremost: *the ten best songs of the year.* Both *best* and *better* can be combined with *had* to mean *should* or *ought to: You had best* (or *better*) *study.* In informal contexts, *had* is sometimes omitted with *better: You better study.* This locution is not appropriate in formal prose, though. Avoid altogether the nonstandard inverted form *you better had.*

be·stead (bĭ-stĕd′) *Archaic.* —*tr.v.* **-stead·ed** or **-stead,** **-stead·ing.** To be of service to; avail; aid. —*adj.* Placed; located. [BE- + STEAD (to help).]

bes·tial (bĕs′chəl, bĕst′yəl) *adj.* **1.** Of or pertaining to an animal. **2.** Having the qualities or manner of a brute; savagely cruel. **3.** Subhuman in intelligence. —See Syns at **fierce.** [Middle English, from Old French, from Late Latin *bēstiālis,* from Latin *bēstia,* beast.] —**bes′tial·ly** *adv.*

bes·ti·al·i·ty (bĕs′chē-ăl′ĭ-tē, bĕs′tē-) *n., pl.* **-ties. 1.** The quality of being bestial; animal nature. **2.** Conduct or an action marked by brutality.

be·stir (bĭ-stûr′) *tr.v.* **-stirred, -stir·ring.** To cause to become active; rouse.

best man. The bridegroom's chief attendant at a wedding.

be·stow (bĭ-stō′) *tr.v.* **1.** To present as a gift or honor; confer: *an award bestowed on the best player in the tournament.* **2.** *Archaic.* To apply; use. **3.** *Archaic.* To store; to house. [Middle English *bestowen,* to stow away.] —**bestow′al** *n.*

be·strew (bĭ-strōō′) *tr.v.* **-strewed, -strewed** or **-strewn** (-strōōn′), **-strew·ing. 1.** To strew (a surface) with things so as to cover it: *bestrew the path with flower petals.* **2.** To scatter or cast things about. **3.** To lie scattered over or about: *litter bestrewed the streets.*

be·stride (bĭ-strīd′) *tr.v.* **-strode** (-strōd′), **-strid·den** (-strĭd′n), **-strid·ing. 1.** To sit or stand on with the legs widely spread; straddle. **2.** To step over.

bet (bĕt) *n.* **1.** An agreement between two parties that the one proved wrong about an uncertain outcome will forfeit a stipulated thing or sum to the other; a wager. **2.** The object or amount risked in a wager; the stake. **3.** The person or thing upon which a stake is placed: *That team is a bad bet.* —*v.* **bet** or **bet·ted, bet·ting.** —*tr.v.* **1.** To stake (an object or amount) in a bet. **2.** To make a bet with: *I bet you he won't finish the race.* **3.** To make a bet on (a contestant or an outcome). **4.** To maintain confidently, as if making a bet. —*intr.v.* To make or place a bet: *I bet on every race yesterday and lost them all.* —*idiom.* **you bet.** Of course; surely. [Perh. short for ABET.]

be·ta (bā′tə, bē′-) *n.* **1.** The second letter in the Greek alphabet, written B, β. **2.** The second item in a series or system of classification. [Greek.]

be·take (bĭ-tāk′) *tr.v.* **-took** (-tōōk′), **-tak·en** (-tā′kən), **-tak·ing. 1.** To cause (oneself) to go or move. **2.** *Archaic.* To commit or apply (oneself) to something.

beta particle. A high-speed electron or positron, esp. one emitted in radioactive decay.

beta ray. A stream of beta particles, esp. of electrons.

be·ta·tron (bā′tə-trŏn′, bē′-) *n.* A fixed-radius magnetic induction electron accelerator. [BETA + -TRON.]

be·tel (bēt′l) *n.* A climbing Asiatic plant, *Piper betle,* the leaves of which are chewed with the betel nut to induce both stimulating and narcotic effects. [Portuguese *betel, betle,* from Malayalam *vettila.*]

Be·tel·geuse (bĕt′l-jōōz′, bĕt′l-jœz′) *n.* Also **Be·tel·geux.** A bright-red variable star, 527 light-years from Earth, in the constellation Orion.

betel nut. Also **be·tel·nut** (bĕt′l-nŭt′). The seed of the fruit of the betel palm, chewed with betel leaves and lime, esp. by many people of southeastern Asia.

betel palm. A palm tree, *Areca catechu,* of tropical Asia, with featherlike leaves and orange fruit.

bête noire (bĕt nwär′). Someone or something that one esp. dislikes or avoids. [French, "black beast."]

beth·el (bĕth′əl) *n.* **1.** A holy place. **2.** A chapel for seamen.

[Hebrew *bēth 'Él,* "house of God."]

be·think (bĭ-thĭngk′) v. **-thought** (-thôt′), **-think·ing.** —*tr.v.*
1. *Archaic.* To reflect upon; consider. **2.** To remind (oneself); remember: *I bethought me of oldentimes.* —*intr.v.*
Archaic. To meditate; ponder.

be·thought (bĭ-thôt′) v. The past tense and part participle of **bethink.**

be·tide (bĭ-tīd′) v. **-tid·ed, -tid·ing.** —*tr.v.* To happen to. —*intr.v.* To take place; befall. [Middle English *betiden* : *be-,* thoroughly + *tiden,* to happen, from Old English *tīdan.*]

be·times (bĭ-tīmz′) adv. **1.** In good time; early: *He awoke betimes.* **2.** *Archaic.* Quickly; soon.

be·to·ken (bĭ-tō′kən) tr.v. To give a sign of; portend: *The clouds betoken snow.* [Middle English *betoknen.*]

be·took (bĭ-tŏŏk′) v. The past tense of **betake.**

be·tray (bĭ-trā′) tr.v. **1.** To give aid to an enemy of; commit treason against. **2.** To be disloyal or unfaithful to: *betray a promise.* **3.** To divulge in a breach of confidence: *betray a family secret.* **4.** To make known unintentionally: *trembling hands betrayed his anxiety.* **5.** To show; reveal; indicate: *Careless errors betrayed her haste.* **6.** To deceive; lead astray: *betrayed her naive trust.* —See Syns at **deceive.** [Middle English *betrayen* : *be-,* thoroughly + *trayen,* to betray, from Old French *trair,* from Latin *trādere.*] —**be·tray′al** n. —**be·tray′er** n.

be·troth (bĭ-trŏth′, -trôth′) tr.v. **1.** To promise to give in marriage. **2.** To promise to marry. [Middle English *betrouthen* : *be-,* in relation to + *trouthe,* troth.]

be·troth·al (bĭ-trō′thəl, -trô′thəl) n. **1.** The act of becoming betrothed or of betrothing. **2.** A mutual promise to marry; an engagement.

be·trothed (bĭ-trŏthd′, -trôtht′) n. A person who is engaged to be married.

bet·ter¹ (bĕt′ər) adj. Comparative of **good. 1.** —Used to indicate a higher degree of excellence or quality: *Which of you is the better skater?* Also used adverbially (as the comparative of **well**): *type better than her.* **2.** —Used to indicate a higher degree of appropriateness or suitability: *This style is better on you than the other.* **3.** —Used to indicate higher social standing or respectability: *In politics, the better element constituted his ultimate strength.* **4.** —Used to indicate an improved condition: *Better roads helped transportation to move forward.* **5.**—Used to indicate the greater portion of something specified: *waiting the better part of an hour.* —*adv.* Comparative of **well. 1.** More: *averaging a shade better than 20 miles per gallon.* **2.** In a superior manner: *With a larger brain, you are better able to think and to do things.* **3.** More commonly: *Thomas Jackson, better known as "Stonewall" Jackson.* **4.** To a larger degree: *The pine trees are better adapted to this environment.* **5.** More fully: *Better than any other businessman of his time, he saw the future of railroads.* **6.** —Used as an auxiliary in informal speech: *You better stay here.* —*tr.v.* **1.** To surpass or exceed: *failed to better the high jump record.* **2.** To improve (oneself): *teaching the poor to better themselves.* —*n.* **1.** The superior of two: *Which is the better?* **2. betters.** One's superiors. —*idioms.* **better off. 1.** Comparative of **well off:** *Working people are better off today than they were thirty years ago.* **2.** Better advised: *Although married, she would be better off filing a separate tax return.* **had better.** Ought to: *We had better be leaving now.* **know better than.** To know well enough not to. —See Usage note at **best.** [Middle English *bettre,* from Old English *betera.*]

bet·ter² (bĕt′ər) n. Var. of **bettor.**

bet·ter·ment (bĕt′ər-mənt) n. **1.** An improvement. **2.** Often **betterments.** Any improvement, excluding simple repairs, that adds to the value of real property.

bet·tor (bĕt′ər) n. Also **bet·ter.** A person who bets.

be·tween (bĭ-twēn′) prep. **1.** —Used to indicate: **a.** Spatial separation: *There was only five feet between the houses.* **b.** Intermediate state or interval: *I napped between classes.* **c.** Position or motion of something enclosed by specified things on either side: *flood waters were flowing between the banks.* **2.** —Used to indicate: **a.** Reciprocal action of two or more persons or groups: *Decide between you who will stay with the baby.* **b.** Spatial connection: *a canal between Chicago and La Salle.* **3.** —Used to indicate: **a.** Re-

lation of difference or comparison: *not much to choose between the two cars.* **b.** Relation of quantity or degree: *There are between thirteen and fourteen hundred minerals in the earth's crust.* —*adv.* In an intermediate space, position, or time: *New York, Albany, and several stations between.* —*Note: Between* is often used preceded by *in* to form the adverbial group **in between.** In an intermediate space, position, or time. —*idiom.* **between you and me.** Confidentially. [Middle English *betwene,* from Old English *betwēonum.*]

Usage: **1. between, among.** The preposition *between* is typically followed by words representing two entities: *arguments between the two of them; a treaty between China and Russia. Among* is typically followed by words representing more than two entities: *arguments among the four of them; a war among several countries.* However, *between* also can be used to indicate an interrelationship affecting more than two entities when they are considered as individuals rather than as a group: *commutes between New York, Chicago, and Philadelphia.* **2. between. . .and.** When *between* is used with two objects, *and* is the proper conjunction linking those objects: *choose between wealth and poverty.* (not *wealth or poverty*). **3. between each, every.** *Between* can be used with *each* and *every* followed by singular nouns: *a short intermission between each act; tissue paper between every sweater.* This construction has been used by many great writers including William Shakespeare and Charles Dickens. **4. between you and me.** Since *between* is a preposition, its object must be in the objective case. Thus, in this construction, the second pronoun is *me* (objective case), not *I* (subjective case).

be·twixt (bĭ-twĭkst′) prep. & adv. *Archaic.* Between. —*idiom.* **betwixt and between.** In an intermediate or middle position; neither wholly one nor the other. [Middle English *betwix(te),* from Old English *betwēohs, betwihs.*]

bev·el (bĕv′əl) n. **1.** The angle of a line or surface that meets another at any angle but 90 degrees. **2.** A rule with an adjustable arm, used to measure or draw angles or to fix a surface at an angle. —*adj.* Inclined at an angle; slanted. —*modifier: a bevel edge.* —v. **-eled** or **-elled, -el·ing** or **-el·ling.** —*tr.v.* To cut a bevel (on something): *bevel the edge of the shelf.* —*intr.v.* To be inclined; to slope. [From Old French *baif,* open-mouthed, from *bayer,* to gape.]

bevel gear. Either of a pair of gears with teeth surfaces cut so that the gear shafts are not parallel.

bev·er·age (bĕv′ər-ij, bĕv′rĭj) n. Any of various liquid refreshments, usu. other than water. [Middle English *beverege,* from Old French *bevrage,* from Latin *bibere,* to drink.]

bev·y (bĕv′ē) n., pl. **-ies. 1.** A group of animals or birds, esp. larks or quail; a flock. **2.** A group or assemblage: *a bevy of schoolchildren.* [Middle English.]

be·wail (bĭ-wāl′) tr.v. To express sorrow; cry or complain about. —*intr.v.* To wail or lament.

be·ware (bĭ-wâr′) v. **-wared, -war·ing.** —*tr.v.* To be on guard against; be cautious of: *Beware the approach of strangers.* —*intr.v.* To be wary or careful: *Beware of suspicious-looking people.* [Middle English *be war* : *be* (imper.) + *war(e),* wary.]

be·wil·der (bĭ-wĭl′dər) tr.v. To confuse or befuddle, esp. with numerous conflicting situations, objects, or statements. —See Syns at **confuse.** [BE- + archaic *wilder,* to stray.] —**be·wil′der·ment** n.

be·witch (bĭ-wĭch′) tr.v. **1.** To place under one's power by magic; cast a spell over. **2.** To captivate completely; fascinate; charm. —See Syns at **charm.** [Middle English *bewicchen* : *be-,* thoroughly + *wicchen,* to bewitch, from Old English *wiccian.*] —**be·witch′ing·ly** adv.

be·wray (bĭ-rā′) tr.v. *Archaic.* To disclose, esp. inadvertently; betray. [Middle English *bewreien* : *be-,* thoroughly + *wreien,* to accuse, from Old English *wrēgan.*]

bey (bā) n. **1.** A provincial governor in the Ottoman Empire. **2.** A native ruler of the former kingdom of Tunis. **3.** A Turkish title of respect. [Turkish, prince, lord, gentleman.]

be·yond (bē-ŏnd′, bĭ-yŏnd′) prep. **1.** On the far side of: *A bird called sadly in the forest beyond the hut.* Also used adverbially: *We drove through an archway of trees into* *the bright sunlight beyond.* **2.** Farther than the limit of: *Place a ruler on the top edge of a desk so that half of it sticks out beyond the desk.* **3.** After (a specified time): *No papers will be accepted beyond this deadline.* **4.** Outside the reach or scope of: *beyond hope; beyond recall.* **—idiom. beyond (one).** Outside one's comprehension: *It's beyond me how he could have done this.* [Middle English *beyonde,* from Old English *begeondan* : *be,* by + *geondan,* farther, from *geond,* yonder.]

bez·el (bĕz'əl) *n.* Also **bez·il. 1.** A slanting edge on various cutting tools. **2.** The facets or sides of a cut gem, esp. the exposed area above the girdle or setting. **3.** A groove or flange designed to hold the edge of a watch crystal in place. [Orig. unknown.]

be·zique (bə-zēk') *n.* A card game similar to pinochle, played with a deck of 64 cards. [French *bésigue.*]

Bha·ga·vad-Gi·ta (bŭg'ə-vəd-gē'tə) *n.* A sacred Hindu text in the form of a dialogue that is incorporated into the *Mahabharata,* an ancient Sanskrit epic. [Sanskrit *Bhagavadgītā,* "Song of the Blessed One."]

bhang (băng) *n.* **1.** A hemp plant. **2.** Any of several narcotics made from dried leaves and flowers; hemp. [Hindi *bhāng,* from Sanskrit *bhangā,* hemp.]

bi- or **bin-.** A prefix meaning: **1. a.** Two: **bipolar, binaural. b.** At intervals of two: **bicentennial. 2.** Twice during: **biweekly.** [Latin *bi-, bin-,* from *bis,* twice.]

Bi The symbol for the element bismuth.

bi·a·ly (bē-ä'lē) *n., pl.* **-lys.** A flat, round baked roll topped with onion flakes. [After Bialystok, Poland.]

bi·an·nu·al (bī-ăn'yōō-əl) *adj.* Happening twice each year; semiannual. **—bi·an'nu·al·ly** *adv.*

> **Usage: biannual, biennial.** *Biannual,* the equivalent of *semiannual,* means twice a year: *a biannual meeting. Biennial* means once every two years: *biennial bulbs.* See Also Usage note at **biyearly.**

bi·as (bī'əs) *n.* **1.** A line cutting diagonally across the grain of fabric. **2.** Preference or inclination, esp. one that inhibits impartial judgment; prejudice. **3. a.** A weight or irregularity in a ball that causes it to swerve, as in lawn bowling. **b.** The tendency of such a ball to swerve. **4.** The fixed voltage applied to an electrode. **—adj.** Slanting or diagonal; oblique: *a bias fold.* **—adv.** Obliquely; aslant. **—tr.v. bi·ased** or **bi·assed, bi·as·ing** or **bi·as·sing.** To cause to have a prejudiced view; to prejudice or influence. [From Old French *biais,* oblique.]

bi·ax·i·al (bī-ăk'sē-əl) *adj.* Having two axes. **—bi·ax'i·al'i·ty** (-ăl'ĭ-tē) *n.* **—bi·ax'i·al·ly** *adv.*

bib (bĭb) *n.* **1.** A kind of cloth napkin tied under the chin, worn by small children to protect their clothing during meals. **2.** The part of an apron or pair of overalls worn over the chest. [From Middle English *bibben,* to tipple, drink, perh. from Latin *bibere.*]

bib and tucker. *Informal.* Clothing; outfit.

bib·cock (bĭb'kŏk') *n.* A faucet with a nozzle bent downward.

bi·be·lot (bĭb'lō; *Fr.* bē-blō') *n.* A small decorative object or trinket. [French, from Old French *beubelet,* from *bel,* beautiful, from Latin *bellus,* handsome, fine.]

Bi·ble (bī'bəl) *n.* **1.** The sacred book of Christianity, a collection of ancient writings including the books of both the Old Testament and the New Testament. **2.** The Old Testament, the sacred book of Judaism. **3.** Any book or writings constituting the sacred text of a religion. **4. bible.** Any book considered authoritative in its field: *the bible of French cooking.* [Middle English, from Old French, from Medieval Latin *biblia,* from Greek *biblion,* book, from *biblos,* papyrus, after *Bublos,* Phoenician port from which Egyptian papyrus was exported to Greece.]

Bib·li·cal (bĭb'lĭ-kəl) *adj.* Also **bib·li·cal. 1.** Of or contained in the Bible. **2.** In keeping with or suggestive of the nature of the Bible. **—Bib'li·cal·ly** *adv.*

biblio-. A prefix meaning books: **bibliomania.** [From Greek *biblion,* book.]

bib·li·og·ra·pher (bĭb'lē-ŏg'rə-fər) *n.* **1.** An expert in the cataloguing of printed matter. **2.** A person who compiles a bibliography.

bib·li·og·ra·phy (bĭb'lē-ŏg'rə-fē) *n., pl.* **-phies. 1.** The description and identification of the editions, dates of issue, and authorship of books or other printed material. **2. a.** A

list of the works of a specific author or publisher. **b.** A list of writings relating to a specific subject. **3.** A list of the works cited in or used by a writer in the preparation of a printed work. [BIBLIO- + -GRAPHY.] **—bib'li·o·graph'i·cal** (-ə-grăf'ĭ-kəl) or **bib'li·o·graph'ic** (-ĭk) *adj.* **—bib'li·o·graph'i·cal·ly** *adv.*

bib·li·o·phile (bĭb'lē-ə-fīl') *n.* **1.** A person who loves books. **2.** A book collector. [French, from BIBLIO- + -PHILE.]

bib·u·lous (bĭb'yə-ləs) *adj.* **1.** Given to or marked by convivial drinking. **2.** Very absorbent. [Latin *bibulus,* from *bibere,* to drink.]

bi·cam·er·al (bī-kăm'ər-əl) *adj.* Composed of two legislative houses, chambers, or branches: *a bicameral legislature.* [BI- + Late Latin *camera,* room, chamber.]

bi·car·bon·ate (bī-kär'bə-nāt', -nĭt) *n.* The radical group HCO₃ or a compound, such as sodium bicarbonate, containing it.

bicarbonate of soda. *Chem.* Sodium bicarbonate.

bi·cen·ten·a·ry (bī'sĕn-tĕn'ə-rē, bī-sĕn'tə-nĕr'ē) *n., pl.* **-ries.** A bicentennial. **—bi'cen·ten'a·ry** *adj.*

bi·cen·ten·ni·al (bī'sĕn-tĕn'ē-əl) *adj.* **1.** Happening once every 200 years. **2.** Lasting for 200 years. **—n.** A 200th anniversary or its celebration; bicentenary.

bi·ceps (bī'sĕps') *n., pl.* **biceps.** Any muscle having two heads or points of origin, esp. the large muscle at the front of the upper arm or at the back of the thigh. [From Latin : *bi-,* two + *caput,* head.]

bi·chlo·ride (bī-klôr'īd', -klōr'-) *n. Chem.* Another name for **dichloride.**

bi·chro·mate (bī-krō'māt', -mĭt) *n. Chem.* Another name for **dichromate.**

bick·er (bĭk'ər) *intr.v.* **1.** To engage in a petty quarrel; to squabble. **2.** *Poet.* To flicker; glisten; quiver. **—See Syns at argue. —n.** A petty quarrel; a tiff. [Middle English *bikeren,* to attack.]

bi·cus·pid (bī-kŭs'pĭd) *adj.* Having two points or cusps. **—n.** A bicuspid tooth, esp. a premolar. [BI- + Latin *cuspis,* point, cusp.]

bi·cy·cle (bī'sĭk'əl, -sī-kəl) *n.* A vehicle, usu. designed for one person, consisting of a metal frame mounted upon two wire-spoked wheels, one behind the other. It has a seat, handlebars for steering, and two pedals or a small motor by which it is driven. **—modifier:** *a bicycle shop.* **—intr.v. -cled, -cling.** To ride or travel on a bicycle. [French : *bi-,* two + Greek *kuklos,* circle, wheel.] **—bi'cy·clist** *n.*

bid (bĭd) *v.* For transitive senses 1 & 2: **bade** (băd, bād) or archaic **bad** (băd), **bid·den** (bĭd'n) or **bid, bid·ding.** For remaining senses: **bid, bid, bid·ding. —tr.v. 1. a.** To order; command: *He bid us to come in for dinner.* **b.** To invite to attend; to summon: *We were bidden to the ball.* **2.** To utter (a greeting or salutation): *She bade him goodbye.* **3.** *Cards.* To state one's intention to take (tricks of a certain number or suit). **4.** To offer or propose (an amount) as a price: *I bid ten dollars for the purse.* **—intr.v. 1.** To make an offer to pay or accept a specified price. **2.** To seek to win or attain something; strive: *His slow start bids poorly for a prize.* **—See Syns at command. —phrasal verbs.** In the following phrases the past tense and past participle is **bid. bid fair.** To appear likely; seem. **bid in.** To outbid on one's own property at an auction in order to raise the final selling price. **bid up.** In an auction or card game, to increase the amount bid. **—n. 1. a.** An offer or proposal of a price, as for an item at an auction or for a contract. **b.** The amount offered or proposed. **2.** An invitation, esp. one offering membership in a group or club. **3.** *Cards.* **a.** The act of bidding. **b.** The number of tricks or points declared. **c.** The turn of a player to bid. **4.** An earnest effort: *a bid for first place.* [Partly from Middle English *bidden,* to ask, demand, from Old English *biddan,* and partly from Middle English *beden,* to offer, present, command, from Old English *bēodan.*] **—bid'der** *n.*

bid·da·ble (bĭd'ə-bəl) *adj.* **1.** Worth bidding on: *a biddable whist hand.* **2.** *Archaic.* Docile; obedient.

bid·ding (bĭd'ĭng) *n.* **1.** A demand that something be done; a command. **2.** A request to appear; a summons. **3.** The bids collectively, as at an auction or in playing cards. **—idioms. at the bidding of.** At the service of. **do the bidding of.** To follow the orders of.

bid·dy¹ (bĭd'ē) *n., pl.* **-dies.** A hen; fowl. [Perh. imit.]

BOOKS OF THE BIBLE

Bible translation is one of the world's oldest scholarly activities; the tradition runs back to the 3rd century B.C. As of the present date, at least some book of the Bible has been translated into more than 1,400 languages. Since there are more than 3,000 languages in the world, it is reasonable to assume that the field will continue to expand. English has an uncommonly rich heritage in this respect; since the metrical paraphrases and Gospels of Anglo-Saxon times, the entire book has been translated again and again. The Jewish Publication Society *Holy Scriptures According to the Masoretic Text*, issued in 1916 by a committee of Jewish scholars, is accepted as standard in American Judaism, and its contents are listed here. For Roman Catholics the Douay Version (1582-1610) has for many centuries been the text officially approved for teaching and Church use. To serve two pressing needs facing the Church in the second half of the twentieth century — the need to keep abreast of the times

and the need to deepen theological thought — changes have had to be made. The original texts were re-examined and re-evaluated with the assistance of the pioneer work of the School of Biblical Studies in Jerusalem; the result was the publication in France of *La Bible de Jerusalem* in the early 1960's. The English text of the *Jerusalem Bible*, published in 1966, owes a large debt to the work of the many scholars who collaborated to produce *La Bible de Jerusalem*. The *Jerusalem Bible* has gained wide acceptance in the light of the most recent research in the fields of history, archaeology, and literary criticism. Protestants may use either the King James Bible (or Authorized Version, as it is often called, especially in Great Britain), which appeared in 1611 under the patronage of James I; or they may use the Revised Standard Version (1946-52). The following table presents the contents as listed in the Jerusalem Bible and King James Versions because they have the sanction of general acceptance.

Hebrew Scriptures

Genesis	Joshua	Micah	Zechariah	II Kings	Hosea	Song of Songs	Daniel
Exodus	Judges	Nahum	Malachi	Isaiah	Joel	Ruth	Ezra
Leviticus	I Samuel	Habakkuk	Psalms	Jeremiah	Amos	Lamentations	Nehemiah
Numbers	II Samuel	Zephaniah	Proverbs	Ezekiel	Obadiah	Ecclesiastes	I Chronicles
Deuteronomy	I Kings	Haggai	Job	THE TWELVE	Jonah	Esther	II Chronicles

Old Testament

Jerusalem Version	King James Version	Jerusalem Version	King James Version
Genesis	Genesis	Song of Solomon	Song of Solomon
Exodus	Exodus	Wisdom	
Leviticus	Leviticus	Ecclesiasticus	
Numbers	Numbers	Isaiah	Isaiah
Deuteronomy	Deuteronomy	Jeremiah	Jeremiah
Joshua	Joshua	Lamentations	Lamentations
Judges	Judges	Baruch	
Ruth	Ruth	Ezekiel	Ezekiel
I Samuel	I Samuel	Daniel	Daniel
II Samuel	II Samuel	Hosea	Hosea
I Kings	I Kings	Joel	Joel
II Kings	II Kings	Amos	Amos
I Chronicles	I Chronicles	Obadiah	Obadiah
II Chronicles	II Chronicles	Jonah	Jonah
Ezra	Ezra	Micah	Micah
Nehemiah	Nehemiah	Nahum	Nahum
Tobit		Habakkuk	Habakkuk
Judith		Zephaniah	Zephaniah
Esther	Esther	Haggai	Haggai
Job	Job	Zechariah	Zechariah
Psalms	Psalms	Malachi	Malachi
Proverbs	Proverbs	I Maccabees	
Ecclesiastes	Ecclesiastes	II Maccabees	

New Testament

Matthew	I Corinthians	II Thessalonians	I Peter
Mark	II Corinthians	I Timothy	II Peter
Luke	Galatians	II Timothy	I John
John	Ephesians	Titus	II John
Acts	Philippians	Philemon	III John
	Colossians	Hebrews	Jude
Romans	I Thessalonians	James	Revelation

bid·dy² (bĭd′ē) n., pl. **-dies.** Slang. A garrulous old woman. [Pet form of the name Bridget.]

bide (bīd) v. **bid·ed** or **bode** (bōd), **bid·ed, bid·ing.** —intr.v. **1.** To stay in some condition; remain the same. **2.** To wait; tarry: bide for a while. —tr.v. To await: bide one's time. [Middle English biden, from Old English bīdan.]

bi·en·ni·al (bī-ĕn′ē-əl) adj. **1.** Lasting or living for two years. **2.** Happening every second year. **3.** Having a normal life cycle of two years. —n. **1.** An event that occurs once every two years. **2.** A plant that normally requires two years to reach maturity, producing leaves in the first year, blooming and producing fruit in its second year, and then dying. —See Usage notes at biannual and biyearly. [From Latin biennium, a two-year period : bi-, two + annus, year.] —bi·en′ni·al·ly adv.

bier (bîr) n. A portable stand on which a corpse or coffin is placed prior to burial. [Middle English bere, from Old English bēr, bær.]

biff (bĭf) Slang. —tr.v. To strike or punch. —n. A blow or cuff. [Imit.]

bi·fid (bī′fĭd) adj. Divided or cleft into two parts or lobes; forked. [Latin bifidus : bi-, two + fidere, to split.]

bi·fur·cate (bī′fər-kāt′, bī-fûr′kāt′) v. **-cat·ed, -cat·ing.** —tr.v. To separate into two parts or branches. —intr.v. To separate into two parts; fork. —adj. (bī′fər-kāt′, -kĭt, bī-fûr′kāt′, -kĭt). Forked or divided into two parts. [Medieval Latin bifurcātus, forked, from Latin bifurcus, two-forked.] —bi′fur·cate′ly adv. —bi′fur·ca′tion n.

big (bĭg) adj. **big·ger, big·gest. 1.** Of great size, number, quantity, magnitude, or extent; large: a big country; a big appetite; a big change. **2.** Grown-up. **3.** Pregnant: big with child. **4.** Filled up; brimming over: a heart big with joy. **5.** Prominent in position, wealth, or importance; influential: a big man in the government. **6.** Of great significance; important; momentous: her big chance. **7.** Loud and firm; resounding: a singer with a big voice. **8.** Bountiful; generous: a big person. **9.** Informal. Self-important; boastful; pompous: a big talker. —adv. **1.** Pompously; pretentiously; boastfully: The braggart talks big. **2.** With considerable success: The show went over big. —idiom. **make it big.** Successful: He made it big in Hollywood. [Middle English big, byg, strong, full-grown.] —big′gish adj. —big′ness n.

Syns: big, extensive, good, great, healthy, large, sizable, tidy (Informal) adj. Core meaning: Of considerable size (a big stadium; a big salary increase). See also Syns at generous.

big·a·mist (bĭg′ə-mĭst) n. A person who commits bigamy.
big·a·mous (bĭg′ə-məs) adj. **1.** Involving bigamy. **2.** Guilty of bigamy. —big′a·mous·ly adv.
big·a·my (bĭg′ə-mē) n., pl. **-mies.** The criminal offense of marrying one person while still legally married to another. [Middle English bigamie, from Old French, from bigame, bigamous, from Late Latin bigamus : bi-, two + Greek gamos, marriage.]

big bang. The cosmic explosion that began the universe in the big bang theory.
big bang theory. A cosmological theory holding that the universe originated billions of years ago from the violent eruption of a point source.
Big Dipper. A cluster of seven stars in the constellation Ursa Major, four forming the bowl and three the handle of a dipper-shaped configuration.
big game. 1. Large animals or fish hunted or caught for sport. **2.** Slang. An important objective.
big-heart·ed (bĭg′här′tĭd) adj. Generous; kind. —big′-heart′ed·ly adv. —big′-heart′ed·ness n.
big·horn (bĭg′hôrn′) n. A wild sheep, Ovis canadensis, of the mountains of western North America, that has massive, curved horns in the male. Also called **Rocky Mountain sheep.**
bight (bīt) n. **1.** A loop in a rope. **2.** A bend or curve, esp. in a shoreline. **3.** A wide bay formed by such a bend or curve. [Middle English byght, bend, bay, from Old English byht, bend, angle.]
big·no·ni·a (bĭg-nō′nē-ə) n. A woody vine of the genus Bignonia capreolata of the southeastern United States, that has trumpet-shaped, reddish flowers. [After the Abbé Jean-Paul Bignon (1662–1743), librarian to Louis XV.]

big·ot (bĭg′ət) n. A person rigidly devoted to his or her own group, creed, etc., and who is prejudiced against those holding different views. [French, from Old French, a pejorative term for the Normans.]
big·ot·ed (bĭg′ə-tĭd) adj. Intolerant of other groups, creeds, or opinions; prejudiced.
big·ot·ry (bĭg′ə-trē) n. The attitude or behavior characteristic of a bigot; intolerance; prejudice.
big shot. Slang. An important or influential person.
big time. Slang. The highest level of attainment in a competitive field or profession. —big′-time′ adj.
big top. Informal. **1.** The main tent of a circus. **2.** The circus.
big·wig (bĭg′wĭg′) n. Informal. An important person.
bi·jou (bē′zhoō) n., pl. **-joux** (-zhooz′). **1.** A small, exquisitely made trinket. **2.** Any charming, delicately made thing. [French, from Breton bizou, ring with a stone, from biz, finger.]
bike (bīk) n. A bicycle. —intr.v. **biked, bik·ing.** To ride a bicycle. [Short for BICYCLE.]
bi·ki·ni (bĭ-kē′nē) n. A woman's brief two-piece bathing suit. [French, after Bikini atoll in the Marshall Islands.]
bi·la·bi·al (bī-lā′bē-əl) adj. Phonet. **1.** Pronounced with both lips, esp. the consonants b, p, m, and w. **2.** Pertaining to or having a pair of lips. —n. Phonet. A bilabial sound or consonant.
bi·la·bi·ate (bī-lā′bē-ĭt, -āt′) adj. Bot. Having two lips, as a flower or corolla.
bi·lat·er·al (bī-lăt′ər-əl) adj. **1.** Of or having two sides; two-sided. **2.** Having two sides that correspond point for point. **3.** Affecting or undertaken by two sides equally; reciprocal: a bilateral agreement. —bi·lat′er·al·ism n. —bi·lat′er·al·ly adv.
bil·ber·ry (bĭl′bĕr′ē) n., pl. **-ries. 1.** Any of several shrubby or woody plants of the genus Vaccinium, with edible blue or blackish berries. **2.** The fruit of any of these plants. [Prob. of Scandinavian orig.]
bil·bo (bĭl′bō) n., pl. **-boes.** An iron bar with sliding manacles, formerly used to shackle the feet of prisoners. [Poss. after Bilbao, Spain, famous for its ironworks.]
bile (bīl) n. **1.** Physiol. A bitter, alkaline, yellow or greenish liquid that is secreted by the liver and discharged into the duodenum, and that aids in digestion, chiefly by breaking down fats. **2.** Bitterness of temper; irascibility; ill humor. [French, from Latin bīlis.]
bile duct. The canal through which bile passes from the liver to the gall bladder, in which it is stored, and then into the duodenum.
bilge (bĭlj) n. **1.** The lowest inner part of a ship's hull. **2.** Stagnant water that collects in this part; bilge water. **3.** The bulging part of a barrel. **4.** Slang. Stupid talk; nonsense. —intr.v. **bilged, bilg·ing.** To bulge or swell. [Prob. var. of BULGE.]
bil·i·ar·y (bĭl′ē-ĕr′ē) adj. Of or pertaining to bile.
bi·lin·gual (bī-lĭng′gwəl) adj. **1.** Able to speak two languages with equal skill. **2.** Written or expressed in two languages. —n. A bilingual person. [Latin bilinguis : bi-, two + lingua, tongue.] —bi·lin′gual·ly adv.
bil·ious (bĭl′yəs) adj. **1.** Of, pertaining to, or containing bile. **2.** Of, characterized by, or experiencing gastric disorder caused by a malfunction of the liver or gall bladder. **3.** Of a peevish disposition; sour-tempered. —bil′ious·ly adv. —bil′ious·ness n.
-bility. A suffix indicating quality or state of being: capability. [Middle English -bilite, from Old French, from Latin -bilitās, from -bilis, adjective suffix.]
bilk (bĭlk) tr.v. **1.** To defraud, cheat, or swindle. **2.** To thwart or frustrate. [Perh. a var. of BALK (to refuse to go farther).] —bilk′er n.
bill¹ (bĭl) n. **1.** A list or statement of charges for goods or services: a telephone bill. **2.** A statement or list of particulars, such as a menu. **3.** The entertainment offered by a theater. **4.** An advertising poster or similar public notice. **5.** A piece of legal paper money. **6.** A bill of exchange or a similar commercial note. **7.** A draft of a proposed law presented for approval to a legislative body. **8.** Law. A document presented to a court and containing a formal statement of a case, complaint, or petition. —tr.v. **1.** To give or send a statement of costs or charges to. **2.** To enter

or charge on a statement of costs. **3.** To advertise, announce, or schedule, either by public notice or as part of a program. **—idioms. fill the bill.** *Informal.* To be satisfactory; meet all necessary requirements. **foot the bill.** *Informal.* To pay the complete cost of. [Middle English *bille,* from Norman French, from Medieval Latin *billa,* var. of *bulla,* seal affixed to a document, from Latin, ball, amulet.]

bill² (bĭl) *n.* **1.** The beak of a bird. **2.** A beaklike mouth part, as of a turtle. **3.** The visor of a cap. **—***intr.v.* To touch beaks together. **—idiom. bill and coo.** To kiss and murmur amorously. [Middle English *bile,* from Old English *bile.*]

bill³ (bĭl) *n.* **1.** A billhook. **2.** A spear or similar weapon with a hooked blade and a long handle. [Middle English *bil,* from Old English *bil.*]

bil·la·bong (bĭl′ə-bông′, -bŏng′) *n. Australian.* A channel flowing from the main stream of a river. [Native Australian name : *billa,* river, water + *bong,* dead.]

bill·board (bĭl′bôrd′, -bōrd′) *n.* A structure for the usu. outdoor public display of advertisements.

bil·let (bĭl′ĭt) *n.* **1.** A lodging for troops in a nonmilitary building. **2.** A written order directing that such quarters be provided. **3.** Any assigned quarters. **—***tr.v.* **1.** To quarter (soldiers), esp. in nonmilitary buildings. **2.** To serve (a person) with an order to provide such quarters. [Middle English *bylett,* from Old French *billette,* dim. of *bulle,* document, from Medieval Latin *bulla,* document, bill.]

bil·let-doux (bĭl′ā-dōō′, bĭl′ē-) *n., pl.* **bil·lets-doux** (bĭl′ā-dōōz′, bĭl′ē-). A love letter. [French : *billet,* short note, from Old French *billette,* billet + *doux,* sweet, from Latin *dulcis.*]

bill·fold (bĭl′fōld′) *n.* A folding pocket-sized case for carrying money and personal documents.

bill·hook (bĭl′hŏŏk′) *n.* A long-handled tool with a curved blade, used esp. for pruning and clearing brush.

bil·liard (bĭl′yərd) *n.* A shot in billiards; a carom. [From BILLIARDS.]

bil·liards (bĭl′yərdz) *n. (used with a sing. verb).* **1.** A game played on a rectangular, cloth-covered table with raised, cushioned edges, in which a long, tapering cue is used to hit three small, hard balls against one another or the side cushions of the table. **2.** Any of several similar games, such as one played on a table with pockets. [From French *billard,* bent stick, billiard cue, from Old French, from *bille,* log, from Medieval Latin *billus.*]

bill·ing (bĭl′ĭng) *n.* The relative importance of performers as indicated by the position in which their names are listed on programs, advertisements, etc.

bil·lings·gate (bĭl′ĭngz-gāt′; *Brit.* -gĭt) *n.* Foul-mouthed, abusive language. [After *Billingsgate,* London, famous for its scolding fishmongers.]

bil·lion (bĭl′yən) *n.* **1.** The cardinal number written 1 followed by 9 zeros, usu. written 10⁹. **2.** *Brit.* The cardinal number represented by 1 followed by 12 zeros, usu. written 10¹². **3.** An indefinitely large number. [French : *bi-,* two + *million,* million.]

bil·lion·aire (bĭl′yə-nâr′) *n.* A person whose wealth amounts to at least a billion dollars, pounds, or other monetary units.

bil·lionth (bĭl′yənth) *n.* **1.** The ordinal number one billion in a series. **2.** One of a billion equal parts. **—bil′lionth** *adj. & adv.*

bill of attainder. A former legislative act pronouncing a person guilty of a crime, usu. treason, without trial and subjecting him to capital punishment.

bill of exchange. A written order directing that a specified sum of money be paid to a particular person.

bill of fare. A menu.

bill of health. A certificate given to a ship's master stating whether or not there is infectious disease aboard a ship or in its port of departure. **—idiom. clean bill of health.** *Informal.* A satisfactory report as to condition, esp. when used as a recommendation.

bill of lading. A document listing and acknowledging receipt of goods for shipment.

bill of rights. A formal summary of those rights and liberties considered essential to a people or group of people.

bill of sale. A document certifying that an item of personal property has been formally transferred to a new owner.

bil·low (bĭl′ō) *n.* **1.** A great wave or surge of the sea. **2.** A great rising mass of something: *billows of smoke.* **—***intr.v.* **1.** To surge or roll in billows. **2.** To swell out or bulge: *sails billowing in the wind.* **—***tr.v.* To cause to swell or rise in billows. [From Old Norse *bylgja.*] **—bil′low·y** *adj.*

bil·ly (bĭl′ē) *n., pl.* **-lies.** A short wooden club. Also called **billy club.** [Prob. from the name *Billy,* pet form of *William.*]

billy goat. *Informal.* A male goat.

bi·me·tal·lic (bī′mə-tăl′ĭk) *adj.* **1.** Consisting of two metals. **2.** Of, based on, or employing bimetallism.

bi·met·al·lism (bī-mĕt′l-ĭz′əm) *n.* The use of both gold and silver as the monetary standard of currency.

bi·month·ly (bī-mŭnth′lē) *adj.* **1.** Happening every two months. **2.** Happening twice a month. **—***adv.* **1.** Once every two months. **2.** Twice a month. **—***n., pl.* **-lies.** A publication issued bimonthly.

    ***Usage:* bimonthly, semimonthly.** *Bimonthly* means every two months but it can also mean twice a month. *Semimonthly* means twice a month. Since *bimonthly* is so ambiguous, we suggest that you omit it and use the more specific "every two months" or "twice a month," depending on your intended meaning. For example: *a magazine that came out every two months* (or *twice a month*) rather than *a bimonthly magazine.*

bin (bĭn) *n.* A container or enclosed space for storing food, coal, etc. [Middle English *binne,* from Old English *binn, binne,* basket, crib.]

bin-. Var. of **bi-.**

bi·na·ry (bī′nə-rē) *adj.* **1.** Of or based on the number 2 or the binary numeration system. **2.** Of two different parts or components. **—***n., pl.* **-ries.** Something that is binary, esp. a binary star. [Late Latin *bīnārius,* from *bīnī,* two by two.]

binary digit. Either of the digits 0 or 1, used in representing numbers in the binary numeration system.

binary fission. Fission, esp. of a cell or of an atomic nucleus, that results in just two approximately equal products.

binary numeration system. A system of numeration, based on 2, in which the numerals are represented as sums of powers of 2 and in which all numerals can be written using just the symbols 0 and 1.

binary operation. An operation, such as addition, that is applied to two elements of a set to produce a single element of the set.

binary star. A system made up of two stars orbiting about a common center of mass and appearing as a single object.

billiards

billy goat

bin·au·ral (bī-nôr′əl, bĭn-ôr′əl) *adj.* **1.** Of, having, or hearing with two ears. **2.** Of a system of sound reproduction in which a different sound can be directed to each of the listener's ears. [BIN- + AURAL.]

bind (bīnd) *v.* **bound** (bound), **bind·ing.** —*tr.v.* **1.** To tie or secure, as with a rope: *Bind the pole to a tree.* **2.** To fasten or wrap by encircling with a belt, girdle, etc. **3.** To bandage: *bind a wound.* **4.** To hold or restrain with or as if with bonds: *I'm bound to follow the company policy.* **5.** To compel, obligate, or unite, as with a sense of moral duty: *We're all bound to him by gratitude.* **6.** *Law.* To place under legal obligation by contract or oath: *His contract bound him to the team for two years.* **7.** To hold or employ as an apprentice; to indenture: *He bound his son out to a carpenter.* **8.** To cause to cohere or stick together in a mass: *add water to bind the cement mix.* **9.** To enclose and fasten (a book) between covers. **10.** To furnish with an edge or border for reinforcement or ornamentation: *bind a hem on the skirt.* —*intr.v.* **1.** To tie up or fasten anything. **2.** To be tight and uncomfortable: *The collar binds.* **3.** To become compact or solid; cohere: *Did the mixture bind?* **4.** To be obligatory or compulsory. —*phrasal verb.* **bind over.** *Law.* To hold on bail or place under bond. —See Syns at **tie.** —*n. Informal.* A difficult situation or dilemma. [Middle English *binden,* from Old English *bindan.*]

bind·er (bīn′dər) *n.* **1.** A person who binds books; a bookbinder. **2.** Something used to tie or fasten, such as a cord or rope. **3.** A notebook cover with rings or clamps for holding sheets of paper. **4.** A material used to ensure uniform consistency, solidification, or adhesion to a surface, as the eggs in batter or the gum in paint. **5.** A machine that reaps and ties grain in bundles. **6.** *Law.* A payment or written statement making an agreement legally binding until the completion of a formal contract, esp. an insurance contract.

bind·er·y (bīn′də-rē) *n., pl.* **-ies.** A place where books are bound.

bind·ing (bīn′dĭng) *n.* **1.** The act or process of binding. **2.** Something that binds or is used as a binder. **3.** The cover that holds together the pages of a book. **4.** A strip sewn or attached over or along the edge of something for protection, reinforcement, or ornamentation. —*adj.* **1.** Serving to bind. **2.** Uncomfortably tight and confining. **3.** Having the power to hold to an agreement or commitment; obligatory.

binding energy. 1. The energy released in binding a group of particles into a single system, esp. a group of nucleons into an atomic nucleus. **2.** The work required to remove an atomic electron to an infinitely remote position from its orbit.

bind·weed (bīnd′wēd′) *n.* Any of several trailing or twining plants of the genus *Convolvulus,* with pink or white trumpet-shaped flowers.

binge (bĭnj) *n. Slang.* **1.** A drunken spree or revel. **2.** A period of uncontrolled self-indulgence: *an eating binge.* [Orig. unknown.]

bin·go (bĭng′gō) *n.* A game of chance in which players place markers on a pattern of numbered squares according to numbers drawn and announced by a caller. [Orig. the winner's exclamation.]

bin·na·cle (bĭn′ə-kəl) *n.* The nonmagnetic stand on which a ship's compass case is supported. [Middle English *bitakle,*

from Spanish *bitácula* or Portuguese *bitácola,* from Latin *habitāculum,* little house, from *habitāre,* to dwell, abide, from *habēre,* to have.]

bin·oc·u·lar (bə-nŏk′yə-lər, bī-) *adj.* Of, used by, or involving both eyes: *binocular vision.* —*n.* Often **binoculars.** An optical device, such as a pair of field glasses, designed for both eyes. [BIN- + OCULAR.]

bi·no·mi·al (bī-nō′mē-əl) *adj.* Consisting of or pertaining to two names or terms. —*n.* **1.** *Math.* An expression that is written as a sum or difference of two terms, such as $3a + 2b.$ **2.** *Biol.* A taxonomic plant or animal name consisting of two parts, the first naming the genus and the second naming the species. [BI- + Greek *nomos,* portion, part.]

binomial theorem. A mathematical theorem that specifies the expansion of a binomial to any power without requiring the explicit multiplication of the binomial terms.

bio-. A prefix meaning life or living organisms: **biogenesis.** [Greek, from *bios,* life, mode of life.]

bi·o·as·say (bī′ō-ăs′ā′, -ə-sā′) *n.* Evaluation of a drug by comparison of its effect with that of a standard on a test organism.

bi·o·chem·is·try (bī′ō-kĕm′ĭ-strē) *n.* The chemistry of biological substances and processes. —**bi′o·chem′i·cal** (-ĭ-kəl) *adj.* —**bi′o·chem′ist** *n.*

bi·o·de·grad·a·ble (bī′ō-dĭ-grā′də-bəl) *adj.* Capable of being decomposed by natural biological processes: *a biodegradable detergent.* [BIO- + DEGRAD(E) + -ABLE.]

bi·o·feed·back (bī′ō-fēd′băk′) *n.* A technique in which one seeks to regulate a bodily function thought to be involuntary, as blood pressure, by using an instrument to monitor the function and to signal changes in it.

bi·o·gen·e·sis (bī′ō-jĕn′ĭ-sĭs) *n.* **1.** The theory that living organisms develop only from other living organisms. **2.** The generation of living organisms from other living organisms.

bi·o·ge·og·ra·phy (bī′ō-jē-ŏg′rə-fē) *n.* The biological study of the geographic distribution of plants and animals. —**bi′o·ge′o·graph′ic** or **bi′o·ge′o·graph′i·cal** *adj.*

bi·og·ra·pher (bī-ŏg′rə-fər, bē-) *n.* A person who writes biographies.

bi·o·graph·i·cal (bī′ə-grăf′ĭ-kəl) or **bi·o·graph·ic** (-grăf′ĭk) *adj.* Containing or pertaining to a person's life: *biographical data.* —**bi′o·graph′i·cal·ly** *adv.*

bi·og·ra·phy (bī-ŏg′rə-fē, bē-) *n., pl.* **-phies. 1.** A written account of a person's life; a life history. **2.** Such accounts in general, esp. when considered as a literary form. [New Latin *biographia,* from Medieval Greek : *bias,* life + *graphein,* to write.]

bi·o·log·i·cal (bī′ə-lŏj′ĭ-kəl) or **bi·o·log·ic** (-lŏj′ĭk) *adj.* **1.** Of or pertaining to biology: *the biological sciences.* **2.** Of, caused by, or affecting life or living organisms: *biological processes.* —**bi′o·log′i·cal·ly** *adv.*

biological warfare. Warfare using disease-producing microorganisms, specialized poisons, etc.

bi·ol·o·gist (bī-ŏl′ə-jĭst) *n.* A person who is trained in or specializes in biology.

bi·ol·o·gy (bī-ŏl′ə-jē) *n.* **1.** The scientific study of living things and life processes, including growth, structure, reproduction, and evolution. Among the branches of biology are the sciences of botany, zoology, and ecology. **2.** The life processes of a particular group of living organisms. [BIO- + -LOGY.]

bi·o·lu·mi·nes·cence (bī′ō-lōō′mə-nĕs′əns) *n.* The emission of light by living organisms such as the firefly, various fish, fungi, bacteria, and other organisms. —**bi′o·lu′mi·nes′cent** (-ənt) *adj.*

bi·o·mass (bī′ō-măs′) *n.* The aggregate living matter in a unit area or volume.

bi·ome (bī′ōm′) *n.* A community of living organisms of a single major ecological region.

bi·o·met·rics (bī′ō-mĕt′rĭks) *n.* (*used with a sing. verb*). Also **bi·om·e·try** (bī-ŏm′ĭ-trē). The statistical study of biological data.

bi·o·phys·i·cist (bī′ō-fĭz′ĭ-sĭst) *n.* A person who specializes in biophysics.

bi·o·phys·ics (bī′ō-fĭz′ĭks) *n.* (*used with a sing. verb*). The physics of biological processes. —**bi′o·phys′i·cal** (-ĭ-kəl) *adj.* —**bi′o·phys′i·cal·ly** *adv.*

binnacle

binoculars

bi·op·sy (bī'ŏp'sē) *n., pl.* **-sies.** The study of tissues taken from a living person or organism, esp. in an examination for the presence of a disease. [French *biopsie*: Greek *bios*, life + *opsis*, sight.]

–biosis. A suffix meaning a specific way of living: **symbiosis.** [From Greek *biōsis*, way of life, from *bios*, mode of life.]

bi·o·sphere (bī'ə-sfîr') *n.* The part of the earth and its atmosphere in which living organisms exist. [BIO- + -SPHERE.]

bi·ot·ic (bī-ŏt'ĭk) *adj.* Of or pertaining to living organisms: *plants and animals forming a biotic community.* [Greek *bilotikos*, from *bios*, mode of life.]

bi·o·tin (bī'ə-tĭn) *n.* A colorless crystalline vitamin, $C_{10}H_{16}N_2O_3S$, of the vitamin B complex, found esp. in liver, egg yolk, milk, and yeast. [Greek *biotos*, life + -IN.]

bi·o·tite (bī'ə-tīt') *n.* A dark-brown to black mica, containing iron, potassium, and magnesium, found in igneous and metamorphic rocks. [After Jean Baptiste *Biot* (1774–1862), French physicist.]

bi·par·ti·san (bī-pär'tĭ-zən) *adj.* Of, consisting of, or supported by members of two parties, esp. two major political parties. —**bi·par'ti·san·ism** *n.* —**bi·par'ti·san·ship'** *n.*

bi·par·tite (bī-pär'tīt') *adj.* **1.** Having or consisting of two parts. **2.** Having two corresponding parts, one for each party: *a bipartite treaty.* **3.** *Bot.* Divided into two, almost to the base, as certain leaves.

bi·ped (bī'pĕd') *n.* An animal with two feet. —*adj.* Two-footed. [Latin *bipēs* : *bi-*, two + *pēs*, foot.]

bi·pin·nate (bī-pĭn'āt') *adj.* Having opposite leaflets that are subdivided into opposite leaflets. [BI- + PINNATE.]

bipinnate leaf   **bird of paradise**
George Miksch Sutton

bi·plane (bī'plān') *n.* An early aircraft with two sets of wings, esp. one above and one below the fuselage.

bi·po·lar (bī-pō'lər) *adj.* **1.** Pertaining to or having two poles. **2.** Relating to or involving both of the earth's poles. —**bi'po·lar'i·ty** (-lăr'ĭ-tē) *n.*

birch (bûrch) *n.* **1.** Any of several deciduous trees of the genus *Betula,* common in the Northern Hemisphere, with white, yellowish, or gray bark that can be separated from the wood in sheets. **2.** The hard, close-grained wood of any of these trees. **3.** A rod from a birch tree, used to administer a whipping. —*tr.v.* To whip with a birch rod. [Middle English *birche,* from Old English *birce, beorc(e).*]

bird (bûrd) *n.* **1.** Any member of the class Aves, which includes warm-blooded, egg-laying, feathered vertebrates with forelimbs modified to form wings. **2.** A bird hunted as game. **3.** A target, a clay pigeon. **4.** A shuttlecock. **5.** *Slang.* One who is odd or remarkable. **6.** *Brit. Slang.* A young woman. —*intr.v.* **1.** To observe and identify birds in their natural surroundings. **2.** To trap or shoot birds. —*idiom.* **for the birds.** *Slang.* Objectionable or worthless. [Middle English *byrd, bryd,* young bird, from Old English *brid.*]

bird·bath (bûrd'băth', -bäth') *n.* A wide, shallow basin filled with water for birds to bathe in or drink.

bird·call (bûrd'kôl') *n.* **1.** The song of a bird. **2. a.** An imitation of the song of a bird. **b.** A small device for producing this.

bird dog. 1. A dog used to hunt game birds. **2.** *Slang.* A person who seeks out something for another.

bird·house (bûrd'hous') *n.* **1.** An aviary. **2.** A small box made as a nesting place for birds.

bird·ie (bûr'dē) *n.* **1.** *Informal.* A small bird. **2.** *Golf.* One stroke under par for any hole. **3.** A shuttlecock. —*tr.v.* **-ied, -ie·ing.** To shoot (a hole in golf) in one stroke under par.

bird·lime (bûrd'līm') *n.* A sticky substance smeared on branches or twigs to capture small birds.

bird of paradise. Any of various birds of the family Paradisaeidae, native to New Guinea and adjacent areas, usu. having brilliant plumage.

bird of passage. 1. A migratory bird. **2.** A transient person.

bird of prey. Any of various predatory carnivorous birds such as the eagle or hawk.

bird·seed (bûrd'sēd') *n.* A mixture of various kinds of seeds used for feeding birds, esp. caged birds.

bird's-eye (bûrdz'ī') *adj.* **1.** Patterned with spots thought to resemble birds' eyes: *bird's-eye maple.* **2.** Seen from high above: *a bird's-eye view.*

bi·reme (bī'rēm') *n.* An ancient galley equipped with two tiers of oars on each side. [Latin *birēmis* : *bi-,* two + *rēmus,* oar.]

bi·ret·ta (bə-rĕt'ə) *n.* A stiff square cap that is worn by Roman Catholic clergy and is black for a priest, purple for a bishop, and red for a cardinal. [Italian *berretta* or Spanish *birreta,* from Medieval Latin *birretum,* from Late Latin *birrus,* hooded cloak.]

birth (bûrth) *n.* **1.** The fact of being born; the beginning. **2.** Any beginning or origin: *The birth of the labor movement.* **3.** The act of bearing young; parturition. **4.** Ancestry; parentage: *a man of noble birth.* **5.** Origin; lineage: *a Southerner by birth.* —*idiom.* **give birth to.** To bring into being: *give birth to a girl. Poverty and tyranny gave birth to the revolution.* [Middle English *birth,* from Old Norse *burdhr.*]

birth control. Control of the number of children conceived, esp. by planned use of contraception.

birth·day (bûrth'dā') *n.* **1.** The day of a person's birth. **2.** The anniversary of that day.

birth·mark (bûrth'märk') *n.* A mark or blemish present on the body from birth.

birth·place (bûrth'plās') *n.* The place where someone is born or where something originates.

birth·rate (bûrth'rāt') *n.* The number of births per thousand of a given population in a given interval of time, usu. one year.

birth·right (bûrth'rīt') *n.* A right or privilege to which a person is entitled by birth.

birth·stone (bûrth'stōn') *n.* A jewel associated with a specific month and thought to bring good luck to a person born in that month.

bis·cuit (bĭs'kĭt) *n., pl.* **-cuits** or **biscuit. 1.** A small cake of shortened bread leavened with baking powder or soda. **2.** *Brit.* A thin, crisp cracker of unleavened bread. **3.** Pottery that has been fired once but not glazed. [Middle English *besquite,* from Old French *bescuit*: Latin *bis-,* twice + *coquere,* to cook.]

bi·sect (bī'sĕkt', bī-sĕkt') *tr.v.* **1.** To cut or divide into two equal parts. **2.** *Geom.* To divide (a figure) into two equal parts. —*intr.v.* To split; fork: *The road bisects at the light.* [BI- + SECT.] —**bi·sec'tion** *n.*

bi·sec·tor (bī'sĕk'tər, bī-sĕk'-) *n.* Something that bisects, esp. a straight line, ray, or line segment that bisects an angle or a line segment.

bi·sex·u·al (bī-sĕk'shōō-əl) *adj.* **1.** Of or pertaining to both sexes. **2.** Having both male and female organs; hermaphroditic. —*n.* **1.** A bisexual organism; a hermaphrodite. **2.** A person who is sexually attracted to members of both sexes. —**bi·sex'u·al·ism** or **bi'sex·u·al'i·ty** (-ăl'ĭ-tē) *n.* —**bi·sex'u·al·ly** *adv.*

bish·op (bĭsh'əp) *n.* **1.** A high-ranking Christian clergyman, usu. in charge of a diocese. **2.** A miter-shaped chessman that can move diagonally across any number of unoccupied spaces of the same color. [Middle English *bishop,* from Old English *bisceop,* ult. from Late Latin *episcopus,*

bison

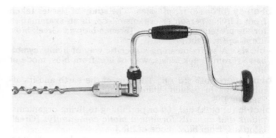

bit drill

from Greek *episkopos,* guardian, overseer: *epi-,* on, over + *skopos,* one who watches.]

bish·op·ric (bĭsh′ə-prĭk) *n.* The office, rank or diocese of a bishop. [Middle English *bisshopriche,* from Old English *bisceoprīce : bisceop,* bishop + *rīce,* realm.]

bis·muth (bĭz′məth) *n. Symbol* **Bi** A white, crystalline, brittle, metallic element used in medicines and esp. in various low-melting alloys. Atomic number 83, atomic weight 208.980, melting point 271.3°C, boiling point 1,560°C, specific gravity 9.747, valences 3, 5. [From German *Wismut.*]

bi·son (bī′sən, -zən) *n.* **1.** A hoofed mammal, *Bison bison,* of western North America, with a dark-brown coat, a shaggy mane, and short, curved horns; buffalo. **2.** A similar, somewhat smaller animal, *B. bonasus,* of Europe; wisent. [Latin *bisōn.*]

bisque (bĭsk) *n.* **1.** A thick, rich soup made from meat, fish, or shellfish. **2.** Any thick cream soup. **3.** Ice cream mixed with crushed macaroons or nuts. [French.]

bis·tro (bē′strō, bĭs′trō) *n., pl.* **-tros.** A small bar, tavern, or nightclub. [French.]

bi·sul·fate (bī-sŭl′fāt′) *n. Chem.* The inorganic acid group HSO_4 or any compound containing it.

bi·sul·fide (bī-sŭl′fīd′) *n. Chem.* A **disulfide.**

bi·sul·fite (bī-sŭl′fīt′) *n. Chem.* The inorganic acid group HSO_3 or any compound containing it.

bit[1] (bĭt) *n.* **1.** A small piece, portion, or amount: *a bit of food in his moustache.* **2.** A brief amount of time; moment: *I'll return in a bit.* **3.** An entertainment routine; an act. **4.** *Slang.* A particular kind of behavior or activity: *do the intellectual bit.* **5.** *Informal.* An amount equal to ⅛ of a dollar. Used only in even multiples: *two bits a head.* **—idioms. bit by bit.** Little by little; gradually. **do one's bit.** To make one's contribution. [Middle English *bit,* from Old English *bita,* piece bitten off, morsel.]

bit[2] (bĭt) *n.* **1.** The sharp part of a tool, as the blade of a knife. **2.** A pointed and threaded tool for drilling and boring that is secured in a brace, bitstock, or drill press. **3.** The part of a key that enters the lock and engages the bolt or tumblers. **4.** The metal mouthpiece of a bridle, serving to control, curb, and direct an animal. *—tr.v.* **bit·ted, bit·ting. 1.** To place a bit in the mouth of (a horse). **2.** To check or control, as if with a bit; curb. [Middle English *bitt,* cutting edge, from Old English *bite,* a sting, bite.]

bit[3] (bĭt) *n. Computers.* **1.** A single character of a language having just two characters, such as either of the binary digits 0 or 1. **2.** A unit of information equivalent to the choice of either of two equally likely alternatives. **3.** A unit of information storage capacity, as of a computer memory. [**B**(INARY) (DIG)IT.]

bit[4] (bĭt) *v.* The past tense and alternate past participle of **bite.**

bitch (bĭch) *n.* **1.** A female dog or other canine animal. **2.** *Slang.* A complaint. *—intr.v. Slang.* To complain; grumble. [Middle English *bicche,* from Old English *bicce,* female dog.]

bite (bīt) *v.* **bit** (bĭt), **bit·ten** (bĭt′n) or **bit, bit·ing.** *—tr.v.* **1.** To cut, grip, or tear with or as if with the teeth: *bite a piece of celery.* **2.** To pierce the skin of with the teeth, fangs, or stinger. **3.** To cut into with a sharp instrument: *The axe bit the tree.* **4.** To grip, grab, or seize: *The wheels bit the gravel as the car pulled out.* **5.** To eat into; corrode. **6.** To cause to sting or smart: *The icy wind was biting my face.* *—intr.v.* **1.** To grip, cut into, or injure something with or as if with the teeth: *The tires won't bite. The baby*

can't bite because he has no teeth. **2.** To have a stinging effect or a sharp taste. **3.** To take or swallow bait: *The fish are biting.* **4.** To be taken in by a ploy or deception. *—n.* **1.** The act of biting. **2.** A wound or injury resulting from biting. **3.** An incisive, penetrating quality: *Her criticism has bite.* **4.** An amount of food taken at one time; mouthful. **5.** *Informal.* A light meal or snack. **6.** A secure grip or hold applied by a tool or machine upon a working surface. **7.** *Dentistry.* The angle at which the upper and lower teeth meet. [Middle English *biten,* from Old English *bītan.*] **—bit′er** *n.*

bit·ing (bī′tĭng) *adj.* **1.** Sharp; cutting; stinging: *biting cold; biting remarks.* **2.** Causing a stinging sensation: *fumes with a biting odor.* **—bit′ing·ly** *adv.*

bitt (bĭt) *n.* A vertical post set on the deck of a ship and used to secure cables. *—tr.v.* To wind (a cable) around a bitt. [Prob. of Low German orig.]

bit·ten (bĭt′n) *v.* The alternate past participle of **bite.** [Middle English *biten,* from Old English *(ge)biten.*]

bit·ter (bĭt′ər) *adj.* **-er, -est. 1.** Having or being a taste that is sharp or unpleasant. **2.** Causing sharp pain to the body or discomfort to the mind; harsh: *a bitter wind; bitter memories.* **3.** Hard to accept, admit, or bear: *the bitter truth.* **4.** Showing or proceeding from strong dislike or animosity: *bitter enemies.* **5.** Resulting from severe grief, anguish, etc.: *cry bitter tears.* **6.** Having or showing a resentful feeling of disappointment: *He was bitter about not being accepted.* [Middle English *bitter,* from Old English *biter.*] **—bit′ter·ly** *adv.* **—bit′ter·ness** *n.*

bit·tern (bĭt′ərn) *n.* Any of several wading birds of the genera *Botaurus* and *Ixobrychus,* similar to the heron, noted for its deep, resonant cry. [Middle English *bitter,* from Old French *butor,* ult. from Latin *būtiō,* bittern + *taurus,* ox, bull.]

bit·ter·root (bĭt′ər-rōōt′, -rŏot′) *n.* A plant, *Lewisia rediviva,* of western North America, that has showy pink or white flowers and a starchy, edible root.

bit·ters (bĭt′ərz) *pl.n.* A bitter, usu. alcoholic liquid made with herbs or roots and used in cocktails or as a tonic.

bit·ter·sweet (bĭt′ər-swēt′) *n.* **1.** A North American woody vine, *Celastrus scandens,* with orange or yellowish fruits that split open to expose seeds enclosed in fleshy scarlet arils. **2.** Also called **nightshade.** A sprawling vine, *Solanum dulcamara,* native to Eurasia, with purple flowers and poisonous scarlet berries. *—adj.* **1.** Bitter and sweet at the same time: *bittersweet chocolate.* **2.** Producing a mixture of pain and pleasure: *bittersweet memories.*

bi·tu·men (bĭ-tōō′mən, -tyōō′-) *n.* Any of various mixtures of hydrocarbons and other substances, occurring naturally or obtained from coal or petroleum, found in asphalt and tar. [Middle English *bithumen,* from Latin *bitūmen.*]

bi·tu·mi·nous (bĭ-tōō′mə-nəs, -tyōō′-, bī-) *adj.* Like or containing bitumen.

bituminous coal. A mineral coal that burns with a smoky, yellow flame, yielding volatile bituminous constituents. Also called **soft coal.**

bi·va·lent (bī-vā′lənt) *adj. Chem.* Having a valence of 2. **—bi·va′lence** *n.*

bi·valve (bī′vălv′) *n.* A mollusk, such as an oyster or clam, with a shell consisting of two hinged parts. *—adj.* **1.** Having such a shell. **2.** Consisting of two similar separable parts.

biv·ou·ac (bĭv′ōō-ăk′, bĭv′wăk′) *n.* A temporary encampment made by soldiers in the field. *—intr.v.* **-acked, -ack·**

ing. To encamp in a bivouac. [French, earlier *biwacht*, prob. from dial. German *biwacht*, "supplementary night watch," from German *Beiwache: bei*, by + *Wache*, watch.]

bi·week·ly (bī-wēk′lē) *adj.* **1.** Happening every two weeks. **2.** Happening twice a week. —*adv.* **1.** Once every two weeks. **2.** Twice a week. —*n., pl.* **-lies.** A publication issued every two weeks.

> *Usage:* **biweekly, semiweekly.** *Biweekly* means every two weeks but it can also mean twice a week. *Semiweekly* means twice a week. Since *biweekly* is so ambiguous, we suggest that you omit it and use the more specific "every two weeks" or "twice a week," depending on your intended meaning. For example: *a magazine that came out once every two weeks* (or *twice a week*) rather than *a biweekly magazine*.

bi·year·ly (bī-yîr′lē) *adj.* **1.** Happening every two years. **2.** Happening twice a year. —*adv.* **1.** Every two years. **2.** Twice a year

> *Usage:* **biyearly, semiyearly.** *Biyearly* means once every two years and as such it is a synonym of *biennial*. *Biyearly* can also mean twice a year, and as such it is a synonym of *biannual*. Since *biyearly* is so ambiguous, we suggest that you omit it and use the more specific "every two years" or "twice a year," depending on your intended meaning. For example: *had a family reunion every two years* (or *twice a year*) rather than *had biyearly family reunions.* See also Usage note at **biannual.**

bi·zarre (bĭ-zär′) *adj.* Strikingly unconventional and far-fetched in manner, style, or appearance; odd; eccentric; grotesque: *a bizarre hat; a bizarre idea.* —See Syns at **fantastic.** [French, orig "handsome," "brave," from Spanish *bizarro*, from Basque *bizar*, beard.] —**bi·zarre′ly** *adv.*

Bk The symbol for the element Berkelium.

blab (blăb) *v.* **blabbed, blab·bing.** —*tr.v.* To reveal (a secret), esp. through careless talk. —*intr.v.* **1.** To talk of secret matters. **2.** To chatter or babble. —*n.* **1.** A person who blabs. **2.** Lengthy chatter. [Middle English *blabben.*]

blab·ber (blăb′ər) *intr.v.* To chatter. —*n.* **1.** Idle chatter. **2.** One who blabs. [Middle English *blabberen.*]

blab·ber·mouth (blăb′ər-mouth′) *n. Slang.* A person who chatters indiscreetly and at length.

black (blăk) *n.* **1. a.** The darkest of all colors; the opposite of white. **b.** Clothing of this color, esp. for mourning. **2.** Often **Black.** Any member of a Negroid people; a Negro. —*adj.* **-er, -est. 1.** Of or nearly of the color black. **2.** Without light: *a black moonless night.* **3.** Often **Black.** Belonging to an ethnic group having dark skin, esp. Negroid. **4.** Gloomy; depressing: *a black day; black thoughts.* **5.** Deserving of or indicating censure or dishonor: *the industry's blackest record as a polluter of the rivers.* **6.** Evil; wicked: *black deeds.* **7.** Angry; sullen: *a black look on his face.* **8.** Served without cream or milk: *black coffee.* **9.** Of or designating a form of humor dealing with the abnormal and grotesque aspects of life and society and evoking a sense of the comedy of human despair and failure. —*tr.v.* **1.** To blacken. **2.** To put black dye, paint, or polish on. —*phrasal verb.* **black out. 1.** To put out or conceal all lights that might help enemy aircraft find a target during an air raid at night. **2.** To lose consciousness temporarily. **3.** To produce or undergo a blackout: *The city was blacked out by the power failure. The government blacked out the news issuing from the rebel provinces.* **4.** To forbid the transmission of (a television program). —*idiom.* **in the black.** Making a profit; prosperous. [Middle English *blak*, from Old English *blæc.*] —**black′ly** *adv.* —**black′ness** *n.*

black-and-blue (blăk′ən-bloo′) *adj.* Discolored from coagulation of broken blood vessels beneath the skin.

black and white. 1. Print or writing: *I got her promise in black and white.* **2.** A picture or photograph in tones of black and white.

black·ball (blăk′bôl′) *n.* **1.** A small, black ball used as a negative ballot. **2.** A negative vote that blocks the admission of an applicant to an organization. —*tr.v.* **1.** To vote against. **2.** To exclude; ostracize.

black bear. Either of two black or dark-brown bears, *Euarctos* (or *Ursus*) *americanus* of North America or *Selenarctos thibetanus* of Asia.

black belt. 1. The rank of expert in a system of self-defense such as judo or karate. **2.** A region of rich soil.

blackberry

black-eyed Susan

black·ber·ry (blăk′bĕr′ē) *n.* **1.** Any of several woody plants of the genus *Rubus*, with canelike, usu. thorny stems and black, glossy, edible berries. **2.** The fruit of any of these plants.

black·bird (blăk′bûrd′) *n.* **1.** Any of various New World birds of the family Icteridae, with black or predominantly black plumage in the male. **2.** An Old World songbird, *Turdus merula*, of which the male is black with a yellow bill. Also called **merle.**

black·board (blăk′bôrd′, -bōrd′) *n.* A panel, once black, now often colored, for writing on with chalk.

black·bod·y (blăk′bŏd′ē) *n. Physics.* A theoretical object that absorbs completely any radiant energy that strikes it.

black box. A usu. electronic device with known performance characteristics but unknown constituents.

black·cap (blăk′kăp′) *n.* **1.** The black raspberry. **2.** Any of various black-crowned birds, such as the chickadee or the European warbler, *Sylvia atricapilla.*

black·en (blăk′ən) *tr.v.* **1.** To make black. **2.** To sully; defame: *blacken one's reputation.* —*intr.v.* To become black or dark. —**black′en·er** *n.*

black eye. 1. A bruised discoloration of the skin around the eye, resulting from a blow. **2.** A severe or critical defeat; bad setback.

black-eyed pea (blăk′īd′). The edible seed of the cowpea.

black-eyed Su·san (soo′zən). Any of several North American plants of the genus *Rudbeckia*, esp. one that has flowers with orange-yellow rays and dark-brown centers.

black·fish (blăk′fĭsh′) *n., pl.* **blackfish** or **-fish·es. 1.** Any of various dark-colored fishes, such as: **a.** A freshwater fish, *Dallia pectoralis*, of far northern regions. **b.** The tautog. **2.** The pilot whale.

black flag. Jolly Roger.

black fly. Any of various small, dark-colored, biting flies of the family Simuliidae.

black grouse. A Eurasian game bird, *Lyrurus tetrix*, of which the male is black with white markings.

black·guard (blăg′ərd, -ärd′) *n.* A low, unprincipled person; scoundrel. —*tr.v.* To abuse or revile. —**black′guard·ly** *adj. & adv.*

black·head (blăk′hĕd′) *n.* A small, dark, oily plug that clogs a pore in the skin.

black·heart (blăk′härt′) *n.* A disease of potatoes and other plants, in which the inner tissues darken.

black hole. A small theoretical celestial body believed to be a collapsed star that has a tremendous gravitational field.

black·ing (blăk′ĭng) *n.* **1.** Lamp black. **2.** A black paste or liquid used as shoe polish.

black·jack¹ (blăk′jăk′) *n.* A small leather-covered club with a short flexible shaft. —*tr.v.* To strike with a blackjack. [BLACK + JACK (tool).]

black·jack² (blăk′jăk′) *n.* A card game in which the object is to accumulate cards with a total count nearer to 21 than that of the dealer. Also called **twenty-one.** [BLACK + JACK (knave in cards).]

black lead. Graphite.

black·leg (blăk′lĕg′) *n.* **1.** *Vet. Med.* An infectious, usu. fatal, gas gangrene that affects sheep and cattle. **2.** A bacterial or fungous plant disease that causes the stems of plants to turn black. **3.** Someone who cheats at cards, esp. a professional gambler; cardsharp. **4.** *Brit.* A strikebreaker; scab.

black light. Any invisible form of light such as infrared, or esp., ultraviolet light.

black·list (blăk′lĭst′) *n.* A list of persons or organizations to be disapproved, boycotted, or suspected of disloyalty. —*tr.v.* To place (a name) on a blacklist.

black lung. A disease, often fatal, of the lungs caused by extensive exposure to coal dust.

black magic. Magic as practiced in league with the Devil; witchcraft.

black·mail (blăk′māl′) *n.* **1.** The extortion of money or something of value from a person by the threat of exposure of something criminal or discreditable about him. **2.** Money or something of value extorted in this manner. —*tr.v.* **1.** To extort money or something of value from (a person) by means of blackmail. **2.** To coerce by means of blackmail. [BLACK + *mail,* tribute, from Middle English *maill,* from Old English *māl,* agreement, from Old Norse *māl.*] —**black′mail′er** *n.*

black market. **1.** The illegal business of buying or selling goods in violation of price controls, rationing, etc. **2.** The place where this trading is carried on.

black·out (blăk′out′) *n.* **1.** The act of putting out or concealing all lights that might help enemy aircraft find a target during a night raid. **2.** A temporary loss of consciousness. **3.** A suppression or stoppage: *a news blackout; an electric-power blackout.* **4.** The act of prohibiting the transmission of a television program in the area adjacent to its place of origin.

black pepper. A seasoning, **pepper.**

Black Power. A cultural and political movement among black Americans that emphasizes racial pride and tries to achieve social equality by creating black political and cultural institutions.

black sheep. A person considered undesirable or disgraceful by his family or group.

black·smith (blăk′smĭth′) *n.* **1.** A person who forges and shapes iron with an anvil and hammer. **2.** A person who makes, repairs, and fits horseshoes. [Middle English *blaksmith,* "a worker in black metal" (iron).]

black·snake (blăk′snăk′) *n.* **1.** Any of various dark-colored, chiefly nonvenomous snakes of North America. **2.** *Western U.S.* A long, tapering, braided rawhide or leather whip with a snapper on the end.

black spruce. An evergreen tree, *Picea mariana,* of northern North America, growing mostly in bogs.

black·thorn (blăk′thôrn′) *n.* A thorny Eurasian shrub, *Prunus spinosa,* with clusters of white flowers and bluish-black, plumlike fruit. Also called **sloe.**

black tie. **1.** A black bow tie worn with a dinner jacket or tuxedo as part of men's semiformal evening clothes. **2.** Semiformal evening clothes for men.

black·top (blăk′tŏp′) *n.* A bituminous material, such as asphalt, used to pave roads. —*tr.v.* **-topped, -top·ping.** To pave with blacktop.

black walnut. **1.** A deciduous tree, *Juglans nigra,* of eastern North America, with dark, hard wood and edible nuts. **2.** The grained wood of this tree, used for cabinetwork.

black widow. A New World spider, *Latrodectus mactans,* of which the poisonous female is black with red markings. [From the fact that the female eats its mate.]

blad·der (blăd′ər) *n.* **1.** *Anat.* Any of various distensible membranous sacs found in most animals in which a gas or liquid is stored, esp. the urinary bladder. **2.** Anything resembling such a sac: *the inner bladder of a football.* [Middle English *bladdre,* from Old English *blǣdre.*]

blad·der·wort (blăd′ər-wûrt′, -wôrt′) *n.* Any of various aquatic plants of the genus *Utricularia,* with violet or yellow flowers, and, in most species, small bladders that trap minute aquatic animals.

blade (blād) *n.* **1.** The flat, sharp-edged part of a cutting instrument, such as a knife, saw, razor, or sword. **2.** The thin, flat part of something, such as an oar, bone, etc.: *a shoulder blade.* **3.** A thin, narrow leaf of a grass or similar plant. **4.** The broad, flattened part of a leaf, extending from the stalk. **5.** The metal part of an ice skate. **6.** A dashing young man: *a gay blade.* [Middle English, from Old English *blæd,* leaf, blade.]

blam·a·ble (blā′mə-bəl) *adj.* Also **blame·a·ble.** Deserving of blame; culpable. —**blam′a·bly** *adv.*

blame (blām) *tr.v.* **blamed, blam·ing. 1.** To hold (someone or something) at fault; to think of as guilty or responsible:

He blamed me for the error. **2.** To find fault with; censure: *I won't blame you if you don't come.* —*n.* **1.** Responsibility or guilt for a fault: *The blame for the accident is mine.* **2.** Condemnation or censure, as for a fault: *not a murmur of approbation or blame, nor the least applause.* —**idiom. be to blame.** To deserve censure; be at fault. [Middle English *blamen,* from Old French *blamer, blasmer,* from Late Latin *blasphēmāre,* to blaspheme.] —**blam′er** *n.*

　　Syns: blame, censure, condemn, criticize, denounce, pan *(Informal),* rap *(Slang)* *v. Core meaning:* To find fault with *(blamed the Administration for the recession).*

blame·a·ble (blā′mə-bəl) *adj.* Var. of **blamable.**

blame·less (blām′lĭs) *adj.* Free from blame; innocent. —**blame′less·ly** *adv.* —**blame′less·ness** *n.*

blame·wor·thy (blām′wûr′thē) *adj.* Deserving blame.

blanch (blănch) *tr.v.* **1.** To remove color from; to bleach. **2.** To whiten (a growing food plant, such as celery) by covering to cut off direct light. **3.** To whiten (a metal) by soaking in acid or coating with tin. **4.** To loosen the skin of (almonds, tomatoes, etc.) by scalding. **5.** To cause to turn pale. —*intr.v.* To turn white or become pale: *blanched in fear.* [Middle English *blaunchen,* from Old French *blanchir,* from *blanc,* white.]

blanc·mange (blə-mänj′; *Fr.* blän-mänzh′) *n.* A flavored and sweetened milk pudding, thickened with cornstarch. [Middle English *blancmanger,* dish of chopped chicken or fish with rice, from Old French, "white food" : *blanc,* white + *mangier,* to eat.]

bland (blănd) *adj.* **1.** Pleasant or soothing in manner; gentle: *a bland smile.* **2.** Free of irritation; soothing: *a bland diet.* **3.** Lacking a distinctive character; mediocre; dull: *a bland speech.* [Latin *blandus,* flattering.] —**bland′ly** *adv.* —**bland′ness** *n.*

blan·dish (blăn′dĭsh) *tr.v.* To coax by flattery; cajole. [Middle English *blandishen,* from Old French *blandir,* from Latin *blandīrī,* from *blandus,* flattering, bland.]

blan·dish·ment (blăn′dĭsh-mənt) *n.* Often **blandishments.** A word or act meant to coax or flatter.

blank (blăngk) *adj.* **1.** Bearing no writing, print, or marking: *blank paper.* **2.** Not finished or filled in: *a blank questionnaire.* **3.** Having no finishing grooves or cuts: *a blank key.* **4.** Expressing nothing; vacuous; vacant: *a blank expression.* **5.** Appearing confused or dazed; bewildered: *a blank stare.* **6.** Devoid of activity or character; empty: *a blank and boring lecture.* **7.** Utter; complete: *a blank refusal.* —*n.* **1.** An empty space; a void: *Her mind is a blank on that subject.* **2. a.** An empty space on a document to be filled in. **b.** A document having one or more such spaces. **3.** An unfinished material, part, or article, such as a key form, stored for eventual finishing. **4.** A gun cartridge with a charge of powder but no bullet. —*tr.v.* **1.** To omit; delete; invalidate: *blank out a passage in a book.* **2.** *Sports.* To prevent (an opponent) from scoring. —**idioms. draw a blank.** To fail utterly, esp. to fail to come up with an idea, answer, or solution. **go blank.** To become suddenly empty or void: *His mind went blank.* [Middle English *bla(u)nk,* white, not written on, from Old French *blanc.*] —**blank′ly** *adv.* —**blank′ness** *n.*

blank check. **1.** A signed check without the amount filled in. **2.** Total freedom of action; carte blanche.

blan·ket (blăng′kĭt) *n.* **1.** A large piece of wool or other thick cloth used as a covering, for warmth, etc., esp. on a bed. **2.** Any thick covering: *a blanket of snow.* —*adj.* Covering a wide range of conditions or requirements: *a blanket insurance policy.* —*tr.v.* To cover with or as if with a blanket: *Snow blanketed the city.* [Middle English, orig., a white woolen material, from Old French *blanquet,* from *blanc,* white.]

blank verse. Verse consisting of unrhymed lines, usu. in iambic pentameter.

blare (blâr) *v.* **blared, blar·ing.** —*intr.v.* To sound loudly and insistently: *The automobile horns blared.* —*tr.v.* To utter or exclaim loudly: *The radio blared the news.* —*n.* A loud, strident noise: *the blare of a siren.* [Middle English *bleren,* to bellow, from Middle Dutch.]

blar·ney (blär′nē) *n.* Smooth, flattering talk.

Blarney Stone. A famous stone located in Blarney Castle, Ireland, supposed to impart great powers of eloquence and persuasion to anyone kissing it.

ă pat　ā pay　â care　ä father　ĕ pet　ē be　hw which　ĭ pit　ī tie　î pier　ŏ pot　ō toe　ô paw, for　oi noise
ōō took　ōō boot　ou out　th thin　*th* this　ŭ cut　û urge　zh vision　ə about, item, edible, gallop, circus

bla·sé (blä-zā′, blä′zā) *adj.* Uninterested, unexcited, or bored because of constant exposure or indulgence. [French *blaser*, to blunt, surfeit, from Middle Dutch *blasen*, to blow up, cause to swell.]

blas·pheme (blăs-fēm′, blăs′fēm′) *v.* **-phemed, -phem·ing.** —*tr.v.* To speak of (God or something sacred) in an irreverent or impious manner. —*intr.v.* To speak blasphemy. [Middle English *blasfemen*, from Old French *blasfemer*, from Late Latin *blasphēmāre*, from Greek *blasphēmein*, from *blasphēmos*, evil-speaking.] —**blas·phem′er** *n.*

blas·phe·mous (blăs′fə-məs) *adj.* Disrespectful and impious: *blasphemous talk.* —**blas′phe·mous·ly** *adv.*

blas·phe·my (blăs′fə-mē) *n., pl.* **-mies. 1.** Any contemptuous or profane act, utterance, or writing, esp. concerning God. **2.** *Theol.* The act of claiming for oneself the attributes and rights of God.

blast (blăst) *n.* **1.** A strong gust of wind. **2.** Any strong rush or stream of air, gas, steam, etc., from an opening. **3. a.** The act of blowing a whistle, trumpet, etc. **b.** The noise made by this. **4. a.** An explosion: *an atomic blast; a blast of dynamite.* **b.** The quantity of explosive used at one time. **c.** The sound of or a sound like an explosion. **5.** Any disease of plants that results in failure of flowers to open or of fruit or seeds to mature. **6.** A violent verbal attack; denunciation. **7.** *Slang.* A big or wild party. —*tr.v.* **1.** To tear to pieces by or as by an explosion; blow up. **2.** To cause to deteriorate; to ruin: *blast one's hopes.* **3.** To make, dislodge, or open (something) by or as by an explosion: *blast a channel through the reefs.* **4.** *Slang.* To attack or criticize vigorously. **5.** *Slang.* To damn: *Blast you!* —*intr.v.* **1.** To detonate explosives. **2.** To emit a sudden loud noise: *Trumpets blasted through the night.* **3.** *Slang.* To attack or criticize with vigor: *He blasted away at the government.* **4.** To wither before flowering or bearing fruit or seeds. **5.** *Slang.* To shoot. —See Syns at **explode.** —*phrasal verb.* **blast off.** To begin flight. [Middle English *blast,* from Old English *blæst.*] —**blast′er** *n.*

blast furnace. Any furnace in which combustion is intensified by a blast of air.

blasto-. A prefix meaning growth, budding, or germination: **blastoderm.** [From Greek *blastos,* bud.]

blas·to·coel or **blas·to·coele** (blăs′tə-sēl′) *n.* The cavity of a blastula. [BLASTO- + -CELE.]

blas·to·derm (blăs′tə-dûrm′) *n.* The layer of cells surrounding the blastocoel. It gives rise to the germinal disc from which the embryo develops in most placental vertebrates. [BLASTO- + -DERM.] —**blas′to·derm′ic** (-dûr′mĭk) *adj.*

blast·off (blăst′ôf′, -ŏf′) *n.* Also **blast-off.** The launching of a rocket or space vehicle.

blas·to·mere (blăs′tə-mîr′) *n.* A cell formed during the cleavage of a fertilized ovum. [BLASTO- + -MERE.] —**blas′to·mer′ic** *adj.*

blas·to·pore (blăs′tə-pôr′, -pōr′) *n.* The mouthlike opening into the primitive intestinal cavity of the gastrula. [BLASTO- + PORE (orifice).]

blas·tu·la (blăs′chōō-lə) *n., pl.* **-las** or **-lae** (-lē′). An early stage in the development of a metazoan embryo, consisting of a hollow sphere surrounded by a single layer of cells. [From Greek *blastos,* bud, germ.] —**blas′tu·lar** *adj.*

blat (blăt) *v.* **blat·ted, blat·ting.** —*tr.v. Informal.* To blurt out. —*intr.v.* To bleat, as a sheep. [Imit.]

bla·tant (blāt′nt) *adj.* **1.** Unpleasantly loud and noisy: *a blatant group of revelers.* **2.** Offensively conspicuous; obvious: *a blatant lie.* [Prob. from Latin *blatīre,* to blab, gossip.] —**bla′tan·cy** *n.* —**bla′tant·ly** *adv.*

> **Usage: blatant, flagrant.** *Blatant* means conspicuous in a loud, offensive way (*blatant huckstering*), whereas *flagrant* means conspicuously objectionable through a shocking violation of propriety (*a flagrant miscarriage of justice*). *Blatant* stresses the way in which a deed is committed, while *flagrant* stresses the nature or effect of the deed.

blath·er (blăth′ər) *v.* Also **bleth·er** (blĕth′ər). —*intr.v.* To talk nonsense. —*tr.v.* To speak foolishly. —*n.* Absurd or foolish talk; nonsense. [Middle English *blether,* from Old Norse *bladhra,* to prattle.]

blath·er·skite (blăth′ər-skīt′) *n.* A babbling, foolish person. [BLATHER + SKATE (fish).]

blaze¹ (blāz) *n.* **1. a.** A brightly burning fire. **b.** A destructive fire. **2.** Any bright or direct light: *the blaze of day.* **3.** A brilliant or striking display: *a blaze of color.* **4.** A sudden outburst, as of activity, emotion, etc.: *horses running in a blaze of speed; the glorious blaze of the Renaissance.* **5. blazes.** Used as an oath: *What in blazes happened?* —*intr.v.* **blazed, blaz·ing. 1.** To burn brightly: *a fire blazing on the broad hearth.* **2.** To shine or shimmer brightly, as with light, heat, etc.: *The sky blazed with stars.* **3.** To be resplendent: *a garden blazing with flowers.* **4.** To show strong emotion: *tempers blazed.* **5.** To shoot rapidly and steadily: *The fighter planes blazed away at the targets.* [Middle English *blase,* from Old English *blæse,* torch, bright fire.]

blaze² (blāz) *n.* **1.** A white spot on the face of an animal. **2.** A mark cut on a tree to indicate a trail. —*tr.v.* **blazed, blaz·ing. 1.** To mark (a tree) by cutting the bark. **2.** To indicate (a trail) by marking trees in this manner. [Prob. from Middle Low German *bles.*]

blaze³ (blāz) *tr.v.* **blazed, blaz·ing.** *Archaic.* To make known; proclaim: *blazed the news.*

blaz·er (blā′zər) *n.* An informal sports jacket, often striped or brightly colored. [Middle English *blasen,* to blow, from Middle Dutch *blāsen.*]

bla·zon (blā′zən) *n.* **1.** A coat of arms. **2.** The heraldic description or representation of a coat of arms. **3.** An ostentatious or showy display. —*tr.v.* **1.** To describe (a coat of arms) in proper heraldic terms. **2.** To paint or depict (a coat of arms) with accurate heraldic detail. **3.** To adorn or embellish with or as if with blazons. **4.** *Archaic.* To announce; proclaim. [From Middle English *blasoun,* shield, coat of arms, from Old French *blason.*]

bla·zon·ry (blā′zən-rē) *n., pl.* **-ries. 1.** The art of describing or representing armorial bearings. **2.** A coat of arms. **3.** Any showy or brilliant display.

bleach (blēch) *tr.v.* **1.** To remove the color from. **2.** To make white or colorless. —*intr.v.* To become white or colorless. —*n* **1.** Any chemical agent used for bleaching, by either oxidation or reduction. **2.** The degree of bleaching obtained. **3.** The act of bleaching. [Middle English *blechen,* from Old English *blæcan.*]

bleach·er (blē′chər) *n.* **1.** Something or someone that bleaches. **2.** Often **bleachers.** An unroofed outdoor grandstand.

bleachers

bleaching powder. Any powder, such as chlorinated lime, used in solution as a bleach.

bleak (blēk) *adj.* **-er, -est. 1.** Exposed to the elements; unsheltered; barren: *bleak moors.* **2.** Cold and cutting; harsh: *a bleak winter wind.* **3.** Dreary and somber: *a bleak prognosis.* —See Syns at **gloomy.** [Middle English *bleike,* pale, from Old Norse *bleikr,* shining, white.] —**bleak′ly** *adv.* —**bleak′ness** *n.*

blear (blîr) *tr.v.* **1.** To blur (the eyes) with or as with tears. **2.** To blur; dim; obscure. —*adj.* Bleary; indistinct. [Middle English *bleren,* prob. of Low German orig.]

blear-eyed (blîr′īd′) *adj.* Var. of **bleary-eyed.**

blear·y (blîr′ē) *adj.* **-i·er, -i·est. 1.** Blurred or dimmed by or as by tears. Said of the eyes. **2.** Vague or indistinct; blurred: *a bleary memory of the accident.* **3.** Exhausted; worn-out. —**blear′i·ly** *adv.* —**blear′i·ness** *n.*

blear·y-eyed (blîr′ē-īd′) *adj.* Also **blear-eyed** (blîr′īd′). **1.** With bleary eyes. **2.** Dull of mind; groggy.

ă pat	ā pay	â care	ä father	ĕ pet	ē be	hw which	ĭ pit	ī tie	î pier	ŏ pot	ō toe	ô paw, for	oi noise
ŏŏ took	ōō boot	ou out	th thin	*th* this	ŭ cut		û urge	zh vision	ə about, item, edible, gallop, circus				

bleat (blēt) *intr.v.* **1.** To utter the cry of a calf, goat, or sheep. **2.** To utter any similar sound, esp. a whine. —*tr.v.* To utter in a whining voice. —*n.* **1.** The cry of a goat, sheep, or calf. **2.** Any similar sound. [Middle English *bleten,* from Old English *blætan.*] —**bleat′er** *n.*

bleb (blĕb) *n.* **1.** A small blister or pustule. **2.** An air bubble. [Perh. var. of BLOB.]

bleed (blēd) *v.* **bled** (blĕd), **bleed·ing.** —*intr.v.* **1.** To lose or emit blood. **2.** To be wounded in battle. **3.** To feel sympathetic grief or anguish: *My heart bleeds for you.* **4.** To exude sap or similar fluid. **5.** *Slang.* To pay out money, esp. an exorbitant amount: *He bled me on that deal.* **6.** To run or become mixed, as dyes in wet cloth or paper. **7.** *Printing.* To be printed so as to go over the edge or edges of a page. —*tr.v.* **1. a.** To take blood from, esp. as an antique medical practice. **b.** To extract sap or juice from. **2.** To exude (blood, sap, etc.). **3.** To draw or drain liquid or gaseous contents from: *bleed the transmission.* **4.** *Slang.* To obtain or extort money from. **5.** *Printing.* **a.** To print (an illustration, text, etc.) so that it will go over the edge or edges of a page. **b.** To trim (a page, sheet, etc.) too closely so as to mutilate the printed or illustrative matter. —*n.* *Printing.* **1.** Illustrative matter that purposely bleeds. **2.** A page trimmed so as to bleed. [Middle English *bleden,* from Old English *blēdan.*]

bleed·er (blē′dər) *n.* **1.** A hemophiliac. **2.** A person who performs bloodletting.

bleed·ing-heart (blē′dĭng-härt′) *n.* **1.** Any of several plants of the genus *Dicentra,* with pink flowers, esp. *D. spectabilis,* native to Japan. **2.** A person who is excessively sympathetic toward others.

bleeding-heart

blem·ish (blĕm′ĭsh) *tr.v.* To impair or spoil by a flaw; mar. —*n.* A flaw or defect; a stain; disfigurement. [Middle English *blemisshen,* from Old French *blemir, blesmir,* to make pale.]

blench (blĕnch) *intr.v.* To draw back in fear; flinch. [Middle English *blenchen,* to deceive, evade, from Old English *blencan.*]

blend (blĕnd) *v.* **blend·ed** or **blent** (blĕnt), **blend·ing.** —*tr.v.* **1.** To combine or mix so as to make the constituent parts indistinguishable. **2.** To mix (different varieties or grades) so as to obtain a new mixture of some particular quality or consistency: *blend whiskeys.* —*intr.v.* **1.** To form a uniform mixture; intermingle: *These colors blend nicely together.* **2.** To become merged into one; unite: *"Evil dreams and evil waking were blended into a long tunnel of misery"* (J.R.R. Tolkien). **3.** To pass imperceptibly into one another; harmonize: *The chameleon blends in with its surroundings.* —*n.* **1.** Something blended: *a different blend of coffee.* **2.** *Ling.* A word produced by combining parts of other words, such as *smog,* from *smoke* and *fog.* [Middle English *blenden,* from Old Norse *blanda.*]

blended whiskey. Whiskey that is a blend of whiskeys or of whiskey and neutral spirits.

blend·er (blĕn′dər) *n.* **1.** Someone or something that combines or blends. **2.** An electrical appliance with whirling blades, used esp. in cooking.

blen·ny (blĕn′ē) *n., pl.* **-nies.** Any of numerous small, elongated saltwater fishes, chiefly of the families Blenniidae and Clinidae. [Latin *blennius,* from Greek *blennos,* "slime" (from the slimy coating on its scales).]

blent (blĕnt) *v.* A past tense and past participle of **blend.**

bless (blĕs) *tr.v.* **blessed** or **blest** (blĕst), **bless·ing.** **1.** To make holy by religious rite; sanctify. **2.** To honor as holy; glorify: *Bless the Lord.* **3.** To invoke divine favor upon: *The rabbi blessed the young couple.* **4.** To confer well-being or prosperity upon. **5.** To endow or favor, as with talent. **6.** To make the sign of the cross over. **7.** To preserve from evil. Used as an exclamation: *Bless my soul!* [Middle English *blessen,* from Old English *blētsian, blædsian,* "to hallow with blood."]

bless·ed (blĕs′ĭd) *adj.* Also **blest** (blĕst). **1.** Made sacred by a religious rite; consecrated: *a blessed relic.* **2.** Worthy of respect or worship. **3.** Enjoying happiness; fortunate. **4.** Bringing happiness or bliss: *a blessed event.* **5.** *Rom. Cath. Ch.* Enjoying the bliss of heaven, as the beatified. **6.** Used as an intensive: *not a blessed dime.* —**bless′ed·ly** *adv.* —**bless′ed·ness** *n.*

Blessed Virgin. The Virgin Mary.

bless·ing (blĕs′ĭng) *n.* **1. a.** The act of one who blesses. **b.** The prescribed words or ceremony for such an act. **2.** An expression or utterance of good wishes. **3.** A special favor granted by God. **4.** Anything promoting or contributing to happiness, well-being, or prosperity; a boon. **5.** Approbation; approval: *This plan has my blessing.* **6.** A short prayer before or after a meal.

blest (blĕst) *v.* A past tense and a past participle of **bless.** —*adj.* Var. of **blessed.**

bleth·er (blĕth′ər) *v. & n.* Var. of **blather.**

blew (bloo) *v.* Past tense of **blow.** [Middle English, from Old English *blēw.*]

blight (blīt) *n.* **1.** Any of several plant diseases that wither leaves or growing tips or kill an entire plant. **2.** An environmental condition that injures or kills plants or animals, as air pollution. **3.** Something that withers hopes, impairs growth, or halts prosperity. **4.** The condition or result of being blighted. —*tr.v.* **1.** To cause decay; ruin: *Drought blighted the crops.* **2.** To frustrate: *a mishap that blighted his hopes.* —*intr.v.* To suffer blight. [Orig. unknown.]

blimp (blĭmp) *n.* A nonrigid, buoyant aircraft. [Orig. unknown.]

blind (blīnd) *adj.* **-er, -est. 1.** Without the sense of sight; sightless. **2.** Performed without the use of sight: *blind*

blimp
The aircraft

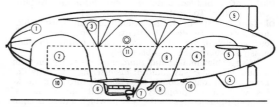

COMPONENTS OF AN AIRSHIP
1. Nose Cone Battens (supports)
2. Forward Ballonet (air bag inside envelope)
3. Catenary Curtain and Suspension Cables (inside envelope)
4. Aft Ballonet
5. Control Surfaces (rudders and elevators)
6. Car — Passenger Compartment
7. Engines
8. Night Sign Lamps
9. Air Scoops (channel air to ballonets)
10. Air Valves (regulate air in ballonets)
11. Helium Valve

blimp
Model drawing

navigation. **3.** Unwilling or unable to perceive or understand: *She was blind to his faults.* **4.** Not based on reason or evidence: *blind faith.* **5.** Without forethought or reason: *in a blind rage.* **6.** Hidden or screened from sight: *a blind intersection.* **7.** Closed at one end: *a blind alley.* **8.** Having no opening: *a blind wall.* **9.** *Informal.* Drunk. —*n.* **1.** Something that shuts out light or hinders vision, as on windows. **2.** A shelter for concealing hunters. **3.** Something that conceals the true nature of an activity, esp. of an illegal or improper one; a subterfuge. —*adv.* **1.** Without being able to see; blindly: *fly blind.* **2.** *Informal.* Into a stupor: *They drank themselves blind.* —*tr.v.* **1.** To deprive of sight. **2.** To deprive (a person) of judgment or reason: *Greed blinded him to the danger.* **3.** To dazzle. [Middle English *blind,* from Old English *blind,* blind, obscure.] —**blind′ly** *adv.* —**blind′ness** *n.*

blind·ers (blīn′dərz) *pl.n.* Either of two leather flaps attached to a horse's bridle to curtail side vision. Also called **blinkers.**

blind·fold (blīnd′fōld′) *tr.v.* **1.** To cover the eyes with or as if with a cloth. **2.** To hamper the sight or comprehension of; mislead; delude. —*n.* A piece of cloth put over the eyes to keep someone from seeing. [Middle English *blindfolde,* past part. of *blindfellen,* to strike blind, from Old English *geblindfellian* : *geblind,* blind + *fellan,* to strike down, fell.]

blind·man's buff (blīnd′mănz′). A game in which one person, blindfolded, tries to catch and identify one of the other players. [*Buff,* short for BUFFET (a blow).]

blind spot. **1.** *Anat.* The small area, insensitive to light, where the optic nerve enters the retina of the eye. **2.** A place that has poorer radio reception than the area surrounding it. **3.** Any part of an area that cannot be observed directly. **4.** A subject about which a person is noticeably ignorant or prejudiced.

blind·worm (blīnd′wûrm′) *n.* A lizard, the slowworm.

blink (blĭngk) *intr.v.* **1.** To close and open one or both eyes rapidly. **2.** To flash on and off; glimmer. —*tr.v.* **1.** To close and open (the eyes or an eye) rapidly. **2.** To signal (a message) with a flashing light. —*phrasal verb.* **blink at.** **1.** To consciously ignore; pretend not to see. **2.** To become startled or dismayed: *I could only blink at the story he told.* —*n.* **1.** A brief closing of the eyes. **2.** A quick look or glimpse; a glance. **3.** A flash of light; a gleam. —*idiom.* **on the blink.** Out of order. [Middle English *blinken.*]

blink·er (blĭng′kər) *n.* **1.** A light that blinks in order to convey a signal. **2.** *Slang.* An eye. **3. blinkers. a.** Goggles. **b.** Another name for **blinders.**

blintz (blĭnts) or **blin·tze** (blĭn′tsə) *n.* A thin, rolled pancake filled with cream cheese or cottage cheese, fruit, or seasoned mashed potatoes, and often served with sour cream. [Yiddish *blintse,* from Russian *blinyets.*]

blip (blĭp) *n.* Anything seen on a radar screen that may indicate that an object has been detected. [Imit.]

bliss (blĭs) *n.* **1.** Extreme happiness; joy. **2.** Religious ecstasy; spiritual joy. [Middle English *blis(se),* from Old English *bliss.*]

bliss·ful (blĭs′fəl) *adj.* Full of or causing bliss. —**bliss′ful·ly** *adv.* —**bliss′ful·ness** *n.*

blis·ter (blĭs′tər) *n.* **1.** A thin, rounded swelling of the skin, containing watery matter, caused by burning or irritation. **2.** A similar swelling on a plant. **3.** An air bubble on a painted surface or in a casting. **4.** A rounded, often transparent structure that projects from an aircraft. —*tr.v.* **1.** To cause a blister or blisters to form upon. **2.** To criticize harshly. —*intr.v.* To form blisters. [Middle English *blester,* poss. from Old French *blestre,* from Middle Dutch *bluyster,* swelling.] —**blis′ter·y** *adj.*

blis·ter·ing (blĭs′tər-ĭng) *adj.* **1.** Hot: *a blistering sun.* **2.** Very strong; intense: *blistering criticism.* **3.** Extremely rapid: *a blistering pace.* —See Syns at **hot.**

blithe (blīth, blīth) *adj.* **-er, -est. 1.** Filled with gaiety; cheerful: *blithe spirits.* **2.** Heedless; casual; carefree: *blithe optimism.* [Middle English *blithe,* from Old English *blīthe.*] —**blithe′ly** *adv.* —**blithe′ness** *n.*

blithe·some (blīth′səm, blīth′-) *adj.* Cheerful; merry. —**blithe′some·ly** *adv.* —**blithe′some·ness** *n.*

blitz (blĭts) *n.* **1. a.** A blitzkrieg. **b.** An intense air raid or series of air raids. **2.** Any intense, swift attack: *a last-min-*

ute *campaign blitz.* **3.** *Football.* A rushing of the passer by the defensive team. —*tr.v.* To subject to a blitz. [From BLITZKRIEG.]

blitz·krieg (blĭts′krēg′) *n.* **1.** A swift, sudden military attack, usu. by air and land forces. **2.** Any swift, concerted effort. Also called **blitz.** [German *Blitzkrieg,* "lightning war:" *Blitz,* lightning + *Krieg,* war.]

bliz·zard (blĭz′ərd) *n.* **1.** A violent windstorm accompanied by intense cold and driving snow. **2.** A very heavy snowstorm with high winds. [Orig. unknown.]

bloat (blōt) *tr.v.* **1.** To cause to swell up or inflate, as with liquid or gas. **2.** To puff up, as with vanity. **3.** To cure (fish) by soaking in brine and half-drying in smoke. —*intr.v.* To become swollen or inflated. [From *bloat,* swollen, earlier *blowt,* soft, flabby, from Middle English *blout,* prob. from Old Norse *blautr,* soft, wet.]

bloat·er (blō′tər) *n.* A herring lightly smoked and salted.

blob (blŏb) *n.* **1.** A soft, formless mass: *a blob of wax.* **2.** A shapeless splotch of color. [Middle English, bubble (imit.).]

bloc (blŏk) *n.* A group of persons, states, or nations, united geographically or by common interests or political aims: *the Communist bloc; the farm bloc in Congress.* [French, from Old French, block.]

block (blŏk) *n.* **1.** A solid piece of wood or other hard substance having one or more flat sides. **2. a.** Such a piece on which chopping or cutting is done. **b.** Such a piece upon which persons are beheaded. **3.** A stand from which articles are displayed at an auction. **4.** A mold or form upon which something is shaped or displayed: *a hat block.* **5.** A pulley or set of pulleys set in a casing. **6.** The metal casing that contains the cylinders of an engine. **7.** A set of like items sold or handled as a unit: *blocks of tickets.* **8.** An obstacle or hindrance. **9. a.** A section of a city or town enclosed by four intersecting streets. **b.** That part of a street which lies between two successive cross streets. **10.** A large building divided into separate units, such as apartments. **11.** A length of railroad track controlled by one set of signals. **12.** *Sports.* An act of obstructing an opponent, esp. in football, a legal act of using one's body to obstruct an opponent and thus protect the teammate who has the ball. **13.** *Med.* Interruption, esp. obstruction, of a neural, digestive, or other physiological process. **14.** *Psychol.* Sudden cessation of a thought ·process without an immediate observable cause, sometimes considered a consequence of repression. **15.** *Slang.* A person's head. —*tr.v.* **1.** To support, strengthen, or retain in place by means of a block or blocks. **2.** To shape, mold, or form with or on a block: *block a hat.* **3.** To stop or impede the passage of or movement through; hinder or obstruct: *block traffic.* **4.** *Sports.* To impede the movement of (one's opponent or the ball) by means of physical interference. **5.** *Med.* To interrupt the proper functioning of (a physiological process). **6.** *Psychol.* To fail to remember; suppress. —*intr.v. Sports.* To obstruct the movement of an opponent. —*phrasal verb.* **block out.** To plan or project broadly without details. —*idiom.* **on the block.** Up for sale, esp. at an auction. [Middle English *blok(ke),* from Old French *bloc,* from Middle Dutch *blok,* trunk of a tree.] —**block′er** *n.*

block·ade (blŏ-kād′) *n.* **1.** The closing off of a city, coast, harbor, or other area to traffic and communication by troops or warships. **2.** The forces employed to close such an area. —*tr.v.* **-ad·ed, -ad·ing.** To set up a blockade against. [From BLOCK (after AMBUSCADE).] —**block·ad′er** *n.*

block·ade-run·ner (blŏ-kād′rŭn′ər) *n.* A ship or person that goes through or past a blockade.

block·age (blŏk′ĭj) *n.* **1.** The act of blocking or obstructing. **2.** An obstruction: *a blockage in the pipe.*

block and tackle. An apparatus of pulley blocks and ropes or cables used for hauling and hoisting.

block·bust·er (blŏk′bŭs′tər) *n. Informal.* **1.** A bomb capable of destroying a city block. **2.** Anything extremely impressive or startling.

block·head (blŏk′hĕd′) *n.* A stupid person.

block·house (blŏk′hous′) *n.* **1.** A fortification made of heavy timbers or concrete, with a projecting upper story and loopholes for firing. **2.** A heavily reinforced building from which the launching of rockets or space vehicles is observed and controlled.

ă pat	ā pay	â care	ä father	ĕ pet	ē be	hw which	ĭ pit	ī tie	î pier	ŏ pot	ō toe	ô paw, for	oi noise
ŏŏ took	ōō boot	ou out	th thin	th this	ŭ cut		û urge	zh vision	ə about, item, edible, gallop, circus				

block·ish (blŏk'ĭsh) *adj.* Stupid; dull.
block letter. **1.** A letter printed or written sans serif. **2.** *Printing.* A sans-serif style of type.
bloke (blōk) *n. Brit. Slang.* A fellow; man. [Orig. unknown.]
blond (blŏnd) *adj.* **-er, -est. 1.** Having fair hair and skin: *a blond boy.* **2.** Light-colored: *blond hair; blond furniture.* —*n.* A blond man or boy. [Old French, prob. of Germanic orig.] —**blond'ish** *adj.* —**blond'ness** *n.*
   Usage: **blond, brunet.** As adjectives, these may be applied to both sexes. As nouns they are usu. restricted to males. *Blonde* and *brunette,* as nouns and adjectives, are applied only to females.
blonde (blŏnd) *adj.* **blond·er, blond·est.** Having fair hair and skin: *a blonde girl.* —*n.* A blonde woman or girl.
blood (blŭd) *n.* **1.** The fluid circulated by the heart in a vertebrate, carrying oxygen, nutrients, hormones, etc., throughout the body and waste materials to excretory organs. **2.** A functionally similar fluid in an invertebrate. **3.** A fluid resembling blood, such as the juice of certain plants. **4.** Life; lifeblood: *Energy is the blood of an industrial nation.* **5.** Bloodshed; murder. **6.** Temperament; temper; disposition: *hot blood; sporting blood.* **7.** Descent from a common ancestor; family relationship; kinship: *related by blood.* **8.** Racial or national ancestry: *Japanese blood.* **9.** Members considered as a class: *the best young blood of the nation.* **10.** A dashing young man; a rake. **11.** Recorded descent from purebred stock. —*modifier: a blood transfusion.* —*adj.* Purebred: *a blood mare.* —*idioms.* **bad blood.** Enmity; hatred. **in cold blood.** Deliberately; coldly. **make (one's) blood boil.** To make extremely angry. **make (one's) blood run cold.** To terrify. [Middle English, from Old English *blōd.*]
blood bank. **1.** A supply of blood plasma or of whole blood for use in transfusions. **2.** A place where a supply of this kind is stored.
blood bath. A savage and indiscriminate killing; a massacre.
blood brother. **1.** Someone who is bound to another by a ceremonial mixing of the blood. **2.** Someone to whom one feels a very close connection.
blood count. A test in which the cells in a sample of a person's blood are classified and counted.
blood·cur·dling (blŭd'kûrd'lĭng) *adj.* Causing great horror; terrifying.
blood·ed (blŭd'ĭd) *adj.* **1.** Having blood or a temperament of a specified kind: *a cold-blooded reptile; a hot-blooded person.* **2.** Of or descending from good stock; thoroughbred: *blooded horses.*
blood group. Any of the four main types, A, B, AB, and O, into which human blood is divided on the basis of the presence or absence of certain antigens. Also called **blood type.**
blood·hound (blŭd'hound') *n.* **1.** A hound with a smooth coat, drooping ears, loose folds of skin around the face, and a keen sense of smell. **2.** *Informal.* Any relentless pursuer.

bloodhound   bloomers

blood·less (blŭd'lĭs) *adj.* **1.** Pale and anemic in color. **2.** Accomplished without killing: *a bloodless revolution.* **3.** Lacking spirit; dull. **4.** Cold-hearted.
blood·let·ting (blŭd'lĕt'ĭng) *n.* **1.** The bleeding of a vein as a therapeutic measure. **2.** Bloodshed.

blood·line (blŭd'līn') *n.* Direct line of descent, esp. of animals; pedigree.
blood·mo·bile (blŭd'mə-bēl') *n.* A motor vehicle equipped for collecting blood from donors.
blood money. **1.** Money paid as compensation to the next of kin of a murder victim. **2.** Money paid to a hired killer. **3.** Money gained at the cost of another's life or livelihood.
blood plasma. The pale-yellow or gray-yellow, protein-containing fluid portion of the blood in which the corpuscles are normally suspended; plasma.
blood platelet. A constituent of blood, a platelet.
blood poisoning. A condition in which the blood contains poisons or poison-producing bacteria.
blood pressure. The pressure that the blood exerts on the walls of the arteries or other blood vessels, primarily maintained by contraction of the left ventricle.
blood pudding. A sausage made from cooked pig's blood and suet.
blood·shed (blŭd'shĕd') *n.* The shedding of blood, esp. the injuring or killing of human beings.
blood·shot (blŭd'shŏt') *adj.* Inflamed and overfilled with blood, often with enlarged blood vessels.
blood·stain (blŭd'stān') *n.* A discoloration caused by blood.
blood·stone (blŭd'stōn') *n.* A variety of deep-green chalcedony flecked with red jasper, often used as a gem. Also called **heliotrope.**
blood·stream (blŭd'strēm') *n.* Also **blood stream.** The blood flowing through a circulatory system.
blood·suck·er (blŭd'sŭk'ər) *n.* **1.** Any animal that sucks blood, as a leech. **2.** *Informal.* One who clings to or preys upon another; parasite. —**blood'suck'ing** *adj.*
blood test. A medical examination of a blood sample, esp. to detect illness.
blood·thirst·y (blŭd'thûr'stē) *adj.* Eager to cause or see bloodshed; cruel. —**blood'thirst'i·ly** *adv.* —**blood'thirst'i·ness** *n.*
blood type. Another name for **blood group.**
blood vessel. Any elastic canal, as an artery, vein, or capillary, through which blood circulates.
blood·worm (blŭd'wûrm') *n.* Any of various segmented worms of the genera *Polycirrus* and *Enoplobranchus,* often used for bait.
blood·y (blŭd'ē) *adj.* **-i·er, -i·est. 1.** Bleeding: *a bloody nose.* **2.** Stained with blood: *bloody bandages.* **3.** Of or containing blood. **4.** Causing or marked by bloodshed: *a bloody fight; a bloody dictatorship.* **5.** *Brit. Slang.* Used as an intensive: *bloody fool.* —*adv. Brit. Slang.* Used as an intensive: *bloody well right.* —*tr.v.* **-ied, -y·ing.** To stain, spot, or cover with or as if with blood. —**blood'i·ly** *adv.* —**blood'i·ness** *n.*
bloody mar·y (mâr'ē). Also **Bloody Mar·y.** A drink made with vodka, tomato juice, and seasonings.
bloom¹ (blōōm) *n.* **1.** The flower or blossoms of a plant. **2.** The condition or time of being in flower: *a rose in bloom.* **3.** A condition or time of great development, vigor, or beauty; prime: *Humanism reached full bloom in the Renaissance.* **4.** A fresh, rosy complexion. **5.** *Bot.* A delicate, powdery coating on some fruits, leaves, and stems: *the bloom on a plum.* **6.** A similar coating, as on newly minted coins. —*intr.v.* **1.** To bear flowers: *The magnolia should bloom soon.* **2.** To shine with health and vigor; to glow. **3.** To grow or flourish: *The record industry is blooming.* [Middle English *blom, blome,* from Old Norse *blōm, blōmi.*]
bloom² (blōōm) *n.* **1.** A bar of steel, usu. over 36 square inches in cross section, prepared for rolling. **2.** A mass of wrought iron ready for further working. [Middle English *blome,* lump of metal, from Old English *blōma.*]
bloo·mer (blōō'mər) *n.* **1.** An outfit designed for women in the 19th cent., consisting of baggy trousers gathered at the ankles and worn under a shorter skirt. **2. bloomers. a.** Baggy trousers gathered at the knee, once worn by women and girls for sports, riding bicycles, etc. **b.** Similar pants worn as underwear. [After Amelia *Bloomer* (1818–94), American suffragette.]
bloom·ing (blōō'mĭng) *adj.* **1.** Flowering; blossoming. **2.** Flourishing, as with health, beauty, or vigor. **3.** *Slang.*

Used as an intensive: *a blooming idiot.*

bloop·er (bloō′pər) *n.* **1.** *Baseball.* A short, weakly hit fly ball. **2.** *Informal.* An embarrassing error or mistake. [From *bloop,* sound of such a hit (imit.).]

blos·som (blŏs′əm) *n.* **1.** A flower, esp. of a plant that yields edible fruit. **2.** The condition or time of flowering: *peach trees in blossom.* —*intr.v.* **1.** To come into flower; to bloom. **2.** To develop; flourish: *She blossomed into a beauty.* [Middle English *blosme,* from Old English *blōstma.*] —**blos′som·y** *adj.*

blot (blŏt) *n.* **1.** A spot; a stain: *a blot of ink.* **2.** A stain on one's reputation or character; a disgrace. **3.** Something that detracts from beauty or excellence. —*v.* **blot·ted,** **blot·ting.** —*tr.v.* **1.** To spot or stain. **2.** To bring moral disgrace to. **3.** To dry or soak up with absorbent material. —*intr.v.* **1.** To spill or spread in a blot or blots. **2.** To become blotted; absorb or soak up: *a paper that blots easily.* —*phrasal verb.* **blot out. 1.** To obliterate; cancel: *I will blot out what you did from my mind.* **2.** To make obscure; darken; hide: *clouds blotting out the moon.* **3.** To destroy utterly; annihilate. [Middle English *blot, blotte.*]

blotch (blŏch) *n.* **1.** A spot or blot; a splotch. **2.** A discoloration on the skin; a blemish. —*tr.v.* To mark with blotches: *Their faces were blotched with insect bites.* [Prob. a blend of BLOT and BOTCH.] —**blotch′i·ness** *n.* —**blotch′y** *adj.*

blot·ter (blŏt′ər) *n.* **1.** A piece or pad of blotting paper. **2.** A book containing daily records of occurrences or transactions: *a police blotter.*

blotting paper. Absorbent paper used to dry a surface or absorb excess ink.

blouse (blous, blouz) *n.* **1.** A woman's or child's outer garment, esp. a loosely fitting shirt, worn on the upper part of the body. **2.** A loose garment resembling a smock, sometimes belted at the waist, and worn esp. by European workers. **3.** The jacket of a U.S. Army uniform. —*v.* **bloused, blous·ing.** —*intr.v.* To hang loose and full. —*tr.v.* To drape loosely. [French.]

blow¹ (blō) *v.* **blew** (bloō), **blown** (blōn), **blow·ing.** —*intr.v.* **1.** To be in motion, as the wind. **2.** To move along or be carried by or as if by the wind: *Her hat blew away.* **3.** To expel or drive a current of air, as from the mouth or from a bellows. **4.** To produce a sound by expelling a current of air, as in playing a musical wind instrument. **5.** To storm: *It blew all night.* **6.** To spout water and air, as a whale. **7.** To break down or fail: *The bulb blew.* **8.** *Slang.* To boast. —*tr.v.* **1.** To cause to move by means of a current of air: *Wind blew the sailboat.* **2.** To expel (air) from the mouth. **3.** To cause air to be expelled from. **4.** To clear out or make free of obstruction by forcing air through. **5.** To shape or form (a pliable material, such as molten glass) by forcing air or gas through the end of a pipe. **6. a.** To cause (a wind instrument) to sound: *blow a trumpet.* **b.** To sound: *A bugle blew taps.* **7.** To cause (a horse) to be out of breath. **8.** To cause to explode. **9.** To lay or deposit eggs in, as a fly. **10.** To melt or disable (a fuse). **11.** *Slang.* To spend (money) freely: *blew my whole paycheck.* **12.** *Slang.* To leave; depart: *Let's blow this place.* **13.** *Slang.* To handle ineptly: *Don't blow this opportunity.* —See Syns at **botch.** —*phrasal verbs.* **blow in.** To arrive. **blow out. 1.** To extinguish or be extinguished by blowing. **2.** To fail suddenly and violently, as a tire. **3.** To melt and open an electric circuit: *The fuse blew out.* **blow over. 1.** To subside; to wane. **2.** To be forgotten. **blow up. 1.** To come into being: *A storm blew up.* **2.** To explode. **3.** To fill with air; inflate. **4.** To enlarge (a photographic image or print). **5.** *Informal.* To lose one's temper. —See Syns at **explode.** —*n.* **1.** A blast of air or wind. **2.** The act of blowing: *a blow on a whistle.* —*idioms.* **blow hot and cold.** To change one's opinion often on a given matter; vacillate. **blow off steam.** To give release to one's anger or other feeling in words or activity. [Middle English *blowen,* from Old English *blāwan.*]

blow² (blō) *n.* **1.** A sudden hard stroke or hit, as with the fist or a weapon. **2.** A sudden unexpected shock or calamity: *His death was a blow to us all.* **3.** A sudden unexpected attack: *The strike was a blow for the working man.* —*idiom.* **come to blows.** To begin to fight. [Middle English *blaw.*]

blow³ (blō) *n.* A mass of blossoms: *peach blow.* —*v.* **blew** (bloō), **blown** (blōn), **blow·ing.** —*intr.v.* To bloom. —*tr.v.* **1.** *Archaic.* To cause to bloom. **2.** *Obs.* To produce (blossoms). [Middle English *blowen,* to blossom, from Old English *blōwan.*]

blow-by-blow (blō′bī-blō′) *adj.* Describing in great detail: *a blow-by-blow account of the meeting.*

blow·er (blō′ər) *n.* A device that produces a flow of air or other gas through a duct or an enclosed space.

blow·fish (blō′fĭsh′) *n., pl.* **blowfish** or **-fish·es.** The puffer.

blow·fly (blō′flī′) *n.* Any of several flies of the family Calliphoridae, that deposit their eggs in carcasses, carrion, or in open sores and wounds.

blow·gun (blō′gŭn′) *n.* A long, narrow pipe through which darts or pellets may be blown; a blowpipe.

blow·hard (blō′härd′) *n.* *Slang.* A boaster; braggart.

blow·hole (blō′hōl′) *n.* **1.** A nostril at the highest point on the head of whales and other cetaceans. **2.** A hole in the ice through which whales, dolphins, and other aquatic mammals come up for air.

blown¹ (blōn) *v.* The past participle of **blow.** —*adj.* **1.** Swollen or inflated; distended. **2.** Out-of-breath. **3.** Flyblown. **4.** Made by blowing: *blown glass.* [Middle English *blowen,* from Old English *(ge)blāwen.*]

blown² (blōn) *v.* The past participle of **blow** (bloom). —*adj.* Completely expanded or opened: *a full-blown flower.* [Middle English *blowen,* from Old English *(ge)blōwen.*]

blow·out (blō′out′) *n.* **1.** A sudden bursting of an automobile tire. **2.** The burning out of a fuse. **3.** *Slang.* A large party or social affair.

blow·pipe (blō′pīp′) *n.* **1.** A narrow tube through which a controlled flow of air is blown into a flame in order to concentrate and direct the heat. **2.** A long, narrow pipe used to blow molten glass. **3.** A blowgun.

blow·sy (blou′zē) *adj.* **-si·er, -si·est.** Var. of **blowzy.**

blow·torch (blō′tôrch′) *n.* A usu. portable gas burner that produces a flame hot enough to melt soft metals.

blow·up (blō′ŭp′) *n.* **1.** An explosion. **2.** A photographic enlargement. **3.** A violent outburst of temper.

blow·y (blō′ē) *adj.* **-i·er, -i·est.** Windy; breezy.

blow·zy (blou′zē) *adj.* **-zi·er, -zi·est.** Also **blow·sy. 1.** Having a coarsely ruddy and bloated appearance. **2.** Disheveled; frowzy; unkempt: *blowzy hair.* [From dial. *blowse,* beggar wench.]

blub·ber¹ (blŭb′ər) *intr.v.* To weep and sob noisily. —*tr.v.* To utter while crying and sobbing. —*n.* A loud weeping. [Middle English *bloberen, blubren,* to bubble, foam (imit.).] —**blub′ber·er** *n.*

blub·ber² (blŭb′ər) *n.* **1.** The thick layer of fat between the skin and the muscle layers of whales, seals, and other sea mammals. **2.** *Slang.* Excessive body fat. —*adj.* Swollen and protruding: *the boxer's blubber ears.* [Middle English *blober, bluber,* foam, bubble, entrails, fish or whale oil.] —**blub′ber·y** *adj.*

blu·cher (bloō′chər, -kər) *n.* **1.** A high shoe or half boot. **2.** A shoe having the vamp and tongue made of one piece and the top lapping over the vamp. [After Gebhard Leberecht von *Blücher* (1742–1819), Prussian field marshal.]

bludg·eon (blŭj′ən) *n.* A short, heavy club that has one end thicker than the other. —*tr.v.* **1.** To hit with or as if with a bludgeon. **2.** To threaten or bully. [Orig. unknown.] —**bludg′eon·er** or **bludg′eon·eer′** (-ə-nîr′) *n.*

blue (bloō) *n.* **1.** Any of a group of colors whose hue is that of the sky on a clear day; the hue lying between green and violet on the spectrum. **2.** Any pigment or dye imparting this color. **3.** Often **Blue. a.** A member of the Union Army in the Civil War. **b.** The Union Army itself. **4. blues.** The blue uniform of the U.S. Navy. **5. the blue. a.** The sea. **b.** The sky. —*adj.* **blu·er, blu·est. 1.** Of the color blue. **2.** Bluish or having parts that are blue or bluish: *blue spruce, blue whale.* **3.** Having a gray or purplish color, as from cold or bruise. **4.** *Informal.* Gloomy; depressed; dreary. **5.** Furious or exasperated; enraged: *blue with anger.* **6.** Indecent; risqué: *a blue joke.* —See Syns at **gloomy.** —*tr.v.* **blued, blu·ing. 1.** To make blue. **2.** To use bluing on. —*idioms.* **once in a blue moon.** Very seldom; rarely. **out of the blue.** At a completely unexpected time. [Middle Eng-

lish *bleu, blewe,* from Old French *bleu,* of Germanic orig.]
—**blue′ness** *n.*

blue baby. A newborn baby who, because of a heart or lung defect, has too little oxygen in its blood and a bluish tint to its skin.

blue·bell (blōō′bĕl′) *n.* Any of various plants with blue, bell-shaped flowers, esp. the harebell, which is the bluebell of Scotland.

blue·ber·ry (blōō′bĕr′ē) *n.* **1.** Any of several North American shrubs of the genus *Vaccinium,* with small, urn-shaped flowers and edible berries. **2.** The juicy blue, purplish, or blackish berry of any of these shrubs.

blueberry

blue·bird (blōō′bûrd′) *n.* Any of several North American birds of the genus *Sialia,* with blue plumage and, in the male of most species, a rust-colored breast.

blue blood. 1. Noble or aristocratic descent. **2.** A member of the aristocracy. —**blue′-blood′ed** (-blŭd′ĭd) *adj.*

blue·bon·net (blōō′bŏn′ĭt) *n.* **1.** A plant, *Lupinus subcarnosus,* of Texas and adjacent regions, with clusters of blue flowers. **2.** Any of several other plants with blue flowers. **3. a.** A broad, blue woolen cap worn in Scotland. **b.** A Scotsman wearing such a cap.

blue book. 1. An official publication of the British government, so named for its blue covers. **2.** An official list of persons in the employ of the U.S. government. **3.** *Informal.* A book listing the names of socially prominent people. **4.** A blank notebook with blue covers in which to write college examinations.

blue·bot·tle (blōō′bŏt′l) *n.* **1.** Any of several flies of the genus *Calliphora,* with a bright metallic-blue body. **2.** A plant, the cornflower.

blue cheese. A tangy cheese made of cow's milk, streaked with a bluish mold.

blue chip. 1. *Finance.* A stock that sells at a high price because of its long record of steady earnings. **2.** A valuable asset held in reserve. —**modifier** (blue′-chip′): *a blue-chip stock portfolio.*

blue·col·lar (blōō′kŏl′ər) *adj.* Of or pertaining to wage earners doing skilled or semi-skilled manual labor.

blue·fish (blōō′fĭsh′) *n., pl.* **bluefish** or **-fish·es. 1.** A food and game fish, *Pomatomus saltatrix,* of temperate and tropical waters. **2.** Any of various other fishes that are predominantly blue in color.

blue·gill (blōō′gĭl′) *n.* An edible freshwater sunfish, *Lepomis macrochirus,* of North America.

blue·grass (blōō′grăs′) *n.* **1.** Any of several lawn and pasture grasses of the genus *Poa,* esp. *P. pratensis,* with bluish or grayish leaves and stems. Also called **Kentucky bluegrass. 2.** A type of folk music that originated in the southern United States, characterized by rapid tempos.

blue-green algae (blōō′grēn′). Any of the algae of the division Cyanophyta, considered to be among the simplest form of plants.

blue gum. A tall timber tree, *Eucalyptus globulus,* native to Australia, with aromatic leaves and outer bark that peels off in shreds.

blue·ing (blōō′ĭng) *n.* Var. of **bluing.**

blue·ish (blōō′ĭsh) *adj.* Var. of **bluish.**

blue·jack·et (blōō′jăk′ĭt) *n.* An enlisted man in the U.S. or British Navy; a sailor. [From the blue jacket of the Navy.]

blue jay. A North American bird, *Cyanocitta cristata,* with

a crested head and predominantly blue plumage.

blue jeans. Blue denim trousers, **jeans.**

blue law. 1. In colonial New England, one of a body of laws designed to enforce certain moral standards, and particularly prohibiting specified forms of entertainment or recreation on Sundays. **2.** Any strict law designed to regulate Sunday activities.

blue-pen·cil (blōō′pĕn′səl) *tr.v.* **-ciled** or **-cilled, -cil·ing** or **cil·ling.** To edit, revise, or correct with or as with a blue pencil.

blue point. A type of edible oyster found chiefly off Blue Point, Great South Bay, Long Island, New York.

blue·print (blōō′prĭnt′) *n.* **1.** A photographic reproduction, as of architectural plans or technical drawings, rendered as white lines on a blue background. **2.** Any carefully designed plan. —*tr.v.* **1.** To make a blueprint of. **2.** To lay a plan for.

blue ribbon. The first prize; highest award or honor. —**blue′-rib′bon** *adj.*

blues (blōōz) *n.* *(used with a sing. or pl. verb).* **1.** A state of depression or melancholy. **2.** A style of jazz evolved from southern American Black secular songs and usu. distinguished by slow tempo and flatted thirds and sevenths.

blue·stock·ing (blōō′stŏk′ĭng) *n.* A pretentiously pedantic or scholarly woman. [After the *Blue Stocking Society,* a predominantly female literary club of 18th-cent. London.]

blue streak. *Informal.* **1.** Anything moving very fast: *She ran like a blue streak.* **2.** A rapid and seemingly interminable stream of words.

blu·ets (blōō′ĭts) *n.* *(used with a sing. or pl. verb).* A slender, low-growing plant, *Houstonia caerulea,* of eastern North America, that has small, light-blue flowers with yellow centers. Also called **innocence** and **Quaker-ladies.** [French *bleuet,* dim. of *bleu,* blue.]

blue vitriol. *Chem.* Copper sulfate.

blue whale. A huge whale, *Sibbaldus musculus,* with a bluish-gray back and grooves along the throat.

bluff¹ (blŭf) *tr.v.* **1.** To mislead, deceive, or hoodwink: *bluff one's way out of a jam.* **2.** To impress, deter, or intimidate, esp. by a false display of confidence: *He bluffed his captors into letting him go.* —*intr.v.* To feign strength when in a condition of weakness. —*n.* **1.** The act or practice of bluffing. **2.** A person who bluffs. —**idiom. call someone's bluff.** To challenge or expose someone's bluff. [Dutch *bluffen,* to boast, from Middle Dutch, to swell up.] —**bluff′er** *n.*

bluff² (blŭf) *n.* A steep headland, promontory, river bank, or cliff. —*adj.* **-er, -est. 1.** Having a rough, blunt but not unkind manner. **2.** Presenting a broad, steep front: *bluff cliffs.* —See Syns at **gruff.** [Orig. unknown.] —**bluff′ly** *adv.* —**bluff′ness** *n.*

blu·ing (blōō′ĭng) *n.* Also **blue·ing.** A blue substance added to rinse water to prevent white fabrics from turning yellow during laundering.

blu·ish (blōō′ĭsh) *adj.* Also **blue·ish.** Somewhat blue.

blun·der (blŭn′dər) *n.* A foolish or stupid mistake. —*intr.v.* **1.** To move awkwardly or clumsily; stumble about. **2.** To make a stupid mistake because of ignorance or confusion. —*tr.v.* **1.** To handle ineptly. **2.** To say stupidly or thoughtlessly. —See Syns at **botch.** [Middle English *blund(e)ren,* to proceed blindly, prob. from Old Norse *blunda,* to shut the eyes.] —**blun′der·er** *n.* —**blun′der·ing·ly** *adv.*

blun·der·buss (blŭn′dər-bŭs′) *n.* **1.** A short musket with a wide muzzle, formerly used to scatter shot at close range. **2.** A stupid, clumsy person. [Alteration of Dutch *donderbus* : *donder,* thunder + *bus,* gun.]

blunt (blŭnt) *adj.* **-er, -est. 1.** Having a thick, dull edge or end; not sharp or pointed. **2.** Abrupt and frank in manner; brusque. —See Syns at **dull** and **gruff.** —*tr.v.* **1.** To dull the edge of. **2.** To make less effective; weaken. —*intr.v.* To become blunt. [Middle English.] —**blunt′ly** *adv.* —**blunt′ness** *n.*

blur (blûr) *v.* **blurred, blur·ring.** —*tr.v.* **1.** To make indistinct in outline or appearance; to obscure: *Clouds blurred the view.* **2.** To smear or stain; to smudge: *Ink blurred the page.* **3.** To lessen the perception of; to dim: *The accident blurred his speech.* —*intr.v.* **1.** To become indistinct. **2.** To make stains or smudges by smearing. —*n.* **1.** A smear or smudge. **2.** An indistinct image to the sight or mind. [Orig. unknown.] **—blur'ry** *adj.*

blurb (blûrb) *n.* A brief, favorable publicity notice, as on a book jacket. [Coined by Frank Gelett Burgess (1866–1951), American humorist and illustrator.]

blurt (blûrt) *tr.v.* To say suddenly and impulsively: *She blurted out the secret.* [Prob. imit.]

blush (blŭsh) *intr.v.* **1.** To become suddenly red in the face from modesty, embarrassment, or shame; to flush. **2.** To feel ashamed or regretful about something: *I blushed at what I'd said.* **3.** To become red or rosy. *—n.* **1.** A sudden reddening of the face from modesty, embarrassment, or shame. **2.** A reddish or rosy color. **—idiom. at** (or **on**) **first blush.** At first sight or glance. [Middle English *blusshen,* from Old English *blyscan.*] **—blush'er** *n.*

blus·ter (blŭs'tər) *intr.v.* **1.** To blow in loud, violent gusts, as wind in a storm. **2.** To speak noisily and boastfully. **3.** To threaten ineffectually. *—tr.v.* To force or bully (someone) with swaggering threats. *—n.* **1.** A violent, gusty wind. **2.** Turbulence or noisy confusion. **3.** Swaggering talk. [Middle English *blusteren.*] **—blus'ter·er** *n.* **—blus'ter·y** *adj.*

bo·a (bō'ə) *n.* **1.** Any of various large, nonpoisonous, chiefly tropical snakes of the family Boidae, which includes the pythons, anaconda, boa constrictor, and other snakes that coil around and crush their prey. **2.** A long, fluffy scarf made of fur, feathers, etc. [From Latin *boa,* a large water snake.]

boar (bôr, bōr) *n.* **1.** Any uncastrated male pig. **2.** Also **wild boar.** A wild pig, *Sus scrofa,* of Eurasia and northern Africa. [Middle English *bor,* from Old English *bār.*]

board (bôrd, bōrd) *n.* **1.** A flat length of sawed lumber; a plank. **2.** A flat piece of wood or similar material adapted for some special use: *a diving board.* **3.** A table top or similar panel on which certain games are played. **4. a.** A table set for serving a meal: *a modest board.* **b.** Food served daily to paying guests: *room and board.* **5.** A group of persons organized to transact or administer some particular business: *board of trustees.* **6.** A bulletin board, blackboard, etc. **7.** The hard pasteboard cover of a book. **8. the boards.** A theater stage. **9. boards.** The wooden structure enclosing an ice-hockey rink. **10.** *Naut.* The side of a ship. *—tr.v.* **1.** To cover or close with boards: *board the window.* **2.** To provide with food and lodging for a charge. **3.** To house where board is furnished: *boarded his friends in an inn.* **4.** To place (an animal) in a kennel or stable. **5.** To go aboard (a ship, train, or plane). **6.** To come alongside (a ship). *—intr.v.* To live as a paying guest. **—idioms. across the board. 1.** Designating a bet that a horse or dog will win, place, or show. **2.** Affecting all members or divisions equally. **go by the board.** To be ruined, unnoticed, or ignored. **on board.** Aboard. **tread the boards.** To perform on or as if on a theater stage. [Middle English *bord,* from Old English *bord,* plank, table, border.]

board·er (bôr'dər, bōr'-) *n.* A person who pays for and receives both meals and lodging at another's home.

board foot. A unit of measure for lumber, equal to the volume of an unplaned board one foot long, one foot wide, and one inch thick.

boarding house. Also **board·ing·house** (bôr'dĭng-hous', bōr'-). A private home that provides meals and lodging for paying guests.

boarding school. A school where pupils are provided with meals and lodging.

board·walk (bôrd'wôk', bōrd'-) *n.* **1.** A walk made of wooden planks. **2.** A public walk or promenade, esp. of planks, along a beach or waterfront.

boast (bōst) *intr.v.* **1.** To brag about one's own accomplishments, talents, or possessions. **2.** To speak with pride. *—tr.v.* **1.** To brag about with excessive pride. **2.** To take pride in the possession of: *The city boasts a modern harbor.* *—n.* **1.** An instance of bragging. **2.** That which one brags about. [Middle English *bosten,* from *bost,* bragging, threat.] **—boast'er** *n.* **—boast'ing·ly** *adv.*

Syns: boast, brag, crow, vaunt *v. Core meaning:* To talk with excessive pride (*boasted about their wealth*).

boast·ful (bōst'fəl) *adj.* Tending to boast or brag. **—boast'ful·ly** *adv.* **—boast'ful·ness** *n.*

boat (bōt) *n.* **1.** A relatively small, usu. open craft of a size that might be carried on a ship. **2.** A ship. **3.** A dish shaped like a boat: *a gravy boat.* *—intr.v.* To travel by boat: *boat around the lake.* **—idiom. in the same boat.** In the same situation. [Middle English *bo(o)t,* from Old English *bāt.*]

boat hook. A pole with a metal point and hook at one end, used to maneuver boats.

boat·house (bōt'hous') *n.* A house in which boats are kept.

boat·man (bōt'mən) *n.* A person who works on, deals with, or operates boats.

boat·swain (bō'sən) *n.* Also **bo's'n, bos'n,** or **bo·sun.** A warrant officer or petty officer in charge of a ship's deck crew, rigging, anchors, and cables.

bob[1] (bŏb) *n.* **1.** A quick jerking movement of the head or body. **2.** A fishing float or cork. **3.** A short haircut on a woman or child. **4.** The docked tail of a horse. *—v.* **bobbed, bob·bing.** *—intr.v.* **1.** To move up and down: *The cork bobbed on the water.* **2.** To curtsy or bow. **3.** To grab at floating or hanging objects with the teeth: *He bobbed for apples.* *—tr.v.* **1.** To move (esp. the head) up and down. **2.** To cut short: *She bobbed her hair.* **—phrasal verb. bob up.** To appear suddenly. [From Middle English *bobbe* (noun), and *bobben* (verb).]

bob[2] (bŏb) *n., pl.* **bob.** *Brit. Slang.* A shilling. [Orig. unknown.]

bob·bin (bŏb'ĭn) *n.* A spool or reel that holds thread or yarn in place for spinning, weaving, knitting, sewing, or the making of lace. [French *bobine.*]

bob·bi·net (bŏb'ə-nĕt') *n.* A machine-woven net fabric with hexagonal meshes. [BOBBI(N) + NET.]

bob·ble (bŏb'əl) *v.* **-bled, -bling.** *—intr.v.* To bob up and down. *—tr.v.* To fumble (a ball). *—n.* A fumble or a miss; a blunder. [Freq. of BOB (verb).]

bob·by (bŏb'ē) *n., pl.* **-bies.** *Brit. Slang.* A policeman. [After Sir Robert Peel (1788–1850), who was Home Secretary of England when the Metropolitan Police Force was created (1828).]

bobby pin. A small metal hair clip with springy ends pressed tightly together to hold the hair in place. [From BOB (lock of hair).]

bobby socks. Also **bobby sox.** *Informal.* Ankle socks worn by girls or women. [From the name *Bobby,* pet form of *Robert.*]

bob·by·sox·er (bŏb'ē-sŏk'sər) *n.* Also **bobby soxer.** *Informal.* A teen-age girl of the 1940's who followed current fads.

bob·cat (bŏb'kăt') *n.* A wild cat, *Lynx rufus,* of North America, with spotted reddish-brown fur, tufted ears, and a short tail. [From its bobbed tail.]

bobcat   bobwhite

bob·o·link (bŏb'ə-lĭngk') *n.* An American migratory songbird, *Dolichonyx oryzivorus,* of which the male has black, white, and yellowish plumage. Also called **reedbird** and **ricebird.** [Imit.]

bob·sled (bŏb'slĕd') *n.* **1.** A long racing sled whose front runners are controlled by a steering wheel. **2. a.** A long sled made of two shorter sleds joined one behind the other. **b.** Either of these two smaller sleds. *—intr.v.* **-sled·ded, -sled·ding.** To ride or race in a bobsled. [From BOB (short).]

bob·tail (bŏb'tāl') *n.* **1.** A short tail or a tail that has been cut short. **2.** An animal, esp. a horse, with such a tail. *—adj.* Having a short tail. *—tr.v.* To cut the tail of (a horse or other animal); to dock.

bob·white (bŏb-hwīt', -wīt') *n.* A brown and white North

American quail, *Colinus virginianus*, with a call that sounds like its name. [Imit.]

bock beer (bŏk). A strong dark beer, the first that is drawn from the vats in springtime. Also called **bock**. [German *Bockbier*, from *Eimbeck*, city in Hanover.]

bode¹ (bōd) *tr.v.* **bod·ed, bod·ing.** 1. To be a sign or omen of (something to come): *A heavy sea boded trouble for the small ship.* 2. *Archaic.* To predict; foretell. [Middle English *boden*, from Old English *bodian*, to announce, proclaim, from *boda*, messenger.]

bode² (bōd) *v.* A past tense of **bide.** [Middle English, from Old English *bād.*]

bod·ice (bŏd′ĭs) *n.* 1. The fitted upper part of a dress. 2. A woman's vest that laces in front, worn over a blouse. [Earlier *bodies*, pl. of BODY.]

bod·ied (bŏd′ēd) *adj.* Having a specified kind of body: *strong-bodied.*

bod·i·less (bŏd′ē-lĭs) *adj.* Having no body, form, or substance: *bodiless fears.*

bod·i·ly (bŏd′l-ē) *adj.* 1. Of or pertaining to the body. 2. Physical as opposed to mental or spiritual: *bodily welfare.* *—adv.* As a complete physical entity: *We carried him bodily from the room.*

bod·kin (bŏd′kĭn) *n.* 1. A small pointed instrument for making holes in fabric or leather. 2. A blunt needle for pulling tape or ribbon through loops or a hem. 3. A long hairpin, usu. with an ornamental head. 4. *Archaic.* A dagger. [Middle English *boidekyn.*]

bod·y (bŏd′ē) *n., pl.* **-ies.** 1. The entire physical structure and substance of a living thing, esp. a human being or animal. 2. The part of this structure that is left after death; a corpse; carcass. 3. The main part of this structure excluding the head and limbs; a trunk; torso. 4. Any well-defined object or collection of matter: *a body of water.* 5. A group of persons considered or acting together: *a governing body.* 6. A collection of related things: *a body of information.* 7. The main or central part of something: *the body of a ship.* 8. Consistency of substance; density; strength: *a wine with fine body.* 9. *Informal.* A person. 10. In a violin, guitar, or other stringed instrument, a hollow chamber whose resonance reinforces the tone; a sound box. *—tr.v.* **-ied, -y·ing.** To give shape to, esp. to represent or manifest: *"Imagination bodies forth the form of things unknown"* (Shakespeare). [Middle English *body*, from Old English *bodig.*]

bod·y·guard (bŏd′ē-gärd′) *n.* A person or group of persons responsible for protecting one or more specific persons against possible attack.

body politic. The whole population of a nation or state, regarded as a political unit.

body stocking. A close-fitting, one-piece garment that covers the torso, and sometimes the arms and legs.

Boer (bôr, bōr, bŏŏr) *n.* A South African of Dutch descent. *—adj.* Of or pertaining to the Boers.

bog (bŏg, bôg) *n.* Soft, water-soaked ground; a marsh; a swamp. *—v.* **bogged, bog·ging.** *—tr.v.* 1. To cause to sink in or as if in a bog. 2. To hinder; slow; impede. *To be hindered and slowed: We bogged down in traffic.* [Scottish and Irish Gaelic *bogach*, from *bog*, soft.] **—bog′gy** *adj.*

bo·gey (bō′gē) *n., pl.* **-geys.** 1. A bogy; hobgoblin. 2. *Golf.* A score of one stroke over par on a hole. *—tr.v.* To shoot (a hole in golf) in one stroke over par. [Orig. unknown.]

bo·gey·man (bō′gē-măn′) *n.* Var. of **boogieman.**

bog·gle (bŏg′əl) *v.* **-gled, -gling.** *—intr.v.* 1. To hesitate or evade as if in fear, doubt, or conscience. 2. To start with fright; shy away from. *—tr.v.* 1. To make a botch of; bungle. 2. To stun or overwhelm with amazement: *it boggles the mind.* [Orig. unknown.]

bo·gie¹ (bō′gē) *n.* 1. A locomotive undercarriage or cart with two, four, or six wheels that swivel so that curves may be negotiated. 2. One of several wheels or supporting and aligning rollers inside the tread of a tractor or tank. [Orig. unknown.]

bo·gie² (bō′gē) *n.* Var. of **bogey** (hobgoblin).

bo·gus (bō′gəs) *adj.* Not genuine; counterfeit; fake: *bogus dollar bills; a bogus deed.* [Orig. unknown.]

bo·gy (bō′gē) *n., pl.* **-gies.** Also **bo·gie** 1. An evil or mischie-

vous spirit; hobgoblin. 2. Something that causes one worry, trouble, or annoyance.

Bo·he·mi·an (bō-hē′mē-ən) *n.* Also **bo·he·mi·an.** A person, esp. one with artistic interests, who disregards conventional standards of behavior. *—modifier: bohemian habits.* [From *Bohemia*, a region of Czechoslovakia.] **—Bo·he′mi·an** *adj.* **—Bo·he′mi·an·ism** *n.*

boil¹ (boil) *intr.v.* 1. To vaporize a liquid by the application of heat. 2. To reach the boiling point. 3. To undergo the action of boiling. 4. To be in a condition of agitation; seethe. 5. To be greatly excited, as with rage or passion: *boiling with desire.* *—tr.v.* 1. To heat to the boiling point. 2. To cook or clean by boiling: *boil the rags.* 3. To separate by evaporation as a result of boiling: *boil the maple sap.* *—phrasal verbs.* **boil away.** To evaporate by boiling. **boil down.** 1. To reduce in bulk or size by boiling. 2. To condense or summarize: *boil down the report for us.* **boil over.** To explode in rage or passion. *—n.* The condition or act of boiling. [Middle English *boillen*, from Old French *bo(u)illir*, from Latin *bullīre.*]

boil² (boil) *n.* A painful, pus-filled swelling of the skin caused by bacterial infection. [Middle English *bile, boyl*, from Old English *bȳl, bȳle.*]

boil·er (boi′lər) *n.* 1. An enclosed vessel in which water is heated and circulated, either as hot water or as steam, for heating or power. 2. A container for boiling liquids. 3. A storage tank for hot water.

boiling point. 1. The temperature at which a liquid boils, esp. under standard atmospheric conditions: *Water boils at 212° Fahrenheit and 100° Celsius.* 2. *Informal.* The point at which a person loses his or her temper.

bois·ter·ous (boi′stər-əs, -strəs) *adj.* 1. Rough and turbulent: *a boisterous storm.* 2. Noisy, high-spirited, and unrestrained: *a boisterous crowd.* [Middle English *boistres*, var. of *boist(e)ous*, rude, fierce, stout.] **—bois′ter·ous·ly** *adv.* **—bois′ter·ous·ness** *n.*

bo·la (bō′lə) *n.* Also **bo·las** (-ləs). A rope with round weights attached, used in South America to catch cattle or game by entangling the legs. [Spanish *bola*, ball, from Latin *bulla*, bubble, round object.]

bold (bōld) *adj.* 1. Fearless and daring; courageous. 2. Requiring or exhibiting courage and bravery: *a bold mission.* 3. Unduly forward and brazen in manner. 4. Clear and distinct to the eye; standing out prominently: *a bold handwriting.* 5. Abrupt; steep, as a cliff. 6. Designating boldface type. *—See Syns at* **brave** *and* **insolent.** *—idiom.* **make bold.** To take the liberty; dare. [Middle English *bold*, from Old English *bald, beald.*] **—bold′ly** *adv.* **—bold′ness** *n.*

bold·face (bōld′fās′) *n. Printing.* Type cut with thick, heavy lines that stand out prominently.

bole (bōl) *n.* The trunk of a tree. [Middle English, from Old Norse *bolr.*]

bo·le·ro (bō-lâr′ō, bə-) *n., pl.* **-ros.** 1. A short, loose jacket, usu. with no front fastening. 2. **a.** A Spanish dance in triple meter. **b.** The music for this dance. [Spanish, prob. from *bola*, ball.]

boll (bōl) *n.* The rounded seed pod or capsule of certain plants, esp. of the cotton plant. [Middle English *bolle*, from Middle Dutch.]

boll weevil. A small, grayish, long-snouted beetle, *Anthonomus grandis*, of Mexico and the southern United States, that lays its eggs in the buds and bolls of the cotton plant, causing great damage.

boll weevil

bo·lo (bō′lō) *n.*, *pl.* **-los.** A long, heavy, single-edged machete used in the Philippines.

bo·lo·gna (bə-lō′nē, -nə, -nyə) *n.* Also *informal* **ba·lo·ney** (-nē) or **bo·lo·ney.** A seasoned smoked sausage made of mixed meats. [After *Bologna,* Italy.]

Bol·she·vik (bōl′shə-vĭk′, bŏl′-) *n.*, *pl.* **-viks** or **-vi·ki** (-vē′kē). **1.** A Communist, esp. a Russian Communist of Lenin's time. **2.** Often **bolshevik.** *Informal.* Any radical. **—*modifier:*** *the Bolshevik revolution.* [Russian *Bol'shevik,* "one of the majority."]

Bol·she·vism (bōl′shə-vĭz′əm, bŏl′-) *n.* Also **bol·she·vism. 1.** The theories and practices developed by the Bolsheviks between 1903 and 1917 with a view to seizing governmental power and establishing the world's first Communist state. **2.** Soviet Communism. **—Bol′she·vist′** *n.* **—Bol′she·vis′tic** *adj.*

bol·ster (bōl′stər) *n.* A long, narrow pillow or cushion. **—*tr.v.* 1.** To support with a pillow. **2.** To strengthen or reinforce: *The award bolstered her pride.* [Middle English *bolster,* from Old English *bolster.*]

bolt¹ (bōlt) *n.* **1.** A threaded rod or pin onto which a nut is screwed, used to hold two parts together. **2.** A sliding bar for fastening a door or gate. **3.** A metal bar or rod in a lock that is pushed out or withdrawn at a turn of the key. **4.** A sliding bar that positions the cartridge in a rifle and closes the breech. **5.** A large roll of cloth. **6.** A flash of lightning or a thunderbolt. **7.** A sudden dash or dart toward or away from something. **—*tr.v.* 1.** To lock with or as if with a bolt or bolts. **2.** To attach or fasten with a bolt or bolts: *bolted the rack to the wall.* **3.** To eat hurriedly and with little chewing; gulp: *bolted his dinner.* **4.** To desert or withdraw support from (a political party). **—*intr.v.* 1.** To move or spring suddenly toward or from something: *a horse that shied and bolted.* **2.** To make off suddenly; run away: *bolted from the room.* **3.** To break away from a political party or its policies. **—*idiom.* bolt from the blue.** A sudden, usu. shocking, surprise. [Middle English *bolt,* from Old English *bolt,* heavy arrow.] **—bolt′er** *n.*

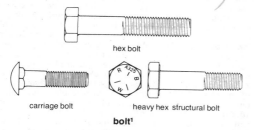

hex bolt

carriage bolt   heavy hex structural bolt

bolt¹

bolt² (bōlt) *tr.v.* To pass through a sieve; sift. [Middle English *bulten, bolten,* from Old French *buleter,* from Middle Dutch *biutelen.*]

bo·lus (bō′ləs) *n.* **1.** A small round mass. **2.** *Pharm.* A large pill or tablet. [Medieval Latin *bōlus,* from Greek *bōlos,* lump, clod.]

bomb (bŏm) *n.* **1.** An explosive weapon constructed to go off upon impact or through a timing mechanism. **2.** Any of various weapons exploded to release smoke, gas, or other destructive materials. **3.** A container for holding a substance under pressure, as a preparation for killing insects, that can be released as a spray or gas. **4.** *Slang.* A dismal failure; complete fiasco. **5. the bomb.** Nuclear weapons in general. **—*modifier:*** *a bomb shelter.* **—*tr.v.*** To attack, damage, or destroy with a bomb or bombs. **—*intr.v.* 1.** To drop a bomb or bombs. **2.** *Slang.* To fail miserably: *The play bombed.* [French *bombe,* from Italian *bomba,* prob. from Latin *bombus,* booming, humming, from Greek *bombos.*]

bom·bard (bŏm-bärd′) *tr.v.* **1.** To attack with bombs, explosive shells, missiles, etc. **2.** To assail or shower (a person), as with questions, insults, etc. **3.** To act on (a target, such as an element, atom, etc.) with high-energy radiation or particles: *Physicists bombard atoms to study them.* [Middle English *bombarde,* cannon, from Old French, from Medieval Latin *bombarda,* prob. from Latin *bombus,* booming.] **—bom·bard′er** *n.* **—bom·bard′ment** *n.*

bom·bar·dier (bŏm′bər-dîr′) *n.* **1.** *Mil.* The member of an aircraft crew who operates the bombing equipment. **2.** *Brit.* A noncommissioned artillery officer. [French, from Old French *bombarde,* bombard.]

bom·bast (bŏm′băst′) *n.* Grandiloquent and pompous speech or writing; wordy, high-flown language. [Earlier *bombace,* cotton padding, from Old French, from Late Latin *bombax,* cotton, silk, alteration of Latin *bombyx,* silkworm, silk, from Greek *bombux.*] **—bom·bast′er** *n.* **—bom·bas′tic** *adj.* **—bom·bas′ti·cal·ly** *adv.*

bom·ba·zine (bŏm′bə-zēn′) *n.* A fine twilled fabric of silk and worsted or cotton. [French *bombasin,* from Late Latin *bombacīnum,* from Latin, *bombȳcīnus,* silken, from *bombyx,* silk.]

bomb bay. The compartment in a military aircraft from which bombs are dropped.

bomb·er (bŏm′ər) *n.* **1.** A military aircraft designed to carry and drop bombs. **2.** A person who attacks with bombs.

bomb·shell (bŏm′shĕl′) *n.* **1.** A bomb. **2.** A great surprise or shock.

bomb·sight (bŏm′sīt′) *n.* A device in a military aircraft for aiming bombs.

bo·na fide (bō′nə fīd′, fī′dē, bŏn′ə). **1.** Done in good faith; sincere: *a bona fide offer.* **2.** Authentic; genuine: *a bona fide Monet.* [Latin, "in good faith."]

bo·nan·za (bə-năn′zə) *n.* **1.** A rich mine, vein, or pocket of ore. **2.** Any source of great profit, wealth, or prosperity. [Spanish, fair weather, prosperity, from Latin *bonus,* good.]

bon·bon (bŏn′bŏn′) *n.* A candy with a center of fondant, fruit, or nuts, usu. coated with chocolate. [French, from *bon,* good, from Latin *bonus.*]

bond (bŏnd) *n.* **1.** Anything that binds, ties, or fastens together, as a cord or rope. **2.** Often **bonds.** A shackle; fetter. **3.** Often **bonds.** A force that unites; a tie; link: *bonds of friendship.* **4.** *Chem.* An attractive force that holds a pair of atoms together in a molecule or compound, produced in general by a transfer or sharing of one or more electrons. **5. a.** Money paid as bail. **b.** A person who provides bail; bondsman. **6.** A certificate of debt issued by a government or corporation that guarantees repayment with interest, on a specified date, of money borrowed from the purchaser of the certificate. **7.** An insurance contract that guarantees payment to an employer in the event of financial loss caused by the actions of an employee. **—*tr.v.* 1.** To join securely, as with glue or cement. **2.** To mortgage or place a guaranteed bond on. **3.** To furnish bond or surety for. **4.** To place (an employee, merchandise, etc.) under bond or guarantee. **—*intr.v.*** To secure or hold something together with or as with a bond or bonds. [Middle English *bond, band,* from Old Norse *band.*] **—bond′a·ble** *adj.* **—bond′er** *n.*

bond·age (bŏn′dĭj) *n.* **1.** The condition of a slave or serf; servitude. **2.** A condition of subjection to any force, power, or influence. [Middle English, from Medieval Latin *bondāgium,* from Middle English *bonde,* serf, peasant, Old English *bōnda,* householder, from Old Norse *bōndi.*]

Syns: **bondage, servitude, slavery** *n.* Core meaning: The condition of being involuntarily under the power of another *(the Israelites who toiled in Egyptian bondage).* BONDAGE can also be used figuratively *(addicts held in bondage by heroin).* SERVITUDE stresses subjection or submission to a master *(involuntary servitude; saw his job as a form of servitude).* SLAVERY implies being owned as a possession and treated as property *(the abolishment of slavery in our country).*

bond·ed (bŏn′dĭd) *adj.* **1.** Guaranteed or secured by a bond. **2.** Stored in a warehouse until taxes or duties are paid.

bond paper. A superior grade of strong white paper made wholly or in part from rag pulp.

bond·ser·vant (bŏnd′sûr′vənt) *n.* **1.** A person obligated to work for another without wages. **2.** A slave or serf. [From Middle English *bonde,* serf.]

bonds·man (bŏndz′mən) *n.* A person who provides bond or surety for another.

bone (bōn) *n.* **1. a.** The hard, dense, calcified tissue that forms the skeleton of most vertebrates. **b.** One of the many distinct structures making up such a skeleton.

---

c. **bones.** The skeleton. **2. bones.** Mortal remains: *God rest his bones.* —*modifier:* bone structure; bone tissue. —*tr.v.* **boned, bon·ing.** To remove the bones from, esp. for cooking. —*phrasal verb.* **bone up.** *Informal.* To study (a subject) intensively; to review; cram. —*idioms.* **bone of contention.** The subject of a dispute. **feel in (one's) bones.** To have an intuition of. **have a bone to pick with.** To have reason to quarrel with. **make no bones about.** To be completely frank about. [Middle English *bon*, from Old English *bān*.]

bone·black (bōn'blăk') *n.* Also **bone black.** A black material containing about 10 per cent charcoal, made by roasting animal bones in an airtight container, and used as a pigment, as a filtering medium, and in whitening sugar. Also called **bone charcoal.**

bone china. Porcelain made of clay mixed with bone ash.

bone-dry (bōn'drī') *adj.* Without a trace of moisture.

bone·fish (bōn'fĭsh') *n., pl.* **bonefish** or **-fish·es.** A saltwater game fish, *Albula vulpes,* of warm waters, that has silvery scales. [From its many small bones.]

bone meal. Bones crushed and ground to a coarse powder, used as fertilizer and animal feed.

bon·er (bō'nər) *n. Slang.* A blunder. [Orig. unknown.]

bon·fire (bŏn'fīr') *n.* A large outdoor fire. [Middle English *banefyre,* a fire in which bones were burned : *bane,* bone + *fyre,* fire.]

bong (bŏng, bông) *n.* A deep ringing sound, as of a bell. —*tr.v.* To announce or proclaim with or as with such a ringing sound. —*intr.v.* To ring. [Imit.]

bongo drums. A pair of connected drums with parchment heads, usu. tuned to different pitches, that are held between the knees and beaten with the hands. Also called **bongos.** [American Spanish *bongó.*]

bon·ho·mie (bŏn'ə-mē') *n.* Also **bon·hom·mie.** A pleasant disposition; geniality. [French, from *bonhomme,* good-natured man: *bon,* good, from Latin *bonus* + *homme,* man, from Latin *homo.*]

bo·ni·to (bə-nē'tō) *n., pl.* **bonito** or **-tos.** Any of several saltwater food and game fishes of the genus *Sarda,* related to and resembling the tuna. [Spanish, "beautiful" (from its appearance), from Latin *bonus,* good.]

bon mot (bŏn' mō') *pl.* **bons mots** (bŏn' mōz'). A clever saying; a terse witticism. [French, "good word."]

bon·net (bŏn'ĭt) *n.* **1.** A hat that is held in place by ribbons tied under the chin, often with a wide brim. **2.** *Scot.* A brimless cap for men. **3.** A feather headdress worn by some American Indians. **4.** A removable metal cover for part or all of a machine. **5.** *Brit.* The hood of an automobile. [Middle English *bonet,* from Old French, from Medieval Latin *abonnis,* cap.]

bonnet   bonsai

bon·ny (bŏn'ē) or **bon·nie** *adj.* **-ni·er, -ni·est.** *Scot.* **1.** Pleasing; pretty; fair. **2.** Healthy; robust. **3.** Cheerful; pleasant. [Perh. from Old French *bon,* good, from Latin *bonus.*] —**bon'ni·ness** *n.*

bon·sai (bŏn'sī', bŏn'-) *n., pl.* **bonsai. 1.** The art of growing dwarfed, ornamentally shaped trees or shrubs in small, shallow pots. **2.** A tree or shrub grown by this method. [Japanese, "potted plant."]

bo·nus (bō'nəs) *n.* Something given or paid in addition to what is usual or expected. [From Latin *bonus,* good.]

bon vi·vant (bŏn' vē-vänt', bôn' vē-vän') *pl.* **bons vi·vants**

(bŏn' vē-vänts', bôn' vē-vän'). *French.* A person who enjoys good food and drink and lives luxuriously.

bon voy·age (bŏn' voi-äzh', bôn' vwä-yäzh'). A phrase used to wish a departing traveler a pleasant journey. [French, "good trip."]

bon·y (bō'nē) *adj.* **-i·er, -i·est. 1.** Of, resembling, or made of bone. **2.** Having many bones. **3.** Having protruding or prominent bones; thin; gaunt: *bony elbows.* **4.** Having a skeleton of bones rather than cartilage: *bony fishes.* —See Syns at **thin.** —**bon'i·ness** *n.*

boo (bōō) *n., pl.* **boos.** A word used to show dislike, scorn, or disapproval. —*interj.* **1.** Used to express dislike or disapproval. **2.** Used to frighten or surprise. —*v.* **booed, boo·ing.** —*intr.v.* To jeer. —*tr.v.* To jeer at (someone or something).

boo·by (bōō'bē) *n., pl.* **-bies. 1.** A stupid or foolish person; dunce; dolt. **2.** Any of several tropical sea birds of the genus *Sula,* with white or brown and white feathers and a long, pointed bill, related to the gannets. [Spanish *bobo,* from Latin *balbus,* stammering.]

booby prize. An award given for the lowest score in a game or contest.

booby trap. 1. A concealed or camouflaged device designed to be triggered by some unsuspecting action of the intended victim. **2.** Any device or situation that catches a person off guard.

boo·dle (bōōd'l) *n. Slang.* Money, esp. counterfeit money. [From Dutch *boedel,* estate, effects, from Middle Dutch *bōdel,* riches, property.]

boog·ie·man (bōōg'ē-măn', bōō'gē-) *n.* Also **boog·y·man** or **bo·gy·man** (bō'gē-). A hobgoblin; a terrifying specter. [*Boogie,* alteration of *booger,* from dialectal *boggart,* specter, hobgoblin.]

boog·ie-woog·ie (bōōg'ē-wōōg'ē, bōō'gē-wōō'gē) *n.* A style of jazz piano playing in which a figure having a distinctive rhythmic and melodic pattern is repeated over and over in the bass. [Imit.]

book (bōōk) *n.* **1.** A set of printed or written pages fastened together along one edge and enclosed between covers. **2.** A long written work or a collection of writings or pictures that may be published between covers. **3.** A main division of a larger written or printed work. **4. the Book** or **the Good Book.** The Bible. **5.** A bound volume of blank pages in which to write, record, or paste things: *an address book.* **6. a.** A volume in which records are kept of money received, owed, and paid. **b. books.** Financial records. **7.** A small packet of similar things bound together: *a book of matches.* **8.** The words or script of a play, musical, or opera; a libretto. **9.** A record of bets placed on a race. **10.** *Cards.* The number of tricks needed before any tricks can have scoring value, as the first six tricks taken by the declaring side in bridge. —*modifier: a book report.* —*tr.v.* **1.** To record charges against (a person) on a police blotter. **2.** To arrange for in advance; reserve (tickets, rooms, etc.). **3.** To hire (entertainers). —*idioms.* **by the book.** According to established rules. **in (one's) book.** In one's opinion. **like a book.** Thoroughly; completely. **make book.** To accept or place bets. **one for the books.** *Informal.* Something noteworthy. **on the books. 1.** Recorded; registered. **2.** Enlisted; enrolled. **throw the book at.** *Slang.* **1.** To make all possible charges against (an offender). **2.** To punish severely; reprimand harshly. [Middle English *bok,* from Old English *bōc,* written document, composition.]

book·bind·er (bōōk'bīn'dər) *n.* A person whose business is binding books; binder.

book·bind·er·y (bōōk'bīn'də-rē) *n.* A business establishment where books are bound.

book·bind·ing (bōōk'bīn'dĭng) *n.* The art or profession of binding books.

book·case (bōōk'kās') *n.* A piece of furniture with shelves for holding books.

book club. 1. An organization that sells books, usu. at a discount, to members. **2.** A club for the reading and discussion of books.

book·ie (bōōk'ē) *n. Slang.* A bookmaker.

book·ish (bōōk'ĭsh) *adj.* **1.** Of, relating to, or resembling a book. **2.** Fond of books and study; studious. **3.** Depending too much on books rather than experience. **4.** Showing off one's learning in a dull, dry, or conceited way.

book·keep·ing (bŏŏk'kē'pĭng) *n.* The work or skill of recording the accounts and transactions of a business. —**book'keep'er** *n.*

book learning. Knowledge gained from books rather than from practical experience.

book·let (bŏŏk'lĭt) *n.* A small bound book or pamphlet, usu. with paper covers.

book·mak·er (bŏŏk'mā'kər) *n.* Someone who accepts and pays off bets, as on a horse race. Also called **bookie.** —**book'mak'ing** *n.*

book·mark (bŏŏk'märk') *n.* An object, such as a ribbon or a strip of leather, placed between the pages of a book to mark one's place.

book·mo·bile (bŏŏk'mə-bēl') *n.* A small truck equipped with shelves of books, used as a mobile lending library.

Book of Common Prayer. The book of services and prayers used in the Anglican Church.

Book of Mormon. The sacred text of the Mormon Church.

book·plate (bŏŏk'plāt') *n.* A label pasted inside a book and bearing the owner's name or other identification.

book·rack (bŏŏk'răk') *n.* 1. A small rack or shelf for books. 2. A frame or rack for supporting an open book; bookstand.

book·sell·er (bŏŏk'sĕl'ər) *n.* A person who sells books.

book·shelf (bŏŏk'shĕlf') *n.* A shelf on which books are kept.

book·shop (bŏŏk'shŏp') *n.* A bookstore.

book·stand (bŏŏk'stănd') *n.* 1. A small counter where books are sold. 2. A bookrack.

book·store (bŏŏk'stôr', -stōr') *n.* A store where books are sold; bookshop.

book value. The worth of an asset or business as shown in the account books, as distinguished from the market value.

book·worm (bŏŏk'wûrm') *n.* 1. The larva of any of various insects that infest books and feed on the paste in the bindings. 2. A person who spends much time reading or studying.

Bool·e·an algebra (bōō'lē-ən). Any of various algebraic systems based on mathematical forms and relationships borrowed from the symbolic logic of George Boole (1815–64), Brit. mathematician.

boom¹ (bōōm) *n.* 1. A deep, hollow sound, as from an explosion. 2. A sudden increase, as in growth or production. 3. **a.** A time of sudden, rapid growth or expansion. **b.** A time of prosperity. —*modifier:* boom times. —*intr.v.* 1. To make a deep, resonant, usu. sustained sound: guns booming at a distant enemy. 2. To flourish or progress rapidly or vigorously: Business boomed. —*tr.v.* 1. To give forth or utter with a deep, resonant sound: "No!" boomed the giant. 2. To cause to flourish. [Middle English bomben, bummen (imit.).]

boom² (bōōm) *n.* 1. *Naut.* A long pole extending from a mast to hold or stretch out the bottom of a sail. 2. **a.** A long pole or similar structure that extends upward and outward from the mast of a derrick and supports the object being lifted or suspended. **b.** A similar support that holds a microphone. 3. **a.** A barrier composed of a chain of floating logs enclosing other free-floating logs. **b.** The area enclosed by such a barrier. [Dutch, tree, pole.]

boo·mer·ang (bōō'mə-răng') *n.* 1. A flat, curved wooden missile that can be thrown so that it returns to the thrower, orig. used as a weapon by Australian aborigines. 2. A statement or course of action that rebounds harmfully against its originator. —*intr.v.* To result in adverse effect upon the originator; to backfire: The scheme boomeranged. [Native Australian word.]

boon¹ (bōōn) *n.* 1. Something beneficial or pleasant that is bestowed; a blessing. 2. *Archaic.* A favor, request, or service. [Middle English bone, prayer, favor, from Old Norse bōn, prayer, request.]

boon² (bōōn) *adj.* 1. Friendly and jolly; convivial; sociable: a boon companion. 2. *Archaic.* Kind; generous. [Middle English bone, "good," from Old French bon, from Latin bonus.]

boon·docks (bōōn'dŏks') *pl.n. Slang.* —**the boondocks.** 1. Wild and dense brush; jungle. 2. Back country; hinterland. [Tagalog bundok, mountain.]

boon·dog·gle (bōōn'dô'gəl, -dŏg'əl). *Informal.* —*intr.v.* **-gled, -gling.** To waste time on pointless and unnecessary work. —*n.* Pointless, unnecessary, and time-wasting work. [Orig. the plaited leather cord worn by Boy Scouts (coined in 1925 by R.H. Link, American scoutmaster).] —**boon'dog'gler** *n.*

boor (bŏŏr) *n.* 1. A peasant. 2. A crude person with rude, clumsy manners; bumpkin. [Dutch boer, farmer, peasant, from Middle Dutch gheboer.]

boor·ish (bŏŏr'ĭsh) *adj.* Like a boor; rude; ill-mannered. —See Syns at **coarse.** —**boor'ish·ly** *adv.* —**boor'ish·ness** *n.*

boost (bōōst) *tr.v.* 1. To lift by or as if by pushing up from behind or below. 2. To increase; to raise: boost sales; boost morale. 3. To encourage or promote; aid: boost one's career by hard work. —See Syns at **raise.** —*n.* 1. A lift or help. 2. An increase: a boost in salary. [Orig. unknown.]

boost·er (bōōst'ər) *n.* 1. Something that increases the power or effectiveness of a system or device: a battery booster. 2. An amplifier for radio signals: a television booster. 3. A rocket used to launch a missile or space vehicle. 4. A dose of a vaccine or serum given to a person who is already immune in order to prolong or strengthen his immunity. Also called **booster shot.** 5. Anything that boosts something: The holiday was a morale booster. 6. An enthusiastic promoter.

boot¹ (bōōt) *n.* 1. A kind of shoe that covers the foot and ankle and usu. part of the leg. 2. A protective sheath for a horse's leg. 3. Something shaped like a boot, as a peninsula. 4. A kick. 5. Any protective covering or sheath, such as a protective flap for an open automobile. 6. A patch for the inner casing of an automobile tire. 7. *Brit.* An automobile trunk. 8. A scabbard on a saddle or vehicle to hold a gun. 9. *U.S. Mil.* A new recruit. —*tr.v.* 1. To put boots on. 2. To kick: boot a football. 3. *Slang.* To discharge; dismiss. —See Syns at **prosper.** —*idioms.* **bet your boots.** To be certain. **lick the boots of.** To flatter insincerely and excessively. **the boot.** *Slang.* Dismissal, as from work. [Middle English bote, from Old French.]

boot² (bōōt) *intr.v. Archaic.* To be of help or benefit; to avail. —*n.* 1. *Archaic.* Advantage; avail. 2. **to boot.** In addition; besides. [Middle English bote, advantage, from Old English bōt.]

boot camp. *U.S. Mil.* A training camp for recruits.

boot·ee (bōō'tē) *n.* A soft baby shoe, usu. knitted.

Bo·ö·tes (bō-ō'tēz) *n.* A constellation in the Northern Hemisphere near Virgo.

booth (bōōth) *n., pl.* **booths** (bōōthz, bōōths). 1. A small enclosed compartment: a telephone booth. 2. A small stall or stand where things are sold or entertainment is provided. 3. A seating compartment consisting of a table enclosed by two facing benches with high backs. [Middle English both, prob. of Scandinavian orig.]

boot·leg (bōōt'lĕg') *v.* **-legged, -leg·ging.** —*tr.v.* To make, sell, or transport (goods) for sale illegally. —*intr.v.* To engage in bootlegging. —*n.* Goods smuggled or illicitly produced or sold. —*adj.* Produced, sold, or transported illegally: bootleg whiskey. [From smugglers' practice of carrying liquor in the legs of tall boots.] —**boot'leg'ger** *n.*

boot·less (bōōt'lĭs) *adj.* Useless; fruitless: a bootless effort. —**boot'less·ly** *adv.* —**boot'less·ness** *n.*

boot·lick (bōōt'lĭk') *tr.v.* To be servile toward. —*intr.v.* To act in a servile manner; to fawn. —**boot'lick'er** *n.*

boo·ty (bōō'tē) *n., pl.* **-ties.** 1. Loot taken from an enemy in war. 2. Any seized or stolen goods: pirates' booty. 3. Treasure. 4. Any large profit or gain. [Middle English bootyne, from Old French butin, from Middle Low German būte, exchange.]

booze (bōōz). *Informal.* —*n.* 1. Alcoholic drink, esp. hard liquor. 2. A drinking spree. —*intr.v.* **boozed, booz·ing.** *Informal.* To drink alcoholic beverages excessively. [Middle English bousen, to carouse, from Middle Dutch būsen.] —**booz'er** *n.*

bop (bŏp). *Informal.* —*tr.v.* **bopped, bop·ping.** To hit or strike. —See Syns at **hit.** —*n.* A blow; a punch. [Imit.]

bo·rac·ic (bə-răs'ĭk) *adj.* Var. of **boric.**

bor·age (bôr'ĭj, bŏr'-) *n.* A plant, Borago officinalis, native to southern Europe and northern Africa, with hairy leaves and star-shaped blue flowers. The young, cucumber-flavored leaves are sometimes used as seasoning. [Middle

English, from Old French *bourrache,* from Medieval Latin *borrāgō.*]

bo·rate (bôr'āt', bōr'-) *n.* A salt of boric acid.

bo·rax (bôr'ăks', -əks, bōr'-) *n.* Sodium borate, either in hydrated or anhydrous form. [Middle English *boras,* from Old French, from Medieval Latin *borax,* from Arabic *būraq,* from Persian *būrah.*]

bo·ra·zon (bôr'ə-zŏn', bōr'-) *n.* A trademark for an extremely hard boron nitride formed at very high pressures and temperatures. [BOR(ON) + AZ(O)- + -ON.]

bor·der (bôr'dər) *n.* 1. The line separating political or geographic divisions such as counties, states, or regions; a boundary. 2. A margin, rim or edge around or along something. 3. A design or decorative strip on the edge or rim of something: *a border of herbs around a flower bed.* —*tr.v.* 1. To put a border or edging on: *border a collar with lace.* 2. To share a boundary with; be next to. —*phrasal verb.* **border on** (or **upon**). 1. To be next to; touch; adjoin. 2. To be almost like; approach: *an act that borders on treason.* [Middle English *bordure,* from Old French, from *border,* to border, from *bord,* side of a vessel, border.] —**bor'der·er** *n.*

bor·der·land (bôr'dər-lănd') *n.* 1. Land on or near a border or frontier. 2. A borderline.

bor·der·line (bôr'dər-līn') *n.* 1. A line that marks a border; dividing line; boundary. 2. A vague or indefinite line between two different conditions: *the borderline between dreams and reality.* —*adj.* Not clearly within a certain class or limit; uncertain; dubious: *a borderline case of paranoia.*

bore¹ (bôr, bōr) *v.* **bored, bor·ing.** —*tr.v.* 1. To make a hole in or through (something), as with a drill or auger. 2. To make (a hole, tunnel, well, etc.) by drilling, digging, or burrowing. —*intr.v.* 1. To make a hole in or through something by or as if by drilling. 2. To be capable of being pierced or drilled. 3. To proceed or advance steadily or laboriously: *"All night they bored through the hot darkness"* (John Steinbeck). —*n.* 1. A hole or passage made by or as if by drilling. 2. The interior diameter of a hole, tube, cylinder, etc. 3. The caliber of a firearm. 4. A drilling tool. [Middle English *boren,* from Old English *borian.*]

bore² (bôr, bōr) *tr.v.* **bored, bor·ing.** To tire with dullness, repetition, or tediousness. —*n.* An uninteresting or tiresome person or thing. [Orig. unknown.]

    Syns: bore, tire *v. Core meaning:* To fatigue with dullness or tedium (*was bored by the long story*).

bore³ (bôr, bōr) *n.* A high and often dangerous wave caused by the surge of a flood tide upstream in a narrowing estuary or by colliding tidal currents. [Middle English *bare,* from Old Norse *bāra,* wave, billow.]

bore⁴ (bôr, bōr) *v.* Past tense of **bear.**

bo·re·al (bôr'ē-əl, bōr'-) *adj.* 1. Pertaining to the north; northern. 2. Of or concerning the north wind. [Middle English *boriall,* from Late Latin *boreālis,* from Latin *Boreās,* the north wind.]

bore·dom (bôr'dəm, bōr'-) *n.* The condition of being bored; tedium.

bor·er (bôr'ər, bōr'-) *n.* 1. A tool used for boring or drilling. 2. An insect or insect larva, such as the corn borer, that bores into plants or wood.

bo·ric (bôr'ĭk, bōr'-) *adj.* Also **bo·rac·ic** (bə-răs'ĭk). Of, pertaining to, derived from, or containing boron.

boric acid. A white or colorless crystalline compound, H_3BO_3, used as an antiseptic, preservative, and in fireproofing compounds, cosmetics, and enamels.

born (bôrn) 1. A past participle of **bear.** —See Usage note at **bear¹.** 2. **be born. a.** To begin one's life. **b.** To come into existence; originate: *The Republican Party was born in 1854.* —*adj.* 1. By birth or natural talent: *a born artist.* 2. Coming or resulting from: *wisdom born of experience.* [Middle English *boren,* from Old English *(ge)boren.*]

borne (bôrn) *v.* A past participle of **bear.** —See Usage note at **bear¹.** [Middle English *boren,* from Old English *(ge)boren.*]

bo·ron (bôr'ŏn', bōr'-) *n. Symbol* **B** A soft, brown, amorphous or crystalline, nonmetallic element, extracted chiefly from kernite and borax, and used in flares, propellant mixtures, nuclear reactor control elements, abrasives, and hard metallic alloys. Atomic number 5, atomic weight 10.811, melting point 2,300°C, specific gravity (crystal)

2.34, valence 3. [BOR(AX) + (CARB)ON.]

bor·ough (bûr'ō, bûr'ō) *n.* 1. A self-governing incorporated town, as in certain U.S. states. 2. One of the five administrative units of New York City. 3. A governmental district in Alaska, corresponding to a county. 4. *Brit.* **a.** A town having a municipal corporation and certain rights, such as self-government. **b.** A town that sends one or more representatives to Parliament. [Middle English *burgh, borugh,* from Old English *burg, burh,* fortress, fortified town.]

bor·row (bôr'ō, bōr'ō) *tr.v.* 1. To obtain (something) on loan with the promise of returning or replacing it later. 2. To adopt or use as one's own: *They borrowed his ideas.* 3. *Math.* To increase a figure in the minuend by ten and make up for it by decreasing the next larger denomination by one. —*intr.v.* To take or receive a loan; obtain or receive something: *He borrowed from the bank.* [Middle English *borwen,* from Old English *borgian.*] —**bor'row·er** *n.*

bor·row·ing (bôr'ō-ĭng, bōr'-) *n.* 1. The act of asking for and accepting loans. 2. The act of taking words, ideas, etc., from another source. 3. A word taken from another language. 4. A sum of money borrowed and owed.

borscht (bôrsht) *n.* Also **borsht** or **borsch** (bôrsh). A Russian beet soup served hot or cold. [Russian *borshch.*]

bor·zoi (bôr'zoi') *n.* A rather large, slenderly built dog of a breed originating in Russia, with a narrow, pointed head and a silky, predominantly white coat. Also called **Russian wolfhound.** [Russian, "swift."]

borzoi

bos·cage (bŏs'kĭj) *n.* A mass of trees or shrubs; thicket; underwood; grove. [Middle English *boskage,* from Old French *boscage,* from *bosc.*]

bosh (bŏsh) *n. Informal.* Foolish or meaningless talk; nonsense. [Turkish *bos,* empty, useless.]

bosk (bŏsk) *n.* A small wooded area or thicket. [Back-formation from BOSKY.]

bosk·y (bŏs'kē) *adj.* **-i·er, -i·est.** 1. Covered with bushes, shrubs, or trees; wooded. 2. Shaded by trees or bushes. [From Middle English *bosk,* from *bosk,* bush, bush, from Old Norse *buskr.*] —**bosk'i·ness** *n.*

bo's'n or **bos'n** (bō'sən) *n.* Vars. of **boatswain.**

bos·om (boŏz'əm, boō'zəm) *n.* 1. The human chest or breast. 2. The part of a garment that covers the chest. 3. The heart or center of anything: *in the bosom of one's family.* 4. The heart or chest considered as the source of emotions and convictions: *a bosom full of sorrows.* —*modifier: a bosom friend.* [Middle English *bosom,* from Old English *bōsm.*]

boss¹ (bôs, bŏs) *n.* 1. The person in charge, who makes decisions. 2. The employer or supervisor of one or more workers. 3. A powerful politician who can influence public policy behind the scenes. 4. The leader of any group. —*tr.v.* 1. To supervise or control. 2. To command in an arrogant or domineering manner. —*intr.v.* To be or act as a boss. —*adj.* 1. Foremost; chief; head. 2. *Slang.* First-rate; topnotch: *Pop music is boss.* [Dutch *baas,* master, from Middle Dutch *baes.*]

boss² (bôs, bŏs) *n.* 1. A raised knoblike ornament projecting from a flat surface. 2. **a.** An enlarged part of a shaft to which another shaft is coupled or to which a wheel or gear is keyed. **b.** A hub, esp. of a propeller. —*tr.v.* 1. To decorate with bosses. 2. To emboss. [Middle English *boce,* from Old French.]

boss·ism (bô'sĭz'əm, bŏs'ĭz'əm) *n.* The control of a political organization by a political boss.

boss·y[1] (bô'sē, bŏs'ē) *adj.* **-i·er, -i·est.** Fond of ordering others around. —See Syns at **dictatorial.** —**boss'i·ly** *adv.* —**boss'i·ness** *n.*

boss·y[2] (bô'sē, bŏs'ē) *n., pl.* **-ies.** *Informal.* A cow or calf.

Bos·ton bull (bô'stən, bŏs'tən). Another name for a **Boston terrier.**

Boston fern. A fern, *Nephrolepis exaltata bostoniensis,* with arching or drooping fronds.

Boston ivy. A climbing woody vine, *Parthenocissus tricuspidata,* native to Asia, that frequently covers the outer walls of buildings.

Boston terrier. A small dog of a breed that originated in New England as a cross between a bull terrier and a bulldog. Also called **Boston bull.**

bo·sun (bō'sən) *n.* Var. of **boatswain.**

bot (bŏt) *n.* Also **bott.** The parasitic larva of a botfly. [Middle English.]

bo·tan·i·cal (bə-tăn'ĭ-kəl) or **bo·tan·ic** (bə-tăn'ĭk) *adj.* **1.** Of plants or plant life. **2.** Pertaining to the science of botany. —*n.* A drug or medicinal preparation obtained from a plant or plants. [French *botanique,* from Late Latin *botanicus,* from Greek *botanikos,* from *botanē,* pasture, herb, plant.] —**bo·tan'i·cal·ly** *adv.*

botanical garden. A place for the study and exhibition of growing plants.

bot·a·nist (bŏt'n-ĭst) *n.* A scientist who specializes in the study of plants.

bot·a·ny (bŏt'n-ē) *n.* **1.** The scientific study of plants. **2.** The plant life of a particular area. **3.** The characteristics of a plant group. [From BOTANICAL.]

botch (bŏch) *tr.v.* To ruin through careless or clumsy work; to bungle. —*n.* A bad job or poor piece of work. [Middle English *bocchen,* to patch up, mend.] —**botch'er** *n.* —**botch'y** *adj.*

    Syns: botch, blow (*Slang*), blunder, bungle, foul up (*Slang*), fumble, goof (up) (*Slang*), louse (*Slang*), mess up, mishandle, mismanage, muddle, muff, snafu (*Slang*), spoil *v.* Core meaning: To harm severely through inept handling (*a repair botched by an incompetent mechanic*).

bot·fly (bŏt'flī') *n.* Also **bot fly.** Any of various winged insects, chiefly of the genera *Gasterophilus* and *Oestrus,* with larvae that are parasitic on man and on sheep, horses, and other animals.

both (bōth) *pron.* The one as well as the other; the two alike. **a.** —Used alone: *If one is guilty, both are.* **b.** —Used with *of* and a pronoun: *both of them.* **c.** —Used in apposition with a pronoun: *You both skate well. They were both crazy.* —*adj.* The two; the one as well as the other. **a.** —Used before an unmodified noun: *both sides of the valley.* **b.** —Used before a noun modified with a demonstrative: *Instead of a plain green or brown skirt, she chose a tweed that emphasized both these colors.* **c.** —Used before a noun modified with a possessive: *Both my parents are gone.* —*conj.* —Used as a correlative conjunction in the construction **both. . .and** to indicate and emphasize a grouping by two: *Both the United States and Great Britain claimed the Oregon Country.* [Middle English *bothe,* from Old Norse *bāthir.*]

    Usage: **both. 1.** In formal compositions, limit usage of *both* to two. Correct: *famous in both America and Europe.* Delete here: *famous in (both) America, Europe, and Asia.* **2.** *Both* is loosely used for *each* here: *Both criticized the other. An image was projected on both halves of the screen* (in formal writing, make it *on each half* or *images on both halves*). **3.** Avoid the phrase *the both;* in this example, delete *the: congratulated (the) both of us.* **4.** Possessive constructions with *both* are illustrated by *the parents of both* and *the fault of both* (preferable to *both their parents, both their fault, or both's fault,* although the last three examples are not unacceptable in the United States). **5.** *Both of* can be used before pronouns (*both of us*). This construction has been used in English since the time of Queen Elizabeth I, and it is standard. Similarly, *both of* can be used with nouns (*both of the children*) esp. in the United States where it is a standard idiom. Alternative wordings are: *both children, both the children.* **6.** *Both* is redundant with *alike, as well as, equal, equally,* and

together; omit *both* in these examples: *are (both) alike; appeared (both) in films as well as on the stage; amounts that are (both) equal; plans that are (both) equally sound; father and son (both) acted together.*

both·er (bŏth'ər) *tr.v.* **1.** To irritate or annoy, esp. repeatedly; pester; harass. **2. a.** To make agitated or nervous; fluster. **b.** To make confused or perplexed; bewilder; puzzle. **3.** To interrupt; disturb: *Don't bother me when I'm working.* **4.** To give trouble to: *His back bothers him constantly.* —*intr.v.* To trouble or concern oneself: *Don't bother with that.* —See Syns at **annoy** —*n.* **1.** An annoying thing; a nuisance. **2.** Trouble: *a lot of bother for nothing.* —*interj.* A word used to express mild annoyance or irritation. [Perh. from Irish *buaidhrim,* I vex.]

both·er·some (bŏth'ər-səm) *adj.* Causing trouble; annoying; troublesome.

bott (bŏt) *n.* Var. of **bot.**

bot·tle (bŏt'l) *n.* **1.** A container, usu. made of glass, with a narrow neck and a mouth that can be corked or capped. **2. a.** A bottle with something in it: *a bottle of soda.* **b.** The amount that a bottle holds: *drink a bottle of milk.* **3.** A bottle of milk with a nipple on it: *Give the baby his bottle.* **4.** A bottle of alcoholic liquor. —*tr.v.* **-tled, -tling.** To put in a bottle or bottles: *This machine bottles soda.* —*phrasal verb.* **bottle up. 1.** To hold in; restrain. **2.** To seal up; to block. [Middle English *botel,* from Old French *botele,* *botaille,* from Medieval Latin *butticula,* dim. of Late Latin *buttis,* cask.] —**bot'tler** *n.*

bot·tle·neck (bŏt'l-něk') *n.* **1.** The narrow part of a bottle near the top. **2.** A narrow route or passage where movement is slowed down. **3.** Any condition that slows or hinders production or progress.

bot·tle-nosed dolphin (bŏt'l-nōzd'). Any of several saltwater mammals of the genus *Tursiops,* with a short, protruding beak. Also called **bottlenose.**

bot·tom (bŏt'əm) *n.* **1.** The lowest part or edge of anything: *the bottom of a page.* **2.** The lowest inside or outside surface: *oars in the bottom of a boat.* **3.** The lowest part of something deep or high: *the bottom of the hill.* **4.** The solid surface under a body of water. **5.** The underlying truth or cause; basis; heart: *get to the bottom of the matter.* **6.** Often **bottoms.** The low, alluvial land that adjoins a river. **7.** The seat of a chair. **8.** *Informal.* The buttocks. —*modifier:* *the bottom drawer.* —*tr.v.* **1.** To provide with an underside or foundation. **2.** To establish on a foundation or basis; to ground; to found: *The theory is bottomed on questionable assumptions.* —*intr.v.* **1.** To be based or grounded. **2.** To rest on or touch the bottom: *The submarine bottomed on the ocean floor.* —*phrasal verb.* **bottom out.** To descend to the lowest point possible, after which only a rise may occur: *Steel stocks bottomed out in the market.* —*idiom.* **at bottom.** Basically. [Middle English *botme,* from Old English *botm.*]

bot·tom·land (bŏt'əm-lănd') *n.* Often **bottomlands.** Low-lying land along a river.

bot·tom·less (bŏt'əm-lĭs) *adj.* **1.** Having no bottom. **2.** Too deep to be measured; unfathomable; limitless: *a bottomless pool; bottomless knowledge.*

bot·u·lism (bŏch'ə-lĭz'əm) *n.* A serious, often fatal form of food poisoning caused by bacteria that grow in improperly canned foods. [German *Botulismus,* "sausage-poisoning," from Latin *botulus,* sausage.]

bou·doir (bōō'dwär', -dwôr') *n.* A woman's private sitting room, dressing room, or bedroom. [French, "place for pouting," from Old French *bouder,* to pout.]

bouf·fant (bōō-fänt') *adj.* Full and puffed-out: *a bouffant hair style; a bouffant skirt.* [French, from *bouffer,* to swell, puff up (the cheeks), from Old French.]

bou·gain·vil·le·a (bōō'gən-vĭl'ē-ə, -vĭl'yə) *n.* Also **bou·gain·vil·lae·a.** Any of several woody tropical American vines of the genus *Bougainvillea,* with inconspicuous flowers surrounded by red, purple, or orange leaves that look like petals. [After Louis Antoine de *Bougainville* (1729–1811), French explorer and scientist.]

bough (bou) *n.* A large branch of a tree. [Middle English, from Old English *bōg, bōh.*]

bought (bôt) *v.* Past tense and past participle of **buy.**

bouil·la·baisse (bōō'yə-bās') *n.* A highly seasoned fish stew made with several kinds of fish and shellfish.

ă pat   ā pay   â care   ä father   ĕ pet   ē be   hw which   ĭ pit   ī tie   î pier   ŏ pot   ō toe   ô paw, for   oi noise
ōō took   ōō boot   ou out   th thin   th this   ŭ cut   û urge   zh vision   ə about, item, edible, gallop, circus

[French, earlier *bouille-abaisse*, from Provençal *bouia-baisso*, "boil (and) settle."]

bouil·lon (bōō'yŏn', bōōl'-, -yən) *n.* A clear, thin soup of liquid in which meat has been boiled: *beef bouillon.* [French, from Old French, from *boulir*, to boil, from Latin *bullīre*.]

boul·der (bōl'dər) *n.* A large, rounded mass of rock lying on the ground or imbedded in the soil. [Middle English *bulder (ston)*, of Scandinavian orig.]

boul·e·vard (bōōl'ə-värd', bōō'lə-) *n.* A broad city street, often lined with trees and landscaped. [French, from Old French *boloart*, rampart, promenade, from Middle Dutch *bolwerc*, from Middle High German, bulwark.]

bounce (bouns) *v.* **bounced, bounc·ing.** —*intr.v.* **1.** To strike a surface and rebound elastically several times in succession: *The ball bounced up and down.* **2.** To bound noisily or enthusiastically: *The child bounced into the room.* **3.** *Informal.* To be sent back by a bank as valueless: *The check bounced.* —*tr.v.* **1.** To cause (a body) to strike a surface and rebound: *bounce a ball off the wall.* **2.** *Slang.* **a.** To throw (someone) out forcefully. **b.** To dismiss from employment. —*n.* **1.** An act of bouncing or a bouncing movement; a bound or rebound. **2.** A reflection. **3.** Capacity to bounce; springiness: *a ball with bounce.* **4.** Liveliness; vivacity. **5. the bounce.** *Slang.* Expulsion; dismissal. **6.** *Brit.* Impudent bluster. [Middle English *bunsen, bonchen*, to beat, stamp.]

bounc·er (boun'sər) *n.* **1.** Someone or something that bounces. **2.** *Slang.* A person employed to throw disorderly persons out of a night club, bar, etc.

bounc·ing (boun'sĭng) *adj.* Large; healthy; thriving: *a bouncing baby; a series of bouncing crops.*

bouncing Bet (bĕt). A plant, *Saponaria officinalis*, native to the Old World, with rounded clusters of fragrant pink or white flowers. Also called **soapwort.** [*Bet*, pet form of the name *Elizabeth*.]

bounc·y (boun'sē) *adj.* **-i·er, -i·est. 1.** Tending to bounce: *a bouncy ball.* **2.** Springy; elastic: *bouncy, spongelike material.* **3.** Lively; energetic: *bouncy tunes.* —**bounc'i·ly** *adv.* —**bounc'i·ness** *n.*

bound¹ (bound) *intr.v.* **1.** To leap forward or upward; to spring: *He bounded over the gate.* **2.** To move by leaping: *The deer bounded away.* **3.** To bounce or rebound: *rocks bounding down the path.* —*n.* **1.** A leap; a jump: *cleared the wall with a bound.* **2.** A bounce. [French *bondir*, to rebound, from Old French, to resound, from Latin *bombīre*, to buzz, from *bombus*, a buzz, from Greek *bombos*.]

bound² (bound) *n.* **1.** Often **bounds.** A boundary; limit: *His joy knew no bounds.* **2. bounds.** The territory on, within, or near limiting lines: *the bounds of the kingdom.* —*tr.v.* **1.** To provide a limit to. **2.** To constitute the boundary or limit of. —*idiom.* **out of bounds.** Beyond the usual, legal, or safe limits; prohibited. [Middle English *bounde*, from Old French *bunde*, from Medieval Latin *bodina*.]

bound³ (bound) *v.* Past tense and past participle of **bind.** —*adj.* **1.** Certain: *We are bound to be late.* **2.** Under obligation; obliged: *bound by a promise; duty bound.* **3.** Confined or held by or as if by bonds; tied: *bound and gagged.* **4.** Enclosed in a cover or binding: *a bound book.* **5.** Resolved: *bound and determined.* —*idiom.* **bound up with.** Closely associated or connected with. [Middle English *bounden, bounden*, from Old English *bundon* (pl.), *(ge)bunden.*]

bound⁴ (bound) *adj.* Ready to start; on the way: *bound for home.* [Middle English *boun*, prepared, ready to go, from Old Norse *būa*, to dwell, prepare.]

bound·a·ry (boun'də-rē, -drē) *n., pl.* **-ries.** Something that indicates a border or limit: *the boundary between the United States and Mexico.* [Earlier *bounder*, from BOUND (limit).]

bound·en (boun'dən) *adj.* Being an obligation; required; obligatory: *your bounden duty.* [From *bounden*, obs. past part. of BIND.]

bound·er (boun'dər) *n. Brit.* A person who behaves dishonorably; cad.

bound·less (bound'lĭs) *adj.* Without limit; infinite: *boundless joy and enthusiasm.* —**bound'less·ly** *adv.* —**bound'less·ness** *n.*

boun·te·ous (boun'tē-əs) *adj.* **1.** Giving generously and

kindly: *bounteous kindness.* **2.** Copious; plentiful: *a bounteous harvest.* See Syns at **generous.** [Middle English *bountevous*, from Old French *bontif*, benevolent, from *bonte*, bounty.] —**boun'te·ous·ly** *adv.* —**boun'te·ous·ness** *n.*

boun·ti·ful (boun'tə-fəl) *adj.* **1.** Generous; bounteous: *a bountiful gentleman.* **2.** Abundant; plentiful: *bountiful rainfall.* —See Syns at **generous.** —**boun'ti·ful·ly** *adv.* —**boun'ti·ful·ness** *n.*

boun·ty (boun'tē) *n., pl.* **-ties. 1.** Generosity in giving: *dependent on a patron's bounty.* **2.** Something that is given liberally. **3.** A reward, inducement, or payment, esp. one given by a government for performing a service for the government, as killing a destructive animal or growing certain crops. [Middle English *bounte*, from Old French *bonte*, from Latin *bonitās*, goodness, from *bonus*, good.]

bou·quet (bō-kā', bōō-) *n.* **1.** A cluster of flowers; nosegay. **2.** (bōō-kā'). A pleasant fragrance, esp. of a wine or a liqueur. [French, from Old North French *bosquet*, clump, from Old French *bosc*, forest.]

bour·bon (bûr'bən) *n.* A whiskey distilled from a fermented mash containing not less than 51 per cent corn. [After *Bourbon* County, Kentucky.]

bour·geois (bōōr-zhwä', bōōr'zhwä') *n., pl.* **bourgeois. 1.** A person who belongs to the middle class or bourgeoisie. **2.** A member of the property-owning class; a capitalist. —*adj.* **1.** Of or typical of the middle class. **2.** Caring too much about respectability and possessions. [French, from Old French *burgeis*, from *bourg*, fortified town, from Late Latin *burgus.*]

bour·geoise (bōōr-zhwäz', bōōr'zhwäz') *n.* A female member of the bourgeoisie. —**bour·geoise'** *adj.*

bour·geoi·sie (bōōr'zhwä-zē') *n.* The middle class as opposed to the aristocracy or the laboring class. [French, from *bourgeois*, bourgeois.]

bourn¹ (bôrn, bōrn, bōōrn) *n.* Also **bourne.** A stream or small brook. [Middle English *burne*, brook.]

bourn² (bôrn, bōrn, bōōrn) *n.* Also **bourne.** *Archaic.* **1.** A boundary, limit, or frontier. **2.** A goal or destination. **3.** A realm; domain. [French *bourne*, from Old French *bonne*, *bodne*, bound, limit.]

bour·rée (bōō-rā', bōō-) *n.* **1.** A quick, lively French dance of the 17th cent. **2.** Music written to accompany or as if to accompany this dance. [French, from *bourrer*, to stuff, from Old French *bourre*, stuffing, fluff, from Late Latin *burra*, shaggy garment.]

bout (bout) *n.* **1.** A contest between opponents; a match: *a wrestling bout.* **2.** A period of time spent in a particular way; a spell: *a bout of the flu.* [Earlier *bought*, a turn (as in plowing), from Middle English *bought*, a bend, from Middle Low German *bucht.*]

bou·tique (bōō-tēk') *n.* A small retail shop that sells gifts, fashionable clothes, etc. [French, from Old Provençal *botica*, ult. from Greek *apothēkē*, storeroom.]

bou·ton·niere or **bou·ton·nière** (bōōt'n-îr', -yâr') *n.* A flower worn in a buttonhole, usu. on a lapel. [Old French, from *bouton*, button.]

bo·vine (bō'vīn', -vēn') *adj.* **1.** Of, pertaining to, or resembling an ox, cow, or other animal of the genus *Bos.* **2.** Dull and placid: *a bovine stare.* —*n.* A bovine animal. [Late Latin *bovīnus*, from Latin *bōs*, ox, cow.]

bow¹ (bō) *n.* **1.** A weapon used to shoot arrows, consisting of a curved strip of wood, metal, etc., with a string stretched tightly from end to end. **2.** A slender, springy rod with horsehair stretched between two raised ends, used in playing the violin, viola, and related stringed instruments. **3.** A knot tied with a loop or loops at either end. **4.** A curve or arch, as of lips or eyebrows. **5. a.** A frame for the lenses of a pair of eyeglasses. **b.** The part of such a frame passing over the ear. **6.** A rainbow. —*tr.v.* **1.** To bend (something) into the shape of a bow. **2.** To play (a stringed instrument) with a bow. —*intr.v.* **1.** To bend into a curve or bow: *His legs bow awkwardly.* **2.** To play a stringed instrument with a bow. [Middle English *bowe*, from Old English *boga.*]

bow² (bou) *intr.v.* **1.** To bend or curve downward; stoop: *He bowed beneath the heavy load.* **2.** To incline the body or head or bend the knee in greeting, consent, courtesy,

---

ă pat   ā pay   â care   ä father   ĕ pet   ē be   hw which   ĭ pit   ī tie   î pier   ŏ pot   ō toe   ô paw, for   oi noise
ōō took   ōō boot   ou out   th thin   th this   ŭ cut   û urge   zh vision   ə about, item, edible, gallop, circus

bowerbird
George Miksch Sutton

bowie knife

bowsprit

etc. **3.** To yield or comply; submit: *They refused to bow without a struggle.* —*tr.v.* **1.** To bend (the head, knee, or body) in order to express greeting, consent, veneration, etc. **2.** To convey (greeting, consent, etc.) by bowing: *They bowed their thanks.* **3.** To escort deferentially: *He bowed us into the restaurant.* **4.** To cause to bend downward; overburden: *Age bowed her back.* —See Syns at **yield.** —*phrasal verb.* **bow out.** To withdraw or resign. —*n.* **1.** A bending of the body or head, as when showing respect or accepting applause. **2.** Any sign of respect, recognition, etc.: *The President's trip was a bow to Europe.* —*idiom.* **bow and scrape.** To behave in a slavish, fawning way. [Middle English *bowen,* from Old English *būgan.*]

bow³ (bou) *n.* **1.** The front section of a ship or boat. **2.** The oar or oarsman closest to the bow of a boat. [Middle English, from Middle Low German *boog.*]

bowd·ler·ize (bŏd′lə-rīz′, boud′-) *tr.v.* **-ized, -iz·ing.** To remove passages considered improper or indecent from (a book, play, etc.) [After Thomas Bowdler (1754–1825), English editor who published an expurgated edition of Shakespeare's works.] —**bowd′ler·i·za′tion** *n.*

bow·el (bou′əl, boul) *n.* **1.** An intestine, esp. of a human being. **2.** Often **bowels.** The part of the digestive tract below the stomach. **3. bowels.** The inmost depths of anything: *in the bowels of the ship.* [Middle English *b(o)uel,* from Old French *bo(u)el,* from Latin *botellus,* from *botulus,* sausage.]

bow·er¹ (bou′ər) *n.* **1.** A shaded, leafy recess; an arbor. **2.** *Poet.* A lady's private chamber; boudoir. **3.** *Poet.* A rustic cottage; a country retreat. [Middle English *bour,* dwelling, inner apartment, from Old English *būr.*] —**bow′er·y** *adj.*

bow·er² (bou′ər) *n.* The heaviest of a ship's anchors, carried at the bow. Also called **bower anchor.**

bow·er·bird (bou′ər-bûrd′) *n.* Any of various birds of the family Ptilonorhynchidae, of Australia and New Guinea. The males build bowers of grasses, twigs, and colored materials to attract females.

bow·fin (bō′fĭn′) *n.* A freshwater fish, *Amia calva,* of central and eastern North America.

bow·head (bō′hĕd′) *n.* A whale, *Balaena mysticetus,* of northern seas, with a large head with a curved top.

bow·ie knife (bō′ē, bōō′ē) *n.* A long single-edged steel hunting knife, with a hilt and a crosspiece, used esp. by frontiersmen. [After Col. James Bowie (1790?-1836), American-born Mexican colonist.]

bowl¹ (bōl) *n.* **1.** A rounded, hollow container or dish that can hold liquid, food, etc. **2. a.** A bowl with something in it: *a bowl of goldfish.* **b.** The amount that a bowl holds: *eat a bowl of soup.* **3.** The curved, hollow part of a spoon, pipe, etc. **4.** Anything shaped like a curved dish or dome: *the blue bowl of the sky.* **5.** A region characterized by a product, crop, or feature: *the rice bowl of Asia.* **6. a.** A bowl-shaped stadium or outdoor theater. **b.** One of several special football games played after the regular season ends: *the Rose Bowl.* [Middle English *bolle,* from Old English *bolla.*]

bowl² (bōl) *n.* **1.** A large, wooden ball weighted or slightly flattened so as to roll with a bias. **2.** A roll or throw of the ball, as in bowling. **3. bowls.** The game of lawn bowling. —*intr.v.* **1.** To play the game of bowling. **2.** To roll a ball or take a turn in bowling: *You bowl first.* **3.** To move

smoothly and rapidly: *The bus bowled along the road.* —*tr.v.* **1.** To throw or roll (a ball) in bowling. **2.** To make (a score) in bowling: *Her brother bowled 137.* —*phrasal verb.* **bowl over. 1.** To knock over. **2.** To take by surprise; astound; stun. [Middle English *boule,* ball, from Old French, from Latin *bulla.*]

bow·leg·ged (bō′lĕg′ĭd, -lĕgd′) *adj.* Having bowlegs.

bow·legs (bō′lĕgz′) *pl.n.* Legs that curve outward at or below the knee.

bowl·er¹ (bō′lər) *n.* A person who bowls.

bowl·er² (bō′lər) *n. Brit.* A man's derby hat. [After John Bowler, 19th-cent. London hatmaker.]

bow·line (bō′lĭn, -līn′) *n.* **1.** A knot forming a loop that does not slip. Also called **bowline knot. 2.** *Naut.* A rope leading forward from the leech of a square sail to hold the leech forward when sailing close-hauled. [Middle English *bouline,* prob. from Middle Low German *bōlīne,* bow line.]

bowl·ing (bō′lĭng) *n.* **1.** A game played by rolling a heavy ball down a wooden alley in an attempt to knock down ten wooden pins at the opposite end; tenpins. **2.** A similar game, such as ninepins or skittles. **3.** Also called **lawn bowling.** A game played on a level lawn, or bowling green, by rolling a wooden ball as close as possible to a target ball.

bowling alley. 1. A long, smooth, level, wooden lane or alley used for bowling. **2.** A building or room containing such alleys.

bowling green. A level grassy area for lawn bowling.

bow·man (bō′mən) *n.* An archer.

bow·sprit (bou′sprĭt′, bō′-) *n.* A long pole or spar extending forward from the bow of a sailing ship, holding chains, ropes, or wires that run to the foremast and sails. [Middle English *bouspret,* from Middle Low German *bōchsprēt.*]

bow·string (bō′strĭng′) *n.* The string of a bow.

bow tie (bō). A small necktie tied in a bow.

box¹ (bŏks) *n.* **1.** A stiff container made of cardboard, wood, metal, etc., usu. having four sides and a top or lid. **2. a.** A box with something in it: *a box of crayons.* **b.** The amount that a box holds: *eat half a box of cereal.* **3.** A rectangle: *Draw a box around the correct answer.* **4.** Anything shaped or enclosed like a box, as a separate seating compartment in a theater or courtroom, or a sentry's shelter. **5.** *Brit.* A small country house in hunting country: *a shooting box.* **6.** *Baseball.* A box stall. **7.** The raised seat for the driver of a coach or carriage. **8.** *Baseball.* **a.** An area marked out by chalk lines where the batter stands. **b.** Any of various designated areas for other team members, such as the catcher and coaches. **9.** Featured printed matter enclosed by a border, white space, etc., placed within or between text columns. **10.** An insulating, enclosing, or protective casing or part in a machine or for a mechanism: *a fire-alarm box.* **11.** A pigeonhole for mail: *a post-office box.* **12.** A chest or trunk. **13.** An awkward or perplexing situation. —*modifier: a box top.* —*tr.v.* **1.** To put or pack in a box. **2.** To enclose in a rectangle: *box the title of the story.* —*phrasal verb.* **box in** (or **up**). To enclose, surround, or hem in. —*idiom.* **box the compass. 1.** To name the points of the compass in proper order. **2.** To make a complete reversal. [Middle English *box,* from Old English *box,* from Late Latin *buxis,* var. of Latin *pyxis,* box (made of boxwood), from Greek *puxis,* from *puxos,* box tree.]

box² (bŏks) *n.* A blow or slap with the hand: *a box on the* ear. —*tr.v.* **1.** To hit with the hand or fist. **2.** To take part in a boxing match with. —*intr.v.* To fight with the fists; to spar. [Middle English.]

box³ (bŏks) *n., pl.* **box** or **box·es. 1.** Any evergreen tree or shrub of the genus *Buxus*, used for hedges, borders, and garden mazes. Also called **boxwood. 2.** The wood of this tree, boxwood. [Middle English *box*, from Old English *box*, from Latin *buxus*, box-tree, from Greek *puxos*.]

box·car (bŏks′kär′) *n.* An enclosed railway car used to carry freight.

box elder. A maple tree, *Acer negundo*, of North America, that has compound leaves with lobed leaflets.

box·er¹ (bŏk′sər) *n.* A person who boxes, esp. professionally.

box·er² (bŏk′sər) *n.* A short-haired dog of a breed developed in Germany, with a brownish coat and a short, square-jawed muzzle. [German *Boxer*, from English *boxer*, pugilist (from its pugnacious nature).]

boxer²

box·ing (bŏk′sĭng) *n.* The sport of fighting with the fists, esp. when padded gloves are worn.

Boxing Day. *Brit.* The first weekday after Christmas, observed as a holiday, when Christmas gifts or boxes were traditionally given to household employees and other service workers.

boxing glove. One of two heavily padded gloves worn by a boxer to protect the fists while boxing.

box kite. A tailless kite consisting of a rectangular, box-shaped frame, covered with cloth or paper bands, and open at the ends.

box office. 1. A ticket office, as of a theater, auditorium, or stadium. **2.** The drawing power of a theatrical entertainment or of a performer.

box pleat. A double pleat formed by two facing folds.

box spring. A bedspring that consists of a frame, containing rows of coil springs, enclosed with cloth.

box stall. An enclosed stall for a single animal; a box.

box turtle. Any of several North American turtles of the genus *Terrapene*, that have a high-domed shell.

box·wood (bŏks′wŏod′) *n.* **1.** A shrub or tree, box. **2.** The hard, light-yellow wood of this tree, used to make musical instruments, rulers, inlays, etc.

box·y (bŏk′sē) *adj.* **-i·er, -i·est.** Like a box; rather square: *a boxy suit.* —**box′i·ness** *n.*

boy (boi) *n.* **1.** A male child or a youth who has not yet reached manhood. **2. a.** A son: *my own sister's boy.* **b.** A brother: *the Jones boys.* **3.** A youth who does some special work: *a shepherd boy.* **4.** *Informal.* A fellow; guy. —*interj.* A word used to express mild astonishment, elation, etc.: *Oh boy!* [Middle English *boye*, male servant, knave.].

bo·yar (bō-yär′) *n.* A member of a former Russian aristocratic order abolished by Peter I. [Russian *boyarin*, from Old Russian, "of the highest rank."]

boy·cott (boi′kŏt′) *tr.v.* To abstain from using, buying, or dealing with, as a protest or means of coercion: *boycott a store; boycott a meeting.* —*n.* The act or an instance of boycotting. [After Charles C. *Boycott* (1832–97), land agent in Ireland, who was ostracized by the tenants for refusing to lower the rents.]

boy·friend (boi′frĕnd′) *n.* Also **boy friend. 1.** *Informal.* A sweetheart or frequent date of a woman or girl. **2.** A male friend.

boy·hood (boi′hŏod′) *n.* The time of being a boy.

boy·ish (boi′ĭsh) *adj.* Of, like, or suitable for a boy: *a boyish prank.* —**boy′ish·ly** *adv.* —**boy′ish·ness** *n.*

Boyle's law (boilz). *Physics.* The principle that at a fixed temperature the pressure of a confined ideal gas varies inversely with its volume. [After Robert *Boyle* (1627–91), English scientist.]

Boy Scout. A member of a worldwide organization of young men and boys, founded to help develop self-reliance, good citizenship, and outdoor skills.

boy·sen·ber·ry (boi′zən-bĕr′ē) *n.* **1.** A prickly bramble hybridized from the loganberry and various blackberries and raspberries. **2.** The large, wine-red, edible berry borne by this plant. [After Rudolph *Boysen*, 20th-cent. American horticulturist.]

boysenberry

Br The symbol for the element bromine.

bra (brä) *n.* A brassiere.

brace (brās) *n.* **1. a.** A device that holds two or more parts together or in place. **b.** A support, as a beam in a building. **2.** *Med.* A device used to support a part of the body. **3.** Often **braces.** An arrangement of wires and bands fixed to crooked teeth in order to straighten them. **4.** Either of the symbols { }, used in printing and writing to connect several lines of text and in mathematics to enclose the listing of the elements of a set. **5.** *Mus.* The symbol {, used to connect several staves. **6.** A rotating handle that holds a drill or bit, used for boring holes. **7.** A pair: *a brace of partridges.* **8. braces.** *Brit.* Suspenders. —See Syns at **couple.** —*tr.v.* **braced, brac·ing. 1.** To support; strengthen; reinforce: *brace a sloping shed with timbers.* **2.** To prepare for a blow, shock, struggle, etc.: *Brace yourselves for the coming test.* **3.** To prop or hold firmly in place: *She braced her feet against the floorboard.* **4.** To fill with energy; refresh; stimulate: *The cold, clear air of the slopes braced the skiers.* —*phrasal verb.* **brace up. 1.** To summon up lost strength or courage. **2.** To straighten up one's body. [Middle English, arm guard, from Old French, the two arms, from Latin *bracchium*, arm, from Greek *brakhíon*.] —**brac′ly** *adv.*

brace·let (brās′lĭt) *n.* **1.** An ornamental band or chain worn around the wrist. **2. bracelets.** *Slang.* Handcuffs. [Middle English, from Old French *bracel*, from armlet, from Latin *bracchiāle*, from *bracchium*, arm.]

brac·er (brā′sər) *n.* **1.** Something or someone that braces. **2.** *Informal.* A stimulating drink; tonic.

brach·i·o·pod (brăk′ē-ə-pŏd′, brā′kē-) *n.* Any of various saltwater invertebrates of the phylum Brachiopoda, with bivalve dorsal and ventral shells and a pair of tentacled, armlike structures on either side of the mouth. [Latin *bracchium*, arm + -POD.]

brack·en (brăk′ən) *n.* **1.** A fern, *Pteridium aquilinum*, with tough stems and branching, finely divided fronds. Also called **brake. 2.** An area overgrown with this fern. **3.** Any large, coarse fern. [Middle English *braken*.]

brack·et (brăk′ĭt) *n.* **1.** A support or fixture in the shape of an L, fastened to a surface vertically and projecting horizontally to support a shelf or other weight. **2.** Any of various similar wall-anchored fixtures used to support loads. **3.** A small shelf or shelves supported by brackets. **4. a.** Either of a pair of symbols, [ ], used to enclose written or printed material or to indicate a mathematical expression considered in some sense a single quantity. **b.** Either of a pair of symbols, < >, similarly used and in mathematics used esp. together to indicate the average of a contained quantity. **5.** A classification or grouping within a series: *the 12-to-18 age bracket.* —*tr.v.* **1.** To support with a bracket or brackets. **2.** To place within brackets. **3.** To classify or group together: *bracket taxpayers according to their earnings.* [Earlier *bragget,* from Old French *braguette,* codpiece, dim. of *brague,* mortise, from Old Provençal *braga,* from Latin *brāca.*]

brack·ish (brăk′ĭsh) *adj.* **1.** Containing some salt; briny: *brackish lake water.* **2.** Bad-tasting; unpalatable. [From British dialectal *brack,* from Dutch *brak,* from Middle Dutch *brac.*] —**brack′ish·ness** *n.*

bract (brăkt) *n.* A leaflike plant part, usu. small but sometimes showy and brightly colored, located either below a flower or on the stalk of a flower cluster. [From Latin *bractea,* metal plate or leaf.]

brad (brăd) *n.* A tapered nail with a small head or a slight side projection instead of a head. [Middle English, from Old Norse *broddr,* spike.]

brae (brā) *n. Scot.* A hillside; a slope. [Middle English *bra,* from Old Norse *brā,* eyelash.]

brag (brăg) *v.* **bragged, brag·ging.** —*intr.v.* To talk boastfully about oneself or one's deeds, possessions, family, etc. —*tr.v.* To assert boastfully: *He bragged that he could run faster than any of us.* See Syns at **boast.** —*n.* **1.** Arrogant or boastful speech. **2.** A braggart; boaster. [Middle English *braggen.*] —**brag′ger** *n.*

brag·ga·do·ci·o (brăg′ə-dō′shē-ō′) *n., pl.* -**os. 1.** A braggart. **2. a.** Empty or pretentious bragging. **b.** Swaggering manner; cockiness. [After *Braggadocchio,* the personification of boasting in Edmund Spenser's *Faerie Queene.*]

brag·gart (brăg′ərt) *n.* A person given to loud, empty boasting; bragger. —*adj.* Boastful. [French *bragard,* from *braguer,* to brag.]

Brah·ma (brä′mə) *n. Hinduism.* **1.** The personification of divine reality in its creative aspect as a member of the Hindu triad. **2.** Var. of **Brahman.**

Brah·man (brä′mən) *n.* **1.** Also **Brah·ma** (-mə). *Hinduism.* The essential divine reality of the universe; the eternal spirit from which all being originates and to which all returns. **2.** Also **Brah·min** (-mən). *Hinduism.* A member of the highest caste, orig. composed of priests but now occupationally diversified. **3.** Also **Brah·ma** or **Brah·min.** One of a breed of domestic cattle developed in the southern United States from stock originating in India, and having a hump between the shoulders and a pendulous dewlap. —**Brah·man′ic** (-măn′ĭk) or **Brah·man′i·cal** *adj.*

Brah·man·ism (brä′mə-nĭz′əm) *n.* Also **Brah·min·ism** (brä′mĭn). **1.** The religious practices and beliefs of ancient India as reflected in the Vedas, the earliest religious texts. **2.** The social caste system of the Brahmans of India. —**Brah′man·ist** *n.*

Brah·min (brä′mən) *n.* **1.** A highly cultured and socially exclusive person, esp. a member of one of the old New England families. **2.** Var. of **Brahman** (caste and cattle). —**Brah·min′ic** (-mĭn′ĭk) or **Brah·min′i·cal** *adj.*

Brah·min·ism (brä′mə-nĭz′əm) *n.* Var. of **Brahmanism.**

braid (brād) *tr.v.* **1.** To interweave three or more strands of (hair, fiber, fabric, etc.); to plait. **2.** To decorate or edge with an ornamental trim. **3.** To make by weaving strands together: *braid a straw rug.* —*n.* **1.** A narrow length of fabric, hair, or other material that has been braided or plaited. **2.** A strip of braided material, used for binding or trimming clothes, making mats, etc. [Middle English *breyden,* to move quickly, braid, from Old English *bregdan.*] —**braid′er** *n.*

brail (brāl) *n.* A line used to furl loose-footed sails. —*tr.v.* To gather in (a sail) with brails. [Middle English *brayle,* from Old French *brail, braiel,* belt, girdle, from Medieval Latin *brācāle,* from Latin *brīaca,* breeches.]

Braille or **braille** (brāl) *n.* A system of writing and printing for the blind, in which varied arrangements of raised dots representing letters and numerals can be identified by touch. [After Louis *Braille* (1809-52), French educator, its inventor.]

brain (brān) *n.* **1.** The portion of the central nervous system consisting of a large mass of gray nerve tissue enclosed in the skull of a vertebrate, responsible for the interpretation of sensory impulses, the coordination and control of bodily activities, and the exercise of emotion and thought. **2.** A functionally similar portion of the invertebrate nervous system. **3. brains.** The brains of an animal used as food. **4.** Often **brains.** Intellectual capacity; intelligence. **5.** *Slang.* A highly intelligent person. **6.** Often **brains.** A person who plans the activities of a group, organization, etc. —*tr.v.* **1.** To smash in the skull of. **2.** *Slang.* To hit on the head. —**idioms. on the brain.** To have an obsession about. **rack** (or **beat**) **(one's) brains.** To try very hard to think of, figure out, or solve something. [Middle English *brain,* from Old English *brægen.*]

brain·child (brān′chīld′) *n. Informal.* An original idea, plan, etc., attributed to a specific person or group.

brain·less (brān′lĭs) *adj.* Lacking intelligence; stupid. —**brain′less·ly** *adv.* —**brain′less·ness** *n.*

brain·storm (brān′stôrm′) *n. Informal.* A sudden inspiration or clever idea.

brain trust. Also *Brit.* **brains trust.** A group of experts who serve as unofficial advisers and policy planners.

brain·wash (brān′wŏsh′, -wôsh′) *tr.v.* To indoctrinate (someone) until he is willing to give up his own beliefs and passively accept an opposing set of beliefs.

brain wave. Any of the rhythmically fluctuating voltages that arise from electrical activity in the brain.

brain·y (brā′nē) *adj.* -**i·er,** -**i·est.** *Informal.* Intelligent; smart. —**brain′i·ness** *n.*

braise (brāz) *tr.v.* **braised, brais·ing.** To brown (meat or vegetables) in fat and then simmer in a small amount of liquid in a covered container. [French *braiser,* from *braise,* hot charcoal, from Old French *brese.*]

brake[1] (brāk) *n.* **1.** Often **brakes.** A device for slowing or stopping motion, as of a vehicle or machine. **2.** Often **brakes.** A restraint that slows or stops an ongoing action or process: *put a brake on rising prices.* **3.** A machine for bending and folding sheet metal. —*v.* **braked, brak·ing.** —*tr.v.* To reduce the speed of with or as if with a brake. —*intr.v.* To operate or apply a brake or brakes. [Middle English, crushing instrument, pestle, from Middle Dutch *braeke.*]

brake[2] (brāk) *n.* **1.** Any of several ferns, esp. bracken. **2.** An area overgrown with dense bushes, briers, etc.; a thicket. [Middle English *(ferne)brake,* from Old English *(fearn)braca,* bed of fern.]

brake[3] (brāk) *v. Archaic.* A past tense of **break.** [Middle English, from Old English *bræc.*]

brake·man (brāk′mən) *n.* Also *Brit.* **brakes·man** (brāks′mən). A railroad employee who assists the conductor and checks on the operation of the train's brakes.

bram·ble (brăm′bəl) *n.* **1.** Any prickly plant or shrub of the genus *Rubus,* esp. the blackberry or the raspberry. **2.** Any prickly shrub or bush. [Middle English *brembel,* from Old English *bræmbel, brēmel.*]

bram·bly (brăm′blē) *adj.* -**bli·er,** -**bli·est.** Full of brambles: *a brambly thicket.* —**bram′bli·ness** *n.*

bran (brăn) *n.* **1.** The outer husks of wheat, rye, and other grain, sifted out from the flour after grinding. **2.** Cereal byproducts used as a food. [Middle English, from Old French.]

branch (brănch) *n.* **1.** One of the woody stem parts dividing out from the trunk, limb, or main stem of a tree or shrub. **2.** Any part going out from a main part like a tree

Braille

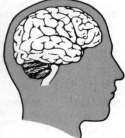

brain

branch: *the branches of an antler.* **3.** A part or division of a larger whole: *Biology is a branch of science.* **4.** A division of government: *the executive branch.* **5.** A local unit or office of a business, institution, etc.: *a bank branch.* **6. a.** A division of a family or tribe. **b.** A subdivision of a family of languages. **7. a.** An arm or offshoot of a larger river or stream. **b.** Any small stream, creek, etc. —*intr.v.* To divide or spread out in branches or branchlike parts: *Small roots branch from a big trunk.* —**phrasal verb.** **branch out.** To expand one's business, activities, etc., into a new area. [Middle English *braunche,* from Old French *branche,* from Late Latin *branca,* foot, paw.]

-branch. *Zool.* A suffix meaning gills: **elasmobranch.** [From Latin *branchia,* gill.]

bran·chi·a (brăng′kē-ə) *n.,* pl. **-chi·ae** (-kē-ē′). *Zool.* A gill or similar breathing organ. [Latin, from Greek *brankhia,* gills.]

bran·chi·al (brăng′kē-əl) *adj.* Of or located near the gills. —**bran′chi·al·ly** *adv.*

brand (brănd) *n.* **1.** A trademark or distinctive name that identifies a product or a manufacturer. **2.** The make of a product thus marked: *a popular brand of soap.* **3.** A distinctive style or type: *his novel brand of crooning.* **4. a.** A mark indicating identity or ownership, burned on the hide of an animal with a hot iron. **b.** An iron used to make such a mark. **5.** A mark formerly burned into the flesh of criminals as a symbol of shame. **6.** Any mark of disgrace or notoriety; a stigma. **7.** A piece of burning or charred wood. **8.** *Archaic.* A sword —*tr.v.* **1.** To mark with or as if with a brand: *Cowboys branded the calves.* **2.** To mark with a label of disgrace or shame; stigmatize: *The tribunal branded them as traitors.* [Middle English *brand,* fire, torch, from Old English *brand,* piece of burning wood.]

bran·dish (brăn′dĭsh) *tr.v.* **1.** To wave or flourish menacingly, as a weapon. **2.** To display ostentatiously: *She brandished her expertise.* —*n.* A menacing or defiant wave or flourish. [Middle English *braundisshen,* from Old French *brandir,* from *brand,* sword.] —**bran′dish·er** *n.*

brand-new (brănd′nōō′, -nyōō′) *adj.* In fresh and unused condition; completely new.

bran·dy (brăn′dē) *n.,* pl. **-dies.** An alcoholic liquor distilled from wine or from fermented fruit juice. —*tr.v.* **-died, -dy·ing.** To mix, flavor, or preserve with brandy. [Earlier *brandy wine,* from Dutch *brandewijn, brantwijn,* "distilled wine."]

brant (brănt) *n.,* pl. **brant** or **brants.** Also *Brit.* **brent** (brĕnt). Any of several wild geese of the genus *Branta,* esp. *B. bernicia,* that breed in arctic regions and have a black neck and head. [Prob. of Scandinavian orig.]

brash¹ (brăsh) *adj.* **-er, -est. 1.** Hasty and unthinking; rash. **2.** Shamelessly bold; impudent; saucy. [Orig. unknown.] —**brash′ly** *adv.* —**brash′ness** *n.*

brash² (brăsh) *n.* A mass or pile of rubble or fragments, as of ice floating in the sea. [Prob. from French *brèche,* breach, from Old French, breach.]

bra·sier (brā′zhər) *n.* Var. of **brazier.**

brass (brăs) *n.* **1.** Any of various alloys that contain chiefly copper and zinc. **2.** Ornaments, objects, or utensils made of such metal. **3. brasses.** *Mus.* **a.** Any brass instrument. **b.** The brass instruments of an orchestra or band. **4.** *Informal.* Blatant self-assurance; effrontery; nerve. **5.** *Slang.* High-ranking military officers or other high officials. **6.** *Brit. Slang.* Money. —**modifier:** *brass buttons; the brass players.* [Middle English *bras,* from Old English *bræs.*]

bras·sard (brə-särd′, brăs′ärd′) *n.* Also **bras·sart** (brə-särt′, brăs′ärt′). **1.** A cloth badge worn around the upper arm. **2.** A piece of armor for the arm. [French, earlier *brassal,* from Provençal *bras,* arm, from Latin *bracchium.*]

brass hat. *Slang.* **1.** A high-ranking military officer. **2.** Any high-ranking official. [From the gold braid on the cap.]

brass·ie (brăs′ē) *n.* Also **brass·y** pl. **-ies.** A wooden golf club with a brass-plated sole, used for long low shots.

bras·siere or **bras·sière** (brə-zîr′) *n.* A woman's undergarment worn to support the breasts. [French *brassière,* from Old French *braciere,* arm guard, from *bras,* arm, from Latin *bracchium.*]

brass instrument. Any of the group of musical instruments that includes the trumpet, trombone, French horn, and tuba, typically made of brass or a similar metal and sounded by pressing the lips and blowing into a cup-shaped or funnel-shaped mouthpiece.

brass knuckles. A weapon consisting of a metal strip or chain with holes or links into which the fingers fit.

brass tacks. *Informal.* Essential facts; basics.

brass·y¹ (brăs′ē) *adj.* **-i·er, -i·est. 1.** Of or decorated with brass. **2.** Having the yellowish color of brass. **3.** Of, like, or characterized by the tone of brass instruments: *a brassy march.* **4.** Cheap and showy; flashy. **5.** *Informal.* Shamelessly bold; brazen; impudent. —**brass′i·ly** *adv.* —**brass′i·ness** *n.*

brass·y² (brăs′ē) *n.pl.* **-ies.** Var. of **brassie.**

brat (brăt) *n.* A child, esp. a nasty or spoiled one. [Prob. from dial. *brat,* coarse garment, from Middle English *brat,* from Old English *bratt,* cloak, from Old Irish *bratt.*] —**brat′ty** *adj.*

bra·va·do (brə-vä′dō) *n.,* pl. **-does** or **-dos.** A show of pretended or defiant courage; false bravery. [Spanish *bravada,* from *bravo,* brave.]

brave (brāv) *adj.* **brav·er, brav·est. 1.** Possessing or showing courage; valiant. **2.** Making a fine display; splendid. **3.** *Archaic.* Excellent. —*n.* **1.** A North American Indian warrior. **2.** A courageous person. —*tr.v.* **braved, brav·ing. 1.** To undergo or face courageously: *The expedition braved many dangers.* **2.** To defy; to challenge: *"Together they would brave Satan and all his legions"* (Emily Brontë). [Old French *brave,* courageous, noble, from Italian and Spanish *bravo,* ult. from Latin *barbarus,* foreign, barbarous.] —**brave′ly** *adv.* —**brave′ness** *n.*

Syns: brave, audacious, bold, courageous, dauntless, fearless, gallant, gutsy (*Informal*), **heroic, intrepid, mettlesome, plucky, stouthearted, unafraid, undaunted, valiant, valorous** *adj. Core meaning:* Having or showing courage (*a brave soldier; a brave rescue*).

brav·er·y (brā′və-rē, brāv′rē) *n.,* pl. **-ies.** The condition or quality of being brave; courage.

bra·vo¹ (brä′vō, brä-vō′) *interj.* Excellent; well done. —*n.,* pl. **-vos.** A shout or cry of approval or praise. [Italian, fine, brave.]

bra·vo² (brä′vō) *n.,* pl. **-voes** or **-vos.** A hired assassin; killer. [Italian, "wild," BRAVE.]

bra·vu·ra (brə-vŏŏr′ə, -vyŏŏr′ə) *n.* **1.** Brilliant technique or style in performance, as in music, dance, etc. **2.** A showy manner or display. [Italian, "bravery," from *bravo,* brave.]

braw (brô) *adj.* **-er, -est.** *Scot.* Fine or splendid. [Scottish, var. of BRAVE.]

brawl (brôl) *n.* **1.** A noisy quarrel or fight. **2.** *Slang.* A loud party. —*intr.v.* **1.** To quarrel noisily. **2.** To flow noisily, as a stream. [Middle English *brawlen.*] —**brawl′er** *n.* —**brawl′ing·ly** *adv.*

brawn (brôn) *n.* **1.** Solid and well-developed muscles. **2.** Muscular strength and power. **3.** *Brit.* A pig. [Middle English, from Norman French *braun,* from Old French *braon,* flesh, muscle.]

brawn·y (brô′nē) *adj.* **-i·er, -i·est.** Strong and muscular. —**brawn′i·ness** *n.*

bray (brā) *n.* **1.** A loud, harsh cry, as of a donkey. **2.** Any sound resembling this: *the bray of trumpets.* —*intr.v.* **1.** To utter a loud, harsh cry, as a donkey. **2.** To sound loudly and harshly: *The foghorn brayed all night.* —*tr.v.* To utter loudly and harshly. [Middle English *brayen,* to make noise, roar, from Old French *braire.*]

braze¹ (brāz) *tr.v.* **brazed, braz·ing.** To make of or decorate with brass. [Middle English *brasen,* from Old English *brasian,* from *bræs,* brass.]

braze² (brāz) *tr.v.* **brazed, braz·ing.** To join (two pieces of metal) together using a hard solder with a high melting point. [Prob. from French *braser,* from Old French, to burn, from *brese,* burning coals.]

bra·zen (brā′zən) *adj.* **1.** Rudely bold; insolent: *a brazen remark.* **2.** Made of or resembling brass: *the sound of a brazen bell.* —See Syns at **impudent.** —*tr.v.* To face or undergo with bold or brash self-assurance: *He brazened out the crisis.* [Middle English *brasen,* from Old English *bræsen,* from *bræs,* brass.] —**bra′zen·ly** *adv.* —**bra′zen·ness** *n.*

bra·zier (brā′zhər) *n.* Also **bra·sier.** A metal pan for holding burning coals or charcoal. [French *brasier,* from *braise,* burning coals, from Old French *brese.*]

Bra·zil nut (brə-zĭl'). **1.** A tree, *Bertholletia excelsa,* of tropical South America, that bears round pods that contain 20 to 30 nuts. **2.** The edible nut of this tree, having a hard, three-sided, dark-brown shell.

Brazil nut

breach (brēch) *n.* **1.** A violation or infraction, as of a law, legal obligation, or promise: *a breach of contract.* **2.** A gap or hole, esp. in a solid structure: *a breach in the dike.* **3.** A disruption of friendly relations; an estrangement: *An argument caused a breach between them.* —*tr.v.* To make a hole or gap in; break through: *Soldiers breached the enemy's line.* —*intr.v.* To leap from the water: *The whale breached.* [Middle English *breche,* from Old French *breche.*]

bread (brĕd) *n.* **1.** A staple food made from moistened, usu. leavened, flour or meal kneaded and baked. **2.** Food in general, regarded as necessary to sustain life. **3.** The necessities of life; livelihood: *earn one's bread.* **4.** *Slang.* Money. —*tr.v.* To coat (food) with bread crumbs before cooking. —**idiom. break bread.** To eat or share a meal. [Middle English *bread,* from Old English *brēad,* crumb.]

bread-and-butter (brĕd'n-bŭt'ər) *adj.* **1.** Influenced by or undertaken out of necessity: *a bread-and-butter job.* **2.** Expressive of thanks for hospitality: *a bread-and-butter note.*

bread and butter. *Informal.* A means of livelihood.

bread·bas·ket (brĕd'băs'kĭt) *n.* **1.** A basket for serving bread, rolls, etc. **2.** A region serving as a major source of grain supply. **3.** *Slang.* The stomach.

bread·board (brĕd'bôrd', -bōrd') *n.* **1.** A board on which bread is sliced. **2.** *Slang.* An experimental model, esp. of an electric or electronic circuit; a prototype.

bread·fruit (brĕd'frōōt') *n.* **1.** A tree, *Artocarpus communis,* of Polynesia, that has deeply lobed leaves and round, usu. seedless fruit. **2.** The edible fruit of this tree that has a texture like that of bread, when baked or roasted.

bread·stuff (brĕd'stŭf') *n.* **1.** Bread. **2.** Flour, meal, or grain used in the making of bread.

breadth (brĕdth) *n.* **1.** The measure or dimension from side to side of something, as distinguished from length or thickness; width. **2.** A piece of something, usu. produced in a standard width: *a breadth of canvas.* **3.** Wide extent or scope: *the breadth of the state.* **4.** Freedom from narrowness, as of views, interests, attitudes, etc.: *the breadth of his intellectual curiosity.* [Middle English *brede,* from Old English *brǣdu.*]

breadth·wise (brĕdth'wīz') *adv. & adj.* Also **breadth·ways** (-wāz'). In the direction of the breadth.

bread·win·ner (brĕd'wĭn'ər) *n.* A person who supports a family or household by his or her earnings.

break (brāk) *v.* **broke** (brōk) or *archaic* **brake** (brāk), **broken** (brō'kən), **break·ing.** —See Usage note at **broke.** —*tr.v.* **1.** To crack or split into two or more fragments with sudden or violent force; to smash. **2.** To crack without actually separating into pieces. **3.** To render unusable or inoperative: *I broke the typewriter.* **4.** To part or pierce the surface of: *break ground for a new hospital.* **5.** To cause to burst: *He broke the balloon.* **6.** To fracture a bone of: *break an arm.* **7.** To force or make a way through; penetrate: *break the sound barrier.* **8.** To force one's way out of; escape from: *break jail.* **9.** To put an end to by force

or strong opposition: *break a strike.* **10.** To fail to conform to; act contrary to; violate: *break a law.* **11.** To discontinue abruptly; interrupt: *A cry broke the silence.* **12.** To call off: *break a date.* **13.** To cause to give up a habit: *finally broke himself of smoking.* **14.** To train to obey; to tame: *break a horse.* **15.** To disrupt or destroy the order, regularity, or continuity of: *break ranks; break the silence.* **16.** To destroy the completeness of: *break a set of books.* **17.** To lessen in force or effect: *break a fall.* **18.** To weaken or destroy, as in spirit or health: *"For a hero loves the world till it breaks him"* (William B. Yeats). **19.** To overwhelm with grief or sorrow: *break one's heart.* **20.** To cause to be without money or to go into bankruptcy: *Bad investments broke him.* **21.** To reduce in rank; demote: *broke him to corporal.* **22.** To reduce to or exchange for smaller monetary units: *break a dollar.* **23.** To surpass or outdo: *break a record.* **24.** To make known, as news. **25.** To find the solution or key to. **26.** *Law.* To invalidate (a will) by judicial action. **27.** *Elect.* To open: *break a circuit.* —*intr.v.* **1.** To become separated into pieces or fragments; come apart: *Glass breaks easily.* **2.** To become unusable or inoperative: *The typewriter broke.* **3.** To give way; to collapse: *The dam broke.* **4.** To diminish or discontinue abruptly: *His fever broke.* **5.** To scatter or disperse. **6.** To run or dash suddenly: *The runner broke for home plate.* **7.** To appear or come into being, esp. suddenly: *The deer broke from the woods.* **8.** To emerge above the surface of water. **9.** To be overwhelmed with sorrow: *His heart broke when she died.* **10.** To begin abruptly to utter or produce something: *flowers breaking into bloom.* **11.** To come to an end: *The game will break in ten minutes.* **12.** To collapse or crash into surf or spray: *The waves are breaking perfectly for surfing.* **13.** To change suddenly in pitch: *His voice broke with emotion.* **14.** *Baseball.* To curve near or over the plate: *The pitch broke away from the batter.* **15.** *Informal.* To occur in a particular way: *Things are breaking well for him.* —See Syns at **separate.** —See Usage note at **broke.** —*phrasal verbs.* **break down. 1.** To shatter or collapse by or as if by breaking. Class barriers often break down during military service. **2.** To fail to function. **3. a.** To decompose chemically. **b.** To analyze or consider in parts: *Break the exercise down into several steps.* **4.** To undergo electrical breakdown. **5.** To become distressed. **6.** To have a mental or physical collapse. **break in. 1.** To enter forcibly or illegally. **2.** To interrupt a conversation. **3. a.** To train or instruct in order to accustom to new work. **b.** To overcome the stiffness of: *break in new shoes.* **break into. 1.** To enter forcibly and illegally. **2.** To start or begin suddenly: *The horse broke into a wild gallop.* **break out. 1.** To be affected with a skin irritation, such as acne or a rash. **2.** To begin suddenly: *A war broke out in the Middle East.* **break up. 1. a.** To break into pieces or fragments. **b.** To separate into smaller parts: *break up a word into syllables.* **2.** To bring or come to an end: *break up a fight. The marriage broke up.* **3.** *Informal.* To burst or cause to burst into laughter. —See Syns at **separate. break with.** To give up or stop following: *He broke with the conservatism of his father.* —*n.* **1.** A result of breaking; a fracture or crack. **2. a.** A gap or opening: *a break in the clouds.* **b.** A beginning: *the break of day.* **3.** An interruption or disruption of regularity, continuity, etc. **4.** *Elect.* Interruption of a flow of current. **5.** A pause or interval, as from work. **6.** A sudden run; a dash: *The soldier made a break for cover.* **7.** An attempt to escape: *a jail break.* **8.** A departure from: *a break with tradition.* **9.** A sudden or marked change: *a break in the weather.* **10.** *Informal.* An unexpected occurrence or chance: *a lucky break.* **11.** *Pros.* A caesura. **12.** *Mus.* **a.** The point at which a register or a tonal quality changes to another register or tonal quality. **b.** A solo jazz cadenza played during the pause between the regular phrases or choruses of a melody. —See Syns at **opportunity.** [Middle English *breken,* from Old English *brecan.*]

break·a·ble (brā'kə-bəl) *adj.* Capable of being broken; fragile. —*n.* Often **breakables.** Articles capable of being broken easily.

break·age (brā'kĭj) *n.* **1.** The act or process of breaking. **2.** A quantity broken. **3. a.** Loss or damage as a result of breaking. **b.** Compensation, as in money, for such a loss or damage.

break·down (brāk'doun') *n.* **1.** The act or process of breaking down and failing to function or the condition resulting from this. **2.** *Elect.* The failure of an insulator or insulating medium to prevent discharge or current flow. **3.** A collapse of physical or mental health. **4.** Disintegration or decomposition into parts, elements, etc. **5.** An analysis, outline, or summary consisting of itemized data or essentials.

break·er (brā′kər) *n.* **1.** A person or thing that breaks. **2.** *Elect.* A circuit breaker. **3.** A wave that crests or breaks into foam, esp. against a shoreline.

break·fast (brĕk′fəst) *n.* The first meal of the day. **—modifier:** *a breakfast tray.* **—intr.v.** To eat breakfast. [Middle English *brekfast*, from *breken faste*, to break (one's) fasting.]

break·front (brāk′frŭnt′) *n.* A high, wide cabinet or bookcase having a central section projecting beyond the end sections.

break·neck (brāk′nĕk′) *adj.* **1.** Reckless; dangerous. **2.** Rapid. —See Syns at **fast**[1].

break·through (brāk′thrōō′) *n.* **1.** An act of breaking through an obstacle or restriction. **2.** *Mil.* An offensive that penetrates an enemy's lines of defense. **3.** A major achievement or success that permits further progress, as in technology.

break·up (brāk′ŭp′) *n.* The act of breaking up; a separation; collapse; dispersal: *the breakup of rock at the earth's surface; the breakup of a marriage.*

break·wa·ter (brāk′wô′tər, -wŏt′ər) *n.* A barrier that protects a harbor or shore from the full impact of waves; a jetty.

breakwater   breastplate

bream (brēm) *n., pl.* **bream** or **breams.** **1.** Any of several European freshwater fishes of the genus *Abramis*, with a flattened body and silvery scales. **2.** Any of several similar or related fishes. [Middle English *breme*, from Old French.]

breast (brĕst) *n.* **1. a.** The human mammary gland. **b.** A corresponding organ in other mammals. **2.** The upper part of the front surface of the body, extending from the neck to the abdomen. **3.** This part of the human body regarded as the seat of affection or emotion. **4.** The section of a garment that covers this part of the body. **5.** Anything likened to this part of the body: *the breast of a hill.* **—tr.v.** To face or advance against boldly: *He breasted every hurdle in his path.* **—idiom. make a clean breast of.** To make a full confession of. [Middle English *brest*, from Old English *brēost*.]

breast·bone (brĕst′bōn′) *n.* The bone to which the collarbone and ribs are joined; the sternum.

breast·plate (brĕst′plāt′) *n.* **1.** A piece of armor plate that covers the breast. **2.** A square cloth set with 12 precious stones representing the 12 tribes of Israel, worn by a Jewish high priest.

breast stroke. A swimming stroke in which one lies face down in the water and extends the arms in front of the head, then sweeps them back laterally while performing a frog kick.

breast·work (brĕst′wûrk′) *n.* A temporary, quickly constructed fortification, usu. breast-high.

breath (brĕth) *n.* **1.** The air inhaled into and exhaled from the lungs in respiration. **2.** The act or process of breathing; respiration. **3.** The ability to breathe, esp. with ease: *short of breath.* **4.** A single cycle of breathing, esp. an inhala-

tion. **5.** Exhaled air, as evidenced by vapor, odor, etc. **6.** A momentary pause or rest. **7. a.** A slight breeze: *not a breath of air.* **b.** A slight gust of fragrant air: *a breath of perfume.* **8.** A trace or suggestion: *The first breath of spring.* **9.** *Phonet.* Exhalation of air without vibrating the vocal cords, as in the articulation of *p* and *s.* **—idioms. catch (one's) breath.** To pause until one's normal breathing is regained. **hold (one's) breath.** To wait anxiously or excitedly. **in the same breath.** At the same time. **save (or waste) (one's) breath.** To refrain from (or engage in) futile talking, esp. when asking or persuading. **take (one's) breath away.** To awe, excite, or surprise greatly. **under (one's) breath.** In a whisper or muted voice. [Middle English *breth*, vapor, air from the lungs, from Old English *brǣth*, odor, exhalation.]

breathe (brēth) *v.* **breathed, breath·ing.** **—intr.v.** **1.** To inhale and exhale air. **2.** To be alive; to live. **3.** To move or blow gently, as air. **4.** To be exhaled or emanated, as a fragrance. **5.** To pause to rest or regain breath, as after action. **—tr.v.** **1.** To inhale and exhale during respiration. **2.** To communicate or impart (a quality); instill: *breathe life into a portrait.* **3.** To give off; emit: *The kitchen breathed an odor of onions.* **4.** To utter, esp. quietly: *Don't breathe a word of this.* **5.** To make apparent; to manifest: *breathed anger.* **6.** To allow (a person or animal) to rest or regain breath. **7.** *Phonet.* To utter with a voiceless exhalation of air. **—idiom. breathe one's last.** To die. [Middle English *brethen*, from *breth*, breath.] **—breath′a·ble** *adj.*

breath·er (brē′thər) *n.* **1.** A person who breathes in a specified manner: *a light breather.* **2.** *Informal.* A short rest period.

breath·ing (brē′thĭng) *n.* **1.** The act or process of respiration. **2.** Either of two marks used in Greek to indicate aspiration of an initial sound (') or the absence of such aspiration (').

breathing space. 1. Sufficient space to permit ease of breathing or movement. **2.** Also **breathing spell.** An opportunity to rest or give thought to a situation.

breath·less (brĕth′lĭs) *adj.* **1.** Not breathing; dead. **2.** Out of breath; panting. **3.** Holding the breath from excitement or suspense: *a breathless audience.* **—breath′less·ly** *adv.* **—breath′less·ness** *n.*

breath·tak·ing (brĕth′tā′kĭng) *adj.* Inspiring awe; exciting: *a breathtaking view; a breathtaking movie.*

breath·y (brĕth′ē) *adj.* **-i·er, -i·est.** Marked by audible or noisy breathing: *a breathy voice.*

bred (brĕd) *v.* Past tense and past participle of **breed.**

breech (brēch) *n.* **1.** The lower rear part of the human trunk; the buttocks. **2.** The part of a firearm to the rear of the barrel or, in a cannon, to the rear of the bore. [Middle English *breech*, from Old English *brēc*, breeches.]

breech·cloth (brēch′klôth′, -klŏth′) *n.* Also **breech·clout** (-klout′). A cloth worn to cover the loins; loincloth.

breech·es (brĭch′ĭz) *pl.n.* **1.** Trousers extending to or just below the knee. **2.** *Informal.* Any trousers. [Pl. of BREECH.]

breeches buoy. An apparatus used for rescue at sea, consisting of canvas breeches attached to a life preserver that is suspended from a pulley running along a line from ship to ship or from ship to shore.

breech·load·er (brēch′lō′dər) *n.* Any gun or firearm loaded at the breech. **—breech′load′ing** *adj.*

breed (brēd) *v.* **bred** (brĕd), **breed·ing.** **—tr.v.** **1.** To produce (offspring); give birth to or hatch. **2.** To bring about; give rise to: *Thunderheads breed storms.* **3. a.** To cause to reproduce; raise. **b.** To develop new or improved strains in (animals or plants). **4.** To rear or train; bring up: *bred his sons to behave like gentlemen.* **—intr.v.** **1.** To produce offspring. **2.** To originate and thrive: *Fads breed in empty heads and full purses.* **—n.** **1.** A genetic strain or type of organism, usu. a domestic animal, with consistent and recognizable inherited characteristics. **2.** A type or kind of person or thing: *a new breed of politicians.* —See Syns at **kind.** [Middle English *breden*, from Old English *brēdan*.]

breed·er (brē′dər) *n.* **1.** A person who breeds animals or plants. **2.** An animal kept to produce offspring. **3.** Anything that causes, creates, or gives birth to something; a source: *War has always been a great machine breeder.* **4.** *Physics.* A breeder reactor.

breeder reactor. A nuclear reactor that produces fissionable material, esp. one that produces more fissionable material than it consumes.

breed·ing (brē′dĭng) n. 1. A line of descent; ancestry: *a man of noble breeding.* 2. Training in the proper forms of social and personal conduct. 3. The producing of offspring or young. 4. The raising of animals or plants, esp. so as to produce new or improved varieties.

breeze (brēz) n. 1. A light air current; gentle wind. 2. *Meteorol.* A wind of from about 6.4 to 49.9 kilometers, or 4 to 31 miles, per hour. 3. *Brit. Informal.* A commotion or disturbance; an argument. 4. *Informal.* An easily accomplished task. —*intr.v.* **breezed, breez·ing.** 1. To blow lightly. 2. *Informal.* To move or do swiftly and effortlessly. [Perh. from Spanish *briza,* northeast wind.]

breeze·way (brēz′wā′) n. A roofed, open-sided passageway connecting two buildings, such as a house and a garage.

breez·y (brē′zē) adj. **-i·er, -i·est.** 1. Exposed to breezes; windy. 2. Fresh and animated; lively; sprightly: *a writer's breezy style.* —**breez′i·ly** adv. —**breez′i·ness** n.

brent (brĕnt) n. *Brit.* Var. of **brant.**

breth·ren (brĕth′rən) n. *Archaic.* Plural of **brother.**

Bret·on (brĕt′n) n. 1. A native or inhabitant of Brittany. 2. The Celtic language of Brittany.

breve (brēv, brĕv) n. 1. A symbol (‑) placed over a vowel to show that it has a short sound, as the (ă) in *bat.* 2. *Pros.* A similar symbol used to indicate that a syllable is short or unstressed. 3. *Mus.* A single note equivalent to two whole notes. [Middle English, var. of *bref,* brief.]

bre·vi·ar·y (brē′vē-ĕr′ē, brĕv′ē-) n., pl. **-ies.** *Eccles.* A book containing the hymns, offices, and prayers for the canonical hours. [Latin *breviārium,* summary, from *breviāre,* to abridge, from *brevis,* brief.]

brev·i·ty (brĕv′ĭ-tē) n. 1. Briefness of duration; shortness. 2. Terseness: *"Brevity is the soul of wit"* (Shakespeare). [Latin *brevitās,* from *brevis,* brief.]

brew (broō) tr.v. 1. To make (ale or beer) from malt and hops by infusion, boiling, and fermentation. 2. To make (a beverage) by boiling, steeping, or mixing various ingredients. 3. To devise or plan; concoct: *brew a scheme.* —*intr.v.* 1. To make ale or beer as an occupation. 2. To be imminent; impend: *A storm is brewing.* —n. 1. A beverage made by brewing. 2. The quantity of beverage brewed at one time. [Middle English *brewen,* from Old English *brēowan.*] —**brew′er** n.

brew·er's yeast (broō′ərz). A yeast, *Saccharomyces cerevisiae,* used in brewing and as a source of B complex vitamins.

brew·er·y (broō′ə-rē, broōr′ē) n., pl. **-ies.** An establishment for the manufacture of malt liquors, such as beer.

brew·ing (broō′ĭng) n. 1. The act, process, or business of producing malt liquors, such as beer. 2. The quantity brewed at one time; a brew.

bri·ar[1] (brī′ər) n. Also **bri·er.** 1. A shrub or small tree, *Erica arborea,* of southern Europe, with a hard, woody root. 2. A pipe made from briarwood or from a similar wood. [French *bruyère,* heath.]

bri·ar[2] (brī′ər) n. Var. of **brier** (thorny shrub).

bri·ar·wood (brī′ər-woōd′) n. Wood from the root of the briar.

bribe (brīb) n. 1. Anything, such as money, property, a favor, etc., offered or given to someone to induce him to act dishonestly. 2. Something offered or serving to influence or persuade. —tr.v. **bribed, brib·ing.** 1. To give, offer, or promise a bribe to. 2. To gain influence over or corrupt by bribery. [Middle English *briben,* to steal, from Old French *briber, brimber,* to beg.] —**brib′a·ble** adj. —**brib′er** n.

brib·er·y (brī′bə-rē) n., pl. **-ies.** The act of giving, offering, or taking a bribe.

bric-a-brac (brĭk′ə-brăk′) n. Small objects displayed in a room as ornaments. [French *bric-à-brac.*]

brick (brĭk) n. 1. An oblong block of clay, baked by the sun or in a kiln until hard and used as building and paving material. 2. These blocks considered collectively as a kind of material. 3. Any object shaped like such a block: *a brick of cheese.* 4. *Informal.* A splendid fellow. —tr.v. 1. To construct, line, or pave with brick. 2. To close or wall with brick. [Middle English *brike, breke.*]

brick·bat (brĭk′băt′) n. 1. A piece of brick, esp. one used as a missile. 2. A blunt remark or criticism.

brick·lay·er (brĭk′lā′ər) n. A person skilled in building walls, chimneys, etc., with bricks. —**brick′lay′ing** n.

brick·work (brĭk′wûrk′) n. 1. A structure made of bricks. 2. Construction with bricks.

brick·yard (brĭk′yärd′) n. A place where bricks are made.

bri·dal (brīd′l) n. A marriage ceremony; a wedding. —adj. Of or pertaining to a bride or a marriage ceremony; nuptial: *a bridal veil; the bridal party.* [Middle English *bridale,* wedding feast, from Old English *brydealu : bryd,* bride + *ealu,* ale.]

bridal wreath. Either of two related shrubs, *Spiraea prunifolia* or *S. vanhouttei,* cultivated for their profuse white flowers.

bride (brīd) n. A woman who has recently been married or is about to be married. [Middle English *bride,* from Old English *bryd.*]

bride·groom (brīd′groom′, -groom′) n. A man who has recently been married or is about to be married. [Alteration of Middle English *bridegome,* from Old English *brydguma : bryd,* bride + *guma,* man.]

brides·maid (brīdz′mād′) n. A woman, usu. young and unmarried, who attends the bride at a wedding.

bridge[1] (brĭj) n. 1. A structure spanning and providing a way across a waterway, railroad, or other obstacle. 2. The upper bony ridge of the human nose. 3. The part of a pair of eyeglasses that rests against this ridge. 4. *Mus.* **a.** A thin, upright piece of wood in some stringed instruments that supports the strings above the sounding board. **b.** A short passage that connects two sections of a composition. 5. A fixed or removable replacement for one or more missing natural teeth, usu. anchored at both ends to natural teeth. 6. *Naut.* A crosswise platform above the main deck of a ship from which the ship is controlled. 7. *Billiards.* A notched piece of wood or a rest made with the hand on which to steady the cue. —*modifier: a bridge tower.* —tr.v. **bridged, bridg·ing.** 1. To build a bridge over: *a plan to bridge the bay.* 2. To cross by or as if by a bridge: *His life bridged three generations.* **idiom. burn (one's) bridges (behind one).** To eliminate the possibility of retreat. [Middle English *brigge,* from Old English *brycg.*] —**bridge′a·ble** adj.

bridge[1]   bridle

bridge[2] (brĭj) n. Any of several card games for four people, derived from whist. [Earlier *biritch,* prob. from Russian *birich,* caller, announcer of official proclamations.]

bridge·head (brĭj′hĕd′) n. A military position established by advance troops in enemy territory to provide protection for the main attacking force.

bridge·work (brĭj′wûrk′) n. *Dentistry.* One or more bridges used to replace missing teeth.

bridg·ing (brĭj′ĭng) n. Wooden braces between beams in a floor or roof, used to reinforce the beams and keep them apart.

bri·dle (brīd′l) n. 1. The straps, bits, and reins fitted about a horse's head, used to control the animal. 2. Any device or condition that controls or restrains free movement; a curb or check. —v. **-dled, -dling.** 1. To put a bridle on. 2. To control or restrain with or as if with a bridle: *Bridle your temper.* —*intr.v.* 1. To lift the head and draw in the chin as an expression of scorn or resentment. 2. To show scorn, anger, or offense: *bridled at the criticism.* [Middle

English *bridel,* from Old English *brĭdel.*]
bridle path. A trail for horseback riding.
brief (brēf) *adj.* **-er, -est. 1.** Short in time or duration: *a brief period.* **2.** Short in length or extent: *a brief skirt.* **3.** Condensed in expression; succinct: *a brief report.* —*n.* **1.** A short or condensed statement. **2.** A condensation or abstract of a large document or series of documents. **3.** *Law.* A document that contains all facts and points of law pertinent to a specific case, filed by an attorney before arguing the case in court. **4. briefs.** Short, tight-fitting underpants. —*tr.v.* To give detailed instructions, information, or advice to: *The squadron commander briefed the pilots before the raid.* —*idiom.* **in brief.** In summary; in a few words. [Middle English *bref,* from Old French, from Latin *brevis.*] —**brief′ly** *adv.* —**brief′ness** *n.*
    Syns: brief, short *adj.* **Core meaning:** Not long in time or duration (*a brief interval*).
brief·case (brēf′kās′) *n.* A portable case of leather or similar material, used for carrying books, papers, etc.
brief·ing (brē′fĭng) *n.* **1.** The act or procedure of giving or receiving detailed instructions, information, or advice. **2.** The instructions, information, or advice conveyed during a briefing.
bri·er¹ (brī′ər) *n.* Also **bri·ar.** Any of various thorny plants or bushes, esp. a rosebush. [Middle English *brere,* from Old English *brær.*] —**bri′er·y** *adj.*
bri·er² (brī′ər) *n.* Var. of **briar** (shrub with woody root).
brig¹ (brĭg) *n.* A two-masted square-rigged sailing ship. [Short for BRIGANTINE.]

brig¹

brig² (brĭg) *n.* **1.** A ship's prison. **2.** *Mil. Slang.* Any guardhouse. [Prob. from BRIG.]
bri·gade (brĭ-gād′) *n.* **1. a.** A military unit consisting of a variable number of combat battalions, with supporting services. **b.** A unit of the U.S. Army composed of two or more regiments. **2.** Any group of persons organized for a specific purpose: *a fire brigade.* [French, from Old French, from Old Italian *brigata,* troop, company, from *brigare,* to fight, from *briga,* strife.]
brig·a·dier (brĭg′ə-dîr′) *n.* Also **brigadier general.** A general of the lowest rank.
brig·and (brĭg′ənd) *n.* A member of a roving band of robbers. [Middle English *brigaunt,* bandit, from Old French *brigand,* from Old Italian *brigante,* from *brigare,* to fight.] —**brig′and·age** (-ən-dĭj), **brig′and·ism** *n.*
brig·an·tine (brĭg′ən-tēn′) *n.* A two-masted sailing ship similar to a brig. [French, from Old French *brigandin,* from Italian *brigantino,* from *brigante,* brigand.]
bright (brīt) *adj.* **-er, -est. 1.** Emitting or reflecting light readily or in large amounts; shining: *bright, sparkling jewels; bright black eyes.* **2.** Containing little or no black, white, or gray; vivid or intense: *a bright green; bright colors.* **3.** Bathed in or exposed to a brilliant, steady light: *a very cold, bright day.* **4.** Quick-witted; smart. **5.** Happy; cheerful: *a bright, smiling face.* **6.** Promising: *a bright future.* —*n.* **brights.** High-beam headlights. —*adv.* In a bright manner. [Middle English *bright,* from Old English *beorht.*] —**bright′ly** *adv.*
    Syns: bright, brilliant, incandescent, luminous, lustrous, radiant, shining *adj.* **Core meaning:** Giving off or reflecting light (*bright street lamps; bright, sparkling diamonds*). See also Syns at **cheerful, clever,** and **favorable.**

bright·en (brīt′n) *tr.v.* **1.** To make bright or brighter. **2.** To make more cheerful: *Praise brightened her day.* —*intr.v.* **1.** To become bright or brighter. **2.** To become more cheerful.
bright·ness (brīt′nĭs) *n.* **1.** The condition or quality of being bright. **2.** The measure of how bright an object or color is.
Bright's disease (brīts). A prolonged inflammation of the kidneys; chronic nephritis. [After Richard *Bright* (1789–1858), British physician.]
brill (brĭl) *n., pl.* **brill** or **brills.** A flatfish, *Scophthalmus rhombus,* of European waters. [Orig. unknown.]
bril·liant (brĭl′yənt) *adj.* **1.** Shining brightly; glittering: *a brilliant sun.* **2.** Bathed in light; luminous: *The day will be cold but brilliant.* **3.** Very vivid in color: *The sky was a brilliant blue.* **4.** Extremely intelligent or inventive: *a brilliant political campaign.* **5.** Splendid; magnificent: *the brilliant court life of Versailles.* **6.** Excellent; wonderful: *a brilliant article; a brilliant performance.* **7. a.** Clear and penetrating, as a musical sound: *a firm, brilliant tone.* **b.** Very rich in quality; sparkling: *Romantic composers created a world of brilliant orchestral color.* —See Syns at **bright** and **intelligent.** —*n.* A precious gem, esp. a diamond, finely cut in any of various forms, with numerous facets, so that it catches the light and sparkles. [French *brillant,* from *briller,* to shine, from Italian *brillare.*] —**bril′liance** or **bril′lian·cy** *n.* —**bril′liant·ly** *adv.*
bril·lian·tine (brĭl′yən-tēn′) *n.* **1.** An oily, perfumed hairdressing. **2.** A glossy, lightweight fabric made from cotton and worsted or cotton and mohair. [French *brillantine,* from *brillant,* brilliant.]
brim (brĭm) *n.* **1.** The rim or uppermost edge of a cup, glass, etc. **2.** A rim on a hat that stands out around the crown. **3.** *Archaic.* A border or edge, esp. one surrounding a body of water. —*v.* **brimmed, brim·ming.** —*tr.v.* To fill to the brim. —*intr.v.* To be full to or as if to the brim: *Fountains brimmed with free water. Her eyes brimmed with mischief.* —*phrasal verb.* **brim over.** To overflow. [Middle English *brimme.*]
brim·ful (brĭm′fŏŏl′) *adj.* Full to or as if to the brim; completely full.
brim·stone (brĭm′stōn′) *n. Obs.* Sulfur. Used in modern speech and writing only in the phrase **fire and brimstone,** suggesting the atmosphere of hell. [Middle English *brimston,* from Old English *brynstān.*]
brin·dle (brĭn′dl) *adj.* Tan, brown, or gray with darker streaks or spots; brindled: *a brindle cow; a bulldog with a brindle coat.* —*n.* A combination of tan, brown, or gray with darker streaks or spots.
brin·dled (brĭn′dld) *adj.* Brindle. [Earlier *brinded, brended,* from Middle English *brende.*]
brine (brīn) *n.* **1.** Water saturated with or containing large amounts of dissolved salt, esp. sodium chloride. **2.** The water of a sea or ocean. **3.** Salt water used for preserving or pickling foods. —*tr.v.* **brined, brin·ing.** To immerse or pickle in brine. [Middle English *brine,* from Old English *brȳne.*]
bring (brĭng) *tr.v.* **brought** (brôt), **bring·ing. 1.** To take with oneself to a place; carry along or escort: *Bring the books upstairs. Soldiers brought the prisoner back for questioning.* **2. a.** To cause to appear: *His account brought into view the details of the accident.* **b.** To be accompanied by: *A cool wind brought relief.* **c.** To cause to occur or happen; result in: *The flood brought death to thousands.* **3.** To sell for: *Diamonds always bring high prices.* **4.** To succeed in persuading; convince: *He could not bring himself to tell her the sad news.* **5.** To call to mind; recall: *bring the past vividly to life.* **6.** To act upon or treat in such a way as to put into a specified situation, location, or condition: *a fox brought to bay by hounds; bring the water to a boil.* **7.** To put forward (a legal action, charges, etc.) against someone in court: *bring suit.* —*phrasal verbs.* **bring about.** To cause to happen. **bring around. 1.** To cause to adopt an opinion or course of action. **2.** To cause to recover consciousness. **bring down. 1.** To cause to fall or collapse: *The revolution brought down the monarchy.* **2.** To kill. **bring forth.** To bear (fruit or young). **bring forward.** To produce; present: *Can you bring forward any proof of your statement?* **bring in. 1.** To give or submit (a verdict). **2.** To produce or yield

---

ă pat	ā pay	â care	ä father	ĕ pet	ē be	hw which	ĭ pit	ī tie	î pier	ŏ pot	ō toe	ô paw, for	oi noise
ŏŏ took	ŏŏ boot	ou out	th thin	*th* this	ŭ cut		û urge	zh vision	ə about, item, edible, gallop, circus				

(profits or income). **bring off.** To accomplish successfully. **bring on.** To result in; cause: *The abuse heaped upon him during the trial brought on a stroke of paralysis.* **bring out.** 1. To reveal or expose: *Notice the different ideas one word can bring out.* 2. To produce or publish: *The company is bringing out new items.* **bring over.** To win over. **bring to.** To cause to recover consciousness. **bring up.** 1. To take care of and educate (a child); rear. 2. To introduce into discussion; mention: *bring up a subject.* [Middle English *bringen,* from Old English *bringan.*]

Usage: 1. **bring, take.** *Bring* indicates movement toward the writer, speaker, or person named: *Bring me your report card, Take* indicates movement away from the writer, speaker, or person named: *Take your report card home.* 2. **brought, brung.** The past tense and past participle of *bring* is *brought*—never *brung,* which is illiterate: *I brought* (not *brung) my work with me. I have brought* (not *have brung) my work with me.*

brink (brĭngk) *n.* 1. a. The upper edge of a steep place: *the brink of the crater.* b. The margin of land bordering a body of water. 2. The verge of something: *on the brink of discovery; at the brink of war.* [Middle English *brinke, brenk.*]

brink·man·ship (brĭngk′mən-shĭp′) *n.* The practice, esp. in international politics, of seeking advantage by creating the impression that one is willing and able to pass the brink of nuclear war rather than concede. [BRINK + (GAMES)MANSHIP.]

brin·y (brī′nē) *adj.* **-i·er, -i·est.** Of or like brine; salty. —*n. Slang.* The sea. —**brin′i·ness** *n.*

bri·o (brē′ō) *n.* Vigor; vivacity. [Italian, "vivacity."]

bri·oche (brē-ōsh′, -ōsh′) *n.* A soft, light-textured roll or bun. [French, from Old French, from *brier,* to knead.]

bri·quette or **bri·quet** (brĭ-kĕt′) *n.* A block of compressed coal dust or charcoal, used for fuel and kindling. [French *briquette,* from *brique,* brick.]

brisk (brĭsk) *adj.* **-er, -est.** 1. Moving or acting quickly; lively; energetic: *a brisk walk; his wife, brisk despite her years.* 2. Fresh and invigorating: *a brisk wind; a brisk morning.* —See Syns at **vigorous.** [Prob. var. of BRUSQUE.] —**brisk′ly** *adv.* —**brisk′ness** *n.*

bris·ket (brĭs′kĭt) *n.* 1. The chest of an animal. 2. The ribs and meat from this part. [Middle English *brusket.*]

bris·tle (brĭs′əl) *n.* A short, coarse, stiff hair or hairlike part. —*v.* **-tled, -tling.** —*intr.v.* 1. To raise the bristles stiffly, as an angry, excited, or frightened animal. 2. To react with agitation to anger, excitement, or fear: *He bristled at being called a coward.* 3. To stand out stiffly like bristles: *His short hair bristled.* 4. To be full of or thick with or as if with bristles: *He's bristling with gossip. The path bristled with thorns.* —*tr.v.* 1. To cause to stand erect like bristles; stiffen: *"Boy, bristle thy courage up"* (Shakespeare). 2. To furnish or supply with bristles; put bristles on. [Middle English *bristil, brustel,* from *brust,* bristle, from Old English *byrst.*] —**bris′tly** (brĭs′lē) *adj.*

Bri·tan·nia (brĭ-tăn′yə, -tăn′ē-ə). 1. *Poet.* Great Britain. 2. A female personification of Great Britain or the British Empire.

bri·tan·nia (brĭ-tăn′yə, -tăn′ē-ə) *n.* A white alloy of tin with copper, antimony, and sometimes bismuth and zinc. It is used in the manufacture of tableware. Also called **Britannia metal.** [From BRITANNIA.]

Bri·tan·nic (brĭ-tăn′ĭk) *adj.* British.

Brit·i·cism (brĭt′ĭ-sĭz′əm) *n.* A word, phrase, or idiom characteristic of or peculiar to British English.

Brit·ish (brĭt′ĭsh) *n.* 1. **the British.** *(used with a pl. verb).* The people of Great Britain. 2. The Celtic language of the ancient Britons. 3. British English. —*adj.* Of Great Britain, the British, or their language.

British English. The English language used in England, as compared with the English spoken elsewhere.

Brit·ish·er (brĭt′ĭ-shər) *n. Informal.* A native or inhabitant of Great Britain.

British thermal unit. *Abbr.* **Btu** or **BTU** The quantity of heat required to raise the temperature of one pound of water by one degree Fahrenheit.

Brit·on (brĭt′n) *n.* 1. A native or inhabitant of Britain. 2. A member of the Celtic people of ancient Britain before the Roman invasion.

Usage: **Briton, Britain.** *Britain* is the country, the island comprising England, Scotland, and Wales. A *Briton* is a native of Britain.

brit·tle (brĭt′l) *adj.* 1. Likely to break because of inelasticity and hardness; fragile: *brittle porcelain.* 2. Difficult to deal with; snappish: *a brittle disposition.* —*n.* A hard candy made of brown sugar and nuts. [Middle English *brotel, britel.*] —**brit′tle·ness** *n.*

broach (brōch) *n.* 1. A tapered and serrated tool used to shape or enlarge a hole. 2. A spit for roasting meat. —*tr.v.* 1. a. To talk or write about for the first time; begin to discuss: *broach a subject.* b. To announce: *He broached his plans about spending the summer in California.* 2. To pierce in order to draw off liquid: *broach a keg.* 3. To shape or enlarge (a hole) with a broach. [Middle English *broche,* pointed rod or pin, from Old French, a spit.] —**broach′er** *n.*

broad (brôd) *adj.* **-er, -est.** 1. Wide from side to side. 2. Large in expanse; spacious: *a broad lawn.* 3. Clear; bright: *broad daylight; the broad gold wake of the afternoon.* 4. Covering a wide scope; general: *a broad vocabulary; a broad topic.* 5. Main or essential: *the broad sense of a word.* 6. Plain and obvious: *a broad hint.* 7. Liberal; tolerant: *a man of broad views.* 8. Coarse; vulgar: *a broad joke.* 9. Indicating the sound of *a* as it is pronounced when the *a* in *bath* or *ask* is pronounced like the *a* in *father.* —*n.* The broad part of something. [Middle English *brood,* from Old English *brād.*] —**broad′ly** *adv.* —**broad′ness** *n.*

Syns: 1. **broad, wide** *adj.* Core meaning: Extending over a large area from side to side (*broad shoulders*). 2. **broad, ample, expansive, extensive, spacious** *adj.* (*a broad lawn*). See also Syns ast **general.**

broad·ax or **broad·axe** (brôd′ăks′) *n.* An ax with a wide, flat head and a short handle, used as a weapon or for cutting timber.

broad·cast (brôd′kăst′) *v.* **-cast** or **-cast·ed, -cast·ing.** —*tr.v.* 1. To transmit (a program) by radio or television. 2. To make known over a wide area: *broadcast rumors.* 3. To sow (seed) over a wide area, esp. by hand; scatter. —*intr.v.* 1. To transmit a radio or television program: *The station broadcasts from noon to midnight.* 2. To participate in a radio or television program. —*n.* 1. Transmission of a radio or television program or signal. 2. a. A radio or television program. b. The duration of such a program. 3. The act of scattering seed. —*adj.* 1. Of or pertaining to transmission by radio or television: *Broadcast time is limited.* 2. Scattered over a wide area. —*adv.* In a scattered manner; far and wide. —**broad′cast′er** *n.*

broad·cast·ing (brôd′kăs′tĭng, -kä′stĭng) *n.* The transmitting of programs by radio or television.

broad·cloth (brôd′klôth′, -klŏth′) *n.* 1. A fine woolen cloth with a smooth, glossy texture. 2. A closely woven silk, cotton, or synthetic cloth with a narrow rib, resembling poplin.

broad·en (brôd′n) *tr.v.* To make broad or broader: *broaden a street.* —*intr.v.* To become broad or broader: *The thruway broadens at the toll booths.*

broad gauge. A railroad track with a width between the rails greater than the standard gauge of 56¹/₂ inches. —*modifier* (**broad-gauge**): *a broad-gauge train.*

broad jump. *Track & Field.* Another name for **long jump.**

broad·leaf (brôd′lēf′) *n.* Any of various tobacco plants having broad leaves. —*adj.* Broad-leaved.

broad-leaved (brôd′lēvd′) *adj.* Also **broad-leafed** (-lēft′). Having comparatively broad leaves rather than narrow, needlelike leaves.

broad·loom (brôd′lōōm′) *n.* A carpet woven on a wide loom.

broad-mind·ed (brôd′mīn′dĭd) *adj.* Having liberal and tolerant views and opinions. —**broad′-mind′ed·ly** *adv.* —**broad′-mind′ed·ness** *n.*

broad·side (brôd′sīd′) *n.* 1. The side of a ship above the water line. 2. A firing of all the guns on one side of a warship. 3. An explosive verbal attack or denunciation. 4. A large sheet of paper printed on one side. —*adv.* 1. With the side turned toward a specified object: *The tugs were broadside to the big ocean liner.* 2. On or along the side facing: *The wave caught them broadside and filled the canoe.*

ă pat   ā pay   â care   ä father   ĕ pet   ē be   hw which   ĭ pit   ī tie   î pier   ŏ pot   ō toe   ô paw, for   oi noise
ōō took   ōō boot   ou out   th thin   th this   ŭ cut   û urge   zh vision   ə about, item, edible, gallop, circus

broad·spec·trum (brôd'spĕk'trəm) *adj.* Widely applicable or effective: *a broad-spectrum drug.*

broad·sword (brôd'sôrd', -sōrd') *n.* A sword with a wide blade for cutting rather than thrusting.

broad·tail (brôd'tāl') *n.* **1.** A breed of sheep, the karakul. **2.** The flat, glossy, rippled fur from the pelt of a prematurely born karakul lamb.

Broad·way (brôd'wā') *n.* **1.** The principal theater district of New York City, located on or near Broadway, a thoroughfare extending the length of Manhattan Island. **2.** The American legitimate stage: *a career in motion pictures and on Broadway.* **—modifier:** *a Broadway musical.*

bro·cade (brō-kād') *n.* A heavy fabric with a rich, raised design woven into it, often with threads of silver, gold, or colored silk. **—modifier:** *a brocade dress.* **—tr.v.** **-cad·ed, -cad·ing.** To weave (cloth) with a raised design. [Earlier *brocado,* from Spanish or Portuguese, from Italian *broccato,* embossed fabric, from *brocco,* twisted thread, shoot, ult. from Latin *brocchus,* projecting.]

brocade   bronchus

broc·co·li (brŏk'ə-lē) *n.* A plant, *Brassica oleracea italica,* closely related to the cabbage and cauliflower, that has densely clustered buds and stalks and is eaten as a vegetable. [Italian, pl. of *broccolo,* cabbage sprout, dim. of *brocco,* shoot, from Latin *brocchus,* projecting.]

bro·chette (brō-shĕt') *n.* A small spit or skewer upon which pieces of meat, fish, or vegetables are roasted or broiled. [French, from Old French, from *broche,* spit.]

bro·chure (brō-shōōr') *n.* A small pamphlet or booklet. [French, "a stitching" (from the loose stitching of the pages), from *brocher,* to stitch.]

bro·gan (brō'gən) *n.* A heavy, ankle-high work shoe. [Irish-Gaelic *brógan,* from *bróg,* shoe.]

brogue[1] (brōg) *n.* A strong dialectal or regional accent, esp. an Irish accent. [From BROGUE (shoe), with reference to the shoes of Irish and Scottish peasants.]

brogue[2] (brōg) *n.* **1.** A heavy shoe of untanned leather, formerly worn in Scotland and Ireland. **2.** A strong oxford shoe, usu. with a pattern of tiny holes for decoration. [Irish and Scottish Gaelic *bróg,* from Old Irish *bróc,* shoe.]

broil[1] (broil) *tr.v.* **1.** To cook by direct heat, as over a grill or under an electric coil. **2.** To expose to great heat. **—intr.v.** To be exposed to great heat: *We broiled on the beach.* [Middle English *broillen, brulen,* from Old French *brul(l)er, brusler,* to burn.]

broil[2] (broil) *n.* A rowdy argument; a brawl. **—intr.v.** To engage in a brawl. [From obs. *broil,* to confound, disturb, from Middle English *broilen,* from Old French *brouiller.*]

broil·er (broi'lər) *n.* **1.** A small electric oven or a specific unit of a stove used for broiling. **2.** A tender young chicken suitable for broiling.

broke (brōk). *v.* The past tense and nonstandard past participle of **break.** **—adj.** *Informal.* Lacking money. **—See** Syns at **poor.** [Middle English *broken* (past part.), from Old English *(ge)brocen;* past tense from the past part. on the model of such verbs as *speak, spoke, spoken.*]

Usage: **broke, broken.** The past tense of *break* is *broke: I broke my arm.* The past participle is *broken: I have broken my arm. My arm is broken.* They are not interchangeable.

bro·ken (brō'kən). *v.* The past participle of **break.** **—adj.** **1.** Shattered or fractured: *broken pieces; a broken leg.* **2.** Out of order; not functioning: *a broken watch.* **3.** Not kept; violated: *a broken promise.* **4.** Spoken imperfectly: *broken English.* **5.** Weakened or exhausted: *broken health.* **6.** Overwhelmed, as by sadness, hardship, etc.: *a broken heart; a broken spirit.* **7.** Tamed and trained: *a broken stallion.* **8.** Divided and disrupted by change: *a broken home.* **9.** Financially ruined; bankrupt. **10.** Stopping and starting at intervals; having gaps; not continuous: *a broken line on a highway.* **11.** Lacking parts; not complete: *a broken set of books.* **12.** Rough; uneven: *patches of broken ground.* **—See** Usage note at **broke.** [Middle English, from Old English *(ge)brocen.*]

bro·ken-down (brō'kən-doun') *adj.* **1.** In poor condition, as from old age: *a broken-down horse.* **2.** Out of working order: *a broken-down car.*

bro·ken-heart·ed (brō'kən-här'tĭd) *adj.* Overwhelmed by grief or despair.

bro·ker (brō'kər) *n.* **1.** A person who acts as an agent for others in negotiating contracts, purchases, or sales in return for a fee or commission. **2.** A stockbroker. [Middle English, peddler, go-between, from Norman French *brocour.*]

bro·ker·age (brō'kər-ĭj) *n.* **1.** The business of a broker. **2.** A fee or commission paid to a broker.

bro·mide (brō'mīd') *n.* **1.** A chemical compound of bromine with another element or radical. **2.** A sedative, potassium bromide. **3. a.** A commonplace remark or notion; platitude. **b.** A tiresome person; bore. [BROM(INE) + -IDE.]

bro·mid·ic (brō-mĭd'ĭk) *adj.* Trite; commonplace.

bro·mine (brō'mēn') *n. Symbol* **Br** A heavy, volatile, corrosive, reddish-brown, nonmetallic liquid element, having a highly irritating vapor. It is used in producing gasoline antiknock mixtures, fumigants, dyes, and photographic chemicals. Atomic weight 79.909; atomic number 35; melting point -7.2°C; boiling point 58.78°C; valences 1, 3, 5, 7. [French *brome,* from Greek *brómos,* stench + -INE.]

bron·chi (brŏng'kī', -kē') *n.* Plural of **bronchus.**

bron·chi·a (brŏng'kē-ə) *pl.n. Sing.* **-chi·um** (-kē-əm). Bronchial tubes smaller than the bronchi and larger than bronchioles. [Late Latin, from Greek *bronkhia,* from *bronkhos,* bronchus.]

bron·chi·al (brŏng'kē-əl) *adj.* Of or pertaining to the bronchi, the bronchia, or the bronchioles.

bronchial tube. A bronchus or any of its branches.

bron·chi·ole (brŏng'kē-ōl') *n.* Any of the fine, thin-walled, tubular extensions of a bronchus.

bron·chi·tis (brŏng-kī'tĭs) *n.* Chronic or acute inflammation of the mucous membrane of the bronchial tubes. **—bron·chit'ic** (-kĭt'ĭk) *adj.*

bron·chi·um (brŏng'kē-əm) *n.* Singular of **bronchia.**

bron·cho·pneu·mo·nia (brŏng'kō-nŏŏ-mōn'yə, -nyŏŏ-) *n.* Inflammation of the lungs spreading from and following infection of the bronchi.

bron·chus (brŏng'kəs) *n., pl.* **-chi** (-kī', -kē'). Either of two main branches of the trachea, leading directly to the lungs. [From Greek *bronkhos,* trachea, windpipe, throat.]

bron·co (brŏng'kō) *n., pl.* **-cos.** A small wild or half-wild horse or pony of western North America. [Mexican Spanish, from Spanish, rough, wild.]

bron·co·bust·er (brŏng'kō-bŭs'tər) *n.* A cowboy who breaks wild horses to the saddle.

bron·to·saur (brŏn'tə-sôr') *n.* Also **bron·to·sau·rus** (brŏn'tə-sôr'əs). A very large, herbivorous dinosaur of the genus *Apatosaurus* (or *Brontosaurus*), of the Jurassic period. [From Greek *brontē,* thunder + -SAUR.]

bronze (brŏnz) *n.* **1. a.** Any of various alloys of copper and tin, sometimes with traces of other metals. **b.** Any of various alloys of copper, with or without tin, and antimony, phosphorus, or other components. **2.** A work of art made of bronze. **3.** A yellowish or olive brown. **—modifier:** *bronze tools; a bronze statue.* **—adj.** Yellowish or olive brown. **—v. bronzed, bronz·ing.** To give the appearance or color of bronze to. **—intr.v.** To become like bronze. [French, from Italian *bronzo.*] **—bronz'y** *adj.*

brooch (brōch, brŏŏch) *n.* A large decorative pin or clasp. [Middle English *broche,* brooch, tool.]

brood (brŏŏd) *n.* **1.** The young of certain animals, esp. a group of young birds, fish, or fowl hatched at one time and cared for by the same mother. **2.** The children in one family. —*tr.v.* To sit on or hatch (eggs). —*intr.v.* **1.** To sit on or hatch eggs. **2.** To hover over: *Smog brooded on the city.* **3.** To think at length and unhappily; worry anxiously. —*adj.* Kept for breeding: *a brood mare.* [Middle English *brood,* from Old English *brōd.*] —**brood'ing·ly** *adv.*

brood·er (brōo'dər) *n.* **1.** Someone or something that broods. **2.** A heated structure in which young chickens or other fowl are raised.

brook¹ (brŏok) *n.* A small, natural stream. [Middle English, from Old English *brōc.*]

brook² (brŏok) *tr.v.* To put up with; bear; tolerate: *We will brook no delay.* [Middle English *brouken,* to enjoy, use, from Old English *brūcan.*]

brook·let (brŏok'lĭt) *n.* A small brook.

brook trout. A freshwater game fish, *Salvelinus fontinalis,* of eastern North America. Also called **speckled trout.**

broom (brōom, brŏom) *n.* **1.** A brush of bound twigs, straw, or synthetic bristles attached to a stick, used for sweeping. **2.** Any shrub of the genus *Cytisus,* native to Eurasia, with compound leaves and yellow or white flowers. **3.** Any of several similar or related shrubs, esp. of the genus *Genista.* [Middle English *broom,* broom made of broom twigs, from Old English *brōm,* broom plant.]

broom·stick (brōom'stĭk', brŏom'-) *n.* The long handle of a broom.

broth (brôth, brŏth) *n., pl.* **broths** (brôths, brŏths, brôthz, brŏthz). **1.** The water in which meat, fish, or vegetables have been boiled; stock. **2.** A thin, clear soup based on stock. [Middle English *broth,* from Old English *broth.*]

broth·el (brôth'əl, brŏ'thəl) *n.* A house of prostitution. [Middle English *brothen,* ruined, from Old English *brothen,* past part. of *brēothan,* to waste away.]

broth·er (brŭth'ər) *n.* **1.** A boy or man having the same mother and father as another person. **2. a.** A kindred human being; a fellow man. **b.** A fellow member of a group, such as a profession or fraternity. **3. a.** A member of a men's Christian religious order who is not a priest, but engages in the work of the order. **b. Brother.** A form of address for such a person: *Brother Luke.* [Middle English, from Old English *brōthor.*]

broth·er·hood (brŭth'ər-hŏod') *n.* **1.** The relationship of being a brother or brothers. **2.** Brotherly feelings or friendship; fellowship. **3.** A group of men united for a common purpose; a fraternity, labor union, etc. **4.** All the members of a specific profession or trade.

broth·er-in-law (brŭth'ər-ĭn-lô') *n., pl.* **broth·ers-in-law.** **1.** The brother of one's husband or wife. **2.** The husband of one's sister. **3.** The husband of the sister of one's husband or wife.

broth·er·ly (brŭth'ər-lē) *adj.* Characteristic of or befitting brothers; fraternal or kind: *brotherly love.* —**broth'er·li·ness** *n.* —**broth'er·ly** *adv.*

brougham (brōom, brŏo'əm, brō'əm) *n.* **1.** A closed four-wheeled carriage with an open driver's seat in front. **2.** An automobile with an open driver's seat. [After Henry Peter Brougham (1778–1868), Scottish jurist.]

brought (brôt) *v.* The past tense and past participle of **bring.**

brou·ha·ha (brōo'hä-hä') *n.* An uproar; a hubbub. [French (prob. imit.).]

brow (brou) *n.* **1.** The forehead. **2.** An eyebrow. **3.** An expression of the face: *a puzzled brow.* **4.** The upper edge of a steep place: *the brow of a precipice.* [Middle English, from Old English *brū.*]

brow·beat (brou'bēt') *tr.v.* **-beat, -beat·en** (-bēt'n), **-beat·ing.** To intimidate or frighten with an overbearing or imperative manner; domineer.

brown (broun) *n.* Any of a group of colors between red and yellow in hue. —*adj.* **-er, -est. 1.** Of the color brown. **2.** Deeply suntanned. —*tr.v.* To make brown, esp. to cook until brown. —*intr.v.* To become brown. [Middle English, from Old English *brūn.*] —**brown'ness** *n.*

brown algae. Brownish, chiefly saltwater algae of the division Phaeophyta.

brown bear. A very large bear, *Ursus arctos,* of Alaska and northern Eurasia, which has brown to yellowish fur.

brown Bet·ty (bĕt'ē). Also **brown bet·ty.** A baked pudding of apples, bread crumbs, brown sugar, butter, and spices.

[*Betty,* pet form of the name *Elizabeth.*]

brown bread. Any bread made of a dark flour, as graham or whole-wheat bread.

brown coal. A type of coal, lignite.

Brown·i·an motion (brou'nē-ən). The random motion of microscopic particles suspended in a liquid or gas, caused by collision with molecules of the liquid or gas. Also called **Brownian movement.** [After Robert *Brown* (1842–95), Scottish botanist.]

brown·ie (brou'nē) *n.* **1.** In folklore, a small elflike creature said to perform household chores at night. **2.** A rich, chewy chocolate cookie. [Dim. of BROWN (from its characterization as a "wee brown man").]

Brown·ie (brou'nē) *n.* A junior Girl Scout. [From BROWNIE (sprite).]

brown·ish (brou'nĭsh) *adj.* Somewhat brown.

brown rice. Unpolished rice grains, retaining the germ and the yellowish outer layer containing the bran.

brown·stone (broun'stōn') *n.* **1.** A brownish-red sandstone once widely used as a building material. **2.** A house built or faced with such stone.

brown study. A condition of deep thought.

brown sugar. Unrefined or partially refined sugar.

brown thrasher. A North American bird, *Toxostoma rufum,* with a reddish-brown back and a dark-streaked breast.

brown trout. A speckled European trout, *Salmo trutta,* naturalized in North America as a game fish.

browse (brouz) *v.* **browsed, brows·ing.** —*intr.v.* **1.** To inspect in a leisurely and casual way: *browse through a book.* **2.** To feed on leaves, young shoots, and other vegetation: *cattle browsing in the pasture.* —*tr.v.* **1.** To nibble; to crop: *The sheep browsed the new grass.* **2.** To graze on: *The heifers browsed the north meadow.* —*n.* Young twigs, leaves, and tender shoots of plants or shrubs that animals eat. [From Old French *broust, brost,* shoot, twig.] —**brows'er** *n.*

bru·cel·lo·sis (brōo'sə-lō'sĭs) *n.* Undulant fever. [After Sir David *Bruce* (1855–1931), British bacteriologist.]

bru·in (brōo'ĭn) *n.* A name or nickname for a bear. [Dutch *bruin,* brown, from Middle Dutch *bruun.*]

bruise (brōoz) *n.* **1.** An injury in which small blood vessels in the skin are broken, producing discoloration but leaving the skin itself unbroken; a contusion. **2.** A similar injury to a fruit, plant, or vegetable. —*v.* **bruised, bruis·ing.** —*tr.v.* **1.** To injure the surface of (the skin) without rupture. **2.** To dent or mar: *bruise an apple.* **3.** To pound into fragments (leaves, food, etc.); crush. **4.** To hurt psychologically; offend: *bruise someone's feelings.* —*intr.v.* To become discolored. [Middle English *brusen,* to crush, from Old English *brȳsan* and Old French *bruisier.*]

bruis·er (brōo'zər) *n. Slang.* A large, powerfully built person.

bruit (brōot) *tr.v.* To spread news of; repeat: *a rumor bruited about town.* —*n. Archaic.* **1.** A rumor. **2.** A din; a clamor. [Middle English, noise, from Old French, from *bruire,* to roar.]

brunch (brŭnch) *n.* A meal eaten late in the morning as a combination of breakfast and lunch. [BR(EAKFAST) + (L)UNCH.]

bru·net (brōo-nĕt') *adj.* Dark or brown in color: *brunet hair.* —*n.* A person, esp. a man or boy, with dark or brown hair. —See Usage note at **blond.** [French, from Old French, from *brun,* brown.]

bru·nette (brōo-nĕt') *adj.* Having dark or brown hair: *Is she blonde or brunette?* —*n.* A girl or woman with dark or brown hair. —See Usage note at **blond.**

Brun·hild (brōon'hĭld', -hĭlt') *n.* In the *Nibelungenlied,* a legendary queen of Iceland who is won as a bride by Gunther.

brunt (brŭnt) *n.* The main impact, force, or burden: *the brunt of the storm.* [Middle English.]

brush¹ (brŭsh) *n.* **1.** An implement consisting of bristles, hairs, or wire fastened to a handle, for use in scrubbing, applying paint, or grooming the hair. **2.** An application of a brush. **3.** Something that resembles a brush, as the bushy tail of a fox. **4.** A brief, sharp fight; a skirmish. **5.** A light touch in passing; a graze. **6.** An electrically conductive part, gen. of graphite, that makes rubbing or sliding contact with another part, such as a commutator, and completes a circuit, as in a motor or generator. —*tr.v.* **1.** To use a brush on, so as to clean, polish, or groom. **2.** To apply with or as if with motions of a brush. **3.** To remove with or as if with motions of a brush: *brush the crumbs off the table.* **4.** To touch lightly in passing; graze against. —*intr.v.* To move past something so as to touch it lightly. —*phrasal verbs.* **brush off** (or **aside**). To dismiss abruptly or curtly. **brush up.** To refresh one's memory of a certain subject. [Middle English *brusshe*, from Old French *broisse, brosse.*]

brush² (brŭsh) *n.* **1. a.** A dense growth of shrubs or small trees; thicket. **b.** Land covered by such growth. **2.** Sparsely populated woodland. **3.** Cut or broken-off branches; brushwood. [Middle English *brusch(e),* from Old French *broce.*] —**brush'y** *adj.*

brush-off (brŭsh'ôf', -ŏf') *n. Slang.* An abrupt or indifferent dismissal.

brush-wood (brŭsh'wŏŏd') *n.* **1.** Cut or broken-off branches; brush. **2.** Dense undergrowth.

brush-work (brŭsh'wûrk') *n.* **1.** Work done with a brush. **2.** The manner in which a painter applies paint with his brush: *Picasso's brushwork.*

brusque (brŭsk) *adj.* Rudely abrupt in manner or speech; curt; blunt. —See Syns at **gruff.** [French, lively, fierce, from Italian *brusco,* sour, sharp.] —**brusque'ly** *adv.* —**brusque'ness** *n.*

Brus-sels sprouts (brŭs'əlz). **1.** A variety of cabbage, *Brassica oleracea gemmifera,* that has a stout stem studded with budlike heads. **2.** The edible heads of this plant.

Brussels sprouts

bru-tal (brŏŏt'l) *adj.* **1.** Characteristic of a brute; savage. **2.** Cruel or heartless: *a brutal insult.* **3.** Harsh; unrelenting: *a brutal winter.* —**bru'tal-ly** *adv.*

bru-tal-i-ty (brŏŏ-tăl'ĭ-tē) *n., pl.* **-ties. 1.** The condition or quality of being brutal. **2.** A brutal act.

bru-tal-ize (brŏŏt'l-īz') *tr.v.* **-ized, -iz-ing. 1.** To make brutal. **2.** To treat brutally. —**bru'tal-i-za'tion** *n.*

brute (brŏŏt) *n.* **1.** An animal as distinct from a man; a beast. **2.** A cruel person. —*adj.* **1.** Of or relating to beasts; animal. **2. a.** Entirely physical or instinctive; not involving mental effort: *brute force.* **b.** Lacking reason or intelligence. **3.** Savage; cruel. **4.** Gross; coarse. [Middle English, from Old French *brut,* rough, from Latin *brūtus,* heavy.]

brut-ish (brŏŏt'ĭsh) *adj.* **1.** Of or resembling a brute. **2.** Crude in feeling or manner: *brutish behavior.* —**brut'ish-ly** *adv.* —**brut'ish-ness** *n.*

Bryn-hild (brĭn'hĭld') *n. Norse Myth.* A Valkyrie who is revived from an enchanted sleep by Sigurd.

bryo-. A prefix meaning moss: **bryophyte.** [Greek *bruon,* moss.]

bry-ol-o-gy (brī-ŏl'ə-jē) *n.* The branch of botany that deals with bryophytes. [BRYO- + -LOGY.]

bry-o-ny (brī'ə-nē) *n., pl.* **-nies.** Either of two European plants, the black bryony or the white bryony. [Latin *bryōnia,* from Greek *bruōnia.*]

bry-o-phyte (brī'ə-fīt') *n.* Any plant of the major botanical division Bryophyta, which includes the mosses and liverworts. [BRYO- + -PHYTE.] —**bry'o-phyt'ic** (-fĭt'ĭk) *adj.*

bry-o-zo-an (brī'ə-zō'ən) *n.* Any of various small aquatic animals of the phylum Bryozoa that reproduce by budding and form mosslike or branching colonies. [From BRYO- + -ZOON.]

bub-ble (bŭb'əl) *n.* **1.** A rounded, more or less spherical object composed of a thin, often transparent wall of liquid or plastic material enclosing a pocket of gas: *a soap bubble.* **2.** A small, rounded pocket of gas that rises to the surface of a liquid or remains trapped in a solid or plastic material. **3.** A glass or plastic dome. **4.** Something that gives early promise of success but suddenly collapses, such as an idea or plan. —*v.* **-bled, -bling.** —*intr.v.* **1.** To form or give off bubbles, as a boiling liquid. **2.** To move or flow with a gurgling sound: *a bubbling brook.* **3.** To display lively activity or emotion: *bubbling with energy.* —*tr.v.* To cause to form bubbles. [Middle English *bobelen* (imit.).] —**bub'bly** *adj.*

bubble chamber. An apparatus for detecting the paths of charged atomic particles by observation of the trails of bubbles that form on ions produced in a superheated liquid.

bubble gum. Chewing gum that can be blown into bubbles.

bu-bo (bŏŏ'bō, byŏŏ'-) *n., pl.* **-boes.** An inflamed swelling of a lymphatic gland, esp. in the armpit or groin. [Middle English, from Medieval Latin *bubo,* from Greek *boubōn.*] —**bu-bon'ic** (byŏŏ-bŏn'ĭk, bŏŏ-) *adj.*

bubonic plague. A very contagious, usu. fatal disease characterized by inflamed lymph nodes (buboes), caused by bacteria transmitted to human beings by fleas and infected rodents.

buc-cal (bŭk'əl) *adj.* Of or pertaining to the cheeks or mouth cavity. [From Latin *bucca,* cheek.]

buc-ca-neer (bŭk'ə-nîr') *n.* A pirate, esp. one who preyed upon Spanish shipping in the West Indies during the 17th cent. [French *boucanier,* pirate, "one who cures meat on a frame," from *boucaner,* to cure meat, from *boucan,* barbecue frame, from Tupi *mocaen.*]

buck¹ (bŭk) *n.* **1.** The adult male of some animals, such as the deer or rabbit. **2.** *Informal.* **a.** A high-spirited young man. **b.** A fop. [Middle English *bukke,* from Old English *buc,* stag, and *bucca,* he-goat.]

buck² (bŭk) *intr.v.* **1.** To leap forward and upward suddenly; rear up: *The bronco bucked.* **2.** To move rapidly forward with the head lowered; to butt. **3.** To move with sudden forward jerks: *Why is the car bucking?* **4.** To resist stubbornly; to balk: *bucked at the sergeant's orders.* —*tr.v.* **1.** To throw (a rider or burden) by bucking. **2.** To butt against with the head. **3.** To oppose directly and stubbornly: *You can't buck the system.* **4.** To contend with or struggle against: *bucking heavy traffic.* —*phrasal verbs.* **buck for.** To strive for: *He's bucking for a promotion.* **buck up.** *Informal.* To gather one's courage or raise one's spirits. —*n.* An act of bucking. [From BUCK (deer).] —**buck'er** *n.*

buck³ (bŭk) *adj. Mil. Slang.* Of the lowest rank in a specified category: *a buck private.* [Perh. from BUCK (young man).]

buck⁴ (bŭk) *n.* **1.** A sawhorse. **2.** A padded frame used for gymnastic vaulting. [Short for SAWBUCK.]

buck⁵ (bŭk) *n. Slang.* A dollar. [Short for BUCKSKIN (a unit of trade with the American Indians).]

buck⁶ (bŭk) *n.* A marker formerly placed before a poker player to indicate that he is to be the next dealer. —*idiom.* **pass the buck.** To shift responsibility or blame to someone else. [Short for earlier *buckhorn knife,* from its use for this purpose.]

buck-a-roo (bŭk'ə-rŏŏ') *n., pl.* **-roos.** Also **buck-er-oo.** A cowboy. [Var. of Spanish *vaquero,* from *vaca,* a cow, from Latin *vacca.*]

buck-board (bŭk'bôrd', -bōrd') *n.* A four-wheeled open carriage with the seat attached to a flexible board extending from the front to the rear axle. [From obs. *buck,* body of a wagon, from Middle English *buke,* belly, from Old English *būc.*]

buck-er-oo (bŭk'ə-rŏŏ') *n.* Var. of **buckaroo.**

buck-et (bŭk'ĭt) *n.* **1.** A round, open container with a curved handle, used for carrying water, coal, sand, etc. **2. a.** A bucket with something in it: *a bucket of water.* **b.** The amount that a bucket holds: *pour a bucket of sand.* **c. buckets.** A great amount. **3.** Something resembling a bucket, such as the scoop on a steam shovel. —*tr.v.* To hold, carry, or put in a bucket. —*idiom.* **kick the bucket.**

Slang. To die. [Middle English *buket,* from Norman French, bucket, tub.]

bucket seat. A seat with a rounded or molded back, as in sports cars and airplanes.

buck·eye (bŭk′ī) *n.* **1.** Any of several North American trees of the genus *Aesculus,* such as the horse chestnut, with compound leaves and erect clusters of white or reddish flowers. **2.** The glossy brown nut of any of these trees. [From the seed's appearance.]

buck·le¹ (bŭk′əl) *n.* **1.** A clasp, esp. a metal frame with a movable tongue for fastening two strap or belt ends. **2.** An ornament that resembles such a clasp. —*v.* **-led, -ling.** —*tr.v.* To fasten or secure with a buckle. —*intr.v.* To become fastened or attached with a buckle. —*phrasal verb.* **buckle down.** To begin working hard and with determination. [Middle English *bocle,* from Old French *boucle,* from Latin *buccula,* cheek strap of a helmet, from *bucca,* cheek.]

buck·le² (bŭk′əl) *v.* **-led, -ling.** —*intr.v.* **1.** To bend, warp, or crumple under pressure or heat. **2.** To collapse: *The roof buckled.* —*tr.v.* To cause to bend, warp, or crumple. —*phrasal verb.* **buckle under.** To surrender to (another's authority); yield. —*n.* A bend, bulge, or other distortion. [Middle English *boclen,* from Old French *boucler,* to fasten with a buckle.]

buck·ler (bŭk′lər) *n.* **1.** A small round shield. **2.** A means of protection; a defense. [Middle English *boc(e)ler,* from Old French *boucler,* from *boucle,* boss on a shield, buckle.]

buck·ram (bŭk′rəm) *n.* A coarse cotton cloth stiffened with glue, used for binding books, lining garments, etc. [Middle English *bokram,* a fine linen, from Old French *boquerant.*]

buck·saw (bŭk′sô′) *n.* A saw usu. set in an H-shaped frame. [From BUCK (sawhorse).]

buck·shot (bŭk′shŏt′) *n.* A large lead shot, used in shotgun shells for hunting game.

buck·skin (bŭk′skĭn′) *n.* **1.** The skin of a male deer. **2.** A strong, grayish-yellow leather made from deerskins or sheepskins. **3.** **buckskins.** Breeches or shoes made from this leather.

buck·thorn (bŭk′thôrn′) *n.* Any shrub or tree of the genus *Rhamnus,* native to Eurasia, with spine-tipped branches and small greenish flowers.

buck·tooth (bŭk′tooth′) *n.* A prominent, projecting upper front tooth. [From BUCK (deer).] —**buck′toothed′** (bŭk′-tootht′) *adj.*

buck·wheat (bŭk′hwēt′, -wēt′) *n.* **1.** Any plant of the genus *Fagopyrum,* with white flowers and small triangular seeds. **2.** The edible seeds of this plant, often ground into cereal grains. **3.** Flour made from this grain. [From Middle Dutch *boec(weite),* "beech (wheat)" (from the resemblance of its seeds to beech nuts).]

bu·col·ic (byoo-kŏl′ĭk) *adj.* **1.** Of or characteristic of shepherds and flocks; pastoral. **2.** Of or characteristic of country life; rustic; rural. —*n.* **1.** A pastoral poem. **2.** A farmer or shepherd; a rustic. [Latin *būcolicus,* from Greek *boukolikos,* from *boukolos,* cowherd.]

bud (bŭd) *n.* **1.** *Bot.* **a.** A small growth on a stem or branch containing an undeveloped shoot, leaves, or flowers. **b.** The stage or condition of having as yet unopened buds: *roses in bud.* **2.** *Biol.* A small outgrowth on an organism, such as a yeast or hydra, that develops into a complete new organism. **3.** A stage of early or incomplete development: *an idea in bud.* —*v.* **bud·ded, bud·ding.** —*intr.v.* **1.** To form or produce a bud or buds. **2.** To begin to develop or grow from or as if from a bud. **3.** To be in an undeveloped stage or condition. —*tr.v.* **1.** To cause to put forth buds. **2.** *Hort.* To graft a bud onto (a plant). —*idioms.* **in the bud.** In an incipient or undeveloped state. **nip in the bud.** To stop (something) in its initial stage. [Middle English *budde.*]

Bud·dha (boo′də, bood′ə) *n.* **1.** Often **buddha.** Any sage who is recognized by Buddhists as having achieved a state of perfect illumination like that of Gautama Buddha. **2.** A representation of Gautama Buddha. [Sanskrit, "awakened," past part. of *bodhati,* he awakes, becomes aware.]

Bud·dhism (boo′dĭz′əm, bood′ĭz′-) *n.* **1.** The doctrine, attributed to Gautama Buddha, that suffering is inseparable from existence but that one can escape or transcend it by the inward extinction of the self and of the senses. This culminates in a state of perfect bliss beyond both suffering and existence called nirvana. **2.** The religion originating in eastern and central Asia represented by the many differing sects that profess this doctrine —**Bud′dhist** *n.* & *adj.*

bud·dy (bŭd′ē) *n., pl.* **-dies.** *Informal.* A close friend; comrade. [Prob. baby-talk for BROTHER.]

budge (bŭj) *v.* **budged, budg·ing.** —*intr.v.* **1.** To move or stir slightly. **2.** To alter a position or attitude: *Once his mind is made up, he won't budge.* —*tr.v.* **1.** To cause to move slightly. **2.** To cause to alter a position or attitude: *She's adamant, and I can't budge her.* [Earlier *bouge,* from Old French *bouger,* from Latin *bullīre,* to boil.]

budg·er·i·gar (bŭj′ə-rē-gär′) *n.* A parakeet, *Melopsittacus undulatus,* native to Australia, that has green, yellow, or blue plumage, often kept as a pet. [Native Australian name : *budgeri,* good + *gar,* cockatoo.]

bud·get (bŭj′ĭt) *n.* **1.** An itemized list of probable expenditures and income for a given period. **2.** The sum of money allocated for a particular purpose or time period: *a $200 budget for gas.* —*tr.v.* **1.** To plan in advance the expenditure of (money, time, etc.). **2.** To enter or plan for in a budget: *The department budgeted two new positions.* [Middle English *budget,* wallet, from Old French *bougette,* from *bouge,* leather bag, from Latin *bulga.*] —**bud′get·ar′y** (bŭj′ĭ-tĕr′ē) *adj.*

budg·ie (bŭj′ē) *n. Informal.* A budgerigar.

bud scale. Any of the small, scalelike leaves that form the protective sheath of a plant bud.

buff¹ (bŭf) *n.* **1.** A soft, thick, undyed leather made from the skins of buffalo, elk, or oxen. **2.** A military coat made of this leather. **3.** A yellowish tan. **4.** A polishing implement covered with a soft material. —*modifier: a buff jerkin.* —*adj.* Yellowish tan. —*tr.v.* To polish or shine with a buff. [Earlier *buffalo,* from Old French *buffle, from Latin būbalus.*]

buff² (bŭf) *n. Informal.* One who is enthusiastic and knowledgeable about a particular subject: *a railroad buff.* [Orig. a New York volunteer fireman, (from the firemen's buff uniforms).]

buf·fa·lo (bŭf′ə-lō′) *n., pl.* **-loes** or **-los** or **buffalo. 1.** Any of several oxlike Old World mammals of the family Bovidae, with outward curving horns, as the water buffalo. **2.** The North American bison. —*tr.v. Slang.* **1.** To intimidate. **2.** To confuse or bewilder. [Portuguese *bufalo,* from Latin *būbalus,* from Greek *boubalos,* African antelope, buffalo.]

buffalo grass. A short grass, *Buchloe dactyloides,* of the plains east of the Rocky Mountains.

buff·er¹ (bŭf′ər) *n.* Something used to shine or polish, as a soft cloth or a machine with a moving head.

buff·er² (bŭf′ər) *n.* **1.** Something that lessens or absorbs the shock of an impact. **2.** Someone or something that protects by intercepting or moderating adverse pressures or influences: *Her secretary serves as a buffer.* **3.** *Chem.* A substance capable of stabilizing the acidity or alkalinity of a solution by neutralizing, within limits, any acid or base that is added. —*tr.v. Chem.* To treat (a solution) with a buffer. [Prob. from *buff,* to deaden the shock of.]

buf·fet¹ (bə-fā′, boo-) *n.* **1.** A large sideboard with drawers and cupboards for storing china, silverware, and table linens. **2. a.** A counter from which food is served. **b.** A restaurant with such a counter. **3.** A meal at which guests serve themselves from various dishes arranged on a table or sideboard. [French.]

buf·fet² (bŭf′ĭt) *tr.v.* **1.** To hit or club, esp. with the hand. **2.** To strike against forcefully; to batter: *Winds buffeted the tent.* **3.** To force (one's way) with or as if with crude blows: *buffeted a path through the mob.* —*intr.v.* To force one's way by struggling: *buffet through the blizzard.* —*n.* A blow or cuff made with or as if with the hand. [Middle English, from Old French, from *buffe,* blow.]

buf·foon (bə-foon′) *n.* **1.** A clown; jester. **2.** A person who makes coarse jokes. [French *bouffon,* from Italian *buffone,* from *buffare,* to puff.] —**buf·foon′er·y** *n.*

bug (bŭg) *n.* **1.** Any of various wingless or four-winged insects of the order Hemiptera, and esp. of the suborder Heteroptera, that have mouth parts adapted for piercing and sucking. **2.** Any insect, spider, or similar organism. **3.** *Informal.* A disease-producing microorganism; a germ. **4.** A

buggy¹

bugle

bulbul
George Miksch Sutton

mechanical, electrical, or other defect or difficulty in a machine. **5.** *Slang.* An enthusiast or devotee; a buff: *a hi-fi bug.* **6.** A small hidden microphone or other device used for eavesdropping. —*v.* **bugged, bug·ging.** —*intr.v.* To protrude; to jut: *His eyes almost bugged out of his head.* —*tr.v.* **1.** *Slang.* To annoy; pester: *Don't bug me.* **2.** To equip (a room, telephone circuit, etc.) with a concealed electronic listening device. —See Syns at **annoy.** [Orig. unknown.]

bug·a·boo (bŭg′ə-bōō′) *n.,* pl. **-boos.** An object of excessive concern or fear. [Perh. of Celtic orig.]

bug·bear (bŭg′bâr′) *n.* **1.** An object of excessive concern or fear. **2.** *Archaic.* A hobgoblin or bogey. [Obs. *bug,* from Middle English *bugge.*]

bug·gy¹ (bŭg′ē) *n.,* pl. **-gies. 1.** A small, light, four-wheeled horse-drawn carriage. **2.** A baby carriage. [Orig. unknown.]

bug·gy² (bŭg′ē) *adj.* **-gi·er, -gi·est. 1.** Infested with bugs. **2.** *Slang.* Crazy.

bu·gle (byōō′gəl) *n.* A brass wind instrument somewhat shorter than a trumpet, and without keys or valves. —*v.* **-gled, -gling.** —*intr.v.* To play a bugle. —*tr.v.* To call by sounding a bugle. [Middle English, buffalo, horn, bugle, from Old French, from Latin *būculus,* from *bōs,* ox.] —**bu′gler** *n.*

build (bĭld) *v.* **built** (bĭlt), **build·ing.** —*tr.v.* **1.** To form by combining materials or parts; to erect; construct. **2.** To build or make according to a definite plan or process; give form to: *a house built from blueprints; a commune built on Marxist principles.* **3.** To establish and strengthen, esp. gradually and steadily: *build a vocabulary.* **4.** To establish a basis for; found or ground: *build an argument on fact.* —*intr.v.* **1.** To construct something or have something constructed. **2.** To be a builder. **3.** To develop an idea, argument, theory, or the like: *We build upon what our forefathers have wrought.* **4.** To progress toward a maximum, as of intensity, excitement, or the like: *The suspense builds from the opening scene.* —*phrasal verb.* **build up. 1.** To construct in stages or by degrees. **2.** To renew the strength or health of. **3.** To establish and strengthen; create and add to: *build up a business.* **4.** To magnify (a person or thing) by extravagant praise or publicity. **5.** To fill up (an area) with buildings. —*n.* The physical make-up of a person or thing: *an athletic build.* [Middle English *bilden,* from Old English *byldan,* from *bold,* a dwelling.]

build·er (bĭl′dər) *n.* **1.** Someone or something that builds: *an empire builder.* **2.** A person who contracts for and supervises the construction of a building.

build·ing (bĭl′dĭng) *n.* **1.** Something that is built; a structure; an edifice. **2.** The act, process, art, or occupation of constructing.

build·up (bĭld′ŭp′) *n.* Also **build-up. 1.** The act of amassing or increasing. **2.** Extravagant praise; widely favorable publicity, esp. by a systematic campaign.

built (bĭlt) *v.* Past tense and past participle of **build.**

built-in (bĭlt′ĭn′) *adj.* **1.** Constructed as a nondetachable part of a larger unit: *a built-in cabinet; a built-in safety device.* **2.** Forming a permanent or essential element or quality: *a built-in escape clause.* **3.** Natural; inherent: *a built-in sense of danger.*

built-up (bĭlt′ŭp′) *adj.* **1.** Made by fastening several layers or sections one on top of the other. **2.** Occupied by several buildings: *a built-up urban section.*

bulb (bŭlb) *n.* **1.** *Bot.* A modified underground stem, such as that of the onion or tulip, usu. surrounded by scalelike

modified leaves, and containing stored food for the undeveloped shoots of the new plant enclosed within it. **2.** Any underground stem or root resembling this, such as a corm, rhizome, or tuber. **3.** Any plant that grows from a bulb. **4.** An incandescent lamp or its glass housing. **5.** *Anat.* Any of various rounded, enlarged, or bulb-shaped structures in the body, esp. the medulla oblongata. [Latin *bulbus,* bulb, onion, from Greek *bolbos,* name of various bulbous plants.]

bul·bar (bŭl′bər, -bär′) *adj.* Of, like, or affecting one of the rounded structures of the body, esp. the medulla oblongata: *bulbar poliomyelitis.*

bul·bous (bŭl′bəs) *adj.* **1.** Resembling a bulb; rounded; swollen. **2.** *Bot.* Bearing or growing from bulbs.

bul·bul (bōōl′bōōl′) *n.* **1.** Any of various chiefly tropical Old World songbirds of the family Pycnonotidae, with grayish or brownish plumage. **2.** A songbird thought to be a nightingale, often mentioned in Persian poetry. [Persian, from Arabic.]

bulge (bŭlj) *n.* A protruding part; a swelling. —*v.* **bulged, bulg·ing.** —*intr.v.* To grow larger or rounder; swell beyond the usual size: *eyes bulging with surprise.* —*tr.v.* To cause to swell out: *Coins bulged his coat.* [Middle English, wallet, pouch, from Old French *bouge,* from Latin *bulga,* leather bag.] —**bulg′y** *adj.*

bulk (bŭlk) *n.* **1.** Great size, mass, or volume: *the whale's monstrous bulk.* **2.** A large mass or portion of matter. **3.** The major portion or greater part of something: *The bulk of the work is done.* —*intr.v.* **1.** To be or appear to be great in size or importance; to loom. **2.** To grow or increase in size or importance. —*tr.v.* To cause to swell or expand. —*idiom.* **in bulk. 1.** Unpackaged; loose. **2.** In large numbers, amounts, or volume. [Middle English *bulke,* from Old Norse *bulki,* cargo.]

> **Syns: bulk, amplitude, magnitude, mass, size, volume** *n.* Core meaning: Great amount or dimension (*the monstrous bulk of a supertanker*).

bulk·head (bŭlk′hĕd′) *n.* **1.** One of the upright partitions that divide the inside of a ship into compartments and serve to prevent the spread of leakage or fire. **2.** An embankment constructed in a mine or tunnel to protect against earth slides, fire, water, or gas; retaining wall. **3.** A horizontal or sloping structure providing access to a cellar stairway or to an elevator shaft. [Orig. unknown.]

bulk·y (bŭl′kē) *adj.* **-i·er, -i·est. 1.** Extremely large; massive. **2.** Clumsy; unwieldy: *a bulky package.* —**bulk′i·ly** *adv.* —**bulk′i·ness** *n.*

bull¹ (bōōl) *n.* **1. a.** An adult male bovine mammal. **b.** The uncastrated adult male of domestic cattle. **2.** The male of certain other mammals, such as the elephant and moose. **3.** An exceptionally large, strong, and aggressive man. **4.** A speculator, esp. one who tries to raise prices of securities and commodities by speculative purchases in order to sell later at a profit. **5.** *Slang.* A policeman or detective. **6.** *Slang.* Empty, foolish talk; nonsense. —*tr.v.* **1.** To push; to force: *bull one's way through a crowd.* **2.** To accomplish or get through on nerve and pretense; to bluff: *I bulled my way through the interview.* —*adj.* **1.** Male. **2.** Resembling a bull; large and strong. **3.** *Stock Market.* Characterized by rising prices: *a bull market.* —*idioms.* **shoot the bull.** *Slang.* **1.** To spend time talking. **2.** To talk foolishly. **take the bull by the horns.** To take prompt and bold action. [Middle English *bule, bole,* from Old English *bula,* from Old Norse *boli.*]

bull² (bōōl) *n.* An official document issued by the pope.

bulldog   bullmastiff   bull terrier

[Middle English *bulle,* from Old French, from Medieval Latin *bulla,* seal.]

bull³ (bŏŏl) *n. Informal.* A foolish blunder, esp. in language. [Orig. unknown.]

bull·dog (bŏŏl'dôg', -dŏg') *n.* **1.** A short-haired dog of a breed characterized by a large head, strong, square jaws with dewlaps, and a stocky body. **2.** *Brit.* A proctor's assistant at Oxford or Cambridge. —*adj.* Resembling or having the qualities of a bulldog; stubborn. —*tr.v.* **-dogged, -dogging.** To throw (a steer) by seizing its horns and twisting its neck.

bull·doze (bŏŏl'dōz') *tr.v.* **-dozed, -doz·ing. 1.** To clear, dig up, or move with a bulldozer. **2.** *Slang.* To bully. [Perh. BULL + DOSE.]

bull·doz·er (bŏŏl'dō'zər) *n.* **1.** A large, powerful tractor having a vertical metal scoop in front for moving earth, rocks, etc., used esp. to clear or grade land. **2.** *Slang.* An overbearing or bullying person.

bul·let (bŏŏl'ĭt) *n.* **1.** A spherical or pointed cylindrical metal projectile that is fired from a pistol, rifle, or other small firearm. **2.** A cartridge. **3.** Any object of similar shape or effect: *The skier shot down the hill like a bullet.* [French *boulette,* from *boule,* ball, from Old French, from Latin *bulla,* bubble, ball.]

bul·le·tin (bŏŏl'ĭ-tn, -tĭn) *n.* **1.** A printed or broadcast statement on a matter of public interest. **2.** A publication, such as a periodical or pamphlet, issued by an organization or society. [French, prob. from Old French *bullette,* from *bulle,* BULL (document).]

bulletin board. A board mounted on a wall, on which notices are posted.

bul·let·proof (bŏŏl'ĭt-prŏŏf') *adj.* Designed to stop or repel bullets: *bulletproof glass.*

bull·fight (bŏŏl'fīt') *n.* A public spectacle, esp. in Spain and Mexico, in which a fighting bull is engaged in a series of traditional maneuvers and then usu. killed. —**bull'fight'er** *n.* —**bull'fight'ing** *n.*

bull·finch (bŏŏl'fĭnch') *n.* A European songbird, *Pyrrhula pyrrhula,* with a short, thick bill and, in the male, a red breast.

bull·frog (bŏŏl'frôg', -frŏg') *n.* Any of several large frogs, chiefly of the genus *Rana,* esp. *R. catesbeiana* of North America, with a deep, resonant croak.

bull·head (bŏŏl'hĕd') *n.* **1.** Any of several North American freshwater catfish of the genus *Ictalurus.* **2.** Any of several large-headed fish of the family Cottidae.

bull·head·ed (bŏŏl'hĕd'ĭd) *adj.* Very stubborn; obstinate; headstrong. —See Syns at **obstinate.** —**bull'head'ed·ly** *adv.* —**bull'head'ed·ness** *n.*

bul·lion (bŏŏl'yən) *n.* Gold or silver bars or ingots. [Middle English, from Norman French, mint.]

bull·ish (bŏŏl'ĭsh) *adj.* **1.** Like a bull; brawny or bullheaded. **2. a.** Causing, expecting, or characterized by rising stock-market prices. **b.** Optimistic or confident. —**bull'ish·ly** *adv.* —**bull'ish·ness** *n.*

bull·mas·tiff (bŏŏl'măs'tĭf) *n.* A heavy-set dog of a breed developed from the bulldog and the mastiff.

bul·lock (bŏŏl'ək) *n.* **1.** A castrated bull; a steer. **2.** A young bull. [Middle English *bullok,* from Old English *bulluc,* from *bula,* bull.]

bull·pen (bŏŏl'pĕn') *n.* **1.** *Baseball.* **a.** An area where relief pitchers warm up during a game. **b.** All the relief pitchers

on a team. **2.** *Informal.* A place for the temporary detention of prisoners.

bull·ring (bŏŏl'rĭng') *n.* A circular arena for bullfights.

bull session. *Informal.* An informal group discussion.

bull's eye. Also **bull's-eye** (bŏŏlz'ī'). **1. a.** The small central circle on a target. **b.** A shot that hits this circle. **2.** Anything that precisely achieves a desired goal. **3.** A thick, circular piece of glass set in a roof, ship's deck, etc., to admit light. **4.** Any circular opening or window. **5. a.** A convex lens used to concentrate light. **b.** A lantern or lamp having such a lens.

bull terrier. A dog of a breed developed by crossing a bulldog and a terrier, with a short, usu. white coat.

bull·whip (bŏŏl'hwĭp', -wĭp') *n.* A long whip of braided rawhide with a knotted end.

bul·ly (bŏŏl'ē) *n., pl.* **-lies.** A person who picks on or beats up smaller or weaker people. —*tr.v.* **-lied, -ly·ing.** To intimidate with superior size or strength. —*adj. Informal.* Excellent; splendid. —*interj.* A word used to express approval: *Bully for you.* [Earlier sweetheart, prob. from Middle Dutch *boele,* lover.]

bul·rush (bŏŏl'rŭsh') *n.* **1.** Any of various grasslike sedges of the genus *Scirpus* that grow in wet places. **2.** Any of various marsh plants, such as the cattail. [Middle English *bulrish.*]

bul·wark (bŏŏl'wərk, bŭl'-, -wôrk') *n.* **1.** A wall or barrier serving as a defensive fortification; rampart. **2.** Any protection or defense: *"We have seen the necessity of the Union, as our bulwark against foreign danger"* (James Madison). **3.** A breakwater. **4. bulwarks.** The part of a ship's side that is above the upper deck. —*tr.v.* **1.** To fortify with a bulwark. **2.** To provide defense or protection for. [Middle English *bulwerke,* from Middle High German *bolwerc:* bole, plank + *werc,* work.]

bum (bŭm) *n.* **1.** A tramp; hobo. **2.** A person who avoids work and seeks to live off others; a loafer. —**on the bum.** *Slang.* **1.** Living as a hobo or tramp. **2.** Out of order; broken. —*v.* **bummed, bum·ming.** *Informal.* —*intr.v.* **1.** To live by begging and scavenging from place to place: *bumming around the country.* **2.** To loaf. —*tr.v.* To acquire by begging or sponging: *bum a cigarette.* —*adj. Slang.* **1.** Worthless: *a bum tip.* **2.** Disabled; malfunctioning: *a bum shoulder.* [From earlier *bummer,* a loafer, prob. from German *bummler,* from *bummeln,* to loaf.]

bum·ble (bŭm'bəl) *v.* **-bled, -bling.** —*intr.v.* To speak or behave in a clumsy manner. —*tr.v.* To bungle; botch: *He bumbled the ball.* [Var. of BUNGLE.]

bum·ble·bee (bŭm'bəl-bē') *n.* Any of various large, hairy bees of the genus *Bombus.* [Middle English *bomblem,* to buzz + BEE.]

bump (bŭmp) *tr.v.* **1.** To strike or collide with. **2.** To cause to knock against an obstacle: *He bumped his knee on the hydrant.* **3.** To knock to a new position; displace: *The loss bumped us into last place.* —*intr.v.* To hit or knock with force: *She bumped into the tree.* —*phrasal verbs.* **bump into.** To meet accidentally or by chance. **bump off.** *Slang.* To murder. —*n.* **1.** A sudden blow, collision, or jolt. **2.** A slight swelling or lump, esp. one caused by a blow, an insect sting, etc. **3.** A small place that rises above the level of the surface surrounding it, esp. on a road. [Imit.]

bump·er¹ (bŭm'pər) *n.* Either of two metal structures, typically horizontal bars, attached to the front and rear of an

---

ă pat   ā pay   â care   ä father   ĕ pet   ē be   hw which
ŏŏ took   ōō boot   ou out   th thin   *th* this   ŭ cut

ĭ pit   ī tie   î pier   ŏ pot   ō toe   ô paw, for   oi noise
û urge   zh vision   ə about, item, edible, gallop, circus

automobile to absorb the impact of a collision.

bump·er² (bŭm′pər) n. A drinking vessel filled to the top. —adj. Unusually full or abundant: a bumper crop. [Perh. from BUMP (lump).]

bump·kin (bŭmp′kĭn, bŭm′-) n. An awkward or unsophisticated person; a yokel. [Orig. unknown.]

bump·tious (bŭmp′shəs) adj. Crudely forward and self-assertive in behavior; pushy. [Perh. a blend of BUMP and FRACTIOUS.] —**bump′tious·ly** adv. —**bump′tious·ness** n.

bump·y (bŭm′pē) adj. -i·er, -i·est. 1. Full of bumps or lumps: a bumpy pillow. 2. Causing jerks and jolts: a bumpy road. —**bump′i·ly** adv. —**bump′i·ness** n.

bun (bŭn) n. 1. A small bread roll, often sweetened or spiced. 2. A roll or coil of hair worn at the back of the head. [Middle English bunne.]

bunch (bŭnch) n. 1. A group of like things growing, fastened, or placed together; a cluster. 2. Informal. A small group of people: a good bunch of students. —tr.v. To gather or form into a cluster or tuft. —intr.v. 1. To form a cluster or tuft. 2. To swell or protrude. [Middle English bunche.] —**bunch′y** adj.

bun·co (bŭng′kō). Also **bun·ko**. Informal. —n., pl. -cos. A swindle in which an unsuspecting person is cheated; confidence game. —tr.v. To swindle, as by a confidence game. [Spanish banca, name of a card game, bank (in gambling).]

bun·dle (bŭn′dl) n. 1. A number of objects bound, wrapped, or otherwise held together. 2. Anything wrapped or tied up for carrying; a package. 3. Biol. A cluster or strand of specialized cells. 4. Bot. A vascular bundle. 5. Slang. A large sum of money. —v. -dled, -dling. —tr.v. 1. To tie, wrap, fold, or otherwise secure together. 2. To send or dispatch quickly and with little fuss: We bundled her off to the doctor. 3. To dress warmly: She bundled us up in heavy coats. —intr.v. 1. To leave hastily. 2. To sleep in the same bed while fully clothed, a custom practiced by engaged couples in early New England. [Middle English bundel, prob. from Middle Dutch.] —**bun′dler** n.

bung (bŭng) n. 1. A stopper for the hole through which a cask, keg, or barrel is filled or emptied. 2. The hole itself; a bunghole. —tr.v. To close (a bunghole) with a cork or stopper. [Middle English bunge, from Middle Dutch bonghe.]

bun·ga·low (bŭng′gə-lō′) n. A small cottage, usu. of one story. [Earlier bungale, from Hindi banglā, "of Bengal."]

bung·hole (bŭng′hōl′) n. The hole in a cask, keg, or barrel through which the liquid is poured or drained.

bun·gle (bŭng′gəl) v. -gled, -gling. —intr.v. To work or act ineptly or inefficiently. —tr.v. To manage (a task) badly; mishandle. —See Syns at **botch**. —n. A clumsy or inept job or performance. [Perh. of Scandinavian orig.] —**bun′gler** n.

bun·ion (bŭn′yən) n. A painful, inflamed swelling at the bursa of the big toe. [Prob. from earlier dial. bunny, swelling, from Old French buigne, bump on the head.]

bunk¹ (bŭngk) n. 1. A narrow bed built like a shelf against a wall. 2. A double-decker bed. 3. Informal. Any place for sleeping. —intr.v. 1. To sleep in a bunk. 2. To sleep, esp. in makeshift quarters: He'll bunk on the sofa tonight. [Poss. short for BUNKER.]

bunk² (bŭngk) n. Slang. Empty talk; nonsense; twaddle. [From Buncombe County, North Carolina, from a congressman's remark that a fatuous speech had been "a speech for Buncombe."]

bun·ker (bŭng′kər) n. 1. A bin or tank for fuel storage, as on a ship. 2. Golf. An obstacle, usu. sand in a shallow depression. 3. A military fortification or earthwork, as a deep trench or tunnel. [Earlier Scottish bonker.]

bunk·house (bŭngk′hous′) n. Sleeping quarters on a ranch or in a camp.

bun·ko (bŭng′kō) n., pl. -kos. Var. of **bunco**.

bun·ny (bŭn′ē) n., pl. -nies. Informal. A rabbit. [From dialectal bun, squirrel.]

Bun·sen burner (bŭn′sən). A small laboratory gas burner consisting of a vertical metal tube and producing a very hot flame from a mixture of gas and air let in through adjustable holes at the base. [After Robert W. Bunsen (1811–99), German chemist, its inventor.]

bunt (bŭnt) tr.v. 1. To strike or push (something) with or as if with the horns or head; to butt. 2. Baseball. To bat (a pitched ball) with a half swing so that the ball rolls slowly in front of the infielders. —intr.v. Baseball. To bunt a pitch. —n. 1. A butt with or as if with the horns or head. 2. Baseball. a. The act of bunting. b. A ball that is bunted. [Prob. of Celtic orig.]

bun·ting¹ (bŭn′tĭng) n. 1. A light cotton or woolen cloth used for making flags. 2. Flags in general. 3. Long strips of cloth with flaglike stripes or colors, used for festive or holiday decoration. [Orig. unknown.]

bun·ting² (bŭn′tĭng) n. Any of various birds of the family Fringillidae, with short, cone-shaped bills. [Middle English buntynge.]

bun·ting³ (bŭn′tĭng) n. A snug-fitting, hooded sleeping bag for infants. [Orig. unknown.]

bunt·line (bŭnt′lĭn, -līn′) n. A rope that keeps a square sail from bellying when it is being hauled up for furling. [Orig. unknown.]

buoy (bōō′ē, boi) n. 1. Naut. A float anchored in water as a warning of danger under the surface or as a marker for a channel. 2. A device made of cork or other buoyant material for keeping a person afloat; life buoy; life preserver. —tr.v. 1. Naut. To mark (a water hazard or a channel) with a buoy. 2. To keep afloat. 3. To cheer; hearten: The news buoyed her spirits. [Middle English boye, prob. from Old French boie.]

buoy

buoy·an·cy (boi′ən-sē, bōō′yən-) n. 1. The tendency or capacity to float or rise in a fluid. 2. The upward force that a fluid exerts on an object less dense than itself. 3. The ability to recover quickly from setbacks. 4. Cheerfulness.

buoy·ant (boi′ənt, bōō′yənt) adj. 1. Capable of floating or of keeping things afloat. 2. Animated; sprightly: a buoyant step. [Spanish buoyante, from boyar, to float, from boya, buoy.] —**buoy′ant·ly** adv.

bur¹ (bûr) n. Also **burr**. 1. The rough, prickly, or spiny covering enclosing the seed, fruit, nut, or flower head of various plants. 2. A persistently clinging or nettlesome person or thing. 3. Any of various rotary cutting tools designed to be attached to a drill. [Middle English burre, prob. of Scandinavian orig.]

bur² (bûr) n. 1. Var. of **burr** (rough edge). 2. Var. of **burr** (guttural trill).

bur·ble (bûr′bəl) intr.v. -bled, -bling. 1. To bubble; to gurgle, as a stream. 2. To speak quickly and excitedly. [Middle English burblen (imit.).]

bur·den¹ (bûr′dn) n. Also archaic **bur·then** (bûr′thən). 1. Something that is carried; a load. 2. Something that is difficult or oppressive to bear physically or emotionally. 3. a. The amount of cargo that a vessel can carry. b. The weight of the cargo carried by a vessel at one time. —tr.v. 1. To load or overload. 2. To weigh down; oppress: Don't burden your mind with useless information. [Middle English, from Old English byrthen.]

bur·den² (bûr′dn) n. 1. The chorus or refrain of a song or other musical composition. 2. The bass accompaniment to a song. 3. A main or recurring idea or theme: the burden of the argument. [Middle English bourdon, from Old French, drone, from Medieval Latin burdo.]

burden of proof. The responsibility of proving a disputed charge or allegation.

bur·den·some (bûr′dn-səm) adj. Hard to bear; heavy.

ă pat	ā pay	â care	ä father	ĕ pet	ē be	hw which	ĭ pit	ī tie	î pier	ŏ pot	ō toe	ô paw, for	oi noise
ŏŏ took	ōō boot	ou out	th thin	th this	ŭ cut		û urge	zh vision	ə about, item, edible, gallop, circus

Syns: burdensome, arduous, backbreaking, demanding, difficult, exacting, formidable, hard, heavy, laborious, onerous, oppressive, rigorous, rough, severe, taxing, tough, trying, weighty *adj. Core meaning:* Imposing a severe test of physical or spiritual strength (*burdensome farm chores*).

bu·reau (byŏŏr′ō) *n., pl.* **-reaus** or **bu·reaux** (byŏŏr′ōz). **1.** A chest of drawers, esp. one with a mirror. **2.** *Brit.* A writing desk or writing table with drawers. **3. a.** A government department or subdivision of a department: *the tax bureau.* **b.** An office, usu. of a large organization, that performs a specific duty: *a news bureau.* **c.** A business that offers information of a specific kind: *a travel bureau.* [French, bureau, woolen material used to cover writing desks, from Old French, from *bure,* coarse woolen stuff.]

bu·reauc·ra·cy (byŏŏ-rŏk′rə-sē) *n., pl.* **-cies. 1.** Government that is administered through bureaus and departments. **2.** The departments and their officials as a group. **3.** Any administration, as of a business, in which the need to follow rules and regulations impairs effective action. [BUREAU + -CRACY.]

bu·reau·crat (byŏŏr′ə-krăt′) *n.* **1.** An official of a bureaucracy. **2.** Someone who insists on rigid adherence to rules, forms, and routines. —**bu′reau·crat′ic** *adj.* —**bu′reau·crat′i·cal·ly** *adv.*

bu·rette (byŏŏ-rĕt′) *n.* Also **bu·ret.** A graduated glass tube for measuring volume, with a stopcock at the bottom, used esp. in laboratory procedures for accurate dispensing of small amounts of fluid. [French, cruet, from Old French, from *buire,* pitcher.]

burg (bûrg) *n.* **1.** A fortified or walled town. **2.** *Informal.* A city or town. [Old English *burg, burh.*]

bur·geon (bûr′jən) *intr.v.* **1.** To put forth new buds, leaves, or greenery; to sprout. **2.** To develop rapidly; flourish. —*tr.v.* To put forth (buds, shoots, etc.). —*n.* A bud, sprout, or newly developing growth. [Middle English *burgenen,* from *burjon,* a bud, from Old French.]

bur·ger (bûr′gər) *n. Informal.* A hamburger.

bur·gess (bûr′jĭs) *n.* **1.** A citizen of an English borough. **2.** Formerly, a member of the English Parliament, representing a town, borough, or university. **3.** A member of the lower house of the colonial legislature of either Virginia or Maryland. [Middle English *burgeis,* from Old French, from Late Latin *burgus,* fortified place.]

burgh (bûrg) *n.* A chartered town or borough in Scotland. [Scottish, var. of BOROUGH.]

burgh·er (bûr′gər) *n.* **1.** A member of the merchant class of a medieval city. **2.** A solid citizen; bourgeois. [From either German *Bürger* or Dutch *burger,* both ult. from Old High German *burg,* castle, city.]

bur·glar (bûr′glər) *n.* A person who commits burglary; a housebreaker. [Norman French *burgler,* from Medieval Latin *burgulator,* prob. var. of *burgātor,* town thief, from Late Latin *burgus,* fortress.]

bur·glar·ize (bûr′glə-rīz′) *tr.v.* **-ized, -iz·ing.** To commit burglary in; break into and rob.

bur·gla·ry (bûr′glə-rē) *n., pl.* **-ries.** The crime of breaking into and entering a building or house with the intention of stealing.

bur·gle (bûr′gəl) *v.* **-gled, -gling.** *Informal.* —*tr.v.* To burglarize. —*intr.v.* To commit burglary. [Back-formation from BURGLAR.]

bur·go·mas·ter (bûr′gə-măs′tər) *n.* In the Netherlands, Flanders, Austria, and Germany, the principal magistrate of a city or town, comparable to a mayor. [From Dutch *burg,* town, from Middle Dutch *burch* + MASTER.]

bur·i·al (bĕr′ē-əl) *n.* The act of placing a dead body in a grave, a tomb, or the sea. —*modifier: burial rites; a burial chamber.* [Middle English *biriel, buryel,* grave, from Old English *byrgels* (pl.).]

bu·rin (byŏŏr′ĭn, bûr′-) *n.* A pointed steel cutting tool used in engraving or in carving stone. [French.]

burl (bûrl) *n.* **1.** A knot or lump in yarn or cloth. **2.** A large, rounded outgrowth on a tree. **3.** The wood from such a growth, usu. with a marked grain, used as decorative veneer. —*tr.v.* To finish (cloth) by removing burls or loose threads. [Middle English *burle,* from Old French *bourle,* from *bourre,* coarse wool, from Late Latin *burra,* shaggy garment.]

bur·lap (bûr′lăp′) *n.* A coarse cloth made of jute, flax, or hemp, used to make bags, sacks, curtains, coverings, etc. [Orig. unknown.]

bur·lesque (bər-lĕsk′) *n.* **1.** A literary or dramatic work that makes a subject appear ridiculous, such as presenting a vulgar or comic treatment of a serious subject or a mock-dignified treatment of a slight or inconsequential subject; a parody. **2.** Any ludicrous or mocking imitation; a travesty. **3.** Vaudeville entertainment characterized by broad, vulgar comedy, dancing, and display or nudity. —*tr.v.* **-lesqued, -lesqu·ing.** To imitate in a way that mocks or makes ridiculous. —See Syns at **imitate.** —*adj.* **1.** Mockingly and ludicrously imitative. **2.** Of, pertaining to, or characteristic of theatrical burlesque. [French, from Italian *burlesco,* from *burla,* joke, ridicule, from Late Latin *burra,* bit of nonsense.] —**bur·lesqu′er** *n.*

bur·ley (bûr′lē) *n., pl.* **-leys.** Also **Bur·ley.** A light-colored tobacco grown chiefly in Kentucky. [Prob. from *Burley,* a proper name.]

bur·ly (bûr′lē) *adj.* **-li·er, -li·est.** Heavy, strong, and muscular; husky: *a burly football player.* [Middle English *burli, borlich,* stately, big.] —**bur′li·ness** *n.*

burn[1] (bûrn) *v.* **burned** or **burnt** (bûrnt), **burn·ing.** —*tr.v.* **1.** *Chem.* To cause to undergo combustion. **2.** *Physics.* To cause to undergo nuclear fission or fusion. **3.** To destroy with fire. **4.** To damage or injure by fire, heat, or a heat-producing agent: *He burned his finger.* **5.** *Slang.* To kill or execute, esp. to electrocute. **6.** To produce by fire or heat: *burn a clearing in the brush.* **7.** To use as a fuel: *burn kerosene for light.* **8.** To brand (an animal). **9.** To impart a sensation of intense heat to: *The chili burned his mouth.* **10.** To harden or impart a finish to by subjecting to intense heat; to fire: *burn the pottery in a kiln.* **11.** To sunburn. **12.** To wear out or exhaust: *She burns a lot of energy playing tennis.* **13.** To waste or squander: *money to burn.* **14.** *Slang.* To anger: *Her snide remarks really burn me.* **15.** *Slang.* **a.** To defeat in a contest, esp. by a narrow margin. **b.** To cheat out of; deny: *They burned us in that deal.* —*intr.v.* **1.** *Chem.* To undergo combustion. **2.** To be on fire; to flame. **3.** To be destroyed, damaged, injured, or changed by or as if by fire: *The house burned to the ground.* **4.** To give off heat or light by or as if by fire: *The sun burned bright in the sky.* **5.** To be produced by or as if by burning: *Her curse burned in my mind.* **6.** *Slang.* To electrocute. **7.** To feel or look hot: *burning with fever.* **8.** To impart a sensation of heat. **9.** To become sunburned. **10.** To be consumed with strong emotion: *burn with anger.* —See Syns at **hot.** —*phrasal verbs.* **burn out. 1.** To stop burning from lack of fuel. **2.** To wear out or fail, esp. because of heat. **burn up. 1.** To consume or be consumed by fire. **2.** *Slang.* To make or become very angry. —*n.* **1.** An injury produced by fire, heat, or a heat-producing agent. **2.** The process or result of firing or burning, as in the manufacture of bricks. **3.** A sunburn. **4.** *Aerospace.* One firing of a rocket. [Middle English *burnen,* from Old English *beornan, bærnan.*]

burn[2] (bûrn) *n.* A small stream or brook in Scotland. [Middle English *burn, burne,* from Old English *burn, burna,* spring, fountain.]

burn·er (bûr′nər) *n.* **1.** One that burns something. **2.** The part of a stove, furnace, or lamp that is lighted to produce a flame. **3.** A device in which something is burned: *an oil burner.*

bur·nish (bûr′nĭsh) *tr.v.* To polish, smooth, or make glossy by or as if by rubbing: *burnish a brass doorknob.* —*n.* A smooth, glossy finish or appearance; luster. [Middle English *burnischen,* from Old French *burnir, brunir,* "to make brown," burnish, from *brun,* brown.] —**bur′nish·er** *n.*

bur·noose (bər-nōōs′) *n.* Also **bur·nous.** A long, hooded cloak worn by Arabs. [French *burnous,* from Arabic *bournous,* from Greek *birros,* cloak with a hood.]

burn·sides (bûrn′sīdz′) *pl.n.* Heavy side whiskers and a moustache, worn with the chin clean-shaven. [After Ambrose E. *Burnside* (1824–81), American army commander.]

burnt (bûrnt) *v.* An alternate past tense and past participle of **burn.** —*adj.* Affected by or as if by burning.

burnt sienna. 1. A reddish-brown pigment. **2.** Dark reddish orange. Also called **sienna.**

burp (bûrp) *n. Informal.* A belch. —*intr.v.* To belch.

ă pat   ā pay   â care   ä father   ĕ pet   ē be   hw which   ĭ pit   ī tie   î pier   ŏ pot   ō toe   ô paw, for   oi noise
ōō took   ōō boot   ou out   th thin   th this   ŭ cut   û urge   zh vision   ə about, item, edible, gallop, circus

—*tr.v.* To cause (a baby) to belch. [Imit.]

burr¹ (bûr). Also **bur.** —*n.* **1.** A rough edge or area remaining on metal or other material after it has been cast, cut, or drilled. **2.** Any rough outgrowth, esp. a burl on a tree. —*tr.v.* **1.** To form a rough edge on. **2.** To remove a rough edge or edges from. [Middle English *burre*, rough edge, bur.]

burr² (bûr). Also **bur.** —*n.* **1.** A rough trilling of the letter *r*, as in Scottish pronunciation. **2.** Any similar pronunciation or speech sound. **3.** A buzzing or whirring sound. —*tr.v.* To pronounce with a burr. —*intr.v.* **1.** To speak with a burr. **2.** To make a buzzing or whirring sound. [Imit.]

burr³ (bûr) *n.* Var. of **bur** (prickly seed).

bur·ro (bûr′ō, boor′ō, bûr′ō) *n., pl.* **-ros.** A small donkey, esp. one used as a pack animal. [Spanish, from *borrico*, donkey, from Late Latin *burricus*, small horse.]

bur·row (bûr′ō, bûr′ō) *n.* **1.** A hole or tunnel dug in the ground by a small animal, such as a rabbit or a mole, for habitation or refuge. **2.** Any similar narrow or snug place. —*intr.v.* **1.** To dig a burrow. **2.** To live or hide in a burrow. **3.** To move or progress through something as if by digging or tunneling: *"Suddenly the train is burrowing through the pinewoods"* (William Styron). **4.** To search or hunt: *He burrowed through the desk for a stamp.* —*tr.v.* **1.** To make by or as if by tunneling. **2.** To dig a burrow in or through. **3.** To hide or seclude (oneself) in a burrow. [Middle English *borow*.] —**bur′row·er** *n.*

bur·sa (bûr′sə) *n., pl.* **-sae** (-sē′) or **-sas.** A saclike body cavity, esp. one located between joints or at points of friction between moving structures. [From Medieval Latin, bag, purse, from Greek.]

bur·sar (bûr′sər, -sär′) *n.* A treasurer, as at a college or university. [Medieval Latin *bursārius*, from *bursa*, purse.]

bur·sa·ry (bûr′sə-rē) *n., pl.* **-ries.** A treasury, esp. of a university or religious order. [Medieval Latin *bursāria*, from *bursa*, purse.]

bur·si·tis (bər-sī′tĭs) *n.* Inflammation of a bursa, esp. in the shoulder, elbow, or knee joints. [From BURS(A) + -ITIS.]

burst (bûrst) *v.* **burst, burst·ing.** —*intr.v.* **1. a.** To come open or fly apart suddenly or violently, esp. from internal pressure. **b.** To explode. **2.** To be full to the point of breaking open; swell: *bursting with pride; a suitcase bursting with clothes.* **3.** To come forth, emerge, or arrive suddenly and in full force: *She burst into the room.* **4.** To give sudden utterance or expression: *burst into laughter.* —*tr.v.* **1.** To cause to come open or fly apart with sudden violence: *burst a balloon.* **2.** To cause to swell or become full to the point of breaking open: *Flood waters burst the dam.* —See Syns at **explode.** —*n.* **1.** A sudden outbreak or outburst; an explosion: *a burst of gunfire; a burst of laughter.* **2.** A sudden, vehement outbreak or occurrence: *a burst of activity.* **3.** An abrupt, intense increase or display: *a burst of speed.* **4.** *Mil.* **a.** The explosion of a projectile or bomb. **b.** The number of bullets fired from an automatic weapon by one pull of the trigger. [Middle English *bersten*, from Old English *berstan.*]

bur·then (bûr′thən) *n. Archaic.* Var. of **burden** (something carried).

bur·y (bĕr′ē) *tr.v.* **-ied, -y·ing.** **1.** To place (a dead body) in a grave, a tomb, or the sea; inter. **2.** To cover or conceal by or as if by covering with earth: *bury treasure; a dog burying a bone.* **3.** To cover from view; hide: *She buried her face in the pillow.* **4.** To embed; sink: *He was found dead with a knife buried in his heart.* **5.** To occupy (oneself) with deep concentration; absorb: *He buried himself in his books.* **6.** To put an end to; abandon: *Help me bury the old quarrel.* [Middle English *berien, burien*, from Old English *byrgan.*]

bus (bŭs) *n., pl.* **bus·es** or **bus·ses.** **1.** A long motor vehicle, sometimes with two decks, for carrying passengers; omnibus. **2.** *Elect.* A conductor, often large and carrying heavy currents, that supplies several circuits. Also called **bus bar.** —*v.* **bused** or **bussed, bus·ing** or **bus·sing.** —*tr.v.* To transport in a bus. —*intr.v.* **1.** To travel in a bus: *I bus to work.* **2.** To work as a bus boy. [Short for OMNIBUS.]

Usage: **bus, busing.** The verb meaning to transport (schoolchildren) in a bus is now standard. The past tense and the past participle are either *bused* or *bussed*, and the present participle and the noun derived from it are either

busing or *bussing.* Choose whichever spelling you feel the most comfortable with.

bus boy. A restaurant employee who clears away dirty dishes and serves as a waiter's assistant.

bus·by (bŭz′bē) *n., pl.* **-bies.** A tall full-dress fur hat worn in certain regiments of the British Army. [Orig. unknown.]

bush (boosh) *n.* **1.** Any low, branching, woody plant, usu. smaller than a tree; shrub. **2.** A thick growth or clump of shrubs; thicket. **3. a.** Land covered with a dense growth of shrubs. **b. the bush.** Land remote from settlement; backland. —*intr.v.* To grow or branch out like a shrub or bush. —*tr.v.* To decorate, protect, or support with shrubs or bushes. —*idiom.* **beat around** (or **about**) **the bush.** To delay in getting to the point. [Middle English *busshe.*]

bush baby. A small primate, the galago.

bush·el (boosh′əl) *n.* **1.** A unit of volume or capacity used in dry measure in the United States and equal to 4 pecks, 35.24 liters, or 2,150.42 cubic inches. **2.** A container with approximately this capacity. [Middle English *busshel, boyschel*, from Old French *boissiel*, from *boisse*, one sixth of a bushel.]

bush·ing (boosh′ĭng) *n.* **1.** A metal tube that acts as a guide or bearing for a moving part. **2.** A lining of insulation for a hole through which an electrical conductor passes. **3.** A fitting that permits pipes of different diameters to be joined. [From earlier *bush*, from Middle Dutch *busse*, bushing of a wheel, wheel box, from Late Latin *buxis*, box.]

bush-league (boosh′lēg′) *adj. Slang.* Second-rate: *a bush-league performance.* —**bush′-leagu′er** *n.*

bush·mas·ter (boosh′măs′tər) *n.* A large, venomous snake, *Lachesis muta*, of tropical America, with brown and grayish markings.

bush pilot. A pilot who flies a small airplane to and from areas inaccessible to larger aircraft or other means of transportation.

bush·whack (boosh′hwăk′, -wăk′) *intr.v.* To live in or travel through the woods. —*tr.v.* To attack suddenly from a place of hiding; to ambush. —**bush′whack′er** *n.*

bush·y (boosh′ē) *adj.* **-i·er, -i·est.** **1.** Overgrown with bushes. **2.** Thick and shaggy. —**bush′i·ness** *n.*

bus·i·ly (bĭz′ə-lē) *adv.* In a busy manner.

busi·ness (bĭz′nĭs) *n.* **1.** The occupation, work, or trade in which a person is engaged. **2.** Any commercial establishment, such as a store or factory. **3.** Volume or amount of commercial trade: *Business is up this year.* **4.** Commercial dealings, policy, or practice: *Extending credit is good business.* **5.** One's rightful or proper concern or interest; responsibility: *"The business of America is business"* (Calvin Coolidge). **6.** Serious work or endeavor that pertains to one's job: *went to Tokyo on business.* **7.** An affair or matter: *a peculiar business.* **8.** An incidental action performed by an actor on the stage to fill a pause between lines or to provide interesting detail. —*modifier:* *business administration; a business suit.* —*idioms.* **give (someone) the business.** To upbraid or treat roughly. **mean business.** To be in dead earnest. [Middle English *bissinesse*, diligence, state of being busy, from Old English *bisignis*, care, solicitude, from *bisig*, busy.]

Syns: **business, commerce, industry, trade, traffic** *n.* Core meaning: Commercial, industrial, or professional activity (*when business is slow*). BUSINESS applies broadly to all gainful activity. INDUSTRY is the production and manufacture of goods (*the plastics industry*), while COMMERCE and TRADE are the exchange and distribution of commodities (*interstate commerce; the publishing trade*). TRAFFIC may suggest illegal trade (*traffic in narcotics.*) See also Syns at **work.**

busi·ness·like (bĭz′nĭs-līk′) *adj.* **1.** Methodical; systematic; efficient. **2.** Purposeful; serious; earnest.

busi·ness·man (bĭz′nĭs-măn′) *n.* A man engaged in business.

busi·ness·wom·an (bĭz′nĭs-woom′ən) *n.* A woman engaged in business.

bus·ing (bŭs′ĭng) *n.* Also **bus·sing.** The transportation of children by bus to schools outside their neighborhoods, esp. as a means of achieving racial integration. —See Usage note at **bus.**

bus·kin (bŭs′kĭn) *n.* **1.** A laced foot and leg covering reaching halfway to the knee. **2.** A thick-soled laced half boot, worn by actors of Greek and Roman tragedies. **3.** Tragedy. [Old French *bouzequin.*]

bus·man's holiday (bŭs'mənz). *Informal.* A vacation on which a person engages in recreation similar to his usual work.

buss (bŭs). *Archaic. tr.v.* To kiss with a loud smacking sound. —*intr.v.* To kiss loudly. —*n.* A smacking kiss. [Perh. imit.]

bus·ses (bŭs'ĭz) *n.* A plural of **bus.**

bust¹ (bŭst) *n.* **1.** A woman's bosom; breast. **2.** A sculpture of a person's head, shoulders, and upper chest. [French *buste,* from Italian *busto,* piece of sculpture.]

bust¹   **bustard**
George Miksch Sutton

bust² (bŭst). *Informal. tr.v.* **1.** To burst or break. **2.** To break up (a trust or monopoly). **3.** To break or tame (a horse). **4.** To cause to become bankrupt. **5.** To reduce the rank of; demote. **6.** To hit or punch. **7.** To place under arrest. —*intr.v.* **1.** To burst or break. **2.** To become bankrupt. —*n.* **1.** A failure; a flop. **2.** A time or period of widespread financial depression. **3.** A punch or blow. **4.** A spree. **5.** An arrest. [Var. of BURST.] —See Syns at **arrest.**

bus·tard (bŭs'tərd) *n.* Any of various large brownish or grayish Old World birds of the family Otididae, inhabiting open, grassy regions of Africa and other parts of the Eastern Hemisphere. [Middle English *bustarde.*]

bus·tle¹ (bŭs'əl) *v.* **-tled, -tling.** —*intr.v.* To hurry energetically and busily. —*n.* Excited activity; commotion; stir. [Prob. var. of obs. *buskle,* from *busk,* to prepare, from Middle English *busken,* from Old Norse *buāsk.*]

bus·tle² (bŭs'əl) *n.* **1.** A frame or pad worn to puff out the back of a woman's skirt. **2.** A gathering of material at the back of a skirt below the waist. [Perh. from German *Buschel,* a bunch, pad.]

bus·y (bĭz'ē) *adj.* **-i·er, -i·est. 1.** Actively engaged in some form of work; occupied. **2.** Crowded with activity. **3.** Meddlesome; prying. **4.** Temporarily in use: *Her phone is busy.* **5.** Cluttered with minute detail; distracting: *a busy design.* —*tr.v.* **-ied, -y·ing.** To make (oneself) busy; occupy (oneself). [Middle English *bisy, busy,* from Old English *bysig, bisig.*] —**bus'y·ness** *n.*

bus·y·bod·y (bĭz'ē-bŏd'ē) *n.,* pl. **-ies.** A person who meddles or pries into the affairs of others.

but (bŭt; *unstressed* bət) *conj.* **1.** Contrary to expectation: *Usually the night was cold, but this night the air was hot and sticky.* **2.** On the contrary. Used to connect coordinate elements: *We offer not a pledge but a request.* **3.** Nevertheless: *He felt something bad was going to happen, but he tried to tell himself he was being silly.* **4.** However: *We know he's crazy, but why would he do such a foolish thing?* Often used with strong emphasis to introduce a new step of an argument: *When something vibrates it may make a sound. But, can you always hear a sound when something vibrates?* **5.** Still: *We don't have anything much to say. But maybe we can think of something.* **6.** Yet: *It is probable but not certain that the tax rate will go up.* **7.** Except for the fact. Used with *that: I would never have heard of him but that my grandmother once knew him.* **8.** —Used with interjectional expressions: *Wow! But that little one in the red jacket skates well!* —*adv.* **1. a.** Only; merely: *This is but one case in many.* **b.** No more than: *They had skated but a few moments when the church bell*

rang. **2.** More than: *He never did hear her name but once again.* **3.** *Informal.* Really; very: *I want that job finished but pronto.* —*prep.* **1.** Except; barring: *The new plan worked in all but a few places.* **2.** Other than: *the whole truth and nothing but the truth.* —*n.* An objection to what one is saying: *no ifs, ands, or buts.* "Yes, but. . ." she began. "No buts!" he shouted. —*Note: But* is often used followed by *for* to form the prepositional group **but for. 1.** Were it not for: *But for me all would have been lost.* **2.** Except for: *The words "big" and "pig" are spelled alike but for one letter.* [Middle English *bute, but,* from Old English *būtan, būte.*]

    Usage: **1. but.** The word *but* can be a conjunction meaning with the exception of: *No one* (subject) *but* (conjunction) *I* (nominative) *heard it.* In this situation, the pronoun following *but* agrees in case with the word that precedes *but.* The word *but* can also function as a preposition meaning except for: *No one* (subject) *heard it but* (preposition) *me* (object). When *but* and the word following it occur at the end of a sentence, *but* is gen. construed as a preposition with its object being in the objective case. **2. but that, but what.** The expressions *but that* and *but what* occur in sentences that begin with negatives and follow words like *doubt, know,* and *question: I don't doubt but that it will fail. I don't know but what I'll go.* Usage studies indicate that these expressions occur on all levels and are standard American idiom. Nevertheless, they are a bit wordy, so we recommend that you avoid them in formal compositions. The sentences can be recast to read: *I don't doubt that it will fail. I might go.* See also Usage note at **cannot.**

bu·ta·di·ene (byōō'tə-dī'ĕn', -dī-ēn') *n.* A colorless, highly flammable hydrocarbon, C_4H_6, obtained from petroleum and used in the manufacture of synthetic rubber. [BU-TA(NE) + DI- + -ENE.]

bu·tane (byōō'tān') *n.* Either of two flammable, gaseous hydrocarbons, C_4H_{10}, produced synthetically from petroleum and used as a household fuel, refrigerant, aerosol propellant, and in the manufacture of synthetic rubber. [BUT(YRIC ACID) + -ANE.]

butch·er (bōōch'ər) *n.* **1.** A person who slaughters and dresses animals for food or market. **2.** A person who sells meats. **3.** A person who cruelly kills without reason. **4.** *Informal.* A person who bungles; botcher. —*tr.v.* **1.** To slaughter or prepare (animals) for market. **2.** To kill (people) cruelly and without reason. **3.** To spoil by botching; to bungle. [Middle English *bo(u)cher,* from Norman French, from Old French *bouchier,* from *boc,* he-goat.] —**butch'er·er** *n.*

butch·er·y (bōōch'ə-rē) *n.,* pl. **-ies. 1.** The trade of a butcher. **2.** A slaughterhouse. **3.** Savage or cruel killing; carnage.

but·ler (bŭt'lər) *n.* The chief male servant of a household. [Middle English *buteler,* servant in charge of the wine cellar, from Old French *bouteillier,* a bottle bearer, from *bouteille,* bottle.]

butler's pantry. A serving and storage room between the kitchen and the dining room.

butt¹ (bŭt) *tr.v.* To hit or push against with the head or horns; ram. —*intr.v.* **1.** To hit or push something with the head or horns. **2.** To project forward or out. —*phrasal verb.* **butt in** (or **into**). *Informal.* To interfere or meddle; intrude. —*n.* A push or blow with the head or horns. [Middle English *butten,* from Norman French *buter.*]

butt² (bŭt) *tr.v.* To attach the ends of; abut. —*intr.v.* To be joined at the ends. [From BUTT (end).]

butt³ (bŭt) *n.* **1.** A person or thing serving as an object of ridicule or contempt. **2.** A target. **3. butts.** A target range. **4.** A mound of earth, a wall, or another obstacle behind a target for stopping the shot. [Middle English *butte,* target, from Old French *but.*]

butt⁴ (bŭt) *n.* **1.** The larger or thicker end of something: *the butt of a rifle.* **2.** An unburned end, as of a cigarette. **3.** A short or broken remnant; a stub. **4.** *Slang.* A cigarette. **5.** *Informal.* The buttocks. [Middle English *but, butte,* thicker end.]

butte (byōot) *n.* A hill that rises sharply from the surrounding area and has a flat top. [French, from Old French *but,* BUTT (mound behind targets).]

ă pat	ā pay	â care	ä father	ĕ pet	ē be	hw which	ĭ pit	ī tie	î pier	ŏ pot	ō toe	ô paw, for	oi noise
ōō took	ōō boot	ou out	th thin	*th* this	ŭ cut		û urge	zh vision	ə about, item, edible, gallop, circus				

but·ter (bŭt'ər) n. **1.** A soft, yellowish or whitish emulsion of butterfat, water, air, and sometimes salt, churned from milk or cream and processed for use in cooking and as a food. **2.** Any of various similar substances, esp.: **a.** A spread made from fruit, nuts, or other foods, as apple butter. **b.** A vegetable fat having a nearly solid consistency at ordinary temperatures, as cocoa butter. —tr.v. **1.** To put butter on or in. **2.** Informal. To flatter: She's always buttering him up. [Middle English buter(e), from Old English butere, from Latin būtyrum, from Greek bouturon, "cow cheese."]

but·ter-and-eggs (bŭt'ər-ən-ĕgz') n. (used with a sing. or pl. verb). A North American plant, Linaria vulgaris, with numerous narrow leaves and a spike of spurred pale-yellow and orange flowers.

but·ter·cup (bŭt'ər-kŭp') n. **1.** Any of various plants of the genus Ranunculus with glossy yellow flowers. **2.** The cup-shaped flower of any of these plants.

buttercup

but·ter·fat (bŭt'ər-făt') n. The oily content of milk from which butter is made, consisting largely of the glycerides of oleic, stearic, and palmitic acids.

but·ter·fin·gers (bŭt'ər-fĭng'gərz) n. (used with a sing. verb). A clumsy or awkward person who drops things.

but·ter·fish (bŭt'ər-fĭsh') n., pl. **butterfish** or **-fish·es. 1.** A saltwater food fish, Poronotus triacanthus, of the North American Atlantic coast, that has a flattened body. **2.** Any of various similar or related fishes. [From its slippery mucous coating.]

but·ter·fly (bŭt'ər-flī') n., pl. **-flies. 1.** Any of various insects of the order Lepidoptera, with slender bodies, knobbed antennae, and four broad, usu. colorful wings. **2.** A frivolous pleasure-seeker: a social butterfly. **3.** A swimming stroke in which both arms are drawn upward out of the water and forward while the legs perform an up-and-down kick. [Middle English butterflie, from Old English buttorflēoge.]

butterfly

but·ter·milk (bŭt'ər-mĭlk') n. **1.** The thick, sour liquid that remains after the butterfat has been removed from whole milk or cream by churning. **2.** A cultured, sour milk made by adding certain microorganisms to sweet milk.

but·ter·nut (bŭt'ər-nŭt') n. **1.** A tree, Juglans cinerea, of eastern North America, with compound leaves and egg-shaped nuts. **2.** The edible, oily nut of this tree. **3.** The hard, grayish-brown wood of this tree. [From the oiliness of the nut.]

butternut squash. A small, pear-shaped winter squash.

but·ter·scotch (bŭt'ər-skŏch') n. **1.** A syrup, sauce, or flavoring made by melting butter, brown sugar, and sometimes artificial flavorings. **2.** A hard, sticky candy made from these ingredients. —modifier: butterscotch ice cream; butterscotch syrup.

but·ter·y¹ (bŭt'ə-rē) adj. **1.** Having the quality, consistency, or flavor of butter. **2.** Resembling, containing, or spread with butter.

but·ter·y² (bŭt'ə-rē, bŭt'rē) n., pl. **-ies.** Brit. A pantry or wine cellar. [Middle English boteri, buttrie, from Old French boterie, from bot, cask, from Latin buttis.]

but·tock (bŭt'ək) n. **1.** Either of the two rounded fleshy parts of the rump. **2. buttocks.** The rump. [Middle English.]

but·ton (bŭt'n) n. **1.** A small disk or knob of plastic, metal, etc., used to join two parts of a garment by fitting through a buttonhole or loop. **2.** Such an object used for decoration. **3.** Any of various objects of similar appearance, esp. a push-button switch. **4.** A round, flat emblem bearing a design or printed information and pinned to the front of a garment: a campaign button. **5.** Any of various knoblike organic structures, as the head of a small mushroom or the tip of a rattlesnake's tail. —tr.v. To fasten with a button or buttons. —intr.v. To be able to be fastened with a button or buttons. —idiom. on the button. Informal. Exactly; precisely. [Middle English boton, from Old French bouton, bud, button, from bouter, to strike against, pierce.] —but'ton·er n.

but·ton·hole (bŭt'n-hōl') n. A slit or hole in a garment or in cloth used to hold and fasten a button. —tr.v. **-holed, -hol·ing. 1.** To make a buttonhole in. **2.** To sew with a buttonhole stitch. **3.** To stop and detain (a person) in conversation, as if by grabbing by the buttonhole in a coat lapel: I buttonholed the boss.

but·ton·hook (bŭt'n-hŏŏk') n. A small hook for buttoning shoes or gloves.

but·ton·wood (bŭt'n-wŏŏd') n. A North American tree, the sycamore. [From its buttonlike fruit.]

but·tress (bŭt'rĭs) n. **1.** A structure, often of brick or stone, built against a wall for support or reinforcement. **2.** Anything that serves to support or reinforce. —tr.v. **1.** To brace or reinforce with a buttress. **2.** To sustain or bolster: buttress an argument with evidence. [Middle English butres, boteras, from Old French (ars) bouterez, thrusting (arch), from bouter, to strike against, butt.]

bu·tyl alcohol (byōōt'l). One of four isomeric alcohols widely used as solvents and in organic synthesis, each having the formula C_4H_9OH. [From BUT(YRIC ACID) + -YL.]

bu·tyr·ic acid (byōō-tĭr'ĭk). Either of two colorless isomeric acids, C_3H_7COOH, occurring in animal milk fats and used in disinfectants, emulsifying agents, and pharmaceuticals. [From Latin būtyrum, butter.]

bux·om (bŭk'səm) adj. Healthily plump and ample of figure, esp. in the bosom. [Middle English buxum, obedient, from Old English būgan, to bend.]

buy (bī) v. **bought** (bôt), **buy·ing.** —tr.v. **1.** To acquire goods in exchange for money or its equivalent; to purchase. **2.** To be capable of purchasing: Money buys less and less everyday. **3.** To acquire by sacrifice, exchange, or trade: You cannot buy his love. **4.** Informal. To bribe. **5.** Slang. To accept the truth or feasibility of; believe: She'll never buy that story. —intr.v. To purchase goods; act as a purchaser: buy on the installment plan. —See Syns at believe. —phrasal verbs. buy in (or into). To purchase stock or interest, as in a company. buy off. To bribe in order to proceed without interference, or to be exempted from an obligation or from prosecution. buy out. To purchase the controlling stock, business rights, or interests of. buy up. To purchase all that is available of. —n. **1.** Anything bought or capable of being bought; a purchase. **2.** Informal. Something that is underpriced; a bargain. [Middle English byen, from Old English bycgan.] —buy'a·ble adj.

buy·er (bī'ər) n. **1.** A person who buys goods; a customer. **2.** A purchasing agent, esp. one who buys for a retail store.

buzz (bŭz) intr.v. **1.** To make a low droning or vibrating sound like that of a bee. **2.** To talk excitedly in low tones. **3.** To move quickly and busily; bustle: We buzzed all over town. —tr.v. **1.** To cause to buzz. **2.** To utter (gossip) in a rapid, low voice. **3.** Informal. To fly a plane low over:

buzzed *the control tower.* **4.** To signal (a person) with a buzzer. **5.** *Informal.* To telephone (a person): *buzz me later.* —*n.* **1.** A rapidly vibrating, humming, or droning sound. **2.** A low murmur, as of many hushed voices speaking at once: *a buzz of talk.* **3.** *Informal.* A telephone call. **4.** *Slang.* A pleasant intoxication, as from alcohol or drugs. [Middle English *bussen,* to drone (imit.).]

buz·zard (bŭz′ərd) *n.* **1.** Any of various North American vultures, such as the turkey buzzard. **2.** *Brit.* Any hawk of the genus *Buteo.* [Middle English *busard,* from Old French *buson,* from Latin *būteō.*]

buzz·er (bŭz′ər) *n.* Any of various electric signaling devices that make a buzzing sound, such as a doorbell.

buzz saw. A circular saw.

by (bī) *prep.* **1.** Through the action or authorship of: *a novel by Cervantes.* **2.** With the help or use of: *crossing by ferry.* **3. a.** In accordance with: *playing by the rules.* **b.** According to: *by his own account.* **4.** Through the method of: *He succeeded by working hard.* **5.** Through the route of; via: *got home by a shortcut.* **6.** During: *sleeping by day.* **7.** In the amount of: *letters by the thousands.* **8.** Past: *A car drove by us.* Also used adverbially: *The Jeep raced by.* **9.** After: *day by day.* **10.** Along: *jogging by the river.* **11.** Next to: *the chair by the window.* **12.** In the presence or name of: *I swear by the book.* **13.** In or at (someone's place): *Come by our house soon.* Also used adverbially: *Come by when you feel like it.* **14.** Not later than: *finish by noon.* **15.** With the difference of or to the extent of: *shorter by three inches.* —*adv.* **1.** On hand; nearby: *stand by.* **2.** Aside: *putting some money by for later.* —*adj.* Var. of **bye.** —*idioms.* **by and by.** Before long; later. **by and large.** On the whole; for the most part. **by the way.** Incidentally. [Middle English *by,* from Old English *bī, be.*]

by– or **bye–.** A prefix meaning: **1.** Close at hand or near: *bystander.* **2.** Out of the way or aside: *bypath.* **3.** Secondary or incidental: *by-product.* [Middle English *by-, bi-,* from *by, by.*]

by-and-by (bī′ən-bī′) *n.* **1.** Some future time or occasion. **2.** The hereafter.

bye (bī) *n.* **1.** A secondary matter; side issue. **2.** *Sports.* The position of one who draws no opponent for a round in a tournament and so advances to the next round. **3.** *Golf.* One or more holes remaining unplayed at the end of a match. **4.** *Cricket.* A run made on a ball not touched by the batsman. —*adj.* Also **by.** Secondary; incidental. —*idiom.* **by the bye.** Incidentally; by the way. [Var. of BY.]

bye-bye (bī′bī′) *interj. Informal.* Good-by. [Baby-talk for (GOOD-)BY.]

by·gone (bī′gôn′, -gŏn′) *adj.* Gone by; past; former: *bygone days.* —*n.* A past occurrence. —*idiom.* **let bygones be bygones.** To forget past differences.

by·law (bī′lô′) *n.* **1.** A secondary law. **2.** A law or rule governing the internal affairs of an organization. [Middle English *bilawe, bylawe,* "village law," prob. from Old Norse *bȳr,* village + *lŏg,* law.]

by-line (bī′līn′) *n.* Also **by·line.** A line at the head of a newspaper or magazine article with the author's name.

by-pass (bī′păs′) Also **by·pass.** —*n.* **1.** A road or highway that passes around or to one side of an obstructed or congested area; a detour. **2.** A pipe or channel to conduct gas or liquid around another pipe or a fixture. **3.** Any means of circumvention. **4.** *Elect.* A shunt. —*tr.v.* **1.** To go around instead of through; avoid (an obstacle). **2.** To proceed heedless of; ignore. **3.** To cause (gas or liquid) to follow a by-pass. —See Syns at **avoid.**

by-path (bī′păth′, -päth′) *n.* A side path.

by-play (bī′plā′) *n.* Action or speech taking place while the main action proceeds, esp. on a theater stage.

by-prod·uct (bī′prŏd′əkt) *n.* **1.** Something produced in the making of something else. **2.** A side effect.

by-road (bī′rōd′) *n.* A side road; back road.

by-stand·er (bī′stăn′dər) *n.* A person who is present at some event without participating in it.

byte (bīt) *n.* A sequence of adjacent binary digits operated upon as a unit and usu. shorter than a word. [Alteration of BIT (unit of information), influenced by BITE (morsel).]

by-way (bī′wā′) *n.* **1.** A road not often used; a side road. **2.** A secondary or overlooked field of study.

by-word (bī′wûrd′) *n.* **1.** A well-known saying; proverb. **2.** One that proverbially represents a type, class, or quality: *Quisling has become a byword for traitor.* **3.** An object of notoriety. **4.** A nickname or epithet.

Byz·an·tine (bĭz′ən-tēn′, -tīn′, bĭ-zăn′tĭn) *adj.* **1.** Of, pertaining to, or characteristic of Byzantium, its inhabitants, or their culture. **2.** Of or designating the style of architecture developed from the 5th cent. A.D. in Byzantium, characterized by round arches, massive domes, intricate spires and minarets, and extensive use of mosaic. **3.** Of the Eastern Orthodox Church or the rites performed in it. —*n.* A native or inhabitant of Byzantium.

Byzantine Empire. The eastern part of the later Roman Empire, founded by Constantine in A.D. 330 and continuing after the fall of Rome as its successor until 1453; its capital was Constantinople. Also called **Eastern Roman Empire.**

By·zan·ti·um (bĭ-zăn′shē-əm, -tē-) *n.* The Byzantine Empire and its culture.

Byzantine

Cc

Phoenician – *About 3,000 years ago the Phoenicians and other Semitic peoples began to use graphic signs to represent individual speech sounds instead of syllables or whole words. They used this symbol to represent the sound of the consonant "g" (as in English "go") and gave it the name gimel, the Phoenician word for "camel."*

Greek – *The Greeks borrowed the Phoenician alphabet with some modifications. They changed the shape and orientation of gimel and altered the name to gamma. They used gamma to represent the sound of the letter "g" (as in English "go"), as gimel did in Phoenician.*

Roman – *The Romans borrowed the alphabet from the Greeks via the Etruscans. Because the Etruscans did not distinguish between the sounds of "g" (as in English "go") and "k," they used gamma for both. The Romans used the letter to represent the sound of "k" and adapted the shape for carving Latin in stone. This monumental script, as it is called, became the basis for modern printed capital letters.*

Medieval – *By medieval times – around 1,200 years ago – the Roman monumental capitals had become adapted to being relatively quickly written on paper, parchment, or vellum. The cursive minuscule alphabet became the basis of modern printed lower-case letters.*

Modern – *Since the invention of printing about 500 years ago many modifications have been made in the shapes and styles of the letter C, but its basic form has remained unchanged. Changes in pronunciation since ancient times, however, have given the letter C several different phonetic values.*

---

c, C (sē) *n., pl.* **c's** *or rare* **cs, C's** *or* **Cs. 1.** The third letter of the modern English alphabet. **2.** *Mus.* **a.** The first tone in the scale of C major. **b.** A note representing this tone.

C The symbol for the element carbon.

Ca The symbol for the element calcium.

cab (kăb) *n.* **1.** A taxicab. **2.** A one-horse vehicle for public hire. **3.** A covered compartment for the operator or driver of a heavy vehicle or machine, such as a truck or locomotive. —*modifier: a cab driver; cab fare.* [Short for TAXI-CAB, and CABRIOLET.]

ca·bal (kə-băl′) *n.* **1.** A small group of people organized to carry out a secret plot or conspiracy. **2.** A secret scheme or plot organized by such a group. —*intr.v.* **-balled, -balling.** To form a cabal; plot; conspire. [French *cabale,* from Medieval Latin *cabala, cabala.*]

cab·a·la (kăb′ə-lə, kə-bä′lə) *n.* Also **cab·ba·la** or **kab·a·la** or **kab·ba·la** (kăb′ə-lə, kə-bä′lə) *n.* **1.** Often **Cabala.** An occult theosophy of rabbinical origin based on an esoteric interpretation of the Hebrew Scriptures. **2.** Any secret or occult doctrine. [Medieval Latin, from Hebrew *qabbālāh,* received doctrine, tradition, from *qābal,* to receive.] —**cab′a·list** *n.* —**cab′a·lis′tic** (kăb′ə-lĭs′tĭk) *adj.* —**cab′a·lis′ti·cal·ly** *adv.*

ca·ban·a (kə-băn′ə, -băn′yə) *n.* Also **ca·ba·ña.** A shelter on a beach, used as a bathhouse. [Spanish *cabaña,* from Late Latin *capanna,* hut, cabin.]

cab·a·ret (kăb′ə-rā′) *n.* **1.** A restaurant providing short programs of live entertainment; nightclub. **2.** The floor show in a cabaret. [French, from Old French, from Middle Dutch *cambret,* ult. from Late Latin *camera,* chamber.]

cab·bage (kăb′ĭj) *n.* An edible plant, *Brassica oleracea capitata,* with a short, thick stalk and a large head formed by tightly overlapping green or reddish leaves. [Middle English *caboche,* from Old French *caboce,* "head."]

cab·ba·la (kăb′ə-lə, kə-bä′lə) *n.* Var. of **cabala.**

cab·by or **cab·bie** (kăb′ē) *n., pl.* **-bies.** *Informal.* A cab driver.

cab·in (kăb′ĭn) *n.* **1.** A small, simply built house; cottage; hut. **2. a.** In a ship, a room used as living quarters. **b.** In a boat, an enclosed compartment serving as a shelter or as living quarters. **c.** In an airplane, the enclosed space for the passengers, crew, or cargo. —*tr.v.* To confine, as in a cabin. —*intr.v.* To live in a cabin or a small area. [Middle English *cabane,* from Old French, from Late Latin *capanna,* hut, cabin.]

cabin class. A class of accommodations on some passenger ships, lower than first class and higher than tourist class.

cabin cruiser. A powerboat with a cabin; cruiser.

cab·i·net (kăb′ə-nĭt) *n.* **1.** An upright case or cupboard with shelves, drawers, or compartments for the keeping or displaying of a collection of objects or materials: *a kitchen cabinet; a filing cabinet; a curio cabinet.* **2.** A small or private room set aside for some specific activity. **3.** Often **Cabinet.** The body of persons appointed by a chief of state or a prime minister to head the executive departments of the government and to act as his official advisers. —*modifier: a cabinet door; a cabinet minister.* [Old French, dim. of Old North French *cabine,* a gambling house.]

cab·i·net·mak·er (kăb′ə-nĭt-mā′kər) *n.* A craftsman who specializes in making fine articles of wooden furniture.

cab·i·net·work (kăb′ə-nĭt-wûrk′) *n.* Finished woodwork or furniture made by a cabinetmaker.

ca·ble (kā′bəl) *n.* **1.** A strong, thick rope of hemp or fiber. **2.** A rope of twisted strands of steel wire or other metal. **3.** *Elect.* A group of insulated conductors that are bound together as a unit. **4.** *Naut.* A heavy rope or chain for mooring or anchoring a ship. **5.** A unit of nautical length equal to about 220 meters, or 720 feet, in the United States and about 185 meters, or 608 feet, in Great Britain. Also called **cable length. 6.** A cablegram. —*v.* **-bled, -bling.**

cabbage

ă pat	ā pay	â care	ä father	ĕ pet	ē be	hw which
ŏŏ took	ōō boot	ou out	th thin	th this	ŭ cut	

ĭ pit	ī tie	î pier	ŏ pot	ō toe	ô paw, for	oi noise
û urge	zh vision	ə about, item, edible, gallop, circus				

—*tr.v.* **1.** To send a cablegram to: *She cabled her husband that she was sailing.* **2.** To send (a message) by cablegram: *He cabled information to us.* —*intr.v.* To send a cablegram. [Middle English, from Norman French, from Medieval Latin *capulum*, rope for fastening cattle, from Latin *capere*, to take.]

cable car. A vehicle pulled by a cable that moves in an endless loop.

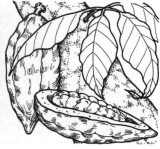

cable car   cacao

ca·ble·gram (kā′bəl-grăm′) *n.* A telegram sent by underwater cable; a cable.

cable length. A cable.

cable television. A commercial television system in which signals are received by a single antenna and delivered to subscribers' receivers by means of a cable.

cab·o·chon (kăb′ə-shŏn′) *n.* A highly polished, convex-cut, unfaceted gem. [Old French, from Old French *caboce*, head, cabbage.]

ca·boo·dle (kə-bōōd′l) *n. Informal.* The lot, group, or bunch. [Perh. a blend of KIT + BOODLE.]

ca·boose (kə-bōōs′) *n.* **1.** The last car on a freight train, with kitchen and sleeping facilities for the train crew. **2.** *Obs.* A ship's galley. [Prob. from Dutch *kabuis*, from Middle Low German *kabūse.*]

cab·ri·o·let (kăb′rē-ə-lā′) *n.* **1.** A two-wheeled one-horse carriage with two seats and a folding top. **2.** An automobile with a collapsible top; a convertible coupe. [French, dim. of *cabriole*, caper (from its bounding motion), from Old French, from Old Italian *capriolo*, roebuck, from Latin *capreolus*, wild goat.]

ca·ca·o (kə-kā′ō, -kä′ō) *n., pl.* **-os.** **1.** An evergreen tropical American tree, *Theobroma cacao*, having yellowish flowers and reddish-brown seed pods. **2.** The seed of this tree, used in making chocolate, cocoa, and cocoa butter. Also called **cacao bean.** [Spanish, from Nahuatl *cacahuatl*, cacao beans.]

cach·a·lot (kăsh′ə-lŏt′, -lō′) *n.* The **sperm whale.** [French, from Spanish, from Portuguese *cacholotte*, "fish with a big head," from *cachola*, head.]

cache (kăsh) *n.* **1.** A hiding place for storing provisions, weapons, etc. **2.** A place for concealing and safekeeping valuables. **3.** A store of goods hidden in a cache. —*tr.v.* **cached, cach·ing.** To store in a hiding place for future use. [French, from *cacher*, to hide, ult. from Latin *cōactāre*, to constrain.]

ca·chet (kă-shā′) *n.* **1.** A seal on a letter or document. **2.** A mark of distinction, individuality, or authenticity. **3. a.** A design stamped on an envelope to commemorate some postal or philatelic event. **b.** A motto forming part of a postal cancellation. [Old French, from *cacher*, to hide, press together.]

ca·chex·i·a (kə-kĕk′sē-ə, kă-) *n.* A general wasting of the body from a chronic disease. [Late Latin, from Greek *kakhexia*, bad condition of the body : *kakos*, bad + *hexis*, condition.]

cach·in·nate (kăk′ə-nāt′) *intr.v.* **-nat·ed, -nat·ing.** To laugh loud, hard, excessively, or convulsively; to guffaw. [From Latin *cachinnāre.*] —**cach′in·na′tion** *n.*

cack·le (kăk′əl) *v.* **-led, -ling.** —*intr.v.* **1.** To make the shrill cry characteristic of a hen after laying an egg. **2.** To laugh or talk in a shrill, broken manner. —*tr.v.* To utter in cackles. —*n.* **1.** The act or sound of cackling. **2.** Shrill, brittle laughter. [Middle English *cakelen.*] —**cack′ler** *n.*

ca·coph·o·nous (kə-kŏf′ə-nəs) *adj.* Having a harsh, unpleasant sound; discordant; dissonant. [Greek *kakophōnos* : *kakos*, bad + *phōnē*, sound.] —**ca·coph′o·nous·ly** *adv.*

ca·coph·o·ny (kə-kŏf′ə-nē) *n., pl.* **-nies.** Harsh, jarring, discordant sound; dissonance.

cac·tus (kăk′təs) *n., pl.* **-ti** (-tī′) or **-tus·es.** Any of a large group of plants of the family Cactaceae, mostly native to arid regions and characterized by thick, fleshy, often prickly stems. [Latin, the cardoon, from Greek *kaktos.*]

cad (kăd) *n.* An ungentlemanly man. [Short for CADDIE.] —**cad′dish** *adj.*

ca·dav·er (kə-dăv′ər) *n.* A dead body, esp. one intended for dissection. [Latin, from *cadere*, to fall, "die."]

ca·dav·er·ous (kə-dăv′ər-əs) *adj.* Resembling a corpse; pale and gaunt. —See Syns at **ghastly.** —**ca·dav′er·ous·ly** *adv.* —**ca·dav′er·ous·ness** *n.*

cad·die (kăd′ē). Also **cad·dy.** —*n., pl.* **-dies.** A person hired by a golfer to carry his clubs. —*intr.v.* **-died, -dy·ing.** To serve as a caddie. [French *cadet*, cadet.]

cad·dis fly (kăd′ĭs). Any of various four-winged insects of the order Trichoptera, found near lakes and streams. [*Caddis*, from obsolete *cad*, var. of *cod*, pod (from the tube in which the larva lives).]

cad·dy[1] (kăd′ē) *n., pl.* **-dies.** A small box or other container, esp. for holding tea. [From Malay *kati*, an Asian unit of weight.]

cad·dy[2] (kăd′ē) *n. & v.* Var. of **caddie.**

ca·dence (kād′ns) *n.* Also **ca·den·cy** (kād′n-sē) *pl.* **-cies.** **1.** Balanced, rhythmic flow, as of poetry or oratory. **2.** The measure or beat of movement, as in dancing or marching. **3.** The general inflection or modulation of the voice. **4.** *Mus.* A progression of chords moving to a harmonic close or point of rest. [Middle English, from Old French, from Old Italian *cadenza*, from *cadere*, to fall, from Latin.]

ca·den·za (kə-děn′zə) *n.* **1.** An elaborate ornamental flourish in an aria or other vocal piece. **2.** A brilliant section, sometimes improvised, of a movement of a concerto in which the soloist exhibits his technique. [Italian, from Old Italian, cadence.]

ca·det (kə-dĕt′) *n.* **1.** A student training to be an officer at a military or naval academy. **2.** A younger son or brother. [French, from dial. *capdet*, chief, from Late Latin *capitellum*, from Latin *caput*, head.] —**ca·det′ship** *n.*

cadge (kăj) *v.* **cadged, cadg·ing.** *Informal.* —*tr.v.* To get by begging. —*intr.v.* To beg. [From Middle English *cadgear*, carrier, from *caggen*, to carry wares.]

cad·mi·um (kăd′mē-əm) *n. Symbol* **Cd** A soft, bluish-white metallic element, occurring primarily in zinc, copper, and lead ores. It is easily cut with a knife and is used in low-friction, fatigue-resistant alloys, solders, dental amalgams, nickel-cadmium storage batteries, and rustproof electroplating. Atomic number 48; atomic weight 112.40; melting point 320.9°C; boiling point 765°C; specific gravity 8.65; valence 2. [From Latin *cadmia*, zinc ore, calamine.] —**cad′mic** (-mĭk) *adj.*

cad·re (kăd′rē) *n.* **1.** A framework. **2.** A nucleus of trained personnel around which a larger organization or military unit can be built and trained. [French, from Italian *quadro*, from Latin *quadrum*, square.]

ca·du·ce·us (kə-dōō′sē-əs, -dyōō′-) *n., pl.* **-ce·i** (-sē-ī′). **1.** An ancient herald's wand or staff. **2.** A winged staff with two serpents twined around it, used as the symbol of the medical profession. [Latin *cādūceus*, from Greek *karukeion*, from *karux*, herald.]

cae·cil·ian (sĭ-sĭl′yən, -sĭl′ē-ən, -sēl′-) *n.* Any of various legless, burrowing, wormlike amphibians of the order Gymnophiona, of tropical regions. [From Latin *caecilia*, lizard, from *caecus*, blind (from the lizard's small eyes).]

cae·cum (sē′kəm) *n., pl.* **-ca** (-kə). Var. of **cecum.**

Cae·sar (sē′zər) *n.* **1.** A title of the Roman emperors after Augustus. **2.** A dictator or autocrat.

Cae·sar·e·an (sĭ-zâr′ē-ən). Also **Cae·sar·i·an** or **Ce·sar·e·an** or **Ce·sar·i·an.** —*adj.* Pertaining to Julius Caesar or the Caesars. —*n.* A **Caesarean section.**

Caesarean section or **caesarean section.** A surgical incision through the abdominal wall and uterus, performed to extract a fetus. [After Julius *Caesar.*]

cae·si·um (sē′zē-əm) *n.* Var. of **cesium.**

cae·su·ra (sĭ-zhŏŏr′ə, -zŏŏr′ə) *n., pl.* **-ras** or **-su·rae** (-zhŏŏr′-ē, -zŏŏr′ē). Also **ce·su·ra**. A pause in a line of verse dictated by sense or natural speech rhythm rather than by metrics. [Latin, "a cutting off," from *caedere*, to cut off.] **—cae·su′ral** (-əl) or **cae·su′ric** (-ĭk) *adj.*

ca·fé (kă-fā′, kə-) *n.* A coffee house, restaurant, or bar. [French, coffee, from Turkish *kahve*.]

café au lait (ō lā′). **1.** Coffee with hot milk. **2.** A light coffee color. [French, "coffee with milk."]

caf·e·te·ri·a (kăf′ĭ-tîr′ē-ə) *n.* A restaurant in which the customers are served at a counter and carry their meals to tables on trays. —*modifier: a cafeteria table.* [American Spanish, coffee shop, from Spanish *cafetero*, coffee maker or seller, from *café*, coffee.]

caf·feine (kă-fēn′, kăf′ēn′, -ē-ĭn) *n.* Also **caf·fein**. A bitter, white alkaloid, $C_8H_{10}N_4O_2 \cdot H_2O$, found in coffee, tea, and cola beverages and used as a stimulant and diuretic. [German *Kaffein*, from *Kaffee*, coffee, from French *café*.]

caf·tan (kăf′tən, kăf-tăn′) *n.* Also **kaf·tan**. In the Near East, a full-length tunic with long sleeves, worn under a coat. [Russian *kaftan*, from Turkish *kaftān*.]

cage (kāj) *n.* **1.** A structure of wire grating or bars for confining birds or animals. **2.** Any enclosure that confines or imprisons. **3.** Any framework having a cagelike appearance or construction: *a cashier's cage; an elevator cage.* **4.** *Baseball.* **a.** A backstop used for batting practices. **b.** A catcher's mask. **5.** *Basketball.* The basket. **6.** *Hockey.* The goal, made of a network frame. —*tr.v.* **caged, cag·ing.** To put in a cage. [Middle English, from Old French, from Latin *cavea*, a hollow, enclosure, from *cavus*, hollow.]

ca·gey (kā′jē) *adj.* **-gi·er, -gi·est.** Also **ca·gy.** Wary; careful; shrewd: *a cagey lawyer.* —See Syns at **shrewd.** [Orig. unknown.] **—ca′gi·ly** *adv.* **—ca′gi·ness** *n.*

ca·hoots (kə-hōōts′) *pl.n. Informal.* —**in cahoots.** Working together secretly: *The teller was in cahoots with the bank robber.* [Orig. unknown.]

cai·man (kā′mən, kă-măn′, kī-) *n., pl.* **-mans.** Also **cay·man.** Any of various tropical American reptiles of the genus *Caiman* and related genera, resembling and closely related to the alligators. [Spanish *caimán*, from Carib *cayman*.]

Cain (kān) *n.* A murderer. —*idiom.* **raise Cain.** *Slang.* To create a great disturbance or uproar; make trouble. [After *Cain*, the eldest son of Adam and Eve, who killed his brother Abel out of jealousy.]

ca·ique (kä-ēk′) *n.* **1.** A long, narrow rowboat used in the Middle East. **2.** A small sailing vessel used in the eastern Mediterranean. [French, from Italian *caicco*, from Turkish *kayık*.]

cairn (kârn) *n.* A mound of stones erected as a landmark or memorial. [Middle English *carne*, of Celtic orig.]

cais·son (kā′sŏn′, -sən) *n.* **1.** A watertight structure within which construction work is done, as in building tunnels, bridges, or dams. **2.** A watertight compartment used to raise a sunken ship; a camel. **3.** *Mil.* **a.** A large box used to hold ammunition. **b.** A horse-drawn two-wheeled vehicle formerly used for carrying ammunition. [French, from Old French *casson*, from Italian *cassa*, chest, box, from Latin *capsa*.]

caisson disease. A painful and often fatal disorder found in divers and persons who work in caissons filled with compressed air. It occurs when such persons return to normal atmospheric pressure too quickly, thus allowing bubbles of nitrogen to accumulate in their blood vessels and tissues. Also called **bends.**

cai·tiff (kā′tĭf) *adj. Obs.* Base and cowardly. [Middle English *caitif*, prisoner, captive, from Old North French, from Latin *captīvus*, captive.]

ca·jole (kə-jōl′) *tr.v.* **-joled, -jol·ing.** To coax; wheedle. [French *cajoler*, "to chatter like a caged jay," ult. from Latin *cavea*, a hollow, enclosure.] **—ca·jol′er** *n.* **—ca·jol′er·y** *n.*

Ca·jun (kā′jən) *n.* A native of Louisiana believed to be descended from the French exiles from Acadia, a colony in eastern Canada.

cake (kāk) *n.* **1.** A sweet baked mixture of flour, liquid, eggs, and other ingredients in loaf or rounded layer form. **2.** A flat, thin mass of dough or batter, baked or fried, as a pancake. **3.** A patty of fried food. **4.** A shaped or molded solid mass of something, such as soap or ice. —*v.* **caked,**

cak·ing. —*tr.v.* To cause to form into a hard mass or crust: *The hot sun caked the riverbed.* —*intr.v.* To become formed into a compact mass or crust: *Mud caked on his shoes.* —*idiom.* **take the cake.** *Informal.* To be unusual or outstanding. [Middle English *cake, kake,* from Old Norse *kaka.*]

cake·walk (kāk′wôk′) *n.* **1.** Formerly, a promenade or walk to music in which the couples performing the most complex and unusual steps won cakes as prizes. **2. a.** A strutting dance based on this. **b.** The music for this dance. —*intr.v.* To perform a cakewalk.

cal·a·bash (kăl′ə-băsh′) *n.* **1.** A vine, *Lagenaria siceraria,* native to the Old World, that bears large, hard-shelled gourds. **2.** A tropical American tree, *Crescentia cujete,* that bears large, rounded fruit. **3.** The fruit of a calabash. **4.** A bowl, tobacco pipe, etc., made from the hollowed-out shell of such a gourd or fruit. [Obs. French *calabasse,* from Spanish *calabaza.*]

cal·a·boose (kăl′ə-bōōs′) *n. Slang.* A jail. [Louisiana French *calabouse,* from Spanish *calabozo,* a dungeon.]

ca·la·di·um (kə-lā′dē-əm) *n.* Any of various tropical plants of the genus *Caladium,* widely cultivated as potted plants for their showy, variegated foliage. [From Malay *kĕladi.*]

cal·a·mine (kăl′ə-mīn′, -mĭn) *n. Pharm.* A pink, odorless, tasteless powder of zinc oxide with a small amount of ferric oxide, dissolved in mineral oils and used in skin lotions. [French, from Medieval Latin *calamīna,* var. of Latin *cadmia,* from Greek *kadmeia.*]

ca·lam·i·tous (kə-lăm′ĭ-təs) *adj.* Causing or involving a disaster. **—ca·lam′i·tous·ly** *adv.*

ca·lam·i·ty (kə-lăm′ĭ-tē) *n., pl.* **-ties. 1.** An event that causes great suffering and misfortune; a disaster. **2.** Great distress. —See Syns at **disaster.** [Middle English *calamite,* from Old French, from Latin *calamitās.*]

cal·a·mus (kăl′ə-məs) *n., pl.* **-mi** (-mī′). **1.** A plant, the **sweet flag,** or its aromatic root. **2.** Any of various tropical Asiatic palms of the genus *Calamus,* from some of which rattan is obtained. **3.** A quill. [Latin, reed, cane, from Greek *kalamos.*]

ca·lash (kə-lăsh′) *n.* Also **ca·lèche** (kə-lĕsh′). **1. a.** A carriage with low wheels and a collapsible or removable top. **b.** The top of such a carriage. **2.** A woman's bonnet that folded back and up to reveal the face, fashionable in the late 18th cent. [French *calèche,* from German *Kalesche,* from Czech *koleso,* wheel.]

calash

calc-. Var. of **calci-.**

cal·ca·ne·us (kăl-kā′nē-əs) *n., pl.* **-ne·i** (-nē-ī′). The large tarsal bone in the human heel. [Latin, "heel," from *calx,* heel.]

cal·car·e·ous (kăl-kâr′ē-əs) *adj.* Of, like, or containing calcium carbonate, calcium, or limestone; chalky. [Latin *calcārius,* from *calx,* lime.]

cal·ces (kăl′sēz′) *n.* A plural of **calx.**

calci- or **calc-.** A prefix meaning lime or calcium: **calciferous.** [From Latin *calx,* lime, limestone.]

cal·ci·cole (kăl′sĭ-kōl′) *n. Bot.* A plant that thrives in soil rich in lime. [French : *calci-,* lime + *-cole,* dweller.] **—cal·cic′o·lous** (-sĭk′ə-ləs) *adj.*

cal·cif·er·ol (kăl-sĭf′ə-rôl′, -rŏl′) *n.* **Vitamin D₂.** [CALCIF(EROUS) + (*ergost*)*erol,* a sterol derived from ergot.]

cal·cif·er·ous (kăl-sĭf′ər-əs) *adj.* Of, forming, or containing calcium or calcium carbonate. [CALCI- + -FEROUS.]

cal·ci·fi·ca·tion (kăl′sə-fĭ-kā′shən) *n.* **1.** Impregnation with calcium or calcium salts, as with calcium carbonate. **2.** Hardening, as of tissue, by such impregnation. **3.** A calcified substance, such as petrified wood.

cal·ci·fy (kăl′sə-fī′) *v.* **-fied, -fy·ing.** —*tr.v.* To make calcareous by deposition of calcium salts. —*intr.v.* To become calcareous. [CALCI- + -FY.]

cal·ci·mine (kăl′sə-mĭn′) *n.* Also **kal·so·mine.** A white or tinted mixture of zinc oxide, water, glue, used to coat walls and ceilings. —*tr.v.* **-mined, -min·ing.** To cover with calcimine. [Alteration of trademark *Kalsomine.*]

cal·cine (kăl′sīn′) *v.* **-cined, -cin·ing.** —*tr.v.* To heat (a substance) to a high temperature but below the melting or fusing point. —*intr.v.* To undergo calcining. [Middle English *calcinen,* from Old French *calciner,* from Medieval Latin *calcīnāre,* from Latin *calx,* lime.] —**cal′ci·na′tion** (kăl′sə-nā′shən) *n.*

cal·cite (kăl′sīt′) *n.* A common crystalline form of calcium carbonate, the basic constituent of limestone, marble, and chalk. [CALC(I)- + -ITE.] —**cal·cit·ic** (-sĭt′ĭk) *adj.*

cal·ci·um (kăl′sē-əm) *n. Symbol* **Ca** A silvery, moderately hard metallic element, constituting approximately three per cent of the earth's crust, a basic component of bone, shells, and leaves. It occurs naturally in limestone, gypsum, and fluorite, and its compounds are used to make plaster, quicklime, Portland cement, and metallurgic and electronic materials. Atomic number 20; atomic weight 40.08; melting point 842 to 848°C; boiling point 1,487°C; specific gravity 1.55; valence 2. [From Latin *calx,* lime, limestone, from Greek *khalix,* pebble.]

calcium carbide. A grayish-black crystalline compound, CaC_2, used to generate acetylene gas, as a dehydrating agent, and in the manufacture of graphite and hydrogen.

calcium carbonate. A colorless or white crystalline compound, $CaCO_3$, occurring naturally as chalk, limestone, marble, and other forms and used in commercial chalk, medicines, and dentifrices.

calcium chloride. A white deliquescent compound, $CaCl_2$, used chiefly as a drying agent, refrigerant, and preservative and for controlling dust and ice on roads.

calcium hydroxide. A soft white powder, $Ca(OH)_2$, used in making mortar, cements, calcium salts, paints, and petrochemicals. Also called **slaked lime.**

calcium oxide. A white caustic lumpy powder, CaO, used as a refractory, as a flux, in manufacturing steel, glassmaking, waste treatment, insecticides, and as an industrial alkali. Also called **lime** and **quicklime.**

calcium phosphate. Any of several phosphate compounds, esp.: **a.** A white crystalline powder, $CaHPO_4$ or $CaHPO_4 \cdot 2H_2O$, used as a food, as a plastic stabilizer, and in glass. **b.** A colorless deliquescent powder, $CaH_4(PO_4)_2 \cdot H_2O$, used in baking powders, as a plant food, plastic stabilizer, and in glass. **c.** A white amorphous powder, $Ca_3(PO_4)_2$, used in ceramics, rubber, fertilizers, and as a food supplement.

cal·cu·la·ble (kăl′kyə-lə-bəl) *adj.* **1.** Capable of being calculated or estimated. **2.** Capable of being counted on; dependable; reliable. —**cal′cu·la·bly** *adv.*

cal·cu·late (kăl′kyə-lāt′) *v.* **-lat·ed, -lat·ing.** —*tr.v.* **1.** To find or determine by using mathematics; compute. **2.** To make an estimate of. **3.** To plan; intend: *actions calculated to provoke a discussion.* **4.** *Informal.* To think; suppose. —*intr.v.* **1.** To execute a mathematical process. **2.** To think; suppose. —*phrasal verb.* **calculate on.** To count, depend, or rely on. [Latin *calculāre,* from *calculus,* small stone (used in reckoning), dim. of *calx,* lime, limestone.] —**cal′cu·la′tive** *adj.*

cal·cu·lat·ed (kăl′kyə-lā′tĭd) *adj.* Undertaken after careful estimation of the likely outcome: *a calculated risk.* —**cal′cu·lat·ed·ly** *adv.*

cal·cu·lat·ing (kăl′kyə-lā′tĭng) *adj.* **1.** Used in or for performing calculations: *a calculating machine.* **2.** Coldly scheming or conniving; shrewd; crafty: *a calculating businessman.*

cal·cu·la·tion (kăl′kyə-lā′shən) *n.* **1.** The act, process, or result of calculating. **2.** An estimate based upon probabilities. **3.** Deliberation; foresight.

cal·cu·la·tor (kăl′kyə-lā′tər) *n.* **1.** A person who performs calculations. **2.** A mechanical or electronic machine that

calculator
automatically performs mathematical operations

cal·cu·lus (kăl′kyə-ləs) *n., pl.* **-li** (-lī′) or **-lus·es.** **1.** *Med.* An abnormal hard mass, usu. of mineral salts, that forms in the body; a stone, as in the urinary bladder, gallbladder, or kidney. **2.** The combined mathematics of differential and integral calculus. [Latin, small stone used in reckoning.]

cal·dron (kôl′drən) *n.* Also **caul·dron.** A large kettle or vat for boiling. [Middle English *caud(e)ron,* from Old North French, from Late Latin *caldāria,* from Latin, warm bath, from *cal(i)dus,* warm.]

ca·lèche (kə-lĕsh′) *n.* Var. of **calash.**

cal·en·dar (kăl′ən-dər) *n.* **1.** Any of various systems of reckoning time in which the beginning, length, and divisions of a year are defined or established. **2.** A chart showing the months, weeks, and days of a specific year. **3.** A list or schedule of dates for planned events, holidays, court cases, legislative hearings, etc.: *a social calendar; a court calendar; a school calendar.* —*tr.v.* To enter on a calendar; to list; schedule. [Middle English *calender,* from Norman French, from Latin *kalendārium,* a moneylender's account book (because monthly interest was due on the calends), from *kalendae,* the calends.]

cal·en·der (kăl′ən-dər) *n.* A machine in which paper or cloth is given a smooth, glossy finish by being pressed between rollers. —*tr.v.* To treat with a calender. [French *calendre,* from Medieval Latin *calendra,* from Latin *cylindrus,* cylinder.]

cal·ends (kăl′əndz, kā′ləndz) *n., pl.* **calends.** Also **kal·ends.** In the ancient Roman calendar, the day of the new moon, the first day of the month. [Middle English *kalendes,* from Latin *kalendae.*]

ca·len·du·la (kə-lĕn′jə-lə) *n.* Any plant of the genus *Calendula,* having orange-yellow flowers, esp. the pot marigold. [From Medieval Latin *calendula,* marigold, from Latin *kalendae,* calends.]

calf¹ (kăf, käf) *n., pl.* **calves** (kăvz, kävz). **1.** The young of cattle; a young cow or bull. **2.** The young of certain other mammals, such as the elephant or whale. **3.** A type of leather made from the hide of a calf; calfskin. [Middle English *calf,* from Old English *cealf.*]

calf² (kăf, käf) *n., pl.* **calves** (kăvz, kävz). The fleshy, muscular back part of the human leg between the knee and ankle. [Middle English, from Old Norse *kalfi.*]

calf·skin (kăf′skĭn′, käf′-) *n.* **1.** The hide of a calf. **2.** Fine leather made from the hide of a calf.

cal·i·ber (kăl′ə-bər) *n.* Also *Brit.* **cal·i·bre.** **1.** The diameter of the inside of a tube, esp. the bore of a firearm. **2.** The diameter of a bullet or other projectile intended for a firearm. **3.** Degree of worth or distinction: *a man of high caliber.* [Old French *calibre,* from Old Italian *calibro,* from Arabic *qālib,* shoemaker's last.]

cal·i·brate (kăl′ə-brāt′) *tr.v.* **-brat·ed, -brat·ing.** **1.** To mark the scale of (a measuring instrument) with graduations: *He built and calibrated an ammeter.* **2.** To check (a measuring instrument) against a standard and adjust it for accuracy. **3.** To determine the caliber of (a tube). —**cal′i·bra′tion** *n.* —**cal′i·bra′tor** *n.*

cal·i·bre (kăl′ə-bər) *n. Brit.* Var. of **caliber.**

cal·i·co (kăl′ĭ-kō′) *n., pl.* **-coes** or **-cos.** **1.** A coarse cloth, usually printed with bright designs. **2.** *Brit.* Plain white cotton cloth. —*adj.* Covered with spots of different colors; mottled: *a calico cat.*

ca·lif (kā′lĭf, kăl′ĭf) *n.* Var. of **caliph.**

California poppy. A plant, *Eschscholtzia californica*, of the Pacific Coast, with bluish-green leaves and orange-yellow flowers.

cal·i·for·ni·um (kăl′ə-fôr′nē-əm) *n. Symbol* **Cf** A synthetic element produced in trace quantities by helium isotope bombardment of curium. All isotopes are radioactive, chiefly by emission of alpha particles. Atomic number 98; mass numbers 244 to 254; half-lives varying from 25 minutes to 800 years. [After *California*, where it was discovered.]

cal·i·per (kăl′ə-pər) *n.* Also **cal·li·per.** **1.** Often **calipers** (*used with a pl. verb*). An instrument consisting essentially of two curved hinged legs or jaws, used to measure internal and external dimensions. **2.** A vernier caliper. [Var. of CALIBER.]

caliper

ca·liph (kā′lĭf, kăl′ĭf) *n.* Also **ca·lif.** The political and religious head of a Moslem state. [Middle English *caliphe, califfe*, from Old French *calife*, from Arabic *khalīfa*, "successor," from *khalafa*, to succeed.]

ca·liph·ate (kā′lĭ-fāt′, kăl′ĭ-, -fĭt) *n.* The office, jurisdiction, or reign of a caliph or the land under his reign.

cal·is·then·ics (kăl′ĭs-thĕn′ĭks) *pl.n.* **1.** Exercises designed to develop muscular tone and to promote physical well-being. **2.** (*used with a sing. verb*). The practice of such exercises. [Greek *kallos*, beauty + *sthenos*, strength.] —**cal′is·then′ic** *adj.*

calk[1] (kôk) *n.* **1.** A pointed extension on the toe or heels of a horseshoe, designed to prevent slipping. **2.** A spiked plate fixed on the bottom of a shoe to prevent slipping. —*tr.v.* **1.** To supply with calks. **2.** To injure with a calk. [Middle English *kakun*, from Middle Dutch *calcoen*, hoof of a horse, from Old Norman French *calcain*, heel, from Latin *calcāneum*, from *calx*.]

calk[2] (kôk) *v.* Var. of **caulk.**

call (kôl) *tr.v.* **1.** To cry out in a loud tone; announce; proclaim: *The town crier called the hours.* **2.** To send for; summon: *call the doctor; call the fire department.* **3.** To convoke or convene (a meeting). **4.** To summon to a particular career or pursuit: *He was called to the priesthood.* **5.** To awaken. **6.** To telephone (someone). **7.** To lure by imitating the characteristic cry of a bird or animal: *a horn to call ducks.* **8.** To name. **9.** To estimate as being; consider: *I call that fair.* **10.** To designate; label: *Nobody calls me a liar.* **11.** To bring to action or under consideration: *call a strike; call a case to court.* **12.** To demand payment of: *call a loan.* **13.** *Baseball.* **a.** To stop (a game) because of bad weather or darkness. **b.** To indicate a decision in regard to (a pitch, ball, strike, or player): *The umpire called him safe.* **14.** *Billiards.* To predict (the outcome of a shot) before playing. **15.** To forecast or predict accurately: *He called the outcome of the election.* **16.** *Poker.* To demand to see the hand of (an opponent) by equaling his bet. **17.** To shout (directions) in rhythm for square dances. —*intr.v.* **1.** To telephone. **2.** To pay a short visit. **3.** To attract attention by shouting: *They called for help.* **4.** To make a characteristic cry or sound, as a bird or animal: *Birds called in the treetops.* —See Syns at **gather.** —*phrasal verbs.* **call back.** To telephone in return. **call down.** **1.** To invoke, as from heaven: *He called down blessings on his people.* **2.** *Informal.* To find fault with; reprimand. —See Syns at **scold. call for. 1.** To go and get or stop for: *I'll call for you at 8 P.M.* **2.** To require; demand: *a job that calls for patience.* **3.** To be appropriate or necessary: *The insult was not called for.* **4.** To ask for; request: *The chairman called for a vote.* **call forth.** To evoke: *The*

music called forth bittersweet memories. **call in. 1.** To take out of circulation: *call in silver dollars.* **2.** To summon for assistance or consultation: *call in a specialist.* **call off. 1.** To cancel or postpone: *call off a trip.* **2.** To order to stop menacing; restrain: *Call off your hounds!* **3.** To read aloud, as from a list: *call off the campers' names.* **call on** (or **upon**). **1.** To pay a short visit to. **2.** To appeal to (someone) to do something: *She called on everyone to contribute.* **3.** To ask (someone) to speak: *Will the teacher call on me?* **call out. 1.** To shout. **2.** To cause to assemble; summon: *call out the guard.* **call up. 1.** To telephone (someone). **2.** To summon into military service: *called up for active duty.* **3.** To remember or cause to remember: *call up old times.* —*n.* **1.** A shout or loud cry: *a call for help.* **2. a.** The typical cry of an animal, esp. a bird: *the call of the screech owl.* **b.** An instrument or sound made to imitate such a sound, used as a lure: *a hunter's moose call; a boy playing a whippoorwill call on the whistle.* **c.** A word habitually used by a person in the performance of his duties: *"Mark Twain" was the call that Samuel Clemens often heard when he was a river pilot. Can you follow the calls in square dancing?* **3.** A signal, as made by a horn, bell, etc.: *a bugle call.* **4. a.** The act of calling on the telephone: *Keep your calls brief.* **b.** An instance of this: *Were there any calls for me?* **5.** A short visit, esp. one made as a formality or for business or professional purposes. **6. a.** An appeal or summons for a certain course of action: *people responding to the call for liberty, equality, and fraternity.* **b.** An appeal or command to assemble, come, etc.: *a draft call; volunteers answering the fire call.* **c.** Attraction or appeal; fascination: *the call of the wild.* **7.** Need or reason; justification: *There was no call for that remark.* **8. a.** Demand, as for a certain product: *There isn't much call for inkstands today.* **b.** A claim of any kind: *Many calls are made on his time. The automobile industry has first call on steel production.* **9.** *Sports.* The decision of an official. —*idioms.* **call into question.** To raise doubts about. **call to mind.** To remind of. **close call.** A narrow escape. **on call. 1.** Available when summoned; ready to respond when needed: *a nurse on call from 4 P.M. to midnight.* **2.** Payable on demand. **within call.** Close enough to come if summoned; accessible. [Middle English *callen*, from Old English *ceallian*, to call, shout.] —**call′er** *n.*

cal·la (kăl′ə) *n.* Any of several tropical or semitropical plants of the genus *Zantedeschia*, esp. *Z. aethiopica*, widely cultivated for its large, usu. white spathe that encloses a yellow spadix. Also called **calla lily** and **arum.** [From Greek *kallaia*, wattle of a cock, prob. from *kallos*, beauty.]

cal·lig·ra·phy (kə-lĭg′rə-fē) *n.* **1.** The art of fine handwriting. **2.** Penmanship; handwriting. [French *calligraphie*, from Greek *kalligraphia* : *kallos*, beauty + *graphē*, writing.] —**cal·lig′ra·pher** or **cal·lig′ra·phist** *n.* —**cal′li·graph′ic** (kăl′ĭ-grăf′ĭk) *adj.*

call·ing (kô′lĭng) *n.* **1.** An inner urge, esp. one that seems to come from a divine source. **2.** An occupation.

cal·li·o·pe (kə-lī′ə-pē, kăl′ē-ōp′) *n.* **1.** A musical instrument fitted with steam whistles, played from a keyboard, usu. at carnivals and circuses. **2. Calliope** (kə-lī′ə-pē). *Gk. Myth.* The Muse of epic poetry.

cal·li·per (kăl′ə-pər) *n.* Var. of **caliper.**

call letters. The series of letters or letters and numbers that identifies a radio or television station.

call loan. A loan repayable on demand at any time.

call number. A set of letters and numbers used to indicate the placement of a library book on the shelves.

cal·los·i·ty (kă-lŏs′ĭ-tē, kə-) *n., pl.* **-ties. 1. a.** A callus. **b.** The condition of having calluses. **2.** Lack of feeling; hardheartedness.

cal·lous (kăl′əs) *adj.* **1.** Having calluses; toughened. **2.** Insensitive; unfeeling: *a callous disregard for our sorrow.* —*tr.v.* To make callous. —*intr.v.* To become callous. —**cal′lous·ly** *adv.* —**cal′lous·ness** *n.*

Usage: **callous, callus.** Only *callus* is the noun denoting thickened skin. *Callous* is an adjective describing hands and feet having calluses and something showing emotional hardness and insensitivity. *Callous* means to make or become callous. *Callus* (verb) means to develop a callus. Thus *callous hands; hands calloused* (or *callused*) *by hard work; callous disregard for others' rights.*

ă pat ā pay â care ä father ĕ pet ē be hw which
ŏŏ took ōō boot ou out th thin th this ŭ cut
ĭ pit ī tie î pier ŏ pot ō toe ô paw, for oi noise
û urge zh vision ə about, item, edible, gallop, circus

cal·low (kăl′ō) *adj.* **1.** Immature; inexperienced: *a callow youth.* **2.** Not yet having feathers; unfledged, as a bird. [Middle English *calwe*, bald, from Old English *calu.*] —**cal′low·ly** *adv.* —**cal′low·ness** *n.*

call-up (kôl′ŭp′) *n.* An order to report for military service.

cal·lus (kăl′əs) *n., pl.* **-lus·es. 1. a.** A localized thickening and enlargement of the horny layer of the skin, usu. because of prolonged pressure or rubbing. **b.** The hard bony tissue that surrounds the ends of a fractured bone. **2.** *Bot.* Hardened tissue that develops over a wound or cut end of a woody stem. —*intr.v.* To form or develop a callus. — See Usage note at **callous.** [Latin *callus, callum.*]

calm (käm) *adj.* **-er, -est. 1.** Nearly or completely motionless; undisturbed: *the pond's calm surface.* **2.** Not excited or agitated; composed; quiet. —*n.* **1.** An absence or cessation of motion; stillness. **2.** Serenity; tranquillity; peace. **3.** *Meteorol.* A condition of little or no wind. —See Syns at **tranquillity.** —*tr.v.* To make calm; to quiet. —*intr.v.* To become calm or quiet. [Middle English *calme,* from Old French, from Old Italian *calma,* from Late Latin *cauma,* heat of the day, from Greek *kauma,* burning heat, from *kaiein,* to burn.] —**calm′ly** *adv.* —**calm′ness** *n.*

Syns: calm, peaceful, placid, serene, tranquil *adj.* Core meaning: Free of movement, noise, or disturbing emotion (*spent a calm night asleep*). While CALM is the most general term implying freedom from agitation, PEACEFUL and TRANQUIL stress undisturbed serenity (*peaceful times; a tranquil lifestyle*). PLACID suggests not being easily shaken physically or emotionally (*a placid lake; a placid disposition*). SERENE suggests a lofty, almost spiritual calm (*a serene smile*).

cal·o·mel (kăl′ə-mĕl′, -məl) *n.* A white, tasteless compound, Hg₂Cl₂, formerly used as a purgative; mercurous chloride. [French, from New Latin *calomelas,* "beautiful black" : Greek *kalos,* beautiful + *melas,* black.]

ca·lor·ic (kə-lôr′ĭk) *adj.* Of or pertaining to heat or calories. —*n.* A hypothetically indestructible, uncreatable fluid formerly thought responsible for the production, possession, and transfer of heat.

cal·o·rie (kăl′ə-rē) *n.* **1.** *Abbr.* **cal** A unit of heat used in physics, chemistry, and related sciences, equal to the amount of heat needed to raise one gram of water one degree Celsius. **2.** Often **Calorie.** *Abbr.* **Cal.** A unit of heat used in biology and related sciences, equal to the amount of heat needed to raise 1,000 grams of water one degree Celsius. [French, from Latin *calor,* heat.]

cal·o·rif·ic (kăl′ə-rĭf′ĭk) *adj.* Pertaining to heat.

cal·o·rim·e·ter (kăl′ə-rĭm′ĭ-tər) *n.* **1.** An instrument that measures and indicates heat. **2.** The part of such an apparatus, usu. a sample container, in which the heat measured causes a change of state. [Latin *calor,* heat + -METER.]

cal·u·met (kăl′yə-mĕt′, kăl′yə-mĕt′) *n.* A long-stemmed ornamented pipe smoked by North American Indians for ceremonial purposes. Also called **peace pipe.** [Canadian French, from French *chalumeau,* a straw, from Late Latin *calamellus,* little reed, from *calamus,* a reed, from Greek *kalamos.*]

ca·lum·ni·ate (kə-lŭm′nē-āt′) *tr.v.* **-at·ed, -at·ing.** To make malicious false statements about; to slander. —**ca·lum′ni·a′tion** *n.* —**ca·lum′ni·a′tor** *n.*

cal·um·ny (kăl′əm-nē) *n., pl.* **-nies. 1.** A false statement maliciously or knowingly made to injure another person's reputation. **2.** The utterance of such statements; slander. [Middle English, from Old French *calomnie,* from Latin *calumnia,* "deception," from *calvī,* to deceive, trick.] —**ca·lum′ni·ous** *adj.*

calve (kăv, käv) *v.* **calved, calv·ing.** —*intr.v.* To give birth to a calf. —*tr.v.* To give birth to (a calf).

calves (kăvz, kävz) *n.* Plural of **calf.**

Cal·vin·ism (kăl′və-nĭz′əm) *n.* The religious doctrines of John Calvin (1509-1564), French religious reformer, that emphasize the omnipotence of God and the salvation of the elect by God's grace alone. —**Cal′vin·ist** *n. & adj.* —**Cal′vin·is′tic** *adj.*

calx (kălks) *n., pl.* **calx·es** or **cal·ces** (kăl′sēz′). **1.** The crumbly residue left after a mineral or metal has been calcined or roasted. **2.** Calcium oxide.

ca·ly·ces (kā′lĭ-sēz′, kăl′ĭ-) *n.* A plural of **calyx.**

ca·lyp·so (kə-lĭp′sō) *n.* A type of folk music that originated in the West Indies, notably in Trinidad, characterized by improvised lyrics on topical or broadly humorous subjects. [After CALYPSO.]

Ca·lyp·so (kə-lĭp′sō) *n. Gk. Myth.* A sea nymph who delayed Odysseus on her island, Ogygia, for seven years.

ca·lyx (kā′lĭks, kăl′ĭks) *n., pl.* **-lyx·es** or **ca·ly·ces** (kā′lĭ-sēz′, kăl′ĭ-). **1.** The outer protective covering of a flower, consisting of leaflike, usu. green segments called sepals. **2.** A cuplike or funnel-shaped animal structure. [Latin, from Greek *kalux.*]

cam (kăm) *n.* A wheel that as it turns transmits back-and-forth motion to another part. [Perh. from French *came,* from German *Kamm,* comb.]

ca·ma·ra·de·rie (kä′mə-rä′də-rē, kăm′ə-räd′ə-) *n.* Good will and warm feeling between or among friends; comradeship. [French, from *camarade.* comrade.]

cam·ber (kăm′bər) *n.* **1. a.** A slightly arched surface, as of a road or a ship's deck. **b.** The condition of being slightly arched. **2.** The adjustment of automobile wheels so that they are closer together at the bottom than at the top. —*tr.v.* To give a slight arch to. —*intr.v.* To arch slightly. [From Middle English *ca(u)mber,* curved, arched, from Old French *cambre,* from Latin *camur,* bent or curved inward.]

cam·bi·um (kăm′bē-əm) *n.* A layer of cells in the stems and roots of vascular plants that gives rise to phloem and xylem. [New Latin, "that which changes into new layers," from Medieval Latin *cambium,* exchange, from Latin *cambiāre,* to exchange.] —**cam′bi·al** (-əl) *adj.*

Cam·bri·a (kăm′brē-ə). The Latin name for Wales.

Cam·bri·an (kăm′brē-ən) *n.* Also **Cambrian period.** A geologic period that began about 600 million years ago and ended about 500 million years ago, characterized by warm seas and desert land areas. [After *Cambria,* where rocks and fossils of this period were found.]

cam·bric (kăm′brĭk) *n.* A finely woven white linen or cotton fabric. [After *Cambrai,* a city in Northern France where the fabric was first made.]

came (kăm) *v.* Past tense of **come.** [Middle English *cam.*]

cam·el (kăm′əl) *n.* A long-necked, humped ruminant mammal of the genus *Camelus,* of northern Africa and western Asia, used in desert regions as a beast of burden. The Arabian camel, or dromedary, has a single hump. The Bactrian camel, of more northern regions, has two humps. [Middle English, ult. from Latin *camēlus,* from Greek *kamēlos.*]

ca·mel·lia (kə-mēl′yə, -mēl′ē-ə) *n.* Any of several shrubs or trees of the genus *Camellia,* native to Asia, esp. *C. japonica,* with shiny evergreen leaves and showy, variously colored flowers. Also called **japonica.** [First described by George Josef *Kamel* (1661-1706), Moravian Jesuit missionary.]

Cam·e·lot (kăm′ə-lŏt′) *n.* In Arthurian legend, the town where King Arthur had his court.

camel's hair. Also **camel hair. 1.** The soft, fine hair of a camel or a substitute for it. **2.** A soft, heavy cloth, usu. light tan, made chiefly of camel's hair.

cam·e·o (kăm′ē-ō′) *n., pl.* **-os.** A gem or medallion with a carved, raised design, esp. one having layers of different colors that are cut so that the design is of one color and the background of another. [Middle English *cameu,* from Italian *cam(m)er* and Old French *camaïeu.*]

caméo

cam·er·a (kăm′ər-ə, kăm′rə) *n.* **1.** Any apparatus for taking photographs, gen. consisting of a lightproof enclosure having an aperture with a shuttered lens through which the image of an object is focused and recorded on a photosensitive film or plate. **2.** The part of a television transmitting apparatus that receives the primary image on a light-sensitive cathode tube and transforms it into electrical impulses. **3.** A **camera obscura. 4.** *Law. pl.* **-er·ae** (-ə-rē'). A judge's private office. [Late Latin, room, from Latin, arched roof, from Greek *kamara*, vault.]

cam·er·al (kăm'ər-əl) *adj.* Of or pertaining to the room used by a judge or a legislative body. [Medieval Latin *camerālis*, from *camera*, office, department of state, from Late Latin, room.]

cam·er·a·man (kăm'ər-ə-măn', kăm'rə-) *n.* A person who operates a motion-picture or television camera.

camera ob·scu·ra (əb-skyŏŏr'ə). A darkened chamber in which the real image of an object is received through a small opening or lens and focused in natural color on a screen inside. [New Latin, "dark chamber."]

cam·i·sole (kăm'ĭ-sōl') *n.* A woman's short, sleeveless undergarment. [French, from Old Provençal *camisolla*, dim. of *camisa*, shirt, from Late Latin *camisia*.]

cam·o·mile (kăm'ə-mīl') *n.* Var. of **chamomile.**

cam·ou·flage (kăm'ə-fläzh', -fläj') *n.* **1.** *Mil.* The method or result of concealing people or things from the enemy by making them appear to be part of the natural surroundings. **2.** Any means of concealment; dissimulation. —*tr.v.* **-flaged, -flag·ing.** To conceal by altering the appearance; disguise: *camouflage a bunker.* [French, from *camoufler*, to disguise.]

camp¹ (kămp) *n.* **1.** A place where a group of people, as vacationers, soldiers, or prisoners, live temporarily in tents, cabins, huts, or other informal shelters. **2.** A group of people who have the same ideas or beliefs; a faction: *people in different political camps.* —*intr.v.* **1.** To make or set up a camp: *Let's camp down here for the night.* **2.** To live in or as if in a camp: *He and his friends camped for a month in the Rocky Mountains. We camped in the apartment until the furniture arrived.* [Old French, from Old North French, from Latin *campus*, open field.]

camp² (kămp) *n.* Artificiality of manner or style, appreciated for its humor, triteness, or vulgarity. —*adj.* Having the qualities of such a manner or style: *a camp movie.* [Orig. unknown.] —**camp'y** *adj.*

cam·paign (kăm-pān') *n.* **1.** A series of military operations undertaken to achieve a specific objective within a given area. **2.** An organized activity or operation to attain some political, social, or commercial goal: *an advertising campaign; a Presidential campaign.* —*intr.v.* To engage in a campaign. [French *campagne*, from Old French, battlefield, ult. from Latin *campus*, field.] —**cam·paign'er** *n.*

cam·pa·ni·le (kăm'pə-nē'lē) *n.* A bell tower, esp. one near but not attached to a church. [Italian, from *campana*, bell, from Late Latin *campāna*, bell.]

cam·pan·u·la (kăm-păn'yə-lə) *n.* Any of various plants of the genus *Campanula*, which includes the bellflowers. [Dim. of Late Latin *campāna*, bell.]

camp·er (kăm'pər) *n.* **1.** A person who camps outdoors or who attends a camp. **2.** A vehicle resembling or an automobile-and-trailer combination, designed to serve as a dwelling and used for camping or on long motor trips.

Camp Fire Girl. A member of an organization for girls that provides recreation and develops practical skills.

cam·phor (kăm'fər) *n.* A white, crystalline compound, $C_{10}H_{16}O$, obtained from the wood of the camphor tree of eastern Asia and used as an insect repellent, in industry in making films, plastics, and explosives, and in medicine as a stimulant. [Middle English *ca(u)mfre*, from Old French *camphre*, ult. from Malay *kāpūr*, chalk.] —**cam·phor'ic** (kăm-fôr'ĭk, -fŏr'-) *adj.*

cam·phor·ate (kăm'fə-rāt') *tr.v.* **-at·ed, -at·ing.** To treat or impregnate with camphor.

camphor tree. An evergreen tree, *Cinnamomum camphora*, native to eastern Asia, having aromatic wood that is a source of camphor.

cam·pi·on (kăm'pē-ən) *n.* Any of various plants of the genus *Lychnis* or related genera, with red, pink, or white flowers. [Prob. from obs. *campion*, champion.]

cam·pus (kăm'pəs) *n., pl.* **-pus·es. 1.** The grounds of a school, college, or university. **2.** A school, such as a col-

lege, university, or boarding school, considered as an entity. [Latin *campus*, field, plain.]

cam·shaft (kăm'shăft') *n.* A turning shaft fitted with one or more cams as in a gasoline engine.

camshaft   Canada goose

can¹ (kăn; kən *when unstressed*) *v.aux.* Past tense **could** (kŏŏd; kəd *when unstressed*). —Used with verbs to indicate that the subject: **1.** Knows how to: *She can skate well.* **2. a.** Is able or enabled to: *a place where people can put their ideas to work.* **b.** Will be able to: *I'll take you where you can find out about him.* **c.** Is inherently able or designed to: *Green plants can make their own food.* **3.** Feels free to: *We cannot accept this money.* **4.** Is logically or by rules enabled to: *You cannot punch or kick your opponent in judo.* **5.** Has permission to: *If you eat your vegetables, you can have dessert.* **6.** Is asked or invited to: *If you want to come, you can meet us there.* **7.** Has to or will have to: *If you don't behave, you can leave the room.* **8.** May possibly: *What can he have to say to me?* **9.** May sometimes: *Guessing at someone else's thoughts can prove disastrous.* [Middle English, from Old English *can*, first and third person pres. indic. of *cunnan*, to know how.]

Usage: can, may. Although the distinction is not often observed in everyday speech, these auxiliary verbs have different functions, esp. in formal writing. *Can* is used to indicate ability to do something; *may*, to ask, grant, or deny permission to do it.

can² (kăn) *n.* **1.** A small, airtight container, usu. made of tin, in which food and beverages are preserved. **2. a.** A can with something in it: *a can of peaches.* **b.** The amount that a can holds: *drink a can of beer.* **3.** A much larger container of similar shape: *a garbage can.* —*tr.v.* **canned, can·ning. 1.** To seal food in a can or jar for future use; to preserve. **2.** *Slang.* **a.** To dismiss from employment or from school. **b.** To quit or dispense with: *can the chatter.* [Middle English *canne*, from Old English *canne*.] —**can'ner** *n.*

Ca·naan (kā'nən). In the Bible, the Promised Land.

Can·a·da balsam (kăn'ə-də). A viscous, yellowish, transparent resin obtained from the balsam fir and used as a mounting cement for microscopic specimens.

Canada goose. A common wild goose, *Branta canadensis*, of North America, with grayish plumage, a black neck and head, and a white face patch.

Ca·na·di·an French (kə-nā'dē-ən). The French language as spoken and written in Canada.

ca·naille (kə-nī', -nāl') *n.* The common people; rabble; riffraff. [French, from Italian *canaglia*, "pack of dogs," from *cane*, dog, from Latin *canis.*]

ca·nal (kə-năl') *n.* **1.** A waterway that is wholly or partly manmade, used for irrigation, shipping, or travel. **2.** *Anat.* A tube or duct in the body. **3.** *Astron.* One of the markings resembling straight lines on the surface of Mars. [Middle English, tube, from Latin *canālis*, channel, from *canna*, reed, from Greek *kanna.*]

ca·nal·ize (kə-năl'īz', kăn'l-īz') *tr.v.* **-ized, -iz·ing. 1.** To furnish with, build, or convert into a canal or canals. **2.** To channel into a particular direction; provide an outlet for. —**ca·nal'i·za'tion** *n.*

can·a·pé (kăn'ə-pā', -pē) *n.* A cracker or small, thin piece of bread or toast spread with cheese, meat, fish, etc., and served as an appetizer. [French, couch ("seat" for the relish), from Medieval Latin *canapeum.*]

ca·nard (kə-närd') *n.* A false or unfounded story; a hoax. [French *canard*, "duck" (from *vendre des canards à moi-*

tié, "to half-sell ducks," swindle, deceive).]

ca·nar·y (kə-nâr′ē) *n.*, *pl.* **-ies. 1.** A songbird, *Serinus cana-ria*, native to the Canary Islands, that is greenish to yellow and is bred as a cage bird. **2.** A sweet white wine from the Canary Islands. **3.** Also **canary yellow.** A light, bright yellow. —*adj.* Light, bright yellow.

ca·nas·ta (kə-năs′tə) *n.* A card game for two to six players, related to rummy and requiring two decks of cards, including the four jokers. [Spanish, "basket," from Latin *canistrum*, canister.]

can·can (kăn′kăn′) *n.* An exuberant dance performed by women and marked by high kicking. [French.]

can·cel (kăn′səl) *v.* **-celed** or **-celled, -cel·ing** or **-cel·ling.** —*tr.v.* **1.** To cross out with lines or other markings. **2.** To mark or perforate (a postage stamp, check, etc.) to indicate that it may not be used again. **3. a.** To abandon or give up (an idea, activity, etc.); call off: *cancel an appointment; cancel a TV series.* **b.** To declare no longer in effect; annul: *cancel a magazine subscription; cancel a contract.* **4.** To equalize or make up for; neutralize; offset: *Two opposing votes cancel each other.* **5.** *Math.* **a.** To remove a common factor from the numerator and denominator of a fractional expression. **b.** To remove a common factor or term from both members of an equation or inequality. —*intr.v.* To balance or neutralize one another: *The two forces canceled out.* —*n.* Cancellation. [Middle English *cancellen*, from Old French *canceller*, from Latin *cancellāre*, to make like a lattice, cross out, from *cancellī*, lattice, from *cancer, carcer*, jail.] —**can′cel·er** *n.*

can·cel·la·tion (kăn′sə-lā′shən) *n.* Also **can·ce·la·tion. 1.** The act of canceling. **2.** Marks or perforations indicating canceling. **3.** Something that has been canceled.

can·cer (kăn′sər) *n.* **1. a.** Any of various malignant cell growths that invade nearby cells and tend to spread to new sites. **b.** The diseased condition characterized by such growths. **2.** A pernicious, spreading evil. **3. Cancer.** A constellation in the Northern Hemisphere near Leo and Gemini. **4. Cancer.** The fourth sign of the zodiac. —*modifier: a cancer cell; a cancer clinic.* [Latin, crab, creeping ulcer.] —**can′cer·ous** -sər-əs) *adj.*

can·del·a (kăn-dĕl′ə) *n.* *Abbr.* **cd** *Physics.* A unit of luminous intensity equal to 1/60 of the intensity of the light emitted per square centimeter by a blackbody heated to a temperature of 1,773°C. Also called **candle.** [Latin *candēla*, candle.]

can·de·la·brum (kăn′dl-ä′brəm, -ăb′rəm, -ä′brəm) *n.*, *pl.* **-bra** (-brə) or **-brums.** Also **can·de·la·bra** *pl.* **-bras.** A large candlestick with arms for holding several candles. [Latin *candēlābrum*, from *candēla*, candle.]

candelabrum   **candlesticks**

can·des·cent (kăn-dĕs′ənt) *adj.* Glowing or dazzling with great heat; incandescent. [Latin, from *candēscere*, to shine, glow.] —**can·des′cent·ly** *adv.*

can·did (kăn′dĭd) *adj.* **1.** Direct and frank; straightforward; open: *a candid opinion.* **2.** Not posed or rehearsed: *a candid photograph.* **3.** Without prejudice; impartial; fair: *a candid view of the issues.* [French *candide*, from Latin *candidus*, glowing, white, pure, from *candēre*, to glow.] —**can′did·ly** *adv.* —**can′did·ness** *n.*

can·di·da·cy (kăn′dĭ-də-sē) *n.*, *pl.* **-cies.** The fact or condition of being a candidate.

can·di·date (kăn′dĭ-dāt′, -dĭt) *n.* **1.** A person who seeks or is nominated for an office, prize, honor, etc. **2.** A person

who seems likely to gain a certain position or come to a certain fate: *a candidate for the gallows.* [Latin *candidātus*, "(Roman candidate) clothed in a white toga," from *candidus*, white.]

can·dle (kăn′dl) *n.* **1.** A solid, usu. cylindrical mass of tallow, wax, or other fatty substance with an embedded wick that is burned to provide light. **2.** Anything resembling a candle in use or shape. **3.** *Physics.* **a.** An **international candle. b.** A candela. —*modifier: candle wax.* —*tr.v.* **-dled, -dling.** To examine (an egg) for fertilization and freshness in front of a light. —*idiom.* **not hold a candle to.** To be not nearly as good as. [Middle English *candel*, from Old English *candel*, from Latin *candēla*, from *candēre*, to shine.] —**can′dler** *n.*

can·dle·light (kăn′dl-līt′) *n.* **1.** Illumination from a candle or candles. **2.** Dusk; twilight.

Can·dle·mas (kăn′dl-məs) *n.* A church festival celebrated on February 2 as the feast of the purification of the Virgin Mary and the presentation of the infant Christ in the temple. [Middle English *candelmasse*, from Old English *candelmæsse*, from *candel*, candle (from the blessing of candles at this feast).]

can·dle·pin (kăn′dl-pĭn′) *n.* **1.** A slender bowling pin used in a variation of the game of tenpins. **2. candlepins.** (*used with a sing. verb*). A bowling game using a ball smaller than in tenpins.

can·dle·pow·er (kăn′dl-pou′ər) *n.* The brightness or intensity of a source of light as expressed in candelas.

can·dle·stick (kăn′dl-stĭk′) *n.* A holder, often ornamental, with a cup or spike for a candle.

can·dle·wick (kăn′dl-wĭk′) *n.* The wick of a candle.

can·dor (kăn′dər) *n.* Also *Brit.* **can·dour. 1.** Frankness of expression; sincerity; straightforwardness. **2.** Freedom from prejudice; impartiality. [Latin *candor*, whiteness, purity, from *candēre*, to glow, be white.]

can·dy (kăn′dē) *n.*, *pl.* **-dies. 1.** A sweet food made of sugar or syrup and often mixed with ingredients such as fruit, nuts, butter, or chocolate. **2.** A single piece of such a confection. —*v.* **-died, -dy·ing.** —*tr.v.* **1.** To cook, preserve, or coat with sugar or syrup: *candy apples.* **2.** To turn to sugar. —*intr.v.* **1.** To crystallize, as sugar: *The molasses candied along the edges of the barrel.* **2.** To become coated with sugar or syrup. [From French (*sucre*) *candi*, ult. from Arabic *qand*, cane sugar.]

can·dy·tuft (kăn′dē-tŭft′) *n.* Any of various plants of the genus *Iberis*, with clusters of white, red, or purplish flowers. [*Candy*, obs. var. of *Candia*, a Greek seaport + TUFT.]

cane (kān) *n.* **1.** A stick used as an aid in walking. **2.** A rod used for flogging. **3. a.** A slender, jointed stem, woody but usu. flexible, as of bamboo, rattan, or certain palm trees. **b.** Any plant having such a stem. **c.** Such stems, or strips of such stems, woven together to make chair seats or other objects. **4. Sugar cane.** —*tr.v.* **caned, can·ing. 1.** To make or repair (furniture) with cane. **2.** To hit or beat with a walking stick. [Middle English, from Old French, from Latin *canna*, from Greek *kanna*, reed, cane.]

cane·brake (kān′brāk′) *n.* A dense thicket of cane.

cane sugar. A sugar obtained from the juice of sugar cane; sucrose.

ca·nine (kā′nīn′) *adj.* **1.** Of, pertaining to, or characteristic of a member of the family Canidae, which includes dogs, wolves, foxes, and jackals. **2.** Of or designating one of the pointed conical teeth between the incisors and the first bicuspids. —*n.* **1.** A canine animal. **2.** A canine tooth; eyetooth. [Latin *canīnus*, from *canis*, dog.]

Ca·nis Ma·jor (kā′nĭs mā′jər, kăn′ĭs). A constellation in the Southern Hemisphere near Puppis and Lepus. It contains the star Sirius.

Canis Mi·nor (mī′nər). A constellation in the equatorial region of the Southern Hemisphere near Hydra and Monoceros. It contains the star Procyon.

can·is·ter (kăn′ĭ-stər) *n.* **1.** A container, usu. of thin metal, for holding coffee, tea, flour, spices, etc. **2.** Also **canister shot.** A metallic cylinder filled with shot or tear gas that bursts and scatters its contents when fired from a gun. [Latin *canistrum*, reed basket, from Greek *kanastron*, from *kanna*, reed.]

can·ker (kăng′kər) *n.* **1.** An ulcerous sore in the mouth or on the lips. **2.** A diseased area in a plant. **3.** Any of several animal diseases characterized by chronic inflammatory processes. **4.** Any source of spreading corruption or debilitation. —*tr.v.* **1.** To attack or infect with canker. **2.** To cause to decay or become corrupt. —*intr.v.* To become infected with or as if with canker. [Middle English, from Old English *cancer* and Norman French *cancre*, both from Latin *cancer*, crab.] —**can'ker·ous** *adj.*

canker sore. A small, painful ulcer usu. of the mouth.

can·ker·worm (kăng'kər-wûrm') *n.* The larva of either of two moths, *Paleacrita vernata* or *Alsophila pometaria*, that damage fruit trees and shade trees by feeding on their leaves.

can·na (kăn'ə) *n.* Any of various tropical plants of the genus *Canna*, with large leaves and showy red or yellow flowers. [From Latin *canna*, reed, cane.]

can·na·bis (kăn'ə-bĭs) *n.* The hemp plant; marijuana. [From Latin, hemp, from Greek *kannabis*.]

canned (kănd) *adj.* **1.** Preserved and sealed in an airtight can or jar: *canned vegetables.* **2.** *Informal.* Recorded or taped: *canned laughter.*

can·nel (kăn'əl) *n.* Also **cannel coal.** A form of bituminous coal that burns with a bright, smoky flame. [From dial. *cannel coal,* "candle coal" (from its bright flame).]

can·ner·y (kăn'ə-rē) *n., pl.* **-ies.** A factory where meat, vegetables, or other foods are canned.

can·ni·bal (kăn'ə-bəl) *n.* **1.** A person who eats the flesh of human beings. **2.** Any animal that feeds on others of its own kind. [From Spanish *Canibalis, Caríbales,* Caribs.] —**can'ni·bal·ism** *n.* —**can'ni·bal·is'tic** *adj.*

can·ni·bal·ize (kăn'ə-bə-līz') *tr.v.* **-ized, -iz·ing.** To remove serviceable parts from (damaged or worn-out equipment) for use in the repair of other equipment.

can·non (kăn'ən) *n., pl.* **cannon** or **-nons. 1.** A weapon for firing projectiles, consisting of a heavy metal tube mounted on a carriage. **2.** Any heavy firearm whose caliber is .60 or larger. [Middle English *canon,* from Old French, from Italian *cannone,* "large tube," from *canna,* reed, tube, from Latin, reed, cane.]

can·non·ade (kăn'ə-nād') *v.* **-ad·ed, -ad·ing.** —*tr.v.* To assault or bombard with cannon fire. —*intr.v.* To deliver heavy artillery fire. —*n.* An extended, usu. heavy discharge of artillery.

can·non·ball (kăn'ən-bôl') *n.* Also **cannon ball. 1.** A round projectile for firing from a cannon. **2.** Something, such as a fast train, moving with great speed.

can·non·eer (kăn'ə-nîr') *n.* A gunner or artilleryman.

can·non·ry (kăn'ən-rē) *n., pl.* **-ries. 1.** Artillery; cannons collectively. **2.** Artillery fire.

can·not (kăn'ŏt', kă-nŏt', kə-) *v.* The negative form of **can.**
   Usage: **cannot** but. Though it is a form of double negative, this expression is acceptable in examples such as *We cannot but regret this action.* The same sense is expressed by *can but regret, can only regret, must regret,* and *cannot help regretting.*

can·ny (kăn'ē) *adj.* **-ni·er, -ni·est. 1.** Careful and shrewd in actions and dealings, esp. where one's own interests are concerned. **2.** Careful in the use of material resources; thrifty; frugal. **3.** *Scot.* **a.** Pleasant; attractive. **b.** Gentle; mild; steady. [From CAN (to know how, be able).] —**can'ni·ly** *adv.* —**can'ni·ness** *n.*

ca·noe (kə-nōō') *n.* A light, slender boat with pointed ends that is moved by paddles. —*v.* **-noed, -noe·ing.** —*tr.v.* To carry or send by canoe. —*intr.v.* To travel in or paddle a canoe. [Earlier *canoa,* from Spanish, from Arawakan.] —**ca·noe'ist** *n.*

can·on¹ (kăn'ən) *n.* **1.** A law or code of laws established by a church council. **2.** A basic principle or standard; criterion: *the canons of good behavior.* **3.** The books of the Bible officially recognized by a Christian church. **4.** *Rom. Cath. Ch.* **a.** Often **Canon.** The most important part of the Mass. **b.** The accepted calendar of saints. **5.** An authoritative list, as of the works of an author. **6.** *Mus.* A composition or passage in which a melody is introduced by one part and restated by a second part before the first has finished its statement. [Middle English *cano(u)n,* from Old English and Old French *canon,* from Late Latin *canōn,* from Latin, measuring line, rule, model, from Greek *kanōn,* rod, rule.]

can·on² (kăn'ən) *n.* A clergyman serving in a cathedral or

collegiate church. [Middle English *cano(u)n,* from Norman French *canunie,* from Late Latin *canōnicus,* one living under a rule, from *canōn,* canon, rule.]

ca·ñon (kăn'yən) *n.* Var. of **canyon.**

ca·non·i·cal (kə-nŏn'ĭ-kəl) or **ca·non·ic** (-nŏn'ĭk) *adj.* **1.** Pertaining to, required by, or abiding by canon law. **2.** Of or appearing in the Biblical canon. **3.** Authoritative; officially approved; orthodox. **4.** Of or like a musical canon. —**ca·non'i·cal·ly** *adv.*

can·on·ize (kăn'ə-nīz') *tr.v.* **-ized, -iz·ing. 1.** *Rom. Cath. Ch.* To declare (a deceased person) to be a saint and entitled to be fully honored as such. **2.** To include in the Biblical canon. **3.** To approve as being within canon law. **4.** To glorify; exalt. —**can'on·i·za'tion** *n.*

canon law. The body of officially established rules governing a Christian church.

Ca·no·pus (kə-nō'pəs) *n.* A star in the constellation Carina, the second-brightest star in the sky.

can·o·py (kăn'ə-pē) *n., pl.* **-pies. 1.** A cloth covering fastened or held horizontally over a bed, entrance, sacred object, or carried over an important person. **2.** *Archit.* An ornamental rooflike structure. **3.** Any high covering: *"spreads out into a vast canopy of foliage"* (Thomas Huxley). **4.** *Aviation.* **a.** The transparent, movable enclosure over an aircraft's cockpit. **b.** The hemispherical surface of a parachute. —*tr.v.* **-pied, -py·ing.** To spread over with or as if with a canopy. [Middle English *canape, canope,* from Medieval Latin *canapeum, canopeum,* (couch with a) mosquito net, from Latin *cōnōpeum,* mosquito net, from Greek *kōnōpion,* after the city *Kanōpos.*]

canopy

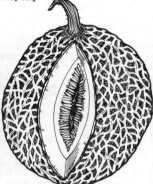
cantaloupe

canst (kănst). *Archaic.* A form of the present tense of **can,** used with *thou.*

cant¹ (kănt) *n.* **1.** Deviation from a vertical or horizontal plane or surface; inclination; slant; slope: *the cant of a roof.* **2.** A slanted edge or surface. —*tr.v.* **1.** To set at an oblique angle; cause to slant or tilt: *canted the mainmast.* **2.** To give a slanting edge to; to bevel. —*intr.v.* To tilt to one side; to slant. [Middle English, side, edge, from Norman French, from Latin *cant(h)us,* rim of a wheel.]

cant² (kănt) *n.* **1.** Whining or singsong speech, as used by beggars. **2.** Hypocritically pious language; insincere talk. **3.** The special vocabulary used by a certain group or class of people; argot; jargon. —See Syns at **language.** —*intr.v.* **1.** To speak in a whining, pleading tone. **2.** To talk insincerely. [Prob. from Norman French, singing, jargon, from *canter,* to sing, tell, from Latin *canere,* to sing.]

can't (kănt, känt). Contraction of **cannot.**

can·ta·bi·le (kän-tä'bē-lā', - bĭ-, kən-). *Mus.* —*adj.* Smooth and lyrical; songlike. —*adv.* Smoothly and lyrically. Used as a direction. —*n.* A cantabile passage or movement. [Italian, from Late Latin *cantābilis,* singable, from Latin *cantāre,* freq. of *canere,* to sing.]

Can·ta·brig·i·an (kăn'tə-brĭj'ē-ən) *adj.* Of or pertaining to Cambridge, England, or Cambridge University. —*n.* **1.** A native or resident of Cambridge. **2.** A student or graduate of Cambridge University.

can·ta·loupe or **can·ta·loup** (kăn'tl-ōp') *n.* A variety of melon, *Cucumis melo cantalupensis,* having fruit with a

ă pat ā pay â care ä father ĕ pet ē be hw which
ŏŏ took ōō boot ou out th thin *th* this ŭ cut
ĭ pit ī tie î pier ŏ pot ō toe ô paw, for oi noise
û urge zh vision ə about, item, edible, gallop, circus

ribbed, rough rind and orange flesh. [After *Cantalupo*, a papal villa near Rome.]

can·tan·ker·ous (kăn-tăng′kər-əs) *adj*. Ill-tempered and quarrelsome. —See Syns at **irritable**. [Prob. from Middle English *contekour*, rioter, brawler, from *contek*, quarrel, strife, from Norman French *contek*.] —**can·tan′ker·ous·ly** *adv*. —**can·tan′ker·ous·ness** *n*.

can·ta·ta (kən-tä′tə) *n. Mus*. A vocal and instrumental composition consisting of a number of short pieces. [Italian *cantata*, "sung," ult. from Latin *canere*, to sing.]

can·teen (kăn-tēn′) *n*. **1.** A small container for carrying drinking water, used by military personnel, campers, etc. **2. a.** A store for on-base military personnel. **b.** *Brit*. A club for soldiers. **3.** A recreation hall or cafeteria in an institution, factory, etc. **4.** A temporary or mobile eating place, esp. one set up in an emergency. [French *cantine*, from Italian *cantina*, a wine cellar, from *canto*, edge, from Latin *cant(h)us*, rim of a wheel.]

can·ter (kăn′tər) *n*. A gait slower than the gallop but faster than the trot. —*intr.v.* To move or ride at a canter. —*tr.v.* To cause (a horse) to go at a canter. [Short for *Canterbury gallop*, the slow pace at which pilgrims rode to Canterbury, England.]

Can·ter·bur·y bells (kăn′tər-bĕr′ē). (*used with a sing. or pl. verb*). A plant, *Campanula medium*, widely cultivated for its bell-shaped violet-blue flowers.

cant hook. A wooden lever with a metal point and a hinged hook near the end, used by lumbermen to handle logs. [From CANT (angle).]

can·ti·cle (kăn′tĭ-kəl) *n*. A song or chant, esp. a hymn with words from a Biblical text. [Middle English, from Latin *canticulum*, from *canere*, to sing.]

can·ti·le·ver (kăn′tl-ē′vər, -ĕv′ər) *n*. **1.** A projecting beam or other structure supported only at one end. **2.** A bracket or block supporting a balcony or cornice. —*tr.v.* To extend outward or build as a cantilever. [Poss. CANT (slope) + LEVER (beam, bar).]

cantilever

can·to (kăn′tō) *n., pl.* **-tos.** One of the principal divisions of a long poem. [Italian, from Latin *cantus*, song, from *canere*, to sing.]

can·ton (kăn′tən, -tŏn′) *n*. **1.** A small division of a country, esp. one of the states of Switzerland. **2.** A division of a flag occupying the upper corner next to the staff. —*tr.v.* **1.** To divide into parts, esp. into cantons. **2.** To assign quarters to (troops); billet. [French, corner, subdivision, from Old French *canton*, from Italian *canto*, from Latin *cant(h)us*, rim of a wheel.] —**can′ton·al** *adj*.

Can·ton·ese (kăn′tə-nēz′, -nēs′) *n., pl.* **Cantonese.** **1.** The Chinese dialect spoken in and around Canton, China. **2.** A native or inhabitant of Canton. —*adj*. Of Canton, the Cantonese, or their dialect.

Canton flannel. A heavy, soft cotton cloth with a woolly nap on one side, used mainly for baby clothes. Also called **flannelette.** [After *Canton*, China.]

can·ton·ment (kăn-tōn′mənt, -tŏn′-) *n*. **1.** A group of temporary buildings for housing troops. **2.** The assignment of troops to temporary quarters.

can·tor (kăn′tər) *n*. **1.** The official who leads the congregation in prayer and sings the music used in a Jewish religious service. **2.** The person who leads a church choir or congregation in singing; precentor. [Latin, singer, from *canere*, to sing.]

can·vas (kăn′vəs) *n*. **1.** A heavy, coarse, closely woven fabric of cotton, hemp, or flax, used for making tents and sails. **2. a.** A piece of canvas on which a painting, esp. an oil painting, is made. **b.** A painting of this kind. **3.** *Naut*. **a.** A sail. **b.** Sails collectively. **4. a.** A tent, esp. a circus tent. **b.** Tents in general. **5.** A fabric of coarse open weave, used as a foundation for needlework. **6.** The floor of a ring in which boxing or wrestling takes place. —*modifier: a canvas bag.* [Middle English *canevas*, from Norman French, from Latin *cannabis*, hemp, from Greek *kannabis*.]

Usage: **canvas, canvass.** The material associated with sails, tents, and paintings is *canvas*. *Canvass* (noun and verb) refers to the acts of examining, soliciting sales orders or votes, and surveying public opinion by polling.

can·vas·back (kăn′vəs-băk′) *n*. A North American duck, *Aythya valisneria*, with a reddish head and neck and a whitish back.

can·vass (kăn′vəs) *tr.v.* **1. a.** To go through (a region) or go to (persons) to solicit votes, orders, subscriptions, etc. **b.** To conduct a survey (of public opinion) on a given subject; to poll. **2.** To examine carefully or discuss thoroughly; scrutinize. —*intr.v.* **1.** To solicit political support, sales orders, opinions, etc. **2.** To make a thorough examination or conduct a detailed discussion. —*n.* **1. a.** A solicitation of votes, sales orders, opinions, etc. **b.** A survey of public opinion. **2.** An examination or discussion. —See Usage note at **canvas.** [From obs. *canvas*, to toss a person in a canvas sheet.] —**can′vass·er** *n*.

can·yon (kăn′yən) *n*. Also **ca·ñon.** A narrow chasm with steep cliff walls. [American Spanish *cañon*, from Spanish, pipe, tube, from *caña*, tube, cane, from Latin *canna*, a reed, from Greek *kanna*.]

caou·tchouc (kou′chŏŏk′, kou-chŏŏk′) *n*. Natural rubber. [French, from obs. Spanish *cauchuc*, from Quechua.]

cap (kăp) *n*. **1.** A close-fitting head covering, usu. soft and having no brim but sometimes having a visor. **2. a.** A special head covering worn to indicate rank, occupation, or membership in a particular group: *a cardinal's cap.* **b.** A graduate's mortarboard. **3.** Any of numerous objects similar to a head covering in form, use, or position: *a bottle cap.* **4.** *Archit*. The top part, or pileus, of a mushroom or similar fungus. **6. a.** A percussion cap. **b.** A small explosive charge enclosed in paper for use in a toy gun. —*tr.v.* **capped, cap·ping.** **1.** To put a cap on. **2.** To lie over or on top of; serve as a cap for; cover: *Snow capped the hills.* **3.** To apply the finishing touch to; complete: *cap a meal with dessert.* **4.** To surpass; outdo: *Each joke capped the one before.* [Middle English *cappe*, from Old English *cæppe*, from Late Latin *cappa*, hood, from Latin *caput*, head.]

ca·pa·bil·i·ty (kā′pə-bĭl′ĭ-tē) *n., pl.* **-ties.** **1.** The quality of being capable; ability. **2.** Often **capabilities.** Potential ability: *live up to one's capabilities.* **3.** Estimated maximum power to be used, treated, or developed for a specific purpose: *America's technological capability.* —See Syns at **ability.**

ca·pa·ble (kā′pə-bəl) *adj*. **1.** Having capacity or ability; competent; able: *a capable administrator.* **2. capable of. a.** Having the mental or physical capacity for; qualified for: *He is capable of running a marathon.* **b.** Open to; susceptible to: *an error capable of remedy.* [French, from Old French, from Late Latin *capābilis*, "able to hold," from *capere*, to hold.] —**ca′pa·ble·ness** *n*. —**ca′pa·bly** *adv*.

ca·pa·cious (kə-pā′shəs) *adj*. Able to contain a large quantity; spacious; roomy: *a capacious suitcase.* [From Latin *capāx*, able to hold, from *capere*, to hold.] —**ca·pa′cious·ly** *adv*. —**ca·pa′cious·ness** *n*.

ca·pac·i·tance (kə-păs′ĭ-təns) *n*. **1.** The ability of a conductor or dielectric to store electric charge. **2.** A measure of this ability equal to the ratio of stored charge to electric potential. [CAPACIT(Y) + -ANCE.]

ca·pac·i·tor (kə-păs′ĭ-tər) *n*. An electric circuit element used to store charge temporarily, consisting in general of two metallic plates separated by a dielectric or nonconductor.

ca·pac·i·ty (kə-păs′ĭ-tē) *n., pl.* **-ties.** **1.** The ability to receive, hold, or absorb: *a jug with a capacity of three quarts; a theater with a small seating capacity.* **2.** The maximum amount that can be contained: *a trunk filled to capacity*. **3.** The maximum or optimum amount of production: *factories operating below capacity*. **4.** The ability to do something; faculty; aptitude: *a capacity for self-expression*. **5.** The quality of being suitable for or receptive to specified treatment: *the capacity of elastic to be stretched*. **6.** The position in which one functions; role: *his capacity as host*. **7.** *Law.* Legal qualification or authority: *the capacity to make an arrest*. **8.** *Elect.* Capacitance. **—adj.** As large or numerous as possible in a given setting: *a capacity crowd on opening night*. [Middle English *capa-cite*, from Old French, from Latin *capácitās*, from *capáx*, capacious.]

cap-a-pie or **cap-à-pie** (kăp'ə-pē') *adv.* From head to foot. [Old French *(de) cap a pie*, (from) head to foot.]

ca-par-i-son (kə-păr'ĭ-sən) *n.* **1.** A cover, usu. decorative, placed over a horse's saddle or harness. **2.** Richly ornamented clothing; finery. **—tr.v.** To outfit with a caparison. [Old French *caparaçon*, from Spanish *caparazón*, saddle blanket, prob. from *capa*, cape.]

cape¹ (kāp) *n.* A sleeveless garment fastened at the throat and worn hanging over the shoulders. [French, ult. from Late Latin *cappa*, hood, cloak, from Latin *caput*, head.]

cape² (kāp) *n.* A point or head of land projecting into a sea or other body of water; promontory. [Middle English *cap*, from Old French, from Old Provençal, from Latin *caput*, head.]

cap-e-lin (kăp'ə-lĭn, kăp'lĭn) *n.* Also **cap-lin** (kăp'lĭn). A small, edible saltwater fish, *Mallotus villosus*, of northern waters, related to and resembling the smelts. [Canadian French *capelan*, from French, codfish, from Old Provençal *cappellan*, from Medieval Latin *cappellānus*, chaplain.]

Ca-pel-la (kə-pĕl'ə) *n.* A double star in Auriga, the brightest star in the constellation, approximately 46 light-years from Earth.

ca-per¹ (kā'pər) *n.* **1.** A playful leap or hop; a skip. **2.** An antic; prank. **3.** *Slang.* A criminal escapade. **—intr.v.** To leap or frisk about. [Short for CAPRIOLE.]

ca-per² (kā'pər) *n.* **1.** A spiny, trailing shrub, *Capparis spinosa*, of the Mediterranean region. **2.** A pickled flower bud of the caper, used as a condiment. [From Middle English *caperis*, from Latin *capparis*, from Greek *kapparis*.]

cap-er-cail-lie (kăp'ər-kāl'yē, -kā'lē) *n.* Also **cap-er-cail-zie** (-kāl'zē). A large grouse, *Tetrao urogallus*, of northern Europe, with dark plumage and a fanlike tail. [Scottish Gaelic *capalcoille*, "horse of the woods" : *capall*, horse + *coille*, forest.]

cap-il-lar-i-ty (kăp'ə-lăr'ĭ-tē) *n., pl.* **-ties.** The interaction between contacting surfaces of a liquid and a solid that distorts the liquid surface from a planar shape.

cap-il-lar-y (kăp'ə-lĕr'ē) *n., pl.* **-ies. 1.** *Anat.* Any of the tiny blood vessels that connect the arteries and veins. **2.** Any tube with a small inside diameter. **—adj. 1.** Pertaining to or resembling a hair; fine and slender. **2.** Having a very small inside diameter: *a capillary tube*. **3.** *Anat.* In, of, or pertaining to the capillaries. **4.** Of or pertaining to capillarity: *capillary attraction*. [Latin *capillāris*, from *capillus*, hair.]

cap-i-tal¹ (kăp'ĭ-tl) *n.* **1.** A town or city that is the official seat of government in a state, nation, or other political entity. **2.** Wealth in the form of money or property, owned, used, or accumulated in business by an individual, partnership, or corporation. **3.** Any form of material wealth used or available for use in the production of more wealth. **4. a.** *Accounting.* The remaining assets of a business after all liabilities have been deducted; net worth. **b.** The funds contributed to a business by the owners or stockholders. **5.** Capitalists considered as a group or class. **6.** Any asset or advantage. **7.** A **capital letter. —modifier:** *capital investments.* **—adj. 1.** First and foremost; chief; principal: *a capital priority; a capital selling point.* **2.** Of or pertaining to a political capital: *a capital city.* **3.** First-rate; excellent: *a capital fellow.* **4.** Extremely serious; fatal: *a capital blunder.* **5.** Involving death or calling for the death penalty: *capital punishment.* **6.** Of or pertaining to monetary capital. **7.** Designating an upper-case letter. **—See Syns at excellent and primary.** [Middle English, from Old French, from Latin *capitālis*, "of the head," important, from *caput*, head.]

Usage: **capital, capitol.** Congress and state legislatures meet in the building called *the capitol*. The town or city that is the seat of a government is a *capital*. The latter term is also the noun used in finance, accounting, and architecture; it is the adjective meaning chief and first-rate. *Capital letter* and *capital punishment* are written thus.

cap-i-tal² (kăp'ĭ-tl) *n.* *Archit.* The top part, or head, of a pillar or column. [Middle English *capitale*, from Norman French *capitel*, from Late Latin *capitellum*, "small head," from Latin *caput*, head.]

capital²   Capitol

capital goods. Goods used in the production of commodities; producers' goods.

cap-i-tal-ism (kăp'ĭ-tl-ĭz'əm) *n.* **1.** An economic system, marked by a free market and open competition, in which goods are produced for profit, labor is performed for wages, and the means of production and distribution are privately owned. **2.** A political or social system regarded as being based on capitalism.

cap-i-tal-ist (kăp'ĭ-tl-ĭst) *n.* **1.** A person who invests capital in business, esp. one having a major interest in an important enterprise. **2.** A person who supports capitalism. **3.** Any person of great wealth. **—cap-i-tal-is-tic** *adj.* **—cap-i-tal-is-ti-cal-ly** *adv.*

cap-i-tal-i-za-tion (kăp'ĭ-tl-ĭ-zā'shən) *n.* **1.** The act, practice, or result of capitalizing. **2. a.** The total value of owners' shares in a business firm; total investment of owners. **b.** The authorized or outstanding stock or bonds in a corporation. **3.** The process of converting anticipated future income into present value.

cap-i-tal-ize (kăp'ĭ-tl-īz') *v.* **-ized, -iz-ing. —tr.v. 1.** To convert into capital. **2.** To supply with capital; to finance. **3.** To estimate the present value of (a stock, annuity, or real estate, for example). **4.** *Accounting.* To include (expenditures) in business accounts as assets instead of expenses. **5.** To write or print in upper-case letters. **—intr.v.** To turn to advantage; profit by; exploit: *capitalize on an opponent's error.*

capital letter. An upper-case letter; a letter written or printed in a size larger than and often in a form differing from its corresponding lower-case letter.

cap-i-tal-ly (kăp'ĭ-tl-ē) *adv.* In an excellent manner.

capital punishment. The infliction of the death penalty for the commission of certain crimes.

capital stock. 1. The total amount of stock authorized for issue by a corporation. **2.** The total value of the permanently invested capital of a corporation.

cap-i-ta-tion (kăp'ĭ-tā'shən) *n.* A tax fixed at an equal sum per person; a per capita or poll tax. [Late Latin *capitātiō*, from *caput*, head, person.]

cap-i-tol (kăp'ĭ-tl) *n.* **1.** The building in which a state legislature assembles. **2. Capitol.** The building in Washington, D.C., occupied by the Congress of the United States. **—See** Usage note at **capital¹.**

ca-pit-u-late (kə-pĭch'ə-lāt') *intr.v.* **-lat-ed, -lat-ing. 1.** To surrender, often under stated conditions; come to terms. **2.** To give up all resistance; give in; acquiesce. **—See** Syns at **yield.** [From Medieval Latin *capitulāre*, to draw up under chapters, from Late Latin *capitulum*, chapter, from Latin, heading, from *caput*, head.]

ca-pit-u-la-tion (kə-pĭch'ə-lā'shən) *n.* **1.** The act of capitulating. **2.** A document, treaty, etc., containing the terms of a surrender. **3.** A statement or enumeration of the main parts of a subject; summary. —**ca·pit′u·la·to′ry** (-lə-tôr′ē, -tōr′ē) *adj.*

cap·lin (kăp′lĭn) *n.* Var. of **capelin.**

ca·pon (kā′pŏn′, -pən) *n.* A rooster castrated to improve the quality of its flesh for food. [Middle English, ult. from Latin *capō.*]

ca·pric·cio (kə-prē′chō, -chē-ō′) *n., pl.* **-cios.** *Mus.* An instrumental work written in a fanciful, improvisatory style and a free form. [Italian, caprice.]

ca·price (kə-prēs′) *n.* **1. a.** An impulsive change of mind; a whim. **b.** An inclination to change one's mind impulsively. **2.** *Mus.* A capriccio. [French, from Italian *capriccio,* "head with hair standing on end" : Latin *caput,* head + *ēricius,* hedgehog.]

ca·pri·cious (kə-prĭsh′əs, -prē′shəs) *adj.* **1.** Characterized by or subject to sudden, unpredictable changes; fickle. **2.** Often changing; irregular: *capricious currents.* —**ca·pri′cious·ly** *adv.* —**ca·pri′cious·ness** *n.*
Syns: **capricious, changeable, erratic, fickle, inconsistent, inconstant, mercurial, tempermental, uncertain, unpredictable, unstable, unsteady, variable, volatile, whimsical** *adj. Core meaning:* Following no predictable pattern (*a capricious flirt; a capricious storm*).

Cap·ri·corn (kăp′rĭ-kôrn′) *n.* **1.** A constellation in the equatorial region of the Southern Hemisphere, near Aquarius and Sagittarius. **2.** The tenth sign of the zodiac.

cap·ri·ole (kăp′rē-ōl′) *n.* **1.** An upward leap made by a trained horse without moving forward and with all feet off the ground. **2.** A leap or jump. [French, from Italian *capriola,* "leap of a goat," from *capriolo,* wild goat, from Latin *caper,* goat.]

cap·si·cum (kăp′sĭ-kəm) *n.* Any of various tropical plants of the genus *Capsicum,* such as pepper and chili, cultivated for their pungent seeds. [Prob. from Latin *capsa,* box (from its podlike fruit).]

cap·size (kăp′sīz′, kăp-sīz′) *v.* **-sized, -siz·ing.** —*intr.v.* To overturn. —*tr.v.* To cause to turn over. [Orig. unknown.]

cap·stan (kăp′stən, -stăn′) *n.* **1.** *Naut.* An apparatus consisting of a vertical cylinder rotated manually or by motor, used for hoisting weights, as an anchor, by winding in a cable. **2.** *Electronics.* A small cylindrical pulley used to regulate the speed of magnetic tape in a tape recorder. [Middle English, from Old Provençal *cabestre,* rope noose, from Latin *capistrum,* halter, from *capere,* to take, seize.]

cap·stone (kăp′stōn′) *n.* **1.** The top stone of a structure or wall. **2.** The crowning or final stroke; culmination; acme: *The novel was the capstone of her career.*

cap·su·lar (kăp′sə-lər, -syōō-) *adj.* Of, resembling, or enclosed in a capsule.

cap·su·late (kăp′sə-lāt′, -syōō-, -lĭt) *adj.* Also **cap·su·lat·ed** (-lā′tĭd). In or formed into a capsule.

cap·sule (kăp′səl, -syōōl) *n.* **1.** *Pharm.* A soluble container, usu. of gelatin, enclosing a dose of an oral medicine. **2.** *Anat.* A fibrous, membranous, or fatty sac or similar structure enclosing an organ or part, such as the sac surrounding the kidney. **3.** *Bot.* A fruit that contains two or more seed cases that dries and splits open. **4.** A pressurized compartment of an aircraft or spacecraft, esp. one designed to accommodate a crew or to be ejected if required. —*adj.* Condensed; brief; concise: *a capsule description.* [French, from Latin *capsula,* dim. of *capsa,* box, chest.]

cap·tain (kăp′tən) *n.* **1.** One who commands, leads, or guides others, specif.: **a.** The officer in command of a ship; skipper. **b.** A precinct chief in a police or fire department. **c.** The designated leader of a team or crew in sports. **2. a.** A commissioned officer in the Army, Air Force, or Marine Corps who ranks below a major and above a first lieutenant. **b.** A commissioned officer in the Navy who ranks below a commodore or rear admiral and above a commander. **3.** A figure in the forefront; leader: *a captain of industry.* —*tr.v.* To command or direct. [Middle English *capitane,* from Old French *capitain(e),* from Late Latin *capitāneus,* chief, from Latin *caput,* head.] —**cap′tain·cy** *n.* —**cap′tain·ship′** *n.*

cap·tion (kăp′shən) *n.* **1.** A title, short explanation, or description accompanying an illustration or photograph. **2.** A subtitle in a motion picture. **3.** A heading, as of a

document. —*tr.v.* To furnish a caption for. [Middle English *capcioun,* capture, from Latin *captiō,* from *capere,* to seize, take.]

cap·tious (kăp′shəs) *adj.* **1.** Inclined to find fault and criticize trivial defects; carping. **2.** Intended to entrap or confuse. [Middle English *capcious,* from Old French *captieux,* from Latin *captiōsus,* "ensnaring," from *captiō,* seizure.] —**cap′tious·ly** *adv.*

cap·ti·vate (kăp′tĭ-vāt′) *tr.v.* **-vat·ed, -vat·ing.** **1.** *Archaic.* To capture. **2.** To fascinate or charm with wit, beauty, intelligence, etc.; enrapture: *The play captivated the audience.* [Late Latin *captīvāre,* to capture, from Latin *captīvus,* captive.] —**cap′ti·va′tion** *n.* —**cap′ti·va′tor** *n.*

cap·tive (kăp′tĭv) *n.* **1.** Someone who is forcibly confined as a prisoner. **2.** Someone who is enslaved by a strong emotion or passion. —*adj.* **1.** Held as prisoner. **2.** Under restraint or control: *a captive nation.* **3.** Captivated; enraptured. **4.** Constrained by the situation to be present or attentive: *a captive audience.* [Middle English *captif,* from Latin *captīvus,* from *capere,* to seize.]

cap·tiv·i·ty (kăp-tĭv′ĭ-tē) *n., pl.* **-ties.** The period or condition of being captive.

cap·tor (kăp′tər, -tôr′) *n.* One who takes or keeps a captive. [Late Latin, from Latin *capere,* to seize.]

cap·ture (kăp′chər) *tr.v.* **-tured, -tur·ing.** **1.** To take captive; seize or catch by force or craft: *capture a wild horse; capture a city.* **2.** To win possession or control of, as in a contest: *The Yankees captured another pennant.* **3.** To succeed in preserving in a fixed form: *capture a likeness in a painting.* —*n.* **1.** The act of capturing; seizure. **2.** One that is seized, caught, or won; a catch or prize. [French, from Old French, from Latin *captūra,* from *capere,* to seize.]

cap·u·chin (kăp′yōō-chĭn, kə-pyōō′-, -shĭn) *n.* **1. Capuchin.** A monk belonging to the Order of Friars Minor Capuchins, a branch that broke away from the Franciscans in 1525. **2.** Any of several long-tailed monkeys of the genus *Cebus,* of Central and South America, many of which have hoodlike tufts of hair on the head. [French, from Old French, from Italian *cappuccino,* "hooded one," from *cappuccio,* hood, from Late Latin *cappa,* from Latin *caput,* head.]

cap·y·ba·ra (kăp′ĭ-bä′rə, -băr′ə) *n.* A large, short-tailed, semiaquatic rodent, *Hydrochoerus hydrochaeris,* of tropical South America, often attaining a length of 1¼ meters, or 4 feet. [Portuguese *capibara,* from Tupi.]

car (kär) *n.* **1.** An automobile. **2.** A conveyance with wheels that runs along tracks, as a railroad car. **3.** *Archaic.* A chariot. **4.** A boxlike enclosure for passengers on a conveyance, as an elevator car or cable car. [Middle English *car(re),* cart, wagon, from Norman French, ult. from Latin *carrus,* two-wheeled wagon.]

car·a·bao (kär′ə-bou′, kä′rə-) *n., pl.* **-baos.** The **water buffalo.** [Visayan *karabáw.*]

car·a·cole (kär′ə-kōl′) *n.* Also **car·a·col** (-kŏl′). A half turn to either side performed by a horseman. [French, from Spanish *caracol,* snail, winding stair.]

car·a·cul (kär′ə-kəl) *n.* Var. of **karakul.**

ca·rafe (kə-răf′, -räf′) *n.* A glass bottle for serving water or wine at the table; decanter. [French, from Italian *caraffa,* from Spanish *garaffa,* from Arabic *gharrāf,* from *gharafa,* to dip.]

car·a·mel (kär′ə-məl, -měl′, kär′məl) *n.* **1.** A smooth, chewy candy made of sugar, butter, cream or milk, and flavoring. **2.** Burnt sugar, used for coloring and sweetening foods. [French, from Old Spanish, prob. from Latin *calamus,* reed, cane, from Greek *kalamos.*]

car·a·pace (kär′ə-pās′) *n. Zool.* A hard bony or chitinous

carapace

outer covering, such as the upper shell of a turtle or the exoskeleton of a crustacean. [French, from Spanish *carapacho*.]

car·at (kăr′ət) *n.* **1.** A unit of weight for precious stones, equal to 200 milligrams. **2.** Var. of **karat.** [French, from Old French, from Medieval Latin *carratus*, from Arabic *qīrāt*, from Greek *keration*, "little horn," carat, from *keras*, horn.]

car·a·van (kăr′ə-văn′) *n.* **1.** A company of travelers journeying together, esp. across a desert. **2.** A single file of vehicles or pack animals. **3.** *Brit.* A trailer or home on wheels. [French *caravane* or Italian *caravana*, from Persian *kārwān*.]

car·a·van·sa·ry (kăr′ə-văn′sə-rē) *n.*, *pl.* **-ries.** Also **car·a·van·se·rai** (-rī′). **1.** In the Near or Far East, an inn for accommodating caravans. **2.** Any large inn or hostelry. [Persian *kārwān*, caravan + *sarāī*, palace, inn.]

car·a·vel (kăr′ə-věl′) *n.* A small, light sailing ship of the kind used by the Spanish and Portuguese in the 15th and 16th cent. [Old French *caravelle*, from Old Portuguese *cáravo*, ship, from Late Latin *cārabus*, a small wicker boat, from Greek *karabos*, light ship.]

car·a·way (kăr′ə-wā′) *n.* **1.** A plant, *Carum carvi*, with finely divided leaves and clusters of small, whitish flowers. **2.** The pungent, aromatic seeds of the caraway, used in baking and cooking. [Middle English, prob. from Old Spanish *alcarahueya* and Medieval Latin *carvi*, both from Arabic *alkarawyā*.]

carb-. Var. of **carbo-.**

car·bide (kär′bīd′) *n.* A binary carbon compound, esp. calcium carbide, consisting of carbon and another element. [CARB(O)- + -IDE.]

car·bine (kär′bīn′, -bēn′) *n.* A light shoulder rifle with a short barrel, orig. for cavalry use. [French *carabine*, carbine, from Old French *carabin*, cavalryman.]

carbine

carbo- or **carb-.** A prefix meaning carbon: *carbohydrate*. [From French *carbone*, carbon.]

car·bo·hy·drate (kär′bō-hī′drāt′, -bə-) *n.* Any of a group of chemical compounds, including sugars, starches, and cellulose, containing carbon, hydrogen, and oxygen only, with the ratio of hydrogen to oxygen atoms usu. 2:1. [CARBO- + HYDRATE.]

car·bo·lat·ed (kär′bə-lā′tĭd) *adj.* Containing or treated with carbolic acid.

car·bol·ic acid (kär-bŏl′ĭk). An organic compound, phenol. [CARB(O)- + Latin *oleum*, oil + -IC.]

car·bon (kär′bən) *n. Symbol* **C** **1.** *Chem.* A naturally abundant nonmetallic element that occurs in many inorganic and in all organic compounds, exists in amorphous, graphitic, and diamond allotropes, and is capable of chemical self-bonding to form an enormous number of chemically, biologically, and commercially important long-chain molecules. Atomic number 6; atomic weight 12.01115; boiling point 4,827°C; specific gravity of amorphous carbon 1.8 to 2.1, of diamond 3.15 to 3.53, of graphite 1.9 to 2.3; valences 2, 3, 4. **2. a.** A sheet of carbon paper. **b.** A copy made by using carbon paper. **3.** *Elect.* Either of two rods through which current flows to form an arc in lighting or in welding. [French *carbone*, from Latin *carbō*, charcoal.]

carbon 14. A naturally radioactive carbon isotope with atomic mass 14 and half-life 5,700 years, used in dating ancient carbon-containing objects.

car·bo·na·ceous (kär′bə-nā′shəs) *adj.* Consisting of, containing, pertaining to, or yielding carbon.

car·bo·na·do (kär′bə-nā′dō, -nä′-) *n.*, *pl.* **-does.** A form of opaque or dark-colored diamond used in industrial drills for its exceptional hardness. [Portuguese, "carbonated."]

car·bon·ate (kär′bə-nāt′) *tr.v.* **-at·ed, -at·ing. 1.** To charge or impregnate with carbon dioxide gas, as a beverage. **2.** To

change into a carbonate. —*n.* (kär′bə-nāt′, -nĭt). A salt or ester of carbonic acid. —**car′bon·a′tion** *n.*

carbon black. Any of various finely divided forms of carbon derived from the incomplete combustion of hydrocarbons and used principally in rubber and ink.

carbon copy. 1. A replica, as of a letter, made by using carbon paper. **2.** *Informal.* Any close copy or reproduction; duplicate: *He's a carbon copy of his brother.*

carbon cycle. *Biol.* The cycle of natural processes in which atmospheric carbon in the form of carbon dioxide is converted to carbohydrates by photosynthesis, metabolized by animals, and ultimately returned to the atmosphere as a carbon dioxide waste or decomposition product.

carbon dating *n.* The estimation of age, as of a fossil, by determination of C14 content.

carbon dioxide. A colorless, odorless, incombustible gas, CO_2, formed during respiration, combustion, and organic decomposition and used in refrigeration, carbonated beverages, fire extinguishers, and aerosols.

carbon disulfide. A clear, flammable liquid, CS_2, used to manufacture cellophane, as a solvent for fats, and in fumigants and pesticides.

car·bon·ic acid (kär-bŏn′ĭk). A weak, unstable acid, H_2CO_3, present in solutions of carbon dioxide in water.

car·bon·if·er·ous (kär′bə-nĭf′ər-əs) *adj.* Producing, containing, or pertaining to carbon or coal. [CARBON + -FEROUS.]

Car·bon·if·er·ous (kär′bə-nĭf′ər-əs) *n. Geol.* A division of the Paleozoic era following the Devonian and preceding the Permian, including the Mississippian and Pennsylvanian periods. It was characterized by dense plant growth that eventually sank into swamps and later hardened into coal.

car·bon·ize (kär′bə-nīz′) *tr.v.* **-ized, -iz·ing. 1.** To reduce or convert (a substance that contains carbon) to carbon alone, as by applying heat. **2.** To treat, coat, or combine with carbon. —**car′bon·i·za′tion** *n.*

carbon monoxide. A colorless, odorless, highly poisonous gas, CO, formed by the incomplete combustion of carbon.

carbon paper. A lightweight paper faced on one side with a dark waxy pigment that is transferred by the impact of typewriter keys or by writing pressure to any copying surface, as paper.

carbon tetrachloride. A poisonous, nonflammable, colorless liquid, CCl_4, used as a solvent.

car·bon·yl (kär′bə-nĭl′, -nēl′) *n.* **1.** The bivalent radical CO. **2.** A metal compound, such as $Ni(CO)_4$, containing the CO group. [CARBON + -YL.] —**car′bon·yl′ic** *adj.*

Car·bo·run·dum (kär′bə-rŭn′dəm) *n.* A trademark for a silicon carbide abrasive.

car·box·yl (kär-bŏk′səl) *n.* A univalent radical, COOH, characteristic of all organic acids. [CARB(O)- + OX(Y)- + -YL.] —**car′box·yl′ic** (-sĭl′ĭk) *adj.*

car·boy (kär′boi′) *n.* A large bottle, usu. encased in a protective basket or crate. [Persian *qarāba*, from Arabic *qarrābah*.]

car·bun·cle (kär′bŭng′kəl) *n.* **1.** A painful, localized, pusproducing infection of the skin and tissue below it. **2.** A deep-red garnet without facets. [Middle English, from Old French, from Latin *carbunculus*, small glowing ember, tumor, from *carbō*, charcoal, ember.] —**car·bun′cu·lar** (-kyə-lər) *adj.*

car·bu·re·tor (kär′bə-rā′tər, -byə-) *n.* Also *Brit.* **car·bu·ret·tor** (-rĕt′ər). A device used in gasoline engines that vaporizes or atomizes the gasoline and mixes it with air. [From obs. carburet, carbide, from French *carbure*, from Latin *carbō*, carbon.]

car·cass (kär′kəs) *n.* Also *archaic* **car·case. 1.** The dead body of an animal, esp. one slaughtered and gutted. **2.** The body of a human being, esp. when used humorously or disparagingly. **3.** Something from which the life, substance, or character is gone: *the carcass of a once-glorious empire.* **4.** A framework or basic structure, as of a ruined building. [French *carcasse*, from Old French *c(h)arcois*.]

car·cin·o·gen (kär-sĭn′ə-jən, kär′sə-nə-jĕn′) *n.* A cancer-causing substance. [Greek *karkinos*, cancer, crab + -GEN.] —**car′cin·o·gen′ic** (kär′sə-nə-jĕn′ĭk) *adj.*

ă **pat**　ā **pay**　â **care**　ä **father**　ĕ **pet**　ē **be**　hw **which**　ĭ **pit**　ī **tie**　î **pier**　ŏ **pot**　ō **toe**　ô **paw, for**　oi **noise**

ōō **took**　ōō **boot**　ou **out**　th **thin**　*th* **this**　ŭ **cut**　û **urge**　zh **vision**　ə **about, item, edible, gallop, circus**

car·ci·no·ma (kär′sə-nō′mə) *n.*, *pl.* **-mas** or **-ma·ta** (-mə-tə). A malignant tumor derived from epithelial tissue. [Latin *carcinōma*, from Greek *karkinōma*, from *karkinos*, cancer, crab.] **—car′ci·nom′a·tous** (-nŏm′ə-təs, -nō′mə-) *adj.*

card[1] (kärd) *n.* **1.** A small, flat piece of stiff paper or thin pasteboard, usu. rectangular, with numerous uses: **a.** One of a set of 52 bearing numbers, symbols, and figures, used in various games and for telling fortunes. **b.** One used to send messages; a post card. **c.** One printed with a suitable illustration and greeting, as for Christmas. **d.** One bearing a person's name and other information, used for purposes of identification or classification, as a calling card or draft card. **2.** A notice or advertisement printed on cardboard. **3.** A program of events, as at horse races. **4.** A circular piece of paper bearing the 32 points of a compass. **5.** *Informal.* An amusing or eccentric person. *—tr.v.* **1.** To furnish with or attach to a card. **2.** To list on a card or cards; to catalogue. **3.** *Informal.* To check the identification of. **—idioms. have a card up (one's) sleeve.** To have a secret resource or plan held in reserve. **in the cards.** Likely or destined to occur. **put (or lay) (one's) cards on the table.** To make a frank and clear revelation, as of one's motives. [Middle English *carde*, from Old French *carte*, from Latin *charta*, leaf of papyrus, from Greek *khartēs*.]

card[2] (kärd) *n.* **1.** A wire-toothed brush used to comb out fibers, as of wool, prior to spinning. **2.** A similar device used to raise the nap on a fabric. *—tr.v.* To comb out or brush with a card. [Middle English *carde*, from Old French, from *carder*, to card, from Old Provençal *cardar*, from Latin *cārere*, to card.] **—card′er** *n.*

car·da·mom or **car·da·mum** (kär′də-məm) *n.* Also **car·da·mon** (-mən). **1.** A tropical Asiatic perennial plant, *Elettaria cardamomum*, with large, hairy leaves and capsular fruit whose seeds are used as a condiment and in medicine. **2.** An East Indian plant, *Amomum cardamomum*, the seeds of which are used as an inferior substitute for true cardamom seed. [Latin *cardamōmum*, from Greek *kardamōmon*.]

card·board (kärd′bôrd′, -bōrd′) *n.* A stiff pasteboard made of paper pulp.

card catalog. A listing, esp. of books in a library, made with a separate card for each item and arranged in alphabetical order. Also called **catalog.**

cardi-. Var. of **cardio-.**

car·di·ac (kär′dē-ăk′) *adj.* **1.** Of, near, or pertaining to the heart: *a cardiac disorder; a cardiac patient.* **2.** Of or pertaining to the opening of the esophagus into the stomach. *—n.* A person with a heart disorder. [Latin *cardiacus*, from Greek *kardiakos*, from *kardia*, heart.]

cardiac muscle. The striated muscle of the heart.

car·di·gan (kär′dĭ-gən) *n.* A sweater or knitted jacket without a collar, opening down the front. [After James Thomas Brudenell (1797–1868), seventh Earl of *Cardigan*, British soldier.]

car·di·nal (kär′dn-əl, kärd′nəl) *adj.* **1.** Of foremost importance; primary; pivotal: *the cardinal element of a plan.* **2.** Of a dark to deep or vivid red color. —See Syns at **primary.** *—n.* **1.** An official of the Roman Catholic Church whose rank is just below that of the pope. **2.** Dark to deep or vivid red, as a cardinal's cassock. **3.** A North American bird, *Richmondena cardinalis*, with a crested head, a short, thick bill, and bright-red plumage in the male. **4.** A **cardinal number.** [Middle English, from Old French, from Late Latin *cardinālis*, from Latin, principal, from *cardo*, hinge.]

car·di·nal·ate (kär′dn-əl-ĭt, kärd′nəl-, -āt′) *n.* *Rom. Cath. Ch.* The position, rank, dignity, or term of a cardinal.

cardinal number. A number, such as 3 or 11 or 412, used to indicate how many elements are in a set without indicating their relative order.

cardinal point. One of the four principal directions on a compass: north, south, east, or west.

cardio- or **cardi-.** A prefix meaning the heart: **cardiogram.** [Greek *kardia*, heart.]

car·di·o·gram (kär′dē-ə-grăm′) *n.* The curve traced by a cardiograph, used in the diagnosis of heart defects. [CARDIO- + -GRAM.]

car·di·o·graph (kär′dē-ə-grăf′) *n.* An instrument used to record graphically the mechanical movements of the heart. [CARDIO- + -GRAPH.]

car·di·ol·o·gy (kär′dē-ŏl′ə-jē) *n.* The study of the diseases and functioning of the heart. [CARDI(O)- + -LOGY.] **—car′di·ol′o·gist** *n.*

car·di·o·vas·cu·lar (kär′dē-ō-văs′kyə-lər) *adj.* Pertaining to or involving the heart and the blood vessels.

cards (kärdz) *pl.n.* *(used with a sing. verb).* **1.** Any game, as bridge, pinochle, or poker, played with cards. **2.** The playing of such games: *He's terrible at cards.*

card·sharp (kärd′shärp′) *n.* A person expert in cheating at cards.

care (kâr) *n.* **1.** Mental distress caused by fear, doubt, anxiety, etc.; trouble; worry. **2.** Mental suffering; grief. **3.** An object or source of worry, attention, or solicitude: *troubled by the cares involved in raising a large family.* **4.** Caution in avoiding harm, damage, etc.; heedfulness: *handling with care.* **5.** Supervision; charge: *in the care of a nurse.* **6.** Attentiveness to detail; painstaking application; conscientiousness: *a report prepared with great care.* —See Syns at **anxiety.** *—v.* **cared, car·ing.** *—intr.v.* **1.** To have a strong feeling, interest, or opinion; be concerned or anxious: *I don't care about going.* **2.** To object; to mind: *I won't care if you borrow my car.* **3.** To like: *I don't care for brussels sprouts.* **4.** To have an inclination: *Would you care to come?* *—tr.v.* To wish; be inclined: *We don't care to attend.* [Middle English *care*, from Old English *caru, cearu.*]

ca·reen (kə-rēn′) *intr.v.* **1.** To lurch or swerve while in motion. **2.** *Naut.* To turn a ship on its side for cleaning, caulking, or repairing. *—tr.v.* *Naut.* **1.** To cause (a ship) to lean to one side; to tilt. **2.** To lean (a ship) on one side for cleaning, caulking, or repairing. [From French *(en) carène*, "(on) the keel," from Old French *carene*, from Old Italian *carena*, from Latin *carīna.*]

ca·reer (kə-rîr′) *n.* **1.** A chosen pursuit; a profession; occupation: *a military career; a career in medicine.* **2.** The general progress or course of one's life, esp. in one's profession: *an officer with a distinguished career.* **3. a.** Speed: *"My hasting days fly on with full career." (Milton).* **b.** The moment of highest pitch or peak activity: *The republic was now in the full career of its triumphs.* *—intr.v.* To move or run at full speed; go headlong; rush. [French *carrière*, course, career, from Old French, from Old Provençal *carriera*, street, from Latin *carrus*, a kind of vehicle.]

care·free (kâr′frē′) *adj.* Free of worries and responsibilities; untroubled.

care·ful (kâr′fəl) *adj.* **1.** Cautious in thought, speech, or action; circumspect; prudent: *Be careful what you sign your name to.* **2.** Thorough; painstaking; conscientious: *careful investigation.* **3.** Showing care; solicitous; protective: *I try to be careful of other people's feelings.* **4.** *Archaic.* Full of cares or anxiety. **—care′ful·ly** *adv.* **—care′ful·ness** *n.*
　　Syns: **1. careful, cautious, circumspect, prudent** *adj.* Core meaning: Trying attentively to avoid danger, risk, or error (*a careful driver*). **2. careful, meticulous, scrupulous** *adj.* Core meaning: Marked by attention to all aspects or details (*a careful writer; careful writing*).

care·less (kâr′lĭs) *adj.* **1.** Not taking enough care or caution; inattentive; negligent: *careless about one's appearance.* **2.** Marked by or resulting from lack of thought, thoroughness, or application: *a careless job.* **3.** Resulting from negligence: *a careless and inexcusable mistake.* **4.** Inconsiderate: *a careless remark.* **5.** Unconcerned; indifferent: *careless about her health.* **6.** Unstudied; effortless:

cardinal

careless grandeur. **—care′less·ly** *adv.* **—care′less·ness** *n.*

Syns: 1. careless, heedless, inattentive, thoughtless, unmindful *adj.* *Core meaning:* Lacking or marked by a lack of care (*a careless remark*). **2. careless, sloppy, slovenly, untidy** *adj.* *Core meaning:* Indifferent to accuracy or neatness (*a careless writer*).

ca·ress (kə-rĕs′) *n.* A gentle touch or gesture of fondness, tenderness, or love. *—tr.v.* To touch or stroke in an affectionate or loving manner. [French *caresse*, from Italian *carezza*, endearment, from *caro*, dear, from Latin *cārus*.] **—ca·ress′er** *n.*

car·et (kăr′ĭt) *n.* A proofreading symbol used to indicate where something is to be inserted in a line of printed or written matter. [Latin, "there is lacking," from *carēre*, to be without.]

care·tak·er (kâr′tā′kər) *n.* A person employed to look after or take charge of goods, property, or a person.

care·worn (kâr′wôrn′, -wōrn′) *adj.* Showing signs of worry or care. —See Syns at **haggard.**

car·fare (kär′fâr′) *n.* Fare charged a passenger, as on a streetcar or bus.

car·go (kär′gō) *n., pl.* **-goes** or **-gos.** The freight carried by a ship, airplane, or other vehicle. *—modifier: a cargo plane.* [Spanish, from *cargar*, to load, from Late Latin *carricāre*, from Latin *carrus*, a kind of vehicle.]

car·hop (kär′hŏp′) *n.* A waitress or waiter at a drive-in restaurant.

Car·ib (kăr′ĭb) *n., pl.* **Carib** or **-ibs. 1. a.** A group of peoples of American Indians of northern South America and the Lesser Antilles. **b.** A member of one of these peoples. **2.** Any of the languages of the Carib. **—Car′ib** *adj.*

Car·i·ban (kăr′ə-bən, kə-rē′bən) *n., pl.* **Cariban** or **-bans.** A language family of the Lesser Antilles and South America, comprising the languages spoken by the Caribs. **—Car′i·ban** *adj.*

ca·ri·be (kə-rē′bē) *n.* A fish, the piranha. [American Spanish, Carib.]

car·i·bou (kăr′ə-bōō′) *n., pl.* **caribou** or **-bous.** A deer, *Rangifer tarandus,* of arctic regions of the New World, both sexes of which have antlers. [Canadian French, of Algonquian orig.]

car·i·ca·ture (kăr′ĭ-kə-chŏŏr′, -chər) *n.* **1. a.** A picture or description in which the subject's distinctive features or peculiarities are deliberately exaggerated or distorted to produce a comic or grotesque effect. **b.** The art of creating such representations. **2.** An imitation or copy so inferior as to be absurd. *—tr.v.* **-tured, -tur·ing.** To represent or imitate in or as if in a caricature; satirize. [French, from Italian *caricatura*, "exaggeration," from *caricare,* to load, from Late Latin *carricāre,* from Latin *carrus,* a kind of vehicle.] **—car′i·ca·tur·ist** *n.*

car·ies (kâr′ēz) *n., pl.* **caries.** Decay of a bone or tooth. [Latin *cariēs.*]

car·il·lon (kăr′ə-lŏn′, -lən) *n.* A set of bells hung in a tower and played from a keyboard. [French, var. of Old French *carignon, quarregnon,* ult. from Late Latin *quaterniō,* set of four (bells), from *quaternī,* four each, from *quater,* four times.]

car·il·lon·neur (kăr′ə-lə-nûr′, kär′ē-ə-) *n.* A person who plays a carillon.

Ca·ri·na (kə-rī′nə) *n.* A constellation in the Southern Hemisphere near Volans and Vela and that contains the star Canopus.

car·load (kär′lōd′) *n.* The amount a car carries or is able to carry.

Car·lo·vin·gi·an (kär′lə-vĭn′jē-ən) *adj. & n.* Var. of **Carolingian.**

car·min·a·tive (kär-mĭn′ə-tĭv, kär′mə-nā′tĭv) *adj.* Helping or serving to expel gas from the stomach and intestines. *—n.* A carminative drug. [Middle English, from Medieval Latin *carminātīvus,* from *carmināre,* to card wool, to comb out impurities, from Latin *carmen,* a card for wool, from *cārere,* to card.]

car·mine (kär′mĭn, -mīn′) *n.* **1.** A strong to vivid red color. **2.** A crimson pigment derived from cochineal. *—adj.* Vivid-red or purplish-red. [French *carmin,* from Medieval Latin *carminium* : Arabic *qirmiz, kermes* + Latin *minium,* cinnabar.]

car·nage (kär′nĭj) *n.* **1.** Massive slaughter, esp. in war; massacre. **2.** *Obs.* Corpses, esp. of men killed in battle. [Old French, from Medieval Latin *carnāticum,* from Latin *carō,* flesh, meat.]

car·nal (kär′nəl) *adj.* **1.** Relating to the desires and appetites of the flesh or body; sensual; animal. **2.** Worldly or earthly; not spiritual. [Middle English, from Medieval Latin *carnālis,* from Latin *carō,* flesh.] **—car·nal′i·ty** (kär-năl′ĭ-tē) *n.* **—car′nal·ly** *adv.*

car·nas·si·al (kär-năs′ē-əl) *adj.* Adapted for cutting flesh: *carnassial teeth. —n.* The last upper premolar and the first lower molar teeth in carnivorous mammals. [From French *carnassier,* carnivorous, from Provençal *carn,* flesh, from Latin *carō.*]

car·na·tion (kär-nā′shən) *n.* **1.** A plant, *Dianthus caryophyllus,* native to Eurasia, widely cultivated for its fragrant white, pink, or red flowers with fringed petals. **2.** The flower of the carnation. [Old French, flesh-colored, carnation, from Latin *carō,* flesh.]

carnation

car·nel·ian (kär-nēl′yən) *n.* A reddish variety of clear chalcedony, used in jewelry. [Middle English *corneline,* from Old French, prob. "cherry-colored," from *cornelle,* cherry.]

car·ney (kär′nē) *n.* Var. of **carny.**

car·ni·val (kär′nə-vəl) *n.* **1.** The season just before Lent, marked by merrymaking and feasting. **2.** Any time of revelry; a festival. **3.** A traveling amusement show. [Italian *carnevale,* from Old Italian *carnelevare,* "the putting away of flesh," Shrovetide : Latin *carō,* flesh + *levāre,* to raise, remove.]

car·ni·vore (kär′nə-vôr′, -vōr′) *n.* **1.** *Zool.* Any animal belonging to the order Carnivora, which includes predominantly flesh-eating mammals such as dogs, cats, and bears. **2.** Any flesh-eating or predatory organism, such as a bird of prey or an insectivorous plant.

car·niv·o·rous (kär-nĭv′ər-əs) *adj.* **1.** Belonging or pertaining to the carnivores. **2.** Flesh-eating or predatory. **3.** *Bot.* Having leaves or other parts capable of trapping and absorbing insects or other small organisms, as do the pitcher plant and the Venus's-flytrap. [Latin *carnivorus* : *carō,* flesh + *vorāre,* to devour.] **—car·niv′o·rous·ly** *adv.* **—car·niv′o·rous·ness** *n.*

car·no·tite (kär′nə-tīt′) *n.* A yellow mineral, used mainly as an ore of uranium and vanadium, with composition $K_2(UO_2)_2(VO_4)_2 \cdot 3H_2O$. [After M. A. Carnot (d. 1920), French inspector general of mines.]

car·ny (kär′nē) *n., pl.* **-nies.** Also **car·ney** *pl.* **-neys.** *Slang.* **1.** A carnival. **2.** A person who works with a carnival.

car·ob (kăr′əb) *n.* **1.** An evergreen tree, *Ceratonia siliqua,* of the Mediterranean region, with compound leaves and edible pods. **2.** A flavoring made from the pod of the carob. [Old French *caro(u)be,* from Medieval Latin *carrūbium,* from Arabic *kharrūbah.*]

car·ol (kăr′əl) *n.* **1.** A song of praise or joy, esp. for Christmas. **2.** An old round dance often accompanied by singing. *—v.* **-oled** or **-olled, -ol·ing** or **-ol·ling.** *—tr.v.* **1.** To celebrate in song. **2.** To sing joyously. *—intr.v.* **1.** To sing in a joyous manner; warble. **2.** To sing Christmas songs. [Middle English *carolen,* from Old French *caroler,* perh. from Late Latin *choraula,* choral song.] **—car′ol·er** *n.*

Car·o·lin·gi·an (kăr′ə-lĭn′jē-ən). Also **Car·o·lin·vin·gi·an** (kăr′lə-vĭn′jē-ən). *—adj.* Related to or belonging to the Frankish dynasty that was founded by Pepin the Short in A.D.

751 and that lasted until A.D. 987 in France and A.D. 911 in Germany. —*n.* A member of the Carolingian dynasty. [Prob. a blend of Medieval Latin *Carolus*, Charles (the Great) and *Mérovingien*, Merovingian.]

car·om (kăr′əm) *n.* **1. a.** *Billiards.* A shot in which the cue ball strikes two other balls in succession. **b.** *Pool.* A shot in which the cue ball is bounced off a cushion in order to strike another ball or in which a ball struck by the cue ball is bounced off a cushion in order to reach the pocket. **2.** Any collision followed by a rebound. —*intr.v.* **1.** To collide with and rebound. **2.** To make a carom, as in billiards or pool. [Spanish *carambola*, a kind of fruit, from Portuguese, from Marathi *karambal*.]

car·o·tene (kăr′ə-tēn′) *n.* An orange-yellow to red hydrocarbon pigment, $C_{40}H_{56}$, existing in three isomeric forms, occurring in many plants, and converted to vitamin A by the liver. [German *Karotin*, from Latin *carōta*, carrot.]

ca·rot·e·noid (kə-rŏt′n-oid′) *n.* Any of a class of yellow- to deep-red pigments, such as the carotenes, occurring in many vegetable oils and some animal fats.

ca·rot·id (kə-rŏt′ĭd) *n.* Either of the two major arteries in the neck that carry blood to the head. [French *carotide*, from Greek *karótides*, from *karoun*, to stupefy (from the belief that pressure on the carotids causes a stupor).] —**ca·rot′id** *adj.*

ca·rouse (kə-rouz′) *n.* Boisterous, drunken merrymaking; a carousal. —*intr.v.* **-roused, -rous·ing.** To drink heavily, usu. while having a noisy and merry time. [Old French *carrousse*, from (*boire*) *carous*, (to drink) all out, from German *garaus*: Old High German *garo*, complete + *ūz*, out.] —**ca·rous′al** *n.* —**ca·rous′er** *n.*

car·ou·sel or **car·rou·sel** (kăr′ə-sĕl′, -zĕl′) *n.* A merry-go-round. [French *carrousel*, prob. from Italian dial. *carosello*, a kind of tournament.]

carp¹ (kärp) *intr.v.* To find fault and complain constantly, esp. about petty grievances. [Middle English *carpen*, from Old Norse *karpa*, to boast.] —**carp′er** *n.*

carp² (kärp) *n., pl.* **carp** or **carps. 1.** An edible freshwater fish, *Cyprinus carpio.* **2.** Any of various other fishes of the family Cyprinidae. [Middle English *carpe*, from Old French, from Late Latin *carpa*.]

-carp. *Bot.* A suffix meaning fruit or similar reproductive structure: **endocarp.** [From Greek *karpos*, fruit.]

car·pal (kär′pəl) *adj. Anat.* Of, pertaining to, or near the carpus. —*n.* Any bone of the carpus.

car·pel (kär′pəl) *n. Bot.* The central, seed-bearing female organ of a flower, consisting of a modified leaf forming one or more sections of the pistil. [From Greek *karpos*, fruit.]

car·pen·ter (kär′pən-tər) *n.* One whose occupation is constructing and repairing wooden objects and structures. —*tr.v.* To make, build, or repair. —*intr.v.* To work as a carpenter. [Middle English, from Norman French, from Latin *carpentārius* (*artifex*), carriage(-maker), from *carpentum*, two-wheeled carriage.]

car·pen·try (kär′pən-trē) *n.* **1.** The work, trade, or business of a carpenter. **2.** The work or objects made by a carpenter.

car·pet (kär′pĭt) *n.* **1. a.** A heavy usu. woven covering for a floor. **b.** The fabric used for this. **2.** A surface of similar function or appearance: *a carpet of leaves.* —*tr.v.* To cover with or as if with a carpet: *"The pool was carpeted with green sponge."* (Rachel Carson). —*idiom.* **on the carpet.** In the position of being reprimanded by one in authority. [Middle English *carpete*, from Old French *carpite*, from Old Italian *carpire*, to pluck, tear, from Latin *carpere*.]

car·pet·bag (kär′pĭt-băg′) *n.* A kind of traveling bag orig. made of carpet fabric.

car·pet·bag·ger (kär′pĭt-băg′ər) *n.* A Northerner who went to the South after the Civil War to gain political or financial advantage by exploiting postwar conditions. —**car′pet·bag′ger·y** *n.*

car·pet·ing (kär′pĭ-tĭng) *n.* **1.** Material or fabric used for carpets. **2.** A carpet or carpets.

carp·ing (kär′pĭng) *adj.* Naggingly critical; faultfinding; complaining. —**carp′ing·ly** *adv.*

car·pi (kär′pī) *n.* The plural of **carpus.**

car·port (kär′pôrt′, -pōrt′) *n.* A roof projecting from the side of a building, used as a shelter for an automobile.

car·pus (kär′pəs) *n., pl.* **-pi** (-pī′). *Anat.* **1.** The wrist. **2.** The bones of the wrist. [From Greek *karpos*, wrist.]

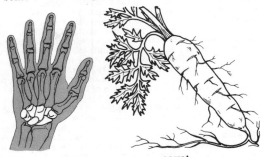

carpus   carrot

car·rack (kăr′ək) *n.* A large type of merchant ship used in the 14th, 15th, and 16th cent.; galleon. [Middle English *caryk*, from Old French *caraque*, from Old Spanish *carraca*, from Arabic *qurqūr*.]

car·rel (kăr′əl) *n.* Also **car·rell.** A nook near the stacks in a library, used for private study. [Orig. unknown.]

car·riage (kăr′ĭj) *n.* **1.** A four-wheeled passenger vehicle, usu. drawn by horses. **2.** *Brit.* A railroad car for passengers. **3.** A wheeled vehicle for a baby that is pushed by someone on foot; a perambulator. **4.** A wheeled support or frame for moving a heavy object, such as a cannon. **5.** A moving part of a machine for holding or shifting another part. **6. a.** The act or process of transporting or carrying. **b.** (kăr′ē-ĭj). The cost of or charge for transporting. **7.** Posture; bearing. [Middle English *cariage*, from Old North French, from *carier*, to transport in a vehicle, carry.]

carriage trade. Wealthy patrons, as of a restaurant.

car·ri·er (kăr′ē-ər) *n.* **1.** Someone or something that transports or conveys. **2.** A person or business that deals in transporting passengers or goods. **3.** A mechanism or device by which something is conveyed or conducted. **4.** *Med.* A person or animal at least temporarily immune to an infection that it transmits directly or indirectly to others. **5.** *Electronics.* **a.** A **carrier wave. b.** A charge-carrying entity, esp. an electron or a hole in a semiconductor. **6.** An aircraft carrier.

carrier pigeon. A homing pigeon, esp. one trained to carry messages.

carrier wave. An electromagnetic wave that can be modulated in frequency, amplitude, phase, or otherwise to transmit radio or telephonic signals.

car·ri·on (kăr′ē-ən) *n.* Dead and decaying flesh. [Middle English *carion, caroine*, ult. from Latin *carō*, flesh.]

car·rot (kăr′ət) *n.* **1.** A widely cultivated plant, *Daucus carota sativa*, with finely divided leaves, flat clusters of small white flowers, and an edible, yellow-orange root. **2.** The long, tapering root of the carrot, eaten as a vegetable. [Old French *carotte*, from Latin *carōta*, from Greek *karōton*.]

car·rou·sel (kăr′ə-sĕl′, -zĕl′) *n.* Var. of **carousel.**

car·ry (kăr′ē) *v.* **-ried, -ry·ing.** —*tr.v.* **1.** To bear in one's hands or arms, on one's shoulders or back, etc., while moving: *carry the groceries into the house.* **2.** To transport or convey: *Railroads carry coal.* **3. a.** To sustain the weight of; bear: *These columns were designed to carry the roof.* **b.** To maintain through personal effort, talent, etc.: *This production established the fact that a few performers could carry a Broadway show.* **4.** To keep, wear, or hold on one's person: *carry a gun. I never carry much money with me.* **5.** To act as the means by which (a person or thing) moves or is moved from one place to another: *A pipe carries water.* **6.** To hold and move (the body or a part of the body) in a certain way: *She carries herself very gracefully.* **7.** To transmit (a disease): *Mosquitoes carry malaria.* **8.** To be pregnant with: *carrying a child.* **9.** To have in stock; have for sale: *Drugstores carry a great variety of products.* **10.** To sing (a tune, melody, etc.) on key. **11.** To put (a digit) into the next column to the left, as in performing addition. **12.** To have as a usual or necessary attribute, accompaniment, consequence, etc.; involve: *a* *crime that carries a heavy penalty. The offer carries a money-back guarantee.* **13.** To contain: *The report carried a grim warning.* **14.** To win the sympathy, agreement, etc., of: *He carried his audience with him.* **15.** To win a majority of the votes in: *In 1936 President Roosevelt carried 46 states. The bill carried the state legislature.* **16.** To prolong, extend, or continue in space, time, or degree: *carry a fence around a field; carry demands too far.* **17.** To print or broadcast: *All the papers carried the story. All the major networks carried the speech.* **18.** *Football.* To run with (the ball). —*intr.v.* **1.** To act as a bearer: *teach a dog to fetch and carry.* **2.** To be capable of being transmitted or conveyed: *a voice that carries well; smoke that carried for miles.* **3.** To be accepted or approved: *The proposal carried by a wide margin.* —*phrasal verbs.* **carry away.** To move or excite greatly: *carried away by the music.* **carry forward.** **1.** To progress with: *carry forward the program.* **2.** *Accounting.* To transfer (an entry) to the next column, page, book, or to another account. **carry off.** **1.** To cause the death of: *The epidemic carried off thousands.* **2.** To handle (a situation, for example) successfully: *carried off first prize.* **carry on.** **1.** To conduct; administer: *carry on the affairs of state.* **2.** To engage in: *carry on a conversation.* **3.** To continue despite difficulties or setbacks: *carry on in the face of disaster.* **4.** To behave in an excited, improper, or silly manner; act hysterically or childishly. **carry out.** **1.** To put into practice or effect: *carry out a plan.* **2.** To follow or obey: *carry out instructions.* **3.** To bring to a conclusion; accomplish. **carry through.** **1.** To accomplish; complete. **2.** To enable to endure; sustain: *Fortitude carried him through the ordeal.* —*n.,* pl. **-ries.** **1.** A portage, as between two navigable rivers or other bodies of water. **2. a.** The range of a gun or projectile. **b.** *Golf & Baseball.* The lift of a ball that makes it travel a considerable distance. **3.** *Football.* A rush with the ball. [Middle English *carien,* from Old North French *carier,* to transport in a vehicle, from *car(re),* vehicle, from Latin *carrus.*]

car·ry·all (kăr′ē-ôl′) *n.* **1. a.** A covered one-horse carriage with two seats. **b.** A closed automobile with two lengthwise seats facing each other. **2.** A large bag, basket, or pocketbook.

carrying charge. The interest charged on the balance owed when paying in installments.

car·sick (kär′sĭk′) *adj.* Nauseated by the motion of a car or other vehicle.

cart (kärt) *n.* **1.** A two-wheeled vehicle drawn by a horse or other animal and used for transporting goods. **2.** An open two-wheeled business or pleasure carriage, such as a dog cart. **3.** Any small, light vehicle moved by hand, as a golf cart. —*tr.v.* **1. a.** To convey in a cart. **b.** To convey laboriously; lug: *cart the old newspapers to the dump.* **2.** To remove or transport (a person or thing) in an unceremonious manner or by force: *He was carted off to jail.* [Middle English *carte, cart,* from Old Norse *kartr.*] —**cart′er** *n.*

cart·age (kär′tĭj) *n.* **1.** The act or process of transporting by cart. **2.** The cost of transporting by cart.

carte blanche (kärt′ blänsh′, blänch′). Complete power or freedom of action; unconditional authority. [French, "blank card."]

car·tel (kär-tĕl′) *n.* A combination of independent business organizations formed to regulate or monopolize production, pricing, and marketing of goods by the members. [Old French, from Old Italian *cartello,* letter of defiance, placard, from *carta,* card.]

Car·te·sian coordinates (kär-tē′zhən). The numbers locating a point in a Cartesian coordinate system, as the abscissa and the ordinate in a plane system.

Cartesian coordinate system. **1.** A two-dimensional coordinate system in which the coordinates of a point are its distances from two intersecting, usu. perpendicular straight lines, the distance from each being measured along a straight line parallel to the other. **2.** A three-dimensional coordinate system in which the coordinates of a point are its distances from each of three intersecting, usu. mutually perpendicular planes along lines parallel to the intersection of the other two.

car·ti·lage (kär′tl-ĭj) *n.* **1.** A tough white fibrous connective tissue attached to the surfaces of bones in regions near joints. It forms a large part of the skeleton of fetal and young vertebrates and is largely converted to bone with maturation. **2.** A part or structure composed of cartilage. [From Latin *cartilāgo.*]

car·ti·lag·i·nous (kär′tl-ăj′ə-nəs) *adj.* **1.** Of or pertaining to cartilage. **2.** Having a skeleton consisting mainly of cartilage.

car·tog·ra·phy (kär-tŏg′rə-fē) *n.* The art or technique of making maps or charts. [French *cartographie,* from *carte,* map, card.] —**car·tog′ra·pher** *n.* —**car′to·graph′ic** (kär′tə-grăf′ĭk) or **car′to·graph′i·cal** *adj.*

car·ton (kär′tn) *n.* A cardboard box or other container made in various sizes and used to hold goods, liquids, etc.: *a packing carton; a carton of milk.* [French, from Italian *cartone,* pasteboard, from *carta,* card.]

car·toon (kär-tōōn′) *n.* **1.** A drawing, as in a newspaper or magazine, depicting a humorous situation, often accompanied by a caption; a pictorial joke. **2.** A drawing satirizing or commenting on a subject of current public interest, usu. accompanied by words. **3.** A preliminary sketch, as for a fresco, mosaic, tapestry, etc. **4.** An **animated cartoon.** [Italian *cartone,* pasteboard, carton.] —**car·toon′ist** *n.*

car·tridge (kär′trĭj) *n.* **1. a.** A tubular container of metal or cardboard and metal containing the propellant powder and bullet or shot of a small firearm. **b.** Such a container loaded with shotgun pellets or fitted with a projectile, such as a bullet. Also called **round.** **2.** A small, readily removable unit of equipment, esp.: **a.** A phonograph pickup. **b.** A cassette for certain tape recorders and players. **c.** A case with photographic film that can be loaded directly into a camera. [From French *cartouche,* cartridge, from Italian *cartoccio,* from *carta,* card.]

cart·wheel (kärt′hwēl′, -wēl′) *n.* **1.** The wheel of a cart. **2.** A handspring in which the body turns sideways with the limbs spread like the spokes of a wheel.

car·un·cle (kăr′ŭng′kəl, kə-rŭng′-) *n.* **1.** *Anat.* A fleshy, naked outgrowth, such as a fowl's wattles. **2.** *Bot.* An outgrowth on a seed. [Obs. French *caruncule,* from Latin *caruncula,* from *carō,* flesh.]

carve (kärv) *v.* **carved, carv·ing.** —*tr.v.* **1. a.** To divide into pieces by cutting; slice: *carve a fowl.* **b.** To divide by parceling out: *carve up an estate.* **2.** To cut (something) into a desired shape; fashion by cutting: *carve the wood into a figure.* **3.** To produce or form by cutting: *carve initials in the bark.* **4.** To decorate by carving. —*intr.v.* To slice and serve meat or poultry. —*phrasal verb.* **carve out.** **1.** To form by or as if by carving: *Rushing water carved out gullies in the hill.* **2.** To achieve by exertion or ability: *carve out a career.* [Middle English *kerven,* from Old English *ceorfan.*] —**carv′er** *n.*

carv·ing (kär′vĭng) *n.* **1.** The act or process of cutting wood, stone, or other material to form a figure or design. **2.** An object or design formed by such cutting.

car·y·at·id (kăr′ē-ăt′ĭd) *n.,* pl. **-ids** or **-at·i·des** (-ăt′ĭ-dēz′). *Archit.* A supporting column sculptured in the form of a woman. [Latin *Caryātidēs* (pl.), from Greek *Karuatidēs,* priestesses of Artemis at *Karuai,* Greece.]

caryatid

car·y·op·sis (kăr′ē-ŏp′sĭs) *n.,* pl. **-op·ses** (-ŏp′sēz′) or **-op·si·des** (-ŏp′sĭ-dēz′). *Bot.* A one-seeded dry fruit having its outer coat fused to its surface, as a grain of barley. [Greek *karuon,* kernel + *opsis,* appearance.]

ca·sa·ba (kə-sä′bə) *n.* Also **cas·sa·ba.** A variety of winter melon with a yellow rind and whitish flesh. [From *Kassaba,* former name of Turgutlu, Turkey.]

cas·cade (kă-skād′) n. **1.** A waterfall or a series of small waterfalls over steep rocks. **2.** Anything resembling a cascade: *a cascade of sparks.* **3.** Any succession of processes, operations, or units: *a cascade of amplifier stages.* —*intr.v.* **-cad·ed, -cad·ing.** To fall in or like a cascade. [French, from Italian *cascata,* from *cascare,* to fall, from Latin *cadere.*]

cas·car·a (kă-skăr′ə) n. **1.** A buckthorn shrub or tree, *Rhamnus purshiana,* of northwestern North America. **2.** The dried bark of the cascara, used as a stimulant and laxative. Also called **cascara sagrada.** [Spanish *cáscara,* bark, from *cascar,* to break off, ult. from Latin *quatere,* to shake.]

case¹ (kās) n. **1.** An instance or example of the existence or occurrence of something: *a case of mistaken identity.* **2. a.** An occurrence of disease or disorder: *a case of the measles.* **b.** A client, as of a physician, psychiatrist, or attorney. **3.** A set of circumstances or state of affairs; the situation: *In that case there is nothing to be done.* **4.** A set of reasons, arguments, or supporting facts offered in justification or support of something: *the case for socialized medicine.* **5.** A question or problem; a matter: *a case of honor.* **6.** *Law.* **a.** An action or suit or just grounds for an action. **b.** The facts or evidence offered in support of a claim. **7.** *Informal.* A peculiar or eccentric person: *a head case.* **8.** *Ling.* **a.** The syntactic relationship of a noun, pronoun, or adjective to the other words of a sentence, indicated in inflected languages by the assumption of declensional endings and in noninflected languages by the position of the words within the sentence. **b.** The form or position of a word that indicates this relationship. **c.** Such forms, positions, or relationships collectively. **9.** *Ling.* **a.** A pattern of inflection of nouns, pronouns, and adjectives to express different syntactic functions in a sentence; for example, *I* and *him* are in the nominative and objective cases respectively in *I like him.* **b.** The form of such an inflected word. —*tr.v.* **cased, cas·ing.** *Slang.* To examine carefully, as in planning a crime: *case the bank before robbing it.* —*idioms.* **in any case.** Regardless of what occurred or will occur. **in case.** If it happens that; if: *in case the need arises.* [Middle English *cas,* an occurrence, from Old French, from Latin *cāsus,* fall, event, past part. of *cadere,* to fall.]

case² (kās) n. **1.** A container or receptacle, esp. for shipping or protection. **2.** A decorative or protective covering or cover. **3.** A set or pair, as of pistols. **4.** The frame or framework of a window, door, or stairway. **5.** *Printing.* A shallow, compartmented tray for storing type or type matrices. —*tr.v.* **cased, cas·ing.** To put into, cover, or protect with a case. [Middle English, from Old North French *casse,* from Latin *capsa,* chest, case.]

case·hard·en (kās′här′dn) *tr.v.* **1.** To harden the surface of (iron or steel), usu. by treating with heat. **2.** To harden the spirit or emotions of; make callous. [From CASE (covering).]

case history. An organized set of facts relevant to the development of an individual or group condition under study or treatment, esp. in sociology or medicine.

ca·sein (kā′sēn, kā′sē-ĭn) n. Any of several white, tasteless, odorless milk and cheese proteins, used to make plastics, adhesives, paints, and foods. [Prob. from French *caséine,* from Latin *cāseus,* cheese.]

case·mate (kās′māt′) n. *Mil.* **1.** On a warship, a fortified enclosure for artillery. **2.** On a rampart, an armored compartment for artillery. [Old French, from Italian *casamatta.*]

case·ment (kās′mənt) n. **1. a.** A window sash that opens outward by means of hinges. **b.** A window with such sashes. **2.** A case or covering. [Middle English.]

case·work (kās′wûrk′) n. The part of a social worker's duties dealing with the problems of a particular case. —**case′work·er** n.

cash¹ (kăsh) n. **1.** Money in the form of currency; bills or coins. **2.** Payment for goods or services in money or by check as opposed to credit or delayed payment: *paid for the new clothes in cash.* —*tr.v.* To exchange for or convert into ready money: *cash a check.* —*idioms.* **cash in on.** To take advantage of. **cash in (one's) chips.** To die. [Old French *casse,* money box, case.]

cash² (kăsh) n., pl. **cash.** Any of various Oriental coins of small denomination, esp. a copper and lead coin with a square hole in its center. [Portuguese *caixa,* from Tamil *kācu,* a small copper coin, from Sanskrit *karsa,* a certain weight.]

cash·book (kăsh′bŏŏk′) n. A book in which a record of cash receipts and expenditures is kept.

cash crop. A crop grown esp. for sale and usu. providing an important source of income.

cash·ew (kăsh′ōō, kə-shōō′) n. **1.** A tropical American evergreen tree, *Anacardium occidentale,* bearing kidney-shaped nuts that protrude from a fleshy receptacle. **2.** The nut of the cashew, edible only when roasted. [Portuguese *cajú, acajú,* from Tupi *acajú.*]

cashew   cask

cash·ier¹ (kă-shîr′) n. **1.** The officer of a bank or business concern in charge of paying and receiving money. **2.** An employee whose major function is to handle cash transactions, as in a restaurant or supermarket. [Dutch *cassier,* from French *caissier,* from *caisse,* money box, case.]

ca·shier² (kă-shîr′) *tr.v.* To dismiss from a position of command or responsibility, esp. for disciplinary reasons. [Dutch *casseren,* from Old French *casser,* to discharge, from Latin *quassāre,* to break in pieces, from *quatere,* to shake.]

cashier's check. A check drawn by a bank on its own funds and signed by the bank's cashier.

cash·mere (kăzh′mîr′, kăsh′-) n. Also **kash·mir. 1.** Fine, downy wool growing beneath the outer hair of the Cashmere goat. **2.** A soft fabric made from this wool or from similar fibers. —*modifier: a cashmere sweater.* [After *Kashmir,* India.]

Cashmere goat. A goat native to the Himalayan regions of India and Tibet, prized for its wool.

cash register. A machine that tabulates the amount of sales transactions, makes a record of them, and has a drawer or drawers in which cash may be kept.

cas·ing (kā′sĭng) n. **1.** A protective case or covering, as for an automobile tire, rocket, etc. **2.** The cleaned intestines of cattle, sheep, or hogs, used for wrapping sausage meat. **3.** The frame or framework for a window or door.

ca·si·no (kə-sē′nō) n., pl. **-nos. 1.** A public room or house for entertainment, esp. for gambling. **2.** Var. of **cassino.** [Italian, dim. of *casa,* house, from Latin *casa.*]

cask (kăsk) n. **1.** A barrel of any size. **2.** The amount that a cask holds. [Spanish *casco,* helmet, cask.]

cas·ket (kăs′kĭt) n. **1.** A small case or chest for jewels or other valuables. **2.** A coffin. [Middle English, from Old French *cassette,* small box, dim. of *casse,* case.]

casque (kăsk) n. **1.** A helmet or other armor for the head. **2.** *Zool.* A helmetlike structure or outgrowth. [French, from Spanish *casco,* cask.]

cas·sa·ba (kə-sä′bə) n. Var. of **casaba.**

Cas·san·dra (kə-săn′drə) n. **1.** *Gk. Myth.* A daughter of Priam, king of Troy, endowed with the gift of prophecy by Apollo, who after she rejected his love decreed that her prophecies never be believed. **2.** Anyone who utters unheeded prophecies.

cas·sa·va (kə-sä′və) n. **1.** Any of various tropical American plants of the genus *Manihot,* esp. *M. esculenta* (or *M. utilissima*), with a large, starchy root. Also called **manioc. 2.** A starch derived from the root of the cassava, used to make tapioca. [Spanish *cazabe,* cassava bread, from Taino *caçábi.*]

cas·se·role (kăs'ə-rōl') *n.* **1.** A dish in which food is both baked and served. **2.** Food prepared and served in such a dish: *a tuna casserole.* [French, saucepan, from Old French, from *casse,* ladle, from Medieval Latin *cattia,* dipper, from Greek *kauthos,* ladle.]

cas·sette (kə-sĕt', kă-) *n.* **1.** A light-proof camera cartridge, usually metal, for daylight loading of photographic film. **2.** A small cartridge containing magnetic tape for use in a tape recorder, in certain electric typewriters, etc. [French, small box, from Old French, dim. of *casse,* case, box.]

cas·sia (kăsh'ə) *n.* **1.** Any of various chiefly tropical trees, shrubs, and plants of the genus *Cassia,* with compound leaves, usu. yellow flowers, and long pods. **2.** A tree, *Cinnamomum cassia,* of tropical Asia, having bark similar to cinnamon but of inferior quality. [Middle English, from Old English, from Latin, a kind of plant, from Greek *kas(-s)ia.*]

cas·si·mere (kăz'ə-mîr', kăs'-) *n.* A twilled woolen cloth. [From *Cassimere,* var. of *Kashmir,* India.]

cas·si·no (kə-sē'nō) *n.* Also **ca·si·no.** A card game for two to four players in which cards on the table are matched by cards in the hand. [From CASINO.]

Cas·si·o·pe·ia (kăs'ē-ə-pē'ə) *n.* A W-shaped constellation in the Northern Hemisphere near Cepheus.

cas·sit·er·ite (kə-sĭt'ə-rīt') *n.* A light-yellow, red-brown, or black mineral, SnO$_2$, an important tin ore. [French *casiterite,* from Greek *kassiteros,* tin.]

cas·sock (kăs'ək) *n.* A long garment, usu. black, reaching to the feet and worn by clergymen and others assisting in church services. [Old French *casaque,* from Persian *kazagand,* padded jacket.]

cas·so·war·y (kăs'ə-wĕr'ē) *n.,* pl. **-ies.** Any of several large, flightless birds of the genus *Casuarius,* of New Guinea and adjacent areas, with a large, horny casque on the head and brightly colored wattles. [Malay *kešuari.*]

cassowary
George Miksch Sutton

caster

cast (kăst) *v.* **cast, cast·ing.** —*tr.v.* **1.** To throw: *cast dice. The fishermen cast their nets at dawn.* **2.** To throw off; shed: *The snake cast its skin.* **3.** To cause to fall upon something: *cast a shadow; cast a spell; cast doubt on his honesty.* **4.** To turn or direct: *cast a glance in her direction. Try to cast your mind back several years.* **5.** To deposit (a ballot); give (a vote): *The chairman cast his vote and broke the tie.* **6. a.** To assign a certain role to: *The director cast him as Romeo.* **b.** To choose actors for: *cast a new play.* **7. a.** To form (an object) by pouring a molten or soft material into a mold and allowing it to harden: *The artist cast the sculpture in bronze.* **b.** To pour (a material) in forming an object in this way. —*intr.v.* **1.** To throw, esp. to throw out a lure or bait at the end of a fishing line. **2.** To receive form or shape in a mold: *Some metals cast easily.* **3.** *Naut.* **a.** To veer to leeward from a former course; fall off. **b.** To put about; tack. —*phrasal verbs.* **cast about.** To search or look for: *cast about for an answer.* **cast aside.** To discard or reject as useless. **cast down. 1.** To bend and turn downward; lower the eyes or head. **2.** To make sad; discourage. **cast off. 1.** To discard or reject. **2.** To let go or set loose, esp. to release a ship from its mooring. **cast on.** To make the first row of stitches in knitting. —*n.* **1.** The act of throwing or casting: *a cast of*

the dice. **2.** The actors in a play, movie, etc.: *There were only four people in the cast.* **3.** A hard, stiff bandage, usu. of gauze and plaster, used to keep a broken or damaged bone or joint from moving. **4. a.** An object cast in or as if in a mold. **b.** An impression formed in a mold: *a cast in plaster of a face.* **5.** A hue or shade: *The cloth has a slightly reddish cast.* **6.** Outward form, quality, or appearance: *This puts a different cast on the matter.* **7.** A slight squint or strabismus: *a cast in her left eye.* —*idioms.* **cast down.** Low in spirit; depressed. **cast lots.** To draw lots in order to determine something by chance. **cast (one's) lot with.** To join or side with for better or for worse. [Middle English *casten,* to throw, from Old Norse *kasta.*]

cas·ta·nets (kăs'tə-nĕts') *pl.n.* A pair of shells of ivory or hardwood, held in the palm of the hand and clapped together with the fingers to make a sharp click. [Spanish *castañeta,* from *castaña,* chestnut.]

cast·a·way (kăst'ə-wā') *adj.* **1.** Shipwrecked; cast adrift or ashore. **2.** Discarded; thrown away. —**cast'a·way'** *n.*

caste (kăst) *n.* **1.** One of the major hereditary classes into which Hindu society is divided. Each caste is distinctly separated from the others by restrictions placed upon occupation and marriage. **2.** Any social class distinguished from others by rank, profession, etc. [Portuguese *casta,* from *casto,* pure, chaste, from Latin *castus.*]

cas·tel·lat·ed (kăs'tə-lā'tĭd) *adj.* Having battlements in the style of a castle. [From Medieval Latin *castellāre,* to fortify as a castle, from Latin *castellum,* castle.]

cast·er (kăs'tər) *n.* **1.** A person or thing that casts. **2.** Also **cas·tor.** A small wheel on a swivel, attached to the underside of a heavy object to make it easier to move. **3.** Also **cas·tor.** A small bottle or cruet for condiments.

cas·ti·gate (kăs'tĭ-gāt') *tr.v.* **-gat·ed, -gat·ing. 1.** To punish or chastise. **2.** To criticize severely. —See Syns at **scold.** [Latin *castīgāre,* to correct, punish : *castus,* pure + *agere,* to do, make.] —**cas'ti·ga'tion** *n.* —**cas'ti·ga'tor** *n.*

Cas·tile soap (kă-stēl') Also **castile soap.** A fine, hard soap made with olive oil and sodium hydroxide.

cast·ing (kăs'tĭng) *n.* **1.** The act or process of making casts or molds. **2.** That which is cast in a mold, as a metal piece.

cast iron. A hard, brittle nonmalleable iron-carbon alloy containing 2.0 to 4.5 per cent carbon and varying amounts of silicon, sulfur, manganese, and phosphorus.

cas·tle (kăs'əl) *n.* **1.** A fort or fortified group of buildings usu. dominating the surrounding country. **2.** Any building similar to or resembling a castle. **3.** Any place of privacy, security, or refuge: *A man's home is his castle.* **4.** *Chess.* The rook. —*v.* **-tled, -tling.** —*tr.v. Chess.* To move (the king) two or three spaces toward a rook and place the rook on the other side. —*intr.v. Chess.* To move the king and rook in this manner. [Middle English *castel,* ult. from Latin *castellum,* castle, dim. of *castrum,* fortified place.]

cast·off (kăst'ôf', -ŏf') *adj.* Discarded; rejected.

cast·off (kăst'ôf', -ŏf') *n.* Someone or something that has been discarded or thrown away.

cas·tor[1] (kăs'tər) *n.* **1.** An oily, brown, odorous substance obtained from skin glands of the beaver and used in perfume. **2.** A beaver hat. [Middle English, beaver, from Latin, from Greek *kastōr.*]

cas·tor[2] (kăs'tər) *n.* Var. of **caster** (wheel and cruet).

Cas·tor (kăs'tər) *n.* A double star in the constellation Gemini, the brightest star in the group, approx. 46 light-years from Earth.

Castor and Pol·lux (pŏl'əks). *Gk. Myth.* The twin sons of Leda and brothers of Helen and Clytemnestra, transformed by Zeus into the constellation Gemini.

castor bean. 1. The castor-oil plant. **2.** A seed of the castor-oil plant. [CASTOR (OIL) + BEAN.]

castor oil. An oil extracted from castor-oil plant seeds and used as a cathartic and a fine lubricant.

cas·tor-oil plant (kăs'tər-oil'). A large plant, *Ricinus communis,* grown for ornament and for the extraction of castor oil from its poisonous seeds.

cas·trate (kăs'trāt') *tr.v.* **-trat·ed, -trat·ing. 1.** To remove the testicles of; geld. **2.** To remove the ovaries of; spay. [From Latin *castrāre.*] —**cas·tra'tion** *n.*

cas·u·al (kăzh'ōō-əl) *adj.* **1.** Happening by chance; not planned; accidental: *a casual meeting.* **2. a.** Showing little

---

ă pat | ā pay | â care | ä father | ĕ pet | ē be | hw which | ĭ pit | ī tie | î pier | ŏ pot | ō toe | ô paw, for | oi noise
ōō took | ōō boot | ou out | th thin | th this | ŭ cut | û urge | zh vision | ə about, item, edible, gallop, circus

interest; unconcerned; nonchalant: *a casual manner.* **b.** Offhand; passing: *a casual remark.* **3. a.** Without ceremony or formality. **b.** Suited for everyday wear or use; informal. **4.** Not serious or thorough; superficial: *a casual inspection; a casual reader of a newspaper.* **5.** Not close or intimate: *a casual friendship.* —See Syns at **accidental** and **informal.** —*n.* **1.** A person who receives temporary welfare relief. **2.** A person who works at irregular intervals. **3.** *Mil.* A soldier temporarily attached to a unit while awaiting permanent assignment. [Middle English *casuel*, from Old French, from Late Latin *cāsuālis*, from Latin *cāsus*, chance, case.] —**cas′u·al·ly** *adv.* —**cas′u·al·ness** *n.*

cas·u·al·ty (kăzh′ōō-əl-tē) *n., pl.* **-ties. 1.** Someone who is injured or killed in an accident. **2. a.** Someone who is injured, killed, captured, or missing in action against an enemy. **b.** Often **casualties.** Loss in numbers through injury, death, or other cause. **3.** An unfortunate accident, esp. one involving loss of life. **4.** A person or thing that is destroyed or cast away. [Middle English *casuelte*, from *casuel*, casual.]

cas·u·ist (kăzh′ōō-ĭst) *n.* One who determines what is right and wrong in matters of conscience or conduct. [French *casuiste*, from Spanish *casuista*, from Latin *cāsus*, chance, case.] —**cas′u·is′tic** *adj.*

cas·u·ist·ry (kăzh′ōō-ĭ-strē) *n.* The determination of right and wrong in questions of conduct or conscience by the application of general principles of ethics.

cat (kăt) *n.* **1. a.** A carnivorous mammal, *Felis catus* (or *F. domesticus*), domesticated since early times as a catcher of rats and mice and as a pet. **b.** Any of the other animals of the family Felidae, which includes the lion, tiger, leopard, and lynx. **2.** The fur of a domestic cat. **3.** A spiteful or gossiping woman. **4.** A cat-o′-nine-tails. **5.** A catfish. **6.** *Slang.* A person. —*idiom.* **let the cat out of the bag.** To let a secret be known. [Middle English *cat(te)*, from Old English *cat(t)*.]

ca·tab·o·lism (kə-tăb′ə-lĭz′əm) *n.* The phase of metabolism in which tissues are broken down and the complex molecules of protoplasm are changed into simpler ones. [From Greek *katabolē*, a throwing down, from *kataballein*, to throw down : *kata-*, down + *ballein*, to throw.] —**cat′a·bol′ic** (kăt′ə-bŏl′ĭk) *adj.*

cat·a·clysm (kăt′ə-klĭz′əm) *n.* **1.** A violent and sudden change in the earth′s crust, such as an earthquake. **2.** A devastating flood. **3.** Any violent upheaval or disaster. —See Syns at **disaster.** [French *cataclysme*, from Latin *cataclysmos*, deluge, flood, from Greek *kataklusmos*, from *katakluzein*, to deluge, inundate : *kata-*, down + *kluzein*, to wash.] —**cat′a·clys′mic** (-klĭz′mĭk) or **cat′a·clys′mal** (-klĭz′məl) *adj.*

cat·a·combs (kăt′ə-kōmz′) *pl.n.* A series of underground chambers with recesses for graves. [From Old French *catacombe*, a subterranean chamber, prob. from Old Italian *catacomba*, from Late Latin *catacumba*.]

ca·tad·ro·mous (kə-tăd′rə-məs) *adj.* Of or pertaining to fish that live in fresh water but migrate down river to breed in salt waters. [Greek *katadromos* : *kata-*, down + *dromos*, running.]

cat·a·falque (kăt′ə-fălk′, -fôlk′) *n.* The raised structure upon which a coffin rests during a state funeral. [French, from Italian *catafalco* : Latin *cata-*, down from + *fala*, scaffold.]

catafalque

Cat·a·lan (kăt′l-ăn′, -ən) *adj.* Of or pertaining to Catalonia, its people, language, or culture. —*n.* **1.** A native or inhabi-

tant of Catalonia. **2.** The Romance language of Catalonia.

cat·a·lase (kăt′l-ās′, -āz′) *n.* An enzyme that catalyzes the decomposition of hydrogen peroxide into water and oxygen. [CATAL(YSIS) + -ASE.]

cat·a·lep·sy (kăt′l-ĕp′sē) *n.* A condition characterized by muscular rigidity, lack of awareness of environment, and lack of response to external stimuli. [Ult. from Greek *katalēpsis*, "a seizing," from *katalambanein*, to seize : *kata-*, down from + *lambanein*, to take.] —**cat′a·lep′tic** (-ĕp′tĭk) *adj.*

cat·a·log or **cat·a·logue** (kăt′l-ôg′, -ŏg′) *n.* **1.** A list, usu. in alphabetical order, often with descriptions of the items listed. **2.** A publication containing such a list: *a mail-order catalog; a college catalog.* **3.** A **card catalog.** —*v.* **-loged** or **-logued**, **-log·ing** or **-logu·ing**. —*tr.v.* To list in a catalog; make a catalog of. —*intr.v.* To make a catalog. [Middle English *cateloge*, from Old French *catalogue*, from Late Latin *catalogus*, an enumeration, from Greek *katalegein*, to recount, enumerate : *kata-*, thoroughly + *legein*, to gather.] —**cat′a·logu′er** *n.*

ca·tal·pa (kə-tăl′pə, -tôl′-) *n.* Any of several chiefly North American trees of the genus *Catalpa*, with large leaves, showy clusters of whitish flowers, and long, slender pods. [Creek *kutuhlpa*, "head with wings" (from the shape of its flowers).]

ca·tal·y·sis (kə-tăl′ĭ-sĭs) *n.* The action of a catalyst, esp. in modifying the rate of a chemical reaction. [Greek *katalusis*, dissolution, from *kataluein*, to dissolve : *kata-*, down + *luein*, to loosen, release.] —**cat′a·lyt′ic** (kăt′l-ĭt′ĭk) *adj.* —**cat′a·lyt′i·cal·ly** *adv.*

cat·a·lyst (kăt′l-ĭst) *n.* **1.** *Chem.* A substance, usu. present in small amounts, that modifies, esp. increases, the rate of a chemical reaction without being consumed in the process. **2.** One that precipitates a process or event, esp. without being changed by the consequences. —See Syns at **stimulus.** [From CATALYSIS.]

catalytic converter. A reaction chamber typically containing a finely divided platinum-iridium catalyst into which exhaust gases from an automotive engine are passed together with excess air so that carbon monoxide and hydrocarbon pollutants are oxidized to carbon dioxide and water.

cat·a·lyze (kăt′l-īz′) *tr.v.* **-lyzed, -lyz·ing.** To modify the rate of (a chemical reaction) as a catalyst. —**cat′a·lyz′er** *n.*

cat·a·ma·ran (kăt′ə-mə-răn′) *n.* **1.** A boat with two parallel hulls. **2.** A raft of logs or floats lashed together. [Tamil *kattumaram* : *kattu-*, to tie + *maram*, tree, timber.]

cat·a·mount (kăt′ə-mount′) *n.* Also **cat·a·moun·tain** (kăt′ə-moun′tən). Any of various wild felines, such as a mountain lion or a lynx. [Short for *catamountain*, var. of earlier *cat of the mountain*.]

cat·a·pult (kăt′ə-pŭlt′, -pŏŏlt′) *n.* **1.** An ancient military machine for hurling large stones, arrows, or other missiles. **2.** A mechanism for launching aircraft without a runway, as from the deck of a ship. **3.** A slingshot. —*tr.v.* To hurl or launch from or as if from a catapult. —*intr.v.* To become catapulted; spring up abruptly: *The rescue team catapulted into action.* [Old French *catapulte*, from Latin *catapulta*, from Greek *katapaltēs* : *kata-*, down + *pallein*, to sway, brandish.]

cat·a·ract (kăt′ə-răkt′) *n.* **1.** A very large waterfall. **2.** A great downpour. **3.** *Path.* An opaque condition in the lens or capsule of the eye, causing partial or total blindness. [Middle English *cataracte*, floodgate, from Old French, from Latin *catarractēs*, waterfall, from Greek *katar(rh)aktēs*, from *katarassein*, to dash down : *kata-*, down + *rassein*, to strike.]

ca·tarrh (kə-tär′) *n.* Inflammation of mucous membranes, esp. of the nose and throat. [Old French *catarrhe*, from Late Latin *catarrhus*, from Greek *katarrhous*, a flowing down, from *katarrhein*, to flow down : *kata-*, down + *rhein*, to flow.] —**ca·tarrh′al** (-əl) *adj.*

ca·tas·tro·phe (kə-tăs′trə-fē) *n.* **1.** A great and sudden calamity; disaster. **2.** A sudden violent change in the earth′s surface; cataclysm. **3.** The dénouement of a play, esp. of a tragedy. —See Syns at **disaster.** [Greek *katastrophē*, from *katastrephein*, to turn down, overturn : *kata-*, down + *strephein*, to turn.] —**cat′a·stroph′ic** (kăt′ə-strŏf′ĭk) *adj.*

cat·call (kăt′kôl′) *n.* A harsh or shrill call or whistle expressing disapproval or derision. —*intr.v.* To sound catcalls.

catch (kăch) *v.* **caught** (kôt), **catch·ing.** —*tr.v.* **1.** To capture or seize, esp. after a chase: *catch a criminal.* **2.** To take by trapping or snaring: *catch wild game.* **3.** To come upon suddenly, unexpectedly, or accidentally: *caught them in the act.* **4. a.** To lay hold of forcibly or suddenly; grasp: *She caught my arm as I was getting into the car.* **b.** To get hold of or grasp so as to stop the motion of: *catch a ball.* **5. a.** To overtake: *Traffic caught us in the tunnel.* **b.** To reach in time to board: *catch a plane.* **6. a.** To entangle; grip: *caught the fish in a net.* **b.** To cause to become suddenly or accidentally hooked, entangled, etc.: *I caught my sweater on the fence.* **7.** To hit; strike: *The punch caught me in the jaw.* **8.** To check (oneself) in some sort of action: *I was going to tell her about the surprise, but I caught myself in time.* **9.** To become subject to or contract, as by exposure or contagion: *catch a cold.* **10.** To become affected by or imbued with: *I caught the joyous mood of the crowd.* **11.** To take or get suddenly, momentarily, or quickly: *I caught sight of the car before it turned the corner.* **12.** To seize mentally or by the senses; apprehend: *I catch your drift.* **13.** To apprehend and reproduce accurately by or as if by artistic means: *The book caught the feeling of Victorian England.* **14.** To attract and fix; arrest: *That dress will catch their attention.* **15.** *Informal.* To see (a play, motion picture, etc.): *Let's catch a movie.* —*intr.v.* **1.** To become held, entangled, or fastened: *The lock wouldn't catch.* **2.** To act or move so as to hold someone or something. **3.** To be communicable or infectious; to spread. **4.** To take fire; kindle; burn: *The charcoal won't catch.* **5.** *Baseball.* To play catcher. —*phrasal verbs.* **catch on.** *Informal.* **1.** To understand or perceive. **2.** To become popular. **catch up. 1.** To come up from behind; overtake. **2.** To become involved with, often unwillingly: *caught up in the scandal.* **3.** To bring up to date: *catch up on one's correspondence.* **4.** To absorb completely; engross: *He is caught up in his work.* —*n.* **1.** The act of catching: *a great catch in the end zone.* **2.** Something that catches, esp. a device for fastening or for checking motion: *I broke the catch on the trunk.* **3.** Something that is caught. **4.** The amount of something caught, esp. fish. **5.** A choking or stoppage of the breath or voice. **6.** A stop or break in a mechanism. **7.** *Informal.* A person or thing worth catching. **8.** *Informal.* A tricky or unsuspected condition or drawback: *What's the catch?* **9.** A game of throwing and catching a ball. —*adj.* Designed to attract attention: *a catch phrase.* —*idioms.* **catch it.** *Informal.* To receive some form of punishment or scolding. **catch (one's) breath.** To rest so as to be able to continue. [Middle English *cacchen,* from Old North French *cachier,* to hunt, from Latin *captāre,* to chase, strive to seize, from *capere,* to seize.]

catch·all (kăch′ôl′) *n.* A box, closet, or other receptacle for odds and ends.

catch·er (kăch′ər) *n.* **1.** Someone or something that catches. **2.** *Baseball.* The player whose position is behind home plate and who signals for and receives pitches.

catch·ing (kăch′ĭng) *adj.* **1.** Infectious; contagious. **2.** Attractive; alluring.

catch·pen·ny (kăch′pĕn′ē) *adj.* Designed and made to sell without concern for quality; cheap.

catch·pole (kăch′pōl′) *n.* Also **catch·poll.** Formerly, a sheriff's officer, esp. one who arrested debtors. [Middle English *cacchepol,* from Old North French *cachepol,* "chicken chaser" : Old French *chacier,* to hunt, chase + *poul, pol,* rooster, from Latin *pullus,* young fowl.]

Catch-22 (kăch′twĕn-tē-tōō′) *n.* A paradox in which seeming alternatives actually cancel each other out, leaving no means of escape from a dilemma. [After *Catch-22* (1961), a novel by Joseph Heller (b. 1923), U.S. author.]

catch·up (kăch′əp, kĕch′-) *n.* Var. of **ketchup.**

catch·word (kăch′wûrd′) *n.* **1.** An often repeated word or slogan. **2.** *Printing.* A word placed at the head of a column or page, as in a dictionary or encyclopedia, to indicate the first or last entry on the page.

catch·y (kăch′ē) *adj.* **-i·er, -i·est. 1.** Attractive; alluring: *a catchy outfit.* **2.** Easily remembered: *a catchy tune.* **3.** Tricky; deceptive: *a catchy question.*

cat·e·chism (kăt′ĭ-kĭz′əm) *n.* **1.** A short book giving, in question-and-answer form, a brief summary of the basic principles of a religion. **2.** A question-and-answer examination, as of a political figure. [Late Latin *catēchismus,* from Late Greek *katēkhismos,* from *katēkhizein,* to catechize.]

cat·e·chist (kăt′ĭ-kĭst) *n.* A person who catechizes. —**cat′·e·chis′tic** (-kĭs′tĭk) or **cat′e·chis′ti·cal** (-kĭs′-tĭ-kəl) *adj.*

cat·e·chize (kăt′ĭ-kīz′) *tr.v.* **-chized, -chiz·ing. 1.** To teach orally (the principles of a religious creed) by means of questions and answers. **2.** To question searchingly or persistently. [Late Latin *catēchizāre,* from Late Greek *katēkhizein,* from Greek *katēkhein,* to teach by word of mouth : *kata-,* according to + *ēkhein,* to sound.] —**cat′e·chi·za′tion** (-kĭ-zā′shən) *n.* —**cat′e·chiz′er** *n.*

cat·e·chu·men (kăt′ĭ-kyōō′mən) *n.* **1.** One who is being taught the principles of Christianity; a neophyte. **2.** One who is being instructed in any subject at an elementary level. [Middle English *cathecumyn,* from Old French *cathecumene,* from Late Latin *catēchūmenus,* from Greek *katēkhein.*]

cat·e·gor·i·cal (kăt′ĭ-gôr′ĭ-kəl, -gŏr′-) or **cat·e·gor·ic** (-ĭk) *adj.* **1.** Without exception or qualification; absolute: *The answer to your request is a categorical no.* **2.** Of, concerning, or included in a category. —See Syns at **explicit.** —**cat′e·gor′i·cal·ly** *adv.* —**cat′e·gor′i·cal·ness** *n.*

cat·e·go·rize (kăt′ĭ-gə-rīz′) *tr.v.* **-rized, -riz·ing.** To put into categories; classify. —**cat′e·go·ri·za′tion** *n.*

cat·e·go·ry (kăt′ĭ-gôr′ē, -gŏr′ē) *n., pl.* **-ries.** A specifically defined division in a system of classification; a class. [Late Latin *catēgoria,* accusation, predicament, from Greek *katēgoria,* from *katēgorein,* to accuse : *kata-,* against + *agorein,* to speak publicly, from *agora,* assembly.]

cat·e·nate (kăt′n-āt′) *tr.v.* **-nat·ed, -nat·ing.** To connect in a series of ties or links; form into a chain. [From Latin *catēna,* chain.] —**cat′e·na′tion** *n.*

ca·ter (kā′tər) *intr.v.* **1.** To provide food, services, or entertainment. **2.** To provide anything wished for or needed: *politicians who cater to special interests.* —*tr.v.* To provide food service for: *cater a wedding.* —See Syns at **baby.** [From Middle English *catour,* short for *acatour,* from Norman French *acater,* to buy, from Latin *acceptāre,* to accept.] —**ca′ter·er** *n.*

cat·er-cor·nered (kăt′ər-kôr′nərd, kăt′ē-) *adj. & adv.* Var. of **cat·ty-cor·nered.**

cat·er·pil·lar (kăt′ər-pĭl′ər, kăt′ə-) *n.* **1. a.** The wormlike, often hairy or spiny larva of a butterfly or moth. **b.** Any of various similar insect larvae. **2. Caterpillar.** A trademark for a tractor equipped with a pair of endless chain treads. [Middle English *catyrpel,* prob. from Old French *catepelose,* "hairy cat."]

caterpillar

cat·er·waul (kăt′ər-wôl′) *intr.v.* To cry or screech like a cat. —*n.* A cry or screech like a cat's. [Middle English *caterw(r)awen,* perh. from Low German *katerwaulen* : *kater,* tomcat + *waulen,* to screech.]

cat·fish (kăt′fĭsh′) *n., pl.* **catfish** or **-fish·es.** Any of numerous scaleless fishes of the order Siluriformes, that characteristically has whiskerlike barbels.

cat·gut (kăt′gŭt′) *n.* A tough cord made from the dried intestines of certain animals, used for stringing musical instruments and rackets and for surgical sutures.

ca·thar·sis (kə-thär′sĭs) *n., pl.* **-ses** (-sēz′). **1.** *Med.* Purgation, esp. for the digestive system. **2.** A purifying or figurative cleansing or release of the emotions or of tension. [From Greek *katharsis,* from *kathairein,* to purge, purify, from *katharos,* pure.]

ca·thar·tic (kə-thär′tĭk) *adj.* Inducing catharsis; purgative; cleansing; purifying. —*n.* A cathartic agent or medicine, esp. a laxative.

ca·the·dral (kə-thē′drəl) *n.* **1.** The principal church of a bishop's see. **2.** Any large or important church. [Middle English *cathedral,* of a bishop's throne, from Old French, from Latin *cathedra,* chair, from Greek *kathedra,* seat : *kata-,* down + *hedra,* seat.]

cathedral

cath·e·ter (kăth′ĭ-tər) *n. Med.* A slender tube inserted into a body channel, as a vein, to distend or maintain an opening to an internal cavity. [Late Latin *catheter,* from Greek *katheter,* something inserted, from *kathienai,* send down : *kata-,* down + *hienai,* to send.]

cath·ode (kăth′ōd) *n.* **1.** Any negatively charged electrode, as of an electrolytic cell, storage battery, or electron tube. **2.** The positively charged terminal of a primary cell or of a storage battery that is supplying current. [Greek *kathodos,* way down : *kata-,* down + *hodos,* way.] —**ca·thod′ic** (kā-thŏd′ĭk) *adj.* —**ca·thod′i·cal·ly** *adv.*

cathode ray. **1.** A stream of electrons emitted by the cathode in electrical discharge tubes. **2.** An electron in such a stream.

cath·ode-ray tube (kăth′ōd-rā′). A vacuum tube in which a hot cathode emits electrons that are accelerated as a beam through a relatively high voltage anode, further focused or deflected electrostatically or electromagnetically, and allowed to fall on a fluorescent screen.

cath·o·lic (kăth′ə-lĭk, kăth′lĭk) *adj.* **1.** Universal; general; all-inclusive. **2.** Broad and comprehensive in interests, sympathies, etc.; liberal: *a person with catholic taste in literature.* [Old French *catholique,* from Late Latin *catholicus,* from Greek *katholikos,* from *katholou,* in general : *kata-,* according to + *holos,* whole.] —**ca·thol′i·cal·ly** (kə-thŏl′ĭ-klē) *adv.*

Cath·o·lic (kăth′ə-lĭk, kăth′lĭk) *adj.* **1.** Of or belonging to the whole body of Christians or the universal Christian church. **2.** Of or belonging to the ancient undivided Christian church. **3. a.** Of or designating those churches that have claimed to be representatives of the ancient undivided church: *Roman Catholic, Eastern Orthodox, Anglican,* and *Old Catholic.* **b.** Of or concerning the Roman Catholic Church. **4.** Pertaining to the Western Church as opposed to the Eastern Orthodox Church. —*n.* A member of any Catholic church, esp. Roman Catholic.

cat·i·on (kăt′ī′ən) *n.* An ion having a positive charge and, in electrolytes, characteristically moving toward a negative electrode. [Greek *kation,* from *katiena,* to go down : *kata-,* down + *ienai,* to go.] —**cat′i·on′ic** (kăt′ī-ŏn′ĭk) *adj.*

cat·kin (kăt′kĭn′) *n. Bot.* A dense, often drooping flower cluster, such as that of a birch or willow, consisting of small, scalelike flowers. [From its resemblance to a kitten's tail.]

cat nap. A short nap; light sleep.

cat·nip (kăt′nĭp′) *n.* A hairy, aromatic plant, *Nepeta cataria,* to which cats are strongly attracted.

cat-o'-nine-tails (kăt′ə-nīn′tālz′) *n.* A whip consisting of nine knotted cords fastened to a handle. [So called because it leaves marks like the scratches of a cat.]

cat's cradle. A child's game in which an intricately looped string is transferred from the hands of one player to the next.

cat's-eye (kăts′ī′) *n.* Any of various semiprecious gems displaying a band of reflected light.

cat's-paw (kăts′pô′) *n.* Also **cats·paw.** **1.** A person used by another as a dupe or tool. **2.** A light breeze that ruffles small areas of a water surface. [From a fable about a monkey that used a cat's paw to pull chestnuts out of the fire.]

cat·sup (kăt′səp, kăch′əp, kĕch′-) *n.* Var. of **ketchup.**

cat·tail (kăt′tāl′) *n.* Any of several marsh plants of the genus *Typha,* with long, straplike leaves and a dense, cylindrical head of minute brown flowers.

cat·tle (kăt′l) *pl. n.* **1.** Various animals of the genus *Bos,* esp. those of the domesticated species *B. taurus,* raised for meat and dairy products. **2.** Human beings considered or treated as having little importance. [Middle English *catel,* property, livestock, from Old North French, from Medieval Latin *capitāle,* property, from Latin *capitālis,* chief, from *caput,* head.]

cat·ty (kăt′ē) *adj.* **-ti·er, -ti·est.** **1.** Catlike; stealthy. **2.** Subtly cruel or malicious; spiteful: *a catty remark.* —**cat′ti·ly** *adv.* —**cat′ti·ness** *n.*

cat·ty-cor·nered (kăt′ē-kôr′nərd) *adj. & adv.* Also **cat·er-cor·nered** (kăt′ər-kôr′nərd, kăt′ē-), **cat·ty-cor·ner** (kăt′-ē-kôr′nər). Diagonally. [From obs. *cater,* four at dice, from Middle English, from Old French *quatre,* four, from Latin *quattuor.*]

cat·walk (kăt′wôk′) *n.* A narrow platform or pathway, as on the sides of a bridge.

Cau·ca·sian (kô-kā′zhən, -kăzh′ən) *n.* **1.** A native or inhabitant of the Caucasus. **2.** A member of the Caucasoid ethnic division. **3.** A group of isolated languages spoken in the area of the Caucasus. —*adj.* Also **Cau·cas·ic** (kô-kăs′ĭk). **1.** Of or pertaining to the Caucasus region, its people, or their languages and culture. **2.** Caucasoid.

Cau·ca·soid (kô′kə-soid′) *adj.* **1.** *Anthropol.* Of, pertaining to, or designating a major ethnic division of the human species having certain distinctive physical characteristics such as skin color varying from very light to brown and fine hair ranging from straight to wavy or curly. This division is considered to include groups of peoples indigenous to or inhabiting Europe, northern Africa, southwestern Asia, and the Indian subcontinent and persons of this ancestry in other parts of the world. **2.** Of, pertaining to, or characteristic of Caucasoids. —**Cau′ca·soid′** *n.*

cau·cus (kô′kəs) *n., pl.* **-cus·es** or **-cus·ses.** **1.** A meeting of the members of a political party or a division within a party to decide upon questions of policy and the selection of candidates for office. **2.** A meeting of any organization or division of an organization to decide policy or position. —*intr.v.* **-cused** or **-cussed, -cus·ing** or **-cus·sing.** To assemble in or hold a caucus. [Earlier *corcas,* prob. of Algonquian orig.]

cau·dal (kôd′l) *adj.* **1.** *Anat.* Of, at, or near the tail or hind parts; posterior. **2.** *Zool.* Taillike. [Latin *cauda,* tail.] —**cau′dal·ly** *adv.*

caudal fin. The tail fin of a fish.

cau·date (kô′dāt′) *adj.* Having a tail. [Latin *cauda,* tail.]

cau·dle (kôd′l) *n.* A warm beverage consisting of wine or ale mixed with sugar, eggs, bread, and various spices. [Middle English *caudel,* from Old North French, from *chaud,* warm, from Latin *cal(i)dus.*]

caught (kôt) *v.* Past tense and past participle of **catch.**

caul (kôl) *n.* A portion of the membrane that surrounds a fetus and sometimes covers its head at birth. [Middle English *calle,* prob. from Old French *cale,* cap.]

caul·dron (kôl′drən) *n.* Var. of **caldron.**

cau·li·flow·er (kô′lĭ-flou′ər, kŏl′ĭ-) *n.* **1.** A plant, *Brassica oleracea botrytis,* related to the cabbage and having an enlarged flower head. **2.** The flower head of this plant, eaten as a vegetable. [Earlier *colie-florie,* prob. from Italian *cavolofiore,* "flowered cabbage."]

cauliflower ear. An ear deformed by repeated blows.

caulk (kôk) *tr.v.* Also **calk.** **1.** *Naut.* To make (a boat) watertight by packing seams with oakum or tar. **2.** To make (pipe joints, seams, etc.) watertight or airtight by filling in cracks. [Middle English *ca(u)lken,* from Old North French *cauquer,* to trample, tread, from Latin *calcāre,* from *calx,* a heel.] —**caulk′er** *n.*

caus·al (kô′zəl) *adj.* **1.** Being or constituting a cause. **2.** Indicating or expressing a cause. —**caus′al·ly** *adv.*

cau·sal·i·ty (kô-zăl′ĭ-tē) *n., pl.* **-ties.** **1.** The relationship between cause and effect. **2.** A causal agency, force, or quality.

cau·sa·tion (kô-zā'shən) *n.* **1.** The act or process of causing. **2.** A cause. **3.** Causality.

caus·a·tive (kô'zə-tĭv) *adj.* **1.** Functioning as a cause; effective. **2.** *Gram.* Designating a verb or verbal affix that expresses causation. —**caus'a·tive·ly** *adv.*

cause (kôz) *n.* **1.** A person or thing that produces an effect, result, or consequence or that is responsible for an action or result: *research into the cause of cancer.* **2.** A reason or basis for an action, decision, or feeling; ground; reason: *no cause for alarm.* **3.** A goal or principle served with dedication and zeal: *the cause of peace; a noble cause.* **4.** The interests of a person or group engaged in a struggle: *"The cause of America is in great measure the cause of all mankind."* (Thomas Paine). **5.** *Law.* **a.** The ground for legal action. **b.** A lawsuit. —*tr.v.* **caused, caus·ing.** To be the cause of; make happen; bring about: *Germs cause disease.* [Middle English, from Old French, from Latin *causa,* reason, motive, lawsuit.] —**cause'less** *adj.*

cause cé·lè·bre (kōz' să-lĕb'rə) *pl.* **causes cé·lè·bres** (kōz' sā-lĕb'rə). *French.* An issue arousing heated public debate and partisanship; controversy.

cau·se·rie (kōz-rē') *n. French.* **1.** A chat. **2.** A short, conversational piece of writing.

cause·way (kôz'wā') *n.* A raised roadway, as across water. [Middle English *caucewei* : Old North French *cauciee,* ult. from Latin *calx,* limestone, small stone: Greek *khalix,* small stone + *wei,* way.]

caus·tic (kô'stĭk) *adj.* **1.** Able to burn, corrode, dissolve, or otherwise eat away by chemical action. **2.** Marked by sharp and bitter wit; cutting; sarcastic: *caustic remarks.* —See Syns at **sarcastic.** —*n.* A caustic material or substance. [Latin *causticus,* from Greek *kaustikos,* from *kaiein,* to burn.] —**caus'ti·cal·ly** *adv.* —**caus·tic'i·ty** (kô-stĭs'ĭ-tē) *n.*

caustic potash. Potassium hydroxide.

caustic soda. Sodium hydroxide.

cau·ter·ize (kô'tə-rīz') *tr.v.* **-ized, -iz·ing.** To burn or sear (a wound, dead tissue, etc.) with a caustic or a hot instrument in order to stop bleeding or prevent infection. [Old French *cauteriser,* from Late Latin *cautērizāre,* to brand, from Greek *kautēriazein,* from *kautērion,* branding iron.] —**cau'ter·i·za'tion** *n.*

cau·tion (kô'shən) *n.* **1.** Forethought or care so as to avoid danger or harm: *Drive with caution.* **2.** A warning; admonishment: *a word of caution.* **3.** *Informal.* Someone or something that is striking or alarming. —See Syns at **prudence.** —*tr.v.* To warn against danger; put on guard. [Middle English *caucion,* from Old French *caution,* from Latin *cautiō,* from *cavēre,* to watch, take heed.] —**cau'tion·ar'y** (-shə-nĕr'ē) *adj.*

cau·tious (kô'shəs) *adj.* Showing or practicing caution; wary. —See Syns at **careful.** —**cau'tious·ly** *adv.* —**cau'tious·ness** *n.*

cav·al·cade (kăv'əl-kād', kăv'əl-kād') *n.* **1.** A ceremonial procession, esp. of horsemen or horse-drawn carriages. **2.** A colorful procession or display. [French, from Old French, from Old Italian *cavalcare,* to ride on horseback, from Latin *caballus,* horse.]

cav·a·lier (kăv'ə-lîr') *n.* **1.** An armed horseman; knight. **2.** A gallant or chivalrous gentleman. **3. Cavalier.** A supporter of Charles I of England in his struggles against Parliament; a Royalist. —*adj.* Haughty; arrogant; disdainful: *The professor was annoyed by his student's cavalier attitude toward school.* [Old French, from Old Italian *cavaliere,* from Latin *caballus,* horse.]

cav·al·ry (kăv'əl-rē) *n., pl.* **-ries.** Troops trained to fight on horseback or in armored vehicles. [Old French *cavallerie,* from Old Italian *cavalleria,* cavalry, chivalry, from *cavaliere,* cavalier.] —**cav'al·ry·man** *n.*

cave (kāv) *n.* A hollow beneath the earth's surface, often having an opening in the side of a hill or cliff. —*intr.v.* **caved, cav·ing.** —**cave in. 1.** To fall in; collapse: *The ground caved in.* **2.** To yield or submit: *They caved in to our demands.* [Middle English, from Old French, from Latin *cava,* from *cavus,* hollow.]

ca·ve·at (kā'vē-ăt', kăv'ē-, kä'vē-ät') *n.* A warning or caution. [Latin, "let him beware," from *cavēre,* to beware.]

caveat emp·tor (ĕmp'tôr'). *Latin.* Let the buyer beware.

cave man. 1. A prehistoric man who lived in caves. **2.** *Informal.* One who is crude or brutal.

cav·ern (kăv'ərn) *n.* A large cave. [Middle English *caverne,* from Old French, from Latin *caverna,* from *cavus,* hollow.]

cav·ern·ous (kăv'ər-nəs) *adj.* **1.** Filled with caverns. **2.** Like a cavern in depth, vastness, or obscurity. **3.** Filled with cavities; porous. —**cav'ern·ous·ly** *adv.*

cav·i·ar (kăv'ē-är') *n.* Also **cav·i·are.** The roe of a sturgeon or other large fish, salted, seasoned, and eaten as a relish or delicacy. [Prob. from French, from Old Italian *caviaro,* from Turkish *havyār.*]

cav·il (kăv'əl) *intr.v.* **-iled** or **-illed, -il·ing** or **-il·ling.** To find fault unnecessarily; raise trivial objections. —*n.* A captious or trivial objection. [Old French *caviller,* from Latin *cavillārī,* to criticize, from *cavilla,* a jeering.] —**cav'il·er** *n.*

cav·i·ty (kăv'ĭ-tē) *n., pl.* **-ties. 1.** A hollow or hole. **2.** A hollow area within the body. **3.** A pitted area in a tooth caused by decay. [French *cavité,* from Late Latin *cavitās,* hollowness, from Latin *cavus,* hollow.]

ca·vort (kə-vôrt') *intr.v.* To bound or prance about playfully; to caper. [Perh. var. of CURVET.]

ca·vy (kā'vē) *n., pl.* **-vies.** Any of various short-tailed or apparently tailless South American rodents of the family Caviidae, which includes the guinea pig and the capybara. [Prob. from Galibi *cabiai.*]

caw (kô) *n.* The hoarse, raucous sound uttered by a crow or similar bird. [Imit.] —**caw** *v.*

cay (kē, kā) *n.* A small, low islet composed largely of coral or sand; a key. [Spanish *cayo,* prob. from Old French *quai,* cay, quay.]

cay·enne pepper (kī-ĕn', kā-). A condiment made from the very pungent fruit of a variety of the plant *Capsicum frutescens.* [Earlier *kian, chian,* from Tupi *kyinha.*]

cay·man (kā'mən, kā-măn', kī-) *n.* Var. of **caiman.**

cay·use (kī-yōōs') *n.* A horse, esp. an Indian pony, of the western United States. [After the Cayuse Indians.]

C clef. *Mus.* A clef sign used to form any of three clefs, soprano, alto, or tenor, by locating the tone C (261.7 cycles per second) on, respectively, the lowest line, the middle line, or the fourth (next to the highest) line of the staff.

Ce The symbol for the element cerium.

cease (sēs) *v.* **ceased, ceas·ing.** —*tr.v.* To put an end to; discontinue: *The factory ceased production.* —*intr.v.* To come to an end; stop: *The noise ceased.* —See Syns at **stop.** [Middle English *ces(s)en,* from Old French *cesser,* from Latin *cessāre,* from *cēdere,* to cede.]

cease-fire (sēs'fīr') *n.* **1.** An order to cease firing. **2.** A suspension of active hostilities; truce.

cease·less (sēs'lĭs) *adj.* Without stop; endless. —See Syns at **continuous.** —**cease'less·ly** *adv.*

ce·ca (sē'kə) *n.* Plural of **cecum.**

ce·cro·pi·a moth (sĭ-krō'pē-ə). A large North American moth, *Hyalophora cecropia,* having wings with red, white, and black markings. [After Cecrops, a legendary Greek king portrayed as half-man, half-dragon.]

cecropia moth

ce·cum (sē'kəm) *n., pl.* **-ca** (-kə). Also **cae·cum. 1.** A cavity with only one opening. **2.** *Anat.* The large blind pouch forming the beginning of the large intestine. [From Latin *(intestinum) caecum,* blind (intestine), from *caecus,* blind.] —**ce'cal** (sē'kəl) *adj.*

ă pat   ā pay   â care   ä father   ĕ pet   ē be   hw which
ōō took   ōō boot   ou out   th thin   th this   ŭ cut

ĭ pit   ī tie   î pier   ŏ pot   ō toe   ô paw, for   oi noise
û urge   zh vision   ə about, item, edible, gallop, circus

ce·dar (sē'dər) *n.* **1. a.** Any of several coniferous evergreen trees of the genus *Cedrus*, native to the Old World. **b.** Any of various similar evergreen trees, mostly of the genera *Thuja, Chamaecyparis,* and *Juniperus.* **2.** The wood of a cedar. [Middle English *cedre,* from Old French, from Latin *cedrus,* cedar, juniper, from Greek *kedros.*]

cedar waxwing. A North American bird, *Bombycilla cedrorum,* with a crested head and predominantly brown plumage. Also called **cedarbird.** [Prob. so called because it eats the berries of the red cedar.]

cede (sēd) *tr.v.* **ced·ed, ced·ing. 1.** To surrender possession of officially or formally. **2.** To yield; grant: *ceded the business to their children.* [Old French *ceder,* from Latin *cēdere,* to withdraw, yield.]

ce·dil·la (sĭ-dĭl'ə) *n.* A mark (ç) placed beneath the letter *c* to indicate that the letter is to be pronounced (s). [Obs. Spanish *cedilla,* dim. of *ceda,* the letter zee, from Late Latin *zēta,* zeta (because a small *z* was used to indicate a sibilant *c*).]

ceil·ing (sē'lĭng) *n.* **1.** The interior upper surface of a room. **2. a.** A vertical boundary of atmospheric visibility, measured from sea level to the lowest cloud layer. **b.** The maximum height at which an airplane can maintain horizontal flight under normal operating conditions. **3.** A maximum limit: *wage and price ceilings.* [Middle English *celing.*]

cel·an·dine (sĕl'ən-dīn', -dēn') *n.* A plant, *Chelidonium majus,* native to Eurasia, with deeply divided leaves and yellow flowers. [Middle English *celidoine,* from Old French, from Medieval Latin *celidonia,* from Latin *chelidonia,* from Greek *khelidōn,* swallow.]

–cele or **–coel** or **–coele.** A suffix meaning a hollow chamber: **blastocoel.** [From Greek *koilos,* hollow.]

cel·e·brant (sĕl'ə-brənt) *n.* **1.** The priest officiating at the celebration of the Eucharist. **2.** A participant in any celebration.

cel·e·brate (sĕl'ə-brāt') *v.* **-brat·ed, -brat·ing.** *—tr.v.* **1.** To observe (a day or event) with ceremonies of respect, festivity, or rejoicing: *celebrate their anniversary.* **2.** To perform (a religious ceremony): *celebrate Mass.* **3.** To extol or praise; to honor. *—intr.v.* To observe an occasion with appropriate ceremony, festivity, or merrymaking. [From Latin *celebrāre,* to fill, celebrate, from *celeber,* numerous.] **—cel'e·bra'tion** *n.* **—cel'e·bra'tor** *n.*

cel·e·brat·ed (sĕl'ə-brā'tĭd) *adj.* Famous.

ce·leb·ri·ty (sĭ-lĕb'rə-tē) *n., pl.* **-ties. 1.** A famous person. **2.** Renown; fame. [Latin *celebritās,* from *celeber,* numerous.]

ce·ler·i·ty (sə-lĕr'ĭ-tē) *n.* Swiftness; quickness; speed. —See Syns at **haste.** [Middle English *celerite,* from Old French, from Latin *celer,* swift.]

cel·er·y (sĕl'ə-rē) *n.* A plant, *Apium graveolens dulce,* native to Eurasia and widely cultivated for its edible stalks. [French *céleri,* from Italian *selero,* from Late Latin *selīnum,* from Greek *selinon.*]

ce·les·ta (sə-lĕs'tə) *n.* Also **ce·leste** (sə-lĕst'). A musical instrument having a keyboard and metal plates struck by hammers that produce bell-like tones. [French *célesta,* from *céleste,* celestial.]

ce·les·tial (sə-lĕs'chəl) *adj.* **1.** Of or pertaining to the sky or the heavens: *Planets are celestial bodies.* **2.** Of, from, or suggestive of heaven; spiritual; divine: *celestial beings; celestial radiance.* [Middle English, from Old French, from Latin *caelestis,* from *caelum,* sky, heaven.]

celestial equator. A great circle on the celestial sphere in the same plane as the earth's equator.

celestial globe. A model of the celestial sphere showing the stars and other celestial bodies.

celestial navigation. Ship or aircraft navigation based on the positions of celestial bodies.

celestial pole. Either of two diametrically opposite points at which the extensions of the earth's axis intersect the celestial sphere.

celestial sphere. An imaginary sphere of infinite extent with the earth at its center. The stars, planets, and other heavenly bodies appear to be located on its imaginary surface.

ce·li·ac (sē'lē-ăk') *adj.* Also **coe·li·ac.** Of or relating to the abdomen. [Latin *coeliacus,* from Greek *koiliakos,* from *koilia,* abdomen, from *koilos,* hollow.]

cel·i·ba·cy (sĕl'ə-bə-sē) *n.* The condition of being unmarried, esp. by reason of religious vows. [Latin *caelibātus,* from *caelebs,* unmarried.]

cel·i·bate (sĕl'ə-bĭt) *n.* One who remains unmarried, esp. by religious vow. *—adj.* Unmarried. [From Latin *caelebs,* unmarried.]

cell (sĕl) *n.* **1.** A narrow, confining room, as in a prison, asylum, or convent. **2.** A small and humble abode, such as a cave or hut. **3.** The primary organizational unit of a movement, esp. of a communist political party. **4.** *Biol.* The smallest unit of living substance, consisting in general of a tiny mass of cytoplasm enclosed by a membrane and containing a nucleus and various other structures. **5.** *Biol.* A small, enclosed cavity or space, such as a compartment in a honeycomb or within a plant ovary or an area bordered by veins in an insect's wing. **6.** *Elect.* **a.** A single unit for electrolysis or for conversion of chemical into electric energy, usu. consisting of a container with electrodes and an electrolyte. **b.** A single unit that converts radiant energy into electric energy: *a solar cell.* [Middle English *celle,* from Old French, from Latin *cella,* storeroom, chamber.]

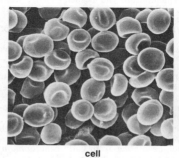

cell
Red blood cells

cello

cel·lar (sĕl'ər) *n.* **1.** A room used for storage, usu. under a building. **2.** A stock of wines. [Middle English *celer,* from Norman French, from Late Latin *cellārium,* storehouse, from Latin *cella,* storeroom, cell.]

cel·list (chĕl'ĭst) *n.* Also **'cel·list.** A person who plays the cello.

cel·lo (chĕl'ō) *n., pl.* **-los.** Also **'cel·lo.** A four-stringed instrument of the violin family, pitched lower than the viola but higher than the double bass. Also called **violoncello.** [Short for VIOLONCELLO.]

cel·lo·phane (sĕl'ə-fān') *n.* A thin, flexible, transparent cellulose material made from wood pulp and used as a moistureproof wrapping. [From CELLULOSE.]

cel·lu·lar (sĕl'yə-lər) *adj.* **1.** Pertaining to or resembling a cell. **2.** Consisting of or containing a cell or cells.

cel·lu·lase (sĕl'yə-lās', -lāz') *n.* Any of several enzymes, found in fungi, bacteria, and lower animals, that hydrolyze cellulose. [CELLUL(OSE) + -ASE.]

Cel·lu·loid (sĕl'yə-loid') *n.* A trademark for a colorless, flammable material made from nitrocellulose and camphor and used for toys, toilet articles, etc.

cel·lu·lose (sĕl'yə-lōs', -lōz') *n.* An amorphous carbohydrate polymer, $(C_6H_{10}O_5)_x$, the main constituent of all plant tissues and fibers, used in the manufacture of many fibrous products, including paper, textiles, and explosives. [French, from *cellule,* biological cell, from Latin *cella,* cell.] **—cel'lu·los'ic** (-lō'sĭk, -zĭk) *adj.*

cellulose acetate. A cellulose resin used in lacquers, photographic film, and cigarette filters.

cellulose nitrate. A tough thermoplastic, nitrocellulose.

ce·lom (sē'ləm) *n.* Var. of **coelom.**

Cel·si·us (sĕl'sē-əs, -shəs) *adj.* Of or pertaining to a temperature scale that registers the freezing point of water as 0°C and the boiling point as 100°C under normal atmospheric pressure. Also called **centigrade.** [After Anders Celsius (1701–44), Swedish astronomer, inventor of the scale.]

Celt (kĕlt, sĕlt) *n.* Also **Kelt** (kĕlt). **1.** One of an ancient people of western and central Europe, including the Britons and the Gauls. **2.** A speaker or a descendant of speakers of a Celtic language.

Celt·ic (kĕl′tĭk, sĕl′-). Also **Kelt·ic** (kĕl′tĭk). —*n.* A branch of the Indo-European family of languages consisting of Cornish, Welsh, Breton, Irish Gaelic, Scottish Gaelic, and Manx. —*adj.* Of or pertaining to the Celtic people and languages.

cel·tuce (sĕl′təs) *n.* **1.** A plant, *Lactuca sativa,* closely related to lettuce and having a composite, greenish flower head. **2.** The edible leaf stalks of this plant.

cem·ba·lo (chĕm′bə-lō′) *n., pl.* **-los.** A harpsichord. [Italian, short for *clavicembalo,* from Medieval Latin *clāvicymbalum* : Latin *clāvis,* key + *cymbalum,* cymbal.] —**cem′ba·list** *n.*

ce·ment (sĭ-mĕnt′) *n.* **1.** Any of various construction materials, consisting essentially of powdered rock and clay substances, that form a paste when mixed with water and can be molded or poured to set as a solid mass. **2.** Any substance that hardens to act as an adhesive; glue. **3.** Anything, such as an ideology, concern, or feeling, that serves to join firmly or unite. —*tr.v.* **1.** To bind with or as if with cement. **2.** To cover or coat with cement. **3.** To make binding; strengthen. —*intr.v.* To become cemented. [Middle English *siment, cyment,* from Old French *ciment,* from Latin *caementum,* rough quarried stone, from *caedere,* to cut.] —*ce·ment′er* *n.*

ce·men·ta·tion (sē′mĕn-tā′shən) *n.* The process or result of cementing.

ce·men·tum (sĭ-mĕn′təm) *n.* A bony substance covering the root of a tooth. [From Latin *caementum,* cement.]

cem·e·ter·y (sĕm′ĭ-tĕr′ē) *n., pl.* **-ies.** A place for burying the dead; graveyard. [Middle English *cimitery,* from Late Latin *coemētērium,* from Greek *koimētērion,* burial place, from *koiman,* to put to sleep.]

-cene. A suffix meaning a recent geological period: **Eocene.** [From Greek *kairos,* new, fresh.]

cen·o·taph (sĕn′ə-tăf′) *n.* A monument or empty tomb erected in honor of a dead person whose remains lie elsewhere. [Old French *cenotaphe,* from Latin *cenotaphium,* from Greek *kenotaphion,* empty tomb : *kenos,* empty + *taphos,* tomb.]

cenotaph   centaur

Ce·no·zo·ic (sē′nə-zō′ĭk, sĕn′ə-) *n.* Also **Cenozoic era.** The latest era of geologic time that began about 63 million years ago and extends to the present, characterized by the evolution of birds and mammals and of the continents in their present form. [Greek *kainos,* new, fresh + -ZOIC.]

cen·ser (sĕn′sər) *n.* A vessel in which incense is burned, esp. one swung on chains in a religious ceremony. [Middle English *censer,* from Old French *censier,* from *encens,* incense.]

cen·sor (sĕn′sər) *n.* **1.** A person authorized to examine literature, plays, etc., and who may remove or suppress sections considered morally or otherwise objectionable. **2.** In ancient Rome, one of two officials responsible for supervising the public census and public behavior and morals. —*tr.v.* To examine and expurgate. [Latin *cēnsor,* from *cēnsēre,* to assess, estimate, judge.] —**cen·so′ri·al** (sĕn-sôr′ē-əl, -sōr′-) *adj.*

cen·so·ri·ous (sĕn-sôr′ē-əs, -sōr′-) *adj.* Tending to reprimand or censure; very critical. —**cen·so′ri·ous·ly** *adv.* —**cen·so′ri·ous·ness** *n.*

cen·sor·ship (sĕn′sər-shĭp′) *n.* **1.** The act or process of censoring. **2.** The office or authority of a censor.

cen·sure (sĕn′shər) *n.* An expression of blame or disapproval. —*tr.v.* **-sured, -sur·ing.** To criticize severely; blame: *The House censured the representative for misuse of funds.* —See Syns at **blame.** [Latin *cēnsūra,* censorship, from *cēnsor,* censor.] —**cen′sur·a·ble** *adj.* —**cen′sur·er** *n.*

cen·sus (sĕn′səs) *n.* An official count of population, often including statistics on age, sex, etc. [Latin *cēnsus,* registration of citizens, from *cēnsēre,* to assess, tax.]

cent (sĕnt) *n.* **1.** A monetary unit equal to 1/100 of the dollar of the United States and Canada. **2.** A coin worth one cent. Also called **penny.** [Old French, "hundred," from Latin *centum.*]

cent-. Var. of **centi-.**

cen·taur (sĕn′tôr′) *n. Gk. Myth.* One of a race of monsters having the head, arms, and trunk of a man and the body and legs of a horse.

Cen·tau·rus (sĕn-tôr′əs) *n.* A constellation in the Southern Hemisphere near Vela and Lupus.

cen·ta·vo (sĕn-tä′vō) *n., pl.* **-vos.** A monetary unit equal to 1/100 of the basic monetary unit of Mexico and many other Latin American countries. [Spanish, "a hundredth," from Latin *centum.*]

cen·te·nar·i·an (sĕn′tə-nâr′ē-ən) *n.* A person 100 years old or older. —**cen′te·nar′i·an** *adj.*

cen·te·nar·y (sĕn-tĕn′ə-rē, sĕn′tə-nĕr′ē) *n., pl.* **-ries. 1.** A 100-year period. **2.** A 100th anniversary. [Latin *centēnārius,* of a hundred, from *centēnī,* a hundred each, from *centum,* hundred.] —**cen·ten′a·ry** *adj.*

cen·ten·ni·al (sĕn-tĕn′ē-əl) *adj.* **1.** Of or pertaining to an age or period of 100 years. **2.** Occurring once every 100 years. **3.** Of or pertaining to a 100th anniversary. —*n.* A 100th anniversary or a celebration of this. [Latin *centum,* hundred + (BI)ENNIAL.]

cen·ter (sĕn′tər). Also *Brit.* **cen·tre.** —*n.* **1.** A point equidistant from all points on the sides or outer boundaries of anything; middle. **2.** *Geom.* **a.** A point equidistant from the vertexes of a regular polygon. **b.** A point equidistant from all points on the circumference of a circle or on the surface of a sphere. **3.** A point around which something, such as a wheel, revolves; axis. **4.** A place of concentrated activity or influence: *a financial center; a shopping center.* **5.** A person or thing that is the chief object of attention, interest, activity, or emotion. **6.** A person, object, or group occupying a middle position. **7.** A political policy or group representing a compromise between the right and the left. **8. a.** *Football.* The player who lines up over and snaps the ball to the quarterback. **b.** *Basketball, Hockey, & Lacrosse.* A player who holds a middle position on the field, court, or forward line. —*modifier: a center point; a center section.* —*tr.v.* **1.** To place in or on a center: *center the vase on the table.* **2.** To gather or concentrate at a center: *center the discussion on the important issues.* **3.** *Football.* To pass (the ball) from the line to a back. —*intr.v.* **1.** To be concentrated: *Executive power centers in the President.* **2.** To have a central theme, interest, or concern; focus: *Attention centered on the baby. The debate centered on inflation.* [Middle English *centre,* from Old French, from Latin *centrum,* center, stationary point of a compass, from Greek *kentron,* sharp point, from *kentein,* to prick.]

center field. *Baseball.* The middle part of the outfield, behind second base.

center of gravity. A point in a material body through which the force equal to the sum of all the gravitational forces acting on the body acts. In a uniform gravitational field this point coincides with the center of mass.

center of mass. A point in a material body or system of material bodies that behaves as if all of the mass of the body or system were concentrated at that point and all external forces acted on that point only.

cen·ter·piece (sĕn′tər-pēs′) *n.* A decorative object or arrangement placed at the center of a dining table.

cen·tes·i·mal (sĕn-tĕs′ə-məl) *adj.* **1.** Hundredth. **2.** Pertaining to or divided into hundredths. [From Latin *centēsimus,* hundredth, from *centum,* hundred.]

centi- or **cent-.** A prefix meaning a hundredth: **centimeter.** [French, from Latin *centum,* hundred.]

cen·ti·grade (sĕn′tĭ-grād′, sän′-) *adj.* Celsius. [French :

centi-, hundred + *grade*, degree.]

cen·ti·gram (sĕn'tĭ-grăm') *n.* A unit of mass or weight equal to one hundredth (10⁻²) of a gram.

cen·time (sän'tēm'; *Fr.* săn-tēm') *n.* A monetary unit equal to ¹/₁₀₀ of the franc of France, Belgium, many other countries. [French, from *cent*, hundred, from Latin *centum*.]

cen·ti·me·ter (sĕn'tə-mē'tər, sän'-) *n.* Also **cen·ti·me·tre.** A unit of length equal to ¹/₁₀₀ of a meter or 0.3937 inch.

cen·ti·me·ter-gram-sec·ond system (sĕn'tə-mē'-tər-grăm'sĕk'ənd). A coherent system of units for mechanics, electricity, and magnetism, in which the basic units of length, mass, and time are the centimeter, gram, and second.

cen·ti·pede (sĕn'tə-pēd') *n.* Any of various wormlike arthropods of the class Chilopoda, having numerous body segments, each with a pair of legs, the front pair modified into venomous biting organs. [Latin *centipeda : centum*, hundred + *pes*, foot.]

centr-. Var. of **centro-**.

cen·tral (sĕn'trəl) *adj.* **1.** At, in, near, or being the center. **2.** Main; principal: *the central character; the central idea.* **3.** Having the dominant or controlling power or influence. —*n.* **1.** A telephone exchange. **2.** A telephone operator. —**cen'tral·ly** *adv.*

central angle. An angle having radii as sides and the center of a circle as its vertex.

cen·tral·ism (sĕn'trə-lĭz'əm) *n.* The assignment of power and authority to a central leadership in an organization. —**cen'tral·is'tic** (sĕn'trə-lĭs'tĭk) *adj.*

cen·tral·i·ty (sĕn-trăl'ĭ-tē) *n.* **1.** The condition or quality of being central. **2.** The tendency to be or remain at the center.

cen·tral·ize (sĕn'trə-līz') *v.* **-ized, -iz·ing.** —*tr.v.* To bring or come under a single, central authority. —*intr.v.* To come together at a center. —**cen'tral·i·za'tion** *n.*

central nervous system. The portion of the vertebrate nervous system consisting of the brain and spinal cord.

Central Powers. The alliance of Germany, Austria-Hungary, Bulgaria, and Turkey in World War I.

Central Standard Time. The local civil time of the 90th meridian west of Greenwich, England, six hours earlier than Greenwich time, observed in the central United States.

cen·tre (sĕn'tər) *n. & v.* Brit. var. of **center**.

cen·tric (sĕn'trĭk) or **cen·tri·cal** (sĕn'trĭ-kəl) *adj.* At, of, or having a center. —**cen'tri·cal·ly** *adv.* —**cen·tric'i·ty** (-trĭs'ĭ-tē) *n.*

cen·trif·u·gal (sĕn-trĭf'yə-gəl, -trĭf'ə-) *adj.* **1.** Moving or directed away from a center or axis. **2.** Operated by means of centrifugal force. [From Latin *centrum*, center + *fugere*, to flee.] —**cen·trif'u·gal·ly** *adv.*

centrifugal force. The apparent force, as observed from a body that is moving in a curve or rotating, that acts outward from the center of the curve or the axis of rotation.

cen·tri·fuge (sĕn'trə-fyōoj') *n.* Any apparatus or device consisting essentially of a chamber whirled about a central axis in such a way that centrifugal force propels its contents toward its outer wall. —*tr.v.* **-fuged, -fug·ing.** To separate, dehydrate, or test by means of a centrifuge.

cen·tri·ole (sĕn'trē-ōl') *n.* A tiny cylindrical organelle considered a pole of the mitotic figure and located at the center of a centrosome. [Latin *centrum*, center + *-OLE*.]

cen·trip·e·tal (sĕn-trĭp'ĭ-tl) *adj.* **1.** Directed or moving toward a center or axis. **2.** Operated by centripetal force. [From Latin *centrum*, center + *petere*, to seek.] —**cen·trip'e·tal·ly** *adv.*

centripetal force. The force acting on a body that moves in a curve or rotates about an axis that acts toward the center of the curve or the axis of rotation.

cen·trist (sĕn'trĭst) *n.* A person who takes a position in the political center; a moderate. [CENTR(O)- + -IST.] —**cen'trism** *n.*

centro- or **centr-.** A prefix meaning center: **centrist**. [From Greek *kentron*, center.]

cen·tro·some (sĕn'trə-sōm') *n.* A small mass of cytoplasm containing the centriole. [CENTRO- + -SOME (body).]

cen·tu·ri·on (sĕn-tōōr'ē-ən, -tyōōr'-) *n.* An officer commanding a century in the ancient Roman army. [From Latin *centuriō*, from *centuria*, century.]

cen·tu·ry (sĕn'chə-rē) *n., pl.* **-ries. 1.** A period of 100 years. **2.** Each of the successive periods of 100 years before or since the advent of the Christian era. **3.** A unit of the ancient Roman army, orig. consisting of 100 men. [Latin *centuria*, a group of a hundred, from *centum*, hundred.]

century plant. Any of several fleshy plants of the genus *Agave*, some species of which bloom only once in 10 to 20 years and then die.

cephal-. Var. of **cephalo-**.

ce·phal·ic (sə-făl'ĭk) *adj.* **1.** Of or relating to the head or skull. **2.** Located on, in, or near the head. [Old French *cephalique*, from Latin *cephalicus*, from Greek *kephalikos*, from *kephalē*, head.]

cephalo- or **cephal-.** A prefix meaning head: **cephalopod**. [Latin, from Greek *kephalo-*, from *kephalē*, head.]

ceph·a·lo·pod (sĕf'ə-lə-pŏd') *n.* Any of various mollusks of the class Cephalopoda, such as an octopus or nautilus, with a beaked head, an internal shell in some species, and prehensile tentacles. [CEPHALO- + -POD.]

ceph·a·lo·tho·rax (sĕf'ə-lə-thôr'ăks', -thōr'-) *n.* The anterior section of arachnids and many crustaceans, consisting of the fused head and thorax. [CEPHALO- + THORAX.]

-cephalous. A suffix meaning a head: **hydrocephalous**. [From Greek *kephalē*, head.]

-cephalus. A suffix meaning an abnormality of the head: **hydrocephalus**.

Ce·phe·id (sē'fē-ĭd, sĕf'ē-) *n.* Any of a class of intrinsically variable stars with highly regular light variations. [After the constellation *Cepheus*, which contains such a variable star.]

Ce·pheus (sē'fyōōs', -fē-əs) *n.* **1.** *Gk. Myth.* An Ethiopian king, father of Andromeda. **2.** A constellation in the Northern Hemisphere near Cassiopeia and Draco.

ce·ram·ic (sə-răm'ĭk) *n.* **1.** Any of various hard, brittle, heat-resistant and corrosion-resistant materials made by firing clay or other minerals and consisting of one or more metals in combination with a nonmetal, usu. oxygen. **2.** Often **ceramics. a.** Objects made of ceramic. **b.** (*used with a sing. verb*). The art or technique of making objects of ceramic, esp. from fired clay or porcelain. [Prob. French *céramique*, "of pottery," from Greek *keramos*, potter's clay, earthenware.] —**ce·ram'ist** *n.*

Cer·ber·us (sûr'bər-əs) *n. Gk. & Rom. Myth.* The three-headed dog guarding the entrance of Hades.

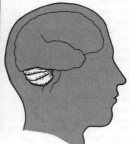

Cerberus   cerebellum

cere (sîr) *n.* A fleshy or waxlike swelling at the base of the upper part of the beak in certain birds, such as parrots. [Middle English *sere*, from Old French *cire*, from Medieval Latin *cēra*, from Latin, wax.]

ce·re·al (sîr'ē-əl) *n.* **1.** An edible grain such as wheat, oats, or corn. **2.** A grass producing such a grain. **3.** A food prepared from such a grain. —*modifier: cereal grains.* [Latin *cereālis*, of grain, "of Ceres."]

cer·e·bel·lum (sĕr'ə-bĕl'əm) *n., pl.* **-lums** or **-bel·la** (-bĕl'ə). The structure of the brain responsible for regulation and coordination of complex voluntary muscular movement, located at the rear of the skull. [Medieval Latin, from Latin, dim. of *cerebrum*, brain.] —**cer'e·bel'lar** (-bĕl'ər) *adj.*

cer·e·bra (sĕr'ə-brə, sə-rē'-) *n.* A plural of **cerebrum**.

cer·e·bral (sĕr'ə-brəl, sə-rē'-) *adj.* **1.** Of or pertaining to the brain or cerebrum. **2.** Appealing to the intellect.

cerebral cortex. The outer layer of gray tissue that covers the two parts of the cerebrum, responsible for most of the higher functions of the nervous system.

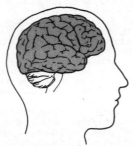

cerebral cortex

cerebral hemisphere. Either hemisphere of the cerebrum of the brain, divided by the longitudinal cerebral fissure.

cerebral palsy. Weakness and lack of coordination of the muscles, resulting from damage to the brain usu. at or before birth.

cer·e·brate (sĕr′ə-brāt′) *intr.v.* **-brat·ed, -brat·ing.** To think; ponder. [Back-formation from CEREBRATION.]

cer·e·bra·tion (sĕr′ə-brā′shən) *n.* The action of thinking; thought. [From Latin *cerebrum*, cerebrum.]

cer·e·bro·spi·nal (sĕr′ə-brō-spī′nəl, sə-rē′-) *adj.* Of or pertaining to the brain and spinal cord. [CEREBR(UM) + SPINAL.]

cerebrospinal fluid. The serumlike fluid that bathes the lateral ventricles of the brain and the cavity of the spinal cord.

cerebrospinal meningitis. An acute infectious epidemic meningitis that is often fatal. Also called **spinal meningitis.**

cer·e·brum (sĕr′ə-brəm, sə-rē′-) *n.,* pl. **-brums** or **-bra** (-brə). The large, rounded structure of the brain that fills most of the skull and is divided by a deep groove into two parts that are joined at the bottom. [Latin, brain.]

cere·cloth (sîr′klôth′, -klŏth′) *n.* Cloth coated with wax, formerly used for wrapping the dead.

cere·ment (sîr′mənt) *n.* Also **cere·ments** (-məntz). A shroud used to wrap a dead body.

cer·e·mo·ni·al (sĕr′ə-mō′nē-əl) *adj.* Of or characterized by ceremony. —*n.* **1.** A ceremony. **2.** The formal rules of ceremony observed in social life, religious worship, etc. —**cer′e·mo′ni·al·ly** *adv.*

Usage: **ceremonial, ceremonious.** *Ceremonial* is applied principally to things and *ceremonious* to persons and things. In addition, *ceremonial* is essentially a general categorizing term referring to ceremony: *ceremonial garb; a ceremonial occasion. Ceremonious* stresses formality and display: *a ceremonious welcome; a ceremonious person.*

cer·e·mo·ni·ous (sĕr′ə-mō′nē-əs) *adj.* **1.** Fond of ceremony; formally polite. **2.** Characterized by ceremony; rigidly formal. —See Usage note at **ceremonial.** —**cer′e·mo′ni·ous·ly** *adv.* —**cer′e·mo′ni·ous·ness** *n.*

cer·e·mo·ny (sĕr′ə-mō′nē) *n.,* pl. **-nies. 1.** A formal act or set of acts performed as prescribed by ritual, custom, or etiquette: *a wedding ceremony.* **2.** A conventional social gesture or act without intrinsic purpose: *The chairman ignored the ceremony of asking for comments.* **3.** Strict observance of formalities or etiquette: *was welcomed with ceremony.* [Middle English *ceremonie,* from Old French, from Latin *caerimōnia,* sacredness, religious rite.]

Ce·res (sîr′ēz′) *n.* **1.** *Rom. Myth.* The goddess of agriculture, identified with the Greek goddess Demeter. **2.** The first asteroid to be discovered (1801), having an orbit between Mars and Saturn.

ce·re·us (sîr′ē-əs) *n.* Any of several tall tropical American cacti of the genus *Cereus* or other genera. [Latin, candle (from its shape).]

ce·rise (sə-rēs′, -rēz′) *n.* Deep to vivid purplish red. [French, from Old French, cherry.]

ce·ri·um (sîr′ē-əm) *n. Symbol* **Ce** A lustrous, iron-gray, malleable, metallic rare-earth element that occurs chiefly in the minerals monazite and bastnaesite, exists in four allotropic states, is a constituent of lighter flint alloys, and is used in various metallurgical and nuclear applications. Atomic number 58; atomic weight 140.12; melting point 795°C; boiling point 3,468°C; specific gravity 6.67 to 8.23; valences 3, 4. [After the asteroid *Ceres.*]

cer·met (sûr′mĕt′) *n.* A material consisting of ceramic particles bonded with metal and used in high-strength and high-temperature applications. [CER(AMIC) + MET(AL).]

cer·tain (sûr′tn) *adj.* **1.** Having no doubt; positive: *Are you certain that you left the book here?* **2.** Established beyond doubt or question; definite: *Whether he will do it is not certain.* **3.** Sure to come or happen; inevitable: *certain death.* **4.** Not named or specified but assumed to be known: *There are certain laws for automobile safety.* **5.** Named but not familiar or well-known: *a certain Mr. Smith.* **6.** Some but not much; limited: *to a certain degree.* —*idiom.* **for certain.** Surely; without doubt: *It will happen for certain.* [Middle English, from Old French, ult. from Latin *cernere,* to decide, determine.] —**cer′tain·ly** *adv.*

Usage: **certain.** Although *certain* seems to be an absolute term incapable of comparison, the word is frequently qualified by *more* and *most: Nothing could be more certain than that.*

cer·tain·ty (sûr′tn-tē) *n.,* pl. **-ties. 1.** The fact, condition, or quality of being certain: *We feel no certainty that she will arrive tonight.* **2.** A clearly established fact.

Syns: **certainty, certitude, confidence, conviction, surety** *n.* Core meaning: Freedom from doubt (*denied the rumor with absolute certainty*).

cer·tif·i·cate (sər-tĭf′ĭ-kĭt) *n.* **1.** A document testifying to a fact, qualification, or promise: *a birth certificate.* **2.** A document issued to a person completing a course of study not leading to a diploma. **3.** A document certifying that a person may officially practice in certain professions, such as teaching. —*tr.v.* (sər-tĭf′ĭ-kāt′) **-cat·ed, -cat·ing.** To furnish with, testify to, or authorize by a certificate. [Middle English *certificat,* from Old French, from Late Latin *certificāre,* certify.]

cer·ti·fi·ca·tion (sûr′tə-fĭ-kā′shən) *n.* **1.** The act of certifying or certificating. **2.** The condition of being certified. **3.** A certified document or statement.

cer·ti·fied (sûr′tə-fīd′) *adj.* **1.** Guaranteed in writing; vouched for; endorsed. **2.** Holding a certificate.

certified check. A check guaranteed by a bank to be covered by sufficient funds on deposit.

certified mail. Uninsured first-class mail whose delivery is recorded by having the addressee sign for it.

certified public accountant. A public accountant who has received a certificate stating that he has met the state's legal requirements.

cer·ti·fy (sûr′tə-fī′) *v.* **-fied, -fy·ing.** —*tr.v.* **1. a.** To confirm formally as true, accurate, or genuine; testify to or vouch for in writing. **b.** To guarantee as meeting a standard; attest: *certify a teacher.* **2.** To assure or make certain; tell positively. —*intr.v.* To testify: *certify to the facts.* [Middle English *certifien,* from Old French *certifier,* from Late Latin *certificāre,* to make certain : Latin *certus,* certain + *facere,* to make.] —**cer′ti·fi′a·ble** *adj.* —**cer′ti·fi′a·bly** *adv.* —**cer′ti·fi′er** *n.*

cer·ti·tude (sûr′tĭ-tōōd′, -tyōōd′) *n.* The condition of being certain; complete assurance. —See Syns at **certainty.** [Middle English, from Late Latin *certitūdō,* from Latin *certus,* certain.]

ce·ru·le·an (sə-rōō′lē-ən) *adj.* Sky-blue; azure. [From Latin *caeruleus,* from Latin *caelum,* sky.]

ce·ru·men (sə-rōō′mən) *n.* A yellowish waxy secretion of the external ear; earwax. [From Latin *cēra,* wax.]

cer·vi·cal (sûr′vĭ-kəl) *adj.* Of or pertaining to a neck or a cervix.

cer·vi·ces (sûr′vĭ-sēz′, sûr-vī′sēz′) *n.* A plural of **cervix.**

cer·vine (sûr′vīn′) *adj.* Of, resembling, or characteristic of a deer. [Latin *cervīnus,* from *cerbus,* deer.]

cer·vix (sûr′vĭks) *n.,* pl. **-vix·es** or **-vi·ces** (-vĭ-sēz′, sûr-vī′sēz′). **1.** The neck. **2.** Any neck-shaped anatomical structure, as the narrow outer end of the uterus. [Latin *cervīx,* neck.]

Ce·sar·e·an or **Ce·sar·i·an** (sĭ-zâr′ē-ən) *adj.* Vars. of **Caesarean.**

ă pat   ā pay   â care   ä father   ĕ pet   ē be   hw which
ŏŏ took   ōō boot   ou out   th thin   *th* this   ŭ cut
ĭ pit   ī tie   î pier   ŏ pot   ō toe   ô paw, for   oi noise
û urge   zh vision   ə about, item, edible, gallop, circus

ce·si·um (sē′zē-əm) n. Also **cae·si·um.** *Symbol* **Cs** A soft, silvery-white ductile metal, liquid at room temperature, the most electropositive and alkaline of the elements. It is used in photoelectric cells and to catalyze hydrogenation of some organic compounds. Atomic number 55; atomic weight 132.905; melting point 28.5°C; boiling point 690°C; specific gravity 1.87; valence 1. [From Latin *caesius*, bluish-gray (from its blue spectral lines).]

ces·sa·tion (sĕ-sā′shən) n. The act of ceasing or stopping; a halt; discontinuance. [Middle English *cessacioun*, from Latin *cessāre*, to cease.]

ces·sion (sĕsh′ən) n. **1.** An act of ceding; a surrendering, as of territory to another country by treaty. **2.** A ceded territory. [Middle English, from Old French, from Latin *cessiō*, from *cēdere*, to yield.]

cess·pool (sĕs′pōōl′) n. **1.** A covered hole or pit for receiving sediment or drained sewage. **2.** A filthy place. [Var. of earlier *cesperalle*, drainpipe, from Middle English *suspiral*, from Old French *souspirail*, breathing hole, from Latin *suspīrāre*, to breathe out.]

ces·tode (sĕs′tōd′) n. Any flatworm of the class Cestoda, which includes tapeworms. [New Latin *Cestoidea*, "ribbon-shaped ones" : Latin *cestus*, belt + -OID.]

ce·su·ra (sĭ-zhōōr′ə, -zōōr′ə) n. Var. of **caesura.**

ce·ta·cean (sĭ-tā′shən) adj. Also **ce·ta·ceous** (-shəs). Of or belonging to the order Cetacea, which includes fishlike aquatic mammals such as the whale and porpoise. —n. An aquatic mammal of the order Cetacea. [From Latin *cētus*, whale, from Greek *kētos*.]

Ce·tus (sē′təs) n. A constellation in the equatorial region of the Southern Hemisphere near Aquarius and Eridanus.

Cf The symbol for the element californium.

cha-cha (chä′chä′) n. Also **cha-cha-cha** (chä-chä-chä′). A rhythmic ballroom dance that originated in Latin America. [American Spanish *cha-cha-cha.*]

chae·tog·nath (kē′tŏg-năth′) n. Any of various marine worms of the phylum Chaetognatha, which includes the arrow worms. [New Latin *Chaetognatha*, "bristle-jaw" (so named from the spines at the jaws) : Greek *khaitē*, long hair + *gnathos*, jaw.]

chafe (chāf) v. **chafed, chaf·ing.** —tr.v. **1.** To wear away or irritate by rubbing: *This collar chafes my neck.* **2.** To annoy; vex: *Arrogance always chafes me.* **3.** To heat or warm by rubbing. —intr.v. **1.** To become worn or sore from rubbing: *Her skin chafes easily.* **2.** To be or become annoyed; feel irritation or impatience: *chafe at the delay.* —See Syns at **annoy.** —n. **1.** Warmth, wear, or soreness produced by friction. **2.** Annoyance; irritation; vexation. [Middle English *chaufen*, from Old French *chauf(f)er*, to warm (by rubbing), from Latin *calefacere* : *calēre*, to be warm + *facere*, to make.]

cha·fer (chā′fər) n. Any of various beetles of the family Scarabaeidae. [Middle English *cheaffer*, from Old English *ceafor*.]

chaff¹ (chăf) n. **1.** The husks of grain after separation from the seed. **2.** Finely cut straw or hay used as fodder. **3.** Trivial or worthless matter. [Middle English *chaf(f)*, from Old English *ceaf*.]

chaff² (chăf) tr.v. To make fun of good-naturedly; to tease. —intr.v. To engage in good-natured teasing. —n. Good-natured teasing; banter. [Prob. from CHAFF (trivia).]

chaf·fer (chăf′ər) intr.v. **1.** To bargain or haggle. **2.** To bandy words. [Middle English *cheapfare*, trade, merchandise.] —**chaf′fer·er** n.

chaf·finch (chăf′ĭnch) n. A small European songbird, *Fringilla coelebs*, with predominantly reddish-brown plumage. [Middle English *chaffynche*, from Old English *ceaffinc*.]

chafing dish. A dish set above a heating device, used to cook or maintain the warmth of food at the table.

cha·grin (shə-grĭn′) n. A feeling of embarrassment or humiliation caused by failure or disappointment. —tr.v. To cause to feel chagrin. [French, grief.]

chain (chān) n. **1.** A connected, flexible series of links, usu. of metal, used for binding, connecting, transmitting motion, etc. **2. chains.** Bonds, fetters, or shackles. **3. chains.** Captivity or oppression; bondage. **4.** Any series of connected or related things. **5.** A number of establishments, such as stores or theaters, under common ownership or management. **6.** A mountain range. **7.** *Chem.* A group of atoms bonded in a spatial configuration resembling a chain. **8. a.** A measuring instrument for surveying or engineering, consisting of 100 linked pieces of iron or steel. **b.** The length of this instrument as a unit of length, equal to 100 links or about 20 meters or 66 feet. —tr.v. **1.** To bind or make fast with a chain or chains. **2.** To bind or fetter; confine. [Middle English *chayne*, from Old French *chaine*, from Latin *catēna*.]

chain gang. A group of convicts chained together.

chain mail. Flexible armor of joined metal links or scales.

chain reaction. **1.** A series of events, each of which induces or otherwise influences its successor: *the chain reaction of decaying cities, poverty, and delinquency.* **2.** *Physics.* A multistage nuclear reaction of this kind, esp. a self-sustaining series of fissions in which the average number of neutrons produced per unit of time exceeds the number absorbed or lost. **3.** *Chem.* A series of reactions in which one product of a reacting set is a reactant in the following set.

chain saw. A power saw with teeth linked in an endless chain.

chain-smoke (chān′smōk′) v. **-smoked, -smok·ing.** —intr.v. To smoke cigarettes or cigars in continuing succession. —tr.v. To smoke (cigarettes or cigars) in continuing succession. —**chain smoker.**

chain stitch. A decorative stitch in which loops are connected like the links of a chain.

chain store. Any of a number of retail stores under the same ownership.

chair (châr) n. **1.** A piece of furniture consisting of a seat, legs, back, and often arms, designed to accommodate one person. **2.** A seat of office, authority, or dignity, as that of a bishop. **3.** The office or position of a person having authority: *named to the chair in Renaissance literature at the university.* **4.** The person who presides over a meeting: *All questions should be addressed to the chair.* **5.** *Slang.* The electric chair. **6.** A seat carried about on poles; a sedan chair. —tr.v. **1.** To install in a position of authority. **2.** To preside over (a meeting). [Middle English *chaiere*, from Old French *chaiere*, from Latin *cathedra*, from Greek *kathedra*, : *kata-*, down + *hedra*, seat.]

   Usage: chair, chairman, chairperson. These three nouns are interchangeably used to refer to one who presides over a group. The terms *chair* and *chairman* can also be used as verbs.

chair lift. A cable-suspended, power-driven chair assembly used to transport people up or down mountains.

chair·man (châr′mən) n. **-men** (-mĭn). One who presides over an assembly, meeting, committee, or board; chair. —tr.v. **-manned, -man·ning.** To act as chairman of. —**chair′man·ship′** n. —See Usage note at **chair.**

chair·per·son (châr′pûr′sən) n. A person who presides over an assembly, meeting, committee, or board; chair. —See Usage note at **chair.**

chair·wom·an (châr′wŏom′ən) n. A woman who presides over an assembly, meeting, committee, or board; chair.

chaise (shāz) n. **1.** Any of various light, open carriages, often with a collapsible hood, esp. a two-wheeled carriage drawn by one horse. **2.** A **post chaise.** [French, chair, seat, from Old French, var. of *chaiere*, chair.]

chaise longue (shāz lông′) pl. **chaise longues** or **chaises longues** (shāz lông′). A reclining chair with a seat long enough to support the outstretched legs of the sitter. [French, "long chair."]

chal·ced·o·ny (kăl-sĕd′n-ē) n., pl. **-nies.** A translucent to

chafing dish

transparent milky or grayish quartz with distinctive microscopic crystals arranged in slender fibers in parallel bands, used as a gemstone. [Middle English *calcedonie*, from Late Latin *chalcēdonius*, from Greek *khalkēdōn*, a mystical stone.]

chal·cid (kăl′sĭd) *n.* Any of various minute wasps of the superfamily Chalcidoidea, of which the larvae of many species are parasitic on the larval stages of other insects. [From New Latin *Chalcis*, "copper (fly)" (from its metallic color and sheen), from Greek *khalkos*, copper.]

chal·co·cite (kăl′kə-sīt′) *n.* An important copper ore, essentially CuS_2. [French *chalcos(ine)*, from Greek *khalkos*, copper.]

chal·co·py·rite (kăl′kə-pī′rīt′) *n.* An important copper ore, essentially $CuFeS_2$. [New Latin *chalcopyrites* : Greek *khalkos*, copper + PYRITE.]

Chal·de·an (kăl-dē′ən) *n.* **1. a.** A member of an ancient Semitic people who ruled in Babylonia. **b.** The Semitic language of the Chaldeans. **2.** A person versed in occult learning; an astrologer, soothsayer, or sorcerer. —**Chal·da′ic** (-dā′ĭk) *n. & adj.* —**Chal·de′an** *adj.*

cha·let (shă-lā′) *n.* **1.** A dwelling with a gently sloping overhanging roof, common in Alpine regions. **2.** A house built in this style. [French.]

chal·ice (chăl′ĭs) *n.* **1.** A cup or goblet. **2.** A cup for the consecrated wine of the Eucharist. **3.** A cup-shaped blossom. [Middle English, from Norman French, from Latin *calix*, cup, goblet.]

chalice   chameleon

chalk (chôk) *n.* **1.** A soft mineral composed chiefly of compact calcium carbonate, $CaCO_3$, generally gray-white or yellow-white and derived mainly from fossil seashells. **2.** A piece of chalk or a chalklike substance, frequently colored, used for marking on a blackboard or other surface. —*tr.v.* **1.** To mark, draw, or write with chalk. **2.** To smear or cover with chalk. —*phrasal verb.* **chalk up. 1.** To earn or score. **2.** To credit: *Chalk that up to experience.* [Middle English, from Old English *cealc*, from Latin *calx*, stone, from Greek *khalix*.]

chalk·board (chôk′bôrd′, -bōrd′) *n.* A panel, usu. green or black, for writing on with chalk; a blackboard.

chalk·y (chô′kē) *adj.* **-i·er, -i·est. 1.** Of or containing chalk. **2.** Resembling chalk. —**chalk′i·ness** *n.*

chal·lenge (chăl′ənj) *n.* **1.** A call to engage in a contest or fight. **2.** A demand for an explanation; a calling into question. **3.** A sentry's demand for identification. **4.** The quality of requiring full use of one's abilities, energy, or resources: *a career that offers a challenge.* **5.** A claim that a vote is invalid or that a voter is unqualified. **6.** *Law.* A formal objection, esp. to the qualifications of a juror or jury. —*v.* **-lenged, -leng·ing.** —*tr.v.* **1.** To call to engage in a contest or fight. **2.** To take exception to; dispute: *I challenge his statement.* **3.** To order to halt and be identified. **4.** *Law.* To object formally to (a juror or jury, for example). **5.** To have due claim to; call for. **6.** To summon to action, effort, or use; stimulate. [Middle English *c(h)alenge*, accusation, challenge, from Old French, from Latin *calumnia*, false accusation, from *calvī*, to deceive.] —**chal′lenge·a·ble** *adj.* —**chal′leng·er** *n.*

chal·lis (shăl′ē) *n.* Also **chal·lie.** A lightweight fabric of wool, cotton, or rayon, usu. having a printed pattern. [Poss. from the surname *Challis*.]

cham·ber (chām′bər) *n.* **1.** A room in a house, esp. a bed-

room. **2.** Often **chambers.** A judge's office. **3.** A room in a palace or official residence where an important personage receives visitors. **4.** A hall for the meeting of an assembly, esp. a legislative assembly. **5.** A legislative, judicial, or deliberative assembly. **6.** A board or council. **7.** Any enclosed space or compartment; cavity. **8. a.** An enclosed space at the bore of a gun that holds the charge. **b.** The part of a cylinder of a revolver that receives the cartridge. —*tr.v.* To put in or as if in a chamber; enclose; confine. [Middle English *chambre*, from Old French, from Latin *camera*, vault, arched roof, from Greek *kamara*, chamber.]

cham·bered nautilus (chām′bərd). A cephalopod mollusk, *Nautilus pompilius*, of the Pacific and Indian oceans, with a coiled and partitioned shell lined with a pearly layer.

cham·ber·lain (chām′bər-lĭn) *n.* **1.** An official who manages the household of a sovereign or nobleman; a chief steward. **2.** An official who receives the rents and fees of a municipality; a treasurer. [Middle English *chamberleyn*, from Old French *chamberlenc*, ult. from Late Latin *camera*, chamber.]

cham·ber·maid (chām′bər-mād′) *n.* A woman who cleans and cares for bedrooms, now chiefly in hotels.

chamber music. Music appropriate for performance in a private room or small concert hall and composed for a small group of instruments such as a trio or quartet.

chamber of commerce. An association of businessmen and merchants for the promotion of business interests in its community.

chamber pot. A portable vessel used as a toilet.

cham·bray (shăm′brā′) *n.* A fine, lightweight type of gingham cloth, woven with white threads across a colored warp. [After *Cambrai*, France.]

cha·me·leon (kə-mēl′yən, -mē′lē-ən) *n.* Any of various tropical Old World lizards of the family Chamaeleonidae, characterized by their ability to change color. [Middle English *camelion*, from Latin *chamaeleōn*, from Greek *khamaileōn*, "ground lion" : *khamai*, on the ground + *leōn*, lion.]

cham·fer (chăm′fər) *tr.v.* **1.** To cut off the edge or corner of; bevel. **2.** To cut a groove in; flute. —*n.* A flat surface made by cutting off the edge or corner of something, as a block of wood. [Perh. a back-formation from *chamfering*, beveling, from French *chanfrein*, from Old French *chanfraindre*, to break the edge off : Latin *canthus*, iron ring of a wheel + *frangere*, to break.]

cham·ois (shăm′ē) *n., pl.* **cham·ois** (shăm′ēz). **1.** A hoofed mammal, *Rupicapra rupicapra*, of mountainous regions of Europe, having upright horns with backward-hooked tips. **2.** Also **cham·my** or **sham·my.** *pl.* **-mies.** The soft leather made from the hide of this animal or others such as deer or sheep. [Old French, prob. from Late Latin *camox*.]

cham·o·mile or **cam·o·mile** (kăm′ə-mīl′) *n.* **1.** Any of various plants of the genus *Anthemis*, esp. *A. nobilis*, an aromatic plant with finely dissected leaves and white flowers. **2.** Any of several similar plants of the genus *Matricaria*, esp. *M. chamomilla*. [Middle English *camomille*, from Old French, from Latin *chamaemēlon*, from Greek *khamaemēlon*, "earth-apple" : *khamai*, on the ground + *mēlon*, apple.]

champ¹ (chămp) *v.* Also **chomp** (chŏmp). —*tr.v.* **1.** To bite upon with restlessness or impatience: *champ a pencil.* **2.** To chew upon noisily: *He champs his food like a wild animal.* —*intr.v.* To work the jaws and teeth vigorously: *champ on the bit.* —*idiom.* **champ at the bit.** To be impatient. [Perh. imit.]

champ² (chămp) *n. Informal.* A champion.

cham·pagne (shăm-pān′) *n.* A sparkling white wine produced in Champagne, a region of France.

cham·paign (shăm-pān′) *n.* Level and open country; a plain. [Middle English *champayn*, from Old French *champagne*, ult. from Latin *campus*, plain, field.]

cham·pi·on (chăm′pē-ən) *n.* **1.** Someone or something acknowledged as the best of all, having defeated others in competition. **2.** A person who fights for or defends a cause, movement, etc. —*tr.v.* To fight for or defend (a cause, movement, etc.); support. [Middle English *champi(o)un*, from Old French *champion*, prob. ult. from Latin *campus*, field.]

cham·pi·on·ship (chăm′pē-ən-shĭp′) *n.* **1. a.** The position or title of a champion. **b.** A contest held to determine a champion. **2.** Defense or support: *He was well known for his championship of human rights.*

chance (chăns) *n.* **1. a.** A force that controls the happening of events without any causes that can be seen or understood; the way things happen: *Let's leave our next meeting to chance.* **b.** An unexpected or fortuitous event; accident. **2.** The likelihood that something will happen; probability; possibility: *She has little chance of winning.* **3.** An opportunity: *She will not give him a chance to talk.* **4.** A risk or gamble: *You're taking a chance by disobeying instructions.* **5.** A raffle or lottery ticket. —See Syns at **opportunity.** —*modifier:* a *chance meeting with a friend.* —See Syns at **accidental.** —*v.* **chanced, chanc·ing.** —*intr.v.* To happen by accident; occur by chance: *It chanced that she was there too.* —*tr.v.* To take the risk or hazard of: *He chanced another throw of the dice.* —*phrasal verb.* **chance on** (or **upon**). To find or meet accidentally; happen upon: *chanced on an old friend today.* [Middle English, from Old French, from Latin *cadere,* to fall, happen.]

chan·cel (chăn′səl) *n.* The space around the altar of a church for the clergy and choir. [Middle English *chauncel,* from Old French *chancel,* from Late Latin *cancellus,* altar, from Latin *cancer,* lattice.]

chan·cel·ler·y (chăn′sə-lə-rē, -slə-rē) *n., pl.* **-ies. 1.** The rank or position of a chancellor. **2.** The office or department of a chancellor or the building in which it is located. **3.** The official place of business of an embassy or consulate.

chan·cel·lor (chăn′sə-lər, -slər) *n.* **1.** The chief minister of state in some European countries. **2.** The head of a university. **3.** The presiding judge of a court of equity. [Middle English *cha(u)nceler,* from Norman French *chanceler,* from Old French *chancelier,* from Late Latin *cancellārius,* secretary, doorkeeper, from *cancellus,* grating, altar, from Latin *cancer,* lattice.] —**chan′cel·lor·ship′** *n.*

Chancellor of the Exchequer. In the British government, the highest minister of finance and a member of the Cabinet.

chan·cer·y (chăn′sə-rē) *n., pl.* **-ies. 1.** A court of equity. **2.** An office for the collection and safekeeping of official documents. **3.** The office of an embassy or consulate; chancellery. [Middle English *chancerie,* from *chancelerie,* chancellery.]

chan·cre (shăng′kər) *n.* A dull-red, hard, insensitive sore that forms on the skin and is an early sign of syphilis. [French, from Latin *cancer,* ulcer, cancer.]

chanc·y (chăn′sē) *adj.* **-i·er, -i·est.** Uncertain as to outcome; risky; hazardous.

chan·de·lier (shăn′də-lîr′) *n.* A branched fixture, usu. suspended from a ceiling, that holds a number of light bulbs or candles. [French, from Old French, from Latin *candēlābrum,* candelabrum.]

chandelier

chan·dler (chănd′lər) *n.* **1.** A person who makes or sells candles. **2.** A dealer in goods or equipment of a specified kind, esp. for ships. [Middle English *chandeler,* from Old French *chandelier,* from *c(h)andelle,* candle, from Latin *candēla,* candle.] —**chan′dler·y** *n.*

change (chānj) *v.* **changed, chang·ing.** —*tr.v.* **1.** To cause to be different; alter: *change the spelling of a word.* **2.** To give a completely different form or appearance to; transform: *Irrigation changed the desert to fertile land.* **3.** To give and receive reciprocally; interchange: *Will you change places with me?* **4.** To exchange for or replace by another, usu. of the same kind or category: *change one's shirt.* **5.** To lay aside, abandon, or leave for another; switch: *change planes.* **6.** To give or receive the equivalent of (money) in lower denominations or in foreign currency: *change a dollar.* **7.** To put fresh clothes or coverings on: *change a bed.* —*intr.v.* **1.** To become different or altered: *Some insects change as they mature.* **2.** To make an exchange. **3.** To transfer from one vehicle to another: *When he flew to the Coast he changed in Chicago.* **4.** To put on other clothing: *She changed for the party.* **5.** To become deeper in tone: *As the vocal cords thicken, boys' voices change.* —*n.* **1.** The act, process, or result of changing: *the change of seasons.* **2. a.** The money of smaller denomination exchanged for a unit of higher denomination: *Will you give me change for a dollar?* **b.** The money returned when the amount given in paying for something exceeds what is due. **c.** Coins: *change jingling in one's pocket.* **3.** Something different that can be used, done, etc., for variety; a break in one's routine: *eat early for a change.* **4.** A different or fresh set of clothing. [Middle English *changen,* from Old French *changier,* from Late Latin *cambiāre.*] —**chang′er** *n.* —**change′less** *adj.*

Syns: change, alter, modify, mutate, turn, vary *v.* Core meaning: To make or become different (*an event that changed the world; a face that had changed with age; changed the liquid into gas*).

change·a·ble (chānj′ə-bəl) *adj.* **1.** Liable to change: *changeable moods.* **2.** Capable of being altered: *changeable behavior.* **3.** Changing color or appearance when seen from different angles: *changeable taffeta.* —See Syns at **capricious.** —**change′a·bil′i·ty** or **change′a·ble·ness** *n.* —**change′a·bly** *adv.*

change·ful (chānj′fəl) *adj.* Given to frequent changes; variable.

change·ling (chānj′lĭng) *n.* A child secretly exchanged for another.

change of life. The menopause.

change·o·ver (chānj′ō′vər) *n.* A change from one activity, system, way of doing something, etc., to another, esp. in equipment or production techniques.

chan·nel (chăn′əl) *n.* **1.** The depression or cut in the earth through which a river or stream passes. **2.** A part of a river or harbor deep enough to form a passage for ships. **3.** A broad strait: *the English Channel.* **4.** A tubular passage for liquids. **5.** Any course or way through which news, ideas, etc., may travel: *opening new channels of information.* **6.** A band of radio-wave frequencies reserved for broadcasting or communication: *a television channel.* **7.** A trench, furrow, or groove. **8. channels.** Official routes of communication: *go through channels to get a final decision.* —*tr.v.* **-neled** or **-nelled, -nel·ing** or **-nel·ling. 1.** To make or cut channels in or through. **2.** To form a channel or groove in. **3.** To direct or guide along a desired course or route. [Middle English *chanel,* from Old French, from Latin *canālis,* canal.]

chan·nel·ize (chăn′ə-līz′) *tr.v.* **-ized, -iz·ing.** To channel. —**chan′nel·i·za′tion** *n.*

chan·son (shäN-sôN′) *n.* A song, esp. a French one. [French, from Old French, from Latin *cantāre,* to sing.]

chant (chănt) *n.* **1. a.** A short, simple melody in which a number of syllables or words are sung on the same note and the rhythm is controlled largely by the words. **b.** A melody of this kind, traditionally used with a religious text: *a Gregorian chant.* **2.** A monotonous rhythmic call or shout: *the chant of the crowd at the campaign rally.* —*tr.v.* **1.** To sing or intone to a chant. **2.** To call out in a monotonous, rhythmic way. —*intr.v.* **1.** To sing, esp. in the manner of a chant. **2.** To speak or shout monotonously. [Middle English, prob. from *chanten,* to sing, from Old French *chanter,* from Latin *cantāre,* from *canere,* to sing.]

chan·teuse (shän-tœz′) *n.* A woman singer, esp. a nightclub singer. [French, fem. of *chanteur,* singer.]

chan·tey (shăn′tē, chăn′-) *n., pl.* **-teys.** Also **chan·ty** (shăn′tē) *pl.* **-ties.** A song sung by sailors to the rhythm of their movements while working. [Prob. from French *chantez,* imper. of *chanter,* to sing.]

ă pat   ā pay   â care   ä father   ĕ pet   ē be   hw which
ŏŏ took   ōō boot   ou out   th thin   *th* this   ŭ cut
ĭ pit   ī tie   î pier   ŏ pot   ō toe   ô paw, for   oi noise
û urge   zh vision   ə about, item, edible, gallop, circus

chan·ti·cleer (chăn′tĭ-klîr′, shăn′-) *n.* A cock or rooster. [Middle English *Chantecleer*, from Old French *Chantecler* (the cock in the fable *Reynard the Fox*) : *chanter*, to sing + *cler*, clear.]

chan·ty (shăn′tē) *n.*, *pl.* **-ties.** Var. of **chantey**.

Cha·nu·kah (κHä′nŏŏ-kə) *n.* Also **Ha·nuk·kah** or **Ha·nu·kah.** A Jewish festival, usu. in Dec., lasting eight days. It commemorates the victory of the Maccabees over the Syrians in 165 B.C. and the rededication of the Temple at Jerusalem. Also **Feast of Lights.** [Hebrew *hanukkāh*, "dedication."]

cha·os (kā′ŏs′) *n.* **1.** Any condition or place of great disorder or confusion. **2.** Often **Chaos.** The shapeless and disordered state of matter and space supposed to have existed before the creation of the universe. **3.** *Obs.* A vast abyss or chasm. [Latin, from Greek *khaos*, empty space, chaos.]

cha·ot·ic (kā-ŏt′ĭk) *adj.* In a state of chaos; in great disorder or confusion. **—cha·ot′i·cal·ly** *adv.*

chap¹ (chăp) *v.* **chapped, chap·ping.** **—tr.v.** To cause (the skin) to split or roughen, esp. as a result of cold or exposure. **—intr.v.** To split or become rough and sore. **—n.** A soreness and roughening of the skin caused by cold or exposure. [Middle English *chappen*.]

chap² (chăp) *n. Informal.* A man or boy; a fellow. [Short for CHAPMAN.]

chap·ar·ral (shăp′ə-răl′, chăp′-) *n.* A dense growth of tangled, often thorny shrubs and small trees, esp. in the southwestern United States and Mexico. [Spanish, from *chaparro*, evergreen oak.]

cha·peau (shă-pō′) *n.*, *pl.* **-peaux** (-pōz′) or **-peaus** (-pōz′). A hat. [French, from Old French *chapel*, from Late Latin *cappa*, head covering, from Latin *caput*, head.]

chap·el (chăp′əl) *n.* **1. a.** A small church. **b.** A small place, with its own altar, within a church. **2.** A place for religious services in a school, hospital, etc. **3.** Religious services held at a chapel. **4.** In England, any place of worship for those not connected with or not members of the Established Church. [Middle English, from Old French *chapele*, from Medieval Latin *capella*, (orig. a shrine containing the cape of St. Martin of Tours), dim. of Late Latin *cappa*, cape.]

chap·er·on (shăp′ə-rōn′) *n.* Also **chap·er·one.** **1.** An older person who attends and supervises a dance or party for young unmarried people. **2.** An older or married woman who accompanies a young unmarried woman in public. **—tr.v.** To act as a chaperon. [French, "hood," protection, from Old French *chape*, cape, from Late Latin *cappa*.] **—chap′er·on·age** (-rō′nĭj) *n.*

chap·fall·en (chăp′fô′lən, chŏp′-) *adj.* Dejected; disheartened; crestfallen. [From *chaps*, var. of CHOPS.]

chap·lain (chăp′lən) *n.* **1.** A clergyman attached to a chapel. **2.** A clergyman or layman who conducts religious services for a legislative assembly or other organization. **3.** A clergyman attached to a military unit. [Middle English *chapeleyn*, from Old French *chapelain*, from Medieval Latin *cappellānus*, from *capella*, chapel.] **—chap′lain·cy** or **chap′lain·ship′** *n.*

chap·let (chăp′lĭt) *n.* **1.** A wreath or garland for the head. **2.** *Rom. Cath. Ch.* A string of prayer beads having one third the number of a rosary's beads. **3.** Any string of beads. [Middle English *chapelet*, from Old French, dim. of *chapel*, chapeau.]

chap·man (chăp′mən) *n. Brit.* A peddler. [Middle English, from Old English *cēapman* : *cēap*, trade + *man*, man.]

chaps¹ (chăps, shăps) *pl.n.* Heavy leather trousers without a seat, worn by cowboys to protect their legs. [Short for Mexican Spanish *chaparreras*.]

chaps² (chăps) *n.* Var. of **chops**.

chap·ter (chăp′tər) *n.* **1.** Any of the main divisions of a book or other writing, usu. numbered or titled. **2.** A period or sequence of events, as in history or a person's life, that marks a distinct change of pattern. **3.** A local branch of a club, fraternity, etc. **4.** *Eccles.* The members or representatives of a religious house, community, or order. [Middle English *chapitre*, from Old French, from Late Latin *capitulum*, from Latin, small head, from *caput*, head.]

char¹ (chär) *v.* **charred, char·ring. —tr.v.** **1.** To burn the surface of; scorch. **2.** To reduce to charcoal by incomplete combustion. **—intr.v.** **1.** To become scorched. **2.** To be-come reduced to charcoal. **—n.** A substance that has been charred; charcoal. [Back-formation from CHARCOAL.]

char² (chär) *n.*, *pl.* **char** or **chars.** Also **charr.** Any of several fishes of the genus *Salvelinus*, related to the trout. [Orig. unknown.]

char³ (chär) *n.* Also *Brit.* **chare** (châr). **1.** A chore or odd job, esp. a household task. **2.** A charwoman. **—intr.v.** **charred** or **chared, char·ring** or **char·ing.** **1.** To do small jobs, tasks, or chores. **2.** To work as a charwoman. [Middle English *char(re)*, piece of work, from Old English *cerr*, *cyrr*, piece of work, a turning.]

char·a·banc (shăr′ə-băng′) *n. Brit.* A large bus, often used for sightseeing. [French *char à bancs*, "carriage with benches."]

char·a·cin (kăr′ə-sĭn) *n.* Any of numerous chiefly tropical freshwater fishes of the family Characidae. [From Greek *kharax*, a kind of fish.]

char·ac·ter (kăr′ĭk-tər) *n.* **1.** The combination of qualities or features that makes one person, group, or thing different from another. **2.** One such distinguishing feature or attribute; a characteristic. **3.** The combined moral or ethical structure of a person or group. **4.** Moral or ethical strength; integrity; fortitude. **5.** A person portrayed in a novel, play, movie, etc. **6.** *Informal.* A person who is appealingly odd, humorous, or eccentric. **7.** A person; individual: *He's a tough character.* **8.** Status; role; capacity: *in his character as father.* **9.** A symbol, such as a letter or number, used in representing information, as in printing or writing. **—idiom. in** (or **out of**) **character.** Consistent (or not consistent) with someone's general character or behavior. [Middle English *caracter*, from Old French *caractere*, from Latin *charactēr*, character, mark, from Greek *kharaktēr*, engraved mark, brand, from *kharassein*, to brand, from *kharax*, pointed stake.]

char·ac·ter·is·tic (kăr′ĭk-tə-rĭs′tĭk) *adj.* Indicating a special feature of or showing the character of a person or thing; typical: *the characteristic quiet of the countryside.* **—n.** **1.** Something characteristic of a person or thing; a feature or quality. **2.** *Math.* The integral part of a logarithm as distinguished from the mantissa. **—char·ac·ter·is′ti·cal·ly** *adv.*

Syns: characteristic, distinctive, individual, peculiar, typical, vintage *adj.* Core meaning: Serving to identify or set apart an individual or group (*the zebra's characteristic stripes; behavior characteristic of psychopaths*).

char·ac·ter·ize (kăr′ĭk-tə-rīz′) *tr.v.* **-ized, -iz·ing.** **1.** To describe the character or qualities of; portray. **2.** To be a characteristic or quality of. **—char′ac·ter·i·za′tion** *n.* **—char′ac·ter·iz′er** *n.*

cha·rade (shə-rād′) *n.* **1. a. charades** (*used with a sing. or pl. verb*). A game in which words or phrases are acted out in pantomime until guessed by the other players. **b.** An instance of acting out a word or phrase in this way. **2.** Something thought to resemble a charade, as a pretense. [French, from Provençal *charrado*, chat, from *charra*, to chat.]

char·coal (chär′kōl′) *n.* **1.** A black, porous material composed chiefly of carbon, produced by heating wood or sometimes bone until the lighter materials in it are driven off as smoke. It is used as a fuel, a filtering material, and for drawing. **2.** A stick of this material, used for drawing. **—modifier:** *a charcoal fire; a charcoal drawing.* **—tr.v.** To draw, write, or blacken with charcoal. [Middle English *charcole*, perh. from Old French *charbon*, charcoal, carbon + *cole*, coal.]

chard (chärd) *n.* A variety of beet, *Beta vulgaris cicla*, with large, succulent leaves that are eaten as a vegetable. Also **Swiss chard.** [French *carde*, edible stalks of the cardoon, from Old French, cardoon, from Latin *carduus*, artichoke.]

chare (châr) *n. & v. Brit.* Var. of **char** (chore).

charge (chärj) *v.* **charged, charg·ing. —tr.v.** **1.** To entrust with a duty, responsibility, task, or obligation. **2.** To place an order or injunction upon; command. **3.** To instruct, warn, or urge authoritatively: *charged the jury.* **4.** To blame; accuse: *They charged him with the crime.* **5.** To set or ask (a given amount) as a price or payment: *The grocer charged a dollar for a dozen eggs.* **6.** To hold financially liable; demand payment from: *charged her for the balance due.* **7.** To postpone payment on by recording the amount owed: *Charge the groceries to my account.* **8.** To attack violently: *The soldiers charged the fort.* **9.** To fill; load: *charge a gun.* **10.** *Elect.* **a.** To make (something) electrically positive or negative. **b.** To pass or receive electrical energy into (a device, such as a storage battery or capacitor, that is capable of storing it). **11.** To excite or intensify: *The argument was charged with emotion.* —*intr.v.* **1.** To rush in or as if in a forceful attack: *The bullfighter stepped aside as the bull charged.* **2.** To demand or ask payment: *The hospital charged for the x-rays.* —See Syns at **command.** —*n.* **1.** An amount asked or made as payment. **2.** Care; supervision; control: *the scientist in charge of the experiment.* **3.** Someone or something for which one is responsible. **4.** A duty, responsibility, or obligation. **5.** An order or command: *a judge's charge to the jury.* **6.** An accusation, esp. one made formally, as in a legal case: *arrested on a false charge.* **7.** A rushing, forceful attack: *a cavalry charge.* **8. a.** The property of matter that accounts for all electrical effects and by which objects not in contact can exert forces on each other independent of gravity. It occurs in two forms, positive charge and negative charge, with like charges repelling each other and unlike charges attracting each other. **b.** A measure of this property. **c.** The amount of this property possessed by an object or particle or enclosed within a region of space. **d.** The amount of electricity, as measured by this property, that can be drawn from a storage battery or the like. **9.** An amount of explosive to be set off at one time. **10.** *Informal.* A feeling of pleasant excitement; a thrill. **11.** *Heraldry.* A bearing or figure. [Middle English *chargen,* to load, from Old French *chargier,* from Late Latin *carricāre,* from Latin *carrus,* a kind of vehicle.] —**charge'a·ble** *adj.*

charge account. A business arrangement, as with a store, in which a customer receives goods or services and pays for them at a later time.

char·gé d'af·faires (shär-zhā' də-fâr') *pl.* **char·gés d'affaires** (shär-zhā', shär-zhāz'). **1.** A governmental official temporarily placed in charge of diplomatic affairs while the ambassador or minister is absent. **2.** A diplomatic representative of the lowest rank. [French, "(one) charged with affairs."]

charg·er[1] (chär'jər) *n.* **1.** One that charges. **2.** A horse trained for battle; a war-horse. **3.** A device used to charge electric storage batteries.

char·ger[2] (chär'jər) *n.* *Archaic.* A large, shallow dish; platter. [Middle English *chargeour.*]

char·i·ot (chăr'ē-ət) *n.* A horse-drawn two-wheeled vehicle, used in ancient times in battle, processions, etc. [Middle English, from Old French, from *char,* vehicle, from Latin *carrus.*]

chariot

charm

char·i·o·teer (chăr'ē-ə-tîr') *n.* A person who drives a chariot.

cha·ris·ma (kə-rĭz'mə) *n.* **1.** A rare quality or power of individuals who show exceptional ability for winning the devotion of large numbers of people. **2.** *Theol.* A divinely inspired gift or power, such as the ability to perform miracles. [Greek *kharisma,* favor, divine gift, from *kharizesthai,* to favor, from *kharis,* grace, favor.] —**char·is·mat·ic** (kăr'ĭz-măt'ĭk) *adj.*

char·i·ta·ble (chăr'ĭ-tə-bəl) *adj.* **1.** Showing love or good will; full of kindness. **2.** Generous in giving help to the needy. **3.** Tolerant or lenient in judging others. **4.** Of, for,

or concerned with helping the needy: *a charitable organization.* —**char'i·ta·bly** *adv.*

char·i·ty (chăr'ĭ-tē) *n., pl.* **-ties. 1.** Good will or brotherly love toward others: *"With malice toward none, with charity for all"* (Abraham Lincoln). **2.** Tolerance and leniency in judging others. **3.** A kind or generous act. **4.** Help or relief to the needy: *raising money for charity.* **5.** An institution or fund established to help the needy: *a ten-dollar donation to a charity.* [Middle English *charite,* Christian love, from Old French, from Latin *cāritās,* love, regard, from *cārus,* dear.]

char·la·tan (shär'lə-tən) *n.* A person who deceives others by falsely claiming to have expert knowledge or skill in a special subject or field of activity; a quack. —See Syns at **impostor.** [French, from Italian *cerretano,* inhabitant of *Cerreto,* village near Spoleto, Italy, famous for its quacks.] —**char'la·tan·ism** *n.* —**char'la·tan·ry** *n.*

char·ley horse (chär'lē). *Informal.* A muscle cramp or stiffness, esp. in the leg. [Orig. unknown.]

char·lotte russe (shär'lət rōōs'). A cold dessert of Bavarian cream set in a mold lined with ladyfingers. [French, "Russian *charlotte*" (a cold dessert).]

charm (chärm) *n.* **1.** The power or ability to please, delight, or attract; appeal. **2.** A personal quality or manner that attracts or wins over others: *What others try to accomplish with force or threats, Roland does with charm.* **3.** A saying, action, etc., supposed to have magical power; a magic spell. **4.** An object kept or worn for its supposed magical effect, as in warding off evil; an amulet. **5.** A trinket or small ornament worn hanging on a bracelet, chain, etc. —*tr.v.* **1.** To please, attract, or delight; fascinate. **2.** To win over; beguile: *He charmed his opponents into letting him have his way.* **3.** To act upon with or as if with magic; bewitch. —*intr.v.* **1.** To be alluring or pleasing. **2.** To act as an amulet or charm. **3.** To use spells. —*idiom.* **like a charm.** Exceedingly well; perfectly. [Middle English *charme,* chant, magic spell, from Old French, from Latin *carmen,* song, incantation.]

Syns: **charm, bewitch, enchant, enthrall, entrance, spellbind, witch** *v.* *Core meaning:* To act on with or as if with magic (*charmed her captors into releasing her unharmed*).

charm·ing (chär'mĭng) *adj.* Delightful; attractive; very pleasing: *a charming girl; charming manners.*

char·nel (chär'nəl) *n.* Often **charnel house.** A building, room, or vault in which the bones or bodies of the dead are placed. —*adj.* Resembling, suggesting, or suitable for receiving the dead. [Middle English, from Old French, from Late Latin *carnālis,* carnal, from Latin *carō,* flesh.]

Char·on (kâr'ən, kăr'-) *n.* *Gk. Myth.* The ferryman who conveyed the dead to Hades over the river Styx.

charr (chär) *n.* Var. of **char** (fish).

chart (chärt) *n.* **1.** Something written or drawn, as a table or graph, that presents information in an organized, easily viewed form. **2.** A map showing coastlines, water depths, or other information of use to navigators. **3.** An outline map on which special information, as weather data, can be plotted. —*tr.v.* **1.** To show or record on a chart; make a chart of: *chart the daily changes in temperature.* **2.** To plan by or as if by means of a chart: *chart a course.* [Old French *charte,* from Latin *charta,* papyrus leaf, paper.]

char·ter (chär'tər) *n.* **1.** Often **Charter.** A written grant or document from a ruler, government, etc., giving certain rights to the people, a group or organization. **2.** A document, such as a constitution, stating the principles, function, and form of a governing body or organization: *The United Nations is governed by a charter.* **3.** The hiring or renting of a bus, aircraft, boat, etc., for a special use. —*tr.v.* **1.** To grant a charter to. **2.** To hire or rent by charter. [Middle English *chartre,* from Old French, from Latin *chartula,* dim. of *charta,* papyrus leaf.] —**char'ter·er** *n.*

char·treuse (shär-trōōz', -trōōs', -trœz') *n.* **1. a.** A yellow, pale-green, or white liqueur made by the Carthusian monks. **b.** Chartreuse. A trademark for this liqueur. **2.** A light yellowish green. —*adj.* Light yellowish green. [French, after *la Grande Chartreuse,* a Carthusian monastery near Grenoble, where it was first made.]

char·wom·an (chär'wŏŏm'ən) *n.* *Brit.* A woman employed to do cleaning in an office building or a household. [CHAR (chore) + WOMAN.]

char·y (châr′ē) *adj.* **-i·er, -i·est. 1.** Cautious; wary: *chary of walking on thin ice.* **2.** Not free or wasteful; sparing: *chary of compliments.* [Middle English *charig*, cherished, dear, from Old English *cearig*, sorrowful.] **—char′i·ly** *adv.* **—char′i·ness** *n.*

Cha·ryb·dis (kə-rĭb′dĭs) *n. Gk. Myth.* A whirlpool off the Sicilian coast, opposite the cave of Scylla.

chase¹ (chās) *v.* **chased, chas·ing. —tr.v. 1.** To go quickly after and try to catch or overtake; pursue: *The policeman chased the thief.* **2.** To follow (game) in order to capture or kill; to hunt. **3.** To put to flight; drive away: *chased off the dog. —intr.v.* **1.** To go or follow in pursuit. **2.** *Informal.* To go hurriedly; rush: *chased aimlessly about the city. —n.* **1.** The act of chasing; rapid pursuit. **2. the chase.** The sport of hunting game. **3.** A person or thing that is hunted or pursued; a quarry. **4.** *Brit.* A privately owned, unenclosed game preserve. [Middle English *chacen*, from Old French *chasser*, from Latin *captāre*, to seize, from *capere*, to take.]

chase² (chās) *n. Printing.* A rectangular steel or iron frame into which pages or columns of type are locked for printing or plate making. [Prob. from French *châsse*, a case, frame, from Latin *capsa*, box, case.]

chase²

chase³ (chās) *n.* **1.** A groove cut in any object; slot. **2.** A trench or channel for drainpipes or wiring. *—tr.v.* **chased, chas·ing. 1.** To decorate (metal) with engraved or embossed designs. **2.** To groove; indent. [Old French *chas*, "enclosure," from Latin *capsa*, box.]

chas·er (chā′sər) *n.* **1.** A person or thing that chases or pursues. **2.** A gun on the bow or stern of a ship, used during pursuit or flight. **3.** *Informal.* A drink of water, beer, etc., taken after hard liquor.

chasm (kăz′əm) *n.* **1.** A deep crack in the earth's surface; a gorge. **2.** Any marked difference of opinion, interests, loyalty, etc.: *chasms in communication.* [Latin *chasma*, from Greek *khasma*.]

chas·seur (shă-sûr′) *n.* A soldier, esp. one of certain light cavalry or infantry troops of the French army, trained for rapid maneuvers. [French, from Old French *chaceour*, from *chacier*, to chase.]

Chas·si·dim (кнä-sē′dĭm) *pl.n.* The less frequently used singular is **Chas·sid** (кнä′sĭd). Also **Has·si·dim** or **Ha·si·dim.** An Orthodox Jewish group, founded in Poland in about 1750, emphasizing joyous and intense devotion to God. [Hebrew *hasīdhīm*, "pious ones," from *hāsīdh*, pious.] **—Chas·si′dic** (-dĭk) *adj.*

chas·sis (shăs′ē, chăs′ē) *n., pl.* **chassis** (shăs′ēz, chăs′ēz). **1.** The metal frame of an automobile or similar vehicle, including the engine, wheels, axles, gears, brakes, and steering system but excluding the body. **2.** The structure that holds and supports the parts of a radio, phonograph, or other piece of electronic equipment. [French *châssis*, from Old French *chassis*, ult. from Latin *capsa*, box.]

chaste (chāst) *adj.* **1.** Not having experienced sexual intercourse or not having engaged in sexual intercourse with a person to whom one is not married. **2.** Morally pure; virtuous. **3.** Not ornate or extreme in literary or artistic style; simple. [Middle English, from Old French, from Latin *castus*, morally pure.] **—chaste′ly** *adv.* **—chaste′ness** *n.*

chas·ten (chā′sən) *tr.v.* **1.** To punish in order to discipline or correct; chastise. **2.** To cause to become subdued or meek; temper: *a spirit chastened by experience.* **3.** To re-

fine; purify. [Var. of obs. *chaste*, from Middle English *chasten*, from Old French *chastier*, from Latin *castigāre*, to castigate.] **—chas′ten·er** *n.*

chas·tise (chăs-tīz′) *tr.v.* **-tised, -tis·ing.** To punish for misbehavior or wrongdoing: *the firm manner of a strict mother chastising a bad boy.* [Middle English *chastisen*, var. of *chasten*, to chasten.] **—chas·tis′a·ble** *adj.* **—chas·tise′ment** (chăs-tīz′mənt, chăs′tĭz-) *n.* **—chas·tis′er** *n.*

chas·ti·ty (chăs′tĭ-tē) *n.* **1.** The condition or quality of being chaste; moral purity. **2.** Celibacy; virginity.

chas·u·ble (chăz′ə-bəl, chăzh′-, chăs′-) *n.* A long, sleeveless vestment worn over the alb by the priest at Mass. [French, from Old French, from Late Latin *casubla*, hooded garment.]

chat (chăt) *intr.v.* **chat·ted, chat·ting.** To converse in a relaxed, friendly, informal manner. *—n.* **1.** A relaxed, friendly, informal conversation. **2.** Any of several birds known for their chattering call, esp. a North American bird, *Icteria virens.* [Middle English *chatten*, short for *chatteren*, to chatter.]

cha·teau or **châ·teau** (shă-tō′) *n., pl.* **-teaux** (-tōz′). **1.** A French castle or manor house. **2.** A large, impressive country house. [French *château*, from Old French *chastel*, from Latin *castellum*, castle.]

chat·e·laine (shăt′l-ān′) *n.* **1.** The lady or mistress of a castle, chateau, or large, fashionable household. **2.** A clasp or chain worn by a woman at the waist for holding keys or a watch.

chat·tel (chăt′l) *n.* **1.** An article of personal property that can be moved or transferred from place to place, as distinguished from a house or land. **2.** A slave. [Middle English *chatel*, property, goods, from Old French, from Medieval Latin *capitāle*, capital.]

chat·ter (chăt′ər) *intr.v.* **1.** To utter rapid, wordless sounds that resemble speech, as some animals and birds do. **2.** To talk rapidly and at length about something unimportant; jabber. **3.** To make a rapid series of rattling or clicking noises: *His teeth chattered with cold. The machine gun chattered. —tr.v.* To utter in a rapid and aimless way. *—n.* **1.** Aimless talk about unimportant matters. **2.** The sharp, rapid sounds made by some birds or animals. **3.** Any series of quick rattling or clicking sounds. [Middle English *chat(t)eren* (imit.).] **—chat′ter·er** *n.*

chat·ter·box (chăt′ər-bŏks′) *n.* An extremely talkative person.

chat·ty (chăt′ē) *adj.* **-ti·er, -ti·est. 1.** Fond of or full of informal conversation. **2.** Having the tone or effect of informal conversation: *a chatty book about life in the White House.* **—chat′ti·ly** *adv.* **—chat′ti·ness** *n.*

chauf·feur (shō′fər, shō-fûr′) *n.* A person who is hired to drive an automobile. [French, stoker, from *chauffer*, to warm, from Old French *chaufer*.]

chau·vin·ism (shō′və-nĭz′əm) *n.* **1.** Militant and boastful devotion to one's country or a cause; fanatical patriotism. **2.** Prejudiced belief in the superiority of one's own group: *male chauvinism.* [French *chauvinisme*, after Nicolas Chauvin, legendary French soldier extremely devoted to Napoleon.] **—chau′vin·ist** *n.* **—chau′vin·is′tic** *adj.* **—chau′vin·is′ti·cal·ly** *adv.*

cheap (chēp) *adj.* **-er, -est. 1.** Low in price; inexpensive or comparatively inexpensive: *Tomatoes are cheap this week.* **2.** Charging low prices: *a cheap restaurant.* **3.** Requiring little effort: *a cheap victory.* **4.** Of or considered of little value: *Life was very cheap.* **5.** Of poor quality; inferior: *cheap, badly made shoes.* **6.** In low or poor taste; vulgar: *cheap humor.* **7.** Not spending or giving money generously; stingy. **8.** *Econ.* **a.** Obtainable at a low rate of interest. **b.** Devalued, as in buying power. *—adv.* At a low price; inexpensively. [From Middle English *chep*, sale, bargain, from Old English *cēap*, ult. from Latin *caupō*, trader.] **—cheap′ly** *adv.* **—cheap′ness** *n.*

Syns: 1. cheap, inexpensive, low *adj. Core meaning:* Low in price (*cheap vegetables*). **2. cheap, cheesy** (*Slang*), **common, crummy** (*Slang*), **lousy** (*Slang*), **paltry, poor, rotten** (*Informal*), **shoddy** *adj. Core meaning:* Of very inferior quality (*cheap merchandise*). See also Syns at **stingy.**

cheap·en (chē′pən) *tr.v.* **1.** To make cheap or cheaper. **2.** To disparage; belittle. *—intr.v.* To become cheap or cheaper. **—See Syns at lower. —cheap′en·er** *n.*

cheap·skate (chēp′skāt′) n. Slang. A stingy person; miser. [CHEAP + SKATE (chap).]

cheat (chēt) tr.v. **1.** To deprive of something dishonestly or unfairly; defraud or swindle: cheated the Indians of their land. **2.** To elude or escape as if by trickery or deception: The mountain climbers cheated death. —intr.v. **1.** To act dishonestly; practice fraud: cheat at cards. **2.** Informal. To be unfaithful to one's spouse. —n. **1.** A person who cheats; swindler. **2.** The action of someone who cheats; a fraud or swindle. [Middle English cheten, to revert, short for acheten, var. of escheten, from eschete, revision of land, from Old French : Latin ex-, out + cadere, to fall.] —cheat′er n.

check (chĕk) tr.v. **1.** To stop, restrain, or control: She checked a sudden impulse to giggle. **2.** To test, examine, or make sure of, as for correctness or good condition: He checked the number in the telephone directory. **3.** To note or consult for information, permission, etc.: He checked the temperature each morning. **4.** To mark with a sign to show that something has been noted or chosen or is correct: Read the sentences below, and check the statements that are true. **5.** To place for temporary safekeeping: They checked their baggage at the airport. **6.** To mark with a pattern of squares: Her apron is checked in white and blue. **7.** Chess. To move so as to place (the opponent's king) under direct attack. **8.** Ice Hockey. To impede an opponent in control of the puck, either by using the body to block the opponent or by jabbing at the puck with the hockey stick. —intr.v. **1.** To come to an abrupt halt; stop; pause. **2.** To correspond item for item; agree: His list checked with hers. **3.** To make an investigation to determine accuracy or verification: check on the date of the conference. **4.** To crack in a pattern of checks, as paint. **5.** Chess. To place an opponent's king in check. —See Syns at stop. —phrasal verbs. check in. To register, as at a hotel. check out. **1.** To leave after going through a required procedure, as after paying a hotel bill. **2.** To take after having counted or recorded and, often, after paying: check out groceries at a supermarket; check out books from the library. —n. **1.** A stop; halt. **2.** A restraint or control: keeping a check on one's impulses. **3.** Careful examination or investigation to determine accuracy, efficiency, etc., or to control or regulate: keeping close check on his lands and possessions. **4.** A standard for testing or comparing. **5.** A mark made to show that something has been noted or selected or is accurate. **6.** Also Brit. cheque. A written order to a bank to pay a certain amount from funds on deposit. **7.** A ticket or slip for identifying and claiming something: a baggage check. **8.** A bill at a restaurant. **9. a.** A pattern of squares resembling a checkerboard. **b.** A single square in such a pattern. **c.** A fabric printed or woven with such a pattern. **10.** Chess. The situation of the king when under threat of direct attack by an opponent's piece. **11.** Ice Hockey. The act of impeding an opponent in control of the puck, either by blocking his progress with the body or by jabbing at the puck with the stick. —idiom. in check. Under restraint; in control. [Middle English chek, attack, check at chess, from Old French eschec, from Arabic shāh, king, check at chess, from Persian, king.] —check′a·ble adj.

check·book (chĕk′bŏŏk′) n. A book or booklet containing blank checks, given by a bank to a depositor who has a checking account.

check·er (chĕk′ər) n. Also chiefly Brit. chequ·er. **1. a. checkers** (used with a sing. verb). A game played on a checkerboard by two players, each using 12 pieces. Each player tries to capture all of his opponent's pieces. Also Brit. **draughts. b.** One of the round, flat pieces used in this game. **2.** One of the squares in a pattern of many squares. **3.** A person who receives items for temporary storage or safekeeping: a baggage checker. **4.** A cashier. —tr.v. To mark with a pattern of squares. [Middle English, from cheker, chessboard, from Old French eschequier, from eschec, check.]

check·er·ber·ry (chĕk′ər-bĕr′ē) n. **1.** A plant, the wintergreen. **2.** The red, edible, spicy berry of this plant. [Checker, a kind of fruit + BERRY.]

check·er·board (chĕk′ər-bôrd′, -bōrd′) n. A game board divided into 64 squares of alternating colors, on which the game of checkers or chess may be played.

check·ered (chĕk′ərd) adj. **1.** Marked with or divided into squares. **2.** Having light and dark patches, as a pattern of sunlight and shadows. **3.** Full of many changes; varied: his checkered career.

checking account. A bank account from which money may be withdrawn or payments made from the amount on deposit by writing checks.

check·mate (chĕk′māt′) tr.v. **-mat·ed, -mat·ing. 1.** Chess. To move so as to place (an opponent's king) under an attack from which there is no escape, thus ending the game. **2.** To defeat or foil by or as if by making such a move. —n. **1.** A chess move or position that places an opponent's king under direct and inescapable attack. **2.** A situation in which one is completely foiled or defeated. —interj. Chess. A call declaring the checkmate of an opponent's king. [Middle English chekmate, from Old French eschec mat, from Arabic shāh māt, "the king is dead."]

check-off (chĕk′ôf′, -ŏf′) n. The collecting of dues from members of a union by authorized deduction from their wages.

check·out (chĕk′out′) n. **1.** The act or process of checking out, as at a supermarket, library, or hotel. **2.** A place where something, such as merchandise, may be paid for, taken out, etc. **3.** A test or inspection, as of a machine, for working condition, accuracy, etc.

check·point (chĕk′point′) n. A place where surface traffic is stopped for inspection.

check·rein (chĕk′rān′) n. A short rein connected from a horse's bit to the saddle to keep a horse from lowering its head.

check·room (chĕk′rōōm′, -rŏŏm′) n. A room where coats, packages, etc., may be left temporarily.

check·up (chĕk′ŭp′) n. A thorough examination or inspection, as for health or general working conditions.

Ched·dar (chĕd′ər) n. Also ched·dar. Any of several types of firm, usu. yellowish cheese. [After Cheddar, a village in Somerset, England.]

cheek (chēk) n. The part of the face below the eye and between the nose and ear on either side. **2.** Impudence. —idiom. cheek by jowl. In close contact. [Middle English che(e)ke, from Old English cēce.]

cheek·bone (chēk′bōn′) n. A small, four-cornered bone on the side of the face just below the eye, forming the outermost point of the cheek; the zygomatic bone.

cheek·y (chē′kē) adj. **-i·er, -i·est.** Saucy; impertinent. —See Syns at impudent. —cheek′i·ly adv. —cheek′i·ness n.

cheep (chēp) n. A faint, shrill sound like that of a young bird; chirp. —tr.v. To utter with a chirp. —intr.v. To chirp; peep. [Imit.] —cheep′er n.

cheer (chîr) tr.v. **1.** To make happier or more cheerful: After the cold rain the warm fire cheered us. **2.** To encourage by or as if by shouting; urge: The fans cheered the runner on. **3.** To salute or acclaim by shouting; applaud: The crowd cheered the President. —intr.v. **1.** To shout cheers; applaud. **2.** To become cheerful: In spite of my disappointment I soon cheered up. —See Syns at encourage. —n. **1.** A shout of praise, approval, encouragement, etc.: The crowd gave a loud cheer for the winning team. **2.** Good spirits; gaiety; happiness: Father was full of cheer. [Middle English chere, cheer, disposition, face, from Old French ch(i)ere, face, from Late Latin cara, from Greek karē, head.] —cheer′er n. —cheer′ing·ly adv.

cheer·ful (chîr′fəl) adj. **1.** In good spirits; happy; gay: He was cheerful at breakfast. **2.** Producing a feeling of cheer; pleasant and bright: a cozy, cheerful room. **3.** Willing; good-humored: his cheerful acceptance of responsibility. —cheer′ful·ly adv. —cheer′ful·ness n.
Syns: cheerful, bright, cheery, chipper (Informal), happy, sunny adj. Core meaning: Being in or showing good spirits (a cheerful person; a cheerful smile). See also Syns at glad.

cheer·lead·er (chîr′lē′dər) n. A person who starts and leads the cheering of spectators at a game.

cheer·less (chîr′lĭs) adj. Lacking cheer; depressing. —See Syns at gloomy. —cheer′less·ly adv. —cheer′less·ness n.

cheer·y (chîr′ē) adj. **-i·er, -i·est.** Bright and cheerful: a cheery smile; a cheery fire. —See Syns at cheerful and glad. —cheer′i·ly adv. —cheer′i·ness n.

cheese (chēz) n. A food, soft to firm in texture, made from the pressed curd of milk, often seasoned and aged. [Middle English *chese,* from Old English *cēse,* from Latin *cāseus.*]

cheese·burg·er (chēz'bûr'gər) *n.* A hamburger topped with melted cheese.

cheese·cake (chēz'kāk') *n.* **1.** Also **cheese cake.** A cake made of cream or cottage cheese, eggs, milk and sugar. **2.** *Slang.* **a.** A photograph of a pretty girl scantily clothed. **b.** Such photographs collectively.

cheese·cloth (chēz'klôth', -klŏth') *n.* A thin, loosely woven cotton gauze, orig. used for wrapping cheese.

chees·y (chē'zē) *adj.* **-i·er, -i·est. 1.** Like cheese. **2.** *Slang.* Of poor quality; shoddy; inadequate. —See Syns at **cheap.** —**chees'i·ness** *n.*

chee·tah (chē'tə) *n.* Also **che·tah.** A long-legged, swift-running wild cat, *Acinonyx jubatus,* of Africa and southwestern Asia, with black-spotted, tawny fur and nonretractile claws. It is sometimes trained to hunt game. [Hindi *cītā,* from Sanskrit *citrakāya,* tiger : *citra,* speckled + *kāya,* body.]

cheetah

chef (shěf) *n.* A cook, esp. the chief cook of a restaurant. [French, from Old French *chief,* chief.]

chef-d'oeu·vre (shě-dœ'vr'ə) *n., pl.* **chefs-d'oeu·vre** (shě-). A masterpiece, esp. in art or literature. [French, "chief work."]

che·la (kē'lə) *n., pl.* **-lae** (-lē). A pincerlike claw, as of a lobster, crab, or similar crustacean. [From Latin *chēlē,* from Greek *khēlē,* claw.]

che·lo·ni·an (kǐ-lō'nē-ən). *Zool.* —*adj.* Of or belonging to the order Chelonia, which includes the turtles and tortoises. —*n.* A member of the Chelonia. [From Greek *khelōnē,* tortoise.]

chem- or **chemi-**. Var. of **chemo-.**

chem·i·cal (kěm'ĭ-kəl) *adj.* **1.** Of or involving chemistry: *a chemical discovery.* **2.** Used in or produced by means of chemistry: *a chemical symbol; a chemical change.* —*n.* Any of the substances classed as elements or the compounds formed from them. [Earlier *chimical,* from *chimic,* an alchemist, ult. from Medieval Latin *alchimia,* alchemy.] —**chem'i·cal·ly** *adv.*

chemical bond. Any of several forces or mechanisms, esp. the ionic bond, covalent bond, and metallic bond, by which atoms or ions are bound in a molecule or crystal.

chemical engineering. Engineering that is concerned with the industrial production of chemicals and chemical products. —**chemical engineer.**

Chemical Mace. A trademark for a mixture of organic chemicals used in aerosol form as a weapon that disables by intense irritation of the eyes, respiratory tract, and skin. Also called **Mace.**

chemical warfare. Warfare involving the use of chemicals such as poisons and irritants that act directly against human beings, crops, and plants.

che·mise (shə-mēz') *n.* **1.** A woman's loose, shirtlike undergarment. **2.** A dress that hangs straight from the shoulders. Also called **shift.** [Middle English, from Old French, shirt, from Late Latin *camīsia,* linen shirt.]

chem·ist (kěm'ĭst) *n.* **1.** A scientist who specializes in chemistry. **2.** *Brit.* A pharmacist. [From Medieval Latin *alchymista,* alchemist.]

chem·is·try (kěm'ĭ-strē) *n., pl.* **-tries. 1.** The scientific study of the composition, structure, properties, and reactions of matter, esp. at the level of atomic and molecular systems. **2.** The composition, structure, properties, and reactions of a substance or a system of substances: *the chemistry of the blood.* **3.** Behavior or functioning, as of a complex of emotions: *the chemistry of love.*

chemo- or **chemi-** or **chem-.** A prefix meaning chemicals or chemical reactions: **chemotherapy.** [From Greek *khēmela,* alchemy.]

che·mo·re·cep·tion (kē'mō-rǐ-sěp'shən, kěm'ō-) *n.* The reaction of a sense organ to a chemical stimulus. —**che'mo·re·cep'tive** *adj.* —**che'mo·re·cep'tor** *n.*

che·mo·syn·the·sis (kē'mō-sǐn'thə-sǐs, kěm'ō-) *n.* A process, as carried on by some living things, in which nutrients or other organic substances are manufactured using the energy of chemical reactions.

che·mo·ther·a·py (kē'mō-thěr'ə-pē, kěm'ō-) *n.* The use of chemicals in treating diseases. —**che'mo·ther'a·peu'tic** (-thěr'ə-pyoo'tǐk)) *adj.*

chem·ur·gy (kěm'ər-jē, kě-mûr'-) *n.* The development of new industrial chemical products from organic raw materials, esp. from those of agricultural origin. [CHEM(O)- + -URGY.] —**chem·ur'gic** (kě-mûr'jǐk) or **chem·ur'gi·cal** *adj.*

che·nille (shə-nēl') *n.* Fabric with a fuzzy, velvety pile, used for making bedspreads, rugs, or curtains. [French, "caterpillar" (from its hairy pile), from Latin *canīcula,* dim. of *canis,* dog.]

cheque (chěk) *n. Brit.* Var. of **check** (bank).

chequ·er (chěk'ər) *n. & v. Brit.* Var. of **checker.**

cher·ish (chěr'ĭsh) *tr.v.* **1.** To care for tenderly and affectionately; love: *The old man cherished the foundling as if she were his own.* **2.** To value highly; hold dear: *Americans cherish freedom.* —See Syns at **appreciate** and **love.** [Middle English *cherissen,* from Old French *cherir,* from *cher,* dear, from Latin *cārus.*]

Cher·o·kee (chěr'ə-kē', chěr'ə-kē') *n., pl.* **Cherokee** or **-kees. 1.** An Iroquoian-speaking tribe of North American Indians, formerly inhabiting North Carolina and northern Georgia and now settled in Oklahoma. **2.** A member of this tribe. —**Cher'o·kee'** *adj.*

Cherokee rose. A climbing rose, *Rosa laevigata,* of Chinese origin, with large, white, fragrant flowers.

cher·ry (chěr'ē) *n., pl.* **-ries. 1. a.** Any of several trees of the genus *Prunus,* having small, fleshy, globe-shaped or heart-shaped fruit with a small, hard stone, esp. *P. avium,* the common sweet cherry, and *P. cerasus,* the sour cherry. **b.** The fruit or wood of any of these trees. **2.** A deep or purplish red. —*adj.* Deep or purplish red. [Middle English *chery,* from Old French *cerise,* from Latin *cerasus,* cherry tree, from Greek *kerasos.*]

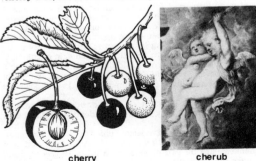

cherry   cherub

cher·ub (chěr'əb) *n.* **1.** *pl.* **cher·u·bim** (chěr'ə-bǐm, -yə-bǐm). *Theol.* One of the second order of angels. **2.** An angelic cherub portrayed as a winged child. **3.** Any person, esp. a child, with an innocent or chubby face. [Hebrew *kərūbh.*]

che·ru·bic (chə-roo'bǐk) *adj.* Of, resembling, or suggestive of a cherub: *a cherubic child; a cherubic smile.*

cher·u·bim (chěr'ə-bǐm, -yə-bǐm) *n.* Plural of **cherub** (angel).

cher·vil (chûr'vəl) *n.* **1.** An aromatic plant, *Anthriscus cerefolium,* native to Eurasia, with leaves used in soups and salads. **2.** Any of several related plants, esp. *Chaerophyllum bulbosum,* with an edible root. [Middle English *cherville,* from Old English *cerfille,* from Latin *chaerephylla,* from Greek *khairephullon* : *khairein*, to delight in + *phullon*, leaf.]

Chesh·ire cat (chĕsh′ər). In *Alice's Adventures in Wonderland* by Lewis Carroll, a grinning cat that gradually disappeared until only its grin remained visible.

chess (chĕs) *n.* A game played on a chessboard between two players, each starting with 16 pieces. The object of the game is to put the opponent's king out of action. [Middle English *ches*, short for Old French *esches*, pl. of *eschec*, check (at chess).]

chess·board (chĕs′bôrd′, -bōrd′) *n.* A board with 64 squares in alternating colors, used in playing chess.

chess·man (chĕs′măn′, -mən) *n.* One of the pieces used in the game of chess.

chest (chĕst) *n.* **1.** The part of the body between the neck and the abdomen, enclosed by the ribs and the breastbone. **2.** A sturdy box with a lid and often a lock, used for holding or storing things. **3.** A piece of furniture with several drawers, used chiefly for keeping clothes; a bureau or dresser. [Middle English, from Old English *cest, cist*, box, from Latin *cista*, from Greek *kistē*.]

ches·ter·field (chĕs′tər-fēld′) *n.* **1.** A single-breasted or double-breasted overcoat, usu. with concealed buttons and a velvet collar. **2.** A large, overstuffed sofa with upright armrests. [Named after a 19th-cent. Earl of *Chesterfield*.]

chest·nut (chĕs′nŭt′, -nət) *n.* **1. a.** Any of several trees of the genus *Castanea*, of the Northern Hemisphere, bearing nuts enclosed in a prickly bur. **b.** The nut of any of these trees, edible when cooked. **c.** The hard wood of these trees, used in furniture and as a building material. **2.** The **horse chestnut. 3.** A reddish brown. **4.** A reddish-brown horse. **5. a.** An old and stale joke. **b.** Anything lacking freshness or originality, as a song or story. —*adj.* Reddish brown. [Middle English *chesten*, chestnut, from Old French *chastaigne*, from Latin *castanea*, from Greek *kastanea* + NUT.]

chestnut   chevron

chestnut blight. A destructive disease of the native American chestnut tree, caused by a fungus, *Endothia parasitica*.

che·tah (chē′tə) *n.* Var. of **cheetah.**

che·val-de-frise (shə-văl′də-frēz′) *n., pl.* **che·vaux-de-frise** (shə-vō′-). **1.** An obstacle composed of barbed wire or spikes attached to a wooden frame. **2.** An obstacle in the form of jagged glass or spikes set in the masonry on the top of a wall. [French, "Frisian horse" (from its having been used in Friesland to compensate for a lack of cavalry).]

che·val glass (shə-văl′). A long mirror mounted on swivels in a frame. [From French *cheval*, support, horse, from Latin *caballus*.]

chev·a·lier (shĕv′ə-lîr′) *n.* **1.** A member of certain orders of knighthood or merit, as the Legion of Honor in France. **2.** A knight or nobleman. [Middle English *chevaler*, from Old French *chevalier*, from Late Latin *caballārius*, horseman, from Latin *caballus*, horse.]

Chev·i·ot (shĕv′ē-ət, chĕv′-) *n.* **1.** One of a breed of sheep with short, thick wool, orig. raised in the Cheviot Hills of England and Scotland. **2. cheviot.** A rough wool cloth used chiefly for suits, overcoats, etc.

chev·ron (shĕv′rən) *n.* **1.** A badge made up of stripes meeting at an angle, worn on the sleeve of a military, naval, or police uniform to show rank, merit, or length of service.

2. Any V-shaped pattern. [Middle English, from Old French *chevron*, beam, rafter, ult. from Latin *caper*, goat.]

chew (chōō) *tr.v.* To bite and grind with the teeth; masticate. —*intr.v.* To make a crushing and grinding motion with the teeth. —*phrasal verb.* **chew out.** *Slang.* To scold; reprimand. —See Syns at **scold.** —*n.* The act of chewing. **2.** Something held in the mouth and chewed. —*idiom.* **chew the fat (or rag).** *Slang.* To talk casually or idly; to chat. [Middle English *chewen*, from Old English *cēowan*.] —**chew′er** *n.*

chewing gum. A sweetened, flavored preparation for chewing, usu. made of chicle.

che·wink (chĭ-wĭngk′) *n.* A bird, the towhee. [Imit.]

chew·y (chōō′ē) *adj.* **-i·er, -i·est.** Needing much chewing: *chewy candy.*

Chey·enne (shī-ăn′, -ĕn′) *n., pl.* **Cheyenne** or **-ennes. 1.** A tribe of Algonquian-speaking North American Indians, formerly inhabiting central Minnesota and the Dakotas, now settled in Montana and Oklahoma. **2.** A member of this tribe. —**Chey·enne′** *adj.*

chi (kī) *n.* Also **khi.** The 22nd letter of the Greek alphabet, written X, χ. In English it is represented as *kh* or *ch*. [Greek.]

chi·a·ro·scu·ro (kē-är′ə-skŏŏr′ō, -skyŏŏr′ō) *n., pl.* **-ros.** Also **chi·a·roo·scu·ro** (kē-är′ə-ō-skŏŏr′ō, -skyŏŏr′ō). **1.** The technique of using light and shade in pictorial representation. **2.** The arrangement of light and dark elements in a pictorial work of art. [Italian : *chiaro*, clear, from Latin *clārus* + *oscuro*, dark, from Latin *obscūrus*.] —**chi·a′ro·scu′rist** *n.*

chi·as·mus (kī-ăz′məs) *n., pl.* **-mi** (-mī′). A rhetorical inversion of the second of two parallel structures, as *He went to the theater, but home went she.* [From Greek *khiasmos*, from *khiazein*, to mark with the letter chi, from *khi*, chi.]

chic (shēk) *adj.* Stylish; fashionable. —*n.* Style and elegance in dress or manner. [French, from German *Schick*, skill.] —**chic′ly** *adv.*

chi·cane (shĭ-kān′) *v.* **-caned, -can·ing.** —*tr.v.* To trick or deceive in order to outwit or gain an advantage. —*intr.v.* To use tricks or chicanery. —*n.* Chicanery. [French *chicaner*, from Old French, to quibble.]

chi·can·er·y (shĭ-kā′nə-rē) *n., pl.* **-ies. 1.** Deception by trickery or sophistry. **2.** A trick; subterfuge.

Chi·ca·no (shĭ-kä′nō, chĭ-) *n., pl.* **-nos.** A Mexican-American. —*adj.* Of or pertaining to Mexican-Americans.

chick (chĭk) *n.* **1.** A young chicken. **2.** The young of any bird. **3.** A child. **4.** *Slang.* A girl; young woman. [Middle English *chike*, short for *chiken*, chicken.]

chick·a·dee (chĭk′ə-dē′) *n.* Any of several small, plump North American birds of the genus *Parus*, with predominantly gray plumage and a dark-crowned head. [Imit. of its cry.]

chick·a·ree (chĭk′ə-rē′) *n.* A small, reddish-gray squirrel, *Tamiascurus douglasi*, of northwestern North America, closely related to the red squirrel. [Imit. of its cry.]

chick·en (chĭk′ən) *n.* **1. a.** The common domestic fowl raised for eggs or food; a hen or rooster. **b.** Any of various similar or related birds, such as the prairie chicken. **2.** The meat of the common domestic fowl. —*adj. Slang.* Afraid; cowardly. —See Syns at **cowardly.** —*intr.v. Slang.* To act in a cowardly manner; lose one's nerve: *chickened out at the last minute.* [Middle English *chiken*, from Old English *cīcen.*]

chicken hawk. Any of various hawks that prey on or have the reputation of preying on chickens.

chick·en-heart·ed (chĭk′ən-här′tĭd) *adj.* Cowardly; timid.

chicken pox. A contagious virus disease, mainly of children, characterized by skin eruption and mild fever.

chick·pea (chĭk′pē′) *n.* **1.** A bushy plant, *Cicer arietinum*, grown in the Mediterranean region and central Asia and bearing edible seeds. **2.** One of the pealike seeds of this plant. [From Middle English *chiche*, chickpea, from Old French, from Latin *cicer* + PEA.]

chick·weed (chĭk′wēd′) *n.* Any of various plants of the genera *Cerastium* and *Stellaria*, esp. *S. media*, a weedy plant with small white flowers.

chic·le (chĭk′əl) *n.* The coagulated milky juice of the sapodilla, a tropical American tree, used as the principal ingredient of chewing gum. [Spanish, from Nahuatl *chictli*.]

chic·o·ry (chĭk′ə-rē) *n., pl.* **-ries.** **1.** A plant, *Cichorium intybus*, with blue, daisylike flowers and leaves that are used in salads. **2.** The root of this plant, dried, roasted, and ground and added to or used for mixing with coffee or as a substitute for coffee. [Middle English *cicoree*, from Old French, from Latin *cichorium*, from Greek *kikhora*.]

chide (chīd) *v.* **chid·ed** or **chid** (chĭd), **chid·ed** or **chid** or **chid·den** (chĭd′n), **chid·ing.** *—intr.v.* To scold; rebuke; reprimand. *—tr.v.* To state one's disapproval of. —See Syns at **scold.** [Middle English *chiden*, from Old English *cīdan*, to quarrel.] **—chid′ing·ly** *adv.*

chief (chēf) *n.* **1.** A person with the highest rank or authority; a leader: *the chief of the fire department.* **2.** Often **Chief.** The chief engineer of a ship. **3.** *Heraldry.* The upper section of a shield. *—adj.* **1.** Highest in rank or authority: *the chief engineer.* **2.** Most important; main; principal: *the country's chief crop.* —See Syns at **primary.** *—idiom.* **in chief.** With the highest rank or greatest authority: *the commander in chief.* [Middle English, from Old French, from Latin *caput*, head.]

chief justice. Also **Chief Justice.** The presiding judge of a court of several judges, esp. of the U.S. Supreme Court.

chief·ly (chēf′lē) *adv.* **1.** Mostly; mainly. **2.** Above all; especially. *—adj.* Of or like a chief.

chief of staff. **1.** *Mil.* The senior staff officer at the division level or higher. **2. Chief of Staff.** The ranking officer of the U.S. Army, Navy, or Air Force, responsible to the secretary of his branch and to the President.

chief of state. The person who serves as the formal head of a nation.

chief·tain (chēf′tən) *n.* The leader of a clan, tribe, or similar group. [Middle English *chieftaine*, from Old French *chevetain*, from Late Latin *capitāneus*, from Latin *caput*, head.]

chif·fon (shĭ-fŏn′, shĭf′ŏn′) *n.* A soft, sheer, airy fabric of silk or rayon, used for scarfs, veils, dresses, etc. [French, "rag," ult. from Middle English *chip*, chip.]

chif·fo·nier (shĭf′ə-nîr′) *n.* Also **chif·fon·nier.** A narrow, high chest of drawers, often with a mirror attached. [French *chiffonnier*, "bureau for rags."]

chig·ger (chĭg′ər) *n.* **1.** Any of various small six-legged larvae of mites of the family Trombidiidae that cling to the skin of a human being or animal and cause intensely irritating itching. Also called **chigoe.** **2.** A flea, the **chigoe.** [Var. of CHIGOE.]

chi·gnon (shēn-yŏn′, shēn-yŏn′) *n.* A roll or knot of hair worn at the back of the head or the nape of the neck. [French, var. of Old French *chaignon*, chain.]

chignon

Chihuahua

chig·oe (chĭg′ō, chē′gō) *n. Zool.* **1.** A small tropical flea, *Tunga penetrans*, of which the fertile female burrows under the skin, causing intense irritation and sores that may become severely infected. Also called **chigger.** **2.** A mite, the **chigger.** [Cariban *chigo*.]

Chi·hua·hua (chĭ-wä′wä, -wə) *n.* A very small dog of a breed that originated in Mexico, with pointed ears and a smooth coat. [From *Chihuahua*, a state of Mexico.]

chil·blain (chĭl′blān′) *n.* An inflammation of the hands, feet, or ears, resulting from exposure to damp cold. [CHIL(L) + BLAIN.]

child (chīld) *n., pl.* **chil·dren** (chĭl′drən). **1.** A person from the time of birth to the stage of physical maturity; a young boy or girl. **2.** A son or daughter; an offspring. **3.** An older person who behaves like a child; an immature person.

4. Often **children.** A descendant: *children of Abraham.* **5.** The figurative offspring of anything: *a child of nature.* —See Syns at **descendant.** *—idiom.* **with child.** Pregnant. [Middle English *child(e)*, from Old English *cild*.]

child·bear·ing (chīld′bâr′ĭng) *n.* Pregnancy and childbirth. *—modifier: childbearing years.*

childbed fever (chīld′bĕd′). Infection of the lining of the uterus and the bloodstream after childbirth.

child·birth (chīld′bûrth′) *n.* The act or process of giving birth to a child.

childe (chīld) *n. Archaic.* A youth of noble birth.

child·hood (chīld′hŏŏd′) *n.* The time or condition of being a child.

child·ish (chīl′dĭsh) *adj.* **1.** Of, typical of, or for a child: *a high, childish voice.* **2.** Thoughtless or foolish in a manner not suitable for a mature person: *childish remarks.* **—child′ish·ly** *adv.* **—child′ish·ness** *n.*

Usage: childish, childlike When applied to adults, *childish* is usu. a derogatory term (*childish behavior for a twenty-one year-old*); applied to children, the word lacks that connotation (*the childish simplicity of the little girl's dress*). *Childlike* is generally favorable on all age levels, suggesting endearing traits characteristic of children (*childlike trust*).

child·less (chīld′lĭs) *adj.* Having no children.

child·like (chīld′līk′) *adj.* Like or befitting a child, as in innocence. —See Usage note at **childish.**

chil·dren (chĭl′drən) *n.* Plural of **child.**

child's play. **1.** Anything that is very easy to do. **2.** A trivial matter.

chil·e (chĭl′ē) *n.* Var. of **chili.**

chil·e con car·ne (chĭl′ē kŏn kär′nē). Also **chil·i con car·ne.** A highly spiced dish made of red peppers, meat, and sometimes beans. Also called **chili.** [Spanish, "chili with meat."]

chil·i (chĭl′ē) *n., pl.* **-ies.** Also **chil·e, chil·li.** **1. a.** The very pungent fruit of several varieties of a woody plant, *Capsicum frutescens.* **b.** A condiment made from the dried fruits of this plant. **2. Chile con carne.** [Spanish, from Nahuatl *chilli*.]

chill (chĭl) *n.* **1.** A moderate but penetrating coldness: *a chill in the air.* **2.** A sensation of coldness, as with a fever. **3.** A checking or dampening of enthusiasm, spirit, or joy: *The bad news put a chill on the celebration.* *—adj.* **1.** Cold; chilly: *a chill wind.* **2.** Discouraging or unfriendly: *a chilly response.* —See Syns at **cold.** *—tr.v.* **1.** To lower in temperature; make cold. **2.** To affect with cold: *The icy wind chilled his face.* **3.** To harden a metallic surface by rapid cooling. *—intr.v.* **1.** To become cold. **2.** To be seized with cold. [Middle English *chile, chele,* frost, from Old English *c(i)ele*.] **—chill′ness** *n.*

chil·li (chĭl′ē) *n.* Var. of **chili.**

chill·y (chĭl′ē) *adj.* **-i·er, -i·est.** **1.** Cool or cold enough to cause shivering. **2.** Seized with cold; shivering. **3.** Distant and cool; unfriendly. —See Syns at **cold.** **—chill′i·ly** *adv.* **—chill′i·ness** *n.*

chi·mae·ra (kī-mîr′ə, kə-) *n.* Var. of **chimera.**

chime (chīm) *n.* **1.** An apparatus for striking a bell or bells to produce a musical sound. **2.** Often **chimes.** A set of bells tuned to different pitches and rung to make musical sounds. **3.** A musical sound produced by or as if by bells or chimes. *—v.* **chimed, chim·ing.** *—intr.v.* **1.** To sound with a harmonious ring when struck. **2.** To sound together in harmony or agreement: *Spring peepers chimed in the marsh.* *—tr.v.* **1.** To produce (music) by striking: *chime the bells.* **2.** To indicate (the hour) by ringing bells: *The clock chimed 3 o'clock.* *—phrasal verb.* **chime in.** To break into, as a conversation; interrupt. [Middle English *cymbal, chime,* perh. from Old French *chimbe,* from Latin *cymbalum,* cymbal.]

chi·me·ra (kī-mîr′ə, kə-) *n.* Also **chi·mae·ra.** **1. Chimera.** *Gk. Myth.* A fire-breathing she-monster with the head of a lion, the body of a goat, and the tail of a serpent. **2.** A creation of the imagination; a fantastic idea or fancy. **3.** *Biol.* An organism, esp. a plant, that contains tissues from at least two genetically distinct parents.

chi·mer·i·cal (kī-mĕr′ĭ-kəl, -mîr′-, kə-) or **chi·mer·ic** (-ĭk) *adj.* **1.** Imaginary; unreal. **2.** Given to unrealistic fantasies; fanciful. **—chi·mer′i·cal·ly** *adv.*

chim·ney (chĭm′nē) *n., pl.* **-neys. 1. a.** The usu. vertical structure containing a flue through which smoke and gases escape; flue. **b.** The part of such a structure that rises above a roof. **2.** A glass tube for enclosing the flame of a lamp. [Middle English *chimenee,* from Old French *cheminee,* from Late Latin *caminata,* from Latin *camīnus,* furnace, from Greek *kaminos.*]

chim·ney·piece (chĭm′nē-pēs′) *n.* **1.** The mantel of a fireplace. **2.** A decoration over a fireplace.

chimney pot. A pipe, usu. earthenware or metal, placed on the top of a chimney to improve the draft.

chimney sweep. Also **chimney sweeper.** A worker employed to clean soot from chimneys.

chimney swift. A small, dark, swallowlike New World bird, *Chaetura pelagica,* that often nests in chimneys.

chimney sweep   chimpanzee   chin
                                        Chinning

chimp (chĭmp) *n. Informal.* A chimpanzee.

chim·pan·zee (chĭm′păn-zē′, chĭm-păn′zē) *n.* An anthropoid ape, *Pan troglodytes,* of tropical Africa, having dark hair, gregarious, somewhat arboreal habits, and a high degree of intelligence. [From a native West African name.]

chin (chĭn) *n.* The lowest part of the face, formed by the center part of the front of the lower jaw. *—tr.v.* **chinned, chin·ning.** To pull (oneself) up with the arms while grasping an overhead horizontal bar until one's chin is level with the bar. [Middle English, from Old English *cin(n).*]

chi·na (chī′nə) *n.* **1.** High-quality porcelain or ceramic ware, often made in China. **2.** Any porcelain ware.

chi·na·ber·ry (chī′nə-bĕr′ē) *n.* **1.** A spreading tree, *Melia azedarach,* native to Asia, widely grown for its white or purple flower clusters. **2.** A soapberry tree, *Sapindus marginatus* (or *S. saponaria*), of the West Indies, Mexico, and the southwestern United States. **3.** The fruit of these trees.

Chi·na·town (chī′nə-toun′) *n.* A neighborhood inhabited by Chinese people.

chinch (chĭnch) *n.* A bedbug. [Spanish *chinche,* from Latin *cīmex,* bug.]

chinch bug. A small black and white insect, *Blissus leucopterus,* that is very destructive to grains and grasses.

chin·chil·la (chĭn-chĭl′ə) *n.* **1. a.** A squirrellike rodent, *Chinchilla laniger,* native to South America and widely raised in captivity for its soft pale-gray fur. **b.** The fur of this animal. **2.** A thick, twilled cloth of wool and cotton, used for coats. [Spanish, prob. from Aymara.]

chine (chīn) *n.* **1.** The backbone; spine. **2.** A cut of meat containing part of the backbone. **3.** A ridge or crest. **4.** The line of intersection between the side and bottom of a flatbottom or V-bottom boat. [Middle English *chyne,* from Old French *eschine.*]

Chi·nese (chī-nēz′, -nēs′) *adj.* Of or pertaining to China, its culture, people, or languages. *—n., pl.* **Chinese. 1. a.** A native or inhabitant of China. **b.** A person of Chinese ancestry. **2.** One of a group of related languages and dialects spoken in China, including Mandarin and Cantonese. **3.** Mandarin, the standard language of China.

Chinese cabbage. A plant, *Brassica pekinensis,* native to China, related to the common cabbage, and having a cylindrical head of crisp, edible leaves.

Chinese lantern. A decorative, collapsible lantern of thin, brightly colored paper.

Chinese puzzle. 1. A very intricate puzzle. **2.** Any very difficult problem.

chink¹ (chĭngk) *n.* A crack or fissure; narrow opening. *—tr.v.* To fill cracks or chinks in. [Perh. from Middle English *chine,* crack, from Old English *cinu, cine.*]

chink² (chĭngk) *n.* A short, clinking sound, as of pieces of metal striking together. *—tr.v.* To strike (something) and make a chink. *—intr.v.* To produce a chink. [Imit.]

chi·no (chē′nō, shē′-) *n., pl.* **-nos. 1.** A coarse, twilled cotton fabric used for uniforms and sports clothes. **2. chinos.** Trousers of this material. [American Spanish, "toasted" (from its orig. tan color).]

Chi·nook (shə-nŏŏk′, chə-) *n., pl.* **Chinook** or **-nooks. 1. a.** A tribe of North American Indians formerly inhabiting the Columbia River basin in Oregon. **b.** A member of this tribe. **c.** The language of the Chinook. **2. chinook.** A moist, warm wind blowing from the sea on the Oregon and Washington coasts. **3. chinook.** A warm, dry wind that descends from the eastern slopes of the Rocky Mountains, causing a rapid rise in temperature.

Chinook Jargon. A language combining English, French, Chinook, and other Indian dialects that was formerly used by Indians and fur traders of the Pacific Northwest.

chintz (chĭnts) *n.* A printed and glazed cotton fabric, usu. of bright colors. [From Hindi *chīnt,* from Sanskrit *citra,* many-colored, bright.]

chintz·y (chĭnt′sē) *adj.* **-i·er, -i·est.** Gaudy; cheap.

chip (chĭp) *n.* **1.** A small piece broken or cut off: *a chip of wood.* **2.** A crack or other mark caused by chipping: *a chip in the table.* **3.** A small disk or counter used in poker and other games to represent money. **4.** *Electronics.* A minute square of a thin semiconducting material, such as silicon or germanium, doped and otherwise processed to have specified electrical characteristics, esp. such a square before attachment of electrical leads and packaging as an electronic component or integrated circuit. **5.** A thin slice of food: *a potato chip.* **6. chips.** *Brit.* French-fried potatoes. **7.** A fragment of dried animal dung used as fuel. *—v.* **chipped, chip·ping.** *—tr.v.* **1.** To break a small piece from: *chip a tooth.* **2.** To shape or carve by cutting or chopping: *chipped his name in the stone. —intr.v.* To become broken off. *—phrasal verb.* **chip in.** *Informal.* To contribute money, labor, etc.: *We all chipped in to buy her a present. —idioms.* **a chip off the old block.** A child that resembles either of its parents. **a chip on (one's) shoulder.** A persistent feeling of resentment or bitterness. [Middle English, from Old English *cipp,* beam, piece cut off a beam.]

chip·munk (chĭp′mŭngk′) *n.* A small rodent, *Tamias striatus,* of eastern North America, or any of several similar rodents of the genus *Eutamias,* of western North America and northern Asia, resembling a squirrel but smaller and having a striped back. [Var. of earlier *chitmunk,* of Algonquian orig.]

chipped beef. Dried beef smoked and sliced very thin.

Chip·pen·dale (chĭp′ən-dāl′) *adj.* Of, pertaining to, or designating a style of furniture characterized by flowing lines and rococo ornamentation. [After Thomas *Chippendale* (1718–79), English cabinetmaker.]

chip·per (chĭp′ər) *adj. Informal.* Active; cheerful; brisk; lively. *—See Syns at* **cheerful.** [Orig. unknown.]

chipping sparrow. A small North American sparrow, *Spizella passerina,* with a reddish-brown crown.

chiro-. A prefix meaning hand: **chiropractic.** [Latin, from Greek *kheir,* hand.]

chi·rog·ra·phy (kī-rŏg′rə-fē) *n.* Penmanship. [French *chirographie,* from Old French *chirographe,* autograph, ult. from Greek *kheirographos,* written with one's own hand.] **—chi·rog′ra·pher** or **chi′·ro·graph′ic** (kī′rə-grăf′ĭk) or **chi′·ro·graph′i·cal** *adj.*

chi·rop·o·dy (kə-rŏp′ə-dē, shə-) *n.* Podiatry. [CHIRO- + -POD.] **—chi·rop′o·dist** *n.*

chi·ro·prac·tic (kī′rə-prăk′tĭk) *n.* A system of therapy based on manipulation of the spinal column and other bodily structures, usu. without drugs or surgery. [CHIRO- + Greek *praktikos,* effective, active.] **—chi′·ro·prac′tor** *n.*

chi·rop·ter·an (kī-rŏp′tər-ən) *n.* A flying mammal of the order Chiroptera, which includes the bats. [CHIRO- + Greek *pteron,* wing.] **—chi·rop′ter·an** *adj.*

ă pat   ā pay   â care   ä father   ĕ pet   ē be   hw which   ĭ pit   ī tie   î pier   ŏ pot   ō toe   ô paw, for   oi noise
ŏŏ took   ōō boot   ou out   th thin   *th* this   ŭ cut   û urge   zh vision   ə about, item, edible, gallop, circus

chirp (chûrp) *n.* A short, high-pitched sound, as that made by a small bird; a tweet; a peep. —*intr.v.* **1.** To utter a chirp. **2.** To speak in a quick, sprightly manner. —*tr.v.* To utter with a chirp. [Middle English *chirpen.*] —**chirp'er** *n.*

chirr (chûr) *n.* A harsh, trilling sound, as that made by a cricket. —*intr.v.* To make a chirr. [Imit.]

chir·rup (chûr'əp, chîr'-) *n.* **1.** A series of chirps; a twitter. **2.** A series of clucks or clicking sounds, as those made to urge on a horse. —*intr.v.* **1.** To utter a series of chirps. **2.** To make clicking, clucking sounds, as in urging on a horse. [Var. of CHIRP.]

chis·el (chĭz'əl) *n.* A metal tool with a sharp, beveled edge, used to cut and shape stone, wood, or metal. —*v.* **-eled**, **-el·ing** or **-el·ling.** —*tr.v.* **1.** To shape or cut with a chisel. **2.** *Slang.* **a.** To cheat or swindle. **b.** To obtain by deception. —*intr.v.* **1.** To use a chisel. **2.** *Slang.* To use unethical methods; cheat. [Middle English, from Old North French, ult. from Latin *caedere,* to cut.] —**chis'el·er** *n.*

chisel

chit·chat (chĭt'chăt') *n.* Casual conversation; small talk. [From CHAT.]

chi·tin (kī'tĭn) *n.* A horny substance that is the principal component of crustacean shells and insect exoskeletons. [French *chitine,* from New Latin *chiton,* mollusk.]

chit·lins or **chit·lings** (chĭt'lĭnz) *n.* Var. of **chitterlings.**

chi·ton (kīt'n, kī'tŏn) *n.* **1.** A tunic worn by men and women in ancient Greece. **2.** Any of various marine mollusks of the class Amphineyra, living on rocks and having shells consisting of eight overlapping transverse plates. [From Greek *khitōn,* tunic.]

chit·ter (chĭt'ər) *intr.v.* To twitter or chatter, as a bird. [Middle English *chiteren* (imit.).]

chit·ter·lings (chĭt'lĭnz) *pl.n.* Also **chit·lins** or **chit·lings.** The small intestines of pigs, cooked and eaten as food. [Middle English *chiterling.*]

chi·val·ric (shĭ-văl'rĭk, shĭv'əl-) *adj.* Chivalrous.

chiv·al·rous (shĭv'əl-rəs) *adj.* **1.** Having the qualities of gallantry, honor, etc., attributed to an ideal knight. **2.** Of or pertaining to chivalry. —**chiv'al·rous·ly** *adv.*

chiv·al·ry (shĭv'əl-rē) *n., pl.* **-ries. 1.** The qualities and principles idealized by knighthood, as bravery, courtesy, honesty, honor, and devotion to the weak. **2.** The medieval institution of knighthood that took these ideals as the basis for a code of behavior. **3.** A group of knights or gallant gentlemen. [Middle English *chivalrie,* from Old French *chevalerie,* from Late Latin *caballārius,* horseman, cavalier.]

chive (chīv) *n.* **1.** A plant, *Allium schoenoprasum,* native to Eurasia and related to the onion, with purplish flowers and hollow, grasslike leaves. **2.** Often **chives.** The leaves of this plant, used as a seasoning. [Middle English *cyve, cheve,* from Old French *cive,* from Latin *cēpa,* onion.]

chlor-. Var. of **chloro-.**

chlo·ral (klôr'əl, klōr'-) *n.* A colorless, oily liquid, CCl₃CHO, used to manufacture DDT and chloral hydrate. [CHLOR(O)- + AL(COHOL).]

chloral hydrate. A colorless crystalline compound, CCl₃CH(OH)₂, used as a sedative and hypnotic.

chlor·am·phen·i·col (klôr'ăm-fĕn'ĭ-kôl, klōr'-, -kōl') *n.* An antibiotic, C₁₁H₁₂Cl₂N₂O₅, derived from a soil bacterium or synthesized.

chlo·rate (klôr'āt, klōr'-) *n.* The inorganic group ClO₃ or a compound containing it. [CHLOR(O)- + -ATE.]

chlor·dane (klôr'dān', klōr'-) *n.* Also **chlor·dan** (-dăn'). A colorless, odorless viscous liquid, C₁₀H₆Cl₈, used as an insecticide.

chlo·rel·la (klə-rĕl'ə) *n.* Any of various green algae of the genus *Chlorella,* widely used in studies of photosynthesis. [CHLOR(O)- + *-ella,* dim. suffix.]

chlo·ric acid (klôr'ĭk, klōr'-). A strongly oxidizing unstable acid, HClO₃·7H₂O. [CHLOR(O)- + -IC.]

chlo·ride (klôr'īd', klōr'-) *n.* Any binary compound of chlorine. [CHLOR(O)- + -IDE.]

chlo·rin·ate (klôr'ə-nāt, klōr'-) *tr.v.* **-at·ed, -at·ing.** To treat or combine with chlorine or with a chlorine compound. —**chlo'ri·na'tion** *n.*

chlorinated lime. A white powder of varying composition, as CaCl(ClO)·4H₂O, produced by chlorinating slaked lime and used as a bleach.

chlo·rine (klôr'ēn', klōr'-, -ĭn) *n. Symbol* **Cl** A highly irritating, greenish-yellow gaseous halogen, capable of combining with nearly all other elements, produced principally by electrolysis of sodium chloride and used widely to purify water, as a disinfectant, a bleaching agent, and in the manufacture of many important compounds including chloroform and carbon tetrachloride. Atomic number 17; atomic weight 35.45; freezing point –100.98°C; boiling point –34.6°C; specific gravity 1.56 (–33.6°C); valences 1, 3, 5, 7. [CHLOR(O)- + -INE.]

chlo·rite¹ (klôr'īt', klōr'-) *n.* A generally green or black secondary mineral, (Mg, Fe, Al)₆(Si, Al)₄O₁₀(OH)₈, often formed by metamorphic alteration of primary dark rock minerals. [Latin *chlorītis,* a green precious stone, from Greek *khlōritis,* from *khlōros,* greenish yellow.]

chlo·rite² (klôr'īt', klōr'-) *n.* The inorganic group ClO₂ or a compound containing it. [CHLOR(O)- + -ITE.]

chloro- or **chlor-.** A prefix meaning: **1.** Green: **chlorosis. 2.** Chlorine: **chloroform.** [From Greek *khlōros,* greenish yellow.]

chlo·ro·form (klôr'ə-fôrm', klōr'-) *n.* A clear, colorless heavy liquid, CHCl₃, used in refrigerants, propellants, and resins and as an anesthetic. —*tr.v.* To anesthetize or kill with chloroform. [CHLORO- + FORM(YL).]

Chlo·ro·my·ce·tin (klôr'ō-mī-sēt'n, klōr'-) *n.* A trademark for chloramphenicol.

chlo·ro·phyll (klôr'ə-fĭl, klōr'-) *n.* Also **chlo·ro·phyl.** Any of several green pigments composed of carbon, hydrogen, magnesium, nitrogen, and oxygen, found in green plants and other living things that carry on photosynthesis. Chlorophyll appears to absorb light and so provide the energy used in photosynthesis. [CHLORO- + -PHYLL.]

chlo·ro·plast (klôr'ə-plăst', klōr'-) *n.* A plastid within a plant cell that contains chlorophyll and is the center of photosynthesis in plants. [CHLORO- + -PLAST.]

chlo·ro·prene (klôr'ə-prēn', klōr'-) *n.* A colorless liquid, C₄H₅Cl, used in the manufacture of synthetic rubber. [CHLORO- + (ISO)PRENE.]

chlo·ro·quine (klôr'ə-kwīn', klōr'-) *n.* A synthetic drug used in the treatment of malaria.

chlo·ro·sis (klə-rō'sĭs) *n.* **1.** *Bot.* An abnormal condition of plants, characterized by absence of or deficiency in green pigment. **2.** *Path.* An iron-deficiency anemia characterized by greenish skin color. [CHLOR(O) + -OSIS.]

chlor·tet·ra·cy·cline (klôr'tĕt-rə-sī'klēn', klōr'-) *n.* An antibiotic, C₂₂H₂₃ClN₂O₈, obtained from a soil bacterium.

chock (chŏk) *n.* **1.** A block or wedge placed under something, as a boat or wheel, to keep it from moving. **2.** *Naut.* A heavy fitting of metal or wood with two jaws curving inward, through which a rope or cable may be run. —*tr.v.* **1.** To fit with or secure by a chock. **2.** To place (a boat) on chocks. [Orig. unknown.]

chock-a-block (chŏk'ə-blŏk') *adj.* Squeezed together; jammed.

chock-full (chŏk'fŏŏl', chŭk'-) *adj.* Also **chuck-full.** Completely filled; stuffed. [Middle English *chokkeful.*]

choc·o·late (chô'kə-lĭt, chŏk'ə-, chôk'lĭt, chŏk'-) *n.* **1.** Husked, roasted, and ground cacao seeds, often combined with a sweetener or flavoring agent. **2.** A candy or beverage made from this. [Spanish, from Aztec *xocolatl* : *xococ,* bitter + *atl,* water.]

Choc·taw (chŏk'tô') *n., pl.* **Choctaw** or **-taws. 1.** A tribe of Muskhogean-speaking Indians, formerly living in southern Mississippi and Alabama, now settled in Oklahoma. **2.** A member of this tribe. **3.** The language of the Choctaw.

choice (chois) *n.* **1.** The act of choosing: *Have you made a*

choice yet? **2.** The power, right, or liberty of choosing: *You have no choice in this matter.* **3.** The person or thing chosen. **4.** A number or variety from which to choose: *a wide choice of styles and colors.* **5.** Something that is best or preferable above others; the best part. —*adj.* **1.** Of fine quality; select; excellent: *choice tidbits; a choice selection.* **2.** Of the U.S. Government grade of meat higher than *good* and lower than *prime.* [Middle English *chois,* from Old French, from *choisir,* to choose.]
   Syns: **1. choice, election, preference, selection** *n. Core meaning:* The act of choosing from a number of alternatives (*a price that influenced my choice of rugs*). **2. choice, alternative, option** *n. Core meaning:* The right or power of choosing (*had two choices: to go or to stay*).

choir (kwīr) *n.* **1. a.** An organized company of singers, esp. in a church. **b.** The part of a church used by such singers. **2.** Any musical group or band or a section of one. [From Middle English *quere,* from Old French *cuer,* from Medieval Latin *chorus,* chorus.]

choke (chōk) *v.* **choked, chok·ing.** —*tr.v.* **1.** To interfere with or terminate normal breathing of (a person or animal), esp. by squeezing, blocking, or breaking the windpipe or by polluting the air. **2.** To stop by or as if by strangling; to silence; suppress: *choke back tears.* **3.** To reduce the air intake of (a carburetor), thereby enriching the fuel mixture. **4.** To check or slow down the movement, growth, or action of. **5.** To block up or obstruct by filling or crowding; to clog; congest. **6.** To fill completely; to jam; pack. —*intr.v.* **1.** To become suffocated; have difficulty in breathing, swallowing, or speaking. **2.** To be blocked up or obstructed. —*phrasal verb.* **choke up.** *Informal.* To be unable to speak because of strong emotion. —*n.* **1.** The act or sound of choking. **2.** That which constricts or chokes; a narrow part, such as the chokebore of a gun. **3.** A device used in an internal-combustion engine to enrich the fuel mixture by reducing the flow of air to the carburetor. [Middle English *choken,* short for *achoken,* from Old English *ācēocian.*]

choke·bore (chōk′bôr′, -bōr′) *n.* **1.** A shotgun bore that narrows toward the muzzle to prevent wide scattering of the shot. **2.** A gun with a bore of this kind.

choke·cher·ry (chōk′chĕr′ē) *n.* **1.** A North American shrub or tree, *Prunus virginiana,* with very astringent dark-red or blackish fruit. **2.** The fruit of this shrub. [From the bitter fruit.]

chol·er (kŏl′ər, kō′lər) *n.* Anger; irritability. [Middle English *coler(a),* from Old French *colere,* from Latin *cholera,* bilious diarrhea, from Greek *kholera,* from *kholē,* bile, gall.]

chol·er·a (kŏl′ər-ə) *n.* An acute infectious epidemic disease, often fatal, characterized by watery diarrhea, vomiting, cramps, and suppression of urine. Also called **Asiatic cholera.** [Latin *cholera,* bilious diarrhea.]

chol·er·ic (kŏl′ə-rĭk, kə-lĕr′ĭk) *adj.* **1.** Easily angered; bad-tempered. **2.** Showing or expressing anger.

cho·les·ter·ol (kə-lĕs′tə-rôl′, -rōl′) *n.* A white soapy crystalline substance, $C_{27}H_{45}OH$, present in most animal and plant tissues and substances and required in many bodily processes, occurring notably in bile, gallstones, the brain, blood cells, plasma, egg yolk, and seeds. [Greek *kholē,* bile, gall + *stereos,* hard, solid + -OL (so called because first found in gallstones).]

chomp (chŏmp) *v.* Var. of **champ** (bite).

choose (chōōz) *v.* **chose** (chōz), **cho·sen** (chō′zən), **choos·ing.** —*tr.v.* **1.** To select from a number of possible alternatives; decide upon and pick out: *He chose the red sweater.* **2.** To want; desire: *choose to go.* —*intr.v.* To make a choice; select; decide: *You may do as you choose.* [Middle English *chosen,* from Old English *cēosan.*]
   Syns: **1. choose, cull, elect, pick, select, single (out)** *v. Core meaning:* To make a choice from a number of alternatives (*chose only the best students*). **2. choose, desire, like, please, want, will, wish** *v. Core meaning:* To have the desire or inclination to (*thought they could do as they chose*).

choos·y (chōō′zē) *adj.* **-i·er, -i·est.** Also **choos·ey.** Unwilling to settle for less than the best; hard to please. —**choos′i·ness** *n.*

chop¹ (chŏp) *v.* **chopped, chop·ping.** —*tr.v.* **1.** To cut by

striking with a heavy, sharp tool, such as an axe: *chop wood.* **2.** To cut into bits; mince: *chop onions.* **3.** *Sports.* To hit or hit at with a short, swift downward stroke. —*intr.v.* To make heavy, cutting strokes. —*n.* **1.** The act of chopping. **2.** A swift, short, cutting blow or stroke: *I took a chop at the ball.* **3.** A chopped-off piece, esp. a cut of meat, usu. taken from the rib, shoulder, or loin and containing a bone. **4.** A short, irregular motion of waves. [Middle English *choppen,* var. of *chappen,* to split.]

chop² (chŏp) *intr.v.* **chopped, chop·ping.** To swerve, as a ship in the wind. [Orig. "to exchange," from Middle English *chappen,* to barter, trade, from Old English *cēapian,* ult. from Latin *caupō,* trader.]

chop·house (chŏp′hous′) *n.* A restaurant that specializes in serving chops and steaks.

chop·per (chŏp′ər) *n. Slang.* A helicopter.

chop·py (chŏp′ē) *adj.* **-pi·er, -pi·est.** Abruptly shifting or breaking, as waves.

chops (chŏps) *pl.n.* The jaws, cheeks, or jowls of animals or man. [Orig. unknown.]

chop·sticks (chŏp′stĭks′) *pl.n.* A pair of slender sticks used as eating utensils chiefly in Oriental countries. [Pidgin English *chop,* fast + STICK(s).]

chopsticks

chop su·ey (chŏp sōō′ē). A Chinese-American dish consisting of small pieces of meat or chicken cooked with bean sprouts and other vegetables and served with rice. [Cantonese *tsap sui,* "mixed pieces."]

cho·ral (kôr′əl, kōr′-) *adj.* **1.** Of or pertaining to a chorus or choir. **2.** Written for performance by a chorus. —*n.* Var. of **chorale.**

cho·rale (kə-răl′, -räl′) *n.* Also **cho·ral.** **1.** A Protestant hymn tune. **2.** A harmonized hymn, esp. one for organ: *a Bach chorale.* **3.** A chorus or choir. [German *Choral(gesang),* "choral (song)."]

chord¹ (kôrd) *n.* **1.** A combination of three or more musical tones sounded simultaneously. **2.** An emotional feeling or response: *Her words struck a sympathetic chord.* [Short for ACCORD (influenced by Latin *chorda,* rope).]

chord² (kôrd) *n.* A line segment that joins two points on a curve. [From CORD (influenced by Latin *chorda,* rope).]

chor·date (kôr′dāt′, -dĭt) *n.* Any of numerous animals belonging to the phylum Chordata, which includes all vertebrates and certain marine animals having a spinal column or notochord, as the lancelets. [From Latin *chorda,* rope.]

chore (chôr, chōr) *n.* **1. chores.** Any daily or routine domestic tasks. **2.** An unpleasant or burdensome task. [Var. of CHAR (chore).]

cho·re·a (kô-rē′ə, kō-) *n.* A nervous disorder, esp. of children, marked by uncontrollable and irregular movements of the arm, leg, and face muscles. Also called **St. Vitus' dance.** [Latin, dance, from Greek *khoreia,* choral dance, from *khoros,* chorus.]

cho·re·o·graph (kôr′ē-ə-grăf′, kōr′-) *tr.v.* To create the choreography of (a ballet or other stage work). —*intr.v.* To serve as a choreographer. —**cho′re·og′ra·pher** (kôr′-ē-ŏg′rə-fər, kōr′-) *n.*

cho·re·og·ra·phy (kôr′ē-ŏg′rə-fē, kōr′-) *n.* **1.** The art of creating and arranging ballets or dances. **2.** The art of dancing. [French *chorégraphie,* from Greek *khoros,* dance.] —**cho′re·o·graph′ic** (kôr′ē-ə-grăf′ĭk, kōr′-) *adj.*

cho·ric (kôr′ĭk, kōr′-, kŏr′-) *adj.* Of or pertaining to a chorus, esp. a Greek chorus.

cho·ri·on (kôr′ē-ŏn′, kōr′-) *n.* The outer membrane that encloses the embryo of a reptile, bird, or mammal. [Greek *khorion,* afterbirth.]

cho·ris·ter (kôr′ĭ-stər, kōr′-, kŏr′-) *n.* A choir singer. [In Middle English *queristre,* from Medieval Latin *chorista,* from *chorus,* chorus.]

cho·roid (kôr′oid′, kōr′-) *n.* Also **cho·roi·de·a** (kô-roi′dē-ə, kō-). The dark-brown vascular membrane of the eye between the sclera and the retina. [Greek *khorioeidēs,* resembling an afterbirth : *khorion,* afterbirth + *eidos,* form.]

chor·tle (chôr′tl) *intr.v.* **-tled, -tling.** To chuckle throatily. —*n.* A snorting, joyful chuckle. [Blend of CHUCKLE and SNORT, coined by Lewis Carroll.] —**chor′tler** *n.*

cho·rus (kôr′əs, kōr′-) *n., pl.* **-rus·es. 1. a.** A body of singers who perform choral compositions. **b.** A body of vocalists and dancers who support the soloists and leading actors in operas, musical comedies, and revues. **2.** A composition in four or more parts written for a large number of singers. **3. a.** In drama or poetry recitation, a group of persons who speak or sing a given part or composition in unison. **b.** In Elizabethan drama, an actor who recites the prologue and epilogue to a play and sometimes comments on the action. **4. a.** In Greek poetry and drama, a ceremonial dance performed to the singing of odes. **b.** The portion of a drama consisting of choric dance and ode. **c.** The body of actors whose choric performance comments upon and accompanies the action of the play. **5.** Any simultaneous speech, song, or other utterance made by a number of persons or animals: *a chorus of boos from the bleachers.* —*v.* **-rused** or **-russed, -rus·ing** or **-rus·sing.** —*tr.v.* To sing or utter in chorus. —*intr.v.* To speak or sing in chorus. —*idiom.* **in chorus.** With simultaneous utterance; all together. [Latin, from Greek *khoros,* dance, chorus.]

chose (chōz) *v.* Past tense of **choose.**

cho·sen (chō′zən) *v.* Past participle of **choose.** —*adj.* Selected from or preferred above others.

chough (chŭf) *n.* A crowlike Old World bird of the genus *Pyrrhocorax,* with black plumage and red legs. [Middle English *choge, chowe.*]

chow[1] (chou) *n.* Also **chow chow.** A heavy-set dog with a long, dense, reddish-brown or black coat and a blackish tongue. [Perh. from Cantonese *kao,* dog.]

chow[1]

chow[2] (chou) *n. Slang.* Food; victuals. [Pidgin English, prob. from Mandarin *ch'ao*[3], to stir, fry, cook.]

chow·der (chou′dər) *n.* A thick soup or stew containing fish or shellfish, esp. clams, and vegetables, often in a milk base. [French *chaudière,* stew pot, from Old French, from Late Latin *caldāria,* caldron.]

chow mein (chou′ mān′). A Chinese-American dish consisting of any of various combinations of stewed vegetables and meat, served over fried noodles. [Cantonese, "fried noodles."]

chrism (krĭz′əm) *n.* A mixture of oil and balsam consecrated by a bishop and used for anointing in various church sacraments, such as baptism and confirmation. [Middle English *crisme,* from Old English *crisma,* from Late Latin *chrisma,* from Greek *khrisma,* ointment, from *khriein,* to anoint.] —**chris′mal** (krĭz′məl) *adj.*

Christ (krīst) *n.* Jesus, the son of Mary, regarded by Christians as being the Son of God and the Messiah foretold by the prophets of the Old Testament. [Middle English *Crist,*

from Old English *Crist,* from Latin *Christus,* from Greek *Khristos,* "the anointed (one)," from *khriein,* to anoint.]

chris·ten (krĭs′ən) *tr.v.* **1.** To baptize. **2.** To give a name to at baptism. **3.** To name and dedicate ceremonially: *christen a ship.* [Middle English *cristen,* from Old English *cristnian,* from *Cristen,* Christian.]

Chris·ten·dom (krĭs′ən-dəm) *n.* **1.** Christians collectively. **2.** The Christian world.

chris·ten·ing (krĭs′ə-nĭng) *n.* The Christian sacrament of baptism, including the bestowal of a name.

Chris·tian (krĭs′chən) *n.* A person who believes in Christ or follows the religion based on his teachings. —*adj.* **1.** Professing belief in Jesus as Christ or following the religion based on his teachings. **2.** Pertaining to or derived from Jesus or his teachings. **3.** Manifesting the qualities or spirit of Christ; Christlike. **4.** Pertaining to or characteristic of Christianity or its adherents. [Middle English *Cristen,* from Old English *Cristen,* from Latin *Christiānus,* from Greek *Khristianos,* from *Khristos,* Christ.]

Christian era. The period beginning with the birth of Jesus (conventionally in A.D. 1).

chris·ti·a·ni·a (krĭs′tē-ä′nē-ə, -chē-ăn′ē-ə) *n.* A ski turn in which the body is swung from a crouching position to change direction or to make a stop. [Norwegian, from *Christiania,* former name for Oslo.]

Chris·ti·an·i·ty (krĭs′chē-ăn′ĭ-tē) *n.* **1.** The Christian religion, founded on the teachings of Jesus. **2.** Christians as a group; Christendom. **3.** The condition or fact of being a Christian.

Chris·tian·ize (krĭs′chə-nīz′) *v.* **-ized, -iz·ing.** —*tr.v.* To convert to Christianity. —*intr.v.* To adopt Christianity. —**Chris′tian·i·za′tion** *n.* —**Chris′tian·iz′er** *n.*

Christian name. A name given at birth or baptism.

Christian Science. The church and the religious system founded by Mary Baker Eddy that emphasizes healing through spiritual means as an important element of Christianity and teaches pure divine goodness as underlying the scientific reality of existence. Also officially called **Church of Christ, Scientist.** —**Christian Scientist.**

Christ·like (krīst′līk′) *adj.* Having the spiritual qualities or attributes of Christ. —**Christ′like′ness** *n.*

Christ·mas (krĭs′məs) *n.* **1.** December 25, a holiday celebrated by Christians as the anniversary of the birth of Jesus. **2.** Also **Christmastide.** The Christian church festival extending from December 24 (Christmas Eve) through January 6 (Epiphany). [Middle English *Cristesmasse,* from Old English *Cristesmæsse.*]

Christ·mas·tide (krĭs′məs-tīd′) *n.* The festival and season of Christmas.

Christmas tree. An evergreen or artificial tree decorated during the Christmas season.

chrom-. Var. of **chromo-.**

chromat-. Var. of **chromato-.**

chro·mate (krō′māt′) *n.* A salt or ester of chromic acid.

chro·mat·ic (krō-măt′ĭk) *adj.* **1.** Of or pertaining to colors or color. **2.** *Mus.* Of, pertaining to, or based on all the tones of the chromatic scale, as a melody or chord. —**chro·mat′i·cal·ly** *adv.* —**chro·mat′i·cism** *n.*

chromatic aberration. A distortion of the color of an image that is caused by different degrees to which a lens bends light of different wavelengths.

chro·mat·ics (krō-măt′ĭks) *n.* (used with a sing. verb). The scientific study of color.

chromatic scale. A musical scale consisting of 12 semitones.

chro·ma·tid (krō′mə-tĭd) *n.* Either of a pair of longitudinal strands of a chromosome.

chro·ma·tin (krō′mə-tĭn) *n. Genetics.* A complex of nucleic acids and proteins present in chromosomes that stains intensely with basic dyes.

chromato- or **chromat-.** A prefix meaning color, staining, or pigmentation: **chromatin.** [From Greek *khrōma,* color.]

chro·mat·o·gram (krō-măt′ə-grăm′) *n.* The pattern formed on the adsorbent medium in chromatography.

chro·ma·tog·ra·phy (krō′mə-tŏg′rə-fē) *n.* Chemical analysis of a complex mixture by percolation through a selectively adsorbing medium, yielding identifiable layers.

chrome (krōm) *n.* **1. a.** Chromium. **b.** Anything plated with a chromium alloy. **2.** A pigment containing chromium. [French, from Greek *khrōma*, color (from the brilliant colors of chromium compounds).]

chro·mic (krō′mĭk) *adj.* Of, pertaining to, or containing chromium, esp. with valence 3.

chro·mite (krō′mīt′) *n.* A widely distributed black to brownish-black chromium ore, $FeCr_2O_4$.

chro·mi·um (krō′mē-əm) *n. Symbol* **Cr** A lustrous, hard, steel-gray metallic element, resistant to tarnish and corrosion and found primarily in chromite. It is used as a catalyst, to harden steel alloys, to produce stainless steels, in corrosion-resistant decorative platings, and as pigment in glass. Atomic number 24; atomic weight 51.996; melting point 1,890°C; boiling point 2,482°C; specific gravity 7.18; valences 2, 3, 6.

chromo– or **chrom–.** A prefix meaning: **1.** Color or pigment: **chromosome. 2.** Chromium or chromic acid: **chromite.** [Greek *khrōma*, color.]

chro·mo·some (krō′mə-sōm′) *n.* Any of the elongated, chromatin-containing bodies of the cell nuclei of plants and animals. Composed mainly of DNA, they are responsible for the determination and transmission of hereditary characteristics. [CHROMO- + -SOME (body).] —**chro′mo·som′al** (-sō′məl) *adj.*

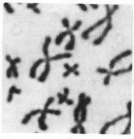

chromosome   chuck²

chro·mo·sphere (krō′mə-sfîr′) *n.* A transparent layer of gas, primarily hydrogen, several thousand kilometers in depth, that surrounds the photosphere of the sun.

chron–. Var. of **chrono–.**

chron·ic (krŏn′ĭk) *adj.* **1.** Of long duration; continuing; constant: *chronic money problems.* **2.** Prolonged; lingering, as certain diseases: *chronic colitis.* **3.** Subject to a disease or habit for a long time; inveterate: *a chronic alcoholic; a chronic liar.* [French *chronique,* from Latin *chronicus,* from Greek *khronos,* time.] —**chron′i·cal·ly** *adv.*

chron·i·cle (krŏn′ĭ-kəl) *n.* A straightforward record of historical events in order of occurrence. —*tr.v.* **-cled, -cling.** To record in, or in the form of, a chronicle. [Middle English *cronicle,* ult. from Greek *(biblia) khronika,* "chronological (books)," from *khronos,* time.] —**chron′i·cler** (-klər) *n.*

Chron·i·cles (krŏn′ĭ-kəlz) *n.* See table at Bible.

chrono– or **chron–.** A prefix meaning time: **chronometer.** [From Greek *khronos,* time.]

chron·o·log·i·cal (krŏn′ə-lŏj′ĭ-kəl, krō′nə-) or **chron·o·log·ic** (-lŏj′ĭk) *adj.* **1.** Arranged in order of time of occurrence. **2.** In accordance with or relating to chronology. —**chron′o·log′i·cal·ly** *adv.*

chro·nol·o·gy (krə-nŏl′ə-jē) *n., pl.* **-gies. 1.** The science that deals with the determination of dates and the sequence of events. **2.** A chronological list or table. **3.** The arrangement of events in time. [CHRONO- + -LOGY.] —**chro·nol′o·gist** *n.*

chro·nom·e·ter (krə-nŏm′ĭ-tər) *n.* An exceptionally precise clock or other timepiece, esp. as used in navigation. [CHRONO- + -METER.]

chron·o·scope (krŏn′ə-skōp′, krō′nə-) *n.* An optical instrument for measuring small time intervals. [CHRONO- + -SCOPE.]

chrys–. Var. of **chryso–.**

chrys·a·lid (krĭs′ə-lĭd) *n.* A chrysalis.

chrys·a·lis (krĭs′ə-lĭs) *n., pl.* **-lis·es** or **chry·sal·i·des** (krĭ-săl′ĭ-dēz′). The pupal stage in the development of a moth or butterfly, enclosed in a firm case or cocoon. [Latin *chrusallis,* from Greek *khrusallis,* the golden pupa of a butterfly, from *khrusos,* gold.]

chry·san·the·mum (krĭ-săn′thə-məm) *n.* **1.** Any of several plants of the genus *Chrysanthemum,* the cultivated forms esp. having showy flowers of various colors and sizes. **2.** The flower of any of these plants. [Latin *chrusanthemum,* from Greek *khrusanthemon,* "gold flower."]

chryso– or **chrys–.** A prefix meaning gold or the color of gold: **chrysotile.** [From Greek *khrusos,* gold.]

chrys·o·lite (krĭs′ə-līt′) *n.* A mineral, olivine. [Middle English *crisolite,* from Old French, from Latin *chrūsolithus,* from Greek *khrusolithos,* "goldstone."]

chrys·o·prase (krĭs′ə-prāz′) *n.* An apple-green chalcedony used as a gemstone. [Middle English *crisopase,* from Old French *crisopace,* from Latin *chrūsoprasus,* from Greek *khrusoprasos,* "gold green."]

chrys·o·tile (krĭs′ə-tīl′) *n.* A fibrous mineral variety of serpentine forming part of commercial asbestos. [CHRYSO- + Greek *tilos,* fine hair.]

chub·by (chŭb′ē) *adj.* **-bi·er, -bi·est.** Rounded and plump. —**chub′bi·ness** *n.*

chuck¹ (chŭk) *tr.v.* **1.** To pat or squeeze fondly or playfully, esp. under the chin. **2.** To throw; toss: *Chuck the ball over here.* **3.** *Informal.* To throw out; discard: *chuck an old suit* —*n.* **1.** An affectionate pat or squeeze under the chin. **2.** A throw, toss, or pitch. [Perh. from Old French *choquer,* to strike, shock.]

chuck² (chŭk) *n.* **1.** A cut of beef extending from the neck to the ribs and including the shoulder blade. **2.** A clamp that holds a tool, or the material being worked, in a machine such as a drill or a lathe. [Var. of CHOCK.]

chuck-full (chŏk′fŏol′, chŭk′-) *adj.* Var. of **chock-full.**

chuck·le (chŭk′əl) *intr.v.* **-led, -ling. 1.** To laugh quietly or to oneself. **2.** To cluck or chuck, as a hen. —*n.* A quiet laugh. [Prob. imit.] —**chuck′ler** *n.*

chug (chŭg) *n.* A dull explosive sound, usu. short and repeated, made by or as if by a laboring or slowly running engine. —*intr.v.* **chugged, chug·ging. 1.** To make chugs. **2.** To travel or move while making chugs. [Imit.]

chuk·ka (chŭk′ə) *n.* A short, ankle-length boot with two pairs of eyelets. [From CHUKKER.]

chuk·ker (chŭk′ər) *n.* Also **chuk·kar.** One of the periods of play in a polo match. [Hindi *cakkar,* circle, turn.]

chum (chŭm) *n.* An intimate friend or companion. —*intr.v.* **chummed, chum·ming.** To be a close friend. [Perh. from *chamber fellow,* roommate.]

chum·my (chŭm′ē) *adj.* **-mi·er, -mi·est.** *Informal.* Intimate; friendly. —See Syns at **friendly.** —**chum′mi·ly** *adv.* —**chum′mi·ness** *n.*

chump (chŭmp) *n.* One who is easily tricked or deceived; a dupe. [Prob. a blend of CHUNK and LUMP or STUMP.]

chunk (chŭngk) *n.* **1.** A thick mass or piece of something: *a chunk of ice; a chunk of bread.* **2.** A fair or substantial amount: *That car cost a chunk of cash.* [Prob. a var. of CHUCK.]

chunk·y (chŭng′kē) *adj.* **-i·er, -i·est. 1.** Short and thick; thickset; stocky. **2.** In chunks. —**chunk′i·ness** *n.*

church (chûrch) *n.* **1. Church.** All Christians regarded as a spiritual body. **2.** A building for public worship. **3.** A congregation. **4.** Public divine worship in a church; a religious service. **5.** Ecclesiastical power as distinguished from the secular: *the separation of church and state.* **6.** The clerical profession; clergy. [Middle English *chirche,* from Old English *ciric,* ult. from Late Greek *(dōma) kuriakon,* the Lord's (house), from Greek *kurios,* lord.]

church·go·er (chûrch′gō′ər) *n.* One who attends church regularly. —**church′go′ing** *adj. & n.*

church·man (chûrch′mən) *n.* **1.** A clergyman; priest. **2.** A member of a church.

Church of Christ, Scientist. The official name of the Christian Science Church.

Church of England. The episcopal and liturgical national church of England, which withdrew its recognition of papal authority in the 16th cent

Church of Jesus Christ of Latter-day Saints. The official name of the Mormon Church.

church·wom·an (chûrch'wŏom'ən) n. A female member of a church.

church·yard (chûrch'yärd') n. A yard adjacent to a church, often used as a burial ground.

churl (chûrl) n. 1. A rude, surly person. 2. A medieval peasant. [Middle English *churl*, man, husband, from Old English *ceorl*, free man of the lowest rank.]

churl·ish (chûr'lĭsh) adj. Rude; boorish. —See Syns at **coarse.** —**churl'ish·ly** adv. —**churl'ish·ness** n.

churn (chûrn) n. A container or device in which cream or milk is agitated to separate the oily globules from the other parts, used to make butter. —tr.v. 1. To stir or agitate (milk or cream) in a churn in order to make butter. 2. To make by the agitation of milk or cream. 3. To swirl or agitate vigorously: *Wind churned up the piles of leaves.* —intr.v. 1. To make butter by operating a churn. 2. To move with great agitation: *Waves churned and beat against the boat.* [Middle English *chírne*, from Old English *cyrin, cyrn.*]

churr (chûr) n. The sharp whirring sound made by some insects and birds. —intr.v. To make a churr. [Imit.]

chute (shōōt) n. 1. An inclined or vertical trough, passage, or channel down which things may be dropped or slid: *a laundry chute.* 2. A waterfall or rapid. 3. *Informal.* A parachute. [French, a fall, from Old French *cheoir,* to fall, from Latin *cadere.*]

chut·ney (chŭt'nē) n. A pungent relish made of fruits, spices, and herbs. [Hindi *caṭnī.*]

chutz·pah (кнŏŏt'spə) n. *Slang.* Brazenness; gall; nerve. [Yiddish.]

chyle (kīl) n. A thick white or pale-yellow fluid, consisting of lymph and finely emulsified fat, absorbed by lymph-carrying vessels from the intestine in digestion. [Latin *chÿlus,* juice, from Greek *khulos,* from *khein,* to pour.] —**chy'lous** (kī'ləs) adj.

chyme (kīm) n. The semifluid mass of partly digested food that is passed from the stomach to the duodenum. [Late Latin *chÿmus,* from Greek *khumos,* juice, from *khein,* to pour.] —**chy'mous** (kī'məs) adj.

ci·bo·ri·um (sĭ-bôr'ē-əm, -bōr'-) n., pl. **-bo·ri·a** (-bôr'ē-ə, -bōr'-). 1. A vaulted canopy placed over an altar. 2. A covered receptacle for holding the consecrated wafers of the Eucharist. [Medieval Latin *cibōrium,* from Latin, drinking vessel, from Greek *kibōrion,* the seed vessel of the Indian lotus, a cup.]

ci·ca·da (sĭ-kā'də, -kä'-) n., pl. **-das** or **-dae** (-dē'). Any of various insects of the family Cicadidae, having a broad head, membranous wings, and, in the male, a pair of resonating organs that produce a characteristic high-pitched, droning sound. [Latin *cicāda.*]

cic·a·trix (sĭk'ə-trĭks', sĭ-kā'trĭks) n., pl. **cic·a·tri·ces** (sĭk'ə-trī'sēz', sĭ-kā'trĭ-sēz'). 1. A scar formed of fibrous connective tissue on a healing wound. 2. *Bot.* A scar left where a leaf or a branch has been detached. [Middle English *cicatrice,* from Latin *cicātrix.*] —**cic'a·tri'cial** (sĭk'ə-trĭsh'əl) adj.

cic·e·ro·ne (sĭs'ə-rō'nē) n., pl. **-nes** or **-ni** (-nē). A guide who conducts sightseers. [Italian, orig. "a learned antiquarian," from *Cicerone,* Marcus Tullius Cicero (106–43 B.C.), Roman statesman.]

–cide. A suffix meaning: 1. Killer of: **insecticide.** 2. Murder or killing of: **genocide.** [French, from Latin *caedere,* to kill.]

ci·der (sī'dər) n. Also *Brit.* **cy·der.** The juice pressed from apples or, formerly, from other fruits, used to produce vinegar or as a beverage. [Middle English *sidre,* from Old French, from Medieval Latin *sícera,* from Greek *sikera,* strong drink, from Hebrew *shlekār.*]

ci·gar (sĭ-gär') n. A small, compact roll of tobacco leaves prepared for smoking. [Spanish *cigarro.*]

cig·a·rette (sĭg'ə-rĕt', sĭg'ə-rĕt') n. Also **cig·a·ret.** A small roll of finely cut tobacco for smoking, usu. enclosed in a wrapper of thin paper. —*modifier: a cigarette holder.* [French, dim. of *cigare,* cigar.]

cil·i·a (sĭl'ē-ə) pl.n. *Sing.* **-i·um** (-ē-əm). 1. Hairlike processes extending from a cell surface and often capable of rhythmical motion. 2. The eyelashes. [New Latin *cilium,* eyelash, from Latin, the lower eyelid.]

cil·i·ar·y (sĭl'ē-ĕr'ē) adj. 1. Of, pertaining to, or resembling

cilia. 2. Of or pertaining to the ciliary body.

ciliary body. The thickened part of the vascular layer of the eye that connects the choroid with the iris.

cil·i·ate (sĭl'ē-ĭt, -āt') adj. Also **cil·i·at·ed** (-ā'tĭd). Having cilia. —n. Any of various protozoans of the class Ciliata, having numerous cilia.

cinch (sĭnch) n. 1. A girth for holding a pack or saddle on a horse. 2. *Informal.* A firm grip. 3. *Slang.* Something easy to accomplish; a sure thing. —tr.v. 1. To put a saddle girth on. 2. *Slang.* To make certain of: *cinch a victory.* [Spanish *cincha,* "girdle," from Latin *cingula,* from *cingere,* to gird.]

cin·cho·na (sĭn-kō'nə, -chō'-, sĭng-) n. 1. Any of various trees and shrubs of the genus Cinchona, native to South America, whose bark yields quinine and other medicinal alkaloids. 2. The dried bark of any of these trees. In this sense, also called **Peruvian bark.** [After Francisca Henriquez de Ribera, countess of Chinchón (1576–1639), who introduced it into Europe.]

cin·der (sĭn'dər) n. 1. A burned or partly burned substance, such as coal or wood, that is not reduced to ashes but cannot be burned further. 2. A partly charred substance that can burn further but without flame. 3. **cinders.** Ashes. 4. Volcanic scoria. [Middle English *cinder, sinder,* from Old English *sinder,* dross.] —**cin'der·y** adj.

cinder block. A hollow, concrete building block made with coal cinders.

cin·e·ma (sĭn'ə-mə) n. 1. **A motion picture.** 2. A motion picture theater. 3. **the cinema. a.** Motion pictures collectively. **b.** The motion-picture industry. 4. The art of making motion pictures. [From Greek *kinēma,* motion, from *kinein,* to move.] —**cin'e·mat'ic** (sĭn'ə-mǎt'ĭk) adj. —**cin'e·mat'i·cal·ly** adv.

cin·e·ma·tog·ra·phy (sĭn'ə-mə-tŏg'rə-fē) n. The making of motion pictures. —**cin'e·ma·tog'ra·pher** n.

cin·e·rar·i·a (sĭn'ə-râr'ē-ə) n. A plant, Senecio cruentis, native to the Canary Islands and widely cultivated as a house plant, with flat clusters of blue or purplish daisylike flowers. [From Latin *cinerārius,* of ashes (from the ash-colored down on its leaves).]

cin·e·rar·i·um (sĭn'ə-râr'ē-əm) n., pl. **-i·a** (ē-ə). A place for keeping the ashes of a cremated body. [Latin, from *cinis,* ashes.] —**cin'er·ar'y** (sĭn'ə-rĕr'ē) adj.

cin·na·bar (sĭn'ə-bär') n. 1. A heavy reddish mercuric sulfide, HgS, that is the principal ore of mercury. 2. Red mercuric sulfide used as a pigment. [Middle English *cynoper,* from Old French *cenobre,* from Latin *cinnābaris,* from Greek *kinnabari.*]

cin·na·mon (sĭn'ə-mən) n. 1. **a.** Either of two trees, Cinnamomum zeylanicum or C. lourerii, of tropical Asia, with very aromatic bark. **b.** The yellowish-brown bark of either of these trees, dried and often ground, used as a spice. 2. Any of several trees yielding a spice similar to this. [Middle English *sinamome,* from Old French *cinnamome,* from Latin *cinna(mo)mum,* from Greek *kinna(mō)mon,* from Hebrew *qinnāmown.*]

ci·pher (sī'fər) n. Also **cy·pher. 1. a.** The mathematical symbol (0) denoting absence of quantity; zero. **b.** The number zero. 2. Any Arabic numeral or figure; a number. 3. The Arabic system of numerical notation. 4. A person or thing without influence or value; a nonentity. **5. a.** Any systematic, secret code in which letters, words, or units of text are arbitrarily transposed or substituted according to a predetermined key. **b.** The key to such a system. **c.** A message in cipher. 6. A design combining or interweaving letters or initials; monogram. —intr.v. To solve problems in arithmetic; calculate. —tr.v. 1. To put (a message) in secret writing. 2. To solve (a problem) by means of arithmetic. [Middle English *cifre,* from Old French, from Medieval Latin *cifra,* from Arabic *ṣifr.*]

cir·ca (sûr'kə) prep. About: *a house built circa 1750.* [Latin *circā,* from *circus,* circle.]

Cir·ce (sûr'sē) n. *Gk. Myth.* An enchantress described in the *Odyssey* who turns men into swine.

cir·cle (sûr'kəl) n. 1. A closed plane curve all of whose points are equidistant from a given fixed point, the center. 2. A region of a plane having such a curve as its outer boundary. 3. Anything shaped like a circle, as a ring or halo. 4. A circular course, circuit, or orbit. 5. A curved section or tier of seats in a theater. 6. A series or process that finishes at its starting point or continuously repeats itself; cycle. **7.** A group of people sharing an interest, activity, or achievement: *a wide circle of friends; a sewing circle.* **8.** A sphere of influence or interest; domain; realm: *He is an authority in the scientific circle.* **9.** *Logic.* A fallacy in reasoning in which the premise is used to prove the conclusion and the conclusion used to prove the premise. Also called **vicious circle.** —*v.* **-cled, -cling.** —*tr.v.* **1.** To make or form a circle around; enclose: *Police circled the area.* **2.** To move in a circle around: *The matador circled the bull.* —*intr.v.* To move in circles; revolve: *Crows circled overhead.* —See Syns at **surround.** [Middle English *cercle,* from Old French, from Latin *circulus,* dim. of *circus,* ring.] —**cir′cler** (-klər) *n.*

Syns: circle, crowd, gang, set *n. Core meaning:* A particular social group (*invited only our circle*).

cir·clet (sûr′klĭt) *n.* A small circle, esp. a circular ornament.

cir·cuit (sûr′kĭt) *n.* **1. a.** A closed curve, such as a circle or an ellipse. **b.** Any path that forms such a curve. **c.** A region having such a curve as its outer boundary. **2.** A closed path through which an electric current flows or may flow. **3.** A connection of electrical or electronic parts or devices intended to accomplish some purpose: *a radio circuit.* **4. a.** A regular route followed by a judge from town to town for the purpose of trying cases in each one of them. **b.** The district or area visited by such a judge. **c.** A similar route, such as that of a minister or salesman. —*tr.v.* To make a circuit of. —*intr.v.* To move about in a circuit. [Middle English, from Old French, from Latin *circuitus,* from *circumire,* to go around : *circum-,* around + *īre,* to go.]

circuit breaker. An automatic switch that interrupts a suddenly overloaded electric circuit.

cir·cu·i·tous (sər-kyōō′ĭ-təs) *adj.* Being or taking a roundabout, lengthy course. —See Syns at **indirect.** [Medieval Latin *circuitōsus,* from Latin *circuitus,* circuit.] —**cir·cu′i·tous·ly** *adv.* —**cir·cu′i·ty** or **cir·cu′i·tous·ness** *n.*

cir·cuit·ry (sûr′kĭ-trē) *n.* **1.** The design of or detailed plan for an electric or electronic circuit. **2.** Electric or electronic circuits in general.

cir·cu·lar (sûr′kyə-lər) *adj.* **1.** Of or pertaining to a circle. **2.** Shaped like or nearly like a circle; round. **3.** Forming or moving in a circle: *circular motion.* **4.** Circuitous; indirect; roundabout. **5.** Addressed or distributed to a large number of persons. —See Syns at **indirect.** —*n.* A printed advertisement, notice, etc., intended for public distribution. —**cir·cu·lar′i·ty** (sûr′kyə-lăr′ĭ-tē) or **cir·cu·lar·ness** *n.* —**cir′cu·lar·ly** *adv.*

circular saw. A power saw whose blade is a toothed metal disk that cuts as the blade rotates at a high speed. Also called **buzz saw.**

cir·cu·late (sûr′kyə-lāt) *v.* **-lat·ed, -lat·ing.** —*intr.v.* **1.** To move in or flow through a circle or circuit: *Blood circulates through the body.* **2.** To move around, as from person to person or place to place: *The guest of honor circulated at the party and talked with almost everybody there.* **3.** To move about or flow freely; be diffused: *The fan helps the air circulate.* **4.** To spread or distribute widely; disseminate: *Rumors tend to circulate quickly.* —*tr.v.* To cause to move about or be distributed: *The heart circulates the blood.* —**cir′cu·la′tive** (-lā′tĭv) *adj.* —**cir′cu·la′tor** *n.* —**cir′cu·la·to′ry** (-lə-tôr′ē, -tōr′ē) *adj.*

cir·cu·la·tion (sûr′kyə-lā′shən) *n.* **1.** The act or process of circulating. **2.** The movement of blood through the blood vessels of the body as a result of the heart's pumping action: *a person with poor circulation.* **3.** The passage of something, such as money or news, from person to person or from place to place: *There aren't many two-dollar bills in circulation.* **4. a.** The distribution of printed matter, such as newspapers: *This magazine has wide circulation.* **b.** The number of copies of a newspaper, magazine, etc., sold or distributed to the public: *a daily circulation of 400,000.*

circulatory system. The heart, blood vessels, and lymphatic system of the body.

circum-. A prefix meaning around or on all sides: **circumnavigate.** [Latin, from *circum,* around, from *circus,* circle.]

cir·cum·cen·ter of a triangle (sûr′kəm-sĕn′tər). The center of a circle that passes through the vertices of a triangle.

cir·cum·cise (sûr′kəm-sīz′) *tr.v.* **-cised, -cis·ing.** To remove the foreskin of (a boy or man) by surgery. [Middle English *circumcisen,* from Latin *circumcīdere,* "to cut around" : *circum,* around + *caedere,* to cut.] —**cir′cum·ci′sion** (-sĭzh′ən) *n.*

cir·cum·fer·ence (sər-kŭm′fər-əns) *n.* **1.** The boundary line of any closed curvilinear figure, esp. a circle. **2.** The length of such a boundary. [Middle English, from Old French, from Latin *circumferentia,* from *circumferre,* to carry around : *circum,* around + *ferre,* to carry.] —**cir′cum·fer·en′tial** (-fə-rĕn′shəl) *adj.*

cir·cum·flex (sûr′kəm-flĕks′) *n.* A mark (^) used over a vowel in certain languages or in phonetic keys to indicate quality of pronunciation. —*adj.* Marked with a circumflex. [Latin *circumflexus,* from *circumflectere,* to bend around : *circum,* around + *flectere,* to bend.]

cir·cum·lo·cu·tion (sûr′kəm-lō-kyōō′shən) *n.* **1.** A wordy or roundabout expression; for example, *the husband of my mother's sister* is a circumlocution for *my uncle.* **2.** The use of such expressions in speech or writing. [Middle English *circumlocucioun,* from Latin *circumloquī,* "to speak in a roundabout way" : *circum,* around + *loquī,* to speak.]

cir·cum·nav·i·gate (sûr′kəm-năv′ĭ-gāt′) *tr.v.* **-gat·ed, -gat·ing.** To sail completely around: *circumnavigate the earth.* —**cir·cum·nav′i·ga′tor** *n.*

cir·cum·scribe (sûr′kəm-skrīb′) *tr.v.* **-scribed, -scrib·ing.** **1.** To draw a line around; encircle. **2.** To confine within or as if within bounds; to limit; restrict: *Old age circumscribes one's activities.* **3.** *Geom.* **a.** To enclose (a polygon) with a plane curve so that the curve passes through every vertex of the polygon. **b.** To enclose (a plane curve) with a polygon so that each side of the polygon is tangent to the curve. **c.** To be a geometric figure that encloses another in one of these ways: *The circle circumscribes the triangle.* [Middle English *circumscriben,* from Latin *circumscrībere* : *circum,* around + *scrībere,* to write.] —**cir′cum·scrip′tion** (sûr′kəm-skrĭp′shən) *n.*

cir·cum·spect (sûr′kəm-spĕkt′) *adj.* Heedful of circumstances or consequences; prudent; cautious. —See Syns at **careful.** [Middle English, from Latin *circumspicere,* to look around, take heed : *circum,* around + *specere,* to look.] —**cir′cum·spect′ly** *adv.*

cir·cum·spec·tion (sûr′kəm-spĕk′shən) *n.* The act or condition of being circumspect; carefulness; caution. —See Syns at **prudence.**

cir·cum·stance (sûr′kəm-stăns′) *n.* **1. a.** Often **circumstances.** One of the conditions, facts, or events connected with and usu. affecting another event, a person, or a course of action: *Write a few lines giving the circumstances of why the car stopped.* **b.** The sum of all these conditions, facts, or events that are beyond one's control: *a victim of circumstance.* **2. circumstances.** Financial condition: *a man in comfortable circumstances.* **3.** Formal display; ceremony: *pomp and circumstance.* —**idioms. under no circumstances.** Never: *Under no circumstances should you use the laboratory without supervision.* **under** (or **in**) **the circumstances.** Given these conditions: *Under the circumstances that was the best solution I could find.* [Middle English, from Old French, from Latin *circumstāntia,* accessory details, from *circumstāre,* to stand around, be accessory : *circum,* around + *stāre,* to stand.]

cir·cum·stan·tial (sûr′kəm-stăn′shəl) *adj.* **1.** Of or dependent upon circumstances: *a circumstantial solution to the plot of the mystery novel.* **2.** Not of primary importance; incidental: *circumstantial matters.* **3.** Full of facts or details; complete: *a circumstantial account.* —**cir′cum·stan′tial·ly** *adv.*

circumstantial evidence. Evidence not bearing directly on the facts in a legal dispute but on various attendant circumstances from which a judge or jury might infer the occurrence of the facts in dispute.

cir·cum·vent (sûr′kəm-vĕnt′, sûr′kəm-vĕnt′) *tr.v.* **1.** To get the better of or overcome by ingenuity: *circumvent an enemy army.* **2.** To avoid by or as if by passing around: *circumvent a problem.* [From Latin *circumvenīre* : *circum,* around + *venīre,* to come.] —**cir′cum·ven′tion** *n.* —**cir′cum·ven′tive** *adj.*

cir·cus (sûr′kəs) *n., pl.* **-cus·es. 1. a.** A public entertainment with performances by acrobats, clowns, and trained ani-

---

| ă pat | ā pay | â care | ä father | ĕ pet | ē be | hw which | ĭ pit | ī tie | î pier | ŏ pot | ō toe | ô paw, for | oi noise |
| ōō took | ōō boot | ou out | th thin | th this | ŭ cut | | û urge | zh vision | ə about, item, edible, gallop, circus |

mals. **b.** The traveling company that puts on the circus. **c.** A circular arena, surrounded by tiers of seats and often covered by a tent, in which the circus is performed. **2.** An open-air arena used by the ancient Romans for athletic contests and public spectacles. **3.** *Informal.* A place or activity in which there is wild confusion or disorder. [Latin *circus,* ring, circle.]

cirque (sûrk) *n.* A steep hollow, often containing a small lake, that is at the upper end of some mountain valleys. [French, from Latin *circus,* ring, circle.]

cir·rate (sĭr'āt') *adj.* Also **cir·rose** (-ōs') or **cir·rous** (-əs). *Biol.* Having or of the nature of a cirrus or cirri.

cir·rho·sis (sĭ-rō'sĭs) *n.* A chronic disease of the liver marked by progressive destruction and regeneration of liver cells and increased connective-tissue formation, the entire organ shrinking and hardening in the process. [New Latin, "orange-colored disease" (from the color of the diseased liver) : Greek *kirrhos,* orange + -OSIS.] —**cir·rhot'ic** (sĭ-rŏt'ĭk) *adj.*

cir·ri (sĭr'ī) *n.* Plural of **cirrus.**

cir·ro·cu·mu·lus (sĭr'ō-kyōō'myə-ləs) *n.* A cloud composed of a series of small, regularly arranged parts in the form of ripples or grains, found typically about five miles above the earth. [CIRR(US) + CUMULUS.]

cir·rose (sĭr'ōs') or **cir·rous** (-əs) *adj. Biol.* Vars. of **cirrate.**

cir·ro·stra·tus (sĭr'ō-strā'təs, -străt'əs) *n.* A thin, hazy cloud, often covering the sky and producing a halo effect, found typically about six miles above the earth. [CIRR(US) + STRATUS.]

cir·rus (sĭr'əs) *n., pl.* **cir·ri** (sĭr'ī). **1.** A type of cloud composed of white, fleecy patches or bands, found at heights of about seven miles above the earth. **2.** *Bot.* A tendril or similar part. **3.** *Zool.* A slender, flexible appendage, such as a tentacle. [From Latin *cirrus,* curl, filament, tuft.]

cis·tern (sĭs'tərn) *n.* A large tank or reservoir for holding water or other liquid, esp. rainwater. [Middle English *cisterne,* from Old French, from Latin *cisterna,* water tank, from *cista,* box, from Greek *kistē,* basket.]

cit·a·del (sĭt'ə-dl, -děl') *n.* **1.** A fortress in a commanding position in or near a city. **2.** Any stronghold or fortified place. [Old French *citadelle,* from Old Italian *citadella,* from Latin *cīvitās,* citizenry, city.]

ci·ta·tion (sī-tā'shən) *n.* **1.** The act of citing. **2.** A reference or quotation. **3.** *Law.* A reference to previous court decisions or authoritative writings. **4.** A summons to appear in court. **5.** An official commendation for bravery, esp. in military service.

cite (sīt) *tr.v.* **cit·ed, cit·ing. 1.** To quote or mention as an authority or example: *Let me cite two cases of what I have in mind.* **2.** To summon to appear in court. **3.** To mention and commend for meritorious action: *The policeman was cited for bravery beyond the call of duty.* **4.** To call to attention or enumerate; to mention. [Middle English *citen,* to summon, from Old French *citer,* from Latin *citāre,* from *ciēre.*]

cith·a·ra (sĭth'ər-ə, kĭth'-) *n.* An ancient musical instrument resembling the lyre. [Latin, from Greek *kithara.*]

cith·er (sĭth'ər, sĭth'-) or **cith·ern** (-ərn) *n.* A cittern. [French *cithare,* from Latin *cithara,* cithara.]

cit·i·fied (sĭt'ə-fīd') *adj.* Having customs, manners, or fashions attributed to city people.

cit·i·fy (sĭt'ə-fī') *tr.v.* **-fied, -fy·ing. 1.** To cause to become like a city; make urban. **2.** To mark with the styles and manners of the city. —**cit'i·fi·ca'tion** *n.*

cit·i·zen (sĭt'ī-zən) *n.* **1.** A person owing loyalty to and entitled by birth or naturalization to the protection of a given country. **2.** A resident of a city or town, esp. one entitled to vote and enjoy other privileges there. **3.** A civilian as distinguished from a person employed by the military, the police, etc. [Middle English *citisein,* from Old French *citeien,* from *cite,* city.]

cit·i·zen·ry (sĭt'ī-zən-rē) *n., pl.* **-ries.** Citizens in general.

cit·i·zen·ship (sĭt'ī-zən-shĭp') *n.* The status of a citizen with its duties, rights, and privileges.

cit·rate (sĭt'rāt', sī'trāt') *n.* A salt or ester of citric acid.

cit·ric (sĭt'rĭk) *adj.* Of or obtained from citrus fruits.

citric acid. A colorless translucent crystalline acid, $C_6H_8O_7 \cdot H_2O$, principally derived by fermentation of carbohydrates or from lemon, lime, and pineapple juices, and used to prepare citrates, in flavorings, and in metal polishes.

cit·rine (sĭt'rĭn, -rēn') *n.* **1.** A pale-yellow variety of quartz, resembling topaz. **2.** A light yellow. —*adj.* Light yellow. [Middle English, from Old French *citrin,* from Medieval Latin *citrīnus,* from Latin *citrus,* citrus.]

cit·ro·nel·la (sĭt'rə-něl'ə) *n.* **1.** A tropical Eurasian grass, *Cymbopogon nardus,* with bluish-green, lemon-scented leaves. **2.** A light-yellow aromatic oil obtained from citronella and used in insect repellents and perfumes. [From French *citronnelle,* lemon oil, dim. of *citron,* citron.]

cit·rus (sĭt'rəs) *adj.* Also **cit·rous. 1.** Of or pertaining to trees or shrubs of the genus *Citrus,* many of which bear edible fruit, such as the orange, lemon, lime, and grapefruit. **2.** Of or characteristic of the fruits of these trees or shrubs. —*n., pl.* **-rus·es** or **citrus.** A citrus tree or shrub. [Latin, citron tree, citrus tree.]

cit·tern (sĭt'ərn) *n.* A 16th-cent. guitar with a pear-shaped body. Also called **cither** or **cithern.** [Middle English *giterne,* a medieval stringed instrument.]

cit·y (sĭt'ē) *n., pl.* **-ies. 1.** A center of population, commerce, and culture; a large and important town. **2.** In the United States, an incorporated municipality with definite boundaries and legal powers set forth in a charter granted by the state. **3.** In Canada, a municipality of high rank, usu. determined by population but varying by province. **4.** In Great Britain, a large incorporated town, usu. the seat of a bishop, with its title conferred by the Crown. **5.** All the people living in a city. —*modifier: a city life; city government.* [Middle English *cite,* from Old French, from Latin *cīvitās,* citizenry, state, city, from *cīvis,* citizen.]

city hall. 1. The building in which the administrative offices of a municipal government are located. **2.** A municipal government, esp. its officials.

civ·et (sĭv'ĭt) *n.* **1.** Also **civet cat.** Any of various catlike animals of the family Viverridae, of Africa and Asia, having scent glands that secrete a fluid with a strong, musky odor. **2.** This fluid, used in the manufacture of perfumes. **3.** The fur of a civet. [French *civette,* from Old French, from Italian *zibetto,* from Arabic *zabād.*]

civet

civ·ic (sĭv'ĭk) *adj.* **1.** Of a city or community: *a civic event.* **2.** Of a citizen or citizens: *civic duties.* **3.** Of the public. — See Syns at **public.** [Latin *civicus,* from *cīvis,* citizen.]

civ·ics (sĭv'ĭks) *n.* (*used with a sing. verb*). The branch of political science that deals with the working of local and national government and the rights and duties of citizens.

civ·il (sĭv'əl) *adj.* **1.** Of a citizen or citizens: *civil rights.* **2.** Of a branch of government other than the legislative, judicial, or military: *civil service.* **3. a.** Within a country or community: *civil war.* **b.** Of the internal affairs of a country or community and its citizens: *civil disorder.* **4.** Of the general public and its affairs as distinguished from military or church affairs: *a civil marriage; civil authorities.* **5.** Polite; courteous: *a civil reply.* **6.** Designating or according to legally recognized divisions of time: *a civil year.* **7.** *Law.* Pertaining to the rights of private individuals and to legal proceedings concerning these rights as distinguished from criminal, military, or international rights, courts, or legal proceedings. —See Syns at **polite** and **public.** [Middle English, from Old French, from Latin *cīvīlis,* from *cīvis,* citizen.] —**civ'il·ly** *adv.*

civil engineer. An engineer trained in the design and construction of projects such as bridges, roads, dams, etc.

ci·vil·ian (sĭ-vĭl′yən) n. A person not serving in the armed forces. —*modifier: a civilian government.*

ci·vil·i·ty (sĭ-vĭl′ĭ-tē) n., pl. **-ties.** 1. Politeness; courtesy. 2. An act or expression of courtesy.

civ·i·li·za·tion (sĭv′ə-lə-zā′shən) n. 1. A condition of human society marked by an advanced stage of development in the arts, sciences, religion, government, etc.: *man's progression from barbarism to civilization.* 2. A culture and society developed by a particular nation, region, or period: *the civilization of ancient Rome.* 3. *Informal.* Modern society with its conveniences: *return to civilization after two weeks of camping.*

civ·i·lize (sĭv′ə-līz′) tr.v. **-lized, -liz·ing.** To bring from a primitive to a highly developed state of society and culture; educate. —**civ′i·liz′a·ble** adj. —**civ′i·liz′er** n.

civil law. 1. The body of law dealing with the rights of private citizens in a particular state or nation, as distinguished from criminal law, military law, or international law. 2. Any system of law having its origin in Roman law as distinguished from common law or canon law.

civil liberty. The legal guarantee of individual rights such as freedom of speech, thought, and action.

civil rights. Rights belonging to an individual by virtue of his status as a citizen. —*modifier:* **(civil-rights):** *the civil-rights movement for racial equality.*

civil service. 1. All branches of public service that are not legislative, judicial, or military. 2. In general, the persons employed by the civil branch of the government. —**civil servant.**

civil war. 1. A war between factions or regions of one country. 2. **Civil War.** In the United States, the war between the Union (the North) and the Confederacy (the South), lasting from 1861 to 1865.

Cl The symbol for the element chlorine.

clab·ber (klăb′ər) n. Sour, curdled milk. —tr.v. To cause to curdle. —intr.v. To become curdled. [Short for earlier *bonnyclabber,* from Irish : *bainne,* milk + *clabair,* thick sour milk.]

clack (klăk) intr.v. 1. To make an abrupt, dry sound of objects struck together: *Typewriters clacked in every office.* 2. To chatter thoughtlessly or at length. 3. To cackle or cluck, as a hen does. —tr.v. 1. To cause to make an abrupt, dry sound. 2. To blab (something): *clacked the rumor all around town.* —n. 1. A clacking sound. 2. Something that makes a clacking sound. 3. Thoughtless, prolonged talk; chatter. [Middle English *clacken,* from Old Norse *klaka.*] —**clack′er** n.

clad (klăd) v. A past tense and past participle of **clothe.**

claim (klām) tr.v. 1. To demand or ask for as one's own or one's due; assert one's right to: *claim luggage; claim a reward.* 2. To state to be true; assert or maintain: *He claimed that he could study better with the radio turned on.* 3. To deserve or call for; require: *political matters that claim all her attention.* —n. 1. A demand or request for something as one's rightful due: *file a claim for losses.* 2. A basis for demanding something; the right to ask for: *Columbus gave Spain a claim to all land he discovered.* 3. A statement of something as fact; assertion: *an advertisement that makes false claims concerning certain foods.* 4. Something claimed, esp. a tract of land claimed by a miner or homesteader. —*idiom.* **lay claim to.** To assert one's right to or ownership of. [Middle English *claimen,* from Old French *clamer,* to cry, appeal, from Latin *clāmāre,* to call.] —**claim′a·ble** adj.

claim·ant (klā′mənt) n. A person making a claim.

clair·voy·ance (klâr-voi′əns) n. The supposed power to perceive things that are out of the range of human senses. [French, "clear-seeing" : *clair,* clear + *voir,* to see, from Latin *vidēre.*] —**clair·voy·ant** (klâr-voi′ənt) n.

clam (klăm) n. 1. Any of various usu. burrowing saltwater and freshwater bivalve mollusks of the class Pelecypoda, including members of the genera *Venus, Mya,* and others, many of which are edible. 2. *Informal.* An uncommunicative person. —*modifier: a clam shell; clam juice.* —intr.v. **clammed, clam·ming.** To hunt for clams. —*phrasal verb.* **clam up.** To refuse to talk; remain silent. [Short for *clamshell,* "bivalve that shuts tight like a clamp," from Middle English *clam,* clamp, from Old English *clamm,* bond.]

clam·bake (klăm′bāk′) n. 1. A seashore picnic where clams, fish, corn, and other foods are baked in layers on buried hot stones. 2. *Informal.* A party, esp. a noisy and lively one.

clam·ber (klăm′bər, klăm′ər) —intr.v. To climb with difficulty, esp. on all fours; scramble. —n. The act of clambering. [Middle English *clambren,* from Old Norse *klembra,* to grip.] —**clam′ber·er** n.

clam·my (klăm′ē) adj. **-mi·er, -mi·est.** Unpleasantly damp, sticky, and usu. cold. [Middle English, from *clammen,* to stick, from Old English *clǣman.*] —**clam′mi·ly** adv. —**clam′mi·ness** n.

clam·or (klăm′ər). Also *Brit.* **clam·our.** —n. 1. A loud outcry or shouting; hubbub: *the clamor of a crowd.* 2. A vehement expression of discontent or protest; public outcry: *a clamor for less pollution.* 3. Any loud and sustained noise; din; blare: *the clamor of auto horns in the city.* —intr.v. 1. To make a clamor: *The children clamored for ice cream.* 2. To make importunate demands or complaints. —tr.v. To exclaim insistently and noisily: *They clamored their objections.* [Middle English *clamour,* from Old French, from Latin *clāmor,* from *clāmāre,* to cry out.] —**clam′or·er** n.

clam·or·ous (klăm′ər-əs) adj. Making, full of, or characterized by clamor: *a clamorous party.* —**clam′or·ous·ly** adv. —**clam′or·ous·ness** n.

clam·our n. & v. *Brit.* Var. of **clamor.**

clamp (klămp) n. A device for gripping or fastening things together, generally consisting of two parts that can be brought together by turning a screw. —tr.v. To grip, fasten, or support with or as if with a clamp. —*phrasal verb.* **clamp down.** *Informal.* To become more strict or repressive. [Middle English, from Middle Dutch *clampe.*]

clan (klăn) n. 1. A group of families, as in the Scottish Highlands, claiming a common ancestor. 2. Any numerous group of relatives, friends, or associates. [Middle English, from Scottish Gaelic *clann,* children, family, from Latin *planta,* shoot, plant.]

clan·des·tine (klăn-dĕs′tĭn) adj. Done secretly or kept secret, usu. for some unlawful purpose: *a clandestine meeting.* —See Syns at **secret.** [French *clandestin,* from Old French, from Latin *clandestīnus,* from *clam,* in secret.] —**clan·des′tine·ly** adv.

clang (klăng) intr.v. To make a loud, ringing, metallic sound: *The bells clanged for the victory.* —tr.v. To cause to clang: *clang a bell.* —n. A clanging sound. [Latin *clangere,* to sound.]

clan·gor (klăng′ər, -gər). Also *Brit.* **clan·gour.** —n. A clang or repeated clanging; loud ringing; din. —intr.v. To make a clangor. —**clan′gor·ous** adj. —**clan′gor·ous·ly** adv.

clank (klăngk) n. A metallic sound, sharp and hard but not as resonant as a clang: *The gate closed with a clank.* —intr.v. To make a clank. [Imit.]

clan·nish (klăn′ĭsh) adj. 1. Of, pertaining to, or characteristic of a clan. 2. Inclined to cling together and exclude outsiders: *a clannish people.* —**clan′nish·ly** adv.

clans·man (klănz′mən) n. A person belonging to a clan.

clap (klăp) v. **clapped, clap·ping.** —intr.v. 1. To strike the palms of the hands together with an abrupt loud sound, as in applauding: *The audience clapped with enthusiasm.* 2. To come together suddenly with a sharp noise: *The door clapped shut.* —tr.v. 1. **a.** To strike (the hands) together with a brisk movement and an abrupt loud sound. **b.** To applaud in this manner. 2. To tap with the open hand, as in greeting: *clapped him on the shoulder.* 3. To put, move, or send promptly or suddenly: *clapped him in jail.* 4. To flap (the wings). 5. *Informal.* To put together hastily: *clap together a plan.* —n. 1. The act or sound of clapping the hands: *She responded to the news with a clap of joy.* 2. A loud, sharp, or explosive noise: *a clap of thunder.* 3. A sharp blow with the open hand; a slap. [Middle English *clappen,* from Old English *clappian,* to throb, beat.]

clap·board (klăb′ərd, klăp′bôrd′, -bōrd′) n. A long, narrow board with one edge thicker than the other, used to cover the outer walls of a frame house. —*modifier: a clapboard house.* —tr.v. To cover with clapboards. [From Middle Dutch *clappen,* to crack, split + BOARD.]

clap·per (klăp′ər) n. 1. **a.** Someone or something that claps. **b.** The hammerlike object, hung inside a bell, that strikes the bell to make it sound. 2. **clappers.** A percussion instrument consisting of two flat pieces of wood held between the fingers and struck together.

clap·trap (klăp′trăp′) *n.* Pretentious, insincere, or empty speech or writing. [CLAP + TRAP ("a trick to win applause").]

claque (klăk) *n.* **1.** A group of persons hired to applaud at a performance. **2.** Any group of adulating or fawning admirers. [French, from *claquer,* to clap.]

clar·et (klăr′ĭt) *n.* **1.** A dry red table wine. **2.** A dark purplish red. —*adj.* Dark purplish red. [Middle English, from Old French, from Medieval Latin *(vīnum) clārātum,* "clarified (wine)."]

clar·i·fy (klăr′ə-fī′) *v.* **-fied, -fy·ing.** —*tr.v.* **1.** To make clear or easier to understand; elucidate. **2.** To make clear by removing impurities, often by heating gently: *clarify butter.* —*intr.v.* To become clear. [Middle English *clarifien,* from Old French *clarifier,* from Late Latin *clārificāre* : Latin *clārus,* clear + *facere,* to make.] —**clar′i·fi·ca′tion** *n.* —**clar′i·fi′er** *n.*

Syns: clarify, clear up, elucidate, illuminate *v.* *Core meaning:* To make clear or clearer *(clarified the meaning of the phrase).*

clar·i·net (klăr′ə-nĕt′) *n.* A woodwind instrument with a single-reed mouthpiece, a cylindrical body, and a flaring bell. [French *clarinette,* from Italian *clarinetto,* dim. of *clarino,* trumpet, from Latin *clārus,* clear.] —**clar′i·net′ist** or **clar′i·net′tist** *n.*

clar·i·on (klăr′ē-ən) *n.* **1.** A medieval valveless trumpet with a clear, shrill tone. **2.** The sound made by this instrument or a similar sound. —*adj.* Shrill and clear. [Middle English *clarioun,* from Medieval Latin *clāriō,* trumpet, from Latin *clārus,* clear.]

clar·i·ty (klăr′ĭ-tē) *n.* **1.** Distinctness, as of shape, outline, or sound: *an actor renowned for the clarity of his speech; a photograph remarkable for its clarity.* **2.** Great precision and terseness: *a young writer striving to achieve clarity of style.* [Middle English *clarite,* from Latin *clāritās,* from *clārus,* clear.]

clash (klăsh) *intr.v.* **1.** To collide with a loud, harsh noise: *The cymbals clashed loudly.* **2.** To strike or meet violently: *where the warm air of the Gulf Stream clashes against the winds of the Arctic. The armies clashed in battle.* **3.** To be strongly out of harmony; come into conflict: *Orange and purple clash. The candidates clashed on that issue.* —*tr.v.* To strike together with a harsh, metallic noise: *The knights clashed their swords swiftly.* —*n.* **1.** A conflict, opposition, or disagreement: *a clash of cultures; a clash between political parties.* **2.** A loud, harsh metallic sound: *a clash of cymbals; a clash of weapons.* —See Syns at **conflict.** [Imit.]

clasp (klăsp) *n.* **1.** A fastener, such as a hook or buckle, used to hold two objects or parts together. **2.** An embrace; a hug. **3.** A grip or grasp of the hand. —*tr.v.* **1.** To fasten with or as if with a clasp: *clasp a necklace.* **2.** To hold in a tight grasp; embrace. **3.** To grip firmly in or with the hand. [Middle English *claspe,* from *claspen,* to grip, grasp.] —**clasp′er** *n.*

class (klăs) *n.* **1.** A set or collection. **2.** A group of persons having approx. the same economic and social standing: *the middle class; the working class.* **3.** *Biol.* A group of animals or plants having certain similar characteristics, ranking taxonomically between an order and a phylum. **4. a.** A group of students or alumni graduated in the same year: *the class of 1961.* **b.** A group of students meeting together for instruction. **c.** The period during which such a group meets: *before class; during class.* **5. a.** A grade of mail: *a letter sent first class.* **b.** The quality of accommodations on a public vehicle: *travel first class.* **6.** *Slang.* Great style or quality: *This new restaurant has class.* —*tr.v.* To arrange, group, or rate according to qualities or characteristics; assign to a class; classify: *class insects; class a book as a mystery novel.* [French *classe,* from Latin *classis,* one of the six divisions of the Roman people.]

class action. A lawsuit in which the plaintiff or plaintiffs bring suit both on their own behalf and on behalf of many others who have the same claim against the defendant.

class-con·scious (klăs′kŏn′shəs) *adj.* Aware of belonging to a particular socioeconomic class. —**class′-con′scious·ness** *n.*

clas·sic (klăs′ĭk) *adj.* **1.** Of the highest rank or class. **2. a.** Long regarded as or serving as an outstanding example of its kind; model: *a classic case of neglect. The Derby is a classic horse race.* **b.** Well-known and typical: *the classic situation of boy meets girl.* **3.** Of ancient Greece and Rome or their literature or art; classical: *classic times; classic styles of architecture.* **4.** Of or in accordance with established principles and methods in the arts and sciences: *a classic chemical experiment.* **5.** Of lasting historical or literary significance. —*n.* **1.** An artist, author, or work traditionally considered to be of the highest rank: *Shakespeare is a classic. Gulliver's Travels is a classic.* **2. the classics.** The literature of ancient Greece and Rome. **3.** A traditional, famous event, as in sports: *The World Series is baseball's fall classic.*

clas·si·cal (klăs′ĭ-kəl) *adj.* **1. a.** Of or pertaining to the culture of ancient Greece and Rome: *classical architecture; a classical scholar.* **b.** In the style of ancient Greek and Roman art, literature, etc.: *a building having classical elements well integrated with modern designs.* **2. a.** Of the musical style that prevailed in Europe in the late part of the 18th cent. **b.** Of concert music or all music other than popular music and folk music. **3.** Standard or traditional rather than new or experimental: *classical methods of navigation.* **4.** Of physics in which the theory of relativity and quantum mechanics are not applied: *the classical theory of light.* —**clas′si·cal·ly** *adv.*

clas·si·cism (klăs′ĭ-sĭz′əm) *n.* **1.** Esthetic attitudes and principles based on the culture, art, and literature of ancient Greece and Rome and characterized by emphasis on form, simplicity, proportion, and restrained emotion. **2.** The use of such rules or principles in artistic creation. —**clas′si·cist** *n.*

clas·si·fi·ca·tion (klăs′ə-fĭ-kā′shən) *n.* **1.** The act or result of classifying; arrangement: *the classification of books according to subject.* **2.** A category, name, or rating: *Nouns have four classifications: common, proper, collective, and abstract.* **3.** *Biol.* The systematic grouping of plants and animals into categories based on shared characteristics or traits; taxonomy.

class·si·fied (klăs′ə-fīd′) *adj.* Available only to authorized persons; secret: *classified information.*

classified advertisement. An advertisement, usu. brief and in small type, printed in a newspaper.

clas·si·fy (klăs′ə-fī′) *tr.v.* **-fied, -fy·ing.** **1.** To arrange in classes or assign to a class; sort; categorize: *A librarian classifies books.* **2.** To designate (information) as secret and available only to authorized persons. —**clas′si·fi′a·ble** *adj.* —**clas′si·fi′er** *n.*

class·y (klăs′ē) *adj.* **-i·er, -i·est.** *Slang.* Stylish; elegant: *a classy hat.*

clat·ter (klăt′ər) *intr.v.* **1.** To make or move with a rattling sound: *clatter along on roller skates.* **2.** To talk rapidly and noisily; chatter. —*tr.v.* To cause to make a rattling sound: *clattered the dishes angrily.* —*n.* **1.** A rattling sound or sounds: *the clatter of dishes in the kitchen.* **2.** A loud disturbance; commotion: *the clatter of the protesters.* **3.** Noisy talk; chatter. [Middle English *clatren,* from Old English *clatrian.*] —**clat′ter·er** *n.*

clause (klôz) *n.* **1.** *Gram.* A sentence or part of a sentence that contains its own subject and a verb or verb phrase and forms part of a compound or complex sentence. **2.** A distinct section, stipulation, or provision of a document. [Middle English, from Old French, from Medieval Latin *clausa,* conclusion of a legal argument, from Latin *claudere,* to close.]

claus·tro·pho·bi·a (klô′strə-fō′bē-ə) *n.* An abnormal fear of being enclosed in a small space. [Latin *claustrum,* enclosed place + -PHOBIA.] —**claus′tro·pho′bic** (-fō′bĭk) *adj.*

clave (klāv) *v. Archaic.* **1.** Past tense of **cleave** (to split). **2.** Past tense of **cleave** (to cling). [Middle English *claue, claue.*]

clav·i·chord (klăv′ĭ-kôrd′) *n.* An early musical keyboard instrument with a soft sound produced by small metal hammers that strike the strings as keys are pushed. [Medieval Latin *clāvichordium* : Latin *clāvis,* key + *chorda,* chord.]

clav·i·cle (klăv′ĭ-kəl) *n.* A bone that connects the sternum and the scapula; the collarbone. [Latin *clāvicula,* "small key" (from its shape), from *clāvis*, key.] **—cla·vic'u·lar** (klă-vĭk'yə-lər) *adj.*

cla·vier (klə-vîr', klă'vē-ər, klăv'ē-) *n.* **1.** A keyboard of a musical instrument such as a piano. **2.** Any stringed keyboard musical instrument, such as a harpsichord. [German *Klavier,* piano, from French *clavier,* keyboard, from Latin *clāvis,* key.]

claw (klô) *n.* **1.** A sharp, often curved nail on the toe of a mammal, reptile, or bird. **2.** A chela or similar pincerlike part, as of a lobster or crab, used for grasping. **3.** Anything resembling a claw, as the forked end of the head of a hammer. **—tr.v.** To scratch or dig with or as if with claws. **—intr.v.** To make scratching or digging motions with or as if with claws. [Middle English *clawe,* from Old English *clawu.*]

claw hammer. A hammer having a head with one end forked for removing nails.

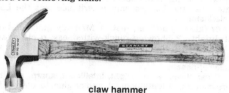

claw hammer

clay (klā) *n.* **1.** A firm, fine-grained earth that is soft and pliable when wet and that consists mainly of various silicates of aluminum. When fired at high temperatures, it becomes a hard, stony material and is used in making bricks, pottery, and tiles. **2.** Moist earth; mud. **3.** The human body as distinguished from the spirit. **—modifier:** *a clay pot; a clay pipe.* [Middle English *cley,* clay, from Old English *clæg.*] **—clay'ey** (klā'ē) *adj.* **—clay'ish** (klā'ĭsh) *adj.*

clay pigeon. A disk-shaped target of brittle, claylike material hurled by a trap in skeet and trapshooting.

clean (klēn) *adj.* **-er, -est. 1.** Free from dirt, stain, or impurities; unsoiled: *clean clothing; a clean glass; clean water.* **2.** Free from guilt or wrongdoing: *a clean life; a clean record.* **3.** Having a smooth edge or surface; even; regular: *a clean break in a bone; a clean line.* **4.** Entire; thorough; complete: *a clean escape.* **5.** Blank: *a clean page.* **6.** Free from clumsiness; skillful; adroit: *a clean throw.* **7.** Obeying the rules; sportsmanlike; fair: *a clean fighter.* **8.** Producing little radioactive fallout or contamination: *a clean nuclear bomb.* **—adv. 1. a.** So as to be clean: *wash clothes clean.* **b.** In a clean manner: *play the game clean.* **2.** *Informal.* Entirely; completely: *He clean forgot he ever had a trouble in the world.* **—tr.v. 1.** To rid of dirt, stain, etc.: *clean a room.* **2.** To remove (dirt or impurities) from something: *clean the jam stain with bleach.* **3.** To prepare (fowl, fish, etc.) for cooking. **—intr.v.** To undergo or perform the act of cleaning: *I clean on Saturdays.* **—phrasal verbs. clean out. 1.** To rid of dirt, trash, etc.: *clean out the garage.* **2.** *Informal.* To deprive completely, as of money; remove everything from: *A bad year for sales cleaned out the company's treasury. The gamblers cleaned him out at poker.* **clean up. 1.** To rid of dirt or disorder: *clean up one's room.* **2.** *Informal.* To make a large sum of money in a short period of time. **—idioms. a clean bill of health. 1.** A diagnosis that one is in very good health. **2.** A statement of soundness: *The company got a clean bill of health from the government.* **a clean slate.** A fresh start. **come clean.** To admit the truth; confess: *The suspect finally came clean.* [Middle English *clene,* from Old English *clæne.*] **—clean'a·ble** *adj.* **—clean'ness** *n.*

Syns: clean, antiseptic, cleanly, immaculate, spotless, stainless *adj.* Core meaning: Free from dirt, stain, or impurities (*clean clothes; clean water*).

clean-cut (klēn'kŭt') *adj.* **1.** Having a distinct, sharp outline: *a car with clean-cut lines.* **2.** Neat and trim in appearance; wholesome: *a clean-cut boy.*

clean·er (klē'nər) *n.* **1.** A person or establishment whose work or business is cleaning. **2.** A machine or substance used in cleaning.

clean·ly (klēn'lē) *adj.* **-li·er, -li·est.** Habitually and carefully neat and clean: *A cat is a very cleanly animal.* **—See Syns**

at **clean. —adv.** (klēn'lē). In a clean manner: *The stems had been severed cleanly by a knife.* **—clean'li·ness** (klēn'lē-nĭs) *n.*

cleanse (klēnz) *tr.v.* **cleansed, cleans·ing.** To free from dirt, defilement, or guilt; clean: *cleanse a wound; cleanse a person of sin.* [Middle English *clensen,* from Old English *clǣnsian.*]

cleans·er (klēn'zər) *n.* **1.** One that cleans; a cleaner. **2.** A soap, detergent, or other preparation used for cleaning: *a tooth cleanser.*

clean-shav·en (klēn'shā'vən) *adj.* **1.** Having the beard or hair shaved off. **2.** Having recently shaved.

clean-up (klēn'ŭp') *n.* **1.** The act or process of cleaning up. **2.** *Informal.* A large profit. **—adj.** Fourth in a baseball batting order: *the cleanup batter.*

clear (klîr) *adj.* **-er, -est. 1.** Free from clouds, mist, or haze: *a clear day.* **2.** Free from anything that dims, darkens, or obscures; transparent: *clear water.* **3.** Free from obstruction or hindrance; open: *a clear view. The road was clear.* **4.** Easily perceived by the eye or ear; distinct: *a clear picture; a clear sound; a clear voice.* **5.** Plain or evident to the mind; easily understood: *Make it clear what you mean.* **6.** Obvious; unmistakable: *a clear case of cheating.* **7.** Free from doubt or confusion; certain: *Are you clear about what has to be done?* **8.** Free from guilt; untroubled: *a clear conscience.* **9.** Having no blemishes: *a clear skin.* **10.** Freed from contact or connection; disengaged: *We are now clear of danger.* **11.** Without charges or deductions; net: *He earned a clear $15,000.* **—adv. 1.** Out of the way: *He jumped clear of the oncoming car.* **2.** Distinctly; clearly: *Speak loud and clear before an audience.* **3.** *Informal.* All the way; entirely: *She cried clear through the night.* **—tr.v. 1.** To make clean, light, or bright: *clear the windshield of mist.* **2.** To make free of obstruction: *clear the road of snow; clear the way.* **3.** To remove or get rid of: *clear snow from the road.* **4.** To pass by, under, or over without contact: *The runner cleared every hurdle.* **5.** To free from a legal charge or imputation of guilt; acquit: *The jury cleared him of the murder charge.* **6.** To free (the throat) of phlegm by coughing. **7.** To gain official approval in: *The bill cleared the Senate.* **8.** To get (a ship or its cargo) free by fulfilling customs and harbor requirements. **9.** To give (an aircraft) clearance or authorization: *cleared the plane for cruising at 30,000 ft.* **—intr.v. 1.** To become clean, fair, or bright: *The day cleared.* **2.** To pass through a clearinghouse: *All checks cleared yesterday.* **3.** To comply with customs and harbor requirements in discharging a cargo or in leaving or entering a port. **—See Syns at vindicate. —phrasal verbs. clear away.** To take away; remove: *clear away the dishes.* **clear off.** To remove something from in order to make clear: *clear off a table.* **clear out.** *Informal.* To leave a place, often quickly: *The thieves cleared out before the police arrived.* **clear up.** To make or become free, as of confusion, blemishes, clouds, etc.: *clear up a mystery. His skin cleared up. The sky cleared up.* **See** Syns at clarify. **—n. 1.** A clear or open space. **2.** Clearance. **—idioms. clear the air.** To dispel emotional tensions or differences: *His joke cleared the air.* **in the clear.** Free from burdens or dangers: *Once that is done, we will be in the clear.* [Middle English *clere,* from Old French *cler,* from Latin *clārus,* bright, clear.] **—clear'ly** *adv.* **—clear'ness** *n.*

clear·ance (klîr'əns) *n.* **1.** The act of clearing. **2.** A space cleared; a clearing. **3.** A sale to dispose of merchandise at reduced prices. **4.** An intervening distance or space, as between a road and the ceiling of a tunnel. **5.** Permission for an airplane, ship, or other vehicle to proceed, as after an inspection of cargo. **6.** Official certification that a person is trustworthy and free from suspicion, guilt, etc.: *You need clearance to handle classified material.* **7.** The passage of checks and other bills of exchange through a clearinghouse.

clear-cut (klîr'kŭt') *adj.* **1.** Distinctly and sharply defined or outlined. **2.** Plain; evident: *a clear-cut victory.* **—See** Syns at explicit.

clear·ing (klîr'ĭng) *n.* An area of land from which trees and other obstructions have been removed.

clear·ing·house (klîr'ĭng-hous') *n.* An office where banks exchange checks and drafts and settle accounts.

clear·sight·ed (klîr'sī'tĭd) *adj.* **1.** Having sharp, clear vision. **2.** Perceptive; discerning. **—clear'-sight'ed·ly** *adv.* **—clear'-sight'ed·ness** *n.*

clear·sto·ry (klîr'stôr'ē, -stōr'ē) *n.* Var. of **clerestory.**

cleat (klēt) *n.* **1.** A strip of wood or iron used to strengthen or support the surface to which it is attached. **2.** A piece of iron, rubber, or leather attached to the sole of a shoe to prevent slipping. **3.** A piece of metal or wood with projecting arms or ends on which a rope can be wound or secured. **4.** A wedge-shaped piece of wood or other material fastened onto something, such as a spar, to act as a support or to prevent slipping. **—tr.v.** **1.** To supply, support, or strengthen with a cleat or cleats. **2.** To secure (rope or other material) to or with a cleat. [Middle English *clete.*]

cleav·age (klē'vĭj) *n.* **1. a.** The act of splitting. **b.** A split. **2.** The tendency of rocks, minerals, and crystals to split smoothly along definite planes. **3. a.** The series of cell divisions by which a fertilized egg becomes a blastula. **b.** Any stage in this series of divisions. **4.** *Informal.* The separation between a woman's breasts.

cleave[1] (klēv) *v.* **cleft** (klĕft) or **cleaved** or **clove** (klōv) or *archaic* **clave** (klāv), **cleft** or **cleaved** or **clo·ven** (klō'vən) or *archaic* **clove, cleav·ing.** **—tr.v.** **1.** To split or separate, as by a sudden blow: *The ax cleft the piece of wood.* **2.** To make or accomplish by or as if by cutting: *a ship cleaving the waves.* **3.** To pierce or penetrate. **—intr.v.** **1.** To split or separate, esp. along a natural line of division. **2.** To make one's way; penetrate; pass: *cleave through the wilderness.* [Middle English *cleven,* from Old English *clēofan.*]

cleave[2] (klēv) *intr.v.* **cleaved** or *archaic* **clave** (klāv) or **clove** (klōv), **cleaved, cleav·ing.** **1.** To adhere, cling, or stick fast: *Barnacles cleave to a hull.* **2.** To be faithful: *"Cleave to that which is good"* (Romans 12:9). [Middle English *clevien,* from Old English *cleofian.*]

cleav·er (klē'vər) *n.* A knife or hatchet used by butchers for cutting meat, consisting of a broad, heavy blade and a short handle.

clef (klĕf) *n.* A symbol on a musical staff that indicates which pitch each of the various lines and spaces represents.

cleft (klĕft) *v.* A past tense and past participle of **cleave** (to split). **—adj.** **1.** Split or partially split: *a cleft chin.* **2.** *Bot.* Having deeply divided lobes or divisions: *a cleft leaf.* **—n.** **1.** A crack; crevice; split. **2.** A hollow or indentation. [Middle English *clift,* rift, fissure, from Old English *geclyft.*]

cleft palate. A split in the roof of the mouth occurring as a birth defect.

clem·a·tis (klĕm'ə-tĭs) *n.* Any of various plants or vines of the genus *Clematis,* of eastern Asia and North America, with white or variously colored flowers and plumelike seeds. [Latin *clēmatis,* from Greek *klēmatis,* from *klēma,* twig.]

clem·en·cy (klĕm'ən-sē) *n., pl.* **-cies.** **1.** Leniency; mercy, esp. toward an offender. **2.** A merciful, kind, or lenient act. **3.** Mildness, esp. of weather.

clem·ent (klĕm'ənt) *adj.* **1.** Lenient or merciful: *a clement ruler.* **2.** Pleasant; mild: *a clement climate; clement weather.* [Middle English, from Latin *clēmēns,* mild, gentle.] **—clem'ent·ly** *adv.*

clench (klĕnch) *tr.v.* **1.** To bring together (a hand or the teeth) tightly: *clench one's fist.* **2.** To grasp or grip tightly: *The halfback clenched the football.* **3.** To clinch (a nail, bolt, etc.). **—n.** **1.** A tight grip or grasp. **2.** Anything that clenches or holds fast, as a mechanical device. **3.** *Naut.* A clinch. [Middle English *clenchen,* from Old English *beclencan.*]

clere·sto·ry (klîr'stôr'ē, -stōr'ē) *n.* Also **clear·sto·ry.** **1.** The upper part of the nave, transepts, and choir of a church, containing windows. **2.** Any similar windowed wall or construction used for light and ventilation. [Middle English : *clere,* lighted, clear + *story,* story of a building.]

cler·gy (klûr'jē) *n., pl.* **-gies.** Ministers, priests, and rabbis in general as distinguished from the laity. [Middle English *clergie,* from Old French, from *clerc,* ecclesiastic, clerk.]

cler·gy·man (klûr'jē-mən) *n.* A member of the clergy.

cler·ic (klĕr'ĭk) *n.* A member of the clergy. [Medieval Latin *clēricus,* clerk.]

cler·i·cal (klĕr'ĭ-kəl) *adj.* **1.** Of or pertaining to clerks or office workers: *clerical jobs.* **2.** Of, relating to, or characteristic of the clergy or a clergyman: *clerical attire.* **—n.** **1.** A clergyman. **2.** **clericals.** The distinctive garb of a clergyman. **—cler'i·cal·ly** *adv.*

cler·i·cal·ism (klĕr'ĭ-kə-lĭz'əm) *n.* A policy of supporting the power or influence of the clergy in political or secular matters. **—cler'i·cal·ist** *n.*

clerk (klûrk; *Brit.* klärk) *n.* **1.** A person who works in an office performing such tasks as keeping records and filing. **2.** A person who keeps the records and performs the regular business of a court or legislative body. **3.** A salesperson in a store. **4.** *Anglican Church.* A lay minister who helps the parish clergyman perform his duties. **5.** *Archaic.* A clergyman. **6.** *Archaic.* **a.** A literate person. **b.** A scholar. **—intr.v.** To work or serve as a clerk. [Middle English, ult. from Greek *klērikos,* of inheritance, cleric, from *klēros,* inheritance (with reference to Deuteronomy 18:2, which states that the Levites only inheritance was the Lord).] **—clerk'ship'** *n.*

clev·er (klĕv'ər) *adj.* **-er, -est.** **1.** Mentally quick and original; bright. **2.** Showing quick-wittedness: *a clever story.* **3.** Nimble with the hands; dexterous; adroit. [Prob. from Middle English *cliver,* dexterous.] **—clev'er·ly** *adv.* **—clev'er·ness** *n.*

Syns: clever, alert, bright, intelligent, sharp, smart *adj.* **Core meaning:** Mentally quick and original (*a clever child*).

clev·is (klĕv'ĭs) *n.* A U-shaped metal piece with holes in each end through which a pin or bolt is run, used for attaching parts. [Prob. pl. of *clevi,* "cleft instrument," of Scandinavian orig.]

clew (klōō) *n.* **1.** A ball of yarn or thread. **2.** *Gk. Myth.* The ball of thread used by Theseus as a guide through the labyrinth of Minos on Crete. **3.** *Naut.* **a.** One of the two lower corners of a square sail. **b.** The lower aft corner of a fore-and-aft sail. **—tr.v.** To roll or coil into a ball. [Middle English *clewe(n),* from Old English *cliewen.*]

cli·ché (klē-shā', klĭ-) *n.* A trite or overused expression or idea. "Quiet as a mouse" is a cliché. [French, stereotype, from *clicher,* to stereotype.]

click (klĭk) *n.* **1.** A brief, sharp sound: *the click of a door latch.* **2.** A mechanical device that snaps into position, such as a pawl. **3.** *Phonet.* A speech sound, common in some African languages, produced by drawing air into the mouth and clicking the tongue. **—intr.v.** **1.** To make one or a series of clicks. **2.** *Informal.* **a.** To be completely successful. **b.** To function well together. **—tr.** To cause to click. [Imit.]

cli·ent (klī'ənt) *n.* **1.** Someone or something for whom professional services are rendered, as by a lawyer or accountant. **2.** A customer or patron. [Middle English, from Old French, from Latin *cliēns,* dependent, follower.]

cli·en·tele (klī'ən-tĕl', klē'ən-) *n.* Clients or customers in general.

cliff (klĭf) *n.* A high, steep, or overhanging face of rock. [Middle English *clif,* from Old English.]

cliff dweller. **1.** A member of certain prehistoric Indian tribes of the southwestern United States who lived in caves in the sides of cliffs. **2.** A person who lives in an apartment house, esp. in a city. **—cliff dwelling.**

cliff·hang·er (klĭf'hăng'ər) *n.* **1.** A melodrama presented in episodes of which each ends in suspense. **2.** Any contest whose outcome is uncertain until the end.

cli·mac·ter·ic (klī-măk'tər-ĭk, klī'măk-tĕr'ĭk) *n.* **1.** A period of life when physiological changes, esp. menopause, take place in the body. **2.** Any critical period. **—adj.** Also **cli·mac·ter·i·cal** (klī'măk-tĕr'ĭ-kəl). Pertaining to a critical stage, period, or year. [Latin *clīmactĕricus,* from Greek *klimaktērikos,* from *klimaktēr,* rung of a ladder, crisis, from *klimax,* ladder.]

cli·mac·tic (klī-măk'tĭk) *adj.* Of, pertaining to, or forming a climax. **—cli·mac'ti·cal·ly** *adv.*

cli·mate (klī'mĭt) *n.* **1.** The general or average weather conditions of a certain region, including temperature, rainfall, and wind. **2.** A region having certain weather conditions: *living in a polar climate.* **3.** A general atmosphere or attitude: *a climate of fear.* [Middle English *climat,* from Old French, from Late Latin *clīma,* from Greek *klima,* sloping surface of the earth.] **—cli·mat'ic** (klī-măt'ĭk) *adj.*

cli·ma·tol·o·gy (klī'mə-tŏl'ə-jē) *n.* The scientific study of

climate. —**cli·ma·to·log·ic** (-tə-lŏj'ĭk) or **cli'ma·to·log'i·cal** *adj.* —**cli'ma·tol'o·gist** *n.*

cli·max (klī'măks') *n.* **1.** That point in a series of events marked by greatest intensity or effect, usu. occurring at or near the end; culmination. **2.** Often **climax community.** The stage at which a community of plants and animals reaches its full development and tends to change no further. —*intr.v.* To come to a climax: *The movie climaxed in realistic scenes of the invasion.* —*tr.v.* To bring to a climax: *His brilliant portrayal of Hamlet climaxed a distinguished career.* [Latin, rhetorical climax, from Greek *klimax,* ladder.]

climb (klīm) *v.* **climbed** or *archaic* **clomb** (klōm), **climb·ing.** —*tr.v.* To move up or mount, esp. by using the hands and feet; ascend: *climb a ladder; climb a tree.* —*intr.v.* **1.** To go up, over, or through, esp. by using the hands and feet. **2.** To go higher; to rise: *The sun climbed in the sky. The rocket climbed steadily. His fever began to climb.* **3.** To rise slowly or with effort in rank, status, or fortune: *She climbed to a top executive position.* **4.** To slant or slope upward: *The hill climbs steeply to the summit.* **5.** To get in or out of: *climb into a cab; climb out of a wet suit.* **6.** To grow upward by clinging to or twining around something, as a vine does. —*phrasal verbs.* **climb down.** To move downward; descend, esp. by means of the hands and feet. **climb up.** To move upward; ascend, esp. by means of the hands and feet. —See Syns at **rise.** —*n.* **1.** The act of climbing; an ascent: *a hard climb up the mountain; Hitler's climb to power.* **2.** A place to be climbed: *That hill was a good climb.* [Middle English *climben,* from Old English *climban.*] —**climb'a·ble** (klī'mə-bəl) *adj.*

climb·er (klī'mər) *n.* **1.** Something or someone that climbs: *a mountain climber.* **2.** *Informal.* A person trying to gain a higher social or professional position. **3.** A plant, such as a vine, that climbs.

climbing irons. Iron bars with spikes or spurs attached, which are strapped to a shoe or boot and used in climbing telegraph poles, trees, etc.

clime (klīm) *n. Poet.* Climate.

clinch (klīnch) *tr.v.* **1. a.** To fix or secure (a nail, bolt, etc.) by bending down or flattening the end that has been driven through something; clench. **b.** To fasten together in this way. **2.** To settle definitely and conclusively; make final: *clinch a deal.* **3.** *Naut.* To fasten with a knot in a rope made by a half hitch with the end of the rope fastened back by seizing. —*intr.v.* **1.** To be held together securely. **2.** *Boxing.* To hold the opponent's body with one or both arms to prevent or hinder his punches. **3.** *Slang.* To embrace. —*n.* **1.** The act of clinching. **2.** Something that clinches, as a clinched nail. **3.** The clinched part of a nail, bolt, rivet, etc. **4.** *Boxing.* The act or an instance of clinching. **5.** *Naut.* A knot in a rope made by a half hitch with the end of the rope fastened back by seizing. Also called **clench. 6.** *Slang.* An embrace. [Var. of CLENCH.]

clinch·er (klĭn'chər) *n.* **1.** Someone or something that clinches. **2.** *Informal.* A decisive point, fact, or remark.

cling (klĭng) *intr.v.* **clung** (klŭng), **cling·ing. 1.** To hold tight or adhere to something: *cling to a rope. Dirt clings to a surface.* **2.** To stay near; remain close: *The children cling to their mother.* **3.** To remain attached; refuse to abandon: *cling to old-fashioned ideas; cling to a hope.* —*n.* A clingstone peach. —*modifier: canned cling peaches.* [Middle English *clingen,* from Old English *clingan.*]

cling·stone (klĭng'stōn') *n.* A fruit, esp. a peach, with pulp that does not separate easily from the stone.

clin·ic (klĭn'ĭk) *n.* **1.** A training session for medical students in which they observe while patients are examined and treated. **2.** An institution associated with a hospital or medical school that deals mainly with outpatients. **3.** A medical institution run by several specialists working in cooperation. **4.** An institution that provides special counseling or training: *a language clinic; a tennis clinic.* [Obs. French *clinique,* orig. a bedridden person, from Greek *klinikos,* physician who visits bedridden persons, from *klinē,* bed.]

clin·i·cal (klĭn'ĭ-kəl) *adj.* **1.** Of or connected with a clinic. **2.** Of or related to direct examination and treatment of patients. **3.** Very objective; not emotional; analytical: *a clinical attitude.* —**clin'i·cal·ly** *adv.*

clink¹ (klĭngk) *intr.v.* To make a light, sharp, ringing sound: *The ice clinked in the glass.* —*tr.v.* To cause to clink: *clink glasses after a toast.* —*n.* A light, sharp, ringing sound. [Middle English *clinken,* from Middle Dutch.]

clink² (klĭngk) *n. Slang.* A prison; a jail. [After *The Clink,* a prison in London.]

clink·er (klĭng'kər) *n.* **1.** A lump of incombustible matter that remains after coal has burned. **2.** An extremely hard burned brick. **3.** *Slang.* A mistake or error, esp. in a musical performance. [Earlier *klincard,* from obs. Dutch *klinckaerd,* "one that clinks."]

Cli·o (klī'ō) *n. Gk. Myth.* The Muse of history.

clip¹ (klĭp) *v.* **clipped, clip·ping.** —*tr.v.* **1.** To cut with scissors or shears: *clip an ad out of the newspaper; clip a hedge.* **2.** To make shorter by cutting; trim: *clipped his beard.* **3.** To cut off the edge of: *clip a coin.* **4.** To fail to pronounce or write fully: *He clipped his words when speaking.* **5.** *Informal.* To strike with a quick, sharp blow. **6.** *Slang.* To cheat, overcharge, or swindle. —*intr.v.* **1.** To cut something. **2.** *Informal.* To move rapidly: *The horse clipped around the ring.* —See Syns at **attach** and **hit.** —*n.* **1.** The act of clipping. **2.** The wool clipped from sheep at one shearing. **3.** Something clipped off, as a sequence clipped from a movie film. **4.** *Informal.* A quick, sharp blow. **5.** *Informal.* A brisk pace: *move along at a good clip.* **6. clips.** A pair of shears. [Middle English *clippen,* from Old Norse *klippa,* to cut short.]

clip² (klĭp) *n.* **1.** A device for gripping something or for holding things together; clasp; fastener: *a paper clip.* **2.** A piece of jewelry that fastens with a clasp or clip. **3.** A metal container or frame for holding cartridges to be loaded into some rifles or pistols. —*tr.v.* **clipped, clip·ping. 1.** To grip securely; fasten: *clip on an earring; clip the papers together.* **2.** *Football.* To block (an opponent) illegally. [Middle English *clipp,* from *clippen,* to embrace, fasten, from Old English *clyppan.*]

clip·board (klĭp'bôrd', -bōrd') *n.* A portable writing board with a spring clip at the top for holding papers or a writing pad.

clip·per (klĭp'ər) *n.* **1.** A person who cuts, shears, or clips. **2. clippers.** An instrument or tool for cutting, clipping, or shearing: *a barber's clippers.* **3.** A sharp-bowed sailing vessel of the mid-19th cent., with tall masts and sharp lines, built for great speed.

clip·ping (klĭp'ĭng) *n.* Something that is cut off or out, esp. an item from a newspaper.

clique (klēk, klĭk) *n.* An exclusive group of friends or associates who stick together and remain aloof from others. [French, from Old French, prob. "a group of applauders," from *cliquer,* to click, clap.]

cliqu·ish (klē'kĭsh, klĭk'ĭsh) *adj.* Also **cliqu·ey** or **cliqu·y** (klē'kē, klĭk'ē). Of, like, or characteristic of a clique; exclusive. —**cliqu'ish·ly** *adv.* —**cliqu'ish·ness** *n.*

clit·o·ris (klĭt'ər-ĭs, klī'tər-) *n.* A small cylindrical organ that forms part of the external female reproductive system, homologous with the penis. [Greek *kleitoris,* "small hill," from *kleinein,* to lean, incline.] —**clit'o·ral** (-əl) *adj.*

clo·a·ca (klō-ā'kə) *n., pl.* **-cae** (-sē'). The cavity into which the intestinal, genital, and urinary tracts open in vertebrates such as fish, reptiles, and birds. [Latin *cloāca,* sewer, canal.] —**clo·a'cal** (-kəl) *adj.*

cloak (klōk) *n.* **1.** A loose outer garment or wrap, usu. sleeveless. **2.** Something that covers or conceals. —*tr.v.* **1.** To cover with a cloak. **2.** To cover up; hide; conceal. [Middle English *cloke,* from Old French *cloque,* "bell-shaped garment."]

cloak-and-dag·ger (klōk'ən-dăg'ər) *adj.* Marked by melodramatic intrigue and spying.

clob·ber (klŏb'ər) *tr.v. Slang.* **1.** To hit or pound with great force; batter or maul. **2.** To defeat completely. —See Syns at **defeat** and **hit.** [Orig. unknown.]

clock¹ (klŏk) *n.* **1.** An instrument for measuring or indicating time, consisting of a numbered dial with moving hands or pointers. **2.** A time clock. —*tr.v.* To record the time or speed of, as with a stopwatch. [Middle English *clok,* from Middle Dutch *clocke,* bell, clock, from Old French *cloche, cloque,* bell, from Late Latin *clocca.*] —**clock'er** *n.*

clock² (klŏk) *n.* An embroidered or woven design on the side of a stocking or sock, at and above the ankle. [Perh. orig. "a bell-shaped ornament," from Middle Dutch *clocke*, bell, clock.]

clock·wise (klŏk'wīz') *adv.* In the same direction as the rotating hands of a clock: *turn clockwise.* —*adj.: a clockwise movement.*

clock·work (klŏk'wûrk') *n.* The mechanism of a clock or any similar mechanism. —*idiom.* **like clockwork.** With machinelike regularity and precision; perfectly.

clod (klŏd) *n.* **1.** A lump of earth or clay. **2.** A dull, ignorant, or stupid person; a dolt. [Middle English *clodde*, from Old English *clott*, lump.] —**clod'dish** *adj.* —**clod'dish·ly** *adv.* —**clod'dish·ness** *n.*

clod·hop·per (klŏd'hŏp'ər) *n.* **1.** A clumsy country fellow; a lout or bumpkin. **2. clodhoppers.** Big, heavy shoes. [Orig. "farmer" : CLOD (earth) + HOPPER.]

clog (klŏg) *n.* **1.** An obstacle or hindrance. **2.** A heavy shoe, usu. having a wooden sole. **3.** A block or other weight attached to the leg of an animal to hinder movement. —*v.* **clogged, clog·ging.** —*tr.v.* **1.** To block up; obstruct: *Heavy traffic clogged the highway.* **2.** To impede or encumber (an animal) with a clog. —*intr.v.* **1.** To become obstructed or choked up: *The pipes clogged with rust.* **2.** To do a clog dance. [Middle English *clogge*, block of wood.]

cloi·son·né (kloi'zə-nā', klə-wä'-) *n.* **1.** A kind of enamelware in which the surface decoration is formed by different colors of enamel separated by thin strips of metal set on edge. **2.** The process or method of producing cloisonné. [French, from *cloisonner*, to partition, from Old French *cloison*, partition, from Latin *claudere*, to close.] —**cloi'son·né'** *adj.*

cloisonne — cloister

clois·ter (kloi'stər) *n.* **1.** A monastery or convent. **2.** Life in a monastery or convent. **3.** A covered walk along the side of a building, as a convent, with open arches facing into a courtyard. —*tr.v.* To confine in or as if in a cloister; seclude. [Middle English *cloistre*, from Old French, var. of *clostre*, from Latin *claustrum*, enclosed place, from *claudere*, to close.]

clois·tral (kloi'strəl) *adj.* **1.** Of, resembling, or suggesting a cloister; secluded. **2.** Living in a cloister.

clomb (klōm) *v. Archaic.* Past tense and past participle of **climb.** [Middle English *clombe(n), clombe,* from Old English *clumbon* (pl.), *(ge)clumben.*]

clomp (klŏmp) *intr.v.* To walk heavily and noisily.

clone (klōn) *n.* **1.** A group of genetically identical cells descended from a single common ancestor. **2.** One or more organisms descended asexually from a single ancestor. —*v.* **cloned, clon·ing.** —*intr.v.* To create a genetic duplicate of an individual organism through asexual reproduction. —*tr.v.* **1.** To duplicate (an organism) asexually by cloning. **2.** To create (a new organism) by cloning. [Greek *klōn*, twig, shoot.] —**clon'al** (klō'nəl) *adj.* —**clon'al·ly** *adv.*

clop (klŏp) *n.* The drumming sound of a horse's hoofs as they strike the pavement. —*intr.v.* **clopped, clop·ping.** To make or move with a clop. [Imit.]

close (klōs) *adj.* **clos·er, clos·est. 1.** Near in space or time: *The airport is close to town. My birthday is close to yours.* **2.** Near in relationship; intimate: *a close friend. They worked together in close harmony.* **3.** With little or no space in between; tight; compact: *a close fit; a close weave.* **4.** Rigorous; strict: *keeping a close watch on the prisoner.* **5.** Confining; narrow; crowded: *close quarters.*

6. Very short or near to the surface: *a close haircut; a close shave.* **7.** Lacking fresh air; stuffy: *It's very close in this room.* **8.** Almost even: *a close race; a close election.* **9.** Thorough; careful: *Pay close attention.* **10.** Stingy; miserly: *He is very close with his money.* **11.** Secretive: *She is very close about her personal life.* —*adv.* Near: *stick close together. She stood close by.* —See Syns at **near** and **stingy.** —*v.* (klōz) **closed, clos·ing.** —*tr.v.* **1.** To shut: *close one's eyes; close the door.* **2.** To declare not open to the public: *The mayor closed all streets for snow removal.* **3.** To fill or stop up: *closed the cracks in the wall with plaster.* **4.** To bring to an end: *close a letter; close a business deal.* **5.** To join or unite; bring into contact: *close a circuit.* **6.** To draw together: *It took eight stitches to close the wound.* **7.** To enclose on all sides; shut in: *The yard was closed by a wire fence.* —*intr.v.* **1.** To become shut: *The store closes at six o'clock.* **2.** To finish or conclude: *The play closed after ten performances.* **3.** To engage in close quarters; to grapple: *The policeman closed with the thief.* **4.** To reach an agreement; come to terms. **5.** To come together: *His arms closed about her.* —See Syns at **end.** —*phrasal verbs.* **close down.** To stop operating: *close down a factory.* **close in.** To surround and advance upon: *The enemy is closing in on us.* **close out.** To sell at a reduced price in order to dispose of quickly. —*n.* (klōz). **1.** The act of closing. **2.** A conclusion; finish: *the close of day. The meeting came to a close.* **3.** An enclosed place, esp. land surrounding a building. —*idiom.* **close call (or shave).** *Informal.* A narrow escape. [Middle English *clos*, from Old French, from Latin *claudere*, to close.] —**close'ly** (klōs'lē) *adv.* —**close'ness** (klōs'nĭs) *n.* —**clos'er** (klō'zər) *n.*

closed-cir·cuit television (klōzd'sûr'kĭt). Television that is transmitted by cable to receivers connected directly to the cable.

closed curve. A curve that can be thought of as having its beginning and end at any one of its points, as the circle and ellipse.

closed shop. A company or business in which only union members or people who agree to join the union within a certain time may be hired; union shop.

close-fist·ed (klōs'fĭs'tĭd) *adj.* Stingy; miserly.

close-hauled (klōs'hôld') *adv. '& adj. Naut.* With sails trimmed flat for sailing as close to the wind as possible.

close-mouthed (klōs'mouthd', -moutht') *adj.* Not talking much; giving away very little information; discreet.

clos·et (klŏz'ĭt) *n.* **1.** A small room or cabinet for hanging clothes, storing linens or supplies, etc. **2.** A small private room for study or prayer. —*tr.v.* To enclose in a private room, as for discussion: *He closeted himself with an adviser.* [Middle English, from Old French, dim. of *clos*, enclosure, from Latin *claudere*, to close.]

close-up (klōs'ŭp') *n.* **1.** A picture taken at close range. **2.** A close or intimate look or view.

clo·sure (klō'zhər) *n.* **1.** The act of closing or the condition of being closed. **2.** Something that closes or shuts. **3.** A finish; conclusion. **4.** Var. of **cloture.** **5.** The property of a set of numbers in which when a given mathematical operation is performed on any pair of them, the result is also a member of the set.

clot (klŏt) *n.* A thick or solid mass or lump formed from a liquid: *a blood clot.* —*v.* **clot·ted, clot·ting.** —*intr.v.* To form into clots. —*tr.v.* To cause to clot; fill or cover with clots. [Middle English, from Old English *clott*, lump.]

cloth (klôth, klŏth) *n.*, *pl.* **cloths** (klôthz, klŏths, klôthz, klŏths). **1.** Material produced by joining natural or manmade fibers, as by weaving, knitting, or matting them together. **2.** A piece of cloth used for a special purpose, as a tablecloth, washcloth, or dishcloth. **3. the cloth.** The clergy. —*modifier: a cloth cap.* [Middle English, from Old English *clāth.*]

clothe (klōth) *tr.v.* **clothed** or **clad** (klăd), **cloth·ing. 1.** To put clothes on or provide clothes for; dress: *feed and clothe a family.* **2.** To cover as if with clothes: *trees clad in leafy splendor.* —See Syns at **wrap.**

clothes (klōz, klōthz) *pl.n.* **1.** Coverings worn on the body; garments, as shirts, trousers, or dresses; wearing apparel. **2.** Bedclothes. —See Syns at **dress.**

cloth·ier (klōth'yər, klō'thē-ər) *n.* One who makes or sells clothing or cloth.

cloth·ing (klō'thǐng) n. 1. Clothes collectively; wearing apparel; attire. 2. A covering. —See Syns at **dress**. —*modifier: a clothing store.*

clo·ture (klō'chər) n. Also **clo·sure** (klō'zhər). A rule or procedure in a legislative body by which debate is ended and an immediate vote is taken on the matter under discussion. [French *clôture,* var. of Old French *closure,* closure.]

cloud (kloud) n. 1. a. A visible body of indefinite shape formed of very fine water droplets or ice particles suspended in the atmosphere above the earth's surface. b. Any similar mass in the air, as of steam, smoke, or dust. 2. A large moving body of things on the ground or in the air; a swarm: *a cloud of locusts.* 3. Anything that darkens or fills with gloom. 4. An appearance of dimness or milkiness, as in glass or a liquid. 5. Something that depresses or makes gloomy: *The bad news cast a cloud over the proceedings.* —*modifier: cloud formations.* —tr.v. 1. To cover with or as if with clouds: *Mist clouded the hills.* 2. To make gloomy, sullen, or troubled: *Suspicion and fear clouded their minds.* 3. To cast aspersions on; blacken; sully: *Scandal clouded his reputation.* —intr.v. To become cloudy or overcast: *The sky clouded over.* —**idioms. in the clouds.** 1. Imaginary; unreal; fanciful. 2. Impractical. **under a cloud.** 1. Under suspicion. 2. In a gloomy state of mind; depressed. [Middle English *cloud,* hill, mass of earth, cloud, from Old English *clūd,* rock, hill.] —**cloud'less** adj.

cloud·burst (kloud'bûrst') n. A sudden rainstorm.

cloud chamber. A device in which the paths of charged subatomic particles are made visible as trails of droplets in a supersaturated vapor.

cloud seeding. A technique of stimulating rainfall, esp. by distributing quantities of dry ice crystals or silver iodide smoke through clouds.

cloud·y (klou'dē) adj. **-i·er, -i·est.** 1. Full of or covered with clouds; overcast: *a cloudy day.* 2. Of or like a cloud or clouds. 3. Marked with indistinct masses or streaks: *cloudy marble.* 4. Not transparent, as certain liquids; murky. 5. Obscure or confused; vague: *cloudy memories.* 6. Troubled; gloomy: *a cloudy expression.* —See Syns at **vague**. —**cloud'i·ly** adv. —**cloud'i·ness** n.

clout (klout) n. 1. A blow, esp. with the fist. 2. *Baseball.* A long, powerful hit. 3. *Informal.* Power, prestige, or influence; pull: *political clout.* 4. An archery target. 5. *Archaic.* A piece of cloth used for mending; patch. —See Syns at **power**. —tr.v. To hit, esp. with the fist. —See Syns at **hit**. [Middle English, from Old English *clūt,* patch.]

clove¹ (klōv) n. 1. An East Indian evergreen tree, *Eugenia aromatica,* whose aromatic unopened flower buds are used as a spice. 2. Often **cloves.** A spice consisting of the dried flower buds of the clove. [Middle English *clowe (of gilofre),* "nail-shaped bud (of clove)," from Old French *clou,* nail, from Latin *clāvus.*]

clove² (klōv) n. One of the small sections of a separable bulb, such as that of garlic. [Middle English, from Old English *clufu.*]

clove³ (klōv) v. 1. A past tense and archaic past participle of **cleave** (to split). 2. *Archaic.* Past tense of **cleave** (to cling). [1. Middle English *clove* (past part.), from Old English *(ge)clofen;* past tense from past part. 2. Middle English *clof.*]

clo·ven (klō'vən) v. A past participle of **cleave** (to split). —adj. Split; divided. [Middle English *cloven,* from Old English *(ge)clofen.*]

cloven hoof. 1. A divided or cleft hoof, as in deer or cattle. 2. The symbol of Satan, usu. depicted with such hoofs.

clo·ven-hoofed (klō'vən-hōoft', -hōof', -hōovd', -hōovd') adj. 1. Having cloven hoofs, as cattle do. 2. Satanic; devilish.

clo·ver (klō'vər) n. Any plant of the genus *Trifolium,* having compound leaves with three leaflets and tight heads of small flowers. —**idiom. in clover.** Living a care-free life of ease, comfort, or prosperity. [Middle English, from Old English *clæfre.*]

clo·ver·leaf (klō'vər-lēf') n. A highway interchange at which two highways crossing each other on different levels are provided with curving access and exit ramps, enabling vehicles to go in any of four directions.

clown (kloun) n. 1. A buffoon or jester who entertains by jokes, antics, and tricks, as in a circus or play. 2. A coarse,

rude person; boor. —intr.v. 1. To behave like a clown. 2. To perform as a jester or clown. [Prob. of Low German orig.] —**clown'ish** adj. —**clown'ish·ly** adv. —**clown'ish·ness** n.

cloy (kloi) tr.v. To displease or make weary with too much of something, esp. of something too rich or sweet; surfeit. —intr.v. To cause to feel surfeited. [Short for obs. *accloy,* to nail, clog, from Middle English *acloien,* to obstruct, from Old French *encloer,* to nail : Latin *in,* in + Latin *clāvus,* nail.]

cloy·ing (kloi'ǐng) adj. Excessive to the point of being distasteful: *cloying praise.* —**cloy'ing·ly** adv.

club¹ (klŭb) n. 1. A stout, heavy stick, usu. thicker at one end than at the other, suitable for use as a weapon; cudgel. 2. A stick used to drive a ball in certain games, esp. golf. 3. a. A black figure on a playing card, shaped like a trefoil or clover leaf. b. A card marked with such figures. c. **clubs.** The suit so marked. —tr.v. **clubbed, club·bing.** To strike or beat with or as if with a club. [Middle English *clubbe,* from Old Norse *klubba,* billet, club.]

club² (klŭb) n. 1. A group of people organized for a common purpose, esp. a group that meets regularly: *a chess club.* 2. The room, building, or other facilities used for the meetings of a club: *I'll meet you at the racquetball club.* —*modifier: club regulations.* —v. **clubbed, club·bing.** —tr.v. To contribute for a joint or common purpose: *clubbing our money to buy new equipment.* —intr.v. To join or combine for a common purpose: *We clubbed together on the fundraising drive.* [Prob. from *club,* to gather into a mass.]

club car. A railroad passenger car equipped with lounge chairs, tables, a buffet or bar, and other extra comforts.

club·foot (klŭb'fŏot') n., pl. **-feet** (-fēt'). 1. A congenital deformity of the foot, marked by a misshapen appearance often resembling a club. Also called **talipes**. 2. A foot so deformed. —**club'foot'ed** adj.

club soda. A carbonated unflavored water used in various alcoholic and nonalcoholic drinks.

club steak. A small beefsteak.

cluck (klŭk) n. The low, short, throaty sound made by or resembling that made by a hen when brooding or calling her chicks. —intr.v. 1. To utter a cluck. 2. To make a similar sound. —tr.v. 1. To call by clucking. 2. To express by clucking: *He clucked disapproval.* [Imit.]

clue (klōo) n. Anything that guides or directs in the solution of a problem or mystery. —tr.v. **clued, clue·ing** or **clu·ing.** To give (someone) guiding information: *Clue me in on what happened.* [Var. of CLEW.]

clump (klŭmp) n. 1. A clustered mass; lump. 2. A thick grouping, as of trees or bushes. 3. A heavy dull sound; a thud, as of footsteps. —intr.v. 1. To walk with a heavy dull sound. 2. To gather into or form clumps of. [Low German *klump,* from Middle Low German *klumpe.*] —**clump'y** adj.

clum·sy (klŭm'zē) adj. **-si·er, -si·est.** 1. Lacking physical coordination, skill, or grace; awkward. 2. Awkwardly made; unwieldy: *clumsy wooden shoes.* 3. Gauche; inept: *a clumsy excuse.* [From obs. *clumse,* to be numb with cold, from Middle English *clumsen.*] —**clum'si·ly** adv. —**clum'si·ness** n.

clung (klŭng) v. Past tense and past participle of **cling**. [Middle English *clong, clunge(n),* from Old English *clungon* (pl.), *(ge)clungen.*]

clus·ter (klŭs'tər) n. A group of the same or similar things growing or gathered closely together; bunch: *a cluster of birch trees.* —intr.v. To gather or grow into clusters: *Everyone clustered around the fire.* —tr.v. To cause to grow or form into clusters. [Middle English, from Old English *clyster.*]

clutch (klŭch) tr.v. 1. To grasp and hold tightly: *clutching a baby in his arms.* 2. To seize or snatch. —intr.v. To attempt to grasp or seize: *clutch at the ring.* —n. 1. The hand, claw, talon, paw, etc., in the act of grasping. 2. A tight grasp. 3. Often **clutches.** Control or power: *the clutches of sin.* 4. *Machinery.* a. Any of various devices for engaging and disengaging two working parts of a shaft or of a shaft and a driving mechanism. b. The lever, pedal, or other apparatus that activates such a device. —**idiom. in the clutch.** In a tense or critical situation. [Middle Eng-

---

lish *clicchen,* from Old English *clyccan.*]

clut·ter (klŭt'ər) *n.* **1.** A confused or disordered collection; a litter; a jumble. **2.** A confused noise; clatter. —*tr.v.* To litter or pile in a disordered state: *clutter the garage with tools and cartons.* [Middle English *clotteren,* to clot, heap, from *clot,* clot.]

Clydes·dale (klīdz'dāl') *n.* A large, powerful draft horse of a breed developed in the Clyde valley, Scotland.

Clydesdale

Cly·tem·nes·tra (klī'təm-nĕs'trə, klĭt'əm-) *n. Gk. Myth.* The wife of Agamemnon.

co-. A prefix meaning: **1.** Joint, jointly, together, or mutually: *copilot.* **2.** Same; similar: *coextend.* **3.** Complement of an angle: *cosine.* [Middle English, from Latin *com-,* with.]

Co The symbol for the element cobalt.

coach (kōch) *n.* **1.** A large closed carriage with four wheels. **2.** A motorbus. **3.** A railroad passenger car. **4.** A low-priced class of passenger accommodations on a train or airplane. **5. a.** A person who trains athletes or athletic teams. **b.** *Baseball.* One of a number of assistants to the manager, esp. one of two who stand near first and third base and direct the batter and baserunner. **c.** A person who provides individual instruction in a certain sport: *a swimming coach.* **6.** A person who gives private instruction, as in singing or acting. —*tr.v.* To teach or train; tutor: *coach a team; coach the actors.* —*intr.v.* **1.** To act as a coach. **2.** To ride in a coach. [French *coche,* Hungarian *kocsi,* after *Kocs,* a town in Hungary.]

co·ad·ju·tor (kō'ə-jōō'tər, kō-ăj'ə-tər) *n.* **1.** A coworker; assistant. **2.** The assistant to a bishop. [Middle English *coadjutour,* from Old French *coadjuteur,* from Latin *coadjūtor* : *cō-,* together + *adjūtor,* assistant, from *adjūtāre,* to assist.]

co·ag·u·lant (kō-ăg'yə-lənt) *n.* An agent that causes coagulation. —*modifier: a coagulant drug.*

co·ag·u·lase (kō-ăg'yə-lās', -lāz') *n.* An enzyme that causes blood clotting. [COAGUL(ATE) + -ASE.]

co·ag·u·late (kō-ăg'yə-lāt') *v.* **-lat·ed, -lat·ing.** —*tr.v.* To cause transformation of (a liquid) into a soft, semisolid, or solid mass; congeal. —*intr.v.* To become coagulated: *Egg whites coagulate when heated.* [Middle English *coagulaten,* from Latin *coāgulāre,* to curdle, from *cōgere,* to drive together : *cō-,* together + *agere,* to drive.] —**co·ag'u·la'tion** *n.*

coal (kōl) *n.* **1. a.** A natural dark-brown to black solid used as a fuel, formed from fossilized plants, and consisting mainly of carbon with various organic and some inorganic compounds. **b.** A piece of this substance. **2.** A glowing or charred piece of coal, wood, or other solid fuel; ember. **3.** Charcoal. —*tr.v.* **1.** To burn a combustible solid to a charcoal residue. **2.** To provide with coal. —*intr.v.* To take on coal. —*idiom.* **rake (haul, take,** or **call) over the coals.** To reprimand; scold. [Middle English *cole,* from Old English *col.*]

coal·er (kō'lər) *n.* A ship, train, or other means of carrying or supplying coal.

co·a·lesce (kō'ə-lĕs') *intr.v.* **-lesced, -lesc·ing. 1.** To grow together so as to form one body; fuse: *The edges of the gash coalesced.* **2.** To come together so as to form one whole; unite: *The many rebel units coalesced to fight the invading army.* [Latin *coalēscere,* to grow together : *cō-,* together + *alēre,* to nourish.] —**co'a·les'cence** *n.*

co·a·li·tion (kō'ə-lĭsh'ən) *n.* **1.** An alliance, esp. a temporary one, of factions, parties, or nations. **2.** A combination or fusion into one body; union. —*modifier: a coalition government.* [French, from Medieval Latin *coalitiō,* from Latin *coalēscere,* to coalesce.]

coal tar. A thick, viscous black liquid obtained by heating coal in the absence of air and used as a raw material for many dyes, drugs, organic chemicals, and industrial materials. —**coal'-tar'** *adj.*

coarse (kôrs, kōrs) *adj.* **coars·er, coars·est. 1.** Of low, common, or inferior quality; base. **2.** Lacking in delicacy or refinement: *coarse language.* **3.** Consisting of large particles; not fine in texture: *coarse sand.* **4.** Rough; harsh: *coarse cloth.* [Middle English *co(a)rs,* ordinary, coarse, prob. from *co(u)rs,* course.]

Syns: 1. coarse, grainy, granular, rough *adj.* Core meaning: Marked by the presence of large particles (*coarse sand*). **2. coarse, boorish, churlish, crass, crude, earthy, gross, rough, rude, uncouth, vulgar** *adj.* Core meaning: Lacking delicacy or refinement (*coarse language and manners*).

coarse-grained (kôrs'grānd', kōrs'-) *adj.* **1.** Having a rough or coarse texture. **2.** Not refined; crude.

coars·en (kôr'sən, kōr'-) *intr.v.* To become coarse. —*tr.v.* To make coarse.

coast (kōst) *n.* **1.** The land next to the sea; the seashore. **2.** A hill or other slope down which one may coast, as on a sled. **3.** The act of sliding or coasting; a slide. **4. the Coast.** In the United States, the Pacific Coast. —*intr.v.* **1. a.** To slide down an inclined slope, as on a sled. **b.** To move effortlessly and smoothly. **2.** To move without further acceleration: *The car coasted down the hill.* **3.** To sail near or along a coast. **4.** To act or move aimlessly or with little effort: *coast through school; coast through life.* —*tr.v.* To sail or move along the coast or border of. —See Syns at **slide.** [Middle English *cost,* from Old French *coste,* from Latin *costa,* rib, side.]

coast·al (kō'stəl) *adj.* On, along, or near a coast.

coast·er (kō'stər) *n.* **1.** Someone or something that coasts. **2.** A vessel engaged in coastal trade. **3.** A coasting sled or toboggan. **4.** A small tray or disk used to protect a table top or other surface. **5.** A small tray on wheels for passing something, such as a wine decanter, around a table.

coast guard. Also **Coast Guard. 1.** The military or naval coastal patrol of a nation, responsible for the protection of life and property at sea, coastal defense, and enforcement of customs, immigration, and navigation laws. **2.** A member of a coast guard.

coast·line (kōst'līn') *n.* The shape or outline of a coast.

coat (kōt) *n.* **1.** An outer garment covering the body from the shoulders to the waist or below, worn primarily for protection from cold or inclement weather. **2.** A garment extending to just below the waist and usu. forming the top part of a suit. **3.** A natural or outer covering, such as the fur of an animal. **4.** A layer of some material covering something else; coating: *a coat of wax.* —*tr.v.* **1.** To provide or cover with a coat. **2.** To cover with a layer: *coat the chicken with flour.* [Middle English *cote,* from Old French.]

coat·ing (kō'tĭng) *n.* **1.** A layer of a substance spread on a surface, as for protection or decoration. **2.** Cloth for making coats.

coat of arms. 1. A shield blazoned with heraldic bearings that serves as the insignia of a nation, family, etc. **2.** A representation of such an insignia.

coat of mail *pl.* **coats of mail.** An armored coat made of chain mail, interlinked rings, or overlapping metal plates, worn in the Middle Ages.

coat·tail (kōt'tāl') *n.* Often **coattails.** The loose rear flap of a man's coat, esp. the lower back part of a swallow-tailed coat. —*idiom.* **on (someone's) coattails.** With the help or on the success of another: *a candidate elected on the coattails of his party's landslide.*

co·au·thor (kō-ô'thər, kō'ô'-) *n.* A collaborating or joint author. —*tr.v.* To write (a book, article, etc.) as a collaborating author with one or more people.

coax (kōks) *tr.v.* **1.** To persuade or try to persuade by pleading or flattery; cajole: *coax her into giving you the money.* **2.** To obtain by persistent persuasion: *We coaxed the secret out of him.* [Earlier *coaks,* to fool, from *cokes,* fool.] —**coax'er** *n.*

co·ax·i·al (kō-ăk'sē-əl) *adj.* Having or mounted on a common axis.

coaxial cable. A high-frequency telephone, telegraph, and

ă pat	ā pay	â care	ä father	ĕ pet	ē be	hw which	ĭ pit	ī tie	î pier	ŏ pot	ō toe	ô paw, for	oi noise
ŏŏ took	ōō boot	ou out	th thin	th this	ŭ cut		û urge	zh vision	ə about, item, edible, gallop, circus				

television transmission cable consisting of a conducting outer metal tube enclosing and insulated from a central conducting core.

cob (kŏb) *n.* **1.** The central core of an ear of corn; corncob. **2.** A male swan. **3.** A thick-set, short-legged horse. [Middle English *cobbe*, lump, round object.]

co·balt (kō′bôlt′) *n.* **Symbol Co** A hard, brittle metallic element, found associated with nickel, silver, lead, copper, and iron ores and resembling nickel and iron in appearance. It is used chiefly for magnetic alloys, high-temperature alloys, and in the form of its salts for blue glass and ceramic pigments. Atomic number 27; atomic weight 58.9332; melting point 1,495°C; boiling point 2,900°C; specific gravity 8.9; valences 2, 3. [German *Kobalt*, from Middle High German *kobolt*, an underground goblin (from the belief that cobalt injures silver ores).]

cobalt 60. A radioactive isotope of cobalt with mass number 60 and exceptionally intense gamma-ray activity, used in radiotherapy, metallurgy, and materials testing.

cob·ble[1] (kŏb′əl) *n.* A cobblestone. *—tr.v.* **-bled, -bling.** To pave with cobblestones. [Back-formation from COBBLE-STONE.]

cob·ble[2] (kŏb′əl) *tr.v.* **-bled, -bling. 1.** To make or mend (boots or shoes). **2.** To put together clumsily; bungle. [Prob. back-formation from COBBLER.]

cob·bler[1] (kŏb′lər) *n.* **1.** One who mends boots and shoes. **2.** *Archaic.* One who is clumsy at his work; a bungler. [Middle English *cobelere*.]

cob·bler[2] (kŏb′lər) *n.* **1.** A deep-dish fruit pie with a thick top crust. **2.** An iced drink made of wine or liqueur, sugar, and citrus fruit. [Orig. unknown.]

cob·ble·stone (kŏb′əl-stōn′) *n.* A naturally rounded stone, formerly used for paving streets and walls; a cobble. [Middle English *cobelston* : *cobel*, prob. dim. of *cob*, lump + *ston*, stone.]

CO·BOL or **Co·bol** (kō′bôl′) *n.* A language based on English words and phrases, used in programming digital computers for various business applications. [CO(MMON) B(USINESS) O(RIENTED) L(ANGUAGE).]

co·bra (kō′brə) *n.* Any of several venomous snakes of the genus *Naja* and related genera, of Asia and Africa, capable of expanding the skin of the neck to form a flattened hood. [Short for Portuguese *cobra (de capello)*, "snake (with a hood)."]

cob·web (kŏb′wĕb′) *n.* **1. a.** The web spun by a spider to catch its prey. **b.** A single thread of such a web. **2.** Something resembling a cobweb in gauziness or flimsiness. **3.** An intricate plot; a snare: *caught in a cobweb of espionage and intrigue.* **4. cobwebs.** Confusion; disorder: *cobwebs in the brain.* [Middle English *coppeweb* : *coppe*, short for *attorcoppe*, spider, from Old English *āttorcoppe* + *web*, web.]

co·ca (kō′kə) *n.* **1.** A South American tree, *Erythroxylon coca*, having leaves that contain cocaine and related alkaloids. **2.** The dried leaves of the coca or related plants, chewed by people of the Andes for their stimulating effect. [Spanish, from Quechua *kúka, cuca*.]

co·caine (kō-kān′) *n.* Also **co·cain.** A colorless or white crystalline narcotic alkaloid, $C_{17}H_{21}NO_4$, extracted from coca leaves and used as a surface anesthetic. [COCA + -INE.]

coc·cus (kŏk′əs) *n.*, *pl.* **coc·ci** (kŏk′sī′, kŏk′ī′). A bacterium with a spherical or oval shape. [From Greek *kokkos*, kermes berry, pit.] *—***coc·coid′** (-oid′) or **coc·cal** (-əl) *adj.*

-coccus A suffix indicating a microorganism that is spheroidal in shape: *streptococcus.* [From COCCUS.]

coc·cyx (kŏk′sĭks) *n.*, *pl.* **coc·cy·ges** (kŏk-sī′jēz, kŏk′sĭ-jēz′). A small bone at the base of the spinal column, consisting of several fused rudimentary vertebrae. [Greek *kokkux*, cuckoo, coccyx (from its resemblance to a cuckoo's beak).]

coch·i·neal (kŏch′ə-nēl′, kŏch′ə-nēl′) *n.* A brilliant-red dye made by drying and pulverizing the bodies of the females of a tropical American scale insect, *Dactylopius coccus*. [French *cochenille*, from Spanish *cochinilla*, from Latin *coccinus*, scarlet, from Greek *kokkos*, kermes berry.]

coch·le·a (kŏk′lē-ə) *n.*, *pl.* **-le·ae** (-lē-ē′). A spiral tube of the inner ear resembling a snail shell and containing nerve endings essential for hearing. [From Latin, snail shell,

from Greek *kokhlos*, land snail.] *—***coch′le·ar** (-lē-ər) *adj.*

cock[1] (kŏk) *n.* **1.** The adult male of the domestic fowl; a rooster. **2.** Any male bird. **3.** A weather vane shaped like a rooster; weathercock. **4.** A faucet or valve by which the flow of a liquid or gas can be regulated. **5. a.** The hammer in a firearm. **b.** Its position when ready for firing. **6.** A tilting or jaunty turning upward: *the cock of a hat.* *—tr.v.* **1.** To set the hammer of (a firearm) in a position ready for firing. **2.** To tilt or turn up or to one side: *The cat cocked her ears.* **3.** To raise or draw back in preparation to throw or hit: *Cock your arm and toss the ball.* *—intr.v.* **1.** To set the hammer of a firearm in a position for firing. **2.** To turn or stick up. *—modifier: a cock lobster.* [Middle English *cok*, from Old English *cocc*, from Late Latin *coccus*, from Latin *coco*, cackling.]

cock[2] (kŏk) *n.* A cone-shaped pile of straw or hay. *—tr.v.* To arrange (straw or hay) in cocks. [Middle English *cok*, from Old English *cocc*.]

cock·ade (kŏ-kād′) *n.* A rosette or knot of ribbon usu. worn on the hat as a badge. [French *cocarde*, jauntily tilted hat, from Old French *coquard*, strutting, from *coq*, cock.]

cockade   cockatoo
                           George Miksch Sutton

Cock·aigne (kŏ-kān′) *n.* An imaginary land of easy and luxurious living. [Middle English *cockayne*, from Old French *(pais de) quoquaigne*, "(land of) delicacies."]

cock-and-bull story (kŏk′ən-bŏŏl′). A highly improbable tale or account passed off as being true.

cock·a·too (kŏk′ə-tōō′) *n.* Any of various parrots of the genus *Kakatoe* and related genera, of Australia and adjacent areas, characterized by a long, erectile crest. [Dutch *kaketoe*, from Malay *kakatua*.]

cock·a·trice (kŏk′ə-trĭs, -trīs′) *n.* A mythical serpent hatched from a cock's egg and having the power to kill by its glance. [Middle English *cocatrice*, crocodile, from Old French *cocatris*, from Late Latin *calcātrix*, "the tracker," from *calcāre*, to track, from *calx*, heel.]

cocked hat. A three-cornered hat with the brim turned up; a tricorn.

cock·er (kŏk′ər) *n.* A cocker spaniel.

cock·er·el (kŏk′ər-əl) *n.* A young rooster. [Middle English *cokerelle*, dim. of *cok*, cock.]

cocker spaniel. A dog with long, drooping ears and a variously colored silky coat. [From its having been used for hunting woodcocks.]

cock·eyed (kŏk′īd′) *adj.* **1.** Cross-eyed. **2.** *Slang.* **a.** Crooked; askew. **b.** Foolish; ridiculous; absurd: *a cock-eyed scheme.* **c.** Drunk.

cock·fight (kŏk′fīt′) *n.* A fight between gamecocks that are usu. fitted with metal spurs. *—***cock′fight′ing** *n.*

cock·le (kŏk′əl) *n.* **1. a.** Any of various bivalve mollusks of the family Cardiidae, having rounded or heart-shaped shells with radiating ribs. **b.** The shell of any of these mollusks; a cockleshell. **2.** A wrinkle or pucker. *—v.* **-led, -ling.** *—tr.v.* To cause to wrinkle or pucker. *—intr.v.* To become wrinkled or puckered. *—idiom.* **cockles of (one's) heart.** One's innermost feelings. [Middle English *cokille*, from Old French *coquille*, shell, ult. from Greek *konkhē*, mussel, conch.]

cock·le·bur (kŏk′əl-bûr′) *n.* **1.** Any of several coarse weeds of the genus *Xanthium*, bearing prickly burs. **2.** The bur of any of these plants.

ă pat	ā pay	â care	ä father	ĕ pet	ē be	hw which	ĭ pit	ī tie	î pier	ŏ pot	ō toe	ô paw, for	oi noise
ŏŏ took	ōō boot	ou out	th thin	*th* this	ŭ cut		û urge	zh vision	ə about, item, edible, gallop, circus				

cock·le·shell (kŏk'əl-shĕl') *n.* **1.** The shell of a cockle. **2.** A small, light boat.

cock·ney (kŏk'nē) *n., pl.* **-neys. 1.** Often **Cockney.** A native of the East End of London. **2.** The dialect or accent of cockneys. —*adj.* Of or like cockneys or their dialect. [Middle English *cokeney,* "cock's egg," pampered brat.]

cock·pit (kŏk'pĭt') *n.* **1.** A pit or enclosed space for cockfights. **2. a.** The space in the fuselage of a small airplane containing seats for the pilot and copilot. **b.** The space in a large airliner set apart for the pilot and crew.

cock·roach (kŏk'rōch') *n.* Any of various oval, flat-bodied insects of the family Blattidae, several species of which are common household pests. Also called **roach.** [Earlier *cacarootch,* from Spanish *cucaracha.*]

cocks·comb (kŏks'kōm') *n.* **1.** The fleshy comb on the head of a rooster. **2.** The cap of a jester, decorated to resemble the comb of a rooster. **3.** Any of several plants of the genus *Celosia,* with a showy crested or rolled flower cluster. **4.** Also **cox·comb.** A pretentious fop.

cock·sure (kŏk'shŏŏr') *adj.* **1.** Completely sure; certain. **2.** Too sure; overconfident. [Orig. unknown.] —**cock'sure'ly** *adv.* —**cock'sure'ness** *n.*

cock·swain (kŏk'sən, -swān') *n.* Var. of **coxswain.**

cock·tail (kŏk'tāl') *n.* **1.** Any of various mixed alcoholic drinks consisting chiefly of brandy, whiskey, or gin combined with fruit juices or other liquors. **2.** An appetizer, such as seafood, served with a sharp sauce: *a clam cocktail.* [Orig. unknown.]

cock·y (kŏk'ē) *adj.* **-i·er, -i·est.** *Informal.* **1.** Cheerfully self-assertive or self-confident. **2.** Conceited; arrogant. —**cock'i·ly** *adv.* —**cock'i·ness** *n.*

co·co (kō'kō) *n., pl.* **-cos. 1.** A tree, the **coconut palm. 2.** Its fruit, the coconut. [Spanish, from Portuguese, "goblin," coconut shell.]

co·coa (kō'kō) *n.* **1. a.** A powder made from cacao seeds after they have been roasted, ground, and freed of most of their fatty oil. **b.** A beverage made by combining this powder with water or milk and sugar. **2.** Moderate brown to reddish brown. [Var. of CACAO.]

cocoa butter. A yellowish-white, waxy solid obtained from cacao seeds and used in making cosmetics, confections, and soap.

co·coa·nut (kō'kə-nŭt', -nət) *n.* Var. of **coconut.**

co·co·nut (kō'kə-nŭt', -nət) *n.* Also **co·coa·nut.** The fruit of the coconut palm, a large seed with a thick, hard shell that encloses edible white meat and has a milky fluid filling the hollow center. [COCO + NUT.]

coconut palm. A tall palm tree, *Cocos nucifera,* native to the East Indies, bearing coconuts as fruit.

co·coon (kə-kōōn') *n.* **1. a.** A caselike covering of silk or similar fibrous material spun by the larvae of moths and other insects as protection for their pupal stage. **b.** Any similar protective covering or structure, such as that of a spider or earthworm. **2.** A protective plastic coating placed over stored inactive military or naval equipment. [French *cocon,* from Provençal *cocoun,* from *coco,* eggshell, from Latin *coccum,* kermes berry, from Greek *kokkos.*]

cod (kŏd) *n., pl.* **cod** or **cods.** Any of various saltwater fishes of the family Gadidae, esp. *Gadus morhua,* an important food fish of Northern Atlantic waters. [Middle English.]

co·da (kō'də) *n. Mus.* A passage at the end of a movement or composition that brings it to a formal close. [Italian, "tail," from Latin *cōda, cauda.*]

cod·dle (kŏd'l) *tr.v.* **-dled, -dling. 1.** To cook in water just below the boiling point. **2.** To treat indulgently; to baby. —See Syns at **baby.** [Var. of CAUDLE.] —**cod'dler** *n.*

code (kŏd) *n.* **1.** A systematically arranged and comprehensive collection of laws: *a judicial code.* **2.** Any systematic collection of regulations and rules of procedure or conduct: *a moral code; the military code.* **3.** A system of signals used to represent letters or numbers in transmitting messages. **4.** A system of symbols, letters, or words given certain arbitrary meanings, used for transmitting messages requiring secrecy or brevity; a cipher. **5.** A system of numbers used to represent a geographic area, such as a zip code or area code. —*tr.v.* **cod·ed, cod·ing. 1.** To systematize and arrange (laws and regulations) into a code. **2.** To put (a text, numbers, etc.) into code. [Middle English, from Old French, from Latin *cōdex, codex.*]

co·deine (kō'dēn', -dē-ĭn) *n.* An alkaloid narcotic, $C_{18}H_{21}NO_3$, derived from opium or morphine, used for relieving pain and coughing, as an analgesic, and as a hypnotic. [French *codéine,* from Greek *kōdeia,* poppyhead, from *koos,* cavity.]

co·dex (kō'dĕks') *n., pl.* **co·di·ces** (kō'dĭ-sēz', kŏd'ĭ-). A manuscript volume, esp. of a classic work or of the Scriptures. [Latin *cōdex, caudex,* tree trunk, board, writing tablet.]

cod·fish (kŏd'fĭsh') *n., pl.* **codfish** or **-fish·es.** The cod.

codg·er (kŏj'ər) *n. Informal.* An odd or somewhat eccentric old man. [Poss. from *cadger,* carrier, peddler, from Middle English *cadgear.*]

co·di·ces (kō'dĭ-sēz', kŏd'ĭ-) *n.* Plural of **codex.**

cod·i·cil (kŏd'ĭ-səl) *n.* **1.** *Law.* A supplement or appendix to a will. **2.** Any supplement or appendix. [Middle English, from Old French *codicille,* from Latin *cōdicillus,* dim. of *cōdex,* codex.] —**cod'i·cil'la·ry** (kŏd'ĭ-sĭl'ə-rē) *adj.*

cod·i·fy (kŏd'ə-fī', kō'də-) *tr.v.* **-fied, -fy·ing. 1.** To reduce (laws) to a code. **2.** To arrange or systematize: *codify the store's inventory procedure.* —**cod'i·fi·ca'tion** *n.*

cod-liv·er oil (kŏd'lĭv'ər). An oil obtained from the livers of cod and containing a rich supply of vitamins A and D.

co-ed or **co·ed** (kō'ĕd'). *Informal.* —*n.* A woman student attending a co-educational college or university. —*adj.* Co-educational. [Short for *co-educational student.*]

co·ed·u·ca·tion or **co·ed·u·ca·tion** (kō'ĕj-ōō-kā'shən) *n.* The system of education in which both men and women attend the same institution or classes. —**co'·ed·u·ca'tion·al** or **co'ed·u·ca'tion·al** *adj.*

co·ef·fi·cient (kō'ə-fĭsh'ənt) *n.* **1.** *Math.* **a.** A numerical factor of an elementary algebraic term, as 4 in the term 4x. **b.** The product of all but one of the factors of an expression, the product being regarded as a distinct entity with respect to the excluded factor and to a designated operation. **2.** A numerical measure of a physical or chemical property that is constant for a system under specified conditions. [CO- (together) + EFFICIENT.]

-coel. Var. of **-cele.**

coe·la·canth (sē'lə-kănth') *n.* Any of various fishes of the order Coelacanthiformes that were believed to be extinct and were known only in fossil form until a living species, *Latimeria chalumnae,* of African seas, was identified in 1938. [From New Latin *coelacanthus,* "hollow-spined" : Greek *koilos,* hollow + *akanthos,* spine, thorn.]

-coele. Var. of **-cele.**

coe·len·ter·ate (sĭ-lĕn'tə-rāt', -tər-ĭt) *n.* Any invertebrate animal of the phylum Coelenterata, characterized by a radially symmetrical body with a saclike internal cavity and including the jellyfishes, hydras, sea anemones, and corals. [New Latin *coelenterata,* "hollow-intestined ones" : Greek *koilos,* hollow + ENTERON + -ATE.]

coe·li·ac (sē'lē-ăk') *adj.* Var. of **celiac.**

coe·lom (sē'ləm) *n.* Also **ce·lom** or **coe·lome.** The body cavity in all animals higher than the coelenterates and certain primitive worms. [German *Koelom,* from Greek *koilōma,* cavity, from *koilos,* hollow.]

co·e·qual (kō-ē'kwəl) *adj.* Equal with one another, as in rank, value, or size. —*n.* An equal. —**co'e·qual'i·ty** (kō'ē-kwŏl'ĭ-tē) *n.* —**co·e'qual·ly** *adv.*

co·erce (kō-ûrs') *tr.v.* **-erced, -erc·ing. 1.** To force to act or think in a given manner by pressure, threats, or intimidation; compel: *coerced his brother into doing his bidding.* **2.** To dominate, restrain, or control by force: *coerced the strikers into compliance.* **3.** To bring about by force: *efforts to coerce agreement.* [Middle English *cohercen,* from Old French *cohercier,* from Latin *coercēre,* to enclose together : *cō-,* together + *arcēre,* to enclose.] —**co·erc'er** *n.* —**co·erc'i·ble** *adj.*

co·er·cion (kō-ûr'shən) *n.* The act or practice of coercing: *The despot ruled by coercion.*

co·er·cive (kō-ûr'sĭv) *adj.* Characterized by or inclined to coercion. —**co·er'cive·ly** *adv.* —**co·er'cive·ness** *n.*

co·e·val (kō-ē'vəl) *adj.* Originating or existing during the same period of time; lasting through the same era. —*n.* One of the same era or period. [Latin *coaevus* : *cō-,* same + *aevum,* age.] —**co·e'val·ly** *adv.*

ă pat	ā pay	â care	ä father	ĕ pet	ē be	hw which	ĭ pit	ī tie	î pier	ŏ pot	ō toe	ô paw, for	oi noise
ŏŏ took	ōō boot	ou out	th thin	*th* this	ŭ cut		û urge	zh vision	ə about, item, edible, gallop, circus				

co·ex·ist (kō′ĭg-zĭst′) *intr.v.* **1.** To exist together, at the same time, or in the same place. **2.** To live in peace with another or others despite differences, esp. as a matter of policy, as countries. **—co·ex·is·tence** (kō′ĭg-zĭs′təns) *n.*

co·ex·ten·sive (kō′ĭk-stĕn′sĭv) *adj.* Occupying the same space; having the same limits or boundaries: *Washington, D.C., is coextensive with the District of Columbia.* **—co·ex·ten′sive·ly** *adv.*

cof·fee (kô′fē, kŏf′ē) *n.* **1. a.** Any of several trees of the genus *Coffea*, native to eastern Asia and Africa, bearing berries containing beans used in the preparation of a beverage. **b.** The seeds or beans of the coffee tree. **c.** An aromatic, mildly stimulating beverage prepared from coffee beans. **2.** A dark yellowish brown. **—modifier:** *a coffee cup.* **—adj.** Dark yellowish brown. [Italian *caffè*, from Turkish *kahve*, from Arabic *qahwah*.]

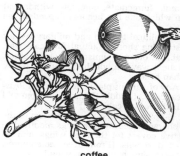

coffee   cog

coffee shop. A small restaurant in which light meals are served.

coffee table. A long, low table, often placed before a sofa.

cof·fer (kô′fər, kŏf′ər) *n.* **1.** A strongbox. **2. coffers.** Financial resources; funds. **3.** A decorative sunken panel in a ceiling, dome, or vault. **4.** A cofferdam. [Middle English *cof(f)re*, box, chest, from Old French, from Latin *cophinus*, basket, coffin.]

cof·fer·dam (kô′fər-dăm′, kŏf′ər-) *n.* **1.** A temporary watertight enclosure built in the water and pumped dry to expose the bottom so that construction, as of piers, may be undertaken. **2.** A watertight chamber attached to a ship's side for making repairs below the water line.

cof·fin (kô′fĭn, kŏf′ĭn) *n.* An oblong box in which a corpse is buried. **—tr.v.** To place in or as if in a coffin. [Middle English, box, basket, from Old French *cofin*, from Latin *cophinus*, from Greek *kophinus*.]

cog (kŏg) *n.* **1.** Any of a series of teeth or notches on the rim of a wheel that can mesh with similar notches on another wheel and allow motion to be transmitted from one wheel to the other. **2.** A cogwheel. **3.** *Informal.* A subordinate member of an organization who performs necessary but usu. minor or routine functions. [Middle English *cogge*, prob. of Scandinavian orig.]

co·gent (kō′jənt) *adj.* Forcefully convincing due to validity: *a cogent argument.* **—See Syns at valid.** [Latin *cōgere*, to force : *cō-*, together + *agere*, to drive.] **—co′gen·cy** (-jən-sē) *n.* **—co′gent·ly** *adv.*

cog·i·tate (kŏj′ĭ-tāt′) *v.* **-tat·ed, -tat·ing.** **—intr.v.** To take careful and unhurried thought; meditate; ponder. **—tr.v.** To think carefully about; consider intently. [Latin *cōgitāre* : *cō-* (intensive) + *agitāre*, to consider, agitate.] **—cog′i·ta′tion** *n.* **—cog′i·ta′tor** *n.*

co·gnac (kōn′yăk′, kŏn′-) *n.* **1.** A brandy produced in the vicinity of Cognac in western France. **2.** Any fine brandy.

cog·nate (kŏg′nāt′) *adj.* **1.** Related by blood; having a common ancestor. **2.** Related in origin, as certain words in different languages derived from the same root. **3.** Related or analogous in nature, character, or function. **—n.** A person or thing cognate with another. [Latin *cōgnātus* : *cō-*, same + *gnāscī, nāscī*, to be born.] **—cog·na′tion** (kŏg-nā′shən) *n.*

cog·ni·tion (kŏg-nĭsh′ən) *n.* **1.** The mental process or faculty by which knowledge is acquired. **2.** That which comes to be known, as through perception, reasoning, or intuition; knowledge. [Middle English *cognicioun*, from Latin *cognitiō*, from *cognōscere*, to get to know : *cō-* (intensive) + *gnōscere*, to know.] **—cog′ni·tive** (kŏg′nĭ-tĭv) *adj.*

cog·ni·za·ble (kŏg′nə-zə-bəl, kŏg-nī′-) *adj.* **1.** Capable of being known or perceived: *a cognizable phenomenon.* **2.** Capable of being tried before or coming within the jurisdiction of a particular court of law.

cog·ni·zance (kŏg′nĭ-zəns) *n.* **1.** Conscious knowledge or recognition: *full cognizance of all the data on the subject.* **2.** The range of what one can know or understand: *facts beyond the cognizance of most children.* **3.** *Law.* **a.** The examination of a case by a court. **b.** The right or power of a court's jurisdiction. **—idiom. take cognizance of.** To take notice of; acknowledge. [Middle English *co(g)nisaunce*, ult. from Latin *cognōscere*, to learn.]

cog·ni·zant (kŏg′nĭ-zənt) *adj.* Fully informed; conscious: *I am cognizant of the problem.* **—See Syns at aware.**

cog·no·men (kŏg-nō′mən) *n., pl.* **-mens** or **-nom·i·na** (-nŏm′ə-nə). **1.** A family name; surname. **2.** The third and usu. last name of a citizen of ancient Rome, as *Caesar* in *Caius Julius Caesar.* **3.** Any name, esp. a descriptive nickname. **—See Syns at name.** [Latin *cōgnōmen*, "additional name" : *cō-*, together + *nōmen*, name.]

co·gno·scen·te (kŏn′yə-shĕn′tē) *n., pl.* **-ti** (-tē). A person of superior knowledge or taste; connoisseur. [Obs. Italian, "the knowing one," from Latin *cognōscere*, to get to know.]

cog·wheel (kŏg′hwēl′, -wēl′) *n.* One of a set of cogged wheels within a given mechanism.

co·hab·it (kō-hăb′ĭt) *intr.v.* To live together in a sexual relationship when not legally married. [Late Latin *cohabitāre* : *cō-*, together + *habitāre*, to inhabit.] **—co·hab′i·ta′tion** *n.*

co·here (kō-hîr′) *intr.v.* **-hered, -her·ing.** **1.** To stick or hold together in a mass, as mud or wet sand. **2.** To be logically connected. [Latin *cohaerēre* : *cō-*, together + *haerēre*, to cling to.]

co·her·ent (kō-hîr′ənt, -hĕr′-) *adj.* **1.** Sticking together; cohering. **2.** Logically connected: *coherent speech: a coherent proposal for restructuring the organization.* **3.** *Physics.* Of or pertaining to waves, as the light of a laser, with a continuous relationship among phases. **—co·her′ence** or **co·her′en·cy** *n.* **—co·her′ent·ly** *adv.*

co·he·sion (kō-hē′zhən) *n.* **1.** The process or condition of cohering: *a breakdown in the cohesion of the alliance.* **2.** *Physics.* The mutual attraction by which the elements of a body are held together.

co·he·sive (kō-hē′sĭv, -zĭv) *adj.* **1.** Tending to cohere; sticking together: *the cohesive nature of water.* **2.** Producing cohesion: *cohesive forces.* **—co·he′sive·ly** *adv.* **—co·he′sive·ness** *n.*

co·hort (kō′hôrt′) *n.* **1.** A group or band united in some struggle. **2.** *Informal.* A companion or associate. **3.** One of the 10 divisions of a Roman legion, consisting of 300 to 600 men. [Middle English, from Old French *cohorte*, from Latin *cohors*, enclosed yard.]

coif (koif) *n.* **1.** A tight-fitting cap worn under a veil, as by nuns. **2.** A white skullcap formerly worn under a wig by English lawyers. **3.** A heavy skullcap of steel or leather formerly worn under a helmet or mail hood. **4.** (*also* kwŏf). A coiffure. [Middle English *coyfe*, from Old French *coiffe, coife.*]

coif·feur (kwä-fûr′) *n.* A hairdresser. [French, from *coiffer*, to arrange the hair.]

coif·fure (kwä-fyŏŏr′) *n.* A way of arranging the hair; hair style.

coil (koil) *n.* **1.** A series of connected spirals or concentric rings formed by gathering or winding: *a coil of rope.* **2.** An individual spiral or ring within such a series. **3.** A spiral pipe or series of spiral pipes, as in a radiator. **4.** A wound spiral of two or more turns of insulated wire, used to produce inductance in a circuit. **—tr.v.** To wind into a shape resembling a coil. **—intr.v.** **1.** To form coils. **2.** To move in a spiral course. **—See Syns at wind.** [Middle English *coilen*, to collect, from Old French *coillir*, from Latin *colligere* : *com-*, together + *legere*, to gather.]

coin (koin) *n.* **1.** A small piece of metal, usu. flat and circular, issued by a government for use as money. **2.** Metal money collectively. **—tr.v.** **1.** To make (coins) from metal; mint; strike: *coin silver dollars.* **2.** To make coins from (metal): *coin gold.* **3.** To invent (a word or phrase). [Middle English *coyne,* wedge, design stamped on a coiner's die, from Old French *coing,* wedge, from Latin *cuneus.*] —**coin′er** *n.*

coin·age (koi′nĭj) *n.* **1.** The process or right of making coins. **2. a.** Metal currency. **b.** A system of metal currency. **3. a.** A coined word or phrase. **b.** The invention of new words.

co·in·cide (kō′ĭn-sīd′) *intr.v.* **-cid·ed, -cid·ing. 1.** To occupy the same position simultaneously: *Points A and B coincide.* **2.** To happen at the same time or during the same period: *The prime minister's visit coincides with the anniversary of her election.* **3.** To correspond exactly; be identical: *Their outlooks and goals coincided.* —See Syns at **agree.** [Medieval Latin *coincidere* : *cō-,* together + *incidere,* to happen.]

co·in·ci·dence (kō-ĭn′sĭ-dəns, -dĕns′) *n.* **1.** A combination of events or circumstances that, though accidental, is so remarkable that it seems to have been planned or arranged: *By a strange coincidence John Adams and Thomas Jefferson both died on the 50th anniversary of the signing of the Declaration of Independence.* **2.** The condition of occupying the same point in space or time: *a curious coincidence of events.*

co·in·ci·dent (kō-ĭn′sĭ-dənt) *adj.* **1.** Occupying the same position. **2.** Happening at the same time. **3.** Matching point for point; coinciding: *coincident circles.*

co·in·ci·den·tal (kō-ĭn′sĭ-dĕn′tl) *adj.* Occurring as or resulting from coincidence. —**co·in′ci·den′tal·ly** *adv.*

co·i·tus (kō′ĭ-təs) *n.* Also **co·i·tion** (kō-ĭsh′ən). Sexual intercourse. [Latin *coitus,* "meeting," from *coīre,* to come together : *cō-,* together + *īre,* to go.] —**co′i·tal** (kō′ĭ-tl) *adj.*

coke (kōk) *n.* The solid residue, chiefly carbon, that remains after the coal gas and coal tar have been removed from bituminous coal by heat, used as a fuel and in making steel. —*v.* **coked, cok·ing.** —*tr.v.* To convert or change into coke. —*intr.v.* To become coke. [Middle English.]

col-. Var. of **com-.**

co·la (kō′lə) *n.* A carbonated soft drink containing an extract prepared from kola nuts.

col·an·der (kŭl′ən-dər, kŏl′-) *n.* A kitchen utensil with a perforated bottom for draining food. [Middle English *colyndore, culatre,* from Old Provençal *colador,* from Latin *cōlāre,* to strain, from *cōlum,* sieve, filter.]

cola nut. Var. of **kola nut.**

col·chi·cum (kŏl′chĭ-kəm, -kĭ-) *n.* **1.** Any of various bulbous plants of the genus *Colchicum,* such as the autumn crocus. [From Latin, a poisonous root, from Greek *Kolkhikos,* belonging to the witch Medea of Colchis.]

cold (kōld) *adj.* **-er, -est. 1.** Having a low temperature: *cold coffee; cold water.* **2.** Having a temperature lower than normal body temperature: *cold hands.* **3.** Feeling no warmth; uncomfortably chilled: *I'm cold.* **4.** Not affected by emotion; objective: *cold logic.* **5.** Without appeal to the senses or feelings: *cold decor.* **6. a.** Not enthusiastic or interested; indifferent: *a cold audience.* **b.** Not cordial or friendly; aloof: *a cold person.* **7.** Designating a color or tone that suggests little warmth, such as pale gray. **8.** *Informal.* Unconscious; insensible: *knocked cold.* **9.** *Informal.* Dead. —*adv. Informal.* Completely; thoroughly: *cold sober.* —*n.* **1.** The relative lack of warmth. **2.** The sensation resulting from lack of warmth. **3.** A viral infection characterized by inflammation of the mucous membranes of the respiratory passages and accompanying fever, chills, coughing, and sneezing. **4.** A condition of low air temperature; cold weather. —*idioms.* **get** (or **have**) **cold feet.** To lack courage; be or become timid or fearful. **in cold blood.** Without feeling or regret. **out in the cold.** Neglected; abandoned; ignored. **throw cold water on.** To dampen enthusiasm for. [Middle English *cold, cald,* from Old English *ceald.*] —**cold′ly** *adv.* —**cold′ness** *n.*

Syns: 1. cold, chill, chilly, cool, nippy *adj. Core meaning:* Marked by a low temperature (*a cold winter*). **2. cold, chill, frigid, glacial, icy** *adj. Core meaning:* Lacking all friendliness and warmth (*a cold stare*).

cold·blood·ed (kōld′blŭd′ĭd) *adj.* **1.** Having a body temperature that changes according to the temperature of the surroundings, as fish, frogs, and reptiles. **2. a.** Having no feeling or emotion: *a cold-blooded killer.* **b.** Done without

feeling or emotion: *a cold-blooded murder.* —**cold′-blood′ed·ly** *adv.* —**cold′-blood′ed·ness** *n.*

cold cuts. Slices of assorted cold meats.

cold feet. *Slang.* Failure of nerve.

cold front. The forward edge of a cold air mass.

cold·heart·ed (kōld′här′tĭd) *adj.* Lacking sympathy or feeling; callous. —**cold′-heart′ed·ly** *adv.* —**cold′-heart′ed·ness** *n.*

cold shoulder. *Informal.* Deliberate coldness or disregard; a snub.

cold·shoul·der (kōld′shōl′dər) *tr.v. Informal.* To give (someone) the cold shoulder; to slight; to snub.

cold sore. A small sore on the lips that often accompanies a fever or cold.

cold storage. The protective storage of foods, furs, etc., in a refrigerated place.

cold turkey. *Informal.* Immediate, complete withdrawal from something on which one has become dependent, as an addictive drug.

cold war. A state of political tension and military rivalry between nations, stopping short of actual full-scale war.

cold wave. 1. An abrupt onset of unusually cold weather. **2.** A form of permanent wave in which the hair is set by chemicals rather than heat.

cole (kōl) *n. Rare.* Any of various plants of the genus *Brassica,* such as the cabbage. [Middle English *col,* from Old English *cāl,* from Latin *caulis,* cabbage.]

co·le·op·ter·an (kō′lē-ŏp′tər-ən, kŏl′ē-) *n.* Any insect of the order Coleoptera, characterized by forewings modified to form tough protective covers for the hind wings, and including the beetles and weevils. [From Greek *koleopteros,* sheath-winged : *koleon,* sheath + *pteron,* wing.]

cole·slaw (kōl′slô′) *n.* Also **cole slaw.** A salad of finely shredded raw cabbage with a dressing. Also called **slaw.** [Dutch *koolsla* : *kool,* cabbage + *sla,* short for *salade,* salad.]

co·le·us (kō′lē-əs) *n.* Any of various plants of the genus *Coleus,* native to Eurasia and Africa, cultivated for their showy leaves. [From Greek *koleon,* sheath (from the way its filaments are joined).]

col·ic (kŏl′ĭk) *n.* A sharp, acute pain in the abdomen. [Middle English *colike,* from Old French *colique,* from Latin *cōlicus,* from Greek *kōlikos,* suffering in the colon, from *kōlon,* colon.] —**col′ick·y** (kŏl′ĭ-kē) *adj.*

co·li·form (kō′lə-fôrm′, kŏl′ə-) *adj.* Of, pertaining to, or resembling the colon bacillus.

col·i·se·um (kŏl′ĭ-sē′əm) *n.* A large amphitheater for public entertainment or assemblies. [After the *Colosseum,* an amphitheater in Rome.]

co·li·tis (kō-lī′tĭs, kə-) *n.* An inflammation of the mucous membrane that lines the colon.

col·lab·o·rate (kə-lăb′ə-rāt′) *intr.v.* **-rat·ed, -rat·ing. 1.** To work together, esp. in a joint intellectual effort. **2.** To cooperate treasonably, as with an enemy occupying one's country. [Late Latin *collabōrāre* : Latin *com-,* together + *labōrāre,* to work, from *labor,* labor.] —**col·lab′o·ra′tion** *n.* —**col·lab′o·ra′tor** *n.*

col·lab·o·ra·tion·ist (kə-lăb′ə-rā′shə-nĭst) *n.* A person who collaborates with an enemy occupying his country.

col·lage (kō-läzh′, kə-) *n.* An artistic composition of materials and objects pasted over a surface. [French, from *coller,* to glue, from *colle,* glue, from Greek *kolla.*]

col·la·gen (kŏl′ə-jən) *n.* The fibrous albuminlike constituent of bone, cartilage, and connective tissue. [Greek *kolla,* glue + -GEN.]

col·lapse (kə-lăps′) *v.* **-lapsed, -laps·ing.** —*intr.v.* **1.** To fall down or inward suddenly; cave in: *The rickety bridge collapsed during the hurricane.* **2.** To cease to function; break down suddenly in health or strength: *The Russian monarchy collapsed in 1917.* **3.** To fold compactly: *These chairs collapse for storage.* —*tr.v.* To cause to collapse. —*n.* **1.** The act of falling down or inward. **2.** An abrupt failure of function, strength, or health; breakdown: *a financial collapse; a mental collapse.* [From Latin *collāpsus,* past part. of *collābī,* to fall together : *com-,* together + *lābī,* to slide, fall.]

col·laps·i·ble (kə-lăp′sə-bəl) *adj.* Capable of being collapsed or folded compactly: *a collapsible tent.*

ă pat	ā pay	â care	ä father	ĕ pet	ē be	hw which	ĭ pit	ī tie	î pier	ŏ pot	ō toe	ô paw, for	oi noise
ōō took	ōō boot	ou out	th thin	*th* this	ŭ cut	û urge	zh vision	ə about, item, edible, gallop, circus					

col·lar (kŏl'ər) n. **1.** The part of a garment that stands up or folds down around the neck. **2.** A necklace. **3.** A leather or metal band put around the neck of an animal. **4.** The cushioned part of a harness that presses against the shoulders of a draft animal. **5.** *Informal.* An arrest. **6.** *Biol.* An encircling structure or bandlike marking suggestive of a collar. **7.** *Machinery.* Any of various ringlike devices used to limit, guide, or secure a part. —*tr.v.* **1.** To furnish with a collar. **2.** *Informal.* **a.** To seize or detain. **b.** To arrest. —See Syns at **arrest.** [Middle English *coler,* from Norman French, from Latin *collum,* neck.]

col·lar·bone (kŏl'ər-bōn') n. The clavicle.

col·lard (kŏl'ərd) n. **1.** A variety of kale, *Brassica oleracea acephala,* having a crown of edible leaves. **2. collards.** The leaves of this plant used as a vegetable. [Var. of *colewort,* from COLE + WORT.]

col·late (kə-lāt', kō-, kŏl'āt') tr.v. **-lat·ed, -lat·ing. 1.** To examine and compare (texts) carefully in order to note points of disagreement. **2.** To assemble in proper numerical or logical sequence: *collate the pages of a book.* [Latin *collātus,* past part. of *conferre,* to bring together.] —**col·la'tor** n.

col·lat·er·al (kə-lăt'ər-əl) adj. **1.** Situated or running side by side; parallel. **2.** Coinciding in tendency or effect; concomitant. **3.** Serving to support or corroborate; additional: *collateral evidence.* **4.** Of a secondary nature; subordinate: *collateral questions and issues.* **5.** Of, designating, or guaranteed by a security pledged against the performance of an obligation: *a collateral loan.* **6.** Having an ancestor in common but descended from a different line. —*n.* **1.** Property acceptable as security for a loan or other obligation. **2.** A collateral relative. [Middle English, from Medieval Latin *collaterālis* : *com-,* together + *laterālis,* of the side, lateral.] —**col·lat'er·al·ly** adv.

col·la·tion (kə-lā'shən, kō-, kō-) n. **1.** The act or process of collating. **2.** A light meal.

col·league (kŏl'ēg') n. A fellow member of a profession, staff, or academic faculty; associate. —See Syns at **partner.** [French *collègue,* from Old French, from Latin *collēga,* one chosen to serve with another : *com-,* together + *lēgāre,* to choose.]

col·lect[1] (kə-lĕkt') tr.v. **1.** To bring together in a group; gather; assemble: *He collected firewood.* **2.** To accumulate as a hobby or for study: *collect stamps.* **3.** To call for and obtain payment of: *collect taxes.* **4.** To recover control of: *collect one's thoughts.* —*intr.v.* **1.** To gather together; congregate; accumulate: *A large group collected to watch the fireworks. Leaves collect on the lawn.* **2.** To take in payments or donations: *collect for charity.* —See Syns at **gather.** —*adj.* With payment to be made by the receiver: *a collect call.* —*adv.* So that the receiver is charged: *send a telegram collect.* [Middle English *collecten,* from Latin *colligere,* to gather together : *com-,* together + *legere,* to gather.] —**col·lect'i·ble** or **col·lect'a·ble** adj.

col·lect[2] (kŏl'ĭkt, -ĕkt') n. *Eccles.* A brief formal prayer used before the epistle at Mass and varying with the day. [Middle English *collecte,* from Old French, from Medieval Latin *(ōrātiō ad) collēctam,* "(prayer at) the congregation," from Late Latin *collēcta,* assembly, from Latin *collēctus,* collected.]

col·lect·ed (kə-lĕk'tĭd) adj. **1.** Self-possessed; composed. **2.** Brought or placed together from various sources: *the collected poems of W.H. Auden.* —**col·lect'ed·ly** adv.

col·lec·tion (kə-lĕk'shən) n. **1.** The act or process of collecting. **2.** A group of objects or works to be seen, studied, or kept together: *an art collection.* **3.** An accumulation; deposit. **4. a.** A collecting of money, as in church. **b.** The sum collected.

col·lec·tive (kə-lĕk'tĭv) adj. **1.** Formed by collecting; assembled or accumulated into a whole. **2.** Of a number of persons or nations considered or acting as one: *the collective opinion of the committee; our collective security.* —*n.* **1.** A business or undertaking set up on the principle of ownership and control of the means of production and distribution by the workers involved, usu. under the supervision of a government. **2.** A collective noun. —**col·lec'tive·ly** adv.

collective bargaining. Negotiation between the representatives of organized workers and their employer or employers to determine wages, hours, rules, and working conditions.

collective noun. A noun that denotes a collection of persons or things regarded as a unit.
   Usage: A collective noun takes a singular verb when it refers to the collection as a whole and a plural verb when it refers to the members of the collection as separate persons or things: *The orchestra was playing. The orchestra have all gone home.* A collective noun should not be treated as both singular and plural in the same construction: *The family is determined to press its* (not *their*) *claim.*

col·lec·tiv·ism (kə-lĕk'tə-vĭz'əm) n. The principle or system of ownership and control of the means of production and distribution by the people collectively. —**col·lec'tiv·ist** n.

col·lec·tor (kə-lĕk'tər) n. **1.** A person or thing that collects. **2.** A person employed to collect taxes, duties, or other payments. **3.** A person who collects something, such as stamps. —**col·lec'tor·ship'** n.

col·leen (kŏ-lēn', kŏl'ēn') n. An Irish girl. [Irish *cailín,* dim. of *caile,* girl, from Old Irish *calé.*]

col·lege (kŏl'ĭj) n. **1.** A school of higher learning that grants a bachelor's degree in liberal arts or science or both. **2.** Any of the undergraduate divisions or schools of a university. **3.** A technical or professional school, often affiliated with a university, offering a bachelor's or master's degree: *teachers college.* **4.** The building or buildings occupied by any such school. **5.** A company or assembly, esp. a body of persons having a common purpose or common duties: *a college of surgeons; the electoral college.* [Middle English, from Old French, from Latin *collēgium,* corporate institution, from *collēga,* colleague.]

col·le·gian (kə-lē'jən, -jē-ən) n. A college student or a recent college graduate.

col·le·giate (kə-lē'jĭt, -jē-ĭt) adj. **1.** Of, pertaining to, or resembling a college. **2.** Of, for, or typical of college students.

col·le·gi·um (kə-lē'jē-əm, -lĕg'ē-) n., pl. **-gi·a** (-lē'jē-ə, -lĕg'ē-ə) or **-gi·ums.** An executive or governing council in which all members have equal authority, specif. one supervising an industry, commissariat, or other organization in the Soviet Union. [Russian *kollegya,* from Latin *collēgium,* college.]

col·lide (kə-līd') intr.v. **-lid·ed, -lid·ing. 1.** To come together with violent, direct impact: *The cars collided.* **2.** To meet in opposition; clash; conflict: *The President and Senate collided over a tax cut.* [Latin *collidere* : *com-,* together + *laedere,* to strike, injure.]

col·lie (kŏl'ē) n. A large dog of a breed that originated in Scotland as a sheep dog, and has long hair and a long, narrow muzzle. [Scottish, poss. from *colly,* "black like coal," from *coll,* var. of COAL.]

collie

col·lier (kŏl'yər) n. *Brit.* **1.** A coal miner. **2.** A coal ship. [Middle English *colier,* from *col, cole,* coal.]

col·lier·y (kŏl'yə-rē) n., pl. **-ies.** *Brit.* A coal mine.

col·li·mate (kŏl'ə-māt') tr.v. **-mat·ed, -mat·ing. 1.** To make parallel; line up. **2.** To adjust the line of sight of (a transit, telescope, or other optical device). [From New Latin *collimare,* to adjust, alteration of Latin *collīneāre,* to direct in a straight line : *com-* (intensive) + *līnea,* line.] —**col'li·ma'tion** n.

col·lin·e·ar (kə-lĭn'ē-ər, kō-) adj. **1.** Lying on the same line. **2.** Containing a common line; coaxial. [COM- + LINEAR.]

---

col·li·sion (kə-lĭzh′ən) *n.* **1.** The act or process of colliding; a direct, violent striking together; a crash. **2.** A clash of ideas or interests; a conflict. [Middle English, from Latin *collīsiō*, from *collīdere*, to collide.]

col·lo·cate (kŏl′ə-kāt′) *tr.v.* **-cat·ed, -cat·ing.** To place together or in proper order; arrange. [From Latin *collocāre* : *com-*, together + *locāre*, to locate.] **—col′lo·ca′tion** *n.*

col·lo·di·on (kə-lō′dē-ən) *n.* Also **col·lo·di·um** (kə-lō′dē-əm). A highly flammable colorless or yellowish syrupy solution of nitrocellulose in ether and alcohol, used to hold surgical dressings, as a coating for the skin, and in making photographic plates. [From Greek *kollōdēs*, gluelike, from *kolla*, glue.]

col·loid (kŏl′oid′) *n.* **1.** *Chem.* A suspension of finely divided particles in a continuous medium, such as an atmospheric fog, a paint, or foam rubber, containing suspended particles that are approx. 5 to 5,000 angstroms in size, do not settle out of the substance rapidly, and are not readily filtered. **2.** The particulate matter so suspended. **—adj.** Colloidal.

col·loi·dal (kə-loi′dl) *adj.* Of, relating to, or having the nature of a colloid; colloid. [French *colloide*, from Greek *kolla*, glue.]

col·lo·qui·al (kə-lō′kwē-əl) *adj.* **1.** Used in or suitable to spoken language or to writing that seeks the effect of speech; informal in style of expression. **2.** Relating to conversation; conversational. [From COLLOQUY.] **—col·lo′qui·al·ly** *adv.* **—col·lo′qui·al·ness** *n.*

col·lo·qui·al·ism (kə-lō′kwē-ə-lĭz′əm) *n.* **1.** Colloquial style or quality. **2.** A colloquial expression; for example, *I'm still in there pitching* is a colloquialism.

col·lo·qui·um (kə-lō′kwē-əm) *n., pl.* **-ums** or **-qui·a** (-kwē-ə). **1.** An informal meeting for discussion. **2.** An academic seminar, usu. led by a different lecturer at each meeting. [Latin *colloquium*, colloquy.]

col·lo·quy (kŏl′ə-kwē) *n., pl.* **-quies. 1.** A conversation, esp. a formal one. **2.** A written dialogue. [Latin *colloquium*, conversation, from *colloquī*, to converse : *com-*, together + *loquī*, to speak.]

col·lude (kə-lōōd′) *intr.v.* **-lud·ed, -lud·ing.** To be in collusion; act together secretly; connive. [Latin *collūdere* : *com-*, together + *lūdere*, to play, from *lūdus*, game.]

col·lu·sion (kə-lōō′zhən) *n.* Secret agreement between two or more persons for a deceitful or fraudulent purpose. — See Syns at **plot. —col·lu′sive** (-sĭv) *adj.* **—col·lu′sive·ly** *adv.*

co·logne (kə-lōn′) *n.* A scented liquid made of alcohol and fragrant oils. Also called **eau de cologne.** [French *eau de cologne*, "water of *Cologne*," West Germany.]

co·lon¹ (kō′lən) *n.* **1.** A punctuation mark (:) used after a word introducing a quotation, explanation, example, or series. **2.** The sign (:) used between numbers or groups of numbers in expressions of time (2:30 A.M.) and ratios (1:2). [Latin *cōlon*, unit of verses, from Greek *kōlon*, limb.]

co·lon² (kō′lən) *n.* The section of the large intestine extending from the cecum to the rectum. [Middle English, from Latin, from Greek *kolon*, large intestine.] **—co·lon′ic** (kə-lŏn′ĭk) *adj.*

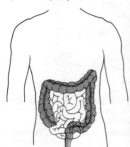

colon²

Colonial
A Colonial house

colo·nel (kûr′nəl) *n.* An officer in the U.S. Army, Air Force, or Marine Corps ranking immediately above a lieutenant colonel and below a brigadier general. [French, from Italian *colonnello*, "commander of a column," from Latin *columna*, column.] **—colo′nel·cy** (-sē) or **colo′nel·ship′** (-shĭp′) *n.*

co·lo·ni·al (kə-lō′nē-əl) *adj.* **1.** Of or possessing colonies: *colonial rule. France and England were colonial powers.* **2.** Often **Colonial.** Of the 13 original American colonies: *the Colonial period; in colonial times.* **3.** Often **Colonial.** Of the style of architecture often found in the American colonies. **4.** Living in, forming, or consisting of a colony: *colonial organisms.* **—n.** An inhabitant of a colony. **—co·lo′ni·al·ly** *adv.*

co·lo·ni·al·ism (kə-lō′nē-ə-lĭz′əm) *n.* A governmental policy of acquiring or maintaining foreign territory as colonies. **—co·lo′ni·al·ist** *n.*

col·o·nist (kŏl′ə-nĭst) *n.* **1.** An original settler or founder of a colony. **2.** An inhabitant of a colony.

col·o·nize (kŏl′ə-nīz′) *v.* **-nized, -niz·ing. —tr.v. 1. a.** To establish a colony or colonies in. **b.** To migrate to and settle in; occupy as a colony. **2.** To establish in a new settlement; form a colony of. **—intr. 1.** To set up or form a colony. **2.** To settle in a colony or colonies. **—col′o·ni·za′tion** *n.* **—col′o·niz′er** *n.*

col·on·nade (kŏl′ə-nād′) *n. Archit.* A series of columns placed at regular intervals. [French, from Italian *colonnato*, from *colonna*, column, from Latin *columna.*] **—col′on·nad′ed** *adj.*

col·o·ny (kŏl′ə-nē) *n., pl.* **-nies. 1.** A group of people who settle in a distant land but remain subject to their native country. **2.** A territory ruled by a distant power. **3.** A group of people of the same nationality, religion, interests, etc., living together in one area: *the American colony in Paris.* **4.** A group of the same kind of animals, plants, or one-celled organisms living or growing together in close association: *a colony of ants; a colony of bacteria.* **5. the Colonies.** The 13 British colonies that became the original United States of America. [Middle English *colonie*, from Old French, from Latin *colōnia*, farm, settlement, from *colōnus*, settler, from *colere*, to inhabit.]

col·o·phon (kŏl′ə-fŏn′, -fən) *n.* **1.** An inscription placed usu. at the end of a book, giving facts pertaining to its publication. **2.** A publisher's emblem or trademark placed usu. on the title page of a book. [Latin *colophōn*, from Greek *kolophōn*, summit, finishing.]

col·or (kŭl′ər) *n.* Also *Brit.* **col·our. —n. 1.** The property by which the sense of vision can distinguish things, such as a red rose and a yellow rose, that are alike in size, shape, and texture. The color of a thing depends mainly on the wavelengths of the light that it emits, reflects, or transmits. **2.** A dye, pigment, paint, or other color substance. **3.** The general appearance of the skin; complexion: *Ill health made her color poor.* **4.** The complexion of a person not classed as a Caucasoid, esp. that of a Negro: *discrimination based on color.* **5. colors.** A flag or banner, as of a country or military unit. **6.** Vivid and interesting detail, as of a scene or its description in writing: *the abundant color of a bullfighting ring.* **7.** Traits of personality or behavior that appeal to the eye or mind: *a political figure with a great deal of color.* **8.** Musical tone quality. **—modifier:** *color photography; color television.* **—tr.v. 1.** To impart color to or change the color of. **2.** To influence, esp. by distortion or exaggeration: *Self-interest colored his judgment.* **—intr. 1.** To take on color or change color. **2.** To become red in the face; to blush. **—idioms. lose color.** To become pale. **show (one's) true colors.** To reveal one's actual nature or character. **with flying colors.** With great success. [Middle English *colour*, from Old French, from Latin *color.*] **—col′or·er** *n.*

Col·o·ra·do potato beetle (kŏl′ə-rä′dō, -răd′ō). The **potato beetle.**

col·or·a·tion (kŭl′ə-rā′shən) *n.* **1.** Arrangement of colors: *Protective coloration helps some animals to hide from their enemies.* **2.** The sum of the beliefs or principles of a person, group, etc.: *Spain's political coloration caused her to be isolated.*

col·or·a·tu·ra (kŭl′ər-ə-tōōr′ə, -tyōōr′ə) *n.* **1. a.** Florid ornamental trills and runs in vocal music. **b.** Music characterized by such ornamentation. **2.** A singer, esp. a soprano, who specializes in the performance of coloratura. [Obs. Italian, "coloring."]

col·or·blind (kŭl′ər-blīnd′) adj. Partially or totally unable to see differences in colors. —**col′or·blind′ness** n.

col·ored (kŭl′ərd) adj. **1.** Having color. **2.** Often **Colored.** Negro or of any ethnic group other than Caucasoid; dark-skinned. The word "colored" is often considered offensive. **3.** Not strictly factual or objective; distorted by prejudice or self-interest.

col·or·fast (kŭl′ər-făst′) adj. Having color that will not run or fade with washing or wear: a colorfast fabric. —**col′or·fast′ness** n.

col·or·ful (kŭl′ər-fəl) adj. **1.** Full of color or colors: insects that fly on colorful wings. **2.** Rich in variety or vivid detail: colorful language; a colorful narrative. **3.** Exciting the senses or the imagination: colorful ballets; a colorful political style. —**col′or·ful·ly** adv. —**col′or·ful·ness** n.

color guard. The flag's ceremonial escort.

col·or·im·e·ter (kŭl′ə-rĭm′ĭ-tər) n. Any of various instruments used to determine or specify colors, as by comparison with spectroscopic or visual standards. —**col′or·i·met′ric** (kŭl′ər-ə-mĕt′rĭk) adj. —**col′or·i·met′ri·cal·ly** adv. —**col′or·im′e·try** n.

col·or·ing (kŭl′ər-ĭng) n. **1.** The manner or process of applying color: laws regulating the coloring of margarine. **2.** A substance used to color something: a food coloring; a hair coloring. **3.** Appearance with respect to color: animals protected by their coloring. —**modifier:** coloring matter; a coloring agent.

col·or·ist (kŭl′ər-ĭst) n. **1.** An artist who is skilled in achieving special effects with color. **2.** A hairdresser who specializes in dyeing hair.

col·or·less (kŭl′ər-lĭs) adj. **1.** Without color: Most bacteria are colorless. **2.** Weak in color; pallid: a frail, colorless invalid. **3.** Lacking variety or interest; dull: A story with no description would be colorless. **4.** Lacking individuality or distinction: a colorless candidate. —**col′or·less·ly** adv. —**col′or·less·ness** n.

color line. A barrier, created by custom, law, or economic differences, that separates nonwhite persons from whites.

co·los·sal (kə-lŏs′əl) adj. Enormous in size, extent, or degree; gigantic; tremendous: colossal statues, many times life-size; a risk requiring colossal self-confidence. —See Syns at **giant.** [From Latin colossus, colossus.] —**co·los′sal·ly** adv.

Co·los·sians (kə-lŏsh′ənz, -lŏs′ē-ənz) pl.n. (used with a sing. verb). See table at **Bible.**

co·los·sus (kə-lŏs′əs) n., pl. **-los·si** (-lŏs′ī′) or **-sus·es. 1.** A huge statue. **2.** Anything of enormous size or importance. [Latin, from Greek kolossos.]

co·los·trum (kə-lŏs′trəm) n. The first milk secreted by the mammary glands for a few days immediately after childbirth. [Latin.]

col·our (kŭl′ər) n. & v. Brit. Var. of **color.**

colt (kōlt) n. **1.** A young horse or related animal such as a zebra, esp. a male. **2.** A youthful or inexperienced person; a novice; beginner. [Middle English, from Old English, young ass or camel.]

col·ter (kōl′tər) n. Also **coul·ter.** A blade or wheel on a plow for making vertical cuts in the sod. [Middle English culter, ult. from Latin, knife, plowshare.]

colt·ish (kōl′tĭsh) adj. **1.** Of or like a colt. **2.** Lively and playful; frisky. —**colt′ish·ly** adv. —**colt′ish·ness** n.

Co·lum·bi·a (kə-lŭm′bē-ə) n. Poet. A feminine personification of the United States. [After Christopher Columbus (1451–1506), Italian explorer.]

col·um·bine (kŏl′əm-bīn′) n. Any of several plants of the genus Aquilegia, with variously colored flowers that have five spurred petals. [Middle English, from Latin columbīnus, dovelike, from columba, dove.]

co·lum·bi·um (kə-lŭm′bē-əm) n. Symbol **Cb** The former name of the element niobium. [After Columbia, because it was discovered in a mineral found in Connecticut.]

Co·lum·bus Day (kə-lŭm′bəs). Oct. 12, a holiday celebrated officially on the second Monday in Oct. in the United States in honor of Christopher Columbus.

col·umn (kŏl′əm) n. **1.** A pillar or upright structure, usu. shaped like a cylinder, used in a building as a support or as a decoration. **2.** Anything that resembles a pillar in shape or use: a column of mercury in a thermometer; the spinal

column. **3.** One of two or more vertical sections of a page, lying side by side but separated from each other, in which lines of print are arranged. **4.** A feature article that appears regularly in a newspaper or magazine. **5.** A formation, as of soldiers or trucks, in which members or rows follow one behind the other. [Middle English columpne, from Old French colomne, from Latin columna.]

co·lum·nar (kə-lŭm′nər) adj. **1.** Having the shape of a column. **2.** Having or constructed with columns.

co·lum·ni·a·tion (kə-lŭm′nē-ā′shən) n. The use or arrangement of columns in a building.

col·um·nist (kŏl′əm-nĭst, -ə-mĭst) n. A writer of a newspaper or magazine column.

col·za (kŏl′zə, kōl′-) n. A plant, **rape.** [French, from Dutch koolzaad, "cabbage seed."]

com- or **col-** or **con-.** A prefix meaning with, together, or jointly: **commingle.** [Latin, from cum, with.]

co·ma¹ (kō′mə) n., pl. **-mas.** A deep, prolonged unconsciousness, usu. the result of injury, disease, or poison. [Greek kōma, deep sleep, lethargy.]

co·ma² (kō′mə) n., pl. **-mae** (-mē). **1.** Astron. The nebulous luminescent cloud containing the nucleus and constituting the major portion of the head of a comet. **2.** Bot. A tuft of hairs, as on some seeds. [Latin, hair, from Greek komē.]

Co·man·che (kə-măn′chē) n., pl. **Comanche** or **-ches. 1.** A tribe of North American Indians, formerly ranging over the western plains from Wyoming to Texas, now living in Oklahoma. **2.** A member of this tribe. **3.** The language of the Comanche. —**Co·man′che** adj.

co·ma·tose (kō′mə-tōs′, kŏm′ə-) adj. Pathol. **1.** Of, pertaining to, or affected with coma; deeply unconscious. **2.** Of or like a coma: a comatose trance.

comb (kōm) n. **1.** A strip of plastic, bone, or hard rubber, having teeth and used to arrange or fasten the hair. **2.** Something resembling a comb in shape or use, as a card for arranging and cleansing wool. **3.** A curry comb. **4.** The brightly colored ridge of flesh on the top of the head of a rooster, hen, or certain other birds. **5.** A honeycomb. —tr.v. **1.** To dress or arrange with or as if with a comb. **2.** To card (wool or other fiber). **3.** To search (something) thoroughly: combed many books for information. —intr.v. **1.** To search thoroughly. **2.** To roll and break: The waves combed thunderously. [Middle English, from Old English comb, camb.]

com·bat (kəm-băt′, kŏm′băt′) v. **-bat·ed** or **-bat·ted, -bat·ing** or **-bat·ting.** —tr.v. **1.** To fight against in battle; contend with: combat the enemy. **2.** To oppose vigorously; resist: new drugs that combat infection. —intr.v. To engage in fighting; contend; struggle: combat with new difficulties at every step of the project. —See Syns at **repel.** —n. (kŏm′băt′). Fighting, esp. armed battle: killed in combat. —modifier: combat boots; a combat unit; combat deaths. [Old French combattre : Latin com-, with + battuere, beat.]

com·bat·ant (kəm-băt′nt, kŏm′bə-tnt) n. A person engaged in fighting or armed combat. —adj. Engaging in combat.

com·bat·ive (kəm-băt′ĭv) adj. Eager to fight; belligerent. —**com·bat′ive·ly** adv. —**com·bat′ive·ness** n.

comb·er (kō′mər) n. **1.** A person or instrument that combs. **2.** A long wave of the sea that has reached its peak or broken into foam; breaker.

com·bi·na·tion (kŏm′bə-nā′shən) n. **1. a.** The act or process of combining. **b.** The condition of being combined. **2.** Something that results from combining two or more things; a compound: An alloy is a combination of metals. **3.** An alliance or association of persons or parties for a common purpose. **4.** The sequence of numbers or letters that opens a combination lock. **5.** A one-piece undergarment consisting of an undershirt or chemise and drawers. **6.** Math. One or more elements selected from a set without regard to order of selection. —**com′bi·na′tion·al** adj.

combination lock. A lock that can be opened only by turning the dial with which it is equipped to a particular sequence of positions.

com·bine (kəm-bīn′) v. **-bined, -bin·ing.** —tr.v. **1.** To bring into a state of unity; merge; blend: The novel combines an interesting story and a message. **2.** To join (two or more substances) to make a single substance, as a chemical compound. **3.** To possess or exhibit in combination.

ă pat	ā pay	â care	ä father	ĕ pet	ē be	hw which	ĭ pit	ī tie	î pier	ŏ pot	ō toe	ô paw, for	oi noise
ōō took	ōō boot	ou out	th thin	th this	ŭ cut		û urge	zh vision	ə about, item, edible, gallop, circus				

—*intr.v.* **1.** To become united; coalesce. **2.** To join forces for a common purpose. **3.** To form a chemical compound. —*n.* (kŏm′bīn′). **1.** A power-operated harvesting machine that cuts, threshes, and cleans grain. **2.** An association of persons or companies united for the furtherance of commercial or political interests. **3.** A combination. [Middle English *combinen*, from Old French *combiner*, from Late Latin *combīnāre* : Latin *com-*, together + *bīnī*, two at a time.] —**com·bin′a·ble** *adj.* —**com·bin′er** *n.*

comb·ings (kō′mĭngz) *pl.n.* Hairs, wool, or other material removed with a comb.

combining form. A word element that combines with other words or word elements to create new words; for example, *-logy*, as in *gynecology*; *macro-*, as in *macrochemistry*; *Sino-*, as in *Sino-Soviet*.

com·bo (kŏm′bō) *n., pl.* **-bos. 1.** A small group of musicians. **2.** *Slang.* The result or product of combining; a combination. [Short for COMBINATION.]

com·bus·ti·ble (kəm-bŭs′tə-bəl) *adj.* **1.** Capable of catching fire and burning. **2.** Easily aroused or stirred to action; explosive: *his combustible nature; a combustible situation.* —*n.* A combustible substance. —**com·bus′ti·bil′i·ty** *n.* —**com·bus′ti·bly** *adv.*

com·bus·tion (kəm-bŭs′chən) *n.* **1.** The process of burning. **2.** A chemical reaction, esp. a combining with oxygen, that goes on rapidly and produces light and heat. **3.** Violent anger or agitation: *combustion building up to the revolution point.* [Middle English, from Old French, from Late Latin *combustiō*, from Latin *combūrere*, to burn up, from *com-* (intensive) + *ūrere*, to burn.] —**com·bus′tive** (-tĭv) *adj.*

come (kŭm) *intr.v.* **came** (kām), **come, com·ing. 1.** To advance toward the speaker or toward a place that is indicated; to approach. **2.** To reach a particular point; arrive. **3.** To arrive at a particular result or end: *came to an agreement; plans that came to nothing.* **4.** To move toward or arrive at a particular condition: *a job coming along well; came to her wits' end.* **5.** To move or be brought to a particular position: *came to a sudden stop.* **6.** To extend; reach: *water that came to my waist.* **7. a.** To exist at a particular point or place: *The date of birth comes after the name in this listing.* **b.** To have priority; to rank: *Your work should come first.* **8.** To happen: *How did she come to be asked?* **9.** To happen as a result; derive; proceed: *This comes of your stubbornness. Success comes from hard work.* **10.** To occur in the mind: *The thought came to her.* **11.** To issue from; descend: *She comes from a good family.* **12.** To be a native or have been a resident of: *Joe comes from Chicago.* **13.** To become: *The catch came open.* **14.** To be available or obtainable: *shoes that come in many styles.* **15.** To prove or turn out to be: *a dream that came true.* —*phrasal verbs.* **come about.** To occur; take place; happen. **come across. 1.** To meet by chance. **2.** *Slang.* To do or give what is wanted: *came across with my money.* **come again.** *Slang.* To say something once more; to repeat. **come around (or round). 1.** To recover; revive. **2.** To change one's opinion or position: *She came around after she heard the whole story.* **come back.** To return to past success after a period of misfortune. **come by.** To acquire; get. **come down. 1.** To lose wealth or position. **2.** To be descended from or handed down by: *a custom that comes down from colonial times.* **come down on (or upon). 1.** To attack. **2.** *Informal.* To criticize; to scold. **come down with.** To become ill: *came down with a cold.* **come in for.** *Informal.* To receive; get: *His work came in for criticism.* **come into.** To inherit: *Ann came into a small fortune.* **come off. 1.** To happen; occur: *The trip came off on schedule.* **2.** To be found to be; turn out: *a party that came off successfully.* **come out. 1.** To become known: *The whole story came out in the trial.* **2.** To be issued or brought out: *His new book just came out.* **3.** To declare publicly: *He has come out for the tax proposal.* **4.** To make a formal social debut. **5.** To result; end up; turn out. **come out with. 1.** To disclose publicly; declare. **2.** To put into words; say. **come over. 1.** To happen to; seize; possess: *Strange feelings came over me.* **2.** To change sides. **3.** *Informal.* To visit. **come through. 1.** To succeed. **2.** *Informal.* To do as expected. **3.** To wear through, as cloth. **come to. 1.** To regain consciousness: *He came to in the hospital.* **2.** To amount to: *The bill came to $11.50.* **come up.** To manifest itself; arise:

The question didn't come up. **come up to.** To equal: *This book doesn't come up to yours.* **come up with.** *Informal.* To propose; produce: *Come up with some new ideas.* —*idiom.* **how come?** *Informal.* Why? [Middle English *comen*, from Old English *cuman*.]

come·back (kŭm′băk′) *n.* **1.** A return to former prosperity or status. **2.** A reply, esp. a quick witty one; a retort.

co·me·di·an (kə-mē′dē-ən) *n.* **1.** A professional entertainer who tells jokes or performs various other comic acts. **2.** A person who amuses or tries to be amusing; a clown. **3.** An actor in comedy.

co·me·dic (kə-mē′dĭk) *adj.* Of or relating to comedy.

co·me·di·enne (kə-mē′dē-ĕn′) *n.* A female comedian.

come·down (kŭm′doun′) *n.* A decline or drop in status, position, or self-esteem.

com·e·dy (kŏm′ĭ-dē) *n., pl.* **-dies. 1.** A play, motion picture, etc., in which the story and characters are humorous and that ends happily. **2.** The branch of drama made up of such plays. **3.** Any literary composition having a comedic theme or using the methods of comedy. **4.** The branch of literature dealing with comedies. **5.** Anything, such as an occurrence in real life, that resembles a comedy. [Middle English *comedie*, from Old French, from Latin *cōmoedia*, from Greek *kōmōidia*, from *kōmōidos*, "a singer in the revels" : *kōmos*, revel + *ōidos*, singer.]

comedy of manners. A comedy that satirizes the ways of fashionable society.

come-hith·er (kŭm-hĭth′ər) *adj.* Seductive; alluring; beguiling: *a come-hither look.*

come·ly (kŭm′lē) *adj.* **-li·er, -li·est.** Having a pleasing appearance. —See Syns at **beautiful.** [Middle English *come-li(ch)*, from Old English *cȳmlic*, lovely.] —**come′li·ness** *n.*

come-on (kŭm′ŏn′, -ôn′) *n.* Something offered to attract or allure; an inducement.

com·er (kŭm′ər) *n.* **1.** Someone or something that arrives or comes. **2.** *Informal.* Someone or something that shows promise of attaining success.

co·mes·ti·ble (kə-mĕs′tə-bəl) *adj.* Fit to be eaten; edible. —*n.* Anything that can be eaten as food. [Old French, from Medieval Latin *comestibilis*, from Latin *comedere*, to eat up : *com-* (intensive) + *edere*, eat.]

com·et (kŏm′ĭt) *n.* A celestial body that travels around the sun in an immense elongated orbit and appears characteristically as an object with a glowing head attached to a long, vaporous tail that always points away from the sun. [Middle English *comete*, from Old English *cōmēta*, from Latin *comēta*, from Greek (*astēr*) *komētēs*, "long-haired (star)," from *komē*, hair.]

come·up·pance (kŭm-ŭp′əns) *n.* Also **come·up·ance.** *Informal.* Punishment or retribution that one deserves. [From the phrase *come up.*]

com·fit (kŭm′fĭt, kŏm′-) *n.* A candy; confection; sweetmeat. [Middle English *confit*, from Old French, from Latin *confectum*, "preparation," from *conficere*, to prepare : *com-* (intensive) + *facere*, to make.]

com·fort (kŭm′fərt) *tr.v.* **1.** To soothe in time of grief or fear; to console. **2.** To ease physically; relieve, as of pain. —*n.* **1.** A condition of ease or well-being: *For comfort we kept the room cool.* **2.** Relief in time of grief or fear: *The frightened child held the toy bear for comfort.* **3.** A person who gives relief from grief or worry: *The child was a comfort to me.* **4.** A thing that gives ease or well-being: *comforts such as air conditioning.* **5.** The capacity or ability to give physical ease and well-being: *The comfort of a chair depends on the purpose for which it is intended.* [Middle English *comforten*, from Old French *conforter*, from Late Latin *confortāre*, to strengthen : *com-* (intensive) + *fortis*, strong.] —**com′fort·ing·ly** *adv.*

com·fort·a·ble (kŭm′fər-tə-bəl, kŭmf′tə-bəl) *adj.* **1.** Providing or giving comfort: *a comfortable home.* **2.** In a state of comfort: *comfortable despite the storm; not comfortable in his company.* **3.** *Informal.* Sufficient; adequate: *comfortable earnings.* —**com′fort·a·ble·ness** *n.* —**com′fort·a·bly** *adv.*

com·fort·er (kŭm′fər-tər) *n.* **1.** Someone or something that comforts. **2. the Comforter.** The Holy Spirit. **3.** A thick, warm quilt used as a bedcover. **4.** *Brit.* A woolen neck scarf.

comfort station. A public toilet or restroom.

ă pat	ā pay	â care	ä father	ĕ pet	ē be	hw which	ĭ pit	ī tie	î pier	ŏ pot	ō toe	ô paw, for	oi noise
ōō took	ōō boot	ou out	th thin	*th* this	ŭ cut		û urge	zh vision	ə about, item, edible, gallop, circus				

com·fy (kŭm′fē) adj. **-fi·er, -fi·est.** *Informal.* Comfortable.

com·ic (kŏm′ĭk) adj. **1.** Of, characteristic of, or pertaining to comedy. **2.** Of or pertaining to comic strips. **3.** Funny; amusing; humorous. —See Syns at **laughable.** —n. **1.** A person, esp. an entertainer, who is funny or amusing. **2. comics.** *Informal.* Comic strips. **3.** *Informal.* A comic book. [Latin *cōmicus,* from Greek *kōmikos,* from *kōmos,* revel, merrymaking.]

com·i·cal (kŏm′ĭ-kəl) adj. Causing amusement; funny. — See Syns at **laughable.** —**com′i·cal′i·ty** (-kăl′ĭ-tē) or **com′i·cal·ness** n. —**com′i·cal·ly** adv.

com·ing (kŭm′ĭng) adj. **1.** Approaching; next: *during the coming season.* **2.** *Informal.* Showing promise of fame or success: *a coming woman in politics.* —n. Arrival; advent: *With the coming of spring, days become longer.*

com·i·ty (kŏm′ĭ-tē) n., pl. **-ties.** Civility; courtesy. [Latin *cōmitās,* from *cōmis,* courteous.]

com·ma (kŏm′ə) n. A punctuation mark (,) used to indicate a separation of ideas or of elements within a sentence. [Latin, from Greek *komma,* a cut, section, clause, from *koptein,* to cut.]

     Usage: **1.** A **comma** can be used to separate independent clauses not connected by a conjunction if they are short and closely related: *I came, I saw, I conquered. It was not only false, it was libelous.* Otherwise a semicolon or period must be used. **2.** When independent clauses are joined by a conjunction, a comma usually precedes the conjunction if the clauses are lengthy and esp. if they have different subjects or if confusion might result from omission of the comma: *It snowed yesterday, and today the road is closed.* **3.** Restrictive, or defining, clauses are never set off by commas: *The book that you requested is still missing.* Nonrestrictive clauses are generally set off: *The book, which was a gift from the teacher, is no longer in print.* Similarly, terms in apposition preceded by a *are* separated by a comma: *a Whitman poem, "Song of Myself"*; but those preceded by defining terms are often not separated: *the poem "Maud Muller"; my son Joe.* **4.** Two adjectives in succession are not separated by commas when the second precedes a noun with which it forms a sort of compound: *a rare second chance; an ugly old man.* The elements of a series can be separated by commas: *colored red, white, and blue.* The comma may be omitted before *and* if there is no possibility of confusion. **5.** When commas are used to set off a parenthetical passage, two are necessary: *Mr. Hay, of Montana, is the junior, not the senior, partner.* **6.** Normally a single comma does not appear between the subject and its verb, though subject and verb may be separated by a passage set off by two commas: *The air, heavy with moisture, was like a warm blanket.*

comma fault. *Gram.* A comma splice.

com·mand (kə-mănd′) tr.v. **1.** To direct with authority; give orders to: *He commanded me to leave.* **2.** To have control or authority over; to rule: *Pershing commanded our overseas army.* **3.** To have at one's disposal: *He commands seven languages.* **4.** To deserve and receive as due; require: *His bravery commanded respect.* **5.** To dominate by position; to overlook: *a hill that commands the approach to the city.* —intr.v. **1.** To give commands: *Beggars are in no position to command.* **2.** To exercise authority as a commander; be in control. —n. **1.** An order or direction: *commands that were always clear.* **2.** The possession or exercise of authority to command: *all the strength at his command. The admiral was in command.* **3.** Ability to control or use; mastery: *command of the seas; a command of four languages.* **4.** *Mil.* **a.** The extent or range of authority of one in command. **b.** The forces and areas under the control of one officer. **c.** A group of officers or officials with authority to command: *the German high command at Stalingrad.* **5.** *Brit.* An invitation from the reigning monarch. —See Syns at **ability.** —*modifier:* a *command performance; the command post; command headquarters; a command ship.* [Middle English *com-(m)aunden,* from Old French *comander:* Latin *com-*(intensive) + *mandāre,* to entrust, order.]

     Syns: **command, bid, charge, direct, enjoin, instruct, order, require, tell** *v.* Core meaning: To give orders to (*commanded the soldiers to march*).

com·man·dant (kŏm′ən-dănt′, -dänt′) n. A commanding officer of a military organization.

com·man·deer (kŏm′ən-dîr′) tr.v. **1.** To force into military service. **2.** To seize (property) for public use, esp. for military use; confiscate. **3.** *Informal.* To take arbitrarily or by force. [Afrikaans *kommanderen,* from French *commander,* to command.]

com·mand·er (kə-măn′dər) n. **1.** A person who commands; leader. **2.** An officer in the Navy ranking below a captain and above a lieutenant commander. **3.** An officer of any rank in command of a military unit. **4.** A chief or an officer in certain knightly or fraternal orders.

commander in chief pl. **commanders in chief. 1.** Often **Commander in Chief.** The supreme commander of all the armed forces of a nation. **2.** The officer commanding a major armed force.

com·mand·ing (kə-măn′dĭng) adj. **1.** Having command; in charge: *the commanding general.* **2.** Having the air of command; impressive: *a clear, commanding voice.* **3.** Dominating by reason of position: *a commanding lead.* —**com·mand′ing·ly** adv.

com·mand·ment (kə-mănd′mənt) n. **1.** A command; an order. **2.** Often **Commandment.** Any of the Ten Commandments.

command module. The portion of a spacecraft in which the astronauts live and operate controls during a flight.

com·man·do (kə-măn′dō, kə-män′-) n., pl. **-dos** or **-does.** A member of a small fighting force specially trained for making quick, destructive raids into enemy territory. —*modifier:* a *commando attack.* [Afrikaans *kommando,* from Dutch *commando,* unit of troops, from Spanish *comandar,* to command.]

comma splice. Improper use of a comma between independent clauses not joined by a conjunction. Also called **comma fault.**

com·me·di·a dell'ar·te (kə-mā′dē-ə děl-är′tē). A type of comedy developed in Italy in the 16th cent. and characterized by improvisation from a plot outline and the use of stock characters. [Italian, "comedy of art."]

com·mem·o·rate (kə-měm′ə-rāt′) tr.v. **-rat·ed, -rat·ing. 1.** To honor the memory of: *A large crowd gathered at the park to commemorate the victory.* **2.** To be a memorial to, as a holiday or ceremony: *a day that commemorates the end of World War II.* [From Latin *commemorāre,* to call to mind clearly : *com-* (intensive) + *memor,* mindful.] —**com·mem′o·ra′tion** n. —**com·mem′o·ra′tor** n.

com·mem·o·ra·tive (kə-měm′ər-ə-tĭv, -ə-rā′tĭv) adj. Serving to commemorate. —n. Anything that commemorates.

com·mence (kə-měns′) v. **-menced, -menc·ing.** —tr.v. To begin; start. —intr.v. To come into existence; have a beginning. —See Syns at **begin.** [Middle English *commencen,* from Old French *comencer* : Late Latin *com-* (intensive) + *initiāre,* to begin, initiate.] —**com·menc′er** n.

com·mence·ment (kə-měns′mənt) n. **1.** A beginning; a start. **2.** A graduation ceremony at which academic degrees or diplomas are conferred.

com·mend (kə-měnd′) tr.v. **1.** To speak highly of; praise: *The mayor commended the commission for its painstaking report.* **2.** To represent as worthy, qualified, or desirable; recommend: *commend someone for employment.* **3.** To put in the care of another; entrust: *commend him to his mother's care.* —See Syns at **praise.** [Middle English *commenden,* from Latin *commendāre,* to commit to one's charge : *com-* (intensive) + *mandāre,* to entrust.] —**com·mend′a·ble** adj. —**com·mend′a·ble·ness** n. —**com·mend′a·bly** adv.

com·men·da·tion (kŏm′ən-dā′shən) n. **1.** Recommendation or praise. **2.** An official award or citation.

com·men·da·to·ry (kə-měn′də-tôr′ē, -tōr′ē) adj. Serving to recommend or praise; approving.

com·men·sal (kə-měn′səl) adj. Describing or living in a relationship in which two different kinds of organisms live in close attachment or partnership and in which one usu. benefits from the association and the other is not harmed. —n. A plant or animal living in a commensal relationship. [Middle English, from Medieval Latin *commensālis* : Latin *com-,* together + *mēnsa,* table.] —**com·men′sal·ism** n. —**com·men′sal·ly** adv.

com·men·su·ra·ble (kə-měn′sər-ə-bəl, -shər-) adj. **1.** Able

---

â pat	ā pay	â care	ä father	ĕ pet	ē be	hw which	ĭ pit	ī tie	î pier	ŏ pot	ō toe	ô paw, for	oi noise
ōō took	ōō boot	ou out	th thin	*th* this	ŭ cut		û urge	zh vision	ə about, item, edible, gallop, circus				

to be measured by a common standard or unit. **2.** Properly proportioned; fitting; suitable: *Congress invoked harsh measures commensurable to the danger of the situation.* **3.** *Math.* Exactly divisible by the same unit an integral number of times, as two quantities. [Late Latin *commēn-sūrābilis* : Latin *com-*, same + *mēnsūra*, measure.] **—com·men′su·ra·bil′i·ty** *n.* **—com·men′su·ra·bly** *adv.*

com·men·su·rate (kə-měn′sər-ĭt, -shə-) *adj.* **1.** Of the same size, extent, or length of time. **2.** Corresponding in size or degree; proportionate: *a salary commensurate with his long service.* **3.** *Math.* Commensurable. **—com·men′su·rate·ly** *adv.* **—com·men′su·ra′tion** *n.*

com·ment (kŏm′ĕnt′) *n.* **1.** A note or remark that explains, interprets, or gives an opinion on something: *a critic's comment on a play; the mayor's comment on the governor's speech.* **2.** Talk; gossip: *Her divorce caused much comment in the town.* *—intr.v.* To make a comment; to remark. [Middle English, from Latin *commentum*, contrivance, interpretation, from *comminīscī*, to contrive by thought.]

com·men·tar·y (kŏm′ən-tĕr′ē) *n.*, *pl.* **-ies. 1.** A series of explanations or interpretations. **2.** Anything that illustrates or reflects on something else: *The scandal is a sad commentary on our city government.* **3.** Often **commentaries.** A personal narrative; memoir.

com·men·tate (kŏm′ən-tāt′) *v.* **-tat·ed, -tat·ing.** *—tr.v.* To make a commentary on. *—intr.v.* To serve as a commentator.

com·men·ta·tor (kŏm′ən-tā′tər) *n.* **1.** An author of commentaries. **2.** A writer or broadcaster who reports and gives his opinion of events in the news.

com·merce (kŏm′ərs) *n.* **1.** The buying and selling of goods, esp. on a large scale, as between nations; business. **2.** Intellectual exchange or social intercourse. —See Syns at **business.** [Old French, from Latin *commercium* : *com-* (collective) + *merx*, merchandise.]

com·mer·cial (kə-mûr′shəl) *adj.* **1.** Of, pertaining to, or engaged in commerce: *commercial capitals; a commercial airport.* **2. a.** Having profit as its chief aim: *too scholarly to be a good commercial book.* **b.** Intended to be self-supporting; not having a subsidy: *the commercial theaters of Europe, distinguished from state theaters.* **3.** Sponsored by an advertiser or supported by advertising: *a commercial message; commercial television.* *—n.* An advertisement on radio or television. **—com·mer′cial·ly** *adv.*

commercial bank. A bank the principal functions of which are to receive demand deposits and to make short-term loans.

com·mer·cial·ism (kə-mûr′shə-lĭz′əm) *n.* The practices of commerce or business, esp. those that give chief importance to the making of profit. **—com·mer′cial·ist** *n.* **—com·mer′cial·is′tic** *adj.*

com·mer·cial·ize (kə-mûr′shə-līz′) *tr.v.* **-ized, -iz·ing. 1.** To make commercial; apply methods of business to: *commercialize agriculture.* **2.** To do, make, exploit, etc., mainly for profit: *commercializing the island's tourist attractions.* **—com·mer′cial·i·za′tion** *n.*

com·mi·na·tion (kŏm′ə-nā′shən) *n.* A formal denunciation. [Middle English *comminacioun*, from Old French *commi-nation*, from Latin *comminātiō*, from *comminārī*, to threaten : *com-* (intensive) + *minae*, threats.]

com·min·gle (kə-mǐng′gəl) *v.* **-gled, -gling.** *—intr.v.* To blend together; mix: *cities where people of many nationalities commingle.* *—tr.v.* To mix together; combine: *a story that commingles tragedy and comedy.*

com·mi·nute (kŏm′ə-nōōt′, -nyōōt′) *tr.v.* **-nut·ed, -nut·ing.** To reduce to powder; pulverize. [From Latin *comminuere* : *com-* (intensive) + *minuere*, to lessen.] **—com′mi·nu′tion** *n.*

com·mis·er·ate (kə-mǐz′ə-rāt′) *v.* **-at·ed, -at·ing.** *—tr.v.* To feel or express sympathy for. *—intr.v.* To feel or express sympathy: *One defeated candidate commiserates with another.* [From Latin *commiserārī* : *com-*, with + *miserārī*, to pity.] **—com·mis′er·a′tive** *adj.* **—com·mis′er·a′tive·ly** *adv.* **—com·mis′er·a′tor** *n.*

com·mis·er·a·tion (kə-mǐz′ə-rā′shən) *n.* A feeling or expression of sympathy for another; compassion.

com·mis·sar (kŏm′ĭ-sär′) *n.* **1.** A former name for the head of a commissariat in the Soviet Union. **2.** An official of the Communist Party in charge of political indoctrination and the enforcement of party loyalty. [Russian *komissar*, from German *Kommissar*, commissioner, from Medieval Latin *commissārius*, commissary.]

com·mis·sar·i·at (kŏm′ĭ-sâr′ē-ət) *n.* **1. a.** A department of an army in charge of providing food and other supplies for the troops. **b.** The officers in charge of this department. **2.** A food supply. **3.** A former name for any major government department in the Soviet Union. [Russian *komissa-riat*, from Medieval Latin *commissārius*, commissary.]

com·mis·sar·y (kŏm′ĭ-sĕr′ē) *n.*, *pl.* **-ies. 1.** A store maintained by a company or an army post for the sale of food and supplies to its employees or personnel. **2.** A lunchroom or cafeteria that serves the employees of a company or the personnel of an institution. **3.** A person to whom a special duty is given by a superior; a representative; deputy. [Middle English *commissarie*, from Medieval Latin *commissārius*, commissioner, agent, from *committere*, to commit.]

com·mis·sion (kə-mǐsh′ən) *n.* **1. a.** The act of granting authority to someone to carry out a certain job or duty. **b.** The job or duty assigned by such a grant: *Investigating charges of fraud in the last election was their commission.* **2.** Often **Commission.** A group of people who have been given authority by law to perform certain duties: *The Federal Trade Commission investigates false advertising.* **3.** The act of committing or perpetrating: *statistics on the commission of crime.* **4.** Money in the form of a fee or a percentage of a sale price paid to a salesman or agent for his services. **5.** Appointment to one of several ranks of commissioned officers in the armed forces. *—tr.v.* **1.** To grant a commission to: *The king commissioned the composer to write an opera.* **2.** To place an order for: *commissioned a portrait of himself by a leading artist.* **3.** To put (a ship) into active service. *—idioms.* **in commission. 1.** In active service, as a ship. **2.** In use or in usable condition. **out of commission. 1.** Not in active service. **2.** Not in use or in working condition.

commissioned officer. An officer appointed to one of several ranks in the armed forces. The lowest rank held by commissioned officers in the U.S. Army, Air Force, and Marine Corps is second lieutenant, and ensign in the Navy.

com·mis·sion·er (kə-mǐsh′ə-nər) *n.* **1.** A member of a commission. **2.** An official in charge of a governmental department: *a police commissioner.* **3.** An official chosen as administrative head of an organized professional sport: *a baseball commissioner.*

com·mis·sure (kŏm′ə-shoor′) *n.* **1.** A line or place at which two things are joined; seam; juncture. **2.** *Anat.* A tract of nerve fibers passing from one side to the other of the spinal cord or brain. [Middle English, from Old French, from Latin *commissūra*, from *committere*, to join, commit.] **—com′mis·su′ral** (kŏm′ə-shoor′əl, kə-mǐsh′ər-əl) *adj.*

com·mit (kə-mǐt′) *tr.v.* **-mit·ted, -mit·ting. 1.** To do, perform, or perpetrate: *commit perjury; commit suicide.* **2.** To place in the charge or keeping of another; entrust: *commit all administrative functions to one person.* **3.** To place in confinement or custody, as by an official act: *He was convicted and committed to prison.* **4.** To put in a certain condition or form, as for future use or preservation: *committed the secret code to memory; seldom committed anything to writing.* **5. a.** To pledge (oneself) to a position: *The decision must be ethical if we are to commit ourselves to it.* **b.** To bind or obligate: *We are committed to follow the terms of the will.* [Middle English *committen*, from Latin *committere*, to join, connect, entrust : *com-*, together + *mittere*, to send, put.] **—com·mit′ta·ble** *adj.*

com·mit·ment (kə-mǐt′mənt) *n.* **1.** The act of committing; a giving in charge or entrusting: *commitment of children to foster homes.* **2.** Official consignment, as to a prison or mental hospital: *the commitment of criminals to labor camps.* **3.** A pledge or obligation, as to follow a certain course of action: *our treaty commitments to protect small nations; a commitment to work for peaceful change.* **4.** The state of being bound emotionally or intellectually to some course of action: *a deep commitment to liberal policies.*

com·mit·tal (kə-mǐt′l) *n.* **1.** The act of entrusting. **2.** The act of committing to confinement. **3.** The act of pledging oneself to a particular position.

com·mit·tee (kə-mĭt'ē) n. A group of people chosen to do a particular job or fulfill specified duties: *the membership committee of our club*. [Middle English *committe*, trustee, from *committen*, to commit.]

com·mit·tee·man (kə-mĭt'ē-mən, -măn') n. 1. A committee member. 2. A ward or precinct party leader.

committee of the whole. A committee consisting of all the members of a legislative house.

com·mit·tee·wom·an (kə-mĭt'ē-wŏŏm'ən) n. 1. A member of a committee. 2. A ward or precinct party leader.

com·mix (kə-mĭks', kŏ-) tr.v. To mix together. —*intr.v.* To mix; blend. —**com·mix·ture** (kə-mĭks'chər, kŏ-) n.

com·mode (kə-mōd') n. 1. A low cabinet or chest of drawers, often elaborately decorated. 2. a. A movable stand containing a washbowl. b. A chair enclosing a chamber pot. 3. A toilet. [French, "convenient," from Latin *commodus*, commodious.]

com·mo·di·ous (kə-mō'dē-əs) adj. Having plenty of room; spacious. [Middle English, from Old French *commodieux*, from Medieval Latin *commodiōsus*, from Latin *commodus*, convenient, "(conforming) with (due) measure" : *com-*, with + *modus*, measure.] —**com·mo'di·ous·ly** adv. —**com·mo'di·ous·ness** n.

com·mod·i·ty (kə-mŏd'ĭ-tē) n., pl. **-ties.** 1. Anything that is useful or can be turned to commercial or other advantage. 2. An article of trade or commerce that can be transported, esp. an agricultural or mining product. [Middle English *commodite*, profit, from Old French *commodite*, from Latin *commoditās*, advantage, convenience, from *commodus*, convenient.]

com·mo·dore (kŏm'ə-dôr', -dōr') n. 1. An officer in the U.S. Navy ranking above a captain and below a rear admiral. This rank was last used in World War II. 2. a. The senior captain of a naval squadron or merchant fleet. b. The presiding officer of a yacht club. [From Dutch *komandeur*, commander.]

com·mon (kŏm'ən) adj. **-er, -est.** 1. a. Belonging to or shared equally by two or more: *common interests; angles with a common side.* b. Of or pertaining to the community as a whole; public: *the common good; common knowledge.* 2. Found or occurring often and in many places; usual; widespread: *when gas stations became common.* 3. Of the most widely known kind; without distinction; average: *a common soldier; the common man.* 4. Of no special quality; standard; plain: *a matter of common courtesy.* 5. Of mediocre or inferior quality; not costly or rare: *common cloth.* 6. Unrefined or coarse in manner; vulgar: *behavior that branded her as common.* —*n.* Often **commons.** A tract of land belonging to or used by a community as a whole. —*idiom.* **in common.** Equally with or by all; jointly: *qualities they have in common.* [Middle English *commun(e)*, from Old French, from Latin *commūnis.*] —**com'mon·ly** adv. —**com'mon·ness** n.

    Syns: **common, everyday, familiar, frequent, regular, routine, widespread** adj. Core meaning: Occurring quite often (*tropical storms—a common occurrence in Florida*). See also Syns at **cheap** and **ordinary**.

com·mon·age (kŏm'ə-nĭj) n. 1. The right to pasture animals on common land. 2. The state of being held in common.

com·mon·al·ty (kŏm'ə-nəl-tē) n., pl. **-ties.** Also **com·mon·al·i·ty** (kŏm'ĭ-năl'ə-tē). The common people as opposed to the upper classes.

common denominator. A number that contains the denominator of each of a set of fractions as a factor.

common divisor. A **common factor.**

com·mon·er (kŏm'ə-nər) n. A person without noble rank or title.

common factor. A number that is a factor of two or more numbers, esp. when all of the numbers are integers. For example, 3 is a common factor of 9 and 15.

common fraction. A fraction whose numerator and denominator are both integers.

common law. The system of law based on court decisions and on customs and usages rather than on an organized body of written laws or statutes.

common-law marriage. A marriage existing only by mutual agreement between a man and a woman without a civil or religious ceremony.

common logarithm. A logarithm for which the number 10 is used as the base.

common multiple. A number that contains each of a set of given numbers as a factor.

common noun. A noun that represents one or more members of a class and that can be used immediately following the definite article; for example, *book*.

com·mon·place (kŏm'ən-plās') adj. Ordinary; common; uninteresting: *reporting a commonplace occurrence in an exciting way.* —See Syns at **ordinary.** —*n.* 1. A statement or remark that is dull or worn out through use. 2. Something ordinary or common. —**com'mon·place'ness** n.

com·mons (kŏm'ənz) n. 1. *(used with a pl. verb).* The common people as distinguished from the aristocracy or nobility. 2. *(used with a sing. verb).* A place for dining.

common stock. Ordinary shares of a corporation on which dividends are paid only after all dividends on preferred stock have been paid.

com·mon·weal (kŏm'ən-wēl') n. Also **common weal.** 1. The public good or welfare. 2. *Archaic.* A commonwealth.

com·mon·wealth (kŏm'ən-wĕlth') n. 1. The people of a nation or state. 2. A nation or state governed by the people; a republic. 3. **Commonwealth. a.** The official title of some U.S. states, including Kentucky, Maryland, Massachusetts, Pennsylvania, and Virginia. b. The official title of Puerto Rico. c. The official title of some democratic countries, such as Australia.

com·mo·tion (kə-mō'shən) n. 1. Violent or turbulent motion; agitation; tumult. 2. Political or social disturbance or insurrection; disorder. [Middle English *commocioun*, from Old French *commotion*, from Latin *commōtiō*, from *commovēre*, to move violently : *com-* (intensive) + *movēre*, move.]

com·mu·nal (kə-myōō'nəl, kŏm'yə-nəl) adj. 1. Of or pertaining to a commune or community. 2. Of, pertaining to, or belonging to the people of a community; public. —**com·mu'nal·ly** adv.

com·mu·nal·ism (kə-myōō'nə-lĭz'əm, kŏm'yə-nə-) n. 1. A theory or system of government in which each commune is virtually an autonomous unit loosely bound in a federation. 2. Belief in or practice of communal ownership, as of goods and property. 3. Strong devotion to the interests of one's own ethnic group rather than those of society as a whole. —**com·mu'nal·ist** n. —**com·mu'nal·is'tic** adj.

com·mu·nal·ize (kə-myōō'nə-līz', kŏm'yə-nə-) tr.v. **-ized, -iz·ing.** To convert into communal property.

com·mune[1] (kə-myōōn') intr.v. **-muned, -mun·ing.** 1. To converse intimately; exchange thoughts and feelings: *commune with friends.* 2. To receive the Eucharist. [Middle English *communen*, to share, communicate, from Old French *comuner*, from *comun*, common.]

com·mune[2] (kŏm'yōōn) n. 1. The smallest local political division of various European countries, such as France, Belgium, Italy, and Switzerland, governed by a mayor and municipal council. 2. A unit of the state organized on a local or community level in some Communist countries. 3. a. A local community organized with a government promoting local interests. b. A municipal corporation in the Middle Ages. 4. a. A small, often rural community whose members have common interests and whose property is often shared or owned jointly. b. The members of a commune. [French, from Medieval Latin *communia*, community, from Latin *commūnis*, common.]

com·mu·ni·ca·ble (kə-myōō'nĭ-kə-bəl) adj. 1. Capable of being communicated or transmitted: *communicable diseases.* 2. Communicative. —**com·mu'ni·ca·bil'i·ty,** **com·mu'ni·ca·ble·ness** n. —**com·mu'ni·ca·bly** adv.

com·mu·ni·cant (kə-myōō'nĭ-kənt) n. 1. A person who receives or is entitled to receive Communion. 2. One who communicates. —*adj.* Communicating.

com·mu·ni·cate (kə-myōō'nĭ-kāt') v. **-cat·ed, -cat·ing.** —*tr.v.* 1. To make known; impart: *communicate information.* 2. To transmit, as a disease. —*intr.v.* 1. To interchange or exchange of thoughts, ideas, etc.: *A difference in age often makes it difficult to communicate.* 2. To receive Communion. [Latin *commūnicāre*, "to make common, share,"] —**com·mu'ni·ca'tor** n.

com·mu·ni·ca·tion (kə-myōō′nĭ-kā′shən) *n.* **1.** The act of communicating; transmission. **2.** The exchange of thoughts, messages, or information, as by speech, signals, or writing. **3.** Something communicated; a message. **4. communications.** A system for sending and receiving messages, as by mail, telephone, or television. **5. communications.** The art and technology of communicating.

communications satellite. An artificial satellite used to aid communications, as by reflecting or relaying a radio signal.

com·mu·ni·ca·tive (kə-myōō′nĭ-kā′tĭv, -kə-tĭv) *adj.* Inclined to communicate readily; not secretive or reticent; talkative. **—com·mu′ni·ca′tive·ness** *n.*

com·mun·ion (kə-myōōn′yən) *n.* **1.** A sharing of thoughts or feelings; intimate talk. **2. a.** A religious or spiritual fellowship. **b.** A body of Christians with a common religious faith who practice the same rites; denomination. **3. Communion. a.** The Eucharist. **b.** The consecrated elements of the Eucharist. **c.** The part of the Mass in which the sacrament of the Eucharist is received. [Middle English communioun, from Old French communion, from Latin, participation by all, from *commūnis*, common.]

com·mu·ni·qué (kə-myōō′nĭ-kā′, kə-myōō′nĭ-kā′) *n.* An official announcement or bulletin. [French, from *communiquer*, to inform, communicate.]

com·mu·nism (kŏm′yə-nĭz′əm) *n.* **1.** Any social system characterized by the absence of classes and by common ownership of the means of production and common sharing of labor and products. **2. Communism. a.** The international movement aimed at the eventual establishment of this society. **b.** The doctrines of this movement; Marxism-Leninism. **c.** The political and economic system of any country governed by a Communist party. [French communisme, from Old French *commun*, common.]

Com·mu·nist (kŏm′yə-nĭst) *n.* **1.** A member of a Communist Party. **2. communist.** A communalist. **3.** Often **communist.** A person who believes in or advocates communism. **—adj.** Often **communist.** Pertaining to, characteristic of, or resembling communism or Commu-

...nis·tic (kŏm′yə-nĭs′tĭk) *adj.* Based on or favoring ...inciples of communism. **—com′mu·nis′ti·cal·ly** *adv.*

...ist Party. A Marxist-Leninist party, esp. the official party of the Soviet Union or one allied with this

...ty (kə-myōō′nĭ-tē) *n.*, *pl.* **-ties. 1. a.** A group of ...in the same locality and under the same gov- ...the district or locality in which they live. **2.** A ...having common interests: *New York's His- ...ty; the scientific community.* **3.** Similarity ...ess: *a community of interests.* **4.** Society ...blic. **5.** *Ecol.* **a.** A group of plants and ...specific region under relatively similar ...gion in which they live. **6.** Common ...ation. [Middle English *communite*, ...nete, from Latin *commūnitās*, from

...elfare fund financed by private ...arious charitable organizations. ...erty owned jointly by a hus-

...v. **-nized, -niz·ing. 1.** To put ...under public ownership or ...Communist principles or

...t. **1.** A substitution or ... payment for another. ...to a less severe one. ...versing of the direc- ..., from Old French, ...e, commute.]

...tĭv) *adj.* **1.** Per- ...ubstitution, in- ...property

...matical ...ives the ...the numbers

com·mu·ta·tor (kŏm′yə-tā′tər) *n.* A cylindrical arrangement of insulated metal bars connected to the coils of an electric motor or generator to provide a unidirectional current from the generator or a reversal of current into the coils of the motor.

com·mute (kə-myōōt′) *v.* **-mut·ed, -mut·ing. —tr.v. 1.** To substitute; exchange; interchange. **2.** To change (a penalty, debt, or payment) to a less severe one. **—intr.v.** To travel as a commuter. **—n.** *Informal.* The distance traveled by a commuter: *a 22-mile commute.* [Middle English commuten, from Latin *commūtāre*, to exchange : com-, mutually + *mutāre*, to change.] **—com·mut′er** *n.*

com·pact¹ (kəm-păkt′, kŏm-, kŏm′păkt′) *adj.* **1.** Closely and firmly united or packed together; solid; dense: *compact clusters of flowers.* **2.** Packed into or arranged within a relatively small space: *compact living quarters.* **—tr.v.** (kəm-păkt′) To press or join firmly together; condense; consolidate. **—n.** (kŏm′păkt′). **1.** A small case containing a mirror and cosmetics. **2.** A small automobile. [Middle English, from Latin *compactus*, past part. of *compingere*, to join together : com-, together + *pangere*, to fasten.] **—com·pact′er** *n.* **—com·pact′ly** *adv.* **—com·pact′ness** *n.*

com·pact² (kŏm′păkt′) *n.* An agreement or covenant; a contract. [Latin *compactum*, from *compacīscī*, to agree together : com-, together + *pacīscī*, to agree.]

com·pac·tor (kəm-păk′tər, kŏm′păk′-) *n.* A device that compresses refuse into relatively small packages.

com·pan·ion (kəm-păn′yən) *n.* **1.** A person who accompanies or associates with another; comrade. **2.** A person employed to assist, live with, or travel with another. **3.** One of a pair or set of things; mate; match. [Middle English compai(g)noun, from Old French compaignon, "one who eats bread with another" : Latin com-, together + *pānis*, bread.]

com·pan·ion·a·ble (kəm-păn′yə-nə-bəl) *adj.* Suited to be a good companion; sociable; friendly. **—com·pan′ion·a·bly** *adv.*

com·pan·ion·ship (kəm-păn′yən-shĭp′) *n.* The relationship of companions; friendly feeling; fellowship.

com·pan·ion·way (kəm-păn′yən-wā′) *n.* A staircase leading from a ship's deck to the cabins or area below. [Obs. Dutch *kompanje*, from Old French *compagne*, from Italian *(camera della) campagna*, ship's storeroom, from campagna, open country or sea + WAY.]

com·pa·ny (kŭm′pə-nē) *n.*, *pl.* **-nies. 1.** A group of people; a gathering. **2.** People assembled for a social purpose. **3.** A guest or guests: *company for the weekend.* **4.** Companionship; fellowship: *grateful for her company.* **5.** One's companions or associates: *move in fast company.* **6.** A business enterprise; firm. **7.** A partner or partners not specifically named in a firm's title: *Rogers and Company.* **8.** A troupe of dramatic or musical performers: *a repertory company.* **9.** *Mil.* A subdivision of a regiment or battalion, usu. under the command of a captain. **10.** A ship's crew and officers. **—idioms. keep company.** To carry on courtship. **keep (someone) company.** To accompany. **part company.** To end an association or friendship. [Middle English compaignie, from Old French compagnie, from compain, companion.]

Usage: **company.** This collective noun takes a singular verb when it means a unit as a whole: *a company that has fired its top management; an infantry company that was ambushed.* If *company* means the individual members of the group, it takes a plural verb: *The company are arriving in their cars.*

com·pa·ra·ble (kŏm′pər-ə-bəl) *adj.* **1.** Capable of being compared: *two errors of comparable magnitude.* **2.** Worthy of comparison: *a genius comparable to Einstein.* **—See** Syns at **like. —com′pa·ra·bil′i·ty** *n.* **—com′pa·ra·bly** *adv.*

com·par·a·tive (kəm-păr′ə-tĭv) *adj.* **1.** Of, based on, or involving comparison: *a comparative study of customs and mores.* **2.** Estimated by comparison; relative: *a comparative newcomer.* **3.** *Gram.* Designating a degree of comparison of adjectives and adverbs higher than positive and lower than superlative. **—n.** *Gram.* **1.** The comparative degree. **2.** An adjective or adverb expressing the comparative degree; for example, *brighter* is the comparative of *bright; more slowly* is the comparative of *slowly.* **—com·par′a·tive·ly** *adv.*

com·pare (kəm-pâr′) v. **-pared, -par·ing.** —tr.v. **1.** To represent as similar, equal, or analogous; liken: *compared his eyes to sapphires.* **2.** To examine in order to note the similarities or differences of: *compare their writing styles.* **3.** To form the positive, comparative, or superlative degrees of (an adjective or adverb). —intr.v. To be worthy of comparison: *prices that compare with anyone's.* —n. Comparison: *a pianist who is beyond compare.* [Middle English *comparen,* from Old French *comparer,* from Latin *comparāre,* to pair, from *compar,* like, equal : *com-,* mutually + *pār,* equal.]

Usage: compare, contrast. To *compare* is to examine in order to note similarities or differences or to liken: *compare the copy with the original.* To *contrast* is to set in opposition in order to show or emphasize differences: *contrast summer and winter.*

com·par·i·son (kəm-păr′ĭ-sən) n. **1.** The act of comparing or being compared. **2.** The condition of being capable or worthy of being compared; similarity; likeness: *There is no comparison between the two books.* **3.** *Gram.* The modification or inflection of an adjective or adverb to denote the three degrees (positive, comparative, and superlative).

com·part·ment (kəm-pärt′mənt) n. **1.** One of the parts or spaces into which an area is subdivided. **2.** A separate room, section, or chamber: *a storage compartment.* [From Late Latin *compartīri,* to divide : *com-,* with + *pars,* part.]

com·part·men·tal·ize (kŏm′pärt-mĕn′tl-īz′, kəm-pärt′-) tr.v. **-ized, -iz·ing.** To divide or partition into compartments or categories.

com·pass (kŭm′pəs, kŏm′-) n. **1. a.** A device used to determine geographical direction, usu. consisting of a magnetic needle mounted or suspended so that it can align itself with the magnetic field of the earth. **b.** Any other device for determining geographical direction, as a radio compass or a gyrocompass. **2.** Also **compasses.** A device used for drawing circles or arcs of circles, usu. consisting of a pair of rigid arms hinged together in a V shape, one of the arms holding a sharp point that serves as an anchor and the other holding a pencil or other drawing tool. **3.** An enclosing line or boundary; circumference; girth. **4.** An enclosed space or area. **5.** A range or scope; extent: *not within the compass of your authority.* —tr.v. **1.** To go around; make a circuit of; circle: *compass the oceans.* **2.** To surround; encircle: *Clouds compassed the city.* **3.** To understand; comprehend: *I could barely compass his intricate argument.* **4.** To achieve; obtain; accomplish: *He managed to compass his life's ambition.* **5.** To scheme; plot: *compass his downfall.* —See Syns at **surround.** [Middle English *compas,* from Old French, from *compasser,* to measure (with compasses) : Latin *com-* (intensive) + *passus,* pace.] —**com′pass·a·ble** adj.

compass
A magnetic needle

compass
A drawing device

compass card. A freely pivoting circular disk carrying the magnetic needles of a mariner's compass and marked with the 32 points of the compass and the 360 degrees of the circle.

com·pas·sion (kəm-păsh′ən) n. The deep feeling of sharing the suffering of another, together with a desire to give aid or show mercy. [Middle English *compassioun,* from Old French *compassion,* from Late Latin *compassiō,* from *compatī,* to sympathize with : *com-,* with + *patī,* to suffer.]

com·pas·sion·ate (kəm-păsh′ə-nĭt) adj. Feeling or showing compassion; sympathetic. —**com·pas′sion·ate·ly** adv.

com·pat·i·ble (kəm-păt′ə-bəl) adj. **1.** Capable of living or performing in harmonious, agreeable, or congenial combination with another or others: *compatible roommates; on compatible terms.* **2.** Capable of orderly, efficient integration and operation with other elements in a system: *compatible acids.* [Middle English, from Old French, from Late Latin *compatī,* to sympathize with.] —**com·pat′i·bil′i·ty** or **com·pat′i·ble·ness** n. —**com·pat′i·bly** adv.

com·pa·tri·ot (kəm-pā′trē-ət, -ŏt′) n. **1.** A fellow countryman. **2.** *Informal.* A colleague.

com·peer (kəm-pîr′, kŏm′pîr′) n. **1.** A person of equal status or rank; a peer or equal. **2.** A comrade, companion, or associate.

com·pel (kəm-pĕl′) tr.v. **-pelled, -pel·ling. 1.** To force, drive, or constrain: *Duty compelled me to volunteer. Lack of funds compels us to economize.* **2.** To make necessary; to exact: *The energy crisis compels fuel conservation.* [Middle English *compellen,* from Old French *compeller,* from Latin *compellere* : *com-,* together + *pellere,* to drive.] —**com·pel′la·ble** adj. —**com·pel′la·bly** adv. —**com·pel′ler** n.

com·pend (kŏm′pĕnd′) n. Var. of **compendium.**

com·pen·di·ous (kəm-pĕn′dē-əs) adj. Containing or stating briefly and concisely all the essential facts or information on a subject; terse; succinct. [Middle English, from Latin *compendiōsus,* from *compendium,* compendium.] —**com·pen′di·ous·ly** adv. —**com·pen′di·ous·ness** n.

com·pen·di·um (kəm-pĕn′dē-əm) n., pl. **-ums** or **-di·a** (-dē-ə). Also **com·pend** (kŏm′pĕnd′). An organized, detailed, complete summary; an abstract. [Latin, "that which is weighed together," gain, abridgment, from *compendere,* to weigh together : *com-,* together + *pendere,* to weigh.]

com·pen·sate (kŏm′pən-sāt′) v. **-sat·ed, -sat·ing.** —tr.v. **1.** To make up for or offset; counterbalance: *His lack of speed is compensated by powerful hitting.* **2.** To make payment or reparation to; recompense or reimburse: *We compensated her for the time she worked.* —intr.v. To provide or serve as a substitute or counterbalance: *We can't compensate for the wasted time.* [Latin *compensāre,* to weigh one thing against another : *com-,* mutually + *pensāre,* freq. of *pendere,* to weigh.] —**com′pen·sa′tive** (-sā′tĭv, kəm-pĕn′sə-tĭv) adj. —**com·pen′sa·to·ry** (kəm-pĕn′sə-tôr′ē, -tōr′ē) adj.

com·pen·sa·tion (kŏm′pən-sā′shən) n. **1.** The act of compensating. **2.** Something given or received as an equivalent or as reparation for a loss, service, or debt; a recompense; an indemnity. **3.** *Biol.* The counterbalancing of any functional defect by the supplementary development and activation of another organ or another part of the defective structure.

com·pete (kəm-pēt′) intr.v. **-pet·ed, -pet·ing. 1.** To strive or contend with another or others, as for a prize: *compete in a race.* **2.** To strive successfully; be compared favorably: *Many countries produce fine wines, but none can compete with France in quality and variety.* [Latin *competere,* "to strive together" : *com-,* together + *petere,* to seek, strive.]

com·pe·tence (kŏm′pĭ-təns) n. Also **com·pe·ten·cy** (-tən-sē). **1.** The state or condition of being competent. **2.** Sufficient means for a comfortable existence. **3.** *Law.* The quality or condition of being legally qualified, eligible, or admissible. —See Syns at **ability.**

com·pe·tent (kŏm′pĭ-tənt) adj. **1.** Properly or well qualified; capable: *a competent worker.* **2.** Adequate for the purpose; sufficient: *a competent job.* **3.** *Law.* Legally qualified or fit; admissible. [Middle English, from Old French, from Latin *competere,* to be competent, compete.] —**com′pe·tent·ly** adv.

com·pe·ti·tion (kŏm′pĭ-tĭsh′ən) n. **1.** The act of competing in or as if in a contest: *won the race in competition with ten runners.* **2.** A contest or similar test of skill or ability: *a skating competition.* **3.** Rivalry or struggle to win an advantage, success, profit, etc., from others or others: *laws intended to protect a nation's business against foreign competition.* **4.** The one or ones against whom one competes: *Is the competition as good as our team?*

com·pet·i·tive (kəm-pĕt′ĭ-tĭv) adj. Also **com·pet·i·to·ry**

(-tôr′ē, -tōr′ē). **1.** Of, involving, or determined by competition: *competitive games; a product priced so as to be competitive with others.* **2.** Liking or inclined to compete: *a competitive person.* —**com·pet′i·tive·ly** *adv.* —**com·pet′i·tive·ness** *n.*

com·pet·i·tor (kəm-pĕt′ĭ-tər) *n.* A person who competes, as in sports or business; rival.

com·pet·i·to·ry (kəm-pĕt′ĭ-tôr′ē, -tōr′ē) *adj.* Var. of **competitive.**

com·pi·la·tion (kŏm′pə-lā′shən) *n.* **1.** The act of collecting or compiling. **2.** Something compiled, such as a set of data, a report, or an anthology.

com·pile (kəm-pīl′) *tr.v.* **-piled, -pil·ing. 1.** To gather into a single collection, set, or record: *compile test results.* **2.** To put together or compose from materials gathered from several sources: *compile an encyclopedia.* [Middle English *compilen,* from Old French *compiler,* from Latin *compīlāre,* "to heap together," plunder : *com-,* together + *pīlāre,* to plunder.] —**com·pil′er** *n.*

com·pla·cen·cy (kəm-plā′sən-sē) *n.* Also **com·pla·cence** (-səns). **1.** A feeling of contentment or satisfaction; gratification. **2.** Self-satisfaction; smugness.

com·pla·cent (kəm-plā′sənt) *adj.* **1.** Contented to a fault; self-satisfied; smug: *the team had won so often they had become complacent.* **2.** Showing contentment or self-satisfaction. [Orig. "pleasing," from Latin *complacēre,* to please : *com-* (intensive) + *placēre,* to please.] —**com·pla′cent·ly** *adv.*

com·plain (kəm-plān′) *intr.v.* **1.** To express feelings of pain, dissatisfaction, or resentment: *complain about a headache. She works hard but never complains.* **2.** To describe one's pains, problems, or dissatisfactions. **3.** To make a formal accusation or bring a formal charge. [Middle English *complainen,* from Old French *complaindre* : Latin *com-* (intensive) + *plangere,* to lament.] —**com·plain′er** *n.*

com·plain·ant (kəm-plā′nənt) *n.* A person who makes a complaint or files a formal charge, as in a court of law; plaintiff.

com·plaint (kəm-plānt′) *n.* **1.** An expression of pain, dissatisfaction, resentment, discontent, or grief. **2.** A cause or reason for complaining; grievance: *The union issued a list of its complaints and demands.* **3.** A cause of physical pain or discomfort; malady; illness: *Colds are a common winter complaint.* **4.** *Law.* A formal statement or accusation in a civil action, setting forth the claim on which relief is sought.

com·plai·sance (kəm-plā′səns, -zəns) *n.* Willing inclination to oblige or comply with the wishes of others.

com·plai·sant (kəm-plā′sənt, -zənt) *adj.* Showing a desire or willingness to please; cheerfully obliging. —See Syns at **amiable.** [French, pleasing, agreeable, from Old French *complaire,* to please, from Latin *complacēre.*] —**com·plai′sant·ly** *adv.*

com·ple·ment (kŏm′plə-mənt) *n.* **1.** Something that completes, makes up a whole, or brings to perfection: *The necklace is a wonderful complement to the new dress.* **2.** The quantity or number needed to make up a whole: *shelves with a full complement of books.* **3.** Either of two parts that complete the whole or mutually complete each other. **4.** *Geom.* An angle related to another with the sum of their measures being 90°. **5.** *Gram.* A word or group of words that completes a predicate or sentence. **6.** The full crew of officers and men required to man a ship. **7.** The heat-sensitive substance found in normal blood serum that destroys antigens. —*tr.v.* (kŏm′plə-mĕnt′). To add or serve as a complement to: *That tie complements your suit.* [Middle English, from Latin *complēmentum,* from *complēre,* to complete.]

com·ple·men·ta·ry (kŏm′plə-mĕn′tə-rē, -trē) *adj.* **1.** Forming or serving as a complement; completing. **2.** Supplying what is lacking or needed. —**com′ple·men·ta·ri·ness** *n.*

com·plete (kəm-plēt′) *adj.* **1.** Having all necessary or normal parts; entire; whole. **2.** *Bot.* Having all characteristic floral parts, including sepals, petals, stamens, and a pistil. **3.** Concluded; ended. **4.** Thorough; consummate; perfect: *complete control.* **5.** Fully or additionally equipped or supplied: *an auditorium complete with public-address system.* **6.** Skilled; accomplished: *a complete musician.* —See Syns

at **utter** and **whole.** —*tr.v.* **-plet·ed, -plet·ing. 1.** To make whole or complete. **2.** To bring to an end; conclude. —See Syns at **end.** [Middle English *complet(e),* from Old French, from Latin *complēre,* to fill up : *com-* (intensive) + *plēre,* to fill.] —**com·plete′ly** *adv.* —**com·plete′ness** *n.*

com·ple·tion (kəm-plē′shən) *n.* **1.** The act of concluding, perfecting, or making entire. **2.** The condition of being completed: *carry plans through to completion.*

com·plex (kəm-plĕks′, kŏm′plĕks′) *adj.* **1. a.** Consisting of two or more parts: *complex components.* **b.** Consisting of many interconnected or interwoven parts, elements, or factors: *the complex sound of a symphony orchestra.* **2.** Difficult to understand or master; intricate; complicated: *complex problems; complex ideas.* —*n.* (kŏm′plĕks′). **1.** A whole composed of intricate or interconnected parts: *a complex of cities and suburbs.* **2.** A connected group of repressed emotions, desires, and memories that influences a person's personality and behavior. **3.** *Informal.* An exaggerated or obsessive concern or fear: *a complex about being short.* [Latin *complexus,* past part. of *complectī,* to entwine : *com-,* together + *plectere,* to twine, braid.] —**com·plex′ly** *adv.* —**com·plex′ness** *n.*

   Syns: complex, complicated, elaborate, intricate, involved, knotty, labyrinthine *adj. Core meaning:* Difficult to understand because of intricacy (*inflation—a complex problem*).

complex fraction. A fraction in which the numerator or denominator or both contain fractions. Also called **compound fraction.**

com·plex·ion (kəm-plĕk′shən) *n.* **1.** The natural color, texture, and appearance of the skin, esp. of the face. **2.** General character, aspect, or appearance: *The latest findings have substantially altered the complexion of the problem.* [Middle English *complexioun,* physical constitution, from Old French *complexion,* from Medieval Latin *complexiō,* "combination of corporeal humors," from Latin *complexus,* complex.]

com·plex·i·ty (kəm-plĕk′sĭ-tē) *n., pl.* **-ties. 1.** The condition of being intricate or complex. **2.** Something intricate or complex.

complex number. A number that can be expressed as $a + bi$, where a and b are real numbers and $i^2 = -1$.

complex sentence. A sentence containing an independent clause and one or more dependent clauses.

com·pli·ance (kəm-plī′əns) *n.* Also **com·pli·an·cy** (-ən-sē). **1.** A act of complying with a wish, request, or demand; acquiescence. **2.** A disposition or tendency to yield to others.

com·pli·ant (kəm-plī′ənt) *adj.* Yielding readily to others. [COMPL(Y) + -ANT.] —**com·pli′ant·ly** *adv.*

com·pli·cate (kŏm′plĭ-kāt′) *tr.v.* **-cat·ed, -cat·ing.** To make complex, intricate, or perplexing. [From Latin *complicāre,* to fold together : *com-,* together + *plicāre,* to fold.]

com·pli·cat·ed (kŏm′plĭ-kā′tĭd) *adj.* **1.** Containing intricately combined or involved parts. **2.** Not easy to understand or deal with. —See Syns at **complex.**

com·pli·ca·tion (kŏm′plĭ-kā′shən) *n.* **1.** The act of complicating. **2.** A confused or intricate relationship of parts, as in a procedure. **3.** Any factor, condition, or element that complicates: *Rising unemployment adds another complication to the economic problem.* **4.** A character or situation that complicates the plot in a film, drama, etc. **5.** *Med.* A condition occurring during the course of a disease and aggravating it.

com·plic·i·ty (kəm-plĭs′ĭ-tē) *n.* Involvement as an accomplice in a crime or wrongdoing.

com·pli·ment (kŏm′plə-mənt) *n.* **1.** An expression of praise, admiration, or congratulation. **2.** A formal act of civility, courtesy, or respect. **3. compliments.** Good wishes; regards: *Extend my compliments to your parents.* —*tr.v.* To pay a compliment to: *I complimented her for her performance.* [French, from Spanish *cumplimiento,* from *cumplir,* to complete, behave properly, from Latin *complēre,* to fill up, complete.]

com·pli·men·ta·ry (kŏm′plə-mĕn′tə-rē, -trē) *adj.* **1.** Expressing, using, or resembling a compliment: *The book received many complimentary reviews.* **2.** Given free as a favor or courtesy: *complimentary tickets to the show.* —**com′pli·men·ta·ri·ly** *adv.*

ă pat	ā pay	â care	ä father	ĕ pet	ē be	hw which	ĭ pit	ī tie	î pier	ŏ pot	ō toe	ô paw, for	oi noise
ŏŏ took	ōō boot	ou out	th thin	*th* this	ŭ cut		û urge	zh vision	ə about, item, edible, gallop, circus				

com·ply (kəm-plī′) *intr.v.* **-plied, -ply·ing.** To act in accordance with a command, request, rule, wish, etc.: *comply with the new regulations.* —See Syns. at **obey.** [Italian *complire,* from Spanish *cumplir,* to complete, do what is proper.]

com·po·nent (kəm-pō′nənt) *n.* **1.** A constituent part or ingredient; element: *the components of a computer. Many components make up a person's personality.* **2.** *Math.* One of a set of two or more vectors having a sum equal to a given vector. —*adj.* Being or functioning as a component; constituent: *the component parts of an amplifier.* [From Latin *compōnere,* to place together : *com-,* together + *pōnere,* to put.]

com·port (kəm-pôrt′, -pōrt′) *tr.v.* To conduct or behave (oneself) in a particular manner: *comport oneself with grace and dignity.* —*intr.v.* To agree, correspond, or harmonize: *actions that comport with the principles of democracy.* [Old French *comporter,* to support, from Latin *comportāre,* to bring together : *com-,* together + *portāre,* to carry, bear.]

com·port·ment (kəm-pôrt′mənt, -pōrt′-) *n.* Bearing; deportment.

com·pose (kəm-pōz′) *v.* **-posed, -pos·ing.** —*tr.v.* **1.** To make up; constitute or form: *an exhibit composed of French Impressionist paintings.* **2.** To make or create by putting together parts or elements: *We composed the party platform from moderate and liberal positions.* **3.** To create or produce (a literary or musical piece). **4.** To make (one's mind or body) calm or tranquil; to quiet: *Compose yourself and deal with the situation.* **5.** To settle or adjust, as a point of disagreement: *composed their differences.* **6.** *Printing.* To arrange or set (type or matter to be printed). —*intr.v.* **1.** To create literary or musical pieces. **2.** *Printing.* To set type. [Middle English, from Old French *composer* : *com-,* together + *poser,* to place, pose.]

Usage: **compose, comprise.** *Compose* means to make up the constituent parts of something and therefore to constitute or form it: *Five boroughs compose New York City. New York City is composed of five boroughs. Comprise* means to consist of or be made up of: *New York City comprises five boroughs.* Remember: the whole comprises the parts; the parts do not comprise the whole, nor is the whole comprised of its parts. See also Usage note at **include.**

com·posed (kəm-pōzd′) *adj.* Calm; serene; self-possessed. —**com·pos′ed·ly** (-pō′zĭd-lē) *adv.*

com·pos·er (kəm-pō′zər) *n.* A person who composes, esp. one who composes music.

com·pos·ite (kəm-pŏz′ĭt) *adj.* **1.** Made up of distinctly different parts or elements: *a composite face made from various photographs.* **2.** *Bot.* Of, belonging to, or characteristic of the Compositae, a large plant family characterized by flower heads consisting of many small, densely clustered flowers that give the impression of a single bloom. —*n.* **1.** A composite structure or entity. **2.** A complex material, such as wood or fiber glass, in which two or more distinct substances, esp. metals, ceramics, glasses, and polymers, combine to produce some structural or functional properties not present in any individual component. **3.** *Bot.* A composite plant. [Latin *compositus,* past part. of *compōnere,* to compose.] —**com·pos′ite·ly** *adv.* —**com·pos′ite·ness** *n.*

com·po·si·tion (kŏm′pə-zĭsh′ən) *n.* **1.** A putting together of parts or elements to form a whole; a combining. **2.** The manner in which such parts are combined or related; constitution; make-up: *the composition of a mineral.* **3.** The result or product of composing; mixture; compound: *Her special fruit punch is a vile composition.* **4.** The arrangement of artistic parts so as to form a unified whole: *the composition of a painting.* **5.** Any work of art, literature, or music or its structure or organization. **6.** A short essay, esp. one written as a school exercise. **7.** *Printing.* The setting of type. [Middle English *composicioun,* from Old French *composition,* from Latin *compositiō,* from *compōnere,* to put together, arrange.] —**com′po·si′tion·al** *adj.*

com·pos·i·tor (kəm-pŏz′ĭ-tər) *n.* *Printing.* A person who arranges or sets type; a typesetter.

com·post (kŏm′pōst′) *n.* **1.** A mixture of decaying organic matter, such as leaves and manure, used as fertilizer. **2.** A

composition; mixture. [Middle English, stew, compote, from Old French *composte,* stewed fruit, and *compost,* mixture, from Latin *compositus,* put together, composite.]

com·po·sure (kəm-pō′zhər) *n.* Self-possession; calmness; tranquillity. [From **compose.**]

com·pote (kŏm′pōt′) *n.* **1.** Fruit stewed or cooked in syrup. **2.** A long-stemmed dish used for holding fruit, nuts, or candy. [French, from Old French *composte,* stewed fruit.]

compote   **compound eye**

com·pound¹ (kŏm′pound′) *n.* **1.** A combination of two or more parts, ingredients, etc. **2.** Also **compound word.** A word consisting of a combination of two or more other words and forming a single unit with its own meaning. A compound word may be written without a space or hyphen, as *everybody* or *loudspeaker,* or with a hyphen or hyphens, as *baby-sitter* or *heart-to-heart.* **3.** A pure, homogeneous substance that consists of atoms of at least two different elements combined in definite proportions, usu. having properties different from any of the elements it contains. —*tr.v.* (kŏm-pound′, kəm-). **1.** To combine; mix. **2.** To produce or create by combining two or more ingredients or parts: *Pharmacists compound medicines.* **3.** To compute (interest) on the principal and accrued interest. **4.** *Law.* To agree, for payment or other consideration, not to prosecute: *compound a felony.* **5.** To add to; increase or intensify: *Strong winds compounded the difficulty of fighting the forest fire.* —*adj.* (kŏm′pound′, kŏm-pound′). Consisting of two or more substances, ingredients, elements, or parts. [Middle English *compounen,* from Old French *compon(d)re,* from Latin *compōnere,* to put together, compose.] —**com·pound′a·ble** *adj.* —**com·pound′er** *n.*

com·pound² (kŏm′pound) *n.* **1.** A residence or group of residences set off and enclosed by a barrier, esp.: **a.** In the Orient, such a group of residences for Europeans. **b.** In Africa, a group of huts for native workers. **2.** A compound used for confining prisoners of war. [From Malay *kampong,* village, cluster of buildings.]

com·pound-com·plex sentence (kŏm′pound-kŏm′plĕks′-). A sentence consisting of at least two coordinate independent clauses and one or more dependent clauses.

compound eye. The eye of most insects and some crustaceans, composed of many light-sensitive elements, each with its own refractive system and each of which forms part of an image.

compound fraction. A complex fraction.

compound fracture. A fracture in which broken bone cuts through soft tissue and makes an open wound.

compound interest. Interest computed on the accumulated unpaid interest as well as on the original principal.

compound leaf. A leaf consisting of two or more separate leaflets borne on a single leafstalk.

compound sentence. A sentence of two or more coordinate independent clauses.

com·pre·hend (kŏm′prĭ-hĕnd′) *tr.v.* **1.** To grasp mentally; understand or know. **2.** To take in, include, or embrace: *The metropolitan area of Boston comprehends the surrounding suburbs.* —See Syns at **understand.** [Middle English *comprehenden,* from Latin *comprehendere,* to grasp mentally : *com-,* together in mind + *prehendere,* to seize, grasp.]

com·pre·hen·si·ble (kŏm′prĭ-hĕn′sə-bəl) *adj.* Also **com·pre·**

hend·i·ble (-hĕn′də-bəl). Capable of being comprehended or understood; intelligible. —**com′pre·hen′si·bil′i·ty** n. —**com′pre·hen′si·bly** adv.

com·pre·hen·sion (kŏm′prĭ-hĕn′shən) n. **1.** The act or fact of comprehending or understanding. **2.** The ability to understand. **3.** Comprehensiveness.

com·pre·hen·sive (kŏm′prĭ-hĕn′sĭv) adj. Covering a subject or matter completely or almost completely; including or comprehending much; large in scope or content: a comprehensive history of the Revolution. —See Syns at **general**. —n. Often **comprehensives**. Informal. Examinations covering the entire field of major study given in the final undergraduate or graduate year. —**com′pre·hen′sive·ly** adv. —**com′pre·hen′sive·ness** n.

com·press (kəm-prĕs′) tr.v. **1.** To put pressure on so as to force into smaller space; condense; compact. **2.** To squeeze or press together: He compressed his lips into a thin, tight line. **3.** To shorten or condense as if by squeezing or pressing: A proverb often compresses the wisdom of centuries into a single sentence. —See Syns at **contract**. —n. (kŏm′prĕs′). **1.** A soft pad of gauze, cotton, or other material, often moistened or medicated, applied to some part of the body, esp. to a wound or injury. **2.** A machine or establishment for baling cotton. [Middle English compressen, from Old French compresser, from Latin compressus, past part. of comprimere, to press together : com-, together + premere, to press.] —**com·press′i·bil′i·ty** n. —**com·press′i·ble** adj.

com·pres·sion (kəm-prĕsh′ən) n. **1. a.** The act or process of compressing. **b.** The condition of being compressed. **2.** The process by which the gaseous substance in a heat engine is compressed, as the fuel mixture in the cylinder of an internal-combustion engine.

com·pres·sor (kəm-prĕs′ər) n. Something that compresses, esp. a device used to compress gases.

com·prise (kəm-prīz′) tr.v. -**prised**, -**pris·ing**. **1.** To consist of; be composed of; include: The Union comprises fifty states. **2.** To make up; form; constitute: Native tribes comprise the bulk of the island's population. —See Usage note at **compose**. [Middle English comprisen, from Old French comprendre, to comprehend.]

com·pro·mise (kŏm′prə-mīz′) n. **1.** A settlement of differences in which each side gives up some of its claims and agrees to some of the demands of the other. **2.** An adjustment, agreement, or choice reached by yielding on certain details or matters or principle or by combining qualities of different things: He chose a medium-sized car as a compromise between the comfort of a large one and the economy of a small one. —**modifier**: a compromise agreement. —v. -**mised**, -**mis·ing**. —tr.v. **1.** To settle by making concessions and adjustments. **2.** To expose to danger, suspicion, or dishonor: She will not compromise herself by abandoning what she believes in. —intr.v. To make a compromise. [Middle English compromis, from Old French, from Latin comprōmissum, from comprōmittere, to promise mutually : com-, mutually + prōmittere, to promise.] —**com′pro·mis′er** n.

comp·trol·ler (kən-trō′lər) n. A business executive or government official who supervises financial affairs; controller.

com·pul·sion (kəm-pŭl′shən) n. **1.** Force or influence that compels or makes it necessary for someone to do something; coercion; constraint: Following a vote, the minority yielded to the wishes of the majority without compulsion. **2.** The condition of being compelled. **3. a.** An often unreasonable urge or impulse that is practically impossible to control: a compulsion to overeat. **b.** An action done in response to such an urge: Overeating is a compulsion with her. [Middle English compulsioun, from Old French compulsion, from Late Latin compulsiō, from Latin compellere, to compel.]

com·pul·sive (kəm-pŭl′sĭv) adj. **1.** Of, having, or resulting from a strong, irresistible impulse: a compulsive gambler. When she is nervous she has a compulsive desire to talk. **2.** Compelling; compulsory. —**com·pul′sive·ly** adv. —**com·pul′sive·ness** n.

com·pul·so·ry (kəm-pŭl′sə-rē) adj. **1.** Employing or exerting compulsion; coercive: compulsory powers of the law. **2.** Obligatory; required.

Syns: compulsory, imperative, mandatory, necessary, obligatory adj. Core meaning: Required by laws, rules or regulations (compulsory attendance at classes).

com·punc·tion (kəm-pŭngk′shən) n. A strong uneasiness caused by a sense of guilt; remorse: He felt no compunctions about lying to her. —See Syns at **qualm**. [Middle English, from Old French componction, from Late Latin compunctiō, "prick of conscience," from Latin compungere, to prick hard : com- (intensive) + pungere, to prick, sting.]

com·pu·ta·tion (kŏm′pyōō-tā′shən) n. The act, process, method, or result of computing.

com·pute (kəm-pyōōt′) v. -**put·ed**, -**put·ing**. —tr.v. To determine or calculate by mathematics, esp. by numerical methods. —intr.v. To determine an amount or number. [Latin computāre, to reckon together : com-, together + putāre, to think, reckon.] —**com·put′a·bil′i·ty** n. —**com·put′a·ble** adj.

com·put·er (kəm-pyōō′tər) n. **1.** A person who computes. **2.** A device that computes, esp. an electronic machine that performs high-speed mathematical or logical calculations and assembles, stores, correlates, or otherwise processes and prints data.

com·put·er·ize (kəm-pyōō′tə-rīz′) tr.v. -**ized**, -**iz·ing**. **1.** To process or store (information) with or in an electronic computer or system of computers. **2.** To convert (a process, operation, or device) so that it can make use of or be controlled by an electronic computer or system of electronic computers.

computer language. A code used to provide data and instructions to computers.

com·rade (kŏm′răd′, -rəd) n. **1.** A friend, associate, or companion, esp. one who shares one's activities. **2.** Often **Comrade.** A fellow member, as in a political party, esp. the Communist Party. [From Old French camarade, roommate, from Spanish camarada, from Late Latin camera, room, from Latin, arched roof, from Greek kamara, vault.] —**com′rade·ship′** n.

con¹ (kŏn) n. An argument, opinion, etc., against something: discussing the pros and cons of the subject. —adv. Against: arguing pro and con. [Middle English, short for contra, against, from Latin contrā.]

con² (kŏn) tr.v. **conned, con·ning.** To study or examine carefully, esp. to memorize. [Middle English connen, to know how, be able, from Old English cunnan.]

con³ (kŏn) tr.v. **conned, con·ning.** Also **conn.** To direct the steering or course of (a vessel). —n. **1.** The station or post of a person who cons. **2.** The act or process of conning. [Middle English conduen, to guide, from Old French conduire, to conduct, from Latin condūcere : com-, together + dūcere, to lead.]

con⁴ (kŏn) tr.v. **conned, con·ning.** Slang. To swindle or defraud (a victim); to dupe. —n. Slang. A swindle. [Short for CONFIDENCE.]

con-. Var. of **com-.**

con·cat·e·nate (kŏn-kăt′n-āt′, kən-) tr.v. -**nat·ed**, -**nat·ing**. To connect or link in a series or chain. —adj. (-ĭt, -āt′). Connected or linked in a series. [From Late Latin concatēnāre : com-, together + catēnāre, to link, chain.] —**con·cat′e·na′tion** n.

con·cave (kŏn-kāv′, kŏn′kāv′) adj. Curved like the inner surface of a sphere. —n. A concave surface or line. [Middle English, from Old French, from Latin concavus, vaulted, hollow.] —**con·cave′ly** adv. —**con·cave′ness** n.

con·cav·i·ty (kŏn-kăv′ĭ-tē) n., pl. -**ties**. **1.** The condition of being concave. **2.** A concave surface or structure.

con·ca·vo-con·cave (kŏn-kā′vō-kŏn-kāv′) adj. Concave on both surfaces, as certain lenses.

con·ca·vo-con·vex (kŏn-kā′vō-kŏn-vĕks′) adj. **1.** Concave on one side and convex on the other. **2.** Designating a lens with greater concave than convex curvature.

con·ceal (kən-sēl′) tr.v. To hide or keep from observation, discovery, or understanding; keep secret: concealed the note under the mattress. She laughed to conceal her disappointment. —See Syns at **hide**. [Middle English concelen, from Old French conceler, from Latin concēlāre : com- (intensive) + cēlāre, to hide.] —**con·ceal′a·ble** adj. —**con·ceal′er** n.

con·ceal·ment (kən-sēl′mənt) n. **1. a.** The act of conceal-

ă pat	ā pay	â care	ä father	ĕ pet	ē be	hw which		ĭ pit	ī tie	î pier	ŏ pot	ō toe	ô paw, for	oi noise
ōō took	ōō boot	ou out	th thin	th this	ŭ cut		û urge	zh vision	ə about, item, edible, gallop, circus			

ing. **b.** The condition of being concealed. **2.** A means of concealing.

con·cede (kən-sēd′) v. **-ced·ed, -ced·ing.** —*tr.v.* **1.** To admit as true or real, often unwilling or hesitantly; acknowledge: *Frank was about to concede defeat when suddenly his opponent faltered.* **2. a.** To give; yield; grant: *After many years the government conceded the right to vote to all citizens.* **b.** To give up on (something in which one has had a strong claim or interest), often before results have been fully established: *The candidate conceded the election before all the votes had been counted.* —*intr.v.* To make a concession; yield. —See Syns at **acknowledge.** [French *concéder,* from Latin *concēdere,* to yield : *com-* (intensive) + *cēdere,* to go away, withdraw.] —**con·ced′er** *n.*

con·ceit (kən-sēt′) n. **1.** Too high an opinion of one's abilities, worth, or personality; vanity. **2.** An ingenious or witty thought or expression. **3.** An elaborate or extended metaphor, used esp. as a poetic device. [Middle English *conceite,* concept, from *conceiven,* to conceive.]

con·ceit·ed (kən-sē′tĭd) adj. Holding too high an opinion of oneself; vain. —**con·ceit′ed·ly** adv. —**con·ceit′ed·ness** *n.*

con·ceiv·a·ble (kən-sē′və-bəl) adj. Capable of being thought of; imaginable; possible: *It is conceivable that life exists on other planets.* —**con·ceiv′a·bly** adv.

con·ceive (kən-sēv′) v. **-ceived, -ceiv·ing.** —*tr.v.* **1.** To become pregnant with: *conceive a child.* **2.** To form or develop in the mind; devise: *conceive a plan for doubling the profits of the company.* **3.** To think or believe; hold an opinion; imagine: *We could not conceive that such a tragedy could happen.* **4.** To apprehend mentally; understand: *I can't conceive your meaning.* —*intr.v.* **1.** To become pregnant. **2.** To form an idea: *Ancient peoples conceived of the earth as flat.* [Middle English *conceiven,* from Old French *conceivre,* from Latin *concipere,* to take to oneself : *com-,* comprehensively + *capere,* to take.] —**con·ceiv′er** *n.*

con·cen·trate (kŏn′sən-trāt′) v. **-trat·ed, -trat·ing.** —*tr.v.* **1.** To bring, direct, or draw toward a common center or objective; focus: *concentrate your eyes on the screen; concentrate our efforts to finishing on time.* **2.** To draw or gather together in or toward one place or point: *The population of the country is concentrated in large cities.* **3.** *Chem.* To increase the concentration of (a solution or mixture). —*intr.v.* **1.** To converge toward a center: *Clouds concentrated overhead.* **2.** To direct one's thoughts or attention: *concentrate on the problem at hand.* —*n.* A substance or product made by increasing the proportion of a substance in a solution or mixture: *orange-juice concentrate.* [Prob. from Old French *concentrer* : *com-,* same + *centre,* center.] —**con′cen·tra′tor** *n.*

con·cen·tra·tion (kŏn′sən-trā′shən) n. **1.** Close, undivided attention: *a task requiring patience and concentration.* **2.** A close gathering or dense grouping: *a heavy concentration of troops on the border.* **3.** The act or process of concentrating or the condition of being concentrated. **4.** *Chem.* The amount of a particular substance contained in a given amount of a solution or mixture: *the concentration of salt in sea water.*

concentration camp. A camp where prisoners of war, enemy aliens, and political prisoners are confined.

con·cen·tric (kən-sĕn′trĭk) or **con·cen·tri·cal** (-trĭ-kəl) adj. Having a center in common: *a set of concentric circles.* —**con·cen′tri·cal·ly** (-trĭ-kə-lē, -trĭk-lē) adv. —**con·cen·tric′i·ty** (kŏn′sĕn-trĭs′ĭ-tē) *n.*

con·cept (kŏn′sĕpt′) n. **1.** A general idea or understanding, esp. one derived from specific instances: *no concept of how the stock market operates.* **2.** A thought or notion. [Late Latin *conceptus,* a thing conceived, past part. of *concipere,* to take to oneself, conceive.]

con·cep·tion (kən-sĕp′shən) n. **1. a.** The fusing of a sperm and egg to form a zygote that is capable of developing into a new organism. **b.** The entity so formed; an embryo; fetus. **2.** A beginning; a start: *We were in on the project from its conception.* **3.** The ability to form or understand mental concepts. **4.** Something that is mentally conceived; a concept, plan, design, idea, or thought: *modern conceptions about how the universe was formed.* [Middle English *concepcioun,* from Old French *conception,* from Latin

conceptiō, from *concipere,* to conceive.] —**con·cep′tion·al** *adj.*

con·cep·tu·al (kən-sĕp′chōō-əl) adj. Of, involving, or based on concepts: *He is an excellent conceptual thinker but a poor administrator.* —**con·cep′tu·al·ly** adv.

con·cep·tu·al·ize (kən-sĕp′chōō-ə-līz′) v. **-ized, -iz·ing.** —*tr.v.* To form concepts of. —*intr.v.* To form concepts. —**con·cep′tu·al·i·za′tion** *n.*

con·cern (kən-sûrn′) tr.v. **1.** To be about; have to do with: *an article concerning the energy crisis.* **2.** To have an effect on; be of interest or importance to: *a problem that concerns us all.* **3.** To engage the attention of; involve: *concerned herself with his well-being.* **4.** To cause worry in; to trouble: *His unreliability concerns me.* —*n.* **1.** A matter that relates to or affects someone or something; a thing of interest or importance: *Unemployment is the President's major concern.* **2.** Regard for or interest in someone or something: *The doctor's concern sped her recovery.* **3.** Anxiety; worry: *filled with concern about his illness.* **4.** A business establishment; a company: *a concern that deals in retail sales.* —See Syns at **anxiety.** [Middle English *concernen,* from Old French *concerner,* from Medieval Latin *concernere,* to relate to, from Latin, to mix in a sieve : *com-,* together + *cernere,* to sift.]

con·cerned (kən-sûrnd′) adj. **1.** Interested or affected. **2.** Anxious; troubled; disturbed.

con·cern·ing (kən-sûr′nĭng) prep. In reference to, regarding.

con·cert (kŏn′sûrt′, -sərt) n. **1.** A musical performance given by one or more singers or instrumentalists or both. **2.** Agreement in purpose, feeling, or action. —*v.* (kən-sûrt′). —*tr.v.* **1.** To plan or arrange by mutual agreement. **2.** To contrive or devise. —*intr.v.* To act or contrive together. —**idiom. in concert.** All together; in agreement: *working in concert.* [French, from Italian *concerto,* from Old Italian *concertare,* to harmonize.]

con·cert·ed (kən-sûr′tĭd) adj. **1.** Planned or accomplished together; combined: *a concerted fund-raising drive.* **2.** Using all available energies and resources: *a concerted effort.*

con·cer·ti·na (kŏn′sər-tē′nə) n. A small, hexagonal accordion with bellows and with buttons for keys. [CONCERT + Italian *-ina* (fem. dim. suffix).]

concertina

con·cert·ize (kŏn′sər-tīz′) intr.v. **-ized, -iz·ing.** To give or perform in concerts.

con·cert·mas·ter (kŏn′sərt-măs′tər) n. The first violinist and assistant conductor in a symphony orchestra.

con·cer·to (kən-chĕr′tō) n., pl. **-tos** or **-ti** (-tē). A composition for an orchestra and one or more solo instruments, typically in three movements. [Italian, "concert".]

concerto gros·so (grō′sō) pl. **con·cer·ti grossi** (kən-chĕr′tē grō′sē). A composition for a small group of solo instruments and a full orchestra. [Italian, "great concerto."]

con·ces·sion (kən-sĕsh′ən) n. **1.** The act of conceding or yielding: *settle a dispute by mutual concession.* **2.** Something yielded or conceded: *Higher wages was the major concession demanded.* **3.** Something granted by a government or controlling authority, as a land tract or franchise, to be used for a specific purpose. **4. a.** The privilege of operating a subsidiary business in a certain place: *bidding for an oil concession in the Middle East.* **b.** The place allotted for such a business: *the parking concession at the ball park.* [Middle English, from Old French, from Latin *concessiō,* from *concēdere,* to concede.]

con·ces·sion·aire (kən-sĕsh′ə-nâr′) n. The operator or holder of a concession.

ă pat	ā pay	â care	ä father	ĕ pet	ē be	hw which	ĭ pit	ī tie	î pier	ŏ pot	ō toe	ô paw, for	oi noise
ōō took	ōō boot	ou out	th thin	*th* this	ŭ cut	û urge	zh vision	ə about, item, edible, gallop, circus

con·ces·sive (kən-sĕs'ĭv) *adj.* **1.** Of the nature of or containing a concession; tending to concede. **2.** *Gram.* Expressing concession, as the conjunction *though.*

conch (kŏngk, kŏnch) *n.*, *pl.* **conchs** (kŏngks) or **conch·es** (kŏn'chĭz). **1.** Any of various tropical saltwater gastropod mollusks of the genus *Strombus* and other genera, with large spiral shells and edible flesh. **2.** The shell of a conch used esp. in making cameos. [Middle English *conche*, seashell, from Latin *concha*, mussel, from Greek *konkhē.*]

conch

con·chol·o·gy (kŏng-kŏl'ə-jē) *n.* The branch of zoology concerned with the study of mollusks and shells. **—con·chol'o·gist** *n.*

con·cil·i·ate (kən-sĭl'ē-āt') *tr.v.* **-at·ed, -at·ing. 1.** To overcome the distrust or anger of; win over; placate: *His apology failed to conciliate her for the insult.* **2.** To gain, win, or secure (favor, friendship, good will, etc.) by friendly overtures. **3.** To make consistent; reconcile. [From Latin *conciliāre*, to bring together, unite, from *concilium*, union, gathering.] **—con·cil'i·a'tion** *n.* **—con·cil'i·a'tor** *n.* **—con·cil'i·a·to'ry** (-ə-tôr'ē, -tōr'ē) *adj.*

con·cise (kən-sīs') *adj.* Expressing much in few words; brief and clear. [Latin *concīdere*, to cut up : *com-* (intensive) + *caedere*, to cut.] **—con·cise'ly** *adv.* **—con·cise'ness** *n.*

Syns: concise, laconic, pithy, succinct, terse *adj.* *Core meaning:* Stating much in few words (*a concise paragraph*). CONCISE implies clarity and compactness through the removal of all unnecessary words, but TERSE adds to *concise* the sense that something is brief and to the point (*a terse reply*). LACONIC often suggests brevity that is almost rude (*a laconic response that merely answered the question*). PITHY implies that something is precisely meaningful and has a telling effect (*a pithy comment*). SUCCINCT strongly emphasizes compactness and the elimination of all elaboration (*a succinct explanation*).

con·clave (kŏn'klāv', kŏng'-) *n.* **1.** A confidential or secret meeting. **2. a.** The private rooms in which the cardinals of the Roman Catholic Church meet to elect a pope. **b.** The meeting so held. [Middle English, from Old French, from Latin *conclāve*, "room locked with a key" : *com-*, together + *clāvis*, key.]

con·clude (kən-klōōd') *v.* **-clud·ed, -clud·ing. —tr.v. 1.** To bring to an end; close; finish: *conclude a meeting; conclude the concert with a Sousa march.* **2.** To come to an agreement or settlement of; settle finally: *conclude a peace treaty.* **3.** To reach a decision or form an opinion about; infer or deduce: *The jury concluded that he was guilty as charged.* **—intr.v. 1.** To come to an end; close: *The debate concluded amicably.* **2.** To form a final judgment; come to a decision or an agreement. **—See Syns at decide** and **end.** [Middle English *concluden*, from Latin *conclūdere*, to shut up closely : *com-* (intensive) + *claudere*, to shut.]

con·clu·sion (kən-klōō'zhən) *n.* **1.** The close or closing part of something; the end; the finish. **2.** The outcome or result of an act or process: *a satisfactory conclusion to the dispute.* **3.** A judgment, decision, or opinion based on experience, examination of facts or results, etc.: *insufficient data to reach a conclusion.* **4.** A final arrangement or settlement, as of a treaty. **5.** *Logic.* In a syllogism, the proposition that must necessarily follow from the major and minor premises. **—idiom. in conclusion.** In closing; as a final statement.

con·clu·sive (kən-klōō'sĭv) *adj.* Putting an end to doubt, question, or uncertainty; decisive; final: *conclusive evidence.* **—con·clu'sive·ly** *adv.* **—con·clu'sive·ness** *n.*

con·coct (kən-kŏkt') *tr.v.* **1.** To prepare by mixing ingredients: *concoct a stew from leftovers.* **2.** To invent; contrive: *concoct an excuse.* [Latin *concoquere*, to cook together : *com-*, together + *coquere*, to cook.] **—con·coct'er** or **con·coc'tor** *n.* **—con·coc'tion** *n.*

con·com·i·tance (kən-kŏm'ĭ-təns) *n.* Also **con·com·i·tan·cy** (-tən-sē) *pl.* **-cies.** Occurrence together or in connection with another; accompaniment.

con·com·i·tant (kən-kŏm'ĭ-tənt) *adj.* Existing or occurring concurrently; accompanying; attendant: *a concomitant development.* **—n.** An accompanying state, circumstance, or thing. [From Latin *concomitārī*, to accompany : *com-*, together + *comes*, companion.]

con·cord (kŏn'kôrd', kŏng'-) *n.* **1.** Agreement of interests or feelings; concurrence; accord: *two tribes living in peace and concord.* **2.** A treaty establishing peaceful relations. **3.** *Gram.* Agreement between words in person, number, gender, and case. **—See Syns at harmony.** [Middle English, from Old French *concorde*, from Latin *concors*, "of the same mind" : *com-*, same, mutually + *cors*, heart, mind.]

con·cor·dance (kən-kôr'dns) *n.* **1.** A state of agreement; harmony; concord. **2.** An alphabetical index of all the words in a written work or collection of works, showing where they occur.

con·cor·dant (kən-kôr'dnt) *adj.* Harmonious; agreeing. **—con·cor'dant·ly** *adv.*

con·cor·dat (kən-kôr'dăt') *n.* **1.** A formal agreement; a compact. **2.** An agreement between the pope and a government for the regulation of church affairs.

con·course (kŏn'kôrs', -kōrs', kŏng'-) *n.* **1.** A large open space for the gathering or passage of crowds, as in a railroad station. **2.** A wide avenue or thoroughfare. [Middle English, from Old French *concours*, from Latin *concursus*, from the past part. of *concurrere*, to run together : *com-*, together + *currere*, to run.]

con·crete (kŏn'krēt', kŏn-krēt') *n.* A building material made of sand, pebbles, crushed stone, etc., held together by a mass of cement or mortar. **—modifier:** *concrete walls; a concrete walk.* **—adj.** (kŏn-krēt', kŏn'krēt'). **1.** Relating to an actual, specific thing or instance; particular: *I don't want theories and guesses, I want concrete evidence.* **2.** Existing in reality or in real experience; perceptible by the senses; real: *concrete objects such as trees.* **3.** Formed by the coalescence of separate particles or parts into one mass; solid. **—v.** (kŏn'krēt', kŏn-krēt') **-cret·ed, -cret·ing. —tr.v. 1.** To form into a mass by coalescence or cohesion of particles. **2.** To build, treat, or cover with concrete. **—intr.v.** To harden; solidify. [Middle English *concret*, from Old French, from Latin *concrēscere*, to grow together, harden.] **—con·crete'ly** *adv.* **—con·crete'ness** *n.*

con·cre·tion (kən-krē'shən) *n.* **1.** The act or process of growing together or becoming united in one mass. **2.** A solid or concrete mass. **3.** *Geol.* A rounded mass of mineral matter found in sedimentary rock. **4.** *Path.* **a.** A solid mass of inorganic material formed in a cavity or tissue of the body; calculus. **b.** An abnormal fusion of otherwise adjacent parts, as of toes.

con·cu·bine (kŏng'kyə-bīn', kŏn'-) *n.* **1.** A woman who cohabits with a man without being married to him. **2.** In certain polygamous societies, a secondary wife, usu. of inferior status. [Middle English, from Old French, from Latin *concubīna*, "one to sleep with" : *com-*, together + *cubāre*, to lie down.]

con·cu·pis·cence (kŏn-kyōō'pĭ-səns) *n.* A strong desire, esp. sexual desire; lust. [From Latin *concupere*, to have a strong desire for : *com-* (intensive) + *cupere*, to desire.] **—con·cu'pis·cent** *adj.*

con·cur (kən-kûr') *intr.v.* **-curred, -cur·ring. 1.** To have the same opinion; agree: *concur with an assessment.* **2.** To act together; cooperate: *nations concurring to prevent terrorism.* **3.** To occur at the same time; coincide: *Happiness and success do not always concur.* [Middle English *concurren*, from Latin *concurrere*, to run together : *com-*, together + *currere*, to run.]

con·cur·rence (kən-kûr'əns) *n.* Also **con·cur·ren·cy** (-ən-sē) *pl.* **-cies. 1.** Agreement in opinion; accordance. **2.** Cooperation or combination, as of agents, circumstances, events, efforts, etc. **3.** Simultaneous occurrence; coincidence. **4.** A joining or coming together; convergence.

con·cur·rent (kən-kûr′ənt) *adj.* **1.** Happening at the same time or place: *concurrent investigations.* **2.** Acting in conjunction. **3.** Meeting at or tending to meet at the same point: *concurrent lines.* **4.** In accordance; agreeing; harmonious. —*n.* Something that concurs. —**con·cur′rent·ly** *adv.*

con·cus·sion (kən-kŭsh′ən) *n.* **1.** A violent jarring; a shock: *a concussion from the explosion.* **2.** An injury to a soft tissue of the body, esp. the brain, resulting from a violent blow. [From Late Latin *concussus,* past part. of *concutere,* to shake violently, from Latin *com-* (intensive) + *quatere,* to shake.] —**con·cus′sive** (-kŭs′ĭv) *adj.*

con·demn (kən-dĕm′) *tr.v.* **1.** To express disapproval of; denounce. **2. a.** To judge to be guilty and state the punishment for; convict: *arrested, tried, and condemned in a day.* **b.** To sentence to a particular kind of punishment: *condemn a criminal to death.* **3.** To declare unfit for use: *condemn an old building.* **4.** *Law.* To declare legally appropriated for public use under the right of eminent domain. —See Syns at **blame.** [Middle English *condem(p)nen,* from Old French *condem(p)ner,* from Latin *condemnāre : com-* (intensive) + *damnum,* damage.] —**con·demn′a·ble** (-dĕm′nə-bəl) *adj.*

con·dem·na·tion (kŏn′dĕm-nā′shən, -dəm-) *n.* **1.** The act of condemning. **2.** The condition of being condemned. **3.** Severe disapproval; strong censure. —**con·dem′na·to·ry** (kən-dĕm′nə-tôr′ē, -tōr′ē) *adj.*

con·den·sa·tion (kŏn′dĕn-sā′shən, -dən-) *n.* **1.** The act of condensing. **2.** The condition of being condensed. **3.** A product of condensing. **4. a.** The physical process by which part or all of a gas or mixture of gases is reduced to a liquid or, sometimes, solid: *the condensation of steam into water.* **b.** The liquid or solid so formed: *condensation on the bathroom mirror.* **5.** *Chem.* A chemical reaction in which water or another simple substance is released by the combination of two or more molecules.

con·dense (kən-dĕns′) *v.* **-densed, -dens·ing.** —*tr.v.* **1.** To reduce (a gas) to a liquid or, sometimes, solid form. **2.** To make more concentrated, compact, or dense; reduce the volume of. **3.** To shorten or make more concise; abridge: *condense a novel; condense a report.* —*intr.v.* **1.** To become more compact. **2.** To undergo condensation. [Middle English *condensen,* from Old French *condenser,* from Latin *condēnsāre : com-* (intensive) + *dēnsus,* dense.]

condensed milk. Cow's milk with sugar added, reduced by evaporation to a thick consistency.

con·dens·er (kən-dĕn′sər) *n.* **1.** Someone or something that condenses. **2.** *Physics.* An apparatus used to condense a gas or vapor. **3.** A capacitor. **4.** A mirror, lens, or combination of lenses used to gather light and direct it upon an object or projection lens.

con·de·scend (kŏn′dĭ-sĕnd′) *intr.v.* **1.** To agree to do something one regards as beneath one's rank or dignity: *The president condescended to type his own letter.* **2.** To treat people in a patronizing or superior manner. [Middle English *condescenden,* from Old French *condescendre,* from Medieval Latin *condēscendere,* to stoop to : Latin *com-* (intensive) + *dēscendere,* to descend.]

con·de·scend·ing (kŏn′dĭ-sĕn′dĭng) *adj.* Marked by an air of superiority; patronizing: *gave a condescending nod.* —**con′de·scend′ing·ly** *adv.*

con·de·scen·sion (kŏn′dĭ-sĕn′shən) *n.* **1.** The act of condescending. **2.** Patronizing behavior or manner.

con·dign (kən-dīn′) *adj.* Deserved; merited, as punishment or censure. [Middle English *condigne,* from Old French, from Latin *condignus,* wholly worthy : *com-* (intensive) + *dignus,* worthy.] —**con·dign′ly** *adv.*

con·di·ment (kŏn′də-mənt) *n.* A seasoning for food, such as mustard or various spices. [Middle English, from Old French, from Latin *condīmentum,* from *condīre,* to season, preserve.]

con·di·tion (kən-dĭsh′ən) *n.* **1.** The particular state of being of a person or thing: *restore an old house to its original condition; the improving condition of the economy.* **2. a.** A state of health: *stay in good condition.* **b.** A state of readi-

ness or physical fitness: *getting in condition for the tournament.* **3.** *Informal.* A disease or ailment: *a heart condition.* **4.** Rank or social position; status: *a person of high condition.* **5.** Something indispensable to the appearance or occurrence of something else; a prerequisite: *Compatibility is a condition of a successful partnership.* **6.** Something that restricts or modifies something else; a qualification: *I'll agree if you meet my condition.* **7.** Often **conditions.** The existing circumstances: *poor driving conditions.* **8.** *Gram.* The dependent clause of a conditional sentence. **9.** *Law.* A provision making the effect of a legal instrument contingent upon the occurrence of some uncertain future event. **10.** An unsatisfactory grade given a student that may be raised by doing further work. —*tr.v.* **1.** To put into good or proper condition; make fit: *condition the body.* **2.** To make conditional: *He conditioned the parole on the prisoner's promise to get a job.* **3.** To accustom (a person) to; adapt: *Our ears have been conditioned to melody, harmony, and rhythm in music.* **4.** *Psychol.* To cause to respond in a specific manner to a specific stimulus. **5.** To give the grade of condition to (a student). —*idiom.* **on (the) condition that.** If; provided. [Middle English *condicioun,* from Old French *condicion,* from Latin *conditiō,* agreement, prob. from *condīcere,* to talk together, agree : *com-,* together + *dīcere,* to talk.]

con·di·tion·al (kən-dĭsh′ə-nəl) *adj.* **1.** Imposing, depending on, or containing a condition or conditions; tentative: *conditional approval.* **2.** *Gram.* Stating or implying a condition; for example, in the sentence *We'll go swimming if it's sunny tomorrow, if it's sunny tomorrow* is a conditional clause. —*n.* *Gram.* A mood, tense, clause, or word expressing a condition. —**con·di′tion·al·ly** *adv.*

con·di·tioned (kən-dĭsh′ənd) *adj.* **1.** Subject to or dependent upon conditions or stipulations. **2. a.** Physically fit; in good physical condition. **b.** Prepared for a specific action or process. **3.** *Psychol.* Exhibiting or trained to exhibit a conditioned response.

conditioned response. A new or changed response that an organism produces as a result of a particular stimulus after it has been given training of a certain type.

con·di·tion·er (kən-dĭsh′ə-nər) *n.* A device or substance used to improve something in some way: *an air conditioner; a bottle of hair conditioner.*

con·dole (kən-dōl′) *intr.v.* **-doled, -dol·ing.** To express sympathy with one in pain, grief, or misfortune. [Late Latin *condolēre* : Latin *com-,* together + *dolēre,* to feel pain, grieve.] —**con·dol′er** *n.*

con·do·lence (kən-dō′ləns) *n.* Sympathy or an expression of sympathy for a person who has experienced sorrow or misfortune.

con·do·min·i·um (kŏn′də-mĭn′ē-əm) *n., pl.* **-ums. 1. a.** Joint sovereignty, esp. joint rule of a territory by two or more states. **b.** The territory so governed. **2. a.** An apartment building in which the apartments are owned individually. **b.** An apartment in such a building. [From COM- (together) + *dominium,* ownership of property, from Latin, property.]

con·done (kən-dōn′) *tr.v.* **-doned, -don·ing.** To forgive, overlook, or disregard (an offense) without protest or censure. [Latin *condōnāre,* to give up, forgive : *com-* (intensive) + *dōnum,* gift.] —**con·don′er** *n.*

con·dor (kŏn′dôr, -dər) *n.* Either of two very large New World vultures, *Vultur gryphus* of the Andes or *Gymnogyps californianus* of the mountains of California. [Spanish *cóndor,* from Quechua *kúntur.*]

condor
California condor

con·duce (kən-dōōs', -dyōōs') *intr.v.* **-duced, -duc·ing.** To contribute or lead: *A negative attitude conduces to failure.* [Middle English *conducen,* from Latin *condūcere,* to lead together : *com-,* together + *dūcere,* to lead.]

con·du·cive (kən-dōō'sĭv, -dyōō-) *adj.* Tending to cause or bring about: *poor working conditions not conducive to productivity.* **—con·du'cive·ness** *n.*

con·duct (kən-dŭkt') *tr.v.* **1.** To direct the course of; control: *conduct an experiment; conduct a business.* **2.** To lead or guide: *conduct a tour.* **3.** To lead an orchestra or other musical group. **4.** To serve as a medium or channel for conveying; transmit: *Most metals conduct heat.* **5.** To behave: *She conducted herself well during the service.* **—n.** (kŏn'dŭkt'). **1.** The way a person acts; behavior. **2.** The act of directing or controlling; management. **3.** The act of leading or guiding. [Middle English *conducten,* from Medieval Latin *condūcere,* to escort, from Latin, to lead together.] **—con·duct'i·bil'i·ty** *n.* **—con·duct'i·ble** *adj.*

con·duc·tance (kən-dŭk'təns) *n.* The measure of a material's ability to conduct electric charge, expressed in mhos.

con·duc·tion (kən-dŭk'shən) *n.* The transmission or conveying of something through a medium or passage, esp. of electric charge or heat through a conducting medium.

con·duc·tive (kən-dŭk'tĭv) *adj.* Having conductivity.

con·duc·tiv·i·ty (kŏn'dŭk-tĭv'ĭ-tē) *n.* **1.** The ability or power to conduct or transmit. **2.** A measure of the ability of a material to conduct an electric charge.

con·duc·tor (kən-dŭk'tər) *n.* **1.** A person who conducts or leads. **2.** The person in charge of a railroad train, bus, or streetcar. **3.** The director of a musical ensemble. **4.** *Physics.* A substance or medium that conducts heat, light, sound, or, esp., an electric charge.

con·duit (kŏn'dĭt, -dōō-ĭt) *n.* **1.** A channel or pipe for conveying water or other fluids. **2.** A tube or duct for enclosing electric wires or cable. [Middle English, from Old French, conveyance, from Latin *conductus,* past part. of *condūcere,* to lead together.]

cone (kōn) *n.* **1.** *Geom.* **a.** A surface formed by all the rays that begin at a given point and pass through a curve not in the same plane as the point or by all the line segments connecting such a point and such a curve. **b.** Any surface of this kind in which the given curve is a circle, esp. one in which the line connecting the given point and the center of the circle is perpendicular to the plane of the circle; a right circular cone. **2. a.** Any figure having such a surface as its outer boundary; a solid cone. **b.** Anything having the shape of such a figure: *an ice-cream cone.* **3.** A rounded or long cluster of woody scales containing the seeds of a pine, fir, hemlock, or related tree. **4.** Any of the structures in the retina of the eye that are sensitive to light and that perceive differences between colors. **5.** Any of various gastropod mollusks of the family Conidae, of tropical seas, with a conical, often vividly marked shell. [French *cône,* from Latin *cōnus,* from Greek *kōnos.*]

Con·es·to·ga wagon (kŏn'ĭ-stō'gə). A heavy covered wagon with broad wheels, used by American pioneers. [After *Conestoga,* Pennsylvania.]

co·ney (kō'nē, kŭn'ē) *n.* Var. of **cony.**

con·fab (kŏn'făb'). *Informal.* **—n.** A confabulation. **—intr.v.** (kən-făb', kŏn'făb') **-fabbed, -fab·bing.** To confabulate.

con·fab·u·late (kən-făb'yə-lāt') *intr.v.* **-lat·ed, -lat·ing.** To talk informally; to chat. **—con·fab'u·la'tion** *n.* **—con·fab'u·la'tor** *n.* **—con·fab'u·la·to·ry** (-lə-tôr'ē, -tōr'ē) *adj.*

con·fec·tion (kən-fĕk'shən) *n.* **1.** A sweet preparation, such as candy or preserves. **2.** A sweetened medicinal compound. **3.** A stylish article of women's clothing. [From Latin *conficere,* to prepare : *com-* (intensive) + *facere,* to make.]

con·fec·tion·er (kən-fĕk'shə-nər) *n.* A person who makes or sells candy, preserves, and other confections.

confectioners' sugar. A powdery sugar with some cornstarch added, used in making candy, icing, etc.

con·fec·tion·er·y (kən-fĕk'shə-nĕr'ē) *n., pl.* **-ies. 1.** Candies and other confections collectively. **2.** The art or occupation of a confectioner. **3.** A confectioner's shop.

con·fed·er·a·cy (kən-fĕd'ər-ə-sē) *n., pl.* **-cies.** A political union of several peoples, parties, or states: *a powerful confederacy of Creek Indians.*

con·fed·er·ate (kən-fĕd'ər-ĭt) *adj.* Belonging to a confederacy. **—n. 1.** An associate in an activity; an accomplice to a crime or plot. **2.** A member of a confederacy. **—See Syns at partner. —v.** (kən-fĕd'ə-rāt') **-at·ed, -at·ing. —tr.v.** To form into a confederacy. **—intr.v.** To become part of a confederacy. [Middle English *confederat,* from Latin *confoederātus,* from past part. of *confoederāre,* to unite in a league : *com-,* together + *foedus,* league.]

con·fed·er·a·tion (kən-fĕd'ə-rā'shən) *n.* A confederacy.

con·fer (kən-fûr') *v.* **-ferred, -fer·ring. —intr.v.** To hold a conference; consult together: *The President conferred with his advisers.* **—tr.v.** To bestow (an honor, degree, etc.): *The general conferred medals on the two marines.* [Latin *conferre,* to bring together : *com-,* together + *ferre,* to bring.] **—con·fer'ment** or **con·fer'ral** *n.* **—con·fer'rer** *n.*

con·fer·ence (kŏn'fər-əns, -frəns) *n.* **1.** A meeting to discuss a subject or a number of subjects: *a news conference; a peace conference; a summit conference.* **2.** A regional association of athletic teams. **3.** A meeting of committees to settle differences between two legislative bodies. **—modifier:** *a conference room.*

con·fer·ree (kŏn'fə-rē') *n.* Var. of **conferee.**

con·fess (kən-fĕs') *tr.v.* **1. a.** To make known (one's sins) to a priest or to God. **b.** To hear the confession of. **2.** To disclose or admit (a fault): *He confessed his mistake.* **3.** To admit conversationally: *I must confess that I was surprised.* **4.** To acknowledge belief or faith in. **—intr.v. 1.** To admit or acknowledge a crime or deed: *The suspect confessed to the robbery.* **2.** To tell one's sins to a priest. **—** See Syns at **acknowledge.** [Middle English *confessen,* from Old French *confesser,* from Late Latin *confessus,* past part. of *confitērī,* to acknowledge : *com-* (intensive) + *fatērī,* to confess.] **—con·fess'ed·ly** (-ĭd-lē) *adv.*

con·fes·sion (kən-fĕsh'ən) *n.* **1.** An act of confessing. **2.** A formal declaration of guilt. **3.** Something confessed. **4.** The disclosure of sins to a priest for absolution. **5.** An avowal of belief in the doctrines of a particular faith. **6.** A church or religious group that adheres to a particular creed.

con·fes·sion·al (kən-fĕsh'ə-nəl) *adj.* Of, pertaining to, or resembling confession. **—n.** A small booth in which a priest hears confessions.

con·fes·sor (kən-fĕs'ər) *n.* **1.** A priest who hears confessions. **2.** A person who confesses.

con·fet·ti (kən-fĕt'ē) *n.* (*used with a sing. verb*). Small pieces of colored paper scattered about on festive occasions. [Italian, pl. of *confetto,* confection, candy, from Latin *confectus,* past part. of *conficere,* to put together : *com-,* together + *facere,* to make.]

con·fi·dant (kŏn'fĭ-dănt', -dänt', kŏn'fĭ-dănt', -dänt') *n.* A person to whom one confides personal matters or secrets.

con·fi·dante (kŏn'fĭ-dănt', -dänt', kŏn'fĭ-dănt', -dänt') *n.* A female confidant.

con·fide (kən-fīd') *v.* **-fid·ed, -fid·ing. —tr.v. 1.** To tell (something) in confidence: *confide a secret to a friend.* **2.** To put into another's keeping. **—intr.v.** To tell or share one's secrets: *I know I can confide in you.* [Middle English *confiden,* from Old French *confider,* from Latin *confidere* : *com-* (intensive) + *fīdere,* to trust.] **—con·fid'er** *n.*

con·fi·dence (kŏn'fĭ-dəns) *n.* **1.** A feeling of assurance, esp. of self-assurance: *states his case with confidence. He lacks confidence in himself.* **2.** Trust or reliance: *I am placing my confidence in you.* **3.** A trusting relationship: *I have decided to take you into my confidence.* **4.** The assurance that someone will keep a secret: *I am telling you this in strict confidence.* **5.** Something confided; a secret.

Syns: 1. confidence, aplomb, assurance, security, self-confidence, self-possession *n. Core meaning:* A firm belief in one's own powers (*a person who had a lot of confidence in himself*). **2. confidence, faith, reliance, trust** *n. Core meaning:* Complete belief in the trustworthiness of another (*had confidence in the President*). See also Syns at **certainty.**

con·fi·dent (kŏn'fĭ-dənt) *adj.* **1.** Feeling or showing confidence; sure of oneself: *The team is confident of victory on Sunday. Mr. Jones approached the lectern with a confident air.*

con·fi·den·tial (kŏn'fĭ-dĕn'shəl) *adj.* **1.** Told in confidence; secret: *confidential information.* **2.** Entrusted with private matters: *a confidential secretary.* **3.** Showing confidence or intimacy: *a confidential tone of voice.* —**con·fi·den·ti·al·i·ty** (-shē-ăl′ĭ-tē) or **con′fi·den′tial·ness** *n.* —**con·fi·den′tial·ly** *adv.*

con·fid·ing (kən-fī′dĭng) *adj.* Having a tendency to confide; trusting. —**con·fid′ing·ly** *adv.*

con·fig·u·ra·tion (kən-fĭg′yə-rā′shən) *n.* **1.** The arrangement of the parts or elements of something. **2.** The figure formed by such an arrangement; outline; contour. [From Latin *configūrāre,* "to form together," fashion after : *com-,* together + *figūra,* shape, figure.] —**con·fig′u·ra′tive** (-rā′tĭv) or **con·fig′u·ra′tion·al** *adj.* —**con·fig′u·ra′tion·al·ly** *adv.*

con·fine (kən-fīn′) *tr.v.* **-fined, -fin·ing. 1.** To limit in area or extent: *Nineteenth-century New York was confined to Manhattan.* **2.** To restrict in movement: *He was confined to bed.* **3.** To imprison: *The Nazis confined many people in concentration camps.* **4.** To restrict (speech, activity, etc.): *Confine your answers to the questions asked.* [Old French *confiner,* from *confin,* boundary, limit, from Latin *confīnis,* having the same border : *com-,* together + *fīnis,* border, end.] —**con·fin′a·ble** or **con·fine′a·ble** *adj.* —**con·fin′er** *n.*

con·fine·ment (kən-fīn′mənt) *n.* **1.** The act of confining or a condition of being confined. **2.** Childbirth.

con·fines (kŏn′fīnz′) *pl.n.* The limits of a space or area; borders: *within the confines of one county.*

con·firm (kən-fûrm′) *tr.v.* **1.** To give moral strength to: *"confirm thy soul in self-control, thy liberty in law"* ("America the Beautiful"). **2.** To support or establish the validity of: *The news confirmed the rumors. Experiments confirmed the theory.* **3.** To give or get definite evidence: *We have confirmed that man can travel to the moon.* **4.** To make (an appointment or action) binding: *confirmed the governor in office; confirm your plane reservations.* **5.** To admit to full membership in a church. —See Syns at **prove.** [Middle English *confirmen,* from Old French *confirmer,* from Latin *confirmāre* : *com-* (intensive) + *firmus,* firm.] —**con·firm′a·ble** *adj.* —**con·fir′ma·to·ry** (kən-fûr′mə-tôr′ē, -tōr′ē) or **con·fir′ma·tive** (-mə-tĭv) *adj.* —**con·firm′er** *n.*

con·fir·ma·tion (kŏn′fər-mā′shən) *n.* **1.** The act of confirming: *senatorial confirmation of an ambassador.* **2.** Something that confirms; proof: *This was confirmation of his suspicions.* **3.** A Christian ceremony in which a young person is made a full member of a church. **4.** In Judaism, a ceremony marking the completion of a young person's religious training.

con·firmed (kən-fûrmd′) *adj.* **1.** Ratified; verified. **2.** Firmly settled in habit or condition; inveterate: *a confirmed bachelor.* **3.** Having received the rite of confirmation. —**con·firm′ed·ly** (-fûr′mĭd-lē) *adv.*

con·fis·cate (kŏn′fĭ-skāt′) *tr.v.* **-cat·ed, -cat·ing. 1.** To seize (private property) so that it may be withheld, redistributed, or destroyed: *confiscated and burned the illegal drugs.* **2.** To seize by or as if by authority: *The teacher confiscated the chewing gum.* [From Latin *confiscāre,* to lay up in a chest, confiscate : *com-* (collective) + *fiscus,* chest, treasury.] —**con′fis·ca′tion** *n.* —**con′fis·ca′tor** *n.*

con·fla·gra·tion (kŏn′flə-grā′shən) *n.* A large, destructive fire. [Latin *conflagrātiō,* from *conflagrāre,* to burn up : *com-* (intensive) + *flagrāre,* to burn.]

con·flict (kŏn′flĭkt′) *n.* **1.** Prolonged fighting; warfare: *Armed conflict could erupt at any time.* **2.** A clash of opposing ideas, interests, etc.: *a personality conflict.* **3.** *Psychol.* The opposition or simultaneous functioning of mutually exclusive impulses, desires, or tendencies. —*intr.v.* (kən-flĭkt′). To be in opposition; differ; clash: *State regulations may not conflict with federal laws.* [Middle English, from Latin *conflīctus,* from the past part. of *conflīgere,* to clash together, contend : *com-,* together + *flīgere,* to strike.] —**con·flic′tive** *adj.*

> **Syns: 1. conflict, belligerency, hostilities, strife, war, warfare** *n. Core meaning:* A state of open, prolonged fighting *(the conflict in Vietnam).* **2. conflict, clash, contention, difficulty, disaccord, discord, dissension, dissent, dissidence, friction, strife** *n. Core meaning:* A state of disagreement and disharmony *(family conflicts).*

con·flu·ence (kŏn′flōō-əns) *n.* Also **con·flux** (-flŭks′). **1. a.** A flowing together of two or more streams. **b.** The point where such streams come together. **2.** A crowd.

con·flu·ent (kŏn′flōō-ənt) *adj.* **1.** Flowing together: *confluent creeks.* **2.** *Pathol.* Merging together so as to form a mass. —*n.* One of two or more confluent streams. [Middle English, from Latin *confluere,* to flow together : *com-,* together + *fluere,* to flow.]

con·flux (kŏn′flŭks′) *n.* Var. of **confluence.**

con·form (kən-fôrm′) *intr.v.* **1.** To have the same form or character: *The pattern conforms with her measurements.* **2.** To act or be in accord or agreement; comply: *The plans must conform to the building code.* **3.** To act in accordance with current attitudes or practices: *conformed to the rules and customs of society.* —*tr.v.* To bring into agreement or correspondence; make similar. —See Syns at **agree.** [Middle English *conformen,* from Old French *conformer,* from Latin *conformāre,* "to have the same form" : *com-,* same + *forma,* form.] —**con·form′er** *n.*

con·form·a·ble (kən-fôr′mə-bəl) *adj.* **1.** Corresponding; similar: *conformable to your wishes.* **2.** Quick to comply; submissive. —**con·form′a·bil′i·ty** or **con·form′a·ble·ness** *n.* —**con·form′a·bly** *adv.*

con·for·mance (kən-fôr′məns) *n.* Var. of **conformity.**

con·for·ma·tion (kŏn′fər-mā′shən) *n.* **1.** The way something is formed; shape or structure. **2.** The act or condition of conforming.

con·form·ist (kən-fôr′mĭst) *n.* A person who conforms to current attitudes or practices. —**con·form′ism** *n.*

con·for·mi·ty (kən-fôr′mĭ-tē) *n., pl.* **-ties.** Also **con·for·mance** (-məns). **1.** Similarity in form or character; correspondence; agreement. **2.** Action or behavior in agreement with current customs, rules, principles, etc.

con·found (kən-found′, kŏn-) *tr.v.* **1.** To bewilder, puzzle, or perplex: *The pitcher confounded the batters with his knuckle ball.* **2.** To mix up; mistake (one thing) for another: *confound fiction and fact.* **3.** *Archaic.* To cause to be ashamed; abash. **4.** *Archaic.* To defeat; overthrow. — See Syns at **confuse.** —*interj.* A word used to express annoyance: *Confound it!* [Middle English *confounden,* from Old French *confondre,* from Latin *confundere,* to mix up : *com-,* together + *fundere,* to pour.] —**con·found′er** *n.*

con·found·ed (kən-foun′dĭd, kŏn-) *adj.* **1.** Bewildered; puzzled. **2.** Used as an intensive: *my confounded brother!* —**con·found′ed·ly** *adv.*

con·fra·ter·ni·ty (kŏn′frə-tûr′nĭ-tē) *n., pl.* **-ties.** An association of men united in some common purpose or profession. [Middle English *confraternite,* from Old French, from Medieval Latin *confrāter,* colleague, confrere.]

con·frere (kŏn′frâr′) *n.* A fellow member of a fraternity or profession; colleague. [Middle English, from Old French, from Medieval Latin *confrāter,* colleague, fellow member : Latin *com-,* together + *frāter,* brother.]

con·front (kən-frŭnt′) *tr.v.* **1.** To come face to face with: *allow the defendant to confront his accuser. The problems that confront us seem overwhelming.* **2.** To meet or face boldly or defiantly: *A couple of hoodlums confronted him on the street.* **3.** To bring face to face: *When confronted with all the evidence, the suspect confessed.* **4.** To bring close together for comparison or examination; compare: *confronted both sides of the issue before making the decision.* [Old French *confronter,* from Medieval Latin *confrontāre,* to have a common border : Latin *com-,* together + *frōns,* forehead, front.] —**con′fron·ta′tion** (kŏn′frən-tā′shən) *n.* —**con·front′er** *n.*

Con·fu·cian·ism (kən-fyōō′shə-nĭz′əm) *n.* The principles of conduct based on the teachings of the Chinese philosopher Confucius, which stress personal virtue, devotion to family and ancestors, and social harmony and justice. —**Con·fu′cian·ist** *n.*

con·fuse (kən-fyōōz′) *tr.v.* **-fused, -fus·ing. 1.** To mislead; mix up; throw off: *The purpose of camouflage is to confuse the enemy.* **2.** To fail to distinguish between; mistake for something else: *Don't confuse the words "principal" and "principle."* **3.** To make unclear; blur: *Such statements merely confuse the issue.* [Middle English *confusen,* from *confus,* confused, from Old French, from Latin *confūsus,* past part. of *confundere,* to pour together, mix : *com-,* together + *fundere,* to pour.] —**con·fus′ed·ly** (-fyōō′zĭd-lē) *adv.* —**con·fus′ing·ly** *adv.*

> **Syns: 1. confuse, addle, befuddle, bewilder, confound,**

| ă pat | ā pay | â care | ä father | ĕ pet | ē be | hw which | ĭ pit | ī tie | î pier | ŏ pot | ō toe | ô paw, for | oi noise |
| ōō took | ōō boot | ou out | th thin | th this | ŭ cut | | û urge | zh vision | ə about, item, edible, gallop, circus |

fuddle, mix up, perplex, throw *v. Core meaning:* To cause to be unclear in mind or intent (*camouflage that confused the enemy; was confused by the maze of freeways*). **2. confuse, ball up** (*Slang*), **disorder, jumble, muddle, scramble, snafu** (*Slang*), **snarl** *v. Core meaning:* To put into total disorder (*had hopelessly confused their finances*).

con·fu·sion (kən-fyōō′zhən) *n.* **1.** The act of confusing. **2.** The condition of being confused. **—con·fu′sion·al** *adj.*

con·fu·ta·tion (kŏn′fyŏō-tā′shən) *n.* **1.** An act of confuting. **2.** Something that confutes. **—con·fu′ta·tive** (kən-fyōō′-tə-tĭv) *adj.*

con·fute (kən-fyōōt′) *tr.v.* **-fut·ed, -fut·ing.** To prove to be wrong or false; refute. [Latin *confūtāre,* to suppress, restrain.] **—con·fut′a·ble** *adj.* **—con·fut′er** *n.*

con·gé (kŏn′zhā′, -jā′, kŏn-zhā′) *n.* Also **con·gee** (kŏn′jē). **1.** Formal or authoritative permission to depart. **2.** An abrupt dismissal. **3.** *Archaic.* A leave-taking. [French, from Old French *congie,* from Latin *commeātus,* "a going to and fro" : *com-,* back and forth + *meāre,* to go.]

con·geal (kən-jēl′) *intr.v.* **1.** To change from a liquid to a solid, as by freezing. **2.** To coagulate; jell. **—tr.v.** To cause to solidify or coagulate. [Middle English *congelen,* from Old French *congeler,* from Latin *congelāre,* to freeze solid : *com-,* together + *gelāre,* to freeze.] **—con·geal′a·ble** *adj.* **—con·geal′ment** *n.*

con·gee (kŏn′jē) *n.* Var. of **congé.**

con·ge·ner (kŏn′jə-nər) *n.* **1.** A member of the same kind, class, or group. **2.** A plant or animal belonging to the same genus as another or others. [Latin, of the same race : *com-,* same + *genus,* race, kind.] **—con′ge·ner′ic** (kŏn′-jə-nĕr′ĭk) or **con·gen′er·ous** (kən-jĕn′ər-əs, kŏn-) *adj.*

con·gen·ial (kən-jēn′yəl) *adj.* **1.** Having the same tastes, habits, etc.: *two congenial persons.* **2.** Of a pleasant disposition; friendly: *a congenial host.* **3.** Suited to one's nature; pleasant; agreeable: *congenial work; congenial surroundings.* **—See Syns at friendly. —con·ge′ni·al′i·ty** (-jē′nē-ăl′-ĭ-tē) or **con·gen′ial·ness** *n.* **—con·gen′ial·ly** *adv.*

con·gen·i·tal (kən-jĕn′ĭ-tl) *adj.* **1.** Existing at birth but not hereditary: *a congenital defect.* **2.** Having a specified character as if by nature: *a congenital thief.* [From Latin *congenitus,* born together with : *com-,* together + *gignere,* to beget.] **—con·gen′i·tal·ly** *adv.*

con·ger (kŏng′gər) *n.* Any of various large, scaleless saltwater eels of the family Congridae, esp. *Conger oceanicus,* of Atlantic waters. [Middle English *congre,* from Old French, from Latin *conger,* from Greek *gongros.*]

conger

con·ge·ries (kŏn′jə-rēz′, kən-jîr′ēz′) *n.* (*used with a sing. verb*). A collection of things heaped together; an aggregation; a heap. [Latin *congeriēs,* heap, pile, from *congerere,* to bring together, congest.]

con·gest (kən-jĕst′) *tr.v.* **1.** To overfill or overcrowd. **2.** *Path.* To cause excessive blood to accumulate in (a vessel or organ of the body). **—intr.v.** To become congested. [Latin *congerere,* to bring together, heap up : *com-,* together + *gerere,* to carry.]

con·ges·tion (kən-jĕs′chən) *n.* **1.** A condition of overcrowding. **2.** A condition in which too much blood collects in an organ or tissue of the body.

con·ges·tive (kən-jĕs′tĭv) *adj.* Of or involving congestion: *congestive heart failure.*

con·glom·er·ate (kən-glŏm′ə-rāt′) *v.* **-at·ed, -at·ing. —tr.v.** To collect into an adhering or rounded mass. **—intr.v.** To

form into an adhering or rounded mass. **—n.** (kən-glŏm′-ər-ĭt). **1.** A collected heterogeneous mass; a cluster. **2.** *Geol.* A rock consisting of pebbles and gravel embedded in a loosely cementing material. **3.** A business corporation made up of a number of different companies that operate in widely diversified fields. **—adj.** (kən-glŏm′ər-ĭt). **1.** Gathered into a mass; clustered. **2.** *Geol.* Made up of loosely cemented heterogeneous material. [From Latin *conglomerāre,* to roll together : *com-,* together + *glomus,* ball.]

con·glom·er·a·tion (kən-glŏm′ə-rā′shən) *n.* **1.** The process of conglomerating or condition of being conglomerated. **2.** A collection or accumulation of many different things.

con·grat·u·late (kən-grăch′ə-lāt′) *tr.v.* **-lat·ed, -lat·ing.** To express praise or acknowledgment for the achievement or good fortune of. [From Latin *congrātulārī,* to rejoice with someone : *com-,* with + *grātulārī,* to rejoice, from *grātus,* pleasing.] **—con·grat′u·la′tor** *n.*

con·grat·u·la·tion (kən-grăch′ə-lā′shən) *n.* **1.** The act of congratulating. **2. congratulations.** An expression of congratulation.

con·grat·u·la·to·ry (kən-grăch′ə-lə-tôr′ē, -tōr′ē) *adj.* Conveying or expressing congratulations: *a congratulatory handshake.*

con·gre·gate (kŏng′grĭ-gāt′) *v.* **-gat·ed, -gat·ing. —intr.v.** To come together in a crowd; assemble: *Salmon congregate here in huge numbers.* **—tr.v.** To bring together in a crowd; collect. **—adj.** (kŏng′grĭ-gĭt). Gathered; assembled. [Middle English *congregaten,* from Latin *congregāre,* to assemble : *com-,* together + *grex,* herd, flock.] **—con′gre·ga′tor** *n.*

con·gre·ga·tion (kŏng′grĭ-gā′shən) *n.* **1.** An act of congregating. **2.** A body of assembled people or things; gathering. **3. a.** A group of people gathered for religious worship. **b.** The members of a specific religious group who regularly worship at a common church. **4.** *Rom. Cath. Ch.* **a.** A religious institute in which only simple vows, not solemn vows, are taken. **b.** A division of the Curia.

con·gre·ga·tion·al (kŏng′grĭ-gā′shə-nəl) *adj.* **1.** Of or pertaining to a congregation. **2. Congregational.** Of or pertaining to Congregationalism or Congregationalists.

con·gre·ga·tion·al·ism (kŏng′grĭ-gā′shə-nə-lĭz′əm) *n.* **1.** A type of church government in which each local congregation is self-governing. **2. Congregationalism.** The system of government and religious beliefs of a Protestant denomination in which each member church is self-governing. **—con′gre·ga′tion·al·ist** *n.*

con·gress (kŏng′grĭs) *n.* **1.** A formal meeting of persons representing various nations, organizations, or professions to discuss problems. **2.** The legislative bodies of certain nations, esp. republics. **3. Congress.** In the United States, the Senate and House of Representatives, the two assemblies whose members are elected to make the laws of the nation. **4.** A coming together; a meeting. **5.** Sexual intercourse. [Middle English *congresse,* a coming together, from Latin *congressus,* past part. of *congredī,* to come together : *com-,* together + *gradī,* to go.]

con·gres·sion·al (kən-grĕsh′ə-nəl) *adj.* **1.** Of or pertaining to a congress. **2. Congressional.** Of or pertaining to the Congress of the United States.

con·gress·man or **Con·gress·man** (kŏng′grĭs-mən) *n.* A member of the U.S. Congress, esp. of the House of Representatives.

con·gress·wom·an or **Con·gress·wom·an** (kŏng′-grĭs-wŏom′ən) *n.* A female member of the U.S. Congress, esp. of the House of Representatives.

con·gru·ence (kŏng′grŏō-əns, kən-grōō′əns) *n.* Also **con·gru·en·cy** (kŏng′grōō-ən-sē, kən-grōō′ən-sē). **1.** The condition of being congruent. **2.** A mathematical statement that two quantities are congruent.

con·gru·ent (kŏng′grōō-ənt, kən-grōō′ənt) *adj.* **1.** Corresponding; congruous. **2.** *Geom.* Coinciding exactly when superimposed: *congruent triangles.* **3.** *Math.* Having a difference divisible by a modulus: *congruent numbers.* [Middle English, from Latin *congruere,* to meet together, agree.] **—con′gru·ent·ly** *adv.*

con·gru·i·ty (kən-grōō′ĭ-tē, kŏn-) *n., pl.* **-ties. 1.** Agreement; harmony. **2.** Exact coincidence when superimposed, as of geometric figures.

ă pat   ā pay   â care   ä father   ĕ pet   ē be   hw which   ĭ pit   ī tie   î pier   ŏ pot   ō toe   ô paw, for   oi noise
ōō took   ōō boot   ou out   th thin   th this   ŭ cut   û urge   zh vision   ə about, item, edible, gallop, circus

con·gru·ous (kŏng′grōō-əs) *adj.* **1.** Corresponding in character or kind; harmonious. **2.** *Geom.* Congruent. [Latin *congruus,* from *congruere,* to agree.]

con·ic (kŏn′ĭk) or **con·i·cal** (-ĭ-kəl) *adj.* **1.** Shaped like a cone. **2.** Pertaining to a cone. —*n. Math.* A **conic section.**

conic section. Any of a group of plane curves, including the circle, ellipse, hyperbola, and parabola, that can be formed by the intersection of a plane and a right circular conical surface.

con·i·fer (kŏn′ə-fər, kō′nə-) *n.* Any of various predominantly evergreen cone-bearing trees, such as a pine, spruce, or fir. [Latin *cōnifer,* cone-bearing.]

co·nif·er·ous (kō-nĭf′ər-əs, kə-) *adj.* **1.** Bearing cones: *coniferous trees such as pines and hemlocks.* **2.** Of or composed of conifers: *a coniferous forest.*

con·jec·tur·al (kən-jĕk′chər-əl) *adj.* **1.** Based on or involving conjecture. **2.** Inclined to conjecture.

con·jec·ture (kən-jĕk′chər) *n.* **1.** The formation of an opinion or conclusion from incomplete or insufficient evidence; guesswork: *The origin of language is a matter of pure conjecture.* **2.** A statement, opinion, or conclusion based on guesswork; a guess: *Make a conjecture about the outcome of the election.* —*v.* **-tured, -tur·ing.** —*tr.v.* To infer from inconclusive evidence; to guess. —*intr.v.* To make a conjecture. [Middle English, from Old French, from Latin *conjectūra,* conclusion, from *conjicere,* "to throw together," conjecture : *com-,* together + *jacere,* to throw.] —**con·jec′tur·er** *n.*

con·join (kən-join′) *tr.v.* To join together; connect; unite. —*intr.v.* To become joined or connected. —**con·join′er** *n.*

con·joint (kən-joint′) *adj.* **1.** Joined together; combined; associated. **2.** Of or pertaining to two or more joined or associated persons or things. —**con·joint′ly** *adv.*

con·ju·gal (kŏn′jōō-gəl, -jə-) *adj.* Of of pertaining to marriage or the marital relationship. [Old French, from Latin *conjugālis,* from *conjux,* a spouse, from *conjungere,* to join together : *com-,* together + *jungere,* to join.] —**con′ju·gal·ly** *adv.*

con·ju·gate (kŏn′jə-gāt′) *v.* **-gat·ed, -gat·ing.** —*tr.v. Gram.* To give the various inflected forms of (a verb). —*intr.v.* **1.** *Biol.* To undergo conjugation, as in the process of reproduction. **2.** *Gram.* To inflect a verb. —*adj.* (kŏn′jə-gĭt, -gāt′). **1.** Joined together, esp. in a pair or pairs; coupled. **2.** Pertaining to words having the same derivation and usu. a related meaning. —*n.* (kŏn′jə-gĭt, -gāt′). One of two or more conjugate words. [Middle English *conjugat,* joined, from Latin *conjugāre,* to yoke together : *com-,* together + *jugum,* yoke.] —**con′ju·ga·tive** *adj.* —**con′ju·ga·tor** *n.*

con·ju·ga·tion (kŏn′jə-gā′shən) *n.* **1.** *Gram.* **a.** The inflection of a particular verb. **b.** A presentation of the complete set of inflected forms of a verb. **2.** *Biol.* **a.** A type of sexual reproduction in which single-celled organisms of the same species join together and exchange nuclear material before undergoing fission. **b.** The union of sex cells. —**con′ju·ga′tion·al** *adj.* —**con′ju·ga′tion·al·ly** *adv.*

con·junct (kən-jŭngkt′, kŏn′jŭngkt′) *adj.* Joined together; united. [Middle English, from Latin *conjungere,* to join together : *com-,* together + *jungere,* to join.] —**con·junct′ly** *adv.*

con·junc·tion (kən-jŭngk′shən) *n.* **1.** Combination or association: *The local police acted in conjunction with the FBI.* **2.** The occurrence together of two events, conditions, etc. **3.** *Gram.* A word, such as *and, but, or,* etc., that connects other words, phrases, or clauses in a sentence. **4.** The relative position of two planets or other celestial bodies when they are located along the same meridian on the celestial sphere. —**con·junc′tion·al** *adj.* —**con·junc′tion·al·ly** *adv.*

con·junc·ti·va (kŏn′jŭngk-tī′və) *n., pl.* **-vas** or **-vae** (-vē′). The mucous membrane that lines the inside of the eyelid and covers the surface of the eyeball. [Middle English, from Medieval Latin *(membrāna) conjunctīva,* "the connective (membrane)," from Latin *conjungere,* to join together.] —**con·junc′ti·val** *adj.*

con·junc·tive (kən-jŭngk′tĭv) *adj.* **1.** Joining; associative; connective. **2.** Joined together; combined. **3.** *Gram.* **a.** Of or used as a conjunction. **b.** Serving to connect elements of meaning and construction in a sentence. —*n. Gram.* A connective word, esp. a conjunction. —**con·junc′tive·ly** *adv.*

con·junc·ti·vi·tis (kən-jŭngk′tə-vī′tĭs) *n.* Inflammation, often very contagious, of the conjunctiva.

con·junc·ture (kən-jŭngk′chər) *n.* **1.** A combination of circumstances or events. **2.** A critical set of circumstances; crisis.

con·jure (kŏn′jər, kən-jōōr′) *v.* **-jured, -jur·ing.** —*tr.v.* **1.** To call upon or entreat solemnly, esp. by an oath. **2.** To summon (a spirit) by oath or magic spell. **3.** To produce as if by magic: *conjure a miracle.* —*intr.v.* **1.** To practice magic; perform magic tricks. **2.** To summon a spirit by oath or magic spell. —*phrasal verb.* **conjure up.** To call to mind; evoke: *The mention of Africa conjures up images of jungles and wild animals.* [Middle English *conjuren,* from Old French *conjurer,* from Latin, to swear together, conspire : *com-,* together + *jūrāre,* to swear.]

con·jur·er or **con·ju·ror** (kŏn′jər-ər, kŭn′-) *n.* A magician, esp. one who claims to be able to summon spirits.

conk (kŏngk, kŏngk). *Slang.* —*tr.v.* To hit, esp. on the head. —*phrasal verb.* **conk out.** **1.** To fail suddenly: *The engine conked out.* **2.** To tire after exertion. [Prob. var. of CONCH.]

conn (kŏn) *v. & n.* Var. of **con** (to direct the steering of).

con·nate (kŏn′āt′) *adj.* **1.** Part of or existing in someone or something from birth; inborn; innate. **2.** Coexisting since or associated in birth or origin; congnate; related. **3.** *Biol.* Congenitally or firmly united, as parts or organs. [Late Latin *connātus,* past part. of *connascī,* to be born together : *com-,* together + *nascī,* to be born.] —**con′nate′ly** *adv.*

con·nect (kə-nĕkt′) *tr.v.* **1.** To join or fasten together; link; unite: *Capillaries connect the arteries and veins.* **2.** To associate or think of as related: *no reason to connect the two events.* **3.** To plug into an electrical circuit: *connect a television set.* **4.** To link by telephone: *I'll connect you with the switchboard.* —*intr.v.* **1.** To become joined or united: *Route 11 connects with Route 20 near Syracuse.* **2.** To meet so that passengers can easily transfer from one plane, train, or bus to another. **3.** *Informal.* To be successful. **4.** *Informal.* To make solid contact with a baseball: *The batter connected for a home run.* —See Syns at **attach** and **join.** [Middle English *connecten,* from Latin *connectere* : *com-,* together + *nectere,* to bind, tie.] —**con·nec′tor** or **con·nect′er** *n.*

con·nec·tion (kə-nĕk′shən) *n.* Also *Brit.* **con·nex·ion.** **1.** The act of connecting or condition of being connected. **2.** Something that connects or joins; a link: *There are excellent road and rail connections between the two cities.* **3.** A relationship: *the connection between the sun and the seasons.* **4.** An association in the mind: *I knew I had met him somewhere, but I couldn't make the connection.* **5.** Context: *In this connection I might mention the following incidents.* **6.** A distant relative. **7.** Often **connections.** An associate or acquaintance with whom one has a mutually beneficial relationship. **8.** A transfer from one plane, train, or bus to another: *I missed my connection in Chicago.* —*idiom.* **in connection with.** With reference to: *He is here in connection with his work.*

con·nec·tive (kə-nĕk′tĭv) *adj.* Connecting or serving or tending to connect. —*n.* **1.** Anything that connects. **2.** *Gram.* A word, such as a conjunction, that connects words, phrases, clauses, and sentences. —**con·nec′tive·ly** *adv.* —**con′nec·tiv′i·ty** *n.*

connective tissue. Any of the various tissues that form the framework and support of the animal body, including such tissues as bone, cartilage, mucous membrane, and fat.

con·nex·ion (kə-nĕk′shən) *n. Brit.* Var. of **connection.**

con·ning tower. (kŏn′ĭng). **1.** A raised, enclosed structure on the deck of a submarine, used for observation and as an entrance. **2.** The armored pilothouse of a warship.

con·nip·tion (kə-nĭp′shən) *n. Informal.* A fit of anger or other violent emotion; tantrum. [Orig. unknown.]

con·nive (kə-nīv′) *intr.v.* **-nived, -niv·ing.** **1.** To pretend not to notice something that should be reported or condemned: *The chief connived at wrongdoing in the police department.* **2.** To cooperate secretly or underhandedly: *The detective was accused of conniving with racketeers.* [French *conniver,* from Latin *connīvēre,* to close the eyes, be indulgent.] —**con·niv′ance** *n.* —**con·niv′er** *n.*

con·nois·seur (kŏn′ə-sûr′) *n.* A person with a thorough knowledge of or appreciation for a certain subject in which good taste is needed for appraisal; an expert: *a connoisseur of art.* [From Old French *connoisseor,* from *connoistre,* to know, from Latin *cognōscere,* to get acquainted with : *co-,* together + *gnōscere,* to know.] —**con′nois·seur′ship′** *n.*

con·no·ta·tion (kŏn′ə-tā′shən) *n.* A secondary meaning suggested by a word in addition to its literal meaning.

con·no·ta·tive (kŏn′ə-tā′tĭv, kə-nō′tə-tĭv) *adj.* Having a connotation. —**con′no·ta′tive·ly** *adv.*

con·note (kə-nōt′) *tr.v.* **-not·ed, -not·ing.** **1.** To suggest or imply in addition to literal meaning: *The word "orient" often connotes mystery.* **2.** To involve as a condition or consequence: *poverty connotes misery.* [Medieval Latin *connotāre,* "to mark in addition" : Latin *com-,* together with + *nota,* a mark, note.]

con·nu·bi·al (kə-nōō′bē-əl, -nyōō′-) *adj.* Of or pertaining to marriage or the relationship between husband and wife; conjugal. [Latin *connūbiālis,* from *connūbium,* marriage : *com-,* together + *nūbere,* to marry.] —**con·nu′bi·al·ly** *adv.*

con·quer (kŏng′kər) *tr.v.* **1.** To win mastery over by war: *In 1066 the Norman French conquered England.* **2.** To gain control over (a hostile environment, challenge, etc.): *Scientists have always battled to conquer disease.* **3.** To gain great recognition from (a group): *went to Paris to conquer the operatic world.* —*intr.v.* To be victorious; win: *Then conquer we must, for our cause is just.* —See Syns at **defeat.** [Middle English *conqueren,* from Old French *conquerre,* from Latin *conquīrere,* to search for, win : *com-* (intensive) + *quaerere,* to seek.] —**con′quer·a·ble** *adj.* —**con′quer·or** *n.*

con·quest (kŏn′kwĕst′, kŏng′-) *n.* **1.** The act or process of conquering. **2.** Something conquered. **3.** Someone whose favor is won. **4. the Conquest.** The Norman Conquest of England. —See Syns at **victory.**

con·quis·ta·dor (kŏn-kwĭs′tə-dôr′, kŏng-kēs′-) *n., pl.* **-dors** or **-do·res** (-dôr′ās, -ēz). One of the Spanish conquerors of Mexico and Peru in the 16th cent. [Spanish, from *conquistar,* to conquer.]

con·san·guin·e·ous (kŏn′săng-gwĭn′ē-əs) *adj.* Also **con·san·guine** (kŏn-săng′gwĭn, kən-). Of the same descent; related by blood. [Latin *consanguineus* : *com-,* joint + *sanguis,* blood.] —**con′san·guin′e·ous·ly** *adv.*

con·san·guin·i·ty (kŏn′săng-gwĭn′ĭ-tē) *n.* Relationship by descent from the same ancestor.

con·science (kŏn′shəns) *n.* **1.** The faculty of recognizing the distinction between right and wrong in regard to one's own conduct. **2.** Conformity to one's own sense of right conduct. —**idioms. in (all) conscience.** In all fairness. **on (one's) conscience.** Causing one to feel guilty. [Middle English, from Old French, from Latin *conscientia,* from *conscīre,* to know well : *com-* (intensive) + *scīre,* to know.]

con·sci·en·tious (kŏn′shē-ĕn′shəs) *adj.* **1.** Governed by or done according to conscience; scrupulous. **2.** Thorough and painstaking; careful; meticulous: *a conscientious worker; a conscientious job.* —**con′sci·en′tious·ly** *adv.* —**con′sci·en′tious·ness** *n.*

conscientious objector. A person who refuses to serve in the armed forces on the basis of moral or religious beliefs.

con·scious (kŏn′shəs) *adj.* **1.** Using one's mental powers; capable of thought, will, or perception: *Man is a conscious being.* **2.** Able to perceive and understand what is happening: *He is badly injured but still conscious.* **3.** Having or showing self-consciousness; aware: *He is conscious of his shortcomings.* **4.** Done with awareness; intentional; deliberate: *a conscious insult; make a conscious effort to speak more distinctly.* [Latin *conscius,* knowing with others, aware of : *com-,* with + *scīre,* to know.] —**con′scious·ly** *adv.*

con·scious·ness (kŏn′shəs-nĭs) *n.* **1.** The condition of being conscious: *regain consciousness.* **2.** Awareness: *The Puritans had a mighty consciousness of sin.* **3.** All the ideas, opinions, feelings, etc., held or thought to be held by a person or group: *Lengthy wars were not a part of the American consciousness.* **4.** A critical awareness of one's own identity and situation.

con·script (kən-skrĭpt′) *tr.v.* To enroll compulsorily for service in the armed forces; to draft. —*n.* (kŏn′skrĭpt′). A person who is drafted into the armed forces. —*adj.* (kŏn′-

skrĭpt′). Conscripted; drafted. [Old French, enlisted, from Latin *conscriptus,* past part. of *conscrībere,* to write together, enroll : *com-,* together + *scrībere,* to write.] —**con′scrip′tion** *n.*

con·se·crate (kŏn′sĭ-krāt′) *tr.v.* **-crat·ed, -crat·ing.** **1.** To declare or set apart as sacred: *consecrate a church.* **2.** *Theol.* To change the substance of (the elements of the Eucharist) into the true presence of Christ. **3.** To dedicate to some worthy service or goal: *consecrated his life to improving the lot of the poor.* **4.** To make venerable: *a tradition consecrated by time.* —See Syns at **devote.** [Middle English *consecraten,* from Latin *consecrāre* : *com-* (intensive) + *sacer,* sacred.] —**con′se·cra′tion** *n.* —**con′se·cra′tor** *n.*

con·sec·u·tive (kən-sĕk′yə-tĭv) *adj.* Following in order without break or interruption; successive: *It rained for five consecutive days.* [French *consécutif,* from Medieval Latin *consecutīvus,* from Latin *consequī,* to follow up : *com-,* together + *sequī,* to follow.] —**con·sec′u·tive·ly** *adv.* —**con·sec′u·tive·ness** *n.*

con·sen·sus (kən-sĕn′səs) *n.* Collective opinion or concord; general agreement: *The consensus among the voters is that the new program is a good one.* [Latin, from *consentīre,* to agree, consent.]

Usage: **consensus.** The stock phrase *consensus of opinion* is widely used, but careful writers say simply *consensus* to avoid redundancy.

con·sent (kən-sĕnt′) *intr.v.* To give assent or permission; agree: *She gave him no peace until he consented.* —*n.* Agreement and acceptance: *"Governments . . . deriving their just powers from the consent of the governed"* (Declaration of Independence). [Middle English *consenten,* from Old French *consentir,* from Latin *consentīre,* to agree : *com-,* together + *sentīre,* to feel.]

con·se·quence (kŏn′sĭ-kwĕns′, -kwəns) *n.* **1.** Something that follows from an action or condition; an effect; a result: *Have you considered the consequences of your decision?* **2.** A logical result or inference. **3.** Significance; importance: *an issue of no consequence.*

con·se·quent (kŏn′sĭ-kwĕnt′, -kwənt) *adj.* **1.** Following as an effect, result, or conclusion. **2.** Following as a logical conclusion. **3.** Logically correct or consistent. —See Usage note at **consequential.** —*n.* **1.** *Logic.* The conclusion, as of a syllogism. **2.** The second term of a ratio. [Middle English, from Old French, from Latin *consequī,* to follow up : *com-,* together + *sequī,* to follow.]

con·se·quen·tial (kŏn′sĭ-kwĕn′shəl) *adj.* **1.** Following as an effect, result, or conclusion; resultant; consequent. **2.** Having consequence; significant. **3.** Conceited; pompous. —See Syns at **important.** —**con′se·quen′ti·al′i·ty** (-shē-ăl′ĭ-tē) or **con′se·quen′tial·ness** *n.* —**con′se·quen′tial·ly** *adv.*

Usage: **consequential, consequent.** These two adjectives both mean resultant: *poverty in the cities and the consequent* (or *consequential*) *increase in crime.* In addition, both adjectives once meant important or self-important, but in modern English this meaning is now confined to *consequential: consequential foreign-policy decisions; considered himself a consequential person deserving of more respect.*

con·se·quent·ly (kŏn′sĭ-kwĕnt′lē, -kwənt-) *adv.* As a result; therefore.

con·ser·van·cy (kən-sûr′vən-sē) *n., pl.* **-cies.** **1.** Conservation, esp. of natural resources. **2.** *Brit.* A commission supervising fisheries, navigation, forests, etc.

con·ser·va·tion (kŏn′sər-vā′shən) *n.* **1.** The act or process of conserving; a saving. **2.** The controlled use and systematic protection of natural resources. —**con′ser·va′tion·al** *adj.*

con·ser·va·tion·ist (kŏn′sər-vā′shə-nĭst) *n.* **1.** A trained conservation worker. **2.** An active supporter of conservation.

conservation of energy. A principle of physics that the total energy of a self-contained system remains constant regardless of what changes occur inside the system.

conservation of mass. A principle of physics that the mass of a self-contained system remains constant regardless of the interaction of its parts.

conservation of mass-en·er·gy (măs′ĕn′ər-jē). A principle of physics that mass can be converted to energy and vice versa and that with this fact taken into account the total amount of mass and energy in a self-contained system remains constant regardless of changes in the system. The relation between mass and energy is given by Einstein's equation $E = mc^2$, where E is energy, m mass, and c the speed of light.

con·serv·a·tism (kən-sûr′və-tĭz′əm) *n.* **1.** The tendency in politics to maintain the existing order and to resist or oppose change. **2.** The principles and practices of persons or groups that have such a tendency.

con·serv·a·tive (kən-sûr′və-tĭv) *adj.* **1.** Tending to oppose change; favoring traditional values. **2.** Traditional in manner or style; not showy: *a conservative dark suit.* **3.** Moderate; cautious; restrained: *a conservative estimate.* **4.** Belonging to a conservative party or political group. **5. Conservative.** Belonging to that branch of Judaism standing midway between Orthodox and Reform in its willingness to accept changes in traditional ritual and custom. —*n.* **1.** Someone who is conservative. **2.** Often **Conservative.** A member or supporter of a conservative party. —**con·serv′a·tive·ly** *adv.* —**con·serv′a·tive·ness** *n.*

con·ser·va·tor (kən-sûr′və-tər, kŏn′sər-vā′tər) *n.* **1.** A protector. **2.** *Law.* One responsible for the person or property of an incompetent.

con·serv·a·to·ry (kən-sûr′və-tôr′ē, -tōr′ē) *n., pl.* **-ries. 1.** A glass-enclosed room or greenhouse in which plants are grown. **2.** A school of music or drama.

conservatory

con·serve (kən-sûrv′) *tr.v.* **-served, -serv·ing. 1.** To use (a supply) carefully; protect from loss or depletion; preserve: *conserve energy.* **2.** To take systematic measures to keep (a resource) in good condition: *conserve our forests.* **3.** To preserve (fruits) by cooking with sugar. —*n.* (kŏn′sûrv′). Often **conserves.** A jam made of fruits stewed in sugar. [Middle English *conserven,* from Old French *conserver,* from Latin *conservāre* : *com-* (intensive) + *servāre,* to keep, preserve.] —**con·serv′er** *n.*

con·sid·er (kən-sĭd′ər) *tr.v.* **1.** To deliberate upon; examine; study: *The committee met to consider the question of lowering taxes.* **2.** To think over; reflect on; contemplate: *consider an offer.* **3.** To regard as; deem to be: *Greenland is considered part of North America.* **4.** To take into account; bear in mind: *He plays well if you consider the fact that he is a beginner.* **5.** To be thoughtful of; show consideration for: *consider the feelings of other people.* —*intr.v.* To think carefully; reflect: *Give me time to consider.* —See Syns at **believe.** [Middle English *consideren,* from Old French *considerer,* from Latin *considerāre,* to observe (the stars), from *sidus,* star.]

con·sid·er·a·ble (kən-sĭd′ər-ə-bəl) *adj.* **1.** Fairly large or great in amount, extent, or degree; respectable: *considerable income.* **2.** Worthy of consideration; important; significant: *a considerable issue.* —*n. Informal.* A considerable amount, extent, or degree. —**con·sid′er·a·bly** *adv.*

con·sid·er·ate (kən-sĭd′ər-ĭt) *adj.* **1.** Having regard for the needs or feelings of others; thoughtful. **2.** Characterized by careful thought; deliberate. —**con·sid′er·ate·ly** *adv.* —**con·sid′er·ate·ness** *n.*

con·sid·er·a·tion (kən-sĭd′ə-rā′shən) *n.* **1.** Careful thought; deliberation: *We shall give your proposal every consideration.* **2.** A factor to be considered in making a decision: *The health of the community is the most important consideration.* **3.** A thoughtful opinion. **4.** Thoughtful concern

for others: *He shows no consideration for people's feelings.* **5.** A payment for a service rendered: *He agreed to do it for a small consideration.* **6.** High regard. —**idioms. in consideration of. 1.** In view of; on account of. **2.** In return for. **take into consideration.** To take into account; allow for.

con·sid·ered (kən-sĭd′ərd) *adj.* **1.** Reached after careful thought: *This is my considered opinion.* **2.** Respected; esteemed.

con·sid·er·ing (kən-sĭd′ər-ĭng) *prep.* In view of: *Considering the mistakes that were made, it was a wonder that the job got done at all.* —*conj.* Inasmuch as; because: *Considering there's more than enough to eat, he's welcome to join us for supper.*

con·sign (kən-sīn′) *tr.v.* **1.** To give over to the care of another; entrust: *consign an orphan to a guardian.* **2.** To deliver (merchandise) for sale. **3.** To assign to a lower or less important position; relegate: *The pitcher was consigned to the bullpen.* [Middle English *consignen,* to certify by a seal, from Old French *consigner,* from Latin *consignāre* : *com-* (intensive) + *signum,* seal, mark.] —**con·sign′a·ble** *adj.* —**con·sign′or** or **con·sign′er** *n.*

con·sign·ee (kŏn′sī-nē′, kən-sī′nē′) *n.* A person, such as an agent, to whom merchandise is consigned.

con·sign·ment (kən-sīn′mənt) *n.* **1.** The delivery of something for sale or safekeeping. **2.** Something that is consigned, as for sale: *receive a consignment of umbrellas.* —**idiom. on consignment.** Sent to a retailer who is expected to pay following sale.

con·sist (kən-sĭst′) *intr.v.* **1.** To be made up or composed: *New York City consists of five boroughs.* **2.** To have a basis; be inherent; to lie; to rest: *The beauty of his style consists in its simplicity.* [Old French *consister,* from Latin *consistere,* to stand still : *com-* (intensive) + *sistere,* to cause to stand.]

con·sis·ten·cy (kən-sĭs′tən-sē) *n., pl.* **-cies.** Also **con·sis·tence** (-təns). **1.** Agreement or compatibility among things or parts: *His statements lack consistency.* **2.** The condition of holding together; firmness. **3.** Degree of firmness, stiffness, or thickness: *mix water and clay to the consistency of thick cream.*

con·sis·tent (kən-sĭs′tənt) *adj.* **1.** In agreement; not contradictory. **2.** Marked by consistency; uniform: *follow a consistent policy.* —**con·sis′tent·ly** *adv.*

con·sis·to·ry (kən-sĭs′tə-rē) *n., pl.* **-ries. 1.** *Rom. Cath. Ch.* A session of cardinals presided over by the pope for the solemn promulgation of papal acts, as the canonization of a saint. **2.** The governing assembly of certain Protestant churches. **3.** In the Anglican Church, a diocesan court presided over by the bishop's chancellor or commissary. **4.** The meeting place or meeting of a consistory. [Middle English *consistorie,* from Old French, from Medieval Latin *consistōrium,* from Late Latin, place of assembly, from Latin *consistere,* to take one's place.]

con·so·la·tion (kŏn′sə-lā′shən) *n.* **1.** Comfort during a time of disappointment or sorrow. **2.** Something that consoles: *His presence is my one consolation.* —**con·so′la·to·ry** (kən-sō′lə-tôr′ē, -tōr′ē, -sŏl′ə-) *adj.*

consolation prize. A prize given to someone who participates in but does not win a contest.

con·sole[1] (kən-sōl′) *tr.v.* **-soled, -sol·ing.** To comfort in time of disappointment or sorrow; to solace. [French *consoler,* from Old French, from Latin *consolārī* : *com-* (intensive) + *sōlārī,* to comfort.] —**con·sol′a·ble** *adj.* —**con·sol′er** *n.* —**con·sol′ing·ly** *adv.*

con·sole[2] (kŏn′sōl′) *n.* **1.** A cabinet for a radio or television set, designed to stand on the floor. **2.** The part of an organ facing the player, containing the keyboard, stops, and pedals. **3.** A panel housing the controls for electrical or mechanical equipment. **4.** A decorative bracket for supporting a cornice, shelf, or other object. **5.** A **console table.** [French, short for *consolateur,* a carved human figure used to support cornices, from Latin *consōlātor,* one that consoles.]

console table. 1. A table supported by decorative consoles fixed to a wall. **2.** A small table designed to be set against a wall. Also called **console.**

con·sol·i·date (kən-sŏl′ĭ-dāt′) *v.* **-dat·ed, -dat·ing.** —*tr.v.* **1.** To make firm or coherent; form into a compact mass;

solidify. **2.** To make secure and strong; strengthen: *consolidated his political base.* **3.** To unite into one system or body; combine; merge: *consolidated four small companies into one large one.* —*intr.v.* To become solidified or united: *His power consolidated during the struggle.* [From Latin *consolidāre* : *com-* (intensive) + *solidus,* solid.] —**con·sol'i·da'tion** *n.* —**con·sol'i·da'tor** *n.*

con·som·mé (kŏn'sə-mā') *n.* A clear soup made of meat or vegetable broth. [French, "concentrate," from Old French *consommer,* to sum up, from Latin *consummāre* : *com-* (intensive) + *summa,* sum.]

con·so·nance (kŏn'sə-nəns) *n.* **1.** Agreement; harmony; accord. **2.** *Pros.* A repetition of the final consonant sounds of words, as *rain* and *tone.* **3.** *Mus.* A simultaneous combination of sounds conventionally regarded as pleasing and final in effect.

con·so·nant (kŏn'sə-nənt) *n.* **1.** A speech sound made by a partial or complete obstruction of the flow of air as it escapes through the mouth. **2.** A letter of the alphabet representing such a sound, as *b, m, s,* or *t.* —*adj.* **1.** *Mus.* **a.** Of or having consonance or consonances. **b.** Consisting chiefly of consonances. **2.** In agreement; in keeping: *remarks consonant with his beliefs.* [Middle English, from Old French, from Latin (*littera*) *consonāns,* "(letter) sounded with (a vowel)," from *consonāre,* to sound at the same time : *com-,* together + *sonāre,* to sound.] —**con'so·nant·ly** *adv.*

con·so·nan·tal (kŏn'sə-năn'tl) *adj.* Of, relating to, or containing a consonant. —**con'so·nan'tal·ly** *adv.*

con·sort (kŏn'sôrt') *n.* **1.** A husband or wife, esp. of a monarch. **2.** A companion or partner. **3.** A ship accompanying another in travel. —*intr.v.* (kən-sôrt'). **1.** To keep company; to associate: *consort with gangsters.* **2.** To be in accord or agreement. [Middle English, from Old French, from Latin *consors,* "one who shares the same fate," companion : *com-,* together + *sors,* fate.]

con·sor·ti·um (kən-sôr'tē-əm, -shē-) *n., pl.* **-ti·a** (-tē-ə, -shē-ə). **1.** An association, as of banks or capitalists, for effecting a venture requiring extensive financial resources, esp. in international finance. **2.** An association or partnership. [Latin, fellowship, from *consors,* partner, consort.]

con·spec·tus (kən-spĕk'təs) *n.* **1.** A general survey of a subject. **2.** A synopsis. [Latin, "view," from the past part. of *conspicere,* to look at.]

con·spic·u·ous (kən-spĭk'yōō-əs) *adj.* **1.** Easy to notice; obvious: *a conspicuous error.* **2.** Attracting attention by being unusual or remarkable: *a conspicuous flower.* [Latin *conspicuus,* from *conspicere,* to observe : *com-* (intensive) + *specere,* to look.] —**con·spic'u·ous·ly** *adv.* —**con·spic'u·ous·ness** *n.*

con·spir·a·cy (kən-spîr'ə-sē) *n., pl.* **-cies.** **1.** An agreement to perform together an illegal or evil act. **2.** A combining or acting together, as if by evil design: *a conspiracy of natural forces.* **3.** *Law.* An agreement between two or more persons to commit a crime or to accomplish a legal purpose through illegal action. —See Syns at **plot.** [Middle English *conspiracie,* from Norman French, from Latin *conspīrātiō,* from *conspīrāre,* to conspire.]

con·spir·a·tor (kən-spîr'ə-tər) *n.* A person who takes part in a conspiracy; plotter.

con·spir·a·to·ri·al (kən-spîr'ə-tôr'ē-əl, -tōr'-) *adj.* Of or characteristic of conspirators or a conspiracy. —**con·spir'a·to'ri·al·ly** *adv.*

con·spire (kən-spīr') *intr.v.* **-spired, -spir·ing.** **1.** To plan together secretly to commit an illegal or evil act: *conspire to kidnap a public official.* **2.** To work or act together; combine: *Many factors conspired against his election.* [Middle English *conspiren,* from Old French *conspirer,* from Latin *conspīrāre,* "to breathe together," plot : *com-,* together + *spīrāre,* to breathe, blow.]

con·sta·ble (kŏn'stə-bəl, kŭn'-) *n.* **1.** A public officer in a town or village with less authority and smaller jurisdiction than a sheriff. **2.** In medieval monarchies, an officer of high rank, usu. serving as military commander in the ruler's absence. **3.** The governor of a royal castle. **4.** *Brit.* A policeman. [Middle English, from Old French, from Late Latin *comes stabulī,* "count of the stable."]

con·stab·u·lar·y (kən-stăb'yə-lĕr'ē) *n., pl.* **-ies.** **1.** The body of constables of a district or city. **2.** The district under the

jurisdiction of a constable. **3.** An armed police force organized like a military unit. —*adj.* Also **con·stab·u·lar** (-lər). Of or pertaining to constables or to constabularies.

con·stan·cy (kŏn'stən-sē) *n.* **1.** Steadfastness in loyalty, affection, etc.; faithfulness. **2.** An unchanging quality or state; uniformity.

con·stant (kŏn'stənt) *adj.* **1.** Not changing; remaining the same: *maintain a constant speed.* **2.** Happening all the time; persistent: *constant interruptions; constant arguments; constant reminders.* **3.** Without interruption; continuous: *in constant use.* **4.** Steadfast in loyalty, affection, etc.; faithful: *a constant friend.* —See Syns at **continuous** and **faithful.** —*n.* **1.** Something that never changes. **2. a.** A symbol whose value does not change during the course of a mathematical discussion, problem, or analysis. **b.** A number, such as π, that has a fixed value. [Middle English, from Old French, from Latin *constāre,* to stand together : *com-,* together + *stāre,* to stand.] —**con'stant·ly** *adv.*

con·stel·la·tion (kŏn'stə-lā'shən) *n.* **1.** *Astron.* **a.** Any of 88 groups of stars that are thought to resemble and are named after various mythological characters, inanimate objects, and animals. **b.** The region of the celestial sphere occupied by such a group. **2.** *Astrol.* The position of the stars at the time of one's birth, regarded as determining one's character or fate. **3.** A group or gathering of distinguished persons or things. [Middle English *constellacioun,* from Old French *constellation,* from Late Latin *constellātiō,* group of stars : Latin *com-,* together + *stella,* star.]

con·ster·na·tion (kŏn'stər-nā'shən) *n.* Great alarm, shock, or amazement; dismay. [From Latin *consternāre,* to stretch out, overcome, perplex : *com-* (intensive) + *sternere,* to spread out.]

con·sti·pate (kŏn'stə-pāt') *tr.v.* **-pat·ed, -pat·ing.** To cause constipation in. [Latin *constipāre,* to press together : *com-,* together + *stīpāre,* to press.]

con·sti·pa·tion (kŏn'stə-pā'shən) *n.* Difficult, incomplete, or infrequent movement of the bowels.

con·stit·u·en·cy (kən-stĭch'ōō-ən-sē) *n., pl.* **-cies.** **1.** A body of voters. **2.** A district represented by a delegate elected to a legislature. **3.** Any group of supporters.

con·stit·u·ent (kən-stĭch'ōō-ənt) *adj.* **1.** Making up part of a whole: *An atom is a constituent part of a molecule.* **2.** Empowered to elect or designate. **3.** Authorized to draw up or change a constitution: *a constituent assembly.* —*n.* **1.** Someone represented by another; a client. **2.** Someone represented by an elected official; a voter. **3.** A constituent part; component. **4.** *Gram.* One of the functional elements into which a construction or compound may be divided by analysis. [Latin *constituere,* to constitute.] —**con·stit'u·ent·ly** *adv.*

con·sti·tute (kŏn'stĭ-tōōt,' -tyōōt') *tr.v.* **-tut·ed, -tut·ing.** **1.** To make up; form: *Ten members constitute a quorum.* **2.** To set up; establish: *Governments are constituted by the people.* **3.** To appoint, as to an office; designate: *The assembly constituted him ambassador to the king.* [Middle English *constituten,* from Latin *constituere,* to cause to stand : *com-* (intensive) + *statuere,* to set up.]

con·sti·tu·tion (kŏn'stĭ-tōō'shən, -tyōō'-) *n.* **1.** The basic law of a politically organized body, such as a nation or state. **2. the Constitution.** The written constitution of the United States, adopted in 1787 and put into effect in 1789. **3.** The way in which something or someone is made up, esp. the physical make-up of a person: *a boy with a strong constitution.* **4.** The act or process of setting up.

con·sti·tu·tion·al (kŏn'stĭ-tōō'shə-nəl, -tyōō'-) *adj.* **1.** Of a constitution: *a constitutional amendment.* **2.** Consistent with or permissible according to a constitution: *The proposed law is not constitutional.* **3.** Established by or operating under a constitution: *a constitutional monarchy.* **4.** Basic or inherent in one's make-up: *a constitutional inability to say "yes."* —*n.* A walk taken for one's health. —**con'sti·tu'tion·al·ly** *adv.*

con·sti·tu·tion·al·ism (kŏn'stĭ-tōō'shə-nə-lĭz'əm, -tyōō'-) *n.* **1.** Government in which power is distributed and limited by a system of laws that must be obeyed by the rulers. **2.** Advocacy of such government. —**con'sti·tu'tion·al·ist** *n.*

con·sti·tu·tion·al·i·ty (kŏn'stĭ-tōō'shə-nă-lĭ'ə-m, -tyōō'-) *n.* Validity according to a constitution: *The Supreme Court*

ă pat	ā pay	â care	ä father	ĕ pet	ē be	hw which	ĭ pit	ī tie	î pier	ŏ pot	ō toe	ô paw, for	oi noise
ŏŏ took	ōō boot	ou out	th thin	*th* this	ŭ cut		û urge	zh vision	ə about, item, edible, gallop, circus				

upheld the constitutionality of the law.

con·sti·tu·tive (kŏn'stĭ-tōō'tĭv, -tyōō-) adj. **1.** Making a thing what it is; essential. **2.** Having power to institute, establish, or enact. —**con'sti·tu'tive·ly** adv.

con·strain (kən-strān') tr.v. **1.** To compel by physical or moral force; oblige: I feel constrained to object. **2.** To keep within close bounds; confine. **3.** To check the freedom or mobility of; restrain. [Middle English constreinen, from Old French constraindre, from Latin constringere, to draw tightly together : com-, together + stringere, to draw tight.] —**con·strain'er** n.

con·strained (kən-strānd') adj. Forced; unnatural: a constrained expression. —**con·strain'ed·ly** (-strā'nĭd-lē) adv.

con·straint (kən-strānt') n. **1.** The threat or use of force to control the action of others: acting under constraint. **2.** Something that restricts or hampers. **3.** The condition of holding back one's natural feelings or behavior; lack of ease; a forced or unnatural manner: "All constraint had vanished between the two, and they began to talk" (Edith Wharton).

con·strict (kən-strĭkt') tr.v. **1.** To make smaller or narrower, as by shrinking or contracting: constrict a blood vessel. **2.** To squeeze or compress: A python constricts its prey. —intr.v. To become contracted or compressed: His muscles constricted. —See Syns at **contract**. [From Latin constringere, to draw tightly together, constrain.] —**con·stric'tive·ly** adv. —**con·stric·tion** (kən-strĭk'shən) n.

con·stric·tor (kən-strĭk'tər) n. **1.** A muscle that contracts or compresses a part or organ of the body. **2.** Any of various snakes, such as a python or boa, that coil around and crush their prey.

con·struct (kən-strŭkt') tr.v. **1.** To build; erect; make: construct new houses. **2.** To compose; devise: construct a sentence. **3.** To draw (a required geometric figure), usu. using no more than a straightedge and a compass as aids. —See Syns at **make**. —n. (kŏn'strŭkt'). Something constructed or synthesized from simple elements, esp. a mental concept. [From Latin construere, to build : com-, together + struere, to pile up.] —**con·struc'tor** or **con·struct'er** n. —**con·struct'i·ble** adj.

con·struc·tion (kən-strŭk'shən) n. **1.** The act or process of constructing. **2.** The business or work of building. **3.** A structure or building. **4.** The way in which something is put together; design: A chisel is a tool of simple construction. **5.** The interpretation or explanation given a certain statement. **6.** Gram. **a.** The arrangement of words to form a meaningful phrase, clause, or sentence. **b.** The group of words so arranged. —**con·struc'tion·al** adj. —**con·struc'tion·al·ly** adv.

con·struc·tion·ist (kən-strŭk'shə-nĭst) n. A person who construes or interprets a legal text or document in a specified way.

con·struc·tive (kən-strŭk'tĭv) adj. **1.** Serving a useful purpose or helping to improve: constructive suggestions. **2.** Of or pertaining to construction; structural. **3.** Law. Based on an interpretation; not directly expressed. —**con·struc'tive·ly** adv. —**con·struc'tive·ness** n.

con·strue (kən-strōō') v. -strued, -stru·ing. —tr.v. **1.** Gram. **a.** To analyze the structure of (a clause or sentence). **b.** To use syntactically: The noun "fish" can be construed as singular or plural. **2.** To place a certain meaning on; interpret. —intr.v. To analyze grammatical structure. —n. (kŏn'strōō'). An interpretation or translation. [Middle English construen, from Late Latin construere, from Latin, to construct.]

con·sub·stan·ti·a·tion (kŏn'səb-stăn'shē-ā'shən) n. The Lutheran doctrine that the body and blood of Christ coexist with the elements of bread and wine during the Eucharist. [From COM- + SUBSTANTIATION.]

con·sul (kŏn'səl) n. **1.** An official appointed by a government to reside in a foreign city and represent its commercial interests and give assistance to its citizens there. **2.** Either of the two chief magistrates of the Roman Republic, elected for a term of one year. [Middle English, from Latin.] —**con'su·lar** adj.

con·su·late (kŏn'sə-lĭt) n. **1.** The building or offices occupied by a consul. **2.** The office or term of office of a consul. **3.** Government by consuls.

consul general pl. **consuls general.** A consular officer of the highest rank.

con·sult (kən-sŭlt') tr.v. **1.** To seek advice or information of: consult a doctor. **2.** To have regard for; consider. —intr.v. **1.** To exchange views; confer: The U.S. consulted with the Canadian government. **2.** To give expert advice as a professional. [Old French consulter, from Latin consulere, to take counsel.]

con·sul·tant (kən-sŭl'tənt) n. **1.** A person who gives expert or professional advice. **2.** A person who consults another.

con·sul·ta·tion (kŏn'səl-tā'shən) n. **1.** The act or procedure of consulting. **2.** A conference at which advice is given or views are exchanged.

con·sume (kən-sōōm') v. -sumed, -sum·ing. —tr.v. **1.** To eat or drink up; ingest. **2.** To expend; use up. **3.** To waste; squander. **4.** To destroy, as by fire. **5.** To absorb; engross. —intr.v. To be destroyed, expended, or wasted. —See Syns at **waste**. [Middle English consumen, from Old French consumer, from Latin consūmere : com- (intensive) + sūmere, to take up.] —**con·sum'a·ble** adj. & n.

con·sum·ed·ly (kən-sōō'mĭd-lē) adv. Excessively.

con·sum·er (kən-sōō'mər) n. **1.** Someone or something that consumes. **2.** Someone who buys and uses goods and services: The manufacturers passed on the price increase to the consumers.

consumer goods. Goods, such as food and clothing, that satisfy human wants.

con·sum·er·ism (kən-sōō'mə-rĭz'əm) n. The movement seeking to protect the rights of consumers by requiring honest packaging, labeling, and advertising, fair pricing, and improved safety standards. —**con·sum'er·ist** n.

con·sum·ing (kən-sōō'mĭng) adj. **1.** Destroying as by fire: the consuming flames of hell. **2.** Overwhelming: a consuming desire to see her again.

con·sum·mate (kŏn'sə-māt') tr.v. -mat·ed, -mat·ing. **1.** To bring to completion; conclude: consummate a business deal. **2.** To fulfill (a marriage) with the first act of sexual intercourse after the ceremony. —adj. (kən-sŭm'ĭt). **1.** Complete or perfect in every respect: consummate happiness. **2.** Highly skilled; polished: a consummate artist. **3.** Complete; utter: a consummate bore. —See Syns at **utter**. [Middle English consummaten, from Latin consummāre, to bring together, sum up : com-, together + summa, a sum.] —**con·sum'mate·ly** adv. —**con'sum·ma'tion** n. —**con'sum·ma'tor** n.

con·sump·tion (kən-sŭmp'shən) n. **1. a.** The act or process of consuming. **b.** The amount consumed. **2.** Econ. The using up of consumer goods and services. **3.** Pathol. **a.** A wasting away of tissues. **b.** Tuberculosis of the lungs.

con·sump·tive (kən-sŭmp'tĭv) adj. **1.** Tending to consume; wasteful; destructive. **2.** Pathol. Of or suffering from consumption. —n. A person afflicted with consumption. —**con·sump'tive·ly** adv.

con·tact (kŏn'tăkt') n. **1.** The condition of touching or coming together: physical contact; body contact. **2.** The condition of being in touch: He put me in contact with the right people. **3.** An acquaintance who is in a position to be of help: He has numerous contacts in the government. **4.** Elect. **a.** A connection of two conductors in a way that allows a flow of current. **b.** A movable part that opens or closes a circuit: the contacts of a switch. **5.** Informal. A contact lens. —v. (kŏn'tăkt, kən-tăkt'). —tr.v. **1.** To bring or put in contact with. **2.** Informal. To get in touch with; communicate with. —intr.v. To be in or come into contact. —adj. (kŏn'tăkt'). **1.** Of, sustaining, or making contact. **2.** Caused or transmitted by touching: a contact skin rash. [Latin contāctus, from the past part. of contingere, to touch : com-, together + tangere, to touch.]

Usage: As a verb meaning to get in touch with, **contact** is informal. In formal writing preferable alternatives include more specific verbs such as write, telephone, and call. As a noun meaning an acquaintance (who might be of use) or connection, contact is better established and appropriate to all levels.

contact lens. A tiny lens designed to correct a defect in vision, worn directly on the cornea of the eye.

con·ta·gion (kən-tā'jən) n. **1. a.** The transmission of disease by direct or indirect contact. **b.** A disease that is or can be transmitted in this way. **2.** Harmful or corrupting influence. **3.** The tendency to spread, as of an influence: *the contagion of laughter.* [Middle English *contagioun,* from Old French *contagion,* from Latin *contāgiō,* from *contingere,* to touch, contact.]

con·ta·gious (kən-tā′jəs) *adj.* **1.** Transmissible by direct or indirect contact: *a contagious disease.* **2.** Carrying or capable of carrying disease. **3.** Spreading or tending to spread; catching: *contagious laughter.* **—con·ta′gious·ly** *adv.* **—con·ta′gious·ness** *n.*

con·tain (kən-tān′) *tr.v.* **1.** To have within itself; hold: *Orange juice contains vitamin C. The document contains important information.* **2.** To consist of; comprise; include: *A gallon contains four quarts.* **3.** To hold back; restrain: *I could scarcely contain my laughter.* **4.** *Math.* To be exactly divisible by. **5.** To restrict the strategic power of (a nation or bloc), as by encircling it with hostile alliances. [Middle English *conteinen,* from Old French *contenir,* from Latin *continēre,* to hold together, enclose : *com-,* together + *tenēre,* to hold.] **—con·tain′a·ble** *adj.*

con·tain·er (kən-tā′nər) *n.* Anything, as a box, can, jar, or barrel, in which material is held or carried; receptacle.

con·tain·ment (kən-tān′mənt) *n.* The policy of attempting to prevent the expansion of an opposing power or ideology.

con·tain·er·ize (kən-tā′nə-rīz′) *tr.v.* **-ized, -iz·ing.** To package (cargo) in standardized containers to facilitate shipping and handling. **—con·tain′er·i·za′tion** *n.*

container ship. A ship used for carrying cargo that has been previously containerized.

con·tam·i·nate (kən-tăm′ə-nāt′) *tr.v.* **-nat·ed, -nat·ing.** To make impure, corrupt, or less good by contact or mixture; to foul; pollute. [Middle English *contaminaten,* from Latin *contāmināre.*] **—con·tam′i·nant** *n.* **—con·tam′i·na·tive** *adj.* **—con·tam′i·na·tor** *n.*

con·tam·i·na·tion (kən-tăm′ə-nā′shən) *n.* **1. a.** The act or process of contaminating. **b.** The condition of being contaminated. **2.** Someone or something that contaminates.

con·tem·plate (kŏn′təm-plāt′) *v.* **-plat·ed, -plat·ing.** *—tr.v.* **1.** To look at, often quietly and solemnly: *The men contemplated the treasure in blissful silence.* **2.** To think about, esp. in a detached way: *I contemplated my strange situation.* **3.** To think about doing (something): *The student contemplated a career in science.* **4.** To expect: *They contemplated various kinds of trouble.* *—intr.v.* To ponder; meditate. [From Latin *contemplārī,* to observe carefully : *com-* (intensive) + *templum,* open space marked out by augurs for observation.] **—con′tem·pla′tor** *n.*

con·tem·pla·tion (kŏn′təm-plā′shən) *n.* **1.** Thoughtful observation or meditation. **2.** Intention or expectation.

con·tem·pla·tive (kən-tĕm′plə-tĭv) *adj.* Of or devoted to contemplation. *—n.* **1.** A person given to contemplation. **2.** A member of a religious order dedicated to meditation. **—con·tem′pla·tive·ly** *adv.* **—con·tem′pla·tive·ness** *n.*

con·tem·po·ra·ne·ous (kən-tĕm′pə-rā′nē-əs) *adj.* Originating, existing, or happening at the same time. *—See Usage note at* **contemporary.** [Latin *contemporāneus* : *com-,* same + *tempus,* time.] **—con·tem′po·ra′ne·ous·ly** *adv.* **—con·tem′po·ra′ne·ous·ness** *n.*

con·tem·po·rar·y (kən-tĕm′pə-rĕr′ē) *adj.* **1.** Living or happening during the same period of time. **2.** Current; modern: *contemporary history; a contemporary composer.* *—n., pl.* **-ies. 1.** A person of the same age as another: *John and I are contemporaries.* **2.** A person living at the same time as another: *a composer much admired by his contemporaries.* **3.** A person of the present age; a modern.

Usage: **1. contemporary, contemporaneous.** Both adjectives refer to persons or things that exist or occur at the same time, but *contemporaneous* applies more often to things: *volcanic eruptions contemporaneous with earthquakes; contemporary poets and artists.* **2.** Sometimes the use of *contemporary* can cause confusion over the time meant; when used in a context having no other reference to time, it indicates the time of the writer or speaker: *contemporary theologians.* When used with persons or things of the past, *contemporary* logically pertains to the same time, though often the intended meaning is otherwise. As a result, *modern* or *period* may be preferable in some contexts, depending on the intended meaning: *a Shakespearean play in period* (rather than *contemporary*) *dress; a*

Shakespearean *play in modern* (rather than *contemporary*) *dress.*

con·tempt (kən-tĕmpt′) *n.* **1. a.** A feeling that someone or something is inferior and undesirable; scorn: *The English used to regard foreigners with contempt.* **b.** The condition of being regarded in this way: *The League of Nations rapidly fell into contempt.* **2.** Open disrespect or willful disobedience of the authority of a court of law or a legislative body. [Middle English, from Latin *contemptus,* from past part. of *contemnere,* to contemn.]

con·tempt·i·ble (kən-tĕmp′tə-bəl) *adj.* Deserving contempt; despicable: *a contemptible trick.* **—con·tempt′i·bil′i·ty** or **con·tempt′i·ble·ness** *n.* **—con·tempt′i·bly** *adv.*

con·temp·tu·ous (kən-tĕmp′chōō-əs) *adj.* Manifesting or feeling contempt; scornful; disdainful: *a person who was contemptuous of our efforts.* **—con·temp′tu·ous·ly** *adv.* **—con·temp′tu·ous·ness** *n.*

con·tend (kən-tĕnd′) *intr.v.* **1.** To fight, as in battle: *The Greek cities contended for supremacy.* **2.** To compete, as in a race; vie: *I could not contend with him in speed.* **3.** To strive in controversy or debate; to dispute: *The candidates contended on almost every issue.* *—tr.v.* To maintain or assert: *The police contend that they are not adequately protected.* *—See Syns at* **argue.** [Middle English *contenden,* from Old French *contendre,* from Latin *contendere,* to strain : *com-,* with + *tendere,* to stretch, strain, strive.] **—con·tend′er** *n.*

con·tent¹ (kŏn′tĕnt′) *n.* **1.** Often **contents.** Something that is contained in a receptacle: *empty a jar of its contents.* **2.** Often **contents.** Subject matter, as of a speech: *The contents of the letter were not revealed.* **3.** The meaning or significance of a literary or artistic work as distinguished from its form: *the content of a sonnet.* **4.** The proportion of a substance contained in something: *Eggs have a high protein content.* [Middle English, from Latin *contentus,* past part. of *continēre,* to contain.]

con·tent² (kən-tĕnt′) *adj.* **1.** Not desiring more than what one has; satisfied: *content with one's lot in life.* **2.** Resigned to circumstances; assenting: *had to be content with the answer.* *—tr.v.* To make content or satisfied: *My own home contents me.* *—n.* **1.** Contentment; satisfaction. **2.** *Brit.* An affirmative vote or voter in the House of Lords. [Middle English, from Old French, from Latin *contentus,* restrained, past part. of *continēre,* to restrain, contain.]

con·tent·ed (kən-tĕn′tĭd) *adj.* **1.** Satisfied with things as they are; content. **2.** Showing contentment: *a contented look on her face.* **—con·tent′ed·ly** *adv.* **—con·tent′ed·ness** *n.*

con·ten·tion (kən-tĕn′shən) *n.* **1.** A battle, competition, or dispute: *They played in fierce but friendly contention.* **2.** A claim or argument: *His contention was that the proceedings were invalid.* *—See Syns at* **conflict.** **—idiom. in (or out of) contention.** In a position (or having no chance) to win: *Three teams are still in contention for the pennant.* [Middle English *contencioun,* from Old French *contention,* from Latin *contentiō,* from *contendere,* to contend.]

con·ten·tious (kən-tĕn′shəs) *adj.* **1.** Inclined to argue; quarrelsome. **2.** Involving contention. **—con·ten′tious·ly** *adv.* **—con·ten′tious·ness** *n.*

con·tent·ment (kən-tĕnt′mənt) *n.* The condition or quality of being contented; satisfaction.

con·ter·mi·nous (kən-tûr′mə-nəs) *adj.* **1.** Having a boundary in common; contiguous. **2.** Contained in the same boundaries; coextensive. [Latin *conterminus* : *com-,* together + *terminus,* boundary, limit.] **—con·ter′mi·nous·ly** *adv.* **—con·ter′mi·nous·ness** *n.*

con·test (kŏn′tĕst′) *n.* **1.** A struggle for superiority or victory between two or more rivals: *A contest developed for the position of majority leader in the Senate.* **2.** Any competition, esp. between entrants who perform separately and are rated by a panel of judges: *a beauty contest; a skating contest.* *—v.* (kən-tĕst′, kŏn′tĕst′) *—tr.v.* **1.** To compete or strive for: *contest a prize.* **2.** To attempt to disprove or invalidate; to dispute; to challenge: *contest a will.* *—intr.v.* To struggle or compete; contend: *contested with his adversary.* [Old French *conteste,* from *contester,* from Latin *contestārī,* bring in by calling witnesses (from both parties) : *com-,* together + *testis,* a witness.] **—con·test′a·ble** *adj.* **—con·test′er** *n.*

ă pat   ā pay   âr care   ä father   ĕ pet   ē be   hw which   ĭ pit   ī tie   îr pier   ŏ pot   ō toe   ô paw, for   oi noise
ōō took   ōō boot   ou out   th thin   th this   ŭ cut   û urge   zh vision   ə about, item, edible, gallop, circus

con·test·ant (kən-tĕs′tənt, kŏn′tĕs′tənt) n. **1.** Someone who takes part in a contest; competitor. **2.** Someone who contests something, such as an election or a will.

con·text (kŏn′tĕkst′) n. **1.** The setting of words and ideas in which a particular word or statement appears: *In some contexts "mad" means "insane"; in other contexts it means "angry."* **2.** A general setting or set of circumstances in which a particular event occurs; a situation: *in the context of modern city life.* [Middle English, from Latin *contextus,* sequence of words, from the past part. of *contexere,* to weave : *com-,* together + *texere,* to join, weave, plait.]

con·tex·tu·al (kən-tĕks′chŏō-əl) adj. Of, pertaining to, or depending upon a context: *a special contextual meaning.* —**con·tex′tu·al·ly** adv.

con·ti·gu·i·ty (kŏn′tĭ-gyŏō′ĭ-tē) n., pl. **-ties. 1.** The condition of being contiguous. **2.** A continuous mass or series.

con·tig·u·ous (kən-tĭg′yŏō-əs) adj. **1.** Having a common edge or boundary; touching. **2.** Nearby; neighboring; adjacent. [Latin *contiguus,* from *contingere,* to touch on all sides, to contact.] —**con·tig′u·ous·ly** adv. —**con·tig′u·ous·ness** n.

con·ti·nence (kŏn′tə-nəns) n. Also **con·ti·nen·cy** (-nən-sē). Self-restraint, esp. with regard to passions and desires; moderation.

con·ti·nent[1] (kŏn′tə-nənt) adj. Self-restrained; moderate. [Middle English, from Old French, from Latin *continēre,* to contain.] —**con′ti·nent·ly** adv.

con·ti·nent[2] (kŏn′tə-nənt) n. **1.** One of the principal land masses of the earth, usu. regarded as including Africa, Antarctica, Asia, Australia, Europe, North America, and South America. **2. the Continent.** The mainland of Europe. [Latin *(terra) continēns,* "continuous (land)," from *continēre,* to contain.]

con·ti·nen·tal (kŏn′tə-nĕn′tl) adj. **1.** Of or like a continent: *continental limits; a continental state.* **2.** Often **Continental.** Of the mainland of Europe. **3. Continental.** Of the American colonies during and just after the Revolutionary War. —n. **1.** Often **Continental.** An inhabitant of the mainland of Europe. **2. Continental.** A soldier in the Continental army during the Revolutionary War. **3.** A piece of paper money issued by the Continental Congress during the Revolutionary War. —**con′ti·nen′tal·ly** adv.

continental divide. An extensive region of high ground from each side of which the river systems of a continent flow in opposite directions.

continental shelf. A portion of the edge of a continent covered to a gen. shallow depth by the ocean and extending to a point where it slopes steeply downward to the ocean depths.

con·tin·gen·cy (kən-tĭn′jən-sē) n., pl. **-cies. 1.** An event that may occur but is not intended; a possibility. **2.** The condition of being contigent.

con·tin·gent (kən-tĭn′jənt) adj. **1.** Liable to occur but not with certainty; possible. **2.** Dependent upon circumstances not yet known; conditional: *The success of the picnic is contingent upon the weather.* **3.** Happening by chance; accidental. —n. **1.** A contingent event or condition. **2.** A share or quota contributed to a general effort: *The division included a contingent from New York.* **3.** A representative group forming part of a gathering; a delegation: *The Maine contingent at the Democratic convention.* [Middle English, from Old French, from Latin *contingere,* to touch on all sides, happen, contact.] —**con·tin′gent·ly** adv.

con·tin·u·al (kən-tĭn′yŏō-əl) adj. **1.** Repeated regularly and frequently: *the continual banging of the shutters.* **2. a.** Not interrupted or broken; steady: *a continual noise.* **b.** Continuing over a long period of time; incessant: *a continual diet of vegetables.* —See Syns at **continuous.** —**con·tin′u·al·ly** adv.

Usage: **continual, continuous. 1.** *Continual* can refer to uninterrupted action but is now largely restricted to what is intermittent or repeated at intervals: *the baby's continual crying. Continuous* implies either action without interruption in time or unbroken extent in space: *a continuous vigil; a continuous slope of terrain.* **2.** The traditional idea is that *continuous* should refer only to unbroken continuity, while *continual* can also be used of intermittent or repetitive effects. In the materials from which this Dictio-

nary was made, the distinction did not seem to be observed. Both words were almost always used to express unbroken continuity (*continuous talking; continual talking*), and both were also occasionally used of repetitive effects (*continual rain showers; continuous rain showers*). In the case of the adverbs derived from *continuous* and *continual,* the distinction seems to have more force; while *continually* was used about equally in both senses, *continuously* was used only to mean "without a break."

con·tin·u·ance (kən-tĭn′yŏō-əns) n. **1.** The act or an example of continuing or lasting: *the continuance of the circumstances that led to the fight.* **2.** The time during which something exists or lasts; duration. **3.** A continuation; sequel. **4.** Postponement or adjournment of legal proceedings to a future date.

con·tin·u·a·tion (kən-tĭn′yŏō-ā′shən) n. **1. a.** The act or process of continuing: *The enormous profits of the slave trade became the most convincing argument for its continuation.* **b.** An example of this: *Today's fair weather is a continuation of yesterday's.* **2.** An extension to a further point: *The Mediterranean is a continuation of the Atlantic.* **3.** A sequel, as in a television series.

con·tin·ue (kən-tĭn′yŏō) v. **-ued, -u·ing.** —intr.v. **1.** To go on with a particular action or in a particular condition; persist: *The rain continued for days.* **2.** To exist over a prolonged period; last. **3.** To remain in the same state, capacity, or place: *She will continue as representative for another two years.* **4.** To go on after an interruption; resume: *The program will continue after station identification.* —tr.v. **1.** To carry forward; persist in: *The police continued their investigation.* **2.** To carry further in time, space, or development; extend: *The magazine will continue the story in the next issue.* **3.** To cause to remain or last; retain. **4.** To carry on after an interruption; resume: *continued painting after a coffee break.* **5.** *Law.* To postpone or adjourn (legal proceedings). [Middle English *continuen,* from Old French *continuer,* from Latin *continuāre,* from *continēre,* to hold together, contain.] —**con·tin′u·er** n.

con·ti·nu·i·ty (kŏn′tə-nŏō′ĭ-tē, -nyŏō′-) n., pl. **-ties. 1.** The condition of being continuous. **2.** An uninterrupted succession; unbroken course: *You interrupted the continuity of my thoughts.* **3.** A detailed script consulted to avoid errors and discrepancies from shot to shot in a film. **4.** A script for all the spoken parts of a radio or television program.

con·tin·u·o (kən-tĭn′yŏō-ō) n., pl. **-os.** A typically keyboard accompaniment for a solo instrument in which numerals indicate the successive chords required. [Italian, "continuous."]

con·tin·u·ous (kən-tĭn′yŏō-əs) adj. Continuing without interruption or cessation; unbroken: *Living cells need a continuous supply of oxygen.* —See Usage note at **continual.** —**con·tin′u·ous·ly** adv. —**con·tin′u·ous·ness** n.

Syns: **continuous, ceaseless, constant, continual, endless, eternal, everlasting, incessant, interminable, nonstop, perpetual, relentless, round-the-clock, timeless** *adj.* Core meaning: Existing or happening without interruption or end (*irritated by their continuous chattering*).

con·tin·u·um (kən-tĭn′yŏō-əm) n., pl. **-u·a** (-yŏō-ə) or **-u·ums. 1.** Something in which no part can be distinguished from neighboring parts except by arbitrary division. **2.** *Math.* A set having the same number of points as all the real numbers in an interval.

con·tort (kən-tôrt′) tr.v. To twist or bend severely out of shape. —intr.v. To become twisted into a strained shape or expression. [From Latin *contorquēre,* to twist together : *com-,* together + *torquēre,* to twist.]

con·tor·tion (kən-tôr′shən) n. **1.** The act or result of contorting; a twisted position or expression: *violent body contortions.* **2.** An unduly or unnecessarily complicated or awkward action: *going through all sorts of contortions to justify a wrong decision.*

con·tor·tion·ist (kən-tôr′shə-nĭst) n. A person who performs acrobatic feats involving contorted, grotesque postures and positions. —**con·tor′tion·is′tic** adj.

con·tour (kŏn′tŏōr′) n. **1.** The outline of a figure, body, or mass: *the contour of the Florida coast.* **2.** A **contour line. 3.** Often **contours.** The surface of a curving form: *the con-*

tours of her body. —*adj.* **1.** Following the contour lines of uneven terrain to limit erosion of topsoil: *contour plowing.* **2.** Shaped to fit the outline or form of something: *contour sheets.* —*tr.v.* **1.** To give a curving shape or outline to; represent in contour. **2.** To build or construct (a road) to follow the contour of the land. [French, from Italian *contorno,* from *contornare,* to go around : *con-* (intensive) + *tornare,* to turn in a lathe, from Latin *tornus,* lathe, from Greek *tornos.*]

contour line. A line drawn on a map in such a way that each point on the line is at the same elevation above sea level.

contour map. A map that shows elevations above sea level and surface features of the land by means of contour lines.

contra-. A prefix meaning: **1.** Against, opposing, or contrary: **contradistinction.** **2.** Pitched next below a specified musical instrument: **contrabassoon.** [Middle English, from Latin *contrā-,* from *contrā,* against.]

con·tra·band (kŏn′trə-bănd′) *n.* **1.** Goods prohibited by law or treaty from being imported or exported. **2.** Illegal traffic in contraband; smuggling. **3.** Smuggled goods. **4.** *International Law.* Goods that may be seized and confiscated by a belligerent if shipped to another belligerent by a neutral. [French *contrebande,* from Italian *contrabbando* : Late Latin *contrā-,* against + *bannum,* proclamation.]

con·tra·bass (kŏn′trə-bās′) *n.* A **double bass.**

con·tra·bas·soon (kŏn′trə-bə-sōōn′) *n.* The largest and lowest-pitched of the double-reed wind instruments, sounding about an octave below the bassoon.

con·tra·cep·tion (kŏn′trə-sĕp′shən) *n.* The prevention of conception. [CONTRA- + (CON)CEPTION.]

con·tra·cep·tive (kŏn′trə-sĕp′tĭv) *adj.* Capable of preventing conception. —*n.* A contraceptive agent or device.

con·tract (kŏn′trăkt′) *n.* **1. a.** An agreement between two or more parties, esp. one that is written and enforceable by law. **b.** A document stating the terms of such an agreement. **2. Contract bridge.** —*v.* (kən-trăkt′, kŏn′trăkt′). —*tr.v.* **1.** To enter into by contract; establish or settle by formal agreement: *contract a marriage.* **2.** To acquire or incur: *contract a debt.* **3.** To reduce in size by drawing together; shrink: *contract one's muscles.* **4.** To shorten (a word or words) by omitting or combining some of the letters or sounds; for example, *I'm* for *I am.* —*intr.v.* **1.** To enter into or make a contract: *contract for garbage collection.* **2.** To become reduced in size by or as if by being drawn together: *The pupils of his eyes contracted.* [Middle English, from Old French, from Latin *contractus,* from the past part. of *contrahere,* to draw together : *com-,* together + *trahere,* to draw.] —**con·tract′i·bil′i·ty** or **con·tract′i·ble·ness** *n.* —**con·tract′i·ble** *adj.*

    Syns: contract, compress, constrict, shrink *v.* *Core meaning:* To reduce in size by or as if by drawing together (*contract an arm muscle*).

contract bridge. A form of auction bridge in which tricks in excess of the contract may not count toward game. Also called **contract.**

con·trac·tile (kən-trăk′təl, -tīl′) *adj.* Able to contract, be compressed, or cause contraction: *contractile muscle fibers.*

con·trac·tion (kən-trăk′shən) *n.* **1.** The act or process of contracting: *contraction of a disease.* **2.** A shortened word or words formed by omitting or combining some of the letters or sounds. For example, *isn't* is a contraction of *is not.* **3. a.** The process by which a muscle becomes shorter or more tense. **b.** An act of squeezing or tightening by a muscle or a muscular organ: *contractions of the stomach.*

con·trac·tor (kŏn′trăk′tər, kən-trăk′-) *n.* **1.** A person who agrees to furnish materials or perform services at a specified price, esp. for construction. **2.** Something that contracts, esp. a muscle.

con·trac·tu·al (kən-trăk′chōō-əl) *adj.* Of, connected with, or having the nature of a contract: *a contractual obligation.* —**con·trac′tu·al·ly** *adv.*

con·tra·dict (kŏn′trə-dĭkt′) *tr.v.* **1.** To assert or express the opposite of (a statement): *The witness seemed to contradict his previous testimony.* **2.** To deny the statement of: *She contradicted her father.* **3.** To be contrary to; be inconsistent with: *magic tricks that contradict what the eye*

sees. —*intr.v.* To utter a contradictory statement. —See Syns at **deny.** [Latin *contrādīcere,* to speak against : *contrā-,* against + *dīcere,* to speak.] —**con′tra·dict′a·ble** *adj.* —**con′tra·dict′er** or **con′tra·dic′tor** *n.*

con·tra·dic·tion (kŏn′trə-dĭk′shən) *n.* **1.** The act of contradicting or the condition of being contradicted: *He can't stand contradiction.* **2.** An inconsistency; discrepancy: *There's a contradiction in what you're saying.* **3.** *Math. & Logic.* **a.** A statement that contains or depends on two ideas that cannot both be true at once. **b.** A statement that contradicts something.

con·tra·dic·to·ry (kŏn′trə-dĭk′tə-rē) *adj.* **1.** In opposition; opposing. **2.** Having elements or parts not in agreement: *In many ways he was a contradictory political figure.* **3.** In the habit of contradicting. —**con′tra·dic′to·ri·ly** *adv.* —**con′tra·dic′to·ri·ness** *n.*

con·tra·dis·tinc·tion (kŏn′trə-dĭ-stĭngk′shən) *n.* Distinction by contrasting or opposing qualities: *science in contradistinction to art.* —**con′tra·dis·tinc′tive** *adj.* —**con′tra·dis·tinc′tive·ly** *adv.*

con·trail (kŏn′trāl′) *n.* A visible trail of water droplets or ice crystals sometimes forming in the wake of an aircraft. [CON(DENSATION) + TRAIL.]

con·tral·to (kən-trăl′tō) *n., pl.* **-tos.** *Mus.* **1.** The lowest female voice or voice part, intermediate in range between soprano and tenor. **2.** A woman having such a voice. —*modifier:* *a contralto voice; a contralto aria.* [Italian.]

con·trap·tion (kən-trăp′shən) *n.* *Informal.* A mechanical device; gadget. [Perh. blend of CONTRIVE and TRAP + -TION.]

con·tra·pun·tal (kŏn′trə-pŭn′tl) *adj.* *Mus.* Of, using, or involving counterpoint: *complex contrapuntal writing.* [From Italian *contrapunto* : Latin *contrā-,* against + *punctus,* point.] —**con′tra·pun′tal·ly** *adv.*

con·tra·ri·e·ty (kŏn′trə-rī′ĭ-tē) *n., pl.* **-ties.** **1.** The condition or quality of being contrary. **2.** Something contrary; a discrepancy or inconsistency.

con·trar·i·wise (kŏn′trĕr′ē-wīz′) *adv.* **1.** From a contrasting point of view. **2.** In the opposite way or reverse order. **3.** (*also* kən-trâr′ē-wīz′). Perversely.

con·trar·y (kŏn′trĕr′ē) *adj.* **1.** Completely different; opposed: *contrary points of view.* **2.** Opposite in direction or position: *play scales in contrary motion.* **3.** Adverse; unfavorable: *a contrary wind.* **4.** (*also* kən-trâr′ē). Stubbornly opposed to others; willful: *He's just a contrary person.* —*n., pl.* **-ies.** The opposite: *I believe the contrary to be true.* —*adv.* In opposition; counter: *He acted contrary to all advice.* —**idioms. on the contrary.** In opposition to the previous statement; conversely. **to the contrary.** To the opposite; to a contrasting effect. [Middle English *contrarie,* from Old French *contraire,* from Latin *contrārius,* from *contrā,* against.] —**con′trar′i·ly** *adv.* —**con′trar′i·ness** *n.*

    Syns: contrary, balky, difficult, impossible, ornery, perverse, wayward *adj.* *Core meaning:* Given to acting in opposition to a prevailing order or prescribed authority (*a contrary child who refused to obey*).

con·trast (kən-trăst′) *tr.v.* To set in opposition in order to show or emphasize differences: *The poem contrasts good and evil.* —*intr.v.* To show differences when compared: *Black contrasts with white.* —See Usage note at **compare.** —*n.* (kŏn′trăst′). **1.** Comparison, esp. in order to reveal differences. **2.** Striking difference between things compared: *the contrast between father and son.* **3.** Something that is strikingly different from something else: *What a contrast he is to his father!* [French *contraster,* from Italian *contrastare,* from Medieval Latin *contrāstāre* : Latin *contrā-,* against + *stāre,* to stand.] —**con·trast′a·ble** *adj.*

con·tra·vene (kŏn′trə-vēn′) *tr.v.* **-vened, -ven·ing.** **1.** To act or be counter to; violate; infringe. **2.** To oppose in argument. [Old French *contravenir,* from Late Latin *contrāvenīre,* to come against : Latin *contrā-,* against + *venīre,* to come.] —**con′tra·ven′er** *n.*

con·tra·ven·tion (kŏn′trə-vĕn′shən) *n.* An act of contravening; a violation; infringement.

con·tre·temps (kŏn′trə-tŏn′, kôn′trə-tän′) *n., pl.* **contretemps** (-tŏnz′, -tänz′). An inopportune or embarrassing occurrence; a mishap. [French : Latin *contra-* + *tempus,* time.]

con·trib·ute (kən-trĭb′yōōt) *v.* **-ut·ed, -ut·ing.** —*tr.v.* **1.** To give or supply in common with others: *contribute time and money to the heart fund.* **2.** To submit for publication: *He contributes a poem every issue.* —*intr.v.* **1.** To make a contribution: *contributed to the heart fund yearly.* **2.** To act as a determining factor; aid in bringing about: *Exercise contributes to better health.* **3.** To submit material for publication: *He contributes regularly to several magazines.* [From Latin *contribuere,* to bring together, unite : *com-,* together + *tribuere,* to allot, grant.] —**con·trib'u·tive** *adj.* —**con·trib'u·tive·ly** *adv.*

con·tri·bu·tion (kŏn'trĭ-byōō'shən) *n.* **1.** The act of contributing. **2.** Something contributed.

con·trib·u·tor (kən-trĭb'yə-tər) *n.* A person who donates or supplies something: *a contributor of funds.*

con·trib·u·to·ry (kən-trĭb'yə-tôr'ē, -tōr'ē) *adj.* **1.** Pertaining to or involving contribution. **2.** Contributing toward a result: *a contributory fact.*

con·trite (kən-trīt', kŏn'trīt') *adj.* **1.** Repentant for one's sins; penitent. **2.** Feeling or caused by contrition: *contrite words; contrite tears.* [Middle English *contrit,* from Old French, from Medieval Latin *contritus,* "broken in spirit," from Latin *conterere,* to bruise : *com-* (intensive) + *terere,* to rub, grind.] —**con·trite'ly** *adv.* —**con·trite'ness** *n.*

con·tri·tion (kən-trĭsh'ən) *n.* Sincere remorse or repentance: *Full of contrition and shame, he tried to make amends for his disloyalty.*

con·triv·ance (kən-trī'vəns) *n.* **1. a.** The act of contriving. **b.** The ability to contrive. **2.** Something that is contrived, as a mechanical device or a clever plan.

con·trive (kən-trīv') *v.* **-trived, -triv·ing.** —*tr.v.* **1.** To devise with cleverness or ingenuity: *contrive a new scheme.* **2.** To bring about through clever planning: *contrive a victory.* **3.** To invent or make, esp. by improvisation: *Scarlett contrives a dress out of an old curtain.* —*intr.v.* To plot or scheme: *contrive to gain admission.* [Middle English *contreven,* from Old French *controver,* from Late Latin *contropāre,* to represent figuratively : *com-,* together + *tropus,* figure of speech, from Greek *tropos,* turn, style.] —**con·triv'ed·ly** (-trī'vĭd-lē) *adv.* —**con·triv'er** *n.*

con·trol (kən-trōl') *tr.v.* **-trolled, -trol·ling.** **1.** To exercise authority or influence over; direct: *The Romans controlled a huge empire.* **2.** To regulate the operation of: *control a machine.* **3.** To hold in check; restrain: *control one's emotions.* **4.** To check or regulate (a scientific experiment) by conducting a similar experiment in which the factor whose effect is being studied is not present. —*n.* **1.** Authority or power to regulate, direct, or dominate: *the coach's control over the team.* **2.** A means of restraint: *a price control.* **3.** Something with which a scientific experiment can be compared in order to check its results. **4.** Often **controls.** The knobs, levers, pedals, etc., that are used in setting and regulating the operating conditions of a machine. **5.** *Spiritualism.* A spirit presumed to act through a medium. — See Syns at **power.** [Middle English *controllen,* from Old French *cont(r)eroller,* from Medieval Latin *contrārotulāre,* to check by a duplicate register, from *contrārotulus,* duplicate register : Latin *contrā,* against, opposite + *rotulus,* roll, from *rota,* wheel.] —**con·trol'la·bil'i·ty** *n.* —**con·trol'la·ble** *adj.*

con·trol·ler (kən-trō'lər) *n.* **1.** Someone or something that controls, esp. an automatic device that regulates the operation of a machine. **2.** A person who regulates a flow of traffic, esp. air traffic. **3.** An executive or official who supervises financial affairs; comptroller.

control tower. A tower at an airport from which the movements of aircraft and other vehicles are controlled.

control tower

con·tro·ver·sial (kŏn'trə-vûr'shəl, -sē-əl) *adj.* **1.** Of, subject to, or marked by controversy: *a controversial issue.* **2.** Fond of controversy; disputatious. —**con'tro·ver'sial·ist** *n.* —**con'tro·ver'sial·ly** *adv.*

con·tro·ver·sy (kŏn'trə-vûr'sē) *n., pl.* **-sies.** **1.** Argument; debate: *He is the subject of much controversy.* **2.** A public dispute between sides holding opposing views: *the controversy over state aid to private schools.* [Middle English *controversie,* from Latin *contrōversia,* from *contrōversus,* turned against : *contrā-,* against + *vertere,* to turn.]

con·tro·vert (kŏn'trə-vûrt') *tr.v.* **1.** To contradict; deny: *The facts controvert his assertions.* **2.** To argue or dispute about; to debate. —**con'tro·vert'i·ble** *adj.*

con·tu·ma·cious (kŏn'tōō-mā'shəs, -tyōō-) *adj.* Stubbornly disobedient or rebellious; insubordinate. —**con'tu·ma'cious·ly** *adv.* —**con'tu·ma'cious·ness** *n.*

con·tu·ma·cy (kŏn'tōō-mə-sē, -tyōō-) *n., pl.* **-cies.** Stubborn or contemptuous resistance to authority; rebelliousness; disobedience; insubordination. [Middle English *contumacie,* from Latin *contumācia,* from *contumāx,* disobedient.]

con·tu·me·ly (kŏn'tōō-mə-lē, -tyōō-, -təm-lē) *n., pl.* **-lies.** **1.** Rudeness in behavior or speech; insolence. **2.** An insulting remark or act. [Middle English *contumelie,* from Old French, from Latin *contumēlia,* insult, reproach.] —**con·tu·me'li·ous** (kŏn'tōō-mē'lē-əs) *adj.* —**con'tu·me'li·ous·ly** *adv.*

con·tuse (kən-tōōz', -tyōōz') *tr.v.* **-tused, -tus·ing.** To injure without breaking the skin; to bruise. [Middle English *contusen,* from Old French *contuser,* from Latin *contundere,* to beat, pound : *com-* (intensive) + *tundere,* to beat.] —**con·tu'sion** *n.*

co·nun·drum (kə-nŭn'drəm) *n.* **1.** A riddle in which a question is answered by a pun. **2.** A baffling problem. [Orig. unknown.]

con·va·lesce (kŏn'və-lĕs') *intr.v.* **-lesced, -lesc·ing.** To regain health and strength after illness or injury; recuperate. [Latin *convalēscere* : *com-* (intensive) + *valēre,* to be strong or well.]

con·va·les·cence (kŏn'və-lĕs'əns) *n.* **1.** Gradual return to health and strength after illness or injury. **2.** The time needed for convalescing.

con·va·les·cent (kŏn'və-lĕs'ənt) *adj.* **1.** Of or for convalescence: *a convalescent home.* **2.** Gradually returning to health and strength after illness or injury. —*n.* A convalescent patient.

con·vec·tion (kən-vĕk'shən) *n.* **1.** The act or process of transmitting or conveying. **2.** *Physics.* **a.** The transfer of heat by fluid motion between regions of unequal density that result from nonuniform heating. **b.** Fluid motion caused by an external force such as gravity. [Late Latin *convectiō,* from *convehere,* to carry together : *com-,* together + *vehere,* to carry.] —**con·vec'tion·al** *adj.* —**con·vec'tive** *adj.*

con·vene (kən-vēn') *v.* **-vened, -ven·ing.** —*intr.v.* To assemble, usu. for an official purpose; meet formally: *Congress will convene next month.* —*tr.v.* To cause to assemble; convoke: *The governor convened the legislature.* —See Syns at **gather.** [Middle English *convenen,* from Old French *convenir,* to come together, from Latin *convenīre* : *com-,* together + *venīre,* to come.] —**con·ven'a·ble** *adj.* —**con·ven'er** *n.*

con·ven·ience (kən-vēn'yəns) *n.* **1.** The condition or quality of being convenient; suitability or handiness: *the convenience of traveling by airplane.* **2.** Personal comfort; material advantage: *a limousine provided for his convenience.* **3.** Anything that increases comfort or makes work less difficult: *a kitchen with all the modern conveniences.* *"If one's own car is a convenience, everybody else's is a nuisance"* (J. W. Krutch). **4.** *Brit.* A lavatory. —**idiom. at (one's) convenience.** When it is convenient for one.

con·ven·ient (kən-vēn'yənt) *adj.* **1.** Suited to one's comfort, needs, or purpose: *a convenient closet.* **2.** Easy to reach; accessible: *a convenient location; a home convenient to the shopping center.* [Middle English, from Latin *convenīre,* to be suitable.] —**con·ven'ient·ly** *adv.*

    Syns: 1. convenient, appropriate, fit[1], good, suitable, useful *adj.* Core meaning: Suited to one's end or purpose (*a convenient excuse*). **2. convenient, accessible, handy, nearby** *adj.* **Core meaning:** Within easy reach (*a convenient location for the desk*).

con·vent (kŏn′vənt, -vĕnt′) *n.* **1.** A community of nuns. **2.** A building occupied by nuns; a nunnery. [Middle English *covent*, from Old French, from Medieval Latin *conventus*, from Latin, a coming together, assembly, from *convenīre*, to come together, convene.]

con·ven·ti·cle (kən-vĕn′tǐ-kəl) *n.* A religious meeting, esp. a secret or illegal one, as those held by Dissenters in England and Scotland in the 16th and 17th cent. [Middle English, from Latin *conventiculum*, a place of meeting, dim. of *conventus*, assembly.]

con·ven·tion (kən-vĕn′shən) *n.* **1.** A formal assembly or meeting: *a teachers' convention; a constitutional convention.* **2.** A widely accepted practice; custom: *the convention of a handshake to seal a bargain.* **3.** A formal agreement or compact, as between nations: *the Geneva Conventions on treatment of war prisoners.* **4.** A widely used and accepted device or technique, as in drama, literature, or painting: *the theatrical convention of the "aside."* [Middle English *convencioun*, from Old French *convention*, from Latin *conventiō*, assembly, from *convenīre*, to come together, convene.]

con·ven·tion·al (kən-vĕn′shə-nəl) *adj.* **1.** Following accepted practice, customs, or taste: *a conventional greeting; a conventional plan for a house.* **2.** Using means other than nuclear weapons or energy. **—con·ven′tion·al·ism** *n.*

con·ven·tion·al·i·ty (kən-vĕn′shə-năl′ĭ-tē) *n., pl.* **-ties.** **1.** The state, quality, or character of being conventional. **2.** A conventional act, principle, or practice. **3. the conventionalities.** The rules of conventional social behavior.

con·verge (kən-vûrj′) *v.* **-verged, -verg·ing.** **—intr.v.** **1.** To approach the same point from different directions; come together in one place: *The three roads converged.* **2.** To tend or move toward union or toward a common conclusion or result. **3.** *Math.* To approach a limit. **—tr.v.** To cause to converge. [Late Latin *convergere*, to incline together : Latin *com-*, together + *vergere*, to turn, incline.]

con·ver·gence (kən-vûr′jəns) *n.* Also **con·ver·gen·cy** (-jən-sē) *pl.* **-cies.** **1.** The act, condition, quality, or fact of converging. **2.** *Math.* The property or manner of approaching a limit such as a point, line, surface, or value. **3.** The point or degree of converging. **4.** *Physiol.* The coordinated turning of the eyes inward to focus on a nearby point. **5.** *Biol.* The adaptive evolution of superficially similar structures, such as the wings of birds and insects, in unrelated species subjected to similar environments.

con·ver·gent (kən-vûr′jənt) *adj.* Tending to converge; merging: *convergent forces; convergent paths.*

con·ver·sant (kən-vûr′-sənt, kŏn′vər-) *adj.* Familiar, as by study or experience: *conversant with medieval history.* — See Syns at **aware.** **—con·ver′sant·ly** *adv.*

con·ver·sa·tion (kŏn′vər-sā′shən) *n.* A spoken exchange between people of thoughts and feelings.

con·ver·sa·tion·al (kŏn′vər-sā′shə-nəl) *adj.* **1.** Of, pertaining to, or in the style of conversation: *in a normal conversational tone.* **2.** Adept at or given to conversation. **—con′ver·sa′tion·al·ly** *adv.*

con·ver·sa·tion·al·ist (kŏn′vər-sā′shə-nə-lĭst) *n.* A person given to or skilled in conversation.

conversation piece. **1.** A kind of genre painting, esp. popular in the 18th cent., depicting a group of fashionable people. **2.** An unusual object that arouses comment.

con·verse¹ (kən-vûrs′) *intr.v.* **-versed, -vers·ing.** To engage in conversation; talk: *converse about family matters.* **—n.** (kŏn′vûrs′). Conversation. [Middle English *conversen*, to dwell, associate with, from Old French *converser*, from Latin *conversārī*, to associate with : *com-*, with + *versārī*, to live, occupy oneself, from *vertere*, to turn.]

con·verse² (kŏn′vûrs′) *n.* **1.** The opposite or reverse of something: *Dark is the converse of light.* **2.** *Logic.* Either of a pair of conditionals in which the hypothesis and conclusion of one are, respectively, the conclusion and hypothesis of the other. **—adj.** (kən-vûrs′, kŏn′vûrs′). Opposite; contrary: *a converse statement.* [From Latin *convertere*, to turn around.] **—con·verse′ly** (kən-vûrs′lē) *adv.*

con·ver·sion (kən-vûr′zhən, -shən) *n.* **1.** The act or process of changing a thing into another form, substance, or product: *the conversion of electricity to heat.* **2.** A change from one use or purpose to another: *the conversion of an ocean liner into a museum.* **3.** A change in which a person adopts a new religion or new beliefs: *the boy's conversion to Catholicism.* **4.** *Law.* **a.** The unlawful appropriation of another's property. **b.** The changing of real property to personal property or vice versa. **5.** *Logic.* The interchange of the subject and predicate of a proposition. **6.** *Football.* A score made on a try for a point or points after a touchdown. **—con·ver′sion·al** *adj.*

con·vert (kən-vûrt′) *tr.v.* **1.** To change into another form, substance, or condition; transform; transmute: *convert water into ice; convert carbon dioxide into sugar.* **2.** To persuade or induce to adopt a particular religion, faith, or belief: *convert the Indians to Christianity.* **3.** To change from one use, function, or purpose to another; adapt to a new or different purpose: *convert a home into a library.* **4.** To exchange for something of equal value: *convert dollars into francs; convert bonds into cash.* **5.** *Finance.* To exchange (a security, bond, etc.) by substituting an equivalent of another form. **6.** To express (a quantity) in alternative units: *convert 100 yards into meters.* **7.** *Logic.* To transform (a proposition) by conversion. **8.** *Law.* **a.** To appropriate without right (another's property) to one's own use. **b.** To change (property) from real to personal, from joint to separate, or vice versa. **—intr.v.** **1.** To be converted: *Electricity converts into other forms of energy.* **2.** *Football.* To score a point or points after a touchdown. **—n.** (kŏn′vûrt′). A person who has adopted a new religion or belief. [Middle English *converten*, from Old French *convertir*, from Medieval Latin *convertere*, from Latin, to turn around, transform : *com-* (intensive) + *vertere*, to turn.]

con·vert·er (kən-vûr′tər) *n.* Also **con·ver·tor.** **1.** Someone or something that converts. **2.** A mechanical device that changes alternating current to direct current or vice versa. **3.** An electronic device that changes the frequency of a radio signal. **4.** A device that transforms information from one code to another.

con·vert·i·ble (kən-vûr′tə-bəl) *adj.* **1.** Capable of being converted. **2.** Having a top that may be folded back or removed, as an automobile. **3.** *Finance.* Capable of being lawfully exchanged for gold or another currency: *dollars convertible into pounds.* **—n.** **1.** A convertible automobile. **2.** Something that can be converted. **—con·vert′i·bil′i·ty** or **con·vert′i·ble·ness** *n.* **—con·vert′i·bly** *adv.*

convertible

con·ver·tor (kən-vûr′tər) *n.* Var. of **converter.**

con·vex (kŏn-vĕks′, kŏn′vĕks′) *adj.* Having a surface that curves or bulges outward, as the outer boundary of a circle or sphere. [Latin *convexus*, arched, convex.] **—con·vex′ly** *adv.*

con·vex·i·ty (kŏn-vĕk′sĭ-tē) *n., pl.* **-ties.** **1.** The condition of being convex. **2.** A convex surface, body, part, or line.

con·vex·o-con·cave (kŏn-vĕk′sō-kŏn-kāv′) *adj.* Having greater convex than concave curvature: *a convexo-concave lens.*

con·vey (kən-vā′) *tr.v.* **1.** To take or carry from one place to another; to transport: *A helicopter conveyed us to the city.* **2.** To serve as a means of transmission for; transmit: *Cables convey electrical power.* **3.** To make known; communicate; impart: *Words convey meaning.* **4.** *Law.* To transfer ownership of or title to. [Middle English *conveien*, from Old French *conveier*, from Medieval Latin *conviāre*, to go with, escort : Latin *com-*, with + *via*, way.] **—con·vey′a·ble** *adj.*

con·vey·ance (kən-vā′əns) *n.* **1.** The act of transporting, transmitting, or communicating. **2.** A means of conveying, esp. a vehicle such as an automobile or bus. **3.** *Law.* **a.** The transfer of title to property from one person to another. **b.** The document by which this transfer is effected.

con·vey·anc·ing (kən-vā′ən-sĭng) *n.* The branch of legal practice dealing with the conveyance of property or real estate. —**con·vey′anc·er** *n.*

con·vey·er or **con·vey·or** (kən-vā′ər) *n.* **1.** Someone or something that conveys. **2.** A mechanical device, such as a continuous moving belt, that transports materials or packages from one place to another.

con·vict (kən-vĭkt′) *tr.v.* To find or prove (someone) guilty of an offense, esp. in a court of law. —*n.* (kŏn′vĭkt′). **1.** A person found or declared guilty of an offense or crime. **2.** A person serving a sentence of imprisonment. [Middle English *convicten*, from Latin *convincere*, to prove guilty, refute.]

con·vic·tion (kən-vĭk′shən) *n.* **1.** The act or process of finding or proving guilty. **2.** The condition of being convicted. **3.** The act or process of convincing or persuading. **4.** The condition of being convinced or persuaded. **5.** A strong opinion or belief: *act according to your convictions.* —See Syns at **belief** and **certainty.**

con·vince (kən-vĭns′) *tr.v.* **-vinced, -vinc·ing.** To cause (someone) to believe or feel certain; persuade. [Latin *convincere*, to overcome, prove guilty : *com-* (intensive) + *vincere*, to conquer.] —**con·vinc′er** *n.*

con·vinc·ing (kən-vĭn′sĭng) *adj.* **1.** Serving to convince; persuasive: *a convincing argument.* **2.** Believable; plausible: *a convincing story.* —**con·vinc′ing·ly** *adv.* —**con·vinc′-ing·ness** *n.*

con·viv·i·al (kən-vĭv′ē-əl) *adj.* Fond of feasting, drinking, and good company; sociable; jovial: *a convivial man.* [Late Latin *convīviālis*, from Latin *convīvium*, "a living together," banquet : *com-*, together + *vīvere*, to live.] —**con·viv′i·al′i·ty** (-vĭv′ē-ăl′ĭ-tē) *n.* —**con·viv′i·al·ly** *adv.*

con·vo·ca·tion (kŏn′və-kā′shən) *n.* **1.** The act of convoking or calling together. **2.** A summoned assembly, as of clergymen and laymen. —**con′vo·ca′tion·al** *adj.*

con·voke (kən-vōk′) *tr.v.* **-voked, -vok·ing.** To call together; cause to assemble; convene: *The President convoked the new Congress.* —See Syns at **gather.** [Old French *convoquer*, from Latin *convocāre*, to call together : *com-*, together + *vocāre*, to call.] —**con·vok′er** *n.*

con·vo·lute (kŏn′və-lōōt′) *adj.* Rolled or folded together with one part over another; twisted; coiled: *the convolute shape of a conch shell.* —*v.* **-lut·ed, -lut·ing.** —*tr.v.* To coil around; twist or wind around. —*intr.v.* To coil up. [Latin *convolvere*, to roll together : *com-*, together + *volvere*, to roll.] —**con′vo·lute′ly** *adv.*

con·vo·lut·ed (kŏn′və-lōō′tĭd) *adj.* **1.** Having convolutions; coiled; twisted: *a convoluted path.* **2.** Intricate; complicated: *a convoluted argument.*

con·vo·lu·tion (kŏn′və-lōō′shən) *n.* **1.** A tortuous winding, folding, or twisting together. **2.** One of the convex folds of the surface of the brain.

con·vol·vu·lus (kən-vŏl′vyə-ləs) *n.,* *pl.* **-lus·es** or **-li** (-lī′). Any of several trailing or twining plants of the genus *Convolvulus,* which includes the bindweeds. [Latin *convolvulus,* bindweed, from *convolvere,* to interweave.]

con·voy (kŏn′voi′, kən-voi′) *tr.v.* To accompany as a protective escort: *The destroyers convoyed the aircraft carrier.* —*n.* (kŏn′voi′). **1.** The act of convoying or the condition of being convoyed. **2. a.** A group of ships or vehicles, protected on their way by an armed escort. **b.** The escort itself. **3.** A column of military trucks, tanks, etc. **4.** A group, as of vehicles or people, traveling together for convenience. [Middle English *convoyen,* from Old French *convoier,* to convey.]

con·vulse (kən-vŭls′) *tr.v.* **-vulsed, -vuls·ing. 1.** To disturb or agitate violently: *"At that moment Darwin was convulsing society"* (Henry Adams). **2.** To cause to laugh uproariously: *His quips convulsed the audience.* **3.** To cause (a person or animal) to have convulsions. [Latin *convulsus,* past part. of *convellere,* to pull violently : *com-* (intensive) + *vellere,* to pull.]

con·vul·sion (kən-vŭl′shən) *n.* **1.** Often **convulsions.** A violent involuntary muscular contraction or an irregular series of such contractions; a fit; seizure. **2.** A violent turmoil

or upheaval: *convulsions of the earth's crust.* **3.** An uncontrolled fit of laughter.

con·vul·sive (kən-vŭl′sĭv) *adj.* **1.** Of or like a convulsion or convulsions. **2.** Having or causing convulsions. —**con·vul′sive·ly** *adv.* —**con·vul′sive·ness** *n.*

co·ny (kō′nē, kŭn′ē) *n.,* *pl.* **-nies.** Also **co·ney** *pl.* **-neys. 1.** A rabbit, esp. the common European rabbit *Oryctolagus cuniculus.* **2.** The fur of a rabbit. **3.** A rabbitlike animal, such as the hyrax. [Middle English *coni(n)g,* from Old French *conin,* from Latin *cunīculus,* rabbit.]

coo (kōō) *n.* **1.** The low, murmuring sound made by a pigeon or dove. **2.** A sound similar to a coo. —*intr.v.* **1.** To make the characteristic murmuring sound of a pigeon or dove. **2.** To talk lovingly or fondly. [Imit.]

cook (kōōk) *tr.v.* **1.** To prepare (food) for eating by applying heat. **2.** To prepare or treat by heating. —*intr.v.* **1.** To prepare food for eating by applying heat. **2.** To undergo cooking. **3.** *Slang.* To happen, develop, or take place: *What's cooking in town?* —*phrasal verb.* **cook up.** *Informal.* To invent; concoct: *cook up an excuse.* —*n.* A person who prepares food for eating. [Middle English *coken,* from *cok(e),* a cook, from Old English *cōc,* from Late Latin *cōcus,* from Latin *coquus.*]

cook·er·y (kōōk′ə-rē) *n.,* *pl.* **-ies. 1.** The art or practice of preparing food. **2.** A place for cooking.

cook·ie or **cook·y** (kōōk′ē) *n.,* *pl.* **-ies.** A small, usu. flat cake made from sweetened dough. [Dutch *koekje,* dim. of *koek,* cake, from Middle Dutch *koeke.*]

cook·out (kōōk′out′) *n.* A meal cooked and eaten outdoors.

cook·y (kōōk′ē) *n.* Var. of **cookie.**

cool (kōōl) *adj.* **-er, -est. 1.** Moderately cold; neither warm nor very cold: *cool weather.* **2.** Giving or allowing relief from heat: *a cool breeze; a cool blouse.* **3.** Calm; unexcited: *a cool head in a crisis.* **4.** Indifferent or disdainful; unenthusiastic: *a cool reception.* **5.** Calmly audacious or bold; impudent. **6.** Designating or characteristic of colors, such as blue and green, that produce the impression of coolness. **7.** *Slang.* Excellent; first-rate; superior. **8.** *Informal.* Entire; full: *He lost a cool million.* —See Syns at **cold.** —*tr.v.* **1.** To make less warm: *cool a room by opening the windows.* **2.** To make less ardent, intense, or zealous: *cool one's passion.* —*intr.v.* **1.** To become less warm: *Let the pie cool before serving.* **2.** To become less calm: *Her anger cooled.* —*phrasal verb.* **cool off.** To become less heated or excited. —*n.* **1.** Anything that is cool or moderately cold: *the cool of early morning.* **2.** *Slang.* Calmness of mind; composure: *lost his cool.* —*idioms.* **cool it.** *Slang.* To calm down; relax. **cool (one's) heels.** *Informal.* To be kept waiting. [Middle English *col,* from Old English *cōl.*] —**cool′ly** *adv.* —**cool′ness** *n.*

cool·ant (kōō′lənt) *n.* Something that cools, esp. a fluid that circulates through a machine or over some of its parts in order to draw off heat.

cool·er (kōō′lər) *n.* **1.** A device or container that cools or keeps something cool. **2.** *Slang.* Jail.

cool-head·ed (kōōl′hĕd′ĭd) *adj.* Not easily excited or flustered; calm. —**cool′-head′ed·ly** *adv.* —**cool′-head′ed·ness** *n.*

coo·lie (kōō′lē) *n.* An unskilled Oriental laborer.

coon (kōōn) *n.* *Informal.* A raccoon. [Short for RACCOON.]

coon·skin (kōōn′skĭn′) *n.* The pelt of a raccoon.

coop (kōōp) *n.* **1.** A cage for poultry or small animals. **2.** *Slang.* Any place of confinement. —*tr.v.* To confine; shut in: *He has been cooped up in the house all day.* —*idiom.* **fly the coop.** *Slang.* To escape. [Middle English *c(o)upe,* wicker basket, chicken coop, prob. from Middle Low German *kūpe,* basket.]

co-op (kō′ŏp′, kō-ŏp′) *n.* A cooperative.

coo·per (kōō′pər) *n.* A person who makes wooden barrels, tubs, and casks. —*tr.v.* To repair or make (casks or barrels). —*intr.v.* To work as a cooper. [Middle English *couper,* prob. from Middle Low German *kūpe,* barrel, coop.]

coo·per·age (kōō′pər-ĭj) *n.* A cooper's work, shop, or products.

co·op·er·ate (kō-ŏp′ə-rāt′) *intr.v.* **-at·ed, -at·ing.** To work or act with another or others toward a common end or purpose. [Latin *cooperārī* : *co-,* together + *operārī,* to work.] —**co·op′er·a′tor** *n.*

co·op·er·a·tion (kō-ŏp′ə-rā′shən) *n.* **1.** Joint action: *This* *treaty will promote international cooperation.* **2.** Assistance; support: *The principal sought the cooperation of the students.* **3.** Willingness to cooperate: *Please show more cooperation.*

co·op·er·a·tive (kō-ŏp′ər-ə-tĭv, -ə-rā′tĭv) *adj.* **1.** Done in cooperation with others: *a cooperative effort; cooperative farming.* **2.** Willing to help or cooperate: *a cooperative patient.* —*n.* An enterprise, building, etc., owned jointly by those who use its facilities or services: *a consumers' cooperative.* Also called **co-op.** —**co·op′er·a·tive·ly** *adv.* —**co·op′er·a·tive·ness** *n.*

co-opt (kō-ŏpt′) *tr.v.* **1.** To elect as a fellow member of a group or body: *The school board co-opted Dr. Smith.* **2.** To appropriate or imitate for one's own purposes: *The administration co-opted the students' demands.* **3.** To win over through subtle bribery: *The students claimed that the administration was trying to co-opt them.* **4.** To take over (an independent minority, movement, etc.) through assimilation into an established group or culture. [Latin *cooptāre* : *co-*, together + *optāre*, to choose, elect.] —**co′-op·ta′tion** (kō-ŏp-tā′shən) *n.* —**co-op′ta·tive** (-tə-tĭv) *adj.*

co·or·di·nate (kō-ôr′dn-ĭt, -āt′) *n.* Also **co-or·di·nate.** **1.** Someone or something that is equal in importance, rank, or degree. **2.** *Math.* **a.** One of a set of numbers that determines the location of a point in a space of a given dimension. **b.** Any of a set of two or more magnitudes used to determine the position of a point, line, curve, or plane. —*adj.* **1.** Of equal importance, rank, or degree; not subordinate. **2.** Of or involving coordination. **3.** Of or based on coordinates. —*v.* (kō-ôr′dn-āt′) **-nat·ed, -nat·ing.** —*tr.v.* **1.** To place in the same order, class, or rank. **2.** To cause to work together efficiently in a common action, cause, or effort: *The nervous system coordinates all the body's activities.* —*intr.v.* To work together harmoniously: *When an acrobat's muscles no longer coordinate perfectly, he is through.* [Back-formation from COORDINATION.] —**co·or′di·nate·ly** *adv.* —**co·or′di·nate·ness** *n.* —**co·or′di·na′tive** *adj.*

coordinate conjunction. A conjunction that connects two grammatical elements having identical construction, for example, *and* in *books and pencils.*

co·or·di·na·tion (kō-ôr′dn-ā′shən) *n.* **1.** An act of coordinating or a condition of being coordinated. **2.** The organized action of muscles or groups of muscles in the performance of complicated movements or tasks. [French, from Late Latin *coōrdinātiō*, arrangement in the same order : Latin *co-*, same + *ōrdināre*, to arrange in order, from *ōrdō*, order.]

co·or·di·na·tor (kō-ôr′dn-ā′tər) *n.* **1.** Someone or something that coordinates. **2.** *Gram.* A form that connects a word or word group.

coot (kōōt) *n.* **1.** Any of several dark-gray water birds of the genus *Fulica,* esp. *F. americana,* of the New World, and *F. atra,* of the Old World. **2.** *Informal.* A foolish old man. [Middle English *cote,* prob. from Middle Dutch *coet.*]

coot

coo·tie (kōō′tē) *n. Slang.* A louse that is a parasite on the skin of human beings. [Prob. from Malay *kutu,* louse.]

cop (kŏp) *n. Informal.* A police officer; policeman. —*tr.v.* **copped, cop·ping.** *Slang.* **1.** To steal. **2.** To seize; catch. —**idioms. cop a plea.** *Slang.* To plead guilty. **cop out.** *Slang.* To fail or refuse to commit oneself: *Don't cop out on the pollution issue.* [Short for *copper,* policeman, from *cop, cap,* to catcn, prob. from Dutch *kapen.*]

co·pa·cet·ic or **co·pa·set·ic** (kō′pə-sĕt′ĭk) *adj.* Also **co·pe·set·ic** or **co·pe·set·tic.** *Slang.* Excellent; first-rate. [Orig. unknown.]

co·pal (kō′pəl) *n.* A brittle, aromatic, yellow to red resin of recent or fossil origin, obtained from various tropical trees and used in varnishes. [Spanish, from Nahuatl *copalli,* resin.]

co·pe·set·ic or **co·pe·set·tic** (kō′pə-sĕt′ĭk) *adj.* Var. of **copacetic.**

cope[1] (kōp) *intr.v.* **coped, cop·ing.** **1.** To contend or strive, esp. successfully: *coped with heavy traffic.* **2.** *Informal.* To contend with difficulties and act to overcome them. [Middle English *co(u)pen,* to contend with, from Old French *couper,* to strike, from *coup,* a blow, from Late Latin *colpus,* from Latin *colaphus,* from Greek *kolaphos.*]

Usage: cope. In formal American usage *cope* is typically used with *with: cope with unhealthy living conditions.* This verb is also used without the preposition *with* in British English and in informal American English to mean to get along satisfactorily by overcoming obstacles: *One must be able to cope.*

cope[2] (kōp) *n.* **1.** A long cloak, cape, or mantle worn by priests or bishops. **2.** Something that provides covering in the form of an arch, vault, or canopy: *Over them vast and high extended the cope of a cedar.* **3.** The top, as of a flask or mold. —*tr.v.* **coped, cop·ing.** **1.** To cover or dress in a cope. **2.** To provide with coping, as a wall. [Middle English *cope,* from Old English *(cantel)cāp,* from Late Latin *cāpa,* cloak, head covering, from Latin *caput,* head.]

co·peck (kō′pĕk′) *n.* Var. of **kopeck.**

cop·i·er (kŏp′ē-ər) *n.* **1.** Any of various office machines that make copies. **2.** A copyist or transcriber.

co·pi·lot (kō′pī′lət) *n.* The second or relief pilot of an aircraft.

cop·ing (kō′pĭng) *n.* The top part of a wall or roof, usu. slanted for drainage. [From COPE (vestment).]

coping saw. A narrow, short-bladed saw set in an open frame, used for cutting designs in wood.

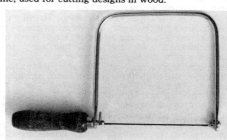

coping saw

co·pi·ous (kō′pē-əs) *adj.* **1.** Large in quantity; abundant: *copious footnotes; a copious rainfall.* **2.** Abounding in matter, thoughts, or words; wordy: *"I found our speech copious without order, and energetic without rules"* (Samuel Johnson). —See Syns at **generous.** [Middle English, from Old French *copieux,* from Latin *cōpiōsus,* from *cō-pia,* abundance.] —**co′pi·ous·ly** *adv.* —**co′pi·ous·ness** *n.*

co·pla·nar (kō-plā′nər) *adj.* Lying or occurring in the same plane: *coplanar points.*

co·pol·y·mer (kō-pŏl′ə-mər) *n.* A polymer of two or more different monomers.

co·pol·y·mer·ize (kō-pŏl′ə-mə-rīz′) *v.* **-ized, -iz·ing.** —*tr.v.* To polymerize (different monomers) together. —*intr.v.* To react to form a copolymer. —**co·pol′y·mer·i·za′tion** *n.*

cop-out (kŏp′out′) *n. Slang.* **1.** A failure or refusal to commit oneself. **2.** A person who cops out.

cop·per (kŏp′ər) *n.* **1.** *Symbol* **Cu** A ductile, malleable, reddish-brown metallic element that is an excellent conductor of heat and electricity and is widely used for electrical wiring, water piping, and corrosion-resistant parts either pure or in alloys such as brass and bronze. Atomic number 29; atomic weight 63.54; melting point 1,083°C; boiling point 2,595°C; specific gravity 8.96; valence 1, 2. **2.** A coin made of copper or a copper alloy. **3.** *Brit.* A large boiler or pot. **4.** A reddish brown. —*tr.v.* To coat or finish

ă pat	ā pay	â care	ä father	ĕ pet	ē be	hw which	ĭ pit	ī tie	î pier	ŏ pot	ō toe	ô paw, for	oi noise
ŏŏ took	ōō boot	ou out	th thin	*th* this	ŭ cut		û urge	zh vision	ə about, item, edible, gallop, circus

with a layer of copper. —*adj.* Reddish brown. [Middle English *coper*, from Old English *coper*, Latin *Cyprium (aes)*, "(metal) of Cyprus."] —**cop′per·y** *adj.*

cop·per·as (kŏp′ər-əs) *n.* A greenish, crystalline ferrous sulfate, $FeSO_4 \cdot 7H_2O$, used in the manufacture of fertilizers and inks and in water purification. [Middle English *coperose*, from Old French *co(u)perose*, from Medieval Latin *cup(e)rosa*, prob. short for *aqua cup(e)rosa*, "copper water."]

cop·per·head (kŏp′ər-hĕd′) *n.* **1.** A venomous snake, *Agkistrodon contortrix* (or *Ancistron contortrix*), of eastern United States, having reddish-brown markings. **2. Copperhead.** During the Civil War, a Northerner who sympathized with the South.

copperhead

cop·per·smith (kŏp′ər-smĭth′) *n.* A worker or manufacturer of objects in copper.

copper sulfate. A poisonous blue crystalline copper salt, $CuSO_4 \cdot 5H_2O$, used in agriculture, electroplating, and the manufacture of germicides. Also called **blue vitriol.**

cop·pice (kŏp′ĭs) *n. Brit.* A thicket; copse.

cop·ra (kŏp′rə) *n.* Dried coconut meat from which coconut oil is extracted. [Portuguese, from Malayalam *koppara*.]

cop·ro·lite (kŏp′rə-līt′) *n.* Fossilized excrement. [Greek *kopros*, dung + -LITE.]

copse (kŏps) *n.* A thicket of small trees or shrubs. [Short for *coppice*, Middle English *copice*, from Old French *co(u)peiz*, "cut wood," from *couper*, to cut, strike.]

Copt (kŏpt) *n.* **1.** A native of Egypt descended from ancient Egyptian stock. **2.** A member of the Coptic Church.

cop·ter (kŏp′tər) *n. Informal.* A helicopter.

Cop·tic Church (kŏp′tĭk). The Christian church of Egypt, adhering to the Monophysite doctrine.

cop·u·la (kŏp′yə-lə) *n., pl.* **-las** or **-lae** (-lē). A verb, usu. a form of *be*, that identifies the predicate of a sentence with the subject. [Latin *cōpula*, link, bond.]

cop·u·late (kŏp′yə-lāt′) *intr.v.* **-lat·ed, -lat·ing.** To engage in sexual intercourse. [From Latin *cōpulāre*, to link, from *cōpula*, link, bond.] —**cop′u·la′tion** *n.*

cop·u·la·tive (kŏp′yə-lā′tĭv, -lə-) *adj.* **1.** Serving to connect coordinate words or clauses: *a copulative conjunction.* **2.** Serving as a copula: *a copulative verb.* —*n.* A copulative word. —**cop′u·la′tive·ly** *adv.*

cop·y (kŏp′ē) *n., pl.* **-ies.** **1.** An imitation or reproduction of something original; a duplicate. **2.** One specimen or example of a printed text or picture: *an autographed copy of a novel.* **3.** A manuscript or other material to be set in type. **4.** Suitable source material, as for journalism: *Celebrities make good copy.* —*v.* **-ied, -y·ing.** —*tr.v.* **1.** To make a copy or copies of; transcribe; reproduce. **2.** To follow as a model or pattern; imitate: *copied her accent.* —*intr.v.* To make one or more copies or reproductions. [Middle English *copie*, from Old French, from Medieval Latin *cōpia*, transcript, from Latin, abundance, power.]

cop·y·book (kŏp′ē-bŏŏk′) *n.* A book of models of penmanship for imitation.

cop·y·cat (kŏp′ē-kăt′) *n.* A mimic; an imitator.

cop·y·right (kŏp′ē-rīt′) *n.* The legal right to exclusive publication, production, sale, or distribution of a literary, musical, dramatic, or artistic work. —*adj.* Also **cop′y·right·ed** (-rī′tĭd). Protected by copyright. —*tr.v.* To secure a copyright for.

cop·y·writ·er (kŏp′ē-rī′tər) *n.* One who writes copy, esp. for advertising.

coq au vin (kôk′ ō văn′). *French.* A hearty dish of chicken cooked in red wine.

co·quet (kō-kĕt′) *intr.v.* **-quet·ted, -quet·ting.** **1.** To flirt. **2.** To trifle or not take seriously; dally.

co·quet·ry (kō′kĭ-trē, kō-kĕt′rē) *n., pl.* **-ries.** Flirtation; dalliance.

co·quette (kō-kĕt′) *n.* A woman who flirts with men. [French, fem. of *coquet*, flirtatious man, dim. of *coq*, cock.] —**co·quet′tish** *adj.* —**co·quet′tish·ly** *adv.* —**co·quet′tish·ness** *n.*

cor·a·cle (kôr′ə-kəl, kŏr′-) *n.* A small boat made of waterproof material stretched over a wicker or wooden frame. [Earlier *corougle*, from Welsh *corwgl*.]

cor·a·coid (kôr′ə-koid′, kŏr′-) *n.* A bone or cartilage that projects from the scapula toward the sternum. [New Latin *coracoides*, "(bone) shaped like a crow's beak," from Greek *korax*, raven.]

cor·al (kôr′əl, kŏr′-) *n.* **1. a.** A hard, stony substance, often white, pink, or reddish, formed by the skeletons of tiny sea animals massed together in great numbers. **b.** One of the tiny animals that form this substance. **c.** A mass of this substance, often branched or rounded in shape. **2.** A yellowish pink or reddish orange. —*modifier: a coral bracelet.* —*adj.* Yellowish pink or reddish orange. [Middle English, from Old French, from Latin *coralium*, from Greek *korallion*.]

cor·al·line (kôr′ə-lĭn, -līn′, kŏr′-) *adj.* Of, consisting of, or resembling coral.

coral snake. Any of various venomous snakes of the genus *Micrurus*, of tropical America and the southern United States, that characteristically have brilliant red, black, and yellow banded markings.

cor·bel (kôr′bəl, -bĕl′) *n.* A bracket projecting from the face of a wall and used to support a cornice or an arch. —*tr.v.* **-beled** or **-belled, -bel·ing** or **-bel·ling.** To provide a corbel. [Middle English, from Old French, dim. of *corp*, raven, from Latin *corvus*.]

cord (kôrd) *n.* **1.** A string or small rope of twisted strands or fibers. **2.** An insulated, flexible electric wire fitted with a plug or plugs. **3.** *Anat.* Any structure resembling a cord: *spinal cord.* **4. a.** A raised rib on the surface of cloth. **b.** A fabric or cloth, such as corduroy, with such ribs. **5.** A unit of quantity for cut fuel wood, equal to 128 cubic feet in a stack measuring 4 by 4 by 8 feet. —*tr.v.* **1.** To fasten or bind with a cord. **2.** To furnish with a cord. **3.** To pile (wood) in cords. [Middle English, from Old French *corde*, from Latin *chorda*, catgut, cord, from Greek *khordē*.]

cord·age (kôr′dĭj) *n.* **1. a.** Cords or ropes in general. **b.** The ropes in the rigging of a ship. **2.** The amount of wood in an area, as measured in cords.

cor·date (kôr′dāt′) *adj.* Having a heart-shaped outline: *a cordate leaf.* [From New Latin *cordatus*, from Latin *cor*, heart.]

cord·ed (kôr′dĭd) *adj.* **1.** Tied or bound with cords. **2.** Ribbed or twilled, as corduroy. **3.** Stacked in cords, as firewood.

cor·dial (kôr′jəl) *adj.* Hearty; sincere: *cordial relations; a cordial welcome.* —See Syns at **amiable.** —*n.* **1.** A stimulant, such as a medicine or drink. **2.** A liqueur. [Middle English, of the heart, from Medieval Latin *cordiālis*, from Latin *cor*, heart.] —**cor′dial·ness** *n.* —**cor′dial·ly** *adv.*

cor·di·al·i·ty (kôr-jăl′ĭ-tē, kôr′jē-ăl′-) *n.* Heartiness; sincerity.

cor·dil·le·ra (kôr′dĭl-yâr′ə, kôr-dĭl′ər-ə) *n.* A chain of mountains, esp. the principal mountain range or system of a large land mass. [Spanish, from *cordilla*, dim. of *cuerda*, cord.]

cord·ite (kôr′dīt′) *n.* A smokeless explosive powder consisting of nitrocellulose, nitroglycerin, and petrolatum. [From CORD.]

cor·don (kôr′dn) *n.* **1.** A line of people, military posts, ships, etc., stationed around an area to enclose or guard it. **2.** A ribbon, usu. worn diagonally across the breast as a badge of honor or a decoration. —*tr.v.* To form a cordon around (an area) so as to prevent communication or contact: *cordon off the mountain path.* [French, from Old French, dim. of *corde*, cord.]

cor·do·van (kôr′də-vən) *n.* A fine-grained leather made originally of goatskin but now more frequently of split horsehide. —*modifier: cordovan shoes.* [Spanish *cordobán*, after *Córdoba*, Spain.]

cor·du·roy (kôr′də-roi′, kôr′də-roi′) *n.* **1.** A durable cut-pile fabric, usu. made of cotton, with vertical ribs or wales. **2. corduroys.** Corduroy trousers. —*modifier:* a corduroy suit. —*adj.* Made of logs laid crosswise on the ground: *a corduroy road.* [Orig. unknown.]

cord·wood (kôrd′wŏŏd′) *n.* Wood sold or cut and piled in cords.

core (kôr, kōr) *n.* **1.** The hard or fibrous central part of certain fruits, such as the apple or pear, containing the seeds. **2.** The innermost or most important part of anything; heart: *get right to the core of the problem.* **3.** *Electricity.* A soft iron rod inside a coil or transformer that intensifies and provides a path for the magnetic field produced by the windings. **4.** The central part of the earth. **5.** An internal computer memory. —See Syns at **heart**. —*tr.v.* **cored, cor·ing.** To remove the core of: *core apples.* [Middle English *coor*.]

CORE (kôr, kōr) *n.* Congress of Racial Equality.

co·re·op·sis (kôr′ē-ŏp′sĭs, kōr′-) *n.* Any of several plants of the genus *Coreopsis*, with daisylike yellow or variegated flowers. [New Latin, "resembling a bedbug" (from the shape of the seed) : Greek *koris*, bedbug + *opsis*, appearance.]

co·re·spon·dent (kō′rĭ-spŏn′dənt) *n.* *Law.* A person charged with having committed adultery with the defendant in a suit for divorce. [CO- + RESPONDENT.]

co·ri·an·der (kôr′ē-ăn′dər, kōr′-) *n.* **1.** An herb, *Coriandrum sativum,* that is widely cultivated for its aromatic seeds. **2.** The dried ripe seeds of the coriander, used esp. as a condiment. [Middle English *coriandre,* from Old French, from Latin *coriandrum,* from Greek *koriandron.*]

Co·rin·thi·an (kə-rĭn′thē-ən) *adj.* **1.** Of or pertaining to ancient Corinth. **2.** Pertaining to or designating the most ornate of the three classical orders of architecture, characterized by a slender fluted column with an ornate bell-shaped capital decorated with designs of acanthus leaves. —*n.* **Corinthians.** See table at **Bible.**

Corinthian

corn¹

co·ri·um (kôr′ē-əm, kōr′-) *n., pl.* **-ri·a** (-ē-ə). The layer of the skin beneath the epidermis, containing nerve endings, sweat glands, and blood and lymph vessels. Also called **derma** and **dermis.** [Latin, skin, hide.]

cork (kôrk) *n.* **1.** The light, porous, elastic outer bark of the cork oak. **2.** Something made of cork, esp. a bottle stopper. **3.** A bottle stopper made of other material, such as plastic. **4.** *Bot.* A tissue of dead cells that forms on the outer side of the cambium in the stems of woody plants. —*tr.v.* **1.** To stop or seal with or as if with a cork. **2.** To hold back; restrain or check. [Middle English, from Dutch *kurk* or Low German *korck,* from Spanish *alcorque,* cork sole or shoe.]

cork·er (kôr′kər) *n. Slang.* Someone or something that is remarkable or astounding.

cork oak. An evergreen oak tree, *Quercus suber,* of the Mediterranean region, with porous outer bark that is the source of cork.

cork·screw (kôrk′skrōō′) *n.* **1.** A device for drawing corks from bottles, consisting of a pointed metal spiral attached to a handle. **2.** A spiral. —*adj.* Spiral in shape; twisted. —*tr.v.* To cause to move in a spiral course. —*intr.v.* To move in a spiral course.

cork·y (kôr′kē) *adj.* **-i·er, -i·est. 1.** Of or like cork. **2.** *Informal.* Lively; buoyant.

corm (kôrm) *n.* A rounded underground stem, such as that of the gladiolus, similar to a bulb but without scales. [Greek *kormos,* a trimmed tree trunk, from *keirein,* to shear.]

cor·mo·rant (kôr′mər-ənt) *n.* **1.** Any of several widely distributed aquatic birds of the genus *Phalacrocorax,* with dark plumage, webbed feet, a hooked bill, and a distensible pouch. **2.** A greedy or rapacious person. [Middle English *cormeraunt,* from Old French *cormoran* : *corp,* raven, from Latin *corvus* + *marenc,* of the sea, from Latin *marīnus,* marine.]

corn¹ (kôrn) *n.* **1. a.** Any of several varieties of a tall, widely cultivated cereal plant, *Zea mays,* bearing seeds or kernels on large ears. **b.** The seeds or kernels of this plant. **c.** The ears of this plant. Also called **Indian corn** and **maize. 2.** *Brit.* **a.** Any of several cereal plants producing edible seed, as wheat, rye, oats, or barley. **b.** The seeds of such a plant or crop; grain. **3.** A seed or fruit of various cereal plants. **4.** *Slang.* Anything considered trite, outdated, melodramatic, or too sentimental. —*tr.v.* **1.** To preserve and season with granulated salt. **2.** To preserve in brine. [Middle English, from Old English.]

corn² (kôrn) *n.* A horny thickening of the skin, usu. on or near a toe, resulting from pressure or friction. [Middle English *corne,* from Old French *corne,* corn on the foot, horn, from Latin *cornū,* horn.]

Corn Belt. A region in the midwestern United States where the chief products are corn and corn-fed livestock.

corn borer. 1. The larva of a moth, *Pyrausta nubilalis,* native to the Old World, that feeds on and destroys corn and other plants. **2.** Any of various similar insect larvae that infest corn.

corn bread. Also **corn-bread** (kôrn′brĕd′). A kind of bread made from cornmeal.

corn·cob (kôrn′kŏb′) *n.* The woody core of an ear of corn, on which the kernels grow.

corn·crib (kôrn′krĭb′) *n.* A structure for storing and drying ears of corn, with slatted sides for ventilation.

cor·ne·a (kôr′nē-ə) *n.* The tough, transparent membrane that forms the forward portion of the outer coat of the eyeball, covering the iris and lens. [Medieval Latin *cornea* (*tēla*), "horny (tissue)," from Latin *cornū,* horn.] —**cor′ne·al** *adj.*

cor·nel (kôr′nəl, -nĕl′) *n.* Any of various shrubs, trees, or plants of the genus.*Cornus,* which includes the dogwoods. [From German *Kornel(beere),* cornel (berry), Latin *cornus,* cornel tree.]

cor·ner (kôr′nər) *n.* **1. a.** The position at which two lines or surfaces meet: *the upper left-hand corner of the page.* **b.** The area formed by the intersection of two lines, edges, surfaces, etc.: *the corner of the room.* **2.** The place where two roads or streets meet: *Meet me at the corner of Oak and Pine.* **3.** A region, esp. a remote one: *from all corners of the world.* **4.** A threatening or embarrassing position, esp. one from which escape is difficult or impossible: *got himself a corner by accepting two invitations for the same evening.* **5.** A guard or decoration fitted on various kinds of corners, as of a bookbinding. **6.** A monopoly of a stock or commodity, created by purchasing all or most of the available supply in order to raise its price. —*modifier:* a *corner drugstore.* —*tr.v.* **1.** To drive into a threatening or difficult position: *The dog cornered the cat.* **2.** To gain control of: *He cornered the market on wheat.* **3.** To put or locate in a corner. —*intr.v.* **1.** To come together or be situated on or at a corner. **2.** To turn, as at a corner: *The truck corners poorly.* —*idiom.* **cut corners.** *Informal.* To reduce expenses; economize. [Middle English, from Old French *cornere,* from Latin *cornū,* horn, extremity.]

cor·ner·back (kôr′nər-băk′) *n.* Also **corner back.** *Football.* Either of two defensive halfbacks stationed a short distance behind the linebackers and relatively near the sidelines.

cor·ner·stone (kôr′nər-stōn′) *n.* Also **corner stone. 1. a.** A stone at one of the corners of a building's foundation. **b.** Such a stone often inscribed and set in place with a special ceremony. **2.** The fundamental basis of something: *Liberty is the cornerstone of the republic.*

cor·ner·wise (kôr′nər-wīz′) *adv.* Also **cor·ner·ways** (-wāz′). **1.** So as to form a corner. **2.** From corner to corner; on a diagonal.

cor·net (kôr-nět′, kôr′nĭt) n. **1.** A musical wind instrument of the trumpet class, having three valves operated by pistons. **2.** A piece of paper twisted into a cone and used to hold small wares such as candy. **3.** A headdress, often cone-shaped, worn by women in the 12th and 13th cent. [Middle English, from Old French, dim. of corn, horn, from Latin cornū.]

cor·net·ist (kôr-nět′ĭst) n. Also **cor·net·tist.** One who plays a cornet.

corn-fed (kôrn′fĕd′) adj. **1.** Fed on corn. **2.** Slang. Healthy and strong but unsophisticated.

corn·flow·er (kôrn′flou′ər) n. A garden plant, Centaurea cyanus, native to Eurasia, with blue, purple, pink, or white flowers. Also called **bachelor's-button, bluebottle.** [So called because it is found in cornfields.]

cor·nice (kôr′nĭs) n. **1.** Archit. **a.** A horizontal molded projection that crowns or completes a building or wall. **b.** The uppermost part of an entablature. **2.** The ornamental molding at the top of the walls of a room. **3.** An ornamental horizontal molding or frame used to conceal curtain rods, picture hooks, etc. —tr.v. **-niced, -nic·ing.** To supply or decorate with a cornice. [Old French, from Italian, prob. from Greek korōnis, curved line, from korōnos, curved.]

cornice

Cor·nish (kôr′nĭsh) adj. Of or pertaining to Cornwall, England, or Cornish. —n. The extinct Celtic language of Cornwall.

corn·meal (kôrn′mēl′) n. Also **corn meal.** Coarse meal made from ground corn kernels. Also called **Indian meal.** —modifier: cornmeal mush.

corn pone (pōn). Southern U.S. Corn bread made without milk or eggs.

corn·stalk (kôrn′stôk′) n. A stalk of corn, esp. maize.

corn·starch (kôrn′stärch′) n. **1.** Starch prepared from corn. **2.** A purified starchy flour made from corn, used as a thickener in cooking.

corn sugar. A sugar, dextrose.

cor·nu·co·pi·a (kôr′nə-kō′pē-ə) n. **1.** A cone-shaped container overflowing with fruit, flowers, and corn, signifying prosperity; horn of plenty. **2.** An overflowing store; abundance. [Late Latin cornūcōpia, horn of plenty : Latin cornū, horn + cōpia, plenty.]

corn whiskey. Whiskey distilled from corn.

corn·y (kôr′nē) adj. **-i·er, -i·est.** Slang. Trite, outdated, melodramatic, or mawkishly sentimental.

co·rol·la (kə-rŏl′ə) n. The outer part of a flower, consisting of fused or separate petals. [Latin, dim. of corōna, garland, corona.]

cor·ol·lar·y (kôr′ə-lĕr′ē, kŏr′-) n., pl. **-ies. 1.** A proposition that clearly follows from one already proven and hence requires no proof. **2.** A deduction or inference. **3.** A natural consequence or effect; a result. [Middle English corolarie, from Latin corollārium, money paid for a garland, gratuity, a corollary, from corolla, dim. of corōna, garland, corona.]

co·ro·na (kə-rō′nə) n., pl. **-nas** or **-nae** (-nē). **1. a.** A faintly colored luminous ring around a celestial body visible through a haze or thin cloud, esp. around the moon or sun, caused by diffraction of light from suspended matter in the intervening medium. **b.** The mass of highly ionized gas outside the chromosphere of the sun appearing as a luminous, irregularly shaped ring during an eclipse. **2.** A crownlike upper part or structure, such as the top of the head. **3.** Bot. A crownlike part of a flower, usu. between the petals and stamens but sometimes an appendage of the corolla, as in daffodils. [Latin corōna, garland, crown, from Greek korōnē, something curved, crown, from korōnos, curved.]

Corona Aus·tra·lis (ô-strā′lĭs). A constellation in the Southern Hemisphere near Sagittarius.

Corona Bo·re·al·is (bôr′ē-ăl′ĭs, -ā′lĭs, bōr′-). A constellation in the Northern Hemisphere near Hercules and Boötes.

cor·o·nar·y (kôr′ə-nĕr-ē, kŏr′-) adj. **1.** Of of pertaining to either of two arteries that originate in the aorta and supply blood directly to the heart tissues. **3.** Of or pertaining to the heart. —n., pl. **-ies.** Informal. A **coronary thrombosis.** [Latin corōnārius, of a garland, from corōna, garland, corona.]

coronary thrombosis. The blockage of a coronary artery by a blood clot, often leading to destruction of heart muscle. Also called **coronary.**

cor·o·na·tion (kôr′ə-nā′shən, kŏr′-) n. The act or ceremony of crowning a sovereign or the consort of a sovereign. [Middle English coronacioun, from Old French coronation, from Medieval Latin corōnātiō, from Latin corōnāre, to crown, from corōna, corona.]

cor·o·ner (kôr′ə-nər, kŏr′-) n. A public officer whose primary function is to investigate by inquest any death thought to be of other than natural causes. [Middle English, officer maintaining the record of the crown's pleas, from Old French coro(u)ne, crown, from Latin corōna, crown, corona.]

cor·o·net (kôr′ə-nět′, kŏr′-) n. **1.** A small crown worn by nobles below the rank of sovereign. **2.** A headband decorated with gold or jewels. [Middle English coronette, from Old French, dim. of corone, crown, from Latin corōna, crown, corona.]

cor·po·ra (kôr′pər-ə) n. Plural of **corpus.**

cor·po·ral[1] (kôr′pər-əl) adj. Of the body; bodily: corporal punishment. [Middle English, from Old French, from Latin corporālis, from corpus, body.] —**cor·po·ral·i·ty** (-pə-răl′ĭ-tē) n. —**cor·po·ral·ly** adv.

cor·po·ral[2] (kôr′pər-əl, -prəl) n. A noncommissioned officer of the lowest rank in the U.S. Army, Air Force, or Marine Corps. [Obs. French, var. of caporal, from Italian capo, chief, head, from Latin capot.]

cor·po·ral[3] (kôr′pər-əl) n. Also **cor·po·ra·le** (kôr′pə-rā′lē). Eccles. A white linen cloth on which the consecrated elements are placed during the celebration of the Eucharist. [Middle English corporale, from Old French corporal, from Latin corporālis, of the body (of Christ), corporal.]

cor·po·rate (kôr′pər-ĭt, -prĭt) adj. **1.** Formed into a corporation; incorporated. **2.** Of a corporation: corporate wealth; corporate structure. **3.** United or combined into one body; collective: corporate effort. [From Latin corporāre, to make into a body, from corpus, body.] —**cor·po·rate·ly** adv.

cor·po·ra·tion (kôr′pə-rā′shən) n. **1.** A body of persons acting under a legal charter as a separate entity with its own rights, privileges and liabilities distinct from those of its individual members. **2.** Any group of people combined into or acting as one body.

cor·po·re·al (kôr-pôr′ē-əl, -pōr′-) adj. **1.** Of, pertaining to, or characteristic of the body. **2.** Of a material nature; tangible. [From Latin corporeus, of the body, from corpus, corpus.] —**cor·po·re·al·ly** adv. —**cor·po·re·al·ness** n.

corps (kôr, kōr) n., pl. **corps** (kôrz, kōrz). **1. a.** Often **Corps.** A section or branch of the armed forces having a specialized function: the Marine Corps. **b.** A tactical unit of ground combat forces composed of two or more divisions. **2.** Any group of persons acting together or associated under common direction: the press corps; a drum and bugle corps. [French, from Latin corpus, body.]

corps de bal·let (kôr′ də bă-lā′). The dancers in a ballet troupe who perform as a group with no solo parts. [French, "ballet troupe."]

corpse (kôrps) n. A dead body, esp. of a human being. [Middle English corps, cors, from Old French, from Latin corpus, body.]

corps·man (kôr′mən, kōr′-) n. An enlisted man trained as a medical assistant.

cor·pu·lence (kôr′pyə-ləns) *n.* Fatness; obesity. [Middle English, from Latin *corpulentia*, from *corpulentus*, from *corpus*, body.]

cor·pu·lent (kôr′pyə-lənt) *adj.* Having a large, overweight body; fat. —See Syns at **fat**. —**cor′pu·lent·ly** *adv.*

cor·pus (kôr′pəs) *n., pl.* **-po·ra** (-p-ərə). **1.** A collection of writings of a specific kind or on a specific subject. **2.** *Anat.* A structure constituting the main part of an organ. [Middle English, from Latin, body, substance.]

Corpus Chris·ti (krĭs′tē, -tī′). *Rom. Cath. Ch.* A festival celebrated in honor of the Eucharist on the first Thursday after Trinity Sunday. [Middle English, from Medieval Latin, "body of Christ."]

cor·pus·cle (kôr′pə-səl, -pŭs′-əl) *n.* **1.** *Biol.* A cell that is capable of free movement in a fluid or matrix as distinguished from a cell fixed in tissue. **2.** Any minute particle. [Latin *corpusculum*, dim. of *corpus*, body.] —**cor·pus′cu·lar** (kôr-pŭs′kyə-lər) *adj.*

corpus de·lic·ti (də-lĭk′tī′). **1.** *Law.* Evidence of the fact that a crime has been committed, as the discovered corpse of a murder victim. **2.** Loosely, the victim's corpse in a murder case. [New Latin, "body of the crime."]

corpus ju·ris (jŏor′ĭs). The body of all the laws of a nation or state. [Late Latin, "body of law."]

cor·ral (kə-răl′) *n.* **1.** An enclosure for confining livestock. **2.** An enclosure formed by a circle of wagons for defense against attack during an encampment. —*tr.v.* **-ralled, -ral·ling. 1.** To drive into and hold in a corral. **2.** To arrange (wagons) in a corral. **3.** *Informal.* To seize; capture: *corral the robbers.* [Spanish.]

cor·rect (kə-rĕkt′) *tr.v.* **1.** To remove the errors or mistakes from: *corrected the manuscript.* **2.** To indicate or mark the errors in: *correct the exams.* **3.** To admonish or punish for the purpose of improving: *She corrected him for his rudeness.* **4.** To remove, remedy, or counteract. **5.** To adjust so as to meet a standard or other required condition: *correct a wrong impression; correct the wheel alignment.* —See Syns at **punish**. —*adj.* **1.** Free from error or fault; true or accurate: *correct spelling.* **2.** Conforming to standards; proper: *correct behavior.* —See Syns at **accurate**. [Middle English *correcten*, from Latin *corrigere*, to make straight : *com-* (intensive) + *regere*, to lead straight, rule.] —**cor·rect′a·ble** or **cor·rect′i·ble** *adj.* —**cor·rect′ly** *adv.* —**cor·rect′ness** *n.*

Syns: *correct, amend, mend, rectify, remedy, right* v. Core meaning: To make right what is wrong (*correct an error*).

cor·rec·tion (kə-rĕk′shən) *n.* **1.** The act or process of correcting. **2.** Something offered or substituted for a mistake or fault; an improvement: *He made sound corrections in my report.* **3.** Punishment intended to improve. **4.** An amount or quantity that is added or subtracted to make correct: *I need a correction of the prescription for my glasses.* —**cor·rec′tion·al** *adj.*

cor·rec·tive (kə-rĕk′tĭv) *adj.* Tending or intended to correct: *corrective lenses; corrective measures.* —*n.* Something that corrects. —**cor·rec′tive·ly** *adv.*

cor·re·late (kôr′ə-lāt′, kŏr′-) *v.* **-lat·ed, -lat·ing.** —*tr.v.* To put or bring into a complementary, parallel, or reciprocal relationship: *correlate ideals with practical requirements.* —*intr.v.* To have systematic connection: *Our facts do not correlate.* —*adj.* Related by a correlation. —*n.* (kôr′ə-lĭt, -lāt′, kŏr′-) Either of two correlate entities; a correlative. [Back-formation from CORRELATION.]

cor·re·la·tion (kôr′ə-lā′shən, kŏr′-) *n.* **1.** A complementary, parallel, or reciprocal relationship: *a direct correlation between recession and unemployment.* **2.** The act of correlating or the condition of being correlated. [Medieval Latin *correlātiō* : *com-*, together + *relātiō*, relation.] —**cor′re·la′tion·al** *adj.*

cor·rel·a·tive (kə-rĕl′ə-tĭv) *adj.* **1.** Related; corresponding. **2.** Reciprocally related. —*n.* **1.** Either of two correlative entities; a correlate. **2.** *Gram.* A correlative word or expression. —**cor·rel′a·tive·ly** *adv.*

correlative conjunction. A conjunction that regularly occurs as part of a pair of conjunctions and that indicates a reciprocal or complementary relation; for example, *both* and *and*, as in *feeling both tired and discouraged.*

cor·re·spond (kôr′ĭ-spŏnd′, kŏr′-) *intr.v.* **1.** To be in agreement, harmony, or conformity; be consistent or compatible; match: *Our goals do not correspond.* **2.** To be similar, parallel, equivalent, or equal: *The eyelids correspond to the shutter of a camera.* **3.** To communicate by letter, usu. over a period of time. —See Syns at **agree**. [Old French *correspondre*, from Medieval Latin *correspondēre* : Latin *com-*, together, mutually + *respondēre*, to respond.]

cor·re·spon·dence (kôr′ĭ-spŏn′dəns, kŏr′-) *n.* Also **cor·re·spon·den·cy** (-dən-sē) *pl.* **-cies. 1.** The act, fact, or condition of agreeing or conforming: *a correspondence between the myths and folktales of different peoples.* **2. a.** Communication by the exchange of letters: *Their correspondence continued throughout their lives.* **b.** The letters written or received: *All correspondence should be sent to the main office.*

cor·re·spon·dent (kôr′ĭ-spŏn′dənt, kŏr′-) *n.* **1.** One who communicates by means of letters. **2.** Someone employed by a publication or a radio or television network to supply news or articles, esp. from a distant place. **3.** A person or firm having regular business relations with another. **4.** A thing that corresponds; a correlative. —*adj.* Corresponding.

cor·re·spond·ing (kôr′ĭ-spŏn′dĭng, kŏr′-) *adj.* **1.** Agreeing or conforming; consistent. **2.** Analogous; equivalent. —See Syns at **like**. —**cor·re·spond′ing·ly** *adv.*

cor·ri·da (kô-rē′də) *n.* A bullfight. [Spanish, "a running," from *correr*, to run, from Latin *currere*.]

cor·ri·dor (kôr′ĭ-dər, -dôr′, kŏr′-) *n.* **1.** A narrow hallway or passageway, usu. with rooms opening onto it. **2.** A narrow strip of land, esp. one that allows passage through a foreign country. [Old French, from Old Italian *corridore*, "a run," from *correre*, to run, from Latin *currere*.]

cor·ri·gen·dum (kôr′ə-jĕn′dəm, kŏr′-) *n., pl.* **-da** (-də). **1.** An error to be corrected, esp. a printer's error. **2. corrigenda.** A list of errors with their corrections, in a book. [Latin, from *corrigere*, to correct.]

cor·ri·gi·ble (kôr′ə-jə-bəl, kŏr′-) *adj.* Capable of being corrected. [Middle English, from Old French, from Medieval Latin *corrigibilis*, from Latin *corrigere*, to correct.] —**cor′ri·gi·bil′i·ty** *n.* —**cor′ri·gi·bly** *adv.*

cor·rob·o·rate (kə-rŏb′ə-rāt′) *tr.v.* **-rat·ed, -rat·ing.** To support or confirm by new evidence; attest the truth or accuracy of: *His account corroborates the defendant's alibi.* [From Latin *corrōborāre* : *com-*, with + *rōborāre*, to strengthen, from *rōbur*, hard oak.] —**cor·rob′o·ra′tion** *n.* —**cor·rob′o·ra′tive** *adj.* —**cor·rob′o·ra′tor** *n.*

cor·rode (kə-rōd′) *v.* **-rod·ed, -rod·ing.** —*tr.v.* To dissolve or wear away gradually, esp. by chemical action: *acid corroding metal.* —*intr.v.* To become corroded: *a manmade substance that will not corrode.* [Middle English *corroden*, from Latin *corrōdere*, to gnaw to pieces : *com-* (intensive) + *rōdere*, to gnaw.] —**cor·rod′i·ble** or **cor·ro·si·ble** (-rō′sə-bəl) *adj.*

cor·ro·sion (kə-rō′zhən) *n.* **1.** The act or process of corroding, esp. of metals. **2.** A substance, such as rust, produced by corroding. **3.** The condition of being corroded. [Middle English *corosioun*, from Old French *corrosion*, from Late Latin *corrōsiō*, from Latin *corrōdere*, to corrode.]

cor·ro·sive (kə-rō′sĭv) *adj.* **1.** Capable of producing or tending to produce corrosion: *a corrosive acid.* **2.** Destructive to the feelings; harsh: *corrosive criticism.* —*n.* A corrosive substance. —**cor·ro′sive·ly** *adv.* —**cor·ro′sive·ness** *n.*

cor·ru·gate (kôr′ə-gāt′, kŏr′-) *v.* **-gat·ed, -gat·ing.** —*tr.v.* To shape into folds or parallel and alternating ridges and grooves. —*intr.v.* To become corrugated. [Latin *corrūgāre*, to make full of wrinkles : *com-*, together + *rūga*, wrinkle.]

cor·ru·ga·tion (kôr′ə-gā′shən, kŏr′-) *n.* **1.** The act of corrugating or the condition of being corrugated. **2.** A groove or ridge on a corrugated surface.

cor·rupt (kə-rŭpt′) *adj.* **1.** Lacking in moral restraint; depraved: *the corrupt court of an aging Roman emperor.* **2.** Marked by or open to bribery, the selling of political favors, etc.; dishonest: *a corrupt judge.* **3.** Decaying; putrid. **4.** Containing errors or alterations, as a text: *a corrupt translation.* —*tr.v.* **1.** To destroy or subvert the honesty or integrity of, as by bribing. **2.** To ruin the morality of; to pervert or debase: *Many fear that permissiveness will corrupt the youth of America.* **3.** To cause to become

ă pat   ā pay   â care   ä father   ĕ pet   ē be   hw which   ĭ pit   ī tie   î pier   ŏ pot   ō toe   ô paw, for   oi noise
ŏŏ took   ōō boot   ou out   th thin   th this   ŭ cut   û urge   zh vision   ə about, item, edible, gallop, circus

rotten; spoil. **4.** To change the original form of (a text, language, etc.). —*intr.v.* To become corrupt. [Middle English, from Old French, from Latin *corruptus,* past part. of *corrumpere,* to break to pieces, ruin : *com-,* completely + *rumpere,* to break.] —**cor·rupt'er** or **cor·rup'tor** *n.* —**cor·rupt'ly** *adv.* —**cor·rupt'ness** *n.*

cor·rupt·i·ble (kə-rŭp'tə-bəl) *adj.* Capable of being corrupted. —**cor·rupt'i·bil'i·ty** or **cor·rupt'i·ble·ness** *n.*

cor·rup·tion (kə-rŭp'shən) *n.* **1.** The act or result of corrupting. **2.** The condition of being corrupt. **3.** Moral depravity; immorality. **4.** Decay; rottenness. —See Syns at **dishonesty.**

cor·sage (kôr-säzh') *n.* A small bouquet of flowers worn by a woman. [Old French, torso, bust, from *cors,* body, from Latin *corpus,* corpus.]

cor·sair (kôr'sâr') *n.* **1.** A pirate or privateer, esp. along the Barbary Coast. **2.** A swift pirate ship, often operating with official sanction. [Old French *corsaire,* pirate, from Old Provençal *corsari,* from Medieval Latin *cursus,* plunder, from Latin, "a run," course, from the past part. of *currere,* to run.]

corse (kôrs) *n. Archaic.* A corpse.

corse·let *n.* **1.** Also **cors·let** (kôrs'lĭt). Body armor, esp. a breastplate. **2.** (kôr'-sə-lĕt'). A light corset with few or no stays. [Old French, dim. of *cors,* corpse.]

cor·set (kôr'sĭt) *n.* A close-fitting undergarment, often reinforced by stays, worn to support and shape the waist and hips. [Middle English, from Old French, dim. of *cors,* corpse.]

cors·let (kôrs'lĭt) *n.* Var. of **corselet** (armor).

cor·tege or **cor·tège** (kôr-tĕzh', -tāzh') *n.* **1.** A train of attendants; retinue, as of a distinguished person. **2.** A ceremonial procession, esp. a funeral procession. [French *cortège,* from Italian *corteggiare,* to pay honor, to court, from *corte,* court, from Latin *cohors.*]

cor·tex (kôr'tĕks') *n., pl.* **-ti·ces** (-tĭ-sēz') or **-tex·es.** **1.** *Anat.* The outer layer of an organ or part, esp. of the cerebrum or adrenal glands. **2.** *Bot.* A layer of tissue in roots and stems lying between the epidermis and the vascular tissue. [Latin, bark, shell, rind.]

cor·ti·cal (kôr'tĭ-kəl) *adj.* **1.** Of, pertaining to, or consisting of a cortex. **2.** Of, pertaining to, or associated with the cerebral cortex. —**cor'ti·cal·ly** *adv.*

cor·ti·cate (kôr'tĭ-kāt') *adj.* Also **cor·ti·cat·ed** (-kā'tĭd). Having a cortex or similar specialized outer layer.

cor·ti·co·tro·pin (kôr'tĭ-kō-trōp'ĭn, -trō'pĭn) *n.* An anterior pituitary hormone, ACTH. [*Cortico-,* cortex + -TROP(IC) + -IN.]

cor·tin (kôr'tn) *n.* An adrenal cortex extract that contains several hormones and is used in medicine. [CORT(EX) + -IN.]

cor·ti·sone (kôr'tĭ-sōn', -zōn') *n.* A hormone produced by the adrenal cortex, active in carbohydrate metabolism and used to treat rheumatoid arthritis, diseases of connective tissue, and gout. [Short for *corticosterone* : cortico-, cortex + STER(OL) + -ONE.]

co·run·dum (kə-rŭn'dəm) *n.* An extremely hard mineral, aluminum oxide, occurring in gem varieties such as ruby and sapphire and in a common gray, brown, or blue form used chiefly in abrasives. [Tamil *kuruntam,* prob. ult. from Sanskrit *kuruvinda,* ruby.]

cor·us·cate (kôr'ə-skāt', kôr'-) *intr.v.* **-cat·ed, -cat·ing.** To give forth flashes of light; to sparkle; glitter. [From Latin *coruscāre,* to thrust, glitter.] —**cor'us·ca'tion** *n.*

cor·vée (kôr-vā') *n.* **1.** A day of unpaid work required of a vassal by his feudal lord. **2.** Labor exacted for little or no pay or instead of taxes and used for public works. [Middle English *corve,* from Old French, from Late Latin *(opera) corrogāta,* "(works) collected," from Latin *corrogāre,* to summon together, collect : *com-,* together + *rogāre,* to ask.]

cor·vette (kôr-vĕt') *n.* Also **cor·vet.** **1.** A fast, lightly armed warship, smaller than a destroyer. **2.** Formerly, a warship smaller than a frigate. [French, from Old French, prob. from Middle Dutch *corf,* basket, kind of small ship.]

Cor·vus (kôr'vəs) *n.* A constellation in the Southern Hemisphere near Crater and Virgo.

cor·ymb (kôr'ĭm, -ĭmb, kôr'-) *n.* A flat-topped flower cluster in which the individual stalks grow upward from various points of the main stem to approx. the same height. [French *corymbe,* from Latin *corymbus,* cluster, from Greek *korumbos.*]

cos (kôs, kŏs) *n.* A type of lettuce, romaine. [After *Kos,* a Greek island.]

co·se·cant (kō-sē'kănt', -kənt) *n. Abbr.* **cosec** and **csc** The secant of the complement of a directed angle or arc.

co·sig·na·to·ry (kō-sĭg'nə-tôr'ē, -tōr'ē) *adj.* Signed jointly with another or others. —*n., pl.* **-ries.** A person who cosigns.

co·sine (kō'sīn') *n. Abbr.* **cos** In a right triangle, the function of an acute angle that is the ratio of the adjacent side to the hypotenuse. [CO- + SINE.]

cosm-. Var. of **cosmo-.**

cos·met·ic (kŏz-mĕt'ĭk) *n.* A preparation, such as skin cream, designed to beautify the body. —*modifier: a cosmetic case.* —*adj.* **1.** Serving to beautify the body. **2.** Serving to correct physical defects: *cosmetic surgery.* **3.** Decorative or superficial rather than functional: *a cosmetic rather than a substantive change.* [French *cosmétique,* "of adornment," from Greek *kosmētikos,* skilled in arranging, from *kosmein,* to arrange, from *kosmos,* order.] —**cos·met'i·cal·ly** *adv.*

cos·mic (kŏz'mĭk) *adj.* **1.** Of or pertaining to the universe, esp. as distinct from the earth and often the solar system: *a theory of cosmic creation.* **2.** Infinitely or inconceivably extended; vast; grand: *an issue of cosmic dimensions.* [Greek *kosmikos,* of the universe, from *kosmos,* cosmos.] —**cos'mi·cal·ly** *adv.*

cosmic ray. A stream of ionizing radiation consisting of high-energy atomic nuclei, alpha particles, fragments, particles, and some electromagnetic waves, that enter the atmosphere from outer space.

cosmo- or **cosm-.** A prefix meaning world or universe: *cosmology.* [From Greek *kosmos,* cosmos.]

cos·mog·o·ny (kŏz-mŏg'ə-nē) *n., pl.* **-nies. 1.** The astrophysical study of the evolution of the universe. **2.** A specific theory or model of the evolution of the universe. [Greek *kosmogonia,* the creation of the world : *cosmos,* world + *gonos,* creation.]

cos·mog·ra·phy (kŏz-mŏg'rə-fē) *n., pl.* **-phies. 1.** The scientific study of the general features and constitution of nature. **2.** A description of the world or universe. [Greek *kosmographia.*]

cos·mol·o·gy (kŏz-mŏl'ə-jē) *n.* **1.** A branch of philosophy dealing with the origin, processes, and structure of the universe. **2. a.** The scientific study of the structure and dynamics of the universe. **b.** A specific theory or model of this structure and dynamics: *an ancient Egyptian cosmology.* [COSMO- + -LOGY.] —**cos'mo·log'ic** (-ə-lŏj'ĭk) or **cos'mo·log'i·cal** *adj.*

cos·mo·naut (kŏz'mə-nôt') *n.* An astronaut, esp. one from the Soviet Union. [Russian *kosmonavt : cosmos,* universe + Greek *nautēs,* sailor.]

cos·mo·pol·i·tan (kŏz'mə-pŏl'ĭ-tn) *adj.* **1.** Of the entire world or from many different parts of the world: *a cosmopolitan group of people.* **2.** Showing worldly experience, education, cultivation, etc.; at home in all parts of the world or in many spheres of interest: *a cosmopolitan person.* **3.** Having a population composed of elements from all parts of the world, from all social levels, etc.; sophisticated: *San Francisco is a very cosmopolitan city.* **4.** *Biol.* Growing or living in all or most parts of the world; widely distributed. —*n.* A cosmopolite. [French *cosmopolitain,* from Old French, from Greek *kosmopolitēs,* cosmopolite.] —**cos'mo·pol'i·tan·ism** *n.*

cos·mop·o·lite (kŏz-mŏp'ə-līt') *n.* A cosmopolitan person. [Greek *kosmopolitēs,* citizen of the world : *cosmos,* world + *politēs,* citizen, from *polis,* city.]

cos·mos (kŏz'məs, -mŏs') *n.* **1.** The universe regarded as an orderly, harmonious whole. **2.** Any system regarded as ordered, harmonious, and whole. **3.** Any of various tropical American plants of the genus *Cosmos,* with variously colored daisylike flowers. [Greek *kosmos,* order, the universe, the world.]

Cos·sack (kŏs'ăk) *n.* A member of a people of the southern Soviet Union in Europe and adjacent parts of Asia, noted as cavalrymen. —**Cos'sack'** *adj.*

cos·set (kŏs′ĭt) *tr.v.* To pamper; fondle; pet. —*n.* A pet, esp. a pet lamb. [Orig. unknown.]

cost (kôst) *n.* **1.** An amount paid or required in payment for a purchase. **2.** A loss, sacrifice, or penalty: *She stood by her principles at the cost of her job.* **3. costs.** The charges fixed for litigation in court, usu. payable by the losing party. —*intr.v.* To require payment, effort, or loss: *It really costs to live in the city.* —*tr.v.* **1.** To have as a price or expenditure: *A subscription costs five dollars.* **2.** To cause to lose: *The strike cost him his job.* —*idiom.* **at all costs.** Whatever the cost may be. [Middle English, from Old French, from *coster*, to cost, from Latin *constāre*, to stand at a particular price : *com-*, with + *stāre*, to stand.]

cos·ta (kŏs′tə) *n.*, *pl.* **-tae** (-tē). A rib or a riblike part of an organism. [Latin, rib.] —**cos′tal** *adj.*

co·star (kō′stär′). Also **co-star.** —*n.* A starring actor or actress given equal status with another or others in a play or motion picture. —*v.* (kō′stär′) **-starred, -star·ring.** —*intr.v.* To act as a costar. —*tr.v.* To present as a costar.

cos·ter·mon·ger (kŏs′tər-mŭng′gər, -mŏng′g-) *n. Brit.* One who sells fruit, vegetables, fish, etc., from a cart in the streets. [Earlier *costardmonger*, apple seller : COSTARD + -MONGER.]

cost·ly (kôst′lē) *adj.* **-li·er, -li·est. 1.** Of high price or value: *costly jewelry; a costly campaign.* **2.** Involving great loss or sacrifice: *a costly war.* —See Syns at **expensive.** —**cost′li·ness** *n.*

cos·tume (kŏs′tōōm′, -tyōōm′) *n.* **1.** A style of dress characteristic of a particular country, period, or people: *a Greek girl in native costume.* **2.** A set of clothes appropriate for a particular occasion or season: *a skating costume.* **3.** An outfit worn by one playing a part, as in a play, or dressing up in disguise, as a masquerade. —*modifier: a costume party.* —*tr.v.* **-tumed, -tum·ing.** To dress in or furnish with a costume or costumes. [French, from Italian, custom, dress, from Latin *consuētūdō*.]

co·sy (kō′zē) *adj.* Var. of **cozy.**

cot[1] (kŏt) *n.* A narrow bed, esp. a collapsible one. [Hindi *khāt*, bedstead, couch, from Sanskrit *khāṭvā*.]

cot[2] (kŏt) *n.* **1.** A small house; cottage. **2.** A small shelter, esp. for animals. [Middle English *cot(e)*, from Old English *cot*.]

co·tan·gent (kō-tăn′jənt) *n. Abbr.* **ctn** The tangent of the complement of a directed angle or arc.

cote (kōt) *n.* A small shed or shelter for sheep or birds. [Middle English, from Old English.]

co·te·rie (kō′tə-rē) *n.* A small group of persons who share interests and associate frequently; circle. [French, from Old French, an association of peasant tenants, prob. from *cotier*, cottager, perh. from Middle English *cot*, cottage.]

co·ter·mi·nous (kō-tûr′mə-nəs) *adj.* Var. of **conterminous.**

co·tid·al (kō-tīd′l) *adj.* **1.** Indicating coincidence of the tides. **2.** Denoting lines on a map that show where high or low tides occur simultaneously.

co·til·lion (kō-tīl′yən, kə-) *n.* **1. a.** A lively, intricate ballroom dance led by one couple and having varied patterns and steps and frequent changing of partners. **b.** A quadrille. **c.** Music for these dances. **2.** A formal ball, esp. one at which young women are presented to society. [French *cotillon*, peasant dress, from Old French, petticoat, dim. of *cote*, coat.]

cot·tage (kŏt′ĭj) *n.* **1.** A small, single-storied house. **2.** A small summer house used during vacations. [Middle English *cotage*, from *cot(e)*, cot, cottage.]

cottage cheese. A soft, white cheese made of strained and seasoned curds of skim milk. Also called **pot cheese.**

cot·tag·er (kŏt′ĭ-jər) *n.* A person who lives in a cottage.

cot·ter[1] (kŏt′ər) *n.* **1.** A bolt, wedge, key, or pin inserted through a slot in order to hold parts together. **2. A cotter pin.** [Short for dial. *cotterel.*]

cot·ter[2] (kŏt′ər) *n.* Also **cot·tor.** A peasant farmer occupying a small holding. [From *cot*, cottage, from Middle English *cot*, from Old English *cot.*]

cotter pin. A split cotter inserted through holes in two or more pieces to fasten and prevent excessive sliding and rotation and secured by bending the ends.

cot·ton (kŏt′n) *n.* **1.** Any of various plants or shrubs of the genus *Gossypium*, cultivated in warm climates for the fi-

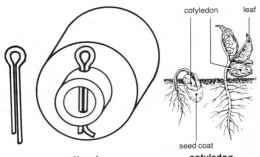

cotter pin

cotyledon

ber surrounding their seeds. **2.** The soft, white, downy fiber attached to the seeds of the cotton plant, used esp. in making textiles. **3.** Cotton plants collectively. **4.** The crop of cotton plants. **5.** Thread or cloth manufactured from cotton fiber. **6.** Any of various soft, downy substances resembling cotton found in other plants. —*modifier: a cotton fabric.* —*intr.v. Informal.* To take a liking; become friendly: *The new horse doesn't cotton to riders.* [Middle English *cotoun*, from Old French, from Arabic *qutn*.]

cotton candy. Spun sugar.

cotton gin. A machine that separates the seeds, seed hulls, and other small objects from the fibers of cotton.

cot·ton·mouth (kŏt′n-mouth′) *n.* A snake, the **water moccasin.** [From the cottony substance lining its mouth.]

cot·ton·seed (kŏt′n-sēd′) *n.*, *pl.* **cottonseed** or **-seeds.** The seed of cotton, used as a source of oil and meal.

cot·ton·tail (kŏt′n-tāl′) *n.* Any of several New World rabbits of the genus *Sylvilagus*, having grayish or brownish fur and a tail with a white underside.

cotton wool. 1. Cotton in its natural or raw state. **2.** *Brit.* Absorbent cotton.

cot·ton·y (kŏt′n-ē) *adj.* **1.** Of or resembling cotton. **2.** Covered with cottonlike down or fibers; nappy.

cot·tor (kŏt′ər) *n.* Var. of **cotter** (farmer).

cot·y·le·don (kŏt′l-ēd′n) *n.* **1.** *Bot.* A leaflike part of a plant embryo within a seed that contains stored food for the newly developing plant and often appears above the ground from a sprouting seed. **2.** *Anat.* A lobule of the placenta, esp. of ruminants. [Latin *cotylēdon*, a kind of plant, from Greek *kotulēdōn*, cup-shaped hollow, from *kotulē*, anything hollow, cup.] —**cot′y·le′don·al** or **cot′y·le′do·nous** *adj.*

couch (kouch) *n.* A piece of furniture, commonly upholstered and often having a back, on which one may sit or recline; sofa. —*tr.v.* **1.** To word in a certain manner; phrase: *couched the speech in lofty phrases.* **2.** To lower (a spear or lance) to the position of attack. —*intr.v.* **1.** To lie down; recline. **2.** To lie in ambush or concealment; lurk. [Middle English *couche*, from Old French, from *coucher*, to lay down, from Latin *collocāre*, to place together, put : *com-*, together + *locāre*, to place, locate.]

couch·ant (kou′chənt) *adj. Heraldry.* Lying down with the head raised. [Middle English, from Old French, pres. part. of *coucher*, to lay down.]

couch grass. Quack grass.

cou·gar (kōō′gər) *n.* The **mountain lion.** [French *couguar*, from Portuguese *cuguardo*, from Tupi *suasuarana*, "like a deer" (from its color) : *suasú*, deer + *ran*, similar to.]

cough (kôf, kŏf) *intr.v.* **1.** To expel air from the lungs suddenly and noisily. **2.** To sputter or choke noisily, as a gasoline engine. —*tr.v.* To expel by coughing: *He coughed up blood.* —*n.* **1.** A sudden and noisy effort to expel air from the lungs. **2.** An illness marked by frequent coughing. [Middle English *coughen*.]

could (kŏŏd; kəd *when unstressed*) *v.* Past tense of **can.**

could·n't (kŏŏd′nt). Contraction of could not.

cou·lee (kōō′lē) *n.* **1.** *Western U.S.* A deep gulch or ravine formed by rainstorms or melting snow. **2. a.** A stream of molten lava. **b.** A sheet of solidified lava. [Canadian French *coulée*, from French, a flow, a flow of lava, from *couler*, to flow, from Latin *cōlāre*, to strain, filter, from *cōlum*, a sieve.]

cou·lomb (kōō'lŏm', -lōm') n. Abbr. **C** A unit of electric charge equal to the quantity of charge transferred in one second by a steady current of one ampere. [After Charles Augustin de *Coulomb* (1736–1806), French physicist.]

coul·ter (kōl'tər) n. Var. of **colter.**

coun·cil (koun'səl) n. **1.** An assembly of persons called together for consultation, deliberation, or discussion: *a special lawyers' council revising the code of ethics.* **2.** A body of people elected or appointed to serve in an administrative, legislative, or advisory capacity: *a city council.* **3.** The discussion or deliberation that takes place in a council: *governors meeting in council.* **—modifier:** *a council chamber.* [Middle English *co(u)nceil,* from Norman French *concilie,* from Latin *concilium,* assembly.]

coun·cil·man (koun'səl-mən) n. A member of a council, esp. the local governing body of a city or town.

coun·cil·or (koun'sə-lər) n. Also **coun·cil·lor.** A member of a council.

coun·cil·wom·an (koun'səl-wōōm'ən) n. A member of a council, esp. the local governing body of a city or town.

coun·sel (koun'səl) n. **1.** An exchange of opinions and ideas; a consultation; discussion: *union leaders meeting for counsel before contract negotiations.* **2.** Advice or guidance, esp. as solicited from a knowledgeable person: *I sought her counsel.* **3.** A deliberate resolution; plan; scheme. **4.** A private opinion or purpose: *keep one's own counsel.* **5.** pl. **counsel.** A lawyer or group of lawyers, esp. an attorney engaged to conduct a case in court. **—v. -seled** or **-selled, -sel·ing** or **-sel·ling.** **—tr.v. 1.** To give counsel to; advise: *He counsels the parents of disturbed children.* **2.** To urge the adoption of; recommend. **—intr.v.** To give or take counsel or advice. [Middle English *counseil, conseil,* from Old French *conseil,* from Latin *consilium,* deliberation, consultation.]

coun·sel·or (koun'sə-lər, -slər) n. Also **coun·sel·lor.** **1.** A person who gives counsel; an adviser: *a career counselor.* **2.** An attorney, esp. a trial lawyer. Also called **counselor-at-law.** **3.** A person supervising children at a summer camp. **—coun'se·lor·ship'** n.

count¹ (kount) tr.v. **1.** To name or list (the units or people of a group) one by one in order to determine a total; to number: *count the pearls on the string.* **2.** To recite numerals in ascending order up to and including: *count three before firing.* **3.** To include in a reckoning; take account of: *ten dogs, counting the puppies.* **4.** To believe or consider to be; deem: *He counts himself lucky.* **—intr.v. 1.** To recite or list numbers in order or enumerate items by units or groups: *count by tens.* **2.** To have importance; merit consideration: *Quality counts for everything in this business.* **3.** To have importance; be of value: *His opinions count for little.* **4.** Mus. To keep time by counting beats. **—phrasal verbs. count in.** To include: *count me in.* **count off. 1.** To separate into groups by counting: *We counted off four groups of students to help with the job.* **2.** To call out numbers so as to divide into groups, maintain the order of a line, etc.: *Count off by twos.* **count on** (or **upon**). To rely on; depend on: *You can count on her help.* **count out.** To exclude: *If there's any roughness, you can count me out.* **—n. 1.** The act of counting or calculating: *Take a quick count of who's here.* **2.** A number reached by counting. **3.** Law. Any of the separate and distinct charges in an indictment. **4.** Boxing. The counting from one to ten seconds, during which time a fighter who is down must rise or be declared the loser. [Middle English *counten,* from Old French *conter,* from Latin *computāre,* to sum up : *com-,* together + *putāre,* to reckon.]

count² (kount) n. In some European countries, a nobleman whose rank corresponds to that of an earl in England. [Middle English *counte,* from Old French *conte, comte,* from Late Latin *comes,* occupant of a state office, from Latin, companion.]

count·down (kount'doun') n. The act or process of counting intervals of time backward from some optionally chosen point to indicate the time remaining until a scheduled event, as the firing of a rocket, is to take place.

coun·te·nance (koun'tə-nəns) n. **1.** Appearance, esp. the expression of the face: *a grave and troubled countenance.* **2.** The face or facial features: *a beautiful countenance.* **3.** Support or approval in general; encouragement: *He re-*

fused to give countenance to her plan. **5.** Composure; bearing; self-control: *kept his countenance in front of his accusers.* **—tr.v. -nanced, -nanc·ing.** To give or express approval to; condone: *The committee countenanced our reorganizational strategy.* [Middle English *contenaunce,* behavior, demeanor, from Old French *contenance,* from *contenir,* to behave.]

coun·ter¹ (koun'tər) adj. Contrary; opposing: *His views are counter to those of the other experts.* **—tr.v. 1.** To move or act in opposition to; oppose: *We developed a new marketing plan to counter the competition's.* **2.** Boxing. To meet or return (a blow) by another blow. **—intr.v. 1.** To move or act in opposition: *He countered with his own suggestion.* **2.** Boxing. To give a return blow while receiving or parrying one. **—n. 1.** Someone or something that is counter; an opposite; a contrary. **2.** Boxing. A blow given while receiving or parrying another. **3.** A stiff piece of leather around the heel of a shoe. **4.** The portion of a ship's stern extending from the water line to the extreme outward swell. **—adv.** In a contrary manner or direction: *a method that runs counter to past practices.* [Middle English *countre,* from Old French *contre,* from Latin *contrā,* contrary to, against.]

count·er² (koun'tər) n. **1.** A table or similar flat surface on which money is counted, business is transacted, or food is served. **2.** A piece, as of wood or ivory, used for keeping a count or a place in games. **3.** An imitation coin; token. [Middle English *contour,* from Old French *comptour,* from Medieval Latin *computātōrium,* place of accounts, from Latin *computāre,* to count.]

count·er³ (koun'tər) n. Someone or something that counts, esp. an electrical or electronic device that automatically counts things or occurrences of events.

counter–. A prefix meaning: **1.** Opposition, as in direction or purpose: **counteract.** **2.** Reciprocation: **countersign.** [Middle English *countre-,* from Norman French, from Old French *contre-,* from Latin *contrā,* opposite to, counter.]

coun·ter·act (koun'tər-ăkt') tr.v. To oppose and lessen the effects of by contrary action; to check: *a tax cut to counteract inflation.* **—coun'ter·ac'tion** n.

coun·ter·at·tack (koun'tər-ə-tăk') n. A return attack. **—v.** (koun'tər-ə-tăk'). **—intr.v.** To deliver a counterattack. **—tr.v.** To make a counterattack against.

coun·ter·bal·ance (koun'tər-băl'əns) n. **1.** Any force or influence equally counteracting another: *The athlete's experience is a counterbalance to his lack of speed.* **2.** A weight that acts to balance another; a counterpoise. **—tr.v.** (koun'tər-băl'əns, koun'tər-băl'əns) **-anced, -anc·ing.** **1.** To act as a counterbalance to; to counterpoise. **2.** To oppose with an equal force; offset.

coun·ter·claim (koun'tər-klām') n. A claim filed in opposition to another claim, esp. in a lawsuit. **—tr.v.** To make a counterclaim against. **—intr.v.** To plead a counterclaim. **—coun'ter·claim'ant** n.

coun·ter·clock·wise (koun'tər-klŏk'wīz') adv. & adj. In a direction opposite to that of the movement of the hands of a clock.

coun·ter·cul·ture (koun'tər-kŭl'chər) n. A culture created by or for the alienated young in opposition to traditional lifestyles, values, and assumptions.

coun·ter·es·pi·o·nage (koun'tər-ĕs'pē-ə-näzh', -nĭj) n. Espionage undertaken to counteract enemy espionage.

coun·ter·feit (koun'tər-fĭt') tr.v. **1.** To make a copy of, usu. with the intent to defraud; to forge: *counterfeit money; counterfeit a signature.* **2.** To make a pretense of; feign: *She counterfeited interest in his story.* **—intr.v. 1.** To feign; dissemble. **2.** To make imitations or counterfeits. **—adj. 1.** Made in imitation of what is genuine, usu. with the intent to defraud: *a counterfeit dollar bill.* **2.** Simulated; feigned; pretended: *counterfeit illness.* **—n.** A fraudulent imitation or facsimile. [Middle English *countrefeten,* from Old French *contrefaire,* Medieval Latin *contrāfacere,* to make in contrast to : Latin *contrā-,* opposite to + *facere,* to make.] **—coun'ter·feit·er** n.

coun·ter·foil (koun'tər-foil') n. The part of a check or other commercial paper retained by the issuer as a record of a transaction.

coun·ter·in·tel·li·gence (koun'tər-ĭn-tĕl'ə-jəns) n. The branch of an intelligence service charged with keeping valuable information from an enemy, preventing subversion and sabotage, and gathering political and military information.

coun·ter·ir·ri·tant (koun′tər-îr′ĭ-tənt) *n.* An agent used to induce local inflammation to counteract general or deep inflammation.

coun·ter·man (koun′tər-măn′, -mən) *n.* A person who tends a counter, as in a luncheonette.

coun·ter·mand (koun′tər-mănd′) *tr.v.* **1.** To cancel or reverse (a command). **2.** To recall by a contrary order. —*n.* An order or command reversing another. [Middle English *countremaunden*, from Old French *contremander* : *contre-*, opposite, from Latin *contra-* + *mander*, to command, from Latin *mandāre*.]

coun·ter·march (koun′tər-märch′) *n.* A march back or in a reverse direction. —*intr.v.* To execute a countermarch.

coun·ter·mea·sure (koun′tər-mězh′ər) *n.* A measure or action taken to oppose or offset another.

coun·ter·of·fen·sive (koun′tər-ə-fěn′sĭv) *n.* A large-scale attack by an army, designed to stop the offensive of an enemy force.

coun·ter·part (koun′tər-pärt′) *n.* **1.** A person or thing exactly or very much like another, as in function: *An automobile is the modern counterpart of the horse and buggy.* **2.** A person or thing that is a natural complement to another: *A fine wine is the perfect counterpart to a delicious dinner.*

coun·ter·plot (koun′tər-plŏt′) *n.* A plot intended to frustrate another plot. —*v.* (koun′tər-plŏt′) **-plot·ted, -plot·ting.** —*tr.v.* To oppose and frustrate by another plot. —*intr.v.* To devise a counterplot.

coun·ter·point (koun′tər-point′) *n.* **1. a.** A musical technique in which two or more melodic lines are combined in such a way that they establish a harmonic relationship while retaining their individuality. **b.** Music incorporating or consisting of such writing. **2.** A secondary melody designed to go along with a principal melody. **3.** A contrasting but parallel element, item, or theme.

coun·ter·poise (koun′tər-poiz′) *n.* **1.** A weight that balances another weight. **2.** Any force or influence that balances or equally counteracts another. **3.** The state of being balanced or in equilibrium. —*tr.v.* **-poised, -pois·ing.** To oppose or act against with an equal weight, force, or power; to counterbalance.

Counter Reformation. A reform movement within the Roman Catholic Church during the 16th and 17th cent. in response to the Protestant Reformation.

coun·ter·rev·o·lu·tion (koun′tər-rĕv′ə-lōō′shən) *n.* A movement arising in opposition to a revolution. —**coun′ter·rev′o·lu′tion·ar′y** *adj. & n.* —**coun′ter·rev′o·lu′tion·ist** *n.*

coun·ter·sign (koun′tər-sīn′) *tr.v.* To sign (a previously signed document) in order to authenticate or confirm it: *countersign a check.* —*n.* **1.** A second or confirming signature, as on a previously signed document. **2.** A secret sign or signal to be given to a sentry in order to obtain passage; password.

coun·ter·sink (koun′tər-sĭngk′) *tr.v.* **-sank** (-săngk′) or **-sunk** (-sŭngk), **-sunk, -sink·ing.** **1.** To enlarge the top part of (a hole) so that a screw or bolthead will lie flush with or below the surface. **2.** To drive a screw or bolt into (such a hole). —*n.* **1.** A tool for making such a hole. **2.** A hole so made.

coun·ter·spy (koun′tər-spī′) *n.* A spy working in opposition to enemy espionage.

coun·ter·ten·or (koun′tər-tĕn′ər) *n.* **1.** An adult male voice with a range above that of tenor. **2.** A singer with such a voice.

coun·ter·weight (koun′tər-wāt′) *n.* A weight used as a counterbalance. —**coun′ter·weight′ed** (-wā′tĭd) *adj.*

count·ess (koun′tĭs) *n.* **1. a.** In various European countries, the wife or widow of a count. **b.** In Great Britain, the wife or widow of an earl. **2.** A woman holding the title of count or earl in her own right. [Middle English *countes(se)*, from Old French *contesse*, fem. of *conte*, count.]

count·less (kount′lĭs) *adj.* Too many to be counted; infinite; innumerable.

coun·try (kŭn′trē) *n., pl.* **-tries.** **1.** A large tract of land distinguishable by features of topography, biology, or culture: *mountain country; farming country.* **2.** A district outside

of cities and towns; rural area: *take a vacation in the country.* **3. a.** A nation or state: *all the countries of the world.* **b.** The territory of a nation or state; land: *the country of France.* **c.** The people of a nation or state: *More than half of the country lives in industrialized, urban areas.* **4.** The land of a person's birth or citizenship or to which a person owes allegiance. —*modifier: a country boy; country life.* —See Syns at **nation.** [Middle English *cuntree, contre,* from Old French *contree,* from Medieval Latin *(terra) contrāta,* "(land) lying opposite or before one," from Latin *contrā,* against, opposite.]

country club. A suburban club with facilities for golf, other outdoor sports, and social activities.

coun·try·man (kŭn′trē-mən) *n.* **1.** A man from one's own country. **2.** A man from a particular region. **3.** A man who lives in the country; a rustic.

country music. Folk music of the rural United States, esp. the southern or southwestern United States.

coun·try·side (kŭn′trē-sīd′) *n.* **1.** A rural region. **2.** The inhabitants of such an area.

coun·try·wom·an (kŭn′trē-wŏŏm′ən) *n.* **1.** A woman from one's own country. **2.** A woman from a particular region. **3.** A woman who lives in the country; a rustic.

coun·ty (koun′tē) *n., pl.* **-ties.** **1.** In the United States, an administrative subdivision of a state. **2.** In Great Britain and Ireland, a territorial division exercising administrative, judicial, and political functions. **3.** The people living in a county. **4.** *Archaic.* A count or earl. [Middle English *co(u)nte,* from Norman French *counté,* from Medieval Latin *comitātus,* territory of a count, from Latin *comes,* count.]

county seat. A town or city that is the center of government in its county.

coup (kōō) *n., pl.* **coups** (kōōz). **1.** A brilliantly executed stratagem; masterstroke. **2.** A coup d'état. [French, from Old French, from Late Latin *colpus,* from Latin *colaphus,* blow, from Greek *kolaphos.*]

coup de grâce (kōō′ də gräs′) *pl.* **coups de grâce** (kōō′ də gräs′). **1.** A death blow or finishing stroke, as delivered to end the misery of someone who is mortally wounded. **2.** Any finishing or decisive stroke. [French, "stroke of mercy."]

coup d'é·tat (kōō′ dā-tä′) *pl.* **coups d'état** (kōō′ dā-tä′). The sudden overthrow of a government by a group of persons in or previously in positions of authority in deliberate violation of constitutional forms.

cou·pé (kōō-pā′) *n.* **1.** A closed four-wheel carriage with two seats inside and one outside. **2.** Also **coupe** (kōōp). A closed two-door automobile. [French, short for *(carrosse) coupé,* "cut-off (carriage)," from *couper,* to cut off, from Old French *coup,* coup.]

coupé

cou·ple (kŭp′əl) *n.* **1.** Two items of the same kind; a pair. **2.** Something that joins two things together; connection; link. **3.** *(used with a sing. or pl. verb).* A man and woman united in some way, as by marriage or betrothal. **4.** *Informal.* A few; several: *a couple of days.* —*v.* **-pled, -pling.** —*tr.v.* **1.** To link together; join. **2.** *Elect.* To link (two circuits or currents) as by magnetic induction. —*intr.v.* To form pairs. —See Syns at **attach.** [Middle English, pair, bond, from Old French, from Latin *cōpula,* bond, link.]

Syns: **couple, brace, doublet, pair** *n. Core meaning:* Two of the same kind together (*a couple of songs*). COUPLE also can mean two closely associated persons (*a married* couple). PAIR stresses the close association and often reciprocal dependence of things (*a pair of gloves*); sometimes it means a single thing with interdependent parts (*a pair of scissors*). BRACE and DOUBLET refer to two like things (*a brace of pistols; shot a doublet of grouse*).

Usage: couple. When the noun means a man and woman united, it may be used with either a singular or plural verb, but the plural construction is more common. Whatever the choice, it should be expressed consistently within the context: *The couple are changing their voting residence* (or *is changing its*).

cou·pler (kŭp′lər) *n.* **1.** Something that links or connects. **2.** A device for coupling two railroad cars. **3.** A device connecting two organ keyboards so that they may be played together.

cou·plet (kŭp′lĭt) *n.* A unit of verse consisting of two successive lines, usu. rhyming and having the same meter. [Old French *couplet*, dim. of *co(u)ple*, couple.]

cou·pling (kŭp′lĭng) *n.* **1.** The act of forming couples. **2.** Something that links or connects, esp. a device for linking machine parts. **3.** A railroad coupler.

cou·pon (kōō′pŏn′, kyōō′-) *n.* **1.** One of a number of small, negotiable certificates attached to a bond that represent sums of interest due at stated maturities. **2.** A detachable part of a ticket, advertisement, etc., that entitles the bearer to certain benefits, such as a cash refund or a gift. **3.** A printed form, as in an advertisement, on which to write one's name and address when sending away for something. [French, from Old French *colpon*, "a piece cut off," from *couper*, to cut off, from *coup*, a blow.]

cour·age (kûr′ĭj, kŭr′-) *n.* The quality of mind or spirit that enables one to face danger with confidence, resolution, and firm control of oneself; bravery; valor. [Middle English *corage*, heart (as the seat of feeling), courage, from Old French, from Latin *cor*, heart.]

cou·ra·geous (kə-rā′jəs) *adj.* Having or characterized by courage; valiant. —See Syns at **brave.** —**cou·ra′geous·ly** *adv.* —**cou·ra′geous·ness** *n.*

cou·rante (kōō-ränt′) *n.* A French dance of the 17th cent., characterized by running and gliding steps to an accompaniment in triple time. [French, "running (dance)," from *courir*, to run, from Old French *courre*, from Latin *currere*.]

cou·ri·er (kōōr′ē-ər, kûr′-) *n.* A messenger, esp. one on urgent or official diplomatic business. [Old French *courrier*, from Old Italian *corriere*, from *correre*, to run, from Latin *currere*.]

course (kôrs, kōrs) *n.* **1.** Onward movement in a particular direction; progress; advance: *the course of events.* **2.** The direction of continuing movement: *a northern course.* **3.** The route or path taken by something that moves, as a stream, river, etc. **4.** A designated area of land or water on which a race is held or a sport played: *a golf course.* **5.** Movement in time; duration: *in the course of a year.* **6.** A mode of action or behavior: *He followed the only proper course to correct the problem.* **7.** A typical or natural manner of proceeding; passage from stage to stage: *The fad ran its course.* **8.** A systematic or orderly succession; sequence: *a course of medical treatments.* **9.** *Archit.* A continuous layer of building material, such as brick or tile, on a wall or roof of a building. **10. a.** A complete body of prescribed studies constituting a curriculum and leading toward an advanced degree: *a premed course.* **b.** A unit of such a curriculum: *a course in anatomy.* **11.** A part of a meal served as a unit at one time. **12.** The lowest sail on any mast of a square-rigged ship. **13.** A point on the compass, esp. the one toward which a ship is sailing. —*v.* **coursed, cours·ing.** —*tr.v.* **1.** To move swiftly through or over; traverse: *horses coursing the hills.* **2.** To pursue; hunt: *course the retreating attackers.* **3.** To set (hounds) to chase game; send into pursuit. —*intr.v.* **1.** To proceed on a course; follow a direction: *The schooner coursed along the coast.* **2. a.** To move swiftly; race: *a canoe coursing down the rapids.* **b.** To run; flow: *"Big tears now coursed down her face"* (Iris Murdoch). **3.** To hunt game with hounds. —*idioms.* **in due course.** In proper order; at the right time. **of course.** Without any doubt; certainly. [Middle English *cours*, from Old French, from Latin *cursus*, from the past part. of *currere*, to run.]

cours·er (kôr′sər, kōr′-) *n. Poet.* A swift horse.

court (kôrt, kōrt) *n.* **1.** An extent of open ground partially or completely enclosed by walls or buildings; courtyard. **2.** A short street, esp. an alley walled by buildings on three sides. **3.** A large, open section of a building, often with a glass roof or skylight. **4. a.** The place of residence of a sovereign or dignitary; a royal mansion or palace. **b.** The retinue of a sovereign. **c.** A sovereign's governing body, including the council of ministers and state advisers. **d.** A formal meeting called for and presided over by a sovereign. **5. a.** A person or body of persons appointed to hear and submit a decision on civil cases. **b.** The building, hall, or room in which cases are heard and determined. **c.** The regular session of a judicial assembly. **d.** Any similar authorized tribunal having military or ecclesiastical jurisdiction. **6.** An open, level area, marked with appropriate lines, upon which tennis, handball, basketball, or other games are played. —*tr.v.* **1.** To attempt to gain the favor of by flattery or attention: *court the boss for a promotion.* **2.** To attempt to gain the affections or love of; woo: *He courted her all through college.* **3.** To attempt to gain; seek: *He courts fame and position.* **4.** To invite, often unwittingly or foolishly: *court disaster.* —*intr.v.* To pay court; woo: *They courted for six months.* —*idioms.* **out of court.** Without a trial: *settled out of court.* **pay court to.** **1.** To flatter with solicitous overtures in an attempt to obtain something. **2.** To woo. [Middle English, from Old French *cort*, from Latin *cohors*, enclosure, court.]

cour·te·ous (kûr′tē-əs) *adj.* Characterized by graciousness and good manners; considerate. —See Syns at **polite.** [Middle English *curteis*, having manners befitting a courtly gentleman, from Old French, from *cort*, court.] —**cour′te·ous·ly** *adv.* —**cour′te·ous·ness** *n.*

cour·te·san (kôr′tĭ-zən, kōr′-) *n.* Also **cour·te·zan.** A prostitute, esp. one who associates with men of rank or wealth. [Old French *courtisane*, from Old Italian *cortigiana*, "female courtier," from *corte*, court.]

cour·te·sy (kûr′tĭ-sē) *n., pl.* **-sies. 1.** Polite behavior; gracious manner or manners. **2.** A polite gesture or remark: *He saluted me, and I returned the courtesy.* **3.** Consent or favor; indulgence: *received a fruit basket by courtesy of the hotel.* [Middle English *curteisie*, from Old French, from *curteis*, courteous.]

cour·te·zan (kôr′tĭ-zən, kōr′-) *n.* Var. of **courtesan.**

court·house (kôrt′hous′, kōrt′-) *n.* A building in which courts of law are held.

court·i·er (kôr′tē-ər, kōr′-) *n.* **1.** An attendant at the court of a sovereign. **2.** A person who seeks favor, esp. by flattery or sycophancy.

court·ly (kôrt′lē, kōrt′-) *adj.* **-li·er, -li·est. 1.** Suitable for a royal court; stately; dignified. **2.** Elegant in manners; polite; refined. **3.** Flattering; obsequious. —**court′li·ness** *n.*

courtly love. A code of chivalrous and romantic devotion to a married lady that developed as a secular counterpart to the cult of the Virgin and exerted an important influence in medieval and Renaissance literature.

court-mar·tial (kôrt′mär′shəl, kōrt′-) *n., pl.* **courts-mar·tial. 1.** A military or naval court of officers appointed to try persons for offenses under military law. **2.** A trial by court-martial. —*tr.v.* **-tialed** or **-tialled, -tial·ing** or **-tial·ling.** To try by court-martial.

Court of St. James's jām′zĭz). The British royal court.

court·room (kôrt′rōōm′, -rōōm′, kōrt′-) *n.* A room in which court proceedings are carried on.

court·ship (kôrt′shĭp′, kōrt′-) *n.* The act or period of wooing or courting.

court tennis. Tennis played in a large indoor court with high cement walls off which the ball may be played.

court·yard (kôrt′yärd′, kōrt′-) *n.* An open space surrounded by walls or buildings, adjoining or within a large building.

cous·in (kŭz′ĭn) *n.* **1.** A child of one's aunt or uncle. **2.** A relative descended from a common ancestor, such as a grandfather, by two or more steps in a diverging line. **3.** A member of a kindred group or country: *our Canadian cousins.* **4.** A title of address used by a sovereign to a nobleman or to another sovereign. [Middle English *cosin(e)*, from Old French *cousin*, from Latin *consōbrīnus*, maternal first cousin : *com-*, together + *sōbrīnus*, maternal cousin.]

ă pat	ā pay	â care	ä father	ĕ pet	ē be	hw which	ĭ pit	ī tie	î pier	ŏ pot	ō toe	ô paw, for	oi noise
ōō took	ōō boot	ou out	th thin	th this	ŭ cut		û urge	zh vision	ə about, item, edible, gallop, circus				

cous·in-ger·man (kŭz′ĭn-jûr′mən) *n., pl.* **cous·ins-ger·man.** A first cousin.

couth (ko͞oth) *adj.* Refined; suave; well-mannered. [Middle English, familiar, known, from Old English *cūth.*]

cou·ture (ko͞o-to͞or′) *n.* The business of a couturier or the work of dressmaking and fashion design. [French, tailoring, sewing, from Old French *cousture,* from Latin *consuere,* to sew together : *com-,* together + *suere,* to sew.]

cou·tu·ri·er (ko͞o-to͞or′ē-ər, -ē-ā′) *n.* A male fashion designer, esp. of women's clothing. [French.]

cou·tu·ri·ère (ko͞o-to͞or′ē-âr′). A female fashion designer, esp. of women's clothing. [French.]

co·va·lence (kō-vā′ləns) *n.* The number of electron pairs an atom can share with other atoms.

co·va·lent bond (kō-vā′lənt). A chemical bond formed by the sharing of one or more electrons, esp. pairs of electrons, between atoms.

cove (kōv) *n.* **1.** A small, sheltered bay in a shoreline. **2.** A recess or small valley in the side of a mountain. **3.** A narrow gap or pass between hills or woods. [Middle English , closet, chamber, cave, from Old English *cofa.*]

cov·en (kŭv′ən, kō′vən) *n.* An assembly of 13 witches. [Var. of *covent,* a gathering, convent.]

cov·e·nant (kŭv′ə-nənt) *n.* **1.** A binding agreement made by two or more persons or parties; a compact; contract. **2.** A solemn agreement or vow made by members of a church to defend and support its faith and doctrine. **3.** *Theol.* God's promises to man as recorded in the Old and New Testaments. **4.** *Law.* A formal sealed agreement or contract. —*tr.v.* To promise by a covenant. —*intr.v.* To enter into a covenant. [Middle English, from Old French, from *co(n)venir,* to convene.]

cov·e·nant·er (kŭv′ə-nən-tər) *n.* **1.** A person who makes a covenant. **2. Covenanter** (*also* kŭv′ə-nän′tər). A Scottish Presbyterian who supported either of the agreements intended to defend and extend Presbyterianism.

cov·er (kŭv′ər) *tr.v.* **1.** To place something upon, over, or in front of, so as to protect, shut in, or conceal; overlay: *cover a table. She covered her eyes.* **2.** To put a covering on; clothe: *covered the princess in silk.* **3.** To put a cap, hat, etc., on (one's head). **4.** To occupy the surface of; spread over: *Dust covered the table.* **5.** To extend over; occupy: *a farm covering more than 100 acres; an assignment covering a period of weeks.* **6.** To sit on (eggs); incubate; brood. **7.** To hide or screen from view or knowledge; conceal: *cover up a crime. She covered her embarrassment by laughing.* **8.** To protect or shield from harm, injury, or danger; to shelter: *Dense ground fog covered the retreating soldiers.* **9.** To be sufficient to defray (a charge or expense); meet or offset (a liability): *My insurance will cover the repairs.* **10.** To make provision for; allow for: *Federal law does not cover all crimes.* **11.** To deal with; treat of: *Today's lecture covers the last year of the Civil War.* **12.** To travel or pass over; traverse: *I hope to cover 300 miles tomorrow.* **13.** To hold within the range and aim of a firearm: *I covered the robber till help arrived.* **14. a.** To overlook and dominate from a strategic position; have within range: *The fort on the mountain covered the valley below.* **b.** To protect (a soldier, position, etc.) by occupying a position from which an enemy troop can be fired upon: *Cover me when I make a run for it.* **15.** To secure and report the details of (an event or situation): *cover the convention.* **16.** *Sports.* To be responsible for guarding the play of (an opponent) or for defending (an area or position): *cover left field.* **17.** To match (an opponent's stake) in a wager. —*intr.v.* **1.** To spread over a surface to protect or conceal something. **2.** *Informal.* To act as a substitute or replacement during someone's absence: *He's covering for the night manager.* **3.** To hide something in order to save someone from censure or punishment: *cover for a colleague.* —*n.* **1.** Something that covers or is laid, placed, or spread over or upon something else: *the cover on a bed; book covers.* **2. a.** Shelter of any kind: *seek cover during a storm.* **b.** Natural or artificial protection by other armed units: *under a cover of mortar fire.* **3.** Vegetation covering an area, often serving to provide shade, prevent erosion, or serve as protective concealment for wild animals. **4.** Something that screens, conceals, or disguises, as a pretext: *That business is a cover for illegal activity.* **5.** A table setting for one person.

6. A cover charge. **7.** Funds sufficient to meet an obligation or secure against loss. *—idioms.* **under cover. 1.** Operating secretly or under a guise; covert. **2.** Hidden; protected. **3.** Within an envelope. **under separate cover.** Within a separate envelope. [Middle English *coveren,* from Old French *covrir,* from Latin *cooperīre,* to cover completely : *co-,* completely + *operīre,* to cover.] **—cov′er·er** *n.*

cov·er·age (kŭv′ər-ĭj) *n.* **1.** The extent to or way in which something is observed, analyzed, and reported, as by a newspaper or a television station. **2.** The extent of protection given by an insurance policy. **3.** The amount of funds reserved to meet liabilities.

cov·er·alls (kŭv′ər-ôlz′) *pl.n.* A loose-fitting one-piece garment worn by workmen to protect their clothes.

cover charge. A fixed amount added to the bill at a nightclub for entertainment or services.

cover crop. A crop, such as winter rye, planted to prevent erosion in winter and provide humus or nitrogen when plowed under.

covered wagon. A large wagon covered with an arched canvas top, used by American pioneers for prairie travel.

covered wagon

cov·er·ing (kŭv′ər-ĭng) *n.* Something that covers for protection, concealment, or warmth.

cov·er·let (kŭv′ər-lĭt) *n.* An ornamental cloth covering for a bed; a bedspread.

cov·ert (kŭv′ərt, kō′vərt) *adj.* **1.** Covered or covered over; sheltered. **2.** Concealed; hidden; secret: *espionage agents in covert operations.* —See Syns at **secret.** —*n.* **1.** A covered place or shelter; hiding place. **2.** Thick underbrush or woodland affording cover for game; cover. **3.** *Zool.* One of the feathers covering the bases of the longer main feathers of a bird's wings or tail. [Middle English, from Old French, from *covrir,* to cover.] **—cov′ert·ly** *adv.* **—cov′ert·ness** *n.*

cov·er·ture (kŭv′ər-chər) *n.* A covering; shelter.

cov·er-up (kŭv′ər-ŭp′) *n.* Also **cov·er·up.** An effort or strategy designed to conceal something, such as a crime or scandal, that could be harmful or embarrassing if known: *presidential aides participating in the Watergate cover-up.*

cov·et (kŭv′ĭt) *tr.v.* **1.** To desire (that which is another's): *He covets his boss's job.* **2.** To wish for excessively; crave: *covet wealth.* [Middle English *coveiten,* from Old French *coveitier,* from Latin *cupiditās,* desire, from *cupere,* to desire.] **—cov′et·er** *n.*

cov·et·ous (kŭv′ĭ-təs) *adj.* **1.** Excessively desirous, esp. of something belonging to another; avaricious; greedy. **2.** Very desirous; eager for acquisition: *covetous of learning.* **—cov′et·ous·ly** *adv.* **—cov′et·ous·ness** *n.*

cov·ey (kŭv′ē) *n., pl.* **-eys. 1.** A family or small flock of partridges, grouse, or other birds. **2.** A small party or group, as of persons. [Middle English *covei(e),* from Old French *covee,* a brood, from *cover,* to hatch, sit on (eggs), from Latin *cubāre,* to lie down (on).]

cow¹ (kou) *n., pl.* **cows** or *archaic* **kine** (kīn). **1.** The mature female of cattle of the genus *Bos.* **2.** The mature female of other animals, such as whales, elephants, or moose. **3.** *Informal.* Any domesticated bovine. [From Middle English *cou,* (pl. *kin*), from Old English *cū,* (pl. *cȳ*).]

cow² (kou) *tr.v.* To frighten with or subdue by threats or a show of force; intimidate. [Orig. unknown.]

cow·ard (kou′ərd) *n.* One who lacks courage in the face of danger, pain, or hardship; an ignobly frightened or timid person. [Middle English *couherde,* from Old French *couard,* "one with his tail between his legs," from *coue,* tail, from Latin *cauda,* tail.]

cow·ard·ice (kou'ǝr-dĭs) n. Lack of courage or a shameful show of fear when facing danger, pain, hardship, or a conflict.

cow·ard·ly (kou'ǝrd-lē) adj. 1. Lacking courage. 2. Showing cowardice; befitting a coward: a cowardly thing to do. —adv. In the manner of a coward; basely; meanly. —**cow'ard·li·ness** n.

    Syns: cowardly, chicken (Slang), craven, dastardly, yellow (Slang) adj. Core meaning: Ignobly fearful (a cowardly soldier who fled under fire).

cow·bane (kou'bān') n. 1. A plant, Oxypolis rigidior, of the southeastern and central United States, with poisonous roots and foliage and clusters of small white flowers. 2. Any of several related plants.

cow·boy (kou'boi') n. A hired man, esp. in the western United States, who tends cattle and performs many of his duties on horseback. —**modifier:** a cowboy movie.

cow·catch·er (kou'kăch'ǝr) n. The iron grille on the front of a locomotive or streetcar that serves to clear the track of obstructions.

cow·er (kou'ǝr) intr.v. To crouch or draw back, as from fear or pain; cringe. —See Syns at recoil. [Middle English couren.]

cow·girl (kou'gûrl') n. A woman who performs the same duties as a cowboy.

cow·hand (kou'hǎnd') n. A cowboy.

cow·herd (kou'hûrd') n. A person who herds or tends cattle.

cow·hide (kou'hīd') n. 1. a. The hide of a cow. b. The leather made from this hide. 2. A strong, heavy, flexible whip, usu. made of braided leather. —**modifier:** a cowhide belt. —tr.v. -hid·ed, -hid·ing. To whip with a cowhide.

cowl (koul) n. 1. a. The hood worn by monks. b. A robe or cloak having such a hood. 2. A hood-shaped covering used to increase the draft of a chimney. 3. The top portion of the front part of an automobile body, supporting the windshield and dashboard. 4. An aircraft cowling. —tr.v. 1. To put a cowl on. 2. To make a monk of. 3. To cover with a cowl. [Middle English coule, Old English cugele, from Late Latin cuculla, from Latin cucullus, hood.]

cow·lick (kou'lĭk') n. A tuft of hair that stands up from the head and will not lie flat. [So called because it appears to have been licked by a cow.]

cowl·ing (kou'lĭng) n. A removable metal covering for an aircraft engine.

cow·man (kou'mǝn) n. 1. The owner of a cattle ranch. 2. Brit. A person who tends cows.

co·work·er (kō'wûrk'ǝr) n. A fellow worker.

cow·pea (kou'pē') n. 1. A vine, Vigna sinensis, bearing long, hanging pods and grown in the southern United States for soil improvement and as animal feed. 2. The edible, pealike seed of this plant; black-eyed pea.

cow·poke (kou'pōk') n. Informal. A cowboy.

cow·pox (kou'pŏks') n. A contagious skin disease of cattle caused by a virus that is isolated and used to vaccinate humans against smallpox.

cow·punch·er (kou'pŭn'chǝr) n. Informal. A cowboy.

cow·ry (kou'rē) n., pl. -ries. Also cow·rie. Any of various tropical saltwater mollusks of the family Cypraeidae, with glossy, often brightly marked shells. [Hindi kaurī, from Sanskrit kaparda.]

cow·skin (kou'skĭn') n. 1. The hide of a cow. 2. Leather made from cowskin.

cow·slip (kou'slĭp') n. An Old World primrose, Primula veris, with fragrant yellow flowers. [Middle English cowslyppe, from Old English cūslyppe, "cow dung" (prob. because some varieties are found in cow pastures) : cū, cow + slyppe, slime, paste.]

cox (kŏks). Informal. —n. A coxswain. —tr.v. To serve as coxswain for (a boat). —intr.v. To act as coxswain.

cox·comb (kŏks'kōm') n. 1. A conceited dandy; fop. 2. Var. of cockscomb. [Middle English cokkes comb, "cock's comb."]

cox·swain (kŏk'sǝn, -swān') n. Also cock·swain. A person who steers a boat or racing shell or has charge of its crew. [Middle English cok swain : cok, cockboat + swain, attendant, boy, from Old Norse sveinn.]

coy (koi) adj. -er, -est. 1. Shy and demure; retiring. 2. Pre-tending to be shy or modest so as to attract the interest of others. [Middle English, from Old French coi, shy, quiet, from Latin quiētus, quiet.] —**coy'ly** adv. —**coy'ness** n.

coy·o·te (kī-ō'tē, kī'ōt') n. 1. A wolflike carnivorous animal, Canis latrans, common in western North America and ranging eastward to Pennsylvania and New York. 2. Slang. A contemptible sneak. [Mexican Spanish, from Nahuatl coyotl.]

coz·en (kŭz'ǝn) tr.v. To deceive by means of a petty trick or fraud. —intr.v. To act with intent to deceive. [Poss. from obs. Italian cozzonare, "to be a horse trader," from cozzone, broker, from Latin coctiō.] —**coz'en·er** n.

co·zy (kō'zē) adj. -zi·er, -zi·est. Also co·sy, -si·er, -si·est. 1. Snug and comfortable; warm. 2. Informal. Marked by close association for devious or illicit purposes: a cozy agreement. —n., pl. -zies. Also co·sy pl. -sies. A padded or knitted covering placed over a teapot to keep the tea hot. [Scottish cosie.] —**co'zi·ly** adv. —**co'zi·ness** n.

Cr The symbol for the element chromium.

crab¹ (krăb) n. 1. Any of various predominantly saltwater crustaceans of the section Brachyura within the order Decapoda, having a broad, flattened cephalothorax covered by a hard carapace and having the small abdomen concealed beneath it, and five pairs of legs, of which the anterior pair are large and pincerlike. 2. Any of various similar related crustaceans. 3. The crab louse. 4. Crab. The constellation and sign of the zodiac Cancer. 5. Any of various machines for handling or hoisting heavy weights. —intr.v. crabbed, crab·bing. To hunt or catch crabs. [Middle English crab(be), from Old English crabba.]

crab² (krăb) n. 1. The crab apple or its fruit. 2. Informal. A quarrelsome, ill-tempered person. —v. crabbed, crab·bing. Informal. —intr.v. To criticize; find fault. —tr.v. 1. To interfere with and ruin. 2. To find fault with; complain irritably about. [Middle English crab(be).]

crab apple. 1. Any of several trees of the genus Pyrus, with white, pink, or red flowers and small, applelike fruit. 2. The tart fruit of any of these trees.

crab·bed (krăb'ĭd) adj. 1. Irritable; ill-tempered. 2. Difficult to understand; complicated. 3. Difficult to read, as handwriting. [Middle English.] —**crab'bed·ly** adv. —**crab'bed·ness** n.

crab·by (krăb'ē) adj. -bi·er, -bi·est. Grouchy; ill-tempered. —**crab'bi·ly** adv. —**crab'bi·ness** n.

crab·grass (krăb'grăs') n. Any of various coarse grasses of the genus Digitaria, which tend to spread and displace other grasses in lawns.

crab louse. A body louse that infests the pubic region and causes severe itching.

crack (krăk) intr.v. 1. a. To break with a sharp, snapping sound: The tree limb cracked. b. To make such a sound; to snap: She fired and the rifle cracked. 2. To break without dividing into parts; split slightly: The veneer on the dresser cracked. 3. To change sharply in pitch or timbre; break: Her voice cracked. 4. To break down; give out: The prisoner cracked under prolonged interrogation. 5. Chem. To decompose into simpler compounds. —tr.v. 1. To break with a sharp, snapping sound: crack an egg. 2. To cause to make a sharp, snapping sound; to snap: crack the whip. 3. To cause to break without dividing into parts; split slightly: A stone cracked the windshield. 4. To strike with a sudden, sharp sound: He cracked the dog with a newspaper. 5. To break open or into: crack a safe. 6. To discover the solution to, esp. after considerable effort: crack a secret code. 7. To cause (the voice) to crack. 8. Informal. To tell (a joke). 9. To impair mentally: Many years in prison camp cracked his mind. 10. To reduce (petroleum) to simpler compounds by cracking. —**phrasal verbs. crack down.** Informal. To become more severe or strict. **crack up.** Informal. 1. To crash; collide. 2. To have a mental or physical breakdown. 3. To break up; disintegrate. 4. To laugh or cause to laugh boisterously. —n. 1. A sharp, snapping sound: the crack of a firearm. 2. A partial split or break; fissure: a crack in a teapot. 3. A slight, narrow space: The window was open a crack. 4. A sharp, resounding blow: gave the horse a crack on the rump. 5. A cracking tone or sound: a crack in her voice. 6. An attempt; a chance: gave him a crack at the job. 7. A flippant or sarcastic remark. 8. A moment; instant: at the crack of dawn. —adj. Excelling in skill or achievement; superior; first-rate: *a crack marksman.* —**idioms. crack a book.** *Slang.* To open a book for studying. **crack a smile.** *Informal.* To smile. **cracked up to be.** *Slang.* Believed to be. [Middle English *craken,* from Old English *cracian.*]

crack·brain (krăk′brān′) *n.* A foolish or crazy person. —**crack′brained′** *adj.*

crack·down (krăk′doun′) *n.* An action taken to stop an illegal or disapproved activity: *a crackdown on gambling.*

cracked (krăkt) *adj.* **1.** Having a crack or cracks: *a cracked dish.* **2.** Broken into pieces: *cracked ice.* **3.** *Slang.* Crazy; insane.

crack·er (krăk′ər) *n.* **1.** A thin, crisp wafer or biscuit. **2.** A firecracker. **3.** A party favor with a weak explosive that makes a sharp popping noise when pulled at one or both ends. **4.** Someone or something that cracks.

crack·er·jack (krăk′ər-jăk′) *n. Slang.* Someone or something of excellent quality or ability. [From CRACK (proficient) + JACK (man).]

crack·ers (krăk′ərz) *adj. Brit. Slang.* Insane.

crack·ing (krăk′ĭng) *n.* The process of decomposing complex hydrocarbons into simpler compounds, usu. by means of heat and often various catalysts, esp. the decomposition of petroleum to extract a substance such as gasoline.

crack·le (krăk′əl) *v.* **-led, -ling.** —*intr.v.* To make a succession of slight sharp, snapping noises, as a small fire does. —*tr.v.* To crush (paper, cellophane, etc.) with such sounds. —*n.* **1.** The act or sound of crackling. **2.** A network of fine cracks on the surface of glazed pottery, china, or glassware. [Freq. of CRACK.]

crack·ling (krăk′lĭng) *n.* **1.** A succession of slight sharp, snapping noises. **2. cracklings.** The crisp bits that remain after rendering pork fat.

crack·ly (krăk′lē) *adj.* Likely to crackle; crisp.

crack·nel (krăk′nəl) *n.* **1.** A hard, crisp biscuit. **2. cracknels.** Crisp bits of fried pork fat. [Middle English *crak(e)nel,* prob. from Old French *craquelin,* from Middle Dutch *krākelinc,* from *krāken,* to crack.]

crack·pot (krăk′pŏt′) *n.* An eccentric person, esp. one espousing bizarre ideas. —*modifier:* *a crackpot scheme.*

crack·up (krăk′ŭp′) *n.* **1.** *Informal.* A collision, as of an airplane or automobile. **2.** *Informal.* A mental or physical breakdown.

-cracy. A suffix meaning government or rule: **technocracy.** [Old French *-cratie,* from Late Latin *-cratia,* from Greek *-kratia,* from *kratos,* strength, power.]

cra·dle (krād′l) *n.* **1.** A small, low bed for an infant, often with rockers. **2.** A place of origin; birthplace: *Philadelphia is known as the cradle of liberty.* **3.** Infancy: *showed an interest in music almost from the cradle.* **4.** A framework of wood or metal used to support something, as a ship undergoing repair. **5.** The part of a telephone that contains the connecting switch upon which the receiver and mouthpiece unit is supported. **6.** A frame projecting above a scythe, used to catch grain as it is cut so that it can be laid flat. **7.** A low, flat framework that rolls on casters, used by a mechanic working beneath an automobile. **8.** A boxlike device furnished with rockers, used for washing gold-bearing dirt. —*v.* **-dled, -dling.** —*tr.v.* **1.** To place into, rock, or hold in or as if in a cradle: *cradled the baby in his arms.* **2.** To care for or nurture in infancy: *cradled the young nation through its first decade.* **3.** To reap (grain) with a cradle. **4.** To place or support (a ship) in a cradle. **5.** To wash (gold-bearing dirt) in a cradle. —*intr.v.* **1.** To lie in or as if in a cradle: *The rifle cradled on my knees.* **2.** To reap grain with a cradle. —*idiom.* **rob the cradle.** *Informal.* To have as a spouse or sweetheart one much younger than oneself. [Middle English *cradel,* from Old English *cradol, cradel.*] —**cra′dler** *n.*

cra·dle·song (krād′l-sông′, -sŏng′) *n.* A lullaby.

craft (krăft) *n.* **1.** Skill or ability in something, esp. in the arts or work done with the hands. **2.** Skill in evasion or deception; cunning; guile: *an espionage ploy conceived with brilliance and carried out with craft.* **3. a.** An occupation or trade, esp. one requiring manual dexterity. **b.** The membership of such an occupation or trade; a guild. **4.** *pl.* **craft.** A boat, ship, or aircraft. —See Syns at **ability.** —*tr.v.* To make by hand. [Middle English, strength, skill, from Old English *cræft.*]

-craft. A suffix meaning work, art, or practice of: **stagecraft.** [From CRAFT.]

crafts·man (krăfts′mən) *n., pl.* **-men** (-mĭn). **1.** A skilled worker, esp. one who practices a craft. **2.** An artist considered with regard to technique. —**crafts′man·ship′** *n.*

craft·y (krăf′tē) *adj.* **-i·er, -i·est.** Skilled in underhandedness and deception; shrewd; cunning. —**craft′i·ly** *adv.* —**craft′i·ness** *n.*

crag (krăg) *n.* A steeply projecting mass of rock forming part of a rugged cliff or headland. [Middle English.]

crag·gy (krăg′ē) *adj.* **-gi·er, -gi·est.** Also **crag·ged** (krăg′ĭd). **1.** Having crags; steep and rugged: *a craggy mountain.* **2.** Rugged in appearance: *a craggy face.* —**crag′gi·ly** *adv.* —**crag′gi·ness** *n.*

cram (krăm) *v.* **crammed, cram·ming.** —*tr.v.* **1.** To force, press, or squeeze (persons or things) into an insufficient space; to stuff. **2.** To fill too tightly. **3.** To gorge with food. **4.** *Informal.* To study (a subject) intensively, esp. just before an examination. —*intr.v.* **1.** To gorge oneself with food. **2.** *Informal.* To make an intensive last-minute review of a subject, as in studying for an examination. [Middle English *crammen,* from Old English *crammian.*] —**cram′mer** *n.*

cramp¹ (krămp) *n.* **1.** A sudden involuntary muscular contraction causing severe pain. **2.** A temporary partial paralysis of muscles used to excess: *a leg cramp.* **3. cramps.** Sharp, persistent pains in the abdomen. —*tr.v.* To cause to be affected with or as if with a cramp. —*intr.v.* To be affected with a cramp. [Middle English *crampe,* from Old French.]

cramp² (krămp) *n.* **1.** An iron bar bent at both ends, used to hold together blocks of stone or timber in building. **2.** A frame with an adjustable part to hold pieces together; a clamp. **3.** Anything that compresses or restrains: *put a cramp on his style.* —*tr.v.* **1.** To hold together with a cramp. **2.** To restrict; hamper: *Lack of money cramped his style.* **3.** To jam (the wheels of a car) hard to the right or left. [Middle Dutch *crampe,* hook.]

cram·pon (krăm′pŏn, -pŏn′) *n.* **1.** A hinged pair of curved iron bars for raising heavy objects, such as stones or timber. **2.** Often **crampons.** An iron spike attached to the shoe to prevent slipping when climbing or walking on ice.

crampon   crane

cran·ber·ry (krăn′bĕr′ē) *n.* **1.** A slender, trailing North American shrub, *Vaccinium macrocarpon,* growing in damp ground and bearing tart red berries. **2.** The edible berry of the cranberry. —*modifier:* *cranberry juice.* [From Low German *kraan,* crane + BERRY.]

crane (krān) *n.* **1. a.** Any of various large wading birds of the family Gruidae, with a long neck, long legs, and a long bill. **b.** Any similar bird, such as a heron. **2.** A machine for hoisting and moving heavy objects by means of cables attached to a movable boom. **3.** Any of various devices with a swinging arm, as one in a fireplace for suspending a pot. —*v.* **craned, cran·ing.** —*tr.v.* To hoist or move (something) with or as if with a crane. **2.** To strain and stretch (the neck). —*intr.v.* To stretch one's neck, as for a better view. [Middle English, from Old English *cran.*]

cra·ni·al (krā′nē-əl) *adj.* Of or pertaining to the skull. [From CRANIUM.]

cranial nerve. Any of several nerves that arise in pairs from the brainstem and reach the periphery through openings in the skull.

cra·ni·um (krā'nē-əm) *n., pl.* **-ums** or **-ni·a** (-nē-ə). **1.** The skull of a vertebrate. **2.** The part of the skull enclosing the brain. [Medieval Latin *crānium,* from Greek *kranion.*]

crank (krăngk) *n.* **1.** A device for converting motion in a straight line into rotary motion, consisting of a rod or handle attached at right angles to a shaft that is free to turn. **2.** *Informal.* **a.** An irritable person; a grouch. **b.** A person with odd or eccentric ideas. **3.** A peculiar or eccentric idea or action. *—tr.v.* **1.** To start or operate (a device) by turning a crank. **2.** To make into the shape of a crank; twist; bend. *—intr.v.* **1.** To turn a crank. **2.** To twist; wind. [Middle English, from Old English *cranc.*]

crank·case (krăngk'kās') *n.* The metal case enclosing the crankshaft and associated parts in an engine.

crank·shaft (krăngk'shăft') *n.* A shaft that turns or is turned by a crank.

crank·y (krăng'kē) *adj.* **-i·er, -i·est. 1.** Ill-tempered; irritable; peevish. **2.** Eccentric; odd. **3.** Full of bends and turns; crooked. **—crank'i·ly** *adv.* **—crank'i·ness** *n.*

cran·ny (krăn'ē) *n., pl.* **-nies.** A small opening, as in a wall or rock face; crevice; fissure. [Middle English *crani,* from Old French *cran, cren,* notch.]

crape (krāp) *n.* Var. of **crepe.**

crap·pie (krăp'ē) *n.* Either of two edible North American freshwater fishes, that are related to the sunfishes. [Canadian French *crapet.*]

craps (krăps) *n.* (*used with a sing. or pl. verb*). A gambling game played with a pair of dice. [Louisiana French, from French *crabs,* from obs. English slang *crabs,* lowest throw at hazard, pl. of *crab.*]

crap·shoot·er (krăp'shōō'tər) *n.* A person who plays craps.

crash¹ (krăsh) *intr.v.* **1.** To fall or collide noisily; smash: *The truck crashed against a tree.* **2.** To undergo sudden damage or destruction on impact: *The falling chimney crashed on the street.* **3.** To make a sudden loud noise: *I jumped when the thunder crashed.* **4.** To move noisily or so as to cause damage: *frightened birds crashing into branches.* **5.** To fail suddenly, as a business or an economy. *—tr.v.* **1.** To cause to crash: *He crashed the bike.* **2.** To dash to pieces; smash. **3.** *Informal.* To join or enter without invitation: *crash a party. —n.* **1.** A sudden loud noise, as of something breaking: *a crash of thunder.* **2.** A wrecking; smashing: *a car crash.* **3.** A sudden, severe decline in business or the economy: *the stock-market crash of 1929. —modifier: Help came too late for the crash victims. —adj. Informal.* Of or characterized by an intensive effort to produce or accomplish something: *a crash program.* [Middle English *crashen,* blend of *crasen,* to craze, and *dashen,* to dash.] **—crash'er** *n.*

crash² (krăsh) *n.* A coarse, light, unevenly woven fabric of cotton or linen, used for towels, curtains, etc. [Russian *krashenina,* a kind of colored linen, from *krashenie,* coloring, from *krasa,* beauty.]

crash dive. A rapid submerging of a submarine.

crash helmet. A padded helmet, as one worn by a motorcyclist, to protect the head.

crash-land (krăsh'lănd') *tr.v.* To land and damage (an aircraft) under emergency conditions. *—intr.v.* To crash-land an aircraft. **—crash landing.**

crass (krăs) *adj.* **-er, -est.** Grossly ignorant; unfeeling; stupid: *a crass person; crass ignorance.* —See Syns at **coarse.** [Latin *crassus,* fat, gross, dense.] **—crass'ly** *adv.* **—crass'ness** *n.*

-crat. A suffix indicating a participant in or supporter of a class or form of government: **technocrat.** [French *-crate,* from Greek *-kratēs,* from *-kratia,* *-cracy.*]

crate (krāt) *n.* **1.** A container, esp. a slatted wooden case or box for storing or shipping things. **2.** *Slang.* An old, badly used, rickety vehicle, as an automobile. *—tr.v.* **crat·ed, crat·ing.** To pack into a crate. [Latin *crātis,* wickerwork.]

cra·ter (krā'tər) *n.* **1.** A bowl-shaped depression at the mouth of a volcano or geyser. **2.** Any pit resembling a crater, esp. when formed by an explosion or by the impact of a meteor. [Latin *crātēr,* bowl, crater, from Greek *kratēr,* mixing vessel.]

cra·vat (krə-văt') *n.* A necktie or a scarf worn as a necktie. [French *cravate,* orig. a neckband worn by Croatian mercenaries in the service of France, from *Cravate,* a Croatian.]

crave (krāv) *tr.v.* **craved, crav·ing. 1.** To have an intense desire for: *crave success; crave an ice-cream soda.* **2.** To beg earnestly for; implore: *I crave your forgiveness.* [Middle English *craven,* from Old English *crafian,* to beg, demand.]

cra·ven (krā'vən) *adj.* Characterized by abject fear; cowardly. —See Syns at **cowardly.** *—n.* A coward. [Middle English *cravant.*] **—cra'ven·ly** *adv.* **—cra'ven·ness** *n.*

crav·ing (krā'vĭng) *n.* A consuming desire; longing.

craw (krô) *n.* **1.** The crop of a bird. **2.** The stomach, esp. of an animal. [Middle English *crawe.*]

craw·fish (krô'fĭsh') *n.* Var. of **crayfish.**

crawl¹ (krôl) *intr.v.* **1.** To move slowly on the hands and knees or by dragging oneself; creep: *The baby crawled across the room.* **2.** To advance slowly, feebly, or laboriously: *Time crawls.* **3.** To proceed or act servilely: *I won't crawl to get the promotion.* **4. a.** To be covered with crawling things: *The sidewalk crawled with ants.* **b.** To shiver as if covered with crawling things: *His skin crawled in horror.* **5.** To swim the crawl. *—n.* **1.** A very slow pace: *traffic moving at a crawl.* **2.** A rapid swimming stroke performed face down and consisting of alternating overarm strokes and a flutter kick. [Middle English *craulen,* from Old Norse *krafla,* to crawl, creep.] **—crawl'er** *n.*

crawl² (krôl) *n.* A pen in shallow water, as for confining fish or turtles. [Dutch *kraal, kraal.*]

crawl·y (krô'lē) *adj.* **-i·er, -i·est.** *Informal.* **1.** Creepy: *an eerie, crawly novel.* **2.** Feeling as if things are crawling over one's skin.

cray·fish (krā'fĭsh') *n., pl.* **crayfish** or **-fish·es.** Also **craw·fish** (krô'-). **1.** Any of various freshwater crustaceans of the genera *Cambarus* and *Astacus,* that resemble a lobster but are considerably smaller. **2.** Any similar crustacean. [By folk etymology (influenced by *fish*) from earlier *crevis, cravis,* Middle English *crevise,* from Old French.]

cray·on (krā'ŏn', -ən) *n.* **1.** A stick of colored wax, charcoal, or chalk, used for drawing. **2.** A drawing made with crayons. *—tr.v.* To draw, color, or decorate with crayons. [French, from *craie,* chalk, from Latin *crēta.*]

craze (krāz) *v.* **crazed, craz·ing.** *—tr.v.* **1.** To make insane; derange: *The man was crazed by his wife's death.* **2.** To produce a network of fine cracks in (a ceramic). *—intr.v.* **1.** To become insane or deranged. **2.** To become covered with fine cracks. *—n.* **1.** A popular fashion; a rage; fad. **2.** A pattern of fine cracks. —See Syns at **insane.** [Middle English *crasen,* to shatter, render insane.]

cra·zy (krā'zē) *adj.* **-zi·er, -zi·est. 1.** Affected with or suggestive of madness; demented. **2.** *Informal.* Full of enthusiasm or excitement: *crazy about dogs.* **3.** *Informal.* Immoderately fond; infatuated: *They're crazy about each other.* **4.** *Informal.* Not sensible; impractical: *a crazy stunt.* —See Syns at **foolish** and **insane. —idiom. like crazy.** *Informal.* Very much: *It hurts like crazy.* [From CRAZE.] **—cra'zi·ly** *adv.* **—cra'zi·ness** *n.*

crazy quilt. A patchwork quilt arranged in no definite pattern.

creak (krēk) *intr.v.* **1.** To make a grating or squeaking sound: *The screen door creaked when I opened it.* **2.** To move with such a sound or sounds: *The old wagon creaked down the road.* *—n.* A grating or squeaking sound. [Middle English *creken.*]

creak·y (krē'kē) *adj.* **-i·er, -i·est.** Tending or liable to creak: *a creaky door.* **—creak'i·ly** *adv.* **—creak'i·ness** *n.*

cream (krēm) *n.* **1.** The yellowish fatty part of unhomogenized milk that tends to separate and rise to the surface. **2.** The color of cream, a pale yellow to yellowish white. **3.** Any of various foods resembling or containing cream: *ice cream.* **4.** A cosmetic or other preparation that is soft and creamy: *shaving cream; a skin cream.* **4.** The choicest part: *the cream of the litter.* **—modifier:** *a cream pitcher.* *—intr.v.* **1.** To form cream. **2.** To form foam or froth. *—tr.v.* **1.** To allow the cream to separate from (milk). **2.** To remove the cream from; to skim. **3.** To select or remove the best part from: *He creamed the profits and sold out.* **4.** To beat into a creamy consistency. **5.** To prepare or cook in or with a cream sauce. **6.** *Slang.* To defeat overwhelmingly: *We creamed them by 21 points.* **—adj.** Yellowish white. [Middle English *creme, creime,* from Old French *cresme, craime,* blend of Late Latin *chrisma,* ointment, and Late Latin *crāmum*, cream.]

cream cheese. A soft white cheese made of cream and milk.

cream·er (krē'mər) *n.* **1.** A small jug or pitcher for cream. **2.** A machine or device for separating cream from milk.

cream·er·y (krē'mə-rē) *n., pl.* **-ies.** An establishment where dairy products are prepared or sold.

cream of tartar. Potassium bitartrate.

cream puff. A shell of light pastry filled with whipped cream, custard, or ice cream.

crease (krēs) *n.* **1.** A fold, wrinkle, or line usu. made by pressure. **2.** *Hockey & Lacrosse.* A rectangular area marked off in front of the goal cage. —*v.* **creased, creas·ing.** —*tr.v.* **1.** To make a fold or wrinkle in. **2.** To graze with a bullet; wound superficially. —*intr.v.* To become wrinkled. [Earlier *creast,* from Middle English *crest,* ridge, crest.]

cre·ate (krē-āt') *tr.v.* **-at·ed, -at·ing. 1.** To cause to exist; bring into being; originate: *created a new style in contemporary fashion.* **2.** To give rise to; bring about; produce: *Her remark created a stir.* **3.** To invest with office or title; appoint: *The king created him a knight.* [Middle English *createn,* from Latin *creāre.*]

cre·a·tine (krē'ə-tēn, -tǐn) *n.* Also **cre·a·tin** (-tǐn). A nitrogenous organic acid, $C_4H_9N_3O_2$, found mainly in the muscle tissue of many vertebrates and acting in muscular contraction. [Greek *kreas,* flesh + -INE.]

cre·a·tion (krē-ā'shən) *n.* **1.** The act or process of creating: *the creation of an empire; the creation of a canyon by erosion.* **2.** Something produced by invention and imagination: *an artist's creation.* **3.** The universe, the world, and all created beings and things. **4. the Creation.** The biblical story of the earth's origin as told in the Old Testament. **5. a.** Everywhere: *He wandered all over creation.* **b.** All creatures or a class of creatures: *all creation.*

cre·a·tive (krē-ā'tǐv) *adj.* **1.** Having the ability or power to create things. **2.** Characterized by originality and expressiveness; imaginative: *creative writing.* —**cre·a'tiv·ly** *adv.* —**cre·a'tiv'i·ty** or **cre·a'tive·ness** *n.*

cre·a·tor (krē-ā'tər) *n.* **1.** Someone that creates. **2. the Creator.** God.

crea·ture (krē'chər) *n.* **1.** A living being, esp. an animal. **2.** A human being: *The prisoners of war were pathetic creatures.* **3.** Someone or something dependent upon, subservient to, or influenced by another; tool: *The board is composed of the president's creatures.* **4.** Anything created. —**crea'tur·al** *adj.*

crèche (krĕsh) *n.* **1.** A representation of the Nativity, usu. consisting of figures of the infant Jesus, Mary, Joseph, shepherds, and the Magi. **2.** *Brit.* A day nursery. [French, from Old French *creche,* manger, crib.]

cre·dence (krēd'ns) *n.* Acceptance as true or valid; belief. [Middle English, from Old French, from Medieval Latin *crēdentia,* belief, trust, from Latin *crēdere,* to believe.]

cre·den·tial (krǐ-dĕn'shəl) *n.* **1.** Something that entitles a person to confidence, credit, or authority. **2. credentials.** A letter or other written evidence attesting to a person's qualifications, authority, or right to credit.

cre·den·za (krǐ-dĕn'zə) *n.* A buffet or sideboard, esp. one without legs. [Italian, from Medieval Latin *crēdentia,* table.]

cred·i·ble (krĕd'ə-bəl) *adj.* **1.** Believable; plausible: *a credible explanation.* **2.** Worthy of confidence; reliable: *a credible witness.* [Middle English, from Latin *crēdibilis,* from *crēdere,* to believe, entrust.] —**cred'i·bil'i·ty** or **cred'i·ble·ness** *n.* —**cred'i·bly** *adv.*

cred·it (krĕd'ĭt) *n.* **1.** Belief or confidence; trust: *place full credit in the truthfulness of the state records.* **2.** The quality or condition of being trustworthy or credible: *"One of no less credit than Aristotle"* (Walton). **3.** A source of honor or distinction: *He is a credit to his family.* **4.** Approval for some act, ability, or quality; praise: *deserves credit for running a successful campaign.* **5.** Influence based on the good opinion or confidence of others. **6.** Often **credits.** An acknowledgment of work done, as in the production of a motion picture, play, or book. **7. a.** Official certification that a student has successfully completed a course of study: *receive credit for a course.* **b.** A unit of study so certified: *She has six credits in biology.* **8.** Reputation for financial responsibility, entitling a person to be trusted in buying or borrowing: *His credit is good everywhere.* **9. a.** A system for the purchase of goods or services in which the amount is charged and payment is made at a later time, often in installments: *buy on credit.* **b.** Confidence in a buyer's ability and intention to fulfill financial obligations at some future time: *The store extended credit to him.* **c.** The time allowed for payment of a debt: *You have credit for three months on this bill.* **10.** *Accounting.* **a.** The acknowledgment of payment by a debtor by entry of the sum in an account. **b.** The right-hand side of an account on which such amounts are entered. **c.** An entry on this side. **11.** The balance or amount of money remaining in a person's account. **12.** An amount placed by a bank at the disposal of a client, against which he may draw: *The bank halved the company's credit.* —**modifier:** *a credit risk; a credit rating.* —*tr.v.* **1.** To believe; trust: *"She refused steadfastly to credit the reports of his death"* (Agatha Christie). **2.** To give honor to (a person) for something: *credit him with the invention.* **3.** To ascribe (something) to a person; attribute to: *credit the invention to him.* **4.** *Accounting.* **a.** To give credit for (a sum paid). **b.** To give credit to (a payer). **5.** To give or award credits to (a student). [Old French, from Old Italian *credito,* from Latin *crēditum,* "something entrusted," loan, from *crēdere,* to believe, entrust.]

cred·it·a·ble (krĕd'ĭ-tə-bəl) *adj.* Deserving commendation; praiseworthy: *a creditable effort.* —**cred'it·a·ble·ness** *n.* —**cred'it·a·bly** *adv.*

credit card. A card issued by business concerns authorizing the holder to buy goods or services on credit.

cred·i·tor (krĕd'ĭ-tər) *n.* A person or firm to whom money or its equivalent is owed.

credit union. A cooperative organization that makes loans to its members at low interest rates.

cre·do (krē'dō, krā'-) *n., pl.* **-dos.** A statement of belief; creed. [Latin *crēdo,* "I believe," the first word of the Apostles' Creed, from *crēdere,* to believe.]

cre·du·li·ty (krǐ-dōō'lǐ-tē, -dyōō'-) *n.* A tendency to believe too readily.

cred·u·lous (krĕj'ə-ləs) *adj.* **1.** Tending to believe too readily; gullible. **2.** Arising from or characterized by credulity. [Latin *crēdulus,* from *crēdere,* to believe.] —**cred'u·lous·ly** *adv.* —**cred'u·lous·ness** *n.*

Cree (krē) *n., pl.* **Cree** or **Crees. 1.** A tribe of Algonquian-speaking Indians formerly living in Ontario, Manitoba, and Saskatchewan. **2.** A member of this tribe. **3.** The language of the Cree.

creed (krēd) *n.* **1.** A formal statement of religious belief; confession of faith. **2.** Any statement or system of belief, principles, or opinions that guides a person's actions: *His artistic creed was art for art's sake.* [Middle English *crede,* from Old English *crēda,* from Latin *crēdo,* "I believe."]

creek (krēk, krĭk) *n.* **1.** A small stream, often a shallow tributary to a river. **2.** *Brit.* A small inlet in a shoreline. —*idiom.* **up the** (or **a**) **creek.** In a difficult position or situation. [Middle English *creke, crike.*]

Creek (krēk) *n., pl.* **Creek** or **Creeks. 1.** A confederacy of several Muskhogean-speaking Indian tribes, formerly inhabiting parts of Georgia, Alabama, and northern Florida. **2.** A member of any of these tribes. **3.** The language of the Creek.

creel (krēl) *n.* A wicker basket used for carrying fish. [Middle English *crel, crelle.*]

creep (krēp) *intr.v.* **crept** (krĕpt), **creep·ing. 1.** To move with the body close to the ground, as a baby on hands and knees. **2.** To move stealthily, cautiously, or very slowly: *soldiers creeping up the mountain.* **3.** To advance or spread slowly: *A reddish glow crept into his cheeks.* **4.** *Bot.* To grow along a surface, sending out roots at intervals or clinging by means of suckers or tendrils: *Ivy crept up the trellis.* **5.** To slip out of place from pressure or wear; shift gradually. **6.** To have a tingling sensation: *made my flesh creep.* —See Syns at **sneak.** —*n.* **1.** A creeping motion or progress: *Traffic moved at a creep.* **2.** *Slang.* An obnoxious or undesirable person. —*idiom.* **the creeps.** *Informal.* A sensation of fear or repugnance, as if things were crawling on one's skin. [Middle English *crepen,* from Old English *crēopan.*]

ă pat	ā pay	â care	ä father	ĕ pet	ē be	hw which	ĭ pit	ī tie	î pier	ŏ pot	ō toe	ô paw, for	oi noise
ōō took	ōō boot	ou out	th thin	*th* this	ŭ cut		û urge	zh vision	ə about, item, edible, gallop, circus				

creep·er (krē′pər) *n.* **1.** Someone or something that creeps. **2.** *Bot.* A plant that creeps. **3.** A grappling device for dragging lakes, rivers, etc. **4.** Often **creepers.** A metal frame with spikes, attached to a shoe or boot to prevent slipping.

creep·y (krē′pē) *adj.* **-i·er, -i·est.** *Informal.* Inducing or having a sensation of repugnance or fear, as of things crawling on one's skin: *a creepy story; a creepy, old house.* **—creep′i·ness** *n.*

cre·mate (krē′māt′, krĭ-māt′) *tr.v.* **-mat·ed, -mat·ing.** To burn (a corpse) to ashes. [From Latin *cremāre*, to burn, consume by fire.] **—cre·ma′tion** *n.*

cre·ma·to·ri·um (krē′mə-tôr′ē-əm, -tōr′-) *n.*, *pl.* **-ums** or **-to·ri·a** (-tôr′ē-ə, -tōr′-). A crematory.

cre·ma·to·ry (krē′mə-tôr′ē, -tōr′ē, krĕm′ə-) *n.*, *pl.* **-ries.** A furnace or establishment for the cremation of corpses. **—adj.** Of or pertaining to cremation.

crème de la crème (krĕm′ də lä krĕm′). The essence of excellence. [French, "cream of the cream."]

cre·nate (krē′nāt′) *adj.* Also **cre·nat·ed** (-nā′tĭd). Having a margin or edge with rounded or scalloped projections: *a crenate leaf.* [Prob. from Late Latin *crēna*, notch.] **—cre′nate·ly** *adv.* **—cre·na′tion** *n.*

cren·e·lat·ed (krĕn′ə-lā′tĭd) *adj.* Having battlements: *a crenelated fort.* [From French *crenel*, a crenelation, from Old French.] **—cren′e·la′tion** *n.*

cre·o·dont (krē′ə-dŏnt′) *n.* Any of various extinct carnivorous mammals of the suborder Creodonta of the Paleocene to Pliocene epochs. [New Latin *Creodondta*, "flesh-toothed ones."]

Cre·ole (krē′ōl′) *n.* **1.** Any person of European descent born in the West Indies or Spanish America. **2. a.** A person descended from or culturally related to the original French settlers of the southern United States, esp. Louisiana. **b.** The French dialect spoken by the Creoles. **3.** A person descended from or culturally related to the Spanish and Portuguese settlers of the Gulf States. **4.** Any person of mixed European and Negro ancestry who speaks a Creole dialect. **—adj.** Of, relating to, or characteristic of the Creoles or their language or culture.

Cre·on (krē′ŏn′) *n. Gk. Myth.* King of Thebes, successor to Oedipus, and uncle of Antigone.

cre·o·sol (krē′ə-sōl′, -sôl′) *n.* A colorless aromatic liquid, $C_8H_{10}O_2$, that is a constituent of creosote and is obtained from beechwood tar. [CREOS(OTE) + -OL.]

cre·o·sote (krē′ə-sōt′) *n.* **1.** A colorless to yellowish oily liquid obtained by the destructive distillation of wood tar, esp. from beechwood. **2.** A yellowish to greenish-brown oily liquid obtained from coal tar and used as a wood preservative and disinfectant. **—tr.v. -sot·ed, -sot·ing.** To treat or paint with creosote. [German *Kreosot*, "flesh preserver" (from its antiseptic qualities) : Greek *kreas*, flesh + *sōtēr*, preserver, from *saos*, safe.]

crepe (krāp) *n.* Also **crape, crêpe. 1.** A light, soft, thin fabric of silk, cotton, wool, or other fiber, with a crinkled surface. **2.** Crepe paper. **3.** Crepe rubber. **4.** A very thin pancake. [French *crêpe*, from Old French *crespe*, crisp, curly, from Latin *crispus.*]

crêpe de Chine (krăp′ də shēn′). A silk crepe used for clothing. [French, "crepe of China."]

crepe paper. Crinkled tissue paper, resembling crepe, used for decorations.

crepe rubber. Rubber with a crinkled texture, used for shoe soles.

crêpe su·zette (krăp′ sōō-zĕt′) *pl.* **crêpe su·zettes** (krăp′ sōō-zĕts′). A thin dessert pancake usu. rolled with hot orange or tangerine sauce and often served with a flaming brandy or curaçao sauce. [French : *crepe*, pancake + *Suzette*, pet form of the name *Suzanne.*]

crep·i·tate (krĕp′ĭ-tāt′) *intr.v.* **-tat·ed, -tat·ing.** To make a rattling sound; crackle. [Latin *crepitāre*, to crackle, from *crepāre*, to crack, creak.] **—crep′i·ta′tion** *n.*

crept (krĕpt) *v.* Past tense and past participle of **creep.**

cre·pus·cu·lar (krĭ-pŭs′kyə-lər) *adj.* **1.** Of or like twilight. **2.** *Zool.* Becoming active at twilight or before sunrise, as certain insects. [From Latin *crepusculum*, twilight, from *creper*, dusky, dark.]

cres·cen·do (krə-shĕn′dō, -sĕn′-) *n.*, *pl.* **-dos. 1.** A gradual increase in the volume or intensity of sound. **2.** A musical passage played in a crescendo. **—adj.** Gradually increasing in volume or intensity. **—adv.** With a crescendo. [Italian, "increasing," from *crescere*, to increase, from Latin *crēscere*, to grow.]

cres·cent (krĕs′ənt) *n.* **1.** The figure of the moon as it appears in its first quarter, with concave and convex edges terminating in points. **2.** Something shaped like a crescent. **—adj. 1.** Crescent-shaped. **2.** Increasing; waxing, as the moon. [Middle English *cressaunt*, from Old French *creissant*, "waxing," "increasing," from Latin *crēscere*, to grow.]

cre·sol (krē′sōl′, -sôl′) *n.* Any of three isomeric phenols, $CH_3C_6H_4OH$, used in resins and as a disinfectant. [Var. of CREOSOL.]

cress (krĕs) *n.* Any of various related plants of the mustard family, such as watercress, with pungent leaves often used in salads and as a garnish. [Middle English *cresse*, from Old English *cærse.*]

Cres·si·da (krĕs′ĭ-də) *n.* In medieval romances, a Trojan lady who first returns the love of Troilus but later forsakes him for Diomedes.

crest (krĕst) *n.* **1.** A tuft, ridge, or similar projection on the head of a bird or other animal. **2.** A plume or farlike ornament used as decoration on top of a helmet. **3.** The top of something, as a mountain or wave; peak; summit. **4.** *Heraldry.* A device placed above the shield on a coat of arms. **—tr.v.** To reach the top of: *The hikers crested the mountain before dusk.* **—intr.v.** To form into a crest: *waves cresting at 10 feet after the hurricane.* [Middle English *creste*, from Old French, from Latin *crista*, crest, plume.]

crest

crest·ed (krĕs′tĭd) *adj.* Having a crest or a certain kind of crest: *the crested head of a bluejay.*

crest·fall·en (krĕst′fô′lən) *adj.* Dejected; dispirited; depressed. **—crest′fall′en·ly** *adv.*

Cre·ta·ceous (krĭ-tā′shəs) *n.* Also **Cretaceous period.** A geologic period that began 135 million years ago and ended 63 million years ago, characterized by the development of flowering plants and the disappearance of dinosaurs. **—modifier:** *a Cretaceous rock.* **—adj. cretaceous.** Of, like, or containing chalk. [Latin *crētāceus*, from *crēta*, chalk, clay.]

cre·tin (krēt′n) *n.* A person afflicted with cretinism. [French *crétin*, idiot, from dial. French *crestin*, Christian, human being, idiot (who is nonetheless human).] **—cre′tin·oid′** *adj.* **—cre′tin·ous** *adj.*

cre·tin·ism (krēt′n-ĭz′əm) *n.* **Myxedema,** a thyroid-deficiency disease.

cre·tonne (krĭ-tŏn′, krē′tŏn′) *n.* A heavy cotton, linen, or rayon fabric, colorfully printed and used for draperies and slipcovers. [French, after *Creton*, village in Normandy.]

cre·vasse (krə-văs′) *n.* **1.** A deep fissure, as in a glacier; chasm. **2.** A crack in a dike or levee. [French, from Old French *crevace*, crevice.]

crev·ice (krĕv′ĭs) *n.* A narrow crack or opening; fissure; cleft. [Middle English, from Old French *crevace*, from *crever*, to split, from Latin *crepāre*, to rattle, crack.]

crew¹ (krōō) *n.* **1.** A group of people working together: *the clean-up crew; the stage crew at the theater.* **2. a.** All the persons manning a ship, aircraft, etc. **b.** All of the persons manning a ship or aircraft except the officers. **3.** A company; a crowd. **4.** A team of oarsmen. [Middle English *creue*, military reinforcement, from Old French, an increase, from *creistre*, to grow, from Latin *crēscere.*]

crew² (krōō) *v.* A past tense of **crow.** [Middle English, from Old English *crēow.*]

crew cut. A close-cropped man's haircut.

crew·el (krōō′əl) *n.* Loosely twisted worsted yarn used for embroidery. [Middle English *crule.*]

crib (krĭb) *n.* **1.** A child's bed with high sides. **2.** A small building, usu. with slatted sides, for storing corn. **3.** A rack or trough for fodder; manger. **4.** A cattle stall or pen. **5.** *Informal.* A petty theft, as of another's work, ideas, or writings; plagiarism. **6.** *Informal.* A list of answers, notes, or information, consulted dishonestly by students during an examination. —*v.* **cribbed, crib·bing.** —*tr.v.* **1.** To confine in or as in a crib. **2.** To furnish with a crib. **3.** *Informal.* To plagiarize. **4.** *Informal.* To steal. —*intr.v. Informal.* To use a crib in examinations; cheat. [Middle English, manger, stall, basket, from Old English *cribb,* manger.] —**crib′ber** *n.*

crib·bage (krĭb′ĭj) *n.* A card game in which the score is kept by inserting pegs into holes arranged in rows on a small board. [Poss. from CRIB, (basket).]

crick (krĭk) *n.* A painful cramp or muscle spasm, as in the back or neck. —*tr.v.* To cause a crick in by turning or wrenching. [Middle English *crike, crykke.*]

crick·et¹ (krĭk′ĭt) *n.* Any of various insects of the family Gryllidae, with long antennae and legs adapted for leaping. The males of many species produce a shrill, chirping sound by rubbing the front wings together. [Middle English *criket,* from Old French *criquet,* from *criquer,* to click, creak.]

crick·et² (krĭk′ĭt) *n.* **1.** An outdoor game, popular in Great Britain, played with bats, a ball, and wickets by two teams of 11 players each. **2.** Good sportsmanship; fair play: *It's not cricket to cheat at cards.* —*intr.v.* To play cricket. [Prob. from Old French *criquet,* wicket or bat in a ball game.] —**crick′et·er** *n.*

cri·er (krī′ər) *n.* **1.** A person who cries. **2.** A person who shouts out public announcements. **3.** A hawker or peddler.

crime (krīm) *n.* **1.** An act committed or omitted in violation of a law for which punishment is imposed upon conviction. **2.** Unlawful activity in general: *Crime in the suburbs is on the rise.* **3.** Any serious wrongdoing or offense, esp. against morality; a sin. **4.** An unjust or senseless act or condition: *It's a crime that so many people live in poverty.* **5.** *Informal.* A shame; a pity: *It's a crime to waste food.* —*modifier:* crime *prevention.* [Middle English, from Old French, from Latin *crimen,* verdict, judgment, crime.]

crim·i·nal (krĭm′ə-nəl) *n.* A person who has committed or been legally convicted of a crime. —*adj.* **1.** Of, involving, or having the nature of crime. **2.** Pertaining to the administration of penal law as distinguished from civil law. **3.** Guilty of crime. —**crim′i·nal·ly** *adv.*

Syns: criminal, illegal, illegitimate, illicit, lawless, unlawful, wrongful *adj.* *Core meaning:* Of, relating to, or being a crime (*criminal activities such as blackmail and extortion*).

crim·i·nal·i·ty (krĭm′ə-nǎl′ĭ-tē) *n., pl.* **-ties. 1.** The fact or condition of being criminal. **2.** A criminal action or practice.

crim·i·nol·o·gy (krĭm′ə-nŏl′ə-jē) *n.* The scientific study of crime, criminals, and criminal behavior. —**crim′i·no·log′i·cal** (-nə-lŏj′ĭ-kəl) *adj.* —**crim′i·no·log′i·cal·ly** *adv.* —**crim′i·nol′o·gist** *n.*

crimp (krĭmp) *tr.v.* **1.** To press or bend into small, regular folds or ridges: *Moisture crimped the plywood.* **2.** To form (hair) into tight curls or waves. —*n.* **1.** Something that has been crimped. **2.** Often **crimps.** Tightly curled or waved hair. [Middle English *crimpen,* to wrinkle, shrivel, from Old English *gecrympan,* to curl.] —**crimp′er** *n.*

crim·son (krĭm′zən, -sən) *n.* A vivid purplish red. —*adj.* Vivid purplish red. —*intr.v.* To become crimson: *The sky crimsoned.* —*tr.v.* To make crimson: *Fire crimsoned the sky.* [Middle English *cremesin,* from Spanish, from Arabic *qirmiz,* kermes insect (from which red dye was obtained).]

cringe (krĭnj) *intr.v.* **cringed, cring·ing. 1.** To shrink back, as in fear; cower. **2.** To fawn. **3.** To be filled with disgust or discomfort: *I cringed when he told that embarrassing story.* [Middle English *crengen.*]

crin·kle (krĭng′kəl) *v.* **-kled, -kling.** —*intr.v.* **1.** To form into wrinkles or ripples. **2.** To make a soft, crackling sound; to rustle. —*tr.v.* To cause to wrinkle or rustle. —*n.* A wrinkle or ripple. [Middle English *crinkelen.*] —**crin′kly** *adj.*

crin·o·line (krĭn′ə-lĭn) *n.* **1.** A coarse, stiff cotton fabric used to line and stiffen garments. **2.** A petticoat made of crinoline. **3.** A hoop skirt. [French, from Italian *crinolino* : Latin *crinis,* hair + *linum,* flax.]

crip·ple (krĭp′əl) *n.* Someone with a bodily defect that hinders normal functioning or movement. —*tr.v.* **-pled, -pling. 1.** To make into a cripple. **2.** To disable or damage: *The storm crippled the fishing fleet.* [Middle English *crepel,* from Old English *crypel.*] —**crip′pler** *n.*

cri·sis (krī′sĭs) *n., pl.* **-ses** (-sēz′). **1. a.** A crucial point or situation in the course of anything; turning point: *a crisis in the peace negotiations.* **b.** An unstable condition in political, international, or economic affairs; a time of danger: *the hostage crisis in Iran.* **2.** A sudden change in the course of an acute disease, either toward improvement or deterioration. [Latin, from Greek *krisis,* turning point, from *krinein,* to separate, decide.]

crisp (krĭsp) *adj.* **-er, -est. 1.** Firm or crusty but easily broken or crumbled, esp. from cooking: *crisp fried chicken.* **2.** Firm and fresh: *crisp celery.* **3.** Brisk; invigorating; bracing: *crisp autumn air.* **4.** Animated; stimulating. **5.** Concise; pithy; sharp: *a crisp writing style.* **6.** Having small curls, waves, or ripples, as hair. —*tr.v.* To make crisp. —*intr.v.* To become crisp. [Middle English, from Old English, curly, from Latin *crispus,* curly.]

crisp·y (krĭs′pē) *adj.* **-i·er, -i·est.** Crisp. —**crisp′i·ness** *n.*

criss·cross (krĭs′krôs′, -krŏs′) *tr.v.* **1.** To mark with crossing lines. **2.** To move crosswise through or over: *He crisscrossed the country on business trips.* —*intr.v.* To move crosswise or in crisscrosses: *Trails crisscrossed through the underbrush.* —*n.* A mark or pattern made of crossing lines. —*adj.* Crossing one another: *crisscross lines.* —*adv.* In crossing directions: *skis lying crisscross on the snow.* [Var. of earlier *christcross,* the figure of a cross.]

cri·te·ri·on (krī-tîr′ē-ən) *n., pl.* **-te·ri·a** (-tîr′ē-ə) or **-ons.** A standard, rule, or test on which a judgment or decision can be based. [Greek *kritērion,* a means for judging, from *kritēs,* a judge, from *krinein,* to choose.]

Usage: criteria. This is the most common plural form of the noun *criterion.* It may not be used in any of these expressions: *a criteria; one criteria; the only* (sole) *criteria.* Use *criterion* in all these.

crit·ic (krĭt′ĭk) *n.* **1.** A person who forms and expresses judgments of the merits and faults of anything: *critics of the administration's economic policy.* **2.** A specialist in the judgment of the worth of literary or artistic works, esp. someone who does this professionally and reports through the media. **3.** A person who finds fault. [Latin *criticus,* from Greek *kritikos,* able to discern, critical, from *krinein,* to separate, choose.]

crit·i·cal (krĭt′ĭ-kəl) *adj.* **1.** Of or pertaining to critics or criticism: *critical writings on Milton.* **2.** Inclined to judge severely; likely to find fault. **3.** Characterized by careful evaluation and judgment: *a critical reading.* **4.** Forming or of the nature of a crisis; crucial: *a critical point in the campaign.* **5. a.** *Med.* Of or involving the crisis stage of a disease. **b.** Extremely serious or dangerous: *in critical condition.* —**crit′i·cal·ly** *adv.*

Syns: critical, acute, crucial, desperate, dire *adj.* *Core meaning:* So serious as to be at the point of crisis (*a critical shortage of fuel*).

critical mass. The smallest mass of a fissionable material, such as plutonium 239 or uranium 235, that will sustain a nuclear chain reaction.

critical point. The conditions of temperature and pressure in which the liquid and gaseous forms of a pure, stable substance have the same density.

critical temperature. The temperature above which a gas cannot be liquefied.

crit·i·cism (krĭt′ĭ-sĭz′əm) *n.* **1.** The act of forming and expressing judgments about the worth of something. **2.** Unfavorable judgment; censure; disapproval. **3. a.** The skill or profession of analyzing and passing discriminating judgments and evaluations, esp. of literary or other artistic works. **b.** A review or other article expressing such judgment and evaluation.

crit·i·cize (krĭt′ĭ-sīz′) *v.* **-cized, -ciz·ing.** —*tr.v.* **1.** To judge the merits and faults of; analyze and evaluate: *criticize the new production of "Macbeth."* **2.** To judge with severity;

ă pat   ā pay   â care   ä father   ĕ pet   ē be   hw which   ĭ pit   ī tie   î pier   ŏ pot   ō toe   ô paw, for   oi noise
ŏŏ took   ōō boot   ou out   th thin   *th* this   ŭ cut   û urge   zh vision   ə about, item, edible, gallop, circus

find fault with; censure: *criticize the governor's judicial appointments.* —*intr.v.* To act as a critic: *He rarely criticizes or praises.* —See Syns at **blame.** —**crit'i·ciz'er** *n.*

cri·tique (krĭ-tēk') *n.* **1.** A critical review or commentary, esp. an evaluation of a literary or other artistic work. **2.** The art of criticism. [French, criticism.]

crit·ter (krĭt'ər) *n. Informal.* Any living creature, esp. a domestic animal. [Var. of CREATURE.]

croak (krōk) *n.* A low, hoarse sound, such as that made by a frog or crow. —*intr.v.* **1.** To make a croak. **2.** To speak with a low, hoarse voice. **3.** To mutter discontentedly; grumble. **4.** *Slang.* To die. —*tr.v.* **1.** To utter by croaking. **2.** *Slang.* To kill. —See Syns at **die.** [Middle English croken.]

cro·chet (krō-shā') *v.* **-cheted** (-shād') **-chet·ing** (-shā'ĭng). —*intr.v.* To make a piece of needlework by looping thread with a hooked needle. —*tr.v.* To make or decorate (a fabric) by looping thread with a hooked needle. —*n.* A kind of needlework made by crocheting. [French, a hook, from Old French croc(he).]

cro·ci (krō'sī) *n.* A plural of **crocus.**

crock (krŏk) *n.* An earthenware vessel. [Middle English crokke, from Old English crocc(a).]

crock·er·y (krŏk'ə-rē) *n.* Pots, plates, jars, etc., made of earthenware.

croc·o·dile (krŏk'ə-dīl') *n.* **1.** Any of various large aquatic reptiles of the genus *Crocodylus* and related genera, of tropical regions, with thick, armorlike skin and long, tapering jaws. **2.** Leather made from crocodile skin. —*modifier:* *A crocodile belt.* [Middle English cocodril, from Old French, from Latin crocodīlus, from Greek krokodilos, lizard, crocodile.]

crocodile

crocodile tears. False tears; an insincere display of grief. [From the belief that crocodiles weep after eating their victims.]

cro·cus (krō'kəs) *n., pl.* **-cus·es** or **-ci** (-sī'). **1.** Any plant of the genus *Crocus,* widely cultivated in gardens having showy, variously colored flowers and grasslike leaves. **2.** A red variety of iron oxide, Fe_2O_3, used in the form of an abrasive powder for polishing. [Latin, saffron, from Greek krokos.]

croft (krôft, krŏft) *n. Brit. & Scot.* **1.** A small enclosed field or pasture. **2.** A small farm, esp. a tenant farm. [Middle English, from Old English.]

croft·er (krôf'tər, krŏf'-) *n. Brit. & Scottish.* A person who rents and cultivates a croft; tenant farmer.

crois·sant (krwä-sän') *n.* A rich, crescent-shaped roll of leavened dough or puff pastry. [French, from Old French croissant, creissant, crescent.]

Cro-Mag·non man (krō-măg'nən, -măn'yən). An early form of modern man, *Homo sapiens,* characterized by a robust physique and known from skeletal parts found in the Cro-Magnon cave in southern France.

crom·lech (krŏm'lĕk') *n.* **1.** A prehistoric monument consisting of monoliths encircling a mound. **2.** A dolmen. [Welsh : crwn, arched + llech, flat stone.]

crone (krōn) *n.* A withered, witchlike old woman. [Middle English, from Middle Dutch caroonje, old ewe, dead body, ult. from Latin carō, flesh.]

Cro·nus (krō'nəs) *n. Gk. Myth.* A Titan who ruled the universe until dethroned by his son Zeus, identified with the Roman god Saturn.

cro·ny (krō'nē) *n., pl.* **-nies.** A close friend or companion. [Earlier chrony, "old companion," from Greek khronios, long-lasting, from khronos, time.]

crook (krŏŏk) *n.* **1.** Something bent or curved: *carried the bag in the crook of her arm.* **2.** An implement or tool with a bent or curved part, as a bishop's crosier. **3.** A curve or bend; a turn: *a crook in the road.* **4.** *Informal.* A person who makes his living by dishonest methods; a thief. —*tr.v.* To curve or bend: *He crooked his arm around the light pole.* —*intr.v.* To become curved or bent: *The trail crooks to the right.* —*idiom.* **by hook or by crook.** By any means possible: *We'll get there by hook or by crook.* [Middle English crok, from Old Norse krókr, a hook.]

crook·ed (krŏŏk'ĭd) *adj.* **1. a.** Having an irregular shape: *crooked fingers.* **b.** Following an irregular course: *a crooked street.* **c.** At an irregular angle: *a crooked picture on the wall.* **2.** *Informal.* Dishonest or unscrupulous; fraudulent: *a crooked merchant.* —**crook'ed·ly** *adv.* —**crook'ed·ness** *n.*

croon (krōōn) *intr.v.* **1.** To sing or hum softly. **2.** To sing popular songs in a soft, sentimental manner. —*tr.v.* To produce an effect on (someone) by crooning: *crooning the baby to sleep.* —*n.* A soft singing or humming. [Middle English croynen, to boom, sing, from Middle Dutch krōnen, to groan, lament.] —**croon'er** *n.*

crop (krŏp) *n.* **1. a.** Cultivated plants or agricultural produce, such as grain, vegetables, or fruit. **b.** The total yield of such produce of a particular season, place, or kind: *Drought killed most of the corn crop.* **3.** A group, quantity, or supply appearing or produced at one time: *a new crop of college graduates.* **4.** A short haircut. **5.** An earmark on an animal. **6. a.** A short whip used in horseback riding, with a loop serving as a lash. **b.** The stock of a whip. **7.** *Zool.* **a.** A pouchlike enlargement of a bird's esophagus, in which food is stored or partially digested; craw. **b.** A similar organ in earthworms, insects, and other invertebrates. —*v.* **cropped, crop·ping.** —*tr.v.* **1.** To cut off the stems or top of (a plant). **2.** To cut or clip very short. **3.** To reap; harvest. **4.** To cause to grow or yield a crop or crops: *cropped all his fields with wheat.* —*intr.v.* To yield a crop or crops. —*phrasal verb.* **crop up** (or **out**). To appear or develop unexpectedly: *Her name cropped up early in our investigation.* [Middle English, from Old English cropp, cluster, ear of corn.]

crop·per¹ (krŏp'ər) *n.* A person who works land in return for a share of the yield; sharecropper.

crop·per² (krŏp'ər) *n.* **1.** A heavy fall; tumble. **2.** A disastrous failure; fiasco. —*idiom.* **come a cropper. 1.** To fall heavily. **2.** To fail miserably; come to ruin. [From the phrase *neck and crop,* "completely."]

cro·quet (krō-kā') *n.* An outdoor game in which the players drive wooden balls through a series of wickets using long-handled mallets. —*modifier:* *a croquet set.* [Perh. from French crochet, a hook.]

cro·quette (krō-kĕt') *n.* A small cake of minced food, often coated with bread crumbs and fried in deep fat. [French, from croquer, to crack (imit.).]

cro·sier (krō'zhər) *n.* Also **cro·zier.** A staff with a crook or cross at the end, carried by or before an abbot, bishop, or archbishop as a symbol of office. [Middle English crocer, from Old French crossier, staff-bearer, from crosse, bishop's staff.]

cross (krôs, krŏs) *n.* **1.** An upright post with a transverse piece near the top, used in former times as an instrument of execution for certain types of criminals. **2.** Any trial or affliction: *Everyone has his own cross to bear.* **3. a. the Cross.** The cross upon which Christ was crucified. **b.** A symbolic representation of this cross. **4.** A crucifix. **5.** A sign made by tracing the outline of a cross with the hand upon the forehead and chest as a devotional act. **6.** Any of various medals or emblems shaped like a cross. **7.** Any mark or pattern formed by the intersection of two lines, esp. such a mark (X) used as a signature. **8.** *Biol.* **a.** A plant or animal produced by crossbreeding; a hybrid. **b.** The process of crossbreeding; hybridization. **9.** Someone or something that combines the qualities of two things: *This novel is a cross between romance and satire.* **10.** *Slang.* A contest whose outcome has been dishonestly prearranged. —*tr.v.* **1.** To go or extend across; pass from one side of to the other: *I crossed the room to greet him.* **2.** To carry or convey across. **3.** To extend or pass through or over; intersect: *I'll meet you where the trail crosses the*

brook. **4.** To make or put a line across: *Cross your T's.*
5. To place crosswise: *cross one's legs.* **6.** To encounter in passing: *His path crossed mine.* **7.** To delete or eliminate by or as if by drawing a line through: *crossing names off a list.* **8.** *Informal.* To thwart or obstruct; interfere with: *Do not cross me.* **9.** To make the sign of the cross on (oneself). **10.** *Biol.* To crossbreed or cross-fertilize (plants or animals). —*intr.v.* **1.** To lie or pass across; intersect: *I found him where the old Indian paths cross.* **2.** To move or extend from one side to another: *We crossed at the corner.* **3.** To meet and pass: *Our paths crossed.* **4.** *Biol.* To crossbreed or cross-fertilize. —*adj.* **1.** Lying or passing crosswise; intersecting: *a cross street.* **2.** Contrary or counter; opposing: *cross winds; cross purposes.* **3.** Showing ill humor; annoyed. **4.** Involving interchange; reciprocal. **5.** Crossbred; hybrid. —See Syns at **irritable.** [Middle English *cros,* from Old English, from Old Irish *cross,* from Latin *crux.*] —**cross'ly** *adv.* —**cross'ness** *n.*

cross·bar (krôs'bär', krŏs'-) *n.* A horizontal bar, line, or stripe.

cross·beam (krôs'bēm', krŏs'-) *n.* A horizontal beam or girder.

cross·bones (krôs'bōnz', krŏs'-) *n.* A representation of two bones placed crosswise, usu. under a skull, symbolizing danger or death.

cross·bow (krôs'bō', krŏs'-) *n.* A medieval weapon consisting of a bow fixed crosswise on a wooden stock, with grooves on the stock to direct the projectile.

cross·breed (krôs'brēd', krŏs'-) *v.* **-bred** (-brĕd'), **-breed·ing.** —*tr.v.* To produce (a hybrid animal or plant) by mating individuals of different varieties or breeds; hybridize. —*intr.v.* To mate so as to produce a hybrid; interbreed. —*n.* A hybrid produced by crossbreeding.

cross·coun·try (krôs'kŭn'trē, krŏs'-) *adj.* **1.** Moving across open country rather than following roads: *a cross-country race.* **2.** From one side of a country to the other: *a cross-country trip.* —*adv.:* *travel cross-country.*

cross·cur·rent (krôs'kûr'ənt, -kŭr'-, krŏs'-) *n.* **1.** A current flowing across another current. **2.** A conflicting movement, tendency, etc.: *a crosscurrent of dissent.*

crosscut saw. **1.** A hand saw for cutting wood across the grain. **2.** A large saw designed for two men.

crosse (krôs, krŏs) *n.* A lacrosse stick. [French, from Old French, staff.]

cross·ex·am·ine (krôs'ĭg-zăm'ĭn, krŏs'-) *tr.v.* **-ined, -in·ing.** **1.** *Law.* To question in court (a witness already examined by the opposing side). **2.** To question (someone) closely, esp. in order to check the resulting answers against answers previously made. —**cross'-ex·am'i·na'tion** *n.* —**cross'-ex·am'in·er** *n.*

cross·eye (krôs'ī', krŏs'ī') *n.* A form of strabismus in which one or both eyes turn inward toward the nose. —**cross'-eyed'** *adj.*

cross·fer·til·i·za·tion (krôs'fûr'tl-ĭ-zā'shən, krŏs'-) *n.* **1.** *Biol.* Fertilization by the union of gametes from different individuals, often of different varieties or species. **2.** *Bot.* Fertilization of the ovule of one plant or flower by pollen nuclei from another.

cross·fer·til·ize (krôs'fûr'tl-īz', krŏs'-) *v.* **-ized, -iz·ing.** —*tr.v.* To fertilize by means of cross-fertilization. —*intr.v.* To be fertilized by means of cross-fertilization.

cross·fire (krôs'fīr', krŏs'-) *n.* **1.** Lines of fire from two or more positions crossing each other at a single point: *soldiers caught in the crossfire.* **2.** Any situation in which a number of things originating from different sources come together: *a crossfire of charges and countercharges.* **3.** A rapid, often heated argument.

cross·grained (krôs'grānd', krŏs'-) *adj.* **1.** Having an irregular, transverse, or diagonal grain: *cross-grained wood.* **2.** Stubborn; contrary.

cross·hatch (krôs'hăch', krŏs'-) *tr.v.* To mark with two or more sets of intersecting parallel lines.

cross·ing (krô'sĭng, krŏs'ĭng) *n.* **1.** A place at which roads, lines, or tracks intersect; an intersection. **2.** The place at which something, such as a river or railroad, may be crossed. **3.** A voyage across an ocean.

crossing over. The exchange of genetic material between homologous chromosomes.

cross·o·ver (krôs'ō'vər, krŏs'-) *n.* **1.** A place at which a

crossing is made. **2.** A connecting track by which a train can be transferred from one line to another.

cross·piece (krôs'pēs, krŏs'-) *n.* A horizontal bar, beam, etc., used as a crossbar or crossbeam.

cross·pol·li·nate (krôs'pŏl'ə-nāt', krŏs'-) *tr.v.* **-nat·ed, -nat·ing.** To cross-fertilize (a plant or flower). —**cross'-pol·li·na'tion** *n.*

cross·pur·pose (krôs'pûr'pəs, krŏs'-) *n.* A conflicting or contrary purpose. —*idiom.* **be at cross-purposes.** To have or act under a misunderstanding of each other's purposes.

cross·re·fer (krôs'rĭ-fûr', krŏs'-) *v.* **-ferred, -fer·ring.** —*tr.v.* To refer (a reader) from one part or passage to another. —*intr.v.* To make a cross-reference.

cross·ref·er·ence (krôs'rĕf'ər-əns, -rĕf'rəns, krŏs'-) *n.* A reference from one part of a book, index, catalogue, or file to another part containing related information.

cross·road (krôs'rōd', krŏs'-) *n.* **1.** A road that intersects another road. **2.** **crossroads. a.** A place where two or more roads meet. **b.** *(used with a sing. verb).* A crucial point or place.

cross section. **1. a.** A section formed by a plane cutting through an object, usu. at right angles to an axis. **b.** A piece so cut or a graphic representation of such a piece. **2.** *Physics.* A measure of the probability of occurrence of a particular atomic or nuclear reaction. **3.** A representative sample meant to be typical of the whole: *This novel presents a cross section of city life.* —**cross'-sec'tion·al** *adj.*

cross·stitch (krôs'stĭch', krŏs'-) *n.* **1.** A needlework stitch forming an X. **2.** Needlework made with the cross-stitch. —*tr.v.* To embroider with cross-stitches. —*intr.v.* To work in cross-stitch.

cross·talk (krôs'tôk', krŏs'-) *n.* Noise or garbled sounds heard on a telephone or other electronic receiver, caused by interference from another channel.

cross·town (krôs'toun', krŏs'-) *adj.* Running across a city or town: *a cross-town bus.* —*adv.* Across a city or town: *We drove cross-town.*

cross·tree (krôs'trē', krŏs'-) *n.* One of the two horizontal crosspieces at the upper ends of the lower masts in fore-and-aft-rigged vessels, serving to spread the shrouds.

cross·walk (krôs'wôk', krŏs'-) *n.* A path marked off for pedestrians crossing a street.

cross·way (krôs'wā', krŏs'-) *n.* A crossroad.

cross·wise (krôs'wīz', krŏs'-) *adv.* Also **cross·ways** (-wāz'). So as to cross: *logs laid crosswise on the fire.* —*adj.* Crossing: *a crosswise direction.*

cross·word puzzle (krôs'wûrd', krŏs'-). A puzzle in which an arrangement of numbered squares is to be filled with words running both across and down in answer to correspondingly numbered clues.

crotch (krŏch) *n.* **1.** The angle or region of the angle formed by the junction of parts or members, as two branches, limbs, or legs. **2.** The region of a garment where the leg seams meet. [Poss. var. of CRUTCH.]

crotch·et (krŏch'ĭt) *n.* **1.** A small hook or hooklike structure. **2.** An odd, whimsical, or stubborn notion. **3.** *Mus.* A quarter note. [Middle English *crochet,* from Old French.]

crotch·et·y (krŏch'ĭ-tē) *adj.* Capriciously stubborn or eccentric; cantankerous. —**crotch'et·i·ness** *n.*

cro·ton (krōt'n) *n.* **1.** Any of various chiefly tropical plants, shrubs, or trees of the genus *Croton.* **2.** Any of various tropical plants of the genus *Codiaeum,* esp. one frequently grown as a house plant for its showy, varicolored foliage. [Greek *krotŏn,* castor oil plant.]

crouch (krouch) *intr.v.* **1.** To lower the body by bending or squatting. **2.** To bend or cower in a servile or timid manner; cringe. —*tr.v.* To cause to bend low. —*n.* The act or posture of crouching. [Middle English *cro(u)chen,* from Old French *crochir,* to be bent, from *croc(he),* a hook.]

croup (krōōp) *n.* A diseased condition that affects the larynx in children, characterized by respiratory difficulty and a harsh cough. [Prob. imit. of coughing.] —**croup'y** *adj.*

crou·pi·er (krōō'pē-ər, -pē-ā') *n.* An attendant at a gaming table who collects and pays bets. [French, orig. "rider on the rump (behind another rider)," from *croupe,* rump.]

crou·ton (krōō'tŏn', krōō-tŏn') *n.* A small crisp piece of toasted or fried bread, used as a garnish. [French *croûton,* from *croûte,* crust, from Latin *crusta.*]

ă pat ā pay â care ä father ĕ pet ē be hw which ĭ pit ī tie î pier ŏ pot ō toe ô paw, for oi noise
ōō took ōō boot ou out th thin th this ŭ cut û urge zh vision ə about, item, edible, gallop, circus

crow¹ (krō) *n.* **1.** Any of several large, glossy black birds of the genus *Corvus*, having a characteristic raucous call. **2.** A crowbar. **—idioms. as the crow flies.** In a straight line. **eat crow.** *Informal.* To be forced into a humiliating situation, as from having been in error. [Middle English *croue*, from Old English *crāwe*.]

crow² (krō) *n.* **1.** The loud, shrill cry of a rooster. **2.** A loud, wordless sound of pleasure or delight. *—intr.v.* **1.** *Past tense* **crowed** or **crew** (krōō). To utter the loud, shrill cry of a rooster. **2.** To make a loud, wordless sound of pleasure: *The baby kicked and crowed.* **3.** To boast; exult. —See Syns at **boast.** [Middle English *crouen,* from Old English *crāwan.*]

crow·bar (krō'bär') *n.* A metal bar, of iron or steel, with the working end shaped like a forked chisel, used as a lever.

crowd (kroud) *n.* **1.** A large number of persons gathered together; throng. **2.** People in general: *She's independent; she never follows the crowd.* **3.** A particular social group; clique; set: *the college crowd.* **4.** An audience: *a new film attracting sell-out crowds.* **5.** A large number of things grouped or considered together: *a crowd of pigeons in the square.* —See Syns at **circle.** *—intr.v.* **1.** To congregate in a close space; throng: *We all crowded around the table.* **2.** To advance by shoving: *Everyone crowded into the dining room.* *—tr.v.* **1.** To press; shove; push: *Don't crowd the people ahead of you.* **2.** To fill by massing together in: *Shoppers crowded the store.* [From Middle English *crowden,* to crowd, press, from Old English *crūdan,* to hasten.] **—crowd'er** *n.*

crown (kroun) *n.* **1.** An ornamental head covering, often made of precious metal set with jewels, worn as a symbol of sovereignty. **2.** The person, authority, or government of a monarch. **3.** A wreath worn on the head as a symbol of victory, honor, or distinction. **4.** Anything resembling a crown in shape. **5.** Any of various coins formerly in use in England and on the Continent. **6.** The top or highest part of the head. **7.** The top or upper part of a hat. **8.** The highest point or summit of anything: *the crown of a hill. The two Picassos were the crown of his collection.* **9. a.** The part of a tooth that projects beyond the gum line. **b.** A gold, porcelain, or plastic substitute for the natural crown of a tooth. **10. a.** The upper part of a tree, bush, or plant. **b.** A flower part, the corona. **11.** The crest of an animal, esp. of a bird. *—modifier: the crown jewels. —tr.v.* **1.** To invest with royal power: *crown a new queen.* **2.** To put a wreath upon the head of: *crown the marathon victor with laurel.* **3.** To confer honor, dignity, or reward upon: *Speakers crowned the former leader with praise.* **4.** To form the topmost part of; cover the top of: *Snow crowned the mountain peaks.* **5.** To be the highest achievement of: *The Nobel Prize crowned his career.* **6.** To put a crown on (a tooth). **7.** *Checkers.* To make (a piece that has reached the last row) into a king by placing another piece upon it. **8.** *Informal.* To hit on the head. [Middle English *crowne, coroune,* from Old French *corone,* from Latin *corōna,* garland, wreath, from Greek *korōnē,* anything curved, from *korōnos,* curved.]

crown

cruet

crown prince. The heir apparent to a throne.
crown princess. **1.** The wife of a crown prince. **2.** A female heir apparent to a throne.
crow's-foot (krōz'fŏŏt') *n.* **1.** Often **crow's-feet.** Any of the

wrinkles at the outer corner of the eye. **2.** A three-pointed embroidery stitch.

crow's-nest (krōz'nĕst') *n.* **1.** A small lookout platform with a high protective railing, located near the top of a ship's mast. **2.** Any similar lookout.

cro·zier (krō'zhər) *n.* Var. of **crosier.**

cru·ces (krōō'sēz) *n.* Plural of **crux.**

cru·cial (krōō'shəl) *adj.* **1.** Of supreme importance; critical; decisive: *a crucial decision.* **2.** Severe; trying. —See Syns at **critical.** [Old French, cross-shaped, from Latin *crux,* cross.] **—cru'cial·ly** *adv.*

cru·ci·ble (krōō'sə-bəl) *n.* **1.** A vessel made of a substance with a very high melting point, such as graphite or porcelain, used for melting and calcining materials at high temperatures. **2.** A severe test or trial. [Middle English *crusible,* from Medieval Latin *crucibulum.*]

cru·ci·fix (krōō'sə-fĭks') *n.* An image of Christ on the cross. [Middle English, from Old French, from Late Latin *crucifigere,* to crucify.]

cru·ci·fix·ion (krōō'sə-fĭk'shən) *n.* **1.** The act of crucifying or condition of being crucified. **2.** A representation of Christ on the cross. **3. the Crucifixion.** The crucifying of Christ on Calvary.

cru·ci·form (krōō'sə-fôrm') *adj.* Cross-shaped. [Latin *crux,* cross + -FORM.]

cru·ci·fy (krōō'sə-fī') *tr.v.* **-fied, -fy·ing.** **1.** To put (a person) to death by nailing or binding to a cross. **2.** To torment, as by devastating criticism; persecute: *a politican crucified by the press.* [Middle English *crucifien,* from Old French *crucifier,* from Late Latin *crucifigere* : Latin *crux,* cross + *figere,* to fasten.]

crud (krŭd) *n. Slang.* **1.** An encrustation of filth or refuse. **2.** A worthless or contemptible person. **3.** Nonsense. [Middle English *crudde,* curd.] **—crud'dy** *adj.*

crude (krōōd) *adj.* **crud·er, crud·est.** **1.** In an unrefined or natural state; raw: *crude ore.* **2.** Lacking tact, refinement, or taste: *a crude expression; a crude person.* **3.** Not carefully or completely made; rough: *a crude sketch.* **4.** Displaying a lack of knowledge or skill: *a crude attempt.* **5.** Undisguised or unadorned; blunt: *the crude truth.* —See Syns at **coarse.** *—n.* Petroleum in its unrefined state. [Middle English, from Latin *crūdus,* bloody, raw.] **—crude'ly** *adv.* **—crude'ness** *n.*

crude oil. A natural hydrocarbon mixture, petroleum.

cru·di·ty (krōō'dĭ-tē) *n., pl.* **-ties** **1.** The condition or quality of being crude; crudeness: *the crudity of the drawing.* **2.** A rude or vulgar remark or action.

cru·el (krōō'əl) *adj.* **-el·er** or **-el·ler, -el·est** or **-el·lest.** **1.** Likely or disposed to inflict pain or suffering; merciless: *a cruel despot.* **2.** Causing suffering; painful: *a cruel storm.* —See Syns at **fierce.** [Middle English, from Old French, from Latin *crūdēlis,* morally unfeeling, cruel.] **—cru'el·ly** *adv.* **—cru'el·ness** *n.*

cru·el·ty (krōō'əl-tē) *n., pl.* **-ties.** **1.** The quality or condition of being cruel. **2.** Something, such as a cruel action or remark, that causes pain or suffering.

cru·et (krōō'ĭt) *n.* A small glass bottle for holding vinegar, oil, or other condiments at the table. [Middle English, from Old French *crue,* flask.]

cruise (krōōz) *v.* **cruised, cruis·ing.** *—intr.v.* **1.** To sail or travel about in an unhurried way, as for pleasure. **2.** To travel at a maximally efficient speed. *—tr.v.* To cruise or journey over: *a police car cruising the streets.* *—n.* A sea voyage for pleasure. [Perh. Dutch *kruisen,* to sail to and fro, from Middle Dutch *crucen,* to cross, from Latin *crux,* cross.]

cruis·er (krōō'zər) *n.* **1.** One of a class of fast, medium-sized warships with a long cruising range and less armor and firepower than a battleship. **2.** A large motorboat whose cabin is equipped with living facilities. **3.** A police squad car.

crul·ler (krŭl'ər) *n.* Also **krul·ler.** A small cake of sweet dough, usu. twisted, fried in deep fat. [Dutch *krulle,* from *krul,* curly, from Middle Dutch *crulle.*]

crumb (krŭm) *n.* **1.** A small piece broken or fallen from cake, bread, or other baked goods. **2.** Any small fragment or scrap: *not a crumb of evidence.* **3.** *Slang.* A contemptible, untrustworthy, or loathsome person. *—tr.v.* **1.** To break into small pieces or crumbs; crumble. **2.** To cover or prepare (food) with bread crumbs. **3.** To brush (a table or cloth) clear of crumbs. [Middle English *crome*, from Old English *cruma*.]

crum·ble (krŭm'bəl) *v.* **-bled, -bling.** —*tr.v.* To break or cause to break into small parts or crumbs: *crumbled crackers into his soup.* —*intr.v.* **1.** To fall into tiny pieces: *The dirt crumbled at my touch.* **2.** To collapse or be destroyed; disintegrate: *His dreams crumbled when the bank refused the loan.* [Earlier *crimble*, from Middle English *cremelen.*]

crum·bly (krŭm'blē) *adj.* **-bli·er, -bli·est.** Easily crumbled; friable.

crum·my (krŭm'ē) *adj.* **-mi·er, -mi·est.** *Slang.* Also **crumb·y.** **1.** Miserable; wretched. **2.** Shabby; cheap. —See Syns at **cheap.** [From CRUMB.]

crum·pet (krŭm'pĭt) *n.* A light, soft bread baked on a griddle. [Prob. from Middle English *crompid* (*cake*), "curled cake," from *crampen*, to curl, from Old English *crump*, crooked.]

crum·ple (krŭm'pəl) *v.* **-pled, -pling.** —*tr.v.* To crush together or press into wrinkles; rumple: *crumple paper.* —*intr.v.* **1.** To become wrinkled or shriveled: *Tinfoil crumples easily.* **2.** To fall down: *A shot rang out, and he crumpled to the floor.* [Prob. from obs. *crump*, to curl up, from Middle English *crampen.*]

crunch (krŭnch) *tr.v.* **1.** To chew with a noisy crackling sound. **2.** To crush, grind, or tread noisily: *tires crunching the snow.* —*intr.v.* **1.** To chew noisily with a crackling sound. **2.** To move with a crushing sound: *Tanks crunched through the brush.* **3.** To produce or emit a crushing sound: *Gravel crunched under the tires.* —*n.* **1.** The act or sound of crunching. **2.** A critical situation: *He didn't have what it takes when the crunch came.* [Imit.] —**crunch'y** *adj.*

cru·ral (krŏŏr'əl) *adj.* Of or pertaining to the leg, shank, or thigh. [Latin *crūrālis*, from *crūs*, leg.]

cru·sade (krŏŏ-sād') *n.* **1.** Often **Crusade.** Any of the military expeditions undertaken by European Christians in the 11th, 12th, and 13th cent. to recover the Holy Land from the Moslems. **2.** Any holy war undertaken with papal sanction. **3.** Any vigorous concerted movement for a cause or against an abuse: *a crusade for civil rights.* —*intr.v.* **-sad·ed, -sad·ing.** To engage in a crusade. [From Old French *croiser*, to bear the cross, and Spanish *cruzar*, to bear the cross, both from Latin *crux*, cross.] —**cru·sad'er** *n.*

cruse (krŏŏz, krŏŏs) *n.* A small jar or pot for holding water, wine, or oil. [Middle English *crouse.*]

crush (krŭsh) *tr.v.* **1.** To press, squeeze, or bear down on with great force so as to break or injure. **2.** To extract or obtain by pressing or squeezing: *crush juice from a grape.* **3.** To crumple or rumple: *Don't crush the wrapping paper.* **4.** To hug with force. **5.** To break, pound, or grind (stone, ore, etc.) into small fragments or powder. **6.** To press upon, shove, or crowd: *Fans crushed the gates.* **7.** To put down; subdue: *crush a rebellion.* **8.** To overwhelm; destroy: *Debt was crushing them.* —*intr.v.* To be or become crushed: *Protesters crushed into the embassy fence.* —*n.* **1.** The act of crushing or the condition of being crushed. **2.** A great crowd or throng: *We were separated in the crush outside the stadium.* **3.** A substance prepared by or as if by crushing: *raspberry crush.* **4. a.** An infatuation. **b.** The object of it. [Middle English *crushen*, from Old French *croissir.*]

crust (krŭst) *n.* **1.** The hard outer portion or surface area of bread. **2.** A piece of bread consisting mostly of crust. **3.** A pastry shell, as of a pie or tart. **4.** Any hard, crisp covering or surface: *a crust of ice on the ground.* **5.** The outermost solid layer of a planet or moon. **6.** *Pathol.* A coating or dry outer layer, as of pus or blood; scab. **7.** *Slang.* Insolence; audacity; gall. —*tr.v.* To cover with a crust. —*intr.v.* **1.** To become covered with a crust. **2.** To harden into a crust. [Middle English *cruste*, from Old French *crouste*, from Latin *crusta*, shell.]

crus·ta·cean (krŭ-stā'shən) *n.* Any of various predominantly aquatic arthropods of the class Crustacea, including lobsters, crabs, shrimps, and barnacles, characteristically having a segmented body, a chitinous exoskeleton, and paired, jointed limbs.

crus·ta·ceous (krŭ-stā'shəs) *adj.* Having, resembling, or constituting a hard crust or shell. [Latin *crusta*, shell, crust + -ACEOUS.]

crust·y (krŭs'tē) *adj.* **-i·er, -i·est.** **1.** Like or having a crust. **2.** Surly; curt; rude. —**crust'i·ness** *n.*

crutch (krŭch) *n.* **1.** A staff or support used by the lame or infirm as an aid in walking, usu. having a crosspiece to fit under the armpit. **2.** Anything depended upon for support: *using drugs as a crutch.* [Middle English *crucche*, from Old English *crycc.*]

crux (krŭks, krŏŏks) *n., pl.* **crux·es** or **cru·ces** (krŏŏ'sēz). **1.** A basic or essential point: *the crux of the problem.* **2.** A puzzling problem. [Latin, cross.]

cry (krī) *v.* **cried, cry·ing.** —*intr.v.* **1.** To shed tears and make sobbing sounds expressive of grief, sorrow, or pain; weep. **2.** To shout: *They were crying for help.* **3.** To utter a characteristic sound or call, as an animal. —*tr.v.* **1.** To utter loudly. **2.** To announce for sale; to hawk: *a peddler crying his wares.* **3.** To beg for; beseech; implore: *cry forgiveness.* **4.** To bring into a particular condition by weeping: *cry oneself to sleep.* —*phrasal verb.* **cry off.** To break or withdraw from a promise, agreement, or undertaking. —*n., pl.* **cries.** **1.** A loud call; shout: *a cry for help.* **2.** Any loud sound expressive of fear, distress, pain, etc.: *a cry of anger.* **3.** A fit of weeping: *He needs to have a good cry.* **4.** An urgent entreaty or appeal. **5.** A public or general demand or complaint; a clamor; an outcry: *a widespread cry for justice.* **6.** A call to action; slogan: *a battle cry.* **7.** The characteristic call or utterance of an animal or bird. —**idioms. a far cry.** A greatly different thing; a long way. **in full cry.** In hot pursuit, as hounds hunting. [Middle English *crien*, from Old French *crier*, from Latin *quirītāre*, to cry out, to implore the aid of the Roman citizens, from *Quirīs*, a Roman citizen.]

cry·ba·by (krī'bā'bē) *n.* A person who cries or complains frequently with little cause.

cry·ing (krī'ĭng) *adj.* So bad as to demand immediate remedy: *a crying shame; a crying need.* —See Syns at **outrageous.**

cryo-. A prefix meaning cold, freezing, or frost: *cryogen.* [From Greek *kruos*, icy cold, frost.]

cry·o·gen (krī'ə-jən) *n.* A refrigerant used to obtain very low temperatures. [CRYO- + -GEN.]

cry·o·gen·ics (krī'ə-jĕn'ĭks) *n.* (used with a sing. verb). The scientific study of phenomena that occur at very low temperatures. [From CRYO- + -GENIC.] —**cry·o·gen'ic** *adj.*

cry·o·lite (krī'ə-līt') *n.* A white, vitreous natural fluoride of aluminum and sodium, Na_3AlF_6, used chiefly as an electrolyte in aluminum refining and in electrical insulation. [CRYO- + -LITE.]

cry·o·sur·ger·y (krī'ə-sûr'jə-rē) *n.* Surgery performed by local or general application of extreme cold.

crypt (krĭpt) *n.* An underground vault, esp. one beneath a church that is used as a burial place. [Latin *crypta*, from Greek *kruptē*, from *kruptein*, to hide.]

cryp·tic (krĭp'tĭk) or **cryp·ti·cal** (-tĭ-kəl) *adj.* **1.** Having an ambiguous or hidden meaning; enigmatic: *a cryptic message.* **2.** *Biol.* Tending to conceal or camouflage: *cryptic coloring.* [Late Latin *crypticus*, from Greek *kruptikos*, from *kruptein*, to hide.]

crypto- or **crypt-.** A prefix meaning hidden or secret: *cryptography.* [Greek *kruptos*, hidden, from *kruptein*, to hide.]

cryp·to·gam (krĭp'tə-găm') *n.* *Bot.* Any of the flowerless and seedless plants that reproduce by spores, as fungi, algae, mosses, and ferns. [French *cryptogame.*]

cryp·to·gram (krĭp'tə-grăm') *n.* Something written in a secret code or cipher; cryptograph. [French *cryptogramme.*] —**cryp'to·gram'mic** *adj.*

cryp·to·graph (krĭp'tə-grăf') *n.* **1.** A cryptogram. **2.** A device used to encode and decode messages and documents. [Back-formation from CRYPTOGRAPHY.]

cryp·tog·ra·phy (krĭp-tŏg'rə-fē) *n.* The study or process of writing in or deciphering secret code. [CRYPTO- + -GRAPHY.] —**cryp·tog'ra·pher** or **cryp·tog'ra·phist** *n.* —**cryp'to·graph'ic** (-tə-grăf'ĭk) *adj.*

crys·tal (krĭs'təl) *n.* **1. a.** A three-dimensional structure composed of atoms, molecules, or ions arranged in basic units that are repeated throughout the structure. **b.** The

---

ă pat	ā pay	â care	ä father	ĕ pet	ē be	hw which
ĭ pit	ī tie	î pier	ŏ pot	ō toe	ô paw, for	oi noise
ŏŏ took	ŏŏ boot	ou out	th thin	th this	ŭ cut	
û urge	zh vision	ə about, item, edible, gallop, circus				

basic unit of such a structure. **c.** A body, such as a piece of quartz, having such a structure, often having characteristic visible plane faces. **d.** Any body having such a structure and used in an electronic circuit because it has some special desired property. **2. a.** A clear, colorless glass of high quality. **b.** An object made of this glass. **3.** A transparent cover that protects the face of a watch or clock. —*modifier:* a crystal vase. —*adj.* Clear; transparent. [Middle English *cristal,* from Old French, from Latin *crystallum,* rock crystal, crystal, from Greek *krustallos,* ice.]

crystal gazing. Divination by gazing into a glass or crystal ball. —**crys′tal-gaz′er** *n.*

crys·tal·line (krĭs′tə-lĭn) *adj.* **1.** Pertaining to or made of crystal. **2.** Resembling crystal; transparent.

crystalline lens. The lens of the vertebrate eye.

crys·tal·lize (krĭs′tə-līz′) *v.* **-lized, -liz·ing.** —*tr.v.* **1.** To cause to form crystals or assume a crystalline structure. **2.** To give a definite and permanent form to: *The scientist finally crystallized her ideas.* **3.** To coat with sugar. —*intr.v.* **1.** To assume a crystalline form. **2.** To take on a definite and permanent form: *New factions crystallized during the revolution.* —**crys′tal-li-za′tion** *n.* —**crys′tal-liz′er** *n.*

crys·tal·log·ra·phy (krĭs′tə-lŏg′rə-fē) *n.* The science of crystal structure and phenomena. —**crys′tal-lo-graph′ic** (-lō-grăf′ĭk) or **crys′tal-lo-graph′i-cal** *adj.*

crys·tal·loid (krĭs′tə-loid′) *adj.* Also **crys·tal·loi·dal** (krĭs′tə-loid′l). Resembling or having properties of a crystal or crystalloid. —*n.* A water-soluble crystalline substance capable of diffusion through a semipermeable membrane.

Cs The symbol for the element cesium.

cub (kŭb) *n.* **1.** The young of certain animals, such as the bear, wolf, or lion. **2.** An inexperienced, awkward, or ill-mannered young person. **3.** A beginner or learner, esp. in newspaper reporting. **4. Cub.** A Cub Scout. [Orig. unknown.]

cub·by·hole (kŭb′ē-hōl′) *n.* **1.** A snug or cramped space or room. **2.** A small compartment. **3.** A small cupboard or closet. [*Cubby,* from obs. *cub,* a stall.]

cube (kyōōb) *n.* **1. a.** *Geom.* A solid having six congruent square faces. **b.** Anything having this shape or almost this shape: *a sugar cube.* **2.** The product that results when the same number is used three times as a factor. —*tr.v.* **cubed, cub·ing. 1.** To raise (a quantity or number) to the third power. **2.** To express or determine the volume of (a container or space) in cubic units. **3.** To form or cut into a cube. [Old French, from Latin *cubus,* a die, cube, from Greek *kubos.*]

cube root. A number whose cube is equal to a given number: *The cube root of 8 is 2.*

cu·bic (kyōō′bĭk) *adj.* **1.** Having the shape of a cube. **2. a.** Having three dimensions. **b.** Having a volume equal to a cube whose edge is of a stated length: *a cubic foot.* **3.** *Math.* Of the third power, order, or degree.

cu·bi·cal (kyōō′bĭ-kəl) *adj.* **1.** Cubic. **2.** Of or pertaining to volume. —**cu′bi-cal-ly** *adv.* —**cu′bi-cal-ness** *n.*

cu·bi·cle (kyōō′bĭ-kəl) *n.* Any small room or compartment, esp. a sleeping compartment. [Latin *cubiculum,* sleeping chamber, from *cubāre,* to lie down, to sleep.]

cubic measure. A unit, as a cubic foot, or a system of units used to measure volume or capacity.

cu·bi·form (kyōō′bə-fôrm′) *adj.* Having the shape of a cube.

cub·ism (kyōō′bĭz′əm) *n.* A style of 20th-cent. art in which the subject matter is portrayed by geometric forms without realistic detail. —**cub′ist** *n.* —**cu·bis′tic** *adj.*

cu·bit (kyōō′bĭt) *n.* An ancient unit of linear measure equal to the length of the forearm from the tip of the middle finger to the elbow, or from 43 to 56 centimeters or 17 to 22 inches. [Middle English *cubite,* from Latin *cubitum,* cubit, elbow.]

cu·boid (kyōō′boid′) *adj.* Also **cu·boi·dal** (kyōō-boid′l). Having the shape of a cube.

Cub Scout. A member of the junior division of the Boy Scouts.

cuck·old (kŭk′əld) *n.* A man whose wife has committed adultery. —*tr.v.* To make a cuckold of. [Middle English *cukeweld,* from Old French *cucualt,* from *cucu,* cuckoo.] —**cuck′old-ry** *n.*

cuckoo
George Miksch Sutton

cuckoo clock

cuck·oo (kōō′kōō, kook′ōō) *n.* **1.** An Old World bird, *Cuculus canorus,* that has grayish plumage and a characteristic two-note call. **2.** The call or cry of a cuckoo. —*tr.v.* To repeat again and again. —*adj.* Crazy; foolish. [Middle English *cuccu.*]

cuckoo clock. A wall clock with a mechanical cuckoo that pops out at regular intervals to announce the time.

cu·cum·ber (kyōō′kŭm′bər) *n.* **1.** A vine, *Cucumis sativus,* cultivated for its edible fruit. **2.** The usu. cylindrical fruit of the cucumber, eaten as a vegetable. [Middle English *cucumer,* from Old French *cocombre,* from Latin *cucumis.*]

cud (kŭd) *n.* **1.** Food regurgitated from the first stomach to the mouth of a ruminant and chewed again. **2.** Something that can be held in the mouth and chewed, as a quid of tobacco. [Middle English *cud(de),* from Old English *cwudu, cudu.*]

cud·dle (kŭd′l) *v.* **-dled, -dling.** —*tr.v.* To fondle in the arms; hug tenderly. —*intr.v.* To nestle; snuggle. —*n.* A hug or embrace. [Orig. unknown.] —**cud′dly** *adj.*

cudg·el (kŭj′əl) *n.* A short, heavy club. —*tr.v.* **-eled, -el·ing** or **-elled, -el·ling.** To beat or strike with a cudgel. —*idiom.* **cudgel (one's) brains.** To think hard. [Middle English *cuggel,* from Old English *cycgel.*]

cue¹ (kyōō) *n.* The long, tapered rod used to propel the ball in billiards and pool. [French *queue,* tail, from Old French *coue,* from Latin *cauda,* tail.]

cue² (kyōō) *n.* **1.** A word or signal given to remind an actor or singer to speak, sing, or move in a prescribed way during a performance. **2.** Any hint or reminder, as a signal for action. —*tr.v.* **cued, cu·ing.** To give (a performer) a cue. [Orig. unknown.]

cue ball. The white ball that is propelled with the cue in billiards and pool.

cuff¹ (kŭf) *n.* **1.** A fold or band used as trimming at the bottom of a sleeve. **2.** The turned-up fold at the bottom of a trouser leg. **3.** A handcuff. —*idioms.* **off the cuff.** *Informal.* Extemporaneously; **on the cuff.** *Informal.* **1.** Without immediate payment; on credit. **2.** Without payment; gratis. [Middle English *cuffe,* glove, mitten.]

cuff² (kŭf) *tr.v.* To strike with the open hand; slap. —*n.* A blow or slap with the open hand. [Orig. unknown.]

cuff links. A pair of linked buttons or a similar device used to fasten the cuffs of a shirt.

cui·rass (kwĭ-răs′) *n.* **1.** A piece of armor for protecting the breast and back. **2.** *Zool.* A protective covering of bony plates or scales. [Middle English *curace,* cuirass, from Old French *cuirasse,* from Latin *coriāceus,* of leather, from *corium,* hide, skin.]

cuish (kwĭsh) *n.* Var. of **cuisse.**

cui·sine (kwĭ-zēn′) *n.* A characteristic manner or style of preparing food: *French cuisine; a restaurant with an excellent cuisine.* [French, from Late Latin *coquīna,* a kitchen, cookery, from *coquere,* to cook.]

cuisse (kwĭs) *n.* Also **cuish** (kwĭsh). Plate armor worn to protect the thigh. [Back-formation from Middle English *cussues,* from Old French *cuisse,* thigh, from Latin *coxa,* thigh, hip.]

cul-de-sac (kŭl′dĭ-săk′, kōōl′-) *n., pl.* **cul-de-sacs. 1.** A dead-end street; impasse. **2.** *Anat.* A saclike cavity or tube open only at one end. [French, "bottom of the sack," blind alley.]

-cule. A suffix meaning small: **molecule.** [French, from New Latin *-cula,* from Latin *-culus, -cula, -culum.*]

cu·li·nar·y (kyōo'lə-nĕr'ē, kŭl'ə-) *adj.* Of or pertaining to a kitchen or to cookery: *culinary ware; culinary skill.* [Latin *culīnārius,* from *culīna,* kitchen.]

cull (kŭl) *tr.v.* **1.** To pick out from others: *cull passages from a poet's work.* **2.** To gather or search through; collect: *cull the forest for firewood.* —See Syns at **choose.** —*n.* Something rejected because of inferior quality. [Middle English *collen,* from Old French *cuillir,* from Latin *colligere,* to collect.] —**cull'er** *n.*

cul·mi·nate (kŭl'mə-nāt') *intr.v.* **-nat·ed, -nat·ing.** To reach the highest point or degree; come to full effect; climax: *A series of wildcat strikes culminated in the shutdown of the factory.* [From Late Latin *culmināre,* from Latin *culmen,* top, summit.] —**cul'mi·na'tion** *n.*

cu·lottes (kōo-lŏts', kyōo-) *pl.n.* A woman's full trousers cut to resemble a skirt. [French, breeches, dim. of *cul,* backside, from Latin *cūlus.*]

cul·pa·ble (kŭl'pə-bəl) *adj.* Responsible for wrong or error; deserving censure; blameworthy: *culpable behavior.* [Middle English *coupable,* from Old French, from Latin *culpābilis,* from *culpāre,* to blame, from *culpa,* fault.] —**cul'pa·bil'i·ty** *n.* —**cul'pa·bly** *adv.*

cul·prit (kŭl'prĭt) *n.* **1.** A person charged with an offense or crime. **2.** A person guilty of a fault or crime. [Orig. unknown.]

cult (kŭlt) *n.* **1.** A system or community of religious worship and ritual, esp. one focusing upon a single deity or spirit: *the cult of Dionysus.* **2. a.** Obsessive devotion or veneration for a person, principle, or ideal. **b.** The object of such devotion. **3.** A group of persons sharing a common interest: *a fashionable political cult.* [French *culte,* from Latin *cultus,* cultivation, worship, from the past part. of *colere,* to cultivate.] —**cult'ism** *n.* —**cult'ist** *n.*

cul·ti·va·ble (kŭl'tə-və-bəl) *adj.* Also **cul·ti·vat·a·ble** (-vā'-tə-bəl). Capable of being cultivated.

cul·ti·vate (kŭl'tə-vāt') *tr.v.* **-vat·ed, -vat·ing. 1. a.** To improve and prepare (land) for raising crops, as by plowing or fertilizing. **b.** To loosen or dig (soil) around growing plants. **2.** To grow or tend (a plant or crop): *cultivate roses.* **3.** To form and refine, as by education: *cultivate a love of music; cultivate one's mind.* **4.** To seek the acquaintance or good will of: *cultivate influential people in business.* [Medieval Latin *cultīvāre,* from *cultīvus,* tilled, from Latin *cultus,* past part. of *colere,* to till, cultivate.]

cul·ti·vat·ed (kŭl'tə-vā'tĭd) *adj.* Cultured; refined. —See Syns at **refined.**

cul·ti·va·tion (kŭl'tə-vā'shən) *n.* **1.** The act or process of tilling or growing. **2.** Development, as by education. **3.** Culture; refinement: *a woman of immense cultivation.*

cul·ti·va·tor (kŭl'tə-vā'tər) *n.* **1.** Someone who cultivates. **2.** An implement or machine for loosening the earth and destroying weeds around growing plants.

cul·tur·al (kŭl'chər-əl) *adj.* **1.** Of or relating to culture: *New York City is a great cultural center.* **2.** *Bot.* Obtained by specialized breeding, as certain plants.

cul·ture (kŭl'chər) *n.* **1.** The result of intellectual development, as evidenced by a high degree of taste, refinement, appreciation of the arts, etc.: *a man of great culture and charm.* **2.** Intellectual and artistic activity and the works produced by this: *Our libraries and museums bring culture to the people.* **3.** The arts, beliefs, customs, institutions, and all other products of human work and thought created by a people or group at a particular time: *The culture of western Europe owes much to Greece.* **4.** Development of the mind or body through special training: *He believes in physical culture.* **5.** The raising of animals or growing of plants, esp. for use or improved development: *bee culture; African violet culture.* **6. a.** The growing of microorganisms or tissues in a specially prepared nutrient substance. **b.** Such a growth, as of bacteria or tissue. —*tr.v.* **-tured, -tur·ing. 1.** To grow (microorganisms, tissues, etc.) in a specially prepared nutrient substance. **2.** To cultivate. [Middle English, cultivation, tillage, from Old French, from Latin *cultūra,* from *cultus,* cultivation, from *colere,* to till.]

cul·tured (kŭl'chərd) *adj.* **1.** Well-educated; refined: *The*

professor is a cultured man. **2.** Grown or produced under artificial and controlled conditions: *cultured pearls.* —See Syns at **refined.**

cul·vert (kŭl'vərt) *n.* A sewer or drain crossing under a road or embankment. [Orig. unknown.]

cum (kōom, kŭm) *prep.* Combined with; together with; plus: *an attic-cum-studio.* [Latin.]

cum·ber (kŭm'bər) *tr.v.* **1.** To weigh down; burden. **2.** To hamper; obstruct. —*n.* A hindrance; encumbrance. [Middle English *combren.*] —**cum'ber·er** *n.*

cum·ber·some (kŭm'bər-səm) *adj.* **1.** Heavy and awkward to carry, wear, etc.; burdensome: *cumbersome baggage.* **2.** Clumsy and inefficient: *a cumbersome method of plowing.* —See Syns at **heavy.** —**cum'ber·some·ly** *adv.* —**cum'ber·some·ness** *n.*

cum·brous (kŭm'brəs) *adj.* Cumbersome. —**cum'brous·ly** *adv.* —**cum'brous·ness** *n.*

cum·in (kŭm'ĭn) *n.* Also **cum·min. 1.** An Old World plant, *Cuminum cyminum,* with finely divided leaves and small white or pinkish flowers. **2.** The aromatic seeds of the cumin, used as a condiment. [Middle English *comin,* from Old French *cumin,* from Latin *cumīnum,* from Greek *kuminon.*]

cum lau·de (kōom lou'də, lou'dē, kŭm lô'dē). With honor: *graduated cum laude from Harvard.* [New Latin, "with praise."]

cum·mer·bund (kŭm'ər-bŭnd') *n.* A broad, pleated sash worn around the waist. [Hindi *kamarband,* from Persian, loinband, waistband : *kamar,* loins, waist + *band,* band.]

cum·min (kŭm'ĭn) *n.* Var. of **cumin.**

cum·quat (kŭm'kwŏt') *n.* Var. of **kumquat.**

cu·mu·late (kyōo'myə-lāt') *tr.v. & intr.v.* **-lat·ed, -lat·ing.** To accumulate. [From Latin *cumulāre,* from *cumulus,* heap.] —**cu'mu·la'tion** *n.*

cu·mu·la·tive (kyōo'myə-lā'tĭv, -lə-tĭv) *adj.* **1.** Increasing or enlarging by successive addition: *the cumulative bad effects of cigarette smoking.* **2.** Acquired by or resulting from accumulation: *cumulative learning.* **3.** *Finance.* Of or pertaining to interest or a dividend that increases if not paid when due. **4.** *Law.* Designating additional or supporting evidence. —**cu'mu·la'tive·ly** *adv.*

cu·mu·li (kyōo'myə-lī') *n.* Plural of **cumulus.**

cu·mu·lo·nim·bus (kyōo'myə-lō-nĭm'bəs) *n., pl.* **-bus·es** or **-bi** (-bī'). *Meteorol.* A very dense cloud with massive projections that billow upward. [CUMUL(US) + NIMBUS.]

cu·mu·lus (kyōo'myə-ləs) *n., pl.* **-li** (-lī'). **1.** *Meteorol.* A dense, white, fluffy cloud that billows upward from a flat base and occurs at an average height of about 3¼ kilometers or 2 miles. **2.** A pile, mound, or heap. [Latin, heap, mass.] —**cu'mu·lous** *adj.*

cunc·ta·tion (kŭngk-tā'shən) *n.* A delay. [Latin *cūnctātiō,* from *cūnctārī,* to delay.] —**cunc'ta·tive** (kŭngk'tā'tĭv, -tə-) *adj.* —**cunc'ta·tor** *n.*

cu·ne·ate (kyōo'nē-āt', -ĭt) *adj.* Wedge-shaped, as a triangular leaf that tapers toward the base. [Latin *cuneātus,* from *cuneus,* wedge.] —**cu'ne·ate·ly** *adv.*

cu·ne·i·form (kyōo'nē-ə-fôrm', kyōo-nē'-) *adj.* **1.** Wedge-shaped. **2. a.** Of or designating wedge-shaped characters used in writing. **b.** Of or designating documents or inscriptions written in such characters. —*n.* Cuneiform writing. [French *cunéiforme,* from Latin *cuneus,* wedge.]

cun·ner (kŭn'ər) *n.* A saltwater fish, *Tautogolabrus adspersus,* of North American Atlantic waters. [Orig. unknown.]

cun·ning (kŭn'ĭng) *adj.* **1.** Shrewd; crafty; sly: *a cunning scheme.* **2.** *Informal.* Delicately pleasing; charming; cute: *a cunning little child.* —*n.* Slyness; craftiness; guile: *The fox is an animal of great cunning.* [Middle English *conning,* perh. from *connen,* to know, from Old English *cunnan.*] —**cun'ning·ly** *adv.* —**cun'ning·ness** *n.*

cup (kŭp) *n.* **1.** A small, open container, usu. with a handle, from which to drink. **2. a.** A cup with something in it: *a cup of tea.* **b.** The amount that a cup holds: *drink a cup of coffee.* **3.** The chalice or the wine used in the celebration of the Eucharist. **4.** *Cooking.* A measure equal to about 237 milliliters or 8 ounces or 16 tablespoons. **5.** Something similar in shape to a cup. **6.** A cup-shaped vessel awarded as a prize or trophy. **7.** *Golf.* A hole or the metal container inside a hole. **8.** Any of various beverages usu. combining wine, fruit, and spices. —*tr.v.* **cupped, cup·ping. 1.** To place in or as in a cup. **2.** To form or shape like a cup: *cup one's hands.* **—idiom. (one's) cup of tea.** *Informal.* Something or someone that is suitable. [Middle English *cuppe*, from Old English *cuppe*, from Late Latin *cuppa*, drinking vessel.]

cup·board (kŭb′ərd) *n.* A closet or cabinet, usu. with shelves for storing food, dishes, etc.

cup·cake (kŭp′kāk′) *n.* A small cake baked in a cup-shaped container.

cu·pel (kyōō′pəl, kyōō-pĕl′) *n.* A small, shallow, porous vessel used in assaying to separate precious metals from less valuable elements such as lead. **—tr.v. -peled** or **-pelled, -pel·ing** or **-pel·ling.** To separate from base metals in a cupel. [French *coupelle*, dim. of *coupe*, cup, from Late Latin *cuppa*, cup.]

cup·ful (kŭp′fŏŏl′) *n., pl.* **-fuls. 1.** The amount a cup will hold. **2.** *Cooking.* A measure of capacity equal to about 237 milliliters or 8 ounces or 16 tablespoons.

Cu·pid (kyōō′pĭd) *n.* **1.** The Roman god of love, identified with the Greek Eros. **2. cupid.** A representation of Cupid, portrayed as a winged boy with a bow and arrow and used as a symbol of love.

cu·pid·i·ty (kyōō-pĭd′ĭ-tē) *n.* Excessive desire, esp. for wealth; greed. [Middle English *cupidite*, from Old French, from Latin *cupiditās*, from *cupere*, to desire.]

cu·po·la (kyōō′pə-lə) *n.* A small dome on top of a roof. [Italian, from Late Latin *cūpula*, dim. of Latin *cūpa*, tub, vat.]

cup·ping (kŭp′ĭng) *n.* A therapeutic process, rarely used in modern medicine, in which glass cups, partially evacuated by heating, are applied to the skin to draw blood toward or through the surface.

cu·pre·ous (kyōō′prē-əs) *adj.* Of, concerning, resembling, or containing copper; coppery.

cu·pric (kyōō′prĭk) *adj.* Of or containing divalent copper.

cu·prous (kyōō′prəs) *adj.* Of or containing univalent copper.

cur (kûr) *n.* **1.** A dog of mixed breed; a mongrel. **2.** A hateful or cowardly person. [Middle English *curre*, short for *kur(dogge)*, "growling dog."]

cur·a·ble (kyŏŏr′ə-bəl) *adj.* Capable of being cured. **—cur′a·bil′i·ty** or **cur′a·ble·ness** *n.* **—cur′a·bly** *adv.*

cu·ra·cy (kyŏŏr′ə-sē) *n., pl.* **-cies.** The office, duties, or term of office of a curate.

cu·ra·re (kyŏŏ-rä′rē, kŏŏ-) *n.* Also **u·ra·ri** (ŏŏ-rä′rē, yŏŏ-). **1.** Any of various resinous extracts obtained from several species of South American trees of the genera *Chondodendron* and *Strychnos.* It is used medicinally as a muscle relaxant and by some South American Indians as an arrow poison. **2.** Any of the trees from which these substances are obtained. [Portuguese and Spanish, from Cariban *kurari*.]

cu·ras·sow (kyŏŏr′ə-sō′) *n.* Any of several long-tailed, crested tropical American birds of the family Cracidae, related to the pheasants and domestic fowl. [Var. of *Curaçao*, an island of the Netherlands Antilles.]

cu·rate (kyŏŏr′ĭt) *n.* **1.** A clergyman who assists a rector or vicar. **2.** A clergyman who has charge of a parish. [Middle English *curat*, from Medieval Latin *cūrātus*, "one having a (spiritual) cure or charge," from *cūra*, cure.]

cur·a·tive (kyŏŏr′ə-tĭv) *adj.* Serving or tending to cure: *curative medicine.* **—n.** Something that cures; a remedy. **—cur′a·tive·ly** *adv.* **—cur′a·tive·ness** *n.*

cu·ra·tor (kyŏŏ-rā′tər, kyŏŏr′ə-tər) *n.* The person in charge of a museum, library, etc. [Middle English *curatour*, from Old French *curateur*, from Latin *cūrātōr*, overseer, from *cūra*, care, cure.] **—cu′ra·to′ri·al** (kyŏŏr′ə-tôr′ē-əl, -tōr′-) *adj.* **—cu·ra′tor·ship′** *n.*

curb (kûrb) *n.* **1.** Also *Brit.* **kerb.** A concrete or stone rim along the edge of a sidewalk. **2.** Something that checks or restrains: *a curb on spending.* **3.** A chain or strap used together with a bit to restrain a horse. **—tr.v. 1.** To check, restrain, or control: *curb one's temper; curb inflation.* **2.** To walk (a dog) in the gutter so as not to soil the sidewalk. [Old French *courbe*, a curved object, horse's bit, from Latin *curvus*, curved.]

curb·ing (kûr′bĭng) *n.* **1.** The material used to construct a curb. **2.** A curb.

curb·stone (kûrb′stōn′) *n.* A stone or row of stones that constitutes a curb.

curd (kûrd) *n.* **1.** Often **curds.** The thick part of milk that separates from the whey, used to make cheese. **2.** A food, such as beancurd, that resembles curd. **—tr.v.** To cause to thicken. **—intr.v.** To become curd. [Middle English *curd, crudde.*]

cur·dle (kûr′dl) *v.* **-dled, -dling. —intr.v.** To become curd; coagulate; thicken: *Add vinegar until the milk starts to curdle.* **—tr.v.** To cause to change into curd: *Be careful not to curdle the sauce.*

cure (kyŏŏr) *n.* **1.** A method or course of medical treatment designed to restore health. **2.** Restoration of health; recovery from disease. **3.** A drug or some similar agent that restores health; a remedy. **4.** The act or process of preserving a product, such as fish, meat, or tobacco. **—v. cured, cur·ing. —tr.v. 1.** To restore to good health. **2.** To get rid of; to remedy: *cure an evil.* **3.** To preserve (meat, fish, etc.), as by salting, smoking, or aging. **4.** To prepare, preserve, or finish (a substance) by a chemical or physical process. **5.** To vulcanize (rubber). **—intr.v. 1.** To effect a cure or recovery. **2.** To be prepared, preserved, or finished by a chemical or physical process. [Middle English, from Old French, from Latin *cūra*, care, spiritual charge, from Old French, from Latin *cūra*, care, charge; healing.] **—cure′less** *adj.* **—cur′er** *n.*

cure-all (kyŏŏr′ôl′) *n.* Something that cures all diseases or evils; a panacea.

cu·rette (kyŏŏ-rĕt′) *n.* Also **cu·ret.** A scooplike surgical instrument used to remove dead tissue or growths from cavities of the body. [French, from *curer*, to cure, from Old French, from Latin *cūrāre*, from *cūra*, cure.]

cur·few (kûr′fyōō) *n.* **1.** An order or regulation requiring specified groups of people to retire from the streets at a certain hour. **2. a.** The period during which a curfew is in effect. **b.** A signal, as a bell, announcing it. [Middle English *curfeu, coeverfeu*, from Old French *cuevrefeu*, "a covering of the fire" : *co(u)vrir*, to cover + *feu*, fire, from Latin *focus*, hearth.]

cu·ri·a (kyŏŏr′ē-ə) *n., pl.* **-ri·ae** (-ē-ē′). **1.** One of the ten primitive subdivisions of a tribe in early Rome. **2.** Often **Curia.** The central administration governing the Roman Catholic Church. **3.** In medieval Europe: **a.** A feudal assembly or council. **b.** A royal court of justice. [Latin *cūria*, council.] **—cu′ri·al** *adj.*

cu·rie (kyŏŏr′ē, kyŏŏ-rē′) *n. Abbr.* **Ci** A unit of radioactivity, the amount of any nuclide that undergoes exactly 3.7 x 10^{10} radioactive disintegrations per second. [After Marie *Curie* (1867–1934), Polish-born French chemist.]

cu·ri·o (kyŏŏr′ē-ō′) *n., pl.* **-os.** A rare or unusual object of art. [Short for CURIOSITY.]

cu·ri·os·i·ty (kyŏŏr′ē-ŏs′ĭ-tē) *n., pl.* **-ties. 1.** A desire to know or learn: *He burned with curiosity over what was in the box.* **2.** Something unusual or extraordinary: *The octagonal house was a real curiosity.*

cu·ri·ous (kyŏŏr′ē-əs) *adj.* **1.** Eager to acquire information or knowledge: *A scientist is always curious to learn more.* **2.** Excessively inquisitive; prying; nosy. **3.** Interesting because unusual or extraordinary; singular; odd: *a curious fact.* [Middle English, from Old French *curios*, from Latin *cūriōsus*, careful, diligent, from *cūra*, care, cure.] **—cu′ri·ous·ly** *adv.* **—cu′ri·ous·ness** *n.*

cu·ri·um (kyŏŏr′ē-əm) *n. Symbol* **Cm** A silvery, metallic radioactive transuranic element, first produced by bombarding plutonium with helium ions. It has 13 isotopes with mass numbers ranging from 238 to 250 and half-lives ranging from 64 minutes to 16.4 million years. Atomic number 96. [After Marie *Curie* (1867–1934) and Pierre *Curie* (1859–1906), French chemists.]

curl (kûrl) *tr.v.* **1.** To twist into ringlets or coils: *curl one's hair.* **2.** To form into the spiral shape of a ringlet or coil; to wind: *Curl the paper around the pencil.* **—intr.v. 1.** To form ringlets or coils: *Her hair curls naturally.* **2.** To assume a curved shape: *His lips curled into a smile.* **3.** To move in a curve or spiral: *Smoke curled from the chimney.* **4.** To play the game of curling. **—See Syns at wind. —phrasal verb. curl up.** To sit or lie cozily with the legs drawn up. **—n. 1.** A coil or ringlet of hair. **2.** Something with a spiral or coiled shape: *a curl of smoke.* **3.** The act of curling or the condition of being curled. [Middle English curlen, *crullen*, from *crulle*, curly, from Middle Dutch.]

curl·er (kûr′lər) *n.* **1.** Something or someone that curls. **2.** A pin, roller, etc., on which hair is wound for curling. **3.** A player of curling.

cur·lew (kûrl′yōō, kûr′lōō) *n.* Any of several brownish, long-legged shore birds of the genus *Numenius*, with long, slender, downward-curving bills. [Middle English *curleu*, from Old French *courlieu*.]

curl·i·cue (kûr′lĭ-kyōō′) *n.* Also **curl·y·cue.** A fancy twist or curl, such as a flourish made with a pen. [CURLY + CUE.]

curl·ing (kûr′lĭng) *n.* A game, played on ice, in which two four-player teams slide heavy stones toward a mark in the center of a circle at either end.

curl·y (kûr′lē) *adj.* **-i·er, -i·est. 1.** Having curls or tending to curl. **2.** Having a wavy grain or markings, as wood: *curly maple.* **—curl′i·ness** *n.*

curl·y·cue (kûr′lĭ-kyōō′) *n.* Var. of **curlicue.**

cur·mudg·eon (kər-mŭj′ən) *n.* A cantankerous person. [Orig. unknown.] **—cur·mudg′eon·ly** *adj.*

cur·rant (kûr′ənt, kŭr′-) *n.* **1. a.** Any of various usu. prickly shrubs of the genus *Ribes*, bearing clusters of red, black, or greenish fruit. **b.** The small, sour fruit of any of these plants. **2.** A small, dried seedless grape of the Mediterranean region. [Middle English *(raysons of) coraunte,* (raisins of) Corinth.]

currant

cur·ren·cy (kûr′ən-sē, kŭr′-) *n., pl.* **-cies. 1.** Any form of money in actual use as a medium of exchange. **2.** General acceptance; widespread use or circulation: *Many newly formed words and expressions have short currency.* [Medieval Latin *currentia,* "a flowing," from Latin *currere,* to run.]

cur·rent (kûr′ənt, kŭr′-) *adj.* **1.** Belonging to the present time; present-day: *the current issue; current events.* **2.** In general or widespread use; commonly accepted; prevalent: *a word that is no longer current.* —See Syns at **modern.** *—n.* **1.** A steady and smooth onward movement, as of water. **2.** The part of any body of liquid or gas that has a continuous onward movement: *a river current.* **3.** *Symbol* **i, I a.** A flow of electric charge. **b.** The amount of electric charge that passes a point in a unit of time, usu. expressed in amperes. **4.** A general tendency, movement, or course, as of events, opinions, etc. [Middle English *curraunt,* from Old French *corant,* from *courre,* to run, from Latin *currere.*] **—cur′rent·ly** *adv.* **—cur′rent·ness** *n.*

cur·ric·u·lum (kə-rĭk′yə-ləm) *n., pl.* **-la** (-lə) or **-lums. 1.** All the courses of study offered by a particular educational institution. **2.** A particular course of study, often in a special field. [Latin, a running, course, from *currere,* to run.] **—cur·ric′u·lar** (-lər) *adj.*

cur·rie (kûr′ē, kŭr′ē) *n.* Var. of **curry** (condiment).

cur·ry[1] (kûr′ē, kŭr′ē) *tr.v.* **-ried, -ry·ing. 1.** To groom (a horse) with a currycomb. **2.** To prepare (tanned hides) for use by soaking, coloring, or other processes. *—idiom.* **curry favor.** To seek or gain favor by flattery. [Middle English *curreien,* from Old French *co(n)reer,* to prepare, equip.]

cur·ry[2] (kûr′ē, kŭr′ē) *n., pl.* **-ries.** Also **cur·rie. 1.** A condiment, **curry powder. 2.** A heavily spiced sauce or relish made with curry powder. **3.** A dish seasoned with curry powder. *—tr.v.* **-ried, -ry·ing.** To season with curry. [Tamil *kari,* relish, sauce.]

cur·ry·comb (kûr′ē-kōm′, kŭr′-) *n.* A comb with metal teeth, used for grooming horses. *—tr.v.* To groom with a currycomb.

curry powder. A blended condiment prepared from cumin, coriander, turmeric, and other pungent spices.

curse (kûrs) *n.* **1. a.** An appeal to a supernatural power to bring down evil or harm upon someone or something. **b.** The evil thus invoked. **2.** A word or group of words expressing great hatred or anger; an oath: *shout curses.* **3.** Something that causes great evil or harm; a scourge: *Mankind's greatest curse is poverty.* *—v.* **cursed** or **curst** (kûrst), **curs·ing.** *—tr.v.* **1.** To place a curse on; to damn: *The old gypsy cursed the soldiers as they led her to the stake.* **2.** To swear at; abuse profanely: *He cursed the day he was born.* **3.** To bring evil upon; afflict. *—intr.v.* To utter curses; swear: *He cursed like a trooper.* [Middle English *curs(e),* from Old English *curs.*] **—curs′er** *n.*

cur·sive (kûr′sĭv) *adj.* Of or designating handwriting or printing in which the letters are joined together; flowing: *cursive writing.* *—n.* **1.** A cursive character or letter. **2.** A kind of type that imitates handwriting. [Medieval Latin *(scripta) cursīva,* "flowing (script)," from Latin *cursus,* past part. of *currere,* to run.]

cur·so·ri·al (kûr-sôr′ē-əl, -sōr′-) *adj. Zool.* Adapted to or specialized for running: *cursorial birds; cursorial legs.* [From Late Latin *cursōrius,* of running.]

cur·so·ry (kûr′sə-rē) *adj.* Hasty and superficial; not thorough. [Late Latin *cursōrius,* of running, from Latin *cursor,* a runner, from *currere,* to run.] **—cur′so·ri·ly** *adv.*

curst (kûrst) *v.* A past tense and past participle of **curse.**

curt (kûrt) *adj.* **-er, -est.** Rudely brief and abrupt in speech or manner; brusque: *a curt reply.* —See Syns at **gruff.** [Latin *curtus,* cut short.] **—curt′ly** *adv.* **—curt′ness** *n.*

cur·tail (kər-tāl′) *tr.v.* To cut short; reduce: *We must curtail our spending.* [Var. of obs. *curtal,* to dock the tail of a horse, from French *courtault,* horse with docked tail, from Latin *curtus,* cut short.] **—cur·tail′er** *n.* **—cur·tail′ment** *n.*

cur·tain (kûr′tn) *n.* **1.** A piece of cloth or similar material hanging in a window or other opening as a decoration, shade, or screen: *a curtain in the doorway; the curtain in a theater that hides the stage from view.* **2.** Something that acts as a screen or cover: *hidden by a curtain of black smoke; a curtain of secrecy.* **3. curtains.** *Slang.* **a.** The end; ruin. **b.** Death. *—tr.v.* To provide or shut off with or as if with a curtain. [Middle English *curtin(e),* from Old French, from Late Latin *cortīna,* enclosure, curtain, from Latin *cohors,* enclosure.]

curtain wall. An exterior wall, as of a skyscraper, that does not support a roof.

curt·sy or **curt·sey** (kûrt′sē) *n., pl.* **-sies** or **-seys.** A gesture of respect or reverence made by women and girls by bending the knees and lowering the body while keeping one foot forward. *—intr.v.* **-sied** or **-seyed, -sy·ing** or **-sey·ing.** To make a curtsy. [Var. of COURTESY.]

cur·va·ceous (kûr-vā′shəs) *adj.* Having a full or voluptuous figure; shapely.

cur·va·ture (kûr′və-chŏor′, -chər) *n.* **1. a.** An act of curving or the condition of being curved. **b.** The degree to which something is curved. **2.** *Math.* The ratio of the change in tangent inclination over a given arc to the length of the arc. **3.** A curving or bending of a body part, esp. an abnormal one: *curvature of the spine.*

curve (kûrv) *n.* **1. a.** A line that deviates from straightness in a smooth, continuous way. **b.** A surface that deviates from flatness in a similar way. **2.** Anything that has the general shape of a curve: *a curve in the road.* **3. a.** A line representing data on a graph. **b.** A trend derived from or as if from such a graph. **4.** *Math.* **a.** The graph of a function on a coordinate plane. **b.** The intersection of two surfaces in three dimensions. **5.** Also **curve ball.** *Baseball.* A pitched ball that veers to one side as it approaches the batter. *—v.* **curved, curv·ing.** *—intr.v.* To move in or take the shape of a curve. *—tr.v.* To cause to curve. [From earlier *curve (line),* "curved (line)," from Middle English *curve,* curved, from Latin *curvus.*] **—curv′ed·ly** (kûr′vĭd-lē) *adv.* **—curv′ed·ness** *n.*

cur·vet (kûr-vĕt′, kûr′vĭt) *n.* A light leap by a horse in which the forelegs come down as the hind legs are raised. *—intr.v.* **-vet·ted, -vet·ed, -vet·ting** or **-vet·ing. 1.** To leap in a curvet. **2.** To prance; frolic. [Italian *corvetta,* "curving leap," from Old Italian *corva,* a curve, from Latin *curvus,* curved.]

cur·vi·lin·e·ar (kûr′və-lĭn′ē-ər) *adj.* Also **cur·vi·lin·e·al** (-əl). Formed, bounded, or characterized by curved lines. [Latin *curvus,* curved + LINEAR.]

cush·ion (ko͝osh′ən) *n.* **1.** A pad or pillow with a soft filling, used to sit, lie, or rest on. **2.** Anything used to absorb or soften the impact of something: *a savings account that was her cushion against unemployment.* **3.** The rim bordering a billiard table. —*tr.v.* **1.** To provide with a cushion or cushions.. **2.** To place or seat on a cushion. **3.** To protect against or absorb the impact of: *cushion a blow.* [Middle English *cuisshen,* from Old French *coissin,* "hip rest," cushion, from Latin *coxa,* hip.]

cush·y (ko͝osh′ē) *adj.* **-i·er, -i·est.** *Slang.* Comfortable; undemanding: *a cushy job.* [From Hindi *khush,* from Persian *khōsh,* pleasant.]

cusp (kŭsp) *n.* **1.** A point or pointed end. **2.** *Anat.* **a.** A prominence on the chewing surface of a tooth. **b.** A fold or flap of a heart valve. **3.** *Geom.* A point at which a curve crosses itself and at which the two tangents to the curve coincide. **4.** Either point of a crescent moon. [Latin *cuspis,* a point, spear.]

cus·pid (kŭs′pĭd) *n.* A tooth having a single point; canine tooth. [Back-formation from BICUSPID.]

cus·pi·date (kŭs′pĭ-dāt′) *adj.* **1.** Having a cusp or cusps. **2.** *Biol.* Terminating in or tipped with a sharp point: *a cuspidate leaf.* [Latin *cuspidātus,* from *cuspidāre,* to make pointed, from *cuspis,* point.]

cus·pi·dor (kŭs′pĭ-dôr′) *n.* A spittoon. [Portuguese, from *cuspir,* to spit, from Latin *conspuere,* to spit upon : *com-,* with + *spuere,* to spit.]

cuss (kŭs). *Informal.* —*intr.v.* To curse. —*tr.v.* To shout curses at. —*n.* **1.** A curse. **2.** An odd person: *He's a silly old cuss.* [Var. of CURSE.]

cuss·ed (kŭs′ĭd) *adj. Informal.* **1.** Cursed. **2.** Perverse; stubborn. —**cuss′ed·ly** *adv.* —**cuss′ed·ness** *n.*

cus·tard (kŭs′tərd) *n.* A puddinglike dessert of milk, sugar, eggs, and flavoring. [Middle English *crustade,* a kind of pie, prob. from Old Provençal *croustado,* from *crosta,* crust.]

custard apple. **1. a.** A tropical American tree, *Annona reticulata,* that bears large, heart-shaped fruit. **b.** The fruit of this tree, having edible, fleshy pulp. **2.** Any of several related trees or fruit, esp. the papaw. [So called because its pulp resembles custard.]

cus·to·di·an (kŭ-stō′dē-ən) *n.* **1.** A person who has charge of or protects someone or something; a caretaker. **2.** A person who takes care of a building; a janitor. —**cus·to′di·an·ship′** *n.*

cus·to·dy (kŭs′tə-dē) *n., pl.* **-dies.** **1.** The right of caring for or guarding, esp. when granted by a court: *The mother was given custody of the children.* **2.** The condition of being detained or held under guard, esp. by the police: *a criminal in protective custody.* [Middle English *custodie,* from Latin *custōdia,* from *custōs,* guard, protector.] —**cus·to′di·al** (kŭ-stō′dē-əl) *adj.*

cus·tom (kŭs′təm) *n.* **1.** An accepted practice or convention followed by tradition: *tribal customs.* **2.** A habitual practice of an individual: *His custom was to think a moment before he spoke.* **3.** *Law.* A common tradition or usage so long established that it has the force or validity of law. **4.** Habitual patronage, as of a store. —*adj.* **1.** Made to order: *expensive cars that were beautiful, sleek custom jobs.* **2.** Making or selling made-to-order goods: *a custom tailor; a custom shop.* [Middle English *custume,* from Old French *costume,* from Latin *consuētūdō,* a being accustomed, from *consuēscere,* to accustom : *com-,* with + *suēscere,* to become accustomed.]

cus·tom·ar·y (kŭs′tə-mĕr′ē) *adj.* Established by custom; usual; habitual: *sit in one's customary place.* —**cus′tom·ar′i·ly** *adv.* —**cus′tom·ar′i·ness** *n.*

cus·tom-built (kŭs′təm-bĭlt′) *adj.* Built according to the specifications of the buyer: *a custom-built car.*

cus·tom·er (kŭs′tə-mər) *n.* **1.** A person who buys goods or services, esp. on a regular basis. **2.** *Informal.* A person: *a real tough customer.*

cus·tom·house (kŭs′təm-hous′) *n.* Also **cus·toms·house** (kŭs′təmz-hous′). A government building or office where customs are levied and collected and ships are cleared for entering or leaving the country.

cus·tom-made (kŭs′təm-mād′) *adj.* Made according to the specifications of the buyer: *custom-made suits.*

cus·toms (kŭs′təmz) *n. (used with a sing. verb).* **1. a.** A duty or tax imposed on goods imported from another country. **b.** The government agency that collects such taxes. **2.** The inspection of goods and baggage entering a country.

cus·toms·house (kŭs′təmz-hous′) *n.* Var. of **customhouse.**

cut (kŭt) *v.* **cut, cut·ting.** —*tr.v.* **1.** To penetrate with or as if with a sharp edge or instrument: *He held the coins so tightly that they cut his hands.* **2.** To form, shape, or divide by penetrating or separating: *Cut the cake in half.* **3.** To separate from the main body of something; detach: *Cut the meat away from the legs of the chicken.* **4.** To shorten; trim: *cut hair.* **5.** To reap; harvest: *cut wheat.* **6.** To cause to fall by sawing: *Each year lumberjacks cut millions of trees.* **7.** To grow (teeth) through the gums: *The baby cut two new teeth.* **8.** To interrupt: *cut electric power for two hours.* **9.** To reduce the size or amount of: *cut taxes; cut down noise.* **10.** To lessen the strength of; dilute: *He cut the drink with water.* **11.** To eliminate; remove: *He cut the third act from the play.* **12.** To edit (film or audio tape). **13.** To hurt: *His remark cut me deeply.* **14.** *Informal.* To be absent from purposely: *I cut my first class today.* **15.** To change the direction of abruptly: *He cut the wheels to the right.* **16.** To divide (a deck of cards) in two, as before dealing. **17.** To dissolve by breaking down the fat of: *Soap cuts grease.* **18.** *Sports.* To strike (a ball) so that it spins irregularly or is deflected. **19.** To record a performance on (a phonograph record). —*intr.v.* **1. a.** To allow penetration or separation, as with a sharp instrument: *Butter cuts easily.* **b.** To perform the action of penetrating or separating: *This knife does not cut well.* **2.** To use a sharp-edged instrument. **3.** To grow through the gums, as teeth. **4.** To penetrate injuriously. **5.** To change direction abruptly: *cut to the left.* **6.** To go directly and often hastily: *cut across the field.* **7.** To divide a pack of cards into two parts. —***phrasal verbs.*** **cut in.** **1.** To interrupt. **2.** To interrupt a dancing couple in order to dance with one of them. **cut off.** **1.** To separate: *The aborigines were cut off from contact with more advanced cultures.* **2.** To stop; discontinue: *He cut off the ignition.* **cut out.** **1.** To be suited: *He is not cut out for city life.* **2.** *Informal.* To stop; cease: *Cut that out right now!* **3.** *Informal.* To depart. **cut up.** *Informal.* To misbehave. —*n.* **1.** The result of cutting; an opening; a slit, wound, etc.: *a cut in the material; a cut on his hand.* **2.** A piece of meat that has been cut from the animal: *cuts of fresh pork.* **3.** A reduction: *a pay cut.* **4.** The style in which something, as clothes or gems, is cut. **5.** A wounding remark; an insult: *That was an unkind cut directed at her.* **6.** The act of shortening or trimming something: *Her hair needs a cut.* **7. a.** The act of cutting out a part, esp. in order to shorten or improve: *Who will make the cuts in the new movie?* **b.** The part that is cut out. **8.** *Informal.* A share of profits or earnings. **9.** *Informal.* An unexcused absence, as from class. **10.** *Sports.* A stroke that causes a ball to spin irregularly or to deflect. **11.** The act of dividing a deck of cards into two parts, as before dealing. **12.** A sharp transition between shots or scenes in a film. —***idiom.*** **a cut above.** A little better than. [Middle English *cutten, kitten.*]

cut-and-dried (kŭt′n-drīd′) *adj.* **1.** In accordance with a formula; prearranged: *There are no cut-and-dried rules for writing.* **2.** Lacking freshness or imagination; ordinary; routine.

cu·ta·ne·ous (kyo͞o-tā′nē-əs) *adj.* Of, involving, or affecting the skin. [From Latin *cutis,* skin.] —**cu·ta′ne·ous·ly** *adv.*

cut·a·way (kŭt′ə-wā′) *n.* A man's formal daytime coat cut so that the front edges slope away from the waist to form tails at the back.

cut·back (kŭt′băk′) *n.* A decrease; curtailment: *a cutback in production.*

cute (kyo͞ot) *adj.* **cut·er, cut·est.** **1.** Delightfully pretty or dainty. **2.** Obviously contrived to charm; affected. [Short for ACUTE.] —**cute′ly** *adv.* —**cute′ness** *n.*

cut·ey (kyo͞o′tē) *n. Slang.* Var. of **cutie.**

cut glass. Glassware shaped or decorated by cutting instruments or abrasive wheels.

cu·ti·cle (kyōō′tĭ-kəl) n. **1.** The outer layer of skin; the epidermis. **2.** The strip of hardened skin at the base of a fingernail or toenail. **3.** Zool. The noncellular, often horny protective outer covering in many invertebrates. **4.** Bot. The layer of cutin covering the epidermis of plants. [Latin cutīcula, dim. of cutis, skin.] **—cu·tic′u·lar** (-tĭk′yə-lər) adj.

cut·ie (kyōō′tē) n. Also **cut·ey.** Slang. A cute person.

cu·tin (kyōōt′n) n. Bot. A waxlike, water-repellent material that is present in the walls of some plant cells and forms the cuticle that covers the epidermis. [Latin cut(is), skin + -IN.]

cu·tis (kyōō′tĭs) n. Anat. The corium. [Latin, skin.]

cut·lass (kŭt′ləs) n. Also **cut·las.** A short, heavy sword with a curved single-edged blade, once used as a weapon by sailors. [Var. of earlier coutelace, from Old French coutelas, from coutel, knife, from Latin culter.]

cut·ler (kŭt′lər) n. A person who makes, repairs, or sells knives or other cutting instruments. [Middle English, from Old French coutelier, from coutel, knife.]

cut·ler·y (kŭt′lə-rē) n. **1.** Cutting instruments and tools, esp. implements used as tableware. **2.** The occupation of a cutler.

cut·let (kŭt′lĭt) n. A thin slice of meat, usu. veal or lamb, cut from the leg or ribs. [French côtelette, from Old French costelette, dim. of coste, rib, from Latin costa.]

cut·off (kŭt′ôf′, -ŏf′) n. **1.** An indicated limit or stopping point. **2.** A cutting off of something, as a flow of steam, water, etc. **3.** A device used to stop a flow, as of a liquid or gas. **4.** A short cut or by-pass. **5.** A new channel cut by a river across the neck of an oxbow.

cut·out (kŭt′out′) n. **1.** Something cut out or intended to be cut out. **2.** Elect. A device that acts as a by-pass or cutoff, esp. in an electric circuit.

cut·purse (kŭt′pûrs′) n. Archaic. A pickpocket.

cut-rate (kŭt′rāt′) adj. Sold or on sale at a reduced price.

cut·ter (kŭt′ər) n. **1.** A worker whose job involves cutting some material, as stone. **2.** A device for cutting. **3.** A Coast Guard vessel of more than 20 meters or 65 feet in length. **4.** A ship's boat used for transporting stores or passengers. **5.** A kind of fast single-masted sailing vessel. **6.** A small sleigh.

cutter

cut·throat (kŭt′thrōt′) n. Someone who cuts throats; a murderer. **—adj. 1.** Cruel; murderous. **2.** Ruthless; merciless: cutthroat competition.

cut·ting (kŭt′ĭng) n. **1.** A part cut off. **2.** Brit. A clipping, as from a newspaper. **3.** The editing of film or audio tape. **4.** A stem, twig, leaf, etc., removed from a plant and placed in soil, sand, or water to form roots and develop into a new plant. **—adj. 1.** Capable of or designed for cutting: a cutting blade. **2.** Sharply penetrating; piercing and cold: a cutting wind. **3.** Sarcastic and insulting: a cutting remark.

cut·tle·bone (kŭt′l-bōn′) n. The chalky shell inside the body of the cuttlefish, used to supply calcium to caged birds.

cut·tle·fish (kŭt′l-fĭsh′) n., pl. **cuttlefish** or **-fish·es.** Any of various squidlike cephalopod saltwater mollusks of the genus Sepia, that have ten arms, a calcareous internal shell, and secrete a dark, inky fluid. [Middle English codel, cuttlefish, from Old English cudele + FISH.]

cut-up (kŭt′ŭp′) n. Informal. A mischievous person; prankster.

cut·wa·ter (kŭt′wô′tər) n. The forward part of a ship's prow.

-cy. A suffix indicating: **1.** A quality or condition: **bankruptcy. 2.** Office or rank: **baronetcy.** [Middle English -cie, from Old French, from Latin -cia, -tia, and Greek -kia, -tiā.]

cyan-. Var. of cyano-.

cy·an·a·mide (sī-ăn′ə-mīd) n. Also **cy·an·a·mid. 1.** An irritating caustic acidic crystalline compound, $NCNH_2$, prepared by treating calcium cyanamide with sulfuric acid. **2.** A salt or ester of cyanamide. [CYAN(O)- + AMIDE.]

cy·a·nate (sī′ə-nāt′, -nĭt) n. A salt or ester of cyanic acid. [CYAN(O)- + -ATE.]

cy·an·ic (sī-ăn′ĭk) adj. **1.** Pertaining to or containing cyanogen. **2.** Blue or bluish. [CYAN(O)- + -IC.]

cy·a·nide (sī′ə-nīd′) n. Also **cy·an·id** (-nĭd). Any of various salts or esters of hydrogen cyanide containing a CN group, esp. the extremely poisonous compounds potassium cyanide and sodium cyanide. [CYAN(O)- + -IDE.]

cyano- or **cyan-.** A prefix meaning: **1.** A blue or dark-blue coloring: **cyanic. 2.** Chem. Cyanide or cyanogen: **cyanate.** [German zyan-, from Greek kuanos, dark-blue enamel, the color blue.]

cy·an·o·gen (sī-ăn′ə-jən) n. **1.** A colorless, flammable, highly poisonous gas, C_2N_2, used as a rocket propellant, fumigant, military weapon, and in welding. **2.** The univalent radical CN found in simple and complex cyanide compounds. [CYANO- + -GEN.]

cy·a·no·sis (sī′ə-nō′sĭs) n. A condition in which the skin appears blue as a result of too little oxygen in the blood. [CYAN(O)- + -OSIS.] **—cy′a·not′ic** (-nŏt′ĭk) adj.

cy·ber·net·ics (sī′bər-nĕt′ĭks) n. (used with a sing. verb). The scientific study of the control processes of electronic, mechanical, and biological systems, esp. the mathematical study of the way in which the information essential to these processes is transmitted. [From Greek kubernētēs, pilot, governor, from kuberman, to steer, govern.] **—cy′ber·net′ic** adj. **—cy′ber·net′i·cist** n.

cycl-. Var. of cyclo-.

cyc·la·mate (sīk′lə-māt′, sī′klə-) n. A salt of cyclamic acid, esp. the sodium and calcium salts, used formerly as noncaloric sweetening agents.

cyc·la·men (sīk′lə-mən, sī′klə-) n. Any of several plants of the genus Cyclamen, with showy white, pink, or red flowers with petals that are turned back. [From Greek kuklaminos, prob. from kuklos, a circle.]

cyc·la·mic acid (sīk′lə-mĭk, sī′klə-). A sour-sweet crystalline acid, $C_6H_{13}NO_3S$.

cy·cle (sī′kəl) n. **1. a.** A single occurrence of an event or series of events that is regularly repeated. **b.** The time during which this event or series of events occurs. **c.** A regularly repeated series of events. **2.** A series of poems, songs, etc., that deal with a single theme or hero. **3.** The orbit of a celestial body. **4.** A long period of time; an age; eon. **5.** A bicycle, tricycle, or motorcycle. **6.** Bot. A circular arrangement of flower parts such as petals or sepals. **—intr.v. -cled, -cling. 1.** To occur in or pass through a cycle. **2.** To move in or as if in a circle. **3.** To ride a bicycle, tricycle, or motorcycle. [French, from Late Latin cyclus, from Greek kuklos, circle.]

cy·clic (sī′klĭk, sĭk′lĭk) or **cy·cli·cal** (sī′klĭ-kəl, sĭk′lĭ-) adj. **1.** Of or occurring in cycles. **2.** Chem. Of compounds that have atoms arranged in a ring. **—cy′cli·cal·ly** adv.

cyclic AMP. A mononucleotide of adenosine that acts as a mediator in the cell in the synthesis of enzymes.

cy·clist (sī′klĭst) n. A person who rides a bicycle, motorcycle, or similar vehicle.

cyclo- or **cycl-.** A prefix meaning a circle: **cyclometer.** [From Greek kuklos, circle, cycle.]

cy·cloid (sī′kloid′) adj. **1.** Resembling a circle. **2.** Zool. Thin, rounded, and smooth-edged, as fish scales. **—n.** Geom. The curve traced by a point on the circumference of a circle that rolls along a straight line. [French cycloïde, from Greek kukloeidēs, from kuklos, circle.] **—cy·cloi′dal** (sī-kloid′l) adj.

cy·clom·e·ter (sī-klŏm′ĭ-tər) n. **1.** An instrument that records the revolutions of a wheel in order to indicate distance traveled. **2.** An instrument that measures circular arcs. [CYCLO- + -METER.] **—cy′clo·met′ric** (-klə-mĕt′rĭk) adj. **—cy·clom′e·try** n.

cy·clone (sī′klōn′) n. **1.** An atmospheric disturbance consisting of a mass of rapidly rotating air. In the Southern Hemisphere the direction of rotation is clockwise, while in the Northern Hemisphere it is counterclockwise. **2.** Any violent rotating windstorm, such as a tornado. [Prob. from Greek *kuklōma*, coil, wheel, from *kuklos*, circle, cycle.] —**cy·clon′ic** (-klŏn′ĭk) or **cy·clon′i·cal** *adj.*

cyclone cellar. An underground shelter used for protection from violent windstorms.

cy·clo·pae·di·a (sī′klə-pē′dē-ə) *n.* Var. of **cyclopedia.**

cy·clo·pe·an (sī′klə-pē′ən, sī-klō′pē-ən) *adj.* **1.** Often **Cyclo-pean.** Of, pertaining to, or suggestive of the Cyclopes. **2.** Pertaining to or designating a primitive style of masonry characterized by the use of massive stones of irregular shape. **3.** Huge or massive; gigantic.

cy·clo·pe·di·a (sī′klə-pē′dē-ə) *n.* Also **cy·clo·pae·di·a.** An encyclopedia. [Short for ENCYCLOPEDIA.] —**cy′clo·pe′dic** *adj.*

Cy·clops (sī′klŏps′) *n., pl.* **Cy·clo·pes** (sī-klō′pēz). *Gk. Myth.* **1.** Any of the three one-eyed Titans who forged thunderbolts for Zeus. **2.** Any of a race of one-eyed giants reputedly descended from these Titans.

cy·clo·ram·a (sī′klə-răm′ə, -rä′mə) *n.* **1.** A large composite picture placed on the interior walls of a cylindrical room so as to appear in natural perspective to a spectator standing in the center. **2.** A large curtain or wall, usu. concave, placed or hung at the rear of a stage. [CYCL(O)- + (PAN)ORAMA.] —**cy′clo·ram′ic** *adj.*

cy·clo·sis (sī-klō′sĭs) *n., pl.* **-ses** (-sēz). The streaming circulatory motion of protoplasm within cells and cell structures. [Greek *kuklōsis*, a surrounding, from *kukloun*, to surround, from *kuklos*, a circle, cycle.]

cy·clo·stome (sī′klə-stōm′) *n.* Any of various primitive eel-like vertebrates of the class Agnatha, such as a lamprey, that lack jaws and true teeth and have a circular, sucking mouth. [CYCLO- + Greek *stoma*, mouth.] —**cy·clos′to·mate′** (sī-klŏs′tə-māt′, -mət) or **cy′clo·stom′a·tous** (sī′-klō-stŏm′ə-təs, stō′mə-) *adj.*

cy·clo·thy·mi·a (sī′klə-thī′mē-ə) *n.* A form of manic-depressive psychosis characterized by alternating periods of activity and excitement and periods of inactivity and depression. [From German *Zyklothymie* : Greek *kuklos*, cycle + *thumos*, soul.] —**cy′clo·thy′mic** *adj.*

cy·clo·tron (sī′klə-trŏn′) *n.* An accelerator capable of giving atomic particles energies of up to several tens of millions of electron volts. It accelerates the particles in a spiral path by means of a fixed magnetic field and a variable electric field. [CYCLO- + -TRON.]

cy·der (sī′dər) *n. Brit.* Var. of **cider.**

cyg·net (sĭg′nĭt) *n.* A young swan. [Middle English *sygnett*, dim. of Old French *cygne*, swan, from Latin *cycnus*, from Greek *kuknos.*]

Cyg·nus (sĭg′nəs) *n.* A constellation in the Northern Hemisphere near Lyra, containing the star Deneb. Also called **Northern Cross.**

cyl·in·der (sĭl′ən-dər) *n.* **1. a.** A **cylindrical surface. b.** A figure bounded by a surface of this kind and by two parallel planes that intersect the surface, esp. when the given curve used to generate the surface is a circle and the given line is perpendicular to the plane of the circle; a right circular cylinder. **2.** Any object or container having the shape of a cylinder. **3.** The chamber in which a piston moves

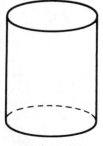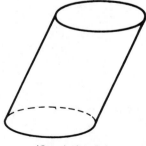

right circular cylinder   oblique circular cylinder

cylinder

back and forth, as in an engine. **4.** The chamber of a revolver that holds the cartridges. **4.** A roller, as one used in a printing press. [Old French *cylindre*, from Latin *cylindrus*, from Greek *kulindros*, roller, cylinder, from *kulindein*, to revolve, roll.]

cy·lin·dri·cal (sə-lĭn′drĭ-kəl) or **cy·lin·dric** (-drĭk) *adj.* Of or shaped like a cylinder. —**cy·lin′dri·cal′i·ty** (-kăl′ĭ-tē) *n.* —**cy·lin′dri·cal·ly** *adv.*

cylindrical surface. A surface that contains all the lines that intersect a given plane curve and that are parallel to a given line.

cym·bal (sĭm′bəl) *n.* **1.** One of a pair of concave brass plates that are struck together as percussion instruments. **2.** A single brass plate, sounded by hitting with a drumstick and often part of a set of drums. [Middle English, from Old French *symbale*, from Latin *cymbalum*, from Greek *kumbalon*, from *kumbē*, hollow of a vessel, a cup.] —**cym′bal·ist** *n.*

cyme (sīm) *n. Bot.* An often flat-topped flower cluster that blooms from the center toward the edges and whose main axis is always terminated by a flower. [Latin *cūma*, young cabbage sprout, from Greek *kuma*, anything swollen.]

cy·mose (sī′mōs′) *adj. Bot.* Pertaining to, resembling, or bearing a cyme. —**cy′mose′ly** *adv.*

Cym·ry (kĭm′rē) *n.* Also **Cym·ri** or **Kym·ry.** The branch of the Celtic people to which the Welsh, the Cornish, and the Bretons belong. —**Cym′ric** (-rĭk) *adj.*

cyn·ic (sĭn′ĭk) *n.* **1. Cynic.** A member of a sect of ancient Greek philosophers who believed virtue to be the only good and self-control to be the only means of achieving virtue. **2.** A person who believes all men are motivated by selfishness. —*adj.* **1. Cynic.** Of or pertaining to the Cynics or their doctrines. **2.** Cynical. [Latin *cynicus*, from Greek *kunikos*, doglike, Cynical, from *kuōn*, dog.]

cyn·i·cal (sĭn′ĭ-kəl) *adj.* **1.** Contemptuous of the motives or virtue of others; mocking and sneering: *a cynical remark.* **2.** Cynical. Of or pertaining to the Cynics or their doctrines. —**cyn′i·cal·ly** *adv.*

cyn·i·cism (sĭn′ĭ-sĭz′əm) *n.* **1.** A cynical attitude or character. **2.** A cynical comment or act. **3. Cynicism.** The beliefs and doctrines of the Cynics.

cy·no·sure (sī′nə-shŏŏr′, sĭn′ə-) *n.* Someone or something that serves as a focus of attention and admiration; a center of interest or attraction. [French, Ursa Minor (which contains the guiding star Polaris), from Latin *cynosūra*, from Greek *kunosoura*, "the dog's tail," Ursa Minor.]

cy·pher (sī′fər) *n. & v.* Var. of **cipher.**

cy·press (sī′prəs) *n.* **1.** Any evergreen tree of the genus *Cupressus*, growing in warm climates and having small, compressed needles. **2.** Any of several similar or related trees, such as one of the genus *Chamaecyparis*. **3.** The wood of any of these trees. [Middle English *cipres*, from Old French, from Late Latin *cypressus*, from Greek *kuparissos.*]

Cy·ril·lic alphabet (sĭ-rĭl′ĭk). A Slavic alphabet ascribed to Saint Cyril, 9th-cent. Greek Christian theologian, and used for Russian and various other Slavic languages.

cyst (sĭst) *n.* **1.** *Path.* An abnormal membranous sac containing a gaseous, liquid, or semisolid substance. **2.** *Anat.* Any sac or vesicle in the body. **3.** *Biol.* A capsulelike membrane of certain organisms in a resting stage. **4.** *Bot.* Any of various cells of nonsexual origin in green algae that germinate and produce new plants after a resting period. [From Greek *kustis*, bladder, pouch.]

cys·tic (sĭs′tĭk) *adj.* **1.** Of, pertaining to, or like a cyst. **2.** Having, containing, or enclosed in a cyst. **3.** Pertaining to the gall bladder or urinary bladder.

cystic fibrosis. A congenital disease of mucous glands throughout the body, usu. developing in childhood and resulting in disorders of the lungs and pancreas.

cys·ti·tis (sĭ-stī′tĭs) *n.* Inflammation of the urinary bladder. [Greek *kustis*, bladder + -ITIS.]

cys·to·scope (sĭs′tə-skōp′) *n.* A tubular instrument used to examine the urinary bladder. [Greek *kustis*, bladder + -SCOPE.] —**cys′to·scop′ic** (-skŏp′ĭk) *adj.*

cyt-. Var. of **cyto-.**

-cyte. A suffix meaning a cell: **leukocyte.** [From Greek *kutos*, hollow vessel.]

cyto– or **cyt–.** A prefix meaning cell: **cytogenesis.** [From Greek *kutos,* hollow vessel.]

cy·to·chem·is·try (sī'tō-kĕm'ĭ-strē) *n.* The chemistry of plant and animal cells. **—cy'to·chem'i·cal** *adj.*

cy·to·gen·e·sis (sī'tō-jĕn'ĭ-sĭs) *n.* The formation and development of cells. [CYTO- + -GENESIS.] **—cy'to·ge·net'ic** (sī'-tō-jə-nĕt'ĭk) *adj.*

cy·to·ge·net·ics (sī'tō-jə-nĕt'ĭks) *n.* *(used with a sing. verb).* The study of heredity by cytological and genetic methods. **—cy'to·ge·net'i·cal** *adj.* **—cy'to·ge·net'i·cal·ly** *adv.* **—cy'to·ge·net'i·cist** *n.*

cy·tol·o·gy (sī-tŏl'ə-jē) *n.* The scientific study of the formation, structure, and function of cells. [CYTO- + -LOGY.] **—cy'to·log'ic** (-tə-lŏj'ĭk) or **cy'to·log'i·cal** *adj.* **—cy·tol'o·gist** *n.*

cy·to·plasm (sī'tə-plăz'əm) *n.* The protoplasm outside a cell nucleus. [CYTO- + -PLASM.] **—cy'to·plas'mic** (-plăz'-mĭk) *adj.* **—cy'to·plas'mi·cal·ly** *adv.*

cy·to·plast (sī'tə-plăst') *n.* The cytoplasm within a single cell. [CYTO- + -PLAST.] **—cy'to·plas'tic** *adj.*

cy·to·sine (sī'tə-sēn') *n.* A pyrimidine base, $C_4H_5N_3O$, that is an essential constituent of both ribonucleic and deoxyribonucleic acids. [CYT(O)- + -OS(E) + -INE.]

czar (zär) *n.* Also **tsar** or **tzar. 1.** A king or emperor, esp. one of the former emperors of Russia. **2.** A tyrant; autocrat. **3.** *Informal.* One in authority; leader: *a czar of finance.* [Polish, from Russian *tsar',* from Gothic *kaisar,* from Latin *Caesar,* emperor, Caesar.] **—czar'dom** *n.*

czar·das (chär'däsh') *n.* **1.** An intricate Hungarian dance characterized by variations in tempo. **2.** Music for the czardas. [Hungarian *csárdás.*]

czar·e·vitch (zär'ə-vĭch') *n.* The eldest son of a Russian czar.

cza·rev·na (zä-rĕv'nə) *n.* **1.** The daughter of a Russian czar. **2.** The wife of a czarevitch.

cza·ri·na (zä-rē'nə) *n.* Also **cza·rit·za** (zä-rĭt'sə). The wife of a czar; an empress of Russia.

czar·ism (zär'ĭz'əm) *n.* The system of government in Russia under the czars; absolute monarchy; autocracy. **—czar'ist** *n.*

cza·rit·sa (zä-rĭt'sə) *n.* Var. of **czarina.**

Czech (chĕk) *n.* **1.** A native or inhabitant of Czechoslovakia, esp. a Bohemian, Moravian, or Slovak. **2.** The Slavic language of these people. **—Czech** *adj.*

ă pat   ā pay   â care   ä father   ĕ pet   ē be   hw which   ĭ pit   ī tie   î pier   ŏ pot   ō toe   ô paw, for   oi noise
ŏŏ took   ōō boot   ou out   th thin   th this   ŭ cut   û urge   zh vision   ə about, item, edible, gallop, circus

| Phoenician | Greek | Roman | Medieval | Modern |

Phoenician – *About 3,000 years ago the Phoenicians and other Semitic peoples began to use graphic signs to represent individual speech sounds instead of syllables or whole words. They used this symbol to represent the sound of the consonant "d" and gave it the name* dāleth, *the Phoenician word for "door."*

Greek – *The Greeks borrowed the Phoenician alphabet with some modifications. They kept the basic triangular shape of* dāleth *but changed its name to delta. They used* delta *to represent the sound of the letter "d," as* dāleth *did in Phoenician.*

Roman – *The Romans borrowed the alphabet from the*

Greeks via the Etruscans and adapted it for carving Latin in stone. This monumental script, as it is called, became the basis for modern printed capital letters.

Medieval – *By medieval times – around 1,200 years ago – the Roman monumental capitals had become adapted to being relatively quickly written on paper, parchment, or vellum. The cursive minuscule alphabet became the basis of modern printed lower-case letters.*

Modern – *Since the invention of printing about 500 years ago many modifications have been made in the shapes and styles of the letter D, but its basic form and its phonetic value remain unchanged.*

---

d, D (dē) *n., pl.* **d's** or **D's. 1.** The fourth letter of the modern alphabet. **2. D** The lowest passing grade given to a student. **3. D** The Roman numeral for the number 500. **4. D** *Mus.* The second tone in the scale of C major.

D The symbol for deuterium.

dab[1] (dăb) *v.* **dabbed, dab·bing.** *—tr.v.* **1.** To apply with short, light strokes. **2.** To cover lightly: *dab the face with cold cream.* *—intr.v.* To pat quickly and lightly: *dabbed at her eyes.* *—n.* **1.** A small amount, lump, or mass. **2.** A light, poling stroke or pat. [Middle English *dabben*, prob. from Middle Dutch.] **—dab'ber** *n.*

dab[2] (dăb) *n.* Any of various flatfishes, chiefly of the genera *Limanda* and *Hippoglossoides*, related to the flounders. [Middle English *dabbe.*]

dab·ble (dăb'əl) *v.* **-bled, -bling.** *—tr.v.* **1.** To splash or spatter with or as with a liquid. **2.** To splash in and out of water playfully. *—intr.v.* **1.** To splash liquid gently and playfully. **2.** To undertake something superficially or without serious intent: *He dabbled in magic.* **3.** To go head down, tail up in shallow water, as some ducks diving for food. [Dutch *dabbelen*, freq. of *dabben*, to dab.] **—dab'-bler** *n.*

da ca·po (dä kä'pō, də). *Mus.* From the beginning. Used as a direction to repeat a passage. [Italian.]

dace (dās) *n., pl.* **dace** or **dac·es.** Any of various small freshwater fishes of the family Cyprinidae, related to the minnows. [Middle English *dars*, from Old French *dars.*]

da·cha (dä'chə) *n.* A Russian country house. [Russian.]

dachs·hund (däks'hŏŏnt', däks'hŏŏnd') *n.* A small dog of a breed developed in Germany for hunting badgers, with a long body, drooping ears, and very short legs. [German.]

Da·cron (dā'krŏn', dăk'rŏn') *n.* A trademark for a synthetic polyester textile fiber or fabric that resists stretching and wrinkling. **—modifier:** *a Dacron shirt.*

dac·tyl (dăk'təl) *n.* **1.** *Pros.* In accentual verse, a metrical foot consisting of one accented syllable followed by two unaccented, and in quantitative verse, of one long syllable followed by two short. **2.** *Zool.* A finger, toe, or similar part or structure; digit. [Middle English *dactil*, from Latin *dactylus*, from Greek *daktulos*, finger, dactyl.] **—dac·tyl'ic** (dăk-tĭl'ĭk) *adj.* **—dac·tyl'i·cal·ly** *adv.*

dactylo-. A prefix meaning finger or toe: **dactylogram.** [From Greek *daktulos*, finger.]

dac·tyl·o·gram (dăk-tĭl'ə-grăm') *n.* A fingerprint. **—dac'ty·log'ra·phy** *n.*

dad (dăd) *n. Informal.* Father. [Of baby-talk orig.]

Da·da (dä'dä) *n.* Also **da·da, Da·da·ism** (-ĭz'əm). A western European artistic and literary movement (1916–23) that sought the discovery of authentic reality through the abolition of traditional cultural and aesthetic forms. [French *dada*, pet theme, hobbyhorse.] **—Da'da·ist** *n.* **—Da'da·is'-tic** *adj.*

dad·dy (dăd'ē) *n., pl.* **-dies.** *Informal.* Father.

daddy long·legs (lông'lĕgz', lŏng'-) *pl.* **daddy longlegs. 1.** Any of various arachnids of the order Phalangida, with long, slender legs. **2.** *Brit.* An insect, the **crane fly.**

da·do (dā'dō) *n., pl.* **-does. 1.** *Archit.* The section of a pedestal between the base and crown. **2.** The lower portion of the wall of a room, decorated differently from the upper section, as with panels. [Italian, a die, cube.]

Daed·a·lus (dĕd'l-əs) *n. Gk. Myth.* A legendary artist and inventor, builder of the Labyrinth and father of Icarus.

dae·mon (dē'mən) *n.* Var. of **demon.**

daf·fo·dil (dăf'ə-dĭl) *n.* **1.** A bulbous plant, *Narcissus pseudo-narcissus*, with showy, usu. yellow flowers with a trumpet-shaped central crown. **2.** Its flower. **3.** A brilliant to vivid yellow. [From Latin *asphodeius*, asphodel.]

daf·fy (dăf'ē) *adj.* **-fi·er, -fi·est.** *Informal.* **1.** Silly; foolish; zany. **2.** Crazy. [From obs. English *daff*, fool.]

daft (dăft) *adj.* **-er, -est. 1.** Crazy; mad. **2.** Foolish; stupid. [Middle English *dafte*, gentle, foolish.] **—daft'ly** *adv.* **—daft'ness** *n.*

dag·ger (dăg'ər) *n.* **1.** A short pointed weapon for stabbing. **2.** Something that looks or stabs like a dagger. **3.** A dagger-shaped symbol (†) used as a reference mark in printing. [Middle English *daggere*, from Old French *dague.*]

da·guerre·o·type (də-gâr'ə-tīp') *n.* **1.** An early photographic process in which an image was formed on a silver-coated metal plate. **2.** A photograph made by this process. [Invented by Louis Jacques Mandé *Daguerre* (1787–1851), French artist.]

dahl·ia (dăl'yə, däl'-, dāl'-) *n.* **1.** Any of several plants of the genus *Dahlia*, with tuberous roots and showy, variously colored flowers. **2.** The flower of any of these plants. [After Anders *Dahl*, 18th-cent. Swedish botanist.]

dai·ly (dā'lē) *adj.* **1.** Done, happening, or appearing every day or weekday. **2.** For each day: *a daily walk.* **3.** Day-to-day; everyday: *for daily use.* *—adv.* **1.** Every day: *Exercise daily.* **2.** Once a day: *Wind the clock daily.* *—n., pl.* **-lies.** A newspaper published every day or every weekday. [Middle English *daili*, from Old English *dælic*, from *dæg*, day.]

daily double. A bet won by choosing both winners of two specified races on one day, as in horse racing.

| ă pat | ā pay | â care | ä father | ĕ pet | ē be | hw which | ĭ pit | ī tie | î pier | ŏ pot | ō toe | ô paw, for | oi noise |
| ŏŏ took | ōō boot | ou out | th thin | *th* this | ŭ cut | | û urge | zh vision | ə about, item, edible, gallop, circus |

dai·mio (dī'myō') *n., pl.* **-mio** or **-mios.** Also **dai·myo.** A hereditary nobleman in feudal Japan. [Japanese *daimyō.*]

dain·ty (dān'tē) *adj.* **-ti·er, -ti·est.** 1. Lovely in a fine, delicate way; exquisite: *dainty embroidery.* 2. Light, graceful, and precise: *dainty little steps.* 3. Very careful in choosing; finicky: *a dainty eater.* 5. Delicious; choice; tasty: *dainty appetizers.* —*n., pl.* **-ties.** A choice, delicious food; a delicacy. [Middle English *deinte,* pleasant, from Old French *deintie,* pleasure, from Latin *dīgnitās,* dignity, from *dīgnus,* worthy.] —**dain'ti·ly** *adv.* —**dain'ti·ness** *n.*

dai·qui·ri (dī'kə-rē, dăk'ə-) *n., pl.* **-ris.** An iced cocktail of rum, lime or lemon juice, and sugar. [After *Daiquiri,* Cuba.]

dair·y (dâr'ē) *n., pl.* **-ies.** 1. A room or building where milk and cream are stored or made into butter and cheese. 2. A business that prepares or sells milk and milk products. 3. A dairy farm. 4. The dairy business; dairying. 5. Dairy products. [Middle English *daierie,* from *daie,* dairymaid, from Old English *dæge,* breadmaker.]

dairy cattle. Cows raised for milk rather than meat.

dairy farm. A farm for producing milk and milk products.

dair·y·ing (dâr'ē-ĭng) *n.* The business of running a dairy farm, company, or store.

dair·y·man (dâr'ē-mən) *n.* A person who owns, manages, or works in a dairy.

da·is (dā'ĭs, dās) *n.* A raised platform for a throne, a speaker, or a group of honored guests. [Middle English *deis,* from Old French, from Latin *discus,* disk.]

dai·sy (dā'zē) *n., pl.* **-sies.** 1. Any of several related plants with rayed flowers. 2. A European plant, *Bellis perennis,* with flowers with pink or white rays. 3. The flower of any of these plants. [Middle English *daisie,* from Old English *dægesēage,* "day's eye" daisy.]

Da·ko·ta (də-kō'tə) *n., pl.* **-tas.** 1. A large group of North American Indian tribes, commonly called Sioux. 2. A member of any of these tribes. 3. The Siouan language of the Dakota people.

Da·lai La·ma (dä-lī' lä'mə). The political and spiritual ruler of the Lamaist religion. Also called **Grand Lama.**

dale (dāl) *n.* A valley. [From Old English *dæl.*]

dal·li·ance (dăl'ē-əns) *n.* 1. Playful flirting. 2. Dawdling and wasting of time.

dal·ly (dăl'ē) *v.* **-lied, -ly·ing.** —*intr.* 1. To flirt playfully. 2. To waste time; dawdle. —*tr.* To waste (time): *dallied away the hours.* —See Syns at **delay.** [Middle English *dalien,* from Norman French *dalier.*] —**dal'li·er** *n.*

Dal·ma·tian (dăl-mā'shən) *n.* A dog of a breed believed to have originated in Dalmatia, with a short white coat covered with black or dark-brown spots. Also called **coach dog.**

Dalmatian   dam¹

dam¹ (dăm) *n.* 1. A barrier built across a waterway to control the flow. 2. A body of water controlled by such a barrier. —*tr.v.* **dammed, dam·ming.** 1. To build a dam across. 2. To hold back; to check. [Middle English.]

dam² (dăm) *n.* 1. Archaic. A female parent of a four-footed animal. 2. *Archaic.* A mother. [Middle English, dam, lady.]

dam·age (dăm'ĭj) *n.* 1. a. Injury that causes loss or harm to a person or thing. b. The loss caused or the cost of repair. 2. **damages. a.** *Law.* Money to be paid to make up for an injury or loss. b. Individual injuries to property or persons. —*v.* **-aged, -ag·ing.** —*tr.v.* To cause injury to. —*intr.v.* To suffer or be susceptible to damage. [Middle English, from Old French, from *dam,* loss, from Latin *damnum.*]

—dam'age·a·ble *adj.* —**dam'ag·ing·ly** *adv.*

dam·as·cene (dăm'ə-sēn', dăm'ə-sēn') *tr.v.* **-cened, -cen·ing.** To decorate (metal) with wavy patterns of inlay or etching. —*n.* Etched or inlaid work in metal. [Middle English, from Old French *damasquiner,* "to decorate in the manner of Damascus blades or steel."]

Da·mas·cus steel (də-măs'kəs). An early form of steel with wavy markings, developed in the Near East and used for making sword blades. Also called **damask.**

dam·ask (dăm'əsk) *n.* 1. A rich glossy fabric woven with patterns that show on both sides, used esp. as a linen for tablecloths. 2. Damascus steel. —*modifier:* a damask curtain. —*tr.v.* 1. To damascene. 2. To decorate or weave with rich patterns. [Middle English, from Medieval Latin *(pannus de) damasco,* "(cloth of) Damascus."]

damask rose. A rose, *Rosa damascena,* native to Asia, with fragrant red or pink flowers used as a source of attar. [Medieval Latin *rosa Damascēna,* "rose of Damascus."]

dame (dām) *n.* 1. Dame. A title formerly given to the mistress of a household or to a schoolmistress who taught children in her home. 2. Dame. In Great Britain: a. A title of honor corresponding to a knight's title of *Sir.* b. The legal title of a knight's or baronet's wife. 3. Any lady or wife. 4. *Slang.* A woman. [Middle English, from Old French, from Latin *domina,* lady.]

damn (dăm) *tr.v.* 1. To condemn as being very bad. 2. To condemn to everlasting punishment. 3. To swear at by using the word "damn." —*intr.v.* To swear; to curse. —*interj.* A word used to express anger, irritation, or disappointment. —*adj. & adv. Informal.* Used as an intensive: *You're damn right.* —*n. Informal.* The least bit; a jot: *not worth a damn.* [Middle English *dam(p)nen,* from Old French *dam(p)ner,* from Latin *dammum,* damage.] —**damn'ing** *adj.* —**damn'ing·ly** *adv.*

dam·na·ble (dăm'nə-bəl) *adj.* Deserving condemnation; odious: *a damnable traitor.* —**dam'na·bly** *adv.*

dam·na·tion (dăm-nā'shən) *n.* The act of damning or the condition of being damned.

damned (dămd) *adj.* **-er, -est.** 1. Condemned or doomed: *damned souls.* 2. *Informal.* a. Dreadful; awful: *this damned weather.* b. Used as an intensive: *a damned fool.* —*adv. Informal.* Used as an intensive: *a damned good idea.*

Dam·o·cles (dăm'ə-klēz') *n.* A courtier of Dionysius the Elder, tyrant of Syracuse, who forced Damocles to sit at a banquet under a sword suspended by a single hair, to demonstrate the precariousness of a king's fortunes.

dam·oi·selle (dăm'ə-zĕl') *n.* Var. of **damosel.**

Da·mon and Pyth·i·as (dā'mən; pĭth'ē-əs). *Rom. Myth.* Two friends so devoted that Damon pledged his life as a hostage for the condemned Pythias.

dam·o·sel (dăm'ə-zĕl') *n.* Also **dam·oi·selle** or **dam·o·zel.** *Archaic.* A damsel. [Var. of *damsel.*]

damp (dămp) *adj.* **-er, -est.** 1. Slightly wet; moist: *damp ground.* 2. Humid: *damp air.* —*n.* 1. Moisture in the air; humidity. 2. Fog; mist. 3. Any foul or poisonous gas that pollutes the air in a mine. —*tr.v.* 1. To make damp; moisten. 2. To put out (a fire) by cutting off its air supply. 3. To discourage; cool; lessen: *tried to damp his anger.* 4. *Physics.* To reduce the strength of (a wave or vibration). [Middle English, poison gas, from Middle Low German *vapor.*] —**damp'ish** *adj.* —**damp'ly** *adv.* —**damp'ness** *n.*

damp·en (dăm'pən) *tr.v.* 1. To moisten; make damp. 2. To diminish or depress: *dampen one's spirits.* —*intr.v.* To become wet or moist. —**damp'en·er** *n.*

damp·er (dăm'pər) *n.* 1. A movable plate in the flue of a furnace or stove for controlling the draft. 2. Any device that weakens or eliminates waves or vibrations. 3. One of a set of pads that can be made to press against the strings of a keyboard musical instrument to stop them from sounding. 4. A depressing or restraining influence.

dam·sel (dăm'zəl) *n.* A young woman or girl; maiden. [Middle English *damisele,* from Old French *dameisele,* from Latin *domina,* lady, dame.]

dam·sel·fly (dăm'zəl-flī') *n.* Any of various slender-bodied, often brightly colored insects of the order Odonata, related to the dragonflies but differing in having wings that are folded together over the back when at rest.

dam·son (dăm'zən) *n.* A Eurasian tree, *Prunus insititia,*

---

cultivated for its bluish-black, juicy plum. [Middle English, from Latin (*prūnum*) *Damascēnum*, "(plum) of Damascus."]

Dan·a·e or **Dan·a·ë** (dăn'ə-ē') *n. Gk. Myth.* The mother of Perseus by Zeus, who visited her in the form of a shower of gold during her imprisonment.

dance (dăns) *v.* **danced, danc·ing.** —*intr.v.* **1.** To move with rhythmic steps and motions, as when keeping time to music. **2.** To leap, skip, or prance about. **3.** To bob up and down: *daffodils dancing in the breeze.* —*tr.v.* **1.** To engage in or perform (a special set of steps and motions): *dance the minuet.* **2.** To cause to dance. —*n.* **1.** A set of rhythmic steps and motions, usu. performed to music. **2.** A party at which people dance. **3.** One round or turn of dancing. **4.** Often **the dance.** The art of dancing. **5.** A piece of music designed as an accompaniment for dancing. [Middle English *dansen, dauncen,* from Old French *danser, dancier.*] —**danc'er** *n.* —**danc'ing·ly** *adv.*

dan·de·li·on (dăn'dl-ī'ən) *n.* **1.** A plant, *Taraxacum officinale,* native to Eurasia, common as a weed in North America, with many-rayed yellow flowers. **2.** Any of several similar, related plants. [Middle English *dent-de-lion,* "lion's tooth."]

dan·der¹ (dăn'dər) *n. Informal.* Temper: *His dander is up.* [Orig. unknown.]

dan·der² (dăn'dər) *n.* Tiny particles from hair or fur, sometimes a cause of allergy in human beings. [From DANDRUFF.]

Dan·die Din·mont (dăn'dē dĭn'mŏnt'). A small terrier of a breed developed in England, with a rough grayish or brownish coat and short legs. [After *Dandie Dinmont,* owner of two such dogs in *Guy Mannering,* a novel by Sir Walter Scott.]

dan·dle (dăn'dl) *tr.v.* **-dled, -dling.** To move up and down on the knees or in the arms playfully. [Orig. unknown.] —**dan'dler** *n.*

dan·druff (dăn'drəf) *n.* Small white scales of dead skin shed from the scalp. [Orig. unknown.]

dan·dy (dăn'dē) *n., pl.* **-dies. 1.** A man who prides himself on his elegant clothes and manners. **2.** *Informal.* Something very good of its kind: *This horse is a dandy.* —*adj.* **-di·er, -di·est. 1.** Like or dressed like a dandy; foppish. **2.** *Informal.* Very good; fine: *That's a dandy idea!* —See Syns at **excellent.** [Orig. unknown.] —**dan'di·fy** *v.* —**dan'dy·ism** *n.*

Dane (dān) *n.* A native or inhabitant of Denmark or a person of Danish ancestry.

Dane·law (dān'lô') *n.* Also **Dane·lagh. 1.** The body of law established by the Danish invaders and settlers in northeastern England in the 9th and 10th cent. **2.** The sections of England under jurisdiction of this law. [Middle English *Dene laue,* from Old English *Dena lagu,* "Danes' law."]

dan·ger (dān'jər) *n.* **1.** Exposure or liability to evil, injury, or harm. **2.** A possible cause or chance of harm; a threat or hazard: *Fog is a danger to pilots.* [Middle English *daunger,* from Old French *dangier,* from Latin *dominium,* sovereignty, from *dominus,* lord, master.]

Syns: **danger, hazard, jeopardy, peril, risk** *n. Core meaning:* Exposure to possible harm, loss, or injury (*high flood waters that put the town in danger*).

dan·ger·ous (dān'jər-əs) *adj.* **1.** Full of risk; hazardous: *a dangerous job.* **2.** Able or likely to cause harm: *a dangerous animal.* —**dan'ger·ous·ly** *adv.* —**dan'ger·ous·ness** *n.*

dan·gle (dăng'gəl) *v.* **-gled, -gling.** —*intr.v.* **1.** To hang loosely and swing to and fro. **2.** To hang uncertainly or insecurely. **3.** To hover after someone; be a hanger-on. —*tr.v.* To cause to swing loosely. —*n.* Something that is dangled. [Prob. of Scandinavian orig.] —**dan'gler** *n.*

dangling participle. *Gram.* A participle that is not clearly connected with the word it modifies, so that it seems to modify the wrong word. For example, in the sentence "Sitting at my desk, a loud noise startled me," *sitting* is a dangling participle. (The *noise* doesn't sit.)

Dan·iel (dăn'yəl) *n.* See table at **Bible.**

Dan·ish (dā'nĭsh) *adj.* Of or pertaining to Denmark, the Danes, or their language or culture. —*n.* **1.** The North Germanic language of the Danes. **2.** Danish pastry.

Danish pastry. A sweet pastry made with raised dough.

dank (dăngk) *adj.* **-er, -est.** Uncomfortably damp; chilly

and wet. [Middle English.] —**dank'ly** *adv.* —**dank'ness** *n.*

dan·seur (dän-sœr') *n., pl.* **-seurs** (-sœr'). A male ballet dancer. [French, from Old French, from *danser,* to dance.]

dan·seuse (dän-sœz') *n., pl.* **-seuses** (-sœz'). A female ballet dancer.

Daph·ne (dăf'nē) *n. Gk. Myth.* A nymph who chose metamorphosis into a laurel in order to escape from Apollo.

daph·ni·a (dăf'nē-ə) *n., pl.* **-ni·a.** Any of various tiny freshwater crustaceans of the genus *Daphnia,* used as food for aquarium fish. [Perh. from Latin *Daphnē,* Daphne.]

dap·per (dăp'ər) *adj.* **1.** Neatly dressed; trim. **2.** Small and active. [Middle English *dapyr,* elegant, from Middle Dutch *dapper,* quick.] —**dap'per·ly** *adv.* —**dap'per·ness** *n.*

dap·ple (dăp'əl) *n.* **1.** Mottled or spotted marking, as on a horse's skin. **2.** An animal with a mottled or spotted skin or coat. —*tr.v.* **-pled, -pling.** To mark with spots, streaks, or patches of a different color or shade: *Sunlight filtering through the leaves dappled the ground.* —*adj.* Also **dap·pled.** Spotted. [Prob. from *dapple-gray.*]

Dar·by and Joan (där'bē; jōn). Any elderly married couple who live a happy life together and are seldom apart. [After the elderly couple in a popular 18th-cent. English ballad.]

dare (dâr) *v.* **dared** or *archaic* **durst** (dûrst), **dar·ing.** —*intr.v.* To have courage or boldness; be so bold as: *He did not dare to speak to her.* **Note:** The verb **dare** is often used without *to* in negative and interrogative sentences or in sentences that indicate doubt: *He dare not speak to her. Dare he speak up?* —*tr.v.* **1.** To have the strength or courage to face or risk; meet defiantly: *Earlier explorers dared the perils of crossing the ocean.* **2.** To challenge; defy: *He dared me to fight him.* —*idiom.* **dare say** or **dare-say** (dâr'sā') To think (it) very likely. —*n.* A challenge. [Middle English *dar,* from Old English *dear,* first and third person pres. indicative of *durran,* to dare.] —**dar'er** *n.*

dare·dev·il (dâr'dĕv'əl) *n.* A person who takes risks with reckless boldness. —*modifier: a daredevil stunt pilot.*

dar·ing (dâr'ĭng) *adj.* **1.** Fearless; adventurous; bold. **2.** Going somewhat beyond accepted custom: *a daring outfit.* —*n.* Audacious bravery; boldness; courage. —**dar'ing·ly** *adv.*

Dar·jee·ling (där-jē'lĭng) *n.* A fine variety of black tea from Darjeeling, India. Also called **Darjeeling tea.**

dark (därk) *adj.* **-er, -est. 1.** Without light or with very little light: *a dark tunnel.* **2.** Having no lights on: *a dark house.* **3.** Dim, gray, or cloudy rather than bright. **4.** Reflecting little of the light that strikes it: *a dark color.* **5.** Of a deep shade closer to black or brown than to white. **6.** Having a deep, low sound: *a dark, velvety tone.* **7.** Hopeless; dismal; despairing. **8.** Sullen; threatening: *a dark scowl.* **9.** Evil; ominous: *dark deeds.* **10.** Unexplored; mysterious; unknown: *darkest Africa.* **11.** Secret; hidden: *a dark scheme.* **12.** Without knowledge or learning; ignorant: *dark ages.* —*n.* **1.** Absence of light. **2.** Night or nightfall. **3.** A dark shade or color. —*idiom.* **in the dark.** In secret. **2.** In ignorance; uninformed. [Middle English *derk,* from Old English *deorc.*] —**dark'ish** *adj.* —**dark'ly** *adv.* —**dark'ness** *n.*

Syns: **dark, dim, dusky, murky, obscure** *adj. Core meaning:* Lacking brightness (*a dark underground passage*).

Dark Ages. The early part of the Middle Ages from about A.D. 500 to about A.D. 1000.

dark·en (där'kən) *tr.v.* **1.** To make dark or darker: *Clouds darkened the sky.* **2.** To fill with sadness: *The news darkened her face.* —*intr.v.* **1.** To become dark or darker. **2.** To grow clouded, sad, or sombre. —**dark'en·er** *n.*

dark horse. **1.** A little-known entrant in a horse race, contest, etc. **2.** A person who receives unexpected support as a candidate for the nomination in a political convention.

dark lantern. A lantern whose light can be blocked by a panel or other device.

dark·ling (där'klĭng). *Poet.* —*adv.* In the dark. —*adj.* **1.** Happening in the dark or the night. **2.** Dim; obscure. —See Syns at **gloomy.** [Middle English *derkeling.*]

dark·room (därk'rōōm', -rōōm') *n.* A room in which photographic materials are processed, either in total darkness or under light to which they are not sensitive.

dark·some (därk'səm) *adj. Poet.* Dark; darkish; somber.

dar·ling (där'lĭng) *n.* **1.** A dearly loved person; beloved. **2.** A favorite. —*adj.* **1.** Dearest; beloved. **2.** *Informal.*

Charming; adorable. [Middle English *dereling,* from Old English *dēorling.*]

darn¹ (därn) *tr.v.* To mend by weaving thread or yarn across a hole. —*intr.v.* To mend or repair a hole or garment by darning. —*n.* A place repaired by darning. [French *darner,* prob. from Norman French *darne,* piece.] —**darn'er** *n.*

darn² (därn) *v. & interj. & adj. & adv.* Damn.

dar·nel (där'nəl) *n.* Any of several grasses of the genus *Lolium,* native to the Old World. [Middle English.]

darning needle. 1. A long, large-eyed needle used in darning. 2. *Informal.* A dragonfly.

dart (därt) *intr.v.* To move suddenly and swiftly. —*tr.v.* To shoot out or send forth with a swift, sudden movement. —See Syns at **rush.** —*n.* 1. A small, arrowlike missile with a sharp point, either thrown at a target by hand or shot from a blowgun, crossbow, etc. 2. **darts.** *(used with a sing. verb).* A game in which darts are thrown at a target. 3. Anything resembling a dart: *darts of flame.* 4. A quick, rapid movement: *made a dart for the car.* 5. A tapered tuck taken in a garment to make it fit better. [Middle English, from Old French.]

dart·er (där'tər) *n.* Any of various small, often brightly colored freshwater fishes of the family Percidae, of eastern North America.

Dar·win·ism (där'wə-nĭz'əm) *n.* A theory of biological evolution developed by Charles Darwin and others, stating that species of plants and animals develop through natural selection of variations that increase the organism's ability to survive and reproduce. —**Dar·win'i·an** (-wĭn'ē-ən) *adj.* —**Dar'win·ist** *n.* —**Dar'win·is'tic** *adj.*

dash (dăsh) *tr.v.* 1. To break or smash by striking violently: *The storm dashed the ship against the rocks.* 2. To hurl, knock, or thrust with sudden violence: *He dashed the glass to the ground.* 3. To splash; bespatter. 4. To complete hastily; finish off: *dash off a letter.* 5. To add an altering element to; mix. 6. To destroy; ruin: *His dreams were dashed.* —*intr.v.* 1. To strike violently; smash: *Salt spray dashed against the deck.* 2. To move with haste; rush: *dashed down the stairs.* —See Syns at **rush.** —*n.* 1. A quick run or rush: *a dash for shelter.* 2. A short, fast race. 3. A splash. 4. A small amount; a bit: *a dash of spice.* 5. Lively spirit or style. 6. A swift, short, forceful stroke: *an artist's dashes of color.* 7. A punctuation mark (—) used to show a pause, break, or omission or to set off part of a sentence from the rest. 8. In Morse code, the long sound or signal used in combination with the dot. —See Syns at **spirit.** [Middle English *dashen,* of Scandinavian orig.] —**dash'er** *n.*

dash·board (dăsh'bôrd', -bôrd') *n.* 1. A panel beneath the windshield of an automobile, containing instruments, dials, and controls. 2. A screen on the front of an open vehicle, as a carriage, to keep out snow, rain, or dirt.

da·shi·ki (də-shē'kē) *n.* A loose, often brightly colored African tunic, usu. worn by men. [From Yoruba *danshiki.*]

dashiki   **date²**

dash·ing (dăsh'ĭng) *adj.* 1. Brave, bold, and daring. 2. Showy or stylish: *a dashing jacket.* —**dash'ing·ly** *adv.*

das·tard (dăs'tərd) *n.* A mean, sneaking coward. [Middle English.]

das·tard·ly (dăs'tərd-lē) *adj.* Cowardly, low, and mean. — See Syns at **cowardly.** —**das'tard·li·ness** *n.*

da·ta (dā'tə, dăt'ə, dä'tə) *pl.n.* The less frequently used sing.

is **da·tum** (dā'təm, dăt'əm, dä'təm). Information, esp. when used for analysis or as the basis for a decision.

data processing. Sorting, classification, and analysis of information, esp. when done by machines. —**data processor.**

date¹ (dāt) *n.* 1. a. Time stated in terms of the month, day, and year or any of these: *The date was May 13, 1851.* b. A statement of calendar time, as on a document. 2. The day of the month. 3. The time when something happened or is to happen. 4. A time or period in history: *Egyptian tombs of an early date.* 5. **dates.** The years of a person's birth and death. 6. *Informal.* a. An appointment, esp. an engagement to go out socially with a member of the opposite sex. b. A person's companion on a date. —*v.* **dat·ed, dat·ing.** —*tr.v.* 1. To mark or supply with a date: *to date a letter.* 2. To determine the age, time, or origin of; assign a date to: *date a fossil.* 3. To betray the age of. 4. *Informal.* To go on a date with. —*intr.v.* 1. To have origin in a particular time in the past: *This statue dates from 500 B.C.* 2. To become old-fashioned. 3. *Informal.* To go on dates with a companion or as a couple. —**idioms. out of date.** No longer current, valid, or useful. **up to date.** Up to the present time. **up to date.** In line with current knowledge, modern methods, or recent styles. [Middle English, from Old French, from Medieval Latin *data,* "given," "issued" (as a letter) from Latin, *dare,* to give.]

date² (dāt) *n.* The sweet, oblong, edible fruit of the date palm tree that contains a narrow, hard seed. [Middle English, from Old French, from Latin *dactylus,* from Greek *daktulos,* "finger."]

date·line (dāt'līn') *n.* A phrase at the beginning of a news story or report that gives its date and place of its origin.

date line. The **International Date Line.**

da·tive (dā'tĭv) *adj.* Designating or belonging to a grammatical case in certain inflected Indo-European languages that marks the indirect object of a verb and the object of any of certain verbs and prepositions. —*n.* 1. The dative case. 2. A word or form in the dative case. [Middle English *datif,* from Latin *(cāsus) datīvus,* "(case) of giving" from *dare,* to give.]

da·tum (dā'təm, dăt'əm, dä'təm) *n., pl.* **-ta** (-tə) or **-tums.** An item of information; a unit of data. [Latin, "something given," from *dare,* to give.]

daub (dôb) *tr.v.* 1. To cover, coat, or smear with an adhesive substance, such as plaster or mud. 2. To apply paint to with hasty or crude strokes. —*intr.v.* To apply paint or coloring with crude, unskillful strokes. —*n.* 1. Something daubed on: *a daub of grease.* 2. Any soft, sticky coating material, such as plaster or mud. 3. A crude painting. [Middle English *dauben,* from Old French *dauber,* from Latin *dēalbāre,* to whitewash.] —**daub'er** *n.* —**daub'ing·ly** *adv.*

daugh·ter (dô'tər) *n.* 1. A female offspring. 2. Any female descendant: *all the daughters of Eve.* 3. A girl or woman considered as if in a relationship of child to parent: *a daughter of the nation.* 4. Anything regarded as a female descendant: *"Culturally Japan is a daughter of Chinese civilization"* (Edwin Reischauer). [Middle English *doughter,* from Old English *dohtor.*] —**daugh'ter·ly** *adj.*

daughter cell. Any of the offspring cells formed when a cell undergoes division.

daugh·ter-in-law (dô'tər-ĭn-lô') *n., pl.* **daugh·ters-in-law.** The wife of one's son.

daunt (dônt, dänt) *tr.v.* 1. To intimidate. 2. To discourage or dishearten. [Middle English *daunten,* from Old French *danter,* from Latin *domitāre,* to tame, subdue.]

daunt·less (dônt'lĭs, dänt'-) *adj.* Courageous; fearless. — See Syns at **brave.** —**daunt'less·ly** *adv.* —**daunt'less·ness** *n.*

dau·phin (dô'fĭn) *n.* The eldest son of a king of France. Used as a title from 1349 to 1830. [French, from Old French *dalphin* (title of the lords of Dauphiné).]

dav·en·port (dăv'ən-pôrt', -pôrt') *n.* A large sofa, often convertible into a bed. [Orig. unknown.]

dav·it (dăv'ĭt, dā'vĭt) *n.* One of a pair of curved arms, usu. made of steel tubing, attached to the side of a ship, used esp. for lowering and hoisting boats. [Middle English *daviot,* from Old French dim. of *David,* David.]

Da·vy Jones (dā'vē jōnz'). The spirit of the sea.

Davy Jones's locker (jōn′zĭz, jōnz). The bottom of the sea, regarded as the grave of persons drowned or buried at sea.

daw (dô) n. A bird, the jackdaw. [Middle English *dawe.*]

daw·dle (dôd′l) v. **-dled, -dling.** —*intr.v.* **1.** To take more time than necessary; linger: *dawdle over lunch.* **2.** To move aimlessly; loiter: *dawdling on the way to work.* —*tr.v.* To waste (time) by idling: *dawdling away the hours.* [Orig. unknown.] —**daw′dler** n.

dawn (dôn) n. **1.** The first appearance of daylight in the morning. **2.** The first appearance of anything; beginning: *before the dawn of recorded history.* —*intr.v.* **1.** To begin to grow light in the morning: *We rose when the day dawned.* **2.** To come into existence: *A new age is dawning.* —*phrasal verb.* **dawn on.** To come as a realization to. [Middle English *daunen,* from Old English *dagian,* to become day.]

day (dā) n. **1.** The time of light between sunrise and sunset. **2. a.** The 24-hour period during which the earth makes one complete rotation on its axis. **b.** The period during which any celestial body makes a similar rotation. **3.** One of the numbered 24-hour periods into which a week, month, or year is divided. **4.** The part of the day devoted to work or study: *the eight-hour day; the school day.* **5.** Often **Day.** A day devoted to some special purpose, event, or observance: *graduation day; New Year's Day.* **6.** Often **days. a.** A particular period of time; age; era: *the present day.* **b.** The period of someone's youth, career, achievement, or success: *a great singer in his day.* **7. days.** Life; lifetime. —*idiom.* **call it a day.** *Informal.* To stop one's work or activity. [Middle English, from Old English *dæg.*]

day bed. A couch or sofa convertible into a bed.

day·book (dā′bŏŏk′) n. A journal or diary.

day·break (dā′brāk′) n. Dawn.

day care. The providing of daytime supervision, training, medical care, etc., esp. for children of preschool age.

day·dream (dā′drēm′) n. A dreamlike musing while awake, esp. one of wish fulfillment. —*v.* **-dreamed** or **-dreamt** (-drĕmt′), **-dream·ing.** —*intr.v.* To have daydreams. —*tr.v.* To imagine in a daydream. —**day′dream′-er** n.

day labor. Labor hired and paid by the day. —**day laborer.**

day letter. A telegram sent during the day, usu. less expensive but slower than a regular telegram.

day·light (dā′līt′) n. **1.** The light of day. **2.** Dawn. **3.** Daytime. **4.** Exposure to public notice. **5.** An understanding or insight into what was formerly obscure. **6. daylights.** *Slang.* Wits; sense: *scared the daylights out of me.* —*idiom.* **see daylight.** To approach the end of a difficult endeavor.

day·light-sav·ing time (dā′līt-sā′vĭng). Time during which clocks are set one hour ahead of standard time, used in spring, summer, and fall to provide extra daylight.

day lily. Any of various plants of the genus *Hemerocallis,* native to Eurasia, with sword-shaped leaves and short-lived, orange, yellow, or red funnel-shaped flowers.

day nursery. A nursery providing day care for children of preschool age, esp. while their mothers are at work.

Day of Atonement. Yom Kippur.

Day of Judgment. The Judgment Day.

day school. 1. A private school for pupils living at home. **2.** A school that holds classes during the day.

day·star (dā′stär′) n. **1.** The morning star. **2.** The sun.

day·time (dā′tīm′) n. The time between dawn and dark.

daze (dāz) *tr.v.* **dazed, daz·ing. 1.** To stun or confuse, as with a blow, shock, or surprise. **2.** To dazzle, as with strong light. —*n.* A stunned or confused condition: *He fell flat and lay there in a daze.* [Middle English *dasen,* ult. from Old Norse *dasask,* to tire.] —**daz′ed·ly** (dā′zĭd-lē) *adv.*

daz·zle (dăz′əl) v. **-zled, -zling.** —*tr.v.* **1.** To dim the vision of; blind with intense light. **2.** To impress or astonish with a spectacular display. —*intr.v.* **1.** To become blinded. **2.** To inspire admiration or wonder: *That opera never fails to dazzle.* —*n.* The act of dazzling or the condition of being dazzled. [Freq. of daze.] —**daz′zler** n. —**daz′zling·ly** *adv.*

D-day (dē′dā′) n. The unnamed day on which a military

offensive is to be launched. [*D* (abbr. for *day*) + DAY.]

DDT A colorless contact insecticide, $(ClC_6H_4)_2CHCCl_3$, that is poisonous to human beings and animals and that remains in the environment for many years. [Abbr. of D(ICHLORO)D(IPHENYL)T(RICHLOROETHANE).]

de-. A prefix meaning: **1.** Reversal or undoing: **decode. 2.** Removal: **delouse. 3.** Degradation, reduction: **degrade. 4.** Disparagement: **demean.** [Latin *dē-,* from *dē,* from.]

dea·con (dē′kən) n. **1.** In the Anglican, Greek Orthodox, and Roman Catholic churches, a clergyman ranking just below a priest. **2.** In various other Christian churches, a layman who assists the minister in various functions. [Middle English *dek(e)n,* from Old English *dīacon,* from Late Latin *diāconus,* from Greek *diakonos,* servant.]

dea·con·ess (dē′kə-nĭs) n. A woman appointed or elected to serve as an assistant in a church.

dea·con·ry (dē′kən-rē) n., pl. **-ries. 1.** The office or position of a deacon. **2.** Deacons collectively.

de·ac·ti·vate (dē-ăk′tə-vāt′) *tr.v.* **-vat·ed, -vat·ing. 1.** To render inactive; make harmless or ineffective. **2.** *Mil.* To remove from active status. —**de·ac′ti·va′tion** n.

dead (dĕd) adj. **-er, -est. 1.** No longer alive or living. **2.** Having lost life: *dead of typhoid fever.* **3.** Marked for certain death; doomed: *A solitary baboon is a dead baboon.* **4.** Lacking life or living things; inanimate: *the dead, cold moon.* **5.** Insensible; numb: *His frostbitten toes felt dead.* **6.** Not moving or circulating; motionless: *dull dead heat.* **7.** No longer used or needed for use: *a dead language; dead files.* **8.** Out of operation, esp. because of a fault or breakdown: *The radio went dead.* **9. a.** Not connected to a source of electric power: *a dead circuit.* **b.** Drained of electricity; discharged: *a dead battery.* **10.** Without activity, interest, or excitement: *This town is dead after 9:00 P.M.* **11.** No longer active: *a dead volcano.* **12.** Having little or no bounce: *a dead ball.* **13. a.** Complete; total; absolute: *dead silence.* **b.** Abrupt: *a dead stop.* **14. a.** Exact: *dead center.* **b.** Sure; certain: *a dead shot.* —*n.* **1.** Those who have died; dead people: *mourn the dead; bury our dead.* **2.** The darkest, coldest, or most silent part: *the dead of night; the dead of winter.* —*adv.* **1. a.** Completely; absolutely: *Surface winds were dead calm.* **b.** Abruptly: *stopped dead in her tracks.* **2.** Straight; directly: *dead ahead.* [Middle England *ded,* from Old English *dēad.*] —**dead′ness** n.

Syns: dead, deceased, extinct, lifeless *adj.* Core meaning: Without life or continuing existence. DEAD has the widest use; it applies to whatever once had—but no longer has—physical life (*a dead person*), function (*a dead doorbell*), currency (*a dead issue*), or usefulness (*a dead language*). DECEASED is a formal term that is used only for dead people (*the deceased spouse*). EXTINCT describes both what is burned out (*an extinct volcano*) and what has died out (*The dodo is extinct, and so are the Tudors*). LIFELESS can describe what once had physical life (*a lifeless body*), what does not support life (*a lifeless planet*), and what lacks spirit or brightness (*lifeless colors*).

dead·beat (dĕd′bēt′) n. *Slang.* **1.** A person who does not pay his debts. **2.** A lazy or lethargic person; loafer.

dead·en (dĕd′n) *tr.v.* **1.** To make less intense, keen, or strong: *deaden pain; deaden engine noise.* **2.** To take away feeling or sensation from: *deaden a tooth.* **3.** To discourage and depress. —**dead′en·er** n.

dead end. 1. A street, alley, or other passage that is closed at one end. **2.** An impasse.

dead·eye (dĕd′ī′) n. **1.** *Naut.* A flat hardwood disk with a grooved perimeter, pierced by three holes through which the lanyards are passed, used on a ship to fasten the shrouds. **2.** *Slang.* An expert marksman.

dead heat. A race in which two or more contestants finish at the same time; a tie.

dead letter. 1. A letter that is not delivered or claimed, usu. because the address is incorrect or illegible. **2.** A law or directive still in effect but no longer enforced.

dead·line (dĕd′līn′) n. A set time by which something must be done, finished, or settled, as completion of a task.

dead·lock (dĕd′lŏk′) n. A standstill that occurs when opposing forces are equally strong and neither will give way. —*tr.v.* To bring to a deadlock. —*intr.v.* To come to a deadlock.

dead·ly (dĕd′lē) adj. **-li·er, -li·est. 1.** Causing or capable of causing death: *deadly diseases.* **2.** Aiming to kill: *a deadly enemy.* **3.** Suggesting death: *deadly silence.* **4.** Absolute; utter: *deadly earnestness.* **5.** Extreme; terrible: *deadly strain.* **6.** Extremely acurate or effective: *a deadly shot.* **7.** *Informal.* Dull and boring: *a deadly party.* —See Syns at **fatal.** —*adv.* **1.** Completely: *I'm deadly serious.* **2.** So as to resemble death: *It was deadly cold.* —**dead′li·ness** *n.*

deadly nightshade. A plant, the belladonna.

deadly sins. The **seven deadly sins.**

dead·pan (dĕd′păn′) adj. & adv. *Informal.* With a blank face or manner that betrays no emotion or amusement.

dead reckoning. A method of estimating the position of a ship or aircraft from its course and speed, its travel time, and the known winds and currents, and without astronomical observations or other navigational aids.

Dead Sea Scrolls. Parchment scrolls, dated from about 100 B.C. to about A.D. 100, containing Hebrew and Aramaic Scriptural texts and liturgical and communal writings, found in 1947 in caves near the Dead Sea.

dead weight. 1. The unrelieved weight of a heavy, motionless mass. **2.** An oppressive burden or difficulty.

dead·wood (dĕd′wŏŏd′) n. **1.** Dead branches or wood on a tree. **2.** Anything burdensome or superfluous.

deaf (dĕf) adj. **-er, -est. 1.** Lacking the ability to hear, either completely or in part. **2.** Unwilling to listen. [Middle English, from Old English *dēaf.*] —**deaf′ness** *n.*

deaf·en (dĕf′ən) tr.v. **1.** To make deaf, esp. temporarily. **2.** To resound loudly; stun with noise. —**deaf′en·ing·ly** *adv.*

deaf-mute (dĕf′myōōt′) n. Also **deaf mute.** A person who can neither speak nor hear.

deal[1] (dēl) v. **dealt** (dĕlt), **deal·ing.** —*tr.v.* **1.** To give to as one's share; apportion: *He dealt me a large plateful.* **2.** To distribute or pass out among several people: *He dealt out the dinner rations.* **3.** To administer; deliver; give: *deal a blow.* **4.** *Card Games.* To distribute (cards) among players. —*intr.v.* **1.** To be concerned; treat: *a book dealing with the Middle Ages.* **2.** To do business; trade or bargain: *a merchant who deals in diamonds.* **3.** *Card Games.* To distribute playing cards: *It's your turn to deal.* —*n.* **1.** *Informal.* An agreement or bargain, as in business or politics. **2.** *Card Games.* **a.** The distribution of playing cards. **b.** A player's turn to deal. **c.** A hand of cards dealt. **3.** *Informal.* Treatment received, esp. as the result of an agreement: *got a bad deal.* **4.** *Informal.* A bargain or favorable sale. **5.** *Slang.* An important issue: *make a big deal out of nothing.* —**idiom. a great (or good) deal. 1.** A considerable amount; a lot. **2.** Much; considerably: *a good deal thinner.* [Middle English *delen,* from Old English *dǣlan.*] —**deal′er** *n.*

deal[2] (dēl) n. A fir or pine board cut to standard dimensions. —*modifier: a deal floor.* [Middle English *dele,* from Middle Low German or Middle Dutch *dele.*]

deal·er·ship (dē′lər-shĭp′) n. **1.** An individual, agency, or distributor that has authorization to sell a particular item in a certain area. **2.** Authorization to sell in this way.

deal·ings (dē′lĭngz) pl.n. Agreements or relations with others, esp. when involving money or trade.

dealt (dĕlt) v. Past tense and past participle of **deal.**

dean (dēn) n. **1.** An official of a college or university in charge of a certain school or faculty. **2.** An official of a college or high school who counsels students and enforces rules: *dean of women.* **3.** The head clergyman in charge of a cathedral. **4.** *Brit.* A priest who oversees a group of parishes. **5.** The oldest or most respected member of a group or profession: *the dean of American medicine.* [Middle English *deen,* from Norman French, from Late Latin *decānus,* "(one) set over ten," from Latin *decem,* ten.] —**dean′ship′** *n.*

dean·er·y (dē′nə-rē) n., pl. **-ies. 1.** The office, jurisdiction, or authority of a dean. **2.** A dean's official residence.

dear (dîr) adj. **-er, -est. 1. a.** Loved and cherished: *my dearest friend.* **b.** Greatly valued; precious: *everything dear to them.* **2.** Highly esteemed or regarded. Often used as a term of address: *Dear Sir.* **3.** Close to the heart: *your dearest interests.* **4.** Expensive; costly. **5.** Earnest; ardent. —See Syns at **expensive.** —*adv.* **1.** At a high cost. **2.** Fondly or affectionately. —*n.* A dearly loved person. [Middle English *dere,* from Old English *dēore.*] —**dear′ly** *adv.* —**dear′ness** *n.*

dear·ie (dîr′ē) n. Var. of **deary.**

dearth (dûrth) n. **1.** Lack; scarcity. **2.** Shortage of food; famine. [Middle English *dearth(e),* costliness, scarcity, from *dere,* dear, expensive.]

dear·y (dîr′ē) n., pl. **-ies.** Also **dear·ie.** *Informal.* Darling.

death (dĕth) n. **1. a.** The act or fact of dying. **b.** The end of life: *remain true until death.* **2.** The condition of being dead. **3.** A cause of dying: *Such a fall is certain death.* **4.** Often **Death.** The destroyer of life, usu. represented as a skeleton with a scythe. **5.** Destruction or extinction: *the death of a dream; the death of stars.* **6.** Execution. —**idioms. put to death.** To kill or execute. **to death.** To an extreme degree: *bored to death.* [Middle English, from Old English *dēath.*] —**death′like′** *adj.*

death·bed (dĕth′bĕd′) n. **1.** The bed on which a person dies. **2.** A dying person's last hours of life.

death·blow (dĕth′blō′) n. A fatal blow or event.

death cup. A poisonous mushroom, *Amanita phalloides,* with a prominent cuplike swelling at the base.

death duty. *Brit.* An inheritance tax.

death·less (dĕth′lĭs) adj. Undying; immortal.

death·ly (dĕth′lē) adj. **1.** Suggesting death: *a deathly pallor.* **2.** Causing death; fatal. —See Syns at **ghastly.** —*adv.* **1.** So as to resemble death: *deathly pale.* **2.** Very: *deathly ill.*

death rate. The number of deaths in a given unit of population in a given period of time; mortality rate.

death row. A cell-block or other part of a prison in which prisoners condemned to death await execution.

death's-head (dĕths′hĕd′) n. The human skull or a representation of it as a symbol of death.

death·watch (dĕth′wŏch′) n. **1.** A vigil kept beside a dying or dead person. **2.** Any of several beetles of the family Anobiidae that strike their heads against the wood into which they burrow with a hollow, clicking sound.

de·ba·cle (dĭ-bä′kəl, -băk′əl) n. **1.** A sudden, disastrous collapse, downfall, or defeat. **2.** The breaking up of ice in a river. **3.** A violent flood. [French, from *débâcler,* to unbar, from Old French *desbacler.*]

de·bar (dē-bär′) tr.v. **-barred, -bar·ring.** To forbid, prohibit, exclude, or bar. [Middle English *debarren,* from Old French *desbarrer,* to unbar.] —**de·bar′ment** *n.*

de·bark (dĭ-bärk′) tr.v. To unload, as from a ship. —*intr.v.* To disembark. [French *débarquer,* from Old French.] —**de·bar·ka·tion** (dē′bär-kā′shən) *n.*

de·base (dĭ-bās′) tr.v. **-based, -bas·ing.** To lower in character, quality, dignity, or value; adulterate. —**de·base′ment** *n.* —**de·bas′er** *n.*

de·bat·a·ble (dĭ-bā′tə-bəl) adj. Open to question, argument, or dispute: *a debatable theory.* —**de·bat′a·bly** *adv.*

de·bate (dĭ-bāt′) n. **1. a.** A discussion or consideration of the arguments for and against something. **b.** An argument or dispute between persons holding opposing views. **2.** A formal contest in which opponents argue for opposite sides of an issue. —*v.* **-bat·ed, -bat·ing.** —*intr.v.* **1.** To deliberate; consider. **2.** To engage in argument; discuss opposing points. **3.** To engage in a formal debate. —*tr.v.* **1.** To present or discuss arguments for and against: *debate a motion.* **2.** To engage (someone) in a formal debate. **3.** To deliberate upon; consider: *debating what to do.* **4.** To call into question; argue about; dispute. [Middle English *debaten,* from Old French *debattre,* to challenge, contest.] —**de·bat′er** *n.*

de·bauch (dĭ-bôch′) tr.v. To lead away from good toward evil; corrupt; pervert. —*intr.v.* To indulge in dissipation. —*n.* Debauchery. [French *débaucher,* from Old French *desbaucher,* separate.] —**de·bauch′er** *n.*

de·bauch·ee (dĭ-bô′chē, dĕb′ə-chē′, -shē′) n. A person who habitually indulges in dissipation or debauchery; libertine.

de·bauch·er·y (dĭ-bô′chə-rē) n., pl. **-ies.** Extreme indulgence in sensual pleasures; intemperance.

de·ben·ture (dĭ-bĕn′chər) n. An unsecured bond, issued by a civil or governmental corporation or agency and backed only by the credit standing of the issuer. [Middle English *debentur,* from Latin, "they are due."]

de·bil·i·tate (dĭ-bĭl′ĭ-tāt′) tr.v. **-tat·ed, -tat·ing.** To make feeble; weaken: *The disease debilitated her body.* [Latin *dēbilitāre,* from *dēbilis,* weak.] —**de·bil′i·ta′tion** *n.*

ă pat   ā pay   â care   ä father   ĕ pet   ē be   hw which   ĭ pit   ī tie   î pier   ŏ pot   ō toe   ô paw, for   oi noise
ŏŏ took   ōō boot   ou out   th thin   *th* this   ŭ cut   û urge   zh vision   ə about, item, edible, gallop, circus

de·bil·i·ty (dĭ-bĭl′ĭ-tē) n., pl. **-ties.** A condition of abnormal bodily weakness; feebleness.

deb·it (dĕb′ĭt) n. **1.** An item of debt charged to and recorded in an account. **2.** The left-hand side of an account or an accounting ledger where bookkeeping entries are made. —tr.v. **1.** To charge with or as a debt. **2.** To enter (a sum) as a debit. [Middle English debite, from Old French, from Latin dēbitum.]

deb·o·nair or **deb·o·naire** (dĕb′ə-nâr′) adj. Gracious and charming: polite and debonair. [Middle English debonaire, from Old French, from de bon aire, "of good disposition".] —**deb′o·nair′ly** adv. —**deb′o·nair′ness** n.

de·bouch (dĭ-bouch′, -bōōsh′) intr.v. Mil. To march from a narrow or confined area into the open. —tr.v. To cause to emerge or issue. [French déboucher : dé-, out of + bouche, mouth.] —**de·bouch′ment** n.

de·brief (dē-brēf′) tr.v. To question in order to obtain knowledge or intelligence gathered on a mission. —**de·brief′ing** n.

de·bris or **dé·bris** (də-brē′, dā′brē′) n. **1.** The remains of something broken, destroyed, or discarded. **2.** Geol. An accumulation of relatively large rock fragments. [French, from Old French de(s)brisier, to break to pieces.]

debt (dĕt) n. **1.** Something, such as money, goods, or services, owed by one person to another: a $200 debt. **2.** The condition of owing; indebtedness: in debt for over a year. **3.** Theol. A sin; a trespass. [Middle English det(te), from Old French, from Latin dēbitum, from dēbēre, to owe.]

debt·or (dĕt′ər) n. **1.** A person who owes something to another. **2.** A person guilty of a trespass or sin; sinner.

de·bunk (dē-bŭngk′) tr.v. Informal. To expose or ridicule the falseness or pretensions of: debunk a ridiculous theory. [DE- + BUNK (nonsense).] —**de·bunk′er** n.

de·but or **dé·but** (dā-byōō′, dĭ-, dā′byōō′) n. **1.** A first public appearance, as of an actor. **2.** The formal presentation of a girl to society. [French, from débuter, to begin.]

deb·u·tante or **dé·bu·tante** (dĕb′yōō-tänt′, dā′byōō-, dĕb′yōō-tänt′) n. A young woman making a debut into society. [French, from débuter, to begin.]

deca- or **dec-** or **deka-**. Abbr. **da** A prefix meaning ten: **decahedron.** [Greek deka-, from deka, ten.]

dec·ade (dĕk′ād′, dĕ-kād′) n. **1.** A group of ten. **2.** A period of ten years. [Middle English, from Old French, from Late Latin decas, from Greek dekas, from deka, ten.]

dec·a·dence (dĕk′ə-dəns, dĭ-kād′ns) n. A process, condition, or period of deterioration or decline, as in morals or art. [Old French, from Medieval Latin decadentia.]

dec·a·dent (dĕk′ə-dənt, dĭ-kād′nt) adj. Marked by or in a condition of decadence. —n. A person in a process of mental or moral decline. —**dec′a·dent·ly** adv.

dec·a·gon (dĕk′ə-gŏn′) n. A plane geometric figure having ten sides and ten angles.

dec·a·gram (dĕk′ə-grăm′) n. Also **dec·a·gramme** or **dek·a·gram.** Abbr. **dag** Ten grams.

dec·a·he·dron (dĕk′ə-hē′drən) n., pl. **-drons** or **-dra** (-drə) A solid geometric figure bounded by ten plane faces.

de·cal (dē′kăl′, dĭ-kăl′) n. A picture or design transferred by the process of decalcomania.

de·cal·ci·fy (dē-kăl′sə-fī′) tr.v. **-fied, -fy·ing.** To remove calcium or calcareous matter from. —**de·cal′ci·fi·ca′tion** n.

de·cal·co·ma·ni·a (dē-kăl′kə-mā′nē-ə) n. **1.** The process of transferring pictures or designs printed on specially prepared paper to glass, metal, or other material. **2.** A picture so transferred; a decal. [French : décalquer, to transfer by tracing + manie, mania.]

Dec·a·logue or **Dec·a·log** (dĕk′ə-lôg′, -lŏg′) n. Also **dec·a·logue** or **dec·a·log.** The Ten Commandments. [Middle English decalog, from Old French decalogue, from Late Latin decalogus, from Greek dekalogos : DECA- + logos, word.]

dec·a·me·ter or **dek·a·me·ter** (dĕk′ə-mē′tər) n. Also **dec·a·me·tre.** Abbr. **dam** Ten meters.

de·camp (dĭ-kămp′) intr.v. **1.** To depart or break camp. **2.** To depart suddenly; run away. [French décamper, from Old French descamper.] —**de·camp′ment** n.

de·cant (dĭ-kănt′) tr.v. **1.** To pour off (a liquid, esp. wine) without disturbing the sediment. **2.** To pour (a liquid) from one container into another. [Medieval Latin dēcanthāre :

Latin dē-, from + canthus, rim.] —**de′can·ta′tion** (dē′-kăn-tā′shən) n.

de·cant·er (dĭ-kăn′tər) n. **1.** A decorative bottle for serving liquids, esp. wine. **2.** A vessel used for decanting.

de·cap·i·tate (dĭ-kăp′ĭ-tāt′) tr.v. **-tat·ed, -tat·ing.** To cut off the head of; behead. [From Late Latin dēcapitāre.] —**de·cap′i·ta′tion** n. —**de·cap′i·ta′tor** n.

dec·a·pod (dĕk′ə-pŏd′) n. **1.** Any crustacean of the order Decapoda, such as a crab, lobster, or shrimp, that characteristically have five pairs of locomotor appendages, each joined to a segment of the thorax. **2.** A cephalopod mollusk, such as a squid or cuttlefish, with ten armlike tentacles. —adj. Of or pertaining to the Decapoda or a decapod. [DECA- + -POD.] —**de·cap′o·dal** (dĭ-kăp′ə-dəl) or **de·cap′o·dan** (-ə-dən) or **de·cap′o·dous** (-ə-dəs) adj.

dec·a·syl·la·ble (dĕk′ə-sĭl′ə-bəl) n. A line of verse having ten syllables. —**dec′a·syl·lab′ic** (-sə-lăb′ĭk) adj.

de·cath·lon (dĭ-kăth′lən, -lŏn′) n. An athletic contest in which contestants compete in ten different track and field events. [French : deca-, ten + Greek athlon, contest.]

de·cay (dĭ-kā′) intr.v. **1.** To rot; decompose. **2.** Physics. To lose radioactive atoms as a result of nuclear disintegrations. **3.** To fall into ruin, as an untended building. **4.** To decline in health or vigor; waste away. **5.** To decline from a condition of normality, excellence, or prosperity: The empire decayed. —tr.v. To cause to become rotten: Fungi decay wood. —n. **1.** The destruction or decomposition of organic matter as a result of bacterial or fungal action; rot. **2.** Physics. Radioactive decay. **3.** A gradual deterioration to an inferior condition, as of health or mental capability. [Middle English decayen, from Old North French decair.]

de·cease (dĭ-sēs′) intr.v. **-ceased, -ceas·ing.** To die. —See Syns at **die.** —n. Death. [Middle English decesen, to die, from deces, death, from Old French, from Latin dēcēdere, to depart.]

de·ceased (dĭ-sēst′) adj. No longer living; dead. —See Syns at **dead.** —n. **the deceased.** A dead person.

de·ce·dent (dĭ-sēd′nt) n. Law. The deceased.

de·ceit (dĭ-sēt′) n. **1.** The act or practice of deceiving; dishonesty; deception. **2.** A stratagem, trick, or wile. [Middle English, from Old French, from Latin dēcipere, to deceive.]

de·ceit·ful (dĭ-sēt′fəl) adj. **1.** Practicing deceit; false; lying. **2.** Deliberately misleading; deceptive: a deceitful advertisement. —**de·ceit′ful·ly** adv. —**de·ceit′ful·ness** n.

de·ceive (dĭ-sēv′) v. **-ceived, -ceiv·ing.** —tr.v. To make believe something that is not true; mislead. —intr.v. To practice deceit. [Middle English deceiven, from Old French deceivre, from Latin dēcipere.] —**de·ceiv′er** n. —**de·ceiv′ing·ly** adv.

Syns: deceive, betray, delude, double-cross, mislead v. Core meaning: To cause to accept what is false, esp. by trickery or misrepresentation (a child who deceived his parents). DECEIVE involves lying or the deliberately concealing truth. BETRAY implies disloyalty or treachery that brings another into danger or to disadvantage: betrayed his friend; betraying the confidence of the voters. To MISLEAD is to cause another to gain a wrong impression (misled by false rumors); it does not always imply intent to harm. DELUDE refers to deceiving or misleading to the point of rendering a person unable to make sound judgments (was deluded into thinking she was not ill). DOUBLE-CROSS, a slang term, implies betrayal of a confidence or the willful breaking of a pledge.

de·cel·er·ate (dē-sĕl′ə-rāt′) v. **-at·ed, -at·ing.** —tr.v. To decrease the speed of. —intr.v. To decrease in speed. [DE- + (AC)CELERATE.] —**de·cel·er·a′tion** n. —**de·cel′er·a′tor** n.

De·cem·ber (dĭ-sĕm′bər) n. The 12th and last month of the year, after November and before January. It has 31 days. [Middle English decembre, from Old French, from Latin December, "the tenth month," from decem, ten.]

de·cem·vir (dĭ-sĕm′vər) n., pl. **-virs** or **-vi·ri** (-və-rī′). A member of one of two bodies of ten Roman magistrates, one appointed in 451 B.C. and the other in 450 B.C., to draw up a code of laws. [Middle English, from Latin decem virī, ten men.] —**de·cem′vi·rate** (-də-sĕm′vər-ĭt) n.

de·cen·cy (dē′sən-sē) n., pl. **-cies. 1.** The condition of being decent; propriety. **2.** Conformity to prevailing standards of propriety or modesty. **3. decencies.** The proprieties.

de·cen·ni·al (dĭ-sĕn′ē-əl) adj. **1.** Of or lasting for ten years.

ă pat	ā pay	â care	ä father	ĕ pet	ē be	hw which
ī pit	ī tie	î pier	ŏ pot	ō toe	ô paw, for	oi noise
ōō took	ōō boot	ou out	th thin	th this	ŭ cut	
û urge	zh vision	ə about, item, edible, gallop, circus				

2. Occurring once every ten years. —*n.* A tenth anniversary or its celebration. —**de·cen'ni·al·ly** *adv.*

de·cent (dē'sənt) *adj.* **1.** Conforming to the standards of propriety; proper. **2.** Kind; considerate: *It was decent of her to call.* **3.** *Adequate; passable: a decent salary.* **4.** *Informal.* Properly or modestly dressed. [From Latin *decēre,* to be fitting.] —**de'cent·ly** *adv.* —**de'cent·ness** *n.*

de·cen·tral·ize (dē-sĕn'trə-līz') *tr.v.* **-ized, -iz·ing. 1.** To distribute the functions or powers of (a government, central authority, etc.) among several local authorities. **2.** To cause to withdraw from an area of concentration: *decentralize an industry.* —**de·cen'tral·i·za'tion** *n.*

de·cep·tion (dĭ-sĕp'shən) *n.* **1.** The act of deceiving. **2.** Something that deceives, as a trick or lie. [Middle English *decepcioun,* from Old French *deception,* from Latin *decipere,* deceive.]

de·cep·tive (dĭ-sĕp'tĭv) *adj.* Intended or tending to deceive; disingenuous. —**de·cep'tive·ly** *adv.* —**de·cep'tive·ness** *n.*

deci-. *Symbol* **d** A prefix meaning one-tenth: *decimeter.* [French, from Latin *decimus,* tenth, from *decem,* ten.]

dec·i·bel (dĕs'ə-bəl, -bĕl') *n. Abbr.* **dB.** A unit used to express relative difference in power, usu. between acoustic or electric signals, equal to ten times the common logarithm of the ratio of the two levels.

de·cide (dĭ-sīd') *v.* **-cid·ed, -cid·ing.** —*tr.v.* **1.** To cause to make or reach a decision: *What decided you to leave that company?* **2.** To determine or settle: *The court decided the case.* —*intr.v.* **1.** To pronounce a judgment or verdict. **2.** To make up one's mind. [Middle English *deciden,* from Old French *decider,* from Latin *dēcīdere,* to cut off.] —**de·cid'a·ble** *adj.* —**de·cid'er** *n.*

Syns: *decide, conclude, determine, resolve, settle* **v. Core meaning:** To make up or cause to make up one's mind (*decided to buy the house*). See also Syns at **judge.**

de·cid·ed (dĭ-sī'dĭd) *adj.* **1.** Clear-cut; definite: *a decided advantage.* **2.** Resolute; unhesitating: *a decided tone of voice.* —See Syns at **explicit.** —**de·cid'ed·ly** *adv.* —**de·cid'ed·ness** *n.*

de·cid·u·ous (dĭ-sĭj'ōō-əs) *adj.* **1.** Falling off or shed at the end of a season or growing period: *deciduous antlers.* **2.** Shedding leaves at the end of the growing season: *deciduous trees.* [Latin *dēciduus,* from *dēcidere,* to fall off.] —**de·cid'u·ous·ly** *adv.* —**de·cid'u·ous·ness** *n.*

dec·i·gram (dĕs'ĭ-grăm') *n.* Also **dec·i·gramme.** *Abbr.* **dg** One-tenth (10⁻¹) of a gram.

dec·i·li·ter (dĕs'ə-lē'tər) *n.* Also **dec·i·li·tre.** *Abbr.* **dl** One-tenth (10⁻¹) of a liter.

dec·il·lion (dĭ-sĭl'yən) *n.* **1.** The cardinal number represented by 1 followed by 33 zeros, usu. written 10^{33}. **2.** *Brit.* The cardinal number represented by 1 followed by 60 zeros, usu. written 10^{60}. [DEC- + (M)ILLION.] —**de·cil'lionth** *adj. & n.*

dec·i·mal (dĕs'ə-məl) *n.* **1.** A numeral in the decimal system of numeration. **2.** A numeral based on 10, used with a decimal point in expressing a decimal fraction. —*adj.* **1.** Of or based on 10. **2.** Of, expressed as, or capable of being expressed as a decimal. [Medieval Latin *decimālis,* of tithes, from Latin *decem,* ten.] —**dec'i·mal·ly** *adv.*

decimal point. A period placed at the left of a decimal fraction, or between the fractional and integral parts of a decimal mixed numeral.

decimal system of numeration. A number system based on 10.

dec·i·mate (dĕs'ə-māt') *tr.v.* **-mat·ed, -mat·ing. 1.** To destroy or kill a large part of: *Disease decimated the village.* **2.** To kill one in every ten of. —**dec'i·ma'tion** *n.* —**dec'i·ma'tor** *n.*

dec·i·me·ter (dĕs'ə-mē'tər) *n.* Also **dec·i·me·tre.** *Abbr.* **dm** One-tenth (10⁻¹) of a meter.

de·ci·pher (dĭ-sī'fər) *tr.v.* **1.** To change a message from a code or cipher to ordinary language; decode. **2.** To read or interpret (something hard to understand or illegible). —**de·ci'pher·a·ble** *adj.* —**de·ci'pher·ment** *n.*

de·ci·sion (dĭ-sĭzh'ən) *n.* **1.** A final or definite conclusion or choice; a judgment: *a jury's decision.* **2.** Firmness of character or action; determination: *a man of decision.* [Old French *decision,* from Latin *dēcīdere,* to decide.]

de·ci·sive (dĭ-sī'sĭv) *adj.* **1.** Having the power to decide; conclusive: *a decisive argument; a decisive victory.*

2. Characterized by decision and firmness; resolute: *a decisive person.* —**de·ci'sive·ly** *adv.* —**de·ci'sive·ness** *n.*

deck (dĕk) *n.* **1.** One of the horizontal partitions dividing a ship into different levels. **2.** Any platform like the deck of a ship: *a sun deck.* **3.** A pack of playing cards. —*tr.v.* **1.** To furnish with a deck. **2.** To clothe with finery: *She decked herself out for a party.* [Middle English *dekke,* from Middle Dutch *dec, decke,* roof, covering.]

deck hand. A seaman assigned to routine work.

deckle edge. The rough edge of handmade paper. —**deck'le-edged'** *adj.*

de·claim (dĭ-klām') *tr.v.* **1.** To deliver formal recitation. **2.** To speak loudly and vehemently; inveigh: *declaimed against pollution of the lake.* —*tr.v.* To recite formally: *declaim a poem.* [Middle English *declamen,* from Latin *dēclāmāre.*] —**dec'la·ma'tion** *n.* —**de·claim'er** *n.*

dec·lam·a·to·ry (dĭ-klăm'ə-tôr'ē, -tōr'ē) *adj.* **1.** Of or pertaining to declamation. **2.** Loud and rhetorical, esp. when bombastic: *a long declamatory explanation.* —**de·clam'a·to'ri·ly** *adv.*

dec·la·ra·tion (dĕk'lə-rā'shən) *n.* **1.** A formal statement or announcement. **2.** Such a statement in written form. **3.** The act or process of declaring. **4.** *Card Games.* **a.** A bid, esp. the final bid of a hand. **b.** An announcement by a player of points made.

Declaration of Independence. A proclamation by the Second Continental Congress declaring the 13 American colonies politically independent from Great Britain, formally adopted July 4, 1776.

de·clar·a·tive (dĭ-klăr'ə-tĭv, -klâr'-) *adj.* Also **de·clar·a·to·ry** (-tôr'ē, -tōr'ē). Making a statement: *a declarative sentence.*

de·clare (dĭ-klâr') *v.* **-clared, -clar·ing.** —*tr.v.* **1.** To state officially or formally: *declare war.* **2.** To state with emphasis or authority; affirm: *He declared his loyalty.* **3.** To make a full statement of (dutiable goods) when entering a country at customs. **4.** *Bridge.* To designate (a trump suit or no-trump) with the final bid of a hand. —*intr.v.* To proclaim one's choice, opinion, or resolution. —See Syns at **assert.** [Middle English *declaren,* from Old French *declarer,* from Latin *dēclārāre,* to make clear.] —**de·clar'er** *n.*

de·clas·si·fy (dē-klăs'ə-fī') *tr.v.* **-fied, -fy·ing.** To remove official security classification from (a document). —**de·clas'si·fi'a·ble** *adj.* —**de·clas'si·fi·ca'tion** *n.*

de·clen·sion (dĭ-klĕn'shən) *n.* **1.** In certain languages, the inflection of nouns, pronouns, and adjectives in such categories as case, number, or gender. **2.** A class of words with the same or a similar system of inflections. **3.** A descending slope; descent. **4.** A decline or decrease; deterioration. [From Middle English *declinson,* from Old French *declinaison,* from Latin *dēclīnātiō,* from Latin, declination.] —**de·clen'sion·al** *adj.*

dec·li·na·tion (dĕk'lə-nā'shən) *n.* **1.** A sloping or bending downward. **2.** A falling off, esp. from prosperity or vigor. **3.** A refusal to accept. [Middle English *declinacioun,* from Old French *declination,* from Latin *dēclīnātiō,* from *dēclīnāre,* to decline.] —**dec'li·na'tion·al** *adj.*

de·cline (dĭ-klīn') *v.* **-clined, -clin·ing.** —*intr.v.* **1.** To refuse to do or accept something. **2.** To become less or decrease, as in strength, value, etc. **3.** To slope downward. **4.** To draw to a gradual close; wane. —*tr.v.* **1.** To refuse (something). **2.** To cause to slope downward. **3.** In certain languages, to give the inflected forms of (a noun, pronoun, or adjective). —See Syns at **reject.** —*n.* **1.** The process or result of declining; deterioration: *a period of economic decline.* **2.** A change to a lower level or condition. **3.** A downward slope. [Middle English *declinen,* from Old French *decliner,* from Latin *dēclīnāre,* to turn aside, go down.] —**de·clin'a·ble** *adj.* —**de·clin'er** *n.*

de·cliv·i·ty (dĭ-klĭv'ĭ-tē) *n., pl.* **-ties.** A downward slope, as of a hill. [Latin *dēclīvitās,* from *dēclīvis,* sloping down.]

de·coct (dĭ-kŏkt') *tr.v.* To extract (the flavor or active principle of) by boiling, usu. in water. [Middle English *decocten,* from Latin *dēcoquere,* to boil down.] —**de·coc'tion** *n.*

de·code (dē-kōd') *tr.v.* **-cod·ed, -cod·ing.** To convert from a code to a form suitable for use. —**de·cod'er** *n.*

dé·colle·tage (dā'kŏl-täzh') *n.* A low neckline on a garment. [French.]

ă pat	ā pay	â care	ä father	ĕ pet	ē be	hw which	ĭ pit	ī tie	î pier	ŏ pot	ō toe	ô paw, for	oi noise
ŏŏ took	ōō boot	ou out	th thin	th this	ŭ cut		û urge	zh vision	ə about, item, edible, gallop, circus				

dé·col·le·té (dā′kôl-tā′) *adj.* **1.** Having a low neckline. **2.** Wearing a dress with a low neckline. [French.]

de·col·or·ize (dē-kŭl′ə-rīz′) *tr.v.* **-ized, -iz·ing.** To remove color from. **—de·col′or·i·za′tion** *n.* **—de·col′or·iz′er** *n.*

de·com·pose (dē′kəm-pōz′) *v.* **-posed, -pos·ing.** *—tr.v.* **1.** To separate into component parts or basic elements. **2.** To cause to rot. *—intr.v.* **1.** To break down into component parts; disintegrate. **2.** To decay; rot. **—de′com·pos′a·ble** *adj.* **—de′com·pos′er** *n.* **—de′com·po·si′tion** *n.*

de·com·press (dē′kəm-prĕs′) *tr.v.* To release (as a diver) from pressure or compression: **—de′com·pres′sion** *n.*

de·con·tam·i·nate (dē′kən-tăm′ə-nāt′) *tr.v.* **-nat·ed, -nat·ing. 1.** To free of contamination. **2.** To make safe by freeing of harmful substances, such as poisons or radioactive materials. **—de′con·tam′i·nant** *n.* **—de′con·tam′i·na′tion** *n.*

de·con·trol (dē′kən-trōl′) *tr.v.* **-trolled, -trol·ling.** To free from control, esp. from government control.

dé·cor or **de·cor** (dā′kôr′, dā-kôr′) *n.* **1.** A decorative style or scheme, as of a room. **2.** Stage scenery. [French.]

dec·o·rate (dĕk′ə-rāt′) *tr.v.* **-rat·ed, -rat·ing. 1.** To furnish with something attractive: *decorate an office.* **2.** To confer a medal or honor upon. [Latin *decorāre,* from *decus,* ornament.]

dec·o·ra·tion (dĕk′ə-rā′shən) *n.* **1.** The act or process of decorating. **2.** Something that adorns or beautifies; an ornament. **3.** A medal awarded for bravery or heroism.

Decoration Day. Memorial Day.

dec·o·ra·tive (dĕk′ər-ə-tĭv, -ə-rā′-) *adj.* Serving to decorate; ornamental: *a decorative design.* **—dec′o·ra·tive·ly** *adv.* **—dec′o·ra·tive·ness** *n.*

dec·o·ra·tor (dĕk′ə-rā′tər) *n.* A person who decorates, esp. an interior decorator.

dec·o·rous (dĕk′ər-əs, -kôr′-, -kōr′-) *adj.* Characterized by or showing decorum; proper: *decorous language; decorous behavior.* [Latin *decōrus,* from *decor,* seemliness, beauty.] **—dec′o·rous·ly** *adv.* **—dec′o·rous·ness** *n.*

de·co·rum (dĭ-kôr′əm, -kōr′-) *n.* Appropriateness of behavior or conduct; propriety. —See Syns at **manner(s).** [Latin.]

de·coy (dē′koi′, dĭ-koi′) *n.* **1.** An artificial bird used to entice game into a trap or within shooting range. **2.** Someone or something that lures another into danger, deception, or a trap. **3.** Any means used to mislead; deception. *—tr.v.* (dĭ-koi′). To lure into danger or a trap by or as if by a decoy. [Poss. from Dutch *de kooi,* "the cage."] **—de·coy′er** *n.*

decoy

de·crease (dĭ-krēs′) *v.* **-creased, -creas·ing.** *—intr.v.* To grow or become gradually less or smaller; dwindle. *—tr.v.* To cause to grow or become less or smaller; reduce. *—n.* (dē′krēs, dĭ-krēs). **1.** The act or process of decreasing. **2.** The amount by which something decreases. [Middle English *decresen,* from Old French *de(s)creistre,* ult. from Latin *dēcrēscere.*] **—de·creas′ing·ly** *adv.*

    Syns: **decrease, abate, diminish, dwindle, ebb, lessen, reduce** *v. Core meaning:* To grow or cause to grow less (*an appetite that decreased; pain gradually decreasing*).

de·cree (dĭ-krē′) *n.* **1.** An authoritative order; edict. **2.** The judgment of a court of equity, probate, or divorce. *—v.* **-creed, -cree·ing.** *—tr.v.* To ordain, establish, or decide by decree. *—intr.v.* To issue a decree. —See Syns at **judge.** [Middle English *decre(t),* from Old French, from Latin *dēcrētum,* from *dēcernere,* to decide.]

dec·re·ment (dĕk′rə-mənt) *n.* **1.** A gradual decrease. **2.** The amount lost by gradual diminution or waste. [Latin *decrēmentum,* from *dēcrēscere,* to decrease.]

de·crep·it (dĭ-krĕp′ĭt) *adj.* Weakened or broken-down by old age, illness, or hard use. [Middle English, from Old

French, from Latin *dēcrepitus,* very old.] **—de·crep′it·ly** *adv.*

de·crep·i·tude (dĭ-krĕp′ĭ-tood′, -tyood′) *n.* The condition of being decrepit; weakness.

de·cre·scen·do (dē′krə-shĕn′dō, dā′-) *Mus.* *—n., pl.* **-dos. 1.** A gradual decrease in loudness; diminuendo. **2.** A decrescendo passage. *—adj.* Gradually decreasing in loudness. *—adv.* With a decrescendo. [Italian, decreasing.]

de·crim·i·nal·ize (dē-krĭm′ə-nə-līz′) *tr.v.* **-ized, -iz·ing.** To make no longer illegal or criminal. **—de·crim′i·nal·i·za′tion** *n.*

de·cry (dĭ-krī′) *tr.v.* **-cried, -cry·ing. 1.** To condemn or censure: *decried the President's action.* **2.** To disparage or belittle publicly: *decried his opponent's qualifications.* [French *décrier,* from Old French *descrier,* "to cry down."] **—de·cri′er** *n.*

de·cum·bent (dĭ-kŭm′bənt) *adj.* **1.** Reclining; prostrate. **2.** *Bot.* Lying or growing along the ground but erect at or near the apex. [Latin *decumbēns,* from *decumbere,* to lie down.] **—de·cum′bence** or **de·cum′ben·cy** *n.*

ded·i·cate (dĕd′ĭ-kāt′) *tr.v.* **-cat·ed, -cat·ing. 1.** To set apart for a special purpose: *dedicate a church.* **2.** To commit (oneself) fully to something; devote: *dedicated himself to research.* **3.** To inscribe (a book, performance, etc.) to someone as a mark of respect or affection. —See Syns at **devote.** [Middle English *dedicaten,* from Latin *dēdicāre,* to proclaim.] **—ded′i·ca′tor** *n.*

ded·i·ca·tion (dĕd′ĭ-kā′shən) *n.* **1.** The act of dedicating or the condition of being dedicated. **2.** A note in a literary or other composition dedicating it to someone. **—ded′i·ca′tive** or **ded′i·ca·to·ry** (-kə-tôr′ē, -tōr′ē) *adj.*

de·duce (dĭ-dōos′, -dyōos′) *tr.v.* **-duced, -duc·ing. 1.** To reach (a conclusion) by reasoning from known facts. **2.** To trace the origin or derivation of. [Middle English *deducen,* from Latin *dēdūcere,* to lead away, infer logically.] **—de·duc′i·ble** *adj.*

de·duct (dĭ-dŭkt′) *tr.v.* To take away (a quantity from another); subtract. [Latin *deductus,* past part. of *dēdūcere,* to lead away, deduce.]

de·duct·i·ble (dĭ-dŭk′tə-bəl) *adj.* **1.** Capable of being deducted. **2.** Allowable as a tax deduction.

de·duc·tion (dĭ-dŭk′shən) *n.* **1.** The act of deducting; subtraction. **2.** Something that is or may be deducted: *tax deductions.* **3. a.** The act or process of reasoning, esp. a logical method in which a conclusion necessarily follows from the propositions stated. **b.** A conclusion reached by this method.

de·duc·tive (dĭ-dŭk′tĭv) *adj.* **1.** Of or based on deduction. **2.** Involving deduction in reasoning. **—de·duc′tive·ly** *adv.*

deed (dēd) *n.* **1.** An act or thing done; action. **2.** Action in general: *bold in deed.* **3.** A legal document showing ownership, esp. pertaining to property. *—tr.v.* To transfer (property) by a deed. [Middle English *dede,* form Old English *dǣd.*]

deem (dēm) *tr.v.* To judge; consider; think: *We deem it advisable to wait.* —See Syns at **believe.** [Middle English *demen,* from Old English *dēman.*]

deep (dēp) *adj.* **-er, -est. 1.** Extending far downward below a surface: *a deep hole.* **2.** Extending far backward from front to rear, or inward from the outside: *a deep closet.* **3.** Far distant down or in: *deep in the woods.* **4.** Extreme; profound; intense: *a deep silence.* **5.** Very much absorbed or involved: *deep in thought.* **6.** Showing much thought or feeling: *a deep understanding; a deep love.* **7.** Difficult to understand or penetrate: *a deep mystery.* **8.** Rich and vivid: *a deep red.* **9.** Low in pitch: *a deep voice.* **10.** Coming from or located at a depth: *a deep sigh.* *—adv.* **1.** Far down or into: *dig deep.* **2.** Well on in time; late: *work deep into the night.* *—n.* **1.** A deep place, esp. one in the ocean. **2.** The most intense or extreme part: *the deep of night.* **—idioms. in deep.** *Informal.* Completely committed. **the deep.** *Poet.* The ocean. [Middle English *dep,* from Old English *dēop.*] **—deep′ly** *adv.* **—deep′ness** *n.*

    Syns: **deep, esoteric, heavy** (*Slang*), **profound** *adj. Core meaning:* Beyond an average person's understanding (*a deep book*).

deep·en (dē′pən) *tr.v.* To make deep or deeper. *—intr.v.* To become deep or deeper. **—deep′en·er** *n.*

deep-fry (dēp′frī′) *tr.v.* **-fried, -fry·ing.** To fry by immersing in a deep pan of fat or oil.

---

deep-root-ed (dēp′rōō′tĭd, -rŏŏt′ĭd) *adj.* Deep-seated.

deep-sea (dēp′sē′) *adj.* Of deep parts of the sea.

deep-seat-ed (dēp′sē′tĭd) *adj.* Deeply entrenched; ingrained: *a deep-seated problem.*

deep-set (dēp′sĕt′) *adj.* Placed or set deeply: *deep-set eyes.*

deer (dîr) *n., pl.* **deer.** Any of several cloven-hoofed ruminant animals of the family Cervidae, with deciduous antlers borne only by the males. [Middle English *der,* animal, from Old English *dēor.*]

deer-hound (dîr′hound′) *n.* A large hunting dog of a breed developed in Scotland, with a wiry coat.

deer mouse. Any of various New World mice of the genus *Peromyscus,* with large ears and white markings.

deer-skin (dîr′skĭn′) *n.* **1.** The skin of a deer. **2.** Leather made from this skin.

de-es-ca-late (dē-ĕs′kə-lāt′) *tr.v.* **-lat-ed, -lat-ing.** To lessen the scope or intensity of. **—de′-es′ca-la′tion** *n.*

de-face (dĭ-fās′) *tr.v.* **-faced, -fac-ing.** To spoil or mar the surface or appearance of. [Middle English *defacen,* from Old French *desfacier.*] **—de-face′ment** *n.* **—de-fac′er** *n.*

de fac-to (dē fāk′tō, dä). **1.** In existence; real: *de facto segregation.* **2.** Actually exercising power: *a de facto ruler.* [Latin, "on account of the fact."]

Usage: **De facto** and **de jure** are lawyers' Latin for "in fact" and "in law." They are used as a contrasted pair in situations where it must be recognized that the effective reality is not the legal reality.

de-fal-cate (dĭ-făl′kāt′, -fôl′-, dĕf′əl-kāt′) *intr.v.* **-cat-ed, -cat-ing.** To misuse funds; embezzle. [Medieval Latin *defalcāre,* to cut off.] **—de′fal-ca′tion** *n.* **—de-fal′ca-tor** *n.*

def-a-ma-tion (dĕf′ə-mā′shən) *n.* Slander or libel; calumny. **—de-fam′a-to-ry** (dĭ-făm′ə-tôr′ē, -tōr′ē) *adj.*

de-fame (dĭ-fām′) *tr.v.* **-famed, -fam-ing.** To attack the good name of by slander or libel. [Middle English *defamen,* from Old French *defamer,* from Latin *diffāmāre.*] **—de-fam′er** *n.*

de-fault (dĭ-fôlt′) *n.* **1.** A failure to do what is required, esp. a failure to pay a debt. **2.** The failure of one or more competitors or teams to participate in or complete a contest: *win by default.* **3.** Failure to make a required appearance in court. **—intr.v. 1.** To fail to do what is required: *default on a contract.* **2.** To fail to pay money when it is due. **3.** *Law.* **a.** To fail to appear in court when summoned. **b.** To lose a case by not appearing. **4.** *Sports.* To fail to compete in or complete a scheduled contest. [Middle English *defaute,* from Old French, lack.] **—de-fault′er** *n.*

de-feat (dĭ-fēt′) *tr.v.* **1.** To win victory over; beat. **2.** To prevent the success of; thwart: *defeat one's purposes.* **—n. 1.** The condition of being defeated; frustration from failure to win: *admit defeat.* **2.** The act of defeating. [Middle English *defeten,* from Old French *desfait,* from Medieval Latin *disfacere,* to undo, destroy.]

Syns: **defeat, beat, best, clobber** (Slang), **conquer, drub** (Slang), **lick** (Slang), **overcome, rout, shellac** (Slang), **subdue, thrash, trim** (Informal), **triumph (over), trounce, vanquish, whip** (Informal) *v. Core meaning:* To win a victory over (*Allies that defeated the Axis; a team that defeated its rival in soccer*).

de-feat-ism (dĭ-fē′tĭz′əm) *n.* An attitude of expecting the defeat of one's efforts or hopes. **—de-feat′ist** *n.*

def-e-cate (dĕf′ĭ-kāt′) *v.* **-cat-ed, -cat-ing. —intr.v.** To empty the bowels of waste matter. **—tr.v.** To clarify (a chemical solution). [From Latin *dēfaecāre.*] **—def′e-ca′tion** *n.* **—def′e-ca′tor** *n.*

de-fect (dē′fĕkt′, dĭ-fĕkt′) *n.* **1.** A lack of something necessary for completion or perfection; a deficiency. **2.** An imperfection; a failing. **—intr.v.** (dĭ-fĕkt′). To desert one's country, party, etc., in order to adopt or join another. [Middle English, from Old French, from Latin *dēficere,* to fail.] **—de-fec′tion** *n.* **—de-fec′tor** *n.*

de-fec-tive (dĭ-fĕk′tĭv) *adj.* **1.** Having a defect or flaw; faulty. **2.** *Gram.* Lacking one or more of the inflected forms normal for a particular category of word. In English, *may* is a defective verb. **—See Syns at imperfect. —n.** A person whose mental or physical development is below normal. **—de-fec′tive-ly** *adv.* **—de-fec′tive-ness** *n.*

Usage: **defective, deficient.** *Defective* describes something that has a discernible fault, and is therefore primarily concerned with quality: *a defective tire. Deficient* is ap-

plied to what has insufficiency or incompleteness: *a deficient diet; deficient in judgment.*

de-fence (dĭ-fĕns′) *n. Brit.* Var. of **defense.**

de-fend (dĭ-fĕnd′) *tr.v.* **1.** To protect from attack, harm, or challenge; to guard. **2.** To support, as by argument; justify: *Defend your answers.* **3. a.** To argue the case of (the defendant) in a court of law. **b.** To contest (a legal action or claim). **—intr.v.** To make a defense. [Middle English *defenden,* from Old French *defendre,* from Latin *dēfendere.*] **—de-fend′a-ble** *adj.* **—de-fend′er** *n.*

Syns: **1. defend, guard, protect, safeguard, secure, shield** *v. Core meaning:* To keep safe from danger or harm (*defended the castle against attackers*). **2. defend, justify, maintain, vindicate** *v. Core meaning:* To support against arguments or criticism (*defended his theses*).

de-fen-dant (dĭ-fĕn′dənt) *n. Law.* A person against whom a suit or criminal charge is brought.

de-fense (dĭ-fĕns′) *n.* Also *Brit.* **de-fence. 1.** The act of defending against attack, harm, or challenge; protection. **2.** A means of defending. **3.** Capacity for defense. **4.** *Sports.* The team or those players on the team attempting to stop the opposition from scoring. **5.** The reply of a defendant to the complaints against him. **6.** A defending individual or group, esp. in a law court. [Middle English *defens(e),* from Old French, from Latin *dēfendere,* to defend.] **—de-fense′less** *adj.* **—de-fense′less-ly** *adv.* **—de-fense′less-ness** *n.*

defense mechanism. Any physical or psychological reaction of an organism used in self-defense, as against germs.

de-fen-si-ble (dĭ-fĕn′sə-bəl) *adj.* Capable of being defended or justified. **—de-fen′si-bil′i-ty —de-fen′si-bly** *adv.*

de-fen-sive (dĭ-fĕn′sĭv) *adj.* Of, intended, or done for defense. **—idiom. on the defensive.** Expecting or being subjected to attack. **—de-fen′sive-ly** *adv.* **—de-fen′sive-ness** *n.*

de-fer¹ (dĭ-fûr′) *v.* **-ferred, -fer-ring. —tr.v.** To put off; postpone: *defer judgment.* **—intr.v.** To procrastinate; delay. [Middle English *differen,* from Old French *differer,* from Latin *differre.*] **—de-fer′ra-ble** *adj.* **—de-fer′rer** *n.*

de-fer² (dĭ-fûr′) *intr.v.* **-ferred, -fer-ring.** To comply with or submit to the opinion or decision of another. [Middle English *deferren,* from Old French *def(f)erer,* from Latin *dēferre,* to submit.] **—de-fer′rer** *n.*

def-er-ence (dĕf′ər-əns) *n.* **1.** Submission or courteous yielding to the opinion, wishes, or judgment of another. **2.** Courteous respect. **—See Syns at honor.**

def-er-en-tial (dĕf′ə-rĕn′shəl) *adj.* Marked by courteous respect: *deferential behavior.* **—def′er-en′tial-ly** *adv.*

de-fer-ment (dĭ-fûr′mənt) *n.* Also **de-fer-ral** (-fûr′əl). **1.** The act or an example of deferring or putting off. **2.** The postponement of compulsory military service.

de-fi-ance (dĭ-fī′əns) *n.* **1.** Resolute resistance to an opposing force or authority. **2.** Intentionally provocative behavior or attitude; a challenge. [Middle English *defiaunce,* from Old French *desfiance,* from *desfier,* to defy.]

de-fi-ant (dĭ-fī′ənt) *adj.* Marked by defiance; openly resisting authority: *a defiant attitude.* **—de-fi′ant-ly** *adv.*

de-fi-cien-cy (dĭ-fĭsh′ən-sē) *n., pl.* **-cies. 1.** A lack; shortage: *a vitamin deficiency.* **2.** A shortcoming; drawback; defect.

Syns: **deficiency, insufficiency, lack, scarcity, shortage** *n. Core meaning:* Inadequacy in amount or degree (*a deficiency in fuel oil*).

deficiency disease. A disease, such as pellagra, that results from a diet lacking in essential nutrients.

de-fi-cient (dĭ-fĭsh′ənt) *adj.* **1.** Lacking an important element; inadequate: *a deficient diet.* **2.** Defective; imperfect. **—See Usage note at defective.** [Latin *dēficiēns,* from *dēficere,* to fail, lack.] **—de-fi′cient-ly** *adv.*

def-i-cit (dĕf′ĭ-sĭt) *n.* The amount by which a sum of money falls short of the required or expected amount; a shortage. [French, from Latin *dēficit,* "it is lacking."]

deficit spending. A government policy of spending money obtained by borrowing.

de-file¹ (dĭ-fīl′) *tr.v.* **-filed, -fil-ing. 1.** To make filthy or dirty; pollute. **2.** To render impure; corrupt. **3.** To profane or sully (a good name, reputation, etc.). **4.** To desecrate: *defile a holy place.* **5.** To violate the chastity of. [Middle English *defilen,* alteration of *defoulen,* to injure, from Old French *defouler.*] **—de-file′ment** *n.* **—de-fil′er** *n.*

de-file² (dĭ-fīl′) *intr.v.* **-filed, -fil-ing.** To march in single file or in files or columns. —*n.* A narrow gorge or pass that prevents the easy passage of a group. [French *défiler.*]

de·fine (dĭ-fīn′) *v.* **-fined, -fin·ing.** —*tr.v.* **1.** To state the meaning of (a word, phrase, etc.). **2.** To describe the nature or basic qualities of; explain: *define one's duties.* **3.** To make clear the outline of: *a shape defined by a line.* **4.** To specify or fix definitely: *defining the borders between the two countries.* —*intr.v.* To make a definition. [Middle English *diffinen,* from Old French *definer,* from Latin *dēfīnīre,* to set bounds to.] —**de·fin′a·ble** *adj.* —**de·fin′a·bly** *adv.* —**de·fin′er** *n.*

def·i·nite (dĕf′ə-nĭt) *adj.* **1.** Clearly defined; precise; exact: *a definite time.* **2.** Known positively; sure: *It's not definite that he'll go.* **3.** *Gram.* Limiting or particularizing. **4.** *Bot.* Determinate. —See Syns at **explicit.** [Middle English *diffinite,* from Latin *dēfīnīre,* to determine, define.] —**def′i·nite·ly** *adv.* —**def′i·nite·ness** *n.*

Usage: **definite, definitive.** Although both words refer to the condition of being defined precisely or set forth explicitly, *definitive* is applied to what is final, a sense that *definite* does not have. For example, a *definite* decision is precise and unequivocal; a *definitive* decision is usu. beyond change or appeal.

definite article. *Gram.* The word **the,** used to introduce an identified or immediately identifiable noun or noun phrase.

def·i·ni·tion (dĕf′ə-nĭsh′ən) *n.* **1.** The act of stating a precise meaning or significance, as of a word, phrase, term, etc. **2.** The statement of such a meaning. **3.** The act of determining the outline, extent, or limits. **4.** The act of making clear and definite: *a definition of one's purposes.* **5.** The condition of being clearly outlined or determined. —**def′i·ni′tion·al** *adj.*

de·fin·i·tive (dĭ-fĭn′ĭ-tĭv) *adj.* **1.** Precisely defining or outlining. **2.** Final; conclusive. **3.** Authoritative and complete: *a definitive biography.* —See Usage note at **definite.** —**de·fin′i·tive·ly** *adv.* —**de·fin′i·tive·ness** *n.*

de·flate (dĭ-flāt′) *v.* **-flat·ed, -flat·ing.** —*tr.v.* **1.** To release contained air or gas from. **2.** To reduce the confidence, pride, happiness, etc., of. **3.** *Econ.* To reduce the value or amount of (currency). —*intr.v.* To be or become deflated. [DE- + (IN)FLATE.] —**de·fla′tor** *n.*

de·fla·tion (dĭ-flā′shən) *n.* **1.** The act of deflating or condition of being deflated. **2.** *Econ.* A reduction in the general price level brought on by a decrease in the amount of money in circulation or in the amount of spending. —**de·fla′tion·ar·y** (-shə-nĕr′ē) *adj.*

de·flect (dĭ-flĕkt′) *tr.v.* To cause to swerve or turn aside: *The tree deflected the car.* —*intr.v.* To swerve or turn aside: *The bullet deflected off the rock.* [Latin *dēflectere.*] —**de·flect′a·ble** *adj.* —**de·flec′tion** *n.* —**de·flec′tive** *adj.* —**de·flec′tor** *n.*

de·flow·er (dē-flou′ər) *tr.v.* **1.** To strip of flowers. **2.** To take away the virginity of. **3.** To spoil the appearance of.

de·fo·li·ant (dē-fō′lē-ənt) *n.* A chemical sprayed or dusted on plants to make their leaves fall off.

de·fo·li·ate (dē-fō′lē-āt′) *tr.v.* **-at·ed, -at·ing.** To deprive of leaves, esp. by the use of a chemical. —**de·fo′li·a′tion** *n.* —**de·fo′li·a′tor** *n.*

de·for·est (dē-fôr′ĭst, -fŏr′-) *tr.v.* To clear away the forests from. —**de·for·es·ta′tion** *n.* —**de·for′est·er** *n.*

de·form (dĭ-fôrm′) *tr.v.* **1.** To spoil the natural form or appearance of; disfigure: *Anger deformed his face.* **2.** To become changed in shape. —*intr.v.* To become deformed. —**de·form′a·bil′i·ty** *n.* —**de′for·ma′tion** (dē′fôr-mā′shən, dĕf′ər-) *n.*

de·for·mi·ty (dĭ-fôr′mĭ-tē) *n., pl.* **-ties. 1.** The condition of being deformed. **2.** A part of the body that is deformed or misshapen. **3.** A deformed person or thing. **4.** A moral distortion or flaw.

de·fraud (dĭ-frôd′) *tr.v.* To take from or deprive of by trickery or fraud. —**de·fraud·a′tion** (dē′frô-dā′shən) *n.* —**de·fraud′er** *n.*

de·fray (dĭ-frā′) *tr.v.* To pay or provide for payment of (costs or expenses): *Contributions will defray the cost of a political campaign.* [French *défrayer,* from Old French *desfrayer.*] —**de·fray′a·ble** *adj.* —**de·fray′al** *n.*

de·frost (dē-frôst′, -frŏst′) *tr.v.* **1.** To remove ice or frost from: *defrost a windshield.* **2.** To cause to thaw: *defrost a steak.* —*intr.v.* **1.** To become free of ice or frost. **2.** To become unfrozen; thaw. —**de·frost′er** (-frô′stər, -frŏs′tər) *n.*

deft (dĕft) *adj.* **-er, -est.** Quick and skillful; adroit: *a deft motion; deft hands.* [Middle English *defte.*] —**deft′ly** *adv.* —**deft′ness** *n.*

de·funct (dĭ-fŭngkt′) *adj.* No longer in existence, operation, or use; dead: *a defunct law; a defunct organization.* [Latin *dēfunctus,* from *dēfungī,* to die.] —**de·funct′ness** *n.*

de·fuse (dē-fyōoz′) *tr.v.* **-fused, -fus·ing. 1.** To remove the fuse from (an explosive). **2.** To make less dangerous.

de·fy (dĭ-fī′) *tr.v.* **-fied, -fy·ing. 1.** To oppose or challenge openly or boldly: *defy the law; defy tradition.* **2.** To withstand; be beyond: *defy belief; defy description; defy solution.* **3.** To challenge or dare (someone) to perform something that is thought to be impossible. [Middle English *defien,* from Old French *desfier,* to renounce (one's faith).] —**de·fi′er** *n.*

de·gauss (dē-gous′) *tr.v.* To neutralize the magnetic field of, as of a ship or television receiver.

de·gen·er·a·cy (dĭ-jĕn′ər-ə-sē) *n., pl.* **-cies. 1.** The condition of being degenerate. **2.** The process of degenerating.

de·gen·er·ate (dĭ-jĕn′ər-ĭt) *adj.* In a much worse or lower condition for having lost what is considered normal or desirable, as mental or moral qualities: *a degenerate person.* —*n.* A morally or psychologically abnormal person. —*intr.v.* (dĭ-jĕn′ə-rāt′). **-at·ed, -at·ing.** To become degenerated; deteriorate: *the debate degenerated into squabbling.* [Latin *dēgenerāre,* to fall from one's ancestral quality.] —**de·gen′er·ate·ly** *adv.* —**de·gen′er·ate·ness** *n.* —**de·gen′er·a·tive** (-ər-ə-tĭv′) *adj.*

de·gen·er·a·tion (dĭ-jĕn′ə-rā′shən) *n.* **1. a.** The process of degenerating. **b.** The condition of being degenerate. **2.** The deterioration, usu. permanent, of specific cells or organs of the body, often as a result of disease or injury.

de·glu·ti·tion (dē′glōo-tĭsh′ən) *n.* The act or process of swallowing. [French, from Latin *dēglūtīre,* to swallow.]

de·grade (dĭ-grād′) *tr.v.* **-grad·ed, -grad·ing. 1.** To reduce in rank, status, or position. **2.** To bring shame, disgrace, or contempt upon. **3.** To lower in moral or intellectual character; debase. **4.** *Chem.* To decompose (a compound) by stages. —**deg′ra·da′tion** (dĕg′rə-dā′shən) *n.* —**de·grad′er** *n.*

de·gree (dĭ-grē′) *n.* **1.** One of a series of steps or stages in a process, course of action, etc. **2.** Relative intensity, amount, or extent of something: *a high degree of accuracy; various degrees of skill in reading.* **3.** Relative social or official rank, position, etc. **4.** One of the forms used in the comparison of an adjective or adverb. For example, the superlative degree of "new" is "newest." **5.** A classification according to seriousness, as of a burn. **6. a.** An academic title awarded by a college or university after completion of a required course of study. **b.** A similar title granted as an honor. **7.** One of the units into which a temperature scale is divided. **8.** A unit of arc or angular measure equal to $\frac{1}{360}$ of a complete revolution. **9. a.** The sum of all the exponents of the variables in an algebraic term. **b.** In a polynomial in simple form, the degree of the term of the highest degree. For example, $x^3 + 2xy + x$ is of the third degree. **10.** *Mus.* **a.** One of the tones of a scale. **b.** A line or space of a staff. [Middle English *degre,* from Old French *degre,* from Latin *dē-,* down + *gradus,* a step.]

de·gree-day (dĭ-grē′dā′) *n.* **1.** An indication of the extent of departure from a standard of mean daily temperature. **2.** A unit used in estimating quantities of fuel and power consumption, based on a daily ratio of consumption and the mean temperature below 65°F.

de·hisce (dĭ-hĭs′) *intr.v.* **-hisced, -his·cing.** To burst or split open along a line or slit, as the ripe capsules or pods of some plants do. [Latin *dēhiscere.*] —**de·his′cence** *n.* —**de·his′cent** *adj.*

de·hu·man·ize (dē-hyōo′mə-nīz′) *tr.v.* **-ized, -iz·ing.** To deprive of human qualities or attributes, esp. to render mechanical and routine. —**de·hu′man·i·za′tion** *n.*

de·hu·mid·i·fy (dē′hyōo-mĭd′ə-fī′) *tr.v.* **-fied, -fy·ing.** To remove moisture from (as the air). —**de·hu′mid′i·fi·er** *n.*

de·hy·drate (dē-hī′drāt′) *v.* **-drat·ed, -drat·ing.** —*tr.v.* To remove water from. —*intr.v.* To lose water or moisture. —**de·hy′dra′tion** *n.*

de·ice (dē-īs′) *tr.v.* **-iced, -ic·ing.** To keep free of ice; melt ice from. —**de·ic′er** *n.*

---

de·i·fy (dē′ə-fī′) *tr.v.* **-fied, -fy·ing. 1.** To make a god of. **2.** To revere as a god: *He deifies money.* **3.** To idealize; exalt: *deify a war hero.* [Middle English *deifien*, from Old French *deifier*, from Late Latin *deificāre*, from Latin *deus*, god.] —**de′i·fi·ca′tion** *n.* —**de′i·fi′er** *n.*

deign (dān) *tr.v.* To condescend to give or grant: *deign an answer; deign to answer.* [Middle English *deinen*, from Old French *deignier*, to regard as worthy, from Latin *dignus*, worthy.]

de·ism (dē′ĭz′əm) *n.* The belief, based solely on reason, that God created the universe and then after setting it in motion, abandoned it, assumed no control over life, exerted no influence on natural laws, and gave no supernatural revelation. [French *déisme*, from Latin *deus*, god.] —**de′ist** *n.* —**de·is′tic** (dē-ĭs′tĭk) *adj.* —**de·is′ti·cal·ly** *adv.*

de·i·ty (dē′ĭ-tē) *n., pl.* **-ties. 1.** A god or goddess. **2.** Divinity. **3. the Deity.** God. [Middle English *deite*, from Old French, from Latin *deus*, god.]

dé·jà vu (dā′zhä vü′). The illusion of having already experienced something actually being experienced for the first time. [French, "already seen."]

de·ject (dĭ-jěkt′) *tr.v.* To dishearten; dispirit. [Middle English *dejecten*, from Latin *dejicere*, to cast down.]

de·ject·ed (dĭ-jěk′tĭd) *adj.* Depressed; disheartened. —**de·ject′ed·ly** *adv.* —**de·ject′ed·ness** *n.*

de·jec·tion (dĭ-jěk′shən) *n.* The condition of being dejected; sadness; melancholy.

de ju·re (dē jŏŏr′ē, dā yŏŏr′ā). *Latin.* According to law; by right. —See Usage note at **de facto.**

deka-. Var. of **deca-.**

dek·a·gram (dĭk′ə-grăm′) *n.* Var. of **decagram.**

dek·a·me·ter (děk′ə-mē′tər) *n.* Var. of **decameter.**

de·lay (dĭ-lā′) *tr.v.* **1.** To postpone until a later time; defer. **2.** To cause to be late or detained; hinder: *Fog delayed the takeoff.* —*intr.v.* To procrastinate or tarry; linger. —*n.* **1.** The act of delaying or condition of being delayed; postponement. **2.** The period of time someone or something is delayed. [Middle English *delaien*, from Old French *delaier.*] —**de·lay′er** *n.*

Syns: 1. delay, detain, retard, slow *v. Core meaning:* To cause to be later or slower than expected or desired (*was delayed by heavy traffic*). **2. delay, dally, dawdle, dilly-dally, drag, lag, linger, loiter, poke, procrastinate, tarry** *v. Core meaning:* To go or move slowly so that progress is hindered (*didn't hurry but didn't delay either*).

de·lec·ta·ble (dĭ-lĕk′tə-bəl) *adj.* Greatly pleasing, esp. to the taste. —See Syns at **delicious.** [Middle English, from Old French, from Latin *dēlectāre*, to delight.] —**de·lec′ta·bly** *adv.*

de·lec·ta·tion (dē′lĕk-tā′shən) *n.* Pleasure; delight.

del·e·ga·cy (dĕl′ĭ-gə-sē) *n., pl.* **-cies. 1.** The authority or position of a delegate. **2.** The act of delegating or being delegated. **3.** A body of delegates; delegation.

del·e·gate (dĕl′ĭ-gāt′, -gĭt) *n.* **1.** A person authorized to act as representative for another; deputy; agent. **2.** A representative of a Territory in the U.S. House of Representatives who is entitled to speak but not vote. **3.** A member of the lower house of the Maryland, Virginia, and West Virginia legislatures. —*tr.v.* (dĕl′ĭ-gāt′) **-gat·ed, -gat·ing. 1.** To authorize and send as one's representative. **2.** To commit or entrust to another: *delegate responsibility to an assistant.* [Middle English *delegat*, from Medieval Latin *dēlēgātus*, from Latin *dēlēgāre*, to send away.]

del·e·ga·tion (dĕl′ĭ-gā′shən) *n.* **1.** A person or group elected or appointed to represent another. **2.** The act of delegating. **3.** The condition of being delegated.

de·lete (dĭ-lēt′) *tr.v.* **-let·ed, -let·ing.** To strike out or remove, esp. from printed matter. [Latin *dēlētum*, from *dēlēre*, wipe out.]

del·e·te·ri·ous (dĕl′ĭ-tîr′ē-əs) *adj.* Harmful; injurious. [Medieval Latin *dēlētērius*, from Greek *dēlētērios*, to harm.] —**del′e·te′ri·ous·ly** *adv.* —**del′e·te′ri·ous·ness** *n.*

de·le·tion (dĭ-lē′shən) *n.* **1.** An act of deleting. **2.** A word, passage, etc. that has been deleted.

delft (dĕlft) *n.* Also **delf** (dĕlf). A style of glazed earthenware, usu. blue and white. Also called **delftware.** [After *Delft*, the Netherlands.]

del·i (dĕl′ē) *n., pl.* **-is.** *Informal.* A delicatessen.

de·lib·er·ate (dĭ-lĭb′ər-ĭt) *adj.* **1.** Premeditated; intentional: *a deliberate lie.* **2.** Careful and thorough in deciding: *a deliberate choice.* **3.** Leisurely or slow in motion or manner: *a deliberate pace.* —See Syns at **voluntary.** —*v.* (dĭ-lĭb′ə-rāt′) **-at·ed, -at·ing.** —*intr.v.* **1.** To think about or consider carefully. **2.** To consult with another as a process in reaching a decision: *a President deliberating with the cabinet.* —*tr.v.* To consider (a matter) by carefully weighing alternatives or the like: *deliberated the alternatives.* [From Latin *dēlīberāre*, to weigh well.] —**de·lib′er·ate·ly** *adv.* —**de·lib′er·ate·ness** *n.*

de·lib·er·a·tion (dĭ-lĭb′ə-rā′shən) *n.* **1.** The act of deliberating. **2.** Often **deliberations.** Formal discussion and debate of all sides of an issue. **3.** Slowness and care in decision or action: *act with deliberation.*

de·lib·er·a·tive (dĭ-lĭb′ə-rā′tĭv, -ər-ə-tĭv) *adj.* **1.** Assembled or organized for deliberation or debate: *a deliberative legislature.* **2.** Characterized by deliberation or debate. —**de·lib′er·a′tive·ly** *adv.* —**de·lib′er·a′tive·ness** *n.*

del·i·ca·cy (dĕl′ĭ-kə-sē) *n., pl.* **-cies. 1.** Something pleasing and appealing, esp. a choice food. **2.** Exquisite fineness or daintiness of quality, appearance, or structure: *silk gauze of great delicacy.* **3.** Frailty of bodily constitution or health. **4.** Consideration of the feelings of others; tact. **5.** The need for tact in treatment or handling: *a topic of some delicacy.* **6.** Sensitivity to what is proper; propriety. **7.** Sensitivity of perception, feeling, or taste; refinement. **8.** Accuracy of response or reaction: *the delicacy of a sophisticated microscope.*

del·i·cate (dĕl′ĭ-kĭt) *adj.* **1.** Exquisitely or pleasingly fine: *delicate lace; a delicate violin passage.* **2.** Frail in constitution or health. **3.** Easily broken or damaged. **4.** Considerate of the feelings of others. **5.** Requiring tactful treatment: *a delicate subject.* **6.** Showing sensitivity to what is proper. **7.** Refined in perception, feeling, or taste. **8.** Accurate in response or reaction: *a delicate musical instrument.* **9.** Requiring great skill and expertise: *delicate surgery.* **10.** Very subtle in difference or distinction: *a delicate pink; a delicate flavor.* [Middle English *delicat*, from Latin *dēlicātus*.] —**del′i·cate·ly** *adv.* —**del′i·cate·ness** *n.*

del·i·ca·tes·sen (dĕl′ĭ-kə-tĕs′ən) *n.* A shop that sells prepared foods, such as smoked meats and salads, ready for serving. [German, from French *délicatesse*, delicacy.]

de·li·cious (dĭ-lĭsh′əs) *adj.* Very pleasing or enjoyable, esp. to taste or smell. [Middle English, from Old French, from Late Latin *dēliciōsus*, pleasing, from Latin *dēlicere*, to delight.] —**de·li′cious·ly** *adv.* —**de·li′cious·ness** *n.*

Syns: delicious, delectable, luscious, savory, scrumptious (Slang)**, tasty, yummy** (Slang) *adj. Core meaning:* Very pleasing to the taste (*a delicious cake*).

de·light (dĭ-līt′) *intr.v.* To take or give great pleasure: *He delights in golfing.* —*tr.v.* To please greatly: *Her company delights me.* —*n.* **1.** Great pleasure; joy. **2.** Something that gives great pleasure: *Her writing is a delight to read.* [Middle English *deliten*, from Old French *deleitier*, from Latin *dēlectāre*, freq. of *dēlicere*, to allure.]

de·light·ed (dĭ-lī′tĭd) *adj.* Greatly pleased; very happy. —**de·light′ed·ly** *adv.* —**de·light′ed·ness** *n.*

de·light·ful (dĭ-līt′fəl) *adj.* Giving delight; greatly pleasing. —**de·light′ful·ly** *adv.* —**de·light′ful·ness** *n.*

de·lim·it (dĭ-lĭm′ĭt) *tr.v.* To establish the limit or boundaries of; demarcate. [French *délimiter*, from Latin *dēlīmitāre*.] —**de·lim′i·ta′tion** *n.* —**de·lim′i·ta′tive** *adj.*

de·lin·e·ate (dĭ-lĭn′ē-āt′) *tr.v.* **-at·ed, -at·ing. 1.** To draw or trace the outline of; sketch out: *This map clearly delineates the rivers and mountains.* **2.** To represent pictorially; depict. **3.** To describe in words; portray: *delineate the characters in a play.* [From Latin *dēlīneāre*, to sketch out.] —**de·lin′e·a′tion** *n.* —**de·lin′e·a′tive** *adj.*

de·lin·quen·cy (dĭ-lĭng′kwən-sē) *n., pl.* **-cies. 1.** Negligence or failure in doing what is required. **2.** An offense.

de·lin·quent (dĭ-lĭng′kwənt) *adj.* **1.** Failing or neglecting to do what is required by law or obligation. **2.** Overdue in payment: *a delinquent account.* —*n.* **1.** A delinquent person. **2.** A juvenile delinquent. [Latin *dēlinquēns*, from *dēlinquere*, to offend.] —**de·lin′quent·ly** *adv.*

del·i·quesce (dĕl′ĭ-kwĕs′) *intr.v.* **-quesced, -quesc·ing. 1.** To melt away. **2.** *Chem.* To dissolve and become liquid by absorbing moisture from the air, as do certain com-

---

ă pat ā pay â care ä father ĕ pet ē be hw which ĭ pit ī tie î pier ŏ pot ō toe ô paw, for oi noise
ōō took ōō boot ou out th thin th this ŭ cut û urge zh vision ə about, item, edible, gallop, circus

pounds. **3.** *Bot.* To become fluid or soft on maturing, as do certain fungi. [From Latin *dēliquēscere*.]

del·i·ques·cence (dĕl'ĭ-kwĕs'əns) *n.* **1.** The act or process of deliquescing. **2.** The liquid resulting from deliquescing. **3.** The ability to deliquesce. —**del'i·ques'cent** *adj.*

de·lir·i·ous (dĭ-lîr'ē-əs) *adj.* **1.** Suffering from delirium. **2.** Of or characteristic of delirium: *a delirious speech.* —**de·lir'i·ous·ly** *adv.* —**de·lir'i·ous·ness** *n.*

de·lir·i·um (dĭ-lîr'ē-əm) *n.,* pl. **-ums** or **-i·a** (-ē-ə). **1.** A condition of temporary mental confusion resulting from high fever, intoxication, or shock, and characterized by anxiety, tremors, hallucinations, delusions, and incoherence. **2.** Uncontrolled excitement or emotion. [Latin, from *dēlīrāre*, to deviate.]

delirium tre·mens (trē'mənz). A violent delirium caused by poisoning from excessive drinking of alcoholic beverages. Also called **D.T.'s.** [New Latin, "trembling delirium."]

de·liv·er (dĭ-lĭv'ər) *tr.v.* **1.** To take to a specified person or place. **2. a.** To send against; strike: *deliver a blow.* **b.** To throw or hurl: *The pitcher delivered the ball.* **3.** To give or utter: *deliver a speech.* **4.** To liberate or rescue; set free. **5.** To surrender; hand over: *deliver a criminal to the authorities.* **6. a.** To assist in the birth of: *The doctor delivered the baby.* **b.** To assist (a female) in giving birth: *deliver a woman of a child.* **7.** To secure or supply (something promised or desired): *deliver votes to a candidate.* —See Syns at **save.** —*idiom.* **deliver oneself.** To pronounce; utter. [Middle English *deliv(e)ren*, from Old French *delivrer*, from Late Latin *dēlīberāre.*] —**de·liv'er·a·bil'i·ty** *n.* —**de·liv'er·a·ble** *adj.* —**de·liv'er·er** *n.*

de·liv·er·ance (dĭ-lĭv'ər-əns) *n.* **1.** The act of delivering or the condition of being delivered; a rescue. **2.** A publicly expressed opinion or judgment, as the verdict of a jury.

de·liv·er·y (dĭ-lĭv'ə-rē) *n.,* pl. **1.** The act of delivering or conveying. **2.** That which is delivered. **3.** The act of releasing or rescuing. **4.** The act of giving birth. **5.** A giving up; surrender. **6.** A manner of speaking or singing: *It was a good speech, but her delivery was poor.* **7.** The act or manner of throwing or discharging, esp. a ball in certain sports: *a pitcher with a herky-jerky delivery.*

dell (dĕl) *n.* A small, secluded wooded valley. [Middle English *del,* from Old English *dell.*]

de·louse (dē-lous') *tr.v.* **-loused, -lous·ing.** To rid of lice by physical or chemical means.

Del·phic (dĕl'fĭk) *adj.* Also **Del·phi·an** (dĕl'fē-ən). **1.** Of or pertaining to ancient Delphi or to the oracle of Apollo at Delphi. **2.** Ambiguous; obscure in meaning; oracular.

del·phin·i·um (dĕl-fĭn'ē-əm) *n.* Any plant of the genus *Delphinium,* esp. any of several tall cultivated varieties with spikes of showy, variously colored flowers. [From Greek *delphinion,* larkspur, dim. of *delphis,* dolphin.]

del·ta (dĕl'tə) *n.* **1.** The fourth letter in the Greek alphabet, written Δ, δ, transliterated in English as *d, D.* **2.** Anything resembling the shape of a triangle. **3.** A usu. triangular mass of sand, mud, and earth formed by deposits at the mouth of a river. [Middle English, from Greek.]

del·toid (dĕl'toid') *n.* A thick, triangular muscle covering the shoulder joint, used to raise the arm from the side. —*adj.* Triangular. [From Greek *deltoeidēs,* triangular.]

de·lude (dĭ-lood') *tr.v.* **-lud·ed, -lud·ing.** To deceive the mind or judgment of: *left false clues to delude his pursuers.* —See Syns at **deceive.** [Middle English *deluden,* from Latin *dēlūdere.*] —**de·lud'er** *n.* —**de·lud'ing·ly** *adv.*

del·uge (dĕl'yōoj) *n.* **1.** A great flood or downpour. **2.** An overwhelming influx of something: *a deluge of mail.* **3. the Deluge.** In the Old Testament, the Flood. —*tr.v.* **-uged, -ug·ing.** **1.** To overrun with water; inundate. **2.** To inundate in overwhelming numbers: *a beach deluged with people.* [Middle English, from Old French, from Latin *dīluvium,* flood, from *dīluere,* to wash away.]

de·lu·sion (dĭ-loo'zhən) *n.* **1. a.** The act of deluding; deception. **b.** The condition of being deluded. **2.** A false belief held in spite of evidence to the contrary, esp. as a condition of certain forms of mental illness. [Middle English *delusioun,* from Latin *dēlūdere,* to delude.]

Usage: **delusion, allusion, illusion.** These words are often confused and misused. A *delusion* is a false belief, held without reservation, that comes from self-deception, the imposition of another person, or mental disorder: *had delusions of grandeur.* An *illusion* is a false impression that may result from faulty observation, wishful thinking, or false perception that one eventually recognizes as false—or that one knows all along is false: *optical illusions.* An *allusion* is an indirect reference: *made an allusion to an earlier statement.*

de·lu·sive (dĭ-loo'sĭv) *adj.* Also **de·lu·so·ry** (-loo'sə-rē). **1.** Tending to deceive; deceptive. **2.** Like a delusion; false. —**de·lu'sive·ly** *adv.* —**de·lu'sive·ness** *n.*

de luxe (də lōoks', lŭks'). Also **de·luxe.** Exceptionally elegant or luxurious: *a de luxe model.* [French, "of luxury."]

delve (dĕlv) *intr.v.* **delved, delv·ing.** **1.** To search deeply and laboriously to obtain information: *delving into the candidate's background.* **2.** *Archaic.* To dig the ground. [Middle English *delven,* to dig, from Old English *delfan.*]

de·mag·net·ize (dē-măg'nĭ-tīz') *tr.v.* **-ized, -iz·ing.** To remove magnetic properties from. —**de·mag'net·i·za'tion** *n.*

dem·a·gogue (dĕm'ə-gŏg', -gŏg') *n.* Also **dem·a·gog.** A leader who obtains power or personal ends by means of impassioned appeals to the emotions and prejudices of the populace. [Greek *dēmagōgos,* popular leader.] —**dem'a·gog'ic** (-gŏj'ĭk) or **dem'a·gog'i·cal** (-gŏj'ĭ-kəl) *adj.* —**dem'a·gog'i·cal·ly** *adv.*

dem·a·gogu·er·y (dĕm'ə-gô'gə-rē, -gŏg'ə-) *n.* The principles, practices, or rhetoric of a demagogue.

dem·a·go·gy (dĕm'ə-gō'jē, -gô'jē, -gŏj'ē) *n.* The quality or character of demagogues.

de·mand (dĭ-mănd') *tr.v.* **1.** To ask for urgently or insistently: *demand a raise.* **2.** To claim as just or due: *demand one's rights.* **3.** To need or require: *work demanding great concentration.* —*intr.v.* To make a demand. —*n.* **1.** The act of demanding. **2.** Something that is demanded. **3. a.** The condition of being sought after: *an actor in great demand.* **b.** A requirement, need, or claim: *an increased demand for capital goods.* **4.** *Archaic.* A question or inquiry. **5.** *Econ.* **a.** The desire to possess something combined with the ability to purchase it. **b.** The amount of any commodity that people are ready to buy at a given time for a given price. —*idiom.* **on demand.** On presentation: *a banknote payable on demand.* [Middle English *demaunden,* from Old French *demander,* to ask, from Latin *dēmandāre,* to entrust.] —**de·mand'a·ble** *adj.* —**de·mand'er** *n.*

de·mand·ing (dĭ-măn'dĭng, dĭ-män'-) *adj.* Requiring careful attention or constant effort. —See Syns at **burdensome.** —**de·mand'ing·ly** *adv.*

de·mar·cate (dĭ-mär'kāt', dē'mär-kāt') *tr.v.* **-cat·ed, -cat·ing.** **1.** To set the boundaries of; delimit. **2.** To separate clearly; discriminate. [Back-formation from DEMARCATION.]

de·mar·ca·tion (dē'mär-kā'shən) *n.* **1.** The setting or marking of boundaries or limits. **2.** A separation; distinction: *line of demarcation.* [Spanish *demarcadión,* from *demarcar,* to mark out the boundary.]

deme (dēm) *n.* One of the townships of ancient Attica. [Greek *dēmos,* common people.]

de·mean¹ (dĭ-mēn') *tr.v.* To lower in dignity or stature; debase; degrade: *Such a trivial job demeans a person of his intelligence.*

de·mean² (dĭ-mēn') *tr.v.* To conduct or behave (oneself) in a particular manner: *demeaned herself with great propriety.* [Middle English *demeinen,* from Old French *demener.*]

de·mean·or (dĭ-mē'nər) *n.* Also *Brit.* **de·mean·our.** The way in which one behaves or conducts oneself; deportment.

de·ment·ed (dĭ-mĕn'tĭd) *adj.* **1.** Mentally disordered; insane. **2.** *Informal.* Foolish; crazy: *a demented scheme.*

de·men·tia (dĭ-mĕn'shə) *n.* Deterioration of mental faculties along with emotional disturbance resulting from organic brain disorder. See Syns at **insanity.** [Latin *dēmentia,* madness, from *dēmēns,* mad.]

dementia prae·cox (prē'kŏks'). Schizophrenia.

de·mer·it (dĭ-mĕr'ĭt) *n.* **1.** A quality that deserves blame or censure; a fault. **2.** A mark made against a person's record for bad conduct or poor work. [Middle English *demerite,* offense, guilt, from Old French, fault.]

de·mesne (dĭ-mān', -mēn') *n.* **1.** *Law.* Possession and use of one's own land. **2.** Lands retained by a feudal lord for his own use. **3.** The lands of an estate. **4.** Any district; ter-

---

| ă pat | ā pay | â care | ä father | ĕ pet | ē be | hw which | ĭ pit | ī tie | î pier | ŏ pot | ō toe | ô paw, for | oi noise |
| ōō took | ōō boot | ou out | th thin | th this | ŭ cut | û urge | zh vision | ə about, item, edible, gallop, circus |

ritory. **5.** A realm; domain. [Middle English, from Old French *demaine,* domain.]

De·me·ter (dĭ-mē′tər) *n. Gk. Myth.* The goddess of agriculture and fertility. Identified with the Roman goddess Ceres.

Demeter   demijohn

demi-. A prefix meaning: **1.** Half: **demisemiquaver. 2.** Less than full status: **demigod.** [French, from *demi,* half, from Medieval Latin *dīmedius,* from Latin *dīmidius.*]

dem·i·god (dĕm′ē-gŏd′) *n. Myth.* **1. a.** The offspring of a god and a mortal. **b.** An inferior or minor deity. **2.** A person with godlike attributes.

dem·i·john (dĕm′ē-jŏn′) *n.* A large, narrow-necked bottle made of glass or earthenware, usu. encased in wickerwork. [Prob. from French *dame-Jeanne,* "Lady Jane."]

de·mil·i·ta·rize (dē-mĭl′ĭ-tə-rīz′) *tr.v.* **-rized, -riz·ing. 1.** To prohibit military forces or installations in: *demilitarize the border region of the divided country.* **2.** To replace military control of with civilian control. **—de·mil′i·ta·ri·za′tion** *n.*

dem·i·mon·daine (dĕm′ē-mŏn-dān′, -mŏn′dān′) *n.* A woman belonging to the demimonde.

dem·i·monde (dĕm′ē-mŏnd′, dĕm′ē-mŏnd′) *n.* **1.** The social class of those who are kept by wealthy lovers or protectors. **2.** Any group that exists on the fringes of respectability. [French, "half-world."]

de·mise (dĭ-mīz′) *n.* **1.** Death. **2.** The end or cessation of something: *the demise of a great newspaper.* **3.** The transfer of an estate by lease or will. **4.** The transfer of a ruler's authority by death or abdication. **—v. -mised, -mis·ing. —tr.v. 1.** To transfer (an estate) by will or lease. **2.** To transfer (sovereignty) by abdication or will. **—intr.v. 1.** To be transferred by will or descent. **2.** To die. —See Syns at **die.** [Middle English, transfer of property, from Old French, from fem. past part. of *demettre,* to remove.] **—de·mis′a·ble** *adj.*

dem·i·sem·i·qua·ver (dĕm′ē-sĕm′ē-kwā′vər) *n. Brit.* A **thirty-second note.** [DEMI- + SEMI- + QUAVER (eighth note).]

dem·i·tasse (dĕm′ē-tăs′, -täs′) *n.* **1.** A small cup of strong black coffee. **2.** The cup itself. [French : *demi-,* half + *tasse,* cup.]

de·mo·bi·lize (dē-mō′bə-līz′) *tr.v.* **-lized, -liz·ing. 1.** To discharge from military service or use, as an army. **2.** To change (an army, economy, etc.) from a wartime to peacetime condition. **—de·mo′bi·li·za′tion** *n.*

de·moc·ra·cy (dĭ-mŏk′rə-sē) *n., pl.* **-cies. 1.** Government by the people, exercised either directly or through elected representatives. **2.** A nation or social unit with this form of government. **3.** Social and political equality and respect for the individual within the community. [Old French *democratie,* from Late Latin *dēmocratia,* from Greek *dēmokratia.*]

dem·o·crat (dĕm′ə-krăt′) *n.* **1.** An advocate of democracy. **2. Democrat.** A member of the Democratic Party.

dem·o·crat·ic (dĕm′ə-krăt′ĭk) *adj.* **1.** Of, characterized by, or advocating political, economic, or social democracy. **2.** Of, pertaining to, or appealing to the masses: *democratic art forms.* **3.** Practicing social equality; not snobbish: *"A proper democratic scorn for bloated dukes and lords"* (George Du Maurier). **4. Democratic.** Of or pertain-

ing to the Democratic Party. —See Syns at **public. —dem′o·crat′i·cal·ly** *adv.*

Democratic Party. One of the two major political parties in the United States, originating from a split in the Democratic-Republican Party under Andrew Jackson in 1828.

Dem·o·crat·ic-Re·pub·li·can Party (dĕm′ə-krăt′ĭk-rĭ-pŭb′-lĭ-kən). A U.S. political party opposed to the Federalist Party, founded in 1792 and dissolved in 1828.

de·moc·ra·tize (dĭ-mŏk′rə-tīz′) *tr.v.* **-tized, -tiz·ing.** To make democratic. **—de·moc′ra·ti·za′tion** *n.*

dé·mo·dé (dā′mō-dā′) *adj. French.* Out of fashion.

de·mod·u·late (dē-mŏj′ōō-lāt′, -mŏd′yə-) *tr.v.* **-lat·ed, -lat·ing.** To extract (information) from a modulated carrier wave. **—de·mod′u·la′tion** *n.* **—de·mod′u·la′tor** *n.*

de·mog·ra·phy (dĭ-mŏg′rə-fē) *n.* The study of human populations, including size, growth, density, distribution, and vital statistics. [Greek *dēmos,* people + -GRAPHY.] **—de·mog′ra·pher** *n.* **—dem′o·graph′ic** (dĕm′ə-grăf′ĭk) *adj.* **—dem′o·graph′i·cal·ly** *adv.*

dem·oi·selle (dĕm′wä-zĕl′) *n.* A young lady. [French, from Old French *dameisele,* damsel.]

de·mol·ish (dĭ-mŏl′ĭsh) *tr.v.* **1.** To tear down completely; raze. **2.** To do away with completely; put an end to: *this new discovery demolishes our theory.* —See Syns at **destroy.** [From Old French *demolir,* from Latin *dēmōlīrī.*]

dem·o·li·tion (dĕm′ə-lĭsh′ən) *n.* The act of demolishing, esp. the destruction of a building by explosives. [Old French, from Latin *dēmōlīrī,* to demolish.] **—dem′o·li′tion·ist** *n.*

de·mon (dē′mən) *n.* **1.** A devil or evil being. **2.** A persistently tormenting person, force, or passion. **3.** Also **dae·mon.** *Gk. Myth.* A demigod. **4.** Also **dae·mon.** An attendant spirit; a genius. **5.** Someone who is extremely zealous or skillful in a given activity: *a demon for work.* [Middle English, from Late Latin *daemōn,* from Latin, spirit, from Greek *daimōn,* god.]

de·mon·e·tize (dē-mŏn′ĭ-tīz′, -mŭn′-) *tr.v.* **-tized, -tiz·ing. 1.** To divest (currency) of its standard monetary value. **2.** To stop using as money. **—de·mon′e·ti·za′tion** *n.*

de·mo·ni·ac (dĭ-mō′nē-ăk′) or **de·mo·ni·a·cal** (dē′mə-nī′-ə-kəl) *adj.* **1.** Of, like, or suggestive of a demon; fiendish. **2.** Caused by or as if by a demon; frenzied; wild: *a mad, demoniac dance.* **—n.** Someone who is or seems to be possessed by a demon. **—de′mo·ni′a·cal·ly** (dē′mə-nī′-ə-kə-lē) *adv.*

de·mon·ic (dĭ-mŏn′ĭk) *adj.* **1.** Befitting a demon; fiendish; devilish. **2.** Inspired by a spiritual force or genius.

de·mon·ol·o·gy (dē′mə-nŏl′ə-jē) *n.* **1.** The study of demons. **2.** A treatise on demons or demon worship.

de·mon·stra·ble (dĭ-mŏn′strə-bəl) *adj.* Capable of being shown or proved: *a demonstrable theory.* **—de·mon′stra·bil′i·ty** *n.* **—de·mon′stra·bly** *adv.*

dem·on·strate (dĕm′ən-strāt′) *v.* **-strat·ed, -strat·ing. —tr.v. 1.** To make apparent or prove by reasoning. **2.** To illustrate by experiment or practical application: *demonstrate the effects of a drug.* **3.** To show or reveal publicly: *demonstrated his political strength.* **4.** To display and explain (a product). **—intr.v.** To present or participate in a demonstration. —See Syns at **prove** and **show.** [From Latin *dēmonstrāre,* to point out.]

dem·on·stra·tion (dĕm′ən-strā′shən) *n.* **1.** The act of making evident or proving. **2.** Conclusive evidence; proof. **3.** An illustration or explanation, as of a theory or product, by example. **4.** A manifestation, as of one's feelings. **5.** A public display of group opinion, as by a rally or march.

de·mon·stra·tive (dĭ-mŏn′strə-tĭv) *adj.* **1.** Serving to show or prove. **2.** Characterized by demonstration. **3.** Marked by the open expression of emotion: *a demonstrative husband.* **4.** *Gram.* Specifying or singling out the person or thing referred to. For example, *these* is a demonstrative pronoun. **—n.** *Gram.* A demonstrative pronoun or adjective. **—de·mon′stra·tive·ly** *adv.* **—de·mon′stra·tive·ness** *n.*

dem·on·stra·tor (dĕm′ən-strā′tər) *n.* **1.** A sample used in a demonstration. **2.** A person who takes part in a public demonstration.

de·mor·al·ize (dĭ-môr′ə-līz′, -mŏr′-) *tr.v.* **-ized, -iz·ing. 1.** To weaken the confidence or morale of; dishearten. **2.** To debase the morals of; to corrupt. **—de·mor′al·i·za′tion** *n.*

de·mote (dĭ-mōt′) tr.v. **-mot·ed, -mot·ing.** To lower in rank or grade. [DE- + (PRO)MOTE.] —**de·mo′tion** n.

de·mot·ic (dĭ-mŏt′ĭk) adj. **1.** Of or pertaining to the common people; popular. **2.** Of, pertaining to, or written in the simplified form of ancient Egyptian hieratic writing. [Greek dēmotikos, from dēmos, common people.]

de·mul·cent (dĭ-mŭl′sənt) adj. Soothing. —n. A soothing, usu. jellylike or oily substance, used esp. to relieve pain in inflamed or irritated mucous membranes. [Latin dēmulcēns, pres. part. of dēmulcēre, to soothe.]

de·mur (dĭ-mûr′) intr.v. **-murred, -mur·ring. 1.** To take exception; object: demurred at her invitation. **2.** Law. To enter a demurrer. —n. Also **de·mur·ral** (dĭ-mûr′əl). Law. An objection. [Middle English demuren, to delay, from French demurer, from Latin dēmorārī.]

de·mure (dĭ-myŏor′) adj. **-mur·er, -mur·est. 1.** Quiet in manner; modest; shy. **2.** Feigning modesty or shyness; coy. —See Syns at **modest.** [Middle English, from Old French demore, from demorer, to delay.] —**de·mure′ly** adv. —**de·mure′ness** n.

de·mur·rage (dĭ-mûr′ĭj) n. **1.** The detention of a ship, freight car, or other cargo conveyance for failure to load or unload by the scheduled time of departure. **2.** The compensation paid for this detention.

de·mur·ral (dĭ-mûr′əl) n. Var. of demur.

de·mur·rer (dĭ-mûr′ər) n. **1.** Law. A plea to dismiss a lawsuit on the grounds that the opposition's statements are insufficient to sustain the claim. **2.** An objection.

den (dĕn) n. **1.** The shelter or retreat of a wild animal; lair. **2.** A small, usu. secluded place, esp. when used as a hideout or for an illegal activity: a den of thieves. **3.** A small secluded room for study or relaxation. **4.** A unit of about eight to ten Cub Scouts. [Middle English, from Old English denn.]

de·nar·i·us (dĭ-nâr′ē-əs) n., pl. **-nar·i·i** (-nâr′ē-ī′). **1.** An ancient Roman silver coin. **2.** An ancient Roman gold coin. [Middle English, from Latin dēnārius.]

de·na·tion·al·ize (dē-năsh′ə-nə-līz′) tr.v. **-ized, -iz·ing. 1.** To deprive of national rights, status, or characteristics. **2.** To return to private ownership. —**de·na′tion·al·i·za′tion** n.

de·na·ture (dē-nā′chər) tr.v. **-tured, -tur·ing. 1.** To change the nature or natural qualities of. **2.** To make unfit to eat or drink, as alcohol, without destroying its usefulness for other purposes. **3.** To change the structure of (a protein) so as to destroy or alter its natural properties. —**de·na′tur·a′tion** n.

dendr– or **dendri–.** Vars. of dendro–.

den·drite (dĕn′drīt) n. **1.** A branching or treelike mark in a mineral. **2.** A branched part of a nerve cell that transmits impulses toward the cell body. —**den·drit′ic** (dĕn-drĭt′ĭk) or **den·drit′i·cal** (-ĭ-kəl) adj.

dendro– or **dendri–** or **dendr–.** A prefix meaning tree: dendrology. [From Greek dendron, tree.]

den·drol·o·gy (dĕn-drŏl′ə-jē) n. The botanical study of trees. [DENDRO- + -LOGY.] —**den·drol′o·gist** n.

Den·eb (dĕn′ĕb′) n. The brightest star in the constellation Cygnus, approx. 1,630 light-years from Earth.

den·gue (dĕng′gē, gā) n. A severe infectious disease of tropical and subtropical regions, transmitted by mosquitoes and characterized by fever, rash, and severe pains in the joints. [Spanish, of African orig.]

de·ni·al (dĭ-nī′əl) n. **1.** A refusal to comply or satisfy a request. **2.** A statement that an accusation or allegation is false. **3.** A rejection, as of a doctrine or belief. **4.** A refusal or disavowal of responsibility for: a denial of the child. **5.** Abstinence; self-denial.

de·ni·er[1] (dĭ-nī′ər) n. Someone who denies.

den·ier[2]. n. **1.** (dĕn′yər). A unit of fineness for rayon, nylon, and silk yarns, based on a standard of 50 milligrams per 450 meters of yarn. **2.** (də-nîr′, dən-yā′). A small coin, of varying value, once current in western Europe. [Middle English denere, a small coin, from Old French denier, from Latin dēnārius, denarius.]

den·i·grate (dĕn′ĭ-grāt′) tr.v. **-grat·ed, -grat·ing.** To belittle or slander the character of; defame. [From Latin dēnigrāre, to blacken.] —**den′i·gra′tion** n. —**den′i·gra′tor** n.

den·im (dĕn′əm) n. **1.** A coarse, heavy cotton cloth used for work clothes and sportswear. **2.** denims. Overalls or trousers made of coarse denim. [French (serge) de Nîmes, serge of Nîmes, city in southern France.]

de·ni·tri·fy (dē-nī′trə-fī′) tr.v. **-fied, -fy·ing. 1.** To remove nitrogen or its compounds from. **2.** To convert (a nitrate) into a compound having a lower level of oxidation, as by bacterial action on soil. —**de·ni′tri·fi·ca′tion** n.

den·i·zen (dĕn′ĭ-zən) n. **1.** An inhabitant; resident. **2.** Ecol. An animal or plant that becomes naturalized in a region to which it is not native. [Middle English denisein, from Old French denzein, from deinz, within, from Late Latin dēintus, from within.]

de·nom·i·nate (dĭ-nŏm′ə-nāt′) tr.v. **-nat·ed, -nat·ing.** To give a name to; designate. [From Latin dēnōmināre.]

de·nom·i·nate number (dĭ-nŏm′ə-nĭt). A number that designates a quantity as a multiple of a unit. In the expression 12 kilograms, 12 is a denominate number.

de·nom·i·na·tion (dĭ-nŏm′ə-nā′shən) n. **1.** The act of naming. **2.** A name; designation. **3.** The name of a class or group; classification. **4.** A class of units having specified values: bills of small denomination. **5.** An organized group of religious congregations. —See Syns at **name.** —**de·nom′i·na′tion·al** adj. —**de·nom′i·na′tion·al·ly** adv.

de·nom·i·na·tion·al·ism (dĭ-nŏm′ə-nā′shə-nə-lĭz′əm) n. Strict adherence to a denomination and its principles.

de·nom·i·na·tive (dĭ-nŏm′ə-nā′tĭv, -nə-tĭv) Gram. —adj. Formed from a noun or adjective. —n. A word derived from a noun or adjective.

de·nom·i·na·tor (dĭ-nŏm′ə-nā′tər) n. **1.** The quantity below the line in a fraction indicating how many subsets a whole set is to be divided into. For example, in the fraction 2/7, 7 is the denominator. **2.** A characteristic or quality held in common.

de·no·ta·tion (dē′nō-tā′shən) n. **1.** The act of denoting; indication. **2.** A symbol or reference that denotes. **3.** The exact meaning of a word, as opposed to its connotation.

de·no·ta·tive (dē′nō-tə-tĭv, dĕ′nō-tā′-) adj. **1.** Able to denote; designative. **2.** Explicit. —**de·no′ta·tive·ly** adv.

de·note (dĭ-nōt′) tr.v. **-not·ed, -not·ing. 1.** To be a sign or symbol of: The blue areas on the map denote water. **2.** To mean explicitly; signify: The prefix "multi-" denotes "many" or "much." [Old French denoter, from Latin dēnotāre.]

dé·noue·ment (dā′nōō-mäN′) n. Also **de·noue·ment. 1.** The solution, clarification, or unraveling of the plot of a literary work. **2.** Any outcome or final solution. [French, "an untying."]

de·nounce (dĭ-nouns′) tr.v. **-nounced, -nounc·ing. 1.** To condemn or attack openly, esp. as evil; to censure. **2.** To accuse formally; inform against. **3.** To give formal announcement of the ending of (a treaty). —See Syns at **blame.** [Middle English denouncen, from Old French denoncier, announce, from Latin dēnūntiāre.] —**de·nounce′ment** n. —**de·nounc′er** n.

de no·vo (dĭ nō′vō, dā). Once again; anew. [Latin.]

dense (dĕns) adj. **dens·er, dens·est. 1.** Having relatively high density. **2.** Crowded closely together: a dense neighborhood. **3.** Thick; impenetrable: a dense fog. **4.** Difficult to comprehend; profound: a dense treatise. **5.** Thickheaded; stupid. **6.** Photog. Opaque, with good contrast between light and dark areas, as of a developed negative. —See Syns at **stupid.** [Latin dēnsus, thick.] —**dense′ly** adv. —**dense′ness** n.

den·si·ty (dĕn′sĭ-tē) n., pl. **-ties. 1.** The quality or condition of being dense. **2.** Physics. **a.** The amount of something per unit measure, esp. per unit length, area, or volume: charge density; energy density. **b.** The mass per unit volume of a substance under specified or standard conditions of pressure and temperature. **3.** The number of inhabitants per unit geographical region. **4.** The degree of optical opacity of a medium or material, as of a photographic negative. **5.** Stupidity; dullness.

dent (dĕnt) n. **1.** A hollow place or depression in a surface made by pressure or a blow. **2.** Meaningful progress; headway. —tr.v. To make a dent in. —intr.v. To become dented. [Middle English, blow, from Old English dynt.]

dent–. Var. of denti–.

den·tal (dĕn′tl) adj. **1.** Of or pertaining to the teeth or dentistry. **2.** Phonet. Produced with the tip of the tongue near or against the upper front teeth. —n. Phonet. A dental consonant. [From Latin dēns, tooth.]

dental floss. A thread used to clean between the teeth.

dental hygienist. A person who assists a dentist.

den·tate (dĕn′tāt′) adj. Edged with pointed or toothlike projections, esp. certain leaves. **—den·ta′tion** n.

denti- or **dent-.** A prefix meaning tooth: **dentine.** [From Latin *dēns,* tooth.]

den·ti·frice (dĕn′tə-frĭs) n. A substance, such as a powder or paste, for cleaning the teeth. [Old French, from Latin *dentifricium* : denti-, tooth + *fricāre,* to rub.]

den·tine (dĕn′tēn′) n. Also **den·tin** (-tĭn), The calcified part of a tooth, beneath the enamel, that contains the pulp chamber and root canals.

den·tist (dĕn′tĭst) n. A person whose profession is dentistry.

den·tist·ry (dĕn′tĭ-strē) n. The diagnosis, prevention, and treatment of diseases of the teeth and gums.

den·ti·tion (dĕn-tĭsh′ən) n. 1. The type, number, and arrangement of teeth, esp. in animals. 2. The process of cutting of teeth; a teething.

den·ture (dĕn′chər) n. A set of artificial teeth.

de·nude (dĭ-nōōd′, -nyōōd′) tr.v. **-nud·ed, -nud·ing. 1.** To strip the covering of: *floods denuded the land of topsoil.* **2.** *Geol.* To expose (rock strata) by erosion. [Latin *dēnūdāre.*] **—den′u·da′tion** (dĕn′yōō-dā′shən) n.

de·nun·ci·a·tion (dĭ-nŭn′sē-ā′shən, -shē-) n. **1.** The act of denouncing; open condemnation or censure. **2.** The act of accusing another publicly of a crime.

de·ny (dĭ-nī′) tr.v. **-nied, -ny·ing. 1.** To declare untrue; contradict: *deny an accusation.* **2.** To refuse to believe; reject: *deny a judge's decision.* **3.** To refuse to recognize or acknowledge; disavow: *deny an illegitimate child.* **4.** To refuse to grant: *deny permission.* [Middle English *denien,* from Old French *denier,* from Latin *dēnegāre.*]

Syns: deny, contradict v. Core meaning: To dispute the truth, reality, or worth of (*couldn't deny that he was arrogant*). DENY is the most general and usu. implies an open declaration that something is untrue (*denied the charge*). To CONTRADICT is to assert that the opposite of a given statement is true (*a child who contradicted her mother*).

de·o·dar (dē′ə-där′) n. A tall cedar, *Cedrus deodara,* native to the Himalayas, with drooping branches and wood valued as timber. [Hindi *dē′odār,* from Sanskrit *devadāru.*]

de·o·dor·ant (dē-ō′dər-ənt) n. A preparation applied to counteract body odors. **—modifier:** *a deodorant spray.*

de·o·dor·ize (dē-ō′də-rīz′) tr.v. **-ized, -iz·ing.** To cover or absorb the odor of. **—de·o′dor·i·za′tion** n. **—de·o′dor·iz′er** n.

De·o vo·len·te (dē′ō və-lĕn′tē, dā′ō). Latin. God willing.

de·ox·i·dize (dē-ŏk′sĭ-dīz′) tr.v. **-dized, -diz·ing.** To chemically remove oxygen from. **—de·ox′i·di·za′tion** n. **—de·ox′i·diz′er** n.

de·ox·y·ri·bo·nu·cle·ic acid (dē-ŏk′sē-rī′bō-nōō-klē′ĭk, -nyōō-). **DNA.**

de·part (dĭ-pärt′) intr.v. **1.** To go away; leave. **2.** To vary or deviate: *depart from custom.* **3.** To die. **—tr.v.** To leave: *depart this life.* **—See Syns at die.** [Middle English *departen,* divide, from Old French *departir.*]

de·part·ed (dĭ-pär′tĭd) adj. **1.** Dead; deceased. **2.** Bygone; past. **—n.** One or more persons who have died.

de·part·ment (dĭ-pärt′mənt) n. **1.** A distinct usu. specialized division of an organization, government, or business. **2.** Often **Department.** One of the principal executive divisions of the Federal government of the United States, headed by a cabinet officer. **3.** A division of a school or college dealing with a particular field of knowledge. **5.** *Informal.* An area of expertise; sphere: *Cleaning up isn't my department.* [French *département,* from Old French, *departir,* to divide.] **—de′part·men′tal** (dē′pärt-mĕn′tl) adj. **—de′part·men′tal·ly** adv.

de·par·men·tal·ize (dē′pärt-mĕn′tl-īz′) tr.v. **-ized, -iz·ing.** To divide into departments. **—de′part·men′tal·i·za′tion** n.

department store. A large retail store offering a variety of merchandise, organized in separate departments.

de·par·ture (dĭ-pär′chər) n. **1.** The act of leaving. **2.** A starting out, as on a trip or a new course of action. **3.** A deviation or divergence: *a departure from tradition.*

de·pend (dĭ-pĕnd′) intr.v. **1.** To rely, as for support: *depends on his scholarship.* **2.** To place trust: *You can de-*

pend on her reliability. **3.** To be determined, conditioned, or dependent. **4.** To hang down: *tinsel depending from the Christmas tree.* [Middle English *dependen,* from Old French *dependre,* to hang down, from Latin *dēpendēre.*]

de·pend·a·ble (dĭ-pĕn′də-bəl) adj. Capable of being depended upon; trustworthy. **—de·pend′a·bil′i·ty** n. **—de·pend′a·bly** adv.

de·pend·ance (dĭ-pĕn′dəns) n. Var. of **dependence.**

de·pend·an·cy (dĭ-pĕn′dən-sē) n. Var. of **dependency.**

de·pend·ant (dĭ-pĕn′dənt) adj. Var. of **dependent.**

de·pend·ence (dĭ-pĕn′dəns) n. Also **de·pend·ance. 1.** The condition of being dependent, esp. for support. **2.** The condition of being determined, influenced, or controlled by something else; subservience: *dependence on foreign oil.* **3.** Trust; reliance.

de·pend·en·cy (dĭ-pĕn′dən-sē) n., pl. **-cies.** Also **de·pend·an·cy. 1.** Dependence. **2.** Anything dependent or subordinate. **3.** A territory or state under the jurisdiction of another country from which it is separated geographically.

de·pend·ent (dĭ-pĕn′dənt) adj. Also **de·pend·ant. 1.** Determined or influenced by something or someone else; contingent. **2.** Subordinate. **3.** Relying on or requiring the aid of another for support: *dependent children.* **4.** Hanging down. **—See Syns at subordinate. —n.** Someone who relies on another for support. **—de·pend′ent·ly** adv.

dependent clause. A clause that cannot stand alone as a full sentence and that acts as a noun, adjective, or adverb within a sentence. For example, in the sentence *When I saw him he was feeling fine,* the clause *when I saw him* is a dependent clause. Also called **subordinate clause.**

de·pict (dĭ-pĭkt′) tr.v. **1.** To represent in a picture. **2.** To represent in words. [Latin *dēpingere.*] **—de·pic′tion** n.

dep·i·late (dĕp′ə-lāt′) tr.v. **-lat·ed, -lat·ing.** To remove hair from (the body). [From Latin *dēpilāre.*] **—dep′i·la′tion** n.

de·pil·a·to·ry (dĭ-pĭl′ə-tôr′ē, -tōr′ē) adj. Able to remove hair. **—n.,** pl. **-ries.** An agent used to remove hair.

de·plane (dē-plān′) intr.v. **-planed, -plan·ing.** To disembark from an airplane.

de·plete (dĭ-plēt′) tr.v. **-plet·ed, -plet·ing.** To reduce the amount of until little or none remains; exhaust: *depleting our oil supplies.* [Latin, past part. of *dēplēre,* to empty.] **—de·ple′tion** n.

de·plor·a·ble (dĭ-plôr′ə-bəl, -plōr′-) adj. **1.** Worthy of reproach: *deplorable behavior.* **2.** Lamentable; grievous. **3.** Wretched; bad. **—de·plor′a·bly** adv.

de·plore (dĭ-plôr′, -plōr′) tr.v. **-plored, -plor·ing. 1.** To feel or express strong disapproval of. **2.** To feel or express deep sorrow over; to lament. [Old French *deplorer,* from Latin *dēplōrāre.*]

de·ploy (dĭ-ploi′) tr.v. **1.** To position according to a strategic plan: *deploy missiles; deploy chess pieces.* **2.** To spread out (troops) to form an extended front. **—intr.v.** To be or become deployed. [French *déployer,* from Latin *displicāre,* to scatter.] **—de·ploy′ment** n.

de·po·lar·ize (dē-pō′lə-rīz′) tr.v. **-ized, -iz·ing.** To eliminate or counteract the polarization of. **—de·po′lar·i·za′tion** n.

de·po·nent (dĭ-pō′nənt) adj. Denoting a verb of active meaning but passive form. **—n. 1.** A deponent verb. **2.** *Law.* A person who testifies under oath, esp. in writing. [Late Latin *dēpōnēns,* "laying aside," from Latin *dēpōnere,* to put down.]

de·pop·u·late (dē-pŏp′yə-lāt′) tr.v. **-lat·ed, -lat·ing.** To reduce sharply the population of, as by expulsion or massacre. **—de·pop′u·la′tion** n.

de·port¹ (dĭ-pôrt′, -pōrt′) tr.v. To behave or conduct (oneself): *He deported himself commendably.* [From Old French *deporter.*]

de·port² (dĭ-pôrt′, -pōrt′) tr.v. To expel from a country. [French *déporter,* from Latin *dēportāre.*] **—de′por·ta′tion** (dē′pôr-tā′shən, -pōr-) n.

de·por·tee (dē′pôr-tē′, -pōr-) n. A deported person.

de·port·ment (dĭ-pôrt′mənt, -pōrt′-) n. Conduct; behavior; demeanor: *aristocratic deportment.*

de·pose (dĭ-pōz′) v. **-posed, -pos·ing. —tr.v. 1.** To remove from office or a position of power. **2.** *Law.* To declare under oath, esp. in writing. **—intr.v.** *Law.* To testify, esp. in writing. [Middle English *deposen,* from Old French *deposer.*] **—de·pos′a·ble** adj. **—de·pos′al** n.

de·pos·it (dĭ-pŏz'ĭt) tr.v. **1.** To place in a bank or other repository for safekeeping. **2.** To lay or set down: *deposit the packages on the table.* **3.** To put down or place, esp. in layers, by a natural process: *silt and gravel deposited by the river.* **4.** To give (money) as partial payment or security. *—n.* **1.** Something entrusted for safekeeping, esp. money in a bank. **2.** The condition of being deposited: *a thousand dollars on deposit.* **3.** A sum of money given as initial payment of a cost or debt or as security for an item acquired for temporary use. **4.** Something deposited, esp. mineral or sandy matter settled by moving water. [Latin *dēpositus,* from *dēpōnere,* to put aside.] **—de·pos'i·tor** *n.*

de·pos·i·tar·y (dĭ-pŏz'ĭ-tĕr'ē) n., pl. **-ies. 1.** A person or group entrusted with something. **2.** A repository.

dep·o·si·tion (dĕp'ə-zĭsh'ən) n. **1.** The act of deposing, as from high office. **2.** *Law.* Testimony under oath, esp. a written statement admissible in court. **3.** A deposit.

de·pos·i·to·ry (dĭ-pŏz'ĭ-tôr'ē, -tōr'ē) n., pl. **-ries.** 1. A place where something is held for safekeeping. **2.** A trustee.

de·pot (dē'pō) n. **1.** A railroad or bus station. **2.** A warehouse or storehouse. **3.** An installation where military material is stored or where military troops are assembled and assigned. [French *dépôt,* from Old French *depost,* from Latin *dēpositum,* deposit, from *dēpōnere,* to deposit.]

de·prave (dĭ-prāv') tr.v. **-praved, -prav·ing.** To make morally bad; debase. [Middle English *depraven,* from Old French *depraver,* to pervert, from Latin *dēprāvāre.*] **—dep'ra·va'tion** (dĕp'rə-vā'shən) n.

de·praved (dĭ-prāvd') adj. Morally corrupt; perverted.

de·prav·i·ty (dĭ-prăv'ĭ-tē) n., pl. **-ties. 1.** Moral corruption; a depraved condition. **2.** A wicked or perverse act.

dep·re·cate (dĕp'rĭ-kāt') tr.v. **-cat·ed, -cat·ing. 1.** To express disapproval of; protest or plead against. **2.** To depreciate; belittle. [From Latin *dēprecārī,* to ward off by prayer.] **—dep're·ca'tion** n. **—dep're·ca'tor** n.

dep·re·ca·to·ry (dĕp'rĭ-kə-tôr'ē, -tōr'ē) adj. Expressing disapproval; disparaging.

de·pre·ci·ate (dĭ-prē'shē-āt') v. **-at·ed, -at·ing.** *—tr.v.* **1.** To lower the price or value of: *depreciate equipment for tax purposes.* **2.** To deprecate; belittle. *—intr.v.* To diminish in price or value. [From Medieval Latin *dēpreciāre,* Late Latin *dēpretiāre.*] **—de·pre'ci·a'tor** n. **—de·pre'ci·a·to'ry** (-shə-tôr'ē, -tōr-) adj.

de·pre·ci·a·tion (dĭ-prē'shē-ā'shən) n. **1.** A decrease or loss in value because of wear, age, or other cause. **2.** *Accounting.* An allowance made for this loss. **3.** A reduction in the purchasing value of money. **4.** A disparaging; a belittling.

dep·re·da·tion (dĕp'rĭ-dā'shən) n. The act or an instance of destruction, plunder, or ravaging.

de·press (dĭ-prĕs') tr.v. **1.** To make sad or dejected; sadden. **2.** To press down; lower: *depress a pedal.* **3.** To lower prices in (a stock market). [Middle English *depressen,* from Old French *depresser,* from Latin *deprimere.*]

de·pres·sant (dĭ-prĕs'ənt) adj. Tending to slow vital body processes. *—n.* A depressant drug.

de·pressed (dĭ-prĕst') adj. **1.** Gloomy; dejected. **2.** *Bot.* Flattened downward, as if pressed from above. **3.** Suffering economic hardship.

Syns: depressed, backward, disadvantaged, underprivileged *adj.* *Core meaning:* Economically and socially below standard (*a program of aid to all depressed areas*). See also Syns at **gloomy.**

de·pres·sion (dĭ-prĕsh'ən) n. **1.** A mental condition of gloom, sadness, or melancholy; dejection. **2.** An area that is sunk below its surroundings; a hollow. **3.** A region of low barometric pressure. **4.** *Econ.* A period of drastic decline in the national economy, characterized by decreasing business activity and unemployment. **5.** An act of pressing down.

de·pres·sive (dĭ-prĕs'ĭv) adj. **1.** Causing depression. **2.** Of or characterized by mental depression.

de·pres·sor (dĭ-prĕs'ər) n. **1.** Someone or something that depresses. **2.** A nerve that lowers arterial blood pressure. **3.** Any of several muscles that cause contraction of a body part. **4.** Any instrument, such as a tongue depressor, used to depress a part.

de·prive (dĭ-prīv') tr.v. **-prived, -priv·ing. 1.** To take something away from; divest: *He was deprived of his rights.* **2.** To keep from the possession of something; deny: *de-*

prived of sleep by the disturbance. [Middle English *depriven,* from Old French *depriver,* from Medieval Latin *dēprīvāre.*] **—dep·ri·va'tion** (dĕp'rə-vā'shən) n.

depth (dĕpth) n. **1.** The quality of being deep. **2.** The distance or dimension downward, backward, or inward. **3.** Often **depths.** The inner or most remote or inaccessible part: *the depths of Siberia.* **4.** The most profound or intense part or stage: *the depth of despair.* **5.** The severest or worst part: *the depth of winter.* **6.** Intellectual complexity or penetration; profundity: *a novel of great depth.* **7.** The range of one's understanding or competence: *beyond one's depth.* **8.** Richness; intensity; darkness: *depth of color.* [Middle English *depthe,* prob. from *dep,* deep.]

depth charge. Any charge designed for explosion under water, used esp. against submarines.

dep·u·ta·tion (dĕp'yə-tā'shən) n. **1.** A person or group appointed to represent others. **2.** The act of deputing.

de·pute (dĭ-pyōot') tr.v. **-put·ed, -put·ing.** To delegate. [Middle English *deputen,* from Old French *deputer,* from Late Latin *dēpūtāre,* allot, from Latin, to consider.]

dep·u·tize (dĕp'yə-tīz') v. **-tized, -tiz·ing.** *—tr.v.* To appoint as a deputy. *—intr.v.* To serve as a deputy.

dep·u·ty (dĕp'yə-tē) n., pl. **-ties. 1.** A person named or empowered to act for another. **2.** An assistant exercising full authority in the absence of his superior. **3.** A representative in a legislative body in certain countries, such as France. *—modifier: a deputy attorney general.* [Middle English *depute,* from Old French, from *deputer,* to depute.]

de·rail (dē-rāl') tr.v. To cause (a train) to run off the rails. *—intr.v.* To run off the rails. **—de·rail'ment** n.

de·range (dĭ-rānj') tr.v. **-ranged, -rang·ing. 1.** To disturb the order of; disarrange. **2.** To disturb the condition or functioning of; upset. **3.** To make insane. [French *déranger,* from Old French *desrengier* : *de-* + *reng, renc,* line.] **—de·range'ment** n.

Der·by n. **1.** (där'bē). Any of various horse races, usu. for three-year-olds, held annually. **2.** *derby.* Any formal race open to all contestants. **3.** A stiff felt hat with a round crown and narrow brim. Also *Brit.* **bowler.** [Founded in 1780 by Edward Smith Stanley (1752–1834), 12th Earl of *Derby.*]

der·e·lict (dĕr'ə-lĭkt) n. **1.** A homeless or jobless person. **2.** Abandoned property, esp. a ship abandoned at sea. *—adj.* **1.** Neglectful of duty or obligation; remiss. **2.** Deserted by an owner or guardian; abandoned. [Latin *dērelictus,* from *dērelinquere,* to abandon.]

der·e·lic·tion (dĕr'ə-lĭk'shən) n. **1.** Willful failure or neglect, as of duty. **2.** Abandonment.

de·ride (dĭ-rīd') tr.v. **-rid·ed, -rid·ing.** To speak of or treat with contempt or scorn; scoff at; mock. —See Syns at **ridicule.** [Latin *dērīdēre.*] **—de·rid'er** n.

de ri·gueur (də rē-gûr'). Required by the current fashion or custom; socially obligatory. [French.]

de·ri·sion (dĭ-rĭzh'ən) n. Ridicule; scorn. [Middle English *derisioun,* from Old French *derision,* from Latin *dērīdēre,* to deride.]

de·ri·sive (dĭ-rī'sĭv) adj. Also **de·ri·so·ry** (-sə-rē). Mocking; ridiculing. **—de·ri'sive·ly** adv. **—de·ri'sive·ness** n.

der·i·va·tion (dĕr'ə-vā'shən) n. **1.** The act or process of deriving or the condition or fact of being derived. **2.** Something derived; a derivative: *The word "vodka" is a derivation from Russian.* **3.** The form or source from which something is derived; origin. **4.** The historical origin and development of a word; etymology. **5.** The morphological process by which new words are formed from existing words, chiefly by the addition of affixes. —See Syns at **origin.**

de·riv·a·tive (dĭ-rĭv'ə-tĭv) adj. **1.** Resulting from derivation. **2.** Copied or adapted from others; not original: *a derivative novel.* *—n.* **1.** Something derived. **2.** A word formed from another by derivation. **3.** *Math.* The limit, as the increment in the argument of a function as it approaches zero, of the ratio of the increment in its value to the corresponding increment in the argument. **4.** *Chem.* Any compound derived or obtained from known or hypothetical substances by a well-defined process and containing essential elements of the original substance. **—de·riv'a·tive·ly** adv.

de·rive (dĭ-rīv') v. **-rived, -riv·ing.** *—tr.v.* **1.** To obtain or receive from a source. **2.** To arrive at by reasoning; infer.

ă pat	ā pay	â care	ä father	ĕ pet	ē be	hw which	ĭ pit	ī tie	î pier	ŏ pot	ō toe	ô paw, for	oi noise

ŏŏ took   ŏŏ boot   ou out   th thin   th this   ŭ cut   û urge   zh vision   ə about, item, edible, gallop, circus

3. To trace the origin or development of. **4.** *Chem.* To produce or obtain (a compound) from another substance by chemical reaction. —*intr.v.* To issue from a source; originate. [Middle English *deriven*, to spring from, from Old French *deriver*, from Latin *dērīvāre*, to draw off.] —**de·riv'a·ble** *adj.* —**de·riv'er** *n.*

-derm. *Biol.* A suffix meaning skin: echinoderm. [From Greek *derma*, skin.]

der·ma (dûr'mə) *n.* The corium. [From Greek *derma*, skin.]

der·mal (dûr'məl) *adj.* Of or involving the skin.

der·ma·ti·tis (dûr'mə-tī'tĭs) *n.* Inflammation of the skin. [From Greek *derma*, skin + -ITIS.]

der·ma·tol·o·gy (dûr'mə-tŏl'ə-jē) *n.* The medical study of the skin, its diseases, and their treatment. [From Greek *derma*, skin + -LOGY.] —**der'ma·to·log'i·cal** (-tə-lŏj'ĭ-kəl) *adj.* —**der'ma·tol'o·gist** *n.*

der·mis (dûr'mĭs) *n.* The corium. [From Late Latin -*dermis*, from Greek *derma*, skin.

der·o·gate (dĕr'ə-gāt') *v.* **-gat·ed, -gat·ing.** —*intr.v.* To detract; take away: *a grave error that will derogate from his reputation.* —*tr.v.* To disparage; belittle. [From Latin *dērogāre*, to restrict, disparage.] —**der'o·ga'tion** *n.*

de·rog·a·to·ry (dĭ-rŏg'ə-tôr'ē, -tōr'ē) *adj.* Tending to derogate; disparaging. —**de·rog'a·to·ri·ly** *adv.*

der·rick (dĕr'ĭk) *n.* **1.** A large crane for hoisting and moving heavy objects, consisting of a movable boom attached to a base and equipped with cables and pulleys. **2.** A tall framework over the opening of an oil well or other drilled hole, used to support boring equipment or to hoist and lower pipe lengths. [Earlier *derick*, a hangman, the gallows, after *Derick*, 17th cent. English hangman.]

der·ri·ère (dĕr'ē-âr') *n.* The buttocks; the rear. [French, "the rear."]

der·ring-do (dĕr'ĭng-dōo') *n.* Daring spirit and action; valor. [Middle English *durring don*, "daring to do."] pres. part. of *durren*, from Old English *durran*, to dare + *don*, to do.]

der·rin·ger (dĕr'ĭn-jər) *n.* A short-barreled pistol with a large bore. [Invented by Henry *Deringer*, 19th-cent. American gunsmith.]

der·vish (dûr'vĭsh) *n.* A member of any of various Moslem orders of ascetics, some of which use whirling dances and howling to achieve a collective ecstasy. [Turkish *dervis*, mendicant, from Persian *dārvīsh*.]

de·sal·i·nate (dē-săl'ə-nāt') *tr.v.* **-nat·ed, -nat·ing.** To remove salt from, esp. sea water. —**de·sal'i·na'tion** *n.*

de·salt (dē-sôlt') *tr.v.* To desalinate.

des·cant (dĕs'kănt) *n.* **1.** Also **dis·cant** (dĭs'kănt'). A melody or counterpoint sung above a musical theme. **2.** The highest part sung in part music. **3.** A discussion or discourse on a subject. —*intr.v.* (dĕ-skănt'). **1.** To comment at length; discourse. **2.** To sing or play a descant. [Old North French, from Medieval Latin *discantus*, refrain.]

de·scend (dĭ-sĕnd') *intr.v.* **1.** To move from a higher to a lower place; come or go down. **2.** To slope, extend, or incline downward. **3.** To be derived from ancestors. **4.** To pass by inheritance or transmission as property or title. **5.** To lower oneself in behavior; to stoop. **6.** To arrive in an overwhelming manner: *Thieves descended on the travelers.* —*tr.v.* To move from a higher to a lower part of; go down: *descend the stairs.* —See Syns at **fall.** [Middle English *descenden*, from Old French *descendre*, from Latin *dēscendere*.]

de·scen·dant (dĭ-sĕn'dənt) *n.* A person or animal descended from specified ancestors. —*adj.* Descendent.

   Syns: **descendant, child, offspring, scion** *n. Core meaning:* One descended directly from the same parents or ancestors (Elizabeth II—*a descendant of George III*).

de·scen·dent (dĭ-sĕn'dənt) *adj.* Also **de·scen·dant. 1.** Moving downward. **2.** Proceeding by descent from an ancestor.

de·scent (dĭ-sĕnt') *n.* **1.** The act or an instance of descending. **2.** A downward incline or passage. **3.** Family origin; ancestry. **4.** A decline, as in status. **5.** A sudden attack. **6.** *Law.* Transference of property by inheritance. [Middle English, from Old French, from *descendre*, to descend.]

de·scribe (dĭ-skrīb') *tr.v.* **1.** To move from a higher to a lower place; come or go down. **2.** To give a verbal account of; tell about in detail. **3.** To trace the outline of: *describe a circle.* [Latin *dēscrībere*, to write down.]

—**de·scrib'a·ble** *adj.* —**de·scrib'er** *n.*

de·scrip·tion (dĭ-skrĭp'shən) *n.* **1.** The act of describing; verbal representation. **2.** A statement or account describing something. **3.** The act of tracing a figure. **4.** A kind; sort: *costumes of every description.*

de·scrip·tive (dĭ-skrĭp'tĭv) *adj.* Serving to describe. —**de·scrip'tive·ly** *adv.* —**de·scrip'tive·ness** *n.*

de·scry (dĭ-skrī') *tr.v.* **-scried, -scry·ing. 1.** To espy or catch sight of. **2.** To discover by careful observation. [Middle English *descrien*, cry out, proclaim, catch sight of, from Old French *descrier*, to decry.] —**de·scri'er** *n.*

des·e·crate (dĕs'ĭ-krāt') *tr.v.* **-crat·ed, -crat·ing.** To abuse the sacredness of; to profane. [DE- + (CON)SECRATE.] —**des'e·crat'er** or **des'e·cra'tor** *n.* —**des'e·cra'tion** *n.*

de·seg·re·gate (dē-sĕg'rĭ-gāt') *v.* **-gat·ed, -gat·ing.** —*tr.v.* To abolish racial segregation in. —*intr.v.* To become desegregated. —**de·seg're·ga'tion** *n.*

de·sen·si·tize (dē-sĕn'sĭ-tīz') *tr.v.* **-tized, -tiz·ing.** To make less sensitive or insensitive, as to light or pain. —**de·sen'si·ti·za'tion** *n.* —**de·sen'si·tiz'er** *n.*

des·ert¹ (dĕz'ərt) *n.* **1.** A dry, barren region, often covered with sand, and with little or no vegetation. **2.** Any unproductive area, activity, or sphere; wasteland: *an intellectual desert.* —*modifier:* a desert island. —See Usage note at **dessert.** [Middle English, from Old French, from Late Latin *dēsertum*, from Latin *dēserere*, to abandon.]

de·sert² (dĭ-zûrt') *n.* Often **deserts.** That which is deserved or merited, esp. a punishment: *received his just deserts.* —See Usage note at **dessert.** [Middle English *deserte*, from *desert*, from *deserve*, to deserve.]

de·sert³ (dĭ-zûrt') *tr.v.* **1.** To forsake or leave; abandon. **2.** To abandon (the army or an army post) illegally and with no intention of returning. **3.** To fail (one) in time of need: *His courage deserted him at the last moment.* —*intr.v.* To forsake one's duty or post. —See Syns at **abandon.** [French *déserter*, from Late Latin *dēsertāre*, from Latin *dēserere*, to abandon.] —**de·sert'er** *n.*

de·ser·tion (dĭ-zûr'shən) *n.* **1.** The act of deserting. **2.** The condition of being deserted. **3.** *Law.* Willful abandonment of one's spouse or children, forsaking all legal obligation.

de·serve (dĭ-zûrv') *v.* **-served, -serv·ing.** —*tr.v.* To be worthy of; to merit: *deserves better treatment than that.* —*intr.v.* To be worthy. [Middle English *deserven*, from Old French *deservir*, from Latin *dēservīre*, to serve well.]

de·served (dĭ-zûrvd') *adj.* Merited or earned: *a deserved vacation.* —**de·serv'ed·ness** (-zûr'vĭd-nĭs) *n.*

de·serv·ed·ly (dĭ-zûr'vĭd-lē) *adv.* As is right and fair.

de·serv·ing (dĭ-zûr'vĭng) *adj.* Worthy of reward, praise, or aid; meritorious: *a deserving student.* —**de·serv'ing·ly** *adv.*

des·ha·bille (dĕs'ə-bēl') *n.* Var. of **dishabille.**

des·ic·cate (dĕs'ĭ-kāt') *v.* **-cat·ed, -cat·ing.** —*tr.v.* **1.** To make thoroughly dry. **2.** To preserve (foods) by removing the moisture. —*intr.v.* To become dry. [From Latin *dēsiccāre*.] —**des'ic·ca'tion** *n.*

de·sid·e·ra·tum (dĭ-sĭd'ə-rä'təm, -rā'-) *n., pl.* **-ta** (-tə). Something needed and desired. [Latin *dēsīderātum*, from *dēsīderāre*, to desire.]

de·sign (dĭ-zīn') *tr.v.* **1.** To conceive in the mind; invent; contrive: *design a strategy.* **2.** To draw up plans for, esp. by means of sketches, drawings, etc. **3.** To have as a goal or purpose; intend. —*intr.v.* **1.** To make or execute plans. **2.** To create designs. —*n.* **1.** A drawing or sketch giving the details of how something is to be made. **2.** The arrangement of the forms, parts, or details of something according to a plan. **3.** A decorative pattern. **4.** The art of creating designs. **5.** A plan or project; an undertaking. **6.** A reasoned purpose; intention. **7.** Often **designs.** A sinister or hostile scheme; crafty plot. [Old French *designer*, from Latin *dēsignāre*, to designate.]

des·ig·nate (dĕz'ĭg-nāt') *tr.v.* **-nat·ed, -nat·ing. 1.** To indicate or specify; point out. **2.** To give a name or title to; characterize. **3.** To select for a particular duty, office, or purpose; appoint. —*adj.* (dĕz'ĭg-nĭt). Appointed but not yet installed in office: *the commissioner-designate.* [From Latin *dēsignāre*.] —**des'ig·na'tor** *n.*

designated hitter. *Baseball.* A player designated at the start of a game to bat instead of the pitcher in the lineup.

des·ig·na·tion (dĕz'ĭg-nā'shən) *n.* **1.** The act of designating. **2.** Nomination or appointment. **3.** A distinguishing name or mark; title. —See Syns at **name**.

de·sign·ed·ly (dĭ-zī′nĭd-lē) *adv.* On purpose; intentionally.

de·sign·er (dĭ-zī′nər) *n.* A person who creates the design of objects or manufactured goods, as clothing or books.

de·sign·ing (dĭ-zī′nĭng) *adj.* Conniving; artful; crafty.

de·sir·a·ble (dĭ-zīr′ə-bəl) *adj.* **1.** Of such quality as to be desired; attractive; fine: *a desirable location.* **2.** Worth wanting or doing; advantageous: *a desirable reform.* —**de·sir′a·bil′i·ty** or **de·sir′a·ble·ness** *n.* —**de·sir′a·bly** *adv.*

de·sire (dĭ-zīr′) *tr.v.* **-sired, -sir·ing. 1.** To wish or long for; want; crave: *desire success.* **2.** To express a wish for: *we desire job information.* —See Syns at **choose**. —*n.* **1.** A wish, longing, or craving. **2.** A request; a petition. **3.** Something or someone longed for: *gained his heart's desire.* **4.** Sexual appetite; passion. [Middle English *desiren,* from Old French *desirer,* from Latin *dēsīderāre.*] —**de·sir′er** *n.*

de·sir·ous (dĭ-zīr′əs) *adj.* Having desire; wishing: *desirous of peace.* —**de·sir′ous·ly** *adv.* —**de·sir′ous·ness** *n.*

de·sist (dĭ-zĭst′, -sĭst′) *intr.v.* To cease doing or trying to do something; to stop; abstain. —See Syns at **abandon** and **stop**. [Old French *desister,* from Latin *dēsistere.*]

desk (dĕsk) *n.* **1.** A piece of furniture usu. with a flat top for writing and a number of drawers. **2.** A table, counter, or booth at which specified, usu. public services or functions are performed. **3.** A department of a large organization in charge of a specific operation: *city desk.* **4.** A music stand in an orchestra. [Middle English *deske,* from Medieval Latin *desca,* from Latin *discus,* disk.]

des·o·late (dĕs′ə-lĭt) *adj.* **1.** Devoid of inhabitants; deserted. **2.** Rendered unfit for habitation or use. **3.** Dreary; dismal; gloomy. **4.** Without friends or hope; forlorn; lonely. —*tr.v.* (dĕs′ə-lāt′) **-lat·ed, -lat·ing. 1.** To rid or deprive of inhabitants. **2.** To lay waste; devastate. **3.** To forsake; abandon. **4.** To make lonely, forlorn, or wretched. [Middle English *desolat,* from Latin *dēsōlātus,* from *dēsōlāre,* to abandon.] —**des′o·late·ly** *adv.* —**des′o·late·ness** *n.*

des·o·la·tion (dĕs′ə-lā′shən) *n.* **1.** The act of making desolate. **2.** The condition of being desolate; ruin. **3.** A wasteland. **4.** Loneliness or misery; wretchedness.

de·spair (dĭ-spâr′) *n.* **1.** Utter lack of hope. **2.** Someone or something that causes great grief or torment. —*intr.v.* To lose all hope; to be overcome by a sense of futility or defeat. [Middle English *despeiren,* from Old French *desperer,* from Latin *dēspērāre.*]

des·patch (dĭ-spăch′) *v. & n.* Var. of **dispatch**.

des·per·a·do (dĕs′pə-rä′dō, -rä′) *n., pl.* **-does** or **-dos.** A desperate, dangerous criminal. [From DESPERATE.]

des·per·ate (dĕs′pər-ĭt, -prĭt) *adj.* **1.** Reckless or violent because of despair: *a desperate criminal.* **2.** Undertaken as a last resort: *desperate measures.* **3.** Nearly hopeless; critical; grave: *a desperate illness.* **4.** Extreme; very great: *in desperate need; a desperate urge.* —See Syns at **critical** and **intense**. [Latin *dēspērātus,* from *dēspērāre,* to despair.] —**des′per·ate·ly** *adv.* —**des′per·ate·ness** *n.*

des·per·a·tion (dĕs′pə-rā′shən) *n.* **1.** The condition of being desperate. **2.** Despair or recklessness arising from it.

des·pi·ca·ble (dĕs′pĭ-kə-bəl, dĭ-spĭk′ə-) *adj.* Deserving contempt or disdain; mean; vile: *a despicable person; a despicable act.* [Late Latin *dēspicābilis,* from Latin *dēspicārī,* to despise.] —**des′pi·ca·ble·ness** *n.* —**des′pi·ca·bly** *adv.*

de·spise (dĭ-spīz′) *tr.v.* **-spised, -spis·ing.** To regard with contempt or disdain. [Middle English *despisen,* from Old French *despire,* from Latin *dēspicere,* to look down on.] —**de·spis′er** *n.*

    Syns: despise, abhor, disdain, scorn *v. Core meaning:* To regard with utter contempt and disdain (*despised the idle rich*). See also Syns at **hate**.

de·spite (dĭ-spīt′) *prep.* In spite of; notwithstanding: *win despite overwhelming odds.* —*n.* **1.** Contemptuous defiance or disregard. **2.** An act of such defiance; insult; offense. —*idiom.* **in despite of.** In spite of. [Short for *in despite of,* from Middle English *despit,* spite, from Old French, from Latin *dēspicere,* to despise.]

de·spite·ful (dĭ-spīt′fəl) *adj. Archaic.* Malicious; spiteful.

de·spoil (dĭ-spoil′) *tr.v.* To deprive of possessions by force; plunder; ravage: *Bandits despoiled the town.* [Middle English *despoilen,* from Old French *despoiller,* from Latin *dēspoliāre.*] —**de·spoil′er** *n.* —**de·spoil′ment** *n.*

de·spo·li·a·tion (dĭ-spō′lē-ā′shən) *n.* The act of despoiling or the condition of being despoiled; plunder. [Late Latin *dēspoliātiō,* from Latin *dēspoliāre,* to despoil.]

de·spond (dĭ-spŏnd′) *intr.v.* To become disheartened; lose hope. [Latin *dēspondēre.*] —**de·spond′ing·ly** *adv.*

de·spon·den·cy (dĭ-spŏn′dən-sē) *n., pl.* **-cies.** Also **de·spon·dence** (-dəns). Depression of spirits from loss of hope, confidence, or courage; dejection.

de·spon·dent (dĭ-spŏn′dənt) *adj.* In low spirits; depressed; disheartened; dejected. —**de·spon′dent·ly** *adv.*

des·pot (dĕs′pət) *n.* **1.** A ruler with absolute power. **2.** A ruler or leader who wields power oppressively or tyrannically; tyrant. [Old French, from Greek *despotēs.*]

des·pot·ic (dĕs-pŏt′ĭk) *adj.* Tyrannical; authoritarian. —See Syns at **absolute**. —**des·pot′i·cal·ly** *adv.*

des·pot·ism (dĕs′pə-tĭz′əm) *n.* **1.** Rule by a despot; absolute power or authority. **2.** The actions of a despot; tyranny; oppression. **3.** A state or government so ruled.

des·sert (dĭ-zûrt′) *n.* **1.** The last course of a lunch or dinner, often consisting of fruit, ice cream, or pastry. **2.** *Brit.* Fresh fruit, nuts, or sweetmeats served after the sweet course of a dinner. —*modifier: a dessert dish.* [Old French, from *desservir,* to clear the table.]

    Usage: **dessert, desert.** *Dessert* has only the sense of last course of a meal. The noun *desert* denotes an arid region and that which is deserved: *nomads living in the desert; just deserts.*

des·ti·na·tion (dĕs′tə-nā′shən) *n.* **1.** The place or point to which someone or something is going or directed. **2.** The purpose for which anything is created or intended. **3.** An act of appointing or setting aside for a specific purpose.

des·tine (dĕs′tĭn) *tr.v.* **-tined, -tin·ing. 1.** To determine (a fate or outcome) beforehand: *a plan destined to fail.* **2.** To assign or set apart for a specific end, use, or purpose: *a trust fund destined to pay for her education.* **3.** To direct toward a given destination: *a flight destined for Tokyo.* [Middle English *destinen,* from Old French *destiner,* from Latin *dēstināre.*]

des·ti·ny (dĕs′tə-nē) *n., pl.* **-nies. 1.** The inevitable fate to which a particular person or thing is destined; one's lot; fortune. **2.** The course of events considered to be predetermined by a power or agency beyond the power or control of man.

des·ti·tute (dĕs′tĭ-tōōt′, -tyōōt′) *adj.* **1.** Altogether lacking; devoid: *destitute of experience.* **2.** Completely impoverished; penniless: *destitute villagers.* —See Syns at **poor**. [Middle English *destitut,* from Latin *dēstitūtus,* from *dēstituere,* to desert.]

des·ti·tu·tion (dĕs′tĭ-tōō′shən, -tyōō′-) *n.* **1.** Extreme poverty. **2.** Any deprivation or lack; deficiency.

de·stroy (dĭ-stroi′) *tr.v.* **1.** To ruin completely; spoil: *ancient manuscripts destroyed by fire.* **2.** To tear down or break up; demolish. **3.** To kill: *destroy a rabid dog.* **4.** To render useless or ineffective: *destroyed the prosecution's chief witness.* **5.** To subdue or defeat completely. [Middle English *destruyen,* from Old French *destruire,* from Latin *dēstruere.*]

    Syns: 1. destroy, demolish, level, raze, tear down *v. Core meaning:* To break up so that rebuilding is impossible (*destroy a condemned building*). **2. destroy, dynamite, finish, ruin, shatter, smash, total, torpedo** *v. Core meaning:* To cause the complete ruin of (*drugs that destroyed their health; news that destroyed our hopes*). See also Syns at **kill**.

de·stroy·er (dĭ-stroi′ər) *n.* **1.** Someone or something that destroys. **2.** A small, fast heavily armed warship.

destroyer escort. A warship, usu. smaller than a destroyer, used to escort merchant vessels.

destroying angel. Any of several poisonous mushrooms of the genus *Amanita.*

de·struct (dĭ-strŭkt′) *n.* The intentional destruction of a space vehicle, rocket, or missile after launching.

de·struc·ti·ble (dĭ-strŭk′tə-bəl) *adj.* Capable of being destroyed. —**de·struc′ti·bil′i·ty** *n.*

de·struc·tion (dĭ-strŭk′shən) *n.* **1.** The act of destroying. **2.** The condition or fact of being destroyed; ruin. **3.** The cause of destroying. [Middle English *destruccioun,* from Old French *destruction,* from Latin *dēstructiō,* from *dēstructus,* past part. of *dēstruere,* to destroy.]

de·struc·tive (dĭ-strŭk'tĭv) adj. 1. Causing destruction; ruinous: a destructive storm. 2. Designed or tending to disprove or discredit: destructive criticism. —**de·struc'tive·ly** adv. —**de·struc'tive·ness** n.

destructive distillation. The chemical decomposition by heat and distillation of organic substances such as wood, coal, and oil shale to produce useful by-products such as coke, charcoal, oils, and gases.

des·ue·tude (dĕs'wĭ-tōōd', -tyōōd') n. The condition of disuse: words fallen into desuetude. [French from Latin dēsuētūdō, from dēsuēscere, to put out of use.]

des·ul·to·ry (dĕs'əl-tôr'ē, -tōr'ē) adj. 1. Moving from one thing to another; disconnected: a desultory discourse. 2. Occurring haphazardly; random: desultory rifle shots. [Latin dēsultōrius, of a leaper, from dēsultor, a leaper, from dēsilīre, to leap down.] —**des'ul·to'ri·ly** adv. —**des'ul·to'ri·ness** n.

de·tach (dĭ-tăch') tr.v. 1. To separate; disconnect: detach a coupon. 2. To send (troops, ships, etc.) on a special mission. [French détacher, from Old French destachier : des-, apart + atachier, var. of estachier, to attach.] —**de·tach'a·bil'i·ty** n. —**de·tach'a·ble** adj. —**de·tach'a·bly** adv.

    Syns: detach, disconnect, disengage, uncouple, unfasten v. **Core meaning:** To separate one thing from another (detached the side panels from the truck).

de·tached (dĭ-tăcht') adj. 1. Separate from others; disconnected. 2. Free from emotional involvement.

de·tach·ment (dĭ-tăch'mənt) n. 1. The act or process of detaching; separation. 2. Absence of prejudice or bias; disinterest; impartiality. 3. The condition of remaining indifferent to worldly affairs or the concerns of others; aloofness. 4. Mil. **a.** The dispatch of troops or ships from a larger unit for a special duty. **b.** A small permanent unit organized for special duties.

de·tail (dĭ-tāl', dē'tāl') n. 1. An individual part or item: discussed every detail of the plan. 2. Items considered separately and in relation to a whole: careful attention to detail. 3. The act of dealing with things item by item: the details of a bookkeeper's ledger. 4. Mil. **a.** The selection of one or more troops for a particular duty. **b.** The personnel or duty assigned. —tr.v. (dĭ-tāl'). 1. To report or relate in detail. 2. Mil. To select and dispatch for a particular duty. [French, from Old French, piece cut off, from detailler, to cut up.]

de·tain (dĭ-tān') tr.v. 1. To keep from proceeding; to delay. 2. To keep in custody; confine. —See Syns at **arrest** and **delay.** [Middle English deteynen, from Old French detenir, from Latin dētinēre, to keep back.] —**de·tain'ment** n.

de·tect (dĭ-tĕkt') tr.v. 1. To discover the existence, presence, or fact of: detect smoke. 2. To discover the true nature of: detect the motives behind her inquiry. 3. To demodulate. [Middle English detecten, from Latin dētegere, to uncover.] —**de·tect'a·ble** or **de·tect'i·ble** adj.

de·tec·tion (dĭ-tĕk'shən) n. 1. The act of finding out or the fact of being found out; discovery. 2. Demodulation.

de·tec·tive (dĭ-tĕk'tĭv) n. A person, usu. a policeman, whose work is investigating crimes, obtaining evidence, and similar duties. —modifier: a detective story.

de·tec·tor (dĭ-tĕk'tər) n. Someone or something that detects, esp. a mechanical, electrical, or chemical device that automatically identifies and registers a stimulus.

dé·tente (dā-tänt', -tänt') n. A relaxing or easing, as of tension between nations. [French, a loosening.]

de·ten·tion (dĭ-tĕn'shən) n. 1. The act of detaining. 2. The condition of being detained. 3. A keeping in confinement, esp. a temporary custody while awaiting trial. 4. A forced or punitive delay. [Old French, from Late Latin dētentiō, from Latin dētinēre, to detain.]

de·ter (dĭ-tûr') tr.v. -terred, -ter·ring. To prevent or discourage (someone) from acting by means of fear or doubt. [Latin dēterrēre, to frighten from.] —**de·ter'ment** n.

de·ter·gent (dĭ-tûr'jənt) n. A cleansing agent, esp. a synthetic one that is chemically different from but resembles soap in its capacity to act as an emulsifier. —modifier: a detergent soap. [From Latin dētergēre, to wipe off.]

de·te·ri·o·rate (dĭ-tîr'ē-ə-rāt') v. -rat·ed, -rat·ing. —tr.v. To lower in quality, character, or value. —intr.v. To degenerate. [From Late Latin dēteriōrāre, from Latin dēterior, worse.] —**de·te'ri·o·ra'tion** n.

de·ter·mi·na·ble (dĭ-tûr'mə-nə-bəl) adj. 1. Capable of being fixed or determined. 2. Law. Liable to be terminated.

de·ter·mi·nant (dĭ-tûr'mə-nənt) n. 1. An influencing or determining factor. 2. Math. A square array of quantities, or elements, having a value determined by a rule of combination for the elements and used esp. in solving certain classes of simultaneous equations. —adj. Tending or serving to determine: determinant factors.

de·ter·mi·nate (dĭ-tûr'mə-nĭt) adj. 1. Precisely limited or defined; definite. 2. Settled; final: a determinate ruling. 3. Firm in purpose; resolute. 4. Bot. Terminating in a flower that blooms in a sequence beginning with the uppermost or central flower.

de·ter·mi·na·tion (dĭ-tûr'mə-nā'shən) n. 1. **a.** The act of making or arriving at a decision. 2. The decision arrived at. 3. Firmness of purpose; resoluteness. 4. **a.** The act of settling a dispute, suit, or other question by an authoritative decision. **b.** The decision. 5. The calculation of the extent, quality, position, or character of anything: the determination of the age of a fossil.

de·ter·mi·na·tive (dĭ-tûr'mə-nā'tĭv, -nə-tĭv) adj. Serving to determine. —n. Something that determines.

de·ter·mine (dĭ-tûr'mĭn) v. -mined, -min·ing. —tr.v. 1. To decide or settle (a dispute, question, etc.) conclusively and authoritatively: The Supreme Court will determine the constitutionality of the law. 2. To establish or ascertain definitely: polling to determine public opinion. 3. To be the cause of; decide the course of: Unemployment problems help determine economic policy. 4. To define or fix the bounds of: determine fishing limits. 5. Geom. To fix or define the position, form, or configuration of. —intr.v. To reach a decision. —See Syns at **decide** and **judge.** [Middle English determinen, from Old French determiner, from Latin dētermināre, to limit.]

de·ter·mined (dĭ-tûr'mĭnd) adj. Marked by or showing determination or fixed purpose; resolute; unwavering; firm. —**de·ter'mined·ly** adv. —**de·ter'mined·ness** n.

de·ter·min·er (dĭ-tûr'mə-nər) n. 1. Someone or something that determines. 2. Gram. A word belonging to a group of noun modifiers, gen. considered to include articles, demonstrative pronouns, demonstrative adjectives, and possessive adjectives, that occupy either the first position in a noun phrase or the second or third position after another determiner. Determiners, unlike adjectives, cannot be compared, and they do not normally appear after a linking verb. Many determiners can stand in the place of the noun phrase that they introduce.

de·ter·min·ism (dĭ-tûr'mə-nĭz'əm) n. The philosophical doctrine that every human, social, and historical act is the inevitable consequence of antecedents completely independent of the human will.

de·ter·rence (dĭ-tûr'əns, -tûr'-) n. The action or a means of deterring.

de·ter·rent (dĭ-tûr'ənt, -tûr'-) n. Someone or something that deters. —adj. Tending to deter or restrain.

de·test (dĭ-tĕst') tr.v. To dislike intensely; abhor; loathe. —See Syns at **hate.** [Latin dētestārī, to curse.]

de·test·a·ble (dĭ-tĕs'tə-bəl) adj. Deserving abhorrence; abominable. —**de·test'a·ble·ness** n. —**de·test'a·bly** adv.

de·tes·ta·tion (dē'tĕ-stā'shən) n. 1. Intense hatred or abhorrence. 2. Someone or something that is detested.

de·throne (dē-thrōn') tr.v. -throned, -thron·ing. To remove from a throne; depose. —**de·throne'ment** n.

det·o·nate (dĕt'n-āt') v. -nat·ed, -nat·ing. —tr.v. To cause to explode. —intr.v. To explode suddenly and violently. —See Syns at **explode.** [From Latin dētonāre, to thunder down.] —**det'o·na'tion** n.

det·o·na·tor (dĕt'n-ā'tər) n. A device, such as a fuse or percussion cap, used to set off explosives.

de·tour (dē'tŏŏr', dĭ-tŏŏr') n. 1. A road used temporarily instead of a main route. 2. A deviation from a direct course of action. —tr.v. To cause to go by a detour. —intr.v. To go by a roundabout way. [French, from Old French destor, from destorner, to turn away.]

de·tox·i·fy (dē-tŏk'sə-fī') tr.v. -fied, -fy·ing. To remove poison or the effects of poison from. —**de·tox'i·fi·ca'tion** n.

de·tract (dĭ-trăkt') intr.v. To take away from; diminish: Rust detracts from the car's value. —tr.v. To distract or divert: detract attention. [Middle English detracten, from

Latin *dētractus,* from *dētrahere,* to draw away.]

de·trac·tion (dĭ-trăk'shən) *n.* A lessening or belittling, esp. of the reputation of a person; slander. —**de·trac'tive** *adj.* —**de·trac'tor** *n.*

de·train (dē-trān') *tr.v.* To cause to leave a railroad train. —*intr.v.* To leave a railroad train. —**de·train'ment** *n.*

det·ri·ment (dĕt'rə-mənt) *n.* **1.** Damage, harm, or loss: *a detriment to safety.* **2.** Something that causes damage, harm, or loss. —See Syns at **harm.** [Middle English, from Old French, from Latin *dētrīmentum,* from *dēterere,* to wear away.]

det·ri·men·tal (dĕt'rə-mĕn'tl) *adj.* Causing damage, harm, or loss; injurious. —**det'ri·men'tal·ly** *adv.*

de·tri·tus (dĭ-trī'təs) *n.* **1.** Loose fragments, particles, or grains formed by the disintegration of rocks. **2.** Any disintegrated matter; debris: *the detritus of a past civilization.* [French, from Latin *dēterere,* to wear away.]

deuce[1] (dōōs, dyōōs) *n.* **1.** A playing card or side of a die bearing two spots. **2.** A cast of the dice totaling two. **3.** *Tennis.* A score in which each player or side has 40 points. [Old French *deus,* two, from Latin *duo.*]

deuce[2] (dōōs, dyōōs) *n. Informal.* Bad luck; the devil. Used as a mild oath. [Prob. from Low German *duus,* deuce.]

deuc·ed (dōō'sĭd, dyōō'-) *adj. Informal.* Darned; confounded; extreme. —**deuc'ed·ly** *adv.*

deu·te·ri·um (dōō-tîr'ē-əm, dyōō-) *n.* Symbol **D** An isotope of hydrogen having an atomic weight of 2.0141. Also called **heavy hydrogen.**

deutero– or **deuter–** or **deuto–.** A prefix meaning second or secondary: **deuterium.** [From Greek *deuteros,* second.]

deu·ter·on (dōō'tə-rŏn', dyōō'-) *n.* Symbol **d** The nucleus of a deuterium atom, a composite of a proton and a neutron. [DEUTER(IUM) + -ON.]

Deu·ter·on·o·my (dōō'tə-rŏn'ə-mē, dyōō'-) *n.* See table at **Bible.**

Deut·sche mark (doi'chə märk'). Also **deut·sche·mark.** The basic monetary unit of West Germany. [German.]

de·val·u·ate (dē-văl'yōō-āt') *tr.v.* **-at·ed, -at·ing.** Also **de·val·ue** (-yōō), **-ued, -u·ing. 1.** To lessen the value of. **2.** To lower the exchange value of (currency). —**de·val'u·a'tion** *n.*

dev·as·tate (dĕv'ə-stāt') *tr.v.* **-tat·ed, -tat·ing. 1.** To lay waste; ruin. **2.** *Informal.* To overwhelm; confound. [From Latin *dēvāstāre.*] —**dev'as·tat'ing·ly** *adv.*

dev·as·ta·tion (dĕv'ə-stā'shən) *n.* **1.** The act of devastating. **2.** The condition of being devastated; ruin; destruction.

de·vel·op (dĭ-vĕl'əp) *tr.v.* **1.** To expand or realize the potentialities of: *develop industry.* **2.** To elaborate or enlarge: *The book develops a theory she formulated earlier.* **3.** *Mus.* To unfold (a theme) with rhythmic and harmonic variations. **4.** To disclose or make known gradually. **5.** To make more available: *develop natural resources.* **6.** To convert (a tract of land) to a specific purpose, as by building extensively. **7.** To come to have gradually; acquire: *develop a taste for opera.* **8.** To become affected with; contract: *develop a disease.* **9.** *Photography.* To process (a photosensitive material) with chemicals in order to render a recorded image visible. —*intr.v.* **1.** To grow; expand: *Nations develop in a variety of ways.* **2.** To come gradually into existence or activity: *Rituals often develop over centuries.* **3.** To be disclosed. **4.** *Biol.* **a.** To progress from earlier to later stages of individual maturation. **b.** To progress from earlier to later or from simpler to more complex stages of evolution. [French *développer,* from Old French *desvelopper.*] —**de·vel'op·a·ble** *adj.*

de·vel·op·er (dĭ-vĕl'ə-pər) *n.* **1.** Someone who develops, esp. someone who builds houses on formerly unused land. **2.** *Photography.* A chemical used to render visible the image recorded on a photosensitive surface.

de·vel·op·ment (dĭ-vĕl'əp-mənt) *n.* **1.** The act or process of developing. **2.** A developed state or form: *His development as a concert pianist is far from complete.* **3.** A product or result of developing: *industrial development.* **4.** An event, occurrence, or happening: *a development in the war.* **5.** A group of dwellings or other buildings, usu. built by the same contractor. —**de·vel'op·men'tal** (-vĕl'əp-mĕn'tl) *adj.* —**de·vel'op·men'tal·ly** *adv.*

de·vi·ant (dē'vē-ənt) *n.* A person whose behavior differs from accepted social or moral standards. —*adj.* Differing

from a norm or from the accepted standards of society: *deviant behavior.* —**de'vi·ance** *n.*

de·vi·ate (dē'vē-āt') *v.* **-at·ed, -at·ing.** —*intr.v.* To differ or move away from an established course or prescribed mode of behavior: *methods that deviate from conventional diplomacy.* —*tr.v.* To cause to turn aside or differ. —*n.* (dē'vē-ĭt). A deviant. [From Late Latin *dēviāre.*]

de·vi·a·tion (dē'vē-ā'shən) *n.* **1.** The act of deviating or turning aside. **2.** The amount by which something has deviated: *a deviation of 20 per cent.*

de·vice (dĭ-vīs') *n.* **1.** Something devised for a particular purpose, esp. a machine. **2.** An artistic contrivance in a literary work used to achieve a particular effect: *the traditional device of mistaken identity.* **3.** A plan or scheme; trick. **4.** A graphic symbol or motto, esp. in heraldry. [Middle English *devise,* from Old French *devis,* contrivance, and *devise,* design, both from *deviser,* to divide.]

dev·il (dĕv'əl) *n.* **1.** Often **Devil.** The major spirit of evil, ruler of Hell, and foe of God; Satan. **2.** Any subordinate evil spirit. **3.** A wicked, cruel, or ill-tempered person. **4.** An unfortunate or pitiful person; wretch: *poor devil.* **5.** A person who is energetic, mischievous, daring, or clever. —*tr.v.* **-iled** or **-illed, -il·ing** or **-il·ling. 1.** To prepare (food) with pungent seasoning or condiments. **2.** To annoy, torment, or harass. [Middle English *devel,* from Old English *dēofol,* from Late Latin *diabolus,* from Greek *diabolos,* slanderer.]

dev·il·fish (dĕv'əl-fĭsh') *n., pl.* **devilfish** or **-fish·es. 1.** The manta. **2.** An octopus, or a similar cephalopod.

dev·il·ish (dĕv'ə-lĭsh) *adj.* **1.** Of or characteristic of a devil; fiendish. **2.** Mischievous or playful. **3.** *Informal.* Excessive; extreme: *devilish heat.* —*adv. Informal.* Extremely; very. —**dev'il·ish·ly** *adv.* —**dev'il·ish·ness** *n.*

devil's advocate. 1. *Rom. Cath. Ch.* An official appointed to present arguments against a proposed canonization or beatification. **2.** A person who supports an issue or position with which he or she does not necessarily agree, as to determine its validity or for the sake of argument. **3.** An adverse critic, esp. of a good cause.

dev·il's-food cake (dĕv'əlz-fōōd'). A rich chocolate cake.

dev·il·try (dĕv'əl-trē) *n., pl.* **-tries. 1.** Wanton or reckless mischief. **2.** Wickedness. **3.** Evil magic.

de·vi·ous (dē'vē-əs) *adj.* **1.** Deviating from the straight or direct course. **2.** Done or acting in an underhand manner; not straightforward. [Latin *dēvius,* off the main road.] —**de'vi·ous·ly** *adv.* —**de'vi·ous·ness** *n.*

de·vise (dĭ-vīz') *tr.v.* **-vised, -vis·ing. 1.** To form or arrange in the mind; contrive: *devise an escape plan.* **2.** *Law.* To transmit or give (real property) by will. —*n.* **1.** The act of transmitting or giving real property by will. **2.** A will or clause in a will devising real property. [Middle English *devisen,* to divide, from Old French *deviser,* from Latin *dīvidere.*] —**de·vis'a·ble** *adj.* —**de·vis'er** *n.*

de·vi·tal·ize (dē-vīt'l-īz') *tr.v.* **-ized, -iz·ing.** To lower or destroy the life or vitality of.

de·void (dĭ-void') *adj.* Completely lacking; destitute: *a novel devoid of wit.* [Middle English *devoide,* from *devoiden,* to get rid of, from Old French *desvuidier.*]

dev·o·lu·tion (dĕv'ə-lōō'shən) *n.* **1.** A passing down through successive stages. **2.** The passing to a successor of anything, such as properties, rights, titles, and qualities. **3.** *Biol.* Degeneration to a lower or simpler form. [Medieval Latin *dēvolūtiō,* from Latin *dēvolvere,* to roll down.] —**dev'o·lu'tion·ar'y** (-shə-nĕr'ē) *adj.*

de·volve (dĭ-vŏlv') *v.* **-volved, -volv·ing.** —*tr.v.* To pass on or delegate (as authority) to a successor or substitute. —*intr.v.* To be passed on to a substitute or successor; be conferred. [Middle English *devolven,* from Latin *dēvolvere,* to roll down.]

Dev·on (dĕv'ən) *n.* Any of a breed of reddish cattle developed in Devonshire, England, and raised for beef.

De·vo·ni·an (dĭ-vō'nē-ən) *n.* Also **Devonian period.** A geologic period that began 405 million years ago and ended 345 million years ago, characterized by the appearance of forests and amphibians. [After Devon, England.]

de·vote (dĭ-vōt') *tr.v.* **-vot·ed, -vot·ing. 1.** To give or apply entirely to a particular activity, pursuit, cause, or person: *devoted his life to politics.* **2.** To set apart by or as if by a vow or solemn act. **3.** To set apart for a specific purpose or

---

ă pat	ā pay	â care	ä father	ĕ pet	ē be	hw which	ĭ pit	ī tie	î pier	ŏ pot	ō toe	ô paw, for	oi noise
ōō took	ōō boot	ou out	th thin	*th* this	ŭ cut	û urge	zh vision	ə about, item, edible, gallop, circus

use. [From Latin *dēvovēre*, to vow.]

Syns: devote, consecrate, dedicate *v. Core meaning:* To give over by or as if by a vow to a higher purpose (*a nurse who devoted her life to healing the sick*).

de·vot·ed (dĭ-vō'tĭd) *adj.* **1.** Loving; affectionate: *A devoted father.* **2.** Dedicated to a purpose; ardent: *a devoted nurse.* **—de·vot'ed·ly** *adv.* **—de·vot'ed·ness** *n.*

dev·o·tee (dĕv'ə-tē', -tā') *n.* **1.** A zealous follower or enthusiast: *a devotee of sports.* **2.** An ardent or fanatic adherent of a religion; zealot.

de·vo·tion (dĭ-vō'shən) *n.* **1.** Ardent attachment or affection. **2.** Religious ardor; piety. **3.** Often **devotions.** An act of religious observance, esp. when private. **4.** The act of devoting or the condition of being devoted.

de·vo·tion·al (dĭ-vō'shə-nəl) *adj.* **1.** Of or pertaining to religious devotion. **2.** Used in worship. *—n.* A short service of worship. **—de·vo'tion·al·ly** *adv.*

de·vour (dĭ-vour') *tr.v.* **1.** To eat up greedily. **2.** To destroy, consume, or waste: *Fire devoured the forest.* **3.** To take in eagerly: *devour a novel.* **4.** To swallow up; engulf: *We were devoured by the crowd.* —See Syns at **waste.** [Middle English *devouren,* from Old French *devourer,* from Latin *dēvorāre.*] **—de·vour'er** *n.* **—de·vour'ing·ly** *adv.*

de·vout (dĭ-vout') *adj.* **1.** Deeply religious; pious. **2.** Displaying reverence or piety. **3.** Sincere; earnest: *a devout wish for her success.* [Middle English, from Old French *devout,* from Late Latin *dēvōtus,* from Latin *dēvovēre,* to vow.] **—de·vout'ly** *adv.* **—de·vout'ness** *n.*

dew (dōo, dyōo) *n.* **1.** Water droplets condensed from the air, usu. at night, onto cool surfaces. **2.** Anything moist, refreshing, or pure. **3.** Any moisture appearing in small drops. *—tr.v.* To wet with or as with dew. [Middle English *deu,* from Old English *dēaw.*]

dew·ber·ry (dōo'bĕr'ē, dyōo'-) *n.* **1.** Any of several trailing forms of the blackberry of the genus *Rubus.* **2.** The edible fruit of any of these plants.

dew·claw (dōo'klô', dyōo'-) *n.* A vestigial digit, claw, or hoof on the foot of certain mammals.

dew·drop (dōo'drŏp', dyōo'-) *n.* A drop of dew.

Dew·ey decimal system (dōo'ē, dyōo'ē). A system used in libraries of classification of books and other publications into ten categories. [Devised in 1876 by Melvis *Dewey* (1851-1931), American librarian.]

dew·fall (dōo'fôl', dyōo'-) *n.* **1.** The formation of dew. **2.** The time of evening when dew begins to form.

dew·lap (dōo'lăp', dyōo'-) *n.* **1.** A fold of loose skin hanging from the neck of certain animals. **2.** Any similar part, such as the wattle of a bird or a fold of skin hanging from the throat of an aged person. [Middle English *dewlappe.*]

dewlap

dhow

dew point. The temperature at which air becomes saturated and produces dew.

dew·y (dōo'ē, dyōo'ē) *adj.* **-i·er, -i·est. 1.** Moist with dew. **2.** Of or resembling dew. **3.** *Poet.* Suggestive of dew; refreshing; pure. **—dew'i·ly** *adv.* **—dew'i·ness** *n.*

dex·ter (dĕk'stər) *adj.* **1.** Of or located on the right side. **2.** *Heraldry.* Located on the wearer's right and the observer's left. [Latin, on the right side.]

dex·ter·i·ty (dĕk-stĕr'ĭ-tē) *n.* **1.** Skill in the use of the hands or body; adroitness. **2.** Mental skill or cleverness.

dex·ter·ous (dĕk'strəs) *adj.* Also **dex·trous. 1.** Adroit or skillful in the use of the hands or mind. **2.** Done with dexterity. **—dex'ter·ous·ly** *adv.* **—dex'ter·ous·ness** *n.*

dextr-. Var. of **dextro-.**

dex·tral (dĕk'strəl) *adj.* **1.** On the right side; right. **2.** Right-handed. **—dex·tral'i·ty** *n.* **—dex'tral·ly** *adv.*

dex·trin (dĕk'strĭn) *n.* Also **dex·trine** (dĕk'strĭn, -strēn'). A powder formed by the hydrolysis of starch, having colloidal properties, and used mainly as an adhesive.

dextro- or **dextr-.** *Abbr.* **d 1.** A prefix meaning on or toward the right-hand side: **dextral. 2.** Turning the plane of the polarization to the right: **dextrose.** [Latin, from *dexter,* on the right side.]

dex·trose (dĕk'strōs') *n.* A colorless sugar, $C_6H_{12}O_6 \cdot H_2O$, found in animal and plant tissue and also made synthetically from starch. Also called **corn sugar, grape sugar,** and **glucose.** [DEXTR(O)- + -OSE.]

dex·trous (dĕk'strəs) *adj.* Var. of **dexterous.**

dey (dā) *n.* Formerly, a title held by a ruler of Tunis or Tripoli. [French, from Turkish *dayi,* maternal uncle.]

dhar·ma (dûr'mə, där'-) *n. Hinduism & Buddhism.* **1.** The ultimate law of all things. **2.** Individual right conduct in conformity to this law. [Sanskrit, law.]

dhow (dou) *n.* A usu. lateen-rigged, single-masted Arabian vessel. [Arabic *dāw.*]

Di The symbol for the element didymium.

di-. A prefix meaning: **1.** Twice, double, or two: **dicotyledon. 2.** Having two atoms, molecules, or radicals: **dichloride.** [From Greek *di-,* two, twice.]

di·a·be·tes (dī'ə-bē'tĭs, -tēz) *n.* Any of several metabolic disorders marked by excessive discharge of urine, esp. one in which too little insulin is produced in the pancreas, resulting in an abnormally high level of sugar in the blood and urine. Also called **diabetes mel·li·tus** (mə-lī'təs). [Middle English *diabete,* from Medieval Latin *diabētēs,* from Greek, from *diabainein,* to go through.]

di·a·bet·ic (dī'ə-bĕt'ĭk) *adj.* Of, relating to, or having diabetes. *—n.* A person afflicted with diabetes.

di·a·bol·ic (dī'ə-bŏl'ĭk) or **di·a·bol·i·cal** (-ĭ-kəl) *adj.* Of or characteristic of the devil; satanic; fiendish; hellish. [Middle English *deabolik,* from Old French *diabolique,* from Late Latin *diabolicus,* from *diabolus,* devil.] **—di'a·bol'i·cal·ly** *adv.* **—di'a·bol'i·cal·ness** *n.*

di·ac·o·nate (dī-ăk'ə-nĭt, -nāt') *n.* **1.** The rank or office of a deacon. **2.** Deacons. [From Late Latin *diāconus,* deacon.]

di·a·crit·ic (dī'ə-krĭt'ĭk) *n.* A diacritical mark.

di·a·crit·i·cal (dī'ə-krĭt'ĭ-kəl) *adj.* Marking a distinction. [Greek *diakritikos,* distinguishing.] **—di'a·crit'i·cal·ly** *adv.*

diacritical mark. A mark added to a letter to indicate a certain feature of pronunciation. For example, in French *façon,* the cedilla indicates that the *c* does not have its regular value (k), but a sibilant value (s).

di·a·dem (dī'ə-dĕm') *n.* **1.** A crown or headband worn as a sign of royalty. **2.** Royal power or dignity. [Middle English *diademe,* from Old French, from Latin *diadēma,* from Greek *diadein,* to bind on either side.]

di·aer·e·sis (dī-ĕr'ĭ-sĭs) *n.* Var. of **dieresis.**

di·ag·nose (dī'əg-nōs', -nōz') *v.* **-nosed, -nos·ing.** *—tr.v.* To identify by diagnosis, as a disease or problem. *—intr.v.* To make a diagnosis.

di·ag·no·sis (dī'əg-nō'sĭs) *n., pl.* **-ses** (-sēz'). **1.** *Med.* **a.** The act or process of identifying a disease through examination. **b.** The conclusion reached from such an examination. **2. a.** A critical analysis of the nature of something. **b.** The conclusion reached by such analysis. **3.** *Biol.* A precise and detailed description for taxonomic classification. [From Greek discernment.] **—di'ag·nos'tic** (-nŏs'tĭk) *adj.* **—di'ag·nos'ti·cal·ly** *adv.* **—di'ag·nos·ti'cian** (-stĭsh'ən) *n.*

di·ag·o·nal (dī-ăg'ə-nəl) *adj. Abbr.* **diag. 1.** *Geom.* **a.** Joining two vertices of a polygon that are not adjacent. **b.** Joining two vertices of a polyhedron that are not in the same face. **2.** Having a slanted or oblique direction. **3.** Having oblique lines or markings: *a diagonal weave.* *—n. Abbr.* **diag. 1.** *Geom.* A diagonal line or plane. **2.** Anything arranged obliquely, such as a row, course, or part. **3.** A fabric woven with diagonal lines. [Latin *diagōnālis,* from Greek *diagōnios,* from angle.] **—di·ag'o·nal·ly** *adv.*

di·a·gram (dī'ə-grăm') *n.* **1.** A plan, sketch, drawing, or outline designed to demonstrate or explain how something works or to clarify the relationship between the parts of a whole. **2.** *Math.* A graphic representation of an algebraic or geometric relationship. *—tr.v.* **-grammed** or **-gramed,**

-gram·ming or **-gram·ing.** To indicate or represent by or as if by a diagram: *diagram a football play; diagram a sentence.* [Latin *diagramma*, from Greek, from *diagraphein*, to delineate.] —**di·a·gram·mat·ic** (-grə-măt′ĭk) or **di·a·gram·mat′i·cal** (-ĭ-kəl) *adj.* —**di·a·gram·mat′i·cal·ly** *adv.*

di·al (dī′əl) *n.* **1.** A graduated, usu. circular figure, such as the face of a clock, with a scale of measure arranged along its circumference and one or more movable pointers that indicate the measure that is to be read from the scale. **2.** A movable control knob or other device on a receiver that selects a setting on a television or radio station. **3.** A movable wheel mounted over a circular scale of numbers and letters and used to signal the number to which a telephone call is made. **4.** A sundial. —*v.* **-aled** or **-alled**, **-al·ing** or **-al·ling.** —*tr.v.* **1.** To control or select by means of a dial. **2.** To use a dial. **3.** To point to, indicate, or register by means of a dial. —*intr.v.* To use a dial. [Middle English *diall*, from Medieval Latin *diāle*, from *diālis*, daily, from Latin *diēs*, day.]

di·a·lect (dī′ə-lĕkt′) *n.* **1.** A regional variety of a language, distinguished by pronunciation, grammar, or vocabulary: *Cockney is a dialect of English.* **2.** The language peculiar to an occupational group or a particular social class; jargon: *a scientific dialect.* **3.** A language considered as part of a larger family: *Mandarin is a dialect of Chinese.* —See Syns at **language.** [French *dialecte*, from Latin *dialectus*, from Greek *dialektos*, speech.] —**di·a·lec′tal** *adj.*

di·a·lec·tic (dī′ə-lĕk′tĭk) *n.* **1.** Also **dialectics.** A method of logical argument in which contradictory facts or ideas are systematically examined or debated for the purpose of resolving the contradictions between them and arriving at some truth. **2.** Any logical argumentation. [Middle English *dialetik*, from Old French *dialetique*, from Latin *dialectica*, from Greek *dialektikē* (*tekhnē*), (the art) of debate.] —**di·a·lec′ti·cal** or **di·a·lec′tic** *adj.* —**di·a·lec·ti′cian** (-lĕk-tĭsh′ən) *n.*

dialectical materialism. The theory of reality formulated by Karl Marx, that views matter as the sole subject of change and all change as the product of a constant conflict between forces in events, ideas, and movements.

di·a·lec·tol·o·gy (dī′ə-lĕk-tŏl′ə-jē) *n.* The study of dialects. —**di·a·lec′to·log′i·cal** (-tə-lŏj′ĭ-kəl) *adj.* —**di·a·lec·tol′o·gist** *n.*

di·a·logue or **di·a·log** (dī′ə-lôg′, -lŏg′) *n.* **1.** A conversation between two or more people. **2.** A conversational passage in a play or narrative. **3.** A literary work written in the form of a conversation: *the dialogues of Plato.* **4.** An exchange of ideas or opinions; discussion. [Middle English, from Old French, from Latin *dialogus*, from Greek *dialogos*, from *dialegesthai*, to converse.]

di·al·y·sis (dī-ăl′ĭ-sĭs) *n.*, *pl.* **-ses** (-sēz′). The separation of smaller molecules from larger molecules, or of crystalloid particles from colloidal particles, in a solution by using a semipermeable membrane. [From Greek *dialusis*, from *dialuein*, to tear apart.] —**di·a·lyt′ic** (dī′ə-lĭt′ĭk) *adj.*

di·a·lyze (dī′ə-līz′) *v.* **-lyzed**, **-lyz·ing.** —*tr.v.* To subject to dialysis. —*intr.v.* To undergo dialysis.

di·a·mag·net·ic (dī′ə-măg-nĕt′ĭk) *adj.* Of or pertaining to a substance in which the magnetic field is in the opposite direction to and weaker than the magnetizing field. [From Greek *dia-*, in different directions + MAGNETIC.] —**di′a·mag′net·ism** (-nə-tĭz′əm) *n.*

di·am·e·ter (dī-ăm′ĭ-tər) *n.* **1.** *Math.* **a.** A straight line segment passing through the center of a figure, esp. of a circle or sphere. **2.** The length of such a segment. **3.** The thickness or width of anything. [Middle English *diametre*, from Old French, from Latin *diametros*, from Greek *diametros* (*grammē*), "(line) that measures through."]

di·a·met·ri·cal (dī′ə-mĕt′rĭ-kəl) *adj.* **1.** Of, pertaining to, or along a diameter. **2.** Also **di·a·met·ric** (-rĭk). Exactly opposite; contrary: *diametric views.* —**di′a·met′ri·cal·ly** (-rĭk-lē, -rĭk-ə-lē) *adv.*

dia·mond (dī′mənd, dī′ə-) *n.* **1.** An extremely hard, colorless or white crystalline form of carbon, the hardest of all known substances, used as a gemstone when pure with lesser varieties used in cutting tools and as abrasives. **2.** A figure with four equal sides forming two inner obtuse angles and two inner acute angles; a rhombus. **3. a.** A red, lozenge-shaped figure on certain playing cards. **b.** A playing card with this figure. **c. diamonds.** The suit of cards

represented by this figure. **4.** *Baseball.* **a.** The infield. **b.** The whole playing field. —*modifier:* a diamond ring. [Middle English *diamaunt*, from Old French *diamant*, from Late Latin *diamas*, from Latin *adamas*, from Greek.]

dia·mond·back (dī′mənd-băk′, dī′ə-) *n.* **1.** Any of several large, venomous rattlesnakes of the genus *Crotalus*, of the southern and western United States and Mexico. **2.** Any of several edible turtles of the genus *Malaclemys*, of the southern Atlantic and Gulf coasts of the United States, with roughly diamond-shaped, ridged markings on its shell. Also called **diamondback terrapin.**

diamondback   Diana

Di·an·a (dī-ăn′ə) *n. Rom. Myth.* The goddess of chastity, hunting, and the moon, identified with the Greek goddess Artemis.

di·a·pa·son (dī′ə-pā′zən, -sən) *n.* **1.** A full, rich outpouring of harmonious sound. **2.** Either of the two principal stops on a pipe organ. **3.** The entire range of any instrument or voice. **4.** A standard indication of musical pitch. [Middle English *dyapason*, from Latin *diapāsōn*, from Greek *dia pasōn*, through all (the notes).]

di·a·per (dī′ə-pər, dī′pər) *n.* **1.** A piece of cloth or other absorbent material, folded and pinned around a baby to serve as underpants. **2. a.** A regularly repeated pattern of small diamonds or other geometric figures. **b.** A piece of such cloth with such a pattern woven in it. —*tr.v.* **1.** To put a diaper on (a baby). **2.** To weave or decorate in a diamond-shaped pattern. [Middle English *diapre*, linen cloth with diamond pattern, from Old French, from Medieval Latin *diasprum*, from Medieval Greek *diaspros*, made of diaper, pure white.]

di·aph·a·nous (dī-ăf′ə-nəs) *adj.* **1.** Of such fine texture as to be translucent. **2.** Characterized by delicacy of form. [Medieval Latin *diaphanus*, from Greek *diaphanēs*, from *diaphainein*, to show through.] —**di′a·pha·ne′i·ty** (dī′-ə-fə-nē′ĭ-tē) or **di·aph′a·nous·ness** *n.* —**di·aph′a·nous·ly** *adv.*

di·a·pho·re·sis (dī′ə-fə-rē′sĭs) *n.* Copious perspiration, esp. when medically induced. [Late Latin *diaphorēsis*, from Greek, from *diaphorein*, to dissipate.] —**di′a·pho·ret′ic** (-rĕt′ĭk) *adj. & n.*

di·a·phragm (dī′ə-frăm′) *n.* **1.** *Anat.* A muscular membrane that separates the organs of the chest from those of the abdomen and acts in forcing air into and out of the lungs. **2.** Any similar membrane that divides or separates. **3.** A thin disk, as in a microphone, whose vibrations convert electric signals to sound waves or sound waves to electric signals. **4.** A contraceptive device consisting of a flexible disk that covers the uterine cervix. **5.** *Optics.* A disk used to restrict the amount of light that passes through a lens or optical system. [Middle English *diafragma*, from Late Latin *diaphragma*, from Greek, from *diaphrassein*, to barricade.] —**di′a·phrag·mat′ic** (dī′ə-frăg-măt′ĭk) *adj.*

di·a·rist (dī′ə-rĭst) *n.* A person who keeps a diary.

di·ar·rhe·a or **di·ar·rhoe·a** (dī′ə-rē′ə) *n.* A condition in which bowel movements are abnormally frequent. [Middle English *diaria*, from Late Latin *diarrhœa*, from Greek *diarrhoia*, "a flowing through."] —**di′ar·rhet′ic** (-rĕt′ĭk) *adj.*

di·a·ry (dī′ə-rē) *n.*, *pl.* **-ries.** **1.** A daily record, esp. a personal record of events, experiences, and observations. **2.** A book for keeping such a record; journal. [Latin *diārium*, daily allowance, journal, from *diēs*, day.]

Di·as·po·ra (dī-ăs′pər-ə) *n.* **1.** The body of Jews living dispersed among the Gentiles after the Babylonian captivity. **2. the diaspora.** The body of Jews or Jewish communities outside of Palestine or modern Israel. **3.** Often **diaspora.** A dispersion of any homogeneous people outside of their homeland. [Greek, "dispersion."]

di·a·stase (dī′ə-stās′) *n.* An amylase or a mixture of amylases found in certain germinating grains such as malt. [French, from Greek *diastasis,* separation.]

di·as·to·le (dī-ăs′tə-lē) *n. Physiol.* The normal rhythmically occurring relaxation and dilatation of the heart cavities during which the cavities fill with blood. [Greek *diastolē,* dilatation, separation.] —**di′a·stol′ic** (dī′ə-stŏl′ĭk) *adj.*

di·a·ther·my (dī′ə-thûr′mē) *n.* The therapeutic generation of local heat in body tissues by high-frequency electromagnetic waves. [Greek *dia-,* across + *thermē,* heat.]

di·a·tom (dī′ə-tŏm′, -təm) *n.* Any of various minute, single-celled or colonial algae of the class Bacillariophyceae, with cell walls consisting mainly of silica. [From Greek *diatomē,* cut in half.]

di·a·to·ma·ceous (dī′ə-tə-mā′shəs) *adj.* Consisting of diatoms or their skeletal remains: *diatomaceous earth.*

di·a·tom·ic (dī′ə-tŏm′ĭk) *adj.* **1.** Made up of two atoms in a molecule. **2.** Having two replaceable atoms or radicals.

di·a·ton·ic (dī′ə-tŏn′ĭk) *adj. Mus.* Of or using the eight tones of a standard major or minor scale without chromatic variations. [Old French *diatonique,* from Late Latin *diatonicus,* from Greek *diatonos,* "at the interval of a tone."] —**di′a·ton′i·cal·ly** *adv.* —**di′a·ton′i·cism** (-ĭ-sĭz′əm) *n.*

di·a·tribe (dī′ə-trīb′) *n.* A bitter and abusive criticism or denunciation; invective. [Latin *diatriba,* learned discourse, from Greek *diatribē,* "a wearing away."]

di·ba·sic (dī-bā′sĭk) *adj.* **1.** Containing two replaceable hydrogen atoms. **2.** Designating salts, or acids forming salts, with two atoms of a univalent metal.

dib·ble (dĭb′əl) *n.* A pointed implement used to make holes in soil, esp. for planting bulbs or seedlings. —*tr.v.* **-bled, -bling. 1.** To make holes in (soil) with a dibble. **2.** To plant by means of a dibble. [Middle English *debylle.*]

dice (dīs) *pl.n. Sing.* **die** (dī). **1.** Small cubes of ivory, bone, or plastic, marked on each side with a number of small dots, varying from one to six, and used in games of chance. **2.** *(used with a sing. verb)* Any game of chance that uses dice. —*v.* **diced, dic·ing.** —*intr.v.* To play or gamble with dice. —*tr.v.* **1.** To lose (money) by gambling with dice. **2.** To cut (food) into cubes. **3.** To decorate with dicelike figures. [Pl. of DIE.]

di·chlo·ride (dī-klôr′īd′, -klōr′-) *n.* A binary chemical compound containing two chlorine atoms per molecule. Also called **bichloride.**

di·chlo·ro·di·phen·yl·tri·chlo·ro·eth·ane (dī-klôr′ō-dī-fĕn′əl-trī-klôr′ō-ĕth′ān′, -klōr′-) *n.* DDT.

di·chot·o·mous (dī-kŏt′ə-məs) *adj.* **1.** Divided or dividing into two parts or classifications. **2.** Characterized by dichotomy. —**di·chot′o·mous·ly** *adv.*

di·chot·o·my (dī-kŏt′ə-mē) *n., pl.* **-mies. 1.** Division into two usu. contradictory parts or opinions. **2.** *Logic.* The division or subdivision of a class into two mutually exclusive groups. **3.** *Bot.* Branching characterized by successive forking into two approx. equal divisions. [Greek *dikhotomia,* from *dikhotomos,* divided.]

di·chro·mate (dī-krō′māt′) *n.* A chromate with two chromium atoms in the molecule. Also called **bichromate.**

di·chro·mat·ic (dī′krō-măt′ĭk) *adj.* **1.** Having or showing two colors. **2.** *Zool.* Having two distinct color phases in the adult, as certain species of birds.

dick·cis·sel (dĭk-sĭs′əl, dĭk′sĭs′-) *n.* A small finch, *Spiza americana,* of central North America, of which the male has a yellow breast marked with black. [Imit. of its note.]

dick·ens (dĭk′ənz) *interj.* Devil; deuce. Used as an oath.

Dick·en·si·an (dĭ-kĕn′zē-ən) *adj.* Of or characteristic of Charles Dickens, his novels, characters, or literary style.

dick·er (dĭk′ər) *intr.v.* To bargain; barter. —*tr.v.* To trade or exchange. [Orig. unknown.]

dick·ey (dĭk′ē) *n., pl.* **-eys.** Also **dick·y** *pl.* **-ies. 1.** A separate shirt front like a bib, often with a collar, worn under a jacket, sweater, etc. **2.** A shirt collar. **3.** A bib. **4.** A donkey. **5.** Any small bird. [From *Dick,* nickname for *Richard.*]

Dick test (dĭk). A test of a person's susceptibility to scarlet fever. [After George Frederick *Dick* (1881–1967), American physician.]

dick·y (dĭk′ē) *n.* Var. of **dickey.**

di·cli·nous (dī-klī′nəs) *adj. Bot.* Having stamens and pistils in separate flowers. [DI- (two) + Greek *klinē,* bed.]

di·cot·y·le·don (dī-kŏt′l-ēd′n) *n. Bot.* Any plant of the subclass Dicotyledonae, one of the two major divisions of angiosperms (flowering plants), characterized by a pair of embryonic seed leaves (cotyledons) that appear at germination. Also called **diocot.** —**di·cot′y·le′don·ous** (-ēd′n-əs) *adj.*

dic·ta (kĭk′tə) *n.* A plural of **dictum.**

Dic·ta·phone (dĭk′tə-fōn′) *n.* A trademark for a small machine that records and reproduces dictation for typing.

dic·tate (dĭk′tāt′, dĭk-tāt′) *v.* **-tat·ed, -tat·ing.** —*tr.v.* **1.** To say or read aloud (something) to be recorded or written by another. **2.** To prescribe with authority; impose; require: *dictate peace terms.* —*intr.v.* **1.** To say or read aloud material to be recorded by another. **2.** To issue orders or commands. —*n.* (dĭk′tāt′). An order; directive. [From Latin *dictāre,* freq. of *dīcere,* to say, tell.]

dic·ta·tion (dĭk-tā′shən) *n.* **1.** The act of dictating material to another to be written down. **2.** The material dictated.

dic·ta·tor (dĭk′tā′tər, dĭk-tā′-) *n.* **1.** A ruler who has complete authority and unlimited power, esp. a tyrant. **2.** A person who dictates. **3.** In ancient Rome, a magistrate appointed temporarily to deal with an immediate crisis or emergency.

dic·ta·to·ri·al (dĭk′tə-tôr′ē-əl, -tōr-) *adj.* Of, pertaining to, or characteristic of a dictator or dictatorship; autocratic. —**dic·ta·to′ri·al·ly** *adv.* —**dic′ta·to′ri·al·ness** *n.*

Syns: dictatorial, bossy, dogmatic, imperious, masterful, overbearing *adj.* **Core meaning:** Tending to assert authority and control over others (*a dictatorial store manager*). See also Syns at **absolute.**

dic·ta·tor·ship (dĭk-tā′tər-shĭp′, dĭk′tā′-) *n.* **1.** The position or rule of a dictator. **2. a.** A form of government in which one person or class has complete authority and unlimited power. **b.** A country having such a government.

dic·tion (dĭk′shən) *n.* **1.** The choice and use of words in speaking or writing. **2.** The quality of speech or singing judged by clarity and distinctness of pronunciation. [Latin *dictiō,* to say.]

dic·tion·ar·y (dĭk′shə-nĕr′ē; *Brit.* dĭk′shə-nə-rē) *n., pl.* **-ies. 1.** A book containing an alphabetical list of words with information given for each word, including meaning, pronunciation, etymology, usage, and synonyms. **2.** A similar book limited to one category of words: *a medical dictionary.* **3.** A book containing an alphabetical list of words translated into another language: *A Russian-English dictionary.*

dic·tum (dĭk′təm) *n., pl.* **-ta** (tə) or **-tums. 1.** An authoritative pronouncement. **2.** A popular saying; a maxim. [Latin, from *dīcere,* to say.]

did (dĭd) *v.* Past tense of **do.**

di·dac·tic (dī-dăk′tĭk) or **di·dac·ti·cal** (-tĭ-kəl) *adj.* **1.** Intended to instruct or teach: *a didactic story.* **2.** Morally instructive. **3.** Inclined to moralize excessively. [Greek *didaktikos,* skillful in teaching, from *didaskein,* to teach.] —**di·dac′ti·cal·ly** *adv.* —**di·dac′ti·cism** (-tĭ-sĭz′əm) *n.*

di·dac·tics (dī-dăk′tĭks) *n. (used with a sing. verb).* The art or science of teaching or instruction; pedagogy.

did·n't (dĭd′nt). Contraction of did not.

di·do (dī′dō) *n., pl.* **-dos** or **-does.** *Informal.* A mischievous prank or antic; caper. [Orig. unknown.]

Di·do (dī′dō) *n. Rom. Myth.* Queen of Carthage.

didst (dĭdst) *v. Archaic.* Past tense of **do,** used with *thou.*

die¹ (dī) *intr.v.* **died, dy·ing. 1.** To cease living. **2.** To lose force or vitality: *The noise died down.* **3.** To cease existing; become extinct: *Old ideas die hard.* **4.** *Informal.* To desire greatly: *I'm dying to go.* [Middle English *d(e)ien,* from Old Norse *deyja.*]

Syns: die, croak (*Slang*), **decease, demise, depart, expire, go, pass away, perish, succumb** *v.* **Core meaning:** To become dead (*died young*).

die² (dī) *n.* **1.** *pl.* **dies.** Any one of several types of machine parts or devices that shape materials that are being worked, gen. by stamping, cutting or punching. **2.** *pl.* **dice**

(dīs). **a.** One of a pair of dice. **b.** Any small block or cube. [Middle English *dee*, from Old French *de*, ult. from Latin *dare*, to give.]

di·e·cious (dī-ē′shəs) *adj.* Var. of **dioecious.**

die-hard (dī′härd′) *n.* Also **die-hard.** A person who stubbornly refuses to abandon a position or resists change.

di·e·lec·tric (dī′ĭ-lĕk′trĭk) *n.* A nonconductor of direct current. —*adj.* Of, like, or characteristic of a dielectric. [From Greek *dia-*, through + ELECTRIC.] —**di′e·lec′tri·cal·ly** *adv.*

di·er·e·sis (dī-ĕr′ĭ-sĭs) *n., pl.* **-ses** (-sēz′). Also **di·aer·e·sis.** A mark (¨) placed over the second of two adjacent vowels to indicate that it is pronounced in a separate syllable. [Late Latin *diaeresis*, from Greek *diairesis*, separation.]

die·sel (dē′zəl, -səl) *n.* A vehicle powered by a diesel engine.

diesel engine or **Diesel engine.** An internal-combustion engine in which the fuel is sprayed directly into the cylinder and ignited by the heat of air that has been highly compressed by the piston. [After Rudolf *Diesel* (1858–1913), German mechanical engineer, its inventor.]

Di·es I·rae (dē′ās ē′rā′). A medieval Latin hymn describing the Day of Judgment, used in some Masses for the dead. [Latin, "day of wrath."]

di·et[1] (dī′ĭt) *n.* **1.** The usual food and drink consumed by a person or animal. **2.** A regulated selection of foods, often prescribed for medical reasons. **3.** Anything taken or provided regularly: *a diet of detective novels.* —*intr.v.* To eat and drink a prescribed selection of foods. [Middle English *diete*, from Old French, from Latin *diaeta*, from Greek *diaita*, mode of life.] —**di′et·er** *n.*

di·et[2] (dī′ĭt) *n.* **1.** A deliberative assembly; legislature. **2. Diet.** The general legislative assembly of certain countries, such as Japan. [Middle English *diete*, day for meeting, from Medieval Latin *diēta*, from Latin *diēs*, day.]

di·e·tar·y (dī′ĭ-tĕr′ē) *adj.* Of or involving diet.

di·e·tet·ic (dī′ĭ-tĕt′ĭk) *adj.* **1.** Of diet or its regulation. **2.** Prepared or processed for use in special diets: *dietetic food.*

di·e·tet·ics (dī′ĭ-tĕt′ĭks) *n.* (used with a sing. verb). The scientific study of diet and its relation to health.

di·e·ti·tian (dī′ĭ-tĭsh′ən) *n.* Also **di·e·ti·cian.** A person who specializes in dietetics.

dif·fer (dĭf′ər) *intr.v.* **1.** To be unlike in form, quality, amount, or nature. **2.** To be of a different opinion; disagree. —See Syns at **disagree.** [Middle English *differen*, from Old French *differer*, from Latin *differre.*]

dif·fer·ence (dĭf′ər-əns, dĭf′rəns) *n.* **1.** The condition of being unlike or different; variation: *a striking difference in their looks.* **2.** A degree or amount of variation: *a difference of two feet.* **3.** A disagreement; quarrel. **4. a.** The amount by which one number or quantity is greater or less than another. **b.** The number that results when one number is subtracted from another; remainder.

dif·fer·ent (dĭf′ər-ənt, dĭf′rənt) *adj.* **1.** Unlike in form, quality, amount, or nature. **2.** Distinct; separate. **3.** Unusual. —**dif′fer·ent·ly** *adv.* —**dif′fer·ent·ness** *n.*

   Syns: **different, disparate, dissimilar, unlike** *adj.* Core meaning: Not like another (*two different ways of studying; siblings who were very different*).

   Usage: **different from, than.** Both *different* + *from* and *different* + *than* occur in standard American English: *different from ours; different than ours.* Although the use of *than* was once frowned on, it has a long history of use by distinguished writers. *Different* + *to* is used in British English.

dif·fer·en·ti·a (dĭf′ə-rĕn′shē-ə) *n., pl.* **-ti·ae** (-shē-ē′, -shē-ī′). An attribute that characterizes and distinguishes a species from others of the same genus. [Latin, difference.]

dif·fer·en·tial (dĭf′ə-rĕn′shəl) *adj.* **1.** Of, showing, or constituting a difference; distinctive. **2.** Dependent on or making use of a difference or distinction. **3.** *Math.* Of or involving differentiation or rates of change. **4.** Involving differences in speed or direction of motion. —*n.* **1.** *Math.* An infinitesimal increment in a variable. **2.** A **differential gear. 3.** An amount or degree of difference between similar kinds or individuals: *a wage differential.*

differential calculus. The mathematics of the variation of a function with respect to changes in independent variables.

differential gear. An arrangement of gears that allows one turning shaft to drive two others at two different speeds.

dif·fer·en·ti·ate (dĭf′ə-rĕn′shē-āt′) *v.* **-at·ed, -at·ing.** —*tr.v.* **1.** To serve as a distinction between: *The colors differentiate them.* **2.** To understand or show the differences in or between: *Differentiate the specimens shown here.* **3.** To develop differences in by alteration or modification. —*intr.v.* **1.** To become different, distinct, or specialized. **2.** To make distinctions; to discriminate. —**dif·fer·en′ti·a′tion** *n.*

dif·fi·cult (dĭf′ĭ-kŭlt′, -kəlt) *adj.* **1.** Hard to do, accomplish, or perform; arduous: *a difficult operation.* **2.** Hard to understand or solve: *a difficult puzzle.* **3.** Hard to please, manage, or satisfy: *a difficult child.* —**dif′fi·cult′ly** *adv.*

   Syns: **difficult, hard, knotty, tough** *adj.* Core meaning: Not easy to do, achieve, or master (*difficult problems in physics*). See also Syns at **burdensome** and **contrary.**

dif·fi·cul·ty (dĭf′ĭ-kŭl′tē, -kəl-tē) *n., pl.* **-ties. 1.** The condition or quality of being difficult: *the difficulty of the experiment.* **2.** Great effort and trouble: *He walked with difficulty.* **3. difficulties. a.** A troublesome or embarrassing state of affairs: *financial difficulties.* **b.** Problems or conflicts: *getting help for emotional difficulties.* —See Syns at **conflict.** [Middle English *difficulte*, from Latin *difficultās*, from *difficilis*, difficult.]

dif·fi·dence (dĭf′ĭ-dəns, -dĕns) *n.* The condition or quality of being diffident.

dif·fi·dent (dĭf′ĭ-dənt, -dĕnt′) *adj.* Lacking self-confidence; timid. —See Syns at **modest.** [Middle English, from Latin *diffīdens*, from *diffīdere*, to mistrust.] —**dif′fi·dent·ly** *adv.*

dif·fract (dĭ-frăkt′) *tr.v.* To cause to undergo diffraction. —*intr.v.* To undergo diffraction.

dif·frac·tion (dĭ-frăk′shən) *n.* The bending or deflection of light or other radiation as it passes an obstacle such as the edge of a slit or aperture. [New Latin *diffractio*, "a breaking up," from Latin *diffringere*, to break to pieces.]

diffraction grating. A surface, usu. glass or polished metal, with a large number of fine parallel grooves cut into it, used to produce spectra of reflected or transmitted light.

dif·fuse (dĭ-fyōōz′) *v.* **-fused, -fus·ing.** —*tr.v.* **1.** To pour out and cause to spread, as a gas or liquid. **2.** To spread about or scatter; disseminate: *diffuse ideas; diffuse knowledge.* —*intr.v.* **1.** To spread out or soften. **2.** *Physics.* To undergo diffusion. —See Syns at **spread.** —*adj.* (dĭ-fyōōs′). **1.** Widely spread or scattered; dispersed. **2.** Characterized by an excess of words; wordy. [Middle English, dispersed, from Old French *diffus*, from Latin *diffundere*, to pour out, spread.] —**dif·fuse′ly** *adv.* —**dif·fuse′ness** (dĭ-fyōōs′nĭs) *n.* —**dif·fus′i·ble** *adj.*

dif·fu·sion (dĭ-fyōō′zhən) *n.* **1.** The process of diffusing or the condition of being diffused. **2.** The gradual mixing of two or more substances as a result of random motion of their molecules. **3.** The spreading out of light or other radiation as it passes through a translucent material or is reflected off a rough surface.

dif·fu·sive (dĭ-fyōō′sĭv, -zĭv) *adj.* Characterized by diffusion; tending to diffuse. —**dif·fu′sive·ly** *adv.*

dig (dĭg) *v.* **dug** (dŭg) or *archaic* **digged** (dĭgd), **dig·ging.** —*tr.v.* **1.** To break up, turn over, or remove (earth, sand, etc.) with a tool or the hands. **2.** To make (an excavation) by or as by digging. **3.** To obtain by digging. **4.** To learn or discover by research or investigation: *dig up information.* **5.** To force or thrust against: *dig a gun into his back.* **6.** *Slang.* To understand, appreciate, or enjoy. —*intr.v.* **1.** To loosen or turn over the earth. **2.** To proceed along one's way by or as by digging. —See Syns at **like.** —*phrasal verb.* **dig in. 1.** *Mil.* To dig holes or trenches. **2.** *Informal.* To begin to work or eat in earnest. —*n.* **1.** A poke; a punch. **2.** A sarcastic remark; a gibe. **3.** An archaeological excavation. **4. digs.** *Informal.* Diggings. [Middle English *diggen*.] —**dig′ger** *n.*

di·gest (dĭ-jĕst′, dī-) *tr.v.* **1.** To change (food) into a form that is easily absorbed into the body. **2.** To absorb mentally; comprehend. **3.** To organize into a systematic arrangement, usu. by summarizing or classifying. **4.** To soften or disintegrate by means of chemical action, heat, or moisture. —*intr.v.* **1.** To become assimilated into the body. **2.** To undergo exposure to heat, liquids, or chemical agents. —*n.* (dī′jĕst′). A systematic organization or arrangement of summarized written materials or data; a synopsis. [Middle English *digesten*, from Latin *dīgestus*, from *dīgere*, to divide, distribute, digest.] —**di·gest'er** *n.*

di·gest·i·ble (dĭ-jĕs'tə-bəl, dī-) *adj.* Capable of being digested. —**di·gest'i·bil'i·ty** —**di·gest'i·bly** *adv.*

di·ges·tion (dĭ-jĕs'chən, dī-) *n.* **1. a.** The processes by which food is changed into simple substances that the body can absorb. **b.** The ability to digest. **2.** The absorption of ideas; comprehension.

di·ges·tive (dĭ-jĕs'tĭv, dī-) *adj.* Of, aiding, or active in digestion. —*n.* Any substance that aids digestion. —**di·ges'tive·ly** *adv.*

digestive system. The alimentary canal along with the glands, such as the liver, salivary glands, and pancreas, that produce substances needed in digestion.

digger wasp. Any of various wasps of the family Sphecidae that burrow into the ground to build nests.

dig·gings (dĭg'ĭngz) *pl.n.* **1.** An excavation site. **2.** Lodgings.

dight (dīt) *tr.v.* **dight** or **dight·ed**, **dight·ing.** *Archaic.* To dress; adorn. [Middle English *dighten*, from Old English *dihtan*, to arrange, from Latin *dictāre*, to dictate.]

dig·it (dĭj'ĭt) *n.* **1.** A finger or toe. **2. a.** Any of the Arabic numerals 0–9 used in the decimal system of numeration. **b.** Such a symbol used in any system of numeration. [Middle English, from Latin *digitus*, finger.]

dig·i·tal (dĭj'ĭ-təl) *adj.* **1.** Of, like, or involving a digit, esp. a finger. **2.** Having digits. **3.** Expressed as a series of digits, esp. for use by a computer: *digital information.* **4.** Using or giving a readout in digits: *a digital clock.* —**dig'i·tal·ly** *adv.*

digital computer. A computer that performs operations on data represented as series of digits.

dig·i·tal·is (dĭj'ĭ-tăl'ĭs) *n.* **1.** A plant, the foxglove. **2.** A drug prepared from the seeds and dried leaves of this plant, used as a powerful heart stimulant. [From Latin *digitālis*, digital.]

dig·i·tate (dĭj'ĭ-tāt') *adj.* **1.** Having digits. **2.** *Bot.* Having radiating fingerlike lobes or leaflets. —**dig'i·tate'ly** *adv.*

dig·i·ti·grade (dĭj'ĭ-tĭ-grād') *adj.* Walking on the toes, as horses, cats, and dogs. [DIGIT + Latin *gradus*, step.]

dig·ni·fied (dĭg'nə-fīd') *adj.* Having or expressing dignity; poised. —**dig'ni·fied'ly** *adv.*

dig·ni·fy (dĭg'nə-fī') *tr.v.* **-fied, -fy·ing. 1.** To give dignity or honor to. **2.** To add to the status of; make seem important. [Middle English *dignifien*, from Old French *dignifier*, from Late Latin *dignificāre.*]

dig·ni·tar·y (dĭg'nĭ-tĕr'ē) *n., pl.* **-ies.** A person of high rank or position. [From DIGNITY.]

dig·ni·ty (dĭg'nĭ-tē) *n., pl.* **-ties. 1.** The condition of being worthy or honorable: *a certain dignity in every man.* **2.** The respect and honor that go with an important position or station. **3.** A high office or rank. **4.** Nobility of character. —See Syns at **honor.** [Middle English *dignite*, from Old French, from Latin *dignitās*, from *dignus*, worthy.]

di·graph (dī'grăf') *n.* A pair of letters that represents one sound, as the *ea* in *beat.* —**di·graph'ic** *adj.*

di·gress (dĭ-grĕs', dī-) *intr.v.* To stray from the main subject in writing or speaking. [Latin *dīgressus*, from *dīgredī*, to go aside.] —**di·gres'sion** *n.* —**di·gres'sion·al** *adj.*

di·gres·sive (dĭ-grĕs'ĭv, dī-) *adj.* Marked by digression; rambling. —**di·gres'sive·ly** *adv.* —**di·gres'sive·ness** *n.*

di·he·dral (dī-hē'drəl) *adj.* Formed by a pair of planes or sections of planes that intersect. —*n.* A dihedral angle.

dike (dīk). Also **dyke.** —*n.* **1.** A wall or embankment of earth and rock built to hold back water and prevent floods. **2.** *Brit.* A low dividing wall, often of sod. **3.** A barrier, esp. one for protection. **4.** A causeway. **5.** A ditch or channel. **6.** *Geol.* A long mass of igneous rock that cuts across the structure of adjoining rock. —*tr.v.* **diked, dik·ing. 1.** To protect, enclose, or provide with a dike. **2.** To drain with ditches. [Middle English, from Old English *dīc*, moat, ditch.] —**dik'er** *n.*

di·lap·i·dat·ed (dĭ-lăp'ĭ-dā'tĭd) *adj.* In a condition of partial ruin or disrepair: *a dilapidated house.* [From Latin *dīlapidāre*, to destroy : *dis-*, apart + *lapidāre*, to throw stones, from *lapis*, stone.]

di·lap·i·da·tion (dĭ-lăp'ĭ-dā'shən) *n.* A condition of partial ruin or disrepair.

di·late (dī-lāt', dĭ-, dī'lāt', dĭ-lāt') *v.* **-lat·ed, -lat·ing.** —*tr.v.* To make wider or larger: *The horse dilated its nostrils.* —*intr.v.* To become wider or larger; expand: *eyes dilated with fear.* [Middle English *dilaten*, from Old French *dilater*, from Latin *dīlātāre*, to enlarge.] —**di·lat'a·ble** *adj.* —**di·la'tion** *n.* —**di·la'tive** *adj.* —**di·la'tor** *n.*

dil·a·to·ry (dĭl'ə-tôr'ē, -tōr'ē) *adj.* **1.** Tending or intended to cause delay: *dilatory maneuvers.* **2.** Characterized by procrastination. —See Syns at **slow.** [Middle English *dilatorie*, from Latin *dīlātōrius*, from *differre*, to postpone.] —**dil'a·to'ri·ly** *adv.* —**dil'a·to'ri·ness** *n.*

di·lem·ma (dĭ-lĕm'ə) *n.* A situation that requires a choice between courses of action that are equally difficult or unpleasant. [Latin, from Greek, ambiguous proposition.]

dil·et·tante (dĭl'ĭ-tänt', -tän'tē, -tănt', -tăn'tē, dĭl'ĭ-tänt') *n., pl.* **-tantes** or **-tan·ti** (-tän'tē, -tăn'-). **1.** A person with an amateurish or superficial interest in an art or branch of knowledge. **2.** A lover of the arts. —See Syns at **amateur.** —*adj.* Superficial or amateurish. [Italian *dilettante*, "amateur."] —**dil'et·tan'tism** *n.*

dil·i·gence¹ (dĭl'ə-jəns) *n.* **1.** Long, steady effort in one's job or studies. **2.** Careful attention.

dil·i·gence² (dĭl'ə-jəns) *n.* A stagecoach. [French, from *diligence*, "speed."]

dil·i·gent (dĭl'ə-jənt) *adj.* Done with or characterized by great effort and care; assiduous. [Middle English, from Old French, from Latin *dīligēns*, from *dīligere*, to love.] —**dil'i·gent·ly** *adv.*

dill (dĭl) *n.* **1.** An aromatic herb, *Anethum graveolens*, native to the Old World, with very fine leaves and small yellow flowers. **2.** The leaves or seeds of this plant used as seasoning. [Middle English *dile*, from Old English.]

dill pickle. A cucumber pickled and flavored with dill.

dil·ly-dal·ly (dĭl'ē-dăl'ē) *intr.v.* **-lied, -ly·ing. 1.** To waste time. **2.** To vacillate. —See Syns at **delay.** [From DALLY.]

di·lute (dĭ-lōōt', dī-) *tr.v.* **-lut·ed, -lut·ing. 1.** To make (a solution) thinner, as by adding a solvent. **2.** To make weaker or less potent, as by mixing or dispersing. —*adj.* Weakened; diluted: *dilute acid.* [Latin *dīlūtus*, from *dīluere*, to dissolve.] —**di·lut'er** *n.*

di·lu·tion (dĭ-lōō'shən, dī-) *n.* **1.** The act of diluting or the condition of being diluted. **2.** A diluted substance.

di·lu·vi·al (dĭ-lōō'vē-əl) *adj.* Also **di·lu·vi·an** (-ən). Of or produced by a flood. [Late Latin *dīluviālis*, from Latin *dīluvium*, flood, from *dīluere*, to wash away.]

dim (dĭm) *adj.* **dim·mer, dim·mest. 1.** Faintly lighted: *a dim corner of the big hall.* **2.** Obscure or indistinct; faint: *a dim light.* **3.** Lacking brightness or luster; dull: *dim colors.* **4.** Lacking sharpness or clarity in sight or understanding. **5.** Negative or unpromising; unfavorable: *a dim view of the situation.* —See Syns at **dark.** —*v.* **dimmed, dim·ming.** —*tr.v.* **1.** To make dim. **2.** To put on low beam: *dim the headlights.* —*intr.v.* To become dim. [Middle English *dim(me)*, from Old English *dimm.*] —**dim'ly** *adv.* —**dim'ness** *n.*

dime (dīm) *n.* A U.S. or Canadian coin worth ten cents. [Middle English, a tenth part, from Old French, from Latin *decima (pars)*, tenth (part).]

di·men·sion (dĭ-mĕn'shən) *n.* **1.** The measure of how far something extends in space. **2.** Any of the physical properties, esp. mass, length, and time, that are considered basic and from which other measures are derived. **3.** The smallest number of independent coordinates that give the location of a unique point in a mathematical space: *a space of*

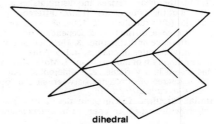

dihedral

four dimensions. **4.** Often **dimensions.** Extent; scope: *Wagner added new dimensions to opera.* [Middle English *dimensio(u)n,* from Old French *dimension,* from Latin *dīmēnsiō,* from *dīmētīrī,* to measure carefully.] —**di·men'·sion·al** *adj.* —**di·men'sion·al'i·ty** (-měn'shə-năl'ĭ-tē) *n.* —**di·men'sion·al·ly** *adv.*

dime store. A five-and-ten-cent store.

di·min·ish (dĭ-mĭn'ĭsh) *tr.v.* **1.** To reduce the apparent or actual size of; make smaller or less. **2.** To detract from the authority, rank, or prestige of. —*intr.v.* To become smaller or less: *His influence diminished steadily.* —See Syns at **decrease.** [Middle English *deminishen,* blend of *diminuen,* to reduce, lessen, and *minishen,* to make smaller, both ult. from Latin *minuere,* to lessen.] —**di·min'ish·a·ble** *adj.* —**di·min'ish·ment** *n.*

di·min·u·en·do (dĭ-mĭn'yōō-ěn'dō) *n., pl.* **-dos.** Decrescendo. [Italian, "diminishing."] —**di·min'u·en'do** *adj. & adv.*

dim·i·nu·tion (dĭm'ə-nōō'shən, -nyōō'-) *n.* **1.** The act or process of diminishing. **2.** The resulting decrease.

di·min·u·tive (dĭ-mĭn'yə-tĭv) *adj.* **1.** Of very small size; tiny. **2.** Expressing smallness, youth, familiarity, or affection, as *-let* in *booklet, -ette* in *dinette,* and *-kin* in *lambkin.* —*n.* A diminutive suffix, word, or name. —**di·min'u·tive·ly** *adv.* —**di·min'u·tive·ness** *n.*

dim·i·ty (dĭm'ĭ-tē) *n., pl.* **-ties.** A thin, crisp cotton cloth with raised threads that form checks or stripes in the weave. [Middle English *demyt,* from Medieval Latin *dimitum,* from Medieval Greek *dimitos,* double-threaded.]

dim·mer (dĭm'ər) *n.* A rheostat or other device used to reduce the brightness of electric lights.

di·mor·phic (dĭ-môr'fĭk) *adj.* Also **di·mor·phous** (-fəs). Occurring in two different forms, as the crystals of a mineral. —**di·mor'phism'** (-fĭz'əm) *n.*

dim·ple (dĭm'pəl) *n.* **1.** A small natural indentation in the flesh of the human body, esp. on the cheek. **2.** Any slight depression in a surface. —*v.* **-pled, -pling. 1.** —*tr.v.* To produce dimples in: *The rain dimpled the pool.* —*intr.v.* To form dimples by smiling. [Middle English.]

din (dĭn) *n.* Loud, confused, prolonged noise. —*v.* **dinned, din·ning.** —*tr.v.* **1.** To stun with deafening noise. **2.** To impart by wearying repetition: *din an idea into her head.* —*intr.v.* To make a din: *Jets dinned overhead.* [Middle English *dine,* from Old English *dyne.*]

di·nar (dĭ-när', dē'när) *n.* Any of several units of gold and silver currency used in the Middle East from the 8th to 19th cent. [Arabic *dīnār,* from Late Greek *dēnarion,* denarius, from Latin *dēnārius,* to denarius.]

dine (dīn) *v.* **dined, din·ing.** —*intr.v.* To eat dinner. —*tr.v.* To give dinner to: *We dined the visiting mayors.* [Middle English *dinen,* from Old French *di(s)ner.*]

din·er (dī'nər) *n.* **1.** A person eating dinner. **2.** A railroad car in which meals are served. **3.** A restaurant that has a long counter and booths, orig. shaped like a railroad car.

di·nette (dī-nět') *n.* A nook or alcove for informal meals.

ding (dĭng) *n.* A ringing sound. —*intr.v.* To ring or clang. —*tr.v.* To cause to clang, as by striking. [Prob. imit.]

ding-dong (dĭng'dông', -dŏng') *n.* The peal of a bell or any series of similar repeated sounds. —*adj.* Characterized by a hammering exchange, as of blows. [Imit.]

din·ghy (dĭng'ē) *n., pl.* **-ghies.** Also **din·gey** pl. **-eys.** A small boat, esp. a rowboat. [Hindi *dīngī,* dim. of *dēṅgā,* boat.]

din·gle (dĭng'gəl) *n.* A small, wooded valley; a dell. [Middle English.]

din·go (dĭng'gō) *n., pl.* **-goes.** A wild dog, *Canis dingo,* of Australia, with a yellowish-brown coat. [Native Australian name.]

din·gus (dĭng'əs) *n. Slang.* A gadget or other article whose name is unknown or forgotten. [German *Dings,* thing.]

din·gy (dĭn'jē) *adj.* **-gi·er, -gi·est. 1.** Dirty; soiled; grimy: *a dingy coat.* **2.** Drab; squalid: *a dingy room.* [Orig. unknown.] —**din'gi·ly** *adv.* —**din'gi·ness** *n.*

dining car. A railroad car in which meals are served.

dining room. A room in which meals are served.

din·key (dĭng'kē) *n., pl.* **-keys.** Also **din·ky** pl. **-kies.** *Informal.* A small locomotive used in a railroad yard. [Prob. from *dinky,* small, from Scottish *dink,* trim, neat.]

din·ky (dĭng'kē) *adj.* **-ki·er, -ki·est.** *Informal.* Of small size

or consequence; insignificant. —*n., pl.* **-kies.** *Informal.* Var. of **dinkey.** [Prob. from Scottish *dink,* trim, neat.]

din·ner (dĭn'ər) *n.* **1.** The main meal of the day, served at noon or in the evening. **2.** A formal meal in honor of a person or an occasion. [Middle English *diner,* from Old French *di(s)ner,* from *di(s)ner,* to dine.]

dinner jacket. A tuxedo.

di·no·flag·el·late (dī'nō-flăj'ə-lĭt, -lāt', -flə-jěl'ĭt) *n.* Any of numerous, minute saltwater organisms of the order Dinoflagellata that form one of the main constituents of plankton. [Greek *dinos,* whirlpool + FLAGELLUM.]

di·no·saur (dī'nə-sôr') *n.* Any of various extinct, often gigantic reptiles of the orders Saurischia and Ornithischia, that existed millions of years ago. [Greek *deinos,* monstrous + -SAUR.] —**di'no·sau'ri·an** (-sôr'ē-ən) *adj.*

dint (dĭnt) *n.* **1.** Force, power, or exertion: *He succeeded by dint of hard work.* **2.** A dent. —*tr.v.* **1.** To put a dent in. **2.** To impress or drive in forcibly. [Middle English, from Old English *dynt.*]

di·oc·e·san (dī-ŏs'ĭ-sən) *adj.* Of or pertaining to a diocese. —*n.* A bishop of a diocese.

di·o·cese (dī'ə-sĭs, -sēs', -sēz') *n.* The district or churches under the leadership of a bishop; a bishopric. [Middle English *diocise,* from Old French, from Late Latin *diocēsis,* from Latin *dioecēsis,* jurisdiction, from Greek *dioikēsis,* administration, from *dioikein,* to manage.]

di·ode (dī'ōd') *n.* **1.** An electron tube that has two electrodes, esp. a tube that allows current to flow in one direction only. **2.** A semiconductor with two terminals, used as a rectifier.

di·oe·cious (dī-ē'shəs) *adj.* Also **di·e·cious.** Having male and female flowers borne on separate plants. [DI- + Greek *oikia,* dwelling.] —**di·oe'cious·ly** *adv.*

Di·o·me·des (dī'ə-mē'dēz) *n. Gk. Myth.* A prince of Argos and, in the Homeric poems, one of the chief heroes at Troy.

Di·o·nys·i·a (dī'ə-nĭz'ē-ə, -nĭzh'-, -nĭs'-) *pl.n.* Any of various festivals of ancient Attica in honor of Dionysus, esp. one in which the tragedy is thought to have had its origin.

Di·o·nys·i·an (dī'ə-nĭz'ē-ən, -nĭzh'-, -nĭs'ē-ən, -nĭsh'-, -nĭzh'-ən, -nĭsh'-) *adj.* **1.** Of or relating to Dionysus or the Dionysia. **2.** Of an ecstatic, orgiastic, or irrational character.

Di·o·ny·sus (dī'ə-nī'səs) *n. Gk. Myth.* Bacchus.

di·o·ram·a (dī'ə-răm'ə, -rä'mə) *n.* **1.** A three-dimensional miniature scene with painted modeled figures and background. **2.** A scene reproduced on cloth transparencies with various lights shining through the cloths to produce changes in effect, and viewed through a small opening. [Greek *dia-,* through + (PAN)ORAMA.] —**di'o·ram'ic** *adj.*

di·o·rite (dī'ə-rīt') *n.* Any of various granite-textured, igneous rocks rich in plagioglase. [French, from Greek *diorizein,* to distinguish.] —**di'o·rit'ic** (-rĭt'ĭk) *adj.*

di·ox·ide (dī-ŏk'sīd') *n.* An oxide containing two atoms of oxygen per molecule.

dip (dĭp) *v.* **dipped, dip·ping.** —*tr.v.* **1.** To plunge briefly into a liquid. **2.** To color or dye by putting into a liquid: *dip Easter eggs.* **3.** To immerse (an animal) in a disinfectant solution. **4.** To cause to drop or sink suddenly: *The colt dipped its head.* **5.** To scoop up by plunging the hand or a container into and out of a liquid; to bail; ladle. **6.** To lower and raise (a flag) in salute. —*intr.v.* **1.** To plunge into water or other liquid and come out quickly. **2.** To plunge the hand, a container, etc., into a liquid, esp. for the purpose of taking something up or out. **3.** To drop or sink suddenly.

dingo

4. To sink or appear to sink; decline: *Wheat prices dipped temporarily.* **5.** *Geol.* To lie at an angle to the horizontal plane, as a rock stratum or vein. **6.** To read or study here and there; browse. —*n.* **1.** A brief plunge or immersion: *a dip in the sea.* **2.** A liquid into which something is dipped. **3.** A creamy food mixture into which crackers, chips, etc. may be dipped. **4.** An amount taken up by dipping; a scoop: *a double dip of ice cream.* **5.** A decline or drop: *a dip in the price of sugar.* **6.** *Geol.* The downward inclination of a rock stratum or vein in reference to the plane of the horizon. **7.** A hollow; depression. [Middle English *dippen,* from Old English *dyppan.*]

diph·the·ri·a (dĭf-thîr′ē-ə, dĭp-) *n.* A serious contagious bacterial disease marked by high fever, weakness, and the formation in the throat and other air passages of false membranes that cause difficulty in breathing. [From French *diphthérie,* from Greek *diphthera,* piece of leather.] —**diph′the·rit′ic** (dĭf′thə-rĭt′ĭk) or **diph·ther′ic** (-thĕr′ĭk) or **diph·the′ri·al** (-thîr′ē-əl) *adj.*

diph·thong (dĭf′thông′, -thŏng′, dĭp′-) *n.* **1.** A complex speech sound beginning with one vowel sound and moving to another vowel or semivowel position within the same syllable. For example, *oy* in the word *boy* is a diphthong. **2.** A digraph. **3.** A ligature. [Middle English *diptonge,* from Old French *diptongue,* from Late Latin *dipthongus,* from Greek *diphthongos* : DI- (two) + *phthongos,* voice, sound.]

diph·thong·ize (dĭf′thông·īz′, -thŏng′, dĭp′-) *v.* **-ized, -iz·ing.** —*tr.v.* To pronounce as a diphthong. —*intr.v.* To become a diphthong. —**diph′thong·i·za′tion** *n.*

diplo– or **dipl–.** A prefix meaning double: *diploid.* [Greek, from *diploos,* double.]

dip·lo·blas·tic (dĭp′lō-blăs′tĭk) *adj.* Having two distinct cellular layers, as embryos and lower invertebrate animals such as sponges and coelenterates. [DIPLO- + Greek *blastos,* bud.]

dip·lo·coc·cus (dĭp′lō-kŏk′əs) *n., pl.* **-coc·ci** (-kŏk′sī′, -kŏk′ī′). Any of various paired spherical bacteria of the genus *Diplococcus,* some of which are disease-causing. [DIPLO- + -COCCUS.] —**dip′lo·coc′cal** *adj.*

dip·loid (dĭp′loid′) *adj.* **1.** Double or twofold. **2.** Having double the basic number of chromosomes. —*n.* A diploid cell.

di·plo·ma (dĭ-plō′mə) *n.* **1.** A document showing that a person has earned a degree from or completed a course of study at a school, college, or university. **2.** A certificate conferring a privilege or honor. [Latin, from Greek *diplōma,* folded paper, document, from *diploos,* double.]

di·plo·ma·cy (dĭ-plō′mə-sē) *n., pl.* **-cies.** **1.** The art or practice of conducting international relations without use of warfare. **2.** Skill in dealing with others; tact.

dip·lo·mat (dĭp′lə-măt′) *n.* A person skilled or working in diplomacy.

dip·lo·mat·ic (dĭp′lə-măt′ĭk) *adj.* **1.** Of or pertaining to diplomacy or diplomats. **2.** Tactful; politic. [French *diplomatique,* from Latin *diplōma,* document.] —**dip′lo·mat′i·cal·ly** *adv.*

diplomatic immunity. Exemption from legal processes granted to diplomatic personnel in a foreign country.

dip·lo·ma·tist (dĭ-plō′mə-tĭst) *n.* A diplomat.

dip needle. A magnetic needle used to indicate the local inclination of the earth's magnetic field.

di·pole (dī′pōl′) *n.* **1.** *Physics.* A pair of electric charges or magnetic poles, of equal magnitude but of opposite sign or polarity, separated by a small distance. **2.** *Electronics.* An antenna consisting of two equal rods extending outward in a straight line. —**di′po·lar** (-pō′lər, dī-po′-) *adj.*

dip·per (dĭp′ər) *n.* **1.** Someone or something that dips, esp. a long-handled cup for taking up water. **2. Dipper.** Either of two dipper-shaped star groups, the **Big Dipper** or the **Little Dipper. 3.** A bird, the **water ouzel.**

dip·so·ma·ni·a (dĭp′sə-mā′nē-ə, -mān′yə) *n.* An uncontrollable craving for alcoholic liquors. [Greek *dipsa,* thirst + -MANIA.] —**dip′so·ma′ni·ac′** (-nē-ăk′) *n.*

dip·stick (dĭp′stĭk′) *n.* A graduated rod for measuring the depth of liquid in a container, as of oil in a crankcase.

dip·ter·ous (dĭp′tər-əs) *adj.* Also **dip·ter·an** (-ən). Of or belonging to the Diptera, a large order of insects that have only a single pair of wings, including true flies and mosqui-

toes. **2.** *Bot.* Having two winglike parts. [From Greek *dipteros,* having two wings.]

dip·tych (dĭp′tĭk) *n.* **1.** An ancient writing tablet with two leaves hinged together. **2.** A pair of painted or carved panels hinged together. [Late Latin *diptycha,* from Greek *diptukhos,* double-folded.]

dire (dīr) *adj.* **dir·er, dir·est.** **1.** Warning of disaster: *dire predictions.* **2.** Dreadful; disastrous: *a dire catastrophe.* **3.** Urgent; grave: *in dire need.* —See Syns at **critical.** [Latin *dīrus,* fearful, ill-omened.] —**dire′ly** *adv.* —**dire′ness** *n.*

di·rect (dĭ-rĕkt′, dī-) *tr.v.* **1.** To conduct the affairs of; manage: *He directs a large business.* **2.** To determine; control: *Instinct directs much of an animal's behavior.* **3.** To instruct, order, or command: *directed him to answer.* **4.** To aim, point, or guide to or toward: *Direct him to the post office.* **5.** To address to a destination, person, or audience. **6.** To conduct (a musical composition or group of musicians). **7.** To guide and supervise the dramatic presentation and acting of: *direct a film.* —*intr.v.* **1.** To give commands, orders, or directions. **2.** To conduct a performance or rehearsal. —See Syns at **command.** —*adj.* **1.** Proceeding or lying in a straight course or line. **2.** Straightforward; candid; frank: *plain, direct talk.* **3.** Without intervening persons, conditions, or agencies; immediate: *direct sunlight; a direct answer.* **4.** By action of the voters, rather than through elected representatives. **5.** Of unbroken descent or lineage: *a direct descendant of King David.* **6.** Consisting of the exact words of the writer or speaker: *a direct citation.* **7.** Absolute; total: *direct opposites.* —*adv.* In a straight line; directly: *He flew direct to New York.* [Middle English *directen,* from Latin *dīrectus,* from *dīrigere,* to direct.]

　Syns: direct, straight, through *adj.* Core meaning: In an uninterrupted line or course (*a direct flight*).

direct current. An electric current flowing in one direction.

di·rec·tion (dĭ-rĕk′shən, dī-) *n.* **1.** Management or guidance of a process, activity, performance, or production. **2. directions.** Instructions for doing something. **3.** An order or command. **4.** A word or phrase in a musical score indicating how a particular passage is to be played or sung. **5.** The act or art of directing a musical or dramatic performance. **6.** The line or course along which a person or thing moves, points, or lies. **7.** A course or area of development; trend.

di·rec·tion·al (dĭ-rĕk′shə-nəl, dī-) *adj.* **1.** Of or indicating direction: *an automobile's directional lights.* **2.** *Electronics.* Able to receive or send signals in one direction only. **3.** Of or pertaining to guidance in effort or behavior: *directional training.*

di·rec·tive (dĭ-rĕk′tĭv, dī-) *n.* An order or instruction, esp. one issued by a governmental or military unit. —*adj.* Serving to direct, indicate, or point out; directing.

di·rect·ly (dĭ-rĕkt′lē, dī-) *adv.* **1.** In a direct line; straight: *Drive directly north.* **2.** In a direct manner: *spoke directly.* **3.** Without anything or anyone intervening: *spoke directly to the President.* **4.** Without delay; instantly: *went directly there.*

direct object. In English and some other languages, the word or words designating the person or thing that receives the action of a verb. For example, in the sentence *He broke the dish,* the direct object is *the dish.*

di·rec·tor (dĭ-rĕk′tər, dī-) *n.* **1.** A person who supervises, controls, or manages something. **2.** A member of a group of persons who control the affairs of a corporation or institution. **3.** A person who supervises or guides the performers in a play, film, etc. —**di·rec′to′ri·al** *adj.* —**di·rec′tor·ship′** *n.*

di·rec·tor·ate (dĭ-rĕk′tər-ĭt, dī-) *n.* **1.** The office or position of a director. **2.** A board of directors.

di·rec·to·ry (dĭ-rĕk′tə-rē, dī-) *n., pl.* **-ries.** **1.** An alphabetical or classified list of names, addresses, and other facts about a specific group of persons or organizations. **2.** A book of rules or directions, esp. for use in church worship. **3.** A group or body of directors; directorate.

direct primary. A preliminary election in which a party's candidates for office are nominated by popular vote.

di·rec·trix (dĭ-rĕk′trĭks, dī-) *n., pl.* **-trix·es** or **-tri·ces** (-trī-sēz′). *Geom.* The fixed curve traversed by a generatrix in generating a conic or a cylinder.

direct tax. A tax, such as an income or property tax, levied directly on the taxpayer.

dire·ful (dīr′fəl) adj. Dreadful; dire. —**dire′ful·ly** adv.

dirge (dûrj) n. A sad, solemn piece of music, such as a funeral hymn or lament. [Latin dirige, from the first word in a Medieval Latin antiphon in the Office of the Dead.]

dir·i·gi·ble (dĭr′ə-jə-bəl, dĭ-rĭj′ə-) n. An early type of rigid lighter-than-air craft that could be steered. [From Latin dīrigere, to direct.]

dirk (dûrk) n. A dagger. —tr.v. To stab with a dirk. [Scottish durk.]

dirn·dl (dûrn′dəl) n. **1.** A dress with a full, gathered skirt and a tight bodice. **2.** A full, gathered skirt of this type. —modifier: a dirndl skirt. [German.]

dirt (dûrt) n. **1.** Earth or soil. **2.** A filthy or soiling substance, such as mud. **3.** Obscene language. **4.** Malicious or scandalous gossip. [Middle English, filth, from Old Norse drit.]

dirt-cheap (dûrt′chēp′) adj. Very cheap. —adv. At a very cheap price.

dirt·y (dûr′tē) adj. -i·er, -i·est. **1.** Soiled; grimy. **2.** Dull in color. **3.** Dark or threatening: a dirty look. **4.** Stormy and disagreeable: dirty weather. **5.** Dishonorable; unfair: a dirty deal; a dirty fighter. **6.** Obscene or indecent: dirty jokes. —v. -ied, -ing. —tr.v. To make soiled and grimy. —intr.v. To become dirty. —**dirt′i·ly** adv. —**dirt′i·ness** n.

    Syns: dirty, filthy, grimy, grubby, soiled, unclean adj. Core meaning: Covered with dirt (dirty clothes).

dirty work. Informal. **1.** Foul play; deceit. **2.** A difficult or distasteful chore or task.

dis–. A prefix meaning: **1.** Negation, lack, invalidation, or deprivation: distrust, disuse. **2.** Reversal: disunite, disapprove. **3.** Removal or rejection: disbar, discard. [Latin from dis, apart, asunder.]

dis·a·bil·i·ty (dĭs′ĭ-bĭl′ĭ-tē) n., pl. -ties. **1.** The condition of lacking a physical or mental capacity. **2.** Something that disables, as an injury. **3.** A legal incapacity or disqualification.

dis·a·ble (dĭs-ā′bəl) tr.v. -bled, -bling. **1.** To weaken or destroy the normal capacity or abilities of; to cripple; incapacitate. **2.** To render legally disqualified.

dis·a·buse (dĭs′ə-byōōz′) tr.v. -bused, -bus·ing. To free from a falsehood or misconception. [French désabuser.]

di·sac·cha·ride (dī-săk′ə-rīd′) n. Any of a class of carbohydrates, including lactose and sucrose, that yield two monosaccharides on hydrolysis.

dis·ac·cord (dĭs′ə-kôrd′) n. Lack of accord; disagreement. —See Syns at **conflict.** —intr.v. To disagree. —See Syns at **disagree.**

dis·ad·van·tage (dĭs′əd-văn′tĭj) n. **1.** An unfavorable condition or circumstance; a handicap: Lack of experience was a disadvantage. **2.** Damage; harm; loss: The ruling worked to our disadvantage. —tr.v. -taged, -tag·ing. To put at a disadvantage; set back.

dis·ad·van·taged (dĭs′əd-văn′tĭjd) adj. Suffering under severe economic and social disadvantage: disadvantaged children. —See Syns at **depressed.**

dis·ad·van·ta·geous (dĭs-ăd′vən-tā′jəs) adj. Detrimental; unfavorable. —See Syns at **unfavorable.** —**dis′ad′van·ta′geous·ly** adv. —**dis′ad·van·ta′geous·ness** n.

dis·af·fect (dĭs′ə-fĕkt′) tr.v. To alienate the affection or loyalty of. —See Syns at **estrange.** —**dis′af·fect′ed·ly** (-fĕk′tĭd-lē) adv. —**dis′af·fec′tion** n.

dis·af·fil·i·ate (dĭs′ə-fĭl′ē-āt′) v. -at·ed, -at·ing. —tr.v. To disassociate from an alliance or affiliation. —intr.v. To sever an affiliation or association. —**dis′af·fil′i·a′tion** n.

dis·af·firm (dĭs′ə-fûrm′) tr.v. **1.** To deny; contradict. **2.** Law. a. To repudiate. b. To set aside; reverse. —**dis′af·fir′mance** (-fûr′məns) or **dis′af·fir·ma′tion** (dĭs′ăf′ər-mā′shən) n.

dis·a·gree (dĭs′ə-grē′) intr.v. -greed, -gree·ing. **1.** To fail to correspond: Our totals disagree. **2.** To have a different opinion: We disagree on what happened. **3.** To dispute; quarrel. **4.** To have bad effects: Fried food disagrees with her.

    Syns: disagree, differ, disaccord, dissent v. Core meaning: To be of different opinion (parents disagreeing about money).

dis·a·gree·a·ble (dĭs′ə-grē′ə-bəl) adj. **1.** Unpleasant; distasteful: a disagreeable odor. **2.** Quarrelsome; bad-tempered. —See Syns at **irritable** and **unpleasant.** —**dis′a·gree′a·ble·ness** n. —**dis′a·gree′a·bly** adv.

dis·a·gree·ment (dĭs′ə-grē′mənt) n. **1.** A failure to agree; difference; inconsistency. **2.** A difference of opinion. **3.** A dispute or quarrel caused by a difference of opinion.

dis·al·low (dĭs′ə-lou′) tr.v. **1.** To refuse to allow. **2.** To reject as invalid, untrue, or improper. —See Syns at **forbid.** —**dis′al·low′a·ble** adj. —**dis′al·low′ance** n.

dis·ap·pear (dĭs′ə-pîr′) intr.v. **1.** To pass out of sight; vanish. **2.** To cease to exist: Whole countries disappeared as boundaries changed. —**dis′ap·pear′ance** n.

dis·ap·point (dĭs′ə-point′) tr.v. **1.** To fail to satisfy the hope, desire, or expectation of. **2.** To fail to keep an appointment with or a promise to. [Middle English disappointen, to dispossess, from Old French desapointier.] —**dis′ap·point′ing·ly** adv.

dis·ap·point·ed (dĭs′ə-poin′tĭd) adj. Made unhappy by the failure of one's hopes or expectations.

dis·ap·point·ment (dĭs′ə-point′mənt) n. **1.** The act of disappointing or the condition of being disappointed. **2.** A person or thing that disappoints.

dis·ap·pro·ba·tion (dĭs-ăp′rə-bā′shən) n. Moral disapproval; condemnation.

dis·ap·prov·al (dĭs′ə-prōō′vəl) n. Dislike or unfavorable judgment of something; condemnation.

dis·ap·prove (dĭs′ə-prōōv′) v. -proved, -prov·ing. —tr.v. **1.** To have an unfavorable opinion of; to censure; condemn: disapproved his behavior. **2.** To refuse to approve: disapprove a request. —intr.v. To have an unfavorable opinion: disapproves of drinking. —**dis′ap·prov′ing·ly** adv.

dis·arm (dĭs-ärm′) tr.v. **1.** To take weapons from; render harmless. **2.** To overcome the suspicion or antagonism of: Her kind words disarmed him. —intr.v. To reduce or abolish one's armed forces or supply of weapons.

dis·ar·ma·ment (dĭs-är′mə-mənt) n. A reduction of a country's armed forces or weapons of war.

dis·ar·range (dĭs′ə-rānj′) tr.v. -ranged, -rang·ing. To upset the arrangement of; to disorder. —**dis′ar·range′ment** n.

dis·ar·ray (dĭs′ə-rā′) n. **1.** A condition of disorder or confusion. **2.** Disordered or insufficient dress. —tr.v. To throw into confusion; to upset.

dis·as·sem·ble (dĭs′ə-sĕm′bəl) tr.v. -bled, -bling. To take apart: He disassembled the engine.

dis·as·so·ci·ate (dĭs′ə-sō′shē-āt′, -sē-) tr.v. -at·ed, -at·ing. To dissociate. —**dis′as·so·ci·a′tion** n.

dis·as·ter (dĭ-zăs′tər) n. Great destruction, distress, or misfortune. [French désastre, from Italian disastro, from disastrato, "ill-starred."]

    Syns: disaster, calamity, cataclysm, catastrophe, tragedy n. Core meaning: A grave occurrence having ruinous results (floods, plane crashes, and other disasters).

dis·as·trous (dĭ-zăs′trəs) adj. Causing disaster; calamitous; ruinous. —**dis·as′trous·ly** adv.

dis·a·vow (dĭs′ə-vou′) tr.v. To disclaim or deny knowledge of, responsibility for, or association with. —**dis′a·vow′** n.

dis·band (dĭs-bănd′) tr.v. To break up; dissolve: disband a committee. —intr.v. To become disbanded: The protesters disbanded after the march. —**dis·band′ment** n.

dis·bar (dĭs-bär′) tr.v. -barred, -bar·ring. To expel (a lawyer) from the legal profession by official action or procedure. —**dis·bar′ment** n.

dis·be·lief (dĭs′bĭ-lēf′) n. The refusal to believe.

dis·be·lieve (dĭs′bĭ-lēv′) tr.v. -lieved, -liev·ing. To refuse to believe in; reject. —intr.v. To withhold belief. —**dis′be·liev′er** n. —**dis′be·liev′ing·ly** adv.

dis·bud (dĭs-bŭd′) tr.v. -bud·ded, -bud·ding. To remove buds from (a plant) to promote better blooms.

dis·bur·sal (dĭs-bûr′səl) n. Var. of **disbursement.**

dis·burse (dĭs-bûrs′) tr.v. -bursed, -burs·ing. To pay out; expend, as from a fund. [Old French desbourser.] —**dis·burs′a·ble** adj. —**dis·burse′ment** n. —**dis·burs′er** n.

disc (dĭsk) n. **1.** Also **disk.** Informal. A phonograph record. **2.** Var. of **disk.**

dis·cant (dĭs′kănt′) n. Var. of **descant** (melody).

dis·card (dĭs-kärd′) tr.v. **1.** To throw away; reject; dismiss. **2.** Card Games. **a.** To throw out (an undesired card or cards) from one's hand. **b.** To play (a card other than a trump and different in suit from the card led). —*intr.v.* *Card Games.* To discard a card. —*n.* (dĭs'kärd'). **1.** The act of discarding. **2.** A person or thing discarded.

disc brake. A brake that derives its stopping power from the friction of two pads pressing in unison against the opposite sides of a rotating disc.

dis·cern (dĭ-sûrn', -zûrn') *tr.v.* **1.** To detect or perceive with the eye or mind: *We could discern only a heap of rocks.* **2.** To perceive the distinctions of; to discriminate. —*intr.v.* To discriminate or distinguish: *discern between fact and rumor.* [Middle English *discernen,* from Old French *discerner,* from Latin *discernere,* to separate by sifting.] —**dis·cern'er** *n.*

dis·cern·i·ble (dĭ-sûr'nə-bəl, -zûr'-) *adj.* Recognizable; distinguishable. —See Syns at **perceptible.** —**dis·cern'i·bly** *adv.*

dis·cern·ing (dĭ-sûr'nĭng, -zûr'-) *adj.* Showing insight and judgment; perceptive: *a discerning literary critic.* —See Syns at **wise.** —**dis·cern'ing·ly** *adv.*

dis·cern·ment (dĭ-sûrn'mənt, -zûrn'-) *n.* Keenness in detecting, distinguishing, or selecting.

dis·charge (dĭs-chärj') *v.* **-charged, -charg·ing.** —*tr.v.* **1.** To relieve of a burden or of contents; unload. **2.** To release or dismiss, as from confinement or duty. **3.** To dismiss from employment. **4.** To send or pour forth; emit: *The broken water main discharged torrents into the street.* **5.** To shoot or fire (a projectile or weapon). **6.** To perform the obligations or requirements of (an office, duty, or task). **7.** To comply with the terms of (a debt or promise). **8.** *Law.* To set aside; dismiss; annul. —*intr.v.* **1.** To get rid of a burden, load, or weight. **2.** To fire: *The gun discharged by mistake.* **3.** To pour forth contents. —*n.* (dĭs'chärj', dĭs-chärj'). **1.** The act of unloading. **2. a.** Dismissal or release from employment, service, or confinement. **b.** A certificate showing such release. **3.** An act of pouring or flowing forth; emission: *a steady discharge of pus.* **4.** Something poured or flowing forth. **5.** An act of firing a weapon or projectile. **6.** Performance or fulfillment. **7.** A legal annulment or acquittal; dismissal. **8. a.** The release of stored energy, as in a capacitor, by the flow of electric current between two points. **b.** The conversion of chemical energy to electric energy in a storage battery. [Middle English *dischargen,* from Old French *deschargier,* from Late Latin *discarricāne* : *dis-* (reversal) + *carricāne,* to load.] —**dis·charge'a·ble** *adj.* —**dis·charg'er** *n.*

discharge tube. A tube that is fitted with electrodes and contains a gas in which an electrical discharge is induced by high applied potentials.

dis·ci·ple (dĭ-sī'pəl) *n.* **1. a.** A person who accepts the teachings of a master and often assists in spreading them. **b.** Any active adherent. **2. Disciple.** A member of the Disciples of Christ. [Middle English, from Old English *discipul,* from Latin *discipulus,* pupil, from *discere,* to learn.] —**dis·ci'ple·ship'** *n.*

Disciples of Christ. A Christian denomination, founded in 1809, that accepts the Bible as the only rule of Christian faith and practice, rejects denominational creeds, and practices baptism by immersion.

dis·ci·pli·nal (dĭs'ə-plə-nəl) *adj.* Var. of **disciplinary.**

dis·ci·pli·nar·i·an (dĭs'ə-plə-nâr'ē-ən) *n.* A person who enforces or believes in strict discipline. —*adj.* Disciplinary.

dis·ci·pli·nar·y (dĭs'ə-plə-nĕr'ē) *adj.* Of, pertaining to, or used for discipline: *disciplinary problems.*

dis·ci·pline (dĭs'ə-plĭn) *n.* **1. a.** Training that molds or perfects a specific skill, behavior, etc. **b.** Control that results from such training. **2.** Punishment. **3.** A branch of knowledge or of teaching. —*tr.v.* **-plined, -plin·ing. 1.** To train by instruction and control. **2.** To punish in order to reform or train. —See Syns at **punish.** [Middle English, from Old French, from Latin *disciplīna,* instruction, from *discipulus,* disciple.] —**dis·ci'plin·er** *n.*

disc jockey. Also **disk jockey.** A radio announcer who presents and comments on phonograph records.

dis·claim (dĭs-klām') *tr.v.* **1.** To deny or renounce any claim to or connection with; disown. **2.** *Law.* To renounce one's right or claim to. —*intr.v. Law.* To renounce a legal right or claim. [Middle English *discla(i)men,* from Old French *desclamer.*]

dis·claim·er (dĭs-klā'mər) *n.* A denial, as of a claim, a connection, knowledge, or responsibility; a disavowal.

dis·close (dĭs-klōz') *tr.v.* **-closed, -clos·ing. 1.** To expose to view; uncover. **2.** To make known; divulge. [Middle English *disclosen,* from Old French *desclore.*] —**dis·clos'er** *n.*

dis·clo·sure (dĭs-klō'zhər) *n.* **1.** The act or process of disclosing. **2.** Something that is disclosed; a revelation.

dis·co (dĭs'kō) *n., pl.* **-cos.** *Informal.* A discotheque.

disco-. A prefix meaning a phonograph record: *discography.* [From DISC.]

dis·cog·ra·phy (dĭ-skŏg'rə-fē) *n., pl.* **-phies.** A descriptive catalogue of phonograph records. —**dis·cog'ra·pher** *n.*

dis·coid (dĭs'koid) *adj.* Also **dis·coi·dal** (dĭ-skoid'l). **1.** Having the shape of a disk. **2.** *Bot.* Having disk flowers but no ray flowers. —*n.* A disk or an object shaped like a disk. [Late Latin *discoides,* from Greek *diskoeidēs.*]

dis·col·or (dĭs-kŭl'ər) *tr.v.* To alter or spoil the proper color of. —*intr.v.* To become changed or spoiled in color. —**dis·col·or·a'tion** (-ə-rā'shən) *n.*

dis·com·bob·u·late (dĭs'kəm-bŏb'yə-lāt') *tr.v.* **-lat·ed, -lat·ing.** To confuse; upset. [Perh. alteration of DISCOMPOSE.]

dis·com·fit (dĭs-kŭm'fĭt) *tr.v.* To make uneasy, uncertain, or confused; disconcert. [Middle English *discomfiten,* from Old French *desconfire,* to defeat.] —**dis·com'fi·ture** (-fĭ-chŏŏr') *n.*

dis·com·fort (dĭs-kŭm'fərt) *n.* **1.** The condition of being uncomfortable in body or mind. **2.** Something that disturbs comfort. —*tr.v.* To make uncomfortable.

dis·com·mode (dĭs'kə-mōd') *tr.v.* **-mod·ed, -mod·ing.** To put to inconvenience; disturb. [French *discommoder.*]

dis·com·pose (dĭs'kəm-pōz') *tr.v.* **-posed, -pos·ing. 1.** To disturb the composure or calm of; agitate. **2.** To disorder; disarrange. —**dis'com·po'sure** (-pō'zhər) *n.*

dis·con·cert (dĭs'kən-sûrt') *tr.v.* **1.** To upset the composure of; perturb. **2.** To frustrate by throwing into disorder or confusion; upset. [Obs. French *disconcerter,* from Old French *desconcerter.*] —**dis'con·cert'ed·ly** (-sûr'tĭd-lē) *adv.* —**dis'con·cert'ed·ness** *n.* —**dis'con·cert'ing·ly** *adv.*

dis·con·nect (dĭs'kə-nĕkt') *tr.v.* To break or interrupt the connection of or between. —See Syns at **detach.** —**dis'con·nec'tion** *n.*

dis·con·nect·ed (dĭs'kə-nĕk'tĭd) *adj.* **1.** Not connected; detached. **2.** Lacking order or logic; incoherent. —**dis'con·nect'ed·ly** *adv.* —**dis'con·nect'ed·ness** *n.*

dis·con·so·late (dĭs-kŏn'sə-lĭt) *adj.* **1.** Beyond consolation; hopelessly sad. **2.** Cheerless; gloomy; dismal. [Middle English, from Medieval Latin *disconsōlātus.*] —**dis·con'so·late·ly** *adv.* —**dis·con'so·late·ness** *n.*

dis·con·tent (dĭs'kən-tĕnt') *n.* The absence of contentment; dissatisfaction. —*adj.* Discontented. —*tr.v.* To cause dissatisfaction in; make discontented.

dis·con·tent·ed (dĭs'kən-tĕn'tĭd) *adj.* Not satisfied; unhappy. —**dis'con·tent'ed·ly** *adv.* —**dis'con·tent'ed·ness** *n.*

dis·con·tin·u·ance (dĭs'kən-tĭn'yōō-əns) *n.* The act of discontinuing or the condition of being discontinued.

dis·con·tin·ue (dĭs'kən-tĭn'yōō) *v.* **-ued, -u·ing.** —*tr.v.* **1.** To put a stop to; terminate. **2.** To cease from; give up. —*intr.v.* To come to an end. —See Syns at **abandon** and **stop.** —**dis'con·tin'u·a'tion** *n.*

dis·con·tin·u·ous (dĭs'kən-tĭn'yōō-əs) *adj.* Marked by breaks or interruptions. —**dis·con·ti·nu'i·ty** (dĭs-kŏn'tə-nōō'ĭ-tē, -nyōō'-) *n.* —**dis'con·tin'u·ous·ly** *adv.*

dis·cord (dĭs'kôrd') *n.* **1.** Lack of agreement or accord; dissension: *discord within the government.* **2.** A confused or harsh mingling of sounds. **3.** *Mus.* A combination of simultaneously sounded tones that is considered to sound harsh or unpleasant; dissonance. —See Syns at **conflict.** [Middle English, from Old French *descorde,* from Latin *discordia,* strife.]

dis·cor·dant (dĭs-kôr'dnt) *adj.* **1.** Not in agreement or accord. **2.** Disagreeable in sound; harsh or dissonant. —See Syns at **harsh.** —**dis·cor'dance** or **dis·cor'dan·cy** *n.* —**dis·cor'dant·ly** *adv.*

dis·co·theque (dĭs'kə-tĕk', dĭs'kə-tĕk') *n.* Also **dis·co·thèque.** A nightclub that features dancing to amplified recorded music. [French : *disco-,* disc + (*biblio*)*thèque,* library.]

dis·count (dĭs'kount', dĭs-kount') *tr.v.* **1.** To deduct or sub-

---

ă pat ā pay â care ä father ĕ pet ē be hw which ĭ pit ī tie î pier ŏ pot ō toe ô paw, for oi noise
ōō took ōō boot ou out th thin *th* this ŭ cut û urge zh vision ə about, item, edible, gallop, circus

tract from a cost or price. **2.** To advance money as a loan on (a commercial paper not immediately payable) after deducting the interest. **3.** To reduce in cost, quantity, or value. **4.** To disregard or doubt (something) as being an exaggeration or not trustworthy: *discounted their fears.* **5.** To anticipate and make allowance for. —*intr.v.* To lend money after deduction of interest. —*n.* (dĭs′kount′). **1.** A reduction from the full or standard amount of a price or debt. **2.** The interest deducted in advance in lending a bill, note, or other commercial paper. **3.** The rate of interest deducted in such a transaction. [Old French *desconter*, from Medieval Latin *discomputāre.*] —**dis·count′a·ble** *adj.* —**dis′count′er** *n.*

dis·coun·te·nance (dĭs-koun′tə-nəns) *tr.v.* **-nanced, -nanc·ing.** **1.** To view or treat with disfavor. **2.** To abash; disconcert. —*n.* Disfavor; disapproval.

dis·cour·age (dĭ-skûr′ĭj, -skûr′-) *tr.v.* **-aged, -ag·ing.** **1.** To make less hopeful or enthusiastic; depress. **2.** To try to dissuade. **3.** To try to prevent, check, or hinder: *They lit a fire to discourage mosquitoes.* [Middle English *discoragen,* from Old French *descoragier.*] —**dis·cour′ag·ing·ly** *adv.*

    Syns: 1. discourage, dishearten, dispirit *v.* Core meaning: To make less hopeful or enthusiastic (*problems that discouraged me*). **2. discourage, dissuade** *v.* Core meaning: To persuade (another) not to do something (*discouraged me from driving in the blizzard*).

dis·cour·age·ment (dĭ-skûr′ĭj-mənt, -skûr′-) *n.* **1.** The act of discouraging. **2.** A condition of being discouraged. **3.** Something that discourages.

dis·course (dĭs′kôrs′, -kōrs′) *n.* **1.** Verbal exchange; conversation. **2.** A formal discussion of a subject, either spoken or written. —See Syns at **speech.** —*intr.v.* (dĭ-skôrs′, -skōrs′) **-coursed, -cours·ing.** **1.** To speak or write formally and at length. **2.** To engage in conversation or discussion; converse. [Middle English *discours,* from Late Latin *discursus,* conversation, from Latin *discurrere,* to run back and forth, speak at length.] —**dis·cours′er** *n.*

dis·cour·te·ous (dĭs-kûr′tē-əs) *adj.* Lacking courtesy; not polite. —See Syns at **rude.** —**dis·cour′te·ous·ly** *adv.* —**dis·cour′te·ous·ness** *n.*

dis·cour·te·sy (dĭs-kûr′tĭ-sē) *n., pl.* **-sies. 1.** Lack of courtesy; rudeness. **2.** An act or statement that is rude.

dis·cov·er (dĭ-skŭv′ər) *tr.v.* **1.** To arrive at through observation or study; obtain knowledge of. **2.** To be the first to find, learn of, or observe. **3.** *Archaic.* To reveal; expose. [Middle English *discoveren,* from Old French *descovrir,* from Late Latin *discooperīre,* to uncover, disclose.] —**dis·cov′er·a·ble** *adj.* —**dis·cov′er·er** *n.*

dis·cov·er·y (dĭ-skŭv′ə-rē) *n., pl.* **-ies. 1.** The act of discovering. **2.** Something that has been discovered.

dis·cred·it (dĭs-krĕd′ĭt) *tr.v.* **1.** To damage in reputation; to disgrace: *behavior that discredits him.* **2.** To cast doubt on; cause to be distrusted: *discredit a claim.* **3.** To refuse to believe in: *discredit a story as mere rumor.* —See Syns at **disprove.** —*n.* **1.** Loss or damage to one's reputation. **2.** Lack or loss of trust or belief; doubt. **3.** Someone or something that brings disgrace or distrust. —See Syns at **disgrace.**

dis·cred·it·a·ble (dĭs-krĕd′ĭ-tə-bəl) *adj.* Deserving of or resulting in disgrace; blameworthy. —**dis·cred′it·a·bly** *adv.*

dis·creet (dĭ-skrēt′) *adj.* Having or showing caution or self-restraint in one's speech or behavior; showing good judgment; prudent: *a discreet girl; a discreet silence.* [Middle English, from Old French *discret,* from Medieval Latin *discrētus,* from Latin *discernere,* to discern.] —**dis·creet′ly** *adv.* —**dis·creet′ness** *n.*

dis·crep·an·cy (dĭ-skrĕp′ən-sē) *n., pl.* **-cies.** Also **dis·crep·ance** (-əns). **1.** Lack of agreement; difference; inconsistency: *great discrepancies between their accounts.* **2.** An example of such disagreement.

dis·crep·ant (dĭ-skrĕp′ənt) *adj.* Showing discrepancy; disagreeing. [Middle English *discrepaunt,* from Latin *discrepāns,* from *discrepāre,* to vary.] —**dis·crep′ant·ly** *adv.*

dis·crete (dĭ-skrēt′) *adj.* **1.** Individually distinct; separate. **2.** Consisting of unconnected distinct parts. —See Syns at **single.** [Middle English, from Latin *discrētus,* separate.] —**dis·crete′ly** *adv.* —**dis·crete′ness** *n.*

dis·cre·tion (dĭ-skrĕsh′ən) *n.* **1.** The quality of being discreet; prudence. **2.** Freedom of action or judgment: *leave the choice to your discretion.* —**dis·cre′tion·ar·y** (-ə-nĕr′ē) *adj.*

dis·crim·i·nate (dĭ-skrĭm′ə-nāt′) *v.* **-nat·ed, -nat·ing.** —*intr.v.* **1.** To make a clear distinction; distinguish; differentiate. **2.** To act on the basis of prejudice: *discriminate against women.* —*tr.v.* **1.** To perceive the distinguishing features of: *discriminate good qualities from bad.* **2.** To serve to mark; differentiate. —*adj.* (dĭ-skrĭm′ə-nĭt). Discriminating. [From Latin *discrīmināre,* to distinguish, from *discrīmen,* distinction.] —**dis·crim′i·nate·ly** *adv.*

dis·crim·i·nat·ing (dĭ-skrĭm′ə-nā′tĭng) *adj.* **1.** Able to recognize small or fine distinctions; discerning: *a discriminating critic.* **2.** Serving to distinguish; distinctive. —**dis·crim′i·nat′ing·ly** *adv.*

dis·crim·i·na·tion (dĭ-skrĭm′ə-nā′shən) *n.* **1.** The act of discriminating. **2.** The ability to recognize small or fine distinctions. **3.** Acts or attitudes based on prejudice.

dis·crim·i·na·tive (dĭ-skrĭm′ə-nā′tĭv, -ə-nə-tĭv) *adj.* **1.** Drawing distinctions; discriminating. **2.** Discriminatory. —**dis·crim′i·na′tive·ly** *adv.*

dis·crim·i·na·to·ry (dĭ-skrĭm′ə-nə-tôr′ē, -tōr′ē) *adj.* **1.** Marked by prejudice; biased. **2.** Discriminating.

dis·cur·sive (dĭ-skûr′sĭv) *adj.* Covering a wide field of subjects; rambling; digressive. [Medieval Latin *discursīvus,* from Latin *discursus,* "a running back and forth."] —**dis·cur′sive·ly** *adv.* —**dis·cur′sive·ness** *n.*

dis·cus (dĭs′kəs) *n., pl.* **-es. 1.** A disk, usu. wooden with a metal rim, that is thrown for distance in athletic contests. **2.** The event in which this disk is thrown. [Latin.]

discus

dis·cuss (dĭ-skŭs′) *tr.v.* **1.** To speak together about; debate: *discussed the matter for hours.* **2.** To examine (a subject) by means of speech or writing; treat of. [Middle English *discussen,* from Late Latin *discutere,* from Latin, to break up, scatter.] —**dis·cuss′i·ble** *adj.*

dis·cus·sion (dĭ-skŭsh′ən) *n.* **1.** A conversation in which ideas and opinions are exchanged. **2.** An examination or presentation of a subject, as in a lecture or book.

dis·dain (dĭs-dān′) *tr.v.* **1.** To treat as inferior; show contempt for. **2.** To refuse aloofly: *She disdained to answer the letter.* —See Syns at **despise.** —*n.* Mild contempt and aloofness. [Middle English *desdeynen,* from Old French *desdeignier,* from Latin *dēdignārī,* to scorn.]

dis·dain·ful (dĭs-dān′fəl) *adj.* Feeling or showing disdain; scornful and haughty. —See Syns at **arrogant.** —**dis·dain′ful·ly** *adv.* —**dis·dain′ful·ness** *n.*

dis·ease (dĭ-zēz′) *n.* **1.** Any condition of an organism that makes it unable to function in the normal, proper way. **2.** A harmful tendency. [Middle English *disese,* from Old French *desaise,* discomfort.] —**dis·eased** (dĭ-zēzd′) *adj.*

dis·em·bark (dĭs′ĕm-bärk′) *intr.v.* To go ashore from a ship. —*tr.v.* To put ashore from a ship. —**dis′em′bar′ka′tion** *n.*

dis·em·bod·y (dĭs′ĕm-bŏd′ē) *tr.v.* **-ied, -y·ing.** To free (the soul or spirit) from the body. —**dis′em·bod′i·ment** *n.*

dis·em·bow·el (dĭs′ĕm-bou′əl) *tr.v.* **-eled** or **-elled, -el·ing** or **-el·ling.** To remove the entrails from. —**dis′em·bow′el·ment** *n.*

dis·en·chant (dĭs′ĕn-chănt′) *tr.v.* To free from false belief; disillusion. —**dis′en·chant′ment** *n.*

dis·en·cum·ber (dĭs′ĕn-kŭm′bər) *tr.v.* To free from something that hinders or burdens. —**dis′en·cum′ber·ment** *n.*

dis·en·fran·chise (dĭs′ĕn-frăn′chīz′) *v.* **-chised, -chis·ing.**

Var. of **disfranchise**. —**dis′en·fran′chise′ment** n.

dis·en·gage (dĭs′ĕn-gāj′) v. **-gaged, -gag·ing.** —tr.v. **1.** To release or make free from entanglement or connection: *disengage a clutch.* **2.** To free or release (oneself) as from a previous involvement or course of action. —intr.v. To free or become free; get loose. —See Syns at **detach**. —**dis′en·gage′ment** n.

dis·en·tan·gle (dĭs′ĕn-tăng′gəl) v. **-gled, -gling.** —tr.v. To free from entanglement or confusion; extricate. —intr.v. To become free of entanglement. —**dis′en·tan′gle·ment** n.

dis·es·tab·lish (dĭs′ĭ-stăb′lĭsh) tr.v. **1.** To alter the status of (something established by authority or general acceptance). **2.** To deprive (a church) of official governmental support. —**dis′es·tab′lish·ment** n.

dis·es·teem (dĭs′ĭ-stēm′) tr.v. To have little regard for; hold in disfavor. —n. Lack of esteem.

dis·fa·vor (dĭs-fā′vər) n. **1.** Dislike or low regard; disapproval. **2.** The condition of being disliked or disapproved of: *in disfavor at work.* —tr.v. To view or treat with dislike or disapproval.

dis·fig·ure (dĭs-fĭg′yər) tr.v. **-ured, -ur·ing.** To spoil the appearance or shape of; mar. —**dis·fig′ure·ment** n.

dis·fran·chise (dĭs-frăn′chīz′) tr.v. **-chised, -chis·ing.** Also **dis·en·fran·chise** (dĭs′ĕn-frăn′chīz′). To deprive (an individual) of a right of citizenship, esp. the right to vote. —**dis·fran′chise′ment** (-chīz′mənt, -chəz-, -chĭz-mənt) n.

dis·gorge (dĭs-gôrj′) v. **-gorged, -gorg·ing.** —tr.v. **1.** To vomit. **2.** To discharge violently; spew. —intr.v. To discharge or pour forth contents. —**dis·gorge′ment** n.

dis·grace (dĭs-grās′) n. **1.** Loss of honor, respect, or reputation. **2.** The condition of being strongly and gen. disapproved: *She couldn't bear the disgrace of the scandal.* **3.** Something that brings shame, dishonor, or disfavor. —tr.v. **-graced, -grac·ing.** To bring shame or dishonor upon. [French *disgrâce*, from Italian *disgrazia*.] —**dis·grac′er** n.

    Syns: disgrace, discredit, dishonor, disrepute, ignominy, shame n. Core meaning: Loss or damage to one's reputation (*expelled from school in disgrace*).

dis·grace·ful (dĭs-grās′fəl) adj. Worthy of or causing shame or disfavor. —**dis·grace′ful·ly** adv. —**dis·grace′ful·ness** n.

dis·grun·tle (dĭs-grŭn′tl) tr.v. **-tled, -tling.** To make discontented; to upset. [DIS- (intensive) + dial. *gruntle*, to grumble.] —**dis·grun′tle·ment** n.

dis·guise (dĭs-gīz′) n. **1.** Clothes or accessories worn to conceal one's true identity. **2.** Any form of concealment or camouflage. —tr.v. **-guised, -guis·ing. 1.** To change the manner or appearance of in order to prevent recognition. **2.** To conceal or obscure by false show; misrepresent: *disguise one's feelings.* [Middle English *disg(u)isen*, from Old French *desguisier*.] —**dis·guis′er** n.

dis·gust (dĭs-gŭst′) tr.v. To make (someone) feel sick, annoyed, offended, etc. —See Syns at **repel**. —n. A feeling of sickness, extreme annoyance, etc. [Old French *desgouster*.] —**dis·gust′ed·ly** adv.

dish (dĭsh) n. **1. a.** A flat or shallow container for holding or serving food. **b.** The amount that a dish holds. **2.** A particular variety or preparation of food: *an interesting dish.* **3.** Anything with the concave shape of a dish. —tr.v. **1.** To serve (food) in or as if in a dish. **2.** To hollow out; make concave. **3.** *Informal.* To give out; dispense; distribute: *dish out advice.* [Middle English, from Old English *disc*, from Latin *discus*, disk.]

dis·ha·bille (dĭs′ə-bēl′) n. Also **des·ha·bille** (dĕs′-). The condition of being dressed in a sloppy or casual way. [French *déshabillé*, from *déshabiller*, to undress.]

dis·har·mo·ny (dĭs-här′mə-nē) n., pl. **-nies.** Lack of harmony; discord. —**dis·har·mo′ni·ous** (-mō′nē-əs) adj.

dish·cloth (dĭsh′klôth′, -klŏth′) n. A cloth or rag used for washing dishes.

dis·heart·en (dĭs-härt′n) tr.v. To shake or destroy the courage or spirit of. —See Syns at **discourage**. —**dis·heart′en·ing·ly** adv. —**dis·heart′en·ment** n.

di·shev·el (dĭ-shĕv′əl) tr.v. **-eled** or **-elled, -el·ing** or **-el·ling.** To put into disarray or disorder, esp. hair or clothing. —**di·shev′el·ment** n.

di·shev·eled (dĭ-shĕv′əld) adj. Not orderly; untidy; disarranged. [Middle English *discheveled*, from Old French

deschevele, from *descheveler*, to disarrange the hair.]

dis·hon·est (dĭs-ŏn′ĭst) adj. **1.** Inclined to lie, cheat, defraud, or deceive. **2.** Showing or resulting from fraud: *a dishonest answer.* —**dis·hon′est·ly** adv.

dis·hon·es·ty (dĭs-ŏn′ĭ-stē) n., pl. **-ties. 1.** Lack of honesty or integrity. **2.** A dishonest act or statement.

    Syns: dishonesty, corruption n. Core meaning: Lack of integrity (*cheating—a form of dishonesty*).

dis·hon·or (dĭs-ŏn′ər) n. **1.** Loss of honor, respect, or reputation; disgrace; shame. **2.** Something that causes loss of honor. **3.** Failure to pay a note, bill, or other commercial obligation. —See Syns at **disgrace**. —tr.v. **1.** To deprive of honor; to disgrace. **2.** To fail to pay. —**dis·hon′or·er** n.

dis·hon·or·a·ble (dĭs-ŏn′ər-ə-bəl) adj. Shameful; unworthy. —**dis·hon′or·a·ble·ness** n. —**dis·hon′or·a·bly** adv.

dish·rag (dĭsh′răg′) n. A dishcloth.

dish·tow·el (dĭsh′tou′əl) n. A towel for drying dishes.

dish·wash·er (dĭsh′wŏsh′ər, -wô′shər) n. A machine or person that washes dishes.

dish·wa·ter (dĭsh′wô′tər, -wŏt′ər) n. Water in which dishes are being or have been washed.

dis·il·lu·sion (dĭs′ĭ-lōō′zhən) tr.v. To deprive of a false idea, belief, or hope. —n. The condition of being deprived of a false idea, belief, or hope. —**dis′il·lu′sion·ment** n.

dis·in·cline (dĭs′ĭn-klīn′) v. **-clined, -clin·ing.** —tr.v. To make reluctant. —intr.v. To be reluctant. —**dis·in′cli·na′tion** (dĭs-ĭn′klə-nā′shən) n.

dis·in·fect (dĭs′ĭn-fĕkt′) tr.v. To rid of microorganisms capable of causing diseases. —**dis′in·fec′tion** n.

dis·in·fec·tant (dĭs′ĭn-fĕk′tənt) n. A substance that kills disease-causing microorganisms. —adj. Capable of acting as a disinfectant: *a disinfectant bath.*

dis·in·gen·u·ous (dĭs′ĭn-jĕn′yōō-əs) adj. Not straightforward; crafty. —**dis′in·gen′u·ous·ly** adv. —**dis′in·gen′u·ous·ness** n.

dis·in·her·it (dĭs′ĭn-hĕr′ĭt) tr.v. To take from (a person) the right to inherit: *disinherited his youngest son.*

dis·in·te·grate (dĭs-ĭn′tĭ-grāt′) v. **-grat·ed, -grat·ing.** —intr.v. **1.** To separate into separate pieces; to fragment. **2.** To decay or undergo a transformation, as an atomic nucleus. —tr.v. To cause to separate into components; destroy. —**dis·in′te·gra′tion** n. —**dis·in′te·gra′tor** n.

dis·in·ter (dĭs′ĭn-tûr′) tr.v. **-terred, -ter·ring. 1.** To dig up or remove from or as if from a grave or tomb; exhume. **2.** To remove from obscurity; expose. —**dis′in·ter′ment** n.

dis·in·ter·est (dĭs-ĭn′trĭst, -ĭn′tər-ĭst) n. **1.** Freedom from bias or self-interest; impartiality. **2.** Lack of interest.

    Syns: disinterest, apathy, indifference, unconcern n. Core meaning: Lack of interest (*viewed the show with utter disinterest*).

dis·in·ter·est·ed (dĭs-ĭn′trī-stĭd, -tə-rĕs′tĭd) adj. **1.** Free of bias and self-interest; impartial. **2.** Uninterested; indifferent. —**dis·in′ter·est·ed·ly** adv. —**dis·in′ter·est·ed·ness** n.

dis·join (dĭs-join′) tr.v. To disconnect. —intr.v. To become disconnected. —See Syns at **separate**.

dis·joint (dĭs-joint′) tr.v. **1.** To take apart at the joints. **2.** To separate; disjoin. —intr.v. To come apart at the joints. —adj. *Math.* Containing no elements in common.

dis·joint·ed (dĭs-join′tĭd) adj. **1.** Separated at the joints. **2.** Lacking order or coherence; disconnected: *a disjointed speech.* —**dis·joint′ed·ly** adv. —**dis·joint′ed·ness** n.

dis·junc·tion (dĭs-jŭngk′shən) n. **1.** The act of disjoining or the condition of being disjointed. **2.** *Logic.* A proposition that presents two or more alternative terms, with the assertion that only one is true.

dis·junc·tive (dĭs-jŭngk′tĭv) adj. **1.** Causing or serving to separate or divide. **2.** *Gram.* Serving to establish a relationship of contrast or opposition, as the conjunction *but* in the phrase *poor but comfortable.* —n. *Gram.* A disjunctive conjunction.

disk (dĭsk) n. Also **disc. 1.** Any thin, flat, circular plate. **2.** Anything that resembles such a plate, as a celestial body or a part of an organism. **3.** The central part of a composite flower, as the daisy, containing many tiny, densely clustered flowers. **4.** Var. of **disc** (phonograph record). —tr.v. To work (soil) with a harrow fitted with angled disks. [Latin *discus*, quoit, from Greek *diskos*, from *dikein*, to throw.]

disk flower. Any of the tiny tubular flowers forming the center of the flower head of certain composite plants.

disk jockey. A disc jockey.

dis·like (dĭs-līk') *tr.v.* **-liked, -lik·ing.** To regard with disfavor. —*n.* An attitude or feeling of disfavor; antipathy.

dis·lo·cate (dĭs'lō-kāt', dĭs-lō'kāt') *tr.v.* **-cat·ed, -cat·ing.** **1.** To move out of its normal position, esp. to displace (a bone) from a socket or joint. **2.** To throw into disorder; upset. —**dis'lo·ca'tion** *n.*

dis·lodge (dĭs-lŏj') *v.* **-lodged, -lodg·ing.** —*tr.v.* To remove or force out from a position previously occupied. —*intr.v.* To move or go from a dwelling or former position.

dis·loy·al (dĭs-loi'əl) *adj.* Lacking in loyalty. —See Syns at **faithless.** —**dis·loy'al·ly** *adv.*

dis·loy·al·ty (dĭs-loi'əl-tē) *n., pl.* **-ties.** Lack of loyalty.

dis·mal (dĭz'məl) *adj.* Causing or showing gloom or depression; dreary: *a dismal fog; a dismal face.* —See Syns at **gloomy.** [Middle English, unlucky days, from Medieval Latin *diēs malī,* "evil days."] —**dis'mal·ly** *adv.* —**dis'mal·ness** *n.*

dis·man·tle (dĭs-măn'tl) *tr.v.* **-tled, -tling.** **1.** To strip of furnishing or equipment. **2.** To take apart. [Old French *desmanteler.*] —**dis·man'tle·ment** *n.*

dis·may (dĭs-mā') *tr.v.* To fill with dread or apprehension; daunt. —*n.* A sudden loss of courage or confidence in the face of trouble or danger. [Middle English *dismayen,* from Old French *dismaye,* troubled.]

dis·mem·ber (dĭs-mĕm'bər) *tr.v.* **1.** To cut, tear, or pull off the limbs of. **2.** To divide into pieces: *dismember a large company.* —**dis·mem'ber·er** *n.* —**dis·mem'ber·ment** *n.*

dis·miss (dĭs-mĭs') *tr.v.* **1.** To discharge, as from employment. **2.** To direct or allow to leave: *dismiss troops.* **3.** To put out of one's mind; ignore. **4.** To refuse to accept or recognize; repudiate: *dismiss one's obligations.* **5.** *Law.* To put (a claim or action) out of court without further hearing. —See Syns at **reject.** [Middle English *dismissen,* from Latin *dīmittere.*] —**dis·miss'i·ble** *adj.*

dis·miss·al (dĭs-mĭs'əl) *n.* The act of dismissing or the condition of being dismissed.

dis·mount (dĭs-mount') *intr.v.* To get off or down, as from a horse. —*tr.v.* **1.** To remove (a thing) from its support, setting, or mounting: *dismounted the machine gun.* **2.** To unseat, as from a horse. —**dis·mount'a·ble** *adj.*

dis·o·be·di·ence (dĭs'ə-bē'dē-əns) *n.* Refusal or failure to obey. —**dis'o·be'di·ent** *adj.* —**dis'o·be'di·ent·ly** *adv.*

dis·o·bey (dĭs'ə-bā') *intr.v.* To refuse or fail to follow an order or rule. —*tr.v.* To refuse or fail to obey.

dis·o·blige (dĭs'ə-blīj') *tr.v.* **-bliged, -blig·ing.** **1.** To refuse or fail to comply with the wishes of. **2.** To inconvenience.

dis·or·der (dĭs-ôr'dər) *n.* **1.** A lack of order or regular arrangement. **2.** A public disturbance. **3.** An upset of health or function in body or mind. —*tr.v.* **1.** To throw into disorder. **2.** To upset the physical or mental health of. —See Syns at **confuse.** —**dis·or'dered** *adj.*

dis·or·der·ly (dĭs-ôr'dər-lē) *adj.* **1.** Not neat or tidy. **2.** Unruly; riotous: *a disorderly crowd.* **3.** Disturbing the public peace: *disorderly conduct.* —**dis·or'der·li·ness** *n.*
> **Syns: 1. disorderly, messy** *adj.* Core meaning: Lacking regular, logical order (*a disorderly desk overflowing with papers*). **2. disorderly, riotous, rowdy, unruly** *adj.* Core meaning: Upsetting civil order (*dispersed the disorderly mob*).

dis·or·gan·ize (dĭs-ôr'gə-nīz') *tr.v.* **-ized, -iz·ing.** To destroy the organization or order of. —**dis·or'gan·i·za'tion** *n.*

dis·o·ri·ent (dĭs-ôr'ē-ĕnt', -ōr'-) *tr.v.* To cause (a person) to lose awareness of his position or relationship with his surroundings. —**dis·o'ri·en·ta'tion** *n.*

dis·own (dĭs-ōn') *tr.v.* To refuse to claim or accept as one's own; repudiate; reject.

dis·par·age (dĭ-spăr'ĭj) *tr.v.* **-aged, -ag·ing.** To speak of as unimportant or inferior; belittle: *disparaged his work.* [Middle English *disparagen,* to degrade, from Old French *desparager,* to deprive one of his rank.] —**dis·par'age·ment** *n.* —**dis·par'ag·ing·ly** *adv.*

dis·pa·rate (dĭs'pər-ĭt, dĭ-spăr'-) *adj.* Completely distinct or different in kind; entirely dissimilar. —See Syns at **different.** [Latin *disparātus,* past part. of *disparāre,* to separate.] —**dis'pa·rate·ly** *adv.* —**dis'pa·rate·ness** *n.*

dis·par·i·ty (dĭ-spăr'ĭ-tē) *n., pl.* **-ties.** **1.** Inequality; difference. **2.** Lack of similarity; unlikeness: *a marked disparity between their stories.*

dis·pas·sion·ate (dĭs-păsh'ə-nĭt) *adj.* Not influenced by strong personal feelings; impartial. —See Syns at **fair¹.** —**dis·pas'sion·ate·ly** *adv.* —**dis·pas'sion·ate·ness** *n.*

dis·patch (dĭ-spăch') Also **des·patch.** —*tr.v.* **1.** To send off to a specific destination or on specific business: *dispatch a letter; dispatch an ambulance.* **2.** To complete or dispose of promptly: *dispatched his business and left.* **3.** To put to death. —See Syns at **kill** and **send.** —*n.* Also **des·patch.** **1.** The act of sending off. **2.** Quickness and efficiency in performance. **3.** A message, esp. an official communication. **4.** A news report sent to a newspaper or broadcasting station. **5.** A putting to death. —See Syns at **haste.** [Spanish *despachar* or Italian *dispacciare,* from Old French *despeechier,* to set free, unshackle.] —**dis·patch'er** *n.*

dis·pel (dĭ-spĕl') *tr.v.* **-pelled, -pel·ling.** To rid of by or as if by scattering; drive away. —See Syns at **scatter.** [Middle English *dispellen,* from Latin *dispellere.*]

dis·pen·sa·ble (dĭ-spĕn'sə-bəl) *adj.* Capable of being dispensed with; not essential. —**dis·pen'sa·bil'i·ty** *n.*

dis·pen·sa·ry (dĭ-spĕn'sə-rē) *n., pl.* **-ries.** **1.** A room in which medicine and medical supplies are dispensed. **2.** A medical clinic.

dis·pen·sa·tion (dĭs'pən-sā'shən, -pĕn-) *n.* **1.** The act of dispensing or giving out. **2.** Something that is distributed or given out. **3.** Any official exemption or release from an obligation or rule. **4.** A system for ordering or administering affairs. **5.** *Theol.* A religious system considered to have been divinely revealed or appointed. —**dis'pen·sa'tion·al** *adj.*

dis·pen·sa·to·ry (dĭ-spĕn'sə-tôr'ē, -tōr'ē) *n., pl.* **-ries.** A book that describes the preparation, uses, and contents of medicines. **2.** *Archaic.* A dispensary.

dis·pense (dĭ-spĕns') *tr.v.* **-pensed, -pens·ing.** **1.** To deal out in parts or portions. **2.** To prepare and give out (medicines). **3.** To carry out; administer: *dispense justice.* —*phrasal verb.* **dispense with. 1.** To manage without; forgo. **2.** To dispose of. [Middle English *dispensen,* from Medieval Latin *dispensāre,* to exempt, from Latin, to pay out, freq. of *dispendere,* to weigh out.] —**dis·pen'ser** *n.*

dis·per·sal (dĭ-spûr'səl) *n.* **1.** The act or process of dispersing. **2.** The condition of being dispersed.

dis·perse (dĭ-spûrs') *v.* **-persed, -pers·ing.** —*tr.v.* **1.** To break up and scatter in various directions: *disperse a crowd.* **2.** To cause to vanish: *Wind dispersed the smoke.* **3.** To spread about or disseminate: *disperse knowledge.* **4.** To cause (light or other radiation) to separate into component parts, as in forming a spectrum. —*intr.v.* To move or scatter in different directions. —See Syns at **scatter** and **spread.** [Middle English *dispersen,* from Old French *disperser,* from Latin *dispergere.*] —**dis·pers'er** *n.* —**dis·pers'i·ble** *adj.*

dis·per·sion (dĭ-spûr'zhən, -shən) *n.* **1. a.** The act of dispersing. **b.** The condition of being dispersed. **2.** The breaking up of light into components, usu. according to wavelength. **3.** *Chem.* A suspension, such as smog, made up of tiny particles of one substance distributed throughout another substance. —**dis·per'sive** *adj.*

dis·pir·it (dĭ-spĭr'ĭt) *tr.v.* **-it·ed, -it·ing.** To lower in spirits; dishearten. —See Syns at **discourage.** [DI(S)- + SPIRIT.] —**dis·pir'it·ed·ly** *adv.*

dis·place (dĭs-plās') *tr.v.* **-placed, -plac·ing.** **1.** To remove from the usual place or position of. **2.** To take the place of; supplant. **3.** To fill the space of (a quantity of liquid, gas, etc.). —**dis·place'a·ble** *adj.*

displaced person. A person who has been driven from his homeland by war.

dis·place·ment (dĭs-plās'mənt) *n.* **1. a.** The weight or volume of fluid displaced by a body floating in it, often used as a measure of the weight or bulk of ships. **b.** The measure of the distance that a body has been moved through space, usu. expressed as a vector. **2.** The act of displacing or the condition of being displaced.

dis·play (dĭ-splā') *tr.v.* **1.** To put on view; exhibit: *displaying the latest fashions.* **2.** To show evidence of: *display fear.* **3.** To exhibit ostentatiously; show off; flaunt. **4.** To spread out; unfurl: *display the flag.* —See Syns at **show.**

ă pat   ā pay   â care   ä father   ĕ pet   ē be   hw which   ĭ pit   ī tie   î pier   ŏ pot   ō toe   ô paw, for   oi noise
ōō took   ōō boot   ou out   th thin   th this   ŭ cut   û urge   zh vision   ə about, item, edible, gallop, circus

—*n.* **1.** The act of displaying, esp. a public exhibition. **2.** A demonstration of the existence of something: *an ugly display of temper.* **3.** Anything that is exhibited. **4.** A show or pretense designed for effect: *a big display of his wealth.* [Middle English *displayen,* from Norman French *despleier,* from Medieval Latin *displicāre,* from Latin, to scatter.]

dis·please (dĭs-plēz′) *v.* **-pleased, -pleas·ing.** —*tr.v.* To cause annoyance or dissatisfaction to. —*intr.v.* To cause annoyance or dissatisfaction. —**dis·pleas′ing·ly** *adv.*

dis·pleas·ure (dĭs-plĕzh′ər) *n.* The condition or feeling of being displeased; annoyance or anger; dissatisfaction.

dis·port (dĭ-spôrt′, -pōrt′) *intr.v.* To play; to sport. —*tr.v.* To entertain (oneself) by sport or play. [Middle English *disporten,* from Old French *desporter,* to amuse.]

dis·pos·al (dĭs-pō′zəl) *n.* **1.** A particular order, distribution, or placement: *the disposal of barriers for defense.* **2.** The act of throwing out or away. **3.** An apparatus for getting rid of something: *a garbage disposal.* **4.** The act or method of attending to or settling a matter: *the principal's disposal of my application.* **5.** The act of transferring ownership by sale or gift. **6.** The power to use something: *limousines put at their disposal.*

dis·pose (dĭ-spōz′) *tr.v.* **-posed, -pos·ing.** **1.** To place in a particular order; arrange. **2.** To make willing; to incline: *a cheerful man very disposed to laughter.* —**phrasal verb.** **dispose of.** To get rid of, as by attending to or selling, destroying or throwing away, or eating or drinking. [Middle English *disposen,* from Old French *disposer,* from Latin *dispōnere,* to arrange.] —**dis·pos′a·ble** (-spō′zə-bəl) *adj.* —**dis·pos′er** *n.*

dis·po·si·tion (dĭs′pə-zĭsh′ən) *n.* **1.** One's usual mood or attitude; temperament. **2.** A tendency or inclination: *a disposition to argue.* **3.** Arrangement or distribution: *the disposition of books on the library shelves.* **4.** A final settlement: *the disposition of an estate.* **4.** An act of disposing of.

Syns: **disposition, humor, nature, temper, temperament** *n.* Core meaning: A person's usual manner of emotional response (*an affectionate disposition*).

dis·pos·sess (dĭs′pə-zĕs′) *tr.v.* To deprive of possession of, as land or buildings. —**dis′pos·ses′sion** *n.*

dis·praise (dĭs-prāz′) *tr.v.* **-praised, -prais·ing.** To express disapproval of; disparage; censure. —*n.* Reproach; censure. —**dis·prais′er** *n.* —**dis·prais′ing·ly** *adv.*

dis·proof (dĭs-prōōf′) *n.* **1.** An act of disproving. **2.** Evidence that disproves.

dis·pro·por·tion (dĭs′prə-pôr′shən, -pōr′-) *n.* **1.** A lack of proper proportion or harmonious relationship. **2.** An instance of this, as in size. —*tr.v.* To make disproportionate. —**dis′pro·por′tion·al** or **dis′pro·por′tion·ate** *adj.* —**dis′pro·por′tion·al·ly** or **dis′pro·por′tion·ate·ly** *adv.*

dis·prove (dĭs-prōōv′) *tr.v.* **-proved, -prov·ing.** To prove to be false. —**dis·prov′a·ble** *adj.* —**dis·prov′al** *n.*

Syns: **disprove, belie, discredit, rebut, refute** *v.* Core meaning: To show to be false (*evidence that disproved the theory*).

dis·pu·ta·tion (dĭs′pyōō-tā′shən) *n.* **1.** The act of disputing; an argument or debate. **2.** An academic exercise that consists of a formal debate or an oral defense of a thesis.

dis·pu·ta·tious (dĭs′pyōō-tā′shəs) *adj.* Inclined to dispute; argumentative; contentious. —**dis′pu·ta′tious·ly** *adv.* —**dis′pu·ta′tious·ness** *n.*

dis·pute (dĭ-spyōōt′) *v.* **-put·ed, -put·ing.** —*tr.v.* **1.** To argue about; to debate. **2.** To question the truth or validity of; to doubt. **3.** To strive to win; contest for. **4.** To strive against; oppose; resist. —*intr.v.* **1.** To argue; discuss; to debate: *men forever disputed in their search for truth.* **2.** To quarrel vehemently. —See Syns at **argue** and **resist.** —*n.* **1.** A verbal controversy; a debate. **2.** A quarrel. [Middle English *disputen,* from Old French *desputer,* from Late Latin *disputāre,* from Latin, to discuss.] —**dis·put′a·ble** *adj.* —**dis·put′a·bly** *adv.* —**dis·put′ant** or **dis·put′er** *n.*

dis·qual·i·fy (dĭs-kwŏl′ə-fī′) *tr.v.* **-fied, -fy·ing.** **1.** To render unfit or unqualified; disable: *Lack of experience disqualified him for the job.* **2.** To declare ineligible, unsuitable, or unworthy, as to hold a position or win a contest. **3.** To deprive of legal rights, powers, or privileges. —**dis·qual′i·fi·ca′tion** (-fĭ-kā′shən) *n.*

dis·qui·et (dĭs-kwī′ĭt) *tr.v.* To make uneasy; to trouble; to

worry. —*n.* Disquietude. —**dis·qui′et·ing·ly** *adv.*

dis·qui·e·tude (dĭs-kwī′ĭ-tōōd′, -tyōōd′) *n.* A condition of worry or uneasiness. —See Syns at **anxiety.**

dis·qui·si·tion (dĭs′kwĭ-zĭsh′ən) *n.* A formal discourse or treatise, often in writing; dissertation. [Latin *disquīsītiō,* inquiry, from *disquīrere,* to inquire diligently.]

dis·re·gard (dĭs′rĭ-gärd′) *tr.v.* To pay no attention to; ignore. —*n.* A lack of thoughtful attention or due regard, esp. when willful. —**dis′re·gard′ful** *adj.*

dis·rel·ish (dĭs-rĕl′ĭsh) *tr.v.* To have distaste for; dislike: *I disrelish formal affairs.* —*n.* Distaste; aversion.

dis·re·pair (dĭs′rĭ-pâr′) *n.* The condition of being neglected or in need of repairs: *a house in disrepair.*

dis·rep·u·ta·ble (dĭs-rĕp′yə-tə-bəl) *adj.* Not respectable in character, action, or appearance: *a disreputable establishment; a disreputable businessman.* —**dis·rep′u·ta·ble·ness** *n.* —**dis·rep′u·ta·bly** *adv.*

dis·re·pute (dĭs′rĭ-pyōōt′) *n.* The absence or loss of reputation; discredit; disfavor. —See Syns at **disgrace.**

dis·re·spect (dĭs′rĭ-spĕkt′) *n.* Lack of respect, esteem, or courtesy; rudeness. —*tr.v.* To show a lack of respect for.

dis·re·spect·ful (dĭs′rĭ-spĕkt′fəl) *adj.* Rude; discourteous. —**dis′re·spect′ful·ly** *adv.* —**dis′re·spect′ful·ness** *n.*

dis·robe (dĭs-rōb′) *v.* **-robed, -rob·ing.** —*tr.v.* To remove the clothing from: *disrobe the dummy.* —*intr.v.* To undress oneself. —See Syns at **undress.**

dis·rupt (dĭs-rŭpt′) *tr.v.* **1.** To throw into confusion or disorder. **2.** To interrupt or impede the progress or continuity of: *Floods disrupted communications.* **3.** To break or burst; rupture. [Latin *disruptus,* from *disrumpere,* to break asunder.] —**dis·rupt′er** or **dis·rup′tor** *n.* —**dis·rup′tion** *n.* —**dis·rup′tive** *adj.* —**dis·rup′tive·ly** *adv.*

dis·sat·is·fac·tion (dĭs-săt′ĭs-făk′shən) *n.* The condition or feeling of being displeased or not satisfied; discontent.

dis·sat·is·fac·to·ry (dĭs-săt′ĭs-făk′tə-rē) *adj.* Causing dissatisfaction; unsatisfactory.

dis·sat·is·fied (dĭs-săt′ĭs-fīd′) *adj.* Feeling or showing a lack of contentment; displeased; discontented.

dis·sat·is·fy (dĭs-săt′ĭs-fī′) *tr.v.* **-fied, -fy·ing.** To fail to meet the expectations or fulfill the desires of; to disappoint.

dis·sect (dĭ-sĕkt′, dī-, dī′sĕkt′) *tr.v.* **1.** To cut apart or separate (tissue), esp. for anatomical study or in surgery. **2.** To examine, analyze, or criticize in minute detail. [Latin *dissectus,* from *dissecāre,* to cut apart.] —**dis·sec′tion** *n.*

dis·sect·ed (dĭ-sĕk′tĭd, dī-) *adj.* *Bot.* Divided into numerous narrow segments or lobes: *dissected leaves.*

dis·sem·ble (dĭ-sĕm′bəl) *v.* **-bled, -bling.** —*tr.v.* **1.** To disguise or conceal the real nature of, as feelings or motives. **2.** To make a false show of; feign. —*intr.v.* To conceal one's real motives, nature, or feelings under a pretense. [Middle English *dissemblen,* from Old French *dessembler,* to be different.] —**dis·sem′bler** *n.*

dis·sem·i·nate (dĭ-sĕm′ə-nāt′) *tr.v.* **-nat·ed, -nat·ing.** To spread widely; distribute: *disseminate information.* [From Latin *dissēmināre.*] —**dis·sem′i·na′tion** *n.* —**dis·sem′i·na′tor** *n.*

dis·sen·sion (dĭ-sĕn′shən) *n.* A difference of opinion, esp. one that causes a dispute or strife within a group. —See Syns at **conflict.** [Middle English *dissencioun,* from Old French *dissension,* from Latin *dissentīre,* to dissent.]

dis·sent (dĭ-sĕnt′) *intr.v.* **1.** To disagree; differ. **2.** To withhold assent or approval. —See Syns at **disagree.** —*n.* **1.** Difference of opinion. **2.** The refusal to conform to the authority or doctrine of an established church; nonconformity. —See Syns at **conflict.** [Middle English *dissenten,* from Latin *dissentīre.*]

dis·sent·er (dĭ-sĕn′tər) *n.* **1.** Someone who dissents. **2.** Often **Dissenter.** Someone who refuses to accept the doctrines or usages of an established or national church, esp. a Protestant who dissents from the Church of England.

dis·ser·ta·tion (dĭs′ər-tā′shən) *n.* A lengthy and formal treatise or discourse on a subject, esp. one written by a candidate for the doctoral degree at a university; thesis. [Latin *dissertātiō,* discourse, from *disserere,* to discuss : *dis-,* apart + *serere,* to join.]

dis·serv·ice (dĭs-sûr′vĭs) *n.* A harmful action; an ill turn.

dis·si·dence (dĭs′ĭ-dəns) *n.* Disagreement, as of opinion or belief; difference; dissent. —See Syns at **conflict.**

dis·si·dent (dĭs′ĭ-dənt) *adj.* Disagreeing, as in opinion or belief. —*n.* Someone who disagrees: *a political.dissident.* [Latin *dissidēns,* from *dissidēre,* to disagree.]

dis·sim·i·lar (dĭ-sĭm′ə-lər) *adj.* Unlike; distinct. —See Syns at **different.** —**dis·sim′i·lar·ly** *adv.*

dis·sim·i·lar·i·ty (dĭ-sĭm′ə-lăr′ĭ-tē) *n., pl.* **-ties.** 1. The quality of being unlike; difference. 2. A point of distinction.

dis·si·mil·i·tude (dĭs′ĭ-mĭl′ĭ-tōōd′, -tyōōd′) *n.* Lack of resemblance; difference; dissimilarity.

dis·sim·u·late (dĭ-sĭm′yə-lāt′) *v.* **-lat·ed, -lat·ing.** —*tr.v.* To disguise under a feigned appearance; dissemble. —*intr.v.* To conceal one's true feelings or intentions. —**dis·sim′u·la′tion** *n.* —**dis·sim′u·la′tor** *n.*

dis·si·pate (dĭs′ə-pāt′) *v.* **-pat·ed, -pat·ing.** —*tr.v.* 1. To break up and drive away: *Wind dissipated the clouds. Experience dissipated his illusions.* 2. To expend foolishly; squander: *dissipated his inheritance.* —*intr.v.* 1. To vanish by dispersion. 2. To indulge in extravagant pursuit of pleasure. —See Syns at **scatter.** [Middle English *dissipaten,* from Latin *dissipāre.*]

dis·si·pat·ed (dĭs′ə-pā′tĭd) *adj.* 1. Inclined to dissipation; dissolute. 2. Wasted; squandered: *a dissipated fortune.*

dis·si·pa·tion (dĭs′ə-pā′shən) *n.* 1. The act of scattering or the condition of being scattered; dispersion. 2. Wasteful use or expenditure. 3. Dissolute self-indulgence.

dis·so·ci·ate (dĭ-sō′shē-āt′, -sē-) *v.* **-at·ed, -at·ing.** —*tr.v.* 1. To remove from association; to separate. 2. *Chem.* To cause to undergo dissociation. —*intr.v.* 1. To cease associating; to part. 2. *Chem.* To undergo dissociation. [From Latin *dissociāre.*] —**dis·so′ci·a·tive** *adj.*

dis·so·ci·a·tion (dĭ-sō′sē-ā′shən, -shē-) *n.* 1. The act of dissociating or the condition of being dissociated. 2. *Chem.* The process in which some change in physical condition causes a molecule to split into simpler groups of atoms, single atoms, or ions.

dis·sol·u·ble (dĭ-sŏl′yə-bəl) *adj.* Capable of being dissolved. [Latin *dissolūbilis,* from *dissolvere,* to dissolve.] —**dis·sol′u·bil′i·ty** *or* **dis·sol′u·ble·ness** *n.*

dis·so·lute (dĭs′ə-lōōt′) *adj.* Lacking in moral restraint; wanton. [Middle English, from Latin *dissolūtus,* loose, licentious, from *dissolvere,* to dissolve.] —**dis′so·lute′ly** *adv.* —**dis′so·lute′ness** *n.*

dis·so·lu·tion (dĭs′ə-lōō′shən) *n.* 1. The act or process of breaking up into parts, esp. the changing from a solid to a liquid. 2. An act of ending a formal or legal bond or tie. 3. Formal dismissal of an assembly or legislature.

dis·solve (dĭ-zŏlv′) *v.* **-solved, -solv·ing.** —*tr.v.* 1. To cause to pass into solution: *Dissolve the tablet in water.* 2. To cause to fade away or disappear; dispel: *dissolved her anger with kind words.* 3. To break into component parts; disintegrate. 4. To bring to an end; terminate: *dissolve a partnership; dissolve parliament.* —*intr.v.* 1. To pass into solution: *Sugar dissolves in water.* 2. To break up or disperse. 3. To collapse emotionally or psychologically. 4. To fade away or disappear: *His resentment dissolved slowly.* 5. *Motion Pictures & TV.* To shift scenes by having one scene fade out while the next appears behind it and grows clearer as the first dims. [Middle English *dissolven,* from Latin *dissolvere.*] —**dis·solv′a·ble** *adj.* —**dis·solv′er** *n.*

dis·so·nance (dĭs′ə-nəns) *n.* Also **dis·so·nan·cy** (-nən-sē). 1. A harsh or disagreeable combination of sounds. 2. Lack of agreement or consistency. 3. *Mus.* A combination of tones that sounds harsh and is often suggestive of an unrelieved tension.

dis·so·nant (dĭs′ə-nənt) *adj.* 1. Harsh or inharmonious in sound; discordant. 2. Disagreeing or at variance. [Middle English *dissonaunt,* from Old French *dissonant,* from Latin *dissonāre,* to be inharmonious.] —**dis′so·nant·ly** *adv.*

dis·suade (dĭ-swād′) *tr.v.* **-suad·ed, -suad·ing.** To discourage or deter (a person) from a purpose or course of action. —See Syns at **discourage.** [Latin *dissuādēre.*]

dis·sua·sion (dĭ-swā′zhən) *n.* The act of dissuading. [Latin *dissuāsiō,* from *dissuādēre,* to dissuade.] —**dis·sua′sive** *adj.* —**dis·sua′sive·ly** *adv.* —**dis·sua′sive·ness** *n.*

dis·taff (dĭs′tăf′) *n., pl.* **-taffs.** 1. A staff having a cleft end that holds flax, wool, etc. in spinning. 2. Women in general. —*adj.* Female. [Middle English *distaf,* from Old English *distæf* : *dis-,* bunch of flax + STAFF.]

distaff side. The female line or branch of a family.

dis·tal (dĭs′təl) *adj.* Anatomically located far from the origin or line of attachment, as a bone. [DIST(ANT) + -AL.]

dis·tance (dĭs′təns) *n.* 1. *Geom.* **a.** The length of a line segment joining two points. **b.** The length of the shortest line segment that can connect a given point and a given line, a given point and a given surface, a pair of given lines, or a pair of given surfaces. 2. The extent of space, esp. between two points. 3. The interval separating any two specified instants in time. 4. The fact or condition of being apart in space or time; remoteness. 5. A stretch of space without definite limits: *a plane flying some distance off its course.* 6. A point removed in space or time: *clouds appearing in the distance.* 7. The degree of difference that separates two things in relationship: *a substantial distance between their positions.* 8. Chilliness of manner; aloofness; reserve. —*tr.v.* **-tanced, -tanc·ing.** 1. To place or keep at a distance. 2. To leave behind; outrun; outstrip.

dis·tant (dĭs′tənt) *adj.* 1. Far removed in space or time: *a distant peak; the distant past.* 2. Located at, coming from, or going to a distance: *distant lands.* 3. Far apart in relationship: *a distant cousin.* 4. Aloof or unfriendly in manner; cool. —See Syns at **far.** [Middle English *distaunt,* from Old French, from Latin *distāre,* to be remote.] —**dis′tant·ly** *adv.*

dis·taste (dĭs-tāst′) *n.* Disfavor.

dis·taste·ful (dĭs-tāst′fəl) *adj.* Unpleasant; disagreeable. —**dis·taste′ful·ly** *adv.* —**dis·taste′ful·ness** *n.*

dis·taves (dĭs-tāvz′) *n. Rare.* A plural of **distaff.**

dis·tem·per[1] (dĭs-tĕm′pər) *n.* 1. A very contagious virus disease that occurs in dogs and certain other mammals, characterized by a watery discharge from the eyes and nose and often partial paralysis and death. 2. Any illness or disease; an ailment: *"He died . . . of a broken heart, a distemper which kills many more than is generally imagined"* (Fielding). 3. Ill humor; testiness. 4. Disorder or disturbance, esp. of a social or political nature. —*tr.v.* To upset or disturb; to disorder.

dis·tem·per[2] (dĭs-tĕm′pər) *n.* A process of painting in which pigments are mixed with water and a glue-size or casein binder, used for flat wall decoration or for scenic and poster painting. [Middle English *distemperen,* to dissolve, from Medieval Latin *distemperāre.*]

dis·tend (dĭ-stĕnd′) *intr.v.* To become expanded or swollen; to bulge out. —*tr.v.* To cause to expand; dilate. [Middle English *distenden,* from Latin *distendere.*]

dis·ten·tion *or* **dis·ten·sion** (dĭ-stĕn′shən) *n.* The act of distending or the condition of being distended.

dis·till (dĭ-stĭl′) *tr.v.* 1. To subject (a substance) to distillation. 2. To extract (a distillate) by distillation. 3. To purify or refine by or as if by distillation. 4. To separate or extract (the core) of: *distill a lesson from the crisis.* 5. To exude or give off in drops. —*intr.v.* 1. To undergo or be produced by distillation. 2. To fall or exude in drops. [Middle English *distillen,* from Old French *distiller,* from Latin *distillāre.*] —**dis·till′a·ble** *adj.*

dis·til·late (dĭs′tə-lāt′, -lĭt, dĭ-stĭl′ĭt) *n.* 1. The liquid condensed from vapor in distillation. 2. Any essence or pure form.

dis·til·la·tion (dĭs′tə-lā′shən) *n.* 1. Any one of several processes in which a complex mixture or substance is broken up into relatively pure or individual components by being heated until the components vaporize one by one and are made to condense individually. 2. The act of distilling or the condition of being distilled. 3. A distillate.

dis·till·er (dĭ-stĭl′ər) *n.* 1. Someone or something that distills. 2. A producer of alcoholic liquors.

dis·till·er·y (dĭ-stĭl′ə-rē) *n., pl.* **-ies.** An establishment or plant for distilling, esp. alcoholic liquors.

dis·tinct (dĭ-stĭngkt′) *adj.* 1. Distinguished from all others; individual; separate: *distinct personalities; on two distinct occasions.* 2. Easily perceived; clear; plain: *a distinct odor.* 3. Well-defined; explicit; unquestionable: *a distinct disadvantage.* —See Syns at **clear.** [Middle English, different, from Old French, from Latin *distinguere,* to distinguish.] —**dis·tinct′ly** *adv.* —**dis·tinct′ness** *n.*

   Usage: **distinct, distinctive.** *Distinct* applies to what is clearcut, and *distinctive* to what sets a person or thing apart from others. *Distinct* speech is clear; *distinctive* speech calls attention to the style of delivery.

---

dis·tinc·tion (dĭ-stĭngk'shən) *n.* **1.** The act of distinguishing; differentiation. **2.** The condition or fact of being dissimilar or distinct; a difference: *a clear distinction between the candidates' positions.* **3.** A distinguishing factor, attribute, or characteristic: *the distinction of being the youngest general in the army.* **4.** Excellence or eminence: *a man of distinction.* **5.** Recognition of achievement or superiority; honor: *graduate with distinction.*

dis·tinc·tive (dĭ-stĭngk'tĭv) *adj.* Serving to distinguish or set apart from others:*distinctive habits.* —See Syns at **characteristic** and Usage note at **distinct.** —**dis·tinc'tive·ly** *adv.* —**dis·tinc'tive·ness** *n.*

dis·tin·gué (dēs'tăng-gā', dĭs'-, dĭ-stăng'gā') *adj.* Distinguished in appearance or manner. [French.]

dis·tin·guish (dĭ-stĭng'gwĭsh) *tr.v.* **a.** To recognize as being different or distinct: *distinguish the types of crab.* **b.** To recognize differences; discriminate: *distinguish fact and opinion.* **2.** To perceive distinctly; make out: *distinguished three shots.* **3.** To make noticeable or different; set apart: *simple, clear-cut forms that distinguish the architect's style.* **4.** To cause (oneself) to be eminent or recognized: *He distinguished himself as a statesman.* —*intr.v.* To perceive or indicate differences; discriminate: *distinguish between right and wrong.* [Middle English *distinguen,* from Old French *distinguer,* from Latin *distinguere.*] —**dis·tin'guish·a·ble** *adj.* —**dis·tin'guish·a·bly** *adv.*

dis·tin·guished (dĭ-stĭng'gwĭsht) *adj.* **1.** Characterized by excellence or distinction; eminent; renowned: *a distinguished composer.* **2.** Dignified in conduct or appearance.

dis·tort (dĭ-stôrt') *tr.v.* **1.** To twist out of a proper or natural shape; contort. **2.** To give a false account of; misrepresent. [Latin *distortus,* from *distorquere.*]

dis·tor·tion (dĭ-stôr'shən) *n.* **1. a.** The act of distorting. **b.** The condition of being distorted. **2.** Something distorted. **3.** A distorted image produced by an imperfection in a lens or other optical system. **4.** Any unwanted change in an electrical or electromagnetic signal.

dis·tract (dĭ-străkt') *tr.v.* **1.** To turn away the attention or interest of; to sidetrack; divert. **2.** To upset emotionally or pull in conflicting directions; unsettle; bewilder. [Middle English *distracten,* from Latin *distrahere,* to draw away.] —**dis·tract'ing·ly** *adv.*

dis·trac·tion (dĭ-străk'shən) *n.* **1.** The act of distracting or the condition of being distracted. **2.** Something that distracts, esp. an amusement. **3.** Extreme mental or emotional disturbance.

dis·traught (dĭ-strôt') *adj.* **1.** Anxious or agitated; harried; worried. **2.** Crazed; mad. [Middle English *distraught,* distracted, from Latin *distrahere,* to distract.]

dis·tress (dĭ-strĕs') *n.* **1.** Pain or suffering of mind or body; sorrow. **2.** Severe psychological strain, usu. from exhaustion or crisis. **3.** The condition of being in need of immediate assistance. —*tr.v.* To cause anxiety or suffering to; to worry. [Middle English *distressen,* from Old French *destresser,* from *destresse,* narrow passage, from Latin *distringere,* to draw tight.] —**dis·tress'ing·ly** *adv.*

Syns: distress, agony, anguish, hurt, misery, pain, woe *n.* Core meaning: A state of suffering (*felt great distress over the death in the family*).

dis·tress·ful (dĭ-strĕs'fəl) *adj.* **1.** Causing distress. **2.** Experiencing or showing distress. —**dis·tress'ful·ly** *adv.*

dis·trib·u·tar·y (dĭ-strĭb'yə-tĕr'ē) *n., pl.* **-ies.** A branch of a river that flows away from the main stream.

dis·trib·ute (dĭ-strĭb'yōōt) *tr.v.* **-ut·ed, -ut·ing. 1.** To divide and give out in portions; parcel out. **2.** To hand or send out; deliver: *distribute circulars.* **3.** To spread or scatter over an area: *franchises distributed across the state.* **4.** To market, esp. as a wholesaler. **5.** To separate into categories; classify. **6.** To apply (multiplication by a given factor) to each of the terms that make up a mathematical expression. [Middle English *distributen,* from Latin *distribuere.*]

dis·tri·bu·tion (dĭs'trə-byōō'shən) *n.* **1.** The act of distributing or the condition of being distributed. **2.** Something distributed. **3.** The way in which a thing is distributed. **4.** Division into categories; classification. **5.** The process of marketing and merchandising goods. **6.** Any array of objects or events in space or time.

dis·trib·u·tive (dĭ-strĭb'yə-tĭv) *adj.* **1.** Of or pertaining to distribution. **2.** Of or pertaining to the distributive prop-

erty. **3.** *Gram.* Referring to each individual or entity of a group separately rather than collectively, for example, *every* in the sentence *every employee attended the meeting.* —*n.* A distributive word or term. —**dis·trib'u·tive·ly** *adv.*

distributive property. The property of a mathematical operation, ♦, that with respect to another operation, •, is stated as $(a \blacklozenge b) \bullet (a \blacklozenge c) = a \blacklozenge (b \bullet c)$.

dis·trib·u·tor (dĭ-strĭb'yə-tər) *n.* **1.** Someone or something that distributes. **2.** A business that markets or sells merchandise, esp. a wholesaler. **3.** A device that applies electric current in proper sequence to the spark plugs of an engine.

dis·trict (dĭs'trĭkt) *n.* **1.** A part of a geographical unit marked out by law for a particular purpose: *a school district.* **2.** A distinctive area: *the lake district.* —*tr.v.* To mark off or divide into districts. [French, from Medieval Latin *districtus,* (area of) jurisdiction, from Latin *distringere,* to detain.]

district attorney. The prosecuting attorney of a given judicial district.

dis·trust (dĭs-trŭst') *n.* Lack of trust; misgiving; suspicion. —*tr.v.* To lack confidence in; to doubt or suspect.

Syns: distrust, doubt, mistrust, suspicion *n.* Core meaning: Lack of trust (*regarded the new student with distrust*).

dis·trust·ful (dĭs-trŭst'fəl) *adj.* Feeling or showing doubt; suspicious. —**dis·trust'ful·ly** *adv.* —**dis·trust'ful·ness** *n.*

dis·turb (dĭ-stûrb') *tr.v.* **1.** To destroy the tranquillity or settled condition of. **2.** To trouble emotionally or mentally. **3.** To intrude upon; interrupt. **4.** To put out of order; disarrange. —See Syns at **annoy.** [Middle English *destourben,* from Old French *destorber,* from Latin *disturbāre.*] —**dis·turb'er** *n.* —**dis·turb'ing·ly** *adv.*

dis·tur·bance (dĭ-stûr'bəns) *n.* **1.** The act of disturbing or the condition of being disturbed. **2.** Something that disturbs. **3.** A public disorder. **4.** Abnormal or improper function: *emotional disturbances.*

di·sul·fide (dī-sŭl'fīd') *n.* A chemical compound containing two sulfur atoms combined with other elements or radicals. Also called **bisulfide.**

dis·un·ion (dĭs-yōōn'yən) *n.* Lack of unity; discord.

dis·u·nite (dĭs'yōō-nīt') *v.* **-nit·ed, -nit·ing.** —*tr.v.* **1.** To separate or sever. **2.** To cause dissension among. —*intr.v.* To become separate.

dis·u·ni·ty (dĭs-yōō'nĭ-tē) *n., pl.* **-ties.** Lack of unity or agreement; discord; dissension.

dis·use (dĭs-yōōs') *n.* The condition of not being used or of being no longer in use; desuetude.

di·syl·la·ble (dī'sĭl'ə-bəl) *n.* A word with two syllables. —**di'syl·lab'ic** (-lăb'ĭk) *adj.*

ditch (dĭch) *n.* A long narrow trench or furrow dug in the ground, as for irrigation, drainage, or a boundary line. —*tr.v.* **1.** To dig or make a ditch in or around. **2.** To drive (a vehicle) into a ditch. **3.** *Slang.* To throw aside; to discard. **4.** *Slang.* To escape from or avoid. [Middle English *dich,* from Old English *dīc,* moat, ditch.]

dith·er (dĭth'ər) *n.* A condition of agitation, nervous excitement, or indecision. [From Middle English *didderen.*]

dith·y·ramb (dĭth'ĭ-răm', -rămb') *n.* **1.** In ancient Greece, a frenzied and impassioned choric hymn and dance in honor of Dionysus. **2.** An irregular poetic expression. [Latin *dīthyrambus,* from Greek *dithurambos.*] —**dith'y·ram'bic** (-răm'bĭk) *adj.*

dit·to (dĭt'ō) *n., pl.* **-tos. 1.** The same as stated above or before. Used to avoid repeating a word and indicated by a pair of small marks (') placed under the word that would otherwise be repeated. **2.** A duplicate or copy. —*adv.* As before. —*tr.v.* **-toed, -to·ing.** To duplicate or repeat. [Italian dial. *ditto,* "said."]

dit·ty (dĭt'ē) *n., pl.* **-ties.** A short, simple song or the lyrics for it. [Middle English *ditti,* from Old French *ditie,* composition, from Latin *dictātum,* something dictated, from *dictāre,* to dictate, freq. of *dīcere,* to say.]

ditty bag. A bag used by sailors to carry small items such as sewing implements. [Orig. unknown.]

di·u·ret·ic (dī'ə-rĕt'ĭk) *adj.* Tending to increase the discharge of urine. —*n.* A diuretic drug. [Middle English *diuretik,* from Late Latin *diurēticus,* from Greek *diourētikos,* from *diourein,* to pass urine.]

di·ur·nal (dī-ûr'nəl) *adj.* **1.** Pertaining to or occurring in a

---

day or each day; daily. **2.** Occurring or active during the daytime rather than at night: *diurnal birds of prey.* **3.** *Bot.* Opening during daylight hours and closing at night: *diurnal flowers.* [Middle English, from Latin *diurnālis,* from *diurnus,* of a day, daily, from *diēs,* day.] —**di·ur′nal·ly** *adv.*

di·va (dē′və) *n., pl.* **-vas.** A prima donna. [Italian, "goddess."]

di·va·gate (dī′və-gāt′, dĭv′ə-) *intr.v.* **-gat·ed, -gat·ing.** To wander or drift about. [From Late Latin *dīvagārī.*] —**di′va·ga′tion** *n.*

di·va·lent (dī-vā′lənt) *adj.* Bivalent.

di·van (dī-văn′, dī′văn′) *n.* A long couch, usu. without a back or arms, and often designed to be used as a bed. [French, from Turkish, from Persian, register.]

dive (dīv) *intr.v.* **dived** or **dove** (dōv), **dived, div·ing.** **1.** To plunge headfirst into water, esp. for sport. **2.** To go toward the bottom of a body of water; submerge. **3.** To fall through the air. **4.** To drop sharply and rapidly; plummet: *stock prices dived.* **5.** To lunge, leap, or dash. **6.** To plunge into some question, activity, or study. —*n.* **1.** A headlong plunge into water, esp. one executed with athletic skill and form. **2.** A nearly vertical descent at an accelerated speed through water or space. **3.** A quick, pronounced drop: *a dive in prices.* **4.** *Slang.* A disreputable or run-down bar or nightclub. **5.** *Slang.* A knockout feigned by prearrangement between prize fighters. [Middle English *diven,* from Old English *dȳfan,* to dip, immerse.]

dive bomber. A bomber that releases its bombs at the end of a steep dive toward its target.

div·er (dī′vər) *n.* **1.** A person who dives into water. **2.** A person who works under water, esp. one equipped with breathing apparatus. **3.** Any of several diving birds, esp. the loon.

di·verge (dī-vûrj′, dĭ-) *intr.v.* **-verged, -verg·ing.** **1.** To go or extend in different directions from a common point; branch out. **2.** To differ, as in opinion or manner. **3.** To turn aside from a course or norm; to deviate. [Late Latin *dīvergere,* to turn aside.]

di·ver·gence (dī-vûr′jəns, dĭ-) *n.* Also **di·ver·gen·cy** (-jən-sē) *pl.* **-cies.** **1.** The act of diverging or the condition of being diverged. **2.** Departure from a course or norm; deviation. **3.** Difference, as of opinion.

di·ver·gent (dī-vûr′jənt, dĭ-) *adj.* **1.** Drawing or moving apart from a common point. **2.** Departing from convention; deviant. **3.** Differing. —**di·ver′gent·ly** *adv.*

di·vers (dī′vərz) *adj.* Various; several; sundry.

di·verse (dī-vûrs′, dĭ-, dī′vûrs′) *adj.* **1.** Distinct in kind; disparate; unlike. **2.** Having variety in form: *a nation of diverse people.* [Middle English, from Old French *divers,* from Latin *dīversus,* from *dīvertere,* to turn aside.] —**di·verse′ly** *adv.* —**di·verse′ness** *n.*

di·ver·si·fy (dī-vûr′sə-fī′, dĭ-) *v.* **-fied, -fy·ing.** —*tr.v.* **1. a.** To make diverse; give variety to; vary. **b.** To extend (activities) into disparate fields, as a business enterprise. **2.** To distribute (investments) among several companies in order to average the risk of loss. —*intr.v.* To spread out activities or investments, as a business. —**di·ver′si·fi·ca′tion** (-fĭ-kā′shən) *n.*

di·ver·sion (dī-vûr′zhən, -shən, dĭ-) *n.* **1.** An act or instance of diverting. **2.** Something that distracts the mind and relaxes or entertains. **3.** A military maneuver to divert the enemy's attention from the planned point of attack. —See Syns at **recreation.** —**di·ver′sion·ar′y** (-zhə-něr′ē) *adj.*

di·ver·si·ty (dī-vûr′sĭ-tē, dĭ-) *n., pl.* **-ties. 1.** The fact or quality of being diverse; difference. **2.** Variety; multiformity.

di·vert (dī-vûrt′, dĭ-) *tr.v.* **1.** To turn aside from a course or direction. **2.** To distract. **3.** To amuse or entertain. —See Syns at **amuse.** [Middle English *diverten,* from Old French *divertir,* from Latin *dīvertere,* to turn aside.]

di·ver·tic·u·li·tis (dī′vûr-tĭk′yə-lī′tĭs) *n.* Inflammation of a diverticulum.

di·ver·tic·u·lum (dī′vûr-tĭk′yə-ləm) *n., pl.* **-la** (-lə). A pouch or sac branching out from a hollow organ or structure, such as the intestine. [From Latin *dēverticulum,* bypath, from *dēvertere,* to turn aside.]

di·ver·ti·men·to (dī-věr′tə-měn′tō) *n., pl.* **-tos** or **-ti** (-tē). *Mus.* A light instrumental work, usu. with several short movements. [Italian, "diversion."]

di·ver·tisse·ment (də-vûr′tĭs-mənt; *Fr.* dē-věr′tēs-mäN′) *n.*

A short ballet or other performance, usu. given as an interlude in the opera or theater. [French, "diversion."]

di·vest (dī-věst′, dĭ-) *tr.v.* **1.** To strip, as of clothes. **2.** To deprive, as of rights. [Var. of earlier *devest,* from Old French *desvestir,* to undress.]

di·vide (dī-vīd′) *v.* **-vid·ed, -vid·ing.** —*tr.v.* **1.** To separate into parts, sections, or groups. **2.** To separate and group according to kind; classify. **3.** To separate into opposing factions; disunite. **4.** To separate from; cut off. **5.** To apportion or distribute among a number. **6.** *Math.* **a.** To subject to the process of division. **b.** To be an exact divisor of. —*intr.v.* **1.** To become separated into parts; branch. **2.** To form into factions. **3.** To perform the mathematical operation of division. —See Syns at **separate.** —*n.* A ridge separating two areas of land each drained by a different river system; watershed. [Middle English *dividen,* from Latin *dīvidere.*]

di·vid·ed (dī-vī′dĭd) *adj.* **1.** Separated into parts, pieces, or areas. **2.** In disagreement: *a divided opinion.* **3.** Pulled by conflicting interests: *divided loyalties.* **4.** Having the lanes for opposing traffic separated. Said of a highway. **5.** *Bot.* Having indentations extending to the midrib or base and forming distinct divisions: *divided leaves.*

div·i·dend (dĭv′ĭ-dĕnd′) *n.* **1.** *Math.* A number or quantity to be divided. **2.** A share of profits received by a stockholder. **3.** *Informal.* A share of a surplus; bonus. [French, from Latin *dīvidendum,* "thing to be divided."]

di·vid·er (dī-vī′dər) *n.* **1.** Something that divides, esp. a partition. **2. dividers.** A device resembling a compass, used for dividing lines and transferring measurements.

div·i·na·tion (dĭv′ə-nā′shən) *n.* **1.** The art or act of foretelling future events or revealing occult knowledge by means of alleged supernatural agency. **2.** A clever presentiment.

di·vine[1] (dī-vīn′) *adj.* **-vin·er, -vin·est. 1.** Being or having the nature of a god: *a divine being.* **2.** Of, relating to, or coming from a god: *divine love.* **3.** In the service or worship of a deity: *divine rights.* **4.** Superhuman; godlike: *divine beauty.* **5.** Supremely good; magnificent. —*n.* **1.** A clergyman. **2.** A person learned in theology. [Middle English, from Old French *devin,* from Latin *dīvīnus,* from *dīvus,* god.] —**di·vine′ly** *adv.*

di·vine[2] (dī-vīn′) *v.* **-vined, -vin·ing.** —*tr.v.* **1.** To foretell or prophesy. **2.** To know or guess by intuition or reflection. —*intr.v.* **1.** To practice divination. **2.** To guess. [Middle English *divinen,* from Old French *deviner,* from Latin *dīvīnāre,* from *dīvīnus,* soothsayer, "(one) inspired by the gods."] —**di·vin′er** *n.*

divine right of kings. The doctrine that monarchs derive their right to rule from and are accountable only to God.

diving bell. A large vessel for underwater work, open on the bottom and supplied with air under pressure.

diving board. A flexible board from which a dive may be executed, secured at one end and projecting over water.

diving suit. A heavy waterproof garment with a detachable air-fed helmet, used for underwater work.

divining rod. A forked branch or stick that allegedly indicates underground water or minerals by bending downward when held over a source.

di·vin·i·ty (dī-vĭn′ĭ-tē) *n., pl.* **-ties. 1.** The condition or quality of being divine. **2. a. the Divinity.** God; the godhead. **b.** A god or goddess; a deity. **3.** Godlike character.

di·vis·i·ble (dī-vĭz′ə-bəl) *adj.* Capable of being divided. —**di·vis′i·bil′i·ty** *n.*

di·vi·sion (dī-vĭzh′ən) *n.* Abbr. **div. 1.** The act or process of dividing or the condition of being divided. **2.** Something that serves to divide or keep separate, as a boundary or partition. **3.** One of the parts, sections, or groups into which something is divided: *the sales division.* **4.** *Mil.* A self-contained administrative and tactical unit that is smaller than a corps. **5.** A major taxonomic category that corresponds approx. to a phylum, used esp. in botany. **6.** Disagreement; disunion. **7.** *Math.* The operation of determining how many times one quantity is contained in another. —**di·vi′sion·al** *adj.*

division of labor. The distribution of tasks among members of a group to increase efficiency.

di·vi·sive (dī-vī′sĭv) *adj.* Creating or tending to create discord or dissension. —**di·vi′sive·ly** *adv.* —**di·vi′sive·ness** *n.*

di·vi·sor (dī-vī′zər) *n. Math.* The quantity by which another quantity, the dividend, is to be divided.

di·vorce (dĭ-vôrs′, -vōrs′) *n.* **1.** The legal dissolution of a marriage. **2.** A complete separation of things. —*tr.v.* **-vorced, -vorc·ing. 1.** To dissolve the marriage between. **2.** To shed (one's spouse) by legal divorce. **3.** To separate or remove. —See Syns at **separate.** [Middle English, from Old French, from Latin *dīvortium,* separation, from *dīvertere,* to turn aside.]

di·vor·cé (dĭ-vôr-sā′, -sē′, -vôr-, -vôr′sā′, -sē′, -vôr′-) *n.* A divorced man.

di·vor·cée (dĭ-vôr-sā′, -sē′, -vōr-, -vôr′sā′, -sē′, -vōr′-) *n.* A divorced woman. [French.]

div·ot (dĭv′ət) *n.* A piece of turf torn up by a golf club in striking the ball. [Scottish *deva(i)t.*]

di·vulge (dĭ-vŭlj′) *tr.v.* **-vulged, -vulg·ing.** To disclose (a secret); make known; reveal. [Middle English *divulgen,* from Latin *dīvulgāre,* to spread abroad among the people.] —**di·vul′gence** *n.* —**di·vulg′er** *n.*

Dix·ie (dĭk′sē) *n.* The Southern states, esp. those states that joined the Confederacy. [Orig. unknown.]

Dix·ie·crat (dĭk′sē-krăt′) *n.* A member of a group of conservative Southern Democrats who dissented from the national party and formed the States' Rights Party in 1948.

Dix·ie·land (dĭk′sē-lănd′) *n.* A style of instrumental jazz associated with New Orleans and characterized by a fast two-beat rhythm and improvised solos.

diz·zy (dĭz′ē) *adj.* **-zi·er, -zi·est. 1.** Having a whirling sensation. **2.** Bewildered or confused. **3.** Producing or tending to produce giddiness: *a dizzy height.* **4.** *Informal.* Scatterbrained; silly; foolish. —*tr.v.* **-zied, -zy·ing.** To make dizzy; confuse; bewilder. [Middle English *dysy,* from Old English *dysig,* foolish.] —**diz′zi·ly** *adv.* —**diz′zi·ness** *n.*

DNA A nucleic acid that is the main constituent of the chromosomes of living cells, consisting of two long chains of phosphate and sugar units twisted into a double helix and joined by hydrogen bonds. The sequence of the bonds determines individual heredity characteristics; deoxyribonucleic acid. [D(EOXYRIBO)N(UCLEIC)A(CID).]

do¹ (do͞o) *v.* **did** (dĭd) or *archaic* **didst** (dĭdst), **done** (dŭn), **do·ing, does** (dŭz). Present tense, first person, **do;** second person, **do** or *archaic* **do·est** (do͞o′ĭst), **dost** (dŭst); third person singular, **does** or *archaic* **do·eth** (do͞o′əth), **doth** (dŭth); third person plural, **do.** —*tr.v.* **1.** To perform or execute: *do a good job.* **2.** To carry out the requirements of; fulfill; complete. **3.** To produce by a creative effort: *did some sketches.* **4.** To act so as to bring about: *It won't do any good.* **b.** To act so as to confer: *do honor to someone.* **5.** To bring or put forth: *I'll do what I can.* **6.** To deal with so as to prepare, make ready, or put in order: *did the dishes; did her hair.* **7.** To render or give: *She did me a big favor.* **8.** To work at: *She's a surgeon; what do you do?* **9.** To work out or at: *do homework; do a math problem.* **10.** To present or perform; stage: *We're going to do Romeo and Juliet.* **11.** To have the role of; play: *He did Caliban in summer stock.* **12.** To cover (a specified distance) in traveling: *do a mile in four minutes.* **13.** To travel through, esp. as a tourist: *do Europe on five dollars a day.* **14.** To meet the needs of sufficiently: *This room will do us very nicely.* **15.** To furnish or decorate: *an apartment done in a severe, modern style.* **16.** *Informal.* To serve out in prison. **17.** *Slang.* To cheat or swindle: *did him out of his share.* —*intr.v.* **1.** To behave or conduct oneself; to act: *They do as they are told.* **2.** To act effectively or energetically; strive: *Do or die.* **3.** To get along; fare: *doing well at school.* **4.** To be adequate: *This coat will do for another season.* **5.** Used as an auxiliary: **a.** In questions, negative statements, and inverted phrases: *Do you understand? I did not sleep well. Little did he suspect.* **b.** As a substitute to avoid repetition of an antecedent verb: *She tries as hard as they do.* **c.** For emphasis: *I do want to be sure.* —*phrasal verbs.* **do away with. 1.** To dispose of; eliminate. **2.** To destroy; kill. **do for.** To take care of. **do in.** *Slang.* **1.** To tire completely; exhaust. **2.** To kill. —See Syns at **murder. do up.** To dress up; deck out. —*n., pl.* **do's** or **dos.** A statement of what should be done: *do's and don'ts.* [Middle English *don,* from Old English *dōn.*]

do² (dō) *n., pl.* **dos.** *Mus.* The first tone of the diatonic scale. [Italian.]

do·a·ble (do͞o′ə-bəl) *adj.* Capable of being done.

dob·bin (dŏb′ĭn) *n.* A horse, esp. a workhorse. [From *Dobbin,* alteration of *Robin,* pet form of *Robert.*]

Do·ber·man pin·scher (dō′bər-mən pĭn′shər). A fairly large dog of a breed originating in Germany, with a smooth, short, usu. black coat. [German : *Dobermann,* after Ludwig *Dobermann,* 19th-cent. German dog-breeder + *Pinscher,* terrier.]

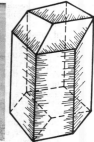

Doberman pinscher   dodecahedron

dob·son fly (dŏb′sən). An insect, *Corydalus cornutus,* having four large wings and whose larval form is the hellgrammite. [Perh. from the name *Dobson.*]

do·cent (dō′sənt, dō-sĕnt′) *n.* A teacher or lecturer who is not a regular faculty member. [Obs. German *Docent,* from Latin *docēre,* to teach.]

doc·ile (dŏs′əl, -īl′) *adj.* Easily managed or taught: *a docile child.* —See Syns at **gentle.** [Latin *docilis,* from *docēre,* to teach.] —**doc′ile·ly** *adv.* —**do·cil′i·ty** (dŏ-sĭl′ĭ-tē, dō-) *n.*

dock¹ (dŏk) *n.* **1.** A landing pier for ships or boats. **2.** The area of water between two piers or alongside a pier that receives a ship. **3.** Often **docks.** A group of piers on a harbor or other waterway. **4.** A loading platform for trucks or trains. —*tr.v.* **1.** To maneuver into or next to a dock. **2.** *Aerospace.* To couple (as two or more spacecraft) in space. —*intr.v.* To move or come into a dock. [Middle Low German and Middle Dutch *docke.*]

dock² (dŏk) *n.* **1.** The solid or fleshy part of an animal's tail. **2.** The stump of an animal's tail after it has been bobbed or clipped. —*tr.v.* **1.** To clip short or cut off. **2.** To withhold a part of the wages or salary of (an employee) as punishment. [Middle English *dok,* trimmed hair (of a tail).]

dock³ (dŏk) *n.* An enclosed place where the defendant stands or sits in a criminal court. [Flemish *dok,* cage.]

dock⁴ (dŏk) *n.* Any of various weedy plants of the genus *Rumex,* with clusters of small greenish or reddish flowers. [Middle English, from Old English *docce.*]

dock·age (dŏk′ĭj) *n.* **1.** A charge for docking privileges. **2.** Facilities for docking vessels. **3.** The docking of ships.

dock·et (dŏk′ĭt) *n.* **1.** *Law.* **a.** A brief entry of the proceedings in a court of justice. **b.** The book containing such entries. **c.** A calendar of the cases awaiting action in a court. **2.** Any list of things to be done; an agenda. —*tr.v.* To enter in a docket. [Middle English *doggette.*]

dock·hand (dŏk′hănd′) *n.* A dock worker; longshoreman.

dock·yard (dŏk′yärd′) *n.* A shipyard.

doc·tor (dŏk′tər) *n.* **1.** A person trained in the healing arts and licensed to practice, esp. a physician, surgeon, dentist, or veterinarian. **2.** A person who holds the highest academic degree awarded by a college or university. **3.** *Archaic.* A learned person; teacher. —*tr.v.* **1.** To give medical treatment to. **2.** To repair, esp. in a makeshift manner. **3.** To change or falsify (evidence) so as to make it favorable to oneself: *doctor evidence.* **4.** To add ingredients to (food) in order to improve its taste or appearance. —*intr.v.* To practice medicine. [Middle English *doctour,* teacher, from Old French *docteur,* from Medieval Latin *doctor,* from Latin *docēre,* to teach.]

doc·tor·al (dŏk′tər-əl) *adj.* Of a doctor or doctorate.

doc·tor·ate (dŏk′tər-ĭt) *n.* The degree or status of a doctor.

doc·tri·naire (dŏk′trə-nâr′) *n.* A person who holds to a theory without regard to whether it is practical. —*adj.* Obstinately devoted to speculative, impractical doctrines. [French, from *doctrine,* doctrine.]

doc·trine (dŏk′trĭn) *n.* **1.** Something that is taught. **2.** A principle or creed of principles presented for acceptance or belief, as by a religious or political group; dogma; theory. [Middle English, from Old French, from Latin *doctrīna*, teaching, learning, from *doctor*, teacher.] —**doc·tri'nal** *adj.*

doc·u·ment (dŏk'yə-mənt) *n.* An official or original paper that can serve as evidence, information, or proof about something. —*tr.v.* (dŏk'yə-mĕnt'). To support, as a claim or statement, with evidence or information. [Middle English, instruction, from Old French, from Latin *documentum*, lesson, from *docēre*, to teach.] —**doc'u·ment'a·ble** *adj.*

doc·u·men·ta·ry (dŏk'yə-mĕn'tə-rē) *adj.* **1.** Consisting of or based upon documents: *documentary evidence.* **2.** Presenting facts objectively. —*n.*, *pl.* **-ries.** A film presentation of a factual account of some subject.

doc·u·men·ta·tion (dŏk'yə-mĕn-tā'shən) *n.* **1.** The supplying of documents or supporting references or records. **2.** The documents or references supplied.

dod·der¹ (dŏd'ər) *intr.v.* **1.** To shake or tremble, as from age. **2.** To move in a feeble manner. [From Middle English *dadiren*.]

dod·der² (dŏd'ər) *n.* Any of various parasitic vines of the genus *Cuscuta*, with a few minute, scalelike leaves, and small whitish flowers. [Middle English *doder*.]

do·dec·a·gon (dō-dĕk'ə-gŏn') *n.* A polygon with 12 sides. [Greek *dōdeka*, twelve + -GON.]

do·dec·a·he·dron (dō-dĕk'ə-hē'drən, dō'dĕk-) *n.*, *pl.* **-drons** or **-dra** (-drə). A solid figure with 12 faces. [Greek *dōdeka*, twelve + -HEDRON.]

dodge (dŏj) *v.* **dodged, dodg·ing.** —*tr.v.* **1.** To avoid by moving quickly aside. **2.** To evade by cunning, trickery, or deceit. —*intr.v.* **1.** To move aside quickly. **2.** To practice trickery or cunning; prevaricate. —See Syns at **avoid.** —*n.* **1.** A quick move or shift. **2.** A clever or evasive plan or device; stratagem. [Orig. unknown.]

dodg·er (dŏj'ər) *n.* **1.** A person who dodges or evades, esp. a shifty or dishonest person. **2.** A small printed handbill. **3.** A corncake.

do·do (dō'dō) *n.*, *pl.* **-does** or **-dos.** A large flightless bird, *Raphus cucullatus*, of the island of Mauritius in the Indian Ocean, that has been extinct since the late 17th cent. [Portuguese *doudo*, from *doudo*, stupid.]

doe (dō) *n.*, *pl.* **does** or **doe. 1.** An adult female deer. **2.** The female of certain other animals, such as the kangaroo. [Middle English *do*, from Old English *dā*.]

do·er (dōo'ər) *n.* **1.** A person who does something, as an agent. **2.** An esp. active and energetic person.

does (dŭz) *v.* Present tense, third person singular of **do.**

doe·skin (dō'skĭn') *n.* **1.** The skin of a doe, deer, or goat. **2.** Leather made from this and used esp. for gloves. **3.** A fine, soft, smooth woolen fabric.

does·n't (dŭz'ənt). Contraction of does not.

do·est (dōo'ĭst) *v. Archaic.* Second person singular, present tense of **do.**

do·eth (dōo'əth) *v. Archaic.* Third person singular, present tense of **do.**

doff (dŏf, dôf) *tr.v.* **1.** To take off, as clothes. **2.** To lift or tip (one's hat). **3.** To throw out or away; discard. [Middle English *doffen*, "do off."]

dog (dôg, dŏg) *n.* **1.** A domesticated carnivorous mammal, *Canis familiaris*, prob. derived from several wild species. **2.** Any of various other animals of the family Canidae. **3.** A male canine animal. **4.** *Informal.* A fellow: *you lucky dog.* **5.** A hopelessly inferior product or creation: *That play was some dog.* **6.** A contemptible person. **7. dogs.** *Slang.* The feet. **8.** Any of various metallic devices used for gripping or holding heavy objects. —*adv.* Totally; completely: *dog-tired.* —*tr.v.* **dogged, dog·ging.** To track or follow after like a dog. [Middle English, from Old English *docga*.]

dog·bane (dôg'bān', dŏg'-) *n.* Any of several usu. poisonous plants of the genus *Apocynum*, with milky juice.

dog·cart (dôg'kärt', dŏg'-) *n.* **1.** A vehicle drawn by one horse and accommodating two persons seated back to back. **2.** A small cart pulled by dogs.

dog·catch·er (dôg'kăch'ər, dŏg'-) *n.* Someone appointed or elected to impound stray dogs.

dog days. The hot, sultry period between mid-July and September. [After the *Dog Star* Sirius, which rises and sets with the sun during this time.]

doge (dōj) *n.* The elected chief magistrate of the former republics of Venice and Genoa. [French, from Italian, from Latin *dux*, leader, from *dūcere*, to lead.]

dog-ear (dôg'îr', dŏg'-) *n.* A turned-down corner of the page of a book. —**dog'-eared'** *adj.*

dog-eat-dog (dôg'ĕt-dôg', dŏg'ĕt-dŏg') *adj.* Ruthlessly competitive or acquisitive: *a dog-eat-dog society.*

dog·face (dôg'fās', dŏg'-) *n. Slang.* An infantryman.

dog·fight (dôg'fīt', dŏg'-) *n.* **1.** A violent fight; a brawl. **2.** An aerial battle between fighter planes.

dog·ged (dôg'gĭd, dŏg'ĭd) *adj.* Not yielding readily; willful; stubborn: *dogged efforts.* —See Syns at **obstinate.** —**dog'·ged·ly** *adv.* —**dog'ged·ness** *n.*

dog·ger·el (dô'gər-əl, dŏg'ər-) *n.* Verse of a loose, irregular rhythm or of a trivial nature with little artistic value. [Middle English *dogerel*, worthless.]

dog·house (dôg'hous', dŏg'-) *n.* A small house or shelter for a dog. —**idiom. in the doghouse.** *Slang.* In disfavor.

do·gie (dō'gē) *n.* Also **do·gy** *pl.* **-gies.** *Western U.S.* A motherless or stray calf. [Orig. unknown.]

dog·ma (dôg'mə, dŏg'-) *n.*, *pl.* **-mas** or **-ma·ta** (-mə-tə). **1.** *Theol.* A system of doctrines proclaimed true, as by a religious sect. **2.** A principle, belief, or idea, esp. one authoritatively considered to be absolute truth. **3.** A system of such principles or beliefs. [Latin, from Greek, belief, from *dokein*, to seem.]

dog·mat·ic (dôg-măt'ĭk, dŏg'-) *adj.* **1.** Of or pertaining to dogma. **2.** Expressing principles, beliefs, etc., in an authoritative, often arrogant way. —See Syns at **dictatorial.** —**dog·mat'i·cal·ly** *adv.*

dog·ma·tism (dôg'mə-tĭz'əm, dŏg'-) *n.* Dogmatic assertion of opinion or belief.

dog·ma·tist (dôg'mə-tĭst, dŏg'-) *n.* **1.** An arrogantly assertive person. **2.** One who expresses or sets forth dogma.

dog·ma·tize (dôg'mə-tīz', dŏg'-) *intr.v.* **-tized, -tiz·ing.** To express oneself dogmatically in writing or speech.

dog paddle. A crude swimming stroke in which the arms and legs remain submerged and paddle in alternation.

dog rose. A prickly wild rose, *Rosa canina*, native to Europe, with fragrant pink or white flowers.

Dog Star. 1. The star Sirius. **2.** The star Procyon.

dog tag. 1. An identification disk attached to a dog's collar. **2.** A military identification tag worn around the neck.

dog·tooth violet (dôg'tōoth', dŏg'-). Any of several flowering plants of the genus *Erythronium*. Also called **adder's-tongue.**

dog·watch (dôg'wŏch', dŏg'-) *n.* Either of two periods of watch duty on a ship, from 4 to 6 or from 6 to 8 P.M.

dog·wood (dôg'wŏod', dŏg'-) *n.* Any of several trees or shrubs of the genus *Cornus*, with small greenish flowers surrounded by showy white or pink petallike leaves.

do·gy (dō'gē) *n.*, *pl.* **-gies.** Var. of **dogie.**

doi·ly (doi'lē) *n.*, *pl.* **-lies.** A small ornamental mat, usu. of lace. [After *Doyly* or *Doily*, an 18th-cent. London draper.]

do·ing (dōo'ĭng) *n.* **1.** The act of performing something. **2. doings.** Activities, esp. social activities.

doit (doit) *n.* A former Dutch coin. [Dutch *duit*.]

do-it-your·self (dōo'ĭt-yər-sĕlf') *adj. Informal.* Of or designed to be done by an amateur.

dol·ce (dōl'chā') *adv. Mus.* Gently and sweetly. [Italian, "sweet."]

dol·drums (dōl'drəmz', dôl'-, dŏl'-) *n.* (used with a sing. verb). **1.** Ocean regions near the equator, marked by calms or light winds. **2.** A period of inactivity, listlessness, or depression. [Perh. ult. from Middle English *dol*, dull.]

dole¹ (dōl) *n.* **1. a.** The distribution of goods, esp. of money, food, or clothing as charity. **b.** The money, food, or clothing distributed. **2.** *Brit.* The distribution by the government of relief payments to the unemployed. —*tr.v.* **doled, dol·ing.** To distribute in small portions. [Middle English *dol(e)*, division, from Old English *dāl*, portion.]

dole² (dōl) *n. Archaic.* Grief; sorrow; dolor. [Middle English *dol*, from Old French, from Late Latin *dolus*, pain.]

dole·ful (dōl'fəl) *adj.* Filled with grief; mournful; melancholy. —**dole'ful·ly** *adv.* —**dole'ful·ness** *n.*

doll (dŏl) *n.* **1.** A child's toy representing a human being. **2.** A pretty child. **3.** *Slang.* An attractive or sexy person. **4.** Any person regarded with fond familiarity. —*intr.v.*

| ă pat | ā pay | â care | ä father | ĕ pet | ē be | hw which | ĭ pit | ī tie | î pier | ŏ pot | ō toe | ô paw, for | oi noise |
| ōo took | ōo boot | ou out | th thin | th this | ŭ cut | | û urge | zh vision | ə about, item, edible, gallop, circus |

Slang. To dress up or adorn oneself smartly, as for a special occasion. —*tr.v.* To dress (oneself) up smartly, esp. for ostentation. [From *Doll,* pet name for *Dorothy.*]

dol·lar (dŏl′ər) *n.* **1.** The basic monetary unit of the United States, Canada, and certain other countries, equal to 100 cents. **2.** A coin or note worth one dollar. [Low German *daler, taler,* from German *Taler,* short for *Joachimstaler,* a coin made with metal from *Joachimsthal, Jachymov,* town in the Erzgebirge Mountains, Czechoslovakia.]

dollar diplomacy. A policy aimed at furthering the interests of the United States abroad by encouraging the investment of U.S. capital in foreign countries.

dol·lop (dŏl′əp) *n.* A large lump, helping, or portion, as of ice cream or brandy. [Orig. unknown.]

dol·ly (dŏl′ē) *n., pl.* **-lies. 1.** A doll. **2.** A low mobile platform that rolls on casters, used for moving heavy loads. **3.** A similar wheeled apparatus used to move a motion-picture or television camera about a set. [From *Dolly,* pet form of *Dorothy.*]

dol·man (dŏl′mən, dōl′-) *n.* **1.** A woman's cloak or coat with dolman sleeves. **2.** A jacket worn like a cape as part of a hussar's uniform. [French, from German *Dolman,* from Turkish *dolaman,* from *dolamak,* to wind.]

dolman sleeve. A full sleeve that is very wide at the armhole and narrow at the wrist.

dol·men (dōl′mən, dŏl′-) *n.* A prehistoric structure consisting of two or more massive upright stones supporting a horizontal stone. Also called **cromlech.** [French.]

dol·o·mite (dō′lə-mīt′, dŏl′ə-) *n.* A light-colored mineral, CaMg $(CO_3)_2$, used as ceramic material and in fertilizer. [French, after Déodat de *Dolomieu* (1705–1801), French geologist.]

do·lor (dō′lər) *n. Poet.* Sorrow; grief. [Middle English *dolour,* from Latin *dolor,* from *dolēre,* to grieve.]

do·lor·ous (dō′lər-əs, dŏl′ər-) *adj.* Causing or expressing sorrow. —**do′lor·ous·ly** *adv.* —**do′lor·ous·ness** *n.*

dol·phin (dŏl′fĭn, dôl′-) *n.* **1.** Any of various saltwater mammals, chiefly of the family Delphinidae, related to the whales but gen. smaller and having a beaklike snout. **2.** Either of two saltwater fishes with iridescent coloring. [Middle English, from Old French *dalfin,* from Latin *delphinus,* from Greek *delphis.*]

dolphin

dolt (dōlt) *n.* A dullard; blockhead. [Orig. unknown.] —**dolt′ish** *adj.* —**dolt′ish·ly** *adv.* —**dolt′ish·ness** *n.*

-dom. A suffix meaning: **1.** The condition of being: **boredom. 2.** The domain, position, or rank of: **dukedom.** [Middle English, from Old English.]

do·main (dō-mān′) *n.* **1.** A territory over which control or rule is exercised. **2.** A sphere of interest, activity, or function. **3.** *Physics.* Any of numerous contiguous regions in a magnetic material in which the direction of spontaneous magnetization is uniform and different from that in neighboring regions. **4.** *Math.* The set of possible values of an independent variable of a function. [French *domaine,* from Old French *demaine,* from Latin *dominium,* property, from *dominus,* lord.]

dome (dōm) *n.* **1.** A hemispherical roof or vault. **2.** Any object or structure resembling the shape of this. **3.** *Poet.* A large, stately building. **4.** *Slang.* The head. —*v.* **domed, dom·ing.** —*tr.v.* **1.** To cover with or as with a dome. **2.** To shape like a dome. —*intr.v.* To assume the shape of a dome by rising or swelling. [French *dôme,* from Italian *duomo,* (domed) cathedral, from Latin *domus,* house.]

do·mes·tic (də-měs′tĭk) *adj.* **1.** Of or pertaining to the family or household. **2.** Fond of home life and household affairs. **3.** Living with human beings; tame. **4.** Of or pertaining to a country's internal affairs: *domestic policy.* **5.** Produced in or native to a particular country. —*n.* A

household servant. [Old French *domestique,* from Latin *domesticus,* from *domus,* house.] —**do·mes′ti·cal·ly** *adv.*

do·mes·ti·cate (də-měs′tĭ-kāt′) *tr.v.* **-cat·ed, -cat·ing. 1.** To train to live with and be of use to man; to tame. **2.** To accommodate to surroundings; adapt: *Old World traditions domesticated in America.* —**do·mes′ti·ca′tion** *n.*

do·mes·tic·i·ty (dō′mě-stĭs′ĭ-tē) *n., pl.* **-ties. 1.** The quality or condition of being domestic. **2.** Home life or devotion to it. **3. domesticities.** Household affairs.

domestic science. Home economics.

dom·i·cile (dŏm′ĭ-sīl′, -səl, dō′mĭ-) *n.* Also **dom·i·cil** (-səl). **1.** A residence; home. **2.** One's legal residence. —*tr.v.* **-ciled, -cil·ing.** To establish (a person or oneself) in a residence. [Old French, from Latin *domicilium,* abode.] —**dom′i·cil′i·ar·y** (dŏm′ĭ-sĭl′ē-ěr′ē, dō′mĭ-) *adj.*

dom·i·nance (dŏm′ə-nəns) *n.* Also **dom·i·nan·cy** (-nən-sē). The condition or fact of being dominant.

dom·i·nant (dŏm′ə-nənt) *adj.* **1.** Exercising the most influence or control; governing. **2.** Most prominent in position or prevalence: *the dominant building in the skyline.* **3.** *Genetics.* Producing a typical effect whether paired with an identical or a dissimilar gene. **4.** *Mus.* Relating to or based upon the fifth tone of a diatonic scale. —See Syns at **primary.** —*n.* **1.** *Genetics.* A dominant gene. **2.** *Mus.* The fifth tone of a diatonic scale. —**dom′i·nant·ly** *adv.*

dom·i·nate (dŏm′ə-nāt′) *v.* **-nat·ed, -nat·ing.** —*tr.v.* **1.** To control or rule by superior authority or power. **2.** To occupy the most prominent position in: *Ambition dominates his life.* **3.** To overlook from a height: *a tower dominating the town.* —*intr.v.* To be dominant in position or authority. [From Latin *dominārī,* to be master, from *dominus,* master.] —**dom′i·na′tor** *n.*

dom·i·na·tion (dŏm′ə-nā′shən) *n.* **1.** The act of dominating or the condition of being dominated; rule. **2.** Supremacy or control over another.

dom·i·neer (dŏm′ə-nîr′) *tr.v.* To rule over arbitrarily or arrogantly; tyrannize. —*intr.v.* To govern tyrannically. [Dutch *domineren,* from French *dominer,* from Latin *dominārī,* to dominate.] —**dom′i·neer′ing** *adj.* —**dom′i·neer′ing·ly** *adv.*

Do·min·i·can (də-mĭn′ĭ-kən) *adj.* Of or pertaining to the order of preaching friars established in 1215 by Saint Dominic. —*n.* A friar of the order of Saint Dominic.

dom·i·nie (dŏm′ĭ-nē, dō′mə-) *n.* **1.** A clergyman. **2.** *Scot.* A schoolmaster. [From obs. *domine,* form of address to ministers, from Latin *dominus,* master.]

do·min·ion (də-mĭn′yən) *n.* **1.** Control; rule; sovereignty. **2.** A realm; domain. **3.** Often **Dominion.** One of the self-governing nations within the British Commonwealth. [Middle English *dominioun,* from Old French *dominion,* from Medieval Latin *dominiō,* from Latin *dominium,* lordship, from *dominus,* master.]

Dominion Day. July 1, a legal holiday in Canada, the anniversary of the Dominion's formation in 1867.

dom·i·no¹ (dŏm′ə-nō′) *n., pl.* **-noes** or **-nos. 1.** A hooded cape worn by clergymen. **2.** A hooded robe worn with an eye mask at a masquerade. [French, from Latin *(benedicamos) domino,* "(let us bless) the Lord."]

dom·i·no² (dŏm′ə-nō′) *n., pl.* **-noes** or **-nos. 1.** A small, rectangular block or tile whose face is divided into halves, each half being blank or marked by one to six dots. **2. dominoes.** *(used with a sing. verb).* The game played with a set, usu. 28, of these pieces. [French.]

don¹ (dŏn) *n.* **1. Don.** Sir. A Spanish title formerly affixed to a Christian name. **2.** A Spanish gentleman. **3.** *Brit.* A head, tutor, or fellow at a college of Oxford or Cambridge. [Spanish, from Latin *dominus,* lord, master.]

don² (dŏn) *tr.v.* **donned, don·ning.** To put on; dress in. [Middle English, "do on."]

do·ña (dōn′yə) *n.* **1. Doña.** Lady. A Spanish title of courtesy used with a woman's given name. **2.** A Spanish gentlewoman. [Spanish, lady, from Latin *domina.*]

do·nate (dō′nāt′, dō-nāt′) *tr.v.* **-nat·ed, -nat·ing.** To present as a gift to a fund or cause. —**do′na′tor** *n.*

do·na·tion (dō-nā′shən) *n.* **1.** The act of giving something to a fund or cause. **2.** A gift or grant; contribution. [Middle English *donacioun,* from Old French, from Latin *dōnātiō,* from *dōnāre,* to give, from *dōnum,* gift.]

done (dŭn) *v.* Past participle of **do.** —*adj.* **1.** Completely accomplished or finished. **2.** Cooked adequately. **3.** Socially acceptable. [Middle English, from Old English *(ge)dōn.*]

do·nee (dō-nē′) *n.* A recipient of a gift. [DON(OR) + -EE.]

don·jon (dŏn′jən, dŭn′-) *n.* The fortified main tower of a castle; a keep. [Var. of DUNGEON.]

Don Juan (dŏn wŏn′, jōō′ən) *n.* **1.** A libertine; profligate. **2.** A man obsessed with seducing women. [After *Don Juan,* legendary Spanish nobleman and libertine.]

don·key (dŏng′kē, dŭng′-, dŏng′-) *n., pl.* **-keys. 1.** The domesticated ass. **2.** An obstinate, sluggish, or stupid person. [Orig. unknown.]

donkey engine. A small auxiliary steam engine used for hoisting or pumping, esp. aboard ship.

don·na (dŏn′ə) *n.* **1. Donna.** Lady. An Italian title of courtesy used with a woman's given name. **2.** An Italian gentlewoman. [Italian, lady, from Latin *domina.*]

don·nish (dŏn′ĭsh) *adj.* Resembling or characteristic of a university don; very learned; bookish.

don·ny·brook (dŏn′ē-brŏŏk′) *n.* A brawl or uproar; free-for-all. [After the annual fair held at *Donnybrook,* Ireland, noted for its brawls.]

do·nor (dō′nər) *n.* **1.** Someone who contributes something. **2.** A person or animal from whom blood, tissue, an organ, etc. is taken for use in a transfusion or transplant. [Old French *doneur,* from Latin *dōnātor,* from *donum,* gift.]

don't (dōnt). Contraction of *do not.* —*n.* A statement of what should not be done.

do·nut (dō′nŭt′, -nət) *n.* Var. of **doughnut.**

doo·dad (dōō′dăd′) *n. Informal.* Any unnamed or nameless gadget or trinket. [Orig. unknown.]

doo·dle (dōōd′l). *Informal.* —*v.* **-dled, -dling.** —*intr.v.* To scribble mechanically or idly while thinking about something else. —*tr.v.* To draw (figures) while preoccupied. —*n.* A figure, design, or scribble drawn or written absentmindedly. [English dial. *doodle,* to trifle.]

doo·dle·bug (dōōd′l-bŭg′) *n.* **1.** The larva of an insect, the ant lion. **2.** A divining rod.

doo·hick·ey (dōō′hĭk′ē) *n., pl.* **-eys.** *Informal.* Any gadget or part whose name one cannot recall. [Orig. unknown.]

doom (dōōm) *n.* **1.** A terrible and inescapable fate, esp. an end in ruin or tragedy. **2.** Disaster; ruin; extinction. **3.** Condemnation to a severe penalty. **4.** The Last Judgment. —*tr.v.* **1.** To destine to an unhappy end: *a scheme doomed to failure.* **2.** To condemn to ruination or death. [Middle English *dom,* judgment, from Old English *dōm.*]

dooms·day (dōōmz′dā′) *n.* **1.** The day of the Last Judgment. **2.** Any dreaded day of judgment or reckoning. [Middle English *domesday,* from Old English *dōmes dæg.*]

door (dôr, dōr) *n.* **1.** Any movable structure used to close off an entrance, typically consisting of a panel that swings on hinges, slides, or rotates. **2.** The entranceway to a room, building, or passage. **3.** Any means of approach or access. [Middle English *dor,* from Old English *duru,* gate, door.]

door·bell (dôr′bĕl′, dōr′-) *n.* A buzzer or bell outside a door, used as a signal for admission.

door·jamb (dôr′jăm′, dōr′-) *n.* Either of the two vertical pieces framing a doorway and supporting the lintel.

door·keep·er (dôr′kē′pər, dōr′-) *n.* A person employed to guard an entrance or gateway.

door·knob (dôr′nŏb′, dōr′-) *n.* A knob-shaped handle for opening and closing a door.

door·man (dôr′măn′, -mən, dōr′-) *n.* An attendant employed to attend the entrance of a building.

door·mat (dôr′măt′, dōr′-) *n.* A mat placed before a doorway for wiping the shoes.

door·nail (dôr′nāl′, dōr′-) *n.* A large-headed nail. —*idiom.* **dead as a doornail.** Dead.

door·sill (dôr′sĭl′, dōr′-) *n.* The threshold of a doorway.

door·step (dôr′stĕp′, dōr′-) *n.* A step or steps leading to a door.

door·way (dôr′wā′, dōr′-) *n.* The entranceway to a room or building.

door·yard (dôr′yärd′, dōr′-) *n.* A yard in front of the door of a house.

dope (dōp) *n.* **1.** Any of various usu. liquid preparations added to produce desired properties; an additive. **2.** *Infor-*

mal. Any of several narcotics, stimulants, or other drugs. **3.** *Slang.* A very stupid person. **4.** *Slang.* Factual information, esp. of a private nature. —*tr.v.* **doped, dop·ing.** **1.** To add or apply dope to. **2.** *Informal.* To figure out (an outcome or puzzle) by calculation and guesswork. [Dutch *doop,* sauce, from *doopen,* to dip, to mix.]

dop·ey (dō′pē) *adj.* **-pi·er, -pi·est.** *Slang.* **1.** Dazed or lethargic, as if drugged. **2.** Stupid.

Dop·pler effect (dŏp′lər). An apparent change in the frequency of waves, as of sound, occurring when the source and observer are in motion relative to one another, the frequency increasing when the source and observer approach one another and decreasing when they move apart. [After Christian *Doppler* (1803–53), Austrian physicist.]

Do·ri·an (dôr′ē-ən, dōr′-) *n.* One of a Hellenic people that invaded Greece around 1100 B.C. and remained culturally distinct within the Greek world. —**Do′ri·an** *adj.*

Dor·ic (dôr′ĭk, dōr′-) *n.* The Greek dialect of the Dorians. —*adj.* **1.** Of or relating to the Doric dialect. **2.** Of or belonging to an order of ancient Greek and Roman architecture characterized by a heavy column with a plain, saucer-shaped top, or capital.

dorm (dôrm). *n.*

dor·mant (dôr′mənt) *adj.* **1.** Asleep or lying as if asleep; sluggish. **2.** Latent or inactive but capable of being activated: *dormant worker unrest.* **3.** Temporarily inactive: *a dormant volcano.* **4.** *Biol.* In a relatively inactive or resting condition in which some processes are slowed down or suspended. —See Syns at **inactive.** [Middle English *dormaunt,* from Old French *dormant,* from *dormir,* to sleep, from Latin *dormīre.*] —**dor′man·cy** *n.*

dor·mer (dôr′mər) *n.* **1.** A window set vertically in a small gable projecting from a sloping roof. Also called **dormer window. 2.** The gable holding such a window. [Old French *dormeor,* dormitory, from *dormir,* to sleep.]

dor·mi·to·ry (dôr′mĭ-tôr′ē, -tōr′ē) *n., pl.* **-ries. 1.** A room providing sleeping quarters for a number of persons. **2.** A building for housing a number of persons, as at a school or resort. [Latin *dormītōrium,* from *dormīre,* to sleep.]

dor·mouse (dôr′mous′) *n.* Any of various small, squirrel-like Old World rodents of the family Gliridae. [Middle English *dormowse.*]

dor·sal (dôr′səl) *adj.* Of, toward, on, in, or near the back of an animal. [Late Latin *dorsālis,* from Latin *dorsum,* back.]

dorsal fin. The main fin on the dorsal surface of fishes or certain saltwater mammals.

do·ry (dôr′ē, dōr′ē) *n., pl.* **-ries.** A small, narrow, flat-bottomed fishing boat with high sides and a sharp prow. [Of South American Indian orig.]

dos·age (dō′sĭj) *n.* **1.** The administration of a medicine or other therapeutic agent in prescribed amounts. **2.** The amount administered.

dose (dōs) *n.* **1.** A specified quantity of a medicine or other therapeutic agent prescribed to be taken at one time or at stated intervals. **2.** *Informal.* An amount, esp. of something unpleasant, to which one is subjected. —*tr.v.* **dosed, dos·ing.** To give a dose, as of medicine. [French, from Late Latin *dosis,* from Greek, from *didonai,* to give.]

do·sim·e·ter (dō-sĭm′ĭ-tər) *n.* A device that measures doses of x-rays or radioactivity. [DOS(E) + -METER.]

dos·si·er (dŏs′ē-ā′, dŏs′sē-ā′) *n.* A collection of papers or documents pertaining to a particular person or subject; a file. [French, from Old French, bundle of papers having a label on the back, from *dos,* back, from Latin *dorsum.*]

dost (dŭst) *v. Archaic.* Second person singular present tense of **do.**

dot[1] (dŏt) *n.* **1.** A tiny round mark; a spot. **2.** In certain codes, a short sound or signal used in combination with the dash to represent letters or numbers. **3.** *Mus.* A mark after a note indicating an increase in time value by half. —*tr.v.* **dot·ted, dot·ting. 1.** To mark with a dot. **2.** To form or make with dots. **3.** To cover with or as if with dots: *Campfires dotted the night.* [Ult. from Old English *dott,* head of a boil.]

dot[2] (dŏt) *n.* A woman's marriage portion; dowry. [French, from Latin *dōs,* dowry.]

do·tage (dō′tĭj) *n.* **1.** A condition of feeble-mindedness, often caused by old age. **2.** Foolish or excessive fondness.

ă pat	ā pay	â care	ä father	ĕ pet	ē be	hw which	ĭ pit	ī tie	î pier	ŏ pot	ō toe	ô paw, for	oi noise
ōō took	ōō boot	ou out	th thin	th this	ŭ cut		û urge	zh vision	ə about, item, edible, gallop, circus				

do·tard (dō′tərd) *n.* A senile person.

dote (dōt) *intr.v.* **dot·ed, dot·ing. 1.** To be foolish or feeble-minded. **2.** To lavish excessive love on. [Middle English *doten,* from Middle Dutch, to be silly.] —**dot′er** *n.*

doth (dŭth) *v. Archaic.* Third person singular present tense of **do.**

dotted swiss. A crisp cotton fabric, embellished with woven, flocked, or embroidered dots.

dot·ty (dŏt′ē) *adj.* **-ti·er, -ti·est.** Eccentric; daft; crazy. [From Middle English *doten,* to dote.]

Dou·ay Bible (dōō-ā′, dōō′ā). An English translation of the Latin Vulgate Bible by Roman Catholic scholars.

dou·ble (dŭb′əl) *adj.* **1.** Twice as much: *a double dose.* **2.** Composed of two like parts. **3.** Composed of two unlike parts; dual: *a double meaning.* **4.** Characterized by duplicity; deceitful: *He led a double life.* **5.** *Bot.* Having many more than the usual number of petals. —*adv.* **1.** To twice the amount. **2.** Two together: *ride double on a horse.* —*n.* **1.** Something increased twofold. **2.** Someone or something that resembles or can substitute for another; counterpart. **3. doubles.** A game that has two players on each side. **4.** *Baseball.* A two-base hit. **5.** *Bridge.* **a.** A bid indicating strength to one's partner; request for a bid. **b.** A bid doubling one's opponent's bid, thus increasing the penalty for failure to fulfill the contract. —*v.* **-bled, -bling.** —*tr.v.* **1.** To make twice as great. **2.** To be twice as much as: *Their staff doubles ours.* **3.** To fold in two. **4.** *Baseball.* To advance (a runner) by making a two-base hit. **5.** *Bridge.* To challenge (an opponent's bid) with a double. —*intr.v.* **1.** To be increased twofold: *The population doubled in 10 years.* **2.** To turn sharply backward; reverse: *double back on one's trail.* **3.** To serve in an additional capacity. **4.** To replace an actor in the execution of a given action or in the actor's absence. **5.** *Baseball.* To make a two-base hit. **6.** *Bridge.* To announce a double. —*idiom.* **on the double.** Immediately or quickly. [Middle English, from Old French, from Latin *duplus,* twofold.]

double bar. A double vertical or heavy black line drawn to separate the main sections of a musical composition.

dou·ble-bar·reled (dŭb′əl-băr′əld) *adj.* **1.** Having two parallel barrels. **2.** Serving two purposes.

double bass. The largest member of the violin family, shaped like a cello. Also called **bass viol, contrabass,** and **string bass.**

double bassoon. The contrabassoon.

double boiler. A cooking utensil consisting of two nested pots, designed to cook or heat food in the upper pan by the action of water boiling in the lower.

dou·ble-breast·ed (dŭb′əl-brĕs′tĭd) *adj.* Describing a coat with one lapel that laps over the other across the breast, and usu. with two rows of buttons.

dou·ble-cross (dŭb′əl-krôs′, -krŏs′) *tr.v. Slang.* To betray by doing the opposite of what was agreed on. —See Syns at **deceive.** —*n. Slang.* An instance of such betrayal; treachery. —**dou′ble-cross′er** *n.*

double dagger. In printing, a reference mark (‡).

dou·ble-deal·ing (dŭb′əl-dē′lĭng) *adj.* Characterized by duplicity. —*n.* Treachery; duplicity. —**dou′ble-deal′er** *n.*

dou·ble-deck·er (dŭb′əl-dĕk′ər) *n.* **1.** Something with two tiers, as a bus or bed. **2.** A sandwich with two layers.

dou·ble-en·ten·dre (dŭb′əl-än-tän′drə; *Fr.* dōō-blän-tän′dr′ə) *n.* A word or phrase with a double meaning, esp. when one is risqué. [French, "double meaning."]

double entry. A method of bookkeeping in which a transaction is entered both as a debit to one account and a credit to another account, so that both totals are equal.

dou·ble-head·er (dŭb′′l-hĕd′ər) *n.* Two games or events held in succession on the same program.

dou·ble-joint·ed (dŭb′′l-join′tĭd) *adj.* Having unusually flexible joints permitting connected parts, such as limbs or fingers, to be bent at unusual angles.

double knit. A jerseylike fabric knitted with two sets of needles so that a double thickness of fabric is produced in which the two sides of the fabric are interlocked.

double negative. A syntactic construction in which two negatives are used when only one should be; for example, the sentence *He didn't say nothing.* —See Usage note at **help,** Usage note **2** at **neither,** and Usage note **1** at **scarcely.**

dou·ble-park (dŭb′əl-pärk′) *tr.v.* To park alongside another vehicle already parked parallel to the curb.

double play. *Baseball.* A play in which two players are put out.

dou·ble-quick (dŭb′əl-kwĭk′) *adj.* Very quick; rapid. —*n.* (dŭb′əl-kwĭk′). **Double time.** —*intr.v.* To Double-time.

dou·ble-space (dŭb′əl-spās′) *v.* **-spaced, -spac·ing.** —*intr.v.* To type so that there is a full space between lines. —*tr.v.* To type (copy) in this way.

double star. A binary star.

dou·blet (dŭb′lĭt) *n.* **1.** A close-fitting jacket, with or without sleeves, worn by men between the 15th and 17th centuries. **2.** A counterfeit gem. **3.** A pair of similar things. **4.** *Ling.* One of two words derived from the same source but through different routes. —See Syns at **couple.** [Middle English, from Old French, from *double,* double.]

doublet

double talk. 1. Meaningless speech that consists of nonsense syllables mixed with intelligible words; gibberish. **2.** Deliberately ambiguous or evasive language.

dou·ble-time (dŭb′əl-tīm′) *intr.v.* **-timed, -tim·ing. 1.** To march in double time. **2.** To jog or run.

double time. 1. *Mil.* A rapid marching pace of 180 three-foot steps per minute. **2.** A wage rate that is double the normal rate.

dou·bloon (dŭ-blōōn′) *n.* An obsolete Spanish gold coin. [Spanish *doblón,* coin, from Latin *dupla,* double.]

dou·bly (dŭb′lē) *adv.* **1.** To a double degree; twice. **2.** In a twofold manner.

doubt (dout) *tr.v.* **1.** To be uncertain about. **2.** To be suspicious of; distrust. —*intr.v.* To be undecided, unsure, or skeptical. —*n.* **1.** Often **doubts.** A lack of conviction or certainty. **2.** An uncertain condition or state of affairs: *an outcome still in doubt.* —*idioms.* **no doubt. 1.** Certainly. **2.** Probably. **without doubt.** Certainly. [Middle English *d(o)uten,* from Old French *douter,* from Latin *dubitāre,* to waver.] —**doubt′er** *n.*

Syns: doubt, question, skepticism, uncertainty *n. Core meaning:* Lack of conviction or certainty *(had doubts about their willingness to help).* See also Syns at **distrust.**

doubt·ful (dout′fəl) *adj.* **1.** Subject to or tending to cause doubt; uncertain; unclear: *a doubtful legal claim.* **2.** Experiencing or showing doubt. **3.** Of uncertain outcome; undecided. **4.** Questionable in character; suspicious. —**doubt′ful·ly** *adv.* —**doubt′ful·ness** *n.*

doubting Thom·as (tŏm′əs). Someone who habitually expresses or feels doubts. [After Saint *Thomas,* who doubted Jesus' resurrection until he had proof.]

doubt·less (dout′lĭs) *adj.* Certain; assured: *doubtless of ultimate victory.* —*adv.* **1.** Certainly; assuredly. **2.** Presumably; probably. —**doubt′less·ly** *adv.*

douche (dōōsh) *n.* **1.** A stream of water or air applied to a part or cavity of the body for cleansing or medicinal purposes. **2.** The application of a douche. **3.** An instrument for applying a douche. —*v.* **douched, douch·ing.** —*tr.v.* To cleanse or treat by means of a douche. —*intr.v.* To be cleansed or treated by a douche. [French.]

dough (dō) *n.* **1.** A soft, thick mixture of flour or meal, liquids, and various dry ingredients that is baked as bread, pastry, or the like. **2.** Any similar pasty mass. **3.** *Slang.* Money. [Middle English *dogh,* from Old English *dāg.*]

dough·boy (dō′boi′) *n.* An American infantryman in World War I.

ă pat   ā pay   â care   ä father   ĕ pet   ē be   hw which
ōō took   ōō boot   ou out   th thin   *th* this   ŭ cut
ĭ pit   ī tie   î pier   ŏ pot   ō toe   ô paw, for   oi noise
û urge   zh vision   ə about, item, edible, gallop, circus

dough·nut (dō′nŭt′, -nət) *n.* Also **do·nut.** A small, ring-shaped cake made of dough that is fried in deep fat.

dough·ty (dou′tē) *adj.* **-ti·er, -ti·est.** Stouthearted; courageous; brave. [Middle English, from Old English *dohtig.*] —**dough′ti·ly** *adv.* —**dough′ti·ness** *n.*

dough·y (dō′ē) *adj.* **-i·er, -i·est.** Having the consistency or appearance of dough.

Doug·las fir (dŭg′ləs). A tall evergreen timber tree, *Pseudotsuga taxifolia,* of northwestern North America.

dour (dŏor, dour) *adj.* **1.** Stern; harsh; forbidding. **2.** Glum; sullen. [Middle English, perh. from Latin *dūrus,* hard.]

douse (dous) *tr.v.* **doused, dous·ing. 1.** To plunge into liquid; immerse. **2.** To wet thoroughly; drench. **3.** To put out; extinguish. —See Syns at **extinguish.** [Perh. from earlier *douse,* to strike, smite.]

dove¹ (dŭv) *n.* **1.** Any of various birds of the family Columbidae, which includes the pigeons, esp. an undomesticated species, such as the mourning dove. **2.** A person who advocates peace and conciliation. [Middle English.]

dove² (dōv) *v.* A past tense of **dive.**

dove·cote (dŭv′kŏt′, -kōt′) *n.* Also **dove·cot** (-kŏt′). A roost for domesticated pigeons.

dove·kie (dŭv′kē) *n.* A small black-and-white auk, *Plautus alle,* of arctic and northern Atlantic regions.

dove·tail (dŭv′tāl′) *n.* A fan-shaped tenon that forms a tight interlocking joint when fitted into a corresponding mortise. —*tr.v.* **1.** To cut into or join by means of dovetails. **2.** To connect or combine precisely or harmoniously. —*intr.v.* To combine or interlock into a unified whole: *Both their accounts of the battle dovetail.*

dow·a·ger (dou′ə-jər) *n.* **1.** A widow who holds a title or property derived from her dead husband. **2.** An elderly woman of high social station. [Old French *douagiere,* from *douage,* dower, from *douer,* to endow, from Latin *dōtāre,* from *dōs,* dowry.]

dow·dy (dou′dē) *adj.* **-di·er, -di·est.** Lacking in stylishness or neatness; shabby. —*n., pl.* **-dies.** A dowdy woman. [From Middle English *doude,* slut.] —**dow′di·ness** *n.*

dow·el (dou′əl) *n.* A usu. round pin that fits tightly into a corresponding hole to fasten or align two adjacent pieces. —*tr.v.* **-eled** or **-elled, -el·ing** or **-el·ling.** To fasten or equip with dowels. [Middle English *dowle,* from Middle Low German *dövel,* peg.]

dow·er (dou′ər) *n.* **1.** The part or interest of a deceased man's real estate allotted by law to his widow for her lifetime. **2.** A dowry. —*tr.v.* To provide with a dower; endow. [Middle English *dowere,* from Old French *douaire,* from Medieval Latin *dōtārium,* from *dōs,* dowry.]

down¹ (doun) *adv.* **1. a.** From a higher to a lower place. **b.** From an upright position to a horizontal position. **2.** In or to a lower position or condition: *going down to Florida. Stock prices are coming down.* **3.** From an earlier to a later time: *down through the ages.* **4.** In partial payment at the time of purchase: *five dollars down.* **5.** In writing. —*adj.* **1. a.** Moving or directed downward: *a down elevator.* **b.** In a low position; not up: *The blinds are down.* **2.** In a lower position or condition: *Productivity is down.* **3.** Sick; not feeling well: *down with a cold.* **4.** Depressed or dejected. **5.** Being the first installment in a series of payments: *a down payment.* —*prep.* In a descending direction upon, along, through, or into: *down the stairs; down the years.* —*n.* **1. a.** A downward movement; descent. **b.** A low or bad phase: *ups and downs.* **2.** Football. Any of a series of four plays during which a team must advance at least ten yards to retain possession of the ball. —*tr.v.* **1.** To bring, strike, or throw down. **2.** To swallow hastily. [Middle English *doun,* from Old English *dūne,* short for *adūne : a,* off + *dūn,* hill.]

down² (doun) *n.* **1.** Fine, soft, fluffy feathers as on a young bird. **2.** Any soft, silky, or feathery substance. [Middle English *doun,* from Old Norse *dūnn.*]

down³ (doun) *n.* Often **downs.** An expanse of rolling, grassy upland used for grazing, esp. in southern England. [Middle English *doun,* hill, from Old English *dūn.*]

down·beat (doun′bēt′) *n. Mus.* The downward stroke made by a conductor to indicate the first beat of a measure.

down·cast (doun′kăst′) *adj.* **1.** Directed downward: *downcast eyes.* **2.** Depressed; dejected; sad.

down·er (dou′nər) *n. Slang.* **1.** A depressant drug, esp. a barbiturate. **2.** A depressing experience.

down·fall (doun′fôl′) *n.* **1.** A sudden fall from a high position; ruin. **2.** Something causing this. **3.** A heavy, usu. sudden fall of rain or snow. —**down′fall′en** *adj.*

down·grade (doun′grād′) *n.* A descending slope in a road. —*tr.v.* **-grad·ed, -grad·ing.** To lower the status, importance, or reputation of. —See Syns at **lower.** —*idiom.* **on the downgrade.** Declining; losing status.

down·heart·ed (doun′här′tĭd) *adj.* Low in spirit; depressed; discouraged. —See Syns at **gloomy.** —**down′heart′ed·ly** *adv.* —**down′heart′ed·ness** *n.*

down·hill (doun′hĭl′) *adv.* Down the slope of a hill. —*adj.* Sloping downhill.

Down·ing Street (dou′nĭng). The British government, specif. the Prime Minister's residence. [After No. 10 *Downing Street,* London, the Prime Minister's residence.]

down·pour (doun′pôr′, -pōr′) *n.* A heavy fall of rain.

down·range (doun′rānj′) *adv.* In a direction away from the launch site and along the flight line of a missile test range.

down·right (doun′rīt′) *adj.* **1.** Thoroughgoing; utter: *a downright lie.* **2.** Frank; candid: *a downright answer.* —*adv.* Thoroughly; absolutely.

Down's syndrome (dounz). A congenital disorder characterized by moderate to severe mental retardation, a short, flattened skull, and slanting eyes. Also called **mongolism.**

down·stage (doun′stāj′) *adv.* Toward or at the front part of a stage. —*n.* (doun′stāj′). The front half of a stage.

down·stairs (doun′stârz′) *adv.* **1.** Down the stairs. **2.** To or on a lower floor. —*adj.* (doun′stârz′). Located on a lower or main floor: *a downstairs bedroom.* —*n.* (doun′stârz′). (used with a sing. verb). The lower or main floor.

down·stream (doun′strēm′) *adv.* Down a stream. —*adj.* (doun′strēm′). In the direction of a stream's current.

down·swing (doun′swĭng′) *n.* **1.** A swing downward, as of a golf club. **2.** A business decline.

down-to-earth (doun′tōō-ûrth′, -tə-) *adj.* Realistic; sensible.

down·town (doun′toun′) *adv.* To, toward, or in the lower part or the business center of a city or town. —*adj.* (doun′toun′). Of or in the lower part or business center of a city or town. —*n.* (doun′toun′). The lower part or business center of a city or town.

down·trod·den (doun′trŏd′n) *adj.* Oppressed; tyrannized.

down·turn (doun′tûrn′) *n.* A tendency downward, esp. in business or economic activity.

down·ward (doun′wərd) *adv.* Also **down·wards** (-wərdz). **1.** From a higher to a lower place, level, or condition. **2.** From an earlier to a more recent time. —*adj.* Descending from a higher to a lower place, level, or condition.

down·wind (doun′wĭnd′) *adv.* In the direction in which the wind blows; leeward. —**down′wind′** *adj.*

down·y (dou′nē) *adj.* **-i·er, -i·est. 1.** Made of or covered with down. **2.** Resembling down; soft and fluffy.

dow·ry (dou′rē) *n., pl.* **-ries. 1.** Money or property brought by a bride to her husband at marriage; dower. **2.** A natural endowment or gift. [Var. of DOWER.]

dowse (douz) *intr.v.* **dowsed, dows·ing.** To use a divining rod, esp. to find water. [Orig. unknown.] —**dows′er** *n.*

dox·ol·o·gy (dŏk-sŏl′ə-jē) *n., pl.* **-gies.** A liturgical formula of praise to God. [Medieval Latin *doxologia,* from Greek, praise.]

doze (dōz) *intr.v.* **dozed, doz·ing.** To sleep lightly. —*n.* A nap. [Prob. of Scandinavian orig.] —**doz′er** *n.*

doz·en (dŭz′ən) *n., pl.* **dozen** or **-ens.** A set of 12. —*adj.* Twelve. [Old French *doze,* twelve, from Latin *duodecim.*]

doz·enth (dŭz′ənth) *adj.* Twelfth.

drab (drăb) *adj.* **drab·ber, drab·best. 1.** Of a dull light brown. **2.** Of a commonplace character; dull; dreary. —*n.* Moderate to grayish brown. [Var. of obs. *drap,* cloth, from Old French.] —**drab′ly** *adv.* —**drab′ness** *n.*

drachm (drăm) *n. Brit.* **1.** A dram. **2.** A drachma.

drach·ma (drăk′mə) *n., pl.* **-mas** or **-mae** (-mē). **1.** The basic monetary unit of Greece. **2.** A silver coin of ancient Greece. **3.** One of several modern units of weight, esp. the dram. **4.** A unit of weight of ancient Greece. [Latin, from Greek *drakhmē.*]

Dra·co (drā′kō) *n.* A constellation in the polar region of the Northern Hemisphere near Cepheus and Ursa Major.

ă pat   ā pay   â care   ä father   ĕ pet   ē be   hw which
ōō took   ōō boot   ou out   th thin   *th* this   ŭ cut

ĭ pit   ī tie   î pier   ŏ pot   ō toe   ô paw, for   oi noise
û urge   zh vision   ə about, item, edible, gallop, circus

dra·co·ni·an (drā-kō′nē-ən, drə-) *adj.* **1.** Of or pertaining to a law or code of extreme severity. **2.** Harsh; rigorous. [After *Draco*, Athenian lawgiver.]

draft (drăft, dräft). Also *Brit.* **draught** (drăft) —*n.* **1.** A current of air, esp. in an enclosed area. **2.** A device in a flue that controls the circulation of air. **3.** A pull or traction of a load, as by horses or oxen. **4. a.** The act or an example of drawing in a fishnet. **b.** The amount of fish drawn in. **5.** A preliminary outline, plan, or picture; a version. **6.** The selection of personnel 'from a pool for a specific duty. **7. a.** Compulsory assignment to military service. **b.** The group of men so assigned. **8. a.** A gulp, swallow, or drink of something. **b.** The amount taken in a single swallow. **9.** A document for the transfer of money: *a bank draft*. **10.** The depth of a vessel's keel below the water line. —*modifier*: *a draft card; a team of draft horses.* —*tr.v.* **1. a.** To select for a specific duty. **b.** To assign to military service. **2.** To draw up a preliminary plan, sketch, or version of. [Middle English *draught*, a pulling.] —**draft′er** *n.*

draft board. A local board of civilians in charge of the selection of men for compulsory military service.

draft·ee (drăf-tē′, dräf-) *n.* A person who is drafted into the armed forces.

drafts·man (drăfts′mən, dräfts′-) *n.* A person whose occupation is drawing plans or designs, as of buildings or machinery. —**drafts′man·ship′** *n.*

draft·y (drăf′tē, dräf′-) *adj.* **-i·er, -i·est.** Having or exposed to drafts of air. —**draft′i·ly** *adv.* —**draft′i·ness** *n.*

drag (drăg) *v.* **dragged, drag·ging.** —*tr.v.* **1.** To draw along, pull, or haul by force. **2.** To cause to trail along the ground. **3.** To search the bottom of (a body of water), as with a grappling hook or net. **4.** To bring forcibly to or into: *dragged the protesters away.* **5.** To move with great reluctance, weariness, or difficulty: *dragged herself to work.* —*intr.v.* **1.** To trail along the ground. **2.** To move slowly or with effort. **3.** To lag behind. **4.** To pass or proceed slowly, tediously, or laboriously: *Time dragged.* **5.** To search or dredge the bottom of a body of water. **6.** *Slang.* To draw on a cigarette. —See Syns at **delay.** —*n.* **1.** Something pulled along the ground, as a harrow. **2.** A device for dragging under water. **3.** A heavy sledge or cart for conveying loads. **4.** A large four-horse coach with seats inside and on top. **5.** Something that stops or slows motion, as a sea anchor. **6.** The force that tends to slow a body that is in motion through a fluid, as air or water. **7.** *Slang.* Something or someone bothersome or tiresome. **8.** *Slang.* A puff on a cigarette, pipe, or cigar. [Middle English *draggen*, from Old English *dragan* or Old Norse *draga*.]

drag·ger (drăg′ər) *n.* Something or someone that drags, esp. a fishing vessel that tows submerged nets.

drag·gle (drăg′əl) *v.* **-gled, -gling.** —*tr.v.* To make wet and dirty by dragging. —*intr.v.* **1.** To become muddy by being trailed. **2.** To follow slowly; straggle. [From DRAG.]

drag·gy (drăg′ē) *adj.* **-gi·er, -gi·est. 1.** Dull and listless. **2.** *Slang.* Obnoxiously tiresome.

drag·net (drăg′nĕt′) *n.* **1.** A large net towed along a river or sea bottom. **2.** A system of actions used in the apprehension of criminal suspects.

drag·o·man (drăg′ə-mən) *n., pl.* **-mans** or **-men.** An interpreter or guide in countries where Arabic, Turkish, or Persian is spoken. [Middle English *drogman*, from Old French *drugeman*, ult. from Arabic *targumān*, interpreter.]

drag·on (drăg′ən) *n.* **1.** An imaginary giant reptile, usu. represented as a winged, fire-breathing monster. **2.** A fiercely intractable person. [Middle English, from Old French, from Latin *dracō*, serpent, from Greek *drakōn*.]

drag·on·fly (drăg′ən-flī′) *n.* Any of various large insects of the order Odonata, with a long, slender body. Also called **darning needle.**

dra·goon (drə-gōon′, dră-) *n.* A heavily armed cavalryman. —*tr.v.* To coerce by violent measures; harass. [French *dragon*, carbine, from Old French, dragon.]

drag race. An acceleration race between cars.

drain (drān) *tr.v.* **1.** To draw off (a liquid) gradually. **2.** To cause liquid to go out from. **3.** To remove water through natural channels from (a tract of land). **4.** To drink all the contents of. **5.** To consume totally; to fatigue or exhaust. —*intr.v.* **1.** To flow off or go out of. **2.** To become empty or dry by the drawing off of liquid. —*n.* **1.** A pipe or channel by which liquid is drained off. **2.** Something that drains or exhausts. [Middle English *dreinen*, from Old English *drēahnian.*] —**drain′a·ble** *adj.* —**drain′er** *n.*

drain·age (drā′nĭj) *n.* **1.** The action or a given method of draining, esp. water or waste material. **2.** A natural or artificial system of drains. **3.** Material that is drained off.

drain·pipe (drān′pīp′) *n.* A pipe for drainage.

drake (drāk) *n.* A male duck. [Middle English.]

dram (drăm) *n.* **1. a.** *Abbr.* **dr** A unit of avoirdupois weight equal to 27.344 grains, 0.0625 ounce, or 1.772 grams. **b.** A unit of apothecary weight equal to 60 grains. **2.** A small drink, as of alcohol. **3.** A bit. [Middle English, from Old French *dragme*, from Medieval Latin *dragma*, from Latin *drachma*, drachma.]

dra·ma (drä′mə, drăm′ə) *n.* **1.** A play in prose or verse, esp. one telling a serious story. **2.** Plays of a given type or period. **3.** The art and practice of writing and producing plays. **4.** A situation that involves conflicts and builds to a climax. **5.** The condition or quality of being dramatic. [Late Latin, from Greek, from *drān*, to do.]

Dram·a·mine (drăm′ə-mēn′) *n.* A trademark for a compound used to treat motion sickness.

dra·mat·ic (drə-măt′ĭk) *adj.* **1.** Of drama or the theater. **2.** Characteristic of a drama; building to a climax. **3.** Striking in appearance or effect; stirring. [Late Latin *drāmaticus*, from Greek *dramatikos.*] —**dra·mat′i·cal·ly** *adv.*

dra·mat·ics (drə-măt′ĭks) *n.* **1.** (*used with a sing. or pl. verb*). The art or practice of acting or staging plays. **2.** (*used with a pl. verb*). Exaggerated behavior.

dram·a·tis per·so·nae (drăm′ə-tĭs pər-sō′nē, drä′mə-tĭs pər-sō′nī′). The characters in a play or story. [New Latin.]

dram·a·tist (drăm′ə-tĭst, drä′mə-) *n.* A playwright.

dram·a·tize (drăm′ə-tīz′, drä′mə-) *tr.v.* **-tized, -tiz·ing. 1.** To adapt for theatrical presentation. **2.** To present in a dramatic or highly emotional way. —**dram′a·ti·za′tion** *n.*

dram·a·tur·gy (drăm′ə-tûr′jē, drä′mə-) *n.* The art of the theater. —**dram′a·tur′gic** or **dram′a·tur′gi·cal** *adj.*

drank (drăngk) *v.* Past tense of **drink.**

drape (drāp) *v.* **draped, drap·ing.** —*tr.v.* **1.** To cover or hang with or as if with cloth in loose folds. **2.** To arrange or let fall in loose, graceful folds: *She draped the veil over her head.* **3.** To hang or rest limply: *He draped his legs over the chair.* —*intr.v.* To fall or hang in loose folds. —*n.* **1.** Often **drapes.** Long, heavy curtains that hang straight in loose folds. **2.** The way in which cloth falls or hangs: *the drape of a Roman toga.* [Middle English *drapen*, from Old French *draper*, from *drap*, cloth, from Late Latin *drappus.*]

drap·er (drā′pər) *n. Brit.* A dealer in cloth and dry goods.

drap·er·y (drā′pə-rē) *n., pl.* **-ies. 1.** Cloth or clothing arranged in loose folds. **2.** Often **draperies.** Long, heavy curtains that hang straight in loose folds; drapes. **3.** Cloth; fabric. **4.** *Brit.* The business of a draper.

dras·tic (drăs′tĭk) *adj.* Violently effective; extreme or severe: *drastic measures.* [Greek *drastikos*, active, efficient, from *drān*, to do.] —**dras′ti·cal·ly** *adv.*

draught (drăft) *n. & v. Brit.* Var. of **draft.**

draughts (drăfts, dräfts) *n.* (*used with a sing. verb*). *Brit.* The game of checkers. [Middle English *draughtes*, pl. of *draught*, a move at chess.]

draw (drô) *v.* **drew** (drōo), **drawn** (drôn), **draw·ing.** —*tr.v.* **1. a.** To pull or move (something) in a given direction or to a given position. **b.** To pull or move so as to cover or uncover: *draw the drapes.* **c.** To cause to move, as by pulling or hauling. **d.** To cause to move in a given direction, as by leading: *She drew us into the room.* **2. a.** To pull out; extract; remove. **b.** To earn; bring: *draw interest.* **c.** To withdraw (money). **3.** To cause to flow. **4.** To suck or take in (air or water). **5. a.** To produce by marking a surface with a pen, pencil, crayon, etc.. **b.** To represent (figures or pictures) by marking in such a way; sketch. **6.** To represent in words. **7. a.** To get as a response; elicit: *draw laughter.* **b.** To get in return for: *draw a salary.* **8.** To get by chance or in a chance drawing. **9.** To attract; entice. **10.** To deduce from evidence at hand; formulate: *Draw a conclusion.* **11.** To eviscerate; disembowel. **12.** To displace (a specified depth of water) in floating. **13.** To force (a card) to be played. **14.** To end (a game) in a draw. **15.** To compose or write up in set form, as a will or contract. **16.** *Med.* To cause to soften and drain: *draw a boil.* —*intr.v.* **1.** To proceed; to move: *The boat drew near the shore.* **2.** To represent forms and figures; to sketch. **3.** To be an attraction. **4.** To take in a draft of air. **5.** To pull out a weapon for use. —See Syns at **attract.** —*phrasal verbs.* **draw on** (or **upon**). To use as a source; call upon. **draw out.** To extend in length; stretch: *fibers drawn out into long strands.* —*n.* **1.** An act of drawing. **2.** A special advantage; edge: *have the draw on one's enemies.* **3.** A contest ending in a tie. **4.** A natural drainage basin; gully. [Middle English *drawen,* from Old English *dragan.*]

draw·back (drô'băk') *n.* A disadvantage or inconvenience.

draw·bar (drô'bär') *n.* A bar across the rear of a tractor for hitching machinery.

draw·bridge (drô'brĭj') *n.* A bridge that can be raised or turned aside either to prevent or permit traffic.

drawbridge

draw·ee (drô-ē') *n.* A person on whom an order for the payment of money is drawn.

draw·er *n.* **1.** (drô'ər). **a.** A person who draws. **b.** A person who draws an order for the payment of money. **2. drawer** (drôr). A sliding boxlike compartment in a bureau or table. **3. drawers** (drôrz). Underpants.

draw·ing (drô'ĭng) *n.* **1.** The act or an example of drawing. **2.** The art of representing forms and figures by means of lines. **3.** A portrayal of forms and figures by means of lines. **4.** A selection of something by drawing lots.

drawing card. An attraction drawing large audiences.

drawing room. **1.** A living room; parlor. **2.** A formal reception room. **3.** A formal reception. **4.** A private room on a railroad sleeping car. [Short for *withdrawing room.*]

draw·knife (drô'nīf') *n.* A woodworking tool that has a blade and two handles, used to shave surfaces.

drawl (drôl) *intr.v.* To speak with lengthened or drawn-out vowels. —*tr.v.* To utter with drawn-out vowels. —*n.* A drawling manner of speaking. [Poss. from DRAW.]

drawn (drôn) *v.* Past participle of **draw.**

drawn butter. Melted butter, often used as a sauce.

draw·shave (drô'shāv') *n.* A drawknife.

draw·string (drô'strĭng') *n.* A cord or ribbon run through a hem or casing and pulled to tighten or close an opening.

dray (drā) *n.* A low, heavy cart without sides, used for hauling. —*tr.v.* To haul by dray. [Middle English *draye,* prob. from Old English *dræge,* dragnet.]

dray·age (drā'ĭj) *n.* **1.** Transport by dray. **2.** A charge for transport by dray.

dray·man (drā'mən) *n.* A driver of a dray.

dread (drĕd) *n.* **1.** Profound fear; terror. **2.** Anxious or fearful anticipation. **3.** *Archaic.* Awe; reverence. **4.** The object of fear, awe, or reverence. —*tr.v.* **1.** To be in terror of. **2.** To anticipate with anxiety or reluctance. **3.** *Archaic.* To hold in awe or reverence. —*intr.v.* To be very afraid. —*adj.* Terrifying; fearsome; dreadful. [Middle English *drēden,* to fear, from Old English *drǣdan.*]

dread·ful (drĕd'fəl) *adj.* **1.** Inspiring dread or great fear; terrible. **2.** Extremely unpleasant; distasteful or shocking. —**dread'ful·ly** *adv.* —**dread'ful·ness** *n.*

dread·nought (drĕd'nôt') *n.* A heavily armed battleship.

dream (drēm) *n.* **1.** A series of mental images, ideas, and emotions that occur while sleeping. **2.** A daydream; reverie. **3.** A dreamlike condition; a trance. **4.** A wild fancy or hope. **5.** A hope or aspiration: *dreams of peace.* **6.** Something or someone that is extremely beautiful, fine, or pleasant. —*v.* **dreamed** or **dreamt** (drĕmt), **dream·ing.** —*intr.v.* **1.** To experience dreams in sleep. **2.** To daydream. **3.** To have a deep aspiration. **4.** To consider something feasible or practical. —*tr.v.* **1.** To experience

dreams of in sleep. **2.** To pass idly or in reverie. [From Old English *drēam,* joy, gladness, music.]

dream·er (drē'mər) *n.* **1.** A person who dreams. **2. a.** A visionary. **b.** An idealist. **3.** A habitually impractical person.

dream·land (drēm'lănd') *n.* An ideal or imaginary land.

dreamt (drĕmt) *v.* A past tense and past participle of **dream.**

dream·y (drē'mē) *adj.* **-i·er, -i·est.** **1.** Like a dream; vague; hazy: *a dreamy look.* **2.** Given to daydreams or reverie. **3.** Soothing; serene: *dreamy music.* **4.** *Informal.* Delightful; wonderful. —**dream'i·ly** *adv.* —**dream'i·ness** *n.*

drear·y (drîr'ē) *adj.* **-i·er, -i·est.** **1.** Bleak; dismal. **2.** Boring; dull: *dreary tasks.* —See Syns at **gloomy.** [Middle English *dreri,* from Old English *drēorig,* bloody, sad, from *drēor,* blood.] —**drear'i·ly** *adv.* —**drear'i·ness** *n.*

dredge¹ (drĕj) *n.* **1.** Any of various machines that use scooping or suction devices to remove mud, silt, etc. from the bottom of a body of water. **2.** A ship or barge equipped with such a machine. **3.** An implement that consists of a net on a frame, used for gathering shellfish. —*v.* **dredged, dredg·ing.** —*tr.v.* **1.** To clean out or deepen the bed of (a harbor or channel). **2.** To fish or dig up with or as if with a dredge. —*intr.v.* To use a dredge. [Scottish *dreg,* to dredge.] —**dredg'er** *n.*

dredge² (drĕj) *tr.v.* **dredged, dredg·ing.** To coat (food) by sprinkling with flour, sugar, etc. [Perh. from obs. *dredge,* sweetmeat.]

dregs (drĕgz) *pl.n.* **1.** The sediment of a liquid. **2.** The least desirable portion of something: *the dregs of society.* **3.** A small amount; residue. [From Middle English *dreg.*]

drench (drĕnch) *tr.v.* **1.** To wet through and through; saturate. **2.** To administer liquid medicine to (an animal). —*n.* A large dose of liquid medicine. [Middle English, from Old English *drencan,* to give to drink, to soak.]

dress (drĕs) *n.* **1.** An outer garment worn by women, consisting of a one-piece top and skirt. **2.** Clothing, apparel, or attire. **3.** Outer covering or appearance. —*tr.v.* **1.** To put clothes on. **2.** To decorate or trim; adorn. **3.** To arrange or style (the hair). **4.** To apply medicine, bandages, etc., to. **5.** To groom; curry. **6.** To make ready for use: *dress a hide.* **7.** To cultivate: *dress the soil.* **8.** To prepare for cooking or sale: *dress a turkey.* —*intr.v.* **1.** To put on clothes. **2.** To choose clothes to wear: *He dresses with elegance.* **3.** To wear formal clothes. **4.** To get into proper alignment, as troops. —*phrasal verb.* **dress down.** To scold; reprimand. —See Syns at **scold.** —*adj.* **1.** Suitable for formal occasions or business wear: *a dress shirt.* **2.** Calling for formal clothes: *a dress reception.* [Middle English *dressen,* to prepare, from Old French *dresser,* from Latin *dīrigere,* to direct.]

Syns: dress, attire, clothes, clothing, garb, garments *n.* **Core meaning:** Articles worn to cover the body (*inexpensive dress*).

dres·sage (drə-säzh', drĕ-) *n.* The guiding of a horse through a series of complex maneuvers by slight movements of the hands, legs, and weight.

dress circle. The first tier of seats in a theater.

dress·er¹ (drĕs'ər) *n.* **1.** Someone or something that dresses. **2.** A wardrobe assistant, as for an actor; valet.

dress·er² (drĕs'ər) *n.* **1.** A chest of drawers, usu. with a mirror. **2.** A cupboard for dishes or kitchen utensils.

dress·ing (drĕs'ĭng) *n.* **1.** Medicine or bandages applied to a wound. **2.** A sauce for certain dishes, such as salads. **3.** A stuffing, as for poultry or fish. **4.** Manure used to dress soil. **5.** The act or an instance of dressing.

dressing gown. A robe worn informally at home.

dressing room. A room in a theater or a home for changing costumes or clothes and making up.

dressing table. A low table with a mirror at which a person sits while making up. Also called **vanity.**

dress·mak·er (drĕs'mā'kər) *n.* A person who makes dresses and other garments. —**dress'mak'ing** *n.*

dress rehearsal. A final rehearsal, as of a play, with costumes and stage properties.

dress·y (drĕs'ē) *adj.* **-i·er, -i·est.** **1.** Fancy, as clothing. **2.** Elegant; stylish. —**dress'i·ly** *adv.* —**dress'i·ness** *n.*

drew (droō) *v.* Past tense of **draw.**

drib·ble (drĭb'əl) *v.* **-bled, -bling.** —*intr.v.* **1.** To flow or fall in drops. **2.** To drool; slobber. **3.** *Sports.* To dribble a ball.

| ă pat | ā pay | â care | ä father | ĕ pet | ē be | hw which | ĭ pit | ī tie | î pier | ŏ pot | ō toe | ô paw, for | oi noise |
| ōō took | ōō boot | ou out | th thin | th this | ŭ cut | | û urge | zh vision | ə about, item, edible, gallop, circus |

—*tr.v.* **1.** To drip or trickle. **2.** *Sports.* To move (a ball) by repeated light bounces or kicks. —*n.* **1.** A trickle; a drip: *a dribble of milk.* **2.** A small quantity; a bit. **3.** *Sports.* The act of moving a ball by dribbling. [Freq. of earlier *drib*, to drip.] —**drib'bler** *n.*

drib·let (drĭb'lĭt) *n.* A small amount or portion.

dri·er[1] (drī'ər) *n.* **1.** A substance added to paint, varnish, ink, etc., to make it harden or dry more quickly. **2.** Var. of **dryer** (appliance).

dri·er[2] (drī'ər) *adj.* A comparative of **dry.**

dri·est (drī'ĭst) *adj.* A superlative of **dry.**

drift (drĭft) *intr.v.* **1.** To be carried along by or as if by currents of water or air. **2. a.** To move unhurriedly with no apparent effort. **b.** To live or move, as from place to place or job to job, without definite goals. **3.** To move from a set course. **4.** To accumulate or cause to accumulate in piles. —*tr.v.* To cause to be carried along by or as if by a current. —See Syns at **slide.** —*n.* **1.** The act or process of drifting. **2.** Something that drifts, as a current of air or water. **3.** The amount by which something drifts away from a set or proper course. **4.** A mass of material, as sand or snow, deposited by a current of air or water. **5.** *Geol.* Fragments of rock that are carried and deposited by or from ice, esp. a glacier. **6.** A general meaning or direction. **7.** A gradual shift in opinion or direction. **8.** Lateral displacement or deviation of an object or vehicle from a planned course, esp. as a result of wind, ocean current, etc. **9.** The rate of flow of a water current. [Middle English *drift*, the act of driving.] —**drift'er** *n.*

drift·age (drĭf'tĭj) *n.* **1.** Deviation from a set course caused by drifting. **2.** Anything that has been carried along or deposited by air or water currents.

drift·wood (drĭft'wŏŏd') *n.* Wood floating in or washed up by the water.

drill[1] (drĭl) *n.* **1. a.** Any of several tools used to make holes in solid materials, usu. by a rotating action or by repeated striking. **b.** The piece of machinery that provides the rotary or striking action. **2.** A means of teaching or training involving continuous repetition of a single exercise. **3.** A specific exercise repeatedly practiced. **4.** Any of several saltwater gastropod mollusks of the genus *Urosalpinx* that drill holes into the shells of bivalve mollusks. —*tr.v.* **1.** To make (a hole) with a drill. **2.** To teach or train by continuous repetition. —*intr.v.* **1.** To make a hole with a drill. **2.** To engage in repetitious physical or mental exercises. [Dutch, from *drillen*, to drill.]

drill[2] (drĭl) *n.* **1.** A trench or furrow in which seeds are planted. **2.** An implement for planting seeds in holes or furrows. —*tr.v.* To sow (seeds) in rows. [Orig. unknown.]

drill[3] (drĭl) *n.* A strong cotton or linen twilled cloth. [Back-formation from *drilling*, from German *Drillich*, from Old High German *drilich*, from Latin *trilix*, triple-twilled.]

drill[4] (drĭl) *n.* A monkey, *Mandrillus leucophaeus*, that resembles the mandrill. [Native West African name.]

drill·mas·ter (drĭl'măs'tər) *n.* A military drill instructor.

drill press. A stationary drilling machine in which the drill is forced into the metal by power or a hand lever.

drink (drĭngk) *v.* **drank** (drăngk), **drunk** (drŭngk), **drink·ing.** —*tr.v.* **1.** To swallow (liquid). **2.** To soak up (liquid or moisture); absorb. **3. a.** To propose (a toast). **b.** To toast (something or someone). **4.** To take in eagerly: *She drank in my story.* —*intr.v.* **1.** To swallow liquid. **2.** To use alcoholic beverages, esp. habitually or in excess. **3.** To salute with a toast. —*n.* **1. a.** A liquid for drinking; a beverage. **b.** An alcoholic beverage. **2.** Beverages in general: *food and drink.* **3.** An amount of liquid swallowed, as a glassful: *a drink of water.* **4.** Excessive use of alcoholic beverages. **5. the drink.** *Slang.* A body of water; the sea. [Middle English *drinken*, from Old English *drincan.*] —**drink'a·ble** *adj.* —**drink'er** *n.*

drip (drĭp) *v.* **dripped, drip·ping.** —*intr.v.* **1.** To fall in drops. **2.** To shed drops. —*tr.v.* To let fall in or as if in drops. —*n.* **1.** Liquid that falls in drops. **2.** The sound made by dripping liquid. **3.** The process of forming and falling in drops. **4.** A projection on a cornice or sill that protects the area below from rainwater. **5.** *Slang.* An unpleasant or dull person. [Middle English *drippen*, perh. from Middle Danish *drippe.*]

drip-dry (drĭp'drī') *adj.* Made of a fabric that will not wrinkle if hung up dripping wet to dry.

drip·pings (drĭp'ĭngz) *n.* The fat and juice from roasting meat, often used in making gravy.

drive (drīv) *v.* **drove** (drōv), **driv·en** (drĭv'ən), **driv·ing.** —*tr.v.* **1. a.** To set and keep in motion; propel by force. **b.** To force to leave or retreat; expel. **2. a.** To force into a particular condition: *He drives me crazy.* **b.** To be or supply the motivating force to; spur. **3.** To force to go through or penetrate: *drive a nail.* **4. a.** To guide, control, and direct (a vehicle). **b.** To transport in a vehicle. **5.** To supply the power to move, as an automobile engine. **6.** To chase (game) into the open or into traps or nets. —*intr.v.* **1.** To move along or advance quickly as if pushed by an impelling force. **2.** To rush or advance violently against: *rain is driving against the house.* **3.** To operate a vehicle. **4.** To go or be transported in a vehicle. **5.** To make an effort to achieve a particular objective. —*n.* **1.** A ride, trip, or journey in a vehicle. **2. a.** A road for automobiles. **b.** A driveway. **3. a.** The means for transmitting motion to a machine. **b.** The means by which automotive power is applied to a roadway. **4. a.** An organized effort to accomplish something. **b.** A massive and sustained military offensive. **5. a.** Energy; push; initiative. **b.** A strong motivating instinct. **6.** *Sports.* A ball that is hit hard. **7. a.** The act of driving cattle. **b.** The act of driving logs down a river. —**idiom. drive at.** To mean to do or say. [Middle English *driven*, from Old English *drīfan.*]

drive-in (drīv'ĭn') *n.* A business establishment designed to service customers who stay in their cars.

driv·el (drĭv'əl) *v.* **-eled** or **-elled, -el·ing** or **-el·ling.** —*intr.v.* **1.** To slobber; drool. **2.** To talk stupidly, childishly, or senselessly. —*tr.v.* To say (something) stupidly. —*n.* Nonsense talk. [Old English *dreflian.*] —**driv'el·er** *n.*

driv·en (drĭv'ən) *v.* Past participle of **drive.**

driv·er (drī'vər) *n.* **1.** A person who drives a car, truck, or other vehicle. **2.** A wooden-headed golf club used for making long shots from the tee.

driver ant. Any of various rapacious tropical Old World ants of the subfamily Dorylinae.

drive·way (drīv'wā') *n.* A private road that connects a house, garage, or other building with the street.

driz·zle (drĭz'əl) *v.* **-zled, -zling.** —*intr.v.* To rain gently in fine, mistlike drops. —*tr.v.* To let fall in fine drops or particles. —*n.* A fine, gentle, misty rain. [Perh. from Middle English *dresen*, to fall.] —**driz'zly** *adj.*

drogue parachute. A parachute used to slow down a fast-moving object, as a space vehicle during re-entry.

droll (drōl) *adj.* **-er, -est.** Amusingly odd; comical. [French *drôle.*] —**droll'ly** *adv.* —**droll'ness** *n.*

droll·er·y (drō'lə-rē) *n., pl.* **-ies. 1.** A droll quality. **2.** Odd or quaint behavior. **3.** Something droll, as a story.

-drome. A suffix meaning a large field or arena: *airdrome.* [Old French, from Latin, from Greek race, course.]

drom·e·dar·y (drŏm'ĭ-dĕr'ē, drŭm'-) *n., pl.* **-ies.** The one-humped domesticated camel, *Camelus dromedarius*, of northern Africa and western Asia. [Middle English, from Old French *dromedaire*, from Late Latin *dromedārius*, from Greek *dromas*, dromedary, runner.]

drone[1] (drōn) *n.* **1.** A stingless male bee, esp. a honeybee, who performs no work and produces no honey. **2.** Someone who is lazy; a loafer. **3.** An unmanned aircraft operated by remote control. [Middle English *drone.*]

drone[2] (drōn) *v.* **droned, dron·ing.** —*intr.v.* **1.** To make a continuous low, dull humming sound. **2.** To speak in a monotonous tone. —*tr.v.* To utter in a monotonous low tone. —*n.* **1.** A continuous low humming or buzzing sound. **2.** Something, such as one of the pipes of a bagpipe, that produces a single sustained tone. [From DRONE (bee).]

drool (drōōl) *intr.v.* **1.** To let saliva run from the mouth; to drivel. **2.** *Informal.* To show great desire, as if watering at the mouth. **3.** *Informal.* To talk nonsense. —*tr.v.* To let run from the mouth. —*n.* **1.** Saliva flowing from the mouth; dribble. **2.** *Informal.* Silly talk; nonsense. [Alteration of DRIVEL.]

droop (drōōp) *intr.v.* **1.** To bend or hang downward; sag. **2.** To sag in dejection, exhaustion, or lifelessness. —*tr.v.* To let bend or hang down. —*n.* The act or condition of drooping. [Middle English *droupen*, from Old Norse *drūpa.*] —**droop'ing·ly** *adv.*

droop·y (drōō'pē) *adj.* **-i·er, -i·est. 1.** Bending or hanging downward. **2.** Sad; dejected. —**droop'i·ly** *adv.*

drop (drŏp) —*v.* **dropped** or *archaic* **dropt** (drŏpt), **drop·ping.** —*intr.v.* **1.** To fall in drops. **2.** To fall from a higher to a lower place or position. **3.** To become less, as in number or amount; decrease; decline. **4.** To descend; sink. **5.** To fall or sink into a condition of exhaustion or death. **6.** To pass into some specified condition: *He dropped into sleep.* —*tr.v.* **1.** To let fall by releasing hold of. **2.** To lower, as by a rope: *drop anchor.* **3.** To let fall in drops: *He dropped oil on the salad.* **4.** To decrease; reduce. **5.** To cause to fall, as by hitting or shooting. **6.** To say or offer casually: *drop a hint.* **7.** To write to: *drop me a line.* **8.** To cease consideration or treatment of: *Let's drop the discussion.* **9.** To resign from; quit officially: *drop a course in school.* **10.** To terminate an association or relationship; reject: *The coach dropped him from the team.* **11.** To leave out (a letter) in speaking or writing: *drops his h's.* **12.** To leave or set down at a particular place; deliver. **13.** To lower the level of (the voice). **14.** To lose (a game or contest). —See Syns at **fall** and **lower.** —*phrasal verbs.* **drop by** (or **in** or **over**). To visit informally. **drop off. 1.** To fall asleep. **2.** To decrease. **drop out.** To withdraw from participation in a school, club, game, or organized society. —*n.* **1.** A tiny, rounded mass of liquid. **2.** Something resembling this: *a cough drop.* **3.** A small amount of liquid. **4.** A sudden fall or decrease: *a drop in temperature.* **5.** A steep or sheer descent. **6.** Something arranged to fall or be lowered, as a drop curtain. **7.** A delivery by parachute. [Middle English, from Old English *dropa.*]

drop-forge (drŏp'fôrj', -fōrj') *tr.v.* **-forged, -forg·ing.** To forge between dies by the force of a drop hammer.

drop hammer. A machine used to forge or stamp metal, consisting of an anvil or base aligned with a hammer that is forced down upon the molten metal.

drop leaf. A wing on a table, hinged for folding down.

drop·let (drŏp'lĭt) *n.* A tiny drop.

drop·out (drŏp'out') *n.* Someone who quits, as from school.

drop·per (drŏp'ər) *n.* A small tube with a suction bulb at one end for drawing in a liquid and releasing it in drops.

drop·pings (drŏp'ĭngz) *pl. n.* The dung of animals.

drop·sy (drŏp'sē) *n.* Pathological accumulation of diluted lymph in body tissues and cavities. [Middle English *ydropesie,* from Old French, from Latin *hydrōpisis,* from Greek *hudrōpisis,* from *hudōr,* water.] —**drop'si·cal** (-sĭ-kəl) *adj.*

dropt (drŏpt) *v. Archaic.* Past tense and past participle of **drop.**

drosh·ky (drŏsh'kē) *n., pl.* **-kies.** Also **dros·ky** (drŏs'kē). An open, four-wheeled, horse-drawn carriage formerly common in Russia. [Russian *drozhki,* dim. of *drogi,* wagon.]

dro·soph·i·la (drō-sŏf'ə-lə, drə-) *n., pl.* **-las.** A fruit fly, *Drosophila melanogaster,* used extensively in genetic studies. [Greek *drosos,* dew + -PHILA.]

dross (drôs, drŏs) *n.* **1.** The waste material that rises to the surface of a molten metal. **2.** Worthless material mixed with or contained in a substance; impurity. [Middle English *dros,* from Old English *drōs,* dregs.]

drought (drout) *n.* Also **drouth** (drouth). **1.** A long period with little or no rain. **2.** A dearth of anything. [Middle English, from Old English *drūgath.*] —**drought'y** *adj.*

drove[1] (drōv) *v.* Past tense of **drive.**

drove[2] (drōv) *n.* **1.** A number of animals being driven in a group. **2.** A crowd or throng. [Middle English *drove,* from Old English *drāf,* from *drifan,* to drive.]

drov·er (drō'vər) *n.* A person who drives cattle, sheep, or horses to market or to grazing lands.

drown (droun) *intr.v.* To die by submerging and suffocating in water or other liquid. —*tr.v.* **1.** To kill by submerging and suffocating in water or other liquid. **2.** To drench thoroughly. **3. a.** To drive out; extinguish. **b.** To overpower or blur. [Middle English *dr(o)unen.*]

drowse (drouz) *v.* **drowsed, drows·ing.** —*intr.v.* To be half-asleep; to doze. —*tr.v.* To pass (time) drowsing. —*n.* The condition of being half asleep.

drows·y (drou'zē) *adj.* **-i·er, -i·est. 1.** Sleepy. **2.** Causing sleepiness. [Perh. ult. from Old English *drūsian,* to be sluggish.] —**drows'i·ly** *adv.* —**drows'i·ness** *n.*

drub (drŭb) *tr.v.* **drubbed, drub·bing. 1.** To beat with or as with a stick. **2.** To instill (as an idea or lesson) forcefully. **3.** *Slang.* To defeat thoroughly. —See Syns at **defeat.** [Arabic *dáraba,* to beat.] —**drub'ber** *n.*

drudge (drŭj) *n.* Also **drudg·er** (drŭj'ər). A person who does tiresome or menial work. —*intr.v.* **drudged, drudg·ing.** To do tiresome or menial work. [Perh. from Middle English *druggen,* to labor.] —**drudg'ing·ly** *adv.*

drudg·er·y (drŭj'ə-rē) *n., pl.* **-ies.** Tiresome or menial work. —See Syns at **labor.**

drug (drŭg) *n.* **1.** A substance that has some special effect on the life processes of an organism, esp. a substance used in medicine. **2.** A narcotic. —*tr.v.* **drugged, drug·ging. 1.** To administer a drug to. **2.** To mix a drug into. **3.** To make dull or sleepy with or as if with a drug. [Middle English *drogge,* from Old French *drogue,* chemical material.]

drug·gist (drŭg'ĭst) *n.* **1.** A pharmacist. **2.** Someone who owns or operates a drugstore.

drug·store (drŭg'stôr', -stōr') *n.* Also **drug store.** A store where prescriptions are filled and drugs are sold.

dru·id (drōō'ĭd) *n.* Also **Dru·id.** A member of an order of priests of the ancient Celtic religion of Gaul and Britain, who appear in Welsh and Irish legend as prophets and sorcerers. [Latin *druides,* druids, of Celtic orig.] —**dru·id'ic** (drōō-ĭd'ĭk) or **dru·id'i·cal** (-ĭ-kəl) *adj.* —**dru'id·ism'** *n.*

drum (drŭm) *n.* **1.** A musical percussion instrument that consists of a hollow container, such as a tube or bowl, with a membrane stretched across one or more of its openings, and is played by beating on the membrane with the hands or with sticks. **2.** Anything having a gen. cylindrical shape, such as a large oil container, a large spool of wire, or a machine part. **3.** Any of various saltwater and freshwater fishes of the family Sciaenidae that make a drumming sound. —*v.* **drummed, drum·ming.** —*intr.v.* **1.** To play a drum. **2.** To thump or tap rhythmically or continually. —*tr.v.* **1.** To perform (a musical part or piece) on or as if on a drum. **2.** To summon by or as if by beating a drum. —*phrasal verbs.* **drum into.** To instill by constant repetition. **drum out.** To expel or dismiss in disgrace. **drum up.** To obtain, stimulate, or create (business, sales, etc.) by soliciting, advertising, etc. [Perh. from Dutch *trom.*]

drum·beat (drŭm'bēt') *n.* The sound made by beating a drum.

drum·lin (drŭm'lĭn) *n.* A long, low hill, rounded at one end and pointed at the other, formed from material left by a glacier. [From Irish Gaelic *druim,* ridge.]

drum major. A uniformed man who leads a marching band, often keeping time with a baton.

drum majorette. A uniformed girl who prances and twirls a baton at the head of a marching band.

drum·mer (drŭm'ər) *n.* **1.** A person who plays a drum, as in a band. **2.** A traveling salesman.

drum·stick (drŭm'stĭk') *n.* **1.** A stick for beating a drum. **2.** The lower part of the leg of a cooked fowl.

drunk (drŭngk) *v.* Past participle of **drink.** —*adj.* **1.** Overcome by alcohol; intoxicated. **2.** Overcome by emotion: *drunk with happiness.* —*n.* **1.** A drunkard. **2.** A drinking spree. [Middle English *drunken,* from Old English *(ge)druncen.*]

drunk·ard (drŭng'kərd) *n.* A person who is habitually drunk.

drunk·en (drŭng'kən) *adj.* **1.** Drunk; intoxicated. **2.** Of, caused by, or happening during intoxication: *a drunken rage.* —**drunk'en·ly** *adv.* —**drunk'en·ness** *n.*

drunk·om·e·ter (drŭng'kə-mē'tər, drŭng-kŏm'ĭ-tər) *n.* An instrument that indicates the amount of alcohol in a person's blood by analysis of the breath.

drupe (drōōp) *n. Bot.* A fleshy fruit, as a peach or cherry, with a single hard stone that encloses a seed. [From Latin *drūpa,* overripe olive, from Greek *druppa,* from *drupepēs,* overripe.] —**dru·pa'ceous** (drōō-pā'shəs) *adj.*

drupe·let (drōōp'lĭt) *n. Bot.* A small drupe, such as one of the many subdivisions of the raspberry or the blackberry.

dry (drī) *adj.* **dri·er** or **dry·er, dri·est** or **dry·est. 1.** Free from liquid or moisture. **2.** Containing relatively little moisture: *dry air.* **3.** Not under water: *dry land.* **4.** Not liquid; solid. **5.** Marked by little or no rainfall; arid: *the dry season.* **6.** Thirsty. **7.** Lacking a mucous or watery discharge: *a dry cough.* **8.** Having all or almost all the water drained away,

---

evaporated, etc.: *a dry riverbed.* **9.** Not shedding tears. **10.** No longer yielding liquid, esp. milk: *a dry cow.* **11.** Brittle from drying out. **12.** Quietly ironic: *a dry wit.* **13.** Matter-of-fact; tedious: *a dry lecture.* **14.** Plain; unadorned: *dry facts.* **15.** Not sweet: *a dry wine.* **16.** *Informal.* Prohibiting the sale of alcoholic beverages: *a dry county.* —*v.* **dried, dry·ing.** —*tr.v.* **1.** To make dry. **2.** To preserve (meat or other foods, for example) by extracting the moisture. —*intr.v.* To become dry. [Middle English, from Old English *drȳge.*] —**dry′ly** or **dri′ly** *adv.* —**dry′ness** *n.*

dry·ad (drī′əd, -ăd′) *n.* Also **Dry·ad.** *Gk. Myth.* A wood nymph. [Latin *dryas,* from Greek *druas,* from *drus,* tree.]

dry cell. An electric cell that has an electrolyte in the form of a moist paste and that is sealed to prevent spilling.

dry-clean (drī′klēn′) *tr.v.* To clean (clothing or fabrics) by using chemicals that dissolve or absorb dirt and grease.

dry dock. A large floating or stationary basin into which a ship can be moved and the water pumped out, used for maintenance, repair, etc.

dry·er (drī′ər) *n.* An appliance that removes moisture.

dry·est (drī′ĭst) *adj.* A superlative of **dry.**

dry farming. Farming practiced in arid areas without irrigation by the maintenance of a fine surface tilth or mulch that protects the natural moisture of the soil.

dry fly. An artificial fly used in fishing that floats on the water's surface when cast.

dry goods. Cloth, clothing, linens, sewing articles, etc., as opposed to liquids, hardware, etc.

dry ice. Solid carbon dioxide used primarily as a cooling agent.

dry measure. A system of units for measuring dry quantities such as grains, fruits, and vegetables by volume.

dry point. **1.** A technique of engraving in which a hard steel needle is used to etch lines in the metal plate, and acid is not used. **2.** An engraving made this way.

dry rot. A fungous disease of seasoned timber that causes it to become brittle and crumble into powder.

dry run. **1.** *Mil.* A combat exercise without live ammunition. **2.** A trial run or rehearsal.

D.T.'s (dē-tēz′) *pl.n.* **Delirium tremens.**

du·al (dōō′əl, dyōō′-) *adj.* **1.** Composed of two parts; double; twofold. **2.** Having a double nature, character, or purpose. [Latin *duālis,* from *duo,* two.] —**du·al′i·ty** (dōō-ăl′ĭ-tē, dyōō-) *n.* —**du′al·ly** *adv.*

du·al·ism (dōō′ə-lĭz′əm, dyōō′-) *n.* **1.** The concept that the world consists of or is governed by two fundamental entities, such as mind and matter. **2.** *Theol.* The concept that the world is ruled by the antagonistic forces of good and evil. —**du′al·ist** *n.* —**du′al·is′tic·al·ly** *adv.*

du·al-pur·pose (dōō′əl-pûr′pəs, dyōō′-) *adj.* Having two functions or designed to serve two purposes.

dub¹ (dŭb) *tr.v.* **dubbed, dub·bing.** **1.** To confer knighthood on. **2.** To give a nickname to. [Middle English *dubben,* from Old English *dubbian.*]

dub² (dŭb) *tr.v.* **dubbed, dub·bing.** **1.** To insert (new sounds) into an existing recording. **2.** To provide (a film) with a new sound track, often in a different language.

du·bi·e·ty (dōō-bī′ĭ-tē, dyōō-) *n.,* pl. **-ties.** **1.** The condition or quality of being dubious. **2.** An uncertainty. [Late Latin *dubietās,* from Latin *dubius,* dubious.]

du·bi·ous (dōō′bē-əs, dyōō′-) *adj.* **1.** Doubtful; uncertain. **2.** Questionable; suspicious: *a dubious character.* [Latin *dubius.*] —**du′bi·ous·ly** *adv.* —**du′bi·ous·ness** *n.*

du·bi·ta·ble (dōō′bĭ-tə-bəl, dyōō′-) *adj.* Open to doubt or question; uncertain. —**du′bi·ta·bly** *adv.*

du·cal (dōō′kəl, dyōō′-) *adj.* Of a duke or dukedom.

duc·at (dŭk′ət) *n.* **1.** Any of various gold coins formerly used in Europe. **2.** *Slang.* An admission ticket. [Middle English, from Old French, from Old Italian *ducato,* duchy (word used on one of the early ducats).]

duch·ess (dŭch′ĭs) *n.* **1.** The wife or widow of a duke. **2.** A woman holding a rank equal to that of a duke in her own right. [Middle English *duchesse,* from Old French, from Medieval Latin *ducissa,* from Latin *dux,* leader.]

duch·y (dŭch′ē) *n.,* pl. **-ies.** The territory ruled by a duke or duchess; a dukedom. [Middle English *duchie,* from Old French *duche,* from *duc,* duke.]

duck¹ (dŭk) *n.* **1.** Any of various wild or domesticated aquatic birds of the family Anatidae, characteristically having a broad, flat bill, short legs, and webbed feet. **2.** The female of one of these birds, as distinguished from a drake. **3.** The flesh of this bird used as food. **4.** *Slang.* A person, esp. a peculiar one. **5.** *Brit. Informal.* Dear; darling. [Middle English *doke,* from Old English *duce.*]

duck¹

duck² (dŭk) *tr.v.* **1.** To lower quickly, esp. so as to avoid something. **2.** To evade; dodge: *duck a tough question.* **3.** To push suddenly under water. —*intr.v.* **1.** To lower the head or body. **2.** To move swiftly, esp. so as to escape being seen. **3.** To submerge the head or body briefly in water. —See Syns at **avoid.** —*n.* The act of ducking. [Middle English *douken.*] —**duck′er** *n.*

duck³ (dŭk) *n.* **1.** A very durable, closely woven cotton fabric. **2. ducks.** Clothing made of this fabric. [Dutch *doek.*]

duck⁴ (dŭk) *n.* An amphibious military truck used during World War II. [From *DUKW,* its code designation.]

duck·bill (dŭk′bĭl′) *n.* A mammal, the platypus. Also called **duck-billed platypus.**

duck·ling (dŭk′lĭng) *n.* A young duck.

duck·pin (dŭk′pĭn′) *n.* **1.** A bowling pin, shorter and squatter than a tenpin. **2. duckpins** (*used with a sing. verb*). A bowling game played with these pins and small balls.

duck·weed (dŭk′wēd′) *n.* Any of various small, free-floating, stemless aquatic plants of the genus *Lemna.*

duct (dŭkt) *n.* **1.** Any tube or similar passage through which a substance, esp. a fluid, is conveyed. **2.** A tube in the body through which a fluid passes, esp. a secretion. **3.** *Elect.* A tube or pipe for carrying cables or wires. [Latin *ductus,* a conducting, from *dūcere,* to lead.]

duc·tile (dŭk′tĭl) *adj.* **1.** Capable of being drawn into a fine strand or wire or of being hammered thin: *a ductile metal.* **2.** Easily controlled or influenced. [Old French, from Latin *ductilis,* from *dūcere,* to lead.] —**duc·til′i·ty** *n.*

duct·less gland (dŭkt′lĭs). An **endocrine gland.**

dud (dŭd) *n. Informal.* **1.** A bomb, shell, or round that fails to explode. **2.** Someone or something that turns out to be a failure. [Middle English *dudde,* article of clothing, thing.]

dude (dōōd, dyōōd) *n.* **1.** *Informal.* An Easterner or city person who vacations on a Western ranch. **2.** *Informal.* A dandy. **3.** *Slang.* A fellow; chap. [Orig. unknown.]

dude ranch. A resort patterned after a Western ranch with horseback riding and other outdoor activities.

dudg·eon (dŭj′ən) *n.* A sullen or angry feeling; resentment: *She stalked in high dudgeon.* [Orig. unknown.]

duds (dŭdz) *pl.n. Informal.* **1.** Clothes; clothing. **2.** Personal belongings. [Pl. of earlier *dud,* article of clothing, from Middle English *dudde.*]

due (dōō, dyōō) *adj.* **1.** Payable immediately or on demand. **2.** Owed as a debt; owing. **3.** Fitting or appropriate: *due esteem.* **4.** Sufficient or adequate: *due cause to worry.* **5.** Expected or scheduled, esp. appointed to arrive. —See Syns at **just** and **suitable.** —*n.* **1.** Something that is owed or deserved. **2. dues.** A charge or fee for membership. —*adv.* Straight; directly: *due west.* —*Note: Due* is often used followed by *to* to form the prepositional group **due to.** **1.** Caused by: *hesitation due to fear.* **2.** Because of: *postponed due to rain.* [Middle English, from Old French *deu,* from Latin *dēbēre,* to owe.]

du·el (dōō′əl, dyōō′-) *n.* **1.** A prearranged formal combat between two persons, fought with deadly weapons, typically to settle a point of honor. **2.** Any struggle between two contending persons, groups, or ideas. —*v.* **-eled** or **-elled, -el·ing** or **-el·ling.** —*tr.v.* To fight with in a duel.

ă pat ā pay â care ä father ĕ pet ē be hw which ĭ pit ī tie î pier ŏ pot ō toe ô paw, for oi noise
ōō took ōō boot ou out th thin *th* this ŭ cut û urge zh vision ə about, item, edible, gallop, circus

—*intr.v.* To fight a duel. [Medieval Latin *duellum,* from Latin, war.] —**du'el·er** or **du'el·ist** *n.*

du·en·na (dōo-ĕn'ə, dyōo-) *n.* **1.** An elderly woman retained by a Spanish or Portuguese family to act as governess and companion to the daughters. **2.** Any chaperon. [Spanish *duena,* from Latin *domina,* lady.]

due process of law. A manner of proceeding in judicial or other governmental activity that does not violate the legal rights of the individual. Also called **due process.**

du·et (dōo-ĕt', dyōo-) *n.* **1.** A musical composition for two voices or instruments. **2.** The two performers presenting such a composition. [Italian *duetto,* from Latin, two.]

duff (dŭf) *n.* A stiff flour pudding boiled in a cloth bag or steamed. [English dial. var. of DOUGH.]

duf·fel (dŭf'əl) *n.* Clothing and equipment carried by a camper. [Dutch, from *Duffel,* town near Antwerp, Belgium.]

duffel bag. A large cloth bag, usu. of canvas, used for carrying clothes and personal belongings.

duf·fer (dŭf'ər) *n.* An inept, incompetent, or dull-witted person. [Orig. unknown.]

dug¹ (dŭg) *n.* An udder, breast, or teat of a female animal.

dug² (dŭg) *v.* Past tense and past participle of **dig.**

du·gong (dōo'gŏng') *n.* A plant-eating tropical sea mammal, *Dugong dugon,* with flipperlike forelimbs and a deeply notched tail fin. [Var. of Malay *duyong.*]

dug·out (dŭg'out') *n.* **1.** A boat or canoe made by hollowing out a log. **2.** A pit dug into the ground or on a hillside and used as a shelter. **3.** *Baseball.* A long, low shelter at the side of a field that houses the players' bench.

dugout

dulcimer

duke (dōok, dyōok) *n.* **1.** A nobleman with the highest hereditary rank, esp. in Great Britain. **2.** A prince who rules an independent duchy. [Middle English, from Old French *duc,* from Latin *dux,* leader, from *dūcere,* to lead.]

duke·dom (dōok'dəm, dyōok'-) *n.* **1.** A duchy. **2.** The office, rank, or title of a duke.

dukes (dōoks, dyōoks) *pl.n. Slang.* The fists. [From *Duke of Yorks,* rhyming slang for "forks" (fingers).]

dul·cet (dŭl'sĭt) *adj.* Pleasing to the ear; gently melodious: *sweet dulcet tones.* [From Middle English *doucet,* from Old French, from Latin *dulcis,* sweet.]

dul·ci·mer (dŭl'sə-mər) *n.* A musical instrument with wire strings of graduated lengths stretched over a sound box, played with two padded hammers or by plucking. [Middle English *dowcemere,* from Old French *doulcemer.*]

dull (dŭl) *adj.* **-er, -est. 1.** Not having a sharp edge or point; blunt. **2.** Not keenly or intensely felt: *a dull ache.* **3.** Unexciting; boring. **4.** Not brisk or active; sluggish: *Business is dull.* **5.** Lacking mental agility; slow to learn. **6.** Lacking responsiveness or alertness; insensitive: *a dull, glassy stare.* **7.** Not bright or vivid; dim. **8.** Cloudy or overcast; gloomy. **9.** Not loud or piercing; muffled: *a dull sound.* —*tr.v.* To make dull. —*intr.v.* To become dull. [Middle English *dul,* from Middle Low German.] —**dul'ly** *adv.* —**dull'ness** or **dul'ness** *n.*

dull·ard (dŭl'ərd) *n.* A dull or stupid person; dolt.

dulse (dŭls) *n.* A coarse, reddish-brown edible seaweed. [Irish Gaelic *duileasg.*]

du·ly (dōo'lē, dyōo'-) *adv.* **1.** In a proper manner; rightfully; fittingly: *a duly elected candidate.* **2.** At the expected time; punctually. [Middle English *duely,* from *due,* due.]

Du·ma (dōo'mə) *n.* A Russian national parliament, con-

vened and dissolved four times between 1905 and 1917. [Russian *duma,* thought.]

dumb (dŭm) *adj.* **-er, -est. 1.** Lacking the power or faculty of speech; mute. **2.** Temporarily speechless with shock or fear. **3.** Unwilling to speak. **4.** Not producing or accompanied by speech or sound. **5.** *Informal.* Ignorant. —See Syns at **stupid.** [Middle English, from Old English.] —**dumb'ly** *adv.* —**dumb'ness** *n.*

dumb·bell (dŭm'bĕl') *n.* **1.** A weight lifted for muscular exercise, consisting of a short bar with a metal ball at each end. **2.** *Slang.* A dull, stupid person; dolt.

dumb·found (dŭm'found') *v.* Var. of **dumfound.**

dumb show. A pantomime.

dumb·wait·er (dŭm'wā'tər) *n.* **1.** A small elevator used to convey food or other goods from one floor to another. **2.** *Brit.* A portable serving table.

dum·dum bullet (dŭm'dŭm'). A bullet with a soft nose designed to expand upon contact, inflicting a gaping wound. [After *Dum-Dum,* a town near Calcutta, India.]

dum·found (dŭm'found') *tr.v.* Also **dumb·found.** To strike dumb with astonishment. [DUM(B) + (CON)FOUND.]

dum·my (dŭm'ē) *n., pl.* **-mies. 1.** An imitation of a real or original object. **2.** A model of the human figure, esp. one used to display clothes. **3.** A figure of a person or an animal used by a ventriloquist. **4.** *Informal.* A blockhead; dolt. **5.** A person or agency secretly in the service of another; a front. **6.** *Printing.* A model of or sample page from a work being published. **7.** *Bridge.* **a.** The partner who exposes his hand to be played by the declarer. **b.** The hand thus exposed. —*modifier: a dummy pocket; a dummy company.* [Earlier *dummie,* dumb person, from *dumb,* dumb.]

dump (dŭmp) *tr.v.* **1.** To release or throw down in a large mass; drop heavily. **2.** To empty or unload (material). **3.** To empty out (a container). **4.** To get rid of by or as if by dumping; dispose of. **5.** To place (goods) on the market, esp. in a foreign country, in large quantities and at a low price. **6.** To reproduce (data stored internally in a computer) onto an external storage medium, as a printout. —*n.* **1.** A place where garbage or refuse is dumped. **2.** A storage place for goods or supplies; depot: *an ammunition dump.* **3.** An unordered accumulation; pile. **4.** *Slang.* A poorly maintained or disreputable place. [Middle English *dumpen,* to drop, fall, plunge, prob. of Scandinavian orig.]

dump·ling (dŭmp'lĭng) *n.* **1.** A small ball of dough cooked with stew or soup. **2.** Sweetened dough wrapped around fruit, baked and served as a dessert. [Orig. unknown.]

dumps (dŭmps) *pl.n. Informal.* A gloomy, melancholy state of mind. [From Dutch *domp,* haze, exhalation.]

dump truck. A heavy-duty truck that tilts and dumps loose material.

dump·y (dŭm'pē) *adj.* **-i·er, -i·est.** Short and stout; squat. [From obs. *dump,* a shapeless mass.] —**dump'i·ness** *n.*

dun¹ (dŭn) *tr.v.* **dunned, dun·ning.** To ask (a debtor) persistently for payment. —*n.* **1.** Someone who duns. **2.** A persistent demand for payment. [Orig. unknown.]

dun² (dŭn) *n.* **1.** A dull grayish-brown color. **2.** A dun-colored horse. —*adj.* A dull grayish brown. [Middle English *dun,* from Old English *dunn.*]

dunce (dŭns) *n.* A stupid person. [After John *Duns Scotus* (1265?–1308), Scottish philosopher and theologian.]

dun·der·head (dŭn'dər-hĕd') *n.* A numbskull; dunce. [Perh. Dutch *donder,* thunder + HEAD.]

dune (dōon, dyōon) *n.* A hill or ridge of wind-blown sand. [French, from Old French, from Middle Dutch *dūne.*]

dung (dŭng) *n.* **1.** The excrement of animals; manure. **2.** Anything foul or abhorrent. —*tr.v.* To fertilize with manure. [Middle English, from Old English.]

dun·ga·ree (dŭng'gə-rē') *n.* **1.** A sturdy, usu. blue denim fabric. **2. dungarees.** Overalls or trousers made from this fabric. [Hindi *dungrī.*]

dung beetle. Any of various beetles of the family Scarabaeidae, that form balls of dung on which they feed and in which they lay their eggs.

dun·geon (dŭn'jən) *n.* **1.** A dark, often underground prison or cell. **2.** A donjon. [Middle English *donjon,* from Old French, castle tower, from Medieval Latin *dominiō,* lordship, dominion, from Latin *dominus,* master.]

dung·hill (dŭng'hĭl') *n.* **1.** A heap of animal excrement.

2. A foul, degraded place or condition.

dunk (dŭngk) *tr.v.* **1.** To plunge into liquid; immerse. **2.** To dip (food) into coffee or other liquid before eating it. **3.** *Basketball.* To slam (a ball) through the basket from above. —*intr.v.* To go under water; submerge oneself briefly. —*n. Basketball.* A shot made by jumping into the air and slamming the ball down through the basket. [Pennsylvania Dutch *dunke,* from Middle High German *dunken,* from Old High German *dunkōn.*] —**dunk′er** *n.*

dun·lin (dŭn′lĭn) *n.* A brown and white sandpiper, *Erolia alpina,* of northern regions. [From DUN (color).]

dun·nage (dŭn′ĭj) *n.* **1.** Loose packing material protecting a ship's cargo from damage during transport. **2.** Personal belongings or baggage. [Middle English *dennage.*]

du·o (dōō′ō, dyōō′ō) *n., pl.* **-os** (-ōz). **1.** *Mus.* A duet. **2.** *Mus.* Two performers singing or playing together. **3.** A pair. [Italian, two, from Latin.]

du·o·dec·i·mal (dōō′ō-dĕs′ə-məl, dyōō′-) *adj.* Of, pertaining to, or based on the number 12. —*n.* A twelfth. [From Latin *duodecim,* twelve.]

duodecimal system. A system of numeration in which 12 is the base.

du·o·de·num (dōō′ə-dē′nəm, dyōō′-, dōō-ŏd′n-əm, dyōō-) *n., pl.* **-o·de·na** (dōō′ə-dē′nə, dyōō′-, dōō-ŏd′n-ə, dyōō-). The beginning portion of the small intestine, extending from the pylorus to the jejunum. [Middle English, from Medieval Latin, *intestinum duodenum digitōrum,* "intestine twelve fingers long."] —**du′o·de′nal** *adj.*

dupe (dōōp, dyōōp) *n.* A person who is easily deceived. —*tr.v.* **duped, dup·ing.** To deceive or trick. [French.] —**dup′er** *n.*

du·ple (dōō′pəl, dyōō′-) *adj.* **1.** Double; consisting of two. **2.** *Mus.* Having two beats or a multiple of two beats to the measure. [Latin *duplus.*]

du·plex (dōō′plĕks, dyōō′-) *adj.* Twofold, esp. having two parts independently performing the same function. —*n.* A duplex apartment or house. [Latin, twofold.]

duplex apartment. An apartment having rooms on two adjoining floors connected by an inner staircase.

du·pli·cate (dōō′plĭ-kĭt, dyōō′-) *n.* Anything that corresponds exactly to something else; a copy; a double. —*modifier:* a duplicate key. —*tr.v.* (dōō′plĭ-kāt′, dyōō′-) **-cat·ed, -cat·ing. 1.** To make an identical copy of. **2.** To make or perform again; repeat. [Middle English, from Latin *duplicāre,* to make twofold, from *duplex,* twofold.]

du·pli·ca·tion (dōō′plĭ-kā′shən, dyōō′-) *n.* **1. a.** The act or procedure of duplicating. **b.** The condition of being duplicated. **2.** A duplicate; replica.

du·pli·ca·tor (dōō′plĭ-kā′tər, dyōō′-) *n.* A machine that reproduces printed or written material.

du·plic·i·ty (dōō-plĭs′ĭ-tē, dyōō-) *n., pl.* **-ties.** Deliberate deceptiveness in behavior or speech; double-dealing. [Middle English, from Old French, from Latin *duplex,* twofold.]

du·ra·ble (dōōr′ə-bəl, dyōōr′-) *adj.* Able to withstand wear or decay. [Middle English, from Old French, from Latin *dūrāre,* to last, endure.] —**du′ra·bil′i·ty** *n.*

du·ral·u·min (dōō-răl′yə-mĭn, dyōō-) *n.* A strong alloy of aluminum containing copper, manganese, and magnesium.

du·ra ma·ter (dōōr′ə mā′tər, dyōōr′ə-). A tough fibrous membrane that is the outermost covering of the brain and the spinal cord. [Middle English, from Medieval Latin *dūra mater (cerebrī),* "hard mother (of the brain)."]

du·ra·men (dōō-rā′mən, dyōō-) *n.* Heartwood. [From Latin, hardness, from *dūrāre,* to harden, from *dūrus,* hard.]

du·rance (dōōr′əns, dyōōr′-) *n.* Forced confinement; imprisonment. [Middle English *duraunce,* duration, from Old French *durer,* to last, from Latin *dūrāre.*]

du·ra·tion (dōō-rā′shən, dyōō-) *n.* **1.** Continuance in time: *a life of long duration.* **2.** The period of time during which something exists or persists: *the duration of the war.* [Medieval Latin *dūrātiō,* from Latin *dūrāre,* to last.]

du·ress (dōō-rĕs′, dyōō-) *n.* **1.** Constraint by threat; coercion: *confessed under duress.* **2.** *Law.* Illegal coercion or confinement. [Middle English *duresse,* hardness, from Old French *dure(s)ce,* from Latin *dūritia,* from *dūrus,* hard.]

du·ri·an (dōōr′ē-ən, dyōōr′-) *n.* **1.** A tree, *Durio zibethinus,* of southeastern Asia, bearing edible fruit. **2.** The fruit of this tree, with a hard, prickly rind and soft pulp with an offensive odor but a pleasant taste. [Malay.]

dur·ing (dōōr′ĭng, dyōōr′-) *prep.* **1.** Throughout the course of: *He phoned during dinner.* **2.** At some time in: *born during the summer.* [Middle English, from *duren,* to last, from Old French *durer,* from Latin *dūrāre.*]

dur·ra (dōōr′ə) *n.* A cereal grain, *Sorghum vulgare durra,* of Asia and northern Africa. [Arabic *dhurah,* grain.]

durst (dûrst) *v. Archaic.* A past tense of **dare.**

du·rum (dōōr′əm, dyōōr′-) *n.* A hardy wheat, *Triticum aestivum durum,* used chiefly in making pasta. Also called **durum wheat.** [From Latin *dūrus,* hard.]

dusk (dŭsk) *n.* **1.** The time of evening immediately before darkness; twilight. **2.** Partial darkness; shade. [Middle English *dusky,* from Old English *dox.*]

dusk·y (dŭs′kē) *adj.* **-i·er, -i·est. 1.** Dark in color. **2.** Lacking adequate light; dim. —See Syns at **dark.** —**dusk′i·ly** *adv.* —**dusk′i·ness** *n.*

dust (dŭst) *n.* **1.** Matter in the form of fine, dry particles. **2.** A cloud of such matter. **3.** Such matter regarded as the result of disintegration, as a dead body or ruined building. **4.** Earth, esp. when regarded as the substance of the grave. **5.** A low, poor, or debased condition. —*tr.v.* **1.** To remove dust from by wiping, brushing, or beating. **2.** To cover or sprinkle with a dustlike substance. —*intr.v.* To clean by removing dust. —*idiom.* **bite the dust.** To die, esp. violently. [Middle English, from Old English *dūst.*]

dust·bin (dŭst′bĭn′) *n. Brit.* A can for trash or garbage.

dust bowl. Any region reduced to aridity by drought and dust storms.

dust devil. A small whirlwind that swirls dust and debris.

dust·er (dŭs′tər) *n.* **1.** Something or someone that dusts. **2.** A cloth or brush used to remove dust. **3.** A device for sifting or spreading a powdered substance. **4.** A smock worn to protect one's clothing from dust. **5.** A woman's loose dress-length housecoat.

dust jacket. A removable paper cover for a book.

dust·man (dŭst′mən) *n. Brit.* A garbage collector.

dust·pan (dŭst′păn′) *n.* A short-handled, shovellike pan into which dust is swept.

dust storm. A severe windstorm that sweeps clouds of dust across an extensive arid region.

dust·y (dŭs′tē) *adj.* **-i·er, -i·est. 1.** Covered or filled with dust. **2.** Like dust; powdery: *dusty soil.* **3.** Of the color of dust; grayish. —**dust′i·ly** *adv.* —**dust′i·ness** *n.*

Dutch (dŭch) *n.* **1. the Dutch** (*used with a pl. verb*). The people of the Netherlands. **2.** The Germanic language of the Netherlands. —*adj.* Of the Netherlands, the Dutch, or their language. —*adv.* So that each person pays his own way. —*idiom.* **in Dutch.** *Informal.* In trouble; in disfavor.

Dutch door. A door divided in half horizontally so that either part may be left open or closed.

Dutch elm disease. A disease of elm trees caused by a fungus, *Ceratocystis ulmi,* and resulting in brown streaks in the wood and eventual death of the tree.

Dutch·man (dŭch′mən) *n.* **1.** A native or inhabitant of the Netherlands. **2.** *Archaic.* A German.

Dutch·man's-breech·es (dŭch′mənz-brĭch′ĭz) *n.* (*used with a sing. or pl. verb*). A woodland plant, *Dicentra cucullaria,* of eastern North America, with finely divided leaves and yellowish-white flowers with two spurs. [From its breeches-shaped blossoms.]

Dutchman's-breeches

Dutch oven. 1. A large, heavy pot or kettle, usu. of cast iron and with a tight lid, used for slow cooking. **2.** A metal

---

ă pat ā pay â care ä father ĕ pet ē be hw which ĭ pit ī tie î pier ŏ pot ō toe ô paw, for oi noise
ŏŏ took ōō boot ou out th thin th this ŭ cut û urge zh vision ə about, item, edible, gallop, circus

utensil open on one side and equipped with shelves, that is placed before an open fire for baking or roasting food. **3.** A wall oven in which food is baked by preheated walls.

Dutch treat. *Informal.* An outing, as for dinner or a movie, for which each pays his own expenses.

Dutch uncle. *Informal.* A stern and candid critic.

du·te·ous (dōō'tē-əs, dyōō'-) *adj.* Obedient; dutiful. [From DUTY.] —**du'te·ous·ly** *adv.*

du·ti·a·ble (dōō'tē-ə-bəl, dyōō'-) *adj.* Subject to import tax.

du·ti·ful (dōō'tĭ-fəl, dyōō'-) *adj.* **1.** Careful to perform one's duties. **2.** Expressing or filled with a sense of duty: *dutiful words.* —**du'ti·ful·ly** *adv.* —**du'ti·ful·ness** *n.*

du·ty (dōō'tē, dyōō'-) *n., pl.* **-ties. 1.** An act or a course of action that one ought to or must do. **2. a.** Moral obligation. **b.** The compulsion felt to meet such obligation. **3.** A task assigned or demanded of one, esp. in the armed forces. **4.** A task, assignment, or function. **5.** A tax charged by a government, esp. on imports. [Middle English *duete,* from Norman French, from Old French *deu,* due.]

du·um·vir (dōō-ŭm'vər, dyōō-) *n., pl.* **-virs** or **-vi·ri** (-və-rē). A member of a duumvirate. [Latin *duo,* two + *vir,* man.]

du·um·vi·rate (dōō-ŭm'vər-ĭt, dyōō-) *n.* **1.** Any of various two-man executive boards in the Roman Republic. **2.** Any regime or partnership of two people.

dwarf (dwôrf) *n., pl.* **dwarfs** or **dwarves** (dwôrvz). **1.** An adult person, animal, or plant of below normal size. **2.** In legend, a tiny, often ugly, person sometimes possessing magical powers. **3.** A **dwarf star.** —*tr.v.* **1.** To check the natural growth or development of; to stunt: *dwarf a tree.* **2.** To cause to appear small by comparison. —*adj.* Of an unusually small type or variety: *a dwarf tree.* [Middle English *dwerf,* from Old English *dweorg.*]

dwarf·ism (dwôr'fĭz'əm) *n.* A pathological condition of arrested growth that has various causes.

dwarf star. A star with relatively low mass and average or below average luminosity.

dwarves (dwôrvz) *n.* A plural of **dwarf.**

dwell (dwĕl) *intr.v.* **dwelt** (dwĕlt) or **dwelled, dwell·ing. 1.** To live as a resident; reside. **2.** To exist in some place or condition: *dwell in peace.* **3.** To remain or be present in: *Her example will dwell in our hearts and minds.* **4.** To linger over or emphasize in thought, speech, or writing. [Middle English *dwellen,* to reside, from Old English *dwellan,* to delay.] —**dwell'er** *n.*

dwell·ing (dwĕl'ĭng) *n.* A place to live in; residence; abode.

dwelt (dwĕlt) *v.* A past tense and past participle of **dwell.**

dwin·dle (dwĭn'dəl) *v.* **-dled, -dling.** —*intr.v.* To become gradually less until little remains; diminish. —*tr.v.* To make smaller or less; cause to shrink. —See Syns at **decrease.** [Freq. of obs. *dwine,* to diminish, from Middle English *dwinen,* from Old English *dwīnan.*]

Dy The symbol for the element **dysprosium.**

dyb·buk (dĭb'ək) *n.* In Jewish folklore, the soul of a dead person that enters and takes control of the body of a living person. [Hebrew *dibbūk,* from *dābak,* to cling.]

dye (dī) *n.* **1.** Any substance used to color cloth, hair, food, or other materials. **2.** A color imparted by dyeing. —*v.* **dyed, dye·ing.** —*tr.v.* To color (a material) with or as if with a dye. —*intr.v.* To take on or impart color. [Middle English *deie,* from Old English *dēag,* hue, tinge.] —**dy'er** *n.*

dyed-in-the-wool (dīd'ĭn-thə-wŏŏl') *adj.* Thoroughgoing; out-and-out: *a dyed-in-the-wool liar and cheat.*

dye·stuff (dī'stŭf') *n.* Any material used as or yielding a dye.

dy·ing (dī'ĭng) *adj.* **1.** About to die: *a dying man.* **2.** Done or uttered just before death: *his dying words.* **3.** Drawing to an end: *a dying day.*

dyke (dīk) *n. & v.* Var. of **dike.**

dy·nam·ic (dī-năm'ĭk) or **dy·nam·i·cal** (-ĭ-kəl) *adj.* **1.** Marked by energy and vigor; forceful. **2.** Characterized

by or tending to produce continuous change or progress. **3. a.** Of or pertaining to energy, force, or motion in relation to force. **b.** Of or pertaining to dynamics. —See Syns at **vigorous.** [French *dynamique,* from Greek *dunamikos,* powerful, from *dunamis,* power, from *dunasthai,* to be able.] —**dy·nam'i·cal·ly** *adv.*

dy·nam·ics (dī-năm'ĭks) *pl.n.* **1.** *(used with a sing. verb).* The branch of mechanics that deals with the relationship between bodies in motion and the forces affecting their motion. **2.** The physical, intellectual, or moral forces that produce motion, activity, and change in any sphere. **3.** *(used with a sing. verb).* The psychological aspect or conduct of an interpersonal relationship. **4.** *(used with a sing. verb).* Variation in force or intensity, esp. in musical sound.

dy·na·mism (dī'nə-mĭz'əm) *n.* **1.** Any of various theories or philosophical systems that explain the universe in terms of the interaction of force or energy. **2.** The quality or condition of being dynamic; vigor.

dy·na·mite (dī'nə-mīt') *n.* A powerful explosive made of nitroglycerin combined with an absorbent material. —*tr.v.* **-mit·ed, -mit·ing.** To blow up with dynamite. —See Syns at **destroy.** —**dy'na·mit'er** *n.*

dy·na·mo (dī'nə-mō') *n., pl.* **-mos. 1.** A generator. **2.** *Informal.* An extremely energetic and forceful person. [Short for *dynamo electric machine.*]

dynamo-. A prefix meaning power: **dynamoelectric.** [Greek *dunamo-,* from *dunamis,* power, from *dunasthai,* to be able.]

dy·na·mom·e·ter (dī'nə-mŏm'ĭ-tər) *n.* Any of several instruments used to measure force or power.

dy·na·mo·tor (dī'nə-mō'tər) *n.* A rotating electric machine with two armatures, used to convert alternating to direct current.

dy·nast (dī'năst', -nəst) *n.* A lord or ruler, esp. a hereditary ruler. [Latin *dynastēs,* from Greek *dunastēs,* from *dunasthai,* to be able.]

dy·nas·ty (dī'nə-stē) *n., pl.* **-ties. 1.** A succession of rulers from the same family or line. **2.** A family or group that maintains power, wealth, or position for several generations. —**dy·nas'tic** (dī-năs'tĭk) *adj.* —**dy·nas'ti·cal·ly** *adv.*

dyne (dīn) *n. Abbr.* **dyn** *Physics.* A centimeter-gram-second unit of force, equal to the force required to produce an acceleration of one centimeter per second per second to a mass of one gram. [French, from Greek *dunamis,* power.]

dys-. A prefix meaning diseased, difficult, faulty, or bad: **dyslexia.** [From Greek *dus-.*]

dys·en·ter·y (dĭs'ən-tĕr'ē) *n.* An infection of the lower intestinal tract producing pain, fever, and severe diarrhea, often with blood and mucus. [Middle English *dissenterie,* from Latin *dysenteria,* from Greek *dusenteria.*] —**dys'en·ter'ic** (dĭs'ən-tĕr'ĭk) *adj.*

dys·func·tion (dĭs-fŭngk'shən) *n.* Any disorder in the functioning of a bodily system or organ.

dys·gen·ic (dĭs-jĕn'ĭk) *adj.* Pertaining to or causing the deterioration of hereditary qualities.

dys·lex·i·a (dĭs-lĕk'sē-ə) *n.* Impairment of the ability to read, esp. in children. [DYS- + Greek *lexis,* speech, from *legein,* to speak.] —**dys·lex'ic** *adj.*

dys·pep·sia (dĭs-pĕp'shə, -sē-ə) *n.* Disturbed digestion; indigestion. [Latin, from Greek *duspepsia.*]

dys·pep·tic (dĭs-pĕp'tĭk) or **dys·pep·ti·cal** (-tĭ-kəl) *adj.* **1.** Pertaining to or having dyspepsia. **2.** Morose or despondent. —*n.* A person who suffers from dyspepsia.

dys·pro·si·um (dĭs-prō'zē-əm) *n. Symbol* **Dy** A soft, silvery rare-earth metal used in nuclear research. Atomic number 66; atomic weight 162.50; melting point 1,407°C; boiling point 2,600°C; specific gravity 8.536; valence 3. [From Greek *dusprositos,* difficult to approach.]

ă pat	ā pay	â care	ä father	ĕ pet	ē be	hw which	ĭ pit	ī tie	î pier	ŏ pot	ō toe	ô paw, for	oi noise
ōō took	ōō boot	ou out	th thin	th this	ŭ cut	û urge	zh vision	ə about, item, edible, gallop, circus

Ee

Phoenician – About 3,000 years ago the Phoenicians and other Semitic peoples began to use graphic signs to represent individual speech sounds instead of syllables or whole words. They used this symbol to represent the sound of the consonant "h" and gave it the name hē.

Greek – The Greeks borrowed the Phoenician alphabet with some modifications. They reversed the orientation of hē, they used it to stand for the vowel "e," and they gave it the name epsilon, or "simple e," to distinguish it from long "e," which they called ēta.

Roman – The Romans borrowed the alphabet from the Greeks via the Etruscans and adapted it for carving Latin in stone. This monumental script, as it is called, became the basis for modern printed capital letters.

Medieval – By medieval times – around 1,200 years ago – the Roman monumental capitals had become adapted to being relatively quickly written on paper, parchment, or vellum. The linear shape of E became rounded and could be written with fewer pen strokes. The cursive minuscule alphabet became the basis of modern printed lower-case letters.

Modern – Since the invention of printing about 500 years ago modifications have been made in the shape and style of the letter E, but its basic form has remained unchanged.

---

e, E (ē) *n., pl.* **e's** or **E's.** The fifth letter of the English alphabet.

each (ēch) *adj.* Being one of two or more persons or things considered individually; every: *Each person has cast a vote.* —*pron.* Every one of a group of persons, objects, or things considered individually: *Each has presented his gift.* —*adv.* For or to each one; apiece: *ten cents each.* [Middle English *ech,* from Old English *ǣlc, ǣghwilc.*]
   Usage: **1. each.** When the pronoun *each* is used as a subject without intervening words, it takes a singular verb: *Each is involved to some extent.* If plural words intervene between *each* and its verb, a plural verb may occur: *Each of them is involved* or *Each of them are involved.* . . . If a plural verb is used, any other pronouns referring to the verb should agree with it in number: *Each of the four of them are liable for their actions.* Similarly, if a singular verb is used, the related pronouns should be singular: *Each of them is liable for his or her actions.* When *each* occurs after a plural subject with which it is in apposition, the verb is gen. plural: *They each need expert advice.* **2. each + every.** Since *each* refers to the individual one and *every* refers to a total group of individuals, the phrase "each and every," often used in conversation and business writing, is illogical and should be avoided in formal compositions. It is preferable to use *each* and *every* singly and not in combination. If, however, the expression is used, it takes a singular verb: *Each and every student must do his part,* but preferably *Each student* (or *Every student*) *must do his part.*

each other. 1. Each the other. Used as a compound reciprocal pronoun: *They met each other on the beach.* **2.** One another.
   Usage: **each other, one another.** The pronouns *each other* and *one another* are interchangeable in modern English, regardless of whether the reference is to two or to more than two individuals: *The two boxers pounded each other* (or *one another*) *mercilessly for three rounds. The three kittens played with each other* (or *one another*) *for hours.* The possessive forms of these pronouns are: *each other's* and *one another's* (not *each others'* or *one anothers'*). If the possessive form of either of these pronouns is followed by a noun representing the thing possessed, that noun is plural in form: *Our student government president and the neighboring academy's senior class president will visit each other's schools* (not *each other's school*). Neither pronoun can be used as the subject of a clause of sentence: *Each of us knew what the other felt* (not *We knew what each other felt*).

ea·ger (ē'gər) *adj.* **-er, -est. 1.** Full of strong and impatient desire: *eager for fame.* **2.** Enthusiastically expectant; keenly interested: *eager sports fans.* [Middle English *egre,* sharp, keen, from Old French *aigre,* from Latin *ācer.*] —**ea'ger·ly** *adv.* —**ea'ger·ness** *n.*

eager beaver. *Informal.* An overzealous person.

ea·gle (ē'gəl) *n.* **1.** Any of various large birds of prey of the family Accipitridae, with a powerful hooked bill, long, broad wings, and strong, soaring flight. **2.** A representation of an eagle used as an emblem, insignia, seal, etc. **3.** A former gold coin of the United States with a face value of ten dollars. **4.** *Golf.* A score of two below par on any hole. [Middle English *egle,* from Old French, from Latin *aquila.*]

ea·glet (ē'glĭt) *n.* A young eagle.

-ean. A suffix meaning pertaining to or derived from: **Caesarean, Tyrolean.** [Var. of -IAN.]

ear¹ (ĭr) *n.* **1.** *Anat.* **a.** In vertebrates, the organ of hearing, responsible for maintaining equilibrium and sensing sound and in man divided into the external ear, the middle ear, and the internal ear. **b.** The visible outer part of this organ. **2.** The sense of hearing. **3.** The ability to distinguish tones or sounds accurately or acutely: *the precise ear of a musician.* **4.** Attention, esp. favorable attention; heed: *Give me your ear.* **5.** Anything resembling the outer ear in shape or position. —*idioms.* **all ears.** Listening eagerly and attentively. **bend (someone's) ear.** *Informal.* To talk to someone for too long a time. **fall on deaf ears.** To be ignored: *His advice fell on deaf ears.* **give (or lend) an ear.** To pay close attention to. **have (or keep) an ear to the ground.** To give attention to or watch the trends of public opinion. **in one ear and out the other.** Heard but without influence or ef-

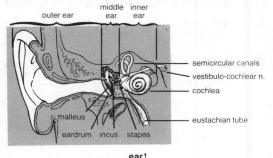

ear¹

fect. **turn a deaf ear.** To be unwilling to listen or pay attention. **up to one's (or the) ears.** Deeply involved or committed: *up to one's ears in debt.* [Middle English *ere*, from Old English *ēare*.] —**eared** *adj.* —**ear'less** *adj.*

ear² (îr) *n.* The seed-bearing spike of a cereal plant, as corn. —*intr.v.* To form or grow ears, as corn. [Middle English *ere*, from Old English *ēar*.]

ear·drum (îr'drŭm') *n.* **1.** The thin membrane that separates the outer and middle ear and vibrates when struck by sound waves; the tympanic membrane. **2.** The cavity of the middle ear; the tympanum.

ear·flap (îr'flăp') *n.* Either of two cloth or fur tabs on a cap that may be turned down over the ears; earlap.

ear·ful (îr'fŏŏl') *n.* **1.** An interesting piece of news or gossip. **2.** A scolding.

earl (ûrl) *n.* A British peer above a viscount and below a marquis in rank. [Middle English *erl*, from Old English *eorl*, warrior, chief, nobleman.] —**earl'dom** *n.*

ear·lap (îr'lăp') *n.* An earflap.

ear·lobe (îr'lōb') *n.* The soft, fleshy tissue at the bottom of the outer ear.

ear·ly (ûr'lē) *adj.* **-li·er, -li·est. 1.** Near the beginning of a given series, period of time, or course of events: *in the early evening.* **2.** In or belonging to a distant or remote period or stage of development; primitive. **3.** Occurring, developing, or appearing before the expected or usual time: *an early fall.* **4.** Occurring in the near future: *an early settlement of the strike.* —*adv.* **-li·er, -li·est. 1.** Near the beginning of a given series, period of time, or course of events: *started early in the morning.* **2.** Far back in time: *as early as the 10th century.* **3.** Before the expected or usual time: *They left early.* **4.** So as to allow enough time: *Send your invitations early.* [Middle English *erly*, from Old English *ǣlīce*, from *ǣr*, before.] —**ear'li·ness** *n.*

Syns: 1. early, first, initial *adj. Core meaning:* At or near the start of a period, development, or series (*early Impressionism; early stages of cancer*). **2. early, ancient, primitive** *adj. Core meaning:* Of, existing, or occurring in a distant period (*early man; early fossils*). **3. early, premature, untimely** *adj. Core meaning:* Developing or appearing before the expected time (*an early death; an early frost*).

early bird. *Informal.* A person who awakens, arrives, or starts being active before most others.

ear·mark (îr'märk') *n.* **1.** An identifying mark on the ear of an animal to indicate ownership. **2.** Any identifying mark, feature, or characteristic: *Careful observation of details is one of the earmarks of a good scientist.* —*tr.v.* **1.** To mark the ear of (an animal) for identification. **2.** To place an identifying or distinctive mark on. **3.** To reserve or set aside: *earmarked some money for a summer vacation.*

ear·muff (îr'mŭf') *n.* Either of a pair of warm fur or cloth coverings for the ears.

earn (ûrn) *tr.v.* **1.** To gain or receive (salary, wages, etc.) in return for one's services or labor. **2.** To acquire or deserve as a result of one's efforts or behavior: *earn a reputation for honesty.* **3.** To produce (interest, profit, etc.). [Middle English *ernen*, from Old English *earnian*, to earn, merit.] —**earn'er** *n.*

ear·nest¹ (ûr'nĭst) *adj.* **1.** Serious and determined in purpose: *earnest students.* **2.** Showing or expressing deep sincerity or feeling: *an earnest prayer.* —*idiom.* **in earnest.** With serious purpose or intent. [Middle English *ernest*, from Old English *eornost*, zeal, seriousness.] —**ear'nest·ly** *adv.* —**ear'nest·ness** *n.*

ear·nest² (ûr'nĭst) *n.* Something, as a promise or money paid in advance, given as an assurance or indication of one's intentions. [Middle English *ernest*, from Old French *erres*, pl. of *erre*, pledge, from Latin *arra*, short for *arrabō*, from Greek *arrabōn*, from Hebrew *ērābhōn*, from *ārabh*, he pledged.]

earn·ings (ûr'nĭngz) *pl.n.* Money earned in payment for work or as profit.

ear·phone (îr'fōn') *n.* A device that converts electric signals into audible sound and that is made to be worn near or in contact with the ear.

ear·ring (îr'rĭng, îr'ĭng) *n.* An ornament or jewel worn clipped to or suspended from the earlobe.

ear·shot (îr'shŏt') *n.* The range or distance within which sound can be heard.

earth (ûrth) *n.* **1.** Often **Earth.** The planet on which human beings live, the third planet of the solar system in order of increasing distance from the sun. **2.** The solid surface of the world; the land. **3.** Soil or dirt, esp. where cultivable or productive. **4.** The dwelling place of mortal men as distinguished from heaven and hell. **5.** All of the human inhabitants of the world: *The earth received the news with joy.* **6.** The lair of a burrowing animal such as the badger. **7.** *Chem.* Any of several metallic oxides, such as iron oxide, that are difficult to reduce. —*tr.v.* To cover or heap up (plants, seeds, or roots) with soil for protection. —*idioms.* **come back (or down) to earth.** To return to reality. **down to earth.** Sensible; realistic. [Middle English *erthe*, from Old English *eorthe*.]

earth·bound or **earth-bound** (ûrth'bound') *adj.* **1.** Headed for the earth: *an earthbound meteor.* **2.** Unimaginative or ordinary: *earthbound concerns.*

earth·en (ûr'thən, -thən) *adj.* **1.** Made of earth: *an earthen floor.* **2.** Made of baked clay: *an earthen vase.*

earth·en·ware (ûr'thən-wâr', -thən-) *n.* Pottery made of coarse, porous baked clay.

earth·ling (ûrth'lĭng) *n.* A human being.

earth·ly (ûrth'lē) *adj.* **1.** Of or relating to the earth, esp. the material world, rather than heavenly or spiritual: *earthly pleasures.* **2.** Possible; imaginable: *nonsense with no earthly meaning.* —**earth'li·ness** *n.*

earth·quake (ûrth'kwāk') *n.* A series of waves or vibrations in the crust of the earth, caused by the sudden shifting of rock under great strain along geologic faults and by volcanic action.

earth science. Any of several sciences, such as geology and meteorology, that are concerned with the origin, structure, and physical nature of the earth.

earth·shak·ing (ûrth'shā'kĭng) *adj.* Having enormous consequences or importance: *an earthshaking discovery.*

earth·ward (ûrth'wərd) *adv.* Also **earth·wards** (-wərdz). To or toward the earth: *snowflakes drifting earthward.*

earth·work (ûrth'wûrk') *n.* Often **earthworks.** An embankment or other structure, esp. a military fortification, made of earth.

earth·worm (ûrth'wûrm') *n.* Any of various segmented worms of the class Oligochaeta, that burrow into and help aerate and enrich soil.

earth·y (ûr'thē) *adj.* **-i·er, -i·est. 1.** Consisting of or resembling earth or soil: *an earthy smell.* **2.** Crude or coarse; unrefined: *earthy humor.* **3.** Uninhibited or hearty; lusty: *an earthy woman.* —See Syns at **coarse.** —**earth'i·ness** *n.*

ear·wax (îr'wăks') *n.* The waxlike substance produced by certain glands lining the canal of the outer ear; cerumen.

ear·wig (îr'wĭg') *n.* Any of various insects of the order Dermaptera, with pincerlike appendages protruding from the rear of the body. [Middle English *erwigge*, from Old English *ēarwicga*, ear insect.]

ease (ēz) *n.* **1.** Freedom from pain, worry, or discomfort: *The medication will allow her to rest with ease.* **2.** Freedom from constraint, embarrassment, or awkwardness; naturalness; self-assurance: *the ease with which he can speak before an audience.* **3.** Freedom from difficulty, hard work, or great effort; readiness; skill: *play tennis with ease.* **4.** Freedom from financial difficulty; comfort: *a life of ease.* —*v.* **eased, eas·ing.** —*tr.v.* **1.** To free from pain, worry, or trouble; relieve: *medication to ease pain.* **2.** To make less troublesome or difficult: *using shortcuts to ease the workload.* **3.** To slacken the strain, pressure, or tension of; loosen: *ease off a cable.* **4.** To move or fit into place or position slowly and carefully: *ease the pie into the oven.* —*intr.v.* **1.** To lessen in discomfort, stress, pressure, etc.; let up: *ease up on the gas pedal.* **2.** To move carefully and slowly: *The tug eased into the narrow docking space.* —*idiom.* **at ease. 1.** Free from strain or discomfort; relaxed; comfortable: *The guests were all at ease and enjoying themselves.* **2.** Standing silently with the legs apart and the hands clasped behind the back. [Middle English *ese*, from Old French *aise*, comfort, convenience, from Latin *adjacēns*, nearby, adjacent, from *adjacēre*, to lie near : *ad-*, near to + *jacēre*, to lie, from *jacere*, to throw.]

Syns: ease, easiness, facility, readiness *n. Core meaning:* The ability to perform without apparent effort (*translated the document with ease*).

ease·ful (ēz′fəl) *adj.* Giving or characterized by comfort and peace; restful. —**ease′ful·ly** *adv.* —**ease′ful·ness** *n.*

ea·sel (ē′zəl) *n.* A stand or rack, usu. in the form of an upright tripod, used to support an artist's canvas or to display a picture or sign. [Dutch *ezel*, ass, from Middle Dutch *esel*, ult. from Latin *asinus*.]

ease·ment (ēz′mənt) *n.* A right given a person to make limited use of another's real property.

eas·i·ly (ē′zə-lē) *adv.* **1.** Without difficulty; with ease; readily: *a problem easily solved.* **2.** Without doubt; surely: *easily the best play this season.*

eas·i·ness (ē′zē-nĭs) *n.* **1.** The condition or quality of being easy. **2.** Ease of manner; self-assurance; poise. —See Syns at **ease.**

east (ēst) *n.* **1. a.** The direction toward which the earth rotates on its axis; the direction from which the sun is seen to rise: *a wind blowing from the east.* **b.** Often **East.** A region or part of the earth in this direction: *the highlands of the east.* **2. the East. a.** Asia and the nearby islands of the Indian and Pacific oceans; the Orient. **b.** The part of the United States along or near the Atlantic coast. —*adj.* **1.** Of, in, or toward the east: *the east bank of the river.* **2.** Often **East.** Forming or belonging to a region, country, etc., toward the east: *East Germany.* **3.** From the east: *an east wind.* —*adv.* In a direction to or toward the east: *a river flowing east.* [Middle English, from Old English *ēast.*]

east·bound (ēst′bound′) *adj.* Going toward the east.

Eas·ter (ē′stər) *n.* **1.** A festival in the Christian Church commemorating the Resurrection of Christ, celebrated on the first Sunday following the first full moon on or after Mar. 21. **2.** The Sunday on which this festival is held. [Middle English *ester*, from Old English *ēastre.*]

Easter lily. Any of various white-flowered lilies that bloom around Easter.

east·er·ly (ē′stər-lē) *adj.* **1.** In or toward the east. **2.** From the east: *easterly winds.* —*n., pl.* **-lies.** A storm or wind from the east.

east·ern (ē′stərn) *adj.* **1.** Toward, in, or to the east: *an eastern exposure.* **2.** Coming from the east: *an eastern wind.* **3.** Often **Eastern.** Of, pertaining to, or characteristic of eastern regions or the East. **4. Eastern.** Of, pertaining to, or characteristic of the Orient: *Eastern philosophy.* [Middle English *esterne*, from Old English *ēasterne.*]

Eastern Daylight-Saving Time. Daylight-saving time as reckoned in the region between the meridians at 67.5° and 82.5° west of Greenwich, England. The eastern United States is in this region.

east·ern·er (ē′stər-nər) *n.* Often **East·ern·er.** A native or inhabitant of the east, esp. of the eastern United States.

Eastern Hemisphere. The half of the earth that includes Europe, Africa, Asia, and Australia.

east·ern·most (ē′stərn-mōst′) *adj.* Farthest east.

Eastern Orthodox Church. The body of modern churches, including the Greek and Russian Orthodox, derived from the early Christian Church established during the Byzantine Empire.

Eastern Standard Time. Standard time as reckoned in the region between the meridians at 67.5° and 82.5° west of Greenwich, England. The eastern United States is in this region.

Eas·ter·tide (ē′stər-tīd′) *n.* **1.** The Easter season, extending in different churches from Easter to Ascension Day, Whitsunday, or Trinity Sunday. **2.** The week following Easter Sunday.

east·ward (ēst′wərd) *adv.* Also **east·wards** (-wərdz). To or toward the east: *a river flowing eastward.* —*n.* A direction or region to the east.

eas·y (ē′zē) *adj.* **-i·er, -i·est. 1.** Not difficult; requiring little or no effort, trouble, etc.: *an easy task; handwriting that is easy to read.* **2.** Free from worry, anxiety, trouble, or pain: *an easy mind.* **3.** Characterized by rest or comfort; pleasant and relaxing: *an easy flight.* **4.** Relaxed; easygoing; informal: *an easy, sociable manner.* **5.** Not strict or demanding; lenient: *an easy teacher.* **6.** Readily persuaded or influenced; compliant: *The huckster thought this was a particularly easy crowd.* **7.** Not strenuous, hurried, or forced; moderate: *an easy walk around the block.* **8.** Econ. **a.** Small in demand and therefore readily obtainable: *Com-* modities are easier. **b.** Plentiful and therefore obtainable at low interest rates: *easy money.* —*adv.* Informal. Without strain or difficulty; in a relaxed, comfortable manner. —*idioms.* **go easy on.** Informal. **1.** To use moderately or carefully: *go easy on the liquor.* **2.** To be lenient or sympathetic to: *go easy on first offenders.* **take it easy.** Informal. **1.** To refrain from exertion; relax. **2.** To refrain from anger or violence; stay calm. [Middle English *esy*, from Old French *aisie*, past part. of *aisier*, to put at ease, from *aise*, ease.]

   Syns: easy, effortless, facile, ready, royal, simple, smooth *adj.* *Core meaning:* Posing no difficulty (*an easy solution to the problem*). See also Syns at **amiable** and **informal.**

eas·y·go·ing (ē′zē-gō′ĭng) *adj.* **1.** Living without intense concern; relaxed; informal. **2.** Having or moving at an even gait, as a horse. —See Syns at **amiable** and **informal.**

eat (ēt) *v.* **ate** (āt), **eat·en** (ēt′n), **eat·ing.** —*tr.v.* **1.** To take (solid food) into the body as nourishment by chewing and swallowing. **2.** To consume or destroy by or as if by eating: *Unexpected expenses ate up his savings.* **3.** To wear, corrode, or break by or as if by eating: *Rust ate away the iron pipes.* —*intr.v.* **1.** To consume food; have or take a meal or meals: *I ate before I left.* **2.** To wear away or corrode by or as if by eating or gnawing: *rust eating through metal.* —*phrasal verb.* **eat up. 1.** To use up; consume: *Wage increases were eaten up by the rise in the cost of living.* **2.** To enjoy greatly; be greedy for: *She eats up compliments.* —*n.* **eats.** *Slang.* Food. —*idioms.* **eat (one's) heart out.** To undergo bitter, hopeless anguish or longing. **eat (one's) words.** To retract something that one has said. [Middle English *eten*, from Old English *etan.*] —**eat′er** *n.*

eat·a·ble (ē′tə-bəl) *adj.* Fit to be eaten; edible. —*n.* Often **eatables.** Something fit to be eaten; food.

eat·en (ēt′n) *v.* Past participle of **eat.** [Middle English *eten*, from Old English *(ge)eten.*]

eat·er·y (ē′tə-rē) *n., pl.* **-ies.** Informal. A lunchroom; diner.

eau de co·logne (ō′ də kə-lōn′) *pl.* **eaux de cologne** (ō′, ōz′). Cologne.

eau de vie (ō′ də vē′) *pl.* **eaux de vie** (ō′, ōz′). Brandy.

eaves (ēvz) *n.* (used with a pl. verb). The projecting overhang at the lower edge of a roof. [Middle English *eves*, from Old English *efes*, eaves, edge, border.]

eaves·drop (ēvz′drŏp′) *intr.v.* **-dropped, -drop·ping.** To listen secretly to the private conversation of others. [Back-formation from *eavesdropper*, Middle English *evesdropper*, from *evesdrop*, water from the eaves.] —**eaves′drop′per** *n.*

ebb (ĕb) *intr.v.* **1.** To fall back or recede, as the tide does after reaching its highest point. **2.** To fade or fall away; weaken; diminish: *His popularity ebbed as conditions worsened. The fish ceased to struggle as its strength ebbed.* —See Syns at **decrease.** —*n.* **1.** A retreating or receding motion, as of the tide as it falls back from its highest point. **2.** A low point or condition: *His fortunes were at their lowest ebb.* [Middle English *ebbe*, from Old English *ebba*, low tide.]

ebb tide. 1. The receding of a tide from its highest point. **2.** The time period during which this occurs.

eb·on (ĕb′ən) *Archaic & Poet.* —*adj.* Black. —*n.* Ebony. [Middle English *eban*, ebony, from Latin *ebenus*, from Greek *ebenos.*]

eb·o·nite (ĕb′ə-nīt′) *n.* A type of hard rubber, esp. when colored black. [EBON + -ITE.]

eb·o·ny (ĕb′ə-nē) *n., pl.* **-nies. 1.** The hard black or blackish heartwood of any of several tropical trees of the genus *Diospyros*, used esp. for piano keys, cabinets, and carvings. **2.** A tree, native to southern Asia and Africa, having this wood. —*modifier:* *an ebony cabinet.* —*adj.* Suggesting ebony; black: *ebony hair.* [Middle English *hebenyf*, from Late Latin *ebeninus*, (made) of ebony, from Greek *ebeninos*, from *ebenos*, ebony tree, from Egyptian *hebni.*]

e·bul·lient (ĭ-bōōl′yənt, ĭ-bŭl′-) *adj.* **1.** Overflowing with excitement or enthusiasm; exuberant. **2.** Boiling or bubbling over: *Liquid nitrogen becomes ebullient when exposed to air.* [Latin *ēbulliēns*, pres. part. of *ēbullīre*, to boil over: *ex-*, completely + *bullīre*, to boil.] —**e·bul′lience** or **e·bul′lien·cy** *n.* —**e·bul′lient·ly** *adv.*

---

eb·ul·li·tion (ĕb′ə-lĭsh′ən) n. **1.** The bubbling or boiling of a liquid. **2.** A sudden, violent outpouring, as of emotion or violence. [Late Latin *ēbullītiō*, from Latin *ēbullīre*, to boil over.]

ec·cen·tric (ĭk-sĕn′trĭk) adj. **1.** Departing or deviating from the conventional norm, model, or practice; odd; peculiar: *an eccentric person; an eccentric habit.* **2.** Deviating from the form of a circle in the way that an ellipse does: *an eccentric orbit.* **3.** Not at or in the center: *an eccentric pivot.* **4.** Not having the same center: *two eccentric circles.* —See Syns at **strange.** —n. **1.** One who deviates markedly from a normal, conventional, or established course or pattern. **2.** *Machinery.* A disk or wheel having its axis of revolution displaced from its center so that it has a reciprocating motion. [Middle English *excentryke*, not having the same center, from Late Latin *eccentricus*, from Greek *ekkentros* : *ex-*, out + *kentron*, point, center, from *kentein*, to prick.] —**ec·cen′tri·cal·ly** adv.

ec·cen·tric·i·ty (ĕk′sĕn-trĭs′ĭ-tē) n., pl. **-ties. 1.** Deviation from a conventional or established norm or practice, esp. peculiar or whimsical behavior. **2.** The condition or quality of being eccentric.
> *Syns:* **eccentricity, idiosyncrasy, peculiarity, quirk** n.
> *Core meaning:* Peculiar behavior (*a hermit with more than one eccentricity*).

Ec·cle·si·as·tes (ĭ-klē′zē-ăs′tēz′) n. See table at **Bible.**

ec·cle·si·as·tic (ĭ-klē′zē-ăs′tĭk) adj. Ecclesiastical. —n. A clergyman; priest. [Medieval Latin *ecclēsiasticus*, from Greek *ekklēsiastikos*, from *ekklēsia*, assembly, church, from *ekkalein*, to summon : *ek-*, out + *kalein*, to call.]

ec·cle·si·as·ti·cal (ĭ-klē′zē-ăs′tĭ-kəl) adj. Of or pertaining to a church, esp. as an organized institution.

ec·dy·sis (ĕk′dĭ-sĭs) n., pl. **-ses** (-sēz′). The shedding of an outer layer of skin, as in insects and snakes. [From Greek *ekdusis*, a stripping, from *ekduein*, to take off : *ex-*, out + *duein*, to put on, enter.]

ech·e·lon (ĕsh′ə-lŏn′) n. **1.** A formation of troops, ships, or aircraft in which units are arranged in a steplike fashion. **2.** A subdivision of a military or naval force: *a command echelon.* **3.** A level of command or authority: *the lowest echelon of the business.* [French *échelon*, "rung of a ladder," from Old French *eschelon*, from *eschile*, ladder, from Latin *scālae*, ladder, stairs.]

ech·id·na (ĭ-kĭd′nə) n. Any of several burrowing, egg-laying mammals of the genera *Tachyglossus* and *Zaglossus*, of Australia, Tasmania, and New Guinea, with a spiny coat, a slender snout, and a sticky tongue used for catching insects. Also called **spiny anteater.** [Latin, viper, from Greek *ekhidna*.]

echidna

e·chi·no·derm (ĭ-kī′nə-dûrm′) n. Any of numerous sea animals of the phylum Echinodermata, which includes starfish, sea urchins, and sea cucumbers, with a spiny or rough outer covering and parts that radiate from the center. [ECHINUS + -DERM.]

e·chi·nus (ĭ-kī′nəs) n., pl. **-ni** (-nī′). **1.** A sea urchin. **2.** A curved molding just below the abacus of a Doric capital. [Latin, from Greek *ekhinos*.]

ech·o (ĕk′ō) n., pl. **-oes. 1. a.** Repetition of a sound by reflection of sound waves from a surface. **b.** A sound produced in this manner. **2.** Any repetition or imitation of something, as of the opinions of another. **3.** Someone who imitates another, as in opinions. **4.** *Electronics.* A reflected wave received by a radio or radar. —tr.v. **1.** To repeat by

or as if by an echo: *The canyon echoed her cry.* **2.** To repeat or imitate: *followers echoing the thoughts of the leader.* —intr.v. **1.** To be repeated by or as if by an echo: *shouts echoing through the streets.* **2.** To resound with or emit an echo; reverberate: *woods echoing with hunting cries.* [Middle English *ecco*, from Old French *echo*, from Latin *ēchō*, from Greek *ēkhō*.] —**ech′o·er** n.

Ech·o (ĕk′ō) n. *Gk. Myth.* A nymph whose unrequited love for Narcissus caused her to pine away until nothing but her voice remained.

é·clair (ā-klâr′, ā′klâr′) n. A light, oblong pastry with cream or custard filling, usu. iced with chocolate. [French, "lightning," from Old French *esclair*, from *esclairier*, to flash, from Latin *exclārāre* : *ex-*, completely + *clārāre*, to brighten, from *clārus*, clear.]

é·clat (ā-klä′, ā′klä′) n. **1.** Great brilliance, as of performance or achievement. **2.** Conspicuous success or acclaim. [French, explosion, from *éclater*, to burst, explode, from Old French *esclater*.]

ec·lec·tic (ĭ-klĕk′tĭk) adj. **1.** Choosing what appears to be the best from diverse sources, systems, or styles: *an eclectic musician.* **2.** Consisting of elements taken from diverse sources: *eclectic architecture.* —n. Someone who uses an eclectic system or method. [Greek *eklektikos*, from *eklektos*, selected, from *eklegein*, to single out : *ex-*, out + *legein*, to choose.] —**ec·lec′ti·cal·ly** adv.

ec·lec·ti·cism (ĭ-klĕk′tĭ-sĭz′əm) n. **1.** An eclectic system or method. **2.** Free selection, as of ideas, from diverse sources.

e·clipse (ĭ-klĭps′) n. **1. a.** The partial or complete obscuring by another celestial body of part or all of the light that reaches an observer from a given celestial body. **b.** The period of time during which such an obscuring occurs. **2.** A decline into obscurity or disuse; downfall: *a reputation in eclipse.* —tr.v. **e·clipsed, e·clips·ing. 1.** To cause an eclipse or obscuring of; darken. **2.** To obscure or overshadow the importance, fame, or reputation of; reduce in importance by comparison. [Middle English, from Old French, from Latin *eclīpsis*, from Greek *ekleipsis*, cessation, from *ekleipein*, to leave out, abandon : *ek-*, *ex-*, out + *leipein*, to leave.]

e·clip·tic (ĭ-klĭp′tĭk) n. The apparent path of the sun among the stars; the circle formed by the intersection of the plane of the earth's orbit and the celestial sphere. —adj. Of or pertaining to eclipses or the ecliptic. [Middle English *ecliptik*, from Late Latin *eclīpticus*, from Latin, of an eclipse.]

e·col·o·gy (ĭ-kŏl′ə-jē) n. **1.** The science of the relationships between organisms and their environments. **2.** The relationship between organisms and their environment. [German *Ökologie* : *öko-*, from Greek *oikos*, house + *-logie*, from Greek *-logia*, study of.] —**ec′o·log′i·cal** (ĕk′ə-lŏj′ĭ-kəl, ē′kə-) adj. —**ec′o·log′i·cal·ly** adv. —**e·col′o·gist** n.

ec·o·nom·ic (ĕk′ə-nŏm′ĭk, ē′kə-) adj. **1.** Of or pertaining to the production, development, and management of material wealth, as of a country or business enterprise: *the government's economic policy.* **2.** Of or pertaining to the science of economics: *economic doctrines.* **3.** Of or pertaining to money matters; financial: *My economic situation forbids me from buying a car.*

ec·o·nom·i·cal (ĕk′ə-nŏm′ĭ-kəl, ē′kə-) adj. **1.** Not wasteful or extravagant; prudent in the management or use of resources; frugal: *an economical person.* **2.** Operating inexpensively or at a saving: *an economical engine.* **3.** Economic. —**ec′o·nom′i·cal·ly** adv.

ec·o·nom·ics (ĕk′ə-nŏm′ĭks, ē′kə-) n. **1.** *(used with a sing. verb).* The science that deals with the production, distribution, development, and consumption of goods and services. **2.** *(used with a pl. verb).* Economic condition or an aspect of it, as of a country or individual: *the economics of a large agricultural region.*

e·con·o·mist (ĭ-kŏn′ə-mĭst) n. A person who specializes in economics.

e·con·o·mize (ĭ-kŏn′ə-mīz′) v. **-mized, -miz·ing.** —intr.v. To be frugal; practice economy: *He's always trying to economize.* —tr.v. To use or manage with thrift: *economize energy.* —**e·con′o·miz′er** n.

e·con·o·my (ĭ-kŏn′ə-mē) n., pl. **-mies. 1.** The careful or thrifty use or management of resources, as of income, ma-

ă pat | ā pay | â care | ä father | ĕ pet | ē be | hw which
ŏŏ took | ōō boot | ou out | th thin | th this | ŭ cut
ĭ pit | ī tie | î pier | ŏ pot | ō toe | ô paw, for | oi noise
û urge | zh vision | ə about, item, edible, gallop, circus

terials, or labor. **2.** An example of this; a saving: *the economies of mass production.* **3.** The management of the resources of a country, community, or business: *the American economy.* **4. a.** A system for the management and development of resources: *an agricultural economy.* **b.** The economic system of a country, region, state, etc.: *Tobacco is the center of their economy.* **5.** The functional arrangement of elements or parts within a structure or system: *the economy of an organism.* [Old French *economie,* management of a household, from Latin *oeconomia,* from Greek *oikonomia* : *oikos,* house + *-nomos,* managing.]

ec·o·sys·tem (ĕk′ō-sĭs′təm) *n.* The plants and animals of an ecological community, together with their environment, forming an interacting system of activities and functions regarded as a unit. [ECO(LOGY) + SYSTEM.]

ec·ru (ĕk′rōō, ā′krōō) *n.* Pale yellow or light yellowish brown; light tan. [French *écru* : *é-,* completely, from Latin *ex-* + *cru,* crude, raw, from Latin *crudus.*]

ec·sta·sy (ĕk′stə-sē) *n., pl.* **-sies.** **1.** A condition of extraordinary joy or delight; rapture; *the ecstasy of romantic love.* **2.** A condition of experiencing an emotion so intensely that one is carried beyond thought and self-control: *an ecstasy of anger.* [Middle English *extasie,* from Old French, from Late Latin *extasis,* from Greek *ekstasis,* from *existanai,* to displace, drive out of one's senses : *ex-,* out + *histanai,* to place.]

ec·stat·ic (ĭk-stăt′ĭk) *adj.* **1.** Of or marked by ecstasy. **2.** In a state of ecstasy; enraptured. —**ec·stat′i·cal·ly** *adv.*

ecto-. A prefix meaning outside or external: **ectoderm.** [Greek *ekto-,* from *ektos,* outside, from *ek, ex,* out.]

ec·to·derm (ĕk′tə-dûrm′) *n.* The outermost of the three layers of cells found in an early embryo, developing in time into the outer skin and nervous system. [ECTO- + -DERM.]

ec·to·morph (ĕk′tə-môrf′) *n.* An individual with a thin body build. —**ec′to·mor′phic** *adj.*

-ectomy. A suffix meaning removal by surgery: **tonsillectomy.** [From Greek *ek-, ex-,* out + *-tomia,* a cutting.]

ec·to·plasm (ĕk′tə-plăz′əm) *n.* **1.** *Biol.* A part of the cytoplasm distinguishable in some cells as a relatively rigid layer on the outside by the cell membrane. **2.** The alleged spirit or emanation called forth by a spiritualistic medium. [ECTO- + -PLASM.]

ec·u·men·i·cal (ĕk′yə-mĕn′ĭ-kəl) *adj.* **1.** Worldwide in range or applicability; universal. **2.** Of or pertaining to the worldwide Christian church, esp. in regard to unity. [From Late Latin *oecūmenicus,* from Greek *oikoumenikos,* of the whole world, from *oikoumenē,* the inhabited world, from *oikein,* to inhabit, from *oikos,* house.] —**ec′u·men′i·cal·ly** *adv.*

ec·u·me·nism (ĕk′yə-mə-nĭz′əm, ĭ-kyōō′-) *n.* A movement seeking to achieve worldwide unity among religions.

ec·ze·ma (ĕk′sə-mə, ĕg-zē′-) *n.* A noncontagious inflammation of the skin, marked by redness, itching, and the formation of sores that discharge fluid and become crusted and scaly. [From Greek *ekzema,* eruption : *ex-,* out + *zema,* boiling, from *zeein,* to boil.]

-ed¹. A suffix indicating the past tense of regular verbs: **called, lived, rotted.** [Middle English *-ede,* from Old English *-ode, -ede, -ade.*]

-ed². A suffix indicating past participles of regular verbs: **healed, hated, petted.** [Middle English *-ed,* from Old English *-od, -ed, -ad.*]

-ed³. A suffix forming adjectives from nouns: **forked, left-handed.** [Middle English *-ede,* from Old English *-ede.*]

e·da·cious (ĭ-dā′shəs) *adj.* Characterized by gluttony; voracious. [From Latin *edax,* gluttonous, from *edere,* to eat.]

Ed·da (ĕd′ə) *n.* **1.** A collection of Old Norse poems called the Elder or Poetic Edda, assembled in the early 13th cent. **2.** A manual of Icelandic poetry, the Younger or Prose Edda, compiled a generation later. [Old Norse *edda.*]

ed·dy (ĕd′ē) *n., pl.* **-dies.** **1.** A current, as of water or air, that moves contrary to the main current, esp. in a circular motion. **2.** A movement that runs contrary to the main current or tradition, as of life, art, or philosophy. —*intr.v.* **-died, -dy·ing.** To move in a circular motion: *"A whirlpool can exist only as long as the water continues to eddy"* (Fritz Kahn). [Middle English *ydy,* from Old Norse *idha,* whirlpool.]

e·del·weiss (ā′dəl-vīs′, -wīs′) *n.* A plant, *Leontopodium alpinum,* of mountainous regions, esp. of the Alps, having leaves covered with whitish down and small flowers surrounded by petallike leaves. [German *Edelweiss* : *edel,* noble + *weiss,* white.]

e·de·ma (ĭ-dē′mə) *n., pl.* **-mas** or **-ma·ta** (-mə-tə). *Pathol.* An excessive accumulation of serous fluid in the tissues. [From Greek *oidēma,* tumor, swelling, from *oidein,* to swell.]

E·den (ēd′n) *n.* **1.** In the Old Testament, the first home of Adam and Eve; Paradise. Also called **Garden of Eden.** **2.** Any delightful place or region; paradise. **3.** A state of bliss or ultimate happiness.

e·den·tate (ē-dĕn′tāt′) *n.* Any of various mammals of the order Edentata, such as the anteater, sloth, or armadillo, having few or no teeth. —*adj.* **1.** Lacking teeth. **2.** Of or belonging to the order Edentata. [Latin *edentātus,* toothless, from *edentāre,* to take out the teeth : *ex-,* out + *dēns,* tooth.]

edge (ĕj) *n.* **1.** The line or point where an object, area, etc., begins or ends: *the edge of a sheet of paper.* **2.** A dividing line or point of transition; a border: *Science stood on the edge of another major discovery.* **3.** A rim, brink, or crest, as of a cliff or ridge. **4.** The usu. thin, sharpened side of the blade of a knife, tool, etc. **5.** A margin of superiority; an advantage: *We had a slight edge over the other team.* **6.** A line or line segment formed by the intersection of two surfaces of a three-dimensional figure, as a polyhedron. **7.** A trace of hardness or harshness, often expressive of annoyance, displeasure, etc.: *His voice had a menacing edge.* **8.** Keenness, as of desire or enjoyment; zest: *"His simplicity sets off the satire, and gives it a finer edge"* (William Hazlitt). —*v.* **edged, edg·ing.** —*tr.v.* **1.** To give an edge to; sharpen. **2.** To put a border or edge on: *She edged the sleeve with lace.* **3.** To advance or move gradually: *He edged his way through the crowd.* —*intr.v.* To advance or move gradually or hesitantly. —*idioms.* **on edge.** Highly tense or nervous; irritable. **take the edge off.** To soften or dull, as the pleasure, excitement, or force of. [Middle English *egge,* from Old English *ecg,* edge, point, sword.]

edge·wise (ĕj′wīz′) *adv.* Also **edge·ways** (-wāz′). **1.** With the edge foreward. **2.** On, by, with, or toward the edge.

edg·ing (ĕj′ĭng) *n.* Something that forms or serves as an edge; a trimming; a border.

edg·y (ĕj′ē) *adj.* **-i·er, -i·est.** **1.** Experiencing and exhibiting nervousness. **2.** Having a sharp edge. —**edg′i·ness** *n.*

Syns: *edgy, jittery (Informal), jumpy, nervous, restive, restless, skittish, tense, uneasy, uptight (Slang) adj.* Core meaning: Feeling or showing nervous tension (*pilots edgy before the combat mission*).

ed·i·ble (ĕd′ə-bəl) *adj.* Capable of being eaten; fit to eat. —*n.* Often **edibles.** Something fit to be eaten; food. [Late Latin *edibilis,* from Latin *edere,* to eat.] —**ed′i·bil′i·ty** or **ed′i·ble·ness** *n.*

e·dict (ē′dĭkt′) *n.* **1.** A decree or proclamation issued by an authority. **2.** Any formal proclamation, command, or decree. [Latin *ēdictum,* from *ēdīcere,* to speak out, proclaim : *ex-,* out + *dīcere,* to speak.]

ed·i·fi·ca·tion (ĕd′ə-fĭ-kā′shən) *n.* Intellectual, moral, or spiritual improvement; enlightenment.

ed·i·fice (ĕd′ə-fĭs) *n.* A building, esp. one of imposing appearance or size. [Middle English, from Old French, from Latin *aedificium,* from *aedificāre,* to build : *aedēs,* building, house + *facere,* to make.]

ed·i·fy (ĕd′ə-fī′) *tr.v.* **-fied, -fy·ing.** To instruct or enlighten so as to encourage intellectual, moral, or spiritual improvement. [Middle English *edifien,* from Old French *edifier,* from Latin *aedificāre,* to build, instruct.] —**ed′i·fi′er** *n.*

ed·it (ĕd′ĭt) *tr.v.* **1.** To make (written material) ready for publication by correcting, revising, or marking directions for a printer. **2.** To prepare an edition of for publication: *edit a collection of short stories.* **3.** To supervise the publication of (a newspaper or magazine). **4.** To omit or eliminate; delete: *edited out her remarks about religion.* **5.** To put together the parts of (film, electronic tape, or sound track) by cutting, combining, and splicing. [Back-formation from EDITOR.]

e·di·tion (ĭ-dĭsh′ən) *n.* **1. a.** The entire number of copies of a publication printed from a single typesetting and having

ă pat	ā pay	â care	ä father	ĕ pet	ē be	hw which	ĭ pit	ī tie	î pier	ŏ pot	ō toe	ô paw, for	oi noise
ŏŏ took	ōō boot	ou out	th thin	*th* this	ŭ cut	û urge	zh vision	ə about, item, edible, gallop, circus					

the same content. **b.** A single copy from this group. **2.** Any of the various forms in which something is issued or produced: *a paperback edition.* **3.** All the copies of a single press run of a newspaper: *the morning edition.* [Old French, from Latin *ēditiō*, a bringing forth, publication, from *ēdere*, to bring forth, publish : *ex-*, out + *dāre*, to give.]

ed·i·tor (ĕd′ĭ-tər) *n.* **1.** A person who edits. **2.** A person who writes editorials. [Late Latin, publisher, from Latin *ēdere*, to bring forth, publish : *ex-*, out + *dāre*, to give.] —**ed′i·tor·ship′** *n.*

ed·i·to·ri·al (ĕd′ĭ-tôr′ē-əl, -tōr′-) *n.* **1.** An article in a newspaper or periodical expressing the opinion of its editors or publishers. **2.** A commentary on radio or television expressing the opinion of the station or network. —*adj.* **1.** Of, concerning, or characteristic of an editor or editing. **2.** Expressing opinion rather than reporting news: *an editorial page.*

ed·i·to·ri·al·ize (ĕd′ĭ-tôr′ē-ə-līz′, -tōr′-) *intr.v.* **-ized, -iz·ing.** **1.** To express an opinion in or as if in an editorial. **2.** To express an opinion in what is supposedly an objective report of facts.

ed·u·ca·ble (ĕj′ə-kə-bəl) *adj.* Capable of being educated. [EDUC(ATE) + -ABLE.]

ed·u·cate (ĕj′ə-kāt′) *v.* **-cat·ed, -cat·ing.** —*tr.v.* **1.** To provide with knowledge or training, esp. through formal schooling; teach. **2.** To provide with training for some particular purpose: *educated him for the priesthood.* **3.** To provide with information; inform: *educate the public about energy conservation.* **4.** To train or develop, as a taste or skill. —*intr.v.* To teach or instruct a person or group: *educating through the use of visual aids.* [Middle English *educaten*, from Latin *ēducāre*, to bring up, educate : *ex-*, out + *dūcere*, to lead.]

ed·u·cat·ed (ĕj′ə-kā′tĭd) *adj.* **1.** Having an education, esp. one above the average. **2.** Showing evidence of having been taught or instructed; cultivated; cultured: *educated tastes.* **3.** Based on experience or some factual knowledge: *an educated guess.*

ed·u·ca·tion (ĕj′ə-kā′shən) *n.* **1.** The act or process of imparting or obtaining knowledge or skill; systematic instruction. **2.** The knowledge or skill obtained or developed by such a process; learning. **3.** A program of instruction of a specified kind or level: *driver education; a college education.* **4.** The field of study that is concerned with teaching and learning; the theory of teaching; pedagogy. —See Syns at **knowledge.**

ed·u·ca·tion·al (ĕj′ə-kā′shə-nəl) *adj.* **1.** Of or relating to education: *an educational system.* **2.** Serving to educate; instructive: *an educational television program.* —**ed′u·ca′tion·al·ly** *adv.*

ed·u·ca·tive (ĕj′ə-kā′tĭv) *adj.* **1.** Tending to educate; educational. **2.** Of or pertaining to education.

ed·u·ca·tor (ĕj′ə-kā′tər) *n.* **1.** A person trained in teaching; a teacher. **2.** A specialist in the theory and practice of education.

e·duce (ĭ-dōōs′, ĭ-dyōōs′) *tr.v.* **e·duced, e·duc·ing.** **1.** To draw or bring out; elicit; evoke: *The crisis educed amazing strength in her.* **2.** To assume from given facts; deduce. [Latin *ēdūcere* : *ex-*, out + *dūcere*, to lead.] —**e·duc′i·ble** *adj.*

-ee[1]. A suffix meaning: **1.** The recipient of an action: **addressee.** **2.** One who is in a specified condition: **standee.** [Middle English *-e*, from Old French *-e*, from Latin *-ātus.*]

-ee[2]. A suffix meaning: **1.** A particular type of: **bootee.** **2.** Something resembling or suggestive of: **goatee.** [Var. of -y.]

eel (ēl) *n., pl.* **eel** or **eels.** **1.** Any of various long, scaleless, snakelike saltwater or freshwater fishes of the order Anguilliformes (or Apodes), characteristically migrating from fresh water to the Sargasso Sea to spawn. **2.** Any of several similar or related fishes, such as the electric eel. [Middle English *ele*, from Old English *ǣl.*]

eel·pout (ēl′pout′) *n., pl.* **eelpout** or **-pouts.** Any of various saltwater fishes of the family Zoarcidae, with an elongated body and a large head. [From Old English *ǣlepūte* : *ǣle*, eel + *pūte*, a kind of fish.]

e'en[1] (ēn) *n. Poet.* Evening.

e'en[2] (ēn) *adv. Poet.* Even.

-eer. A suffix meaning: **1.** One who works with or is concerned with: **auctioneer.** **2.** One who makes or composes: **balladeer.** [Old French *-ier*, from Latin *-ārius.*]

e'er (âr) *adv. Poet.* Ever.

ee·rie or **ee·ry** (îr′ē) *adj.* **-ri·er, -ri·est.** **1.** Inspiring fear or dread without being openly threatening; strangely unsettling; weird: *an eerie old house.* **2.** Supernatural in aspect or character; uncanny; mysterious: *an eerie glow.* —See Syns at **weird.** [Middle English *eri*, fearful, cowardly, from Old English *earg*, cowardly, timid.]

ef·face (ĭ-fās′) *tr.v.* **-faced, -fac·ing.** **1.** To remove by or as if by rubbing out; obliterate; erase: *gravestone markings effaced by weather; memories effaced by time.* **2.** To conduct (oneself) in an inconspicuous or humble manner. [Old French *effacer* : *ef-*, out, from Latin *ex-* + *face*, face.] —**ef·face′ment** *n.*

ef·fect (ĭ-fĕkt′) *n.* **1.** Something brought about by a cause or agent; result. **2.** The power or capacity to achieve a desired result; influence: *Advice has no effect on him.* **3.** The manner in which something acts upon or influences an object: *the effect of a drug on the nervous system.* **4.** The condition of being in full force or operation: *The new regulations go into effect tomorrow.* **5. a.** An artistic technique that produces a specific impression: *a film's striking special effects.* **b.** The impression produced by an artistic technique, a way of behaving, etc.: *She cries just for effect.* **6.** The basic meaning of something said or written; purport: *He said he approved or something to that effect.* **7. effects.** Physical belongings; goods; property. —*tr.v.* To produce as a result; bring about; accomplish: *Technology has effected many changes.* —*idioms.* **in effect. 1.** In fact; actually. **2.** In essence; virtually. **3.** In active force; in operation. **take effect.** To become operative; gain active force. [Middle English, from Old French, from Latin *effectus*, past part. of *efficere*, to accomplish : *ex-*, out + *facere*, to do.]

Usage: effect, affect. Each is a verb and a noun. As a verb *effect* means to bring about or make: *layoffs designed to effect savings.* As a verb *affect* is used mainly to mean to influence or cause a change in and to simulate or imitate so as to make a desired impression: *drugs that affect the central nervous system; affected illness to gain sympathy.* As a noun *effect* is used to mean a result or an influence: *a plea to no effect; the effect of drugs on the central nervous system,* whereas *affect* as a noun is confined to psychology. Don't confuse and misuse these words.

ef·fec·tive (ĭ-fĕk′tĭv) *adj.* **1.** Having the intended or desired effect; serving the purpose: *two vaccines effective against polio.* **2.** Producing the desired impression; striking: *an effective speech.* **3.** Operative; in effect: *The law will be effective immediately.* **4.** Prepared for action: *We have eight effective troop divisions.* —**ef·fec′tive·ly** *adv.* —**ef·fec′tive·ness** *n.*

ef·fec·tor (ĭ-fĕk′tər) *n.* An organ at the end of a nerve, as a gland or muscle, that activates in response to a stimulus.

ef·fec·tu·al (ĭ-fĕk′chōō-əl) *adj.* Producing or sufficient to produce a desired effect; fully adequate: *effectual methods.* —**ef·fec′tu·al′i·ty** or **ef·fec′tu·al·ness** *n.* —**ef·fec′tu·al·ly** *adv.*

ef·fec·tu·ate (ĭ-fĕk′chōō-āt′) *tr.v.* **-at·ed, -at·ing.** To cause; bring about; effect: *effectuate improvement.* [From Medieval Latin *effectuāre*, from Latin *efficere*, to accomplish, effect.]

ef·fem·i·nate (ĭ-fĕm′ə-nĭt) *adj.* Having qualities associated more with women than men; unmanly. [Middle English *effeminat*, from Latin *effēminātus*, past part. of *effēmināre*, to make effeminate : *ex-*, out of + *fēmina*, woman.] —**ef·fem′i·na·cy** or **ef·fem′i·nate·ness** *n.* —**ef·fem′i·nate·ly** *adv.*

ef·fer·ent (ĕf′ər-ənt) *adj.* Directed away from a central organ or area, esp. carrying impulses from the central nervous system to the muscular and glandular systems. [French *efférent*, from Latin *efferens*, pres. part. of *efferre*, to carry away : *ex-*, away from + *ferre*, to carry.]

ef·fer·vesce (ĕf′ər-vĕs′) *intr.v.* **-vesced, -vesc·ing.** **1.** To give off gas in small bubbles, as a carbonated liquid does. **2.** To come out of a liquid in small bubbles. **3.** To show high spirits; be lively. [Latin *effervēscere*, to boil over : *ex-*, completely + *fervēscere*, to start to boil, from *fervēre*, to be hot, boil.]

ă **pat**	ā **pay**	â **care**	ä **father**	ĕ **pet**	ē **be**	hw **which**	ĭ **pit**	ī **tie**	î **pier**	ŏ **pot**	ō **toe**	ô **paw, for**	oi **noise**
ōō **took**	ōō **boot**	ou **out**	th **thin**	*th* **this**	ŭ **cut**	û **urge**	zh **vision**	ə **about, item, edible, gallop, circus**

ef·fer·ves·cence (ĕf'ər-vĕs'əns) n. Also **ef·fer·ves·cen·cy** (-ən-sē). **1.** The act or process of effervescing. **2.** Bubbles of gas formed in liquid. **3.** Sparkling high spirits; liveliness; vivacity.

ef·fer·ves·cent (ĕf'ər-vĕs'ənt) adj. **1.** Giving off small bubbles of gas. **2.** High-spirited; vivacious; lively.

ef·fete (ĭ-fēt') adj. **1.** Having lost vitality, strength, character, vigor, etc.; spent; degenerate: an effete civilization. **2.** Decadent and soft as a result of self-indulgence and lack of discipline: an effete people. [Latin effētus, worn out by childbearing : ex-, out + fētus, offspring.] —**ef·fete'ly** adv. —**ef·fete'ness** n.

ef·fi·ca·cious (ĕf'ĭ-kā'shəs) adj. Capable of producing a desired effect: an efficacious medicine. [Latin efficāx, effective, from efficere, to effect.] —**ef'fi·ca'cious·ly** adv.

ef·fi·ca·cy (ĕf'ĭ-kə-sē) n. Power or capacity to produce a desired effect; effectiveness: a method whose efficacy has been proven time and again. [Latin efficācia, from efficāx, efficacious.]

ef·fi·cien·cy (ĭ-fĭsh'ən-sē) n., pl. **-cies. 1.** The condition or quality of being efficient. **2.** The effectiveness of something; the measure of how well something operates. **3.** The fraction of the energy put into a machine that appears in the form of useful output.

ef·fi·cient (ĭ-fĭsh'ənt) adj. Acting or producing effectively with a minimum of waste, expense, or effort: an efficient automobile. [Middle English, from Old French, from Latin efficiēns, pres. part. of efficere, to effect.] —**ef·fi'cient·ly** adv.

ef·fi·gy (ĕf'ə-jē) n., pl. **-gies. 1.** A painted or sculptured representation of a person, as on a stone wall or monument. **2.** A crude image or dummy fashioned in the likeness of a hated or despised person. [Middle English effigie, from Latin effigiēs, likeness, image, from effingere, to form, portray : ex-, out of + fingere, to fashion, shape.]

ef·flo·resce (ĕf'lə-rĕs') intr.v. **-resced, -resc·ing. 1.** To blossom; flower; bloom. **2.** Chem. **a.** To change from a crystal form to a powder by losing water of crystallization when exposed to air. **b.** To become covered with a powdery deposit, as by evaporation. [Latin efflōrēscere, to blossom out : ex-, out + flōrēscere, to begin to blossom, from flōs, flower.]

ef·flo·res·cence (ĕf'lə-rĕs'əns) n. **1.** A flowering or blooming forth. **2.** The culmination or fulfillment of something, as of an artistic career. **3.** Chem. **a.** The process of efflorescing. **b.** The deposit that results from this process. —**ef'flo·res'cent** adj.

ef·flu·ence (ĕf'lōō-əns) n. **1.** The act or an instance of flowing out. **2.** Something that flows out or forth; an emanation.

ef·flu·ent (ĕf'lōō-ənt) adj. Flowing out or forth. —n. **1.** Something that flows out or forth, as a stream flowing out of a lake. **2.** The liquid outflow of a sewer, storage tank, irrigation canal, or other channel. [Middle English, from Latin effluēns, pres. part. of effluere, to flow out : ex-, out + fluere, to flow.]

ef·flu·vi·um (ĭ-flōō'vē-əm) n., pl. **-vi·a** (-vē-ə) or **-ums.** An invisible or barely visible flow of gas or smoke, esp. one that is foul or harmful. [Latin, from effluere, to flow out.] —**ef·flu'vi·al** adj.

ef·flux (ĕf'lŭks') n. **1.** An outward flowing. **2.** Something that flows out or forth; an emanation. [Latin efflūxus, past part. of effluere, to flow out.]

ef·fort (ĕf'ərt) n. **1.** The use of physical or mental energy to do something: Much time and effort went into this project. **2.** A difficult or tiring exertion of the strength or will: It was an effort to get up. **3.** An attempt, esp. an earnest attempt: Make an effort to arrive promptly. **4.** Something done or produced through exertion; an achievement: This ballet is her latest effort. [Old French, from esforcier, to force : Latin ex-, out + fortis, strong.]
Syns: effort, exertion, pains, strain, struggle, trouble n. **Core meaning:** The use of energy to do something (a job that isn't worth the effort).

ef·fort·less (ĕf'ərt-lĭs) adj. Requiring or showing little or no effort or difficulty. —See Syns at easy. —**ef'fort·less·ly** adv. —**ef'fort·less·ness** n.

ef·fron·ter·y (ĭ-frŭn'tə-rē) n., pl. **-ies.** Impudent and insulting boldness or insolence; audacity. [French effronterie,

from effronté, shameless, from Late Latin effrōns : ex-, out of + frōns, forehead.]

ef·ful·gent (ĭ-fōōl'jənt, ĭ-fŭl'-) adj. Shining brilliantly; radiant. [Latin effulgēns, pres. part. of effulgēre, to shine out : ex-, out + fulgēre, to shine.] —**ef·ful'gence** n.

ef·fuse (ĭ-fyōōz') v. **-fused, -fus·ing. —tr.v.** To pour or spread out. **—intr.v. 1.** To spread or flow out. **2.** To exude; emanate. [Latin effūsus, past part. of effundere, to pour out : ex-, out + fundere, to pour.]

ef·fu·sion (ĭ-fyōō'zhən) n. **1.** The act of effusing. **2.** The passage of a gas through tiny holes as a result of pressure applied to it. **3.** Pathol. A seepage of fluid into a cavity of the body. **4.** An unrestrained outpouring of feeling, as in speech or writing.

ef·fu·sive (ĭ-fyōō'sĭv) adj. Unrestrained or excessive in emotional expression; gushy: an effusive display of gratitude. —**ef·fu'sive·ly** adv. —**ef·fu'sive·ness** n.

eft (ĕft) n. A newt, esp. the immature land-dwelling form of a North American species, Diemictylus viridescens. [Middle English evete, from Old English efeta, lizard.]

e·gal·i·tar·i·an (ĭ-găl'ĭ-târ'ē-ən) adj. Of, pertaining to, or advocating the doctrine of equal political, economic, and legal rights for all citizens. —n. Someone who holds or advances egalitarian opinions. [French égalitaire, from égalité, equality, from Latin aequālitās, from aequālis, equal.] —**e·gal'i·tar'i·an·ism** n.

egg¹ (ĕg) n. **1.** One of the female reproductive cells of a plant or animal, uniting with a male reproductive cell in the process of sexual reproduction. **2.** One of the female reproductive cells of various animals, consisting usu. of an embryo surrounded by nutrient material with a protective, membranous covering and often deposited externally. **3.** The oval, hard-shelled ovum of a bird, esp. that of a domestic fowl, used as food. **4.** Something having the characteristically ovoid shape of a hen's egg. **5.** Slang. A fellow; a person: He's a good egg. —**idioms. lay an egg.** To fail completely, esp. before an audience. **put (or have) all (one's) eggs in one basket.** To risk everything on a single venture, act, etc. [Middle English egge, from Old Norse egg.]

egg² (ĕg) tr.v. —**egg on.** To encourage or incite with taunts, dares, etc.; urge: Egged on by him, I played a shameful trick on the old man. [Middle English eggen, from Old English eggian, from Old Norse eggja.]

egg·beat·er (ĕg'bē'tər) n. A kitchen utensil with rotating blades for beating eggs, whipping cream, etc.

egg·head (ĕg'hĕd') n. Slang. An intellectual; highbrow.

egg·nog (ĕg'nŏg') n. A drink consisting of milk and beaten eggs, often mixed with rum, brandy, or other liquor. [EGG + nog, ale.]

egg·plant (ĕg'plănt') n. **1.** A tropical Old World plant, Solanum melongena, cultivated for its edible fruit. **2.** The oval-shaped fruit of the eggplant, with glossy, dark-purple skin. [From the shape of its fruit.]

egg·shell (ĕg'shĕl') n. **1.** The thin, brittle outer covering of a bird's egg. **2.** A light, yellowish tan. —adj. Light, yellowish tan.

egg white. The albumen of an egg.

e·gis (ē'jĭs) n. Var. of aegis.

eg·lan·tine (ĕg'lən-tīn', -tēn') n. A rose, the sweetbrier. [Middle English eglentyn, from Old French aiglent, from Latin aculeus, dim. of acus, needle.]

e·go (ē'gō, ĕg'ō) n. **1.** The self or part of the human mind that is conscious of being separate or distinct from the external world and from other selves. **2.** Psychoanal. The conscious component or part of the personality that controls behavior and is most in touch with external reality. **3. a.** Self-love; conceit; egotism. **b.** Self-confidence; self-esteem. [Latin, I.]

e·go·cen·tric (ē'gō-sĕn'trĭk, ĕg'ō-) adj. Thinking or acting with the view that one's self is the center or object of all experience; selfish; self-centered. —n. An egocentric person. [EGO + CENTRIC.] —**e'go·cen·tric'i·ty** (-trĭs'ĭ-tē) n.

e·go·ism (ē'gō-ĭz'əm, ĕg'ō-) n. **1.** The condition or quality of thinking or acting with only oneself and one's own interests in mind; preoccupation with one's own welfare and advancement. **2.** Conceit; egotism.

e·go·ist (ē'gō-ĭst, ĕg'ō-) n. A self-centered person. —**e'go·is'tic** or **e'go·is'ti·cal** adj. —**e'go·is'ti·cal·ly** adv.

ă pat   ā pay   â care   ä father   ĕ pet   ē be   hw which   ĭ pit   ī tie   î pier   ŏ pot   ō toe   ô paw, for   oi noise
ōō took   ōō boot   ou out   th thin   th this   ŭ cut   û urge   zh vision   ə about, item, edible, gallop, circus

e·go·ma·ni·a (ē'gō-mā'nē-ə, -mān'yə, ĕg'ō-) *n.* Obsessive preoccupation with the self; extreme egotism. [EGO + -MANIA.] —**e'go·ma'ni·ac'** (-nē-ăk') *n.*

e·go·tism (ē'gə-tĭz'əm, ĕg'ə-) *n.* **1.** The tendency to speak or write of oneself excessively and boastfully. **2.** An inflated or extreme sense of self-importance; conceit. [EGO + -ISM (by analogy with nouns such as NEPOTISM).]

e·go·tist (ē'gə-tĭst, ĕg'ə-) *n.* **1.** A conceited, boastful person. **2.** A person who acts selfishly; an egoist. —**e'go·tis'tic** or **e'go·tis'ti·cal** *adj.* —**e'go·tis'ti·cal·ly** *adv.*

ego trip. *Slang.* **1.** An experience that boosts or gratifies the ego. **2.** An act of self-aggrandizement or self-indulgence.

e·gre·gious (ĭ-grē'jəs, -jē-əs) *adj.* Conspicuously bad; flagrant; blatant: *an egregious error.* [Latin *ēgregius*, distinguished : *ex-*, out of + *grex*, herd, flock.] —**e·gre'gious·ly** *adv.* —**e·gre'gious·ness** *n.*

e·gress (ē'grĕs') *n.* **1.** A path or means of going out; an exit. **2.** The right to go out: *He was denied egress.* **3.** The act of going out. [Latin *ēgressus*, from the past part. of *ēgredī*, to go out: *ex-*, out + *gradī*, to go, step.]

e·gret (ē'grĭt, ĕg'rĭt) *n.* Any of several usu. white wading birds of the genera *Bubulcus, Casmerodius, Leucophoyx,* and related genera, having long, showy, drooping plumes during the breeding season. [Middle English *egrete,* from Old French *aigrette,* from Old Provençal *aigreta,* from *aigron,* heron.]

egret   eider

E·gyp·tian (ĭ-jĭp'shən) *n.* **1.** A native or inhabitant of Egypt. **2.** The extinct Hamitic language of the ancient Egyptians. —*adj.* Of or pertaining to Egypt, its people, or its culture.

E·gyp·tol·o·gy (ē'jĭp-tŏl'ə-jē) *n.* The study of ancient Egyptian civilization. —**E'gyp·tol'o·gist** *n.*

eh (ā, ĕ) *interj.* **1.** A word used interrogatively: *Eh? What was that?* **2.** A word used in asking for confirmation: *He is a shrewd one, eh?*

ei·der (ī'dər) *n.* Any of several sea ducks of the genus *Somateria,* of northern regions, with soft, fine down on its breast. Also called **eider duck.** [Icelandic *ædhur,* from Old Norse *ædhr.*]

ei·der·down (ī'dər-doun') *n.* **1.** The soft, fine down of the eider, used for stuffing quilts and pillows. **2.** A quilt stuffed with eiderdown.

eider duck. An eider.

ei·det·ic (ī-dĕt'ĭk) *adj.* Of or characterized by the ability to recall images, esp. images experienced in childhood, vividly and in great detail. [Greek *eidētikos,* relating to images or knowledge, from *eidēsis,* knowledge, from *eidos,* form, shape.] —**ei·det'i·cal·ly** *adv.*

eight (āt) *n.* **1.** The cardinal number, written 8 or in Roman numerals VIII, that is equal to the sum of 7 + 1. **2.** The eighth in a set or sequence. **3.** Something having eight parts, units, or members. [Middle English *eighte,* from Old English *eahta.*] —**eight** *adj. & pron.*

eight ball. **1.** A black pool ball bearing the number eight. **2.** A pool game in which the eight ball must be pocketed last. —**idiom. behind the eight ball.** *Slang.* In an unfavorable or uncomfortable position; in trouble.

eight·een (ā-tēn') *n.* The cardinal number, written 18 or in Roman numerals XVIII, that is equal to the sum of 17 + 1. [Middle English *eightetene,* from Old English *eahtatīene.*] —**eight·een'** *adj. & pron.*

eight·eenth (ā-tēnth') *n.* **1.** The ordinal number that

matches the number 18 in a series, written 18th. **2.** One of 18 equal parts, written 1/18. —**eight·eenth'** *adj. & adv.*

eighth (ātth, āth) *n.* **1.** The ordinal number that matches the number eight in a series, written 8th. **2.** One of eight equal parts, written 1/8. [Middle English *eighthe,* from Old English *eahtotha,* from *eahta,* eight.] —**eighth** *adj. & adv.*

eighth note. *Mus.* A note having one-eighth the time value of a whole note. Also *Brit.* **quaver.**

eight·i·eth (ā'tē-ĭth) *n.* **1.** The ordinal number that matches the number 80 in a series, written 80th. **2.** One of 80 equal parts, written 1/80. —**eight'i·eth** *adj. & adv.*

eight·y (ā'tē) *n.* The cardinal number, written 80 or in Roman numerals LXXX, that is equal to the product of 8×10. [Middle English *eigh(te)ty,* from Old English *(hund)eahtatig : hund,* hundred + *eahta,* eight + *-tig,* ten.] —**eight'y** *adj. & pron.*

–ein. Var. of **–in** (neutral chemical compound).

ein·stein·i·um (īn-stī'nē-əm) *n. Symbol* **Es** A synthetic radioactive element first discovered in the debris of a hydrogen-bomb explosion and later produced by nuclear bombardment. It has 12 known isotopes with half-lives ranging between 1.2 minutes and 270 days and mass numbers from 245 to 256. Atomic number 99. [After Albert *Einstein* (1879–1955), German-born American physicist.]

ei·ther (ē'thər, ī'thər) *pron.* **1.** One or the other of two: *To get there you can take either of the two roads.* **2.** One of more than two: *Of the three satellites either is capable of reversing its course.* —*adj.* **1.** One or the other; any one of two: *When two words are joined in a compound, the spelling of either word is seldom changed.* **2.** The one and the other: *Candles stood on either side of the centerpiece.* —*conj.* —Used correlatively with *or* to introduce alternatives: *A statement using an equal sign may be either true or false.* —*adv.* Likewise; also; any more than the other. Used as an intensive following negative statements: *He didn't want to be late for school, but he didn't want to meet those boys again either.* [Middle English *aither,* from Old English *ægther, æghwæther.*]

e·jac·u·late (ĭ-jăk'yə-lāt') *v.* **-lat·ed, -lat·ing.** —*tr.v.* **1.** To eject or discharge abruptly, esp. to discharge semen. **2.** To utter suddenly and passionately; exclaim. —*intr.v.* To eject a fluid. [From Latin *ējaculārī : ex-,* out + *jaculārī,* to shoot, from *jaculum,* dart, from *jacere,* to throw.] —**e·jac'u·la·to'ry** (-lə-tōr'ē, -tôr'ē) *adj.*

e·jac·u·la·tion (ĭ-jăk'yə-lā'shən) *n.* **1.** The act or process of ejaculating. **2.** An abrupt discharge of fluid, esp. an emission of seminal fluid. **3.** A sudden, emphatic utterance; an exclamation.

e·ject (ĭ-jĕkt') *tr.v.* **1.** To discharge or throw out forcefully; expel: *The rifle ejects empty shells after firing.* **2.** To compel to leave; evict: *The directors ejected him from the chairmanship.* —*intr.v.* To catapult oneself from a disabled aircraft: *The pilot ejected over water.* [Middle English *ejecten,* from Latin *ējectus,* past part. of *ejicere : ex-,* out + *jacere,* to throw.] —**e·jec'tion** *n.*

ejection seat. A seat designed to eject clear of an aircraft and parachute to the ground in an emergency.

e·jec·tor (ĭ-jĕk'tər) *n.* Someone or something that ejects, esp. a machine part that ejects waste material.

eke[1] (ēk) *tr.v.* **eked, ek·ing.** **1.** To make (money, a living, etc.) with great effort or strain: *eke out a livelihood.* **2.** To supplement with great effort; strain to fill out: *He eked out his income by working at night.* **3.** To make (something) last by economy: *eked out the fuel oil by keeping the thermostat low.* [Middle English *eken,* from Old English *ēacan,* to increase.]

eke[2] (ēk) *adv. Archaic.* Also. [Middle English, from Old English *eac.*]

e·lab·o·rate (ĭ-lăb'ər-ĭt) *adj.* **1.** Planned or executed with painstaking attention to detail: *elaborate preparations.* **2.** Very detailed or ornate: *elaborate costumes.* **3.** Hard to understand because of complexity: *an elaborate plan.* —*v.* (ĭ-lăb'ə-rāt') **-rat·ed, -rat·ing.** —*tr.v.* To work out with care and detail; develop thoroughly: *elaborate a scientific theory.* —*intr.v.* To express oneself at greater length or in greater detail: *elaborate on a proposal.* [Latin *ēlabōrātus,* past part. of *ēlabōrāre,* to work out: *ex-,* out + *labōrāre,* to work, from *labor,* work.] —**e·lab'o·rate·ly** *adv.* —**e·lab'o·rate·ness** *n.* —**e·lab'o·ra'tion** (ĭ-lăb'ə-rā'shən) *n.*

Syns: elaborate, fancy, intricate *adj. Core meaning:* Complexly detailed (*an elaborate mural*). See also Syns at **complex.**

E·laine (ĭ-lān′) *n. Arthurian legend.* **1.** A woman who died of unrequited love for Lancelot. **2.** The mother of Galahad by Lancelot.

é·lan (ā-län′, ā-län′) *n.* **1.** Enthusiasm; zest; dash. **2.** Style; flair: *She plays the piano with élan.* —See Syns at **spirit.** [French, from Old French *eslan,* a dash, from *eslancer,* to rush : *es-,* out, from Latin *ex-* + *lancer,* to throw, from Latin *lancea,* lance.]

e·land (ē′lənd) *n.* Either of two large African antelopes, *Taurotragus oryx* or *T. derbianus,* with a light-brown or grayish coat and spirally twisted horns. [Afrikaans, from Dutch *eland,* elk, from obs. German *elend,* from Lithuanian *ellenis,* stag.]

e·lapse (ĭ-lăps′) *intr.v.* **e·lapsed, e·laps·ing.** To pass or slip by: *Months elapsed before I went.* [Latin *ēlapsus,* past part. of *ēlābī* : *ex-,* away + *lābī,* to slip, glide.]

e·las·mo·branch (ĭ-lăz′mə-brăngk′) *n.* Any of numerous fishes of the class Chondrichthyes, with a cartilaginous skeleton and including the sharks, rays, and skates. [New Latin *Elasmobranchii,* "plate-gilled ones."]

e·las·tic (ĭ-lăs′tĭk) *adj.* **1.** *Physics.* **a.** Capable of returning to an original or normal shape or arrangement after being deformed. **b.** Occurring without loss of momentum: *an elastic collision.* **2.** Capable of adapting or being adapted to change or a variety of circumstances; flexible: *an elastic schedule.* **3.** Quick to recover or revive: *an elastic spirit.* **4.** Springy; firm: *elastic turf.* —See Syns at **flexible.** —*n.* **1.** A fabric or tape woven with strands of real or imitation rubber to make it stretch. **2.** A **rubber band.** [From Late Greek *elastikos,* from Greek *elastos,* beaten, from *elaunein,* to drive.] —**e·las′ti·cal·ly** *adv.*

e·las·tic·i·ty (ĭ-lă-stĭs′ĭ-tē, ē′lă-) *n.* The condition or property of being elastic; resiliency; flexibility.

e·late (ĭ-lāt′) *tr.v.* **e·lat·ed, e·lat·ing.** To raise the spirits of; fill with happiness or joy. [Latin *ēlātus,* past part. of *efferre,* to bring out, lift up : *ex-,* out + *ferre,* to carry.]

e·lat·ed (ĭ-lā′tĭd) *adj.* Upraised in spirits; lively and joyful. —**e·lat′ed·ly** *adv.* —**e·lat′ed·ness** *n.*

e·la·tion (ĭ-lā′shən) *n.* An intense feeling of happiness or joy; jubilation.

E layer. A region of the ionosphere, occurring between about 55 and 95 miles, or 89 and 153 kilometers, above the earth and influencing long-distance radio communications by reflecting certain radio waves strongly.

el·bow (ĕl′bō′) *n.* **1. a.** The joint or bend between the forearm and the upper arm. **b.** The bone that projects at the outer part of this joint. **2.** Anything, esp. a length of pipe, that bends sharply or has a sharp angle in it. **3.** The part of a sleeve that covers the elbow: *a jacket with worn elbows.* —*tr.v.* **1.** To push or jostle with or as if with the elbows. **2.** To make (one's way) by such pushing or jostling. —*intr.v.* To move by pushing or jostling. —*idiom.* **rub elbows with.** To associate with (wealthy or prominent people). [Middle English *elbowe,* from Old English *elnboga.*]

elbow grease. *Informal.* Strenuous physical effort.

el·bow·room (ĕl′bō-rōōm′, -rōōm′) *n.* Room enough to move around or function in; ample space.

eld·er¹ (ĕl′dər) *adj.* A comparative of **old,** used only in reference to members of a specific family or organization as an indication of age or seniority: *the elder Harris; the elder partner.* —*n.* **1.** An older person. **2.** An ancestor; predecessor; forefather. **3.** An older, influential member of a family, tribe, or community. **4.** One of the governing officers of certain Christian churches. [Middle English *eldre,* from Old English *eldra.*]

el·der² (ĕl′dər) *n.* Any of various shrubs or small trees of the genus *Sambucus,* with clusters of small white flowers and red or blackish berrylike fruit. Also called **elderberry.** [Middle English *eldre,* from Old English *ellaern.*]

el·der·ber·ry (ĕl′dər-bĕr′ē) *n.* **1.** The small, edible fruit of an elder, sometimes used to make wine or preserves. **2.** A shrub or tree, the elder.

eld·er·ly (ĕl′dər-lē) *adj.* **1.** Approaching old age; old. **2.** Of, pertaining to, or characteristic of old age. —See Syns at **old.** —**el′der·li·ness** *n.*

eld·est (ĕl′dĭst) *adj.* A superlative of **old,** used only in ref-

erence to members of a specific family or organization as an indication of age or seniority: *my eldest brother; the eldest board member.* [Middle English, from Old English *eldesta.*]

El Do·ra·do (ĕl′ də-rä′dō). **1.** A legendary city of great wealth in South America, sought after by 16th-cent. explorers. **2.** Any place of fabulous wealth. [Spanish, "the gilded (land).'']

e·lect (ĭ-lĕkt′) *tr.v.* **1.** To select by vote for an office or membership. **2.** To make a choice; pick out: *elect an art course.* —*intr.v.* To make a choice, esp. with deliberation. —See Syns at **choose.** —*adj.* **1.** Chosen deliberately; singled out: *an elect group of scientists.* **2.** Elected but not yet installed in office: *the governor-elect.* —*n.* **1. the elect.** A selected or favored person or group, esp. the members of a wealthy or privileged group. **2.** *Theol.* Those selected by the divine will for salvation. [Middle English *electen,* from Latin *ēlectus,* past part. of *ēligere,* to select : *ex-,* out + *legere,* to choose.]

e·lec·tion (ĭ-lĕk′shən) *n.* **1.** The act or process of electing. **2.** The fact of being elected. **3.** *Theol.* Predestined salvation, esp. as conceived by Calvinists. —See Syns at **choice.**

e·lec·tion·eer (ĭ-lĕk′shə-nîr′) *intr.v.* To work actively for a particular candidate or political party.

e·lec·tive (ĭ-lĕk′tĭv) *adj.* **1.** Of or pertaining to a selection by vote. **2.** Filled or obtained by election: *an elective office.* **3.** Having the power or authority to elect: *an elective assembly.* **4.** Capable of being chosen; optional: *an elective course.* —*n.* An optional course in an academic curriculum. —**e·lec′tive·ly** *adv.*

e·lec·tor (ĭ-lĕk′tər) *n.* **1.** A qualified voter. **2.** A member of the Electoral College of the United States. **3. Elector.** One of the German princes in the Holy Roman Empire entitled to elect the emperor.

e·lec·tor·al (ĭ-lĕk′tər-əl) *adj.* **1.** Of or pertaining to electors, esp. the members of the Electoral College. **2.** Of or pertaining to election: *electoral reforms.*

Electoral College. A group of electors chosen to elect the President and Vice President of the United States.

e·lec·tor·ate (ĭ-lĕk′tər-ĭt) *n.* **1.** All those persons qualified to vote in an election. **2.** The rank or territory of an Elector of the Holy Roman Empire.

electr-. Var. of **electro-.**

E·lec·tra (ĭ-lĕk′trə) *n.* Also **E·lek·tra.** *Gk. Myth.* A daughter of Clytemnestra and Agamemnon. With her brother Orestes she avenged the murder of Agamemnon by killing their mother and her lover.

e·lec·tric (ĭ-lĕk′trĭk) or **e·lec·tri·cal** (-trĭ-kəl) *adj.* **1. a.** Of, derived from, producing, or produced by electricity. **b.** Powered or operated by electricity. **2.** Charged with emotion; exciting; thrilling. [New Latin *electricus,* like amber (because amber produces sparks when rubbed), from Latin *ēlectrum,* amber, from Greek *ēlektron.*] —**e·lec′tri·cal·ly** *adv.*

electrical engineering. Engineering that deals with the practical use of electricity and its effects. —**electrical engineer.**

electric cell. A device, usu. consisting of electrodes of dissimilar substances immersed in an electrolyte, in which chemical energy is changed into electrical energy.

electric chair. **1.** A chair used to restrain and electrocute a person sentenced to death. **2.** Execution by means of electrocution.

electric charge. **1.** The basic property of matter from which electric phenomena result; charge. **2.** The measure of this property.

electric eel. A long, eellike freshwater fish, *Electrophorus electricus,* of northern South America, with organs capable of producing a powerful electric shock.

electric eye. A photoelectric cell.

electric field. A region of space, such as that around an object that has collected an electric charge, in which a unit of electric charge is acted on by a measurable force at any point.

e·lec·tri·cian (ĭ-lĕk-trĭsh′ən, ē′lĕk-) *n.* A person whose occupation is the installation, repair, or operation of electric equipment and circuitry.

e·lec·tric·i·ty (ĭ-lĕk-trĭs′ĭ-tē, ē′lĕk-) *n.* **1. a.** The physical phenomena that arise from the existence of electric

ă pat	ā pay	â care	ä father	ĕ pet	ē be	hw which	ĭ pit	ī tie	î pier	ŏ pot	ō toe	ô paw, for	oi noise
ōō took	ōō boot	ou out	th thin	*th* this	ŭ cut		û urge	zh vision	ə about, item, edible, gallop, circus				

charges and interactions that involve them. **b.** The scientific study of such phenomena. **2.** Electric current used or regarded as a source of power. **3.** Intense emotional excitement.

e·lec·tri·fy (ĭ-lĕk'trə-fī') *tr.v.* **-fied, -fy·ing. 1.** To produce electric charge on or in (a conductor). **2.** To wire or equip (a building, room, etc.) for the use of electric power. **3.** To thrill, startle greatly, or shock: *acting that electrified the audience.* [ELECTRI(C) + -FY.] **—e·lec'tri·fi·ca'tion** *n.*

electro- or **electr-.** A prefix meaning: **1.** Electric: **electromagnet. 2.** Electrically: **electrocute. 3.** Electrolysis: **electrolyte.**

e·lec·tro·car·di·o·gram (ĭ-lĕk'trō-kär'dē-ə-grăm') *n.* The curve traced by an electrocardiograph, used in studying the heart and diagnosing its diseases.

e·lec·tro·car·di·o·graph (ĭ-lĕk'trō-kär'dē-ə-grăf') *n.* An instrument that records the electrical activity of the heart, usu. in the form of a curve traced on a chart.

e·lec·tro·chem·is·try (ĭ-lĕk'trō-kĕm'ĭ-strē) *n.* The science that deals with the interaction of electricity and chemical reactions or changes. **—e·lec'tro·chem'i·cal** (-kĕm'ĭ-kəl) *adj.*

e·lec·tro·cute (ĭ-lĕk'trə-kyōōt') *tr.v.* **-cut·ed, -cut·ing.** To kill with electricity, esp. to execute by passing a high-voltage electric current through the body of. [ELECTRO- + (EXE)-CUTE.] **—e·lec'tro·cu'tion** *n.*

e·lec·trode (ĭ-lĕk'trōd') *n.* A solid electric conductor through which an electric current enters or leaves a medium such as an electrolyte, a nonmetallic solid, a molten metal, a gas, or a vacuum. [ELECTR(O)- + -ODE.]

e·lec·tro·dy·nam·ics (ĭ-lĕk'trō-dī-năm'ĭks) *n.* *(used with a sing. verb).* The scientific study of the relationships between electric, magnetic, and mechanical phenomena. **—e·lec'tro·dy·nam'ic** *adj.*

e·lec·tro·en·ceph·a·lo·gram (ĭ-lĕk'trō-ĕn-sĕf'ə-lə-grăm') *n.* The curve traced by an electroencephalograph, used in studying the brain and diagnosing its diseases.

e·lec·tro·en·ceph·a·lo·graph (ĭ-lĕk'trō-ĕn-sĕf'ə-lə-grăf') *n.* An instrument that records the electrical activity of the brain, usu. in the form of a curve on a graph.

e·lec·trol·y·sis (ĭ-lĕk-trŏl'ĭ-sĭs, ē'lĕk-) *n.* **1.** A chemical change, esp. decomposition, produced in an electrolyte by an electric current. **2.** Destruction of living tissue, such as the roots of hairs, by an electric current. [ELECTRO- + -LY-SIS.]

e·lec·tro·lyte (ĭ-lĕk'trə-līt') *n.* **1.** A substance that when dissolved or melted becomes electrically conductive by breaking apart into ions. **2.** A solution that conducts electricity, esp. a solution used in an electric cell or battery. [ELECTRO- + -LYTE.]

e·lec·tro·lyt·ic (ĭ-lĕk'trə-lĭt'ĭk) *adj.* **1.** Of, pertaining to, or caused by electrolysis. **2.** Of, pertaining to, or using an electrolyte.

electrolytic cell. 1. A cell containing an electrolyte through which an external electric current is passed in order to produce an electrochemical reaction. **2.** A cell containing an electrolyte in which an electrochemical reaction produces an electromotive force.

e·lec·tro·lyze (ĭ-lĕk'trə-līz') *tr.v.* **-lyzed, -lyz·ing.** To decompose by electrolysis. [Back-formation from ELECTROLYSIS.]

e·lec·tro·mag·net (ĭ-lĕk'trō-măg'nĭt) *n.* A device consisting essentially of a soft-iron core with a coil of insulated wire wound onto it. When an electric current passes through the coil, the core becomes a magnet.

e·lec·tro·mag·net·ic (ĭ-lĕk'trō-măg-nĕt'ĭk) *adj.* Of or involving electromagnetism. **—e·lec'tro·mag·net'i·cal·ly** *adv.*

electromagnetic field. The field of force associated with an electric charge in motion, having both electric and magnetic components and containing a definite amount of electromagnetic energy.

electromagnetic radiation. A series of electromagnetic waves.

electromagnetic spectrum. The entire range of electromagnetic wave frequency including, in order of decreasing frequency, cosmic rays, gamma rays, x-rays, ultraviolet radiation, visible light, infrared radiation, microwaves, radio waves, and electric currents.

electromagnetic wave. A wave that travels through space as a system of electric and magnetic fields that vary

periodically with position and time, including radio waves, light waves, x-rays, and gamma rays.

e·lec·tro·mag·net·ism (ĭ-lĕk'trō-măg'nĭ-tĭz'əm) *n.* **1.** Magnetism that arises from the motion of an electric charge. **2.** The scientific study of electricity and magnetism and the relationships between them.

e·lec·tro·met·al·lur·gy (ĭ-lĕk'trō-mĕt'l-ûr'jē) *n.* The use of electricity to purify metals or to reduce metallic compounds to metals.

e·lec·trom·e·ter (ĭ-lĕk-trŏm'ĭ-tər, ē'lĕk-) *n.* An instrument for detecting or measuring potential differences, electric charge, or, indirectly, electric current by means of mechanical forces exerted between electrically charged bodies.

e·lec·tro·mo·tive (ĭ-lĕk'trō-mō'tĭv) *adj.* Of, pertaining to, or tending to produce an electric current.

electromotive force. *Abbr.* **emf, EMF 1.** A force that tends to produce an electric current. **2.** The energy per unit of charge that is converted into electrical form by a battery, generator, or any other similar device.

e·lec·tron (ĭ-lĕk'trŏn') *n.* A subatomic particle commonly found as one of a group surrounding the nucleus of an atom and having a unit negative electric charge of about 1.602×10^{-19} coulomb and a mass, when at rest, of 9.1066×10^{-28} gram. [ELECTR(O)- + -ON.]

e·lec·tro·neg·a·tive (ĭ-lĕk'trō-nĕg'ə-tĭv) *adj.* **1.** Having a negative electric charge. **2.** Tending to attract electrons to form a chemical bond.

electron gun. A source of electrons and a series of electrodes that forms the electrons into a high-speed beam, as in a cathode-ray tube.

e·lec·tron·ic (ĭ-lĕk-trŏn'ĭk, ē'lĕk-) *adj.* **1.** Of, pertaining to, or involving electrons. **2.** Of, pertaining to, based on, or operated by a controlled flow of electrons or other carriers of electric charge, as in an electron tube or semiconductor. **3.** Of or involved in electronics: *an electronic technician.* **—e·lec·tron'i·cal·ly** *adv.*

electronic music. Music produced entirely or in part by manipulating sounds with electronic devices.

e·lec·tron·ics (ĭ-lĕk-trŏn'ĭks, ē'lĕk-) *n.* **1.** *(used with a sing. verb).* **a.** The science and technology concerned with the development and practical application of electronic devices and systems. **b.** The commercial industry of electronic devices and systems. **2.** *(used with a pl. verb).* The part of something that is composed mainly of electronic devices.

electron microscope. A microscope that uses a beam of electrons rather than a beam of visible light to produce magnified images and has magnification power far exceeding that of a conventional microscope.

electron tube. A sealed, enclosed space, containing either a vacuum or a small amount of gas, in which electrons act as the main carriers of current between at least two electrodes, often with one or more other electrodes controlling the electron flow.

electron volt. A unit of energy equal to the energy gained by an electron that is accelerated by a potential difference of one volt. An electron volt equals about 1.602×10^{-19} joule.

e·lec·troph·o·rus (ĭ-lĕk-trŏf'ər-əs, ē'lĕk-) *n.*, *pl.* **-o·ri** (-ə-rī'). A device for generating static electricity through the process of induction. [ELECTRO- + -PHOROUS.]

e·lec·tro·plate (ĭ-lĕk'trə-plāt') *tr.v.* **-plat·ed, -plat·ing.** To coat or cover with a thin layer of metal by means of an electrolytic process.

e·lec·tro·pos·i·tive (ĭ-lĕk'trō-pŏz'ĭ-tĭv) *adj.* **1.** Having a positive electric charge. **2.** Tending to release electrons to form a chemical bond.

e·lec·tro·scope (ĭ-lĕk'trə-skōp') *n.* An instrument used to detect the presence of electric charges and to determine whether they are positive or negative.

e·lec·tro·shock (ĭ-lĕk'trō-shŏk') *n.* A form of shock therapy in which an electric current is passed through the brain.

e·lec·tro·stat·ic (ĭ-lĕk'trō-stăt'ĭk) *adj.* **1.** Of, pertaining to, produced by, or caused by static electric charges. **2.** Of or pertaining to electrostatics.

electrostatic generator. Any of several machines that collect large amounts of static electric charge, creating

---

ă pat	ā pay	â care	ä father	ĕ pet	ē be	hw which	ĭ pit	ī tie	î pier	ŏ pot	ō toe	ô paw, for	oi noise
ōō took	ōō boot	ou out	th thin	th this	ŭ cut		û urge	zh vision	ə about, item, edible, gallop, circus				

large differences of electric potential.

e·lec·tro·stat·ics (ĭ-lĕk′trō-stăt′ĭks) *n. (used with a sing. verb).* The scientific study of static electricity.

e·lec·tro·ther·a·py (ĭ-lĕk′trō-thĕr′ə-pē) *n.* Any form of medical treatment in which electric currents, radio waves, etc., are applied to body tissues.

e·lec·tro·type (ĭ-lĕk′trə-tīp′) *n.* **1.** A duplicate metal plate used in letterpress printing, made by electroplating a mold of the original plate. **2.** The process of making such a plate. —*tr.v.* **-typed, -typ·ing.** To make an electrotype of. —**e·lec′tro·typ′er** *n.*

e·lec·tro·va·lence (ĭ-lĕk′trō-vā′ləns) *n.* Also **e·lec·tro·va·len·cy** (-lən-sē). Valence characterized by the transfer of electrons from atoms of one element to atoms of another. —**e·lec′tro·va′lent** *adj.*

e·lec·trum (ĭ-lĕk′trəm) *n.* A natural pale yellow alloy of silver and gold. [Middle English, from Latin *ēlectrum,* amber, from Greek *ēlektron.*]

el·ee·mos·y·nar·y (ĕl′ə-mŏs′ə-nĕr′ē, ĕl′ē-ə-) *adj.* **1.** Of or pertaining to alms or the giving of alms; charitable. **2.** Dependent upon or supported by charity. **3.** Contributed as charity; gratuitous; free. [Medieval Latin *eleēmosynārius,* from Late Latin *eleēmosyna,* alms.]

el·e·gance (ĕl′ĭ-gəns) *n.* Also **el·e·gan·cy** (-gən-sē) *pl.* **-cies. 1.** Refinement and grace in movement, appearance, or manners. **2.** Tasteful richness in form, decoration, or presentation: *nothing remaining of the mansion's Victorian elegance.* **3.** Something that is a luxury: *an elegance we could ill afford.*

el·e·gant (ĕl′ĭ-gənt) *adj.* **1.** Characterized by elegance; refined and tasteful: *an elegant restaurant.* **2.** Excellent; splendid: *an elegant idea.* [Old French, from Latin *ēlegāns,* choice, fine, pres. part. of *ēligere,* to select : *ex-,* out + *legere,* to choose.] —**el′e·gant·ly** *adv.*

    Syns: elegant, exquisite, graceful *adj. Core meaning:* So tastefully beautiful as to draw attention and admiration (*an elegant ball gown; an elegant lady*).

el·e·gi·ac (ĕl′ə-jī′ək, ĭ-lē′jē-ăk′) *adj.* **1.** Of, pertaining to, or suitable for an elegy or elegies. **2.** Expressing sorrow; mournful. [French *élégiaque,* from Late Latin *elegīacus,* from Greek *elegeiakos,* from *elegeia,* elegy.]

el·e·gize (ĕl′ə-jīz′) *v.* **-gized, -giz·ing.** —*intr.v.* To compose an elegy. —*tr.v.* To compose an elegy on.

el·e·gy (ĕl′ə-jē) *n., pl.* **-gies. 1.** A mournful poem, esp. one composed to lament one who is dead. **2.** A mournful musical composition. [French *élégie,* from Latin *elegīa,* from Greek *elegeia,* from *elegos,* lament.]

E·lek·tra (ĭ-lĕk′trə) *n.* Var. of **Electra.**

el·e·ment (ĕl′ə-mənt) *n.* **1.** *Chem. & Physics.* Any substance composed of atoms that all have the same number of protons in their nuclei and that cannot be broken down into a less complex substance by chemical means. **2. a.** A fundamental or essential part of a whole: *the basic elements of music.* **b.** A basic assumption or proposition: *Freedom of speech is one of the crucial elements of democracy.* **3.** A trace or suggestion: *An element of mystery pervades the story.* **4.** *Math.* Any of the members of a set. **5.** *Geom.* **a.** Any line on the surface of a cone that passes through its vertex. **b.** Any of the straight lines contained in the curved surface of a cylinder. **6. elements.** Earth, air, fire, and water, formerly regarded as the fundamental components of the universe. **7. elements.** The forces that collectively constitute the weather, esp. cold, wind, rain, or other inclement influences. **8.** An environment to which someone or something is suited or adapted: *The business world is her element.* **9. elements.** The bread and wine of the Eucharist. [Middle English, from Old French, from Latin *elementum,* first principle.]

el·e·men·tal (ĕl′ə-mĕn′tl) *adj.* **1.** Of, pertaining to, or being an element. **2.** Fundamental or essential; indispensable. **3.** Not complex or refined; rudimentary; simple: *elemental logic; the elemental life of early man.* **4.** Of or resembling a force of nature in power or effect: *the elemental fury of the hurricane.* —**el′e·men′tal·ly** *adv.*

el·e·men·ta·ry (ĕl′ə-mĕn′tə-rē, -trē) *adj.* **1.** Fundamental, essential, or irreducible: *elementary truths.* **2.** Of, involving, or introducing the fundamental or simplest aspects of a subject: *an elementary text-book.*

elementary particle. A subatomic particle.

elementary school. A school attended for the first six to eight years of a child's formal education. Also called **grade school** and **grammar school.**

el·e·phant (ĕl′ə-fənt) *n.* Either of two very large herbivorous mammals, *Elephas maximus,* of south-central Asia, or *Loxodonta africana,* of Africa, with thick, almost hairless skin, a long flexible trunk, long curved tusks, and, in the African species, large fan-shaped ears. [Middle English *elifaunt,* from Old French *elifant,* from Latin *elephantus,* from Greek *elephas.*]

el·e·phan·ti·a·sis (ĕl′ə-fən-tī′ə-sĭs) *n.* A chronic, often extreme enlargement and hardening of the cutaneous and subcutaneous tissue, esp. of the lower body, as a result of the blockage of lymph ducts by parasitic worms. [Latin *elephantiāsis* : Greek *elephas,* elephant (so called because the affected skin resembles an elephant's hide) + *-iasis,* disease.]

el·e·phan·tine (ĕl′ə-făn′tēn′, -tīn′, ĕl′ə-fən-) *adj.* **1.** Of or pertaining to an elephant. **2.** Like an elephant; ponderous. **3.** Gigantic. —See Syns at **giant.**

el·e·vate (ĕl′ə-vāt′) *tr.v.* **-vat·ed, -vat·ing. 1.** To raise to a higher place or position; lift up. **2.** To promote to a higher rank: *elevated her to department manager.* **3.** To raise to a higher moral, cultural, or intellectual level: *elevated the simple folk song to heights of beauty.* **4.** To lift the spirits of; elate. —See Syns at **raise.** [Middle English *elevaten,* from Latin *ēlevāre* : *ex-,* up + *levāre,* to lighten, raise.]

el·e·vat·ed (ĕl′ə-vā′tĭd) *adj.* **1.** Raised above a given level: *an elevated platform.* **2.** Exalted; lofty: *elevated thought.* **3.** Elated; high-spirited; joyful.

elevated railway. A railway that operates on a track raised high above the ground.

el·e·va·tion (ĕl′ə-vā′shən) *n.* **1.** The act of elevating or the condition of being elevated. **2.** An elevated place or position. **3.** A height, esp. as measured from some special reference, such as sea level: *The elevation of that peak is 5,227 feet.* **4.** Loftiness, grandeur, or dignity, as of thought or feeling. **5.** A scale drawing of the side, front, or rear of a given structure.

el·e·va·tor (ĕl′ə-vā′tər) *n.* **1.** A platform or enclosure raised and lowered in a vertical shaft to transport freight or people. **2.** A granary equipped with devices for hoisting and discharging grain. **3.** Any device that raises or hoists. **4.** A movable airfoil, usu. attached to the tail assembly of an aircraft, used to turn the nose of the craft upward or downward.

el·ev·en (ĭ-lĕv′ən) *n.* **1.** The cardinal number, written 11 or in Roman numerals XI, that is equal to the sum of 10 + 1. **2.** The eleventh in a set or sequence. **3.** Something having eleven parts, units, or members. [Middle English *ellevene,* from Old English *endleofan.*]

el·ev·enth (ĭ-lĕv′ənth) *n.* **1.** The ordinal number that matches the number 11 in a series, written 11th. **2.** One of 11 equal parts, written $^{1}/_{11}$. —**el·ev′enth** *adj. & adv.*

elf (ĕlf) *n., pl.* **elves** (ĕlvz). **1.** In Germanic folklore, a small, magic-wielding creature, often mischievous but rarely evil. **2.** A mischievous child. [Middle English, from Old English *ælf.*]

elf·in (ĕl′fĭn) *adj.* **1.** Of or pertaining to an elf or elves: *the elfin king.* **2.** Suggestive of an elf or elves; sprightly; prankish; mischievous: *an elfin smile.*

elf·ish (ĕl′fĭsh) *adj.* Also **el·vish** (ĕl′vĭsh). Of, pertaining to, or resembling an elf or elves; elfin: *elfish tricks.* —**elf′ish·ly** *adv.* —**elf′ish·ness** *n.*

e·lic·it (ĭ-lĭs′ĭt) *tr.v.* To bring out; draw forth; evoke; educe: *could not elicit a response from her.* [Latin *ēlicitus,* past part. of *ēlicere* : *ex-,* out + *lacere,* to allure, deceive.] —**e·lic′i·ta′tion** *n.*

e·lide (ĭ-līd′) *tr.v.* **e·lid·ed, e·lid·ing. 1.** To omit or slur over (a vowel or syllable) in pronunciation. **2.** To eliminate or ignore; leave out. [Latin *ēlīdere,* to strike out : *ex-,* out + *laedere,* to strike, hurt.]

el·i·gi·ble (ĕl′ĭ-jə-bəl) *adj.* **1.** Qualified for an office, position, function, privilege, etc. **2.** Suitable or desirable, esp. for marriage: *an eligible bachelor.* —*n.* An eligible person. [Middle English, from Old French, from Late Latin *ēligibilis,* from Latin *ēligere,* to choose, elect.] —**el′i·gi·bil′i·ty** *n.* —**el′i·gi·bly** *adv.*

e·lim·i·nate (ĭ-lĭm′ə-nāt′) *tr.v.* **-nat·ed, -nat·ing. 1.** To get rid of; remove. **2.** To leave out or omit from consideration; disregard; reject. **3.** To remove from competition by defeating. **4.** *Math.* To remove (an unknown quantity) by combining equations. **5.** To excrete (waste products) from the body. [From Latin *ēlīmināre*, to banish : *ex-*, out + *līmen*, threshold.] —**e·lim′i·na′tion** *n.*

e·li·sion (ĭ-lĭzh′ən) *n.* **1.** The act of eliding. **2.** The omission of an unstressed vowel or syllable in pronunciation. [Latin *ēlīsiō*, from *ēlīsus*, past part. of *ēlīdere*, to elide.]

e·lite or **é·lite** (ĭ-lēt′, ā-lēt′) *n.* **1.** (*used with a pl. verb*). **a.** The best or superior members of a society or group. **b.** A small but powerful group: *the power elite within the administration.* **2.** A size of type on a typewriter, equal to ten points. [French *élite*, from Old French *eslite*, past part. of *eslire*, to choose, from Latin *ēligere*, to elect.] —**e·lite′** *adj.*

e·lit·ism or **é·lit·ism** (ĭ-lē′tĭz′əm, ā-lē′-) *n.* A sense of being part of a superior or privileged group. —**e·lit′ist** *n.*

e·lix·ir (ĭ-lĭk′sər) *n.* **1.** A sweetened solution of alcohol and water, containing medicine. **2.** Any medicinal potion thought to have general curative or restorative powers; panacea. **3.** In medieval alchemy, a substance believed to have the power to change base metals into gold. [Middle English, from Medieval Latin, from Arabic *al-iksīr*, "the elixir."]

elk (ĕlk) *n., pl.* **elks** or **elk. 1.** A wapiti. **2.** A large deer, *Alces alces*, of northern Europe and Asia, with large antlers, related to the North American moose. [Middle English *elke*, from Old Norse *elgr*.]

ell (ĕl) *n.* A wing or extension of a building at right angles to the main structure. [From its resemblance to the letter L.]

el·lipse (ĭ-lĭps′) *n.* A closed plane curve formed by: **a.** The locus of points the sum of the distances of each of which from two fixed points is the same constant. **b.** A conic section neither parallel to an element nor parallel to the axis of the intersected cone. [Back-formation from ELLIPSIS.]

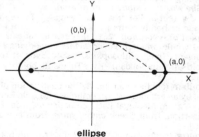

ellipse

el·lip·sis (ĭ-lĭp′sĭs) *n., pl.* **-ses** (-sēz′). **1.** *Gram.* The omission of a word or words necessary for the complete syntactic construction of a sentence but not necessary for understanding it; for example, *Stop laughing* for *You stop laughing.* **2.** A mark or series of marks (. . . or ***) used in writing or printing to indicate an omission of a word or words. [Latin *ellipsis*, from Greek *elleipsis*, defect, from *elleipein*, to leave behind : *en-*, in + *leipein*, to leave.]

el·lip·soid (ĭ-lĭp′soid′) *n.* A geometric surface whose plane sections are all either ellipses or circles. [ELLIPS(E) + -OID.] —**el·lip′soid′** or **el′lip·soi′dal** *adj.*

el·lip·tic (ĭ-lĭp′tĭk) or **el·lip·ti·cal** (-tĭ-kəl) *adj.* **1.** Of, pertaining to, or having the shape of an ellipse. **2.** *Gram.* Containing an ellipsis. [Greek *elleiptikos*, defective, from *elleipein*, to fall short.] —**el·lip′ti·cal·ly** *adv.*

elm (ĕlm) *n.* **1.** Any of various tall, sturdy deciduous trees of the genus *Ulmus*, of the Northern Hemisphere, characteristically having arching or curving branches and widely planted as shade trees. **2.** The hard wood of any of these trees. [Middle English, from Old English.]

el·o·cu·tion (ĕl′ə-kyoo′shən) *n.* **1.** The art of public speaking, emphasizing pronunciation, inflection, and delivery. **2.** A style of public speaking. [Middle English *elocucion*, from Latin *ēlocūtiō*, from *ēloquī*, to speak out : *ex-*, out + *loquī*, to speak.] —**el′o·cu′tion·ar′y** (-shə-nĕr′ē) *adj.* —**el′o·cu′tion·ist** *n.*

e·lon·gate (ĭ-lông′gāt′, ĭ-lŏng′-) *v.* **-gat·ed, -gat·ing.** —*tr.v.* To make longer; extend; lengthen. —*intr.v.* To grow in length. —*adj.* **1.** Lengthened; extended. **2.** Slender or tapered: *an elongate leaf; an elongate neck.* **3.** Long. —See Syns at **long.** [From Late Latin *ēlongāre* : Latin *ex-*, out + *longus*, long.]

e·lon·ga·tion (ĭ-lông-gā′shən, ĭ-lŏng-, ē′lông-, ē′lŏng-) *n.* **1.** The act of elongating or the condition of being elongated. **2.** Something that is elongated.

e·lope (ĭ-lōp′) *intr.v.* **e·loped, e·lop·ing. 1.** To run away secretly with a lover, esp. to get married. **2.** To run away; abscond. [Anglo-French *aloper*, perh. ult. from Old English *a-* (away) + *hlēapan*, to run.] —**e·lope′ment** *n.* —**e·lop′er** *n.*

el·o·quence (ĕl′ə-kwəns) *n.* **1.** Fluent, persuasive, and expressive discourse: *His speech rolled on in mighty surges of eloquence.* **2.** The ability to express an intended meaning or to persuade: *He was carried away by the crowd's enthusiasm and his own eloquence.*

el·o·quent (ĕl′ə-kwənt) *adj.* **1.** Fluent, persuasive, and expressive in discourse: *an eloquent appeal for human rights.* **2.** Clearly and movingly expressive of some emotion, condition, etc.: *an eloquent smile.* [Middle English, from Old French, from Latin *ēloquēns*, pres. part. of *ēloquī*, to speak out : *ex-*, out + *loquī*, to speak.] —**el′o·quent·ly** *adv.*

else (ĕls) *adj.* **1.** Other; different: *somebody else.* **2.** In addition; further; more: *Would you like anything else?* —*adv.* **1.** Differently: *How else could it be done?* **2.** Otherwise: *Be careful or else you will make a mistake.* [Middle English *elles*, from Old English otherwise, else.]

***Usage:* else.** The possessive forms of combinations with *else* are usu. written: *anyone* (or *anybody*) *else's; everyone* (or *everybody*) *else's; no one* (or *nobody*) *else's; someone* (or *somebody*) *else's.* Both *who else's* (followed by a noun) and *whose else* are in use, but not *whose else's: Who else's work might it be? Whose else could it be?*

else·where (ĕls′hwâr′, -wâr′) *adv.* Somewhere or anywhere else: *He decided to go elsewhere.*

e·lu·ci·date (ĭ-loo′sĭ-dāt′) *tr.v.* **-dat·ed, -dat·ing.** To make clear or plain: *elucidate the meaning of the phrase.* —See Syns at **clarify.** [From Late Latin *ēlūcidāre* : Latin *ex-*, completely + *lūcidus*, bright, clear, from *lūcēre*, to shine.] —**e·lu′ci·da′tion** *n.*

e·lude (ĭ-lood′) *tr.v.* **e·lud·ed, e·lud·ing. 1.** To get away from, as by artfulness, cunning, or daring; evade: *elude capture.* **2.** To escape understanding or detection by; baffle: *The meaning of her glance eluded him.* —See Syns at **avoid** and Usage note at **allude.** [Latin *ēlūdere*, to cheat, deceive : *ex-*, away + *lūdere*, to play, from *lūdus*, play.]

e·lu·sion (ĭ-loo′zhən) *n.* The act of eluding; escape or evasion. [Medieval Latin *ēlūsiō*, from Latin *ēlūsus*, past part. of *ēlūdere*, to elude.]

e·lu·sive (ĭ-loo′sĭv, -zĭv) *adj.* Tending to elude capture, grasp, understanding, or explanation: *an elusive theory.* —**e·lu′sive·ly** *adv.* —**e·lu′sive·ness** *n.*

el·ver (ĕl′vər) *n.* A young eel. [Var. of *eelfare*, "the passage of young eels up a river."]

elves (ĕlvz) *n.* Plural of **elf.**

el·vish (ĕl′vĭsh) *adj.* Var. of **elfish.**

E·ly·sian (ĭ-lĭzh′ən) *adj.* **1.** Of, pertaining to, or suggestive of Elysium. **2.** Blissful; delightful.

Elysian Fields. Elysium.

E·lys·i·um (ĭ-lĭz′ē-əm, ĭ-lĭzh′-) *n.* **1.** *Gk. Myth.* A land of idyllic happiness where the virtuous dwelt after death. **2.** Any place or condition of happiness; paradise.

em (ĕm) *n. Printing.* A unit of measure describing the line space occupied by the body size of a piece of type that is as long as it is wide, esp. of a pica M.

'em (əm) *pron. Informal.* Them. [Middle English *hem*, from Old English *him, heom*, dative and accusative pl. of *hē, he.*]

em-¹. Var. of **en-** (put into).

em-². Var. of **en-** (into).

e·ma·ci·ate (ĭ-mā′shē-āt′) *tr.v.* **-at·ed, -at·ing.** To make thin and wasted, as by starvation or illness. [From Latin *ēmaciāre* : *ex-*, completely + *maciāre*, to make thin, from *macer*, thin.] —**e·ma′ci·a′tion** *n.*

em·a·nate (ĕm′ə-nāt′) *v.* **-nat·ed, -nat·ing.** —*intr.v.* To come forth, as from a source; originate: *light emanating*

---

from the window. —*tr.v.* To send forth; emit: *Radioactive substances emanate gamma rays.* [From Latin *ēmānāre*, flow out : *ex-*, out + *mānāre*, to flow.]

em·a·na·tion (ĕm′ə-nā′shən) *n.* **1.** An act or instance of emanating. **2. a.** Something that emanates from a source: *the heavy, sweet emanations of magnolias.* **b.** *Chem.* A gaseous substance produced by the disintegration of radioactive material.

e·man·ci·pate (ĭ-măn′sə-pāt′) *tr.v.* **-pat·ed, -pat·ing.** To free from oppression, bondage, or restraint; liberate: *emancipate serfs.* —See syns at **free.** [From Latin *ēmancipāre* : *ex-*, out of + *mancipium*, ownership, from *manceps*, purchaser.] —**e·man′ci·pa′tor** *n.*

e·man·ci·pa·tion (ĭ-măn′sə-pā′shən) *n.* **1.** The act of emancipating or the condition of being emancipated: *the emancipation of slaves.* **2. Emancipation.** The formal abolition of slavery in the United States.

e·mas·cu·late (ĭ-măs′kyə-lāt′) *tr.v.* **-lat·ed, -lat·ing. 1.** To castrate (a male animal). **2.** To deprive of strength or vigor; make weak: *emasculate a language; emasculate a law.* —*adj.* (ĭ-măs′kyə-lĭt, -lāt′). Deprived of strength or vigor; ineffectual. [From Latin *ēmasculāre* : *ex-* (removal) + *masculus*, male, manly.] —**e·mas′cu·la′tion** *n.* —**e·mas′cu·la′tor** *n.*

em·balm (ĕm-bäm′) *tr.v.* **1.** To prevent or retard the decay of (a corpse) by treatment with preservatives. **2.** To preserve as if by embalming. **3.** *Archaic.* To make fragrant. [Middle English *embalmen*, from Old French *embaumer* : *en-*, to put on + *basme*, balm.] —**em·balm′er** *n.* —**em·balm′ment** *n.*

em·bank (ĕm-băngk′) *tr.v.* To confine, support, or protect with an embankment, dam, etc.

em·bank·ment (ĕm-băngk′mənt) *n.* **1.** The act of embanking. **2.** A mound of earth or stone built to hold back water or to support a roadway.

em·bar·go (ĕm-bär′gō) *n., pl.* **-goes. 1.** An order by a government prohibiting merchant ships from entering or leaving its ports. **2.** A suspension by a government of foreign trade or of foreign trade in a particular commodity: *a grain embargo.* **3.** Any prohibition or restriction. —*tr.v.* To impose an embargo upon. [Spanish, from *embargar*, to impede, restrain.]

em·bark (ĕm-bärk′) *intr.v.* **1.** To go aboard a vessel, esp. at the start of a journey: *vacationers embarking for Europe.* **2.** To set out on a venture; commence: *embarking on a plan to develop solar energy.* —*tr.v.* **1.** To cause to board a vessel. **2.** To enlist or invest in a commercial enterprise. [Old French *embarquer*, from Late Latin *imbarcāre* : *in-*, in + *barca*, bark.] —**em′bar·ka′tion** *n.*

em·bar·rass (ĕm-băr′əs) *tr.v.* **1.** To cause to feel self-conscious, ill at ease, or ashamed; disconcert: *His poor performance embarrassed him.* **2.** To hamper with debt or financial difficulties. **3.** To beset with difficulties; impede: *Pride, envy, and greed embarrass all mankind.* [French *embarrasser*, from Spanish *embarazar*, from Italian *imbarazzare*, from *imbarrare*, to impede.] —**em·bar′rass·ing·ly** *adv.*

em·bar·rass·ment (ĕm-băr′əs-mənt) *n.* **1.** The act of embarrassing or the condition of being embarrassed. **2.** Something that embarrasses. **3.** An overabundance: *an embarrassment of riches.*

em·bas·sage (ĕm′bə-sĭj) *n. Archaic.* An embassy.

em·bas·sy (ĕm′bə-sē) *n., pl.* **-sies. 1.** The position, function, or assignment of an ambassador. **2.** A mission to a foreign government headed by an ambassador. **3.** An ambassador and his staff. **4.** The official headquarters of an ambassador and his staff. [Middle English, from Old French *ambassee*, from Old Italian *ambasciata*, from Old Provençal *ambaissada*, from Medieval Latin *ambactia*.]

em·bat·tle (ĕm-băt′l) *tr.v.* **-tled, -tling. 1.** To prepare or furnish for battle. **2.** To prepare to struggle or resist; be ready to wage war. **3.** To fortify. [Middle English *embatailen*, from Old French *embataillier* : *en-*, in + *bataille*, battle.]

em·bed (ĕm-bĕd′) *v.* **-bed·ded, -bed·ding.** Also **im·bed** (ĭm-). —*tr.v.* **1.** To fix firmly in a surrounding mass: *They embedded the pilings deep into the subsoil.* **2.** To instill or fix in the memory: *a name embedded in the minds of millions.* —*intr.v.* To become embedded.

em·bel·lish (ĕm-bĕl′ĭsh) *tr.v.* **1.** To make more beautiful, as by ornamentation; adorn: *a gold bracelet embellished with diamonds.* **2.** To add fanciful or fictitious details to: *embellish the truth.* [Middle English *embelisshen*, from Old French *embellir* : *en-* (causative) + *bel*, beautiful, from Latin *bellus*.] —**em·bel′lish·ment** *n.*

em·ber (ĕm′bər) *n.* **1.** A small piece of live coal or wood, as in a dying fire. **2. embers.** The smoldering coal or ash of a dying fire. [Middle English *embre*, from Old English *æmerge*, embers, ashes.]

em·bez·zle (ĕm-bĕz′əl) *tr.v.* **-zled, -zling.** To take (money or property) for one's own use in violation of a trust: *He embezzled the union's pension fund.* [Middle English *embesilen*, from Norman French *enbesiler* : Old French *en-* (intensive) + *besiller*, to do away with, destroy.] —**em·bez′zle·ment** *n.* —**em·bez′zler** *n.*

em·bit·ter (ĕm-bĭt′ər) *tr.v.* To cause bitter feelings, harsh resentments, and animosities in.

em·bla·zon (ĕm-blā′zən) *tr.v.* **1.** To ornament richly, esp. with heraldic devices: *emblazon a tapestry with fleurs-de-lis.* **2.** To make resplendent with brilliant colors: *emblazon the hall with gay streamers.* **3.** To celebrate; exalt: *His heroism was emblazoned in song and verse.* —**em·bla′zon·ment** *n.*

em·bla·zon·ry (ĕm-blā′zən-rē) *n., pl.* **-ries. 1.** The art of emblazoning with heraldic devices. **2.** Heraldic devices collectively.

em·blem (ĕm′bləm) *n.* **1.** An object or a personification of an object that comes to represent an abstract meaning; a symbol: *A dove is the emblem of peace.* **2.** An identifying badge, design, or device: *The wolf patch was an emblem of his platoon.* [Middle English, from Latin *emblēma*, inlaid work, from Greek, insertion, from *emballein*, to insert : *en-*, in + *ballein*, to throw.]

em·blem·at·ic (ĕm′blə-măt′ĭk) or **em·blem·at·i·cal** (-ĭ-kəl) *adj.* Of, relating to, or serving as an emblem; symbolic.

em·bod·i·ment (ĕm-bŏd′ē-mənt) *n.* **1.** The act of embodying or the condition of being embodied. **2.** Someone or something that embodies something else; a perfect example: *She was the embodiment of kindness.*

em·bod·y (ĕm-bŏd′ē) *tr.v.* **-ied, -y·ing. 1.** To represent in concrete or bodily form; personify: *The general embodied the spirit of revolution.* **2.** To make or include as part of a united whole: *modern governments embodying the ideas of ancient Greek philosophies.* —See Syns at **represent.**

em·bold·en (ĕm-bōl′dən) *tr.v.* To instill boldness in; encourage.

em·bo·lism (ĕm′bə-lĭz′əm) *n.* **1.** The obstruction of a blood vessel by an embolus. **2.** An embolus. [Middle English *embolisme*, from Medieval Latin *embolismus*, from Late Latin, insertion, from Greek *embolismos*, from *emballein*, to insert.]

em·bo·lus (ĕm′bə-ləs) *n., pl.* **-li** (-lī′). An air bubble, detached blood clot, or other mass of material that blocks a blood vessel. [From Latin, piston, from Greek *embolos*, something inserted, stopper, from *emballein*, to insert.]

em·bos·om (ĕm-bŏoz′əm, -bōo′zəm) *tr.v.* **1.** To clasp to or hold in the bosom; cherish. **2.** To envelop or enclose protectively; to shelter.

em·boss (ĕm-bôs′, -bŏs′) *tr.v.* **1.** To cause (a design) to stand out by raising it above the surrounding surface: *emboss a head on a coin.* **2.** To decorate with a raised design: *emboss leather.* [Middle English *embosen*, from Old French *embocer* : *en-*, in + *boce*, boss, knob.] —**em·boss′er** *n.*

em·bou·chure (äm′bŏo-shŏor′) *n.* **1.** The mouth of a river. **2. a.** The mouthpiece of a wind instrument. **b.** The manner in which the lips and tongue are applied to such a mouthpiece. [French, from Old French *emboucher*, to stop up : *en-*, in + *bouche*, mouth, from Latin *bucca*, puffed-out cheek.]

em·bow·er (ĕm-bou′ər) *tr.v.* To enclose or shelter in or as if in a bower.

em·brace (ĕm-brās′) *v.* **-braced, -brac·ing.** —*tr.v.* **1.** To clasp or hold with the arms, usu. as a sign of affection; to hug. **2.** To encircle or surround: *a small lake embraced by mountains.* **3.** To include or take in; encompass: *a course embracing all aspects of Shakespeare's work.* **4.** To take up willingly; adopt: *embrace Christianity.* **5.** To avail oneself of; accept eagerly: *embrace an opportunity.* —*intr.v.*

ă pat	ā pay	â care	ä father	ĕ pet	ē be	hw which	ĭ pit ī tie î pier ŏ pot ō toe ô paw, for oi noise
ŏŏ took	ōŏ boot	ou out	th thin	th this	ŭ cut	û urge	zh vision ə about, item, edible, gallop, circus

To clasp or hold each other in the arms: *The couple embraced.* —*n.* The act of embracing. [Middle English *embracen,* from Old French *embracer* : Latin *in-,* in + *bracchium,* arm, from Greek *brakhiōn.*] —**em·brace′ment** *n.* —**em·brac′er** *n.*

em·bra·sure (ĕm-brā′zhər) *n.* **1.** An opening in a wall for a door or window. **2.** An opening for a gun in a wall or parapet. [French, from *embraser,* to set on fire, fire a gun.]

em·bro·cate (ĕm′brə-kāt′) *tr.v.* **-cat·ed, -cat·ing.** To moisten and rub (a part of the body) with a lotion or liniment. [From Medieval Latin *embrocāre,* from Late Latin *embrocha,* lotion, from Greek *embrokhē,* from *embrekhein,* to moisten with a lotion : *en-,* in + *brekhein,* to wet.]

em·bro·ca·tion (ĕm′brə-kā′shən) *n.* **1.** The act of embrocating. **2.** A liniment or lotion.

em·broi·der (ĕm-broi′dər) *tr.v.* **1.** To work (a design) into fabric with a needle and yarn. **2.** To decorate (cloth) by sewing on designs with thread. **3.** To add imaginary, fictitious details to (a narrative) for added interest; embellish: *She embroidered her autobiography heavily.* —*intr.v.* To make embroidery. [Middle English *embroderen,* from Norman French *enbrouder* : Old French *en-,* in + *brouder,* to embroider.] —**em·broi′der·er** *n.*

em·broi·der·y (ĕm-broi′də-rē) *n., pl.* **-ies. 1.** The art or act of embroidering. **2.** An embroidered fabric or design. **3.** An embellishment.

em·broil (ĕm-broil′) *tr.v.* **1.** To involve in argument, contention, or conflict: *"These considerations are additional admonitions to avoid . . . any step that may embroil us with Great Britain."* (Alexander Hamilton). **2.** To throw into confusion or disorder; entangle: *price hikes that further embroil the economy.* [French *embrouiller* : Old French *en-,* in + *brouiller,* to mix, confuse.] —**em·broil′ment** *n.*

em·bry·o (ĕm′brē-ō′) *n., pl.* **-os. 1.** *Biol.* **a.** An organism in its early stages of development, esp. before it has reached a distinctively recognizable form. **b.** Such an organism at any time before full development or birth. **2.** *Bot.* The rudimentary plant contained within a seed. **3.** A rudimentary or beginning stage of something: *the embryo of a new foreign policy.* [Medieval Latin, from Greek *embruon* : *en-,* in + *bruein,* to grow.]

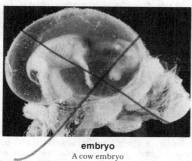

embryo
A cow embryo

em·bry·ol·o·gy (ĕm′brē-ŏl′ə-jē) *n.* The science dealing with the formation, early growth, and development of embryos. —**em′bry·o·log′ic** (-ə-lŏj′ĭk) or **em′bry·o·log′i·cal** *adj.* —**em′bry·ol′o·gist** *n.*

em·bry·on·ic (ĕm′brē-ŏn′ĭk) *adj.* **1.** Of, pertaining to, or in the condition of being an embryo. **2.** In an early, undeveloped state: *an embryonic theory.*

em·cee (ĕm′sē′). *Informal.* —*n.* A master of ceremonies. —*v.* **-ceed, -cee·ing.** —*tr.v* To serve as master of ceremonies of. —*intr.v.* To act as master of ceremonies. [Pronunciation of M.C., initials of *master of ceremonies.*]

e·meer (ē-mîr′) *n.* Var. of **emir.**

e·mend (ĭ-mĕnd′) *tr.v.* To improve or correct (a text) by editing. [Middle English *emenden,* from Latin *ēmendāre* : *ex-,* out + *mendum,* fault.]

e·men·date (ē′mĕn-dāt′, ĭ-mĕn′-) *tr.v.* **-dat·ed, -dat·ing.** To emend (a text).

e·men·da·tion (ĭ-mĕn-dā′shən, ē′mĕn-) *n.* **1.** The act of emending. **2.** An alteration that improves something, esp. a written work. —**e·men′da·to′ry** (ĭ-mĕn′də-tôr′ē, -tōr′ē) *adj.*

em·er·ald (ĕm′ər-əld, ĕm′rəld) *n.* **1.** A brilliant, transparent green beryl used as a gem. **2.** A dark yellowish green. —*modifier:* *an emerald necklace.* —*adj.* Dark yellowish-green. [Middle English *emeraude,* from Old French *esmeraude,* from Latin *smaragdus,* a kind of precious stone.]

e·merge (ĭ-mûrj′) *intr.v.* **e·merged, e·merg·ing. 1.** To come into view; appear: *The butterfly emerged from the cocoon.* **2.** To come into existence; crop up: *A new spirit of freedom emerged.* **3.** To become known, revealed, or evident: *Startling new facts emerged as the trial progressed.* [Latin *ēmergere* : *ex-,* out of + *mergere,* to dip, immerse.]

e·mer·gence (ĭ-mûr′jəns) *n.* The act or process of emerging.

e·mer·gen·cy (ĭ-mûr′jən-sē) *n., pl.* **-cies.** A serious situation or occurrence that develops suddenly and unexpectedly and demands immediate attention. —*modifier: an emergency aircraft landing.*

e·mer·gent (ĭ-mûr′jənt) *adj.* Coming into existence, view, or attention.

e·mer·i·tus (ĭ-mĕr′ĭ-təs) *adj.* Retired but retaining an honorary title corresponding to that held before retirement: *a professor emeritus.* —*n., pl.* **-ti** (-tī′). One who is emeritus. [Latin *ēmeritus,* past part. of *ēmerērī,* to earn by service : *ex-,* out of + *merērī,* to deserve.]

e·mer·sion (ĭ-mûr′zhən, -shən) *n.* The act or process of emerging; emergence. [From Latin *ēmersus,* past part. of *ēmergere,* to emerge.]

em·er·y (ĕm′ə-rē, ĕm′rē) *n.* A fine-grained impure form of the mineral corundum used in grinding and polishing. [Middle English, from Old French *emeri,* ult. from Greek *smuris,* emery powder.]

emery board. A flat strip of cardboard or wood coated with powdered emery, used to file fingernails.

e·met·ic (ĭ-mĕt′ĭk) *adj.* Causing vomiting. —*n.* An emetic drug or medicine. [Latin *emeticus,* from Greek *emetikos,* inclined to vomit, from *emetos,* vomiting, from *emein,* to vomit.]

-emia. A suffix meaning blood: *leukemia.* [From Greek *haima,* blood.]

em·i·grant (ĕm′ĭ-grənt) *n.* Someone who emigrates. —*modifier: an emigrant family.*

em·i·grate (ĕm′ĭ-grāt′) *intr.v.* **-grat·ed, -grat·ing.** To leave one country or region to settle in another. [From Latin *ēmigrāre* : *ex-,* away + *migrāre,* to move.] —**em′i·gra′tion** *n.*

é·mi·gré (ĕm′ĭ-grā′) *n.* An emigrant, esp. one who has fled his country during a revolution. [French, past part. of *émigrer,* to emigrate, from Latin *ēmigrāre.*]

em·i·nence (ĕm′ə-nəns) *n.* **1.** A position of great distinction or superiority: *a woman of eminence in medicine.* **2.** A rise or elevation of ground; hill. **3. Eminence.** A title of honor given to cardinals in the Roman Catholic Church.

em·i·nent (ĕm′ə-nənt) *adj.* **1. a.** Outstanding or superior in performance, rank, or character; distinguished: *an eminent historian.* **b.** Well-known and respected. **2.** Remarkable; noteworthy: *an eminent achievement.* **3.** Towering above others; projecting; prominent. —See Syns at **famous.** [Middle English, from Old French, from Latin *ēminēns,* pres. part. of *ēminēre,* to stand out.] —**em′i·nent·ly** *adv.*

eminent domain. *Law.* The right of a government to take private property for public use, usu. with compensation to the owner.

e·mir (ē-mîr′) *n.* Also **e·meer.** An Arabian prince, chieftain, or governor. [French *émir,* from Spanish *emir,* from Arabic *'amīr,* commander, from *amara,* he commanded.] —**e·mir′ate** *n.*

em·is·sar·y (ĕm′ĭ-sĕr′ē) *n., pl.* **-ies.** A messenger or agent sent to represent or advance the interests of another, esp. one representing a government. [Latin *ēmissārius,* from *ēmissus,* past part. of *emittere,* to send out, emit.]

e·mis·sion (ĭ-mĭsh′ən) *n.* **1.** The act or process of emitting. **2.** Something that is emitted: *the radioactive emissions of radium.* [From Latin *ēmissus,* past part. of *ēmittere,* to emit.]

e·mis·sive (ĭ-mĭs′ĭv) *adj.* Emitting or tending to emit; radiating: *a hot, highly emissive star.*

e·mit (ĭ-mĭt′) *tr.v.* **e·mit·ted, e·mit·ting. 1.** To release, give off, or send out (light, heat, etc.). **2.** To utter; express:

emitted a cry of surprise. **3.** To put into circulation, as paper currency. [Latin *ēmittere,* to send out : *ex-,* out + *mittere,* to send.]

e·mol·lient (ĭ-mŏl′yənt) *adj.* Acting to produce softness and smoothness, esp. of the skin. —*n.* An emollient agent or substance. [Latin *ēmolliēns,* pres. part. of *ēmollīre,* to soften : *ex-,* completely + *mollīre,* to soften, from *mollis,* soft.]

e·mol·u·ment (ĭ-mŏl′yə-mənt) *n.* Compensation or profit derived from one's employment or office; wages. [Middle English, from Latin *ēmolumentum,* from *ēmolere,* to grind out : *ex-,* out + *molere,* to grind.]

e·mote (ĭ-mōt′) *intr.v.* **e·mot·ed, e·mot·ing.** To express emotion in an exaggerated and theatrical manner. [Back-formation from EMOTION.]

e·mo·tion (ĭ-mō′shən) *n.* **1.** A mental condition marked by excitement or stimulation of the passions or sensibilities, as love, fear, rage, or joy, and often involving physiological changes, as laughter, tears, or nervousness. **2.** A strong, complex feeling, as joy, sorrow, hate, or love. [French *émotion,* from Old French *esmovoir,* to excite, from Latin *ēmovēre* : *ex-,* out + *movēre,* to move.]

e·mo·tion·al (ĭ-mō′shə-nəl) *adj.* **1.** Of or pertaining to emotion: *emotional conflict; emotional satisfaction.* **2.** Easily affected or stirred by emotion: *a sensitive, emotional child.* **3.** Capable of stirring the emotions: *an emotional appeal.* **4.** Showing emotion; agitated; excited: *an emotional outburst.* —**e·mo′tion·al·ly** *adv.*

e·mo·tion·al·ism (ĭ-mō′shə-nə-lĭz′əm) *n.* **1.** A tendency to encourage or yield to emotion: *the emotionalism of adolescent girls.* **2.** Undue display of emotion. **3.** An artistic attitude that places value on emotional expression: *the emotionalism of the romantic composers.*

e·mo·tive (ĭ-mō′tĭv) *adj.* **1.** Of or relating to emotion. **2.** Expressing, appealing to, or exciting emotion. —**e·mo′tive·ly** *adv.*

em·path·ic (ĕm-păth′ĭk) *adj.* Also **em·pa·thet·ic** (ĕm′pə-thĕt′ĭk). Of, pertaining to, or characterized by empathy. —**em·path′i·cal·ly** *adv.*

em·pa·thize (ĕm′pə-thīz′) *intr.v.* **-thized, -thiz·ing.** To feel or experience empathy.

em·pa·thy (ĕm′pə-thē) *n.* Identification with and understanding of another's situation, feelings, and motives. [EN-(in) + -PATHY.]

em·per·or (ĕm′pər-ər) *n.* A male ruler of an empire. [Middle English *emperour,* from Old French *empereor,* from Latin *imperātor,* from *imperāre,* to command : *in-,* against + *parāre,* to prepare.]

em·pha·sis (ĕm′fə-sĭs) *n., pl.* **-ses** (-sēz′). **1.** Special importance or significance placed upon or imparted to something: *a strong emphasis on productivity.* **2.** Stress given to a syllable, word, or phrase. **3.** Force or intensity of expression: *spoke of human rights with emphasis.* [Latin, from Greek *emphainein,* to indicate : *en-,* in + *phainein,* to show.]

em·pha·size (ĕm′fə-sīz′) *tr.v.* **-sized, -siz·ing.** To give emphasis to; stress: *emphasize a point; emphasized the automobile's fuel economy.* [From EMPHASIS.]

em·phat·ic (ĕm-făt′ĭk) *adj.* **1.** Expressed or performed with emphasis: *an emphatic refusal.* **2.** Bold and forceful in expression or action: *an emphatic person.* **3.** Striking or significant; definite: *an emphatic victory.* [Late Latin *emphaticus,* from Greek *emphatikos,* from *emphainein,* to indicate.] —**em·phat′i·cal·ly** *adv.*

em·phy·se·ma (ĕm′fĭ-sē′mə) *n.* A disease in which the air sacs of the lungs lose their elasticity, resulting in an often severe loss of breathing ability. [From Greek *emphysēma,* inflation, from *emphysan,* to blow in : *en-,* in + *physan,* to blow, from *physai,* bellows.]

em·pire (ĕm′pīr′) *n.* **1. a.** A political union of territories or nations ruled by one single central government. **b.** The territory included in such a union. **2.** Absolute dominion, power, or authority. **3.** An extensive enterprise controlled by a single person, family, or financial group: *a vast publishing empire.* [Middle English, from Old French, from Latin *imperium,* dominion, empire, from *imperāre,* to command.]

Em·pire (ŏm-pîr′, ĕm′pīr′) *adj.* Of or characteristic of a 19th-cent. French style of art, architecture, and decor marked by elaborate ornamentation.

em·pir·ic (ĕm-pîr′ĭk) *n.* A person who believes that practical experience is the sole source of knowledge. [Latin *empiricus,* from Greek *empeirikos,* from *empeirā,* experience : *en-,* in + *peira,* trial.]

em·pir·i·cal (ĕm-pîr′ĭ-kəl) *adj.* **1.** Relying upon or based on observation or experiment rather than theory: *empirical methods; empirical knowledge.* **2.** Guided by practical experience rather than theory, esp. in medicine. —**em·pir′i·cal·ly** *adv.*

em·pir·i·cism (ĕm-pîr′ĭ-sĭz′əm) *n.* **1.** The philosophical view that experience, esp. of the senses, is the only source of knowledge. **2.** The employment of empirical methods, as in medicine. —**em·pir′i·cist** *n.*

em·place (ĕm-plās′) *tr.v.* **-placed, -plac·ing.** To put in place or position.

em·place·ment (ĕm-plās′mənt) *n.* **1.** A prepared position for guns, as a mounting or platform, within a fortification. **2.** A putting into position; placement. [French, place, situation, from obs. *emplacer,* to place in (a position) : *em-,* in + *placer,* to place.]

em·ploy (ĕm-ploi′) *tr.v.* **1.** To engage the services of; provide with a job and livelihood. **2.** To make use of; put to use: *They employed all their skills to build the bridge.* **3.** To devote or apply (one's time or energies) to some activity: *employed all his leisure in fishing.* —*n.* The condition of being employed: *He was in the employ of the government.* [Middle English *emploien,* from Old French *employer,* from Latin *implicāre,* to involve : *in-,* in + *plicāre,* to fold.] —**em·ploy′a·ble** *adj.*

em·ploy·ee (ĕm-ploi′ē, ĕm′ploi-ē′) *n.* Also **em·ploy·e** or **em·ploy·é.** A person who works for another person or business in return for salary, wages, or other compensation.

em·ploy·er (ĕm-ploi′ər) *n.* A person or business that employs persons for salary, wages, or other compensation.

em·ploy·ment (ĕm-ploi′mənt) *n.* **1.** The act of employing or using. **2.** The condition of being employed. **3.** The work in which one is engaged; business; profession. —See Syns at **work.**

em·po·ri·um (ĕm-pôr′ē-əm, -pōr′-) *n., pl.* **-ums** or **-po·ri·a** (-pôr′ē-ə, -pōr′-). **1.** A large retail store carrying a wide variety of merchandise. **2.** A place that is an important trade center. [Latin, from Greek *emporion,* market, from *emporos,* merchant, traveler : *en-,* in + *poros,* journey.]

em·pow·er (ĕm-pou′ər) *tr.v.* To give legal power or official authority to; authorize: *The Senate is constitutionally empowered to declare war.*

em·press (ĕm′prĭs) *n.* **1.** A female ruler of an empire. **2.** The wife or widow of an emperor. [Middle English *emperesse,* from Old French, fem. of *emperor,* emperor.]

em·prise (ĕm-prīz′) *n.* Also **em·prize.** **1.** An undertaking, esp. of a chivalrous or adventurous nature. **2.** Chivalrous daring or prowess; adventurousness. [Middle English, from Old French, from *emprendre,* to undertake : Latin *in-,* in + *prehendere,* to take, seize.]

emp·ty (ĕmp′tē) *adj.* **-ti·er, -ti·est.** **1.** Containing nothing: *an empty bottle.* **2.** Having no occupants or inhabitants; vacant; unoccupied: *an empty apartment; an empty lot.* **3.** Lacking purpose or substance; meaningless: *an empty life.* **4.** Not having something; devoid; lacking: *a life empty of adventure; streets empty of traffic.* **5.** Having no value, effect, or meaning; meaningless or vain: *empty promises; empty pleasures.* **6.** Needing food; hungry: *an empty stomach.* —*v.* **-tied, -ty·ing.** —*tr.v.* **1.** To remove the contents of; make empty: *empty one's pockets.* **2.** To transfer, take out, or pour off: *empty the ashes into a pail.* —*intr.v.* **1.** To become empty: *The business district empties at night.* **2.** To discharge or flow: *The river empties into a bay.* —*n., pl.* **-ties.** An empty container, esp. a bottle. [Middle English, from Old English *æmettig,* empty, unoccupied, from *æmetta,* rest, leisure.] —**emp′ti·ly** *adv.* —**emp′ti·ness** *n.*

Syns: empty, bare, vacant *adj. Core meaning:* Not containing anything (*an empty cupboard*).

emp·ty-hand·ed (ĕmp′tē-hăn′dĭd) *adj.* **1.** Bearing no gifts, possessions, etc.: *They arrived empty-handed.* **2.** Having gained or accomplished nothing.

emp·ty-head·ed (ĕmp′tē-hĕd′ĭd) *adj.* Lacking sense; foolish; scatterbrained.

empty set. *Math.* The set that has no members; the null set.

em·py·re·al (ĕm′pī-rē′əl, ĕm-pîr′ē-əl) *adj.* Of or pertaining to the empyrean; celestial. [Middle English *imperyale*, from Late Latin *empyrius*, from Greek *empurios*, fiery : *en-*, in + *pur*, fire.]

em·py·re·an (ĕm′pī-rē′ən, ĕm-pîr′ē-ən) *n.* **1.** The highest reaches of heaven, believed by the ancients to be a realm of pure fire and light. **2.** The sky or firmament. —*adj.* Heavenly; celestial. [From Late Latin *empyreus*, empyreal.]

e·mu (ē′myōō) *n.* A large, flightless Australian bird, *Dromiceius novaehollandiae*, related to and resembling the ostrich. [Portuguese *ema*.]

em·u·late (ĕm′yə-lāt′) *tr.v.* **-lat·ed, -lat·ing.** **1.** To strive to equal or excel, esp. through imitation: *trying to emulate his father's success.* **2.** To compete with successfully: *California is emulating France as a producer of fine wines.* [From Latin *aemulārī*, from *aemulus*, emulous.] —**em′u·la·tive** *adj.* —**em′u·la·tor** *n.*

em·u·la·tion (ĕm′yə-lā′shən) *n.* Effort or ambition to equal or surpass another.

e·mul·si·fy (ĭ-mŭl′sə-fī′) *tr.v.* **-fied, -fy·ing.** To make into an emulsion. [EMULSI(ON) + -FY.] —**e·mul′si·fi·ca′tion** *n.* —**e·mul′si·fi′er** *n.*

e·mul·sion (ĭ-mŭl′shən) *n.* **1.** *Chem.* A suspension of small droplets of one liquid in a second liquid with which the first does not mix. **2.** The light-sensitive coating of a photographic film or plate, usu. made of fine grains of a silver salt suspended in a thin layer of gelatin. [From Latin *ēmulsus*, past part. of *ēmulgēre*, to drain out : *ex-*, out + *mulgēre*, to milk.] —**e·mul′sive** *adj.*

en (ĕn) *n. Printing.* A unit of measure equal to half the width of an em.

en–¹. Also **em-** before *b*, *p*, and sometimes *m*. **1.** A prefix used to form verbs from nouns and meaning: **a.** To put into or on: **enthrone. b.** To go into or on: **entrain. c.** To cover or imbue with: **enrobe. d.** To provide with: **empower. 2.** A prefix used to form verbs from nouns and adjectives and meaning causing to become or resemble: **enable.** [Middle English, from Old French, from Latin *in-*, *im-*.]

en–². Also **em-** before *b*, *m*, *p*, or *ph*. A prefix used to form nouns and adjectives and meaning in, into, or within: **empathy.** [Middle English *en-*, from Latin, from Greek.]

–en¹. **1.** A suffix used to form verbs from adjectives and meaning being, becoming, or causing to be: **cheapen. 2.** A suffix used to form verbs from nouns and meaning causing to have or gain: **lengthen.** [Middle English *-nen*, *-nien*, from Old English *-nian*.]

–en². A suffix meaning made of or resembling: **wooden, earthen, ashen.** [Middle English, from Old English.]

en·a·ble (ĕn-ā′bəl) *tr.v.* **-bled, -bling.** **1.** To give the means, knowledge, ability, or opportunity to do something; make possible: *a loan that enables us to expand the business.* **2.** To give legal power, capacity, or sanction to; permit.

en·act (ĕn-ăkt′) *tr.v.* **1.** To make (a bill) into a law. **2.** To act out, as on a stage; perform. —**en·act′ment** *n.*

e·nam·el (ĭ-năm′əl) *n.* **1.** A glassy, usu. opaque protective or decorative coating baked on metal, glass, or ceramic ware. **2.** An object with an enameled surface, as a piece of jewelry. **3.** A paint that dries to a hard, glossy surface. **4.** Any glossy, hard coating resembling enamel. **5.** *Anat.* The hard substance that covers the exposed portion of a tooth. —*tr.v.* **-eled** or **-elled, -el·ing** or **-el·ling. 1.** To coat, inlay, or decorate with enamel. **2.** To give a glossy or brilliant surface to. [Middle English *enamelen*, from Norman French *enameler* : *en-*, in + *amail*, enamel, from Old French *esmail*.] —**e·nam′el·er** *n.*

en·am·or (ĭ-năm′ər) *tr.v.* Also *Brit.* **en·am·our.** To inspire with love; charm; captivate: *He was enamored of the countryside.* [Middle English *enamouren*, from Old French *enamourer* : *en-*, in + *amour*, love, from Latin *amor*, from *amāre*, to love.]

en bloc (äN blôk′) As one; all together; as a whole. [French, "in a lump."]

en·camp (ĕn-kămp′) *intr.v.* To set up or live in a camp. —*tr.v.* To provide quarters for in a camp.

en·camp·ment (ĕn-kămp′mənt) *n.* **1.** The act of camping. **2.** A camp or campsite.

en·cap·su·late (ĕn-kăp′sə-lāt′) *v.* **-lat·ed, -lat·ing.** —*tr.v.* **1.** To encase in a capsule. **2.** To express the essence of; condense. —*intr.v.* To become encapsulated. —**en·cap′su·la′tion** *n.*

en·case (ĕn-kās′) *tr.v.* **-cased, -cas·ing.** Also **in·case** (ĭn-). To enclose in or as if in a case. —**en·case′ment** *n.*

en·caus·tic (ĕn-kô′stĭk) *n.* A painting process in which colored beeswax is applied to a surface and fixed with heat. [Latin *encausticus*, from Greek *enkaustikos*, from *enkaiein*, to burn in : *en-*, in + *kaiein*, to burn.]

–ence or **–ency.** A suffix meaning action, state, quality, or condition: **reference.** [Middle English, from Old French, from Latin *-entia*, from *-ēns*, pres. part. suffix.]

encephal-. Var. of **encephalo-.**

en·ce·phal·ic (ĕn′sə-făl′ĭk) *adj.* **1.** Of or pertaining to the brain. **2.** Located within the cranial cavity.

en·ceph·a·li·tis (ĕn-sĕf′ə-lī′tĭs) *n.* Inflammation of the brain. [ENCEPHAL(O)- + -ITIS.] —**en·ceph′a·lit′ic** (-lĭt′ĭk) *adj.*

encephalo- or **encephal-.** A prefix meaning the brain: **encephalitis.** [From Greek *(muelos) enkephalos*, "(marrow) in the head," from *en-*, in + *kephalē*, head.]

en·ceph·a·lon (ĕn-sĕf′ə-lŏn′) *n., pl.* **-la** (-lə). The brain of a vertebrate. [From Greek *enkephalon.*]

en·chain (ĕn-chān′) *tr.v.* To bind with or as if with chains; fetter. [Middle English *encheynen*, from Old French *enchaeiner* : *en-*, in + *chaeine*, chain.]

en·chant (ĕn-chănt′) *tr.v.* **1.** To cast under a spell; bewitch. **2.** To delight completely; charm. —See Syns at **charm.** [Middle English *enchanten*, Old French *enchanter*, from Latin *incantāre*, to chant (magic words) : *in-* (intensive) + *cantāre*, to sing.] —**en·chant′er** *n.*

en·chant·ing (ĕn-chăn′tĭng) *adj.* Very charming; delightful; attractive. —**en·chant′ing·ly** *adv.*

en·chant·ment (ĕn-chănt′mənt) *n.* **1. a.** An act of enchanting. **b.** The condition of being enchanted. **2.** Something that enchants; an irresistible charm.

en·chant·ress (ĕn-chăn′trĭs) *n.* **1.** A woman of unusual appeal, charm, or fascination. **2.** A sorceress.

en·chase (ĕn-chās′) *tr.v.* **-chased, -chas·ing. 1.** To set or mount: *enchase a jewel.* **2.** To decorate or ornament (a surface) by inlaying, engraving, or carving. **3.** To engrave or carve (a design) in a surface. [Middle English *enchasen*, from Old French *enchasser* : *en-*, in + *chasse*, case, from Latin *capsa*, box.]

en·chi·la·da (ĕn′chə-lä′də) *n.* A tortilla rolled and stuffed with a meat or cheese filling and served with a sauce spiced with chili. [American Spanish.]

en·cir·cle (ĕn-sûr′kəl) *tr.v.* **-cled, -cling. 1.** To form a circle around; surround. **2.** To move to go around; make a circuit of: *moons encircling a planet.* —See Syns at **surround.** —**en·cir′cle·ment** *n.*

en·clave (ĕn′klāv′, ŏn′-) *n.* **1.** A small territory lying entirely within the boundaries of another country. **2.** A district within a city or country inhabited by a minority group. [French, from Old French *enclaver*, to enclose : Latin *in-*, in + *clāvis*, key.]

en·clit·ic (ĕn-klĭt′ĭk) *adj. Ling.* Of or pertaining to a word that does not have an independent accent in a sentence and is pronounced as part of the preceding word; for example, *'em* in informal English *Give 'em the works.* —*n.* An enclitic word. [Late Latin *encliticus*, from Greek *enklitikos*, "leaning (on the preceding word for accent)," from *enklinein*, to lean on : *en-*, in + *klinein*, to lean.]

en·close (ĕn-klōz′) *tr.v.* **-closed, -clos·ing.** Also **in·close** (ĭn-). **1.** To surround on all sides; close in. **2.** To include with a package or letter. **3.** To contain, esp. so as to shelter or hide: *"every one of those darkly clustered houses encloses its own secret"* (Dickens). —See Syns at **surround.** [Middle English *enclosen*, from Old French *enclose*, past part. of *enclore*, ult. from Latin *inclūdere*, to include.]

en·clo·sure (ĕn-klō′zhər) *n.* **1.** The act of enclosing or the condition of being enclosed. **2.** An area, object, or item that is enclosed. **3.** Something that encloses, as a wall or fence.

en·code (ĕn-kōd′) *tr.v.* **-cod·ed, -cod·ing.** To put (a message) into code. —**en·cod′er** *n.*

en·co·mi·ast (ĕn-kō′mē-ăst′, -əst) *n.* A person who delivers or writes encomiums; eulogist. [Greek *enkōmiastēs*, from enkōmiazein, to praise, from enkōmion, encomium.]

en·co·mi·um (ĕn-kō′mē-əm) n., pl. **-ums** or **-mi·a** (-mē-ə). A formal expression of lofty praise; tribute; eulogy. [Latin *encōmium*, from Greek *enkōmion (epos)*, "(speech) in praise of a victor," from *enkōmios*, belonging to the victory procession : *en-*, in + *kōmos*, celebration.]

en·com·pass (ĕn-kŭm′pəs, -kŏm′-) tr.v. **1.** To form a circle or ring about; surround. **2.** To comprise or contain; include: *The report encompassed a wide variety of subjects.* —**en·com′pass·ment** n.

en·core (ŏn′kôr′, -kōr′) n. **1.** A demand or request by an audience, expressed by extended applause, for an additional performance. **2.** An additional performance in response to such a demand. —tr.v. **-cored, -cor·ing.** To demand an encore of or from. —interj. A word used to demand an additional performance. [French, again.]

en·coun·ter (ĕn-koun′tər) n. **1.** A casual or unexpected meeting. **2.** A hostile confrontation or engagement, as between enemies; a clash. —tr.v. **1.** To meet casually or unexpectedly. **2.** To meet in battle. **3.** To come up against; be faced with: *encounter difficulties; encounter opposition to a plan.* [Middle English *encountre*, from Old French *encontre*, from *encontrer*, to meet : Latin *in-*, in + *contrā*, opposite, against.]

en·cour·age (ĕn-kûr′ĭj, -kŭr′-) tr.v. **-aged, -ag·ing. 1.** To inspire with hope, courage, or confidence; hearten. **2.** To help to bring about; foster: *afraid that the team's success would encourage complacency.* **3.** To urge or inspire: *encouraged us to ask questions.* [Middle English *encoragen*, from Old French *encorager* : *en-* (causative) + *corage*, courage.] —**en·cour′ag·er** n. —**en·cour′ag·ing·ly** adv.

Syns: encourage, cheer, hearten, nerve v. Core meaning: To give strength and confidence to (*were encouraged by the doctor's findings*).

en·cour·age·ment (ĕn-kûr′ĭj-mənt, -kŭr′-) n. **1.** The act of encouraging or the condition of being encouraged. **2.** Something that encourages.

en·croach (ĕn-krōch′) intr.v. **1.** To intrude or infringe gradually or insidiously upon the property or rights of another; trespass: *encroach on the fields of a neighboring farm.* **2.** To advance beyond proper or usual limits: *a river encroaching on the shore.* [Middle English *encroachen*, from Old French *encrochier*, to seize : *en-*, in + *croc*, hook.] —**en·croach′ment** n.

en·crust (ĕn-krŭst′) tr.v. Also **in·crust** (ĭn-). **1.** To cover with or as if with a crust or hard layer: *Ice encrusted the windowsill.* **2.** To adorn with a solid covering of jewels or other ornaments: *encrust a crown with diamonds.* —**en′crust·a′tion** n.

en·cum·ber (ĕn-kŭm′bər) tr.v. **1.** To weigh down excessively; lay too much upon; burden: *encumber a mule with gear.* **2.** To hinder, as with useless articles or unwanted additions: *junk encumbering the attic; a knight encumbered with armor.* **3.** To handicap or burden, as with obligations or legal claims: *encumbered with debts.* —See Syns at **hinder.** [Middle English *encombren*, from Old French *encombrer*, to block up : *en-*, in + *combre*, hindrance.]

en·cum·brance (ĕn-kŭm′brəns) n. **1.** Something or someone that encumbers or hinders; a burden. **2.** *Law.* A lien or claim upon property.

-ency. Var. of **-ence.**

en·cyc·li·cal (ĕn-sĭk′lĭ-kəl) n. *Rom. Cath. Ch.* A letter written by the pope, addressed to the bishops, usu. concerned with matters of doctrine, morals, or discipline. —adj. Intended for general or wide circulation. Said of letters. [Late Latin *encyclicus*, from Greek *enkuklios*, circular : *en-*, in + *kuklos*, circle.]

en·cy·clo·pe·di·a (ĕn-sī′klə-pē′dē-ə) or **en·cy·clo·pae·di·a** n. A comprehensive reference work containing articles, usu. arranged alphabetically, on a wide range of subjects or on numerous aspects of one particular field. [Medieval Latin *encyclopaedia*, general education course, from Greek *enkuklios paideia*, general education : *enkuklios*, circular, general + *paideia*, education, from *pais*, child.]

en·cy·clo·pe·dic (ĕn-sī′klə-pē′dĭk) or **en·cy·clo·pae·dic** adj. **1.** Of, pertaining to, or like an encyclopedia. **2.** Having or covering a wide range of information; comprehensive: *encyclopedic knowledge.*

en·cy·clo·pe·dist (ĕn-sī′klə-pē′dĭst) or **en·cy·clo·pae·dist** n. A person who writes for or compiles an encyclopedia.

en·cyst (ĕn-sĭst′) tr.v. To enclose in a cyst or sac. —intr.v. To become enclosed in a cyst or sac. —**en·cyst′ment** n.

end (ĕnd) n. **1. a.** Either extremity of something that has length: *opposite ends of the table.* **b.** The outermost or extreme edge or limit of a space or area; a boundary: *a cabin at the end of the lake.* **2.** The point at which an action, event, or process ceases or is completed; a finish; conclusion: *the end of a day.* **3. a.** A result or consequence; outcome. **b.** A purpose or goal; an aim. **4. a.** Death or ruin: *a violent end.* **b.** The cause or agent of this: *Greed will be the end of her.* **5.** A point that marks the extent or limit of something: *the end of one's patience.* **6. ends.** A remainder or remnant. **7.** *Informal.* A share in a responsibility: *your end of the bargain.* **8.** *Football.* **a.** Either of the players, on both offense and defense, stationed at the outermost position at the line of scrimmage. **b.** The position played by such a player. —modifier: *the end result; the end product.* —tr.v. **1.** To bring to an end; finish; conclude. **2.** To form the end or concluding part of. **3.** To cause the death or ruin of; destroy. —intr.v. To come to an end; cease: *The negotiations ended with no agreement.* —**phrasal verb.** end up. To finish in a certain situation or place: *end up in jail.* —idioms. hold (or keep) (one's) end up. To do one's share. make (both) ends meet. To manage to live within one's means. [Middle English *ende*, from Old English.]

Syns: end, close, complete, conclude, finish, terminate, wind up (*Informal*), wrap up v. Core meaning: To bring to a natural or proper end (*ended the letter with thanks*).

end-. Var. of **endo-.**

en·dan·ger (ĕn-dān′jər) tr.v. To expose to danger or harm; imperil. —**en·dan′ger·ment** n.

endangered species. A species in danger of extinction.

en·dear (ĕn-dîr′) tr.v. To make beloved, dear, or admired: *The actor endeared himself to the audience.*

en·dear·ment (ĕn-dîr′mənt) n. A word or expression of affection.

en·deav·or (ĕn-dĕv′ər) Also *Brit.* **en·deav·our.** —intr.v. To make an earnest effort or attempt; strive: *endeavoring to keep up with the latest research in his field.* —n. **1.** An earnest effort or attempt. **2.** An undertaking: *a new business endeavor.* [Middle English *endevour*, from *endeveren*, to exert oneself, from the phrase *putten in dever*, to put in duty, make it one's duty, from Old French *devoir*, duty.]

en·dem·ic (ĕn-dĕm′ĭk) adj. Prevalent in or peculiar to a particular locality or people; native: *an endemic disease; problems endemic to socialist economies.* —See Syns at **native.** [French *endémique*, from Greek *endēmios*, dwelling in a place, indigenous : *en-*, in + *dēmos*, people.]

en·dive (ĕn′dīv′, ŏn′dēv′) n. **1.** A plant, *Cichorium endivia*, cultivated for its crisp leaves, used in salads. **2.** A variety of the common chicory, *Cichorium intybus*, with whitish leaves used in salads. [Middle English, from Old French, from Medieval Latin *endiva*, from Latin *entibus*, chicory, from Greek *entubioi*.]

endive

end·less (ĕnd′lĭs) adj. **1.** Having or seeming to have no end; infinite: *endless stretches of sandy beaches.* **2.** Constant; incessant: *endless arguments.* **3.** Formed with the ends joined; continuous: *an endless ring.* —See Syns at **continuous.** —**end′less·ly** adv. —**end′less·ness** n.

ă pat	ā pay	â care	ä father	ĕ pet	ē be	hw which	ĭ pit	ī tie	î pier	ŏ pot	ō toe	ô paw, for	oi noise
ōō took	ōō boot	ou out	th thin	th this	ŭ cut	û urge	zh vision	ə about, item, edible, gallop, circus

end·most (ĕnd′mōst′) *adj.* Being at or closest to the end; last.

endo- or **end-.** A prefix meaning inside or within: **endo·carp.** [Greek, from *endon,* within.]

en·do·blast (ĕn′də-blăst′) *n.* Also **en·to·blast** (ĕn′tə-). The inner layer of the blastoderm. [ENDO- + -BLAST.]

en·do·car·di·tis (ĕn′dō-kär-dī′tĭs) *n.* Inflammation of the endocardium. [ENDOCARD(IUM) + -ITIS.]

en·do·car·di·um (ĕn′dō-kär′dē-əm) *n., pl.* **-di·a** (-dē-ə). The thin membrane that lines the interior of the heart. [ENDO- + Greek *kardia,* heart.] —**en′do·car′di·al** *adj.*

en·do·carp (ĕn′də-kärp′) *n. Bot.* The often hard or leathery inner layer of the ripened ovary or fruit of many plants. [ENDO- + -CARP.]

en·do·crine (ĕn′də-krĭn, -krēn′, -krīn′) *adj.* **1.** Secreting internally rather than through a duct. **2.** Of or pertaining to any of the ductless or endocrine glands. —*n.* **1.** The internal secretion of a gland. **2.** An **endocrine gland.** [ENDO- + Greek *krīnein,* to separate.]

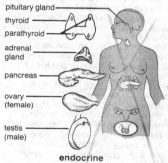

endocrine

endocrine gland. Any of the ductless glands, such as the thyroid or adrenal, whose secretions pass directly into the blood stream.

en·do·cri·nol·o·gy (ĕn′də-krə-nŏl′ə-jē) *n.* The medical study of the endocrine glands, their functions, and their diseases. [ENDOCRIN(E) + -LOGY.] —**en′do·cri·nol′o·gist** *n.*

en·do·derm (ĕn′də-dûrm′) *n.* The innermost of the three primary germ layers of an embryo, which later develops into the respiratory and digestive systems and associated structures. [ENDO- + -DERM.] —**en′do·der′mal** *adj.*

en·do·der·mis (ĕn′də-dûr′mĭs) *n.* The innermost layer of the cortex in many plants. [ENDO- + Greek *derma,* skin.]

en·dog·a·my (ĕn-dŏg′ə-mē) *n.* Marriage within one's own group, class, or tribe in accordance with set custom or law; inbreeding. [ENDO- + -GAMY.] —**en·dog′a·mous** *adj.*

en·dog·e·nous (ĕn-dŏj′ə-nəs) *adj.* Originating within an organ or part. [ENDO- + -GEN + -OUS.]

en·do·lymph (ĕn′də-lĭmf′) *n.* The fluid in the inner ear. [ENDO- + LYMPH.]

en·do·morph (ĕn′də-môrf′) *n.* An endomorphic person. [ENDO- + -MORPH.]

en·do·mor·phic (ĕn′də-môr′fĭk) *adj. Physiol.* Characterized by prominence of the abdomen and other soft, rounded body parts. —**en′do·mor′phy** *n.*

en·do·plasm (ĕn′də-plăz′əm) *n.* The inner, relatively viscous portion of the continuous phase of cytoplasm. [ENDO- + PLASM.]

en·dorse (ĕn-dôrs′) *tr.v.* **-dorsed, -dors·ing.** Also **in·dorse** (ĭn-). **1.** To write one's signature on the back of (a check) in order to receive or be credited with the money indicated. **2.** To give approval of; support: *Many senators have already endorsed the new bill.* [Middle English *endosen,* from Old French *endosser,* "to put on the back of" : *en-,* to put on + *dos,* back, from Latin *dorsum.*] —**en·dors′er** or **en·dor′sor** *n.*

en·dors·ee (ĕn′dôr-sē′) *n.* One to whom ownership of a check, money order, stock certificate, etc., is transferred by endorsement.

en·dorse·ment (ĕn-dôrs′mənt) *n.* **1.** An act of endorsing. **2.** Something that endorses or validates, esp. a signature on the back of a check. **3.** Approval; sanction; support: *Her candidacy has my full endorsement.* **4.** An amend-

ment to a contract, such as an insurance policy, permitting a change in the original terms.

en·do·skel·e·ton (ĕn′dō-skĕl′ĭ-tən) *n.* An internal supporting structure or framework for the body, as the skeleton in man and other vertebrates. —**en′do·skel′e·tal** *adj.*

en·do·sperm (ĕn′də-spûrm′) *n.* The tissue of a plant seed that contains nourishment for the developing embryo. [ENDO- + -SPERM.]

en·do·ther·mic (ĕn′dō-thûr′mĭk) *adj.* Also **en·do·ther·mal** (-məl). Characterized by or causing the absorption of heat: *an endothermic chemical reaction.* [ENDO- + THERM + -IC.]

en·dow (ĕn-dou′) *tr.v.* **1.** To provide with property, income, or a source of income: *endow a college.* **2.** To provide or equip with a talent, ability, quality, right, etc.: *a woman endowed with both beauty and charm.* [Middle English *endowen,* from Norman French *endouer* : Old French *en-* (intensive) + *douer,* to provide with a dowry, from Latin *dōtāre,* from *dōs,* dowry.]

en·dow·ment (ĕn-dou′mənt) *n.* **1.** An act of endowing. **2.** Funds or property donated to an institution, individual, or group as a source of income. **3.** A natural gift, talent, ability, or quality.

en·due (ĕn-dōo′, -dyōo′) *tr.v.* **-dued, -du·ing.** Also **in·due** (ĭn-). To provide with some quality or trait: *a performance endued with passion and power.* [Middle English *enduen,* from Old French *enduire,* to lead in, induct, from Latin *indūcere* : *in-,* in + *dūcere,* to lead.]

en·dur·ance (ĕn-dōor′əns, -dyōor′-) *n.* **1.** The act or power of withstanding hardship, such as stress, strain, or use: *a real test of an athlete's endurance.* **2.** The condition or fact of persevering; continuing survival: *the endurance of a tradition.*

en·dure (ĕn-dōor′, -dyōor′) *v.* **-dured, -dur·ing.** —*tr.v.* **1.** To undergo; bear up under: *endure an Arctic winter.* **2.** To bear with tolerance; put up with: *endure a boring lecture.* —*intr.v.* **1.** To continue to exist; last: *His name will endure forever.* **2.** To suffer patiently without yielding; persevere; hold out. [Middle English *enduren,* from Old French *endurer,* from Latin *indūrāre,* to harden : *in-* (intensive) + *dūrāre,* to harden, from *dūrus,* hard.] —**en·dur′a·ble** *adj.*

end·wise (ĕnd′wīz′) *adv.* Also **end·ways** (-wāz′). **1.** On end. **2.** With the end foremost. **3.** Lengthwise. **4.** End to end.

end zone. *Football.* The area beyond the goal line at each end of the field.

-ene. A suffix meaning unsaturation of an organic compound, esp. one having a double bond: *ethylene.* [From Greek *-ēnē,* fem. patronymic suffix.]

en·e·ma (ĕn′ə-mə) *n.* **1.** The injection of a liquid into the rectum through the anus for cleansing, as a laxative, or for other therapeutic purposes. **2.** The liquid used in this way. [Late Latin, from Greek, from *enienai,* to inject : *en-,* in + *hienai,* to send, throw.]

en·e·my (ĕn′ə-mē) *n., pl.* **-mies. 1.** A person, animal, or group that shows hostility toward or opposes the purposes or interests of another; a foe; an opponent. **2.** A hostile power or military force or a member or unit of such a force. **3.** Something destructive or injurious in its effects: *Fear is our chief enemy.* —*modifier:* *enemy soldiers.* [Middle English *enemi,* from Old French, from Latin *inimīcus* : *in-,* not + *amīcus,* friend.]

en·er·get·ic (ĕn′ər-jĕt′ĭk) *adj.* Having, exerting, or displaying energy; vigorous. —See Syns at **vigorous.** [Greek *energētikos,* active, from *energein,* to be active, from *energos,* active.] —**en′er·get′i·cal·ly** *adv.*

en·er·gize (ĕn′ər-jīz′) *v.* **-gized, -giz·ing.** —*tr.v.* To give or supply energy or power to; activate; charge. —*intr.v.* To release or put out energy. —**en′er·giz′er** *n.*

en·er·gy (ĕn′ər-jē) *n., pl.* **-gies. 1.** *Physics.* The capability for doing work, esp. the work that a material body or system can perform on another such body by undergoing a change in condition. **2.** The ability to act or put forth effort with either the mind or the body: *He lacked energy to finish the job.* **3.** Strength and vigor; force: *a book of amazing frankness and energy.* **4. energies.** Powers available for working or efficiently put to work: *He devoted all his energies to a worthy cause.* [Late Latin *energīa,* from Greek *energeia,* from *energos,* active : *en-,* at + *ergon,* work.]

ă pat   ā pay   â care   ä father   ĕ pet   ē be   hw which   ĭ pit   ī tie   î pier   ŏ pot   ō toe   ô paw, for   oi noise
ōō took   ōō boot   ou out   th thin   th this   ŭ cut   û urge   zh vision   ə about, item, edible, gallop, circus

energy level. The energy characteristic of a stationary state of any mechanical system.

en·er·vate (ĕn'ər-vāt') *tr.v.* **-vat·ed, -vat·ing.** To deprive of strength or vitality; debilitate; weaken: *enervated by disease; a culture enervated by luxury.* [From Latin *ēnervāre* : *ex-* (removal) + *nervus,* sinew, nerve.] **—en'er·va'tion** *n.* **—en'er·va'tor** *n.*

en·fant ter·ri·ble (äN-fän' tĕ-rē'blə) *pl.* **en·fants ter·ri·bles** (äN-fän' tĕ-rē'blə). A person, esp. a youth, whose unconventional behavior and ideas are a source of embarrassment or dismay. [French, "terrible child."]

en·fee·ble (ĕn-fē'bəl) *tr.v.* **-bled, -bling.** To make feeble; weaken. [Middle English *enfeblen,* from Old French *enfebler* : *en-* (causative) + *feble,* feeble.] **—en·fee'ble·ment** *n.*

en·fi·lade (ĕn'fə-lād', -läd') *n.* **1.** The firing of a gun or guns so as to sweep the length of a target, such as a column of troops. **2.** A position under enfilade. **—tr.v. -lad·ed, -lad·ing.** To rake with gunfire. [French, series, from *enfiler,* to thread, from Old French : *en-,* in + *fil,* thread, from Latin *fīlum.*]

en·fold (ĕn-fōld') *tr.v.* Also **in·fold** (ĭn-). **1.** To cover with or as if with folds; envelop. **2.** To embrace. **—See Syns at wrap.**

en·force (ĕn-fôrs', -fōrs') *tr.v.* **-forced, -forc·ing. 1.** To compel observance of or obedience to: *enforce a regulation.* **2.** To give force to; reinforce: *enforce one's opinion with numerous arguments.* [Middle English *enforcen,* from Old French *enforcier* : Latin *in-* (causative) + *fortis,* strong.] **—en·force'a·ble** *adj.* **—en·force'ment** *n.* **—en·forc'er** *n.*

en·fran·chise (ĕn-frăn'chīz') *tr.v.* **-chised, -chis·ing. 1.** To endow with the rights of citizenship, esp. the right to vote. **2.** To free, as from slavery. [Middle English *enfraunchisen,* from Old French *enfranchir* : *en-* (causative) + *franc,* free.] **—en·fran'chise'ment** *n.*

en·gage (ĕn-gāj') *v.* **-gaged, -gag·ing. —tr.v. 1.** To obtain or contract for the services of; hire; employ: *engage a lawyer.* **2.** To contract for the use of; reserve: *engage a hotel room.* **3.** To attract and hold; engross: *The project engaged her interest for months.* **4.** To require the use of; occupy: *Studying engages most of a student's time.* **5.** To pledge, esp. to promise to marry. **6.** To enter into conflict with: *We have engaged the enemy.* **7.** To cause to interlock; mesh: *engage the gears.* **8.** To draw into; involve: *engage someone in conversation.* **—intr.v. 1.** To involve oneself; participate: *scientists engaged in cancer research.* **2.** To assume an obligation; pledge; agree: *He engaged to address the convention.* **3.** To enter into conflict. **4.** To become meshed or interlocked: *The clutch engaged with the flywheel.* [Middle English *engagen,* from Old French *engager* : *en-,* in + *gage,* pledge.]

en·gaged (ĕn-gājd') *adj.* **1.** Pledged to marry; betrothed. **2.** Employed; occupied; busy. **3.** Arranged so as to transmit power, as gears or mechanical parts.

en·gage·ment (ĕn-gāj'mənt) *n.* **1.** An act of engaging or the condition of being engaged. **2.** Betrothal. **3.** A promise to appear at a certain time, as for business or social activity; an appointment. **4. a.** Employment, esp. for a set length of time. **b.** The period of such employment. **5.** A battle or encounter. **6.** The condition of being in gear.

en·gag·ing (ĕn-gā'jĭng) *adj.* Tending to attract; charming; pleasing: *an engaging smile.* **—en·gag'ing·ly** *adv.*

en·gen·der (ĕn-jĕn'dər) *tr.v.* **1.** To give rise to; cause; produce: *His manner engenders confidence and trust.* **2.** To procreate; propagate; beget. **—intr.v.** To come into existence. [Middle English *engenderen,* from Old French *engenderer,* from Latin *ingenerāre* : *in-,* in + *generāre,* to generate.]

en·gine (ĕn'jĭn) *n.* **1.** A machine that converts energy into mechanical motion. **2.** Any mechanical device, instrument, or tool: *engines of war and destruction.* **3.** A locomotive. [Middle English *engin,* from Old French, skill, invention, from Latin *ingenium,* inborn talent, skill.]

engine block. The cast metal block containing the cylinders of an internal-combustion engine.

en·gi·neer (ĕn'jə-nîr') *n.* **1.** A person trained in, skilled at, or professionally engaged in a branch of engineering: *a mining engineer.* **2.** A person who skillfully or shrewdly manages an enterprise: *The campaign manager was the*

engineer of the stunning victory. **3.** A person who operates an engine, esp. a locomotive. **—tr.v. 1.** To plan, construct, and manage as an engineer. **2.** To plan or accomplish by skill or contrivance; to maneuver: *engineer a military takeover.* [Middle English *enginer,* from Old French *engineor,* from Medieval Latin *ingeniātor,* contriver, from *ingeniāre,* to contrive, from Latin *ingenium,* talent.]

en·gi·neer·ing (ĕn'jə-nîr'ĭng) *n.* The application of scientific principles to practical purposes, as the design, construction, and operation of efficient and economical structures, equipment, and systems.

en·gine·ry (ĕn'jən-rē) *n.* Machinery.

Eng·lish (ĭng'glĭsh) *adj.* Of, pertaining to, derived from, or characteristic of England and its inhabitants. **—n. 1. the English.** The people of England collectively. **2.** The Germanic language of the peoples of Britain, the United States, and many other countries, divided historically into Old English, Middle English, and Modern English. **3.** The English language of a particular time, region, person, or group of people: *American English; Shakespeare's English.* **4.** A course or individual class in the study of English literature, language, or composition. **5.** Often **english.** The spin given to a ball by striking it on one side or releasing it with a sharp twist. **—tr.v.** To translate into English. **—Eng'lish·man** *n.* **—Eng'lish·wom'an** *n.*

English horn. A double-reed woodwind instrument similar to but larger and lower in pitch and timbre than the oboe.

English muffin. A griddle-baked muffin made of yeast dough, usu. served toasted.

English setter. A dog of a breed that has a silky white coat usu. with black or brownish markings.

English sheepdog. An **Old English sheepdog.**

en·gorge (ĕn-gôrj') *tr.v.* **-gorged, -gorg·ing. 1.** To devour greedily. **2.** To congest or fill with blood, as a bodily organ. [Old French *engorgier* : *en-,* in + *gorge,* throat.] **—en·gorge'ment** *n.*

en·graft (ĕn-grăft') *tr.v.* Also **in·graft** (ĭn-). **1.** To graft (a shoot) onto or into another tree or plant. **2.** To plant firmly; establish; root. **—en·graft'ment** *n.*

en·grave (ĕn-grāv') *tr.v.* **-graved, -grav·ing. 1.** To carve, cut, or etch (a design or letters) into a material or a surface: *engrave a name on a plaque.* **2.** To carve, cut, or etch a design or letters into (a material or surface): *engrave a plate.* **3. a.** To carve, cut, or etch (a design or letters) into a block, plate, or other surface used for printing. **b.** To print from a block or plate made by such a process: *engrave wedding invitations.* **4.** To impress deeply; fix permanently: *The old man's threat was engraved in her mind.* [EN- + GRAVE (to carve).] **—en·grav'er** *n.*

en·grav·ing (ĕn-grā'vĭng) *n.* **1. a.** The art or technique of cutting letters or designs into a surface. **b.** The letters or designs engraved. **2.** An engraved surface for printing. **3.** A print made from an engraved plate.

en·gross (ĕn-grōs') *tr.v.* **1.** To occupy the complete attention of; absorb wholly: *He is engrossed in a new project.* **2.** To acquire most or all of (a commodity). **3.** To prepare the text of (an official document). [Middle English *engrossen,* partly from Old French *en gros,* in large quantity, and partly from Medieval Latin *ingrossāre.*] **—en·gross'er** *n.*

en·gulf (ĕn-gŭlf') *tr.v.* Also **in·gulf** (ĭn-). To swallow up or overwhelm by or as if by overflowing and enclosing: *The floodwaters engulfed the surrounding farmlands.* [EN- + GULF.]

en·hance (ĕn-hăns') *tr.v.* **-hanced, -hanc·ing.** To increase or make greater, as in value, beauty, reputation, etc.: *The use of contrast enhances the forceful effect of the poem. The new garden enhances the house.* [Middle English *enhauncen,* from Norman French *enhauncer,* var. of Old French *enhaucer* : Latin *in-* (intensive) + *altus,* high.] **—en·hance'ment** *n.*

en·har·mon·ic (ĕn'här-mŏn'ĭk) *adj.* Of or involving the use of two different names, such as F♯ and G♭, for the same musical tone. [Late Latin *enharmonicus,* from Greek *enarmonikos,* in harmony : *en-,* in + *harmonia,* harmony.]

E·nid (ē'nĭd) *n.* In Arthurian legend, the loyal wife of Geraint.

e·nig·ma (ĭ-nĭg'mə) *n.* **1.** Ambiguous or cryptic speech or writing. **2.** Someone or something that is puzzling, ambiguous, or inexplicable: *Her strange behavior was an enigma to everyone.* [Latin *aenigma,* from Greek *ainigma,* from *ainissesthai,* to speak in riddles, hint, from *ainos,* tale, story.]

en·ig·mat·ic (ĕn'ĭg-măt'ĭk) or **en·ig·mat·i·cal** (-ĭ-kəl) *adj.* Of or resembling an enigma; puzzling; mysterious: *an enigmatic smile.* —**en'ig·mat'i·cal·ly** *adv.*

en·join (ĕn-join') *tr.v.* **1.** To direct, order, or impose with authority and emphasis; command: *"The regulations enjoin the attendance of almost the entire ship's company."* (Melville). **2.** To prohibit, esp. by legal action: *The court enjoined him from visiting his children.* —See Syns at **command** and **forbid.** [Middle English *enjoinen,* from Old French *enjoindre,* from Latin *injungere,* to join to, impose : *in-,* in, to + *jungere,* to join.]

en·join·der (ĕn-join'dər) *n.* An authoritative request or injunction: *an enjoinder to cease picketing.*

en·joy (ĕn-joi') *tr.v.* **1.** To experience joy in; receive pleasure from; relish: *enjoy good food.* **2.** To have the use of; benefit from: *enjoy good health.* **3. enjoy oneself.** To have a pleasant time. —See Syns at **like.** [Middle English *enjoien,* from Old French *enjoir* : *en-,* in + *joir,* to rejoice, from Latin *gaudēre.*]

en·joy·a·ble (ĕn-joi'ə-bəl) *adj.* Giving enjoyment. —See Syns at **pleasant.** —**en·joy'a·ble·ness** *n.* —**en·joy'a·bly** *adv.*

en·joy·ment (ĕn-joi'mənt) *n.* **1.** The act or condition of enjoying something. **2.** Pleasure; joy. **3.** The use or possession of something beneficial or pleasurable: *enjoyment of the right to vote.*

en·lace (ĕn-lās') *tr.v.* **-laced, -lac·ing. 1.** To wrap or wind about with or as if with laces; encircle. **2.** To entangle; entwine. —**en·lace'ment** *n.*

en·large (ĕn-lärj') *v.* **-larged, -larg·ing.** —*tr.v.* **1.** To make larger: *enlarge a photograph; enlarge a building.* **2.** To give greater scope to; expand: *enlarge one's mind by reading.* —*intr.v.* **1.** To become larger; grow. **2.** To speak or write at greater length or in greater detail: *enlarge on an idea.* —See Syns at **increase.** [Middle English *enlargen,* from Old French *enlargier* : *en-,* in + *large,* large.] —**en·larg'er** *n.*

en·large·ment (ĕn-lärj'mənt) *n.* **1.** An act of enlarging or the condition of being enlarged. **2.** Something that enlarges: *an enlargement added to the dining room.* **3.** A reproduction or copy larger than the original, esp. a magnified print of a photographic negative.

en·light·en (ĕn-līt'n) *tr.v.* **1.** To give knowledge or insight to; edify; instruct. **2.** To give information to; inform. —**en·light'en·er** *n.*

en·light·en·ment (ĕn-līt'n-mənt) *n.* **1.** An act of enlightening or the condition of being enlightened. **2. the Enlightenment.** A philosophical movement in 18th-cent. Europe, concerned with the critical examination of previously accepted doctrines, beliefs, and institutions from the point of view of rationalism and empirical science.

en·list (ĕn-lĭst') *tr.v.* **1.** To persuade (someone) to enter the armed forces; induct. **2.** To engage the assistance or cooperation of: *enlist the advice of an attorney.* —*intr.v.* **1.** To enter the armed forces voluntarily. **2.** To participate actively in some cause or enterprise. [EN- + LIST (roster).] —**en·list'ment** *n.*

enlisted man. A person in the armed forces who is not a warrant officer or a commissioned officer.

en·liv·en (ĕn-lī'vən) *tr.v.* To make lively or spirited; animate: *enliven a party with music.* —**en·liv'en·ment** *n.*

en masse (ŏn măs'). In a group or body; all together: *marched en masse to city hall.* [French, "in a body."]

en·mesh (ĕn-mĕsh') *tr.v.* To entangle or catch in or as if in a net: *enmeshed in a family quarrel.*

en·mi·ty (ĕn'mĭ-tē) *n., pl.* **-ties.** Deep hatred or hostility, as between enemies or opponents; antagonism. [Middle English *enemite,* from Old French *enemiste,* from Latin *inimīcus,* enemy.]

en·no·ble (ĕn-nō'bəl) *tr.v.* **-bled, -bling. 1.** To invest with nobility or stature; add to the honor of: *a great poet whose humility ennobled him.* **2.** To confer a rank of nobility upon. [Middle English *ennoblen,* from Old French *ennoblir* : *en-,* in + *noble,* noble.] —**en·no'ble·ment** *n.* —**en·no'bler** *n.*

en·nui (ŏn-wē', ŏn'wē) *n.* Listlessness and dissatisfaction resulting from inactivity or lack of interest; boredom. [French, from Old French *enui,* from Latin *in odiō,* "in hate," odious : *in,* in + *odium,* hate.]

e·nor·mi·ty (ĭ-nôr'mĭ-tē) *n., pl.* **-ties. 1.** Extreme wickedness or outrageousness passing all moral bounds: *the enormity of the Nazis' contempt for human life.* **2.** A monstrous offense or evil; an outrage.

e·nor·mous (ĭ-nôr'məs) *adj.* **1.** Of very great size, extent, number, or degree; immense; vast. **2.** *Archaic.* Very wicked; heinous. —See Syns at **giant.** [Middle English *enorme,* from Latin *ēnormis,* unusual, immense : *ex-,* out of + *norma,* pattern, rule.] —**e·nor'mous·ly** *adv.* —**e·nor'mous·ness** *n.*

e·nough (ĭ-nŭf') *adj.* Sufficient to meet a need or satisfy a desire; adequate: *not enough time; enough room for all.* —*n.* An adequate quantity: *He ate enough for two.* —*adv.* **1.** To a satisfactory amount or degree; sufficiently: *Are you warm enough?* **2.** Very; fully; quite: *glad enough to leave.* **3.** Tolerably; rather: *She sang well enough.* [Middle English *inough,* from Old English *genōg.*]

e·now (ĭ-nou') *adj. & adv. Archaic.* Enough.

en pas·sant (än' pä-sän'). **1.** *French.* In passing; by the way; incidentally. **2.** *Chess.* The capture of a pawn that has made an initial move of two squares by an opponent's pawn that occupies the adjacent square on the forward diagonal to the square that is crossed.

en·quire (ĕn-kwīr') *v.* Var. of **inquire.**

en·rage (ĕn-rāj') *tr.v.* **-raged, -rag·ing.** To put in a rage; infuriate; anger.

en·rapt (ĕn-răpt') *adj.* Enraptured; enthralled. [EN- + RAPT.]

en·rap·ture (ĕn-răp'chər) *tr.v.* **-tured, -tur·ing.** To fill with rapture or delight; captivate; enchant.

en·rich (ĕn-rĭch') *tr.v.* **1.** To make rich or richer: *enriched himself at the expense of his employees.* **2.** To make fuller, more meaningful, or more rewarding: *Foreign words have enriched the English language.* **3.** To add fertilizer to (soil) to increase its productivity. **4.** To add nutrients to (foodstuffs) during processing. **5.** To add to the beauty or character of; embellish; adorn: *enriched the walls with carved moldings.* **6.** *Physics.* To increase the ratio of radioactive isotopes in. [Middle English *enrichen,* from Old French *enricher* : *en-* (causative) + *riche,* rich.] —**en·rich'er** *n.* —**en·rich'ment** *n.*

en·roll or **en·rol** (ĕn-rōl') *v.* **-rolled, -roll·ing.** —*tr.v.* To enter the name of in a register, record, or roll. —*intr.v.* To place one's name on a roll or register: *enroll in college.* [Middle English *enrollen,* from Old French *enroller* : *en-,* in + *rolle,* roll.]

en·roll·ment or **en·rol·ment** (ĕn-rōl'mənt) *n.* **1.** The act of enrolling or the condition of being enrolled. **2.** The number of people enrolled.

en route (ŏn rōōt', ĕn). On the route; on or along the way: *stopped to eat en route.* [French, "on the way."]

en·sconce (ĕn-skŏns') *tr.v.* **-sconced, -sconc·ing. 1.** To settle securely or comfortably: *She ensconced herself in the armchair.* **2.** To place or conceal in a secure place: *ensconced the family heirlooms in the basement cupboard.* [EN- + SCONCE.]

en·sem·ble (ŏn-sŏm'bəl) *n.* **1.** A unit or group of complementary parts that contribute to a single effect. **2.** A complete outfit of coordinated clothing: *A hat was the final piece for her new ensemble.* **3.** A group of musicians, singers, dancers, or actors who perform together. **4.** The quality of performance by a group of actors or musicians, esp. in regard to the achievement of unity of style and technique. [French, "together," from Latin *insimul,* at the same time : *in-,* in + *simul,* at the same time.]

en·shrine (ĕn-shrīn') *tr.v.* **-shrined, -shrin·ing. 1.** To enclose in or as if in a shrine. **2.** To cherish as sacred: *His name is enshrined in our hearts.* —**en·shrine'ment** *n.*

en·shroud (ĕn-shroud') *tr.v.* To cover with or as if with a shroud. —See Syns at **wrap.**

en·sign (ĕn'sən) *n.* **1.** (*also* ĕn'sīn'). **a.** A national flag or banner, often with a special insignia, displayed on ships and aircraft. **b.** Any flag or banner, as of a military unit. **2.** (*also* ĕn'sīn'). A standard-bearer. **3.** A commissioned officer of the lowest rank in the U.S. Navy, ranking below a lieutenant. **4.** (*also* ĕn'sīn'). A badge or emblem of rank. [Middle English *ensigne*, from Old French *enseigne*, from Latin *insignia*, insignia.]

en·si·lage (ĕn'sə-lĭj) *n.* **1.** The process of storing and preserving green fodder in a silo. **2.** Fodder preserved in this manner; silage.

en·sile (ĕn-sīl') *tr.v.* **-siled, -sil·ing.** To store (fodder) in a silo for preservation. [French *ensiler* : *en-*, in + *silo*, silo, from Old Spanish.]

en·slave (ĕn-slāv') *tr.v.* **-slaved, -slav·ing.** To make a slave of; reduce to slavery, bondage, or dependence. **—en·slave'ment** *n.* **—en·slav'er** *n.*

en·snare (ĕn-snâr') *tr.v.* **-snared, -snar·ing.** Also **in·snare** (ĭn-). To catch in or as if in a snare.

en·sue (ĕn-sōō') *intr.v.* **-sued, -su·ing.** **1.** To take place subsequently; follow: *The popularity of the group's first album guaranteed an audience for records that ensued.* **2.** To follow as a consequence; to result: *Angry words were exchanged, and a fight ensued.* [Middle English *ensuen*, from Old French *ensuivre*, from Latin *insequī* : *in-*, in, onward + *sequī*, to follow.]

en·sure (ĕn-shōōr') *tr.v.* **-sured, -sur·ing.** To make sure or certain of; insure: *measures taken to ensure compliance.*
Usage: ensure, insure. These verbs mean to make secure or certain, and they may be applied to the act of making something certain: *Success is ensured* (or *insured*). *Ensure* and *insure* also mean to make secure from harm: *ensure* (or *insure*) *a country against invasion.* In American usage, only *insure* is now in wide use in the sense of guaranteeing life or property against risk.

-ent. **1.** A suffix meaning having a specified quality: **effervescent.** **2.** A suffix used to form nouns of agency: **referent.** [Middle English, from Old French, from Latin *-ens.*]

en·tab·la·ture (ĕn-tăb'lə-chŏŏr', -chər) *n.* In Greek and Roman architecture, the upper section of a structure, resting on the capital and including the architrave, frieze, and cornice. [Obs. French, from Italian *intavolatura*, from *intavolare*, to put on the table : *in-*, in + *tavola*, table, from Latin *tabula.*]

en·tail (ĕn-tāl') *tr.v.* **1.** To have as a necessary consequence; involve: *a project entailing great expense.* **2.** To limit the inheritance of (property) to a specified, unalterable succession of heirs. **—n.** (ĕn'tāl', ĕn-tāl'). **1.** The act of entailing or the condition of being entailed. **2.** An entailed estate. **3.** A specified order of succession, as to an estate. [Middle English *entaillen, entailen* : *en-*, in + *taille*, limitation, from Old French, division, from *taillier*, to cut.] **—en·tail'ment** *n.*

en·tan·gle (ĕn-tăng'gəl) *tr.v.* **-gled, -gling.** **1.** To make tangled; snarl: *entangled a kite in the tree.* **2.** To involve, as in something complicated or difficult: *entangled in legal disputes.* **—en·tan'gle·ment** *n.*

en·tente (ŏn-tŏnt') *n.* **1.** An agreement, usu. broad and unformalized, between two or more governments or powers for cooperative action or policy. **2.** The parties to an entente. [French, "understanding," from Old French *entendre*, to understand, intend.]

en·ter (ĕn'tər) *tr.v.* **1.** To come or go into: *enter a building.* **2.** To penetrate; pierce: *The bullet entered her lung.* **3.** To begin; embark upon: *Our work is now entering a new phase.* **4.** To become a member of or participant in: *a country entering the United Nations.* **5.** To take up; make a beginning in: *enter a profession.* **6.** To register or enroll in: *enter college.* **7.** To inscribe; record: *Enter the total amount in the box below.* **8.** To submit formally for consideration: *enter a protest.* **9.** *Law.* To place formally before a court or on the record: *enter a plea.* **—intr.v.** **1.** To come or go in, esp. to make an entry on stage. **2.** To gain entry; penetrate: *The bullet entered below his thigh.* **—phrasal verb. enter into.** **1.** To take part in: *enter into a conversation.* **2.** To be a component or part of: *factors entering into a decision.* **3.** To consider; delve into: *The police entered into the details of the crime.* **4.** To become party to (a contract). [Middle English *entren*, from Old French *entrer*, from Latin *intrāre*, from *intrā*, within.]

enter-. Var. of *entero-.*

en·ter·ic (ĕn-tĕr'ĭk) *adj.* Of or within the intestine. [Greek *enterikos*, from *enteron*, intestine.]

en·ter·i·tis (ĕn'tə-rī'tĭs) *n.* Inflammation of the intestinal tract. [ENTER(O)- + -ITIS.]

entero- or **enter-.** A prefix meaning intestine: **enteritis.** [From Greek *enteron*, intestine.]

en·ter·on (ĕn'tə-rŏn') *n.* The intestine. [Greek, intestine, entrails.]

en·ter·prise (ĕn'tər-prīz') *n.* **1. a.** An undertaking or venture, esp. one of great scope, complexity, and risk. **b.** Readiness to participate in such an undertaking; boldness; initiative. **2.** A business organization. [Middle English, from Old French *entreprise*, from *entreprendre*, to undertake : *entre-*, between, from Latin *inter-* + *prendre*, to take, from Latin *prehendere.*]

en·ter·pris·ing (ĕn'tər-prī'zĭng) *adj.* Showing imagination, initiative, and readiness to undertake challenging or risky projects.

en·ter·tain (ĕn'tər-tān') *tr.v.* **1.** To hold the attention of; amuse. **2.** To have as a guest; extend hospitality to: *entertain friends at dinner.* **3.** To contemplate; consider: *entertain an idea; entertain an offer.* **4.** To hold in mind; to harbor: *I entertain few illusions.* **—intr.v.** **1.** To have guests, as for dinner or a party: *We rarely entertain.* **2.** To provide entertainment. **—See Syns at amuse.** [Middle English *entertinen*, to maintain, from Old French *entretenir* : Latin *inter-*, between + *tenēre*, to hold.]

en·ter·tain·er (ĕn'tər-tā'nər) *n.* A person, such as a singer or dancer, who performs for an audience.

en·ter·tain·ing (ĕn'tər-tā'nĭng) *adj.* Amusing; agreeably diverting. **—en'ter·tain'ing·ly** *adv.*

en·ter·tain·ment (ĕn'tər-tān'mənt) *n.* **1.** The act of entertaining. **2.** The art, field, or profession of entertaining. **3.** Something that entertains, as a performance or show. **4.** The pleasure afforded by being entertained; amusement. **—See Syns at recreation.**

en·thrall or **en·thral** (ĕn-thrôl') *tr.v.* **-thralled, thrall·ing.** **1.** To hold spellbound; captivate; charm: *The music enthralled me.* **2.** To enslave. **—See Syns at charm.** **—en·thrall'ment** *n.*

en·throne (ĕn-thrōn') *tr.v.* **-throned, -thron·ing.** **1. a.** To invest with sovereign power. **b.** To invest with the authority of high office. **2.** To raise to a lofty position; revere. **—en·throne'ment** *n.*

en·thuse (ĕn-thōōz') *v.* **-thused, -thus·ing.** *Informal.* **—tr.v.** To make enthusiastic. **—intr.v.** To show enthusiasm. [Back-formation from ENTHUSIASM.]
Usage: enthuse. This verb, a back-formation from *enthusiasm*, is informal: *She enthused* (showed enthusiasm) *over the rise in membership. She was even more enthused* (made more enthusiastic) *by the caliber of the newcomers.* More acceptable wordings are indicated within the parentheses.

en·thu·si·asm (ĕn-thōō'zē-ăz'əm) *n.* **1.** Great or fervent interest or excitement. **2.** A subject or activity that inspires a lively interest. **—See Syns at passion.** [Late Latin *enthūsiasmus*, from Greek *enthousiasmos*, inspiration, from *enthous, entheos*, possessed by a god : *en-*, in + *theos*, god.]

en·thu·si·ast (ĕn-thōō'zē-ăst') *n.* A person with a keen interest in a particular hobby or activity.

en·thu·si·as·tic (ĕn-thōō'zē-ăs'tĭk) *adj.* Having or showing enthusiasm; eager; ardent. **—en·thu'si·as'ti·cal·ly** *adv.*

en·tice (ĕn-tīs') *tr.v.* **-ticed, -tic·ing.** To attract by arousing hope or desire; lure. [Middle English *enticen*, from Old French *enticier* : Latin *in-*, in + *tītiō*, firebrand.] **—en·tice'ment** *n.* **—en·tic'er** *n.* **—en·tic'ing·ly** *adv.*

en·tire (ĕn-tīr') *adj.* **1.** Having no part missing or excepted; whole: *an entire set of the encyclopedia; the entire country.* **2.** Without reservation or limitation; total; complete: *my entire approval; his entire attention.* **3.** All in one piece; unbroken; intact. **4.** *Bot.* Not indented or toothed, as the edge of a leaf. **—See Syns at whole.** [Middle English *entier*, from Old French, from Latin *integer*, intact.]

en·tire·ly (ĕn-tīr'lē) *adv.* **1.** Without exception; wholly; completely: *entirely satisfied.* **2.** Solely or exclusively: *entirely my fault.*

en·tire·ty (ĕn-tīr'tē) *n.*, *pl.* **-ties.** **1.** The condition of being entire; completeness: *a film shown in its entirety.* **2.** Something that is entire; a whole.

en·ti·tle (ĕn-tīt'l) *tr.v.* **-tled, -tling.** **1.** To give a name or title to; designate: *entitle a book.* **2.** To give (a person) a right or privilege: *This coupon entitles you to a discount.* [Middle English *entitlen*, from Old French *entiteler*, from Late

ă pat ā pay â care ä father ĕ pet ē be hw which
ŏŏ took ōō boot ou out th thin th this ŭ cut
ĭ pit ī tie î pier ŏ pot ō toe ô paw, for oi noise
û urge zh vision ə about, item, edible, gallop, circus

Latin *intitulāre* : *in-*, in + *titulus*, title.] —**en·ti′tle·ment** *n.*

en·ti·ty (ĕn′tĭ-tē) *n.*, *pl.* -**ties.** **1.** The fact of existence; being. **2.** Something that exists independently and may be distinguished from other things. [Medieval Latin *entitās*, from Latin *ēns*, pres. part of *esse*, to be.]

en·to·blast (ĕn′tə-blăst′) *n.* Var. of **endoblast.**

en·tomb (ĕn-tōōm′) *tr.v.* **1.** To place in or as if in a tomb; bury. **2.** To serve as a tomb for. [Middle English *entoumben*, from Old French *entomber* : *en-*, in + *tombe*, tomb, from Late Latin *tumba*.] —**en·tomb′ment** *n.*

entomo-. A prefix meaning insect: *entomology*. [From Greek *entomon*, insect, from *entemnein*, to cut up : *en-*, in + *temnein*, to cut.]

en·to·mol·o·gy (ĕn′tə-mŏl′ə-jē) *n.* The scientific study of insects. —**en′to·mo·log′ic** (-mə-lŏj′ĭk) or **en′to·mo·log′i·cal** *adj.* —**en′to·mo·log′i·cal·ly** *adv.* —**en′to·mol′o·gist** *n.*

en·tou·rage (ŏn′tōō-räzh′) *n.* A group of attendants, followers, or associates who accompany an important or influential person; retinue. [French, from *entourer*, to surround, from Old French *entour*, surroundings : *en-*, in + *tour*, circuit.]

en·tr′acte (ŏn′trăkt′, än-trăkt′) *n.* **1.** The interval between two acts of a theatrical performance. **2.** An entertainment provided during this interval. [French : *entr(e)-*, between + *acte*, act.]

en·trails (ĕn′trālz′, -trəlz) *pl.n.* The internal organs, esp. the intestines; viscera. [Middle English *entrailles*, from Old French, from Medieval Latin *intrālia*, from Latin *interāneus*, internal, from *inter*, within.]

en·train (ĕn-trān′) *tr.v.* To put on a train. —*intr.v.* To board a train.

en·trance[1] (ĕn′trəns) *n.* **1.** The act or an instance of entering: *an actor's entrance on stage; a candidate's entrance into politics.* **2.** Any place or means that affords entry. **3.** The permission or right to enter; admission. [Middle English *entraunce*, from Old French *entrance*, from *entrer*, to enter.]

en·trance[2] (ĕn-trăns′) *tr.v.* -**tranced,** -**tranc·ing.** **1.** To put into a trance. **2.** To fill with delight, wonder, or enchantment; fascinate: *a child entranced by his own reflection.* —See Syns at **charm.** —**en·trance′ment** *n.* —**en·tranc′ing·ly** *adv.*

en·trant (ĕn′trənt) *n.* **1.** A person who enters a competition. **2.** A new member, as of a profession or organization. [French, from *entrer*, to enter.]

en·trap (ĕn-trăp′) *tr.v.* -**trapped,** -**trap·ping.** **1.** To catch in or as if in a trap. **2.** To lure into danger, difficulty, or self-incrimination by deceptive means. —**en·trap′ment** *n.*

en·treat (ĕn-trēt′) *tr.v.* To ask earnestly; beseech; implore; beg. —*intr.v.* To make an earnest request; plead. [Middle English *entreten*, to plead with, from Old French *entraitier* : *en-*, in + *traitier*, *traiter*, to treat.] —**en·treat′ing·ly** *adv.* —**en·treat′ment** *n.*

en·treat·y (ĕn-trē′tē) *n.*, *pl.* -**ies.** An earnest request or petition; a plea.

en·trée or **en·tree** (ŏn′trā′, ŏn-trā′) *n.* **1.** The power, right, or liberty to enter; admittance. **2. a.** The main course of a meal. **b.** A dish served in formal dining immediately before the main course or between any two principal courses. [French, from Old French *entree*, entry.]

en·trench (ĕn-trĕnch′) *v.* Also **in·trench** (ĭn-). —*tr.v.* **1.** To place in a trench, esp. in order to fortify or defend. **2.** To implant or establish firmly: *ideas entrenched in his mind.* —*intr.v.* **1.** To dig or occupy a trench or trenches. **2.** To encroach, infringe, or trespass: *She's entrenching on my privileges.*

en·trench·ment (ĕn-trĕnch′mənt) *n.* Also **in·trench·ment** (ĭn-). **1.** The act of entrenching or the condition of being entrenched. **2.** A system of trenches and mounds used for defense.

en·tre nous (ŏn′trə nōō′). Between ourselves; confidentially. [French, "between ourselves."]

en·tre·pre·neur (ŏn′trə-prə-nûr′) *n.* A person who organizes, operates, and assumes the risk of a business venture. [French, from Old French, from *entreprendre*, to undertake.]

en·tro·py (ĕn′trə-pē) *n.* The gradual reduction by stages of energy and matter to a final uniform condition of chemical inactivity. [German *Entropie* : Greek *en-*, in + *tropē*, a turning, change.]

en·trust (ĕn-trŭst′) *tr.v.* Also **in·trust** (ĭn-). **1.** To turn over (something) for safekeeping, care, or action: *entrust a sale to a broker.* **2.** To charge (someone) with a task or responsibility involving trust: *entrusted him with a difficult assignment.*

en·try (ĕn′trē) *n.*, *pl.* -**tries. 1.** The act or right of entering. **2.** A place that affords entrance. **3. a.** The inclusion of an item in a diary, register, list, or other record. **b.** An item thus entered. **4. a.** A word, term, or phrase entered or defined in a dictionary. **b.** Such an entry along with the text related to it. **5.** Someone or something entered in a race or contest. [Middle English *entre*, from Old French *entree*, from Latin *intrāre*, to enter.]

en·twine (ĕn-twīn′) *v.* -**twined,** -**twin·ing.** —*tr.v.* To twine or twist around or about. —*intr.v.* To twine or twist together.

e·nu·mer·ate (ĭ-nōō′mə-rāt′, ĭ-nyōō′-) *tr.v.* -**at·ed,** -**at·ing. 1.** To count off or name one by one; to list. **2.** To determine the number of; to count. [From Latin *ēnumerāre*, to count out : *ex-*, out + *numerus*, number.] —**e·nu′mer·a′tion** *n.* —**e·nu′mer·a′tor** *n.*

e·nun·ci·ate (ĭ-nŭn′sē-āt′, -shē-) *v.* -**at·ed,** -**at·ing.** —*tr.v.* **1.** To pronounce, esp. with clarity or in a particular manner: *She does not enunciate words clearly.* **2.** To state or set forth thoroughly or systematically: *enunciate the details of a proposal.* **3.** To announce; proclaim: *enunciated his goal.* —*intr.v.* To pronounce words or sounds, esp. with clarity or in a particular manner. [From Latin *ēnuntiāre* : *ex-*, out + *nuntiāre*, to announce, from *nuntius*, message, messenger.] —**e·nun′ci·a·ble** (-ə-bəl) *adj.* —**e·nun′ci·a′tion** *n.* —**e·nun′ci·a′tor** *n.*

en·vel·op (ĕn-vĕl′əp) *tr.v.* To cover with or as if with a garment or other material. —See Syns at **wrap.** [Middle English *enveloupen*, from Old French *enveloper* : *en-*, in + *veloper*, to wrap up.] —**en·vel′op·ment** *n.*

en·ve·lope (ĕn′və-lōp′, ŏn′-) *n.* **1.** Something that envelops, as a cover or wrapping. **2.** A flat, folded paper container, used esp. for mailing letters. **3.** The bag containing the gas in a balloon. [French *enveloppe*, from Old French *envelope*, from *enveloper*, to envelop.]

en·ven·om (ĕn-vĕn′əm) *tr.v.* **1.** To put venom into or on; make poisonous. **2.** To fill with hate; embitter.

en·vi·a·ble (ĕn′vē-ə-bəl) *adj.* Arousing strong envy; highly desirable. —**en′vi·a·bly** *adv.*

en·vi·ous (ĕn′vē-əs) *adj.* Feeling, expressing, or marked by envy. —**en′vi·ous·ly** *adv.* —**en′vi·ous·ness** *n.*

en·vi·ron·ment (ĕn-vī′rən-mənt) *n.* **1.** Something that surrounds; surroundings. **2.** The combination of external physical conditions that affect and influence the growth and development of organisms. **3.** The social and cultural conditions that affect the nature of an individual or community. —**en·vi′ron·men′tal** (-mĕn′tl) *adj.* —**en·vi′ron·men′tal·ly** *adv.*

en·vi·ron·men·tal·ist (ĕn-vī′rən-mĕn′tl-ĭst) *n.* A person who seeks to protect the natural environment. —**en·vi′ron·men′tal·ism** *n.*

en·vi·rons (ĕn-vī′rənz) *pl.n.* The surrounding areas, esp. of a city; outskirts. [From Middle English *environen*, to surround, from Old French *environer* : *en-*, in + *viron*, circle, from *virer*, to turn.]

en·vis·age (ĕn-vĭz′ĭj) *tr.v.* -**aged,** -**ag·ing.** To picture in the mind, esp. as a future possibility; conceive; visualize. [French *envisager* : Old French *en-*, in + *visage*, face, visage.]

en·vi·sion (ĕn-vĭzh′ən) *tr.v.* To picture in the mind; foresee or imagine.

en·voi (ĕn′voi′, ŏn′-) *n.* Also **en·voy.** A short concluding stanza of certain verse forms, often serving as a dedication or summary. [Middle English *envoie*, from Old French *envoy*, from *envoier*, to send.]

en·voy[1] (ĕn′voi′, ŏn′-) *n.* **1. a.** A diplomat assigned to a foreign embassy, ranking next below the ambassador. **b.** A government representative sent on a special diplomatic mission. **2.** A messenger or other agent sent on a mission. [From French *envoyé*, one who is sent, from *envoyer*, to send, from Old French *envoier*, from Late Latin *inviāre*, to put on the way : Latin *in-*, in + *via*, way.]

en·voy² (ĕn'voi', ŏn'-) *n.* Var. of **envoi.**

en·vy (ĕn'vē) *n., pl.* **-vies. 1.** A feeling of discontent and resentment aroused by the contemplation of another's desirable possessions, achievements, or qualities, with a strong desire to have them for oneself. **2.** The object of such a feeling. —*tr.v.* **-vied, -vy·ing.** To feel envy toward or because of: *Everyone envies her. I envy his success.* [Middle English *envie,* from Old French, from Latin *invidia,* from *invidēre,* to look at with malice : *in-,* in, upon + *vidēre,* to see.] —**en'vi·er** *n.* —**en'vy·ing·ly** *adv.*

en·wrap (ĕn-răp') *tr.v.* **-wrapped, -wrap·ping.** To wrap up; enclose; enfold.

en·wreathe (ĕn-rēth') *tr.v.* **-wreathed, -wreath·ing.** To enclose or surround with or as if with a wreath.

en·zo·ot·ic (ĕn'zō-ŏt'ĭk) *adj.* Of a disease affecting or peculiar to animals of a specific area or limited district. —*n.* An enzootic disease. [EN- (within) + ZO(O)- + -OTIC.]

en·zyme (ĕn'zīm') *n.* Any of numerous proteins that are produced in the cells of living organisms and function as catalysts in the chemical processes of those organisms. [German *Enzym,* from Greek *enzumos,* leavened : *en-,* in + *zumē,* leaven.] —**en'zy·mat'ic** (ĕn'zə-măt'ĭk) *adj.*

eo-. A prefix meaning: **1.** An early period of time: **Eocene. 2.** An early form or representative: **eohippus.** [Greek *ēō-,* from *ēōs,* dawn.]

E·o·cene (ē'ə-sēn') *n.* Also **Eocene epoch.** The second oldest of the five major geologic epochs of the Cenozoic era or Tertiary period, extending from the end of the Paleocene to the beginning of the Oligocene and characterized by the rise of mammals. —*modifier:* an *Eocene fossil.*

e·o·hip·pus (ē'ō-hĭp'əs) *n.* A small, extinct mammal of the genus *Hyracotherium* (or *Eohippus*), of the Eocene epoch, an early ancestor of the horse, with four-toed front feet and three-toed hind feet. [EO- + Greek *hippos,* horse.]

e·o·li·an (ē-ō'lē-ən) *adj.* Pertaining to, caused by, or carried by the wind. [After *Aeolus,* god of the winds.]

e·o·lith (ē'ə-lĭth') *n.* Any of the stone artifacts dating from the Eolithic era, alleged to have been used as a tool by early man.

E·o·lith·ic (ē'ə-lĭth'ĭk) *n. Anthropol.* The era considered to be the earliest period of human culture preceding the Paleolithic; the earliest part of the Stone Age. —*modifier:* an *Eolithic flint.*

e·on (ē'ŏn', ē'ən) *n.* **1.** An indefinitely long period of time; an age; eternity. **2.** *Geol.* The longest division of geologic time, containing two or more eras. [Late Latin *aeōn,* age, from Greek *aiōn.*]

E·os (ē'ŏs') *n. Gk. Myth.* The goddess of the dawn, identified with the Roman goddess Aurora.

e·o·sin (ē'ĭ-sən) *n.* A red crystalline powder used esp. in textile dyeing. [Greek *ēōs,* dawn + -IN (from its color).]

-eous. A suffix meaning like or resembling: **beauteous.** [Latin *-eus.*]

ep-. Var. of **epi-.**

ep·au·let or **ep·au·lette** (ĕp'ə-lĕt', ĕp'ə-lĕt') *n.* A shoulder ornament, esp. on certain military dress uniforms. [French *épaulette,* dim. of *épaule,* shoulder, from Old French *espaule,* from Latin *spatula.*]

epaulet

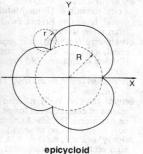

epicycloid

é·pée or **e·pee** (ā-pā') *n.* A fencing sword with a bowl-shaped guard and a long, narrow blade that has no cutting edge and tapers to a blunt point. [French, from Latin *spatha,* sword, blade.]

e·phed·rine (ĭ-fĕd'rĭn, ĕf'ĭ-drēn') *n.* A white, odorless, powdered or crystalline alkaloid, $C_{10}H_{15}NO$, extracted from a certain shrub or made synthetically, used as a drug to treat allergies and asthma and as a vasoconstrictor. [From Latin *ephedra,* horsetail, from Greek *ephedros,* sitting upon : *epi,* upon + *hedra,* seat.]

e·phem·er·al (ĭ-fĕm'ər-əl) *adj.* **1.** Lasting for a brief time; short-lived. **2.** Living or lasting only one day, as certain flowers or adult insects. [Greek *ephēmeros* : *epi,* on + *hēmera,* day.] —**e·phem'er·al·ly** *adv.*

e·phem·er·id (ĭ-fĕm'ər-ĭd) *n.* An insect of the order Ephemeroptera, which includes the mayflies.

e·phem·er·is (ĭ-fĕm'ər-ĭs) *n., pl.* **eph·e·mer·i·des** (ĕf'ə-mĕr'ĭ-dēz'). A table giving the predicted positions of one or more celestial bodies at a number of specific times during a given period. [Late Latin *ephēmeris,* diary, from Greek, from *ephēmeros,* ephemeral.]

eph·or (ĕf'ôr', -ər) *n., pl.* **-ors** or **-o·ri** (-ə-rī'). One of a body of five elected magistrates in ancient Sparta with supervisory power over the king. [Latin *ephorus,* from Greek *ephoros,* from *ephoran,* to oversee : *epi,* over + *horan,* to see.]

epi- or **ep-.** A prefix meaning: **1.** On; upon: **epiphyte. 2.** Over; above: **epicenter. 3.** Around; covering: **epicanthic fold. 4.** To, toward, or near: **epicalyx. 5.** Besides; in addition: **epoxy. 6.** Among: **epizootic.** [Greek *epi-,* from *epi,* upon, over, at, after.]

ep·ic (ĕp'ĭk) *n.* **1.** A long narrative poem, such as *Beowulf* or the *Iliad,* that celebrates the deeds and achievements of a historical or legendary hero or episodes of a people's heroic tradition. **2.** A literary or dramatic work that imitates or suggests the characteristics of epic poetry. **3.** A tradition, movement, or series of historical events similar to an epic in subject, grandeur, and scope: *the epic of the Old West.* —*adj.* **1.** Of or resembling an epic: *an epic poem.* **2.** Resembling an epic in subject, grandeur, or scope; heroic: *an epic achievement; an epic journey.* [Latin *epicus,* from Greek *epikos,* from *epos,* song, word.]

ep·i·ca·lyx (ĕp'ĭ-kā'lĭks, -kăl'ĭks) *n., pl.* **-lyx·es** or **-ca·ly·ces** (-kā'lĭ-sēz', -kăl'ĭ-sēz'). *Bot.* A set of bracts close to and resembling a calyx. [EPI- + CALYX.]

ep·i·can·thic fold (ĕp'ĭ-kăn'thĭk). A fold of skin on the upper eyelid that tends to cover the inner corner of the eye, characteristic of many Mongolian peoples. [EPI- + Greek *kanthos,* corner of the eye.]

ep·i·carp (ĕp'ĭ-kärp') *n. Bot.* An exocarp.

ep·i·cen·ter (ĕp'ĭ-sĕn'tər) *n.* **1.** The part of the earth's surface directly above the point where an earthquake begins. **2.** A focal point.

ep·i·cot·yl (ĕp'ĭ-kŏt'l) *n. Bot.* The part of the stem of a seedling or plant embryo that is above the cotyledons. [EPI- + COTYL(EDON).]

ep·i·cure (ĕp'ĭ-kyoor') *n.* **1.** A person with refined taste in food and wine. **2.** *Archaic.* A person devoted to sensuous pleasure. [After *Epicurus* (342?–270 B.C.), Greek philosopher, who considered pleasure (defined as freedom from pain) to be the highest good.]

ep·i·cu·re·an (ĕp'ĭ-kyoo-rē'ən) *adj.* **1.** Devoted to the pursuit of sensuous pleasure and luxury; hedonistic. **2.** Suited to the tastes of an epicure: *an epicurean meal.* —*n.* **1.** A follower of Epicurus. **2.** An epicure.

ep·i·cy·cle (ĕp'ĭ-sī'kəl) *n.* In the Ptolemaic system, a small circle the center of which moves on the circumference of a larger circle at whose center is the earth, and the circumference of which describes the orbit of one of the planets around the earth. [Middle English *epicicle,* from Late Latin *epicyclus,* from Greek *epikuklos* : *epi-,* on + *kuklos,* circle, cycle.]

ep·i·cy·cloid (ĕp'ĭ-sī'kloid') *n.* The curve described by a point fixed on the circumference of a circle as it rolls on the outside of the circumference of a fixed circle.

ep·i·dem·ic (ĕp'ĭ-dĕm'ĭk) *adj.* Also **ep·i·dem·i·cal** (-ĭ-kəl). Spreading rapidly and widely among the inhabitants of an area: *an epidemic disease.* —*n.* **1.** A contagious disease that spreads rapidly: *an influenza epidemic.* **2.** A temporary, widespread popularity, as of a fashion or a fad. **3.** A rapid spread or development: *an epidemic of violence in the cities.* [French *épidémique,* from *épidémie,* from Old French *espydymie,* from Late Latin *epidēmia,* from Greek epidēmia (nosos), "(illness) prevalent among people" : epi-, among + dēmos, people.]

ep·i·de·mi·ol·o·gy (ĕp′ĭ-dē′mē-ŏl′ə-jē, -dĕm′ē-) n. The study of epidemics and epidemic diseases. —**ep′i·de′mi·o·log′ic** (-ə-lŏj′ĭk) or **ep′i·de′mi·o·log′i·cal** adj. —**ep′i·de′mi·ol′·o·gist** n.

ep·i·der·mis (ĕp′ĭ-dûr′mĭs) n. **1.** Anat. The outer protective layer of the skin, having neither blood vessels nor nerves. **2.** Bot. The outermost layer of cells or protective covering of a plant or plant part. [Late Latin, from Greek : epi-, over + derma, skin.] —**ep′i·der′mal** adj.

ep·i·glot·tis (ĕp′ĭ-glŏt′ĭs) n., pl. **-tis·es** or **-glot·ti·des** (-glŏt′-ĭ-dēz′). An elastic flap of cartilage located at the base of the tongue that folds over the glottis to prevent food from entering the windpipe during swallowing.

ep·i·gram (ĕp′ĭ-grăm′) n. **1.** A short, witty poem expressing a single thought. **2.** A concisely and cleverly worded statement making a pointed observation and often concluding with a satirical twist. [Old French epigramme, from Latin epigramma, from Greek, inscription, from epigraphein, to write on : epi-, on + graphein, to write.] —**ep′i·gram′ma·tist** n.

ep·i·gram·mat·ic (ĕp′ĭ-grə-măt′ĭk) adj. **1.** Of, relating to, or like an epigram. **2.** Full of or using epigrams; terse; witty. —**ep′i·gram·mat′i·cal·ly** adv.

ep·i·graph (ĕp′ĭ-grăf′) n. **1.** An inscription, as on a statue or building. **2.** A quotation at the beginning of a book or chapter. [Greek epigraphē, from epigraphos, written on, from epigraphein, to write on.]

e·pig·ra·phy (ĭ-pĭg′rə-fē) n. **1.** Inscriptions in general. **2.** The study of inscriptions, esp. the deciphering and interpretation of ancient inscriptions. —**e·pig′ra·pher** or **e·pig′·ra·phist** n.

e·pig·y·nous (ĭ-pĭj′ə-nəs) adj. Bot. Having floral parts or organs attached to or near the top of the ovary. [EPI- + -GYNOUS.]

ep·i·lep·sy (ĕp′ə-lĕp′sē) n. A disorder of the nervous system in which there are recurring seizures marked by disturbances of consciousness or convulsions or both. [Old French epilepsie, from Late Latin epilēpsia, from Greek, from epilambanein, to take besides, seize upon : epi-, besides, in addition to + lambanein, to take hold of.]

ep·i·lep·tic (ĕp′ə-lĕp′tĭk) adj. Of, pertaining to, or suffering from epilepsy. —n. A person who has epilepsy.

ep·i·logue or **ep·i·log** (ĕp′ə-lôg′, -lŏg′) n. **1.** A short poem or speech spoken directly to the audience following the conclusion of a play. **2.** A short section at the end of any literary work, often dealing with the future of its characters. [Middle English epiloge, from Old French epilogue, from Latin epilogus, from Greek epilogos : epi-, in addition + legein, to say.]

ep·i·neph·rine (ĕp′ə-nĕf′rēn′, -rĭn) or **ep·i·neph·rin** (-rĭn) n. An adrenal hormone that constricts blood vessels and raises blood pressure. Also called **adrenaline**. [EPI- + NEPHR(O)- + -INE.]

e·piph·a·ny (ĭ-pĭf′ə-nē) n., pl. **-nies**. **1.** A manifestation or appearance of a divine being. **2. Epiphany.** A Christian festival occurring on January 6 and celebrating the visit of the Magi to the Christ child, the first revelation of Christ to the Gentiles. **3.** A sudden flash of recognition or understanding of the meaning or essence of something. [Greek epiphaneia, appearance, from epiphanēs, appearing, manifest : epi-, to + phainein, to show.]

ep·i·phyte (ĕp′ə-fīt′) n. A plant, as Spanish moss, that grows on another plant or object that provides support but not nourishment. [EPI- + -PHYTE.] —**ep′i·phyt′ic** (-fĭt′ĭk) adj.

e·pis·co·pa·cy (ĭ-pĭs′kə-pə-sē) n., pl. **-cies**. **1.** The government of a church by bishops. **2.** An episcopate.

e·pis·co·pal (ĭ-pĭs′kə-pəl) adj. **1.** Of or pertaining to a bishop or bishops. **2.** Governed by bishops. **3. Episcopal.** Of or pertaining to the Anglican Church or the Protestant Episcopal Church. [Middle English, from Old French, from Late Latin episcopālis, from episcopus, bishop, from Greek episkopos, overseer : epi-, over + skopos, watcher.]

E·pis·co·pa·li·an (ĭ-pĭs′kə-pālē-ən, -pāl′yən) n. A member of the Protestant Episcopal Church. —adj. Of, pertaining to, or belonging to the Protestant Episcopal Church. —**E·pis′co·pa′li·an·ism** n.

e·pis·co·pate (ĭ-pĭs′kə-pĭt, -pāt′) n. **1.** The rank, position, or term of office of a bishop. **2.** The area of jurisdiction of a bishop. **3.** Bishops in general.

ep·i·sode (ĕp′ĭ-sōd′) n. **1.** An incident or series of related events in the course of a continuous experience: an episode from her childhood. **2.** An incident that forms a distinct part of a story. **3.** An installment in a serialized novel, play, or radio or television program. **4.** Mus. A passage between statements of a main subject or theme. [Greek epeisodion, addition, from epeisodios, coming in besides : epi-, besides + eis, into + hodos, way, road.]

ep·i·sod·ic (ĕp′ĭ-sŏd′ĭk) or **ep·i·sod·i·cal** (-ĭ-kəl) adj. **1.** Pertaining to or resembling an episode; incidental. **2.** Presented in episodes; somewhat uneven or disjointed: an episodic narrative.

e·pis·te·mol·o·gy (ĭ-pĭs′tə-mŏl′ə-jē) n. The branch of philosophy that deals with the nature and theory of knowledge. [Greek epistēmē, knowledge, understanding + -LOGY.] —**e·pis′te·mo·log′i·cal** (-mə-lŏj′ĭ-kəl) adj. —**e·pis′te·mol′o·gist** n.

e·pis·tle (ĭ-pĭs′əl) n. **1.** A letter, esp. a formal one. **2.** Often **Epistle. a.** In the New Testament, a letter written by an Apostle. **b.** An excerpt from one of these letters, read as part of a religious service. [Middle English, from Old French, from Latin epistola, from Greek epistolē, from epistellein, to send to : epi-, over + stellein, to send.]

e·pis·to·lar·y (ĭ-pĭs′tə-lĕr′ē) adj. **1.** Of or associated with letters or letter writing. **2.** In the form of a letter or letters: an epistolary novel. **3.** Carried on by or made up of letters: an epistolary friendship.

ep·i·taph (ĕp′ĭ-tăf′) n. **1.** An inscription on a tombstone or monument in memory of the person buried there. **2.** A brief eulogy written for a deceased person. [Middle English epitaphe, from Old French, from Latin epitaphium, funeral oration, from Greek epitaphion : epi-, over + taphos, tomb.]

ep·i·the·li·um (ĕp′ə-thē′lē-əm) n., pl. **-ums** or **-li·a** (-lē-ə). A thin, membranous tissue, usu. in a single layer, that covers most internal surfaces and organs and the outer surface of an animal body. [EPI- + Greek thēlē, nipple.] —**ep′i·the′li·al** adj.

ep·i·thet (ĕp′ə-thĕt′) n. **1.** A term, as the Lion-Hearted in Richard the Lion-Hearted, used to characterize the nature of a person or thing. **2.** An abusive or insulting word or phrase. [Latin epitheton, from Greek : epi-, on + tithenai, to place, put.]

e·pit·o·me (ĭ-pĭt′ə-mē) n. **1.** A summary of a book, article, etc. **2.** Someone or something that is the typical or perfect example of an entire class or type: She is the epitome of tactfulness and diplomacy. [Latin epitomē, from Greek : epi-, upon + temnein, to cut.]

e·pit·o·mize (ĭ-pĭt′ə-mīz′) tr.v. **-mized, -miz·ing. 1.** To make an epitome of; sum up. **2.** To typify or represent perfectly an entire class or type. —See Syns at **represent.**

ep·i·zo·ot·ic (ĕp′ĭ-zō-ŏt′ĭk) adj. Of or being a disease that is prevalent among or attacks a large number of animals simultaneously. —n. An epizootic disease. [EPI- + ZO(O)- + -OTIC.]

e plu·ri·bus u·num (ē plŏŏr′ə-bəs yŏŏ′nəm). Latin. One out of many. The motto of the United States.

ep·och (ĕp′ək) n. **1.** A particular period of history, esp. one regarded as being in some way characteristic, remarkable, or memorable; an era. **2.** Geol. A unit of geologic time that is a division of a period. [Greek epokhē, pause.]

ep·och·al (ĕp′ə-kəl) adj. **1.** Of or characteristic of a geologic epoch. **2.** Epoch-making.

ep·och-mak·ing (ĕp′ək-mā′kĭng) adj. Highly significant or important; momentous.

ep·o·nym (ĕp′ə-nĭm′) n. A real or mythical person whose name is the source of the name of a city, country, era, institution, etc.: "Romulus" is the eponym of Rome.

e·pon·y·mous (ĭ-pŏn′ə-məs) adj. Giving one's name to something, as a city, country, era, or institution. [Greek epōnumos : epi-, to + onoma, name.]

ep·ox·y (ĕp′ŏk′sē, ĭ-pŏk′-) n., pl. **-ies**. Any of various usu. thermosetting resins made by polymerization, characterized by toughness and strong adhesion and used esp. in surface coatings and adhesives. Also called **epoxy resin.** [EP(I)- + OXY(GEN).]

ă pat   ā pay   â care   ä father   ĕ pet   ē be   hw which   ĭ pit   ī tie   î pier   ŏ pot   ō toe   ô paw, for   oi noise
ŏŏ took   ōŏ boot   ou out   th thin   th this   ŭ cut   û urge   zh vision   ə about, item, edible, gallop, circus

ep·si·lon (ĕp′sə-lŏn′) *n.* The fifth letter in the Greek alphabet, written E, ε, and transliterated in English as *E, e.* [Greek *e psilon,* "simple e."]

Ep·som salts (ĕp′səm). Also **Epsom salt.** A colorless, crystalline compound, $MgSO_4 \cdot 7H_2O$, that is a hydrated magnesium sulfate, used esp. as a cathartic. [First obtained from the mineral springs in *Epsom,* England.]

eq·ua·bil·i·ty (ĕk′wə-bĭl′ĭ-tē, ē′kwə-) *n.* The quality or condition of being equable.

eq·ua·ble (ĕk′wə-bəl, ē′kwə-) *adj.* **1.** Unvarying; steady; even: *an equable climate.* **2.** Even-tempered; serene: *an equable disposition.* **—eq′ua·bly** *adv.*

e·qual (ē′kwəl) *adj.* **1.** Having the same capability, quantity, effect, etc., as another: *equal strength; equal importance.* **2.** *Math.* **a.** Alike in meaning or value; equivalent. **b.** Capable of being substituted one for the other. **3.** Having the same privileges, status, or rights: *All men are created equal.* **4.** Having the necessary strength, ability, or determination: *equal to the task.* —See Syns at **same.** *—n.* Someone or something that is equal to another. *—tr.v.* **e·qualed** or **e·qualled, e·qual·ing** or **e·qual·ling. 1.** To be equal to, esp. in value. **2.** To do, make, or produce something equal to: *He equaled the world's record in the mile run.* **—phrasal verb. equal out.** To be of equal value; reach a balance: *The pros and cons equal out.* [Latin *aequālis,* from *aequus,* even, level.]

e·qual·i·ty (ĭ-kwŏl′ĭ-tē) *n., pl.* **-ties. 1.** The condition of being equal, esp. the condition of enjoying equal political, economic, and social rights. **2.** *Math.* A statement, usu. an equation, that one thing equals another.

e·qual·ize (ē′kwə-līz′) *tr.v.* **-ized, -iz·ing. 1.** To make equal: *a law that equalizes opportunity.* **2.** To make uniform: *equalize the temperatures in the two rooms.* **—e·qual·i·za·tion** *n.* **—e′qual·iz′er** *n.*

e·qual·ly (ē′kwə-lē) *adv.* **1.** In an equal manner: *They divided the inheritance equally.* **2.** To an equal degree: *equally attractive.*

e·quate (ĭ-kwāt′) *tr.v.* **e·quat·ed, e·quat·ing. 1.** To make, treat, or regard as equal or equivalent: *Many people equate wisdom with old age.* **2.** To reduce to a standard or average; equalize; balance: *equate profit and loss.* **3.** To show or state the equality of; express in an equation. [Middle English *equaten,* from Latin *aequāre,* from *aequus,* equal.]

e·qua·tion (ĭ-kwā′zhən, -shən) *n.* **1.** The process or act of equating. **2.** The condition of being equal; a balanced state; equilibrium. **3.** *Math.* A statement that two expressions are equal. For example, $y = 2 + 8$ and $x + y = 18$ are equations. **4.** *Chem.* A representation of a chemical reaction with the chemical symbols for the reacting atomic or molecular substances on the left and those of the product of the chemical change on the right. In chemical equations, the two sides are separated by the signs (=), (→), or, if a reversible reaction, (⇌). **—e·qua′tion·al** *adj.*

e·qua·tor (ĭ-kwā′tər) *n.* **1.** The great circle whose plane is perpendicular to the earth's axis of rotation, whose circumference coincides with the earth's surface, and which divides the earth into the Northern Hemisphere and the Southern Hemisphere. **2.** A similar circle on any celestial body: *the sun's equator.* [Middle English, from Medieval Latin *(circulus) aequator (diei et nocis),* (circle) equalizing (day and night), from Latin *aequāre,* to equate.]

e·qua·to·ri·al (ē′kwə-tôr′ē-əl, -tōr′-, ĕk′wə-) *adj.* **1.** Of, relating to, or near the equator. **2.** Characteristic of the equator or the regions near it: *equatorial heat.*

eq·uer·ry (ĕk′wə-rē) *n., pl.* **-ries. 1.** An officer in charge of the horses in a royal or noble household. **2.** In England, a personal attendant to a member of the royal family. [Earlier *escurie,* from Old French, from *escier,* riding master, squire.]

e·ques·tri·an (ĭ-kwĕs′trē-ən) *adj.* **1.** Of or pertaining to horseback riding or horsemanship. **2.** Representing a person on horseback: *an equestrian statue.* *—n.* A person who rides a horse or performs on horseback. [From Latin *equester,* from *equus,* horse.]

e·ques·tri·enne (ĭ-kwĕs′trē-ĕn′) *n.* A female equestrian.

equi-. A prefix meaning equality: *equiangular.* [Middle English, from Latin *aequi-,* from *aequus,* equal.]

e·qui·an·gu·lar (ē′kwē-ăng′gyə-lər, ĕk′wē-) *adj.* Having all

angles equal: *an equiangular triangle.*

e·qui·dis·tant (ē′kwə-dĭs′tənt, ĕk′wə-) *adj.* Equally distant.

e·qui·lat·er·al (ē′kwə-lăt′ər-əl, ĕk′wə-) *adj.* Having all sides equal. *—n.* A geometric figure with equal sides.

e·quil·i·brant (ĭ-kwĭl′ə-brənt) *n.* A force capable of balancing a system of forces to produce equilibrium.

e·quil·i·brate (ĭ-kwĭl′ə-brāt′) *v.* **-brat·ed, -brat·ing.** *—intr.v.* To be in or bring about a condition of equilibrium. *—tr.v.* To maintain in or bring into a condition of equilibrium. [From Latin *aequilibrāre,* to balance, from *aequilibris,* in perfect balance, from *aequilibrium,* equilibrium.] **—e·quil′i·bra′tion** *n.*

e·qui·lib·ri·um (ē′kwə-lĭb′rē-əm, ĕk′wə-) *n.* **1.** A condition of balance between opposites: *The death rate and the birth rate were in equilibrium.* **2.** *Physics.* A condition in which all the forces and torques acting on a physical system cancel each other. **3.** *Chem.* A condition in which a reaction and its corresponding reverse reaction go on at equal rates. **4.** Mental balance or psychological stability. [Latin *aequilībrium,* even balance : *equi-,* equal + *lībra,* balance.]

e·quine (ē′kwīn′) *adj.* **1.** Of, pertaining to, or characteristic of a horse. **2.** Of or belonging to the family Equidae, which includes the horses, asses, and zebras. *—n.* A member of the Equidae. [Latin *equīnus,* from *equus,* horse.]

e·qui·noc·tial (ē′kwə-nŏk′shəl, ĕk′wə-) *adj.* **1.** Of or pertaining to an equinox. **2.** Occurring at or near an equinox: *an equinoctial storm.* **3.** Equatorial. *—n.* **1.** A violent storm occurring at or near the time of an equinox. **2.** Also **equinoctial circle.** The **celestial equator.** [Middle English *equinoxial,* from Old French, from Latin *aequinoctiālis,* from *aequinoctium,* equinox.]

equinoctial circle. The **celestial equator.**

e·qui·nox (ē′kwə-nŏks′, ĕk′wə-) *n.* **1.** Either of the two times during a year when the sun crosses the celestial equator and the length of day and night are approx. equal; the vernal equinox and the autumnal equinox. **2.** The position of the sun at these times; either of two points on the celestial sphere where the ecliptic intersects the celestial equator. [Middle English, from Old French, from Medieval Latin *aequinoxium,* var. of Latin *aequinoctium* : *aequi-,* equal + *nox,* night.]

e·quip (ĭ-kwĭp′) *tr.v.* **e·quipped, e·quip·ping. 1.** To supply with the necessary materials for an undertaking, as tools or provisions. **2.** To supply with intellectual, emotional, or spiritual essentials. [Old French *esquiper,* to embark.]

eq·ui·page (ĕk′wə-pĭj) *n.* **1.** Equipment or furnishings, as of a military unit. **2.** An elegantly equipped horse-drawn carriage, usu. attended by footmen.

e·quip·ment (ĭ-kwĭp′mənt) *n.* **1.** The things used in or provided for a particular purpose; furnishings; gear. **2.** The act of equipping or the condition of being equipped.

e·qui·poise (ē′kwə-poiz′, ĕk′wə-) *n.* **1.** Equality in distribution, as of weight, relationship, or emotional forces; balance; equilibrium. **2.** A weight or force that balances another; a counterbalance.

e·qui·po·ten·tial (ē′kwə-pə-tĕn′shəl, ĕk′wə-) *adj.* Having equal power or potential.

eq·ui·ta·ble (ĕk′wĭ-tə-bəl) *adj.* **1.** Just and fair; impartial: *an equitable decision.* **2.** *Law.* Concerned with or valid in equity as distinguished from civil and common law. —See Syns at **fair.** [French *équitable,* from Old French, from *equite,* equity.] **—eq′ui·ta·ble·ness** *n.* **—eq′ui·ta·bly** *adv.*

eq·ui·ta·tion (ĕk′wĭ-tā′shən) *n.* The practice of riding a horse; horsemanship. [Old French, from Latin *equitātiō,* riding, from *equitāre,* to ride.]

eq·ui·ty (ĕk′wĭ-tē) *n., pl.* **-ties. 1.** The condition or quality of being just, impartial, and fair. **2.** Something that is just, impartial, and fair. **3.** The value of a business or property beyond any mortgage or liability. **4.** *Law.* **a.** Justice applied in circumstances not covered by civil or common law. **b.** A system of rules and principles supplementing civil and common law and overriding such law in cases where a fair or just solution cannot be provided. **c.** A right or claim considered appropriate for a court of equity. [Middle English *equite,* from Old French, from Latin *aequitās,* from *aequus,* equal.]

e·quiv·a·lence (ĭ-kwĭv′ə-ləns) *n.* Also **e·quiv·a·len·cy** (-lən-sē) *pl.* **-cies.** The condition or property of being equivalent; equality.

e·quiv·a·lent (ĭ-kwĭv'ə-lənt) *adj.* **1.** Equal in amount, degree, value, force, meaning, etc. **2.** Having similar or identical functions or effects: *Their accounting department is equivalent to our financial bureau.* **3.** *Math.* **a.** Equal in numerical value or meaning: *equivalent fractions.* **b.** Having the same solution set: *equivalent sets.* **4.** *Geom.* Equal in area or volume but unlike in shape. **5.** *Chem.* Having the same ability to combine. —See Syns at **like** and **same.** —*n.* That which is equivalent. [Middle English, from Old French, from Late Latin *aequivalēns,* pres. part. of *aequivalēre,* to be equal in value.] —**e·quiv'a·lent·ly** *adv.*

e·quiv·o·cal (ĭ-kwĭv'ə-kəl) *adj.* **1.** Capable of two or more interpretations; ambiguous: *an equivocal statement.* **2.** Of uncertain outcome or worth; inconclusive: *an equivocal result.* [Late Latin *aequivocus : aequi-,* equal + Latin *vōx,* voice.] —**e·quiv'o·cal·ly** *adv.*

e·quiv·o·cate (ĭ-kwĭv'ə-kāt') *intr.v.* **-cat·ed, -cat·ing.** To use equivocal language intentionally; hedge.

Er The symbol for the element erbium.

-er¹ **1.** A suffix indicating: **a.** Someone or something performing an action: **helper. b.** A native or resident: **Vermonter. 2.** A suffix used to form informal shortenings for certain phrases: **homer** for **home run.** [Middle English *-ere, -er,* partly from Old English *-ere* and partly from Old French *-ier,* from Latin *-ārius.*]

-er² or **-r.** A suffix indicating the comparative degree of adjectives and adverbs: **whiter, slower.** [Middle English *-ere, -re,* from Old English *-ra, -ora.*]

e·ra (ĭr'ə, ĕr'ə) *n.* **1.** A period of time with a specific point in history as its beginning: *the Christian era; the Napoleonic era.* **2.** A period of time distinguished by specific aspects, events, or people: *the Colonial era of U.S. history.* **3.** *Geol.* A division of geologic time comprising one or more periods. [Late Latin *aera,* from Latin, counters for calculating, from *aes,* brass, copper, money.]

e·rad·i·cate (ĭ-rădʹĭ-kāt') *tr.v.* **-cat·ed, -cat·ing.** To remove all traces of; destroy completely; abolish: *eradicate poverty.* [From Latin *ērādicāre : ex-,* out + *rādix,* root.] —**e·rad'i·ca·ble** *adj.* —**e·rad'i·ca'tion** *n.* —**e·rad'i·ca'tor** *n.*

e·rase (ĭ-rās') *v.* **e·rased, e·ras·ing.** —*tr.v.* **1.** To remove (something written or drawn); rub, wipe, scrape, or blot out. **2.** To remove writing or a recording from: *erase a blackboard; erase a tape.* **3.** To remove all traces of: *Time erases hurt feelings.* —*intr.v.* To be capable of being erased: *a soft pencil that erases easily.* [Latin *ērāsus,* past part. of *ērādere,* to scrape off : *ex-,* out + *rādere,* to scrape.] —**e·ras'a·ble** *adj.*

e·ras·er (ĭ-rā'sər) *n.* Something that erases, as a piece of rubber, cloth, or felt.

e·ra·sure (ĭ-rā'shər) *n.* **1.** The act of erasing. **2.** Something that has been erased. **3.** A mark or blank space where something has been erased.

Er·a·to (ĕr'ə-tō') *n. Gk. Myth.* The Muse of lyric poetry and mime.

er·bi·um (ûr'bē-əm) *n. Symbol* **Er** A soft, silvery rare-earth element. Atomic number 68; atomic weight 167.26; melting point 1,497°C; boiling point 2,900°C; specific gravity 9.051; valance 3. [After *Ytterby,* Sweden, where it was discovered.]

ere (âr) *Archaic.* —*prep.* Previous to; before. —*conj.* **1.** Before. **2.** Sooner than; rather than. [Middle English *ar, er,* from Old English *ǣr,* before.]

e·rect (ĭ-rĕkt') *adj.* **1.** Directed or pointing upward; vertical: *an erect steeple.* **2.** Standing upright: *erect posture.* —*tr.v.* **1.** To build; put up; construct: *erect a skyscraper.* **2.** To raise upright; set on end: *erect a Christmas tree for decorating.* **3.** To put together; assemble: *erect a model airport.* **4.** To set up; establish: *erect a dynasty.* **5.** *Geom.* To construct (a perpendicular, altitude, etc.) from or upon a given base. [Middle English, from Latin *ērectus,* past part. of *ērigere,* to raise up : *ex-,* out + *regere,* to direct, to set.] —**e·rect'ly** *adv.* —**e·rect'ness** *n.* —**e·rec'tor** *n.*

e·rec·tile (ĭ-rĕk'təl, -tīl') *adj.* **1.** Capable of being erected. **2.** *Physiol.* Of vascular tissue that is capable of filling with blood and becoming rigid.

e·rec·tion (ĭ-rĕk'shən) *n.* **1.** The act of erecting or the condition of being erected. **2.** Something erected, as a building. **3.** *Physiol.* The condition of erectile tissue when filled with blood.

ere·long (âr-lông', -lŏng') *adv. Archaic.* Before long; soon.

er·e·mite (ĕr'ə-mīt') *n.* A hermit, esp. a religious recluse. [Middle English *(h)ermite,* hermit.]

ere·while (âr-hwīl', -wīl') *adv. Archaic.* Some time ago; formerly.

erg (ûrg) *n.* A centimeter-gram-second unit of energy or work equal to the work done by a force of one dyne acting over a distance of one centimeter and equal to 10^{-7} joule. [Greek *ergon,* work.]

er·go (ûr'gō, âr'-) *conj. & adv.* Consequently; therefore. [Latin *ergō,* therefore.]

er·got (ûr'gət, -gŏt') *n.* **1.** A fungus of the genus *Claviceps* that infects rye and various other cereal plants and forms hard, black masses that replace many of the seeds of the host plant. **2.** The disease caused by such a fungus. **3.** The dried fungus, used in the preparation of certain drugs. [French, "cock's spur" (from its shape), from Old French *argot.*]

er·got·ism (ûr'gə-tĭz'əm) *n.* Poisoning that results from eating ergot-infected grain.

E·rid·a·nus (ĭ-rĭd'n-əs) *n.* A constellation located in the Southern Hemisphere and containing the star Achernar.

Er·in (ĕr'ĭn) *n. Poet.* Ireland.

er·mine (ûr'mĭn) *n.* **1.** A weasel, *Mustela erminea,* of northern regions, with a black tail tip and brownish fur that turns white in winter. **2.** The valuable white fur of the ermine. [Middle English *ermin,* from Old French, from Medieval Latin *(mūs) Armenius,* "Armenian (mouse)."]

erne or **ern** (ûrn) *n.* Any of several sea eagles, esp. *Haliaeetus albicella,* of the Old World. [Middle English *ern,* eagle, from Old English *earn.*]

e·rode (ĭ-rōd') *v.* **e·rod·ed, e·rod·ing.** —*tr.v.* **1.** To wear away gradually by or as if by abrasion and dissolution: *rains eroding the slopes; rejections eroding her self-confidence.* **2.** To eat into or away; corrode: *Salt eroded the dented fender.* **3.** To make or form by wearing away: *The river eroded a deep gorge.* —*intr.v.* To become eroded or worn. [Latin *ērōdere,* to gnaw off, eat away : *ex-,* off + *rōdere,* to gnaw.]

e·rog·e·nous (ĭ-rŏj'ə-nəs) *adj.* Arousing sexual desire. [Greek *erōs,* sexual desire + -GEN + -OUS.]

Er·os (ĭr'ŏs', ĕr'-) *n. Gk. Myth.* The god of love, son of Aphrodite.

e·ro·sion (ĭ-rō'zhən) *n.* The process of eroding or the condition of being eroded.

e·ro·sive (ĭ-rō'sĭv, -zĭv) *adj.* Causing erosion; eroding.

e·rot·ic (ĭ-rŏt'ĭk) *adj.* **1.** Of, concerning or tending to arouse sexual desire. **2.** Dominated by sexual desire. [Greek *erōtikos,* of or caused by love, from *erōs,* love, desire.] —**e·rot'i·cal·ly** *adv.*

e·rot·i·cism (ĭ-rŏt'ĭ-sĭz'əm) *n.* **1.** Erotic quality or character. **2.** Preoccupation with sex, esp. in literature and art.

err (ûr, ĕr) *intr.v.* **1.** To make an error or mistake; be incorrect: *We erred in thinking him ready for so much responsibility.* **2.** To violate accepted moral standards; to sin. [Middle English *erren,* to wander about, from Old French *errer,* from Latin *errāre.*]

er·rand (ĕr'ənd) *n.* **1.** A short trip taken to perform a specific task. **2.** The purpose or object of such a trip. [Middle English *erend,* business, message, from Old English *ǣrende,* message.]

er·rant (ĕr'ənt) *adj.* **1.** Roving, esp. in search of adventure: *the knights errant of medieval legend.* **2.** Straying from proper moral standards; erring: *errant behavior.* [Middle English *erraunt,* from Old French *errant,* pres. part of both *errer,* to err, and *errer,* to travel.] —**er'rant·ry** *n.*

er·rat·ic (ĭ-răt'ĭk) *adj.* **1.** Without a fixed or regular course; wandering. **2.** Irregular or uneven in character or quality: *His work has been erratic.* **3.** Unconventional; odd; eccentric: *erratic behavior.* —See Syns at **capricious.** [Middle English *erratik,* from Old French *erratique,* from Latin *errāticus,* wandering, straying, from *errāre,* to wander.] —**er·rat'i·cal·ly** *adv.*

er·ra·tum (ĭ-rä'təm, ĭ-rā'-) *n., pl.* **-ta** (-tə). An error in printed or written matter. [Latin *errātum,* error.]

Usage: **erratum, errata.** The plural form *errata* is regularly employed as a collective noun meaning a list of errors. In this sense the word can be construed as either singular or plural, and the verb that follows it should agree in number with it: *The errata* (i.e., all the errors) *are listed separately. The errata* (i.e., the list of errors) *is in the appendix.*

er·ro·ne·ous (ĭ-rō'nē-əs) *adj.* Containing or derived from error; mistaken; false: *an erroneous conclusion.* —See Syns at **false.** [Middle English, from Old French *erroneus* or Latin *errōneus*, wandering, from *errāre*, to wander, err.] —**er·ro'ne·ous·ly** *adv.* —**er·ro'ne·ous·ness** *n.*

er·ror (ĕr'ər) *n.* **1.** An act, statement, or belief that deviates from what is correct, right, or true; a mistake: *an error in addition.* **2.** The condition of being incorrect or wrong: *His statement is in error.* **3.** A deviation from an accepted code of behavior; a transgression: *refused to see the error of their ways.* **4.** A mistake caused by accident or ignorance: *an error in judgment.* **5.** The difference between a computed, estimated, or observed value and a correct value. **6.** *Baseball.* A defensive misplay by a player on a play that normally should have resulted in an out or prevented an advance by a base runner. [Middle English *errour*, from Old French, from Latin *error*, from *errāre*, to err.]

Syns: error, lapse, miscue, misstep, mistake, slip, slip-up *(Informal) n.* *Core meaning:* An unintentional deviation from what is correct, right, or true (*an error in judgment*).

er·satz (ĕr'zäts, ĕr-zäts') *adj.* Serving as a substitute; artificial: *ersatz mink.* —See Syns at **artificial.** —*n.* A substitute, esp. an inferior imitation. [German, from *Ersatz*, replacement, from *ersetzen*, to replace.]

Erse (ûrs) *n.* The Gaelic language, esp. **Irish Gaelic.** —*adj.* Of or pertaining to the Scottish or Irish Celts or their language.

erst (ûrst) *adv.* *Archaic.* Formerly. [Middle English *erest*, formerly, first, earliest, from Old English *ærest*.]

erst·while (ûrst'hwīl', -wīl') *adj.* Former. —*adv.* *Archaic.* Formerly.

e·ruct (ĭ-rŭkt') *intr.v.* To belch. —*tr.v.* To belch (gas from the stomach). [Latin *ēructāre* : *ex-*, out + *ructāre*, to belch.] —**e·ruc'ta'tion** *n.*

er·u·dite (ĕr'yə-dīt', ĕr'ə-) *adj.* Marked by erudition; learned; scholarly. [Middle English *erudit*, from Latin *ērudītus*, past part. of *ērudīre*, to polish, teach : *ex-*, out + *rudis*, rough, rude.] —**er'u·dite'ly** *adv.*

er·u·di·tion (ĕr'yə-dĭsh'ən, ĕr'ə-) *n.* Extensive knowledge, esp. when acquired by scholarship; learning. —See Syns at **knowledge.**

e·rupt (ĭ-rŭpt') *intr.v.* **1.** To burst forth violently from limits or restraint; explode: *Lava erupted. Tempers erupted during the debate.* **2.** To become violently active: *Fighting erupted along the border.* **3.** To force out or release suddenly, as something pent up: *The geyser erupts periodically.* **4. a.** To pierce the gum: *A new tooth erupted.* **b.** To appear on the skin, as a skin blemish. —*tr.v.* To eject violently (steam, lava, etc.). [Latin *ēruptus*, past part of *ērumpere*, to erupt : *ex-*, out + *rumpere*, to break.]

e·rup·tion (ĭ-rŭp'shən) *n.* **1.** The fact or an example of erupting, esp. the discharge from a volcano or geyser. **2.** A sudden, often violent outburst: *a spontaneous eruption of applause.* **3.** A rash or other blemish on the skin. —**e·rup'tive** *adj.*

-ery or **-ry.** A suffix indicating: **1.** A certain activity: *bakery.* **2.** Certain things or persons: *nunnery.* **3.** A collection or class of objects: *finery.* **4.** A craft, study, or practice: *husbandry.* **5. a.** Certain characteristics: *snobbery.* **b.** A kind of behavior: *knavery.* **6.** Condition or status: *slavery.* [Middle English *-erie*, from Old French.]

er·y·sip·e·las (ĕr'ĭ-sĭp'ə-ləs, ĭr'ĭ-) *n.* An acute disease of the skin caused by a streptococcus and marked by spreading inflammation. [Middle English *erisipila*, from Latin *erysipelas*, from Greek *erusipelas*, "red skin" : *eruthros*, red + *-pelas*, skin.]

erythro- or **erythr-.** A prefix meaning red: *erythrocyte.* [From Greek *eruthros*, red.]

e·ryth·ro·cyte (ĭ-rĭth'rə-sīt') *n.* A red blood cell. [ERYTHRO- + -CYTE.]

e·ryth·ro·my·cin (ĭ-rĭth'rə-mī'sĭn) *n.* An antibiotic drug similar in activity to penicillin. [ERYTHRO- + -MYCIN.]

Es The symbol for the element einsteinium.

-es¹. Var. of **-s** (plural suffix).

-es². Var. of **-s** (verb suffix).

es·ca·drille (ĕs'kə-drĭl') *n.* A unit of an air command, esp. in France during World War I. [French, from Spanish *escuadrilla*, dim. of *escuadra*, squadron, from *escuadrar*, to square.]

es·ca·lade (ĕs'kə-lād', -läd') *n.* The act of scaling a fortified wall with ladders. [French, from Italian *scalata*, from *scalare*, to climb, from *scala*, ladder, from Late Latin *scāla*, from Latin *scālae*, steps.]

es·ca·late (ĕs'kə-lāt') *v.* **-lat·ed, -lat·ing.** —*tr.v.* To increase or intensify. —*intr.v.* To increase in intensity or extent. [Back-formation from ESCALATOR.] —**es'ca·la'tion** *n.*

es·ca·la·tor (ĕs'kə-lā'tər) *n.* A moving stairway consisting of steps attached to a continuously circulating belt. [From a trademark.]

escalator clause. A provision in a contract stipulating an increase or decrease, as in wages, benefits, or prices, under certain conditions, such as changes in the cost of living or in production costs.

es·cal·lop (ĭ-skŏl'əp, ĭ-skăl'-) *n.* Var. of **scallop** (thin slice).

es·ca·pade (ĕs'kə-pād') *n.* A carefree or reckless adventure; a fling; caper. [French, from Old French, from Old Italian *scappata*, from the past part. of *scappare*, to escape.]

es·cape (ĭ-skāp') *intr.v.* **-caped, -cap·ing.** **1.** To break loose from confinement; get free: *escape from prison.* **2.** To issue from confinement or an enclosure: *gas escaping from a pipe.* **3.** To avoid capture, danger, or harm: *barely escaped with his life.* —*tr.v.* **1.** To break loose from; get free of. **2.** To succeed in avoiding: *escape injury; could not escape financial ruin.* **3.** To elude the memory or mind of: *Her name escapes me.* **4.** To issue involuntarily from: *A sigh escaped her lips.* —See Syns at **avoid.** —*n.* **1.** The act or an instance of escaping. **2.** A means of escaping: *a fire escape.* **3.** A means of obtaining temporary freedom from worry, care, or unpleasantness: *Reading is his escape from business problems.* **4.** A gradual outflow from an enclosure; a leakage. —*modifier:* *an escape attempt; an escape clause.* [Middle English *escapen*, from Old North French *escaper.*] —**es·cap'er** *n.*

es·cap·ee (ĕs'kā-pē', ĭ-skā'pē') *n.* Someone who has escaped, esp. an escaped prisoner.

es·cape·ment (ĭ-skāp'mənt) *n.* **1.** A mechanism used esp. in timepieces to control the wheel movement and provide periodic energy impulses to a pendulum or balance. **2.** The mechanism in a typewriter that controls the lateral movement of the carriage.

escape velocity. The minimum velocity that a body such as a rocket must attain to escape from the gravitational field of another body such as the earth.

es·cap·ism (ĭ-skā'pĭz'əm) *n.* The tendency to avoid reality by engaging in fantasy, daydreams, or other forms of distraction. —**es·cap'ist** *n.*

es·car (ĕs'kär, -kər) *n.* Var. of **esker.**

es·car·got (ĕs'kär-gō') *n.* An edible snail, esp. when cooked. [French, snail, from Old French, from Old Provençal *escaragol.*]

es·ca·role (ĕs'kə-rōl') *n.* A variety of *Cichorium endivia* with densely clustered, ruffled leaves used in salads. [French, from Old French *scariole*, from Late Latin *escariola*, from Latin *escārius*, of food, from *esca*, food, from *edere*, to eat.]

es·carp·ment (ĭ-skärp'mənt) *n.* **1.** A steep slope or long cliff resulting from erosion or faulting. **2.** A steep slope in front of a fortification.

-escence. A suffix indicating a beginning or continuing state: *luminescence.* [Old French, from Latin *-ēscentia.*]

-escent. A suffix meaning beginning to be: *luminescent, phosphorescent.* [Old French, from Latin *-ēscēns.*]

es·cha·tol·o·gy (ĕs'kə-tŏl'ə-jē) *n.* The branch of theology concerned with ultimate or last things, such as death, judgment, heaven, and hell. [Greek *eskhatos*, last, extreme + -LOGY.] —**es'cha·to·log'i·cal** (-tə-lŏj'ĭ-kəl) *adj.*

es·cheat (ĕs-chēt') *n.* **1.** The reversion of land to the state when there are no legal heirs or claimants. **2.** Property so reverted. —*intr.v.* To revert by escheat. —*tr.v.* To cause (property) to revert to by escheat. [Middle English *eschete*, from Old French *eschete*, from *escheoir*, to fall out : Latin *ex-*, out + *cadere*, to fall.] —**es·cheat'a·ble** *adj.*

ă pat ā pay â care ä father ĕ pet ē be hw which ĭ pit ī tie î pier ŏ pot ō toe ô paw, for oi noise
ōō took ōō boot ou out th thin th this ŭ cut û urge zh vision ə about, item, edible, gallop, circus

es·chew (ĕs-chōō′) *tr.v.* To avoid (something); abstain from; shun: *eschew temptation.* —See Syns at **avoid.** [Middle English *escheuen,* from Old French *eschiuver,* to shun, avoid.]

es·cort (ĕs′kôrt′) *n.* **1.** One or more persons who accompany another to give guidance or protection or to pay honor. **2.** One or more planes, ships, etc., accompanying another or others to provide protection. **3.** A man who acts as the companion of a woman in public. **4.** Accompaniment by a person or group of vehicles. —*tr.v.* (ĭ-skôrt′) To accompany as an escort. [French *escorte,* from Old French *(e)scorte,* from Old Italian *scorta,* an escorting, from *scorgere,* to show, guide : Latin *ex-,* out + *corrigere,* to set right, correct.]

es·cri·toire (ĕs′krĭ-twär′) *n.* A writing desk or table. [French, from Old French *escriptoire,* a study, from Medieval Latin *scriptorium,* scriptorium.]

es·crow (ĕs′krō′, ĭ-skrō′) *n.* A written agreement, such as a deed or bond, put into the custody of a third party until certain conditions are fulfilled. [Old French *escroe,* strip of parchment, scroll.]

es·cu·lent (ĕs′kyə-lənt) *adj.* Suitable for eating; edible. —*n.* Something edible, esp. a vegetable. [Latin *esculentus,* from *esca,* food, from *edere,* to eat.]

es·cutch·eon (ĭ-skŭch′ən) *n.* Also **scutch·eon** (skŭch′ən). **1.** A shield or shield-shaped emblem bearing a coat of arms. **2.** Any ornamental shield-shaped emblem, esp. a plate surrounding the keyhole of a door. [Middle English *escochon,* from Old French *escuchon, escusson,* from Latin *scūtum,* shield.]

-ese. A suffix meaning: **1.** A native or inhabitant: **Sudanese. 2.** A language or dialect: **Japanese. 3.** A literary style or diction: **journalese.** [Old French *-eis* and Italian *-ese,* from Latin *-ēnsis,* "originating in."]

es·ker (ĕs′kər) *n.* Also **es·car** (ĕs′kär′, -kər). A long, narrow ridge of coarse gravel deposited by a stream flowing in a trough or tunnel in a decaying glacier. [Irish *eiscir,* ridge, from Old Irish *escir.*]

Es·ki·mo (ĕs′kə-mō′) *n., pl.* **-mos** or **Eskimo.** Also **Es·qui·mau** *pl.* **-maux** (-mōz′). **1.** One of a people native to the Arctic coastal regions of North America and to parts of Greenland and Siberia. **2.** The language of the Eskimos. —*adj.* Of, pertaining to, or concerning the Eskimos or their language.

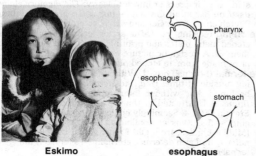

Eskimo   **esophagus**

e·soph·a·gus (ĭ-sŏf′ə-gəs) *n., pl.* **-gi** (-jī′). Also **oe·soph·a·gus.** A muscular tube through which food passes from the pharynx to the stomach; gullet. [Middle English *ysophagus,* from Greek *oisophagos,* gullet.] —**e·soph′a·ge′al** (ĭ-sŏf′ə-jē′əl) *adj.*

es·o·ter·ic (ĕs′ə-tĕr′ĭk) *adj.* **1.** Intended for or understood by only a small group: *an esoteric cult.* **2.** Difficult to understand; abstruse: *an esoteric theory.* **3.** Not publicly disclosed; confidential: *an esoteric reason.* —See Syns at **deep.** [Late Latin *esōtericus,* from Greek *esōterikos,* from *esōterō,* comp. of *esō,* within.] —**es′o·ter′i·cal·ly** *adv.*

es·pa·drille (ĕs′pə-drĭl′) *n.* A sandal with a flexible sole and a canvas upper. [French, var. of *espardille,* from Provençal *espardilho,* dim. of *espart,* esparto, from Latin *spartum.*]

es·pal·ier (ĭ-spăl′yər, -yā′) *n.* **1.** A tree or shrub trained to grow horizontally against a wall or framework, often in a pattern. **2.** A trellis or other framework upon which such a plant is grown. —*tr.v.* To train on or provide with an espalier. [French, from Italian *spalliera,* applied to shoulder supports, from *spalla,* shoulder, from Latin *spatula,* broad piece, flat piece.]

es·pe·cial (ĭ-spĕsh′əl) *adj.* Standing above or apart from others; particular; exceptional. [Middle English, from Old French, from Latin *speciālis,* from *speciēs,* a view, appearance.]

es·pe·cial·ly (ĭ-spĕsh′ə-lē) *adv.* To an extent or degree deserving of special emphasis; particularly: *an especially talented songwriter.*

Es·pe·ran·to (ĕs′pə-rän′tō, -răn′-) *n.* An artificial international language invented in 1887, based on word roots common to many European languages.

es·pi·o·nage (ĕs′pē-ə-näzh′, -nĭj) *n.* The act or practice of spying, esp. the use of spies by one government to obtain military or political information about another. [French, from Old French, from *espionner,* to spy, from *espion,* spy, from Old Italian *spione,* from *spia.*]

es·pla·nade (ĕs′plə-näd′, -nād′) *n.* A flat, open stretch of pavement or grass used as a promenade. [French, from Italian *spianala,* from *spianare,* to level, from Latin *explānāre,* to flatten, explain.]

es·pou·sal (ĭ-spou′zəl) *n.* **1.** Adoption of or support for an idea or cause: *espousal of women's rights.* **2.** Often **espousals. a.** An engagement; betrothal. **b.** A wedding ceremony.

es·pouse (ĭ-spouz′) *tr.v.* **-poused, -pous·ing. 1.** To give one's loyalty or support to (an idea or cause); adopt. **2.** To marry. [Middle English *espousen,* from Old French *espouser,* from Late Latin *spōnsāre,* from Latin *spondēre,* to promise solemnly.]

es·pres·so (ĕ-sprĕs′ō) *n., pl.* **-sos.** A strong coffee brewed by forcing steam under pressure through long-roasted, powdered beans. [Italian *(caffe) expresso,* "pressed out (coffee)," from *exprimere,* to press out, express, from Latin *exprimere.*]

es·prit (ĕ-sprē′) *n.* Liveliness of mind and expression; spirit. —See Syns at **spirit.** [French, from Latin *spīritus,* spirit.]

es·prit de corps (ĕ-sprē′ də kôr′). A spirit of devotion and enthusiasm among members of a group for one another, their group, and its purposes. [French, "team spirit."]

es·py (ĭ-spī′) *tr.v.* **-pied, -py·ing.** To catch sight of; glimpse. [Middle English *(e)spien,* from Old French *espier,* to spy.]

-esque. A suffix indicating manner or quality: **statuesque, Lincolnesque.** [French, from Italian *-esco.*]

Es·qui·mau (ĕs′kə-mō′) *n. & adj.* Var. of **Eskimo.**

es·quire (ĭ-skwīr′, ĕs′kwīr′) *n.* **1.** A candidate for knighthood in medieval times, serving a knight as attendant and shield-bearer. **2.** A member of the English gentry ranking just below a knight. **3. Esquire.** A title of courtesy used after the full name of a person, esp. an attorney: *Martin Chuzzlewit, Esq.* [Middle English, from Old French *esquier,* from Late Latin *scūtārius,* from Latin *scūtum,* shield.]

-ess. A suffix meaning a female: **lioness.** [Middle English *-esse,* from Old French, from Late Latin *-issa,* from Greek.]

es·say (ĕs′ā′) *n.* **1.** A short literary composition on a single subject, usu. presenting the personal views of the author. **2.** (*also* ĕ-sā′). An attempt; an endeavor. —*tr.v.* (ĕ-sā′). To make an attempt at; try. [Old French *essaier,* from *essai,* a trial, from Late Latin *exagium,* a weighing, balance, from Latin *exigere,* to weigh out, examine.] —**es·say′er** *n.*

es·say·ist (ĕs′ā′ĭst) *n.* A writer of essays.

es·sence (ĕs′əns) *n.* **1. a.** The quality or qualities of a thing that give it its identity; the fundamental nature of a thing: *The essence of religion is faith.* **b.** The innermost and most essential part. **2. a.** An extract of a substance that contains its fundamental properties in concentrated form: *essence of vanilla.* **b.** Such an extract in a solution of alcohol. **3.** A perfume or scent. —See Syns at **heart.** [Middle English, from Old French, from Latin *essentia,* from *esse,* to be.]

es·sen·tial (ĭ-sĕn′shəl) *adj.* **1.** Constituting or part of the essence of something; basic or indispensable: *The computer is an essential component of modern technology.* **2.** Of, being, or containing an essence, as a plant or spice. —*n.* A fundamental, necessary, or indispensable part, item, or principle: *took only the essentials on his trip.*

ă pat	ā pay	â care	ä father	ĕ pet	ē be	hw which
ŏŏ took	ōō boot	ou out	th thin	*th* this	ŭ cut	

ĭ pit	ī tie	î pier	ŏ pot	ō toe	ô paw, for	oi noise
û urge	zh vision	ə about, item, edible, gallop, circus				

—es·sen·ti·al·i·ty (-shē-ăl´ĭ-tē) or **es·sen´tial·ness** n. **—es·sen´tial·ly** adv.

essential oil. A volatile oil, usu. with the characteristic odor or flavor of the plant from which it is obtained, used to make perfumes and flavorings.

-est¹. A suffix indicating the superlative degree of adjectives and adverbs: **greatest, earliest.** [Middle English, from Old English -est, -ost.]

-est² or **-st.** A suffix indicating the archaic second person singular present and past indicative forms of verbs: **comest, lovedest.** [Middle English, from Old English -est, -ast.]

es·tab·lish (ĭ-stăb´lĭsh) tr.v. **1.** To settle securely in a position or condition; install: quickly established himself in a successful law firm. **2.** To create on a permanent basis; found: establish a business; establish a scholarship. **3.** To cause to be recognized or accepted: establish a reputation. **4.** To prove the validity or truth of: established her guilt. —See Syns at **create.** [Middle English establissen, from Old French establir, from Latin stabilīre, to make firm, from stabilis, firm.] **—es·tab´lish·er** n.

established church. A church that is officially recognized and given support as a state institution by a government.

es·tab·lish·ment (ĭ-stăb´lĭsh-mənt) n. **1.** The act of establishing or the condition or fact of being established. **2. a.** A business firm, club, institution, or residence, including its members or residents. **b.** Any organized military or civil group, such as a government or political party. **3.** The act of recognizing a church as an official state institution. **4. the Establishment.** An exclusive or powerful group who control or strongly influence a government, a society, or a field of activity.

es·tate (ĭ-stāt´) n. **1.** A large piece of rural land, usu. with a large house. **2.** The whole of one's possessions, esp. all of the property and debts left by a deceased person. **3.** A condition of social standing or status, esp. of a high and wealthy order; a rank. **4.** Any of the three distinct sociopolitical classes, the clergy, nobility, and commoners, in early modern Europe. [Middle English estat, state, condition, from Old French, state.]

es·teem (ĭ-stēm´) tr.v. **1.** To place a high value on; respect; prize: He's not much esteemed by his colleagues. **2.** To judge to be; regard as; consider: That was esteemed the best. —See Syns at **appreciate.** —n. Favorable regard; respect: She is held in high esteem. —See Syns at **favor.** [Middle English estemen, from Old French estimer, from Latin aestimāre, to estimate.]

es·ter (ĕs´tər) n. Any of the large group of chemical compounds formed when an acid and an alcohol interact so that the hydrogen characteristic of the acid and the hydroxyl group of the alcohol combine to form water, leaving the remaining radicals or groups bound together. [German Ester, short for Essigäther, "vinegar ether."]

es·the·sia (ĕs-thē´zhə, -zhē-ə) n. The ability to receive sense impressions. [Back-formation from ANESTHESIA.]

es·thete (ĕs´thēt´) n. Var. of **aesthete.**

es·thet·ic (ĕs-thĕt´ĭk) adj. Var. of **aesthetic.**

es·thet·i·cism (ĕs-thĕt´ĭ-sĭz´əm) n. Var. of **aestheticism.**

es·thet·ics (ĕs-thĕt´ĭks) n. Var. of **aesthetics.**

es·ti·ma·ble (ĕs´tə-mə-bəl) adj. **1.** Capable of being estimated or evaluated. **2.** Deserving of esteem; admirable. **—es´ti·ma·bly** adv.

es·ti·mate (ĕs´tə-māt´) tr.v. **-mat·ed, -mat·ing. 1.** To make a judgment as to the likely or approximate cost, quantity, or extent of: estimate the distance to the city. **2.** To form an opinion about; evaluate: "While an author is yet living we estimate his powers by his worst performance" (Samuel Johnson). —n. (ĕs´tə-mĭt). **1.** A rough calculation. **2.** A preliminary calculation submitted by a contractor or workman of the cost of work to be undertaken. **3.** An evaluation; opinion. [From Latin aestimāre.]

es·ti·ma·tion (ĕs´tə-mā´shən) n. **1.** The act or an example of estimating. **2.** An opinion reached by estimating; judgment. **3.** Favorable regard; esteem. —See Syns at **favor.**

es·ti·vate (ĕs´tə-vāt´) v. Var. of **aestivate.**

Es·to·ni·an (ĕ-stō´nē-ən) adj. Pertaining to or characteristic of Estonia, its people, or their language. —n. **1.** A native or inhabitant of Estonia. **2.** The Finno-Ugric language of Estonia.

es·top (ĕ-stŏp´) tr.v. **-topped, -top·ping. 1.** Law. To prohibit

or impede by estoppel. **2.** Archaic. To stop up; plug up. [Middle English estoppen, from Old French estoper, from Late Latin stuppāre, to stop up.]

es·top·pel (ĕ-stŏp´əl) n. Law. A restraint on a person to prevent him from contradicting his own previous assertions. [Old French estoupail, from estouper, to estop.]

es·tra·di·ol (ĕs´trə-dī´ôl´, -ōl´) n. An estrogenic hormone, $C_{18}H_{24}O_2$, used medicinally.

es·trange (ĭ-strānj´) tr.v. **-tranged, -trang·ing. 1.** To destroy the affection or friendliness of; make unsympathetic; alienate: His cruel treatment estranged his wife. **2.** To remove from an accustomed place; put at a distance, esp. an emotional or psychological distance: estranged himself from his family. [Old French estranger, from Medieval Latin extrāneāre, from Latin extrāneus, strange.] **—es·trange´ment** n.

Syns: estrange, alienate, disaffect v. Core meaning: To make distant, hostile, or unsympathetic (a mean person who had estranged all his former friends).

es·tro·gen (ĕs´trə-jən) n. Any of several hormones, produced chiefly in the ovaries, that act to regulate certain female reproductive functions and maintain female secondary sex characteristics. [ESTR(US) + -GEN.] **—es´tro·gen´ic** (-jĕn´ĭk) adj.

es·trus (ĕs´trəs) n. A regularly recurrent period of ovulation and sexual excitement in female mammals other than humans; heat. [From Latin oestrus, gadfly, frenzy, from Greek oistros.]

es·tu·ar·y (ĕs´chōō-ĕr´ē) n., pl. **-ies. 1.** The wide lower part of a river where its current is met and influenced by the tides. **2.** An arm of the sea that meets the mouth of a river. [Latin aestuārium, estuary, tidal channel, from aestus, heat, swell, surge, tide.]

-et. A suffix meaning small: **spinneret.** [Middle English, from Old French.]

e·ta (ā´tə, ē´tə) n. The seventh letter of the Greek alphabet, written H, η, and transliterated in English as long e (ē). [Late Latin ēta, from Greek.]

é·ta·gère (ā´tä-zhâr´) n. A piece of furniture with open shelves for ornaments or bric-a-brac; whatnot.

et cet·er·a (ĕt sĕt´ər-ə, -sĕt´rə). Also **et·cet·er·a.** Abbr. **etc.** And other unspecified things; and so forth. —See Usage note at **and.** [Latin, "and other (things)."]

etch (ĕch) tr.v. **1.** To make (a pattern) on a metal plate with acid. **2.** To impress or imprint clearly: The memory etched itself on her mind forever. —intr.v. To practice etching. [Dutch etsen, from German ätzen, to etch, bite, feed.]

etch·ing (ĕch´ĭng) n. **1.** The art or technique of preparing etched metal plates and printing designs and pictures with them. **2.** A design or picture etched on such a plate. **3.** A print made from an etched plate.

e·ter·nal (ĭ-tûr´nəl) adj. **1.** Without beginning or end; existing outside of time: God, the eternal Father. **2.** Having a beginning but without interruption or end: an eternal flame. **3.** Unaffected by time; lasting; timeless: Rome, the Eternal City. **4.** Seemingly endless; incessant: eternal nagging. —See Syns at **continuous.** —n. **the Eternal.** God. [Middle English, from Old French, from Late Latin aeternālis, from Latin aeternus, eternal.] **—e·ter´nal·ly** adv. **—e·ter´nal·ness** n.

e·ter·ni·ty (ĭ-tûr´nĭ-tē) n., pl. **-ties. 1.** The totality of time without beginning or end; infinite time. **2.** The condition or quality of being eternal; timelessness. **3. a.** The endless period of time following death. **b.** The afterlife; immortality. **4.** A very long or seemingly very long time: It seemed an eternity before she called. [Middle English eternite, from Old French, from Latin aeternitās, from aeternus, eternal.]

-eth¹ or **-th.** A suffix indicating the archaic third person singular present indicative form of verbs: **leadeth, doth.** [Middle English, from Old English -eth, -th.]

-eth². Var. of **-th** (in ordinal numbers).

eth·ane (ĕth´ān´) n. A colorless, odorless gas, C_2H_6, occurring in natural gas and used as a fuel and refrigerant. [ETH(YL) + -ANE.]

eth·a·nol (ĕth´ə-nôl´, -nōl´) n. Chem. An alcohol. [ETHAN(E) + -OL.]

e·ther (ē´thər) n. **1.** Any of a class of organic chemical compounds composed of two hydrocarbon groups linked by an oxygen atom. **2.** The volatile, highly flammable ether,

| ă pat | ā pay | â care | ä father | ĕ pet | ē be | hw which | ĭ pit | ī tie | î pier | ŏ pot | ō toe | ô paw, for | oi noise |
| ōō took | ōō boot | ou out | th thin | th this | ŭ cut | | û urge | zh vision | ə about, item, edible, gallop, circus |

$C_4H_{10}O$, formed from ethanol. **3.** A massless material, now known to be nonexistent, once thought to fill space and act as a medium for electromagnetic waves. **4.** The clear sky; the heavens. [Middle English, from Latin *aethēr*, the upper or bright air, from Greek *aithēr*.]

e·the·re·al (ĭ-thîr′ē-əl) *adj.* **1.** Highly refined and delicate; exquisite: *ethereal music.* **2.** Of or pertaining to heaven or the heavens; heavenly: *ethereal beings.* **3.** Of or pertaining to the upper regions of the earth's atmosphere or the space beyond. **4.** *Chem.* Of or pertaining to ether. [From Latin *aetherius*, from Greek *aitherios*, from *aithēr*, ether.] —**e·the′re·al·ly** *adv.*

e·ther·ize (ē′thə-rīz′) *tr.v.* **-ized, -iz·ing. 1.** To subject to the fumes of ether; anesthetize. **2.** *Chem.* To convert into an ether.

eth·ic (ĕth′ĭk) *n.* A principle of right or good conduct or a body of such principles. [Middle English *et(h)ik*, the science of ethics, from Old French *ethique*, from Latin *ēthicē*, from Greek *ēthikē*, from *ēthos*, moral custom.]

eth·i·cal (ĕth′ĭ-kəl) *adj.* **1.** Of, pertaining to, or dealing with ethics. **2.** In accordance with accepted principles of right and wrong, esp. standards governing the conduct of a group. **3.** Designating a drug available only by a physician's prescription. —**eth′i·cal·ly** *adv.*

eth·ics (ĕth′ĭks) *n.* **1.** *(used with a sing. verb).* The branch of philosophy that deals with the general nature of good and bad and the specific moral obligations of and choices to be made by the individual in his relationship with others. **2.** The rules or standards governing conduct, esp. of the members of a profession.

eth·moid (ĕth′moid′) *adj.* Of or pertaining to a light spongy bone that forms part of the walls of the upper nasal cavity. —*n.* The ethmoid bone. [French *ethmoïde*, from Old French, from Greek *ēthmoeidēs*, perforated (from the bone's many perforations) : *ēthmos*, strainer, from *ēthein*, to strain, to sift + *eidos*, shape.]

ethn-. Var. of **ethno-.**

eth·nic (ĕth′nĭk) *adj.* Of or pertaining to a group of people recognized as a class on the basis of certain distinctive characteristics, such as religion, language, ancestry, culture, or national origin. —*n. Informal.* A member of a particular ethnic group. [Late Latin *ethnicus*, heathen, foreign, from Greek *ethnikos*, of a national group, foreign, from *ethnos*, people, nation.] —**eth′ni·cal·ly** *adv.*

eth·nic·i·ty (ĕth-nĭs′ĭ-tē) *n.* **1.** The condition of belonging to a particular ethnic group. **2.** Ethnic pride.

ethno- or **ethn-.** A prefix meaning race or people: **ethnocentrism.** [French, from Late Greek, from Greek *ethnos*, people.]

eth·no·cen·trism (ĕth′nō-sĕn′trĭz′əm) *n.* The belief in the superiority of one's own ethnic group. [ETHNO- + CENTR(O)- + -ISM.] —**eth′no·cen′tric** *adj.*

eth·nol·o·gy (ĕth-nŏl′ə-jē) *n.* **1.** The branch of anthropology that deals with the characteristics, history, and development of human cultures. **2.** The branch of anthropology that deals with the characteristics and origins of ethnic groups and the relations among them. [ETHNO- + -LOGY.] —**eth′no·log′ic** (ĕth′nə-lŏj′ĭk) or **eth′no·log′i·cal** *adj.* —**eth′no·log′i·cal·ly** *adv.*

e·thol·o·gy (ē-thŏl′ə-jē) *n.* The scientific study of animal behavior. [Latin *ēthologia*, the art of depicting character, from Greek *ēthologia* : *ēthos*, ethos + *-logia*, study of.] —**e′tho·log′i·cal** (ē′thə-lŏj′ĭ-kəl) *adj.*

e·thos (ē′thŏs′) *n.* The character or attitude peculiar to a specific culture or group. [From Greek *ēthos*, custom, usage, trait.]

eth·yl (ĕth′əl) *n.* A univalent organic radical, C_2H_5. [ETH(ER) + -YL.]

ethyl alcohol. *Chem.* An alcohol.

eth·yl·ene (ĕth′ə-lēn′) *n.* A colorless, flammable gas, C_2H_4, derived from natural gas and petroleum and used in organic compounds, esp. to color citrus fruits and as an anesthetic. [ETHYL + -ENE.]

ethylene glycol. A colorless, syrupy, poisonous alcohol, $C_2H_6O_2$, used as an antifreeze.

e·ti·o·late (ē′tē-ə-lāt′) *tr.v.* **-lat·ed, -lat·ing.** To cause (a plant) to develop without normal green coloring by preventing exposure to sunlight; blanch. [French *étioler*, from *eteule*, a stalk, from Old French *estuble*, from Latin *sti-*

pula, stalk, straw, stubble.] —**e′ti·o·la′tion** *n.*

e·ti·ol·o·gy (ē′tē-ŏl′ə-jē) *n.* **1.** The causes or origins of something. **2.** The medical study of the causes of disease. [Late Latin *aetiologia*, from Greek *aitiologia*, a giving the cause of : *aitia*, cause + *logia*, study of.] —**e′ti·o·log′ic** (-ə-lŏj′ĭk) or **e′ti·o·log′i·cal** *adj.* —**e′ti·o·log′i·cal·ly** *adv.* —**e′ti·ol′o·gist** *n.*

et·i·quette (ĕt′ĭ-kĕt′, -kĭt) *n.* The body of rules governing correct behavior among people, in a profession, etc.: *court etiquette; military etiquette.* —See Syns at **manner(s).** [French, prescribed routine, label, ticket, from Old French *estiqu(i)er,* to attach, from Middle Dutch *steken.*]

E·trus·can (ĭ-trŭs′kən) *adj.* Of or pertaining to Etruria, its inhabitants, or their language or culture. —*n.* **1.** A person who lived in ancient Etruria. **2.** The pre-Roman extinct language of the Etruscans.

–ette. A suffix meaning: **1.** Small: **kitchenette. 2.** Female: **usherette.** [Middle English, from Old French.]

é·tude or **e·tude** (ā′tōōd′, -tyōōd′) *n.* **1.** A piece of music used for practice in developing a given point of technique. **2.** A piece of music embodying some point of technique but intended for performance. [French *étude*, study, from Old French *estudie.*]

et·y·mol·o·gy (ĕt′ə-mŏl′ə-jē) *n., pl.* **-gies. 1.** The origin and historical development of a word, as shown by study of its basic elements, earliest known use, and changes in form and meaning. **2.** The branch of linguistics that studies the derivation of words. [Middle English *ethimologie*, from Old French, from Medieval Latin *ethimologia*, from Latin *etymologia*, from Greek *etumologiā* : *etumon*, etymon + *-logia*, study of.] —**et′y·mo·log′i·cal** (-mə-lŏj′ĭ-kəl) *adj.* —**et′y·mol′o·gist** (-jĭst) *n.*

et·y·mon (ĕt′ə-mŏn′, -mən) *n., pl.* **-mons** or **-ma** (-mə). **1.** An earlier form of a word. **2.** A foreign word from which a borrowed word is derived. [Latin, origin of a word, from Greek *etumon*, true sense of a word, etymology, from *etumos*, true, real.]

Eu The symbol for the element europium.

eu-. A prefix meaning well, pleasant, or beneficial: **eucalyptus.** [Middle English, from Latin, from Greek, from *eus,* good.]

eu·ca·lyp·tus (yōō′kə-lĭp′təs) *n., pl.* **-tus·es** or **-ti** (-tī′). Any of numerous trees of the genus *Eucalyptus,* native to Australia, with aromatic leaves that yield an oil used medicinally and wood used as timber. [EU- + Greek *kaluptos,* covered (from the flower, which is covered before it opens), from *kaluptein,* to hide.]

eucalyptus

Eu·cha·rist (yōō′kər-ĭst) *n.* **1.** The Christian sacrament commemorating Christ's Last Supper. Also called **Communion** and **Holy Communion. 2.** The consecrated elements of bread and wine used in this sacrament. [Middle English *eukarist,* from Old French *eucariste,* from Late Latin *eucharistia,* from Greek *eukharistia,* gratitude, from *eukharistos,* grateful : *eu-,* well, good + *kharis,* favor, grace.] —**Eu′cha·ris′tic** *adj.*

eu·chre (yōō′kər) *n.* A card game in which each player is dealt 5 cards and the player making the trump is required to take at least 3 tricks to win. [Orig. unknown.]

Eu·clid·e·an (yōō-klĭd′ē-ən) *adj.* Also **Eu·clid·i·an.** Of or pertaining to Euclid's geometric principles.

eu·gen·ic (yōō-jĕn′ĭk) *adj.* **1.** Pertaining to the improvement of a breed or race through eugenics. **2.** Of or pertaining to eugenics.

eu·gen·ics (yōō-jĕn′ĭks) *n. (used with a sing. verb).* The study of hereditary improvement of a breed or race, esp. of human beings, by genetic control. [From Greek *eugenēs*, well-born.]

eu·lo·gize (yōō′lə-jīz′) *tr.v.* **-gized, -giz·ing.** To write or deliver a eulogy about or for; praise highly; extol. —**eu′lo·gist** (-jĭst) *or* **eu′lo·giz′er** *n.*

eu·lo·gy (yōō′lə-jē) *n., pl.* **-gies.** A public speech or written tribute praising the virtues or achievements of a person or thing, esp. a person who has recently died. [Middle English *euloge*, from Medieval Latin *eulogium*, from Greek, praise, eulogy.] —**eu′lo·gis′tic** *adj.*

Eu·men·i·des (yōō-mĕn′ĭ-dēz′) *pl.n. Gk. Myth.* The Furies.

eu·nuch (yōō′nək) *n.* A castrated man, esp. one who was employed as a harem attendant in certain Oriental courts. [Middle English *eunuke*, from Latin *eunūchus*, from Greek *eunoukhos* : *eunē*, bed + *ekhein*, to have, to hold.]

eu·on·y·mus (yōō-ŏn′ə-məs) *n.* Any of various trees, shrubs, or vines of the genus *Euonymus*, many of which are cultivated for their decorative foliage or fruits. [Latin *euōnymus*, a kind of tree, from Greek *euōnumos* : *eu-*, good + *onoma*, name.]

eu·phe·mism (yōō′fə-mĭz′əm) *n.* **1.** The substitution of an inoffensive term for one considered offensively explicit. **2.** A word or phrase thus substituted; for example, *to pass away* is a euphemism for *to die.* [Greek *euphēmismos*, from *euphēmia*, use of good words : *eu-*, good + *phēmē*, speech, saying.] —**eu′phe·mist** *n.* —**eu′phe·mis′tic** (-mĭs′tĭk) *adj.* —**eu′phe·mis′ti·cal·ly** *adv.*

eu·pho·ni·ous (yōō-fō′nē-əs) *adj.* Pertaining to or characterized by euphony; agreeable to the ear: *euphonious verse; euphonious music.* —**eu·pho′ni·ous·ly** *adv.*

eu·pho·ni·um (yōō-fō′nē-əm) *n.* A brass wind instrument similar to the tuba but with a somewhat higher pitch and a mellower sound.

eu·pho·ny (yōō′fə-nē) *n., pl.* **-nies.** Pleasing or agreeable sound, esp. of words that please the ear. [French *euphonie*, from Late Latin *euphōnia*, from Greek, from *euphōnos*, sweet-voiced, euphonious : *eu-*, good + *phōnē*, sound.]

eu·phor·bi·a (yōō-fôr′bē-ə) *n.* Any plant of the genus *Euphorbia*, which includes the spurges. [After *Euphorbus*, 1st-cent. Greek physician.]

eu·pho·ri·a (yōō-fôr′ē-ə, -fōr′-) *n.* **1.** A feeling of great happiness or well-being; bliss. **2.** *Psychiat.* An exaggerated sense of well-being. [Greek, from *euphoros*, easy to bear : *eu-*, well + *pherein*, to bear.] —**eu·phor′ic** (-fôr′ĭk, -fōr′-) *adj.*

eu·phu·ism (yōō′fyōō-ĭz′əm) *n.* An affectedly elegant style of speech or writing, esp. a literary style used in the late 16th and early 17th cent. in England, characterized by elaborate alliteration, antitheses, and similes. [After *Euphues*, a character in two works by John Lyly.] —**eu′phu·ist** *n.* —**eu′phu·is′tic** *or* **eu′phu·is′ti·cal** *adj.* —**eu′phu·is′ti·cal·ly** *adv.*

Eur·a·sian (yōō-rā′zhən, -shən) *n.* A person of mixed European and Asian ancestry. —*adj.* **1.** Of, pertaining to, or originating in Eurasia. **2.** Of mixed European and Asian ancestry.

eu·re·ka (yōō-rē′kə) *interj.* A word used to express triumph upon finding or discovering something. [Greek *heurēka*, "I have found (it)" (supposedly exclaimed by Archimedes upon discovering how to measure the volume of an irregular solid and thereby determine the purity of a gold object), perfect indicative of *heuriskein*, to find.]

Eu·ro·pa (yōō-rō′pə) *n. Gk. Myth.* A Phoenician princess abducted to Crete by Zeus, in the guise of a white bull.

Eu·ro·pe·an (yōōr′ə-pē′ən) *n.* **1.** A native or inhabitant of Europe. **2.** A person of European descent. —*adj.* Of Europe or its peoples, cultures, or languages.

European plan. A system of hotel management in which the payment for room and services is separate from the payment for meals.

eu·ro·pi·um (yōō-rō′pē-əm) *n. Symbol* **Eu** A silvery-white, soft rare-earth element, used to absorb neutrons in research. Atomic number 63; atomic weight 151.96; melting point 826°C; boiling point 1,439°C; specific gravity 5.259; valences 2, 3. [After *Europe*.]

Eu·ryd·i·ce (yōō-rĭd′ĭ-sē) *n. Gk. Myth.* The wife of Or-

pheus, who was permitted by Pluto to follow her husband out of Hades provided that he did not look back at her; Orpheus did look back, and Eurydice was doomed to return.

Eu·sta·chian tube (yōō-stā′shən, -shē-ən, -stā′kē-ən). The narrow tube that connects the middle ear and the pharynx and allows the pressures on both sides of the eardrum to equalize. [After Bartolommeo *Eustachio* (1524?–74), Italian anatomist.]

Eu·ter·pe (yōō-tûr′pē) *n. Gk. Myth.* The Muse of lyric poetry and music.

eu·tha·na·sia (yōō′thə-nā′zhə, -shə) *n.* **1.** The act of inducing the painless death of a person, usu. one in the terminal stage of an incurable disease; mercy killing. **2.** An easy or painless death. [Greek : *eu-*, good + *thanatos*, death.]

eu·then·ics (yōō-thĕn′ĭks) *n. (used with a sing. or pl. verb).* The study of the improvement of human functioning and well-being by the control or adjustment of environmental conditions. [From Greek *euthenein*, to flourish, thrive.]

e·vac·u·ate (ĭ-văk′yōō-āt′) *tr.v.* **-at·ed, -at·ing.** **1.** To withdraw or send away from a threatened area: *evacuated the inhabitants from the flood zone.* **2.** To withdraw or depart from; vacate: *residents evacuating a burning building.* **3. a.** To cause to be empty. **b.** To create a vacuum in (a container). **4.** To discharge (waste matter), esp. from the bowels. [From Latin *ēvacuāre* : *ex-*, out + *vacuus*, empty, from *vacāre*, to be empty.] —**e·vac′u·a′tor** *n.*

e·vac·u·a·tion (ĭ-văk′yōō-ā′shən) *n.* **1.** The act of evacuating or the condition of being evacuated. **2. a.** The discharge of waste matter from bodily passages, esp. from the bowels. **b.** The matter thus discharged.

e·vac·u·ee (ĭ-văk′yōō-ē′) *n.* A person removed from a threatened or dangerous area.

e·vade (ĭ-vād′) *v.* **e·vad·ed, e·vad·ing.** —*tr.v.* **1.** To get away from by cleverness or deceit: *evade arrest.* **2.** To avoid fulfilling, answering, or performing: *evade responsibility.* **3.** To baffle or elude: *The accident evades explanation.* —*intr.v.* To use cleverness or deceit in avoiding or escaping. —See Syns at **avoid.** [Old French *evader*, from Latin *ēvādere*, to go out, escape : *ex-*, out + *vādere*, to go.] —**e·vad′er** *n.*

e·val·u·ate (ĭ-văl′yōō-āt′) *tr.v.* **-at·ed, -at·ing.** **1.** To determine or fix the value or worth of: *evaluate an antique clock.* **2.** To examine and judge; appraise; estimate: *evaluate a new play; evaluate data.* **3.** *Math.* To calculate the numerical value of. [Back-formation from EVALUATION.]

e·val·u·a·tion (ĭ-văl′yōō-ā′shən) *n.* **1.** The act of evaluating or judging. **2.** The result of evaluating; a judgment or appraisal. [French *évaluation*, from Old French *evaluation*, from *evaluer*, to evaluate.]

ev·a·nesce (ĕv′ə-nĕs′) *intr.v.* **-nesced, -nesc·ing.** To disappear gradually; fade away; vanish. [Latin *ēvānēscere*, to vanish : *ex-*, completely + *vānus*, empty, vain.]

ev·a·nes·cence (ĕv′ə-nĕs′əns) *n.* **1.** Gradual disappearing; dissipation. **2.** The condition or quality of being insubstantial or transitory.

ev·a·nes·cent (ĕv′ə-nĕs′ənt) *adj.* Tending to disappear; transitory; fleeting: *evanescent joy.*

e·van·gel (ĭ-văn′jəl) *n.* **1.** Evangel. The Christian gospel, esp. any of the four Gospels of the New Testament. **2.** An evangelist. [Middle English *evangelie*, from Old French *evangile*, from Late Latin *evangelium*, from Greek *euangelion*, good news : *eu-*, good + *angelos*, messenger.]

e·van·gel·i·cal (ē′văn-jĕl′ĭ-kəl) *or* **e·van·gel·ic** (-jĕl′ĭk) *adj.* **1.** Of or in accordance with the Christian gospel, esp. the four Gospels of the New Testament. **2.** Of or being a Protestant group emphasizing the belief that salvation is achieved through faith in Christ. —*n.* A member of an evangelical church or party. —**e′van·gel′i·cal·ism** *n.* —**e′van·gel′i·cal·ly** *adv.*

e·van·gel·ism (ĭ-văn′jə-lĭz′əm) *n.* **1.** The practice of preaching and spreading the gospel, as through missionary work. **2.** Militant zeal for any cause.

e·van·gel·ist (ĭ-văn′jə-lĭst) *n.* **1.** Often **Evangelist.** Any of the authors of the four New Testament Gospels; Matthew, Mark, Luke, or John. **2.** A person who practices evangelism, esp. a zealous preacher. **3.** A Mormon patriarch. —**e·van′gel·is′tic** *adj.* —**e·van′gel·is′ti·cal·ly** *adv.*

e·van·gel·ize (ĭ-văn′jə-līz′) *v.* **-ized, -iz·ing.** —*tr.v.* **1.** To preach the gospel to. **2.** To convert to Christianity. —*intr.v.* To be an evangelist. —**e·van′gel·i·za′tion** *n.*

e·vap·o·rate (ĭ-văp′ə-rāt′) *v.* **-rat·ed, -rat·ing.** —*tr.v.* **1.** To convert or change into a vapor. **2.** To remove or draw moisture from, as by heating, leaving only the dry solid residue. —*intr.v.* **1.** To change into vapor: *Alcohol evaporates quickly.* **2.** To produce vapor: *Smoke rose from the beaker as the nitrogen evaporated.* **3.** To disappear; vanish; fade: *His fears evaporated.* [Middle English *evaporaten,* from Latin *ēvāporāre* : *ex-,* out + *vapor,* steam, vapor.] —**e·vap′o·ra′tion** *n.* —**e·vap′o·ra′tive** *adj.* —**e·vap′o·ra′tor** *n.*

evaporated milk. Concentrated, unsweetened milk made by evaporating some of the water from whole milk.

e·va·sion (ĭ-vā′zhən) *n.* **1.** The act of avoiding, evading, or escaping; dodging: *income-tax evasion.* **2.** A means of evading; an excuse. [Middle English *evasioun,* from Old French *evasion,* from Late Latin *ēvāsiō,* from Latin *ēvāsus,* past part. of *ēvādere,* to evade.]

e·va·sive (ĭ-vā′sĭv) *adj.* Tending to evade; characterized by evasion; vague or ambiguous : *an evasive statement.* —**e·va′sive·ly** *adv.* —**e·va′sive·ness** *n.*

eve (ēv) *n.* **1.** Often **Eve.** The evening or day preceding a special day, such as a holiday. **2.** The period immediately preceding a certain event: *the eve of war.* **3.** *Poet.* Evening. [Middle English, var. of *even,* evening.]

e·ven¹ (ē′vən) *adj.* **-er, -est. 1. a.** Having a horizontal surface; flat: *an even floor.* **b.** Having no irregularities, roughness, or indentations; smooth: *an even board.* **2.** At the same height or depth; parallel; level: *The picture is even with the window.* **3.** Having no variations; uniform; regular: *an even rate of speed.* **4.** Not easily disturbed; tranquil; calm: *an even temper.* **5.** Equally matched or balanced, as a competition: *an even fight.* **6.** Equal or identical in degree, extent, or amount: *even amounts of oil and vinegar.* **7.** Having equal probability: *an even chance of winning.* **8. a.** Having an equal score: *The teams are even.* **b.** Being equal for each opponent: *an even score.* **9.** Neither owing nor being owed; having nothing due: *Give him five dollars, and you will be even.* **10.** Having taken or gained full revenge: *After hitting his brother back he said they were even.* **11.** Exactly divisible by 2. **12.** Having an even number in a series. **13.** Having an exact amount, extent, or number: *an even pound.* —*adv.* **1.** To a higher degree or extent; yet; still: *an even worse condition.* **2.** In the exact manner; precisely; just: *She didn't show how upset she was, even as I had predicted.* **3.** At the same time as; just: *Even as we watched, the building collapsed.* **4.** In spite of; nevertheless; notwithstanding: *Even with his head start I soon overtook him.* **5.** Indeed; in fact; moreover: *unhappy, even weeping.* **6.** Although seemingly improbable: *Even old ladies were playing poker.* **7.** To the fullest degree; completely: *loyal even unto death.* **8.** *Nonstandard.* Smoothly; evenly. —*tr.v.* To make level, smooth, or equal: *even the score.* —*intr.v.* To become even or smooth. —**idioms. break even.** *Informal.* To have neither losses nor gains. **get even.** To take revenge. [Middle English, from Old English *efen,* even, level.] —**e′ven·ly** *adv.* —**e′ven·ness** *n.*

e·ven² (ē′vən) *n. Archaic & Poet.* Evening. [Middle English, from Old English *æfen.*]

e·ven·hand·ed (ē′vən-hăn′dĭd) *adj.* Dealing fairly with all; impartial; just. —**e′ven·hand′ed·ly** *adv.* —**e′ven·hand′ed·ness** *n.*

e·ven·ing (ēv′nĭng) *n.* The period just after sunset; late afternoon and early night. —*modifier:* *an evening bath; an evening meal.* [Middle English, from Old English *æfnung,* from *æfnian,* to become evening, from *æfen,* evening.]

evening dress. Formal clothing worn for evening social events.

evening star. A planet, esp. Mercury or Venus, that shines brightly in the western sky after sunset.

e·ven·song (ē′vən-sông′, -sŏng′) *n.* **1.** An evening prayer service that is read or sung. **2.** *Rom. Cath. Ch.* A vesper service. **3.** *Archaic.* Evening.

e·vent (ĭ-vĕnt′) *n.* **1.** An occurrence, incident, or experience, esp. one of significance. **2.** An actual outcome or final result. **3.** One of the items in a program of sports: *the relay event.* —**idioms. at all events.** In any case; anyhow.

in any event. In any case; anyhow. **in the event.** In case; if it should happen. [Latin *ēventus,* from the past part. of *ēvenīre,* to come out, happen : *ex-,* out + *venīre,* to come.]

e·vent·ful (ĭ-vĕnt′fəl) *adj.* **1.** Full of events: *an eventful week.* **2.** Important; momentous: *an eventful decision.*

e·ven·tide (ē′vən-tīd′) *n. Poet.* Evening. [Middle English, from Old English *æfentīd* : *æfen,* evening + *tīd,* time.]

e·ven·tu·al (ĭ-vĕn′chōō-əl) *adj.* Occurring at an unspecified time in the future; ultimate: *his eventual death.* [From EVENT.] —**e·ven′tu·al·ly** *adv.*

e·ven·tu·al·i·ty (ĭ-vĕn′chōō-ăl′ĭ-tē) *n., pl.* **-ties.** Something that may occur; a contingency; possibility.

e·ven·tu·ate (ĭ-vĕn′chōō-āt′) *intr.v.* **-at·ed, -at·ing.** To result ultimately; culminate: *The disputes eventuated in a strike.*

ev·er (ĕv′ər) *adv.* **1.** At all times; always; constantly: *He is ever courteous.* **2.** At any time: *Have you ever seen a circus?* **3.** In any possible way or case; at all: *How could you ever treat him that way?* —**idioms. ever and ever** (or **anon**). Now and then; occasionally. **ever so.** *Informal.* To an extreme degree; very: *ever so glad.* **ever so often.** Frequently. **for ever and a day.** Always; forever. [Middle English, from Old English *æfre.*]

ev·er·glade (ĕv′ər-glād′) *n.* A tract of swampy marsh land, covered in places with tall grass.

ev·er·green (ĕv′ər-grēn′) *adj. Bot.* Having foliage that remains green throughout the year. —*n.* **1.** An evergreen tree, shrub, or plant. **2. evergreens.** Twigs or branches of evergreen plants used as decorations.

ev·er·last·ing (ĕv′ər-lăs′tĭng) *adj.* **1.** Lasting or enduring forever; eternal: *everlasting God.* **2.** Continuing indefinitely or for a long time; perpetual: *everlasting bliss.* **3.** Going on too long; tedious; wearisome: *an everlasting speech.* —See Syns at **continuous.** —*n.* **1. the Everlasting.** God. **2.** Eternity. **3.** Any of various plants, such as the strawflower, that retain form and color long after they are dry. —**ev′er·last′ing·ly** *adv.*

ev·er·more (ĕv′ər-môr′, -mōr′) *adv.* At all times; forever.

e·vert (ĭ-vûrt′) *tr.v.* To turn inside out or outward. [Latin *ēvertere,* to turn out, overturn : *ex-,* out + *vertere,* to turn.] —**e·ver′sion** *n.*

ev·er·y (ĕv′rē) *adj.* **1.** Each without exception: *every student in the class.* **2.** Each in a specified series: *every third seat; every two hours.* **3.** Entire; utmost: *was given every care.* —See Usage note **2** at **each.** —*adv.* More or less; periodically: *every once in a while.* —**idioms. every bit.** *Informal.* In all ways; quite; equally: *He is every bit as mean as she is.* **every so often.** Occasionally. —See Usage note **3** at **ever. every which way.** *Informal.* In complete disorder; chaotic. [Middle English, from Old English *æfre ælc,* every, each one : *æfre,* ever + *ælc,* each.]

eve·ry·bod·y (ĕv′rē-bŏd′ē) *pron.* Every person; everyone.

Usage: **everybody, everyone, every one. 1. everybody, everyone.** When used as subjects these pronouns take singular verbs, with accompanying personal pronouns and pronominal adjectives often but not invariably agreeing with the verbs in number. In recent years plural pronominal forms have been increasingly used by many writers to avoid forms of the masculine *he* or forms of the sometimes cumbersome *he or she.* In fact, these plurals have been used by reputable speakers and writers for several hundred years. All of these examples are acceptable: *Everybody raised his* (or *her*) *hand. Everybody raised his or her hand. Everybody raised their hands* (or *hand*). *Everyone is entitled to sufficient time to make up his* (or *her*) *mind. Everyone is entitled to sufficient time to make up his or her mind. Everyone is entitled to sufficient time to make up their minds* (or *mind*). **2. everyone, every one.** These two terms are distinguished in usage. *Everyone* is the choice when *everybody* can be substituted for it—when the sense is that of every individual considered indefinitely: *Everyone was aware of her presence. Every one* refers to each individual of a specific group; it is typically followed by *of,* or else *of* and an object are implied: *Every one of them is at fault* (or *Every one is to blame*). *There were four choices, every one of which presented serious problems.*

eve·ry·day (ĕv′rē-dā′) *adj.* **1.** Suitable for ordinary or routine occasions: *an everyday suit.* **2.** Commonplace; ordinary: *everyday worries.* —See Syns at **common.**

ă pat ā pay â care ä father ĕ pet ē be hw which ĭ pit ī tie î pier ŏ pot ō toe ô paw, for oi noise
ōō took ōō boot ou out th thin th this ŭ cut û urge zh vision ə about, item, edible, gallop, circus

eve·ry·one (ĕv′rē-wŭn′) *pron.* Every person; everybody. —See Usage note at **everybody.**

eve·ry·thing (ĕv′rē-thĭng′) *pron.* **1.** All that exists or pertains to a given instance; entirety; totality: *everything in this room.* **2.** All relevant items or factors: *Tell him everything.* **3.** The most important fact or consideration: *Her children are everything to her.*

eve·ry·where (ĕv′rē-hwâr′, -wâr′) *adv.* In every place; in all places.
   Usage: **everywhere.** This is the only acceptable spelling—not "everywheres."

e·vict (ĭ-vĭkt′) *tr.v.* To expel (an occupant) from property by legal process; put out. [Middle English *evicten,* from Latin *ēvictus,* past part. of *ēvincere,* to conquer, overcome : *ex-,* completely + *vincere,* to conquer.] —**e·vic′tion** *n.* —**e·vic′tor** *n.*

ev·i·dence (ĕv′ĭ-dəns) *n.* **1.** Something that furnishes proof; the data on which a judgment or conclusion is based. **2.** Something that serves to indicate, suggest, or make evident: *His reaction was evidence of guilt.* **3.** *Law.* The statements and objects admissible as testimony in a court of law. —See Syns at **sign.** —*tr.v.* **-denced, -denc·ing.** To indicate clearly; demonstrate; prove: *Downed power lines evidenced the storm's ferocity.* —See Syns at **show.** —*idiom.* **in evidence.** Present and plainly visible; conspicuous: *He was very much in evidence at the convention.* [Middle English, from Old French, from Late Latin *ēvidentia,* from Latin *ēvidēns,* evident.]

ev·i·dent (ĕv′ĭ-dənt) *adj.* Easily seen or understood; clear; obvious: *It was evident that he was only interested in himself.* [Middle English, from Old French, from Latin *ēvidēns: ex-,* completely + *vidēns,* pres. part. of *vidēre,* to see.]

ev·i·den·tial (ĕv′ĭ-dĕn′shəl) *adj.* Pertaining to, providing, or having the nature of evidence. —**ev′i·den′tial·ly** *adv.*

ev·i·dent·ly (ĕv′ĭ-dənt-lē, -dĕnt′-) *adv.* **1.** Obviously; clearly: *He was evidently dead.* **2.** Apparently or seemingly; probably: *She's evidently going to be late.*

e·vil (ē′vəl) *adj.* **-er, -est. 1.** Morally bad or wrong; wicked: *an evil tyrant; evil deeds.* **2.** Causing harm or trouble; harmful; injurious: *an evil habit.* **3.** Characterized by or indicating future misfortune; foreboding; ominous: *evil omens.* **4.** Resulting from bad conduct or character; infamous: *an evil reputation.* **5.** Spiteful; malicious: *an evil temper.* —See Syns at **malevolent.** —*n.* **1.** That which is morally bad or wrong; wickedness; sin. **2.** That which causes misfortune, suffering, or difficulty: *High interest rates are a necessary evil required to drive down inflation.* **3.** Often **evils.** Anything that is undesirable because of its harmful nature or effect: *the evils of war.* [Middle English *evel, yvel,* from Old English *yfel.*] —**e′vil·ly** *adv.* —**e′vil·ness** *n.*

e·vil-mind·ed (ē′vəl-mīn′dĭd) *adj.* Having evil thoughts or intentions; malicious. —**e′vil-mind′ed·ness** *n.*

e·vince (ĭ-vĭns′) *tr.v.* **e·vinced, e·vinc·ing. 1.** To demonstrate clearly or convincingly; make evident. **2.** To show or exhibit; manifest: *evince surprise at the news.* —See Syns at **show.** [Latin *ēvincere : ex-,* completely + *vincere,* to conquer.] —**e·vinc′i·ble** *adj.*

e·vis·cer·ate (ĭ-vĭs′ə-rāt′) *tr.v.* **-at·ed, -at·ing. 1.** To remove the entrails of; disembowel. **2.** To take away a vital or essential part of: *Many claim that Supreme Court decisions have eviscerated the police's power to collect evidence.* [From Latin *ēviscerāre : ex-,* out + *viscera,* viscera.] —**e·vis′cer·a′tion** *n.*

ev·o·ca·tion (ĕv′ō-kā′shən) *n.* The act of calling forth or conjuring up: *an evocation of childhood memories.*

e·voc·a·tive (ĭ-vŏk′ə-tĭv) *adj.* Tending or having the power to evoke. —**e·voc′a·tive·ly** *adv.*

e·voke (ĭ-vōk′) *tr.v.* **e·voked, e·vok·ing.** To summon or call forth; elicit; inspire: *evoke memories; evoke curiosity.* [Latin *ēvocāre,* to call forth, to call out, summon : *ex-,* out + *vocāre,* to call.]

ev·o·lu·tion (ĕv′ə-lōō′shən) *n.* **1.** A gradual process in which something changes or develops into a different, esp. more complex, form: *the evolution of jazz.* **2.** *Biol.* **a.** The theory that groups of organisms, such as species, may change or develop over a long period of time and through natural processes so that descendants differ morphologically and physiologically. **b.** The historical development of a related group of organisms: *plant evolution.* **3.** *Math.* The operation of finding a square root, cube root, or other root of a number. [Latin *ēvolūtiō,* an opening, an unrolling, from *ēvolūtus,* past part. of *ēvolvere,* to roll out, to open, evolve.]

ev·o·lu·tion·ar·y (ĕv′ə-lōō′shə-nĕr′ē) *adj.* **1.** Of, pertaining to, or resulting from evolution. **2.** Of or in accord with the theory of biological evolution; Darwinian.

ev·o·lu·tion·ism (ĕv′ə-lōō′shə-nĭz′əm) *n.* Acceptance of the theory of biological evolution. —**ev′o·lu′tion·ist** *n.*

e·volve (ĭ-vŏlv′) *v.* **e·volved, e·volv·ing.** —*tr.v.* **1.** To develop or work out; arrive at gradually: *evolve a plan.* **2.** *Biol.* To develop by evolutionary processes from a primitive to a more highly organized form. **3.** To yield, give, or throw off (gas, vapor, heat, etc.). —*intr.v.* **1.** To be developed; come forth; emerge: *The plot evolves in many subtle ways.* **2.** To be part of or subject to the process of biological evolution. [Latin *ēvolvere,* to roll out, unfold : *ex-,* out + *volvere,* to roll.] —**e·volve′ment** *n.*

ewe (yōō) *n.* A female sheep. [Middle English, from Old English *ēowu.*]

ew·er (yōō′ər) *n.* A large, wide-mouthed pitcher or jug. [Middle English, from Norman French, from Old North French *eviere,* from Latin *aquārius,* relating to water, from *aqua,* water.]

ewer

ex (ĕks) *prep. Finance.* Without; not including; not participating in: *ex dividend.* [Latin *ex,* out, from.]

ex-. A prefix meaning: **1.** Out of or from: *exurbia.* **2.** Former: *ex-president.* [Middle English, from Old French, from Latin.]

ex·ac·er·bate (ĭg-zăs′ər-bāt′, ĭk-săs′-) *tr.v.* **-bat·ed, -bat·ing.** To increase the severity of; aggravate: *exacerbate tensions; exacerbate pain.* [From Latin *exacerbāre : ex-,* completely + *acerbus,* bitter, harsh.] —**ex·ac′er·ba′tion** *n.*

ex·act (ĭg-zăkt′) *adj.* **1.** Accurate and precise; correct: *the exact time; an exact measurement.* **2.** Strictly and completely in accord with fact: *an exact description; her exact words.* **3.** Characterized by accuracy or precision: *an exact reading.* —See Syns at **correct.** —*tr.v.* **1.** To demand and obtain by or as if by force or authority: *exact justice; exact payment.* **2.** To call for or require: *exact great effort.* [Latin *exactus,* past part. of *exigere,* to require, examine : *ex-,* out + *agere,* to lead, to drive.] —**ex·act′ness** *n.*

ex·act·ing (ĭg-zăk′tĭng) *adj.* **1.** Making severe or rigorous demands: *an exacting taskmaster.* **2.** Requiring great care or effort: *an exacting task.* —See Syns at **burdensome.** —**ex·act′ing·ly** *adv.*

ex·ac·tion (ĭg-zăk′shən) *n.* **1.** The act of exacting. **2.** Something that is exacted, as a sum of money.

ex·act·i·tude (ĭg-zăk′tĭ-tōōd′, -tyōōd′) *n.* The condition or quality of being exact; precision.

ex·act·ly (ĭg-zăkt′lē) *adv.* **1.** In an exact manner; precisely: *Follow the recipe exactly.* **2.** In all respects; just: *Do exactly as you please.* **3.** Quite so; as you say: *"Exactly," he replied, "I feel the same."*

ex·ag·ger·ate (ĭg-zăj′ə-rāt′) *v.* **-at·ed, -at·ing.** —*tr.v.* **1.** To enlarge or increase (something) beyond normal bounds: *exaggerate the details of a map.* **2.** To make (something) appear greater than it is; overstate: *exaggerate the value of an antique.* —*intr.v.* To make something appear greater

than it is; overstate. [From Latin *exaggerāre* : *ex-*, completely + *aggerāre*, to pile up, from *agger*, pile, heap.]
—ex·ag·ger·a·tive or **ex·ag·ger·a·to·ry** (-ə-tôr′ē, -tōr′ē) *adj.*
—ex·ag·ger·a·tor *n.*

ex·ag·ger·a·tion (ĭg-zăj′ə-rā′shən) *n.* **1.** The act of exaggerating. **2.** An example of exaggerating; an overstatement.

ex·alt (ĭg-zôlt′) *tr.v.* **1.** To raise in rank, character, status, etc.; elevate: *exalted the general to a place among the peers.* **2.** To praise; honor; glorify: *exalted his achievements in medical research.* **3.** To fill with an intensified feeling such as joy, pride, or delight; elate. [Middle English *exalten*, from Old French *exalter*, from Latin *exaltāre* : *ex-*, up + *altus*, high.]

ex·al·ta·tion (ĕg′zôl-tā′shən) *n.* **1.** The act of exalting or the condition of being exalted. **2.** A feeling of intense exhilaration and well-being; elation.

ex·am (ĭg-zăm′) *n. Informal.* An examination.

ex·am·i·na·tion (ĭg-zăm′ə-nā′shən) *n.* **1.** The act or process of examining; an inspection; analysis. **2.** A set of questions or exercises designed to test knowledge or skills. **3.** A formal interrogation, as of a witness in a trial; official inquiry. **4.** An inspection of part or all of the body, as by a dentist or physician. **—ex·am′i·na′tion·al** *adj.*

ex·am·ine (ĭg-zăm′ĭn) *tr.v.* **-ined, -in·ing.** **1.** To inspect or scrutinize in detail: *examining cells under a microscope.* **2.** To determine the qualifications, ability, knowledge, etc., by questioning or testing. **3.** To interrogate or question formally to elicit facts, information, etc. **4.** To study the state of health of. [Middle English *examinen*, from Old French *examiner*, from Latin *exāmināre*, from *exāmen*, a weighing, consideration, from *exigere*, to examine : *ex-*, out + *agere*, to lead.] **—ex·am′in·er** *n.*

ex·am·in·ee (ĭg-zăm′ə-nē′) *n.* A person who is examined.

ex·am·ple (ĭg-zăm′pəl) *n.* **1.** One particular thing that is representative of a group as a whole; a sample; specimen: *a fine example of Beethoven's late sonatas.* **2.** Someone or something worthy of imitation; a model; exemplar: *His life is an example of dedication.* **3.** Someone or something that serves or is intended to serve as a warning: *Let his punishment be an example to you.* **4.** A problem shown with its solution to illustrate a principle or method. —See Syns at **ideal. —idioms. for example.** Serving as an illustration, a model, or an instance. **set an example.** To be or provide a model of behavior worthy of imitation. [Middle English *exaumple*, from Old French *example*, from Latin *exemplum*, sample, from *eximere*, to take out : *ex-*, out + *emere*, to take.]

ex·as·per·ate (ĭg-zăs′pə-rāt′) *tr.v.* **-at·ed, -at·ing.** To make angry or irritated; provoke; irk. [From Latin *exasperāre* : *ex-*, entirely + *asper*, rough.]

ex·as·per·a·tion (ĭg-zăs′pə-rā′shən) *n.* An act of exasperating or the condition of being exasperated.

Ex·cal·i·bur (ĭk-skăl′ə-bər). In English legend, King Arthur's sword.

ex ca·the·dra (ĕks′ kə-thē′drə). *Latin.* With authority; from a position of authority.

ex·ca·vate (ĕk′skə-vāt′) *tr.v.* **-vat·ed, -vat·ing.** **1.** To make a cavity or hole in; dig out: *excavate the mountainside.* **2.** To form by hollowing out: *excavate a tunnel.* **3.** To remove by digging or scooping out: *excavate soil.* **4.** To uncover by digging: *excavate an ancient temple.* [From Latin *excavāre*: *ex-*, out + *cavus*, hollow.] **—ex′ca·va′tor** *n.*

ex·ca·va·tion (ĕk′skə-vā′shən) *n.* **1.** The act or process of excavating. **2.** A cavity formed by excavating. **3.** Something, as ruins, uncovered by excavating.

ex·ceed (ĭk-sēd′) *tr.v.* **1.** To be greater than; surpass: *success exceeding all expectations.* **2.** To go beyond the proper limits of: *exceed one's authority.* —See Syns at **surpass.** [Middle English *exceden*, from Old French *exceder*, from Latin *excēdere*, to depart, go out, surpass : *ex-*, out + *cēdere*, to go.]

ex·ceed·ing (ĭk-sē′dĭng) *adj.* Extreme; extraordinary. *—adv. Archaic.* Exceedingly.

ex·ceed·ing·ly (ĭk-sē′dĭng-lē) *adv.* To an unusual degree; extremely: *exceedingly dangerous.*

ex·cel (ĭk-sĕl′) *v.* **-celled, -cel·ling. —***tr.v.* To be superior to; surpass: *Her beauty excels that of others.* *—intr.v.* To be or do better than others: *He excels in wit.* —See Syns at **surpass.** [Middle English *excellen*, from Latin *excellere.*]

ex·cel·lence (ĕk′sə-ləns) *n.* **1.** The quality or condition of being excellent; superiority: *artistic excellence.* **2.** Something in which a person or thing excels.

Ex·cel·len·cy (ĕk′sə-lən-sē) *n., pl.* **-cies.** A title or form of address for certain high officials, such as ambassadors, bishops, or governors: *His Excellency.*

ex·cel·lent (ĕk′sə-lənt) *adj.* Of the highest or finest quality; exceptionally good; superb. **—ex′cel·lent·ly** *adv.*

    Syns: **excellent, capital, dandy** *(Informal),* **fine, first-class, great, prime, splendid, super** *(Slang),* **superb, swell** *(Informal),* **terrific** *(Informal),* **top, topflight, topnotch** *(Informal) adj.* Core meaning: Exceptionally good of its kind *(an excellent picture).*

ex·cel·si·or (ĭk-sĕl′sē-ər) *n.* Slender, curved wood shavings used esp. for packing. [From a trade name.]

ex·cept (ĭk-sĕpt′) *prep.* Other than; but: *All the eggs except one broke.* *—conj.* **1.** Only: *He would buy the suit except that it costs too much.* **2.** Otherwise than: *He would not open his mouth except to yell.* *—tr.v.* To leave out; exclude. —See Usage note at **accept.** [Middle English, from Latin *exceptus*, past part. of *excipere* : *ex-*, out + *capere*, to take.]

    Usage: **except. 1.** When the word means other than or but, it is a preposition. A pronoun following *except*, used in this meaning, is therefore in the objective case: *No one except me was affected. Every member of the committee was implicated except him.* **2.** As a conjunction *except* can mean if it were not for the fact that. In that sense, esp. in formal writing, *except* is followed by *that: She would have accepted the invitation except that the trip was very expensive.* See also Usage note at **excepting.**

ex·cept·ing (ĭk-sĕp′tĭng) *prep.* Excluding; except.

    Usage: **excepting, except.** As prepositions, both words mean excluding. However, *excepting* is the choice in negative constructions and *except*, the choice in positive constructions. Examples: *All students, not excepting part-time ones, must be familiar with the rules* (negative construction). *No one except me was affected* (positive construction). *Every member except him was implicated* (positive construction).

ex·cep·tion (ĭk-sĕp′shən) *n.* **1.** The act of excepting or the condition of being excepted. **2.** Someone or something that is excepted: *"Americans want to be liked — and senators are no exception"* (John F. Kennedy). **3.** An objection or criticism; opposition. **4.** *Law.* A formal objection taken during the course of a legal proceeding. **—idiom. take exception.** To object to.

ex·cep·tion·a·ble (ĭk-sĕp′shə-nə-bəl) *adj.* Liable or likely to cause objection. **—ex·cep′tion·a·bly** *adv.*

ex·cep·tion·al (ĭk-sĕp′shə-nəl) *adj.* Being an exception; uncommon; extraordinary: *exceptional beauty.* —See Syns at **uncommon. —ex·cep′tion·al·ly** *adv.*

ex·cerpt (ĕk′sûrpt′) *n.* A passage or scene selected from a speech, book, film, play, etc. *—tr.v.* (ĭk-sûrpt′). To select, quote, or take out (a passage or scene) from a speech, book, film, play, etc. [Latin *excerptum*, from the past part. of *excerpere*, to pick out, excerpt : *ex-*, out + *carpere*, to pick, pluck.]

ex·cess (ĭk-sĕs′, ĕk′sĕs′) *n.* **1.** The condition of exceeding what is normal or sufficient: *overcome by an excess of grief.* **2.** An amount or quantity beyond what is normal or sufficient: *an excess of praise.* **3.** The amount or quantity by which something exceeds another: *an excess of imports over exports.* **4.** Intemperance; overindulgence. *—adj.* Exceeding what is required or usual: *excess fat.* **—idiom. to excess.** To an extreme degree or extent: *generous to excess.* [Middle English, from Old French *exces*, from Latin *excessus*, past part. of *excēdere*, to exceed.]

    Syns: **excess, glut, overage, overflow, overstock, superfluity, surplus** *n.* Core meaning: An amount beyond what is needed or appropriate *(an excess of grain).*

ex·ces·sive (ĭk-sĕs′ĭv) *adj.* Exceeding what is usual, necessary, or proper; extreme; inordinate: *excessive praise; excessive grief.* **—ex·ces′sive·ly** *adv.*

ex·change (ĭks-chānj′) *v.* **-changed, -chang·ing.** **—***tr.v.* **1.** To give and receive reciprocally; interchange: *exchange ideas.* **2.** To give up for something else: *exchange a business career for a government position.* **3.** To give, provide, or transfer in return for something of equal value; to trade

---

ă pat   ā pay   â care   ä father   ĕ pet   ē be   hw which   ĭ pit   ī tie   î pier   ŏ pot   ō toe   ô paw, for   oi noise
ōō took   ōō boot   ou out   th thin   *th* this   ŭ cut   û urge   zh vision   ə about, item, edible, gallop, circus

or swap: *exchanged food for oil.* **4.** To replace with something more satisfactory: *exchange defective merchandise.* —*intr.v.* To make an exchange. —*n.* **1.** An act of exchanging. **2.** An act of giving up one thing for something else. **3.** The replacement or substitution of one thing for another. **4.** Someone or something that is exchanged. **5.** A place where things are exchanged, esp. a center where securities and commodities are bought and sold: *a stock exchange.* **6.** A **telephone exchange. 7.** A system of payments using negotiable drafts, bills of exchange, etc., instead of money. **8.** A **bill of exchange. 9.** The amount of difference in the actual value of two or more currencies or between values of the same currency at two or more places. [Middle English *eschaungen,* from Old French *eschangier* : Late Latin *ex-,* completely + *cambiāre,* to exchange, barter.] —**ex·change′a·ble** *adj.*

ex·cheq·uer (ĭks-chĕk′ər, ĕks′chĕk′ər) *n.* **1. Exchequer.** The British governmental department in charge of the collection and care of the national revenue. **2.** A treasury, as of a nation or an organization. [Middle English *escheker,* from Old French *eschequier,* chessboard, counting table (usu. covered with a checkered cloth), from *eschec,* check (at chess).]

ex·cise¹ (ĕk′sīz′, ĭk-sīz′) *n.* A tax on the production, sale, or consumption of certain commodities within a country. Also called **excise tax.** [Obs. Dutch *excijs,* from Middle Dutch, prob. from Old French *acceis* : Latin *ad-,* against, to + *cēnsus,* tax, census.]

ex·cise² (ĭk-sīz′) *tr.v.* **-cised, -cis·ing.** To remove by or as if by cutting: *excise a tumor.* [Latin *excīsus,* past part. of *excīdere,* to cut out : *ex-,* out + *caedere,* to cut.] —**ex·ci′sion** (ĭk-sĭzh′ən) *n.*

ex·cit·a·ble (ĭk-sī′tə-bəl) *adj.* **1.** Capable of being excited; easily excited. **2.** Capable of responding to stimuli: *an excitable aural nerve.* —**ex·cit′a·bil′i·ty** or **ex·cit′a·ble·ness** *n.* —**ex·cit′a·bly** *adv.*

ex·ci·ta·tion (ĕk′sī-tā′shən, -sī-) *n.* **1. a.** A process in which an atom, molecule, or other physical system absorbs energy and changes its internal structure. **b.** The condition of an atom, molecule, etc., that has undergone this process. **2.** Stimulation, as of a nerve, muscle, etc. **3.** The act of exciting or condition of being excited.

ex·cite (ĭk-sīt′) *tr.v.* **-cit·ed, -cit·ing.** **1.** To stir to activity; put into motion. **2.** To call forth or elicit; induce: *excite interest.* **3.** To arouse strong feeling in (a person); provoke: *excited him to anger.* **4.** *Biol.* To produce increased activity in (an organism or part); stimulate. **5.** *Physics.* To raise (an atom, molecule, etc.) to a higher energy level. —See Syns at **provoke.** [Middle English *exciten,* from Old French *exciter,* from Latin *excitāre,* from *exciēre,* to call or bring out : *ex-,* out + *ciēre,* to call, put in motion.]

ex·cit·ed (ĭk-sī′tĭd) *adj.* **1.** Emotionally aroused; stirred. **2.** *Physics.* At an energy level higher than normal: *an excited atom.* —**ex·cit′ed·ly** *adv.*

ex·cite·ment (ĭk-sīt′mənt) *n.* **1.** The condition of being excited. **2.** Something that excites.

ex·cit·ing (ĭk-sī′tĭng) *adj.* Creating excitement; rousing. —**ex·cit′ing·ly** *adv.*

ex·claim (ĭk-sklām′) *intr.v.* To cry out or speak suddenly, as from surprise or emotion. —*tr.v.* To cry out or speak suddenly. [Old French *exclamer,* from Latin *exclāmāre* : *ex-,* out + *clāmāre,* to call.]

ex·cla·ma·tion (ĕks′klə-mā′shən) *n.* **1.** A sudden, forceful utterance; an outcry. **2.** An interjection.

exclamation point. A punctuation mark (!) used after an exclamation. Also called **exclamation mark.**

ex·clam·a·to·ry (ĭk-sklăm′ə-tôr′ē, -tōr′ē) *adj.* Of, containing, using, or being an exclamation.

ex·clude (ĭk-sklōōd′) *tr.v.* **-clud·ed, -clud·ing.** **1.** To prevent from entering a place, group, activity, etc.: *exclude a person from a job.* **2.** To fail to notice or consider; disregard: *can't exclude the possibility of a wildcat strike.* **3.** To put out; expel. [Middle English *excluden,* from Latin *exclūdere* : *ex-,* out + *claudere,* to shut.]

ex·clu·sion (ĭk-sklōō′zhən) *n.* The act of excluding or the condition of being excluded. [Latin *exclūsiō,* from *exclūsus,* past part. of *exclūdere,* to exclude.]

ex·clu·sive (ĭk-sklōō′sĭv) *adj.* **1.** Not divided or shared with others: *exclusive publishing rights.* **2.** Regarded as unre-

lated; incompatible: *two ideas that are mutually exclusive.* **3.** Undivided; concentrated: *giving the thought his exclusive attention.* **4.** Admitting only certain people to membership, participation, etc.; select. **5.** Catering to a wealthy or fashionable class: *exclusive shops.* —*n.* A news item granted to or obtained by only one person or source. —**idiom. exclusive of.** Not including; besides: *exclusive of other factors.* —**ex·clu′sive·ly** *adv.* —**ex·clu′sive·ness** *n.*

ex·com·mu·ni·cate (ĕks′kə-myōō′nĭ-kāt′) *tr.v.* **-cat·ed, -cat·ing.** To exclude from membership in a church by ecclesiastical authority. [Middle English *excommunicaten,* from Late Latin *excommūnicāre,* to put out of the (church) community : *ex-,* out + *commūnicāre,* to communicate.] —**ex′com·mu′ni·ca′tion** *n.*

ex·co·ri·ate (ĭk-skôr′ē-āt′, -skōr′-) *tr.v.* **-at·ed, -at·ing.** **1.** To tear or wear off the skin of; abrade. **2.** To censure strongly; denounce severely. [Middle English *excoriaten,* from Latin *excoriāre,* to strip of skin : *ex-,* removal from + *corium,* skin, hide, leather.] —**ex·co′ri·a′tion** *n.*

ex·cre·ment (ĕk′skrə-mənt) *n.* Waste material expelled from the body, esp. from the intestinal tract. [Latin *excrēmentum,* from *excrētus,* past part. of *excernere,* to sift out : *ex-,* out + *cernere,* to sift.] —**ex′cre·men′tal** (ĕk′-skrə-mĕn′tĭl) *adj.*

ex·cres·cence (ĭk-skrĕs′əns) *n.* **1.** An abnormal outgrowth, as a wart. **2.** A normal outgrowth, as a toenail. [Middle English, from Latin *excrēscentia,* from *excrēscens,* pres. part. of *excrēscere,* to grow out : *ex-,* out + *crēscere,* to grow.]

ex·cres·cent (ĭk-skrĕs′ənt) *adj.* Of or forming an excrescence, esp. one that is abnormal.

ex·cre·ta (ĭk-skrē′tə) *pl.n.* Waste matter, such as sweat, urine, or feces, expelled from the body. [From Latin *excrēta,* past part. of *excernere,* to sift out.]

ex·crete (ĭk-skrēt′) *tr.v.* **-cret·ed, -cret·ing.** To separate and eliminate (waste matter) from the blood, tissues, or organs, esp. as sweat or urine. [Latin *excrētus,* past part. of *excernere,* to sift out.]

ex·cre·tion (ĭk-skrē′shən) *n.* **1.** The act or process of excreting. **2.** The matter excreted.

ex·cre·to·ry (ĕk′skrĭ-tôr′ē, -tōr′ē) *adj.* Also **ex·cre·tive** (-tĭv). Of, pertaining to, or used in excretion.

ex·cru·ci·ate (ĭk-skrōō′shē-āt′) *tr.v.* **-at·ed, -at·ing.** To afflict with severe pain or mental distress. [From Latin *excruciāre* : *ex-,* completely + *cruciāre,* to torment, crucify, from *crux,* cross.] —**ex·cru′ci·a′tion** *n.*

ex·cru·ci·at·ing (ĭk-skrōō′shē-ā′tĭng) *adj.* Intensely painful or distressing. —**ex·cru′ci·at′ing·ly** *adv.*

ex·cul·pate (ĕk′skəl-pāt′, ĭk-skŭl′-) *tr.v.* **-pat·ed, -pat·ing.** To clear of guilt or blame; exonerate. [From Medieval Latin *exculpāre* : Latin *ex-,* away + *culpa,* guilt, blame.] —**ex′-cul·pa′tion** *n.* —**ex·cul′pa·to′ry** (ĭk-skŭl′pə-tôr′ē, -tōr′ē) *adj.*

ex·cur·sion (ĭk-skûr′zhən) *n.* **1.** A usu. brief journey, esp. one taken for pleasure or for a specific purpose. **2.** A pleasure tour, as on a boat, usu. at a reduced fare that includes a return trip. **3.** A digression from the main topic. [Latin *excursiō,* from *excursus,* past part. of *excurrere,* to run out : *ex-,* out + *currere,* to run.]

ex·cur·sion·ist (ĭk-skûr′zhə-nĭst) *n.* A person who goes on an excursion.

ex·cur·sive (ĭk-skûr′sĭv) *adj.* Given to or characterized by digression; rambling. —**ex·cur′sive·ly** *adv.* —**ex·cur′sive·ness** *n.*

ex·cuse (ĭk-skyōōz′) *tr.v.* **-cused, -cus·ing.** **1.** To pardon; forgive. **2.** To serve as apology for; justify; vindicate: *Nothing excuses such rudeness.* **3.** To free or release, as from an obligation or duty; exempt: *excused him from jury duty.* **4.** To request forgiveness; apologize: *excused herself for losing her temper.* —See Syns at **pardon.** —*n.* (ĭk-skyōōs′) **1.** Something offered as grounds for excusing; a reason or explanation. **2.** Something that serves to excuse; a justification. **3.** An act of excusing. **4.** *Informal.* Something that falls short of expectations: *a poor excuse for a poet.* [Middle English *excusen,* from Old French *excuser,* from Latin *excūsāre* : *ex-,* out from + *causa,* accusation, cause.] —**ex·cus′a·ble** *adj.* —**ex·cus′a·bly** *adv.* —**ex·cus′er** *n.*

ex·e·cra·ble (ĕk′sĭ-krə-bəl) *adj.* **1.** Detestable; abhorrent: *Rape is an execrable crime.* **2.** Extremely inferior; very bad: *execrable taste.* [Middle English, from Old French, from Latin *ex(s)ecrābilis,* from *ex(s)ecrārī,* to execrate.] —**ex'e·cra·bly** *adv.*

ex·e·crate (ĕk'sĭ-krāt') *t.r.v.* -**crat·ed, -crat·ing. 1.** To protest vehemently against; denounce. **2.** To loathe; hate; detest. [Latin *ex(s)ecrārī,* to curse : *ex-,* opposing + *sacer,* sacred.] —**ex'e·cra'tion** *n.*

ex·e·cute (ĕk'sĭ-kyōōt') *t.r.v.* -**cut·ed, -cut·ing. 1.** To carry out; put into effect. **2.** To make or produce (a work of art), esp. in accordance with a design. **3.** To make valid or legal, as by signing: *execute a deed.* **4.** To perform or carry out what is required by: *execute a will.* **5.** To subject to capital punishment. [Middle English *executen,* from Old French *executer,* from Medieval Latin *ex(s)equī,* to execute, follow to the end : *ex-,* completely + *sequī,* to follow.] —**ex'e·cut'er** *n.*

ex·e·cu·tion (ĕk'sĭ-kyōō'shən) *n.* **1.** The act of executing or carrying out. **2.** The manner, style, or result of performance. **3.** The act of performing or carrying out what is necessary or required. **4.** The infliction of capital punishment. **5.** A legal writ empowering an officer to enforce a court judgment.

ex·e·cu·tion·er (ĕk'sĭ-kyōō'shə-nər) *n.* Someone who administers capital punishment.

ex·ec·u·tive (ĭg-zĕk'yə-tĭv) *n.* **1.** A person or group that has administrative or managerial authority in an organization. **2.** The chief officer of a government or political division. **3.** The branch of government concerned with putting a country's laws into effect. —*adj.* **1.** Of, pertaining to, or capable of carrying out plans, duties, etc.: *an executive committee.* **2.** Of or pertaining to the branch of government concerned with the enforcement and administration of a nation's laws. **3.** Of or pertaining to an executive.

ex·ec·u·tor (ĭg-zĕk'yə-tər) *n.* **1.** (*also* ĕk'sĭ-kyōō'tər). A person who carries out or performs something. **2.** A person designated to execute the terms of a will.

ex·ec·u·trix (ĭg-zĕk'yə-trĭks') *n., pl.* -**trix·es** *or* -**tri·ces** (ĭg-zĕk'yə-trī'sēz'). A female executor.

ex·e·ge·sis (ĕk'sə-jē'sĭs) *n., pl.* -**ses** (-sēz'). Critical explanation or analysis of a text, esp. interpretation of the Bible. [From Greek *exēgēsis,* from *exēgeisthai,* to expound : *ex-,* out of + *hēgeisthai,* to lead.] —**ex'e·get'ic** (-jĕt'ĭk) *or* **ex'·e·get'i·cal** (-ĭ-kəl) *adj.*

ex·em·plar (ĭg-zĕm'plär', -plər) *n.* **1.** One that is worthy of being imitated; a model. **2.** Someone or something considered typical or representative; example. —See Syns at **ideal.** [Middle English, from Old French *exemplaire,* from Late Latin *exemplārium,* from Latin *exemplum,* example.]

ex·em·pla·ry (ĭg-zĕm'plə-rē) *adj.* **1.** Worthy of imitation; commendable. **2.** Serving as a model or archetype. **3.** Serving as an illustration; typical. **4.** Serving as a warning.

ex·em·pli·fi·ca·tion (ĭg-zĕm'plə-fĭ-kā'shən) *n.* **1.** The act of exemplifying. **2.** Someone or something that exemplifies; an example.

ex·em·pli·fy (ĭg-zĕm'plə-fī') *t.r.v.* -**fied, -fy·ing. 1.** To demonstrate by example; illustrate. **2.** To serve as an example of. —See Syns at **represent.** [Middle English *exemplifien,* from Old French *exemplifier,* from Medieval Latin *exemplificāre* : Latin *exemplum,* example + *facere,* to make.]

ex·em·pli gra·ti·a (ĭg-zĕm'plī grā'shē-ə). *Latin.* For the sake of example; for example.

ex·empt (ĭg-zĕmpt') *t.r.v.* To free from an obligation or duty required of others. —*adj.* Freed from an obligation or duty required of others. [Middle English *exempten,* from Latin *exemptus,* past part. of *eximere,* to exempt.]

ex·emp·tion (ĭg-zĕmp'shən) *n.* **1.** The act of exempting or the condition of being exempt. **2.** A fixed deduction from the annual taxable income of a person.

ex·e·quies (ĕk'sĭ-kwēz') *pl.n.* Funeral rites. [Middle English, from Old French, from Latin *exequiae,* from *exsequi,* to follow.]

ex·er·cise (ĕk'sər-sīz') *n.* **1.** The act of using or putting into play or effect: *the exercise of power.* **2.** The fulfillment or performance of a duty, office, function, etc. **3.** Activity that requires physical exertion, esp. when performed to develop or maintain physical fitness. **4.** A lesson, problem, task, etc., designed to develop or improve understanding or skill: *a piano exercise.* **5. exercises.** A ceremony that includes speeches, awards, etc. —*v.* -**cised, -cis·ing.** —*tr.v.* **1.** To make use of; to employ: *exercise one's rights.* **2.** To bring to bear; exert: *exercise influence.* **3.** To put through exercises: *exercise the memory.* **4.** To carry out the functions of; perform: *exercise the duties of the presidency.* **5.** To absorb the attention of, esp. to worry, upset, or make anxious. —*intr.v.* To do exercise: *exercise an hour each day.* [Middle English, from Old French *exercice,* from Latin *exercitium,* from *exercēre,* to drill, practice : *ex-,* out + *arcēre,* to enclose, restrain.] —**ex'er·cis'er** *n.*

ex·ert (ĭg-zûrt') *t.r.v.* **1.** To put into effect; bring to bear: *exert influence.* **2. exert (oneself).** To make a strenuous effort. [Latin *exsertus,* past part. of *exserere,* to stretch out: *ex-,* out + *serere,* to join.]

ex·er·tion (ĭg-zûr'shən) *n.* An act of exerting, esp. a strenuous effort. —See Syns at **effort.**

ex·e·unt (ĕk'sē-ənt, -ōŏnt'). *Latin.* They go out. Used as a stage direction to indicate that two or more actors leave the stage.

ex·fo·li·ate (-fō'lē-āt') *v.* -**at·ed, -at·ing.** —*tr.v.* To remove (skin, bark, etc.) in flakes or scales. —*intr.v.* To come off as flakes or scales. [From Latin *exfoliāre,* to strip of leaves : *ex-,* from + *folium,* leaf.] —**ex·fo'li·a'tion** *n.* —**ex·fo'li·a'tive** *adj.*

ex·ha·la·tion (ĕks'hə-lā'shən, ĕk'sə-) *n.* **1.** The act or process of exhaling. **2.** Something that is exhaled.

ex·hale (ĕks-hāl', ĕk-sāl') *v.* -**haled, -hal·ing.** —*intr.v.* **1.** To breathe out. **2.** To be given off as vapor. —*tr.v.* **1.** To blow forth or breathe out (air, vapor, smoke, etc.). **2.** To draw out or off; evaporate. [Middle English *exalen,* from Old French *exhaler,* from Latin *exhālāre* : *ex-,* out + *hālāre,* to breathe.]

ex·haust (ĭg-zôst') *t.r.v.* **1.** To draw off or release (a liquid or gas). **2.** To drain the contents of; empty. **3.** To use up; consume: *exhaust one's money.* **4.** To wear out completely; to tire: *exhaust oneself through work.* **5.** To study, investigate, or deal with completely and comprehensively: *exhaust a topic; exhaust all possibilities.* —*intr.v.* To escape or pass out, as steam or gases. —*n.* **1.** The escape or release of waste gases or vapors, as from an engine. **2.** The vapors or gases released. **3.** A device or system that pumps such gases out or allows them to escape. [Latin *exhaustus,* past part. of *exhaurīre,* to exhaust : *ex-,* out + *haurīre,* to draw up.] —**ex·haust'i·bil'i·ty** *n.* —**ex·haust'i·ble** *adj.*

ex·haus·tion (ĭg-zôs'chən) *n.* **1.** The act or process of exhausting. **2.** The condition of being exhausted; extreme fatigue.

ex·haus·tive (ĭg-zô'stĭv) *adj.* Comprehensive; thorough: *exhaustive tests.* —**ex·haus'tive·ly** *adv.* —**ex·haus'tive·ness** *n.*

ex·hib·it (ĭg-zĭb'ĭt) *t.r.v.* **1.** To give evidence of; to show: *exhibit courage.* **2.** To present for the public to view: *exhibit photographs.* **3.** *Law.* To submit (evidence or documents) in a court. —See Syns at **show.** —*intr.v.* To put something on display; have an exhibition. —*n.* **1.** An act of exhibiting. **2.** Something exhibited; a display. **3.** *Law.* Something formally introduced as evidence in court. [Middle English *exhibiten,* from Latin *exhibitus,* past part. of *exhibēre,* to exhibit : *ex-,* out + *habēre,* to hold.] —**ex·hib'i·tor** *n.*

ex·hi·bi·tion (ĕk'sə-bĭsh'ən) *n.* **1.** An act of exhibiting. **2.** A display for the public, as of art objects.

ex·hi·bi·tion·ism (ĕk'sə-bĭsh'ə-nĭz'əm) *n.* **1.** The act or practice of flaunting oneself in order to attract attention. **2.** Compulsive exposure of the sexual organs in public. —**ex'hi·bi'tion·ist** *n.* —**ex'hi·bi'tion·is'tic** *adj.*

ex·hil·a·rate (ĭg-zĭl'ə-rāt') *t.r.v.* -**rat·ed, -rat·ing. 1.** To make cheerful; elate. **2.** To invigorate; stimulate. [From Latin *exhilarāre* : *ex-,* completely + *hilaris,* cheerful, happy, from Greek *hilaros.*] —**ex·hil'a·ra'tion** *n.* —**ex·hil'a·ra'tive** *adj.*

ex·hort (ĭg-zôrt') *t.r.v.* To urge by strong argument, advice, or appeal; admonish earnestly. —*intr.v.* To make urgent appeal. —See Syns at **urge.** [Middle English *exhorten,* from Old French *exhorter,* from Latin *exhortārī* : *ex-,* completely + *hortārī,* to encourage.] —**ex·hort'er** *n.*

ă pat ā pay â care ä father ĕ pet ē be hw which
ōō took ōō boot ou out th thin th this ŭ cut

ĭ pit ī tie î pier ŏ pot ō toe ô paw, for oi noise
û urge zh vision ə about, item, edible, gallop, circus

ex·hor·ta·tion (ĕg′zôr-tā′shən, ĕk′sôr-) *n.* **1.** An act of exhorting. **2.** A speech intended to exhort.

ex·hor·ta·tive (ĭg-zôr′tə-tĭv) *adj.* Also **ex·hor·ta·to·ry** (-tôr′ē, -tōr′ē). Serving to exhort.

ex·hume (ĭg-zyōōm′, ĕks-hyōōm′) *tr.v.* **-humed, -hum·ing.** **1.** To dig up or remove from a grave. **2.** To bring to light; uncover; disclose: *exhume an old custom.* [French *exhumer,* from Medieval Latin *exhumāre* : Latin *ex-,* out of + *humus,* earth.] **—ex·hu·ma′tion** *n.*

ex·i·gen·cy (ĕk′sə-jən-sē, ĕg′zə-) *n.,* pl. **-cies.** Also **ex·i·gence** (-jəns). **1.** A situation demanding swift attention or action. **2.** Often **exigencies.** Urgent demands or requirements; pressing needs. —See Syns at **need.**

ex·i·gent (ĕk′sə-jənt, ĕg′zə-) *adj.* **1.** Requiring immediate attention or remedy; urgent. **2.** Excessively demanding; exacting. [Latin *exigēns,* pres. part. of *exigere,* to demand.] **—ex′i·gent·ly** *adv.*

ex·ig·u·ous (ĭg-zĭg′yōō-əs, ĭk-sĭg′-) *adj.* Scanty; meager. [Latin *exiguus,* from *exigere,* to weigh exactly, demand.] **—ex·ig′u·ous·ly** *adv.* **—ex·ig′u·ous·ness** *n.*

ex·ile (ĕg′zīl′, ĕk′sīl′) *n.* **1.** Enforced removal or voluntary separation from one's native country. **2. a.** The condition of being exiled. **b.** The period of time in exile. **3.** Someone who has been separated from his country by either legal authority or voluntary action. —*tr.v.* **-iled, -il·ing.** To send (someone) into exile; banish. [Middle English *exil,* from Old French, from Latin *exilium,* from *exul,* one who is exiled.]

ex·ist (ĭg-zĭst′) *intr.v.* **1.** To have material or spiritual being; to be: *I don't believe ghosts exist.* **2.** To continue to live: *Man cannot exist without food and water.* **3.** To be present; occur: *Completely free trade has never existed.* [Latin *exsistere* : *ex-,* out + *sistere,* to stand, place.]

ex·is·tence (ĭg-zĭs′təns) *n.* **1.** The fact or condition of existing; being. **2.** The fact or condition of continued being; life: *a very unhappy existence.* **3.** Occurrence; presence: *the existence of life on other planets.* **4.** A manner of existing: *a meager existence.*

ex·is·tent (ĭg-zĭs′tənt) *adj.* **1.** Having life or being; existing: *existent animals.* **2.** Occurring or present at the moment; current: *existent rules and regulations.*

ex·is·ten·tial (ĕg′zĭ-stĕn′shəl, ĕk′sĭ-) *adj.* **1.** Of, pertaining to, or dealing with existence. **2.** Based on experience.

ex·is·ten·tial·ism (ĕg′zĭ-stĕn′shə-lĭz′əm, ĕk′sĭ-) *n.* A 20th-cent. philosophy that views the individual as being unique and alone in an indifferent and even hostile universe. **—ex′is·ten′tial·ist** *n.*

ex·it¹ (ĕg′zĭt, ĕk′sĭt). *Latin.* He (or she) goes out. Used as a stage direction.

ex·it² (ĕg′zĭt, ĕk′sĭt) *n.* **1.** A passage or way out. **2.** The act of going away or out. **3.** The departure of a performer from the stage. —*intr.v.* To make one's exit; leave. [Latin *exitus,* exit, departure, from *exīre,* to go out : *ex-,* out + *īre,* to go.]

ex li·bris (ĕks lī′brĭs, lē′-). *Latin.* From the library of. Used on bookplates before the owner's name.

exo-. A prefix meaning outside of, external, or beyond: *exoskeleton.* [Greek *exō,* outside of, from *ex,* out of.]

ex·o·bi·ol·o·gy (ĕk′sō-bī-ŏl′ə-jē) *n.* **1.** A branch of biology that deals with the search for and study of extraterrestrial life. **2.** A branch of biology that deals with the effects of extraterrestrial space on living organisms. **—ex′o·bi·ol′o·gist** *n.*

ex·o·crine (ĕk′sə-krĭn, -krēn, -krīn′) *adj.* Having or secreting through a duct: *an exocrine gland.* [EXO- + Greek *krinein,* to separate.]

ex·o·dus (ĕk′sə-dəs) *n.* **1.** A mass departure or wave of emigration: *the exodus from the north to the sunbelt.* **2. Exodus.** See table at **Bible.** [Late Latin, from Greek *exodos,* a going out : *ex-,* out + *hodos,* way.]

ex of·fi·ci·o (ĕks′ ə-fĭsh′ē-ō′). By virtue of one's office or position: *The mayor is ex officio a member of the city council.* [Latin.]

ex·og·a·my (ĕk-sŏg′ə-mē) *n.* Marriage outside of one's tribe, family, clan, or other social unit. [EXO- + -GAMY.] **—ex·og′a·mous** (ĕk-sŏg′ə-məs) *adj.*

ex·og·e·nous (ĕk-sŏj′ə-nəs) *n.* Having a cause external to the body: *an exogenous disease.* [French *exogène,* having additional layers.]

ex·on·er·ate (ĭg-zŏn′ə-rāt′) *tr.v.* **-at·ed, -at·ing.** To free from a charge; declare blameless. —See Syns at **vindicate.** [Middle English *exoneraten,* from Latin *exonerāre,* to free from a burden : *ex-,* from + *onus,* load, burden.] **—ex·on′er·a′tion** *n.*

ex·or·bi·tant (ĭg-zôr′bĭ-tənt) *adj.* Exceeding reasonable or proper limits; excessive: *exorbitant prices.* [Middle English, from Old French, from Late Latin *exorbitāns,* pres. part. of *exorbitāre,* to deviate : Latin *ex-,* out of + *orbita,* route, orbit.] **—ex·or′bi·tance** *n.* **—ex·or′bi·tant·ly** *adv.*

ex·or·cise (ĕk′sôr-sīz′, -sər-) *tr.v.* **-cised, -cis·ing.** **1.** To expel (an evil spirit) by or as if by incantation or prayer. **2.** To free from evil spirits. [Middle English *exorcisen,* from Old French *exorciser,* from Late Latin *exorcīzāre,* from Greek *exorkizein,* to exorcise (an evil spirit) with an oath : *ex-,* away + *horkos,* oath.] **—ex·or′cis·er** *n.*

ex·or·cism (ĕk′sôr-sĭz′əm, -sər-) *n.* **1.** The act or practice of exorcising. **2.** A formula or ritual used in exorcising. **—ex′or·cist** *n.*

ex·or·di·um (ĭg-zôr′dē-əm, ĭk-sôr′-) *n.,* pl. **-ums** or **-di·a** (-dē-ə). A beginning or introductory part, esp. of a speech or treatise. [Latin, from *exōrdīrī,* to begin : *ex-,* completely + *ōrdīrī,* to begin.]

ex·o·skel·e·ton (ĕk′sō-skĕl′ĭ-tən) *n.* An external protective or supporting structure of many invertebrates, such as insects and crustaceans.

ex·o·sphere (ĕk′sō-sfîr′) *n.* The outermost layer of the atmosphere, estimated to begin 300 to 600 miles above the earth.

ex·o·ther·mic (ĕk′sō-thûr′mĭk) *adj.* Also **ex·o·ther·mal** (-məl). Releasing or giving off heat: *an exothermic chemical reaction.* [EXO- + THERM(O)- + -IC.]

ex·ot·ic (ĭg-zŏt′ĭk) *adj.* **1.** From another part of the world; foreign: *exotic birds.* **2.** Strikingly and intriguingly unusual or beautiful: *an exotic design.* —See Syns at **foreign.** —*n.* Someone or something that is exotic. [Latin *exōticus,* from Greek *exōtikos,* from *exō,* outside, from *ex,* out.] **—ex·ot′i·cal·ly** *adv.*

ex·pand (ĭk-spănd′) *tr.v.* **1.** To open up or out; spread out; unfold: *a bird expanding its wings.* **2.** To increase in one or more dimensions; cause to swell: *Inhaling expands the lungs.* **3.** To increase in scope; extend; enlarge: *expand one's knowledge.* **4.** *Math.* To write (a quantity) as a sum of terms, as a continued product, or as another extended form. —*intr.v.* **1.** To open up; unfold. **2.** To become larger or wider: *Gases expand when heated.* —See Syns at **increase** and **spread.** [Middle English *expanden,* from Latin *expandere* : *ex-,* out + *pandere,* to spread.]

expanding universe theory. Big bang theory.

ex·panse (ĭk-spăns′) *n.* A wide and open extent, as of land, sky, or water: *an expanse of desert.* [Latin *expansum,* from *expandere,* to expand.]

ex·pan·si·ble (ĭk-spăn′sə-bəl) *adj.* Capable of expanding or of being expanded. **—ex·pan′si·bil′i·ty** *n.*

ex·pan·sion (ĭk-spăn′shən) *n.* **1.** The act or process of expanding; an increase in extent, size, number, volume, etc. **2.** Something formed or produced by expanding. **3.** *Math.* **a.** A number or other mathematical expression written in an expanded form; for example, $a^2 + b^2$ is the expansion of $(a + b)^2$. **b.** The process of finding this expanded form.

ex·pan·sive (ĭk-spăn′sĭv) *adj.* **1. a.** Capable of expanding. **b.** Tending to expand. **2.** Wide; sweeping; comprehensive: *an expansive lake.* **3.** Kind and generous; outgoing: *an expansive mood.* **4.** Grand in scale: *an expansive style of living.* —See Syns at **broad** and **general.** **—ex·pan′sive·ly** *adv.* **—ex·pan′sive·ness** *n.*

ex parte (ĕks pär′tē). *Law.* From or on one side only; partisan. [Latin.]

ex·pa·ti·ate (ĭk-spā′shē-āt′) *intr.v.* **-at·ed, -at·ing.** To speak or write at length; elaborate: *expatiated on the subject he knew best.* [From Latin *exspatiārī* : *ex-,* out + *spatiārī,* to spread, from *spatium,* space.] **—ex·pa′ti·a′tion** *n.*

ex·pa·tri·ate (ĕks-pā′trē-āt′) *v.* **-at·ed, -at·ing.** —*tr.v.* To banish (a person) from his native land; exile. —*intr.v.* To leave one's homeland to reside in another country. —*n.* (-ĭt, -āt′). An expatriated person. —*modifier:* an expatriate poet. [From Medieval Latin *expatriāre* : Latin *ex-,* out of + *patria,* native land, from *pater,* father.] **—ex·pa′tri·a′tion** *n.*

ă pat   ā pay   â care   ä father   ĕ pet   ē be   hw which   ĭ pit   ī tie   î pier   ŏ pot   ō toe   ô paw, for   oi noise
ŏŏ took   ōō boot   ou out   th thin   *th* this   ŭ cut   û urge   zh vision   ə about, item, edible, gallop, circus

ex·pect (ĭk-spĕkt') *tr.v.* **1.** To look forward to the occurrence or appearance of something or someone: *expect visitors; expect trouble.* **2.** To consider reasonable, proper, or just: *expect an apology.* **3.** To consider necessary; require: *The entrance committee expects a high-school diploma.* **4.** *Informal.* To think or suppose. **5.** To be pregnant. —See Usage note at **anticipate.** [Latin *exspectāre* : *ex-*, out + *specere*, to see, look at.]

ex·pec·tan·cy (ĭk-spĕk'tən-sē) *n., pl.* **-cies.** Also **ex·pec·tance** (-təns). **1.** The act or condition of expecting; anticipation. **2.** Something expected, esp. as a result of calculation from known facts or statistics: *a life expectancy of 70 years.*

ex·pec·tant (ĭk-spĕk'tənt) *adj.* **1.** Filled with or marked by expectation: *an expectant pause.* **2.** Awaiting the birth of a child: *an expectant mother.* —**ex·pec'tant·ly** *adv.*

ex·pec·ta·tion (ĕk'spĕk-tā'shən) *n.* **1.** The act or condition of expecting; anticipation: *"Ten boys sat before him, their hands folded, their eyes bright with expectation"* (Evelyn Waugh). **2. expectations.** Prospects; hopes: *fall short of expectations.*

ex·pec·to·rant (ĭk-spĕk'tər-ənt) *adj.* Easing or increasing secretion or discharge from the mucous membranes of the respiratory system. —**ex·pec'to·rant** *n.*

ex·pec·to·rate (ĭk-spĕk'tə-rāt') *v.* **-rat·ed, -rat·ing.** —*tr.v.* **1.** To eject from the mouth. **2.** To cough up and eject by spitting. —*intr.v.* **1.** To spit. **2.** To cough up and spit mucus or phlegm from the chest and lungs. [From Latin *expectorāre*, to drive from the breast : *ex-*, from, out of + *pectus*, breast.] —**ex·pec'to·ra'tion** *n.*

ex·pe·di·en·cy (ĭk-spē'dē-ən-sē) *n., pl.* **-cies.** Also **ex·pe·di·ence** (-dē-əns). **1.** Appropriateness to the purpose at hand. **2.** Adherence to self-serving means; selfish practicality: *plans based on sheer expediency.*

ex·pe·di·ent (ĭk-spē'dē-ənt) *n.* Something that answers an immediate purpose; a means to an end. —*adj.* **1.** Suited to a particular purpose; appropriate. **2.** Serving narrow or selfish interests; useful and practical though perhaps unprincipled. [Middle English, from Old French, from Latin *expediēns*, pres. part. of *expedīre*, to free, make ready.] —**ex·pe'di·ent·ly** *adv.*

ex·pe·dite (ĕk'spĭ-dīt') *tr.v.* **-dit·ed, -dit·ing.** **1.** To speed or ease the progress of; help along; assist; facilitate. **2.** To perform quickly and efficiently. [Latin *expedītus*, past part. of *expedīre*, to free, extricate.] —**ex'pe·dit'er** or **ex'pe·di'tor** *n.*

Syns: expedite, accelerate, hasten, hurry, quicken, speed, step up *v.* *Core meaning:* To increase the speed of (*expedite a delivery; expedite tax reform*).

ex·pe·di·tion (ĕk'spĭ-dĭsh'ən) *n.* **1. a.** A journey undertaken with a definite objective: *an expedition to the South Pole.* **b.** A group making such a journey. **2.** Speed in performance; dispatch; promptness. —See Syns at **haste.** [Middle English *expedicioun*, from Old French *expedition*, from Latin *expedītiō*, from *expedīre*, to extricate.]

ex·pe·di·tion·ar·y (ĕk'spĭ-dĭsh'ə-nĕr'ē) *adj.* Of or being an expedition, esp. a military expedition.

ex·pe·di·tious (ĕk'spĭ-dĭsh'əs) *adj.* Acting or done with speed and efficiency. —**ex'pe·di'tious·ly** *adv.* —**ex'pe·di'tious·ness** *n.*

ex·pel (ĭk-spĕl') *tr.v.* **-pelled, -pel·ling.** **1.** To force or drive out; eject forcefully: *expel air from the lungs.* **2.** To dismiss by official decision: *expel a student from school.* [Middle English *expellen*, from Latin *expellere* : *ex-*, out + *pellere*, to drive.] —**ex·pel'la·ble** *adj.*

ex·pend (ĭk-spĕnd') *tr.v.* **1.** To put out; spend: *expended a million dollars on promotion.* **2.** To use up; waste: *expend time and energy.* —See Syns at **waste.** [Middle English *expenden*, from Latin *expendere*, to pay out : *ex*, out + *pendere*, to weigh, pay.]

ex·pend·a·ble (ĭk-spĕn'də-bəl) *adj.* Subject to being sacrificed or used up to gain an objective: *gasoline and other expendable supplies.*

ex·pen·di·ture (ĭk-spĕn'də-chər) *n.* **1.** The act or process of expending; outlay. **2.** Something that is expended.

ex·pense (ĭk-spĕns') *n.* **1.** The cost involved in some activity; a price: *the expense of going to college.* **2. expenses. a.** Charges incurred while performing one's job. **b.** Money allotted for payment of such charges. **3.** Something requiring the expenditure of money: *Rent is his greatest expense.* **4.** Loss; sacrifice: *finished the project at the expense of her health.* [Middle English, from Old French *espense*, from Late Latin *expensa*, from Latin *expendere*, to expend.]

ex·pen·sive (ĭk-spĕn'sĭv) *adj.* **1.** High-priced; costly: *an expensive dress.* **2.** Achieved or gained at great cost, loss, or sacrifice: *an expensive victory.*

Syns: expensive, costly, dear, high *adj. Core meaning:* Bringing a large price (*an expensive fur*).

ex·pe·ri·ence (ĭk-spîr'ē-əns) *n.* **1.** The apprehension or perception of an object, thought, emotion, or event through the senses or mind. **2.** Knowledge or skill derived from active participation in events or activities: *gained experience on his previous job.* **3. a.** An event or series of events participated in or lived through: *the experience of being in an earthquake.* **b.** The totality of such events in the past of an individual or group: *the experience of the Great Depression.* —*tr.v.* **-enced, -enc·ing.** To participate in or partake of personally; undergo: *"Everyone experiences this feeling of loneliness, of not belonging"* (Brendan Behan). [Middle English, from Old French, from Latin *experientia*, from *experīrī*, to try, test.]

ex·pe·ri·enced (ĭk-spîr'ē-ənst) *adj.* Skilled or knowledgeable through long or wide experience: *an experienced teacher.*

ex·per·i·ment (ĭk-spĕr'ə-mənt, -mĕnt') *n.* **1.** A test made to demonstrate a known truth, examine the validity of a hypothesis, or determine the nature of something not yet known. **2.** The process of conducting such a test. —*intr.v.* To conduct an experiment or experiments. [Middle English, from Old French, from Latin *experīmentum*, from *experīrī*, to try, test.]

ex·per·i·men·tal (ĭk-spĕr'ə-mĕn'tl) *adj.* **1.** Of, pertaining to, or based on experiment: *experimental procedures.* **2.** In the process of being tested; tentative: *an experimental drug.* **3.** Proven by experience; empirical. —**ex·per'i·men'tal·ly** *adv.*

ex·per·i·men·ta·tion (ĭk-spĕr'ə-mĕn-tā'shən) *n.* The act, process, or practice of experimenting.

ex·pert (ĕk'spûrt) *n.* A person with a high degree of knowledge, skill, and experience in a certain subject. —*adj.* (ĭk-spûrt', ĕk'spûrt'). **1.** Having great knowledge, skill, and experience in a particular field. **2.** Given by an expert: *an expert opinion.* [Middle English, from Old French, from Latin *expertus*, past part. of *experīrī*, to try.] —**ex·pert'ly** *adv.* —**ex·pert'ness** *n.*

ex·per·tise (ĕk'spər-tēz') *n.* Expert skill or knowledge. —See Syns at **ability.** [French, survey, evaluation, from Old French, expertness, from *expert*, expert.]

ex·pi·ate (ĕk'spē-āt') *tr.v.* **-at·ed, -at·ing.** To atone or make amends for; redress: *expiate a crime.* [From Latin *expiāre* : *ex-*, completely + *piāre*, to appease, atone, from *pius*, devout.] —**ex'pi·a·ble** *adj.* —**ex'pi·a'tion** *n.* —**ex'pi·a'tor** *n.* —**ex'pi·a·to·ry** (-ə-tôr'ē, -tōr'ē) *adj.*

ex·pi·ra·tion (ĕk'spə-rā'shən) *n.* **1.** The act or process of breathing out. **2.** The process of coming to a close; termination: *the expiration of a lease.*

ex·pi·ra·to·ry (ĭk-spīr'ə-tôr'ē, -tōr'ē) *adj.* Of, pertaining to, or involving the expiration of air from the lungs.

ex·pire (ĭk-spīr') *v.* **-pired, -pir·ing.** —*intr.v.* **1.** To come to an end; terminate: *His membership expired.* **2.** To die. **3.** To breathe out; exhale. —*tr.v.* To breathe out. —See Syns at **die.** [Middle English *expiren*, from Old French *exspirer*, from Latin *exspīrāre* : *ex-*, out + *spīrāre*, to breathe.]

ex·pi·ry (ĭk-spīr'ē) *n., pl.* **-ries.** An expiration, esp. of a contract or agreement. [From EXPIRE.]

ex·plain (ĭk-splān') *tr.v.* **1.** To make plain or clear; clarify; elucidate: *explain the meaning of a poem.* **2.** To offer reasons for; account for: *explain his erratic behavior.* —*intr.v.* To give an explanation: *Give me a chance to explain.* [Middle English *explanen*, from Latin *explānāre* : *ex-*, completely + *plānus*, plain, flat.] —**ex·plain'a·ble** *adj.* —**ex·plain'er** *n.*

ex·pla·na·tion (ĕk'splə-nā'shən) *n.* **1.** The act or process of explaining; clarification. **2.** A statement, fact, etc., that serves to explain.

ex·plan·a·to·ry (ĭk-splăn'ə-tôr'ē, -tōr'ē) *adj.* Also **ex·plan·a·**

tive (-ə-tĭv). Serving or intended to explain: *explanatory footnotes.* —**ex·plan'a·to'ri·ly** *adv.*

ex·ple·tive (ĕks'plĭ-tĭv) *adj.* Also **ex·ple·to·ry** (-tôr'ē, -tōr'ē). Added or inserted in order to fill out something: *an expletive phrase.* —*n.* **1.** An exclamation or oath, esp. one that is profane or obscene. **2.** *Gram.* A word or phrase added to a sentence in order to ease syntax or rhythm, as the word *there* in the sentence *There are many reasons given.* [Late Latin *explētivus,* from Latin *explētus,* past part. of *explēre,* to fill out : *ex-,* out + *plēre,* to fill.]

ex·pli·ca·ble (ĕk'splĭ-kə-bəl) *adj.* Capable of being explained; explainable.

ex·pli·cate (ĕk'splĭ-kāt') *tr.v.* **-cat·ed, -cat·ing.** To make clear the meaning of; explain: *explicate a scientific theory.* [From Latin *explicāre,* to unfold, explicate : *ex-* (reversal) + *plicāre,* to fold.] —**ex'pli·ca'tive** *adj.* —**ex'pli·ca'tor** *n.*

ex·pli·ca·tion (ĕk'splĭ-kā'shən) *n.* **1.** The act of explicating. **2.** A detailed analysis or interpretation.

ex·plic·it (ĭk-splĭs'ĭt) *adj.* Clearly defined; specific; precise: *explicit directions.* [French *explicite,* from Latin *explicitus,* past part. of *explicāre,* to explicate.] —**ex·plic'it·ly** *adv.* —**ex·plic'it·ness** *n.*

Syns: **explicit, categorical, clear-cut, decided, definite, express, positive, precise, specific, unequivocal** *adj.* Core meaning: Clearly, fully, and sometimes emphatically expressed (*an explicit order; an explicit denial*).

ex·plode (ĭk-splōd') *v.* **-plod·ed, -plod·ing.** —*intr.v.* **1.** To release mechanical, chemical, or nuclear energy in an explosion. **2.** To burst and be destroyed by explosion. **3.** To burst forth suddenly: *explode with anger.* **4.** To increase suddenly, sharply, and without control: *World population is exploding.* —*tr.v.* **1.** To cause to burst violently and noisily; detonate. **2.** To expose as false; refute: *explode a theory.* [Latin *explōdere,* to drive out by clapping : *ex-,* out + *plaudere,* to clap.] —**ex·plod'er** *n.*

Syns: **explode, blast, blow up, burst, detonate, go off** *v.* Core meaning: To release energy violently and suddenly, esp. with a loud noise (*a bomb that exploded in midair*).

ex·ploit (ĕk'sploit') *n.* An act or deed, esp. a heroic feat. —*tr.v.* (ĭk-sploit') **1.** To make the greatest possible use of; turn to advantage: *exploit coal resources.* **2.** To make use of selfishly or unethically: *exploit unskilled laborers.* [Middle English *esploit,* from Old French, achievement, from Latin *explicitus,* explicit.] —**ex·ploit'a·ble** *adj.* —**ex·ploit'er** *n.*

ex·ploi·ta·tion (ĕk'sploi-tā'shən) *n.* **1.** The act of exploiting. **2.** The utilization of another person for selfish purposes.

ex·plo·ra·tion (ĕk'splə-rā'shən) *n.* The act or an example of exploring. —**ex·plor'a·to'ry** (ĭk-splôr'ə-tôr'ē, -splōr'ə-tōr'ē) *adj.*

ex·plore (ĭk-splôr', -splōr') *v.* **-plored, -plor·ing.** —*tr.v.* **1.** To travel into or wander through (an unknown or unfamiliar place, region, etc.) for the purpose of discovery: *De Soto explored a vast region in North America.* **2.** To look into; investigate: *explore the possibilities of a cease-fire.* **3.** To make a medical examination of (an organ or part of the body). —*intr.v.* To conduct a systematic search: *explore for oil.* [Latin *explōrāre,* to search out, explore : *ex-,* out + *plōrāre,* cry aloud.]

ex·plor·er (ĭk-splôr'ər, -splōr'-) *n.* A person who explores, esp. one who explores a geographical area.

ex·plo·sion (ĭk-splō'zhən) *n.* **1. a.** A sudden, violent release of energy from a confined space, esp. with the production of a shock wave and a loud, sharp sound, as well as heat, light, flames, and flying debris. **b.** The sound made by such a release of energy. **2.** A sudden outbreak: *an explosion of laughter.* **3.** A sudden and sharp increase: *the population explosion.* [Latin *explōsiō,* from *explōsus,* past part. of *explōdere,* to explode.]

ex·plo·sive (ĭk-splō'sĭv) *adj.* **1.** Of, pertaining to, or of the nature of an explosion. **2.** Capable of exploding or tending to explode. —*n.* A substance, esp. a prepared chemical, that explodes or is capable of explosion. —**ex·plo'sive·ly** *adv.* —**ex·plo'sive·ness** *n.*

ex·po·nent (ĭk-spō'nənt) *n.* **1.** A person who explains or interprets something: *a leading exponent of new teaching methods.* **2.** A person who speaks for, represents, or advocates: *an exponent of international cooperation.* **3.** *Math.* A number or symbol, such as the *2* in $(x + y)^2$, that indi-

cates the number of times an expression is used as a factor. [Latin *expōnēns,* pres. part. of *expōnere,* to expound.]

ex·po·nen·tial (ĕk'spə-nĕn'shəl) *adj.* **1.** Of, containing, or involving one or more exponents. **2.** *Math.* Of or defined by a function that has an independent variable as an exponent: *an exponential increase.* —*n.* Also **exponential function.** *Math.* A function, such as $f(x) = ab^x$, that contains an independent variable used as an exponent. —**ex'po·nen'tial·ly** *adv.*

ex·port (ĭk-spôrt', -spōrt', ĕk'spôrt', -spōrt') *tr.v.* To send or carry (goods, products, etc.) to another country for trade or sale. —*intr.v.* To send or carry merchandise abroad, esp. for sale or trade. —*n.* (ĕk'spôrt, -spōrt). **1.** The act or process of exporting. **2.** Something that is exported. —*modifier:* *an export tax; the export trade.* [Latin *exportāre,* to carry out or away : *ex-,* out + *portāre,* to carry.] —**ex·port'a·ble** *adj.* —**ex·port'er** *n.*

ex·pose (ĭk-spōz') *tr.v.* **-posed, -pos·ing.** **1.** To uncover; lay bare: *expose one's back to the sun.* **2.** To lay open or subject, as to a force, influence, etc.: *expose an opponent to ridicule.* **3.** To make visible; reveal: *Cleaning exposed the grain of the wood.* **4.** To disclose; make known: *expose a plot.* **5.** To subject (a photographic film or plate) to the action of light. **6.** To put out or abandon without food or shelter. [Middle English *exposen,* from Old French *exposer,* from Latin *expōnere* : *ex-,* out + *pōnere,* to place.] —**ex·pos'er** *n.*

ex·po·sé (ĕk'spō-zā') *n.* An exposure or revelation, as through a newspaper article, of a fraud or crime. [French, from the past part. of *exposer,* to expose.]

ex·po·si·tion (ĕk'spə-zĭsh'ən) *n.* **1.** A written or oral presentation of informative or explanatory material. **2.** Often **Exposition.** A large public exhibition or fair. **3.** The opening section of a musical composition, such as a sonata, in which the themes are first stated. —**ex·pos'i·tive** (ĭk-spŏz'ĭ-tĭv) or **ex·pos'i·to'ry** (-tôr'ē, -tōr'ē) *adj.* —**ex·pos'i·tor** *n.*

ex post fac·to (ĕks' pōst făk'tō). Enacted after an event but applying to it nonetheless; retroactive: *an ex post facto law.* [Medieval Latin, "from what is done afterwards."]

ex·pos·tu·late (ĭk-spŏs'chə-lāt') *intr.v.* **-lat·ed, -lat·ing.** To reason earnestly with someone in an effort to dissuade or correct; remonstrate. [From Latin *expostulāre,* to demand strongly : *ex-,* completely + *postulāre,* to demand.] —**ex·pos'tu·la'tion** *n.* —**ex·pos'tu·la'tor** *n.* —**ex·pos'tu·la·to'ry** (-lə-tôr'ē, -tōr'ē) *adj.*

ex·po·sure (ĭk-spō'zhər) *n.* **1.** The act or an example of exposing: *the exposure of a scandal.* **2.** The condition of being exposed: *exposure to measles.* **3.** A location or position in relation to the sun, direction, etc.: *a northern exposure.* **4.** Injury due to a lack of protection from excessive sun, cold, wind, rain, etc. **5. a.** The act or process of exposing a photographic film or plate. **b.** The length of time for which such a film or plate is exposed. **c.** The amount of light to which a film or plate is exposed. **d.** An exposed film or plate or an exposed section of a roll of film.

exposure meter. A light meter.

ex·pound (ĭk-spound') *tr.v.* To set forth or explain in detail: *expounded his viewpoint.* —*intr.v.* To make a detailed statement; explain a point of view: *expound on the probabilities of continued inflation.* [Middle English *expoun(d)en,* from Old French *espondre,* from Latin *expōnere,* to put forth, expose : *ex-,* out + *pōnere,* to place, put.] —**ex·pound'er** *n.*

ex·press (ĭk-sprĕs') *tr.v.* **1.** To make known; show; reveal: *a painting that expresses the artist's inner conflicts.* **2.** To put into words; state: *expresses her ideas clearly.* **3.** To be a sign of; signify: *The minus sign expresses subtraction.* **4. express (oneself).** *Informal.* To give expression or vent to one's thoughts, feelings, hopes, etc. **5.** To squeeze or press out: *express juice from an orange.* —*adj.* **1.** Clearly stated; definite: *one's express wishes.* **2.** Of or sent by rapid direct transportation: *an express package.* **3.** Direct, rapid, and usu. not making local stops: *an express train.* —See Syns at **explicit.** —*adv.* By express transportation: *send a package express.* —*n.* **1.** An express train, bus, etc. **2. a.** A rapid, efficient system for the delivery of goods and mail. **b.** A company that deals in such transport. [Middle English *expressen,* from Old French *expresser* : Latin *ex-,* out + *pressāre,* to press, from *premere.*] —**ex·press'er** *n.* —**ex·press'i·ble** *adj.*

ă pat	ā pay	â care	ä father	ĕ pet	ē be	hw which		ĭ pit	ī tie	î pier	ŏ pot	ō toe	ô paw, for	oi noise
ōō took	ōō boot	ou out	th thin	*th* this	ŭ cut		û urge	zh vision	ə about, item, edible, gallop, circus

ex·pres·sion (ĭk-sprĕsh'ən) n. **1.** The act or process of expressing. **2.** Something that serves to express an idea, feeling, etc.: *flowers as an expression of gratitude.* **3.** *Math.* A symbol or an arrangement of symbols that has some meaning: *an algebraic expression.* **4.** A vivid or emphatic manner of speaking: *tried to put expression in his voice.* **5.** A particular word, phrase, or saying: *a slang expression.* **6.** The outward manifestation of an inner mood: *tears as an expression of grief.* **7.** A facial aspect or look that conveys a special mood or feeling: *a worried expression on her face.* **8.** The act of removing a liquid by squeezing.

ex·pres·sion·ism (ĭk-sprĕsh'ə-nĭz'əm) n. A movement in the fine arts that emphasized the expression of inner experience rather than solely realistic portrayal. **—ex·pres'sion·ist** n. **—ex·pres'sion·is'tic** adj.

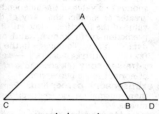

expressionism   exterior angle

ex·pres·sion·less (ĭk-sprĕsh'ən-lĭs) adj. Not revealing feelings or emotion; impassive.

ex·pres·sive (ĭk-sprĕs'ĭv) adj. **1.** Expressing or tending to express: *music expressive of one's mood.* **2.** Full of meaning; significant: *an expressive glance.* **—ex·pres'sive·ly** adv. **—ex·pres'sive·ness** n.

ex·press·ly (ĭk-sprĕs'lē) adv. **1.** Especially; particularly: *a ship designed expressly for exploring the Arctic waters.* **2.** Without any doubt; definitely; plainly; explicitly: *The rules expressly forbid it.*

ex·press·way (ĭk-sprĕs'wā') n. A multilane highway designed for fast travel.

ex·pro·pri·ate (ĕks-prō'prē-āt') tr.v. **-at·ed, -at·ing.** To acquire (land or other property), esp. for public use, by taking it away from the original owner. [From Medieval Latin *expropriāre* : Latin *ex-*, from + *proprius*, one's own.] **—ex·pro'pri·a'tion** n. **—ex·pro'pri·a'tor** n.

ex·pul·sion (ĭk-spŭl'shən) n. The act of expelling or the condition of being expelled.

ex·punge (ĭk-spŭnj') tr.v. **-punged, -pung·ing. 1.** To remove completely; erase; delete. **2.** To destroy; annihilate. [Latin *expungere* : *ex-*, out + *pungere*, to prick.] **—ex·pung'er** n.

ex·pur·gate (ĕk'spər-gāt') tr.v. **-gat·ed, -gat·ing. 1.** To remove obscene, objectionable, or erroneous passages from. **2.** To cleanse or clean; purge. [From Latin *expurgāre*, to purify : *ex-*, out + *purgāre*, to purge.] **—ex'pur·ga'tion** n. **—ex'pur·ga'tor** n.

ex·qui·site (ĕk'skwĭ-zĭt, ĭk-skwĭz'ĭt) adj. **1.** Beautifully made or designed: *an exquisite chalice.* **2.** Of special beauty, charm, and elegance: *an exquisite sunset.* **3.** Keenly perceptive or discriminating; refined: *exquisite taste in art.* **4.** Intense; keen: *takes exquisite pleasure in his meals.* **—See Syns at elegant.** [Middle English *exquisit*, from Latin *exquīsītus*, chosen, exquisite, past part. of *exquīrere*, to search out : *ex-*, out + *quaerere*, to seek.] **—ex'qui·site·ly** adv. **—ex'qui·site·ness** n.

ex·tant (ĕk'stənt, ĭk-stănt') adj. Still in existence; not destroyed, lost, or extinct. [Latin *exstāns*, pres. part. of *exstāre*, to stand out, exist, be prominent : *ex-*, out + *stāre*, to stand.]

ex·tem·po·ra·ne·ous (ĭk-stĕm'pə-rā'nē-əs) adj. **1.** Done, made, or spoken with little or no advance preparation or practice; impromptu: *extemporaneous remarks.* **2.** Made or adapted for immediate needs; improvised: *an extemporaneous shelter.* [Late Latin *extemporāneus*, from Latin *ex tempore*, extempore.] **—ex·tem'po·ra'ne·ous·ly** adv. **—ex·tem'po·ra'ne·ous·ness** n.

ex·tem·po·rar·y (ĭk-stĕm'pə-rĕr'ē) adj. Extemporaneous. [From Latin *ex tempore*, extempore.] **—ex·tem'po·rar'i·ly** (-rârʹə-lē) adv.

ex·tem·po·re (ĭk-stĕm'pə-rē) adj. Extemporaneous. —adv. Extemporaneously. [Latin *ex tempore*, "out of the time."]

ex·tem·po·rize (ĭk-stĕm'pə-rīz') v. **-rized, -riz·ing.** —tr.v. To perform, utter, or do extemporaneously. —intr.v. To perform or make extemporaneously; improvise. **—ex·tem'po·ri·za'tion** n. **—ex·tem'po·riz'er** n.

ex·tend (ĭk-stĕnd') tr.v. **1.** To straighten or stretch out to full length: *extend the leg.* **2.** To make longer; lengthen; prolong: *extend the sides of an angle; extend a visit.* **3.** To enlarge the area of; expand: *extend the boundaries.* **4.** To expand the influence or meaning of; broaden: *extend one's responsibilities.* **5.** To offer or grant: *extend my greetings.* **6.** To grant additional time for payment or delivery of: *extend a loan; extend a deadline.* —intr.v. To be or become extended; stretch or reach: *a beach that extends for miles.* —See Syns at **increase, offer,** and **spread.** [Middle English *extenden*, from Latin *extendere* : *ex-*, out + *tendere*, to stretch.] **—ex·tend'i·bil'i·ty** n. **—ex·tend'i·ble** adj.

ex·tend·ed (ĭk-stĕn'dĭd) adj. **1.** Stretched or spread out. **2.** Continued for a long period of time; prolonged: *extended peace talks.* —See Syns at **long.**

ex·ten·si·ble (ĭk-stĕn'sə-bəl) adj. Capable of being extended. [From Latin *extensus*, past part. of *extendere*, to extend.] **—ex·ten'si·bil'i·ty** n.

ex·ten·sion (ĭk-stĕn'shən) n. **1.** The act of extending or the condition of being extended. **2. a.** A part that extends from a main part; a prolongation. **b.** A structure that is built onto a main structure; an addition. **3.** Something that develops, grows, or follows from something else: *a logical extension of his ideas.* **4.** An additional period of time granted, as for meeting an obligation. **5.** Any of a network of telephones to which calls can be directed through a switchboard and that can call each other. **—modifier:** an *extension cord.*

ex·ten·sive (ĭk-stĕn'sĭv) adj. **1.** Large in area; vast; broad. **2.** Having a wide range; far-reaching; comprehensive: *an extensive library.* **3.** Large in amount: *extensive wealth.* —See Syns at **big, broad,** and **general. —ex·ten'sive·ly** adv. **—ex·ten'sive·ness** n.

ex·tent (ĭk-stĕnt') n. **1.** The area or distance over which something extends; size. **2.** The scope or range of something: *the extent of his knowledge.* **3.** The point or degree to which something extends: *To a certain extent he led a happy life.* —See Syns at **range.** [Middle English *extente*, from Norman French, from Medieval Latin *extenta*, from Latin, past part. of *extendere*, to extend.]

ex·ten·u·ate (ĭk-stĕn'yōō-āt') tr.v. **-at·ed, -at·ing.** To lessen or attempt to lessen the seriousness of (an offense, error, etc.) by providing partial excuses or justifications. [From Latin *extenuāre* : *ex-*, out + *tenuāre*, to make thin, from *tenuis*, thin.] **—ex·ten'u·a'tion** n. **—ex·ten'u·a'tor** n.

ex·te·ri·or (ĭk-stîr'ē-ər) adj. **1.** Outer; external: *an exterior wall.* **2.** Suitable for use outside: *an exterior paint.* —n. **1.** A part or surface that is outside: *the exterior of a house.* **2.** An outward appearance; aspect: *a friendly exterior.* [Latin, comp. of *exterus*, outward, outside.] **—ex·te'ri·or·ly** adv.

exterior angle. The angle formed between a side of a polygon and an extended adjacent side.

ex·ter·mi·nate (ĭk-stûr'mə-nāt') tr.v. **-nat·ed, -nat·ing.** To get rid of by destroying completely; wipe out: *exterminate termites.* [From Latin *extermināre*, to drive out : *ex-*, out of + *termināre*, to limit, end.] **—ex·ter'mi·na'tion** n. **—ex·ter'mi·na'tor** n.

ex·ter·nal (ĭk-stûr'nəl) adj. **1.** Of, being on, or connected with the outside or an outer part; exterior. **2.** Of, on, or for the outer surface of the body: *a medicine for external use only.* **3.** Acting or coming from the outside: *an external force.* **4.** For outward show; superficial: *an external display of politeness.* **5.** Of or pertaining to foreign affairs or foreign countries: *external policy.* —n. **1.** An exterior part or surface. **2. externals.** Outward appearances. [Middle English, from Latin *externus*, from *exterus*, outward.] **—ex·ter'nal·ly** adv.

external ear. The parts of the ear that are outside the head; the outer ear.

ex·ter·nal·ize (ĭk-stûr′nə-līz′) *tr.v.* **-ized, -iz·ing. 1.** To make external. **2.** To attribute (a feeling, opinion, etc.) to others or to one's environment. **—ex·ter′nal·i·za′tion** *n.*

ex·tinct (ĭk-stĭngkt′) *adj.* **1.** No longer existing in living form: *extinct birds such as the dodo.* **2.** Not likely to erupt; inactive: *an extinct volcano.* **3.** Not burning; extinguished. —See Syns at **dead.** [Middle English, from Latin *exstinctus,* past part. of *exstinguere,* to extinguish.]

ex·tinc·tion (ĭk-stĭngk′shən) *n.* **1.** The act or process of extinguishing or making extinct. **2.** The condition of being extinguished or extinct. **—ex·tinc′tive** *adj.*

ex·tin·guish (ĭk-stĭng′gwĭsh) *tr.v.* **1.** To put out (a fire or flame). **2.** To put an end to; destroy. **3.** To obscure; eclipse. [Latin *ex(s)tinguere* : *ex-,* out + *stinguere,* to quench.] **—ex·tin′guish·a·ble** *adj.* **—ex·tin′guish·er** *n.* **—ex·tin′guish·ment** *n.*

Syns: extinguish, douse, quench *v. Core meaning:* To cause to stop burning (*extinguished the lamp; extinguished the flames*).

ex·tir·pate (ĕk′stər-pāt′, ĭk-stûr′-) *tr.v.* **-pat·ed, -pat·ing. 1.** To remove completely by rooting up or cutting out: *extirpate a tumor.* **2.** To destroy the whole of: *extirpate an evil.* [From Latin *ex(s)tirpāre,* to pluck up by the roots : *ex-,* out + *stirps,* root, stem.] **—ex′tir·pa′tion** *n.* **—ex′tir·pa′tor** *n.*

ex·tol or **ex·toll** (ĭk-stōl′) *tr.v.* **-tolled, -tol·ling.** To praise lavishly; laud; eulogize. [Middle English *extollen,* to lift up, praise, from Latin *extollere* : *ex-,* up + *tollere,* to lift, raise.] **—ex·tol′ler** *n.* **—ex·tol′ment** *n.*

ex·tort (ĭk-stôrt′) *tr.v.* To obtain by threats or other coercive means; exact; wring: *extort a confession from a prisoner.* [Latin *extortus,* past part. of *extorquēre,* to twist out : *ex-,* out +*torquēre,* to twist.] **—ex·tort′er** *n.* **—ex·tor′tive** *adj.*

ex·tor·tion (ĭk-stôr′shən) *n.* **1.** The act or crime of extorting. **2.** Something that is extorted. **—ex·tor′tion·ate** (-ĭt) *adj.* **—ex·tor′tion·ist** *n.*

ex·tra (ĕk′strə) *adj.* **1.** More than what is usual, normal, expected, or necessary; additional: *extra money.* **2.** Better than ordinary; superior: *extra fineness.* **—adv.** Especially; unusually: *extra quiet.* **—n. 1.** Something more than what is usual or necessary. **2.** Often **extras.** Something additional, as an accessory for which an added charge is made: *buy all the extras with a new car.* **3.** A special edition of a newspaper. **4.** A motion-picture actor hired to play a minor part, as in a crowd scene. [Prob. short for EXTRAORDINARY.]

extra-. A prefix meaning outside a boundary or scope: **extrasensory.** [Middle English, from Latin *extrā,* outside, above, beyond, without, from *exterus,* outward.]

ex·tract (ĭk-străkt′) *tr.v.* **1.** To draw out or forth forcibly: *extract a tooth.* **2.** To obtain despite resistance, as by a threat: *extract a confession.* **3.** To obtain by a chemical or physical process: *extract a metal from an ore; extract juice from an orange.* **4.** To remove, select, or quote (a passage from a literary work). **5.** *Math.* To determine or calculate (a root of a number). **—n.** (ĕk′străkt). **1.** Something drawn or pulled out. **2.** A passage from a literary work; an excerpt. **3.** A concentrated substance prepared by extracting; essence: *vanilla extract.* [Middle English *extracten,* from Latin *extractus,* past part. of *extrahere,* to draw out : *ex-,* out + *trahere,* to draw.] **—ex·tract′i·ble** or **ex·tract′a·ble** *adj.* **—ex·trac′tor** *n.*

ex·trac·tion (ĭk-străk′shən) *n.* **1.** The act or process of extracting. **2.** Something obtained by extracting; an extract. **3.** Origin; descent; lineage.

ex·trac·tive (ĭk-străk′tĭv) *adj.* **1.** Of, involving, or resulting from extraction: *an extractive product. Mining is an extractive industry.* **2.** Capable of being extracted. **—n.** Something that can be extracted.

ex·tra·cur·ric·u·lar (ĕk′strə-kə-rĭk′yə-lər) *adj.* Not part of a regular course of study.

ex·tra·dite (ĕk′strə-dīt′) *tr.v.* **-dit·ed, -dit·ing.** To surrender or obtain the surrender of (an alleged criminal) for trial by another judicial authority. [Back-formation from EXTRADITION.] **—ex′tra·dit′a·ble** *adj.*

ex·tra·di·tion (ĕk′strə-dĭsh′ən) *n.* The legal surrender of an alleged criminal to the jurisdiction of another state, country, or government for trial. [French : Latin *ex-,* out + *trāditiō,* a surrendering.]

ex·tra·dos (ĕk′strə-dŏs′, -dōs′) *n., pl.* **-dos** (-dōz′) or **-dos·es.** The upper or exterior curve of an arch. [French : Latin *extrā,* outside + French *dos,* back, from Latin *dorsum.*]

ex·tra·mu·ral (ĕk′strə-myŏŏr′əl) *adj.* Of or between participants, teams, etc., from more than one school; interscholastic: *extramural sports.*

ex·tra·ne·ous (ĭk-strā′nē-əs) *adj.* **1.** Coming from without; foreign. **2.** Irrelevant; not essential: *an extraneous consideration.* —See Syns at **irrelevant.** [Latin *extrāneus,* strange, from *extrā,* outward.] **—ex·tra′ne·ous·ly** *adv.* **—ex·tra′ne·ous·ness** *n.*

ex·traor·di·nar·y (ĭk-strôr′dn-ĕr′ē, ĕk′strə-ôr′-) *adj.* **1.** Beyond what is ordinary or usual; exceptional; remarkable: *extraordinary authority; an extraordinary event.* **2.** Employed for a special service or occasion: *a diplomat extraordinary.* —See Syns at **uncommon.** **—ex·traor′di·nar′i·ly** (-nâr′ə-lē) *adv.*

ex·trap·o·late (ĭk-străp′ə-lāt′) *v.* **-lat·ed, -lat·ing. —tr.v. 1.** *Math.* To estimate (a value of a function) that corresponds to a value of the independent variable that is either greater or smaller than any of the values for which the value of the function is known. **2.** To make an estimate or prediction of (unknown data) on the basis of available data. **—intr.v.** To engage in the process of extrapolation. [EXTRA- + (INTER)POLATE.] **—ex·trap′o·la′tion** *n.*

ex·tra·sen·so·ry (ĕk′strə-sĕn′sə-rē) *adj.* Outside the range of normal sense perception.

extrasensory perception. Perception by means other than normal sense perceptions, esp. by supernatural means.

ex·tra·ter·res·tri·al (ĕk′strə-tə-rĕs′trē-əl) *adj.* Originating, located, or occurring outside the earth or its atmosphere.

ex·tra·ter·ri·to·ri·al (ĕk′strə-tĕr′ĭ-tôr′ē-əl, -tōr′-) *adj.* Located outside the territorial boundaries of a nation or state.

ex·tra·ter·ri·to·ri·al·i·ty (ĕk′strə-tĕr′ĭ-tôr′ē-ăl′ĭ-tē, -tōr′-) *n.* Immunity from local legal jurisdiction, as is granted to foreign diplomats.

ex·trav·a·gance (ĭk-străv′ə-gəns) *n.* **1.** The quality or condition of being extravagant. **2.** Something that is excessively costly.

ex·trav·a·gant (ĭk-străv′ə-gənt) *adj.* **1.** Lavish, wasteful, or imprudent in the spending of money. **2.** Going beyond reasonable bounds; excessive; unrestrained: *extravagant demands.* **3.** Unreasonably high; exorbitant: *extravagant prices.* [Middle English *extravagaunt,* from Old French *extravagant,* from Medieval Latin *extrāvagāns,* pres. part. of *extrāvagāri,* to wander beyond : Latin *extrā,* beyond + *vagāri,* to wander.] **—ex·trav′a·gant·ly** *adv.*

ex·trav·a·gan·za (ĭk-străv′ə-găn′zə) *n.* A lavish stage or screen production; a spectacular. [Italian *estravaganza,* from *estravagant,* extravagant.]

ex·tra·ve·hic·u·lar activity (ĕk′strə-vē-hĭk′yə-lər). Activity or maneuvers performed by an astronaut outside a spacecraft in space.

ex·treme (ĭk-strēm′) *adj.* **1.** Of the greatest or highest degree; very intense: *extreme pleasure.* **2.** Outermost; farthest: *the extreme end of the room.* **3.** Far beyond what is normal or reasonable; radical: *an extreme conservative.* **4.** Drastic; severe: *extreme measures.* **—n. 1.** The greatest or utmost degree: *eager to the extreme.* **2.** Either of two ends of a scale, range, etc.: *the extremes of wealth and poverty.* **3.** A drastic expedient: *resort to extremes in an emergency.* **4.** *Math.* The first or last term of a ratio or series. [Middle English, from Old French, from Latin *extrēmus.*] **—ex·treme′ly** *adv.* **—ex·treme′ness** *n.*

extremely high frequency. A radio-frequency band with a range of 30,000 to 300,000 megahertz.

ex·trem·ist (ĭk-strē′mĭst) *n.* A person with extreme views, esp. in politics; radical. **—modifier:** *an extremist position.* **—ex·trem′ism** *n.*

ex·trem·i·ty (ĭk-strĕm′ĭ-tē) *n., pl.* **-ties. 1.** The outermost or farthest point or part. **2.** The greatest or utmost degree: *the extremity of despair.* **3.** Extreme danger, need, or distress. **4.** An extreme or severe measure. **5.** A limb or appendage of the body. **6. extremities.** The hands or feet.

ex·tri·cate (ĕk′strĭ-kāt′) *tr.v.* **-cat·ed, -cat·ing.** To free or release from an entanglement or difficulty; disengage: *extricate oneself from an embarrassing situation.* [From Latin *extrīcāre* : *ex-,* out + *trīcae,* perplexities.]

ă pat	ā pay	â care	ä father	ĕ pet	ē be	hw which	ĭ pit	ī tie	î pier	ŏ pot	ō toe	ô paw, for	oi noise
ŏŏ took	ōō boot	ou out	th thin	th this	ŭ cut		û urge	zh vision	ə about, item, edible, gallop, circus				

ex·trin·sic (ĭk-strĭn'sĭk, -zĭk) *adj.* **1.** Not forming an essential part of a thing; extraneous: *a fact extrinsic to the current problem.* **2.** Originating from the outside; external: *extrinsic forces.* [Late Latin *extrinsecus,* outer, from Latin, outwardly : *exterus,* exterior + *secus,* alongside.] —**ex·trin'si·cal·ly** *adv.*

ex·tro·vert (ĕk'strə-vûrt') *n.* An individual whose interest centers on the people and things surrounding him rather than on his own inner thoughts and feelings. [From *extro-,* outside + Latin *vertere,* to turn.] —**ex'tro·ver'sion** (-vûr'zhən) *n.*

ex·trude (ĭk-strōod') *v.* **-trud·ed, -trud·ing.** —*tr.v.* **1.** To push or thrust out: *Expansion extruded the lava.* **2.** To shape (metal, plastic, etc.) by forcing through a die. —*intr.v.* To protrude or project. [From Latin *extrūdere,* thrust out : *ex-,* out + *trūdere,* to thrust.]

ex·tru·sion (ĭk-strōo'zhən) *n.* The act or process of extruding. [Medieval Latin *extrūsiō,* from Latin *extrūsus,* past part. of *extrūdere,* to extrude.]

ex·tru·sive (ĭk-strōo'sĭv, -zĭv) *adj.* **1.** Tending to extrude. **2.** *Geol.* Derived from molten matter.

ex·u·ber·ant (ĭg-zōo'bər-ənt) *adj.* **1.** Full of unrestrained high spirits; lively; joyous. **2.** Lavish; effusive. **3.** Growing or producing abundantly; prolific: *exuberant vegetation.* [Middle English, from Old French, from Latin *exūberāns,* pres. part. of *exūberāre,* to be abundant : *ex-,* completely + *ūberāre,* to be fruitful.] —**ex·u'ber·ance** *n.* —**ex·u'ber·ant·ly** *adv.*

ex·ude (ĭg-zōod', ĭk-sōod') *v.* **-ud·ed, -ud·ing.** —*intr.v.* To come gradually through an opening; ooze forth. —*tr.v.* **1.** To discharge or emit gradually. **2.** To give off; radiate: *exude confidence.* [From Latin *exsūdāre* : *ex-,* out + *sudāre,* to sweat, ooze.] —**ex'u·da'tion** (ĕks'yōo-dā'shən) *n.*

ex·ult (ĭg-zŭlt') *intr.v.* To rejoice greatly; be jubilant or triumphant. [Latin *exsultāre,* freq. of *exsilīre,* to leap up, rejoice : *ex-,* up + *salīre,* to leap.] —**ex·ult'ing·ly** *adv.*

ex·ul·tant (ĭg-zŭl'tənt) *adj.* Feeling great joy; jubilant; triumphant. —**ex·ul'tant·ly** *adv.*

ex·ul·ta·tion (ĕg'zŭl-tā'shən, ĕk'səl-) *n.* **1.** The act of exulting. **2.** The condition of being exultant.

ex·urb (ĕk'sûrb', ĕg'zûrb') *n.* Exurbia.

ex·ur·ban·ite (ĕk-sûr'bə-nīt, ĕg-zûr'-) *n.* A person living in exurbia. [EX- + (SUB)URBANITE.]

ex·ur·bi·a (ĕk-sûr'bē-ə, ĕg-zûr'-) *n.* A mostly rural residential area located beyond the suburbs of a city. [EX- + (SUB)URBIA.]

eye (ī) *n.* **1. a.** An organ of vision. **b.** Either of the pair of organs by which vertebrates see, consisting of a hollow structure located in a fixed socket of the skull that contains a photosensitive retina on which a lens focuses incoming light. **2.** The faculty of seeing; sight; vision: *A marksman must have a sharp eye.* **3.** The ability to judge or estimate; discernment: *a good eye for talent.* **4.** A look; gaze: *cast a disdainful eye on the inept fellow.* **5.** A way of regarding something; point of view: *saw the world with a cynical eye.* **6.** Anything suggestive of an eye in appearance, as an opening in a needle. **7.** The loop to which a hook is linked for fastening. **8.** *Bot.* A bud on a twig or tuber: *the eye of a potato.* **9.** The relatively calm area at the center of a hurricane or similar storm. **10.** Anything

considered as a center or focal point. —*tr.v.* **eyed, eye·ing** or **ey·ing.** To look at; regard: *eyed him suspiciously.* —See Syns at **watch.** —*idioms.* **catch (someone's) eye.** To attract someone's attention. **give (someone) the eye.** *Informal.* To look at with admiration or invitation. **keep an eye on.** To watch carefully; look after. **make eyes at.** To gaze at flirtatiously. **see eye to eye.** To be in agreement. **with an eye to.** With the aim or intent of. [Middle English *eie,* from Old English *ēage.*]

eye·ball (ī'bôl') *n.* The ball-shaped portion of the eye enclosed by the socket and eyelids.

eye·brow (ī'brou') *n.* **1.** The bony ridge of the skull extending over the eye. **2.** The arch of short hairs covering this ridge.

eye·cup (ī'kŭp') *n.* A small cup with a rim shaped to fit over the eye, used for applying a liquid medicine or wash to the eye.

eye·ful (ī'fŏol') *n.* **1.** A good look. **2.** *Informal.* A sight to please the eyes, esp. a beautiful woman.

eye·glass (ī'glăs') *n.* **1. a.** eyeglasses. A pair of lenses worn in front of the eyes to improve faulty vision; glasses; spectacles. **b.** A lens, such as a monocle, worn or held in front of an eye to improve vision. **2.** An eyepiece, as of a microscope. **3.** An eyecup.

eye·lash (ī'lăsh') *n.* **1.** A row of short hairs that forms a fringe on the edge of an eyelid. **2.** Any of the hairs in this row.

eye·let (ī'lĭt') *n.* **1. a.** A small hole for a lace, cord, or hook to fit through. **b.** A metal ring used as a rim to strengthen such a hole; grommet. **2.** A small hole in embroidery with fancy stitches around the edge. [Middle English *oilet,* from Old French *oillet,* dim. of *oil,* eye, from Latin *oculus,* eye.]

eye·lid (ī'lĭd') *n.* Either of two folds of skin and muscle that can be closed over an eye.

eye opener. Something that gives startling new insights; a revelation.

eye·piece (ī'pēs') *n.* The lens or group of lenses closest to the eye in an optical instrument.

eye shadow. A cosmetic used to color the eyelids.

eye·sight (ī'sīt') *n.* **1.** The faculty of sight; vision. **2.** The range of vision; view.

eye·sore (ī'sôr', ī'sōr') *n.* An ugly sight.

eye·spot (ī'spŏt') *n.* In certain one-celled organisms, a colored area that is sensitive to light and functions somewhat like an eye.

eye·stalk (ī'stôk') *n.* A movable, stalklike structure bearing at its tip one of the eyes of a crab, shrimp, or similar crustacean.

eye·strain (ī'strān') *n.* Fatigue of one or more of the muscles of the eye, resulting from weakness, overuse, or errors of refraction.

eye·tooth (ī'tōoth') *n.* Either of the canine teeth of the upper jaw.

eye·wash (ī'wŏsh', -wôsh') *n.* **1.** A medicated solution for washing the eyes. **2.** Nonsense; meaningless talk.

eye·wit·ness (ī'wĭt'nəs) *n.* A person who has personally seen someone or something, such as an accident or a crime, and can bear witness to the fact.

eyr·ie or **eyr·y** (âr'ē, ăr'ē, îr'ē) *n.* Vars. of **aerie.**

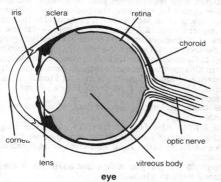

eye

eyestalk

Ff

| Phoenician | Greek | Roman | Medieval | Modern |

Phoenician – About 3,000 years ago the Phoenicians and other Semitic peoples began to use graphic signs to represent individual speech sounds instead of syllables or whole words. They used this symbol, which is the ancestor of the letters U, V, W, and Y as well as F, to represent the sound of the semivowel "w" and gave it the name wāw, the Phoenician word for "hook".

Greek – The Greeks borrowed the Phoenician alphabet with some modifications. They changed the shape of wāw and gave it the name digamma because it looked like one gamma (Γ) on top of another. They used digamma to represent the sound of the semivowel "w," as wāw had in Phoenician. This sound was lost in Greek at an early date and digamma does not appear in the Greek alphabet as it is now known.

Roman – The Romans borrowed the alphabet from the Greeks via the Etruscans. They used digamma to represent the sound of the consonant "f" and adapted the shape for carving Latin in stone. This monumental script, as it is called, became the basis for modern printed capital letters.

Medieval – By medieval times – around 1,200 years ago – the Roman monumental capitals had become adapted to being relatively quickly written on paper, parchment, or vellum. The shape of F became rounded and could be written with fewer pen strokes. The cursive minuscule alphabet became the basis of modern printed lower-case letters.

Modern – Since the invention of printing about 500 years ago modifications have been made in the shape and style of the letter F, but its basic form has remained unchanged.

---

f or **F** (ĕf) n., pl. **f's** or **F's. 1.** The sixth letter of the English alphabet. **2. F** *Mus.* The fourth tone in the scale of C major. **3. F** A failing grade.

F The symbol for the element fluorine.

fa (fä) n. *Mus.* A syllable used to represent the fourth tone of a major scale or sometimes the tone F. [Middle English, from Medieval Latin.]

fa·ble (fā'bəl) n. **1.** A brief tale or story, often with animal characters that speak and act like human beings, that teaches a useful lesson. **2.** A story about legendary persons and feats. **3.** A falsehood; lie. —*tr.v.* **-bled, -bling.** To tell or write about as if true. [Middle English, from Old French, from Latin *fābula*, narration, story, from *fārī*, to speak.] —**fa'bler** n.

fa·bled (fā'bəld) adj. **1.** Described in fiction; imaginary: a *fabled city of solid gold.* **2.** Famous in legend.

fab·ric (făb'rĭk) n. **1.** Cloth or other material produced by knitting, weaving, or felting natural or synthetic fibers. **2.** A system of relations; structure; framework: *the fabric of human society.* [Old French *fabrique*, from Latin *fabrica*, workshop, a trade, from *faber*, workman.]

fab·ri·cate (făb'rĭ-kāt') tr.v. **-cat·ed, -cat·ing. 1. a.** To manufacture; fashion or make. **b.** To construct; build. **2.** To make up; invent. —See Syns at **make.** [Middle English *fabricaten*, from Latin *fabricātus*, past part. of *fabricārī*, to build, from *fabrica*, workshop.] —**fab'ri·ca'tion** n.

fab·u·list (făb'yə-lĭst) n. **1.** A composer of fables. **2.** A liar.

fab·u·lous (făb'yə-ləs) adj. **1.** Belonging to legend; mythical: *the fabulous Phoenix.* **2.** Famous in old stories; fabled: *the fabulous lands of Asia.* **3.** Barely believable; astonishing: *fabulous wealth.* **4.** *Informal.* Extremely exciting or excellent; amazing; wonderful: *a fabulous opportunity.* [Middle English, from Latin *fābulōsus*, from *fābula*, fable.] —**fab'u·lous·ly** adv. —**fab'u·lous·ness** n.

    Syns: fabulous, amazing, astonishing, fantastic, incredible, marvelous, miraculous, phenomenal, stupendous, unbelievable, wonderful, wondrous adj. Core meaning: So remarkable as to cause disbelief (*the fabulous endurance of a long-distance runner*).

fa·cade or **fa·çade** (fə-säd') n. **1.** The main face or front of a building. **2.** The face or front part of anything, esp. an artificial or false front: "*Of most famous people we know only the imposing façade*" (Edith Hamilton). [French, from Italian *facciata*, from *faccia*, face.]

face (fās) n. **1.** The front of the head from the top of the forehead to the bottom of the chin and from ear to ear. **2. a.** The expression of the features of this part of the head: *a sad face.* **b.** A distorted expression: *Don't make faces.* **3.** The surface presented to view; the front: *the face of a building; the sheer face of a mountain.* **4.** The upper or marked side of something, such as a clock or playing card. **5.** *Geom.* A plane surface that bounds a solid figure. **6.** An outward appearance; aspect; look: *The face of the city has changed.* **7.** Standing in the eyes of others; dignity; prestige: *They hushed up the affair to save face.* **8.** *Printing.* Typeface. —**modifier:** *face powder.* —v. **faced, fac·ing.** —*tr.v.* **1.** To turn the face to or toward: *Turn around and face the class.* **2.** To have the front directly opposite to; look out on; front on: *The cathedral faces the square.* **3.** To confront or deal with boldly or bravely: *He has faced danger many times.* **4.** To meet in competition: *The White Sox face the Orioles today.* **5.** To be or have in store for: *We are facing a serious food crisis.* **6.** To recognize; realize: *You've got to face the facts.* **7.** To furnish with a surface or edge of a different material: *face the walls of a building with white marble; face a cloth collar with leather.* —*intr.v.* **1.** To be turned or placed with the front toward a specified direction: *My window faces south..* **2.** To turn the face in a specified direction. —**phrasal verbs. face down.** To overcome or prevail over by a stare or a resolute manner. **face off.** To start play in hockey, lacrosse, and other games by releasing the puck or ball between two opposing players. **face up to. 1.** To recognize the existence or importance of. **2.** To confront bravely. —**idioms. face to face. 1.** In each other's presence. **2.** Directly confronting. **in the face of. 1.** Despite the opposition of; notwithstanding. **2.** Considering the fact of; in view of. **on the face of it.** From all appearances; apparently. **to (one's) face.** In one's presence. [Middle English, from Old French, from Latin *faciēs*, form, shape, face, from *facere*, to make, form.] —**face'a·ble** adj.

face card. A king, queen, or jack of a deck of playing cards.

face lifting. Also **face-lift** (fās'lĭft'). **1.** Plastic surgery to tighten sagging facial muscles and improve the appearance of facial skin. **2.** An alteration or renovation of an exterior.

face·plate (fās'plāt') n. A disk that holds flat or irregularly shaped work in a lathe.

ă pat	ā pay	â care	ä father	ĕ pet	ē be	hw which	ĭ pit	ī tie	î pier	ŏ pot	ō toe	ô paw, for	oi noise
ŏŏ took	ōō boot	ou out	th thin	*th* this	ŭ cut		û urge	zh vision	ə about, item, edible, gallop, circus

fac·et (făs′ĭt) *n.* **1.** A small, flat surface, as on a gem. **2.** A separate side or aspect of anything: *the many facets of a problem.* **3.** One of the lenslike divisions of a compound eye, as of an insect. [French *facette,* dim. of *face,* face.] —**fac′et·ed** or **fac′et·ted** *adj.*

fa·ce·tious (fə-sē′shəs) *adj.* Meant to be funny; humorous and flippant: *a facetious remark.* [Old French *facetieux,* from *facetie,* a jest, from Latin *facētia,* from *facētus,* elegant, fine, witty.] —**fa·ce′tious·ly** *adv.* —**fa·ce′tious·ness** *n.*

face value. The value printed or written on the face, as of a bill, bond, or coin. —*idiom.* **take (or accept) at face value.** To accept as genuine without checking.

fa·cial (fā′shəl) *adj.* Of the face. —*n.* A treatment for the face, usu. consisting of a massage and the application of cosmetic creams. —**fa′cial·ly** *adv.*

fac·ile (făs′əl) *adj.* **1. a.** Done with little effort or difficulty; easy: *a facile triumph.* **b.** Arrived at without due care or effort; superficial: *a facile solution.* **2.** Working, acting, or speaking effortlessly; fluent: *a facile speaker.* **3.** Relaxed in manner; easygoing. **4.** Yielding; compliant. —See Syns at **easy.** [Old French, from Latin *facilis.*] —**fac′ile·ly** *adv.* —**fac′ile·ness** *n.*

fa·cil·i·tate (fə-sĭl′ĭ-tāt′) *tr.v.* **-tat·ed, -tat·ing.** To make easier; assist. [French *faciliter,* from Italian *facilitare,* from *facile,* easy, from Latin *facilis,* facile.] —**fa·cil′i·ta′tion** *n.*

fa·cil·i·ty (fə-sĭl′ĭ-tē) *n., pl.* **-ties. 1.** Ease in moving, acting, or doing, resulting from skill or aptitude: *He reads music with great facility.* **2.** Often **facilities.** Something that provides a service or convenience: *storage facilities.* **3.** An agreeable, pliable disposition. —See Syns at **ease.**

fac·ing (fā′sĭng) *n.* **1.** A lining or trimming that covers the edge, esp. of a garment: *suede facings on cuffs and lapels.* **2.** An outer layer applied to a surface as a decoration or protection.

fac·sim·i·le (făk-sĭm′ə-lē) *n.* **1.** An exact copy or reproduction, as of a document, book, or painting. **2.** A method of transmitting images or printed matter by electronic means. [Latin *fac simile,* "make (it) similar."]

fact (făkt) *n.* **1.** Something that is objectively true and accurate: *stick to the facts.* **2.** Something having real, demonstrable existence: *You must learn to distinguish between fact and fiction.* **3. a.** An act or deed. **b.** A criminal act. —*idioms.* **as a matter of fact.** In truth; actually. **in (point of) fact.** In reality; actually. [Latin *factum,* a deed, from *factus,* past part. of *facere,* to do.]

fact-find·ing (făkt′fīn′dĭng) *n.* The discovery or determination of facts or accurate information. —*modifier: a fact-finding committee.*

fac·tion (făk′shən) *n.* **1.** A united and usu. troublesome minority within a larger group. **2.** Internal discord; conflict within an organization or nation. [Old French, from Latin *factiō,* an acting (together), a making, from *factus,* past part. of *facere,* to do, make.] —**fac′tion·al** *adj.*

fac·tious (făk′shəs) *adj.* **1.** Produced or characterized by faction. **2.** Tending to cause conflict or discord; divisive: "*The . . . injustice with which a factious spirit has tainted our public administration*" (James Madison). —**fac′tious·ly** *adv.* —**fac′tious·ness** *n.*

fac·ti·tious (făk-tĭsh′əs) *adj.* **1.** Not natural. **2.** Lacking authenticity or genuineness; artificial: *speculators responsible for the factitious value of some stocks.* [Latin *factīcius,* made by art, from *facere,* to make, do.] —**fac·ti′tious·ly** *adv.* —**fac·ti′tious·ness** *n.*

fac·tor (făk′tər) *n.* **1. a.** A person who acts for someone else. **b.** A person or firm that accepts accounts receivable as security for short-term loans. **2.** Something that helps bring about a certain result: *Many factors contributed to his success.* **3.** *Biol.* A gene. **4.** *Math.* One of two or more numbers or expressions that have a given product. For example, 2 and 3 are factors of 6, and $a + b$ and $a - b$ are factors of $a^2 - b^2$. —*tr.v.* *Math.* To find the factors of (a number or expression). [Middle English *factour,* from Old French *facteur,* from Latin *factor,* maker, doer, from *factum,* deed.]

fac·to·ri·al (făk-tôr′ē-əl, -tōr′) *n.* The product of all the positive integers from 1 to a given number. For example, 4 factorial, usu. written 4!, is the product 1·2·3·4 = 24; similarly, 5! = 1·2·3·4·5 = 120. —*adj.* Of a factor or factorial

fac·tor·i·za·tion (făk′tər-ĭ-zā′shən) *n.* **1.** The act or process of factoring. **2.** A mathematical expression written in the form of a product and equivalent to another mathematical expression. For example, $5 \times 3 \times 2$ is a factorization of 30, and $(a + b) (a - b)$ is a factorization of $a^2 - b^2$.

fac·to·ry (făk′tə-rē) *n., pl.* **-ries.** A building or group of buildings in which goods are manufactured; a plant. —*modifier: factory workers.* [Medieval Latin *factōria,* establishment for factors, from Latin *factor,* factor.]

fac·to·tum (făk-tō′təm) *n.* An employee or assistant with a wide range of duties. [Medieval Latin *factōtum,* from Latin *fac tōtum,* "do everything."]

fac·tu·al (făk′chōō-əl) *adj.* Based on or containing facts: *a factual account.* —**fac′tu·al·ly** *adv.*

fac·u·la (făk′yə-lə) *n., pl.* **-lae** (-lē). Any of various large bright spots or streaks on the sun's photosphere, most conspicuous at the solar edge or near sunspots. [Latin, dim. of *fax,* flame, torch.]

fac·ul·ty (făk′əl-tē) *n., pl.* **-ties. 1.** One of the powers or capacities of the mind: *the faculty of speech.* **2.** A special aptitude; skill: *He has a faculty for languages.* **3.** The teaching staff of a school, college, or university or of one of its divisions. —See Syns at **ability.** —*modifier: a faculty member.* [Middle English *faculte,* from Old French, from Latin *facultās,* power, capability, from *facul,* easy.]

fad (făd) *n.* A fashion, as in dress, behavior, or speech, that enjoys brief popularity; craze. [Orig. unknown.] —**fad′dish** *adj.* —**fad′dist** *n.*

fade (fād) *v.* **fad·ed, fad·ing.** —*intr.v.* **1.** To lose brightness or brilliance gradually; dim: *The material faded in the wash.* **2.** To lose freshness; wither: *The flowers are beginning to fade.* **3.** To become faint or inaudible; die out. **4.** To disappear slowly; vanish: *All hope of reaching the camp by nightfall soon faded away.* —*tr.v.* **1.** To cause to fade. **2.** *Slang.* To meet the bet of (an opposing player) in a game of dice. —*phrasal verbs.* **fade in.** To make (an image or sound) appear gradually, as in television, films, or radio broadcasting. **fade out.** To make (an image or sound) change or disappear gradually, as in television, films, or radio broadcasting. —*n.* A gradual change from one image or sound to another, as in television, films, or radio broadcasting. [Middle English *faden,* from Old French *fader,* from *fade,* faded, vapid, prob. a blend of Latin *fatuus,* insipid, foolish, and *vapidus,* vapid.]

fa·er·ie (fā′ə-rē, fâr′ē) *n.* Also **fa·er·y** *pl.* **-ies. 1.** A fairy. **2.** The land of the fairies. [Middle English *faierie, fairie,* fairyland, fairy.]

fag¹ (făg) *n. Brit.* A student at an English public school who is required to perform menial tasks for a student in a higher class. —*v.* **fagged, fag·ging.** —*intr.v.* **1.** To work to exhaustion; to toil. **2.** *Brit.* To serve as the fag of another student. —*tr.v.* To exhaust from long work; to fatigue: *He was fagged out by three hours on the tennis courts.* [Orig. unknown.]

fag² (făg) *n. Slang.* A cigarette. [Short for FAG END.]

fag end. *n.* **1.** The frayed, worn, or untwisted end of a piece of cloth or rope. **2.** The last and least useful part of anything: *the fag end of an exhausting day.* [From Middle English *fagge.*]

fag·got (făg′ət) *n. & v.* Var. of **fagot.**

fag·ot or **fag·got** (făg′ət) *n.* **1.** A bundle of twigs, sticks, or branches bound together, esp. for firewood. **2.** A bundle of pieces of iron or steel to be welded or hammered into bars. —*tr.v.* Also **fag·got. 1.** To collect or bind into a fagot; to bundle. **2.** To decorate with fagoting. [Middle English, from Old French, from Italian *fagotto,* ult. from Greek *phakelos.*]

fag·ot·ing or **fag·got·ing** (făg′ə-tĭng) *n.* **1.** A decoration on

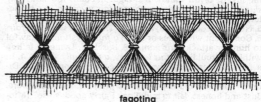

fagoting

cloth made by pulling out horizontal threads and tying the remaining vertical threads into hourglass-shaped bunches. **2.** A stitch that joins hemmed edges.

Fahr·en·heit (făr′ən-hīt′) *adj. Abbr.* **F** Of or concerning a temperature scale that indicates the freezing point of water at 32° and the boiling point of water as 212° under normal atmospheric pressure. [After Gabriel *Fahrenheit* (1686–1736), German physicist.]

fa·ience or **fa·ïence** (fī-äns′, -äns′, fä-) *n.* An often colorfully decorated earthenware with a tin glaze. [French, short for *(vaisselle de) Faïence,* "(vessel of) Faenza," a city in Italy.]

fail (fāl) *v.* —*intr.v.* **1.** To be unsuccessful: *He succeeded where all others had failed.* **2.** To prove deficient or lacking. **3.** To receive less than a passing academic grade: *Under the new system, a student either passes or fails.* **4.** To prove insufficient; give out: *The water supply failed.* **5.** To decline in strength or effectiveness: *Her hearing began to fail.* **6.** To cease functioning properly: *The brakes on the car failed.* **7.** To become bankrupt or insolvent. —*tr.v.* **1.** To disappoint or not meet the expectations of: *Our sentries failed us.* **2.** To abandon; forsake: *His strength failed him.* **3.** To neglect or not do: *The defendant failed to appear in court.* **4. a.** To receive less than a passing academic grade in: *Many students failed the course.* **b.** To give less than a passing academic grade to: *The teacher failed nearly half the class.* —*n.* —**without fail.** Definitely; positively: *The job will be finished tomorrow without fail.* [Middle English *failen,* from Old French *faillir,* from Latin *fallere,* to deceive, disappoint, fail.]

Syns: fail, flunk (Informal) *v. Core meaning:* To receive less than a passing grade (*failed the course*).

fail·ing (fā′lĭng) *n.* **1.** A minor fault or weakness; shortcoming. **2.** Failure. —*prep.* In the absence of; without: *Failing instructions, we shall proceed on our own.*

faille (fīl, fāl) *n.* A ribbed, woven fabric of silk, cotton, or rayon. [French, from Old French *faille.*]

fail-safe (fāl′sāf′) *adj.* Capable of compensating automatically for a failure.

fail·ure (fāl′yər) *n.* **1.** The condition or fact of failing to achieve a desired end: *the failure of an experiment.* **2.** Someone or something that has failed: *I'm a failure as a writer.* **3.** A falling short: *the failure of the sugar-cane harvest.* **4.** An inability to function or perform properly: *an electric power failure; heart failure.* **5.** Omission or neglect of what is requested or expected: *failure to report a change of address.* **6.** A decline in strength; weakening. **7.** The act or fact of becoming bankrupt or insolvent. [Var. of earlier *failer,* from Norman French *failer,* from Old French *faillir,* to fail.]

fain (fān). *Archaic.* —*adv.* Willingly; gladly: *I would fain risk my life for thee.* —*adj.* **1.** Willing; glad. **2.** Obliged or required. [Middle English, from *fain,* joyful, happy, from Old English *fægen.*]

faint (fānt) *adj.* -**er,** -**est.** **1.** Barely perceptible; indistinct; dim: *a faint light; a faint memory.* **2.** Not great; slight: *a faint resemblance.* **3.** Likely to fall unconscious; dizzy and weak: *Hunger made him feel faint.* —*n.* A sudden, usu. short loss of consciousness, often caused by a deficient flow of blood to the brain. —*intr.v.* **1.** To lose consciousness for a short time; swoon. **2.** *Archaic.* To weaken in purpose; languish. [Middle English *feint, faint, faint, feigned,* from Old French, past part. of *feindre, faindre,* feign.] —**faint′ly** *adv.* —**faint′ness** *n.*

faint-heart·ed (fānt′här′tĭd) *adj.* Lacking in conviction or courage; cowardly; timid. —**faint-heart′ed·ly** *adv.* —**faint-heart′ed·ness** *n.*

fair[1] (fâr) *adj.* **fair·er, fair·est. 1.** Pleasing to look at; beautiful; lovely: *a fair maiden.* **2.** Light in color: *fair hair; fair skin.* **3.** Free of clouds or storms: *fair weather.* **4.** Characterized by evenhanded honesty; just: *fair play; a fair trial.* **5.** Neither good nor bad; average: *The movie was only fair.* **6.** Consistent with rules or logic: *a fair question.* **7.** Lawful to hunt or attack: *fair game.* **8.** *Baseball.* Lying or falling within the foul lines: *fair territory; a fair ball.* —*adv.* **1.** In a fair manner; properly: *I believe in playing fair.'* **2.** Directly; squarely; straight: *a blow caught fair in the stomach.* —**idioms. bid fair.** To show promise. **fair and square.** Just and honest. **fair to middling.** Fairly good; so-so. [Mid-

dle English, from Old English *fæger.*] —**fair′ness** *n.*

Syns: fair, dispassionate, equitable, fair-minded, impartial, just, objective *adj. Core meaning:* Free from bias in judgment (*a fair judge*). See also Syns at **beautiful.**

fair[2] (fâr) *n.* **1.** A gathering for the buying and selling of goods; market. **2.** A large exhibition or display, as of farm products or manufactured goods, often accompanied by amusements or entertainments: *a world's fair.* [Middle English *feire,* from Old French, from Late Latin *fēria,* from Latin *fēriæ,* holidays.]

fair catch. *Football.* A catch of a punt by a defensive player who has signaled that he will not run with the ball and who therefore may not be tackled.

fair·ground (fâr′ground′) *n.* Often **fairgrounds.** An open area where fairs are held.

fair·ing[1] (fâr′ĭng) *n.* An auxiliary structure on the external surface of an aircraft that reduces drag. [From *fair,* to make smooth.]

fair·ing[2] (fâr′ĭng) *n. Brit.* A gift, esp. one bought at a fair.

fair·ish (fâr′ĭsh) *adj.* Of moderately good size or quality.

fair·ly (fâr′lē) *adv.* **1.** In a fair manner; equitably. **2.** Moderately; rather: *a fairly good dinner.* **3.** Quite; completely: *The walls fairly shook with his screaming.*

fair-mind·ed (fâr′mīn′dĭd) *adj.* Just and impartial; unprejudiced. —See Syns at **fair**[1]. —**fair′-mind′ed·ness** *n.*

fair-spo·ken (fâr′spō′kən) *adj.* Civil, courteous, and pleasant in speech.

fair-trade (fâr′trād′) *adj.* Of, relating to, or constituting an agreement under which retailers sell a given item at no less than a certain price.

fair·way (fâr′wā′) *n.* **1.** The mowed area of grass of a golf course extending from the tee to the putting green. **2.** A navigable deep-water channel in a river, harbor, or along a coastline.

fair-weath·er (fâr′wĕth′ər) *adj.* **1.** Appropriate to fair weather. **2.** Loyal and dependable only in good times: *fair-weather friends.*

fair·y (fâr′ē) *n., pl.* -**ies.** An imaginery being supposed to have magical powers. —*modifier: a fairy story.* [Middle English *fairie,* from Old French *faerie,* enchantment, from *fae,* fairy, from Latin *fāta,* the Fates, pl. of *fātum,* fate.]

fair·y·land (fâr′ē-lănd′) *n.* **1.** The land of the fairies. **2.** A delightful or enchanting place.

fairy ring. A circle of mushrooms in a grassy area. [From the folklore belief that the circle is produced by dancing fairies.]

fairy tale. 1. A children's story about fairies and magical events. **2.** A highly fanciful story usu. intended to mislead.

fait ac·com·pli (fĕt′ä-kôN-plē′, fāt′-) *pl.* **faits ac·com·plis** (fĕt′ä-kôN-plē′, fāt′-). *French.* Something already done that cannot be undone.

faith (fāth) *n.* **1.** Confidence or trust in a person, idea, or thing: *You must have faith in yourself.* **2.** Belief not based on logical proof or material evidence: *faith in miracles.* **3.** Belief in God: *a man of great faith.* **4.** A religion: *people of every faith.* **5.** A promise or pledge of loyalty: *break faith with one's supporters.* **6.** Any set of principles or beliefs: *"Realism had been his literary faith from his earliest days"* (Alfred Kazin). —See Syns at **confidence.** —*idioms.* **bad faith.** Deceit; insincerity. **good faith.** Sincerity; honesty: *promises made in good faith.* **in faith.** Indeed; truly. [Middle English *feith,* from Old French *feid, feit,* from Latin *fidēs.*]

faith·ful (fāth′fəl) *adj.* **1.** Loyal to the person, cause, or idea to which one is bound; dutiful. **2.** Worthy of trust; consistently reliable: *a faithful guide.* **3.** Accurate; exact: *a faithful reproduction.* —*n.* **1.** A member of a religious group. **2.** A loyal follower. —**faith′ful·ly** *adv.* —**faith′ful·ness** *n.*

Syns: faithful, constant, fast[1]**, firm**[1]**, loyal, liege, resolute, staunch, steadfast, steady, true** *adj. Core meaning:* Firmly and devotedly supportive of a person or cause (*a faithful party member; a faithful friend*). See also Syns at **accurate.**

faith·less (fāth′lĭs) *adj.* **1.** Breaking faith; disloyal. **2.** Lacking faith. —**faith′less·ly** *adv.* —**faith′less·ness** *n.*

Syns: faithless, disloyal, false, false-hearted, traitorous, treacherous, unfaithful, untrue *adj. Core meaning:* Not true to duty or obligation (*a faithless spouse*).

ă pat	ā pay	â care	ä father	ĕ pet	ē be	hw which
ŏŏ took	ōō boot	ou out	th thin	th this	ŭ cut

ĭ pit   ī tie   î pier   ŏ pot   ō toe   ô paw, for   oi noise
û urge   zh vision   ə about, item, edible, gallop, circus

fake (fāk) *n.* Someone or something that is not genuine or authentic; fraud. —See Syns at **impostor.** —*v.* **faked, fak·ing.** —*tr.v.* **1.** To make in order to deceive; counterfeit or forge: *fake a ten-dollar bill.* **2.** To simulate or put on an act; pretend; feign: *fake illness.* —*intr.v.* **1.** To engage in faking. **2.** *Sports.* To make a deceptive maneuver: *The halfback faked to his left and ran to the right.* —*adj.* False; counterfeit. [Orig. unknown.] —**fak'er** *n.* —**fak'er·y** *n.*

fa·kir (fə-kîr') *n.* **1.** A Moslem religious beggar. **2.** A Hindu holy man or worker of miracles. [Arabic *faqīr,* from *faqura,* he was poor.]

Fa·lange (fā'lănj', fə-lănj') *n.* The fascist party that was the official ruling party of Spain after 1939. [Spanish, from *falange,* phalanx, from Latin *phalanx,* phalanx.] —**Fa·lan'gist** (fə-lăn'gĭst, fā'lăn'jĭst) *n.*

fal·cate (făl'kāt') *adj.* Curved and tapering to a point; sickle-shaped; hooked. [Latin *falcātus,* from *falx,* sickle.]

fal·chion (fôl'chən) *n.* A short, broad sword with a slightly curved blade, used in medieval times. [Middle English *fauchoun,* from Old French *fauchon,* from Latin *falx,* sickle.]

fal·con (făl'kən, fôl'-, fô'kən) *n.* **1.** Any of various birds of prey of the family Falconidae, esp. of the genus *Falco,* with long, pointed, powerful wings adapted for swift flight. **2.** Any of several species of these birds or related birds such as hawks, trained to hunt small game. [Middle English *faucoun,* from Old French *faucon,* from Late Latin *falcō.*]

fal·con·er (făl'kə-nər, fôl'-, fô'kə-) *n.* A person who breeds, trains, or uses falcons for hunting.

fal·con·ry (făl'kən-rē, fôl'-, fô'kən-) *n.* **1.** The sport of hunting with falcons. **2.** The art of training falcons for hunting.

fal·de·ral or **fal·de·rol** (făl'də-răl') *n.* Vars. of **folderol.**

fall (fôl) *v.* **fell** (fĕl), **fall·en** (fô'lən), **fall·ing.** —*intr.v.* **1. a.** To descend or move downward freely as a result of gravitational force: *The snow fell silently to the ground.* **b.** To hang down freely: *a skirt which fell in smooth folds.* **c.** To stretch or extend downward. **2. a.** To drop suddenly and involuntarily from an upright position: *She slipped and fell.* **b.** To drop down wounded or dead: *Many soldiers fell at Waterloo.* **3.** To come or occur as if descending suddenly: *Darkness fell upon the scene.* **4.** To diminish, as in value or intensity: *Prices fell on the stock exchange. The temperature fell below freezing.* **5.** To perform an immoral or wrong act; sin. **6.** To suffer defeat, destruction, or capture: *Paris fell in 1940.* **7.** To come to rest at a specified place: *The major stress falls on the first vowel in the word "travel."* **8. a.** To come to pass; happen: *Disasters fell upon the tiny village.* **b.** To occur on a particular date: *Thanksgiving always falls on a Thursday.* **9.** To pass from one state or condition into another: *fall asleep.* **10.** To come as a right, assignment, or duty: *The estate fell to the eldest surviving son.* **11.** To come by chance: *fall into a trap; fall into bad company.* **12.** To come within the limits or scope esp. of a certain category or class: *Most languages fall into groups or families.* **13.** To be uttered: *A sigh fell from her lips.* **14.** To assume a look of disappointment, shame or hurt: *His face fell when she refused to dance.* —*tr.v.* To cut down (a tree); fell. —*phrasal verbs.* **fall away.** To withdraw friendship or support; part company. **fall back.** To give ground; retreat. **fall back on.** To turn to for help; resort to. **fall behind.** To fail to keep up with: *He fell behind in his work.* **fall for.** *Informal.* **1.** To become infatuated or fall in love with: *He falls for every girl he meets.* **2.** To be taken in by: *Some people fall for anything you say.* **fall in.** To take one's place in a military formation. **fall in with. 1.** To meet by chance: *The boy fell in with another boy he liked very much.* **2.** To agree to: *He immediately fell in with my suggestions.* **fall on** (or **upon**). To attack suddenly: *The troops fell upon the enemy at dusk.* —See Syns at **attack. fall out. 1.** To become estranged; quarrel: *She has fallen out with her next-door neighbors.* **2.** To occur. **fall through.** To fail; collapse: *Their plans for a vacation fell through.* **fall to.** To begin, esp. with vigor: *The villagers fell to work at daybreak.* —*n.* **1.** The action of falling as a result of gravitational force: *the fall of a spacecraft toward the moon.* **2.** A sudden drop from a relatively erect to a less erect position: *He took a bad fall.* **3. a.** Something that has fallen: *a sudden fall of snow.* **b.** The amount of what has fallen: *a fall of two inches of rain.* **c.** The distance that something falls: *a fall of three stories.* **4.** Often **Fall.** Autumn. **5.** Often **falls.** A waterfall; cascade. **6.** A downward movement or slope: *the fall of a river toward its mouth.* **7.** A woman's hair piece with long hair that hangs down loose. **8.** A capture, overthrow, or collapse: *the fall of a government; the fall of the Alamo.* **9.** A reduction in value, amount, or degree: *a fall in prices.* **10.** A decline in status, rank, or importance: *a fall from favor.* **11. a.** A loss of virtue or innocence; a yielding to temptation. **b. the Fall.** The sin of Adam and Eve in eating the forbidden fruit in the Garden of Eden. **12.** *Wrestling.* **a.** The act of pinning one's opponent to the ground. **b.** A wrestling match. —*modifier: a fall day.* —*idioms.* **fall flat.** *Informal* To produce no result; fail. **fall short.** To fail to reach or attain: *The campaign fell short of expectations.* [Middle English *fallen,* from Old English *feallan.*]

   Syns: 1. fall, descend, drop *v. Core meaning:* To move downward in response to gravity (*apples falling from a tree*). **2. fall, drop, pitch, plunge, spill, sprawl, topple, tumble** *v. Core meaning:* To come to the ground suddenly and involuntarily (*stumbled and fell*).

fal·la·cious (fə-lā'shəs) *adj.* **1.** Containing fundamental errors in reasoning; illogical: *fallacious arguments.* **2.** Not real or sound; deceptive; delusive: *fallacious hopes.* —**fal·la'cious·ly** *adv.*

fal·la·cy (făl'ə-sē) *n., pl.* **-cies. 1.** A false idea or notion. **2.** A fallacious belief or argument. [Latin *fallācia,* deceit, trick, from *fallāx,* deceitful, from *fallere,* to deceive.]

fall·en (fô'lən) *v.* Past participle of **fall.**

fall guy. *Slang.* **1.** A dupe. **2.** A scapegoat.

fal·li·ble (făl'ə-bəl) *adj.* Capable of erring or of being erroneous: *all men are fallible.* [Middle English, from Medieval Latin *fallibilis,* from Latin *fallere,* to deceive.] —**fal'li·bil'i·ty** *n.* —**fal'li·bly** *adv.*

fall·ing-out (fô'lĭng-out') *n., pl.* **fall·ings-out** or **fall·ing-outs.** A disagreement; quarrel.

falling star. A meteor.

fall line. *Geog.* An imaginary line that connects the waterfalls of nearly parallel rivers and marks the boundary between two land levels.

Fal·lo·pi·an tube (fə-lō'pē-ən). Either of a pair of slender tubes found in the female reproductive system of human beings and higher vertebrates that carry egg cells from the ovaries to the uterus. [After Gabriello *Fallopio* (1523–1562), Italian anatomist.]

fall·out (fôl'out') *n.* **1. a.** The slow fall of tiny particles of radioactive material from the atmosphere after a nuclear explosion. **b.** The particles that fall in this way. **2.** An incidental result or side effect: *the technological fallout of the space program.*

fal·low (făl'ō) *adj.* Unseeded during a growing season: *a fallow field.* —*n.* **1.** Fallow land. **2.** The condition or period of being fallow. —*tr.v.* To plow (land) without seeding it. [Middle English *falow, falwe,* from Old English *fealh,* arable land.] —**fal'low·ness** *n.*

fallow deer. Either of two Eurasian deer, *Dama dama* or *D. mesopotamica,* with a yellowish coat spotted with white in summer, and broad, flattened antlers in the male. [From obs. *fallow,* reddish-yellow, from Middle English *falwe,* sallow, from Old English *fealo.*]

false (fôls) *adj.* **fals·er, fals·est. 1. a.** Contrary to fact or truth; erroneous: *a false assumption.* **b.** Arising from mistaken ideas: *false hopes.* **2.** Marked by an intent to deceive; untruthful: *a false accusation.* **3.** Unfaithful; disloyal: *a false friend.* **4. a.** Not natural; artificial: *false teeth.* **b.** Not real or genuine: *a false name.* **5.** *Mus.* Wrong in pitch. [Middle English *fals,* from Old French, from Latin *falsus,* past part. of *fallere,* to deceive.] —**false'ly** *adv.*

   Syns: false, erroneous, inaccurate, incorrect, specious, untruthful, wrong *adj. Core meaning:* Lacking truth (*a rumor that was false*). See also Syns at **faithless.**

false arrest. *Law.* An unlawful or unjustifiable arrest.

false-heart·ed (fôls'här'tĭd) *adj.* Having a deceitful nature; disloyal: *a false-hearted lover.* —See Syns at **faithless.**

false·hood (fôls'hŏŏd) *n.* **1.** Lack of conformity with truth or fact. **2.** The act of lying. **3.** An untrue statement; lie. —See Syns at **lie.**

---

false rib. Any of the five lower pairs of ribs that do not join directly to the breastbone.

fal·set·to (fôl-sĕt'ō) n., pl. **-tos. 1.** An artificially produced high voice used esp. by a tenor. **2.** A singer of falsetto. —adv. In falsetto: sing falsetto. [Italian, dim. of falso, false, from Latin falsus, false.]

fal·si·fy (fôl'sə-fī') v. **-fied, -fy·ing.** —tr.v. **1.** To represent untruthfully; lie: falsify the facts. **2.** To make false in order to deceive: falsify a passport. **3.** To prove to be false. —intr.v. To make untrue statements; lie. [Middle English falsifien, from Old French falsifier, from Medieval Latin falsificāre, from Latin falsus, false + facere, to make.] —fal'si·fi·ca'tion n. —fal'si·fi'er n.

fal·si·ty (fôl'sĭ-tē) n., pl. **-ties. 1.** The condition of being false. **2.** Something false; a lie. —See Syns at **lie.**

fal·ter (fôl'tər) intr.v. **1.** To perform haltingly or unsteadily: The engine faltered. **2.** To speak hesitatingly; stammer. **3.** To waver in purpose or action; hesitate. —See Syns at **hesitate.** —n. **1.** An unsteadiness in speech or action. **2.** A faltering sound. [Middle English falteren.] —fal'ter·ing·ly adv.

fame (fām) n. Great reputation and recognition; renown. [Middle English, from Old French, from Latin fāma, talk, reputation.]

famed (fāmd) adj. Having great fame; renowned. —See Syns at **famous.**

fa·mil·ial (fə-mĭl'yəl) adj. Of, pertaining to, or characteristic of a family.

fa·mil·iar (fə-mĭl'yər) adj. **1.** Often encountered; common: the familiar voice of his wife. **2.** Having a good knowledge; well-acquainted: I am not familiar with the details of the case. **3.** Close; intimate: on familiar terms with his colleagues. **4.** Natural and unstudied; informal: wrote in a familiar style. **5.** Unduly forward; bold. —See Syns at **common.** —n. **1.** A close friend or associate. **2.** A spirit believed to attend to a person. **3.** A person who frequents a place. [Middle English familial, from Old French familier, from Latin familiāris, from familia, family.] —fa·mil'iar·ly adv.

fa·mil·iar·i·ty (fə-mĭl'ē-ăr'ĭ-tē) n., pl. **-ties. 1.** Substantial acquaintance with or knowledge of something: His familiarity with the city helped him get around. **2.** Close friendship; intimacy. **3. a.** Undue liberty or forwardness. **b.** A sexual liberty or impropriety.

fa·mil·iar·ize (fə-mĭl'yə-rīz') tr.v. **-ized, -iz·ing. 1.** To make well-known or familiar. **2.** To make acquainted with. —fa·mil'iar·i·za'tion n.

fam·i·ly (făm'ə-lē, făm'lē) n., pl. **-lies. 1.** Parents and their children. **2.** A group of persons related by blood or marriage. **3.** The members of one household. **4.** A group of things with common characteristics. **5.** Biol. A group of related plants or animals ranking between a genus and an order. **6.** A language group descended from the same parent language. —modifier: a family reunion. [Middle English familie, from Latin familia, family, household, servants of a household, from famulus, servant.]

family name. A person's last name; surname.

family tree. 1. A genealogical record or diagram. **2.** The history of the descent of a family or individual from an ancestor.

fam·ine (făm'ĭn) n. **1.** A severe shortage of food. **2.** A great scarcity. [Middle English famine, from Old French, from Latin fames, hunger.]

fam·ish (făm'ĭsh) Archaic. —tr.v. To cause to suffer severe hunger. —intr.v. To suffer severe hunger. [Middle English famishen, prob. var. of famen, from Old French afamer : Latin ad-, toward + fames, hunger.]

fa·mous (fā'məs) adj. Well-known; renowned: a famous musician. [Middle English, from Old French famous, from Latin fāmōsus, from fāma, fame.] —fa'mous·ness n.

Syns: famous, eminent, famed, renowned adj. Core meaning: Widely and favorably known (a famous pianist).

fa·mous·ly (fā'məs-lē) adv. Very well; excellently: The two got along famously.

fan¹ (făn) n. **1. a.** A usu. wedge-shaped device for creating a cool breeze, made of a light material such as silk or paper. **b.** An electrical device that circulates air by means of rapidly rotating thin, rigid blades, attached to a central hub. **2.** Anything shaped like or resembling a fan. **3.** A machine for winnowing. —v. **fanned, fan·ning.** —tr.v. **1.** To blow upon with or as with a fan: He sat fanning himself under a tree. **2.** To stir up as if by fanning: fan resentment. **3.** To open out something to a fan shape. **4.** To winnow. **5.** Baseball. To cause to strike out. —intr.v. **1.** To spread like a fan: The searchers fanned out in several directions. **2.** Baseball. To strike out. [Middle English fan(ne), from Old English fann, from Latin vannus.]

fan² (făn) n. Informal. An enthusiastic devotee or admirer. —modifier: a fan club. [Short for FANATIC.]

fa·nat·ic (fə-năt'ĭk) n. A person who has an excessive and uncritical attachment to a view or position. [From Latin fānāticus, of a temple, inspired by a god, mad, from fānum, temple.]

fa·nat·i·cal (fə-năt'ĭ-kəl) or **fa·nat·ic** (-ĭk) adj. Characterized by excessive and unreasonable devotion. —fa·nat'i·cal·ly adv. —fa·nat'i·cism n.

fan·ci·er (făn'sē-ər) n. A person who has a special enthusiasm for or interest in something: a horse fancier.

fan·ci·ful (făn'sĭ-fəl) adj. **1.** Full of fancy; imaginary. **2.** Tending to indulge in fancy: a fanciful mind. **3.** Quaint or original in design; imaginative. —fan'ci·ful·ly adv. —fan'ci·ful·ness n.

fan·cy (făn'sē) n., pl. **-cies. 1.** Imagination, esp. of a playful or whimsical sort. **2.** An unfounded opinion. **3.** A notion; whim: a sudden fancy to buy a parrot. **4.** A fondness or inclination: take a fancy to someone. —See Syns at **imagination.** —adj. **-ci·er, -ci·est. 1.** Not plain; elaborate in design. **2.** Marked by great technical skill: fancy footwork. **3.** Based on imagination. **4. a.** Of superior grade; fine: fancy groceries. **b.** Bred for special traits. —See Syns at **elaborate.** —tr.v. **-cied, -cy·ing. 1.** To imagine: He fancies himself an actor. **2.** To be fond of; like. **3.** To have an unfounded belief. [Middle English fantsy, from fantasie, fancy, fantasy.] —fan'ci·ly adv. —fan'ci·ness n.

fancy dress. A masquerade costume. —modifier (fancy-dress): a fancy-dress ball.

fan·cy-free (făn'sē-frē') adj. Not in love; unattached.

fan·cy·work (făn'sē-wûrk') n. Decorative needlework, such as embroidery.

fan·dan·go (făn-dăng'gō) n., pl. **-gos. 1.** A lively dance of Spanish origin. **2.** Music for such a dance. [Spanish.]

fan·fare (făn'fâr') n. **1.** A flourish of trumpets. **2.** A spectacular display. [French (imit.).]

fang (făng) n. A long, pointed tooth, such as that with which a poisonous snake injects its venom or a meat-eating animal seizes and tears its prey. [Middle English fang, prey, spoils, from Old English fang, plunder.] —fanged adj.

fan·jet (făn'jĕt') n. An aircraft powered by turbofan engines.

fan·light (făn'līt') n. A half-circle window, often with radiating sash bars like the ribs of an open fan.

fanlight   fantail

fan mail. Letters to a public figure from admirers.

fan·tail (făn'tāl') n. **1.** A domesticated pigeon with a rounded, fan-shaped tail. **2.** A goldfish with a fanlike double tail fin. **3.** Something that resembles a fan in shape. —fan'tailed' adj.

fan-tan (făn'tăn') n. **1.** A Chinese game in which the players bet on the number of counters that will remain when a hidden pile of them has been divided by four. **2.** A card game in which the cards are played in a certain sequence. [Cantonese fan t'an, "repeated division."]

ă pat   ā pay   â care   ä father   ĕ pet   ē be   hw which   ĭ pit   ī tie   î pier   ŏ pot   ō toe   ô paw, for   oi noise
ōō took   ōō boot   ou out   th thin   th this   ŭ cut   û urge   zh vision   ə about, item, edible, gallop, circus

fan·ta·sia (făn-tā′zhə, -zhē-ə, făn′tə-zē′ə) *n. Mus.* A free-form composition structured according to the composer's fancy. [Italian, fantasy, from Latin *phantasia.*]

fan·ta·size (făn′tə-sīz′) *intr.v.* **-sized, -siz·ing.** To indulge in fantasies; daydream.

fan·tas·tic (făn-tăs′tĭk) or **fan·tas·ti·cal** (-tĭ-kəl) *adj.* **1.** Of, relating to, or based on fantasy; unreal. **2. a.** Arising from or as if from unrestrained fancy. **b.** Strange; bizarre: *fantastic designs.* **3.** Extraordinary; unbelievable: *fantastic prices.* **4.** Remarkable; superb: *He did a fantastic job.* [Middle English *fantastik,* from Old French *fantastique,* from Medieval Latin *fantasticus,* from Late Latin *phantasticus,* imaginary, ult. from Greek *phantazein,* to make visible.] **—fan·tas′ti·cal·ly** *adv.*

    Syns: fantastic, bizarre, grotesque *adj. Core meaning:* Having no reference to reality or common sense (*a fantastic tale*). See also Syns at **fabulous.**

fan·ta·sy (făn′tə-sē, -zē) *n., pl.* **-sies.** Also **phan·ta·sy. 1.** The creative imagination; unrestrained fancy. **2. a.** A work, such as a story or play that is based on fantastic or unreal elements: *a romantic fantasy.* **b.** *Mus.* A fantasia. **3.** *Psychol.* A mental image or daydream that fulfills a wish. —See Syns at **imagination.** [Middle English *fantasie,* fancy, fantasy, from Old French, from Latin *phantasia,* from Greek, appearance, perception, faculty of imagination, from *phantazein,* to make visible, from *phainein,* to show.]

far (fär) *adv.* **far·ther** (fär′thər) or **fur·ther** (fûr′thər), **farth·est** (fär′thĭst) or **fur·thest** (fûr′thĭst). **1.** To or at a considerable distance: *walked too far; a party that went on far into the night.* **2. a.** To a considerable degree: *a far better writer.* **b.** By a great interval: *He's far from happy.* —*adj.* **far·ther** or **fur·ther, farth·est** or **fur·thest. 1.** At considerable distance: *a far country.* **2.** More distant or remote: *the far corner.* **3.** Extensive or long: *a far trek.* —*idioms.* **as far as.** To the distance, extent, or degree that: *as far as I know.* **by far.** To a considerable degree: *His grades are better than hers by far.* **far and away.** By a great margin: *He's far and away the best skier on the team.* **far and wide.** Everywhere. **go far.** To be successful: *That boy will go far.* **in so far** (or **insofar**) **as.** To the degree or extent that; as long as. **so far. 1.** Up to now: *We haven't heard from him so far.* **2.** To a certain limit: *You can only go so far on 25 cents.* **so far as.** To the extent that: *so far as I can tell.* **so far so good.** Free from difficulty up to the present. [Middle English *fer,* from Old English *feor(r),* far, distant, remote.]

    Syns: far, distant, faraway, far-off, remote, removed *adj. Core meaning:* Widely separated from others in space, time, or relationship (*the far north; a far country; the far past*).

far·ad (făr′əd, -ăd′) *n.* A unit of capacitance equal to that of a capacitor that will accumulate a charge of 1 coulomb when a potential difference of 1 volt is applied to it. [After Michael *Faraday* (1791–1867), British chemist and physicist.]

far·a·way (făr′ə-wā′) *adj.* **1.** Very distant; remote: *faraway lands.* **2.** Dreamy or abstracted: *a faraway smile.* —See Syns at **far.**

farce (färs) *n.* **1.** A comic play with a story and characters greatly exaggerated to cause laughter. **2.** Humor typical of a farce. **3.** Something that is ridiculous or laughable, esp. a mockery. [Middle English *farse,* stuffing, farce, from Old French *farce,* stuffing, farce, from *farcir,* to stuff, from Latin *farcīre.*]

far·ceur (fär-sûr′) *n.* Also **farc·er** (fär′sər). A person who acts in or writes a farce. [French, from Old French, author or actor of farce, from *farce,* farce.]

far·ci·cal (fär′sĭ-kəl) *adj.* Of, pertaining to, or resembling farce. —**far′ci·cal′i·ty** (-kăl′ĭ-tē) or **far′ci·cal·ness** *n.* —**far′ci·cal·ly** *adv.*

fare (fâr) *intr.v.* **fared, far·ing. 1.** To get along; progress: *How did he fare?* **2.** To travel; go. —*n.* **1. a.** The money a passenger pays for traveling on a vehicle. **b.** A passenger who pays a fare. **2.** Food and drink. [From Middle English *faren,* to travel, go, fare, from Old English *faran.*] —**far′er** *n.*

fare·well (fâr-wĕl′) *interj.* Good-by. —*n.* **1.** An acknowledgment at parting; good-by. **2.** The act of departing.

—*modifier: a farewell party.* [Middle English *fare well : fare,* go, fare, imper. of *faren,* to fare + *well,* well.]

far-fetched (fär′fĕcht′) *adj.* Hard to believe; implausible.

far-flung (fär′flŭng′) *adj.* Extending over a vast area; wide-ranging: *a far-flung empire.*

fa·ri·na (fə-rē′nə) *n.* A finely ground meal made from cereal grains, nuts, or potatoes and used as a cooked cereal or in puddings. [Latin *farīna,* ground corn, meal, from *far,* a kind of grain.]

far·i·na·ceous (făr′ə-nā′shəs) *adj.* **1.** Made from or containing starch. **2.** Having a mealy or powdery texture. [Late Latin *farīnāceus,* mealy, from Latin *farīna.*]

farm (färm) *n.* **1.** An area of land on which crops or animals are raised. **2.** An area or tract of water used for raising aquatic animals: *an oyster farm.* **3.** *Baseball.* Also **farm team.** A minor-league team affiliated with a major-league team for the purpose of training recruits. —*modifier: farm products.* —*tr.v.* To cultivate crops or livestock on. —*intr.v.* To engage in farming. —*phrasal verb.* **farm out. 1.** To send or give out (work) for performance elsewhere. **2.** *Baseball.* To assign (a player) to a farm team. [Middle English *ferme,* lease, rent, from Old French, from Medieval Latin *firma,* fixed payment, from Latin *firmāre,* to fortify, fix, confirm, from *firmus,* firm.] —**farm′er** *n.*

farm·house (färm′hous′) *n.* The house on a farm.

farm·stead (färm′stĕd′) *n.* A farm and its buildings.

farm·yard (färm′yärd′) *n.* An area surrounded by or adjacent to farm buildings.

far·o (făr′ō) *n.* A card game in which the players bet on cards drawn from a dealing box. [Var. of PHARAOH.]

far-off (fär′ôf′, -ŏf′) *adj.* Remote in space or time; distant. —See Syns at **far.**

far-out (fär′out′) *adj. Slang.* Exhibiting new and extremely unconventional ideas.

far-reach·ing (fär′rē′chĭng) *adj.* Having a wide range, influence, or effect: *far-reaching implications.*

far·ri·er (făr′ē-ər) *n.* A person who shoes horses. [Old French *ferrier,* blacksmith, from Latin *ferrārius,* from *ferrum,* iron.]

far·row (făr′ō) *n.* A litter of pigs. —*tr.v.* To give birth to (a farrow). [Middle English *farwen,* ult. from Old English *fearh,* little pig.]

far·see·ing (fär′sē′ĭng) *adj.* **1.** Able to see far; keen-sighted. **2.** Prudent; foresighted.

far·sight·ed (fär′sī′tĭd) *adj.* **1.** Having a defect of vision in which it is easier to see distant objects than those that are nearby. **2.** Planning wisely for the future; foresighted; prudent. —**far·sight′ed·ly** *adv.* —**far·sight′ed·ness** *n.*

far·ther (fär′thər) *adv.* A comparative of **far. 1.** To or at a greater distance: *He went farther than he had expected.* **2.** In addition. **3.** To a greater extent. —*adj.* A comparative of **far. 1.** Remoter; more distant: *a house at the farther end of the street.* **2.** Longer or lengthier: *The trip there is farther than anyone expected.* **3.** Additional. [Middle English *ferther,* var. of *further,* further.]

    Usage: farther, farthest; further, furthest. 1. The adjectives *farther* and *further* meaning additional both occur in standard English although *further* occurs more often: *took a further* (or *farther*) *look; knew nothing further* (or *farther*) *about it.* **2.** When the reference is to physical, measurable distance or space, *farther* is the more common choice though *further* is possible, too: *We went to the farther* (or *further*) *side of the lake. The ride is farther* (or *further*) *than I thought. This is the farthest* (or *furthest*) *point from the center of the city.* **3.** The adverbs *farther* and *further* are interchangeable when meaning to or at a greater physical or temporal distance; however, *farther* occurs a bit more often: *geese flying farther* (or *further*) *north; moving farther* (or *further*) *away; walked farther* (or *further*) *down the hall; a story that goes farther* (or *further*) *back in time to our ancestors.* **4.** The adverbs *farther* and *further* can also mean in addition or moreover. In this case, *further* is by far the more common term: *The soil is further enriched with nitrogen. She disliked the idea in general and felt, further, that the proposal was ill-timed.* **5.** The adverb *further* is also the most common choice when the meaning is to a greater degree or extent, although *farther* is also possible: *went further* (also *farther*) *into debt.*

ă pat	ā pay	â care	ä father	ĕ pet	ē be	hw which	I pit	ī tie	î pier	ŏ pot	ō toe	ô paw, for	oi noise
ŏŏ took	ōō boot	ou out	th thin	th this	ŭ cut		û urge	zh vision	ə about, item, edible, gallop, circus				

far·ther·most (fär′thər-mōst′) adj. Most remote.

far·thest (fär′thĭst) adj. A superlative of **far**. Most remote or distant. —adv. A superlative of **far**. To or at the most distant or remote point in space or time. [Middle English *ferthest*, from *ferther*, farther.]

far·thing (fär′thĭng) n. A former British coin worth one-fourth of a penny. [Middle English *ferthing*, from Old English *fēorthing*.]

far·thin·gale (fär′thĭng-gāl′) n. A support, such as a hoop, that makes a skirt stand out, worn by women in the 16th and 17th cent. [Var. of Old French *verdugale*, from Spanish *verdugado*, from *verdugo*, rod, stick, shoot of a tree, from *verde*, green, from Latin *virdis*, from *virēre*, to be green.]

fas·ces (făs′ēz′) pl.n. A bundle of rods bound together about an ax, carried before ancient Roman magistrates as a symbol of authority. [Latin, pl. of *fascis*, bundle.]

fas·ci·a (făsh′ē-ə) n., pl. **-ci·ae** (-ē-ē′). Anat. A sheet of fibrous tissue beneath the surface of the skin, enveloping the body, enclosing muscles or muscular groups, and separating muscular layers. [From Latin, band, bandage.]

fas·ci·cle (făs′ĭ-kəl) n. 1. A small bundle. 2. Also **fas·ci·cule** (-kyōōl′). One of the separately published parts or installments of a book. 3. Bot. A bundlelike cluster, as of stems, flowers, or leaves. [Latin *fasciculus*, dim. of *fascis*, a bundle.] —**fas′ci·cled** adj. —**fas·cic′u·lar** adj. —**fas·cic′u·late** adj.

fas·ci·nate (făs′ə-nāt′) tr.v. **-nat·ed, -nat·ing.** 1. To capture and hold the interest and attention of; attract irresistibly. 2. To hold motionless; spellbind or mesmerize. [Latin *fascināre*, to enchant, bewitch, from *fascinus*, a bewitching, an amulet.] —**fas′ci·na′tor** n. —**fas′ci·na′tion** n.

fas·cine (fă-sēn′, fə-) n. A bundle of sticks bound together for use, as in building fortresses or reinforcing trenches. [French, from Latin *fascīna*, from *fascis*, bundle.]

fas·cism (făsh′ĭz′əm) n. 1. A political philosophy of the extreme right, marked by strict government control of the economy, nationalism, and suppression of all opposition. 2. A regime that follows or is based on fascism. [Italian *fascismo*, from *fascio*, bundle, group, from Latin *fascis*, bundle.] —**fas′cist** n. —**fas·cis′tic** adj.

fash·ion (făsh′ən) n. 1. A manner of performing; way: *Continue in this fashion until you have finished the job.* 2. a. The prevailing style or custom of a certain time: *the latest fashion; the fashions of the 1940's.* b. The current style: *out of fashion.* —**modifier:** *a fashion show.* —tr.v. To shape or form into; mold: *fashion figures from clay.* — See Syns at **make**. —**idiom. after** (or **in**) **a fashion**. To a limited extent: *She sings after a fashion.* [Middle English *facioun*, from Old French *facon*, from Latin *factiō*, a making, from *factus*, past part. of *facere*, to do.]
  Syns: fashion, craze, mode, rage, style, thing, vogue n. Core meaning: The current custom (*jeans—the fashion of the day*). See also Syns at **method**.

fash·ion·a·ble (făsh′ə-nə-bəl) adj. 1. Conforming to the current style; in fashion: *"It became fashionable to repair your mistakes by turning your back on them and running"* (William Faulkner). 2. Popular with persons who conform to the current fashions: *a fashionable hotel.* —**fash′ion·a·ble·ness** n. —**fash′ion·a·bly** adv.

fast[1] (făst) adj. **fast·er, fast·est.** 1. Moving quickly; swift; rapid. 2. Done quickly: *a fast visit.* 3. Suitable for rapid movement: *the fast lane on a highway.* 4. Ahead of time: *My watch is fast.* 5. Firmly fixed or fastened: *a fast grip.* 6. Permanently dyed: *fast colors.* 7. Loyal; firm: *fast friends.* 8. Deep; sound: *a fast sleep.* 9. Designed for short photographic exposure time: *fast film.* 10. a. Marked by dissipation; wild: *a fast crowd.* b. Unconventional esp. in sexual matters. —adv. 1. Firmly; securely; tightly: *Hold fast to the railing.* 2. Deeply; soundly: *fast asleep.* 3. Quickly; rapidly: *You are driving too fast.* 4. In a dissipated, immoderate way; recklessly. [Middle English *fast*, from Old English *fæst*.]
  Syns: fast, breakneck, fleet[2], quick, rapid, speedy, swift adj. Core meaning: Characterized by great speed (*a fast freight train; a fast pace*). See also Syns at **faithful**.

fast[2] (făst) intr.v. 1. To go without food. 2. To eat very little or avoid certain foods. —n. The act or a period of fasting. —**modifier:** *a fast day.* [Middle English *fasten*, from Old

English *fæstan*, to hold fast, to observe, to abstain from food.]

fas·ten (făs′ən) tr.v. 1. To attach firmly to; join; connect: *fasten the button to the skirt.* 2. To make fast or close securely: *Fasten your seat belts.* 3. To fix or direct steadily: *fastened her attention on the page.* —intr.v. 1. To become attached, fixed, or joined: *The dress fastens in the back.* 2. To take firm hold; cling fast. 3. To fix or focus steadily. —See Syns at **attach**. [Middle English *fastnen*, from Old English *fæstnian*, to make fast.] —**fas′ten·er** n.

fas·ten·ing (făs′ə-nĭng) n. Something that fastens.

fast-food (făst′fōōd′) adj. Specializing in foods prepared and served quickly.

fas·tid·i·ous (fă-stĭd′ē-əs, fə-) adj. 1. Careful in all details; meticulous. 2. Very difficult to please. [Middle English, disdainful, distasteful, from Latin *fastīdiōsus*, from *fastīdium*, a loathing, from *fastus*, disdain.] —**fas·tid′i·ous·ly** adv. —**fas·tid′i·ous·ness** n.

fast·ness (făst′nĭs) n. 1. A fortified or secure place. 2. The condition or quality of being fast and firm.

fat (făt) n. 1. Any of various soft solid or semisolid organic compounds comprising the glyceride esters of fatty acids and associated phosphatides, sterols, alcohols, hydrocarbons, ketones, and related compounds. 2. Tissue, esp. of an animal, that contains a high proportion of such compounds. 3. A solidified animal or vegetable oil. 4. The best part of something: *live off the fat of the land.* —adj. **fat·ter, fat·test.** 1. Having an excess of body fat; too plump; obese: *He decided to go on a diet because he was getting too fat.* 2. Full of fat; greasy. 3. Marked by abundance or amplitude. 4. Yielding a rich profit; lucrative. —v. **fat·ted, fat·ting.** —tr.v. To make fat; fatten. —intr.v. To become fat. —**idiom. chew the fat.** Slang. To have a leisurely conversation; chat. [Middle English, from *fat*, plump, from Old English *fætt*.] —**fat′ly** adv. —**fat′ness** n.
  Syns: fat, corpulent, fleshy, gross, obese, overweight, portly, stout, weighty adj. Core meaning: Having too much flesh (*a fat person who overate*).

fa·tal (fāt′l) adj. 1. Causing or capable of causing death; mortal: *a fatal blow.* 2. Causing ruin or destruction: *"Such doctrines, if true, would be absolutely fatal to my theory"* (Charles Darwin). 3. Controlling one's fate or destiny. [Middle English, fated, fatal, from Old French, from Latin *fātālis*, from *fātum*, fate.] —**fa·tal′ly** adv.
  Syns: fatal, deadly, lethal, mortal adj. Core meaning: Causing or likely to cause death (*cyanide—a fatal poison*).
  Usage: fatal, fateful. Although there is considerable overlapping of meaning between these adjectives, usage has given them rather well-differentiated roles. In the following examples, the word given first is the more common one in that sense, though by definition the other could be substituted: *a fatal* (or *fateful*) *wound* (causing death); *a fatal* (or *fateful*) *mistake* (causing ruin); *a fateful* (or *fatal*) *decision* (controlling destiny). *Fateful* is the choice when the sense is related clearly to the operation of fate: *no escaping a fateful conclusion* (seemingly controlled by fate; predetermined); *a fateful sign* (indicative of impending disaster or trouble).

fa·tal·ism (fāt′l-ĭz′əm) n. 1. The belief that all events are determined in advance by fate and cannot be altered by man. 2. The attitude of a person who accepts fatalism. —**fa′tal·ist** n. —**fa′tal·is′tic** adj. —**fa′tal·is′ti·cal·ly** adv.

fa·tal·i·ty (fā-tăl′ĭ-tē, fə-) n., pl. **-ties.** 1. A death that results esp. from an accident. 2. The ability to cause death: *diseases with a high degree of fatality.* 3. The condition or quality of being governed or determined by fate. 4. A fatal determination; doom. —**modifier:** *fatality rate.*

fat·back (făt′băk′) n. Salt-cured fat from the upper part of a side of pork.

fate (fāt) n. 1. The power or force that is supposed to determine the course of events. 2. An inevitable event predestined as if by fate. 3. Something that happens to or befalls a person or thing: *The fate of the plane's passengers is as yet unknown.* 4. Doom or ruin. [Middle English, from Old French, from Latin *fātum*, from *fātus*, past part. of *fārī*, to speak.]

fat·ed (fā′tĭd) adj. 1. Governed by or as if by fate. 2. Doomed to disaster or destruction.

fate·ful (fāt′fəl) adj. 1. Decisively important; momentous:

the President's fateful decision to go to war. **2.** Involving or controlled by fate: *a fateful meeting foreordained to failure.* **3.** Indicating approaching trouble or disaster; prophetic: *the first fateful signs that he was seriously ill.* **4.** Deadly; fatal: *at the fateful hour of the massacre.* —See Usage note at **fatal.** —**fate'ful·ly** *adv.* —**fate'ful·ness** *n.*

Fates (fāts) *pl.n. Gk. & Rom. Myth.* Any of the three goddesses who govern human destiny.

fat·head (făt'hĕd') *n. Slang.* A stupid person. —**fat'head'ed** *adj.*

fa·ther (fä'thər) *n.* **1. a.** A male parent. **b.** Any male ancestor; forefather. **2.** A man who leads or cares for, as a father does: *the city fathers.* **3.** A man who is a founder or originator. **4. Father. a.** God. **b.** The first member of the Trinity. **5. Father.** A title of respect used for a priest. **6.** Often **Father.** Any of the leaders of the early Christian Church, whose writings on religious observances and doctrines are regarded as authoritative. —*tr.v.* **1.** To be the male parent of; beget. **2.** To act or serve as a father to. **3.** To create, found, or originate. [Middle English *fader,* from Old English *fæder.*]

fa·ther·hood (fä'thər-hōod') *n.* The condition of being a father; paternity.

fa·ther-in-law (fä'thər-ĭn-lô') *n., pl.* **fa·thers-in-law.** The father of one's husband or wife.

fa·ther·land (fä'thər-lănd') *n.* **1.** A person's native land. **2.** The native land of one's ancestors.

fa·ther·less (fä'thər-lĭs) *adj.* Having no father.

fa·ther·ly (fä'thər-lē) *adj.* **1.** Of a father. **2.** Suited to a father: *a fatherly concern.* —*adv.* In a fatherly manner. —**fa'ther·li·ness** *n.*

Father's Day. The third Sunday in June, set aside to honor fathers.

fath·om (făth'əm) *n., pl.* **fath·oms** or **fathom.** A unit of length equal to about 1.83 meters or 6 feet, used mainly in measuring the depth of water. —*tr.v.* **1.** To measure the depth of; to sound. **2.** To understand; comprehend: *"Her simplicity fathomed what clever people falsified"* (Virginia Woolf). —See Syns at **understand.** [Middle English *fadme,* from Old English *fæthm,* a measure of length.] —**fath'om·a·ble** *adj.*

fath·om·less (făth'əm-lĭs) *adj.* **1.** Too deep to be measured. **2.** Too complicated to be understood.

fa·tigue (fə-tēg') *n.* **1.** Weariness resulting from hard work or strain. **2.** *Physiol.* The lessening or failure of the capacity of an organism, organ, or part to function normally because of excessive stimulation or prolonged exertion. **3.** Weakness in a material, such as metal or wood, resulting from prolonged stress. **4.** Also **fatigue duty.** Manual labor, such as barracks, cleaning assigned to soldiers. **5. fatigues.** Clothing worn by soldiers for heavy work or field duty. —*v.* **-tigued, -tigu·ing.** —*tr.v.* **1.** To tire out; exhaust: *fatiguing work.* **2.** To weaken by prolonged stress. —*intr.v.* To be or become exhausted or tired out. [French, from Old French, from *fatiguer,* to fatigue, from Latin *fatīgāre.*] —**fat'i·ga·ble** (făt'ĭ-gə-bəl, fə-tē'gə-bəl) *adj.* —**fa·tigued'** *adj.*

fat·ling (făt'lĭng) *n.* A young animal fattened for slaughter.

fat·ten (făt'n) *tr.v.* **1.** To make fat or fatter. **2.** To increase the size of. —*intr.v.* To grow fat or fatter. —**fat'ten·er** *n.*

fat·ty (făt'ē) *adj.* **-ti·er, -ti·est.** **1.** Of or containing fat. **2.** Greasy. —**fat'ti·ness** *n.*

fatty acid. Any of a large group of monobasic acids having the general formula $C_nH_{2n+1}COOH$, esp. any of a commercially important subgroup obtained from animals and plants, the most abundant of which contain 16 or 18 carbon atoms and include palmitic, stearic, and oleic acids.

fa·tu·i·ty (fə-tōo'ĭ-tē, -tyōo'-) *n., pl.* **-ties.** **1.** Stupidity; self-satisfied foolishness. **2.** A fatuous act, remark, sentiment, etc. [Old French *fatuite,* from Latin *fatuitās,* from *fatuus,* fatuous.]

fat·u·ous (făch'ōo-əs) *adj.* Smugly foolish or silly; inane. [Latin *fatuus,* silly, absurd.] —**fat'u·ous·ly** *adv.* —**fat'u·ous·ness** *n.*

fau·ces (fô'sēz') *pl.n.* The space between the mouth and pharynx bounded by the soft palate, the base of the tongue, and the palatine arches. [Latin *faucēs,* throat.]

fau·cet (fô'sĭt) *n.* A device with an adjustable valve for drawing liquid from a vessel. [Middle English *faucet,* from

Old French *fausset,* plug, from *fausser,* to damage, make false, from Late Latin *falsāre,* to falsify, from Latin *falsus,* false.]

fault (fôlt) *n.* **1.** Responsibility for a mistake or offense: *That is no fault of yours. The mix-up was all my fault.* **2. a.** A defect or shortcoming. **b.** Weakness; failing. **3.** A mistake or error: *faults of grammar.* **4.** *Geol.* A break in a rock formation caused by a disturbance of the earth's crust that cracks the rock and shifts adjoining sections in a direction parallel to the crack. **5.** *Sports.* A bad serve, as in tennis. —*modifier: a fault line.* —*tr.v.* **1.** To find a fault in; criticize or blame: *I cannot fault his performance.* **2.** *Geol.* To produce a fault in. —*intr.v.* **1.** To commit a fault or error. **2.** *Geol.* To shift so as to produce a fault. —*idioms.* **at fault.** Deserving of blame; guilty: *I am at fault, not you.* **find fault with.** To seek and find faults in; criticize. **to a fault.** Excessively: *He is polite to a fault.* [Middle English *faute,* from Old French, from Latin *fallere,* to fail, deceive.]

fault·find·er (fôlt'fīn'dər) *n.* A person who continually seeks to find fault with others; a chronic complainer. —**fault'find'ing** *n.*

fault·less (fôlt'lĭs) *adj.* Without fault or flaw. —See Syns at **perfect.** —**fault'less·ly** *adv.* —**fault'less·ness** *n.*

fault·y (fôl'tē) *adj.* **-i·er, -i·est.** Having a fault or faults; imperfect or defective. —See Syns at **imperfect.** —**fault'i·ly** *adv.* —**fault'i·ness** *n.*

faun (fôn) *n. Rom. Myth.* One of a group of woodland deities represented as having the body of a man and the horns, ears, tail, and sometimes legs of a goat. [Middle English *faun,* from Latin *Faunus,* a Roman god of nature and fertility.]

fau·na (fô'nə) *n., pl.* **-nas** or **-nae** (-nē'). The animals of a particular region or time period. [From Latin *Fauna,* sister of Faunus. See **faun.**] —**fau'nal** *adj.*

trologer.]

fau·vism (fō'vĭz'əm) *n.* An art movement of the early 20th cent., characterized by the use of exuberant colors and the distortion of forms. [French *fauvisme,* from *fauve,* wild beast.]

faux pas (fō' pä') *pl.* **faux pas** (fō' päz', pä'). A social blunder. [French, "false step."]

fa·vor (fā'vər) Also *Brit.* **fa·vour.** —*n.* **1.** A kind or helpful act: *asked a special favor of a friend.* **2.** Approval or support: *The idea of a national health plan is gaining favor with many congressmen.* **3.** A small gift given at a party as a souvenir. **4. a.** Friendly regard shown esp.by a superior. **b.** Partiality. **5.** Advantage; benefit: *a balance in our favor.* —*tr.v.* **1.** To perform a kindness for; oblige: *favored us with a song.* **2.** To regard with approval; like. **3.** To give support to; advocate: *I favor her appointment as director.* **4.** To show partiality toward: *He always seemed to favor his youngest daughter.* **5.** To be beneficial to the success of: *The climate there favors the growing of fruit trees.* **6.** To resemble in appearance: *favors her father.* **7.** To treat with care; be gentle with: *favor a weak ankle.* —*idiom.* **in (one's) favor.** To one's advantage. [Middle English *favour,* from Old French, from Latin *favor,* from *favēre,* to favor, be favorable.] —**fa'vor·er** *n.* —**fa'vor·ing·ly** *adv.*

Syns: favor, admiration, esteem, estimation, honor, regard, respect *n. Core meaning:* A feeling of deference, approval, and liking (*a professor who won the favor of the scientific community*).

fa·vor·a·ble (fā'vər-ə-bəl, fāv'rə-) *adj.* **1.** Helpful; advantageous: *favorable winds; a favorable climate.* **2.** Encouraging; promising: *favorable signs of recovery.* **3.** Expressing approval or satisfaction: *The reviews of the movie were very favorable.* **4.** Pleasing; positive: *The new teacher has made a favorable impression so far.* **5.** Affirmative; as wished for: *hoping to receive a favorable reply.* —**fa'vor·a·ble·ness** *n.* —**fa'vor·a·bly** *adv.*

Syns: favorable, auspicious, bright, propitious *adj. Core meaning:* Indicating future success (*favorable prospects for a labor settlement*).

fa·vored (fā'vərd) *adj.* Having a physical appearance of a particular kind: *well-favored; ill-favored.*

fa·vor·ite (fā'vər-ĭt, fāv'rĭt) *n.* **1.** Someone or something liked or favored above all others: *That song is a favorite of* mine. **2.** The contestant considered most likely to win. —*adj.* Liked best or preferred above all others. [Obs. French *favorit*, from Italian *favorito*, past part. of *favorire*, to favor, from *favore*, favor, from Latin *favor*, favor.]

favorite son. A candidate supported by the delegates from his state at a national political convention.

fa·vor·it·ism (fā′vər-ĭ-tĭz′əm, fāv′rə-) *n.* Unfair preference or partiality for one person or group over another.

fawn¹ (fôn) *n.* **1.** A young deer, esp. one less than a year old. **2.** A light yellowish brown. —*adj.* Light yellowish brown. [Middle English, from Old French *foun, feon*, offspring of an animal, from Latin *fētus*, offspring, a giving birth.]

fawn¹   **F clef**

fawn² (fôn) *intr.v.* **1.** To show friendliness or affection, as a dog does by wagging its tail. **2.** To seek favor by flattery: *The ministers fawned on the young prince.* [Middle English *faunen*, from Old English *fægnian*, to rejoice, from *fægen*, fain.] —**fawn′er** *n.* —**fawn′ing·ly** *adv.*

fay (fā) *n.* **1.** A fairy. **2.** An elf. [Middle English *faie*, one possessing magical powers, from Old French *faie, fae*, from Latin *fāta*, the Fates, pl. of *fātum*, fate.]

faze (fāz) *tr.v.* **fazed, faz·ing.** To upset the composure of; disconcert: *Nothing fazes her.* [Var. of *feeze*, from Middle English *fesen*, to put to flight, from Old English *fēsian*.]

F clef. The bass clef.

Fe The symbol for the element iron. [Latin *ferrum*.]

fe·al·ty (fē′əl-tē) *n., pl.* **-ties. 1.** The loyalty owed by a feudal vassal to his lord. **2.** Loyalty; allegiance. [Middle English *fealtye*, from Old French *fealte*, from Latin *fidēlitās*, faithfulness, from *fidēlis*, faithful, from *fidēs*, faith.]

fear (fîr) *n.* **1.** A feeling of agitation or anxiety caused by the expectation or realization of danger: *fear of the unknown.* **2.** A state or condition of fear: *spent the night in fear.* **3.** Reverence or awe: *fear of God.* **4.** A cause of fear. —*tr.v.* **1.** To be afraid or frightened of. **2.** To be anxious or apprehensive about. **3.** To be in awe of; revere. —*intr.v.* **1.** To be afraid, frightened, or terrified. **2.** To feel anxious or apprehensive. [Middle English *fer*, from Old English *fǣr*, danger, sudden calamity.] —**fear′er** *n.*

fear·ful (fîr′fəl) *adj.* **1.** Filled with fear; afraid. **2.** Causing fear; terrible: *a fearful explosion.* **3.** Indicating or marked by fear: *a fearful expression.* **4.** *Informal.* Very bad; dreadful: *a fearful blunder.* —**fear′ful·ly** *adv.* —**fear′ful·ness** *n.*

fear·less (fîr′lĭs) *adj.* Having no fear; unafraid. —See Syns at **brave.** —**fear′less·ly** *adv.* —**fear′less·ness** *n.*

fear·some (fîr′səm) *adj.* **1.** Causing fear. **2.** Fearful; timid. —**fear′some·ly** *adv.* —**fear′some·ness** *n.*

fea·si·ble (fē′zə-bəl) *adj.* **1.** Capable of being accomplished or carried out. **2.** Capable of being used successfully. **3.** Plausible; likely: *a feasible excuse.* —See Syns at **possible.** [Middle English *fesable*, from Old French *faisible*, from *faire*, to do, from Latin *facere*.] —**fea′si·bil′i·ty** or **fea′si·ble·ness** *n.* —**fea′si·bly** *adv.*

feast (fēst) *n.* **1.** A large, elaborate meal; banquet: *a wedding feast.* **2.** A religious festival: *Chanukah is sometimes called the Feast of Lights.* **3.** Something that gives great pleasure or satisfaction: *That book is a feast for the mind.* —*modifier:* *a feast day.* —*tr.v.* **1.** To give a feast for. **2.** To provide with pleasure; delight. —*intr.v.* To dine lavishly at or as if at a feast. [Middle English *feste*, from Old French, from Latin *fēstus*, joyous, festal.] —**feast′er** *n.*

feat (fēt) *n.* **1.** A deed remarkable esp. for bravery. **2.** An act or the result of skill, endurance, or inventiveness: *The*

new bridge is a remarkable feat of engineering. [Middle English *fete*, from Old French *fait, fet*, from Latin *factum*, deed, from *factus*, past part. of *facere*, to do.]

feath·er (fĕth′ər) *n.* **1.** One of the light specialized structures that grow from the skin of birds and form their outer covering. **2. feathers.** Plumage. **3. feathers.** Clothing; attire. **4.** A feathery tuft or fringe of hair. **5.** Character, kind, or nature: *Birds of a feather flock together.* **6.** The vane of an arrow. —See Syns at **kind.** —*modifier:* *a feather pillow.* —*tr.v.* **1.** To supply, cover, or dress with or as if with feathers: *feather an arrow.* **2.** To turn (an oar) so that its blade is parallel to the surface of the water between strokes. **3.** To turn the blades of (an aircraft propeller) so that they are parallel to the direction of flight. —*intr.v.* **1.** To grow feathers. **2.** To move, spread, or grow like feathers. —*idioms.* **a feather in (one's) cap.** An achievement of which one can be proud. **feather (one's) nest.** To accumulate wealth esp. by abusing a position of trust. **in fine (or good) feather.** In excellent condition or humor. [Middle English *fether*, from Old English *fether*.] —**feath′er·less** *adj.*

feather bed. A mattress stuffed with feathers or down.

feath·er·bed·ding (fĕth′ər-bĕd′ĭng) *n.* The practice, esp. by a labor union, of requiring an employer to hire more workers than are actually needed.

feath·er·brain (fĕth′ər-brān′) *n.* A flighty, empty-headed person. —**feath′er·brained′** *adj.*

feath·er·edge (fĕth′ər-ĕj′) *n.* A thin, fragile edge, as of a board.

feath·er·stitch (fĕth′ər-stĭch′) *n.* An embroidery stitch that produces a decorative zigzag line. —*tr.v.* To embroider in featherstitch. —*tr.v.* To embroider (material) in featherstitch.

feath·er·weight (fĕth′ər-wāt′) *n.* **1.** A boxer weighing between approx. 54 and 57 kilograms or 118 and 127 pounds. **2.** A person of little intelligence or importance.

feath·er·y (fĕth′ə-rē) *adj.* **1.** Covered with or made of feathers. **2.** Like a feather; light, soft, or delicate: *a feathery covering of snow.* —**feath′er·i·ness** *n.*

fea·ture (fē′chər) *n.* **1.** A prominent part or element; characteristic: *Jagged rocks were a feature of the landscape.* **2. a.** A part of the face. **b. features.** The appearance of the face or its parts. **3.** The main film of a motion-picture program. **4.** A special article, column, or section in a newspaper or magazine. **5.** A special attraction or inducement. —*tr.v.* **-tured, -tur·ing. 1.** To give special attention or prominence to: *The exhibit features paintings of colonial times.* **2.** *Informal.* To resemble. **3.** *Informal.* To imagine, picture mentally, or conceive of. [Middle English *feture*, from Old French *feture*, form, from Latin *factūra*, formation, from *factus*, past part. of *facere*, to do, make.]

feb·ri·fuge (fĕb′rə-fyōōj′) *n.* A medicine that reduces a fever. [French *fébrifuge*, from New Latin *febrifugus* : Latin *febris*, fever + *fugāre*, to drive away, from *fugere*, to flee.] —**feb′ri·fuge** *adj.*

feb·rile (fĕb′rəl) *adj.* Of, pertaining to, or characterized by fever; feverish. [French *fébrile*, from Latin *febris*, fever.]

Feb·ru·ar·y (fĕb′rōō-ĕr′ē, fĕb′yōō-) *n., pl.* **-ies** or **-ys.** The second month of the year. [Middle English *februari*, from Latin *februārius*, from *februa*, Roman festival of purification (held on February 15).]

fe·ces (fē′sēz) *pl.n.* Waste excreted from the bowels; excrement. [Middle English, from Latin *faex*, dregs.] —**fe′cal** (-kəl) *adj.*

feck·less (fĕk′lĭs) *adj.* **1.** Lacking vitality; feeble; ineffective. **2.** Careless and irresponsible. [Scottish *feck*, efficacy, short for EFFECT + -LESS.] —**feck′less·ly** *adv.* —**feck′less·ness** *n.*

fe·cund (fē′kənd, fĕk′ənd) *adj.* Productive; fertile; fruitful. —See Syns at **fertile.** [Middle English *fecound*, from Old French *fecond*, from Latin *fēcundus*.] —**fe·cun′di·ty** (fĭ-kŭn′dĭ-tē) *n.*

fe·cun·date (fē′kən-dāt′, fĕk′ən-) *tr.v.* **-dat·ed, -dat·ing.** To fertilize. [From Latin *fēcundāre*, from *fēcundus*, fecund.]

fed (fĕd) *v.* Past tense and past participle of **feed.**

fed·er·al (fĕd′ər-əl) *adj.* **1.** Of, relating to, or constituting a form of government in which separate states are united under one central authority while retaining certain regula-tory powers. **2.** Often **Federal.** Of or relating to the central government of the United States. **3. Federal.** Of or pertaining to the Federalist Party or Federalism. **4. Federal.** Of, relating to, or supporting the Union during the Civil War. —*n.* **Federal.** A supporter of the Union during the Civil War, esp. a Union soldier. [From Latin *foedus,* league, treaty, compact.] —**fed′er·al·ly** *adv.*

fed·er·al·ism (fĕd′ər-ə-lĭz′əm) *n.* **1. a.** Often **Federalism.** The federal form of government, esp. of the U.S. government. **b.** A doctrine advocating such a form of government. **2. Federalism.** The doctrine of the Federalist Party.

fed·er·al·ist (fĕd′ər-ə-lĭst) *n.* **1.** An advocate of federalism. **2. Federalist.** A supporter of the Federalist Party.

Federalist Party. Also **Federal Party.** An American political party of the 1790's that advocated a strong federal government.

fed·er·al·ize (fĕd′ər-ə-līz′) *tr.v.* **-ized, -iz·ing. 1.** To unite in a federal union. **2.** To put under the authority of a federal government. —**fed′er·al·i·za′tion** *n.*

fed·er·ate (fĕd′ə-rāt′) *v.* **-at·ed, -at·ing.** —*tr.v.* To join or bring together in a federation. —*intr.v.* To unite in a federal union. [From Latin *foederāre,* from *foedus,* league, treaty.]

fed·er·a·tion (fĕd′ə-rā′shən) *n.* **1.** The act of federating. **2.** A league or association formed by federating. —**fed′er·a′tive** (fĕd′ə-rā′tĭv, fĕd′ər-ə-tĭv) *adj.*

fe·do·ra (fĭ-dôr′ə, -dōr′ə) *n.* A soft felt hat with a flexible brim and a low crown creased lengthwise. [From *Fédora* (1882), a play by Victorien Sardou (1831–1908), French playwright.]

fed up. Completely exhausted and disgusted: *was fed up with their inefficiency.*

fee (fē) *n.* **1.** A fixed charge: *an admission fee.* **2.** A charge for professional service: *a lawyer's fee.* **3.** A feudal estate in land; fief; feud. [Middle English *fe,* inherited estate, payment, from Old French *fe, fief.*]

fee·ble (fē′bəl) *adj.* **-bler, -blest. 1. a.** Lacking strength; weak or frail. **b.** Indicating weakness or frailty: *a feeble voice.* **2.** Without sufficient force, power, or intensity; inadequate: *a feeble attempt.* [Middle English *feble,* from Old French *feble, fleible,* from Latin *flēbilis,* to be wept over, lamentable, from *flēre,* to weep.] —**fee′ble·ness** *n.* —**fee′bly** *adv.*

fee·ble-mind·ed (fē′bəl-mīn′dĭd) *adj.* Mentally deficient; subnormal in intelligence. —**fee′ble-mind′ed·ly** *adv.* —**fee′ble-mind′ed·ness** *n.*

feed (fēd) *v.* **fed** (fĕd), **feed·ing.** —*tr.v.* **1.** To give food to. **2.** To provide as food. **3.** To produce or furnish food for. **4. a.** To supply with material essential to the function, maintenance, or growth of. **b.** To supply for consumption: *He fed more wood to the fire.* **5.** To minister to; gratify: *The story fed their appetite for the morbid.* **6.** To supply as a cue: *feed lines to an actor.* —*intr.v.* **1.** To eat food. **2.** To become satisfied as if by food: *His ego feeds on flattery.* —*n.* **1. a.** Food for animals or birds; fodder. **b.** The amount of food given at one time. **2.** *Informal.* A meal. **3. a.** Material supplied, as to a machine. **b.** The apparatus that supplies material to a machine. [Middle English *feden,* Old English *fēdan.*]

feed·back (fēd′băk′) *n.* **1.** The return of a part of the output of a system or process to the input. **2. a.** The return of information to the source of a process or action for the purpose of control or correction. **b.** The information so transmitted.

feed·er (fē′dər) *n.* **1.** Someone or something that feeds. **2.** A device for holding animal feed. **3.** Something that feeds materials into a machine. **4.** A branch or tributary. **5.** *Elect.* Any of the medium-voltage lines used to distribute electric power.

feel (fēl) *v.* **felt** (fĕlt), **feel·ing.** —*tr.v.* **1.** To be aware of or perceive through the sense of touch. **2.** To examine by touching. **3.** To find or ascertain by or as if by the sense of touch: *felt his way through the darkened room.* **4.** To be aware of; perceive. **5.** To have or receive an impression of. **6. a.** To experience: *feel compassion.* **b.** To experience the effect of: *feel the loss of someone.* **7.** To have as an opinion; believe: *She felt that his answer was evasive.* —*intr.v.* **1.** To experience or be able to experience sensations of touch. **2.** To seem, esp. to the sense of touch: *The sheets*

felt smooth. **3.** To experience a certain physical or emotional condition: *feel sleepy; feel hot.* **4.** To search for something by the sense of touch: *He felt in his pocket for a quarter.* **5.** To have sympathy or compassion. —*n.* **1.** The sense of touch. **2.** A mental or physical sensation. **3.** The nature or quality of something perceived through or as if through touch: *the feel of a sports car.* —*idioms.* **feel like.** *Informal.* To be in the mood for: *She did not feel like writing in her diary.* **feel (someone) out.** To try cautiously to ascertain a person's position or opinion. [Middle English *felen,* from Old English *fēlan.*]

feel·er (fē′lər) *n.* **1.** Something, such as a cat's whisker or an insect's antenna, used for touching or feeling. **2.** A remark, question, or proposal designed to ascertain or find out.

feeler

feel·ing (fē′lĭng) *n.* **1.** The faculty through which one perceives a sensation, such as roughness or heat, by means of the sense of touch. **2.** A physical sensation: *a dizzy feeling.* **3.** Sensitive awareness or consciousness: *a feeling that danger was near.* **4. a.** The condition or an example of being emotionally affected: *a feeling of irritation.* **b. feelings.** Responsiveness to impressions; sensibilities: *The remark hurt his feelings.* **5.** A capacity to respond esp. with sympathy or appreciation: *a feeling for the downtrodden; a feeling for music.* **6.** Opinion; belief. —See Syns at **belief.** —*adj.* Easily moved emotionally; sensitive. —**feel′ing·ly** *adv.*

fee simple *pl.* **fees simple.** *Law.* An estate in land of which the inheritor has unqualified ownership and power of disposition.

feet (fēt) *n.* Plural of **foot.** —See Usage note at **foot.**

feign (fān) *tr.v.* **1.** To give a false appearance of: *feign sleep.* **2.** To make up and assert as true. —*intr.v.* To make a false show; pretend. [Middle English *feinen,* from Old French *feindre,* from Latin *fingere,* to form, shape, alter.] —**feign′er** *n.*

feint (fānt) *n.* Something that is feigned, as a pretended attack on one position, in order to divert attention away from the real target or objective. —*intr.v.* To make a feint. [French *feinte,* from Old French, from the past part. of *feindre,* to feign.]

feis·ty (fī′stē) *adj.* **-i·er, -i·est.** *Informal.* **1.** Touchy; quarrelsome. **2.** Spirited; frisky. [From dial. *feist,* a small dog.]

feld·spar (fĕld′spär′, fĕl′spär′) *n.* Also **fel·spar** (fĕl′spär′). Any one of a large group of minerals that occur widely in various rocks and are composed largely of silicates. [From obs. German *Feld(spath),* "field(spar)" + SPAR.]

fe·lic·i·tate (fĭ-lĭs′ĭ-tāt′) *tr.v.* **-tat·ed, -tat·ing.** To congratulate. —**fe·lic′i·ta′tion** *n.* —**fe·lic′i·ta′tor** *n.*

fe·lic·i·tous (fĭ-lĭs′ĭ-təs) *adj.* **1.** Well-chosen; apt; appropriate: *a felicitous use of words.* **2.** Having an agreeable manner or style of expression. —**fe·lic′i·tous·ly** *adv.* —**fe·lic′i·tous·ness** *n.*

fe·lic·i·ty (fĭ-lĭs′ĭ-tē) *n., pl.* **-ties. 1.** Great happiness; bliss. **2.** A cause of happiness. **3.** Appropriateness and aptness of expression. [Middle English *felicite,* from Old French, from Latin *fēlīcitās,* from *fēlix,* happy.]

fe·line (fē′līn′) *adj.* **1.** Of or belonging to the family Felidae, which includes the lions, tigers, jaguars, and wild and domestic cats. **2. a.** Of or similar to a cat. **b.** Sly; stealthy. —*n.* A feline animal. [Latin *fēlīnus,* from *fēlēs,* cat.] —**fe′line·ly** *adv.* —**fe′line·ness** or **fe·lin′i·ty** (fĭ-lĭn′ĭ-tē) *n.*

fell¹ (fĕl) *tr.v.* **1.** To cut or knock down. **2.** To kill. **3.** To sew (a seam) by turning under and then stitching down the raw edges. [Middle English *fellen,* from Old English *fellan,* to

felucca   femur

fencing

strike down, fell.] —**fell′a·ble** adj. —**fell′er** n.

fell² (fĕl) adj. **1.** Of a cruel nature; fierce. **2.** Able to destroy; lethal. —See Syns at **fierce.** [Middle English fel, from Old French, from Medieval Latin fellō, wicked person, felon.] —**fell′ness** n.

fell³ (fĕl) n. The hide of an animal; pelt. [Middle English fel, from Old English fell.]

fell⁴ (fĕl) v. Past tense of **fall.** [Middle English, from Old English fēol.]

fel·lah (fĕl′ə) n., pl. **-lahs** or **fel·la·hin** (fĕl′ə-hēn′) or **fel·la·heen.** A peasant or agricultural laborer in Arab countries. [Arabic fellāh, from falaha, to cultivate, till.]

fel·loe (fĕl′ō) n. Var. of **felly.**

fel·low (fĕl′ō) n. **1.** A man or boy. **2.** Informal. A boyfriend. **3.** An individual; person. **4.** A comrade; an associate. **5.** One of a pair. **6.** A member of a learned society. **7.** A person who receives a grant of money for advanced study. —**modifier:** his fellow workers. [Middle English felawe, from Old English fēolaga, from Old Norse fēlagi, partner, fellow : fē, cattle money + lag, a laying down.]

fel·low·ship (fĕl′ō-shĭp′) n. **1.** Friendly association; companionship. **2.** A union or group joined by a common interest. **3.** A grant awarded for advanced study.

fellow traveler. A person who sympathizes with the beliefs and programs of the Communist Party without actually joining it.

fel·ly (fĕl′ē) n., pl. **-lies.** Also **fel·loe** (fĕl′ō). The exterior rim or part of the rim of a wheel supported by the spokes. [Middle English fely, from Old English felg.]

fel·on¹ (fĕl′ən) n. Law. A person who has committed a felony. [Middle English feloun, from Old French felon, from Medieval Latin fellō, scoundrel, faithless person.]

fel·on² (fĕl′ən) n. A pus-filled infection near the nail or the end of a finger or toe. [Middle English feloun, from Old French, poss. from Latin fel, bile, venom.]

fel·o·ny (fĕl′ə-nē) n., pl. **-nies.** Law. A serious crime, such as murder, rape, or burglary, punishable by a more severe sentence than that for a misdemeanor. —**fe·lo′ni·ous** adj. —**fe·lo′ni·ous·ly** adv. —**fe·lo′ni·ous·ness** n.

fel·spar (fĕl′spär′) n. Var. of **feldspar.**

felt¹ (fĕlt) n. **1.** A smooth, firm cloth made by pressing and matting fibers together instead of weaving them. **2.** A material resembling felt. —**modifier:** a felt hat. —tr.v. **1.** To make into felt. **2.** To cover with felt. —intr.v. To mat together. [Middle English, from Old English.]

felt² (fĕlt) v. Past tense and past participle of **feel.**

fe·luc·ca (fə-lōō′kə, -lŭk′ə) n. A narrow, swift sailing vessel with lateen sails, used chiefly in the Mediterranean area. [Italian feluc(c)a, from obs. Spanish faluca, from Arabic fulk, ship.]

fe·male (fē′māl′) adj. **1.** Of or characteristic of the sex that produces egg cells or gives birth to offspring. **2.** Bot. **a.** Pertaining to or designating an organ, such as a pistil or ovary, that functions in producing seeds or spores after fertilization. **b.** Bearing pistils but not stamens: female flowers. **3.** Having a hollow part into which a projecting part, such as a plug or prong, fits. —n. **1.** A female animal or plant. **2.** A woman or girl as opposed to a man or boy. [Middle English, var. (influenced by male, male) of femelle, from Old French, from Latin fēmella, dim. of fēmina, woman, female.] —**fe′male′ness** n.

Syns: female, feminine, womanish, womanly adj. Core meaning: Of, relating to, or suitable to women (female at-

tire; heard female voices in the hall).

fem·i·nine (fĕm′ə-nĭn) adj. **1.** Of or belonging to the female sex. **2.** Marked by or possessing qualities associated with or appropriate to women. **3.** Gram. Of, relating to, or being the gender made up chiefly of words or grammatical forms that refer to or denote females: Lioness has a feminine suffix. —See Syns at **female.** —n. Gram. **1.** The feminine gender. **2.** A word or form of the feminine gender. [Middle English, from Old French, from Latin fēminīnus, from fēmina, female.] —**fem′i·nine·ly** adv. —**fem′i·nine·ness** n.

fem·i·nin·i·ty (fĕm′I-nĭn′ə-tē) n., pl. **-ties. 1.** The quality or condition of being feminine. **2.** Women as a group; womankind. **3.** Womanishness; effeminacy.

fem·i·nism (fĕm′ə-nĭz′əm) n. **1.** A doctrine that advocates the political, social, and economic equality of men and women. **2.** Activity undertaken in support of the doctrine of feminism. —**fem′i·nist** n. & adj. —**fem′i·nis′tic** adj.

femme fa·tale (fĕm′ fə-tăl′, fäm′ fə-tăl′) pl. **femmes fa·tales** (fĕm′ fə-tăl′, fäm′ fə-tăl′). A woman whose seductive charms may lead a man into compromising or dangerous situations.

fem·o·ral (fĕm′ər-əl) adj. Of or pertaining to the thigh or the femur. [From Latin femur, femur.]

fe·mur (fē′mər) n., pl. **-murs** or **fem·o·ra** (fĕm′ər-ə). The long uppermost bone of the hind or lower limb in vertebrates, located between the knee and pelvis in human beings; thighbone. [Latin, thigh.]

fen (fĕn) n. Low, swampy land; bog. [Middle English, from Old English fenn.]

fence (fĕns) n. **1.** A structure, as of boards, posts, or wire, that serves as an enclosure or barrier. **2. a.** A person who receives and sells stolen goods. **b.** A place, such as a shop, where stolen goods are received and sold. —v. **fenced, fenc·ing.** —tr.v. **1.** To surround or close in by means of a fence. **2.** To separate or close off by means of a fence: We fenced off part of the yard for a patio. —intr.v. **1.** To engage in fencing. **2.** To avoid giving direct answers; be evasive. **3.** To act as a fence for stolen goods. [Middle English fens, short for defens, defense.] —**fenc′er** n.

fenc·ing (fĕn′sĭng) n. **1.** The art, practice, or sport of using a foil, épée, or saber; swordplay. **2.** Material used in constructing fences. **3.** All the fences in an area.

fend (fĕnd) tr.v. To keep off; repel: He used an oar to fend off the sharks. —See Syns at **repel.** —**idiom. fend for (oneself).** To get along without help: The boys had to fend for themselves at an early age. [Middle English fenden, short for defenden, to defend.]

fend·er (fĕn′dər) n. **1.** A cover or guard mounted over the wheel of a vehicle. **2.** A device at the front end of a locomotive or streetcar, designed to push aside objects blocking the tracks. **3.** A low screen or frame placed in front of an open fireplace. **4.** A cushioning device, such as a piece of timber or an automobile tire, used on the side of a ship or dock to absorb impact or friction.

fen·es·tra·tion (fĕn′ə-strā′shən) n. The design and placement of windows in a building. [From Latin fenestra, window.]

Fe·ni·an (fē′nē-ən) n. **1. Fenians.** A legendary group of heroic Irish warriors of the 2nd and 3rd cent. **2.** A member of a secret organization of the mid-19th cent. whose goal was the overthrow of British rule in Ireland. [Prob. from Irish féinne, pl. of fiann, legendary body of warriors,

fern
Fiddlehead fern

ferret

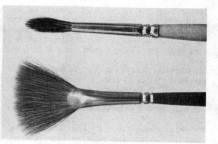

ferrule

after *Fiann,* a legendary hero.]

fen·nec (fĕn′ĭk) *n.* A small fox, *Fennecus zerda,* of desert regions of northern Africa, with fawn-colored fur and large, pointed ears. [Arabic *fanak,* fox.]

fen·nel (fĕn′əl) *n.* **1.** A plant, *Foeniculum vulgare,* native to Eurasia, with finely dissected leaves, clusters of small yellow flowers, and aromatic seeds used as flavoring. **2.** The seeds of this plant. [Middle English *fenel,* from Old English *fenol,* from Latin *fēniculum,* dim. of *fēnum,* hay.]

fen·ny (fĕn′ē) *adj.* **1.** Having the characteristics of a fen; boggy; marshy. **2.** Of, pertaining to, or found in fens.

feoff (fĕf) *n.* Var. of **fief.**

-fer. A suffix meaning agency, bearing, or production: **aquifer.** [Latin, from *ferre,* to carry, bear.]

fe·ral (fîr′əl, fĕr′-) *adj.* **1.** Having reverted to a wild or untamed state from domestication. **2.** Of, relating to, or characteristic of a wild animal; savage. —See Syns at **fierce.** [From Latin *fera,* wild animal, from *ferus,* wild.]

fer-de-lance (fĕr′də-lăns′, -läns′) *n.* A poisonous snake, *Bothrops atrox,* of tropical America and the West Indies, with brown and grayish markings. [French, "iron (head) of a lance."]

fer·ment (fûr′mĕnt′) *n.* **1.** An agent, such as a yeast or enzyme, that causes fermentation. **2.** Fermentation. **3.** A state of agitation; unrest. —*v.* (fər-mĕnt′). —*tr.v.* **1.** To cause to undergo fermentation. **2.** To agitate; excite. —*intr.v.* **1.** To undergo fermentation. **2.** To be agitated; seethe. [Middle English, leaven, yeast, from Old French, from Latin *fermentum.*] —**fer·ment′a·bil′i·ty** *n.* —**fer·ment′a·ble** *adj.* —**fer·ment′er** *n.*

fer·men·ta·tion (fûr′mĕn-tā′shən) *n.* **1.** Any one of a group of chemical reactions, caused by various microorganisms or enzymes, in which relatively complex organic compounds are broken down into simpler compounds, esp. the anaerobic process by which yeasts convert sugar to alcohol and carbon dioxide. **2.** Unrest; commotion; agitation. —**fer·men′ta·tive** (fər-mĕn′tə-tĭv) *adj.*

fer·mi·um (fûr′mē-əm) *n. Symbol* **Fm** A synthetic transuranic metallic element first discovered in the debris of a hydrogen-bomb explosion and later produced by nuclear bombardment. Atomic number 100. [After Enrico *Fermi* (1901–54), Italian-born American physicist.]

fern (fûrn) *n.* Any of a group of plants that have fronds divided into many leaflets and that reproduce by means of spores rather than by producing flowers and seeds. [Middle English, from Old English *fearn.*] —**fern′y** *adj.*

fern·er·y (fûr′nə-rē) *n., pl.* **-ies.** **1.** A place or container in which ferns are grown. **2.** A collection of ferns.

fe·ro·cious (fə-rō′shəs) *adj.* **1.** Marked by extreme cruelty and fierceness; savage. **2.** Extreme; intense: *ferocious energy.* —See Syns at **fierce.** [From Latin *ferōx,* wild, fierce.] —**fe·ro′cious·ly** *adv.* —**fe·ro′cious·ness** *n.*

fe·roc·i·ty (fə-rŏs′ĭ-tē) *n., pl.* **-ties.** The quality or condition of being ferocious.

-ferous. A suffix meaning bearing, producing, or containing: **umbelliferous.** [-FER + -OUS.]

fer·ret (fĕr′ĭt) *n.* **1.** A domesticated, usu. albino form of the European polecat, often trained to hunt rats or rabbits. **2.** A related weasellike North American mammal, *Mustela nigripes,* with yellowish fur and dark feet. —*tr.v.* **1.** To hunt for with a ferret. **2.** To uncover and bring to light by searching: *ferret out a secret.* —*intr.v.* **1.** To hunt with a ferret. **2.** To search intensively. [Middle English *feret,* from Old French *fuiret, furet,* from Latin *fūr,* thief.] —**fer′ret·er** *n.* —**fer′ret·y** *adj.*

fer·ric (fĕr′ĭk) *adj.* Of or containing iron, esp. with valence 3 or with valence higher than in a corresponding ferrous compound. [FERR(O)- + -IC.]

ferric oxide. A dark compound, Fe_2O_3, that occurs naturally as hematite ore and rust, and is used in pigments, polishing compounds, and magnetic tapes.

Fer·ris wheel (fĕr′ĭs). Also **fer·ris wheel.** A large upright, rotating wheel with suspended cars in which passengers ride for amusement. [After George W.G. *Ferris* (1859–96), American engineer, its inventor.]

ferro- or **ferr-.** A prefix meaning: **1.** Iron: **ferromagnetic.** **2.** Iron in alloy: **ferromanganese.** [From Latin *ferrum,* iron.]

fer·ro·con·crete (fĕr′ō-kŏn′krēt′, -kŏn-krēt′) *n.* Reinforced concrete.

fer·ro·mag·net·ic (fĕr′ō-măg-nĕt′ĭk) *adj.* Of or characteristic of substances, such as iron, nickel, cobalt, and various alloys, that have magnetic properties similar to those of iron.

fer·ro·man·ga·nese (fĕr′ō-măng′gə-nēz′, -nēs′) *n.* An alloy of iron and manganese, used in the production of steel.

fer·rous (fĕr′əs) *adj.* Of, pertaining to, or containing iron, esp. with valence 2. [From Latin *ferrum,* iron + -OUS.]

ferrous oxide. A black powdery compound, FeO, used in the manufacture of steel, green heat-absorbing glass, and enamels.

ferrous sulfate. A greenish crystalline compound, $FeSO_4 \cdot 7H_2O$, used as a pigment, fertilizer, feed additive, and in sewage and water treatment.

fer·ru·gi·nous (fə-rōō′jə-nəs, fĕ-) *adj.* **1.** Of, containing, or similar to iron. **2.** Having the color of iron rust. [Latin *ferrūginus,* from *ferrūgō,* iron rust, from *ferrum,* iron.]

fer·rule (fĕr′əl, -ōōl′) *n.* Also **fer·ule.** A metal ring or cap placed around a wooden shaft for reinforcement or to prevent splitting. [Var. of earlier *verrel,* from Middle English *verelle, virol,* from Old French *virelle, virole,* from Latin *viriola,* little bracelet, dim. of *viriae,* bracelets.]

fer·ry (fĕr′ē) *v.* **-ried, -ry·ing.** —*tr.v.* **1.** To transport across a body of water. **2.** To cross (a body of water) on a ferry. **3.** To transport by means of a vehicle, esp. an aircraft, from one point to another. —*intr.v.* To cross a body of water on a ferry. —*n., pl.* **-ries.** **1.** A ferryboat. **2.** The place where a ferryboat embarks. [Middle English *fery,* from Old English *ferian.*]

fer·ry·boat (fĕr′ē-bōt′) *n.* A boat used to ferry passengers, goods, and vehicles.

fer·tile (fûr′tl) *adj.* **1.** Favorable to the growth of crops and plants: *fertile soil.* **2.** Capable of producing offspring. **3.** Capable of developing into a complete organism: *a fertile egg.* **4. a.** Highly productive or active; prolific: *a fertile imagination.* **b.** Rich in possibilities for development or growth. [Middle English, from Old French, from Latin *fertilis,* from *ferre,* to bear, carry, produce.] —**fer′tile·ly** *adv.* —**fer′til′i·ty** *n.*

Syns: fertile, fecund, fruitful, productive, prolific, rich *adj. Core meaning:* Characterized by great productivity (*fertile farm land*).

fer·til·ize (fûr′tl-īz′) *v.* **-ized, -iz·ing.** —*tr.v.* **1.** To make fertile, esp. by impregnating or pollinating. **2.** To apply fertilizer. —*intr.v.* To spread fertilizer. —**fer′til·iz′a·ble** *adj.* —**fer′til·i·za′tion** *n.*

fer·til·iz·er (fûr′tl-ī′zər) n. **1.** A material, such as manure, compost, or a chemical compound, added to soil to increase its fertility. **2.** Something or someone that fertilizes.

fer·ule¹ (fĕr′əl, -ool′) n. A flat stick or ruler used in punishing children. [Latin ferula, giant fennel, rod used to punish.]

fer·ule² (fĕr′əl, -ool′) n. Var. of ferrule.

fer·vent (fûr′vənt) adj. **1.** Showing deep feeling or great emotion. **2.** Extremely hot; glowing. [Middle English, from Old French, from Latin fervēns, pres. part. of fervēre, to boil, glow.] **—fer′ven·cy** or **fer′vent·ness** n. **—fer′vent·ly** adv.

fer·vid (fûr′vĭd) adj. **1.** Fervent; impassioned. **2.** Extremely hot. [Latin fervidus, glowing, from fervēre, to glow, boil.] **—fer′vid·ly** adv. **—fer′vid·ness** n.

fer·vor (fûr′vər) n. Also Brit. **fer·vour. 1.** Intensity of emotion; ardor. **2.** Intense heat. —See Syns at **passion.** [Middle English fervour, from Old French, from Latin fervor, a boiling, from fervēre, to boil.]

fes·tal (fĕs′təl) adj. Of or pertaining to a feast or festival; festive. [Old French, from Latin fēsta, feast.] **—fes′tal·ly** adv.

fes·ter (fĕs′tər) intr.v. **1.** To generate pus. **2.** To decay; rot: "Lilies that fester smell far worse than weeds" (Shakespeare). **3.** To be or become a source of irritation or resentment; rankle: Envy festered for years in her mind. —n. A small, festering sore. [Middle English festre, from Old French, from Latin fistula, fistula.]

fes·ti·val (fĕs′tə-vəl) n. **1.** An occasion or time for celebration, marked esp. by special rituals or customs. **2.** A series of cultural presentations: an international film festival. **3.** Conviviality; revelry. —modifier: a festival day; the festival site. [Middle English, from Old French, from Medieval Latin fēstīvālis, festive.]

fes·tive (fĕs′tĭv) adj. **1.** Of or suited to a feast or festival. **2.** Merry; joyous. —See Syns at **glad.** [Latin festīvus, from fēstus, joyous.] **—fes′tive·ly** adv. **—fes′tive·ness** n.

fes·tiv·i·ty (fĕ-stĭv′ĭ-tē) n., pl. **-ties. 1.** A joyous feast, holiday, or celebration; festival. **2.** Often **festivities.** The activities during a festival or feast: The festivities included parades, banquets, and balls. **3.** The merriment of a celebration or festival: a holiday with much festivity. —See Syns at **gaiety.**

fes·toon (fĕ-stoon′) n. **1.** A decorative chain, as of leaves or flowers, hung between two points. **2.** An ornament in the shape of a festoon. —tr.v. **1.** To decorate with or as with a festoon or festoons: "The aged cobwebs that festoon its dusky beams" (Nathaniel Hawthorne). **2.** To form or make into a festoon. **3.** To join together by festoons. [French feston, from Italian festone, festal ornament, from fēsta, feast, festival, from Latin fēstus, festal.] **—fes·toon′er·y** n.

fe·tal (fēt′l) adj. Also **foe·tal.** Of or relating to a fetus.

fetch (fĕch) tr.v. **1.** To go after and return with; get: Shall I fetch your bags for you? **2.** To cause to come: a blow that fetched blood. **3.** To bring as a price: "Our corn will fetch its price in any market in Europe" (Thomas Paine). **4.** To arrive at; reach. —n. An act or example of fetching. [Middle English fecchen, from Old English feccan, fetian.] **—fetch′er** n.

fetch·ing (fĕch′ĭng) adj. Informal. Very attractive; charming. **—fetch′ing·ly** adv.

fete (fāt, fĕt) or **fête** n. **1.** A festival or feast. **2.** An elaborate party or entertainment. —tr.v. **fet·ed, fet·ing.** To honor with a fete. [French fête, from Old French feste, feast.]

fet·id (fĕt′ĭd, fē′tĭd) adj. Also **foe·tid.** Having an offensive, foul smell. [Middle English, from Latin foetidus, from foetēre, to stink.] **—fet′id·ly** adv. **—fet′id·ness** n.

fet·ish or **fet·ich** (fĕt′ĭsh, fē′tĭsh) n. **1.** An object that is believed to have magical power. **2.** Something to which excessive attention or reverence is given: an age in which hygiene has become a fetish. [French fétiche, from Portuguese feitiço, charm, sorcery, from Latin factītius, made by art, from facere, to make, do.] **—fet′ish·ism** n.

fet·lock (fĕt′lŏk′) n. **1.** A projection above and behind the hoof of a horse. **2.** A tuft of hair on the fetlock. [Middle English fitlok.]

fet·ter (fĕt′ər) n. **1.** A chain or shackle attached to the ankles to restrain movement. **2.** Anything that restricts or restrains. —tr.v. To restrict or restrain with or as if with fetters. [Middle English feter, from Old English fetor.]

fet·tle (fĕt′l) n. Proper or sound condition: in fine fettle. [From Middle English fetlen, to shape, make ready, prob. from Old English fetel, girdle, belt.]

fe·tus (fē′təs) n., pl. **-tus·es.** Also **foe·tus.** The unborn young of a mammal from the time at which the major features of its body have appeared, esp. an unborn human baby after the eighth week of its development. [Latin fētus, offspring.]

feud¹ (fyood) n. A bitter, prolonged quarrel, esp. between two groups, marked by violence and acts of revenge. —intr.v. To carry on a feud. [Middle English fede, feide, from Old French, from Old High German fēhida.]

feud² (fyood) n. A feudal estate; fee. [Medieval Latin feudum.]

feu·dal (fyood′l) adj. **1.** Of or relating to feudalism. **2.** Of or pertaining to lands held in fee. [Medieval Latin feudālis, from feudum, feud (estate).] **—feu′dal·ize** tr.v. **—feu′dal·i·za′tion** n. **—feu′dal·ly** adv.

feu·dal·ism (fyood′l-ĭz′əm) n. A political and economic system in medieval Europe by which a landowner granted land to a vassal in exchange for military service. **—feu′dal·is′tic** adj.

feu·da·to·ry (fyood′ə-tôr′ē, -tōr′ē) n., pl. **-ries. 1.** A vassal. **2.** A feudal fee; fief. —adj. Owing feudal tribute or loyalty. [Medieval Latin feudātōrius, from feudātus, past part. of feudāre, to invest with a feudal estate, from feudum, feud (estate).]

fe·ver (fē′vər) n. **1.** An abnormally high body temperature. **2.** A disease in which fever is one of the main symptoms. **3.** A condition of great agitation or enthusiasm; intensity. **4.** An intense usu. short-lived enthusiasm. [Middle English fever, from Old English fēfor, fēfer, from Latin febris.]

fever blister. A cold sore.

fe·ver·few (fē′vər-fyoo′) n. An aromatic plant, Chrysanthemum parthenium, native to Eurasia, with clusters of buttonlike, white-rayed flowers.

fe·ver·ish (fē′vər-ĭsh) adj. **1. a.** Having a fever, esp. one that is not very high. **b.** Caused by a fever. **2.** Marked by agitation, intense emotion, or activity. **—fe′ver·ish·ly** adv. **—fe′ver·ish·ness** n.

few (fyoo) adj. **few·er, few·est.** Amounting to or consisting of a small number. —n. (used with a pl. verb). **1.** An indefinitely small number of persons or things: Only a few came to my party. **2.** A limited, often select or elite group: the happy few. —pron. (used with a pl. verb). A small number of persons or things: Few of them were able to read. [Middle English fewe, from Old English fēa, fēawe.] **—few′ness** n.

Usage: few, less. Use fewer when referring to numbers or units considered individually and therefore capable of being counted or enumerated: fewer jobs; fewer teachers; no fewer than ten applicants; fourteen fewer seats in Congress. Use less in references to collective quantity and to something abstract: less opportunity; less individual instruction. Less is gen. the choice in sentences setting forth periods of time, sums of money, and measures of distance, weight, and the like; here the sense is collective, even though the nouns qualified by less name things that can be counted or enumerated: less than two months; less than forty years of age; less than $1,000; weighing less than 100 pounds.

fey (fā) adj. **1.** Having visionary powers; clairvoyant. **2.** Appearing as if under a spell; enchanted. [Middle English feie, from Old English fǣge, doomed.]

fez (fĕz) n., pl. **fez·zes.** A brimless red felt hat with a flat top and a black tassel, worn chiefly by men in eastern Mediterranean countries. [French, from Turkish, from Fez, a city in Morocco.]

fi·an·cé (fē-än-sā′, fē-än′sā′) n. A man engaged to be married. [French, past part. of fiancer, to betroth, from Old French fiancier, from fier, to trust, from Latin fīdere.]

fi·an·cée (fē-än-sā′, fē-än′sā′) n. A woman engaged to be married.

fi·as·co (fē-ăs′kō, -äs′-) n., pl. **-coes** or **-cos.** A complete and often ludicrous failure. [French, from Italian.]

fi·at (fē′ăt′, fī′ăt′, -ət) n. An authoritative order or decree. [Latin, "let it be done."]

fib (fĭb) n. A small or trivial lie. —See Syns at **lie.** —intr.v.

ă pat   ā pay   â care   ä father   ĕ pet   ē be   hw which
ŏŏ took   ōō boot   ou out   th thin   th this   ŭ cut
ĭ pit   ī tie   î pier   ŏ pot   ō toe   ô paw, for   oi noise
û urge   zh vision   ə about, item, edible, gallop, circus

fibbed, fib·bing. To tell a fib. [Orig. unknown.] —**fib′ber** n.

fi·ber (fī′bər) n. Also *Brit.* **fi·bre.** **1.** A slender, threadlike strand, as of plant or animal tissue or of man-made material. **2.** A number of fibers forming a single substance: *muscle fiber; flax fiber.* **3.** Inner strength; toughness: *lacking in moral fiber.* [French *fibre,* from Latin *fibra.*]

fi·ber·board (fī′bər-bôrd′, -bōrd′) n. A building material composed of fibers compressed into rigid sheets.

fiber glass. Any of several materials made from glass fibers, such as cloth, thread, or insulation.

fi·bril (fī′brəl, fīb′rəl) n. A tiny, slender, often microscopic fiber, as a root hair. [From Latin *fibra,* fiber.] —**fi′bril·lar** or **fi′bril·lar·y** (-lěr′ē) adj.

fib·ril·la·tion (fīb′rə-lā′shən, fī′brə-) n. An uncoordinated twitching of the muscle fibers of the ventricles of the heart.

fi·brin (fī′brĭn) n. An elastic, insoluble, fibrous protein that forms a blood clot. [FIBR(O)- + -IN.]

fi·brin·o·gen (fī-brĭn′ə-jən) n. A soluble protein normally present in the blood plasma, that is converted to fibrin when blood clots.

fibro– or **fibr–.** A prefix meaning fibrous tissue: **fibrosis.** [From Latin *fibra,* fiber.]

fi·broid (fī′broid′) adj. Like or composed of fibrous tissue. —n. A benign tumor of smooth muscle. [FIBR(O)- + -OID.]

fi·bro·sis (fī-brō′sĭs) n. The formation of excess fibrous tissue. [FIBR(O)- + -OSIS.]

fi·brous (fī′brəs) adj. Of, like, or having fibers.

fi·bro·vas·cu·lar (fī′brō-văs′kyə-lər) adj. *Bot.* Having fibrous tissue and vascular tissue, as in the woody tissue of plants.

fib·u·la (fīb′yə-lə) n., pl. **-lae** (-lē′) or **-las.** The outer and smaller of two bones that support the lower section of the hind or lower limb of vertebrates, located between the ankle and knee in human beings. [Latin *fībula.*]

fibula   fichu   fiddle

fi·chu (fĭsh′ōō, fē′shōō) n. A woman's triangular, light scarf, worn over the shoulders and fastened at the breast. [French, from the past part. of *ficher,* to fix, attach, from Latin *figere.*]

fick·le (fĭk′əl) adj. Changeable, as in affections or loyalties; inconstant. —See Syns at **capricious.** [Middle English *fikel,* false, treacherous, from Old English *ficol.*] —**fick′le·ness** n.

fic·tion (fĭk′shən) n. **1.** A product of the imagination: *Legends are often mixtures of fact and fiction.* **2. a.** A story of imaginary characters and events. **b.** A literary genre that consists of such stories. —**modifier:** *a fiction writer.* [Middle English *ficcioun,* invention, from Old French *fiction,* from Latin *fictiō,* a making, fashioning, from *fictus,* past part. of *fingere,* to touch, form, mold.] —**fic′tion·al** adj. —**fic′tion·al·ly** adv.

fic·ti·tious (fĭk-tĭsh′əs) adj. **1.** Of, relating to, or resembling fiction: *a fictitious account.* **2.** Not genuine, sincere, or authentic: *a fictitious name.* —**fic·ti′tious·ly** adv. —**fic·ti′tious·ness** n.

fid (fĭd) n. **1.** A square bar used as a support for a topmast. **2.** A large, tapering pin used to open the strands of a rope prior to splicing. [Orig. unknown.]

fid·dle (fĭd′l) n. *Informal.* **1.** A violin. **2.** Any member of the violin family. —v. **-dled, -dling.** —*intr.v.* **1.** *Informal.* To play a violin. **2. a.** To move the hands or fingers restlessly or idly. **b.** To meddle or tinker with. —*tr.v. Infor-*

mal. To play (a tune) on a violin. —*idioms.* **fit as a fiddle.** Of sound body; healthy. [Middle English *fithele, fidle,* from Old English *fithele,* from Medieval Latin *vītula,* from Latin *vītulārī,* to celebrate a victory, from *Vītula,* goddess of joy and victory.] —**fid′dler** n.

fid·dle·head (fĭd′l-hěd) n. The coiled young frond of various ferns, considered a delicacy when cooked.

fiddler crab. Any of various burrowing crabs of the genus *Uca,* of coastal areas, with one of the front claws much enlarged in the male. [So called from its fiddle-like large claw.]

fid·dle·sticks (fĭd′l-stĭks′) interj. A word used to express mild annoyance or impatience.

fi·del·i·ty (fĭ-děl′ĭ-tē, fī-) n., pl. **-ties.** **1.** Faithfulness, as to a person or cause; loyalty. **2.** Conformity to truth; accuracy. **3.** The degree to which an electronic system, such as a radio or phonograph, reproduces sound without distortion. [Middle English *fidelite,* from Old French, from Latin *fidēlitās,* from *fidēlis,* faithful, from *fidēs,* faith.]

fidg·et (fĭj′ĭt) intr.v. To move uneasily, nervously, or restlessly. —*tr.v.* To make restless or nervous. —n. **fidgets.** A condition of nervousness or restlessness. [Prob. from obs. *fidge,* to move about restlessly.] —**fidg′et·i·ness** n. —**fidg′et·y** adj.

fi·du·ci·ar·y (fī-dōō′shē-ěr′ē, -dyōō′-, fī-) adj. **1.** Of, pertaining to, or founded upon a trust or confidence. **2.** Having the nature or characteristics of a trust. —n., **-ies.** A person or institution that is a participant in a fiduciary relationship or functions in a fiduciary capacity. [Latin *fīdūciārius,* from *fīdūcia,* trust.]

fie (fī) interj. A word used to express distaste or shock. [Middle English *fi,* from Old French, from Latin *fī,* expression of disgust.]

fief (fēf) n. Also **feoff.** A feudal estate. [French, from Old French *fie(f),* fee.]

field (fēld) n. **1.** An area of open land. **2.** An area of land that is devoted to a particular use or that yields a particular product: *cotton fields; a football field.* **3.** An area of interest, activity, or specialization: *the field of medicine.* **4.** A region of space in which a particular property or effect, such as gravitation or electricity, exists. **5.** The range or scope of the eye or an optical instrument: *the field of vision.* **6.** A scene or place of battle. **7.** All the participants in a race or competition: *a large field in the Kentucky Derby.* **8.** A great expanse: *ice fields that stretched out endlessly below.* **9.** A background area, as of a flag or painting: *a gold dragon on a field of blue.* —**modifier:** *a field hospital.* —*tr.v.* **1.** *Sports.* To retrieve (a ball) and throw it to the proper player. **2.** To put into a field. **3.** To respond to adequately; cope with: *fielded the question expertly.* [Middle English, from Old English *feld.*]

field artillery. Artillery light enough to be mounted for use in the field.

field corn. Any of several varieties of corn used primarily as feed for livestock.

field day. **1.** A day spent outdoors in a planned activity such as athletic competition, nature study, etc. **2.** *Informal.* An occasion of great pleasure or triumph.

field·er (fēl′dər) n. *Sports.* A baseball player stationed in the outfield.

field event. A track event other than a race.

field·fare (fēld′fâr′) n. An Old World thrush, *Turdus pilaris,* with gray and brown plumage. [Middle English *feldefare,* prob. from Late Old English *feldefare,* "field-goer."]

field glasses. Portable binoculars for outdoor use.

field goal. **1.** *Football.* A score of three points made by a place kick that propels the ball above the crossbar of the opposing team's goal posts. **2.** *Basketball.* A score of two points made during regular play by throwing the ball through the basket defended by the opposing team.

field gun. A mobile piece of field artillery; fieldpiece.

field hockey. *Sports.* Hockey.

field magnet. A magnet used to provide a magnetic field that is needed for the operation of a machine such as a generator or motor.

field marshal. An officer of the highest rank in some European armies.

field mouse. Any of various small mice, as of the genera *Apodemus* or *Microtus,* inhabiting meadows and fields.

field·piece (fēld'pēs') *n.* A field gun.

field trial. A test for hunting dogs to determine their competence in pointing and retrieving.

field trip. An organized trip made by a group to observe and learn, as by visiting a museum.

field work. Work done or observations made in the field, as opposed to that done or observed in a laboratory or classroom.

fiend (fēnd) *n.* **1.** An evil spirit; demon. **2.** Often **Fiend.** Satan; the Devil. **3.** An extremely evil or cruel person. **4.** *Informal.* A person devoted to or obsessed with something: *a fresh-air fiend.* [Middle English *fe(o)nd*, enemy, devil, fiend, from Old English *fēond.*]

fiend·ish (fēn'dĭsh) *adj.* Of or like a fiend; evil or cruel. —**fiend'ish·ly** *adv.* —**fiend'ish·ness** *n.*

fierce (fîrs) *adj.* **fierc·er, fierc·est. 1.** Wild and savage; ferocious: *a fierce beast.* **2.** Extremely severe or violent; terrible. **3.** Intense or ardent; extreme: *fierce loyalty.* **4.** *Informal.* Very difficult or unpleasant: *a fierce exam.* [Middle English *f(i)ers*, from Old French, from Latin *ferus*, wild.] —**fierce'ly** *adv.* —**fierce'ness** *n.*
　　Syns: fierce, bestial, cruel, fell², feral, ferocious, inhuman, savage, vicious *adj. Core meaning:* Violently destructive without scruples or restraint (*a fierce interrogator; fierce cannibals*). See also Syns at **intense.**

fier·y (fîr'ē, fī'ə-rē) *adj.* **-i·er, -i·est. 1.** Of, consisting of, or like fire: *the fiery crater of the volcano.* **2.** Very hot. **3. a.** Blazing or glowing like fire. **b.** Reddish in color, like fire. **4. a.** Filled with or exhibiting intense emotion or spirit. **b.** Easily stirred up or provoked: *a fiery temper.* —See Syns at **hot.** [Middle English, from *fiere*, fire.] —**fier'i·ly** *adv.* —**fier'i·ness** *n.*

fi·es·ta (fē-ĕs'tə) *n.* A festival, esp. a religious celebration in a Spanish-speaking country. [Spanish, from Latin *fēstus*, joyous, festive.]

fife (fīf) *n.* A musical instrument similar to a flute but higher in range. [German *Pfeife*, from Old High German *pfīffa*, from Latin *pīpāre*, to chirp.]

fif·teen (fĭf-tēn') *n.* A number, written 15 in Arabic numerals or XV in Roman numerals, equal to the sum of 14 + 1. [Middle English *fiftene*, from Old English *fīftȳne.*] —**fif'teen'** *adj. & pron.*

fif·teenth (fĭf-tēnth') *n.* **1.** The ordinal number that matches the number fifteen in a series. **2.** One of 15 equal parts, written ¹⁄₁₅. —**fif'teenth'** *adj. & adv.*

fifth (fĭfth) *n.* **1.** The ordinal number that matches the number five. **2.** One of five equal parts, written ⅕. **3.** A measure of liquid capacity equal to ⅕ of a gallon or ¾ of a liter, used mainly for alcoholic beverages. **4.** *Mus.* **a.** The interval between two musical tones that are seven semitones apart. **b.** The musical tone five steps above the tonic of a diatonic scale; dominant. [Middle English *fifte*, from Old English *fīfta.*] —**fifth** *adj. & adv.*

fifth column. A secret organization that works within a country to further the military and political aims of an enemy. [First applied in 1936 to rebel sympathizers in Madrid when four columns of rebel troops were attacking that city.] —**fifth columnist.**

fifth wheel. Someone or something that is unnecessary.

fif·ti·eth (fĭf'tē-ĭth) *n.* **1.** The ordinal number that matches the number fifty. **2.** One of fifty equal parts, written ¹⁄₅₀. —**fif'ti·eth** *adj. & adv.*

fif·ty (fĭf'tē) *n.* The cardinal number written 50 in Arabic numerals or L in Roman numerals, equal to the product of 5 × 10. [Middle English *fifti*, from Old English *fīftig.*] —**fif'ty** *adj. & pron.*

fif·ty-fif·ty (fĭf'tē-fĭf'tē). *Informal.* —*adj.* **1.** Equally balanced between favorable and unfavorable: *a fifty-fifty chance to win.* **2.** Shared equally: *a fifty-fifty split.* —**fif'ty-fif'ty** *adv.*

fig (fĭg) *n.* **1. a.** Any of several trees or shrubs of the genus *Ficus*, esp. *F. carica*, native to the Mediterranean region, widely cultivated for its edible fruit. **b.** The sweet, pear-shaped, many-seeded fruit of this tree. **2.** The least bit or amount; a whit: *didn't care a fig for me.* —*modifier:* a *fig tree.* [Middle English *fig(e)*, from Old French *figue*, from Old Provençal *figa*, from Latin *ficus.*]

fight (fīt) *v.* **fought** (fôt), **fight·ing.** —*intr.v.* **1.** To take part in physical combat or battle. **2.** To make a great effort: *fight for freedom; fight against disease and ignorance.* **3.** To take part in boxing. —*tr.v.* **1.** To struggle against in or as if in physical combat or battle. **2.** To box or wrestle with. **3.** To strive or struggle against in order to prevent or defeat: *fight disease; fought the tax increase.* **4.** To carry on or engage in: *fight a battle.* **5.** To achieve or gain with great difficulty: *fought her way to stardom.* —See Syns at **argue** and **resist.** —*n.* **1. a.** A physical conflict. **b.** A quarrel. **2.** A battle between opposing forces. **3.** A boxing or wrestling match. **4.** A vigorous or difficult struggle. **5.** The power or will to fight: *was exhausted and had little fight left.* —*idiom.* **fight shy of.** To keep away from; avoid. [Middle English *fighten*, from Old English *feohtan.*]

fight·er (fī'tər) *n.* **1.** A person or animal that fights. **2.** A boxer or wrestler. **3.** Also **fighter plane.** A fast, maneuverable aircraft used in combat.

fig·ment (fĭg'mənt) *n.* Something made up or invented: *a figment of the imagination.* [Middle English, from Latin *figmentum*, a formation, from *fingere*, to mold, fashion.]

fig·u·ra·tion (fĭg'yə-rā'shən) *n.* **1.** A shape, form, or outline. **2.** The act of representing with figures.

fig·u·ra·tive (fĭg'yər-ə-tĭv) *adj.* **1.** Based on, using, or containing figures of speech; metaphorical. **2.** Representing by a figure; symbolic or emblematic. **3.** Of or relating to representation by a figure. —**fig'ur·a·tive·ly** *adv.*

fig·ure (fĭg'yər) *n.* **1. a.** A written or printed symbol. **b.** A numeral. **2. figures.** Arithmetic calculations: *a good head for figures.* **3.** *Geom.* A subset of a plane or of space, for example, a union of lines or line segments or a union of planes or portions of planes. **4.** An amount expressed in numbers. **5. a.** A diagram, picture, or illustration in a text. **b.** A design or pattern. **6.** The shape or form esp. of a human body. **7.** Something recognized only as a shape or form: *a tall figure in the gloom.* **8.** A representation of a person or animal, as in sculpture or painting. **9.** A well-known or prominent person: *an important public figure.* **10.** The impression someone makes: *He cuts a fine figure in his new suit.* **11.** *Mus.* A short melodic, rhythmic, or harmonic unit; a motif. **12.** A group of movements in a dance. **13.** A **figure of speech.** —*v.* **-ured, -ur·ing.** —*tr.v.* **1.** To calculate. **2.** To make a likeness of; represent. **3.** To decorate with a figure. **4.** *Informal.* **a.** To conclude: *He figured that would happen.* **b.** To consider; believe: *I figure he's an impostor.* —*intr.v.* To be a part of: *figured in all the reports.* —See Syns at **believe.** —*idioms.* **figure on** (or **upon**). *Informal.* To depend on or look forward to: *I figured on relaxing today.* **figure out.** *Informal.* To work out; determine: *figured out the correct answer.* [Middle English, from Old French, from Latin *figūra*, form, shape, figure.]

figure eight. A figure in the shape of the number 8.

fig·ure·head (fĭg'yər-hĕd') *n.* **1.** A leader or head of a country or organization in name only. **2.** A figure on the prow of a ship.

figure of speech. An expression, such as a metaphor or hyperbole, in which the literal meanings of words are distorted to create vivid or dramatic effects.

fig·u·rine (fĭg'yə-rēn') *n.* A small ornamental figure; statuette. [French, from Italian *figurina*, dim. of *figura*, figure, from Latin *figura*.]

fig·wort (fĭg'wûrt', -wôrt') *n.* Any of various plants of the

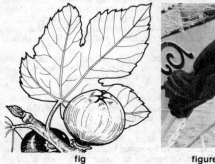

fig   figurehead

ă pat　â pay　â care　ä father　ĕ pet　ē be　hw which
ŏŏ took　ōō boot　ou out　th thin　th this　ŭ cut
ĭ pit　ī tie　î pier　ŏ pot　ō toe　ô paw, for　oi noise
û urge　zh vision　ə about, item, edible, gallop, circus

genus *Scrophularia*, with loose, branching clusters of small greenish or purple flowers. [From obs. *fig*, piles, for which the plant was thought to be a cure.]

fil·a·ment (fĭl′ə-mənt) *n.* **1. a.** *Elect.* A fine wire that is enclosed in the bulb of a lamp and is heated electrically to incandescence. **b.** *Electronics.* An electrically heated wire that heats the cathode of some electron tubes. **2.** Any fine or slender thread, strand, or fiber. **3.** A slender, threadlike part or structure, such as a chainlike series of cells in some algae. [Old French, from Medieval Latin *fīlamentum*, from Late Latin *fīlāre*, to wind threads, spin, from Latin *fīlum*, thread.] **—fil′a·men′tous** *adj.*

fi·lar·i·a (fĭ-lâr′ē-ə) *n.*, *pl.* **-i·ae** (-ē-ē′). Any of various parasitic nematode worms of the superfamily Filarioidea that infest man and other vertebrates and are often transmitted by biting insects. [New Latin *Filaria* (former genus name), "threadworm," from Latin *fīlum*, thread.] **—fi·lar′i·al** *adj.*

fil·a·ri·a·sis (fĭl′ə-rī′ə-sĭs) *n.* Infestation of tissue, esp. of the lymph glands, with filariae.

fil·bert (fĭl′bərt) *n.* **1.** A Eurasian shrub or tree, *Corylus maxima*, a species of hazel, cultivated for its edible nuts. **2.** The rounded, smooth-shelled nut of the filbert. [Middle English, from Norman French *(noix de) filbert*, "nut of Saint Philibert" (d. A.D. 684), Frankish abbot whose feast day in late August marks the ripening season of the nut.]

filch (fĭlch) *tr.v.* To steal furtively; pilfer. [Middle English *filchen*.] **—filch′er** *n.*

file[1] (fīl) *n.* **1. a.** A collection, as of papers or cards, arranged in order. **b.** The container, such as a cabinet or folder, for storing such a collection. **2.** A line of persons, animals, or things positioned one behind the other. **3.** One of the rows of squares that run between two players on the opposite sides of a playing board. **—modifier:** *a file clerk.* **—v. filed, fil·ing.** **—tr.v.** **1.** To arrange or put in a file: *He filed the reports alphabetically.* **2.** To enter or submit for entry in a public or official record: *file a claim.* **3.** To turn in (copy) to a newspaper. **4.** To present for consideration: *file an application for a job.* **—intr.v.** **1.** To move in a file: *The nine justices filed in.* **2.** To enter an application. **3.** To register as a candidate in a political contest. **—idioms. on file.** In a file so as to be available; on hand. [French *fil*, thread (on which documents were strung), from Latin *fīlum*.] **—fil′er** *n.*

file[2] (fīl) *n.* A tool, usu. made of steel, with a series of sharp ridged edges, used in smoothing, shaping or grinding down. **—tr.v. filed, fil·ing.** To smooth, grind, or remove with a file. [Middle English, from Old English *fēol, fīl.*] **—fil′er** *n.*

file·fish (fīl′fĭsh′) *n.*, *pl.* **filefish** or **-fish·es.** Any of various saltwater fishes of the family Balistidae, related to and resembling the triggerfishes. [From the rough scales of some species.]

fi·let[1] (fĭ-lā′, fĭl′ā′) *n.* A lace with a simple pattern of squares. [French, from Old French *filé*, from Old Provençal *filat*, "made of threads," from *fil*, thread, from Latin *fīlum*.]

fi·let[2] (fĭ-lā′, fĭl′ā′) *n. & v.* Var. of **fillet.**

fi·let mi·gnon (fĭl′ā mēn-yōN′, fĭ-lā′) A small, choice cut of beef from the loin. [French, "dainty fillet."]

fil·i·al (fĭl′ē-əl) *adj.* Of or befitting a son or daughter: *filial obedience.* [Middle English, from Late Latin *fīliālis*, from Latin *fīlius*, son.]

fil·i·bus·ter (fĭl′ə-bŭs′tər) *n.* **1. a.** A tactic, such as long speeches or debates, employed in an attempt to delay or prevent legislative action. **b.** An example of this. **2.** An adventurer or mercenary who engages in warfare in a foreign country. **—intr.v.** **1.** To use a filibuster in a legislative body. **2.** To engage in unlawful warfare in a foreign country. [From Spanish *filibustero*, "freebooter."] **—fil′i·bus′ter·er** *n.*

fil·i·gree (fĭl′ə-grē′) *n.* **1.** Lacelike ornamental work of twisted gold or silver wire. **2.** Any lacy, delicate design. **—modifier:** *filigree earrings.* **—tr.v. -greed, -gree·ing.** To decorate with filigree. [Earlier *filigreen*, from French *filigrane*, from Italian *filigrana* : *fili-*, from Latin *filum*, thread + *grana*, grain, from Latin *grānum*.]

fil·ing (fī′lĭng) *n.* Often **filings.** Particles scraped off with a file.

Fil·i·pi·no (fĭl′ə-pē′nō) *n.*, *pl.* **-nos.** A native or inhabitant of

the Philippines. **—Fil′i·pi′no** *adj.*

fill (fĭl) *tr.v.* **1.** To put into as much as can be held: *fill a glass with water.* **2.** To occupy the whole of: *Smoke filled the room.* **3.** To occupy or hold: *He filled a new spot in the World Series.* **4.** To take up all the attention of: *The idea of the circus filled her with excitement.* **5.** To complete: *fill out an application; fill in the blanks.* **6.** To stop; plug up: *fill cavities in teeth.* **7.** To satisfy or meet; fulfill: *fill the requirements for the job.* **8.** To supply the necessary materials for: *fill a prescription; fill an order.* **9.** To cause to swell. **—intr.v.** To become full. **—phrasal verb. fill in.** To substitute for: *The understudy filled in for the star.* **—n.** **1.** An amount needed to make full, complete, or satisfied: *eat one's fill. I like baseball, but I've had my fill today.* **2.** Material, such as gravel or sand, used to fill holes or depressions in the ground. **—idioms. fill (someone's) shoes.** To take someone's position and handle it properly. **fill the bill.** To serve or perform adequately. [Middle English *fillen*, from Old English *fyllan*.]

fill·er (fĭl′ər) *n.* **1.** Something added in order to increase weight or size or to fill space. **2.** A material used to fill pores, cracks, or holes in a surface. **3.** A sheaf of loose papers used to fill a notebook or binder.

fil·let *n.* **1.** (fĭl′ĭt). A narrow strip of material, as a band or ribbon, often worn as a headband. **2.** (fĭ-lā′, fĭl′ā′). Also **fi·let.** A boneless piece of meat or fish. **—tr.v.** **1. fil·let·ed** (fĭl′ĭ-tĭd), **fil·let·ing** (fĭl′ĭ-tĭng). To bind or decorate with or as with a fillet. **2. fi·leted** (fĭ-lād′, fĭl′ād′), **fi·let·ing** (fĭ-lā′ĭng, fĭl′ā′ĭng). Also **fi·let.** To cut into fillets. [Middle English *filet*, from Old French, dim. of *fil*, thread, from Latin *fīlum*.]

fill·ing (fĭl′ĭng) *n.* **1.** Something used to fill a space or cavity: *a gold filling in a tooth.* **2.** An edible mixture used to fill something: *pie filling.* **3.** The threads that cross the warp in weaving; weft.

filling station. A gas station.

fil·lip (fĭl′əp) *n.* A snap or light blow made by pressing a fingertip against the thumb and suddenly releasing it. **—tr.v.** **1.** To strike or propel with a fillip. **2.** To stir; stimulate.

fil·ly (fĭl′ē) *n.*, *pl.* **-lies.** A young female horse. [Middle English *filli*, from Old Norse *fylja*.]

film (fĭlm) *n.* **1.** A thin sheet or strip of flexible cellulose coated with materials that are sensitive to light, used in recording photographic images. **2. a.** A motion picture; movie. **b.** Motion pictures an an art; the cinema. **3.** A thin membrane. **4.** A thin coating, layer, or sheet: *a film of dust.* **—modifier:** *a film festival.* **—tr.v.** **1.** To cover with or as if with a film. **2.** To make a motion picture of: *filmed a dance sequence.* **—intr.v.** To become coated or obscured with or as if with a film. [Middle English *film*, from Old English *filmen.*]

film·ic (fĭl′mĭk) *adj.* Of or relating to motion pictures.

film·strip (fĭlm′strĭp′) *n.* A strip of film with photographs, diagrams, or other graphic matter, prepared for still projection one picture or frame at a time.

film·y (fĭl′mē) *adj.* **-i·er, -i·est.** **1.** Of, resembling, or consisting of film. **2.** Covered by or as if by a film. **—film′i·ly** *adv.* **—film′i·ness** *n.*

fil·ter (fĭl′tər) *n.* **1. a.** A device containing a porous substance through which a liquid or gas is passed in order to remove unwanted components, esp. suspended material. **b.** The porous material used in such a device. **2.** A device that operates on electric currents, electromagnetic waves, sound waves, etc., in a way that allows waves of certain frequencies to pass while those of other frequencies are blocked. **—modifier:** *filter paper.* **—tr.v.** **1.** To pass (a liquid or gas) through a filter: *filter water.* **2.** To remove by passing through a filter. **—intr.v.** To pass through or as if through a filter: *filter through enemy lines; light filtered through the blinds.* [Middle English *filtre*, a piece of felt (used to strain liquid), from Old French, from Medieval Latin *filtrum.*]

fil·ter·a·ble (fĭl′tər-ə-bəl, fĭl′trə-) *adj.* Also **fil·tra·ble.** **1.** Capable of being filtered, esp. capable of being removed by filtering. **2.** Small enough to pass through an exceedingly fine filter: *a filterable virus.* **—fil′ter·a·bil′i·ty** *n.*

filth (fĭlth) *n.* **1.** Foul or dirty matter: *Insects like flies carry filth that spreads disease germs.* **2.** Corruption; foulness.

3. Something that disgusts or offends, esp. obscenity. [Middle English, from Old English *fȳlth*, putrid matter.]

filth·y (fĭl'thē) *adj.* **-i·er, -i·est. 1.** Covered with or full of filth; dirty. **2.** Obscene: *a filthy picture.* **3.** Vile; nasty: *a filthy trick.* —See Syns at **dirty. —filth'i·ly** *adv.* **—filth'i·ness** *n.*

fil·tra·ble (fĭl'tər-ə-bəl, fĭl'trə-) *adj.* Var. of **filterable.**

fil·trate (fĭl'trāt') *v.* **-trat·ed, -trat·ing.** —*tr.v.* To put through a filter. —*intr.v.* To go through a filter. —*n.* Material that has passed through a filter. [From Medieval Latin *filtrāre*, from *filtrum*, filter.]

fil·tra·tion (fĭl-trā'shən) *n.* The act or process of filtering.

fin¹ (fĭn) *n.* **1.** One of the thin, flat parts that extend from the body of a fish or other aquatic animal and are used for moving through and balancing in the water. **2.** Something resembling a fin, as an aircraft, missile, automobile, or boat. **3.** A flexible piece of rubber attached to each foot to give added propulsion while swimming. [Middle English *finne*, from Old English *finn*.]

fin² (fĭn) *n. Slang.* A five-dollar bill. [Yiddish *finf*, five, from Middle High German *vimf*, from Old High German *finf*.]

fi·na·gle (fĭ-nā'gəl) *v.* **-gled, -gling.** *Informal.* —*tr.v.* **1.** To get or achieve by indirect methods; wangle. **2.** To obtain by trickery or deceit. [Orig. unknown.] **—fi·na'gler** *n.*

fi·nal (fī'nəl) *adj.* **1.** Coming at the end; last; concluding. **2.** Ultimate and definitive; decisive: *The decision of the court is final.* **3.** Of, relating to, or constituting an ultimate goal or purpose: *final cause.* —See Syns at **last.** —*n.* **1.** Often **finals.** The last game in a series of games or a tournament. **2.** The last examination of an academic course. [Middle English, from Old French, from Latin *fīnālis*, from *fīnis*, end.] **—fi'nal·ly** *adv.*

fi·na·le (fĭ-nāl'ē, -näl'ē) *n.* The final section of something, esp. of a musical composition. [Italian, "final," from Latin *fīnālis*, final.]

fi·nal·ist (fī'nə-lĭst) *n.* A contestant in the finals of a competition.

fi·nal·i·ty (fī-nāl'ĭ-tē, fĭ-) *n., pl.* **-ties. 1.** The condition or quality of being final. **2.** Something that is final.

fi·nal·ize (fī'nə-līz') *tr.v.* **-ized, -iz·ing.** To put into final form. **—fi'nal·iz'er** *n.*

Usage: **finalize.** Although this verb is used by a broad spectrum of reputable writers, it is nevertheless disliked by other good writers, perhaps because they associate it with bureaucracy and bureaucratic jargon. Alternative, less controversial wordings are: *complete, conclude, make final,* or *put into final form.*

fi·nance (fĭ-nāns', fī-, fī'nāns') *n.* **1.** The management of money, banking, investments, and credit. **2.** The science of the management of money and other assets. **3. finances.** Money and other resources; funds: *His finances were getting low.* **—modifier:** *finance company.* —*v.* **-nanced, -nanc·ing.** —*tr.v.* **1.** To provide the funds or capital for. **2.** To furnish with on credit. [Middle English *finaunce*, end, settlement, payment, from Old French *finance*, from *finer*, to end, settle, from *fin*, end, from Latin *fīnis*.]

fi·nan·cial (fĭ-nān'shəl, fī-) *adj.* Of, pertaining to, or involving finance or finances. **—fi·nan'cial·ly** *adv.*

fin·an·cier (fĭn'ən-sîr', fī-nān'-, fī'nən-) *n.* A person who deals in large-scale financial affairs. [French, from Old French, from *finance*, end.]

fin·back (fĭn'băk') *n.* A whale, the rorqual.

finch (fĭnch) *n.* Any of various small birds of the family Fringillidae, such as the goldfinch or canary, with a short, stout bill for cracking seeds. [Middle English, from Old English *finc*.]

find (fīnd) *v.* **found** (found), **find·ing.** —*tr.v.* **1. a.** To come upon by chance or accident: *I found this on the stairs.* **b.** To meet with; encounter: *find obstacles at every turn.* **2.** To look for and discover: *Help Mary find her pen.* **3.** To come upon as a result of study, observation, or investigation: *found the best person for the post; found that it was an insoluble problem.* **4.** To get or acquire by means of searching or making a great effort: *found the money by economizing.* **5.** To regain or recover: *found her keys.* **6.** To achieve; attain: *found an outlet in hard work.* —*intr.v.* To come to a legal decision or verdict: *The jury found for the defendant.* **—phrasal verb. find out.** To get

information about something; ascertain: *Scientists try to find out as much as they can about the world.* —*n.* **1.** An act of finding. **2.** An unexpectedly valuable discovery. [Middle English *finden*, from Old English *findan*.]

Syns: find, locate, pinpoint, spot *v.* *Core meaning:* To look for and discover (*helped me find the misprints*).

find·er (fīn'dər) *n.* **1.** Someone or something that finds. **2.** A lens on a camera that shows what will appear in a photograph. **3.** *Astron.* A small telescope attached to a larger one to aid in locating an object.

fin de siè·cle (făN' də sē-ĕk'lə). *French.* Of or characteristic of the sophistication and decadence that marked the last part of the 19th cent. [French, "end of the century."]

find·ing (fīn'dĭng) *n.* **1.** The act or an example of discovering. **2. findings.** The results or conclusions of an investigation. **3. findings.** Small articles used in a craft or trade.

fine¹ (fīn) *adj.* **fin·er, fin·est. 1.** Consisting of small particles; not coarse. **2.** Very small in bulk, weight, or size. **3.** Very thin or sharp: *a fine edge.* **4.** Of delicate texture: *fine skin.* **5. a.** Delicately exacting and painstaking. **b.** Marked by refinement and delicacy of workmanship. **6.** Subtle or precise: *a fine shade of meaning.* **7.** Characterized by refinement and elegance: *fine manners.* **8.** Of superior quality, skill, or appearance; admirable; splendid: *a fine day.* **9.** In good health; quite well. **10. a.** Free from foreign matter; pure. **b.** Containing pure metal in a specified proportion or amount: *gold 21 carats fine.* —*interj.* A word used to indicate agreement or acquiescence: *How about taking in a movie? Fine!* —*adv.* **1.** Finely. **2.** Very well; splendidly: *The two of us are getting along just fine.* [Middle English *fin*, from Old French, from Latin *fīnis*, limit, end.] **—fine'ly** *adv.* **—fine'ness** *n.*

fine² (fīn) *n.* A sum of money imposed as a penalty for an offense. —*tr.v.* **fined, fin·ing.** To impose a fine on. [Middle English *fin*, a fine, a payment for completion, from Old French, from Latin *fīnis*, limit, end.]

fi·ne³ (fē'nā') *n. Mus.* The end.

fine arts. The arts of painting, sculpture, and architecture, esp. as presented in an academic curriculum.

fine-drawn (fīn'drôn') *adj.* Drawn to the finest subtlety; extremely fine: *a fine-drawn analysis.*

fine-grained (fīn'grānd') *adj.* Having a fine, smooth grain, as leather or wood.

fin·er·y (fī'nə-rē) *n., pl.* **-ies.** Fine or fancy clothes and ornaments. [From FINE (excellent).]

fi·nesse (fĭ-nĕs') *n.* **1.** Delicacy and refinement of performance or execution: *played the nocturne with finesse.* **2.** Subtlety; tact: *show finesse in handling the situation.* **3.** *Bridge.* The playing of a card in a suit in which one holds a nonsequential higher card to try to win the trick economically. —*v.* **-nessed, -ness·ing.** —*tr.v.* **1.** To accomplish by the use of finesse. **2.** *Bridge.* To play (a card) as a finesse. —*intr.v. Bridge.* To make a finesse. [Old French, delicacy, fineness, from *fin*, fine.]

fin·ger (fĭng'gər) *n.* **1.** Any of the five digits that extend outward from the hand. **2.** The part of a glove that fits over a finger. **3.** Something resembling a finger. **4.** The length or width of a finger. —*tr.v.* **1.** *Mus.* To play (an instrument) by using the fingers in a particular order. **2.** To handle or feel with the fingers; touch. **3.** *Slang.* To inform on. **4.** *Slang.* To designate as an intended victim. —*intr.v.* To handle something with the fingers. **—idioms. keep (one's) fingers crossed.** To hope for the best while watching out for the worst. **put (one's) finger on.** To pin down or define. [Middle English, from Old English.] **—fin'ger·er** *n.*

fin·ger·board (fĭng'gər-bôrd', -bōrd') *n. Mus.* A strip of wood on the neck of a stringed instrument against which the strings are pressed in playing.

finger bowl. A small bowl to hold water for rinsing the fingers at the table after a meal.

fin·ger·ing (fĭng'gər-ĭng) *n. Mus.* **1.** The use of or technique of using the fingers in playing an instrument. **2.** Symbols that indicate which fingers are to be used in playing.

fin·ger·ling (fĭng'gər-lĭng) *n.* A young or small fish, such as a young salmon or trout.

fin·ger·nail (fĭng'gər-nāl') *n.* The thin sheet of horny, transparent material that covers a fingertip.

finger painting. 1. The technique of painting by applying color to moistened paper with the fingers. **2.** A painting so made.

fin·ger·print (fĭng'gər-prĭnt') *n.* An impression formed by the curves in the ridges of the skin that covers the tip of the fingers, used as a way of identifying people. —*tr.v.* To take the fingerprints of.

fin·ger·tip (fĭng'gər-tĭp') *n.* Also **finger tip.** The extreme end or tip of a finger.

fin·i·al (fĭn'ē-əl) *n.* **1.** *Archit.* An ornament fixed to the peak of an arch or arched structure. **2.** Any ornamental terminating part, such as the screw on top of a lampshade. [Middle English, var. of *final,* final.]

fin·i·cal (fĭn'ĭ-kəl) *adj.* Fastidious; finicky. [Prob. from *fine,* delicate.] —**fin'i·cal·ly** *adv.*

fin·ick·y (fĭn'ĭ-kē) *adj.* Difficult to please; very fussy. [From FINICAL.] —**fin'ick·i·ness** *n.*

fi·nis (fĭn'ĭs, fī'nĭs) *n.* The end. [Middle English, from Latin *fīnis.*]

fin·ish (fĭn'ĭsh) *tr.v.* **1.** To reach the end of: *finish a race.* **2.** To bring to an end; terminate: *finish cleaning the room.* **3.** To consume all of; use up: *finish a meal.* **4.** To kill, destroy, or wear out completely: *The crash finished him.* **5.** To put the final touches on; perfect: *finish a painting.* **6.** To give (a surface) a desired texture. —*intr.v.* **1.** To come to an end; stop. **2.** To reach the end of a task, course, relationship, etc.—See Syns at **destroy, end,** and **kill.** —*n.* **1.** The conclusion of something; the end: *a close finish in the election; carry it off to the finish.* **2. a.** The last treatment or coating of a surface. **b.** The surface texture produced. **3.** Smoothness of execution; perfection. **4.** Polish or refinement in speech, manners, etc. [Middle English *finishen,* from Old French *finir,* from Latin *fīnīre,* to limit, complete, from *fīnis,* end.] —**fin'ish·er** *n.*

finishing school. A private school where girls finish their education and are prepared for their entrance into society.

fi·nite (fī'nīt') *adj.* **1.** Having bounds; not infinite; limited. **2.** *Math.* **a.** Having a magnitude that is less than or equal to that of some number that can be reached by counting: *a finite sum.* **b.** Having a finite number as its measure: *a finite region.* **3.** *Gram.* Limited by person, number, and tense; for example, *am* and *is,* are finite verb forms as distinguished from *being.* [Middle English *finit,* from Latin *fīnītus,* past part. of *fīnīre,* to limit, finish.] —**fi'nite·ly** *adv.* —**fi'nite·ness** *n.*

fink (fĭngk) *Slang.* —*n.* **1.** A person who informs against another. **2.** An undesirable person. —*intr.v.* To inform against another. [Orig. unknown.]

Finn (fĭn) *n.* **1.** A native or inhabitant of Finland. **2.** One who speaks Finnish.

fin·nan had·die (fĭn'ən hăd'ē). Smoked haddock. [Earlier *findon haddock,* from earlier *findhorn haddock,* product of *Findhorn,* a fishing port in Scotland.]

Finn·ish (fĭn'ĭsh) *adj.* Of or pertaining to Finland, its language, or its people. —*n.* The language of the Finns.

Fin·no-U·gric (fĭn'ō-ōō'grĭk, -yōō'-) *n.* A subfamily of the Uralic language group, including Finnish and Hungarian. —**Fin'no-U'gric** *adj.*

fin·ny (fĭn'ē) *adj.* **-ni·er, -ni·est. 1.** Having or resembling a fin or fins. **2.** Of or pertaining to fish.

fiord (fyôrd, fyōrd) *n.* Var. of **fjord.**

fir (fûr) *n.* **1.** Any of various evergreen trees of the genus *Abies,* with flat needles and erect cones. **2.** Any of several similar or related trees. **3.** The wood of any of these trees. [Middle English *fir(re),* from Old English *fyrh.*]

fire (fīr) *n.* **1.** A rapid, self-sustaining chemical reaction that releases light and heat, esp. the burning of something with oxygen. **2.** A destructive burning: *insured his house against fire.* **3.** Great enthusiasm; ardor. **4.** Luminosity or brilliance, as of a cut and polished gemstone. **5.** The discharge of a gun or guns: *artillery fire.* —See Syns at **passion.** —*v.* **fired, fir·ing.** —*tr.v.* **1.** To cause to burn; ignite. **2. a.** To add fuel to (something burning). **b.** To maintain or intensify a fire in. **3.** To bake in a kiln: *fire a flowerpot.* **4.** To arouse the emotions of; make enthusiastic or ardent: *He was fired by patriotism.* **5.** To detonate or discharge (a firearm, explosives, or a projectile): *fire a rifle.* **6.** *Informal.* To project or hurl suddenly and forcefully: *fire a ball.* **7.** *Informal.* To discharge from a job; dismiss. —*intr.v.* **1.** To become ignited; flame up. **2.** To discharge; go off:

The mortar fired toward the enemy. **3.** To detonate or shoot a weapon: *He fired at the enemy.* —*idioms.* **catch fire. 1.** To become ignited. **2.** To become excited or enthusiastic. **hang fire. 1.** To fail to fire or to delay firing, as a gun. **2.** To be delayed, as an event or decision. **on fire. 1.** Ignited; burning; ablaze. **2.** Filled with enthusiasm or excitement. **open fire. 1.** To begin shooting. **2.** To begin asking questions. **play with fire.** To take part in a dangerous or risky situation; be foolhardy. **under fire. 1.** Exposed or subjected to enemy attack. **2.** Exposed or subjected to critical attack or censure. [Middle English, from Old English *fȳr.*]

fire·arm (fīr'ärm') *n.* Any weapon capable of firing a missile, esp. a pistol or rifle using an explosive charge as a propellant.

fire·ball (fīr'bôl') *n.* **1.** Any brilliantly burning sphere. **2.** An exceptionally bright meteor. **3.** A highly luminous, intensely hot spherical cloud of dust, gas, and vapor generated by a nuclear explosion.

fire·boat (fīr'bōt') *n.* A boat equipped to fight fires along waterfronts and on ships.

fireboat

fire·box (fīr'bŏks') *n.* **1.** A chamber, as a furnace, in which fuel is burned. **2.** A box containing a device for sending an alarm to a fire station.

fire·brand (fīr'brănd') *n.* **1.** A piece of burning wood. **2.** A person who stirs up trouble or kindles a revolt.

fire·break (fīr'brāk') *n.* A strip of cleared or plowed land used to stop the spread of a fire.

fire·brick (fīr'brĭk') *n.* A brick made of fire clay, used for lining furnaces, chimneys, or fireplaces.

fire·bug (fīr'bŭg') *n. Informal.* A person who deliberately sets fires to property; a pyromaniac.

fire clay. A type of heat-resistant clay used esp. in the making of firebricks and crucibles.

fire·crack·er (fīr'krăk'ər) *n.* A small explosive charge in a cylinder of heavy paper, used to make noise, as at celebrations.

fire·damp (fīr'dămp') *n.* A gas, chiefly methane, that occurs naturally in coal mines and forms an explosive mixture with air.

fire drill. A practice exercise in the use of fire-fighting equipment or the exit procedure to be followed in case of a fire.

fire engine. Any of various large trucks that carry fire-fighters and equipment to a fire.

fire escape. A ladder or outside stairway for emergency exit in the event of fire.

fire extinguisher. A portable apparatus containing chemicals that can be sprayed to extinguish a fire.

fire·fight·er (fīr'fī'tər) *n.* A person who fights fires, esp. for a living.

fire·fly (fīr'flī') *n.* Any of various nocturnal beetles of the family Lampyridae, with luminous abdominal organs that produce a flashing light.

fire·house (fīr'hous') *n.* A **fire station.**

fire irons. The equipment used to tend a fireplace, including a shovel, a poker, and tongs.

fire·light (fīr'līt') *n.* The light from a fire, as in a fireplace or at a campsite.

fire·man (fīr'mən) *n.* **1.** A man employed by a fire department to fight fires. **2.** A man who tends fires; a stoker. **3.** *U.S. Navy.* An enlisted man engaged in the operation of the engineering machinery.

fire·place (fīr'plās') *n.* An open recess for holding a fire at the base of a chimney; hearth.

fire·plug (fīr'plŭg') *n.* A large pipe at which water may be drawn for use in extinguishing a fire; a hydrant.

fire·pow·er (fīr′pou′ər) n. The capacity, as of a weapon, a military unit, or a ship, for discharging fire.

fire·proof (fīr′prōōf′) adj. Capable of withstanding or preventing damage by fire. —tr.v. To make fireproof.

fire sale. A sale of commodities damaged by fire.

fire screen. A metal screen placed in front of an open fireplace to catch sparks.

fire·side (fīr′sīd′) n. **1.** The area immediately around a fireplace or hearth. **2.** Home.

fire station. A building for fire equipment and firefighters. Also called **firehouse.**

fire tower. A tower in which a lookout for fires is posted, usu. in a forest.

fire·trap (fīr′trăp′) n. A building likely to catch fire easily or difficult to escape from in the event of fire.

fire wall. A fireproof wall used in buildings and machinery to prevent the spread of a fire.

fire·wa·ter (fīr′wô′tər, -wŏt′ər) n. Slang. Strong liquor.

fire·weed (fīr′wēd′) n. **1.** A species of willow herb, *Epilobium angustifolium*, with clusters of pinkish-purple flowers. **2.** A weedy North American plant, *Erechtites hieracifolia*, with small white or greenish flowers.

fire·wood (fīr′wōōd′) n. Wood used as fuel.

fire·works (fīr′wûrks′) pl.n. **1. a.** Explosives and combustibles used to produce lights, smoke, and noise for entertainment. **b.** A display of fireworks. **2.** An exciting or dramatic display: *musical fireworks.*

firing line. 1. The line of positions from which gunfire is directed against a target. **2.** The foremost position of an activity or pursuit.

firing pin. The part of the bolt of a firearm that strikes the primer and explodes the charge of the projectile.

firing squad. 1. A detachment assigned to shoot persons condemned to death. **2.** A detachment of soldiers chosen to fire a salute at a military funeral.

fir·kin (fûr′kĭn) n. **1.** A small wooden barrel or keg used esp. for storing butter, cheese, or lard. **2.** Any of several Brit. units of capacity, usu. equal to about 34 liters, ¹/₄ of a barrel, or nine gallons. [Middle English *ferken*, a cask, one-fourth of a barrel.]

firm¹ (fûrm) adj. **-er, -est. 1.** Unyielding to pressure; solid: *firm ground.* **2.** Exhibiting the tone and resiliency characteristic of healthy tissue: *firm muscles.* **3.** Securely fixed in place: *firm building supports.* **4.** Constant and steady: *a firm rapport.* **5.** Not changing; fixed: *a firm belief.* **6.** Strong and sure: *a firm grasp.* **7.** Showing or having resolution or determination: *a firm voice.* —See Syns at **faithful** and **hard.** —adv. Without wavering; resolutely: *The enemy stood firm and refused to surrender.* —tr.v. To make firm. —intr.v. To become firm. [Middle English *ferm*, from Old French *ferme*, from Latin *firmus.*] —**firm′ly** adv. —**firm′ness** n.

firm² (fûrm) n. **1.** A commercial partnership of two or more persons. **2.** The name or title under which such a partnership transacts business. [Italian *firma*, signature, name of a business establishment or partnership, from *firmare*, to sign, "confirm by signature," from Late Latin *firmāre*, to confirm, from Latin, to strengthen, from *firmus*, firm.]

fir·ma·ment (fûr′mə-mənt) n. The expanse of the heavens; sky. [Middle English, from Old French, from Late Latin *firmāmentum*, from Latin, support, from *firmāre*, to make firm, from *firmus*, firm.]

first (fûrst) adj. **1.** Corresponding in order to the number one. **2.** Coming before all others in time, order, rank, importance, etc.: *the first chapter.* **3.** Highest in pitch or having the principal musical part: *first trumpet.* **4.** Of the transmission gear that produces the lowest speeds in an automobile. —n. **1.** In a set of items arranged to match the natural numbers in a one-to-one correspondence, the item that matches the number one. **2.** The beginning; outset: *At first I disliked the idea.* **3.** The first of a specified kind: *an aviation first.* **4.** The member of a set of similar voices or musical instruments that is highest in pitch or has the principal part. **5.** The transmission gear in an automobile that produces the lowest speeds. **6.** The winning position in a contest. —adv. **1.** Before or above all others in time, order, rank, importance, etc.: *Who will speak first?* **2.** For the first time: *When did you first meet Mr.*

Jones? **3.** Before some other specified or implied time: *First finish your work, then you may go.* **4.** In preference; rather: *He said he would quit first.* [Middle English, from Old English *fyrst.*]

Syns: first, initial, maiden, original, prime *adj.* Core meaning: Preceding all others in time (*America's first space flight*). See also Syns at **early** and **primary.**

first aid. Emergency treatment administered to injured or sick persons.

first base. 1. *Baseball.* **a.** The first of the bases in the infield, counterclockwise from home plate. **b.** The fielding position occupied by the first baseman. **2.** *Informal.* The first step in a project involving several steps: *The reform bill never got to first base.*

first baseman. *Baseball.* The infielder stationed at or near first base.

first-born (fûrst′bôrn′) adj. First in order of birth; born first. —n. The first-born child.

first class. 1. The first, highest, or best group of a specified category. **2.** The most luxurious and most expensive class of accommodations on a train, ship, plane, etc. **3.** A class of mail including letters, post cards, and packages sealed against inspection.

first-class (fûrst′klăs′) adj. **1.** Indicating the first, highest, or best group of a specified category: *first-class tickets.* **2.** Of the foremost excellence or highest quality; first-rate: *a first-class mind.* —See Syns at **excellent.** —**first′class′** adv.

first·hand (fûrst′hănd′) adj. Received from the original source: *firsthand information.* —**first′hand′** adv.

first lady. 1. Often **First Lady.** The wife or hostess of the chief executive of a country, state, or city. **2.** The foremost woman of a specified profession or art.

first lieutenant. An officer in the Army, Air Force, and Marine Corps ranking above a second lieutenant and below a captain.

first·ling (fûrst′lĭng) n. **1.** The first of a kind or category. **2.** The first-born offspring.

first·ly (fûrst′lē) adv. To begin with.

first mate. A ship's officer ranking immediately below the captain.

first person. 1. a. A set of grammatical forms designating the speaker or writer of the sentence in which they appear. **b.** One of the forms of this set. **2.** A style of narration in which forms in the first person are used: *a novel written in the first person.*

first-rate (fûrst′rāt′) adj. **1.** Foremost in importance or rank: *a first-rate hotel.* **2.** Foremost in quality: *a first-rate mechanic.* —**first′rate′** adv.

first sergeant. In the U.S. Army, the highest-ranking non-commissioned officer of a company or other military unit.

first-string (fûrst′strĭng′) adj. Being a regular performer as distinguished from a substitute, esp. in sports.

first water. 1. The highest degree of quality or purity in diamonds or pearls. **2.** The foremost rank or quality: *a pianist of the first water.*

firth (fûrth) n. A long, narrow inlet of the sea; fjord. [Middle English *furth*, from Old Norse *fjördhr.*]

fis·cal (fĭs′kəl) adj. **1.** Of or pertaining to the treasury or finances of a nation or branch of government. **2.** Of or pertaining to finances in general. [Old French, from Latin *fiscālis*, from *fiscus*, treasury, basket.] —**fis′cal·ly** adv.

fiscal year. A 12-month period for which an organization plans the use of its funds.

fish (fĭsh) n., pl. **fish** or **fish·es. 1.** Any of numerous cold-blooded aquatic vertebrates of the superclass Pisces, characteristically having fins, gills, and a streamlined body. **2.** The flesh of a fish, used as food. **3.** *Informal.* A person: *a poor fish.* —intr.v. **1.** To catch or try to catch fish. **2.** To look for something by feeling one's way; grope. **3.** To seek something in a sly or indirect way: *fish for compliments.* —tr.v. **1.** To catch or try to catch fish in: *fish a river.* **2.** To pull in the manner of one who fishes: *fished the keys out of her purse.* [Middle English, from Old English *fisc.*]

fish and chips. Fried fillets of fish and French-fried potatoes.

fish·bowl (fĭsh′bōl′) n. **1.** A transparent bowl in which live fish are kept. **2.** An activity or position that operates under or is open to public view.

fish·er (fĭsh′ər) n. **1.** Someone or something that fishes. **2. a.** A carnivorous mammal, *Martes pennanti*, of northern North America, with thick, dark-brown fur. **b.** The fur of this animal.

fish·er·man (fĭsh′ər-mən) n. **1.** Someone who fishes as an occupation or sport. **2.** A commercial fishing vessel.

fish·er·y (fĭsh′ə-rē) n., pl. **-ies. 1.** The industry or occupation of catching, processing, or selling fish or similar aquatic products. **2.** A fishing ground.

fish·hook (fĭsh′hŏŏk′) n. A barbed metal hook used for catching fish.

fish·ing (fĭsh′ĭng) n. The act or practice of catching fish.

fishing rod. A rod used with a line for catching fish.

fishing tackle. Equipment used for catching fish.

fish ladder. A series of pools of water arranged like steps by which fish can pass around or over a dam in moving upstream.

fish·meal (fĭsh′mēl′) n. Ground, dried fish, used as animal feed and fertilizer.

fish·mon·ger (fĭsh′mŭng′gər, -mŏng′-) n. *Brit.* A dealer in fish.

fish·net (fĭsh′nĕt′) n. **1.** A net for catching fish. **2.** A mesh fabric resembling netting used for catching fish.

fish·plate (fĭsh′plāt′) n. A metal plate used to fasten two rails or beams placed end to end, used esp. on railroad tracks. [Earlier *fish*, a piece of wood used to strengthen a ship's mast, fishplate, prob. from Old French *fiche*, peg, nail, joint, from *ficher*, to drive in, fix, from Latin *fīgere*, to fasten, fix + PLATE.]

fish·pond (fĭsh′pŏnd′) n. A pond stocked with edible fish.

fish stick. An oblong, breaded piece of fish fillet.

fish story. *Informal.* An implausible and boastful story. [From stories of fishermen who exaggerate the size of their catch.]

fish·tail (fĭsh′tāl′) adj. Resembling or suggestive of the tail of a fish in shape or movement. —*intr.v.* *Slang.* To swing uncontrollably from side to side.

fish·wife (fĭsh′wīf′) n. **1.** A woman who sells fish. **2.** A coarse, abusive woman; shrew.

fish·y (fĭsh′ē) adj. **-i·er, -i·est. 1.** Resembling or suggestive of fish, esp. in taste or smell. **2.** Of a suspicious or questionable nature: *a fishy excuse.*

fis·sile (fĭs′əl, -īl′) adj. **1.** Capable of being split. **2.** *Physics.* Fissionable, esp. by neutrons of all energies. [Latin *fissilis*, from *fissus*, split.] —**fis·sil′i·ty** (fĭ-sĭl′ĭ-tē) n.

fis·sion (fĭsh′ən) n. **1.** The act or process of splitting into parts. **2.** *Physics.* A nuclear reaction in which an atomic nucleus splits into fragments, usu. two fragments of comparable mass, with the evolution of approximately 100 million to several hundred million electron volts of energy. Also called **nuclear fission. 3.** *Biol.* An asexual reproductive process in which a single cell splits into two or more independent cells. [Latin *fissiō*, from *fissus*, past part. of *findere*, to split.]

fis·sion·a·ble (fĭsh′ə-nə-bəl) adj. Capable of undergoing fission, esp. nuclear fission. —**fis′sion·a·bil′i·ty** n.

fis·sure (fĭsh′ər) n. A narrow crack, usu. of considerable size. —v. **-sured, -sur·ing.** —*tr.v.* To cause a fissure in. —*intr.v.* To form fissures; crack. [Middle English *fissure*, fracture, opening, from Old French, from Latin *fissūra*, from *fissus*, split.]

fist (fĭst) n. **1.** The hand closed tightly, with the fingers bent against the palm. **2.** *Informal.* Grasp; clutch. **3.** *Printing.* An index. [Middle English, from Old English *fȳst*.]

fist·ful (fĭst′fŏŏl′) n. A handful.

fist·ic (fĭs′tĭk) adj. Of or pertaining to boxing.

fist·i·cuffs (fĭs′tĭ-kŭfs′) pl.n. A fist fight. [Earlier *fisty cuff*: *fisty*, from FIST + CUFF (a blow).]

fis·tu·la (fĭs′chŏŏ-lə, -chə-) n., pl. **-las** or **-lae** (-lē′). An abnormal duct or passage from an abscess, cavity, or hollow organ to the surface of the body or to another hollow organ. [Middle English, from Latin *fistula*, pipe, tube, fistula.] —**fis′tu·lous** adj.

fit¹ (fĭt) v. **fit·ted** or **fit, fit·ting.** —*tr.v.* **1.** To be the proper size and shape for: *The shoes fit me.* **2.** To be appropriate or suitable to; be in keeping with: *undignified behavior that does not fit his high position.* **3.** To be in conformity or agreement with: *observations which fit in nicely with my theory.* **4.** To make suitable; adjust. **5.** To make ready; prepare: *Specialized training fitted her for the job.* **6.** To equip; outfit: *fit out a ship.* **7.** To provide a place or time for: *The doctor can fit you in this afternoon.* **8.** To insert or adjust so as to be properly in place: *fit a handle on a door.* —*intr.v.* **1.** To be the proper size and shape: *The hat fits.* **2.** To be suited; belong: *I don't fit in with these people.* **3.** To be in harmony; agree: *Her good mood fit in with the joyful occasion.* —adj. **fit·ter, fit·test. 1.** Suited, adapted, or acceptable for a given circumstance or purpose: *not a fit time for discussion.* **2.** Appropriate; proper: *Do as you see fit.* **3.** Physically sound; healthy: *keep fit.* —See Syns at **healthy** and **convenient.**—n. The manner in which something fits: *a good fit.* [Middle English *fit*, suitable, appropriate.] —**fit′ly** adv. —**fit′ness** n. —**fit′ter** n.

Usage: fit. The past tense and past participle of this verb is *fitted* or *fit.* Both forms are standard although regional and social preferences prevail. In the United States, *fit* is used more often than *fitted* for the past tense: *The punishment fit the crime. That suit fit me well last year.* In the United States, *fitted* is the more common form for the past tense and the past participle when the verb means to make suitable: *The equipment was fitted to their needs. The training fitted her for the ordeal. They fitted him out for the journey. Fitted* is required when the sense is to measure, adjust, or tailor (clothing): *The seamstress fitted my wedding gown. I was fitted for a suit.*

fit² (fĭt) n. **1. a.** A sudden, acute attack of a disease or disorder. **b.** A convulsion. **2.** A sudden outburst: *a fit of rage and jealousy.* **3.** A sudden period of vigorous activity. —**idiom. by (or in) fits and starts.** Irregularly; intermittently. [Middle English *fit*, hardship, painful experience, from Old English *fitt*, conflict.]

fitch (fĭch) n. The fur of the Old World polecat. [Middle English *fiche*, prob. from *ficheux*, polecat.]

fit·ful (fĭt′fəl) adj. Intermittent; irregular: *fitful sleep.* —**fit′ful·ly** adv. —**fit′ful·ness** n.

fit·ting (fĭt′ĭng) n. **1.** The act of trying on clothes for fit. **2.** A small accessory part: *a pipe fitting.* —adj. Suitable; appropriate. —**fit′ting·ly** adv. —**fit′ting·ness** n.

five (fīv) n. **1.** The cardinal number written 5 or in Roman numerals V, equal to the sum of 4 + 1. **2.** The fifth in a set or sequence. **3.** Something having five parts, units, or members, esp. a basketball team. [Middle English, from Old English *fīf*.] —**five** adj. & pron.

five-and-ten-cent store (fīv′ən-tĕn′sĕnt′). A variety store selling inexpensive commodities.

Five-Year Plan (fīv′yîr′). A program for economic development over a five-year period.

fix (fĭks) tr.v. **1.** To place or fasten securely: *fix a pole in the ground.* **2.** To direct or hold steadily: *fixed his sights on the target.* **3.** To set or establish definitely: *fix a time; fix the blame.* **4.** To set right; repair. **5.** To make ready; prepare: *fix a snack.* **6.** To put in order; arrange: *She's fixing her hair.* **7.** To spay or castrate. **8.** *Biol.* To convert (nitrogen) into stable compounds that can be assimilated by living organisms. **9.** To kill and mount for microscopic study. **10.** To prevent discoloration of (a photographic image) by treating with a chemical preservative. **11.** *Informal.* To get even with: *I'll fix her.* **12.** To influence by unlawful means: *fix a horse race.* —*intr.v.* To become stable, attached, or firm. —See Syns at **attach.** —n. **1.** A difficult or embarrassing position: *I'm in a real fix.* **2.** The position, as of a ship or aircraft, as determined by observations or radio. **3.** *Slang.* A dose of a narcotic. [Middle English *fixen*, ult. from Latin *fīxus*, past part. of *fīgere*, to fasten.] —**fix′a·ble** adj. —**fix′er** n.

fix·ate (fĭk′sāt′) v. **-at·ed, -at·ing.** —*tr.v.* **1.** To make fixed. **2.** To focus the eyes or the attention on. —*intr.v.* To focus or concentrate the eyes or the attention.

fix·a·tion (fĭk-sā′shən) n. **1.** The act or process of fixing or fixating. **2.** A strong, usu. unhealthy attachment or interest.

fix·a·tive (fĭk′sə-tĭv) n. A substance used to fix or stabilize. —**fix′a·tive** adj.

fixed (fĭkst) adj. **1.** Firmly in position; stationary. **2.** Not subject to change or variation; constant. **3.** Firmly held in the mind: *a fixed notion.* **4.** *Chem.* **a.** Nonvolatile: *fixed oils.* **b.** In a stable combined form. —**fix′ed·ly** (fĭk′sĭd-lē) adv. —**fix′ed·ness** (-sĭd-nĭs) n.

ă pat	ā pay	â care	ä father	ĕ pet	ē be	hw which
ĭ pit	ī tie	î pier	ŏ pot	ō toe	ô paw, for	oi noise
ōŏ took	ōō boot	ou out	th thin	th this	ŭ cut	
û urge	zh vision	ə about, item, edible, gallop, circus				

fixed star. A star so distant that it seems to stay in the same position with respect to other stars.

fix·ings (fĭk′sĭngz) *pl.n. Informal.* Accessories; trimmings: *a big meal with all the fixings.*

fix·i·ty (fĭk′sĭ-tē) *n., pl.* **-ties.** The quality or condition of being fixed; stability.

fix·ture (fĭks′chər) *n.* **1.** Something installed or fixed as a part of a larger system: *a plumbing fixture.* **2.** Someone or something considered to be permanently established or fixed. [Var. of obs. *fixure,* from Late Latin *fixūra,* from Latin *fixus,* fixed.]

fizz (fĭz) *intr.v.* To make a hissing or bubbling sound. —*n.* A hissing or bubbling sound. [Imit.]

fiz·zle (fĭz′əl) *intr.v.* **-zled, -zling. 1.** To make a hissing or sputtering sound. **2.** *Informal.* To fail or die out, esp. after a hopeful beginning. —*n. Informal.* A failure. [Prob. from obs. *fist,* to break wind.]

fjord or **fiord** (fyôrd, fyōrd) *n.* A long, narrow, often deep inlet of the sea between steep cliffs and slopes. [Norwegian, from Old Norse *fjördhr.*]

fjord

flab·ber·gast (flăb′ər-găst′) *tr.v.* To overwhelm with astonishment; astound. [Orig. unknown.]

flab·by (flăb′ē) *adj.* **-bi·er, -bi·est. 1.** Lacking firmness; loose and soft. **2.** Lacking force or vitality; feeble; ineffectual. [Var. of *flappy,* from *flap.*] —**flab′bi·ly** *adv.* —**flab′bi·ness** *n.*

flac·cid (flăk′sĭd, flăs′ĭd) *adj.* Lacking firmness; soft and limp [French *flaccide,* from Latin *flaccidus,* from *flaccus,* hanging, flabby.] —**flac·cid′i·ty** *n.* —**flac′cid·ly** *adv.*

flac·on (flăk′ən, -ŏn′) *n.* A small stoppered bottle. [French, from Old French *fla(s)con,* flagon.]

flag¹ (flăg) *n.* **1.** A piece of cloth of individual size, color, and design, used as a symbol, signal, or emblem. **2.** *Mus.* A cross stroke on a note of less than a quarter note in value. —*tr.v.* **flagged, flag·ging. 1.** To place on a flag. **2.** To signal or communicate with or as if with a flag. [Orig. Unknown.]

flag² (flăg) *n.* Any of various plants having long bladelike leaves, such as an iris or cattail. [Middle English *flagge,* rush, reed.]

flag³ (flăg) *intr.v.* **flagged, flag·ging. 1.** To hang limply; droop. **2.** To decline in vigor or strength; weaken. [Orig. unknown.]

flag⁴ (flăg) *n.* Flagstone. —*tr.v.* **flagged, flag·ging.** To pave with flags. [Middle English *flagge,* piece of turf, sod, prob. from Old Norse *flaga,* slab of stone.]

Flag Day. June 14, an annual holiday celebrating the adoption in 1777 of the official U.S. flag.

flag·el·lant (flăj′ə-lənt, flə-jĕl′ənt) *n.* A person who whips, esp. one who whips himself as a penance. [Latin *flagelliāns,* pres. part. of *flagellāre,* to flagellate.]

flag·el·late (flăj′ə-lāt′) *tr.v.* **-lat·ed, -lat·ing.** To whip or flog; scourge. —*adj.* **1.** Having flagella, as one-celled organisms of the class Flagellata or Magistophora. **2.** Resembling or having the form of a flagellum; whiplike. [From Latin *flagellāre,* to whip, scourge, from *flagellum,* small whip, dim. of *flagrum,* whip.] —**flag′el·la′tion** *n.*

fla·gel·lum (flə-jĕl′əm) *n., pl.* **-gel·la** (-jĕl′ə). *Biol.* A long, whiplike strand or extension, esp. one in certain cells or one-celled organisms that functions as an organ of locomotion. [Latin, small whip.]

flag·eo·let (flăj′ə-lĕt′, -lā′) *n.* A small flutelike instrument with a cylindrical mouthpiece, four finger holes, and two thumb holes. [French, dim. of Old French *flajol,* ult. from Latin *flāre,* to blow.]

flag·ging (flăg′ĭng) *n.* A pavement laid with flagstones.

fla·gi·tious (flə-jĭsh′əs) *adj.* Guilty of shocking or cruel crimes; vicious. [Middle English *flagicious,* from Latin *flāgitiōsus,* from *flāgitium,* noisy protest, scandal, shameful act, from *flāgitāre,* to demand fiercely.] —**fla·gi′tious·ly** *adv.* —**fla·gi′tious·ness** *n.*

flag·man (flăg′mən) *n.* A person who signals with or carries a flag.

flag officer. A naval officer holding the rank of commodore, rear admiral, vice admiral, or admiral.

flag·on (flăg′ən) *n.* A vessel for liquids that has a handle and spout. [Middle English *flagon, flakon,* from Old French *fla(s)con,* from Late Latin *flascō,* bottle, flask.]

flag·pole (flăg′pōl′) *n.* A pole for displaying a flag.

fla·grant (flā′grənt) *adj.* Outstandingly and conspicuously bad; shocking: *a flagrant miscarriage of justice.* —See Usage note at **blatant.** [Latin *flagrāns,* pres. part. of *flagrāre,* to burn, blaze.] —**fla′gran·cy** *n.* —**fla′grant·ly** *adv.*

flag·ship (flăg′shĭp′) *n.* **1.** A ship bearing the flag of a fleet or squadron commander. **2.** The largest or most important of a group.

flag·staff (flăg′stăf′) *n.* A flagpole.

flag·stone (flăg′stōn′) *n.* A flat, fine-grained, hard, evenly layered stone used esp. in paving; flag. [FLAG (stone) + STONE.]

flail (flāl) *n.* A tool for threshing grain, consisting of a long wooden handle and a free-swinging stick attached to its end. —*tr.v.* To beat with or as with a flail. —*intr.v.* To thrash; wave. [Middle English, ult. from Latin *flagellum,* dim. of *flagrum,* whip.]

flair (flâr) *n.* **1.** A natural talent or aptitude: *a flair for interior decorating.* **2.** Instinctive discernment; keenness. [French, "sense of smell," from Old French, from *flairer,* to emit an odor, to scent, smell, from Latin *frāgrāre,* to emit a smell.]

flak (flăk) *n.* **1. a.** Antiaircraft artillery. **b.** The bursting shells fired from such artillery. **2.** *Slang.* Excessive criticism. [German *Flak,* short for *Fl(ieger)a(bwehr)k(anone),* "aircraft defense gun."]

flake (flāk) *n.* A flat, thin piece: *a flake of snow; plaster flakes.* —*intr.v.* **flaked, flak·ing.** To come off in flakes; chip off: *The paint is flaking.* [Middle English *flake,* of Scandinavian orig.] —**flak′er** *n.*

flak·y (flā′kē) *adj.* **-i·er, -i·est. 1.** Made of or resembling flakes. **2.** Forming or tending to form flakes. —**flak′i·ness** *n.*

flam·beau (flăm′bō′) *n., pl.* **-beaux** (-bōz′) or **-beaus.** A lighted torch. [French, from Old French, from *flambe, flamble,* "small flame," from Latin *flammula,* dim. of *flamma,* flame.]

flam·boy·ant (flăm-boi′ənt) *adj.* **1.** Highly elaborate; ornate. **2.** Exaggerated or high-flown in style or manner; showy: *a flamboyant actor.* **3.** Richly colored; vivid: *a flamboyant costume.* [French, from Old French, pres. part. of *flamboyer,* to blaze, from *flambe,* small flame.] —**flam·boy′ance** or **flam·boy′an·cy** *n.* —**flam·boy′ant·ly** *adv.*

flame (flām) *n.* **1.** The often bright zone of burning gases and fine suspended particles that forms as a result of fire. **2.** A condition of active combustion: *burst into flames.* **3.** Something flamelike in motion, brilliance, intensity, or shape. **4.** A violent or intense passion: *the spreading flames of hate.* **5.** *Informal.* A sweetheart. —*intr.v.* **flamed, flam·ing. 1.** To burn with a flame; blaze. **2.** To have a flamelike color: *Her cheeks flamed with embarrassment.* **3.** To break out passionately: *flaming with jealousy.* —*tr.v.* To treat with or subject to flame. [Middle English *flaume, flam(m)e,* from Old French *flam(m)e,* from Latin *flamma.*]

fla·men·co (flə-mĕng′kō) *n.* A dance style of the Andalusian Gypsies characterized by forceful often improvised rhythms. [Spanish *flamenco,* Gypsy Flemish, from Middle Dutch *Vlāming,* Fleming.]

flame·out (flām′out′) *n.* The failure of a jet aircraft engine in flight.

flame thrower. A weapon that projects burning fuel in a steady stream.

flam·ing (flā′mĭng) *adj.* **1.** On fire; in flames; ablaze. **2.** Flamelike. **3.** Intense; passionate; ardent. —**flam′ing·ly** *adv.*

fla·min·go (flə-mĭng′gō) *n., pl.* **-gos** or **-goes.** Any of several large, gregarious wading birds of the family Phoenicopteridae, of tropical regions, with reddish or pinkish plumage, long legs, a long, flexible neck, and a bill turned downward at the tip. [Perh. Portuguese *flamengo,* from Provençal *flamenc,* prob. "fire bird" (from its bright plumage).]

flam·ma·ble (flăm′ə-bəl) *adj.* Capable of igniting easily and burning very rapidly. [From Latin *flammāre,* to blaze, from *flamma,* flame.] —**flam′ma·bil′i·ty** *n.* —**flam′ma·ble** *n.*

Usage: **flammable, inflammable, inflammatory.** *Flammable* and *inflammable* are interchangeable when they describe something capable of burning: *flammable* (or *inflammable*) *gas.* Nowdays, however, *flammable* is more often used in warnings on combustible materials because it is felt that some people might misinterpret the *in-* in *inflammable* to mean 'nonflammable; noncombustible.' *Inflammatory* applies to what stirs strong emotion: *the inflammatory rhetoric of a revolutionary.*

flange (flănj) *n.* A rim or edge that projects from something, such as a wheel or a pipe, used to strengthen an object, hold it in place, or attach it to something. —*tr.v.* **flanged, flang·ing.** To equip with a flange. [Prob. var. of earlier *flanch.*]

flank (flăngk) *n.* **1.** The fleshy section of the side between the last rib and the hip. **2.** A cut of meat from this section of an animal. **3.** A side or lateral part. **4.** *Mil.* The right or left side of a formation. —*tr.v.* **1.** To protect or guard the flank of. **2.** To attack or maneuver around the flank of. **3.** To be placed or situated at the flank of. [Middle English *fla(u)nke,* from Old French *flanc.*]

flank·er (flăng′kər) *n.* **1.** Someone or something that flanks. **2.** *Football.* An offensive halfback who lines up wide of the formation.

flan·nel (flăn′əl) *n.* **1.** A soft woven cloth of wool or of a blend of wool and cotton or synthetics. **2. Canton flannel. 3. flannels.** Trousers or underclothing made of flannel. [Middle English, prob. from *flanen,* sackcloth, from Welsh *gwlanen,* woolen cloth, from *gwlân,* wool.]

flan·nel·ette or **flan·nel·et** (flăn′ə-lĕt′) *n.* **Canton flannel.**

flap (flăp) *tr.v.* **flapped, flap·ping. 1.** To move (wings or arms) up and down; to beat. **2.** To cause to wave or flutter. **3.** To hit with something broad and flat; to slap. —*intr.v.* **1.** To move arms or wings up and down. **2.** To wave about while fixed at one edge or corner to something stationary; to flutter: *shutters flapping in the storm.* —*n.* **1.** A flat piece attached along one side and hanging loose on the other, often over an opening, as on an envelope or pocket. **2.** A hinged section on the rear edge of an aircraft wing, used primarily to increase lift or drag. **3.** The sound or action of flapping. **4.** A blow given with something flat; a slap. **5.** *Slang.* A condition of agitation, nervous excitement, or distress: *Her speech caused quite a flap.* [Middle English *flappen.*]

flap·jack (flăp′jăk′) *n.* A pancake.

flap·per (flăp′ər) *n.* **1.** Someone or something that flaps. **2.** *Informal.* A young woman, esp. one in the 1920's, who flaunted her disdain for conventional dress and behavior.

flare (flâr) *v.* **flared, flar·ing.** —*intr.v.* **1.** To burn with a bright, wavering light. **2.** To burst into intense, short-lived flame. **3.** To erupt into sudden or intense emotion or activity: *Tempers flared.* **4.** To expand outward in shape, as a skirt. —*tr.v.* **1.** To cause to flare. **2.** To signal with flares. —*n.* **1.** A brief, wavering blaze of light. **2.** A device that produces a bright flame for signaling or illumination. **3.** An outbreak, as of emotion or activity. **4.** An expanding outward, as of a skirt. **5.** A **solar flare.** [Orig. unknown.]

flare-up (flâr′ŭp′) *n.* A sudden outbreak, as of flame or resentment.

flash (flăsh) *intr.v.* **1.** To burst out suddenly in or as if in light or flame: *Fireworks flashed across the sky.* **2.** To appear, occur, or be perceived for an instant only: *A thought flashed through my mind.* **3.** To be lighted intermittently; sparkle. **4.** To move rapidly: *cars flashing by.* —*tr.v.* **1.** To cause (light) to appear suddenly or intermittently. **2.** To

signal with light. **3.** To communicate at great speed. **4.** To exhibit briefly: *She flashed me a smile.* **5.** To display ostentatiously; flaunt: *flash a bankroll.* **6.** To fill suddenly with water. **7.** To cover with a thin protective layer. —*n.* **1.** A sudden, brief display of light. **2.** A brief, unexpected display, as of a mental faculty: *a flash of insight.* **3.** A split second; an instant. **4.** A brief, important news dispatch or transmission. **5.** A flashlight. —See Syns at **moment.** —*adj.* **1.** Happening suddenly or very quickly: *a flash flood.* **2.** Ostentatious; flashy. [Middle English *flashen,* to splash, burst into flame (imit.).]

flash·back (flăsh′băk′) *n.* **1.** The interruption of a story, film, etc., to show or tell about an incident or scene from the past. **2.** The incident shown or told.

flash bulb. A glass bulb filled with finely shredded metal foil that is ignited by electricity to produce a bright flash of light for taking photographs.

flash card. A card marked with information, words, or numbers, used by a teacher in a drill.

flash·cube (flăsh′kyōōb′) *n.* A small cube that contains four flash bulbs and that rotates automatically when a picture is taken.

flash flood. A sudden, violent flood after a heavy rain.

flash gun. A portable device used in photography to hold a flash bulb and fire it electrically.

flash lamp. An electric lamp that produces a bright light for use in photography.

flash·light (flăsh′līt′) *n.* **1.** A small, portable lamp consisting of a bulb and dry batteries. **2.** A brief, brilliant flood of light from a photographic lamp.

flash point. The lowest temperature at which the vapor of a combustible liquid can be made to ignite.

flash·y (flăsh′ē) *adj.* **-i·er, -i·est. 1.** Giving a momentary or superficial impression of brilliance. **2.** Cheap and showy; gaudy. —**flash′i·ly** *adv.* —**flash′i·ness** *n.*

flask (flăsk) *n.* **1.** A container with a flat, slightly curved shape designed to fit in a pocket, used to hold liquor. **2.** A round or cone-shaped container with a long, narrow neck for laboratory use. [Old French *flasque, flaske,* from Late Latin *flascō, flasca.*]

flat¹ (flăt) *adj.* **flat·ter, flat·test. 1.** Having a smooth, level, horizontal surface: *flat land.* **2.** Having no curves or projections: *a flat dish.* **3.** Extending or lying completely in a plane: *a flat geometric figure.* **4.** Lying prone against a surface: *flat on one's back.* **5.** Unequivocal; absolute; downright: *a flat refusal.* **6.** Fixed; uniform; unvarying: *a flat rate.* **7.** Neither more nor less; to the exact measure: *a flat ten minutes.* **8.** Lacking interest or liveliness; stale; dull: *a flat performance.* **9. a.** Lacking zest; flavorless: *a flat meal.* **b.** Having lost a characteristic effervescence; stale: *The soda is flat.* **10.** Having lost contained air; deflated: *a flat tire.* **11.** Not glossy or shiny; mat: *flat paint.* **12.** *Mus.* **a.** Being below the intended pitch. **b.** Being one half step lower than the corresponding natural key: *B flat.* —See Syns at **level, stale,** and **utter.** —*adv.* **1.** So as to be flat: *press the dough flat.* **2.** Exactly: *ran the race in 50 seconds flat.* **3.** *Mus.* Below the intended pitch: *sing flat.* —*n.* **1.** A flat surface or part. **2.** Often **flats.** A stretch of level ground: *the salt flats.* **3.** A shallow frame or box for seeds or seedlings: *a flat of marigolds.* **4.** Stage scenery on a movable wooden frame. **5.** A deflated tire. **6. flats.** Women's shoes with flat heels. **7.** *Mus.* **a.** A sign (♭) affixed to a note to indicate that it is to be lowered by a half step. **b.** A note that is lowered a half step: *B flat.* —*v.* **flat·ted, flat·ting.** —*tr.v.* **1.** To make flat; flatten. **2.** *Mus.* To lower (a note) a semitone. —*intr.v. Mus.* To sing or play below the proper pitch. [Middle English, from Old Norse *flatr.*] —**flat′ly** *adv.* —**flat′ness** *n.*

flat² (flăt) *n.* An apartment on one floor. [Var. of Scottish *flet,* interior of a house, from Middle English *flet,* from Old English *flett,* floor, ground, hall.]

flat·boat (flăt′bōt′) *n.* A flat-bottomed barge for transporting freight on shallow inland waters.

flat·car (flăt′kär′) *n.* A railroad freight car without sides or roof, used for carrying freight.

flat·fish (flăt′fĭsh′) *n., pl.* **flatfish** or **-fish·es.** Any of numerous chiefly saltwater fishes of the order Pleuronectiformes, which includes fishes with a flattened body. In an early stage of development one eye moves to the same side of the body as the other and the fish swims with its eyeless side downward.

flat·foot (flăt′foŏt′) *n.* **1.** *pl.* **-feet** (-fēt′). A condition in which the arch of the foot is flattened so that the entire sole makes contact with the ground. **2.** *pl.* **-foots.** *Slang.* A policeman. —**flat′-foot′ed** *adj.*

flat·i·ron (flăt′ī′ərn) *n.* A heated iron for pressing clothes.

flat·ten (flăt′n) *tr.v.* **1.** To make flat or flatter. **2.** To knock down, as in a fight. —*intr.v.* To become flat or flatter. —**flat′ten·er** *n.*

flat·ter (flăt′ər) *tr.v.* **1.** To compliment excessively and often insincerely, esp. in order to win favor. **2.** To please or gratify: *Winning the prize flattered him.* **3.** To portray too favorably: *The photograph flatters him.* **4.** To persuade (oneself) that something one wants to believe is the case: *flattered herself she was beautiful.* [Middle English *flateren,* from Old French *flater,* to caress with the hand, smooth, flatter.] —**flat′ter·er** *n.*

flat·ter·y (flăt′ə-rē) *n.* **1.** The act or practice of flattering. **2.** Excessive or insincere praise.

flat·top (flăt′tŏp′) *n. Informal.* A U.S. aircraft carrier.

flat·u·lent (flăch′ə-lənt) *adj.* **1.** Of or having excessive gas in the digestive tract. **2.** Producing or likely to produce gas in the digestive tract. **3.** Inflated with self-importance; pompous and pretentious: *flatulent oratory.* [Old French, ult. from Latin *flātus,* a breaking wind.] —**flat′u·lence** *n.* —**flat′u·lent·ly** *adv.*

fla·tus (flā′təs) *n.* Gas generated in the stomach or intestine. [Latin *flātus,* a blowing, from *flāre,* to blow.]

flat·ware (flăt′wâr′) *n.* **1.** Tableware that is fairly flat and formed usu. of a single piece, as plates. **2.** Table utensils such as knives, forks, and spoons.

flat·worm (flăt′wûrm′) *n.* Any worm of the phylum Platyhelminthes.

flaunt (flônt) *tr.v.* To exhibit ostentatiously; show off: *flaunts his knowledge.* —*intr.v.* To wave proudly: *a flag flaunting in the wind.* —**flaunt′ing·ly** *adv.*

flau·tist (flô′tĭst, flou′-) *n.* A flutist. [Italian *flautista,* from *flauto,* flute, from Old Provençal *flaut.*]

fla·vor (flā′vər). Also *Brit.* **fla·vour.** —*n.* **1.** Distinctive taste; savor: *a flavor of smoke in bacon.* **2.** A seasoning; flavoring: *contains no artificial flavors.* **3.** A quality felt to be characteristic of a given thing: *the flavor of the Orient.* —*tr.v.* To give flavor to. [Middle English *flavour,* aroma, var. of Old French *flaor,* from Latin *flātus,* blowing, breeze, from the past part. of *flāre,* to blow.] —**fla′vor·ful** *adj.* —**fla′vor·less** *adj.*

fla·vor·ing (flā′vər-ĭng) *n.* A substance that imparts flavor, as an extract or spice.

fla·vour (flā′vər) *n. & v. Brit.* Var. of **flavor.**

flaw (flô) *n.* **1.** An imperfection, often concealed, that can cause failure: *a flaw in an argument.* **2.** A crack or blemish: *a flaw in a diamond.* —*tr.v.* To make defective. —*intr.v.* To become defective. [Middle English *flawe,* flake, fragment, from Old Norse *flaga,* slab of stone.] —**flaw′less** *adj.* —**flaw′less·ly** *adv.* —**flaw′less·ness** *n.*

flax (flăks) *n.* **1.** Any of several plants of the genus *Linum,* esp. *L. usitatissimum,* with blue flowers and slender stems from which a fine fiber is obtained. **2.** The textile fiber obtained from flax. [Middle English, from Old English *fleax, flæx.*]

flax·en (flăk′sən) *adj.* **1.** Made of or resembling flax. **2.** Having the pale-yellow color of flax fiber.

flax·seed (flăks′sēd′) *n.* The seeds of flax, from which linseed oil is pressed.

flay (flā) *tr.v.* **1.** To strip off the skin of. **2.** To criticize or scold harshly. [Middle English *flen,* from Old English *flēan.*] —**flay′er** *n.*

F layer. The highest zone of the ionosphere, extending variously from about 145 or 190 kilometers, or 90 or 120 miles, upward to about 400 kilometers, or 250 miles.

flea (flē) *n.* Any of various small, wingless, bloodsucking insects of the order Siphonaptera, which have legs adapted for jumping and are parasitic on warm-blooded animals. [Middle English *fle,* from Old English *flēa(h).*]

flea·bane (flē′bān′) *n.* Any of various plants of the genus *Erigeron,* believed to destroy or repel fleas. [From its supposed ability to drive away fleas.]

flea-bit·ten (flē′bĭt′n) *adj.* **1.** Covered with fleas or fleabites. **2.** *Informal.* Shabby or run-down: decrepit.

flea market. A shop or an open market selling antiques, second-hand goods, and curios.

fleck (flĕk) *n.* **1.** A tiny mark or spot. **2.** A small bit or flake. —*tr.v.* To spot or streak: *a path flecked with sunlight.* [Prob. from Middle English *flecked,* spotted, from Old Norse *flekkōttr,* from *flekkr,* spot.]

flec·tion (flĕk′shən) *n.* **1.** The act or process of bending or flexing. **2.** A bent part; a bend. **3.** *Anat.* Var. of **flexion.** [Latin *flexiō,* a bending, from *flexus,* past part. of *flectere,* to bend, flex.]

fled (flĕd) *v.* Past tense and past participle of **flee.**

fledge (flĕj) *v.* **fledged, fledg·ing.** —*tr.v.* To provide (an arrow) with feathers. —*intr.v.* To grow the feathers necessary for flight. [Prob. from obs. *fledge,* feathered, from Middle English *flegge,* from Old English *flycge.*]

fledg·ling or **fledge·ling** (flĕj′lĭng) *n.* **1.** A young bird that has recently acquired its flight feathers. **2.** A young and inexperienced person.

flee (flē) *v.* **fled** (flĕd), **flee·ing.** —*intr.v.* **1.** To run away, as from trouble or danger. **2.** To pass swiftly; vanish. —*tr.v.* To run away from. [Middle English *flen,* from Old English *flēon.*] —**fle′er** *n.*

fleece (flēs) *n.* **1.** The coat of wool of a sheep or similar animal. **2.** Any soft, woolly covering or fabric. —*tr.v.* **fleeced, fleec·ing.** **1.** To shear the fleece from. **2.** To defraud of money or property; to swindle. [Middle English *flees,* from Old English *flēos.*] —**fleec′er** *n.*

fleec·y (flē′sē) *adj.* **-i·er, -i·est.** Of, like, or covered with fleece: *fleecy clouds.* —**fleec′i·ness** *n.*

fleet¹ (flēt) *n.* **1.** A group of warships operating together under one command. **2.** Any group of vehicles, such as taxicabs or fishing boats, owned or operated as a unit. [Middle English *flete,* from Old English *flēot,* from *flēotan,* to float.]

fleet² (flēt) *adj.* **-er, -est.** Moving swiftly; rapid or nimble. —See Syns at **fast¹.** —*intr.v.* To move or pass swiftly. [Prob. from Middle English *fleten,* to flow, from Old English *flēotan,* to float.] —**fleet′ly** *adv.* —**fleet′ness** *n.*

Fleet Admiral. A naval officer, the **Admiral of the Fleet.**

Flem·ing (flĕm′ĭng) *n.* **1.** A native of Flanders. **2.** A Belgian who speaks Flemish.

Flem·ish (flĕm′ĭsh) *adj.* Of or pertaining to Flanders, the Flemings, or their language. —*n.* **1.** The Germanic language of the Flemings. **2.** The Flemings.

flesh (flĕsh) *n.* **1.** The soft tissue of the body, esp. the skeletal muscles. **2.** The meat of animals as distinguished from the edible tissue of fish or fowl. **3.** The pulpy, usu. edible part of a fruit or vegetable. **4.** The body as distinguished from the mind or soul. **5.** Mankind in general; humanity. —*tr.v.* **1.** To fill out (a structure or framework): *fleshed out the novel with a subplot.* **2.** To clean (a hide) of adhering flesh. —*intr.v.* To gain weight; become plump. —*idioms.* **flesh and blood.** A blood relative or relatives. **in the flesh.** In person. [Middle English, from Old English *flǣsc.*]

flesh fly. Any of various flies of the genus *Sarcophaga,* of which the larvae are parasitic in animal tissue.

flesh·ly (flĕsh′lē) *adj.* **-li·er, -li·est.** **1.** Of or pertaining to the body; physical; corporeal. **2.** Carnal; sensual. **3.** Not spiritual; worldly. —**flesh′li·ness** *n.*

flesh·y (flĕsh′ē) *adj.* **-i·er, -i·est.** **1.** Of or resembling flesh.

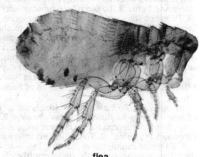

flea

2. Having much flesh; fat. **3.** Firm and pulpy, as fruit. — See Syns at **fat**. —**flesh′i·ness** *n.*

fleur-de-lis or **fleur-de-lys** (flûr′də-lē′, floor′-) *n., pl.* **fleurs-de-lis** or **fleurs-de-lys** (flûr′də-lēz′, floor′-). **1.** An iris, esp. a white-flowered form of *Iris germanica.* **2.** A heraldic device consisting of a stylized three-petaled iris. [Middle English *flour de lice,* from Old French *flor de lis,* lily flower.]

fleur-de-lis

flicker²

flew (floo) *v.* Past tense of **fly**. [Middle English, from Old English *flugon* (pl.).]

flews (flooz) *pl.n.* The pendulous corners of the upper lip of certain dogs. [Orig. unknown.]

flex (flĕks) *tr.v.* **1.** To cause to bend: *flex one's toes.* **2.** To contract (a muscle). —*intr.v.* To bend: *hands flexing nervously.* [Latin *flexus,* past part. of *flectere,* to bend.]

flex·i·ble (flĕk′sə-bəl) *adj.* **1.** Capable of being flexed; pliable. **2.** Capable of or responsive to change; adaptable: *flexible plans.* —**flex′i·bil′i·ty** *n.* —**flex′i·bly** *adv.*

    Syns: **flexible, elastic, plastic, resilient, springy, supple** *adj.* *Core meaning:* Capable of withstanding stress without injury (*a flexible girder*).

flex·ion (flĕk′shən) *n.* Also **flec·tion**. *Anat.* The act of bending a limb. [Var. of FLECTION.]

flex·or (flĕk′sər) *n.* A muscle that acts to flex a joint. [From Latin *flexus,* past part. of *flectere,* to flex.]

flex·ure (flĕk′shər) *n.* **1.** A bend, curve, or turn. **2.** A bending or flexing.

flick¹ (flĭk) *n.* A light, quick blow or stroke: *a flick of a whip.* —*tr.v.* **1.** To strike with a flick. **2.** To cause to move with a light flick; to snap: *flick the light switch.* [Perh. imit.]

flick² (flĭk) *n. Slang.* A motion picture. [Back-formation from FLICKER.]

flick·er¹ (flĭk′ər) *intr.v.* **1.** To give off light that burns or shines unsteadily: *candles flickering in the breeze.* **2.** To move waveringly; flutter: *Shadows flickered on the wall.* —*n.* **1.** A wavering or unsteady light. **2.** A brief or slight sensation, as of emotion: *a flicker of hope.* [Middle English *flikeren,* to flutter, flicker, from Old English *flicorian,* to flutter, hover.]

flick·er² (flĭk′ər) *n.* Any of several large North American woodpeckers of the genus *Colaptes,* with a spotted breast. [Prob. from FLICK (verb).]

flied (flīd) *v.* Past tense and past participle of **fly** (to hit a fly ball).

fli·er (flī′ər) *n.* Also **fly·er**. **1.** Anything that flies, esp. a pilot. **2.** *Informal.* A daring financial venture. **3.** A pamphlet or circular for mass distribution.

flight¹ (flīt) *n.* **1.** The act or process of flying. **2.** A scheduled airline trip or the plane making it. **3.** A group, esp. of birds or aircraft, flying together. **4.** Any swift passage or movement: *the flight of time.* **5.** An effort or display that surpasses the usual bounds: *a flight of imagination.* **8.** A series of stairs rising from one landing to another. [Middle English, from Old English *flyht.*]

flight² (flīt) *n.* An act of running away; an escape. [Middle English *flight.*]

flight deck. The upper deck of an aircraft carrier, used as a runway.

flight feather. One of the large, stiff feathers of a bird's wing or tail that are necessary for flight.

flight·less (flīt′lĭs) *adj.* Incapable of flying, as certain birds.

flight·y (flī′tē) *adj.* **-i·er, -i·est. 1.** Given to capricious or impulsive behavior. **2.** Easily excited; skittish. [Orig. "swift," from *flight.*] —**flight′i·ly** *adv.* —**flight′i·ness** *n.*

flim·flam (flĭm′flăm′). *Informal.* —*n.* **1.** Nonsense. **2.** A deception; a swindle. —*tr.v.* **-flammed, -flam·ming.** To swindle; deceive. [Of Scandinavian orig.]

flim·sy (flĭm′zē) *adj.* **-si·er, -si·est. 1.** Lacking solidity or strength: *flimsy cloth.* **2.** Lacking validity or plausibility; unconvincing: *a flimsy excuse.* [Orig. unknown.] —**flim′si·ly** *adv.* —**flim′si·ness** *n.*

flinch (flĭnch) *intr.v.* To draw back or away, as from pain or fear; shrink; wince. [Old French *flenchir.*] —**flinch** *n.* —**flinch′er** *n.*

fling (flĭng) *v.* **flung** (flŭng), **fling·ing.** —*tr.v.* **1.** To throw with violence or force; hurl. **2.** To put or send suddenly or unexpectedly: *The army was flung into battle.* **3.** To throw (oneself) into some activity with abandon and energy. **4.** To toss aside; discard: *fling propriety to the winds.* —*intr.v.* To move quickly, violently, or impulsively. —*n.* **1.** An act of flinging. **2.** A brief period of indulging one's impulses; a spree. **3.** *Informal.* A brief attempt or try. [Middle English *flingen,* of Scandinavian orig.]

flint (flĭnt) *n.* **1.** A very hard, fine-grained quartz that makes sparks when struck with steel. **2.** A small solid cylinder of a spark-producing alloy, used in lighters to ignite the fuel. [Middle English, from Old English.]

flint glass. A soft, brilliant glass containing an oxide of lead, used for making lenses. Also called **lead glass**.

flint·lock (flĭnt′lŏk′) *n.* **1.** An obsolete gunlock in which a flint embedded in the hammer produces a spark that ignites the charge. **2.** A firearm with a flintlock.

flint·y (flĭn′tē) *adj.* **-i·er, -i·est. 1.** Containing or composed of flint. **2.** Unyielding; hard; stony: *a flinty stare.* —**flint′i·ly** *adv.* —**flint′i·ness** *n.*

flip (flĭp) *v.* **flipped, flip·ping.** —*tr.v.* **1.** To toss (a coin) vertically in the air, giving it a spin. **2.** To strike or move with a light, quick blow; to flick: *flip a switch.* **3.** To reverse or overturn quickly: *flip the hamburgers.* —*intr.v.* **1.** To turn or skim quickly: *flip through the catalog.* **2.** *Slang.* To have a strong reaction; be overwhelmed: *flipped over the new car.* —*n.* **1.** An act of flipping, esp. a quick, turning movement. **2.** A somersault. —*adj.* **flip·per, flip·pest.** *Informal.* Disrespectful; impertinent: *a flip attitude.* [Orig. unknown.]

flip·pant (flĭp′ənt) *adj.* Lacking due respect or seriousness; casually disrespectful; pert: *flippant remarks.* [Prob. from FLIP.] —**flip′pan·cy** *n.* —**flip′pant·ly** *adv.*

flip·per (flĭp′ər) *n.* **1.** A wide, flat limb, as of a seal, adapted for swimming. **2.** A wide, flat, finlike rubber shoe worn for swimming and skin diving.

flirt (flûrt) *intr.v.* **1.** To play lightly or mockingly at courtship. **2.** To deal playfully, casually, or coyly; to toy: *flirt with danger.* —*tr.v.* To toss or move move abruptly or jerkily. —*n.* **1.** A person given to romantic flirting. **2.** An abrupt, jerking movement. [Orig. unknown.]

flir·ta·tion (flûr-tā′shən) *n.* **1.** The act or practice of flirting. **2.** A casual or brief romance.

flir·ta·tious (flûr-tā′shəs) *adj.* **1.** Given to flirting. **2.** Lightheartedly romantic: *a flirtatious glance.* —**flir·ta′tious·ly** *adv.* —**flir·ta′tious·ness** *n.*

flit (flĭt) *intr.v.* **flit·ted, flit·ting. 1.** To move or fly quickly and nimbly; to dart. **2.** To move or pass quickly: *A smile flitted across her face.* [Middle English *flitten,* to convey, from Old Norse *flytja.*] —**flit′ter** *n.*

flit·ter (flĭt′ər) *intr.v.* To flutter. [Freq. of FLIT.]

fliv·ver (flĭv′ər) *n. Slang.* An old or cheap car. [Orig. unknown.]

float (flōt) *intr.v.* **1.** To remain suspended in or on the surface of a liquid without sinking. **2.** To move along on the surface of a liquid: *logs floating down the river.* **3.** To move easily and lightly as if suspended: *clouds floating through the air.* **4.** To move from place to place, esp. at random; to drift: *He floats from town to town.* —*tr.v.* **1.** To cause to remain suspended without sinking or falling. **2. a.** To establish (a business, company, etc.) by selling stocks. **b.** To offer for sale: *float a bond issue.* —*n.* **1.** Something that floats, as: **a.** An anchored raft used for swimming. **b.** A cork or other floating object on a fishing line. **c.** A hollow ball attached to a lever to regulate the water level in a tank. **2.** A large, flat vehicle bearing an exhibit in a parade. **3.** A soft drink with ice cream floating in it. [Middle English *floten,* from Old English *flotian.*]

float·er (flō'tər) *n.* **1.** Something that floats. **2.** A person who wanders; a drifter.

float·ing (flō'tĭng) *adj.* **1.** Buoyed on or suspended in or as if in a fluid. **2.** *Finance.* **a.** Available for use; in circulation: *floating capital.* **b.** Short-term and usu. unfunded: *a floating debt.*

floating rib. One of the four lower ribs that, unlike the other ribs, are not attached at the front.

floc·cu·lent (flŏk'yə-lənt) *adj.* Having a fluffy or woolly appearance. [From Late Latin *flocculus,* dim. of Latin *floccus,* tuft of wool.] —**floc'cu·lence** *n.*

flock¹ (flŏk) *n.* **1.** A group of animals, as birds or sheep, that live, travel, or feed together. **2.** A group of people under the leadership of one person, esp. the members of a congregation. **3.** A large crowd or number. —*intr.v.* To congregate or travel in a flock or crowd. [Middle English *flok,* from Old English *flocc.*]

flock² (flŏk) *n.* **1.** A tuft, as of fiber or hair. **2.** Waste wool or cotton used for stuffing furniture and mattresses. **3.** Pulverized wool or felt applied to paper or cloth to produce a pattern. —*tr.v.* **1.** To stuff with flock. **2.** To decorate with flock. [Middle English *flok,* prob. from Old French *floc,* from Latin *floccus.*]

floe (flō) *n.* A large, flat mass of floating ice. [Prob. from Norwegian *flo,* layer, slab, from Old Norse *flō,* stratum, coating.]

flog (flŏg, flôg) *tr.v.* **flogged, flog·ging.** To beat severely with a whip or rod. [Perh. from Latin *flagellāre,* to whip, from *flagellum,* dim. of *flagrum,* whip.] —**flog'ger** *n.*

flood (flŭd) *n.* **1.** An overflowing of water onto normally dry land; a deluge. **2.** Any abundant flow or outpouring: *a flood of immigrants.* **3. Flood.** The universal deluge recorded in the Old Testament as having occurred during the life of Noah. —*tr.v.* **1.** To cover or submerge with a flood; inundate: *Rains flooded the basement.* **2.** To fill with an abundance or an excess: *Letters flooded the office.* —*intr.v.* **1.** To become inundated: *The fields flood every spring.* **2.** To pour forth; overflow. [Middle English *flod,* from Old English *flōd.*]

flood·gate (flŭd'gāt') *n.* **1.** A gate used to control the flow of a body of water. **2.** Anything that restrains a flood or outpouring.

flood·light (flŭd'līt') *n.* **1.** Artificial light in an intensely bright and broad beam. **2.** A unit that produces such a beam. —*tr.v.* **-light·ed** or **-lit** (-lĭt'), **-light·ing.** To illuminate with a floodlight.

flood plain. A plain bordering a river, subject to flooding.

flood tide. The incoming or rising tide.

floor (flôr, flōr) *n.* **1.** The surface of a room on which one stands. **2.** A bottom or base; lower limit. **3.** The ground or lowermost surface, as of a forest or ocean. **4.** The lower part of a room, such as a legislative chamber, where business is conducted: *the floor of the House.* **5. a.** The right to address an assembly: *The speaker has the floor.* **b.** The body of assembly members: *a motion from the floor.* **6.** A story or level of a building: *living on the fifth floor.* —*tr.v.* **1.** To provide with a floor. **2.** To knock down: *He floored his assailant.* **3.** To stun; overwhelm: *The news floored me.* [Middle English *flor,* from Old English *flōr.*]

floor·board (flôr'bôrd', flōr'bōrd') *n.* **1.** A board in a floor. **2.** The floor of a motor vehicle.

floor·ing (flôr'ĭng, flōr'-) *n.* **1.** Floors in general. **2.** Material used in making floors.

floor leader. The member of a legislative body chosen by fellow party members to be in charge of the party's activities on the floor.

floor plan. A scale diagram of a room or building drawn as if seen from above.

floor show. A series of entertainments presented in a nightclub.

floor·walk·er (flôr'wô'kər, flōr'-) *n.* An employee of a department store who supervises sales personnel and assists customers.

floo·zy (floo'zē) *n., pl.* **-zies.** *Slang.* A slovenly or vulgar woman, esp. a prostitute. [Orig. unknown.]

flop (flŏp) *intr.v.* **flopped, flop·ping.** **1.** To fall heavily and noisily; plop: *flop in a chair.* **2.** To move about in a noisy way; flap: *sheets flopping in the wind.* **3.** *Informal.* To fail utterly. —*n.* **1.** The act of flopping. **2.** The sound of flopping; a dull thud. **3.** *Informal.* An utter failure. [Var. of FLAP.]

flop·house (flŏp'hous') *n.* A cheap hotel or rooming house.

flop·py (flŏp'ē) *adj.* **-pi·er, -pi·est.** Tending to flop: *a dog with floppy ears.* —**flop'pi·ly** *adv.* —**flop'pi·ness** *n.*

flo·ra (flôr'ə, flōr'ə) *n., pl.* **-ras** or **flo·rae** (flôr'ē', flōr'ē'). Plants in general, esp. the plants or plant life of a particular region. [From Latin *Flora,* Roman goddess of flowers, from *flōs,* flower.]

flo·ral (flôr'əl, flōr'-) *adj.* Of, pertaining to, or suggestive of flowers.

flo·res·cence (flô-rĕs'əns, flə-) *n.* The condition, time, or period of blossoming. [From Latin *flōrēscens,* pres. part. of *flōrēscere,* to begin to bloom, from *flōs,* flower.]

flo·ret (flôr'ĭt, flōr'-) *n.* A small flower, usu. part of a dense cluster, esp. one of the disk or ray flowers of a composite plant, such as a daisy. [Middle English *flouret,* from Old French *florete,* dim. of *flo(u)r,* flower.]

flor·id (flôr'ĭd, flōr'-) *adj.* **1.** Flushed with rosy color; ruddy: *a florid complexion.* **2.** Excessively or elaborately embellished; flowery: *a florid style of writing.* [French *floride,* from Latin *flōridus,* from *flōrēre,* to bloom, from *flōs,* flower.] —**flo·rid'i·ty** (flə-rĭd'ĭ-tē) or **flor'id·ness** *n.* —**flor'id·ly** *adv.*

flo·rin (flôr'ĭn, flōr'-) *n.* **1.** A British coin worth two shillings. **2.** A guilder. **3. a.** A gold coin first issued at Florence in 1252. **b.** Any of several similar obsolete European gold coins. [Middle English *flore(i)n,* from Old French *florin,* from Italian *fiorino,* from *fiore,* flower (from the figure of a lily on the coin), from Latin *flōs.*]

flo·rist (flôr'ĭst, flōr'-, flŏr'-) *n.* A person who sells flowers and ornamental plants. [Latin *flōs,* flower + -IST.]

floss (flôs, flŏs) *n.* **1.** Short fibers or waste silk. **2.** A soft, loosely twisted thread used in embroidery. **3.** Any soft, silky, fibrous substance. **4. Dental floss.** [Perh. from French *floche,* from Old French *flosche,* down.]

floss·y (flô'sē, flŏs'ē) *adj.* **-i·er, -i·est.** **1.** Made of or resembling floss. **2.** *Slang.* Ostentatiously stylish; flashy. —**floss'i·ness** *n.*

flo·ta·tion (flō-tā'shən) *n.* **1.** The act or condition of floating. **2.** Any of several processes in which different materials, notably pulverized minerals, are separated by agitation with water, oil, and chemicals that cause some of the particles to float.

flo·til·la (flō-tĭl'ə) *n.* **1.** A fleet of small ships. **2.** *U.S. Navy.* A unit of two or more squadrons of small warships. [Spanish, dim. of *flota,* fleet, from Old French *flote,* from Old Norse *floti,* raft, fleet.]

flot·sam (flŏt'səm) *n.* Any wreckage or cargo that remains afloat after a ship has sunk. [Earlier *flotsen,* from Norman French *floteson,* from *floter,* to float.]

flounce¹ (flouns) *n.* A strip of material, such as a ruffle, attached along its upper edge to a skirt, curtain, etc. —*tr.v.* **flounced, flounc·ing.** To trim with a flounce. [Var. of obs. *frounce,* from Middle English, a wrinkle, crease, from Old French *fronce,* from *froncir,* to wrinkle.]

flounce² (flouns) *intr.v.* **flounced, flounc·ing.** To move with exaggerated motions expressive of displeasure or impatience: *flounced out in a huff.* —*n.* The act or motion of flouncing. [Orig. unknown.]

floun·der¹ (floun'dər) *intr.v.* **1.** To move clumsily or with difficulty, as to regain balance. **2.** To proceed clumsily and in confusion: *floundering through a speech.* [Prob. blend of FOUNDER and BLUNDER.]

Usage: **flounder, founder.** *Flounder* is the verb expressing clumsy movement: *floundered in the snow. Founder* refers to becoming disabled, collapsing or giving way, and sinking below the surface of a body of water: *a ship that foundered in the storm.*

floun·der² (floun'dər) *n., pl.* **flounder** or **-ders.** Any of various saltwater flatfishes of the families Bothidae and Pleuronectidae, important as food fishes. [Middle English, from Norman French *floundre.*]

flour (flour) *n.* **1.** A soft, fine, powdery substance obtained by grinding and sifting the meal of a grain, esp. wheat. **2.** Any similar soft, fine powder. —*tr.v.* To cover or coat

---

ă pat ā pay â care ä father ĕ pet ē be hw which ĭ pit ī tie î pier ŏ pot ō toe ô paw, for oi noise
oo took oo boot ou out th thin *th* this ŭ cut û urge zh vision ə about, item, edible, gallop, circus

with flour. [Middle English, finer meal, farina, flower.] —**flour'y** *adj.*

flour·ish (flûr'ĭsh, flŭr'-) *intr.v.* **1.** To grow well or luxuriantly; thrive. **2.** To fare well; succeed; prosper. —*tr.v.* To wield, wave, or exhibit dramatically: *flourish a baton.* — See Syns at **prosper.** —*n.* **1.** An act of waving or brandishing. **2.** An embellishment or ornamentation, esp. in handwriting. **3.** A dramatic action or gesture: *finished his speech with a flourish.* [Middle English *florishen,* from Old French *florir,* to bloom, from Latin *flōrēre,* from *flōs,* flower.]

flout (flout) *tr.v.* To show contempt for; scoff at; scorn: *flouting authority.* —*intr.v.* To be scornful; jeer. [Prob. from Middle English *flouten,* to play the flute.] —**flout'er** *n.*

flow (flō) *intr.v.* **1.** To move or run steadily and freely in the manner characteristic of a liquid. **2.** To move or proceed steadily and continuously: *traffic flowing over the bridge; sentences that flow.* **3.** To hang loosely and gracefully: *The cape flowed from his shoulders.* **4.** To arise; derive: *Several conclusions flow from this hypothesis.* **5.** To abound or be plentiful: *She was flowing with pride and love.* **6.** To rise, as the tide. **7.** To menstruate. —*n.* **1.** The act or process of flowing. **2.** A flowing mass; a stream: *a lava flow.* **3.** A continuous output or outpouring; a flood: *a flow of ideas.* **4.** A continuous movement or circulation: *the flow of traffic.* **5.** The amount that flows in a given period of time. **6.** The incoming or rise of the tide. **7.** Menstrual discharge. [Middle English *flouen,* from Old English *flōwan.*]

flow chart. A schematic representation of a sequence of operations, as for a computer program.

flow·er (flou'ər) *n.* **1. a.** The part of a seed-bearing plant that contains the reproductive structure, having specialized male and female organs, enclosed in an outer envelope of petals and sepals. **b.** Any such structure having showy or colorful parts; a blossom. **2.** Any similar reproductive organ of other plants, as mosses. **3.** A plant cultivated for its blossoms. **4.** The period of highest development; peak. **5.** The highest example or best representative of something: *the flower of our generation.* **6.** Often **flowers.** *Chem.* A fine powder produced by condensation or sublimation. —*intr.v.* **1.** To produce a flower or flowers; to blossom; bloom. **2.** To develop fully; reach a peak: *Her talents flowered late.* —*tr.v.* To decorate with flowers or with a floral pattern. [Middle English *flo(u)r,* from Old French *flo(u)r,* from Latin *flōs.*]

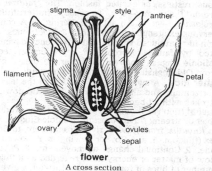

stigma   style   anther

filament

petal

ovary   ovules
sepal

flower
A cross section

flow·ered (flou'ərd) *adj.* Having flowers or a design of flowers: *flowered wallpaper.*

flow·er·et (flou'ər-ĭt) *n.* A small flower. [Middle English *flourette,* from Old French *flo(u)rete,* dim. of *flo(u)r,* flower.]

flower girl. A very young girl who carries flowers at a wedding.

flower head. A tight cluster of tiny flowers.

flow·er·pot (flou'ər-pŏt') *n.* A pot in which plants are grown.

flow·er·y (flou'ə-rē) *adj.* **-i·er, -i·est. 1.** Full of flowers or suggestive of flowers: *a flowery perfume.* **2.** Full of figurative and ornate words and expressions: *a flowery speech.* —**flow'er·i·ness** *n.*

flown (flōn) *v.* Past participle of **fly** (to move through the

air). [Middle English *flowen,* from Old English *(ge)flogen.*]

flu (flōō) *n. Informal.* Influenza.

flub (flŭb) *tr.v.* **flubbed, flub·bing.** To botch or bungle: *flubbed her big speech.* —*n.* An error or blunder. [Orig. unknown.]

fluc·tu·ate (flŭk'chōō-āt') *intr.v.* **-at·ed, -at·ing. 1.** To change or vary, as from one level, condition, or direction to another: *Prices fluctuate according to supply and demand.* **2.** To rise and fall like waves; undulate. [From Latin *fluctuāre,* from *fluctus,* a flowing, from the past part. of *fluere,* to flow.] —**fluc·tu·a'tion** *n.*

flue (flōō) *n.* **1.** A pipe, tube, etc., through which hot air, gas, steam, or smoke may pass, as in a boiler or a chimney. **2.** A **flue pipe.** [Orig. unknown.]

flu·ent (flōō'ənt) *adj.* **1. a.** Capable of speaking or writing effortlessly and smoothly: *fluent in German and French.* **b.** Smoothly and naturally flowing; polished: *speak fluent French.* **2.** Flowing or capable of flowing; fluid. [Latin *fluēns,* pres. part. of *fluere,* to flow.] —**flu'en·cy** *n.* —**flu'ent·ly** *adv.*

flue pipe. An organ pipe that is sounded by means of a current of air striking a lip in the side of the pipe and causing the air within it to vibrate.

fluff (flŭf) *n.* **1.** Light, soft, downy substance: *fluff from a down quilt.* **2.** Something that has a light, soft, or frothy consistency or appearance. **3.** *Informal.* An error or lapse of memory, esp. by an actor or announcer. —*tr.v.* **1.** To make light and puffy by shaking, poking, or patting into a soft, loose mass: *fluffed up her hair.* **2.** *Informal.* To misread or forget (one's lines in a play). [Prob. var. of *flue,* down, from Flemish *vluwe,* from French *velu,* velvety, from Old French,, shaggy.]

fluff·y (flŭf'ē) *adj.* **-i·er, -i·est. 1.** Of, like, or covered with fluff or down. **2.** Light and airy; soft: *fluffy curls.* —**fluff'i·ly** *adv.* —**fluff'i·ness** *n.*

flu·id (flōō'ĭd) *n.* A substance, such as air or water, that flows relatively easily and tends to take on the shape of its container. —*adj.* **1.** Capable of flowing, as a liquid. **2.** Smooth and effortless. **3.** Easily changed or readily changing; adaptable: *fluid living space.* **4.** Convertible into cash: *fluid assets.* [Middle English, from Old French *fluide,* from Latin *fluidus,* from *fluere,* to flow.] —**flu·id'i·ty** (flōō-ĭd'ĭ-tē) or **flu'id·ness** *n.* —**flu'id·ly** *adv.*

fluid dram. *Abbr.* **fl dr** A unit equal to ⅛ of a fluid ounce.

fluid ounce. *Abbr.* **fl oz** **1.** A unit of volume or capacity in the U.S. Customary System, used in liquid measure, equal to 29.574 milliliters, 1.804 cubic inches, or ¹⁄₁₆ of a pint. **2.** A unit of volume or capacity in the British Imperial System, used in liquid and dry measure, equal to 3.552 cubic centimeters, or 1.734 cubic inches.

fluke¹ (flōōk) *n.* **1.** Any of various flatfishes, esp. a flounder. **2.** A trematode, esp. any of various parasitic species. [Middle English, from Old English *flōc.*]

fluke² (flōōk) *n.* **1.** The triangular blade at the end of either arm of an anchor, designed to catch in the ground. **2.** A barb or barbed head, as on an arrow or harpoon. **3.** One of the two horizontally flattened divisions of the tail of a whale or related animal. [Prob. from FLUKE (from its shape).]

fluke³ (flōōk) *n.* Any accidental stroke of good luck. [Orig. unknown.]

fluk·y (flōō'kē) *adj.* **-i·er, -i·est. 1.** Resulting from chance. **2.** Constantly shifting; variable. —See Syns at **accidental.**

flume (flōōm) *n.* **1.** A narrow passage or gorge, usu. with a stream flowing through it. **2.** A channel or chute, usu. inclined, for a stream of water, as for furnishing power. [Earlier, river, from Middle English *flum,* from Old French, from Latin *flūmen,* from *fluere,* to flow.]

flum·mer·y (flŭm'ə-rē) *n., pl.* **-ies. 1.** *Brit.* Any of several soft, light foods, as a custard or blancmange. **2.** Meaningless flattery; humbug. [Welsh *llymru.*]

flum·mox (flŭm'əks) *tr.v. Slang.* To confuse; perplex. [Orig. unknown.]

flung (flŭng) *v.* Past tense and past participle of **fling.** [Middle English *flung, flungen.*]

flunk (flŭngk) *Informal.* —*intr.v.* To fail an examination, course, or other school work. —*tr.v.* **1.** To fail (an examination or course). **2.** To give (someone) a failing grade. —See Syns at **fail.** —*phrasal verb.* **flunk out.** To be expelled from a school or course because of unsatisfactory work. [Orig. unknown.]

flun·ky (flŭng′kē) *n., pl.* **-kies.** Also **flun·key** *pl.* **-keys. 1.** A liveried manservant; a lackey. **2.** A servile or fawning person; a toady. **3.** A person who does menial or trivial work. [Scottish.]

flu·or (flōō′ôr, -ər) *n.* Fluorite. [From Latin, a flowing, fluid, from *fluere,* to flow.]

fluor-. Var. of **fluoro-.**

flu·o·resce (flōō′ə-rĕs′, flōō-rĕs′) *intr.v.* **-resced, -resc·ing.** To undergo, produce, or show fluorescence. [Back-formation from FLUORESCENCE.]

flu·o·res·cence (flōō′ə-rĕs′əns, flōō-rĕs′-) *n.* **1.** The property whereby a substance re-emits usu. visible electromagnetic radiation during exposure to incident radiation. **2.** The radiation so emitted. [FLUOR + -ESCENCE.] **—flu′o·res′cent** *adj.*

fluorescent lamp. An electric lamp that generates light by means of an electric discharge through a gas-filled tube in which the ultraviolet light emitted by the discharge is converted to visible light by fluorescent material that coats the inside.

fluor·i·date (flōōr′ĭ-dāt′, flôr′-, flōr′-) *tr.v.* **-dat·ed, -dat·ing.** To add a fluorine compound to (a water supply) for the purpose of preventing tooth decay. **—fluor′i·da′tion** *n.*

flu·o·ride (flōō′ə-rīd′, flōōr′ĭd′, flôr′-, flōr′-) *n.* Any binary compound of fluorine with another element. [FLUOR(O)- + -IDE.]

flu·o·rine (flōō′ə-rēn′, -rĭn, flōōr′ēn′, -ĭn, flôr′-, flōr′-) *n.* Symbol **F** A pale-yellow, highly corrosive, highly poisonous, gaseous halogen element, the most electronegative and most reactive of all the elements. It is used in a wide variety of industrially important compounds. Atomic number 9; atomic weight 18.9984; freezing point −219.62°C; boiling point −188.14°C; specific gravity of liquid 1.108; valence 1. [French, from New Latin *fluor,* fluor.]

flu·o·rite (flōō′ə-rīt′, flōōr′ĭt′, flôr′-, flōr′-) *n.* A mineral, essentially CaF₂, of different colors, that is often fluorescent in ultraviolet light. Also called **fluorspar.** [Italian : FLUOR + -ITE.]

fluoro– or **fluor-.** A prefix meaning: **1.** Fluorine in compound: **fluorosis. 2.** Fluorescence: **fluoroscope.** [From FLUORINE and FLUORESCENCE.]

fluor·o·car·bon (flōōr′ō-kär′bən) *n.* Any of various inert organic compounds in which fluorine replaces hydrogen, used as aerosol propellants, refrigerants, solvents, lubricants, and in making plastics and resins.

fluor·o·scope (flōōr′ə-skōp′, flôr′-, flōr′-, flōō′ər-ə-) *n.* A mounted fluorescent screen on which the internal structure or parts of an optically opaque object, as of the human body, may be viewed as shadows formed by the transmission of x rays through the object. **—tr.v. -scoped, -scop·ing.** To examine the interior of (an object) with a fluoroscope. [FLUORO- + -SCOPE.] **—fluor′o·scop′ic** (-skōp′ĭk) *adj.* **—fluo·ros′co·py** (flōō-rŏs′kə-pē) *n.*

flu·or·spar (flōō′ər-spär′) *n.* Fluorite. [FLUOR(O)- + SPAR.]

flur·ry (flûr′ē, flŭr′ē) *n., pl.* **-ries. 1.** A sudden gust of wind. **2.** A light snowfall. **3.** A sudden burst of excitement or bustling activity: *a flurry of preparations.* [From obs. *flurr,* to whirl up, scatter.]

flush¹ (flŭsh) *intr.v.* **1.** To turn red in the face; blush. **2.** To glow, esp. with a reddish color. **3.** To flow suddenly and abundantly. **4.** To be cleaned, emptied, or discharged by a rapid, brief gush of water. **—tr.v. 1.** To cause to redden or glow. **2.** To excite or elate, as with a feeling of pride or accomplishment: *flushed with victory.* **3.** To wash out or empty with a sudden, rapid flow of water. **—n. 1.** A blush or glow. **2.** Redness of the skin, as with fever. **3.** A feeling of animation or exhilaration. **4.** A sudden freshness, development, or growth: *the first flush of beauty.* **5.** A brief but copious flow or gushing, as of water. **—adj. 1.** Having a healthy reddish color; glowing. **2.** Abundant; plentiful. **3.** Having an abundant supply of money; prosperous; affluent. **4. a.** Having surfaces in the same plane; even; level: *The first column is flush with the margin.* **b.** Arranged with adjacent sides, surfaces, or edges close together: *a safe flush against the wall.* **—See Syns at level. —adv. 1.** So as to be even, in one plane, or aligned. **2.** Squarely; solidly: *The ball hit him flush on the face.* [Prob. from

flush, to take flight, dart out, from Middle English *flusshen.*]

flush² (flŭsh) *n.* A hand of playing cards in which all the cards are of the same suit. [Prob. from Old French *flus, flux,* from Latin *fluxus,* a flow, flux.]

flush³ (flŭsh) *tr.v.* To frighten (a game bird or animal) from cover. **—intr.v. 1.** To dart out or fly from cover; take flight. [Middle English *flusshen.*]

flus·ter (flŭs′tər) *tr.v.* To make nervous or upset, as by confusing. **—intr.v.** To become nervous or upset, as from confusion. **—n.** A state of agitation, confusion, or excitement. [Middle English *flostren.*]

flute (flōōt) *n.* **1.** A high-pitched woodwind instrument, tubular in shape, with finger holes and keys on the side and a reedless mouthpiece. **2.** *Archit.* One of the long, usu. rounded parallel grooves on the shaft of a column. **3.** A groove in cloth, as in a pleated ruffle. **—v. flut·ed, flut·ing. —tr.v.** To make ornamental flutes in: *a fluted collar.* **—intr.v. 1.** To play a flute. **2.** To make a flutelike tone. [Middle English *floute,* from Old French *flaute, fleute.*]

flute

flut·ing (flōō′tĭng) *n.* **1.** A decorative motif consisting of flutes. **2.** The grooves formed by narrow pleats in cloth, as in a ruffle.

flut·ist (flōō′tĭst) *n.* One who plays the flute. Also called **flautist.**

flut·ter (flŭt′ər) *intr.v.* **1.** To wave or flap rapidly in an irregular manner: *The curtains fluttered in the breeze.* **2. a.** To fly by a quick, light flapping of the wings. **b.** To flap the wings without flying. **3.** To vibrate or beat rapidly or erratically, as the heart. **4.** To move quickly in a nervous, restless, or excited fashion: *The children fluttered around the room.* **—tr.v.** To cause to flutter: *fluttered her eyelashes.* **—n. 1.** An act of fluttering. **2.** A condition of nervous excitement or agitation. **3.** *Electronics.* A distortion in reproduced sound due to frequency deviations created by faulty recording or reproduction techniques. [Middle English *floteren,* to flutter, be tossed by waves, from Old English *floterian.*] **—flut′ter·y** *adj.*

flutter kick. A swimming kick in which the legs are held horizontally and alternately moved up and down in rapid strokes without bending the knees.

flu·vi·al (flōō′vē-əl) *adj.* Of, pertaining to, or produced by a river or stream: *fluvial erosion.* [Middle English, from Latin *fluviālis,* from *fluvius,* river, from *fluere,* to flow.]

flux (flŭks) *n.* **1. a.** A flow or flowing. **b.** A flowing in of the tide. **2.** Continual change or movement. **3.** *Physics.* **a.** A flow of matter or energy as or regarded as a fluid. **b.** The number of lines of force that pass through a given surface located in a magnetic or electric field. **4.** *Med.* The discharge of large quantities of fluid material from a bodily surface or cavity. **5.** *Metallurgy.* **a.** A mineral added to a smelting furnace to promote fusing of metals or to prevent the formation of oxides. **b.** A substance applied in soldering and brazing to portions of a surface to be joined to prevent oxide formation and to facilitate the flowing of solder. **—tr.v. 1.** To melt; fuse. **2.** To apply a flux to. [Middle English, from Old French, from Latin *fluxus,* past part. of *fluere,* to flow.]

fly¹ (flī) *v.* **flew** (flōō), **flown** (flōn), **fly·ing. —intr.v. 1.** To move through the air with the aid of wings or winglike parts. **2. a.** To travel by air. **b.** To pilot an aircraft. **3. a.** To rise in or be carried through the air by the wind. **b.** To float or flutter in the air: *pennants flying.* **4.** To be sent through the air with great speed or force: *bullets flying all around.*

5. a. To rush; run: *He flew down the hall.* **b.** To flee. **6.** To pass by swiftly, as time or youth: *Our vacation flew by.* **7.** Past tense and past participle **flied.** *Baseball.* To hit a fly ball. **8.** To react explosively; burst: *He flew into a rage.* —*tr.v.* **1.** To cause to float or flutter in the air: *fly a flag.* **2.** To pilot (an aircraft). **3.** To carry or transport in an aircraft. **4.** To pass over in an aircraft: *fly the ocean.* **5.** To perform in an aircraft: *He flew 60 combat missions.* —*phrasal verbs.* **fly at.** To rush at angrily or excitedly. **fly out.** *Baseball.* To make an out by hitting a fly ball that is caught. —*n., pl.* **flies. 1.** A cloth flap covering a zipper or a set of buttons, esp. one on the front of trousers. **2.** A cloth flap that covers an entrance or forms a roof extension for a tent or wagon. **3.** A flyleaf. **4.** *Baseball.* A fly ball. **5. flies.** The area directly over the stage of a theater. **6.** *Brit.* A one-horse carriage; a hackney. —*idioms.* **fly in the face (or teeth) of.** To resist or defy openly. **fly off the handle.** To lose control of one's temper. **on the fly.** On the run; in a hurry. [Middle English *flien,* from Old English *flēogan.*]

fly² (flī) *n., pl.* **flies. 1. a.** Any of numerous winged insects of the order Diptera, which includes the housefly. **b.** Any of various other flying insects, such as the caddis fly. **2.** A fishing lure simulating a fly. —*idiom.* **fly in the ointment.** A bad point or drawback. [Middle English *flie,* from Old English *flēoge.*]

fly agaric. A poisonous mushroom, *Amanita muscaria.* [From its use as a poison on flypaper.]

fly ball. *Baseball.* A ball that is batted in a high arc to the outfield.

fly-blown (flī'blōn') *adj.* **1.** Contaminated with the eggs or larvae of flies. **2.** Spoiled; tainted; corrupt.

fly-by-night (flī'bī-nīt') *adj.* **1.** Of unreliable business character: *a fly-by-night operation.* **2.** Dubious and temporary: *a fly-by-night style.*

fly casting. The act of casting a fishing line using artificial flies and a long flexible pole.

fly-catch-er (flī'kăch'ər) *n.* Any of various birds that fly suddenly from a perch to catch flying insects, esp. a member of the New World family Tyrannidae or the Old World family Muscicapidae.

flycatcher
George Miksch Sutton

flying buttress

fly-er (flī'ər) *n.* Var. of **flier.**

fly-ing (flī'ĭng) *adj.* **1.** Swiftly moving: *flying fingers.* **2.** Brief; hurried: *a flying visit.* —*n.* **1.** Flight in an aircraft. **2.** The piloting or navigation of an aircraft.

flying boat. A large seaplane that is kept afloat by its hull rather than by pontoons.

flying buttress. An arch extending from a separate supporting structure to brace part of the main structure of a building.

flying colors. Complete success; triumph: *passed the bar examination with flying colors.*

flying fish. Any of various saltwater fishes of the family Exocoetidae, with enlarged pectoral or pelvic fins that sustain them in brief, gliding flight over the water.

flying fox. Any of various fruit-eating bats of the genus *Pteropus,* chiefly of tropical Africa, Asia, and Australia, with a foxlike muzzle and ears.

flying jib. *Naut.* A light sail that extends beyond the jib and is attached to an extension of the jib boom.

flying machine. An aircraft or other machine designed for flight.

flying saucer. Any of various unidentified flying objects typically reported and described as luminous disks.

flying squirrel. Any of various squirrels of the genera *Pteromys, Glaucomys,* and related genera that have membranes between the forelegs and hind legs that enable them to glide through the air.

flying start. A start in racing in which the participants cross the starting line at full speed.

fly-leaf (flī'lēf') *n.* A blank page at the beginning or end of a book.

fly-pa-per (flī'pā'pər) *n.* Paper coated with a sticky, sometimes poisonous substance for catching flies.

fly-speck (flī'spĕk') *n.* **1.** A speck or stain made by the excrement of a fly. **2.** Any minute spot.

fly swatter. A device used to kill flies or other insects, usu. consisting of a flat square of plastic or wire mesh attached to a long handle.

fly-trap (flī'trăp') *n.* **1.** A trap for catching flies. **2.** A plant that traps insects, as the Venus's-flytrap.

fly-weight (flī'wāt') *n.* A boxer of the lightest weight class, weighing 112 pounds or less.

fly-wheel (flī'hwēl', -wēl') *n.* A heavy-rimmed rotating wheel used to keep a shaft of a machine turning at a steady speed.

Fm The symbol for the element fermium.

f-num-ber (ĕf'nŭm'bər) *n.* The ratio of focal length to the effective aperture diameter in a lens or lens system, used in photography as a measure of the effectiveness of the lens in collecting light. Also called **f-stop.**

foal (fōl) *n.* The young offspring of a horse or other equine animal, esp. one less than a year old. —*intr.v.* To give birth to a foal. [Middle English *fole,* from Old English *fola.*]

foam (fōm) *n.* **1.** A light, frothy mass of bubbles formed in a liquid. **2.** Frothy saliva or sweat, esp. of a horse or other equine. **3.** A thick, chemically produced froth, as shaving cream or certain firefighting substances. —*intr.v.* To form or come forth in foam; froth. —*tr.v.* To cause to foam. [Middle English *fom,* saliva, foam, from Old English *fām.*]

foam rubber. A light, firm, spongy rubber, used in upholstery and for insulation.

foam-y (fō'mē) *adj.* **-i-er, -i-est.** Consisting of, covered with, or resembling foam. —**foam'i-ly** *adv.* —**foam'i-ness** *n.*

fob¹ (fŏb) *n.* **1.** A small pocket at the front waistline of a man's trousers or in the front of a vest. **2.** A short chain or ribbon attached to a pocket watch and worn hanging in front of the vest or waist. **3.** An ornament attached to a watch chain. [Prob. of Germanic orig.]

fob² (fŏb) *tr.v.* **fobbed, fob-bing.** —**fob off. 1.** To dispose of (goods) by fraud or deception. **2.** To put off by deceitful or evasive means. [Middle English *fobben.*]

fo-cal (fō'kəl) *adj.* Of, at, or pertaining to a focus. —**fo'cal-ly** *adv.*

focal length. *Optics.* The distance of the focus from the surface of a lens or mirror.

fo-ci (fō'sī) *n.* A plural of **focus.**

fo'c's'le (fōk'səl) *n.* Var. of **forecastle.**

fo-cus (fō'kəs) *n., pl.* **-cus-es** or **-ci** (-sī'). **1. a.** A point in a system of lenses or other optical system at which rays, esp. of light, converge or from which they appear to diverge. **b.** Focal length. **c.** The distinctness or clarity with which an eye or optical system renders an image. **d.** Adjustment for distinctness or clarity: *out of focus.* **2.** A center of interest or activity: *the focus of a discussion.* **3.** *Geol.* The point of origin of an earthquake. **4.** *Geom.* A fixed point or one of a pair of fixed points used in constructing a curve such as an ellipse, parabola, or hyperbola. —*v.* **-cused** or **-cussed, -cus-ing** or **-cus-sing.** —*tr.v.* **1. a.** To produce a clear image of by adjusting the eyes or an optical instrument. **b.** To adjust (the eyes, a lens, etc.) to produce a clear image. **2.** To concentrate on: *focusing his effort on building a business.* —*intr.v.* To converge at a point of focus; be focused. [Latin *focus,* fireplace, hearth.]

fod-der (fŏd'ər) *n.* Feed for livestock, often of coarsely chopped stalks of corn and hay. —*tr.v.* To feed (animals) with fodder. [Middle English *fodder,* from Old English *fōdor.*]

foe (fō) *n.* **1.** A personal enemy. **2.** An enemy in war. **3.** An adversary; opponent: *political foes.* [Middle English *fo,* from Old English *gefā,* from *gefāh,* at feud with, hostile.]

foehn (fān, fœn) *n.* Also **föhn.** A warm dry wind blowing down the slopes of a mountain range. [German Föhn, ult. from Latin *favōnius,* west wind.]

foe·tal (fēt′l) *adj.* Var. of **fetal.**

foe·tid (fĕt′ĭd, fē′tĭd) *adj.* Var. of **fetid.**

foe·tus (fē′təs) *n.* Var. of **fetus.**

fog (fŏg, fôg) *n.* **1.** A cloudlike mass of condensed water vapor lying close to the surface of the ground. **2.** Any mass of floating material, such as dust or smoke, that forms an obscuring haze. **3.** A condition of mental confusion or bewilderment. **4.** A dark blur on a developed photographic negative. —*v.* **fogged, fog·ging.** —*tr.v.* **1.** To cover with or as if with fog. **2.** To make uncertain or unclear. —*intr.v.* To be covered with or as if with fog. [Prob. back-formation from earlier *foggy,* murky, moist, boggy, from *fog,* rank grass.]

fog·bound (fŏg′bound′, fôg′-) *adj.* Clouded, obscured, or immobilized by fog.

fo·gey (fō′gē) *n.* Var. of **fogy.**

fog·gy (fŏ′gē, fô′gē) *adj.* **-gi·er, -gi·est. 1.** Full of or covered by fog. **2.** Dim or blurred; indistinct. **3.** Vague: *only a foggy idea of what happened.* —See Syns at **vague.** —**fog′gi·ly** *adv.* —**fog′gi·ness** *n.*

fog·horn (fŏg′hôrn′, fôg′-) *n.* A horn, usu. having a deep tone, blown to warn ships of danger in foggy weather.

fo·gy (fō′gē) *n., pl.* **-gies.** Also **fo·gey** *pl.* **-geys.** A person of old-fashioned habits or narrow-minded attitudes. [Orig. unknown.] —**fo′gy·ish** *adj.*

föhn (fān, fœn) *n.* Var. of **foehn.**

foi·ble (foi′bəl) *n.* A minor weakness or failing of character. [Obs. French, from Old French *feble,* feeble.]

foil¹ (foil) *tr.v.* To prevent from being successful; thwart; frustrate. [Orig. to trample, tread upon, from Middle English *foilen.*]

foil² (foil) *n.* **1.** A thin, flexible sheet of metal. **2.** A thin layer of bright metal placed under a displayed gem to lend it brilliance. **3.** A person or thing that by contrast enhances or sets off the distinctive characteristics of another: *a perfect foil for the comedian.* **4.** *Archit.* A leaflike design or space, found esp. in Gothic window tracery. [Middle English *foile,* thin sheet of metal, leaf, from Old French, from Latin *folium.*]

foil³ (foil) *n.* A light, flexible fencing sword with a thin four-sided blade and a blunt point. [Orig. unknown.]

foist (foist) *tr.v.* To pass off as genuine, valuable, or worthy. [Orig. "to introduce a palmed die surreptitiously," from Dutch (dial.) *vuisten,* from *vuist,* fist.]

fold¹ (fōld) *tr.v.* **1.** To bend over or double up so that one part lies on another part: *fold a sheet of paper.* **2.** To bring from an extended to a closed position: *The hawk folded its wings.* **3.** To place together and intertwine: *fold one's arms.* **4.** To surround with the arms; embrace. **5.** *Cooking.* To mix in (an ingredient) by slowly and gently turning one part over another. —*intr.v.* **1.** To become folded. **2.** *Informal.* To close for lack of funds; fail financially. **3.** *Informal.* **a.** To give in; yield. **b.** To collapse. —See Syns at **yield.** —*n.* **1.** A line, layer, pleat, or crease formed by folding. **2.** A folded edge or piece: *the fold of a hem.* **3.** *Geol.* A bend in a layer of rock. [Middle English *folden,* from Old English *faldan, fealdan.*]

fold² (fōld) *n.* **1.** A fenced enclosure for domestic animals, esp. sheep. **2.** A flock of sheep. **3.** A group of people bound together by common beliefs and aims. [Middle English, from Old English *fald, falod.*]

–fold. A suffix meaning: **1.** Division into a specified number of parts: **fivefold. 2.** Multiplication by a specified number: **tenfold.** [Middle English, from Old English *-f(e)ald.*]

fold·er (fōl′dər) *n.* **1.** A folded sheet of heavy paper used as a holder for loose papers. **2.** A booklet or pamphlet made of one or more folded sheets of paper. **3.** A person or machine that folds.

fol·de·rol (fŏl′də-rŏl′) *n.* Also **fal·de·ral** or **fal·de·rol** (făl′də-răl′). **1.** Nonsense. **2.** A trifle; gewgaw. [From *fol-de-rol* and *fal-deral,* a refrain in some old songs.]

fo·li·a·ceous (fō′lē-ā′shəs) *adj.* **1.** Of, relating to, or resembling the leaf of a plant. **2.** Consisting of thin leaflike layers, as certain rocks. [Latin *foliāceus,* from *folium,* leaf.]

fo·li·age (fō′lē-ĭj) *n.* The leaves of growing plants; plant leaves in general. [Middle English *foilage,* from Old French *foillage,* from *foille,* leaf, from Latin *folium.*]

fo·li·ate (fō′lē-ĭt, -āt′) *adj.* Having leaves. —*v.* (fō′lē-āt′) **-at·ed, -at·ing. —tr.v. 1.** To decorate with foils. **2.** To number the leaves of (a book). —*intr.v.* **1.** To produce foliage; put forth leaves. **2.** To split into thin layers. [Latin *foliātus,* bearing leaves, from *folium,* leaf.]

fo·li·a·tion (fō′lē-ā′shən) *n.* **1.** The condition of being in leaf. **2.** *Archit.* The decoration of an opening with cusps and foils. [From Latin *folium,* leaf.]

fo·lic acid (fō′lĭk). A yellowish-orange compound, $C_{19}H_{19}N_7O_6$, a member of the vitamin-B complex, occurring in green plants, fresh fruit, liver, and yeast and used medicinally to treat pernicious anemias. [Latin *fol(ium),* leaf + -IC.]

fo·li·o (fō′lē-ō′) *n., pl.* **-os. 1. a.** A large sheet of paper, folded once in the middle, making two leaves or four pages of a book. **b.** A book of the largest common size, consisting of such folded sheets. **2.** A page number in a book. [From Latin *folium,* leaf.]

folk (fōk) *n., pl.* **folk** or **folks. 1. folk.** A people or nation. **2.** Often **folks.** People of a specified group or kind: *country folk.* **3. folks.** *Informal.* One's family or relatives. **4. folks.** *Informal.* People in general. —*adj.* Of, occurring in, or originating among the common people: *folk art; a folk hero.* [Middle English, from Old English *folc,* the people, nation, tribe.]

Usage: **folk, folks.** *Folk* is the singular and plural form when the noun means a people (i.e., an ethnic group): *the tribal folk of Southwest Asia.* The plural *folk* and often *folks* can be used when describing a specific kind of people: *city folk* (also *folks*). The plural *folks* is informal when applied to one's relatives and to people in general: *Your folks called. Good morning, folks! Folks are a pretty good lot, all told.*

folk etymology. A change in form of a word or phrase so that it resembles a more familiar term mistakenly taken to be analogous, as *sparrowgrass* for *asparagus.*

folk·lore (fōk′lôr′, -lōr′) *n.* The traditional beliefs, practices, legends, and tales of the common people, passed down orally. —**folk′lor′ist** *n.*

folk music. Music originating among the common people of a nation or region.

folk rock. A variety of popular music that combines elements of rock'n'roll and folk music.

folk singer. A singer of folk songs.

folk song. A song belonging to the folk music of a people or area and characterized chiefly by the directness and simplicity of the feelings expressed.

folk·sy (fōk′sē) *adj.* **-si·er, -si·est.** *Informal.* Simple and unpretentious. —**folk′si·ness** *n.*

folk·tale (fōk′tāl′) *n.* Also **folk tale.** A traditional story or local legend handed down by the common people of a country or region from one generation to the next.

folk·way (fōk′wā′) *n.* A way of thinking or acting shared by the members of a group as part of their common culture.

fol·li·cle (fŏl′ĭ-kəl) *n.* **1.** *Anat.* A tiny cavity or sac in the body, such as the depression in the skin from which a hair grows. **2.** *Anat.* One of the structures in an ovary in which the ova are contained. **3.** *Bot.* A dry single-cell fruit such as the milkweed that splits along only one seam to release its seeds. [Latin *folliculus,* little bag, dim. of *follis,* bellows.]

fol·low (fŏl′ō) *tr.v.* **1.** To come or go after; move behind and in the same direction: *Follow the usher.* **2.** To move behind, as when chasing or trailing: *Follow a suspect.* **3.** To move or go along: *following a trail.* **4.** To come after in order, time, or position: *Night follows day.* **5.** To be the result of: *A fight followed the argument.* **6. a.** To act in agreement with; obey: *follow orders.* **b.** To keep to or stick to: *follow a recipe.* **7.** To engage in; work at (a trade or occupation). **8.** To be attentive to: *listen to or watch closely: followed the game on the radio.* **9.** To grasp the meaning or logic of; understand; comprehend: *Do you follow my reasoning?* —*intr.v.* **1.** To come, move, or take place after. **2.** To occur or be evident as a consequence; ensue. —See Syns at **obey** and **understand.** —*phrasal verb.*

follow up. 1. To carry to completion. **2.** To increase the effectiveness of by repetition or further action. [Middle English *fol(o)wen*, from Old English *folgian* and *fylgan*.]

fol·low·er (fŏl'ō-ər) *n.* **1.** Someone or something that follows another or a belief, theory, etc., as a supporter, disciple, adherent, or admirer. **2.** An attendant, servant, or subordinate.

fol·low·ing (fŏl'ō-ĭng) *adj.* **1.** Coming next in time or order: *the following chapter.* **2.** Now to be mentioned or listed: *The following men will report for duty.* —*n.* A group of admirers, adherents, or disciples: *a writer with a large following.*

fol·low-up (fŏl'ō-ŭp') *n.* **1.** The act of repeating or adding to previous action so as to increase effectiveness. **2.** The means used to do this.

fol·ly (fŏl'ē) *n., pl.* **-lies. 1.** A lack of good sense, understanding, or foresight. **2.** An act or example of foolishness. **3.** A costly undertaking having an absurd or ruinous outcome. [Middle English *folie*, from Old French, from *fol*, foolish, from Latin *follis*, bellows.]

fo·ment (fō-mĕnt') *tr.v.* To stir up; arouse; provoke: *foment a rebellion.* [Middle English *fomenten*, from Old French *fomenter*, from Late Latin *fōmentāre*, from Latin *fōmentum*, warm application, from *fovēre*, to warm, cherish.] —**fo·ment'er** *n.*

fo·men·ta·tion (fō'mən-tā'shən) *n.* **1.** The act of fomenting; instigation. **2.** A warm, moist medicinal compress applied to the body to reduce pain.

fond (fŏnd) *adj.* **-er, -est. 1.** Loving or affectionate; tender: *a fond embrace.* **2.** Having a strong affection or liking: *fond of ballet.* **3.** Overly or irrationally affectionate; doting: *a fond grandparent.* **4.** Deeply felt; dear: *my fondest hopes.* [Middle English *fonned*, foolish, prob. from *fon*, a fool.] —**fond'ly** *adv.* —**fond'ness** *n.*

fon·dant (fŏn'dənt) *n.* A sweet, creamy sugar paste, eaten as candy or used in icings or as a filling for other candies. [French, from *fondre*, to melt, from Latin *fundere*, to pour, melt.]

fon·dle (fŏn'dl) *tr.v.* **-dled, -dling.** To handle or stroke with affection; caress lovingly with the hands. [Back-formation from earlier *fondling*, foolish person.]

fon·due (fŏn-dōō') *n.* Also **fon·du.** A hot dish made of melted cheese and wine and eaten with bread. [French, fem. past part. of *fondre*, to melt.]

font¹ (fŏnt) *n.* **1.** A basin holding baptismal or holy water in a church. **2.** A source of abundance; fount. [Middle English, from Old English, from Latin *fons*, fountain.]

font¹

football

font² (fŏnt) *n. Printing.* A complete set of type of one size and face. [Old French, casting, from *fondre*, to melt, cast.]

food (fōōd) *n.* **1.** Any substance taken in and assimilated by an organism to maintain life and growth; nourishment. **2.** A particular kind of nourishment: *plant food.* **3.** Nourishment in solid form as distinguished from liquid nourishment. **4.** Anything that sustains, stimulates, or encourages: *food for thought.* [Middle English *fode*, from Old English *fōda*.]

food chain. A series of plants and animals within an environment of which each kind serves as a source of nourishment for the next in the series.

food poisoning. Poisoning caused by eating food containing natural toxins or contaminated by bacteria, characterized by vomiting, diarrhea, and prostration.

food·stuff (fōōd'stŭf') *n.* Any substance that can be used or prepared for use as food.

fool (fōōl) *n.* **1.** A person who is deficient in judgment, sense, or understanding. **2.** Formerly, a member of a royal or noble household who entertained the court with jests, mimicry, etc.; jester. **3.** A person who can easily be deceived or imposed upon; a dupe. —*tr.v.* **1.** To deceive or trick; dupe. **2.** To take unawares; surprise, esp. pleasantly: *We were sure he would fail, but he fooled us.* —*intr.v.* To act or speak in jest; joke. —*phrasal verbs.* **fool around.** *Informal.* **1.** To waste time; idle. **2.** To mess around; play. **fool with (or around with).** To toy, tamper, or meddle with. [Middle English *fol(e)*, a fool, foolish, from Old French *fol*, from Latin *follis*, bellows, windbag.]

fool·er·y (fōō'lə-rē) *n., pl.* **-ies.** Foolish behavior; nonsense.

fool·har·dy (fōōl'här'dē) *adj.* **-di·er, -di·est.** Foolishly bold or daring; rash. [Middle English *fol-hardi*, from Old French *folhardi* : *fol*, foolish + *hardi*, hardy.] —**fool'har'di·ly** *adv.* —**fool'har'di·ness** *n.*

fool·ish (fōō'lĭsh) *adj.* **1.** Lacking good sense or judgment; silly: *foolish remarks; foolish decision.* **2.** Silly or absurd; ridiculous: *a foolish grin.* —**fool'ish·ly** *adv.* —**fool'ish·ness** *n.*

    Syns: **foolish, absurd, crazy, idiotic, insane, nonsensical, preposterous, silly, wacky** (*Slang*), **zany** *adj.* Core meaning: So senseless as to be laughable (*a foolish attempt to cross the country on a tricycle*).

fool·proof (fōōl'prōōf') *adj.* Designed so as to be proof against error, misuse, or failure.

fools·cap (fōōlz'kăp') *n.* A sheet of writing paper approx. 13x16 inches. [From the watermark of a fool's cap orig. marking this type of paper.]

fool's cap. 1. A gaily decorated cap formerly worn by court jesters and clowns. **2.** A dunce cap.

fool's gold. Pyrite or any similar mineral sometimes mistaken for gold.

fool's paradise. A state of delusive contentment or false hope.

foot (fōōt) *n., pl.* **feet** (fēt). **1.** The lower extremity of the vertebrate leg that is in direct contact with the ground in standing or walking. **2.** A structure used for locomotion or attachment in an invertebrate animal, as the muscular organ extending from the shell of a snail or clam. **3.** Something resembling or suggestive of a foot in position or function: *the foot of a mountain.* **4.** The lower end of an object or the end opposite the head, as of a bed. **5.** The attachment on a sewing machine that clamps down and guides the cloth. **6.** *Pros.* A metric unit consisting of a stressed or unstressed syllable or syllables. **7.** *Symbol* ' *Abbr.* **ft** A unit of length in the U.S. Customary and British Imperial systems, equal to ¹/₃ yard or 12 inches. —*intr.v.* **1.** To go on foot; walk: *Let's foot it to town.* **2.** To dance: *footed it until dawn.* —*tr.v.* **1.** To add (a column of numbers); total: *Foot up the bill.* **2.** *Informal.* To pay: *Can you foot the monthly rent?* —**idioms. at the feet of** or **at (one's) feet.** Fascinated or enchanted by; under the spell of. **on foot. 1.** Walking or running rather than riding. **2.** Under way; in progress. **put (one's) best foot forward.** *Informal.* To make a good first impression. **put (one's) foot down.** *Informal.* To take a firm stand; insist on being obeyed. **put (one's) foot in it.** To make an embarrassing blunder. **put (one's) foot in (one's) mouth.** *Informal.* To say something by mistake that causes embarrassment or hurt feelings. [Middle English *fot*, from Old English *fōt*.] —**foot'less** *adj.*

    Usage: **foot, feet.** *Foot* and *feet* are typically but not invariably distinguished in usage. Here are some very basic guidelines for their use. If the word occurs as a part of a compound preceding the noun it modifies, *foot* is the choice: *a six-foot-tall man* (but *a man who is six feet tall*); *a two-foot space.* If the word occurs after the word it modifies, *feet* is the usual choice: *a man six feet tall; a ledge six feet wide.*

foot·age (fōōt'ĭj) *n.* The length or extent of something as expressed in feet.

foot-and-mouth disease (fōōt'n-mouth') **.** A highly contagious viral disease of cattle and other animals with cloven hoofs, marked by fever and the breaking out of blisters around the mouth and hoofs.

foot·ball (fōōt'bôl') *n.* **1. a.** A game played by two teams of

---

ă pat	ā pay	â care	ä father	ĕ pet	ē be	hw which	ĭ pit	ī tie	î pier	ŏ pot	ō toe	ô paw, for	oi noise
ōō took	ōō boot	ou out	th thin	th this	ŭ cut		û urge	zh vision	ə about, item, edible, gallop, circus

11 players each on a long field with goals at either end, the object being to carry the ball across the opponent's goal line or to kick it between the opponent's goal posts. **b.** The inflated oval ball used in football. **2.** *Brit.* **a.** Soccer or rugby. **b.** The ball used in soccer or rugby.

foot·board (fŏŏt′bôrd′, -bōrd′) *n.* **1.** A board or small raised platform on which to support or rest the feet. **2.** An upright board across the foot of a bedstead.

foot·bridge (fŏŏt′brĭj′) *n.* A narrow bridge for pedestrians only.

foot-can·dle (fŏŏt′kăn′dl) *n. Abbr.* **fc** *Physics.* The illumination of a surface one foot distant from a source of one candela, equal to one lumen per square foot.

foot·ed (fŏŏt′ĭd) *adj.* **1.** Having a foot or feet: *a footed vase.* **2.** Having a specified kind or number of feet: *web-footed; four-footed.*

foot·fall (fŏŏt′fôl′) *n.* **1.** A footstep. **2.** The sound made by a footstep.

foot·gear (fŏŏt′gîr′) *n.* Sturdy footwear.

foot·hill (fŏŏt′hĭl′) *n.* A low hill near the base of a mountain or mountain range.

foot·hold (fŏŏt′hōld′) *n.* **1.** A place providing support for the foot in climbing or standing. **2.** A secure position that provides a base for further advancement.

foot·ing (fŏŏt′ĭng) *n.* **1.** A secure placement of the feet in standing or moving. **2.** A basis; foundation: *a business begun on a good footing.* **3.** A basis for social or business transactions with others; a standing: *We are all on equal footing here.*

foot·lights (fŏŏt′lĭts′) *pl.n.* **1.** Lights placed in a row along the front of a stage floor. **2.** The theater as a profession; the stage.

foot·lock·er (fŏŏt′lŏk′ər) *n.* A small trunk for personal belongings designed to be kept at the foot of a bunk.

foot·loose (fŏŏt′lōōs′) *adj.* Having no attachments or ties; free to do as one pleases.

foot·man (fŏŏt′mən) *n.* A male servant who waits on tables, attends the door, and runs various errands.

foot·note (fŏŏt′nōt′) *n.* **1.** A note at the bottom of a page or the end of a book that comments on or cites a reference for a designated part of the text. **2.** An afterthought. —*tr.v.* **-not·ed, -not·ing.** To furnish with footnotes.

foot·path (fŏŏt′păth′, -päth′) *n.* A narrow path for pedestrians.

foot-pound (fŏŏt′pound′) *n. Abbr.* **ft-lb** A unit of work equal to the energy needed to lift a one-pound weight a distance of 1 foot against the force of the earth's gravity that is equivalent to approx 1.36 joules.

foot-pound-sec·ond (fŏŏt′pound′sĕk′ənd) *adj. Abbr.* **fps** Of, pertaining to, or characteristic of a system of units based on the foot, the pound, and the second as the fundamental units of length, weight, and time.

foot·print (fŏŏt′prĭnt′) *n.* An outline or indentation left by a foot on a surface.

foot·rest (fŏŏt′rĕst′) *n.* A support on which to rest the feet.

foot soldier. An infantryman.

foot·sore (fŏŏt′sôr′, -sōr′) *adj.* Having sore or tired feet.

foot·step (fŏŏt′stĕp′) *n.* **1.** A step with the foot. **2.** The distance covered by one step. **3.** The sound of a foot stepping. **4.** A footprint.

foot·stool (fŏŏt′stōōl′) *n.* A low stool for supporting or resting the feet.

foot·way (fŏŏt′wā′) *n.* A walk or path for pedestrians.

foot·wear (fŏŏt′wâr′) *n.* Coverings for the feet.

foot·work (fŏŏt′wûrk′) *n.* The manner in which the feet are used or maneuvered, as in boxing or fencing.

fop (fŏp) *n.* A vain man who is preoccupied with his clothes and manners; a dandy. [Middle English *foppe,* a fool.] —**fop′pish** *adj.* —**fop′pish·ness** *n.*

fop·per·y (fŏp′ə-rē) *n., pl.* **-ies.** The dress or manner of a fop.

for (fôr; fər *when unstressed*) *prep.* **1.** Directed or sent to: *a letter for you.* **2.** As a result of: *weep for joy.* **3.** To the extent or through the duration of: *sitting still for an hour.* **4.** In order to go to or reach: *starting for home.* **5. a.** With a view to: *swimming for fun.* **b.** So as to find, get, have, keep, or save: *looking for a bargain; fighting for one's life.* **6.** In order to serve in or as: *studying for the ministry.* **7.** In

the amount or at the price of: *a bill for three dollars.* **8.** In response to: *I slapped him for saying that.* **9.** In view of the normal character of: *His book is short for a novel.* **10.** At a stated time: *a date for one o'clock.* **11.** In the service or hire of: *working for a boss.* **12.** In spite of: *For all her experience she does a poor job.* **13.** On behalf or in honor of: *a collection for the poor; a reception for the ambassador.* **14.** In place of: *using artificial flowers for real ones.* **15.** Together with: *one rotten apple for every good one.* **16.** As against: *pound for pound.* **17.** As being: *took him for a fool.* **18.** As the duty or task of; up to: *That's for you to decide.* —*conj.* Because; since. [Middle English, from Old English.]

for·age (fôr′ĭj, fŏr′-) *n.* **1.** Food for domestic animals, esp. plants or grass eaten while grazing. **2.** The act of searching for food or provisions. —*v.* **-aged, -ag·ing.** —*intr.v.* **1.** To search for food or provisions. **2.** To search, as for supplies; rummage. —*tr.v.* **1.** To wander or rummage through, esp. in search of provisions. **2.** To obtain by foraging: *foraged a snack in the refrigerator.* [Middle English, from Old French fo(ur)rage, from feurre, fodder.] —**for′ag·er** *n.*

fo·ra·men (fə-rā′mən) *n., pl.* **-ram·i·na** (-răm′ə-nə) or **-mens.** An opening in a bone or through a membrane. [From Latin *forāmen,* an opening, from *forāre,* to bore.]

foramen mag·num (măg′nəm). The large opening in the base of the skull through which the spinal cord passes and becomes continuous with the medulla oblongata. [New Latin, "large orifice."]

for·as·much as (fôr′əz-mŭch′). Inasmuch as; since.

for·ay (fôr′ā′, fŏr′ā′) *n.* **1.** A sudden raid or military advance. **2.** A first venture or attempt: *his foray into politics.* —*intr.v.* To make a raid. [Middle English *forrai,* from *forraien,* to foray, back-formation from *forreour,* raider, plunderer, from Old French *forrier.*]

for·bad (fər-băd′, fôr-). A past tense of **forbid**.

for·bade (fər-băd′, -bād′, fôr-). A past tense of **forbid**.

for·bear¹ (fôr-bâr′) *v.* **-bore** (-bôr′, -bōr′), **-borne** (-bôrn′, -bōrn′), **-bear·ing.** —*tr.v.* **1.** To refrain from; resist. **2.** To desist from; cease. —*intr.v.* **1.** To hold back; refrain. **2.** To be tolerant or patient. [Middle English *forberen,* from Old English *forberan,* to bear, endure.]

for·bear² (fôr′bâr′, fōr′-) *n.* Var. of **forebear**.

for·bear·ance (fôr-bâr′əns) *n.* **1.** The act of forbearing. **2.** Tolerance and restraint in the face of provocation; patience.

for·bid (fər-bĭd′, fôr-) *tr.v.* **-bade** (-băd′, -bād′) or **-bad** (-băd′), **-bid·den** (-bĭd′n) or **-bid, -bid·ding.** **1.** To command (someone) not to do something: *I forbid you to go.* **2.** To prohibit: *Smoking is forbidden.* **3.** To have the effect of preventing; preclude. [Middle English *forbidden,* from Old English *forbēodan.*]

Syns: forbid, ban, disallow, enjoin, outlaw, prohibit, proscribe *v.* *Core meaning:* To refuse to allow (*smoking forbidden therein; forbade them entry*).

Usage: forbid. This verb is used with an infinitive or a gerund: *forbid her to leave; forbid her leaving.* Avoid use of *from* after forbid: *forbid her from leaving.*

for·bid·ding (fər-bĭd′ĭng, fôr-) *adj.* Tending to frighten off; threatening or ominous: *a black and forbidding sky; a forbidding scowl.*

for·bore (fôr-bôr′, -bōr′) *v.* Past tense of **forbear** (to refrain).

for·borne (fôr-bôrn′, -bōrn′) *v.* Past participle of **forbear** (to refrain).

force (fôrs, fōrs) *n.* **1.** Strength; power; energy: *the force of an explosion; a personality of great force.* **2. a.** Power, pressure, or violence used on something or someone that resists: *use force in driving a nail.* **b.** The use of such power: *a confession obtained by force.* **3. a.** A group of people organized for a particular purpose: *a large labor force; a police force.* **b.** A military branch or unit: *the armed forces.* **4. a.** A capacity for affecting, influencing, or persuading the mind or behavior; efficacy: *the force of logical argumentation.* **b.** Anything or anyone possessing such capacity: *forces of evil; forces of nature.* **5.** *Law.* Legal validity; efficacy. **6.** *Physics.* A vector quantity that tends to produce an acceleration of a body in the direction in which it is applied. —*tr.v.* **forced, forc·ing.** **1.** To compel through pressure or necessity: *She forced him to practice every day.* **2.** To obtain by the use of force or coercion:

force a confession. **3.** To move (something) against resistance. **4.** To move, open, or clear by force: *force one's way through a crowd.* **5.** To break down or open by force: *force a lock.* **6.** To inflict or impose: *force one's will on someone.* **7.** To bring on or produce by an effort: *force one's voice.* **8.** To cause to grow by artificially accelerating the normal processes: *force flowers.* **—idiom. in force. 1.** In full strength. **2.** In effect; operative: *a rule no longer in force.* [Middle English, from Old French, from Latin *fortis,* strong.] **—forc′er** *n.*

forced (fôrst, fōrst) *adj.* **1.** Enforced or imposed; involuntary: *forced labor.* **2.** Produced under strain; not spontaneous; unnatural: *forced laughter.*

force·ful (fôrs′fəl, fōrs′-) *adj.* Marked by or full of force; effective: *a forceful speaker.* **—force′ful·ly** *adv.* **—force′ful·ness** *n.*

force·meat (fôrs′mēt′, fōrs′-) *n.* Finely ground meat or poultry, used in stuffing or as a garnish. [From *force,* var. of FARCE (to stuff).]

for·ceps (fôr′səps) *n.* *(used with a pl. verb).* An instrument resembling a pair of pincers or tongs, used for grasping, manipulating, or extracting, esp. in surgery. [Latin, fire tongs, pincers.]

forc·i·ble (fôr′sə-bəl, fōr′-) *adj.* **1.** Accomplished through the use of force: *a forcible entry.* **2.** Characterized by force; forceful. **—forc′i·bly** *adv.*

ford (fôrd, fōrd) *n.* A shallow place in a body of water where a crossing can be made on foot. **—***tr.v.* To cross (a body of water) at a ford. [Middle English, from Old English.] **—ford′a·ble** *adj.*

fore (fôr, fōr) *adj. & adv.* At, in, or toward the front. **—***n.* The front part. **—***interj. Golf.* A word used to warn those ahead that a ball is about to be driven in their direction. **—idiom. to the fore.** In, into, or toward a position of prominence. [From Middle English, "beforehand," from Old English *for(e).*]

fore–. A prefix meaning: **1.** Before in time: *foresight.* **2.** The front or first part: *foredeck.* [Middle English *for-, fore-,* from Old English *fore-,* from *fore,* in front, beforehand.]

fore and aft. From the bow to the stern of a ship; lengthwise of a ship.

fore–and–aft (fôr′ən-ăft′, fōr′-) *adj.* Parallel with the keel of a ship.

fore·arm¹ (fôr-ärm′, fōr′-) *tr.v.* To prepare or arm in advance of some conflict.

fore·arm² (fôr′ärm′, fōr′-) *n.* The part of the arm between the wrist and elbow.

fore·bear (fôr′bâr′, fōr′-) *n.* Also **fore·bear.** A forefather; ancestor. **—**See Syns at **ancestor.** [Middle English : *fore-,* before + *bear,* from *been,* to be.]

fore·bode (fôr-bōd′, fōr-) *tr.v.* **-bod·ed, -bod·ing. 1.** To give a warning or hint of; portend: *Their harsh words foreboded a fight.* **2.** To have a premonition of (a future misfortune). [FORE- + BODE.]

fore·bod·ing (fôr-bō′dĭng, fōr-) *n.* A feeling that something evil or bad is going to happen; premonition.

fore·brain (fôr′brān′, fōr′-) *n.* The front region of the embryonic brain from which the cerebrum, the thalamus, and the hypothalamus develop.

fore·cast (fôr′kăst′, fōr′-) *v.* **-cast** or **-cast·ed, -cast·ing.** **—***tr.v.* **1.** To calculate or predict in advance, usu. after analyzing available data, esp. to predict (weather conditions). **2.** To serve as an advance indication of; foreshadow: *price rises that forecast inflation.* **—***n.* A prediction, as of coming events or conditions. [Middle English *forecasten,* to devise beforehand.] **—fore′cast′er** *n.*

fore·cas·tle (fōk′səl, fôr′kăs′əl, fōr′-) *n.* Also **fo′c's′le** (fōk′səl). **1.** The section of the upper deck of a ship located forward of the foremast. **2.** The crew's quarters at the bow of a merchant ship. [Middle English *forecastel.*]

fore·close (fôr-klōz′, fōr-) *v.* **-closed, -clos·ing.** **—***tr.v.* **1.** *Law.* To end (a mortgage), taking possession of the mortgaged property when regular payments on the mortgage loan are not met. **2.** To exclude or rule out; bar: *won't foreclose the option of intervention.* **—***intr.v.* To foreclose a mortgage. [Middle English *forclosen,* to shut out, preclude, from Old French *forclore* : *fors-,* outside, from Latin *forīs* + *clore,* to close, from Latin *claudere,* to close.]

fore·clo·sure (fôr-klō′zhər, fōr-) *n.* The act of foreclosing, esp. a legal proceeding by which a mortgage is foreclosed.

fore·deck (fôr′dĕk′, fōr′-) *n.* The forward part of a ship's deck, usu. the main deck.

fore·doom (fôr-dōom′, fōr-) *tr.v.* To doom or condemn beforehand.

fore·fa·ther (fôr′fä′thər, fōr′-) *n.* **1.** An ancestor. **2.** A person from an earlier time and common tradition. **—**See Syns at **ancestor.** [Middle English *forefader,* from Old Norse *forfadhir* : *for-,* before + *fadhir,* father.]

fore·fin·ger (fôr′fĭng′gər, fōr′-) *n.* The index finger.

fore·foot (fôr′fŏot′, fōr′-) *n.* **1.** One of the front feet of an animal. **2.** The part of a ship at which the prow joins the keel.

fore·front (fôr′frŭnt′, fōr′-) *n.* **1.** The foremost part or area of something. **2.** The most important part or advanced position: *in the forefront of politics.*

fore·gath·er (fôr-găth′ər, fōr-) *v.* Var. of **forgather.**

fore·go¹ (fôr-gō′, fōr-) *tr.v.* **-went** (-wĕnt′), **-gone** (-gôn′, -gŏn′), **-go·ing.** To precede or go before, as in time or place. [Middle English *forgon,* from Old English *foregān.*] **—fore·go′er** *n.*

Usage: **forego, forgo.** *Forego,* spelled only as given, is the verb meaning to precede or go before in time or place. *Forgo,* less often spelled *forego,* is the verb meaning to relinquish or abstain from: *forgo* (also *forego*) *wordly pleasures.*

fore·go² (fôr-gō′, fōr-) *v.* Var. of **forgo.**

fore·go·ing (fôr-gō′ĭng, fōr-, fôr′gō′ĭng, fōr′-) *adj.* Said, written, or encountered just before; previous: *the foregoing statements.* **—**See Syns at **last.**

fore·gone (fôr-gôn′, -gŏn′, fōr-) *v.* Part participle of **forego** (to precede). **—***adj.* (fôr′gôn′, -gŏn′, fōr′-). So certain as to be known in advance: *a foregone conclusion.* [Past part. of FOREGO.]

fore·ground (fôr′ground′, fōr′-) *n.* **1.** The part of a view or picture that is seen as nearest to the viewer. **2.** The most important or prominent position.

fore·hand (fôr′hănd′, fōr′-) *n.* *Sports.* A stroke, as of a racket, made with the palm of the hand moving forward. **—***modifier: a forehand shot.* **—***adv.* With a forehand stroke or motion.

forehand

fore·head (fôr′ĭd, fōr′-, fôr′hĕd′, fōr′-) *n.* The part of the face between the eyebrows and the normal hairline. [Middle English *forhed,* from Old English *forehēafod.*]

for·eign (fôr′ĭn, fōr′-) *adj.* **1.** Of, characteristic of, or from a country other than one's own: *a foreign custom.* **2.** Located away from one's native country: *a foreign city.* **3.** Conducted or involved with other nations: *foreign trade.* **4.** Located in an abnormal or improper place: *a foreign object in his eye.* **5.** Not natural; alien: *Jealousy is foreign to her nature.* **6.** Not appropriate or essential; irrelevant: *foreign to his needs.* [Middle English *forein,* from Old French *forein,* from Late Latin *forānus,* from Latin *forās,* out of doors, abroad.] **—for′eign·ness** *n.*

Syns: **foreign, alien, exotic** *adj.* *Core meaning:* Of, from, or characteristic of another place or part of the world (*a foreign species of plants; foreign languages we didn't understand*).

for·eign·er (fôr′ə-nər, fōr′-) *n.* A person from a foreign country.

foreign exchange. 1. The transaction of international monetary business, as between governments or businessmen of different countries. **2.** Negotiable bills drawn in one country to be paid in another country.

fore·knowl·edge (fôr-nŏl′ĭj, fōr-) *n.* Knowledge or awareness of something prior to when it happens or comes into existence; prescience.

fore·leg (fôr′lĕg′, fōr′-) *n.* A front leg of an animal.

fore·limb (fôr′lĭm′, fōr′-) *n.* A front part such as an arm, wing, foreleg, or flipper.

fore·lock (fôr′lŏk′, fōr′-) *n.* A lock of hair that grows or falls on the forehead.

fore·man (fôr′mən, fōr′-) *n.* **1.** A person in charge of a group of workers, as at a factory or ranch. **2.** The chairman and spokesman for a jury.

fore·mast (fôr′məst, -măst′, fōr′-) *n.* The mast closest to the bow of a sailing ship.

fore·most (fôr′mōst′, fōr′-) *adj.* First in rank or position; leading: *the foremost authority on international affairs.* —See Syns at **primary.** —*adv.* In the front or first position. [Var. of Middle English *formost,* from Old English *formest,* superl. of *forma,* first.]

fore·name (fôr′nām′, fōr′-) *n.* A first name; given name.

fore·named (fôr′nāmd′, fōr′-) *adj.* Named earlier; aforesaid.

fore·noon (fôr′nōōn′, fōr′-) *n.* The period between sunrise and noon.

fo·ren·sic (fə-rĕn′sĭk, -zĭk) *adj.* Of, characteristic of, or used in legal proceedings or in public debate or argumentation. [From Latin *forēnsis,* of a market or forum, public, from *forum,* forum.] —**fo·ren′si·cal·ly** *adv.*

fore·or·dain (fôr′ôr-dān′, fōr′-) *tr.v.* To appoint or ordain beforehand; predestine. —**fore′or·dain′ment** or **fore·or′di·na′tion** (-ôr′dn-ā-shən) *n.*

fore·part (fôr′pärt′, fōr′-) *n.* The first or foremost part.

fore·paw (fôr′pô′, fōr′-) *n.* The paw of a foreleg.

fore·quar·ter (fôr′kwôr′tər, fōr′-) *n.* **1.** The front section of a side of meat. **2. forequarters.** The forelegs, shoulders, and adjacent parts of an animal, esp. a horse.

fore·run·ner (fôr′rŭn′ər, fōr′-) *n.* **1.** Something that precedes, as in time; predecessor: *The harpsichord was the forerunner of the piano.* **2.** Something that provides advance notice of the coming of others; harbinger: *buds that are the forerunners of spring.*

fore·sail (fôr′səl, -sāl′, fōr′-) *n.* **1.** The principal square sail hung to the foremast of a square-rigged vessel. **2.** The principal fore-and-aft sail on the foremast of a schooner.

fore·see (fôr-sē′, fōr-) *tr.v.* **-saw** (-sô′), **-seen** (-sēn′), **-see·ing.** To see or know beforehand; anticipate: *a critical development we had not foreseen.* —**fore·see′a·ble** *adj.* —**fore·se′er** *n.*

fore·shad·ow (fôr-shăd′ō, fōr-) *tr.v.* To present a warning, sign, or hint of beforehand; presage: *acrimonious negotiations that foreshadow a strike.*

fore·sheet (fôr′shēt′, fōr′-) *n.* **1.** A rope used in trimming a foresail. **2. foresheets.** The spaces near the bow of an open boat.

fore·shore (fôr′shôr′, fōr′shōr′) *n.* The part of a shore that is covered at high tide.

fore·short·en (fôr-shôr′tn, fōr-) *tr.v.* In drawing or painting, to shorten certain lines in (a figure, design, etc.) so as to give the illusion of depth or distance.

foreshorten

fore·skin (fôr′skĭn′, fōr′-) *n.* The loose fold of skin that covers the end of the penis; prepuce.

for·est (fôr′ĭst, fŏr′-) *n.* **1.** A dense growth of trees, together with other plants, covering a large area. **2.** Something that resembles a forest: *a forest of skyscrapers.* [Middle English, from Old French, from Late Latin *forestis (silva),* outside or unfenced (wood), prob. from Latin *forīs,* outside, outdoors.]

fore·stall (fôr-stôl′, fōr-) *tr.v.* To prevent or delay by taking precautionary measures against beforehand: *called in additional police to forestall a riot.* [Middle English *forestallen,* to forestall, obstruct, from *forestal,* the crime of waylaying on the highway, from Old English *foresteall,* waylaying, interception : *fore-,* in front of + *steall,* position, place.] —**fore·stall′er** *n.*

fore·stay (fôr′stā′, fōr′-) *n.* A rope or cable extending from the head of a ship's foremast to the bowsprit.

for·est·er (fôr′ĭ-stər, fŏr′-) *n.* A person trained in forestry.

for·est·ry (fôr′ĭ-strē, fŏr′-) *n.* The science that deals with the development, maintenance, and management of forests.

fore·swear (fôr-swâr′, fōr-) *v.* Var. of **forswear.**

fore·taste (fôr′tāst′, fōr′-) *n.* A sample of something to come in the future: *a foretaste of doom.* —*tr.v.* (fôr-tāst′, fōr-, fôr′tāst′, fōr′-). **-tast·ed, -tast·ing** To have a foretaste of.

fore·tell (fôr-tĕl′, fōr-) *v.* **-told** (-tōld′), **-tell·ing.** —*tr.v.* To tell of or indicate beforehand; prophesy; predict. —*intr.v.* To tell beforehand. —**fore·tell′er** *n.*

fore·thought (fôr′thôt′, fōr′-) *n.* Thought, planning, or preparation for the future beforehand.

fore·to·ken (fôr-tō′kən, fōr-) *tr.v.* To foreshow; foreshadow; presage. —*n.* (fôr′tō′kən, fōr′-). An advance indication.

fore·told (fôr-tōld′, fōr-) *v.* Past tense and past participle of **foretell.**

for·ev·er (fôr-ĕv′ər, fər-) *adv.* **1.** For everlasting time; eternally. **2.** At all times; incessantly: *He was forever complaining about his job.*

for·ev·er·more (fôr-ĕv′ər-môr′, -mōr′, fər-) *adv.* Forever.

fore·warn (fôr-wôrn′, fōr-) *tr.v.* To warn in advance.

fore·went (fôr-wĕnt′, fōr-) *v.* Past tense of **forego** (to go before).

fore·wom·an (fôr′wŏom′ən, fōr′-) *n.* **1.** A woman in charge of a group of workers, as at a factory or ranch. **2.** A woman who acts as a foreman.

fore·word (fôr′wûrd′, -wərd, fōr′-) *n.* A preface or introductory note, esp. in a book.

fore·yard (fôr′yärd′, fōr′-) *n.* The lowest yard on a foremast.

for·feit (fôr′fĭt) *tr.v.* To lose or lose the right to (something) as a penalty or fine for a failure, error, or offense. —*n.* **1.** Something lost as a penalty for a failure, error, or offense. **2.** A forfeiture. —*adj.* Forfeit or liable to forfeiture. [Middle English *forfet,* forfeit, transgression, from Old French *forfet,* from *for(s)faire,* to commit a crime : *fors-,* beyond, from Latin *forīs,* outside + *faire,* to do, act, from Latin *facere.*]

for·fei·ture (fôr′fĭ-chōŏr′, -chər) *n.* **1.** The act of forfeiting. **2.** Something that is forfeited.

for·gat (fər-găt′, fôr-) *v.* Archaic. Past tense of **forget.**

for·gath·er (fôr-găth′ər, fōr-) *intr.v.* Also **fore·gath·er. 1.** To gather together; assemble. **2.** To meet by accident. [Orig. Scottish : FOR- + GATHER.]

for·gave (fər-gāv′, fôr-) *v.* Past tense of **forgive.**

forge¹ (fôrj, fōrj) *n.* **1.** A furnace or hearth where metal is heated so that it can be worked into shape. **2.** A workshop where pig iron is transformed into wrought iron. —*v.* **forged, forg·ing.** —*tr.v.* **1.** To form (metal) by heating in a forge and beating or hammering into shape. **2.** To give form or shape to; contrive; devise: *forge a treaty.* **3.** To fashion or reproduce for fraudulent purposes; counterfeit: *forge a signature.* —*intr.v.* **1.** To work at a forge. **2.** To make a forgery. [Middle English, from Old French, from Latin *fabrica,* smithy, artisan's workshop, from *faber,* smith.] —**forg′er** *n.*

forge² (fôrj, fōrj) *intr.v.* **forged, forg·ing. 1.** To advance gradually but steadily: *forge through the snow.* **2.** To advance quickly and suddenly: *forge ahead in the race.* [Perh. var. of *force.*]

ă pat   ā pay   â care   ä father   ĕ pet   ē be   hw which
ŏŏ took   ōō boot   ou out   th thin   *th* this   ŭ cut
ĭ pit   ī tie   î pier   ŏ pot   ō toe   ô paw, for   oi noise
û urge   zh vision   ə about, item, edible, gallop, circus

for·ger·y (fôr′jə-rē, fōr′-) *n., pl.* **-ies. 1.** The act or crime of producing something counterfeit or forged. **2.** Something counterfeit, forged, or fraudulent.

for·get (fər-gĕt′, fôr-) *v.* **-got** (-gŏt′) or *archaic* **-gat** (-găt′), **-got·ten** (-gŏt′n) or **-got, -get·ting.** —*tr.v.* **1.** To be unable to remember or call to mind: *forgot the address.* **2.** To treat with inattention; neglect: *forgot those who helped her.* **3.** To banish from one's thoughts: *forget an insult.* —*intr.v.* To fail to remember at the proper or specified moment: *forget about paying taxes.* —*idiom.* **forget (oneself).** To lose one's inhibitions or self-restraint. [Middle English *forgeten,* from Old English *forgietan.*] —**for·get′ta·ble** *adj.* —**for·get′ter** *n.*

for·get·ful (fər-gĕt′fəl, fôr-) *adj.* **1.** Tending or likely to forget. **2.** Neglectful; careless: *forgetful of her duties.* —**for·get′ful·ly** *adv.* —**for·get′ful·ness** *n.*

for·get-me-not (fər-gĕt′mē-nŏt′, fôr-) *n.* Any of various low-growing plants of the genus *Myosotis,* with clusters of small blue flowers.

forget-me-not

for·give (fər-gĭv′, fôr-) *v.* **-gave** (-gāv′), **-giv·en** (-gĭv′ən), **-giv·ing.** —*tr.v.* **1.** To excuse for a fault, injury, or offense; pardon. **2.** To stop feeling anger for or resentment against: *forgive an affront.* **3.** To absolve from payment of (a debt). —See Syns at **pardon.** [Middle English *forgiven,* from Old English *forgiefan.*] —**for·giv′a·ble** *adj.* —**for·giv′er** *n.*

for·give·ness (fər-gĭv′nĭs, fôr-) *n.* The act of forgiving; a pardon.

for·go (fôr-gō′, fōr-) *tr.v.* **-went** (-wĕnt′), **-gone** (-gôn′, -gŏn′), **-go·ing.** Also **fore·go.** To give up; relinquish: *forgo the pleasantries and get down to business.* —See Usage note at **forego¹.** [Middle English *forgon,* from Old English *forgān,* to pass away.] —**for·go′er** *n.*

for·got (fər-gŏt′, fôr-) *v.* Past tense and alternate past participle of **forget.**

for·got·ten (fər-gŏt′n, fôr-) *v.* A past participle of **forget.**

fo·rint (fôr′ĭnt′) *n.* The basic monetary unit of Hungary. [Hungarian, from Italian *fiorino, florin.*]

fork (fôrk) *n.* **1.** A utensil with several tines for use in eating food. **2.** A large farm tool of similar shape used esp. for digging. **3. a.** A separation into two or more branches, as of a road. **b.** The place at which such a separation occurs. **c.** One of the branches of such a separation: *the right fork.* —*tr.v.* **1.** To raise, carry, or pitch with a fork: *fork hay.* **2.** To give the shape of a fork to. —*intr.v.* To divide into two or more branches. [Middle English *forke,* from Old English *forca,* fork (for digging), from Latin *furca,* two-pronged fork, fork-shaped prop.]

forked (fôrkt, fôr′kĭd) *adj.* **1.** Having a fork: *a forked river.* **2.** Shaped like a fork: *a forked tail.*

fork·ful (fôrk′fŏŏl′) *n., pl.* **fork·fuls** or **forks·ful.** As much as a fork will hold or lift.

fork lift. A small industrial vehicle with a power-operated pronged platform that can be raised and lowered for insertion under a load to be lifted and carried.

for·lorn (fôr-lôrn′, fər-) *adj.* **1. a.** Appearing sad because abandoned or deserted: *a forlorn house.* **b.** Feeling lonely or depressed because forsaken or deserted: *a forlorn lover.* **2.** Wretched or pitiful in appearance or condition: *a forlorn refugee.* **3.** Nearly hopeless; desperate: *a forlorn cause.* [Middle English *forloren,* past part. of *forlēsen,* to forfeit, lose, abandon, from Old English *forlēosan.*] —**for·lorn′ly** *adv.* —**for·lorn′ness** *n.*

form (fôrm) *n.* **1.** The contour, shape, or structure of something as distinguished from its substance or color. **2.** The body or outward appearance of a person or animal considered separately from the face or head. **3. a.** The manner in which a thing exists, acts, or manifests itself; kind; type; variety: *Light is a form of energy.* **b.** The particular character or nature of something: *Diplomatic persuasion often takes the form of private talks.* **4. a.** Acceptable manners or behavior: *His acerbic questions were in bad form.* **b.** A usual manner of behaving: *The Soviet condemnation of U.S. imperialism was true to form.* **5.** Fitness of mind or body with regard to health or training: *not in top form.* **6.** A fixed order of words or procedures, as in ceremony, ritual, or other regulated social situation; formula. **7.** A document with blanks for the insertion of details or information. **8.** Style or manner of presenting ideas or concepts; organization: *a muddled lecture with no form.* **9.** The design, structure, or pattern of a work of art: *sonata form.* **10.** A model for making a mold. **11.** A copy of the human figure used for displaying clothes. **12.** Type that has been assembled and secured for printing. **13.** A grade in a British school or in some American private schools. **14. a.** A linguistic form, as a prefix, suffix, etc. **b.** The external aspect of words with regard to their inflections, pronunciation, or spelling: *verb forms.* **15.** *Brit.* A bench. —*tr.v.* **1.** To give form to; shape: *form figurines from clay.* **2.** To make or produce: *Water forms rust on certain metals.* **3.** To fashion, train, or develop by instruction or precept: *form the mind.* **4.** To develop or acquire: *form a habit.* **5.** To constitute or be an element, part, or characteristic of: *Men still form the majority of the army.* **6.** To combine into; establish: *musicians forming a band.* **7.** To develop in the mind; conceive: *form an opinion.* **8.** To put in order; draw up; arrange. —*intr.v.* **1.** To become formed or shaped: *The dew formed into droplets on the windows.* **2.** To be created; come into being; arise: *Buds form in the spring.* [Middle English *forme,* from Old French, from Latin *fōrma,* form, contour, shape.]

-form. A suffix meaning having the form of: *cuneiform.* [From Latin *-fōrmis,* from *fōrma,* form.]

for·mal (fôr′məl) *adj.* **1.** Relating to or concerned with the outward form or structure of something as distinguished from its content: *Unity of time, place, and action are the formal elements of classical Greek tragedy.* **2. a.** Following accepted forms, conventions, or regulations: *a formal requirement.* **b.** Structured according to forms or conventions: *a formal meeting of the committee.* **c.** Officially made or stated: *a formal reprimand.* **3.** Characterized by strict or meticulous observation of forms: *formal diplomatic relations.* **4. a.** Calling for elegant clothes and fine manners: *a formal dance.* **b.** Suitable for occasions when elegant clothes and fine manners are called for: *formal dress.* **5.** Done for the sake of form only: *a purely formal greeting.* —*n.* **1.** An occasion or ceremony requiring formal attire. **2.** Formal attire. [Middle English, from Old French, from Latin *fōrmālis,* of or for form, from *fōrma,* form.] —**for′mal·ly** *adv.*

for·mal·de·hyde (fôr-măl′də-hīd′) *n.* A colorless gaseous compound, HCHO, that has a sharp, irritating odor, used in making plastics and dyes and as a preservative and disinfectant. [German *Formaldehyd.*]

for·mal·ism (fôr′mə-lĭz′əm) *n.* Strict or excessive observance of accepted or recognized forms, esp. in religion or art. —**for′mal·ist** *n.* —**for′mal·is′tic** *adj.*

for·mal·i·ty (fôr-măl′ĭ-tē) *n., pl.* **-ties. 1.** The condition or quality of being formal. **2.** Strict or ceremonious compliance with established forms, rules, or customs. **3.** An established form, rule, or custom. **4.** Something done for the sake of form, custom, or decorum.

for·mal·ize (fôr′mə-līz′) *tr.v.* **-ized, -iz·ing. 1.** To make formal. **2.** To give formal endorsement to: *formalize a treaty.* —**for′mal·i·za′tion** *n.*

for·mat (fôr′măt′) *n.* **1.** A general plan for the organization and arrangement of something. **2.** The form or layout of a publication. [French, from German *Format,* from Latin *fōrmātus,* past part. of *fōrmāre,* to form, from *fōrma,* form.]

for·ma·tion (fôr-mā′shən) *n.* **1.** The act or process of forming: *the formation of labor unions.* **2.** Something that is formed: *a cloud formation.* **3.** The manner or style in

---

| ă pat | ā pay | â care | ä father | ĕ pet | ē be | hw which | ĭ pit | ī tie | î pier | ŏ pot | ō toe | ô paw, for | oi noise |
| ōō took | ōō boot | ou out | th thin | *th* this | ŭ cut | | û urge | zh vision | ə about, item, edible, gallop, circus |

which something is formed: *troops in marching formation.* **4.** *Geol.* A large body of rocks sharing some characteristic, as composition or origin. **—for·ma'tion·al** *adj.*

for·ma·tive (fôr'mǝ-tĭv) *adj.* **1.** Forming or capable of forming: *a formative influence.* **2.** Of or relating to formation or growth: *a formative stage.*

for·mer (fôr'mǝr) *adj.* **1.** Occurring earlier in time or belonging to a period previous to the one specified: *former ages; our former President.* **2.** Coming before in place or order: *the former part of the book.* **3.** Being first or first mentioned of two: *Boston and Hartford are both big; the former city is the bigger of the two.* [Middle English, earlier, from *forme,* first, from Old English *forma.*]

for·mer·ly (fôr'mǝr-lē) *adv.* At a former time; once.

form·fit·ting (fôrm'fĭt'ĭng) *adj.* Closely fitted to the body: *a formfitting jersey.*

for·mic (fôr'mĭk) *adj.* Of or relating to ants. [From Latin *formīca,* ant.]

For·mi·ca (fôr-mī'kǝ) *n.* A trademark for any of various laminated plastic coverings, used esp. for chemical and heat-resistant surfaces, as in kitchens.

formic acid. A colorless caustic fuming liquid, HCOOH, used in dyeing and finishing textiles and in the manufacture of fumigants and insecticides. [From FORMIC (from its natural occurrence in ants).]

for·mi·da·ble (fôr'mĭ-dǝ-bǝl, fôr-mĭd'ǝ-bǝl) *adj.* **1.** Arousing fear, dread, or alarm: *a formidable enemy.* **2.** Admirable or awe-inspiring; impressive: *a formidable talent.* **3.** Difficult to surmount, defeat, or undertake: *a formidable task.* —See Syns at **burdensome.** [Middle English, from Old French, from Latin *formīdābilis,* from *formīdāre,* to dread, from *formīdō,* fright, fear.] **—for'mi·da·bil'i·ty** *n.* **—for'mi·da·bly** *adv.*

form·less (fôrm'lĭs) *adj.* Having no definite form; shapeless. **—form'less·ness** *n.*

for·mu·la (fôr'myǝ-lǝ) *n.,* pl. **-las** or **-lae** (-lē'). **1.** An established set form of words, symbols, or rules for use in a ceremony or procedure. **2.** *Chem.* A set of symbols that show the composition or the composition and structure of a chemical compound. **3.** *Math.* A statement of a rule, principle, etc., esp. in the form of an equation. **4.** A prescription of ingredients in fixed proportion; recipe. **5.** A liquid food prescribed for an infant. [Latin *fōrmula,* dim. of *fōrma,* form.] **—for'mu·la'ic** (fôr'myǝ-lā'ĭk) *adj.*

for·mu·lar·y (fôr'myǝ-lĕr'ē) *n.,* pl. **-ies. 1.** A book or other collection of formulas. **2.** A formula. **3.** A book containing the names of pharmaceutical substances.

for·mu·late (fôr'myǝ-lāt') *tr.v.* **-lat·ed, -lat·ing. 1.** To state as a formula. **2.** To express in systematic terms or concepts: *formulate one's thoughts.* **—for'mu·la'tion** *n.* **—for'mu·la'tor** *n.*

for·ni·cate (fôr'nĭ-kāt') *intr.v.* **-cat·ed, -cat·ing.** To commit fornication. [From Late Latin *fornicārī,* from *fornix,* vault, arch, a vaulted underground dwelling in Rome where prostitutes lived.] **—for'ni·ca'tor** *n.*

for·ni·ca·tion (fôr'nĭ-kā'shǝn) *n.* Sexual intercourse between persons not married to each other.

for·sake (fôr-sāk', fǝr-) *tr.v.* **-sook** (-sŏŏk'), **-sak·en** (-sā'kǝn), **-sak·ing. 1.** To give up; renounce: *forsook the religion of his forebears.* **2.** To leave altogether; desert. —See Syns at **abandon.** [Middle English *forsaken,* to object to, reject, from Old English *forsacan.*]

for·sooth (fôr-sŏŏth', fǝr-) *adv.* Archaic. In truth; indeed. [Middle English *for soth,* from Old English *forsōth : for,* for + *sōth,* truth.]

for·swear (fôr-swâr', fôr-) *v.* **-swore** (-swôr', -swōr'), **-sworn** (-swôrn', -swōrn'), **-swear·ing.** Also **fore·swear.** —*tr.v.* To give up; renounce: *He foreswore gambling.* —*intr.v.* To swear falsely; commit perjury. [Middle English *forsweren,* from Old English *forswerian,* to swear falsely : *for-,* wrongly + *swerian,* to swear.]

for·syth·i·a (fôr-sĭth'ē-ǝ, fǝr-) *n.* Any of several shrubs of the genus *Forsythia,* native to Asia and widely cultivated for their early-blooming yellow flowers. [After William Forsyth (1737–1804), British botanist.]

fort (fôrt, fōrt) *n.* A fortified place stationed with troops; fortification; bastion. [Middle English, from Old English *fort,* from *fort(e),* strong, from Latin *fortis.*]

forte¹ (fôrt, fōrt, fôr'tā') *n.* Something in which a person excels; strong point. [Old French *fort,* from adjective, strong.]

for·te² (fôr'tā'). *Mus.* —*adv.* Loudly; forcefully. Used as a direction. —*n.* A note, passage, or chord played forte. —*adj.* Loud; forceful. [Italian, "strongly."]

forth (fôrth, fōrth) *adv.* **1. a.** Out into view, as from confinement: *children poured forth from the schoolhouse.* **b.** Out: *Let the word go forth.* **2.** Forward or onward: *Putting forth all his strength, he bent the heavy bow.* **—idiom. and so forth.** And the like; et cetera. [Middle English, from Old English.]

forth·com·ing (fôrth-kŭm'ĭng, fōrth-) *adj.* **1.** About to appear; approaching; coming: *the forthcoming elections.* **2.** Available when required or as promised: *State aid was not forthcoming.*

forth·right (fôrth'rīt', fōrth'-) *adj.* Straightforward; frank; candid: *a forthright appraisal.* —See Syns at **plain.** **—forth'right'ly** *adv.* **—forth'right'ness** *n.*

forth·with (fôrth-wĭth', -wĭth', fōrth-) *adv.* At once; immediately: *I expect your answer forthwith.*

for·ti·eth (fôr'tē-ĭth) *n.* **1.** The ordinal number that matches the number 40 in a series, written 40th. **2.** One of 40 equal parts, written ¹/₄₀. **—for'ti·eth** *adj. & adv.*

for·ti·fi·ca·tion (fôr'tǝ-fĭ-kā'shǝn) *n.* **1.** The act, science, or art of fortifying. **2.** Something that serves to defend, strengthen, or fortify, esp. a military defensive work.

for·ti·fy (fôr'tǝ-fī') *v.* **-fied, -fy·ing.** —*tr.v.* **1.** To strengthen and secure (a position or structure) militarily: *fortified the castle with moats.* **2.** To strengthen physically; invigorate: *The cheese fortified him.* **3.** To give moral or mental strength to; encourage: *He fortified his troubled spirit by praying.* **4.** To increase the amount of an important ingredient in (a substance): *fortify bread with vitamins.* —*intr.v.* To prepare defensive works; build fortifications. [Middle English *fortifien,* from Old French *fortifier,* from Late Latin *fortificāre,* from Latin *fortis,* strong.]

for·tis·si·mo (fôr-tĭs'ǝ-mō'). *Mus.* —*adv.* Very loudly. Used as a direction. —*n.,* pl. **-mos.** A note, passage, or chord played fortissimo. —*adj.* Very loud. [Italian, from Latin *fortissimus,* superl. of *fortis,* strong.]

for·ti·tude (fôr'tĭ-tŏŏd', -tyŏŏd') *n.* Strength of mind that allows one to endure pain or adversity with courage. [Middle English, from Old French, from Latin *fortitūdō,* from *fortis,* strong.]

fort·night (fôrt'nīt') *n.* A period of 14 days and nights; two weeks. [Middle English *fourtenight,* from Old English *fēowertīene niht,* fourteen nights.]

fort·night·ly (fôrt'nīt'lē) *adj.* Happening once every two weeks. —*adv.* Once every two weeks. —*n.,* pl. **-lies.** A publication issued every two weeks.

FOR·TRAN or **For·tran** (fôr'trăn') *n.* A computer programming language for problems that can be expressed in algebraic terms. [FOR(MULA) + TRAN(SLATION).]

for·tress (fôr'trĭs) *n.* **1.** A fortified place, esp. a large and permanent military stronghold; a fort. **2.** Any source of refuge or support. [Middle English *forteresse,* from Old French, from Latin *fortis,* strong.]

for·tu·i·tous (fôr-tŏŏ'ĭ-tǝs, -tyŏŏ'-) *adj.* Happening by chance; unplanned. —See Syns at **accidental.** [Latin *fortuitus,* from *forte,* by chance, from *fors,* chance.] **—for·tu'i·tous·ly** *adv.* **—for·tu'i·tous·ness** *n.*

for·tu·i·ty (fôr-tŏŏ'ĭ-tē, -tyŏŏ'-) *n.,* pl. **-ties. 1.** An accidental occurrence; chance. **2.** The condition or quality of being fortuitous.

for·tu·nate (fôr'chǝ-nĭt) *adj.* **1.** Occurring or brought by good fortune or favorable chance. **2.** Having unexpected good fortune; lucky. **—for'tu·nate·ly** *adv.*

Syns: fortunate, happy, lucky, providential *adj.* Core meaning: Characterized by luck or good fortune (*a fortunate turn of events*).

for·tune (fôr'chǝn) *n.* **1.** A supposed force that governs the events of one's life: *Fortune is on our side.* **2.** The good or bad luck that comes to someone; fate: *It is my fortune to be a failure.* **3.** Luck, esp. when good; success: *Fortune accompanied his endeavors.* **4.** An accumulation of material possessions or money; wealth; riches. [Middle English, fortune, chance, from Old French, from Latin *fortūna,* from *fors,* chance, luck.]

fortune cookie. A thin cookie that contains a slip of paper bearing a prediction of fortune or other saying.

fortune hunter. A person who seeks to become wealthy, esp. through marriage. **—for′tune-hunt′ing** n.

for·tune-tell·er (fôr′chən-těl′ər) n. A person who professes to predict future events. **—for′tune-tell′ing** n.

for·ty (fôr′tē) n., pl. **-ties.** The cardinal number written 40 or XL in Roman numerals. [Middle English fourti, from Old English fēowertig.] **—for′ty** adj. & pron.

for·ty-five (fôr′tē-fīv′) n. **1.** A .45-caliber pistol. **2.** A phonograph record designed to be played at 45 rpm.

for·ty-nin·er (fôr′tē-nī′nər) n. A person who took part in the 1849 California gold rush.

forty winks. Informal. A short nap.

fo·rum (fôr′əm, fōr′-) n., pl. **-rums** or **fo·ra** (fôr′ə, fōr′ə). **1.** Often **Forum.** The public square of an ancient Roman city that was the assembly place for public activity. **2. a.** A public meeting place for open discussion. **b.** A medium for open discussion, as a television program. **3.** A court of law; a tribunal. [Middle English, from Latin, place out-of-doors.]

for·ward (fôr′wərd) adj. **1.** At, near, belonging to, or located in the front: the forward part of a train. **2.** Going, tending, or moving toward a position in front: a bad forward fall. **3.** Presumptuous; bold: forward manners. **4.** Progressive, esp. technologically, politically, or economically: a forward new nation. **5.** Mentally, physically, or socially advanced; precocious: a forward child. **—See** Syns at **impudent.** **—adv. 1.** Also **for·wards** (-wərdz). Toward the front; frontward: Please step forward. **2.** In or toward the future; at a future time: I look forward to seeing you. **3.** Into view; forth: Come forward out of the shadows so I can see you. **—n.** Sports. **1.** A player in certain games, such as basketball or soccer, who is part of the front line of offense or defense. **2.** The position itself. **—tr.v. 1.** To send (something mailed) on to a subsequent destination or address. **2.** To advance; promote; advocate: trying to forward their own interests. **—See** Syns at **send.** [Middle English for(e)ward, from Old English foreweard.] **—for′ward·er** n. **—for′ward·ness** n.

Usage: forward, forwards. The adjective is always written forward in all senses: a forward gun emplacement; forward movement; a forward person; a forward country. Forward is the usual form of the adverb. Either forward or forwards is possible when the adverb means toward the front or frontward: Drive forward (or forwards) a bit. But in other adverbial senses the only form is forward: look forward to seeing you (toward the future); came forward from obscurity (into view).

forward pass. Football. A pass thrown in the direction of the opponent's goal.

for·went (fôr-wěnt′, fōr-) v. Past tense of **forgo.**

foss (fŏs) n. Var. of **fosse.**

fos·sa (fŏs′ə) n., pl. **fos·sae** (fŏs′ē′). Anat. A hollow or depression, as in a bone. [Latin, ditch, trench, fem. past part. of fodere, to dig.]

fosse (fŏs) n. Also **foss.** A ditch, esp. a moat around a fortification. [Middle English, from Old French, from Latin fossa.]

fos·sil (fŏs′əl) n. **1.** A remnant or trace of an organism of a past geological age, as a skeleton, footprint, or leaf imprint, embedded in the earth's crust. **2.** Someone or something that is outdated or antiquated, esp. a person with outmoded ideas. **—modifier:** a fossil study; fossil fuel. [From Latin fossilis, dug up, from fossus, past part. of fodere, to dig.]

fos·sil·if·er·ous (fŏs′ə-lĭf′ər-əs) adj. Containing fossils. [FOSSIL + -FEROUS.]

fos·sil·ize (fŏs′ə-līz′) v. **-ized, -iz·ing.** **—tr.v. 1.** To convert into a fossil. **2.** To make outmoded, rigid, or fixed. **—intr.v.** To become a fossil. **—fos′sil·i·za′tion** n.

fos·ter (fô′stər, fŏs′tər) tr.v. **1.** To bring up; rear; nurture: fostered a child. **2.** To promote the development or growth of; cultivate: fostered in him a sense of purpose. **—adj.** Receiving or giving parental care although not related through legal or blood ties: a foster child; a foster mother. [Middle English fostren, from Old English fōstrian, to provide with food, nourish, from fōstor, food.] **—fos′ter·age** n. **—fos′ter·er** n.

foul (foul) adj. **-er, -est. 1.** Offensive to the sense of smell,

taste, etc.; disgusting: a foul flavor. **2.** Full of dirt or mud; dirty; filthy: foul drinking water. **3.** Morally offensive; wicked: foul acts. **4.** Vulgar; obscene: foul language. **5.** Unpleasant; bad: foul weather. **6.** Not according to accepted standards; dishonorable: advance by foul means. **7.** Contrary to the rules of a game or sport. **8.** Baseball. Outside the foul line. **—n. 1.** Anything that is dirty or foul. **2.** Sports. An infraction or violation of the rules of play. **3.** Baseball. A **foul ball.** **—adv.** In a foul manner. **—tr.v. 1.** To make foul; soil: foul the streets with garbage. **2.** To bring into dishonor or disgrace. **3.** To entangle or catch, as a rope: The ship fouled its lines. **4.** Sports. To commit a foul against. **5.** Baseball. To hit (a ball) outside the foul lines. **—intr.v. 1.** To become foul. **2.** Sports. To commit a foul. **3.** Baseball. To hit a ball outside the foul lines. **4.** To become entangled or twisted: The anchor fouled on a rock. **—phrasal verbs. foul out.** Baseball. To make an out by hitting a foul ball that is caught before it touches the ground. **foul up.** Slang. To cause disorder or ruin because of mistakes or poor judgment: foul up a job; fouled himself up. **—See** Syns at **botch.** [Middle English foul, from Old English fūl.] **—foul′ly** adv. **—foul′ness** n.

fou·lard (fōō-lärd′) n. **1.** A lightweight twill or plain-woven fabric of silk or silk and cotton, usu. having a small printed design. **2.** An article of clothing, esp. a necktie, made of foulard. [French.]

foul ball. Baseball. Any batted ball that is not judged a fair ball.

foul line. 1. Baseball. Either of two straight lines extending from the rear of home plate to the boundary of the playing field to indicate the area in which a fair ball can be hit. **2.** Basketball. A line from which a player makes a foul shot. Also called **free-throw line.** **3.** Sports. Any boundary limiting the playing area.

foul-mouthed (foul′mouthd′, -moutht′) adj. Using obscene, coarse, or abusive language.

foul play. Unfair or treacherous action, esp. when it involves violence.

foul shot. Basketball. A **free throw.**

foul tip. Baseball. A pitched ball that is slightly deflected off the bat into the foul zone.

foul-up (foul′ŭp′) n. **1.** A condition of confusion caused by poor judgment or mistakes. **2.** Mechanical trouble.

found[1] (found) tr.v. **1.** To originate or establish; create: founded a school. **2.** To establish the foundation of; lay a base for: founded his argument on logic. [Middle English founden, from Old French fonder, from Latin fundāre, to lay the foundation for, from fundus, bottom.] **—found′er** n.

found[2] (found) tr.v. **1.** To melt (metal, glass, etc.) and pour into a mold. **2.** To make (objects) by founding; to cast. [Middle English founden, from Old French fondre, from Latin fundere, to melt.] **—found′er** n.

found[3] (found) v. Past tense and past participle of **find.** [Middle English founde, founde(n), from Old English fundon (pl.), (ge)funden.]

foun·da·tion (foun-dā′shən) n. **1.** The act of founding or condition of being founded. **2. a.** The basis on which a thing stands, is founded, or is supported: the foundations of modern science. **b.** The base on which a building stands: laying the foundation for a house. **3. a.** Funds for the perpetual support of an institution, such as a hospital or school; an endowment. **b.** An institution supported by such a fund. **4.** A cosmetic used as a base for facial makeup. **—foun·da′tion·al** adj.

foun·der (foun′dər) intr.v. **1.** To become disabled or go lame: My mount foundered. **2.** To fail utterly; collapse: The rescue attempt foundered. **3.** To sink below the water: The ship foundered in heavy seas. **4.** To cave in or fall down: buildings that foundered due to age. **—tr.v.** To cause to founder. **—See** Usage note at **flounder**[1]. [Middle English foundren, to fall to the ground, from Old French fondrer, to submerge, from Latin fundus, bottom.]

found·ling (found′lĭng) n. A child deserted by parents whose identity is not known. [Middle English, prob. from founden, past part. of finden, to find.]

foun·dry (foun′drē) n., pl. **-dries. 1.** An establishment in which metals are cast and molded. **2. a.** The art or operation of founding. **b.** The castings made by founding.

ă pat	ā pay	â care	ä father	ĕ pet	ē be	hw which	ĭ pit	ī tie	î pier	ŏ pot	ō toe	ô paw, for	oi noise
ōō took	ōō boot	ou out	th thin	th this	ŭ cut	û urge	zh vision	ə about, item, edible, gallop, circus

fox

foxglove

fox terrier

fount (fount) *n.* **1.** A fountain. **2.** Any source; wellspring: *a fount of wisdom.* [Prob. a back-formation from FOUNTAIN.]

foun·tain (foun'tən) *n.* **1.** A spring of water from the earth. **2. a.** An artificially created stream of water. **b.** The structure or device from which such a stream rises and flows. **3.** A source; point of origin. **4.** A **soda fountain.** [Middle English *fountaine,* spring, from Old French *fontaine,* from Late Latin *fontāna,* from *fontānus,* of a spring, from *fons,* spring.]

foun·tain·head (foun'tən-hĕd') *n.* **1.** A spring that is the source of a stream. **2.** A primary source or origin.

fountain pen. A pen containing a reservoir of ink that automatically feeds the writing point.

four (fôr, fōr) *n.* A number, written 4 in Arabic numerals or IV in Roman numerals, that is equal to the sum of 3 + 1. It is the positive integer that immediately follows 3. —*idiom.* **on all fours.** On the hands and knees or on all four legs. [Middle English, from Old English *fēower.*] —**four** *adj. & pron.*

four-di·men·sion·al (fôr'dĭ-mĕn'shə-nəl, fōr'-) *adj.* Exhibiting or being specified by four dimensions, esp. the three spatial dimensions and single temporal dimension of relativity theory.

four-flush·er (fôr'flŭsh'ər, fōr'-) *n. Slang.* A person who cannot or does not live up to his claims; bluffer; faker. [From *four-flush,* to bluff in poker with a five-card hand having only four cards of the same suit.]

four·fold (fôr'fōld', fōr'-) *adj.* **1.** Having four units or aspects; quadruple. **2.** Being four times as much or as many. —**four'fold'** *adv.*

four-foot·ed (fôr'fŏot'ĭd, fōr'-) *adj.* Having four feet.

Four-H Club (fôr'āch', fōr'-). A youth organization sponsored by the Department of Agriculture and offering instruction in agriculture and home economics. [From its goal of improving head, heart, hands, and health.]

four hundred. Often **the Four Hundred.** The wealthiest and most exclusive social set.

four-in-hand (fôr'ĭn-hănd', fōr'-) *n.* **1.** A vehicle drawn by four horses and driven by one person. **2.** A necktie tied in a slipknot with the ends left hanging and overlapping.

four-leaf clover (fôr'lēf', fōr'-). Also **four-leaved clover** (-lēvd'). A clover leaf with four leaflets instead of three, considered to be an omen of good luck.

four-o'clock (fôr'ə-klŏk', fōr'-) *n.* Any of several plants of the genus *Mirabilis,* esp. *M. jalapa,* widely cultivated for its tubular, variously colored flowers that open in the late afternoon.

four-post·er (fôr'pō'stər, fōr'-) *n.* A bed with tall corner posts orig. intended to support curtains or a canopy.

four·score (fôr'skôr', fōr'skōr') *adj.* Four times 20; 80.

four·some (fôr'səm, fōr'-) *n.* **1.** A group of four persons; a quartet. **2.** The players in a golf match played by four persons. [Middle English *four-sum,* from Old English *fēowra sum,* one of four.]

four·square (fôr'skwâr', fōr'-) *adj.* **1.** Having four equal sides and four right angles; square. **2.** Forthright; frank. —*adv.* Squarely; forthrightly.

four·teen (fôr-tēn', fōr'-) *n.* The cardinal number, written 14 in Arabic numerals or XIV in Roman numerals, that is equal to the sum of 13 + 1. It is the positive integer that immediately follows 13. [Middle English *fourtene,* from Old English *fēowertīene.*] —**four·teen'** *adj. & pron.*

four·teenth (fôr-tēnth', fōr'-) *n.* **1.** In a set of items arranged to match the natural numbers in a one-to-one correspondence, the item that matches the number fourteen. **2.** One of fourteen equal parts of a unit, written 1/14. —**four·teenth'** *adj. & adv.*

fourth (fôrth, fōrth) *n.* **1.** In a set of items arranged to match the natural numbers in a one-to-one correspondence, the item that matches the number four. **2.** One of four equal parts of a unit, written 1/4; one quarter. **3. a.** A musical interval of five half steps. **b.** The tone of a diatonic scale that is five half steps above the tonic; the subdominant. **4. the Fourth. Independence Day.** [Middle English *fourthe,* from Old English *fēortha.*] —**fourth** *adj. & adv.*

fourth-class (fôrth'klăs', fōrth'-) *adj.* Designating a class of mail consisting of merchandise or certain printed matter weighing over eight ounces and not sealed against inspection.

fourth dimension. A dimension other than the dimensions of length, width, and height, considered to be measured along an axis that meets at right angles all three axes of a three-dimensional coordinate system.

fourth estate. The public press; journalism or journalists in general.

Fourth of July. Independence Day.

fo·ve·a (fō'vē-ə) *n., pl.* **-ve·ae** (-vē-ē'). A shallow cuplike depression or pit in a bone or other organ. [From Latin *fovea,* small pit.] —**fo've·al** or **fo've·ate'** (-āt') *adj.*

fowl (foul) *n., pl.* **fowl** or **fowls. 1.** Any of various birds of the order Galliformes, esp. the common, widely domesticated chicken, *Gallus gallus.* **2.** Any bird used as food or hunted as game. **3.** The edible flesh of such a bird. —*intr.v.* To hunt, trap, or shoot wild fowl. [Middle English *foul,* from Old English *fugol.*] —**fowl'er** *n.*

fowl·ing (fou'lĭng) *n.* The hunting of wild fowl.

fowling piece. A light shotgun for shooting birds and small animals.

fox (fŏks) *n.* **1. a.** Any of various carnivorous mammals of the genus *Vulpes* and related genera, related to the dogs and wolves and characteristically having upright ears, a pointed snout, and a long, bushy tail. **b.** The fur of a fox. **2.** A crafty, sly, or clever person. —*tr.v.* To trick or fool by ingenuity or cunning; outwit. [Middle English, from Old English.]

fox·fire (fŏks'fīr') *n.* A phosphorescent glow produced by certain fungi found on rotting wood.

fox·glove (fŏks'glŭv') *n.* **1.** Any of several plants of the genus *Digitalis,* esp. *D. purpurea,* native to Europe, with a long cluster of large, tubular, pinkish-purple flowers and leaves that are the source of the medicinal drug digitalis. **2.** Any of several similar or related plants. [Middle English *foxes-globe,* from Old English *foxes glōfa,* "fox's glove."]

fox·hole (fŏks'hōl') *n.* A shallow pit dug by a soldier for protection in combat.

fox·hound (fŏks'hound') *n.* A usu. smooth-coated dog trained for fox hunting.

fox·tail (fŏks'tāl') *n.* **1.** Any of several grasses of the genus *Alopecurus,* with dense silky or bristly flowering spikes. **2.** Any of several similar or related plants.

fox terrier. A small dog with a smooth or wiry white coat with dark markings.

fox trot. 1. A ballroom dance in 2/4 or 4/4 time, composed of a variety of slow and fast steps. **2.** The music for the fox trot.

ă pat ā pay â care ä father ĕ pet ē be hw which
ŏŏ took ōō boot ou out th thin *th* this ŭ cut
ĭ pit ī tie î pier ŏ pot ō toe ô paw, for oi noise
û urge zh vision ə about, item, edible, gallop, circus

fox-trot (fŏks′trŏt′) *intr.v.* **-trot·ted, -trot·ting.** To dance a fox trot.

fox·y (fŏk′sē) *adj.* **-i·er, -i·est.** Suggestive of a fox; sly; cunning; clever. **—fox′i·ly** *adv.* **—fox′i·ness** *n.*

foy·er (foi′ər, foi′ā′) *n.* **1.** The lobby or anteroom of a public building, such as a theater or hotel. **2.** The entrance hall or vestibule of a private dwelling. [French, hearth, home, foyer, from Medieval Latin *focārius*, from Latin *focus*, hearth, fireplace.]

Fr The symbol for the element francium.

fra·cas (frā′kəs) *n.* A disorderly uproar; brawl. [French, from Italian *fracasso*, from *fracassare*, to make an uproar.]

frac·tion (frăk′shən) *n.* **1.** A small part of something; scant portion: *a fraction of the populace.* **2.** A disconnected piece of something; fragment; scrap; bit. **3.** *Math.* A number that is equal to a quotient of two other numbers, shown as a numerator over a denominator. **4.** *Chem.* One of the parts into which a mixture of substances can be separated. [Middle English *fraccioun*, from Late Latin *fractiō*, act of breaking, from Latin *fractus*, past part. of *frangere*, to break.]

frac·tion·al (frăk′shə-nəl) *adj.* **1.** Of or constituting a fraction or fractions. **2.** Very small; insignificant. **3.** Being in fractions or pieces; broken; fragmentary. **—frac′tion·al·ly** *adv.*

frac·tion·ate (frăk′shə-nāt′) *tr.v.* **-at·ed, -at·ing.** To separate (a chemical compound) into components, as by distillation or crystallization. **—frac′tion·a′tion** *n.*

frac·tious (frăk′shəs) *adj.* **1.** Inclined to make trouble; unruly. **2.** Having a peevish nature; irritable: *a fractious old man.* [From FRACTION (breaking).] **—frac′tious·ly** *adv.* **—frac′tious·ness** *n.*

frac·ture (frăk′chər) *n.* **1. a.** The act or process of breaking. **b.** The condition of being broken. **2.** A break, rupture, or crack, as in bone or cartilage. **—v.** **-tured, -tur·ing.** **—tr.v.** To break or crack. **—intr.v.** To undergo a fracture. [Middle English, from Old French, from Latin *fractūra*, from *fractus*, past part. of *frangere*, to break.]

frag·ile (frăj′əl, -īl′) *adj.* **1.** Easily broken or damaged; delicate: *a fragile crystal vase.* **2.** Tenuous; flimsy: *a fragile claim to fame.* [Old French, from Latin *fragilis*, from *frangere*, to break.] **—frag′ile·ly** *adv.* **—fra·gil′i·ty** (frə-jĭl′ĭ-tē) or **frag′ile·ness** *n.*

frag·ment (frăg′mənt) *n.* **1.** A part broken off or detached from a whole. **2.** Something incomplete; an odd bit or piece: *a fragment of a conversation.* **—v.** (frăg′mĕnt′). **—tr.v.** To break or separate (something) into fragments. **—intr.v.** To break into pieces. [Middle English, from Latin *fragmentum*, from *frangere*, to break.]

frag·men·ta·ry (frăg′mən-tĕr′ē) *adj.* Consisting of fragments or disconnected parts; broken. **—frag′men·tar′i·ly** (-târ′ə-lē) *adv.* **—frag′men·tar′i·ness** *n.*

frag·men·ta·tion (frăg′mən-tā′shən, -mĕn-) *n.* **1.** The act or process of breaking into fragments. **2.** The scattering of the fragments of an exploding grenade, bomb, or shell; dispersion.

fra·grance (frā′grəns) *n.* **1.** The condition or quality of being fragrant. **2.** A sweet or pleasant odor; scent.

fra·grant (frā′grənt) *adj.* Having a pleasant odor; sweet-smelling. [Middle English, from Old French, from Latin *fragrāns*, pres. part. of *fragrāre*, to emit an odor.]

frail (frāl) *adj.* **-er, -est.** **1.** Having a delicate constitution; physically weak: *a frail old man.* **2.** Not strong or substantial: *a youth of frail build.* **3.** Easily broken or destroyed; fragile. [Middle English, from Old French *fraile*, from Latin *fragilis*, fragile.] **—frail′ly** *adv.* **—frail′ness** *n.*

frail·ty (frāl′tē) *n.,* pl. **-ties.** **1.** The condition or quality of being frail. **2.** Often **frailties.** A fault arising from human weakness; a failing: *human frailties.*

frame (frām) *n.* **1. a.** A basic or skeletal structure that shapes or supports: *a car frame.* **b.** An open structure or rim used to encase, hold, or border: *a door frame; a picture frame.* **c.** The human body: *He has a small frame.* **2.** The general structure of something; system. **3. a.** A round of play in some games, such as bowling. **b.** The box on a score sheet in which the score of such a round of play is entered. **4.** A single exposure on a roll of movie film. **—tr.v.** **framed, fram·ing.** **1.** To put together the various parts of; construct; build: *frame a treaty.* **2.** To put into words; phrase: *framed the question in an odd way.* **3.** To provide with a frame; enclose or encircle: *frame a picture; fair hair framing a beautiful face.* **4.** *Slang.* To set up evidence so as to incriminate (someone) falsely. [Middle English *framen*, to benefit, form, construct, from Old English *framian*, to benefit, avail.] **—fram′er** *n.*

frame house. A house constructed with a wooden framework and covered usu. with wood siding.

frame of mind. Mental state or attitude; mood.

frame of reference. **1.** A set or system of principles, rules, ideas, or values that serve as a basis for the formation of attitudes. **2.** *Physics.* A set of coordinate axes in terms of which position or movement may be specified or with reference to which physical laws may be mathematically stated.

frame-up (frām′ŭp′) *n. Slang.* A conspiracy or scheme involving falsified charges or evidence designed to place guilt on an innocent person.

frame·work (frām′wûrk′) *n.* **1.** A skeletal structure for supporting, shaping, or enclosing something; a frame. **2.** A basic arrangement, form, system, or set of relationships.

franc (frăngk) *n.* The basic monetary unit of France, Belgium, Switzerland, and of various other countries. [Middle English *frank*, from Old French *franc*, from the Latin legend *Francorum rex*, "king of the Franks," on gold coins struck during the reign of Jean le Bon (1350–64).]

fran·chise (frăn′chīz′) *n.* **1.** The right to vote; suffrage. **2.** A privilege or right granted by a government, state, or sovereign. **3.** Authorization granted by a manufacturer to sell his products. **4.** The territory or limits within which some privilege, right, or immunity may be exercised. **—tr.v.** **-chised, -chis·ing.** To endow with a franchise; enfranchise. [Middle English *fraunchise*, freedom, privilege, from Old French *franchise*, from *franc*, free, frank.]

fran·ci·um (frăn′sē-əm) *n. Symbol* **Fr** An extremely unstable radioactive metallic element, having approx. 19 isotopes, the most stable of which is Fr 223 with a half-life of 21 minutes. Atomic number 87; valence 1. [After FRANCE.]

fran·gi·ble (frăn′jə-bəl) *adj.* Easily broken; breakable. [Middle English, from Old French, from Medieval Latin *frangibilis*, from Latin *frangere*, to break.] **—fran′gi·bil′i·ty** or **fran′gi·ble·ness** *n.*

fran·gi·pan·i (frăn′jə-păn′ē, -pä′nē) *n.* Also **fran·gi·pane** (frăn′jə-pān′). **1.** Any of various tropical American shrubs of the genus *Plumeria,* with milky juice and showy, fragrant, variously colored flowers. **2.** A perfume derived from or similar in scent to these flowers. [French *frangipane,* after the Marquis *Frangipani,* 16th-cent. Italian nobleman.]

frank (frăngk) *adj.* **-er, -est.** **1.** Open and sincere in expression; straightforward: *a frank discussion.* **2.** Clearly manifest; evident: *frank enjoyment.* **—tr.v.** **1.** To put an official mark on (a piece of mail) so that it can be sent and delivered free. **2.** To send (mail) free of charge. **—n.** **1.** A mark or signature placed on a piece of mail to indicate the right to send it free of postage. **2.** The right to send mail free. [Middle English, free, generous, from Old French *franc,* free, from Medieval Latin *francus,* from Late Latin *Francus,* Frank.] **—frank′ly** *adv.* **—frank′ness** *n.*

Frank (frăngk) *n.* A member of one of the Germanic tribes of the Rhine region in the early Christian era, esp. one of the Salic Franks who conquered Gaul about A.D. 500 and established an extensive empire that reached its greatest power in the 9th cent.

frank·furt·er (frăngk′fər-tər) *n.* Also **frank·fort·er** or **frank·furt** (frăngk′fərt) or **frank·fort.** A smoked sausage of beef or beef and pork made in long, reddish links. [After *Frankfurt (am Main),* German city.]

frank·in·cense (frăng′kĭn-sĕns′) *n.* An aromatic gum resin from African and Asian trees of the genus *Boswellia,* used chiefly as incense. [Middle English *frank encens,* from Old French *franc encens* : *franc,* superior + *encens,* incense.]

fran·tic (frăn′tĭk) *adj.* Distraught, as from fear, pain, or worry; desperate; frenzied: *a frantic call for help.* [Middle English *frantik,* frenetic.] **—fran′ti·cal·ly** or **fran′tic·ly** *adv.* **—fran′tic·ness** *n.*

frap·pé (fră-pā′, frăp) *n.* **1.** A frozen mixture similar to sherbet. **2.** A beverage poured over shaved ice. **3.** A milk shake that contains ice cream. [French, past part. of *frapper*, to strike, chill, from Old French *fraper*, to strike.]

frat (frăt) *n. Informal.* A college fraternity.

fra·ter·nal (frə-tûr′nəl) *adj.* **1. a.** Of brothers. **b.** Showing comradeship: *a fraternal greeting.* **2.** Consisting of persons joined together by a common purpose or interest: *a fraternal organization.* **3.** *Biol.* Of or concerning a twin or twins developed from separately fertilized egg cells and having distinct hereditary characteristics. [Middle English, from Medieval Latin *frāternālis*, from Latin *frāternus*, from *frāter*, brother.] —**fra·ter′nal·ism** *n.* —**fra·ter′nal·ly** *adv.*

fra·ter·ni·ty (frə-tûr′nĭ-tē) *n., pl.* **-ties. 1.** A group of people associated or linked by similar backgrounds, interests, or occupations: *the medical fraternity.* **2.** A chiefly social organization of male college students. **3.** The relationship of a brother or brothers; brotherhood. [Middle English *fraternite*, from Old French, from Latin *frāternitās*, from *frāternus*, fraternal.]

frat·er·nize (frăt′ər-nīz′) *intr.v.* **-nized, -niz·ing. 1.** To associate with others in a brotherly or congenial way. **2.** To mix intimately with the people of an enemy or conquered country. [French *fraterniser*, from Medieval Latin *frāternizāre*, from Latin *frāternus*, fraternal.] —**frat′er·ni·za′tion** *n.* —**frat′er·niz′er** *n.*

frat·ri·cide (frăt′rĭ-sīd′) *n.* **1.** The act of killing one's brother or sister. **2.** A person who has killed his own brother or sister. [Middle English, from Old French, ult. from Latin *frāter*, brother.] —**frat′ri·cid′al** *adj.*

Frau (frou) *n., pl.* **Frau·en** (frou′ən). A title of polite address for a married woman in a German-speaking country or district. [German.]

fraud (frôd) *n.* **1.** A deception deliberately practiced in order to secure unfair or unlawful gain. **2.** A piece of trickery; a swindle. **3. a.** A person who defrauds; a cheat. **b.** A person who assumes a false pose. —See Syns at **imposter.** [Middle English *fraude*, from Old French, from Latin *fraus.*]

fraud·u·lent (frô′jə-lənt) *adj.* Characterized by, constituting, or gained by fraud: *a fraudulent scheme.* [Middle English, from Old French, from Latin *fraudulentus*, from *fraus*, fraud.] —**fraud′u·lence** *n.* —**fraud′u·lent·ly** *adv.*

fraught (frôt) *adj.* Filled; attended; loaded: *an occasion fraught with peril.* [Middle English, past part. of *fraughten*, to load a ship, from Middle Dutch *vrachten*, from *vracht*, freight.]

Fräu·lein (froi′līn′) *n., pl.* **Fräulein.** A title of polite address for an unmarried girl or woman in a German-speaking country or district. [German, dim. of *Frau*, wife.]

fray[1] (frā) *n.* **1.** A fight or scuffle; brawl. **2.** A heated dispute or contest. [Middle English, fright, commotion, conflict, from *fraien*, to frighten, short for *afraien*, from Old French *affreer*, to affray.]

fray[2] (frā) *tr.v.* **1.** To unravel or wear away (cloth) by rubbing. **2.** To strain or irritate; chafe: *frayed nerves.* —*intr.v.* To become unraveled or threadbare along the edges. [Middle English *fraien*, from Old French *fraier*, from Latin *frī-cāre*, to rub.] —**fray** *n.*

fraz·zle (frăz′əl) *v.* **-zled, -zling.** *Informal.* —*tr.v.* **1.** To fray, ravel, or tatter. **2.** To tire out completely. —*intr.v.* To become frazzled. —*n.* **1.** A frayed or tattered condition. **2.** A condition of nervous exhaustion: *worn to a frazzle.* [Prob. a blend of *fray* (wear) and dial. *fazzle*, to fray.]

freak (frēk) *n.* **1.** A thing or occurrence that is very unusual or irregular. **2.** An abnormally formed organism, esp. a person or animal regarded as a curiosity or monstrosity. **3.** A sudden capricious turn of mind; whim. **4.** *Slang.* **a.** A drug addict. **b.** A fan or enthusiast. —*modifier: a freak accident.* —*phrasal verb.* **freak out.** *Slang.* **1.** To experience the mental and behavioral aberrations induced by drug abuse. **2.** To make or become wild, distressed, or very agitated. [Orig. unknown.] —**freak′i·ly** *adv.*—**freak′y** *adj.*

freak·ish (frē′kĭsh) *adj.* Of or like a freak. —**freak′ish·ly** *adv.* —**freak′ish·ness** *n.*

freak-out (frēk′out′) *n. Slang.* A mental state induced by drugs and characterized by hallucinations and often violent behavior.

freck·le (frĕk′əl) *n.* A small spot of dark pigment in the skin, often caused by exposure to the sun. —*v.* **-led, -ling.**

—*tr.v.* To dot with freckles or spots. —*intr.v.* To become dotted with freckles or spots. [Middle English *frakles* (pl), var. of *fraknes*, from Old Norse *freknur* (pl).] —**freck′ly** *adj.*

free (frē) *adj.* **tre·er, free·est. 1.** At liberty; not imprisoned or enslaved. **2.** Not controlled by obligation or the will of another: *felt free to go.* **3. a.** Having political independence: *a free country.* **b.** Having legal rights that a government may not violate: *a free press.* **4. a.** Not affected by a given condition: *free from worry.* **b.** Not subject to a given condition; exempt: *tax-free income.* **5.** Not bound, confined, or fixed in position: *the free end of a chain.* **6.** Not occupied or busy: *a free hour.* **7.** Costing nothing: *free meals.* **8.** Liberal or lavish: *very free with her money.* **9.** Not literal or exact: *a free translation.* —*adv.* **1.** In a free manner; freely: *The rope swung free.* **2.** Without charge: *We were admitted free.* —*tr.v.* **freed, free·ing. 1.** To set at liberty. **2.** To rid or release: *freed from all suspicion of guilt.* **3.** To unfasten or untangle; detach. —*idioms.* **make free with.** To take liberties with. **set free.** To liberate or release. [Middle English *fre(e)*, from Old English *frēo.*] —**free′ly** *adv.* —**free′ness** *n.*

Syns: free, emancipate, liberate, release *v. Core meaning:* To set at liberty (*free the prisoners*). FREE, LIBERATE and RELEASE are the most general and are often interchangeable (*free an innocent man; liberate slaves; releasing inmates from an internment camp*). EMANCIPATE usually applies more narrowly to setting free from bondage or restraint (*emancipate slaves*).

Usage: free. The word is both an adjective and an adverb. The comparative and superlative forms are *freer* and *freest;* the corresponding forms for the adverb *freely* are *more freely* and *most freely.*

free·board (frē′bôrd′, -bōrd′) *n.* The distance between the water line and the uppermost, fully watertight deck of a ship.

free·boot·er (frē′bōo′tər) *n.* A person who pillages and plunders; pirate; buccaneer. [From Dutch *vrijbuiter*, from *vrijbuit*, free booty : *vrij*, free + *buit*, booty, from *buiten*, to plunder.]

free·born (frē′bôrn′) *adj.* **1.** Born as a free person. **2.** Of or befitting a person born free.

freed·man (frēd′mən) *n.* A person who has been freed from bondage; an emancipated slave.

free·dom (frē′dəm) *n.* **1.** The condition of being free of restraints. **2.** Liberty of the person from slavery, oppression, or incarceration. **3. a.** Political independence. **b.** Possession of civil rights. **4.** Exemption from unpleasant or onerous conditions: *freedom from unfair labor practices.* **5.** The capacity to exercise choice; free will: *freedom to do as he wishes.* **6.** Ease of movement; facility: *A short skirt affords freedom for long strides.* **7.** Frankness or boldness; lack of modesty or reserve: *the new freedom in movies.* **8.** Unrestricted use or access: *I was given the freedom of their research facilities.* [Middle English *fredom*, from Old English *frēodōm.*]

Syns: freedom, autonomy, independence, liberty, sovereignty *n. Core meaning:* The condition of being politically free (*granted the colony its freedom*).

freed·wom·an (frēd′wōom′ən) *n.* A woman who has been freed from bondage; an emancipated slave.

free electron. An electron that is not bound to an atom, esp. an electron in a conductor that is available to move in a current.

free energy. The part of the energy of a physical system that can in theory be made available to do work.

free enterprise. The freedom of private business to operate competitively for profit with little government regulation.

free fall. 1. The fall of a body toward the earth without a drag-producing device such as a parachute. **2.** The unconstrained motion of a body in a gravitational field.

free-for-all (frē′fər-ôl′) *n.* A quarrel, argument, or competition in which one and all take part.

free hand. Full liberty to do or decide as one sees fit.

free·hand (frē′hănd′) *adj.* Drawn by hand without mechanical aids. —**free′hand′** *adv.*

free·hand·ed (frē′hăn′dĭd) *adj.* Openhanded; generous. —**free′hand′ed·ly** *adv.* —**free′hand′ed·ness** *n.*

free·hold (frē′hōld′) n. 1. Law. a. An estate held for life. b. The tenure by which such an estate is held. 2. A tenure of an office or a dignity for life. —**free′hold′er** n.

free lance. A person, esp. a writer, artist, or musician, who does not work for one employer only but sells his services to several employers as those services are needed. —modifier (**free-lance**): a free-lance job.

free-lance (frē′lǎns′) v. **-lanced, -lanc·ing.** —intr.v. To work as a free lance. —tr.v. To produce and sell as a free lance. —**free′lanc′er** n.

free-liv·ing (frē′lĭv′ĭng) adj. 1. Given to self-indulgence. 2. Biol. Living or moving independently; not part of a parasitic or symbiotic relationship.

free-load (frē′lōd′) intr.v. Slang. To live off the generosity or hospitality of others; sponge. —**free′load′er** n.

free love. Belief in or practice of sexual relations without marriage and without formal obligations.

free·man (frē′mən) n. 1. A person not in bondage or slavery. 2. A person who possesses the rights or privileges of a citizen.

free·ma·son (frē′mā′sən) n. 1. A member of a guild of skilled, itinerant masons of the Middle Ages. 2. **Freema·son.** A member of the Free and Accepted Masons, an international secret fraternity.

free·ma·son·ry (frē′mā′sən-rē) n. 1. Tacit fellowship and sympathy among a number of people. 2. **Freemasonry. a.** The institutions, precepts, and rites of the Freemasons. **b.** The Freemasons.

free on board. Delivered by the seller on board or into a carrier without charge to the buyer.

free port. 1. A port open to all commercial vessels. 2. An area in which imported goods can be held or processed before re-export, free of customs duties.

fre·er (frē′ər) adj. Comparative of **free**.

free·sia (frē′zhə, -zhē-ə, -zē-ə) n. Any of several plants of the genus Freesia, native to southern Africa, with clusters of fragrant, variously colored flowers. [After Friedrich H.T. Freese (d. 1876), German physician.]

free silver. The free coinage of silver, esp. at a fixed ratio to gold.

free soil. U.S. territory in which slavery was prohibited prior to the Civil War.

free-soil (frē′soil′) adj. 1. Prohibiting slavery: free-soil states. 2. **Free-Soil.** Of an American political party founded in 1848 to oppose the extension of slavery into U.S. Territories and the admission of slave states into the Union.

free-spo·ken (frē′spō′kən) adj. Candid in expression; outspoken; frank. —**free′-spo′ken·ness** n.

fre·est (frē′ĭst) adj. Superlative of **free**.

free-stand·ing (frē′stǎn′dĭng) adj. Standing independently; free of support or attachment: a freestanding column of marble.

free-stone (frē′stōn′) n. 1. A fruit that has a stone that does not adhere to the pulp. 2. A stone, such as sandstone or limestone, that is soft enough to be cut easily without shattering or splitting.

free-think·er (frē′thĭng′kər) n. A person who has rejected dogma, esp. in religious matters, for rational inquiry and speculation. —**free′think′ing** adj. & n.

free throw. Basketball. A throw from the foul line, awarded to a fouled player and scored as one point if successful; foul shot.

free-throw line (frē′thrō′). Basketball. The **foul line**.

free trade. Trade between nations or states without protective customs tariffs.

free verse. Verse that does not follow a conventional metrical or stanzaic pattern and has either an irregular rhyme or no rhyme.

free·way (frē′wā′) n. 1. A highway that has several lanes and no intersections or stoplights; expressway. 2. A highway without tolls.

free wheel. An automotive transmission device that allows the drive shaft to continue turning when its speed is greater than that of the engine shaft. —**free′-wheel′** adj.

free-wheel·ing (frē′hwē′lĭng, -wē′-) adj. 1. Of or equipped with free wheel. 2. Informal. **a.** Free of restraints or rules in organization, methods, or procedure: a freewheeling real-estate promoter. **b.** Heedless; carefree: a freewheeling life.

free will. 1. The power or discretion to choose. 2. The belief that man's choices ultimately are or can be voluntary and not determined by external causes.

free·will (frē′wĭl′) adj. Done of one's own accord; voluntary.

freeze (frēz) v. **froze** (frōz), **fro·zen** (frō′zən), **freez·ing.** —intr.v. 1. To pass from the liquid to the solid state by loss of heat. 2. To become covered, clogged, or jammed due to the formation of ice: The pipes froze. 3. To become stiff or hard from cold: The ground froze. 4. To be uncomfortably cold. 5. To be harmed, ruined, or killed by cold or frost: The crops froze. 6. To become paralyzed as from fear: She froze in front of the audience. 7. To become icily silent in manner. —tr.v. 1. To cause (a liquid) to become a solid; convert into ice: The cold froze the water. 2. To cause ice to cover, clog, or jam. 3. To cause to harden or stiffen from extreme cold: The winter froze the ground. 4. To preserve (food, serum, etc.) by subjecting to freezing temperatures. 5. To damage, kill, or ruin by cold or by the formation of ice. 6. To make very cold; chill: This raw cold is freezing my bones. 7. To chill with an icy or formal manner. 8. To cause to become fixed or stuck because of cold or frost: The rain and cold froze the leaves to the ground. 9. To make motionless, as from fear: A sudden noise froze him in his tracks. 10. To fix (prices or wages) at a given or current level. 11. Surgery. To anesthetize by freezing. —n. 1. An act of freezing or a condition of being frozen. 2. A period of very cold weather; frost. [Middle English fresen, from Old English frēosan.]

freeze-dry (frēz′drī′) tr.v. **-dried, -dry·ing.** To preserve (food, serum, etc.) by freezing and drying in a vacuum.

freez·er (frē′zər) n. Someone or something that freezes, esp. a thermally insulated cabinet or room that maintains a subfreezing temperature for the rapid freezing and storing of perishable food.

freezing point. The temperature at which a given liquid changes to a solid under a specified pressure, esp. a pressure equal to that of the atmosphere.

F region. The F layer.

freight (frāt) n. 1. Goods carried by a vessel or vehicle, esp. goods transported as cargo. 2. The commercial transportation of goods. 3. The charge for transporting goods by cargo carrier. 4. A railway train carrying goods only. —tr.v. 1. To convey commercially as cargo. 2. To load with cargo. 3. To charge; impregnate. [Middle English, from Middle Dutch vrecht, cargo, fee for a transport vessel.]

freight car. A railway car for carrying freight.

freight·er (frā′tər) n. 1. A vehicle, esp. a ship, for carrying freight. 2. A shipper of cargo.

freight train. A railroad train made up of freight cars.

French (french) adj. Of or characteristic of France or its people, language, or culture. —n. 1. The Romance language of France, western Switzerland, southern Belgium, and various former French possessions. 2. **the French.** (used with a pl. verb). The people of France.

French-Ca·na·di·an (french′kə-nā′dē-ən) n. Also **French Canadian.** 1. A Canadian of French descent. 2. Canadian French. —**French′-Ca·na′di·an** adj.

French cuff. A wide cuff that is folded back and fastened with a cuff link.

French curve. A flat drafting instrument with curved edges and scroll-shaped cutouts, used as a guide in connecting a set of points with a smooth curve.

French door. A door, usu. one of a pair, with glass panes extending the full length.

French fries. Strips of potatoes fried in deep fat.

French fry. To fry (potato strips, onion rings, etc.) in deep fat.

French horn. A valved brass wind instrument with a circular or coiled shape that tapers from a narrow mouthpiece to a flaring bell at the other end.

French Revolution. The revolution in France, lasting from 1789 to 1799, in which the monarchy and aristocracy were overthrown.

French toast. Sliced bread soaked in a milk and egg batter and lightly fried.

ă pat ā pay â care ä father ĕ pet ē be hw which
ōō took ōō boot ou out th thin th this ŭ cut

ĭ pit ī tie î pier ŏ pot ō toe ô paw, for oi noise
û urge zh vision ə about, item, edible, gallop, circus

French window. A casement window extending to the floor and closed by a pair of French doors.

fre·net·ic (frə-nĕt′ĭk) or **fre·net·i·cal** (-ĭ-kəl) *adj.* Also **phre·net·ic** or **phre·net·i·cal.** Frantic; frenzied. [Middle English *frenetik,* frenzied, insane, from Old French *frenetique,* from Latin *phrenēticus,* from Greek *phrenitikos,* from *phrenitis,* brain disease, insanity, from *phrēn,* mind.] **—fre·net′i·cal·ly** *adv.*

fre·num (frē′nəm) *n., pl.* **-nums** or **-na** (-nə). A membranous structure that restrains the movement of or supports a part, as the fold under the tongue. [Latin *frēnum,* bridle.]

fren·zy (frĕn′zē) *n., pl.* **-zies.** 1. A seizure of violent agitation or wild excitement, often accompanied by manic activity. 2. Temporary madness or delirium. *—tr.v.* **-zied, -zy·ing.** To drive into a frenzy; make wild or frantic. [Middle English *frenesie,* from Old French, from Medieval Latin *phrenēsia,* from Latin *phrenēsis,* from Greek, from *phrēn,* mind.] **—fren′zied·ly** *adv.*

fre·quen·cy (frē′kwən-sē) *n., pl.* **-cies.** 1. The number of occurrences of a specified event within a given interval: **a.** The number of complete cycles of a wave that occur within a period of time. **b.** The number of complete oscillations or vibrations that a body undergoes in a given period of time. 2. A fraction representing the number of times a particular event or value has occurred in a given number of opportunities for its occurrence. 3. The condition of occurring repeatedly at short intervals: *The frequency of his calls is proof enough of his interest.* [Latin *frequentia,* crowd, from *frequēns,* frequent.]

frequency modulation. *Abbr.* **FM.** The encoding of a carrier wave by variation of its frequency in accordance with an input signal.

fre·quent (frē′kwənt) *adj.* Occurring or appearing quite often or at close intervals: *frequent errors of judgment; frequent traffic accidents.* —See Syns at **common.** *—tr.v.* (frē-kwĕnt′, frē′kwənt). To pay frequent visits to; be in or at often: *He frequents several restaurants in town.* [Middle English, profuse, ample, from Old French, from Latin *frequēns,* full, frequent.] **—fre·quent′er** *n.* **—fre′quent·ly** *adv.* **—fre′quent·ness** *n.*

fre·quen·ta·tive (frē-kwĕn′tə-tĭv) *adj. Gram.* Expressing or denoting repeated action. *—n.* A frequentative verb: *Flicker is a frequentative of flick.*

fres·co (frĕs′kō) *n., pl.* **-coes** or **-cos.** 1. The art of painting on fresh, moist plaster with colors mixed in water. 2. A painting executed in this manner. *—tr.v.* **-coed, -co·ing.** To paint in fresco. [From Italian *fresco,* fresh.] **—fres′co·er** or **fres′co·ist** *n.*

fresh (frĕsh) *adj.* **-er, -est.** 1. Recently made, produced, or harvested; not stale, spoiled, or withered: *fresh bread; fresh produce.* 2. Not preserved, as by canning, smoking, or freezing: *fresh vegetables.* 3. Containing only a small amount of dissolved salts as compared with sea water: *fresh water.* 4. Additional; new: *fresh evidence.* 5. New and unusual; novel; different; original: *a fresh approach to old problems.* 6. Not yet used or soiled; clean: *a fresh paper towel.* 7. Bright and clear; not dull or faded: *a fresh memory.* 8. Having just arrived; straight: *fresh from Paris.* 9. Revived; rested; refreshed: *fresh as a daisy after a nap.* 10. Giving energy or strength; invigorating: *a fresh spring morning.* 11. *Informal.* Bold and saucy; impudent. *—idiom.* **fresh out.** *Informal.* Having just run out: *fresh out of sugar.* [Middle English, from Old French *freis.*] **—fresh′ly** *adv.* **—fresh′ness** *n.*

Syns: fresh, inventive, new, newfangled, novel, original *adj.* **Core meaning:** Showing marked departure from previous practice (*a fresh style of painting; a fresh approach to an old problem*). See also Syns at **impudent.**

fresh·en (frĕsh′ən) *intr.v.* 1. To make oneself clean and fresh: *freshen up after a day's work.* 2. To become brisk; increase in strength: *The winds began to freshen and fill our sails.* *—tr.v.* To make fresh: *freshened my make-up.* **—fresh′en·er** *n.*

fresh·et (frĕsh′ĭt) *n.* A sudden overflow of a stream resulting from heavy rain or a thaw. [FRESH + -ET.]

fresh·man (frĕsh′mən) *n.* 1. A student in the first-year class of a high school, college, or university. 2. Any beginner; a novice.

fresh·wa·ter (frĕsh′wô′tər, -wŏt′ər) *adj.* 1. Of, living in, or consisting of water that is not salty: *freshwater fish; a freshwater pond.* 2. Accustomed to sailing on inland waters only; inexperienced at sea: *a freshwater sailor.*

fret¹ (frĕt) *v.* **fret·ted, fret·ting.** *—tr.v.* 1. To cause to be uneasy or distressed; annoy; vex. 2. To gnaw or wear away; erode: *a river fretting a channel through rock.* *—intr.v.* 1. To be vexed or troubled; worry: *frets about her wardrobe.* 2. To be worn or eaten away; become corroded: *Over the years the pipes fretted.* 3. To gnaw with or as with the teeth. —See Syns at **annoy.** *—n.* A condition of being troubled; worry. [Middle English *freten,* to devour, irritate, from Old English *fretan,* to devour, consume.]

fret² (frĕt) *n.* One of several ridges, usu. of metal, set across the fingerboard of a guitar or other stringed instrument. [Orig. unknown.] **—fret′ted** *adj.*

fret³ (frĕt) *n.* An ornamental design contained within a band or border, consisting of repeated, symmetrical, and often geometric figures. *—tr.v.* **fret·ted, fret·ting.** To provide with a fret or frets. [Middle English, from Old French *frete,* trellis, embossed work.]

fret³

fret·ful (frĕt′fəl) *adj.* Inclined to fret; peevish; plaintive. **—fret′ful·ly** *adv.* **—fret′ful·ness** *n.*

fret saw. A saw with a narrow, fine-toothed blade, used for cutting patterns in thin wood or metal.

fret·work (frĕt′wûrk′) *n.* 1. Ornamental work consisting of three-dimensional frets. 2. Such ornamental work represented two-dimensionally.

Freu·di·an (froi′dē-ən) *adj.* Pertaining to or in accordance with the psychoanalytic theories of Sigmund Freud. *—n.* Someone who actively applies the psychoanalytic methods or theories of Freud in conducting psychotherapy.

Frey·a (frā′ə) *n.* Also **Frey·ja.** *Norse Myth.* The goddess of love and beauty.

fri·a·ble (frī′ə-bəl) *adj.* Readily crumbled; brittle. [French, from Latin *friābilis,* crumbling, from *friāre,* to crumble.] **—fri′a·bil′i·ty** or **fri′a·ble·ness** *n.*

fri·ar (frī′ər) *n.* A man who is a member of certain Roman Catholic orders. [Middle English *frere,* from Old French, from Latin *frāter,* brother.]

fri·ar·y (frī′ə-rē) *n., pl.* **-ies.** A monastery of friars.

fric·as·see (frĭk′ə-sē′, frĭk′ə-sē′) *n.* Poultry or meat cut into pieces, stewed, and served with a thick gravy. *—tr.v.* **-seed, -see·ing.** To prepare as a fricassee. [French *fricassée,* past part. of *fricasser,* to fry.]

fric·a·tive (frĭk′ə-tĭv) *adj. Phonet.* Produced by the forcing of breath through a constricted passage, as such consonantal sounds as (f) and (v), (s) and (z), (sh) and (zh), (th) and (th). *—n. Phonet.* A fricative consonant. Also called **spirant.** [From Latin *fricāre,* to rub.]

fric·tion (frĭk′shən) *n.* 1. The rubbing of one object or surface against another. 2. A clash, as of persons having dissimilar interests or beliefs. 3. *Physics.* A force that acts to resist or retard the relative motion of two objects that are in contact. —See Syns at **conflict.** [Old French, from Latin *frictiō,* from *frictus,* past part. of *fricāre,* to rub.] **—fric′tion·less** *adj.*

fric·tion·al (frĭk′shə-nəl) *adj.* Of or involving friction: *frictional heating.* **—fric′tion·al·ly** *adv.*

friction tape. A sturdy moisture-resistant adhesive tape used chiefly to insulate electrical conductors.

Fri·day (frī′dē, -dā′) *n.* The sixth day of the week, after Thursday and before Saturday. [Middle English *fridai,* from Old English *frīgedæg.*]

fried (frīd) *v.* Past tense and past participle of **fry** (to cook).

friend (frĕnd) *n.* **1.** A person whom one knows, likes, and trusts; a close acquaintance. **2.** A person, group, or nation that supports, sympathizes with, or patronizes a group, cause, or movement: *friends of the symphony.* **3. Friend.** A member of the Society of Friends; a Quaker. **—idiom. make friends with.** To enter into friendship with. [Middle English *frend,* from Old English *frēond.*] **—friend′less** *adj.* **—friend′less·ness** *n.*

friend·ly (frĕnd′lē) *adj.* **-li·er, -li·est. 1.** Of or befitting a friend. **2.** Favorably disposed; not antagonistic: *a friendly gesture.* **3.** Warm; comforting: *friendly sunlight.* **—friend′li·ness** *n.*

    Syns: friendly, amiable, amicable, chummy (*Informal*), **congenial, warmhearted** *adj.* Core meaning: Of or befitting a friend or friends (*a friendly letter; friendly cooperation*).

friend·ship (frĕnd′shĭp′) *n.* **1.** The condition of being friends. **2.** Friendly feeling; friendliness.

fri·er (frī′ər) *n.* Var. of **fryer.**

frieze[1] (frēz) *n. Archit.* **1.** The horizontal part of an entablature between the architrave and cornice. **2.** Any decora-

frieze[1]

tive horizontal band. [French *frise,* from Old French, from Medieval Latin *frisium, frigium,* fringe, embroidered cloth, from Latin *Phrygium,* of Phrygia, a place noted for its embroidery.]

frieze[2] (frēz) *n.* A coarse, shaggy woolen cloth with an uncut nap. [Middle English *frise,* from Old French, from Middle Dutch *vriese,* perh. from *Vriese,* from Latin *Frīsiī,* Frisian.]

frig·ate (frĭg′ĭt) *n.* **1.** Any of various fast-sailing, square-rigged warships built between the 17th and mid-19th cent. **2.** A U.S. warship intermediate in size between a cruiser and destroyer. [French *frégate,* from Italian *fregata.*]

frigate bird. Any of various tropical sea birds of the genus *Fregata,* having long, powerful wings and dark plumage and characteristically snatching food from other birds in flight. Also called **man-o′-war bird.**

Frig·ga (frĭg′ə) *n. Norse Myth.* The wife of Odin and goddess of the heavens.

fright (frīt) *n.* **1.** Sudden, intense fear, as of something immediately threatening; alarm. **2.** *Informal.* Something extremely unsightly, alarming, or strange. [Middle English, from Old English *fryhto, fyrhto.*]

fright·en (frīt′n) *tr.v.* **1.** To make suddenly afraid; alarm or startle. **2.** To drive or force by arousing fear. —*intr.v.* To become suddenly afraid.

    Syns: frighten, alarm, panic, scare, startle, terrify, terrorize *v.* Core meaning: To fill with fear (*an explosion that frightened us*).

fright·en·ing (frīt′nĭng, frīt′n-ĭng) *adj.* Causing fright or sudden alarm. **—fright′en·ing·ly** *adv.*

fright·ful (frīt′fəl) *adj.* **1.** Causing great disgust or shock; horrifying. **2.** Causing fright; terrifying. **3.** *Informal.* **a.** Excessive; extreme: *a frightful liar.* **b.** Disagreeable; distressing: *frightful weather.* —See Syns at **unspeakable. —fright′ful·ly** *adv.* **—fright′ful·ness** *n.*

frig·id (frĭj′ĭd) *adj.* **1.** Extremely cold. **2.** Lacking warmth of feeling; stiff and formal in manner. [Latin *frigidus,* from *frīgēre,* to be cold, from *frigus,* cold.] **—fri·gid′i·ty** (frĭ-jĭd′ĭ-tē) or **frig′id·ness** *n.* **—frig′id·ly** *adv.*

    Syns: frigid, arctic, frosty, glacial, icy, polar *adj.* Core meaning: Very cold (*a frigid night*). See also Syns at **cold.**

fri·jol (frē-hōl′, frē′hōl′) *n.,* pl. **-jo·les** (frē-hō′lēz, frē′hō′lēz). Also **fri·jo·le** (frē-hō′lē). *Southwestern U.S.* A bean cultivated and used for food. [Spanish, var. of *fresol,* from Lat-

---

in *phaseolus,* dim. of *phasēlus,* kidney bean, from Greek *phasēlos.*]

frill (frĭl) *n.* **1.** A ruffled, gathered, or pleated border, as lace used for trimming. **2.** *Zool.* A ruff of hair or feathers or a similar membranous projection about the neck of an animal or bird. **3.** *Informal.* Something that is fancy or decorative but not essential. —*tr.v.* **1.** To make into a ruffle or frill. **2.** To add a ruffle or frill to. [Orig. unknown.] **—frill′y** *adj.*

fringe (frĭnj) *n.* **1.** A decorative border or edging of hanging threads, cords, or loops. **2.** Something like a fringe along an edge: *a fringe of eyelashes.* **3.** A marginal or peripheral part; an edge: *the fringes of the crowd.* **4.** Those members of a group or political party holding extreme views: *the lunatic fringe.* —*tr.v.* **fringed, fring·ing. 1.** To decorate with a fringe. **2.** To form a fringe along the edge of. [Middle English *frenge,* from Old French, from Late Latin *fimbria.*]

fringe benefit. An employment benefit given in addition to wages or salary.

trip·per·y (frĭp′ə-rē) *n.,* pl. **-ies. 1.** Cheap, showy ornaments or dress. **2.** An ostentatious display, as in behavior. [French *friperie,* from Old French *freperie,* from *frepe, felpe,* frill, from Medieval Latin *faluppa,* fiber.]

frisk (frĭsk) *intr.v.* To move about briskly and playfully; frolic. —*tr.v.* To search (a person) for something concealed, esp. weapons, by passing the hands quickly over clothes or through pockets. [From obs. *frisk,* lively, from Old French *frisque.*] **—frisk′er** *n.*

frisk·y (frĭs′kē) *adj.* **-i·er, -i·est.** Energetic, lively, and playful. **—frisk′i·ly** *adv.* **—frisk′i·ness** *n.*

frit·il·lar·y (frĭt′l-ĕr′ē) *n.,* pl. **-ies. 1.** Any of various bulbous plants of the genus *Fritillaria,* with nodding, often variously colored, often spotted or checkered flowers. **2.** Any of various butterflies of the family Nymphalidae, and esp. of the genera *Speyeria* and *Boloria,* with brownish wings that are marked with black or silvery spots. [From Latin *fritillus,* dice box (from its checkered markings).]

frit·ter[1] (frĭt′ər) *tr.v.* To reduce or squander little by little: *fritter away the day.* [Prob. from obs. *fritter,* to break in pieces.]

frit·ter[2] (frĭt′ər) *n.* A small fried cake made of batter that often contains fruit, vegetables, or fish. [Middle English *friture,* from Old French, from Latin *frictus,* past part. of *frīgere,* to fry.]

fri·vol·i·ty (frĭ-vŏl′ĭ-tē) *n.,* pl. **-ties. 1.** The condition or quality of being frivolous. **2.** A frivolous act or thing.

friv·o·lous (frĭv′ə-ləs) *adj.* **1.** Unworthy of serious attention; insignificant; trivial: *wasting their time on frivolous pursuits.* **2.** Not serious or sensible; silly: *frivolous conversation.* [Middle English, from Latin *frīvolus.*] **—friv′o·lous·ly** *adv.* **—friv′o·lous·ness** *n.*

frizz (frĭz). *tr.v.* To curl (hair) into small, tight curls. —*intr.v.* To be formed into small, tight curls. —*n.* A tight curl of hair or fabric. [French *friser,* to curl.] **—frizz′er** *n.*

friz·zle[1] (frĭz′əl) *v.* **-zled, -zling.** —*tr.v.* To fry until crisp and curled. —*intr.v.* To fry or sear with a sizzling noise. [Perh. blend of FRY and SIZZLE.]

friz·zle[2] (frĭz′əl) *v.* **-zled, -zling.** —*tr.v.* To frizz (hair). —*intr.v.* To form tight curls. —*n.* A small, tight curl. [Orig. unknown.]

friz·zly (frĭz′lē) *adj.* **-zli·er, -zli·est.** Tightly curled.

friz·zy (frĭz′ē) *adj.* **-zi·er, -zi·est.** Tightly curled; frizzly. **—friz′zi·ly** *adv.* **—friz′zi·ness** *n.*

fro (frō) *adv.* **to and fro.** Back and forth. [Middle English, from Old Norse *frā.*]

frock (frŏk) *n.* **1.** A woman′s or girl′s dress. **2.** A long, loose outer garment, such as that worn by artists; a smock. **3.** A robe worn by monks, friars, and other clerics; habit. [Middle English *frok,* from Old French *froc.*]

frock coat. A man′s dress overcoat with knee-length skirts, worn chiefly in the 19th cent.

frog (frôg, frŏg) *n.* **1.** Any of numerous tailless, chiefly aquatic amphibians of the order Salientia, esp. of the family Ranidae, that characteristically have a smooth, moist skin, webbed feet, and long hind legs adapted for leaping. **2.** A wedge-shaped, horny prominence in the sole of a horse′s hoof. **3.** An ornamental looped braid or cord with a button or knot for fastening the front of a garment. **4.** A

---

device on intersecting railroad tracks that permits wheels to cross the junction. **5.** A spiked or perforated object placed in a container and used to support stems in a decorative floral arrangement. **6.** *Informal.* Hoarseness in the throat. [Middle English *frogge,* from Old English *frogga.*]

frog kick. A swimming kick in which the legs are drawn up close beneath one, then thrust outward and together vigorously.

frog·man (frôg'măn', -mən, frŏg'-) *n.* A swimmer provided with breathing apparatus and other equipment to execute underwater maneuvers, esp. military maneuvers.

frol·ic (frŏl'ĭk) *n.* **1.** Gaiety; merriment. **2.** A gay, carefree time. —*intr.v.* **-icked, -ick·ing. 1.** To behave playfully and uninhibitedly; romp. **2.** To engage in merrymaking. [Dutch *vrolijk,* from Middle Dutch *vrolijc : vro,* happy + *-lijc,* -ly.] —**frol'ick·er** *n.*

frol·ic·some (frŏl'ĭk-səm) *adj.* Full of high-spirited fun; frisky; playful.

from (frŭm, frŏm; frəm *when unstressed*) *prep.* **1.** Beginning at a specified place or time: *walked home from the station; from six o'clock on.* **2.** With a specified time or point as the first of two limits: *from age four to age eight.* **3. a.** With a person, place, or thing as the source, cause, or instrument: *a note from the teacher.* **b.** Because of: *faint from hunger.* **4.** Out of: *take a book from the shelf.* **5.** Out of the jurisdiction, control, or possession of: *running away from home.* **6.** So as not to be engaged in: *keep someone from making a mistake.* **7.** Measured by reference to: *far away from home.* **8.** As opposed to: *know right from wrong.* [Middle English, from Old English.]

frond (frŏnd) *n.* **1.** The leaf of a fern, palm tree, etc., usu. divided into smaller leaflets. **2.** A leaflike thallus, as of a seaweed or lichen. [Latin *frōns,* branch, leaf.] —**frond'ed** *adj.*

front (frŭnt) *n.* **1.** The forward part or surface of a thing or place: *a desk at the front of the room.* **2.** The area, location, or position directly before or ahead: *a crowd in front of the lions' cage.* **3.** A foremost position in rank, superiority, or leadership; forefront: *still in front scientifically.* **4.** The first part; beginning; opening: *the front of your book.* **5.** A person's manner or behavior; demeanor; bearing: *trying to keep up a brave front.* **6.** A false appearance or manner; outward show: *He puts up a confident front among strangers.* **7.** Land bordering a lake, river, street, etc. **8.** In warfare, an area where major fighting is taking place. **9.** An area or scene of a particular activity: *life on the home front.* **10.** The boundary between two masses of air that are at different temperatures: *a cold front.* **11.** A group or movement uniting persons or organizations that seek a common goal; a coalition. **12.** An outwardly respectable person or business that serves as a cover for secret or illegal activity. —*adj.* In or facing the front. —*tr.v.* **1.** To face or look out upon: *a building fronting the street.* **2.** To serve as a front for: *fronts a gambling syndicate.* **3.** To meet in opposition; confront. —*intr.v.* **1.** To face or border: *Her property fronts on the highway.* **2.** To act as a front or cover: *He fronts for the mob.* [Middle English, from Old French, from Latin *frōns,* front, forehead.]

front·age (frŭn'tĭj) *n.* **1. a.** The front part of a piece of property, as a lot or building. **b.** The dimensions of such a part. **2.** Land adjacent to a building, street, or body of water.

fron·tal (frŭn'tl) *adj.* **1.** Of, at, or concerning the front. **2.** Of the forehead. **3.** Aimed at the front: *a frontal attack.* —**fron'tal·ly** *adv.*

fron·tier (frŭn-tîr', frŏn-) *n.* **1.** An international border or the area along it. **2.** A region in a country that marks the point of farthest settlement. **3.** Any undeveloped field of activity, as of science: *new frontiers in space.* —*modifier: a frontier town.* [Middle English *frountier,* from Old French *frontiere,* from *front,* front.]

fron·tiers·man (frŭn-tîrz'mən, frŏn-) *n.* A man who lives in an area bordering unsettled territory.

fron·tis·piece (frŭn'tĭ-spēs') *n.* An illustration that faces or immediately precedes the title page of a book. [Var. of earlier *frontispice,* from Old French, from Late Latin *frontispicium,* "examination of the front," building exterior : Latin *frōns,* front + *specere,* to look at.]

front·let (frŭnt'lĭt) *n.* **1.** An ornament or band worn across

the forehead. **2.** The forehead of an animal or bird, esp. when distinctively marked. [Middle English, from Old French *frontelet,* dim. of *frontel,* from Latin *frontāle,* from *frōns,* front.]

front-page (frŭnt'pāj') *adj.* Receiving or worthy of coverage on the front page of a newspaper; important.

front-run·ner (frŭnt'rŭn'ər) *n.* **1.** Someone or something that is leading in a race, contest, or other competition. **2.** A competitor in a race or other contest who performs best when in the lead. —**front'run'ning** *adj.*

frost (frôst, frŏst) *n.* **1.** A deposit or covering of small ice crystals formed from frozen water vapor. **2.** The atmospheric conditions below the freezing point of water. **3.** A cold or icy manner; haughtiness. —*tr.v.* **1.** To cover with or as if with frost. **2.** To cover or decorate (a cake, cupcake, etc.) with icing. —*intr.v.* To become covered with or as if with frost. [Middle English, from Old English *frost, forst.*]

frost·bite (frôst'bīt', frŏst'-) *n.* Local destruction of body tissue as a result of freezing. —*tr.v.* **-bit** (-bĭt'), **-bit·ten** (-bĭt'n), **-bit·ing.** To injure or damage (body tissue) by freezing.

frost·ed (frô'stĭd, frŏs'tĭd) *adj.* **1.** Covered by frost or a surface resembling frost. **2.** Frostbitten. **3.** Covered or decorated with icing.

frost·ing (frô'stĭng, frŏs'tĭng) *n.* **1.** A sweet glaze of sugar and other ingredients used to decorate cakes and cookies; icing. **2.** A roughened or speckled surface imparted to glass or metal.

frost line. The limit to which frost penetrates the earth.

frost·y (frô'stē, frŏs'tē) *adj.* **-i·er, -i·est. 1.** Of or producing frost; freezing: *a frosty night.* **2.** Covered with or as if with frost: *a frosty window.* **3.** Extremely cold in temperature. **4.** Cold in manner: *a frosty tone of voice.* —See Syns at **frigid.** —**frost'i·ly** *adv.* —**frost'i·ness** *n.*

froth (frôth, frŏth) *n.* **1.** A mass of bubbles in or on a liquid; foam. **2.** A salivary foam released as a result of disease or exhaustion. **3.** Something lacking in substance or depth: *a play that is mere froth.* —*tr.v.* **1.** To exude or expel (liquid) in the form of froth. **2.** To cover with froth. **3.** To cause to foam. —*intr.v.* To exude or expel froth; to foam. [Middle English, from Old Norse *frodha.*]

froth·y (frô'thē, frŏth'ē) *adj.* **-i·er, -i·est. 1.** Of, covered with, or resembling froth; foamy. **2.** Playfully frivolous in character or content. —**froth'i·ly** *adv.* —**froth'i·ness** *n.*

frou-frou (frōo'frōo') *n.* **1.** A rustling sound, as of silk. **2.** Showy dress or ornamentation. [French (imit.).]

fro·ward (frô'wərd, frô'ərd) *adj.* Stubbornly contrary and disobedient; obstinate. [Middle English *froward.*] —**fro'ward·ly** *adv.* —**fro'ward·ness** *n.*

frown (froun) *intr.v.* **1.** To wrinkle the brow, as in thought or displeasure; to scowl. **2.** To regard with disapproval or distaste: *frown on smoking.* —*tr.v.* To express (disapproval, distaste, etc.) by wrinkling the brow. —*n.* The act of wrinkling the brow, as in thought or displeasure; a scowl. [Middle English *frounen,* from Old French *froigner.*] —**frown'er** *n.* —**frown'ing·ly** *adv.*

frow·zy (frou'zē) *adj.* **-zi·er, -zi·est.** Also **frow·sy.** Unkempt in appearance; slovenly. [Orig. unknown.] —**frow'zi·ness** *n.*

froze (frōz) *v.* Past tense of **freeze.** [Middle English *frose,* from Old English *frēas.*]

fro·zen (frō'zən) *v.* Past participle of **freeze.** —*adj.* **1.** Made into, covered with, or surrounded by ice: *a frozen pond.* **2.** Very cold: *the frozen wilds of Alaska.* **3.** Preserved by freezing: *frozen foods.* **4.** Rendered immobile: *stood frozen in their tracks.* **5.** Expressive of cold unfriendliness: *a frozen stare.* **6. a.** Kept at an arbitrary level, as wages. **b.** Incapable of being withdrawn, sold, or liquidated; as assets. [Middle English *frosen,* alteration of *froren,* from Old English *(ge)froren.*]

fruc·ti·fy (frŭk'tə-fī', frōok'-) *v.* **-fied, -fy·ing.** —*tr.v.* To cause to produce fruit; make fruitful or productive. —*intr.v.* To bear fruit. [Middle English *fructifien,* from Old French *fructifier,* from Latin *frūctificāre : frūctus,* fruit + *facere,* to make.]

fruc·tose (frŭk'tōs', frōok'-, frŏok'-) *n.* A very sweet sugar, $C_6H_{12}O_6$, found in many fruits and honey and used as a preservative for foodstuffs and as an intravenous nutrient.

Also called **fruit sugar** and **levulose**. [Latin *frūctus*, fruit + -OSE.]

fru·gal (frōō′gəl) *adj.* **1.** Avoiding unnecessary expenditure of money; thrifty. **2.** Not very abundant; meager: *a frugal meal.* [Latin *frūgālis*, back-formation from *frūgālior*, comparative of *frūgī*, useful, worthy, from *frūx*, fruit.] **—fru·gal′i·ty** (-găl′ĭ-tē) or **fru′gal·ness** *n.* **—fru′gal·ly** *adv.*

fruit (frōōt) *n., pl.* **fruit** or **fruits.** **1. a.** The ripened, seed-bearing part of a flowering plant, as a pod, berry, or burr. **b.** An often sweet fleshy or juicy plant part of this kind, as an apple, eaten as food. **2.** The fertile, often spore-bearing structure of a plant that does not bear seeds. **3.** A result; outcome: *the fruit of their labor.* **—modifier:** *fruit trees.* **—intr.v.** To produce fruit. **—tr.v.** To cause to produce fruit. [Middle English, from Old French, from Latin *frūctus*, enjoyment, use, fruit, past part. of *fruī*, to enjoy, to eat fruit.]

fruit·age (frōō′tĭj) *n.* **1.** The process or condition of bearing fruit. **2.** Fruit collectively. **3.** A result or effect.

fruit·cake (frōōt′kāk′) *n.* A heavy, spiced cake that contains citron, nuts, raisins, and preserved fruits.

fruit fly. 1. Any of various small flies of the family Drosophilidae, which have larvae that feed on ripening or fermenting fruit, esp. a common species, *Drosophila melanogaster.* **2.** Any of various flies of the family Tripetidae (or Tephritidae), which have larvae that hatch in and damage plant tissue.

fruit·ful (frōōt′fəl) *adj.* **1.** Producing fruit. **2.** Producing results; profitable: *an arrangement that may prove fruitful.* —See Syns at **fertile.** **—fruit′ful·ly** *adv.* **—fruit′ful·ness** *n.*

fru·i·tion (frōō-ĭsh′ən) *n.* **1.** The achievement of something desired or worked for; accomplishment; realization: *May all your plans reach fruition.* **2.** The condition of bearing fruit. [Middle English *fruicioun,* from Old French *fruition,* from Late Latin *fruitiō,* from *fruī,* to enjoy, eat fruit.]

fruit·less (frōōt′lĭs) *adj.* **1.** Having little or no result; unproductive: *a fruitless experiment.* **2.** Producing no fruit. **—fruit′less·ly** *adv.* **—fruit′less·ness** *n.*

fruit sugar. Fructose.

fruit·y (frōō′tē) *adj.* **-i·er, -i·est. 1.** Tasting or smelling of fruit. **—fruit′i·ness** *n.*

frump (frŭmp) *n.* A dull, plain, unfashionably dressed girl or woman. [Perh. short for dial. *frumple,* to wrinkle, from Middle English *fromplen,* from Middle Dutch *verrompelen.*]

frus·trate (frŭs′trāt′) *tr.v.* **-trat·ed, -trat·ing. 1.** To prevent from accomplishing a purpose or fulfilling a desire; thwart: *injuries that frustrated the athlete.* **2.** To prevent the accomplishment of; nullify: *frustrated the enemy's plan.* [Middle English *frustraten,* from Latin *frūstrātus,* past part. of *frūstrāre,* to disappoint, frustrate, from *frūstra,* in error, uselessly.] **—frus·tra′tion** *n.*

frus·tum (frŭs′təm) *n., pl.* **-tums** or **-ta** (-tə). A part of a solid figure, such as a cone or pyramid, cut off by two parallel planes that cross all the lines contained in its surface, esp. the section between the base and a plane parallel to it. [Latin, piece, piece cut off.]

fry[1] (frī) *v.* **fried, fry·ing. —tr.v.** To cook over direct heat in hot oil or fat. **—intr.v.** To be cooked over direct heat in hot oil or fat. **—n., pl. fries. 1.** A dish of fried food. **2.** A social gathering featuring fried food: *a fish fry.* [Middle English *frien,* from Old French *frire,* from Latin *frīgere.*]

fry[2] (frī) *n., pl.* **fry. 1. a.** A small fish, esp. a recently hatched fish. **b.** The similar young of certain other animals. **2.** Individuals; persons: *young fry.* [Middle English, young offspring, perh. from Norman French *frie,* from Old French *freier,* to spawn, rub, from Latin *fricāre,* to rub.]

fry·er (frī′ər) *n.* Also **fri·er. 1.** A young chicken suitable for frying. **2.** A deep pot for frying foods.

f-stop (ĕf′stŏp′) *n.* **1.** A camera lens aperture setting that is calibrated to a corresponding f-number. **2.** An **f-number.**

fuch·sia (fyōō′shə) *n.* **1.** Any of various chiefly tropical shrubs of the genus *Fuchsia,* widely cultivated for their showy, drooping purplish, reddish, or white flowers. **2.** A vivid purplish red. **—adj.** Vivid purplish red. [After Leonhard *Fuchs* (1501–66), German botanist.]

fud·dle (fŭd′l) *tr.v.* **-dled, -dling.** To muddle or confuse with or as if with liquor; intoxicate. —See Syns at **confuse.** [Orig. unknown.]

fud·dy-dud·dy (fŭd′ē-dŭd′ē) *n., pl.* **-dies.** A person who is old-fashioned, conservative, or very fussy or critical. [Orig. unknown.]

fudge (fŭj) *n.* **1.** A soft rich candy made of sugar, butter, and flavoring. **2.** Nonsense; humbug. **—v. fudged, fudg·ing. —tr.v. 1.** To fake or falsify: *He fudged the truth.* **2.** To evade (an issue, answer, etc.); to dodge. **—intr.v.** To act in a dishonest or indecisive manner. [Orig. unknown.]

fueh·rer (fyŏŏr′ər) *n.* Var. of **führer.**

fu·el (fyōō′əl) *n.* **1.** Anything consumed to produce energy, esp.: **a.** A material such as wood, coal, gas, or oil burned to produce heat. **b.** Fissionable material used in a nuclear reactor. **c.** Nutritive material metabolized by a living organism. **2.** Anything that maintains or heightens an activity or emotion. **—modifier:** *a fuel pump.* **—v. -eled** or **-elled, -el·ing** or **-el·ling. —tr.v.** To provide with fuel. **—intr.v.** To take in fuel. [Middle English *feuel,* from Old French *fouaille,* from Latin *focus,* fire, hearth.] **—fu′el·er** *n.*

fuel cell. A device in which a fuel and an oxidizing agent react and release energy in the form of electricity.

fuel injection. Any of several methods or mechanical systems by which a fuel is vaporized and sprayed into the cylinders or into the air at the cylinder intake ports of an internal-combustion engine.

fuel oil. Any liquid or liquefiable petroleum product with a flash point above 100°F that is used to generate heat or power.

fu·gi·tive (fyōō′jĭ-tĭv) *adj.* **1.** Running or having run away, as from the law or justice: *a fugitive convict.* **2.** Passing quickly; fleeting or elusive: *fugitive dreams.* **—n.** A person who flees; a runaway; refugee. [Middle English *fugitif,* from Old French, from Latin *fugitīvus,* from *fugitus,* past part. of *fugere,* to flee.] **—fu′gi·tive·ly** *adv.* **—fu′gi·tive·ness** *n.*

fugue (fyōōg) *n.* A musical composition in which one or more themes are stated and then developed by means of imitation and elaborate counterpoint. [French *fugue* or Italian *fuga,* flight, from Latin.] **—fu′gal** (fyōō′gəl) *adj.* **—fu′gal·ly** *adv.*

füh·rer (fyŏŏr′ər) *n.* Also **fueh·rer. 1.** A leader, esp. one exercising the powers of a tyrant. **2. Führer.** The title of Adolf Hitler as the leader of Nazi Germany. [German *Führer.*]

-ful. A suffix meaning: **1.** Fullness or abundance: **playful. 2.** Having the characteristics: **masterful. 3.** Tendency or ability: **useful. 4.** The amount or number that will fill: **armful.** [Middle English, from Old English *-ful, -full,* from *full,* full.]

ful·crum (fŏŏl′krəm, fŭl′-) *n., pl.* **-crums** or **-cra** (-krə). The point or point of support on which a lever turns. [Latin, bedpost, support, from *fulcīre,* to prop up.]

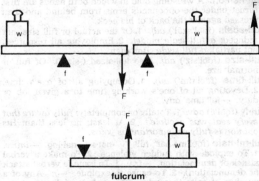

fulcrum
The fulcrums of three basic levers

ful·fill or **ful·fil** (fŏŏl-fĭl′) *tr.v.* **-filled, -fil·ling. 1.** To bring into actuality; effect: *fulfilled the prophecy.* **2.** To carry out (an order, duty, etc.): *fulfilled the terms of the contract.* **3.** To measure up to; satisfy: *fulfilled all requirements.* [Middle English *fulfillen,* Old English *fullfyllan,* to fill full.] **—ful·fill′er** *n.* **—ful·fill′ment** or **ful·fil′ment** *n.*

full[1] (fŏŏl) *adj.* **-er, -est. 1.** Containing all that is normal or possible; filled: *a full bucket.* **2.** Not partial; complete: *full employment.* **3.** Of highest degree or development: *in full bloom.* **4.** Having a great many or a great deal of: *shelves full of books.* **5.** Totally qualified or accepted: *a full member of the club.* **6.** Rounded in shape: *a full figure.* **7.** Not tight or narrow: *a full skirt.* **8.** Abundantly fed. **9.** Having depth and body; rich: *a full flavor.* **10.** Having its illuminated side completely facing the earth: *a full moon.* **11.** Having the same mother and father: *full brothers.* —*adv.* **1.** To a complete extent; entirely: *knew full well that he was wrong.* **2.** Exactly; directly: *a blow that caught him full on the chin.* —*n.* The maximum or complete size, amount, or development. —*idiom.* **in full.** Completely; with nothing lacking: *paid in full.* [Middle English *ful(l),* from Old English *full.*] —**full′ness** or **ful′ness** *n.*

full² (fõol) *tr.v.* To increase the weight and bulk of (cloth) by shrinking and beating or pressing. [Middle English *fullen,* from Old French *fouler,* from Latin *fullō,* a fuller.]

full·back (fõol′băk′) *n.* **1.** *Football.* An offensive backfield player whose position is behind the quarterback and halfbacks. **2.** *Field Hockey, Soccer, & Rugby.* Either of two players stationed near their team's goal.

full-blood·ed (fõol′blŭd′ĭd) *adj.* **1.** Of unmixed ancestry; purebred. **2.** Vigorous and energetic.

full-blown (fõol′blōn′) *adj.* **1.** In full blossom; fully open: *a full-blown tulip.* **2.** Fully developed or matured: *a full-blown beauty.*

full-bod·ied (fõol′bŏd′ēd) *adj.* Having richness and intensity of flavor: *a full-bodied wine.*

full dress. The kind of clothing required for very formal occasions, as a man's white tie and tails. —*modifier* **(full-dress):** *a full-dress banquet.*

full·er (fõol′ər) *n.* A person who fulls cloth. [Middle English *fullere,* from Old English *fullere,* from Latin *fullō.*]

fuller's earth. A highly absorbent claylike substance used in talcum powder, in cleaning woolen cloth, and as a filtering material.

full-fash·ioned (fõol′făsh′ənd) *adj.* Knitted in a shape that conforms closely to body lines.

full-fledged (fõol′flĕjd′) *adj.* **1.** Having fully developed adult plumage. **2.** Having reached full development; mature. **3.** Having full status or rank.

full gainer. A forward dive in which one executes a full back somersault before entering the water.

full-grown (fõol′grōn′) *adj.* Having reached full growth or development; fully mature.

full house. *Poker.* A hand that contains three of a kind and a pair.

full moon. **1.** The phase of the moon when it is seen as a fully lighted disk. **2.** The time of the month at which this occurs.

full nelson. A wrestling hold in which both hands are first thrust under the opponent's arms from behind and then pressed against the back of his neck.

full-scale (fõol′skāl′) *adj.* **1.** Of the actual or full size; not reduced: *a full-scale model.* **2.** Employing all resources; not partial: *a full-scale campaign.*

full-size (fõol′sīz′) *adj.* Also **full-sized** (-sīzd′). Of full or normal size.

full-time (fõol′tīm′) *adj.* **1.** Occupying all of one's time. **2.** Devoting all of one's working time to a given job or duty. —**full′time′** *adv.*

ful·ly (fõol′ē) *adv.* **1.** Totally or completely: *fully aware that every seat was occupied.* **2.** At least; no less than: *His opinion is fully as important as yours.*

ful·mi·nate (fõol′mə-nāt′, fŭl′-) *v.* **-nat·ed, -nat·ing.** —*intr.v.* **1.** To explode with sudden violence. **2.** To make a verbal attack or denunciation. —*tr.v.* **1.** To issue (a verbal attack or denunciation). **2.** To cause to explode. —*n.* Any of a number of salts that when dry explode violently at the slightest shock or friction. [Middle English *fulminaten,* from Medieval Latin *fulminatus,* past part. of *fulmināre,* to censure ecclesiastically, from Latin, to strike with lightning, from *fulmen,* lightning.] —**ful′mi·na′tor** *n.* —**ful′mi·na′tion** *n.*

ful·some (fõol′səm) *adj.* Abundant to the point of being excessive or insincere: *fulsome praise.* [Middle English *fulsom,* abundant.] —**ful′some·ly** *adv.* —**ful′some·ness** *n.*

fum·ble (fŭm′bəl) *v.* **-bled, -bling.** —*intr.v.* **1.** To touch or handle nervously or idly: *fumble with a necktie.* **2.** To grope awkwardly: *fumble for a key.* **3.** To proceed awkwardly and uncertainly; to blunder: *fumble through a speech.* **4. a.** *Baseball.* To mishandle a ground ball. **b.** *Football.* To drop a ball that is in play. —*tr.v.* **1.** To touch or handle nervously or idly. **2.** To make a botch of; bungle: *The actor fumbled his lines.* **3. a.** *Baseball.* To mishandle (a ground ball). **b.** *Football.* To drop (the ball) while in play. —See Syns at **botch.** —*n.* **1.** The act or an example of fumbling. **2.** *Sports.* A ball that has been fumbled. [Perh. of Scandinavian orig.] —**fum′bler** *n.*

fume (fyõom) *n.* **1.** Often **fumes.** Any smoke, vapor, or gas, esp. one that is irritating or disagreeable: *the fumes from a smokestack.* **2.** A state of irritation or anger. —*v.* **fumed, fum·ing.** —*tr.v.* **1.** To subject to or treat with fumes. **2.** To give off in or as if in fumes. —*intr.v.* **1.** To emit fumes. **2.** To rise or dissipate in vapor. **3.** To feel or show agitation or anger: *The crowd fumed over the long wait.* [Middle English, from Old French *fum,* from Latin *fūmus,* smoke, steam.]

fu·mi·gate (fyõo′mĭ-gāt′) *tr.v.* **-gat·ed, -gat·ing.** To treat (a room or an object) with fumes in order to kill germs, insects, rats, or other pests. [Latin *fūmigāre:* *fūmus,* smoke, fume + *agere,* to make, do.] —**fu′mi·ga′tion** *n.* —**fu′mi·ga′tor** *n.*

fun (fŭn) *n.* **1.** Enjoyment, pleasure, or amusement. **2.** Excited, noisy activity; gaiety. —See Syns at **gaiety.** —*intr.v.* **funned, fun·ning.** To behave playfully; to joke. —*idioms.* **for (or in) fun.** As a joke; playfully. **make fun of.** To ridicule. [Perh. from obs. *fun,* to trick, from Middle English *fonnen,* to make fun of, from *fon, fonne,* a fool.]

func·tion (fŭngk′shən) *n.* **1.** The proper, normal, or characteristic activity of a person or thing: *the function of the pancreas.* **2.** The duty, occupation, or role of a person: *in his function as attorney.* **3.** An official ceremony or elaborate social occasion. **4.** Something closely related to another thing and dependent upon it for its existence, value, or significance: *Growth is a function of nutrition.* **5.** *Math.* A rule of correspondence between two sets such that there is a unique element in one set assigned to each element in the other set. —*intr.v.* To have or perform a function; to serve. [Latin *functiō,* activity, performance, from *functus,* past part. of *fungī,* to perform.] —**func′tion·less** *adj.*

func·tion·al (fŭngk′shə-nəl) *adj.* **1.** Of or concerning a function or functions. **2.** Designed for or adapted to a particular purpose, often avoiding additions that are merely decorative; efficient and practical: *functional architecture.* **3.** Capable of performing; operative. **4.** *Path.* Existing with no apparent change in the structure of an organism: *a functional disorder of the brain.* **5.** *Math.* Of, relating to, or indicating a function or functions. —See Syns at **pratical.** —**func′tion·al·ly** *adv.*

func·tion·ar·y (fŭngk′shə-nĕr′ē) *n., pl.* **-ies.** A person who holds a position of authority or trust; an official.

function word. A word that expresses grammatical function rather than content or meaning.

fund (fŭnd) *n.* **1.** A source of supply; a stock: *a fund of good will.* **2.** A sum of money or other resources raised or set aside for a specific purpose. **3. funds.** Available money; ready cash. —*tr.v.* **1.** To furnish money for (a project, the operation of a program, etc.): *fund a housing project.* **2.** To make provision for paying off (a debt). [Blend of French *fond,* bottom, and *fonds,* stock, both from Latin *fundus,* bottom, landed property.]

fun·da·men·tal (fŭn′də-mĕn′tl) *adj.* **1.** Having to do with the foundation; elemental; basic; primary: *a fundamental knowledge of electricity.* **2.** *Physics.* **a.** Of or concerning the component of a regularly recurring wave that is lowest in frequency. **b.** Of or concerning the frequency with which an object vibrates when it moves as a whole. —*n.* **1.** Something that is an elemental or basic part of a system, as a principle or law; an essential: *the fundamentals of mathematics.* **2.** *Physics.* A fundamental frequency, as of a wave or vibration. —**fun′da·men′tal·ly** *adv.*

fun·da·men·tal·ism (fŭn′də-mĕn′tl-ĭz′əm) *n.* **1.** Belief in the Bible as a historical record and statement of prophecy that is not to be questioned. **2.** Often **Fundamentalism.** A movement among U.S. Protestants of the 19th cent. based upon

ă pat   ā pay   â care   ä father   ĕ pet   ē be   hw which
oŏ took   ōō boot   ou out   th thin   th this   ŭ cut
ĭ pit   ī tie   î pier   ŏ pot   ō toe   ô paw, for   oi noise
û urge   zh vision   ə about, item, edible, gallop, circus

this belief. **—fun′da·men′tal·ist** n.

fu·ner·al (fyōō′nər-əl) n. **1.** The ceremonies held in connection with the burial or cremation of the dead. **2.** A procession accompanying a body to the grave. **—modifier:** a funeral director. [Middle English funerelles, rites for a dead person, from Old French funerailles, from Medieval Latin funerālia, from Latin funus, funeral, death.]

fu·ne·re·al (fyōō-nîr′ē-əl) adj. **1.** Of or suitable for a funeral. **2.** Mournful; sorrowful: a funereal tone of voice. [From Latin funereus, from funus, funeral.] **—fu·ne′re·al·ly** adv.

fun·gal (fŭng′gəl) adj. Var. of fungous.

fun·gi (fŭn′jī′) n. A plural of fungus.

fun·gi·cide (fŭn′jĭ-sīd′, fŭng′gĭ-) n. A substance that destroys or inhibits the growth of fungi. [FUNG(US) + -CIDE.]

fun·go (fŭng′gō) n., pl. **-goes.** Baseball. A practice fly ball hit to a fielder with a specially designed bat. [Orig. unknown.]

fun·gous (fŭng′gəs) adj. Also **fun·gal** (-gəl). **1.** Of, typical, or characteristic of a fungus. **2.** Caused by a fungus: a fungous plant disease. [Middle English, from Latin fungōsus, from fungus, fungus.]

fun·gus (fŭng′gəs) n., pl. **fun·gi** (fŭn′jī′) or **-gus·es.** Any of numerous plants of the Thallophyta, including the yeasts, molds, and mushrooms, that lack chlorophyll and obtain their nourishment from living or dead plant or animal substances. [Latin, perh. from Greek sp(h)ongos, sponge.]

fu·nic·u·lar (fyōō-nĭk′yə-lər, fə-) n. A cable railway on a steep incline, esp. one with simultaneously ascending and descending cars counterbalancing one another. [From Latin funiculus, dim. of funis, rope.]

funk (fŭngk) n. **1.** A state of cowardly fright; panic. **2.** A state of extreme depression. **—tr.v. 1.** To try to avoid out of fright; shrink from. **2.** To be afraid of. [Perh. from obs. Flemish fonck, a blow.]

funk·y (fŭng′kē) adj. **-i·er, -i·est.** Slang. **1.** Having a lively, pulsating quality with a mixture of jazz, rock, and blues, often with soul-music overtones: funky music. **2. a.** Marked by self-expression, originality, and modishness; trendy and unconventional: funky clothes. **b.** Outlandishly vulgar or far-out in a humorous manner: a funky movie. [Orig. "smelly," from obs. funk, a strong, offensive smell.] **—funk′i·ness** n.

fun·nel (fŭn′əl) n. **1.** A conical utensil with a narrow tube at the bottom, used to pour liquid or other substances into a small-mouthed container. **2.** Something shaped like a funnel. **3.** A shaft, flue, or stack for the passage of smoke, esp. the smokestack of a ship or locomotive. **—v. -neled** or **-nelled, -nel·ing** or **-nel·ling. —intr.v.** To move through or as if through a funnel: tourists funneling slowly through customs. **—tr.v.** To cause to funnel. [Middle English fonel, from Provençal fonilh, from Latin infundibulum, from infundere, to pour in: in-, in + fundere, to pour.]

fun·ny (fŭn′ē) adj. **-ni·er, -ni·est. 1.** Causing laughter or amusement. **2.** Strange; odd; curious. —See Syns at **laughable. —pl.n. funnies.** Informal. Comic strips. [From FUN.] **—fun′ni·ly** adv. **—fun′ni·ness** n.

funny bone. Informal. **1.** A point near the elbow where a nerve can be pressed against a bone to produce a numb or a tingling feeling in the arm. **2.** A sense of humor.

fur (fûr) n. **1.** The thick coat of soft hair covering the body of any of various animals, such as a rabbit, cat, or fox. **2.** The hair-covered skin or skins of such animals, used for clothing, trimming, etc. **3.** A coat, cape, etc., made of fur. **4.** A fuzzy or fluffy covering that resembles fur. **—modifier:** a fur coat. **—tr.v. furred, fur·ring. 1.** To cover or line with fur. **2.** To line (a wall or floor) with furring. [Middle English furre, from furren, to line with fur, from Old French forrer, from forre, fodder, lining.]

fur·be·low (fûr′bə-lō′) n. **1.** A ruffle or flounce on a garment. **2.** Any small piece of showy ornamentation. [Var. of French falbala, flounce, ruffle.]

fur·bish (fûr′bĭsh) tr.v. **1.** To brighten by cleaning or rubbing; burnish. **2.** To restore to attractive or serviceable condition; renovate. [Middle English furbishen, from Old French fo(u)rbir.] **—fur′bish·er** n.

fur·cate (fûr′kāt′) intr.v. **-cat·ed, -cat·ing.** To divide into branches; to fork. **—adj.** Forked. [Late Latin furcātus, from Latin furca, fork.]

Fu·ries (fyōōr′ēz) pl.n. Gk. & Rom. Myth. The three terri-

ble, winged goddesses with serpentine hair, who pursue and punish doers of unavenged crimes.

fu·ri·ous (fyōōr′ē-əs) adj. **1.** Full of or marked by extreme anger; raging. **2.** Violent in action or appearance; fierce: a furious speed; a furious battle. —See Syns at **angry** and **intense.** [Middle English, from Old French furieus, from Latin furiōsus, from furia, fury.] **—fu′ri·ous·ly** adv.

furl (fûrl) tr.v. To roll up and secure (a flag or sail) to a pole, yard, or mast. **—n. 1.** The act of furling. **2.** Something furled. [Old French ferler, ferlier : fer(m), firm, from Latin firmus, firm + lier, to bind, from Latin ligāre.]

fur·long (fûr′lông′, -lŏng′) n. Abbr. **fur.** A unit of distance, equal to about 201 meters, $^1/_8$ mile or, 220 yards. [Middle English furlong, from Old English furlang : furh, furrow + lang, long.]

fur·lough (fûr′lō) n. A vacation or leave of absence from duty, esp. one granted to enlisted personnel of the armed forces. **—tr.v.** To grant a furlough to. [Dutch verlof, leave, permission, from Middle Dutch.]

fur·nace (fûr′nĭs) n. **1.** An enclosed chamber in which a fuel is consumed, usu. by burning, to produce heat. **2.** Any intensely hot enclosed space. [Middle English furna(i)s, from Old French fornais, from Latin fornāx.]

fur·nish (fûr′nĭsh) tr.v. **1.** To equip with what is needed, esp. with furniture. **2.** To supply; give: furnish money. [Middle English furnisshen, from Old French furnir, fornir.] **—fur′nish·er** n.

fur·nish·ings (fûr′nĭ-shĭngz) pl.n. **1.** Furniture and other equipment for a home or office. **2.** Clothes and accessories: men's furnishings.

fur·ni·ture (fûr′nə-chər) n. **1.** The movable articles, such as chairs and tables, used to make a room or establishment fit for living or working. **2.** Necessary equipment, as for a factory or ship. [Old French fourniture, from fournir, furnir, to furnish.]

fu·ror (fyōōr′ôr′, -ōr′) n. **1.** Violent anger; frenzy. **2.** A state of intense excitement. **3.** A general commotion; public disorder or uproar. [Latin, from furere, to rage.]

fur·ri·er (fûr′ē-ər) n. A person who designs, sells, or repairs furs. [Middle English furrer, from Old French forreor, from forrer, to line with fur.]

fur·ring (fûr′ĭng) n. **1.** A trimming or lining made of fur. **2 a.** The process of preparing a wall, ceiling, or floor with strips of wood or metal to provide a level surface or air space above which a new surface can be applied. **b.** Strips of material used for this.

fur·row (fûr′ō, fŭr′ō) n. **1.** A long, narrow, shallow trench made in the ground by or as if by a plow or other tool. **2.** A deep wrinkle in the skin, as on the forehead. **—tr.v.** To make furrows in; to plow. **—intr.v.** To become furrowed or deeply wrinkled. [Middle English for(o)we, from Old English furh.]

fur·ry (fûr′ē) adj. **-ri·er, -ri·est. 1.** Consisting of or covered with fur. **2.** Resembling fur. **—fur′ri·ness** n.

fur·ther (fûr′thər) adj. **1.** More distant in space, time, or degree: You couldn't be further from the right idea. **2.** Additional: Stay tuned for further bulletins. **—adv. 1.** To a greater extent; more: He was going to explore the matter further. **2.** In addition; furthermore; also: We further see the importance of careful preparation. **3.** At or to a more distant point in space or time: Settlers who went to Colorado traveled further than those who stayed in Indiana. **—tr.v.** To help the progress of; to forward; advance: He furthered the careers of many composers. [Middle English, from Old English furthor.] **—fur′ther·er** n.

fur·ther·ance (fûr′thər-əns) n. The act of furthering, advancing, or helping forward.

fur·ther·more (fûr′thər-môr′, -mōr′) adv. In addition; moreover.

fur·ther·most (fûr′thər-mōst′) adj. Most distant or remote.

fur·thest (fûr′thĭst) adj. Most distant in space, time, or degree: the furthest corner of the earth. **—adv. 1.** To the greatest extent or degree: went furthest toward finding a solution. **2.** At or to the most distant point in space or time: traveled furthest. See Syns at **advance** and Usage note at **farther.** [Middle English, from further, further.]

fur·tive (fûr′tĭv) adj. Done or marked by stealth; surreptitious: a furtive glance. [French furtif, from Old French, from Latin furtīvus, from furtum, theft, from fūr, thief.]

ă pat	ā pay	â care	ä father	ĕ pet	ē be	hw which	ĭ pit	ī tie	î pier	ŏ pot	ō toe	ô paw, for	oi noise
ōō took	ōō boot	ou out	th thin	th this	ŭ cut	û urge	zh vision	ə about, item, edible, gallop, circus

—**fur′tive·ly** adv. —**fur′tive·ness** n.

fu·ry (fyŏŏr′ē) n., pl. **-ries.** 1. Violent rage. 2. An outburst of violent rage. 3. Violent and uncontrolled action; turbulence; agitation: *the blizzard's fury.* 4. A person who often has fits of violent anger. [Middle English *furie,* from Old French *furie,* from Latin *furia,* from *furere,* to rage.]

furze (fûrz) n. Gorse. [Middle English *furse, firse,* from Old English *fyrs.*]

fuse¹ (fyŏŏz) n. 1. A length of easily burned material that is lighted at one end to carry a flame to and detonate an explosive charge at the other. 2. Var. of **fuze.** —tr.v. **fused, fus·ing.** To furnish (an explosive charge) with a fuse. [Italian *fuso,* from Latin *fūsus,* spindle.]

fuse² (fyŏŏz) v. **fused, fus·ing.** —tr.v. 1. To liquefy by heating; melt. 2. To mix together or unite by or as if by melting; blend: *fuse separate images.* —intr.v. 1. To become liquefied by being heated. 2. To become mixed or united by or as if by melting: *joy and sorrow fused into one.* —n. A protective device for an electric circuit that melts when the current becomes too strong and thus opens the circuit. [From Latin *fūsus,* past part. of *fundere,* to pour, melt.]

fu·see (fyŏŏ-zē′) n. Also **fu·zee.** 1. A friction match with a large head that is capable of burning in a wind. 2. A colored flare used as a railway warning signal. [French *fusée,* spindle-shaped figure, from Old French *fusee,* from *fus,* spindle, from Latin *fūsus.*]

fu·se·lage (fyŏŏ′sə-läzh′,-zĭ-) n. The main body of an airplane, to which the wings and tail assembly are attached. [French, from *fuseler,* to shape like a spindle, from *fuseau,* spindle, from Old French *fusel,* spindle, dim. of *fus,* spindle, from Latin *fūsus.*]

fu·sel oil (fyŏŏ′zəl). A clear, colorless, poisonous liquid mixture of amyl alcohols, obtained as a by-product of the fermentation of starch-containing and sugar-containing plant materials and used as a solvent and in the manufacture of explosives and pure amyl alcohols. [From German *Fusel,* bad liquor.]

fus·i·ble (fyŏŏ′zə-bəl) adj. Capable of being fused or melted by heating. —**fus′i·bil′i·ty** or **fus′i·ble·ness** n.

fu·sil (fyŏŏ′zəl) n. A light flintlock musket. [French, musket, from Old French *fuisil,* fusil, steel for a tinderbox, from Latin *focus,* fireplace.]

fu·sil·ier (fyŏŏ′zə-lîr′) n. Also **fu·sil·eer.** 1. A soldier armed with a fusil. 2. **Fusilier.** A soldiers belonging to certain British army regiments: *Royal Fusiliers.* [French, from *fusil,* musket.]

fu·sil·lade (fyŏŏ′sə-lād′, -läd′, -zə-) n. 1. A discharge of many firearms simultaneously or in rapid succession. 2. Any rapid outburst or barrage: *a fusillade of insults.* [French, from *fusiller,* to shoot, from *fusil,* musket.]

fu·sion (fyŏŏ′zhən) n. 1. The act or process of melting by heat. 2. A mixture or blend formed by fusing two or more things: *An alloy is a fusion of several metals.* 3. A reaction in which atomic nuclei combine to form more massive nuclei, gen. leaving some excess mass that is converted into energy. [Latin *fūsiō,* from *fūsus,* past part. of *fundere,* to pour, melt.]

fusion bomb. A bomb, esp. a hydrogen bomb, that derives its energy mainly from the fusion of atomic nuclei.

fuss (fŭs) n. 1. Needlessly nervous or useless activity; commotion; bustle. 2. A state of concern or worry over an unimportant matter. 3. A protest; complaint: *kick up a fuss over a meal.* —intr.v. 1. To get into or be in a state of nervous or useless activity. 2. To show excessive care or concern: *mothers fussing over children.* 3. To protest; object; complaint. [Orig. unknown.] —**fuss′er** n.

fuss-budg·et (fŭs′bŭj′ĭt) n. A person who fusses over unimportant matters.

fuss·y (fŭs′ē) adj. **-i·er, -i·est.** 1. Given to fussing; easily upset. 2. Frequently complaining or making demands; discontented or dissatisfied: *a fussy eater.* 3. Requiring or showing attention to small details: *a fussy, time-consuming chore.* —**fuss′i·ly** adv. —**fuss′i·ness** n.

fus·tian (fŭs′chən) n. 1. *Obs.* A coarse, sturdy cloth made of cotton and flax. 2. Pretentious speech or writing; pompous

language. —adj. 1. Made of fustian. 2. Pompous; ranting; bombastic. [Middle English, from Old French *fustai(g)ne,* from Medieval Latin *fustāneums,* cloth.]

fus·ty (fŭs′tē) adj. **-ti·er, -ti·est.** 1. Smelling of mildew or decay; musty; moldy. 2. Old-fashioned; antique. [Middle English, from Old French *fuste,* barrel, stale odor of a barrel, from *fust,* barrel, tree trunk, club, from Latin *fūstis,* club.] —**fus′ti·ly** adv. —**fus′ti·ness** n.

fu·tile (fyŏŏt′l, fyŏŏ′tīl′) adj. Having no useful result; useless; vain: *futile efforts.* [Latin *fūtilis,* untrustworthy, useless.] —**fu′tile·ly** adv.

fu·til·i·ty (fyŏŏ-tĭl′ĭ-tē) n., pl. **-ties.** 1. The condition or quality of being futile. 2. Lack of importance or purpose: *laugh at the futility of life.*

fu·ture (fyŏŏ′chər) n. 1. The period of time yet to be; time that is to come: *plans for the future.* 2. That which will happen in time to come: *The state's future will depend on overcoming tax problems.* 3. Chance of success or advancement: *a writer with a solid future.* 4. Often **futures.** Commodities or stocks bought or sold upon agreement of delivery in time to come. 5. *Gram.* The **future tense.** —adj. That will be or occur in time to come: *future generations.* [Middle English, from Old French *futur,* from Latin *futūrus,* about to be.]

future perfect tense. A verb tense expressing action completed by a stated time in the future, formed in English by combining *will have* or *shall have* with a past participle.

future shock. The disorientation brought on in people by the overwhelmingly rapid changes in the social structure or technology of modern society.

future tense. A verb tense used to express action in the future, formed in English with the use of the auxiliary verbs *shall* and *will.*

fu·tur·ism (fyŏŏ′chə-rĭz′əm) n. An artistic movement originating in Italy in about 1910 and marked by an attempt to depict the energetic and dynamic motion and force of modern machinery. —**fu′tur·ist** n. —**fu′tur·is′tic** adj.

futurism

fuze (fyŏŏz) n. Also **fuse.** A mechanical or electrical device used to explode a bomb, grenade, or other explosive charge. [Var. of FUSE (detonator).]

fu·zee (fyŏŏ-zē′) n. Var. of **fusee.**

fuzz¹ (fŭz) n. A mass of soft, light particles, fibers, or hairs; fine down. [Perh. back-formation from FUZZY.]

fuzz² (fŭz) n. *Slang.* The police; policemen in general. [Orig. unknown.]

fuzz·y (fŭz′ē) adj. **-i·er, -i·est.** 1. Covered with fuzz. 2. Of or resembling fuzz. 3. Not clear; indistinct; blurred: *a fuzzy snapshot.* 4. Not clearly reasoned or expressed: *fuzzy thinking.* —See Syns at **vague.** [Perh. from Low German *fussig,* spongy.] —**fuzz′i·ly** adv. —**fuzz′i·ness** n.

-fy. A suffix meaning to make or form into: **calcify.** [Middle English *-fien,* from Old French *-fier,* from Latin *-ficāre,* from *-ficus,* from *facere,* to do.]

Gg

ı Γ G ᵹ **Gg**

Phoenician   Greek   Roman   Medieval   Modern

Phoenician – About 3,000 years ago the Phoenicians and other Semitic peoples began to use graphic signs to represent individual speech sounds instead of syllables or whole words. They used this symbol to represent the sound of the consonant "g" (as in English "go") and gave it the name gīmel, the Phoenician word for "camel".

Greek – The Greeks borrowed the Phoenician alphabet with some modifications. They changed the shape and orientation of gīmel, and altered the name to gamma. They used gamma to represent the sound of the consonant "g" (as in English "go"), as gīmel did in Phoenician.

Roman – The Romans borrowed the alphabet from the Greeks via the Etruscans. Because the Etruscans did not distinguish between the sounds of the consonants "g" (as in "go") and "k," they used gamma for both. The Romans, however, did distinguish the two sounds and added a stroke to

the lower curve of the letter C (which represented "k") to identify the sound of "g". They also adapted the alphabet for carving Latin in stone, and this monumental script, as it is called, became the basis for modern printed capital letters.

Medieval – By medieval times – around 1,200 years ago – the Roman monumental capitals had become adapted to being relatively quickly written on paper, parchment, or vellum. The cursive minuscule alphabet became the basis of modern printed lower-case letters.

Modern – Since the invention of printing about 500 years ago modifications have been made in the shape and style of the letter G, but its basic form has remained unchanged. Changes in pronunciation since ancient times, however, have given the letter G several different phonetic values.

---

g, G (jē) n., pl. **g's** or **G's.** The seventh letter of the modern English alphabet.

G (jē) adj. Indicating a rating given motion pictures considered appropriate for all ages to see. [Short for GENERAL.]

Ga The symbol for the element gallium.

gab (găb) intr.v. **gabbed, gab·bing.** Informal. To talk idly or thoughtlessly; chatter: Quit gabbing on the phone and do your homework! —n. Chatter; prattle. [Perh. from Scottish gab, mouthful, lump, mouth, var. of GOB (lump).] —**gab'ber** n.

gab·ar·dine (găb'ər-dēn', găb'ər-dēn') n. **1.** A strong, woven cloth with a smooth surface and slanted ribs, used in making dresses, suits, and coats. **2.** A gaberdine. [Var. of GABERDINE.]

gab·ble (găb'əl) v. **-bled, -bling.** —intr.v. **1.** To speak rapidly and unclearly; jabber. **2.** To make rapid, repeated cackling noises, as a goose or duck. —tr.v. To say quickly and unclearly: She gabbled a long address that I didn't understand. —n. Rapid, confused noise or speech. [Middle Dutch gabbelen (imit.).]

gab·bro (găb'rō) n. A usu. coarse-grained igneous rock composed chiefly of calcic plagioclase and pyroxene. [Italian, from Latin glaber, smooth, bald.]

gab·by (găb'ē) adj. **-bi·er, -bi·est.** Informal. Tending to talk too much. —**gab'bi·ness** n.

gab·er·dine (găb'ər-dēn', găb'ər-dēn') n. **1.** A long, loose cloak of coarse material, worn during the Middle Ages. **2.** Gabardine. [Earlier gawbardine, from Old French gauvardine.]

ga·ble (gā'bəl) n. **1.** The triangular wall section at the ends of a pitched roof, bounded by the two roof slopes. **2.** That end of a building having a gable in the roof section. **3.** Any triangular architectural part, usu. ornamental, as over a door or window. [Middle English, from Old French, prob. from Old Norse gafl.] —**ga'bled** adj.

gable roof. A pitched roof that ends in a gable.

gad[1] (găd) intr.v. **gad·ded, gad·ding.** To move about restlessly; rove: She gadded about town, visiting all the shops. [Middle English gadden, prob. back-formation from gadeling, companion, wanderer, from Old English gædeling.] —**gad'der** n.

gad[2] (găd) n. **1.** Mining. A spike or other pointed tool for breaking rock. **2.** A goad, as for prodding cattle to make them move. —tr.v. **gad·ded, gad·ding. 1.** Mining. To break

up (rock, ore, etc.) with a gad. **2.** To goad (cattle). [Middle English gad(de), from Old Norse gaddr, rod, goad, spike.]

Gad (găd) n. Euphemism for God.

gad·a·bout (găd'ə-bout') n. A person who wanders about looking for fun, excitement, or gossip.

gad·fly (găd'flī') n. **1.** Any of various flies, esp. of the family Tabanidae, that bite or annoy livestock and other animals. **2.** A person who annoys or criticizes others, esp. to get them to reform themselves or their institutions. [GAD (goad, sting) + FLY.]

gadg·et (găj'ĭt) n. Informal. A small specialized mechanical device; a contrivance. [Orig. unknown.]

gadg·et·eer (găj'ĭ-tîr') n. Informal. A person who makes or likes to collect gadgets.

gadg·et·ry (găj'ĭ-trē) n. **1.** Gadgets. **2.** The designing or constructing of gadgets.

gad·o·lin·i·um (găd'l-ĭn'ē-əm) n. Symbol **Gd** A silvery-white, malleable, ductile, metallic rare-earth element obtained from monazite and bastnaesite. It has the highest neutron-absorption cross section known and is useful in improving high-temperature characteristics of iron, chromium, and related metallic alloys. Atomic number 64, atomic weight 157.25, melting point 1,312°C, boiling point approx. 3,000°C, specific gravity from 7.8 to 7.896, valence 3. [After Johann Gadolin (1760–1852), Finnish chemist.]

Gae·a (jē'ə) n. Gk. Myth. The goddess of the earth, who bore and married Uranus and became the mother of the Titans, the Furies, and the Cyclopes.

Gael (gāl) n. **1.** A Celt of Scotland, Ireland, or the Isle of Man. **2.** A Scottish Highlander.

Gael·ic (gā'lĭk) adj. Of or relating to the Gaels or their languages. —n. **1.** A branch of the Celtic languages. **2.** One of the languages of the Gaels.

gaff (găf) n. **1.** An iron hook attached to a pole and used for landing large fish. **2.** Naut. A spar used to extend the top edge of a fore-and-aft sail. **3.** A metal spur attached to the leg of a gamecock during a cockfight. **4.** Slang. Harshness of treatment; abuse. —tr.v. To hook or land (a fish) using a gaff. [Middle English gaffe, from Old French, from Old Provençal gaf.]

gaffe (găf) n. A clumsy social error; a faux pas: It was a gaffe to call him by his nickname, which he hated. [French, from gaffer, to hook, to blunder, from gaffe, hook, gaff.]

---

gaf·fer (găf′ər) n. Informal. An old man. [Alteration of GODFATHER.]

gag (găg) n. **1.** Something forced into or put over a person's mouth to prevent him from speaking or crying out. **2.** Something, such as a law, that limits or censors free expression. **3.** Informal. **a.** A practical joke; a hoax. **b.** A comic remark; a joke. —See Syns at **joke.** —v. **gagged, gag·ging.** —tr.v. **1.** To prevent from speaking or crying out by using a gag: The robbers bound and gagged their captives. **2.** To prevent from speaking out or telling the truth; censor. **3.** To cause to choke or retch. —intr.v. **1.** To choke; to retch from nausea: "The smell of smashed perfume bottles made me gag" (Truman Capote). **2.** Informal. To make jokes or quips. [Middle English gaggen, to suffocate.]

ga·ga (gä′gä′) adj. Slang. Senseless; crazy. [French, from gaga, foolish old man.]

gage¹ (gāj) n. **1.** Something deposited or given as security against an obligation; a pledge. **2.** Something, such as a glove, offered or thrown down as a challenge to fight. —tr.v. **gaged, gag·ing.** Archaic. To offer as a stake in a bet; to wager. [Middle English, from Old French.]

gage² (gāj) n. Var. of **gauge.** —See Usage note at **gauge.**

gag·gle (găg′əl) n. A flock of geese. [Middle English gagelen.]

gag rule. A rule, as in a legislative body, limiting discussion or debate on a given issue.

gai·e·ty (gā′ĭ-tē) n., pl. **-ties.** Also **gay·e·ty. 1.** The condition of being gay or merry· cheerfulness. **2.** Festive or joyful activity; merrymaking. **3.** Gay color or showiness, as of dress; finery. [French gaieté, from Old French gai, gay.]

Syns: 1. gaiety, glee, hilarity, jollity, merriment, mirth n. Core meaning: A state of joyful exuberance (a house that rang with Christmas gaiety). **2. gaiety, festivity, fun, merrymaking, revelry** n. Core meaning: Joyful, exuberant activity (invited the guests to join the gaiety).

gai·ly (gā′lē) adv. Also **gay·ly. 1.** In a joyful, cheerful, or happy manner; merrily. **2.** Colorfully; showily: gaily dressed.

gain (gān) tr.v. **1.** To become the owner of; acquire; get: became rich and gained more property. **2.** To acquire in competition; win: gain a decisive victory. **3.** To secure as profit or payment; earn: gain a living. **4.** To develop an increase of; build up: The movement gained strength. She gained ten pounds in a week of overeating. **5.** To arrive at; reach: After a hard climb we gained the hilltop. —intr.v. **1.** To become better or greater; advance; progress: gaining in strength. **2.** To come nearer; get closer: We are still best, but the other team is gaining on us. **3.** To increase in weight: He gained a lot as he got older. —n. **1.** Often **gains. a.** Something gained or acquired: territorial gains. **b.** Progress; advancement: Economic gains were impressive last year. **2.** The act of acquiring something; attainment: the gain of an advantage. **3.** Benefit: using public funds for personal gain. **4.** Electronics. **a.** An increase in signal power. **b.** The ratio of output to input, as of output power to input power in an antenna. [Old French gaigner, of Germanic orig.]

gain·er (gā′nər) n. **1.** Someone or something that gains. **2.** A dive in which the diver leaves the board facing forward, does a back somersault, and enters the water feet first.

gain·ful (gān′fəl) adj. Providing an income: gainful employment. —**gain′ful·ly** adv. —**gain′ful·ness** n.

gain·say (gān-sā′) tr.v. **-said** (-sĕd′), **-say·ing.** To contradict; deny: Do not gainsay him, even though you disagree. [Middle English gaynsayen, "to say against."] —**gain·say′er** n.

'gainst (gĕnst) prep. Also **gainst.** Poet. Against.

gait (gāt) n. **1.** A way of moving on foot: "That indescribable gait of the long-distance tramp the world over" (Kipling). **2.** Any of the ways a horse can move by lifting the feet in a certain order or rhythm, as a canter, trot, or walk. [Middle English gate, gait, way, passage, from Old Norse gata, path, street.]

gai·ter (gā′tər) n. **1.** A leather or cloth covering for the legs extending from the knee to the instep; a legging. **2.** A smaller covering worn over a shoe and extending from the ankle to the instep; a spat. **3.** An ankle-high shoe with elastic sides and no laces or buckles. **4.** An overshoe with a cloth top. [French guêtre, from Old French guestre, guietre.]

gal (găl) n. Informal. A girl.

ga·la (gā′lə, găl′ə, gä′lə) n. A festive occasion or celebration; festival. —adj. Characterized by celebration; festive: a gala dance. —See Syns at **merry.** [Italian, from Spanish, from Old French gale, pleasure, merrymaking, from galer, to make merry, live a gay life.]

galact-. Var. of **galacto-.**

ga·lac·tic (gə-lăk′tĭk) adj. **1.** Of a galaxy or galaxies. **2.** Often **Galactic.** Of or originating in the Milky Way. [Late Latin galacticus, milky, from Greek galaktikos, from gala, milk.]

galacto– or **galact–.** A prefix meaning milk or milky: **galactose.** [From Greek gala, milk.]

ga·lac·tose (gə-lăk′tōs′) n. A simple sugar, $C_6H_{12}O_6$, commonly occurring in lactose. [GALACT(O)- + -OSE.]

Gal·a·had (găl′ə-hăd′) n. Arthurian Legend. **1.** The purest of the knights of the Round Table, who alone succeeded in the quest for the Holy Grail. **2.** Any man considered to be noble, pure, or chivalrous.

gal·an·tine (găl′ən-tēn′) n. A dish of boned, stuffed meat or fish, cooked and served cold coated with aspic or its own jelly. [Middle English galauntyne, a sauce for fish and poultry, from Old French galantine, galatine, from Medieval Latin galatīna, gelatīna, prob. from Latin gelāre, to freeze.]

Gal·a·te·a (găl′ə-tē′ə) n. Gk. Myth. An ivory statue of a maiden, brought to life by Aphrodite in answer to the pleas of the sculptor, Pygmalion, who had fallen in love with his creation.

Ga·la·tian (gə-lā′shən) adj. Of or pertaining to ancient Galatia or its people. —n. **1.** A native or inhabitant of ancient Galatia. **2. Galatians.** See table at **Bible.**

gal·a·vant (găl′ə-vănt′) intr.v. Var. of **gallivant.**

ga·lax (gā′lăks′) n. A plant, Galax aphylla, of the southeastern United States with glossy leaves and small white flowers. [Prob. from Greek galaxias, galaxy.]

gal·ax·y (găl′ək-sē) n., pl. **-ies. 1.** Astron. **a.** Any of numerous large-scale aggregates of stars, gas, and dust, having one of a group of more or less definite overall structures, containing an average of 100 billion (10^{11}) solar masses, and ranging in diameter from 1,500 to 300,000 light-years. **b.** Often **Galaxy.** The galaxy of which the earth's sun is a part; the Milky Way. **2.** An assembly of brilliant, beautiful, or distinguished persons or things. [Middle English galaxie, the Milky Way, from Old French, from Latin galaxiās, from Greek galaxias (kuklos), "milky (circle)," from gala, milk.]

gale (gāl) n. **1.** A very strong wind, esp. one having a speed between 51.5 and 101.5 kilometers or 32 and 63 miles per hour. **2.** A forceful outburst: gales of laughter. [Orig. unknown.]

ga·le·a (gā′lē-ə) n., pl. **-le·ae** (-lē-ē′). Biol. A helmet-shaped part, such as the upper petal of certain plants or part of the maxilla of an insect. [Latin, leather helmet, from Greek galeē, weasel.] —**ga′le·ate** (-āt′) or **ga′le·at′ed** (-ā′tĭd) adj.

ga·le·na (gə-lē′nə) n. A gray mineral, essentially PbS, the principal ore of lead. [Latin galēna, lead ore.]

Ga·li·bi (gə-lē′bē, găl′ə-bē) n., pl. **Galibi** or **-bis. 1.** A member of the Carib people of French Guiana. **2.** The language of the Galibi.

gaiter

gal·i·ot (găl′ē-ət) *n.* Also **gal·li·ot.** **1.** A swift single-decked ship propelled by sails and oars, formerly used on the Mediterranean. **2.** A single-masted, flat-bottomed Dutch merchant ship or seagoing barge. [Middle English *galiot*, a light galley, and Middle Dutch *galiŏte*, merchant ship, both from Old French *galiote*, from Medieval Latin *galiota*, dim. of *galea*, galley.]

gall¹ (gôl) *n.* **1. a.** Liver bile. **b.** The gallbladder. **2.** Bad feeling; bitterness: *When he spoke of the past, there was gall in his words.* **3.** Something bitter to endure. **4.** Impudence; effrontery: *He had the gall to try to borrow money.* —See Syns at **temerity.** [Middle English *gall(e)*, from Old English *gealla*, bile.]

gall² (gôl) *n.* **1.** A skin sore caused by rubbing, as one under a horse's saddle. **2. a.** Exasperation; irritation; vexation. **b.** The cause of such vexation. —*tr.v.* **1.** To make sore by rubbing; chafe. **2.** To irritate; vex: *Her undeserved luck galls me.* —*intr.v.* To become irritated, chafed, or sore. —See Syns at **annoy.** [Middle English *galle*, from Old English *gealla*, sore place, from Latin *galla*, gallnut.]

gall³ (gôl) *n.* An abnormal swelling on a plant, caused by insects, disease organisms, or external injury. [Middle English *galle*, from Old French, from Latin *galla*, gallnut.]

gal·lant (găl′ənt) *adj.* **1.** Stately; majestic; noble: *"On my word, master, this is a gallant trout"* (Walton). **2.** High-spirited and courageous; daring: *gallant soldiers.* **3.** (*also* gə-lănt′, -länt′). Attentive and complimentary to women; chivalrous. —See Syns at **brave.** —*n.* (gə-lănt′, -länt′, găl′-ənt). **1.** A fashionable young man. **2. a.** A man who charms or pays compliments to women. **b.** A woman's lover. [Middle English *galaunt*, from Old French *galant*, gorgeous, showy, brave, from *galer*, to rejoice.] —**gal′lant·ly** *adv.*

gal·lant·ry (găl′ən-trē) *n., pl.* **-ries. 1.** Bravery; courage. **2.** Polite or complimentary attention to women; courtliness: *"The air of faintly mocking gallantry with which he habitually treated mother"* (Louis Auchincloss). **3.** A gallant act or speech.

gall·blad·der (gôl′blăd′ər) *n.* Also **gall bladder.** A small, pear-shaped, muscular sac located under the right lobe of the liver, in which bile secreted by the liver is stored.

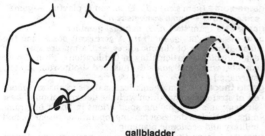

gallbladder

gal·le·on (găl′ē-ən, găl′yən) *n.* A large three-masted sailing ship with a high, square stern, used during the 15th and 16th cent. for trading and warfare. [Spanish *galeon*, from Old French *galion*, from *galie*, galley.]

gal·ler·y (găl′ə-rē, găl′rē) *n. pl.* **-ies. 1. a.** A long, narrow walk or passageway, esp. a roofed one that extends along the wall of a building. **b.** A room or place resembling such a passageway and used for a particular purpose: *a shooting gallery.* **2. a.** An upper floor projecting over the rear part of the main floor of a theater and usu. containing the cheapest seats. **b.** The people occupying these seats. **3.** Any large audience or group of spectators, as at a legislative assembly or sports event. **4.** A large room or building for displaying works of art. **5.** A place where works of art or other objects are displayed and sold, esp. by auction. **6.** An underground tunnel or passageway, as in a mine. **7.** A platform at the stern of certain early sailing ships. —*idiom.* **play to the gallery.** To try to please the general public, esp. by crude or obvious means. [Middle English *galerie*, from Old French, portico, from Italian *galleria*, from Medieval Latin *galeria.*]

gal·ley (găl′ē) *n., pl.* **-leys. 1.** A long, single-decked ship of shallow draft, propelled by sails and oars and used in the Mediterranean until the 17th cent. **2.** An ancient seagoing vessel propelled by oars. **3.** The kitchen of a ship or airliner. **4.** *Printing.* **a.** A long tray, usu. of metal, used for holding type that has been set. **b.** A printer's proof taken from composed type before pages are made to allow for the detection and correction of errors. [Middle English *galeie, galy*, from Old French *galie*, from Medieval Latin *galea*, from Medieval Greek *galea.*]

gall·fly (gôl′flī′) *n.* Any of various small insects of the family Cecidomyiidae that deposit their eggs on plant stems or in the bark of trees, causing the formation of galls in which their larvae grow.

gal·liard (găl′yərd) *n.* **1.** A spirited dance popular in France in the 16th and 17th cent. **2.** The triple-time music for a galliard. [Middle English *galiard, gaillard*, valiant, lively, from Old French *gaillard.*]

Gal·lic (găl′ĭk) *adj.* Of ancient Gaul or modern France; French.

gal·lic acid (găl′ĭk). A colorless crystalline compound, $C_7H_6O_5·H_2O$, derived from tannin and used in photography, as a tanning agent, and in ink and paper manufacture.

Gal·li·cism (găl′ĭ-sĭz′əm) *n.* **1.** A French phrase or idiom appearing in another language. **2.** A characteristic French trait.

gal·li·gas·kins (găl′ĭ-găs′kĭnz) *pl.n.* Also **gal·ly·gas·kins.** Loosely fitting stockings or trousers of a kind worn in the 16th and 17th cent. [Earlier *gallogascaine, garragascoyne*, perh. from Old French *garguesque, greguesque*, from Old Italian *grechesca*, "Grecian breeches," from *greco*, Greek, from Latin *Graecus*, Greek.]

gal·li·na·ceous (găl′ə-nā′shəs) *adj.* Of, belonging to, or characteristic of the order Galliformes, which includes the common domestic fowl as well as the pheasants, turkeys, and grouse. [Latin *gallīnāceus*, of poultry, from *gallīna*, hen, fem. of *gallus*, cock.]

gall·ing (gô′lĭng) *adj.* Causing extreme irritation; exasperating: *a galling delay.* —**gall′ing·ly** *adv.*

gal·li·nule (găl′ə-nōōl′, -nyōōl′) *n.* Any of various wading birds of the genera *Gallinula, Porphyrio*, or *Porphyrula*, frequenting swampy regions and characteristically having dark, iridescent plumage. [From Latin *gallīnula*, chicken, pullet, dim. of *gallīna*, hen, fem. of *gallus*, cock.]

gal·li·ot (găl′ē-ət) *n.* Var. of **galiot.**

gal·li·pot (găl′ə-pŏt′) *n.* A small, glazed earthenware jar formerly used by druggists for medicines. [Middle English *galy pott.*]

gal·li·um (găl′ē-əm) *n. Symbol* **Ga** A rare metallic element that is liquid near room temperature, expands on solidifying, and is found as a trace element in coal, bauxite, and other minerals. It is used in semiconductor technology and as a component of various low-melting alloys. Atomic number 31; atomic weight 69.72; melting point 29.78°C; boiling point 2,403°C; specific gravity 5.907 (20°C); valences 2, 3. [From Latin *gallus*, cock, transl. of the name of its discoverer, Lecoq de Boisbaudran (1838–1912), French chemist.]

gallium arsenide. A dark-gray crystalline compound used in transistors, solar cells, and lasers. [GALLIUM + ARSEN(IC) + -IDE.]

gal·li·vant (găl′ə-vănt′) *intr.v.* Also **gal·a·vant. 1.** To roam about in search of amusement; traipse; gad. **2.** To flirt. [Perh. alteration of GALLANT.]

gall·nut (gôl′nŭt′) *n.* A plant gall with a rounded form like a nut.

gal·lon (găl′ən) *n. Abbr.* **gal. 1. a.** A unit of liquid volume or capacity equal to 4 quarts or 231 cubic inches. **b.** A unit of volume in the British Imperial System, used in liquid and dry measure, equal to 277.420 cubic inches. **2.** A container with such capacity. [Middle English, from Old North French, from Medieval Latin *gallēta*, jug, measure for wine.]

gal·loon (gə-lōōn′) *n.* A narrow band or braid used as trimming and commonly made of lace, metallic thread, or embroidery. [French *galon*, from Old French *galonner*, to decorate with ribbons.]

gal·lop (găl′əp) *n.* **1.** A natural three-beat gait of a horse, faster than a canter and slower than a run. **2.** A fast running pace. **3.** A ride on a horse going at a gallop. —*intr.v.* **1.** To ride a horse at a gallop. **2.** To move fast; dash: *The* *lively story galloped along from incident to incident.* —*tr.v.* To cause to gallop. [Middle English *galopen,* from Old French *galoper,* var. of Old North French *waloper.*] —**gal'lop·er** *n.*

gal·lows (găl'ōz) *n., pl.* **gallows** or **-lows·es. 1.** A framework from which a noose is suspended, used for executing condemned persons by hanging. Also called **gallowstree. 2.** Execution by hanging: *a crime for which he was sent to the gallows.* [Middle English *galwes,* pl. of *galwe,* gallows, cross, from Old English *gealga.*]

gall·stone (gôl'stōn') *n.* A small, hard mass that forms in the gallbladder or in a bile duct.

gal·lows·tree (găl'ōz-trē') *n.* A gallows.

gal·ly·gas·kins (găl'ĭ-găs'kĭnz) *pl.n.* Var. of **galligaskins.**

gal·op (găl'əp) *n.* **1.** A lively dance in duple rhythm, popular in the 19th cent. **2.** The music for the galop. [French, gallop, from Old French *galoper,* to gallop.]

ga·lore (gə-lôr', -lōr') *adj. Informal.* In great numbers; in abundance: *dresses galore; opportunities galore.* [Irish Gaelic *go leór,* enough.]

ga·losh (gə-lŏsh') *n.* Also **ga·loshe.** A waterproof overshoe. [Middle English *galoche,* from Old French, prob. from Late Latin *gallicula,* dim. of Latin *gallica (solea),* "Gaulish (sandal)."]

gal·van·ic (găl-văn'ĭk) *adj.* **1.** Of or pertaining to direct-current electricity, esp. when produced chemically. **2.** Having or suggesting the effect of an electric shock; jolting: *a galvanic command.* [French *galvanique,* from *galvanisme,* galvanism.] —**gal·van'i·cal·ly** *adv.*

gal·va·nism (găl'və-nĭz'əm) *n.* Direct-current electricity, esp. when produced chemically. [French *galvanisme,* from Italian *galvanismo,* after Luigi Galvani (1737–98), Italian physiologist.]

gal·va·nize (găl'və-nīz') *tr.v.* **-nized, -niz·ing. 1.** To stimulate or shock with an electric current. **2.** To arouse to awareness or action; to spur: *"A blast in my ear . . . galvanized me into full consciousness"* (Erskine Childers). **3.** To put a coating of zinc on (iron or steel) as protection against rust. —See Syns at **provoke.** —**gal'va·ni·za'tion** *n.* —**gal'va·niz'er** *n.*

gal·va·nom·e·ter (găl'və-nŏm'ĭ-tər) *n.* A device for detecting or measuring small electric currents by means of mechanical effects produced by the current to be measured. [GALVAN(ISM) + -METER.] —**gal'va·no·met'ric** (-nō-mĕt'rĭk) or **gal'va·no·met'ri·cal** *adj.* —**gal'va·nom'e·try** *n.*

gam¹ (găm) *n.* A school or herd of whales. —See Syns at **flock.** [Perh. short for obs. *gammon,* talk.]

gam² (găm) *n. Slang.* A person's leg, esp. a shapely female leg. [Prob. from obs. *gamb,* leg of an animal, from Old North French *gambe,* from Late Latin *gamba,* hook, leg, from Greek *kampē,* a bend.]

gam·bit (găm'bĭt) *n.* **1.** A chess opening in which a pawn or piece is sacrificed in order to gain a favorable position. **2.** A carefully considered strategy; a maneuver. [Earlier *gamet,* from Italian *gambetto,* "a tripping up," from *gamba,* leg.]

gam·ble (găm'bəl) *v.* **-bled, -bling.** —*intr.v.* **1. a.** To bet money on the outcome of a game, contest, or other event. **b.** To play a game of chance for money or other stakes. **2.** To take a risk in the hope of gaining an advantage; speculate: *The puddle was large, but he decided to gamble and try to leap it.* —*tr.v.* **1.** To put up in gambling; to wager. **2.** To expose to hazard; to risk: *gambled his prestige on the outcome of the talks.* —*n.* **1.** A bet, wager, or other gambling venture. **2.** An act or undertaking of uncertain outcome; a risk. [Prob. from earlier *gamel,* from Middle English *gamenen,* from Old English *gamenian,* to sport, play, from *gamen,* amusement, game.] —**gam'bler** *n.*

gam·bol (găm'bəl) *intr.v.* **-boled** or **-bolled, -bol·ing** or **-bol·ling.** To leap about playfully; to frolic; skip. —*n.* A skipping or frolicking about. [Earlier *gamba(u)de,* from Old French *gambade,* from Italian *gambata,* from *gamba,* leg, from Late Latin, hoof, leg, from Greek *kampē,* bend.]

gam·brel (găm'brəl) *n.* The hock of a horse or other animal. [Old North French *gamberel,* dim. of *gambier,* from *gambe,* leg, from Late Latin *gamba,* hoof, leg.]

gambrel roof. A roof having two slopes on each side, the lower slope steeper than the upper.

game¹ (găm) *n.* **1.** A way of amusing oneself; a pastime;

diversion: *He made a game of avoiding cracks in the sidewalk.* **2.** A sport or other competitive activity governed by specific rules: *the game of tennis.* **3.** A single contest between opposing players or teams: *We lost the first game.* **4.** The total number of points required to win a game: *One hundred points is game in bridge.* **5.** The equipment needed for playing certain games: *Pack the children's games in the car.* **6.** A particular style or manner of playing a game: *His bridge game is only adequate.* **7.** A scheme; plan: *You'll never see through his game.* **8. a.** Wild animals, birds, or fish hunted for food or sport. **b.** The flesh of game, eaten as food. **9. a.** Anything hunted or fit to be hunted; quarry; prey. **b.** An object of ridicule, teasing, or scorn: *The new boy's odd appearance made him fair game in the schoolyard.* **10.** *Informal.* An occupation or business: *the publishing game.* —**modifier:** *a game room; pheasants and other game birds.* —*intr.v.* **gamed, gam·ing.** To play games for money or other stakes; gamble. —*adj.* **gam·er, gam·est. 1.** Plucky; courageous: *a game fighter.* **2.** *Informal.* Ready and willing: *Are you game for a swim?* [Middle English *game(n),* from Old English *gamen,* amusement, sport.] —**game'ly** *adv.* —**game'ness** *n.*

game² (găm) *adj.* **gam·er, gam·est.** Lame: *"To jump with his game leg foremost might mean to collapse under the impact of arrival"* (Aldous Huxley). [Orig. unknown.]

game·cock (găm'kŏk') *n.* A rooster trained for cockfighting.

game fowl. 1. Any bird hunted for game. **2.** Any of several breeds of domestic fowl raised esp. for cockfighting.

game·keep·er (găm'kē'pər) *n.* A person employed to protect and maintain wildlife, esp. on an estate or game preserve.

game laws. Regulations for the protection of game animals, including birds and fish, that limit the hunting seasons and restrict the size and number of animals that may be taken.

games·man·ship (gāmz'mən-shĭp') *n.* The method or art of winning a game or contest by means of unsportsmanlike behavior or other conduct that does not actually break the rules. [From *Gamesmanship,* title of a book by S. Potter.]

game·some (gām'səm) *adj.* Frolicsome; playful. —**game'-some·ly** *adv.* —**game'some·ness** *n.*

game·ster (gām'stər) *n.* A habitual gambler.

gam·ete (găm'ēt', gə-mēt') *n.* A germ cell possessing the haploid number of chromosomes, esp. a mature sperm or egg capable of participating in fertilization. [From Greek *gametē,* wife, and *gametēs,* husband, both from *gamos,* marriage.]

game theory. The mathematical analysis of abstract models of strategic competition with the determination of best strategy as a goal, having applications in linear programming, statistical decision making, operations research, and military and economic planning.

gameto-. A prefix meaning gamete: **gametophyte.** [From New Latin *gameta,* gamete.]

ga·me·to·cyte (gə-mē'tə-sīt') *n.* A cell from which gametes are developed by division; a spermatocyte or an oocyte. [GAMETO- + -CYTE.]

ga·me·to·gen·e·sis (gə-mē'tə-jĕn'ĭ-sĭs, găm'ĭ-tə-) *n.* Also **gam·e·tog·e·ny** (găm'ĭ-tŏj'ə-nē).** The production of gametes. [GAMETO- + -GENESIS.] —**ga·me'to·gen'ic** or **gam'e·tog'e·nous** (găm'ĭ-tŏj'ə-nəs) *adj.*

ga·me·to·phyte (gə-mē'tə-fīt') *n. Bot.* The generation or form that reproduces sexually in a plant characterized by alternation of generations. [GAMETO- + -PHYTE.] —**ga·me'to·phyt'ic** (-fĭt'ĭk) *adj.*

gam·in (găm'ĭn) *n.* A neglected or homeless child who roams about the streets; urchin. [French.]

gam·ing (gā'mĭng) *n.* Gambling.

gam·ma (găm'ə) *n.* **1.** The third letter in the Greek alphabet, written γ, and transliterated in English as *g,* or as *n* before *g, k,* or *kh.* **2.** A gamma ray. [Greek.]

gamma globulin. Any of several globulin fractions of blood serum that are closely associated with immune bodies and used to treat measles, poliomyelitis, infectious hepatitis, and other infectious diseases.

gamma ray. 1. Electromagnetic radiation emitted by ra-

---

dioactive decay and having energies in a range overlapping that of the highest energy x rays, extending up to several hundred thousand electron volts. **2.** Any electromagnetic radiation with energy greater than several hundred thousand electron volts. **3.** A ray of such radiation.

gam·mon¹ (găm′ən) *n.* A victory in backgammon occurring before the loser has removed a single man. —*tr.v.* To defeat in backgammon by scoring a gammon. [Prob. from Middle English *gamen,* game.]

gam·mon² (găm′ən). *Brit. Informal.* —*n.* Misleading or nonsensical talk; blather. —*tr.v.* To mislead by deceptive talk. —*intr.v.* To talk nonsense. [Obs. *gammon,* talk.] —**gam′mon·er** *n.*

gam·mon³ (găm′ən) *n.* **1.** A cured or smoked ham. **2.** The lower or bottom part of a side of bacon. [Old North French *gambon,* from *gambe,* leg, from Late Latin *gamba,* hoof, leg, from Greek *kampē,* a bend.]

gamo-. A prefix meaning: **1.** Sexual union: **gamogenesis. 2.** Union or fusion: **gamopetalous.** [From Greek *gamos,* marriage.]

gam·o·gen·e·sis (găm′ə-jĕn′ĭ-sĭs) *n.* Sexual reproduction. [GAMO- + -GENESIS.] —**gam′o·ge·net′ic** (găm′ə-jə-nĕt′ĭk) *adj.* —**gam′o·ge·net′i·cal·ly** *adv.*

gam·o·pet·al·ous (găm′ə-pĕt′l-əs) *adj. Bot.* Having a corolla with the petals fused or partially fused. [GAMO- + PETALOUS.]

gam·o·sep·al·ous (găm′ə-sĕp′ə-ləs) *adj. Bot.* Having the sepals united or partly united. [GAMO- + -SEPALOUS.]

gam·ut (găm′ət) *n.* **1.** The complete range of anything; entire extent: *The actor's face expressed the gamut of emotion from rage to peaceful content.* **2.** The entire series of recognized musical notes. —See Usage note at **gantlet².** [Middle English, from Medieval Latin *gamma ut* : *gamma,* the note one tone lower than the first note in Guido d'Arezzo's musical scale + *ut,* the lowest note.]

gam·y (gā′mē) *adj.* **-i·er, -i·est. 1.** Having the strong flavor or odor of game, esp. game that is slightly spoiled. **2.** Showing an unyielding spirit; plucky: *a gamy little mare.* —**gam′i·ness** *n.*

-gamy. A suffix meaning marriage or sexual union: **misogamy.** [Greek *-gamia,* from *gamos,* marriage.]

gan·der (găn′dər) *n.* **1.** A male goose. **2.** *Slang.* A quick look; a glance: *He took a gander at his opponent's size and decided not to fight after all.* [Middle English, from Old English *gandra, ganra.*]

gang¹ (găng) *n.* **1.** A group of people, usu. young, who gather together regularly and informally as friends and sometimes compete against or fight other such groups. **2.** A group of criminals or hoodlums who band together for mutual protection and profit. **3.** A group of laborers organized together on one job or under one foreman: *a railroad gang.* **4.** A set, esp. of matched tools: *a gang of chisels.* —See Syns at **circle.** —*intr.v.* To band together as a group or gang. —*tr.v.* To group together into a gang. **2.** *Informal.* To attack as a gang. —*phrasal verb.* **gang up on.** *Informal.* To harass or attack as a group. [Middle English *gang,* a group of persons, from Old English *gang,* a going, journey.]

gang² (găng) *n.* Var. of **gangue.**

gan·gli·a (găng′glē-ə) *n.* A plural of **ganglion.**

gan·gling (găng′glĭng) *adj.* Also **gan·gly** (-glē), **-gli·er, -gli·est.** Tall, thin, and ungraceful; lanky; rangy: *"That gangly, craning look a kid's head has"* (Robert Penn Warren). [From dial. *gang,* to go, straggle, from Middle English *gangen.*]

gan·gli·on (găng′glē-ən) *n., pl.* **-gli·a** (-glē-ə) or **-ons. 1.** *Anat.* A group of nerve cells, such as one located outside the brain or spinal cord, in vertebrates. **2.** Any center of power, activity, or energy. **3.** *Pathol.* A cystic lesion resembling a tumor, occurring in a tendon sheath or joint capsule. [Greek *ganglion,* cystlike tumor, ganglion.] —**gan′gli·on′ic** (-ŏn′ĭk) *adj.*

gan·gly (găng′glē) *adj.* Var. of **gangling.**

gang·plank (găng′plăngk′) *n.* A board or ramp used as a removable footway between a ship and a pier. [Obs. *gang,* passage) + PLANK.]

gang·plow (găng′plou′) *n.* A plow equipped with several blades that make parallel furrows. [GANG (set of tools) + PLOW.]

gan·grene (găng′grēn′, găng-grēn′) *n.* Death and decay of tissue in a part of the body, usu. a limb, due to failure of blood supply, injury, or disease. —*v.* **-grened, -gren·ing.** —*tr.v.* To affect with gangrene. —*intr.v.* To become affected with gangrene. [Old French *gangrine,* from Latin *gangraena,* from Greek *gangraina.*] —**gan′gre·nous** (-grə-nəs) *adj.*

gang·ster (găng′stər) *n.* A member of an organized group of criminals; racketeer. [GANG + -STER.]

gangue (găng) *n.* Also **gang.** The worthless rock or other material in which valuable minerals are found. [French, from German *Gang,* course, lode, vein, from Old High German, a going.]

gang·way (găng′wā′) *n.* **1.** A passageway, as through a crowd or an obstructed area. **2. a.** A passage along either side of a ship's upper deck. **b.** A gangplank. **c.** An opening in the side of a ship through which passengers may board. **3.** *Brit.* An aisle between seating sections, as in a theater. [Obs. *gang,* passage + WAY.]

gan·net (găn′ĭt) *n.* Any of several large sea birds of the family Sulidae, esp. *Morus bassanus,* of northern coastal regions, having white plumage with black wing tips. [Middle English *ganat, ganett,* from Old English *ganot.*]

gannet

gan·oid (găn′oid′) *adj.* Of, pertaining to, or characteristic of certain fishes, such as the sturgeon and the gar, that have armorlike scales consisting of bony plates covered with layers of dentine and enamel. —*n.* A ganoid fish. [From French *ganoïde,* having a shiny surface, from Greek *ganos,* brightness, joy, from *ganusthai,* to rejoice.]

gant·let¹ (gônt′lĭt, gănt′-) *n.* Also **gaunt·let.** A section of railroad track where two sets of tracks are overlapped to afford passage at a narrow place without switching. [Alteration of earlier *gant(e)lope,* from Swedish *gatlopp* : *gata,* road, way + *lop,* course.]

gant·let² (gônt′lĭt, gănt′-) *n.* **1.** Var. of **gauntlet** (glove). **2.** Var. of **gauntlet** (ordeal).

Usage: **gantlet, gauntlet, gamut.** The first two words often occur in the phrase *run the gantlet* (or *gauntlet*). In earlier times a person being punished was sometimes forced to run between two lines of men facing each other and armed with sticks or other weapons with which they beat the runner. The two lines made up the *gantlet (gauntlet).* A figurative sense meaning trial or ordeal then developed: *run the gantlet (gauntlet) of criticism.* Both *gantlet* and *gauntlet* are acceptable spellings for the word meaning ordeal. However, *gauntlet* is the preferred spelling for the word meaning the glove worn with medieval armor; that term is often used in the phrases *fling* (or *throw*) *down the gauntlet* and *take up the gauntlet*—e.g., issue a challenge and accept a challenge. The term *gamut,* meaning the complete range of anything, should not be confused with *gantlet (gauntlet).* Gamut is often used in the phrase *run the gamut,* as: *The critics' comments ran the gamut from high praise to great condemnation.* This phrase simply means to range from one extreme to another.

gan·try (găn′trē) *n., pl.* **-tries. 1.** A support for a barrel lying on its side. **2. a.** A bridgelike framework on which a traveling crane moves. **b.** A similar structure supporting a group of railway signals over several tracks. **3.** *Aerospace.* A large vertical structure used in assembling or servicing rockets on their launching pads. [Prob. from Old North French *gantier,* var. of Old French *chantier,* from Latin

---

ă pat   ā pay   â care   ä father   ĕ pet   ē be   hw which   ĭ pit   ī tie   î pier   ŏ pot   ō toe   ô paw, for   oi noise
ōō took   ōō boot   ou out   th thin   th this   ŭ cut   û urge   zh vision   ə about, item, edible, gallop, circus

canthērius, rafter, from Greek *kanthēlios*, pack ass.]

Gan·y·mede (găn'ə-mēd') *n. Gk. Myth.* A Trojan boy of great beauty whom Zeus carried away to be cupbearer to the gods.

gaol (jāl) *n. Brit.* Var. of **jail.**

gap (găp) *n.* **1.** An opening, as in a wall: *We squeezed through a gap in the fence.* **2.** A break or pass through mountains. **3.** An empty space; blank: *a gap in your knowledge; a gap in his report.* **4.** A wide difference; disparity: *a gap between expenses and income.* **5.** *Elect.* A space traversed by an electric spark; spark gap. —*tr.v.* **gapped, gap·ping.** To make an opening or gap in. [Middle English *gap(pe)*, from Old Norse *gap*, chasm.]

gape (gāp, găp) *intr.v.* **gaped, gap·ing. 1.** To open the mouth wide; to yawn. **2.** To stare wonderingly, as with the mouth open: *The audience gaped as the magician's assistant disappeared.* **3.** To become widely open or separated: *The curtains gaped when the wind blew.*—See Syns at **gaze.** —*n.* **1.** An act of gaping. **2.** A large opening. **3.** *Zool.* The width of the space between the open jaws or mandibles of a vertebrate. **4. gapes.** A fit of yawning: *"Another hour of music was to give pleasure or the gapes, as real or affected taste for it prevailed"* (Jane Austen). [Middle English *gapen*, from Old Norse *gapa*, to open the mouth.] —**gap'er** *n.*

gar (gär) *n.* **1.** Any of several ganoid fishes of the genus *Lepisosteus*, of fresh and brackish waters of North and Central America, with an elongated body and a long snout. **2.** A similar or related fish, such as the needlefish. Also called **garfish.** [Short for *garfish*, from Middle English *garfysshe*.]

ga·rage (gə-räzh', -räj') *n.* **1.** A building or wing of a building in which to park a car or cars. **2.** A commercial establishment where cars are repaired and serviced. —*tr.v.* **-raged, -rag·ing.** To put or keep in a garage. [French, from *garer*, to dock (ships), store in a garage, from Old French, to warn, protect, guard.]

garb (gärb) *n.* Clothing, esp. a distinctive way of dressing: *sailors' garb.*—See Syns at **dress.** —*tr.v.* To dress; clothe: *The judge was garbed in his robes.* [Obs. French *garbe*, graceful appearance, from Italian *garbo*, grace, elegance of dress.]

gar·bage (gär'bǐj) *n.* **1.** Waste material, esp. scraps of food, that is thrown away: *Kitchen garbage should be disposed of in sealed bags.* **2.** Worthless matter; trash: *This program is better than most of the garbage that gets shown on television.* —*modifier: a garbage can.* [Middle English *garbage*, offal of an animal.]

gar·ble (gär'bəl) *tr.v.* **-bled, -bling. 1.** To distort or scramble (an account or message) so that it cannot be understood. **2.** To pronounce indistinctly: *He garbled his words with his mouth full of food.* —*n.* The act of garbling. [Middle English *garbelen*, to sift, select, from Italian *garbellare*, from Arabic *gharbala*, from Late Latin *cribellum*, dim. of *cribrum*, sieve.] —**gar'bler** *n.*

gar·çon (gär-sôN') *n., pl.* **-çons** (-sôN'). A waiter. [French, boy, servant.]

gar·den (gär'dn) *n.* **1.** A plot of land used for growing flowers, vegetables, or fruit. **2.** Often **gardens.** A park or similar place, usu. with plants or animals on public display: *a zoological garden.* **3.** A fertile, well-cultivated region. —*modifier: a garden hose.* —*tr.v.* To cultivate (a plot of ground) as a garden. —*intr.v.* To care for plants in a garden. [Middle English *gardyn*, from Old North French *gardin*.]

gar·den·er (gärd'nər, gär'dn-ər) *n.* A person who works in or tends a garden.

gar·de·nia (gär-dēn'yə, -dē'nē-ə) *n.* **1.** Any of various shrubs and trees of the genus *Gardenia*, esp. *G. jasminoides*, native to China, with glossy evergreen leaves and large, fragrant, usu. white flowers. **2.** The flower of this shrub. [After Dr. Alexander *Garden* (1731-90), Scottish naturalist.]

Garden of Eden. In the Old Testament, Eden.

gar·fish (gär'fǐsh) *n., pl.* **garfish** or **-fish·es.** A gar.

Gar·gan·tu·a (gär-găn'chōō-ə) *n.* A giant king noted for his enormous physical and intellectual appetites, the hero of Rabelais' satire *Gargantua and Pantagruel.*

gar·gan·tu·an or **Gar·gan·tu·an** (gär-găn'chōō-ən) *adj.*

Enormous; huge. —See Syns at **giant.**

gar·gle (gär'gəl) *v.* **-gled, -gling.** —*intr.v.* **1.** To exhale air through a liquid held in the back of the mouth in order to cleanse or medicate the mouth or throat. **2.** To produce the sound of gargling when speaking or singing. —*tr.v.* **1.** To rinse or medicate (the mouth or throat) by gargling. **2.** To circulate or apply (a solution or medicine) by gargling. —*n.* **1.** A medicated solution for gargling. **2.** A gargling sound. [Old French *gargouiller*, from *gargouille*, throat.]

gar·goyle (gär'goil') *n.* **1.** A water spout carved to represent a grotesque human or animal figure and protruding from the gutter of a roof. **2.** Any grotesque ornamental figure. [Middle English *gargoyl*, from Old French *gargouille*, throat, from Latin *gurguliō*, windpipe.]

gar·ish (gâr'ĭsh) *adj.* Too bright and flashy; gaudy: *garish colors.* [Perh. from obs. *gaur*, to stare, from Middle English *gauren*.] —**gar'ish·ly** *adv.* —**gar'ish·ness** *n.*

gar·land (gär'lənd) *n.* **1.** A wreath or ring of flowers, leaves, or other material worn as a crown or collar. **2.** A collection of short literary works, as of ballads or poems; anthology. —*tr.v.* To decorate with a garland. [Middle English, from Old French *gerlande, garlande*, "ornament made with gold threads."]

gar·lic (gär'lĭk) *n.* **1.** A plant, *Allium sativum*, related to the onion, having a bulb with a strong, distinctive odor and flavor. **2.** The bulb of this plant, divisible into separate cloves, and used as a seasoning. —*modifier: garlic dressing.* [Middle English *garlec*, from Old English *gārlēac*, "spear leek" (from its spear-shaped leaves) : *gār*, spear + *lēac*, leek.]

gar·lick·y (gär'li-kē) *adj.* Containing, tasting of, or smelling of garlic: *garlicky breath.*

gar·ment (gär'mənt) *n.* An article of clothing, esp. of outer clothing —See Syns at **dress.** —*tr.v.* To clothe; to dress. [Middle English *gar(ne)ment*, from Old French *garnement*, equipment, from *g(u)arnir*, to furnish, equip.]

gar·ner (gär'nər) *tr.v.* **1.** To gather and store in or as if in a granary. **2.** To amass; acquire. —*n.* A granary. [Middle English granary, from Old French *gernier, grenier*, from Latin *grānārium*, from *grānum*, grain.]

gar·net (gär'nĭt) *n.* **1.** Any of several common, widespread silicate minerals, occurring in two internally isomorphic series, gen. crystallized, often imbedded in igneous and metamorphic rocks, colored red, brown, black, green, yellow, or white, and used as gemstones and abrasives. **2.** A dark to very dark red. —*modifier: garnet earrings.* —*adj.* Dark to very dark red. [Middle English *gernet*, from Old French *grenat*, dark red, garnet, pomegranate-colored, from *pome grenate*, pomegranate.]

gar·nish (gär'nĭsh) *tr.v.* **1.** To furnish with beautifying details; embellish: *a saddle garnished with silver studs.* **2.** To add something to (a food or drink) for extra color or flavor: *garnish mashed potatoes with parsley.* **3.** *Law.* To garnishee. —*n.* **1.** Ornamentation; embellishment. **2.** Something added to a food or drink to give it extra color or flavor. [Middle English *garnysshen*, to equip, adorn, from Old French *guarnir, garnir*.]

gar·nish·ee (gär'nĭ-shē') *Law.* —*n.* A debtor against whom someone has begun a process of garnishment. —*tr.v.* **-eed, -ee·ing.** To attach (a debtor's pay or property) by garnishment.

gardenia   gargoyle

gar·nish·ment (gär′nĭsh-mənt) *n.* **1.** *Law.* A legal proceeding in which money or property due to a debtor is kept from him to be used to pay his debts. **2.** An embellishment.

gar·ni·ture (gär′nĭ-chər) *n.* Something that garnishes or decorates; embellishment. [Old French *garniture*, *garneture*, from *garnir*, to garnish.]

gar·ret (găr′ĭt) *n.* A room on the top floor of a house, typically just under a sloping roof; an attic; a loft. [Middle English *garet(te)*, turret, watchtower, from Old French *garite*, from *g(u)arir*, to defend, protect.]

gar·ri·son (găr′ĭ-sən) *n.* **1.** A military post, esp. a permanent one. **2.** The troops stationed at a garrison. —*tr.v.* **1.** To assign (troops) to a military post. **2.** To supply (a post) with troops. **3.** To occupy as or convert into a garrison. [Middle English *gariso(u)n*, protection, fortress, from Old French *garison*, from *g(u)arir*, to protect.]

gar·rote or **gar·rotte** (gə-rŏt′, -rōt′) *n.* **1. a.** A method of execution by strangulation or by breaking the neck with an iron collar screwed tight. **b.** A collar used for this. **2.** Strangulation, esp. in order to rob. —*tr.v.* **-rot·ed** or **-rot·ted**, **-rot·ing** or **-rot·ting**. **1.** To execute by garrote. **2.** To strangle or throttle in order to rob. [Spanish, cudgel, prob. from Old French *garrot*, earlier *guaroc*, club, turning rod, from *garokier*, to bend down, strangle.] —**gar·rot′er** *n.*

gar·ru·li·ty (gə-rōō′lĭ-tē) *n.* Talkativeness; chattiness: *"Its style is relaxed to the point of garrulity"* (Dwight Macdonald).

gar·ru·lous (găr′ə-ləs, -yə-) *adj.* Habitually talkative; chatty: *a garrulous old man.* —See Syns at **talkative.** [Latin *garrulus*, from *garrīre*, to chatter.] —**gar′ru·lous·ly** *adv.* —**gar′ru·lous·ness** *n.*

gar·ter (gär′tər) *n.* **1. a.** An elastic band worn around the leg to hold up a stocking. **b.** A suspender strap with a fastener attached to a girdle or belt for holding up a stocking. **2.** Garter. **a.** The badge of the Order of the Garter. **b.** The order itself. —*tr.v.* To fasten and hold with a garter. [Middle English *garter*, from Old North French *gartier*, from *garet*, bend of the knee.]

garter snake. Any of various nonvenomous North American snakes of the genus *Thamnophis*, with longitudinal stripes.

garth (gärth) *n.* **1.** A grassy quadrangle surrounded by cloisters. **2.** *Archaic.* A yard, garden, or paddock. [Middle English, from Old Norse *garthr*, yard.]

gas (găs) *n., pl.* **gas·es** or **gas·ses.** **1. a.** The state of matter distinguished from the solid and liquid states by very low density and viscosity, relatively great expansion and contraction with changes in pressure and temperature, the ability to diffuse readily, and the spontaneous tendency to become distributed uniformly throughout any container. **b.** A substance in this state. **c.** A substance in this state at room temperature and atmospheric pressure. **2.** A gaseous fuel such as natural gas. **3. a.** Gasoline. **b.** The speed control of a gasoline engine: *step on the gas.* **4. a.** A poisonous, irritating, or choking gas used as a weapon: *tear gas.* **5.** *Slang.* Thoughtless or boastful talk: *His threats are just a lot of gas.* **6.** *Slang.* Someone or something that provides great fun or amusement. —*modifier: a gas tank in a car; a gas burner.* —*v.* **gassed, gas·sing.** —*tr.v.* **1.** To supply with gas or gasoline. **2.** To treat chemically with gas. **3.** To poison with gas, as in war. —*intr.v.* **1.** To give off gas. **2.** *Slang.* To talk excessively. **3.** *Informal.* To supply one's car with gas. Used with *up.* [Dutch *gas*, an occult principle supposed to be present in all bodies, from Greek *khaos*, chasm, chaos.]

gas chamber. A sealed enclosure in which prisoners are executed by a poisonous gas.

gas·con (găs′kən) *n.* A boastful person; braggart. [French, from Old French *gascon*, Gascon (from the traditional garrulity of the Gascons).]

gas·con·ade (găs′kə-nād′) *n.* Boastfulness; bravado; swagger. —*intr.v.* **-ad·ed**, **-ad·ing.** To boast or swagger. —**gas′con·ad′er** *n.*

gas·e·ous (găs′ē-əs, găsh′əs) *adj.* Of, like, or existing as a gas.

gas gangrene. Gangrene occurring in a wound infected with bacteria and characterized by the presence of gas in the affected tissue.

gash (găsh) *tr.v.* To make a long, deep cut in; slash deeply: *He gashed his arm while sawing a piece of wood.* —*n.* A long, deep cut or wound. [Middle English *garsen*, to cut, slash, from Old North French *garser*, prob. from Late Latin *charaxāre*, from Greek *kharassein*, to carve, cut.]

gas·i·fy (găs′ə-fī′) *v.* **-fied, -fy·ing.** —*tr.v.* To convert into gas. —*intr.v.* To become gas. —**gas′i·fi′a·ble** *adj.* —**gas′i·fi·ca′tion** *n.*

gas·ket (găs′kĭt) *n.* **1.** *Machinery.* A ring or other device, often of soft material, used to form a seal between matched machine parts or around pipe joints to prevent leaking. **2.** *Naut.* A cord or canvas strap used to secure a furled sail to a yard boom or gaff. —*idiom.* **blow a gasket.** *Slang.* To explode with anger. [French *garcette*, "little girl," rope, dim. of *garce*, girl, from *gars*, boy.]

gas·light (găs′līt′) *n.* Also **gas light.** **1.** Light made by burning gas in a lamp. **2.** A gas burner or lamp.

gas main. A major pipeline conveying gas to smaller pipes for distribution to consumers.

gas·o·line (găs′ə-lēn′, găs′ə-lēn′) *n.* Also **gas·o·lene.** A volatile mixture of flammable liquid hydrocarbons derived chiefly from crude petroleum and used principally as a fuel for internal-combustion engines and as a solvent and thinner. —*modifier: a gasoline engine.* [GAS + -OL + -INE.]

gas·om·e·ter (gă-sŏm′ĭ-tər) *n.* An apparatus for measuring gases. [French *gazomètre*, from *gaz*, gas.]

gasp (găsp) *intr.v.* **1.** To draw in or catch the breath sharply: *The crowd gasped in amazement.* **2.** To make violent or labored attempts at breathing: *The diver finally surfaced and gasped for air.* —*tr.v.* To say in a breathless manner: *She gasped out an astonished reply.* —*n.* A sudden, violent, or irregular intake of the breath. [Middle English *ga(y)spen*, from Old Norse *geispa*.]

gas station. An establishment at which vehicles are serviced, as with gasoline, water, etc. Also called **filling station.**

gas·sy (găs′ē) *adj.* **-si·er, -si·est.** **1.** Containing, full of, or resembling gas. **2.** *Slang.* Talkative or boastful; windy.

gastr-. Var. of **gastro-.**

gas·tric (găs′trĭk) *adj.* Of or concerning the stomach. [French *gastrique*, from Greek *gastēr*, belly, womb.]

gastric juice. The colorless, watery, acidic digestive fluid secreted by the stomach glands and containing hydrochloric acid, pepsin, rennin, and mucin.

gas·trin (găs′trĭn) *n.* A secretion of the gastric mucosa that stimulates production of gastric juice. [GASTR(O)- + -IN.]

gas·tri·tis (gă-strī′tĭs) *n.* Chronic or acute inflammation of the stomach. [GASTR(O)- + -ITIS.]

gastro- or **gastr-.** A prefix meaning stomach: **gastritis.** [From Greek *gastēr*, belly, womb.]

gas·tro·in·tes·ti·nal (găs′trō-ĭn-tĕs′tə-nəl) *adj.* Of the stomach and intestines.

gas·tro·nome (găs′trə-nōm′) *n.* A person who enjoys good food and drink. [From GASTRONOMY.]

gas·tro·nom·ic (găs′trə-nŏm′ĭk) or **gas·tro·nom·i·cal** (-ĭ-kəl) *adj.* Of the art or science of good eating. —**gas′tro·nom′i·cal·ly** *adv.*

gas·tron·o·my (gă-strŏn′ə-mē) *n.* **1.** The art or science of good eating. **2.** Cooking, as of a particular region or country. [French *gastronomie*, from Greek *gastronomia* : *gastēr*, belly + *nomos*, law.]

gas·tro·pod (găs′trə-pŏd′) *n.* Any mollusk of the class Gastropoda, such as a snail, slug, cowry, or limpet, characteristically having a single, usu. coiled shell and a ventral muscular mass serving as an organ of locomotion. —*adj.* Of or belonging to the Gastropoda. [GASTRO- + -POD.] —**gas·trop′o·dous** (gŭ-strŏp′ə-dəs) *adj.*

gas·tru·la (găs′trōō-lə) *n., pl.* **-las** or **-lae** (-lē′). An embryo at the stage following the blastula and consisting of ectoderm, endoderm, and archenteron. [New Latin, "small stomach" (from its shape), dim. of Greek *gastēr*, belly, womb.] —**gas′tru·lar** *adj.*

gas·tru·late (găs′trōō-lāt′) *intr.v.* **-lat·ed, -lat·ing.** To form or become a gastrula. —**gas′tru·la′tion** *n.*

gas·works (găs′wûrks′) *n.* (used with a sing. or pl. verb). A factory where gas, esp. for heating and lighting, is produced.

gat¹ (găt) *n.* *Slang.* A pistol. [Short for GATLING GUN.]

ă pat ā pay â care ä father ĕ pet ē be hw which ĭ pit ī tie î pier ŏ pot ō toe ô paw, for oi noise
ōō took ōō boot ou out th thin th this ŭ cut û urge zh vision ə about, item, edible, gallop, circus

gat² (găt) v. *Archaic.* Past tense of **get.** [Middle English, from Old Norse.]

gate (gāt) n. **1.** A structure that may be swung, drawn, or lowered to block an entrance or passageway. **2. a.** An opening in a wall or fence for entrance or exit. **b.** The structure surrounding such an opening, as the monumental entrance to a palace. **3.** A way of getting to something: *Education is the gate to fortune.* **4.** A device for controlling the passage of water or gas through a dam or conduit. **5.** The total admission receipts or attendance at a public spectacle. **—idioms. get the gate.** *Slang.* To be dismissed or thrown out. **give (someone) the gate.** *Slang.* To dismiss or throw out: *The head waiter grabbed the disorderly customer and gave him the gate.* [Middle English *gat*, from Old English *geat.*]

gate·crash·er (gāt'krăsh'ər) n. *Slang.* A person who gains admittance without being invited or enters without paying admission.

gate·post (gāt'pōst') n. An upright post on which a gate is hung or against which a gate is closed.

gate·way (gāt'wā') n. **1.** An opening, as in a wall or fence, that may be closed by a gate. **2.** A way of getting to something; means of access: *a gateway to success.*

gath·er (găth'ər) tr.v. **1.** To bring together in a group; assemble: *The teacher gathered the students around him.* **2.** To pick; collect: *Squirrels gather nuts.* **3.** To obtain from many places or sources; amass gradually: *gather information.* **4.** To prepare (mental or physical powers) for use; summon up; muster: *He took a moment to gather his wits before reciting.* **5.** To gain or increase gradually: *gathering speed.* **6.** To conclude; infer: *I gather from your comments that you didn't like the movie.* **7.** To bring closer: *She gathered the blanket around the child's shivering body.* **8.** To run a thread through (cloth) so as to draw it up into small folds or pleats: *gather material at the waist of a full skirt.* —intr.v. **1.** To come together in a group: *The campers gathered around the fire.* **2.** To accumulate; collect: *The cut hay gathered on each side of the reaper.* **3.** To grow or increase gradually: *Storm clouds gathered.* **4.** To come to a head, as a boil does. —n. **1.** An act of gathering. **2.** One of the small folds or pleats made in cloth by gathering it. [Middle English *gad(e)ren*, from Old English *gad(e)rian*, to put together, come together.] **—gath'er·er** n.

Syns: 1. gather, call, convene, convoke, muster, summon v. *Core meaning:* To bring together *(gathered the faculty for a meeting).* **2. gather, accumulate, amass, collect** v. *Core meaning:* To come together *(a crowd that gathered to watch the parade).* GATHER is the most general term and COLLECT is often interchangeable with it *(crowds collecting along the parade route),* but it is often used to imply the careful selection of related things *(paintings collected by an avid art lover)* ACCUMULATE and AMASS refer to the gradual increase of something over a period of time *(snow accumulating on the sidewalks; a fortune amassed over the years).* ASSEMBLE suggests a convening for a common purpose *(legislators assembling for a joint session of Congress).*

gath·er·ing (găth'ər-ĭng) n. **1.** Something gathered or amassed; a collection. **2.** An assembly of persons; a meeting: *a family gathering.* **3.** A gather in cloth. **4.** A boil or abscess.

Gat·ling gun (găt'lĭng). A 19th-cent. machine gun with a cluster of rotating barrels that fire as the cluster is turned. [Designed by Richard J. *Gatling* (1818–1903), American inventor.]

gauche (gōsh) adj. Lacking social grace; tactless; clumsy. [French, left, clumsy, from Old French *gauchir*, to turn aside, detour.] **—gauche'ly** adv. **—gauche'ness** n.

gau·che·rie (gō'shə-rē') n. **1.** An awkward or tactless action, manner, or expression. **2.** Tactlessness; awkwardness. [French, from *gauche*, left, gauche.]

Gau·cho (gou'chō) n., pl. **-chos.** A cowboy of the South American pampas. [American Spanish, prob. from Quechua *wáhcha*, poor person, vagabond.]

gaud (gôd) n. A gaudy or showy ornament. [Middle English *gaude*, jest, toy, from Old French *gaudir*, to rejoice, from Latin *gaudēre*, to delight in.]

gaud·y (gô'dē) adj. **-i·er, -i·est.** Too brightly colored and showy; garish: *a gaudy outfit.* [From GAUD.]

gauge (gāj) n. Also **gage.** **1. a.** A standard or scale of measurement. **b.** A standard dimension, quantity, or capacity. **2.** An instrument for measuring or testing: *a rain gauge; a pressure gauge.* **3.** A means of estimating or evaluating; a test: *a gauge of character.* **4. a.** The distance between the two rails of a railroad. **b.** The distance between two wheels on an axle. **5.** The diameter of a shotgun barrel. **6.** Thickness or diameter, as of sheet metal or wire. **7.** The fineness of knitted cloth as determined by the number of loops per 1½ inches. **—modifier:** *a narrow-gauge railroad; a 12-gauge shotgun.* —tr.v. **gauged, gaug·ing. 1.** To measure precisely. **2.** To determine the capacity, volume, or contents of. **3.** To evaluate or judge: *It is too early to gauge the damage caused by the hurricane.* [Middle English, from Old North French.] **—gauge'a·ble** adj. **—gaug'er** n.

Usage: gauge, gage. *Gauge* is the first spelling, and *gage* an acceptable alternative, of the noun meaning a standard of measurement, an instrument for measuring or testing, the distance between two rails or between two wheels, the diameter of a shotgun barrel, thickness or diameter, and fineness of knitted cloth. The corresponding verb meaning to measure or evaluate is spelled only *gauge.*

gaunt (gônt) adj. **-er, -est. 1.** Thin and bony; angular: *a gaunt profile.* **2.** Emaciated and haggard; drawn: *the survivors' gaunt faces.* **3.** Bleak and desolate; barren: *the bare, gaunt mountains enclosing Death Valley.* —See Syns at **haggard.** [Middle English, slim, lean, prob. of Scandinavian orig.] **—gaunt'ly** adv. **—gaunt'ness** n.

gaunt·let¹ (gônt'lĭt, gănt'-) n. Also **gant·let. 1.** A protective glove worn with medieval armor. **2.** A protective glove with a flaring cuff used in manual labor. **3.** A challenge to fight or compete: *fling down the gauntlet.* —See Usage note at **gantlet.** [Middle English *gaunt(e)let*, from Old French *gantelet*, dim. of *gant*, glove.]

gaunt·let² (gônt'lĭt, gănt'-) n. Also **gant·let. 1.** An old form of punishment in which two lines of men facing each other and armed with clubs beat a person forced to run between them. **2.** A severe trial; an ordeal: *The candidate had to run the gauntlet of questions from the press.* —See Usage note at **gantlet.** [Earlier *gantlope*, from Swedish *gatlopp: gata*, road + *lop*, course.]

gaunt·let³ (gônt'lĭt, gănt'-) n. Var. of **gantlet** (railroad track).

gauss (gous) n. *Abbr.* **G** The centimeter-gram-second electromagnetic unit of magnetic flux density, equal to one maxwell per square centimeter or 10^{-4} tesla. [After Karl F. *Gauss* (1777–1855), German mathematician, astronomer, and physicist.]

gauze (gôz) n. **1.** A thin, transparent fabric with a loose open weave, used for curtains or clothing. **2.** A loosely woven cloth used esp. for bandages. **—modifier:** *a gauze strip.* [Earlier *gais*, from Old French *gaze.*] **—gauz'i·ness** n. **—gauz'y** adj.

gave (gāv) v. Past tense of **give.** [Middle English *gafe*, from English *gæf.*]

gav·el (găv'əl) n. The mallet or hammer used by a presiding officer or auctioneer to signal for attention or order. [Orig. unknown.]

ga·vi·al (gā'vē-əl) n. A large reptile, *Gavialis gangeticus*, of southern Asia, related to and resembling the crocodiles and having a long, slender snout. [French, from Hindi *ghariyāl.*]

ga·votte (gə-vŏt') n. **1.** A French peasant dance resembling the minuet. **2.** Music for the gavotte, in moderately quick 4/4 time. [French, from Provençal *gavoto*, from *Gavot*, "mountaineer," "rustic."]

Ga·wain (gä'wĭn, wān', gô'-, gə-wān') n. Also **Ga·waine.** A nephew of King Arthur and a knight of the Round Table.

gawk (gôk) n. An awkward, stupid person; oaf. —intr.v. *Informal.* To stare stupidly; gape. —See Syns at **gaze.** [Perh. alteration of obs. *gaw*, to stare, gape, from Middle English *gawen*, from Old Norse *gá*, to heed.]

gawk·y (gô'kē) adj. **-i·er, -i·est.** Awkward; clumsy. —See Syns at **awkward.** **—gawk'i·ly** adv. **—gawk'i·ness** n.

gay (gā) adj. **-er, -est. 1.** Merry; lighthearted: *a gay mood; gay music.* **2.** Bright or lively, esp. in color: *The package was tied with gay ribbons.* **3.** Homosexual. —See Syns at **glad.** —n. A homosexual. [Middle English *gay, gai*, from

gazelle gear gecko

Old French *gai*, from Old Provençal.] **—gay′ness** *n.*

gay·e·ty (gā′i-tē) *n.* Var. of **gaiety.**

gay·ly (gā′lē) *adv.* Var. of **gaily.**

gaze (gāz) *intr.v.* **gazed, gaz·ing.** To look intently or steadily; to stare. **—***n.* A steady, fixed look. [Middle English *gazen*, prob. of Scandinavian orig.] **—gaz′er** *n.*

 Syns: gaze, eye, gape, gawk (*Informal*), **goggle, ogle, peer, stare** *v. Core meaning:* To look intently and fixedly (*gazed in awe at the crown jewels*).

ga·ze·bo (gə-zē′bō, -zā′-) *n., pl.* **-bos** or **-boes.** A small, open-sided, roofed structure in a garden or park, that provides a shady resting place. [Perh. from GAZE + -*ĕbō*, Latin future suffix as in *vidĕbō* (I shall see).]

ga·zelle (gə-zĕl′) *n.* Any of various hoofed mammals of the genus *Gazella* and related genera, of Africa and Asia, with a slender neck and ringed, lyrate horns. [French, from Old French, prob. from Spanish *gacela*, from Arabic *ghazāl*.]

ga·zette (gə-zĕt′) *n.* **1.** A newspaper. **2.** An official journal. **—***tr.v.* **-zet·ted, -zet·ting.** *Brit.* To announce or publish in an official journal. [French, from Italian *gazzetta*, from Venetian *gazeta* (*de la novita*), (newspaper sold for) a small copper coin, from *gazeta*, a small copper coin.]

gaz·et·teer (găz′ĭ-tîr′) *n.* A geographical dictionary or index.

G clef. The **treble clef.**

Gd The symbol for the element gadolinium.

Ge The symbol for the element germanium.

gear (gîr) *n.* **1. a.** A toothed wheel or a similar mechanical device that interlocks with another toothed part in order to transmit motion. **b.** An arrangement of the gears of an automobile or other motor vehicle, used to match a range of road speeds to the possible speeds of the engine. **2.** An assembly of parts that does a particular job in a larger machine: *the landing gear of an aircraft.* **3.** Equipment, such as tools, clothing, etc., needed for a particular activity: *fishing gear.* **4.** One's personal belongings: *The sailor stowed his gear.* **—***tr.v.* **1.** To provide with gears. **2.** To adjust so that the gears are properly engaged or interlocked: *She started and geared the power lawn mower.* **3.** To connect by gears: *gearing the motor to the crankshaft.* **4.** To adjust or adapt: *The producers geared the show to a broad popular audience.* **—***intr.v.* To become engaged or interlocked: *The two wheels gear tightly.* **—idiom. in** (**or out of**) **gear. 1.** Having the gears that transmit power engaged (or not engaged). **2.** Ready (or not ready) for effective operation. [Middle English *gere*, from Old Norse *gervi*, equipment, gear.]

gear·box (gîr′bŏks′) *n.* The transmission of a car or other motor vehicle.

gear·ing (gîr′ĭng) *n.* A system of gears by which motion is transferred within a machine.

gear·shift (gîr′shĭft′) *n.* A device for changing from one gear to another, as in a car.

gear·wheel (gîr′hwēl′, -wēl′) *n.* Also **gear wheel.** A wheel with a toothed rim.

geck·o (gĕk′ō) *n., pl.* **-os** or **-oes.** Any of various usu. small lizards of the family Gekkonidae, of warm regions, having toes with adhesive pads that enable them to climb on vertical surfaces. [Malay *ge'kok* (imit. of its cry).]

gee¹ (jē) *interj.* A word used to express a command, as to a horse or ox, to turn to the right or to go forward. **—***intr.v.* **geed, gee·ing.** To turn to the right.

gee² (jē) *interj.* A word used to express emphasis or as an

exclamation of surprise. [Euphemistic shortening of JESUS.]

geese (gēs) *n.* Plural of **goose.**

Geiger counter (gī′gər). An instrument used to detect, measure, and record nuclear emanations, cosmic rays, and artificially produced subatomic particles. [After Hans *Geiger* (1882–1945), German physicist.]

gei·sha (gā′shə, gē′-) *n., pl.* **geisha** or **-shas.** A Japanese girl trained to provide entertainment, such as singing, dancing, or amusing talk, esp. for men. [Japanese, "artist" : *gei*, art + *sha*, person.]

gel (jĕl) *n.* A colloid in which the disperse phase has combined with the continuous phase to produce a semisolid material such as a jelly. [Short for GELATIN.]

gel·a·tin (jĕl′ə-tən) *n.* Also **gel·a·tine. 1.** A colorless or slightly yellow protein formed by boiling the specially prepared skin, bones, and connective tissue of animals and used in foods, drugs, and photographic film. **2.** A jelly made with gelatin, popular as a dessert or salad base. [French *gélatine*, from Italian *gelatina*, dim. of *gelata*, jelly, from Latin *gelāre*, to freeze, congeal.]

ge·lat·i·nous (jə-lăt′n-əs) *adj.* **1.** Thick and viscous; resembling a gelatin. **2.** Of, like, or containing gelatin. **—ge·lat′i·nous·ly** *adv.* **—ge·lat′i·nous·ness** *n.*

geld (gĕld) *tr.v.* **geld·ed** or **gelt** (gĕlt), **geld·ing.** To castrate (a horse or other animal). [Middle English *gelden*, from Old Norse *gelda.*]

geld·ing (gĕl′dĭng) *n.* A castrated male animal, esp. a horse. [Middle English, from Old Norse *geldingr*, from *gelda*, geld.]

gel·id (jĕl′ĭd) *adj.* Very cold; icy. [Latin *gelidus*, from *gelū*, cold, frost.] **—ge·lid′i·ty** (jə-lĭd′ĭ-tē) or **gel′id·ness** *n.* **—gel′id·ly** *adv.*

gelt (gĕlt) *v.* Alternate past tense and part participle of **geld.**

gem (jĕm) *n.* **1.** A precious or semiprecious stone, esp. one that has been cut and polished. **2.** Something or someone valued for beauty or perfection: *a gem of a poem.* **—***tr.v.* **gemmed, gem·ming.** To adorn with or as if with gems. [Middle English *gemme*, from Old French, from Latin *gemma*, bud, precious stone.]

gem·i·nate (jĕm′ə-nāt′) *v.* **-nat·ed, -nat·ing. —***tr.v.* **1.** To arrange in pairs. **2.** To double. **—***intr.v.* To occur in pairs. **—***adj.* (jĕm′ə-nĭt, -nāt′). Forming a pair; doubled. [From Latin *gemināre*, from *geminus*, twin.] **—gem′i·na′tion** *n.*

Gem·i·ni (jĕm′ə-nī′, -nē′) *n.* **1.** *Astron.* A constellation in the Northern Hemisphere containing the stars Castor and Pollux. **2.** The third sign of the zodiac.

gem·ma (jĕm′ə) *n., pl.* **gem·mae** (jĕm′ē′). An asexual reproductive structure, as in liverworts or the hydra, consisting of a cell or group of cells capable of developing into a new individual; a bud. [Latin, bud, precious stone.]

gem·mate (jĕm′āt′) *adj.* Having or reproducing by gemmae. **—***intr.v.* **-mat·ed, -mat·ing.** To produce gemmae or reproduce by means of gemmae. [From Latin *gemmāre*, to bud, from *gemma*, bud, gemma.] **—gem·ma′tion** (jĕ-mā′shən) *n.*

gem·mip·a·rous (jĕ-mĭp′ər-əs) *adj.* Reproducing by buds or gemmae. [Latin *gemma*, bud, gemma + -PAROUS.]

gem·mol·o·gy (jĕ-mŏl′ə-jē) *n.* Var. of **gemology.**

gem·mule (jĕm′yōōl) *n.* A small gemma or similar structure, esp. a reproductive structure in some sponges that remains dormant through the winter and later develops

---

ă pat ā pay â care ä father ĕ pet ē be hw which ĭ pit ī tie î pier ŏ pot ō toe ô paw, for oi noise
ōō took ōō boot ou out th thin *th* this ŭ cut û urge zh vision ə about, item, edible, gallop, circus

into a new individual. [French, from Latin *gemmula,* dim. of *gemma,* gem.]

gem·ol·o·gy or **gem·mol·o·gy** (jĕ-mŏl′ə-jē) *n.* The study of gems. —**gem′o·log′i·cal** (jĕm′ə-lŏj′ĭ-kəl) *adj.* —**gem·ol′o·gist** *n.*

gems·bok (gĕmz′bŏk′) *n.* An antelope, *Oryx gazella,* of arid regions of southern Africa, with long, sharp, straight horns. [Afrikaans, from Dutch *gemsbok,* male chamois, from German *Gemsbock* : *Gemse,* chamois + *Bock,* hegoat, buck.]

gem·stone (jĕm′stōn′) *n.* A precious or semiprecious stone that can be used as a jewel when cut and polished.

-gen or **-gene.** A suffix meaning: **1.** That which produces; producing: *carcinogen.* **2.** Something produced: *antigen.* [French *-gène,* from Greek *-genēs,* born.]

gen·darme (zhän′därm′) *n.* **1.** *Informal.* A French policeman. **2.** *Slang.* Any policeman. [French, from *gens d'armes,* "men of arms."]

gen·der (jĕn′dər) *n.* **1.** *Gram.* **a.** Any of two or more categories, such as masculine, feminine, and neuter, into which words are divided and that determine agreement with or the selection of modifiers, referents, or grammatical forms. **b.** The classification of a word or grammatical form in such a category. **2.** Classification according to sex; sex. [Middle English *gendre,* from Old French *gen(d)re,* kind, sort, from Latin *genus* race, kind.]

gene (jĕn) *n.* A functional hereditary unit that occupies a fixed location on a chromosome, has a specific influence on phenotype, and is capable of mutation to various allelic forms. [German *Gen,* ult. from Greek *genēs,* born.]

-gene. Var. of **-gen.**

ge·ne·al·o·gy (jē′nē-ăl′ə-jē, -ŏl′-, jĕn′ē-) *n., pl.* **-gies. 1.** A record or table of the descent of a family, group, or person from an ancestor or ancestors. **2.** Direct descent from an ancestor; lineage; pedigree. **3.** The study of ancestry and family histories. [Middle English *genealogie,* from Old French, from Late Latin *genealogia,* from Greek, from *genea,* race, generation.] —**ge′ne·a·log′i·cal** (-ə-lŏj′ĭ-kəl) *adj.* —**ge′ne·a·log′i·cal·ly** *adv.* —**ge′ne·al′o·gist** *n.*

gen·er·a (jĕn′ər-ə) *n.* Plural of **genus.**

gen·er·al (jĕn′ər-əl) *adj.* **1.** Applicable to or involving the whole or every member of a class or category: *a general meeting; the general welfare.* **2.** Widespread; prevalent. **3.** Not restricted or specialized: *a doctor with a general practice.* **4.** True or applicable in most but not all cases: *a general rule to follow.* **5.** Involving only the main or more obvious features of something; not precise or detailed: *discuss the matter in general terms.* **6.** Diversified: *a general store; a general education.* **7.** Highest or superior in rank: *the general manager.* —*n.* **1.** Any of several high-ranking officers in the Army, Air Force, or Marine Corps ranking above a colonel and including, in descending order of rank, **general, lieutenant general, major general,** and **brigadier general. 2.** *Archaic.* The public; the common people: *" 'Twas caviare to the general"* (Shakespeare). —**idiom. in general.** For the most part; on the whole: *He approved of the plan in general but quarreled with certain details.* [Middle English, from Old French, from Latin *generālis,* belonging to a kind or species, relating to all, from *genus,* birth, race, kind.]

Syns: **general, broad, comprehensive, expansive, extensive, global, inclusive, overall, sweeping, widespread** *adj. Core meaning:* Covering a wide scope (*general discontent*). See also Syns at **public.**

general assembly. 1. A legislative body, esp. a U.S. state legislature. **2. General Assembly.** The main body of the United Nations, in which each member nation is represented and has one vote. **3.** The supreme governing body of some religious denominations.

general delivery. A department of a post office that holds mail until it is called for.

gen·er·al·is·si·mo (jĕn′ər-ə-lĭs′ə-mō′) *n., pl.* **-mos.** The commander in chief of all the armed forces in certain countries. [Italian, superlative of *generale,* general, from Latin *generālis,* belonging to a kind, general.]

gen·er·al·i·ty (jĕn′ə-răl′ĭ-tē) *n., pl.* **-ties. 1.** The condition or quality of being general. **2.** An observation or principle that is true or applicable in most but not all cases; a generalization. **3.** A statement or idea that is imprecise or vague. **4.** The greater portion or number; majority.

gen·er·al·i·za·tion (jĕn′ər-ə-lĭ-zā′shən) *n.* **1.** An act of generalizing. **2.** A general principle, statement or idea.

gen·er·al·ize (jĕn′ər-ə-līz′) *v.* **-ized, -iz·ing.** —*intr.v.* **1.** To make a general statement about a broad subject that is more or less accurate or applicable: *We may generalize and say that the best basketball players are tall.* **2.** To come to a general conclusion: *generalizing from insufficient data.* **3.** To speak or think vaguely or imprecisely: *Stop generalizing and come to the point.* —*tr.v.* **1.** To give a general form to; make general: *The anthropologist generalized her conclusions so that they applied to all peoples.* **2.** To draw general conclusions from; sum up: *generalize the available data.* **3.** To infer from many particulars: *generalized a theory of wave motion from the observed phenomena.* **4.** To make indefinite or unspecific: *The painter generalized the portrait so that the sitter could not be recognized.*

gen·er·al·ly (jĕn′ər-ə-lē) *adv.* **1.** For the most part; widely: *generally known.* **2.** As a rule; usually; ordinarily. **3.** In disregard of particular instances and details; not specifically: *generally speaking.*

General of the Air Force. A general having the highest rank in the U.S. Air Force and having an insignia of five stars.

General of the Army. A general having the highest rank in the U.S. Army and having an insignia of five stars.

general practitioner. A physician who does not limit his or her practice to a medical specialty.

gen·er·al-pur·pose (jĕn′ər-əl-pûr′pəs) *adj.* Having more than one use: *a general-purpose pocket knife.*

general relativity. The geometric theory of gravitation developed by Albert Einstein, incorporating and extending the special theory of relativity to accelerated frames of reference and introducing the principle that gravitational and inertial forces are equivalent. Also called "general theory of relativity."

gen·er·al·ship (jĕn′ər-əl-shĭp′) *n.* **1.** The rank or office of a general. **2.** Leadership or skill in the conduct of a war. **3.** Any skillful management or leadership.

general store. A store that sells a large variety of goods but is not divided into departments.

gen·er·ate (jĕn′ə-rāt′) *tr.v.* **-at·ed, -at·ing. 1.** To bring into existence; cause to be; produce: *machines that generate electricity; generating worldwide interest.* **2.** To engender (offspring); beget. **3.** To form (a geometric figure) by describing a curve or surface. —See Syns at **create.** [From Latin *generāre,* from *genus,* birth, race, kind.] —**gen′er·a·tive** (-ə-rā′tĭv, -ər-ə-tĭv) *adj.*

gen·er·a·tion (jĕn′ə-rā′shən) *n.* **1.** The act or process of generating: *the generation of electric power.* **2.** All of the offspring that are at the same stage of descent from a common ancestor. **3.** A group of people who grow up at about the same time, often thought to have similar ideas, customs, etc.: *the younger generation.* **4.** A class of things derived from an earlier class, usu. by making improvements and refinements: *the new generation of computers.* **5.** The average length of time between the birth of parents and the birth of their children; a period of about thirty years.

gen·er·a·tor (jĕn′ə-rā′tər) *n.* **1.** Someone or something that generates. **2.** A machine that converts mechanical energy into electrical energy. **3.** An apparatus that generates vapor or gas. **4.** A generatrix.

gen·er·a·trix (jĕn′ə-rā′trĭks) *n., pl.* **gen·er·a·tri·ces** (jĕn′ər-ə-trī′sēz′). A geometric element that generates a geometric figure, esp. a straight line that generates a surface by moving in a specified fashion.

ge·ner·ic (jĭ-nĕr′ĭk) *adj.* **1.** Of, including, or indicating an entire group, class, or category; general rather than specific: *The generic word "sad" suggests specific words like "mournful," "grieving," and "downhearted."* **2.** Not protected by a trademark and therefore applicable to an entire class of products: *the generic name for a widely prescribed drug.* **3.** Of or relating to a biological genus. [French *générique,* from Latin *genus,* race, species, kind.] —**ge·ner′i·cal·ly** *adv.*

gen·er·os·i·ty (jĕn′ə-rŏs′ĭ-tē) *n., pl.* **-ties. 1.** The condition or quality of being generous; willingness to give or share. **2.** Nobility of thought or behavior; magnanimity. **3.** Ampli-

---

| ă pat | ā pay | â care | ä father | ĕ pet | ē be | hw which | ĭ pit | ī tie | î pier | ŏ pot | ō toe | ô paw, for | oi noise |
| ōō took | ōō boot | ou out | th thin | th this | ŭ cut | | û urge | zh vision | ə about, item, edible, gallop, circus |

tude; abundance. **4.** A generous act.

gen·er·ous (jĕn′ər-əs) *adj.* **1.** Willing to give or share; unselfish. **2.** Lacking pettiness or meanness in thought or behavior; magnanimous: *A generous critic overlooks small faults.* **3.** Showing generosity: *a generous gift; generous praise.* **4.** Characterized by abundance; bountiful; ample. [Old French *genereux,* from Latin *generōsus,* of noble birth, excellent, magnanimous, from *genus,* birth, race, kind.] **—gen′er·ous·ly** *adv.* **—gen′er·ous·ness** *n.*
　　Syns: 1. generous, big, greathearted, magnanimous, unselfish *adj.* *Core meaning:* Willing to give of oneself and one's possessions (*a generous contributor to charity*). **2. generous, handsome, liberal, munificent** *adj.* *Core meaning:* Marked by bounteous giving (*a generous living allowance for the children*). **3. generous, abundant, bounteous, bountiful, copious, liberal, plentiful** *adj.* *Core meaning:* Marked by abundance (*a generous serving of peas*).

gen·e·sis (jĕn′ĭ-sĭs) *n.,* pl. **-ses** (-sēz′). **1.** The coming into being of anything; beginning; origin: *the genesis of a new nation.* **2. Genesis.** See table at **Bible.** [Latin, from Greek, generation, birth, origin.]

–genesis. A suffix meaning generation: **cytogenesis.** [From Latin *genesis,* birth, genesis.]

ge·net·ic (jə-nĕt′ĭk) or **ge·net·i·cal** (-ĭ-kəl) *adj.* **1.** Of or relating to the origin or development of something. **2. a.** Of genetics. **b.** Affecting or affected by genes. [From GENESIS.] **—ge·net′i·cal·ly** *adv.*

ge·net·i·cist (jə-nĕt′ĭ-sĭst) *n.* A scientist who specializes in genetics.

genetic code. The basis of heredity that consists of a series of nucleotide arrangements in RNA and DNA and that specifies the amino acid sequence in the synthesis of proteins.

ge·net·ics (jə-nĕt′ĭks) *n.* **1.** (*used with a sing. verb*). The scientific study of the biological processes involved in the transmission of characteristics from an organism to its offspring. **2.** (*used with a pl. verb*). The genetic make-up of an individual or group.

gen·ial (jĕn′yəl, jē′nē-əl) *adj.* **1.** Having a pleasant or friendly disposition or manner; cordial; kindly. **2.** Favorable to life or growth; warm and pleasant: *"The genial sunshine . . . saturating his miserable body with its warmth"* (Jack London). —See Syns at **amiable.** [Latin *geniālis,* of generation or birth, nuptial, joyous, from *Genius,* deity of generation and birth.] **—ge′ni·al′i·ty** (jē′nē-ăl′ĭ-tē) *n.* **—gen′ial·ly** *adv.* **—gen′ial·ness** *n.*

–genic. A suffix meaning generation or production: **antigenic.** [From -GEN.]

ge·nie (jē′nē) *n.* **1.** A supernatural creature who magically grants the wishes of the one who summons him. **2.** Var. of **jinni.** [French *génie,* spirit, from Latin *genius,* guardian spirit, genius.]

ge·ni·i (jē′nē-ī′) *n.* A plural of **genius** (guardian spirit).

gen·i·tal (jĕn′ĭ-təl) *adj.* **1.** Of or relating to biological reproduction. **2.** Of the genitals. [Middle English *genytal,* from Old French *genital,* from Latin *genitālis,* from *gignere,* to beget, produce.]

gen·i·ta·li·a (jĕn′ĭ-tā′lē-ə, -tāl′yə) *pl.n.* The reproductive organs, esp. the external sex organs. [Latin *genitālia (membra),* genital (meinbers), neut. pl. of *genitālis,* genital.]

gen·i·tals (jĕn′ĭ-təlz) *pl.n.* Genitalia.

gen·i·tive (jĕn′ĭ-tĭv) *adj.* **1.** Of or designating a grammatical case that indicates possession or source. **2.** Of or designating an affix or a construction, such as a prepositional phrase, characteristic of this case. —*n.* **1.** The genitive case. **2.** A genitive form or construction. [Middle English *genitif (case),* from Latin *(casus) genitīvus,* "case of production or origin " from *gignere,* to beget, produce.] **—gen′i·ti′val** *adj.*

gen·i·to·u·ri·nar·y (jĕn′ĭ-tō-yŏŏr′ə-nĕr′ē) *adj.* Of the genital and urinary organs or their functions. [GENIT(AL) + URINARY.]

gen·ius (jēn′yəs) *n.* **1.** Brilliant mental ability or outstanding creative power: *the genius of Leonardo da Vinci.* **2.** A person of the highest mental ability or the greatest creative power. **3.** A strong natural talent or ability: *a genius for leadership.* **4.** Skill at imagining and inventing new things; ingenuity: *the genius of American technology.* **5.** A person who is extremely talented or clever at something; a

wizard: *a mechanical genius.* **6.** The prevailing spirit of a place, person, time, or group: *Her songs are lighthearted in keeping with her genius.* **7.** A person who has great influence over another: *dominated by an elder brother, his evil genius.* **8.** *Rom. Myth.* pl. **ge·ni·i.** The guardian spirit of a person or place. [Latin *genius,* guardian spirit.]

gen·o·cide (jĕn′ə-sīd′) *n.* The deliberate killing off of a racial, political, or cultural group. [Greek *genos,* race + -CIDE.] **—gen′o·cid′al** (-sīd′l) *adj.*

ge·nome (jē′nōm′) *n.* A complete haploid set of chromosomes. [GEN(E) + (CHROMOS)OME.]

gen·o·type (jĕn′ə-tīp′) *n.* **1.** The genetic constitution of an organism, esp. as distinguished from its physical appearance. **2.** A group or class of organisms having the same genetic constitution. **3.** The type species of a genus. [Greek *genos* + TYPE.] **—gen′o·typ′ic** (-tĭp′ĭk) or **gen′o·typ′i·cal** *adj.* **—gen′o·typ′i·cal·ly** *adv.* **—gen′o·ty·pic′i·ty** (-tĭ-pĭs′ĭ-tē) *n.*

gen·re (zhän′rə) *n.* **1.** Type; class; variety. **2.** A style of painting concerned with depicting scenes and subjects of common everyday life. **3.** A particular type or category of literary composition or other artistic work: *studied the detective story as a literary genre.* **—modifier:** *a genre painting.* [French, kind, from Old French *gen(d)re,* from Latin *genus* (stem *gener-*), race, kind.]

gens (jĕnz) *n.,* pl. **gen·tes** (jĕn′tēz′). **1.** A group of ancient Roman families descended from a common male ancestor. **2.** Any clan or tribe. [Latin *gēns,* clan.]

gent (jĕnt) *n. Informal.* A man; fellow. [Short for GENTLEMAN.]

gen·teel (jĕn-tēl′) *adj.* **1.** Refined and polite in manner; well-bred. **2.** Free from vulgarity or rudeness. **3.** Trying to seem refined but in an artificial or prudish way. —See Syns at **polite.** [Old French *gentil,* gentle.] **—gen·teel′ly** *adv.* **—gen·teel′ness** *n.*

gen·tes (jĕn′tēz′) *n.* Plural of **gens.**

gen·tian (jĕn′shən) *n.* **1.** Any of numerous plants of the genus *Gentiana,* characteristically having showy blue flowers. **2.** The dried rhizome and roots of a yellow-flowered European gentian, *G. lutea,* sometimes used as a tonic. [Middle English *gencian,* from Old French *genciane,* from Latin *gentiāna.*]

gentian violet. A purple dye used chiefly as a biological stain and bactericide.

Gen·tile or **gen·tile** (jĕn′tīl′) *n.* **1.** Anyone who is not a Jew. **2.** A Christian as distinguished from a Jew. **3.** A pagan or heathen. **4.** Among Mormons, a person who is not a Mormon. —*adj.* Of or relating to a Gentile. [Middle English *gentil, gentyle,* from Late Latin *gentīles,* pagans, heathens, from *gentīlis,* pagan, from Latin, of the same clan, from *gēns,* clan, gens.]

gen·til·i·ty (jĕn-tĭl′ĭ-tē) *n.* **1.** The condition of being genteel; good manners and breeding. **2.** The condition of coming from a family of distinction or high social standing. **3.** Persons of gentle birth or refinement; the gentry. [Middle English *gentilete,* from Old French, from Latin *gentilitās,* clanship, from *gentīlis,* belonging to a clan, gentle.]

gen·tle (jĕn′tl) *adj.* **-tler, -tlest. 1.** Considerate or kindly in disposition; amiable; patient. **2.** Not harsh, severe, or violent; mild; soft: *a gentle scolding.* **3.** Easily managed or handled; docile. **4.** Gradual; not steep or sudden: *a gentle incline.* **5.** Of good family; well-born. **6.** *Archaic.* Noble; chivalrous: *a gentle knight.* —*tr.v.* **-tled, -tling. 1.** To make gentle; pacify; mollify. **2.** To tame or break (a horse). [Middle English *gentil,* well-born, noble, graceful, from Old French, from Latin *gentīlis,* of the same clan, of noble birth, from *gēns,* clan.] **—gen′tle·ness** *n.* **—gen′tly** *adv.*
　　Syns: 1. gentle, mild, soft, softhearted, tender, tenderhearted *adj.* *Core meaning:* Kind and considerate (*a gentle mother*). **2. gentle, docile, meek, tame** *adj.* *Core meaning:* Easily controlled, led, or handled (*a gentle horse*).

gen·tle·folk (jĕn′tl-fōk′) *pl.n.* Also **gen·tle·folks** (-fōks′). Persons of good family and high social standing.

gen·tle·man (jĕn′tl-mən) *n.* **1.** A man of high or noble birth or of superior social standing. **2.** A man whose fine clothes, manners, and speech mark him as a refined, well-bred person. **3.** Any man spoken of in a polite way: *a very nice old gentleman.* **4. gentlemen.** A word used in speaking or writing to men as members of a group: *Good eve-*

ning, ladies and gentlemen. **5.** A manservant; valet.

gen·tle·man·ly (jĕn'tl-mən-lē) *adj.* Of or like a gentleman; courteous, proper, or polite: *gentlemanly behavior.* —**gen'tle·man·li·ness** *n.*

gentleman's agreement. An unwritten agreement guaranteed only by the honor of the participants.

gen·tle·wom·an (jĕn'tl-wŏŏm'ən) *n.* **1.** A woman of high or noble birth or superior social position. **2.** A polite, gracious, or considerate woman.

gen·try (jĕn'trē) *n.* **1.** Well-bred people of good family and high social standing. **2.** A social class ranking next below the nobility. [Middle English *gentri(se)*, gentle birth, from Old French *genterise*, from *gentil*, gentle.]

gen·u·flect (jĕn'yə-flĕkt') *intr.v.* To bend one knee in a kneeling or half-kneeling position, as in worship. [Late Latin *genuflectere* : Latin *genu*, knee + *flectere*, to bend.] —**gen'u·flec'tion** *n.*

gen·u·ine (jĕn'yŏŏ-ĭn) *adj.* **1.** Actually being what it seems or claims to be; real: *genuine sorrow; genuine leather.* **2.** Free from hypocrisy or dishonesty; sincere: *"She found behind his too incessant flattery a genuine affection for his mates"* (Sinclair Lewis). —See Syns at **true.** [Latin *genuīnus*, native, genuine.] —**gen'u·ine·ly** *adv.* —**gen'u·ine·ness** *n.*

ge·nus (jē'nəs) *n., pl.* **gen·er·a** (jĕn'ər-ə). **1.** *Biol.* A taxonomic category ranking below a family and above a species, used in taxonomic nomenclature, either alone or followed by a Latin adjective or epithet, to form the name of a species. **2.** Any class, group, or kind that can be divided into smaller groups. [Latin *genus*, birth, race, kind.]

-geny. A suffix meaning manner of origin or development: *ontogeny.* [Greek *-geneia*, from *-genēs*, born.]

geo-. A prefix meaning the earth: *geotropism.* [Greek *geō-*, from *gē*, earth.]

ge·o·cen·tric (jē'ō-sĕn'trĭk) *adj.* **1.** Of or measured from the center of the earth. **2.** Having the earth as a center: *a geocentric model of the universe.* —**ge'o·cen'tri·cal·ly** *adv.*

ge·o·chem·is·try (jē'ō-kĕm'ĭ-strē) *n.* The chemistry of the composition and alterations of the earth's crust. —**ge'o·chem'i·cal** *adj.* —**ge'o·chem'ist** *n.*

ge·o·chro·nol·o·gy (jē'ō-krə-nŏl'ə-jē) *n.* The chronology of the earth's history as determined by geological data.

ge·ode (jē'ōd') *n.* A small, hollow, usu. spheroidal rock with crystals lining the inside wall. [Latin *geōdēs*, from Greek, earthlike, from *gē*, earth.]

ge·o·des·ic (jē'ō-dĕs'ĭk, -dē'sĭk) *adj.* **1.** *Math.* Of or pertaining to the geometry of geodesics. **2.** Geodetic. —*n. Math.* In three-dimensional Euclidean space, a curve whose principal normal at any point is the normal to the surface on which the curve occurs; the shortest line between two points on any mathematically derived surface.

geodesic dome. A domed or vaulted structure of lightweight straight elements that form interlocking polygons.

ge·od·e·sy (jē-ŏd'ĭ-sē) *n.* The geological science of the size and shape of the earth. [French *geodesie*, from New Latin *geodaesia*, from Greek *geōdaisia*, "division of the earth" : *gē*, earth + *daiesthai*, to divide.] —**ge·od'e·sist** (-sĭst) *n.*

ge·o·det·ic (jē'ə-dĕt'ĭk) *adj.* **1.** Of or pertaining to geodesy. **2.** Geodesic. —**ge'o·det'i·cal·ly** *adv.*

ge·o·graph·ic (jē'ə-grăf'ĭk) or **ge·o·graph·i·cal** (-ĭ-kəl) *adj.* Of or relating to geography. —**ge'o·graph'i·cal·ly** *adv.*

geographic mile. A nautical mile.

ge·og·ra·phy (jē-ŏg'rə-fē) *n., pl.* **-phies. 1.** The study of the earth and its features and of the distribution on the earth of life, including human life and the effects of human activity. **2.** The location and natural features of any area: *studying the geography of California.* **3.** A book on geography. [Latin *geōgraphia*, from Greek.] —**ge·og'ra·pher** *n.*

ge·o·log·ic (jē'ə-lŏj'ĭk) or **ge·o·log·i·cal** (-ĭ-kəl) *adj.* Of or relating to geology. —**ge'o·log'i·cal·ly** *adv.*

ge·ol·o·gy (jē-ŏl'ə-jē) *n., pl.* **-gies. 1.** The scientific study of the origin, history, and structure of the earth. **2.** The structure of a specific region of the earth's surface: *the geology of the Hudson River valley.* [GEO- + -LOGY.] —**ge·ol'o·gist** (-jĭst) *n.*

ge·o·mag·ne·tism (jē'ō-măg'nĭ-tĭz'əm) *n.* **1.** The magnetism of the earth. **2.** The study of the earth's magnetic field. —**ge'o·mag·net'ic** (-măg-nĕt'ĭk) *adj.* —**ge'o·mag·net'i·cal·ly** *adv.*

ge·om·e·ter (jē-ŏm'ĭ-tər) *n.* A mathematician who specializes in geometry; geometrician.

ge·o·met·ric (jē'ə-mĕt'rĭk) or **ge·o·met·ri·cal** (-rĭ-kəl) *adj.* **1.** Of geometry and its methods and principles. **2.** Using simple shapes formed from straight lines or curves: *a geometric design.* —**ge'o·met'ri·cal·ly** *adv.*

ge·om·e·tri·cian (jē-ŏm'ĭ-trĭsh'ən, jē'ə-mĭ-) *n.* A mathematician who specializes in geometry.

geometric mean. The *n*th root, usually the positive *n*th root, of a product of *n* factors.

geometric progression. A sequence of terms, such as 1, 3, 9, 27, 81, each of which is a constant multiple of the immediately preceding term.

ge·om·e·trid (jē-ŏm'ĭ-trĭd) *n.* Any of various moths of the family Geometridae, whose caterpillars move by looping the body in alternate contractions and expansions. Also called **inchworm** and **measuring worm.** —*adj.* Of or belonging to the Geometridae. [New Latin *Geometridae*, "land measurers'" (from the movement of the caterpillars), from Latin *geōmetrēs*, geometrician, from Greek, from *geōmetrein*, to measure land.]

ge·om·e·try (jē-ŏm'ĭ-trē) *n., pl.* **-tries. 1. a.** The mathematics of the properties, measurement, and relationships of points, lines, angles, surfaces, and solids. **b.** A system of geometry: *Euclidean geometry.* **c.** A geometry restricted to a class of problems or objects: *solid geometry.* **2.** Configuration; arrangement. **3.** A surface shape. **4.** Any physical arrangement suggesting geometric forms or lines. [Middle English, from Old French *geometrie*, from Latin *geōmetria*, from Greek, from *geōmetrein*, to measure land : *gē*, earth + *metrein*, to measure, from *metron*, measure.]

ge·o·mor·phol·o·gy (jē'ō-môr-fŏl'ə-jē) *n.* The geological study of the configuration and evolution of land forms. —**ge'o·mor'pho·log'ic** (-môr'fə-lŏj'ĭk), or **ge'o·mor'pho·log'·i·cal** *adj.* —**ge'o·mor'pho·log'i·cal·ly** *adv.*

ge·o·phys·ics (jē'ō-fĭz'ĭks) *n.* (*used with a sing. verb*). The physics of geological phenomena, including fields such as meteorology, oceanography, geodesy, and seismology. —**ge'o·phys'i·cal** *adj.* —**ge'o·phys'i·cist** (-ĭ-sĭst) *n.*

ge·o·pol·i·tics (jē'ō-pŏl'ĭ-tĭks) *n.* (*used with a sing. verb*). The study of how geography, including such factors as natural resources and population distribution, influences international relations. —**ge'o·po·lit'i·cal** (-pə-lĭt'ĭ-kəl) *adj.*

ge·o·tax·is (jē'ō-tăk'sĭs) *n. Biol.* The movement of an organism in response to the forces of gravity. —**ge'o·tac'tic** (-tăk'tĭk) *adj.* —**ge'o·tac'ti·cal·ly** *adv.*

ge·o·ther·mal (jē'ō-thûr'məl) *adj.* Also **ge·o·ther·mic** (-mĭk). Of or relating to the internal heat of the earth: *geothermal energy.*

ge·ot·ro·pism (jē-ŏt'rə-pĭz'əm) *n. Biol.* The response of a living organism to gravity, as the downward growth of plant roots. [GEO- + -TROPISM.] —**ge'o·trop'ic** (jē'ō-trŏp'ĭk) *adj.* —**ge'o·trop'i·cal·ly** *adv.*

ge·ra·ni·um (jĭ-rā'nē-əm) *n.* **1.** Any of various plants of the genus *Geranium*, with divided leaves and pink or purplish flowers. Also called **cranesbill. 2.** Any of various plants of the genus *Pelargonium*, native chiefly to southern Africa, esp. *P. domesticum*, widely cultivated for its showy clusters of red, pink, or white flowers. [Latin, from Greek *geranion*, "small crane" (from the resemblance of the fruit to a crane's bill), from *geranos*, crane.]

geranium

gerbil

ger·bil (jûr'bĭl) *n.* Any of various small, mouselike rodents of the genus *Gerbillus* and related genera, of arid regions

of Africa and Asia Minor, having long hind legs and a long tail. [French *gerbille*, from New Latin *Gerbillus*, dim. of *gerboa*, jerboa, jerboa.]

ger·fal·con (jûr′făl′kən, -fôl′-, -fô′kən) *n.* Var. of **gyrfalcon.**

ger·i·at·ric (jĕr′ē-ăt′rĭk) *adj.* **1.** Of geriatrics. **2.** Of the aged or their characteristic afflictions: *geriatric problems.* —*n.* An aged person viewed as an object of geriatrics or geriatric care. [Greek *gēras*, old age + -IATRIC.]

ger·i·at·rics (jĕr′ē-ăt′rĭks) *n.* *(used with a sing. verb).* The medical study of the biological processes and diseases of old age. —**ger′i·a·tri′cian** (-ə-trĭsh′ən) *n.*

germ (jûrm) *n.* **1.** *Biol.* A small organic structure or cell from which a new organism may develop. **2.** The beginning or first form from which something larger or more complex develops: *the germ of a new theory.* **3.** *Med.* A microorganism, esp. a pathogen. [French *germe*, from Latin *germen*, offshoot, sprout, fetus.]

    Usage: **germ, bacillus, bacteria, microbe, virus.** These nouns denote minute organisms or agents, invisible to the unaided human eye, some of which are related to the production of disease. They are not interchangeable in careful usage except as indicated. *Germ* and *microbe* are nonscientific terms for such microorganisms; in popular usage they usu. refer to disease-producing bodies. *Bacteria* (plural of *bacterium*) is the scientific term for a large group of microorganisms, only some of which produce disease. Many others are active in processes beneficial or not harmful to human, animal, and plant life. *Bacillus* is the scientific word for a specific class of bacteria that includes some disease-producing microorganisms; only in loose popular usage is the term employed as the equivalent of any bacterium or any pathogenic bacterium. *Virus* is the technical term for any of a group of extremely small infective agents capable of producing certain diseases in human, animal, and plant life.

Ger·man (jûr′mən) *adj.* Of, pertaining to, or characteristic of Germany, its people, or their language. —*n.* **1. a.** A native or citizen of Germany. **b.** A person of German descent. **2.** The Germanic language of Germany, Austria, and part of Switzerland.

ger·mane (jər-mān′) *adj.* Closely or naturally related to the matter being considered; pertinent: *One of the panelists kept raising issues that were not germane to the subject.* —See Syns at **relevant.** [Middle English *germa(i)n*, having the same parents.]

Ger·man·ic (jûr-măn′ĭk) *adj.* **1. a.** Characteristic of Germany, any of the German people, or their culture. **b.** Of or pertaining to Teutons. **c.** Of or pertaining to people who speak a Germanic language. **2.** Of or relating to the Germanic languages. —*n.* A branch of the Indo-European language family, comprising English, German, Dutch, Afrikaans, Flemish, Frisian, the Scandinavian languages, and Gothic.

ger·ma·ni·um (jər-mā′nē-əm) *n. Symbol* **Ge** A brittle, crystalline, gray-white metalloid element, widely used as a semiconductor, as an alloying agent and catalyst, and in certain optical glasses. Atomic number 32; atomic weight 72.59; melting point 937.4°C; boiling point 2,830°C; specific gravity 5.323 (25°C); valences 2, 4. [From Latin *Germānia*, Germany.]

German measles. A mild, contagious, viral disease capable of causing congenital defects in infants born to mothers infected during the first three months of pregnancy. Also called **rubella** and **rubeola.**

German shepherd. A large dog of a breed developed in Germany, having a dense brownish or black coat and often trained to assist the police and the blind.

German silver. An alloy, **nickel silver.**

germ cell. A cell, esp. an egg or sperm cell, having reproduction as its principal function.

ger·mi·cide (jûr′mĭ-sīd′) *n.* Any agent that kills germs. [GERM + -CIDE.] —**ger′mi·cid′al** (-sīd′l) *adj.*

ger·mi·nal (jûr′mə-nəl) *adj.* **1.** Of, pertaining to, or having the nature of a germ cell. **2.** Of or in the earliest stage of development. [French, from Latin *germen*, offshoot.]

ger·mi·nant (jûr′mə-nənt) *adj.* Germinating; sprouting.

ger·mi·nate (jûr′mə-nāt′) *v.* **-nat·ed, -nat·ing.** —*intr.v.* To begin to grow; sprout. —*tr.v.* To cause to sprout. [From Latin *germināre*, to sprout, from *germen*, sprout, germ.]

—**ger′mi·na′tion** *n.* —**ger′mi·na′tive** *adj.* —**ger′mi·na′tor** *n.*

germ layer. Any of three cellular layers, the ectoderm, endoderm, or mesoderm, into which most animal embryos differentiate.

germ plasm. 1. The cytoplasm of a germ cell. **2.** Germ cells collectively. **3.** Hereditary material; genes.

germ theory. The doctrine that infectious diseases are caused by the activity of microorganisms within the body.

germ warfare. The use of disease-causing germs as a weapon in war.

geronto– or **geront–.** A prefix meaning old people or old age: **gerontology.** [French *géronto-*, from Greek *gerōn*, old man.]

ger·on·tol·o·gy (jĕr′ən-tŏl′ə-jē) *n.* The scientific study of aging and the problems of the old. [GERONTO- + -LOGY.] —**ge·ron′to·log′i·cal** (jə-rŏn′tl-ŏj′ĭ-kəl) *adj.* —**ger′on·tol′o·gist** *n.*

ger·ry·man·der (jĕr′ē-măn′dər, gĕr′-) *tr.v.* To divide (a state, county, or city) into voting districts in such a way as to give unfair advantage to one party in elections. —*n.* An act or process of gerrymandering. [Elbridge *Gerry* + (*sala*)*mander*, from the shape of an election district formed (1812) in Massachusetts while Gerry was governor.]

ger·und (jĕr′ənd) *n.* The form of a verb ending in *-ing* when it is used as a noun; a verbal noun. [Late Latin *gerundium*, from Latin *gerundum*, acting, carrying, from *gerere*, to carry, act.] —**ge·run′di·al** (jə-rŭn′dē-əl) *adj.*

ge·run·dive (jə-rŭn′dĭv) *n.* A Latin verbal adjective with the construction of a future passive participle, suggesting fitness or propriety, necessity, or imminence. [Middle English *gerundif*, from Late Latin *gerundivus*, from *gerundium*, gerund.]

ges·so (jĕs′ō) *n.* A mixture of plaster of Paris and glue used as a base for low relief or as a surface for painting. [Italian, gypsum, chalk, from Latin *gypsum*, gypsum.]

gest or **geste** (jĕst) *n. Archaic.* **1.** A feat or exploit; a notable deed. **2.** A story of adventure or exploits, esp. one in verse. [Middle English *geste, jeste*, from Old French, from Latin *gesta*, actions, exploits, from *gestus*, past part. of *gerere*, to act, carry.]

ge·stalt psychology (gə-shtält′, -shtôlt′). Also **Ge·stalt psychology.** A school of psychology holding that human beings behave and perceive in unified patterns, the parts of which cannot be understood in isolation.

Ge·sta·po (gə-stä′pō, -shtä′-) *n.* The secret police force of Nazi Germany. [German, short for *Ge(heime) Sta(ats)po(lizei)*, "secret state police."]

ges·tate (jĕs′tāt′) *tr.v.* **-tat·ed, -tat·ing. 1.** To carry (unborn young) within the uterus for a period following conception. **2.** To conceive and develop (a plan or idea) in the mind. [Back-formation from GESTATION.]

ges·ta·tion (jĕ-stā′shən) *n.* **1.** The period of carrying developing offspring in the uterus after conception; pregnancy. **2.** The development of a plan or idea before it is adopted or expressed. —*modifier:* *a gestation period.* [Latin *gestātiō*, from *gestāre*, freq. of *gerere*, to carry, bear.] —**ges·ta′tion·al** *adj.*

geste (jĕst) *n.* Var. of **gest.**

ges·tic·u·late (jĕ-stĭk′yə-lāt′) *v.* **-lat·ed, -lat·ing.** —*intr.v.* To make vigorous gestures, esp. while speaking, that express or emphasize one's meaning. —*tr.v.* To say or express by gestures. [From Latin *gesticulārī*, from

German shepherd

gesticulus, dim. of *gestus*, action, gest.] **—ges·tic′u·la′tive** *adj.* **—ges·tic′u·la′tor** *n.*

ges·tic·u·la·tion (jĕ-stĭk′yə-lā′shən) *n.* **1.** The act of gesticulating. **2.** A vigorous gesture meant to express or emphasize what a speaker is saying. **—ges·tic′u·la·to′ry** (-lə-tôr′ē, -tōr′ē) *adj.*

ges·ture (jĕs′chər) *n.* **1.** A motion of the limbs or body made to express or help express thought or to emphasize speech. **2.** The use of gestures as a means of communication: *By gesture the strangers let us know that they were hungry.* **3.** An act or expression made as a sign of one's intentions or attitude: *The oldest guest was seated at the head of the table as a gesture of respect.* *—v.* **-tured, -tur·ing.** *—intr.v.* To make or signal with gestures: *The policeman gestured for me to approach him.* *—tr.v.* To express or direct by gestures: *She gestured her agreement.* [Medieval Latin *gestūra*, bearing, carriage, from Latin *gestus*, past part. of *gerere*, to carry, act.] **—ges′tur·er** *n.*

Ge·sund·heit (gə-zŏŏnt′hīt′) *interj.* A word used to wish good health to a person who has just sneezed. [German, "health."]

get (gĕt) *v.* **got** (gŏt) or *archaic* **gat** (găt), **got** or **got·ten** (gŏt′n), **get·ting.** *—tr.v.* **1.** To obtain or acquire: *get a new car.* **2.** To procure; secure: *getting more money.* **3.** To go after; fetch: *getting the mail.* **4.** To reach or make contact with by or as if by radio or telephone. **5.** To earn; gain: *get a reward.* **6.** To receive or come into possession of: *get a present.* **7.** To buy. **8.** To be subjected to: *get a tongue-lashing.* **9.** *Informal.* To meet with; suffer: *He got a few knocks, but he'll recover.* **10.** To catch; contract: *They all got chicken pox at once.* **11.** To have or reach by calculation: *If you add them, you'll get 1,000.* **12.** To have. Used only in the present perfect tense: *I've got a large collection of books.* **13.** To gain understanding or mastery of by study: *I must get this by heart.* **14.** To understand; comprehend: *Do you get his point?* **15.** *Informal.* To register or catch, as by eye or ear: *I'm sorry, I didn't get your name.* **16.** To give birth to; beget. **17.** To prepare or make ready: *get dinner.* **18.** To cause to become or to be in a specified condition: *getting the car started.* **19.** To cause to move, come, or go: *Get that dog out of here!* **20.** To bring or take: *I'll get him in here, and you can talk to him.* **21.** To induce or persuade; prevail upon: *I'll get my friend to show you his house.* **22.** To overpower; destroy: *Frost got our tomato crop.* **23.** To capture or catch: *The police got him.* **24.** *Slang.* To cause harm to: *I'll get you for that remark.* **25.** *Informal.* To strike or hit; affect: *That blow got him on the chin.* **26.** *Slang.* To arouse strong, usu. negative feelings in: *Noisy eaters really get me.* **27.** To have the obligation; must. Used only in the present perfect tense: *I have got to go.* **28.** To be able or allowed: *I asked permission and got to leave school early.* *—intr.v.* **1.** To become or grow. Used as a linking verb: *getting well after a long illness.* **2.** To arrive: *When will we get to New York?* **3.** To go; move: *get out of the car.* **4.** *Informal.* To start: *Get going!* **5.** *Regional & Informal.* To be off; depart: *Now get!* **—See Syns at annoy.** *—phrasal verbs.* **get about** (or **around**). **1.** To move around: *He gets about by himself now.* **2.** *Informal.* To be socially active. **3.** To spread or travel: *The news got around quickly.* **get across. 1.** To make understandable or clear: *Am I getting this across to you?* **2.** To be clear or understandable: *It's not getting across to him.* **get along. 1.** To be on friendly terms. **2.** To manage with reasonable success: *He hasn't much money, but he gets along.* **3.** To make progress; advance: *How's your project getting along?* **4.** To advance in years. **get around. 1.** To evade; circumvent: *trying to get around the rules.* **2.** *Informal.* To convince or gain the favor of by flattering or cajoling.—See Syns at **avoid.** **get around to.** To consider or deal with after a postponement. **get at. 1.** To determine; uncover: *I'm trying to get at the truth.* **2.** To reach; find a way to: *It's under the desk and I can't get at it.* **3.** To lead up to or arrive at: *Do you understand what I'm getting at?* **get away.** To escape; get away with. *Informal.* To succeed in doing without being found out or punished. **get back at.** *Informal.* To retaliate or have revenge against: *He swears he'll get back at him.* **get by. 1.** To pass within range of, esp. without drawing unfavorable attention: *His past record got by the judge altogether.* **2.** To manage; survive: *It will be a hard year, but we'll get by.* **get**

down to. To concentrate on; give full attention to: *Let's get down to the real problems.* **get in. 1.** To arrive: *What time does the train get in?* **2.** To inject, as into a conversation: *He gets in a great many references to himself.* **3.** To receive: *The store got in a new shipment.* **4.** *Slang.* To gain favor: *trying to get in with the new teacher.* **get off. 1.** To get down from or out of. **2.** To write and send: *got off a telegram.* **3.** To escape, as punishment or labor: *He got off scot-free.* **get on. 1.** To climb onto or into; enter. **2.** To get along. **3.** To advance: *It's getting on toward noon. He's getting on in years.* **get out. 1.** To leave. **2.** To become public: *The secret got out.* **get out of. 1.** To derive or draw: *He got very little out of the book.* **2.** To avoid. **3.** To escape. **get over. 1.** To get across; convey. **2.** To recover from. **get through. 1.** To finish or complete. **2.** To undergo and survive: *I wonder if that tree will get through the winter.* **get through to. 1.** To make contact with. **2.** To make understandable or apparent to. **get to. 1.** To reach: *We never got to that point.* **2.** *Informal.* To happen to start: *Then we got to remembering good times.* **3.** To make contact with: *Your message is getting to me.* **4.** *Informal.* To have an effect on: *His conceit really gets to me.* **—See Syns at affect. get together. 1.** To come together; assemble. **2.** To put together; collect. **3.** To agree. **get up. 1.** To arise, as from bed. **2.** To create; make: *got up a makeshift shelter.* **3.** *Informal.* To dress or make up: *was got up as an Arabian princess.* **get with.** *Slang.* To become up to date with: *You have to get with the new styles.* *—n.* **1.** The act of begetting. **2.** Progeny; offspring. **3.** *Tennis.* A return on a shot that seems impossible to reach. **—idioms. get it. 1.** *Informal.* To understand: *I just don't get it.* **2.** *Informal.* To be punished or scolded. **get nowhere.** To make no progress or have no success. **get there.** *Informal.* To attain one's goal: *If you try hard enough, you'll get there.* [Middle English *getten*, from Old Norse *geta*.] **—get′ter** *n.*

Usage: **get.** The past tense is *got*, the past participle *got* or *gotten*. (In British English *got* is virtually the only form of the past participle.) In usage, the constructions *has* (or *have*) *got* and *has* (or *have*) *gotten* are distinguished as follows: *got* indicates possession (*has got two cars*) without indication of time, and *gotten* usu. implies, besides possession, the idea of recent acquisition (*has gotten two cars*). Esp. in writing, the idea of mere possession is better expressed without *got*—by *has* or *have* alone: *has* (or *have*) *two cars.*

get·a·way (gĕt′ə-wā′) *n.* **1.** An act of escaping. **2.** The start, as of a race; takeoff.

get-to·geth·er (gĕt′tə-gĕth′ər) *n.* An informal meeting or small party.

get-up (gĕt′ŭp′) *n.* An outfit or costume, esp. one that is odd or remarkable: *wore an outlandish get-up to the masquerade party.*

get-up-and-go (gĕt′ŭp-ən-go′) *n.* *Informal.* Ambition and energy; drive.

gew·gaw (gyŏŏ′gô′) *n.* A showy but worthless trinket; bauble. [Orig. unknown.]

gey·ser (gī′zər) *n.* A natural hot spring that throws out a spray of steam and water from time to time. [Icelandic *Geysir*, "gusher," the name of a hot spring in Iceland, from *geysa*, to gush, from Old Norse.]

ghast·ly (găst′lē) *adj.* **-li·er, -li·est. 1.** Terrifying; dreadful: *ghastly tales of starvation and disease.* **2.** Having a deathlike pallor: *the ghastly faces of the miners.* **3.** Extremely unpleasant or bad: *a ghastly little book.* *—adv.* Dreadfully; horribly. [Middle English *gastlich*, from Old English *gāstlīc*, spiritual, ghostly, ghastly, from *gāst*, soul, ghost.] **—ghast′li·ness** *n.*

Syns: **1. ghastly, grim, grisly, gruesome, hideous, horrible, horrid, lurid, macabre** *adj. Core meaning:* Shockingly repellent (*the ghastly sight of starving refugees*). **2. ghastly, cadaverous, deathly, ghostly, spectral** *adj. Core meaning:* Gruesomely suggestive of ghosts or death (*the ghastly figure of the Headless Horseman; the ghastly pallor of the dying patient*).

ghat (gôt, gät) *n.* Also **ghaut. 1.** A mountain pass. **2.** A mountain chain. **3.** A flight of steps down to the bank of a river. [Hindi *ghāt*, from Sanskrit *ghaṭṭa*.]

gher·kin (gûr′kĭn) *n.* **1. a.** A tropical American vine, *Cucumis anguria*, bearing prickly, edible fruit. **b.** The fruit of this vine. **2.** A small cucumber, esp. one used for pickling.

| ă pat | ā pay | â care | ä father | ĕ pet | ē be | hw which | ĭ pit | ī tie | î pier | ŏ pot | ō toe | ô paw, for | oi noise |
| ŏŏ took | ŏŏ boot | ou out | th thin | *th* this | ŭ cut | | û urge | zh vision | ə about, item, edible, gallop, circus |

[Dutch *augurkje*, pickled gherkin, ult. from Late Greek *angourion*.]

ghet·to (gĕt′ō) *n.*, *pl.* **-tos** or **-toes**. **1.** A section or quarter in a European city to which Jews are or were restricted. **2.** A slum section of an American city occupied predominantly by blacks or Spanish-speaking people: "*A ghetto can be improved in one way only: out of existence*" (James Baldwin). **—modifier:** *ghetto children.* [Italian *ghetto.*]

ghost (gōst) *n.* **1.** The spirit of a dead person, supposed to haunt or appear to living persons; a phantom; specter. **2.** A slight trace or hint; a vestige: *a ghost of a smile.* **3.** A false image, often faint, produced along with the correct image, as in television or photography. **4.** *Informal.* A person hired to write in another's name; a ghostwriter. *—intr.v. Informal.* To work as a ghostwriter. *—tr.v.* **1.** To haunt. **2.** *Informal.* To write as a ghostwriter. **—idiom. give up the ghost.** To die. [Middle English *gost*, from Old English *gāst.*]

ghost·ly (gōst′lē) *adj.* **-li·er, -li·est. 1.** Of or like a ghost; spectral. **2.** Spiritual. —See Syns at **ghastly. —ghost′li·ness** *n.*

ghost·write (gōst′rīt′) *v.* **-wrote** (-rōt′), **-writ·ten** (-rīt′n), **-writ·ing.** *—intr.v.* To work as a ghostwriter. *—tr.v.* To write (something) as a ghostwriter.

ghost·writ·er (gōst′rī′tər) *n.* A person who writes for and gives credit of authorship to another person who has hired him to do so.

ghoul (gōōl) *n.* **1.** An evil spirit in Moslem folklore that plunders graves and feeds on corpses. **2.** A grave robber. **3.** A person who enjoys loathsome things. [Arabic *ghūl*, from *ghāla*, he took suddenly.] **—ghoul′ish** *adj.* **—ghoul′ish·ly** *adv.* **—ghoul′ish·ness** *n.*

GI (jē′ī′) *n.*, *pl.* **GIs** or **GI's.** An enlisted man in any of the U.S. armed forces. **—modifier:** *GI boots; a GI haircut.* *—tr.v.* **GI'd, GI'ing.** To scrub or clean thoroughly, as in preparation for a military inspection. [Abbreviation for *galvanized iron*, a term used for items such as trash cans, but later taken to be abbreviation for *government issue.*]

gi·ant (jī′ənt) *n.* **1.** A person or thing of extraordinary size or importance: *He is a giant in his field.* **2.** One of the manlike beings of great height and strength in myth and folklore. *—adj.* Of immense size; gigantic; huge: *a giant stadium.* [Middle English *geant*, from Old French, from Latin *gigās*, from Greek *gigas.*]

Syns: giant, colossal, elephantine, enormous, gargantuan, gigantic, herculean, huge, immense, jumbo, mammoth, massive, mighty, monstrous, monumental, mountainous, stupendous, titan, titanic, tremendous, vast *adj. Core meaning:* Of extraordinary size and power (*a giant linebacker; a giant corporation*).

gi·ant·ism (jī′ən-tīz′əm) *n.* **1.** The condition of being a giant. **2.** *Pathol.* **Gigantism.**

gib (gĭb) *n.* An often wedge-shaped piece of wood or metal designed to hold parts of a machine or structure in place or provide a bearing surface. [Orig. unknown.]

gib·ber (jĭb′ər, gĭb′-) *intr.v.* To speak rapidly and unintelligibly; to chatter. *—n.* Senseless talk; gibberish. [Imit.]

gib·ber·ish (jĭb′ər-ĭsh, gĭb′-) *n.* Nonsensical, rapid speech; prattle.

gib·bet (jĭb′ĭt) *n.* **1.** A gallows. **2.** An upright post with a crosspiece, forming a T-shaped structure from which to hang executed criminals for public viewing. *—tr.v.* **-bet·ed** or **-bet·ted, -bet·ing** or **-bet·ting. 1.** To execute by hanging. **2.** To hang on a gibbet for public viewing. **3.** To expose to public ridicule. [Middle English *gibet*, from Old French, dim. of *gibe*, staff, club.]

gib·bon (gĭb′ən) *n.* Any of several arboreal apes of the genera *Hylobates* or *Symphalangus*, of tropical Asia, with a slender body and long arms. [French, perh. from a native word in India.]

gib·bous (gĭb′əs) *adj.* **1.** Rounded; convex; protuberant. **2.** More than half but less than fully illuminated: *the gibbous moon.* **3.** Hunchbacked. [Middle English, from Late Latin *gebbōsus*, humpbacked, from *gibbus*, hump.] **—gib′bous·ly** *adv.* **—gib′bous·ness** *n.*

gibe (jīb) Also **jibe.** *—v.* **gibed, gib·ing.** *—intr.v.* To make heckling or mocking remarks. *—tr.v.* To reproach by taunting; scoff at. —See Syns at **ridicule.** *—n.* A scornful or sarcastic remark; a taunt. [Poss. from Old French *giber*,

to handle roughly.] **—gib′er** *n.* **—gib′ing·ly** *adv.*

Usage: gibe, jibe. As verbs and nouns both words express the sense of taunting or scoffing, but only *jibe* is used for the verb expressing agreement.

gib·let (jĭb′lĭt) *n.* The heart, liver, or gizzard of a fowl. **—modifier:** *giblet gravy.* [Middle English *gibelet*, from Old French, prob. from *gibier*, hunting, game.]

gid (gĭd) *n.* A disease of sheep caused by the presence of the larva of a tapeworm, *Taenia caenurus*, in the brain. [Back-formation from GIDDY.]

gid·dap (gĭ-dăp′) *intr.v.* Also **gid·dy·ap** (gĭd′ē-ăp′). To go ahead or go faster. Used as a command to a horse.

gid·dy (gĭd′ē) *adj.* **-di·er, -di·est. 1. a.** Having a whirling or lightheaded sensation; dizzy. **b.** Causing or capable of causing dizziness: *a giddy climb to the topmast.* **2.** Frivolous and lighthearted; flighty: *giddy young girls.* [Middle English *gidy*, mad, foolish, from Old English *gydig*, possessed by a god, insane.] **—gid′di·ly** *adv.* **—gid′di·ness** *n.*

gid·dy·ap (gĭd′ē-ăp′) *intr.v.* Var. of **giddap.**

gie (gē) *v. Scot.* To give.

gift (gĭft) *n.* **1.** Something given voluntarily and without compensation; a present. **2.** The act, right, or power of giving: *Your request is not in my gift.* **3.** A special ability or facility; talent: *a gift for languages.* [Middle English, from Old Norse *gipt, gift.*]

gift·ed (gĭf′tĭd) *adj.* Endowed with great natural ability; talented: *a gifted artist.* **—gift′ed·ness** *n.*

gig¹ (gĭg) *n.* **1.** A light, two-wheeled carriage drawn by one horse. **2. a.** A long, light ship's boat usu. reserved for use by the captain. **b.** A fast, light rowboat. *—intr.v.* **gigged, gig·ging.** To ride in a gig. [Middle English *gigg*, giddy girl, something that whirls.]

gig² (gĭg) *n.* **1.** A set of hooks that is dragged through a school of fish to hook them in the bodies. **2.** A pronged spear for fishing. *—v.* **gigged, gig·ging.** *—tr.v.* To catch with a gig. *—intr.v.* To fish with a gig. [Short for *fishgig*, from Spanish *fisga*, spear for fishing.]

gig³ (gĭg) *n. Slang.* A mark recorded against someone for a fault or infraction, esp. in the armed services; demerit. *—tr.v.* **gigged, gig·ging.** *Slang.* To give a demerit to. [Orig. unknown.]

gig⁴ (gĭg) *n. Slang.* A job, esp. an engagement for a musician. [Orig. unknown.]

gi·gan·tic (jī-găn′tĭk) *adj.* **1.** Like or as big as a giant: *a gigantic warrior.* **2.** Extremely large or enormous: *a gigantic industrial enterprise; a gigantic earthquake.* —See Syns at **giant.** [From Latin *gigās*, giant.] **—gi·gan′ti·cal·ly** *adv.*

gi·gan·tism (jī-găn′tĭz′əm, jī′gən-) *n.* **1.** Excessive growth of the body or any of its parts as a result of oversecretion of the pituitary growth hormone. Also called **giantism. 2.** Abnormally large size.

gig·gle (gĭg′əl) *intr.v.* **-gled, -gling.** To laugh in a half-suppressed or nervous way. *—n.* A short, silly, or nervous laugh. [Imit.] **—gig′gler** *n.* **—gig′gling·ly** *adv.*

gig·gly (gĭg′lē) *adj.* **-gli·er, -gli·est.** Inclined to giggle.

gig·o·lo (jĭg′ə-lō′, zhĭg′-) *n.*, *pl.* **-los.** A man who is kept as a lover and supported by a woman. [French, from *gigolette*, dance-hall pickup, from *giguer*, to dance, from *gigue*, leg, fiddle, from Old French, from Old High German *giga.*]

gig·ot (jĭg′ət, zhē-gō′) *n.* **1.** A leg of mutton, lamb, or veal for cooking. **2.** A leg-of-mutton sleeve. [Old French, dim. of *gigue*, leg, fiddle.]

Gi·la monster (hē′lə). A venomous lizard, *Heloderma sus-*

gibbon | Gila monster

---

pectum, of the southwestern United States and northern Mexico, with a stout body covered with black and pinkish or yellowish scales. [After the *Gila* River, Arizona.]

gild¹ (gĭld) *tr.v.* **gild·ed** or **gilt** (gĭlt), **gild·ing. 1.** To cover with or as if with a thin layer of gold: *"The lanterns gilded the leaves of the trees"* (Flannery O'Connor). **2.** To give an often deceptively attractive or improved appearance to. **—idiom. gild the lily.** To adorn unnecessarily something already beautiful. [Middle English *gilden,* from Old English *gyldan.*] **—gild'er** *n.*

gild² (gĭld) *n.* Var. of **guild.**

gil·der (gĭl'dər) *n.* Var. of **guilder.**

gill¹ (gĭl) *n.* **1.** The respiratory organ of fishes, larval amphibians, and numerous aquatic invertebrates. **2.** Often **gills.** The wattle of a bird. **3.** Often **gills.** *Informal.* The area around the chin and neck: *green around the gills.* **4.** *Bot.* One of the thin, platelike structures on the underside of the cap of a mushroom or similar fungus. [Middle English *gille.*]

gill² (jĭl) *n. Abbr.* **gi 1.** A unit of volume or capacity in the U.S. Customary System, used in liquid measure, equal to 4 fluid ounces ($^1/_4$ pint) or 7.216 cubic inches. **2.** A unit of volume or capacity in the British Imperial System, used in dry and liquid measure, equal to 5 fluid ounces ($^1/_4$ pint) or 8.670 cubic inches. [Middle English *gille,* from Old French, from Late Latin *gillo,* water pot.]

gill³ (gĭl) *n. Brit.* **1.** A ravine. **2.** A narrow stream. [Middle English *gille,* from Old Norse *gil.*]

gil·lie (gĭl'ē) *n.* Also **gil·ly** *pl.* **-lies.** *Scot.* A professional guide and servant for sportsmen, esp. in fishing and deer-stalking. [Scottish Gaelic *gille,* boy, servant.]

gil·li·flow·er (gĭl'ē-flou'ər) *n.* Var. of **gillyflower.**

gill net (gĭl). A fishnet set vertically in the water so that fish swimming into it are entangled by the gills.

gill slit (gĭl). One of several narrow external openings connecting with the pharynx, present in all vertebrates during embryonic development and characteristic of sharks and related fishes.

gil·ly (gĭl'ē) *n.* Var. of **gillie.**

gil·ly·flow·er (gĭl'ē-flou'ər) *n.* Also **gil·li·flow·er. 1.** The carnation or a similar plant of the genus *Dianthus.* **2.** Any of several other plants having fragrant flowers, as the stock or wallflower. [Alteration of Middle English *gilofre,* from Old French *girofre,* from Medieval Latin *caryophylum,* clove, from Greek *karuophullon* : *karuon,* nut + *phullon,* leaf.]

gilt (gĭlt) *v.* A past tense and past participle of **gild.** *—adj.* **1.** Gilded. **2.** Having the appearance of gold. *—n.* **1.** A thin layer of gold or gold-colored material applied to a surface. **2.** Superficial brilliance; glitter.

gilt-edged (gĭlt'ĕjd') *adj.* Also **gilt-edge** (-ĕj'). **1.** Having gilded edges: *the gilt-edged pages of a Bible.* **2.** Of the highest quality or value: *gilt-edged securities.*

gim·bals (jĭm'bəlz, gĭm'-) *pl.n.* A device consisting of two rings mounted on axes at right angles to each other so that an object such as a ship's compass will remain suspended in a horizontal plane between them regardless of the motion of the ship. [Pl. of *gimbal,* from Old French *gemel,* a ring made of two interlocking rings, from Latin *gemellus,* dim. of *geminus,* twin.]

gim·crack (jĭm'krăk') *n.* A cheap and showy object of little or no use; a knickknack. *—adj.* Cheap and shoddy; flimsy. [Middle English *gibecrake,* ornament, *gimcrack.*] **—gim'crack'er·y** *n.*

gim·let (gĭm'lĭt) *n.* A small hand tool with a pointed spiral tip, used for boring holes. [Middle English, from Old French *guimbelet,* prob. from Middle Dutch *wimmelkijn,* dim. of *wimmel,* auger.]

gim·mick (gĭm'ĭk) *n. Slang.* **1.** A device employed to cheat or deceive: *a magician's gimmick.* **2.** A novel idea, method, or slogan employed to promote a project: *an advertising gimmick.* **3.** An undesirable feature concealed or played down in the promotion of a project; a catch. [Orig. unknown.] **—gim'mick·ry** *n.* **—gim'mick·y** *adj.*

gimp¹ (gĭmp) *n.* A narrow braid or cord of fabric, sometimes stiffened, used to trim or pipe clothes, curtains, or upholstered furniture. *—tr.v.* To trim or edge with gimp. [French *guimpe,* from Old French *guimple,* from Old High German *wimpal.*]

gimp² (gĭmp) *n. Slang.* **1.** A limp or limping gait. **2.** A person who limps; a cripple. *—intr.v. Slang.* To limp. [Orig. unknown.] **—gimp'y** *adj.*

gin¹ (jĭn) *n.* A strong alcoholic beverage made by distilling rye or other grains with juniper berries. [Shortened from Dutch *jenever,* from Middle Dutch *geniver, genever,* juniper, from Old French *geneivre,* from Latin *jūniperus,* juniper.]

gin² (jĭn) *n.* **1.** Any of several machines or devices, as: **a.** A machine for hoisting or moving heavy objects. **b.** A pile driver. **c.** A snare or trap for game. **d.** A pump operated by a windmill. **2.** A **cotton gin.** *—tr.v.* **ginned, gin·ning. 1.** To remove the seeds from (cotton) with a gin. **2.** To trap in a gin. [Middle English *gin,* short for *engin,* engine.]

gin³ (jĭn) *n.* A card game, **gin rummy.**

gin·ger (jĭn'jər) *n.* **1. a.** A plant, *Zingiber officinale,* of tropical Asia, with yellowish-green flowers and a pungent, aromatic rootstock. **b.** The rootstock of this plant, often dried and powdered and used as flavoring, or, in sugared form, as a sweetmeat. **c.** Any of various other plants of the family Zingiberaceae, having variously colored, often fragrant flowers. **2.** A reddish brown. **3.** *Informal.* Liveliness; vigor; pep. **—modifier:** *a ginger cookie.* *—adj.* Reddish brown. [Middle English *gingivere,* from Old English *gingifer* and Old French *gingivre,* from Medieval Latin *gingiber,* from Latin *zinziberi,* from Greek *ziggiberis,* ult. from Sanskrit *śṛṅgaveram.*]

ginger ale. A carbonated soft drink flavored with ginger.

gin·ger·bread (jĭn'jər-brĕd') *n.* **1. a.** A dark molasses cake flavored with ginger. **b.** A soft molasses and ginger cookie cut in various shapes and sometimes elaborately decorated with colored frosting. **2.** Any elaborate ornamentation, esp. in architecture. [Middle English *gingebred,* preserved ginger, alteration of Old French *gingebras,* from Medieval Latin *gingibrātum,* from *gingiber,* ginger.]

gin·ger·ly (jĭn'jər-lē) *adv.* Cautiously; carefully: *He patted the big dog gingerly.* *—adj.* Cautious; careful. [Poss. from Old French *gensor,* compar. of *gent,* pretty, of noble birth, gentle.]

gin·ger·snap (jĭn'jər-snăp') *n.* A flat, brittle cookie spiced with ginger and sweetened with molasses.

gin·ger·y (jĭn'jə-rē) *adj.* **1.** Having the spicy flavor of ginger. **2.** Sharp and pungent; biting: *a gingery remark.*

ging·ham (gĭng'əm) *n.* A light cotton cloth woven in stripes, checks, plaids, or solid colors. [Dutch *gingang,* from Malay *ginggang, gênggang,* "interspace."]

gin·gi·vi·tis (jĭn'jə-vī'tĭs) *n.* Inflammation of the gums. [Latin *gingīva,* gum + -ITIS.]

ging·ko (gĭng'kō) *n.* Var. of **ginkgo.**

gink (gĭngk) *n. Slang.* A man or boy, esp. one considered odd in some way. [Orig. unknown.]

gink·go (gĭng'kō) *n., pl.* **-goes.** Also **ging·ko** *pl.* **-koes.** A tree, *Ginkgo biloba,* native to China, with fan-shaped leaves and fleshy, yellowish fruit, often used as an ornamental street tree. [Japanese *ginkyō.*]

gin rummy. A variety of rummy in which a player may win by matching all his cards or may end the game by melding when his unmatched cards add up to ten points or less. Also called **gin.**

gin·seng (jĭn'sĕng') *n.* **1.** Any of several plants of the genus *Panax,* esp. *P. schinseng,* of eastern Asia, or *P. quinquefolium,* of North America, with small greenish flowers and a forked root believed to have medicinal properties. **2.** The root of either of these plants. [Mandarin *jen² shen¹* : *jen²,* man (from the resemblance of the root to the human form) + *shen¹,* ginseng.]

Gip·sy (jĭp'sē) *n. & adj.* Var. of **Gypsy.**

gi·raffe (jĭ-răf') *n.* An African ruminant mammal, *Giraffa camelopardis,* having a very long neck and legs, a tan coat with brown blotches, and short horns. [Italian *giraffa,* from Arabic *zirāfah.*]

gird (gûrd) *tr.v.* **gird·ed** or **girt** (gûrt), **gird·ing. 1.** To encircle with a belt or band. **2.** To fasten or secure with a belt: *gird on their trusty swords.* **3.** To surround: *an island girded by water.* **4.** To equip or endow. **5.** To prepare (oneself) for action: *We girded ourselves for an attack.* **—See Syns at surround.** [Middle English *girden,* from Old English *gyrdan.*]

gird·er (gûr'dər) *n.* A horizontal beam, as of steel or wood, used as a main support for a building or other structure.

gir·dle (gûr′dl) *n.* **1.** A belt, sash, or band worn around the waist. **2.** An elastic undergarment, lighter than a corset, worn by women to hold in the waist and hips. **3.** Anything that surrounds like a belt: *Just beyond the four inner planets is a girdle of small ones, the asteroids.* —*tr.v.* **-dled,** **-dling.** **1.** To put an encircling garment around: *He girdled his waist with a red sash.* **2.** To encircle or surround: *A moat girdled the castle.* **3.** To remove a beltlike strip of bark from around the trunk of (a tree). [Middle English *girdel,* from Old English *gyrdel.*] —**gir′dler** *n.*

girl (gûrl) *n.* **1.** A female who has not yet reached womanhood. **2.** A young woman. **3.** A daughter: *She's my sister's girl.* **4.** *Informal.* A female servant: *A new girl is reporting for work this morning.* **5.** *Informal.* A female friend: *a bridge game with the girls.* **6.** *Informal.* A sweetheart or girlfriend: *She's my girl, and you can't dance with her.* [Middle English *girle.*]

girl·friend (gûrl′frĕnd′) *n.* Also **girl friend.** **1.** A female friend. **2.** *Informal.* A sweetheart or favored female companion of a man.

girl·hood (gûrl′hŏŏd′) *n.* The condition or time of being a girl.

girl·ish (gûr′lĭsh) *adj.* Of, like, often suitable for a girl or girls. —**girl′ish·ly** *adv.* —**girl′ish·ness** *n.*

Girl Scout. A member of the Girl Scouts, an organization for girls between 7 and 17 that helps to develop physical fitness, good character, and homemaking ability.

girt¹ (gûrt) *tr.v.* **1.** To gird. **2.** To measure the girth of. [Var. of GIRD.]

girt² (gûrt) *v.* A past tense and past participle of **gird.**

girth (gûrth) *n.* **1.** The distance around something; circumference. **2.** The size of something; bulk. **3.** A strap encircling an animal's body to secure a load or saddle upon its back; a cinch. —*tr.v.* **1.** To measure the circumference of. **2.** To encircle. **3.** To secure with a girth. [Middle English *gerth,* from Old Norse *gyŏrdh,* girdle.]

gis·mo (gĭz′mō) *n., pl.* **-mos.** Also **giz·mo.** *Slang.* A mechanical device or part the name of which is forgotten or unknown. [Orig. unknown.]

gist (jĭst) *n.* The central idea; essence: *The news summary gave the gist of the President's speech.* —See Syns at **heart.** [From Old French *(cest action) gist,* (this action) lies, from *gesir,* to lie, from Latin *jacēre,* from *jacere,* to throw.]

give (gĭv) *v.* **gave** (gāv), **giv·en** (gĭv′ən), **giv·ing.** —*tr.v.* **1.** To make a present of: *He gave her flowers for her birthday.* **2.** To deliver in exchange or payment; to pay: *He will give five dollars for the book.* **3.** To put temporarily at another's disposal; entrust: *give them the cottage for a week.* **4.** To place in the hands of: to pass: *Give me the scissors.* **5.** To convey or offer for conveyance: *Give him my best wishes.* **6.** To bestow; confer: *give authority.* **7.** To impart: *give order to chaos.* **8.** To grant: *give permission.* **9.** To contribute; donate: *give one's time.* **10.** To be a source of; afford: *His remark gave offense.* **11.** To expose or subject to: *She gave him the measles.* **12.** To produce; bring forth: *This cow gives three gallons of milk per day.* **13.** To provide (something required or expected): *give one's name and address.* **14.** To administer: *give a spanking.* **15.** To allow: *give odds of five to one.* **16.** To relinquish; yield: *give ground.* **17.** To emit or utter: *give a sigh.* **18.** To allot; assign: *give her five minutes to finish.* **19.** To ascribe to; attribute to: *give him the blame.* **20.** To stage: *give a dinner party.* **21.** To offer: *give a toast.* **22.** To show: *give promise of brilliance.* **23.** To perform for an audience: *give a play.* **24.** To submit for consideration or acceptance; tender: *give an opinion.* **25.** To devote: *give oneself to one's work.* —*intr.v.* **1.** To make gifts or donations: *give generously to charity.* **2.** To be unable to hold up; yield: *The dike gave under the pressure of the flood water.* **3.** To afford a view or access; open: *The French doors give onto a terrace.* —*phrasal verbs.* **give away.** **1.** To make a gift of. **2.** To present (a bride) to the bridegroom at a wedding ceremony. **3.** To reveal or make known, often by accident. **give back.** To return: *Give me back my book.* **give in.** To surrender; yield. **give off.** To send forth; emit; discharge: *Some chemical changes give off energy.* **give out.** **1.** To let (something) be known: *gave out the bad news.* **2.** To distribute: *give out surplus food to the needy.* **3.** To break down; fail: *My watch gave out.* **4.** To become used up; run out: *His supply of gloves gave out.* **give over.** **1.** To hand over. **2.** To devote; make available for a purpose: *The last part of the program is given over to questions from the audience.* **give up.** **1.** To surrender; admit defeat. **2.** To stop; leave off: *give up smoking.* **3.** To part with; relinquish. **4.** To abandon hope for. —See Syns at **abandon.** —*n. Informal.* Elasticity; springiness: *The mattress has lots of give.* [Middle English *given,* from Old English *giefan.*] —**giv′er** *n.*

give-and-take (gĭv′ən-tāk′) *n.* **1.** Willingness on both sides to make concessions; compromise. **2.** A lively exchange: *the give-and-take of our student debates.*

give·a·way (gĭv′ə-wā′) *n. Informal.* **1.** Something given away at no charge. **2.** Something that betrays or exposes, often accidentally.

giv·en (gĭv′ən) *adj.* **1.** Specified; fixed: *a given date.* **2.** Granted as an assumption; acknowledged: *Given their superiority, we can't expect to win.* **3.** Having a tendency; inclined: *He is given to brooding.*

given name. A name given at birth or at baptism as distinguished from a surname.

giz·mo (gĭz′mō) *n.* Var. of **gismo.**

giz·zard (gĭz′ərd) *n.* **1.** An enlargement of the alimentary canal in birds, often having dense muscular walls and containing fine grit eaten to aid in the digestion of seeds. **2.** A similar digestive organ of certain invertebrates, such as the earthworm. [Middle English *giser,* from Old French *giser, gezier,* from Latin *gigeria,* cooked entrails of poultry, poss. from Persian *jigar.*]

gla·brous (glā′brəs) *adj. Biol.* Having no hairs or down; smooth. [From Latin *glaber,* hairless, bald.]

gla·cé (glă-sā′) *adj.* **1.** Having a smooth, glossy surface. **2.** Coated with a sugar glaze; candied. [French, past part. of *glacer,* to ice, glaze, from *glace,* ice, from Latin *glaciēs.*]

gla·cial (glā′shəl) *adj.* **1.** Of, relating to, or derived from a glacier: *glacial deposits.* **2.** Often **Glacial.** Characterized or dominated by the existence of glaciers: *the Glacial periods of the Pleistocene epoch.* **3.** Extremely cold. **4.** Lacking warmth and friendliness; icy. —See Syns at **cold** and **frigid.** [Latin *glaciālis,* icy, from *glaciēs,* ice.] —**gla′cial·ly** *adv.*

glacial epoch. **1.** Any of several periods during the Pleistocene epoch, up to 1,000,000 years ago, when much of the earth's surface was covered by glaciers. **2.** The Pleistocene epoch.

gla·cier (glā′shər) *n.* A large mass of slowly moving ice, formed from snow packed together by the weight of snow above it. [French, from *glace,* ice, from Latin *glaciēs.*]

gla·ci·ol·o·gy (glā′sē-ŏl′ə-jē, glā′shē-) *n.* The scientific study of glaciers. [GLACIER + -LOGY.] —**gla′ci·o·log′ic** (-ə-lŏj′ĭk) or **gla′ci·o·log′i·cal** *adj.* —**gla′ci·ol′o·gist** *n.*

gla·cis (glă-sē′, glăs′ē) *n.* **1.** A gentle slope; an incline. **2.** A slope extending down from a fortification. [French, from Old French *glacier,* to slide, from *glace,* ice, from Latin *glaciēs.*]

glad (glăd) *adj.* **glad·der, glad·dest.** **1.** Experiencing joy and pleasure: *glad to be home again.* **2.** Providing joy and pleasure: *a glad occasion.* **3.** Pleased; willing: *I am glad to go with you.* **4.** *Archaic.* Of a cheerful disposition. [Middle English, joyful, happy, shining, from Old English *glæd.*] —**glad′ly** *adv.* —**glad′ness** *n.*

Syns: 1. glad, cheerful, cheery, festive, gay, joyful, joy·ous *adj.* Core meaning: Providing joy and pleasure *(glad tidings).* **2. glad, happy, ready** *adj.* Core meaning: Eagerly compliant *(glad to help).* See also Syns at **merry.**

glad·den (glăd′n) *tr.v.* To make glad.

glade (glād) *n.* An open space in a forest. [Perh. from obs. *glad,* shining.]

glad·i·a·tor (glăd′ē-ā′tər) *n.* **1.** A man trained to entertain the public by engaging in fights to the death in ancient Roman arenas. **2.** A person who engages in a sensational struggle or controversy. [Middle English, from Latin *gladiātor,* from *gladius,* sword.] —**glad′i·a·to′ri·al** (-ə-tôr′ē-əl, -tōr′-) *adj.*

glad·i·o·lus (glăd′ē-ō′ləs) *n., pl.* **-li** (-lī′, -lē′) or **-lus·es.** **1.** Also **glad·i·o·la** (-lə). Any of various plants of the genus *Gladiolus,* native to tropical regions but widely cultivated elsewhere, with sword-shaped leaves and a spike of showy, variously colored flowers. **2.** *Anat.* The large middle section of the sternum. [Latin, dim. of *gladius,* sword.]

ă pat ā pay â care ä father ĕ pet ē be hw which ĭ pit ī tie î pier ŏ pot ō toe ô paw, for oi noise
ŏŏ took ōŏ boot ou out th thin th this ŭ cut û urge zh vision ə about, item, edible, gallop, circus

glad·some (glăd'səm) *adj.* **1.** Glad; joyful. **2.** Causing gladness. —**glad'some·ly** *adv.* —**glad'some·ness** *n.*

Glad·stone bag (glăd'stōn'). A piece of light hand luggage consisting of two hinged compartments. [After William E. Gladstone (1809–98), British statesman.]

glam·or (glăm'ər) *n.* Var. of glamour.

glam·or·ize (glăm'ə-rīz') *tr.v.* **-ized, -iz·ing.** Also **glam·our·ize. 1.** To make glamorous. **2.** To treat or portray in a romantic manner; idealize or glorify. —**glam'or·i·za'tion** *n.* —**glam'or·iz'er** *n.*

glam·or·ous (glăm'ər-əs) *adj.* Also **glam·our·ous.** Having or showing glamour: *a glamorous Hollywood star.* —**glam'or·ous·ly** *adv.* —**glam'or·ous·ness** *n.*

glam·our (glăm'ər) *n.* Also **glam·or.** An air of romantic charm or excitement surrounding a person or thing and attracting wide interest; allure: *the glamour of the theater.* [Scottish var. of *grammar* (from the association of learning with magic).]

glam·our·ize (glăm'ə-rīz') *tr.v.* Var. of glamorize.

glam·our·ous (glăm'ər-əs) *adj.* Var. of glamorous.

glance (glăns) *v.* **glanced, glanc·ing.** —*intr.v.* **1.** To look briefly or hastily: *She didn't even glance at his new outfit.* **2.** To strike a surface at such an angle as to fly off to one side: *A pebble glanced off the windshield.* **3.** To shine with intermittent rays of light; glitter. **4.** To make a passing reference: *He glanced at his opponent's arguments, then pursued his own.* —*tr.v.* To cause to glance: *glanced the stone over the surface of the pond.* —*n.* **1.** A brief or hasty look. **2.** An oblique movement following impact; deflection. **3.** A quick or intermittent flash of light; a gleam. [Alteration of Middle English *glacen*, from Old French *glacier*, to slide, from glace, ice, from Latin *glaciēs*.]

gland (glănd) *n.* **1.** *Anat.* **a.** An organ that extracts specific substances from the blood and concentrates or alters them for subsequent secretion. **b.** Any of various nonsecretory or excretory organs that resemble such organs. **2.** *Bot.* An organ or structure that secretes a substance. **3.** *Machinery.* A sliding part that is designed to hold something in place. [French *glande*, from Old French, glandular swelling, acorn, from Latin *glāns*, acorn.]

glan·ders (glăn'dərz) *n.* A contagious, often chronic, sometimes fatal disease of horses and other animals, caused by a bacillus, *Actinobacillus mallei.* [Old French *glandres*, pl. of *glandre*, glandular swelling, from Latin *glandula*, dim. of *glāns*, acorn.]

glan·du·lar (glăn'jə-lər) *adj.* **1.** Of, pertaining to, affecting, or resembling a gland or its secretion. **2.** Functioning as a gland. **3.** Having glands. **4.** Resulting from abnormal gland function. [French *glandulaire*, from *glandule*, small gland, from Latin *glandula*, glandular swelling.] —**glan'du·lar·ly** *adv.*

glandular fever. *Pathol.* Mononucleosis.

glare (glâr) *v.* **glared, glar·ing.** —*intr.v.* **1.** To stare fixedly and angrily. **2.** To shine intensely and blindingly; dazzle: *A searing sun glares down on the desert.* **3.** To be conspicuous; stand out: *The mistake glared on the page.* —*tr.v.* To express (an emotion) by staring fixedly and angrily. —*n.* **1.** A fixed, angry stare. **2.** An intense and blinding light: *the sun's glare.* [Middle English *glaren*, prob. from Middle Low German, to gleam.]

glar·ing (glâr'ĭng) *adj.* **1.** Staring fixedly and angrily: *a snake's glaring eyes.* **2.** Shining intensely and blindingly. **3.** Too brightly colored; gaudy; garish. **4.** Painfully conspicuous: *a glaring error.* —**glar'ing·ly** *adv.*

glar·y (glâr'ē) *adj.* **-i·er, -i·est.** Dazzlingly bright.

glass (glăs) *n.* **1.** Any of a large class of materials with highly variable mechanical and optical properties that solidify from the molten state without crystallization, that are typically based on silicon dioxide, boric oxide, aluminum oxide, or phosphorus pentoxide, that are generally transparent or translucent, and that are regarded physically as supercooled liquids rather than true solids. **2.** Objects made of glass; glassware. **3.** Something made of glass, esp.: **a.** A drinking vessel. **b.** A mirror. **c.** A barometer. **d.** A windowpane. **4. a.** Often **glasses.** Any device containing a lens or lenses and used as an aid to vision. **b. glasses.** Eyeglasses. **5.** The quantity that a drinking vessel holds; glassful. —*modifier:* *a glass door.* —*tr.v.* **1.** To place within glass or a glass container: *glass in a balcony.*

2. To provide with glass or glass parts. —*intr.v.* To become like glass: *The pond glassed over.* [Middle English *glas*, from Old English *glæs*.]

glass·ful (glăs'fŏŏl') *n.,* pl. **-fuls.** The quantity that a glass will hold.

glass·house (glăs'hous') *n. Brit.* A greenhouse.

glass·ine (glă-sēn') *n.* A nearly transparent, resilient glazed paper resistant to the passage of air and grease.

glass snake. Any of several slender, limbless, snakelike lizards of the genus *Ophisaurus*, with a tail that breaks or snaps off readily.

glass·ware (glăs'wâr') *n.* Objects, esp. containers, made of glass.

glass wool. Fine-spun fibers of glass used esp. for insulation and in air filters.

glass·y (glăs'ē) *adj.* **-i·er, -i·est. 1.** Of or like glass: *a glassy surface.* **2.** Lifeless; expressionless: *"The face changing to a demon's face with a fixed glassy grin"* (Katherine Anne Porter). —**glass'i·ly** *adv.* —**glass'i·ness** *n.*

Glau·ber's salts (glou'bərz). Also **Glauber's salt.** A hydrated sodium sulfate, $Na_2SO_4 \cdot 10H_2O$, used in paper and glass manufacturing and as a cathartic. [After J.R. Glauber (1604–68), German chemist and physician, its inventor.]

glau·co·ma (glou-kō'mə, glô-) *n.* A disease of the eye characterized by high intraocular pressure, damaged optic disk, hardening of the eyeball, and partial or complete loss of vision. [Latin *glaucōma*, cataract, from Greek *glaukōma*, from *glaukos*, glaucous.] —**glau·co'ma·tous** *adj.*

glau·cous (glô'kəs) *adj. Bot.* Grayish green or bluish green due to a fine, whitish, powdery coating: *glaucous leaves.* [Latin *glaucus*, from Greek *glaukos*, gleaming, bluish green or gray.]

glaze (glāz) *n.* **1.** A thin, smooth, shiny coating, as on paper or cloth. **2.** A thin, glassy coating of ice. **3.** A coating applied to ceramics before firing in a kiln to produce a protective or decorative gloss. **4.** A coating, as of syrup, applied to food. **5.** A glassy film, as over the eyes. —*v.* **glazed, glaz·ing.** —*tr.v.* **1.** To fit or furnish with glass: *glaze a window.* **2.** To apply a glaze to: *glaze pottery.* **3.** To give a smooth, lustrous surface to. —*intr.v.* **1.** To become glazed. **2.** To form a glaze. [Middle English *glāsen*, to provide with glass or a glassy surface, from *glas*, glass.] —**glaz'er** *n.*

gla·zier (glā'zhər) *n.* A person who cuts and fits window glass. [Middle English *glasier*, from *glas*, glass.]

glaz·ing (glā'zĭng) *n.* **1.** Glass set or made to be set in frames. **2.** A glaze.

gleam (glēm) *n.* **1.** A brief beam or flash of light: *gleams of daylight seen through the cracks.* **2.** A steady but subdued shining; a glow: *the gleam of a steel blade.* **3.** A brief or dim indication; trace: *a gleam of intelligence.* —*intr.v.* To give off a gleam; to flash or glow: *"It shone with gold and gleamed with ivory"* (Edith Hamilton). [Middle English *gleem, glem*, from Old English *glǣm*.]

glean (glēn) *intr.v.* To gather grain left behind by reapers. —*tr.v.* **1.** To gather (grain) left behind by reapers. **2.** To collect (knowledge or information) bit by bit: *"Records from which historians glean their knowledge"* (Kemp Malone). [Middle English *glenen*, from Old French *glener*, from Late Latin *glennāre*.] —**glean'er** *n.*

glean·ings (glē'nĭngz) *pl.n.* Things that have been gleaned or picked up bit by bit.

glebe (glēb) *n.* **1.** *Brit.* A plot of land granted to a clergyman as part of his payment. **2.** *Poet.* The soil or earth; land. [Latin *glēba*, clod.]

glee (glē) *n.* **1.** Merriment; joy. **2.** An unaccompanied song for three or more male voices, popular in the 18th cent.— See Syns at **gaiety.** [Middle English *glē*, from Old English *glēo*, merriment, play, music.]

glee club. A group of singers who perform usu. short pieces of choral music.

glee·ful (glē'fəl) *adj.* Full of glee; merry. —**glee'ful·ly** *adv.* —**glee'ful·ness** *n.*

glee·man (glē'mən) *n.* A medieval itinerant singer; minstrel. [Middle English, from Old English *glēoman* : *glēo*, glee + *mann*, man.]

glen (glĕn) *n.* A valley. [Middle English *glen*, from Scottish Gaelic *gle(a)nn*, from Old Irish *glend*.]

ă pat ā pay â care ä father ĕ pet ē be hw which ĭ pit ī tie î pier ŏ pot ō toe ô paw, for oi noise
ŏŏ took ōō boot ou out th thin th this ŭ cut û urge zh vision ə about, item, edible, gallop, circus

Glen·gar·ry (glĕn-gărʹē) *n., pl.* **-ries.** A woolen cap that is creased lengthwise and often has short ribbons at the back. [After *Glengarry,* Scotland.]

glib (glĭb) *adj.* **glib·ber, glib·best. 1.** Performing or performed with careless, often thoughtless ease: *Though a slow writer, she is quite glib in conversation.* **2.** Marked by a quickness or fluency that suggests insincerity: *glib politicians, promising the moon.* —See Syns at **talkative.** [Prob. from Low German *glibbrig,* from Middle Low German *glibberich,* slippery.] —**glibʹly** *adv.* —**glibʹness** *n.*

glide (glīd) *v.* **glid·ed, glid·ing.** —*intr.v.* **1.** To move in a smooth, effortless manner: *The submarine glided silently through the water.* **2.** To move silently and furtively. **3.** To occur or pass without notice: *Precious time had glided by.* **4.** To fly without using propelling power: *hawks gliding on the wind.* **5.** *Phonet.* To articulate a glide. —*tr.v.* To cause to glide: *glided his fingers up the neck of the guitar.* —See Syns at **slide** and **sneak.** —*n.* **1.** A smooth, effortless movement. **2.** An act of flying without propulsion: *The plane descended in a gentle glide.* **3.** *Phonet.* The transitional sound produced when the voice shifts from one speech sound to another. [Middle English *gliden,* from Old English *glīdan.*]

glid·er (glīʹdər) *n.* **1.** Someone or something that glides. **2.** A light, engineless aircraft designed to glide after being towed aloft by an airplane or launched from a catapult. **3.** A swinging couch that hangs in a vertical frame.

glim·mer (glĭmʹər) *n.* **1.** A dim or unsteady light; a flicker: *the glimmer of distant campfires.* **2.** A faint suggestion or indication; a trace: *a glimmer of her old sense of humor.* —*intr.v.* **1.** To give off a dim or unsteady light. **2.** To appear or be indicated faintly: *Hope still glimmered.* [Middle English *glimeren.*]

glimpse (glĭmps) *n.* A brief, incomplete view or look. —*v.* **glimpsed, glimps·ing.** —*tr.v.* To obtain a glimpse of: *We could barely glimpse the driver of the speeding car.* —*intr.v.* To look briefly: *glimpsed at the newspaper headlines.* [Middle English *glimsen, glymsen.*]

glint (glĭnt) *n.* **1.** A small, brief flash of light; a sparkle. **2.** A faint or fleeting indication; a trace. —*intr.v.* **1.** To gleam or flash: *The creek glinted like quicksilver in the moonlight.* **2.** To move abruptly; to dart. —*tr.v.* To cause to gleam or flash. [Middle English *glinten,* to shine, move quickly.]

glis·san·do (glĭ-sänʹdō) *n., pl.* **-di** (-dē) or **-dos.** *Mus.* A rapid glide through a series of consecutive tones, each one blending into the next. [Prob. from GLISSADE.]

glis·ten (glĭsʹən) *intr.v.* To shine or glitter with reflected light: *Sunshine made the snow glisten on the hilltops.* —*n.* A shine or sparkle; glitter. [Middle English *glistnen,* from Old English *glisnian.*]

glit·ter (glĭtʹər) *n.* **1.** A sparkling light or brightness. **2.** Brilliant or showy attractiveness: *the pomp and glitter of the queen's coronation.* **3.** Small pieces of light-reflecting decorative material. —*intr.v.* **1.** To sparkle brilliantly; glisten. **2.** To be brilliantly attractive or colorful. [Middle English *gliteren,* from Old Norse *glitra.*] —**glitʹter·ing·ly** *adv.* —**glitʹter·y** *adj.*

gloat (glōt) *intr.v.* To feel or express great, often malicious pleasure or self-satisfaction: *gloating over his triumph and his opponent's defeat.* [Perh. of Scandinavian orig.] —**gloatʹer** *n.*

glob (glŏb) *n.* **1.** A drop. **2.** A rounded lump or mass. [Middle English *globbe,* large mass, from Latin *globus,* globe.]

glob·al (glōʹbəl) *adj.* **1.** Having the shape of a globe; spherical. **2.** Of or involving the entire earth; worldwide: *a global disarmament treaty.* —See Syns at **general.** —**globʹal·ly** *adv.*

glo·bate (glōʹbāt') *adj.* Having the shape of a globe; globular. [Latin *globātus,* past part. of *globāre,* to form into a globe, from *globus,* globe.]

globe (glōb) *n.* **1.** Any object having the general shape of a sphere, esp. a representation of the earth or the celestial sphere in the form of a hollow ball. **2.** The earth. **3.** An object resembling a globe, as a glass sphere covering a light bulb. —*v.* **globed, glob·ing.** —*intr.v.* To assume the shape of a globe. —*tr.v.* To form into a globe. [Middle English, from Old French, from Latin *globus.*]

globe·trot·ter (glōbʹtrŏt'ər) *n.* A person who travels often

and widely, esp. for sightseeing. —**globeʹtrot'ting** *n. & adj.*

glo·bose (glōʹbōs') *adj.* Also **glo·bous** (-bəs). Spherical; globular. [Latin *globōsus,* from *globus,* globe.] —**gloʹbose'ly** *adv.* —**glo·boseʹness** or **glo·bosʹi·ty** (-bŏsʹĭ-tē) *n.*

glob·u·lar (glŏbʹyə-lər) *adj.* **1.** Having the shape of a globe or globule; spherical. **2.** Consisting of globules. —**globʹu·lar·ly** *adv.* —**globʹu·lar·ness** *n.*

glob·ule (glŏbʹyōōl) *n.* A small, often minute spherical mass, esp. a small drop of liquid. [Latin *globulus,* dim. of *globus,* globe.]

glob·u·lin (glŏbʹyə-lĭn) *n.* Any of a class of simple proteins that are found extensively in blood, milk, muscle, and plant seeds and are insoluble in pure water, soluble in dilute salt solution, and coagulable by heat. [GLOBUL(E) + -IN.]

glock·en·spiel (glŏkʹən-spēl', -shpēl') *n.* A percussion musical instrument having a series of metal bars tuned to the chromatic scale and played with two light hammers. [German *Glockenspiel,* "play of bells."]

glockenspiel

glom·er·ate (glŏmʹər-ĭt, -ə-rāt') *adj.* Formed into a compact, rounded mass; conglomerate. [Latin *glomerātus,* past part. of *glomerāre,* to make into a ball, from *glomus,* ball.]

glom·er·ule (glŏmʹə-rōōl', -ər-yōōl') *n. Bot.* A compact cluster of flowers. [From Latin *glomus,* ball.] —**glo·merʹu·late'** (glō-mĕrʹyə-lāt', -lĭt) *adj.*

gloom (glōōm) *n.* **1.** Partial or total darkness; dimness: *peering into the gloom of the cave.* **2.** An appearance or atmosphere of melancholy or depression: *A gloom pervaded the household.* **3.** Low spirits; dejection; despondency. —*intr.v.* **1.** To be or become dark, shaded, or obscure. **2.** To appear despondent, sad, or mournful. [From Middle English *gloum(b)en,* to look glum, become dark.]

gloom·y (glōōʹmē) *adj.* **-i·er, -i·est. 1.** Dismal, dark, or dreary: *a gloomy, deserted castle.* **2.** Showing or filled with gloom: *gloomy faces.* **3.** Causing or producing gloom or dejection; depressing: *gloomy news.* **4.** Marked by hopelessness; pessimistic: *gloomy predictions.* —**gloomʹi·ly** *adv.* —**gloomʹi·ness** *n.*

    Syns: 1. gloomy, bleak, cheerless, dismal, dreary, glum *(Brit. Regional),* **joyless, somber** *adj.* Core meaning: Dark and depressing *(a gloomy, rainy day).* **2. gloomy, blue** *(Informal),* **depressed, downhearted, low, melancholy, sad, unhappy** *adj.* Core meaning: In poor spirits *(felt gloomy after the exam).* **3. gloomy, dark, dismal, pessimistic** *adj.* Core meaning: Marked by little hopefulness *(gloomy predictions of doom).*

Glo·ri·a (glôrʹē-ə, glōrʹ-) *n.* **1. a.** Any of the Christian hymns of praise to God that begin with the Latin word *Glōria,* meaning "glory." **b.** The music to which one of these hymns is set. **2. gloria.** A ring or disc of light surrounding the head or body of a sacred figure; halo or nimbus. **3. gloria.** A lightweight fabric chiefly of silk, wool, or cotton, used for umbrellas and dresses. [Middle English, from Latin *glōria,* glory.]

glo·ri·fi·ca·tion (glôr'ə-fĭ-kāʹshən, glōr'-) *n.* **1.** The act of glorifying or the condition of being glorified. **2.** *Informal.* An enhanced or glorified version of something.

glo·ri·fy (glôrʹə-fī', glōrʹ-) *tr.v.* **-fied, -fy·ing. 1.** To give honor or high praise to; exalt. **2.** To cause to be or seem more glorious or excellent than is actually the case: *His descriptions glorified the house into a mansion.* **3.** To give glory to, esp. through worship: *glorify God.* [Middle English *glorifien,* from Old French *glorifier,* from Late Latin *glōrifi-*

cāre, from Latin *glória*, glory.] —**glo'ri·fi'er** *n.*

glo·ri·ous (glôr'ē-əs, glōr'-) *adj.* **1.** Having or deserving glory: *a glorious national hero.* **2.** Giving or advancing glory: *a glorious achievement.* **3.** Characterized by great beauty and splendor; magnificent: *a glorious sunset.* —**glo'ri·ous·ly** *adv.* —**glo'ri·ous·ness** *n.*

glo·ry (glôr'ē, glōr'ē) *n., pl.* **-ries. 1.** Great honor or praise granted by common consent; renown: *the days of Solomon's might and glory.* **2.** Something that brings honor or renown. **3.** Adoration or praise offered in worship: *"Glory to God in the highest."* **4.** Great beauty: *The sun was setting in a blaze of glory.* **5.** A condition of splendor, as a period of highest achievement or prosperity: *Paris in its greatest glory.* **6.** A highly praiseworthy asset: *Her hair is her crowning glory.* —*intr.v.* **-ried, -ry·ing.** To rejoice triumphantly; exult: *aggressive kings who gloried in war.* [Middle English *glorie*, from Old French, from Latin *glória*, glory.]

gloss¹ (glôs, glŏs) *n.* **1.** A surface shininess or luster: *the gloss of patent leather.* **2.** A deceptive or superficially attractive appearance. —*tr.v.* **1.** To give a bright shine or luster to. **2.** To make acceptable by deception or superficial treatment: *gloss over a friend's weaknesses.* [Prob. of Scandinavian orig.]

gloss² (glôs, glŏs) *n.* **1. a.** A brief note that explains or translates a difficult word, phrase, or section of a text or manuscript. **b.** A collection of such notes; a glossary. **2.** A commentary or translation printed in the margins or between the lines of a text. —*tr.v.* To provide (a text) with glosses. [Middle English *glose*, from Old French, from Medieval Latin *glósa*, from Latin *glóssa*, word that needs explanation, from Greek *glóssa*, tongue, language.] —**gloss'er** *n.*

glos·sa·ry (glô'sə-rē, glŏs'ə-) *n., pl.* **-ries.** A list of difficult or specialized words with their definitions, often placed at the back of a book. [Latin *glossárium*, from *glóssa*, foreign word.] —**glos·sar'i·al** (glô-sâr'ē-əl, glŏ-) *adj.*

glot·tal (glŏt'l) *adj.* Of or relating to the glottis.

glottal stop. A speech sound produced by momentarily closing the glottis and then releasing the breath explosively.

glot·tis (glŏt'ĭs) *n., pl.* **-tis·es** or **glot·ti·des** (glŏt'ĭ-dēz'). The space between the vocal cords at the upper part of the larynx. [From Greek *glóttis*, from *glótta*, *glóssa*, tongue, language.]

glove (glŭv) *n.* **1.** A fitted covering for the hand having a separate section for each finger and the thumb. **2.** An oversized padded leather covering for the hand, used in baseball. **3.** A boxing glove. —*tr.v.* **gloved, glov·ing.** To cover with or as if with a glove. —*idiom.* **hand in glove.** In a close relationship. [Middle English, from Old English *glóf*.]

glov·er (glŭv'ər) *n.* A person who makes or sells gloves.

glow (glō) *intr.v.* **1.** To shine brightly and steadily, esp. without a flame: *embers glowing in the furnace.* **2.** To have a bright, warm color. **3.** To have a healthful, ruddy color: *His cheeks glowed.* **4.** To be bright or radiant: *glowing with pride.* —*n.* **1.** A light produced by a heated body; incandescence. **2.** Brilliance or warmth of color, esp. redness: *"The evening glow of the city streets when the sun has gone behind the tallest houses"* (Sean O'Faolain). **3.** A sensation of physical warmth. **4.** A warm feeling of passion or emotion; ardor. [Middle English *glowen*, from Old English *glówan*.]

glow·er (glou'ər) *intr.v.* To look or stare angrily or sullenly; to scowl. —*n.* An angry, sullen, or threatening stare. [Middle English *glo(u)ren*, to shine, stare, prob. of Scandinavian orig.] —**glow'er·ing·ly** *adv.*

glow·ing (glō'ĭng) *adj.* **1.** Giving or reflecting bright, usu. steady light: *glowing coals.* **2.** Having a rich, warm color: *a glowing complexion.* **3.** Warmly enthusiastic or favorable: *glowing reports.* —**glow'ing·ly** *adv.*

glow·worm (glō'wûrm') *n.* A firefly, esp. the luminous larva or wingless, grublike female of a firefly.

glox·in·i·a (glŏk-sĭn'ē-ə) *n.* Any of several tropical South American plants of the genus *Sinningia*, esp. *S. speciosa*, cultivated as a house plant for its showy, variously colored flowers. [After Benjamin Peter *Gloxin*, 18th-cent. German botanist and physician.]

glu·cose (gloo'kōs') *n.* **1.** Dextrose.. A colorless to yellowish syrupy mixture of dextrose, maltose, and dextrins with about 20 per cent water, used in confectionery, alcoholic fermentation, tanning, and treating tobacco. [French, from Greek *gleukos*, sweet new wine, must.]

glue (gloo) *n.* **1.** Any of various thick, sticky liquids used to hold things together. **2.** An adhesive obtained by boiling certain animal proteins. —*modifier: a glue pot.* —*tr.v.* **glued, glu·ing.** To stick or fasten together with or as if with glue. [Middle English *gleu*, glue, birdlime, from Old French *glu*, from Late Latin *glūs*, from Latin *glūten*.]

glu·ey (gloo'ē) *adj.* **glu·i·er, glu·i·est. 1.** Like glue; sticky or viscous: *gluey candy.* **2.** Full of or covered with glue. —**glu'i·ness** *n.*

glum (glŭm) *adj.* **glum·mer, glum·mest. 1.** In low spirits; dejected. **2.** *Brit. Regional.* Gloomy; dismal. —See Syns at **gloomy.** [From Middle English *glomen, gloumen*, to look sullen, gloom.] —**glum'ly** *adv.* —**glum'ness** *n.*

glut (glŭt) *v.* **glut·ted, glut·ting.** —*tr.v.* **1.** To fill beyond capacity; to stuff: *glutted himself with fine food.* **2.** To flood (a market) with goods so that supply exceeds demand. —*intr.v.* To eat too much. —*n.* An oversupply. —See Syns at **excess.** [Middle English *glotten, glouten*, prob. from Old French *gloutir*, to swallow, from Latin *gluttīre*.]

glu·ten (gloot'n) *n.* A mixture of plant proteins occurring in cereal grains, chiefly corn and wheat, and used as an adhesive and as a flour substitute. [Latin *glūten*, glue.] —**glu'ten·ous** *adj.*

glu·te·us (gloo'tē-əs, gloo-tē'-) *n., pl.* **-te·i** (gloo'tē-ī', gloo'-tē'ī'). Any of three large muscles of the buttocks: **a.** *gluteus maximus*, which extends the thigh; **b.** *gluteus medius*, which rotates and abducts the thigh; **c.** *gluteus minimus*, which abducts the thigh. [From Greek *gloutos*, buttock.] —**glu'te·al** *adj.*

glu·ti·nous (gloot'n-əs) *adj.* Like glue; sticky; adhesive. [Latin *glūtinōsus*, from *glūten*, glue.] —**glu'ti·nous·ly** *adv.* —**glu'ti·nous·ness** or **glu'ti·nos'i·ty** (-ŏs'ĭ-tē) *n.*

glut·ton (glŭt'n) *n.* **1.** A person who eats too much. **2.** A person with an unusually great capacity to receive or withstand something: *a glutton for punishment.* **3.** A wolverine. [Middle English *glotoun*, from Old French *gluton, gloton*, from Latin *gluttō*.] —**glut'ton·ous** *adj.* —**glut'ton·ous·ly** *adv.*

glut·ton·y (glŭt'n-ē) *n., pl.* **-ies.** Excess in eating or drinking.

glyc·er·in (glĭs'ər-ĭn) *n.* Also **glyc·er·ine** (-ər-ĭn, -ə-rēn'). Glycerol. [French, from Greek *glukeros*, sweet.]

glyc·er·ol (glĭs'ə-rôl', -rŏl', -rōl') *n.* A syrupy, sweet, colorless or yellowish liquid, $C_3H_8O_3$, obtained from fats and oils as a by-product of the manufacture of soaps and fatty acids and used as a solvent, antifreeze and antifrost fluid, plasticizer, and sweetener and in the manufacture of dynamite, cosmetics, liquid soaps, inks, and lubricants. [GLYCER(IN) + -OL.]

gly·co·gen (glī'kə-jən) *n.* A white, sweet-tasting powder, $(C_6H_{10}O_5)_n$, occurring as the chief animal storage carbohydrate, primarily in the liver. [Greek *glukus*, sweet + -GEN.] —**gly'co·gen'ic** (-jĕn'ĭk) *adj.*

gly·col (glī'kôl', -kŏl', -kōl') *n.* **1.** Ethylene glycol. **2.** Any of various dihydric alcohols. [Greek *glukus*, sweet + -OL.]

glyph (glĭf) *n.* **1.** *Archit.* A vertical groove, esp. in a Doric column or frieze. **2.** A symbol used in ancient hieroglyphic writing; a hieroglyph. [Greek *gluphē*, carving, from *gluphein*, to carve.] —**glyph'ic** *adj.*

G-man (jē'măn') *n.* An agent of the Federal Bureau of Investigation. [G(OVERNMENT) MAN.]

gnarl² (närl) *n.* A protruding knot on a tree. —*tr.v.* To make knotted or deformed; to twist. —See Syns at **distort.** [Back-formation from GNARLED.]

gnarled (närld) *adj.* **1.** Having gnarls; knotty or misshapen: *gnarled branches.* **2.** Rugged and roughened, as from work or old age: *the gnarled hands of a carpenter.* [Prob. var. of KNURLED.]

gnash (năsh) *tr.v.* **1.** To grind or strike together: *gnashed his teeth in frustration.* **2.** To bite by grinding the teeth. —*n.* An act of gnashing the teeth. [Middle English *gnasten, gnaisten.*]

gnat (năt) *n.* Any of numerous small, winged insects, esp. one that bites. [Middle English, from Old English *gnæt.*]

gnaw (nô) *tr.v.* **1.** To bite, chew on, or erode with the teeth: *animals gnawing the bark of trees.* **2.** To produce by gnawing: *gnaw a hole.* **3.** To wear away: *waves gnawing the rocky shore.* **4.** To afflict or trouble persistently: *Fear gnawed him.* —*intr.v.* **1.** To bite or chew persistently: *gnawing contentedly on a bone.* **2.** To cause gradual loss or depletion. **3.** To cause persistent pain or distress. [Middle English *gnawen*, from Old English *gnagan*.]

gneiss (nīs) *n.* A banded or foliated metamorphic rock, usu. of the same composition as granite, in which the minerals are arranged in layers. [German *Gneis.* —**gneiss'ic** (nī'sĭk) or **gneiss'oid'** (nī'soid') or **gneiss'ose'** (nī'sōs') *adj.*

gnome (nōm) *n.* **1.** One of a fabled race of dwarflike creatures who live underground and guard treasure hoards. **2.** A shriveled old man. [French, from New Latin *gnomus.*] —**gnom'ish** *adj.*

gno·mon (nō'mŏn') *n.* **1.** An object, such as the style of a sundial, that projects a shadow used as an indicator. **2.** *Geom.* The figure that remains after a parallelogram has been removed from a similar but larger parallelogram with which it has a common corner. [Latin *gnōmōn*, from Greek, one who knows, indicator, interpreter, from *gignōskein*, to know.] —**gno·mon'ic** (nō-mŏn'ĭk) or **gno·mon'i·cal** *adj.*

gnos·tic (nŏs'tĭk) *adj.* **1.** Of, relating to, or possessing intellectual or spiritual knowledge. **2. Gnostic.** Of Gnosticism. —*n.* **Gnostic.** A believer in Gnosticism. [From Greek *gnostikos*, pertaining to knowledge, from *gnosis*, knowledge.]

Gnos·ti·cism (nŏs'tĭ-sĭz'əm) *n.* The doctrines of certain early Christian sects that valued inquiry into spiritual truth above faith and thought salvation attainable only by the few whose faith enabled them to transcend matter.

gnu (nōō, nyōō) *n.* Either of two large African antelopes, *Connochaetes gnou* or *C. taurinus*, with a drooping beard, a long, tufted tail, and curved horns in both sexes. Also called **wildebeest.** [From Kaffir *nqu.*]

gnu

go (gō) *v.* **went** (wĕnt), **gone** (gôn, gŏn), **go·ing.** —*intr.v.* **1.** To move along; proceed: *going on a walk.* **2.** To move to a particular place: *going to the beach.* **3.** To move from a particular place; depart: *time to go.* **4.** To get out of sight; move out of someone's presence: *Go before I really get angry.* **5.** To move or function: *The car won't go.* **6.** To proceed to the performance of an activity: *went to eat.* **7.** Used in the form *be going* with the sense of *will* to indicate indefinite future intent or expectation: *He is going to learn to fly.* **8.** To engage in an activity: *go riding.* **9.** To make a specified sound: *The glass went crack.* **10.** To be customarily located; belong: *The fork goes to the left of the plate.* **11.** To extend; run: *The drapes go from the ceiling to the floor.* **12.** To pass or be given into someone's possession: *The bulk of the estate went to the nephew.* **13.** To be allotted: *money to go for food.* **14.** To serve; to help: *It goes to show he was wrong.* **15.** To be compatible; harmonize: *The rug goes well with this room.* **16.** To proceed in a particular form or sequence: *Is this the way the song goes?* **17.** To be in a specified state of dress or undress: *go barefoot.* **18.** To die. **19.** To come apart; cave in. **20.** To fail: *His hearing is beginning to go.* **21.** To be consumed or used up: *The sale items are going fast.* **22.** To lose effect; disappear. **23.** To be given up or abolished: *Unnecessary expenditures must go.* **24.** To pass: *The hours went slowly.* **25.** To pass in a transaction; be sold or auctioned off: *The portrait will go to the highest bidder.* **26.** To enter into a specified condition; become: *go insane.* **27.** To be or con-tinue to be in a specified condition: *go unchallenged.* **28.** To turn out; fare: *How did your day go?* **29.** To be thought of; be judged: *As monkeys go, this one is well-behaved.* **30.** To pursue a course: *go too far; go to a lot of trouble.* **31.** To act, esp. under guidance or on advice: *go on someone's word.* **32.** To hold out; endure. —*tr.v.* **1.** To proceed along; follow: *go the same way.* **2.** To withstand; endure: *went the distance.* **3.** To wager; bid: *He went five dollars on a bet.* **4.** To furnish: *go bail for a client.* **5.** To take part to the extent of: *go fifty-fifty on a deal.* —See Syns at **die.** —*phrasal verbs.* **go about. 1.** To busy oneself with: *go about one's business.* **2.** To change direction in a sailing vessel; to tack. **go along.** To be in agreement; cooperate: *He went along with the majority.* **go at. 1.** To attack verbally or physically. **2.** To work at diligently or energetically. **go away.** To come to an end; cease. **go back on. 1.** To withdraw from; abandon: *I could never go back on my promise.* **2.** To betray: *go back on an old friend.* **go down. 1.** To be remembered. **2.** To be defeated. **3.** To be believed or accepted: *His version of the incident doesn't go down.* **go for. 1.** To try to obtain. **2.** *Informal.* To enjoy or appreciate. **3.** To pass as; be thought of as. **4.** To attack. **go in for.** *Informal.* To enjoy participating in or partaking of: *She never did go in for make-up.* **go into. 1.** To investigate; inquire about. **2.** To take up or turn to as an occupation, study, or pastime: *going into the ministry.* **go off. 1.** To happen; take place: *went off according to plan.* **2.** To be fired or shot; explode. **3.** To start ringing: *The alarm went off at 6 o'clock.* —See Syns at **explode. go on. 1.** To proceed. **2.** To continue to exist. **3.** To happen. **4.** To approach: *She's 16, going on 17.* **go out.** To be extinguished. **go out for.** To seek to be a member of or participant in: *went out for the tennis team.* **go over. 1.** To check or examine. **2.** To be received: *a speech that went over well.* **go through. 1.** To search or examine thoroughly. **2.** To suffer; undergo; experience. **3.** To use up entirely. **4.** To be passed or approved. **go through with.** To complete or not leave undone: *They decided to go through with the original wedding plans.* **go under. 1.** To fail or be ruined: *My uncle's business almost went under.* **2.** To lose consciousness under an anesthetic: *I went under so fast I didn't know what had hit me.* **go up. 1.** To be built: *New homes are going up all over the place.* **2.** To be blown up, destroyed, etc.: *The woodshed went up in flames.* —*n., pl.* **goes.** *Informal.* **1.** A try; venture: *Let's have a go at it.* **2.** A turn, as in a game. **3.** A bargain; agreement; deal: *You either bring the money and pay cash or it's no go.* **4.** Energy; vitality: *That kid has sure got a lot of go.* —*adj. Informal.* Ready for action: *All systems are go.* —*idioms.* **from the word go.** *Informal.* From the very beginning or from the bottom of the heart: *They're staunch Republicans from the word go.* **go far.** To succeed; prosper greatly: *Speak softly and carry a big stick; you will go far.* **go (someone) one better.** To surpass or outdo. **go together.** To be sweethearts. **on the go.** *Informal.* Perpetually busy. **to go.** To be taken out, as restaurant food and drink: *We want coffee and sandwiches to go.* [Middle English *gon*, from Old English *gān*.]

goad (gōd) *n.* **1.** A long stick with a pointed end used for prodding animals. **2.** Something that prods or urges; stimulus: *His rival's success was a goad to his own efforts.* —*tr.v.* To prod with or as if with a goad; give impetus to; incite. —See Syns at **provoke.** [Middle English *gode*, from Old English *gād.*]

go·a·head (gō'ə-hĕd') *n. Informal.* Permission to proceed.

goal (gōl) *n.* **1.** A desired result or purpose toward which one is working; an objective. **2.** A place one desires or is trying to reach: *His goal was California.* **3.** The finish line of a race. **4. a.** In certain sports, a structure or area into which players must propel the ball or puck in order to score. **b.** The score awarded for this. —*modifier: a goal line; a goal post.* —See Syns at **intention.** [Middle English *gol*, boundary, limit.]

goal·ie (gō'lē) *n.* A goalkeeper.

goal·keep·er (gōl'kē'pər) *n.* A player assigned to protect his team's goal in soccer, hockey, and other sports.

goat (gōt) *n.* **1.** Any of various horned, bearded ruminant mammals of the genus *Capra*, orig. of mountainous regions of the Old World, esp. one of the domesticated forms of *C. hircus.* **2.** A lecherous man. **3.** A scapegoat. —*idiom.*

get (someone's) goat. *Informal.* To make angry or annoyed. [Middle English *gote*, from Old English *gāt*.] —**goat′ish** *adj.*

goat·ee (gō-tē′) *n.* A small chin beard, often trimmed to a point. [From GOAT + -EE.]

goat·skin (gōt′skĭn′) *n.* **1.** The skin of a goat. **2.** Leather made from this skin. **3.** A container, as for wine, made from such leather.

gob[1] (gŏb) *n.* **1.** A small piece or lump. **2. gobs.** *Informal.* A large quantity, as of money. [Middle English *gobbe*, lump, mass, from Old French *gobe*, mouthful, lump, from *gober*, to swallow, gulp.]

gob[2] (gŏb) *n. Slang.* A sailor. [Orig. unknown.]

gob·ble[1] (gŏb′əl) *v.* **-bled, -bling.** —*tr.v.* **1.** To devour in large, greedy gulps. **2.** To snatch greedily; to grab: *gobbled up the few remaining tickets.* —*intr.v.* To eat greedily or rapidly. [Prob. ult. from *gobbe*, lump, gob.]

gob·ble[2] (gŏb′əl) *intr.v.* **-bled, -bling.** To make the throaty, chortling sound of a male turkey. —*n.* The throaty, chortling sound of a male turkey. [Imit.]

gob·ble·dy·gook (gŏb′əl-dē-gōōk′) *n.* Also **gob·ble·de·gook.** Unclear, wordy jargon. [From GOBBLE (to sound like a turkey).]

gob·bler (gŏb′lər) *n.* A male turkey.

go-be·tween (gō′bĭ-twēn′) *n.* A person who acts as a messenger or intermediary between two sides.

gob·let (gŏb′lĭt) *n.* A drinking glass with a stem and base. [Middle English *gobelet*, from Old French, dim. of *gobel*, cup.]

gob·lin (gŏb′lĭn) *n.* **1.** A grotesque, elfin creature of folklore, thought to work mischief or evil. **2.** A haunting ghost. [Middle English *gobelin*, from Old French, from Middle High German *kobolt*.]

go·by (gō′bē) *n., pl.* **-bies** or **goby.** Any of numerous usu. small freshwater and saltwater fishes of the family Gobiidae, whose pelvic fins are united to form a sucking disk. [Latin *gōbius*, var. of *cōbius*, from Greek *kōbios*.]

go-cart (gō′kärt′) *n.* **1.** A small wagon for children to ride in, drive, or pull. **2.** A small frame on casters designed to help support a child learning to walk. **3.** A handcart.

god (gŏd) *n.* **1.** A being of supernatural powers or attributes, believed in and worshiped by a people; esp., a male deity thought to control some part of nature or reality or to personify some force or activity: *Mars, the Roman god of war.* **2.** An image of a supernatural being; idol. **3.** Someone or something that is worshiped or idealized: *Beauty was his god.* **4.** A man godlike in appearance or power. [Middle English, from Old English.]

God (gŏd) *n.* **1.** A being regarded as the perfect, all-powerful, all-knowing originator and ruler of the universe, the principal object of belief and worship in many religions and philosophical systems. **2.** The force, effect, or a manifestation or aspect of God.

god·child (gŏd′chīld′) *n.* A child for whom a person serves as sponsor at baptism.

god·daugh·ter (gŏd′dô′tər) *n.* A female godchild.

god·dess (gŏd′ĭs) *n.* **1.** A female deity: *Aphrodite, goddess of love.* **2.** A woman of great beauty or grace.

god·fa·ther (gŏd′fä′thər) *n.* A man who sponsors a child at its baptism.

god·for·sak·en (gŏd′fər-sā′kən) *adj.* Also **God·for·sak·en.** Appearing as if deprived of God's blessing, as: **1.** Desperate; depraved. **2.** Desolate; forlorn.

god·head (gŏd′hĕd′) *n.* **1.** Divinity; godhood. **2. the Godhead.** God, or the essential and divine nature of God, regarded abstractly. [Middle English *godhede* : *god*, god + *-hede*, var. of *-hode*, -hood.]

god·hood (gŏd′hōōd′) *n.* The quality or condition of being a god; divinity. [Middle English *godhode*, from Old English *godhād*.]

god·less (gŏd′lĭs) *adj.* **1.** Recognizing or worshiping no god. **2.** Irreverent; wicked. —**god′less·ly** *adv.* —**god′less·ness** *n.*

god·like (gŏd′līk′) *adj.* Resembling or of the nature of a god or God: *godlike authority.* —**god′like′ness** *n.*

god·ly (gŏd′lē) *adj.* **-li·er, -li·est. 1.** Having great reverence for God; pious. **2.** Divine. —**god′li·ness** *n.*

god·moth·er (gŏd′mŭth′ər) *n.* A woman who sponsors a child at its baptism.

god·par·ent (gŏd′pâr′ənt, -păr′-) *n.* A godfather or godmother.

God's acre. A churchyard or burial ground.

god·send (gŏd′sĕnd′) *n.* An unexpected stroke of luck; windfall. [Middle English *goddes sand*, God's message.]

god·son (gŏd′sŭn′) *n.* A male godchild.

god·wit (gŏd′wĭt′) *n.* Any of various wading birds of the genus *Limosa*, with a long, slender, slightly upturned bill. [Orig. unknown.]

go-get·ter (gō′gĕt′ər) *n. Informal.* An enterprising, hustling person.

gog·gle (gŏg′əl) *v.* **-gled, -gling.** —*intr.v.* To stare with wide and bulging eyes. —*tr.v.* To roll or bulge (the eyes). —See Syns at **gaze.** —*n.* **1.** A stare or leer. **2. goggles.** A pair of large, usu. tinted eyeglasses with shielding sidepieces, worn as a protection against wind, dust, or glare. [Middle English *gog(e)len*, to roll the eyes.] —**gog′gly** *adj.*

gog·gle-eyed (gŏg′əl-īd′) *adj.* Having prominent or rolling eyes.

go·ing (gō′ĭng) *n.* **1.** Departure: *comings and goings.* **2.** The condition underfoot as it affects one's headway in walking or riding: *The going was rough on the muddy trails.* **3.** *Informal.* Progress toward a goal; headway. —*adj.* **1.** Working; running: *in going order.* **2.** In full operation; flourishing: *a going business.* **3.** Current; prevailing: *The going rates are low.* **4.** Available; to be found: *the best products going.* —**idioms. going over.** *Informal.* **1.** An examination or inspection: *A team of physicians gave the patient a thorough going over.* **2.** A rehearsal. **3.** A severe beating or reprimand. **goings on.** *Informal.* Events or behavior, esp. when regarded with disapproval.

goi·ter (goi′tər) *n.* Also **goi·tre.** A chronic, noncancerous enlargement of the thyroid gland, visible as a swelling at the front of the neck, associated with iodine deficiency. [French *goitre*, from Provençal *goitron*, from Latin *guttur*, throat.] —**goi′trous** (-trəs) *adj.*

gold (gōld) *n.* **1.** *Symbol* **Au** A soft, yellow, corrosion-resistant element, the most malleable and ductile metal, occurring in veins and alluvial deposits and recovered by mining or by panning or sluicing. It is a good thermal and electrical conductor, is generally alloyed to increase its strength, and is used as an international monetary standard, in jewelry, for decoration, and as a plated coating on a wide variety of electrical and mechanical components. Atomic number 79; atomic weight 196.967; melting point 1,063.0°C; boiling point 2,966.0°C; specific gravity 19.32; valences 1, 3. **2.** A deep, strong, or metallic yellow: *when leaves turn to red and gold.* **3.** Money, esp. money in coins of gold. **4.** Something thought of as having great value or goodness: *a heart of gold.* —**modifier:** *a gold ring; a gold coin.* —*adj.* Deep, strong, or metallic yellow. [Middle English, from Old English.]

gold-beat·ing (gōld′bē′tĭng) *n.* The act, art, or process of beating sheets of gold into gold leaf.

gold·brick (gōld′brĭk′) *n.* Also **gold·brick·er** (-brĭk′ər). *Slang.* A person, esp. a soldier, who avoids assigned duties or work; a shirker. —*intr.v. Slang.* To shirk one's assigned duties or responsibilities.

gold·en (gōl′dən) *adj.* **1.** Made of or containing gold: *golden earrings.* **2.** Having the color of gold or a yellow color suggestive of gold: *a golden wheat field.* **3.** Suggestive of gold, as in richness or splendor: *a golden voice.* **4.** Of the greatest value or importance; precious: *golden memories.* **5.** Marked by peace, prosperity, and often creativeness: *a golden age.* **6.** Very favorable or advantageous; excellent: *a golden opportunity.* **7.** Having a promising future; seemingly assured of success: *a golden boy.* —**gold′en·ly** *adv.* —**gold′en·ness** *n.*

golden anniversary. A 50th anniversary, symbolized by gold.

golden eagle. An eagle, *Aquila chrysaetos*, of mountainous areas of the Northern Hemisphere, that has dark plumage with yellowish feathers on the head and neck.

gol·den·eye (gōl′dən-ī′) *n.* Either of two ducks, *Bucephala clangula* or *B. islandica*, of northern regions, with a short black bill, a rounded head, and black and white plumage.

Golden Fleece. *Gk. Myth.* The fleece of the golden ram, stolen by Jason and the Argonauts with Medea's aid.

golden mean. The medium course between extremes.

goldenrod

goldfinch

gondola

gold·en·rod (gŏl′dən-rŏd′) *n.* Any of numerous chiefly North American plants of the genus *Solidago*, with clusters of small yellow flowers that bloom in late summer or fall.

golden rule. The teaching that one should behave toward others as one would have others behave toward oneself.

gold-filled (gōld′fĭld′) *adj.* Made of a hard metal with an outer layer of gold: *a gold-filled watch.*

gold·finch (gōld′fĭnch′) *n.* **1.** Any of several small New World birds of the genus *Spinus*, esp. *S. tristis*, of which the male has yellow plumage with a black forehead, wings, and tail. **2.** A small Old World bird, *Carduelis carduelis*, that has brownish plumage with red, yellow, and black markings.

gold·fish (gōld′fĭsh′) *n., pl.* **goldfish** or **-fish·es.** A freshwater fish, *Carassius auratus*, native to eastern Asia, characteristically having brassy or reddish coloring and bred in many ornamental forms as an aquarium fish.

gold leaf. Gold beaten into extremely thin sheets, used for gilding.

gold mine. **1.** A mine yielding gold ore. **2.** *Informal.* A source of great wealth or profit.

gold rush. A rush of migrants to an area where gold has been discovered, as to California in 1849.

gold·smith (gōld′smĭth′) *n.* **1.** A craftsman who makes objects of gold. **2.** A tradesman who deals in gold articles.

gold standard. A monetary standard under which the basic unit of currency is equal in value to a specified amount of gold.

go·lem (gō′ləm) *n.* In Jewish folklore, an artificially created human being endowed with life by supernatural means. [Yiddish *goylem*, from Hebrew *gōlem*, shapeless thing.]

golf (gŏlf, gôlf) *n.* A game played on an outdoor course that has a series of nine or eighteen holes spaced far apart and in which a player, using various clubs, tries to propel a small ball into each hole with as few strokes as possible. —*modifier: a golf ball.* —*intr.v.* To play golf. [Middle English *golf*.] —**golf′er** *n.*

golf club. **1.** One of a set of clubs having a slender shaft and a head of wood or iron, used in golf. **2.** An organization of golfers or the clubhouse and grounds belonging to it.

golf course. A large tract of land laid out for golf.

Gol·go·tha (gŏl′gə-thə) *n.* **1.** The hill of Calvary, where Jesus was crucified. **2.** **golgotha.** A place or occasion of suffering or agony.

gon-. Var. of **gono-.**

-gon. A suffix meaning a figure having a designated number of angles: **nonagon.** [From Greek *gōnia*, angle.]

go·nad (gō′nǎd′, gŏn′ǎd′) *n.* The organ that produces gametes; a testis or ovary. [From Greek *gonos*, offspring, procreation.] —**go·nad′al** (gō-nǎd′l) or **go·nad′ic** (-nǎd′ĭk) *adj.*

go·nad·o·trop·ic (gə-nǎd′ə-trŏp′ĭk, -trō′pĭk) *adj.* Also **go·nad·o·troph·ic** (-trŏf′ĭk, -trō′fĭk). Acting on or stimulating the gonads, as a hormone. [GONAD + -TROPIC.]

gon·do·la (gŏn′dl-ə, gŏn-dō′lə) *n.* **1.** A long, narrow boat with a high, pointed prow and stern, used for public conveyance on the canals of Venice. **2.** An open, shallow freight car with low sides. **3.** The basket suspended from a balloon. **4.** The cabin of a dirigible. [Italian dial. *gondola*, roll, rock.]

gon·do·lier (gŏn′dl-îr′) *n.* The boatman of a gondola.

gone (gôn, gŏn) *v.* Past participle of **go.** —*adj.* **1.** Past; bygone: *Those days are gone.* **2.** Dying or dead. **3.** Ruined; lost: *a gone cause.* **4.** Carried away; absorbed. **5.** Used up; exhausted. **6.** *Slang.* Infatuated: *gone on the girl.* [Middle English, from Old English. *(ge)gān.*]

gon·er (gô′nər, gŏn′ər) *n.* *Slang.* Someone or something that is ruined or doomed. [From GONE.]

gong (gông, gŏng) *n.* A metal disk that produces a loud, ringing tone when struck with a padded mallet. [Malay *gōng* (imit.).]

go·nid·i·um (gō-nĭd′ē-əm) *n., pl.* **-i·a** (-ē-ə). **1.** An asexually produced reproductive cell that separates from the parent body, as in certain colonial microorganisms. **2.** An algal cell in the thallus of a lichen. [From Greek *gonos*, offspring, seed.]

-gonium. A suffix meaning a reproductive cell or seed: **oogonium.** [From New Latin *gonium*, seed, cell, from Greek *gonos*, seed, procreation.]

gono- or **gon-.** A prefix meaning sexual, reproductive, or procreative: **gonococcus.** [From Greek *gonos*, offspring, seed, procreation.]

gon·o·coc·cus (gŏn′ə-kŏk′əs) *n., pl.* **-coc·ci** (-kŏk′sī′). A bacterium, *Neisseria gonorrhoeae*, that causes gonorrhea. [GONO- + -COCCUS.]

gon·or·rhe·a (gŏn′ə-rē′ə) *n.* An infectious disease of the genitourinary tract, rectum, and cervix, caused by the gonococcus, transmitted chiefly by sexual intercourse, and characterized by acute purulent urethritis with dysuria. [Late Latin *gonorrhoea*, from Greek *gonorrhoia*. —**gon′or·rhe′al** (-rē′əl) or **gon′or·rhe′ic** (-rē′ĭk) *adj.*

goo (gōō) *n.* *Informal.* A sticky, wet substance. [Poss. short for *burgoo*, a thick gruel or stew.]

goo·ber (gōō′bər) *n.* *Regional.* A peanut. [Of African orig.]

good (gŏŏd) *adj.* **bet·ter** (bĕt′ər), **best** (bĕst). **1.** Having positive or desirable qualities; not bad or poor: *a good book.* **2.** Serving the end desired; suitable; serviceable: *a good outdoor paint.* **3.** Not spoiled or ruined: *The milk is still good.* **4.** In excellent condition; whole; sound: *a good tooth.* **5.** Superior to the average: *a good student.* **6.** Designating the U.S. Government grade of meat higher than standard and lower than choice. **7.** Used or suitable for special or formal occasions: *good clothes.* **8.** Beneficial; helpful: *Earthworms are good for the soil.* **9.** Competent; skilled: *a good machinist.* **10.** Complete; thorough: *a good scrubbing.* **11.** Valid or sound: *a good reason.* **12.** Genuine; real: *a good dollar bill.* **13.** Ample; substantial; considerable: *a good income.* **14.** Full: *a good mile from here.* **15.** Pleasant; enjoyable: *having a good time at the party.* **16.** Favorable: *good weather; a good omen.* **17.** Of moral excellence; virtuous; upright: *a good man.* **18.** Benevolent; cheerful; kind: *a good soul.* **19.** Loyal; staunch: *a good Republican.* **20.** Well-behaved; obedient: *a good child.* **21.** Socially correct; proper: *good manners.* —See Syns at **big** and **convenient.** —*n.* **1.** That which is good: *learning to accept the bad with the good.* **2.** Welfare; benefit; well-being: *for the good of the country.* **3.** Goodness; virtue; merit: *There is much good in him.* —*adv. Informal.* Well. —**idioms. a good deal.** A lot; a considerable amount: *You learn a good deal when you collect stamps.* **as good as.** **1.** Equal or equivalent to: *In some stores checks are as good as cash.* **2.** Nearly; almost: *This car is as good as new.* **for good.** Permanently; forever. **good and.** *Informal.*

Very; entirely: *She is good and mad at him.* **good for.**
1. Able to serve or continue performing for: *Our car is
good for two more years.* **2.** Worth: *This ticket is good for
two seats.* **make good. 1.** To fulfill: *made good his promise.*
2. To compensate for. **3.** To be successful: *He could never
make good as an athlete.* **no good.** *Informal.* Useless: *It's
no good arguing with him.* **to the good.** For the best. [Middle English *gode*, *goode*, from Old English *gōd.*]
　　Usage: **good.** In formal usage, as a descriptive word
good is an adjective, not an adverb. As an adjective it can
qualify a noun by preceding the noun (*a good soup; good
news*), or it can follow a linking verb such as *be, feel, seem,
smell, sound,* and *taste: The soup smells good. The news
sounds good.* In all these examples *good* describes a noun.
Adverbs, rather than adjectives, qualify nonlinking verbs;
but the adverb *good* is informal and should be confined to
dialogue or other deliberately nonformal usage, as: *She
speaks good.* On a formal level *well* replaces *good* in such
examples: *speaks well; sings well; dances well; a machine
that runs well* (or *works well*). The expression *good and,*
preceding an adjective, is informal: *good and tired.*

Good Book. The Bible.
good-by or **good-bye** (gŏŏd-bī′) *interj.* A word used to
express farewell. —*n.* An expression of farewell. —*modifier:* *a good-by kiss.* [Contraction of *God be with you.*]
good-for-noth·ing (gŏŏd′fər-nŭth′ĭng) *n.* A person of little
worth or usefulness. —*adj.* Having little worth; useless.
Good Friday. The Friday before Easter, observed by
Christians in commemoration of the Crucifixion of Jesus.
good-heart·ed (gŏŏd′här′tĭd) *adj.* Kind and generous.
—**good′heart′ed·ly** *adv.* —**good′heart′ed·ness** *n.*
good-hu·mored (gŏŏd′hyōō′mərd) *adj.* Cheerful; amiable:
a good-humored disagreement. —**good′-hu′mored·ly** *adv.*
—**good′-hu′mored·ness** *n.*
good-look·ing (gŏŏd′lŏŏk′ĭng) *adj.* Of a pleasing appearance; attractive. —See Syns at **beautiful.**
good looks. Attractive appearance; handsomeness.
good·ly (gŏŏd′lē) *adj.* **-li·er, -li·est. 1.** Of pleasing appearance; comely. **2.** Somewhat large; considerable: *a goodly
sum.* —**good′li·ness** *n.*
good·man (gŏŏd′mən) *n. Archaic.* **1. a.** The male head of a
household; master. **b.** A husband. **2.** A courteous title of
address for a man not of gentle birth.
good-na·tured (gŏŏd′nā′chərd) *adj.* Having an easygoing,
cheerful disposition. —See Syns at **amiable.** —**good′-na′-
tured·ly** *adv.* —**good′-na′tured·ness** *n.*
good·ness (gŏŏd′nĭs) *n.* **1.** The condition or quality of
being good; excellence; merit; worth. **2.** Virtuousness;
moral excellence. **3.** Kindness; benevolence; generosity.
4. The good part of something; essence; strength. —See
Syns at **virtue.** —*interj.* A word used in various phrases to
express surprise: *For goodness sake!*
goods (gŏŏdz) *pl.n.* **1.** Merchandise; wares: *manufactured
goods.* **2.** Personal belongings. **3.** Fabric; material.
4. *Slang.* Incriminating information or evidence: *The detective tailed the suspect and got the goods on him.* —*idiom.*
deliver the goods. *Slang.* To produce what is expected;
carry out a promise. [Pl. of GOOD.]
Good Sa·mar·i·tan (sə-măr′ĭ-tən). **1.** In a New Testament
parable, the only passer-by to aid a man who had been
beaten and robbed. **2.** A compassionate person who unselfishly helps others.
good-sized (gŏŏd′sīzd′) *adj.* Of a fairly large size.
good-tem·pered (gŏŏd′tĕm′pərd) *adj.* Having an even or
mild temper; not easily irritated. —**good′-tem′pered·ly**
adv. —**good′-tem′pered·ness** *n.*
good-wife (gŏŏd′wīf′) *n. Archaic.* **1.** The female head of a
household; mistress. **2.** A courteous title of address for a
woman not of gentle birth.
good-will (gŏŏd′wĭl′) *n.* Also **good will. 1.** An attitude of
kindness or friendliness; benevolence. **2.** Cheerful willingness: *pitched in with goodwill.* **3.** A good relationship, as
of a business enterprise with its customers or a nation with
other nations. —*modifier:* *an ambassador on a goodwill
tour of Latin America.*
good·y¹ (gŏŏd′ē) *n., pl.* **-ies.** *Informal.* Something attractive or delectable, esp. something sweet to eat. —*interj.* A
word used chiefly by children to express delight.
good·y² (gŏŏd′ē) *n., pl.* **-ies.** *Archaic.* A polite title usually

applied to a married woman of humble rank. [Short for
GOODWIFE.]
good·y-good·y (gŏŏd′ē-gŏŏd′ē) *adj.* Affectedly sweet or
good. —*n., pl.* **good·y-good·ies.** A person who is affectedly good or virtuous.
goo·ey (gōō′ē) *adj.* **-i·er, -i·est.** *Informal.* Viscous; sticky.
[From GOO.]
goof (gōōf). *Slang.* —*n.* **1.** An incompetent, foolish, or stupid person. **2.** A careless mistake; a slip. —*intr.v.* **1.** To
make a silly mistake; to blunder. **2.** To waste or kill time:
goofed off all afternoon. —*tr.v.* To spoil; bungle: *Follow
the recipe and don't goof it up.* —See Syns at **botch.** [Poss.
var. of obs. *goff,* dope, from Old French *goffe,* awkward,
from Italian *goffo.*]
goof·y (gōō′fē) *adj.* **-i·er, -i·est.** *Slang.* Silly; ridiculous: *a
goofy hat.* —**goof′i·ly** *adv.* —**goof′i·ness** *n.*
gook (gōōk) *n. Slang.* A dirty, sludgy, or slimy substance.
[Perh. from Scottish *gowk,* simpleton, from Middle English
gowke, cuckoo, from Old Norse *gaukr.*]
goon (gōōn) *n. Slang.* **1.** A thug hired to intimidate or
harm people. **2.** A stupid or oafish person. [From dial.
gooney, gony, fool.]
goo·ney bird (gōō′nē). *Slang.* An albatross, esp. *Diomedea
nigripes,* common on islands of the Pacific. [From dial.
gooney, fool.]
goose (gōōs) *n., pl.* **geese** (gēs). **1. a.** Any of various wild
or domesticated water birds of the family Anatidae, and
esp. of the genera *Anser* and *Branta,* characteristically
having a shorter neck than that of a swan and a shorter,
more pointed bill than that of a duck. **b.** The female of
such a bird as distinguished from a gander. **c.** The flesh of
such a bird, used as food. **2.** *Informal.* A silly person; a
simpleton. **3.** *pl.* **goos·es.** A tailor's pressing iron with a
long, curved handle. —*idiom.* **cook (one's) goose.** *Informal.* To ruin one's chances. [Middle English *goos,* from
Old English *gōs.*]

　　　　　goose　　　　　　　　　　gooseberry

goose·ber·ry (gōōs′bĕr′ē, gōōz′-) *n.* **1. a.** A spiny shrub,
Ribes grossularia, native to Eurasia, with lobed leaves,
greenish flowers, and edible greenish berries. **b.** The fruit
of this plant. **2.** Any of several plants bearing fruit similar
to the gooseberry.
goose bumps. **Goose flesh.**
goose egg. *Slang.* **1.** A zero: *nothing but goose eggs on the
scoreboard.* **2.** A swelling caused by a blow.
goose flesh. Momentary roughness of skin caused by tiny
bumps that form in the crease surrounding the hairs as a
reaction to cold or fear. Also called **goose bumps** and
goose pimples.
goose·neck (gōōs′nĕk′) *n.* A slender, curved object or
part, such as the flexible shaft of a type of desk lamp.
—*modifier:* *a gooseneck lamp.*
goose pimples. **Goose flesh.**
goose step. A stiff-legged, high-kicking step used in parades by some armies.
goose-step (gōōs′stĕp′) *intr.v.* **-stepped, -step·ping.** To
march in a goose step.
go·pher (gō′fər) *n.* **1.** Any of various short-tailed, burrowing mammals of the family Geomyidae, of North America,
with fur-lined external cheek pouches. Also called **pocket
gopher. 2.** A ground **squirrel,** esp. one of the genus *Citellus.* **3.** Any of several burrowing tortoises of the genus
Gopherus, esp. *G. polyphemus,* of the southeastern United

â pay	â care	ä father	ĕ pet	ē be	hw which	ĭ pit	ī tie	î pier	ŏ pot	ō toe	ô paw, for	oi noise
	ōō boot	ou out	th thin	*th* this	ŭ cut		û urge	zh vision		ə about, item, edible, gallop, circus		

States. Also called **gopher tortoise**. [Short for earlier *magopher*.]

Gor·don setter (gôr′dn). A hunting dog of a breed originating in Scotland, with a silky black and tan coat.

gore[1] (gôr, gōr) *tr.v.* **gored, gor·ing.** To pierce or stab with a horn or tusk. [Middle English *gōren*, to pierce, from *gore*, spear, from Old English *gār*.]

gore[2] (gôr, gōr) *n.* **1.** A triangular or tapering piece of cloth, as in a skirt, umbrella or sail. **2.** A small, triangular piece of land. —*tr.v.* **gored, gor·ing. 1.** To make or provide with a gore or gores. **2.** To cut into a gore. [Middle English, from Old English *gāra*, triangular piece of land.]

gore[3] (gôr, gōr) *n.* Blood, esp. dried blood from a wound. [Middle English, from Old English *gor*, dung, dirt.]

gorge (gôrj) *n.* **1.** A deep, narrow passage with steep sides, as between mountains. **2.** The throat; gullet. **3.** A mass obstructing a narrow passage: *The shipping lane was blocked by an ice gorge.* —*v.* **gorged, gorg·ing.** —*tr.v.* **1.** To stuff with food; satiate: *gorged himself on sweets.* **2.** To devour greedily: *broke into a hive and gorged the honey.* —*intr.v.* To eat gluttonously. [Middle English, throat, from Old French, from Latin *gurges*, whirlpool, throat.] —**gorg′er** *n.*

gor·geous (gôr′jəs) *adj.* **1.** Dazzlingly brilliant; magnificent: *gorgeous jewels.* **2.** Strikingly attractive. —See Syns at **beautiful**. [Middle English *gorgeouse*, showy, splendid, from Old French *gorgias*, stylish, fine, elegant.] —**gor′geous·ly** *adv.* —**gor′geous·ness** *n.*

gor·get (gôr′jĭt) *n.* **1.** A piece of armor protecting the throat. **2.** An ornamental collar. **3.** A patch of distinctive color on the throat, esp. of a bird. [Middle English, from Old French, dim. of *gorge*, throat.] GORGE.]

Gor·gon (gôr′gən) *n.* **1.** *Gk. Myth.* Any of the three sisters who had snakes for hair and eyes that if looked into turned the beholder into stone. **2. gorgon.** A repulsively ugly or terrifying woman.

go·ril·la (gə-rĭl′ə) *n.* **1.** A large anthropoid ape, *Gorilla gorilla*, of forests of equatorial Africa, with a stocky body and coarse, dark hair. **2.** A powerful, brutal man; a thug. [From Greek *Gorillai*, name of an African tribe of hairy men.]

gorilla　　　　　　　　goshawk

gor·mand (gôr′mənd) *n.* Var. of **gourmand**.

gor·man·dize (gôr′mən-dīz′) *v.* **-dized, -diz·ing.** —*intr.v.* To eat gluttonously; to gorge. —*tr.v.* To devour (food) gluttonously; to gorge. [From *gourmandise*, "gluttony."] —**gor′man·diz′er** *n.*

gorse (gôrs) *n.* Any of several spiny, thickset shrubs of the genus *Ulex*, esp. *U. europaeus*, native to Europe, with fragrant yellow flowers. Also called **furze** and **whin**. [Middle English *gorst, gors*, from Old English *gorst, gors*.]

gor·y (gôr′ē, gōr′ē) *adj.* **-i·er, -i·est. 1.** Covered with gore; bloody; bloodstained. **2.** Characterized by much bloodshed or physical violence: *a gory battle.* —**gor′i·ly** *adv.* —**gor′i·ness** *n.*

gosh (gŏsh) *interj.* A word used to express mild surprise or delight. [Euphemistic var. of GOD.]

gos·hawk (gŏs′hôk′) *n.* **1.** A large hawk, *Accipiter gentilis*, with broad, rounded wings and gray or brownish plumage. **2.** Any of several similar or related hawks. [Middle English *goshawke*, from Old English *gōshafoc* : *gōs*, goose + *hafoc*, hawk.]

gos·ling (gŏz′lĭng) *n.* A young goose. [Middle English, ear-

lier *gesling*, from Old Norse *gæslingr*.]

gos·pel (gŏs′pəl) *n.* **1.** Often **Gospel. a.** The teachings of Jesus and the Apostles. **b.** The basic Christian teaching that Christ came to save mankind. **2. a. Gospel.** Any of the first four books of the New Testament, describing the life, death, and resurrection of Jesus Christ. **b.** Often **Gospel.** A selection from any of these books included as part of a religious service. **3.** A teaching or doctrine that is fervently believed in: *the gospel of modernism in art.* **4.** Something accepted as unquestionably true: *What her father says is gospel to her.* **5.** A style of singing characterized by strong Christian evangelical feeling and popular or jazz rhythms and phrasing. —*modifier: a gospel singer.* [Middle English, from Old English *godspell*, good news, gospel: *gōd*, good + *spel*, news.]

gos·sa·mer (gŏs′ə-mər) *n.* **1.** A fine film of cobwebs often seen floating in the air or caught on bushes or grass. **2.** A soft, sheer, gauzy cloth. **3.** Anything delicate, light, or insubstantial. —*adj.* Also **gos·sa·mer·y** (-mə-rē). Light, thin, and delicate. [Middle English *gossomer*: perh. *gos*, goose + *somer*, summer (from its appearance in the Indian summer, when geese are in season).]

gos·sip (gŏs′əp) *n.* **1.** Trivial talk, often involving rumors of a personal or sensational nature. **2.** A person who habitually engages in gossip. —*modifier: a gossip columnist.* —*intr.v.* To engage in or spread gossip. [Middle English *godsib*, godparent, godchild, close friend, from Old English *godsibb*: *god*, god + *sibb*, kinsman.] —**gos′sip·er** *n.*

gos·sip·y (gŏs′ə-pē) *adj.* Full of or inclined to gossip.

got (gŏt) *v.* Past tense and a past participle of **get**. —See Usage note at **get**. [Past tense from *get*, formed on the model of such verbs as *steal, stole*; past part. from Middle English *goten*, formed on the model of such verbs as *steal, stolen*.]

Goth (gŏth) *n.* **1.** A member of the Germanic people that orig. settled between the Elbe and Vistula rivers and that invaded the Roman Empire in the early centuries of the Christian era. **2.** An uncivilized person; a barbarian.

Goth·ic (gŏth′ĭk) *adj.* **1. a.** Of the Goths or their language. **b.** Germanic; Teutonic. **2.** Of the Middle Ages; medieval. **3.** Of an architectural style prevalent in western Europe from the 12th through the 15th cent., characterized by pointed arches, flying buttresses, and ornamental carving. **4.** Often **gothic.** Of a style of fiction that originated in the late 18th cent. and that emphasizes the grotesque, mysterious, and desolate: *a Gothic novel.* **5.** Often **gothic.** Barbarous; uncivilized. —*n.* **1.** The extinct Germanic language of the Goths. **2.** Gothic architecture. —**Goth′i·cal·ly** *adv.*

Gothic arch. *Archit.* A pointed arch.

got·ten (gŏt′n) *v.* A past participle of **get**. —See Usage note at **get**. [Middle English *goten*, formed on the model of such verbs as *steal, stolen*.]

gouache (gwŏsh, gōō-äsh′) *n.* **1.** A method of painting using opaque water colors mixed with a preparation of gum. **2.** An opaque pigment prepared in such a way. **3.** A painting executed with such pigments. [French, from Italian *guazzo*, "puddle," from Latin *aquātiō*, watering, from *aquārī*, to bring water to, from *aqua*, water.]

gouge (gouj) *n.* **1.** A chisel with a rounded, troughlike blade. **2.** A scooping or digging action, as with a gouge. **3.** A groove, hole, or indentation scooped with or as if with a gouge. —*tr.v.* **gouged, goug·ing. 1.** To cut or scoop out with or as if with a gouge: *"He began to gouge a small pattern in the sand with his cane"* (Vladimir Nabokov). **2.** To force out with a scooping action: *gouged out his eye.* **3.** To demand excessively high prices from; overcharge deliberately. [Middle English, from Old French, from Late Latin *gubia*.] —**goug′er** *n.*

gourd (gôrd, gōrd, gōōrd) *n.* **1.** Any of several vines of the family Cucurbitaceae, related to the pumpkin, squash, and cucumber, and bearing fruits with a hard rind. **2.** The fruit of such a vine, as a calabash, often of irregular and unusual shape. **3.** The dried and hollowed-out shell of one of these fruits, used as a drinking vessel or utensil. [Middle English *gourde*, from Old French, from Latin *cucurbita*.]

gour·mand (gōōr′mənd, -mänd′) *n.* Also **gor·mand** (gôr′mənd). A person who delights in eating well and heartily. [Middle English *gourmaunt*, glutton, from Old French *gourmant*.]

gour·met (gŏŏr-mā', gŏŏr'mā') n. A person who knows and appreciates fine food and drink; an epicure. —*modifier: a gourmet restaurant.* [French, from Old French *gourmet*, wine merchant's servant.]

gout (gout) n. **1.** A disease in which, as a result of faulty uric-acid metabolism, hard deposits form in joints. **2.** A large blob or clot: *"And makes it bleed great gouts of blood"* (Oscar Wilde). [Middle English *goute*, from Old French, "drop" (from the belief that gout was caused by drops of morbid humors), from Latin *gutta*, drop.] **gou·ty** (gou'tē) adj.

gov·ern (gŭv'ərn) tr.v. **1.** To control the actions or behavior of; guide; direct: *The mind governs the body.* **2.** To direct or manage the public affairs of; rule politically: *governing a nation.* **3.** To control the speed or amount of; regulate: *a valve governing fuel intake.* **4.** To keep under control; restrain: *unable to govern his emotions.* **5.** To decide; determine: *Chance usually governs the outcome of the game.* **6.** Gram. **a.** To require (a word) to be in a particular case or mood: *A preposition governs a pronoun in the objective case.* **b.** To require the use of (a certain case or mood): *Russian prepositions often govern the instrumental case.* —intr.v. **1.** To exercise political authority: *governing cautiously during a crisis.* **2.** To have or exercise a predominating influence; prevail. [Middle English *governen*, from Old French *governer*, from Latin *gubernāre*, to direct, steer, from Greek *kubernan.*] —**gov'ern·a·ble** adj.

gov·ern·ance (gŭv'ər-nəns) n. **1.** The act, process, or power of governing; government. **2.** The condition of being governed.

gov·ern·ess (gŭv'ər-nĭs) n. A woman employed to educate and train the children of a private household.

gov·ern·ment (gŭv'ərn-mənt) n. **1.** The act or process of governing, esp. the political administration of an area: *the government of a state.* **2.** A system by which a political unit is governed: *democratic government.* **3.** A governing body or organization. **4.** Political science. —*modifier: a government official.* —**gov'ern·men'tal** (gŭv'ərn-mĕn'tl) adj. —**gov'ern·men'tal·ly** adv.

Government Issue. Anything issued by the government or a government agency, as U.S. Army equipment.

gov·er·nor (gŭv'ər-nər) n. **1.** A person who governs, esp.: **a.** The chief executive of a state in the United States. **b.** An official appointed to govern a colony or territory. **2.** The manager or administrative head of an organization or institution: *the governors of a bank.* **3.** A military commandant. **4.** A device that automatically regulates the operation of a machine. [Middle English *governour*, from Old French *governeor*, from Latin *gubernātor*, from *gubernāre*, to govern.]

governor general pl. **governors general.** Also **gov·er·nor-gen·er·al** (gŭv'ər-nər-jĕn'ər-əl) pl. **gov·er·nors-gen·er·al** or **gov·er·nor-gen·er·als.** A governor of a large territory who has other, subordinate governors under his jurisdiction. —**gov'er·nor·gen'er·al·ship'** n.

gov·er·nor·ship (gŭv'ər-nər-shĭp') n. The office, term, or jurisdiction of a governor.

gown (goun) n. **1.** A long, loose, flowing garment, as a robe or nightgown. **2.** A long, usu. formal woman's dress. **3.** A special outer robe worn on ceremonial occasions, as by scholars or clergymen. **4.** A university faculty and student body as distinguished from townspeople: *town and gown.* —tr.v. To dress in a gown. [Middle English *goune*, from Old French, from Late Latin *gunna*, robe, fur.]

Graaf·i·an follicle (grä'fē-ən, grŭf'ē-). Anat. Any of the follicles in the mammalian ovary, containing a maturing ovum. [After Regnier de *Graaf* (1641-73), Dutch anatomist.]

grab (grăb) v. **grabbed, grab·bing.** —tr.v. **1.** To take or grasp suddenly; snatch: *grabbed her coat and ran out the door.* **2.** To capture or restrain; arrest. **3.** To seize unlawfully or forcibly: *accused of grabbing the land of neighboring farmers.* **4.** To take hurriedly: *He grabbed a bite to eat.* —intr.v. To make a grasp: *He grabbed for the gun.* —n. **1.** An act of grabbing; sudden seizure. **2.** Anything grabbed. **3.** A mechanical device for gripping an object. —*idiom.* **up for grabs.** *Informal.* Available for anyone to take. [Middle Dutch and Middle Low German *grabben.*] —**grab'ber** n.

grab bag. 1. A container filled with articles, such as party gifts, to be drawn sight unseen. **2.** Any miscellaneous collection of items.

grace (grās) n. **1.** Seemingly effortless beauty or charm of movement, form, or proportion: *learning to dance with grace.* **2.** A characteristic or quality pleasing for its charm or refinement: *the social graces.* **3.** Skill at avoiding the inept or clumsy course: *She accepted the praise with modest grace.* **4. a.** A disposition to be generous or helpful; good will. **b.** Mercy; clemency. **5.** Often **graces.** Favor; acceptance: *trying to stay in the coach's good graces.* **6.** A favor rendered by one who need not do so: *asked a grace of the king.* **7.** Temporary immunity from penalties granted after a deadline has been passed: *a period of grace before a new law is enforced.* **8.** Theol. **a.** Divine love and protection bestowed freely upon mankind. **b.** The state of being protected or sanctified by the favor of God. **9.** A short prayer of blessing or thanksgiving said before or after a meal. **10. Grace.** A title of courtesy used with *his, her,* or *your* for a duke, duchess, or archbishop. **11.** A musical embellishment, such as an appoggiatura. —tr.v. **graced, grac·ing. 1.** To honor; favor: *She graced the meeting with her regal presence.* **2.** To give beauty, elegance, or charm to. [Middle English, from Old French, from Latin *grātia*, pleasure, favor, thanks, from *grātus*, favorable, pleasing.]

grace·ful (grās'fəl) adj. **1.** Showing grace of movement, form, or proportion: *a graceful bow.* **2.** Exhibiting elegance.—See Syns at **elegance.** —**grace'ful·ly** adv. —**grace'ful·ness** n.

grace·less (grās'lĭs) adj. **1.** Lacking grace; clumsy: *mumbled a graceless apology.* **2.** Having no sense of propriety or decency.—See Syns at **awkward.** —**grace'less·ly** adv. —**grace'less·ness** n.

grace note. A musical note, esp. an appoggiatura, added as an embellishment.

Grac·es (grā'sĭz) pl.n. Gk. Myth. Three sister goddesses who dispense charm and beauty.

gra·cious (grā'shəs) adj. **1.** Characterized by kindness and warm courtesy: *a gracious host.* **2.** Merciful; compassionate. **3.** Condescendingly courteous; indulgent. **4.** Leisurely; elegant: *a gracious dinner.* **5.** Graceful: *a gracious willow.* —interj. A word used in various phrases to express surprise or mild emotion: *Goodness gracious!* [Middle English, from Old French, from Latin *grātiōsus,* favorable, pleasing, from *grātia,* grace.] —**gra'cious·ly** adv. —**gra'cious·ness** n.

grack·le (grăk'əl) n. **1.** Any of several New World blackbirds of the family Icteridae, esp. of the genera *Quiscalus* or *Cassidix,* with iridescent blackish plumage. **2.** Any of several Asian mynas of the genus *Gracula.* [From Latin *grāculus,* jackdaw.]

grad (grăd) n. *Informal.* A graduate of a school or college.

gra·date (grā'dāt') v. **-dat·ed, -dat·ing.** —intr.v. To pass gradually from one degree, shade, or tone to another. —tr.v. To cause to pass gradually from one degree, shade, or tone to another. [Back-formation from GRADATION.]

gra·da·tion (grā-dā'shən) n. **1.** A series of gradual, successive stages. **2.** A degree or stage in such a progression: *the gradations in shading from light to dark.* [Latin *gradātiō,* from *gradus,* step, grade.] —**gra·da'tion·al** adj. —**gra·da'tion·al·ly** adv.

grade (grād) n. **1.** A stage or degree in a process. **2.** A position in a scale of size, quality, value, etc.: *a poor grade of lumber; grade AA eggs.* **3.** A standard of quality: *not up to grade.* **4.** A group of persons or things all falling in the same specified limits; a class. **5.** A class at an elementary school or the pupils in it. **6.** A mark showing the quality of a student's work. **7.** A military, naval, or civil-service rank. **8.** The degree of inclination of a slope, road, or other surface. **9.** A slope or gradual inclination, esp. of a road or railroad track. **10.** A domestic animal produced by crossbreeding one of purebred stock with one of ordinary stock. —v. **grad·ed, grad·ing.** —tr.v. **1.** To arrange in grades or classes; to sort: *grading fruit according to size and quality.* **2.** To arrange in a series or according to a scale: *grading the year's ten best films.* **3. a.** To determine the quality of; evaluate: *grading test papers.* **b.** To give a grade to: *grade a student.* **4.** To level or smooth to a desired or horizontal gradient. **5.** To gradate. —intr.v. **1.** To hold a certain relative position; to rank: *This wine grades high.* **2.** To change or progress gradually. **—idioms. at grade. 1.** On the same level. **2.** At the same degree of inclination. **make the grade.** *Informal.* To reach a goal; succeed. [French, from Latin *gradus,* step.]

grade crossing. An intersection, as of roads and railroad tracks, at the same level.

grade school. An elementary school.

gra·di·ent (grā′dē-ənt) *n.* **1.** The degree to which something inclines; slope. **2.** An ascending or descending part; an incline. **3.** *Physics.* The maximum rate at which a variable physical quantity changes in value per unit change in position. **4.** *Math.* A vector having coordinate components that are the partial derivatives of a function with respect to its variables. [From Latin *gradiens,* pres. part. of *gradī,* to walk, from *gradus,* step.]

grad·u·al (grăj′ōō-əl) *adj.* Occurring in small stages or degrees or by even, continuous change. *—n. Rom. Cath. Ch.* **1.** A book containing the choral portions of the Mass. **2.** The antiphon sung between the Epistle and the Gospel of the Mass. [Middle English, from Medieval Latin *gradualis,* step by step, from Latin *gradus,* step, grade.] **—grad′u·al·ly** *adv.* **—grad′u·al·ness** *n.*

grad·u·al·ism (grăj′ōō-ə-lĭz′əm) *n.* The belief in or policy of advancing toward a goal by gradual, often slow stages. **—grad′u·al·ist** *n.* **grad′u·al·is′tic** *adj.*

grad·u·ate (grăj′ōō-āt′) *v.* **-at·ed, -at·ing.** *—intr.v.* **1.** To be granted an academic degree or diploma: *She graduated from college in June.* **2.** To change gradually or by degrees. **3.** To move to a higher or better stage or position. *—tr.v.* **1.** To grant a diploma or degree to: *She was graduated from the state university.* **2.** To arrange or divide into categories, steps, or grades. **3.** To divide into marked intervals, esp. for use in measurement: *graduate a thermometer in Celsius degrees.* *—n.* (grăj′ōō-ĭt, -āt′). **1.** A person who has received an academic degree or diploma. **2.** A container marked with measured lines indicating degrees or quantity. *—modifier: a graduate degree; graduate courses.* [Middle English *graduaten,* from Medieval Latin *graduāre,* from Latin *gradus,* degree, step, grade.] **—grad′u·a′tor** *n.*

Usage: graduate. The idea of successfully completing a course of study is expressed by either *graduated* or *was graduated:* *He graduated* (or *was graduated*) *from college.* Both constructions are acceptable on a formal level, and both require *from. He graduated college* is not acceptable.

graduate student. A student at a school of a university that offers studies beyond the bachelor's degree.

grad·u·a·tion (grăj′ōō-ā′shən) *n.* **1.** The giving or receiving of an academic degree or diploma marking completion of studies. **2.** A ceremony at which degrees or diplomas are given; commencement. **3.** A mark or series of marks on a container or instrument indicating degrees or quantity. *—modifier: graduation day; graduation exercises.*

Graec·o·Ro·man (grēk′ō-rō′mən) *adj.* Var. of **Greco-Roman.**

graf·fi·to (grə-fē′tō) *n.,* pl. **-ti** (-tē). **1.** A crude drawing or inscription scratched on stone, plaster, or some other hard surface. **2. graffiti.** Any unauthorized writing or drawing in a public place, as on a wall or lavatory door. [Italian, dim. of *graffio,* a scratching, from *graffiare,* to scratch, perh. from *grafio,* a pencil, stylus, from Latin *graphium,* from Greek *graphein,* to write.]

graft¹ (grăft) *tr.v.* **1.** *Hort.* **a.** To unite (a shoot or bud) with a growing plant by insertion or placing in close contact. **b.** To join (a plant or plants) by such union. **2.** To transplant or implant (tissue, an organ, etc.) surgically into a bodily part to compensate for a defect. *—intr.v.* **1.** To make a graft. **2.** To be or become grafted. *—n.* **1.** *Hort.* **a.** A detached shoot or bud united or to be united with a growing plant. **b.** The union or point of union of a detached shoot or bud with a growing plant by insertion or attachment. **c.** A plant produced by such union. **2. a.** Material, esp. tissue or an organ, surgically attached to or inserted into a bodily part to compensate for a defect. **b.** The procedure of implanting or transplanting such material. **c.** The configuration or condition resulting from such a procedure. [Middle English *grafte, graff,* from Old French *grafe,* pencil, shoot for grafting (from its pencillike

shape), from Latin *graphium.*] **—graft′er** *n.*

graft² (grăft) *n.* **1.** The unscrupulous use of one's public position to derive profit or advantages. **2.** Money or an advantage gained by such action. *—tr.v.* To gain by graft. *—intr.v.* To practice graft. [Perh. from GRAFT (transplant).] **—graft′er** *n.*

gra·ham (grā′əm) *adj.* Made from or consisting of wholewheat flour: *a graham cracker.* [After Sylvester *Graham* (1794–1851), American vegetarian who urged dietary reform.]

Grail (grāl) *n.* The legendary cup or chalice used by Christ at the Last Supper and later searched for by medieval knights. Also called **Holy Grail.** [Middle English *graal,* from Old French, from Medieval Latin *gradālis,* dish.]

grain (grān) *n.* **1. a.** A small, hard seed or fruit, esp. that produced by a cereal grass such as wheat, barley, rice, or oats. **b.** The seeds of such plants collectively, esp. after having been harvested. **2.** Cereal grasses collectively: *a field of grain.* **3.** A small hard particle similar to a seed: *a grain of sand.* **4.** The very smallest amount; a tiny quantity: *a grain of truth.* **5.** A unit of weight in the U.S. Customary System, an avoirdupois unit equal to 0.002285 ounce or 0.036 dram. **6.** The arrangement, direction, or pattern formed by the constituents in wood, leather, stone, cloth, or other material. **7.** The side of a hide or piece of leather from which the hair or fur is removed. **8.** The relative size of the particles composing a substance or pattern: *a coarse grain.* **9.** Any painted, stamped, or printed design that imitates the pattern found in wood, leather, or stone. **10.** Natural disposition; temperament: *It went against his grain to surrender without a fight.* *—modifier: grain storage.* *—tr.v.* **1.** To form into grains; granulate. **2.** To paint, stamp, or print with a design imitating the grain of wood, leather, or stone. **3.** To give a granular or rough texture to. *—intr.v.* To form grains. **—idiom. with a grain of salt.** With reservations; skeptically. [Middle English, from Old French, from Latin *grānum,* seed.] **—grain′er** *n.*

grain alcohol. *Chem.* An alcohol.

grain elevator. A building equipped with mechanical lifting devices, used for storing grain.

grain·y (grā′nē) *adj.* **-i·er, -i·est. 1.** Made of or resembling grain; granular. **2.** Having a surface pattern of grain: *grainy wood.* —See Syns at **coarse. —grain′i·ness** *n.*

gram (grăm) *n.* Also *Brit.* **gramme.** *Abbr.* **g** A metric unit of mass and weight equal to one-thousandth (10^{-3}) of a kilogram. [French *gramme,* from Late Latin *gramma,* a small unit, from Greek, letter.]

–gram¹. A suffix meaning written or drawn: **cardiogram.** [Latin *-gramma,* something written, from Greek *gramma,* letter, and *grammē,* line.]

–gram². A suffix meaning gram: **kilogram.** [From GRAM.]

gram-at·om (grăm′ăt′əm) *n.* The mass in grams of an element numerically equal to the atomic weight.

gra·mer·cy (grə-mûr′sē) *interj. Archaic.* A word used to express surprise or gratitude. [Middle English *gramercye,* great thanks, from Old French *grand merci.*]

gra·min·e·ous (grə-mĭn′ē-əs) *adj.* **1.** Of, pertaining to, or characteristic of grasses. **2.** Of or belonging to the family Gramineae, which includes the grasses. [From Latin *grāmineus,* grassy, from *grāmen,* grass.]

gram·mar (grăm′ər) *n.* **1.** The study of language as a body of words that exhibit regularity of structure (morphology) and arrangement into sentences (syntax), sometimes including such aspects of language as the pronunciation of words (phonology), the meanings of words (semantics), and the history of words (etymology). **2.** The system of rules used by the speakers of a language for making sentences in that language: *English grammar is quite different from Turkish grammar.* **3. a.** A description of the rules for making sentences in a given language: *I went out and bought a grammar of French.* **b.** Study of these rules or theory about them, esp. as a school subject. **4.** Usage judged with reference to an idea of standard usage. **5.** The basic principles of any area of knowledge: *the grammar of music.* *—modifier: a grammar lesson.* [Middle English *gramere,* from Old French *gramaire,* from Latin *grammatica,* from Greek *grammatikē (tekhnē),* "(art) of the letters," from *gramma,* letter.]

gram·mar·i·an (grə-mâr′ē-ən) *n.* A specialist in grammar.

grammar school. 1. An elementary school. 2. *Brit.* A secondary or preparatory school. 3. A school stressing the study of classical languages.

gram·mat·i·cal (grə-măt′ĭ-kəl) *adj.* 1. Of or relating to grammar: *grammatical principles.* 2. Conforming to the rules of grammar: *a grammatical sentence.* [Late Latin *grammaticālis,* from Latin *grammaticus,* from Greek *grammatikos,* pertaining to letters.] —**gram·mat′i·cal·ly** *adv.*

gramme. (grăm) *n. Brit.* Var. of **gram.**

gram molecule. *Chem.* A mole.

gram·o·phone (grăm′ə-fōn′) *n.* A record player; phonograph. [From *Gramophone,* orig. a trademark.]

gram·pus (grăm′pəs) *n.* 1. A saltwater mammal, *Grampus griseus,* related to and resembling the dolphins but lacking a beaklike snout. 2. Any of several similar cetaceans, such as the killer whale. [Middle English *graspeis,* from Old French *graspois, craspois* : *cras,* fat, from Latin *crassus* + *pois,* fish, from Latin *piscis.*]

gran·a·ry (grăn′ə-rē, grā′nə-) *n., pl.* **-ries.** 1. A building for storing grain. 2. A region yielding large supplies of grain. [Latin *grānārium,* from *grānum,* grain.]

grand (grănd) *adj.* **-er, -est.** 1. Large and impressive in size, scope, or extent: *a truly grand palace.* 2. Magnificent; splendid: *a grand view of the city.* 3. Rich and sumptuous: *grand furnishings.* 4. Having higher rank than others of the same category: *a grand duke.* 5. Most important; principal; main: *the grand ballroom.* 6. Illustrious; outstanding: *a grand assemblage.* 7. Dignified and admirable: *a grand old man.* 8. Stately; regal. 9. Lofty; noble: *a grand purpose.* 10. Inclusive; complete: *the grand total.* 11. *Informal.* Very good or pleasant; fine: *had a grand time.* —*n.* 1. A **grand piano.** 2. *Slang.* A thousand dollars. [French, from Old French, from Latin *grandis,* grand, full-grown.] —**grand′ly** *adv.* —**grand′ness** *n.*

Syns: *grand, baronial, grandiose, imposing, lordly, magnificent, majestic, princely, regal, royal, stately adj.* Core meaning: Large and impressive in size, scope, or extent (*the grand architecture of Buckingham Palace*).

gran·dam (grăn′dăm′, -dəm) *n.* Also **gran·dame** (-dām′, -dəm). 1. A grandmother. 2. An old woman. [Middle English *graundam,* from Norman French *graund dame* : Old French *grand,* grand + *dame,* mother, dame.]

grand·aunt (grănd′ănt′, -änt′) *n.* A sister of one's grandparent; great-aunt.

grand·child (grănd′chīld′, grăn′-) *n.* A child of one's son or daughter.

grand·dad (grăn′dăd′) *n.* Also **grand·dad·dy** (grăn′dăd′ē) *pl.* **-dies.** *Informal.* Grandfather.

grand·daugh·ter (grăn′dô′tər) *n.* The daughter of one's son or daughter.

grand duchess. 1. The wife or widow of a grand duke. 2. A woman ruler of a grand duchy. 3. The daughter of a czar or of one of his male descendants.

grand duchy. A territory ruled by a grand duke or a grand duchess.

gran·deur (grăn′jər, -jōōr′) *n.* Greatness; splendor: *"The world is charged with the grandeur of God"* (Gerard Manley Hopkins). [Middle English, from Old French, from *grand,* grand.]

grand·fa·ther (grănd′fä′thər, grăn′-) *n.* 1. The father of one's mother or father. 2. A forefather; ancestor.

grandfather clock. Also **grandfather's clock.** A pendulum clock enclosed in a tall, narrow cabinet.

grand·fa·ther·ly (grănd′fä′thər-lē, grăn′-) *adj.* Characteristic of or befitting a grandfather; kindly; indulgent.

gran·dil·o·quence (grăn-dĭl′ə-kwəns) *n.* Pompous or bombastic speech or expression. [From Latin *grandiloquus,* speaking loftily : *grandis,* grand + *loqui,* to speak.] —**gran·dil′o·quent** *adj.* —**gran·dil′o·quent·ly** *adv.*

gran·di·ose (grăn′dē-ōs′, grăn′dē-ōs′) *adj.* 1. Characterized by greatness of scope or intent; grand: *grandiose plans to build a city in the desert.* 2. Characterized by pretended or affected grandeur; pompous: *a grandiose writing style.* — See Syns at **grand.** [French, from Italian *grandioso,* from *grande,* great, grand, from Latin *grandis.*] —**gran′di·ose′ly** *adv.* —**gran′di·os′i·ty** (-ŏs′ĭ-tē), or **gran′di·ose′ness** *n.*

grand jury. A jury of 12 to 23 persons that meets to examine evidence of a crime, evaluate accusations, and decide whether an indictment should be made.

Grand La·ma (lä′mə). The **Dalai Lama.**

grand·ma (grănd′mä′, grăn′-, grăm′mä′, grăm′ə) *n.* Also **grand·ma·ma** (grănd′mə-mä′, grăn′-, -mä′mə). *Informal.* Grandmother.

grand mal (grănd′ mäl′, grän′, grän mäl′). A form of epilepsy characterized by severe seizures and loss of consciousness. [French, "great illness."]

grand·moth·er (grănd′mŭth′ər, grăn′-) *n.* 1. The mother of one's father or mother. 2. A female ancestor.

grand·moth·er·ly (grănd′mŭth′ər-lē, grăn′-) *adj.* Characteristic of or befitting a grandmother.

grand·neph·ew (grănd′něf′yōō, -něv′-, grăn′-) *n.* A son of one's nephew or niece.

grand·niece (grănd′nēs′, grăn′-) *n.* A daughter of one's nephew or niece.

grand·pa (grănd′pä′, grăn′-, grăm′pä′, grăm′pə) *n.* Also **grand·pa·pa** (grănd′pə-pä′, grăn′-, -pä′pə). *Informal.* Grandfather.

grand·par·ent (grănd′pâr′ənt, -păr′-, grăn′-) *n.* A parent of one's mother or father; a grandmother or grandfather.

grand piano. A piano whose strings are stretched out in a horizontal frame.

grand·sire (grănd′sīr′) *n. Archaic.* 1. A grandfather. 2. A male ancestor; forefather. 3. An old man.

grand slam. 1. *Bridge.* The taking of all the tricks. 2. *Baseball.* A home run hit when three men are on base.

grand·son (grănd′sŭn′, grăn′-) *n.* The son of one's son or daughter.

grand·stand (grănd′stănd′, grăn′-) *n.* 1. A roofed stand for spectators at a stadium or racetrack. 2. The spectators seated in a grandstand. —*intr.v.* To perform in a showy way so as to win applause or attract attention. —**grand′stand′er** *n.*

grand·un·cle (grănd′ŭng′kəl) *n.* The uncle of one's father or mother; great-uncle.

grange (grānj) *n.* 1. **Grange. a.** The Patrons of Husbandry, an association of farmers founded in the United States in 1867. **b.** One of its branch lodges. 2. *Brit.* A farm with its farmhouse and other buildings. [Middle English, from Old French, from Medieval Latin *grānica,* from Latin *grānum,* grain.]

gran·ite (grăn′ĭt) *n.* 1. A common, coarse-grained, light-colored, hard igneous rock consisting chiefly of quartz, orthoclase or microcline, and mica, used in monuments and for building. 2. Unyielding endurance; firmness: *The fort's defenders displayed a will of granite.* —*modifier: a granite monument.* [Italian *granito,* "grained," from the past part. of *granire,* to impart a grained surface to, from *grano,* grain, from Latin *grānum.*] —**gra·nit′ic** (grə-nĭt′ĭk) or **gran′it·oid′** (grăn′ĭ-toid′) *adj.*

gran·ite·ware (grăn′ĭt-wâr′) *n.* 1. Enameled iron utensils. 2. Earthenware with a speckled glaze resembling granite.

gran·ny or **gran·nie** (grăn′ē) *n., pl.* **-nies.** *Informal.* A grandmother. 2. An old woman. [Short for GRANDMOTHER.]

granny knot. Also **granny's knot.** A knot like a square knot but with the second tie crossed incorrectly.

grant (grănt) *tr.v.* 1. To allow to have; consent to the fulfillment of: *grant a wish.* 2. To permit as a favor or privilege:

grandfather clock   grand piano

ă pat   ā pay   â care   ä father   ĕ pet   ē be   hw which
ōō took   ōō boot   ou out   th thin   th this   ŭ cut
ĭ pit   ī tie   î pier   ŏ pot   ō toe   ô paw, for   oi noise
û urge   zh vision   ə about, item, edible, gallop, circus

grant a kiss. **3. a.** To bestow; confer: *grant aid.* **b.** To transfer (property) by a deed. **4.** To concede; acknowledge. —See Syns at **acknowledge.** —*n.* **1.** The act or an instance of granting. **2.** Something granted: *His land grant covers five acres.* **3.** A transfer of property by deed. —*idiom.* **take for granted. 1.** To assume to be true without question. **2.** To value too lightly: *We take for granted many of the wonders of electricity.* [Middle English *graunten,* from Old French *gr(e)anter, creanter,* to ensure, guarantee, from Latin *crēdere,* to believe, trust.] —**grant'-a·ble** *adj.* —**grant'er** *n.*

grant·ee (grăn-tē′) *n. Law.* A person to whom a grant is made.

gran·tor (grăn′tər) *n. Law.* A person who makes a grant.

gran·u·lar (grăn′yə-lər) *adj.* **1.** Composed of or appearing to be composed of granules or grains. **2.** Rough in texture; grainy. —See Syns at **coarse.** —**gran'u·lar'i·ty** (-lăr′ĭ-tē) *n.* —**gran'u·lar·ly** *adv.*

gran·u·late (grăn′yə-lāt′) *v.* **-lat·ed, -lat·ing.** —*tr.v.* **1.** To form into grains or granules. **2.** To make rough and grainy. —*intr.v.* To become granular or grainy. —**gran'u·la'tive** (-lā′tĭv) *adj.* —**gran'u·la'tor** or **gran'u·lat'er** *n.*

gran·u·la·tion (grăn′yə-lā′shən) *n.* **1. a.** The act or process of granulating. **b.** The condition of being granulated. **2.** *Physiol.* **a.** The formation of small, fleshy, beadlike protuberances on the surface of a wound that is healing. **b.** One of these protuberances.

gran·ule (grăn′yōol) *n.* A small grain or pellet; a particle. [Late Latin *grānulum,* dim. of *grānum,* grain.]

gran·u·lose (grăn′yə-lōs′) *adj.* Having a surface covered with granules. [GRANUL(E) + -OSE.]

grape (grāp) *n.* **1. a.** Any of numerous woody vines of the genus *Vitis,* bearing clusters of edible fruit and widely cultivated in many species and varieties. **b.** The fleshy, smooth-skinned, purple, red, or green fruit of such a vine, eaten raw or dried and widely used in winemaking. **2.** Grapeshot. —*modifier: grape jelly.* [Middle English, from Old French, bunch of grapes, hook.]

grape·fruit (grāp′frōot′) *n.* **1.** An evergreen tropical or semitropical tree, *Citrus paradisi,* cultivated for its edible fruit. **2.** The large, round fruit of this tree, having a yellow rind and juicy, somewhat acid pulp. —*modifier: grapefruit juice.* [So called because the fruit grows in clusters.]

grape hyacinth. Any of various plants of the genus *Muscari,* native to Eurasia, with narrow leaves and dense terminal clusters of rounded, usu. blue flowers.

grape·shot (grāp′shŏt′) *n.* A cluster of small iron balls formerly used as a cannon charge. [From its resemblance to a cluster of grapes.]

grape sugar. Dextrose.

grape·vine (grāp′vīn′) *n.* **1.** A vine on which grapes grow. **2.** An informal means of transmitting information, gossip, or rumor from person to person. **3.** A secret information source.

graph (grăf) *n.* **1.** A drawing that exhibits a relationship, often functional, between two sets of numbers as a set of points having coordinates determined by the relationship. **2.** Any drawing or diagram used to display numerical data. —*tr.v.* **1.** To represent by a graph. **2.** To plot (a function) on a graph. [Short for *graphic formula.*]

-graph. A suffix meaning: **1.** An apparatus that writes or records: **telegraph. 2.** Something drawn or written: **monograph.** [French *-graphe,* from Latin *-graphum,* from Greek *-graphon,* written, from *graphein,* to write.]

graph·eme (grăf′ēm′) *n.* **1.** A letter of an alphabet. **2.** The sum of letters and letter combinations that can be used to represent a single phoneme. [Greek *graphēma,* letter, from *graphein,* to write.] —**gra·phe'mic** (gră-fē′mĭk) *adj.* —**gra·phe'mi·cal·ly** *adv.*

-grapher. A suffix meaning: **1.** A person who writes about a specific subject: **biographer. 2.** One who employs a specific means to write, draw, or record: **stenographer.** [From Greek *graphein,* to write.]

graph·ic (grăf′ĭk) or **graph·i·cal** (-ĭ-kəl) *adj.* **1.** Represented on paper or a substitute; written or drawn: *put down her thoughts in graphic form.* **2.** Of or represented by or as if by a graph. **3.** Described in vivid detail: *a graphic account of the baseball game.* **4.** Of or used in writing: *a graphic symbol.* **5.** Of the graphic arts. **6.** Of

graphics. [Latin *graphicus,* from Greek *graphikos,* from *graphē,* a writing, from *graphein,* to write.] —**graph'i·cal·ly** *adv.* —**graph'ic·ness** *n.*

graphic arts. The arts that involve representing, writing, or printing on flat surfaces, as painting, drawing, engraving, and lithography.

graph·ics (grăf′ĭks) *n. (used with a sing. or pl. verb).* **1.** The making of drawings in accordance with the rules of mathematics, as in engineering or architecture. **2.** The **graphic arts.**

graph·ite (grăf′īt′) *n.* The soft, steel-gray to black, hexagonally crystallized allotrope of carbon, used in lead pencils, lubricants, paints and coatings, and various fabricated forms including molds, bricks, electrodes, crucibles, and rocket nozzles. [German *Graphit,* from Greek *graphein,* to write.] —**gra·phit'ic** (gră-fĭt′ĭk) *adj.*

graph·ol·o·gy (gră-fŏl′ə-jē) *n.* The study of handwriting, esp. as a means of determining character. —**graph'o·log'i·cal** (grăf′ə-lŏj′ĭ-kəl) *adj.* —**graph·ol'o·gist** *n.*

graph paper. Paper ruled into small squares for use in drawing graphs, charts, and diagrams.

-graphy. A suffix meaning: **1.** A specific process or method of writing or representation: **stenography. 2.** A descriptive science of a specific subject or field: **oceanography.** [Latin *-graphia,* from Greek, from *graphein,* to write.]

grap·nel (grăp′nəl) *n.* A small anchor with three or more flukes. Also called **grappling.** [Middle English *grapenel,* ult. from Old French *grapon,* anchor, hook.]

grap·ple (grăp′əl) *v.* **-pled, -pling.** —*tr.v.* **1.** To seize and hold with or as if with a grappling iron. **2.** To seize firmly with the hands. —*intr.v.* **1.** To use a grappling iron, as for dragging. **2.** To struggle at close quarters; to wrestle: *The policeman lunged at the gunman and grappled with him.* **3.** To attempt to cope: *grapple with the political realities of our time.* —*n.* **1.** A grappling iron. **2.** An act of grappling. **3.** A struggle in which the participants try to clutch or grip each other. **4.** A grip; hold. [Middle English *grapel,* from Old French *grapil,* from Old Provençal, dim. of *grapa,* hook.] —**grap'pler** *n.*

grap·pling (grăp′lĭng) *n.* **1.** A grappling iron. **2.** A grapnel.

grappling iron. Also **grappling hook.** An iron bar with claws at one end for grasping and holding, esp. one for drawing and holding an enemy ship alongside. Also called **grapple** and **grappling.**

grasp (grăsp) *tr.v.* **1.** To seize and hold firmly with or as if with the hand. **2.** To take hold of intellectually; comprehend: *"It is this distinction between freedom and license that many parents cannot grasp"* (A.S. Neill). —See Syns at **understand.** —*intr.v.* **1.** To make a motion of seizing; clutch: *grasped at the swinging rope but missed it.* **2.** To show eager willingness or acceptance: *grasped at the opportunity.* —*n.* **1.** An act of grasping. **2.** A firm hold or grip. **3.** The ability to seize or attain; reach: *The Presidency was within his grasp.* **4.** Understanding; comprehension: *"only a vague intuitive grasp of the meaning of greatness in literature"* (Gilbert Highet). [Middle English *graspen.*]

grasp·ing (grăs′pĭng) *adj.* Eager for gain; greedy: *a grasping moneylender.* —**grasp'ing·ly** *adv.* —**grasp'ing·ness** *n.*

grass (grăs) *n.* **1. a.** Any of numerous plants of the family Gramineae, characteristically with narrow leaves, hollow, jointed stems, and spikes or clusters of membranous flowers borne in smaller spikelets. **b.** Such plants collectively. **2.** Any of various plants with slender leaves like those of the true grasses. **3.** Ground, as a meadow or lawn, covered with grass: *a picnic on the grass.* **4.** Grazing land; pasture. **5.** *Slang.* Marijuana. —*tr.v.* To cover with grass; grow grass on. [Middle English *gras,* from Old English *græs.*]

grass·hop·per (grăs′hŏp′ər) *n.* **1.** Any of numerous insects of the families Locustidae (or Acrididae) and Tettigoniidae, often destructive to plants and characteristically having long hind legs adapted for jumping. **2.** A cocktail consisting of crème de menthe, crème de cacao, and cream.

grass·land (grăs′lănd′) *n.* An area, such as a prairie or meadow, of grass or grasslike vegetation.

grass·roots (grăs′rōots′, -rōōts′) *pl.n. (used with a sing. or pl. verb).* People in local, outlying, or rural areas as distinguished from those in major political centers: *The candidate returned to the grassroots to appeal for votes.*

—*modifier:* grassroots support.

grass snake. Any of several greenish snakes, esp. *Natrix natrix*, of Europe, or *Opheodrys vernalis*, of eastern North America.

grass widow. 1. A woman who is divorced or separated from her husband. 2. A woman whose husband is temporarily absent.

grass·y (grăs′ē) adj. **-i·er, -i·est.** 1. Covered with or abounding in grass. 2. Resembling or suggestive of grass, as in color or odor.

grate¹ (grāt) v. **grat·ed, grat·ing.** —*tr.v.* 1. To reduce to small pieces or powder by rubbing against a rough surface: *grate cabbage.* 2. To cause to make a harsh grinding or rasping sound by rubbing: *grate one's teeth.* 3. To irritate or annoy persistently. —*intr.v.* 1. To make a harsh rasping sound by or as if by scraping or grinding. 2. To cause irritation or annoyance: *The constant noise grated on my nerves.* —*n.* A harsh rasping sound made by scraping or rubbing: *the grate of a key in a lock.* [Middle English *graten,* from Old French *grater,* to scrape.]

grate² (grāt) n. 1. **a.** A framework of parallel or crossed bars for blocking an opening; a grill: *a grate over a storm sewer.* **b.** Such a framework of metal, used to hold burning fuel in a stove, furnace, or fireplace. 2. A fireplace. —*tr.v.* **grat·ed, grat·ing.** To equip with a grate. [Middle English *graten,* from Old French, grille, from Latin *crātis,* frame, wicker basket.]

grate·ful (grāt′fəl) adj. 1. Appreciative; thankful. 2. Expressing gratitude: *a grateful smile.* 3. Affording pleasure or comfort; agreeable: *"he left his home to enjoy the grateful air"* (Ronald Firbank). [From obs. *grate,* agreeable, thankful, from Latin *grātus,* pleasing, favorable.] —**grate′ful·ly** adv. —**grate′ful·ness** n.

grat·er (grā′tər) n. 1. Someone or something that grates. 2. A kitchen utensil with rough or sharp-edged slits and perforations on which to shred or grate foods.

grat·i·fi·ca·tion (grăt′ə-fĭ-kā′shən) n. 1. The act of gratifying. 2. The condition of being gratified; satisfaction; pleasure. 3. A source of pleasure or satisfaction.

grat·i·fy (grăt′ə-fī′) tr.v. **-fied, -fy·ing.** 1. To please or satisfy: *His achievement gratified his father.* 2. To give what is desired; indulge: *He gratified his curiosity by reading the old letters.* [Middle English *gratifien,* to favor, from Old French, from Latin *grātificārī,* to reward, do favor to, from *grātus,* favorable, pleasurable.] —**grat′i·fi′er** n.

grat·ing¹ (grā′tĭng) adj. 1. Rasping or scraping in sound. 2. Nerve-racking; irritating. —**grat′ing·ly** adv.

grat·ing² (grā′tĭng) n. A set of bars placed across a window or door or used as a partition; a grate.

grat·is (grăt′ĭs, grā′tĭs) adv. Freely; without charge: *The tickets are provided gratis.* —adj. Free. [Middle English, from Latin *grātīs,* without reward, from *grātia,* favor, from *grātus,* pleasing.]

grat·i·tude (grăt′ĭ-tōōd′, -tyōōd′) n. An appreciative awareness and thankfulness, as for kindness shown or something received. [Middle English, from Old French, from Medieval Latin *grātitūdō,* from *grātus,* favorable.]

gra·tu·i·tous (grə-tōō′ĭ-təs, -tyōō′-) adj. 1. Given or granted without return or expectation of payment: *gratuitous services.* 2. Given or received without cost or obligation; free. 3. Unnecessary or unwarranted; unjustified: *gratuitous criticism.* [Latin *grātuītus,* given as a favor, from *grātus,* favorable, pleasing.] —**gra·tu′i·tous·ly** adv. —**gra·tu′i·tous·ness** n.

gra·tu·i·ty (grə-tōō′ĭ-tē, -tyōō′-) n., pl. **-ties.** A gift, usu. of money, given in return for service; a tip. [Old French *gratuite,* from Medieval Latin *grātuītās,* present, gift, from Latin *grātuītus,* given free, gratuitous.]

grat·u·lant (grăch′ōō-lənt) adj. Congratulatory.

grat·u·late (grăch′ōō-lāt′) tr.v. **-lat·ed, -lat·ing.** Archaic. 1. To greet with pleasure; welcome. 2. To congratulate. [From Latin *grātulārī,* to greet, salute, from *grātus,* pleasing, grateful.] —**grat′u·la′tion** n. —**grat′u·la·to·ry** (-ə-lə-tôr′ē, -tōr′ē) adj.

gra·va·men (grə-vā′mən) n., pl. **-vam·i·na** (-văm′ə-nə). 1. The part of a charge or accusation that weighs most heavily against the accused. 2. A grievance. [Late Latin, from Latin *gravis,* heavy.]

grave¹ (grāv) n. 1. An excavation for the burial of a corpse;

burial place. 2. Any place of burial: *The sea was his grave.* 3. **the grave.** Death. [Middle English, from Old English græf.]

grave² (grāv) adj. **grav·er, grav·est.** 1. Extremely serious; important; weighty: *a grave decision in a time of crisis.* 2. Bringing death or great danger; critical: *a grave wound.* 3. Dignified in appearance or conduct; solemn: *a grave procession.* 4. Somber; dark. Said of colors. 5. (**also** grăv). Of, being, or written with the mark `, as the è in *Sèvres.* —*n.* (grăv, grāv). The grave accent. [Old French, from Latin *gravis,* heavy, weighty.] —**grave′ly** adv. —**grave′ness** n.

grave³ (grāv) tr.v. **graved, grav·en** (grā′vən), **grav·ing.** To sculpt or carve; engrave: *"I wish I could grave my sonnets on an ivory tablet"* (Oscar Wilde). [Middle English *graven,* from Old English *grafan.*]

grave⁴ (grāv) tr.v. **graved, grav·ing.** To clean (the bottom of a wooden ship) by removing barnacles and other matter and coating with pitch. [Middle English *graven,* prob. from Old French *grave,* sand, gravel.]

grave·dig·ger (grāv′dĭg′ər) n. A person whose occupation is digging graves.

grav·el (grăv′əl) n. 1. A loose mixture of rock fragments or pebbles. 2. *Pathol.* The sandlike granular material of urinary calculi. —*modifier:* a gravel driveway. —*tr.v.* **-eled or -elled, -el·ing or -el·ling.** 1. To cover with a surface of gravel: *gravel a driveway.* 2. To confuse; perplex: *His inconsistencies gravel the reader.* 3. *Informal.* To irritate. [Middle English, from Old French *gravele, gravelle,* dim. of *grave,* gravel, sand, pebbly shore.]

grav·en (grā′vən) v. Past participle of **grave** (to carve). [Middle English, from Old English *grafen.*]

graven image. An idol carved in wood or stone.

grav·er (grā′vər) n. 1. A person who carves or engraves; a stonecarver. 2. An engraver's cutting tool; a burin.

grave·stone (grāv′stōn′) n. A stone placed over a grave as a marker; a tombstone.

grave·yard (grāv′yärd′) n. An area set aside as a burial ground; a cemetery.

graveyard shift. A work shift that runs during the early morning hours, as from midnight to 8:00 A.M.

grav·id (grăv′ĭd) adj. 1. Pregnant. 2. Full of ripe eggs: *a fish gravid with roe.* [Latin *gravidus,* pregnant, from *gravis,* heavy.] —**gra·vid′i·ty** (grə-vĭd′ĭ-tē) or **grav′id·ness** n. —**grav′id·ly** adv.

gra·vim·e·ter (grə-vĭm′ĭ-tər) n. Any instrument used to determine specific gravity. [French *gravimètre* : Latin *gravis,* heavy + *-mètre,* meter.]

grav·i·met·ric (grăv′ĭ-mĕt′rĭk) or **grav·i·met·ri·cal** (-rĭ-kəl) adj. Of or pertaining to measurement by weight. [Latin *gravis,* heavy + METRIC.] —**grav′i·met′ri·cal·ly** adv. —**gra·vim′e·try** (grə-vĭm′ĭ-trē) n.

grav·i·tate (grăv′ĭ-tāt′) intr.v. **-tat·ed, -tat·ing.** 1. To move in response to the force of gravity. 2. To move downward; sink; settle. 3. To be attracted as if by an irresistible force: *"My excuse must be that all Celts gravitate towards each other"* (Oscar Wilde). [From Latin *gravitās,* gravity.] —**grav′i·tat′er** n.

grav·i·ta·tion (grăv′ĭ-tā′shən) n. 1. **a.** The attraction that tends to draw together any pair of material objects. **b.** The force involved in this attraction; gravity. 2. The act or process of gravitating. —**grav′i·ta′tion·al** or **grav′i·ta′tive** (-tā′tĭv) adj. —**grav′i·ta′tion·al·ly** adv.

grav·i·ton (grăv′ĭ-tŏn′) n. A particle postulated to be the quantum of gravitational interaction and presumed to have zero electric charge, zero rest mass, and spin 2. [GRAVIT(ATION) + -ON.]

grav·i·ty (grăv′ĭ-tē) n. 1. **a.** The force of gravitation, having a magnitude (F) that is proportional to the product of the masses (m_1, m_2) divided by the square (s^2) of the distance between them. In mathematical notation $F = G (m_1 m_2/s^2)$, where G is a constant. **b.** The force that the earth or another celestial body exerts on any small mass close to its surface. 2. Seriousness; importance: *It was then that the gravity of our deed fell upon us.* 3. Solemnity or dignity of manner. [Old French *gravite,* from Latin *gravitās,* from *gravis,* heavy, serious, grave.]

gra·vure (grə-vyōōr′) n. 1. A method of printing with etched plates or cylinders; esp., photogravure. 2. A plate or reproduction produced by gravure or used in the process. [French, from *graver*, to engrave, dig into, from Old French.]

gra·vy (grā′vē) *n., pl.* **-vies. 1. a.** The juices that drip from cooking meat. **b.** A sauce made by thickening and seasoning these juices. **2.** *Slang.* Money or profit easily or unexpectedly gained: *Half is for expenses; the rest is gravy.* —*modifier:* *a gravy bowl.* [Middle English *gravey,* from Old French *grave.*]

gravy boat. An elongated dish or pitcher for serving gravy.

gravy train. *Slang.* An easy, well-paid job or occupation.

gray (grā). Also **grey.** —*n.* **1.** Any of the colors, all of which have brightness but lack hue, that can be made by mixing black and white in various proportions. **2.** Often **Gray. a.** A Confederate soldier in the U.S. Civil War. **b.** The Confederate Army. —*adj.* **-er, -est. 1.** Of the color gray. **2.** Having gray hair: *an old gray head.* **3.** Lacking in light or cheer; gloomy: *a gray day.* —*tr.v.* To make gray: *Suffering and anxiety grayed her hair.* —*intr.v.* To become gray: *The driftwood grayed in the sand.* [Middle English, from Old English *græg.*] —**gray′ness** *n.*

gray·beard (grā′bîrd′) *n.* An old man.

gray·lag goose (grā′lăg′). A gray goose, *Anser anser,* of marshy areas of the Old World. [GRAY + *lag,* last.]

gray·ling (grā′lĭng) *n., pl.* **grayling** or **-lings. 1.** Any of several freshwater food fishes of the genus *Thymallus,* of the Northern Hemisphere, with a small mouth and a large dorsal fin. **2.** Any of several grayish or brownish butterflies of the family Satyridae, such as the European species *Eumenis semele.*

gray matter. 1. The brownish-gray nerve tissue of the brain and spinal cord, composed of nerve cells and fibers and some supportive tissue. **2.** *Informal.* Brains; intellect.

gray mullet. A mullet.

gray squirrel. A common squirrel, *Sciurus carolinensis,* of eastern North America, with gray or blackish fur and a very bushy tail.

graze¹ (grāz) *v.* **grazed, graz·ing.** —*intr.v.* To feed on growing grasses and herbage: *Cattle were grazing in the pasture.* —*tr.v.* **1.** To feed on (herbage) in a field or on pasture land: *grazing the stubby grass.* **2.** To feed on the herbage of (land): *when buffalo grazed the prairie.* **3.** To put (livestock) out to feed. **4.** To provide enough herbage for: *This field will graze 30 head of cattle.* **5.** To tend (feeding livestock) in a pasture. [Middle English *grasen,* to feed on grass, from Old English *grasian,* from *græs,* grass.] —**graz′er** *n.*

graze² (grāz) *v.* **grazed, graz·ing.** —*tr.v.* **1.** To touch lightly in passing; to skim; brush: *The hydroplane barely grazes the surface of the water.* **2.** To scrape or scratch slightly: *The bullet grazed his shoulder.* —*intr.v.* To scrape or touch a surface lightly in passing. —*n.* **1.** A brushing or scraping along a surface. **2.** A scratch or abrasion resulting from a graze. [Perh. from GRAZE (to feed).]

gra·zier (grā′zhər) *n.* A person who grazes cattle.

graz·ing (grā′zĭng) *n.* Land used for feeding; pasturage. —*modifier:* *grazing animals.*

grease (grēs) *n.* **1.** Animal fat when melted or soft. **2.** Any thick oily or an oily substance, esp. when used as a lubricant. **3. a.** The oily substance present in raw wool. **b.** Raw wool that has not been cleansed of this. —*modifier:* *a grease spot.* —*tr.v.* **greased, greas·ing.** To coat, smear, lubricate, or soil with grease. —*idiom.* **grease (someone's) palm (or hand).** *Slang.* To bribe. [Middle English *grese,* from Old French *graisse,* from Latin *crassus,* fat.]

grease monkey. *Slang.* A mechanic who lubricates machinery.

grease paint. Theatrical make-up.

grease·wood (grēs′wŏŏd′) *n.* **1.** A spiny shrub, *Sarcobatus vermiculatus,* of western North America, with small alternate leaves, white stems, and small greenish flowers. **2.** Any of various similar or related plants, as the creosote bush.

greas·y (grē′sē, -zē) *adj.* **-i·er, -i·est. 1.** Coated or soiled with grease. **2.** Containing grease, esp. too much grease: *greasy soup.* **3.** Slick; unctuous: *a greasy character.* —**greas′i·ly** *adv.* —**greas′i·ness** *n.*

great (grāt) *adj.* **-er, -est. 1.** Extremely large; notably big. **2.** Larger than others of the same kind: *the great auk.*

3. Large in quantity or number: *A great throng awaited him.* **4.** Of considerable duration; long in time or distance. **5.** Remarkable or outstanding in magnitude, degree, or extent: *a great crisis.* **6.** Significant; important; meaningful: *a great work of art.* **7.** Chief or principal: *the great house on the estate.* **8.** Superior in quality or character; noble; excellent: *"For he was great, ere fortune made him so"* (Dryden). **9.** Powerful; influential. **10.** Eminent; distinguished: *a great leader.* **11.** Grand; aristocratic. **12.** *Archaic.* Pregnant: *great with child.* **13.** Enthusiastic: *a great boxing fan.* **14.** Skillful: *He is great at algebra.* **15.** First-rate; very good: *a great book.* **16.** Being one generation removed from the relative specified: *her great-grandfather.* —See Syns at **big** and **excellent.** —*n.* Someone or something that is great: *Many of the nation's greats were there.* —*adv.* *Informal.* Very well. [Middle English *grete,* from Old English *grēat,* thick, coarse.] —**great′ness** *n.*

great-aunt (grāt′ănt′, -änt′) *n.* A grandaunt.

great circle. A circle that is the intersection of the surface of a sphere with a plane passing through the center of the sphere.

great·coat (grāt′kōt′) *n.* A heavy overcoat.

Great Dane. A large and powerful dog of a breed developed in Germany, with a smooth, short coat and a narrow head.

Great Dane   great horned owl

great·er (grā′tər) *adj.* Including the populous suburbs of a specified city: *the greater Los Angeles area.*

great-grand·child (grāt′grănd′chīld′, -grăn′-) *n.* A child of a grandchild.

great-grand·daugh·ter (grāt′grăn′dô′tər) *n.* A daughter of a grandchild.

great-grand·fa·ther (grāt′grănd′fä′thər, -grăn′-) *n.* The father of a grandparent.

great-grand·moth·er (grāt′grănd′mŭth′ər, -grăn′-) *n.* The mother of a grandparent.

great-grand·par·ent (grāt′grănd′pâr′ənt, -păr′-, -grăn′-) *n.* Either of the parents of a grandparent.

great-grand·son (grāt′grănd′sŭn′, -grăn′-) *n.* A son of a grandchild.

great-heart·ed (grāt′här′tĭd) *adj.* **1.** Noble or courageous in spirit; stouthearted. **2.** Great in generosity; magnanimous. —See Syns at **generous.** —**great′heart′ed·ly** *adv.* —**great′heart′ed·ness** *n.*

great horned owl. A large North American owl, *Bubo virginianus,* with brownish plumage and prominent ear tufts.

great·ly (grāt′lē) *adv.* **1.** In a great manner; nobly. **2.** To a great degree; very much: *The states vary greatly in population.*

great-neph·ew (grāt′něf′yŏŏ, -něv′-) *n.* A grandnephew.

great-niece (grāt′nēs′) *n.* A grandniece.

Great Powers. Those nations having the greatest influence in international affairs.

great seal. The principal seal of a government or state, with which official documents are stamped.

Great Spirit. The principal god in the religion of many North American Indian tribes.

great-un·cle (grāt′ŭng′kəl) *n.* A granduncle.

greave (grēv) *n.* Leg armor worn below the knee. [Middle English, from Old French, shin.]

grebe (grēb) *n.* Any of various diving birds of the family Podicipedidae, with lobed, fleshy membranes along each toe and a pointed bill. [French *grèbe.*]

ă pat ā pay â care ä father ĕ pet ē be hw which ĭ pit ī tie î pier ŏ pot ō toe ô paw, for oi noise
ŏŏ took ŏŏ boot ou out th thin th this ŭ cut û urge zh vision ə about, item, edible, gallop, circus

Gre·cian (grē'shən) *adj.* Greek. —*n.* A native of Greece.

Grec·o-Ro·man (grĕk'ō-rō'mən, grē'ko-) *adj.* Also **Graec·o-Ro·man.** Of or relating to both Greece and Rome: *Greco-Roman mythology.*

greed (grēd) *n.* A selfish desire for more than one needs or deserves, as of food, wealth, or power; avarice. [Back-formation from GREEDY.]

greed·y (grē'dē) *adj.* **-i·er, -i·est. 1.** Filled with greed; avaricious: *a man greedy for more and more land.* **2.** Wanting to eat or drink more than is reasonable; gluttonous. [Middle English *gredy*, from Old English *grǣdig*.] —**greed'i·ly** *adv.* —**greed'i·ness** *n.*

Greek (grēk) *n.* **1.** The Indo-European language of Greek people. **2.** A native or inhabitant of Greece. **3.** *Informal.* Something unintelligible: *What the economists say is Greek to me.* —*adj.* **1.** Of, pertaining to, or designating Greece, the Greeks, their language, or their culture. **2.** Of or designating the Greek Orthodox Church.

Greek cross. A cross formed by two bars of equal length crossing at the middle at right angles to each other.

Greek Orthodox Church. A division of the Eastern Orthodox Church.

green (grēn) *n.* **1.** The color of most plant leaves and growing grass. **2. greens. a.** The branches and leaves of green plants used for decoration: *Christmas greens.* **b.** Leafy plants or plant parts eaten as vegetables: *salad greens; turnip greens.* **3.** A grassy lawn or park in the center of a town: *the village green.* **4.** The closely mowed area of grass surrounding a cup on a golf course. —*adj.* **-er, -est. 1.** Of the color green. **2.** Covered with green growth or foliage: *green meadows.* **3.** Not ripe: *a green banana.* **4.** Lacking training or experience; unschooled: *green players.* **5.** Not aged or seasoned: *green wood.* **6.** Pale and sickly in appearance; wan: *He turned green at the thought.* **7.** Easily deceived; gullible. —*tr.v.* To make green. —*intr.v.* To become green. [Middle English *grene*, from Old English *grēne*.] —**green'ly** *adv.* —**green'ness** *n.*

green algae. Any of the numerous algae of the division Chlorophyta, which includes spirogyra, sea lettuce, and others having pronounced green coloring.

green·back (grēn'băk') *n.* A legal-tender note of U.S. currency.

green bean. The **string bean.**

green·belt (grēn'bĕlt') *n.* A belt of recreational parks, farmland, or uncultivated land surrounding a community.

green corn. Young, tender ears of sweet corn.

green·er·y (grē'nə-rē) *n., pl.* **-ies. 1.** Green plants or leaves. **2.** A place where plants are grown.

green-eyed (grēn'īd') *adj.* **1.** Having green eyes. **2.** Jealous.

green·gage (grēn'gāj') *n.* A variety of plum with yellowish-green skin and sweet flesh. [GREEN + *gage*, plum.]

green·gro·cer (grēn'grō'sər) *n. Brit.* A person who sells fresh fruit and vegetables. —**green'gro'cer·y** *n.*

green·horn (grēn'hôrn') *n.* **1.** An inexperienced or immature person; beginner. **2.** A recent immigrant or arrival. **3.** A gullible person. [Orig., a young animal with immature horns.]

green·house (grēn'hous') *n.* A room or building with a glass roof and sides, used for growing plants that need an even, usu. warm temperature.

greenhouse effect. The heating of the earth's atmosphere that occurs when infrared radiation from the sun passes through the atmosphere and strikes the earth's surface. This radiation loses some of its energy and is re-emitted at a longer wavelength that causes it to be absorbed in the atmosphere instead of passing out again.

green·ing (grē'nĭng) *n.* Any of several varieties of apple that have green-skinned fruit and are used chiefly in cooking.

green·ish (grē'nĭsh) *adj.* Somewhat green.

green light. 1. The green-colored light that signals traffic to proceed. **2.** *Informal.* Permission to proceed.

green onion. A young onion with a tender green stalk and a small white bulb, usu. eaten raw; scallion.

green pepper. The unripened green fruit of various pepper plants.

green·room (grēn'rōōm', -rōōm') *n.* A waiting room or lounge in a theater or concert hall for the use of performers when off-stage.

green snake. Any of several nonvenomous North American snakes of the genus *Opheodrys*, with a slender yellow-green body.

green·sward (grēn'swôrd') *n.* Turf covered with green grass.

green thumb. A knack for making plants grow well.

green turtle. A large saltwater turtle, *Chelonia mydas*, that has greenish flesh esteemed as food.

Green·wich time (grĭn'ĭj, -ĭch, grĕn'-). The time at the meridian at Greenwich, England (0° longitude), used as a basis for calculating time throughout most of the world.

green·wood (grēn'wōōd') *n.* A wood or forest when the foliage is green.

greet (grēt) *tr.v.* **1.** To address in a friendly and respectful way; to welcome or salute: *The host greeted his guests at the door.* **2.** To receive with a specified reaction: *greet a joke with laughter.* **3.** To present itself to; be perceived by: *A din greeted our ears.* [Middle English *greten*, from Old English *grētan*.] —**greet'er** *n.*

greet·ing (grē'tĭng) *n.* A gesture or word of welcome or salutation.

gre·gar·i·ous (grĭ-gâr'ē-əs) *adj.* **1.** Tending to move in or form a group with others of the same kind, as a herd, pack, or flock. **2.** Seeking and enjoying the company of others; sociable: *a gregarious man.* **3.** *Bot.* Growing in groups that are close together but not densely clustered or matted. [From Latin *gregārius*, belonging to a flock, from *grex*, herd, flock.] —**gre·gar'i·ous·ly** *adv.* —**gre·gar'i·ous·ness** *n.*

Gre·go·ri·an (grĭ-gôr'ē-ən, -gōr'-) *adj.* Associated with or introduced by Pope Gregory I or Pope Gregory XIII.

Gregorian calendar. The calendar in use throughout most of the world, introduced by Pope Gregory XIII in 1582.

Gregorian chant. The type of plainsong used in the Roman Catholic Church, systematized in about A.D. 600 during the papacy of Gregory I.

grem·lin (grĕm'lĭn) *n.* **1.** An imaginary elf whose mischief is said to cause mechanical failures in aircraft. **2.** Any mischief-maker. [Orig. unknown.]

gre·nade (grə-nād') *n.* **1.** A small bomb detonated by a fuse, designed to be thrown by hand or fired from a launcher-equipped rifle. **2.** A glass container filled with a volatile chemical or a liquid that is dispersed when the glass is thrown and smashed: *a tear-gas grenade.* [French, from Old French *pome grenate*, pomegranate (from its shape).]

gren·a·dier (grĕn'ə-dîr') *n.* **1. a.** A member of the British Grenadier Guards, the first regiment of the royal household infantry. **b.** A soldier formerly bearing grenades. **2.** Any of various fishes of the family Macrouridae, chiefly of the deep ocean, having a long tapering tail and lacking a tail fin. [French, "grenade thrower," from *grenade*, grenade.]

gren·a·dine (grĕn'ə-dēn', grĕn'ə-dēn') *n.* **1.** A thick, sweet syrup made from pomegranates or red currants and used as flavoring, esp. in beverages. **2.** A thin, openwork fabric of silk, cotton, or a synthetic. [French, from Old French *pome grenate*, pomegranate.]

grew (grōō) *v.* Past tense of **grow.** [Middle English, from Old English *grēow.*]

grew·some (grōō'səm) *adj.* Var. of **gruesome.**

grey (grā) *n., adj. & v.* Var. of **gray.**

grey·hound (grā'hound') *n.* A slender, swift-running dog with long legs, a smooth coat, and a narrow head. [Middle English *grehound*, from Old English *grīghund.*]

grib·ble (grĭb'əl) *n.* Any of several small, wood-boring saltwater crustaceans of the genus *Limnoria*, esp. *L. lignorum*, that often damage underwater wooden structures. [Poss. a dim. of GRUB.]

grid (grĭd) *n.* **1.** A framework of parallel or crisscrossed bars. **2.** A pattern of horizontal and vertical lines forming squares of uniform size on a map, chart, or aerial photograph, used as a reference for locating points. **3.** A football field. **4. a.** An interconnected system of electric cables and power stations that distributes electricity over a large area. **b.** A corrugated or perforated conducting plate in a storage battery. **5. a.** A fine wire screen or coil placed between the cathode and anode of an electron tube in a way that allows the voltage applied to it to control the passage of electrons through the tube. **b.** The terminal of an electron tube that connects to its grid. [Short for GRIDIRON.]

grid·dle (grĭd′l) *n.* A flat pan or other flat metal surface used for cooking pancakes, bacon, etc. —*tr.v.* **-dled, -dling.** To cook on a griddle. [Middle English *gredil*, from Old French, from Latin *crāticula,* dim. of *crātis,* wickerwork.]

grid·dle·cake (grĭd′l-kāk′) *n.* A pancake.

grid·i·ron (grĭd′ī′ərn) *n.* **1.** A flat framework of parallel metal bars used for broiling meat or fish. **2.** Any framework or network of crossing straight lines. **3.** A football field. [Middle English *gredire,* perh. var. of *gredile, gredil,* griddle.]

grief (grēf) *n.* **1.** Deep sadness, as over a loss; sorrow. **2.** A cause of sorrow. —See Syns at **sorrow.** —*idiom.* **come to grief.** To meet with failure or defeat. [Middle English *gref,* from Old French *grief, gref,* from *grever,* to grieve.]

griev·ance (grē′vəns) *n.* **1.** An actual or supposed circumstance regarded as just cause for protest: *Taxation without representation was the principal grievance of the American colonists.* **2.** A complaint or protestation based on such a circumstance: *The workers presented their grievances to a panel of judges.* [Middle English *grievaunce,* from Old French *grevance,* from *grever,* to grieve.]

grieve (grēv) *v.* **grieved, griev·ing.** —*tr.v.* To cause to be sorrowful; to distress: *grieved by the news of his teacher's death.* —*intr.v.* To feel grief; mourn. [Middle English *greven,* from Old French *grever,* from Latin *gravāre,* to oppress, weigh upon, from *gravis,* heavy, weighty.]

griev·ous (grē′vəs) *adj.* **1.** Causing grief, pain, or anguish: *a grievous loss.* **2.** Serious; grave: *a grievous crime.* —**griev′ous·ly** *adv.* —**griev′ous·ness** *n.*

grif·fin (grĭf′ĭn) *n.* Also **grif·fon** or **gryph·on** (grĭf′ən). *Gk. Myth.* A fabled beast with the head and wings of an eagle and the body of a lion. [Middle English *griffon,* from Old French *grifoun,* from Late Latin *grȳphus,* from Latin, from Greek *grups.*]

grill (grĭl) *tr.v.* **1.** To broil on a gridiron. **2.** To torture as if by broiling. **3.** *Informal.* To question relentlessly; cross-examine. —*intr.v.* To undergo broiling. —*n.* **1.** A cooking utensil with parallel thin metal bars on which food is broiled. **2.** Food cooked by broiling or grilling. **3.** A grillroom. **4.** Var. of **grille.** [French *griller,* from *gril, grille,* a grating, gridiron, from Old French *grille, grail,* from Latin *crāticula.*]

grille (grĭl) *n.* Also **grill.** A framework of metal bars used as a screen, divider, barrier, or decorative element, as in a window or gateway. [French, grating, grill.]

grilled (grĭld) *adj.* **1.** Broiled on a grill: *a grilled hamburger.* **2.** Having a grille: *a grilled window.*

grim (grĭm) *adj.* **grim·mer, grim·mest. 1.** Unrelenting; rigid; stern: *a grim insistence on continuing.* **2.** Uninviting or unnerving in appearance; forbidding; terrible: *"undoubtedly the grimmest part of him was his iron claw"* (J.M. Barrie). **3.** Ghastly; sinister: *"he made a grim jest at the horrifying nature of his wound"* (Reginald Pound). **4.** Dismal; gloomy. **5.** Ferocious; savage. —See Syns at **ghastly.** [Middle English, from Old English, fierce, severe.] —**grim′ly** *adv.* —**grim′ness** *n.*

grim·ace (grĭm′əs, grĭ-mās′) *n.* A sharp tightening or twisting of the facial features expressive of pain, contempt, or disgust. —*intr.v.* **-aced, -ac·ing.** To make a grimace: *Father grimaced when he saw my report card.* [French, from Old French *grimasse,* from *grimuche.*]

gri·mal·kin (grĭ-mǎl′kĭn, -môl′-) *n.* **1.** A cat, esp. an old female cat. **2.** A shrewish old woman. [Var. of *graymalkin :* GRAY + dial. *malkin,* lewd woman, hussy.]

grime (grīm) *n.* Black dirt or soot, esp. such dirt clinging to or ingrained in a surface. —*tr.v.* **grimed, grim·ing.** To cover with dirt; begrime. [Middle English *grim(e),* from Middle Dutch *grime.*]

grim·y (grī′mē) *adj.* **-i·er, -i·est.** Covered or ingrained with grime: *a grimy old pair of running shoes.* —See Syns at **dirty.** —**grim′i·ly** *adv.* —**grim′i·ness** *n.*

grin (grĭn) *v.* **grinned, grin·ning.** —*intr.v.* To smile broadly, showing the teeth: *grin with delight.* —*tr.v.* To express with a grin: *He grinned a welcome.* —*n.* The expression of the face produced by grinning. [Middle English *grinnen,* from Old English *grennian,* to grimace.] —**grin′ner** *n.*

grind (grīnd) *v.* **ground** (ground), **grind·ing.** —*tr.v.* **1.** To crush into fine particles, esp. by rubbing between two hard surfaces: *grind wheat into flour.* **2.** To shape, sharpen, or refine with friction: *grind a lens.* **3.** To rub together; gnash: *grind the teeth.* **4.** To bear down on harshly; crush. **5. a.** To operate by turning a crank: *grind a pepper mill.* **b.** To produce by turning a crank: *grinding out hamburger; grind out music on a hand organ.* **6.** To produce mechanically or without inspiration: *"The production line grinds out a uniform product"* (Dwight Macdonald). **7.** To instill or teach by persistent repetition: *grind the truth into their heads.* —*intr.v.* **1.** To perform the operation of grinding something. **2.** To be ground. **3.** To move with noisy friction; to grate: *The train ground along the rusty rails.* **4.** *Informal.* To devote oneself to study or work: *She grinds away at her homework.* —*n.* **1.** The act of grinding. **2.** A crunching or grinding noise. **3.** A specific grade or degree of pulverization: *a fine grind of coffee.* **4.** *Informal.* A laborious task, routine, or study. **5.** *Informal.* A student who studies very hard to the exclusion of other activities. [Middle English *grinden,* from Old English *grindan.*] —**grind′ing·ly** *adv.*

grind·er (grīn′dər) *n.* **1.** Someone or something that grinds, esp. a person who sharpens cutting edges. **2.** A molar. **3. grinders.** *Informal.* The teeth. **4.** *Slang.* A hero sandwich.

grind·stone (grīnd′stōn′) *n.* **1.** A stone disk turned on an axle for grinding, polishing, or sharpening tools. **2.** A millstone. —*idiom.* **keep (or have) (one's) nose to the grindstone.** To work hard and steadily.

grip¹ (grĭp) *n.* **1.** A tight hold; a firm grasp: *She held the racket with a steady grip.* **2.** A manner or power of grasping and holding: *With age his hands had lost their grip.* **3.** A prescribed manner of clasping hands, used by members of a fraternal society. **4.** Mastery; command; understanding: *a good grip on French grammar.* **5. a.** A mechanical device that grasps and holds. **b.** A part designed to be grasped and held; a handle. **6.** A suitcase or valise. **7. a.** A stagehand who helps in shifting scenery. **b.** A member of a film production crew who adjusts sets and props and sometimes assists the cameraman. —*tr.v.* **gripped, grip·ping. 1.** To get and maintain a tight hold on; seize firmly: *grip a bat.* **2.** To hold the interest or attention of: *a scene that gripped the entire audience.* —*idiom.* **come to grips. 1.** To engage in combat; to fight. **2.** To try to deal directly or boldly; confront: *He avoided coming to grips with his drinking problem.* [Middle English, partly from Old English *gripa,* grasp, and partly from Old English *gripa,* handful.] —**grip′ping·ly** *adv.*

grip² (grĭp) *n.* Var. of **grippe.**

gripe (grīp) *v.* **griped, grip·ing.** —*tr.v.* **1.** To cause sharp pain in the bowels of. **2.** To irritate; annoy. **3.** To grasp; seize. —*intr.v.* **1.** *Informal.* To complain naggingly; to grumble: *always griping about the food.* **2.** To have sharp pains in the bowels. —*n.* **1.** *Informal.* A complaint. **2. gripes.** Sharp, repeated pains in the bowels. **3.** A grip; grasp. [Middle English *gripen,* from Old English *grīpan.*]

grippe (grĭp) *n.* Also **grip.** *Path.* Influenza. [French, from *gripper,* to seize, from Old French.] —**grip′py** *adj.*

grip·sack (grĭp′săk′) *n.* A small suitcase.

gris·ly (grĭz′lē) *adj.* **-li·er, -li·est.** Horrifying; gruesome: *a grisly murder.* —See Syns at **ghastly.** [Middle English, from Old English *grislīc.*]

grist (grĭst) *n.* **1.** Grain or a quantity of grain for grinding. **2.** Ground grain. —*idiom.* **grist for (one's) mill.** Something that can be turned to one's advantage. [Middle English, from Old English *grist.*]

gris·tle (grĭs′əl) *n.* Cartilage, esp. when present in meat. [Middle English *gristil,* from Old English *gristle.*]

gris·tly (grĭs′lē) *adj.* **-tli·er, -tli·est.** Of, like, or containing gristle. —**gris′tli·ness** *n.*

grist·mill (grĭst′mĭl′) *n.* A mill for grinding grain.

grit (grĭt) *n.* **1.** Tiny rough particles, as of sand or stone. **2.** The texture or structure of stone to be used in grinding. **3.** *Informal.* Indomitable spirit; pluck. —*v.* **grit·ted, grit·ting.** —*tr.v.* To clamp (the teeth) together. —*intr.v.* To make a grinding noise. [Middle English *grete,* from Old English *grēot.*]

grits (grĭts) *pl.n.* Coarsely ground grain, esp. corn. [From

Middle English *gryt*, bran, from Old English *grytt*.]

grit·ty (grĭt'ē) *adj.* **-ti·er, -ti·est. 1.** Containing or resembling grit. **2.** *Informal.* Indomitably spirited; plucky. **—grit'ti·ness** *n.*

griz·zly (grĭz'lē) *adj.* **-zli·er, -zli·est.** Grayish or flecked with gray. **—n.,** *pl.* **-zlies.** A grizzly bear.

grizzly bear. The grayish form of the brown bear, *Ursus arctos,* of northwestern North America, often considered a separate species, *U. horribilis.*

grizzly bear

groan (grōn) *intr.v.* **1.** To utter a deep, prolonged sound expressive of pain, grief, annoyance, or disapproval. **2.** To make a low creaking sound expressive of stress or strain: *"I stretched out . . . hearing the springs groan beneath me"* (Ralph Ellison). **—tr.v.** To utter or convey with groaning. **—n.** A sound made in groaning; a moan: *the groans of wounded men.* [Middle English *gronen,* from Old English *grānian.*]

groat (grōt) *n.* A British silver fourpence piece used from the 14th to the 17th cent. [Middle English *grote,* from Middle Dutch *groot.*]

groats (grōts) *pl.n.* Hulled, usu. crushed or broken grain, esp. oats. [Middle English *grotes,* from Old English *grotan.*]

gro·cer (grō'sər) *n.* A storekeeper who sells foodstuffs and household supplies. [Middle English, from Old French *grossier,* wholesale dealer, from Medieval Latin *grossārius,* from Latin *grossus,* thick, gross.]

gro·cer·y (grō'sə-rē) *n., pl.* **-ies. 1.** A store selling foodstuffs and household supplies. **2. groceries.** The goods sold by a grocer. **—modifier:** *a grocery list.*

grog (grŏg) *n.* Rum or other alcoholic liquor diluted with water. [After Old *Grog,* nickname of Admiral Edward Vernon (1684–1757), who ordered that diluted rum be served to his sailors.]

grog·gy (grŏg'ē) *adj.* **-gi·er, -gi·est.** Unsteady and dazed; shaky: *groggy from lack of sleep.* [From GROG.] **—grog'gi·ly** *adv.* **—grog'gi·ness** *n.*

grog·ram (grŏg'rəm) *n.* **1.** A coarse, often stiffened fabric of silk, mohair, or wool or a blend of these. **2.** A garment of grogram. [Alteration of GROSGRAIN.]

groin (groin) *n.* **1.** The crease where the thigh meets the trunk, together with the area nearby. **2.** *Archit.* The curved edge at the junction of two intersecting vaults. **—tr.v.** To provide or build with groins. [Earlier *gryne,* from Middle English *grynde,* perh. from Old English *grynde,* abyss, depression.]

grom·met (grŏm'ĭt) *n.* **1. a.** A reinforced eyelet, as in a garment, through which a lace or other fastener is passed. **b.** A small metal or plastic ring used to reinforce such an eyelet. **2.** A ring of rope or metal used esp. for securing the edge of a sail. [Obs. French *grom(m)ette, gourmette,* bridle ring, from Old French *gourmel.*]

groom (grōōm, grŏŏm) *n.* **1.** A man or boy employed to take care of horses. **2.** A bridegroom. **3.** *Archaic.* **a.** A man. **b.** A manservant. **—tr.v. 1.** To make neat and trim: *groomed himself carefully in front of the mirror.* **2.** To clean and brush (an animal). **3.** To train, as for a specific position: *groom a candidate for Congress.* [Middle English *grom,* man, servant; sense 2 short for BRIDEGROOM.]

grooms·man (grōōmz'mən, grŏŏmz'-) *n.* The best man or an usher at a wedding.

groove (grōōv) *n.* **1.** A long, narrow furrow or channel: *a drawer that slides on grooves.* **2.** A situation or activity to which one is esp. well suited; niche: *She's finally found her groove.* **3.** A settled, humdrum way of doing things; routine. **—tr.v. grooved, groov·ing.** To cut a groove in. [Middle English *grofe,* from Middle Dutch *groeve,* ditch.]

groov·y (grōō'vē) *adj.* **-i·er, -i·est.** *Slang.* Delightful; satisfying. [From the phrase *in the groove,* exciting, satisfying.]

grope (grōp) *v.* **groped, grop·ing. —intr.v. 1.** To reach about uncertainly; feel one's way: *grope for the light switch.* **2.** To search blindly or uncertainly: *grope for an answer.* **—tr.v.** To make (one's way) by groping. **—n.** The act of groping. [Middle English *gropen,* from Old English *grāpian.*]

gros·beak (grōs'bēk') *n.* Any of various finches of the genera *Hesperiphona, Pinicola,* and related genera, with a thick, rounded bill. [French *gros(bec)* + BEAK.]

gros·grain (grō'grān') *n.* A heavy silk or rayon fabric with narrow horizontal ribs. [French *gros grain,* "coarse grain."]

gross (grōs) *adj.* **-er, -est. 1.** Exclusive of deductions; total; entire: *gross profits.* **2.** Glaringly obvious; flagrant: *gross injustice.* **3. a.** Coarse; vulgar; obscene. **b.** Lacking sensitivity or discernment; unrefined: *a gross buffoon.* **c.** Carnal; sensual: *gross pleasures.* **4. a.** Overweight; corpulent. **b.** Dense; profuse. **5.** Broad; general: *the gross outlines of a plan.* **6.** *Path.* Visible to the naked eye: *a gross lesion.* —See Syns at **coarse, fat,** and **whole. —n. 1.** *pl.* **gross·es.** The entire body or amount; a total. **2.** *pl.* **gross.** A group of 144 or 12 dozen items: *buy a gross of oranges.* **—tr.v.** To earn as a total income or profit before deductions. [Middle English, from Old French *gros,* thick, large, from Latin *grossus.*] **—gross'ly** *adv.* **—gross'ness** *n.*

gross national product. The total market value of all the goods and services produced by a nation during a specified period.

gro·tesque (grō-tĕsk') *adj.* **1.** Characterized by ludicrous or incongruous distortion: *a grotesque face, part man and part rat.* **2.** Extravagant; outlandish; bizarre: *grotesque costumes.* **3.** *Fine Arts.* Of or designating the grotesque or a work executed in this style. —See Syns at **fantastic. —n. 1.** Someone or something that is grotesque. **2. a.** An artistic and decorative style developed in 16th-cent. Italy, characterized by incongruous combinations of animal and human forms. **b.** A work of art executed in this style. [French, from Old Italian *(pittura) grottesca,* "grottolike (painting)," from *grottesco,* of a grotto, from *grotta,* grotto.] **—gro·tesque'ly** *adv.* **—gro·tesque'ness** *n.*

gro·tes·que·ry (grō-tĕs'kə-rē) *n., pl.* **-ries.** Also **gro·tes·que·rie. 1.** The condition of being grotesque; grotesqueness. **2.** Something grotesque.

grot·to (grŏt'ō) *n., pl.* **-toes** or **-tos. 1.** A small cave or cavern. **2.** An artificial structure or excavation made to resemble a cave or cavern. [Italian *grotta, grotto,* from Old Italian, from Latin *crypta,* vault, crypt.]

grouch (grouch) *intr.v.* To complain; grumble. **—n. 1.** A grumbling or sulky mood. **2.** A complaint; grudge. **3.** A habitually complaining or irritable person. [Middle English *grutchen,* to grudge.]

grouch·y (grou'chē) *adj.* **-i·er, -i·est.** Ill-humored; peevish; grumpy. —See Syns at **irritable. —grouch'i·ly** *adv.* **—grouch'i·ness** *n.*

ground¹ (ground) *n.* **1.** The solid surface of the earth. **2.** Soil; earth: *level the ground for a lawn.* **3.** Often **grounds.** An area of land set aside for a particular purpose: *burial grounds.* **4. grounds.** The land surrounding or forming part of a house or other building: *The embassy has beautiful grounds.* **5.** Often **grounds.** The foundation for an argument, belief, or action; basis; premise. **6.** Often **grounds.** The underlying condition prompting some action; a cause; reason: *grounds for suspicion, a legal ground for the lawsuit.* **7.** A surrounding area; background. **8.** The preparatory coat of paint on which a picture is to be painted. **9. grounds.** The sediment at the bottom of a liquid, esp. coffee. **10.** *Elect.* **a.** The position or portion of an electric circuit that is at zero potential with respect to the earth. **b.** A conducting connection to such a position or to the earth. **c.** A large conducting body, such as the earth, used as a return for electric currents and as an arbitrary zero of potential. **—modifier:** *ground transportation.* **—tr.v. 1.** To place or set on the ground. **2.** To cause to run aground. **3.** To provide a basis for; establish; base: *He grounded his argument on facts.* **4.** To supply with basic information; instruct in fundamentals: *ground a pupil in the rules of spelling.* **5.** To prevent (an aircraft or pilot) from flying: *The flight was grounded by a dense fog.* **6.** *Elect.* To connect (an electric circuit) to a ground. —*intr.v.* **1.** To hit or reach the ground. **2.** *Baseball.* To hit a ground ball. **3.** To run aground: *The schooner grounded in shallow water.* —*idioms.* **break ground. 1.** To cut or dig into the soil, as in excavating. **2.** To start in on an undertaking. **cover ground. 1.** To move about or travel rapidly or widely. **2.** To make headway in some work; accomplish a great deal. **cut the ground from under (someone's) feet.** To ruin someone's argument or defense. **from the ground up.** Leaving out nothing; completely; thoroughly: *learn a subject from the ground up.* **gain ground. 1.** To move forward; make progress. **2.** To gain favor or popularity. **hold (or stand) (one's) ground.** To hold one's position in the face of attack or opposition. **lose (or give) ground.** To be forced back; retreat. **run into the ground.** To overdo; overemphasize. **shift (one's) ground.** To change one's argument, tactics, etc. [Middle English, from Old English *grund.*]

Usage: **ground, grounds.** An area of land set aside for a particular purpose is denoted by either the singular or plural form: *burial ground(s); fairground(s).* But in some senses only the plural appears: *baseball grounds. Grounds* is always used to designate land surrounding or forming part of a building: *the rectory grounds.* Either form may be used to denote the foundation for an argument, belief, or action, in the sense of basis or premise: *little ground (or grounds) for dispute.* The plural form is gen. but not always used in the case of an underlying condition that prompts an action: *grounds for impeachment; found a ground for divorce.*

ground² (ground) *v.* Past tense and past participle of **grind.** [Middle English *grounde, grounde(n),* from Old English *grundon* (pl.), *(ge)grunden.*]

ground ball. *Baseball.* A batted ball that rolls or bounces along the ground; grounder.

ground cover. Low-growing plants that form a dense, extensive growth and tend to prevent soil erosion.

ground crew. A team of mechanics and technicians who maintain and service aircraft on the ground.

ground·er (groun'dər) *n. Baseball.* A **ground ball.**

ground floor. The floor of a building at or nearly at ground level. —*idiom.* **get in on the ground floor.** To work with a project or business from its start.

ground glass. Glass that has been subjected to grinding or etching to create a roughened, nontransparent surface. —**ground'-glass'** *adj.*

ground hemlock. A low-growing yew, *Taxus canadensis,* of northeastern North America.

ground hog. A woodchuck.

ground-hog day (ground'hŏg', -hôg'). February 2, which traditionally indicates an early spring if cloudy and six more weeks of winter if sunny. [From the belief that a ground hog returns to hibernation if it sees its shadow.]

ground ivy. A creeping or trailing aromatic plant, *Glechoma hederacea,* native to Eurasia, with rounded, scalloped leaves and small purplish flowers.

ground·less (ground'lĭs) *adj.* Having no ground or foundation; unsubstantiated: *groundless optimism.* —**ground'less·ly** *adv.* —**ground'less·ness** *n.*

ground·ling (ground'lĭng) *n.* **1. a.** A plant or animal living on or close to the ground. **b.** A fish that lives at the bottom of the water. **2.** A person with uncultivated tastes.

ground loop. A sharp, uncontrollable turn of an aircraft in taxiing, landing, or taking off.

ground·mass (ground'măs') *n.* The fine-grained crystalline base of porphyritic rock in which phenocrysts are embedded.

ground·nut (ground'nŭt') *n.* **1.** A climbing vine, *Apios tuberosa,* of eastern North America, with compound leaves, clusters of fragrant brownish flowers, and small, edible tubers. **2.** Any of several other plants having underground tubers or nutlike parts. **3.** The tuber or nutlike part of such a plant. **4.** *Brit.* The peanut.

ground plan. 1. A plan of a floor of a building as if seen from overhead. **2.** A preliminary or basic plan.

ground rule. 1. A rule governing the playing of a game on a particular field, course, or court. **2.** Any basic rule of procedure.

ground·sill (ground'sĭl') *n.* The horizontal timber nearest the ground in the frame of a building.

ground speed. Also **ground·speed** (ground'spēd'). The speed of an airborne aircraft computed in terms of the ground distance traversed in a given period of time.

ground squirrel. Any of various rodents of the genus *Citellus* (or *Spermophilus*) and related genera, related to and resembling the chipmunks. Also called **gopher.**

ground state. *Physics.* The stationary state of least energy in a physical system.

ground swell. 1. A deep swell in the ocean, often caused by a distant storm or earthquake. **2.** A strong, rapid growth or surge, as of public opinion.

ground water. Water beneath the earth's surface between saturated soil and rock that supplies wells and springs.

ground·work (ground'wûrk') *n.* Preliminary work; foundation; basis.

ground zero. The place on the earth's surface directly at, below, or above the explosion of a nuclear bomb.

group (grōōp) *n.* **1.** A number of persons or things gathered or located together: *a group of men on a street corner; a group of islands off the coast of Alaska.* **2.** A number of things classed together because of similar qualities: *a language group.* **3.** A military unit consisting of two or more battalions and a headquarters. **4.** A structure formed of two or more atoms bound together in a particular way that acts as a unit and is found in a number of chemical compounds: *a hydroxyl group.* —*modifier: a group discussion.* —*tr.v.* To arrange in a group or groups: *grouping blocks according to shape.* —*intr.v.* To form or gather in a group: *They grouped on the steps of the library.* [French *groupe,* from Italian *gruppo,* "knot."]

Usage: **group.** Like most collective nouns, *group* can be construed as a singular or a plural in determining the grammatical number of the verb that *group* governs. A singular verb is used when the persons or things forming the group are considered as one or as acting as one or when they are related by membership in a class or category: *A good chamber group always practices its repertoire. This group of animals shares the same characteristics.* A plural verb occurs with *group* when reference is made to its members as acting individually: *The group were divided in their sympathies.* The grammatical number of related pronouns or pronominal adjectives agrees with that of the verb.

grou·per (grōō'pər) *n., pl.* **grou·pers** or **grouper.** Any of various often large fishes of the genera *Epinephelus, Mycteroperca,* and related genera, of warm seas. [Portuguese *garoupa.*]

group·ing (grōō'pĭng) *n.* A collection of people or things arranged in a group.

grouse¹ (grous) *n., pl.* **grouse.** Any of various plump birds of the family Tetraonidae, chiefly of the Northern Hemisphere, with mottled brown or grayish plumage. [Orig. unknown.]

grouse¹
George Miksch Sutton

grouse² (grous). *Informal.* —*intr.v.* **groused, grous·ing.** To complain; to grumble. —*n.* A complaint; grievance. [Orig. unknown.] —**grous'er** *n.*

grout (grout) *n.* **1.** A thin mortar used to fill cracks and

---

ă pat   ā pay   âr care   ä father   ĕ pet   ē be   hw which
ŏŏ took   ōō boot   ou out   th thin   th this   ŭ cut
ĭ pit   ī tie   îr pier   ŏ pot   ō toe   ô paw, for   oi noise
û urge   zh vision   ə about, item, edible, gallop, circus

crevices, as in masonry. **2.** A thin plaster for finishing walls and ceilings. —*tr.v.* To fill or finish with grout. [Middle English, from Old English *grūt.*] —**grout'er** *n.*

grove (grōv) *n.* A small wood or stand of trees lacking dense undergrowth. [Middle English, from Old English *grāf.*]

grov·el (grŭv'əl, grŏv'-) *intr.v.* **-eled** or **-elled, -el·ing** or **-el·ling. 1.** To lie flat or crawl on one's belly, as in abasement; humble oneself: *a slave forced to grovel at his master's feet.* **2.** To behave in a servile or abject manner; cringe: *Tommy groveled before the bully.* [Back-formation from obs. *groveling,* prone, from Middle English *gruflinge,* in prostrate position, from the phrase *on grufe,* on the face, from Old Norse *ā grūfu.*] —**grov'el·er** *n.*

grow (grō) *v.* **grew** (grōō), **grown** (grōn), **grow·ing.** —*intr.v.* **1.** To increase in size by some natural process: *Jerry grew an inch over the summer.* **2. a.** To expand; to gain: *The business grew under new management.* **b.** To increase in amount or degree: *Her anxiety grew.* **3.** To develop and reach maturity: *The seeds sprouted and grew.* **4.** To be capable of growth; flourish: *plants that will only grow in deep shade.* **5.** To become attached by or as if by a natural process: *The trunks of the two trees had grown together.* **6.** To originate or emerge as if by a natural process; develop: *Their love grew out of friendship.* **7.** To come to be by a gradual process or by degrees; become: *grow angry; grow cold; grow rich.* —*tr.v.* **1.** To cause to grow; cultivate; raise: *grow tulips.* **2.** To let grow: *grow a beard.* **3.** To cover with a growth: *a path grown with moss.* —**phrasal verbs. grow on** (or **upon**). To become more pleasurable, acceptable, or essential to: *a style that grows on one.* **grow out of. 1.** To outgrow. **2.** To result or develop from. **grow up.** To reach maturity; become an adult. [Middle English *growen,* from Old English *grōwan.*] —**grow'er** *n.*

growing pains. 1. Pains in the limbs and joints of children, often mistakenly attributed to rapid growth. **2.** Problems arising in the first stages of an enterprise.

growl (groul) *intr.v.* **1.** To utter a low, throaty, menacing sound such as that made by an angry dog. **2.** To make a sound suggestive of this: *The engine growled.* —*tr.v.* To utter by growling: *growl orders.* —*n.* **1.** A low, throaty, menacing sound such as that made by an angry dog. **2.** A gruff, surly utterance. [Perh. imit.] —**growl'er** *n.*

grown (grōn) *v.* Past participle of **grow.** —*adj.* Having full growth; mature; adult. —See Syns at **mature.** [Middle English *growen,* from Old English (ge)*grōwen.*]

grown-up (grōn'ŭp') *adj.* **1.** Adult; mature. **2.** Characteristic of or suitable for an adult. —See Syns at **mature.** —*n.* Var. of **grownup.**

grown·up (grōn'ŭp') *n.* Also **grown-up.** An adult.

growth (grōth) *n.* **1. a.** The process of growing: *the growth of a child; the growth of India's population.* **b.** A stage in the process of growing; size: *reached full growth.* **2.** Development toward a higher or more complex form; evolution: *the growth of commerce.* **3.** An increase, as in size, number, value, or strength; extension or expansion: *population growth.* **4.** Something that grows or has grown: *a new growth of grass.* **5.** An abnormal mass of tissue growing in or on a living organism. —*modifier:* a growth rate.

grub (grŭb) *v.* **grubbed, grub·bing.** —*tr.v.* **1.** To clear of roots and stumps by digging. **2.** To dig up by the roots: *grub up weeds.* **3.** *Slang.* To provide with food. **4.** *Slang.* To obtain by pleading or begging: *grub a cigarette.* —*intr.v.* **1.** To dig in the earth: *grub for potatoes.* **2.** To search laboriously; rummage: *grubbing through the closet for a shoe.* **3.** To work hard; to drudge: *grub for a living.* **4.** *Slang.* To eat. —*n.* **1.** The thick, wormlike larva of certain beetles and other insects. **2.** A drudge. **3.** *Slang.* Food. [Middle English *grubben.*] —**grub'ber** *n.*

grub·by (grŭb'ē) *adj.* **-bi·er, -bi·est. 1.** Dirty; unkempt: *grubby old work clothes.* **2.** Infested with grubs: *grubby wood.* —See Syns at **dirty.** —**grub'bi·ly** *adv.* —**grub'bi·ness** *n.*

grub·stake (grŭb'stāk') *n.* Supplies or funds advanced to a mining prospector or a person starting a business in return for a promised share of the profits. —*tr.v.* **-staked, -stak·ing.** To supply with a grubstake. [GRUB (food) + STAKE (bet).] —**grub'stak·er** *n.*

grudge (grŭj) *tr.v.* **grudged, grudg·ing.** To be reluctant to

give or admit: *"His nature grudged thinking, for it crippled his speed in action"* (T.E. Lawrence). —*n.* A feeling of resentment or rancor provoked by some incident or situation. [Middle English *gruggen,* var. of *grutchen,* from Old French *grouchier, groncier,* of Germanic orig.] —**grudg'er** *n.* —**grudg'ing·ly** *adv.*

gru·el (grōō'əl) *n.* A thin, watery porridge. [Middle English *grewel,* from Old French *gruel,* dim. of *gru,* groats, oatmeal.]

gru·el·ing (grōō'ə-lĭng) *adj.* Also **gru·el·ling.** Demanding and exhausting.

grue·some (grōō'səm) *adj.* Also **grew·some.** Causing horror and repugnance; frightful and shocking. —See Syns at **ghastly.** [From obs. *grue,* to shiver, from Middle English *gruen,* prob. from Middle Dutch *grūwen.*] —**grue'some·ly** *adv.* —**grue'some·ness** *n.*

gruff (grŭf) *adj.* **-er, -est. 1.** Brief and unfriendly; stern: *"Go away!" was the old man's gruff reply.* **2.** Hoarse; harsh: *a gruff voice.* [Dutch *grof,* from Middle Dutch.] —**gruff'ly** *adv.* —**gruff'ness** *n.*

> ***Syns:* gruff, bluff, blunt, brusque, curt** *adj.* Core meaning: Abrupt and sometimes markedly impolite in manner or speech (*a gruff retort*). GRUFF implies rough and often harsh speech, but it does not necessarily suggest intentional rudeness. BRUSQUE emphasizes rude abruptness of manner (*a brusque refusal to help*). BLUNT stresses utter frankness and usu. a disconcerting directness (*a blunt criticism*). BLUFF refers to unpolished, unceremonious manner but usu. implies good nature (*a bluff old sea dog*). CURT refers to briefness and abruptness of speech and manner and usu. implies rudeness (*a curt dismissal*).

grum·ble (grŭm'bəl) *v.* **-bled, -bling.** —*intr.v.* **1.** To complain in a surly manner; mutter discontentedly: *"The governed will always find something to grumble about"* (Crane Brinton). **2.** To rumble or growl. —*tr.v.* To express by grumbling. —*n.* **1.** A muttered complaint. **2.** A rumble. [Freq. of Middle English *grummen,* to grumble, perh. from Middle Dutch *grommen.*] —**grum'bler** *n.* —**grum'bly** *adj.*

grump (grŭmp) *n.* **1.** A cranky, complaining person. **2. grumps.** A fit of ill temper. [From dial. *grump,* ill-tempered.]

grump·y (grŭm'pē) *adj.* **-i·er, -i·est.** Irritable; cranky. —See Syns at **irritable.** —**grump'i·ly** *adv.* —**grump'i·ness** *n.*

grunt (grŭnt) *intr.v.* **1.** To utter a short, deep, guttural sound, as a hog does. **2.** To utter a similar sound, as in disgust, annoyance, indifference, strain, or effort: *He grunted as he lifted the trunk.* —*tr.v.* To utter or express with a short, deep, guttural sound: *grunt approval.* —*n.* **1.** A short, deep, guttural sound. **2.** Any of various chiefly tropical saltwater fishes of the genus *Haemulon* and related genera that produce grunting sounds. [Middle English *grunten,* from Old English *grunnettan.*]

gryph·on (grĭf'ən) *n.* Var. of **griffin.**

G-suit (jē'sōōt') *n.* A garment for pilots and astronauts, designed to counteract the effects of high acceleration by exerting pressure on parts of the body below the chest. [G, short for GRAVITY.]

gua·na·co (gwə-nä'kō) *n., pl.* **-cos.** A brownish South American mammal, *Lama guanicoe,* related to and resembling the domesticated llama. [Spanish, from Quechua *huanaco.*]

gua·nine (gwä'nēn) *n.* A purine, $C_5H_5N_5O$, that is a constituent of both ribonucleic and deoxyribonucleic acids. [From *guano,* in which it is found.]

gua·no (gwä'nō) *n.* The excrement of sea birds or bats, accumulated along certain coastal areas or in caves and used as fertilizer. [Spanish, from Quechua *huanu,* dung.]

Gua·ra·ni (gwä'rə-nē') *n., pl.* **-nis** or **Guarani. 1. a.** A group of South American Indians of Paraguay, Bolivia, and southern Brazil. **b.** A member of one of these tribes. **2.** The language of the Guarani.

guar·an·tee (găr'ən-tē') *n.* **1.** Anything that makes certain a particular condition or outcome: *Money is not always a guarantee of happiness.* **2.** A promise or assurance: *You have my guarantee that I'll finish the job on time.* **3.** A promise or assurance as to the quality or durability of a product or service. **4.** A guaranty. **5.** Something given or held as security; a pledge. **6.** A guarantor. —*tr.v.* **-teed,**

-tee·ing. **1.** To assume responsibility for the debt, default, or miscarriage of; vouch for. **2.** To assume responsibility for the quality or execution of: *Most good plumbers guarantee their work.* **3.** To undertake to accomplish or secure something: *He guaranteed to free the captives.* **4.** To furnish security for. **5. a.** To give a guarantee for: *a product that is guaranteed.* **b.** To make certain; ensure: *His family connections guaranteed his success in business.* [Earlier *garante,* perh. from Spanish, warrant, of Germanic orig.]

guar·an·tor (găr′ən-tər, -tôr′) *n.* A person or company that makes or gives a guarantee.

guar·an·ty (găr′ən-tē) *n., pl.* **-ties.** **1.** An agreement by which one person assumes the responsibility of assuring payment or fulfillment of another's debts or obligations. **2.** Something that guarantees: *His record is a guaranty of his honesty.* **3.** Anything held or provided as security for the execution, completion, or existence of something. —*tr.v.* **-tied, -ty·ing.** To guarantee. [Old French *garantie,* from *garant,* warrant.]

guard (gärd) *tr.v.* **1.** To protect from harm; watch over; defend: *guard a bank; guarding the President.* **2.** To watch over to prevent escape, violence, or indiscretion; keep in check: *guarding a prisoner.* **3.** To keep watch at (a door or gate) to supervise entries and exits. **4.** To furnish (a device or object) with a protective piece. —*intr.v.* To take precautions: *Hospital personnel wore face masks to guard against infection.* —See Syns at **defend.** —*n.* **1.** Something that gives protection; a safeguard; defense: *a guard against tooth decay.* **2.** A person who keeps watch, protects, or controls, as in a prison. **3.** Protection; watch; control: *The prisoner is under close guard.* **4.** A special body of troops, as those connected with the household of a sovereign: *the palace guard.* **5.** Any device attached to a tool, esp. a power tool, to protect the person who operates it. **6.** A defensive position, as in boxing or fencing. **7.** *Football.* Either of the two players on a team's offensive line on each side of the center. **8.** *Basketball.* Either of two players stationed farthest from the opponents' basket. —*modifier: guard duty.* —*idioms.* **off (one's) guard.** Unprepared; not alert. **on (one's) guard.** Alert and watchful; cautious. **stand (or mount) guard.** **1.** To act as a sentry. **2.** To keep watch. [Middle English *garden,* from Old French *garder, guarder,* of Germanic orig.] —**guard′er** *n.*

guard cell. *Bot.* One of the paired epidermal cells that control the opening and closing of a stoma in plant tissue.

guard·ed (gär′dĭd) *adj.* **1.** Protected; defended: *heavily guarded borders.* **2.** Cautious; restrained; prudent: *guarded words.*

guard·house (gärd′hous′) *n.* **1.** A building that accommodates a military guard. **2.** A military jail for soldiers guilty of minor offenses.

guard·i·an (gär′dē-ən) *n.* **1.** Someone or something that guards, protects, or defends. **2.** A person who is legally responsible for the person or property of another person, such as a child, who cannot manage his own affairs. —*modifier: a guardian angel.* [Middle English *gardein,* from Norman French, var. of Old French *gardien,* from *garder,* to guard.] —**guard′i·an·ship′** *n.*

guard·rail (gärd′rāl′) *n.* A protective rail, as on a footpath, staircase, or highway.

guard·room (gärd′rōōm′, -rōōm′) *n.* **1.** A room used by guards on duty. **2.** A room in which prisoners are confined.

guards·man (gärdz′mən) *n.* **1.** Someone who acts as a guard. **2.** A member of any military unit called a guard or guards, esp. a member of the U.S. National Guard.

gua·va (gwä′və) *n.* **1.** Any of various tropical American shrubs and trees of the genus *Psidium,* esp. *P. guajava,* having white flowers and bearing edible fruit. **2.** The fruit of the guava, having a yellow rind and pink flesh and used for jellies and preserves. [Spanish *guava, guayaba,* of South American Indian orig.]

gua·yu·le (gwī-ōō′lē) *n.* A woody plant or shrub, *Parthenium argentatum,* of the southwestern United States and Mexico, with sap that is sometimes used as a source of rubber. [American Spanish, from Nahuatl *cuauhuli* : *cuahuitl,* tree + *uli,* gum.]

gu·ber·na·to·ri·al (gōō′bər-nə-tôr′ē-əl, -tōr′-, gyōō′-) *adj.* Of or relating to a governor or the office of a governor. [From Late Latin *gubernatorius,* from Latin *gubernātor,* governor.]

Gud·run (gōōd′rōōn′) *n.* **1.** The Danish heroine of the 13th-cent. German epic *Gudrun Lied.* **2.** The daughter of the king of the Nibelungs and wife of Sigurd in the *Volsunga Saga.*

Guen·e·vere (gwĕn′ə-vîr′) *n.* Var of **Guinevere.**

guer·don (gûr′dn) *n. Archaic.* A reward. [Middle English, from Old French, from Medieval Latin *widerdōnum,* alteration of Old High German *widarlōn* : *widar,* again + *lōn,* reward, payment.]

gue·ril·la (gə-rĭl′ə) *n.* Var of **guerrilla.**

Guern·sey (gûrn′zē) *n., pl.* **-seys.** One of a breed of brown and white dairy cattle orig. developed on the Isle of Guernsey.

guer·ril·la or **gue·ril·la** (gə-rĭl′ə) *n.* A member of an irregular military force that uses harassing tactics against an enemy army, usu. with the support of the local population. —*modifier: guerrilla warfare; guerrilla tactics.* [Spanish *guerrilla,* dim. of *guerra,* war, of Germanic orig.]

guess (gĕs) *tr.v.* **1. a.** To predict (a result or event) without enough information to be sure: *He guessed that next winter would be mild.* **b.** To assume, presume, or assert (a fact) without enough information to be sure: *She guessed that he was lying.* **2.** To estimate correctly: *good at guessing people's ages.* **3.** To suppose; judge: *I guess you're right.* —*intr.v.* **1.** To make a conjecture: *We can only guess at his motives.* **2.** To make a correct guess: *She wasn't sure but succeeded in guessing.* —*n.* **1.** An act of guessing: *taking a guess.* **2.** A judgment or estimate arrived at by guessing. [Middle English *gessen.*] —**guess′er** *n.*

guess·work (gĕs′wûrk′) *n.* The process or result of making guesses: *came to the right conclusion by guesswork.*

guest (gĕst) *n.* **1.** A visitor who receives hospitality, as at the home or table of another: *inviting guests for dinner.* **2.** A person who is offered some entertainment or service without charge. **3.** A patron of a hotel, restaurant, etc. **4.** A visiting participant, as in a television program. —*modifier: a guest room; a guest speaker.* [Middle English *gest,* from Old Norse *gestr.*]

guff (gŭf) *n. Slang.* Foolish talk; nonsense. [Perh. imit.]

guf·faw (gə-fô′) *n.* A hearty or coarse burst of laughter. —*intr.v.* To laugh heartily or coarsely. [Imit.]

guid·ance (gīd′ns) *n.* **1.** The act or an example of guiding. **2.** Counseling, as on vocational, educational, or marital problems. **3.** Any of various means by which the course of a missile in flight can be controlled.

guide (gīd) *n.* **1.** Someone or something that shows the way by leading, directing, or advising: *Her mother was her guide in dressing.* **2.** A person employed to lead a tour, expedition, or similar group. **3. a.** Any sign or mark that serves to direct. **b.** An example or model to be followed. **4.** A guidebook. **5.** Any device, such as a ruler, line, ring, tab, or bar, that acts as an indicator or that regulates the motion of one's hand, a tool, or a machine part. —*v.* **guid·ed, guid·ing.** —*tr.v.* **1.** To show the way to; to conduct; lead: *The scout guided them through the mountains.* **2.** To direct the course of; to steer: *guide a plank through a saw.* **3.** To manage the affairs of; govern: *guide the nation during a crisis.* —*intr.v.* To serve as a guide. [Middle English *g(u)ide,* from Old French, from Old Provençal *guida,* from *guidar,* to show the way.] —**guid′a·ble** *adj.* —**guid′er** *n.*

guide·book (gīd′bōōk′) *n.* A handbook of information for travelers, tourists, or students.

guided missile. Any missile capable of being guided while it is in flight.

guide·line (gīd′līn′) *n.* A policy or rule, or a statement of such a policy or rule, intended to give practical guidance: *The President presented his new guidelines for the economy.*

guide·post (gīd′pōst′) *n.* A post with a sign giving directions, placed at a fork in a road.

guide word. A word that appears at the top of a page of a dictionary or other reference book, indicating the first or last entry on the page.

gui·don (gī′dŏn′, gīd′n) *n.* **1.** A small flag, often with a forked end, carried as a standard by a regiment or other military unit. **2.** A soldier bearing a guidon. [French, from

guillemot
George Miksch Sutton

guitar

gull¹
George Miksch Sutton

Italian *guidone,* from *guida,* guide, from Old Provençal.]

guild (gĭld) *n.* Also **gild. 1.** An association of persons of the same trade, pursuits, or interests formed for their mutual aid and protection, esp. a medieval society of merchants or artisans. **2.** *Ecol.* One of four groups of plants with a characteristic mode of existence that involves some dependence upon other plant life; the lianas, epiphytes, saprophytes, and parasites. [Middle English *gilde,* from Old Norse *gildi,* payment, fraternity, contribution.]

guil·der (gĭl′dər) *n.* Also **gil·der.** The basic monetary unit of the Netherlands and the Netherlands Antilles. Also called **gulden** or **florin.** [Alteration of Dutch *gulden,* gulden.]

guild·hall (gĭld′hôl′) *n.* **1.** The meeting hall of a guild. **2.** A town hall.

guilds·man (gĭldz′mən) *n.* A member of a guild.

guile (gīl) *n.* Deceitful cunning; craftiness. [Middle English *gile,* from Old French *guile,* of Germanic orig.]

guile·ful (gīl′fəl) *adj.* Full of guile; artfully deceitful; crafty. —**guile′ful·ly** *adv.* —**guile′ful·ness** *n.*

guile·less (gīl′lĭs) *adj.* Free of guile; artless. —**guile′less·ly** *adv.* —**guile′less·ness** *n.*

guil·le·mot (gĭl′ə-mŏt′) *n.* Any of several small sea birds of the genus *Cepphus,* of northern regions, that have black plumage with white markings. [French, dim. of *Guillaume,* William.]

guil·lo·tine (gĭl′ə-tēn′, gē′ə-) *n.* **1.** A machine for beheading condemned prisoners by means of a heavy blade that falls freely between upright posts. **2.** Execution by a guillotine. —*tr.v.* (gĭl′ə-tēn′) **-tined, -tin·ing.** To behead with a guillotine. [After Joseph Ignace *Guillotin* (1738–1814), French doctor who proposed its use.]

guilt (gĭlt) *n.* **1.** The fact of being responsible for a crime or wrongdoing. **2.** Regretful awareness of having done something wrong; remorse. [Middle English *gilt,* from Old English *gylt.*]

guilt·less (gĭlt′lĭs) *adj.* Free from guilt; blameless; innocent. —**guilt′less·ly** *adv.* —**guilt′less·ness** *n.*

guilt·y (gĭl′tē) *adj.* **-i·er, -i·est. 1.** Responsible for a crime or wrongdoing: *guilty of cheating.* **2.** Burdened with or showing a sense of guilt: *a guilty conscience.* —**guilt′i·ly** *adv.* —**guilt′i·ness** *n.*

guimpe (gĭmp, gămp) *n.* **1.** A short blouse worn with a jumper. **2.** A yoke insert for a low-necked dress. **3.** A starched cloth covering the neck and shoulders as part of a nun's habit.

guin·ea (gĭn′ē) *n.* **1.** A former British gold coin worth one pound and one shilling. **2.** The sum of one pound and one shilling. [After *Guinea,* West Africa.]

guinea fowl. Any of several pheasantlike birds of the family Numididae, native to Africa, esp. a widely domesticated species, *Numida meleagris,* having blackish plumage marked with small white spots. [After *Guinea,* West Africa.]

guinea pig. 1. Any of various South American burrowing rodents of the genus *Cavia,* with variously colored hair and no visible tail, widely domesticated as pets and as experimental animals. **2.** A person who is used as a subject in scientific experiments. [Prob. from a confusion of *Guiana,* South America, with *Guinea,* West Africa.]

Guin·e·vere (gwĭn′ə-vîr′) *n.* Also **Guen·e·vere** (gwĕn′-). In Arthurian legend, the wife of King Arthur and the mistress of Lancelot.

guise (gīz) *n.* **1.** Outward appearance; aspect. **2.** False appearance; pretense: *deceived them in the guise of a friend.* **3.** Mode of dress; garb: *in the guise of a beggar.* [Middle English, fashion, manner, from Old French, of Germanic orig.]

gui·tar (gĭ-tär′) *n.* A musical instrument with a large flat-backed sound box, a long fretted neck, and usu. six strings, played by strumming or plucking. —*modifier:* a guitar string. [French *guitare,* from Old French, from Spanish *guitarra,* from Arabic *qītār,* from Greek *kithara,* lyre.] —**gui·tar′ist** *n.*

gulch (gŭlch) *n.* A small, shallow canyon; ravine. [Orig. unknown.]

gul·den (gōōl′dən, gŏŏl′-) *n., pl.* **-dens** or **gulden.** A Dutch monetary unit, the **guilder.** [Dutch *gulden (florijn),* golden (florin), from Middle Dutch.]

gulf (gŭlf) *n.* **1.** A large area of a sea or ocean partially enclosed by land. **2.** A deep, wide hole or gap in the earth; abyss. **3.** A separating distance; wide gap: *the gulf between the Victorian sensibility and our own.* **4.** A whirlpool; an eddy. —*tr.v.* To swallow; engulf. [Middle English *golf,* from Old French *golfe,* from Old Italian *golfo,* ult. from Greek *kolpos, kolphos,* bosom, fold, bay.]

gulf·weed (gŭlf′wēd′) *n.* Any of several brownish seaweeds of the genus *Sargassum,* of tropical Atlantic waters, having rounded air bladders and often forming dense, floating masses. Also called **sargasso.**

gull¹ (gŭl) *n.* Any of various chiefly coastal aquatic birds of the subfamily Larinae, with long wings, webbed feet, and usu. gray and white plumage. [Middle English, prob. from Welsh *gwylan.*]

gull² (gŭl) *n.* A person who is easily fooled; a dupe. —*tr.v.* To deceive; cheat; dupe. [Prob. from dial. *gull,* unfledged bird, from Middle English *golle, gulle,* prob. from *gul,* yellow, pale, from Old Norse *gulr.*]

Gul·lah (gŭl′ə) *n.* **1.** A member of a group of Blacks inhabiting the Sea Islands and coastal area of South Carolina, Georgia, and northern Florida. **2.** The dialect of the Gullahs.

gul·let (gŭl′ĭt) *n.* **1.** The esophagus. **2.** The throat. [Middle English *golet,* from Old French *goulet,* dim. of *gole, goule,* throat, from Latin *gula.*]

gul·li·ble (gŭl′ə-bəl) *adj.* Easily deceived or duped; credulous: *the sale of worthless medicines to gullible people.* [From GULL (dupe).] —**gul′li·bil′i·ty** *n.* —**gul′li·bly** *adv.*

gul·ly (gŭl′ē) *n., pl.* **-lies.** A deep ditch or channel cut in the earth by running water, usu. after a rain. —*tr.v.* **-lied, -ly·ing.** To cut a gully in. [Alteration of GULLET.]

gulp (gŭlp) *tr.v.* **1.** To swallow greedily or rapidly in large amounts: *He gulped down his lunch and ran off.* **2.** To stifle by or as if by swallowing: *gulp down a sob.* —*intr.v.* **1.** To swallow air, as in nervousness. **2.** To swallow food or drink in large mouthfuls. **3.** To make a noise in the throat when swallowing. —*n.* **1.** An act of gulping: *ate the ice cream in a single gulp.* **2.** A large mouthful. [Middle English *gulpen,* from Middle Dutch *gulpen* (imit.).] —**gulp′er** *n.*

gum¹ (gŭm) *n.* **1. a.** Any of various viscous substances that are exuded by certain plants and trees and that dry into water-soluble, noncrystalline, brittle solids. **b.** A similar plant exudate, such as a resin. **2.** A product, such as rubber, made from a plant exudate for use in industry, the arts, etc. **3. a.** Any of various trees, such as one of the genera *Eucalyptus, Liquidambar,* or *Nyssa,* that are a source of gum. Also called **gum tree. b.** The wood of such a tree. Also called **gumwood. 4.** Chewing gum. —*v.* **gummed, gum·ming.** —*tr.v.* To cover, smear, seal, fill, or fix in place with gum. —*intr.v.* To become sticky or clogged with or as if with gum. —**idiom. gum up the works.** *Slang.* To ruin; spoil. [Middle English *gumme, gomme,* from Old French *gomme,* from Latin *gummi, cummi,* from Greek *kommi,* from Egyptian *kemai.*]

gum² (gŭm) *n.* Often **gums.** The firm connective tissue that is covered by mucous membrane and that envelops the alveolar arches of the jaw and surrounds the bases of the teeth. [Middle English *gome,* from Old English *gōma,* palate, jaw.]

gum ar·a·bic (ăr′ə-bĭk). A gum exuded by various African trees of the genus *Acacia,* esp. *A. senegal,* and used in the preparation of pills and emulsions, the manufacture of mucilage and candies, and in general as a thickener and colloidal stabilizer. Also called **acacia.**

gum·bo (gŭm′bō) *n., pl.* **-bos. 1. a.** Okra. **b.** A soup or stew thickened with okra. **2.** A fine silty soil, common in the southern and western United States, that forms an unusually sticky mud when wet. [Louisiana French *gombo,* from Bantu.]

gum·drop (gŭm′drŏp′) *n.* A small, sugar-coated candy made of sweetened, colored, and flavored gum arabic or gelatin.

gum·my (gŭm′ē) *adj.* **-mi·er, -mi·est. 1.** Consisting of, containing, or covered with gum. **2.** Sticky; viscid. —**gum′mi·ness** *n.*

gump·tion (gŭmp′shən) *n. Informal.* **1.** Shrewdness: *"Did you really have the gumption to suspect me just because I brought you up to this bare part of the heath?"* (G.K. Chesterton). **2.** Boldness of enterprise; initiative. [Orig. unknown.]

gum resin. A mixture of gum and resin that exudes from some plants or trees.

gum·shoe (gŭm′shōō′) *n.* **1.** A rubber shoe or overshoe. **2.** *Slang.* A detective. —*intr.v.* **-shoed, -shoe·ing.** *Slang.* To search in a prying or sneaking way; to snoop.

gum tree. The gum.

gun (gŭn) *n.* **1.** A weapon that fires bullets or other projectiles through a metal tube, usu. by the explosion of gunpowder. **2.** A cannon as distinguished from a small firearm. **3.** A portable firearm. **4.** A device that shoots or discharges something: *a spray gun; an electron gun.* **5.** A discharge of a gun as a signal or salute: *the opening gun of the race.* **6.** A person who carries or uses a gun, as a member of a shooting party or a gunfighter. **7.** A mechanism controlling the flow of fuel to an engine; a throttle. —*v.* **gunned, gun·ning.** —*tr.v.* **1.** To fire upon; shoot: *gun down an escaping prisoner.* **2.** To open the throttle of so as to accelerate: *gun an engine.* —*intr.v.* To hunt or shoot with a gun: *gunning for big game.* —*phrasal verb.* **gun for. 1.** To seek to catch, overcome, or destroy: *Black Bart is gunning for the marshal.* **2.** To aim or work hard to gain: *a politician gunning for higher office.* —**idioms. go great guns.** *Slang.* To do very well; make great progress. **jump the gun.** To begin a race before the starting signal. **stick to (one's) guns.** To hold firmly to an opinion or course of action. [Middle English *gunne.*]

gun·boat (gŭn′bōt′) *n.* A small armed vessel.

gun·cot·ton (gŭn′kŏt′n) *n.* An explosive, nitrocellulose.

gun·fight (gŭn′fīt′) *n.* A duel or battle with firearms. —**gun′fight′er** *n.*

gun·fire (gŭn′fīr′) *n.* The firing of guns.

gung ho or **gung-ho** (gŭng′ hō′). *Slang.* Extremely dedicated or enthusiastic: *a gung ho member of the team.* [Pidgin English : prob. Mandarin *kung¹,* work + *ho²,* together.]

gun·lock (gŭn′lŏk′) *n.* A device for igniting the gunpowder in some firearms.

gun·man (gŭn′mən) *n.* **1.** A hired gunfighter or professional killer. **2.** A criminal armed with a gun.

gun metal. 1. An alloy of copper with ten per cent tin. **2.** Metal used for guns. **3.** The dark gray color of gun metal. —**gun′-met′al** *adj.*

Gun·nar (gŏŏn′är′) *n. Norse Myth.* The husband of Bryn-

hild, the brother-in-law of Sigurd, and the brother of Gudrun. Identified with Gunther.

gun·nel¹ (gŭn′əl) *n.* Any of various long, eellike fishes of the family Pholidae, of northern seas. [Orig. unknown.]

gun·nel² (gŭn′əl) *n.* Var. of **gunwale.**

gun·ner (gŭn′ər) *n.* **1.** A soldier, sailor, or airman who aims or fires a gun. **2.** A person who hunts with a gun. **3.** A naval warrant officer having charge of ordnance.

gun·ner·y (gŭn′ə-rē) *n.* **1.** The art and science of constructing and operating guns. **2.** The use of guns.

gun·ny (gŭn′ē) *n.* **1.** A coarse fabric made of jute or hemp. **2.** Burlap. [Hindi *gōnī,* from Sanskrit *goṇī,* sack.]

gunny sack. A sack made of burlap or gunny.

gun·pow·der (gŭn′pou′dər) *n.* Any of various explosive powders used to propel projectiles from guns, esp. a black explosive mixture of potassium nitrate, charcoal, and sulfur.

gun·run·ner (gŭn′rŭn′ər) *n.* A person or ship that smuggles firearms and ammunition. —**gun′run′ning** *n.*

gun·shot (gŭn′shŏt′) *n.* **1.** Shot or a shot fired from a gun. **2.** The range of a gun: *within gunshot.* —**modifier:** *a gunshot wound.*

gun·shy (gŭn′shī′) *adj.* **1.** Afraid of gunfire or other loud noises: *a gun-shy hound dog.* **2.** Extremely mistrustful: *He had been hurt once, and now he was gun-shy.*

gun·sling·er (gŭn′slĭng′ər) *n.* A gunfighter; gunman. —**gun′sling′ing** *n.*

gun·smith (gŭn′smĭth′) *n.* A person who makes or repairs firearms.

gun·stock (gŭn′stŏk′) *n.* The wooden or metal handle of a gun; a stock.

Gun·ther (gŏŏn′tər). *n.* In the *Nibelungenlied,* a king of Burgundy, the husband of Brunhild, and brother of Kriemhild. Identified with Gunnar.

gun·wale (gŭn′əl) *n.* Also **gun·nel.** The upper edge of the side of a ship or boat. [Middle English *gonnewale : gonne,* gun + *wale,* wale (from its former use as a prop for guns).]

gup·py (gŭp′ē) *n., pl.* **-pies.** A small, brightly colored freshwater fish, *Poecilia reticulata* (or *Lebistes reticulatus*), of northern South America and adjacent islands of the West Indies, that is popular in home aquariums. [After R.J.L. Guppy of Trinidad.]

gur·gle (gûr′gəl) *v.* **-gled, -gling.** —*intr.v.* **1.** To flow in a broken, uneven current, making low sounds: *Water trickled, then gurgled from the pump spout.* **2.** To make the sounds of a gently flowing liquid. —*tr.v.* To express or pronounce with such sounds. —*n.* The act or sound of gurgling. [Perh. ult. from Latin *gurgulio,* gullet.] —**gur′gling·ly** *adv.*

gur·nard (gûr′nərd) *n., pl.* **-nards** or **gurnard.** Any of various saltwater fishes of the family Triglidae, and esp. of the Old World genus *Trigla,* with large, fanlike pectoral fins. [Middle English, from Old French *gornart,* from Latin *grundīre, grunnīre,* to grunt.]

gu·ru (gŏŏ′rŏŏ′, gŏŏ-rŏŏ′) *n.* **1.** Often **Guru.** A Hindu spiritual teacher. **2.** *Informal.* A person who is followed as a teacher and regarded as having special knowledge or insight. [Hindi *gurū,* "the venerable one," from Sanskrit *guruh,* heavy, venerable.]

gush (gŭsh) *intr.v.* **1.** To flow forth heavily or violently: *Water gushed from the open fire hydrant.* **2.** To make an excessive display of sentiment or enthusiasm. —*tr.v.* To emit abundantly: *The well gushed oil.* —*n.* **1.** A sudden, violent, or heavy outflow: *a gush of tears.* **2.** An excessive or exaggerated expression: *a gush of sentiment.* [Middle English *guschen, gosshen.*]

gush·er (gŭsh′ər) *n.* **1.** Someone or something that gushes. **2.** A gas or oil well with an abundant natural flow.

gush·y (gŭsh′ē) *adj.* **-i·er, -i·est.** Characterized by excessive displays of sentiment or enthusiasm. —**gush′i·ly** *adv.* —**gush′i·ness** *n.*

gus·set (gŭs′ĭt) *n.* A usu. triangular piece of material inserted in a garment to make it roomier or stronger. [Middle English, from Old French *gousset,* armpit, piece of armor under the armpit, dim. of *gousse,* pod, shell.]

gust (gŭst) *n.* **1.** A sudden, strong rush of wind. **2.** An outburst of emotion: *gusts of rage.* —See Syns at **wind.** —*intr.v.* To blow in sudden, strong rushes. [From Old Norse *gustr.*]

gus·ta·to·ry (gŭs′tə-tôr′ē, -tōr′ē) *adj.* Of or relating to the sense of taste: *wine-tasting, with its olfactory and gustatory sensations.*

gus·to (gŭs′tō) *n.* **1.** Fondness; taste; liking. **2.** Vigorous enjoyment; relish: *set to work with gusto.* —See Syns at **zest.** [Italian, from Latin *gustus,* taste.]

gust·y (gŭs′tē) *adj.* **-i·er, -i·est.** Marked by gusts of wind: *gusty weather.* —**gust′i·ly** *adv.* —**gust′i·ness** *n.*

gut (gŭt) *n.* **1.** The alimentary canal or any of its parts, esp. the stomach or intestines. **2. guts.** The bowels; entrails. **3. guts.** The essential contents of something: *"These hunks of metal are the guts of an atomic bomb"* (Stewart Alsop and Ralph Lapp). **4.** The intestines of certain animals when processed for use as strings for musical instruments or as surgical sutures. **5. guts.** *Slang.* Courage; fortitude. —*tr.v.* **gut·ted, gut·ting.** **1.** To remove the intestines or entrails of; disembowel. **2.** To destroy the contents or interior of: *The fire gutted the store.* —*adj. Slang.* **1.** Arousing or arising from basic emotions; deeply felt: *a gut issue; a gut response.* **2.** Easy: *gut courses.* [Middle English *gut,* from Old English *guttas* (pl.).]

gut·less (gŭt′lĭs) *adj. Slang.* Lacking courage.—**gut′less·ly** *adv.* —**gut′less·ness** *n.*

guts·y (gŭt′sē) *adj.* **-i·er, -i·est.** *Informal* Full of courage; daring; plucky. —See Syns at **brave.** —**guts′i·ness** *n.*

gut·ta-per·cha (gŭt′ə-pûr′chə) *n.* **1.** Any of several tropical trees of the genera *Palaquium* and *Payena* that have sap in the form of milky latex. **2.** A rubbery substance derived from the latex of these trees, used as electrical insulation and for waterproofing. [Malay *gĕtah percha* : *gĕtah,* sap + *percha,* strip of cloth.]

gut·ter (gŭt′ər) *n.* **1.** A channel for draining off water at the edge of a street or road. **2.** A pipe or trough for draining off water under the border of a roof. **3.** A furrow or groove formed by running water. **4.** The trough on either side of a bowling alley. **5.** A place or district where life is most impoverished or squalid: *language of the gutter.* —*tr.v.* To form gutters or furrows in. —*intr.v.* **1.** To flow in small streams or channels. **2.** To melt away rapidly: *The candle guttered and died.* **3.** To flicker. [Middle English *guter, goter,* sewer, trough, drain, from Norman French *gotere,* from Old French *gotiere,* from Latin *gutta,* drop.]

gut·ter·snipe (gŭt′ər-snīp′) *n.* A homeless or neglected child; street urchin.

gut·tur·al (gŭt′ər-əl) *adj.* **1.** Of or relating to the throat. **2.** Having the harsh, grating quality of certain sounds produced deep in the throat: *a guttural growl.* —*n.* A guttural sound. [Old French, from Latin *guttur,* throat.] —**gut′tur·al·ism′, gut′tur·al′i·ty** (gŭt′ə-răl′ĭ-tē) or **gut′tur·al·ness** *n.* —**gut′tur·al·ly** *adv.*

gut·ty (gŭt′ē) *adj.* **-ti·er, -ti·est.** Vivid; bold; stark.

guy¹ (gī) *n.* A rope, cord, or cable used for steadying, guiding, or holding. —*tr.v.* To fasten, guide, or hold with a guy. [Prob. of Low German orig.]

guy² (gī) *n. Informal* A man; fellow. —*tr.v.* To make fun of; mock. [After *Guy Fawkes* (1570–1606), an unsuccessful English regicide whose effigy is ceremonially burned in Britain on Nov. 5.]

guz·zle (gŭz′əl) *tr.v.* **-zled, -zling.** To drink greedily or excessively. [Poss. from Old French *gosiller,* from *gosier,* throat.] —**guz′zler** *n.*

gym (jĭm) *n. Informal.* **1.** A gymnasium. **2.** Gymnastics. **3.** A course or class in physical education.

gym·kha·na (jĭm-kä′nə, -kăn′ə) *n.* A meet with athletic or equestrian contests. [Blend of GYM(NASIUM) + Hindi *(gend)-khānā,* "(ball) house," racket court, from *khāna,* house, from Persian *khāna.*]

gym·na·si·um (jĭm-nā′zē-əm) *n., pl.* **-ums** or **-si·a** (-zē-ə). **1.** A room or building equipped for gymnastics and sports. **2.** (gĭm-nä′zē-ōōm′). An academic high school in various central European countries, esp. Germany. [Latin, school, from Greek *gumnasion,* from *gumnazein,* "to train naked," practice gymnastics, from *gumnos,* naked.]

gym·nast (jĭm′năst′, -nəst) *n.* A person skilled in gymnastic exercises. [Greek *gumnastēs,* from *gumnazein,* to practice gymnastics.]

gym·nas·tic (jĭm-năs′tĭk) *adj.* Of gymnastics. —**gym·nas′ti·cal·ly** *adv.*

gym·nas·tics (jĭm-năs′tĭks) *n. (used with a sing. or pl. verb).* Body-building exercises requiring training and skill, esp. those performed with special apparatus in a gymnasium.

gym·no·sperm (jĭm′nə-spûrm′) *n.* Any of a group of plants, including the pines and other cone-bearing trees, that produce seeds that are not enclosed in a fruit.

gy·ne·col·o·gy (gī′nĭ-kŏl′ə-jē, jī′-, jĭn′ĭ-) *n.* The medical science of disease, reproductive physiology, and endocrinology in females. [Greek *gunē* + -LOGY.] —**gy′ne·co·log′i·cal** (-kə-lŏj′ĭ-kəl) or **gy′ne·co·log′ic** *adj.* —**gy′ne·col′o·gist** *n.*

gy·noe·ci·um (jī-nē′sē-əm, -shē-, gī-) *n., pl.* **-ci·a** (-sē-ə, -shē-ə). *Bot.* The female reproductive organs of a flower; the pistil or pistils collectively. [From Greek *gunaikeios,* pertaining to women, from *gunē,* woman.]

-gynous. A suffix meaning: **1.** Women or females: **monogynous.** **2.** Female organs of plants: **epigynous.** [From Greek *gunē,* woman.]

-gyny. A suffix meaning: **1.** The condition of having women or females: **monogyny.** **2.** The condition of (a plant's) having female organs: **epigyny.** [From Greek *gunē,* woman.]

gyp (jĭp) *tr.v.* **gypped, gyp·ping.** *Informal.* To swindle, cheat, or defraud. —*n. Informal.* **1.** An act of cheating; a swindle. **2.** A person who cheats; a swindler. [Prob. short for GYPSY.] —**gyp′per** *n.*

gyp·soph·i·la (jĭp-sŏf′ə-lə) *n.* Any of various plants of the genus *Gypsophila,* having small white or pink flowers, and including the baby's-breath. [GYPSUM + -PHILA.]

gyp·sum (jĭp′səm) *n.* A white mineral, $CaSO_4 \cdot 2H_2O$, used in the manufacture of plaster of Paris, gypsum plaster and plasterboard, Portland cement, wallboards, and fertilizers. [Latin, from Greek *gupsos.*] —**gyp′se·ous** (-sē-əs) or **gyp·sif′er·ous** (-sĭf′ər-əs) *adj.*

Gyp·sy (jĭp′sē). Also **Gip·sy.** —*n., pl.* **-sies.** **1.** One of a nomadic Caucasoid people orig. migrating from the border region between Iran and India to Europe in the 14th or 15th cent. and now living principally in Europe and the United States. **2.** The Indic language of the Gypsies; Romany. **3.** Often **gypsy.** A person who is like a Gypsy, as in being a wanderer. —*adj.* Of or like Gypsies.

gypsy moth. A moth, *Porthetria dispar,* native to the Old World, having hairy caterpillars that feed on foliage and are very destructive to trees.

gy·rate (jī′rāt′) *intr.v.* **-rat·ed, -rat·ing.** **1.** To revolve on or around a center or axis. **2.** To circle or spiral. —*adj. Biol.* In rings; coiled. [From Latin *gȳrāre,* from *gȳrus,* circle, from Greek *guros.*] —**gy·ra′tion** *n.* —**gy′ra·tor** *n.* —**gy′ra·tor′y** (-rə-tôr′ē, -tōr′ē) *adj.*

gyr·fal·con (jûr′făl′kən, -fôl′-, -fô′kən) *n.* Also **ger·fal·con.** A large falcon, *Falco rusticolus,* of northern regions, with various color phases ranging from black to white. [Middle English *gerfaucoun,* from Old French *gerfaucon,* from Old Norse *geirfalki.*]

gy·ro (jī′rō) *n., pl.* **-ros.** **1.** A gyroscope. **2.** A gyrocompass.

gy·ro·com·pass (jī′rō-kŭm′pəs, -kŏm′-) *n.* A device in which a gyroscope acts to keep a pointer aligned in the direction from south to north, giving a reference for use in navigation.

gy·ro·scope (jī′rə-skōp′) *n.* A device consisting essentially of a disk or wheel that spins rapidly about an axis. Because the spinning motion tends to keep the line of the axis fixed, the device is often used to provide a directional reference, as in navigation instruments, missile guidance systems, etc. [Greek *gyros,* circle + -SCOPE.] —**gy′ro·scop′ic** (-skŏp′ĭk) *adj.* —**gy′ro·scop′i·cal·ly** *adv.*

gy·ro·sta·bi·liz·er (jī′rō-stā′bə-lī′zər) *n.* A device with a heavy gyroscope whose axis spins in a vertical plane to reduce the side-to-side rolling of a ship or airplane.

gyve (jīv) *Archaic.* —*n.* A shackle or fetter, esp. for the leg. —*tr.v.* **gyved, gyv·ing.** To shackle or fetter. [Middle English.]

Phoenician – *About 3,000 years ago the Phoenicians and other Semitic peoples began to use graphic signs to represent individual speech sounds instead of syllables or whole words. They used this symbol to represent a laryngeal consonant that is not found in English or any other Indo-European language, and they gave it the name* hēth.
Greek – *The Greeks borrowed the Phoenician alphabet with some modifications. They changed the shape of* hēth *and altered the name to* ēta. *At first they used it to represent the sound of the aspirate "h," but later used it to represent the vowel "ē."*
Roman – *The Romans borrowed the alphabet from the*

Greeks via the Etruscans. They used ēta *to represent the aspirate "h" and adapted the shape for carving Latin in stone. This monumental script, as it is called, became the basis for modern printed capital letters.*
Medieval – *By medieval times – around 1,200 years ago – the Roman monumental capitals had become adapted to being relatively quickly written on paper, parchment, or vellum. The cursive minuscule alphabet became the basis of modern printed lower-case letters.*
Modern – *Since the invention of printing about 500 years ago modifications have been made in the shape of the letter H, but its basic form has remained unchanged.*

---

h, H (āch) *n., pl.* **h's** *or* **H's.** The eighth letter of the modern English alphabet.

ha (hä) *interj.* Also **hah.** A word used to express surprise, laughter, or triumph. [Middle English.]

ha·ba·ne·ra (ä′bə-nâr′rə, hä′-) *n.* **1.** A slow Cuban dance. **2.** The music for the habanera, in duple time, with a repetitive rhythmic pattern. [Spanish (*danza*) *habanera,* "Havanan (dance)," from *La Habana,* Havana, a city in Cuba.]

ha·be·as cor·pus (hā′bē-əs kôr′pəs). *Law.* One of a variety of writs that may be issued to bring a person before a court or judge, esp. one issued to determine whether a person has been unlawfully imprisoned. [Middle English, from Medieval Latin *habeās corpus,* "you should have the body" (the first words of such a writ).]

hab·er·dash·er (hăb′ər-dăsh′ər) *n.* **1.** A dealer in men's furnishings such as hats, shirts, and socks. **2.** *Brit.* A dealer in sewing notions and small dry goods. [Middle English *haberdassher,* from Norman French *hapertas,* fabric, cloth.]

hab·er·dash·er·y (hăb′ər-dăsh′ə-rē) *n., pl.* **-ies. 1.** The goods a haberdasher sells. **2.** A haberdasher's shop.

hab·er·geon (hăb′ər-jən) *n.* **1.** A short, sleeveless coat of mail. **2.** A hauberk. [Middle English, from Old French *haubergeon,* from *hauberc,* hauberk.]

ha·bil·i·ment (hə-bĭl′ə-mənt) *n.* **1.** The dress or attire typical of an office, rank, or occasion: *the habiliment of a warrior.* **2. habiliments.** Clothes. [Old French (*h*)*abillement,* from *habiller,* to make fit, fit out.]

hab·it (hăb′ĭt) *n.* **1. a.** A constant, often involuntary way of reacting or behaving, acquired through frequent repetition. **b.** An established disposition of the mind or charac-

ter. **2.** Often **habits.** Customary manner or practice: *a man of ascetic habits.* **3.** An addiction. **4.** Characteristic appearance, form, or manner of growth, esp. of a plant. **5. a.** The distinctive clothing or costume worn by members of a religious order. **b.** A riding habit. —*tr.v.* To clothe; dress. [Middle English (*h*)*abit,* from Old French, from Latin *habitus,* condition, appearance, from the past part. of *habēre,* to hold, have.]

hab·it·a·ble (hăb′ĭ-tə-bəl) *adj.* Suitable to live in; inhabitable. [Middle English *abitable,* from Old French (*h*)*abitable,* from Latin *habitābilis,* from *habitāre,* to inhabit, reside, from *habēre,* to have, hold.] —**hab′it·a·bil′i·ty** *or* **hab′it·a·ble·ness** *n.* —**hab′it·a·bly** *adv.*

hab·i·tant (hăb′ĭ-tənt) *n.* Also **ha·bi·tan** (*Fr.* ä′bē-täN′). **1.** An inhabitant. **2.** An inhabitant of French descent in Canada or Louisiana belonging to the small farmer class. [Old French, from the pres. part. of *habiter,* to inhabit, from Latin *habitāre.*]

hab·i·tat (hăb′ĭ-tăt′) *n.* **1.** The area or natural environment in which an organism normally lives or grows. **2.** The place where a person or thing is most likely to be found. [Latin, "it dwells," from *habitāre,* to inhabit.]

hab·i·ta·tion (hăb′ĭ-tā′shən) *n.* **1.** The act of inhabiting. **2.** The condition of being inhabited: *Scientists expect that nuclear energy may open Antarctica to human habitation.* **3. a.** Natural environment or locality. **b.** Dwelling place: *a flimsy habitation of logs and dried mud.* [Middle English *habitacioun,* from Old French *habitation,* from Latin *habitātiō,* from *habitātus,* past part. of *habitāre,* to inhabit.]

hab·it-form·ing (hăb′ĭt-fôr′mĭng) *adj.* **1.** Leading to or causing addiction: *a habit-forming drug.* **2.** Tending to become habitual.

ha·bit·u·al (hə-bĭch′ōō-əl) *adj.* **1. a.** Of the nature of a habit; done constantly or repeatedly. **b.** By habit: *a habitual smoker.* **2.** Customary; usual: *took his habitual place at the table.* —**ha·bit′u·al·ly** *adv.* —**ha·bit′u·al·ness** *n.*

ha·bit·u·ate (hə-bĭch′ōō-āt′) *tr.v.* **-at·ed, -at·ing.** To accustom by frequent repetition or constant exposure. [From Late Latin *habituāre,* from Latin *habitus,* habit.]

hab·i·tude (hăb′ĭ-tōōd′, -tyōōd′) *n.* **1.** A customary behavior or action. **2.** A disposition to act in a customary manner. [Middle English, from Old French, from Latin *habitūdo,* condition, habit, from *habitus,* habit.]

ha·bit·u·é (hə-bĭch′ōō-ā′, hə-bĭch′ōō-ā′) *n.* Someone who frequents a particular place or places of a similar kind: *a habitué of sidewalk cafés.* [French, from the past part. of *habituer,* to frequent, from Late Latin *habituāre,* to make into a habit.]

habit
A nun's habit

habit
A riding habit

ă pat   ā pay   â care   ä father   ĕ pet   ē be   hw which   ĭ pit   ī tie   î pier   ŏ pot   ō toe   ô paw, for   oi noise
ōō took   ōō boot   ou out   th thin   th this   ŭ cut   û urge   zh vision   ə about, item, edible, gallop, circus

ha·ci·en·da (hä′sē-ĕn′də, ä′sē-) n. **1. a.** In Spanish-speaking countries, a large estate; a plantation or large ranch. **b.** The house of the owner of the hacienda. **2.** *Southwestern U.S.* A low, sprawling house with a projecting roof and wide porches. [Spanish, domestic work, landed property, from Latin *facienda*, things to be done, from *facere*, to do.]

hack[1] (hăk) tr.v. **1.** To cut or sever with repeated and irregular blows. **2.** To break up (earth) into clods or ridges. —intr.v. **1.** To chop or chip away at something. **2.** To cough roughly and harshly. —n. **1.** A rough, irregular cut made by hacking. **2.** A tool, such as a hoe, used for chopping or breaking up something. **3.** A rough, dry cough. [Middle English *hacken*, from Old English (tō)*haccian*, to cut to pieces.] —**hack′er** n.

hack[2] (hăk) n. **1.** A horse used for riding or driving; a hackney. **2.** A worn-out horse for hire. **3. a.** A person who performs unpleasant or distasteful tasks for money; a hireling. **b.** A writer hired to turn out routine and commercial literary work. **4.** A carriage or hackney for hire. **5.** *Informal.* **a.** A taxicab. **b.** The driver of a taxicab. —modifier: *a hack writer; a hack discussion.* —tr.v. **1.** To let out for hire. **2.** To employ as a hack. **3.** *Informal.* To write as a hack. **4.** To make banal or hackneyed with indiscriminate use. **5.** *Informal.* To manage or cope with: *took a second job but just couldn't hack it.* —intr.v. **1.** *Informal.* To work as a hack. **2.** To ride on horseback at an ordinary pace. [Short for HACKNEY.]

hack·ber·ry (hăk′bĕr′ē) n. **1.** Any of various trees or shrubs of the genus *Celtis*, having inconspicuous flowers and berrylike, often edible fruit. **2.** The fruit of a hackberry. [Var. of earlier *hagberry*.]

hack·ie (hăk′ē) n. Slang. A taxicab driver.

hack·le[1] (hăk′əl) n. **1.** One of the long, slender, often glossy feathers on the neck of a bird, esp. a male domestic fowl. **2.** hackles. **a.** The erectile hairs at the back of the neck, esp. of a dog. **b.** Temper; rage: *addressed us with a rudeness that made the hackles rise.* **3. a.** A tuft of cock feathers used for trimming an artificial fishing fly. **b.** An artificial fishing fly trimmed with hackles and usu. without wings. —tr.v. -led, -ling. To trim (a fly) with a hackle. [Middle English *hakell*, flax comb.]

hack·le[2] (hăk′əl) tr.v. -led, -ling. To chop roughly; hack. [Freq. of HACK (cut).]

hack·man (hăk′mən) n. The driver of a hack or hired carriage.

hack·ma·tack (hăk′mə-tăk′) n. A tree, the **tamarack.** [Of Algonquian orig.]

hack·ney (hăk′nē) n., pl. -neys. **1.** Often **Hackney.** A horse of a breed developed in England, having a gait characterized by pronounced flexion of the knee. **2.** A horse suited for routine riding or driving. **3.** A coach or carriage for hire. —adj. **1.** Hackneyed; banal. **2.** Hired. [Middle English *hakeney*.]

hack·neyed (hăk′nēd) adj. Lacking in freshness because of overuse; trite; banal.

hack·saw (hăk′sô′) n. Also **hack saw.** A tough, fine-toothed saw stretched taut in a frame, used for cutting metal.

had (hăd) v. Past tense and past participle of **have.**

had·dock (hăd′ək) n., pl. **haddock** or **-docks.** A food fish, *Melanogrammus aeglefinus,* of the northern Atlantic Ocean, related to and resembling the cod. [Middle English *haddok*, from Norman French *hadoc*.]

Ha·des (hā′dēz) n. Gk. Myth. **1.** The god who ruled the underworld, identified with the Roman god Pluto. **2.** The underworld kingdom of Hades, the abode of dead or departed spirits.

had·n't (hăd′nt). Had not.

hadst (hădst) v. Archaic. Past tense and past participle of **have,** used with *thou.*

haf·ni·um (hăf′nē-əm) n. Symbol **Hf** A silvery, metallic element obtained from zirconium ores. Atomic number 72, atomic weight 178.49, melting point 2,150°C, boiling point 5,400°C, specific gravity 13.29, valence 4. [From *Hafnia*, Latin name for Copenhagen, Denmark.]

haft (hăft) n. The handle of a cutting instrument, such as a sword, knife, or sickle. —tr.v. To equip or set into a haft. [Middle English, from Old English *hæft*.]

hag (hăg) n. **1.** An ugly, frightful old woman; crone. **2.** A witch; sorceress. **3.** A hagfish. [Middle English *hagge*, prob. short for Old English *hægtesse*, witch.]

hag·fish (hăg′fĭsh′) n., pl. **hagfish** or **-fishes.** Any of various eel-shaped saltwater fishes of the family Myxinidae, with a jawless sucking mouth and rasping teeth used to bore into and feed on other fishes.

hag·gard (hăg′ərd) adj. **1.** Appearing worn and exhausted from suffering, worry, or deprivation; gaunt. **2.** Wild and unruly. [Old French *hagard*, wild hawk.] —**hag′gard·ly** adv. —**hag′gard·ness** n.
   Syns: haggard, careworn, gaunt, wan, worn adj. Core meaning: Pale and exhausted because of worry, disease, hunger, or fatigue (*the haggard faces of the defeated troops*).

hag·gis (hăg′ĭs) n. A Scottish dish consisting of the minced heart, lungs, and liver of a sheep or calf mixed with suet, onions, oatmeal, and seasonings and boiled in the stomach of the animal. [Middle English *hagese*.]

hag·gle (hăg′əl) v. -gled, -gling. —intr.v. To bargain or dicker over the price or the terms of something. —tr.v. **1.** To cut in a crude, unskillful manner; to hack; mangle. **2.** Archaic. To harass or worry by wrangling. —n. An instance of haggling. [Freq. of dial. *hag*, to cut, from Middle English *haggen*, from Old Norse *höggva*.] —**hag′gler** n.

hag·i·og·ra·phy (hăg′ē-ŏg′rə-fē, hā′jē-) n., pl. -phies. **1.** Biography of saints. **2.** Any idealizing or worshipful biography. [Greek *hagios*, holy + -GRAPHY.] —**hag′i·og′ra·pher** n. —**hag′i·o·graph′ic** (-ə-grăf′ĭk) or **hag′i·o·graph′i·cal** adj.

hag·i·ol·o·gy (hăg′ē-ŏl′ə-jē, hā′jē-) n., pl. -gies. **1.** Literature dealing with the lives of saints. **2.** An authoritative list of saints. [Greek *hagios*, holy + -LOGY.]

hah (hä) interj. Var. of **ha.**

ha-ha (hä′hä′) n. A sound made in imitation of laughter. —interj. Also **haw-haw** (hô′hô′). A word used to express amusement or scorn. [Middle English, from Old English.]

hai·ku (hī′kōō) n., pl. **haiku.** A Japanese lyric poem of a fixed, 17-syllable form, usu. on a subject that is drawn from nature. [Japanese : *hai*, amusement + *ku*, sentence, verse.]

hail[1] (hāl) n. **1. a.** Precipitation in the form of pellets of ice and hard snow. **b.** A hailstone. **c.** Archaic. A hailstorm. **2.** Something that pours down like a shower of hail: *a hail of criticism.* —intr.v. **1.** To precipitate. **2.** To fall like hail. —tr.v. To pour down or out: *hailed blows upon his back.* [Middle English, from Old English *hagol*.]

hail[2] (hāl) tr.v. **1. a.** To salute or greet; to welcome. **b.** To greet or acclaim enthusiastically: *They hailed him as their leader.* **2.** To call out to in order to catch the attention of: *hail a cab.* —intr.v. **1.** To signal or call to a passing ship as a greeting. —n. **1.** The act of hailing. **2.** A shout made to greet or catch the attention of someone. **3.** Hearing distance. —interj. A word used to express a greeting or tribute. —idiom. hail from. To come or originate: *He hails from Boston.* [Middle English *hailen*, from *hail*, "hail" (interjection used as a greeting), from Old English *hāl*, health, safety.] —**hail′er** n.

hail-fel·low (hāl′fĕl′ō) adj. Also **hail-fel·low-well-met** (hāl′-fĕl′ō-wĕl′mĕt′). Heartily friendly and congenial. —n. A boon companion; congenial comrade. [From the archaic greetings *"Hail, fellow!"* and *"Hail, fellow! well met!"*]

hail·stone (hāl′stōn′) n. A hard pellet of snow and ice.

hail·storm (hāl′stôrm′) n. A storm in which hail falls.

hair (hâr) n. **1. a.** One of the fine, threadlike strands that grows from the skin of mammals, including human beings. **b.** A similar fine strand, as on a plant or insect. **c.** A covering of such strands, as on the human head. **2.** A tiny distance or narrow margin: *win by a hair.* —modifier: *a hair dryer.* —idioms. get in (someone's) hair. To upset or annoy. let one's hair down. To drop one's guard or reserve. split hairs. To make distinctions that are too small to be important. turn a hair. To show distress or embarrassment. Used in negative constructions: *accepted the challenge without turning a hair.* [Middle English *haire*, from Old English *hǽr*.] —**haired** (hârd) adj.

hair·breadth (hâr′brĕdth′) adj. Extremely close: *a hairbreadth escape.*

hair·cloth (hâr′klôth′, -klŏth′) n. A stiff, wiry, scratchy fabric with horsehair or camel's hair woven into it, used for upholstering furniture and stiffening garments.

ă pat	ā pay	â care	ä father	ĕ pet	ē be	hw which
ŏŏ took	ōō boot	ou out	th thin	th this	ŭ cut	

ĭ pit	ī tie	î pier	ŏ pot	ō toe	ô paw, for	oi noise
û urge	zh vision	ə about, item, edible, gallop, circus				

hair·cut (hâr′kŭt′) n. **1.** A shortening or shaping of the hair by cutting. **2.** The style in which hair is cut.

hair·do (hâr′dōō′) n., pl. **-dos.** The style in which hair is arranged; coiffure.

hair·dress·er (hâr′drĕs′ər) n. A person who cuts or arranges hair.

hair·dress·ing (hâr′drĕs′ĭng) n. **1.** The occupation of a hairdresser. **2.** The act of dressing or arranging the hair. **3.** A preparation used for dressing or arranging the hair.

hair·less (hâr′lĭs) adj. Having little or no hair.

hair·line (hâr′līn′) n. **1.** The front edge of hair growing above the forehead or on the head. **2.** A very thin line. **3.** Printing. A very fine line on a typeface. —**hair′line′** adj.

hair piece. A small wig or thick bunch of real or artificial hair, as a toupee or fall, worn over a bald spot or as part of a hairdo.

hair·pin (hâr′pĭn′) n. A thin, U-shaped pin, usu. of metal or plastic, used to hold the hair in place.

hair·rais·ing (hâr′rā′zĭng) adj. Horrifying; terrifying.

hair shirt. A coarse haircloth garment worn next to the skin as a penance.

hair·split·ting (hâr′splĭt′ĭng) n. The act or process of making unreasonably fine distinctions; quibbling. —adj. Concerned with subtle but petty distinctions. —**hair′split′ter** n.

hair spray. A preparation sprayed on the hair to keep it neat.

hair·spring (hâr′sprĭng′) n. A fine coiled spring that regulates the movement of the balance wheel in a watch or clock.

hair trigger. A gun trigger adjusted to respond to a very slight pressure.

hair-trig·ger (hâr′trĭg′ər) adj. Responding to the slightest provocation: a hair-trigger temper.

hair·y (hâr′ē) adj. -i·er, -i·est. **1.** Covered with hair: a hairy arm. **2.** Of or like hair: a hairy coat. **3.** Slang. Causing anxiety, apprehension, or fear: a hairy experience. —**hair′i·ness** n.

Hai·tian (hā′shən, -tē-ən) adj. Of or pertaining to Haiti, its people, or its dialect. —n. **1.** A native or inhabitant of Haiti. **2.** The language of the Haitians, composed of French and certain African languages. Also called **Haitian Creole**.

hake (hāk) n., pl. **hake** or **hakes.** Any of various saltwater food fishes of the genera Merluccius and Urophycis, related to and resembling the cod. [Middle English.]

hal-. Var. of **halo-.**

ha·la·tion (hā-lā′shən) n. **1.** A blurring or spreading of light around bright objects or areas on a photographic negative or print. **2.** A ring of light that appears around a bright object on a television screen. [HAL(O) + -ATION.]

ha·la·vah (hä′lə-vä′) n. Var. of **halvah.**

hal·berd (hăl′bərd) n. Also **hal·bert** (-bərt). A weapon, used in the Middle Ages, consisting of a long pole with both a steel spike and an axlike blade mounted as a single piece at one end. [Middle English, from Old French hallebarde, from Middle High German helmbarde: helm, handle + barte, ax.]

hal·berd·ier (hăl′bər-dîr′) n. A soldier, attendant, or guard armed with a halberd.

hal·bert (hăl′bərt) n. Var. of **halberd.**

hal·cy·on (hăl′sē-ən) n. **1.** A legendary bird, identified with the kingfisher, that was supposed to have the power to calm the wind and the waves when nesting on the sea during the winter solstice. **2.** Poet. A kingfisher. —adj. **1.** Calm and peaceful; tranquil. **2.** Prosperous; golden: halcyon years. [Middle English alceon, from Latin (h)alcyon, from Greek alkuōn.]

hale¹ (hāl) adj. **hal·er, hal·est.** Sound in health; vigorous; robust. —See Syns at **healthy.** [Middle English, from Old English hál.] —**hale′ness** n.

hale² (hāl) tr.v. **haled, hal·ing. 1.** To compel to go: hale a man into court. **2.** Archaic. To pull, drag, draw, or hoist. [Middle English halen, from Norman French haler, of Germanic orig.]

half (hăf, häf) n., pl. **halves** (hăvz, hävz). **1. a.** Either of two equal parts into which a thing can be divided, esp. either of a pair of subsets of equal measure that form a unit set when taken together. **b.** A part of something approximately equal to the remainder: the smaller half of a candy bar. **2.** A half-hour. **3.** In football and other sports, either of the two time periods that make up a game. **4.** Brit. A school term; semester. —adj. **1. a.** Being a half: a half hour. **b.** Being approximately a half. **2.** Partial; incomplete: a half-truth. **3.** Having only one parent in common with another person: a half sister. —adv. **1.** To the extent of exactly or nearly a half: a half-empty tank. **2.** Not completely; partly: only half prepared; half asleep. —idioms. **better half.** Informal. One's spouse, esp. one's wife. **by halves.** Partially; imperfectly: Don't do things by halves. **go halves.** To share equally. **in half.** Into halves. [Middle English, from Old English healf.]

Usage: **half.** The word half can be a noun, an adjective, or an adverb. Its usage in a sentence is determined by its grammatical function therein. For example, when half is a noun, it can stand alone: divided the cake in half/into halves. As a noun it also can be followed by of + another noun qualified by a word like a, an, the, this, your, my, or their: half of the group; half of an apple; found half of a dollar bill. Sometimes the of can be omitted, as: half the group; half an apple. But when the noun half is used with a pronoun, it must always be followed by of: half of them; half of it. When half is an adjective, it occurs directly before the noun it modifies: spent a half day in the city; a half peach left on my plate. When half is an adverb, it qualifies a verb or an adjective: We half finished the project. It is half past five.

half-and-half (hăf′ənd-hăf′, häf′ənd-häf′) adj. Being half one thing and half another. —adv. In equal portions. —n. **1.** A mixture of two things in equal portions, esp. a mixture of equal parts of milk and cream. **2.** Brit. A blend of malt liquors, esp. porter and ale.

half·back (hăf′băk′, häf′-) n. **1.** Football. Either of the two players who, along with the fullback and quarterback, make up a team's offensive backfield. **2.** Soccer & Field Hockey. Any of the three players stationed at the beginning of play about halfway between the front line of players and the fullbacks.

half-baked (hăf′bākt′, häf′-) adj. **1.** Only partly baked; not cooked through. **2.** Informal. Not sufficiently thought out; ill-conceived; foolish: a half-baked scheme. **3.** Informal. Lacking good judgment or common sense: a half-baked visionary.

half blood. Also **half-blood** (hăf′blŭd′, häf′-). **1.** The relationship that exists between persons having only one parent in common. **2.** A person related to another in such a way. —**half′-blood′ed** adj.

half boot. A low boot extending just above the ankle.

half-breed (hăf′brēd′, häf′-) n. A person having parents of different ethnic types, esp. one born of a Caucasian and an American Indian.

half brother. A brother related through one parent only.

half-caste (hăf′kăst′, häf′-) n. A person of mixed racial descent; half-breed.

half cock. The position of the hammer of a firearm when it is raised halfway and locked by a catch so that the trigger cannot be pulled.

half-cocked (hăf′kŏkt′, häf′-) adj. **1.** At the position of half cock. **2.** Informal. Inadequately prepared or conceived; not fully thought out. —adv. Informal. Prematurely; hastily; carelessly: fall halfcocked into an argument.

half dollar. A U.S. silver coin worth 50 cents.

half eagle. A U.S. gold coin worth five dollars, last issued in 1929.

half gainer. A dive in which the diver springs from the board facing forward, rotates backward in the air in a half backward somersault, and enters the water headfirst, facing the board.

half-heart·ed (hăf′här′tĭd, häf′-) adj. Done with or possessing little interest or enthusiasm; uninspired: a halfhearted attempt at painting. —**half′heart′ed·ly** adv. —**half′heart′ed·ness** n.

half hitch. A hitch made by looping a rope or strap around an object and then back around itself, bringing the end of the rope through the loop.

half-hour (hăf′our′, häf′-) n. **1.** A period of time equal to 30 minutes. **2.** The point in time halfway between one hour and the next. —modifier: a half-hour broadcast. —**half′hour′ly** adj. & adv.

half-life (hăf'līf', häf'-) *n. Physics.* The time required for half the nuclei in a sample of a specific isotopic species to undergo radioactive decay.

half-mast (hăf'măst', häf'-) *n.* The position about halfway up a mast or pole at which a flag is flown as a symbol of mourning or as a signal of distress. Also called **half-staff.**

half-moon (hăf'mōōn', häf'-) *n.* **1.** The moon when only half its disk is illuminated. **2.** Something shaped like a crescent, as the lunula of the fingernail.

half nel·son (nĕl'sən). A wrestling hold in which one arm is passed under the opponent's arm from behind to the back of his neck.

half note. *Mus.* A note having one half the value of a whole note.

half·pen·ny (hā'pə-nē, hăp'nē) *n.* **1.** *pl.* **-nies.** A British coin worth ¹/₂ of a penny. **2.** *pl.* **-pence** (hā'pəns). The sum of ¹/₂ of a penny. **3.** A small or trifling amount.

half sister. A sister related through one parent only.

half-slip (hăf'slĭp', häf'-) *n.* A woman's underskirt that extends from the waist to the hem of the outer garment.

half sole. A shoe sole extending from the shank to the toe.

half-sole (hăf'sōl', häf'-) *tr.v.* **-soled, -sol·ing.** To fit or repair with a half sole.

half sovereign. A former gold coin of Britain worth ten shillings.

half-staff (hăf'stăf', häf'-) *n.* Half-mast.

half step. **1.** *Mus.* A semitone. **2.** A marching step of 15 in. at quick time and 18 at double time.

half-tim·bered (hăf'tĭm'bərd, häf'-) *adj.* Also **half-tim·ber** (-bər). *Archit.* Having a timber framework with masonry filling the spaces.

half time. The intermission between halves in a game such as football or basketball.

half tone. *Mus.* A semitone.

half·tone (hăf'tōn', häf'-) *n.* **1.** A photoengraving in which various shades of light and dark are produced by extremely small dots that are dark and close together where a dark shade appears and lighter and more widely spaced to make lighter shades. **2.** The method or technique by which such a picture is prepared. **3.** The plate from which such a picture is printed.

half-track (hăf'trăk', häf'-) *n.* A military motor vehicle, often lightly armored, with endless treads in place of wheels. **—half'-track'** or **half'-tracked'** *adj.*

half-truth (hăf'trōōth', häf'-) *n.* A statement, esp. one intended to deceive, that omits some of the facts necessary for a truthful description or account.

half-way (hăf'wā', häf'-) *adj.* **1.** Midway between two points or conditions; in the middle. **2.** Reaching or including only half or a portion; partial: *halfway measures.* **—half'way'** *adv.*

half-wit (hăf'wĭt', häf'-) *n.* **1.** A mentally retarded person. **2.** A stupid or foolish person; simpleton. **—half'-wit'ted** (-wĭt'ĭd) *adj.* **—half'-wit'ted·ly** *adv.* **—half'-wit'ted·ness** *n.*

hal·i·but (hăl'ə-bət, hŏl'-) *n., pl.* **halibut** or **-buts.** Any of several large, edible flatfishes of northern Atlantic or Pacific waters. [Middle English *halybutte* : *hali,* holy (from its being eaten on holy days) + *butte,* flatfish.]

hal·ide (hăl'īd', hā'līd') *n.* A binary compound of a halogen with an electropositive element or radical. [HAL(O)- + -IDE.]

hal·i·dom (hăl'ĭ-dəm) *n. Obs.* **1.** A sanctuary. **2.** A holy relic. [Middle English *halidom,* from Old English *hālig-dōm* : *hālig,* holy + *-dom,* state, condition.]

hal·ite (hăl'īt', hā'līt') *n.* Rock salt. [HAL(O)- + -ITE.]

hal·i·to·sis (hăl'ĭ-tō'sĭs) *n.* A condition in which the breath smells foul or offensive. [Latin *hālitus,* breath + -OSIS.]

hall (hôl) *n.* **1.** A corridor or passageway in a building. **2.** A large entrance room or vestibule in a building; a lobby. **3.** A building for public entertainments, as concerts, lectures, or plays: *Symphony Hall.* **4.** A usu. large building for public purposes: *the town hall.* **5.** A room or building in a school, college, or university, set apart for a special purpose: *a dining hall.* **6.** The main house on a landed estate, esp. the house of a nobleman. **7.** The principal room in a medieval castle, used for dining, entertaining, and sleeping. [Middle English *halle,* from Old English *heall.*]

hal·le·lu·jah (hăl'ə-lōō'yə) *interj.* A word used to express praise or joy. **—n.** **1.** The exclamation of "hallelujah." **2.** A musical composition expressing praise and based on the word *hallelujah.* [Hebrew *hallelūyāh,* praise the Lord : *hallelū,* pl. imper. of *həllēl,* to praise + *yāh,* Yahweh.]

Hal·ley's comet (hăl'ēz). A comet, last seen in 1910, that is visible from the earth approximately every 76 years. [After Edmund *Halley* (1656–1742), British astronomer, who predicted its return after observing it in 1682.]

hal·liard (hăl'yərd) *n.* Var. of **halyard.**

hall·mark (hôl'märk') *n.* **1.** A mark used in England to stamp gold and silver articles that meet established standards of purity. **2.** Any mark indicating quality or excellence. **3.** A distinguishing characteristic, feature, or trait: *Lyricism is the hallmark of her poetry.* **—tr.v.** To mark with a hallmark. [After Goldsmith's *Hall,* London, where gold and silver articles were appraised and stamped.]

hall of fame. Also **Hall of Fame. 1.** A room or building housing memorials to famous or illustrious persons. **2.** A group of persons judged outstanding in a particular category or profession.

hal·loo (hə-lōō'). Also **hal·loa** (hə-lō'). *interj.* **1.** A word used to attract attention. **2.** A word used to urge on hounds in a hunt. **—n.** A shout or call of "halloo." **—intr.v.** To shout or call out "halloo." **—tr.v.** **1.** To urge on by calling or shouting "halloo." **2.** To call out to. [Perh. var. of earlier *hallow,* to shout so as to incite hounds, from Middle English *halowen,* from Old French *halloer.*]

hal·low (hăl'ō) *tr.v.* **1.** To make or set apart as holy; sanctify; consecrate. **2.** To honor or regard as holy; revere. [Middle English *halowen,* from Old English *hālgian.*]

hal·lowed (hăl'ōd) *adj.* **1.** Made or set apart as holy; consecrated. **2.** Highly venerated; considered sacred.

Hal·low·een (hăl'ō-ēn', hŏl'-) *n.* Also **Hal·low·e'en.** October 31, the eve of All Saints' Day, celebrated by children who go in costume from door to door begging treats or playing pranks. [Short for *All Hallow E'en.*]

Hal·low·mas (hăl'ō-məs', -məs) *n.* Also **Hal·low·mass.** *Archaic.* November 1, the feast of All Saints' Day. [Short for *Allhallowmas.*]

hal·lu·ci·nate (hə-lōō'sə-nāt') *intr.v.* **-nat·ed, -nat·ing.** To experience hallucinations. [From Latin *(h)allūcinārī,* to wander in mind, from Greek *aluein,* to wander, be distraught.]

hal·lu·ci·na·tion (hə-lōō'sə-nā'shən) *n.* **1.** An illusion of seeing, hearing, or otherwise sensing something that does not really exist; false perception. **2.** Something, as a vision or image, that occurs as a hallucination.

hal·lu·ci·na·to·ry (hə-lōō'sə-nə-tôr'ē, -tōr'ē) *adj.* **1.** Marked by hallucination: *a hallucinatory vision.* **2.** Hallucinogenic.

hal·lu·ci·no·gen (hə-lōō'sə-nə-jən) *n.* A drug, such as mescaline, that induces hallucination. [HALLUCIN(ATION) + -GEN.]

hal·lu·ci·no·gen·ic (hə-lōō'sə-nə-jĕn'ĭk) *adj.* Producing or tending to produce hallucinations.

hal·lux (hăl'əks) *n., pl.* **hal·lu·ces** (hăl'yə-sēz'). **1.** The inner or first digit on the hind foot of a mammal. **2.** In man, the big toe. [Latin, big toe.]

hall·way (hôl'wā') *n.* **1.** A corridor, passageway, or hall in a building. **2.** An entrance hall; foyer.

ha·lo (hā'lō) *n., pl.* **-los** or **-loes.** **1.** A ring of light surrounding the heads or bodies of sacred figures, as in religious paintings; a nimbus. **2.** The aura of glory surrounding a person, thing, or event regarded with reverence, awe, or sentiment. **3.** A circular band of light around a light source, as the sun or moon, caused by the refraction or reflection of light. **—tr.v.** To surround or invest with a halo. [Medieval Latin *halō,* from Latin *halōs,* from Greek, disk of the sun or moon.]

halo- or **hal-.** A prefix meaning salt or the sea: **halite.** [From Greek *hals,* salt, sea.]

hal·o·gen (hăl'ə-jən) *n.* Any of a group of five chemically related nonmetallic elements that includes fluorine, chlorine, bromine, iodine, and astatine. [HALO- + -GEN.] **—ha·log'e·nous** (hə-lŏj'ə-nəs) *adj.*

hal·o·phyte (hăl'ə-fīt') *n.* A plant that grows in saline soil. [HALO- + -PHYTE.] **—hal'o·phyt'ic** (-fĭt'ĭk) *adj.*

halt¹ (hôlt) *n.* A temporary stop of movement or progress; a pause. **—tr.v.** To bring to a stop. **—intr.v.** To come to a stop; pause. **—See Syns at hesitate and stop.** [German *Halt.*]

ă pat	ā pay	â care	ä father	ĕ pet	ē be	hw which	ĭ pit	ī tie	î pier	ŏ pot	ō toe	ô paw, for	oi noise
ōō took	ōō boot	ou out	th thin	th this	ŭ cut		û urge	zh vision		ə about, item, edible, gallop, circus			

halter   **hammer**   **hammerhead**
George Miksch Sutton

halt² (hôlt) *intr.v.* **1.** To proceed lamely or faultily, as in the development of a logical argument or in the rhythmical structure of a verse. **2.** To proceed or act with uncertainty or indecision; waver. **3.** To limp or hobble. —*adj. Archaic.* Having a limp; lame. [Middle English *halten*, to be lame, from Old English *healtian*.]

hal·ter (hôl'tər) *n.* **1.** A device of rope or leather to be placed around the head or neck in order to lead or secure an animal. **2. a.** A rope with a noose used for execution by hanging. **b.** Death or execution by hanging. **3.** A bodice for women that fastens behind the neck and across the back, leaving the arms, shoulders, and back bare. —*tr.v.* **1.** To put a halter on. **2.** To restrain or control with a halter. **3.** To hang (someone). [Middle English, from Old English *hælftre*.]

halt·ing (hôl'tǐng) *adj.* **1.** Limping; lame. **2.** Imperfect; defective: *a halting verse.* **3.** Hesitant or wavering: *a halting voice.*

hal·vah (häl-vä', häl'vä) *n.* Also **ha·la·vah** (hä'lə-vä'), **hal·va.** A confection of Turkish origin consisting of crushed sesame seeds in a binder of honey. [Yiddish *halva*, from Turkish *helve*, from Arabic *halwā*, sweetmeat.]

halve (hăv, häv) *tr.v.* **halved, halv·ing.** **1. a.** To divide or separate into two equal portions or parts: *halve a cake.* **b.** To divide by two: *halve a number.* **2.** To reduce or lessen by half: *halve prices.* **3.** *Golf.* To play (a game or hole) in the same number of strokes as an opponent. [Middle English *halven*, from *half*, half.]

halves (hăvz, hävz) *n.* Plural of **half.**

hal·yard (hăl'yərd) *n.* Also **hal·liard.** A rope used to raise or lower a sail, flag, or yard. [Var. of Middle English *halier*, from *halen*, to pull.]

ham (hăm) *n.* **1.** The thigh of the hind leg of certain animals, esp. a hog. **2.** The meat from the thigh of a hog, often smoked and dried. **3. hams.** The back part of the thighs and buttocks. **4.** *Slang.* An actor or performer who overacts. **5.** *Informal.* A licensed amateur radio operator. —*intr.v.* **hammed, ham·ming.** To exaggerate in acting; overact. [Middle English, from Old English.]

ham·a·dry·ad (hăm'ə-drī'əd) *n., pl.* **-ads** or **-a·des** (-ə-dēz') *n. Gk. & Rom. Myth.* A wood nymph, esp. a tree spirit. [Latin *hamādryas*, from Greek *hamadruas: hama*, together with + *drus*, tree.]

ham·burg·er (hăm'bûr'gər) *n.* Also **ham·burg** (-bûrg'). **1.** Ground beef. **2.** A cooked patty of ground meat. **3.** A sandwich consisting of a hamburger patty usu. in a roll or bun. [Short for *Hamburger steak*, after *Hamburg*, Germany.]

hame (hām) *n.* One of the two curved wooden or metal pieces of a harness on a draft animal to which the traces are attached. [Middle English.]

Ham·ite (hăm'īt) *n.* A member of a group of related peoples inhabiting northern and northeastern Africa, including the Berbers and the descendants of the ancient Egyptians.

Ha·mit·ic (hă-mǐt'ǐk, hə-) *adj.* Of or relating to the Hamites or the language of the Hamites. —*n.* A group of North African languages related to Semitic.

ham·let (hăm'lǐt) *n.* A small village. [Middle English, from Old French *hamelet*, from *ham*, village, of Germanic orig.]

ham·mer (hăm'ər) *n.* **1.** A hand tool consisting of an iron head attached to a wooden handle, used chiefly for driving in nails or for pounding and shaping metals. **2.** Any of a number of similar devices: **a.** The part of a gun that strikes the firing pin or percussion cap, causing it to go off. **b.** One of the padded wooden pieces that strike the strings of a piano. **c.** A device for striking a bell or gong. **3.** A metal ball weighing 16 pounds, or about 7.26 kilograms, with a long wire handle by which it is thrown for distance in an athletic contest. **4.** The largest of three small bones in the middle ear that transmit vibrations to the inner ear; the malleus. —*tr.v.* **1.** To hit with or as if with a hammer; to strike; pound. **2.** To beat into a shape or flatten with a hammer: *hammered the gold into a thin sheet.* **3.** To put together, fasten, or seal, particularly with nails, by hammering. **4.** To force upon by constant repetition. —*intr.v.* **1.** To deal repeated blows with or as if with a hammer; to pound: *The wind and rain hammered at us mercilessly.* **2.** *Informal.* To work at continuously or diligently: *He hammered away at his homework.* —*idiom.* **hammer and tongs.** With tremendous energy; vigorously. [Middle English *hamer*, from Old English *hamor*.] —**ham'mer·er** *n.*

hammer and sickle. A Communist symbol consisting of a crossed hammer and sickle to represent the alliance of workers and peasants.

ham·mered (hăm'ərd) *adj.* **1.** Created or shaped by hammering. **2.** Having a rough or indented surface as a result of hammering: *hammered gold.*

ham·mer·head (hăm'ər-hĕd') *n.* **1.** The head of a hammer. **2.** Any of several large, predatory sharks whose eyes are set into elongated, fleshy extensions at the sides of the head. **3.** A bird of Africa and southwestern Asia, with brown plumage, a large, bladelike bill, and a long, backward-pointing crest. Also called **hammerkop.**

hammer lock. A wrestling hold in which an opponent's arm is pulled behind his back and twisted upward.

ham·mock¹ (hăm'ək) *n.* A hanging bed of canvas or netting suspended between two supports. [Spanish *hamaca*, from Taino.]

ham·mock² (hăm'ək) *n.* Var. of **hummock.**

ham·per¹ (hăm'pər) *tr.v.* To prevent the free movement, action, or progress of; impede. —See Syns at **hinder.** [Middle English *hamperen*.]

ham·per² (hăm'pər) *n.* A large basket, usu. with a cover. [Middle English *hampere*, from Old French *hanapier*, a case for holding goblets, from *hanap*, goblet.]

ham·ster (hăm'stər) *n.* Any of several Eurasian rodents with large cheek pouches and a short tail, often used in laboratory research. [German *Hamster*, from Old High German *hamustro*, of Slavic orig.]

ham·string (hăm'strǐng') *n.* **1.** Either of two tendons at the rear hollow of the human knee. **2.** The large sinew in the back of the hock of a quadruped. —*tr.v.* **-strung** (-strŭng'), **-string·ing.** **1.** To cripple by cutting the hamstring. **2.** To make ineffective; impede the efficiency of. [HAM (thigh) + STRING.]

hand (hănd) *n.* **1. a.** In humans, the free end of the forelimb, consisting of the palm, four fingers, and an opposable thumb used for grasping and holding. **b.** An anatomical part in another animal, as a monkey, that serves a similar function. **2.** Something suggesting the shape or function of the human hand, esp.: **a.** A pointer on the dial of a clock. **b.** A pointer on a similar instrument, such as a gauge or meter. **3.** A style of handwriting; pen-

ă pat	ā pay	â care	ä father	ĕ pet	ē be	hw which	ĭ pit	ī tie	î pier	ŏ pot	ō toe	ô paw, for	oi noise
ŏŏ took	ōō boot	ou out	th thin	*th* this	ŭ cut		û urge	zh vision	ə about, item, edible, gallop, circus				

manship: *The message was written in a good, clear hand.*
4. a. Side or direction specified according to the way in which one is facing: *At my right hand you see a box.* **b.** One of the two sides of an argument, discussion, issue, etc.: *On the one hand I think you should go; on the other I think you should stay.* **5.** Assistance; help: *Give me a hand with this carton.* **6.** A person who does manual labor: *a hired hand.* **7.** A member of a ship's crew: *All hands on deck!* **8. a.** A person relatively skilled in a particular field: *He is quite a hand at plumbing.* **b.** Workmanship; skill; touch: *a master's hand.* **c.** A manner or way of doing or handling something: *She has a delicate hand with animals.* **9.** *Informal.* A round of applause: *The audience gave her a tremendous hand.* **10. a.** A pledge of marriage or permission to marry: *He asked for the hand of the viscount's daughter.* **b.** An agreement, esp. a business agreement, in which something is pledged with a handshake: *You have my hand on that.* **11.** *Cards.* **a.** A player: *We need four hands for bridge.* **b.** The cards dealt to and held by a player: *Don't look at my hand.* **c.** One round of a game in which all the cards distributed are played out: *I'll sit out for this hand.* **12.** Often **hands. a.** Possession: *These books should be in her hands by noon.* **b.** Control; jurisdiction: *You are in good hands.* **13.** A unit of length equal to 4 in., or 10.16 cm, used esp. to indicate the height of horses. —*modifier: a hand mirror; hand signals; hand tools.* —*tr.v.* To give or pass with or as if with the hands; transmit: *Hand me the flashlight. He handed the teacher a note.* —*phrasal verbs.* **hand down. 1.** To give or pass on, as from father to son: *The tribe handed down the legend from generation to generation.* **2.** To deliver or render (a verdict): *The court handed down a number of important decisions.* **hand in.** To turn in; submit: *Hand in your term papers by May 1.* **hand out.** To give out; distribute: *He stood on the corner, handing out leaflets to passers-by.* **hand over.** To yield control of; deliver up: *Hand over the money.* —*idioms.* **at hand.** Close by; near in time or place: *Spring is nearly at hand.* **at the hand** (or **hands**) **of.** By the action of: *He died at the hands of an assassin.* **by hand.** By using one's hands: *These dresses have been sewn by hand.* **force (someone's) hand.** To force someone to commit himself before he is ready to do so. **from hand to mouth.** With just enough for each day; with nothing set aside for the future: *live from hand to mouth.* **hand and foot.** Completely; totally: *She waits on him hand and foot.* **hand in glove.** In close association: *They worked together hand in glove.* **hand in hand. 1.** Holding each other's hand. **2.** Closely linked or associated; jointly: *Proper diet and good health go hand in hand.* **hand over fist.** *Informal.* At a tremendous rate: *He is making money hand over fist.* **hands down.** By a comfortable margin; easily: *She's sure to win the beauty contest hands down.* **have a hand in.** To have a share or part in: *I can see you had a hand in this. He wants to have a bigger hand in policy making.* **have (one's) hands full.** To be fully occupied; be unable to take on more duties or responsibilities. **in hand.** Under control: *He succeeded in keeping the situation in hand.* **lay hands** (or **a hand**) **on. 1.** To grasp or seize. **2.** To touch or handle, esp. so as to harm. **off (one's) hands.** Out of one's care or responsibility: *At last we were able to get him off our hands.* **on hand.** Available for use: *We always keep a supply of food on hand.* **on (one's) hands.** In one's care or possession, usu. as a responsibility or burden: *We've got my mother-in-law on our hands for the weekend.* **out of hand.** Out of control: *The situation is getting out of hand.* **out of (one's) hands.** Not under one's control or jurisdiction: *The matter is completely out of my hands.* **show** (or **tip**) **(one's) hand.** To reveal one's intentions in a given situation. **take in hand.** To take control of; handle; deal with: *We must try to take the boy in hand.* **throw up (one's) hands.** To give up in despair; concede. [Middle English, from Old English.]

hand·bag (hănd′băg′) *n.* **1.** A bag for carrying articles such as money, keys, and cosmetics; pocketbook. **2.** A small suitcase.
hand·ball (hănd′bôl′) *n.* **1.** A game in which two or more players bat a ball against the wall with their hands. **2.** The small rubber ball used in handball.
hand·bill (hănd′bĭl′) *n.* A printed sheet or pamphlet to be distributed by hand.
hand·book (hănd′bŏŏk′) *n.* **1.** A small reference book that

provides specific information or instruction on a particular subject. **2. a.** A book in which off-track bets are recorded. **b.** A place where off-track bets are taken.
hand·breadth (hănd′brĕdth′) *n.* Also **hand's-breadth** (hăndz′-). A linear measurement based on the width of a hand.
hand·car (hănd′kär′) *n.* A small open railroad car propelled by a hand pump or a small motor.
hand·cart (hănd′kärt′) *n.* A small cart pulled or pushed by hand.
hand·clasp (hănd′klăsp′) *n.* A handshake.
hand·cuff (hănd′kŭf′) *n.* Often **handcuffs.** A device that consists of a pair of metal bracelets chained together that can be locked around the wrists; manacle. —*tr.v.* To put handcuffs on.
hand·ed (hăn′dĭd) *adj.* **1.** Using or designed for use by one hand in preference to the other: *a left-handed pitcher; a left-handed golf club.* **2.** Having or requiring a particular number of hands: *a four-handed card game.*
hand·ful (hănd′fŏŏl′) *n., pl.* **-fuls. 1.** The quantity or number that can be held in the hand. **2.** A small but unspecified quantity or number: *a handful of requests.* **3.** *Informal.* A person or thing too difficult to control or handle easily.
hand grenade. A small grenade to be thrown by hand.
hand·gun (hănd′gŭn′) *n.* A firearm that can be used with one hand; a pistol.
hand·i·cap (hăn′dē-kăp′) *n.* **1. a.** A race or contest in which an advantage or disadvantage is given to a contestant in order to equalize the chances of winning. **b.** Such an advantage or penalty. **2.** Any disadvantage or disability that is a hindrance to progress or success: *overcame the handicap of inexperience.* —*tr.v.* **-capped, -cap·ping. 1.** To assign a handicap to. **2.** To be a disadvantage to. [From earlier *hand in cap,* a lottery game in which players held forfeits in a cap.]
hand·i·capped (hăn′dē-kăpt′) *adj.* Suffering from or affected by a handicap. —*n.* **the handicapped.** Handicapped persons collectively.
hand·i·craft (hăn′dē-krăft′) *n.* **1.** A trade, craft, or occupation, such as basketry or weaving, that requires skilled use of the hands. **2.** The work produced by skilled hands. [Middle English *handie-craft.*]
hand·i·work (hăn′dē-wûrk′) *n.* **1.** Work performed by hand. **2.** Something that is accomplished by a single person's efforts. **3.** The product of a person's work or actions. [Middle English *handiwork,* from Old English *handgeweorc : hand,* hand + *geweorc,* work.]
hand·ker·chief (hăng′kər-chĭf, -chēf′) *n.* **1.** A small square of cloth used esp. for wiping the nose or mouth. **2.** A square piece of cloth worn as a decorative article; kerchief; scarf. [HAND + KERCHIEF.]
han·dle (hăn′dl) *v.* **-dled, -dling.** —*tr.v.* **1.** To touch, lift, or hold with the hands. **2.** To operate with the hands; manipulate. **3.** To conduct, direct, or manage: *handle an investment.* **4.** To manage or represent: *handle a boxer.* **5.** To deal or cope with: *handle a crowd; handle a problem.* **6.** To deal or trade in: *a shop that handles porcelain and glass.* —*intr.v.* To act or function under operation: *a boat that handles beautifully.* —*n.* **1.** A part that is designed to be held or operated with the hand. **2.** An opportunity or means for achieving a purpose. **3.** *Slang.* A person's name. —See Syns at **name.** —*idiom.* **fly off the handle.** *Informal.* To become violently and suddenly angry. [Middle English *handelen,* from Old English *handlian.*]
  Syns: handle, manipulate, ply, wield *v. Core meaning:* To use with or as if with the hands *(handles an ax like a born woodsman).* See also Syns at **sell.**
han·dle·bar (hăn′dl-bär′) *n.* Often **handlebars.** A curved metal steering bar, as on a bicycle.
handlebar mustache *n.* A long, curved mustache resembling a handlebar.
han·dler (hănd′lər) *n.* **1.** A person who handles. **2.** *Sports.* **a.** A person who trains or shows an animal, such as a dog. **b.** A person who acts as the trainer or second of a boxer.
hand·made (hănd′mād′) *adj.* Made or prepared by hand rather than by machine.
hand·maid (hănd′mād′) *n.* Also **hand·maid·en** (hănd′mād′n) A female servant or attendant.

ă pat	ā pay	â care	ä father	ĕ pet	ē be	hw which	ĭ pit	ī tie	î pier	ŏ pot	ō toe	ô paw, for	oi noise
ŏŏ took	ōō boot	ou out	th thin	th this	ŭ cut		û urge	zh vision	ə about, item, edible, gallop, circus				

hand-me-down (hănd′mē-doun′) *adj.* Handed down to one person after being used and discarded by another. —*n.* Something used and then passed down from one person to another.

hand-off (hănd′ôf′, -ŏf′) *n.* A football play in which one player hands the ball to another.

hand organ. A barrel organ operated by turning a crank.

hand-out (hănd′out′) *n.* **1.** Food, clothing, or money given to a beggar. **2.** A folder or leaflet circulated free of charge. **3.** A prepared statement for release to the press.

hand-pick (hănd′pĭk′) *tr.v.* **1.** To gather or pick by hand. **2.** To select personally. —**hand′-picked′** *adj.*

hand-rail (hănd′rāl′) *n.* A narrow rail to be grasped with the hand for support.

hand′s-breadth (hăndz′brĕdth′) *n.* Also **hand′s breadth.** Var. of **handbreadth.**

hand-shake (hănd′shāk′) *n.* The grasping of right hands by two people as in greeting, leave-taking, or congratulation.

hand-some (hăn′səm) *adj.* **-som·er, -som·est. 1.** Pleasing and dignified in form or appearance. **2.** Generous; liberal: *a handsome reward.* —See Syns at **beautiful** and **generous.** [Middle English *handsom,* easy to handle, handy.] —**hand′some·ly** *adv.* —**hand′some·ness** *n.*

hand-spike (hănd′spīk′) *n.* A heavy bar used as a lever.

hand-spring (hănd′sprĭng′) *n.* The act of flipping the body completely forward or backward from an upright position, landing first on the hands, then on the feet.

hand-stand (hănd′stănd′) *n.* The act of balancing on the hands with the feet in the air.

hand-to-hand (hănd′tə-hănd′) *adj.* At close quarters.

hand-to-mouth (hănd′tə-mouth′) *adj.* Having barely enough; with nothing to spare.

hand-work (hănd′wûrk′) *n.* Work done by hand rather than by machine.

hand-writ-ing (hănd′rī′tĭng) *n.* **1.** Writing done with the hand. **2.** The writing characteristic of a particular person.

hand-y (hăn′dē) *adj.* **-i-er, -i-est. 1.** Skillful in using one's hands, esp. in a variety of ways: *He is very handy with a chisel. My father is very handy around the house.* **2.** Within easy reach; accessible: *a handy supply of medicine. Leave the dictionary on the table where it will be handy.* **3.** Useful; convenient: *An alarm clock is a handy thing to have when traveling.* **4.** Easy to use or handle: *a handy reference book.* —**idiom. come in handy.** To be useful, esp. at some specified time: *The money is bound to come in handy someday.* —See Syns at **convenient** and **practical.** [From HAND.] —**hand′i-ly** *adv.* —**hand′i-ness** *n.*

hand-y-man (hăn′dē-măn′) *n.* Also **handy man.** A person hired to perform odd jobs.

hang (hăng) *v.* **hung** (hŭng), **hang·ing.** —*tr.v.* **1.** To fasten from above with no support from below; suspend. **2.** To suspend or fasten so as to allow free movement at or about the point of suspension: *hang a door.* **3.** *Past tense & past participle* **hanged** or **hung.** To put to death by suspending by the neck. **4.** To alter the hem of (a garment) so as to fall evenly at a specified height. **5.** To furnish, decorate, or appoint by hanging: *hang a room with curtains.* **6.** To hold or incline downward; let droop: *hang one's head in sorrow.* **7.** To attach to a wall: *hang wallpaper.* **8.** To deadlock (a jury) by preventing a unanimous verdict. —*intr.v.* **1.** To be attached from above with no support from below. **2.** To die as a result of hanging. **3.** To remain suspended or poised above a place or object; hover. **4.** To hold fast for support; cling. **5.** To incline downward; droop. **6.** To depend: *The fate of the country hung on the outcome of the election.* **7.** To pay close or strict attention: *hang on every word.* **8.** To remain unresolved or uncertain: *The decision of the court is still hanging.* **9.** To fit the body in loose lines. **10.** To be on display, as in a gallery: *Her drawings hang in museums all over the world.* —*phrasal verbs.* **hang around.** *Informal.* **1.** To spend time idly; loiter: *I think I'll hang around a while.* **2.** To keep company: *hang around with odd characters.* **hang back.** To show unwillingness to do something; hesitate; hold back. **hang on. 1.** To cling tightly to something: *"Hang on to the rope," the guide said.* **2.** To remain on the telephone; hold the line. **3.** To last; continue: *This fever keeps hanging on.* **hang onto.** To hold or cling tightly to something: *Hang onto the rope.* **hang out.** *Slang.* To spend one's free time in a certain place. **hang together. 1.** To stand united; stick together. **2.** To constitute a coherent totality. **hang up.** To end a telephone conversation. —*n.* **1.** The way in which something hangs. **2.** The particular meaning or significance. **3.** *Informal.* The proper method of doing or using something: *get the hang of it.* —**idioms. give** (or **care**) **a hang.** To be concerned or anxious. **hang by a thread.** To be in an extremely precarious position. **hang fire.** To be slow in firing, as a gun. **hang over** (one's) **head.** To be or seem to be an imminent danger or threat to. **let it all hang out.** *Slang.* **1.** To be completely relaxed. **2.** To be completely frank or candid. [Middle English *hangen,* partly from Old English *hōn* (past part. *hangen*), and partly from Old English *hangian.*]

Usage: **hanged, hung.** The past tense and past participle *hanged* is used only to refer to capital punishment: *The outlaw was hanged. Hung* is also used in this sense, although *hanged* is more common in formal writing. In all other senses of the verb, the corresponding past tense and past participle is *hung: hung the clothes; hung her head in shame; a jury that was hung; an argument that hung on slim evidence; a listener who hung on every word.*

han-gar (hăng′ər) *n.* A shed or shelter, esp. a structure for housing, servicing, or repairing aircraft. [French, from Old French, prob. from Medieval Latin *angarium,* shed for shoeing horses.]

hang-bird (hăng′bûrd′) *n.* A bird, such as the oriole, that builds a hanging nest.

hang-dog (hăng′dôg′, -dŏg′) *adj.* **1.** Shamefaced or guilty. **2.** Downcast; abject. —*n.* A sneak.

hang-er (hăng′ər) *n.* **1.** One that hangs. **2.** A contrivance to which something hangs or by which something is hung. **3.** A device around which a garment is draped for hanging from a hook or rod.

hang-er-on (hăng′ər-ŏn′, -ôn′) *n., pl.* **hang-ers-on.** A person who hangs around a place, group, or another person in the hope of gain; parasite.

hang-ing (hăng′ĭng) *n.* **1.** An execution on a gallows. **2.** Often **hangings.** Something hung, as draperies or a tapestry. **3.** A downward slope or inclination. —*adj.* **1.** Situated on a sharp declivity. **2.** Projecting downward; overhanging. **3.** Suited for holding an object that hangs. **4. a.** Deserving death by hanging: *a hanging crime.* **b.** Disposed to inflict the sentence of death by hanging: *a hanging judge.*

hang-man (hăng′mən) *n.* A person who hangs condemned prisoners.

hang-nail (hăng′nāl′) *n.* A small piece of dead skin that is partly detached from the rest of the skin at the side or base of a fingernail. [By folk ety. from Middle English *agnail,* sore around the nail, from Old English *angnaegl.*]

hang-out (hăng′out′) *n.* A favorite place for meeting or spending time.

hang-o-ver (hăng′ō′vər) *n.* **1.** Unpleasant aftereffects as a result of drinking too much alcohol. **2.** Something left from an earlier time; holdover: *hangovers from prewar legislation.*

hang-up (hăng′ŭp′) *n. Informal.* **1.** A psychological or emotional problem. **2.** Something that blocks or hinders progress; an obstacle.

hank (hăngk) *n.* **1.** A coil or loop, esp. of hair. **2.** A looped bundle, as of yarn; skein. [Middle English, of Scandinavian orig.]

han-ker (hăng′kər) *intr.v.* To have a longing; crave. [Prob. from dial. Dutch *hankeren.*] —**hank′er-er** *n.*

han-ky-pan-ky (hăng′kē-păng′kē) *n. Slang.* **1.** Devious or mischievous activity. **2.** Foolish talk or action. [Perh. alteration of *hokey-pokey,* trickery, deception, alteration of HOCUS-POCUS.]

Han-sen's disease (hăn′sənz). Leprosy. [After A.G.H. Hansen (1841–1912), Norwegian physician, who discovered the bacillus that causes leprosy.]

han-som (hăn′səm) *n.* A two-wheeled covered carriage with the driver's seat above and behind. [After its designer, Joseph A. Hansom (1803–82), English architect.]

Ha-nuk-kah or **Ha-nu-kah** (KHä′nŏŏ-kä′, -nə-kə, hä′-) *n.* Vars. of **Chanukah.**

hap (hăp) *n. Archaic.* —*n.* **1.** Fortune; chance. **2.** A happening; an occurrence. —*intr.v.* **happed, hap·ping.** To happen. [Middle English, from Old Norse *happ,* good luck, chance.]

hap-haz-ard (hăp-hăz′ərd) *adj.* Dependent upon or charac-

ă pat ā pay â care ä father ĕ pet ē be hw which ĭ pit ī tie î pier ŏ pot ō toe ô paw, for oi noise
ŏŏ took ŏŏ boot ou out th thin th this ŭ cut û urge zh vision ə about, item, edible, gallop, circus

terized by mere chance. [HAP + HAZARD.] —**hap·haz′ard·ly** adv. —**hap·haz′ard·ness** n.

hap·less (hăp′lĭs) adj. Luckless; unfortunate. —See Syns at **unfortunate.** —**hap′less·ly** adv. —**hap′less·ness** n.

hap·loid (hăp′loid′) adj. Genetics. Having the number of chromosomes of a germ cell that is equal to half the number in the normal body cell. [From Greek haplous, single, simple + -OID.]

hap·ly (hăp′lē) adv. Archaic. By chance or accident; perhaps.

hap·pen (hăp′ən) intr.v. **1.** To come to pass; occur; take place. **2.** To take place or occur by chance. **3.** To come upon something by chance. **4.** To appear by chance; turn up. [Middle English happenen, from hap, chance.]

hap·pen·chance (hăp′ən-chăns′) n. Var. of **happenstance.**

hap·pen·ing (hăp′ə-nĭng) n. **1.** Something that happens; an event. **2.** An event or occurrence of particular importance. **3.** An improvised and often spontaneous event or performance.

hap·pen·stance (hăp′ən-stăns′) n. Also **hap·pen·chance** (-chăns′). A chance occurrence; accident. [HAPPEN + (CIR-CUM)STANCE.]

hap·py (hăp′ē) adj. **-pi·er, -pi·est. 1.** Characterized by good luck; fortunate. **2.** Having, showing, or marked by pleasure or joy. **3.** Apt; appropriate; suitable: a happy turn of phrase. **4.** Cheerfully, willing: happy to assist you. —See Syns at **cheerful, fortunate, glad,** and **merry.** [Middle English, from hap, chance.] —**hap′pi·ly** adv. —**hap′pi·ness** n.

hap·py-go-luck·y (hăp′ē-gō-lŭk′ē) adj. Easygoing; lighthearted; carefree.

ha·ra·ki·ri (hä′rə-kîr′ē, hăr′ə-) n. Ritual suicide by disembowelment as formerly practiced by the Japanese upper classes. [Japanese harakiri.]

ha·rangue (hə-răng′) n. A long, pompous speech; tirade. —v. **-rangued, -rangu·ing.** —tr.v. To deliver a harangue to. —intr.v. To deliver a harangue. [Middle English arang, from Old French arenge, from Medieval Latin harenga.] —**ha·rangu′er** n.

ha·rass (hăr′əs, hə-răs′) tr.v. **1.** To bother or torment repeatedly and persistently. **2.** To carry out repeated attacks or raids against. [French harasser, from Old French harer, to set a dog on, from hare, a cry used to set a dog on.] —**har′ass·er** n. —**har′ass·ment** n.

har·bin·ger (här′bən-jər) n. Someone or something that indicates what is to come; a forerunner: dark clouds that were harbingers of rain. [Middle English harbergere, from Old French, from herbergier, to provide lodging for, from herberge, lodging, from Old High German heriberga, lodging.]

har·bor (här′bər). Also Brit. **har·bour.** —n. **1.** A sheltered part of a body of water deep enough to serve as a port for ships. **2.** Any place of shelter; a refuge. —tr.v. **1.** To give shelter to; protect; keep. **2.** To hold a particular thought or feeling in the mind: harbor feelings of resentment. [Middle English herber, from Old English herebeorg.] —**har′bor·er** n.

har·bor·age (här′bər-ĭj) n. **1.** Shelter and anchorage for ships. **2.** Shelter; refuge.

har·bor·mas·ter (här′bər-măs′tər) n. An officer who oversees and enforces the regulations of a harbor.

hard (härd) adj. **-er, -est. 1.** Resistant to pressure; firm; rigid: a hard surface. **2.** Difficult to understand, express, or convey: a hard question. **3.** Requiring great effort; arduous: The book represents years of hard work by the author. **4.** Energetic; industrious; diligent: He's a very hard worker. **5.** Intense; forceful: a hard blow. **6.** Difficult to endure; trying: a hard life. He's had a hard day at the office. **7.** Severe; harsh: a hard winter. **8.** Stern; strict; unrelenting: a hard taskmaster. **9.** Making few or no concessions: a hard bargain; a hard line in foreign policy. **10.** Sharp; probing; searching: He promised to take a hard look at the entire situation. **11.** Unchangeable; real: hard facts; hard evidence. **12.** Causing damage; tending to wear down quickly: Freezing weather is very hard on a car. **13.** Bad: a victim of very hard luck. **14.** Bitter; rancorous; resentful: No hard feelings, I hope! **15. a.** Designating metal currency as against checks or notes: hard cash. **b.** Backed by and thus exchangeable for gold: hard currency. **16.** Designating the sound of the letters c and g as they are pronounced in cat and go. **17.** Having high alco-

holic content; intoxicating: hard liquor. **18.** Having a cloth, cardboard, or leather binding: a hard-bound book. **19.** Containing dissolved salts that interfere with the lathering action of soap: hard water. **20.** Physics. Having high energy and great penetrating power: hard x-rays. —adv. **1.** Intently; earnestly: work hard. **2.** With great force, vigor, or energy: Press hard on the lever. She laughed hard at his jokes. **3.** In such a way as to cause great damage: A number of towns were hard hit by the storm. **4.** With great distress, grief, or bitterness: She took the news very hard. **5.** With resistance; reluctantly: Old superstitions die hard. **6.** Toward or into a solid condition: The cement will set hard within a day. —idioms. **be hard put.** To have great difficulty in doing something: He was hard put to come up with an answer. **hard and fast.** Fixed; rigid: hard and fast rules. **hard by.** Close to; near to: The village lies hard by the river. **hard of hearing.** Partially deaf. **hard up.** Informal. Short of or in need of money. [Middle English, from Old English.]

Syns: hard, firm, solid adj. Core meaning: Unyielding to physical pressure (a hard surface; hard ground). See also Syns at **burdensome** and **difficult.**

hard·back (härd′băk′) adj. Bound in cloth, cardboard, or leather rather than paper: a hardback novel. —n. A hardback book.

hard-bit·ten (härd′bĭt′n) adj. Toughened by experience.

hard-boiled (härd′boild′) adj. **1.** Boiled until both the white and yolk of an egg become hard. **2.** Informal. Callous; tough.

hard cash. Ready money; cash.

hard cider. Fermented cider.

hard coal. Anthracite.

hard-core (härd′kôr′) adj. Also **hard-core. 1.** Stubbornly resistant or inveterate: the hard-core criminal element. **2.** Continuing or persisting for a long time: hard-core poverty cases.

hard·en (här′dn) tr.v. **1.** To make firm or firmer; make solid or hard. **2.** To toughen mentally or physically; make strong. **3.** To make unfeeling, unsympathetic, or callous. —intr.v. **1.** To become hard or rigid to the touch; set. **2. a.** To become strong or hardy. **b.** To become insensitive or unfeeling. **3.** To become firm and unyielding: His resolve hardened.

hard·head·ed (härd′hĕd′ĭd) adj. **1.** Stubborn; willful. **2.** Realistic; tough-minded. —See Syns at **obstinate.** —**hard′head′ed·ly** adv. —**hard′head′ed·ness** n.

hard·heart·ed (härd′här′tĭd) adj. Lacking in feeling; cold. —**hard′heart′ed·ly** adv. —**hard′heart′ed·ness** n.

har·di·hood (här′dē-hŏod′) n. Boldness and daring; audacity. [HARDY + -HOOD.]

hard labor. Compulsory physical labor during a prison term imposed as part of the legal punishment for a crime.

hard·ly (härd′lē) adv. **1.** Barely; scarcely; just. **2.** To almost no degree; almost not. **3.** Probably not; almost certainly not: is hardly likely to make another offer after such a definite refusal. **4.** Harshly; with severity. **5.** With great difficulty; painfully. [Middle English hardli, boldly, hardily, from Old English h(e)ardlīce.]

Usage: hardly. 1. Since the word has senses verging on the negative, it is not used with another negative in the same construction: They could hardly hear (not couldn't hardly). She accepted the verdict with hardly a sign of emotion (not without hardly). **2.** Hardly is followed by clauses introduced by when or before but not by than or until: They had hardly arrived when (or before) the call came.

hard·ness (härd′nĭs) n. **1.** The quality or condition of being hard. **2.** Mineral. The relative resistance of a mineral to scratching.

hard palate. The relatively hard, bony front portion of the palate.

hard·pan (härd′păn′) n. **1.** A layer of hard subsoil or clay. **2.** Hard, unbroken ground. **3.** A foundation; basis.

hard sauce. A creamy dessert sauce of butter and sugar flavored with rum, brandy, or vanilla.

hard sell. Informal. Aggressive, high-pressure salesmanship or advertising.

hard·ship (härd′shĭp′) n. **1.** Extreme privation; suffering. **2.** Something that causes privation or distress.

ă pat ā pay â care ä father ĕ pet ē be hw which ĭ pit ī tie î pier ŏ pot ō toe ô paw, for oi noise
ōō took ōō boot ou out th thin th this ŭ cut û urge zh vision ə about, item, edible, gallop, circus

hard·tack (härd′tăk′) *n.* A hard biscuit or bread made only with flour and water. [HARD + TACK (food).]

hard·top (härd′tŏp′) *n.* An automobile designed to look like a convertible but with a rigidly fixed hard top.

hard·ware (härd′wâr′) *n.* **1.** Metal articles such as locks, tools, and cutlery. **2.** A machine, such as a computer, and its associated physical equipment or parts. **3.** *Informal.* Weapons, esp. military weapons.

hard·wood (härd′wŏŏd′) *n.* **1.** The wood of a broad-leaved flowering tree as distinguished from that of a conifer. **2.** A broad-leaved flowering tree. —*modifier: a hardwood floor.*

har·dy (här′dē) *adj.* **-di·er, -di·est. 1.** Robust; strong: *a hardy mountain climber.* **2.** Courageous; brave. **3.** Brazenly daring; audacious. **4.** Able to withstand unfavorable conditions such as cold weather: *a hardy rosebush.* [Middle English, from Old French *hardi*, from the past part. of *hardir*, to become bold, make hard.] —**har′di·ness** *n.*

hare (hâr) *n.* Any of various mammals of the family Leporidae, and esp. of the genus *Lepus*, related to the rabbit but with longer ears, large hind feet, and long legs adapted for jumping. [Middle English, from Old English *hara*.]

hare·bell (hâr′běl′) *n.* A plant, *Campanula rotundifolia*, with slender stems and leaves and bell-shaped blue flowers. Also called **bluebell.** [Middle English *harebelle*.]

hare·brained (hâr′brānd′) *adj.* Foolish; flighty.
   Usage: harebrained. This adjective is not spelled *hairbrained.*

hare·lip (hâr′lĭp′) *n.* A birth defect in which the upper lip is split into two or more parts. —**hare′lipped′** *adj.*

har·em (hâr′əm, hăr′-) *n.* **1.** Rooms reserved for women members of a Moslem household. **2.** The women who live in a harem. [Arabic *ḥarīm*, sacred, forbidden place, from *harama*, he prohibited.]

hark (härk) *intr.v.* To listen carefully. —*idiom.* **hark back.** To return to a previous point or event. [Middle English *herk(i)en.*]

hark·en (här′kən) *v.* Var. of **hearken.**

har·le·quin (här′lə-kwən, -kən) *n.* A clown; buffoon. —*adj.* Having a pattern of brightly colored diamond shapes; parti-colored. [French, a character in Italian comedy, from Italian *arlecchino.*]

har·lot (här′lət) *n.* A whore or prostitute. [Middle English, vagabond, itinerate jester, male servant, prostitute, from Old French *(h)arlot*, young fellow, vagabond.] —**har′lot·ry** (-lə-trē) *n.*

harm (härm) *n.* Physical or psychological injury or damage. —*tr.v.* To cause harm to; hurt. [Middle English, from Old English *hearm.*]
   Syns: **harm, damage, detriment, hurt, injury, outrage** *n.* Core meaning: The action or result of inflicting loss or pain *(did harm to the hostages).*

harm·ful (härm′fəl) *adj.* Capable of harming or causing harm; injurious. —**harm′ful·ly** *adv.* —**harm′ful·ness** *n.*

harm·less (härm′lĭs) *adj.* Not harmful; not capable of harming. —**harm′less·ly** *adv.* —**harm′less·ness** *n.*

har·mon·ic (här-mŏn′ĭk) *n.* **1.** Any of the pure tones having frequencies that are whole-number multiples (twice, three times, four times, etc.) of a fundamental frequency and that sounding together with the fundamental make up a tone, as of a musical instrument. **2.** A tone produced on a stringed instrument by lightly touching a vibrating string at a given fraction of its length so that both segments vibrate. **3.** Any wave whose frequency is a whole-number multiple of that of another. —*adj.* **1.** Of harmonic motion. **2.** Of musical harmony. [Latin *harmonicus*, harmonious, from Greek *harmonikos*, from *harmonia*, harmony.] —**har·mon′i·cal·ly** *adv.*

har·mon·i·ca (här-mŏn′ĭ-kə) *n.* A small, rectangular musical instrument consisting of a row of tuned reeds that are made to vibrate by the player's breath; a mouth organ. [Var. of earlier *armonica*, from Italian, from *armonico*, harmonious, from Latin *harmonicus.*]

harmonic motion. *Physics.* The simplest type of vibrating motion in which a body, such as a pendulum, moves back and forth across a central point under the influence of a force that tends to return it to that point.

har·mon·ics (här-mŏn′ĭks) *n.* (*used with a sing. verb).* The theory or study of the physical properties and characteristics of musical sound.

har·mo·ni·ous (här-mō′nē-əs) *adj.* **1.** Marked by agreement and good will in feeling or action: *a harmonious relationship.* **2.** Having elements pleasingly or appropriately combined: *a harmonious structure.* **3.** Melodious; pleasing to the ear. —**har·mo′ni·ous·ly** *adv.* —**har·mo′ni·ous·ness** *n.*

har·mo·ni·um (här-mō′nē-əm) *n.* An organlike keyboard instrument that produces tones by means of air forced through free metal reeds.

har·mo·nize (här′mə-nīz′) *v.* **-nized, -niz·ing.** —*tr.v.* **1.** To bring into agreement or harmony; make harmonious. **2.** To provide harmony for (a melody). —*intr.v.* **1.** To be in agreement; be harmonious. **2.** To sing or play in harmony.

har·mo·ny (här′mə-nē) *n., pl.* **-nies. 1.** *Mus.* **a.** A sequence of chords used to accompany a melody: *The piano fills in the harmony.* **b.** The study of the structure, succession, and relationships of combinations of tones that sound at the same time in music. **c.** The structure of music as seen in terms of this study. **d.** A particular chord or a passage based on it: *The tonic harmony persists for six measures.* **2.** A combination of musical sounds considered to be pleasing. **3.** A pleasing combination of the elements that form a whole: *color harmony; the order and harmony of the universe.* **4.** Agreement in feeling or opinion; good will; accord: *live in harmony.* —*modifier: a harmony class; a harmony book.* [Middle English *armonie*, from Old French *(h)armonie*, from Latin *harmonia*, from Greek, agreement, harmony, means of joining, from *harmos*, joint.]
   Syns: **harmony, concord, rapport, unity** *n.* Core meaning: The state of individuals who are in total agreement *(family harmony).*

har·ness (här′nĭs) *n.* **1.** The gear or tackle, other than a yoke, with which a draft animal pulls a vehicle. **2.** Anything resembling a harness, such as the arrangement of straps used to hold a parachute to the body. —*tr.v.* **1.** To put a harness on (a draft animal). **2.** To bring under control and direct the force of: *If he can harness his energy, he will accomplish a great deal.* —*idiom.* **in harness.** On duty. [Middle English, from Old French *harneis*, military equipment.] —**har′ness·er** *n.*

harness   harp

harp (härp) *n.* A musical instrument consisting of an upright, open, triangular frame with 46 strings of graded lengths played by plucking with the fingers. —*intr.v.* To play a harp. —*phrasal verb.* **harp on** (or **upon**). To talk or write about to an excessive and tedious degree; dwell on. [Middle English *harp(e)*, from Old English *hearpe.*] —**harp′er** *n.* —**harp′ist** *n.*

har·poon (här-pōōn′) *n.* A spear with an attached rope and a barbed head used in hunting whales and large fish. —*tr.v.* To strike, kill, or capture with or as if with a harpoon. [French *harpon*, from *harpe*, clamp, dog's claw, from Latin *harpē*, sickle, from Greek *harpē.*] —**har·poon′-er** or **har·poon·eer** (här′pōō-nîr′) *n.*

harp·si·chord (härp′sĭ-kôrd′) *n.* A keyboard instrument whose strings are plucked by means of quills or leather picks. [Obs. French *harpechorde*, from Italian *arpicordo* : *arpi*, harp + *corda*, string.]

har·py (här′pē) *n., pl.* **-pies. 1.** *Gk. Myth.* **Harpy.** A foul, loathsome monster with the head and trunk of a woman and the tail, wings, and talons of a bird. **2.** A predatory person. **3.** A shrewish woman.

har·que·bus (här′kə-bəs, -kwĭ-bŭs′) *n.* A heavy, portable matchlock gun used during the 15th and 16th cent. [Old French *(h)arquebuse*, from Middle Dutch *hakebusse* :

hake, hook + *busse*, box, gun.]

har·ri·dan (hăr′ĭ-dən) *n.* A vicious, scolding old woman. [Poss. var. of French *haridelle*, worn-out horse, jade.]

har·ri·er[1] (hăr′ē-ər) *n.* **1.** Someone or something that harries. **2.** Any of various slender, narrow-winged hawks of the genus *Circus*, which prey on small animals.

har·ri·er[2] (hăr′ē-ər) *n.* **1.** One of a breed of small hounds orig. used in hunting hares. **2.** A cross-country runner. [From HARE.]

har·row (hăr′ō) *n.* A farm instrument consisting of a heavy frame with sharp teeth or upright disks, used to break up and even off plowed ground. —*tr.v.* **1.** To break up and level (soil or land) with a harrow. **2.** To inflict great distress or torment on. [Middle English *harwe*.]

har·row·ing (hăr′ō-ĭng) *adj.* Extremely distressing; agonizing: *a harrowing experience.*

har·ry (hăr′ē) *tr.v.* **-ried, -ry·ing. 1.** To raid, as in a war; to sack; pillage. **2.** To disturb or annoy by or as if by constant attacks; harass. [Middle English *harien*, from Old English *hergian*.]

harsh (härsh) *adj.* **-er, -est. 1.** Unpleasant to the senses, esp. to the sense of hearing. **2.** Extremely severe or exacting; stern. [Middle English *harsk*.] —**harsh′ly** *adv.* —**harsh′ness** *n.*
　Syns: harsh, discordant, hoarse, rough, strident *adj.* *Core meaning:* Disagreeable to the ear (*a harsh voice*).

hart (härt) *n., pl.* **harts** or **hart.** A male deer, esp. a male red deer over five years old. [Middle English *hert*, from Old English *heor(o)t*.]

har·te·beest (här′tə-bēst′, härt′bēst′) *n.* Also **hart·beest** (härt′-). Either of two African antelopes, *Alcelaphus buselaphus* or *A. lichtensteini*, with a brownish coat and ridged, outward-curving horns. [Obs. Afrikaans, from Dutch, deer : *hart*, deer, hart + *beest*, beast.]

har·um-scar·um (hâr′əm-skâr′əm, hăr′əm-skăr′əm) *adj.* Rash; reckless. —*adv.* With abandon; recklessly. [Perh. from HARE + SCARE.]

ha·rus·pex (hə-rŭs′pĕks′, hăr′əs-) *n., pl.* **ha·rus·pi·ces** (hə-rŭs′pĭ-sēz′.) A Roman priest who practiced divination by the inspection of the entrails of animals. [Latin.]

har·vest (här′vĭst) *n.* **1.** The act or process of gathering a crop. **2.** The crop that ripens or is gathered in a season. **3. a.** The amount or measure of the crop gathered in one season. **b.** The time or season of such a gathering. **4.** The result or consequence of any action. —*modifier: a harvest festival.* —*tr.v.* **1.** To gather (a crop). **2.** To gather a crop from. **3.** To receive (the benefits or consequences of an action). —*intr.v.* To gather a crop. [Middle English *hervest*, autumn, from Old English *hærfest*.]

har·vest·er (här′vĭ-stər) *n.* **1.** A person who gathers a crop. **2.** A machine for harvesting crops; a reaper.

harvest moon. The full moon that occurs nearest the autumnal equinox.

has (hăz) *v.* Third person singular present indicative of **have.**

has-been (hăz′bĭn′) *n. Informal.* Someone or something that is no longer famous, successful, or useful.

ha·sen·pfef·fer (hä′zən-fĕf′ər) *n.* A highly seasoned stew made of rabbit meat. [German *Hasenpfeffer* : *Hase*, rabbit + *Pfeffer*, pepper.]

hash (hăsh) *n.* **1.** A dish of chopped meat, potatoes, and sometimes vegetables, usu. browned. **2.** A jumble or hodgepodge. **3.** A reworking or restatement of material already familiar. —*tr.v.* **1.** To chop into pieces; mince. **2.** *Informal.* To make a mess of; mangle. **3.** *Informal.* To discuss carefully; review: *hash over future plans.* —*idioms.* **make a hash of. 1.** To make a mess of; botch. **2.** To defeat soundly. **settle one's hash.** To silence or subdue. [French *hachis*, from *hacher*, to chop up, from Old French *hachier*, from *hache*, ax, hatchet.]

hash·ish (hăsh′ĕsh′, -ĭsh) *n.* Also **ha·sheesh** (hä′shēsh′). A purified extract prepared from the dried flowers of the hemp plant, smoked or chewed as a mild narcotic. [Arabic *ḥashīsh*, hemp, dried grass.]

hash mark. *Mil. Slang.* A service stripe on the sleeve of an enlisted man's uniform.

Ha·sid (KHä′sĭd) *n.* Var. of **Chassid.**

has·n't (hăz′ənt). Contraction of has not.

hasp (hăsp) *n.* A metal fastener that is passed over a staple and secured by a pin, bolt, or padlock. [Middle English, from Old English *hæsp(e), hæpse*, fastening, hinge.]

Has·sid (KHä′sĭd) *n.* Var. of **Chassid.**

has·sle (hăs′əl) *n. Slang.* **1.** An argument or squabble. **2.** Trouble; bother. —*v.* **-sled, -sling.** *Slang.* To argue or fight. —*intr.v.* To bother or harass: *street gangs hassling passers-by.* —See Syns at **argue.** [Perh. blend of HAGGLE + TUSSLE.]

has·sock (hăs′ək) *n.* **1.** A thick cushion used as a footstool or for kneeling. **2.** A dense clump of grass. [Middle English *hassok*, from Old English *hassuc*, clump of matted vegetation.]

hast (hăst). *v. Archaic.* A form of the present tense of **have,** used with *thou.*

has·tate (hăs′tāt′) *adj.* Shaped like the head of an arrow or spear: *a hastate leaf.* [From Latin *hasta*, spear.]

haste (hāst) *n.* **1.** Swiftness; rapidity. **2.** Overeagerness to act. **3.** Rash or headlong action. —*v.* **hast·ed, hast·ing.** *Poet.* —*intr.v.* To hasten. —*tr.v.* To cause to hurry; hasten. —*idiom.* **make haste.** To move swiftly; hurry. [Middle English, from Old French.]
　Syns: haste, celerity, dispatch, expedition, hurry, hustle (*Informal*), **rapidity, speed** *n. Core meaning:* Rapidness of movement or activity (*left the room in great haste*).

has·ten (hā′sən) *intr.v.* To move swiftly. —*tr.v.* **1.** To hurry. **2.** To speed the progress of; expedite. —See Syns at **expedite** and **rush.**

hast·y (hā′stē) *adj.* **-i·er, -i·est. 1.** Characterized by speed; swift; rapid. **2.** Done or made too quickly to be accurate or wise; rash: *a hasty decision.* **3.** Easily angered; irritable. —**hast′i·ly** *adv.* —**hast′i·ness** *n.*

hasty pudding. 1. Cornmeal mush served with maple syrup, brown sugar, or other sweetening. **2.** *Brit.* A mush made with flour or oatmeal.

hat (hăt) *n.* A covering for the head, usu. with a shaped crown and brim. —*tr.v.* **hat·ted, hat·ting.** To supply or cover with a hat. —*idioms.* **at the drop of a hat.** At the slightest pretext or provocation. **pass the hat.** To take up a collection of money. **take (one's) hat off to.** To respect, admire, or congratulate. **talk through (one's) hat. 1.** To talk nonsense. **2.** To bluff. **throw** (or **toss**) **(one's) hat into the ring.** To enter a political race as a candidate for office. **under (one's) hat.** As a secret or in confidence. [Middle English, from Old English *hæt(t)*.]

hat·band (hăt′bănd′) *n.* A band of ribbon or cloth on the crown of a hat just above the brim.

hat·box (hăt′bŏks′) *n.* A round box or case for a hat.

hatch[1] (hăch) *n.* **1. a.** An opening, as in the deck of a ship, in the roof or floor of a building, or in an airplane. **b.** The cover for such an opening. **2.** A hatchway. [Middle English *hacche*, from Old English *hæc(c)*, hatch, wicket.]

hatch[2] (hăch) *intr.v.* **1.** To emerge from or break out of the egg. —*tr.v.* **1.** To produce (young) from an egg. **2.** To cause (an egg) to produce young. **3.** To devise or originate, esp. in secret. —*n.* **1.** The act or an instance of hatching. **2.** The young hatched at one time; a brood. [Middle English *hacchen*.] —**hatch′er** *n.*

hatch[3] (hăch) *tr.v.* To shade by drawing or etching fine parallel or crossed lines on. —*n.* A fine line used in hatching. [Middle English *hachen*, from Old French *hach(i)er*, from *hache*, ax.]

hatch·er·y (hăch′ə-rē) *n., pl.* **-ies.** A place where eggs, esp. those of fish or poultry, are hatched.

hatch·et (hăch′ĭt) *n.* **1.** A small, short-handled ax for use in one hand. **2.** A tomahawk. —*idioms.* **bury the hatchet.** To stop fighting; make peace. **dig up the hatchet.** To begin fighting; declare war. [Middle English, from Old French *hachette*, dim. of *hache*, ax.]

hatch·ing (hăch′ĭng) *n.* The fine lines used to give the impression of shading.

hatch·ment (hăch′mənt) *n. Heraldry.* A panel for the display of the coat of arms of a dead person. [Earlier *(h)achement*, alteration of *achievement*.]

hatch·way (hăch′wā′) *n.* **1.** A hatch leading to a hold, compartment, or cellar. **2.** A ladder or stairway within such an opening.

hate (hāt) *v.* **hat·ed, hat·ing.** —*tr.v.* **1.** To feel animosity or hostility toward. **2.** To detest; wish to avoid. **3.** To feel dislike or distaste for: *hates washing dishes.* —*intr.v.* To feel hatred. —*n.* **1.** Intense dislike or animosity; hatred. **2.** An object of detestation or hatred: *a pet hate.* [Middle English *haten,* from Old English *hatian.*] —**hat′er** *n.*

Syns: hate, abominate, despise, detest, loathe *v. Core meaning:* To feel great hostility and dislike for *(hated the cruel enemy).*

hate·ful (hāt′fəl) *adj.* **1.** Arousing hatred; detestable. **2.** Feeling or showing hatred; full of hate. —**hate′ful·ly** *adv.* —**hate′ful·ness** *n.*

hath (hăth) *v. Archaic.* Third person singular present indicative of **have.**

ha·tred (hā′trĭd) *n.* Violent hostility or animosity. [Middle English : *hate,* hate + Old English *rǣden,* condition.]

hau·berk (hô′bûrk) *n.* A long tunic made of chain mail. [Middle English, from Old French *hauberc.*]

haugh·ty (hô′tē) *adj.* **-ti·er, -ti·est.** Proud and vain to the point of arrogance; scornful and self-satisfied. —See Syns at **arrogant.** [From archaic *haught,* haughty, from Middle English *haute,* from Old French *haut,* high, from Latin *altus.*] —**haugh′ti·ly** *adv.* —**haugh′ti·ness** *n.*

haul (hôl) *tr.v.* **1.** To pull or drag forcibly; to tug. **2.** To transport, as with a truck or cart. **3.** To change the course of (a ship), esp. in order to sail closer into the wind. —*intr.v.* **1.** To pull; to tug. **2.** To provide transportation; to cart. **3. a.** To shift direction: *The wind hauled to the east.* **b.** To change one's mind. **4.** To change the course of a ship. —*phrasal verbs.* **haul off.** To draw back slightly, as in preparation for initiating an action: *hauled off and socked him.* **haul up.** To come to a halt. —*n.* **1.** The act of pulling or dragging. **2.** The act of transporting or carting. **3.** A distance, esp. the distance over which something is pulled or transported. **4.** Something that is pulled or transported; a load. **5.** Everything collected or acquired by a single effort; the take: *a haul of fish.* [Middle English *halen,* to pull, draw, from Old French *haler.*]

haul·age (hô′lĭj) *n.* **1.** The act or process of hauling. **2.** The force required to haul something. **3.** The charge made for hauling.

haunch (hônch, hŏnch) *n.* **1.** The hip, buttock, and upper thigh in man and animals. **2.** The loin and leg of a four-footed animal, esp. as used for food: *a haunch of venison.* [Middle English *ha(u)nche,* from Old French *hanche.*]

haunt (hônt, hŏnt) *tr.v.* **1.** To inhabit, visit, or appear to as a ghost or spirit. **2.** To visit often; to frequent. **3.** To come to mind continually; obsess: *was haunted by the riddle.* —*n.* (hônt, hŏnt). **1.** A place that is habitually visited or frequented. **2.** (*also* hŏnt). *Regional.* A ghost or spirit. [Middle English *haunten,* from Old French *hanter.*]

haunt·ing (hôn′tĭng) *adj.* Continually recurring to the mind; unforgettable. —**haunt′ing·ly** *adv.*

haut·boy (hō′boi′, ō′boi′) *n. Also* **haut·bois** *pl.* **hautbois.** An oboe. [French *hautbois,* "high wood" (from its pitch).]

hau·teur (hō-tûr′, hō-) *n.* Haughtiness; arrogance. [French, from *haut,* high, pious, from Old French.]

have (hăv) *v.*

The six standard forms of the verb *have* are:		
	I	*he/she/it* *we/you/they*
Present Tense	**have**	**has** **have**
Past Tense	**had**	
Present Participle	**having**	
Past Participle	**had**	

1. —Used as an auxiliary verb with a past participle to form the following tenses indicating completed action in the present, past, or future: **a.** Present perfect: *They have already finished their supper.* **b.** Past perfect: *We had just finished supper when he arrived.* **c.** Future perfect: *I will have finished supper by the time they arrive.* **2.** —Used as an auxiliary verb to indicate necessity, obligation, or compulsion: **a.** With an infinitive: *I have to go. She has to hurry.* **b.** With *got* followed by an infinitive: *I've got to go.* **3.** —Used as an auxiliary verb with *got* followed by an object in the present-tense sense of "have, possess, or own": *Burglars stay away because I have got nothing worth stealing.* **4. a.** To be in possession of; own: *She has two cars.* **b.** To possess as a characteristic, quality, or function: *She has blue eyes. A teacher must have patience.* **5.** To be

related or in a particular relationship to: *I have two brothers and one sister.* **6.** To have an intellectual grasp of; know; understand: *has very little French.* **7.** To hold in one's mind; entertain: *I have my doubts about the wisdom of this plan.* **8.** To receive or get: *She had more than a dozen cards on her birthday.* **9.** To accept or take: *I'll have that gray jacket.* **10.** To suffer, experience, or undergo: *have a cold. I had a good summer.* **11.** To allow; permit: *I won't have any child of mine talk like that.* **12.** To cause (something) to be done: *He had a big cake made for the party.* **13.** To induce, order, or compel to: *Have him go home before I throw him out.* **14.** To carry on, perform, or execute: *We had a serious discussion.* **15.** *Informal.* To beat or cheat; get the better of: *I feel I've been had.* **16.** To claim or maintain: *Rumor had it that the ailing leader was actually dead.* **17. a.** To give birth to: *had twins a week ago.* —See Syns at **permit.** —*phrasal verbs.* **have at.** To attack. **have on. 1.** To be wearing: *She has on a red dress and black shoes.* **2.** *Informal.* To be scheduled for: *I have a dinner party on tomorrow.* —*n.* A person or country that possesses a great deal of wealth. —*idioms.* **had as well.** Might as well: *I'd as well go now.* **had better.** To be to one's benefit or advantage to: *He'd better leave town.* **had rather** (*or* **sooner**). To prefer to: *He'd rather read than eat.* **have done with.** To be through with; finish: *Let's have done with this business once and for all.* **have it in for.** To have a grudge against: *I've had it in for him ever since he told on me.* **have it out.** To settle a disagreement; fight it out to the end. **have to do with. 1.** To associate with. **2.** To deal or be concerned with: *The book has to do with the Civil War.* [Middle English *haven,* from Old English *habban.*]

ha·ven (hā′vən) *n.* **1.** A sheltered harbor or anchorage; port. **2.** A place of refuge or rest; sanctuary. [Middle English *haven,* from Old English *hæfen.*]

have-not (hăv′nŏt′) *n.* A person or country that possesses little or no material wealth.

have·n't (hăv′ənt). Contraction of have not.

hav·er·sack (hăv′ər-săk′) *n.* A bag worn over one shoulder, used for carrying supplies. [French *havresac,* from German *Habersack, Haber,* oats + *Sack,* bag, sack.]

hav·oc (hăv′ək) *n.* Widespread destruction; devastation. —*idiom.* **play havoc with.** To destroy or ruin. [Middle English *havok,* from Norman French, var. of Old French *havot,* plunder.]

haw¹ (hô) *n.* An utterance used by a speaker who is fumbling for words. —*intr.v.* To fumble in speaking. [Imit.]

haw² (hô) *n.* **1.** The fruit of a hawthorn. **2.** A hawthorn tree or shrub. [Middle English *haw(e),* from Old English *haga,* hawthorn, hedge.]

Ha·wai·ian (hə-wä′yən) *n.* **1.** A native or resident of Hawaii. **2.** The Polynesian language of Hawaii. —*adj.* Of or relating to Hawaii.

haw-haw (hô′hô′) *interj.* Var. of **ha-ha.**

hawk¹ (hôk) *n.* **1. a.** Any of various birds of prey of the order Falconiformes, and esp. of the genera *Accipiter* and *Buteo,* that characteristically have a short, hooked bill and strong claws adapted for seizing. **b.** Any of various similar birds. **2.** A person who preys on others; a swindler. **3.** *Informal.* A person in favor of using military force or action in order to carry out foreign policy. —*intr.v.* **1.** To hunt with trained hawks. **2.** To hunt in the manner of a hawk. [Middle English *hauk,* from Old English *h(e)afoc.*]

hawk² (hôk) *intr.v.* To peddle goods by calling out. —*tr.v.* To peddle (goods) by calling out. [Back-formation from HAWKER.]

hawk³ (hôk) *intr.v.* To clear the throat by or as if by coughing up phlegm. —*tr.v.* To clear the throat of (phlegm). —*n.* An audible effort to clear the throat by expelling phlegm. [Imit.]

hawk·er (hô′kər) *n.* A person who hawks goods. [Prob. from Middle Low German *hōker.*]

hawk-eyed (hôk′īd′) *adj.* Having very sharp eyesight.

hawks·bill (hôks′bĭl′) *n.* A tropical sea turtle, *Eretmochelys imbricata,* that is a source of tortoiseshell.

hawk·weed (hôk′wēd′) *n.* Any of various often hairy plants of the genus *Hieracium,* with yellow or orange daisylike flowers.

hawse (hôz) *n. Naut.* **1.** The part of a ship where the

ă pat	ā pay	â care	ä father	ĕ pet	ē be	hw which	ĭ pit	ī tie	î pier	ŏ pot	ō toe	ô paw, for	oi noise
ōō took	ōō boot	ou out	th thin	*th* this	ŭ cut		û urge	zh vision	ə about, item, edible, gallop, circus				

hawseholes are located. **2. hawses.** The hawseholes. **3.** The space between the bow of a ship and its anchors. **4.** The arrangement of a ship's anchor cables when both starboard and port anchors are secured. [Middle English *halse,* from Old Norse *hals,* neck, ship's bow.]

hawse·hole (hôz′hōl′) *n.* An opening in the bow of a ship through which a cable or hawser is passed.

haw·ser (hô′zər) *n. Naut.* A cable or rope used in mooring or towing a ship. [Middle English, from Norman French *hauceour,* from Old French *haucier,* to lift, hoist, ult. from Latin *altus,* high.]

haw·thorn (hô′thôrn′) *n.* Any of various thorny trees or shrubs of the genus *Crataegus,* with white or pinkish flowers and reddish fruit. [Middle English *haw(e)thorn,* from Old English *hagathorn.*]

hay (hā) *n.* Grass or other plants, such as clover or alfalfa, cut and dried for fodder. —*intr.v.* To mow and cure grass and herbage for hay. —*tr.v.* **1.** To make (grass) into hay. **2.** To feed with hay. —*idioms.* **hit the hay.** *Slang.* To go to bed. **make hay while the sun shines.** To make the most of every opportunity. **that ain't hay.** *Slang.* That is a large amount of money: *gets $100 an hour and that ain't hay.* [Middle English, from Old English *hīeg.*]

hay fever. A condition characterized by a running nose and sneezing, conjunctivitis, and headaches and caused by an allergy to airborne pollens.

hay·fork (hā′fôrk′) *n.* **1.** A pitchfork. **2.** A machine-operated fork for moving hay.

hay·loft (hā′lôft′, -lŏft′) *n.* A loft for storing hay.

hay·mow (hā′mou′) *n.* **1.** A hayloft. **2.** The hay stored in a hayloft. **3.** *Archaic.* A haystack.

hay·rack (hā′răk′) *n.* **1.** A rack for hay from which livestock feed. **2. a.** A rack fitted to a wagon for carrying hay. **b.** A wagon so fitted.

hay·rick (hā′rĭk′) *n.* A haystack.

hay·seed (hā′sēd′) *n.* **1.** Grass seed shaken out of hay. **2.** Pieces of chaff or straw that fall from hay. **3.** *Slang.* A country bumpkin; yokel.

hay·stack (hā′stăk′) *n.* A large stack of hay stored in the open.

hay·wire (hā′wīr′) *n.* Wire used in baling hay. —*adj. Informal.* **1.** Not functioning properly; broken. **2.** Mentally or emotionally upset; crazy: *went haywire when his wife died.*

haz·ard (hăz′ərd) *n.* **1.** A chance; accident. **2.** A chance of being injured or harmed; danger; risk: *Space travel is full of hazards.* **3.** A possible source of danger: *a fire hazard.* **4.** A dice game similar to craps. **5.** An obstacle on a golf course. —See Syns at **danger.** —*tr.v.* **1.** To expose to danger or harm. **2.** To venture (something); to dare: *hazard a guess.* [Middle English, from Old French *hasard,* from Spanish *azar,* unlucky throw of the dice, accident, from Arabic *yásara,* "he played at dice."]

haz·ard·ous (hăz′ər-dəs) *adj.* **1.** Dangerous; perilous. **2.** Depending on chance; risky.

haze¹ (hāz) *n.* **1. a.** A foglike mixture of moisture, dust, smoke, and vapor suspended in the air. **b.** The atmospheric condition so formed. **2.** A vague or confused state of mind. —*intr.v.* **hazed, haz·ing.** To become misty or hazy; to blur. [Back-formation from HAZY.]

haze² (hāz) *tr.v.* **hazed, haz·ing.** **1.** *Naut.* To persecute or harass with meaningless, difficult, or humiliating tasks. **2.** To initiate, as into a college fraternity, by exacting humiliating performances from or playing rough practical jokes upon. **3.** *Regional.* To drive (cattle or horses) with saddle horses. [Orig. unknown.] —**haz′er** *n.*

ha·zel (hā′zəl) *n.* **1. a.** Any of various shrubs or small trees of the genus *Corylus,* such as *C. avellana* or *C. americana,* that bear edible nuts enclosed in a leafy husk. **b.** The nut of such a tree or shrub, having a smooth brown shell; hazelnut. **2.** A light to strong brown or yellowish brown. [Middle English *hasel,* from Old English *hæsel.*] —**ha′zel** *adj.*

ha·zel·nut (hā′zəl-nŭt′) *n.* The hard-shelled, edible nut of a hazel.

haz·y (hā′zē) *adj.* **-i·er, -i·est.** **1.** Marked by the presence of haze; misty. **2.** Not clearly defined; vague.—See Syns at **vague.** [Orig. unknown.] —**haz′i·ly** *adv.* —**haz′i·ness** *n.*

H-bomb (āch′bŏm′) *n.* A hydrogen bomb.

he (hē) *pron.* **1.** The male that is neither the speaker nor the hearer. **2.** Used to refer to any person whose sex is not specified: *He who hesitates is lost.* —*n.* A male animal or person: *Is the cat a he?* [Middle English, from Old English.]

He The symbol for the element helium.

head (hĕd) *n.* **1. a.** The uppermost or forwardmost part of the body of a vertebrate, containing the brain or principal nerve centers and the eyes, ears, nose, mouth, and jaws. **b.** The corresponding part of any organism. **2.** The seat of the faculty of reason; intelligence, intellect, or mind: *I can do all the figuring in my head.* **3.** A mental ability or aptitude: *He has a good head for mathematics.* **4.** A projection, weight, or fixture at the end of an elongated object: *the head of a pin.* **5.** The working part of a tool: *the head of a hammer.* **6.** A rounded, tightly clustered mass of leaves, buds, or flowers: *a head of cabbage.* **7.** A person who leads, rules, or is in charge of something; a leader; director: *heads of state.* **8.** The foremost or leading position: *The bugler marched at the head of the column.* **9.** The uppermost part of something; the top: *Place the appropriate name at the head of each column.* **10.** The end considered the most important: *The host usually sits at the head of the table.* **11. a.** A person: *The cost was ten dollars a head.* **b.** *pl.* **head.** A single animal: *seven head of cattle.* **12.** Often **heads** (used with a sing. verb). The side of a coin having the principal design and the date. **13.** Any portrait or image of a person's head. **14.** The tip of a boil, pimple, or abscess, in which pus forms. **15.** The pressure exerted by a liquid or gas: *a head of steam.* **16.** The froth or foam that rises to the top in pouring an effervescent liquid, such as beer or ale. **17.** The membrane or skin stretched across a drum, tambourine, etc. **18.** *Naut.* **a.** The forward part of a vessel. **b.** The toilet on a ship. **19. a.** A headline or heading. **b.** A separate topic or category. **20.** Headway; progress. **21.** *Slang.* A habitual drug user: *an acid head.* —*modifier:* *a head covering; the head librarian.* —*tr.v.* **1.** To aim, point, or turn in a certain direction: *He headed the team of horses up the hill.* **2.** To be in charge of; lead: *The minister headed the delegation.* **3.** To be in the first or foremost position of: *Collins heads the list of candidates for the job.* **4.** To remove the head or top of. **5.** To place a heading on: *head each column with a number.* **6.** *Soccer.* To hit (a ball) into the air with one's head. —*intr.v.* **1.** To proceed or go in a certain direction: *head for town.* **2.** To rise; originate, as a stream or river. **3.** To form a head, as lettuce or cabbage. —*phrasal verb.* **head off.** To block the progress or completion of; intercept: *I'll try to head him off before he gets home.* —*idioms.* **come to a head.** **1.** To fill with or give off pus, as a boil or abscess. **2.** To reach a critical point: *The crisis is coming to a head.* **go to (one's) head.** **1.** To make one lightheaded or drunk: *Wine goes to my head.* **2.** To make conceited: *Success went to his head.* **head and shoulders above.** Far superior to: *He is head and shoulders above his classmates in reading ability.* **head over heels.** **1.** Rolling, as in a somersault: *He tripped and fell head over heels.* **2.** Completely; hopelessly: *head over heels in love.* **keep (one's) head.** To remain calm; not lose control of oneself. **lose (one's) head.** To lose one's poise or self-control. **make head or tail of.** To make sense of: *I can't make head or tail of what he is saying.* **off (or out of) (one's) head.** Insane; crazy. **over (one's) head.** **1.** Beyond one's ability to understand or deal with: *The conversation was completely over my head.* **2.** To a higher-ranking per-

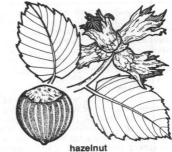

hazelnut

son: *He went over his boss's head and spoke to the manager.* **put heads together.** To consult and plan together. **take it into (one's) head.** To decide suddenly. **turn (one's) head.** To make conceited. [Middle English *heved,* from Old English *héafod.*]

head·ache (hĕd′āk′) *n.* **1.** A pain in the head. **2.** *Informal.* Something, such as a problem, that causes annoyance or trouble. **—head′ach·y** (-ā′kē) *adj.*

head·band (hĕd′bănd′) *n.* A band worn around the head.

head·board (hĕd′bôrd′, -bōrd′) *n.* A board or panel that forms the head, as of a bed.

head·cheese (hĕd′chēz′) *n.* A jellied loaf or sausage made from chopped and boiled parts of the feet, head, and sometimes the tongue and heart, usu. of a hog.

head·dress (hĕd′drĕs′) *n.* **1.** A covering or ornament for the head. **2.** A hairdo; coiffure.

head·ed (hĕd′ĭd) *adj.* **1.** Growing or grown into a head. **2.** Having a head or heading. **3.** Having a specified kind or number of heads: *a thickheaded dolt; a two-headed eagle.*

head·er (hĕd′ər) *n.* **1.** A person or thing that fits a head on an object. **2.** A person or thing that removes a head from an object, esp. a machine that reaps the heads of grain and passes them into a wagon or receptacle. **3.** A floor or roof beam placed between two long beams that supports the ends of the tailpieces. **4.** A brick laid across rather than parallel with a wall. **5.** *Informal.* A headlong dive or fall.

head·first (hĕd′fûrst′) *adv.* Also **head·fore·most** (hĕd′fôr′mōst′, -məst, -fōr′-). **1.** With the head leading; headlong: *go headfirst down the stairs.* **2.** Impetuously; brashly.

head gate. 1. A control gate upstream of a lock or canal. **2.** A floodgate that controls the flow of water in a ditch, sluice, race, or channel.

head·gear (hĕd′gîr′) *n.* **1.** A covering, such as a hat or helmet, for the head. **2.** The part of a harness that fits about a horse's head.

head·hunt·ing (hĕd′hŭn′tĭng) *n.* The custom of cutting off and preserving the heads of an enemy as a trophy. **—head′hunt′er** *n.*

head·ing (hĕd′ĭng) *n.* **1.** The title, subtitle, or topic that stands at the head of a text. **2.** The direction in which a ship or aircraft is moving.

head·land (hĕd′lənd, -lănd′) *n.* A usu. high point of land extending out into a body of water; promontory.

head·less (hĕd′lĭs) *adj.* **1.** Without a head. **2.** Without a leader or director. **3.** Brainless; foolish.

head·light (hĕd′līt′) *n.* A light on the front of a vehicle.

head·line (hĕd′līn′) *n.* The title or caption of a newspaper article, usu. set in large type. **—*tr.v.* -lined, -lin·ing. 1.** To supply (an article or page) with a headline. **2. a.** To present as the chief performer: *The Palace Theater headlines a magician.* **b.** To serve as the headliner of: *He headlines the bill.*

head·lin·er (hĕd′lī′nər) *n.* A performer who receives prominent billing; a star.

head·lock (hĕd′lŏk′) *n.* A wrestling hold in which the head of one wrestler is encircled by the arm of the other.

head·long (hĕd′lông′, -lŏng′) *adv.* **1.** With the head leading; headfirst. **2.** Impetuously; rashly. **—*adj.*** (hĕd′lông′, -lŏng′). **1.** Headfirst; done with the head leading: *a headlong dive.* **2.** Impetuous; rash. [Middle English *hedlong,* var. of *hedling.*]

head·man (hĕd′măn′) *n.* A person who has the highest rank or authority, as in a tribe or clan.

head·mas·ter (hĕd′măs′tər) *n.* Also **head master.** A male school principal, usu. of a private school.

head·mis·tress (hĕd′mĭs′trĭs) *n.* Also **head mistress.** A woman who is the principal, usu. of a private school.

head·most (hĕd′mōst′, -məst) *adj.* Leading; foremost.

head·on (hĕd′ŏn′, -ôn′) *adj.* **1.** Facing forward; frontal. **2.** With the front end foremost: *a head-on collision.* **—head′-on′** *adv.*

head·phone (hĕd′fōn′) *n.* A receiver held to the ear by a headband.

head·piece (hĕd′pēs′) *n.* **1.** A protective covering for the head. **2.** A set of headphones; headset. **3.** A headstall. **4.** *Printing.* An ornamental design, esp. one at the top of a page.

head pin. *Bowling.* The front pin in a triangle of bowling pins.

head·quar·ters (hĕd′kwôr′tərz) *pl.n.* (used with a sing. or pl. verb). **1.** The offices of a commander, as of a military unit, from which official orders are issued. **2.** Any center of operations or administration: *The company has its headquarters in a suburb.*
    Usage: **headquarters.** The noun *headquarters,* plural in form, is more often used with a plural verb: *headquarters are located;* however, a singular one is also possible: *Batallion headquarters has approved the retreat.*

head·rest (hĕd′rĕst′) *n.* A support for the head, as at the back of a chair.

head·sail (hĕd′sāl′, -səl) *n. Naut.* Any sail, such as a jib, set forward of a foremast.

head·set (hĕd′sĕt′) *n.* A pair of headphones.

heads·man (hĕdz′mən) *n.* A public executioner who beheads condemned prisoners.

head·stall (hĕd′stôl′) *n.* The part of a bridle that fits over a horse's head.

head·stand (hĕd′stănd′) *n.* The act of balancing the body with all the weight resting on the top of the head and the arms.

head start. 1. A start before other contestants in a race. **2.** Any early start that confers an advantage.

head·stock (hĕd′stŏk′) *n.* A nonmoving part of a machine or powered tool that supports a revolving part, such as the spindle of a lathe.

head·stone (hĕd′stōn′) *n.* **1.** A memorial stone set at the head of a grave. **2.** Also **head stone.** A keystone.

head·strong (hĕd′strông′, -strŏng′) *adj.* **1.** Inclined to insist on having one's own way; willful; obstinate. **2.** Resulting from willfulness or obstinacy. **—See Syns at obstinate.**

head·wait·er (hĕd′wā′tər) *n.* A waiter in charge of the other waiters in a restaurant, who is often responsible for taking reservations and seating guests.

head·wa·ters (hĕd′wô′tərz, -wŏt′ərz) *pl.n.* The waters from which a river rises.

head·way (hĕd′wā′) *n.* **1.** Movement forward; advance. **2.** Progress toward a goal. **3.** *Archit.* The clear vertical space beneath a ceiling or archway; clearance. **4.** The amount of distance or time that separates two vehicles traveling the same route.

head wind. A wind blowing directly opposite to the course of a plane or ship.

head·work (hĕd′wûrk′) *n.* Mental activity or work. **—head′work′er** *n.*

head·y (hĕd′ē) *adj.* **-i·er, -i·est. 1.** Tending to upset or make dizzy; intoxicating. **2.** Headstrong; obstinate. **—head′i·ly** *adv.* **—head′i·ness** *n.*

heal (hēl) *tr.v.* **1.** To make healthy; cure. **2.** To set right; repair: *healed the rift between us.* **—*intr.v.*** To become whole and sound; return to health. [Middle English *helen,* from Old English *hælen.*] **—heal′a·ble** *adj.* **—heal′er** *n.*

health (hĕlth) *n.* **1.** The overall condition of an organism at any given time: *was in poor health.* **2.** Soundness, esp. of body or mind; freedom from disease or abnormality. **3.** A wish for someone's good health, often expressed as a toast. [Middle English *helthe,* from Old English *hælth.*]

health·ful (hĕlth′fəl) *adj.* Tending to promote good health; beneficial. **—health′ful·ly** *adv.* **—health′ful·ness** *n.*

health·y (hĕl′thē) *adj.* **-i·er, -i·est. 1.** Possessing good health. **2.** Conducive to good health; healthful: *healthy air.* **3.** Indicative of good health; sound: *a healthy attitude.* **4.** Sizable; considerable: *a healthy portion.* **—health′i·ly** *adv.* **—health′i·ness** *n.*
    Syns: healthy, fit, hale, sound, well *adj.* Core meaning: Possessing good health (*a healthy baby*). See also Syns at **big.**

heap (hēp) *n.* **1.** A haphazard or disorderly collection of things; a pile. **2.** Often **heaps.** *Informal.* A great deal; lots. **3.** *Slang.* An old or run-down car; rattletrap. **—*tr.v.* 1.** To put or throw in a heap; pile up. **2.** To fill to overflowing: *heap a plate with vegetables.* **3.** To give or bestow in abundance: *They heaped insults upon him.* [Middle English, from Old English *héap.*]

heap·ing (hē′pĭng) *adj.* Piled high; full to overflowing.

hear (hîr) *v.* **heard** (hûrd), **hear·ing. —*tr.v.* 1.** To perceive (sound) by means of the ear. **2.** To listen to attentively. **3.** To learn; be informed: *heard the good news from a friend.* **4.** To listen to in order to examine officially or for-

mally: *The fourth witness was heard in the afternoon.*
5. To attend (a concert, for example). **6.** To listen to with
favor; heed: *Lord, hear my plea.* —*intr.v.* **1.** To perceive
or be capable of perceiving sound. **2.** To receive news or
information: *heard from my sister yesterday.* **3.** To be familiar with; know of: *I heard about your accident.*
—*phrasal verb.* **hear out.** To listen to the end: *Hear him
out before you make up your mind.* —*idioms.* **hear tell.**
Informal. To learn: *I hear tell you're leaving town.* **not
hear of.** To refuse to consider or allow: *I won't hear of
your going!* [Middle English *heren,* from Old English *hīer-
an.*] —**hear′er** *n.*

hear·ing (hîr′ĭng) *n.* **1.** The sense by which sound is perceived; the capacity to hear. **2.** The range within which a
sound can be heard; earshot. **3.** An opportunity to be
heard. **4.** A session for listening to arguments or testimony.

hearing aid. A small electronic amplifying device that is
worn to aid the hearing of persons who are partially deaf.

heark·en (här′kən) *intr.v.* Also **hark·en.** *Poet.* To listen
carefully or attentively. [Middle English *herk(n)en,* from
Old English *heorcnian,* from *heorcian,* to hark, hear.]

hear·say (hîr′sā′) *n.* **1.** Information heard from another.
2. *Law.* Evidence based on the reports of others rather
than on the personal knowledge of a witness and therefore
gen. not admissible as testimony. Also called **hearsay evidence.**

hearse (hûrs) *n.* A vehicle for carrying a dead person to a
church or cemetery. [Middle English *herse,* a frame for
holding candles at a funeral service, from Old French,
from Latin *hirpex,* harrow, rake.]

heart (härt) *n.* **1. a.** The hollow, muscular organ in vertebrates that receives blood from the veins and pumps it into
the arteries by regular, rhythmic contraction. **b.** A similar
organ in invertebrate animals. **2.** The area that is the approximate location of this organ in the chest; the breast.
3. The vital center of someone's being, emotions, sensitivity, and spirit: *With joy in his heart he sailed for Europe.*
4. a. Emotional state, disposition, or mood: *having a
change of heart.* **b.** Love; affection: *The children won his
heart.* **c.** The capacity to feel sympathy, kindness, concern, etc.; compassion: *He has great heart.* **5.** Inner
strength; courage: *The captain's talk gave him heart.*
6. a. The central part; the center: *the heart of the city.*
b. The essential part; the basis: *the heart of the issue.*
7. Enthusiasm; energy: *His heart is not in his work.*
8. Someone loved or respected: *a dear heart.* **9. a.** A
two-lobed representation of the heart, usu. colored red.
10. a. A red figure, shaped like a heart, on a playing card.
b. A card bearing this figure. **c. hearts.** The suit in a deck
of cards having this figure as its symbol. —*modifier: a
heart disease; a heart transplant.* —*idioms.* **after (one's)
own heart.** Meeting one's preferences or desires; to one's
liking: *He ran away to sea and found a life after his own
heart.* **at heart.** Basically; fundamentally: *She is a good
friend at heart.* **break (someone's) heart.** To cause someone much disappointment or grief. **by heart.** From memory: *He knew the poem by heart.* **have a heart.** Have
sympathy; be considerate: *Have a heart, John; we can't
finish the job today.* **have (one's) heart in the right place.**
To be sincerely concerned or interested; have good intentions. **have the heart.** To have the will to do something

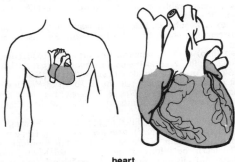

heart

unpleasant. **heart and soul.** All one's being: *She put heart
and soul into the task.* **near** (close, or **dear**) **to (one's) heart.**
Important to or cherished by a person: *That subject is near
to her heart.* **set** (or **have**) **(one's) heart on.** To want more
than anything else: *She set her heart on winning the prize.*
take to heart. To be deeply affected or troubled by: *She
took their mocking laughter to heart.* **to (one's) heart's
content.** To one's entire satisfaction; as much as one
wants: *There you may paint to your heart's content.* **wear
(one's) heart on (one's) sleeve.** To show one's feelings easily. **with all (one's) heart.** **1.** With great sincerity. **2.** Very
gladly. **with (one's) heart in (one's) mouth.** With great fear
or apprehension. [Middle English *hart,* from Old English
heorte.]
  **Syns: heart, core, essence, gist, kernel, marrow, meat,
nub, pith, root, stuff, substance.** *n. Core meaning:* The most
central and material part *(the heart of the matter).*

heart·ache (härt′āk′) *n.* Emotional anguish; sorrow. —See
Syns at **sorrow.**

heart attack. A condition in which the functioning of the
heart is impaired or interrupted, often because of an insufficient supply of blood to the tissues of the heart itself.

heart·beat (härt′bēt′) *n.* A single cycle of contraction and
relaxation of the heart.

heart·break (härt′brāk′) *n.* Intense grief; crushing disappointment; sorrow. —See Syns at **sorrow.**

heart·break·ing (härt′brā′kĭng) *adj.* Causing heartbreak.
—**heart′break′ing·ly** *adv.*

heart·bro·ken (härt′brō′kən) *adj.* Suffering from or displaying heartbreak. —**heart′bro′ken·ly** *adv.* —**heart′bro′-
ken·ness** *n.*

heart·burn (härt′bûrn′) *n.* A burning sensation in the stomach and esophagus, usu. caused by excess stomach acid.

heart·ed (här′tĭd) *adj.* Having a specified kind of heart:
lighthearted; false-hearted.

heart·en (här′tn) *tr.v.* To encourage; cheer. —See Syns at
encourage.

heart·felt (härt′fĕlt′) *adj.* Deeply or sincerely felt; genuine.

hearth (härth) *n.* **1.** The floor of a fireplace, which usu. extends into a room. **2.** The fireside as a symbol of home or
family life. **3.** The lowest part of a blast furnace, from
which the molten metal flows. **4.** The fireplace or brazier
used by a blacksmith. [Middle English *herth,* from Old
English *heorth.*]

hearth·stone (härth′stōn′) *n.* **1.** Stone used in the construction of a hearth. **2.** The fireside; home.

heart·land (härt′lănd′) *n.* An important central region, esp.
one considered to be strategically or economically vital to
a nation.

heart·less (härt′lĭs) *adj.* **1.** Without compassion or feeling.
2. Without enthusiasm; spiritless. —**heart′less·ly** *adv.*
—**heart′less·ness** *n.*

heart-rend·ing (härt′rĕn′dĭng) *adj.* Inciting anguish or
deep sympathy; acutely moving.

hearts·ease (härts′ēz′) *n.* Also **heart's-ease.** **1.** Peace of
mind. **2.** A plant, *Viola tricolor,* native to Eurasia, having
small, spurred, variously colored flowers. Also called
Johnny-jump-up.

heart·sick (härt′sĭk′) *adj.* Profoundly depressed. —**heart′-
sick′ness** *n.*

heart-strick·en (härt′strĭk′ən) *adj.* Also **heart-struck**
(-strŭk′). Overwhelmed with grief, dismay, or remorse.

heart·strings (härt′strĭngz′) *pl.n.* The deepest feelings or
affections: *a performance geared to tug at the heartstrings.*

heart-struck (härt′strŭk′) *adj.* Var. of **heart-stricken.**

heart-to-heart (härt′tə-härt′) *adj.* Candid; frank.

heart·wood (härt′wŏŏd′) *n.* The inactive central wood of a
tree or woody plant, usu. darker and harder than the sapwood.

heart·y (här′tē) *adj.* **-i·er, -i·est. 1.** Showing warmth of feeling; cheerful and friendly: *a hearty welcome.* **2.** Complete
or thorough; unequivocal: *our hearty congratulations.*
3. Vigorous. **4. a.** Enjoying or requiring much food: *a
hearty appetite.* **b.** Providing abundant nourishment; substantial: *a hearty bowl of soup.* —*n., pl.* **-ies.** A good fellow; comrade, esp. a sailor. —**heart′i·ly** *adv.* —**heart′i·ness** *n.*

heat (hēt) *n.* **1.** The energy associated with the motion of
atoms or molecules in solids, which can be transmitted
through solid and fluid media by conduction, through fluid

ă pat	ā pay	â care	ä father	ĕ pet	ē be	hw which	ĭ pit	ī tie	î pier	ŏ pot	ō toe	ô paw, for	oi noise
ŏŏ took	ŏŏ boot	ou out	th thin	*th* this	ŭ cut	û urge	zh vision	ə about, item, edible, gallop, circus					

media by convection, and through empty space by radiation. **2.** The sensation or feeling of being hot. **3.** Intense or excessive warmth. **4.** The warmth provided for a building or room, as by a furnace: *turned off the heat.* **5.** The condition or quality of being warm or hot. **6. a.** Intensity of emotion: *the heat of passion.* **b.** Most intense or active stage: *the heat of battle.* **7.** A time in which a female mammal, other than a woman, is ready to mate. **8.** *Sports.* **a.** A single division in a race or competition. **b.** A preliminary race to determine finalists. **9.** *Informal.* Pressure: *The heat was on to finish before the deadline.* —*tr.v.* **1.** To make warm or hot. **2.** To excite; inflame. —*intr.v.* **1.** To become warm or hot. **2.** To become excited. [Middle English *hete,* from Old English *hǣtu.*]

heat·er (hē′tər) *n.* **1.** An apparatus that heats or provides heat. **2.** *Slang.* A pistol.

heath (hēth) *n.* **1.** Any of various usu. low-growing shrubs of the genus *Erica* and related genera, with small evergreen leaves and small, urn-shaped pink or purplish flowers. **2.** An extensive tract of open, uncultivated land covered with low-growing shrubs such as heather. [Middle English, from Old English *hǣth.*]

hea·then (hē′thən) *n., pl.* **hea·thens** or **heathen.** **1. a.** One who adheres to the religion of a tribe or nation that does not acknowledge the God of Judaism, Christianity, or Islam. **b.** Such persons collectively. —*modifier:* heathen *practices.* **2.** An irreligious, uncivilized, or unenlightened person. [Middle English *hethen,* from Old English *hǣthen.*] —**hea′then·dom** (hē′thən-dəm) or **hea′then·ism** or **hea′then·ry** *n.*

hea·then·ish (hē′thə-nĭsh) *adj.* **1.** Of or having to do with the heathen. **2.** Like or characteristic of the heathen. —**hea′then·ish·ly** *adv.* —**hea′then·ish·ness** *n.*

heath·er (hĕth′ər) *n.* A family of low evergreen shrubs that grow in dense masses and have small evergreen leaves and clusters of small, urn-shaped, pinkish-purple flowers. [Middle English *hadder.*] —**heath′er·y** *adj.*

heat lightning. Intermittent flashes of light without thunder, seen across the horizon, esp. on a hot summer evening, and thought to be cloud reflections of distant lightning.

heat shield. A barrier, as on a spacecraft or missile, that is designed to protect against excessive heat.

heat stroke. A condition caused by exposure to excessively high temperatures and characterized by severe headache, high fever, rapid pulse, and, in serious cases, collapse and coma.

heave (hēv) *v.* **heaved** or *naut.* **hove** (hōv), **heav·ing.** —*tr.v.* **1.** To raise or lift, esp. with great force or effort; hoist. **2. a.** To throw with or as if with great effort; hurl: *heave the shot-put.* **b.** To throw. **3.** To utter painfully, unhappily, or with great effort: *heaved a sigh.* **4.** *Naut.* **a.** To raise (an anchor, net, etc.). **b.** To pull on or haul (a rope, cable, etc.). —*intr.v.* **1.** To rise up, bulge, or be forced upward, esp. from turbulence. **b.** To rise and fall, often rhythmically. **2.** *Informal.* To vomit. **3.** *Naut.* **a.** To move into a specified position: *The tugboat hove alongside.* **b.** To push or pull, as on a capstan bar or line. —*phrasal verb.* **heave to.** To bring a ship about to a standstill. —*n.* **1.** The act or effort of heaving. **2.** A throw: *a heave of 63 feet.* **3. heaves** (*used with a sing. or pl. verb*). A respiratory disease of horses. —*idiom.* **heave into sight** (or **view**). To rise into view; become visible. [Middle English *heven,* from Old English *hebban.*]

heav·en (hĕv′ən) *n.* **1.** Often **heavens.** The sky; firmament. **2.** In many religions, the abode of God, the angels, and the souls of those who are saved. **3. Heaven.** The divine Providence: *Thank Heaven you're safe.* **4.** Often **heavens.** A word used in exclamations: *Oh, for heaven's sake! Good heavens!* **5.** A place or state of great happiness or bliss: *The lake was heaven.* —*idioms.* **in seventh heaven.** Supremely happy. **move heaven and earth.** To do everything possible. [Middle English *heven,* from Old English *heofon.*]

heav·en·ly (hĕv′ən-lē) *adj.* **1.** Sublime; enchanting; lovely. **2.** Of or having to do with the firmament; celestial. **3.** Of or pertaining to the abode of God. —**heav′en·li·ness** *n.*

heav·en·ward (hĕv′ən-wərd) *adv.* Also **heav·en·wards** (-wərdz). Toward heaven. —**heav′en·ward** *adj.*

heav·y (hĕv′ē) *adj.* **-i·er, -i·est.** **1.** Having relatively great weight: *a heavy load.* **2.** Having relatively high density; of a high specific gravity: *a heavy metal.* **3. a.** Large, as in number, yield, or output; substantial: *heavy rainfall; a heavy turnout.* **b.** Intense or sustained: *heavy activity.* **4. a.** Dense or thick: *heavy fog.* **b.** Having considerable thickness, body, or strength: *a heavy coat.* **5. a.** Concerted or powerful; severe: *a heavy punch.* **b.** In turmoil; rough; violent: *heavy seas.* **6.** Indulging to a great or excessive degree: *a heavy drinker.* **7. a.** Of great import or seriousness; grave: *heavy matters of state.* **b.** Causing sorrow; painful: *heavy news.* **8. a.** Hard to do or accomplish; arduous. **b.** Difficult to bear; severe; burdensome: *heavy taxes.* **9. a.** Substantial; hearty: *a heavy breakfast.* **b.** Not easily or quickly digested: *a dessert that was too heavy for a midnight supper.* **10.** Having large or marked physical features; coarse. **11.** Weighed down with concern or sadness; despondent: *a heavy heart.* **12.** Dull; lacking in animation or vivacity. **13.** Awkward or clumsy in movement or performance. **14.** Strong and pervasive; pungent: *a heavy scent.* **15. a.** Weighed down; laden: *trees heavy with plums.* **b.** Marked by or exhibiting weariness. **16.** Involving large-scale manufacturing, as of machinery or armaments: *heavy industry.* **17.** Pregnant. **18.** *Physics.* Designating an isotope with a mass greater than that of other isotopes of the same element. **19.** Bearing heavy arms or armor: *heavy cavalry.* **20.** *Slang.* Of great significance and profundity. —*adv.* Heavily. —*n., pl.* **-vies.** **1.** A serious, tragic, or villainous character in a story or play. **2.** *Informal.* A villain. —*idiom.* **hang heavy.** To pass slowly or tediously: *The time hangs heavy on his hands.* [Middle English *hevi,* from Old English *hefig.*] —**heav′i·ly** *adv.* —**heav′i·ness** *n.*

Syns: 1. heavy, hefty, massive, ponderous, weighty *adj.* Core meaning: Having great physical weight (*a heavy concert-grand piano*). **2. heavy, cumbersome, ponderous** *adj.* Core meaning: Unwieldy, esp. because of excess weight (*heavy sandbags*). See also Syns at **burdensome** and **deep.**

heav·y-du·ty (hĕv′ē-dōō′tē, -dyōō′-) *adj.* Made to withstand hard use or wear.

heav·y-foot·ed (hĕv′ē-fōōt′ĭd) *adj.* Having a heavy, lumbering gait.

heav·y-hand·ed (hĕv′ē-hăn′dĭd) *adj.* **1.** Clumsy; awkward. **2.** Oppressive; harsh. —**heav′y-hand′ed·ly** *adv.* —**heav′y-hand′ed·ness** *n.*

heav·y-heart·ed (hĕv′ē-här′tĭd) *adj.* Melancholy; sad; depressed. —**heav′y-heart′ed·ly** *adv.* —**heav′y-heart′ed·ness** *n.*

heavy hydrogen. Deuterium.

heav·y·set (hĕv′ē-sĕt′) *adj.* Having a heavy, compact build.

heavy water. Any of several isotopic varieties of water, esp. deuterium oxide, which consists chiefly or exclusively of molecules containing hydrogen with mass number greater than 1, and used as a moderator in certain nuclear reactors.

heav·y·weight (hĕv′ē-wāt′) *n.* **1.** A person, animal, or object of above average weight. **2.** A person who competes in the heaviest class, esp. a boxer who weighs more than 175 lb. or 81 kg. **3.** *Informal.* A person of great importance or influence.

He·be (hē′bē) *n. Gk. Myth.* The goddess of youth and spring.

He·bra·ic (hĭ-brā′ĭk) or **He·bra·i·cal** (-ĭ-kəl) *adj.* Of, pertaining to, or characteristic of the Hebrews, their language, or their culture. —**He·bra′i·cal·ly** *adv.*

He·bra·ism (hē′brā-ĭz′əm, -brə-) *n.* **1.** A Hebrew expression or idiom. **2.** The culture, spirit, or character of the Hebrew people. **3.** Judaism.

He·bra·ist (hē′brā-ĭst) *n.* A Hebrew scholar. —**He′bra·is′tic** or **He′bra·is′ti·cal** *adj.* —**He′bra·is′ti·cal·ly** *adv.*

He·brew (hē′brōō) *n.* **1.** A member of a northern Semitic people, esp. an Israelite. **2. a.** The Semitic language of the ancient Hebrews, used in most of the Old Testament. **b.** Any of various later forms of this language, esp. the language of the Israelis. **3. Hebrews.** See table at **Bible.** —*adj.* Of or having to do with the Hebrews.

Hebrew calendar. The lunisolar calendar used by the Jews. See **calendar.**

heck·le (hĕk′əl) *tr.v.* **-led, -ling.** To harass or annoy, as with

ă pat   ā pay   â care   ä father   ĕ pet   ē be   hw which
ōō took   ōō boot   ou out   th thin   th this   ŭ cut
ĭ pit   ī tie   î pier   ŏ pot   ō toe   ô paw, for   oi noise
û urge   zh vision   ə about, item, edible, gallop, circus

questions, taunts, or comments: *heckled the speaker unmercifully.* —**heck′ler** *n.*

hect-. Var. of **hecto-.**

hec·tare (hĕk′târ′) *n.* A metric measure of area equal to 100 ares, or 2.471 acres.

hec·tic (hĕk′tĭk) *adj.* **1.** Marked by intense activity, confusion, or excitement: *a hectic day.* **2.** Marked by a fluctuating and persistent fever. —**hec′ti·cal·ly** *adv.*

hecto- or **hect-.** *Symbol* **h.** A prefix meaning 100 (10²): **hectoliter.** [From Greek *hekaton,* hundred.]

hec·to·gram (hĕk′tə-grăm′) *n.* Also **hec·to·gramme.** A metric unit of mass equal to 100 grams, or 3.527 avoirdupois ounces.]

hec·to·graph (hĕk′tə-grăf′) *n.* A machine using a glycerin-coated layer of gelatin to make copies of typed or written material. —*tr.v.* To copy by means of a hectograph. [HECTO- + -GRAPH.] —**hec′to·graph′ic** *adj.* —**hec′to·graph′i·cal·ly** *adv.*

hec·to·li·ter (hĕk′tə-lē′tər) *n.* Also **hec·to·li·tre.** A metric unit of capacity or volume equal to 100 liters or 26.42 gallons.

hec·to·me·ter (hĕk′tə-mē′tər, hĕk-tŏm′ĭ-tər) *n.* Also **hec·to·me·tre.** A metric unit of length equal to 100 meters, or approx. 328 feet.

hec·tor (hĕk′tər) *tr.v.* To intimidate by blustering. —*intr.v.* To behave like a bully; to swagger. —*n.* A bully. [After HECTOR.]

Hec·tor (hĕk′tər) *n. Gk. Myth.* The greatest of the Trojan warriors, a son of Priam, killed by Achilles in Homer's *Iliad.*

Hec·u·ba (hĕk′yŏŏ-bə) *n. Gk. Myth.* The wife of King Priam in Homer's *Iliad.*

he'd (hēd). **1.** Contraction of he had. **2.** Contraction of he would.

hedge (hĕj) *n.* **1.** A fence or boundary formed by a row of closely planted shrubs or low-growing trees. **2.** A protection, esp. against financial loss. **3.** A purposely indirect statement made to avoid giving a definite response or promise. —*v.* **hedged, hedg·ing.** —*tr.v.* **1.** To enclose or protect with or as if with a hedge. **2.** To restrict. **3.** To protect from loss by counterbalancing one transaction, such as a bet, against another. —*intr.v.* **1.** To plant or cultivate hedges. **2.** To take measures so as to counterbalance against possible loss. **3.** To avoid making a clear, direct response or statement. [Middle English *hegge,* from Old English *hecg.*] —**hedg′er** *n.*

hedge·hog (hĕj′hŏg′, -hôg′) *n.* **1.** Any of several small Old World mammals of the family Erinaceidae, and esp. of the genus *Erinaceus,* with dense, erectile spines on the back and the ability to roll itself into a ball for protection. **2.** A porcupine.

hedge·row (hĕj′rō′) *n.* A hedge.

he·don·ism (hēd′n-ĭz′əm) *n.* **1.** Pursuit of or devotion to pleasure. **2.** The ethical doctrine that only that which gives or brings pleasure is good. [Greek *hēdonē,* pleasure + -ISM.]

he·don·ist (hēd′n-ĭst) *n.* A person who believes in or practices hedonism. —**he′don·is′tic** *adj.* —**he′don·is′ti·cal·ly** *adv.*

-hedral. A suffix meaning (a given number of) surfaces or faces: **dihedral.** [From Greek *hedra,* base, seat.]

-hedron. A suffix indicating a geometric figure having (a given number of) surfaces or faces: **pentahedron.** [From Greek *hedra,* base, seat.]

hee·bie-jee·bies (hē′bē-jē′bēz) *pl.n. Slang.* A feeling of uneasiness or nervousness; the jitters. [Coined by Billy De Beck (1890-1942), American cartoonist.]

heed (hēd) *tr.v.* To pay attention to: *He did not heed our warning.* —*intr.v.* To pay attention. —*n.* Careful attention. [Middle English *heden,* from Old English *hēdan.*]

heed·ful (hēd′fəl) *adj.* Paying heed; mindful. —**heed′ful·ly** *adv.* —**heed′ful·ness** *n.*

heed·less (hēd′lĭs) *adj.* Inattentive; not taking heed. —See Syns at **careless.** —**heed′less·ly** *adv.* —**heed′less·ness** *n.*

hee-haw (hē′hô′) *n.* **1.** The braying sound made by a donkey. **2.** A noisy laugh; a guffaw. —*intr.v.* **1.** To bray. **2.** To laugh noisily; to guffaw. [Imit.]

heel¹ (hēl) *n.* **1. a.** The rounded posterior portion of the human foot under and behind the ankle. **b.** The corresponding part of the hind foot of other vertebrates. **2.** The fleshy rounded base of the human palm nearest the wrist. **3.** That part of footwear, such as a sock, shoe, or stocking, that covers the heel. **4.** The built-up portion of a shoe or boot that is under the heel. **5.** One of the crusty ends of a loaf of bread. **6.** A lower, rearward surface, as of the head of a golf club. **7.** *Naut.* **a.** The lower end of a mast. **b.** The after end of a ship's keel. **8.** The base, as of a cutting or tuber, used in propagation. **9.** *Informal.* A contemptible or dishonorable man. —*tr.v.* **1.** To furnish with a heel. **2.** *Slang.* To furnish, esp. with money. **3.** To follow upon the heels of. —*intr.v.* To follow immediately or closely. —**idioms. down at the heels. 1.** Having one's shoe heels worn down. **2.** Shabby; run-down. **kick up (one's) heels.** To have fun; celebrate. **on (or upon) the heels of.** Immediately following in space or time. **take to (one's) heels.** To flee; run away. [Middle English, from Old English *hēla.*] —**heel′less** *adj.*

heel² (hēl) *intr.v.* To tilt or list to one side: *The schooner heeled over dangerously.* —*tr.v.* To cause (a ship) to tilt to one side. —*n.* A tilt to one side; a list. [From earlier *heeld,* from Middle English *he(e)lden,* from Old English *hieldan.*]

heel-and-toe (hēl′ən-tō′) *adj.* Characterized by a stride in which the heel of one foot touches ground before the toe of the other foot is lifted, as in walking races.

heel·er (hē′lər) *n.* **1.** One who heels shoes. **2.** *Informal.* A ward heeler.

heft (hĕft) *n. Informal.* Weight; heaviness. —*tr.v.* **1.** To determine or estimate the weight of by lifting. **2.** To hoist; to heave up. —*intr.v.* To weigh. [From HEAVE.]

heft·y (hĕf′tē) *adj.* **-i·er, -i·est. 1.** Weighty; heavy. **2.** Large and powerful; bulky; muscular. —See Syns at **heavy.**

he·gem·o·ny (hĭ-jĕm′ə-nē, hĕj′ə-mō′nē) *n., pl.* **-nies.** The dominant influence of one state over others. [Greek *hēgemonia,* authority, rule, from *hēgemōn,* leader, from *hēgeisthai,* to lead.] —**heg′e·mon′ic** (hĕj′ə-mŏn′ĭk) *adj.*

He·gi·ra (hĭ-jī′rə, hĕj′ər-ə) *n.* Also **He·ji·ra. 1.** The flight of Mohammed from Mecca to Medina in A.D. 622. **2. hegira.** Any flight, as from danger or hardship. [Arabic *(al)hijrah,* flight, departure, from *hajara,* to depart.]

heif·er (hĕf′ər) *n.* A young cow, esp. one that has not yet given birth to a calf. [Middle English *heyfre,* from Old English *hēahfore,* young ox.]

heigh (hā, hī) *interj. Archaic.* A word used to express encouragement or to attract attention.

heigh-ho (hī′hō′, hā′-) *interj.* A word used to express fatigue, melancholy, mild surprise, or disappointment.

height (hīt) *n.* **1.** The highest or uppermost point; summit. **2. a.** The highest or most advanced degree; zenith. **b.** The point of highest intensity; climax: *the height of a storm.* **3. a.** The distance from the base to the top of something. **b.** The elevation of something above a given level; altitude. **4. a.** The condition or attribute of being sufficiently or relatively high or tall. **b.** Stature, esp. of the human body. **5.** An eminence, as a hill or mountain. [Middle English *heighth,* from Old English *hēhthu.*]

height·en (hīt′n) *tr.v.* **1.** To increase the quantity, degree, or intensity of. **2.** To make high or higher; to raise. —*intr.v.* **1.** To rise in quantity, degree, or intensity. **2.** To become high or higher; to rise. —**height′en·er** *n.*

hei·nous (hā′nəs) *adj.* Grossly wicked or evil; abominable; vile: *a heinous crime.* —See Syns at **outrageous.** [Middle English *heynous,* hateful, from Old French *haineus,* from *haïne,* hate, from *hair,* to hate.] —**hei′nous·ly** *adv.* —**hei′nous·ness** *n.*

heir (âr) *n.* **1.** *Law.* A person who inherits or is legally entitled to inherit the property, rank, title, or office of another. **2.** A person who receives a heritage, as of ideas, from a predecessor. [Middle English, from Old French, from Latin *hērēs.*]

heir apparent *pl.* **heirs apparent.** *Law.* An heir whose right to inheritance is certain provided he survives his ancestor.

heir·ess (âr′ĭs) *n.* A female heir, esp. one who inherits great wealth.

heir·loom (âr′lŏŏm′) *n.* **1.** A valued possession passed down in a family through succeeding generations. **2.** *Law.* An article of personal property included in an inherited estate. [Middle English *heir lome* : *heir,* heir + *lome,* utensil, tool.]

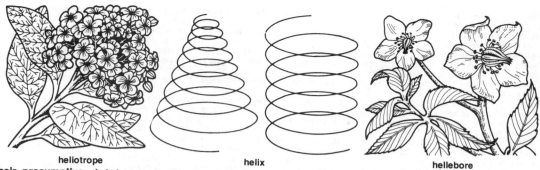

heliotrope · helix · hellebore

heir presumptive *pl.* **heirs presumptive.** *Law.* An heir whose right to inherit may be canceled by the birth of a relative with a stronger claim to the inheritance.

heist (hīst). *Slang.* —*tr.v.* To rob; steal. —See Syns at **rob.** —*n. Slang.* A robbery; burglary. [Dial. var. of HOIST.]

He·ji·ra (hĭ-jī′rə, hĕj′ər-ə) *n.* Var. of **Hegira.**

held (hĕld). *v.* Past tense and past participle of **hold.** [Middle English, from Old English *heold.*]

Hel·en of Troy (hĕl′ən). *Gk. Myth.* The wife of King Menelaus whose abduction by Paris caused the Trojan War.

hel·i·cal (hĕl′ĭ-kəl) *adj.* Of or relating to the shape of a helix. [From Greek *helix,* spiral.] —**hel′i·cal·ly** *adv.*

hel·i·ces (hĕl′ĭ-sēz′, or hē′lĭ-). *n.* A plural of **helix.**

hel·i·con (hĕl′ĭ-kŏn′, -kən) *n.* A large circular brass tuba that fits around the shoulder. [Perh. from Greek *helix,* spiral.]

hel·i·cop·ter (hĕl′ĭ-kŏp′tər) *n.* An aircraft with horizontal blades that rotate about an approx. vertical central axis. [French *hélicoptère:* Greek *helix,* spiral + *pteron,* wing.]

helio-. A prefix meaning the sun: *heliograph.* [From Greek *hēlios,* the sun.]

he·li·o·cen·tric (hē′lē-ō-sĕn′trĭk) or **he·li·o·cen·tri·cal** (-trĭ-kəl) *adj.* **1.** Relative to the sun: *the heliocentric position of a planet.* **2.** Having the sun as a center: *a heliocentric model of the solar system.* —**he′li·o·cen·tric′i·ty** (-sĕn-trĭs′ĭ-tē) *n.*

he·li·o·graph (hē′lē-ə-grăf′) *n.* **1.** An apparatus once used to photograph the sun. **2.** A signaling apparatus that reflects sunlight with a movable mirror to flash coded messages. —*tr.v.* To transmit (messages) by heliograph. —*intr.v.* To signal by heliograph. —**he′li·og′ra·pher** (-ŏg′rə-fər) *n.* —**he′li·o·graph′ic** *adj.* —**he′li·og′ra·phy** *n.*

He·li·os (hē′lē-ŏs′) *n. Gk. Myth.* The sun god who was believed to drive his chariot across the sky from east to west daily.

he·li·o·trope (hē′lē-ə-trōp′, hēl′yə-) *n.* **1.** Any of several plants of the genus *Heliotropium,* with small, fragrant purplish flowers. **2.** The garden heliotrope. **3.** Any of various plants that turn toward the sun. **4.** Bloodstone. **5.** A reddish purple. —*adj.* Reddish purple. [From Latin *hēliotropium,* from Greek *hēliotropion: hēlios,* sun + *tropos,* a turning.]

he·li·ot·ro·pism (hē′lē-ŏt′rə-pĭz′əm) *n. Biol.* Growth or movement of an organism toward or away from the light of the sun.

he·li·port (hĕl′ə-pôrt′, -pōrt′) *n.* A place for helicopters to land and take off. [HELI(COPTER) + PORT.]

he·li·um (hē′lē-əm) *n. Symbol* **He** A colorless, odorless, tasteless inert gaseous element. Atomic number 2, atomic weight 4.0026, boiling point –268.6°C, liquid density at boiling point 7.62 pounds per cubic foot. [From Greek *hēlios,* the sun (the element was first discovered in an examination of the solar spectrum).]

he·lix (hē′lĭks) *n., pl.* **-lix·es** or **hel·i·ces** (hĕl′ĭ-sēz′, hē′lĭ-). **1.** *Geom.* A three-dimensional curve that lies on a cylinder or cone and cuts the elements at a constant angle. **2.** Any spiral form. **3.** *Anat.* The folded rim of skin and cartilage around the outer ear. **4.** *Archit.* A volute on a Corinthian or Ionic capital. [Latin, from Greek, spiral, spiral object.]

hell (hĕl) *n.* **1.** In ancient traditions, the abode of the dead; the underworld. **2.** Often **Hell.** In many religions, the abode of condemned souls and devils; the place of punishment of the wicked after death. **3.** Any place or situation of evil, misery, discord, or destruction: *into the hell of battle.* **4. a.** Torment; anguish: *She went through hell in that job.* **b.** A person or thing that causes trouble, agony, etc.: *He's hell when a job is not properly done.* **5.** Used as an oath: *How the hell can I do that? To hell with it!* —*interj.* A word used to express an emotion, such as anger, impatience, or dismay. [Middle English, from Old English.]

he'll (hĕl). **1.** Contraction of *he will.* **2.** Contraction of *he shall.*

hell·ben·der (hĕl′bĕn′dər) *n.* A large aquatic salamander, *Cryptobranchus alleganiensis,* of eastern and central North America.

hell·bent (hĕl′bĕnt′) *adj.* Impetuously or recklessly determined to do or achieve something: *was hell-bent on winning.* —*adv.* Recklessly and determinedly.

hell·cat (hĕl′kăt′) *n.* A bad-tempered and evil woman; vixen.

hel·le·bore (hĕl′ə-bôr′, -bōr′) *n.* **1.** Any of various plants of the genus *Helleborus,* most species of which are poisonous. **2.** Any of various poisonous plants of the genus *Veratrum,* esp. *V. viride,* with large leaves and greenish flowers. [Middle English *ellebre,* from Old French, from Latin *elleborus,* from Greek *(h)elleboros.*]

Hel·lene (hĕl′ēn) *n.* Also **Hel·le·ni·an** (hə-lē′nē-ən). A Greek.

Hel·len·ic (hə-lĕn′ĭk) *adj.* Of or relating to the ancient Greeks or their language. —*n.* The Greek language.

Hel·le·nism (hĕl′ə-nĭz′əm) *n.* **1.** An idiom, custom, or the like peculiar to the Greeks. **2.** The civilization and culture of ancient Greece. **3.** The adoption of esp. ancient Greek ideas, style, or culture.

Hel·le·nist (hĕl′ə-nĭst) *n.* **1.** One in classical times who adopted the Greek language and culture, esp. a Jew of the Diaspora. **2.** A devotee or student of the language, literature, or culture of ancient Greece.

Hel·le·nis·tic (hĕl′ə-nĭs′tĭk) or **Hel·le·nis·ti·cal** (-tĭ-kəl) *adj.* **1.** Relating to the Hellenists. **2. a.** Of or relating to Greek history and culture from the time of Alexander the Great into the first cent. B.C. **b.** Pertaining to or in the style of the Greek art or architecture of this period.

hell·gram·mite (hĕl′grə-mīt′) *n.* The large, brownish aquatic larva of the dobson fly, often used as fishing bait. [Orig. unknown.]

hel·lion (hĕl′yən) *n. Informal.* A mischievous, troublesome person. [Prob. from dial. *hallion,* a low person.]

hell·ish (hĕl′ĭsh) *adj.* Of, like, or worthy of hell. —**hell′ish·ly** *adv.* —**hell′ish·ness** *n.*

hel·lo (hĕ-lō′, hə-). Also **hul·lo** (hə-). —*interj.* A word used to greet someone, answer the telephone, attract attention, or express surprise. —*n., pl.* **-loes.** A call or greeting of "hello." —*tr.v.* To say or call "hello" to. —*intr.v.* To call "hello." [Var. of earlier *holla,* "stop!", prob. from French *hold.*]

helm¹ (hĕlm) *n.* **1.** *Naut.* The steering gear of a ship, esp. the tiller or wheel. **2.** A position of leadership or control. [Middle English *helme,* from Old English *helma.*]

helm² (hĕlm) *n. Archaic.* A helmet. —*tr.v.* To cover or furnish with a helmet. [Middle English, from Old English.]

hel·met (hĕl′mĭt) *n.* **1.** A piece of armor, usu. of metal, designed to protect the head. **2.** A head covering of hard material, such as leather, metal, or plastic, worn to protect the

| ă pat | ā pay | â care | ä father | ĕ pet | ē be | hw which | ĭ pit | ī tie | î pier | ŏ pot | ō toe | ô paw, for | oi noise |
| ōō took | ōō boot | ou out | th thin | th this | ŭ cut | | û urge | zh vision | ə about, item, edible, gallop, circus |

head. [Middle English, from Old French, dim. of *helme*, helmet.] —**hel′met·ed** *adj.*

hel·minth (hĕl′mĭnth′) *n.* A parasitic worm, esp. an intestinal worm. [Greek *helmis*, parasitic worm.]

helms·man (hĕlmz′mən) *n.* A person who steers a ship.

hel·ot (hĕl′ət, hē′lət) *n.* **1. Helot.** One of a class of serfs in ancient Sparta. **2.** A serf; bondsman. [Latin *hēlōtes*, serfs, helots, from Greek *heilōtes*, pl. of *heilōs*.] —**hel′ot·ism** *n.* —**hel′ot·ry** *n.*

help (hĕlp) *tr.v.* **1.** To give assistance to; to aid: *I helped her find the book. He helped her into her coat.* **2.** To contribute to; further the progress or advancement of. **3.** To give relief to: *help the poor.* **4.** To ease; relieve: *This medicine will help your cold.* **5.** To be able to prevent, change, or rectify: *I cannot help my laziness.* **6.** To refrain from; avoid: *couldn't help laughing.* **7.** To wait on, as in a store or restaurant. —*intr.v.* To be of service; give assistance. —*phrasal verb.* **help out.** To aid with a problem or difficulty. —*n.* **1. a.** The act or an example of helping. **b.** Aid; assistance. **2.** Relief; remedy. **3.** A person or thing that helps. **4. a.** A person employed to help, esp. a farm hand or a servant. **b.** Such employees in general. —*idioms.* **cannot help but.** To be unable to avoid or resist: *He can't help but do what they ask.* **help (oneself) to. 1.** To serve oneself: *Help yourself to the cookies.* **2.** To take or appropriate. [Middle English *helpen*, from Old English *helpan*.] —**help′er** *n.*

　　Syns: help, aid, assist *v. Core meaning:* To provide assistance (*helped the exhausted swimmer*).

　　Usage: help. The expression *cannot help but*, esp. common in speech, is found in examples such as *We cannot help but regret it.* This locution is standard American idiom. Alternative wordings are: *cannot help regretting it* and *can (or cannot) but regret it.*

help·ful (hĕlp′fəl) *adj.* Providing help; useful. —**help′ful·ly** *adv.* —**help′ful·ness** *n.*

help·ing (hĕl′pĭng) *n.* A portion of food for one person.

help·less (hĕlp′lĭs) *adj.* **1.** Unable to manage by oneself; dependent. **2.** Lacking power or strength. **3.** Incapable of being remedied. —See Syns at **powerless.** —**help′less·ly** *adv.* —**help′less·ness** *n.*

help·mate (hĕlp′māt′) *n.* A helper and companion, esp. a spouse. [By folk ety. from HELPMEET.]

help·meet (hĕlp′mēt′) *n.* A helpmate. [From *I will make an help meet for him* (Genesis 2:18, 20) : HELP + MEET (suitable).]

hel·ter-skel·ter (hĕl′tər-skĕl′tər) *adv.* **1.** In disorderly haste; pell-mell. **2.** Haphazardly. —*adj.* **1.** Hurried and confused. **2.** Haphazard. —*n.* Turmoil; confusion. [Orig. unknown.]

helve (hĕlv) *n.* A handle of a tool, such as an ax, chisel, or hammer. [Middle English, from Old English *hielf(e).*]

hem[1] (hĕm) *n.* A smooth, even edge of a garment or piece of cloth, made by folding the raw edge under and sewing it down. —*tr.v.* **hemmed, hem·ming.** To fold back and sew down the edge of: *She hemmed her skirt.* —*phrasal verb.* **hem in.** To surround and shut in; enclose: *a valley hemmed in by mountains.* —See Syns at **surround.** [Middle English, from Old English.] —**hem′mer** *n.*

hem[2] (hĕm) *n.* A short cough or clearing of the throat made to gain attention, hide embarrassment, or fill a pause in speech. —*intr.v.* **hemmed, hem·ming. 1.** To make this sound. **2.** To hesitate in speech. —*idiom.* **hem and haw.** To be hesitant and indecisive. [Imit.]

hem-. Var. of **hemo-.**

he-man (hē′măn′) *n. Informal.* A strong, muscular, virile man.

hem·a·tite (hĕm′ə-tīt′, hē′mə-) *n.* A blackish-red to brick-red mineral, Fe_2O_3, the chief ore of iron. [Latin *haematītēs,* from Greek *(lithos) haimatītēs,* "bloodlike (stone)," red iron ore, from *haima,* blood.]

he·ma·tol·o·gy (hē′mə-tŏl′ə-jē) *n.* The science concerning the generation, anatomy, physiology, pathology, and therapeutics of blood. [From Greek *haima,* blood + -LOGY.] —**he′ma·tol′o·gist** *n.*

he·ma·to·ma (hē′mə-tō′mə) *n.* A localized swelling containing blood. [From Greek *haima,* blood.]

heme (hēm) *n.* The nonprotein, iron-containing pigment of hemoglobin. [From Greek *haima,* blood.]

hemi- or **hem-.** A prefix meaning half: **hemipteran.** [Latin *hēmi-,* from Greek.]

he·mip·ter·an (hĭ-mĭp′tər-ən) *n.* Also **he·mip·ter·on** (-tə-rŏn′). An insect of the order Hemiptera, whose members include true bugs, such as the bedbug, and related forms, such as the plant lice. —*adj.* Of or belonging to the Hemiptera; hemipterous. [HEMI- + Greek *pteron,* wing.]

he·mip·ter·ous (hĭ-mĭp′tər-əs) *adj.* Of or belonging to the Hemiptera.

hem·i·sphere (hĕm′ĭ-sfîr′) *n.* **1. a.** Either of the two halves into which a sphere is divided by a plane that passes through its center. **b.** Either half of a symmetrical object whose shape is roughly that of a sphere: *a hemisphere of the brain.* **2.** Either of the halves into which the earth is divided by the equator or by a great circle that passes through the poles. [Middle English *hemisperie,* from Latin *hēmisphaerium,* from Greek *hēmisphairion* : *hemi-,* half + *sphairion,* dim. of *sphaira,* sphere.] —**hem′i·spher′ic** (-sfîr′ĭk, -sfĕr′ĭk) or **hem′i·spher′i·cal** *adj.*

hem·i·stich (hĕm′ĭ-stĭk′) *n. Pros.* **1.** Half a line of verse, esp. when separated rhythmically from the rest of the line by a caesura. **2.** An incomplete line of verse. [Latin *hēmistichium,* from Greek *hēmistikhion* : *hemi-,* half + *stikhos,* line.]

hem·line (hĕm′lĭn′) *n.* A hem.

hem·lock (hĕm′lŏk′) *n.* **1. a.** Any of various evergreen trees of the genus *Tsuga,* with short, flat needles and small cones. **b.** The wood of such a tree, used as a source of lumber, wood pulp, and tannic acid. **2. a.** Any of several poisonous plants of the genera *Conium* and *Cicuta,* such as the poison hemlock and the water hemlock. **b.** A poison extracted from the poison hemlock. [Middle English *hemlok,* from Old English *hemlic.*]

he·mo·glo·bin (hē′mə-glō′bĭn, hĕm′ə-) *n.* The iron-containing protein in vertebrate red blood cells that transports oxygen from the lungs to other body tissues. [Shortening of earlier *hematoglobulin* : *hemato-,* blood + GLOBULIN.]

he·mo·phil·i·a (hē′mə-fĭl′ē-ə, hĕm′ə-) *n.* A hereditary blood disease, principally of males but transmitted by females, that is characterized by excessive internal or external bleeding. [Greek *haima,* blood + *philia,* friendship.]

he·mo·phil·i·ac (hē′mə-fĭl′ē-ăk′, hĕm′ə-) *n.* A person who suffers from hemophilia.

hem·or·rhage (hĕm′ər-ĭj) *n.* Bleeding, esp. severe or heavy bleeding. —*intr.v.* **-rhaged, -rhag·ing.** To bleed heavily or copiously. [From Old French *hemorragie,* from Latin *haemorrhagia,* from Greek *haimorrhagia* : *hemo-,* blood + *-rrhagia,* excessive discharge.] —**hem′or·rhag′ic** (-răj′ĭk) *adj.*

hem·or·rhoids (hĕm′ə-roidz′) *pl.n.* An itching or painful mass of dilated veins on or within the anus. Also called **piles.** [Middle English *emeroudis,* from Old French *hemorrhoides,* from Latin *haemorrhoida,* from Greek *haimorrhois,* liable to discharge blood, from *haimorrhoos,* flowing with blood.]

hemp (hĕmp) *n.* **1. a.** A tall plant, *Cannabis sativa,* native to Asia, that yields a coarse fiber used to make cordage. **b.** The fiber of this plant. **2.** A drug, such as hashish, derived from hemp. [Middle English *hemp(e),* from Old English *hænep.*]

hem·stitch (hĕm′stĭch′) *n.* Also **hem·stitch·ing** (-ĭng). A decorative stitch usu. bordering a hem, made by drawing out several parallel threads and catching together the cross threads in uniform groups to create a design. —*tr.v.* To ornament by means of a hemstitch. —**hem′stitch′er** *n.*

hen (hĕn) *n.* **1.** A female bird, esp. the adult female of the domestic fowl. **2.** The female of certain aquatic animals, such as an octopus or a lobster. [Middle English, from Old English *henn.*]

hen·bane (hĕn′bān′) *n.* A poisonous plant, *Hyoscyamus niger,* with an unpleasant odor, clammy leaves, and funnel-shaped greenish-yellow flowers.

hence (hĕns) *adv.* **1.** For this reason; as a result; therefore: *handmade and hence expensive.* **2.** From this time; from now: *A year hence he will have forgotten.* **3.** *Archaic.* From this place; away: *an inn two miles hence.* [Middle English *hennes,* from *henne,* from Old English *heonane,* from here, away.]

ă pat　ā pay　â care　ä father　ĕ pet　ē be　hw which　ĭ pit　ī tie　î pier　ŏ pot　ō toe　ô paw, for　oi noise
ōō took　ōō boot　ou out　th thin　th this　ŭ cut　û urge　zh vision　ə about, item, edible, gallop, circus

hence·forth (hĕns′fôrth′) *adv.* From this time on.

hence·for·ward (hĕns-fôr′wərd) *adv.* Henceforth.

hench·man (hĕnch′mən) *n.* **1.** A loyal follower or supporter. **2.** A member of a criminal gang. [Middle English *hengestman*, squire : Old English *hengest*, horse + *man*, man.]

hen·na (hĕn′ə) *n.* **1.** A tree or shrub, *Lawsonia inermis*, with fragrant white or reddish flowers. **2.** A reddish dyestuff obtained from the leaves of the henna plant, used as a cosmetic dye and for coloring leather. **3.** A reddish brown. —*tr.v.* To dye or treat with henna. [Arabic *ḥinnā′*.] —**hen′na** *adj.*

henna   Hercules

hen·ner·y (hĕn′ə-rē) *n., pl.* **-ies. 1.** A poultry farm. **2.** A pen for domestic fowl.

hen·peck (hĕn′pĕk′) *tr.v. Informal.* To dominate (one's husband) by scolding or nagging. —**hen′-pecked′** or **hen′-pecked′** *adj.*

hen·ry (hĕn′rē) *n., pl.* **-ries** or **-rys.** *Physics.* The unit of inductance in which an induced electromotive force of one volt is produced when the current changes at the rate of one ampere per second. [After Joseph *Henry* (1797–1878), American physicist.]

hep (hĕp) *adj.* Var. of **hip** (aware). [Orig. unknown.]

hep·a·rin (hĕp′ər-ĭn) *n.* A complex organic acid that is found esp. in lung and liver tissue and that has the ability in certain circumstances to prevent the clotting of blood. [Greek *hēpar*, liver + -IN.]

he·pat·ic (hĭ-păt′ĭk) *adj.* **1.** Of or resembling the liver. **2.** Acting on or affecting the liver. **3.** Liver-colored. [Middle English *epatik*, from Latin *hēpaticus*, of liver, from Greek *hēpatikos*, from *hēpar*, liver.]

he·pat·i·ca (hĭ-păt′ĭ-kə) *n.* Any of several woodland plants of the genus *Hepatica*, esp. *H. americana*, with three-lobed leaves and white or lavender flowers. [From Medieval Latin *hēpatica*, liverwort, from Latin *hēpaticus*, hepatic.]

hep·a·ti·tis (hĕp′ə-tī′tĭs) *n.* Inflammation of the liver, often caused by a virus, characterized by jaundice and usu. fever. [Greek *hēpar*, liver + -ITIS.]

He·phaes·tus (hĭ-fĕs′təs) *n. Gk. Myth.* The Greek god of fire and metalworking; identified with the Roman god Vulcan.

hepta– or **hept–.** A prefix meaning seven: **heptameter.** [From Greek *hepta*, seven.]

hep·ta·gon (hĕp′tə-gŏn′) *n.* A polygon with seven sides and seven angles. [Greek *heptagonos*, having seven angles.] —**hep·tag′o·nal** (-tăg′ə-nəl) *adj.*

hep·tam·e·ter (hĕp-tăm′ĭ-tər) *n. Pros.* A line of verse consisting of seven metrical feet. [HEPTA- + METER.]

her (hûr; hər, ər *when unstressed*) *pron.* **1.** The objective case of **she,** used: **a.** As the direct object of a verb: *They saw her in the library.* **b.** As the indirect object of a verb: *They gave her a book.* **c.** As the object of a preposition: *This letter is addressed to her.* **2.** The possessive form of **she,** used as a modifier before a noun: *her purse; her tasks; her first rebuff.* [Middle English *hire*, from Old English.]

He·ra (hîr′ə) *n.* Also **He·re** (hîr′ē). *Gk. Myth.* The sister and wife of Zeus; identified with the goddess Juno.

Her·a·cles or **Her·a·kles** (hĕr′ə-klēz′) *n.* Vars. of **Hercules.**

her·ald (hĕr′əld) *n.* **1.** A person who carries or announces important news; a messenger. **2.** A person or thing that gives a sign or indication of what is to follow; harbinger: *The crocus is the herald of spring.* **3.** *Brit.* An official who specializes in heraldry. **4.** In former times, an official responsible for announcing royal proclamations and for carrying messages between sovereigns. —*tr.v.* To proclaim; announce: *heard the cheers that heralded their arrival.* [Middle English *herauld*, from Old French *herault*.]

he·ral·dic (hə-răl′dĭk) *adj.* Of heralds or heraldry. —**he·ral′di·cal·ly** *adv.*

her·ald·ry (hĕr′əl-drē) *n., pl.* **-ries. 1.** The study or art of tracing genealogies, of determining, designing, and granting coats of arms, and of ruling on questions of rank or protocol. **2.** Armorial ensigns or devices. **3.** Heraldic ceremony; pageantry.

herb (ûrb, hûrb) *n.* **1.** A plant without the persistent woody tissue characteristic of shrubs and trees that usu. dies back at the end of each growing season. **2.** A plant whose leaves, roots, seeds, or stems are used medicinally or as flavoring for food. [Middle English *herbe*, from Old French, from Latin *herba*.]

her·ba·ceous (hûr-bā′shəs) *adj.* **1.** Of, like, or consisting of herbs. **2.** Green and leaflike in appearance or texture. [Latin *herbāceus* : *herba*, herb + -*aceus*, of a specific kind.]

herb·age (ûr′bĭj, hûr′-) *n.* **1.** Herbaceous plant growth, such as grass, used for pasturage. **2.** The fleshy parts of herbaceous plants. [Middle English *(h)erbage*, from Old French *(h)erbe*, herb.]

herb·al (hûr′bəl, ûr′-) *adj.* Of, relating to, or containing herbs.

herb·al·ist (hûr′bə-lĭst, ûr′-) *n.* One who grows or deals in herbs, esp. medicinal herbs.

her·bar·i·um (hûr-bâr′ē-əm) *n., pl.* **-ums** or **-i·a** (-ē-ə). **1.** A collection of dried plants, as for use in scientific study. **2.** A place or institution where such a collection is kept. [Late Latin *herbārium*, from Latin *herba*, herb.]

her·bi·cide (hûr′bĭ-sīd′) *n.* A substance used to destroy plants, esp. weeds. [HERB + -CIDE.] —**her′bi·cid′al** (-sīd′l) *adj.*

her·bi·vore (hûr′bə-vôr′, -vōr′) *n.* A plant-eating animal.

her·biv·o·rous (hûr-bĭv′ər-əs) *adj.* Feeding entirely on plants or plant parts: *Cattle and deer are herbivorous animals.* [HERB + -VOROUS.]

her·cu·le·an (hûr′kyə-lē′ən, hûr-kyōō′lē-ən) *adj.* **1.** Of unusual size, power, or difficulty. **2.** Often **Herculean.** Of or resembling Hercules: *Herculean strength.* **3. Herculean.** Of or relating to Hercules. —See Syns at **giant.**

Her·cu·les (hûr′kyə-lēz′) *n.* Also **Her·a·cles** (hĕr′ə-klēz′), or **Her·a·kles.** *Gk. & Rom. Myth.* **1.** The son of Zeus and Alcmene, a hero of extraordinary strength who won immortality by performing the 12 labors demanded by Hera. **2.** *Astron.* A constellation in the Northern Hemisphere near Lyra and Corona Borealis.

herd (hûrd) *n.* **1.** A group of animals of a single kind kept or living together. **2.** A large number of people; crowd: *a herd of shoppers waiting to enter the store.* —*intr.v.* To come together in a herd. —*tr.v.* To gather, keep, or drive in or as if in a herd. [Middle English, from Old English *heord*.] —**herd′er** *n.*

herds·man (hûrdz′mən) *n.* **1.** A person who tends or drives a herd. **2.** A person who owns or breeds livestock.

here (hîr) *adv.* **1.** At or in this place: *Let's stay here.* **2.** At this time; now: *We'll adjourn the meeting here.* **3.** At or on this point or item: *Here I must disagree.* **4.** To this place: *Come here.* —*n.* This place: *Come away from here.* —*interj.* A word used to respond to a roll call, attract attention, command an animal, or rebuke or admonish. —*idioms.* **here and there.** In one place and another: *lived here and there before settling down.* **neither here nor there.** Not important or relevant. [Middle English, from Old English *hēr.*]

Usage: **here. 1.** When the adverb *here* means in this place, it follows (and never precedes) the noun in constructions introduced by *this: this house here* (not *this here house*). **2.** Constructions introduced by the adverb *here* can take a singular or a plural verb, depending on the number of the subject: *Here are three reasons* (plural subject *reasons*) *why the book is poor. Here is the glove* (singular subject *glove*) *that you lost.*

He·re (hîr′ē) *n.* Var. of **Hera.**

here·a·bout (hîr'ə-bout') *adv.* Also **here·a·bouts** (-bouts'). In this vicinity; near or around here.

here·af·ter (hîr-ăf'tər) *adv.* **1.** After this; from now on. **2.** In a future time or state: *win salvation hereafter.* —*n.* The afterlife: *belief in a hereafter.*

here·by (hîr-bī', hîr'bī') *adv.* By this means.

he·red·i·tar·y (hə-rĕd'ĭ-tĕr'ē) *adj.* **1.** *Law.* **a.** Descending from an ancestor to a legal heir; passing down by inheritance. **b.** Having title or possession through inheritance. **2.** Transmitted or capable of being transmitted from parent to offspring by biological inheritance. **3. a.** Appearing in or characteristic of successive generations. **b.** Derived from or fostered by one's ancestors: *a hereditary prejudice.* **4.** Ancestral; traditional: *their hereditary home.* **5.** Of or relating to heredity or inheritance. [Latin *hērēditārius,* from *hērēditās,* heredity.] —**he·red'i·tar'i·ly** (-târ'ə-lē) *adv.* —**he·red'i·tar'i·ness** *n.*

he·red·i·ty (hə-rĕd'ĭ-tē) *n., pl.* **-ties. 1.** The genetic transmission of characteristics from parent to offspring. **2.** The set of of characteristics transmitted to an individual organism by heredity. [Old French *heredite,* from Latin *hērēditās,* inheritance, from *hērēs,* heir.]

Her·e·ford (hĕr'ə-fərd, hûr'fərd) *n.* Any of a breed of beef cattle developed in Herefordshire, England, having a reddish coat with white markings.

here·in (hîr-ĭn') *adv.* In or into this.

here·of (hîr-ŭv', -ŏv') *adv.* Of or concerning this.

here·on (hîr-ŏn', -ôn') *adv.* On this.

her·e·sy (hĕr'ĭ-sē) *n., pl.* **-sies. 1.** An opinion or doctrine at variance with established religious beliefs. **2. a.** A controversial or unorthodox opinion or doctrine, as in politics, philosophy, or science. **b.** Adherence to such opinion. [Middle English *(h)eresie,* from Old French, from Late Latin *haeresis,* from Late Greek *hairesis,* from Greek, faction, from *hairein,* choose.]

her·e·tic (hĕr'ĭ-tĭk) *n.* A person who holds opinions that differ from established beliefs, esp. religious beliefs. [Middle English *(h)eretik,* from Old French *(h)eretique,* from Late Latin *haereticus,* from Greek *hairetikos,* able to choose, factious, from *hairein,* to choose.]

he·ret·i·cal (hə-rĕt'ĭ-kəl) *adj.* Of, relating to, or characterized by heresy. —**he·ret'i·cal·ly** *adv.*

here·to (hîr-tōō') *adv.* To this.

here·to·fore (hîr'tə-fôr', -fōr') *adv.* Before this; previously. [Middle English : *here,* here + *tofore,* before, from Old English *tōforan.*]

here·un·to (hîr-ŭn'tōō, hîr'ŭn-tōō') *adv.* Hereto.

here·up·on (hîr'ə-pŏn', -pôn', hîr'ə-pŏn', -pôn') *adv.* Immediately after this; at this.

here·with (hîr-wĭth', -wĭth') *adv.* **1.** Along with this. **2.** By this means; hereby.

her·i·ta·ble (hĕr'ĭ-tə-bəl) *adj.* **1.** Capable of being inherited. **2.** Capable of inheriting. [Middle English *heretable,* from Old French *heritable,* from *heriter,* to inherit.]

her·i·tage (hĕr'ĭ-tĭj) *n.* **1.** Property that is or can be inherited; inheritance. **2.** Something passed down from preceding generations; tradition. **3.** The status acquired by a person through birth; birthright: *a heritage of affluence and social position.* [Middle English *(h)eritage,* from Old French, from *heriter,* to inherit, from Late Latin *hērēditāre,* from Latin *hērēs,* heir.]

her·maph·ro·dite (hər-măf'rə-dīt') *n.* **1.** One having the sex organs and many of the secondary characteristics of both male and female. **2.** *Biol.* An organism, such as an earthworm, with both male and female reproductive organs in the same individual. [Middle English *hermofrodite,* from Latin *hermaphrodītus,* from Greek *hermaphroditos,* after *Hermaphroditos,* the son of Hermes and Aphrodite.] —**her·maph'ro·dit'ic** (-dĭt'ĭk) *adj.* —**her·maph'ro·dit'i·cal·ly** *adv.*

Her·mes (hûr'mēz) *n.* *Gk. Myth.* The god of commerce, invention, and theft; identified with the Roman god Mercury.

her·met·ic (hər-mĕt'ĭk) or **her·met·i·cal** (-ĭ-kəl) *adj.* **1.** Completely sealed, esp. against the escape or entry of air. **2.** Completely insulated against or resistant to outside influences: *the hermetic confines of a prison.* **3.** Of or relating to the occult sciences, esp. alchemy. [New Latin

hermeticus, magical, from Latin *Hermes Trismegistus,* a Greek name for the Egyptian god Thoth.] —**her·met'i·cal·ly** *adv.*

her·mit (hûr'mĭt) *n.* **1.** A person who lives a solitary existence, esp. from religious motives; recluse. **2.** A spicy cooky made with molasses, raisins, and nuts. [Middle English *(h)ermite,* from Old French, from Late Latin *erēmīta,* from Greek *erēmītēs,* "(one) of the desert," from *erēmia,* desert, solitude, from *erēmos,* deserted, solitary.] —**her·mit'ic** (hər-mĭt'ĭk) or **her·mit'i·cal** *adj.* —**her·mit'i·cal·ly** *adv.*

her·mit·age (hûr'mĭ-tĭj) *n.* **1.** The habitation of a hermit. **2.** A solitary and secluded dwelling; a retreat or hideaway.

hermit crab. Any of various crustaceans having a soft, unarmored abdomen and occupying the empty shell of a univalve mollusk such as a snail.

her·ni·a (hûr'nē-ə) *n., pl.* **-as** or **-ni·ae** (-nē-ē'). A condition in which a structure of the body, as an organ or organic part, protrudes through an opening in the wall of the cavity that normally encloses it; a rupture. [Middle English, from Latin.] —**her'ni·al** (-əl) *adj.*

he·ro (hîr'ō) *n., pl.* **-roes. 1.** In mythology and legend, a man, often of divine ancestry, who has great courage and strength and is celebrated for his bold exploits. **2.** A man noted for his courageous and daring acts, esp. one who has risked or sacrificed his life: *war heroes.* **3.** A man noted for his special achievements in a particular field: *the heroes of medicine.* **4.** The principal male character in a novel, poem, or literary work, as a play. **5.** *Slang.* A large sandwich made with a long crusty roll that has been split lengthwise and filled with a variety of meats and cheeses, lettuce, tomato, and onion. Also called **grinder, hoagie, and submarine.** [Back-formation from Middle English *heroes* (pl.), from Latin *hērōēs,* pl. of *hērōs,* a hero, from Greek.]

he·ro·ic (hĭ-rō'ĭk) or **he·ro·i·cal** (-ĭ-kəl) *adj.* **1.** Of or resembling the heroes of literature, legend, or myth. **2.** Having, showing, or marked by the qualities appropriate to a hero; courageous; noble: *heroic deeds.* **3.** Of a size or scale that is larger than life; grand: *heroic sculpture.* —See Syns at **brave.** —*n.* **1.** A heroic verse or poem. **2. heroics.** Melodramatic behavior or language. —**he·ro'i·cal·ly** *adv.* —**he·ro'i·cal·ness** *n.*

heroic couplet. A verse unit consisting of two rhymed lines in iambic pentameter.

heroic verse. One of several verse forms traditionally used in epic and dramatic poetry, as the dactylic hexameter in Greek and Latin and the iambic pentameter in English.

her·o·in (hĕr'ō-ĭn) *n.* A white, odorless, bitter crystalline compound, $C_{17}H_{17}NO(C_2H_3O_2)_2$, that is derived from morphine and is a highly addictive narcotic. [From a trademark.]

her·o·ine (hĕr'ō-ĭn) *n.* **1.** A woman noted for her courageous and daring achievements. **2.** A woman noted for her special achievements in a particular field. **3.** The principal female character in a novel, poem, or literary work, as a play. [Latin *hērōīna,* from Greek *hērōīnē,* fem. of *hērōs,* hero.]

her·o·ism (hĕr'ō-ĭz'əm) *n.* **1.** Heroic conduct or behavior. **2.** Heroic traits or qualities; courage.

her·on (hĕr'ən) *n.* Any of various wading birds of the family Ardeidae, with a long neck, long legs, and a long, pointed bill. [Middle English *heiroun,* from Old French *hairon.*]

hero worship. Intense or excessive admiration for a hero or for a person regarded as a hero.

her·pes (hûr'pēz') *n.* Any of several viral diseases characterized by the eruption of blisters of the skin or mucous membrane. [Latin *herpēs,* from Greek, shingles, from *herpein,* to creep.] —**her·pet'ic** (-pĕt'ĭk) *adj.*

her·pe·tol·o·gy (hûr'pĭ-tŏl'ə-jē) *n.* The scientific study of reptiles and amphibians as a branch of zoology. [Greek *herpeton,* reptile + -LOGY.] —**her'pe·to·log'ic** (-tə-lŏj'ĭk) or **her'pe·to·log'i·cal** *adj.* —**her'pe·to·log'i·cal·ly** *adv.* —**her'pe·tol'o·gist** *n.*

Herr (hĕr) *n., pl.* **Her·ren** (hĕr'ən). A title placed before the name or professional title of a German, equivalent to the English *Mister.* [German, Lord.]

her·ring (hĕr'ĭng) *n., pl.* **herring** or **-rings.** Any of various fishes of the family Clupeidae, esp. *Clupea harengus,* a

ă pat   ā pay   â care   ä father   ĕ pet   ē be   hw which
ŏŏ took   ōō boot   ou out   th thin   th this   ŭ cut
ĭ pit   ī tie   î pier   ŏ pot   ō toe   ô paw, for   oi noise
û urge   zh vision   ə about, item, edible, gallop, circus

commercially important food fish of Atlantic and Pacific waters. [Middle English *hering*, from Old English *hæring*.]

her·ring·bone (hĕr′ĭng-bōn′) *n.* **1.** A zigzag pattern made up of short parallel lines arranged in rows that slant first one way, then another. **2.** A twilled fabric woven in this pattern. —*modifier:* a herringbone tweed. [From its resemblance to the skeletal structure of a herring.]

hers (hûrz) *pron.* Used to indicate the one or ones belonging to her: *If you can't find your hat, take hers.* [Middle English *hires*, from *hire*, her.]
　　Usage: **hers.** This possessive pronoun is written without an apostrophe: *The money is hers.*

her·self (hər-sĕlf′) *pron.* **1.** That one identical with her. Used: **a.** Reflexively as the direct or indirect object of a verb or as the object of a preposition: *She hurt herself.* **b.** For emphasis: *She herself wasn't certain.* **2.** Her normal or healthy condition or state: *She isn't herself today.*

hertz (hûrts) *n. Symbol* **Hz** A unit of frequency equal to one cycle per second. [After Heinrich *Hertz* (1857–94), German physicist.]

he's (hēz). **1.** Contraction of he is. **2.** Contraction of he has.

hes·i·tan·cy (hĕz′ĭ-tən-sē) *n., pl.* **-cies.** **1.** The condition or quality of being hesitant. **2.** An example of hesitating.

hes·i·tant (hĕz′ĭ-tənt) *adj.* Inclined or tending to hesitate. —**hes′i·tant·ly** *adv.*

hes·i·tate (hĕz′ĭ-tāt′) *intr.v.* **-tat·ed, -tat·ing.** **1.** To be slow to act, speak, or decide; pause in doubt or uncertainty; waver. **2.** To be reluctant: *If there's anything you need, don't hesitate to ask.* **3.** To speak haltingly; falter. [From Latin *haesitāre*, to stick fast, hesitate, from *haerēre*, to hold fast, stick.] —**hes′i·tat·er** *n.* —**hes′i·tat′ing·ly** *adv.*
　　Syns: **hesitate, falter, halt, pause, vacillate, waver** *v.* *Core meaning:* To be irresolute in acting or doing (*hesitated before answering the question*).

hes·i·ta·tion (hĕz′ĭ-tā′shən) *n.* **1.** The act or an example of hesitating. **2.** The condition of being hesitant. **3.** A pause or faltering in speech.

Hes·per·us (hĕs′pər-əs) *n.* The planet Venus in its appearance as the evening star.

hest (hĕst) *n. Archaic.* Command; behest. [Middle English *heste,* var. of *hes,* command, from Old English *hǣs.*]

hetero– or **heter–.** A prefix meaning other: *heterosexual.* [From Greek *heteros,* other.]

het·er·o·dox (hĕt′ər-ə-dŏks′) *adj.* **1.** Not in agreement with accepted beliefs. **2.** Holding unorthodox opinions. [Late Latin *heterodoxus,* from Greek *heterodoxos,* differing in opinion : *heteros-,* other + *doxa,* opinion, from *dokein,* to think.]

het·er·o·dox·y (hĕt′ər-ə-dŏk′sē) *n., pl.* **-ies.** **1.** The condition or quality of being heterodox. **2.** A heterodox belief or doctrine.

het·er·o·dyne (hĕt′ər-ə-dīn′) *tr.v.* **-dyned, -dyn·ing.** To combine (a radio-frequency wave) with a locally generated wave of different frequency in order to produce a new frequency equal to the sum or difference of the two. —*adj.* Of or pertaining to the process of heterodyning. [HETERO- + DYNE.]

het·er·o·ge·ne·i·ty (hĕt′ə-rō-jə-nē′ĭ-tē) *n.* The quality or condition of being heterogeneous.

het·er·o·ge·ne·ous (hĕt′ə-rə-jē′nē-əs, -jēn′yəs) *adj.* Also **het·er·og·e·nous** (hĕt′ə-rŏj′ə-nəs). Consisting of dissimilar elements or parts; not homogeneous: *a heterogeneous collection.* [Medieval Latin *heterogeneus,* from Greek *heterogenēs* : *heteros,* other + *genos,* kind.] —**het′er·o·ge′ne·ous·ly** *adv.* —**het′er·o·ge′ne·ous·ness** *n.*

het·er·o·nym (hĕt′ər-ə-nĭm′) *n.* One of two or more words that are identical in spelling but different in meaning and pronunciation; for example, *row* (a line) and *row* (a fight). [HETER(O)- + -ONYM.]

het·er·o·sex·u·al (hĕt′ə-rō-sĕk′shōō-əl) *adj.* Characterized by attraction to the opposite sex. —*n.* A heterosexual person. —**het′er·o·sex′u·al′i·ty** (-ăl′ĭ-tē) *n.*

het·er·o·zy·gote (hĕt′ə-rō-zī′gōt′) *n.* A zygote that has inherited different alleles at one or more loci. —**het′er·o·zy′gous** (-zī′gəs) *adj.*

heu·ris·tic (hyōō-rĭs′tĭk) *adj.* **1.** Helping to discover or learn; guiding or furthering investigation: *"the historian discovers the past by the judicious use of such a heuristic device as the 'ideal type'"* (Karl J. Weintraub). **2.** Desig-

nating the educational method in which the student is allowed or encouraged to learn independently through his own investigation. [From Greek *heuriskein,* to discover, find.]

hew (hyōō) *v.* **hewed, hewn** (hyōōn) or **hewed, hew·ing.** —*tr.v.* **1.** To make or shape with or as if with an ax: *hew a path through the underbrush.* **2.** To cut down with an ax: *hew trees.* **3.** To strike or cut. —*intr.v.* **1.** To cut by repeated blows, as of an ax. **2.** To adhere or conform to strictly: *hew to the line.* [Middle English *hewen,* from Old English *hēawan.*]

hex (hĕks) *n.* **1.** An evil spell; a curse. **2.** A person or thing that brings bad luck. —*tr.v.* **1.** To put a hex on. **2.** To wish or bring bad luck to. [Pennsylvania Dutch, from German *Hexe,* witch, from Middle High German *hecse.*]

hexa– or **hex–.** A prefix meaning six: *hexagram.* [Greek, from *hex,* six.]

hex·a·gon (hĕk′sə-gŏn′) *n.* A polygon with six sides and six angles. [Late Latin *hexagōnum,* from Greek *hexagōnon,* from *hexagōnos,* six-angled.]

hex·ag·o·nal (hĕk-săg′ə-nəl) *adj.* Having six sides and six angles. —**hex·ag′o·nal·ly** *adv.*

hex·a·gram (hĕk′sə-grăm′) *n.* A six-pointed star made by extending the sides of a regular hexagon so as to form an external equilateral triangle on each of the sides. [HEXA- + -GRAM.]

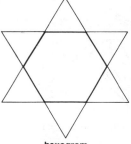

hexagram

hex·a·he·dron (hĕk′sə-hē′drən) *n., pl.* **-drons** or **-dra** (-drə). A polyhedron with six faces. [Greek *hexaedron,* from *hexaedros,* six-sided.] —**hex′a·he′dral** *adj.*

hex·am·e·ter (hĕk-săm′ĭ-tər) *n. Pros.* A line consisting of six metrical feet. [Latin, from Greek *hexametron,* from *hexametros,* having six metrical feet.] —**hex·am′e·tric** (hĕk′sə-mĕt′rĭk) or **hex′a·met′ri·cal** *adj.*

hex·ane (hĕk′sān′) *n.* A colorless, flammable liquid, $CH_3(CH_2)_4CH_3$, used as a solvent. [HEX- + -ANE.]

hex·a·pod (hĕk′sə-pŏd′) *n.* An insect. —*adj.* Also **hex·ap·o·dous** (hĕk-săp′ə-dəs). **1.** Of or pertaining to insects. **2.** Having six legs or feet. [HEXA- + -POD.]

hey (hā) *interj.* A word used to attract attention or to express surprise, appreciation, or pleasure: *Hey, that's nice! Hey you!* [Middle English *hei.*]

hey·day (hā′dā′) *n.* The period of greatest popularity, success, or power; prime. [Earlier *heyda,* prob. from HEY.]

Hf The symbol for the element hafnium.

Hg The symbol for the element mercury. [Latin *hydrargyrum,* "water silver."]

hi (hī) *interj. Informal.* A word used as a greeting. [Middle English *hy.*]

hi·a·tus (hī-ā′təs) *n., pl.* **-tus·es** or **hiatus.** **1.** A gap or interruption in space, time, or continuity: *a hiatus in their narrative.* **2.** A slight pause that occurs when two immediately adjacent vowels in consecutive syllables are pronounced, as in *reality* and *naive.* [Latin *hiātus,* gap, from the past part. of *hiāre,* to gape.]

hi·ba·chi (hĭ-bä′chē) *n., pl.* **-chis.** A portable charcoal-burning brazier with a grill, often used for cooking. [Japanese : *hi,* fire + *bachi,* bowl.]

hi·ber·nal (hī-bûr′nəl) *adj.* Of or pertaining to winter. [Latin *hibernālis,* from *hibernus,* winter.]

hi·ber·nate (hī′bər-nāt′) *intr.v.* **-nat·ed, -nat·ing.** To spend the winter in an inactive state resembling deep sleep, during which the body temperature is lower than normal and breathing and other body processes slow down. [From

---

ă pat	ā pay	â care	ä father	ĕ pet	ē be	hw which	ĭ pit	ī tie	î pier	ŏ pot	ō toe	ô paw, for	oi noise
ōō took	ōō boot	ou out	th thin	th this	ŭ cut		û urge	zh vision	ə about, item, edible, gallop, circus				

Latin *hībernāre,* from *hībernus,* winter.] —**hi'ber·na'tion** *n.* —**hi'ber·na'tor** *n.*

hi·bis·cus (hī-bĭs′kəs, hĭ-) *n.* Any of various chiefly tropical plants, shrubs, or trees of the genus *Hibiscus,* with large, showy, variously colored flowers. [From Greek *hibiskos,* marshmallow.]

hic·cup (hĭk′ŭp). Also **hic·cough** (hĭk′ŭp). —*n.* **1.** A spasm of the diaphragm that causes a sudden inhalation that is quickly cut off by another spasm in the glottis. **2. hiccups.** An attack in which spasms of this kind occur repeatedly. —*intr.v.* **-cupped, -cup·ping. 1.** To make a hiccup. **2.** To have an attack of hiccups. [Imit.]

hick (hĭk) *n. Informal.* A gullible, provincial person; yokel. —*adj.* Provincial; unsophisticated: *a hick town.* [From *Hick,* pet form of *Richard.*]

hick·o·ry (hĭk′ə-rē) *n., pl.* **-ries. 1.** Any of several chiefly North American deciduous trees of the genus *Carya,* with smooth or shaggy bark, compound leaves, and hard, smooth nuts with an edible kernel. **2.** The hard, tough, heavy wood of a hickory tree. [From earlier *pohickery,* from *pawcohiccora,* food prepared from crushed hickory nuts, of Algonquian orig.]

hickory

hieroglyphic

hide[1] (hīd) *v.* **hid** (hĭd), **hid·den** (hĭd′n) or **hid, hid·ing.** —*tr.v.* **1.** To put or keep out of sight; secrete. **2.** To keep secret; conceal. **3.** To cut off from sight; cover up: *Clouds hid the stars.* —*intr.v.* To keep oneself out of sight. [Middle English *hiden,* from Old English *hȳdan.*] —**hid′er** *n.*

    Syns: hide, conceal, secrete, stash *v. Core meaning:* To put (something) out of sight and keep it there *(hid the stolen money in an abandoned mine).*

hide[2] (hīd) *n.* The skin of an animal, esp. of a large animal. —*tr.v.* **hid·ed, hid·ing.** To beat severely; flog. [Middle English, from Old English *hȳd.*]

hide-and-seek (hīd′n-sēk′) *n.* A children's game in which one player tries to find and catch others who are hiding.

hide·a·way (hīd′ə-wā′) *n.* **1.** A hide-out. **2.** A secluded or isolated place.

hide·bound (hīd′bound′) *adj.* **1.** Having abnormally dry, stiff skin that adheres closely to the underlying flesh: *hidebound cattle.* **2.** Stubbornly prejudiced or narrow-minded.

hid·e·ous (hĭd′ē-əs) *adj.* Extremely unpleasant, esp. to the sight; repulsive; revolting: *a hideous mask; a hideous murder.* —See Syns at **ghastly** and **ugly.** [Middle English *hidous,* from Old French, from *hi(s)de,* fear, horror.] —**hid′e·ous·ly** *adv.*

hide-out (hīd′out′) *n.* A place of shelter or concealment.

hid·ing[1] (hī′dĭng) *n.* A place or state of concealment.

hid·ing[2] (hī′dĭng) *n. Informal.* A beating or thrashing.

hie (hī) *intr.v.* **hied, hie·ing** or **hy·ing.** To hasten; hurry. [Middle English *hien,* from Old English *hīgian,* to strive, exert oneself, hurry.]

hi·er·arch (hī′ə-rärk′, hī′rärk′) *n.* A person who occupies a high position in a hierarchy. [Old French *hierarche,* from Medieval Latin *hierarcha,* from Greek *hierarkhēs,* high priest: *hieros,* holy + *archos,* ruler.]

hi·er·ar·chy (hī′ə-rär′kē, hī′rär′-) *n., pl.* **-chies. 1.** A body of persons, as clergy, organized or classified according to rank or authority, with each level subordinate to the one above. **2.** An arrangement of persons or things in a graded series. —**hi′er·ar′chi·cal** or **hi·er·ar′chic** *adj.* —**hi′er·ar′chi·cal·ly** *adv.*

hi·er·at·ic (hī′ə-răt′ĭk, hī-răt′-) *adj.* **1.** Also **hi·er·at·i·cal**

(-ĭ-kəl). Of or relating to priests; sacerdotal. **2.** Of or relating to a simplified cursive style of Egyptian hieroglyphics developed and chiefly used by the priestly class. [Latin *hierāticus,* from Greek *hieratikos,* from *hiereus,* priest, from *hieros,* sacred, supernatural.] —**hi′er·at′i·cal·ly** *adv.*

hi·er·o·glyph (hī′ər-ə-glĭf′, hī′rə-) *n.* A hieroglyphic.

hi·er·o·glyph·ic (hī′ər-ə-glĭf′ĭk, hī′rə-) or **hi·er·o·glyph·i·cal** (-ĭ-kəl) *adj.* **1.** Of or pertaining to a system of writing, as that of ancient Egypt, in which pictorial symbols are used to represent words or sounds. **2.** Written with hieroglyphic symbols. **3.** Hard to read or decipher. —*n.* **1.** A picture or symbol used in hieroglyphic writing. **2. hieroglyphics. a.** Hieroglyphic writing. **b.** Illegible or undecipherable writing. [Old French *hieroglyphique,* from Late Latin *hieroglyphicus,* from Greek *hierogluphikos* : *hieros,* sacred + *gluphē,* carving, engraving, from *gluphein,* to carve.] —**hi′er·o·glyph′i·cal·ly** *adv.* —**hi′er·o·glyph′ist** (-ĭst) *n.*

hi·fa·lu·tin (hī′fə-lōōt′n) *adj. Informal.* Var. of **highfalutin.**

hi-fi (hī′fī′) *n., pl.* **-fi. 1. High** fidelity. **2.** An electronic system for reproducing sound with high fidelity. [HI(GH) FI(DELITY).]

hig·gle·dy-pig·gle·dy (hĭg′əl-dē-pĭg′əl-dē) *adv.* In utter disorder or confusion. —*adj.* Topsy-turvy; jumbled. [Orig. unknown.]

high (hī) *adj.* **-er, -est. 1. a.** Having a relatively great elevation; extending far upward: *a high mountain; a high stool.* **b.** Extending a specified distance upward: *a cabinet 4 feet high and 2 feet wide.* **2.** Far above the horizon: *The sun is high in the sky.* **3.** Far from the equator: *the high latitudes.* **4.** Above average, as in degree, amount, price, quality, or intensity: *high temperature; higher wages; a high standard of living.* **5. a.** Having a musical pitch that corresponds to a relatively great number of cycles per second: *the high tones of a flute.* **b.** Not soft or hushed; piercing: *a high voice.* **6.** Being at or near its peak: *high noon.* **7.** Eminent in rank or status: *a high official.* **8.** Of great importance: *a high priority.* **9.** Excited; elated: *high spirits.* **10.** *Informal.* Intoxicated by alcohol or a narcotic. **11.** Advanced in development or complexity: *higher forms of animal life.* **12.** Favorable: *a high opinion of himself.* **13.** Allowing the greatest output speed: *high gear.* **14.** Luxurious; extravagant: *high living.* —See Syns at **expensive** and **rich.** —*adv.* At, in, or to a high position, price, or level: *fly high in the sky.* —*n.* **1.** A high degree, level, or point: *Prices reached a new high.* **2.** A mass of atmospheric air that exerts greater pressure than the air in the regions surrounding it; anticyclone. **3.** The transmission gear, as of an automobile, that gives the greatest output speed for a given engine speed. **4.** *Informal.* Intoxication or euphoria induced as by a stimulant or narcotic. —*idioms.* **high and dry. 1.** Helpless; alone: *He left me high and dry.* **2.** Out of water, as a ship. **high and low.** Here and there; everywhere. **high and mighty.** Arrogant; domineering. [Middle English, from Old English *hēah.*]

high·ball (hī′bôl′) *n.* A beverage consisting of alcoholic liquor mixed with water or soda and served in a tall glass.

high·born (hī′bôrn′) *adj.* Of noble birth.

high·boy (hī′boi′) *n.* A tall chest of drawers divided into two sections and supported on long legs.

high·bred (hī′brĕd′) *adj.* Of superior breed or stock.

high·brow (hī′brou′) *n. Informal.* A person who has or pretends to have superior learning or culture. —**high′brow′** or **high′browed′** *adj.*

High-Church (hī′chûrch′) *adj.* Favoring or marked by the incorporation of elements, such as the liturgy, usu. associated with Roman Catholicism into the forms of worship of the Anglican Church.

high·er-up (hī′ər-ŭp′, hī′ər-ŭp′) *n. Informal.* A person who has a superior rank, position, or status.

high·fa·lu·tin or **hi·fa·lu·tin** (hī′fə-lōōt′n) *adj. Informal.* Pompous or pretentious. [HIGH + *falutin,* perh. var. of *fluting,* pres. part. of FLUTE.] —**high′fa·lu′tin** *n.*

high fidelity. The electronic reproduction of sound with minimal distortion. Also called **hi-fi.** —**high′-fi·del′i·ty** *adj.*

high-flown (hī′flōn′) *adj.* Pretentious; inflated.

high frequency. *Abbr.* **hf** A radio frequency in the range between 3 and 30 megacycles per second.

High German. German as indigenously spoken and written in southern Germany.

high-grade (hī'grād') *adj.* Of superior quality.

high·hand·ed (hī'hăn'dĭd) *adj.* Arrogant or overbearing in manner. —**high'hand'ed·ly** *adv.* —**high'hand'ed·ness** *n.*

high-hat (hī'hăt') *n. Slang.* A snob. —*tr.v.* **-hatted, -hat· ting.** To treat in a condescending or supercilious way. —**high'-hat'** *adj.*

high·jack (hī'jăk') *v.* Var. of **hijack.**

high jinks. Mischievous pranks.

high jump. 1. A jump for height in a field contest. 2. Such a contest.

high·land (hī'lənd) *n.* 1. Elevated land. 2. **highlands.** A mountainous region or part of a country. —*modifier: a highland shepherd.*

high·land·er (hī'lən-dər) *n.* A person who lives in a high-land area.

Highland fling. A folk dance of the highlands of Scotland.

high·light (hī'līt') *n.* 1. A light or brilliantly lighted area, as in a painting or photograph. 2. An outstanding event or occurrence. —*tr.v.* 1. To give a highlight to. 2. To empha-size; make prominent. 3. To be the highlight of.

high·ly (hī'lē) *adv.* 1. To a great degree; extremely; very: *highly developed; highly valued; highly amusing.* 2. In a good or favorable way: *I think highly of him.* 3. In a high position or rank: *a highly placed official.* 4. At a high sal-ary, cost, etc.: *a highly paid executive.*

high-mind·ed (hī'mīn'dĭd) *adj.* 1. Characterized by ele-vated ideals or conduct; noble. 2. *Archaic.* Disdainfully proud; haughty. —**high'-mind'ed·ly** *adv.* —**high'-mind'ed-ness** *n.*

high·ness (hī'nĭs) *n.* 1. Tallness; height. 2. **Highness.** A ti-tle of honor for royalty: *His Royal Highness.*

high-oc·tane (hī'ŏk'tān') *adj.* Having a high octane num-ber.

high-pitched (hī'pĭcht') *adj.* 1. High in pitch, as a voice or musical tone. 2. Steeply sloped, as a roof.

high-pres·sure (hī'prĕsh'ər) *adj.* 1. Of or pertaining to pressures higher than that of the atmosphere. 2. *Informal.* Using aggressive and persistent methods of persuasion. —*tr.v.* **-sured, -sur·ing.** *Informal.* To convince or influence by using high-pressure methods.

high relief. A sculptural relief in which the forms project from the background by at least half their depth.

high-rise (hī'rīz') *n.* A multistoried building equipped with elevators. —*modifier: a high-rise apartment building.*

high·road (hī'rōd') *n.* 1. *Brit.* A main road; highway. 2. A simple, direct, or sure path: *the highroad to happiness.*

high school. A secondary school that includes grades 9 or 10 through 12 or grades 7 through 12. —*modifier* (high--school): *a high-school teacher.*

high seas. The open waters of an ocean or sea beyond the limits of the territorial jurisdiction of a country.

high-sound·ing (hī'soun'dĭng) *adj.* Pretentious; pompous.

high-spir·it·ed (hī'spĭr'ĭ-tĭd) *adj.* 1. Having a proud or un-broken spirit; brave. 2. Vivacious; lively.

high-strung (hī'strŭng') *adj.* Tending to be extremely ner-vous and sensitive.

hight (hīt) *adj. Archaic.* Named; called. [Middle English *highten,* from *hoten,* to call, be called, from Old English *hātan.*]

high·tail (hī'tāl') *intr.v. Slang.* To go or clear out in a great hurry.

high-ten·sion (hī'tĕn'shən) *adj.* Having a high voltage.

high-test (hī'tĕst') *adj.* 1. Meeting the most exacting re-quirements. 2. Of or pertaining to highly volatile high-octane gasoline.

high tide. 1. a. The highest level of the tide. b. The time at which this occurs. 2. A point of culmination; a climax.

high-toned (hī'tōnd') *adj.* 1. Intellectually, morally, or so-cially superior: *a high-toned lecture.* 2. *Informal.* Preten-tiously elegant or fashionable: *a high-toned country club.*

high water. 1. High tide. 2. The state of a body of water that has reached its highest level.

high·ty-tigh·ty (hī'tē-tī'tē) *adj.* Var. of **hoity-toity.**

high-wa·ter mark (hī'wô'tər, -wŏt'ər). 1. A mark indicating the highest level reached by a body of water. 2. The high-est point, as of achievement; apex.

high·way (hī'wā') *n.* A main public road, esp. one that con-nects towns and cities.

high·way·man (hī'wā'mən) *n.* A robber who holds up trav-elers on a highway.

hi·jack (hī'jăk') *tr.v.* Also **high-jack.** *Informal.* 1. To steal (goods) from a vehicle in transit. 2. To seize control of (a vehicle), esp. in order to go to a place other than the origi-nal or scheduled destination. [Orig. unknown.] —**hi'jack'-er** *n.*

hike (hīk) *v.* **hiked, hik·ing.** —*intr.v.* To go on an extended walk for pleasure or exercise: *hiked for three hours over a mountain trail.* —*tr.v.* 1. To increase or raise in amount: *hiked up prices for the tourist trade.* 2. To pull up or raise with a sudden motion: *He hiked up his pants.* —*n.* 1. A long walk or march. 2. A rise; an upward movement. [Orig. unknown.] —**hik'er** *n.*

hi·la (hī'lə) *n.* Plural of **hilum.**

hi·lar·i·ous (hĭ-lâr'ē-əs, -lăr'-, hī-) *adj.* Boisterously funny; causing merriment. [From Latin *hilarus,* cheerful, from Greek *hilaros.*] —**hi·lar'i·ous·ly** *adv.* —**hi·lar'i·ous·ness** *n.*

hi·lar·i·ty (hĭ-lăr'ĭ-tē, -lâr'-, hī-) *n.* Boisterous merriment. —See Syns at **gaiety.** [Old French *hilarite,* from Latin *hilaritās,* from *hilarus,* cheerful, from Greek *hilaros.*]

hill (hĭl) *n.* 1. A well-defined natural elevation that is smaller than a mountain. 2. A small heap, pile, or mound. 3. An incline, esp. in a road; a slope. —*tr.v.* 1. To form into a heap, pile, or mound. 2. To cover (a plant) with a mound of soil. [Middle English, from Old English *hyll.*]

hill·bil·ly (hĭl'bĭl'ē) *n., pl.* **-lies.** *Informal.* A person from the backwoods or a remote mountain area, esp. of the south-eastern United States. —*modifier: hillbilly music.* [HILL + *Billy,* pet form of *William.*]

hill·ock (hĭl'ək) *n.* A small hill. [Middle English *hilloc.*] —**hill'ock·y** *adj.*

hill·side (hĭl'sīd') *n.* The side or slope of a hill.

hill·top (hĭl'tŏp') *n.* The crest or top of a hill.

hill·y (hĭl'ē) *adj.* **-i·er, -i·est.** 1. Having many hills. 2. Similar to a hill; steep: *hilly terrain.* —**hill'i·ness** *n.*

hilt (hĭlt) *n.* The handle of a weapon or tool, esp. of a sword or dagger. —*idiom.* **to the hilt.** To the limit; completely: *was in debt to the hilt.* [Middle English, from Old English.]

hi·lum (hī'ləm) *n., pl.* **-la** (-lə). *Bot.* The scarlike mark on a seed, such as a bean, at the point of attachment, as to the seed case. [From Latin *hīlum,* trifle.]

him (hĭm) *pron.* The objective case of **he,** used: 1. As the direct object of a verb: *They assisted him.* 2. As the in-direct object of a verb: *They offered him a ride.* 3. As the object of a preposition: *This letter is addressed to him.* [Middle English, from Old English.]

him·self (hĭm-sĕlf') *pron.* 1. That one identical with him. Used: a. Reflexively as the direct or indirect object of a verb or as the object of a preposition: *He hurt himself.* b. For emphasis: *He himself wasn't certain.* 2. His normal or healthy condition or state: *He hasn't been himself lately.* —See Usage note at **herself.**

hind¹ (hīnd) *adj.* Also **hind·er** (hīn'dər). At the back or rear; posterior: *hind legs.* [Middle English *hint,* perh. from Old English *hinder,* behind.]

hind² (hīnd) *n.* A female red deer. [Middle English *hinde,* from Old English *hind.*]

hin·der¹ (hĭn'dər) *tr.v.* 1. To get in the way of; hamper: *Rain and wind hindered the searchers.* 2. To check or delay the progress of. [Middle English *hindren,* from Old English *hindrian.*] —**hin'der·er** *n.*

Syns: *hinder, encumber, hamper, impede, obstruct, re-tard v. Core meaning:* To interfere with the progress of (*hindered the negotiations by making unreasonable de-mands*).

hind·er² (hīn'dər) *adj.* Var. of **hind** (posterior).

hind·er·most (hīn'dər-mōst') *adj.* Var. of **hindmost.**

Hin·di (hĭn'dē) *n.* 1. A group of vernacular Indic dialects spoken in northern India. 2. A literary language based upon these dialects. —**Hin'di** *adj.*

hind·most (hīnd'mōst') *adj.* Also **hind·er·most** (hīn'dər-). Farthest to the rear.

Hin·doo (hĭn'dōō) *n. & adj.* Var. of **Hindu.**

hind·quar·ter (hīnd'kwôr'tər) *n.* 1. The back portion of a side of beef, lamb, veal, or mutton, including the hind leg and loin. 2. Often **hindquarters.** The rear part of a four-footed animal, adjacent to the hind legs; the rump.

hin·drance (hĭn′drəns) n. **1.** An act of hindering or a condition of being hindered. **2.** A person or thing that hinders; an obstacle. [Middle English *hinderaunce,* from *hindren,* to hinder.]

hind·sight (hīnd′sīt′) n. **1.** The rear sight of a firearm. **2.** An understanding of events after they have occurred.

Hin·du (hĭn′dōō). Also **Hin·doo.** —n. **1.** A native of India, esp. of northern India. **2.** A believer in Hinduism. —adj. Of or pertaining to the Hindus or to Hinduism.

Hin·du·ism (hĭn′dōō-ĭz′əm) n. The major religion of India, characterized by belief in a universal spirit, in reincarnation, and in the view that social customs and traditions, such as the caste system, are reflections of essential reality.

Hin·du·sta·ni (hĭn′dōō-stä′nē, -stăn′ē) n. **1.** A subdivision of the Indic branch of languages. **2.** A native of Hindustan. —adj. Of or pertaining to Hindustani or Hindustan.

hinge (hĭnj) n. **1.** A jointed device that permits one part, such as a door or lid, to turn or pivot on a stationary frame. **2.** A structure similar to a hinge, such as an elbow or knee joint or the valves that open and close an oyster shell or clam shell. **3.** A point or circumstance upon which subsequent events turn or depend. —v. **hinged, hing·ing.** —tr.v. To attach by or equip with a hinge. —intr.v. To turn or hang on or as if on a hinge: *plans that hinged upon his consent.* [Middle English *heeng.*]

hin·ny (hĭn′ē) n., pl. **-nies.** A hybrid animal that is the offspring of a male horse and a female donkey. [Latin *hinnus.*]

hint (hĭnt) n. **1.** A slight suggestion or indication. **2.** A statement that conveys information in an indirect fashion. **3.** A barely perceptible amount: *just a hint of color.* —tr.v. To suggest or make known by means of a hint. —intr.v. To give a hint: *He only hinted at the true purpose of his visit.* —See Syns at **suggest.** [Orig. unknown.] —**hint′er** n.

hin·ter·land (hĭn′tər-lănd′) n. **1.** The area inland from a coast. **2.** A region remote from cities and towns; back country. [German *Hinterland* : *hinter,* behind, rear + *Land,* land.]

hip[1] (hĭp) n. **1.** Anat. The part of the human body that projects outward over the hipbone between the waist and the thigh. **2.** The **hip joint.** **3.** Archit. The external angle formed by the meeting of two adjacent sloping sides of a roof. [Middle English, from Old English *hype.*]

hip[2] (hĭp) adj. **hip·per, hip·pest.** Also **hep** (hĕp). Slang. Aware of the most recent developments or trends. —See Syns at **aware.** [Var. of HEP.]

hip[3] (hĭp) n. The fleshy, berrylike, often brightly colored seed case of a rose. [Middle English *hipe,* from Old English *hēope.*]

hip·bone (hĭp′bōn′) n. Anat. Either of the large, flat, irregularly shaped bones that form the two halves of the pelvis.

hip joint. Anat. The joint between the hipbone and the femur.

hip·pie (hĭp′ē) n. Also **hip·py** pl. **-pies.** Informal. A usu. young person who opposes or rejects the conventional standards and customs of society, esp. in matters of dress, personal appearance, and living arrangements. —modifier: *a hippie poet.* [From HIP (aware).]

hip·po (hĭp′ō) n., pl. **-pos.** Informal. A hippopotamus.

Hip·po·crat·ic oath (hĭp′ə-krăt′ĭk). An oath or vow made by new physicians that is attributed to Hippocrates and sets forth a code of ethical conduct. [After *Hippocrates,* Greek physician of the 5th–4th cent. B.C.]

hip·po·drome (hĭp′ə-drōm′) n. **1.** A stadium with an oval racetrack, used for chariot races in ancient Greece and Rome. **2.** An arena for spectacles, such as circuses and horse shows. [Old French, from Latin *hippodromus,* from Greek *hippodromos* : *hippos,* horse + *dromos,* course.]

hip·po·pot·a·mus (hĭp′ə-pŏt′ə-məs) n., pl. **-es** or **-mi** (-mī′). A large, chiefly aquatic African mammal, *Hippopotamus amphibius,* with dark, thick, almost hairless skin, short legs, a broad snout, and a wide mouth. [Latin, from Late Greek *hippopotamos* : *hippos,* horse + *potamos,* river.]

hip·py (hĭp′ē) n. Informal. Var. of **hippie.**

hip roof. A roof with sloping ends and sides.

hip·ster (hĭp′stər) n. Slang. A person who is hip.

hire (hīr) tr.v. **hired, hir·ing.** To engage the services or use

of for a fee: *hired a new salesman; hire a car for the day.* —phrasal verb. **hire out. 1.** To grant one's services in exchange for pay: *He hires out as a field hand when work is slow on his farm.* **2.** To allow the use of for pay: *hired out my cottage for the summer.* —n. **1.** The payment for services or the use of something. **2.** The act or fact of hiring. **3.** The condition or fact of being hired. —idiom. **for hire.** Available for use or services in exchange for payment. [Middle English *hiren,* from Old English *hȳr(i)an.*] —**hir′a·ble** or **hire′a·ble** adj. —**hir′er** n.

hire·ling (hīr′lĭng) n. A person who works for pay, esp. one willing to do any kind of work, however hateful or unpleasant, for money.

hir·sute (hûr′sōōt′, hûr-sōōt′) adj. Hairy. [Latin *hirsūtus.*] —**hir′sute·ness** n.

his (hĭz). **1.** The possessive form of **he,** used as a modifier before a noun: *his wallet; his work; his dismissal.* **2.** Used to indicate: The one or ones belonging to him: *a friend of his. The brown boots are his. He wants to take my car instead of his. If you can't find your hat, take his.* [Middle English, from Old English.]

His·pan·ic (hĭ-spăn′ĭk) adj. Of or pertaining to the language, people, and culture of Spain or Latin America.

his·pid (hĭs′pĭd) adj. Covered with stiff or rough hairs; bristly. [Latin *hispidus.*]

hiss (hĭs) n. **1.** A sharp, sibilant sound similar to a sustained *s.* **2.** This sound as an expression of disapproval, contempt, or dissatisfaction. —intr.v. To utter a hiss. —tr.v. **1.** To utter with a hissing sound. **2.** To show disapproval or scorn for by hissing. [Middle English *hissen.*] —**hiss′er** n.

his·ta·mine (hĭs′tə-mēn′, -mĭn) n. A white crystalline compound, $C_5H_9N_3$, found in plant and animal tissue, that stimulates gastric secretion, is thought to have a major role in allergic reactions, and is used as a drug to cause dilation of the blood vessels. [Greek *histos,* web + AMINE.] —**his′ta·min′ic** (-mĭn′ĭk) adj.

his·tol·o·gy (hĭ-stŏl′ə-jē) n. **1.** The anatomical study of the microscopic structure of animal and plant tissues. **2.** The microscopic structure of tissue. [Greek *histos,* web + -LOGY.] —**his′to·log′i·cal** (hĭs′tə-lŏj′ĭ-kəl) adj. —**his′to·log′i·cal·ly** adv. —**his·tol′o·gist** n.

his·to·ri·an (hĭ-stôr′ē-ən, -stōr′-) n. **1.** A writer or student of history. **2.** A person who makes a record of proceedings: *the historian of the drama club.* [Old French *historien,* from Latin *historia,* history.]

his·tor·ic (hĭ-stôr′ĭk, -stŏr′-) adj. **1.** Having importance, esp. in history; famous; renowned. **2.** Historical. —See Syns at **important.**

his·tor·i·cal (hĭ-stôr′ĭ-kəl, -stŏr′-) adj. **1.** Of, relating to, or of the nature of history. **2.** Based on or concerned with events in history. **3.** Having importance in history; historic. —**his·tor′i·cal·ly** adv. —**his·tor′i·cal·ness** n.

historical present. The present tense used to narrate past events.

his·to·ri·og·ra·pher (hĭ-stôr′ē-ŏg′rə-fər, -stōr′-) n. A usu. official historian.

his·to·ri·og·ra·phy (hĭ-stôr′ē-ŏg′rə-fē, -stōr′-) n. **1.** The principles or methodology of historical study. **2.** The writing of history. **3.** Historical literature.

his·to·ry (hĭs′tə-rē) n., pl. **-ries. 1.** A narrative of events; chronicle. **2.** An account or record of events, as of the life or development of a people or country. **3.** The branch of knowledge that records and analyzes past events. **4.** The events that are the subject matter of history. **5.** An interesting past: *a house with a history.* **6.** A drama based on historical events. [Latin *historia,* from Greek, inquiry, observation, from *histōr,* learned man.]

his·tri·on·ic (hĭs′trē-ŏn′ĭk) or **his·tri·on·i·cal** (-ĭ-kəl) adj. **1.** Of or pertaining to actors or acting. **2.** Overly dramatic or theatrical; affected. [Late Latin *histriōnicus,* theatrical, from *histriō,* actor.] —**his′tri·on′i·cal·ly** adv.

his·tri·on·ics (hĭs′trē-ŏn′ĭks) n. **1.** (used with a sing. verb). Theatrical arts. **2.** (used with a pl. verb). Exaggeratedly dramatic or emotional behavior.

hit (hĭt) v. **hit, hit·ting.** —tr.v. **1.** To strike with or as if with a blow. **2.** To strike against forcefully; crash into: *hit her hand against the wall.* **3.** To propel with a blow: *hit the ball into center court.* **4.** To strike with a missile, as a bullet or arrow: *He fired and hit the target.* **5.** To impress or affect, esp. adversely: *was hit hard by the depression.* **6.** To come upon or discover, often by chance. **7.** To attain, reach, or arrive at: *They hit town last week. The article hit exactly the right note.* **8.** *Baseball.* To achieve (a base hit): *hit a triple.* **9.** *Informal.* To ask for money from: *He hit me for a dollar.* **10.** *Slang.* To take the life of (another). —*intr.v.* **1.** To strike or deal a blow. **2.** To come into forceful contact; collide. **3.** To come upon or stumble across, esp. by accident: *hit upon the answer.* **4.** *Baseball.* To bat. —*n.* **1.** A blow that strikes something aimed at. **2.** A great or popular success: *a Broadway hit.* **3.** *Baseball.* A base hit. —*idioms.* **hit it off.** To get along well together: *We hit it off from the beginning.* **hit the bottle.** To drink to excess. **hit the road.** To depart or set out. [Middle English *hitten,* from Old Norse *hitta,* to hit.] —*hit'ter* n.

    Syns: **hit, bash** (*Informal*), **belt** (*Informal*), **bop** (*Informal*), **clip** (*Informal*), **clobber** (*Slang*), **clout, knock, paste** (*Slang*), **slam, slog, slug** (*Slang*), **smack, smash, smite, sock** (*Slang*), **strike, swat, wallop** (*Informal*), **whack, wham** v. *Core meaning:* To deliver (a powerful blow) suddenly and sharply (*hit the other boxer in the jaw*). See also Syns at **murder.**

hit-and-run (hĭt'n-rŭn') *adj.* **1.** Of or relating to an accident in which the operator of a vehicle who is responsible for the damage or injury flees from the scene in order to escape the consequences. **2.** *Baseball.* Of or relating to a play in which a man on base begins to run to the next base as the pitcher starts to pitch and before the batter attempts to hit the ball.

hitch (hĭch) *tr.v.* **1.** To fasten or tie temporarily, as with a loop, hook, or noose. **2.** To connect or attach, as to a vehicle: *hitched a team of horses to the wagon.* **3.** *Informal.* To join in marriage. **4.** To raise by pulling or jerking. **5.** *Informal.* To secure (a free ride). —*intr.v.* **1.** To move with a limp; to hobble. **2.** To become joined or fastened. **3.** *Informal.* To hitchhike. —*n.* **1.** Any of various knots used as a temporary fastening. **2.** A short pull or jerk; a tug. **3.** A hobble or limp. **4.** An impediment or delay: *a hitch in our plans.* **5.** A term of military service. [Middle English *hytchen,* to move or lift with a jerk.]

hitch-hike (hĭch'hīk') *intr.v.* **-hiked, -hik·ing. 1.** To solicit free rides along a road. **2.** To travel by means of free rides obtained from passing motorists. —*hitch'hik'er* n.

hitching post. A post for tying up an animal, esp. a horse.

hith·er (hĭth'ər) *adv.* To or toward this place: *Come hither.* —*adj.* Located on the near side. [Middle English, from Old English *hider.*]

hith·er·most (hĭth'ər-mōst') *adj.* Nearest to this place or side.

hith·er·to (hĭth'ər-tōō') *adv.* Until this time; up to now: *hitherto unobserved rings of Saturn.*

hith·er·ward (hĭth'ər-wərd) *adv.* Also **hith·er·wards** (-wərdz). Hither.

hit-or-miss (hĭt'ər-mĭs') *adj.* Lacking care or precision; haphazard.

Hit·tite (hĭt'īt') *n.* **1.** A member of an ancient people living in Asia Minor and northern Syria about 2000–1200 B.C. **2.** An extinct Indo-European language spoken by the Hittites. —*adj.* Of the Hittites or their language.

hive (hīv) *n.* **1.** A natural or artificial structure for housing bees, esp. honeybees. **2.** A colony of bees living in a hive. **3.** A place crowded with busy people. —*v.* **hived, hiv·ing.** —*tr.v.* **1.** To collect (bees) into a hive. **2.** To store or accumulate in or as if in a hive. —*intr.v.* **1.** To enter a hive. **2.** To live in close association in or as if in a hive. [Middle English, from Old English *hȳf.*]

hives (hīvz) *n.* (*used with a sing. or pl. verb*). A skin rash marked by itching welts, usu. caused by an allergic reaction. [Orig. unknown.]

h'm or **hm** (hmm) *interj.* Often **hmm, hmmm,** etc. Used to express a question, thoughtful concentration, hesitation prompted by doubt, etc.

ho (hō) *interj.* A word used to express surprise or joy or to attract attention: *Land ho! Westward ho!* [Middle English.]

Ho The symbol for the element holmium.

hoa·gie (hō'gē) *n. Slang.* A hero sandwich. [Orig. unknown.]

hoar (hôr, hōr) *adj.* Hoary. —*n.* Hoarfrost. [Middle English *hoor,* from Old English *hār.*]

hoard (hôrd, hōrd) *n.* A hidden or secret supply stored up for future use: *a miser's hoard.* —*intr.v.* To gather or accumulate a hoard. —*tr.v.* To accumulate or gather into a hoard. [Middle English *hord,* from Old English.] —*hoard'er* n.

hoard·ing (hôr'dĭng, hōr'-) *n. Brit.* **1.** A temporary wooden fence around a building or structure under construction or repair. **2.** A billboard. [From earlier *hoard,* a fence, from Anglo-French *hurdis.*]

hoar·frost (hôr'frôst', -frŏst', hōr'-) *n.* A deposit of ice crystals that forms on an object that is at a temperature below freezing and exposed to moist air; hoar.

hoar·hound (hôr'hound', hōr'-) *n.* Var. of **horehound.**

hoarse (hôrs, hōrs) *adj.* **hoars·er, hoars·est. 1.** Low and husky in sound. **2.** Having a harsh, grating sound. [Middle English *hors,* from Old English *hās.*] —See Syns at **harsh.** —*hoarse'ly* adv. —*hoarse'ness* n.

hoar·y (hôr'ē, hōr'ē) *adj.* **-i·er, -i·est. 1.** Gray or white with or as if with age: *a plant with hoary leaves.* **2.** Very old; ancient. —*hoar'i·ness* n.

hoax (hōks) *n.* Something, as a joke or fraud, that is intended to deceive or trick others. —*tr.v.* To deceive or cheat by using a hoax. [Perh. var. of HOCUS.] —*hoax'er* n.

hob¹ (hŏb) *n.* A shelf or projection at the back or side of the inside of a fireplace for keeping things warm. [Orig. unknown.]

hob² (hŏb) *n.* A hobgoblin, sprite, or elf. —*idiom.* **play** (or **raise**) **hob** (**with**). To make mischief or trouble. [Middle English *hob,* from *Hobbe,* pet form of Robin.]

hob·ble (hŏb'əl) *v.* **-bled, -bling.** —*intr.v.* To walk or move along haltingly or with difficulty; limp. —*tr.v.* **1.** To place a device around the legs of (an animal) so as to hamper but not prevent movement. **2.** To cause to limp. **3.** To hamper the action or progress of; impede. —*n.* **1.** An awkward, clumsy, or irregular walk or gait. **2.** A device, such as a rope or strap, used to hobble an animal. **3.** *Archaic.* An unfortunate or awkward situation. [Middle English *hoblen.*] —*hob'bler* n.

hob·ble·de·hoy (hŏb'əl-dē-hoi') *n.* A gawky, awkward adolescent boy. [Orig. unknown.]

hobble skirt. A long skirt that is so narrow below the knees that it restricts a normal stride.

hob·by (hŏb'ē) *n., pl.* **-bies.** An activity, as stamp-collecting or gardening, carried on not as one's regular work but primarily for pleasure; a pastime. [From earlier *hobby-horse,* a pastime.]

hob·by·horse (hŏb'ē-hôrs') *n.* **1.** A toy consisting of a long stick with an imitation horse's head on one end. **2.** A rocking horse. **3.** A favorite topic.

hob·gob·lin (hŏb'gŏb'lĭn) *n.* **1.** An ugly, mischievous elf or goblin. **2.** A usu. imaginary source of anxiety, fear, or dread: *was haunted by the hobgoblin of poverty.* [HOB (elf) + GOBLIN.]

hob·nail (hŏb'nāl') *n.* A short nail with a thick head that is put on the soles of shoes or boots to protect from wear. [HOB (projection) + NAIL.]

hob·nob (hŏb'nŏb') *intr.v.* **-nobbed, -nob·bing.** To associate familiarly: *He hobnobs with some of your brother's friends.* [Earlier *hob and nob,* to drink together.]

ho·bo (hō'bō) *n., pl.* **-boes** or **-bos.** A tramp. [Orig. unknown.]

Hob·son's choice (hŏb'sənz). An apparently free choice that offers no true alternative. [After Thomas Hobson (d. 1631), English liveryman, who required his customers to take the next available horse.]

hock¹ (hŏk) *n.* The tarsal joint of the hind leg of a four-footed animal, such as a horse, that corresponds to the human ankle. [Middle English *hoch,* from Old English *hōh,* heel.]

hock² (hŏk) *n. Brit.* Rhine wine. [Short for obs. *hockamore,* from German *Hochheimer* (*Wein*), wine of Hochheim, West Germany.]

hock³ (hŏk) *tr.v. Informal.* To pawn. —*n. Informal.* The condition of being pawned. —*idiom.* **in hock.** *Informal.* In debt: *in hock up to her ears.* [From Dutch *hok,* prison.]

hock·ey (hŏk'ē) *n.* **1.** A game played on ice in which two opposing teams of six skaters each use curved sticks to try to drive a flat disk, or puck, into the opponents' goal. Also called **ice hockey**. **2.** A game played on a field in which two opposing teams of eleven players each use curved sticks to attempt to drive a ball into the opponents' goal. Also called **field hockey**. [Orig. unknown.]

ho·cus (hō′kəs) *tr.v.* **-cused** or **-cussed, -cus·ing** or **-cus·sing.** **1.** To fool or deceive; to hoax; cheat. **2.** To put a drug into. [Short for HOCUS-POCUS.]

ho·cus-po·cus (hō′kəs-pō′kəs) *n.* **1.** Nonsense words or phrases used when performing magic tricks. **2.** A trick performed by a magician or juggler. **3.** Any deception or trickery. [From earlier *Hocus Pocus,* a name used for a conjurer and formed in imitation of the Latin-sounding incantations that he used.]

hod (hŏd) *n.* **1.** A V-shaped trough carried over the shoulder for transporting loads, such as bricks or mortar. **2.** A coal scuttle. [Prob. from Middle English *hot,* a basket, from Old French *hotte.*]

hodge·podge (hŏj′pŏj′) *n.* A haphazard mixture; a jumble. [Var. of HOTCHPOTCH.]

Hodg·kin's disease (hŏj′kĭnz). A disease marked by enlargement of the lymph nodes, the spleen, and often of the liver and kidneys. [After Thomas *Hodgkin* (1798–1866), English physician.]

hoe (hō) *n.* A tool with a flat blade attached approximately at a right angle to a long handle, used for weeding, cultivating, and breaking up the soil. *—tr.v.* **hoed, hoe·ing.** To weed, cultivate, or dig up with a hoe. [Middle English *howe,* from Old French *houe.*] **—ho′er** *n.*

hoe·cake (hō′kāk′) *n.* A small, thin cake made of cornmeal.

hoe·down (hō′doun′) *n.* **1.** A square dance. **2.** A party at which hoe-downs are danced. **3.** The music for a hoe-down.

hog (hôg, hŏg) *n.* **1.** A domesticated pig, esp. one weighing over 120 pounds. **2.** Any of various mammals, such as the boar and the wart hog, that are related to the domesticated pig. **3.** A gluttonous, greedy, or filthy person. *—modifier:* a hog *farm.* *—tr.v.* **hogged, hog·ging.** To take more than one's share of. *—idioms.* **high (off or on) the hog.** In a lavish or extravagant manner. **go hog wild.** To react in an intemperate and immoderate manner. [Middle English *hogge,* from Old English *hogg.*]

hog·back (hôg′băk′, hŏg′-) *n.* A sharp ridge with steeply sloping sides, produced by the outcropping edges of sharply tilted rock strata.

hog cholera. A highly infectious, often fatal viral disease of swine.

hog·gish (hô′gĭsh, hŏg′ĭsh) *adj.* Filthy, greedy, or gluttonous. **—hog′gish·ly** *adv.* **—hog′gish·ness** *n.*

hog·nose snake (hôg′nōz′, hŏg′-). Any of several thick-bodied, nonpoisonous North American snakes of the genus *Heterodon* that protect themselves when disturbed by hissing and then by pretending to be dead. Also called **puff adder.**

hogs·head (hôgz′hĕd′, hŏgz′-) *n. Abbr.* **hhd** **1.** A large barrel or cask, esp. one with a capacity ranging from 63 to 140 gallons, or from approx. 238 to 530 liters. **2.** A unit of liquid measure in the United States, equal to 63 gallons, or approx. 238 liters.

hog-tie or **hog·tie** (hôg′tī′, hŏg′-) *tr.v.* **-tied, -ty·ing.** **1.** To tie together the legs of. **2.** To make incapable of movement or action.

hog·wash (hôg′wŏsh′, -wôsh′, hŏg′-) *n.* **1.** Garbage or slop fed to hogs. **2.** False or nonsensical language.

hoi pol·loi (hoi′ pə-loi′). The common people. [Greek *hoi polloi,* "the many."]

hoist (hoist) *tr.v.* To raise or haul up with or as if with the help of a mechanical apparatus. *—See Syns at* **raise.** *—n.* **1.** An apparatus, such as a crane or tackle, for lifting heavy or cumbersome objects. **2.** The act of hoisting; a lift. [Var. of earlier *hoise,* from Middle English *hyssen.*] **—hoist′er** *n.*

hoi·ty-toi·ty (hoi′tē-toi′tē) *adj.* Also **high·ty-tigh·ty** (hī′tē-tī′tē). **1.** Arrogant; haughty. **2.** Giddy; flighty. [From dial. *hoit,* to romp.]

ho·kum (hō′kəm) *n.* Something that is false or worthless; humbug. [Perh. from HOCUS-POCUS.]

hol-. Var. of **holo-.**

hold¹ (hōld) *v.* **held** (hĕld), **hold·ing.** *—tr.v.* **1.** To have and keep in or as if in one's grasp: *held a glass.* **2.** To support; keep up: *a shelf that held a heavy load.* **3.** To put or maintain in a certain position or relationship; keep: *held his head high.* **4.** To contain; have or receive as contents: *The jar holds one pint.* **5.** To have or keep in one's possession or control. **6.** To control; restrain: *The dam held the flood waters.* **7.** To retain the attention or interest of. **8.** To defend against attack or capture: *held the fort.* **9.** To stop or delay: *held dinner for an hour.* **10.** To have or occupy (a position): *held the office of governor.* **11.** To keep or bind to: *held him to his promise.* **12.** To keep in the mind. **13. a.** To consider; judge. **b.** To assert; affirm. **14.** To cause to take place; conduct: *hold a conference.* *—intr.v.* **1.** To maintain a grasp or grip. **2.** To position or continue in the same state. **3.** To adhere closely; keep: *They held to a southwesterly course.* **4.** To remain firm or secure. **5.** To be valid, correct, or true: *His theory holds.* *—See Syns at* **assert** *and* **believe.** *—phrasal verbs.* **hold back.** To keep in one's possession or under one's control. **hold off.** To stop or delay: *Hold off for a minute.* **hold on. 1.** To maintain one's grip; cling. **2.** To keep at; continue. **3.** To wait for someone or something. **hold out. 1.** To last or endure. **2.** To continue to resist: *held out for weeks without supplies.* **hold over. 1.** To postpone or delay action. **2.** To keep or continue, as in a position or situation. **hold up. 1.** To endure: *shoes that have held up under hard wear.* **2.** To obstruct or delay: *What's holding up traffic?* **3.** To rob: *held up a bank.* *—See Syns at* **rob. hold with.** To agree with; support: *don't hold with those views.* *—n.* **1.** The act or a means of grasping; a grip: *a wrestling hold.* **2.** A controlling influence; power. **3.** Something held for support. **4.** A prison cell. **5.** *Archaic.* A fortified place; stronghold. **6.** *Mus.* **a.** The lengthening or extension of a note or pause. **b.** The symbol designating this prolongation; a fermata. **7.** An order or instruction to delay, set aside, or halt. *—idioms.* **hold forth.** To talk at great length. **hold (one's) own.** To maintain one's position; keep on a level of equality: *held his own against the competition.* **hold water.** To survive or stand up to critical examination: *His story doesn't hold water.* [Middle English *holden,* from Old English *healdan.*]

hold² (hōld) *n. Naut.* The lower part of the interior of a ship or airplane, in which cargo is stored. [Var. of HOLE.]

hold·back (hōld′băk′) *n.* A strap or iron between the shaft and the harness on a drawn wagon that allows a horse to stop or back up.

hold·er (hōl′dər) *n.* **1.** A person or thing that holds. **2.** A person who possesses something; an owner: *a ticket holder.* **3.** *Law.* A person who possesses and is legally entitled to the payment of a check, bill, or promissory note.

hold·ing (hōl′dĭng) *n.* **1.** holdings. **a.** Legally owned property, such as land, money, or stocks. **b.** Land rented or leased from another. **2.** *Sports.* An illegal hampering of an opponent's movement with the arms or hands.

holding company. A company that controls a partial or complete interest in other companies.

hold·out (hōld′out′) *n. Informal.* A person who withholds or delays cooperation or agreement.

hold·o·ver (hōld′ō′vər) *n.* A person or thing that remains from an earlier time: *a holdover from the previous administration.*

hold·up (hōld′ŭp′) *n.* **1.** A suspension of activity; delay; interruption. **2.** A robbery, esp. an armed robbery.

hole (hōl) *n.* **1.** A cavity or hollow place in a solid, made by or as if by digging. **2.** An opening or perforation; a gap. **3.** A small, deep pond. **4.** The hollowed-out dwelling place of an animal; a burrow: *a gopher hole.* **5.** An ugly, squalid, or depressing place. **6.** A deep or isolated place of confinement; a dungeon. **7.** A fault; defect: *the holes in his argument.* **8.** A bad or troublesome situation; predicament. **9.** *Golf.* **a.** The small hollow lined with a cup into which the ball must be hit. **b.** One of the 9 or 18 divisions of a golf course, from tee to cup. *—v.* **holed, hol·ing.** *—tr.v.* **1.** To put a hole or holes in; to puncture; perforate. **2.** To drive (a golf ball) into a hole. *—intr.v.* To make a hole or holes. *—phrasal verb.* **hole up. 1.** To hibernate in or as if in a hole. **2.** To hide out or shut oneself up in: *The bandits holed up in the mountains.* *—idiom.* **in the hole.** *Informal.* In debt. [Middle English, from Old English *hol*, hollow place.] —**hole'y** *adj.*

hol·i·day (hŏl'ĭ-dā') *n.* **1.** A day free from work, esp. a day set aside by law, religious custom, or tradition to celebrate or commemorate a particular event. **2.** A **holy day. 3.** *Brit.* A period free from work; a vacation. —*modifier:* holiday *traffic.* [Middle English, from Old English *hāligdæg* : *hālig,* holy + *dæg,* day.]

ho·li·er-than-thou (hō'lē-ər-thən-thou') *adj.* Marked by an attitude of superior and self-righteous piety or virtue.

ho·li·ness (hō'lē-nĭs) *n.* **1.** The condition or quality of being holy; sanctity. **2. Holiness.** A title of address for church dignitaries and esp. for the pope.

hol·land (hŏl'ənd) *n.* A cotton or linen fabric, often glazed, that is used esp. for window shades and upholstery. [Middle English *holand,* from Dutch *Holland,* a province in the Netherlands.]

hol·lan·daise sauce (hŏl'ən-dāz', hŏl'ən-dāz'). A creamy sauce of butter, egg yolks, and lemon juice or vinegar.

hol·ler (hŏl'ər) *intr.v.* To yell or shout. —*n.* A yell or shout. [From French *holà,* "hey."]

hol·low (hŏl'ō) *adj.* **-er, -est. 1.** Having a cavity, hole, or space within: *a hollow wall.* **2.** Shaped by or as if by scooping out; concave: *a hollow basin.* **3.** Caved in or sunken; indented: *hollow cheeks.* **4.** Without substance, worth, or character; shallow; superficial: *a hollow person; hollow arguments.* **5.** Deep, low, and booming; echoing. —*n.* **1.** An indentation or space within something: *the hollow behind a wall; the hollow of one's hand.* **2.** A valley or depression. **3.** A void; emptiness. —*tr.v.* To make hollow by or as if by scooping: *hollow out a pumpkin.* [Middle English *holewe,* from *holh,* hole, from Old English.] —**hol'low·ly** *adv.* —**hol'low·ness** *n.*

hol·low·ware (hŏl'ō-wâr') *n.* Tableware, such as bowls, pitchers, or knife handles, that are bowl-shaped or tubular.

hol·ly (hŏl'ē) *n.,* pl. **-lies. 1.** Any of numerous trees or shrubs of the genus *Ilex,* often with bright-red berries and glossy evergreen leaves with spiny margins. **2.** Branches or leaves of the holly, traditionally used for Christmas decoration. **3.** Any of various similar or related plants. [Middle English *holin,* from Old English *holen.*]

hol·ly·hock (hŏl'ē-hŏk') *n.* A tall plant, *Althaea rosea,* with a long cluster of showy, variously colored flowers. [Middle English *holihoc* : *holi,* holy + *hoc,* a mallow, from Old English.]

hollyhock   holster

Hol·ly·wood (hŏl'ē-wood') *n.* **1.** The U.S. motion-picture industry. **2.** The artificiality usu. considered characteristic of Hollywood. [After *Hollywood,* a district of Los Angeles, California.]

holm (hōm, hōlm) *n. Brit.* **1.** An island in a river. **2.** Low land near a stream. [Middle English, from Old Norse *holmr,* islet, meadow.]

hol·mi·um (hōl'mē-əm) *n. Symbol* **Ho** A relatively soft, malleable, stable rare-earth element. Atomic number 67; atomic weight 164.930; melting point 1,461°C; boiling point 2,600°C; specific gravity 8.803; valence 3. [After Stockholm, Sweden.]

holm oak (hōm, hōlm). A tree, *Quercus ilex,* with prickly evergreen leaves. Also called **ilex.** [From Middle English, var. of *holin,* holly.]

holo- or **hol-.** A prefix meaning whole: **hologram.** [From Greek *holos,* whole, entire.]

hol·o·caust (hŏl'ə-kôst', hō'lə-) *n.* **1.** *Rare.* A sacrifice that is consumed by fire. **2.** Great or total destruction, esp. by fire. **3. Holocaust.** The mass murder of the Jews carried out by the Nazi government of Germany. [Middle English, from Old French *holocauste,* from Latin *holocaustum,* from Greek *holokauston* : *holo-,* whole + *kaustos,* burnt, from *kaein,* to burn.] —**hol'o·caus'tal** or **hol'o·caus'tic** *adj.*

Hol·o·cene (hŏl'ə-sēn', hō'lə-) *adj. Geol.* Of the Recent geologic epoch. —*n. Geol.* The Recent epoch. [HOLO- + -CENE.]

hol·o·gram (hŏl'ə-grăm', hō'lə-) *n.* A photographic film or plate that is a record of the light wave interference pattern of an object illuminated by a split coherent beam of light, such as a laser beam. [HOLO- + -GRAM.]

hol·o·graph (hŏl'ə-grăf', hō'lə-) *n.* **1.** A document written wholly in the handwriting of the person whose signature it bears. **2.** A hologram. [From Late Latin *holographus,* entirely written by the signer, from Greek *holographos,* written in full : *holo-,* whole + *-graphos,* written.] —**hol'o·graph'ic** or **hol'o·graph'i·cal** *adj.* —**hol'o·graph'i·cal·ly** *adv.*

ho·log·ra·phy (hō-lŏg'rə-fē) *n.* The method of producing a three-dimensional image without a lens, using a coherent light beam to illuminate a hologram in order to reconstruct the image.

Hol·stein (hōl'stīn') *n.* Any of a breed of large black and white dairy cattle. [After Holstein, Germany.]

hol·ster (hōl'stər) *n.* A leather case for carrying a pistol. [Dutch.] —**hol'stered** *adj.*

ho·ly (hō'lē) *adj.* **-li·er, -li·est. 1.** Of or associated with God, a divine power, or religious beliefs and traditions and therefore regarded with special reverence; sacred: *The Bible and the Koran are holy books.* **2.** Given a special influence or quality by or as if by God or a divine power; blessed: *a pure and holy feeling; freedom's holy light.* **3.** Living according to a strict or highly moral religious or spiritual system; saintly. **4.** Regarded with or worthy of special respect or awe: *peace, education, and other holy subjects of American politics.* [Middle English, from Old English *hālig.*] —**ho'li·ly** *adv.*

Holy Communion. The Eucharist.

holy day. Also **ho·ly·day** (hō'lē-dā'). A day specified for religious observance.

Holy Father. One of the titles of the pope.

Holy Ghost. The third person of the Christian Trinity. Also called **Holy Spirit.**

Holy Grail. The Grail.

Holy Land. Palestine.

holy of holies. 1. The innermost shrine of a Jewish tabernacle and temple. **2.** Any place considered esp. sacred.

holy orders. *Eccles.* **1.** The sacrament or ceremony of ordination to the priesthood or ministry. **2.** The rank of an ordained Christian minister or priest. **3.** The principal orders of the clergy in the Roman Catholic, Eastern Orthodox, or Anglican Church.

Holy See. *Rom. Cath. Ch.* The court, office, or jurisdiction of the pope.

Holy Spirit. The **Holy Ghost.**

ho·ly·stone (hō'lē-stōn') *n.* A soft sandstone used for scouring the wooden decks of a ship. —*tr.v.* **-stoned, -stoning.** To scrub or scour with a holystone.

Holy Thursday. 1. *Rom. Cath. Ch.* Maundy Thursday. **2.** In the Church of England, Ascension Day.

holy water. Water blessed by a priest.

Holy Week. The week before Easter.

hom·age (hŏm'ĭj, ŏm'-) *n.* **1.** Special honor or respect shown or expressed publicly. **2.** An action or ceremony by which a feudal vassal acknowledged his allegiance to a lord or ruler. —See Syns at **honor.** [Middle English, acknowledgment of a man's allegiance, from Old French, from Medieval Latin *hominaticum,* from Latin *homō,* man.]

hom·bre (ŏm'brā', -brē) *n. Western U.S. Slang.* A man; fellow. [Spanish, from Latin *homō.*]

Hom·burg (hŏm'bûrg') *n.* Also **hom·burg.** A man's felt hat with a soft, dented crown and a shallow, slightly rolled brim. [After *Homburg,* West Germany.]

home (hōm) *n.* **1.** A place, such as a house or apartment, where one lives; residence; habitation. **2.** A house that is a residence or dwelling place. **3.** A dwelling place together with the family that lives there; a household. **4.** The place, as a country or town, in which one was born or in which one lived for a long time. **5.** The native habitat, as of a plant or animal. **6.** A goal or place of safety for players of a game, such as baseball or tag. **7.** An institution for the care of those who cannot take care of themselves: *a nursing home.* **—modifier:** *home cooking.* **—adv. 1.** At, to, or toward the direction of home. **2.** To the point or mark at which something is aimed: *The arrow struck home.* **3.** To the very center. **—v. homed, hom·ing. —intr. v. 1.** To go or return home. **2.** To be guided to a target automatically, as by means of radio waves. **—tr.v.** To guide (a missile or aircraft) to a target automatically. **—idiom. at home. 1.** Comfortable and relaxed; at ease: *at home with strangers.* **2.** Ready and expecting to have visitors: *We are at home every Thursday.* [Middle English, from Old English *hām.*]

home base. 1. *Baseball.* **Home plate. 2.** A base of operations; headquarters. **3.** An objective toward which players of a game, such as baseball or backgammon, progress; home.

home·bod·y (hōm′bŏd′ē) *n.* A person whose principal interests are in domestic matters.

home·bred (hōm′brĕd′) *adj.* Raised, bred, or reared at home; domestic.

home·brew (hōm′brōō′) *n.* An alcoholic beverage made at home. **—home′-brewed′** *adj.*

home·com·ing (hōm′kŭm′ĭng) *n.* **1.** A return home. **2.** In some colleges and universities, an annual celebration for visiting alumni.

home economics. The science and art of home management.

home front. The civilian population of a country at war.

home·land (hōm′lănd′) *n.* One's native land.

home·less (hōm′lĭs) *adj.* Without a home.

home·ly (hōm′lē) *adj.* **-li·er, -li·est. 1.** Characteristic of the home or of home life: *homely warmth.* **2.** Of a simple or unpretentious nature; plain: *homely truths.* **3.** Not handsome or good-looking. —See Syns at **plain. —home′li·ness** *n.*

home·made (hōm′mād′) *adj.* **1.** Made or prepared in the home: *homemade cake.* **2.** Crudely or simply made.

home·mak·er (hōm′mā′kər) *n.* A person who manages a household, esp. a housewife.

homeo- or **homoio-.** A prefix meaning like or similar: *homeostasis.* [From Greek *homoios,* similar, from *homos,* same.]

ho·me·op·a·thy (hō′mē-ŏp′ə-thē, hŏm′ē-) *n.* A system of medical treatment based on the use of small quantities of drugs that in massive doses produce symptoms similar to those of the disease under treatment. [HOMEO- + -PATHY.] **—ho′me·o·path′** (hō′mē-ə-păth′, hŏm′ē-) or **ho′me·op′a·thist** (-ŏp′ə-thĭst) *n.* **—ho′me·o·path′ic** (-ə-păth′ĭk) *adj.* **—ho′me·o·path′i·cal·ly** *adv.*

ho·me·o·sta·sis (hō′mē-ō-stā′sĭs, hŏm′ē-) *n.* In the bodies esp. of higher animals, a tendency to maintain a state of internal equilibrium among the complex of interdependent elements. [HOMEO- + -STASIS.] **—ho′me·o·stat′ic** (-stăt′ĭk) *adj.*

home plate. *Baseball.* The base at which a batter stands to hit the ball and which a runner must cross safely in order to score a run.

hom·er (hō′mər) *Baseball.* **—n.** A home run. **—intr.v.** To hit a home run.

home rule. The principle or practice of self-government with respect to the internal affairs of a political unit, as a city or town, within a larger unit.

home run. *Baseball.* A hit that allows the batter to touch all the bases and score a run.

home·sick (hōm′sĭk′) *adj.* Longing for home. **—home′-sick′ness** *n.*

home·spun (hōm′spŭn′) *adj.* **1.** Spun, woven, or made in the home. **2.** Made of a homespun fabric. **3.** Simple and homely in character. **—n. 1.** A plain coarse woolen cloth made of homespun yarn. **2.** A sturdy fabric similar to homespun. **—modifier:** *a homespun skirt.*

home·stead (hōm′stĕd′) *n.* **1.** A house, esp. a farmhouse, with adjoining buildings and land. **2.** Land granted to a settler, as under the Homestead Act. **—intr.v.** To settle and farm land, esp. under the Homestead Act. **—tr.v.** To claim and settle (land) as a homestead. **—home′stead′er** *n.*

home·stretch (hōm′strĕch′) *n.* **1.** The part of a racetrack from the last turn to the finish line. **2.** The final stage of an undertaking.

home·ward (hōm′wərd) *adv.* Also **home·wards** (-wərdz). Toward home. **—adj.** Directed toward home.

home·work (hōm′wûrk′) *n.* **1.** Work, such as schoolwork, office work, or piecework, that is to be done at home. **2.** Any work of a preparatory or preliminary nature.

hom·ey (hō′mē) *adj.* **-i·er, -i·est.** Also **hom·y.** *Informal.* Having a feeling of home; homelike. **—hom′ey·ness** *n.*

hom·i·cid·al (hŏm′ĭ-sīd′l, hō′mĭ-) *adj.* **1.** Of or relating to homicide. **2.** Marked by a tendency to homicide. **—hom′i·cid′al·ly** *adv.*

hom·i·cide (hŏm′ĭ-sīd′, hō′mĭ-) *n.* **1.** The killing of one person by another. **2.** A person who kills another. [Middle English, from Old French, from Latin *homicīda,* murderer, and *homicīdium,* murder.]

hom·i·let·ic (hŏm′ĭ-lĕt′ĭk) or **hom·i·let·i·cal** (-ĭ-kəl) *adj.* **1.** Relating to or characteristic of a homily. **2.** Pertaining to homiletics. **—hom′i·let′i·cal·ly** *adv.*

hom·i·let·ics (hŏm′ə-lĕt′ĭks) *n.* (used with a sing. verb). The art of preaching. [Greek *homilētikē,* art of conversing, from *homilētikos,* social, affable, ult. from *homilos,* crowd.]

hom·i·ly (hŏm′ə-lē) *n., pl.* **-lies. 1.** A sermon. **2.** A tedious moralizing lecture. [Middle English *omelie,* from Old French, from Late Latin *homīlia,* from Greek *homilia,* discourse, association, from *homilos,* crowd.]

homing pigeon. A pigeon trained to return to its home roost.

hom·i·nid (hŏm′ə-nĭd) *n.* A primate of the family Hominidae, of which modern man, *Homo sapiens,* is the only surviving species. [Latin *homo,* man, human being + -ID.] **—hom′i·nid** *adj.*

hom·i·noid (hŏm′ə-noid′) *adj.* Resembling or related to man. [From Latin *homo,* man, human being + -OID.] **—hom′i·noid′** *n.*

hom·i·ny (hŏm′ə-nē) *n.* Hulled and dried kernels of corn. [Perh. of Algonquian orig.]

hominy grits. A coarse white meal made by grinding hominy.

homo-. A prefix meaning same: *homophone.* [From Greek *homos,* same.]

ho·mo·ge·ne·i·ty (hō′mə-jə-nē′ĭ-tē, hŏm′ə-) *n.* The state or quality of being homogeneous.

ho·mo·ge·ne·ous (hō′mə-jē′nē-əs, -jēn′yəs, hŏm′ə-) *adj.* **1.** Of the same or similar nature or kind. **2.** Uniform throughout in structure or composition. [Medieval Latin *homogeneus,* from Greek *homogenēs* : *homo-,* same + *-genēs,* born.] **—ho′mo·ge′ne·ous·ly** *adv.* **—ho′mo·ge′ne·ous·ness** *n.*

ho·mog·e·nize (hō-mŏj′ə-nīz′, hə-) *tr.v.* **-ized, -iz·ing. 1.** To make homogeneous. **2. a.** To reduce to particles and distribute evenly throughout. **b.** To make (milk) uniform in consistency by breaking up the fat globules into particles of extremely small size. [From HOMOGENEOUS.] **—ho·mog′e·ni·za′tion** *n.* **—ho·mog′e·niz′er** *n.*

hom·o·graph (hŏm′ə-grăf′, hō′mə-) *n.* One of two or more words that have the same spelling but differ in origin, meaning, and sometimes pronunciation. **—hom′o·graph′ic** *adj.*

homoio-. Var. of **homeo-.**

hom·o·log (hŏm′ə-lôg′, -lŏg′, hō′mə-) *n.* Var. of **homologue.**

ho·mol·o·gous (hō-mŏl′ə-gəs, hə-) *adj.* **1.** Corresponding or similar in position, value, structure, or function. **2.** *Biol.* Corresponding in structure and evolutionary origin, as the flippers of a seal and the arms of a human being. **3.** *Genetics.* Having the same linear order of genes as another chromosome. **4.** *Chem.* Belonging to or being a series of organic compounds where successive members differ from preceding members by a regular increment. [Greek *homologos,* agreeing : *homo-,* same + *logos,* word, from *legein,* to speak.]

---

hom·o·logue (hŏm′ə-lôg′, -lŏg′, hō′mə-) *n.* Also **hom·o·log.** Something homologous; a homologous organ or part.

ho·mol·o·gy (hō-mŏl′ə-jē, hə-) *n., pl.* **-gies. 1.** The quality or condition of being homologous. **2.** A homologous relationship or correspondence. [Greek *homologia,* agreement, from *homologos,* homologous.]

hom·o·nym (hŏm′ə-nĭm′, hō′mə-) *n.* One of two or more words that have the same sound and often the same spelling but differ in meaning. [Latin *homōnymum,* from Greek *homōnumon : homos,* same + *onuma,* name.] —**hom′o·nym′ic** *adj.*

hom·o·phone (hŏm′ə-fōn′, hō′mə-) *n.* One of two or more words that have the same sound but differ in spelling, origin, and meaning, as English *sum* and *some.*

hom·o·phon·ic (hŏm′ə-fŏn′ĭk, hō′mə-) *adj.* **1.** Having the same sound. **2.** *Mus.* Having or characterized by a single melodic line with accompaniment. [From Greek *homo-phōnos : homos,* same + *phonē,* sound.]

ho·moph·o·ny (hō-mŏf′ə-nē, hə-) *n.* **1.** The quality or condition of being homophonic. **2.** Homophonic music.

ho·mop·ter·ous (hō-mŏp′tər-əs, hə-) *adj.* Of or belonging to the order Homoptera, which includes insects such as the cicadas, aphids, and scale insects. [HOMO- + Greek *pteron,* wing.]

Ho·mo sa·pi·ens (hō′mō sā′pē-ĕnz′, -ənz). Modern man, the only surviving species of the genus *Homo.* [Latin *homo,* man, human being + *sapiēns,* sapient, wise.]

ho·mo·sex·u·al (hō′mə-sĕk′shōō-əl, -mō-, hŏm′ə-) *adj.* Of, relating to, characteristic of, or exhibiting sexual desire for a member of the same sex. —*n.* A homosexual person. —**ho′mo·sex′u·al′i·ty** (-ăl′ĭ-tē) *n.*

ho·mun·cu·lus (hō-mŭng′kyə-ləs) *n., pl.* **-li** (-lī′). A little man; manikin. [Latin, dim. of *homō,* man, human being.]

hom·y (hō′mē) *adj.* Var. of **homey.**

hone (hōn) *n.* **1.** A fine-grained whetstone for sharpening a tool, such as a razor. **2.** A tool with a rotating abrasive tip for enlarging holes to precise dimensions. —*tr.v.* **honed, hon·ing.** To sharpen on or as if on a hone. [Middle English, from Old English *hān,* stone.]

hon·est (ŏn′ĭst) *adj.* **1.** Marked by or displaying truthfulness and integrity; upright. **2.** Not deceptive or fraudulent; genuine: *honest weight.* **3.** Conforming to fact or to the truth; not false: *honest reporting.* **4.** Frank and straightforward; sincere: *an honest opinion; an honest face.* **5.** Without disguise or pretense: *honest pleasure.* **6.** *Archaic.* Chaste; virtuous. [Middle English, from Old French *honeste,* from Latin *honestus,* honorable, from *honōs,* honor.] —**hon′est·ly** *adv.*

hon·es·ty (ŏn′ĭ-stē) *n.* **1.** The quality or state of being honest; integrity. **2.** Truthfulness; sincerity: *in all honesty.*
Syns: honesty, honor, integrity, rectitude *n.* Core meaning: The quality of truthfulness and uprightness combined with overall moral excellence (*honesty in all business dealings*).

hon·ey (hŭn′ē) *n., pl.* **-eys. 1.** A sweet, thick, syrupy substance made by bees from the nectar of flowers and used as food. **2.** Sweetness; pleasantness. **3.** *Informal.* Darling: *Hello, honey.* **4.** *Informal.* Something remarkably good: *a honey of a cat.* [Middle English *hony,* from Old English *hunig.*]

honey bear. The kinkajou.

hon·ey·bee (hŭn′ē-bē′) *n.* Any of several social bees of the genus *Apis* that produce honey, esp. *A. mellifera,* widely domesticated as a source of honey and beeswax.

hon·ey·comb (hŭn′ē-kōm′) *n.* **1.** A structure of hexagonal, thin-walled cells constructed from beeswax by honeybees to hold honey and eggs. **2.** Something that resembles a honeycomb in structure or pattern. —*tr.v.* **1.** To fill with holes; to riddle: *His story was honeycombed with lies.* **2.** To form in or cover with a honeycomb pattern.

hon·ey·dew (hŭn′ē-dōō′, -dyōō′) *n.* **1.** A sweet, sticky substance excreted by various insects, esp. aphids. **2.** Any sweet, sticky substance sometimes found on the leaves of plants. **3.** A honeydew melon.

honeydew melon. A melon with a smooth, whitish rind and green flesh.

hon·eyed (hŭn′ēd) *adj.* Also **hon·ied. 1.** Full of or sweetened with honey. **2.** Sweet as if full of honey: *honeyed words.*

hon·ey·moon (hŭn′ē-mōōn′) *n.* **1.** A vacation or trip taken by a newly married couple. **2.** The early harmonious period of any relationship. —*intr.v.* To spend a honeymoon. [HONEY + MOON (month).]

hon·ey·suck·le (hŭn′ē-sŭk′əl) *n.* **1.** Any of various shrubs or vines of the genus *Lonicera,* with tubular, often very fragrant yellowish, white, or pink flowers. **2.** Any of various similar or related plants. [Middle English *honysoukel,* from Old English *hunigsūce : hunig,* honey + *sūcan,* to suck.]

hon·ied (hŭn′ēd) *adj.* Var. of **honeyed.**

honk (hŏngk, hŏngk) *n.* **1.** The harsh cry of a goose. **2.** The harsh resonant sound esp. of an automobile horn. —*intr.v.* To make a honk. —*tr.v.* To cause to produce a honk. [Imit.] —**honk′er** *n.*

hon·ky-tonk (hŏng′kē-tôngk′, hŏng′kē-tŏngk′) *n. Slang.* A cheap, noisy saloon or dance hall. [Orig. unknown.]

hon·or (ŏn′ər) *n.* Also *Brit.* **hon·our.** —*n.* **1.** Special respect or high regard; deference. **2.** High standing among others; reputation; good name. **3.** A source or cause of credit or distinction: *was an honor to the profession.* **4.** A mark or token of special distinction: *the place of honor at the table.* **5.** An inner sense of what is right, moral, or ethical; integrity. **6.** A woman's chastity or virtue. **7.** Great privilege: *I have the honor to present the governor.* **8. Honor.** A title of address used esp. for judges: *Your Honor.* **9. honors.** Something given or done esp. as a mark of respect: *military honors.* **10. honors.** Special recognition for outstanding academic achievement: *graduate with honors.* **11. honors.** *Cards.* The four or five highest cards in a suit. —*modifier:* *an honor guard.* —*tr.v.* **1.** To treat or regard with honor and respect. **2.** To confer honor upon: *The ambassador honored us with his presence.* **3.** To accept as valid for payment: *honor a check.* **4.** To bow to in a square dance. —*idiom.* **do the honors.** To perform the social courtesies or civilities usu. of a host. [Middle English *honour,* from Old French *honor,* from Latin.] —**hon′or·er** *n.*
Syns: 1. honor, deference, homage, obeisance *n.* Core meaning: Great respect accorded as a right or as due (*a head of state who received military honors*). **2. honor, dignity, prestige, reputation, repute, status** *n.* Core meaning: A person's high standing among others (*fought the duel to defend his honor*). See also Syns at **favor** and **honesty.**

hon·or·a·ble (ŏn′ər-ə-bəl) *adj.* **1.** Worthy of honor and respect: *an honorable deed.* **2.** Bringing distinction or honor: *honorable mention.* **3.** Possessing or characterized by honor: *an honorable man.* **4.** Of great fame or distinction; illustrious. **5.** Done or attended by marks of respect and honor: *an honorable burial.* **6. Honorable.** Used as a title for a person of high rank, such as a member of the U.S. Congress. —**hon′or·a·ble·ness** *n.* —**hon′or·a·bly** *adv.*

hon·o·rar·i·um (ŏn′ə-râr′ē-əm) *n., pl.* **-ums** or **-i·a** (-ē-ə). A payment made to a professional person for services for which fees are not legally or traditionally required. [Latin *honōrārium,* from *honōrārius,* honorary.]

hon·or·ar·y (ŏn′ə-rĕr′ē) *adj.* **1.** Held or given as an honor, without fulfillment of the usual requirements. **2.** Relying upon honor; not legally enforceable. [Latin *honōrārius,* from *honōrāre,* to honor, from *honor,* honor.]

hon·or·if·ic (ŏn′ə-rĭf′ĭk) *adj.* Conferring or showing respect or honor. [Latin *honōrificus.*]

hon·our (ŏn′ər) *n. & v. Brit.* Var. of **honor.**

hooch (hōōch) *n.* Also **hootch.** *Slang.* Alcoholic liquor, esp.

honeycomb   honeysuckle

cheap or bootleg liquor. [After the *Hoochinoo* Indians of Alaska.]

hood¹ (hŏŏd) *n.* **1.** A loose, pliable covering for the head and neck, often attached to a robe or jacket. **2.** An ornamental fold of cloth hung from the shoulders of an academic or ecclesiastical robe. **3.** A covering placed over the head of a falcon. **4.** A hoodlike covering, as the hinged metal covering of an automobile engine. **5.** A crest, marking, or expandable fold on or near the head of an animal. —*tr.v.* To supply or cover with or as if with a hood. [Middle English, from Old English *hōd.*]

hood² (hŏŏd) *n. Slang.* A hoodlum; thug. [Short for HOODLUM.]

–hood. A suffix meaning: **1.** The state, condition, or quality of being: **manhood. 2.** All the members of a group of a specified nature: **neighborhood.** [Middle English *-hod(e),* from Old English *-hād.*]

hood·ed (hŏŏd′ĭd) *adj.* **1.** Covered with or having a hood. **2.** Shaped like a hood.

hood·lum (hŏŏd′ləm, hŏŏd′-) *n.* **1.** A gangster or thug. **2.** A tough, wild, destructive youth. [Orig. unknown.]

hoo·doo (hŏŏ′dŏŏ) *n.* **1.** Voodoo. **2. a.** Bad luck. **b.** A person or thing that brings bad luck. —*tr.v.* To bring bad luck to. [Perh. var. of VOODOO.] —**hoo′doo·ism** *n.*

hood·wink (hŏŏd′wĭngk′) *tr.v.* **1.** To deceive; cheat. **2.** Archaic. To blindfold.

hoo·ey (hŏŏ′ē) *n. Slang.* Nonsense. [Orig. unknown.]

hoof (hŏŏf, hŏŏf) *n., pl.* **hooves** (hŏŏvz, hŏŏvz) or **hoofs. 1.** The horny sheath covering the toes or lower part of the foot of some mammals such as the horse or deer. **2.** A hoofed foot, esp. of a horse. **3.** *Slang.* The human foot. —*intr.v. Slang.* To dance. —*idioms.* **hoof it.** To go on foot; walk. **on the hoof.** Before butchering; alive. [Middle English, from Old English *hōf.*]

hoofed (hŏŏft, hŏŏft) *adj.* Having hoofs.

hoof·er (hŏŏf′ər, hŏŏ′fər) *n. Slang.* A professional dancer, esp. a tap dancer.

hook (hŏŏk) *n.* **1.** A curved or sharply bent device, often of metal, used to catch, pull, or hold something: *a picture hook.* **2.** A fishhook. **3.** Something that resembles a hook. **4.** *Sports.* A thrown or struck ball that moves in a curve. **5.** *Boxing.* A short, swinging blow delivered with a bent arm. —*tr.v.* **1.** To catch, connect, or fasten with or as if with a hook. **2.** To make or bend into a hook. **3.** To make (a rug) by looping yarn or fabric through canvas with a hook. **4.** *Sports.* To throw or strike (a ball) with a curve. **5.** *Boxing.* To hit with a hook. **6.** *Informal.* To steal. —*intr.v.* **1.** To bend like a hook. **2.** To be fastened or secured with or as if with a hook. —*phrasal verb.* **hook up. 1.** To assemble and install: *hooked up a portable shower.* **2.** To connect to a source of power. —*idioms.* **by hook or (by) crook.** By any means possible. **hook, line, and sinker.** Completely; entirely. **off the hook.** *Slang.* Out of difficulty. **on (one's) own hook.** *Informal.* By one's own efforts. [Middle English, from Old English *hōc.*]

hoo·kah (hŏŏk′ə) *n.* A smoking pipe in which the smoke is cooled by passing through a long tube that is submerged in a container of water. [Urdu, from Arabic *huqqah.*]

hookah

hoop skirt

hook and eye. A fastener consisting of a hook and a loop or bar through which the hook is secured.

hooked (hŏŏkt) *adj.* **1.** Bent or angled like a hook. **2.** Having a hook. **3.** Made by hooking yarn: *a hooked rug.*

4. *Slang.* **a.** Addicted to a narcotic. **b.** Obsessed by or devoted to something.

hook·er (hŏŏk′ər) *n.* **1.** A single-masted fishing boat. **2.** Any old or clumsy boat. [Dutch *hoeker,* from *hoek,* hook, fishhook, from Middle Dutch *hoec.*]

hook·up (hŏŏk′ŭp′) *n.* An arrangement or connection of parts that functions as a unit, as in an electric or electronic system.

hook·worm (hŏŏk′wûrm′) *n.* **1.** Any of numerous small, parasitic nematode worms that use their hooked mouth parts to fasten themselves to the intestinal walls of various hosts, including human beings. **2.** A disease caused by hookworms, marked by weakness and anemia.

hook·y (hŏŏk′ē) *n.* —**play hooky.** *Informal.* To be absent, as from school, without permission or an acceptable excuse. [Per. from *hook,* to escape.]

hoo·li·gan (hŏŏ′lĭ-gən) *n. Informal.* A young ruffian; hoodlum. [Orig. unknown.] —**hoo′li·gan·ism** *n.*

hoop (hŏŏp, hŏŏp) *n.* **1.** A circular band used esp. to bind together the staves of a cask or barrel. **2.** Something that resembles a hoop. **3.** One of the lightweight circular supports for a hoop skirt. **4.** One of a pair of circular wooden or metal frames used to hold material taut for embroidery or similar needlework. **5.** A croquet wicket. —*tr.v.* To hold together or bind with or as if with a hoop. [Middle English, from Old English *hōp.*]

hoop·la (hŏŏp′lä′, hŏŏp′-) *n. Slang.* Great commotion or fuss. [French *houp-là,* an interjection.]

hoop skirt. A long, full, bell-shaped skirt worn over a framework of connected hoops.

hoo·ray (hŏŏ-rā′) *interj., n.,* & *v.* Var. of **hurrah.**

hoose·gow (hŏŏs′gou′) *n. Slang.* A jail. [Spanish *juzgado,* courtroom, from *juzgar,* to judge, from Latin *jūdicāre.*]

hoot (hŏŏt) *intr.v.* **1.** To utter the characteristic cry of an owl. **2.** To make a loud, raucous cry, esp. of derision or contempt. —*tr.v.* **1.** To drive off with jeering cries: *hoot a speaker off a platform.* **2.** To express or convey by hooting: *hooted their disgust.* —*n.* **1.** The characteristic cry of an owl. **2.** A cry of scorn or derision. —*idiom.* **not give a hoot.** To be completely indifferent to: *I don't give a hoot what you think.* [Middle English *h(o)uten.*]

hootch (hŏŏch) *n. Slang.* Var. of **hooch.**

hoo·te·nan·ny (hŏŏt′n-ăn′ē) *n., pl.* **-nies.** Also **hoot·nan·ny** (hŏŏt′năn′ē). An informal performance by folk singers, usu. with the audience joining in. [Orig. unknown.]

hooves (hŏŏvz, hŏŏvz) *n.* A plural of **hoof.**

hop¹ (hŏp) *v.* **hopped, hop·ping.** —*intr.v.* **1.** To move with a short skip or leap or with a springing motion. **2.** To jump on one foot. **3.** To make a quick trip, esp. in an airplane. —*tr.v.* **1.** To move over by hopping. **2.** To jump aboard: *hop a freight.* —*n.* **1.** A motion made by or as if by hopping. **2.** *Informal.* A dance. **3.** A trip, esp. by air. —*idiom.* **hop, skip, and (a) jump.** A short distance. [Middle English *hoppen,* from Old English *hoppian.*]

hop² (hŏp) *n.* **1.** A twining vine with lobed leaves and green, conelike flowers. **2. hops.** The dried, ripe flowers of this plant used as a flavoring in brewing beer. —*tr.v.* **hopped, hop·ping.** To flavor with hops. —*phrasal verb.* **hop up.** *Slang.* **1.** To increase the power or energy of. **2.** To stimulate by means of a drug. —*idiom.* **hop to it.** To move or act quickly. [Middle English *hoppe,* from Middle Dutch.]

hope (hŏp) *v.* **hoped, hop·ing.** —*intr.v.* **1.** To wish for something with expectation. **2.** *Archaic.* To have confidence; trust. —*tr.v.* To look forward to with confidence or expectation: *hoped that his daughter would carry on the tradition.* **2.** To expect and desire. —*n.* **1.** A wish or desire accompanied by some confident expectation. **2.** Something that is hoped for or desired. **3.** A person or a thing that is a source of or reason for hope: *the team's only hope for victory.* **4.** *Archaic.* Trust; confidence. —*idiom.* **hope against hope.** To hope with little reason or justification. [Middle English *hopen,* from Old English *hopian.*]

hope chest. A chest used by a young woman for clothing and household goods, such as linens and silver, collected in anticipation of marriage.

hope·ful (hŏp′fəl) *adj.* **1.** Having or manifesting hope. **2.** Inspiring hope; promising. —*n.* A person who wants to succeed or who shows promise of succeeding, esp. as a political candidate. —**hope'ful·ly** *adv.* —**hope'ful·ness** *n.*

hope·less (hōp'lĭs) *adj.* **1.** Having no hope. **2.** Offering no hope. —**hope'less·ly** *adv.* —**hope'less·ness** *n.*

hop·lite (hŏp'līt) *n.* A heavily armed foot soldier of ancient Greece. [French, from Greek *hoplitēs,* from *hoplon,* weapon.]

hop·per (hŏp'ər) *n.* **1.** Someone or something that hops. **2.** A usu. funnel-shaped container in which materials such as grain or fuel are held ready for dispensing.

hop·scotch (hŏp'skŏch') *n.* A children's game in which players toss a small object into the numbered spaces of a pattern of rectangles outlined on the ground and then hop or jump through the spaces to retrieve the object. [HOP + scotch, line.]

ho·ra (hôr'ə, hōr'ə) *n.* Also **ho·rah.** A traditional round dance of Rumania and Israel. [Hebrew *hôrāh,* from Rumanian *horă.*]

horde (hôrd, hōrd) *n.* **1.** A large group or crowd; swarm. **2.** A nomadic Mongol tribe. **3.** Any nomadic tribe or group. [Old French, from German *Horde,* from Polish *horda,* from Turkish *ordū,* camp.]

hore·hound (hôr'hound', hōr'-) *n.* Also **hoar·hound.** **1.** An aromatic plant, *Marrubium vulgare,* with whitish, downy leaves. **2.** A bitter extract from the leaves of the horehound, used as flavoring and as a cough remedy. **3.** A candy or medicine flavored with horehound extract. [Middle English *horhoune,* from Old English *hārhūne* : *hār,* grey + *hūne,* horehound.]

ho·ri·zon (hə-rī'zən) *n.* **1.** The apparent line along which the earth and sky seem to meet. **2.** The range of a person's knowledge, experience, or interest. [Middle English *orizonte,* from Old French, from Late Latin *horīzōn,* from Greek *horizōn,* from *horizein,* to divide, separate, from *horos,* boundary, limit.]

hor·i·zon·tal (hôr'ĭ-zŏn'tl, hŏr'-) *adj.* **1.** Of, relating to, or near the horizon. **2.** Parallel to or in the plane of the horizon. —*n.* Something, as a line, plane, or object, that is horizontal. [From Late Latin *horīzōn,* horizon.] —**hor'i·zon'tal·ly** *adv.*

hor·mone (hôr'mōn') *n.* A substance produced by living cells that is transported, as by blood or sap, and stimulates other cells by means of chemical action. [Greek *hormōn,* from *horman,* to urge on, from *hormē,* impulse, onrush.] —**hor·mon'al** or **hor·mon'ic** (-mōn'ĭk) *adj.*

horn (hôrn) *n.* **1.** One of the hard, usu. permanent structures projecting from the head of certain mammals, such as cattle, sheep, goats, or antelopes, consisting of a bony core covered with a sheath of keratinous material. **2.** A projecting growth similar to or suggestive of a horn. **3. a.** The hard, smooth, keratinous material that forms the outer covering of an animal horn. **b.** A natural or synthetic substance similar to horn. **4.** A container made from a horn: *a powder horn.* **5.** Something similar to a horn in shape, esp. a cornucopia. **6.** Either of the curved ends of a crescent. **7.** *Mus.* **a.** A wind instrument made of brass, esp. a French horn. **b.** *Informal.* A trumpet. **8.** A usu. electrical device that produces a sound similar to that of a horn: *a fog horn.* —*modifier:* *a horn player.* —*adj.* Made of horn. —*idioms.* **blow** (or **toot**) **(one's) own horn.** To brag or boast about oneself. **horn in.** To join without being invited. **on the horns of a dilemma.** Faced with two equally undesirable alternatives. **pull** (or **draw**) **in (one's) horns.** To act more cautiously than at a previous time. [Middle English, from Old English.]

horn·beam (hôrn'bēm') *n.* **1.** Any of various trees of the genus *Carpinus,* with smooth, grayish bark and hard, white wood. **2.** The wood of the hornbeam. [From its tough, close-grained wood.]

horn·bill (hôrn'bĭl') *n.* Any of various tropical Old World birds of the family Bucerotidae, with a large, curved bill, often with a bony projection on top.

horn·blende (hôrn'blĕnd') *n.* A common green or bluish-green to black mineral formed in the late stages of cooling in igneous rock. [German *Hornblende* : *Horn,* horn + *Blende,* a shiny mineral, from *blenden,* to blind.]

horn·book (hôrn'bŏŏk') *n.* **1.** An early primer consisting of a single page protected by a transparent sheet of horn, formerly used in teaching children to read. **2.** A text that instructs in the basic skills or rudiments of a subject.

horned (hôrnd) *adj.* Having a horn.

horned owl. An owl with hornlike ear tufts.

horned toad. A lizard of the genus *Phrynosoma,* of western North America and Central America, with hornlike projections on the head, a flattened, spiny body, and a short tail.

hor·net (hôr'nĭt) *n.* Any of various large social wasps, chiefly of the genera *Vespa* and *Vespula,* that usu. build a large papery nest. [Middle English *hernet,* from Old English *hyrnet.*]

horn of plenty. A cornucopia.

horn·pipe (hôrn'pīp') *n.* **1.** An obsolete musical instrument with a single reed, finger holes, and a bell and mouthpiece made of horn. **2.** A lively British folk dance orig. accompanied by a hornpipe. **3.** The music for a hornpipe.

horn·pout (hôrn'pout') *n.* A freshwater catfish, *Ictalurus nebulosus* (or *Americus nebulosus*), native to eastern North America.

horn·worm (hôrn'wûrm') *n.* The larva of the hawk moth, with a hornlike posterior segment.

horn·y (hôr'nē) *adj.* **-i·er, -i·est. 1.** Made of horn or a similar substance. **2.** Having horns or hornlike projections. **3.** Tough and calloused: *horny skin.*

hor·o·loge (hôr'ə-lōj', hōr'-) *n.* An instrument that tells the time; timepiece. [Middle English *horologe,* from Old French *orloge,* from Latin *hōrologium,* from Greek *hōrologion* : *hōra,* hour + *-logos,* teller.]

ho·rol·o·ger (hə-rŏl'ə-jər) *n.* Also **ho·rol·o·gist** (-jĭst.) One who practices or is skilled in horology.

ho·rol·o·gy (hə-rŏl'ə-jē) *n.* **1.** The science of measuring time. **2.** The art of making timepieces. [Middle English *horologie,* from Latin *hōrologium,* horologe.]

hor·o·scope (hôr'ə-skōp', hōr'-) *n. Astrol.* **1.** A diagram that shows the position of the planets in relation to the twelve signs of the zodiac at a particular time, such as the moment of a person's birth. **2.** A forecast, as of a person's future, based on a horoscope. [Old French, from Latin *hōroscopus,* from Greek *hōroskopos,* astrologer : *hōra,* hour + *skopos,* observer.]

hor·ren·dous (hô-rĕn'dəs, hŏ-) *adj.* Hideous; dreadful. [From Latin *horrendus,* from *horrēre,* to tremble.] —**hor·ren'dous·ly** *adv.*

hor·ri·ble (hôr'ə-bəl, hŏr'-) *adj.* **1.** Arousing or tending to arouse horror; dreadful. **2.** Very unpleasant; disagreeable. —See Syns at **ghastly.** [Middle English, from Old French, from Latin *horribilis,* from *horrēre,* to tremble.] —**hor·ri·ble·ness** *n.* —**hor'ri·bly** *adv.*

hor·rid (hôr'ĭd, hŏr'-) *adj.* **1.** Causing horror; dreadful. **2.** Extremely disagreeable; offensive. —See Syns at **ghastly.** [Latin *horridus,* from *horrēre,* to tremble.] —**hor'rid·ly** *adv.* —**hor'rid·ness** *n.*

hor·rif·ic (hô-rĭf'ĭk, hŏ-) *adj.* Causing horror; terrifying. [Old French *horrifique,* from Latin *horrificus.*]

hor·ri·fy (hôr'ə-fī', hŏr'-) *tr.v.* **-fied, -fy·ing. 1.** To cause to feel horror. **2.** To cause unpleasant surprise; to shock. [Latin *horrificāre,* from *horrificus* horrific.]

hor·ror (hôr'ər, hŏr'-) *n.* **1.** An intense and painful feeling of repugnance and fear. **2.** Intense dislike; abhorrence. **3.** A person or a thing that causes horror. **4.** *Informal.* Something unpleasant, ugly, or disagreeable: *That hat is a horror.* **5. horrors.** *Slang.* Intense nervous depression or anxiety: *a bad case of the horrors.* [Middle English *(h)or-*

hornbill
George Miksch Sutton

hornet

ă pat ā pay â care ä father ĕ pet ē be hw which ĭ pit ī tie î pier ŏ pot ō toe ô paw, for oi noise
ŏŏ took ōŏ boot ou out th thin *th* this ŭ cut û urge zh vision ə about, item, edible, gallop, circus

rour, from Old French, from Latin *horror*, from *horrēre*, to tremble, bristle, be in horror.]

hors de com·bat (ôr′ də kôN-bä′). *French.* Out of action; disabled.

hors d'oeuvre (ôr dûrv′) *pl.* **hors d'oeuvres** (ôr dûrvz′) or **hors d'oeuvre.** An appetizer served before a meal. [French, side dish, "outside of the work."]

horse (hôrs) *n.* **1.** A large four-legged hoofed mammal, *Equus caballus*, domesticated since prehistoric times and used for riding and for drawing or carrying loads. **2.** An adult male horse; stallion. **3.** Mounted soldiers; cavalry: *a squadron of horse.* **4.** A frame, usu. with four legs, for supporting or holding. **5.** A piece of gymnastic equipment with an upholstered body used esp. for vaulting. **6.** *Slang.* Heroin. —*tr.v.* **horsed, hors·ing.** To provide with a horse. —*phrasal verb.* **horse around.** To indulge in horseplay. —*idioms.* **a horse of another** (or **a different**) **color.** Something else. **be** (or **get**) **on** (one's) **high horse.** To be or become disdainful, superior, or conceited. **hold** (one's) **horses.** To restrain oneself. **the horse's mouth.** The original source. [Middle English *hors*, from Old English.]

horse   horse chestnut

horse·back (hôrs′băk′) *n.* **1.** The back of a horse. **2.** A natural ridge; a hogback. —*modifier: horseback riding.* —*adv.* On the back of a horse.

horse·car (hôrs′kär′) *n.* **1.** A streetcar drawn by horses. **2.** A car for transporting horses.

horse chestnut. 1. Any of several trees of the genus *Aesculus*, esp. *A. hippocastanum*, with palmate leaves, erect clusters of white flowers tinged with red, and brown, shiny nuts enclosed in a spiny bur. **2.** The nut of the horse chestnut.

horse·flesh (hôrs′flĕsh′) *n.* **1.** The flesh of a horse. **2.** Horses collectively, esp. for driving, riding, or racing.

horse·fly (hôrs′flī′) *n.* Also **horse fly.** Any of numerous large flies of the family Tabanidae, the females of which suck the blood of various mammals.

horse·hair (hôrs′hâr′) *n.* **1.** The hair of a horse, esp. from the mane or tail. **2.** Cloth made of horsehair. —*modifier: a horsehair sofa.*

horse·hide (hôrs′hīd′) *n.* **1.** The hide of a horse. **2.** Leather made from the hide of a horse.

horse latitudes. Either of two regions located over the oceans at about 30 degrees north and south latitudes, marked by high barometric pressure, calms, and light, changeable winds.

horse·less carriage (hôrs′lĭs). An automobile.

horse·man (hôrs′mən) *n.* **1.** A man who rides a horse. **2.** A person skilled at horsemanship.

horse·man·ship (hôrs′mən-shĭp′) *n.* The art of horseback riding.

horse opera. A movie or play about the U.S. West.

horse·play (hôrs′plā′) *n.* Rowdy, rough play.

horse·pow·er (hôrs′pou′ər) *n.* A unit of power equal to 745.7 watts, or 33,000 foot-pounds per minute.

horse·rad·ish (hôrs′răd′ĭsh) *n.* **1.** A coarse plant, *Armoracia rusticana* (or *A. lapathifolia*), with a thick, whitish, pungent root. **2.** The shredded or grated root of the horseradish, often used as a condiment.

horse sense. *Informal.* Common sense.

horse·shoe (hôrs′shoo′, hôrsh′-) *n.* **1.** A narrow U-shaped iron plate fitted and nailed to the outer rim of a horse's

hoof. **2.** Something shaped like a horseshoe. **3. horseshoes** (used with a *sing. verb*). A game in which players try to toss horseshoes so that they encircle a stake. —*tr.v.* **-shoed, -shoe·ing.** To shoe (a horse).

horseshoe crab. Any of various North American saltwater arthropods of the class Merostomata, esp. *Limulus polyphemus* (or *Xiphosura polyphemus*), with a large, rounded body and a stiff, pointed tail.

horse·tail (hôrs′tāl′) *n.* Any of various nonflowering plants of the genus *Equisetum*, with a jointed, hollow stem and narrow, sheathlike leaves.

horse trade. A transaction characterized by shrewd and vigorous bargaining.

horse·whip (hôrs′hwĭp′, -wĭp′) *n.* A whip used to control a horse. —*tr.v.* **-whipped, -whip·ping.** To beat with or as if with a horsewhip.

horse·wom·an (hôrs′wŏom′ən) *n.* **1.** A woman who rides a horse. **2.** A woman skilled at horsemanship.

hors·ey (hôr′sē) *adj.* Var. of **horsy.**

horst (hôrst) *n.* *Geol.* A block of the earth's crust that lies between two faults and is higher than the surrounding land. [German *Horst*, from Old High German *hurst*, thicket.]

hors·y (hôr′sē) *adj.* **-i·er, -i·est.** Also **hors·ey. 1.** Of, pertaining to, or characteristic of a horse. **2.** Devoted to horses or horsemanship. **3.** Large and clumsy.

hor·ta·tive (hôr′tə-tĭv′) *adj.* Hortatory. [Late Latin *hortātīvus*, from Latin *hortātus*, past part. of *hortārī*, to exhort.] —**hor·ta·tive·ly** *adv.*

hor·ta·to·ry (hôr′tə-tôr′ē, -tōr′ē) *adj.* Marked by or given to exhortation or strong urging. [Late Latin *hortātōrius*, from *hortātus*, exhortation.]

hor·ti·cul·ture (hôr′tĭ-kŭl′chər) *n.* **1.** The science or art of cultivating fruits, vegetables, and flowers. **2.** The cultivation of a garden. [Latin *hortus*, garden + (AGRI)CULTURE.] —**hor·ti·cul·tur·al** *adj.* —**hor·ti·cul·tur·ist** *n.*

Ho·rus (hôr′əs, hōr′-) *n.* The ancient Egyptian god of the sun, represented as having the head of a hawk.

ho·san·na (hō-zăn′ə) *interj.* A word used to express praise or adoration to God. —*n.* A cry of "hosanna." [Middle English *osanna*, from Late Latin *(h)ōsanna*, from Greek, from Hebrew *hoshaʻnā*, "save us."]

hose (hōz) *n.* **1.** *pl.* **hose.** Stockings or socks. **2.** *pl.* **hose a.** A man's garment that covers the legs and hips and fastens to a doublet by points. **b.** Short full breeches reaching to the knees. **3.** *pl.* **hos·es.** A flexible tube for conveying fluids. —*tr.v.* **hosed, hos·ing.** To water, drench, or wash with a hose. [Middle English *hose*, a stocking, from Old English *hosa*, leg covering.]

ho·sier (hō′zhər) *n.* A maker of or dealer in hosiery. [Middle English *hosyer*, from *hose*, hose.]

ho·sier·y (hō′zhə-rē) *n.* **1. a.** Stockings and socks; hose. **b.** *Brit.* Stockings, socks, and underclothing. **2.** The business of a hosier.

hos·pice (hŏs′pĭs) *n.* A shelter or lodging for travelers, often maintained by monks. [French, from Old French, from Latin *hospitium*, hospitality, from *hospes*, host, guest.]

hos·pi·ta·ble (hŏs′pĭ-tə-bəl, hŏ-spĭt′ə-bəl) *adj.* **1.** Cordial and generous to guests. **2.** Having an open mind; receptive. [From Latin *hospitārī*, to be hospitable to, from *hospes*, host, guest.] —**hos·pi·ta·bly** *adv.*

hos·pi·tal (hŏs′pĭ-təl, -pĭt′l) *n.* **1.** An institution that provides medical or surgical care and treatment for the sick and the injured. **2.** A repair shop for specified items: *a doll hospital.* [Middle English, hospice, from Old French, from Medieval Latin *hospitāle*, from Latin *hospitālis*, of a guest, from *hospes*, host, guest.]

hos·pi·tal·i·ty (hŏs′pĭ-tăl′ĭ-tē) *n., pl.* **-ties. 1.** Cordial and generous reception of guests. **2.** An example of being hospitable. [Middle English *hospitalite*, from Old French, from Latin *hospitālitās*, from *hospitālis*, of a guest.]

hos·pi·tal·i·za·tion (hŏs′pĭ-tə-lĭ-zā′shən, -lī-) *n.* **1.** The state or act of being hospitalized. **2.** The length of time a patient is hospitalized.

hos·pi·tal·ize (hŏs′pĭ-tə-līz′) *tr.v.* **-ized, -iz·ing.** To put into a hospital for treatment.

host¹ (hōst) *n.* **1.** One who entertains guests in a social or business capacity. **2.** *Biol.* An organism that harbors and provides nourishment for a parasite. —*tr.v.* To serve as host for. [Middle English *(h)oste,* from Old French, host, guest, from Latin *hospes,* guest, host, stranger.]

host² (hōst) *n.* **1.** An army. **2.** A great number. [Middle English, from Old French, from Late Latin *hostis,* from Latin, stranger, enemy.]

host³ (hōst) *n.* Also **Host.** *Eccles.* The consecrated bread or wafer of the Eucharist. [Middle English *oste,* from Old French *oiste,* from Latin *hostia,* sacrifice, victim.]

hos·tage (hŏs′tĭj) *n.* A person held as a pledge that certain terms will be fulfilled. [Middle English, from Old French, from Late Latin *obsidātus,* the state of being a hostage, from Latin *obses,* a hostage.]

hos·tel (hŏs′təl) *n.* **1.** A supervised, inexpensive lodging, esp. for youthful travelers. **2.** An inn. [Middle English, from Old French, from Medieval Latin *hospitāle,* hospice.]

hos·tel·ry (hŏs′təl-rē) *n., pl.* **-ries.** An inn; hotel.

host·ess (hōs′tĭs) *n.* **1.** A woman who acts as a host. **2.** A woman whose occupation is to greet and serve patrons, as in a restaurant or on an airplane.

hos·tile (hŏs′təl, -tīl′) *adj.* **1.** Of or pertaining to an enemy. **2.** Feeling or showing enmity; antagonistic. **3.** Not hospitable. —See Syns at **unfriendly.** [Old French, from Latin *hostīlis,* from *hostis,* stranger, enemy.] —**hos′tile·ly** *adv.*

hos·til·i·ty (hŏ-stĭl′ĭ-tē) *n., pl.* **-ties. 1.** The state of being hostile; antagonism; enmity. **2. a.** A hostile act. **b. hostilities.** Open warfare. —See Syns at **conflict.**

hos·tler (hŏs′lər) *n.* Also **os·tler** (ŏs′lər). A person who takes charge of horses, as at an inn; a stableman. [Middle English, from Old French *hostelier,* from *hostel,* hostel.]

hot (hŏt) *adj.* **hot·ter, hot·test. 1.** Having or giving off great heat. **2.** Higher in temperature than is normal or desirable. **3.** Highly spiced: *hot mustard.* **4. a.** Charged or energized with electricity: *a hot wire.* **b.** Radioactive, esp. to a dangerous degree. **5. a.** Marked by intensity or warmth of emotion; fiery: *a hot temper.* **b.** Having or displaying desire or enthusiasm. **c.** Arousing excited interest and attention: *a hot issue.* **6.** *Slang.* Arousing or experiencing sexual excitement. **7.** *Slang.* **a.** Obtained by stealing: *hot goods.* **b.** Wanted by the police. **8.** Close to a successful solution or conclusion: *hot on the trail.* **9.** *Informal.* **a.** New; fresh: *hot off the press.* **b.** Extremely popular: *a hot sales item.* **10.** *Slang.* Very good or impressive. **11.** *Slang.* **a.** Possessing or showing unusual skill. **b.** Unusually lucky. **12.** *Mus.* Marked by strong rhythms and improvisation: *hot jazz.* —**idioms. hot under the collar.** *Informal.* Angry. **in hot water.** *Informal.* In trouble. **make it hot for.** *Informal.* To make things uncomfortable or dangerous for. [Middle English, from Old English *hāt.*]
　　Syns: hot, blistering, fiery, red-hot, sultry, torrid *adj.* Core meaning: Marked by much heat *(a hot summer sun).*

hot air. *Slang.* Empty, often boastful talk.

hot·bed (hŏt′bĕd′) *n.* **1.** A glass-covered bed of soil heated with fermenting manure or by electricity, used for the germination of seeds or for protecting tender plants. **2.** An environment conducive to rapid growth and development, esp. of something bad: *a hotbed of intrigue.*

hot-blood·ed (hŏt′blŭd′ĭd) *adj.* Easily excited or aroused. —**hot′-blood′ed·ness** *n.*

hot cake. A pancake. —**idiom. sell** (or **go**) **like hot cakes.** To be in great demand.

hotch·potch (hŏch′pŏch′) *n.* A hodgepodge. [Var. of *hotchpot,* from Middle English, from Old French *hochepot,* stew : *hocher,* to shake + *pot,* pot.]

hot cross bun. A sweet bun often made with dried fruit and marked on top with a cross, traditionally eaten during Lent.

hot dog. A frankfurter, usu. served in a long soft roll. —**modifier** (hot-dog): *a hot-dog stand.*

ho·tel (hō-tĕl′) *n.* A public house that provides lodging and usu. meals and other services. [French *hôtel,* from Old French *hostel,* hostel.]

hot·foot (hŏt′fŏŏt′) *intr.v.* To go in haste: *hotfoot it out of town.* —*adv.* In haste. —*n., pl.* **-foots.** A trick or joke in which a match is stealthily inserted into the side of someone's shoe and lit.

hot·head (hŏt′hĕd′) *n.* A hotheaded person.

hot·head·ed (hŏt′hĕd′ĭd) *adj.* **1.** Easily angered or excited.

2. Impetuous; rash. —**hot′head′ed·ly** *adv.* —**hot′head′ed·ness** *n.*

hot·house (hŏt′hous′) *n.* A greenhouse. —**modifier:** *hothouse grapes.*

hot line. A communications line for use in a crisis or emergency.

hot pepper. The pungent fruit of any of several varieties of *Capsicum frutescens.*

hot plate. A portable apparatus or device for cooking or warming food.

hot rod. Also **hot·rod** (hŏt′rŏd′) or **hot-rod.** *Slang.* An automobile rebuilt or modified for increased speed and power. —**hot rodder.**

hot·shot (hŏt′shŏt′) *n.* *Slang.* An ostentatiously skillful person.

hot spring. A natural spring of water that is hotter than 37°C or 98°F.

hot toddy. A toddy.

hou·dah (hou′də) *n.* Var. of **howdah.**

hound (hound) *n.* **1.** A dog of any of various breeds used for hunting, characteristically having drooping ears, a short coat, and a deep, resonant voice. **2.** Any dog. **3.** A contemptible person; scoundrel. **4.** An enthusiast or addict: *a coffee hound.* —*tr.v.* **1.** To pursue relentlessly and tenaciously. **2.** To urge insistently; nag. [Middle English, from Old English *hund.*]

hour (our) *n.* **1.** One of the 24 parts of a day. **2. a.** The time of day determined on a 12-hour basis. **b. hours.** The time of day determined on a 24-hour basis: *1700 hours.* **3. a.** A customary time: *the dinner hour.* **b. hours.** A specified time: *bank hours.* **4. a.** The work that can be accomplished in an hour. **b.** The distance that can be traveled in an hour. **5. hours. a.** Times set for daily liturgical devotion. **b.** The prayers for such times. [Middle English, from Old French *hore,* from Latin *hōra,* from Greek, time, season.]

hour·glass (our′glăs′) *n.* An instrument for measuring time that consists of two glass chambers connected by a narrow channel through which a quantity of sand or mercury trickles from the upper chamber to the lower in exactly one hour.

hour·ly (our′lē) *adj.* **1. a.** Every hour. **b.** Frequent; continual. **2.** By the hour as a unit: *hourly pay.* —*adv.* **1.** At or during every hour. **2.** Frequently; continually.

house (hous) *n., pl.* **hous·es** (hou′zĭz). **1. a.** A building used as a dwelling by one or more families. **b.** A household. **2.** Something that serves as a shelter or habitation for an animal. **3. a.** A building used for a particular purpose, as for entertainment: *a movie house.* **b.** The audience or patrons of such an establishment: *a full house.* **4.** A dwelling for a religious community or for students. **5.** Often **House.** A noble family: *the House of Orange.* **6.** A commercial firm: *a brokerage house.* **7. a.** A legislative or deliberative assembly. **b.** The hall where such an assembly meets. **8.** *Astrol.* **a.** One of the 12 parts into which the heavens are divided. **b.** The sign of the zodiac indicating the seat or station of a planet in the heavens. —**modifier:** *house guests.* —*v.* (houz) **housed, hous·ing.** —*tr.v.* **1.** To provide living quarters for; lodge: *The cottage housed ten boys.* **2.** To shelter, keep, or store in or as if in a house. **3.** To contain; to harbor. —*intr.v* To reside; dwell. —**idioms. bring down the house.** *Informal.* To receive enthusiastic applause from an audience. **clean house. 1.** To take care of and clean a house. **2.** To eliminate or discard undesirable people, items, or situations. **keep house.** To clean and manage a house. **on the house.** As a gift from the management; free. [Middle English, from Old English *hūs.*]

house·boat (hous′bōt′) *n.* A barge equipped for use as a home or cruiser.

house·break·ing (hous′brā′kĭng) *n.* The act of unlawfully breaking into another's house for the purpose of committing a felony. —**house′break′er** *n.*

house·bro·ken (hous′brō′kən) *adj.* Trained in habits of excretion appropriate for a house pet.

house·coat (hous′kōt′) *n.* A woman's robe usu. with a long skirt, worn at home.

house·fly (hous′flī′) *n.* A common, widely distributed fly, *Musca domestica,* that frequents human dwellings, breeds in moist or decaying organic matter, and is a transmitter of a wide variety of diseases.

house·hold (hous′hōld′) *n.* The members of a family and others who live under the same roof. —*modifier:* household appliances. [Middle English household : hous, house + hold, possession, property, from Old English heald, from healdan, to hold.]

house·hold·er (hous′hōl′dər) *n.* **1.** A person who occupies or owns a house. **2.** The head of a household.

house·keep·er (hous′kē′pər) *n.* One hired to perform the domestic tasks in a household. —**house′keep′ing** *n.*

house·maid (hous′mād′) *n.* A woman employed to do housework.

housemaid's knee. A chronic inflammatory swelling of the bursa in front of the kneecap.

house·moth·er (hous′mŭth′ər) *n.* A woman employed as supervisor or housekeeper of a residence hall or dormitory for young people.

House of Commons. The lower house of Parliament in the United Kingdom and in Canada.

house of correction. An institution for persons convicted of minor criminal offenses.

House of Lords. The upper house of Parliament in the United Kingdom, made up of members of the nobility and high-ranking clergy.

House of Representatives. The lower branch of the U.S. Congress and of most state legislatures.

house organ. A periodical published by a business organization for its employees or clients.

house physician. A resident physician, as in a hospital.

house·rais·ing (hous′rā′zĭng) *n.* The construction of a house or its framework by a group of neighbors.

house sparrow. A small bird, *Passer domesticus*, with brown and gray plumage and a black throat in the male. Also called **English sparrow.**

house·top (hous′tŏp′) *n.* The roof.

house·warm·ing (hous′wôr′mĭng) *n.* A party to celebrate the occupancy of a new home.

house·wife (hous′wīf′) *n.* **1.** A married woman who supervises the affairs of a household. **2.** A small container for sewing equipment.

house·wife·ly (hous′wīf′lē) *adj.* Of, pertaining to, or suited to a housewife; domestic. —**house′wife·li·ness** *n.*

house·wif·er·y (hous′wī′fə-rē, -wīf′rē) *n.* The function or duties of a housewife; housekeeping.

house·work (hous′wûrk′) *n.* The tasks of housekeeping, as cleaning or cooking. —**house′work′er** *n.*

hous·ing¹ (hou′zĭng) *n.* **1.** Residences or dwelling places for people. **2.** A place to live; a dwelling. **3. a.** Something that covers, protects, or supports. **b.** A frame, bracket, or box for holding or protecting a mechanical part: *a wheel housing.* **4.** A hole, groove, or slot in a piece of wood for the insertion of another piece. **5.** The part of a mast that is below deck or of a bowsprit that is inside the hull.

hous·ing² (hou′zĭng) *n.* **1.** An ornamental or protective covering for a horse. **2.** Often **housings.** Trappings. [Middle English, from house, covering, from Old French houce, from Medieval Latin hultia.]

hove (hōv) *v. Naut.* Past tense and past participle of **heave.** [Middle English, from Old English hóf.]

hov·el (hŭv′əl, hŏv′-) *n.* **1.** A small, miserable dwelling. **2.** An open, low shed. [Middle English.]

hov·er (hŭv′ər, hŏv′-) *intr.v.* **1.** To remain floating or suspended in the air over a particular place: *gulls hovering over the waves.* **2.** To remain or linger in or near a place. **3.** To be in a state of uncertainty; waver: *hover between skepticism and belief.* —*n.* An act or example of hovering. [Middle English hoveren, freq. of hoven, to linger.] —**hov′er·er** *n.* —**hov′er·ing·ly** *adv.*

how (hou) *adv.* **1.** In what manner or way; by what means: *How does this machine work?* **2.** In what state or condition: *How do I look in this jacket?* **3.** To what extent, amount, or degree: *How do you like that?* **4.** For what reason or purpose; why: *How did he happen to buy such an expensive car?* **5.** With what meaning: *How should I interpret this?* **6.** By what name: *How is he called?* **7.** What: *How is that again?* —*conj.* **1.** In what way or manner: *forgot how it was accomplished.* **2.** That: *told them how he had a wife and family to support.* **3.** In whatever way or manner: *did it how he liked.* —*n.* A manner or method of doing or performing: *learn the how of a procedure.* —**idioms. how about.** What do you feel or think about: *How about a cup of tea?* **how come.** *Informal.* For what reason; why: *How come you're so late?* [Middle English, from Old English hū.]

how·be·it (hou-bē′ĭt) *adv. Archaic.* Be that as it may; nevertheless. —*conj. Archaic.* Although.

how·dah (hou′də) *n.* Also **hou·dah.** A seat, usu. fitted with a canopy and railing, placed on the back of an elephant or camel. [Urdu, from Persian haudah, from Arabic haudaj, burden carried by a camel or elephant.]

howdah   howitzer

how·dy (hou′dē) *interj. Informal.* A word used to express greeting. [Short for how-de-do.]

how·e'er (hou-âr′). *Poet.* However.

how·ev·er (hou-ev′ər) *adv.* **1.** By whatever manner or means: *However he did it, it was very clever.* **2.** To whatever degree or extent: *always finished the job, however tired she was.* —*conj.* Nevertheless; yet: *The tickets are expensive; however, we will go.*

Usage: **however.** Avoid using *but* just before *however* when the conjunction means nevertheless, for such usage is redundant: *The votes are in; however* (not *but however*), *they have not yet been counted.*

how·it·zer (hou′ĭt-sər) *n.* A short cannon that delivers shells with medium velocities, usu. at a high trajectory. [Dutch houwitser, from German Haubitze, from Czech houfnice, catapult.]

howl (houl) *intr.v.* **1.** To utter or emit a long, mournful, plaintive sound. **2.** To cry or wail loudly, as in pain, sorrow, or anger. **3.** *Slang.* To laugh heartily. —*tr.v.* To express or utter with a howl. —*phrasal verb.* **howl down.** To suppress or drive away by or as if by howling. —*n.* **1.** A long, wailing cry. **2.** *Slang.* Something uproariously funny or absurd. [Middle English houlen.]

howl·er (hou′lər) *n.* **1.** Someone or something that howls. **2.** *Informal.* An amusing or stupid blunder.

how·so·ev·er (hou′sō-ev′ər) *adv.* **1.** To whatever degree or extent. **2.** By whatever means.

hoy·den (hoid′n) *n.* A high-spirited, often boisterous girl or woman. —*adj.* High-spirited; boisterous. [Orig. unknown.]

hua·ra·che (wə-rä′chē, hŏŏ-rä′-) *n.* Also **hua·ra·cho** (-chō). A flat-heeled sandal with an upper of woven leather strips. [Mexican Spanish.]

hub (hŭb) *n.* **1.** The center portion of a wheel, fan, or propeller. **2.** A center of activity or interest; focal point. [Prob. var. of HOB (a projection).]

hub·bub (hŭb′ŭb) *n.* **1.** A confused babble of loud sounds and voices; uproar. **2.** Confusion; tumult. [Perh. of Irish orig.]

hu·bris (hyōō′brĭs) *n.* Excessive pride; arrogance. [Greek, insolence, outrage.]

huck·a·back (hŭk′ə-băk′) *n.* A coarse absorbent cotton or linen fabric used esp. for toweling. Also called **huck.** [Orig. unknown.]

huck·le·ber·ry (hŭk′əl-bĕr′ē) *n.* **1.** Any of various fruit-bearing shrubs of the genus *Gaylussacia*, related to the blueberries. **2.** The glossy, blackish, many-seeded berry of the huckleberry bush. [Perh. var. of dial. hurtleberry, huckleberry.]

huck·ster (hŭk′stər) *n.* **1.** A person who sells wares in the street; peddler; hawker. **2.** *Slang.* A writer of advertising copy, as for radio or television. —*tr.v.* To sell; peddle. [Middle English *huccstere.*]

hud·dle (hŭd'l) *n.* **1.** A densely packed group or crowd. **2.** *Football.* A brief gathering of a team's players behind the line of scrimmage to prepare for the next play. **3.** A small private conference. —*v.* **-dled, -dling.** —*intr.v.* **1.** To crowd together. **2.** To draw oneself together; curl up. **3.** To gather in a huddle. **4.** To gather for conference or consultation. —*tr.v.* **1.** To crowd together. **2.** To draw (oneself) together; crouch. [Orig. unknown.]

hue (hyōō) *n.* **1.** The property of color that is perceived and measured on a scale ranging from red through yellow, green, and blue to violet. **2.** A particular color as distinct from other colors; tint; shade. **3.** Color: *all the hues of the rainbow.* **4.** Appearance; aspect. [Middle English *hewe,* complexion, appearance, from Old English *hēo, hīw,* appearance, form, color.]

hue and cry. 1. The loud shout formerly used to announce the pursuit of a felon. **2.** Any public clamor, as of protest or demand: *raised a great hue and cry about political corruption.* [Anglo-Norman *hu e cri* : *hu,* noise, from Old French *hue* + *cri,* shout, from Old French *cri.*]

huff (hŭf) *n.* A fit of anger or annoyance; pique. —*intr.v.* To puff; blow. [Imit.]

huff·y (hŭf'ē) *adj.* **-i·er, -i·est. 1.** Easily offended; touchy. **2.** Irritated or annoyed; indignant. **3.** Arrogant; disdainful; haughty. —**huff'i·ly** *adv.* —**huff'i·ness** *n.*

hug (hŭg) *tr.v.* **hugged, hug·ging. 1.** To clasp or hold closely; embrace. **2.** To hold steadfastly to; cherish. **3.** To keep, remain, or be situated close to: *a footpath that hugged the slope.* —*n.* An affectionate clasp or embrace. [Orig. unknown.] —**hug'ger** *n.*

huge (hyōōj) *adj.* **hug·er, hug·est.** Of exceedingly great size, extent, or quantity; tremendous. —See Syns at **giant.** [Middle English, from Old French *ahuge.*] —**huge'ly** *adv.* —**huge'ness** *n.*

hug·ger-mug·ger or **hug·ger-mug·ger** (hŭg'ər-mŭg'ər) *n.* Disorderly confusion; muddle. [Orig. unknown.]

Hu·gue·not (hyōō'gə-nŏt') *n.* A French Protestant of the 16th and 17th cent. [French *huguenot,* alteration (influenced by gate of Roi-*Hugon,* where the Protestants of Tours assembled at night) of dial. French *eyguenot,* from dial. German *Eidgenosse(n),* confederate(s).]

huh (hŭ) *interj.* Used to express interrogation, surprise, contempt, or indifference.

hu·la (hōō'lə) *n.* Also **hu·la-hu·la** (hōō'lə-hōō'lə). A Polynesian dance characterized by rhythmic movements of the hips, arms, and hands and often accompanied by rhythmic drumbeats and chants. [Hawaiian.]

hulk (hŭlk) *n.* **1.** A heavy, unwieldy ship. **2. a.** An old, unseaworthy ship that has been wrecked or abandoned. **b.** An old or unseaworthy ship used as a prison or warehouse. **3.** A person or thing that is bulky, clumsy, or awkward. —*intr.v.* To appear or seem impressively or exaggeratedly large; loom. [Middle English *hulke,* from Old English *hulc,* ship, from Medieval Latin *hulcus,* from Greek *holkas,* merchant vessel, from *helkein,* to pull, tow.]

hulk·ing (hŭl'kĭng) *adj.* Also **hulk·y** (hŭl'kē). Unwieldy or bulky; massive.

hull (hŭl) *n.* **1. a.** The usu. green calyx at the base of a fruit such as the strawberry. **b.** The dry outer covering of certain fruits, seeds, or nuts; husk. **2.** *Naut.* The frame or body of a ship, exclusive of masts, sails, yards, and rigging. **3.** *Aviation.* The central body of a flying boat. **4.** *Aerospace.* The outer casing of a rocket, guided missile, or spaceship. —*tr.v.* To remove the hull from. [Middle English, husk, from Old English *hulu.*]

hul·la·ba·loo (hŭl'ə-bə-lōō') *n.* Also **hul·la·bal·loo.** Great noise or excitement; uproar. [Perh. from the interjection HULLO.]

hul·lo (hə-lō') *interj., n. & v.* Var. of **hello.**

hum (hŭm) *v.* **hummed, hum·ming.** —*intr.v.* **1. a.** To make or emit a continuous low droning sound like that of the speech sound (m) when prolonged. **b.** To emit the continuous droning sound of an insect on the wing. **2.** To be in a state of busy activity. **3.** To sing a tune without opening the lips or articulating words. —*tr.v.* To sing without opening the lips or articulating words. —*n.* The act or sound of humming. —*interj.* Used to indicate hesitation,

surprise, or displeasure. [Middle English *hummen.*] —**hum'mer** *n.*

hu·man (hyōō'mən) *adj.* **1.** Of, relating to, or characteristic of human beings: *human nature; the human voice.* **2.** Made up of people: *formed a human bridge.* —*n.* A human being; a person. [Middle English *humain,* from Old French, from Latin *hūmānus.*] —**hu'man·ness** *n.*

  Syns: human, humane, humanitarian *adj.* Core meaning: Concerned with the welfare of people and the easing of suffering *(the alleviation of poverty—a human concern).* HUMAN is essentially a classifying term relating to individuals or people collectively *(human kindness),* while HUMANE stresses the qualities of kindness and compassion *(humane treatment).* HUMANITARIAN applies to what actively promotes the needs and welfare of people *(humanitarian considerations in the treatment of prisoners).*

human being. A primate mammal of the species *Homo sapiens,* characterized by an upright posture on two feet, a highly developed brain, and the capacity for speech.

hu·mane (hyōō-mān') *adj.* **1.** Characterized by kindness, mercy, or compassion: *a humane judge.* **2.** Marked by an emphasis on humanistic values and concerns: *a humane education.* —See Syns at **human.** [Middle English *humaine,* human.] —**hu·mane'ly** *adv.* —**hu·mane'ness** *n.*

hu·man·ism (hyōō'mə-nĭz'əm) *n.* **1.** A doctrine or attitude that is concerned primarily with human beings and their values, capacities, and achievements. **2.** Often **Humanism.** A cultural and intellectual movement of the Renaissance that emphasized secular concerns as a result of the study of the literature, art, and civilization of ancient Greece and Rome. —**hu'man·ist** *n. & adj.* —**hu'man·is'tic** *adj.* —**hu'man·is'ti·cal·ly** *adv.*

hu·man·i·tar·i·an (hyōō-măn'ĭ-târ'ē-ən) *n.* A person devoted to the promotion of human welfare and the advancement of social reforms; a philanthropist. —**hu·man'i·tar'i·an** *adj.* —**hu·man'i·tar'i·an·ism** *n.*

hu·man·i·ty (hyōō-măn'ĭ-tē) *n., pl.* **-ties. 1.** Human beings collectively; the human race; mankind. **2.** The condition, quality, or fact of being human; human nature; humanness. **3.** The quality of being humane; benevolence; kindness; mercy. **4.** A humane quality or action. **5. humanities.** Those studies, such as philosophy, literature, and the fine arts, concerned with man and his culture as distinguished from the sciences. [Middle English *humanite,* from Old French, from Latin *hūmānitās,* from *hūmānus.*]

hu·man·ize (hyōō'mə-nīz') *tr.v.* **-ized, -iz·ing. 1.** To portray or endow with human characteristics or attributes. **2.** To make humane. —**hu'man·i·za'tion** *n.* —**hu'man·iz'er** *n.*

hu·man·kind (hyōō'mən-kīnd') *n.* The human race; mankind.

hu·man·ly (hyōō'mən-lē) *adv.* **1.** In a human way. **2.** Within the scope of human means, capabilities, or powers. **3.** According to human experience or knowledge.

hu·man·oid (hyōō'mə-noid') *adj.* Resembling a human being in appearance. —**hu'man·oid'** *n.*

hum·ble (hŭm'bəl) *adj.* **-bler, -blest. 1.** Marked by meekness or modesty in behavior, attitude, or spirit. **2.** Showing submissive respect. **3.** Of low rank or station; unpretentious: *a humble cottage.* —*tr.v.* **-bled, -bling. 1.** To humiliate. **2.** To make lower in condition or station. [Middle English, from Old French, from Latin *humilis,* lowly, base, from *humus,* ground, soil.] —**hum'ble·ness** *n.* —**hum'bler** *n.* —**hum'bly** *adv.*

  Syns: humble, lowly, meek, modest *adj.* Core meaning: Having or expressing humility *(had a humble opinion of his own ability).* HUMBLE stresses lack of pride, assertiveness, or pretense *(your humble servant).* MEEK implies patience, humility, and gentleness; it sometimes suggests that a person is easily imposed on *(a meek and dignified manner; the meekest of men).* LOWLY combines the senses of humble and meek *(a lowly beggar child.)* MODEST implies lack of vanity, pretension, or forwardness *(modest despite her fame).*

hum·ble·bee (hŭm'bəl-bē') *n.* A bumblebee. [Middle English *humbylbee.*]

humble pie. A pie formerly made from the edible organs of a deer or hog. —*idiom.* **eat humble pie.** To apologize abjectly in humiliating circumstances. [*Humble,* from Middle English *(h)umbles,* entrails, from Old French

---

ă **pat**   ā **pay**   â **care**   ä **father**   ĕ **pet**   ē **be**   hw **which**
ōō **took**   ōō **boot**   ou **out**   th **thin**   *th* **this**   ŭ **cut**

ĭ **pit**   ī **tie**   î **pier**   ŏ **pot**   ō **toe**   ô **paw, for**   oi **noise**
û **urge**   zh **vision**   ə **about, item, edible, gallop, circus**

nombles, pork loins, ult. from Latin *lumbus,* loin.]

hum·bug (hŭm′bŭg′) *n.* **1.** Something intended to deceive; a hoax; imposture. **2.** One who tries to trick or deceive. **3.** Nonsense; rubbish. —*tr.v.* **-bugged, -bug·ging.** To deceive or trick. [Orig. unknown.] —**hum′bug′ger** *n.* —**hum′bug′ger·y** *n.*

hum·ding·er (hŭm′dĭng′ər) *n. Slang.* Someone or something that is outstanding or superior. [Orig. unknown.]

hum·drum (hŭm′drŭm′) *adj.* Without change, variety, or excitement; monotonous. —*n.* Something or someone dull or unexciting. [Perh. from HUM.]

hu·mec·tant (hyoo-mĕk′tənt) *n.* A substance that promotes moisture retention. [From Latin *(h)ūmectāns,* pres. part. of *(h)ūmectāre,* to moisten, from *(h)ūmectus,* moist, from *(h)ūmēre,* to be moist.] —**hu·mec′tant** *adj.*

hu·mer·al (hyoo′mər-əl) *adj.* **1.** Of, relating to, or located in the region of the humerus or the shoulder. **2.** Of, relating to, or being a body part analogous to the humerus. —**hu′mer·al** *n.*

hu·mer·us (hyoo′mər-əs) *n., pl.* **-mer·i** (-mə-rī′). The long bone of the upper part of the arm or forelimb, extending from the shoulder to the elbow. [Latin, upper arm, shoulder.]

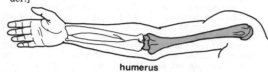

humerus

hu·mid (hyoo′mĭd) *adj.* Containing a large amount of water or water vapor, esp. in the air. [Old French *humide,* from Latin *(h)ūmidus,* from *(h)ūmēre,* to be moist.] —**hu′mid·ly** *adv.*

hu·mid·i·fy (hyoo-mĭd′ə-fī′) *tr.v.* **-fied, -fy·ing.** To make humid. —**hu·mid′i·fi·ca′tion** *n.*

hu·mid·i·ty (hyoo-mĭd′ĭ-tē) *n.* Dampness, esp. of the air. [Middle English *humidite,* from Old French, ult. from Latin *(h)ūmidus,* humid.]

hu·mi·dor (hyoo′mĭ-dôr′) *n.* A container for the storage of cigars that has a device for maintaining the humidity at a constant level. [From HUMID.]

hu·mil·i·ate (hyoo-mĭl′ē-āt′) *tr.v.* **-at·ed, -at·ing.** To lower the pride or dignity of; mortify. [From Late Latin *humiliāre,* from *humilis,* humble.] —**hu·mil′i·a·to′ry** (-ə-tôr′ē, -tōr′ē) *adj.*

hu·mil·i·a·tion (hyoo-mĭl′ē-ā′shən) *n.* **1.** The act of humiliating; degradation. **2.** The condition of being humiliated; disgrace.

hu·mil·i·ty (hyoo-mĭl′ĭ-tē) *n., pl.* **-ties.** The quality or condition of being humble; lack of pride. [Middle English *humilite,* from Old French, from Latin *humilitās,* from *humilis,* humble.]

hum·ming·bird (hŭm′ĭng-bûrd′) *n.* Any of numerous usu. extremely small New World birds of the family Trochilidae, with brilliant plumage and a long, slender bill. [From the humming sound produced by the rapidly vibrating wings.]

hummingbird

hum·mock (hŭm′ək) *n.* Also **ham·mock** (hăm′-). **1.** A low mound or ridge of earth; knoll. **2.** A ridge or hill of ice in an ice field. [Orig. unknown.] —**hum′mock·y** *adj.*

hu·mor (hyoo′mər). Also *Brit.* **hu·mour.** —*n.* **1.** The quality of being amusing or comical: *He saw the humor of the situation.* **2.** The ability to perceive, enjoy, or express

what is comical or funny: *a sense of humor.* **3.** A state of mind; mood; temper: *in a bad humor.* **4.** A sudden inclination or fancy; whim. **5.** *Physiol.* A body fluid, such as blood, lymph, or bile. —See Syns at **disposition.** —*tr.v.* To comply with the wishes or ideas of; indulge. [Middle English *(h)umour,* plant or animal fluid, from Anglo-French, from Latin *(h)ūmor,* liquid, fluid.]

hu·mor·esque (hyoo′mə-rĕsk′) *n.* A whimsical or light-spirited musical composition. [German *Humoreske,* from *Humor,* humor, from English HUMOR.]

hu·mor·ist (hyoo′mər-ĭst) *n.* **1.** A person with a good sense of humor. **2.** A performer or writer who specializes in humor.

hu·mor·less (hyoo′mər-lĭs) *adj.* Without humor or a sense of humor. —**hu′mor·less·ly** *adv.* —**hu′mor·less·ness** *n.*

hu·mor·ous (hyoo′mər-əs) *adj.* Possessing, characterized by, or expressing humor: *a humorous writer; a humorous tale.* —**hu′mor·ous·ly** *adv.* —**hu′mor·ous·ness** *n.*

hu·mour (hyoo′mər) *n.&v.* Var. of **humor.**

hump (hŭmp) *n.* **1.** A rounded mass or lump, as on the back of a camel. **2.** A low mound of earth; hummock. —*tr.v.* To bend or make into a hump. [Orig. unknown.]

hump·back (hŭmp′băk′) *n.* **1.** A hunchback. **2.** An abnormally curved or humped back. **3.** A whalebone whale, *Megaptera novaeangliae,* with a rounded back and long, knobby flippers. —**hump′backed′** *adj.*

humph (hŭmf) *interj.* Used to express doubt, displeasure, or contempt.

hu·mus (hyoo′məs) *n.* A brown or black organic substance that consists of decomposed animal or vegetable matter and contains nutrients for plants. [Latin *humus,* earth, ground, soil.]

Hun (hŭn) *n.* **1.** A member of a nomadic Asiatic people who invaded Europe in the 4th and 5th cent. A.D. under the leadership of Attila. **2.** Often **hun.** Any savage, uncivilized, or destructive person.

hunch (hŭnch) *n.* **1.** An intuitive feeling or guess. **2.** A hump. —*tr.v.* To bend or draw up into a hump: *hunched his shoulders against the wind.* —*intr.v.* To draw oneself up closely into a crouched or cramped posture: *The scared child hunched in a corner.* [Orig. unknown.]

hunch·back (hŭnch′băk′) *n.* **1.** An individual with a humpback. **2.** An abnormally curved or humped back. —**hunch′backed′** *adj.*

hun·dred (hŭn′drĭd) *n., pl.* **-dreds** or **hundred. 1.** The cardinal number written 100 in Arabic numerals or C in Roman numerals, that is equal to the product of 10×10. It is the tenth positive integer after 90. **2. hundreds.** The numbers between 100 and 999: *The dress was valued in the hundreds.* [Middle English, from Old English.] —**hun′dred** *adj. & pron.*

hun·dredth (hŭn′drĭdth) *n.* **1.** The ordinal number that matches the number 100 in a series. Also written 100th. **2.** One of 100 equal parts of a unit, written 1/100, .01 or 10^{-2}. —**hun′dredth** *adj. & adv.*

hun·dred·weight (hŭn′drĭd-wāt′) *n., pl.* **hundredweight** or **-weights.** *Abbr.* **cwt. 1.** A unit of weight equal to approx. 45.6 kilograms, or 100 pounds. **2.** *Brit.* A unit of weight equal to approx. 50.8 kilograms, or 112 pounds. Also called **quintal.**

hung (hŭng) *v.* Past tense and past participle of **hang.** —See Usage note at **hang.** [From *hang,* formed on the model of such verbs as *wring, wrung, wrung.*]

Hun·gar·i·an (hŭng-gâr′ē-ən) *adj.* Of or relating to Hungary, its people, language, or culture. —*n.* **1.** A native or inhabitant of Hungary. **2.** The Finno-Ugric language of Hungary.

hun·ger (hŭng′gər) *n.* **1. a.** A strong desire for food. **b.** The discomfort, weakness, or pain caused by a lack of food. **2.** A strong desire or craving: *a hunger for affection.* —*intr.v.* **1.** To have a need or desire for food. **2.** To have a strong desire or craving. [Middle English, from Old English *hungor.*]

hung jury. A jury unable to agree on a verdict.

hun·gry (hŭng′grē) *adj.* **-gri·er, -gri·est. 1.** Experiencing or showing hunger. **2.** Extremely desirous; avid: *hungry for recognition.* **3.** Lacking richness or fertility: *hungry soil.* [Middle English *hungri,* from Old English *hungrig,* from *hungor,* hunger.] —**hun′gri·ly** *adv.* —**hun′gri·ness** *n.*

hunk (hŭngk) *n. Informal.* A large piece; a chunk: *a hunk of freshly baked bread.* [Perh. from Flemish *hunke,* a piece of food.]

hun·ker (hŭng′kər) *intr.v.* To squat close to the ground; crouch. [Orig. unknown.]

hun·ky-do·ry (hŭng′kē-dôr′ē, -dōr′ē) *adj. Slang.* Extremely satisfactory; fine. [From obs. *hunk,* in good condition, from Dutch *honk,* goal.]

hunt (hŭnt) *tr.v.* **1. a.** To pursue (game) for food or sport. **b.** To seek out; search for. **2.** To search through, as for game or prey. **3.** To make use of in pursuing game. —*intr.v.* **1.** To pursue game or other animals in order to capture or kill them. **2.** To make a search; seek. —*n.* **1.** The act or sport of hunting. **2.** A hunting expedition or outing, usu. with horses and hounds. **3.** A diligent and thorough search or pursuit: *the hunt for the criminal.* [Middle English *hunten,* from Old English *huntian.*]

hunt·er (hŭn′tər) *n.* **1.** A person who hunts. **2.** A dog or horse bred or trained for hunting.

hunt·ing (hŭn′tĭng) *n.* The sport or activity of pursuing game.

hunt·ress (hŭn′trĭs) *n.* A female hunter.

hunts·man (hŭnts′mən) *n.* **1.** A person who hunts; a hunter. **2.** A person who manages the hounds in the hunting field.

hur·dle (hûr′dl) *n.* **1. a.** A barrier used in races that usu. consists of two uprights between which a horizontal bar may be hung at varying heights. **b.** Often **hurdles.** A race in which hurdles must be jumped. **2.** An obstacle or difficulty. **3.** *Brit.* A portable section of fencing used chiefly for folding sheep. —*tr.v.* **-dled, -dling. 1.** To jump or leap over (a barrier) in or as if in a race. **2.** To overcome. —See Syns at **jump.** [Middle English *hurdel,* from Old English *hyrdel.*] —**hur′dler** *n.*

hur·dy-gur·dy (hûr′dē-gûr′dē, hûr′dē-gûr′-) *n., pl.* **-dies.** A musical instrument, such as a barrel organ, played by turning a crank. [Prob. imit.]

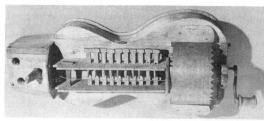

hurdy-gurdy

hurl (hûrl) *tr.v.* **1.** To throw with or as if with great force: *hurl a javelin; hurled insults at each other.* **2.** To send with great vigor; to thrust. —*intr.v.* To pitch a baseball. —*n.* An act or instance of hurling. [Middle English *hurlen,* to be driven with great force, throw, rush on.] —**hurl′er** *n.*

hur·ly-bur·ly (hûr′lē-bûr′lē) *n., pl.* **-lies.** An uproar; commotion. [Earlier *hurling and burling,* from *hurling,* tumult, from Middle English *hurlen,* to throw.]

hur·rah (hōō-rä′, -rô′). Also **hoo·ray** (-rā′) or **hur·ray** (-rā′). —*interj.* A word used to express pleasure, approval, or triumph. —*n.* A shout of "hurrah." —*tr.v.* To applaud, cheer, or approve by shouting "hurrah." —*intr.v.* To shout "hurrah."

hur·ri·cane (hûr′ĭ-kān′, hŭr′-) *n.* A cyclone with heavy rains and winds exceeding 75 mi. per hr., originating in the tropical regions of the Atlantic Ocean or Caribbean Sea and usu. moving northward from its point of origin. [From Spanish *huracan,* from Carib *huracan.*]

hurricane lamp. A lamp that consists of a candle or electric bulb covered by a glass chimney.

hur·ried (hûr′ēd, hŭr′-) *adj.* **1.** Moving or acting rapidly. **2.** Done in great haste: *a hurried tour.* —**hur′ried·ly** *adv.* —**hur′ried·ness** *n.*

hur·ry (hûr′ē, hŭr′ē) *v.* **-ried, -ry·ing.** —*intr.v.* To move or act with haste or speed: *hurried to the store.* —*tr.v.* **1.** To cause to move or act more rapidly; hasten. **2.** To cause to move or act too quickly; to rush: *Don't hurry the cook or dinner will be spoiled.* **3.** To speed the progress or comple-

tion of; expedite. —See Syns at **expedite** and **rush.** —*n., pl.* **-ries. 1.** The act of hurrying. **2.** The need or wish to hurry; a condition of urgency: *Are you in a hurry to leave?* —See Syns at **haste.** [Orig. unknown.]

hur·ry-scur·ry (hûr′ē-skûr′ē, hŭr′ē-skûr′ē). Also **hur·ry-skur·ry.** —*n., pl.* **-ries.** Confused haste; agitation; bustle. —*intr.v.* **-ried, -ry·ing.** To move with undue hurry and confusion. [From HURRY.]

hurt (hûrt) *v.* **hurt, hurt·ing.** —*tr.v.* **1.** To cause physical damage or pain to; injure; wound. **2.** To cause mental or emotional suffering to. **3.** To damage or impair: *hurt his chances for victory.* —*intr.v.* **1.** To have a feeling of pain or discomfort: *His leg hurts.* **2.** To cause suffering, distress, or damage: *The tax bill hurts.* —*n.* **1.** Something that hurts. **2.** Mental suffering; anguish. **3.** A wrong; damage; harm. —See Syns at **distress** and **harm.** [Middle English *hurten,* to strike, harm, from Old French *hurter.*] —**hurt′er** *n.*

hurt·ful (hûrt′fəl) *adj.* Causing hurt or injury. —**hurt′ful·ly** *adv.* —**hurt′ful·ness** *n.*

hur·tle (hûr′tl) *v.* **-tled, -tling.** —*intr.v.* To move with or as if with great speed. —*tr.v.* To throw or fling with great force; hurl. [Middle English *hurtlen,* to dash one thing against another, freq. of *hurten,* to strike.]

hus·band (hŭz′bənd) *n.* A married man. —*tr.v.* To manage or use economically; to conserve: *husband one's energy.* [Middle English, from Old English *hūsbonda,* master of a household, from Old Norse *hūsbōndi : hūs,* house + *bōndi,* pres. part. of *būa,* to dwell.]

hus·band·man (hŭz′bənd-mən) *n.* A person whose occupation is husbandry; a farmer. [Middle English *housbondeman.*]

hus·band·ry (hŭz′bən-drē) *n.* **1. a.** The cultivation of crops and the breeding and raising of livestock; farming; agriculture. **b.** The application of scientific principles esp. to animal breeding. **2.** Good, careful management of resources; economy. [Middle English *housbondrie.*]

hush (hŭsh) *tr.v.* **1.** To make silent or quiet. **2.** To calm; soothe. **3.** To keep from the knowledge of the public; suppress. —*intr.v.* To be or become silent or still. —*n.* A silence or stillness, esp. after noise. [From Middle English *husht,* silent.]

hush-hush (hŭsh′hŭsh′) *adj. Informal.* Secret; confidential. —See Syns at **secret.**

hush money. *Informal.* A bribe or payment made to keep something secret.

hush·pup·py (hŭsh′pŭp′ē) *n.* A fried cornmeal fritter.

husk (hŭsk) *n.* **1.** The dry thin outer covering of certain fruits and seeds, as of an ear of corn or a nut. **2.** A shell or outer layer that is often worthless. —*tr.v.* To remove the husk from. [Middle English *husk(e).*] —**husk′er** *n.*

husk·y¹ (hŭs′kē) *adj.* **-i·er, -i·est.** Hoarse or deep: *a husky voice.* [Orig. "dry as a husk."] —**husk′i·ly** *adv.* —**husk′i·ness** *n.*

husk·y² (hŭs′kē) *adj.* **-i·er, -i·est.** Rugged and strong; burly. —*n., pl.* **-ies.** A husky person. [From HUSK.] —**husk′i·ness** *n.*

hus·ky³ (hŭs′kē) *n., pl.* **-kies.** Often **Husky.** A dog with a dense, furry coat, used in Arctic regions for pulling sleds. [Perh. a shortened var. of ESKIMO.]

hus·sar (hōō-zär′, -sär′) *n.* A member of any of various European units of light cavalry. [Hungarian *huszár,* freebooter, hussar, ult. from Old Italian *corsaro,* corsair.]

hus·sy (hŭz′ē, hŭs′ē) *n., pl.* **-sies. 1.** A saucy or mischievous girl. **2.** An immoral woman. [Var. of HOUSEWIFE.]

hus·tings (hŭs′tĭngz) *n.* (used with a sing. verb). **1.** *Brit.* A platform on which candidates for Parliament formerly stood to make their campaign speeches. **2.** A political campaign. [From Middle English *husting,* an assembly, from Old English *hūsting,* from Old Norse *husthing : hūs,* house + *thing,* assembly.]

hus·tle (hŭs′əl) *v.* **-tled, -tling.** —*tr.v.* **1.** To push or shove roughly. **2.** *Informal.* To move hurriedly or urgently: *hustle the prisoner onto a plane.* **3.** *Informal.* To urge forward; hurry along. **4.** *Informal.* **a.** To gain by energetic effort. **b.** To sell or obtain by questionable means. —*intr.v.* **1.** To jostle; push. **2.** *Informal.* To perform, do, or move energetically and rapidly. **3.** *Slang.* To obtain something by deceitful or underhanded methods. —See Syns at **rush.**

ă pat   ā pay   â care   ä father   ĕ pet   ē be   hw which   ĭ pit   ī tie   î pier   ŏ pot   ō toe   ô paw, for   oi noise
ōō took   ōō boot   ou out   th thin   *th* this   ŭ cut   û urge   zh vision   ə about, item, edible, gallop, circus

hyacinth

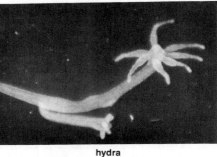

hydra

hydrangea

—*n. Informal.* **1.** An instance or act of hustling. **2.** Busy activity. —See Syns at **haste.** [From Dutch *husselen,* to shake and toss.] —**hus′tler** *n.*

hut (hŭt) *n.* A makeshift or crude dwelling or shelter; a shack. [Old French *hutte,* from Middle High German *hütte.*]

hutch (hŭch) *n.* **1.** A pen or coop for small animals. **2.** A cupboard having drawers for storage and usu. open shelves above. **3.** A chest or bin for storage. **4.** A hut. [Middle English *huche,* chest, from Old French, from Medieval Latin *hutica.*]

huz·za (hə-zä′). Also **huz·zah.** *Archaic.* —*n.* A shout of encouragement or triumph; a cheer. —*interj.* A word used to express joy, encouragement, or triumph.

hy·a·cinth (hī′ə-sĭnth) *n.* **1.** Any of several bulbous plants of the genus *Hyacinthus,* with narrow leaves and a terminal cluster of variously colored, usu. very fragrant flowers. **2.** A deep purplish blue to vivid violet. **3.** A reddish or cinnamon-colored variety of transparent zircon used as a gemstone. Also called **jacinth.** [Latin *hyacinthus,* from Greek *huakinthos,* wild hyacinth.] —**hy′a·cin′thine** (-sĭn′thĭn, -thĭn′) *adj.*

hy·ae·na (hī-ē′nə) *n.* Var. of **hyena.**

hy·a·line (hī′ə-lĭn, -līn′) *adj.* Translucent or transparent like glass. [Late Latin *hyalinus,* from Greek *hualinos,* of crystal or glass, from *hualos,* crystal, glass.]

hy·a·lite (hī′ə-līt′) *n.* A clear, colorless opal. [German *Hyalit,* from Greek *hualos,* glass, crystal.]

hy·brid (hī′brĭd) *n.* **1.** The offspring of genetically different parents, esp. the offspring of plants or animals that are of different varieties, species, or races. **2.** Something of mixed origin or composition. —*modifier: a hybrid tulip.* [Latin *hybrida,* hybrid, mongrel.] —**hy′brid·ism** *n.* —**hy·brid′i·ty** *n.*

hy·brid·ize (hī′brĭ-dīz′) *v.* **-ized, -iz·ing.** —*tr.v.* To cause to produce hybrids; crossbreed. —*intr.v.* To produce hybrids. —**hy′brid·i·za′tion** *n.* —**hy′brid·iz′er** *n.*

hydr-. Variant of **hydro-.**

Hy·dra (hī′drə) *n.* **1.** *Gk. Myth.* A many-headed monster that was slain by Hercules. **2.** A constellation in the equatorial region of the southern sky near Cancer, Libra, and Centaurus. **3. hydra** *pl.* **-dras** or **-drae** (-drē) Any of various small freshwater polyps of the genus *Hydra* and related genera, with a naked, cylindrical body and a mouth opening surrounded by tentacles.

hy·dran·gea (hī-drān′jə, -jē-ə, -drăn′-) *n.* Any of various shrubs or trees of the genus *Hydrangea,* with large, rounded clusters of white, pink, or blue flowers. [New Latin, "water vessel" (from the cuplike shape of the seed pod).]

hy·drant (hī′drənt) *n.* An upright pipe with a nozzle or spout for drawing water from a water main. [HYDR(O)- + -ANT.]

hy·drate (hī′drāt′) *n.* A chemical compound that contains water combined in a definite ratio, the water being retained or regarded as being retained in its molecular state. —*tr.v.* **-drat·ed, -drat·ing.** To combine with water to form a hydrate. [HYDR(O)- + -ATE.] —**hy·dra′tion** *n.*

hy·drau·lic (hī-drô′lĭk) *adj.* **1.** Of, involving, or moved or operated by a liquid, esp. water or oil, under pressure. **2.** Of or pertaining to hydraulics. **3.** Capable of setting and hardening under water, as Portland cement. [Latin *hy-*

draulicus, from Greek *hudraulis,* a musical instrument operated by water : *hudōr,* water + *aulos,* tube, pipe.] —**hy·drau′li·cal·ly** *adv.*

hydraulic ram. A water pump in which the downward flow of naturally running water is intermittently halted by a valve so that the water is forced upward to a higher level.

hy·drau·lics (hī-drô′lĭks) *n.* (*used with a sing. verb*). The science that deals with the dynamic behavior of liquids.

hy·dra·zine (hī′drə-zēn′) *n.* A colorless, fuming, corrosive hygroscopic liquid, H_2NNH_2, used in jet and rocket fuels. [HYDR(O)- + AZ(O)- + -INE.]

hy·dride (hī′drīd′) *n.* A compound of hydrogen with another, more electropositive element or radical. [HYDR(O)- + -IDE.]

hydro- or **hydr-.** A prefix meaning: **1.** Water: **hydroelectric. 2.** Liquid: **hydrostatic. 3.** Hydrogen: **hydrochloride.** [From Greek *hudōr,* water.]

hy·dro·car·bon (hī′drə-kär′bən) *n.* Any of numerous organic compounds, such as benzene and methane, that contain only carbon and hydrogen.

hy·dro·ceph·a·lus (hī′drō-sĕf′ə-ləs) *n.* Also **hy·dro·ceph·a·ly** (-lē). An abnormal condition in which an accumulation of fluid in the cerebral ventricles causes enlargement of the skull and compression of the brain. [Late Latin, from Greek *hudrokephalon* : *hudōr,* water + *kephalē,* head.] —**hy′dro·ce·phal′ic** (-sə-făl′ĭk) or **hy′dro·ceph′a·loid′** (-sĕf′ə-loid′) or **hy′dro·ceph′a·lous** (-ləs) *adj.*

hy·dro·chlo·ric acid (hī′drə-klôr′ĭk, -klōr′-). A clear, colorless, fuming aqueous solution of hydrogen chloride, HCl, used in petroleum production, ore reduction, food processing, and metal cleaning.

hy·dro·chlo·ride (hī′drə-klôr′īd′, -klōr′-) *n.* A compound of hydrochloric acid.

hy·dro·cor·ti·sone (hī′drə-kôr′tĭ-sōn′, -zōn′) *n.* A bitter crystalline hormone, $C_2H_{30}O_5$, derived from the adrenal cortex and used for purposes similar to those of cortisone.

hy·dro·cy·an·ic acid (hī′drō-sī-ăn′ĭk). A colorless aqueous solution of hydrogen cyanide, HCN, used in the manufacture of dyes, fumigants, and plastics.

hy·dro·dy·nam·ics (hī′drō-dī-năm′ĭks) *n.* (*used with a sing. verb*). The science that deals with the dynamics of fluids, esp. incompressible fluids, in motion.

hy·dro·e·lec·tric (hī′drō-ĭ-lĕk′trĭk) *adj.* Of or relating to electricity generated by conversion of the energy of running water. —**hy′dro·e·lec·tric′i·ty** (-ĭ-lĕk-trĭs′ĭ-tē, -ē′lĕk′-) *n.*

hy·dro·flu·or·ic acid (hī′drō-floo-ôr′ĭk, -ŏr′, -floor′ĭk). A colorless, fuming, corrosive aqueous solution of hydrogen fluoride, HF, used to etch or polish glass, pickle certain metals, and clean masonry.

hy·dro·foil (hī′drə-foil′) *n.* **1.** A structure shaped like a wing of an aircraft and attached to the hull of a boat below the water line so that at a certain speed the hull of the boat is lifted clear of the water, allowing the boat to travel faster and use less fuel. **2.** A boat equipped with hydrofoils. [HYDRO- + FOIL.]

hy·dro·gen (hī′drə-jən) *n.* *Symbol* **H** A colorless, highly flammable gaseous element, the lightest of all the elements. Atomic number 1, atomic weight 1.00797, melting point -259.14°C, boiling point -252.5°C, density 0.08988 gram per liter, valence 1. [French *hydrogène,* "water generating."] —**hy·drog′e·nous** (-drŏj′ə-nəs) *adj.*

hy·dro·gen·ate (hī′drə-jə-nāt′, hī-drŏj′ə-) *tr.v.* **-at·ed, -at·ing.**

1. To treat or combine with hydrogen. **2.** To treat (a liquid vegetable oil) with hydrogen and convert it to a solid fat. —**hy′dro·gen·a′tion** n.

hydrogen bomb. A bomb whose explosive power is derived from the sudden release of atomic energy in the fusion of hydrogen nuclei to form helium nuclei. Also called **H-bomb.**

hydrogen chloride. A colorless, fuming, corrosive gas, HC1, used in the manufacture of plastics.

hydrogen fluoride. A colorless, fuming, corrosive liquid or gas, HF, used in the manufacture of hydrofluoric acid, as a reagent and catalyst, and in the refining of uranium and the preparation of many fluorine compounds.

hydrogen ion. The positively charged ion of hydrogen, H+, formed by removal of the electron from atomic hydrogen.

hydrogen peroxide. An unstable compound, H_2O_2, used chiefly in aqueous solution as an antiseptic, bleaching agent, oxidizing agent, and laboratory reagent.

hydrogen sulfide. A colorless, flammable, poisonous gas, H_2S, with a characteristic rotten-egg odor, used as a precipitant, purifier, and reagent.

hy·drog·ra·phy (hī-drŏg′rə-fē) n., pl. **-phies. 1.** The scientific study of the physical conditions, boundaries, flow, and related characteristics of bodies of water, such as oceans, lakes, or rivers. **2.** The mapping of bodies of water. —**hy·drog′ra·pher** n. —**hy′dro·graph′ic** (hī′drə-grăf′ĭk) adj. —**hy′dro·graph′i·cal·ly** adv.

hy·droid (hī′droid′) n. Any of numerous hydrozoan coelenterates, esp. a polyp as distinguished from a jellyfish. [HYDR(A) (genus name) + -OID.] —**hy′droid′** adj.

hy·drol·o·gy (hī-drŏl′ə-jē) n. The scientific study of the properties, distribution, and effects of water on and below the surface of the earth and in the atmosphere. —**hy′dro·log′ic** (hī′drə-lŏj′ĭk) or **hy′dro·log′i·cal** adj. —**hy′dro·log′i·cal·ly** adv. —**hy·drol′o·gist** n.

hy·drol·y·sis (hī-drŏl′ĭ-sĭs) n. Decomposition of a chemical compound by reaction with water, as the catalytic conversion of glucose to starch. —**hy′dro·lyt′ic** (hī′drə-lĭt′ĭk) adj.

hy·dro·lyze (hī′drə-līz′) v. **-lyzed, -lyz·ing.** —tr.v. To subject to hydrolysis. —intr.v. To undergo hydrolysis. [From HYDROLYSIS.]

hy·drom·e·ter (hī-drŏm′ĭ-tər) n. An instrument used to determine the specific gravity of a liquid. —**hy′dro·met′ric** (hī′drə-mĕt′rĭk) or **hy′dro·met′ri·cal** adj. —**hy·drom′e·try** n.

hy·dro·pho·bi·a (hī′drə-fō′bē-ə) n. **1.** Fear of water. **2.** Pathol. Rabies. [Late Latin, from Greek hudrophobia : hudor, water + -phobia, fear.] —**hy′dro·pho′bic** adj.

hy·dro·phyte (hī′drə-fīt′) n. A plant that grows in water or very wet soil. [HYDRO- + -PHYTE.]

hy·dro·pon·ics (hī′drə-pŏn′ĭks) n. (used with a sing. verb). The cultivation of plants in a nutrient solution rather than in soil. [HYDRO- + Greek ponein, to work, labor.] —**hy′dro·pon′ic** adj. —**hy′dro·pon′i·cal·ly** adv.

hy·dro·qui·none (hī′drō-kwĭ-nōn′, -kwĭn′ōn′) n. Also **hy·dro·qui·nol** (-kwĭn′ōl′, -ōl′). A white, crystalline compound, $C_6H_4(OH)_2$, used as a photographic developer, antioxidant, stabilizer, and reagent.

hy·dro·sphere (hī′drə-sfîr′) n. **1.** The water vapor in the atmosphere of the earth. **2.** The water on the surface of the earth and the water vapor in the atmosphere.

hy·dro·stat·ic (hī′drə-stăt′ĭk) or **hy·dro·stat·i·cal** (-ĭ-kəl) adj. Of or pertaining to hydrostatics. —**hy′dro·stat′i·cal·ly** adv.

hy·dro·stat·ics (hī′drə-stăt′ĭks) n. (used with a sing. verb). The science that deals with the characteristics of fluids at rest.

hy·dro·ther·a·py (hī′drə-thĕr′ə-pē) n., pl. **-pies.** The use of water in the treatment of diseases.

hy·drot·ro·pism (hī-drŏt′rə-pĭz′əm) n. Biol. Growth or movement of an organism in response to water.

hy·drous (hī′drəs) adj. Containing water, esp. water of crystallization or hydration.

hy·drox·ide (hī-drŏk′sīd′) n. A chemical compound that consists of an element or radical joined to a hydroxyl group.

hydroxide ion. The negatively charged ion OH-, characteristic of basic hydroxides.

hy·drox·yl (hī-drŏk′sĭl) n. The univalent radical or group, OH, characteristic of bases, certain acids, and alcohols, composed of one atom of oxygen and one of hydrogen. [HYDR(O)- + OX(YGEN) + -YL.]

hy·dro·zo·an (hī′drə-zō′ən) n. Any of numerous coelenterates of the class Hydrozoa, which includes simple and compound polyps and certain jellyfish.

hy·e·na (hī-ē′nə) n. Also **hy·ae·na.** Any of several carnivorous mammals of the genera Hyaena or Crocuta, with powerful jaws, relatively short hind limbs, and coarse hair. [Middle English hyene, from Latin hyaena, from Greek huaina, from hus, swine.]

hy·giene (hī′jēn′) n. **1.** Scientific methods or practices for the promotion of health and the prevention of disease. **2.** The science that deals with the maintenance of good health and the prevention of disease. [French hygiène, ult. from Greek hugieinē, healthful, from hugiēs, healthy.] —**hy·gien′ist** (hī-jē′nĭst, hī′jē′-) n.

hy·gi·en·ic (hī′jē-ĕn′ĭk) adj. **1.** Of or pertaining to hygiene. **2.** Tending to promote good health. **3.** Clean and free of germs; sanitary. —**hy′gi·en′i·cal·ly** adv.

hygro-. A prefix meaning moist or moisture: **hygrometer.** [From Greek hugros, wet, moist.]

hy·grom·e·ter (hī-grŏm′ĭ-tər) n. Any of several instruments that measure atmospheric humidity. —**hy′gro·met′ric** (hī′grə-mĕt′rĭk) adj. —**hy·grom′e·try** n.

hy·gro·scope (hī′grə-skōp′) n. An instrument that measures changes in atmospheric moisture.

hy·gro·scop·ic (hī′grə-skŏp′ĭk) adj. Readily absorbing moisture, as from the atmosphere.

hy·ing (hī′ĭng). v. A present participle of hie.

hy·men (hī′mən) n. A membranous fold of tissue partly closing the external opening of the vagina. [Latin hymen, from Greek humēn, membrane.] —**hy′men·al** adj.

Hy·men (hī′mən) n. Gk. Myth. The god of marriage.

hy·me·ne·al (hī′mə-nē′əl) adj. Of or pertaining to a wedding or marriage. [From Latin hymenaeus, from Greek humēnaios, bridal song, wedding.]

hy·me·nop·ter·on (hī′mə-nŏp′tə-rŏn′) n., pl. **-ter·a** (-tər-ə) or **-ter·ons.** Any insect of the order Hymenoptera, characteristically having two pairs of membranous wings and including the bees, wasps, and ants. —adj. Also **hy·me·nop·ter·ous** (-tər-əs). Of or belonging to the Hymenoptera. [From Greek humenopteros, "membrane-winged": humēn, membrane + pteron, wing.]

hymn (hĭm) n. **1.** A song of praise or thanksgiving, esp. to God. **2.** Any song of praise or joy. [Middle English ymne, from Old French, from Latin hymnus, from Greek humnos, hymn, ode of praise of gods or heroes.]

hym·nal (hĭm′nəl) n. A book or collection of hymns. [Middle English hymnale, from Medieval Latin hymnāle, from Latin hymnus, hymn.]

hym·no·dy (hĭm′nə-dē) n., pl. **-dies. 1.** The singing of hymns. **2.** The composing of hymns. **3.** The hymns of a particular time, place, or church. [From Medieval Latin hymnōdia, from Greek humnōidia : humnos, hymn + ōidē, song.]

hy·oid bone (hī′oid′). A bone or group of bones that is located between the mandible and the larynx at the base of the tongue. [French hyoïde, ult. from Greek huoeides, "in the form of an upsilon."]

hyp-. Variant of **hypo-.**

hype (hīp). Slang. —n. **1.** Something deliberately misleading; deception. **2.** Extravagant or exaggerated claims made esp. in advertising or promotional material. —tr.v. **hyped, hyp·ing.** To publicize or promote by inflated or misleading claims. [Orig. unknown.]

hyped-up (hīpt′ŭp′) adj. Excited or overstimulated by or as if by the hypodermic injection of a drug. [From HYPODERMIC.]

hyper-. A prefix meaning: **1.** Over, above, or beyond: **hypersonic. 2.** Excessive or excessively: **hyperacidity.** [From Greek huper, over, above, beyond, exceeding.]

hy·per·a·cid·i·ty (hī′pər-ə-sĭd′ĭ-tē) n. A condition marked by excessive or abnormal acidity.

hy·per·ac·tive (hī′pər-ăk′tĭv) adj. Excessively or abnormally active.

hy·per·bo·la (hī-pûr′bə-lə) *n. Geom.* A plane curve having two branches, formed by: **a.** A conic section formed by a plane that intersects both halves of a right circular cone. **b.** The locus of points related to two given points such that the difference in the distances of each point from the two given points is a constant. [From Greek *huperbolē*, "a throwing beyond," excess.]

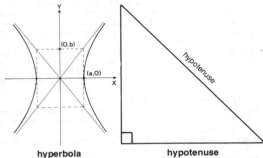

hyperbola   hypotenuse

hy·per·bo·le (hī-pûr′bə-lē) *n.* An exaggerated statement often used as a figure of speech; for example, *I could sleep for a year. This book weighs a ton.* [From Latin *hyperbolē*, from Greek *huperbolē*, excess.]

hy·per·bol·ic (hī′pər-bŏl′ĭk) or **hy·per·bol·i·cal** (-ĭ-kəl) *adj.* **1.** Of, pertaining to, or employing hyperbole. **2.** *Geom.* Of or pertaining to a hyperbola.

hy·per·crit·i·cal (hī′pər-krĭt′ĭ-kəl) *adj.* Overcritical; captious. **—hy′per·crit′i·cal·ly** *adv.* **—hy′per·crit′i·cism** (-krĭt′ĭ-sĭz′əm) *n.*

hy·per·gly·ce·mi·a (hī′pər-glī-sē′mē-ə) *n.* An excess of glucose in the blood. [HYPER- + Greek *glukus*, sweet + -EMIA.] **—hy′per·gly·ce′mic** *adj.*

Hy·pe·ri·on (hī-pîr′ē-ən) *n. Gk. Myth.* A Titan, the son of Gaea and Uranus, and father of Helios, the sun god.

hy·per·o·pi·a (hī′pə-rō′pē-ə) *n.* A pathological condition of the eye in which parallel rays are focused behind the retina, so that vision is better for distant than near objects. Also called **farsightedness.** [HYPER- + -OPIA.] **—hy′per·op′ic** (-rŏp′ĭk) *adj.*

hy·per·sen·si·tive (hī′pər-sĕn′sĭ-tĭv) *adj.* Abnormally sensitive. **—hy′per·sen′si·tive·ness** or **hy′per·sen′si·tiv′i·ty** *n.*

hy·per·son·ic (hī′pər-sŏn′ĭk) *adj.* Of, pertaining to, or relating to speed equal to or exceeding five times the speed of sound. **—hy′per·son′ics** *n.*

hy·per·ten·sion (hī′pər-tĕn′shən) *n.* **1.** Abnormally high arterial blood pressure. **2.** A state of high emotional tension.

hy·per·thy·roid·ism (hī′pər-thī′roi-dĭz′əm) *n.* Pathologically excessive activity of the thyroid.

hy·per·tro·phy (hī-pûr′trə-fē) *n. Pathol.* An increase in the size of an organ or body part as a result of an increase in size, but not in number, of the constituent cells. **—*intr.v.* -phied, -phy·ing.** To grow abnormally large. [HYPER- + Greek *trophē*, food.] **—hy′per·troph′ic** (-trŏf′ĭk) *adj.*

hy·phen (hī′fən) *n.* A punctuation mark (-) used between the parts of a compound word or between syllables of a word, esp. of a word divided at the end of a line. [Late Latin, from Late Greek *huphen*, a sign written below two consecutive letters to show that they belong to the same word : *hupo*, under + *hen*, one.]

hy·phen·ate (hī′fə-nāt′) *tr.v.* **-at·ed, -at·ing.** To divide or connect (syllables or word elements) with a hyphen. **—hy′phen·a′tion** *n.*

hyp·no·sis (hĭp-nō′sĭs) *n., pl.* **-ses** (-sēz′). **1.** An induced sleeplike condition in which an individual is extremely responsive to suggestions made by the hypnotist. **2.** Hypnotism. [Greek *hupnos*, sleep + -OSIS.]

hyp·no·ther·a·py (hĭp′nō-thĕr′ə-pē) *n.* Treatment of illness by the use of hypnotism.

hyp·not·ic (hĭp-nŏt′ĭk) *adj.* **1.** Of or relating to hypnosis. **2.** Causing or producing sleep. **—*n.*** An agent that causes sleep; a soporific. [French *hypnotique,* from Late Latin *hypnōticus,* from Greek *hupnōtikos,* sleepy, from *hupnoun,* to put to sleep, from *hupnos,* sleep.] **—hyp·not′i·cal·ly** *adv.*

hyp·no·tism (hĭp′nə-tĭz′əm) *n.* **1.** The study, practice, or act of inducing hypnosis. **2.** Hypnosis.

hyp·no·tist (hĭp′nə-tĭst) *n.* A person who induces hypnosis.

hyp·no·tize (hĭp′nə-tīz′) *tr.v.* **-tized, -tiz·ing. 1.** To induce hypnosis in. **2.** To fascinate by or as if by hypnosis. **—hyp′no·tiz′a·ble** *adj.* **—hyp′no·ti·za′tion** *n.* **—hyp′no·tiz′er** *n.*

Hyp·nus (hĭp′nəs) *n.* Var. of **Hypnos.**

hypo- or **hyp-.** A prefix meaning: **1.** Below or beneath: *hypodermic.* **2.** Abnormally low: *hypoglycemia.* [From Greek *hupo,* under, beneath.]

hy·po·chlo·rite (hī′pə-klôr′īt′, -klōr′-) *n.* A salt or ester of hypochlorous acid.

hy·po·chlo·rous acid (hī′pə-klôr′əs, -klōr′-). A weak, unstable acid, HOCl, used as a bleach, oxidizer, deodorant, and disinfectant.

hy·po·chon·dri·a (hī′pə-kŏn′drē-ə) *n.* A condition marked by depression and a preoccupation with imaginary illnesses. [Orig. a region of the abdomen (formerly held to be the seat of melancholy), from Late Latin, ult. from Greek *hupokhondrios,* under the cartilage of the breastbone : *hupo-,* under + *khondros,* cartilage.] **—hy′po·chon′dri·ac′** (-ăk′) *n. & adj.* **—hy′po·chon·dri′a·cal** (-kən-drī′ə-kəl) *adj.* **—hy′po·chon·dri′a·cal·ly** *adv.*

hy·po·cot·yl (hī′pə-kŏt′l) *n. Bot.* The part of the axis of a plant embryo or seedling that is below the cotyledons. [HYPO- + COTYL(EDON).]

hy·poc·ri·sy (hĭ-pŏk′rĭ-sē) *n., pl.* **-sies.** The practice or act of professing virtues and beliefs that one does not possess. [Middle English *ypocrisy,* from Old French *ypocrisie,* from Late Latin *hypocrisis,* from Greek *hupokrisis,* playing of a part on the stage, from *hupokrinein,* to answer, play a part.]

hyp·o·crite (hĭp′ə-krĭt′) *n.* A person given to hypocrisy. **—hyp′o·crit′i·cal** *adj.* **—hyp′o·crit′i·cal·ly** *adv.*

hy·po·derm (hī′pə-dûrm′) *n.* Var. of **hypodermis.**

hy·po·der·mic (hī′pə-dûr′mĭk) *adj.* **1.** Of or pertaining to the layer just beneath the epidermis. **2.** Pertaining to the hypodermis. **3.** Injected beneath the skin. **—*n.* 1.** A hypodermic injection. **2.** A hypodermic needle or syringe. **—hy′po·der′mi·cal·ly** *adv.*

hypodermic injection. A subcutaneous, intramuscular, or intravenous injection by means of a hypodermic syringe and needle.

hypodermic needle. 1. A hollow needle used with a hypodermic syringe. **2.** A hypodermic syringe complete with needle.

hypodermic syringe. A syringe fitted with a hypodermic needle for hypodermic injections.

hy·po·der·mis (hī′pə-dûr′mĭs) *n.* Also **hy·po·derm** (hī′pə-dûrm′). **1.** *Zool.* An underlying layer of cells that secretes an overlying chitinous cuticle, as in arthropods. **2.** *Bot.* A layer of cells lying immediately below the epidermis. [HYPO- + DERMIS.]

hy·po·gly·ce·mi·a (hī′pō-glī-sē′mē-ə) *n.* An abnormally low level of sugar in the blood. [HYPO- + Greek *glukus,* sweet + -EMIA.] **—hy′po·gly·ce′mic** *adj.*

hy·poph·y·sis (hī-pŏf′ĭ-sĭs) *n., pl.* **-ses** (-sēz′). *Anat.* The pituitary gland. [From Greek *hupophusis,* attachment underneath, from *hupophuein,* to grow up under : *hupo-,* under + *phuein,* to bring forth, grow.] **—hy′po·phys′e·al** (hī′pə-fĭz′ē-əl, hī-pŏf′ĭ-sē′əl) *adj.*

hy·po·sul·fite (hī′pə-sŭl′fīt′) *n.* **Sodium thiosulfate.**

hy·po·sul·fu·rous acid (hī′pō-sŭl-fyŏŏr′əs, hī′pə-sŭl′fər-əs). An unstable acid, $H_2S_2O_4$, used as a bleaching and reducing agent.

hy·pot·e·nuse (hī-pŏt′n-ōōs′, -yōōs′) *n.* Also **hy·poth·e·nuse** (hī-pŏth′ə-nōōs′, -nyōōs′). *Geom.* The side of a right triangle opposite the right angle. [Latin *hypotēnūsa,* from Greek *hupoteinousa,* from *hupoteinein,* to stretch under : *hupo-,* under + *teinein,* to stretch.]

hy·po·thal·a·mus (hī′pō-thăl′ə-məs) *n.* The part of the brain that lies below the thalamus and regulates bodily temperature, certain metabolic processes, and other autonomic activities. **—hy′po·tha·lam′ic** (-thə-lăm′ĭk) *adj.*

hy·poth·e·cate (hī-pŏth′ĭ-kāt′) *tr.v.* **-cat·ed, -cat·ing.** To pledge (property) as security to a creditor without transfer of title or possession; to mortgage. [From Medieval Latin *hypothēcāre,* from Late Latin *hypothēca,* a pledge, security.] —**hy·poth′e·ca′tion** *n.*

hy·poth·e·nuse (hī-pŏth′ə-nōōs′, -nyōōs′) *n.* Var. of **hypotenuse.**

hy·poth·e·sis (hī-pŏth′ĭ-sĭs) *n., pl.* **-ses** (-sēz′). **1.** An explanation that accounts for a set of facts and that can be tested by further investigation; theory. **2.** Something that is taken to be true for the purpose of argument or investigation; assumption. [Late Latin, from Greek *hupothesis,* proposal, supposition, from *hupotithenai,* to propose : *hupo-,* under + *tithenai,* to place.]

hy·poth·e·size (hī-pŏth′ĭ-sīz′) *v.* **-sized, -siz·ing.** —*tr.v.* To assert as a hypothesis. —*intr.v.* To form a hypothesis.

hy·po·thet·i·cal (hī′pə-thĕt′ĭ-kəl) or **hy·po·thet·ic** (-thĕt′ĭk) *adj.* Of, relating to, or founded on a hypothesis. [From Late Latin *hypotheticus,* from Greek *hupothetikos,* from *hupothesis,* hypothesis.] —**hy′po·thet′i·cal·ly** *adv.*

hy·po·thy·roid·ism (hī′pō-thī′roi-dĭz′əm) *n.* **1.** Deficient activity of the thyroid gland. **2.** A pathological condition resulting from deficient activity of the thyroid, marked by loss of energy and a lowered rate of metabolism. [HYPO- + THYROID + -ISM.]

hy·pox·i·a (hī-pŏk′sē-ə) *n.* Deficiency in the amount of oxygen reaching bodily tissues. [HYP(O)- + OX(Y)- + -IA.]

hy·rax (hī′răks′) *n., pl.* **-rax·es** or **-ra·ces** (-rə-sēz′). Any of several small, herbivorous mammals of the family Procaviidae within the order Hyraoidea, similar in appearance to a woodchuck or rabbit but more closely related to the hoofed mammals. [From Greek *hurax,* shrew mouse.]

hys·sop (hĭs′əp) *n.* **1.** A woody plant, *Hyssopus officinalis,* with spikes of small blue flowers and aromatic leaves that are used in perfumery and as a condiment. **2.** Any of several similar or related plants. **3.** An unidentified plant mentioned in the Bible as the source of twigs used for sprinkling in certain Hebraic purificatory rites. [Middle English *ysop,* from Latin *hyssōpus,* from Greek *hussōpos.*]

hys·ter·ec·to·my (hĭs′tə-rĕk′tə-mē) *n., pl.* **-mies.** Surgical removal of the uterus. [Greek *hustera,* uterus + -ECTOMY.]

hys·te·ri·a (hĭ-stĕr′ē-ə, -stîr′-) *n.* **1.** A neurosis characterized by physical symptoms, such as blindness or paralysis, without apparent organic cause and by episodes of hallucination, somnambulism, or amnesia. **2.** Excessive or uncontrollable emotion, such as fear or panic. [From Latin *hystericus,* hysteric.]

hys·ter·ic (hĭ-stĕr′ĭk) *n.* A person suffering from hysteria. —*adj.* Hysterical. [Latin *hystericus,* from Greek *husterikos,* suffering in the womb (from the belief that hysteria was caused by uterine disorders), from *hustera,* womb.]

hys·ter·i·cal (hĭ-stĕr′ĭ-kəl) *adj.* **1.** Of, characterized by, or arising from hysteria. **2.** Having or prone to having hysterics. —**hys·ter′i·cal·ly** *adv.*

hys·ter·ics (hĭ-stĕr′ĭks) *n. (used with a sing. verb).* **1.** A fit of uncontrollable laughing and crying. **2.** An attack of hysteria.

Ii

Phoenician – About 3,000 years ago the Phoenicians and other Semitic peoples began to use graphic signs to represent individual speech sounds instead of syllables or whole words. They used this symbol to represent the sound of the semivowel "y" and gave it the name yōdh, the Phoenician word for "hand".

Greek – The Greeks borrowed the Phoenician alphabet with some modifications. They changed the shape of yōdh and altered the name to iota. They used iota to represent the sound of the vowel "i".

Roman – The Romans borrowed the alphabet from the Greeks via the Etruscans. They used iota to represent both the vowel "i" and the semivowel "y." In time a hook was added to I to identify the semivowel, and the new symbol

became the letter J. The letter I continued to represent the vowel. The Romans also adapted the alphabet for carving Latin in stone, and this monumental script, as it is called, became the basis for modern printed capital letters.

Medieval – By medieval times – around 1,200 years ago – the Roman monumental capitals had become adapted to being relatively quickly written on paper, parchment, or vellum. The dot was added to I to help distingutsh it from other similarly shaped letters. The cursive minuscule alphabet became the basis for modern printed lower-case letters.

Modern – Since the invention of printing about 500 years ago modifications have been made in the shape and style of the letter I, but its basic form has remained unchanged.

---

i, I (ī) *n., pl.* **i's** or **is, I's** or **Is.** The ninth letter of the modern English alphabet.

I (ī) *pron.* The person who is the speaker or the writer: *I expect to leave soon.* —See Usage note **4** at **between** and Usage note at **me.** [Middle English *i, ich,* from Old English *ic.*]

I The symbol for the element iodine.

–ia¹. A suffix indicating: **1.** Diseases and disorders: **diphtheria. 2.** Plants: **begonia. 3.** Areas and countries: **Manchuria.** [From Latin and Greek.]

–ia². A suffix indicating: **1.** Collective nouns: **trivia. 2.** Something relating or belonging to: **orthodontia.** [From Latin and Greek.]

–ial. A suffix meaning of, pertaining to, or characterized by: **residential.** [Middle English, from Old French, from Latin *-iālis.*]

i·amb (ī′ămb′) *n.* A metrical unit of verse in which a stressed syllable follows an unstressed syllable. The following line from Shakespeare's *Julius Caesar* has five iambs: *O, párdon mé, thou bléeding piéce of eárth.* [French *iambe,* from Latin *iambus,* from Greek *iambos,* metrical foot.] **—i·am′bic** *adj. & n.*

–ian¹. A suffix meaning: **1.** Of or belonging to: **Bostonian. 2.** Characteristic of or resembling: **Johnsonian.** [Old French *-ien,* from Latin *-iānus.*]

–ian². A suffix meaning: **1.** An admirer or follower of: **Chaucerian. 2.** One skilled in or a specialist in: **pediatrician. 3.** One belonging to a certain period of time or place: **Edwardian.** [From -IAN.]

–iana. Var. of **-ana.**

–iatric. A suffix meaning pertaining to a specific kind of medical treatment: **geriatric.** [From Greek *iatrikos,* medical, from *iatros,* healer, from *iasthai,* to heal.]

–iatrics. A suffix meaning a specific kind of medical treatment: **pediatrics.** [From -IATRIC.]

–iatry. A suffix meaning a specific kind of medical treatment: **psychiatry.** [From Greek *iatreia,* the art of healing, from *iatros,* physician.]

i·bex (ī′běks′) *n.* Any of several wild goats of the genus *Capra,* of mountainous regions of the Old World; esp., *C. ibex,* having long, ridged, backward-curving horns. [Latin.]

ib·i·dem (ĭb′ĭ-děm′, ĭ-bī′dəm) *adv. Latin. Abbr.* **ib.** or **ibid.** In the same place. A term used in footnotes and bibliographies to refer to the book, chapter, article, or page cited

just before.

–ibility. Var. of **-ability.**

i·bis (ī′bĭs) *n.* **1.** Any of various long-billed wading birds of the family Threskiornithidae. **2.** The **wood ibis.** [Latin *ibis,* from Greek *ibis,* from Egyptian *hĭb.*]

–ible. Var. of **-able.**

–ic. 1. A suffix meaning of, pertaining to, or characteristic of: **seismic. 2.** Having or taking a valence higher than in corresponding *-ous* compounds: **ferric.** [Middle English *-ic, -ik,* from Latin *-icus.*]

Ic·a·rus (ĭk′ər-əs) *n. Gk. Myth.* The son of Daedalus, who, in escaping from Crete on artificial wings made for him by his father, flew so close to the sun that the wax with which his wings were fastened melted so that he fell into the Aegean Sea.

ice (īs) *n.* **1.** Water frozen solid. **2.** A surface, layer, or mass of frozen water: *skating on the ice.* **3.** Anything resembling frozen water. **4.** A dessert consisting of sweetened and flavored crushed ice. **5.** Cake frosting; icing. **6.** *Slang.* A diamond or diamonds. **—modifier:** ice cubes. **—v. iced, ic·ing. —tr.v. 1.** To coat or slick with ice. **2.** To cause to become ice; freeze. **3.** To chill by setting in or as if in ice. **4.** To cover or decorate with icing. **5.** *Ice Hockey.* To shoot (the puck) far out of defensive territory. **—intr.v.** To turn into or become coated with ice: *The pond iced over. The windows iced up.* **—idioms. break the ice. 1.** To relax a tense or too formal atmosphere. **2.** To make a start;

ibex

ibis
George Miksch Sutton

---

begin. **cut no ice.** *Informal.* To have no influence or effect. **on ice. 1.** In a refrigerator or cooler. **2.** *Informal.* **a.** In reserve or readiness. **b.** Put aside; postponed. **on thin ice.** In a risky situation; on uncertain ground. [Middle English *is,* from Old English *īs.*]

ice age. 1. Any of a series of cold periods during which glaciers covered much of the earth. **2. Ice Age.** The Pleistocene or glacial epoch.

ice bag. A small waterproof bag filled with ice and applied to sore or swollen parts of the body.

ice·berg (īs'bûrg') *n.* A massive floating body of ice that has broken away from a glacier. [Prob. from Danish and Norwegian *isberg* : *is,* ice + *berg,* mountain.]

ice·boat (īs'bōt') *n.* **1.** A boatlike vehicle with runners that sails on ice. **2.** An icebreaker.

ice·bound (īs'bound') *adj.* **1.** Locked in by ice: *an icebound ship.* **2.** Jammed or covered over by ice: *a harbor icebound during the winter.*

ice·box (īs'bŏks') *n.* **1.** An insulated chest or box in which ice is put to cool and preserve food. **2.** A refrigerator.

ice·break·er (īs'brā'kər) *n.* **1.** A sturdy ship built for breaking a passage through icebound waters. **2.** A protective pier or dock apron used as a buffer against floating ice.

icebreaker

ice cap. A mass of ice and snow that covers an area throughout the year: *the polar ice caps.*

ice cream. A smooth, sweet, cold food made of milk products, sugar, eggs, and flavoring. **—modifier (ice-cream):** *an ice-cream cone.*

iced (īst) *adj.* **1.** Covered over with ice. **2.** Chilled with ice: *iced coffee.* **3.** Decorated or coated with icing.

ice floe. A flat expanse of floating ice.

ice hockey. *Sports.* Hockey.

Ice·land·ic (īs-slăn'dĭk) *adj.* Of or pertaining to Iceland, its inhabitants, their language, or their culture. **—n.** The Germanic language of Iceland.

Iceland moss (īs'lənd). A brittle, grayish-brown, edible lichen, *Cetraria islandica,* of northern regions.

ice pack. 1. A floating mass of compacted ice fragments. **2.** An **ice bag.**

ice pick. A hand tool with a sharply pointed spike, used for chipping or breaking ice.

ice skate. 1. A metal runner or blade fitted to the sole of a shoe for skating on ice. **2.** A shoe or light boot with such a runner or blade permanently fixed to it.

ice-skate (īs'skāt') *intr.v.* **-skat·ed, -skat·ing.** To skate on ice. **—ice skater.**

ice water. 1. a. Very cold drinking water. **b.** Such water containing ice. **2.** Melted ice.

ich·neu·mon (ĭk-nōō'mən, -nyōō'-) *n.* A mongoose of the genus *Herpestes,* esp. *H. ichneumon,* of Africa. [Latin, from Greek *ikhneúmōn,* a weasel, from *ikhneúein,* to track, from *ikhnos,* track.]

ichneumon fly. Any of various wasplike insects of the family Ichneumonidae, having larvae that are parasitic on the larvae of other insects. Also called **ichneumon wasp.**

i·chor (ī'kôr) *n.* **1.** *Gk. Myth.* The rarefied fluid said to run in the veins of the gods. **2.** A fluid likened to blood. **3.** *Pathol.* A watery, acrid discharge from a wound or ulcer. [Greek *ikhōr.*] **—i'chor·ous** (ī'kər-əs) *adj.*

ichthyo- or **ichthy-.** A prefix meaning fish: *ichthyology.*

[Latin, from Greek *ikhthuo-,* from *ikhthus,* fish.]

ich·thy·ol·o·gy (ĭk'thē-ŏl'ə-jē) *n.* Zoology specializing in the study of fishes. **—ich'thy·o·log'ic** (-ə-lŏj'ĭk) or **ich'thy·o·log'i·cal** *adj.* **—ich'thy·ol'o·gist** *n.*

ich·thy·o·saur (ĭk'thē-ə-sôr') *n.* Also **ich·thy·o·saur·us** (ĭk'thē-ə-sôr'əs). Any of various extinct fishlike saltwater reptiles of the order Ichthyosauria, of the Triassic to the Cretaceous periods. [ICHTHYO- + -SAUR.]

-ician. A suffix meaning a person who practices or is a specialist in a given field: *mortician.*

i·ci·cle (ī'sĭ-kəl) *n.* A tapering spike of ice formed by the freezing of dripping or falling water. [Middle English *isikel* : *is,* ice + *ikel,* icicle, from Old English *gicel.*]

ic·ing (ī'sĭng) *n.* **1.** A sweet glaze of sugar, butter, and egg whites or milk, often flavored and cooked, used to decorate cakes and cookies. **2.** *Ice Hockey.* The intentional shooting of the puck out of the defensive zone.

i·con (ī'kŏn') *n.* Also **i·kon. 1.** An image; representation. **2.** A picture of a sacred Christian personage, as Christ or the Virgin Mary, painted on a wooden panel and itself regarded as sacred in the tradition of the Eastern Churches. [Latin *īcōn,* from Greek *eikōn,* likeness, image.]

i·con·o·clasm (ī-kŏn'ə-klăz'əm) *n.* **1.** The action or doctrine of destroying sacred images. **2.** The attacking of established or respected institutions, practices, or attitudes. [From ICONOCLAST.]

i·con·o·clast (ī-kŏn'ə-klăst') *n.* **1.** A person who opposes the use or worship of sacred images. **2.** A person who attacks and seeks to overthrow traditional or popular ideas or institutions. [Medieval Latin *īconoclastēs,* from Medieval Greek *eikonoklastēs* : Greek *eikōn,* image + *klastēs,* breaker, from *klan,* to break.] **—i·con'o·clas'tic** (-klăs'tĭk) *adj.*

-ics. A suffix meaning: **1.** The science or art of: **graphics. 2.** The act, practices, or activities of: **athletics.** [From -IC.]

ic·tus (ĭk'təs) *n.,* pl. **-tus·es** or **ictus.** *Pathol.* A sudden attack; a fit; stroke. [Latin, blow, stroke, from the past part. of *īcere,* to strike.]

i·cy (ī'sē) *adj.* **-i·er, -i·est. 1.** Containing or covered with ice; frozen: *an icy road.* **2.** Resembling ice; cold or slippery: *icy fingers.* **3.** Bitterly cold; freezing: *an icy day.* **4.** Chilling in manner; frigid: *an icy smile.* —See Syns at **cold** and **frigid.** **—ic'i·ly** *adv.* **—ic'i·ness** *n.*

id (ĭd) *n.* *Psychoanal.* The division of the psyche associated with instinctual impulses and demands for immediate satisfaction of primitive needs. [Latin, it.]

I'd (īd). Contraction of: **1.** I had. **2.** I would. **3.** I should.

-id. A suffix meaning: **1.** A member of a zoological family: **hominid. 2.** Var. of **-ide.** [Ult. from Latin *-is,* fem. patronymic suffix.]

-ide or **-id.** A suffix meaning chemical compound: **chloride.** [German *-id,* from French *-ide,* from *acide,* acid.]

i·de·a (ī-dē'ə) *n.* **1.** That which exists in the mind as a product of mental activity; a thought; notion: *was kept awake by disturbing ideas.* **2.** An opinion, conviction, or principle: *Upon what do you base your political ideas?* **3.** A plan or method: *a great idea for catching fish.* **4.** The basic meaning or purpose: *The whole idea of studying is to learn.* **5.** Intention; design: *His idea is to retire at forty.* —See Syns at **belief.** [Latin, from Greek, form, model, class, notion.]

i·de·al (ī-dē'əl, ī-dēl') *n.* **1.** A conception of something made perfect: *creating a community that approaches the ideal.* **2.** Someone or something regarded as a standard or model of perfection. **3.** An ultimate goal. **4.** An honorable or worthy principle or aim. **—adj. 1.** Conforming to an ultimate form of perfection or excellence: *The ideal machine requires no fuel at all.* **2.** Considered the best of its kind: *He would make an ideal choice for president.* **3.** Completely or highly satisfactory: *an ideal day for the beach.* **4.** Existing only in the mind; imaginary: *under ideal conditions.* [French *idéal,* from Late Latin *ideālis,* from Latin *idea,* model, idea.]

Syns: ideal, example, exemplar, model, standard *n.* Core meaning: One worthy of imitation (*a person who was the ideal of virtue*).

i·de·al·ism (ī-dē'ə-lĭz'əm) *n.* **1.** The practice of seeing or representing things in ideal form rather than as they usu. exist in real life. **2.** The practice of following one's ideals.

ă pat	ā pay	â care	ä father	ĕ pet	ē be	hw which	ĭ pit	ī tie	î pier	ŏ pot	ō toe	ô paw, for	oi noise
ōō took	ōō boot	ou out	th thin	th this	ŭ cut		û urge	zh vision	ə about, item, edible, gallop, circus				

3. Any of several philosophical beliefs and systems that hold that reality consists of ideas or perceptions.

i·de·al·ist (ī-dē′ə-lĭst) *n.* **1.** A person who pursues ideals, esp. when they conflict with practical or financial considerations. **2.** An artist or writer whose work expresses idealism. **3.** An adherent of a system of philosophical idealism.

i·de·al·is·tic (ī-dē′ə-lĭs′tĭk, ī′dē-) *adj.* Of or appropriate to an idealist or idealism. **—i·de′al·is′ti·cal·ly** *adv.*

i·de·al·ize (ī-dē′ə-līz′) *tr.v.* **-ized, -iz·ing.** To regard as ideal; hold in highest esteem: *idealized his mother; idealizing the Russian peasant.* **—i·de′al·i·za′tion** *n.* **—i·de′al·iz′er** *n.*

i·de·al·ly (ī-dē′ə-lē) *adv.* **1.** In conformity with an ideal; perfectly: *The apartment ideally suits her needs.* **2.** In theory or imagination; theoretically.

i·de·ate (ī′dē-āt′) *v.* **-at·ed, -at·ing.** **—tr.v.** To form an idea of; imagine; conceive. **—intr.v.** To conceive mental images; think. [From IDEA.] **—i′de·a′tion** *n.*

i·dem (ī′dĕm′) *pron. Abbr.* **id.** Something previously mentioned; the same. [Latin, the same, from *id,* it.]

i·den·ti·cal (ī-dĕn′tĭ-kəl) *adj.* **1.** Being the same: *The quotation used the President's identical words.* **2.** Being exactly equal and alike: *identical machine parts.* **—See Syns at same.** [Medieval Latin *identicus,* from Late Latin *identitās,* identity.] **—i·den′ti·cal·ly** *adv.* **i·den′ti·cal·ness** *n.*

identical twin. Either of a pair of twins developed from a single fertilized ovum, having identical genetic constitutions and pronounced mutual resemblance.

i·den·ti·fi·ca·tion (ī-dĕn′tə-fĭ-kā′shən) *n.* **1.** The act of identifying. **2.** The condition of being identified. **3.** Proof of one's identity, as a card or letter bearing one's name and other personal information. **—modifier:** *an identification tag.*

i·den·ti·fy (ī-dĕn′tə-fī′) *v.* **-fied, -fy·ing.** **—tr.v.** **1. a.** To establish the identity of: *Fingerprints are used to identify persons.* **b.** To find out the origin, nature, or definitive characteristics of: *His accent was difficult to identify.* **2.** To determine the classification of: *identifying leaves by their shapes.* **3.** To consider as identical; equate: *Some identify communism with evil.* **4.** To associate; connect: *George Orwell is usually identified with the novel 1984.* **—intr.v.** To feel closely associated with a person, group, or place: *A Swiss always identifies with the canton where he was born.* [Medieval Latin *identificāre* : Late Latin *identitās,* identity + *facere,* to make.] **—i·den′ti·fi′a·ble** *adj.* **—i·den′ti·fi′er** *n.*

i·den·ti·ty (ī-dĕn′tĭ-tē) *n., pl.* **-ties.** **1.** The condition of being a certain person or thing and definitely recognizable as such. **2.** The personality of a particular individual; individuality. **3.** The condition of being exactly the same as something else: *The identity of the signatures was never in doubt.* **4. a.** A mathematical equation that remains true for all values of the variables that it contains. For example, $(x + y)^2 = x^2 + 2xy + y^2$ is true regardless of the values of x and y. **b.** An **identity element.** [Late Latin *identitās,* from Latin *idem,* the same.]

identity element. The element of a set of numbers that when combined with another number in an operation leaves that number unchanged. For example, 0 is the identity element under addition for the real numbers, since if a is any real number, $a + 0 = 0 + a = a$. Similarly, 1 is the identity element under multiplication for the real numbers, since $a \times 1 = 1 \times a = a$.

ideo-. A prefix meaning idea: **ideogram.** [French *idéo-,* from Greek *idea,* form, notion.]

id·e·o·gram (ĭd′ē-ə-grăm′, ī′dē-) *n.* **1.** A character or symbol representing an idea or thing without expressing a particular word or phrase for it, as the characters in Chinese. **2.** A graphic symbol, as &, $, and @.

id·e·o·graph (ĭd′ē-ə-grăf′, ī′dē-) *n.* An ideogram.

i·de·o·log·i·cal (ī′dē-ə-lŏj′ĭ-kəl, ĭd′ē-) Of or relating to ideology: *ideological conflicts.* **—i·de′o·log′i·cal·ly** *adv.*

i·de·ol·o·gy (ī′dē-ŏl′ə-jē, ĭd′ē-) *n., pl.* **-gies.** A group of political and social ideas that help to determine the thinking and behavior of a class, party, nation, etc.

ides (īds) *n.* (used with a sing. verb). In the ancient Roman calendar, the 15th day of Mar., May, July, or Oct. or the 13th day of the other months. [Middle English, from Old French, from Latin *īdūs.*]

id est (ĭd ĕst′). *Abbr.* **i.e.** *Latin.* That is.

idio-. A prefix meaning individuality, peculiarity, isolation, or spontaneity: **idiopathy.** [Greek, from *idios,* personal, separate.]

id·i·o·cy (ĭd′ē-ə-sē) *n., pl.* **-cies.** **1.** A condition of extreme mental retardation. **2.** Extreme folly or stupidity. **3.** A foolish or stupid utterance or deed.

id·i·om (ĭd′ē-əm) *n.* **1.** An expression having a special meaning not obtainable or not clear from the usual meaning of the words in the expression; for example, *fly off the handle* (lose one's temper) and *on pins and needles* (in a condition of anxiety) are idioms. **2.** The accepted pattern of word usage within a language: *an offense to English idiom.* **3.** A regional speech or dialect: *the colorful idiom of the Ozark Mountains.* **4.** A specialized vocabulary used by a group or profession: *legal idiom.* **5.** A style of artistic expression: *a painter searching for a new idiom.* **—See Syns at language.** [Old French *idiome,* from Late Latin *idiōma,* from Greek, peculiarity, idiom, from *idiousthai,* to make one's own, from *idios,* own, private.]

id·i·o·mat·ic (ĭd′ē-ə-măt′ĭk) *adj.* **1.** Peculiar to or in accordance with the accepted pattern of word usage within a language. **2.** Resembling or having the nature of an idiom. **3.** Using many idioms. **—id′i·o·mat′i·cal·ly** *adv.*

id·i·op·a·thy (ĭd′ē-ŏp′ə-thē) *n. Med.* **1.** A disease of unknown origin or cause; a primary disease. **2.** A disease for which no cause is known. [IDIO- + -PATHY.] **—id′i·o·path′ic** (-ə-păth′ĭk) *adj.*

id·i·o·syn·cra·sy (ĭd′ē-ō-sĭng′krə-sē, -sĭn′-) *n., pl.* **-sies.** A peculiar trait or form of behavior; eccentricity. **—See Syns at eccentricity.** [Greek *idiosunkrasia* : *idios,* personal + *sunkrasis,* mixture, temperament.] **—id′i·o·syn·crat′ic** (-sĭn-krăt′ĭk) *adj.* **—id′i·o·syn·crat′i·cal·ly** *adv.*

id·i·ot (ĭd′ē-ət) *n.* **1.** *Psychol.* A mentally deficient person having intelligence in the lowest measurable range, being unable to guard against common dangers, and incapable of learning connected speech. **2.** A very foolish or stupid person. [Middle English, from Old French *idiote,* from Latin *idiōta,* ignorant person, from Greek *idiōtēs,* private person, layman, from *idios,* private.]

id·i·ot·ic (ĭd′ē-ŏt′ĭk) *adj.* **1.** Showing or suffering from idiocy. **2.** Foolish; stupid. **—See Syns at foolish. —id′i·ot′i·cal·ly** *adv.*

i·dle (īd′l) *adj.* **i·dler, i·dlest.** **1.** Not working or devoted to working or producing: *idle employees.* **2.** Avoiding work; lazy; shiftless: *idle boys who do nothing but play.* **3.** Having no foundation in fact; worthless: *idle talk; no idle threat.* **—See Syns at inactive.** **—v. i·dled, i·dling.** **—intr.v.** **1.** To pass time without working or in avoiding work. **2.** To move lazily: *She idled over to her neighbor's for a chat.* **3.** To run at a low speed or out of gear: *The engine idled.* **—tr.v.** **1.** To pass (time) without working or in avoiding work: *idle away the hours.* **2.** To cause to be unemployed or inactive: *a strike that idled the merchant fleet.* **3.** To cause (a motor or machine) to idle. [Middle English *idel,* idle, empty, from Old English *īdel.*] **—i′dle·ness** *n.* **—i′dly** *adv.*

i·dler (īd′lər) *n.* Someone or something that idles.

i·dol (īd′l) *n.* **1.** An image used as an object of worship. **2.** A person or thing worshiped or adored. [Middle English, from Old French *idole, idele,* from Late Latin *īdōlum,* from Greek *eidōlon,* image, apparition, from *eidos,* form.]

i·dol·a·ter (ī-dŏl′ə-tər) *n.* **1.** A person who worships idols or an idol. **2.** A person who blindly admires or adores another. [Middle English *idolatrer,* from Old French *idolatre,* from Late Latin *īdōlolatrēs,* from Greek *eidōlolatreia* : *eidōlon,* idol + *-latrēs,* worshiper.]

i·dol·a·trous (ī-dŏl′ə-trəs) *adj.* **1.** Given to idolatry. **2.** Constituting idolatry: *idolatrous worship.* **—i·dol′a·trous·ly** *adv.* **—i·dol′a·trous·ness** *n.*

i·dol·a·try (ī-dŏl′ə-trē) *n., pl.* **-tries.** **1.** The worship of idols. **2.** Blind admiration or devotion: *a love of famous people that amounted to idolatry.* [Middle English *idolatrie,* from Old French, from Medieval Latin *īdōlatrīa,* from Late Latin *īdōlolatrīa,* from Greek *eidōlolatreia* : *eidōlon,* idol + *-latreia,* service, worship.]

i·dol·ize (īd′l-īz′) *tr.v.* **-ized, -iz·ing.** **1.** To regard with blind admiration or devotion. **2.** To worship as an idol. **—i′dol·i·za′tion** *n.* **—i′dol·iz′er** *n.*

i·dyll (īd′l) *n.* Also **i·dyl.** **1.** A short poem describing a pleasant scene of country life. **2.** A scene, experience, or relationship marked by supreme peacefulness and contentment. [Latin *īdyllium*, from Greek *eidullion*, dim. of *eidos*, form, picture.]

i·dyl·lic (ī-dĭl′ĭk) *adj.* **1.** Of or like an idyll. **2.** Full of quiet beauty and peacefulness: *idyllic countryside.* **—i·dyl′li·cal·ly** *adv.*

-ie. Var. of **-y** (small).

if (ĭf) *conj.* **1.** In the event that: *If I were to go, I would be late.* **2.** Granting that: *Even if that were true, what would we do?* **3.** On condition that: *She will sing only if she is paid.* **4.** Although possibly; even though: *a handsome if useless trinket.* **5.** Whether: *Ask if he will come.* **6.** —Used to introduce an exclamatory clause indicating: **a.** A wish: *If she had only come earlier!* **b.** Surprise, anger, or a similar emotion: *If she ever does that again!* —*n.* A possibility, condition, or stipulation: *I'm not listening to any ifs, ands, or buts.* [Middle English *yif*, from Old English *gif*.]
   Usage: **1. if, whether.** Both *if* and *whether* introduce noun clauses indicating doubt or uncertainty. These clauses commonly follow verbs such as *ask, doubt, know, learn, see,* and *wonder: By Friday we will learn if* (or *whether) the plan has succeeded.* Both *if* and *whether* can occur in the same sentence: *When I see those ominous clouds, I wonder if it will snow or whether the storm will blow over.* But when a noun clause indicating uncertainty occurs at the start of a sentence, *whether* is the correct choice: *Whether the plan has succeeded is uncertain.* **2. if and when.** This expression is a cliché. Use *if* to express possibility: *If you go, call me first.* Use *when* to express certainty: *When you go, call me first.*

ig·loo (ĭg′lōō) *n.* An Eskimo house, sometimes built of blocks of ice or hard snow. [Eskimo *iglu*, house.]

igloo
A summer igloo

ig·ne·ous (ĭg′nē-əs) *adj.* **1.** Of or relating to fire. **2.** *Geol.* **a.** Formed by solidification from a molten or partially molten state: *igneous rocks.* **b.** Of or pertaining to rock so formed. [Latin *igneus,* from *ignis,* fire.]

ig·nis fat·u·us (ĭg′nĭs făch′ōō-əs) *pl.* **ig·nes fat·u·i** (ĭg′nēz făch′ōō-ī′). **1.** A light that hovers over swampy ground at night, possibly caused by spontaneous combustion of gases from rotting organic matter. Also called **will-o'-the-wisp.** **2.** Something that misleads or deludes; a deception. [Medieval Latin, "foolish fire."]

ig·nite (ĭg-nīt′) *v.* **-nit·ed, -nit·ing.** *—tr.v.* **1. a.** To cause to burn. **b.** To set fire to. **2.** To arouse or kindle. *—intr.v.* To begin to burn; catch fire: *Dry leaves ignite readily.* [From Latin *ignīre,* to set on fire, from *ignis,* fire.] **—ig·nit′a·ble** *adj.* **—ig·nit′er** or **ig·ni′tor** *n.*
   Syns: **ignite, kindle, light, torch** (Slang) *v.* Core meaning: To cause to burn or undergo combustion (*ignite a fire*).

ig·ni·tion (ĭg-nĭsh′ən) *n.* **1.** The raising of the temperature of a substance to the point where it will burn continuously. **2. a.** An electrical system, typically powered by a battery or magneto, that provides the spark to ignite the fuel mixture in an internal-combustion engine. **b.** A switch that activates this system.

ig·no·ble (ĭg-nō′bəl) *adj.* **1.** Not having a noble character or purpose; dishonorable. **2.** Not of the nobility; common. [Latin *ignōbilis* : *in-,* not + *nōbilis,* noble.] **—ig′no·bil′i·ty** or **ig·no′ble·ness** *n.* **—ig·no′bly** *adv.*

ig·no·min·i·ous (ĭg′nə-mĭn′ē-əs) *adj.* **1.** Characterized by shame or disgrace: *an ignominious defeat.* **2.** Deserving disgrace or shame; despicable. **3.** Injuring dignity or pride; humiliating. **—ig′no·min′i·ous·ly** *adv.* **—ig′no·min′i·ous·ness** *n.*

ig·no·min·y (ĭg′nə-mĭn′ē, -mə-nē) *n., pl.* **-ies.** **1.** Dishonor; disgrace. **2.** That which causes dishonor; a disgraceful act or shameful conduct. —See Syns at **disgrace.** [Latin *ignōminia* : *in-,* not + *nōmen,* name, reputation.]

ig·no·ra·mus (ĭg′nə-rā′məs) *n.* An ignorant person. [Latin, "we do not know," from *ignōrāre,* to be ignorant.]

ig·no·rance (ĭg′nər-əns) *n.* The condition of being ignorant; lack of knowledge.

ig·no·rant (ĭg′nər-ənt) *adj.* **1.** Without education or knowledge: *an ignorant person.* **2.** Exhibiting lack of education or knowledge: *ignorant assumptions.* **3.** Unaware or uninformed: *Not having seen a newspaper, she was ignorant of the day's events.* [Middle English *ignoraunt,* from Old French *ignorant,* from Latin *ignōrāns,* pres. part. of *ignōrāre,* to be ignorant.] **—ig′no·rant·ly** *adv.*
   Syns: **1. ignorant, illiterate, uneducated, untaught** *adj.* Core meaning: Without education or knowledge (*ignorant youths who had quit school*). **2. ignorant, oblivious, unaware, unconscious, unfamiliar, unknowing, unwitting** *adj.* Core meaning: Not aware or informed (*walked into danger in ignorant bliss; ignorant of the change in plans*).

ig·nore (ĭg-nôr′, -nōr′) *tr.v.* **-nored, -nor·ing.** To pay no attention to; disregard. [French *ignorer,* from Latin *ignōrāre,* not to know, to be ignorant.] **—ig·nor′er** *n.*

i·gua·na (ĭ-gwä′nə) *n.* Any of various large tropical American lizards of the family Iguanidae, often having spiny projections along the back. [Spanish, from Arawak *iwana.*]

i·guan·o·don (ĭ-gwä′nə-dŏn′) *n.* Any of various large dinosaurs of the genus *Iguanodon,* of the Jurassic and Cretaceous periods. [IGUAN(A) + Greek *odōn,* tooth.]

IHS A graphic symbol for Jesus. [From ΙΗΣΟΤΣ or IHSOUS, Jesus (in Greek capitals).]

i·kon (ī′kŏn′) *n.* Var. of **icon.**

il-. Var. of **in-** (not) and **in-** (in).

-ile. A suffix meaning relationship with, similarity to, or capability of: **contractile.** [Middle English, from Old French, from Latin *-ilis.*]

il·e·a (ĭl′ē-ə) *n.* Plural of **ileum.**

il·e·ac (ĭl′ē-ăk′) *adj.* Of or pertaining to the ileum; ileal.

il·e·i·tis (ĭl′ē-ī′tĭs) *n.* Inflammation of the ileum. [ILE(UM) + -ITIS.]

il·e·um (ĭl′ē-əm) *n., pl.* **-e·a** (ĭl′ē-ə). The portion of the small intestine extending from the jejunum to the beginning of the large intestine. [From Latin *īleum,* groin, flank.] **—il′e·al** (-əl) *adj.*

i·lex (ī′lĕks′) *n.* **1.** Any of various trees or shrubs of the genus *Ilex;* a holly. **2.** The holm oak. [Latin *īlex,* holm oak.]

ilk (ĭlk) *n.* Type or kind: *He wanted no dealings with men of that ilk.* —See Syns at **kind.** [Middle English, from Old English *ilca,* same.]

ill (ĭl) *adj.* **worse** (wûrs), **worst** (wûrst). **1.** Not healthy; sick: *grew ill as the ship tossed.* **2.** Not normal; unsound: *ill health.* **3.** Resulting in suffering; distressing: *ill effects.* **4.** Having or showing a wish to harm; hostile: *ill intentions.* **5.** Not favorable: *ill luck.* **6.** Not proper; wrong: *subjected to ill use.* **7.** Inferior; poor; bad: *a piece of really ill behavior.* —See Syns at **sick.** *—adv.* **worse, worst. 1.** In an ill manner; not well: *ill repaid for her work.* **2.** Scarcely or with difficulty: *ill prepared.* *—n.* **1.** Evil; wrongdoing; sin. **2.** Disaster or harm. **3.** Something that causes suffering; an ailment: *seeking a cure for urban ills.* *—idiom.* **ill at ease.** Nervous and uncomfortable. [Middle English, from Old Norse *illr,* bad.]

I'll (īl). Contraction of: **1.** I will. **2.** I shall.

ill-ad·vised (ĭl′əd-vīzd′) *adj.* Done without wise counsel or careful deliberation. **—ill′-ad·vis′ed·ly** (-vī′zĭd-lē) *adv.*

ill-bred (ĭl′brĕd′) *adj.* Badly brought up; ill-mannered.

ill·con·sid·ered (ĭl′kən-sĭd′ərd) *adj.* Done without proper consideration; ill-advised.

il·le·gal (ĭ-lē′gəl) *adj.* **1.** Prohibited by law. **2.** Of or involving a crime. **3.** Prohibited by official rules: *an illegal baseball pitch.* —**il·le·gal·i·ty** (ĭl′ē-găl′ĭ-tē) *n.* —**il·le·gal·ly** *adv.*
    Syns: illegal, illegitimate, illicit, unlawful, wrongful *adj.* *Core meaning:* Prohibited by law (*illegal tax deductions*). See also Syns at **criminal.**

il·leg·i·ble (ĭ-lĕj′ə-bəl) *adj.* Not capable of being read: *an illegible scrawl.* —**il·leg′i·bil′i·ty** or **il·leg′i·ble·ness** *n.* —**il·leg′i·bly** *adv.*

il·le·git·i·mate (ĭl′ə-jĭt′ə-mĭt) *adj.* **1.** Against or not supported by the law; illegal: *an illegitimate claim to property* **2.** Born of parents not married to each other. **3.** Incorrectly deduced. —See Syns at **criminal** and **illegal.** —**il·le·git′i·ma·cy** *n.* —**il·le·git′i·mate·ly** *adv.*

ill-fat·ed (ĭl′fā′tĭd) *adj.* **1.** Destined for misfortune; doomed: *The ill-fated ship never reached port.* **2.** Marked by or causing misfortune: *an ill-fated decision; an ill-fated remark.* —See Syns at **unfortunate.**

ill-fa·vored (ĭl′fā′vərd) *adj.* **1.** Having an ugly or unattractive appearance. **2.** Objectionable; offensive.

ill-got·ten (ĭl′gŏt′n) *adj.* Obtained in an evil manner or by dishonest means.

ill-hu·mored (ĭl′hyoo′mərd) *adj.* Irritable and surly. —**ill′-hu′mored·ly** *adv.*

il·lib·er·al (ĭ-lĭb′ər-əl) *adj.* **1.** Narrow-minded; bigoted. **2.** Ungenerous; stingy. [Latin *illiberālis : in-*, not + *līberālis*, liberal, from *līber*, free.] —**il·lib′er·al′i·ty** (-ə-răl′ĭ-tē) or **il·lib′er·al·ness** *n.* —**il·lib′er·al·ly** *adv.*

il·lic·it (ĭ-lĭs′ĭt) *adj.* Not permitted by custom or law; illegal. —See Syns at **criminal** and **illegal.** [Latin *illicitus : in-*, not + *licitus*, allowed.] —**il·lic′it·ly** *adv.* —**il·lic′it·ness** *n.*

il·lim·it·a·ble (ĭ-lĭm′ĭ-tə-bəl) *adj.* Incapable of being limited; limitless. —**il·lim′it·a·bil′i·ty** or **il·lim′it·a·ble·ness** *n.* —**il·lim′it·a·bly** *adv.*

il·lit·er·a·cy (ĭ-lĭt′ər-ə-sē) *n., pl.* **-cies. 1.** The quality or condition of being unable to read and write. **2.** An error caused by unfamiliarity with language or literature.

il·lit·er·ate (ĭ-lĭt′ər-ĭt) *adj.* **1.** Unable to read and write. **2.** Showing a lack of familiarity with language or literature. **3.** Violating prescribed standards of speech or writing: *illiterate usage.* **4.** Ignorant of the fundamentals of a given art or branch of knowledge: *musically illiterate.* —See Syns at **ignorant.** —*n.* A person who is illiterate. —**il·lit′er·ate·ly** *adv.* —**il·lit′er·ate·ness** *n.*

ill-man·nered (ĭl′măn′ərd) *adj.* Lacking or indicating a lack of good manners; impolite; rude. —See Syns at **rude.** —**ill′-man′nered·ly** *adv.*

ill-na·tured (ĭl′nā′chərd) *adj.* Disagreeable; surly. —**ill′-na′tured·ly** *adv.* —**ill′-na′tured·ness** *n.*

ill·ness (ĭl′nĭs) *n.* **1.** Sickness of body or mind. **2.** A particular sickness or disease; an ailment.

il·log·i·cal (ĭ-lŏj′ĭ-kəl) *adj.* Contradicting or disregarding the principles of logic. —**il·log′i·cal′i·ty** (-kăl′ĭ-tē) or **il·log′i·cal·ness** *n.* —**il·log′i·cal·ly** *adv.*

ill-starred (ĭl′stärd′) *adj.* Ill-fated; unlucky.

ill-tem·pered (ĭl′tĕm′pərd) *adj.* Having a bad temper; irritable. —See Syns at **irritable.** —**ill′-tem′pered·ly** *adv.*

ill-treat (ĭl′trēt′) *tr.v.* To treat harmfully or wrongly; maltreat. —**ill′-treat′ment** *n.*

il·lu·mi·nate (ĭ-loo′mə-nāt′) *tr.v.* **-nat·ed, -nat·ing. 1.** To provide with light; turn or focus light upon: *The full moon illuminated the landscape.* **2.** To decorate or hang with lights. **3.** To make understandable: *clues that illuminate the snarled story.* **4.** To enable to understand; enlighten. **5.** To adorn (a text, page, or initial letter) with designs, pictures, or decorative lettering. —See Syns at **clarify.** [From Latin *illūmināre : in-*, in + *lūmināre*, to light up.] —**il·lu′mi·na′tive** *adj.* —**il·lu′mi·na′tor** *n.*

il·lu·mi·na·tion (ĭ-loo′mə-nā′shən) *n.* **1.** The act of illuminating. **2.** The condition of being illuminated. **3.** A light source. **4.** Light or lights used as decoration. **5.** Spiritual or intellectual enlightenment. **6.** Clarification; elucidation. **7.** The art or act of decorating a text, page, or initial letter with designs, pictures, or lettering.

il·lu·mine (ĭ-loo′mĭn) *tr.v.* **-mined, -min·ing.** To illuminate; give light to. —**il·lu′min·a·ble** *adj.*

ill-use (ĭl′yooz′) *tr.v.* **-used, -us·ing.** To treat badly; abuse. —*n.* (ĭl′yoos′). Bad or unjust treatment.

il·lu·sion (ĭ-loo′zhən) *n.* **1.** An appearance or impression that has no real basis; false perception: *creating the illusion of depth in a painting.* **2.** A mistaken notion or belief. **3.** The condition of being deceived by false perceptions or beliefs. —See Usage note at **allusion.** [Middle English *illusioun*, from Old French *illusion*, from Late Latin *illūsiō*, from Latin, a mocking, jeering, from *illūdere : in-*, against + *lūdere*, to play.] —**il·lu′sion·al** or **il·lu′sion·ar′y** (-zhə-nĕr′ē) *adj.*

illuminate
The Empire State Building at night

illusion
A painting with the illusion of depth

il·lu·sion·ist (ĭ-loo′zhə-nĭst) *n.* An entertainer skilled at producing illusions; conjuror or magician.

il·lu·sive (ĭ-loo′sĭv) *adj.* Of or like an illusion; lacking reality; illusory. —**il·lu′sive·ly** *adv.* —**il·lu′sive·ness** *n.*

il·lu·so·ry (ĭ-loo′sə-rē, -zə-) *adj.* Deceptive; not real; illusive.

il·lus·trate (ĭl′ə-strāt′, ĭ-lŭs′trāt′) *v.* **-trat·ed, -trat·ing.** —*tr.v.* **1. a.** To clarify or explain by using examples, comparisons, etc. **b.** To clarify by serving as an example, comparison, etc.: *The diagram illustrates the arrangement of the solar system.* **2.** To provide with explanatory or decorative pictures, photographs, diagrams, etc.: *illustrate a magazine.* —*intr.v.* To present a clarification, example, or explanation. [From Latin *illūstrāre : in-*, in + *lūstrāre*, to make bright, enlighten.] —**il′lus·tra′tor** *n.*

il·lus·tra·tion (ĭl′ə-strā′shən) *n.* **1. a.** The act of illustrating: *an illustration of how to pitch a tent.* **b.** The condition of being illustrated. **2.** Something, such as a picture, diagram, or chart, serving to clarify, explain, or decorate. **3.** Something serving as an example, comparison, or proof: *A rock falling to the ground is an illustration of gravity.*

il·lus·tra·tive (ĭ-lŭs′trə-tĭv, ĭl′ə-strā′tĭv) *adj.* Acting as an illustration: *pictures and other illustrative material.* —**il·lus′tra·tive·ly** *adv.*

il·lus·tri·ous (ĭ-lŭs′trē-əs) *adj.* Renowned; famous; celebrated. [Latin *illūstris*, shining, clear.] —**il·lus′tri·ous·ly** *adv.* —**il·lus′tri·ous·ness** *n.*

ill will. Unfriendly feeling; hostility; enmity.

il·men·ite (ĭl′mə-nīt′) *n.* A lustrous black-to-brownish titanium ore, essentially $FeTiO_3$. [German *Ilmenit*, after *Ilmen*, range in the Ural Mountains.]

im-.[1] Var. of **in-** (not).

im-.[2] Var. of **in-** (in).

I'm (īm). Contraction of I am.

im·age (ĭm′ĭj) *n.* **1.** A pattern of light and dark areas, often produced with color as well, that duplicates the appearance of some real object or objects, esp. such a pattern formed by one or more lenses, mirrors, or other optical devices. **2.** A mental picture of something not present or real: *Images of snakes, lizards, and frogs came to his mind.* **3.** A reproduction of a person or thing, as a statue or a figure in a painting. **4. a.** A form distinctly like another; a close likeness: *"And God said, 'Let us make man in our image'"* (The Bible, Genesis 1:26). **b.** A person who resembles another: *the very image of his grandfather.* **5.** A personification: *He is the image of health.* **6.** A figure of speech that evokes a mental picture. **7.** The character projected by someone or something to the public; reputation:

As a star she lived expensively, trying to maintain a glamorous image. [Middle English, from Old French, from Latin *imāgō*, copy, likeness.]

im·age·ry (ĭm´ĭj-rē) *n., pl.* **-ries. 1.** Mental pictures or images. **2.** The use of figures of speech or vivid descriptions in writing or speaking to produce mental images.

i·mag·in·a·ble (ĭ-măj´ə-nə-bəl) *adj.* Capable of being conceived of by the imagination. **—i·mag´in·a·bly** *adv.*

i·mag·i·nar·y (ĭ-măj´ə-něr´ē) *adj.* **1.** Having existence only in the imagination; unreal. **2.** *Math.* **a.** Of, pertaining to, or being the coefficient of the imaginary unit in a complex number. **b.** Of, pertaining to, involving, or being an imaginary number. **c.** Involving only a complex number of which the real part is zero. —*n., pl.* **-ies.** *Math.* An **imaginary number. —i·mag´i·nar´i·ly** (-nâr´ə-lē) *adv.* **—i·mag´i·nar´i·ness** *n.*

imaginary number. A complex number in which the real part is zero and the coefficient of the imaginary unit is not zero.

i·mag·i·na·tion (ĭ-măj´ə-nā´shən) *n.* **1. a.** The ability of the mind to conceive ideas or to form images of something not present; the power of mental conception. **b.** Such ability used creatively; inventiveness; creativity: *the lively imagination of the writer.* **2.** The ability to act effectively by using the creative power of the mind; resourcefulness: *Using his imagination, Crusoe survived and prospered on his island.* **—i·mag´i·na´tion·al** *adj.*

Syns: imagination, fancy, fantasy *n. Core meaning:* The power of the mind to form images *(the writer's lively imagination; just a figment of your imagination).*

i·mag·i·na·tive (ĭ-măj´ə-nə-tĭv, -nā´-) *adj.* **1.** Having a strong or creative imagination. **2.** Tending to indulge in the fanciful or in make-believe. **3.** Created by, indicative of, or characterized by imagination: *imaginative writing; an imaginative costume.* **—i·mag´i·na·tive·ly** *adv.* **—i·mag´i·na·tive·ness** *n.*

i·mag·ine (ĭ-măj´ĭn) *v.* **-ined, -in·ing.** —*tr.v.* **1.** To form a mental picture or image of: *Can you imagine a blue horse with a yellow mane?* **2.** To think; suppose: *I imagine you're right.* —*intr.v.* **1.** To use the imagination. **2.** To make a guess; to conjecture. [Middle English *imaginen,* from Old French *imaginer,* from Latin *imāginārī,* to picture to oneself, from *imāgō,* image.] **—i·mag´in·er** *n.*

i·ma·go (ĭ-mā´gō) *n., pl.* **-goes** or **i·mag·i·nes** (ĭ-măj´ə-nēz´). **1.** An insect in its sexually mature adult stage after metamorphosis. **2.** *Psychoanal.* An often idealized image of a person, usu. a parent, formed in childhood and persisting into adulthood. [From Latin *imāgō,* image.]

i·mam (ĭ-mäm´) *n.* **1.** A Moslem prayer leader. **2.** A Moslem scholar, esp. an authority on Islamic law. **3. Imam. a.** A title accorded to Mohammed and his four immediate successors. **b.** One of the leaders regarded by the Shiites as successors of Mohammed. **c.** Any of various religious and temporal leaders claiming descent from Mohammed. [Arabic *imām,* leader, from *amma,* he led.]

im·bal·ance (ĭm-băl´əns) *n.* A lack of balance.

im·be·cile (ĭm´bĭ-sĭl, -səl) *n.* **1.** A feeble-minded person. **2.** A stupid person. —*adj.* Also **im·be·cil·ic** (ĭm´bĭ-sĭl´ĭk). **1.** Lacking in mental ability. **2.** Stupid. [Old French *imbecille,* from Latin *imbēcillus,* feeble : *in-,* not + *bacillum,* dim. of *baculum,* staff, rod.] **—im·be·cil´i·ty** (-sĭl´ĭ-tē) *n.*

im·bed (ĭm-bĕd´) *v.* Var. of **embed.**

im·bibe (ĭm-bīb´) *v.* **-bibed, -bib·ing.** —*tr.v.* **1.** To drink. **2.** To absorb or take in as if by drinking: *"the whole body . . . imbibes delight through every pore"* (Thoreau). —*intr.v.* To drink. [Middle English *enbiben,* to absorb, from Old French *embiber,* from Latin *imbibere : in-,* in + *bibere,* to drink.] **—im·bib´er** *n.*

im·bro·glio (ĭm-brōl´yō) *n., pl.* **-glios. 1.** A confused or difficult situation; entanglement. **2.** A confused heap; a tangle. [Italian *imbroglio,* prob. from French *embrouiller,* to confuse, embroil.]

im·bue (ĭm-byōō´) *tr.v.* **-bued, -bu·ing. 1.** To make thoroughly wet; saturate, as with stain or dye. **2.** To inspire, permeate, or fill: *imbued with a revolutionary spirit.* [Latin *imbuere,* to moisten, stain.]

im·i·ta·ble (ĭm´ĭ-tə-bəl) *adj.* Capable or worthy of being imitated.

im·i·tate (ĭm´ĭ-tāt´) *tr.v.* **-tat·ed, -tat·ing. 1.** To copy the actions, appearance, function, or sounds of; model oneself after: *Little children imitate their parents.* **2.** To reproduce exactly; to copy: *She imitated the old woman's high-pitched laugh.* **3.** To look like; resemble: *Nylon can imitate many other materials.* [From Latin *imitārī.*] **—im´i·ta·tor** *n.*

Syns: imitate, burlesque, mimic, mock, parody *v. Core meaning:* To copy (the manner or expression of another), often mockingly *(a comedian who imitated the President).*

im·i·ta·tion (ĭm´ĭ-tā´shən) *n.* **1.** An act of imitating. **2.** Something derived or copied from an original. *—modifier: imitation leather.* **—im´i·ta´tion·al** *adj.*

im·i·ta·tive (ĭm´ĭ-tā´tĭv) *adj.* **1.** Of or involving imitation: *imitative gifts.* **2.** Not original; derivative; copied. **3.** Tending to imitate. **4.** Onomatopoeic. **—im´i·ta´tive·ly** *adv.* **—im´i·ta´tive·ness** *n.*

im·mac·u·late (ĭ-măk´yə-lĭt) *adj.* **1.** Perfectly clean; spotless. **2.** Free from fault or error: *an immaculate record.* —See Syns at **clean.** [Middle English *immaculat,* from Latin *immaculātus : in-,* not + *maculātus,* past part. of *maculāre,* to stain, blemish, from *macula,* spot.] **—im·mac´u·late·ly** *adv.* **—im·mac´u·late·ness** *n.*

Immaculate Conception. The Roman Catholic doctrine that the Virgin Mary was conceived in her mother's womb free from all stain of original sin.

im·ma·nent (ĭm´ə-nənt) *adj.* Existing or remaining within; inherent: *believed in a God immanent in human beings.* [Late Latin *immanēns,* pres. part. of *immanēre : in-,* in + *manēre,* to remain .] **—im´ma·nence** or **im´ma·nen·cy** *n.* **—im´ma·nent·ly** *adv.*

im·ma·te·ri·al (ĭm´ə-tîr´ē-əl) *adj.* **1.** Having no material body or form: *felt the ghost's immaterial presence.* **2.** Of no importance or relevance. —See Syns at **irrelevant.** **—im´ma·te´ri·al·ly** *adv.* **—im´ma·te´ri·al·ness** *n.*

im·ma·ture (ĭm´ə-tōōr´, -tyōōr´, -chōōr´) *adj.* **1.** Not fully grown or developed; unripe: *immature corn.* **2.** Marked by or suggesting a lack of normal maturity: *She is too immature to be trusted to babysit.* —See Syns at **young.** **—im´ma·ture´ly** *adv.* **—im´ma·tur´i·ty** or **im´ma·ture´ness** *n.*

im·meas·ur·a·ble (ĭ-mězh´ər-ə-bəl) *adj.* **1.** Incapable of being measured. **2.** Vast; limitless. **—im·meas´ur·a·bil´i·ty** or **im·meas´ur·a·ble·ness** *n.* **—im·meas´ur·a·bly** *adv.*

im·me·di·a·cy (ĭ-mē´dē-ə-sē) *n., pl.* **-cies. 1.** The condition or quality of being immediate; directness. **2.** Something immediate, as in importance.

im·me·di·ate (ĭ-mē´dē-ĭt) *adj.* **1.** Taking place at once or very soon; occurring without delay: *needing immediate medical care.* **2.** Close at hand; nearby: *our immediate surroundings; the immediate past.* **3.** Coming next or very soon: *the immediate future; an immediate danger.* **4.** Next in line or relation: *an immediate successor.* **5.** Being or acting without anything intervening; direct: *the immediate cause of death.* —See Syns at **near.** [Late Latin *immediātus : in-,* not + *mediātus,* past part. of *mediāre,* to be in the middle.] **—im·me´di·ate·ness** *n.*

im·me·di·ate·ly (ĭ-mē´dē-ĭt-lē) *adv.* **1.** Without anything intervening; directly: *Take the road immediately after you leave the turnpike.* **2.** Without delay. —*conj.* As soon as; directly: *He phoned immediately he reached home.*

im·med·i·ca·ble (ĭ-měd´ĭ-kə-bəl) *adj.* Incurable.

im·me·mo·ri·al (ĭm´ə-môr´ē-əl, -mōr´-) *adj.* Reaching beyond the limits of memory, tradition, or recorded history: *time immemorial.* **—im´me·mo´ri·al·ly** *adv.*

im·mense (ĭ-měns´) *adj.* **1.** Extremely large; huge: *immense icebergs; an immense span of time.* **2.** *Informal.* Extremely good; excellent. —See Syns at **giant.** [Old French, from Latin *immēnsus : in-,* not + *mēnsus,* past part. of *mētīrī,* to measure.] **—im·mense´ly** *adv.* **—im·mense´ness** *n.*

im·men·si·ty (ĭ-měn´sĭ-tē) *n., pl.* **-ties. 1.** The quality or condition of being immense. **2.** Something immense.

im·merge (ĭ-mûrj´) *v.* **-merged, -merg·ing.** —*tr.v.* To immerse. —*intr.v.* To submerge or disappear in or as if in a liquid. [Latin *immergere,* to immerse.] **—im·mer´gence** *n.*

im·merse (ĭ-mûrs´) *tr.v.* **-mersed, -mers·ing. 1.** To cover completely in a liquid; submerge. **2.** To baptize by submerging in water. **3.** To involve profoundly; absorb. [Latin *immersus,* past part. of *immergere,* to dip in.]

---

im·mer·sion (ĭ-mûr'zhən, -shən) n. **1.** An act of immersing. **2.** The condition of being immersed. **3.** Baptism performed by totally submerging a person in water.

im·mi·grant (ĭm'ĭ-grənt) n. **1.** A person who leaves a country to settle permanently in another. **2.** An organism that appears where it was formerly unknown. —*modifier: an immigrant family.*

im·mi·grate (ĭm'ĭ-grāt') v. **-grat·ed, -grat·ing.** —*intr.v.* To enter and settle in a country or region to which one is not native. —*tr.v.* To send or introduce as immigrants. —**im'·mi·gra'tion** n.

im·mi·nent (ĭm'ə-nənt) adj. About to occur; impending. [Latin *imminēns,* pres. part. of *imminēre,* to project over or toward, threaten : *in-,* toward + *-minēre,* to project.] —**im'mi·nence** n. —**im'mi·nent·ly** adv.

im·mo·bile (ĭ-mō'bəl, -bēl', -bīl') adj. **1.** Not movable; fixed. **2.** Not moving; motionless. —**im'mo·bil'i·ty** n.

im·mo·bi·lize (ĭ-mō'bə-līz') tr.v. **-lized, -liz·ing.** To render incapable of moving; make immobile. —**im·mo'bi·li·za'tion** n. —**im·mo'bi·liz'er** n.

im·mod·er·ate (ĭ-mŏd'ər-ĭt) adj. Not moderate; extreme. —**im·mod'er·ate·ly** adv. —**im·mod'er·ate·ness** or **im·mod'er·a'tion** n.

im·mod·est (ĭ-mŏd'ĭst) adj. **1.** Lacking modesty. **2.** Morally offensive: *immodest language.* **3.** Conceited; boastful: *her immodest description of her own talents.* —**im·mod'est·ly** adv. —**im·mod'es·ty** n.

im·mo·late (ĭm'ə-lāt') tr.v. **-lat·ed, -lat·ing. 1.** To kill as a sacrifice. **2.** To destroy. [From Latin *immolāre,* to sacrifice, orig. "to sprinkle with sacrificial meal" : *in-,* on + *mola,* meal.] —**im'mo·la'tion** n. —**im'mo·la'tor** n.

im·mor·al (ĭ-môr'əl, ĭ-mŏr'-) adj. **1.** Contrary to what is just, right, or good: *considered slavery immoral.* **2.** Contrary to accepted rules of conduct, esp. sexual conduct. —**im·mor'al·ist** n. —**im·mor'al·ly** adv.

im·mo·ral·i·ty (ĭm'ə-răl'ĭ-tē, ĭm'ô-) n., pl. **-ties. 1.** The quality or condition of being immoral. **2.** Behavior that is immoral: *guilty of immorality.*

im·mor·tal (ĭ-môr'tl) adj. **1.** Not subject to death; living forever: *an immortal soul.* **2.** Lasting forever, as in fame: *an immortal poet.* —n. **1.** A being who will not and cannot die. **2.** Someone with enduring fame: *a baseball immortal.* **3. immortals.** The gods of ancient Greece and Rome. [Middle English, from Latin *immortālis* : *in-,* not + *mortālis,* mortal.] —**im·mor'tal·ly** adv.

im·mor·tal·i·ty (ĭm'ôr-tăl'ĭ-tē) n. **1.** The quality or condition of being immortal. **2.** Endless life. **3.** Enduring fame.

im·mor·tal·ize (ĭ-môr'tl-īz') tr.v. **-ized, -iz·ing.** To make immortal.

im·mov·a·ble (ĭ-mōō'və-bəl) adj. **1.** Not capable of moving or of being moved. **2.** Unyielding in principle, purpose, or adherence; steadfast. **3.** Not readily moved emotionally; impassive. —n. **immovables.** Property, such as real estate, that cannot be moved. —**im·mov'a·ble·ness** or **im·mov'a·bil'i·ty** n. —**im·mov'a·bly** adv.

im·mune (ĭ-myōōn') adj. **1. a.** Exempt: *immune from taxation.* **b.** Not susceptible; resistant: *immune to change; immune to persuasion.* **2.** Med. Having immunity. [Latin *immūnis* : *in-,* not + *mūnia,* duties.]

im·mu·ni·ty (ĭ-myōō'nĭ-tē) n., pl. **-ties. 1.** The quality or condition of being immune. **2.** The ability of an animal or plant to resist a disease, esp. a disease caused by microbes, wholly or in part. **3.** Freedom from certain duties, penalties, etc.: *the rights and immunities enjoyed by citizens.*

im·mu·nize (ĭm'yə-nīz') tr.v. **-nized, -niz·ing.** To render immune. —**im'mu·ni·za'tion** n.

im·mu·no·gen·ic (ĭm'yə-nō-jĕn'ĭk) adj. Producing immunity. [From IMMUNE + -GENIC.]

im·mu·nol·o·gy (ĭm'yə-nŏl'ə-jē) n. The medical study of immunity. [From IMMUNE + -LOGY.] —**im'mu·no·log'ic** (-nə-lŏj'ĭk) or **im'mu·no·log'i·cal** adj. —**im'mu·no·log'i·cal·ly** adv. —**im'mu·nol'o·gist** n.

im·mure (ĭ-myōōr') tr.v. **-mured, -mur·ing.** To confine within walls; imprison. [Medieval Latin *immūrāre* : Latin *in-,* in + *mūrus,* wall.] —**im·mure'ment** n.

im·mu·ta·ble (ĭ-myōō'tə-bəl) adj. Not subject to change; unchangeable. —See Syns at **inflexible.** [Middle English, from Latin *immūtābilis* : *in-,* not + *mūtābilis,* mutable.]

—**im·mu'ta·bil'i·ty** or **im·mu'ta·ble·ness** n. —**im·mu'ta·bly** adv.

imp (ĭmp) n. **1.** A mischievous child. **2.** A small demon. [Middle English *impe,* scion, offspring, child, from Old English *impa,* young shoot, sapling, from *impian,* to graft on, from Medieval Latin *impotus,* graft, from Greek *emphutos,* implanted : *en-,* in + *phuein,* plant.]

im·pact (ĭm'păkt) n. **1.** The striking of one body against another; a collision. **2.** An impression made on the senses or feelings: *the emotional impact of a poem.* **3.** The effect of one thing upon another: *the impact of computers on business procedures.* —tr.v. (ĭm-păkt'). **1.** To pack firmly together. **2.** To strike; hit. [From Latin *impactus,* past part. of *impingere,* to dash or strike against, impinge.] —**im·pac'tion** n.

im·pact·ed (ĭm-păk'tĭd) adj. **1.** Wedged together at the broken ends: *The fractured bone was impacted.* **2.** Located inside the gum in such a way that it will not come through the gum in a normal position: *an impacted tooth.*

im·pair (ĭm-pâr') tr.v. To diminish in strength, value, quantity, or quality; to damage. [Middle English *empairen,* from Old French *empeirer.*] —**im·pair'ment** n.

im·pa·la (ĭm-pä'lə, -pă'lə) n. An African antelope, *Aepyceros melampus,* having a reddish coat and ridged, curved horns in the male. [Zulu.]

im·pale (ĭm-pāl') tr.v. **-paled, -pal·ing. 1.** To pierce with a sharp stake or point. **2.** To torture or kill by impaling. [Medieval Latin *impālāre* : Latin *in-,* in + *pālus,* stake, pole.] —**im·pale'ment** n. —**im·pal'er** n.

im·pal·pa·ble (ĭm-păl'pə-bəl) adj. **1.** Not perceptible to the touch; intangible. **2.** Not easily perceived or grasped by the mind: *impalpable hints.* —See Syns at **imperceptible.** —**im·pal'pa·bil'i·ty** n. —**im·pal'pa·bly** adv.

im·pan·el (ĭm-păn'əl) tr.v. **-eled** or **-elled, -el·ing** or **-el·ling.** Also **em·pan·el** (ĕm-). To enroll (a jury) upon a panel or list. —**im·pan'el·ment** n.

im·part (ĭm-pärt') tr.v. **1.** To give; bestow: *impart a backspin to the ball; impart advice.* **2.** To make known; disclose: *Privately she imparted her true feelings.* [Latin *impartīre,* to share with : *in-,* in + *partīre,* to share, divide.]

im·par·tial (ĭm-pär'shəl) adj. Not favoring either side; unprejudiced. —See Syns at **fair¹.** —**im·par'ti·al'i·ty** (-shē-ăl'ĭ-tē) or **im·par'tial·ness** n. —**im·par'tial·ly** adv.

im·pass·a·ble (ĭm-păs'ə-bəl) adj. Impossible to travel across or over: *a deep, impassable gorge.* —**im·pass'a·bil'i·ty** or **im·pass'a·ble·ness** n. —**im·pass'a·bly** adv.

im·passe (ĭm'păs) n. **1.** A road or passage having no exit; dead end. **2.** A difficult situation from which there is no workable escape. **3.** A deadlock. [French : Old French *in-,* not, in- + *passer,* to pass.]

im·pas·sioned (ĭm-păsh'ənd) adj. Filled with passion; ardent.

im·pas·sive (ĭm-păs'ĭv) adj. **1.** Devoid of or not subject to emotion; apathetic. **2.** Revealing no emotion; expressionless. [IN- (not) + Latin *passīvus,* capable of feeling.] —**im·pas'sive·ly** adv. —**im·pas'sive·ness** or **im'pas·siv'i·ty** (ĭm'pă-sĭv'ĭ-tē) n.

im·pa·tience (ĭm-pā'shəns) n. **1.** The inability to wait patiently. **2.** The inability to endure irritation. **3.** Restless eagerness, desire, or anticipation: *their impatience to get home.* —**im·pa'tient** adj. —**im·pa'tient·ly** adv.

im·peach (ĭm-pēch') tr.v. **1.** To charge with misconduct in office before a proper tribunal. **2.** To challenge or discredit; attack: *impeach a man's honesty.* [Middle English *empeachen,* to impede, accuse, from Old French *empescher,* impede, from Late Latin *impedicāre,* to put in fetters : Latin *in-,* in + *pedica,* fetter.] —**im·peach'a·ble** adj. —**im·peach'er** n. —**im·peach'ment** n.

im·pec·ca·ble (ĭm-pĕk'ə-bəl) adj. **1.** Without flaw; faultless: *impeccable table manners.* **2.** Not capable of sin or wrongdoing. —See Syns at **perfect.** [Latin *impeccābilis,* not liable to sin : *in-,* not + *peccāre,* to sin.] —**im·pec'ca·bil'i·ty** n. —**im·pec'ca·bly** adv.

im·pe·cu·ni·ous (ĭm'pĭ-kyōō'nē-əs) adj. Lacking money; penniless. [IN- (not) + obs. *pecunious,* rich, from Middle English *pecunyous,* from Latin *pecūniōsus,* from *pecūnia,*

ă pat	ā pay	â care	ä father	ĕ pet	ē be	hw which	ĭ pit	ī tie	î pier	ŏ pot	ō toe	ô paw, for	oi noise
ōō took	ōō boot	ou out	th thin	th this	ŭ cut		û urge	zh vision	ə about, item, edible, gallop, circus				

money.] **—im·pe·cu′ni·ous·ly** *adv.* **—im′pe·cu′ni·ous·ness** or **im′pe·cu′ni·os′i·ty** (-ŏs′ĭ-tē) *n.*

im·ped·ance (ĭm-pēd′ns) *n. Symbol* **Z** A measure of the total opposition to current flow in an alternating-current circuit, equal to the ratio of the rms electromotive force in the circuit to the rms current produced by it and usu. represented in complex notation as $Z = R + iX$, where R is the ohmic resistance and X is the reactance. [From IM-PEDE.]

im·pede (ĭm-pēd′) *tr.v.* **-ped·ed, -ped·ing.** To obstruct the way of; block. —See Syns at **hinder.** [Latin *impedīre,* to entangle, fetter.] **—im·ped′er** *n.*

im·ped·i·ment (ĭm-pĕd′ə-mənt) *n.* **1.** A hindrance; an obstruction: *One's racial origin should be no impediment to getting a job.* **2.** Something that impedes, esp. an organic defect preventing clear articulation: *a speech impediment.*

im·ped·i·men·ta (ĭm-pĕd′ə-mĕn′tə) *pl.n.* Objects, as provisions or baggage, that impede movement.

im·pel (ĭm-pĕl′) *tr.v.* **-pelled, -pel·ling.** **1.** To urge to action; spur: *the curiosity that impels the research scientist.* **2.** To drive forward; propel. —See Syns at **provoke.** [Latin *impellere,* to drive on or against : *in-,* against + *pellere,* to drive.]

im·pel·ler (ĭm-pĕl′ər) *n.* **1.** Someone or something that impels. **2.** *Mechanics.* **a.** A rotor or rotor blade. **b.** A rotating device used to force a gas in a given direction under pressure.

im·pend (ĭm-pĕnd′) *intr.v.* **1.** To hang or hover menacingly. **2.** To be about to take place: *when war was impending.* [Latin *impendēre : in-,* against + *pendēre,* to hang.]

im·pen·e·tra·ble (ĭm-pĕn′ĭ-trə-bəl) *adj.* **1.** Not capable of being penetrated or entered: *an impenetrable swamp.* **2.** Incomprehensible; unfathomable. **3.** Impervious to reason or persuasion. **—im·pen′e·tra·bil′i·ty** or **im·pen′e·tra·ble·ness** *n.* **—im·pen′e·tra·bly** *adv.*

im·pen·i·tent (ĭm-pĕn′ĭ-tənt) *adj.* Not penitent; unrepentant. **—n.** Someone who is impenitent. **—im·pen′i·tence** *n.* **—im·pen′i·tent·ly** *adv.*

im·per·a·tive (ĭm-pĕr′ə-tĭv) *adj.* **1.** Expressing a command; peremptory: *the imperative tone of a person accustomed to giving orders.* **2.** Having the power or authority to command or control. **3.** *Gram.* Of or being the mood that expresses a command or request: *a verb in the imperative mood.* **4.** Obligatory; mandatory: *It is imperative for mountaineers to be roped together.* —See Syns at **compulsory.** **—n.** **1.** *Gram.* **a.** The imperative mood. **b.** A verb form of the imperative mood. **2. a.** A command; an order. **b.** An obligation. [Late Latin *imperātīvus,* from Latin *imperāre,* to command : *in-,* against + *parāre,* to prepare.] **—im·per′a·tive·ly** *adv.* **—im·per′a·tive·ness** *n.*

im·pe·ra·tor (ĭm′pə-rä′tôr, -tər) *n.* **1.** A supreme commander in ancient Rome. **2.** An emperor. [Latin *imperātor,* emperor.]

im·per·cep·ti·ble (ĭm′pər-sĕp′tə-bəl) *adj.* **1.** Not capable of being perceived by the senses or mind. **2.** Barely perceptible: *an imperceptible nod of the head.* **—im′per·cep′ti·bil′i·ty** or **im′per·cep′ti·ble·ness** *n.* **—im′per·cep′ti·bly** *adv.*

Syns: imperceptible, impalpable, indistinguishable, insensible, intangible, unappreciable, unnoticeable *adj. Core meaning:* Incapable of being seen, measured, or detected by the mind or senses (*an imperceptible flutter of her eyelashes; color—imperceptible to the touch*).

im·per·fect (ĭm-pûr′fĭkt) *adj.* **1.** Not perfect. **2.** Of or being the set of verb forms used in certain languages to express incomplete or continuous action. **3.** Having either stamens or a pistil only: *imperfect flowers.* **—n.** **1.** The imperfect tense. **2.** A verb in this tense. **—im·per′fect·ly** *adv.* **—im·per′fect·ness** *n.*

Syns: imperfect, defective, faulty *adj. Core meaning:* Having a defect or defects (*imperfect crystal; an imperfect memory*).

im·per·fec·tion (ĭm′pər-fĕk′shən) *n.* **1.** The quality or condition of being imperfect. **2.** Something imperfect; a defect; flaw.

im·pe·ri·al (ĭm-pîr′ē-əl) *adj.* **1.** Of or relating to an empire or emperor: *imperial Rome; the imperial court.* **2.** Designating a nation or government having sovereign rights over colonies or dependencies. **3.** Regal; majestic. **4.** Outstanding in size or quality. **5.** Of or relating to the British

Imperial System of weights and measures. [Middle English, from Old French, from Late Latin *imperiālis,* from Latin *imperium,* command, empire.] **—im·pe′ri·al·ly** *adv.*

im·pe·ri·al·ism (ĭm-pîr′ē-ə-lĭz′əm) *n.* **1.** The policy of extending a nation's authority by acquiring foreign lands or by establishing economic and political dominance over other nations. **2.** The system, policies, or practices of an empire. **—im·pe′ri·al·ist** *n. & adj.* **—im·pe′ri·al·is′tic** *adj.* **—im·pe′ri·al·is′ti·cal·ly** *adv.*

im·per·il (ĭm-pĕr′əl) *tr.v.* **-iled** or **-illed, -il·ing** or **-il·ling.** To put in peril; endanger. **—im·per′il·ment** *n.*

im·pe·ri·ous (ĭm-pîr′ē-əs) *adj.* **1.** Domineering; overbearing. **2.** Urgent; pressing. —See Syns at **dictatorial.** [Latin *imperiōsus,* from *imperium,* imperium.] **—im·pe′ri·ous·ly** *adv.* **—im·pe′ri·ous·ness** *n.*

im·per·ish·a·ble (ĭm-pĕr′ĭ-shə-bəl) *adj.* Not perishable. **—im·per′ish·a·bil′i·ty** or **im·per′ish·a·ble·ness** *n.* **—im·per′ish·a·bly** *adv.*

im·pe·ri·um (ĭm-pîr′ē-əm) *n., pl.* **-pe·ri·a** (-pîr′ē-ə). **1.** Absolute rule; supreme power. **2.** A sphere of power; an empire. **3.** The right or power to use the force of a state to enforce the law. [Latin, empire.]

im·per·ma·nent (ĭm-pûr′mə-nənt) *adj.* Not permanent; not lasting or durable. **—im·per′ma·nence** or **im·per′ma·nen·cy** *n.* **—im·per′ma·nent·ly** *adv.*

im·per·me·a·ble (ĭm-pûr′mē-ə-bəl) *adj.* Not permeable. **—im·per′me·a·bil′i·ty** or **im·per′me·a·ble·ness** *n.* **—im·per′me·a·bly** *adv.*

im·per·mis·si·ble (ĭm′pər-mĭs′ə-bəl) *adj.* Not permissible. **—im′per·mis′si·bil′i·ty** *n.* **—im′per·mis′si·bly** *adv.*

im·per·son·al (ĭm-pûr′sə-nəl) *adj.* **1.** Not referring to or intended for any particular person: *an impersonal remark.* **2.** Showing no emotion: *an aloof, impersonal manner.* **3.** Not responsive to or expressive of human personalities: *a large, impersonal corporation.* **4.** *Gram.* Of or being a verb that is used in the third person sing. with no defined subject (as *meseems*) or a purely formal subject (as snowed in *it snowed*). **—im·per′son·al′i·ty** (-năl′ĭ-tē) *n.* **—im·per′son·al·ly** *adv.*

im·per·son·ate (ĭm-pûr′sə-nāt′) *tr.v.* **-at·ed, -at·ing.** To act the character or part of; pretend to be. [IN- (in) + PERSON + -ATE.] **—im·per′son·a′tion** *n.* **—im·per′son·a′tor** *n.*

im·per·ti·nence (ĭm-pûr′tn-əns) *n.* **1.** Discourteousness; insolence. **2.** An impertinent act or remark. **3.** Irrelevance.

im·per·ti·nent (ĭm-pûr′tn-ənt) *adj.* **1.** Impudent; presumptuous; rude. **2.** Not pertinent; irrelevant. —See Syns at **impudent.** [Middle English, irrelevant, from Old French, from Late Latin *impertinēns :* Latin *in-,* not + *pertinēns,* pertinent.] **—im·per′ti·nent·ly** *adv.*

im·per·turb·a·ble (ĭm′pər-tûr′bə-bəl) *adj.* Unshakably calm and collected; not perturbable. **—im′per·turb′a·bil′i·ty** or **im′per·turb′a·ble·ness** *n.* **—im′per·turb′a·bly** *adv.*

im·per·vi·ous (ĭm-pûr′vē-əs) *adj.* **1.** Incapable of being penetrated: *a material impervious to water.* **2.** Incapable of being affected: *He seemed impervious to fear.* [Latin *impervius : in-,* not + *pervius,* pervious.] **—im·per′vi·ous·ly** *adv.* **—im·per′vi·ous·ness** *n.*

im·pe·ti·go (ĭm′pĭ-tē′gō, -tī′-) *n.* A contagious skin disease characterized by superficial pustules that burst and form characteristic thick yellow crusts. [Latin *impetīgō,* from *impetere,* to attack.]

im·pet·u·os·i·ty (ĭm-pĕch′ōō-ŏs′ĭ-tē) *n., pl.* **-ties.** **1.** The quality or condition of being impetuous. **2.** An impetuous act.

im·pet·u·ous (ĭm-pĕch′ōō-əs) *adj.* **1.** Characterized by suddenness and boldness of action; impulsive. **2.** Having or marked by violent force: *impetuous, heaving waves.* [Middle English, from Old French *impetueux,* from Latin *impetuōsus,* from *impetus,* impetus.] **—im·pet′u·ous·ly** *adv.* **—im·pet′u·ous·ness** *n.*

im·pe·tus (ĭm′pĭ-təs) *n., pl.* **-tus·es.** **1.** A driving force; impulse: *Blood circulates under the impetus of the heart's pumping action.* **2.** Something that incites; a stimulus. —See Syns at **stimulus.** [Latin, attack, from *impetere,* to assail, attack : *in-,* against + *petere,* to go toward, seek, attack.]

im·pi·e·ty (ĭm-pī′ĭ-tē) *n., pl.* **-ties.** **1.** The quality or condition of being impious. **2.** An impious act. **3.** Undutifulness.

im·pinge (ĭm-pĭnj') *intr.v.* **-pinged, -ping·ing. 1.** To collide; strike: *Sound waves impinge on the eardrum.* **2.** To encroach; trespass: *impinging on his privacy.* [Latin *impingere,* to push against : *in-,* against + *pangere,* to fasten, drive in.] **—im·pinge'ment** *n.* **—im·ping'er** *n.*

im·pi·ous (ĭm'pē-əs, ĭm-pī'-) *adj.* **1.** Not pious; lacking reverence: *impious behavior in church.* **2.** Lacking due respect: *impious toward one's elders.* **—im'pi·ous·ly** *adv.* **—im'pi·ous·ness** *n.*

imp·ish (ĭm'pĭsh) *adj.* Of or befitting an imp; mischievous: *an impish grin.* **—imp'ish·ly** *adv.* **—imp'ish·ness** *n.*

im·pla·ca·ble (ĭm-plă'kə-bəl, -plăk'ə-) *adj.* **1.** Not capable of being calmed or pacified: *implacable fury.* **2.** Unalterable; inflexible: *implacable opposition.* **—im·pla'ca·bil'i·ty** or **im·pla'ca·ble·ness** *n.* **—im·pla'ca·bly** *adv.*

im·plant (ĭm-plănt') *tr.v.* **1.** To set in firmly, as in the ground; entrench. **2.** To establish decisively, as in the mind or consciousness; instill: *implant ideals.* **3.** *Med.* To insert or embed surgically: *implanting an artificial lens into the eye.* —*n.* (ĭm'plănt'). Something implanted.

im·plan·ta·tion (ĭm'plăn-tā'shən) *n.* **1.** An act of implanting. **2.** The condition of being implanted. **3.** An implanted object.

im·plau·si·ble (ĭm-plô'zə-bəl) *adj.* Not plausible; unlikely to be true: *an implausible excuse.* **—im·plau'si·bil'i·ty** or **im·plau'si·ble·ness** *n.* **—im·plau'si·bly** *adv.*

im·ple·ment (ĭm'plə-mənt) *n.* **1.** A tool or utensil used in doing a task: *rakes, hoes, and other gardening implements.* **2.** A means; an agent. —*tr.v.* (ĭm'plə-mĕnt'). **1.** To put into practical effect; carry out: *implement a plan.* **2.** To supply with implements. [Middle English, from Late Latin *implēmentum,* a filling up, supplement, from Latin *implēre,* to fill up, fulfill : *in-* (intensive) + *plēre,* to fill.] **—im'ple·men·ta'tion** *n.*

im·pli·cate (ĭm'plĭ-kāt') *tr.v.* **-cat·ed, -cat·ing. 1.** To involve or connect with a crime or other disapproved activity: *His testimony implicated several other people in the scandal.* **2.** To imply. [From Latin *implicāre* : *in-,* in + *plicāre,* to fold.]

im·pli·ca·tion (ĭm'plĭ-kā'shən) *n.* **1.** The act of implicating or the condition of being implicated. **2.** The act of implying or the condition of being implied: *conveying ideas by implication.* **3.** Something implied.

im·plic·it (ĭm-plĭs'ĭt) *adj.* **1.** Contained in the nature of something but not clearly apparent; inherent: *The butterfly is implicit in the caterpillar.* **2.** Implied or understood without being directly expressed. **3.** So certain as to need no affirmation; absolute: *implicit obedience.* [Latin *implicitus,* involved, entangled, from *implicāre,* to involve, implicate.] **—im·plic'it·ly** *adv.* **—im·plic'it·ness** *n.*

> **Syns: 1. implicit, implied, tacit, understood, unsaid, unspoken** *adj.* Core meaning: Conveyed indirectly without words or speech (*an implicit agreement*). **2. implicit, unconditional** *adj.* Core meaning: Having no reservations (*implicit trust*).

im·plied (ĭm-plīd') *adj.* Suggested, involved, or understood although not clearly or openly expressed. —See Syns at **implicit.**

im·plode (ĭm-plōd') *intr.v.* **-plod·ed, -plod·ing.** To collapse violently; burst inward. [**IN-** (in) + (**EX**)**PLODE.**]

im·plore (ĭm-plôr', -plōr') *v.* **-plored, -plor·ing.** —*tr.v.* **1.** To appeal to humbly and earnestly; entreat; beseech: *I implore you to have mercy on the defendant.* **2.** To plead or beg for urgently: *I implore your mercy.* —*intr.v.* To make earnest appeal. [Latin *implōrāre,* to invoke with tears : *in-,* in + *plōrāre,* to weep, lament.] **—im'plo·ra'tion** (ĭm'plə-rā'shən) *n.* **—im·plor'er** *n.* **—im·plor'ing·ly** *adv.*

im·plo·sion (ĭm-plō'zhən) *n.* A more or less violent collapse inward, as of a highly evacuated glass vessel. [**IN-** (in) + (**EX**)**PLOSION.**]

im·ply (ĭm-plī') *tr.v.* **-plied, -ply·ing. 1.** To involve or suggest by logical necessity; entail: *His aims imply a good deal of energy.* **2.** To say or express indirectly; suggest without stating: *I asked to borrow the car, and his "Be careful" implied consent.* —See Syns at **suggest.** [Middle English *implien,* from Old French *emplier,* from Latin *implicāre,* to infold, involve, implicate.]

> **Usage: imply, infer.** These verbs are carefully distinguished in modern usage. To *imply* something is to state it

indirectly, to hint or suggest it: *Their comments imply criticism. Your silence implies boredom. Imply,* in another sense, means to involve by logical necessity or to entail: *Continued success generally implies something more than mere luck.* To *infer* is to conclude something from evidence, to deduce: *I inferred from your silence that you were bored. Infer* is often misused for *imply* in the sense of stating indirectly. In addition, the nouns *implication* and *inference* have different meanings and should not be misused: *a story containing implications of scandal; drew four inferences from his testimony.*

im·po·lite (ĭm'pə-līt') *adj.* Not polite; discourteous. —See Syns at **rude.** **—im'po·lite'ly** *adv.* **—im'po·lite'ness** *n.*

im·pol·i·tic (ĭm-pŏl'ĭ-tĭk) *adj.* Not wise or expedient; not politic. **—im·pol'i·tic·ly** *adv.* **—im·pol'i·tic·ness** *n.*

im·pon·der·a·ble (ĭm-pŏn'dər-ə-bəl) *adj.* Incapable of being weighed or measured with preciseness. **—im·pon'der·a·ble·ness** *n.* **—im·pon'der·a·bly** *adv.*

im·port (ĭm-pôrt', -pōrt', ĭm'pôrt', -pōrt') *tr.v.* **1.** To bring or carry in from an outside source; esp., to bring in (goods) from a foreign country for trade or sale. **2.** To mean; signify: *What does the inflation rate import for the economy?* **3.** To imply. —*intr.v.* To be significant; to matter: *It imports little.* —*n.* (ĭm'pôrt', -pōrt'). **1.** Something imported. **2.** The act or business of importing. **3.** Meaning; signification. **4.** Importance; significance. —*modifier:* *the import trade; an import tax.* [Middle English *importen,* from Latin *importāre* : *in-,* in + *portāre,* to carry.] **—im·port'a·ble** *adj.* **—im·port'er** *n.*

im·por·tance (ĭm-pôr'tns) *n.* **1.** The condition or quality of being important; significance. **2.** Personal status; standing.

im·por·tant (ĭm-pôr'tnt) *adj.* **1.** Able to determine or change the course of events or the nature of things; significant: *an important seaport; an important crop; an important message.* **2.** Having rank, fame, or authority; prominent: *celebrities and other important people.* [Old French, from Old Italian *importante,* from Medieval Latin *importāre,* to mean, be significant, from Latin, to carry in, import.] **—im·por'tant·ly** *adv.*

> **Syns: important, consequential, historic, momentous, significant, weighty** *adj.* Core meaning: Having great significance (*an important development in medicine*).

im·por·ta·tion (ĭm'pôr-tā'shən, -pōr-) *n.* **1.** The act or business of importing. **2.** Something imported; an import.

im·por·tu·nate (ĭm-pôr'chə-nĭt) *adj.* Persistent in pressing a request or demand: *an importunate bill-collector.* **—im·por'tu·nate·ly** *adv.* **—im·por'tu·nate·ness** *n.*

im·por·tune (ĭm'pôr-tōōn', -tyōōn', ĭm-pôr'chən) *tr.v.* **-tuned, -tun·ing.** To press with repeated and insistent requests; ask insistently. —*adj.* Importunate. [Medieval Latin *importūnārī,* to be troublesome, from Latin *importūnus,* difficult of access, unsuitable : *in-,* not + *portus,* port, harbor.] **—im·por'tune'ly** *adv.* **—im·por'tun'er** *n.*

im·por·tu·ni·ty (ĭm'pôr-tōō'nĭ-tē, -tyōō'-) *n., pl.* **-ties. 1.** The condition or quality of being importunate. **2.** An insistent demand or request.

im·pose (ĭm-pōz') *tr.v.* **-posed, -pos·ing. 1.** To place (something burdensome) on someone; inflict: *long hours of work that imposed a great strain on us.* **2.** To bring about by exercising authority; force to prevail: *impose a settlement.* **3.** To apply or enact (something to be paid, observed, or followed): *impose a tax.* —*phrasal verb.* **impose on** (or **upon**). To take unfair advantage of: *imposing on them by staying too long; imposing on a friend's good nature.* [Old French *imposer,* from Latin *impōnere* : *in-,* on + *pōnere,* to put, place.] **—im·pos'er** *n.*

im·pos·ing (ĭm-pō'zĭng) *adj.* Impressive or awesome. — See Syns at **grand.** **—im·pos'ing·ly** *adv.*

im·po·si·tion (ĭm'pə-zĭsh'ən) *n.* **1.** The act of imposing. **2.** Something imposed, as a tax, undue burden, or fraud. **3.** An unfair or burdensome demand, as upon someone's time or hospitality.

im·pos·si·bil·i·ty (ĭm-pŏs'ə-bĭl'ĭ-tē) *n., pl.* **-ties. 1.** The condition or quality of being impossible. **2.** Something that is impossible.

im·pos·si·ble (ĭm-pŏs'ə-bəl) *adj.* **1.** Not capable of existing or happening: *It is impossible to be in two places at the same time.* **2.** Having little likelihood of happening or being accomplished: *impossible goals.* **3.** Unacceptable.

4. Not capable of being dealt with or tolerated: *an impossible person.* —See Syns at **contrary.** —**im·pos'si·bly** *adv.*

im·post (ĭm'pōst') *n.* Something imposed or levied, as a tax or duty. [Old French, from Medieval Latin *impositum*, from Latin *impōnere,* impose.]

im·pos·tor (ĭm-pŏs'tər) *n.* A person who deceives by pretending to be someone else. [Old French *imposteur,* from Late Latin *impos(i)tor,* from Latin *impōnere,* to impose.]
Syns: *impostor, charlatan, fake, fraud, phony (Informal),* **pretender, quack** *n. Core meaning:* One who is not what he claims to be *(not a doctor, just an impostor).*

im·pos·ture (ĭm-pŏs'chər) *n.* Deception or fraud, esp. assumption of a false identity. [Late Latin *impostura,* from Latin *impōnere,* to impose.]

im·po·tence (ĭm'pə-təns) *n.* Also **im·po·ten·cy** (-tən-sē). The quality or condition of being impotent.

im·po·tent (ĭm'pə-tənt) *adj.* **1.** Lacking physical strength or vigor; weak. **2.** Powerless; ineffectual. **3.** Incapable of sexual intercourse: *an impotent man.* See Syns at **powerless.** —**im'po·tent·ly** *adv.*

im·pound (ĭm-pound') *tr.v.* **1.** To confine in or as if in a pound: *The city impounds stray dogs.* **2.** To seize and retain in legal custody: *impounding smuggled goods.* **3.** To accumulate (water) in a reservoir. —**im·pound'er** *n.* —**im·pound'ment** *n.*

im·pov·er·ish (ĭm-pŏv'ər-ĭsh, -pŏf'rĭsh) *tr.v.* **1.** To reduce to poverty; make poor. **2.** To deprive of natural richness or strength: *impoverish the soil.* [Middle English *enpoverisen,* from Old French *empovrir* : *en-* (causative) + *povre,* poor.] —**im·pov'er·ish·ment** *n.*

im·prac·ti·ca·ble (ĭm-prăk'tĭ-kə-bəl) *adj.* **1.** Not capable of being done or carried out: *The proposed tunnel under the English Channel has proved impracticable.* **2.** Unfit for passage: *an impracticable road.* —**im·prac'ti·ca·bil'i·ty** or **im·prac'ti·ca·ble·ness** *n.* —**im·prac'ti·ca·bly** *adv.*
Usage: **impracticable, impractical.** *Impracticable* describes what is impossible to carry out: *an impracticable war plan. Impractical* can be used in the same sense, but it is more often applied to what is not desirable or worthwhile: *an impractical gadget.*

im·prac·ti·cal (ĭm-prăk'tĭ-kəl) *adj.* **1.** Unwise to implement or maintain in practice: *The highway was too narrow and turned out to be impractical.* **2.** Incapable of dealing efficiently with practical matters: *an impractical fellow who could never balance his bankbook.* **3.** Not a part of experience, fact, or practice; theoretical. **4.** Impracticable. —See Usage note at **impracticable.** —**im·prac'ti·cal'i·ty** or **im·prac'ti·cal·ness** *n.*

im·pre·cise (ĭm'prĭ-sīs') *adj.* Not precise. —**im'pre·cise'ly** *adv.* —**im'pre·ci'sion** (-sĭzh'ən) *n.*

im·preg·na·ble (ĭm-prĕg'nə-bəl) *adj.* **1.** Unable to be taken by attack: *an impregnable castle.* **2.** Unable to be shaken or criticized: *an impregnable conviction.* [Middle English *imprenable,* from Old French : *in-,* not + *prenable,* from *prendre,* to take, capture.] —**im·preg'na·bil'i·ty** or **im·preg'na·ble·ness** *n.*

im·preg·nate (ĭm-prĕg'nāt') *tr.v.* **-nat·ed, -nat·ing.** **1.** To make pregnant; inseminate. **2.** To fertilize (an ovum). **3.** To fill completely; permeate or saturate. [From Late Latin *impraegnāre* : Latin *in-,* in + *praegnās,* pregnant.] —**im'preg·na'tion** *n.* —**im·preg'na'tor** *n.*

im·pre·sa·ri·o (ĭm'prĭ-sär'ē-ō', -sâr'-) *n., pl.* **-ri·os.** A person who sponsors or produces entertainment; esp., the director of an opera company. [Italian, undertaker, manager, from *impresa,* undertaking, chivalric deed, from *imprendere,* to undertake.]

im·press[1] (ĭm-prĕs') *tr.v.* **1.** To produce or apply with pressure: *impress a design on a surface.* **2.** To mark or stamp with or as if with pressure: *impressed the sand with his broad feet.* **3.** To produce a vivid, often favorable effect on the mind or emotions of: *His sincerity impressed me.* **4.** To establish firmly in the mind: *Impress upon her the importance of choosing carefully.* —*n.* (ĭm'prĕs'). **1.** The act of impressing. **2.** A mark or pattern made by pressure. **3.** A stamp or seal meant to be impressed. [Middle English *impressen,* from Latin *imprimere* : *in-,* in + *premere,* to press.]

im·press[2] (ĭm-prĕs') *tr.v.* **1.** To compel (a person) to serve in a military force. **2.** To confiscate (property). —*n.* (ĭm'-

impressionism

prĕs'). The act of impressing men or property for public service or use. [IN- (intensive) + *press,* to force into service.] —**im·press'ment** *n.*

im·press·i·ble (ĭm-prĕs'ə-bəl) *adj.* Capable of being impressed. —**im·press'i·bly** *adv.*

im·pres·sion (ĭm-prĕsh'ən) *n.* **1.** The act or process of impressing. **2.** An effect, mark, or imprint made on a surface by pressure. **3.** An effect, image, or feeling retained as a consequence of experience: *After the performance we discussed our impressions.* **4.** A vague notion, remembrance, or belief: *I had the impression I had seen him before.* **5.** A humorous imitation of someone's speech or manner. **6.** *Printing.* **a.** All the copies of a publication printed at one time from the same set of type. **b.** A single copy of this printing. **7.** *Dentistry.* An imprint of the teeth and surrounding tissue in material such as wax or plaster, used as a mold in making dentures or inlays.

im·pres·sion·a·ble (ĭm-prĕsh'ə-nə-bəl) *adj.* Readily influenced; suggestible. —**im·pres'sion·a·bil'i·ty** or **im·pres'sion·a·ble·ness** *n.*

im·pres·sion·ism (ĭm-prĕsh'ə-nĭz'əm) *n.* **1.** A style of painting of the late 19th cent., marked by concentration on the impression produced by a scene or object and the use of many small strokes to simulate reflected light. **2.** A musical style of the late 19th cent., using rather vague but colorful harmonies and rhythms to suggest moods, places, and happenings. —**im·pres'sion·ist** *n. & adj.* —**im·pres'sion·is'tic** (-nĭs'tĭk) *adj.*

im·pres·sive (ĭm-prĕs'ĭv) *adj.* Making a strong or vivid impression; commanding attention: *an impressive monument; an impressive ceremony.* —**im·pres'sive·ly** *adv.* —**im·pres'sive·ness** *n.*

im·pri·ma·tur (ĭm'prə-mä'tŏŏr', ĭm-prĭm'ə-tŏŏr', -tyŏŏr') *n.* **1.** Official approval or license to print or publish. **2.** Official approval; sanction. [New Latin, "let it be printed," from Latin *imprimere,* to impress.]

im·print (ĭm-prĭnt', ĭm'prĭnt') *tr.v.* **1.** To produce (a mark or pattern) on a surface. **2.** To stamp or produce a mark on. **3.** To establish firmly, as on the mind or memory. —*n.* (ĭm'prĭnt'). **1.** A mark or pattern made by something pressed on a surface. **2.** A marked influence or effect: *countries that show the imprint of Spanish colonization.* **3.** The publisher's name, often with the date, address, and edition of a publication, printed at the bottom of a title page. [Middle English *imprenten,* from Old French *empreinter,* from *empreinte,* impression, from *empreindre,* to print, from Latin *imprimere,* to impress.]

im·pris·on (ĭm-prĭz'ən) *tr.v.* To put in or as if in prison. [Middle English *emprisonen,* from Old French *emprisoner* : *en-* (causative) + *prison,* prison.] —**im·pris'on·ment** *n.*

im·prob·a·bil·i·ty (ĭm-prŏb'ə-bĭl'ĭ-tē) *n., pl.* **-ties. 1.** The condition of being improbable. **2.** Something that is improbable.

im·prob·a·ble (ĭm-prŏb'ə-bəl) *adj.* Not probable; unlikely. —See Syns at **unlikely.** —**im·prob'a·ble·ness** *n.* —**im·prob'a·bly** *adv.*

im·promp·tu (ĭm-prŏmp'tōō, -tyōō) *adj.* Not rehearsed: *an impromptu speech.* —*adv.* Without rehearsal or preparation. —*n.* Something made or done impromptu, as a speech. [French, from Latin *in promptū,* at hand : *in,* in + *promptus,* ready, prompt.]

ă pat	ā pay	â care	ä father	ĕ pet	ē be	hw which	ĭ pit	ī tie	î pier	ŏ pot	ō toe	ô paw, for	oi noise
ōō took	ōō boot	ou out	th thin	th this	ŭ cut		û urge	zh vision	ə about, item, edible, gallop, circus

im·prop·er (ĭm-prŏp′ər) *adj.* **1.** Not suited to circumstances; unsuitable. **2.** Not conforming to social or moral conventions. **3.** Not consistent with fact or rule; incorrect. **4.** Irregular or abnormal. —See Syns at **unsuitable.** —**im·prop′er·ly** *adv.* —**im·prop′er·ness** *n.*

improper fraction. A fraction in which the numerator is larger than or equal to the denominator.

im·pro·pri·e·ty (ĭm′prə-prī′ĭ-tē) *n., pl.* **-ties. 1.** The quality or condition of being improper. **2.** An improper act or expression.

im·prove (ĭm-prō̅o̅v′) *v.* **-proved, -prov·ing.** —*tr.v.* **1.** To make better: *She improved her tennis serve by practicing.* **2.** To increase the productivity or value of (land). —*intr.v.* To become better: *Living conditions gradually improved.* —*phrasal verb.* **improve on.** To make beneficial additions or changes in: *They improved on his method.* [Norman French *emprouer,* to turn to profit : Old French *en-* (causative) + *prou,* profit, from Late Latin *prōde,* advantageous.] —**im·prov′a·bil′i·ty** *n.* —**im·prov′a·ble** *adj.* —**im·prov′er** *n.*

im·prove·ment (ĭm-prō̅o̅v′mənt) *n.* **1.** The act or procedure of improving. **2.** The condition of being improved. **3.** A change or addition that improves.

im·prov·i·dent (ĭm-prŏv′ĭ-dənt) *adj.* **1.** Not providing for the future; thriftless. **2.** Rash; incautious. —**im·prov′i·dence** *n.* —**im·prov′i·dent·ly** *adv.*

im·prov·i·sa·tion (ĭm-prŏv′ĭ-zā′shən, ĭm′prə-vĭ-) *n.* **1.** The act of improvising. **2.** Something improvised. —**im·prov′i·sa′tion·al** *adj.*

im·prov·i·sa·to·ry (ĭm-prŏv′ĭ-zə-tôr′ē, -tōr′ē, ĭm′prə-vī′zə-) *adj.* Of improvisation or an improviser: *a comedian's improvisatory gifts.*

im·pro·vise (ĭm′prə-vīz′) *v.* **-vised, -vis·ing.** —*tr.v.* **1.** To invent, compose, or recite without preparation: *He sat down and improvised a melody on the piano.* **2.** To make or provide from available materials: *improvised a hasty meal.* —*intr.v.* To invent, compose, recite, or execute something without preparation. [French *improviser,* from Italian *improvvisare,* from *improvviso,* unforeseen, from Latin *imprōvīsus* : *in-,* not + *prōvīdere,* to foresee, provide.] —**im′pro·vis′er** *n.*

im·pru·dent (ĭm-prō̅o̅d′nt) *adj.* Not prudent; unwise or injudicious; rash. —**im·pru′dence** *n.* —**im·pru′dent·ly** *adv.*

im·pu·dence (ĭm′pyə-dəns) *n.* **1.** The quality of being impudent. **2.** Impudent behavior.

im·pu·dent (ĭm′pyə-dənt) *adj.* Impertinent; rude; disrespectful. [Middle English, from Latin *impudēns* : *in-,* not + *pudēre,* to be ashamed.] —**im′pu·dent·ly** *adv.*

> **Syns:** impudent, audacious, bold, brazen, cheeky, forward, fresh *(Informal),* impertinent, insolent, presumptuous, sassy, saucy, smart, wise *adj.* Core meaning: Rude and disrespectful *(an impudent child who sassed the teacher; made impudent remarks).*

im·pugn (ĭm-pyō̅o̅n′) *tr.v.* To oppose or attack as false; cast doubt on: *impugned his right to the throne.* [Middle English *impugnen,* from Old French *impugner,* from Latin *impugnāre,* to fight against.] —**im·pugn′a·ble** *adj.* —**im·pugn′er** *n.*

im·pulse (ĭm′pŭls′) *n.* **1.** A short, sudden burst or flow, as of energy: *an electrical impulse.* **2.** A sudden inclination or urge; a whim: *acting on impulse.* **3.** A strong motivation; a drive or instinct: *A child has the impulse to utter audible sounds.* **4.** A driving force; a thrust; push; impetus: *a new impulse to the economy.* **5.** *Physics.* The product of the average value of a force with the time during which it acts, equal in general to the change in momentum produced by the force in this time interval. **6.** *Physiol.* An instance of the transmission of energy from one neuron to another. —See Syns at **stimulus.** [Latin *impulsus,* from *impellere,* to impel.]

im·pul·sive (ĭm-pŭl′sĭv) *adj.* **1.** Tending to act on impulse rather than thought. **2.** Caused by impulse; uncalculated: *an impulsive act.* **3.** Having power to impel or incite; forceful. —**im·pul′sive·ly** *adv.* —**im·pul′sive·ness** *n.*

im·pu·ni·ty (ĭm-pyō̅o̅′nĭ-tē) *n., pl.* **-ties.** Exemption from punishment or penalty: *The favorite child can often avoid household duties with impunity.* [Latin *impūnitās,* from *impūnis,* not punished : *in-,* not + *poena,* penalty, pain, from Greek *poina,* expiation, punishment.]

im·pure (ĭm-pyō̅o̅r′) *adj.* **1.** Not pure or clean; contaminated. **2.** Not purified by a religious ritual; defiled. **3.** Immoral or obscene; unchaste. —**im·pure′ly** *adv.* —**im·pure′ness** *n.*

im·pu·ri·ty (ĭm-pyō̅o̅r′ĭ-tē) *n., pl.* **-ties. 1.** The quality or condition of being impure, esp.: **a.** Contamination or pollution. **b.** Lack of consistency or homogeneity. **c.** A state of immorality; sin. **2.** Something that renders something else impure; a contaminant.

im·pute (ĭm-pyō̅o̅t′) *tr.v.* **-put·ed, -put·ing. 1.** To ascribe (a crime or fault) to another; charge: *The error was imputed to an accountant.* **2.** To attribute to a cause or source. [Middle English *inputen,* from Old French *imputer,* from Latin *imputāre,* to bring into the reckoning : *in-,* in, into + *putāre,* to reckon, compute, consider.] —**im·put′a·ble** *adj.* —**im′pu·ta′tion** *n.*

in (ĭn) *prep.* **1. a.** Within the confines of; inside: *He's in his room.* **b.** Within the area covered by: *playing in the mud.* **2.** On or affecting some part of: *He was hit in the head.* **3.** Forming a part, aspect, or property of: *a character in a novel.* **4.** During the course of or before the expiration of: *ready in a few minutes.* **5.** At the position or business of: *put in command.* **6.** After the pattern or form of: *going around in circles.* **7.** To or at the condition or situation of; into: *in trouble.* **8.** As an expression of; out of: *said in anger.* **9.** During or as part of the process of: *in hot pursuit.* **10.** With the attribute of: *working in silence.* **11. a.** By means of: *paid in cash.* **b.** With or through the medium of; using: *a text written in French.* **12.** Within the category or class of: *the latest thing in fashion.* **13.** With reference to; as regards: *in my opinion; equal in speed.* —*adv.* **1.** To or toward the inside: *He stepped in.* **2.** To or toward a center or each other: *The group closed in.* **3.** Into a given place or position: *Let her in.* **4.** Indoors: *time to go in.* **5.** Into a given activity together: *joined in and sang.* **6.** Inward: *caved in.* —*adj.* **1.** Fashionable; popular: *the in rock group.* **2.** Exclusive or private: *a member of the in crowd.* **3.** Available or at home: *He wasn't in.* **4.** For coming or going in; entering. **5.** Having power; incumbent. —*n.* **1.** Often **ins.** Those in power or having the advantage. **2.** *Informal.* A means of access or favor. —*idioms.* **all in.** *Informal.* Very tired; exhausted. **have it in for (someone).** *Informal.* To have a grudge against. **in for.** About to get or have: *He's in for a big surprise.* **in on.** Aware of: *She's in on the secret.* **ins and outs. 1.** The twists and turns, as of a road. **2.** The intricacies of an activity or process. **in that.** Inasmuch as; since. [Middle English, from Old English.]

> *Usage:* **in, into, in to.** As a preposition *in* primarily indicates position, location, or condition: *He was in the library. She was in a bad mood.* Used correspondingly, *into* indicates direction or movement to an interior location or, figuratively, change of condition: *She went into the lobby. He flew into a rage. In* is also possible in such examples but conveys the desired sense less clearly and less forcefully: *came into* (or *in*) *the room.* The two-word form *in to* is used in examples in which *in* is an adverb: *We went in to supper. You may go in to see them now.*

in-[1] Also **il-** (before *l*) or **im-** (before *b, m,* and *p*) or **ir-** (before *r*). A prefix meaning not, lacking, or without: **inaction.** [Middle English, from Old French, from Latin.]

in-[2] Also **il-** (before *l*) or **im-** (before *b, m,* and *p*) or **ir-** (before *r*). A prefix meaning: **1.** In, into, within, or inward: **impound. 2.** Intensive action: **impress.** [Middle English, from Old French, from Latin, from *in,* in, within.]

-in. Also **-ein** (for sense 1). A suffix meaning: **1.** A neutral chemical compound, such as glyceride or protein, as distinguished from an alkaloid or basic substance: **globulin. 2.** Enzyme: **pancreatin. 3.** A drug or other pharmaceutical product: **penicillin. 4.** Var. of **-ine** (chemical suffix). [French *-ine,* from Latin *-īna,* belonging to.]

In The symbol for the element indium.

in·a·bil·i·ty (ĭn′ə-bĭl′ĭ-tē) *n.* Lack of ability or means.

in ab·sen·ti·a (ĭn′ ăb-sĕn′shē-ə, -shə) *Latin.* In absence; although not present: *The fugitive was tried and convicted in absentia.*

in·ac·ces·si·ble (ĭn′ăk-sĕs′ə-bəl) *adj.* Not accessible; unapproachable. —**in′ac·ces′si·bil′i·ty** *n.* —**in′ac·ces′si·bly** *adv.*

in·ac·cu·ra·cy (ĭn-ăk′yər-ə-sē) *n., pl.* **-cies. 1.** The quality or condition of being inaccurate. **2.** An error.

in·ac·cu·rate (ĭn-ăk'yər-ĭt) *adj.* **1.** Not accurate. **2.** Mistaken or incorrect. —See Syns at **false.** —**in·ac'cu·rate·ly** *adv.* —**in·ac'cu·rate·ness** *n.*

in·ac·tion (ĭn-ăk'shən) *n.* Lack or absence of action.

in·ac·ti·vate (ĭn-ăk'tə-vāt') *tr.v.* **-vat·ed, -vat·ing.** To render inactive. —**in·ac'ti·va'tion** *n.*

in·ac·tive (ĭn-ăk'tĭv) *adj.* **1.** Not active or not tending to be active: *inactive since his leg injury.* **2. a.** Being out of use: *inactive machines.* **b.** Retired from duty or service. **3. a.** *Chem.* Not readily participating in chemical reactions. **b.** *Biol.* Having no significant effect on or interaction with living organisms. **c.** *Med.* Quiescent, as a disease. **d.** *Physics.* Displaying little or no radioactivity. —**in·ac'tive·ly** *adv.* —**in·ac'tive·ness** or **in'ac·tiv'i·ty** *n.*

 Syns: inactive, dormant, idle, inert, inoperative *adj.* Core meaning: Not involved in or tending toward action or movement (*an inactive life; an inactive volcano*). INACTIVE is very neutral and does not imply favorable or unfavorable judgment. DORMANT refers mainly to suspended activity that may be renewed (*dormant cancer*). IDLE refers to human inactivity (*employees idle because of strikes; idle students*). INERT implies mental or spiritual lethargy (*an inert person unwilling to try*). INOPERATIVE often refers to mechanical inactivity (*a temporarily inoperative drill press*).

in·ad·e·qua·cy (ĭn-ăd'ĭ-kwə-sē) *n., pl.* **-cies. 1.** The quality or condition of being inadequate. **2.** A failing or lack; shortcoming.

in·ad·e·quate (ĭn-ăd'ĭ-kwĭt) *adj.* **1.** Not adequate; insufficient. **2.** Not able; incapable: *felt inadequate to the task.* —**in·ad'e·quate·ly** *adv.*

in·ad·mis·si·ble (ĭn'əd-mĭs'ə-bəl) *adj.* Not admissible. —**in·ad·mis'si·bil'i·ty** *n.* —**in·ad·mis'si·bly** *adv.*

in·ad·ver·tent (ĭn'əd-vûr'tnt) *adj.* **1.** Not duly attentive. **2.** Accidental; unintentional. —See Syns at **accidental.** [Back-formation from INADVERTENCE.] —**in'ad·ver'tence** or **in'ad·ver'ten·cy** *n.* —**in'ad·ver'tent·ly** *adv.*

in·ad·vis·a·ble (ĭn'əd-vī'zə-bəl) *adj.* Unwise; not recommended. —**in'ad·vis'a·bil'i·ty** *n.*

in·al·ien·a·ble (ĭn-āl'yə-nə-bəl) *adj.* Not capable of being given up or taken away: *an inalienable right.* —**in·al'ien·a·bly** *adv.*

in·al·ter·a·ble (ĭn-ôl'tər-ə-bəl) *adj.* Not alterable; unchangeable. —See Syns at **inflexible.** —**in·al'ter·a·bil'i·ty** *n.* —**in·al'ter·a·bly** *adv.*

in·ane (ĭ-nān') *adj.* Lacking sense or substance; silly: *inane chatter.* [Latin *inānis,* empty, vain.] —**in·ane'ly** *adv.*

in·an·i·mate (ĭn-ăn'ə-mĭt) *adj.* **1.** Not living: *an inanimate object.* **2.** Showing no sign of life; lifeless. **3.** Not lively; listless. —**in·an'i·mate·ly** *adv.* —**in·an'i·mate·ness** *n.*

in·a·ni·tion (ĭn'ə-nĭsh'ən) *n.* **1.** Exhaustion and weakness, as from lack of nourishment. **2.** The condition or quality of being empty. [Medieval Latin *inānītiō,* an emptying, from Latin *inānīre,* to make empty, from *inānis,* empty, inane.]

in·an·i·ty (ĭ-năn'ĭ-tē) *n., pl.* **-ties. 1.** The condition or quality of being inane. **2.** Something foolish or absurd: *"his mind was steeled against the inanities she uttered"* (Henry James).

in·ap·pli·ca·ble (ĭn-ăp'lĭ-kə-bəl) *adj.* Not applicable. —See Syns at **irrelevant.** —**in·ap'pli·ca·bil'i·ty** *n.* —**in·ap'pli·ca·bly** *adv.*

in·ap·po·site (ĭn-ăp'ə-zĭt) *adj.* Not appropriate; unsuitable. —**in·ap'po·site·ly** *adv.*

in·ap·pre·cia·ble (ĭn'ə-prē'shə-bəl) *adj.* Not appreciable. —See Syns at **imperceptible.** —**in'ap·pre'cia·bly** *adv.*

in·ap·pro·pri·ate (ĭn'ə-prō'prē-ĭt) *adj.* Not appropriate. —See Syns at **unfortunate** and **unsuitable.** —**in'ap·pro'pri·ate·ly** *adv.* —**in'ap·pro'pri·ate·ness** *n.*

in·apt (ĭn-ăpt') *adj.* **1.** Inappropriate. **2.** Inept. —See Syns at **unsuitable.** —**in·apt'ly** *adv.* —**in·apt'ness** *n.*

in·ap·ti·tude (ĭn-ăp'tĭ-tōōd', -tyōōd') *n.* **1.** Inappropriateness. **2.** Lack of skill; ineptitude.

in·ar·tic·u·late (ĭn'är-tĭk'yə-lĭt) *adj.* **1.** Uttered without the use of normal words or syllables: *an inarticulate cry.* **2.** Unable to speak; speechless: *inarticulate with astonishment.* **3.** Unable to speak with clarity or eloquence. **4.** Unexpressed: *inarticulate sorrow.* —**in'ar·tic'u·late·ly** *adv.* —**in'ar·tic'u·late·ness** *n.*

in·as·much as (ĭn'əz-mŭch'). **1.** Because of the fact that; since. **2.** To the extent that; insofar as.

in·at·ten·tion (ĭn'ə-tĕn'shən) *n.* Lack of attention; heedlessness; neglect.

in·at·ten·tive (ĭn'ə-tĕn'tĭv) *adj.* Showing a lack of attention; negligent. —See Syns at **careless.** —**in'at·ten'tive·ly** *adv.* —**in'at·ten'tive·ness** *n.*

in·au·di·ble (ĭn-ô'də-bəl) *adj.* Not audible; incapable of being heard. —**in·au'di·bly** *adv.*

in·au·gu·ral (ĭ-nô'gyər-əl) *adj.* **1.** Of or relating to an inauguration: *an inaugural ceremony.* **2.** Initial; first: *a new train's inaugural run.* —*n.* A speech made by a President of the United States at his inauguration.

in·au·gu·rate (ĭ-nô'gyə-rāt') *tr.v.* **-rat·ed, -rat·ing. 1.** To install in office by a formal ceremony. **2.** To begin officially; launch: *inaugurate an express mail service.* **3.** To open or begin use of formally with a ceremony; dedicate. —See Syns at **introduce.** [From Latin *inaugurāre,* to take omens from the flight of birds, to consecrate, install : *in,* in + *augurāre,* to augur.] —**in·au'gu·ra'tion** *n.* —**in·au'gu·ra'tor** *n.*

in·aus·pi·cious (ĭn'ô-spĭsh'əs) *adj.* Not auspicious; unfavorable: *an inauspicious beginning.* —**in'aus·pi'cious·ly** *adv.* —**in'aus·pi'cious·ness** *n.*

in between. Between two things, limits, etc.

in-be·tween (ĭn'bĭ-twēn') *adj.* Intermediate: *adolescence, that awkward in-between age.* —*n.* An intermediate: *conservatives, radicals, and in-betweens.*

in·board (ĭn'bôrd', -bōrd') *adj.* **1.** Within the hull or toward the center of a ship: *an inboard motor.* **2.** Relatively close to the fuselage of an aircraft: *the inboard engines.* **3.** Toward the center of a machine. —*n.* A motor attached to the inside of the hull of a boat. —**in'board'** *adv.*

in·born (ĭn'bôrn') *adj.* **1.** Possessed by an organism at birth: *an inborn trait.* **2.** Inherited or hereditary.

in·bound (ĭn'bound') *adj.* Incoming; arriving: *inbound traffic.*

in·bred (ĭn'brĕd') *adj.* **1.** Produced by inbreeding. **2.** Innate; deep-seated.

in·breed (ĭn'brēd', ĭn-brēd') *tr.v.* **-bred** (-brĕd'), **-breed·ing. 1.** To produce by the continued breeding of closely related individuals. **2.** To breed or develop within; engender.

in·breed·ing (ĭn'brē'dĭng) *n.* **1.** The breeding or mating of closely related individuals. **2.** Intermarriage among people who are closely related or from the same social groups.

In·ca (ĭng'kə) *n., pl.* **Inca** or **-cas. 1.** An Indian of the group of Quechuan peoples who ruled Peru before the Spanish conquest. **2.** A king or other member of the royal family of this group of peoples.

in·cal·cu·la·ble (ĭn-kăl'kyə-lə-bəl) *adj.* **1.** Too great to be calculated or conceived: *the incalculable distances of outer space.* **2.** Incapable of being foreseen; unpredictable; uncertain: *"The motions of her mind were as incalculable as the flit of a bird"* (Edith Wharton). —**in·cal'cu·la·bil'i·ty** or **in·cal'cu·la·ble·ness** *n.* —**in·cal'cu·la·bly** *adv.*

in cam·er·a (ĭn kăm'ər-ə). **1.** In secret, private, or closed session. **2.** *Law.* In private with a judge rather than in open court. [Latin, "in the chamber."]

inauguration
Presidential inauguration

in·can·des·cent (ĭn′kən-dĕs′ənt) adj. **1.** Giving off visible light as a result of being heated. **2.** Shining brilliantly; very bright. —See Syns at **bright.** [Latin *incandescens,* pres. part. of *incandescere,* to glow with heat : *in-* (intensive) + *candēre,* to shine.] —**in′can·des′cence** n. —**in′can·des′cent·ly** adv.

incandescent lamp. An electric lamp in which a filament is heated to incandescence by an electric current.

in·can·ta·tion (ĭn′kăn-tā′shən) n. **1.** Ritual recitation of verbal charms or spells to produce a magical effect. **2.** A formula of words or sounds recited or chanted to produce a magical effect. **3.** The casting of spells. [Middle English *incantacioun,* from Old French *incantation,* from Late Latin *incantātiō,* enchantment, spell, from Latin *incantāre,* to enchant.] —**in·can′ta·to′ry** (ĭn-kăn′tə-tôr′ē, -tōr′ē) adj.

in·ca·ble (ĭn-kā′pə-bəl) adj. Not capable; lacking the necessary ability or power: *incapable of singing; incapable of flight.* —See Syns at **powerless.** —**in·ca′pa·bil′i·ty** or **in·ca′pa·ble·ness** n. —**in·ca′pa·bly** adv.

in·ca·pac·i·tate (ĭn′kə-pās′ĭ-tāt′) tr.v. **-tat·ed, -tat·ing. 1.** To deprive of strength or ability; disable. **2.** To make legally ineligible; disqualify. —**in′ca·pac′i·ta′tion** n.

in·ca·pac·i·ty (ĭn′kə-pās′ĭ-tē) n., pl. **-ties. 1.** Lack of capacity; inadequate strength or ability: *incapacity for work.* **2.** A disability; a defect or handicap.

in·car·cer·ate (ĭn-kär′sə-rāt′) tr.v. **-at·ed, -at·ing. 1.** To put in jail. **2.** To shut in; confine. [From Latin *incarcerāre :* *in-,* in + *carcer,* prison.] —**in·car′cer·a′tion** n. —**in·car′cer·a′tor** n.

in·car·nate (ĭn-kär′nĭt, -nāt′) adj. **1.** In a bodily, esp. human, form: *an incarnate devil.* **2.** Personified: *She is wisdom incarnate.* —tr.v. (ĭn-kär′nāt′) **-nat·ed, -nat·ing. 1.** To give bodily, esp. human, form to. **2.** To embody or personify. [From Late Latin *incarnāre,* to make flesh : Latin *in-* (causative) + *carō,* flesh.]

in·car·na·tion (ĭn′kär-nā′shən) n. **1.** The act of taking on or the condition of having taken on bodily form: *the incarnation of the devil in the form of a serpent.* **2. the Incarnation.** The embodiment of God in the human form of Christ. **3.** A person or thing thought to personify a quality or idea: *The wolverine has been considered the incarnation of everything evil.*

in·case (ĭn-kās′) v. Var. of **encase.**

in·cau·tious (ĭn-kô′shəs) adj. Not cautious; rash. —**in·cau′tious·ly** adv. —**in·cau′tious·ness** n.

in·cen·di·ar·y (ĭn-sĕn′dē-ĕr′ē) adj. **1.** Starting or designed to start fires: *an incendiary bomb.* **2.** Of or involving arson: *an incendiary fire.* **3.** Tending to arouse passions or incite violent action; inflammatory: *incendiary pamphlets.* —n., pl. **-ies. 1.** An arsonist. **2.** An incendiary bomb or other explosive. [Latin *incendiārius,* from *incendium,* burning, fire, from *incendere,* to set on fire.] —**in·cen′di·a·rism** (-ə-rĭz′əm) n.

in·cense¹ (ĭn-sĕns′) tr.v. **-censed, -cens·ing.** To cause to be angry; infuriate; enrage. [Middle English *encensen,* from Old French *incenser,* from Latin *incendere,* to set on fire, enrage.]

in·cense² (ĭn′sĕns) n. **1.** A substance, as a gum or wood, that burns with a pleasant odor. **2.** The smoke or odor produced by the burning of such a substance. **3.** Any pleasant smell. [Middle English *insens,* from Old French *encens,* from Late Latin *incensum,* from Latin *incendere,* to set on fire.]

in·cen·tive (ĭn-sĕn′tĭv) n. Something inciting to action or effort, as the fear of punishment or the expectation of reward. —See Syns at **stimulus.** —adj. Inciting; motivating. [Middle English, from Latin *incentīvus,* that sets the tune, from *incinere,* to sing, sound : *in-* (intensive) + *canere,* to sing.]

in·cep·tion (ĭn-sĕp′shən) n. The beginning of something. [Latin *inceptiō,* from *incipere,* to take in hand, begin : *in-,* in + *capere,* to take.]

in·cep·tive (ĭn-sĕp′tĭv) adj. **1.** Incipient; beginning. **2.** Gram. Expressing an action, state, or occurrence in its initial phase: *an inceptive verb suffix.*

in·cer·ti·tude (ĭn-sûr′tĭ-tood′, -tyood′) n. **1.** Uncertainty. **2.** Absence of confidence; doubt. **3.** Insecurity or instability.

in·ces·sant (ĭn-sĕs′ənt) adj. Continuing without interruption; unceasing. —See Syns at **continuous.** [Late Latin *incessāns :* *in-,* not + *cessāns,* pres. part. of *cessāre,* to cease.] —**in·ces′sant·ly** adv.

in·cest (ĭn′sĕst) n. Sexual union between persons who are so closely related that their marriage is illegal or forbidden by custom. [Middle English, from Latin *incestum :* *in-,* not + *castus,* chaste.]

in·ces·tu·ous (ĭn-sĕs′chōo-əs) adj. **1.** Of or involving incest. **2.** Having committed incest. **3.** Resulting from incest. —**in·ces′tu·ous·ly** adv. —**in·ces′tu·ous·ness** n.

inch (ĭnch) n. *Abbr.* **in.** and **in** A unit of length in the U.S. Customary and British Imperial systems, equal to $^{1}/_{12}$ of a foot. —intr.v. To move slowly or by small degrees. —tr.v. To cause to move slowly or by small degrees. —**idioms. every inch.** In every detail; entirely: *He is every inch a hero.* **inch by inch.** Very gradually or slowly. **within an inch of.** Almost to the point of; very near. [Middle English, from Old English *ince,* from Latin *unica,* twelfth part, inch, ounce, from *ūnus,* one.]

in·cho·ate (ĭn-kō′ĭt) adj. Not fully formed; beginning to take shape: *An inchoate idea dawned on him.* [Latin *inchoātus,* past part. of *inchoāre, incohāre,* to begin.] —**in·cho′ate·ly** adv.

in·cho·a·tive (ĭn-kō′ə-tĭv) adj. Gram. Inceptive.

inch·worm (ĭnch′wûrm′) n. A geometrid caterpillar that moves by looping its body in alternate contractions and expansions. Also called **looper** and **measuring worm.**

in·ci·dence (ĭn′sĭ-dəns) n. **1.** The act or manner of occurring; occurrence. **2.** The extent or frequency with which something occurs: *the high incidence of malaria in the tropics.* **3.** *Physics.* The arrival of incident radiation or of an incident projectile at a surface.

in·ci·dent (ĭn′sĭ-dənt) n. **1.** A definite, distinct occurrence; an event. **2.** An event that is connected with but less important than another. **3.** An occurrence or event that causes trouble or interrupts normal procedure. —adj. **1.** Tending to arise or occur as a minor result or accompaniment: *"There is a professional melancholy . . . incident to the occupation of a tailor"* (Lamb). **2.** Related to or dependent on another thing. **3.** *Physics.* Falling upon something; striking: *incident radiation.* [Middle English, from Old French, from Latin *incidere,* to fall upon, happen to : *in-,* on + *cadere,* to fall.]

in·ci·den·tal (ĭn′sĭ-dĕn′tl) adj. **1.** Likely to occur at the same time or as a minor consequence; attendant: *fleabites and other annoyances incidental to an African safari.* **2.** Of a minor, casual, or subordinate nature: *incidental expenses.* —n. A minor item or expense.

in·ci·den·tal·ly (ĭn′sĭ-dĕn′tl-ē) adv. **1.** Casually; by chance. **2.** Apart from the main subject; by the way.

in·cin·er·ate (ĭn-sĭn′ə-rāt′) v. **-at·ed, -at·ing.** —tr.v. To consume by burning. —intr.v. To burn or burn up. [From Medieval Latin *incinerāre :* Latin *in-,* in, into + *cinis,* ashes.] —**in·cin′er·a′tion** n.

in·cin·er·a·tor (ĭn-sĭn′ə-rā′tər) n. A furnace or other device for burning waste.

in·cip·i·ent (ĭn-sĭp′ē-ənt) adj. In an initial or early stage; just beginning to exist or appear: *"that incipient smile which is apt to accompany agreeable recollections"* (George Eliot). [Latin *incipiēns,* beginning, pres. part. of *incipere,* to take in hand, begin : *in-,* in + *capere,* to take.] —**in·cip′i·en·cy** (-ən-sē) or **in·cip′i·ence** (-əns) n. —**in·cip′i·ent·ly** adv.

in·cise (ĭn-sīz′) tr.v. **-cised, -cis·ing. 1.** To cut into or mark with a sharp instrument. **2.** To cut (designs or writing) into a surface; engrave; carve. [Old French *inciser,* from Latin *incidere :* *in-,* into, in + *caedere,* to cut.]

in·ci·sion (ĭn-sĭzh′ən) n. **1.** The act of incising. **2. a.** A surgical cut into soft tissue. **b.** The scar resulting from such a cut. **3.** A notch, as in the edge of a leaf. **4.** Incisiveness.

in·ci·sive (ĭn-sī′sĭv) adj. **1.** Cutting; penetrating. **2.** Direct and effective; telling: *incisive comments.* [Medieval Latin *incīsīvus,* from Latin *incisus,* past part. of *incīdere,* to incise.] —**in·ci′sive·ly** adv. —**in·ci′sive·ness** n.

in·ci·sor (ĭn-sī′zər) n. A tooth adapted for cutting, located in the front of the jaws of mammals.

in·cite (ĭn-sīt′) tr.v. **-cit·ed, -cit·ing.** To provoke to action; stir up; urge on: *inciting the mob to violence.* —See Syns at **provoke.** [Old French *inciter*, from Latin *incitāre* : *in-* (intensive) + *citāre*, to rouse, provoke.] —**in·cite′ment** *n.* —**in·cit′er** *n.*

in·clem·ent (ĭn-klĕm′ənt) *adj.* **1.** Stormy; severe: *inclement weather.* **2.** Unmerciful. —**in·clem′en·cy** (-ən-sē) *n.* —**in·clem′ent·ly** *adv.*

in·clin·a·ble (ĭn-klī′nə-bəl) *adj.* Favorably disposed; amenable.

in·cli·na·tion (ĭn′klə-nā′shən) *n.* **1.** An attitude or disposition toward something: *My inclination is to distrust theories.* **2.** A tendency toward a particular aspect, condition, or character: *Many socialist countries have shown an inclination to dictatorship.* **3.** Something for which one has a preference or leaning: *"I shall indulge the inclination so natural in old men, to be talking of themselves"* (Franklin). **4.** The act of inclining. **5.** The condition of being inclined. **6.** A deviation from a definite direction, esp. from a horizontal or vertical; a slant. **7.** The degree of deviation from a horizontal or vertical.

in·cline (ĭn-klīn′) *v.* **-clined, -clin·ing.** —*intr.v.* **1.** To depart from a true horizontal or vertical direction; to lean; slant. **2.** To be disposed; tend: *She inclines to exaggerate.* **3.** To lower or bend the head or body, as in a nod or bow. —*tr.v.* **1.** To cause to lean, slant, or slope. **2.** To influence to have a certain preference, leaning, or disposition; dispose. **3.** To bend or lower in a nod or bow. —*n.* (ĭn′klīn′). An inclined surface; a slope. [Middle English *inclinen,* from Old French *encliner,* from Latin *inclīnāre* : *in-,* toward + *clīnāre*, to bend, lean.] —**in·clin′er** *n.*

in·clined plane (ĭn-klīnd′). A plane inclined to the horizontal, a simple machine used to raise or lower a load by rolling or sliding.

in·close (ĭn-klōz′) *v.* Var. of **enclose.**

in·clo·sure (ĭn-klō′zhər) *n.* Var. of **enclosure.**

in·clude (ĭn-klōōd′) *tr.v.* **-clud·ed, -clud·ing.** **1.** To have as a part or member; be made up of, at least in part; contain: *The United Nations includes most independent countries.* **2.** To consider with or put into a group, class, or total: *The price of the meal includes service charges.* [Middle English *includen,* from Latin *inclūdere,* to shut in : *in-,* in + *claudere,* to close.] —**in·clud′a·ble** or **in·clud′i·ble** *adj.*

Usage: **include.** Unlike *comprise,* this verb does not imply that all components are enumerated; it usu. implies an incomplete listing: *The cake's ingredients include butter and egg yolks.* When a complete listing is made, *comprise* is a better choice than *include.* See also Usage note at **compose.**

in·clud·ed (ĭn-klōō′dĭd) *adj.* **1.** *Bot.* Not protruding beyond a surrounding part, as stamens that do not project from a corolla. **2.** *Geom.* Formed by and between two intersecting straight lines: *an included angle.*

in·clu·sion (ĭn-klōō′zhən) *n.* **1.** The act of including or the condition of being included. **2.** Something included. **3.** *Mineral.* Any solid, liquid, or gaseous foreign body enclosed in a mineral or rock. **4.** *Biol.* Any nonliving mass in cytoplasm.

in·clu·sive (ĭn-klōō′sĭv) *adj.* **1.** Taking everything into account; including everything; comprehensive: *an inclusive fee.* **2.** Including the specified extremes or limits as well as the area between them: *the numbers one to ten, inclusive.* —See Syns at **general.** —**in·clu′sive·ly** *adv.* —**in·clu′sive·ness** *n.*

in·cog·ni·to (ĭn-kŏg′nĭ-tō′, ĭn′kŏg-nē′tō) *adv. & adj.* With one's identity hidden or disguised: *The movie star traveled incognito.* —*n.* **1.** A person who is incognito. **2.** The condition of being incognito. [Italian, from Latin *incognitus,* unknown.]

in·co·her·ent (ĭn′kō-hîr′ənt) *adj.* **1.** Not coherent; disordered; unconnected: *an incoherent explanation.* **2.** Unable to think or express one's thoughts in a clear or orderly manner: *incoherent with grief.* —**in′co·her′ent·ly** *adv.* —**in′co·her′ence** or **in′co·her′en·cy** *n.*

in·com·bus·ti·ble (ĭn′kəm-bŭs′tə-bəl) *adj.* Incapable of burning. —*n.* An incombustible object or material. [Middle English, from Medieval Latin *incombustibilis* : Latin *in-,* not + *combūrere,* to burn up.] —**in′com·bus′ti·bil′i·ty** *n.* —**in′com·bus′ti·bly** *adv.*

in·come (ĭn′kŭm′) *n.* The amount of money or its equivalent received during a period of time in exchange for labor or services, from the sale of goods or property, or as profit from financial investments.

income tax. A tax on the annual income of a person or business.

in·com·ing (ĭn′kŭm′ĭng) *adj.* **1.** Coming in; entering. **2.** About to come in; next in succession: *the incoming president.* —*n.* The act of coming in; arrival.

in·com·men·su·ra·ble (ĭn′kə-mĕn′shər-ə-bəl, -sər-) *adj.* **1.** Incapable of being measured or judged comparatively; incomparable. **2.** *Math.* Having no common measure. —*n.* Something that is incommensurable. —**in′com·men′su·ra·bil′i·ty** *n.* —**in′com·men′su·ra·bly** *adv.*

in·com·men·su·rate (ĭn′kə-mĕn′shər-ĭt, -sər-) *adj.* **1.** Not commensurate; unequal; disproportionate: *a reward that is incommensurate with his efforts.* **2.** Incommensurable. —**in′com·men′su·rate·ly** *adv.* —**in′com·men′su·rate·ness** *n.*

in·com·mu·ni·ca·ble (ĭn′kə-myōō′nĭ-kə-bəl) *adj.* Not communicable: *incommunicable diseases.* —**in′com·mu′ni·ca·bil′i·ty** *n.* —**in′com·mu′ni·ca·bly** *adv.*

in·com·mu·ni·ca·do (ĭn′kə-myōō′nĭ-kä′dō) *adv. & adj.* Without the means or right of communicating with others: *a prisoner held incommunicado.* [Spanish, past part. of *incomunicar,* to deny communication : *in-,* not, from Latin + *comunicar,* to communicate, from Latin *commūnicāre,* to communicate.]

in·com·pa·ra·ble (ĭn-kŏm′pər-ə-bəl) *adj.* **1.** Incapable of being compared; incommensurable. **2.** Above all comparisons; beyond equal; unsurpassed. —See Syns at **unique.** —**in·com′pa·ra·bil′i·ty** or **in·com′pa·ra·ble·ness** *n.* —**in·com′pa·ra·bly** *adv.*

in·com·pat·i·ble (ĭn′kəm-păt′ə-bəl) *adj.* **1.** Not compatible; not in harmony or agreement: *incompatible colors; conduct incompatible with self-respect.* **2.** Incapable of being held by one person at the same time: *incompatible offices.* —**in′com·pat′i·bil′i·ty** *n.* —**in′com·pat′i·ble·ness** *n.* —**in′com·pat′i·bly** *adv.*

in·com·pe·tent (ĭn-kŏm′pĭ-tənt) *adj.* Not competent. —*n.* An incompetent person. —**in·com′pe·tence** or **in·com′pe·ten·cy** *n.* —**in·com′pe·tent·ly** *adv.*

in·com·plete (ĭn′kəm-plēt′) *adj.* Not complete: *an incomplete set.* —**in′com·plete′ly** *adv.* —**in′com·plete′ness** or **in′com·ple′tion** *n.*

in·com·pre·hen·si·ble (ĭn-kŏm′prĭ-hĕn′sə-bəl, ĭn′kŏm-) *adj.* Incapable of being understood or comprehended. —**in·com′pre·hen′si·bil′i·ty** or **in·com′pre·hen′si·ble·ness** *n.* —**in·com′pre·hen′si·bly** *adv.*

in·com·pre·hen·sion (ĭn-kŏm′prĭ-hĕn′shən, ĭn′kŏm-) *n.* Lack of comprehension or understanding.

in·com·press·i·ble (ĭn′kəm-prĕs′ə-bəl) *adj.* Incapable of being compressed. —**in′com·press′i·bil′i·ty** *n.*

in·con·ceiv·a·ble (ĭn′kən-sē′və-bəl) *adj.* Incapable of being conceived or grasped fully: *the inconceivable size of the universe.* —**in′con·ceiv′a·bil′i·ty** or **in′con·ceiv′a·ble·ness** *n.* —**in′con·ceiv′a·bly** *adv.*

in·con·clu·sive (ĭn′kən-klōō′sĭv) *adj.* Not conclusive. —**in′con·clu′sive·ly** *adv.* —**in′con·clu′sive·ness** *n.*

in·con·gru·ent (ĭn′kən-grōō′ənt, ĭn-kŏng′grōō-ənt) *adj.* **1.** Not congruent. **2.** Incongruous. —**in′con·gru′ence** *n.* —**in′con·gru′ent·ly** *adv.*

in·con·gru·i·ty (ĭn′kən-grōō′ĭ-tē, -kŏn-) *n., pl.* **-ties. 1.** The condition or quality of being incongruous. **2.** Something that is incongruous.

in·con·gru·ous (ĭn-kŏng′grōō-əs) *adj.* **1.** Not consistent with what is logical, customary, or expected; inappropriate: *the incongruous cheerfulness of the executioner.* **2.** Made up of sharply different members, qualities, or parts: *an incongruous group of people.* —**in·con′gru·ous·ly** *adv.* —**in·con′gru·ous·ness** *n.*

in·con·se·quent (ĭn-kŏn′sĭ-kwənt) *adj.* **1.** Not obtained as a result. **2.** Proceeding without logical sequence; haphazard. **3.** Unimportant; insignificant. —**in·con′se·quence** *n.* —**in·con′se·quent·ly** *adv.*

in·con·se·quen·tial (ĭn-kŏn′sĭ-kwĕn′shəl) *adj.* **1.** Without consequence; lacking importance; petty. **2.** Inconsequent. —See Syns at **little.** —**in·con′se·quen′ti·al′i·ty** (-shē-ăl′ĭ-tē) *n.* —**in·con′se·quen′tial·ly** *adv.*

in·con·sid·er·a·ble (ĭn′kən-sĭd′ər-ə-bəl) *adj.* Too small or unimportant to merit consideration; trivial. —**in′con·sid′er·a·ble·ness** *n.* —**in′con·sid′er·a·bly** *adv.*

in·con·sid·er·ate (ĭn′kən-sĭd′ər-ĭt) *adj.* Not considerate; thoughtless. —**in′con·sid′er·ate·ly** *adv.* —**in′con·sid′er·ate·ness** or **in′con·sid·er·a′tion** (-ə-rā′shən) *n.*

in·con·sis·ten·cy (ĭn′kən-sĭs′tən-sē) *n., pl.* -cies. 1. The condition or quality of being inconsistent. 2. Something that is inconsistent.

in·con·sis·tent (ĭn′kən-sĭs′tənt) *adj.* Not consistent, esp.: 1. Not in agreement or harmony; incompatible: *an intersection inconsistent with the road map.* 2. Lacking in correct logical relation; contradictory: *inconsistent statements.* 3. Not regular or predictable; erratic. —See Syns at **capricious.** —**in′con·sis′ten·cy** *n.* —**in′con·sis′tent·ly** *adv.*

in·con·sol·a·ble (ĭn′kən-sō′lə-bəl) *adj.* Incapable of being consoled or comforted; despondent. —**in′con·sol′a·bil′i·ty** or **in′con·sol′a·ble·ness** *n.* —**in′con·sol′a·bly** *adv.*

in·con·so·nant (ĭn-kŏn′sə-nənt) *adj.* Lacking harmony, agreement, or compatibility; discordant. —**in·con′so·nance** *n.* —**in·con′so·nant·ly** *adv.*

in·con·spic·u·ous (ĭn′kən-spĭk′yoo-əs) *adj.* Not readily noticeable. —**in′con·spic′u·ous·ly** *adv.* —**in′con·spic′u·ous·ness** *n.*

in·con·stant (ĭn-kŏn′stənt) *adj.* 1. Not constant. 2. Fickle; faithless. —See Syns at **capricious.** —**in·con′stan·cy** *n.* —**in·con′stant·ly** *adv.*

in·con·test·a·ble (ĭn′kən-tĕs′tə-bəl) *adj.* Incapable of being contested; unquestionable: *incontestable proof.* —**in′con·test′a·bil′i·ty** or **in′con·test′a·ble·ness** *n.* —**in′con·test′a·bly** *adv.*

in·con·ti·nent (ĭn-kŏn′tə-nənt) *adj.* 1. Not continent; unrestrained; uncontrolled. 2. Incapable of holding back. 3. Incapable of controlling the excretion of urine or feces. —**in·con′ti·nence** *n.* —**in·con′ti·nent·ly** *adv.*

in·con·tro·vert·i·ble (ĭn-kŏn′trə-vûr′tə-bəl) *adj.* Indisputable; unquestionable. —**in·con′tro·vert′i·bil′i·ty** or **in·con′tro·vert′i·ble·ness** *n.* —**in·con′tro·vert′i·bly** *adv.*

in·con·ven·ience (ĭn′kən-vēn′yəns) *n.* 1. Lack of ease or comfort; trouble; difficulty. 2. Something that causes difficulty, trouble, or discomfort; an inconvenient thing. —*tr.v.* -ienced, -ienc·ing. To cause inconvenience for; to trouble; bother.

in·con·ven·ient (ĭn′kən-vēn′yənt) *adj.* Not convenient; causing difficulty. —**in′con·ven′ient·ly** *adv.*

in·con·vert·i·ble (ĭn′kən-vûr′tə-bəl) *adj.* Incapable of being converted, esp. not redeemable for gold or silver: *inconvertible paper currency.* —**in′con·vert′i·bil′i·ty** or **in′con·vert′i·ble·ness** *n.* —**in′con·vert′i·bly** *adv.*

in·cor·po·rate (ĭn-kôr′pə-rāt′) *v.* -rat·ed, -rat·ing. —*tr.v.* 1. To form into a legal corporation: *incorporate a business.* 2. To combine or blend into a unified whole; unite: *a new car that incorporates the best features of past models.* 3. To give a material form to; embody: *a bust that incorporates the sculptor's view of the subject.* —*intr.v.* 1. To become united or combined. 2. To form a legal corporation: *We decided to pool our capital and incorporate.* —*adj.* (ĭn-kôr′pər-ĭt). 1. Combined into one united body; merged. 2. Formed into a legal corporation. [Middle English *incorporaten,* from Late Latin *incorporāre,* to form into a body : Latin *in-* (intensive) + *corporāre,* to form into a body.] —**in·cor′po·ra′tion** *n.* —**in·cor′po·ra′tive** *adj.* —**in·cor′po·ra′tor** *n.*

in·cor·po·rat·ed (ĭn-kôr′pə-rā′tĭd) *adj.* 1. United into one body; combined. 2. Organized and maintained as a legal business corporation: *an incorporated village.*

in·cor·po·re·al (ĭn′kôr-pôr′ē-əl, -pōr′-) *adj.* 1. Lacking material form or substance: *an incorporeal phantom.* 2. Spiritual. —**in′cor·po′re·al·ly** *adv.*

in·cor·rect (ĭn′kə-rĕkt′) *adj.* Not correct; wrong or improper. —See Syns at **false.** —**in′cor·rect′ly** *adv.* —**in′cor·rect′ness** *n.*

in·cor·ri·gi·ble (ĭn-kôr′ə-jə-bəl, -kŏr′-) *adj.* Incapable of being corrected or reformed: *an incorrigible criminal; incorrigible dishonesty.* —*n.* A person who cannot be reformed. [Middle English, from Late Latin *incorrigibilis* : Latin *in-,* not + *corrigere,* to correct.] —**in·cor′ri·gi·bil′i·ty** *n.* —**in·cor′ri·gi·bly** *adv.*

in·cor·rupt·i·ble (ĭn′kə-rŭp′tə-bəl) *adj.* Incapable of being corrupted morally. —**in′cor·rupt′i·bil′i·ty** *n.* —**in′cor·rupt′i·bly** *adv.*

in·crease (ĭn-krēs′) *v.* -creased, -creas·ing. —*intr.v.* 1. To become greater or larger. 2. To multiply; reproduce. —*tr.v.* To make greater or larger. —*n.* (ĭn′krēs′). 1. The act of increasing. 2. The amount or rate by which something is increased: *a tax increase of 10 per cent.* [Middle English *encresen,* from Old French *encreistre,* from Latin *incrēscere,* to grow in or on : *in-,* in + *crēscere,* to grow.] —**in·creas′a·ble** *adj.*

Syns: increase, augment, enlarge, expand, extend, magnify, mount, snowball, swell *v. Core meaning:* To become larger or greater (*problems that increased*).

in·creas·ing·ly (ĭn-krē′sĭng-lē) *adv.* More and more: *increasingly difficult.*

in·cred·i·ble (ĭn-krĕd′ə-bəl) *adj.* 1. Unbelievable. 2. Astonishing; amazing. —See Syns at **fabulous.** —**in·cred′i·bil′i·ty** *n.* —**in·cred′i·bly** *adv.*

Usage: incredible, incredulous. What is *incredible* is unbelievable: *incredible wealth.* *Incredulous,* often misused in that sense, properly describes a person or something about a person that shows skepticism or disbelief: *an incredulous expression on her face.*

in·cre·du·li·ty (ĭn′krĭ-doo′lĭ-tē, -dyoo′-) *n.* Disbelief.

in·cred·u·lous (ĭn-krĕj′ə-ləs) *adj.* 1. Disbelieving; skeptical: *incredulous of flying-saucer stories.* 2. Expressing disbelief: *an incredulous stare.* —See Usage note at **incredible.** —**in·cred′u·lous·ly** *adv.* —**in·cred′u·lous·ness** *n.*

in·cre·ment (ĭn′krə-mənt) *n.* 1. An increase in number, size, or extent; growth; enlargement. 2. An added amount, esp. one of a series of regular, usu. small additions or stages. 3. A change, esp. a small change, in the value of a mathematical variable. [Middle English, from Latin *incrēmentum,* from *incrēscere,* to increase.] —**in′cre·men′tal** (-mĕn′tl) *adj.*

in·crim·i·nate (ĭn-krĭm′ə-nāt′) *tr.v.* -nat·ed, -nat·ing. To charge with or involve in a crime or other wrongful act. [From Late Latin *incrīmināre* : Latin *in-,* in + *crīmen,* crime.] —**in·crim′i·na′tion** *n.* —**in·crim′i·na·to′ry** (-nə-tôr′ē, -tōr′ē) *adj.*

in·crust (ĭn-krŭst′) *v.* Var. of **encrust.**

in·cu·bate (ĭn′kyə-bāt′, ĭng′-) *v.* -bat·ed, -bat·ing. —*tr.v.* 1. To warm (eggs), as by bodily heat, so as to promote embryonic development and the hatching of young; to brood. 2. To maintain (a bacterial culture, for example) in the best possible conditions for development. —*intr.v.* 1. To brood eggs. 2. To develop and hatch. 3. To undergo incubation. [From Latin *incubāre,* to hatch, lie down upon : *in-,* on + *cubāre,* to lie down.]

in·cu·ba·tion (ĭn′kyə-bā′shən, ĭng′-) *n.* 1. The act of incubating or the condition of being incubated. 2. *Med.* The development of an infection from the time of its entry into or initiation within an organism up to the time of the first appearance of signs or symptoms. —**in′cu·ba′tion·al** *adj.*

in·cu·ba·tor (ĭn′kyə-bā′tər, ĭng′-) *n.* 1. An enclosed space in which a desired temperature can be maintained, used for incubating eggs, cultures of microorganisms, etc. 2. A device used to supply a prematurely born infant with controlled conditions of temperature, humidity, and oxygen concentration.

incubator

in·cu·bus (ĭn′kyə-bəs, ĭng′-) *n., pl.* -bus·es or -bi (-bī′). 1. An evil spirit believed to descend upon and have sexual intercourse with sleeping women. 2. A nightmare. 3. Something nightmarishly burdensome. [Middle English, from Late Latin, from Latin *incubāre*, to lie down upon, incubate.]

in·cu·des (ĭng-kyōō'dēz) *n*. Plural of **incus.**

in·cul·cate (ĭn-kŭl'kāt') *tr.v.* **-cat·ed, -cat·ing.** To teach or impress by forceful urging or frequent repetition; instill: *inculcate a code of ethics into children.* [From Latin *inculcāre*, to trample in, impress upon : *in-*, in + *calcāre*, to trample, from *calx*, heel.] **—in'cul·ca'tion** *n.* **—in·cul'ca'tor** *n.*

in·cul·pate (ĭn-kŭl'pāt') *tr.v.* **-pat·ed, -pat·ing.** To incriminate. [From Late Latin *inculpāre* : *in-*, on + *culpāre*, to blame, from *culpa*, fault.] **—in'cul·pa'tion** *n.*

in·cum·ben·cy (ĭn-kŭm'bən-sē) *n., pl.* **-cies. 1.** The condition or quality of being incumbent. **2.** The holding and administering of an office: *The senator took advantage of his incumbency to gain frequent press and TV coverage.* **3.** The term of office of an incumbent.

in·cum·bent (ĭn-kŭm'bənt) *adj.* **1.** Lying, leaning, or resting upon something else. **2.** Imposed as an obligation or duty; required: *the responsibilities incumbent upon a good parent.* **3.** Currently holding a specified office: *the incumbent mayor.* *—n.* A person who holds an office: *In some elections the challenger ousts the incumbent.* [Middle English, from Latin *incumbere*, to lean upon : *in-*, on + *cumbere*, to lean, recline.] **—in·cum'bent·ly** *adv.*

in·cu·nab·u·lum (ĭn'kyə-năb'yə-ləm, ĭng'-) *n., pl.* **-la** (-lə). **1.** A book printed from movable type before 1501. **2.** Any early product of an art or craft. [From Latin *incūnābula* (pl.), swaddling clothes, cradle, infancy : *in-*, in + *cūnābula*, cradle, from *cūnae*.]

in·cur (ĭn-kûr') *tr.v.* **-curred, -cur·ring. 1.** To meet with; run into: *incurring difficulties.* **2.** To become liable or subject to as a result of one's actions; bring upon oneself: *incur heavy expenses.* [Latin *incurrere* : *in-*, in + *currere*, to run.]

in·cur·a·ble (ĭn-kyŏŏr'ə-bəl) *adj.* **1.** Not capable of being cured: *an incurable disease.* **2.** Not capable of being reformed or dissuaded; stubborn: *an incurable optimist.* **—in·cur'a·bil'i·ty** or **in·cur'a·ble·ness** *n.* **—in·cur'a·bly** *adv.*

in·cur·i·ous (ĭn-kyŏŏr'ē-əs) *adj.* Not curious; uninterested. —See Syns at **uninterested. —in·cu'ri·os'i·ty** (-ŏs'ĭ-tē) or **in·cu'ri·ous·ness** *n.* **—in·cu'ri·ous·ly** *adv.*

in·cur·sion (ĭn-kûr'zhən, -shən) *n.* A sudden attack on or invasion of enemy territory; a raid. [Middle English, from Old French, from Latin *incursiō*, from *incurrere*, to run into, attack, incur.] **—in·cur'sive** *adj.*

in·cus (ĭng'kəs) *n., pl.* **in·cu·des** (ĭng-kyōō'dēz). An anvil-shaped bone in the mammalian middle ear. Also called **anvil.** [Latin *incūs*, anvil.]

in·debt·ed (ĭn-dĕt'ĭd) *adj.* Owing something, as money or gratitude, to another for a loan, gift, or useful service; beholden: *indebted to a moneylender; a novel indebted to classical models.* [Middle English *endetted*, from Old French *endette*, from *endetter*, to oblige : *en-*, in + *dette*, debt.] **—in·debt'ed·ness** *n.*

in·de·cen·cy (ĭn-dē'sən-sē) *n., pl.* **-cies. 1.** The condition or quality of being indecent. **2.** Something that is indecent.

in·de·cent (ĭn-dē'sənt) *adj.* **1.** Offensive to good taste; unseemly. **2.** Offensive to public moral values; immodest: *indecent exposure.* **—in·de'cent·ly** *adv.*

in·de·ci·pher·a·ble (ĭn'dĭ-sī'fər-ə-bəl) *adj.* Incapable of being deciphered. **—in'de·ci'pher·a·bil'i·ty** or **in'de·ci'pher·a·ble·ness** *n.*

in·de·ci·sion (ĭn'dĭ-sĭzh'ən) *n.* The quality or condition of being unable to make up one's mind; irresolution.

in·de·ci·sive (ĭn'dĭ-sī'sĭv) *adj.* **1.** Not decisive; inconclusive. **2.** Characterized by indecision; vacillating; hesitant. **—in'de·ci'sive·ly** *adv.* **—in'de·ci'sive·ness** *n.*

in·dec·o·rous (ĭn-dĕk'ər-əs) *adj.* Lacking propriety or good taste; unseemly. **—in·dec'o·rous·ly** *adv.* **—in·dec'o·rous·ness** *n.*

in·de·co·rum (ĭn'dĭ-kôr'əm, -kōr'-) *n.* Lack of decorum; lack of propriety or good taste.

in·deed (ĭn-dēd') *adv.* **1.** Without a doubt; certainly; truly. **2.** In fact; in reality. **3.** Admittedly; unquestionably. *—interj.* A word used to express surprise, skepticism, or irony. [Middle English *in dede*, in reality : *in*, in + *dede*, deed.]

in·de·fat·i·ga·ble (ĭn'dĭ-făt'ĭ-gə-bəl) *adj.* Untiring; tireless. [Latin *indēfatigābilis* : *in-*, not + *dēfatigāre*, to fatigue.] **—in'de·fat'i·ga·bil'i·ty** or **in'de·fat'i·ga·ble·ness** *n.* **—in'de·fat'i·ga·bly** *adv.*

in·de·fea·si·ble (ĭn'dĭ-fē'zə-bəl) *adj.* Not capable of being annulled or set aside. **—in'de·fea'si·bil'i·ty** *n.* **—in'de·fea'si·bly** *adv.*

in·de·fen·si·ble (ĭn'dĭ-fĕn'sə-bəl) *adj.* Not capable of being defended: *an indefensible outpost; indefensible behavior.* **—in'de·fen'si·bil'i·ty** or **in'de·fen'si·ble·ness** *n.* **—in'de·fen'si·bly** *adv.*

in·de·fin·a·ble (ĭn'dĭ-fī'nə-bəl) *adj.* Not capable of being defined, described, or analyzed. **—in'de·fin'a·ble·ness** *n.* **—in'de·fin'a·bly** *adv.*

in·def·i·nite (ĭn-dĕf'ə-nĭt) *adj.* Not definite, esp.: **1.** Not fixed: *an indefinite period of time.* **2.** Unclear; vague: *indefinite outlines.* **3.** Not decided; uncertain: *indefinite plans.* —See Syns at **vague. —in·def'i·nite·ly** *adv.* **—in·def'i·nite·ness** *n.*

indefinite article. An article, in English either *a* or *an*, that does not fix the identity of the noun modified.

indefinite pronoun. A pronoun, such as *any* or *some*, that does not specify the identity of its object.

in·del·i·ble (ĭn-dĕl'ə-bəl) *adj.* **1.** Incapable of being removed, erased, or washed away; permanent: *indelible ink.* **2.** Making a mark not easily erased or washed away: *an indelible laundry pencil.* [Latin *indēlēbilis* : *in-*, not + *dēlēre*, to obliterate, delete.] **—in·del'i·bil'i·ty** or **in·del'i·ble·ness** *n.* **—in·del'i·bly** *adv.*

in·del·i·ca·cy (ĭn-dĕl'ĭ-kə-sē) *n., pl.* **-cies. 1.** The quality or condition of being indelicate. **2.** An indelicate act or remark.

in·del·i·cate (ĭn-dĕl'ĭ-kĭt) *adj.* **1.** Offensive to taste or good manners; coarse. **2.** Tactless. **—in·del'i·cate·ly** *adv.* **—in·del'i·cate·ness** *n.*

in·dem·ni·fi·ca·tion (ĭn-dĕm'nə-fĭ-kā'shən) *n.* **1.** The act of indemnifying or the condition of being indemnified. **2.** Something that indemnifies.

in·dem·ni·fy (ĭn-dĕm'nə-fī') *tr.v.* **-fied, -fy·ing. 1.** To protect against possible damage, legal suit, or bodily injury; insure. **2.** To make compensation to for damage or loss suffered. [Latin *indemnis*, uninjured + -FY.] **—in·dem'ni·fi'er** *n.*

in·dem·ni·ty (ĭn-dĕm'nĭ-tē) *n., pl.* **-ties. 1.** Insurance or other security against possible damage, loss, or injury. **2.** A legal exemption from liability for damages. **3.** Compensation for damage, loss, or injury suffered. [Middle English *indempnyte*, from Old French *indemnite*, from Late Latin *indemnitās*, from Latin *indemnis*, unhurt, uninjured : *in-*, not + *damnum*, hurt, harm.]

in·dent¹ (ĭn-dĕnt') *tr.v.* **1.** To set in (the first line of a paragraph) from the margin. **2.** To edge with notches or toothlike projections; make jagged: *Coves and capes indent the shoreline.* **3. a.** To make notches, grooves, or holes in (wood) for the purpose of mortising. **b.** To fit or join together by or as if by mortising. *—intr.v.* **1.** To set the first line of a paragraph in from the margin. **2.** To form an indentation. *—n.* (ĭn'dĕnt', ĭn-dĕnt'). **1.** The act of indenting; indentation. **2.** A recess along an edge or boundary. **3.** A notch or jagged cut. [Middle English *indenten*, to make a toothlike incision into, from Old French *endenter* : *en-*, in + *dent*, tooth, from Latin *dēns*.] **—in·dent'er** *n.*

in·dent² (ĭn-dĕnt') *tr.v.* To make a dent or other impression in: *a potter's tool for indenting clay.* *—n.* (ĭn'dĕnt', ĭn-dĕnt'). An indentation.

in·den·ta·tion (ĭn'dĕn-tā'shən) *n.* **1.** The act of indenting or the condition of being indented. **2.** A notch or jagged cut in an edge. **3.** A deep recess in a border, coastline, or other boundary. **4.** The blank space between a margin and the beginning of an indented line.

in·den·tion (ĭn-dĕn'shən) *n.* **1.** The act of indenting or the condition of being indented. **2.** The blank space between a margin and the beginning of an indented line. **3.** An indentation or dent.

in·den·ture (ĭn-dĕn'chər) *n.* **1.** A deed or contract executed between two or more parties. **2.** Often **indentures.** A contract binding one party into the service of another for a specified term. *—tr.v.* **-tured, -tur·ing.** To bind by inden-

---

| ă pat | ā pay | â care | ä father | ĕ pet | ē be | hw which | ĭ pit | ī tie | î pier | ŏ pot | ō toe | ô paw, for | oi noise |
| ŏŏ took | ōō boot | ou out | th thin | *th* this | ŭ cut | | û urge | zh vision | ə about, item, edible, gallop, circus |

ture. [Middle English *indenture,* from Old French *enden-ture,* from *endenter,* to indent.]

in·de·pend·ence (ĭn′dĭ-pĕn′dəns) *n.* The condition or quality of being independent. —See Syns at **freedom.**

Independence Day. July 4, a U.S. legal holiday celebrating the anniversary of the adoption of the Declaration of Independence in 1776.

in·de·pend·en·cy (ĭn′dĭ-pĕn′dən-sē) *n., pl.* **-cies.** **1.** Independence. **2.** An independent territory or state.

in·de·pend·ent (ĭn′dĭ-pĕn′dənt) *adj.* **1.** Politically autonomous; self-governing: *an independent country.* **2.** Free from the influence, guidance, or control of others; self-reliant: *an independent mind.* **3.** Not determined or influenced by someone or something else; not contingent: *an independent study of air pollution.* **4.** Not dependent on or connected with a larger or controlling group, system, etc.: *an independent food store.* **5.** Not committed to any one political party: *an independent voter.* **6.** Earning one's own living; self-supporting. **7.** Providing or being sufficient income to enable one to live without working: *a man of independent means.* —*n.* Someone or something that is independent, esp. a voter who does not pledge allegiance to any one political party. —**in′de·pend′ent·ly** *adv.*

independent clause. A clause containing a subject, a verb, and sometimes an object and modifiers, capable of standing alone as a complete sentence.

in-depth (ĭn′dĕpth′) *adj.* Detailed; thorough: *an in-depth study.*

in·de·scrib·a·ble (ĭn′dĭ-skrī′bə-bəl) *adj.* **1.** Incapable of being described. **2.** Beyond description: *indescribable delight.* —See Syns at **unspeakable.** —**in′de·scrib′a·bil′i·ty** or **in′de·scrib′a·ble·ness** *n.* —**in′de·scrib′a·bly** *adv.*

in·de·struc·ti·ble (ĭn′dĭ-strŭk′tə-bəl) *adj.* Not capable of being destroyed. —**in′de·struc′ti·bil′i·ty** or **in′de·struc′ti·ble·ness** *n.* —**in′de·struc′ti·bly** *adv.*

in·de·ter·min·a·ble (ĭn′dĭ-tûr′mə-nə-bəl) *adj.* **1.** Not capable of being fixed or measured; not ascertainable. **2.** Incapable of being finally settled or decided. —**in′de·ter′mi·na·bly** *adv.*

in·de·ter·mi·na·cy (ĭn′dĭ-tûr′mə-nə-sē) *n.* The condition or quality of being indeterminate.

in·de·ter·mi·nate (ĭn′dĭ-tûr′mə-nĭt) *adj.* **1.** Incapable of being determined. **2.** Not precisely determined or known: *a person of indeterminate age.* **3.** *Bot.* Not terminating in a flower but continuing to grow at the apex: *an indeterminate inflorescence.* —**in′de·ter′mi·nate·ly** *adv.* —**in′de·ter′mi·nate·ness** *n.*

in·dex (ĭn′dĕks′) *n., pl.* **-dex·es** or **-di·ces** (-dĭ-sēz′). **1.** Anything that serves to guide, point out, or aid reference, as: **a.** An alphabetized listing of names, places, and subjects included in a printed work, giving for each item the pages on which it is mentioned. **b.** A series of notches cut into the edge of a book for easy access to chapters or other divisions. **c.** Any table, file, or catalogue. **2.** Anything that reveals or indicates; a sign: *"Her face . . . was a fair index to her disposition"* (Samuel Butler). **3.** *Printing.* A character used to call attention to a particular paragraph or section. Also called **fist.** **4.** Something that serves as an indicator or pointer, as in a scientific instrument. **5.** *Math.* **a.** A number or symbol, often written as a subscript or superscript to a mathematical expression, that indicates an operation to be performed on, an ordering relation involving, or a use of the associated expression. **b.** A number derived from a formula used to characterize a set of data: *the cost-of-living index.* —*tr.v.* **1.** To furnish with an index. **2.** To enter (an item) in an index. **3.** To indicate or signal. [Latin, forefinger, indicator.]

index finger. The finger next to the thumb.

index number. A number indicating change in magnitude, as of prices or wages, relative to the magnitude at some specified point usu. taken as 100.

index of refraction. The ratio of the speed of light in a vacuum to the speed of light in a medium under consideration.

In·di·an (ĭn′dē-ən) *n.* **1.** A native or inhabitant of India or of the East Indies. **2.** A member of any of the aboriginal peoples of North America, South America, or the West Indies. **3.** Loosely, any of the languages spoken by the American Indians. **4.** A constellation, **Indus.** —*adj.* **1.** Of or pertain-

ing to India or the East Indies, their culture, or their people. **2.** Of or pertaining to the aboriginal people of North America, South America, or the West Indies.

Indian corn. A tall widely cultivated cereal plant, *Zea mays,* that bears seeds on large ears.

Indian file. Single file.

Indian meal. Cornmeal.

Indian summer. A period of mild weather occurring in late autumn or early winter.

Indian turnip. **1.** A plant, the **jack-in-the-pulpit.** **2.** The acrid tuber of this plant.

In·dic (ĭn′dĭk) *adj.* **1.** Of or pertaining to India, its people, or their culture. **2.** Of, pertaining to, or constituting the Indic languages. —*n.* A branch of the Indo-European languages that comprises Sanskrit and its modern descendants.

in·di·cate (ĭn′dĭ-kāt′) *tr.v.* **-cat·ed, -cat·ing.** **1.** To show or point out with precision: *indicate a route.* **2.** To serve as a sign, symptom, or token of; signify: *"The cracking and booming of the ice indicate a change of temperature"* (Thoreau). **3.** To suggest or demonstrate the necessity or advisability of: *The symptoms indicate immediate surgery.* **4.** To state or express briefly: *He indicated his wishes.* [From Latin *indicāre,* to show, from *index,* forefinger, indicator, index.]

in·di·ca·tion (ĭn′dĭ-kā′shən) *n.* **1.** The act of indicating. **2.** Something that indicates; a sign, token, or symptom. —See Syns at **sign.**

in·dic·a·tive (ĭn-dĭk′ə-tĭv) *adj.* **1.** Serving to point out or indicate. **2.** *Gram.* Of or being a verb mood used for statements and questions of fact. —*n. Gram.* **1.** The indicative mood. **2.** A verb in the indicative mood. —**in·dic′a·tive·ly** *adv.*

in·di·ca·tor (ĭn′dĭ-kā′tər) *n.* **1.** Something that indicates, as a pointer, sign, or index. **2.** Any meter, gauge, warning light, etc., that tells something about the operation of a furnace, engine, or other machine or system. **3.** A chemical compound, such as litmus, that shows a characteristic change in color under certain known conditions, used in making chemical tests. —See Syns at **sign.**

in·di·ces (ĭn′dĭ-sēz′) *n.* A plural of **index.**

in·dict (ĭn-dīt′) *tr.v.* **1.** To accuse of a crime or other offense; charge. **2.** To make a formal accusation or indictment against by the findings of a grand jury. [Alteration of Middle English *enditen,* to accuse, from Norman French *enditer,* to dictate.] —**in·dict′a·ble** *adj.* —**in·dict′er** or **in·dic′tor** *n.*

in·dict·ment (ĭn-dīt′mənt) *n.* **1.** The act of indicting or the condition of being indicted. **2.** *Law.* A written statement listing the charges against an accused person, drawn up by the prosecuting attorney and presented by the grand jury.

in·dif·fer·ence (ĭn-dĭf′ər-əns) *n.* **1.** The condition or quality of being indifferent. **2.** Lack of interest or concern. **3.** Lack of importance; insignificance. —See Syns at **disinterest.**

in·dif·fer·ent (ĭn-dĭf′ər-ənt) *adj.* **1.** Having or showing no interest; not caring one way or the other. **2.** Showing no preference; impartial. **3.** Neither good nor bad; mediocre: *The musician gave an indifferent performance.* **4.** Not mattering one way or the other; of no great importance; insignificant. —See Syns at **uninterested.** —**in·dif′fer·ent·ly** *adv.*

in·di·gence (ĭn′də-jəns) *n.* Neediness; poverty.

in·dig·e·nous (ĭn-dĭj′ə-nəs) *adj.* **1.** Occurring or living naturally in an area; not introduced; native. **2.** Intrinsic; innate. —See Syns at **native.** [From Latin *indigena,* native.] —**in·dig′e·nous·ly** *adv.* —**in·dig′e·nous·ness** *n.*

in·di·gent (ĭn′də-jənt) *adj.* Lacking the means to live; poor; needy. —*n.* See at **poor.** —*n.* A destitute or needy person. [Middle English, from Old French, from Latin *indigēns,* pres. part. of *indigēre,* to lack.] —**in′di·gent·ly** *adv.*

in·di·gest·i·ble (ĭn′dĭ-jĕs′tə-bəl, -dī-) *adj.* Difficult or impossible to digest. —**in′di·gest′i·bil′i·ty** *n.* —**in′di·gest′i·bly** *adv.*

in·di·ges·tion (ĭn′dĭ-jĕs′chən, -dī-) *n.* **1.** The inability to digest food. **2.** Discomfort or illness that accompanies the inability to digest food.

in·dig·nant (ĭn-dĭg′nənt) *adj.* Feeling or expressing indignation. —See Syns at **angry.** [Latin *indignāns,* pres. part.

of *indignārī*, to regard as unworthy, from *indignus*, unworthy.] —**in·dig′nant·ly** *adv.*

in·dig·na·tion (ĭn′dĭg-nā′shən) *n.* Anger aroused by something unjust, mean, or unworthy. [Middle English *indignacioun*, from Latin *indignātiō*, from *indignārī*, to regard as unworthy.]

in·dig·ni·ty (ĭn-dĭg′nĭ-tē) *n., pl.* **-ties. 1.** Humiliating, degrading, or abusive treatment. **2.** Something that offends a person's pride and sense of dignity; an affront. [Latin *indignitās*, from *indignus*, unworthy.]

in·di·go (ĭn′dĭ-gō′) *n., pl.* **-gos** or **-goes. 1. a.** Any of various plants of the genus *Indigofera*, some of which yield a blue dyestuff. **b.** Any of several similar or related plants. **2.** A blue dye obtained from indigo or other plants or produced synthetically. **3.** A dark blue. —*adj.* Dark blue. [Earlier *indico*, from Spanish, from Latin *indicum*, from Greek *indikon (pharmakon)*, "Indian (dye)," from *India*, India.]

indigo bunting. A small bird, *Passerina cyanea*, of North and Central America, the male of which has deep-blue plumage.

indigo snake. A nonvenomous bluish-black snake, *Drymarchon corais*, of the southern United States and northern Mexico.

in·di·rect (ĭn′dĭ-rĕkt′, -dī-) *adj.* **1.** Not being or taking a direct course; roundabout: *an indirect route home.* **2.** Not straight to the point, as in speaking; devious. **3.** Not directly planned for; secondary: *indirect benefits.* —**in·di·rect′ly** *adv.* —**in·di·rect′ness** *n.*

Syns: indirect, circuitous, circular, roundabout *adj.* Core meaning: Not going straight to a destination or mark (*an indirect route; an indirect reply*).

indirect discourse. Discourse reporting the words of another without quoting directly, as in *He said that he would be back soon.*

indirect object. A grammatical object indirectly affected by the action of a verb; for example, *me* in *Sing me a song* and *turtle* in *He feeds the turtle lettuce* are indirect objects.

in·dis·creet (ĭn′dĭ-skrēt′) *adj.* Lacking in discretion; imprudent or tactless. —**in′dis·creet′ly** *adv.* —**in′dis·creet′ness** *n.*

in·dis·crete (ĭn′dĭ-skrēt′) *adj.* Not divided or divisible into separate parts; unified.

in·dis·cre·tion (ĭn′dĭ-skrĕsh′ən) *n.* **1.** Lack of discretion. **2.** An indiscreet act or remark.

in·dis·crim·i·nate (ĭn′dĭ-skrĭm′ə-nĭt) *adj.* **1.** Lacking in discrimination; exercising or showing no care in choosing: *an indiscriminate shopper.* **2.** Not sorted out or put in order; confused: *an indiscriminate pile of letters.* —**in′dis·crim′i·nate·ly** *adv.* —**in′dis·crim′i·nate·ness** *n.*

in·dis·crim·i·na·tion (ĭn′dĭ-skrĭm′ə-nā′shən) *n.* The condition or quality of being indiscriminate. —**in′dis·crim′i·na′tive** *adj.*

in·dis·pen·sa·ble (ĭn′dĭ-spĕn′sə-bəl) *adj.* Incapable of being dispensed with; essential; required. —See Syns at **necessary.** —**in′dis·pen′sa·bil′i·ty** or **in′dis·pen′sa·ble·ness** *n.* —**in′dis·pen′sa·bly** *adv.*

in·dis·pose (ĭn′dĭ-spōz′) *tr.v.* **-posed, -pos·ing. 1.** To make unwilling; disincline. **2.** To render unfit; disqualify.

in·dis·posed (ĭn′dĭ-spōzd′) *adj.* **1.** Ill. **2.** Disinclined; unwilling. —See Syns at **sick.**

in·dis·po·si·tion (ĭn′dĭs′pə-zĭsh′ən) *n.* **1.** Disinclination; unwillingness. **2.** A minor ailment.

in·dis·put·a·ble (ĭn′dĭ-spyōō′tə-bəl) *adj.* Beyond doubt; undeniable. —**in′dis·put′a·ble·ness** *n.* —**in′dis·put′a·bly** *adv.*

in·dis·sol·u·ble (ĭn′dĭ-sŏl′yə-bəl) *adj.* **1.** Impossible to break or undo; binding: *an indissoluble contract.* **2.** Incapable of being dissolved. —**in′dis·sol′u·bil′i·ty** or **in′dis·sol′u·ble·ness** *n.* —**in′dis·sol′u·bly** *adv.*

in·dis·tinct (ĭn′dĭ-stĭngkt′) *adj.* Not clearly heard, seen, or understood: *indistinct sounds.* —See Syns at **vague.** —**in′dis·tinct′ly** *adv.* —**in′dis·tinct′ness** *n.*

in·dis·tin·guish·a·ble (ĭn′dĭ-stĭng′gwĭsh-ə-bəl) *adj.* **1.** Not capable of being perceived: *an indistinguishable difference.* **2.** Without distinctive qualities; hard to tell apart from others: *a small town indistinguishable from a thousand others.* —See Syns at **imperceptible.** —**in′dis·tin′guish·a·ble·ness** *n.* —**in′dis·tin′guish·a·bly** *adv.*

in·dite (ĭn-dīt′) *tr.v.* **-dit·ed, -dit·ing.** *Archaic.* **1.** To write; compose. **2.** To set down in writing. [Middle English *enditen*, to compose, write down, from Norman French *enditer*, from Latin *indīcere*, to proclaim : *in-*, toward + *dīcere*, to pronounce.] —**in·dite′ment** *n.* —**in·dit′er** *n.*

in·di·um (ĭn′dē-əm) *n. Symbol* **In** A soft, malleable, silvery-white metallic element found primarily in ores of zinc and tin, used as a plating over silver in making mirrors, in plating aircraft bearings, and in compounds for making transistors. Atomic number 49, atomic weight 114.82, melting point 156.61°C, boiling point 2,000°C, specific gravity 7.31, valences 1, 2, 3. [From Latin *indicum*, indigo (from the indigo-blue color of its spectrum).]

in·di·vid·u·al (ĭn′də-vĭj′ōō-əl) *adj.* **1. a.** Of or relating to a single human being. **b.** By or for one person: *an individual portion.* **2.** Existing as a distinct thing; single; separate: *individual words.* **3.** Having special qualities or identifying traits; distinctive: *"There was nothing individual about him except a deep scar . . . across his right cheek"* (Rebecca West). —See Syns at **characteristic** and **single.** —*n.* **1. a.** A single human being considered separately from a group or from society: *The average score was low, though certain individuals scored high.* **b.** A single organism as distinguished from a group or colony. **2.** An independent, strong-willed person: *learned to think as an individual.* **3.** A particular person: *a disagreeable individual.* [Middle English *indyvyduall*, separate, indivisible, from Medieval Latin *indīviduālis*, from Latin *indīviduus* : *in-*, not + *dīviduus*, divisible.] —**in′di·vid′u·al·ly** *adv.*

in·di·vid·u·al·ism (ĭn′də-vĭj′ōō-ə-lĭz′əm) *n.* **1.** The assertion of one's own will and personality; personal independence. **2.** Self-reliance. **3. a.** The theory that the individual is more important than the state or social group. **b.** The theory that the individual should be free to advance himself economically and should succeed by his own initiative.

in·di·vid·u·al·ist (ĭn′də-vĭj′ōō-ə-lĭst) *n.* **1.** A person who is independent in thought and action. **2.** A person who advocates individualism. —**in′di·vid′u·al·ist** or **in′di·vid′u·al·is′tic** *adj.* —**in′di·vid′u·al·is′ti·cal·ly** *adv.*

in·di·vid·u·al·i·ty (ĭn′də-vĭj′ōō-ăl′ĭ-tē) *n., pl.* **-ties. 1.** The quality of being individual; distinctness: *music in four parts, each having individuality.* **2.** The qualities that make a person or thing different from others; distinctive identity: *expressing one's individuality.*

in·di·vis·i·ble (ĭn′də-vĭz′ə-bəl) *adj.* **1.** Incapable of being divided. **2.** *Math.* Incapable of being divided exactly: *7 is indivisible by 3.* —**in′di·vis′i·ble·ness** or **in′di·vis′i·bil′i·ty** *n.* —**in′di·vis′i·bly** *adv.*

Indo-. A prefix meaning India or East Indian: **Indochina.**

in·doc·tri·nate (ĭn-dŏk′trə-nāt′) *tr.v.* **-nat·ed, -nat·ing. 1.** To instruct in a body of doctrine. **2.** To teach to accept a system of thought uncritically. —**in·doc′tri·na′tion** *n.*

In·do-Eu·ro·pe·an (ĭn′dō-yŏŏr′ə-pē′ən) *adj.* Belonging to or constituting a family of languages that includes the Germanic, Celtic, Italic, Baltic, Slavic, Greek, Armenian, Hittite, Tocharian, Iranian, and Indic groups. —*n.* **1.** The Indo-European family of languages. **2.** A member of any of the peoples who spoke Indo-European languages.

In·do-I·ra·ni·an (ĭn′dō-ĭ-rā′nē-ən) *adj.* Belonging to or constituting the branch of Indo-European made up of the Indic and the Iranian language groups. —*n.* The Indo-Iranian branch of Indo-European.

in·do·lent (ĭn′də-lənt) *adj.* **1.** Disinclined to work; habitually lazy. **2.** Suggesting a calm idleness and ease: *the indolent movements of a cat.* —See Syns at **lazy.** [Late Latin *indolēns*, painless : Latin *in-*, not + *dolēre*, to give pain, feel pain.] —**in′do·lence** *n.*

in·dom·i·ta·ble (ĭn-dŏm′ĭ-tə-bəl) *adj.* Incapable of being overcome or subdued; unconquerable. [Late Latin *indomitābilis* : Latin *in-*, not + *domāre*, to tame.] —**in·dom′i·ta·bly** *adv.*

in·door (ĭn′dôr′, -dōr′) *adj.* Of, situated in, or carried on within a house or other building: *an indoor pool.* [Short for earlier *within-door.*]

Usage: indoor, indoors. *Indoor* is an adjective, and *indoors* an adverb: *indoor sports; an indoor football field,* but: *went indoors; a field built indoors.*

in·doors (ĭn-dôrz′, -dōrz′) *adv.* In or into a house or other building: *staying indoors.* [Short for earlier *withindoors.*]

ă pat	ā pay	â care	ä father	ĕ pet	ē be	hw which	ĭ pit	ī tie	î pier	ŏ pot	ō toe	ô paw, for	oi noise
ŏŏ took	ōō boot	ou out	th thin	*th* this	ŭ cut		û urge	zh vision	ə about, item, edible, gallop, circus				

in·dorse (ĭn-dôrs') v. Var. of **endorse**.

in·dorse·ment (ĭn-dôrs'mənt) n. Var. of **endorsement**.

in·du·bi·ta·ble (ĭn-dōō'bĭ-tə-bəl, -dyōō'-) adj. Too apparent to be doubted; unquestionable. —**in·du'bi·ta·bly** adv.

in·duce (ĭn-dōōs', -dyōōs') tr.v. **-duced, -duc·ing**. **1**. To lead or move by influence or persuasion; to prevail upon: *What finally induced you to give up smoking?* **2**. To stimulate the occurrence of; cause: *induce childbirth*. **3**. To infer by inductive reasoning. **4**. *Physics.* To produce (an electric current or magnetic effect) by induction. [Middle English *inducen*, from Latin *indūcere* : *in-*, in + *dūcere*, to lead.] —**in·duc'er** n. —**in·duc'i·ble** adj.

in·duce·ment (ĭn-dōōs'mənt, -dyōōs'-) n. **1**. The act or process of inducing: *the inducement of sleep*. **2**. Something that induces; an incentive; motive.

in·duct (ĭn-dŭkt') tr.v. **1**. To place formally in an office; install. **2**. To admit as a member; to initiate: *inducted her into the club*. **3**. To call into military service; to draft. **4**. *Physics.* To induce. [Middle English *inducten*, from Medieval Latin *indūcere*, from Latin, to lead in, induce.] —**in·duc·tee'** (ĭn'dŭk-tē') n.

in·duc·tance (ĭn-dŭk'təns) n. **1**. The property of an electric circuit. **2**. A circuit element, as a conducting coil, having inductance in which electromotive force is generated by electromagnetic induction.

in·duc·tion (ĭn-dŭk'shən) n. **1**. The act of inducting into office. **2**. The process of being enrolled in the armed forces. **3**. A method of reasoning or mathematical proof in which a conclusion is reached about all the members of a given set by examining just a few members of the set. **4. a**. The generation of an electromotive force across a circuit element by a magnetic field that changes with time. **b**. The generation of an electromotive force across a circuit element as a current that changes with time passes through it. **c**. The production of an electric charge in an uncharged body by bringing a charged body close to it.

induction coil. A transformer, often used in automotive ignition systems, in which an interrupted low-voltage direct current in the primary is converted into an intermittent high-voltage current in the secondary.

in·duc·tive (ĭn-dŭk'tĭv) adj. **1**. Of or using induction: *inductive reasoning*. **2**. *Elect*. Of or arising from inductance: *inductive reactance*. **3**. Serving to cause or bring on: *a medication inductive of vomiting*. —**in·duc'tive·ly** adv. —**in·duc'tive·ness** n.

in·duc·tor (ĭn-dŭk'tər) n. **1**. A person who inducts. **2**. *Elect*. A device that functions by or introduces inductance into a circuit.

in·due (ĭn-dōō', -dyōō') v. Var. of **endue**.

in·dulge (ĭn-dŭlj') v. **-dulged, -dulg·ing**. —tr.v. **1**. To yield to the desires of, esp. to an excessive degree; humor: *indulge a child; indulged herself on her vacation*. **2**. To gratify or yield to: *indulge a craving for chocolate*. —intr.v. **1**. To allow oneself some special pleasure; give in to a desire or appetite. **2**. To take part; engage: *indulge in sports*. —See Syns at **baby**. [Latin *indulgēre*, to be forbearing, grant as a favor.] —**in·dulg'er** n.

in·dul·gence (ĭn-dŭl'jəns) n. **1**. The act or an example of indulging: *an occasional indulgence in rich food*. **2**. Something indulged in: *Sports cars are an expensive indulgence*. **3. a**. Something granted as a favor or privilege. **b**. Permission to extend the time of payment or performance, as in business. **4**. Liberal or lenient treatment; tolerance: *parental indulgence*. **5**. *Rom. Cath. Ch.* The remission of temporal punishment due for a sin after the guilt has been forgiven.

in·dul·gent (ĭn-dŭl'jənt) adj. Showing, characterized by, or given to indulgence; lenient: *an indulgent employer*. —**in·dul'gent·ly** adv.

in·du·rate (ĭn'dōō-rāt', -dyōō-) v. **-rat·ed, -rat·ing**. —tr.v. **1**. To make hard; harden. **2**. To make callous. —intr.v. **1**. To harden. **2**. To become stubborn or unfeeling. —adj. (ĭn'dōō-rĭt, -dyōō-). Hardened; obstinate; unfeeling. [From Latin *indūrāre*, to harden : *in-* (intensive) + *dūrus*, hard.] —**in·du·ra'tion** n.

in·dus·tri·al (ĭn-dŭs'trē-əl) adj. **1**. Of or having to do with industry: *industrial products; industrial know-how*. **2**. Having highly developed industries: *an industrial nation*. **3**. Used in industry: *industrial diamonds*. —n. in-

dustrials. Stocks or bonds issued by an industrial enterprise. —**in·dus'tri·al·ly** adv.

in·dus·tri·al·ism (ĭn-dŭs'trē-ə-lĭz'əm) n. An economic system in which industries are dominant.

in·dus·tri·al·ist (ĭn-dŭs'trē-ə-lĭst) n. A person who owns or runs a large industrial enterprise.

in·dus·tri·al·ize (ĭn-dŭs'trē-ə-līz') v. **-ized, -iz·ing**. —tr.v. To develop industry in; make industrial rather than agricultural. —intr.v. To become industrial rather than agricultural. —**in·dus'tri·al·i·za'tion** n.

in·dus·tri·ous (ĭn-dŭs'trē-əs) adj. Hard-working; diligent. [From Latin *industriōsus*, from *industria*, skill, industry.] —**in·dus'tri·ous·ly** adv. —**in·dus'tri·ous·ness** n.

in·dus·try (ĭn'də-strē) n., pl. **-tries**. **1**. The production and sale of goods and services on a large scale. **2**. A specific branch of manufacture and trade: *the textile industry*. **3**. Industrial management as distinguished from labor. **4**. Hard work; steady effort; diligence. —See Syns at **business**. [Middle English *industrie*, skill, diligence, from Old French, from Latin *industria*.]

-ine[1]. A suffix meaning: **1**. Of, pertaining to, or belonging to: **saccharine**. **2**. Made of or resembling: **opaline**. [Middle English *-ine*, from Old French *-in*, from Latin *-īnus*, *-inus*, from Greek *-inos*.]

-ine[2] or **-in**. A suffix meaning: **1**. A halogen: **chlorine**. **2**. A basic organic nitrogenous compound: **quinine**. **3**. A mixture of compounds: **gasoline**. [Middle English *-ine*, *-in*, from Old French *-ine*, from Latin *-īna*, adj. suffix.]

in·e·bri·ate (ĭ-nē'brē-āt') tr.v. **-at·ed, -at·ing**. To make drunk; intoxicate. —n. (ĭ-nē'brē-ĭt). An intoxicated person, esp. a drunkard. [From Latin *inēbriāre* : *in-* (intensive) + *ēbriāre*, to intoxicate, from *ēbrius*, drunk.] —**in·e'bri·a'tion** n.

in·ed·i·ble (ĭn-ĕd'ə-bəl) adj. Not suitable for food; not edible.

in·ef·fa·ble (ĭn-ĕf'ə-bəl) adj. **1**. Beyond expression; indescribable or unspeakable: *ineffable delight*. **2**. Too sacred to be uttered: *the ineffable name of God*. —**in·ef'fa·bil'i·ty** n. —**in·ef'fa·ble·ness** n. —**in·ef'fa·bly** adv.

in·ef·fec·tive (ĭn'ĭ-fĕk'tĭv) adj. **1**. Not effective; ineffectual. **2**. Incompetent. —**in·ef·fec'tive·ly** adv. —**in·ef·fec'tive·ness** n.

in·ef·fec·tu·al (ĭn'ĭ-fĕk'chōō-əl) adj. **1**. Not having the desired effect; vain: *ineffectual measures to stop the leak*. **2**. Powerless; impotent: *an ineffectual king*. —**in·ef·fec'tu·al'i·ty** (-ăl'ĭ-tē) or **in·ef·fec'tu·al·ness** n. —**in·ef·fec'tu·al·ly** adv.

in·ef·fi·ca·cious (ĭn-ĕf'ĭ-kā'shəs) adj. Not producing a desired effect or result; ineffective. —**in·ef'fi·ca'cious·ly** adv.

in·ef·fi·cien·cy (ĭn'ĭ-fĭsh'ən-sē) n. The quality, condition, or fact of being inefficient.

in·ef·fi·cient (ĭn'ĭ-fĭsh'ənt) adj. Not efficient, esp.: **1**. Lacking in ability; incompetent. **2**. Wasteful of time, energy, or materials: *an inefficient gasoline engine*. **3**. Not producing the intended result. —**in·ef'fi·cient·ly** adv.

in·e·las·tic (ĭn'ĭ-lăs'tĭk) adj. Not returning to an original shape or original dimensions after being deformed; not elastic. —See Syns at **rigid**. —**in·e·las'tic'i·ty** (-lă-stĭs'ĭ-tē) n.

in·el·e·gant (ĭn-ĕl'ĭ-gənt) adj. **1**. Lacking elegance. **2**. Coarse; vulgar. —**in·el'e·gant·ly** adv. —**in·el'e·gance** n.

in·el·i·gi·ble (ĭn-ĕl'ə-jə-bəl) adj. **1**. Not qualified for some office or privilege: *Those under 18 are ineligible to vote*. **2**. Not worthy of being chosen. —n. A person who is not eligible. —**in·el'i·gi·bil'i·ty** n. —**in·el'i·gi·bly** adv.

in·e·luc·ta·ble (ĭn'ĭ-lŭk'tə-bəl) adj. Not to be avoided or overcome; inescapable. [Latin *inēluctābilis* : *in-*, not + *ēluctāri*, to struggle out.] —**in·e·luc'ta·bly** adv.

in·ept (ĭn-ĕpt') adj. **1**. Not apt or fitting; inappropriate: *an inept comparison*. **2**. Lacking skill or competence: *an inept performance*. —See Syns at **awkward**. [Latin *ineptus* : *in-*, not + *aptus*, apt.] —**in·ept'ly** adv. —**in·ept'ness** n.

in·ep·ti·tude (ĭn-ĕp'tĭ-tōōd', -tyōōd') n. **1**. The quality of being inept. **2**. An inept act or remark.

in·e·qual·i·ty (ĭn'ĭ-kwŏl'ĭ-tē) n., pl. **-ties**. **1**. The condition of being unequal: *the inequality of two line segments*. **2**. Lack of regularity; unevenness. **3. a**. A condition, as of society, in which some people or classes are favored over others. **b.** An example of this condition: *the inequalities that exist in housing, job opportunities, and education.* **4.** A mathematical statement that two numbers are not equal.

in·eq·ui·ta·ble (ĭn-ĕk′wĭ-tə-bəl) *adj.* Not equitable; unfair; unjust. —See Syns at **unfair.** —**in·eq′ui·ta·bly** *adv.*

in·eq·ui·ty (ĭn-ĕk′wĭ-tē) *n., pl.* **-ties. 1.** Lack of equity; injustice; unfairness. **2.** An example of injustice or unfairness.

in·ert (ĭ-nûrt′) *adj.* **1.** Unable to move or act. **2.** Resisting motion or activity; sluggish. **3.** *Chem.* **a.** Exhibiting no chemical activity; totally unreactive. **b.** Exhibiting chemical activity under special or extreme conditions only. —See Syns at **inactive.** [Latin *iners*, inactive, unskilled : *in-*, not + *ars*, skill, art.] —**in·ert′ly** *adv.* —**in·ert′ness** *n.*

in·er·tia (ĭ-nûr′shə, -shē-ə) *n.* **1.** The tendency of a physical body to remain at rest or of a body in motion to stay in motion in a straight line unless disturbed by an external force. **2.** Resistance to motion, action, or change. —**in·er′tial** *adj.*

in·es·cap·a·ble (ĭn′ĭ-skā′pə-bəl) *adj.* Not capable of being avoided, denied, or overlooked: *an inescapable conclusion.* —**in′es·cap′a·bly** *adv.*

in·es·sen·tial (ĭn′ĭ-sĕn′shəl) *adj.* Not essential; unessential. —**in′es·sen′ti·al′i·ty** (-shē-ăl′ĭ-tē) *n.*

in·es·ti·ma·ble (ĭn-ĕs′tə-mə-bəl) *adj.* Too great or valuable to be estimated: *an inestimable service to all.* —**in·es′ti·ma·bly** *adv.*

in·ev·i·ta·ble (ĭn-ĕv′ĭ-tə-bəl) *adj.* Incapable of being avoided or prevented. —**in·ev′i·ta·bil′i·ty** *n.* —**in·ev′i·ta·bly** *adv.*

in·ex·act (ĭn′ĭg-zăkt′) *adj.* Not exact; not quite accurate or precise. —**in′ex·act′ly** *adv.* —**in′ex·act′ness** *n.*

in·ex·ac·ti·tude (ĭn′ĭg-zăk′tĭ-tōōd′, -tyōōd′) *n.* Lack of exactitude; inexactness.

in·ex·cus·a·ble (ĭn′ĭk-skyōō′zə-bəl) *adj.* Not excusable; unpardonable. —**in′ex·cus′a·ble·ness** *n.* —**in′ex·cus′a·bly** *adv.*

in·ex·haust·i·ble (ĭn′ĭg-zô′stə-bəl) *adj.* **1.** Incapable of being used up; limitless: *inexhaustible funds.* **2.** Tireless; indefatigable. —**in′ex·haust′i·bil′i·ty** or **in′ex·haust′i·ble·ness** *n.* —**in′ex·haust′i·bly** *adv.*

in·ex·o·ra·ble (ĭn-ĕk′sər-ə-bəl, -ĕg′zər-) *adj.* Not capable of being persuaded or moderated by pleas; unyielding: *"and more inexorable far/Than empty tigers or the roaring sea"* (Shakespeare). [Latin *inexorabilis* : *in-*, not + *exorāre*, to persuade by entreaty.] —**in·ex′o·ra·ble·ness** *n.* —**in·ex′o·ra·bly** *adv.*

in·ex·pen·sive (ĭn′ĭk-spĕn′sĭv) *adj.* Not expensive; low-priced. —See Syns at **cheap.** —**in′ex·pen′sive·ly** *adv.* —**in′ex·pen′sive·ness** *n.*

in·ex·pe·ri·ence (ĭn′ĭk-spîr′ē-əns) *n.* Lack of experience.

in·ex·pert (ĭn-ĕk′spûrt′, ĭn′ĭk-spûrt′) *adj.* Not expert; unskilled. —**in·ex′pert′ly** *adv.* —**in·ex′pert′ness** *n.*

in·ex·pli·ca·ble (ĭn-ĕk′splĭ-kə-bəl, ĭn′ĭk-splĭk′ə-bəl) *adj.* Not explicable; not possible to explain. —**in′ex·pli·ca·bil′i·ty** or **in·ex′pli·ca·ble·ness** *n.* —**in·ex′pli·ca·bly** *adv.*

in·ex·plic·it (ĭn′ĭk-splĭs′ĭt) *adj.* Not explicit; indefinite.

in·ex·press·i·ble (ĭn′ĭk-sprĕs′ə-bəl) *adj.* Not capable of being expressed; indescribable: *inexpressible joy.* —**in′ex·press′i·bil′i·ty** or **in′ex·press′i·ble·ness** *n.* —**in′ex·press′i·bly** *adv.*

in·ex·pres·sive (ĭn′ĭk-sprĕs′ĭv) *adj.* Lacking expression or expressiveness: *blank, inexpressive eyes.* —**in′ex·pres′sive·ly** *adv.* —**in′ex·pres′sive·ness** *n.*

in·ex·tin·guish·a·ble (ĭn′ĭk-stĭng′gwĭ-shə-bəl) *adj.* Not capable of being extinguished. —**in′ex·tin′guish·a·bly** *adv.*

in ex·tre·mis (ĭn′ ĭk-strē′mĭs). *Latin.* At the point of death.

in·ex·tri·ca·ble (ĭn-ĕk′strĭ-kə-bəl, ĭn′ĭk-strĭk′ə-) *adj.* **1.** Incapable of being disentangled or untied. **2.** Too intricate or complicated to solve. **3.** Incapable of being escaped from: *an inextricable quandary.* —**in·ex′tri·ca·bil′i·ty** or **in·ex′tri·ca·ble·ness** *n.* —**in·ex′tri·ca·bly** *adv.*

in·fal·li·ble (ĭn-făl′ə-bəl) *adj.* **1.** Incapable of making a mistake or being wrong. **2.** Incapable of failing: *an infallible antidote.* —**in·fal′li·bil′i·ty** or **in·fal′li·ble·ness** *n.* —**in·fal′li·bly** *adv.*

in·fa·mous (ĭn′fə-məs) *adj.* **1.** Having an exceedingly bad reputation; notorious: *an infamous racketeer.* **2.** Causing or deserving universal condemnation; loathsome; grossly shocking: *an infamous crime.* [Middle English, from Medieval Latin *infamōsus*, from Latin *infāmis* : *in-*, not + *fāma*, fame.] —**in′fa·mous·ly** *adv.* —**in′fa·mous·ness** *n.*

in·fa·my (ĭn′fə-mē) *n., pl.* **-mies. 1.** Evil fame or reputation. **2.** The condition of being infamous. **3.** An infamous act.

in·fan·cy (ĭn′fən-sē) *n., pl.* **-cies. 1.** The condition or period of being an infant. **2.** The earliest years or stage of something: *television in its infancy.*

in·fant (ĭn′fənt) *n.* **1.** A child in the earliest period of its life; a baby. **2.** *Law.* A person under the legal age of majority; a minor. —*modifier: an infant son.* [Middle English *enfaunt*, from Old French *enfant*, from Latin *infāns*, "(one) unable to speak" : *in-*, not + *fārī*, to speak.]

in·fan·ta (ĭn-făn′tə) *n.* **1.** A daughter of a Spanish or Portuguese king. **2.** The wife of an infante. [Spanish, fem. of *infante*, infante.]

in·fan·te (ĭn-făn′tē) *n.* Any son of a Spanish or Portuguese king other than the heir to the throne. [Spanish and Portuguese, infante, infant.]

in·fan·ti·cide (ĭn-făn′tĭ-sīd′) *n.* **1.** The killing of an infant. **2.** A person who kills an infant.

in·fan·tile (ĭn′fən-tīl′, -tĭl) *adj.* **1.** Of or relating to infants or infancy: *infantile diseases.* **2.** Lacking maturity; childish: *infantile behavior.*

infantile paralysis. Poliomyelitis.

in·fan·til·ism (ĭn′fən-tə-lĭz′əm) *n.* A state of arrested development in an adult, characterized by a retention of infantile mentality accompanied by stunted growth and sexual immaturity.

in·fan·try (ĭn′fən-trē) *n., pl.* **-tries.** The branch of an army made up of units trained to fight on foot. —*modifier: an infantry officer.* [French *infanterie*, from Italian *infanteria*, from *infante*, youth, foot soldier, from Latin *infāns*, infant.] —**in′fan·try·man** *n.*

in·farct (ĭn′färkt′, ĭn-färkt′) *n.* A necrotic area of tissue resulting from failure of local blood supply. [From Latin *infarctus*, past part. of *infarcīre*, to stuff in, cram : *in-*, in + *farcīre*, to stuff.] —**in·farc′tion** *n.*

in·fat·u·ate (ĭn-făch′ōō-āt′) *tr.v.* **-at·ed, -at·ing. 1.** To cause to behave foolishly. **2.** To fill with a strong, foolish passion or attraction. [From Latin *infatuāre* : *in-* (causative) + *fatuus*, fatuous.] —**in·fat′u·a′tion** *n.*

in·fect (ĭn-fĕkt′) *tr.v.* **1.** To contaminate with disease-causing microorganisms. **2.** To communicate a disease to (another person). **3.** To invade and produce infection in. **4.** To corrupt. **5.** To affect as if by contagion: *"His fear infected me, and . . . I followed as fast as I could"* (W.H. Hudson). [Middle English *infecten*, from Latin *inficere*, to work in, dye, taint : *in-*, in + *facere*, to do.]

in·fec·tion (ĭn-fĕk′shən) *n.* **1. a.** The entry of microorganisms into the body or a part of the body where they multiply and damage tissue or cause disease. **b.** The diseased condition resulting from this. **2.** An infectious disease. **3.** Persuasion or corruption by argument or example.

in·fec·tious (ĭn-fĕk′shəs) *adj.* **1.** Capable of causing infection: *infectious bacteria.* **2.** Caused or spread by infection: *an infectious disease.* **3.** Tending to spread easily or catch on: *infectious laughter.* —**in·fec′tious·ly** *adv.* —**in·fec′tious·ness** *n.*

infectious mononucleosis. Mononucleosis.

infantry

in·fe·lic·i·tous (ĭn'fĭ-lĭs'ə-təs) *adj.* **1.** Not happy; unfortunate; sad. **2.** Not well suited to the occasion; inappropriate. —**in'fe·lic'i·tous·ly** *adv.*

in·fe·lic·i·ty (ĭn'fə-lĭs'ĭ-tē) *n., pl.* **-ties. 1.** The quality or condition of being infelicitous. **2.** Something inappropriate or unpleasing: *the verbal infelicities in a bad poem.* [Middle English *infelicite,* from Latin *infēlīcitās,* from *infēlix,* unhappy : *in-,* not + *fēlix,* happy.]

in·fer (ĭn-fûr') *v.* **-ferred, -fer·ring.** —*tr.v.* To conclude from evidence; deduce. —*intr.v.* To draw inferences. —See Usage note at **imply.** [Old French *inferer,* from Latin *inferre,* to bring in, deduce : *in-, in-* + *ferre,* to bear.] —**in·fer'a·ble** *adj.*

in·fer·ence (ĭn'fər-əns) *n.* **1.** The act or process of inferring. **2.** Something inferred; a conclusion.

in·fer·en·tial (ĭn'fə-rĕn'shəl) *adj.* Derived or capable of being derived by inference. —**in'fer·en'tial·ly** *adv.*

in·fe·ri·or (ĭn-fîr'ē-ər) *adj.* **1.** Situated below; lower: *the inferior section of the spine.* **2.** Low or lower in order, degree, or rank: *an inferior post in the company.* **3.** Low or lower in quality, status, or estimation: *inferior merchandise.* **4.** *Bot.* Located below the perianth and other floral parts: *an inferior ovary.* —*n.* A person of lesser rank or status than others. —See Syns at **subordinate.** [Middle English, from Latin *inferior,* comparative of *inferus,* low.] —**in·fe'ri·or'i·ty** (-ôr'ĭ-tē, -ŏr'-) *n.*

Usage: **inferior.** Persons and things are said to be *inferior to* others—not *inferior than.*

inferiority complex. A persistent sense of inadequacy or tendency to belittle oneself.

in·fer·nal (ĭn-fûr'nəl) *adj.* **1.** Of or relating to the world of the dead in classical mythology. **2.** Of or resembling hell. **3.** Abominable; damnable: *an infernal nuisance.* [Middle English, from Old French, from Late Latin *infernālis,* from *infernus,* hell, from Latin *infernus,* lower.] —**in·fer'nal·ly** *adv.*

in·fer·no (ĭn-fûr'nō) *n., pl.* **-nos. 1.** Hell. **2.** Any place likened to hell, as in being very hot or chaotic. [Italian, hell, from Late Latin *infernus.*]

in·fer·tile (ĭn-fûr'tl) *adj.* Not fertile; unproductive; barren. —**in'fer·til'i·ty** (ĭn'fər-tĭl'ĭ-tē) *n.*

in·fest (ĭn-fĕst') *tr.v.* To inhabit or overrun in large numbers so as to be harmful or unpleasant: *Cockroaches infested the building.* [Middle English *infesten,* to attack, molest, trouble, from Old French *infester,* from Latin *infestāre,* from *infestus,* hostile.] —**in'fes·ta'tion** *n.* —**in·fest'er** *n.*

in·fi·del (ĭn'fĭ-dəl, -dĕl') *n.* **1.** A person who has no religious beliefs. **2.** A person who is an unbeliever with respect to some religion, esp. Christianity or Islam. —*adj.* **1.** Of or relating to unbelievers. **2.** Having no religious beliefs. **3.** Not believing in a particular religion, esp. Christianity or Islam. [Middle English *infydel,* from Old French *infidel,* from Latin *infidēlis,* unfaithful : *in-,* not + *fidēs,* faith.]

in·fi·del·i·ty (ĭn'fĭ-dĕl'ĭ-tē) *n., pl.* **-ties. 1.** Lack of religious faith, esp. in Christianity or Islam. **2.** Lack of loyalty; unfaithfulness. **3.** A disloyal act. **4.** Adultery.

in·field (ĭn'fēld') *n.* **1.** *Baseball.* **a.** The area of a baseball field enclosed by the foul lines and the arc of the outfield grass just beyond the bases. **b.** The defensive positions of first base, second base, third base, and shortstop. **2.** The area inside a racetrack or running track.

in·field·er (ĭn'fēl'dər) *n.* A baseball player who plays in the infield.

in·fight·ing (ĭn'fī'tĭng) *n.* **1.** Fighting at close range. **2.** Rivalry among competitors struggling for supremacy within a field or organization: *political infighting.* —**in'fight'er** *n.*

in·fil·trate (ĭn-fĭl'trāt, ĭn'fĭl-) *v.* **-trat·ed, -trat·ing.** —*tr.v.* **1.** To pass (a liquid or gas) into something through small openings. **2.** To fill or saturate with a liquid or gas passed through small openings. **3.** To enter gradually or secretly: *Foreign agents infiltrated the organization.* —*intr.v.* To gain entrance gradually or secretly. —*n.* A substance that accumulates gradually in bodily tissues. —**in·fil·tra·tion** (ĭn'fĭl-trā'shən) *n.*

in·fi·nite (ĭn'fə-nĭt) *adj.* **1.** Having no boundaries or limits; endless. **2.** Immeasurably or uncountably large: *an infinite number.* **3.** *Math.* **a.** Existing beyond or being greater than any arbitrarily large value. **b.** Unlimited in spatial extent. **c.** Of or pertaining to a set capable of being put into

one-to-one correspondence with a proper subset of itself. **4.** Seemingly without limit; immense: *infinite tact.* —*n.* **1.** Something infinite. **2. the Infinite.** God. —**in'fi·nite·ly** *adv.* —**in'fi·nite·ness** *n.*

in·fin·i·tes·i·mal (ĭn'fĭn-ĭ-tĕs'ə-məl) *adj.* **1.** Extremely or incalculably small: *infinitesimal particles of matter.* **2.** *Math.* Capable of having values arbitrarily close to zero. —*n.* **1.** An infinitesimal amount or quantity. **2.** *Math.* A function having values arbitrarily close to zero. [From New Latin *infinitesimus,* a fraction that represents the reciprocal of an infinite quantity, from Latin *infinitus,* infinite.] —**in'fin·i·tes'i·mal·ly** *adv.*

in·fin·i·tive (ĭn-fĭn'ĭ-tĭv) *n.* A verb form that is not inflected to indicate person, number, or tense and that in English is usu. preceded by *to* or by an auxiliary verb. For example, in the phrases *wanted to leave* and *will play tomorrow, leave* and *play* are infinitives. —*adj.* Of or using the infinitive. [Late Latin *infinitīvus,* unlimited (because it has no definite numbers or persons), from Latin *infinitus,* infinite.]

in·fin·i·ty (ĭn-fĭn'ĭ-tē) *n., pl.* **-ties. 1.** A space, distance, period of time, or quantity that is or appears to be without limit or end. **2.** The quality or condition of being infinite. **3.** *Math.* **a.** A quantity, not a number in the usual sense, whose value exceeds that of any chosen number, however large. **b.** A coordinate of a point that is considered to be an infinite distance away from a reference point.

in·firm (ĭn-fûrm') *adj.* **1.** Weak in body, as from old age; feeble. **2.** Lacking moral firmness; irresolute. —**in·firm'ly** *adv.*

in·fir·ma·ry (ĭn-fûr'mə-rē) *n., pl.* **-ries.** A place for the care of the sick or injured, esp. a small hospital or dispensary. [Medieval Latin *infirmāria,* from Latin *infirmus,* infirm.]

in·fir·mi·ty (ĭn-fûr'mĭ-tē) *n., pl.* **-ties. 1.** The condition of being infirm; bodily weakness; frailty. **2.** A disease or disorder that causes infirmity.

in·flame (ĭn-flām') *v.* **-flamed, -flam·ing.** —*tr.v.* **1.** To set on fire; kindle. **2.** To arouse to strong emotion: *His speech inflamed the crowd.* **3.** To produce inflammation in (bodily tissues). —*intr.v.* **1.** To catch fire. **2.** To become excited or aroused. **3.** To be affected by inflammation. —See Syns at **provoke.** [Middle English *inflamen,* from Old French *enflammer,* from Latin *inflammāre* : *in-* (intensive) + *flammāre,* to set on fire, from *flamma,* flame.]

in·flam·ma·ble (ĭn-flăm'ə-bəl) *adj.* **1.** Tending to catch fire easily and burn rapidly; flammable. **2.** Quickly or easily aroused to strong emotion. —See Usage note at **flammable.** —*n.* Something flammable. [French, from Medieval Latin *inflammābilis,* from Latin *inflammāre,* to inflame.] —**in·flam'ma·bly** *adv.*

in·flam·ma·tion (ĭn'flə-mā'shən) *n.* **1.** The act of inflaming or the condition of being inflamed. **2.** Redness, swelling, heat, and pain in a part of the body, resulting from injury, infection, or irritation.

in·flam·ma·to·ry (ĭn-flăm'ə-tôr'ē, -tōr'ē) *adj.* **1.** Tending to arouse strong emotion: *inflammatory language.* **2.** Characterized or caused by inflammation. —See Usage note at **flammable.**

in·flate (ĭn-flāt') *v.* **-flat·ed, -flat·ing.** —*tr.v.* **1.** To fill and swell with a gas: *inflate a tire.* **2.** To cause to increase unduly; puff up: *The initial success inflated his hopes.* **3.** *Econ.* To raise (prices, wages, or currency) to an abnormally high degree. —*intr.v.* To become inflated; swell; expand. [From Latin *inflāre,* to blow into : *in-,* in + *flāre,* to blow.]

in·fla·tion (ĭn-flā'shən) *n.* **1.** The act of inflating or the condition of being inflated. **2.** A sharp, continuing rise in the prices of goods and services, usu. attributed to an abnormal increase in available currency and credit. —**in·fla'tion·ar'y** (-shə-nĕr'ē) *adj.*

in·flect (ĭn-flĕkt') *tr.v.* **1.** To turn from a course or alignment; to bend. **2.** To alter (the voice) in tone or pitch; modulate. **3.** To change the form of (a word) to indicate number, tense, person, degree, etc. —*intr.v.* To be modified by inflection. [Middle English *inflecten,* from Latin *inflectere,* to bend, warp, change : *in-* (intensive) + *flectere,* to bend.]

in·flec·tion (ĭn-flĕk'shən) *n.* Also *Brit.* **in·flex·ion. 1.** The act of inflecting or the condition of being inflected. **2.** A

ă pat	ā pay	â care	ä father	ĕ pet	ē be	hw which	ĭ pit	ī tie	î pier	ŏ pot	ō toe	ô paw, for	oi noise
ŏŏ took	ŏŏ boot	ou out	th thin	th this	ŭ cut	û urge	zh vision	ə about, item, edible, gallop, circus					

change in the pitch of the voice, esp. in speech: *Questions usually end with a rising inflection.* **3. a.** The process by which the form of a word changes to indicate number, tense, person, degree, etc.; for example, the comparative *quicker* is formed from *quick* by inflection. **b.** A word derived by this process; an inflected form; for example, *drives, drove,* and *driven* are all inflections of the word *drive.* **—in·flec′tion·al** *adj.* **—in·flec′tion·al·ly** *adv.*

in·flex·i·ble (ĭn-flĕk′sə-bəl) *adj.* **1.** Not flexible; stiff; rigid. **2.** Incapable of being changed; unalterable: *inflexible standards.* **3.** Obstinate; unyielding. **—in·flex′i·bil′i·ty** or **in·flex′i·ble·ness** *n.* **—in·flex′i·bly** *adv.*
 Syns: inflexible, immutable, inalterable, invariable, ironbound, ironclad, stiff, unchangeable *adj. Core meaning:* Incapable of changing or of being changed *(an inflexible person; inflexible standards).* See also Syns at **rigid.**

in·flex·ion (ĭn-flĕk′shən) *n. Brit.* Var. of **inflection.**

in·flict (ĭn-flĭkt′) *tr.v.* **1.** To cause to be suffered or endured, as by attacking: *inflicting damage; inflict a severe bite.* **2.** To impose: *"malignant Nature, who reserves the right to inflict upon her children the most terrifying jests"* (Thornton Wilder). [Latin *inflictus,* past part. of *infligere : in-,* on + *fligere,* to strike.] **—in·flict′er** or **in·flic′tor** *n.* **—in·flic′tive** *adj.*

in·flic·tion (ĭn-flĭk′shən) *n.* **1.** The act or process of inflicting. **2.** Something inflicted, as blows or punishment.

in·flo·res·cence (ĭn′flə-rĕs′əns) *n.* **1.** *Bot.* A characteristic arrangement of flowers on a stalk or in a cluster. **2.** A flowering. [From Late Latin *inflōrēscere,* to begin to flower : Latin *in-* (intensive) + *flōrēscere,* to begin to flower.] **—in′flo·res′cent** *adj.*

in·flow (ĭn′flō′) *n.* **1.** The act or process of flowing in. **2.** Something that flows in; influx.

in·flu·ence (ĭn′flōō-əns) *n.* **1.** The power to bring about effects or changes, esp. when indirectly or quietly exerted: *a person with great influence in the government.* **2.** An effect or change brought about by such a power: *The book had a great influence on me.* **3.** Someone or something that brings about such effects or changes: *Travel has been a good influence on you.* *—tr.v.* **-enced, -enc·ing.** To have power or influence over; affect: *The weather influences his moods.* [Middle English, from Old French, from Medieval Latin *influentia,* from Latin *influere,* to flow in : *in-,* in + *fluere,* to flow.] **—in′flu·enc·er** *n.*

in·flu·en·tial (ĭn′flōō-ĕn′shəl) *adj.* Having or exercising influence. **—in′flu·en′tial·ly** *adv.*

in·flu·en·za (ĭn′flōō-ĕn′zə) *n.* An acute infectious viral disease characterized by inflammation of the respiratory tract, fever, muscular pain, and irritation in the intestinal tract. Also called **flu** and **grippe.** [Italian, influence, epidemic, from Medieval Latin *influentia,* influence.]

in·flux (ĭn′flŭks′) *n.* **1.** A flowing in; inflow. **2.** A steady stream of people or things coming in: *an influx of migrant workers.* [Late Latin *influxus,* from Latin *influere,* to flow in.]

in·fold (ĭn-fōld′) *tr.v.* **1.** To fold inward. **2.** Var. of **enfold.** **—in·fold′er** *n.* **—in·fold′ment** *n.*

in·form (ĭn-fôrm′) *tr.v.* **1.** To give form or character to. **2.** To inspire with a particular quality or character; imbue. **3.** To impart information to; notify; tell. *—intr.v.* To give often incriminating information: *He informed on the other members of the gang.* [Middle English *enfourmen,* from Old French *enfourmer,* from Latin *informāre,* to give form to, form an idea of : *in-* (intensive) + *formāre,* to form.]

in·for·mal (ĭn-fôr′məl) *adj.* **1.** Not performed or made according to regulations or forms; unofficial: *an informal agreement.* **2.** Marked by lack of ceremony or formality: *an informal dinner.* **3.** Of or for ordinary everyday use; casual: *informal clothes.* **4.** Not suitable for formal writing but frequently used in conversation and ordinary writing: *informal terms like "kid" for "child."* **—in′for·mal′i·ty** (ĭn′-fôr-măl′ĭ-tē) *n.* **—in·for′mal·ly** *adv.*
 Syns: informal, casual, easy, easygoing, relaxed *adj. Core meaning:* Not bound by rigid standards *(an informal lifestyle; an informal host).*

in·for·mant (ĭn-fôr′mənt) *n.* A person who communicates information.

in·for·ma·tion (ĭn′fər-mā′shən) *n.* **1.** The act of informing or the condition of being informed; communication of knowl-

edge. **2.** Knowledge derived from study, experience, or instruction; facts: *a mind full of information.* **3.** Knowledge of a specific event or situation; news; word. **4.** A nonaccidental signal used as an input to a computer or communications system. —See Syns at **knowledge.** **—modifier:** *an information bureau.* **—in′for·ma′tion·al** *adj.*

in·for·ma·tive (ĭn-fôr′mə-tĭv) *adj.* Also **in·for·ma·to·ry** (-tôr′ē, -tōr′ē). Providing or disclosing information; instructive.

in·formed (ĭn-fôrmd′) *adj.* Provided with information; knowledgeable: *well informed on world events.*

in·form·er (ĭn-fôr′mər) *n.* **1.** An informant. **2.** A person who informs against others, esp. to authorities.

infra-. A prefix meaning below, beneath, inferior to: **infrared.** [Latin *infrā,* below, beneath.]

in·frac·tion (ĭn-frăk′shən) *n.* A violation of a rule or regulation.

in·fra·red (ĭn′frə-rĕd′) *adj.* **1.** Of, pertaining to, or being electromagnetic radiation having wavelengths greater than those of visible light and shorter than those of microwaves. **2.** Generating, using, or sensitive to such radiation. [INFRA- + RED.]

in·fra·son·ic (ĭn′frə-sŏn′ĭk) *adj.* **1.** Generating or using waves or vibrations with frequencies below that of audible sound. **2.** Subsonic.

in·fre·quent (ĭn-frē′kwənt) *adj.* **1.** Not frequent; rare. **2.** Not steady; irregular; occasional: *an infrequent guest.* **—in·fre′quence** or **in·fre′quen·cy** *n.* **—in·fre′quent·ly** *adv.*

in·fringe (ĭn-frĭnj′) *v.* **-fringed, -fring·ing.** *—tr.v.* To break or ignore the terms of; violate: *infringe a contract.* *—intr.v.* To trespass; encroach: *infringing on other people's rights.* [Latin *infringere : in-* (intensive) + *frangere,* to break.] **—in·fringe′ment** *n.*

in·fu·ri·ate (ĭn-fyōōr′ē-āt′) *tr.v.* **-at·ed, -at·ing.** To make furious; enrage. [From Medieval Latin *infuriāre,* to enrage : Latin *in-* (intensive) + *furia,* fury.] **—in·fu′ri·at′ing·ly** *adv.*

in·fuse (ĭn-fyōōz′) *tr.v.* **-fused, -fus·ing.** **1.** To fill; imbue; inspire: *The teacher infused the children with a great love of learning.* **2.** To impart or instill: *The coach infused a feeling of pride in his men.* **3.** To steep or soak without boiling in order to extract soluble elements: *infuse tea leaves.* [Middle English *infusen,* from Old French *infuser,* from Latin *infundere,* to pour in : *in-,* in + *fundere,* to pour.] **—in·fus′er** *n.*

in·fu·sion (ĭn-fyōō′zhən) *n.* **1.** The act or process of infusing. **2.** An admixture. **3.** A liquid extract obtained by steeping a substance, as plant leaves, in a liquid. **4.** The introduction of a solution into a vein.

in·fu·so·ri·an (ĭn′fyōō-sôr′ē-ən, -sōr′-) *n.* Any of numerous microscopic organisms, esp. of the phylum Protozoa or the order Rotifera, occurring in stagnant water or in infusions containing organic material. *—adj.* Of or pertaining to infusorians. [New Latin *Infusoria,* "found in infusions," from Latin *infundere,* to infuse.] **—in′fu·so′ri·al** *adj.*

–ing¹. A suffix used to form: **1.** The present participle of verbs: **going.** **2.** Participial adjectives: **crippling.** **3.** Adjectives resembling participial adjectives but not derived from verbs: **swashbuckling.** [Middle English *-inge, -ing.*]

–ing². A suffix used to form nouns from verbs, nouns, and occasionally other parts of speech and meaning: **1.** The act, process, or art of performing an action: **dancing.** **2.** The thing or substance that accomplishes an action: **coating.** **3.** Something necessary for the performance of an action: **mooring.** **4.** The result of an action: **peeling.** **5.** Belonging to, connected with, or having the character of: **boarding.** **6.** An action upon or involving: **berrying.** [Middle English, from Old English *-ung, -ing.*]

in·gen·ious (ĭn-jēn′yəs) *adj.* **1.** Clever at devising things; creative. **2.** Showing originality and resourcefulness: *an ingenious idea.* [French *ingénieux,* from Latin *ingeniōsus,* from *ingenium,* inborn talent, skill.] **—in·gen′ious·ly** *adv.* **—in·gen′ious·ness** *n.*
 Usage: ingenious, ingenuous. Both adjectives describe persons and the attributes and creations of persons. *Ingenious* indicates originality: *an ingenious inventor. Ingenuous* indicates an absence of worldliness or sophistication or a tendency to be open and honest in dealing: *an ingenuous young girl; an ingenuous answer.*

in·gé·nue (ăn′zhə-nōō′, -nyōō′, ŏn′-; Fr. ăN′zhā-nü′) *n.* **1.** An artless, innocent girl or young woman. **2.** An actress play-

ă pat	ā pay	â care	ä father	ĕ pet	ē be	hw which	ĭ pit	ī tie	î pier	ŏ pot	ō toe	ô paw, for	oi noise
ōō took	ōō boot	ou out	th thin	th this	ŭ cut		û urge	zh vision	ə about, item, edible, gallop, circus		

ing an ingénue. [French, guileless, artless, from Latin *ingenuus,* ingenuous.]

in·ge·nu·i·ty (ĭn′jə-nōō′ĭ-tē, -nyōō′-) *n., pl.* **-ties. 1.** Inventive skill or imagination; cleverness. **2.** An ingenious or imaginative device. [Latin *ingenuitās,* frankness, innocence (but influenced in meaning by INGENIOUS).]

in·gen·u·ous (ĭn-jĕn′yōō-əs) *adj.* **1.** Artless; innocent. **2.** Open or honest; frank; candid. —See Usage note at **ingenious.** [Latin *ingenuus,* native, free-born, noble, honest, frank.] —**in·gen′u·ous·ly** *adv.* —**in·gen′u·ous·ness** *n.*

in·gest (ĭn-jĕst′) *tr.v.* To take in by or as if by swallowing: *ingest food.* [Latin *ingerere,* to carry in : *in-,* in + *gerere,* to bear, carry.] —**in·ges′tion** *n.* —**in·ges′tive** *adj.*

in·glo·ri·ous (ĭn-glôr′ē-əs, -glōr′-) *adj.* Dishonorable; shameful: *inglorious defeat.* —**in·glo′ri·ous·ly** *adv.* —**in·glo′ri·ous·ness** *n.*

in·got (ĭng′gət) *n.* **1.** A mass of metal shaped in the form of a bar or block. **2.** A casting mold for metal. [Middle English : *in,* in + Old English *geotan,* to pour, cast in metal.]

ingot

in·graft (ĭn-grăft′) *v.* Var. of **engraft.**

in·grain (ĭn-grān′) *tr.v.* To impress deeply on the mind or nature; to fix. —*n.* Yarn or fiber dyed before use in spinning, weaving, or knitting. [IN- (in) + obs. *grain,* dye.]

in·gra·ti·ate (ĭn-grā′shē-āt′) *tr.v.* **-at·ed, -at·ing.** To bring (oneself) purposely into the good graces of another; try to win favor for. [IN- (in) + Latin *grātia,* grace.] —**in·gra′ti·at′ing·ly** *adv.* —**in·gra′ti·a′tion** *n.* —**in·gra′ti·a·to·ry** (-ə-tôr′ē, -tōr′ē) *adj.*

in·grat·i·tude (ĭn-grăt′ĭ-tōōd′, -tyōōd′) *n.* Lack of gratitude; ungratefulness.

in·gre·di·ent (ĭn-grē′dē-ənt) *n.* **1.** Something added or required to form a mixture or compound: *ingredients for onion soup.* **2.** A component or constituent: *Ambition and energy are important ingredients of success.* [Middle English, from Latin *ingredī,* to enter into.]

in·gress (ĭn′grĕs′) *n.* Also **in·gres·sion** (ĭn-grĕsh′ən). **1.** A going in or entering. **2.** The right or permission to enter. **3.** A means or place of entering; entrance. [Middle English *ingresse,* from Latin *ingredī,* to enter into : *in-,* in, into + *gradī,* to step.]

in·grown (ĭn′grōn′) *adj.* **1.** Grown abnormally into the flesh: *an ingrown toenail.* **2.** Innate; deep-seated: *an ingrown habit.*

in·growth (ĭn′grōth′) *n.* **1.** The act of growing inward. **2.** Something that grows inward or within.

in·gui·nal (ĭng′gwə-nəl) *adj.* Of, relating to, or located in the groin. [Latin *inguinālis,* from *inguen,* groin.]

in·gulf (ĭn-gŭlf′) *v.* Var. of **engulf.**

in·hab·it (ĭn-hăb′ĭt) *tr.v.* To have as a dwelling place; live in. [Middle English *enhabiten,* from Old French *enhabiter,* from Latin *inhabitāre : in-,* in + *habitāre,* to dwell.] —**in·hab′it·a·bil′i·ty** *n.* —**in·hab′it·a·ble** *adj.* —**in·hab′i·ta′tion** *n.* —**in·hab′it·er** *n.*

in·hab·i·tant (ĭn-hăb′ĭ-tənt) *n.* Someone or something that lives permanently in a place; resident.

in·hab·it·ed (ĭn-hăb′ĭ-tĭd) *adj.* Having inhabitants; populated.

in·ha·lant (ĭn-hā′lənt) *adj.* Used in or for inhaling. —*n.* Something that is inhaled, as a medicine.

in·ha·la·tion (ĭn′hə-lā′shən) *n.* The act or an example of inhaling.

in·ha·la·tor (ĭn′hə-lā′tər) *n.* A device that produces a vapor to be inhaled, either to ease breathing or to introduce medication.

in·hale (ĭn-hāl′) *v.* **-haled, -hal·ing.** —*tr.v.* To draw in by breathing: *inhale smoke.* —*intr.v.* To breathe in: *inhaling deeply.* [Latin *inhālāre : in-,* in + *hālāre,* to breathe.]

in·hal·er (ĭn-hā′lər) *n.* **1.** Someone or something that inhales. **2.** An inhalator. **3.** A respirator.

in·har·mon·ic (ĭn′här-mŏn′ĭk) or **in·har·mon·i·cal** (-ĭ-kəl) *adj.* Not harmonic; discordant.

in·har·mo·ni·ous (ĭn′här-mō′nē-əs) *adj.* **1.** Harsh or unpleasant in sound: *the inharmonious noises of city traffic.* **2.** Not in accord or agreement: *inharmonious views.* —**in′har·mo′ni·ous·ly** *adv.* —**in′har·mo′ni·ous·ness** *n.*

in·here (ĭn-hîr′) *intr.v.* **-hered, -her·ing.** To be inherent or innate. [Latin *inhaerēre : in-,* in + *haerēre,* to stick, to remain fixed.] —**in·her′ence** (-hîr′əns, -hĕr′-) or **in·her′en·cy** *n.*

in·her·ent (ĭn-hîr′ənt, -hĕr′-) *adj.* Existing as an essential quality or characteristic; intrinsic: *the stability inherent in a broad-based structure; his inherent laziness.* —**in·her′ent·ly** *adv.*

in·her·it (ĭn-hĕr′ĭt) *tr.v.* **1.** To come into possession of; possess. **2.** To receive (property) from someone after he dies, usu. as provided for in a will. **3.** To receive from a predecessor or a former time: *As he took office the mayor inherited many serious problems.* **4.** To receive (a characteristic or trait) by or as if by genetic transmission from a parent or ancestor: *She inherited her father's dark eyes.* —*intr.v.* To succeed as an heir; take possession of an inheritance: *When the old man died, a remote relative inherited.* [Middle English *enheriten,* from Old French *enheriter,* from Late Latin *inhērēdītāre : in-* (intensive) + *hērēs,* heir.] —**in·her′i·tor** *n.*

in·her·it·a·ble (ĭn-hĕr′ĭ-tə-bəl) *adj.* **1.** Capable of inheriting; having the right to inherit. **2.** Capable of being inherited.

in·her·i·tance (ĭn-hĕr′ĭ-təns) *n.* **1.** The act of inheriting. **2.** Property, money, etc., that is or that will be received by an heir at a person's death; legacy. **3.** Anything received from a predecessor or a former time; heritage: *the cultural inheritance of Rome.* **4.** *Biol.* **a.** The process of genetic transmission of characters or characteristics. **b.** The configuration of characters or characteristics so inherited.

inheritance tax. A tax on inherited property.

in·hib·it (ĭn-hĭb′ĭt) *tr.v.* **1.** To restrain or hold back; prevent: *Caution inhibited him from talking more freely.* **2.** To prohibit; forbid. **3.** To prevent from achieving natural or spontaneous expression; repress. [Middle English *inhibiten,* from Latin *inhibēre : in-,* in + *habēre,* to have, hold.] —**in·hib′it·er** *n.* —**in·hib′i·tive** or **in·hib′i·to·ry** (-tôr′ē, -tōr′ē) *adj.*

in·hi·bi·tion (ĭn′hĭ-bĭsh′ən, ĭn′ĭ-) *n.* **1.** The act of inhibiting or the condition of being inhibited. **2.** The frequent or habitual suppression of a feeling, urge, biological drive, etc.: *His inhibitions made his life joyless.*

in·hib·i·tor (ĭn-hĭb′ĭ-tər) *n.* Something that inhibits, esp. a substance used to retard or halt an undesirable reaction, as rusting.

in·hos·pi·ta·ble (ĭn-hŏs′pĭ-tə-bəl, ĭn′hŏ-spĭt′ə-) *adj.* **1.** Displaying no hospitality; unfriendly. **2.** Not affording shelter or comfort: *an inhospitable climate.* —**in·hos′pi·ta·ble·ness** *n.* —**in·hos′pi·ta·bly** *adv.* —**in·hos′pi·tal′i·ty** (-tăl′ĭ-tē) *n.*

in-house (ĭn′hous′) *adj.* Being or coming from within an organization: *an in-house editor, not a free-lancer.*

in·hu·man (ĭn-hyōō′mən) *adj.* **1.** Not human. **2.** Not possessing desirable human qualities; lacking kindness or pity; brutal: *inhuman treatment.* **3.** Not of ordinary human form; monstrous. —See Syns at **fierce.** —**in·hu′man·ly** *adv.* —**in·hu′man·ness** *n.*

Usage: **inhuman, inhumane, nonhuman.** The first two adjectives refer to individuals or things that are cruel or lacking in compassion: *inhuman (or inhumane) treatment of prisoners; an inhuman (or inhumane) jailer.* Nonhuman categorizes things not human: *pathologists studying tissue samples from nonhuman subjects.* Inhuman also can be used to indicate a nonhuman species: *heard an inhuman scream in the jungle.*

in·hu·mane (ĭn'hyōō-mān') *adj.* Not humane; lacking in pity or compassion. —See Usage note at **inhuman. —in'hu·mane'ly** *adv.*

in·hu·man·i·ty (ĭn'hyōō-mǎn'ĭ-tē) *n., pl.* **-ties. 1.** The quality of being inhumane; unkindness. **2.** An inhuman or cruel act.

in·im·i·cal (ĭ-nĭm'ĭ-kəl) *adj.* **1.** Not conducive; harmful; adverse: *habits inimical to good health.* **2.** Unfriendly; hostile; antagonistic: *"a voice apparently cold and inimical"* (Arnold Bennett). [Late Latin *inimīcālis,* from Latin *inimīcus,* enemy : *in-,* not + *amīcus,* friend.]

in·im·i·ta·ble (ĭ-nĭm'ĭ-tə-bəl) *adj.* Impossible to imitate; matchless; unique: *a singer's inimitable style.* —**in·im'i·ta·bil'i·ty** *n.* —**in·im'i·ta·bly** *adv.*

in·iq·ui·tous (ĭ-nĭk'wĭ-təs) *adj.* Wicked; sinful. —**in·iq'ui·tous·ly** *adv.* —**in·iq'ui·tous·ness** *n.*

in·iq·ui·ty (ĭ-nĭk'wĭ-tē) *n., pl.* **-ties. 1.** Wickedness; sinfulness. **2.** A grossly immoral act; a sin. [Middle English *iniquite,* from Old French, from Latin *iniquitās,* from *iniquus,* unjust : *in-,* not + *aequus,* just, equal.]

in·i·tial (ĭ-nĭsh'əl) *adj.* **1.** Occurring at the very beginning; first: *The initial reaction was unenthusiastic.* **2.** Denoting the first letter or letters of a word. —See Syns at **early** and **first.** —*n.* **1.** The first letter of a name, used as part of a shortened signature or for identification. **2.** The first letter of a word. **3.** A large, often highly decorated letter set at the beginning of a chapter, verse, or paragraph. —*tr.v.* **-tialed** or **-tialled, -tial·ing** or **-tial·ling.** To mark or sign with one's initial or initials. [Latin *initiālis,* from *initium,* beginning.] —**in·i'tial·ly** *adv.*

in·i·ti·ate (ĭ-nĭsh'ē-āt') *tr.v.* **-at·ed, -at·ing. 1.** To begin or originate: *initiate a campaign.* **2.** To introduce (a person) to a new field, interest, skill, etc.: *A friend initiated me into the world of rock music.* **3.** To admit to membership, as with ceremonies or ritual. —See Syns at **introduce.** —*adj.* (ĭ-nĭsh'ē-ĭt). Initiated. —*n.* (ĭ-nĭsh'ē-ĭt). **1.** A person who has been initiated. **2.** A novice; beginner. [From Latin *initiāre,* from *initium,* beginning.] —**in·i'ti·a'tor** *n.*

in·i·ti·a·tion (ĭ-nĭsh'ē-ā'shən) *n.* **1.** The act or process of initiating or the condition or fact of being initiated. **2.** Admission into a club, society, or organization. **3.** A ceremony, ritual, etc., with which a new member is initiated. —*modifier: an initiation fee.*

in·i·ti·a·tive (ĭ-nĭsh'ē-ə-tĭv, ĭ-nĭsh'ə-) *n.* **1.** The ability to begin or to follow through energetically with a plan or task; enterprise and determination. **2.** The first step or action; opening move: *take the initiative.* **3. a.** The power or right to introduce a new legislative measure. **b.** The right and procedure by which citizens can propose a law by petition and have it voted on by the electorate. —*idiom.* **on (one's) own initiative.** Without prompting or direction from others.

in·ject (ĭn-jĕkt') *tr.v.* **1. a.** To force or drive (a liquid or gas) into something: *a mechanism that injects fuel into the cylinders of an engine.* **b.** To introduce (liquid medicine, serum, etc.) into the body, as by using a hypodermic needle. **2.** To introduce into conversation or consideration: *I tried to inject a note of humor.* [From Latin *injicere,* to throw or put in : *in-,* in + *jacere,* to throw.] —**in·jec'tor** *n.*

in·jec·tion (ĭn-jĕk'shən) *n.* **1.** The act of injecting. **2.** Something that is injected, esp. a dose of a liquid medicine.

in·ju·di·cious (ĭn'jōō-dĭsh'əs) *adj.* Lacking or marked by lack of judgment; imprudent: *an injudicious use of resources.* —**in'ju·di'cious·ly** *adv.* —**in'ju·di'cious·ness** *n.*

in·junc·tion (ĭn-jŭngk'shən) *n.* **1.** The act of enjoining. **2.** A command, directive, or order. **3.** A court order prohibiting or requiring a certain action: *An injunction was obtained to delay the strike.* [Late Latin *injunctiō,* from Latin *injungere,* to enjoin : *in-,* in + *jungere,* to join.] —**in·junc'tive** *adj.*

in·jure (ĭn'jər) *tr.v.* **-jured, -jur·ing. 1.** To cause harm or damage to; hurt. **2.** To commit an injustice or offense against; wound; wrong. [Back-formation from INJURY.] —**in'jur·er** *n.*

in·ju·ri·ous (ĭn-jŏŏr'ē-əs) *adj.* Causing injury or damage; harmful: *injurious chemicals.* —**in·ju'ri·ous·ly** *adv.* —**in·ju'ri·ous·ness** *n.*

in·ju·ry (ĭn'jə-rē) *n., pl.* **-ries. 1.** Damage; harm. **2.** A wound or other specific damage to the body: *a leg injury.* **3.** Injus-

tice. —See Syns at **harm.** [Middle English *injurie,* from Norman French, from Latin *injūria,* injustice, wrong, from *injūrius,* unjust : *in-,* not + *jūs,* right, law.]

in·jus·tice (ĭn-jŭs'tĭs) *n.* **1.** The fact, practice, or quality of being unjust; lack of justice. **2.** A specific unjust act; a wrong.

ink (ĭngk) *n.* **1.** A colored liquid used esp. for writing or printing. **2.** A dark liquid secreted by cuttlefish and other cephalopods. —*modifier: an ink spot.* —*tr.v.* To cover or stain with ink. [Middle English *enke,* from Old French *enke,* from Late Latin *encaustum,* from Greek *enkauston,* purple ink, from *enkaiein,* to burn in.]

ink·ling (ĭngk'lĭng) *n.* **1.** A hint or intimation. **2.** A vague idea or notion. [From Middle English *inkle,* to mutter.]

ink·stand (ĭngk'stănd') *n.* **1.** A tray or rack for bottles of ink, pens, and other writing implements. **2.** An inkwell.

inkstand

ink·well (ĭngk'wĕl') *n.* A small container for ink, usu. on the top of a desk.

in·laid (ĭn'lād', ĭn-lād') *adj.* **1.** Set smoothly into a surface in a decorative pattern: *a wall with inlaid mosaic tiles.* **2.** Decorated with a pattern set into a surface: *an inlaid cabinet.*

in·land (ĭn'lənd) *adj.* **1.** Of or located in the interior part of a country or region: *an inland waterway.* **2.** Operating or applying within the borders of a country or region; domestic: *inland tariffs.* —*adv.* In, toward, or into the interior of a country or region. —*n.* The interior of a country or region.

in-law (ĭn'lô') *n.* Any relative by marriage.

in·lay (ĭn'lā', ĭn-lā') *tr.v.* **-laid** (-lād'), **-lay·ing. 1.** To set (pieces of wood, ivory, metal, etc.) into a surface to form a design. **2.** To decorate by setting in such designs. —*n.* (ĭn'lā'). **1.** Contrasting material set into a surface in pieces to form a design. **2.** An inlaid decoration or design. **3.** A filling, as of gold, molded to fit a cavity in a tooth and cemented into place. —**in'lay·er** *n.*

in·let (ĭn'lĕt', -lĭt) *n.* **1.** A bay, cove, estuary, or other recess along a coast. **2.** A narrow passage of water between two land masses. **3.** An opening providing a means of entrance.

in·mate (ĭn'māt') *n.* **1.** A resident in a building or dwelling. **2.** A person confined to an institution such as a prison or asylum.

in me·di·as res (ĭn mĕd'ē-əs rās', mē'dē-əs rēz'). *Latin.* Into the middle of things: *The epic poet traditionally starts his narrative by plunging his audience in medias res.* [Taken from the passage *"in medias res . . . auditorem rapit,"* "(the poet) plunges his hearer into the middle of things" (Horace, *Ars Poetica*).]

in me·mo·ri·am (ĭn' mə-môr'ē-əm, -mōr'-). *Latin.* In memory of; as a memorial to.

in·most (ĭn'mōst') *adj.* Innermost.

inn (ĭn) *n.* **1.** A public lodging house serving food and drink to travelers; hotel. **2.** A tavern or restaurant. [Middle English, from Old English.]

in·nards (ĭn'ərdz) *pl.n. Informal.* **1.** The internal organs of the body, esp. of the abdomen. **2.** The inner parts of a machine, structure, etc. [Var. of INWARDS.]

in·nate (ĭ-nāt', ĭn'āt') *adj.* **1.** Possessed at birth; inborn: *an innate instinct.* **2.** Possessed as an essential characteristic;

inherent: *her innate goodness.* [Middle English *innat,* from Latin *innātus,* past part. of *innāscī,* to be born in : *in-,* in + *nāscī,* to be born.] **—in·nate·ly** *adv.* **—in·nate·ness** *n.*

in·ner (ĭn′ər) *adj.* **1.** Located farther inside: *the inner core of the earth.* **2.** Less apparent; deeper: *the inner meaning of a poem.* **3.** Of the spirit or mind: *"Beethoven's manuscript looks like a bloody record of a tremendous inner battle"* (Leonard Bernstein). **4.** More exclusive or important: *the inner circles of government.* [Middle English, from Old English *innera, innra.*]

inner city. The older, central part of a city, esp. when characterized by crowded, run-down low-income neighborhoods. **—modifier (inner-city):** *inner-city schools.*

inner ear. The innermost part of the ear of a vertebrate, consisting of the cochlea, vestibule, and semicircular canals.

in·ner·most (ĭn′ər-mōst′) *adj.* **1.** Situated or occurring farthest within. **2.** Most intimate: *innermost feelings.*

in·ning (ĭn′ĭng) *n.* **1.** One of the nine divisions of a regulation baseball game, in which each team has a turn at bat. **2.** Often **innings.** An opportunity to act or speak out; turn: *He will get his innings soon.* [From IN.]

in·no·cence (ĭn′ə-səns) *n.* **1.** The condition, quality, or virtue of being innocent, esp. freedom from guilt. **2.** A plant, bluets.

in·no·cent (ĭn′ə-sənt) *adj.* **1.** Uncorrupted by evil, malice, or wrongdoing; sinless; pure: *an innocent child.* **2.** Not guilty of a specific crime; legally blameless: *found innocent of all charges.* **3.** Not intended or intending to cause harm; harmless: *an innocent prank.* **4.** Not experienced or worldly; naive: *innocent tourists.* **5.** Betraying or suggesting no deception or guile; simple; artless: *an innocent smile.* *—n.* A person, esp. a child, who is free of evil or worldly knowledge. [Middle English, from Old French, from Latin *innocēns* : *in-,* not + *nocēre,* to harm, hurt.] **—in′no·cent·ly** *adv.*

in·noc·u·ous (ĭ-nŏk′yōō-əs) *adj.* **1.** Having no adverse effect; harmless: *innocuous bacteria.* **2.** Lacking significance or impact; banal; dull: *an innocuous speech.* [From Latin *innocuus* : *in-,* not + *nocuus,* harmful, from *nocēre,* to harm.] **—in·noc′u·ous·ly** *adv.* **—in·noc′u·ous·ness** *n.*

in·nom·i·nate bone (ĭ-nŏm′ə-nĭt). *Anat.* A large flat bone forming the lateral half of the pelvis. Also called **hipbone.** [From Late Latin *innōminātus,* having no name : Latin *in-,* not + *nōmināre,* to name.]

in·no·vate (ĭn′ə-vāt′) *v.* **-vat·ed, -vat·ing.** *—tr.v.* To begin or introduce (something new). *—intr.v.* To begin or introduce something new; make changes. [From Latin *innovāre,* to renew : *in-* (intensive) + *novus,* new.] **—in′no·va′tive** *adj.* **—in′no·va′tor** *n.*

in·no·va·tion (ĭn′ə-vā′shən) *n.* **1.** The act of innovating: *an age of innovation.* **2.** Something newly introduced; a change. **—in′no·va′tion·al** *adj.*

in·nu·en·do (ĭn′yōō-ĕn′dō) *n.,* pl. **-does.** A subtle, often spiteful reference; an insinuation. [Latin *innuendō,* by hinting, from *innuere,* to nod to, signal to.]

in·nu·mer·a·ble (ĭ-nōō′mər-ə-bəl, ĭ-nyōō′-) *adj.* Too many to be counted or numbered. **—in·nu′mer·a·ble·ness** *n.* **—in·nu′mer·a·bly** *adv.*

in·oc·u·late (ĭ-nŏk′yə-lāt′) *tr.v.* **-lat·ed, -lat·ing. 1.** To transmit a disease to by introducing bacteria or viruses into the body: *inoculate guinea pigs with viruses.* **2.** To introduce antigens, vaccines, the microorganisms of a disease, etc., into in order to immunize, cure, or experiment. [Middle English *inoculaten,* from Latin *inoculāre,* to engraft : *in-,* in + *oculus,* eye, bud.] **—in·oc′u·la′tion** *n.*

in·of·fen·sive (ĭn′ə-fĕn′sĭv) *adj.* Giving no offense; harmless. **—in′of·fen′sive·ly** *adv.*

in·op·er·a·tive (ĭn-ŏp′ər-ə-tĭv) *adj.* Not working or functioning. **—See Syns at inactive.**

in·op·por·tune (ĭn-ŏp′ər-tōōn′, -tyōōn′) *adj.* Not opportune; ill-timed. **—in·op′por·tune′ly** *adv.* **—in·op′por·tune′ness** *n.*

in·or·di·nate (ĭn-ôr′dn-ĭt) *adj.* Exceeding reasonable limits; immoderate; unrestrained: *a speech of inordinate length.* [Middle English *inordinat,* from Latin *inordinātus* : *in-,* not + *ordināre,* to set in order, from *ōrdō,* order.] **—in·or′di·na·cy** (-ə-sē) *or* **in·or′di·nate·ness** *n.* **—in·or′di·nate·ly** *adv.*

in·or·gan·ic (ĭn′ôr-găn′ĭk) *adj.* **1.** Not involving living organisms or the products of their life processes. **2.** Of mineral matter as opposed to the substance of things that are or were alive. **3.** Of or involving chemical compounds that are not classified as organic: *inorganic chemistry.* **4.** Lacking system or structure. **—in′or·gan′i·cal·ly** *adv.*

in·pa·tient (ĭn′pā′shənt) *n.* A patient in a hospital.

in·put (ĭn′pŏŏt) *n.* **1.** Anything put into a system to achieve a result or output, esp.: **a.** Energy, work, or power used to drive a machine. **b.** Current, electromotive force, or power supplied to an electric circuit, network, or device. **c.** Information put into a communications system for transmission or into a data-processing system for processing. **d.** The entirety of basic resources, including materials, equipment, and funds, required to complete a project. **2.** A position, terminal, or station at which any such input enters a system.

in·quest (ĭn′kwĕst′) *n.* **1. a.** A judicial inquiry, esp. one made into the cause of a death. **b.** A jury making such an inquiry. **2.** An investigation. [Middle English *enquest,* from Old French *enqueste.*]

in·quire (ĭn-kwīr′) *v.* **-quired, -quir·ing.** Also **en·quire.** *—intr.v.* **1. a.** To put a question. **b.** To request information: *inquire after another's health; inquire about the date of the sale.* **2.** To make a search or study; investigate: *inquire into a case.* *—tr.v.* To ask about: *inquire the way to the station.* [Middle English *enquiren,* from Old French *enquerrer,* from Latin *inquīrere* : *in-* (intensive) + *quaerere,* to seek, ask.] **—in·quir′er** *n.*

in·quir·y (ĭn-kwīr′ē, ĭn′kwə-rē) *n.,* pl. **-ies. 1.** The act or process of inquiring. **2.** A request for information. **3.** A close examination of some matter; investigation.

in·qui·si·tion (ĭn′kwĭ-zĭsh′ən) *n.* **1.** The act of inquiring into a matter; an investigation. **2.** An inquest. **3. Inquisition.** In the Middle Ages, a tribunal of the Roman Catholic Church established to seek out and punish those people considered guilty of heresy. **4.** Any investigation that violates the privacy or rights of individuals. [Middle English *inquisicioun,* from Old French *inquisition,* from Latin *inquīsītiō,* from *inquīrere,* to inquire.] **—in′qui·si′tion·al** *adj.*

in·quis·i·tive (ĭn-kwĭz′ĭ-tĭv) *adj.* **1.** Unduly inquiring; prying. **2.** Eager to learn. **—See Syns at curious. —in·quis′i·tive·ly** *adv.* **—in·quis′i·tive·ness** *n.*

in·quis·i·tor (ĭn-kwĭz′ĭ-tər) *n.* **1.** A person who inquires; a questioner. **2.** A person who conducts an official inquiry. **3. Inquisitor.** A member of the Inquisition.

in·quis·i·to·ri·al (ĭn-kwĭz′ĭ-tôr′ē-əl, -tōr′-) *adj.* **1.** Of, resembling, or having the function of an inquisitor or inquisition. **2.** Offensively prying. **—in·quis′i·to·ri·al·ly** *adv.*

in re (ĭn rā′, rē′). In the matter or case of; in regard to. [Latin.]

in·road (ĭn′rōd′) *n.* **1.** A hostile invasion; raid. **2.** An advance at another's expense; encroachment: *Japanese products have made heavy inroads into the American economy.* [IN + obs. *road,* raid.]

in·rush (ĭn′rŭsh′) *n.* A sudden rushing in; influx.

in·sane (ĭn-sān′) *adj.* **1.** Of, exhibiting, or afflicted with insanity. **2.** Characteristic of, used by, or for the insane: *an insane asylum.* **3.** Very foolish; rash; wild: *an insane scheme.* **—in·sane′ly** *adv.* **—in·sane′ness** *n.*

  Syns: insane, batty (*Slang*), **crazy, loco** (*Slang*), **loony** (*Informal*), **lunatic, mad, maniacal, nuts** (*Slang*), **screwy** (*Slang*), **touched, unbalanced** *adj.* *Core meaning:* Suffering from or showing irrationality and mental unsoundness (*diagnosed insane by two psychiatrists*). See Also Syns at **foolish.**

in·san·i·tar·y (ĭn-săn′ĭ-tĕr′ē) *adj.* Not sanitary.

in·san·i·ty (ĭn-săn′ĭ-tē) *n.,* pl. **-ties. 1.** Serious mental illness or disorder. **2. a.** *Civil Law.* Unsoundness of mind sufficient, in the judgment of a court, to render a person unfit to maintain a legal relationship or to warrant commitment to a mental hospital. **b.** *Criminal Law.* A degree of mental malfunctioning sufficient to prevent the accused from knowing right from wrong. **3. a.** Extreme foolishness; total folly. **b.** Something foolish.

  Syns: insanity, dementia, lunacy, madness, mania, unbalance *n.* *Core meaning:* Serious mental illness or disorder impairing a person's ability to function normally and safely (*hallucinations and wild suspicions—the first signs of his approaching insanity*).

ă pat ā pay â care ä father ĕ pet ē be hw which ĭ pit ī tie î pier ŏ pot ō toe ô paw, for oi noise
ōō took ōō boot ou out th thin *th* this ŭ cut û urge zh vision ə about, item, edible, gallop, circus

in·sa·ti·a·ble (ĭn-sā'shə-bəl, -shē-ə-) *adj.* Incapable of being satiated; never satisfied: *an insatiable appetite.* —**in·sa'·tia·bil'i·ty** or **in·sa'tia·ble·ness** *n.* —**in·sa'tia·bly** *adv.*

in·scribe (ĭn-skrīb') *tr.v.* **-scribed, -scrib·ing.** **1.** To write, print, carve, or engrave (words or letters) on or in a surface: *inscribed the winners' names on a plaque.* **2.** To mark or engrave (a surface) with words or letters: *inscribe a plaque.* **3.** To enter (a name) on a list or in a register. **4.** To sign or write a brief message in or on (a book or picture) when giving it as a gift. **5. a.** To enclose (a polygon, polyhedron, etc.) in another geometric figure so that every vertex of the enclosed figure touches the enclosing figure. **b.** To enclose (a circle, sphere, etc.) in another geometric figure so that every line or surface of the enclosing figure is tangent to the enclosed figure. [Latin *inscrībere : in-,* in + *scrībere,* to write.] —**in·scrib'er** *n.*

in·scrip·tion (ĭn-skrĭp'shən) *n.* **1.** The act or an instance of inscribing. **2.** Something inscribed: *a wall covered with inscriptions.* **3.** A short, signed message in a book or on a picture given as a gift. **4.** An enrollment or registration of names. [From Latin *inscrībere,* to inscribe.] —**in·scrip'·tion·al** *adj.*

in·scru·ta·ble (ĭn-skrōō'tə-bəl) *adj.* Difficult or impossible to understand or fathom; mysterious; enigmatic: *an inscrutable face.* [Latin *inscrūtābilis : in-,* not + *scrūtārī,* to search. —**in·scru'ta·bil'i·ty** or **in·scru'ta·ble·ness** *n.* —**in·scru'ta·bly** *adv.*

in·sect (ĭn'sĕkt') *n.* **1. a.** Any of numerous usu. small invertebrate animals of the class Insecta (or Hexapoda), having an adult stage characterized by three pairs of legs, a segmented body with three major divisions, and usu. two pairs of wings. **b.** Loosely, any of various similar invertebrate animals such as a spider, centipede, or tick. **2.** A person who is small or contemptible. [Latin *insectum (animale),* "segmented (animal)," from *insecāre,* to cut into.]

in·sec·ti·cide (ĭn-sĕk'tĭ-sīd') *n.* Something, esp. a poison, used to kill insects. —**in·sec'ti·cid'al** (-sīd'l) *adj.*

in·sec·ti·vore (ĭn-sĕk'tə-vôr', -vōr') *n.* **1.** Any of various mammals of the order Insectivora, characteristically feeding on insects, and including the shrews, moles, and hedgehogs. **2.** An organism that feeds on insects.

in·sec·tiv·o·rous (ĭn'sĕk-tĭv'ər-əs) *adj.* **1.** Feeding on insects. **2.** *Bot.* Capable of trapping and absorbing insects, as the pitcher plant or Venus's-flytrap. [INSECT + -VOROUS.]

in·se·cure (ĭn'sĭ-kyŏŏr') *adj.* **1.** Not secure or safe; inadequately guarded or protected: *an insecure fortress.* **2.** Unsure; unstable; shaky: *an insecure hold; a rickety, insecure table.* **3.** Apprehensive or lacking self-confidence: *feeling insecure.* —**in'se·cure'ly** *adv.* —**in'se·cu'ri·ty** or **in'se·cure'ness** *n.*

in·sem·i·nate (ĭn-sĕm'ə-nāt') *tr.v.* **-nat·ed, -nat·ing.** **1.** To sow seed in. **2.** To introduce semen into the uterus of. [From Latin *insēmināre : in-,* in + *sēmināre,* to plant, from *sēmen,* seed.] —**in·sem'i·na'tion** *n.* —**in·sem'i·na'tor** *n.*

in·sen·sate (ĭn-sĕn'sāt', -sĭt) *adj.* **1.** Lifeless; inanimate. **2.** Unconscious. **3.** Lacking sensibility; unfeeling. **4.** Lacking sense; foolish. **5.** Cruel; savage: *insensate slaughter.* —**in·sen'sate'ly** *adv.*

in·sen·si·ble (ĭn-sĕn'sə-bəl) *adj.* **1.** Imperceptible; inappreciable: *an insensible change.* **2.** Deprived of the power of feeling; unconscious: *"Sir Henry lay insensible where he had fallen."* (Arthur Conan Doyle). **3.** Unsusceptible; unaffected: *insensible to the cold.* **4.** Unheeding; unmindful: *I am not insensible of your concern.* —See Syns at **imperceptible.** —**in·sen'si·bil'i·ty** *n.* —**in·sen'si·bly** *adv.*

in·sen·si·tive (ĭn-sĕn'sĭ-tĭv) *adj.* **1.** Not sensitive; numb: *render a tooth insensitive.* **2.** Unfeeling; unresponsive: *insensitive to the sufferings of others.* —**in·sen'si·tiv'i·ty** or **in·sen'si·tive·ness** *n.* —**in·sen'si·tive·ly** *adv.*

in·sep·a·ra·ble (ĭn-sĕp'ər-ə-bəl) *adj.* Incapable of being separated; always together: *inseparable friends.* —**in·sep'·a·ra·bil'i·ty** or **in·sep'a·ra·ble·ness** *n.* —**in·sep'a·ra·bly** *adv.*

in·sert (ĭn-sûrt') *tr.v.* **1.** To put or set into, between, or among another or other things: *insert a key in a lock.* **2.** To introduce into the body or text of something; interpolate: *insert an illustration into a lecture.* **3.** To place into an

orbit, trajectory, or stream. —*n.* (ĭn'sûrt'). Something inserted or meant to be inserted, as into written material. [From Latin *inserere : in-,* in + *serere,* to sow, plant.] —**in·sert'er** *n.*

in·ser·tion (ĭn-sûr'shən) *n.* **1.** The act of inserting. **2.** Something inserted. **3.** A point or mode of attachment. **4.** A strip of lace, embroidery, or other trim to be inserted in a garment, tablecloth, etc. —**in·ser'tion·al** *adj.*

in·set (ĭn-sĕt', ĭn'sĕt') *tr.v.* **-set, -set·ting.** To insert; set in. —*n.* (ĭn'sĕt'). Something set in, as: **1.** A small map or illustration set within a larger one. **2.** A leaf or group of pages inserted in a publication. **3.** A piece of material set into a dress as trim.

in·side (ĭn-sīd', ĭn'sīd') *n.* **1.** The inner or interior part: *the inside of a house.* **2.** An inner side or surface. **3.** The middle part; the part away from the edge. **4. insides.** *Informal.* **a.** The inner organs; entrails. **b.** The inner parts or workings. —*adj.* (ĭn'sīd'). **1.** Inner; interior: *an inside pocket.* **2.** For the interior. **3.** Of or coming from those in authority: *the inside office.* **4.** *Baseball.* Passing too near the body of the batter: *a fast ball, high and inside.* —*adv.* (ĭn-sīd'). Into or in the interior; within: *going inside; staying inside.* —*prep.* (ĭn'sīd'). **1.** Within: *inside an hour.* **2.** Into: *went inside the house.* —*idioms.* **inside of.** Inside: *inside of the cave; inside of an hour.* **inside out.** With the inner surface turned out; reversed: *wearing his socks inside out.*

> **Usage: inside, inside of.** *Inside of* is standard idiom interchangeable with *inside* in American English. Both terms occur in contexts indicating time: *returned inside* (or *inside of) an hour,* and both occur in contexts indicating place: *inside* (or *inside of) the house.*

in·sid·er (ĭn-sī'dər) *n.* **1.** An accepted member of an exclusive group. **2.** Someone who has special knowledge or access to private information.

in·sid·i·ous (ĭn-sĭd'ē-əs) *adj.* **1.** Working or spreading harmfully in a subtle or stealthy manner: *an insidious disease without warning signs.* **2.** Intended to entrap; treacherous: *an insidious plot.* [Latin *insidiōsus,* deceitful, from *insidiae,* ambush, from *insidēre,* to sit in or on, lie in wait for.] —**in·sid'i·ous·ly** *adv.* —**in·sid'i·ous·ness** *n.*

in·sight (ĭn'sīt') *n.* **1.** The capacity to see into the true or hidden nature of things; penetration. **2.** A keen, illuminating perception.

in·sig·ni·a (ĭn-sĭg'nē-ə) *n., pl.* **insignia** or **-ni·as.** **1.** A badge of office, rank, membership, or nationality; emblem. **2.** A distinguishing sign: *the insignia of success.* [Latin, pl. of *insigne,* sign, mark, from *insignis,* distinguished, marked : *in-,* in + *signum,* sign.]

> **Usage: insignia.** Though plural in form, this noun is acceptably used with a singular verb: *This insignia is attractive.* The plural form, meaning more than one such badge or distinguishing sign, is either *insignia* or *insignias: Their insignia* (or *insignias) are brass.*

in·sig·nif·i·cance (ĭn'sĭg-nĭf'ĭ-kəns) *n.* Also **in·sig·nif·i·can·cy** (-kən-sē). The quality or condition of being insignificant.

in·sig·nif·i·cant (ĭn'sĭg-nĭf'ĭ-kənt) *adj.* **1. a.** Not significant. **b.** Trivial: *an insignificant detail.* **2.** Small in size, power, or value: *an insignificant country priest.* —See Syns at **little.** —**in'sig·nif'i·cant·ly** *adv.*

in·sin·cere (ĭn'sĭn-sîr') *adj.* Not sincere; hypocritical. —**in'sin·cere'ly** *adv.* —**in'sin·cer'i·ty** (-sĕr'ĭ-tē) *n.*

in·sin·u·ate (ĭn-sĭn'yōō-āt') *v.* **-at·ed, -at·ing.** —*tr.v.* **1.** To introduce gradually and slyly: *insinuating a political message into the movie; insinuated himself into the king's favor.* **2.** To convey indirectly; hint at: *What are you insinuating?* —*intr.v.* To make insinuations. —See Syns at **suggest.** [From Latin *insinuāre,* to wind one's way into : *in-,* in + *sinus,* curve.] —**in·sin'u·a'tor** *n.*

in·sin·u·a·tion (ĭn-sĭn'yōō-ā'shən) *n.* **1.** The act or practice of insinuating. **2.** An artfully indirect suggestion.

in·sip·id (ĭn-sĭp'ĭd) *adj.* **1.** Lacking flavor or zest; unpalatable: *an insipid cafeteria meal.* **2.** Lacking excitement or interest; unstimulating; vapid: *"I have no taste of those insipid dry discourses"* (Congreve). [Late Latin *insipidus : Latin in-,* not + *sapidus,* tasty.] —**in'si·pid'i·ty** or **in·sip'id·ness** *n.* —**in·sip'id·ly** *adv.*

---

in·sist (ĭn-sĭst′) *intr.v.* To be firm in one's demand; take a strong stand: *I tried to say no, but he insisted on giving me a second helping.* —*tr.v.* To assert or demand vehemently and persistently: *We insist that you accept these gifts.* [Latin *insistere*, to stand on, persist : *in-*, on + *sistere*, to cause to stand, stand firm.] —**in·sis′tence** or **in·sis′ten·cy** *n.*

in·sis·tent (ĭn-sĭs′tənt) *adj.* **1.** Firm in asserting a demand or opinion: *He was insistent that the water be boiled before use.* **2.** Repetitive or continual; persistent: *the wren's insistent melody.* —**in·sis′tent·ly** *adv.*

in si·tu (ĭn sī′tōō, sĭt′ōō). *Latin.* In (its original) place.

in·snare (ĭn-snâr′) *v.* Var. of **ensnare.**

in·so·far as (ĭn′sō-fär′). To the extent that: *"The scientist loves both the truth he discovers and himself insofar as he discovers it."* (Paul Tillich).

in·sole (ĭn′sōl′) *n.* **1.** The inner sole of a shoe or boot. **2.** An extra strip of material put inside a shoe for comfort or protection.

in·so·lence (ĭn′sə-ləns) *n.* **1.** The quality of being insolent. **2.** An insolent act or utterance.

in·so·lent (ĭn′sə-lənt) *adj.* Disrespectfully arrogant; impudent; rude. —See Syns at **arrogant** and **impudent.** [Middle English, from Latin *insolēns* : *in-*, not + *solēre*, to use.] —**in′so·lent·ly** *adv.*

in·sol·u·ble (ĭn-sŏl′yə-bəl) *adj.* **1.** Incapable of being dissolved, esp. in water: *an insoluble salt.* **2.** Incapable of being solved or explained: *an insoluble puzzle.* [Latin *insolūbilis* : *in-*, not + *solvere*, to solve.] —**in·sol′u·bil′i·ty** or **in·sol′u·ble·ness** *n.* —**in·sol′u·bly** *adv.*

in·solv·a·ble (ĭn-sŏl′və-bəl) *adj.* Incapable of being solved. —**in·solv′a·bly** *adv.*

in·sol·vent (ĭn-sŏl′vənt) *adj.* Unable to pay one's debts; bankrupt. —*n.* A person who is insolvent. —**in·sol′ven·cy** *n.*

in·som·ni·a (ĭn-sŏm′nē-ə) *n.* Chronic inability to sleep. [Latin, from *insomnis*, sleepless : *in-*, not + *somnus*, sleep.]

in·som·ni·ac (ĭn-sŏm′nē-ăk′) *n.* A person with insomnia.

in·so·much as (ĭn′sō-mŭch′). Inasmuch as; because; since.

in·sou·ci·ance (ĭn-sōō′sē-əns) *n.* A cheerful lack of concern; carefree indifference.

in·sou·ci·ant (ĭn-sōō′sē-ənt) *adj.* Cheerfully unconcerned; carefree. [French : *in-*, not + *soucier*, to trouble, upset, from Latin *sollicitāre*, to agitate, vex.] —**in·sou′ci·ant·ly** *adv.*

in·spect (ĭn-spĕkt′) *tr.v.* **1.** To examine carefully and critically: *inspecting meat before approving it.* **2.** To review or examine officially: *inspect troops.* [From Latin *inspicere* : *in-*, in + *specere*, to look.]

in·spec·tion (ĭn-spĕk′shən) *n.* **1.** The act or an example of inspecting. **2.** Official examination or review. —**in·spec′tion·al** *adj.*

in·spec·tor (ĭn-spĕk′tər) *n.* **1.** A person, esp. an official, who inspects. **2.** A police officer of the rank next below superintendent. —**in·spec′tor·ship′** *n.*

in·spi·ra·tion (ĭn′spə-rā′shən) *n.* **1. a.** Stimulation of the mind or emotions to a high level of feeling or activity. **b.** The condition of being so stimulated: *a composer's inspiration.* **2.** Someone or something that moves the intellect or emotions of another or that prompts action or invention. **3.** Something that is inspired; a sudden, creative act or idea. **4.** Divine guidance or influence exerted directly upon a person. **5.** The act of breathing in; inhalation.

in·spi·ra·tion·al (ĭn′spə-rā′shə-nəl) *adj.* **1.** Of inspiration. **2.** Providing, or intended to convey inspiration: *inspirational religious literature.* **3.** Resulting from inspiration. —**in′spi·ra′tion·al·ly** *adv.*

in·spire (ĭn-spīr′) *v.* **-spired, -spir·ing.** —*tr.v.* **1.** To fill with noble or reverent emotion; exalt: *hymns that inspire the congregation.* **2.** To affect, guide, or arouse by divine influence. **3.** To stimulate to creativity or action: *a worker inspired by fear of poverty.* **4.** To elicit or create (an emotion, attitude, etc.) in another or others: *tried to inspire confidence in the voters.* **5.** To be the cause or source of: *an invention that inspired many imitations.* **6.** To inhale (air): *inspiring the fresh country air.* —*intr.v.* To stimu-

late energies, ideals, or reverence. **2.** To inhale. —See Syns at **provoke.** [Middle English *inspiren*, from Old French *inspirer*, from Latin *inspīrāre*, to breathe into : *in-*, into + *spīrāre*, to breathe.] —**in·spir′er** *n.* —**in·spir′ing·ly** *adv.*

in·spir·it (ĭn-spĭr′ĭt) *tr.v.* To instill courage or life into; animate; enliven.

in·sta·bil·i·ty (ĭn′stə-bĭl′ĭ-tē) *n., pl.* **-ties.** Lack of stability.

in·stall (ĭn-stôl′) *tr.v.* **1.** To set in position and connect or adjust for use: *install a new refrigerator.* **2.** To put in an office, rank, or position: *a brief ceremony to install the new prime minister.* **3.** To settle; to place: *She installed herself in her favorite chair.* [Old French *installer*, from Medieval Latin *installāre* : *in-* (causative) + *stallum*, place, stall.] —**in·stall′er** *n.*

in·stal·la·tion (ĭn′stə-lā′shən) *n.* **1.** The act of installing or the condition of being installed. **2.** A system of machinery or other apparatus set up for use. **3.** A military base or camp.

in·stall·ment[1] (ĭn-stôl′mənt) *n.* **1.** One of several successive payments in settlement of a debt. **2.** A portion of anything issued at intervals. **3.** A chapter or part of a literary work presented serially. —*modifier: buying on the installment plan.* [Var. of earlier *estallment*, from Norman French *estalement*, from *estaler*, to fix (as payments), from *estal*, place, fixed position.]

in·stall·ment[2] (ĭn-stôl′mənt) *n.* Also **in·stal·ment.** Installation.

in·stance (ĭn′stəns) *n.* **1.** A case or example: *"It may be thought an instance of vanity that I pretend at all to write my life"* (Hume). **2.** An occasion: *In this instance I choose to remain silent.* **3.** Prompting; request: *He called at the instance of his wife.* —*tr.v.* **-stanced, -stanc·ing.** **1.** To offer as an example; cite. **2.** To demonstrate or show by being an example; exemplify. [Middle English *instaunce*, from Old French *instance*, from Latin *instantia*, presence, perseverance, urgency, from *instāns*, instant.]

in·stant (ĭn′stənt) *n.* **1.** A very brief time; a moment. **2.** A particular point in time: *the instant he arrives.* —See Syns at **moment.** —*adj.* **1.** Immediate: *instant attention.* **2.** Imperative; urgent: *an instant need.* **3.** *Archaic.* Of the current month: *your letter of the 12th instant.* **4.** Designed for quick preparation: *instant coffee.* [Middle English, urgent, immediate, from Old French, from Latin *instāns*, pres. part. of *instāre*, to stand upon, be present, persist : *in-*, upon + *stāre*, to stand.]

in·stan·ta·ne·ous (ĭn′stən-tā′nē-əs) *adj.* **1.** Occurring or completed without a detectable lapse of time: *an instantaneous reaction.* **2.** Occurring at a specific instant: *instantaneous velocity.* —**in′stan·ta′ne·ous·ly** *adv.* —**in′stan·ta′ne·ous·ness** *n.*

in·stant·ly (ĭn′stənt-lē) *adv.* **1.** At once. **2.** *Archaic.* Urgently. —*conj.* As soon as.

in·stead (ĭn-stĕd′) *adv.* In the place of that previously mentioned; as a substitute: *Planning to drive, he walked instead.* —*idiom.* **instead of.** In place of; rather than: *I'll have rice instead of potatoes.* [Middle English *in sted (of)* : *in*, in + *sted*, place.]

in·step (ĭn′stĕp′) *n.* **1.** The arched middle part of the human foot. **2.** The part of a shoe or stocking covering the instep.

in·sti·gate (ĭn′stĭ-gāt′) *tr.v.* **-gat·ed, -gat·ing.** **1.** To urge on; goad: *taxes that instigated the colonies to revolt.* **2.** To foment; stir up: *instigate a rebellion.* —See Syns at **provoke.** [From Latin *instīgāre* : *in-* (intensive) + *stīgāre*, to spur on.] —**in′sti·ga′tion** *n.* —**in′sti·ga′tive** *adj.* —**in′sti·ga′tor** *n.*

in·still (ĭn-stĭl′) *tr.v.* **1.** To introduce by gradual, persistent efforts; implant: *"morality . . . may be instilled into their minds"* (Jefferson). **2.** To pour in drop by drop. [Latin *instillāre* : *in-*, in + *stillāre*, to drip.] —**in·stil·la′tion** (ĭn′stə-lā′shən) *n.* —**in·still′er** *n.* —**in·still′ment** or **in·stil′ment** *n.*

in·stinct (ĭn′stĭngkt) *n.* **1.** An inner influence, feeling, or drive that is not learned and that results in complex animal behavior such as building of nests, incubation of eggs, nursing of young, etc. **2.** A powerful motivation or impulse. **3.** A natural talent or ability. —*adj.* (ĭn-stĭngkt′). Filled; imbued: *a spirit instinct with devotion.* [Middle

ă pat	ā pay	â care	ä father	ĕ pet	ē be	hw which	ĭ pit	ī tie	î pier	ŏ pot	ō toe	ô paw, for	oi noise
ŏŏ took	ōō boot	ou out	th thin	th this	ŭ cut	û urge	zh vision	ə about, item, edible, gallop, circus

English, from Latin *instinctus*, instigation, from *instinguere*, to urge on : *in-*, on + *stinguere*, to prick, incite.]

in·stinc·tive (ĭn-stĭngk′tĭv) *adj.* **1.** Of or arising from instinct. **2.** Deep-seated; inveterate: *an instinctive dislike.* —See Syns at **involuntary.** —**in·stinc′tive·ly** *adv.*

in·sti·tute (ĭn′stĭ-tōōt′, -tyōōt′) *tr.v.* **-tut·ed, -tut·ing. 1.** To establish, organize, and set in operation: *institute a new government.* **2.** To initiate; begin. —See Syns at **introduce.** —*n.* **1.** Something instituted, esp. an authoritative rule or precedent. **2.** An organization founded to promote some cause. **3. a.** An educational institution. **b.** The building or buildings of such an institution. [Middle English *instituten*, from Latin *instituere*, to establish, ordain : *in-*, in + *statuere*, to set up, from *stāre*, to stand.]

in·sti·tu·tion (ĭn′stĭ-tōō′shən, -tyōō′-) *n.* **1.** The act or process of instituting: *the institution of a new immigration quota.* **2.** An established custom, practice, or pattern of behavior important in the cultural life of a society: *the institution of marriage.* **3. a.** An organization or foundation, esp. one dedicated to public service. **b.** The building or buildings housing such an organization. **4.** *Informal.* An ever-present feature; fixture. **5.** A place of confinement, as a mental asylum. —**in′sti·tu′tion·al** *adj.*

in·sti·tu·tion·al·ism (ĭn′stĭ-tōō′shə-nə-lĭz′əm, -tyōō′-) *n.* **1.** Belief in established forms, esp. in organized religion. **2.** The system of civic or philanthropic institutions. —**in′sti·tu′tion·al·ist** *n.*

in·sti·tu·tion·al·ize (ĭn′stĭ-tōō′shə-nə-līz′, -tyōō′-) *tr.v.* **-ized, -iz·ing. 1.** To make into or treat as an institution. **2.** To confine (a person) in an institution. —**in′sti·tu′tion·al·i·za′tion** *n.*

in·struct (ĭn-strŭkt′) *tr.v.* **1.** To furnish with knowledge; teach; educate. **2.** To give orders to; to direct: *instructed us to begin work.* —See Syns at **command.** [Middle English *instructen*, from Latin *instruere* : *in-*, in + *struere*, to build.]

in·struc·tion (ĭn-strŭk′shən) *n.* **1.** The act, practice, or profession of instructing; education. **2. a.** Something that is taught; a lesson or series of lessons. **b.** Something learned. **3. instructions.** Directions; orders. —See Syns at **knowledge.** —**in·struc′tion·al** *adj.*

in·struc·tive (ĭn-strŭk′tĭv) *adj.* Conveying or helping to convey knowledge or information: *an instructive example.* —**in·struc′tive·ly** *adv.* —**in·struc′tive·ness** *n.*

in·struc·tor (ĭn-strŭk′tər) *n.* **1.** A person who instructs; a teacher. **2. a.** An academic rank below an assistant professor. **b.** A person who holds such a rank. —**in·struc′tor·ship′** *n.*

in·stru·ment (ĭn′strə-mənt) *n.* **1.** A means by which something is done; agency. **2.** A person used and controlled by another. **3.** A mechanical implement: *a dentist's picks, drills, and other instruments.* **4.** A device for recording or measuring, esp. such a device functioning as part of a control system. **5.** A device for making music. **6.** A legal document. —*modifier: a pilot's instrument panel.* [Middle English, from Latin *instrūmentum*, implement, equipment, tool, from *instruere*, to prepare, equip.]

in·stru·men·tal (ĭn′strə-mĕn′tl) *adj.* **1.** Serving as an instrument; helpful: *A former teacher was instrumental in getting him his first job.* **2.** Performed on or written for a

musical instrument or instruments. —**in′stru·men′tal·ly** *adv.*

in·stru·men·tal·ist (ĭn′strə-mĕn′tl-ĭst) *n.* Someone who plays a musical instrument.

in·stru·men·tal·i·ty (ĭn′strə-mĕn-tăl′ĭ-tē) *n., pl.* **-ties. 1.** The quality or circumstance of being instrumental. **2.** Agency; means.

in·stru·men·ta·tion (ĭn′strə-mĕn-tā′shən) *n.* **1.** The application or use of instruments in the performance of some work. **2.** The arrangement of music for instruments; orchestration. **3.** The study, development, and manufacture of instruments, as for scientific use. **4.** Instrumentality.

in·sub·or·di·nate (ĭn′sə-bôr′dn-ĭt) *adj.* Not submissive to authority; disobedient. —**in′sub·or′di·na′tion** *n.* —**in′sub·or′di·nate·ly** *adv.*

in·sub·stan·tial (ĭn′səb-stăn′shəl) *adj.* **1.** Lacking substance or reality; imaginary. **2.** Not firm; flimsy: *an insubstantial cardboard wall.* —**in′sub·stan′ti·al′i·ty** (-shē-ăl′ĭ-tē) *n.*

in·suf·fer·a·ble (ĭn-sŭf′ər-ə-bəl) *adj.* Incapable of being endured; intolerable. —**in·suf′fer·a·ble·ness** *n.* —**in·suf′fer·a·bly** *adv.*

in·suf·fi·cien·cy (ĭn′sə-fĭsh′ən-sē) *n., pl.* **-cies. 1.** The quality or condition of being insufficient. **2.** Something insufficient. —See Syns at **deficiency.**

in·suf·fi·cient (ĭn′sə-fĭsh′ənt) *adj.* Not sufficient; inadequate. —**in′suf·fi′cient·ly** *adv.*

in·su·lar (ĭn′sə-lər, ĭns′yə-) *adj.* **1.** Of or constituting an island or islands: *an insular nation.* **2. a.** Characteristic or suggestive of the isolated life of an island: *insular customs.* **b.** Narrow-minded; prejudiced. [Late Latin *īnsulāris*, from Latin *īnsula*, island, isle.] —**in′su·lar·ism** or **in′su·lar′i·ty** (-lăr′ĭ-tē) *n.* —**in′su·lar·ly** *adv.*

in·su·late (ĭn′sə-lāt′, ĭns′yə-) *tr.v.* **-lat·ed, -lat·ing. 1.** To detach; isolate. **2.** To prevent the passage of heat, electricity, or sound into or out of, esp. by surrounding or lining with material that blocks such passage. [From Latin *īnsula*, island, isle.]

in·su·la·tion (ĭn′sə-lā′shən, ĭns′yə-) *n.* **1.** The act of insulating or the condition of being insulated. **2.** Material used in insulating.

in·su·la·tor (ĭn′sə-lā′tər, ĭns′yə-) *n.* **1.** A material that insulates. **2.** A device that insulates.

in·su·lin (ĭn′sə-lĭn, ĭns′yə-) *n.* A polypeptide hormone secreted by the islands of Langerhans and functioning to regulate carbohydrate metabolism by controlling blood glucose levels. [From Latin *īnsula*, island.]

in·sult (ĭn-sŭlt′) *tr.v.* To speak to or treat with disrespect or contempt; to affront. —*n.* (ĭn′sŭlt′). **1.** An action or remark that shows disrespect or contempt. **2.** *Med.* An injury, irritation, or trauma. [Old French *insulter*, to triumph over, behave arrogantly, from Latin *insultāre*, to leap on, jump over : *in-*, on, + *saltāre*, to jump.]
    Syns: insult, affront, offend, outrage *v.* *Core meaning:* To cause resentment or hurt by rude, unfeeling behavior (*a guest who insulted the hostess*).

in·su·per·a·ble (ĭn-sōō′pər-ə-bəl) *adj.* Incapable of being overcome; insurmountable: *an insuperable barrier.* —**in·su′per·a·bil′i·ty** or **in·su′per·a·ble·ness** *n.* —**in·su′per·a·bly** *adv.*

in·sup·port·a·ble (ĭn′sə-pôr′tə-bəl, -pōr′-) *adj.* **1.** Unbearable; intolerable: *insupportable pain.* **2.** Lacking grounds or defense; unjustifiable: *an insupportable claim.*

in·sur·ance (ĭn-shoor′əns) *n.* **1.** The act of insuring or the condition of being insured. **2. a.** The business of guaranteeing to cover specified losses in the future, as in case of accident, illness, theft, or death, in return for the continuing payment of regular sums of money. **b.** A contract making such guarantees to the party insured. **c.** The total amount to be paid to the party insured: *bought $10,000 of life insurance.* **d.** A periodic amount paid for such coverage; a premium: *We pay insurance on the first of the month.* **3.** A protective measure or device. —*modifier: an insurance company; insurance premiums.*

in·sure (ĭn-shoor′) *tr.v.* **-sured, -sur·ing. 1.** To protect against risk or loss by means of insurance. **2.** To make sure or certain; to guarantee; ensure. —See Usage note at **ensure.** [Middle English *insuren*, to guarantee, from Norman French *enseurer*, perh. var. of Old French *ass(e)urer*,

instrument
Of an airplane

to assure.] **—in·sur·a·bil·i·ty** *n.* **—in·sur·a·ble** *adj.* **—in·sur′er** *n.*

in·sured (ĭn-sho͝ord′) *n.* A person covered by insurance.

in·sur·gence (ĭn-sûr′jəns) *n.* An uprising; revolt. —See Syns at **rebellion.**

in·sur·gen·cy (ĭn-sûr′jən-sē) *n.* **1.** The quality or circumstance of being insurgent. **2.** An insurgence.

in·sur·gent (ĭn-sûr′jənt) *adj.* Rising in revolt; rebellious: *The insurgent forces overthrew the government.* —*n.* A person who revolts against authority, esp. a member of a political party who rebels against its leadership. [Latin *insurgēns,* from *insurgere,* to rise up : *in-* (intensive) + *surgere,* to rise.]

in·sur·mount·a·ble (ĭn′sər-moun′tə-bəl) *adj.* Incapable of being surmounted; insuperable: *struggling against insurmountable difficulties.* —**in′sur·mount′a·bly** *adv.*

in·sur·rec·tion (ĭn′sə-rĕk′shən) *n.* The act or an example of open revolt against civil authority or a constituted government. —See Syns at **rebellion.** [Middle English *insurrecioun,* from Old French *insurrection,* from Latin *insurrectiō,* from *insurgere,* to rise up.] —**in′sur·rec′tion·al** *adj.* —**in′sur·rec′tion·ar·y** (-shə-nĕr′ē) *adj. & n.* —**in′sur·rec′tion·ist** *n.*

in·tact (ĭn-tăkt′) *adj.* Not broken or impaired in any way. [Middle English *intacte,* untouched, from Latin *intactus* : *in-,* not + *tangere,* to touch.] —**in·tact′ness** *n.*

in·ta·glio (ĭn-tăl′yō, -täl′-) *n., pl.* **-glios. 1. a.** A figure or design carved deep into the surface of hard metal or stone. **b.** The art or process of carving a design in this manner. **2.** A gemstone carved in intaglio. **3.** Printing done with a plate bearing an image in intaglio. **4.** A die incised to produce a design in relief. —*modifier: an intaglio design.* [Italian, from *intagliare,* to engrave : *in-,* in + *tagliare,* to cut.]

in·take (ĭn′tāk′) *n.* **1.** An opening through which a liquid or gas enters a container or pipe. **2. a.** The act or process of taking in: *an efficient air intake.* **b.** Something or the amount of something taken in: *an adequate intake of food.* —*modifier: an intake valve.*

in·tan·gi·ble (ĭn-tăn′jə-bəl) *adj.* **1.** Not capable of being touched; lacking physical substance. **2.** Not capable of being perceived; vague; elusive: *an intangible change.* —See Syns at **imperceptible.** —*n.* Something intangible: *Beauty is an intangible in the art of design.* —**in·tan′gi·bil′i·ty** or **in·tan′gi·ble·ness** *n.* —**in·tan′gi·bly** *adv.*

in·te·ger (ĭn′tĭ-jər) *n.* **1.** Any member of the set of positive whole numbers (1, 2, 3, . . .), negative whole numbers (−1, −2, −3, . . .), and zero (0). **2.** Any intact unit or thing. [Latin, whole, complete, perfect.]

in·te·gral (ĭn′tĭ-grəl, ĭn-tĕg′rəl) *adj.* **1.** Forming a necessary part of a whole; constituent: *Finland was once an integral part of Sweden.* **2.** Whole; entire; intact. **3.** *Math.* **a.** Expressed or expressible as or in terms of integers. **b.** Expressed as or involving integrals. —*n.* A complete unit; a whole. [Middle English, from Late Latin *integrālis,* making up a whole, from Latin *integer,* whole.] —**in′te·gral′i·ty** (-grăl′ĭ-tē) *n.* —**in′te·gral·ly** *adv.*

integral calculus. The mathematical study of integration, the properties of integrals, and their applications.

in·te·grate (ĭn′tĭ-grāt′) *v.* **-grat·ed, -grat·ing.** —*tr.v.* **1.** To make into a whole by bringing all parts together; unify: *Music, dance, painting, and sculpture courses were integrated to form an arts program.* **2.** To join with something else; to unite. **3.** To open to people of all races or ethnic groups without restriction; desegregate: *integrate a school system.* **4.** *Math.* **a.** To calculate the integral of. **b.** To perform integration upon. —*intr.v.* To become integrated or undergo integration. [From Latin *integrāre,* to make complete, from *integer,* whole.] —**in′te·gra′tive** *adj.*

in·te·gra·tion (ĭn′tĭ-grā′shən) *n.* **1. a.** The act or process of integrating. **b.** The condition of being integrated. **2.** Desegregation.

in·te·gra·tion·ist (ĭn′tĭ-grā′shə-nĭst) *n.* A person who believes in or supports racial integration.

in·teg·ri·ty (ĭn-tĕg′rĭ-tē) *n.* **1.** Strict personal honesty and independence: *a man of integrity.* **2.** Completeness; unity: *a movie shown without interruptions to maintain its integrity.* **3.** The state of being unimpaired; soundness. —See Syns at **honesty.** [Middle English *integrite,* from Old

French, from Latin *integritās,* completeness, purity, from *integer,* whole.]

in·teg·u·ment (ĭn-tĕg′yə-mənt) *n.* An outer covering or coat, such as the skin of an animal, the coat of a seed, or the membrane enclosing an organ. [Latin *integumentum,* from *integere,* to cover : *in-,* on + *tegere,* to cover.] —**in·teg′u·men′ta·ry** (-mĕn′tə-rē) *adj.*

in·tel·lect (ĭn′tl-ĕkt′) *n.* **1. a.** The ability of the mind to think, reason, and learn; capacity for knowledge and understanding. **b.** The ability to think abstractly or deeply. **2.** A person of great intellectual ability. [Middle English, from Old French, from Latin *intellectus,* perception, comprehension, from *intellegere,* to perceive, choose between.]

in·tel·lec·tu·al (ĭn′tl-ĕk′choō-əl) *adj.* **1. a.** Of, relating to, or requiring use of the intellect. **b.** Rational rather than emotional. **2. a.** Having superior intelligence. **b.** Given to learning, thinking, and judging ideas. —*n.* A person of trained intelligence, esp. a person devoted to the arts, letters, etc. —**in′tel·lec′tu·al·ly** *adv.*

in·tel·lec·tu·al·ism (ĭn′tl-ĕk′choō-ə-lĭz′əm) *n.* **1.** The use of the intellect. **2.** Devotion to exercise or development of the intellect. **3.** The doctrine that knowledge is the product of pure reason; rationalism. —**in′tel·lec′tu·al·ist** *n.* —**in′tel·lec′tu·al·is′tic** *adj.*

in·tel·lec·tu·al·ize (ĭn′tl-ĕk′choō-ə-līz′) *tr.v.* **-ized, -iz·ing. 1.** To make rational or intellectual. **2.** To avoid emotional insight into (an emotional problem) by performing an intellectual analysis. —**in′tel·lec′tu·al·i·za′tion** *n.*

in·tel·li·gence (ĭn-tĕl′ə-jəns) *n.* **1. a.** The capacity to acquire and apply knowledge and to solve problems. **b.** The faculty of thought and reason. **c.** Superior powers of mind. **2.** *Rare.* An intelligent being. **3.** Received information; news. **4. a.** Secret information, esp. about an enemy. **b.** The work of gathering such information.

in·tel·li·gent (ĭn-tĕl′ə-jənt) *adj.* **1.** Having intelligence: *Man is an intelligent animal.* **2.** Having a high degree of intelligence; mentally acute: *an intelligent leader.* **3.** Showing intelligence; perceptive and sound: *an intelligent choice.* —See Syns at **clever.** [Latin *intelligēns,* from *intelligere,* to perceive, choose between : *inter-,* between + *legere,* to gather, choose.] —**in·tel′li·gent·ly** *adv.*

in·tel·li·gent·si·a (ĭn-tĕl′ə-jĕnt′sē-ə, -gĕnt′-) *n.* The intellectual class within a society. [Russian *intelligentsiya,* from Latin *intelligentia,* intelligence, from *intelligēns,* intelligent.]

in·tel·li·gi·ble (ĭn-tĕl′ə-jə-bəl) *adj.* Comprehensible: *intelligible speech.* [Middle English, from Latin *intelligibilis,* from *intelligere,* to perceive.] —**in·tel′li·gi·bil′i·ty** *n.* —**in·tel′li·gi·bly** *adv.*

in·tem·per·ance (ĭn-tĕm′pər-əns) *n.* Lack of moderation, esp. in the drinking of alcoholic beverages.

in·tem·per·ate (ĭn-tĕm′pər-ĭt) *adj.* Not temperate or moderate: *an intemperate drinker; intemperate language.* —**in·tem′per·ate·ly** *adv.* —**in·tem′per·ate·ness** *n.*

in·tend (ĭn-tĕnd′) *tr.v.* **1.** To have in mind; to plan: *We intended to get an early start but were delayed.* **2.** To design for a specific purpose or destine to a particular use: *a rocket intended for probes of interplanetary space.* **3.** To signify; to mean. [Middle English *entenden,* from Old French *entendre,* from Latin *intendere,* to direct one's mind to : *in,* toward + *tendere,* to stretch, tend.]

Usage: **intend.** This verb is often followed by an infinitive: *intend to go.* It can also be followed by a *that* clause with the verb following in the subjunctive mood: *intended that he call her* (but not *intended for him to call her*).

in·tend·ed (ĭn-tĕn′dĭd) *adj.* **1.** Planned; intentional: *an intended insult.* **2.** Prospective; future: *his intended bride.* —*n.* *Informal.* A person's prospective spouse.

in·tense (ĭn-tĕns′) *adj.* **1.** Of great intensity: *an intense beam of light; an intense odor.* **2.** Extreme in degree, strength, or size: *taking intense care.* **3.** Involving or showing great concentration or strain: *an intense gaze.* **4. a.** Deeply felt; profound: *intense hatred.* **b.** Tending to feel deeply: *an intense person.* [Middle English, from Old French, from Latin *intensus,* stretched tight, from *intendere,* to stretch toward, intend.] —**in·tense′ly** *adv.* —**in·tense′ness** *n.*

Syns: **intense, desperate, fierce, furious, terrible, violent** *adj.* Core meaning: Extreme in degree, strength, or effect (*an intense power struggle*).

in·ten·si·fi·er (ĭn-tĕn′sə-fī′ər) *n.* **1.** Someone or something that intensifies. **2.** A word or word element used for emphasis; an intensive.

in·ten·si·fy (ĭn-tĕn′sə-fī′) *v.* **-fied, -fy·ing.** —*tr.v.* **1.** To make intense or more intense: *intensify the pressure.* **2.** To increase the contrast of (a photographic image). —*intr.v.* To become intense or more intense. [INTENSE + -FY.] —**in·ten′si·fi·ca′tion** *n.*

in·ten·si·ty (ĭn-tĕn′sĭ-tē) *n., pl.* **-ties. 1.** Exceptionally great concentration, power, or force: *emotional intensity; intensity of color.* **2.** Degree; strength: *Her suspicions increased in intensity.* **3.** *Physics.* **a.** The measure of effectiveness of a force field given by the force per unit test element. **b.** The energy transferred by a wave per unit time across a unit area perpendicular to the direction of propagation.

in·ten·sive (ĭn-tĕn′sĭv) *adj.* **1.** Marked by a full and thorough application of resources; concentrated; exhaustive: *intensive training; intensive care.* **2.** Adding emphasis but little new meaning: *"Very" in "very dark" is an intensive adverb.* **3.** Calling for large-scale employment of capital and labor: *intensive agriculture.* —*n.* A word or word element that adds emphasis but contributes little or no new meaning; intensifier. —**in·ten′sive·ly** *adv.*

in·tent (ĭn-tĕnt′) *n.* **1.** Aim; purpose. **2.** The state of mind operative at the time of an action. **3. a.** Meaning; significance. **b.** Connotation. —*adj.* **1.** Firmly fixed; concentrated: *The lookout's eyes were intent on the horizon.* **2.** Having the attention applied; engrossed. **3.** Having the mind fastened upon some purpose; bent: *intent on securing their freedom.* [Middle English *entent,* from Old French, from Latin *intentus,* a stretching out, from *intendere,* to stretch toward, intend.] —**in·tent′ly** *adv.* —**in·tent′ness** *n.*

in·ten·tion (ĭn-tĕn′shən) *n.* **1.** A plan of action; a design: *Our intention is to stay the whole summer.* **2. a.** An aim that guides action; an object: *achieved his intention.* **b. intentions.** Purpose in regard to marriage: *a suitor with honorable intentions.* **3.** The import; meaning.

in·ten·tion·al (ĭn-tĕn′shə-nəl) *adj.* Done deliberately; intended: *an intentional slight.* —See Syns at **voluntary.** —**in·ten·tion·al′i·ty** (-năl′ĭ-tē) *n.* —**in·ten′tion·al·ly** *adv.*

in·ter (ĭn-tûr′) *tr.v.* **-terred, -ter·ring.** To place in a grave; bury. [Middle English *enteren,* from Old French *enterrer:* Latin *in,* in + *terra,* earth, ground.]

inter-. A prefix meaning: **1.** Between or among: **international. 2.** Mutually or together: **interact.** [Middle English *inter-, entre-,* from Old French, from Latin *inter-,* from *inter,* between, among.]

in·ter·act (ĭn′tər-ăkt′) *intr.v.* To act on each other: *gears that interact; people who interact peacefully.* —**in·ter·ac′tion** *n.* —**in·ter·ac′tive** *adj.*

in·ter a·li·a (ĭn′tər ā′lē-ə, ä′lē-ə). *Latin.* Among other things.

in·ter·breed (ĭn′tər-brēd′) *v.* **-bred** (-brĕd′), **-breed·ing.** —*intr.v.* **1.** To breed with another kind or species; crossbreed. **2.** To breed within a narrow range or with closely related types or individuals; inbreed. —*tr.v.* To cause to interbreed.

in·ter·ca·late (ĭn-tûr′kə-lāt′) *tr.v.* **-lat·ed, -lat·ing. 1.** To add (a day or month) to a calendar. **2.** To insert, interpose, or interpolate. [From Latin *intercalāre,* to proclaim the insertion (of a day in the calendar) : *inter-,* among + *calāre,* to call.] —**in·ter·ca·la′tion** *n.*

in·ter·cede (ĭn′tər-sēd′) *intr.v.* **-ced·ed, -ced·ing. 1.** To plead on another's behalf. **2.** To act so as to help unfriendly parties settle a dispute; mediate. [Latin *intercēdere,* to come between : *inter-,* between + *cēdere,* to go.] —**in·ter·ced′er** *n.*

in·ter·cel·lu·lar (ĭn′tər-sĕl′yə-lər) *adj.* Among or between cells.

in·ter·cept (ĭn′tər-sĕpt′) *tr.v.* **1.** To stop or interrupt the progress or course of: *intercept a messenger; intercept a quarterback's pass.* **2.** To intersect. **3.** *Math.* To cut off or bound a part of (a line, plane, surface, or solid). —*n.* (ĭn′tər-sĕpt′). *Math.* The distance from the origin of coordinates along a coordinate axis to the point at which a line, curve, or surface intersects the axis. [From Latin *interci-*

pere : *inter,* between + *capere,* to take, seize.] —**in·ter·cep′tion** *n.* —**in·ter·cep′tive** *adj.*

in·ter·cep·tor (ĭn′tər-sĕp′tər) *n.* Also **in·ter·cept·er. 1.** Someone or something that intercepts. **2.** A fast-climbing, highly maneuverable fighter plane designed to intercept enemy aircraft.

in·ter·ces·sion (ĭn′tər-sĕsh′ən) *n.* **1.** The act or an example of pleading on another's behalf. **2.** The act or an example of trying to help unfriendly parties settle a dispute; mediation. [Old French, from Latin *intercessiō,* from *intercedere,* to intercede.] —**in·ter·ces′sion·al** *adj.* —**in·ter·ces′sor** *n.* —**in·ter·ces′so·ry** *adj.*

in·ter·change (ĭn′tər-chānj′) *v.* **-changed, -chang·ing.** —*tr.v.* **1.** To switch each of (two things) into the place of the other. **2.** To give and receive mutually; to exchange: *interchange ideas.* —*intr.v.* To change places with each other. —*n.* (ĭn′tər-chānj′). **1.** The act or process or an example of interchanging, esp.: **a.** A switch of places. **b.** An exchange. **2.** A highway intersection designed to permit traffic to move freely by means of separate levels from one road to another. —**in·ter·chang′er** *n.*

in·ter·change·a·ble (ĭn′tər-chān′jə-bəl) *adj.* Capable of being interchanged or switched: *The two cars are so much alike that their parts are interchangeable.* —**in·ter·change′a·bil′i·ty** or **in·ter·change′a·ble·ness** *n.* —**in·ter·change′a·bly** *adv.*

in·ter·col·le·giate (ĭn′tər-kə-lē′jĭt, -jē-ĭt) *adj.* Involving or representing two or more colleges.

in·ter·com (ĭn′tər-kŏm′) *n.* A system for two-way communication, as between two rooms, consisting of a microphone and a receiving loudspeaker at each station. [Short for INTERCOMMUNICATION.]

in·ter·com·mu·ni·cate (ĭn′tər-kə-myōō′nĭ-kāt′) *intr.v.* **-cat·ed, -cat·ing. 1.** To communicate with each other. **2.** To be connected or adjoined: *rooms that intercommunicate.* —**in·ter·com·mu·ni·ca′tion** *n.* —**in·ter·com·mu·ni·ca′tive** *adj.*

in·ter·con·nect (ĭn′tər-kə-nĕkt′) *intr.v.* To be connected one to the other. —*tr.v.* To connect (one thing) with another. —**in·ter·con·nec′tion** *n.*

in·ter·con·ti·nen·tal (ĭn′tər-kŏn′tə-nĕn′tl) *adj.* **1.** Extending or traveling from one continent to another: *an intercontinental flight from France to Canada.* **2.** Carried on between continents: *intercontinental warfare.*

in·ter·cos·tal (ĭn′tər-kŏs′təl) *adj.* Located or occurring between the ribs. [INTER- + Latin *costa,* rib.]

in·ter·course (ĭn′tər-kôrs′, -kōrs′) *n.* **1.** Interchange between persons or groups; communication. **2.** The act of mating; coitus. [Middle English *intercurse,* from Old French *entrecours,* from Latin *intercurrere,* to run between : *inter-,* between + *currere,* to run.]

in·ter·de·nom·i·na·tion·al (ĭn′tər-dĭ-nŏm′ə-nā′shə-nəl) *adj.* Involving two or more denominations: *an interdenominational church.*

in·ter·de·pend·ent (ĭn′tər-dĭ-pĕn′dənt) *n.* Mutually dependent. —**in·ter·de·pend′ence** *n.*

in·ter·dict (ĭn′tər-dĭkt′) *tr.v.* **1.** To prohibit; forbid: *The church interdicted certain forms of worship.* **2.** To cut or destroy (an enemy line of communication) by firepower so as to halt an enemy's advance. —*n.* (ĭn′tər-dĭkt′). **1.** A prohibition. **2.** A Roman Catholic Church censure excluding an offending person or district from participation in most sacraments and from Christian burial. [Middle English *entrediten,* to announce ecclesiastical censure, from Old French *entredire,* from Latin *interdīcere,* to forbid : *inter-,* among + *dīcere,* to say.] —**in·ter·dic′tion** *n.* —**in·ter·dic′tive** or **in·ter·dic′to·ry** *adj.* —**in·ter·dic′tive·ly** *adv.* —**in·ter·dic′tor** *n.*

in·ter·est (ĭn′trĭst, -tər-ĭst) *n.* **1. a.** Willingness to give special attention to something; active concern: *arousing the reader's interest.* **b.** The quality of arousing such willingness: *a speech that lacked interest for me.* **c.** A subject that arouses such willingness: *Music, science fiction, and girls were among his interests.* **2.** Often **interests.** Advantage; benefit: *a government decision that is not in the public interest.* **3.** A right, claim, or legal share in something: *an interest in a business.* **4.** A charge paid for borrowing money, usu. a percentage of the amount borrowed: *bank interest of 5.50 per cent.* **5.** An excess or bonus beyond what is expected or due: *She paid back the insult with*

ă pat	ā pay	â care	ä father	ĕ pet	ē be	hw which
ŏŏ took	ōō boot	ou out	th thin	th this	ŭ cut

ĭ pit ī tie î pier ŏ pot ō toe ô paw, for oi noise
û urge zh vision ə about, item, edible, gallop, circus

interest. **—modifier:** *an interest rate of 7 per cent.* **—tr.v.** **1.** To arouse interest in: *tried to interest her students in reading.* **2.** To cause to become involved or concerned: *Can I interest you in a game of chess?* [Middle English, var. of *interesse,* concern, share, from Norman French, from Latin *interesse,* to matter, be of concern : *inter-,* between + *esse,* to be.]

in·ter·est·ed (ĭn′trĭ-stĭd, -tər-ĭ-stĭd, -tə-rĕs′tĭd) *adj.* **1.** Having or showing interest; disposed to participate, learn, or be attentive: *interested in geology.* **2.** Possessing a right, claim, or share: *The interested parties met to settle the dispute.* **3.** Desirous of personal gain; self-seeking. **—in′ter·est·ed·ly** *adv.* **—in′ter·est·ed·ness** *n.*

in·ter·est·ing (ĭn′trĭ-stĭng, -tər-ĭ-stĭng, -tə-rĕs′tĭng) *adj.* Arousing or holding attention: *an interesting story.* **—in′ter·est·ing·ly** *adv.*

in·ter·face (ĭn′tər-fās′) *n.* A surface forming a common boundary between adjacent regions. **—in′ter·fa′cial** (-fā′shəl) *adj.*

in·ter·fere (ĭn′tər-fîr′) *intr.v.* **-fered, -fer·ing.** **1.** To be a hindrance or obstacle; impede: *We might have entered through the window, but a grating interfered.* **2.** *Sports.* To impede illegally the catching of a pass or the playing of a ball or puck. **3.** To intervene or intrude in the affairs of others; meddle. **4.** To strike one hoof against the opposite hoof or leg while moving: *The horse interfered and lost a stride.* **5.** *Physics.* To produce interference with another wave. **6.** *Electronics.* To inhibit or prevent clear reception of broadcast signals. [Old French *(s')entreferir,* to strike each other : *entre-, inter-* + *ferir,* to strike, from Latin *ferīre.*] **—in′ter·fer′er** *n.*

Syns: interfere, meddle, tamper *v. Core meaning:* To involve oneself in the affairs of others *(a neighbor who interfered in my life).* Although INTERFERE and MEDDLE are interchangeable, MEDDLE is the stronger word, implying unwanted, unwarranted intrusion *(meddling in the private lives of others).* TAMPER refers to rash or harmful intervention *(jury tampering; tampered with the machine and broke it).*

in·ter·fer·ence (ĭn′tər-fîr′əns) *n.* **1.** The act or process or an example of interfering. **2.** *Football.* **a.** The tackling or blocking of defensive tacklers to protect the ball carrier. **b.** The players protecting the ball carrier in such a manner. **c.** The illegal obstruction of the receiving of a pass. **3.** An illegal obstruction of a play or player in various other sports. **4.** *Physics.* A physical effect in which two or more waves combine to form a wave in which the disturbance at any point is the algebraic or vector sum of the disturbances due to the interfering waves at that point. **5.** *Electronics.* **a.** The inhibition or prevention of clear reception of broadcast signals. **b.** The distorted portion of a received signal. **—in′ter·fer·en′tial** (-fə-rĕn′shəl) *adj.*

in·ter·fer·on (ĭn′tər-fîr′ŏn′) *n.* A cellular protein produced in response to and acting to prevent replication of an infectious viral form within an infected cell. [INTERFER(E) + -ON.]

in·ter·ga·lac·tic (ĭn′tər-gə-lăk′tĭk) *adj.* Between galaxies.

in·ter·gla·cial (ĭn′tər-glā′shəl) *adj.* Between glacial epochs.

in·ter·im (ĭn′tər-ĭm) *n.* An interval of time between one event, process, or period and another. **—adj.** For or during an interim; temporary: *named interim chairmen.* [Latin, in the meantime, from *inter,* at intervals, among.]

in·te·ri·or (ĭn-tîr′ē-ər) *adj.* **1.** Of or located in the inside; inner. **2.** Of or relating to one's mental or spiritual being: *an interior monologue.* **3.** Situated away from a coast or border; inland: *Interior Canada is sparsely populated.* **4.** Of the insides of houses or other structures: *an interior designer.* **—n.** **1.** The inner part of something; the inside. **2.** One's mental or spiritual being. **3.** A representation of the inside of a building or room, as in a painting. **4.** The inland part of a geographical area. [Latin, comp. of *inter,* in, within.] **—in·te′ri·or′i·ty** (-ôr′ĭ-tē, -ŏr′-) *n.* **—in·te′ri·or·ly** *adv.*

interior angle. **1. a.** Any of four angles formed between two straight lines cut by a transversal. **b.** A vertex angle measured wholly within a polygon. **2.** The angle formed inside a polygon by two adjacent sides.

in·ter·ject (ĭn′tər-jĕkt′) *tr.v.* **1.** To put in between or among other things; insert: *paused in his speech to interject a*

joke. **2.** To exclaim: *"Hurry!" he interjected.* [From Latin *interjicere,* to throw between : *inter-,* between + *jacere,* to throw.] **—in′ter·jec′tor** *n.* **—in′ter·jec′to·ry** *adj.*

in·ter·jec·tion (ĭn′tər-jĕk′shən) *n.* **1.** The act of interjecting. **2.** A phrase or remark that is interjected. **3.** A word that expresses some abrupt or momentary emotion and that stands alone grammatically; for example, the word *Ouch!* and the word *oh,* as in *Oh, what a feast,* are interjections. **4.** Any exclamation. **—in′ter·jec′tion·al** *adj.* **—in′ter·jec′tion·al·ly** *adv.*

in·ter·lin·ing (ĭn′tər-lī′nĭng) *n.* An extra lining between the outer fabric and the regular lining of a garment.

in·ter·lock (ĭn′tər-lŏk′) *tr.v.* To join closely; lock together: *interlocking their arms to form a human chain.* **—intr.v.** To become joined closely; be locked together: *Our eyes interlocked.*

in·ter·loc·u·tor (ĭn′tər-lŏk′yə-tər) *n.* Someone who takes part in a conversation or dialogue.

in·ter·loc·u·to·ry (ĭn′tər-lŏk′yə-tôr′ē, -tōr′ē) *adj.* **1.** Of or relating to a temporary decree made during the course of a suit or trial. **2.** Of or relating to conversation or dialogue.

in·ter·lope (ĭn′tər-lōp′, ĭn′tər-lōp′) *intr.v.* **-loped, -lop·ing.** **1.** To violate the legally established trading rights of others. **2.** To interfere in the affairs of others; intrude; meddle. [INTER- + Dutch *loopen,* to run.] **—in′ter·lop′er** *n.*

in·ter·lude (ĭn′tər-lōōd′) *n.* **1.** An intervening episode, feature, or period of time. **2.** An entertainment between the acts of a play. **3.** A short musical piece inserted between the parts of a longer composition. [Middle English *enterlude,* from Medieval Latin *interlūdium,* performance between acts : Latin *inter-,* between + *lūdus,* play.]

in·ter·mar·ry (ĭn′tər-măr′ē) *intr.v.* **-ried, -ry·ing.** **1.** To marry someone of another religion, nationality, race, or group. **2.** To be bound together by the marriages of members: *The two clans intermarried..* **3.** To marry within one's family, tribe, or clan. **—in′ter·mar′riage** *n.*

in·ter·me·di·ar·y (ĭn′tər-mē′dē-ĕr′ē) *n., pl.* **-ies.** **1.** A person who acts as a mediator or go-between. **2.** An intermediate state or stage. **—adj.** **1.** Acting as a mediator. **2.** In between; intermediate.

in·ter·me·di·ate (ĭn′tər-mē′dē-ĭt) *adj.* Lying, occurring, or being between two extremes; in between; in the middle: *of intermediate size; an intermediate skier.* **—n.** **1.** Someone or something that is intermediate. **2.** An intermediary. **—intr.v.** (-āt′) **-at·ed, -at·ing.** To act as an intermediary; mediate. [Medieval Latin *intermediātus,* from Latin *intermedius: inter-,* between + *medius,* middle.] **—in′ter·me′di·ate·ly** *adv.* **—in′ter·me′di·ate·ness** or **in′ter·me′di·a·cy** (-ə-sē) *n.* **—in′ter·me′di·a′tion** *n.*

in·ter·mez·zo (ĭn′tər-mĕt′sō, -mĕd′zō) *n., pl.* **-zos** or **-zi** (-mĕt′sē, -mĕd′zē). **1.** A piece of music heard between sections of a larger work, acts of a play or opera, etc.; an interlude. **2.** An independent instrumental composition with the brevity of such a piece. [Italian, from Latin *intermedius,* intermediate.]

in·ter·mi·na·ble (ĭn-tûr′mə-nə-bəl) *adj.* Tiresomely long; endless. **—See Syns at continuous. —in·ter′mi·na·bly** *adv.*

in·ter·min·gle (ĭn′tər-mĭng′gəl) *v.* **-gled, -gling. —tr.v.** To mix or mingle. **—intr.v.** To mix with one another.

in·ter·mis·sion (ĭn′tər-mĭsh′ən) *n.* **1. a.** The act of intermit-

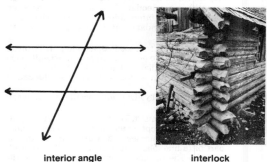

interior angle

interlock
Logs interlocked on a log cabin

ting. **b.** The condition of being intermitted. **2.** A pause or recess. **3.** The period between the acts of a theatrical or musical performance. [Latin *intermissiō,* from *intermittere,* to intermit.]

in·ter·mit·tent (ĭn′tər-mĭt′nt) *adj.* Stopping and starting at intervals; not continuous: *intermittent noises.* —**in′ter·mit′tent·ly** *adv.*

in·ter·mix (ĭn′tər-mĭks′) *tr.v.* To mix together. —*intr.v.* To be or become mixed together. [Back-formation from earlier *intermixt,* intermixed, from Latin *intermiscēre,* to mix together : *inter-,* mutually + *miscēre,* to mix.] —**in′ter·mix′ture** *n.*

in·ter·mo·lec·u·lar (ĭn′tər-mə-lĕk′yə-lər) *adj.* Between molecules.

in·tern (ĭn′tûrn′) *n.* Also **in·terne. 1.** An advanced student or recent graduate, as of a medical school, undergoing supervised practical training. **2.** One who is interned; an internee. —*intr.v.* (ĭn′tûrn′). To train or serve as an intern: *She interned in a large municipal hospital.* —*tr.v.* (ĭn′tûrn′). To detain or confine, esp. in wartime: *Many Japanese-Americans were interned during World War II.* [French *interne,* inmate, resident assistant physician, from Old French, internal, from Latin *internus.*] —**in′tern·ship′** *n.*

in·ter·nal (ĭn-tûr′nəl) *adj.* **1.** Located or existing within the limits or beneath the surface of something; inner; interior. **2.** Intrinsic; inherent. **3.** Located, acting, or effective within the body: *internal bleeding.* **4.** Of or relating to the domestic affairs of a country: *internal political divisions.* [From Latin *internus,* from *inter,* in, within.] —**in·ter′nal·ly** *adv.*

in·ter·nal-com·bus·tion engine (ĭn-tûr′nəl-kəm-bŭs′chən). An engine, such as an automobile's gasoline engine, in which fuel is burned within the engine itself rather than in an outside furnace or burner.

internal revenue. Governmental income from taxes levied within the country.

internal rhyme. Rhyme between words within the same line or between words in different lines but not at the ends of those lines.

in·ter·na·tion·al (ĭn′tər-năsh′ə-nəl) *adj.* Of, relating to, or involving two or more nations or nationalities: *an international incident.* —**in′ter·na′tion·al′i·ty** *n.* —**in′ter·na′tion·al·ly** *adv.*

international candle. A candle, a unit of illumination.

in·ter·na·tion·al·ism (ĭn′tər-năsh′ə-nə-lĭz′əm) *n.* **1.** The condition or quality of being international in character, principles, concern, or attitude. **2.** A theory that promotes cooperation among nations, esp. in politics and economy. —**in′ter·na′tion·al·ist** *n.*

international law. A set of rules gen. regarded and accepted as binding in relations between states and nations. Also called **law of nations.**

International Phonetic Alphabet. A phonetic alphabet sponsored by the International Phonetic Association to provide a uniform, universally comprehensible system of letters and symbols for writing the speech sounds of all languages.

in·terne (ĭn′tûrn′) *n.* Var. of **intern.**

in·ter·nec·ine (ĭn′tər-nĕs′ēn′, -īn′, -ĭn, -nē′sīn′) *adj.* **1.** Destructive or fatal to both sides: *internecine warfare.* **2.** Characterized by bloodshed or carnage. **3.** Involving conflict within a group or nation: *internecine squabbles within the department.* [Latin *internecīnus,* from *internecāre,* to slaughter, massacre : *inter* (intensive) + *necāre,* to kill.]

in·tern·ee (ĭn′tûr-nē′) *n.* A person who is interned, esp. during a war.

in·ter·nist (ĭn′tûr′nĭst, ĭn-tûr′-) *n.* A physician who specializes in internal medicine. [INTERN(AL MEDICINE) + -IST.]

in·tern·ment (ĭn-tûrn′mənt) *n.* The act of interning or the condition of being interned.

in·ter·o·cep·tor (ĭn′tə-rō-sĕp′tər) *n.* A specialized sensory nerve receptor responding to stimuli originating in internal organs. [From INTER(IOR) + (RE)CEPTOR.] —**in′ter·o·cep′tive** *adj.*

in·ter·pel·late (ĭn′tər-pĕl′āt′, ĭn-tûr′pə-lāt′) *tr.v.* **-lat·ed, -lat·ing.** To question formally about government policy or ac-

tion. [From Latin *interpellāre,* to interrupt by speaking.] —**in′ter·pel·la′tion** *n.* —**in′ter·pel′la·tor** *n.*

in·ter·pen·e·trate (ĭn′tər-pĕn′ĭ-trāt′) *v.* **-trat·ed, -trat·ing.** —*tr.v.* To penetrate between. —*intr.v.* To penetrate each other. —**in′ter·pen′e·tra′tion** *n.*

in·ter·plan·e·tar·y (ĭn′tər-plăn′ĭ-tĕr′ē) *adj.* Between planets.

in·ter·play (ĭn′tər-plā′) *n.* Reciprocal action and reaction; interaction: *There is constant interplay between soils and plants.* —*intr.v.* (ĭn′tər-plā′, ĭn′tər-plā′). To act or react on each other; interact.

in·ter·po·late (ĭn-tûr′pə-lāt′) *v.* **-lat·ed, -lat·ing.** —*tr.v.* **1.** To insert or introduce between other things or parts. **2.** To insert (additional or false material) in a text. **3.** To change or falsify (a text) by introducing new or false material. **4.** *Math.* To determine a value of (a function) between known values by a procedure or algorithm different from that specified by the function itself. —*intr.v.* To make insertions or additions. [From Latin *interpolāre* : *inter-,* between + *polīre,* to adorn, polish.] —**in·ter′po·la′tion** *n.* —**in·ter′po·la′tive** *adj.* —**in·ter′po·la′tor** *n.*

in·ter·pose (ĭn′tər-pōz′) *v.* **-posed, -pos·ing.** —*tr.v.* **1.** To insert in an intervening or obstructing position: *interposed a shield to deflect the arrow.* **2.** To introduce or interject (a remark, question, or argument) into a conversation or speech. **3.** To exert (influence or authority) in order to interfere or intervene. —*intr.v.* **1.** To come between; intervene. **2.** To introduce a remark, question, or argument. [Old French *interposer,* from Latin *interpōnere,* to place between : *inter-,* between + *pōnere,* to put, place.] —**in′ter·pos′er** *n.* —**in′ter·po·si′tion** (-pə-zĭsh′ən) *n.*

in·ter·pret (ĭn-tûr′prĭt) *tr.v.* **1.** To explain or clarify the meaning of: *interpreting a dream; interpreting data.* **2.** To see or understand in a certain way: *He interpreted the letter to mean that the deal was off.* **3.** To perform or present according to one's artistic understanding: *an actor interpreting a role.* **4.** To translate (spoken words). —*intr.v.* **1.** To offer an explanation. **2.** To translate orally. [Middle English *interpreten,* from Old French *interpreter,* from Latin *interpretārī,* from *interpres,* interpreter, negotiator.] —**in·ter′pret·a·ble** *adj.*

in·ter·pre·ta·tion (ĭn-tûr′prĭ-tā′shən) *n.* **1. a.** The act or process of interpreting: *the interpretation of the law.* **b.** An example of interpreting; an explanation of the meaning of something unclear: *two different interpretations of a dream.* **2.** An artistic performance or presentation that expresses someone's understanding of the work. **3.** Translation, esp. oral translation. —**in·ter′pre·ta′tion·al** *adj.*

in·ter·pre·ta·tive (ĭn-tûr′prĭ-tā′tĭv) *adj.* Also **in·ter·pre·tive** (-prĭ-tĭv). Of or pertaining to interpretation; explanatory. —**in·ter′pre·ta′tive·ly** *adv.*

in·ter·pret·er (ĭn-tûr′prĭ-tər) *n.* **1.** A person who translates orally from one language into another. **2.** A person who explains or expounds on a certain subject: *medieval interpreters of Aristotle.*

in·ter·pre·tive (ĭn-tûr′prĭ-tĭv) *adj.* Var. of **interpretative.**

in·ter·ra·cial (ĭn′tər-rā′shəl) *adj.* Of or between different races: *interracial cooperation.*

in·ter·reg·num (ĭn′tər-rĕg′nəm) *n., pl.* **-nums** or **-na** (-nə). **1.** The interval of time between two successive reigns or governments. **2.** A gap in continuity. [Latin *interrēgnum* : *inter-,* between + *rēgnum,* reign.] —**in′ter·reg′nal** *adj.*

in·ter·re·late (ĭn′tər-rĭ-lāt′) *v.* **-lat·ed, -lat·ing.** —*tr.v.* To place in mutual relationship: *The lives of bees and clover plants are interrelated.* —*intr.v.* To come into mutual relationship. —**in′ter·re·la′tion** *n.* —**in′ter·re·la′tion·ship′** *n.*

in·ter·ro·gate (ĭn-tĕr′ə-gāt′) *tr.v.* **-gat·ed, -gat·ing.** To question formally or closely. [From Latin *interrogāre,* to consult, question : *inter-,* between + *rogāre,* to ask.] —**in′ter·ro·ga′tion** *n.* —**in·ter·ro·ga′tion·al** *adj.* —**in·ter′ro·ga′tor** *n.*

interrogation point. A question mark.

in·ter·rog·a·tive (ĭn′tə-rŏg′ə-tĭv) *adj.* **1.** Of the nature of a question; asking a question: *an interrogative sentence.* **2.** Used in asking a question: *an interrogative pronoun.* —*n.* **1.** A word or form used in asking a question. **2.** An interrogative sentence or expression. —**in′ter·rog′a·tive·ly** *adv.*

in·ter·rog·a·to·ry (ĭn′tə-rŏg′ə-tôr′ē, -tōr′ē) *adj.* Interroga-

---

| ă pat | ā pay | â care | ä father | ĕ pet | ē be | hw which | ĭ pit | ī tie | î pier | ŏ pot | ō toe | ô paw, for | oi noise |
| ōō took | ōō boot | ou out | th thin | *th* this | ŭ cut | | û urge | zh vision | ə about, item, edible, gallop, circus |

tive. —*n.*, *pl.* **-ries.** *Law.* A formal question, as to an accused person. —**in'ter·rog'a·to'ri·ly** *adv.*

in·ter·rupt (ĭn'tə-rŭpt') *tr.v.* **1.** To break the continuity or uniformity of: *interrupt a program for a special news bulletin.* **2.** To stop the action or speech of (someone) by breaking in. —*intr.v.* To break in on another's speech or action. [Middle English *interrupten*, from Latin *interrumpere*, to break in : *inter-*, between + *rumpere*, to break.] —**in'ter·rup'tion** *n.* —**in'ter·rup'tive** *adj.*

in·ter·rupt·er (ĭn'tə-rŭp'tər) *n.* Also **in·ter·rup·tor.** **1.** Someone or something that interrupts. **2.** *Elect.* A device for periodically and automatically opening or closing an electric circuit.

in·ter·sect (ĭn'tər-sĕkt') *tr.v.* **1.** To cut across or through: *A river intersects the plain.* **2.** To cut at an intersection to: *where Broadway intersects 42nd Street.* —*intr.v.* **1.** To cut across or overlap each other. **2.** To form an intersection: *roads that intersect.* [From Latin *intersecāre* : *inter-*, mutually + *secāre*, to cut.]

in·ter·sec·tion (ĭn'tər-sĕk'shən) *n.* **1. a.** The act or process of intersecting. **b.** A place where things intersect, esp. a place where two or more roads cross. **2.** *Math.* **a.** The point or locus of points common to two or more geometric figures. **b.** A set every member of which is an element of each of two or more given sets.

in·ter·sperse (ĭn'tər-spûrs') *tr.v.* **-spersed, -spers·ing.** **1.** To scatter here and there among other things: *We interspersed fern fronds among the flowers.* **2.** To give variety to by distributing things here and there: *interspersed the serious story with comic remarks.* [From Latin *interspergere* : *inter-*, among + *spargere*, to scatter.] —**in'ter·sper'sion** (-spûr'zhən, -shən) *n.*

in·ter·state (ĭn'tər-stāt') *adj.* Of, between, or connecting two or more states: *interstate commerce; an interstate highway.*

in·ter·stel·lar (ĭn'tər-stĕl'ər) *adj.* Between the stars.

in·ter·stice (ĭn-tûr'stĭs) *n.*, *pl.* **-sti·ces** (-stĭ-sēz', -stĭ-sĭz). A narrow or small space between things or parts: *passing through the interstices of a net.* [French, from Late Latin *interstitium*, from Latin *intersistere*, to stand in the middle of : *inter-*, between + *sistere*, to stand.]

in·ter·sti·tial (ĭn'tər-stĭsh'əl) *adj.* Of or occurring in interstices. —**in'ter·sti'tial·ly** *adv.*

in·ter·tri·bal (ĭn'tər-trī'bəl) *adj.* Between tribes.

in·ter·twine (ĭn'tər-twīn') *v.* **-twined, -twin·ing.** —*tr.v.* To twist or braid together. —*intr.v.* To interweave with one another. —**in'ter·twine'ment** *n.*

in·ter·ur·ban (ĭn'tər-ûr'bən) *adj.* Between urban areas: *an interurban railroad.*

interurban
An interurban elevated train

in·ter·val (ĭn'tər-vəl) *n.* **1.** A period of time between two events or occurrences: *an interval of rest before resuming work.* **2.** A space between two points or objects: *Pierce the meat deeply at one-inch intervals.* **3. a.** The set of all numbers that lie between two given numbers, sometimes including either or both of the given numbers. **b.** A line segment that represents the numbers in this set. **4.** The difference in pitch between two musical tones. **5.** *Brit.* An intermission. [Middle English *intervalle*, from Latin *intervallum*, space between ramparts : *inter-*, between + *vallum*, rampart.]

in·ter·vene (ĭn'tər-vēn') *intr.v.* **-vened, -ven·ing.** **1.** To occur or come between two things, points, or events: *A day of calm intervened between the hectic weeks.* **2. a.** To enter a course of events so as to hinder or change it: *The governor intervened to delay the execution.* **b.** To interfere, usu. with force, in the affairs of another nation. [Latin *intervenīre* : *inter-*, between + *venīre*, to come.]

in·ter·ven·tion (ĭn'tər-vĕn'shən) *n.* **1.** The act or an example of intervening: *an intervention to settle an argument.* **2.** Interference, usu. with force, in the affairs of another nation.

in·ter·view (ĭn'tər-vyōō') *n.* **1. a.** A face-to-face meeting. **b.** Such a meeting arranged for the formal discussion of some matter. **2. a.** A conversation between a reporter and a person from whom he seeks facts or statements. **b.** An account or reproduction of such a conversation. —*tr.v.* To have an interview with: *interview an actress.* [From Old French *entrevue*, from *(s')entrevoir*, to see each other : *entre-*, mutually, each other + *voir*, to see, from Latin *vidēre*.]

in·ter·weave (ĭn'tər-wēv') *v.* **-wove** (-wōv') or **-weaved, -wo·ven** (-wō'vən) or **-wove, -weav·ing.** —*tr.v.* **1.** To weave together. **2.** To intermix: *The author skillfully interweaves two plots.* —*intr.v.* To intertwine.

in·tes·tate (ĭn-tĕs'tāt', -tĭt) *adj.* **1.** Having made no legal will. **2.** Not disposed of by a legal will. —*n.* A person who dies without a legal will. [Middle English, from Latin *intestātus* : *in-*, not + *testārī*, to make a will, from *testis*, witness.] —**in·tes'ta·cy** (-tə-sē) *n.*

intestinal fortitude. Courage; endurance.

in·tes·tine (ĭn-tĕs'tĭn) *n.* The portion of the alimentary canal extending from the outlet of the stomach to the anus; the large intestine and the small intestine. [Latin *intestīnum*, from *intestīnus*, internal, from *intus*, within.] —**in·tes'ti·nal** *adj.* —**in·tes'ti·nal·ly** *adv.*

in·ti·ma·cy (ĭn'tə-mə-sē) *n.*, *pl.* **-cies.** **1.** The condition of being intimate. **2.** An example of being intimate. **3.** Often **intimacies.** Sexual intercourse.

in·ti·mate[1] (ĭn'tə-mĭt) *adj.* **1.** Marked by close acquaintance, association, or familiarity: *an intimate understanding of his craft.* **2.** Coming from or characterizing one's deepest nature: *intimate thoughts.* **3.** Essential; innermost: *the intimate chambers of the organization.* **4.** Characterized by informality and privacy: *an intimate nightclub.* **5.** Very personal; private; secret: *an intimate diary.* —*n.* A close friend or confidant. [Late Latin *intimātus*, past part. of *intimāre*, to put in, announce, hint.] —**in'ti·mate·ly** *adv.* —**in'ti·mate·ness** *n.*

in·ti·mate[2] (ĭn'tə-māt') *tr.v.* **-mat·ed, -mat·ing.** To communicate with a hint or other indirect sign; imply subtly: *He intimated that there was trouble ahead.* See Syns at **suggest.** [From Late Latin *intimāre*, to put or bring in, publish, announce, from Latin *intimus*, inmost, deepest.] —**in'ti·mat'er** *n.* —**in'ti·ma'tion** *n.*

in·tim·i·date (ĭn-tĭm'ĭ-dāt') *tr.v.* **-dat·ed, -dat·ing.** **1.** To make timid; frighten. **2.** To discourage or inhibit by or as if by threats. [From Medieval Latin *intimidāre* : Latin *in-* (causative) + *timidus*, timid.] —**in·tim'i·da'tion** *n.* —**in·tim'i·da'tor** *n.*

in·to (ĭn'tōō) *prep.* **1.** To the inside of: *going into the house.* **2.** To the action or occupation of: *go into banking.* **3.** To the condition or form of: *break into pieces.* **4.** So as to be in or within: *enter into an agreement.* **5.** To a time or place in the course of: *well into the week.* **6.** Against: *ram into a tree.* **7.** Toward; in the direction of: *look into the distance.* **8.** *Informal.* Interested in or involved with: *They are into vegetarianism.* —See Usage note at **in.** [Middle English, from Old English *intō*.]

in·tol·er·a·ble (ĭn-tŏl'ər-ə-bəl) *adj.* **1.** Not capable of being tolerated; unbearable. **2.** Inordinate; extravagant. —**in·tol'er·a·bil'i·ty** or **in·tol'er·a·ble·ness** *n.* —**in·tol'er·a·bly** *adv.*

in·tol·er·ance (ĭn-tŏl'ər-əns) *n.* **1.** The quality or condition of being intolerant. **2.** Inability to withstand or consume: *a great intolerance of loud noises.*

in·tol·er·ant (ĭn-tŏl'ər-ənt) *adj.* **1.** Not tolerant of others; bigoted. **2.** Unable to endure: *intolerant of certain drugs.* —**in·tol'er·ant·ly** *adv.*

ă pat ā pay â care ä father ĕ pet ē be hw which ĭ pit ī tie î pier ŏ pot ō toe ô paw, for oi noise
ōō took ōō boot ou out th thin th this ŭ cut û urge zh vision ə about, item, edible, gallop, circus

in·to·na·tion (ĭn′tō-nā′shən) *n.* **1.** The way in which the speaking voice emphasizes words, makes pauses, or rises and falls in pitch in order to convey meaning. **2. a.** A particular quality or tone of voice: *an angry intonation.* **b.** Expression or expressiveness: *She spoke without intonation.* **3.** The manner in which musical tones are produced, sung, chanted, etc., esp. with respect to accuracy of pitch.

in·tone (ĭn-tōn′) *v.* **-toned, -ton·ing.** —*tr.v.* To recite in a singing or chanting voice, often on a single tone: *intone a prayer.* —*intr.v.* To speak with a given intonation. [Middle English *entonen,* from Old French *entoner,* from Medieval Latin *intonāre* : Latin *in-,* in + *tonus,* tone.] —**in·ton′er** *n.*

in to·to (ĭn tō′tō). *Latin.* Totally; altogether.

in·tox·i·cate (ĭn-tŏk′sĭ-kāt′) *tr.v.* **-cat·ed, -cat·ing. 1.** To disturb the normal physical or mental functioning of by the effect of alcohol or another drug; make drunk. **2.** To stimulate or excite: *The idea intoxicated her.* [From Medieval Latin *intoxicāre,* to poison : Latin *in-,* in + *toxicum,* poison.] —**in·tox′i·ca′tion** *n.* —**in·tox′i·ca′tive** *adj.* —**in·tox′i·ca′tor** *n.*

intra-. A prefix meaning in, within, or inside of: **intracellular.** [Late Latin, from Latin *intrā,* on the inside, within.]

in·tra·cel·lu·lar (ĭn′trə-sĕl′yə-lər) *adj.* Within a cell or cells.

in·trac·ta·ble (ĭn-trăk′tə-bəl) *adj.* **1.** Difficult to manage or govern; stubborn. **2.** Difficult to mold or manipulate. **3.** Difficult to remedy or cure. —See Syns at **obstinate.** —**in·trac′ta·bil′i·ty** or **in·trac′ta·ble·ness** *n.* —**in·trac′ta·bly** *adv.*

in·tra·dos (ĭn-trā′dŏs′, -dōs′, ĭn′trə-dŏs′) *n., pl.* **intrados** (-dŏz′, -dōz′) or **-dos·es.** *Archit.* The inner curve of an arch. [French : *intra-,* within + *dos,* back, from Old French, from Latin *dorsum.*]

in·tra·mo·lec·u·lar (ĭn′trə-mə-lĕk′yə-lər) *adj.* Within a molecule.

in·tra·mu·ral (ĭn′trə-myŏor′əl) *adj.* **1.** Existing or carried on within an institution, esp. a school. **2.** *Anat.* Within the wall of a cavity or organ. [INTRA- + Latin *mūrus,* wall.] —**in′tra·mu′ral·ly** *adv.*

in·tran·si·gent (ĭn-trăn′sə-jənt) *adj.* Also **in·tran·si·geant.** Refusing to moderate an extreme position; uncompromising. [French *intransigeant,* from Spanish *los intransigentes,* "the uncompromising" (name of a party of extreme republicans) : *in-,* not, from Latin + *transigir,* to compromise, from Latin *trānsigere,* to come to an understanding.] —**in·tran′si·gence** or **in·tran′si·gen·cy** *n.* —**in·tran′si·gent** *n.* —**in·tran′si·gent·ly** *adv.*

in·tran·si·tive (ĭn-trăn′sĭ-tĭv) *adj.* Not requiring a direct object to complete its meaning: *an intransitive verb.* —*n.* An intransitive verb. —**in·tran′si·tive·ly** *adv.* —**in·tran′si·tive·ness** or **in·tran′si·tiv′i·ty** *n.*

in·tra·state (ĭn′trə-stāt′) *adj.* Within the boundaries of a state.

in·tra·u·ter·ine (ĭn′trə-yōō′tər-ĭn, -tə-rīn′) *adj.* Within the uterus.

in·tra·ve·nous (ĭn′trə-vē′nəs) *adj.* Within a vein or veins. —**in′tra·ve′nous·ly** *adv.*

in·trench (ĭn-trĕnch′) *v.* Var. of **entrench.**

in·trench·ment (ĭn-trĕnch′mənt) *n.* Var. of **entrenchment.**

in·trep·id (ĭn-trĕp′ĭd) *adj.* Resolutely courageous; fearless; bold: *"thinking is but the intrepid effort of the soul to keep the open independence of her sea"* (Melville). —See Syns at **brave.** [French, *intrépide,* from Latin *intrepidus* : *in-,* not + *trepidus,* agitated, alarmed.] —**in′tre·pid′i·ty** (-trə-pĭd′ĭ-tē) or **in·trep′id·ness** *n.* —**in·trep′id·ly** *adv.*

in·tri·ca·cy (ĭn′trĭ-kə-sē) *n., pl.* **-cies. 1.** The condition or quality of being intricate. **2.** Something intricate.

in·tri·cate (ĭn′trĭ-kĭt) *adj.* **1.** Having many complexly arranged elements: *an intricate design.* **2.** Comprehensible only with painstaking effort: *intricate instructions.* —See Syns at **complex** and **elaborate.** [Middle English, from Latin *intricātus,* entangled : *in-,* in + *trīcae,* trifles, troubles, perplexities.] —**in′tri·cate·ly** *adv.* —**in′tri·cate·ness** *n.*

in·trigue (ĭn′trēg′, ĭn-trēg′) *n.* **1.** A concealed maneuver to achieve a secret purpose; an underhand scheme. **2.** Secret plotting or scheming. **3.** A secret love affair. **4.** Mystery; suspense. —See Syns at **plot.** —*v.* (ĭn-trēg′) **-trigued, -trigu·ing.** —*intr.v.* To engage in secret or underhand schemes; to plot. —*tr.v.* **1.** To insinuate (one's way, for

example) by scheming. **2.** To arouse the interest or curiosity of: *Hibernation has long intrigued biologists.* [French, from Italian *intrigo,* from *intrigare,* to perplex, from Latin *intricāre,* to entangle.] —**in·trigu′er** *n.*

Usage: **intrigue.** As a transitive verb meaning to arouse interest or curiosity, the word occurs on all usage levels: *a tale that intrigued us.* It is still resisted by some usage authorities, however, on the grounds that it is overworked and that it is a vague word displacing more precise terms such as *enchant, excite, interest, mystify, puzzle, fascinate,* and *titillate* that could be used instead, depending on the writer's intended meaning.

in·trin·sic (ĭn-trĭn′sĭk) or **in·trin·si·cal** (-sĭ-kəl) *adj.* Belonging to the essential nature of a thing; inherent: *the intrinsic difficulty of mathematics.* [Old French *intrinseque,* inner, from Late Latin *intrinsecus,* inward, from Latin, inwardly, on the inside : *intrā,* within + *secus,* alongside.] —**in·trin′si·cal·ly** *adv.*

intro-. A prefix meaning: **1.** In or into: **introjection. 2.** Inward: **introvert.** [Latin, from *intrō,* to the inside, inwardly.]

in·tro·duce (ĭn′trə-dōōs′, -dyōōs′) *tr.v.* **-duced, -duc·ing. 1.** To present (a person) by name to another or others in order to establish an acquaintance: *introduce a young person to a grownup.* **2.** To provide with a beginning knowledge or first experience of something: *This class will introduce you to tennis.* **3.** To open or begin: *She wrote a preface to introduce her book.* **4. a.** To bring or put in (something new or different); add: *introduce suspense into a story.* **b.** To bring in and establish in a new place or surroundings: *Dandelions were introduced from Europe.* **5.** To propose, create, or bring into use or acceptance for the first time: *introduce faster, safer methods; introduce legislation in Congress.* **6.** To put inside or into something; insert or inject: *introduce a vaccine into the body.* [Latin *introdūcere,* to lead in : *intrō-,* in + *dūcere,* to lead.] —**in′tro·duc′er** *n.*

Syns: **introduce, inaugurate, initiate, institute, launch, originate** *v.* Core meaning: To bring into use, fashion, or practice (*introduce a new product*).

in·tro·duc·tion (ĭn′trə-dŭk′shən) *n.* **1.** The act of introducing. **2.** The fact of being introduced. **3.** A means of presenting one person to another, as a personal presentation or formal letter. **4.** Something recently introduced: *"He loathed a fork; it is a modern introduction which has still scarcely reached common people."* (D.H. Lawrence). **5.** Anything spoken, written, or otherwise presented in introducing, esp.: **a.** A preface, as in a book. **b.** A short preliminary movement in a musical work. **6.** A basic instructive text or course of study.

in·tro·duc·to·ry (ĭn′trə-dŭk′tə-rē) *adj.* Also **in·tro·duc·tive** (-tĭv). Serving to introduce a person, subject, etc.: *an introductory paragraph.* —**in′tro·duc′to·ri·ly** *adv.*

in·tro·spect (ĭn′trə-spĕkt′) *intr.v.* To turn one's thoughts inward; examine one's own feelings. [From Latin *intrōspicere,* to look into : *intrō-,* into + *specere,* to look.]

in·tro·spec·tion (ĭn′trə-spĕk′shən) *n.* The act or practice of looking inward to examine one's own thoughts and feelings; self-examination.

in·tro·spec·tive (ĭn′trə-spĕk′tĭv) *adj.* Having the habit or involving the practice of looking inward to examine one's own thoughts and feelings: *an introspective man; an introspective philosophy.* —**in′tro·spec′tive·ly** *adv.* —**in′tro·spec′tive·ness** *n.*

in·tro·ver·sion (ĭn′trə-vûr′zhən, -shən) *n.* **1.** The act of introverting or the condition of being introverted. **2.** The directing of one's thoughts and interests inward.

in·tro·vert (ĭn′trə-vûrt′) *tr.v.* **1.** To turn or direct inward. **2.** To concentrate (one's interests) upon oneself. **3.** To turn (a tubular organ or part) inward upon itself. —*intr.v.* To exhibit introversion. —*n.* **1.** A person whose thoughts and interests are directed inward. **2.** An anatomic structure, such as the intestine, that is turned inward upon itself. [INTRO- + Latin *vertere,* to turn.]

in·trude (ĭn-trōōd′) *v.* **-trud·ed, -trud·ing.** —*tr.v.* **1.** To put or force (oneself or something) in without being wanted or asked: *Don't intrude your opinions into a factual report.* **2.** *Geol.* To thrust (molten rock) into a stratum. —*intr.v.* To come in rudely or inappropriately; enter as an improper or unwanted element: *"The flute would be intruding here* like a delicate lady at a club smoker." (Leonard Bernstein). [Latin *intrūdere* : *in-*, in + *trūdere*, to thrust.] —**in·trud'er** n.

in·tru·sion (ĭn-trōō'zhən) n. **1.** The act or fact of intruding; imposition. **2.** An inappropriate or unwelcome addition: "*The fields were a timid intrusion on a landscape hardly marked by man*" (Doris Lessing). **3.** *Law.* Illegal entry upon or appropriation of the property of another. **4.** *Geol.* **a.** The forcing of molten rock into an earlier formation. **b.** The intrusive mass so produced.

in·tru·sive (ĭn-trōō'sĭv) adj. **1.** Intruding or tending to intrude: *a rude, intrusive reporter.* **2.** *Geol.* Designating igneous rock forced into another stratum while in molten state; irruptive. —**in·tru'sive·ly** adv. —**in·tru'sive·ness** n.

in·trust (ĭn-trŭst') v. Var. of **entrust**.

in·tu·it (ĭn-tōō'ĭt, -tyōō'-) tr.v. To know or sense by intuition. —*intr.v.* To acquire knowledge by intuition. [Back-formation from **INTUITION**.]

in·tu·i·tion (ĭn'tōō-ĭsh'ən, -tyōō-) n. **1. a.** The faculty of knowing as if by instinct, without conscious reasoning. **b.** A perception based on this faculty; a sense of something not evident or deducible. **2.** A capacity for guessing accurately; sharp insight. [Middle English *intuycion*, contemplation, from Old French *intuition*, from Late Latin, from Latin *intuērī*, to contemplate : *in-*, on, toward + *tuērī*, to look at.] —**in'tu·i'tion·al** adj.

in·tu·i·tive (ĭn-tōō'ĭ-tĭv, -tyōō'-) adj. **1.** Of or based on intuition; intuitional: *intuitive powers; an intuitive understanding.* **2.** Having or skilled in intuition: *an intuitive mind.* —**in·tu'i·tive·ly** adv. —**in·tu'i·tive·ness** n.

in·tu·mes·cence (ĭn'tōō-mĕs'əns, -tyōō-) n. Also **in·tu·mes·cen·cy** (-ən-sē) pl. **-cies.** **1.** The process or condition of swelling. **2.** A swollen organ or part. —**in'tu·mes'cent** adj.

in·u·lin (ĭn'yə-lĭn) n. A carbohydrate, $(C_6H_{10}O_5)_3$ or $(C_6H_{10}O_5)_4$, found in the roots of many plants and used to manufacture fructose. [Prob. from German *Inulin*, from New Latin *Inula*, genus of plants from which inulin is derived.]

in·un·date (ĭn'ən-dāt') tr.v. **-dat·ed, -dat·ing.** **1.** To cover with water, esp. flood water; to flood: *A tidal wave inundated the port city.* **2.** To overwhelm as if with a flood; to swamp: *inundated with requests.* [From Latin *inundāre* : *in-*, in + *undāre*, to flow, from *unda*, wave.] —**in'un·da'tion** n. —**in'un·da'tor** n. —**in·un'da·to·ry** (ĭ-nŭn'də-dôr'ē, -tôr'ē) adj.

in·ure (ĭn-yōōr') tr.v. **-ured, -ur·ing.** To make used to something undesirable; harden: "*though the food became no more palatable, he soon became sufficiently inured to it*" (John Barth). [Middle English *enewren* : *en-* (causative) + *ure*, use, custom, from Old French *uevre*, custom, work, from Latin *opera*, work.] —**in·ure'ment** n.

in vac·u·o (ĭn văk'yōō-ō'). *Latin.* In a vacuum.

in·vade (ĭn-vād') v. **-vad·ed, -vad·ing.** —*tr.v.* **1.** To enter by force in order to conquer or overrun. **2.** To get into and spread harm through: *Viruses invade cells of the body. Locusts may invade our fields.* **3.** To enter in great numbers; overrun: *On winter weekends skiers invade the mountain town.* **4.** To trespass or intrude upon; violate: *invade someone's privacy.* —*intr.v.* To make an invasion. [Middle English *invaden*, from Latin *invādere* : *in-*, in + *vādere*, to go.] —**in·vad'er** n.

in·va·lid[1] (ĭn'və-lĭd) n. A chronically ill or disabled person. —*adj.* **1.** Disabled by illness or injury; sickly or infirm. **2.** Of or for invalids. —*tr.v.* **1.** To make an invalid of; disable physically. **2.** *Brit.* To release or exempt from duty because of ill health. [Latin *invalidus*, weak, ineffective : *in-*, not + *validus*, strong.]

in·val·id[2] (ĭn-văl'ĭd) adj. **1.** Not legally valid; not in effect: *an invalid passport.* **2.** Falsely based or reasoned; unjustified: *an invalid conclusion.* —**in·val'id·ly** adv.

in·val·i·date (ĭn-văl'ĭ-dāt') tr.v. **-dat·ed, -dat·ing.** To make void; render invalid. —**in·val'i·da'tion** n. —**in·val'i·da'tor** n.

in·va·lid·i·ty (ĭn'və-lĭd'ĭ-tē) n. The condition or quality of being invalid; lack of validity.

in·val·u·a·ble (ĭn-văl'yōō-ə-bəl) adj. **1.** Having great value; priceless: *invaluable paintings.* **2.** Indispensable; much appreciated: *an invaluable service.* —See Syns at **valuable**. —**in·val'u·a·bly** adv.

in·var·i·a·ble (ĭn-vâr'ē-ə-bəl) adj. Not changing or subject to change; constant. —See Syns at **inflexible**. —**in·var'i·a·bil'i·ty** or **in·var'i·a·ble·ness** n. —**in·var'i·a·bly** adv.

in·va·sion (ĭn-vā'zhən) n. **1.** The act of invading or the condition of being invaded; esp., entrance by force: *the invasion of Italy by the Allies.* **2.** The onset of something injurious or harmful, as of a disease. **3.** Any intrusion or encroachment; infringement. —*modifier: an invasion fleet.* [Middle English *invasioune*, from Old French *invasion*, from Latin *invādere*, to invade.]

in·vec·tive (ĭn-vĕk'tĭv) n. Sharp, harsh, insulting words used to attack; violent denunciation or abuse. [Middle English *invectiff*, abusive, vituperative, from Old French *invectif*, from Late Latin *invectīvus* (*ōrātiō*), "abusive (speech)," from Latin *invehere*, to attack.]

in·veigh (ĭn-vā') intr.v. To speak out in angry disapproval; protest vehemently: *The preacher inveighed against modern immorality.* [Latin *invehī*, from *invehere*, to enter, attack : *in-*, in + *vehere*, to carry.] —**in·veigh'er** n.

in·vei·gle (ĭn-vē'gəl, -vā'-) tr.v. **-gled, -gling.** **1.** To lead astray or win over by flattering or deceiving: *inveigled naive investors into buying worthless stock.* **2.** To obtain by artful deceiving or flattery. [Old French *aveugler*, to blind, ult. from Medieval Latin *ab oculīs*, "without eyes."] —**in·vei'gle·ment** n. —**in·vei'gler** n.

in·vent (ĭn-vĕnt') tr.v. **1.** To conceive of or devise first; originate. **2.** To fabricate; make up: *invent an excuse.* [Middle English *inventen*, to come upon, find, from Latin *invenīre* : *in-*, on + *venīre*, to come.] —**in·vent'i·ble** adj. —**in·ven'tor** n.

in·ven·tion (ĭn-vĕn'shən) n. **1.** The act or process of inventing: *the invention of the printing press.* **2.** A new device or process developed from study and experimentation. **3.** Something made up or untrue; a falsehood. **4.** Skill in inventing; inventiveness: "*very unlearned, neither savouring of poetry, wit, nor invention*" (Shakespeare). **5.** A short musical piece developing a single theme.

in·ven·tive (ĭn-vĕn'tĭv) adj. **1.** Of or characterized by invention. **2.** Adept or skillful at inventing; creative; ingenious. —See Syns at **fresh**. —**in·ven'tive·ly** adv. —**in·ven'tive·ness** n.

in·ven·to·ry (ĭn'vən-tôr'ē, -tōr'ē) n., pl. **-ries.** **1.** A detailed list of things in one's view or possession, esp. a periodic survey of all goods and materials in stock. **2.** The process of making such a survey: *taking inventory.* **3.** The items so listed. **4.** The supply of goods on hand; stock. —*tr.v.* **-ried, -ry·ing.** **1.** To make an inventory of. **2.** To include in an inventory. [Medieval Latin *inventōrium*, list, from Latin *invenīre*, to come upon, find.] —**in·ven·to'ri·al** adj. —**in·ven·to'ri·al·ly** adv.

in·verse (ĭn-vûrs', ĭn'vûrs') adj. **1.** Reversed in order, nature, or effect: *CBA is ABC in inverse order.* **2.** Turned upside down; inverted. —*n.* **1.** Something opposite in effect or character: *Division is the inverse of multiplication.* **2.** *Math.* An element x^* in a set S related to a designated element x in S such that $x^* \cdot x = x \cdot x^* = I$, where · is a binary operation defined in S and I is the identity element; esp.: **a.** The reciprocal of a designated quantity. **b.** The negative of a designated quantity. —**in·verse'ly** adv.

in·ver·sion (ĭn-vûr'zhən, -shən) n. **1.** The act of inverting or the condition of being inverted. **2.** An interchange of position, esp. of adjacent objects in a sequence. **3.** A change in normal word order, as the placing of a verb before its subject. **4.** A weather condition in which the air temperature increases with increasing altitude, holding surface air down along with its pollutants.

in·vert (ĭn-vûrt') tr.v. **1.** To turn inside out or upside down: *Invert the jar and let it stand in a pan of water.* **2.** To reverse the position, order, or condition of. —*intr.v.* To be inverted or capable of being inverted. —See Syns at **reverse**. [Latin *invertere*, to turn inside out or upside down : *in-*, in, inward + *vertere*, to turn.] —**in·vert'i·ble** adj.

in·ver·te·brate (ĭn-vûr'tə-brĭt, -brāt') adj. Having no backbone or spinal column; not vertebrate. —*n.* An invertebrate animal.

in·vert·er (ĭn-vûr'tər) n. **1.** Someone or something that inverts. **2.** A device used to convert direct current into alternating current.

in·vest (ĭn-vĕst′) *tr.v.* **1.** To commit (money or capital) in order to gain profit or interest, as by purchasing property, securities, or bonds: *She invested her savings in real estate.* **2.** To spend or utilize (time, money, or effort) for future advantage or benefit: *They invested much energy in their vegetable garden.* **3.** To entrust with a right or power: *invested with the authority to perform marriages.* **4.** To install in office with a ceremony: *invest a new bishop.* **5.** To provide with some enveloping or pervasive quality: *"A charm invests a face/Imperfectly beheld"* (Emily Dickinson). **6.** To cover completely; envelop; shroud. **7.** To surround with hostile troops or ships; besiege. —*intr.v.* To invest money; make an investment: *investing in bonds.* [Old French *investir,* from Medieval Latin *investīre,* from Latin, to clothe in, surround : *in-,* in + *vestīre,* to clothe, from *vestis,* clothes.] —**in·ves′tor** *n.*

in·ves·ti·gate (ĭn-vĕs′tĭ-gāt′) *v.* **-gat·ed, -gat·ing.** —*tr.v.* To look into carefully in a search for facts or the truth; examine systematically. —*intr.v.* To make an investigation. [From Latin *investīgāre,* to trace out, search into : *in-,* in + *vestīgāre,* to trace, track, from *vestīgium,* trace, footprint, vestige.] —**in·ves′ti·ga′tive** or **in·ves′ti·ga·to·ry** (-gə-tôr′ē, -tôr′ē) *adj.*

in·ves·ti·ga·tion (ĭn-vĕs′tĭ-gā′shən) *n.* The act or process or an example of investigating; inquiry.

in·ves·ti·ga·tor (ĭn-vĕs′tĭ-gā′tər) *n.* **1.** Someone who investigates. **2.** A detective. —**in·ves′ti·ga·to′ri·al** (-gə-tôr′ē-əl, -tōr′-) *adj.*

in·ves·ti·ture (ĭn-vĕs′tə-chŏŏr′, -chər) *n.* The act or formal ceremony of conferring upon someone the authority and symbols of a high office. [Middle English, from Medieval Latin *investītūra,* from *investīre,* to invest.]

in·vest·ment (ĭn-vĕst′mənt) *n.* **1.** The act of investing or the condition of being invested. **2.** An amount invested: *interest earned on an investment.* **3.** Property or another possession acquired for future income or benefit. **4.** Investiture.

in·vet·er·ate (ĭn-vĕt′ər-ĭt) *adj.* **1.** Fixed in a habit, custom, or practice; habitual; confirmed: *an inveterate reader.* **2.** Firmly established by having existed for a long time; long-standing; deep-rooted: *inveterate prejudice.* [Latin *inveterātus,* past part. of *inveterāre,* to render old : *in-* (causative) + *vetus,* old.] —**in·vet′er·a·cy** (-ər-ə-sē) or **in·vet′er·ate·ness** *n.* —**in·vet′er·ate·ly** *adv.*

in·vid·i·ous (ĭn-vĭd′ē-əs) *adj.* Tending to stir up bad feeling, envy, or resentment: *invidious comparisons of the three children.* [Latin *invidiōsus,* envious, hostile, from *invidia,* envy.] —**in·vid′i·ous·ly** *adv.* —**in·vid′i·ous·ness** *n.*

in·vig·o·rate (ĭn-vĭg′ə-rāt′) *tr.v.* **-rat·ed, -rat·ing.** To give vigor, strength, or vitality to: *"A few whiffs of the raw, strong scent of phlox invigorated her."* (D.H. Lawrence). —**in·vig′o·rat′ing·ly** *adv.* —**in·vig′o·ra′tion** *n.* —**in·vig′o·ra′tive** *adj.* —**in·vig′o·ra′tor** *n.*

in·vin·ci·ble (ĭn-vĭn′sə-bəl) *adj.* Too strong or great to be defeated or overcome; unconquerable: *an invincible army.* [Middle English, from Latin *invincibilis* : *in-,* not + *vincibilis,* able to be defeated.] —**in·vin′ci·bil′i·ty** or **in·vin′ci·ble·ness** *n.* —**in·vin′ci·bly** *adv.*

in·vi·o·la·ble (ĭn-vī′ə-lə-bəl) *adj.* **1.** Safe from or secured against violation or profanation; kept sacred: *an inviolable sanctuary.* **2.** Incapable of being attacked or seized; impregnable. —**in·vi′o·la·bil′i·ty** or **in·vi′o·la·ble·ness** *n.* —**in·vi′o·la·bly** *adv.*

in·vi·o·late (ĭn-vī′ə-lĭt) *adj.* Not violated; intact: *She kept her honor inviolate.* —**in·vi′o·late·ly** *adv.* —**in·vi′o·late·ness** *n.*

in·vis·i·ble (ĭn-vĭz′ə-bəl) *adj.* **1.** Incapable of being seen; not visible: *Air is odorless and invisible.* **2.** Not accessible to view; hidden: *an invisible camera.* **3.** Not easily noticed or detected; inconspicuous: *"the poor are politically invisible"* (Michael Harrington). —**in·vis′i·bil′i·ty** or **in·vis′i·ble·ness** *n.* —**in·vis′i·bly** *adv.*

in·vi·ta·tion (ĭn′vĭ-tā′shən) *n.* **1.** The act of inviting. **2.** A spoken or written request for a person's presence or participation. **3.** An allurement or enticement.

in·vite (ĭn-vīt′) *tr.v.* **-vit·ed, -vit·ing.** **1.** To ask (a person or persons) to come somewhere to do something: *invite guests to a wedding.* **2.** To ask formally: *The children invited the mayor to talk to their class.* **3.** To tend to bring on; provoke: *To drive recklessly is to invite disaster.* **4.** To tempt, lure, or entice: *The sun invites one to be out in the open air.* **5.** To welcome; encourage: *invite questions.* —*n.* (ĭn′vīt′). *Informal.* An invitation. [Old French *inviter,* from Latin *invītāre.*]

in·vit·ing (ĭn-vī′tĭng) *adj.* Attractive; tempting: *an inviting dessert.* —**in·vit′ing·ly** *adv.* —**in·vit′ing·ness** *n.*

in·vo·ca·tion (ĭn′və-kā′shən) *n.* **1.** The act of invoking, esp. an appeal to a higher power for assistance. **2.** A prayer or other formula used in invoking, as at the opening of a religious service. **3. a.** A conjuring or calling up of a spirit by incantation. **b.** The incantation used in conjuring. [Middle English, from Old French, from Latin *invocātiō,* from *invocāre,* to invoke.]

in·voice (ĭn′vois′) *n.* **1.** A detailed list of goods shipped or services rendered, with an account of all costs; a bill. **2.** The goods or services so itemized. —*tr.v.* **-voiced, -voic·ing.** To make an invoice of; to bill. [Earlier *invoyes,* pl. of *invoy,* invoice, from Old French *envoy,* a sending, shipment of goods.]

in·voke (ĭn-vōk′) *tr.v.* **-voked, -vok·ing.** **1.** To call upon (a higher power) for help, support, or inspiration: *"Stretching out her hands she had the air of a Greek woman who invoked a deity"* (Ford Madox Ford). **2.** To appeal to; to petition. **3.** To call for earnestly: *invoke divine blessing.* **4.** To call up (a spirit) with magic words or spells; conjure. **5.** To resort to; use or apply: *The President invoked his veto power.* [Old French *invoquer,* from Latin *invocāre* : *in-,* in, on + *vocāre,* to call.] —**in·vok′er** *n.*

in·vo·lu·cre (ĭn′və-lōō′kər) *n.* A whorl or series of leaflike scales or bracts beneath or around a flower or flower cluster. [From Latin *involucrum,* wrapper, case, envelope, from *involvere,* to enwrap, involve.] —**in′vo·lu′cral** *adj.*

in·vol·un·tar·y (ĭn-vŏl′ən-tĕr′ē) *adj.* **1.** Not performed willingly or deliberately: *an involuntary service.* **2.** Not subject to control: *an involuntary twitch.* —**in·vol′un·tar′i·ly** (-târ′ə-lē) *adv.* —**in·vol′un·tar′i·ness** *n.*

Syns: **involuntary, automatic, instinctive** *adj. Core meaning:* Not involving or based on conscious choice (*an involuntary exclamation of pain*). INVOLUNTARY refers to what is not subject to the control of the will (*involuntary muscles*). What is AUTOMATIC is done or produced by the body without conscious control or awareness (*automatic reflexes*). INSTINCTIVE actions are directed by unlearned inner drives (*the birds' instinctive seasonal migrations*).

in·vo·lute (ĭn′və-lōōt′) *adj.* Also **in·vo·lut·ed** (-lōō′tĭd). **1.** Intricate; complex. **2.** *Bot.* Having the margins rolled inward. **3.** Having whorls that obscure the axis or other volutions: *an involute cowry shell.* —*n. Math.* **1.** The locus of a fixed point on a taut, inextensible string as it unwinds from a fixed plane curve. **2.** The locus of any point on a tangent line as it rolls but does not slide around a fixed curve. [Latin *involutus,* past part. of *involvere,* to enwrap, involve.]

in·vo·lu·tion (ĭn′və-lōō′shən) *n.* **1.** The act of involving or the condition of being involved. **2.** Anything that is complex or involved. **3.** A complicated grammatical construction. **4.** *Math.* The multiplying of a quantity by itself a specified number of times; raising to a power. [Latin *involūtiō,* from *involvere,* to involve.]

in·volve (ĭn-vŏlv′) *tr.v.* **-volved, -volv·ing.** **1.** To contain or include as a part: *The plot of the play involves a doctor, his patients, and a murder.* **2.** To have as a necessary feature or consequence: *The project will involve hard work.* **3.** To draw in; mix up; implicate: *involved in a scandal.* **4.** To occupy or engross completely; absorb. **5.** To make complex or intricate; complicate: *involved his argument with obscure detail.* **6.** To wrap; envelop: *a castle involved in mist.* **7.** *Math.* To raise (a number) to a specified degree. [Middle English *involven,* from Latin *involvere,* to enwrap : *in-,* in + *volvere,* to roll, turn.] —**in·volve′ment** *n.* —**in·volv′er** *n.*

in·volved (ĭn-vŏlvd′) *adj.* **1.** Complicated; intricate: *a long, involved sentence.* **2.** Confused; tangled. —See Syns at **complex.**

in·vul·ner·a·ble (ĭn-vŭl′nər-ə-bəl) *adj.* **1.** Immune to attack; impregnable: *an invulnerable position.* **2.** Incapable of being damaged, injured, or wounded. [Latin *invulnerābilis*

| ă pat | ā pay | â care | ä father | ĕ pet | ē be | hw which | ĭ pit | ī tie | î pier | ŏ pot | ō toe | ô paw, for | oi noise |
| ŏŏ took | ōō boot | ou out | th thin | *th* this | ŭ cut | û urge | zh vision | ə about, item, edible, gallop, circus |

: in-, not + *vulnerāre*, to wound.] **—in·vul′ner·a·bil′i·ty** or **in·vul′ner·a·ble·ness** *n.* **—in·vul′ner·a·bly** *adv.*

in·ward (ĭn′wərd) *adj.* **1.** Located inside; inner: *inward bleeding.* **2.** Directed or moving toward the interior: *an inward pull on the door.* **3.** Existing in thought or mind. —*adv.* Also **in·wards.** **1.** Toward the inside or center. **2.** Toward the mind or the self: *thoughts turned inward.* —*n.* An inner or central part. [Middle English, from Old English *inweard.*]

in·ward·ly (ĭn′wərd-lē) *adv.* **1.** On or in the inside; within. **2.** Privately; to oneself: *"kept his lips closed with the expression of a man inwardly laughing"* (T.S. Stribling).

in·wards (ĭn′sərdz) *adv.* Var. of **inward.**

in·weave (ĭn-wēv′) *tr.v.* **-wove** (-wōv′) or **-weaved, -wo·ven** (-wō′vən), **-weav·ing.** To weave into a fabric or design.

iod-. Var. of **iodo-.**

i·o·dide (ī′ə-dīd′) *n.* A binary compound of iodine with a more electropositive atom or group. [IOD(O)- + -IDE.]

i·o·dine (ī′ə-dīn′, -dĭn, -dēn′) *n. Symbol* **I** **1.** A lustrous, grayish-black, corrosive, poisonous halogen element having radioactive isotopes, esp. I 131, used as tracers and in thyroid disease diagnosis and therapy, and compounds used as germicides, antiseptics, and dyes. Atomic number 53; atomic weight 126.9044; melting point 113.5°C; boiling point 184.35°C; specific gravity (solid, 20°C) 4.93; valences 1, 3, 5, 7. **2.** A tincture of iodine and sodium iodide, NaI, or potassium iodide, KI, used as an antiseptic for wounds. [French *iode,* from Greek *iōdēs, ioeidēs,* violet-colored + -INE.]

i·o·dize (ī′ə-dīz′) *tr.v.* **-dized, -diz·ing.** To treat or combine with iodine or an iodide. [IOD(O)- + -IZE.]

iodo- or **iod-.** A prefix meaning iodine: **iodide.** [From French *iode,* iodine.]

i·o·do·form (ī-ō′də-fôrm′, ī-ŏd′ə-) *n.* A yellowish iodine compound, CHI₃, used as an antiseptic. [IODO- + FORM(YL).]

i·on (ī′ən, ī′ŏn′) *n.* An atom, group of atoms, or molecule that has acquired or is regarded as having acquired a net electric charge by gaining electrons in or losing electrons from an initially electrically neutral configuration. [From Greek *ion,* something that goes (from the passage of ions to either of the electrodes in electrolysis), from *ienai,* to go.]

-ion. A suffix meaning: **1.** An act or process or the outcome of an act or process: **invention.** **2.** A state of being: **cohesion.** [Middle English *-io(u)n,* from Old French *-ion,* from Latin *-iō.*]

i·on·ic (ī-ŏn′ĭk) *adj.* Of, containing, or involving ions.

I·on·ic (ī-ŏn′ĭk) *adj.* Of or designating an order of classical Greek architecture characterized by two opposed volutes or scroll-shaped forms at the tops of the columns.

i·on·i·za·tion (ī′ə-nĭ-zā′shən) *n.* **1.** The formation of one or more ions by the addition of electrons to or the removal of electrons from an electrically neutral atomic or molecular configuration by heat, electrical discharge, radiation, or chemical reaction. **2.** The condition of being ionized.

ionization chamber. A gas-filled enclosure fitted with electrodes between which electric current flows upon ionization of the gas by incident radiation, the electrodes being maintained at a potential difference just sufficient to collect ions thus produced without causing further ionization.

i·on·ize (ī′ə-nīz′) *v.* **-ized, -iz·ing.** —*tr.v.* To convert totally or partially into ions. —*intr.v.* To become converted totally or partially into ions.

i·on·o·sphere (ī-ŏn′ə-sfîr′) *n.* An electrically conducting set of layers around the earth's atmosphere, extending from altitudes of approx. 30 miles to more than 250 miles, caused by ionization of rarefied atmospheric gases by incident solar radiation. [ION + -SPHERE.]

i·o·ta (ī-ō′tə) *n.* **1.** The ninth letter in the Greek alphabet, written I, i. In English it is represented as I, i. **2.** A very small amount; the least bit: *There is not one iota of truth in that gossip.* [Greek *iōta,* of Semitic orig.]

IOU (ī′ō-yōō′) *n., pl.* **IOU's** or **IOUs.** A promise to pay a debt. [Short for *I owe you.*]

-ious. A suffix meaning characterized by or full of: **sagacious.** [Middle English, partly from Latin *-ius* and partly from Old French *-ieus, -ieux,* from Latin *-iōsus.*]

ip·so fac·to (ĭp′sō făk′tō). *Latin.* By the fact itself; by that very fact: *An alien, ipso facto, has no right to a U.S. passport.*

Ir The symbol for the element iridium.

I·ra·ni·an (ĭ-rā′nē-ən, -rä′-, -răn′ē-ən) *adj.* Of Iran, its inhabitants, or their language. —*n.* **1.** A native or inhabitant of Iran. **2.** A group of languages including Persian, Kurdish, and Pashto, spoken principally in Iran, Afghanistan, and westernmost Pakistan and forming a subbranch of the Indo-Iranian branch of the Indo-European language family.

i·ras·ci·ble (ĭ-răs′ə-bəl, ī-răs′-) *adj.* Prone to outbursts of temper; easily angered. —See Syns at **irritable.** [Old French, from Late Latin *īrāscibilis,* from Latin *īrāscī,* to get angry, from *īra,* anger, ire.] **—i·ras′ci·bil′i·ty** or **i·ras′ci·ble·ness** *n.* **—i·ras′ci·bly** *adv.*

i·rate (ī-rāt′, ī′rāt′) *adj.* **1.** Angry; enraged. **2.** Characterized or occasioned by anger: *an irate phone call.* —See Syns at **angry.** [Latin *īrātus,* from *īra,* anger, ire.] **—i·rate′ly** *adv.*

ire (īr) *n.* Wrath; anger. [Middle English, from Old French, from Latin *īra,* anger.]

ire·ful (īr′fəl) *adj.* Full of ire; angry. **—ire′ful·ly** *adv.* **—ire′ful·ness** *n.*

i·ri·des (ī′rĭ-dēz′, ĭr′ĭ-) *n.* A plural of **iris.**

ir·i·des·cence (ĭr′ĭ-dĕs′əns) *n.* The condition or quality of being iridescent; a display of rainbowlike colors.

ir·i·des·cent (ĭr′ĭ-dĕs′ənt) *adj.* Producing a display of lustrous, rainbowlike colors: *butterflies with iridescent wings.* [Latin *īris,* rainbow, iris + -ESCENT.]

i·rid·ic (ī-rĭd′ĭk, ĭ-rĭd′-) *adj.* Of the iris of the eye.

i·rid·i·um (ī-rĭd′ē-əm, ĭ-rĭd′-) *n. Symbol* **Ir** A very hard and brittle, exceptionally corrosion-resistant whitish-yellow metallic element occurring in platinum ores and used principally to harden platinum and in high-temperature materials, electrical contacts, and wear-resistant bearings. Atomic number 77; atomic weight 192.2; melting point 2,410°C; boiling point 4,527°C; specific gravity 22.42 (17°C); valences 3, 4. [From Latin *īris,* rainbow, iris (from the variety of colors it gives in solution).]

i·ris (ī′rĭs) *n., pl.* **i·ris·es** or **i·ri·des** (ī′rĭ-dēz′, ĭr′ĭ-). **1.** The pigmented, round, contractile membrane of the eye, situated between the cornea and lens and perforated by the pupil. **2.** Any of numerous plants of the genus *Iris,* with narrow sword-shaped leaves and showy, variously colored flowers. **3.** A rainbow or rainbowlike display of colors. [Middle English, rainbow, kind of prismatic crystal, from Latin *īris,* from Greek *iris,* rainbow, iris of the eye.]

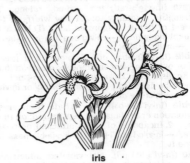

iris

I·rish (ī′rĭsh) *adj.* Of or relating to Ireland, its people, or their language. —*n.* **1. the Irish** (used with a pl. verb). The inhabitants of Ireland and their descendants. **2. Irish Gaelic. 3.** The English spoken in Ireland; Irish English. **4.** *Informal.* Fieriness of temper or passion; high spirit.

Irish Gaelic. The Celtic language of Ireland. Also called **Erse** and **Irish.**

I·rish·ism (ī′rĭ-shĭz′əm) *n.* An Irish expression or custom.

I·rish·man (ī′rĭsh-mən) *n.* A man of Irish birth or descent.

Irish moss. An edible North Atlantic seaweed, *Chondrus crispus,* that yields a mucilaginous substance used medicinally and in preparing jellies.

Irish setter. A setter having a silky reddish-brown coat.

ă pat   ā pay   â care   ä father   ĕ pet   ē be   hw which   ĭ pit   ī tie   î pier   ŏ pot   ō toe   ô paw, for   oi noise
ŏŏ took   ōŏ boot   ou out   th thin   th this   ŭ cut   û urge   zh vision   ə about, item, edible, gallop, circus

I·rish·wom·an (ī'rĭsh-wo͝om'ən) *n.* A woman of Irish birth or descent.

irk (ûrk) *tr.v.* To annoy; irritate: *Nothing irks him so much as to be kept waiting.* —See Syns at **annoy.** [Middle English *irken.*]

irk·some (ûrk'səm) *adj.* Causing annoyance or bother; tedious: *irksome restrictions.* —**irk'some·ly** *adv.* —**irk'some·ness** *n.*

i·ron (ī'ərn) *n.* **1.** *Symbol* **Fe** A silvery-white, lustrous, malleable, ductile, magnetic or magnetizable metallic element occurring abundantly in combined forms, notably in hematite, limonite, magnetite, and taconite and used alloyed in a wide range of important structural materials. Atomic number 26; atomic weight 55.847; melting point 1,535°C; boiling point 3,000°C; specific gravity 7.874 (20°C); valences 2, 3, 4, 6. **2.** Great hardness or strength; firmness: *a will of iron.* **3.** An implement made of iron alloy or similar metal, esp. a bar heated for use in branding, curling hair, or cauterizing. **4.** A golf club with a metal head. **5.** A metal appliance with a handle and a weighted flat bottom, used when heated to press wrinkles from fabric. **6.** A harpoon. **7. irons.** Fetters; shackles: *put a prisoner in irons.* —**modifier:** *an iron horseshoe.* —*adj.* **1.** Extremely hard and strong: *an iron fist.* **2.** Hardy; robust: *an iron constitution.* **3.** Inflexible; unyielding: *an iron will.* —*tr.v.* **1.** To press and smooth with a heated iron. **2.** To remove (creases) by pressing. —*intr.v.* To iron clothes. —*phrasal verb.* **iron out.** To discuss and settle; work out: *iron out our problems.* —*idiom.* **strike while the iron is hot.** To seize a favorable opportunity for action. [Middle English *iren,* from Old English *īsern.*]

i·ron·bound (ī'ərn-bound') *adj.* **1.** Bound with iron. **2.** Rigid and unyielding. **3.** Bound with rocks and cliffs: *an ironbound coast.* —See Syns at **inflexible.**

i·ron·clad (ī'ərn-klăd') *adj.* **1.** Covered with iron plates for protection: *an ironclad battleship.* **2.** Rigid: *an ironclad rule.* —See Syns at **inflexible.** —*n.* A 19th-cent. warship having sides armored with metal plates.

i·ron·ic (ī-rŏn'ĭk) or **i·ron·i·cal** (-ĭ-kəl) *adj.* **1.** Characterized by or showing irony: *an ironic prize for the slowest runner.* **2.** Given to the use of irony: *an ironic observer of human folly.* —**i·ron'i·cal·ly** *adv.* —**i·ron'i·cal·ness** *n.*

i·ron·ing (ī'ər-nĭng) *n.* **1.** The pressing of clothes with a heated iron. **2.** Clothing to be ironed.

iron lung. A tank in which the entire body except the head is enclosed and by means of which pressure is regularly increased and decreased to provide artificial respiration.

iron ore. Any of various minerals, such as hematite or magnetite, from which iron can be commercially extracted.

i·ron·stone (ī'ərn-stōn') *n.* **1.** One of several kinds of iron ore with admixtures of silica and clay. **2.** A hard white pottery used for dishes.

i·ron·work (ī'ərn-wûrk') *n.* Work in iron, as gratings and rails.

i·ron·works (ī'ərn-wûrks') *n.* (used with a sing. verb). A building or establishment where iron is smelted or where heavy iron products are made.

i·ro·ny (ī'rə-nē) *n., pl.* **-nies. 1. a.** The humorous or mocking use of words to convey the opposite of their literal meaning: *Using irony, Mark Antony called Caesar's assassins honorable men.* **b.** An expression or utterance marked by such a deliberate contrast between apparent and intended meaning. **2. a.** Incongruity between what might be expected and what actually occurs: *"Hyde noted the irony of Ireland's copying the nation she most hated."* (Richard Kain). **b.** An occurrence, result, or circumstance notable for such incongruity. [Latin *īrōnia,* from Greek *eirōneia,* dissembling, feigned ignorance, from *eirōn,* dissembler, from *eirein,* to say.]

Ir·o·quoi·an (ĭr'ə-kwoi'ən) *n.* **1.** A family of North American Indian languages spoken in Canada and eastern United States by such tribes as the Iroquois, Cherokee, Conestoga, Erie, and Wyandot. **2.** A member of a tribe using a language of this family. —**Ir'o·quoi'an** *adj.*

ir·ra·di·ant (ĭ-rā'dē-ənt) *adj.* Sending forth radiant light. [Latin *irradiāns,* pres. part. of *irradiāre,* to irradiate.] —**ir·ra'di·ance** or **ir·ra'di·an·cy** *n.*

ir·ra·di·ate (ĭ-rā'dē-āt') *tr.v.* **-at·ed, -at·ing. 1.** To expose to or treat with light or other radiation. **2.** To fill with or as if with light; brighten; illuminate: *A smile irradiated her face.* **3.** To send out in or as if in rays; radiate. [From Latin *irradiāre,* to shine forth : *in-,* toward + *radiāre,* to shine, radiate.] —**ir·ra'di·a'tion** *n.* —**ir·ra'di·a'tive** *adj.* —**ir·ra'di·a'tor** *n.*

ir·ra·tion·al (ĭ-răsh'ə-nəl) *adj.* **1.** Not capable of reasoning or thinking clearly. **2.** Not based on or guided by reason; unreasonable; illogical: *an irrational fear.* **3.** *Math.* Incapable of being expressed as an integer or a quotient of integers. —**ir·ra'tion·al·ly** *adv.* —**ir·ra'tion·al·ness** *n.*

ir·ra·tion·al·i·ty (ĭ-răsh'ə-năl'ĭ-tē) *n., pl.* **-ties. 1.** The condition or quality of being irrational. **2.** An irrational idea or action.

irrational number. A member of the set of real numbers that is not a member of the set of rational numbers.

ir·rec·on·cil·a·ble (ĭ-rĕk'ən-sī'lə-bəl, ĭ-rĕk'ən-sī'-) *adj.* **1.** Not capable of being reconciled: *irreconcilable enemies.* **2.** Incompatible; incongruous. —*n.* A person who will not compromise, adjust, or submit. —**ir·rec'on·cil'a·bil'i·ty** *n.* —**ir·rec'on·cil'a·bly** *adv.*

ir·re·duc·i·ble (ĭr'ĭ-doo'sə-bəl, -dyoo'-) *adj.* Incapable of being reduced to a simpler or smaller form or amount: *an irreducible fraction.* —**ir're·duc'i·bil'i·ty** or **ir're·duc'i·ble·ness** *n.* —**ir're·duc'i·bly** *adv.*

ir·ref·u·ta·ble (ĭ-rĕf'yə-tə-bəl, ĭr'ĭ-fyoo'tə-bəl) *adj.* Incapable of being refuted or disproved: *irrefutable arguments.* —**ir·ref'u·ta·bil'i·ty** *n.* —**ir·ref'u·ta·bly** *adv.*

ir·reg·u·lar (ĭ-rĕg'yə-lər) *adj.* **1.** Not standard or uniform, as in shape, size, length, or arrangement: *an irregular coastline; irregular splotches of color.* **2.** Not following a set pattern or regular schedule: *irregular rhythm.* **3.** Unusual or improper: *a highly irregular procedure.* **4.** *Gram.* Not following the standard pattern of inflected forms; for example, *do* is an irregular verb, with irregular principal parts. **5.** Not up to standard because of flaws or imperfections: *irregular merchandise.* **6.** Not belonging to a permanent, organized military force: *irregular troops.* —*n.* **1.** A person or thing that is irregular. **2.** A soldier, such as a guerrilla, who is not a member of a regular military force. —**ir·reg'u·lar·ly** *adv.*

ir·reg·u·lar·i·ty (ĭ-rĕg'yə-lăr'ĭ-tē) *n., pl.* **-ties. 1.** The quality or condition of being irregular. **2.** An irregular feature, place, practice, etc.: *irregularities in the earth's surface.*

ir·rel·e·vance (ĭ-rĕl'ə-vəns) *n.* Also **ir·rel·e·van·cy** (-vən-sē) *pl.* **-cies. 1.** The quality or condition of being irrelevant. **2.** Something that is irrelevant.

ir·rel·e·vant (ĭ-rĕl'ə-vənt) *adj.* Having no relation to the subject or situation; not relevant or applicable: *an irrelevant question.* —**ir·rel'e·vant·ly** *adv.*

    Syns: irrelevant, extraneous, immaterial, inapplicable *adj.* Core meaning: Not relating to the subject at hand (*avoided irrelevant digressions*).

ir·re·li·gious (ĭr'ĭ-lĭj'əs) *adj.* Hostile or indifferent to religion. —**ir're·li'gious·ly** *adv.* —**ir're·li'gious·ness** *n.*

ir·re·me·di·a·ble (ĭr'ĭ-mē'dē-ə-bəl) *adj.* Impossible to remedy, correct, or repair; incurable. —**ir're·me'di·a·bly** *adv.*

ir·re·mis·si·ble (ĭr'ĭ-mĭs'ə-bəl) *adj.* Not remissible; unpardonable. —**ir're·mis'si·bil'i·ty** *n.* —**ir're·mis'si·bly** *adv.*

ir·rep·a·ra·ble (ĭ-rĕp'ər-ə-bəl) *adj.* Incapable of being repaired, remedied, or set right; beyond repair: *irreparable harm.* —**ir·rep'a·ra·bil'i·ty** or **ir·rep'a·ra·ble·ness** *n.* —**ir·rep'a·ra·bly** *adv.*

ir·re·place·a·ble (ĭr'ĭ-plā'sə-bəl) *adj.* Incapable of being replaced: *irreplaceable natural resources.*

ir·re·press·i·ble (ĭr'ĭ-prĕs'ə-bəl) *adj.* Impossible to hold back, control, or restrain: *irrepressible laughter.* —**ir're·press'i·bil'i·ty** or **ir're·press'i·ble·ness** *n.* —**ir're·press'i·bly** *adv.*

ir·re·proach·a·ble (ĭr'ĭ-prō'chə-bəl) *adj.* Beyond reproach; faultless: *irreproachable manners.* —**ir're·proach'a·ble·ness** *n.* —**ir're·proach'a·bly** *adv.*

ir·re·sist·i·ble (ĭr'ĭ-zĭs'tə-bəl) *adj.* **1.** Too strong, powerful, or compelling to be resisted: *irresistible forces; an irresistible impulse.* **2.** Having an overpowering appeal: *irresistible beauty.* —**ir're·sist'i·bil'i·ty** or **ir're·sist'i·ble·ness** *n.* —**ir're·sist'i·bly** *adv.*

ă pat	ā pay	â care	ä father	ĕ pet	ē be	hw which		ĭ pit	ī tie	î pier	ŏ pot	ō toe	ô paw, for	oi noise
oo took	oo boot	ou out	th thin	th this	ŭ cut		û urge	zh vision	ə about, item, edible, gallop, circus

ir·res·o·lute (ĭ-rĕz′ə-lōōt′) adj. Undecided or showing uncertainty about what to do; indecisive: standing irresolute on the road; a good deal of irresolute discussion. —**ir′res′o·lute′ly** adv. —**ir·res′o·lute′ness** or **ir·res′o·lu′tion** n.

ir·re·spec·tive (ĭr′ĭ-spĕk′tĭv) adj. —**irrespective of.** Regardless of: equal rights for all, irrespective of class or race.
Usage: irrespective. The phrase is irrespective of (regardless of), not irrespectively of.

ir·re·spon·si·ble (ĭr′ĭ-spŏn′sə-bəl) adj. 1. Not liable to be called to account for one's actions. 2. Not mentally or financially fit to assume responsibility. 3. Showing no sense of responsibility; undependable; untrustworthy: too irresponsible to be allowed to drive a car. —**ir′re·spon′si·bil′i·ty** or **ir′re·spon′si·ble·ness** n. —**ir′re·spon′si·bly** adv.

ir·re·triev·a·ble (ĭr′ĭ-trē′və-bəl) adj. Not capable of being retrieved or recovered. —**ir′re·triev′a·ble·ness** or **ir′re·triev′a·bil′i·ty.** —**ir′re·triev′a·bly** adv.

ir·rev·er·ence (ĭ-rĕv′ər-əns) n. 1. Lack of reverence or due respect. 2. A disrespectful act or remark.

ir·rev·er·ent (ĭ-rĕv′ər-ənt) adj. Showing a lack of reverence, as for someone or something held sacred or worthy of respect: irreverent humor. —**ir·rev′er·ent·ly** adv.

ir·re·vers·i·ble (ĭr′ĭ-vûr′sə-bəl) adj. Incapable of being reversed. —**ir′re·vers′i·bil′i·ty** or **ir′re·vers′i·ble·ness** n. —**ir′re·vers′i·bly** adv.

ir·rev·o·ca·ble (ĭ-rĕv′ə-kə-bəl) adj. Incapable of being changed or undone; irreversible: an irrevocable decision. —**ir·rev′o·ca·bil′i·ty** or **ir·rev′o·ca·ble·ness** n. —**ir·rev′o·ca·bly** adv.

ir·ri·gate (ĭr′ĭ-gāt′) tr.v. **-gat·ed, -gat·ing.** 1. To supply (land or crops) with water by means of ditches, pipes, or streams. 2. To wash out (a wound or an opening of the body) with water or a medicated fluid. [From Latin irrigāre : in-, in + rigāre, to wet, water.] —**ir′ri·ga′tion** n. —**ir′ri·ga′tion·al** adj. —**ir′ri·ga′tor** n.

ir·ri·ta·bil·i·ty (ĭr′ĭ-tə-bĭl′ĭ-tē) n. 1. The quality or condition of being irritable; testiness; petulance. 2. Path. Excessive sensitivity. 3. Biol. The capacity to respond to stimuli.

ir·ri·ta·ble (ĭr′ĭ-tə-bəl) adj. 1. Easily annoyed; ill-tempered. 2. Path. Abnormally sensitive. 3. Biol. Responsive to stimuli. [Latin irritābilis, from irritāre, to irritate.] —**ir′ri·ta·ble·ness** n. —**ir′ri·ta·bly** adv.
Syns: irritable, cantankerous, cross, disagreeable, grouchy, grumpy, ill-tempered, irascible, nasty, peevish, petulant, querulous, surly, testy adj. Core meaning: Having or showing a bad temper (irritable people; irritable retorts).

ir·ri·tant (ĭr′ĭ-tənt) adj. Causing irritation. —n. Something that causes irritation: Smoke is an eye irritant. [Latin irritāns, pres. part. of irritāre, to irritate.]

ir·ri·tate (ĭr′ĭ-tāt′) tr.v. **-tat·ed, -tat·ing.** 1. To make angry or impatient, as with many small disturbances; annoy or bother: Joan's habit of mumbling irritated her parents. 2. To chafe or inflame. —See Syns at annoy. [From Latin irritāre.] —**ir′ri·tat′ing·ly** adv. —**ir′ri·ta′tor** n.

ir·rupt (ĭ-rŭpt′) intr.v. 1. To break or burst in; invade: Barbarians would periodically irrupt into Roman provinces. 2. To increase irregularly in number: Locusts irrupt in cycles. [From Latin irrumpere : in-, in + rumpere, to break, burst.] —**ir·rup′tion** n.

ir·rup·tive (ĭ-rŭp′tĭv) adj. 1. Irrupting or tending to irrupt. 2. Geol. Intrusive. —**ir·rup′tive·ly** adv.

is (ĭz) v. The third person singular present indicative of **be.** —**idiom. as is.** In its present condition; without change, repair, etc.: The shopworn merchandise will be sold as is. [Middle English, from Old English.]

is-. Var. of **iso-.**

is·che·mi·a (ĭ-skē′mē-ə) n. A local anemia caused by mechanical obstruction of the blood supply. [From Greek ischaimos, stopping blood : ischein, to restrain + haima, blood.]

is·chi·um (ĭs′kē-əm) n., pl. **-chi·a** (-kē-ə). The lowest of three major bones comprising each half of the pelvis. [Latin, hip joint, from Greek ischīon.]

-ise. Var. of **-ize.**

I·seult (ĭ-sōōlt′, ĭ-zōōlt′) n. Also **I·sol·de** (ĭ-zōl′də). Arthurian Legend. An Irish princess who married the king of Cornwall and had a hopeless love affair with his knight Tristan.

-ish. A suffix meaning: 1. **a.** Of the nationality of: **Finnish. b.** Having the qualities or character of: **childish. c.** Tending to or preoccupied with: **selfish. d.** Informal. Being near in age or time: **fortyish. 2.** Somewhat or rather: **greenish.** [Middle English -is(c)h, from Old English -isc.]

Ish·tar (ĭsh′tär′) n. Assyrian & Babylonian Myth. The goddess of love and fertility and also of war; identified with the Phoenician Astarte.

i·sin·glass (ī′zĭng-glăs′, ī′zən-) n. 1. A transparent, almost pure gelatin prepared from the air bladder of certain fishes, as the sturgeon. 2. The most common form of the mineral mica; muscovite. [Alteration of obs. Dutch huizenblas, from Middle Dutch huusblase : huus, sturgeon + blase, bladder.]

I·sis (ī′sĭs) n. An ancient Egyptian goddess of fertility and sister and wife of Osiris.

Is·lam (ĭs′ləm, ĭz′-, ĭ-släm′) n. 1. A religion based upon the teachings of the prophet Mohammed, embodying a belief in one God (Allah) and having a body of law put forth in the Koran and the Sunna; the Moslem religion. 2. **a.** The Moslem nations of the world. **b.** Moslems as a group or their civilization. —**Is·lam′ic** (-lăm′ĭk, -lä′mĭk) adj.

is·land (ī′lənd) n. 1. A land mass, esp. one smaller than a continent, entirely surrounded by water. 2. Anything like an island in being completely separated or different in character from what surrounds it. 3. Anat. A tissue or cluster of cells separated from surrounding tissue by a groove or differing from surrounding tissue in structure. —tr.v. To make into or as if into an island. [Middle English ilond, from Old English īland.]

is·land·er (ī′lən-dər) n. An inhabitant of an island.

islands of Lang·er·hans (läng′ər-häns′, -hänz′). Also **islets of Langerhans.** Irregular masses of small cells that lie in the interstitial tissue of the pancreas and secrete insulin. [After Paul Langerhans (1847–88), German physician.]

isle (īl) n. An island, esp. a small one. [Middle English, from Old French, from Latin īnsula.]

is·let (ī′lĭt) n. A little island.

ism (ĭz′əm) n. Informal. A distinctive doctrine, system, or theory. [From -ISM.]

-ism. A suffix meaning: 1. An action, practice, or process: **terrorism. 2.** A state or condition of being: **parallelism. 3.** A characteristic behavior or quality: **heroism. 4.** A distinctive usage or feature, esp. of language: **malapropism. 5.** A doctrine, theory, system, or principle: **capitalism.** [Middle English -isme, from Old French, from Latin -ismus, from Greek -ismos, noun suffix.]

is·n't (ĭz′ənt). Contraction of is not.

iso- or **is-.** A prefix meaning: 1. Equal, identical, or similar: **isogonic. 2.** Isomeric: **isopropyl alcohol.** [Greek, from isos, equal.]

i·so·bar (ī′sə-bär′) n. 1. A line on a weather map connecting points of equal barometric pressure. 2. Any of two or more nuclides having the same mass number but different atomic numbers. [ISO- + Greek baros, weight.] —**i′so·bar′ic** (-bär′ĭk, -băr′-) adj.

i·soch·ro·nal (ī-sŏk′rə-nəl) adj. Also **i·soch·ro·nous** (-nəs), **i·so·chron·ic** (ī′sō-krŏn′ĭk). 1. Equal in duration. 2. Characterized by or occurring at equal intervals of time. [From Greek isokhronos : isos, equal + khronos, time.] —**i·soch′ro·nal·ly** adv. —**i·soch′ro·nism** n.

i·so·gam·ete (ī′sō-găm′ēt′, -gə-mēt′) n. A gamete that is morphologically indistinguishable from one with which it unites.

i·so·gloss (ī′sə-glôs′, -glŏs′) n. A line on a map that separates areas in which linguistic features, such as a pronunciation or a form of a word, differ. [ISO- + Greek glōssa, language, tongue.] —**i′so·gloss′al** adj.

i·so·gon·ic (ī′sə-gŏn′ĭk) adj. Also **i·sog·o·nal** (ī-sŏg′ə-nəl). Having equal angles.

isogonic line. A line on a map connecting points of equal magnetic declination.

i·so·late (ī′sə-lāt′, ĭs′ə-) tr.v. **-lat·ed, -lat·ing.** 1. To separate from a group or whole and set apart. 2. To place in quarantine. 3. Chem. To obtain (a substance) in an uncombined form. [From French isolé, isolated, from Italian isolato, from Late Latin īnsulātus, converted into an island, from Latin īnsula, island.] —**i′so·la′tor** n.

i·so·la·tion (ī'sə-lā'shən, ĭs'ə-) n. **1.** The act or process of isolating: *the isolation of polio patients.* **2.** The condition of being isolated: *living in isolation from the world.* —See Syns at **solitude.** —*modifier:* an isolation ward in a hospital.

i·so·la·tion·ism (ī'sə-lā'shə-nĭz'əm, ĭs'ə-) n. A national policy of not taking part in international affairs and of avoiding entanglements with other countries. —**i'so·la'tion·ist** n. & adj.

I·sol·de (ĭ-zōl'də) n. Var. of **Iseult.**

i·so·leu·cine (ī'sə-loo'sēn') n. An essential amino acid, $C_6H_{13}NO_2$, isomeric with leucine.

i·so·mer (ī'sə-mər) n. **1.** *Chem.* **a.** A compound having the same percentage composition and molecular weight as another compound but differing in chemical or physical properties. **b.** Such a compound so differing because of the manner of linkage of its constituent atoms. **c.** Such a compound so differing because of the manner of arrangement of its constituent atoms in space. Also called **stereoisomer. d.** A stereoisomer manifesting one of two structures that rotate the plane of polarization of polarized light either to the left or to the right. **e.** A stereoisomer having no effect on polarized light but exhibiting isomerism because of a structural asymmetry about a double bond in the molecule. **2.** *Physics.* An atom the nucleus of which can exist in any of several bound excited states for a measurable period of time. [Greek *isomerēs*, equally divided : *isos*, equal + *meros*, part.] —**i'so·mer'ic** (-mĕr'ĭk) adj.

i·som·er·ism (ī-sŏm'ə-rĭz'əm) n. **1.** The phenomenon of the existence of isomers. **2.** The complex of chemical and physical phenomena characteristic of or attributable to isomers. **3.** The condition of being an isomer.

i·som·er·ous (ī-sŏm'ər-əs) adj. **1.** Having an equal number of parts, as organs or markings. **2.** Having or designating floral whorls with equal numbers of parts.

i·so·met·ric (ī'sə-mĕt'rĭk) or **i·so·met·ri·cal** (-rĭ-kəl) adj. **1.** Of or exhibiting equality in dimensions or measurements. **2.** Of or being a crystal system of three equal axes at right angles to one another. **3.** Of or involving muscle contractions in which the ends of the muscle are held in place so that there is an increase in tension rather than a shortening of the muscle: *isometric exercises.* —n. **1.** A line connecting isometric points. **2.** *isometrics* (used with a sing. verb). Isometric exercise. [From Greek *isometros*, of equal measure : *isos*, equal + *metron*, measure.]

i·so·morph (ī'sə-môrf') n. An object, organism, or group exhibiting isomorphism.

i·so·mor·phism (ī'sə-môr'fĭz'əm) n. **1.** *Biol.* Similarity in form, as in different kinds of organisms. **2.** *Math.* **a.** A one-to-one correspondence between the elements of two sets such that the result of an operation on elements of one set corresponds to the result of the analogous operation on their images in the other set. **b.** A mapping * of a group G onto another group H such that $(ab)* = (a*)(b*)$ for all a, b in G. **3.** The existence or an instance of the existence of two or more different substances having closely similar crystalline structure, crystalline dimensions, and chemical composition. —**i'so·mor'phic** or **i'so·mor'phous** adj.

i·so·pro·pyl alcohol (ī'sə-prō'pəl). A colorless, flammable liquid alcohol, C_3H_8O, used as a solvent and rubbing compound. [ISO- + PROPYL.]

i·sos·ce·les (ī-sŏs'ə-lēz') adj. Having two equal sides: *an isosceles triangle; an isosceles trapezoid.* [Late Latin *isoscelēs*, from Greek *isoskelēs*, "having equal legs" : *isos*, equal + *skelos*, leg.]

i·so·therm (ī'sə-thûrm') n. A line drawn on a weather map or chart linking all points having the same temperature at a given time or the same average temperature for a given period of time.

i·so·tope (ī'sə-tōp') n. One of two or more atoms the nuclei of which have the same number of protons but different numbers of neutrons. [ISO- + Greek *topos*, place, "position in the periodic table."] —**i'so·top'ic** (-tŏp'ĭk) adj. —**i'so·top'i·cal·ly** adv.

i·so·trop·ic (ī'sə-trŏp'ĭk) adj. Identical in all directions; invariant with respect to direction. —**i·sot'ro·py** (ī-sŏt'rə-pē) or **i·sot'ro·pism'** (-pĭz'əm) n.

Is·ra·el (ĭz'rē-əl) n. **1.** The descendants of Jacob. **2.** The

whole Hebrew people, past, present, and future, regarded as the chosen people of Jehovah by virtue of the covenant of Jacob.

is·su·ance (ĭsh'oo-əns) n. The act of issuing: *the issuance of hunting permits.*

is·sue (ĭsh'oo) n. **1.** The act of putting out; release: *The date of issue is indicated on the first page.* **2.** Something that is put into circulation: *a new issue of postage stamps.* **3.** A single number of a newspaper or magazine: *the June issue.* **4.** A subject being discussed or disputed; a question under debate: *the issue of school integration.* **5.** An outflow or outpouring, as of water, air, or smoke: *The lake has no issue to the sea.* **6.** A result; outcome. **7.** Offspring; children: *He died without issue.* —v. **-sued, -su·ing.** —*intr.v.* **1.** To go or come out: *Water issued from the broken pipe.* **2.** To be born or be descended. **3.** To spring or result: *A number of agreements issued from the conference.* —*tr.v.* **1.** To cause to flow out; emit. **2.** To put out; announce: *issue orders.* **3.** To put in circulation: *issue stamps.* **4.** To give; extend; grant: *The government refused to issue him a patent.* **5.** To give out; distribute: *Each soldier was issued a rifle.* —*idioms.* **at issue. 1.** In question; in dispute: *Your past record is not at issue here.* **2.** At variance; in disagreement. **take issue.** To disagree. [Middle English, from Old French, from Latin *exīre*, to go out : *ex-*, out + *īre*, to go.] —**is'su·er** n.

-ist. A suffix meaning: **1.** A person who does, makes, produces, operates, plays, or sells a specified thing: **dramatist. 2.** A person who is skilled, trained, or employed in a specified field: **machinist. 3.** An adherent or proponent of a doctrine, system, or school of thought: **anarchist. 4.** A person characterized by a certain trait or predilection: **romanticist.** [Middle English *-iste*, from Old French, from Latin *-ista*, *-istēs*, from Greek *-istēs*, noun suffix.]

isth·mus (ĭs'məs) n., pl. **-mus·es. 1.** A narrow strip of land connecting two larger masses of land. **2.** *Anat.* **a.** A narrow strip of tissue joining two larger organs or parts of an organ. **b.** A narrow passage connecting two larger cavities. [Latin, from Greek *isthmos.*]

is·tle (ĭs'lē, ĭst'-) n. Also **ix·tle.** A plant, **pita,** or its fiber. [Mexican Spanish *ixtle,* from Nahuatl *ichtli.*]

it (ĭt) pron. The third person singular neuter pronoun. **1.** Used to refer to a nonhuman being, to an animal or a human being whose sex is unknown, to a group of persons, or to an abstraction. **2.** Used as the subject of an impersonal verb: *It is raining.* **3.** The general situation or state of affairs: *He just couldn't take it.* —n. The player in children's games who must perform a certain act, such as chasing the other players. [Middle English, from Old English *hit.*]

I·tal·ian (ĭ-tăl'yən) adj. Of Italy, its people, or their language. —n. **1.** A native or inhabitant of Italy or a person of Italian descent. **2.** The Romance language of Italy and one of the three official languages of Switzerland.

Italian sonnet. A **Petrarchan sonnet.**

i·tal·ic (ĭ-tăl'ĭk, ī-tăl'-) adj. Of or being a style of printing type with the letters slanting to the right, now chiefly used to set off a word or passage within a text printed in roman type: *This sentence is printed in italic type.* —n. Often **italics.** Italic print or typeface. [After *Italy.*]

i·tal·i·cize (ĭ-tăl'ĭ-sīz', ī-tăl'-) v. **-cized, -ciz·ing.** —*tr.v.* **1.** To print in italic type. **2.** To underscore (written matter) with a single line to indicate italics. —**i·tal'i·ci·za'tion** n.

itch (ĭch) n. **1.** A skin sensation causing a desire to scratch. **2.** Any of various contagious skin diseases marked by intense irritation, eruptions, and itching. **3.** A restless desire or craving for something: *"I am tormented with an everlasting itch for things remote."* (Melville). —*intr.v.* **1.** To feel, have, or produce an itch: *itching all over from a heat rash; a wool shirt that itches.* **2.** To have a strong, restless craving: *just itching to go.* —*tr.v.* To cause to itch. [Middle English *(y)icchen,* from Old English *giccan.*]

itch·y (ĭch'ē) adj. **-i·er, -i·est.** Having or causing an itching sensation: *"that itchy particular red velvet that one associates with hot days on a train"* (Truman Capote). —**itch'i·ness** n.

-ite¹. A suffix meaning: **1.** A person who is a native or resident of a specified place: **New Jerseyite. 2.** An adherent of someone specified: **Luddite. 3.** *Biol.* A part of an organ or body: **somite. 4.** A mineral or rock: **graphite. 5.** A commercial product: **Lucite.** [Middle English, from Old French, from Latin *-ita, -ites,* from Greek *-ites.*]

-ite². A suffix meaning a salt or ester of an acid whose adjectival denomination ends in *-ous:* **sulfite.** [French.]

i·tem (ī′təm) *n.* **1.** A single article or unit in a group, series, or list: *The receipt shows the price of each item you purchased.* **2.** A piece of news or information: *an interesting item in the newspaper.* [Middle English, also, likewise, from Latin, from *ita,* so.]

i·tem·ize (ī′tə-mīz′) *tr.v.* **-ized, -iz·ing.** To set down item by item; to list. **—i′tem·i·za′tion** *n.* **—i′tem·iz′er** *n.*

i·tin·er·ant (ī-tĭn′ər-ənt, ĭ-tĭn′-) *adj.* Traveling from place to place, esp. to perform some duty or work: *an itinerant judge; itinerant labor.* **—***n.* A person who so travels. [Late Latin *itinerāns,* pres. part. of *itinerārī,* to travel, from Latin *iter,* journey.] **—i·tin′er·an·cy** or **i·tin′er·a·cy** *n.*

i·tin·er·ar·y (ī-tĭn′ə-rĕr′ē, ĭ-tĭn′-) *n., pl.* **-ies. 1.** A schedule of places to be visited in the course of a journey: *Their itinerary includes stops in Denver and Salt Lake City.* **2.** An account or record of a journey. **—***adj.* Of or relating to a journey or to a route. [Middle English *itinerarie,* from Late Latin *itinerārium,* course of travel, from *itinerārius,* of traveling, from Latin *iter,* journey.]

-itis. A suffix meaning inflammation of or inflammatory disease: **laryngitis.** [From Greek *-itis,* pertaining to, native.]

it'll (ĭt′l). Contraction of: **1.** It will. **2.** It shall.

its (ĭts). The possessive form of **it,** used as a modifier before a noun: *We opposed the bill and worked for its defeat.* [IT + -'s, possessive ending.]

    Usage: **its, it's.** Do not confuse *its* (the possessive form of the pronoun *it*) with *it's* (the contraction of *it is* and *it has*). Examples: *a city and its people* but *it's not new; it's been done before.*

it's (ĭts). Contraction of: **1.** It is. **2.** It has. **—**See Usage note at **it.**

it·self (ĭt-sĕlf′) *pron.* **1.** That one identical with it. Used: **a.** Reflexively as the direct or indirect object of a verb or the object of a preposition: *This record player turns itself off.* **b.** For emphasis: *The trouble is in the machine itself.* **2.** Its normal, healthy condition: *The computer is acting*

itself again since the program was corrected. **—idiom.** **(all) by itself. 1.** Alone: *a dog left by itself in front of the store.* **2.** Without manipulation or guidance; automatically: *a refrigerator that defrosts by itself.*

-ity. A suffix meaning a state or quality: **authenticity.** [Middle English *-it(i)e,* from Old French *-ite,* from Latin *-itās.*]

-ium. *Chem. & Physics.* A suffix meaning an element or chemical group: **barium.** [From Greek *-ion,* dim. suffix.]

I've (īv). Contraction of I have.

-ive. A suffix meaning having a tendency toward or inclination to perform some action: **disruptive.** [Middle English, from Old French *-if,* from Latin *-īvus.*]

i·vied (ī′vēd) *adj.* Overgrown or covered with ivy.

i·vo·ry (ī′və-rē, īv′rē) *n., pl.* **-ries. 1. a.** The hard, smooth, yellowish-white substance forming the main part of the tusks of the elephant and used as an ornamental material. **b.** A similar substance forming the tusks or teeth of certain other animals, such as the walrus. **2.** An article made of ivory. **3. ivories.** *Slang.* **a.** Piano keys. **b.** Dice. **4.** A yellowish white. **—***modifier: an ivory figurine.* **—***adj.* Yellowish white. [Middle English *ivorie,* from Old French *ivoire,* from Latin *eboreus,* of ivory, from *ebur,* ivory, prob. of Egyptian orig.]

i·vy (ī′vē) *n., pl.* **i·vies. 1.** Any of several woody climbing or trailing plants of the genus *Hedera,* native to the Old World, esp. *H. helix,* with lobed evergreen leaves and berrylike black fruit. **2.** Any of various other climbing or creeping plants, such as Boston ivy or poison ivy. [Middle English *ivye,* from Old English *ifig.*]

i·wis (ī-wĭs′) *adv.* Also **y·wis.** *Archaic.* Certainly; surely. [Middle English, from Old English *gewis,* certain.]

ix·tle (ĭs′lē, ĭst′-) *n.* Var. of **istle.**

-ize. Also **-ise.** A suffix meaning: **1. a.** To cause to be or to become; make into: **dramatize. b.** To make conform with: **Anglicize. c.** To treat or regard as: **idolize. 2.** To cause to acquire a specified quality: **modernize. 3.** To become or become similar to: **materialize. 4. a.** To subject to: **jeopardize. b.** To affect with: **galvanize. 5.** To do or follow some practice: **bowdlerize.** [Middle English *-isen,* from Old French *-iser,* from Late Latin *-izāre,* from Greek *-izein.*]

Phoenician – About 3,000 years ago the Phoenicians and other Semitic peoples began to use graphic signs to represent individual speech sounds instead of syllables or whole words. They used this symbol to represent the sound of the semivowel "y" and gave it the name yōdh, the Phoenician word for "hand".

Greek – The Greeks borrowed the Phoenician alphabet with some modifications. They changed the shape of yōdh and altered its name to iota. They used iota to represent the sound of the vowel "ı".

Roman – The Romans borrowed the alphabet from the Greeks via the Etruscans. They used iota to represent both the vowel "ı" and the semivowel "y." They eventually began to distinguish the two sounds by adding a tail to the semivowel, and they also adapted the alphabet for carving Latin in stone. This monumental script, as it is called, be-

came the basis for modern printed capital letters.

Medieval – By medieval times – around 1,200 years ago – the Roman monumental capitals had become adapted to being relatively quickly written on parchment, paper, or vellum. The dot was retained from the letter I and helped distinguish J (and I) from other similarly shaped letters. During the medieval period and well into modern times the letters I and J were interchangeable. The cursive minuscule alphabet became the basis of modern printed lowercase letters.

Modern – Since the invention of printing about 500 years ago spelling has become more standardized. During the 17th century J and I were finally distinguished and assigned their modern phonetic values. The basic form of the letter J has remained unchanged.

---

j, J (jā) n., pl. **j's** or **js, J's** or **Js. 1.** The tenth letter of the modern English alphabet. **2.** Any of the speech sounds represented by this letter. **3.** Anything shaped like the letter **J.**

jab (jăb) v. **jabbed, jab·bing.** —*tr.v.* **1.** To poke or thrust abruptly, esp. with something sharp. **2.** To punch with short blows. —*intr.v.* **1.** To make an abrupt jabbing motion. **2.** To deliver a quick punch. —*n.* A quick stab or blow. [Var. of JOB.]

jab·ber (jăb′ər) *intr.v.* To talk rapidly, unintelligibly, or idly. —*tr.v.* To utter rapidly or unintelligibly. —*n.* Rapid or babbling talk. [Middle English *jaberen.*] —**jab′ber·er** *n.*

jab·ot (zhă-bō′, jă-) *n.* An ornamental series of ruffles or frills down the front of a shirt. [French, frill, ruffle.]

jabot

ja·cinth (jā′sĭnth, jăs′ĭnth) *n.* A variety of hyacinth. [Middle English *iacynth,* from Old French *iacinte,* from Medieval Latin *jacintus,* from Latin *hyacinthus,* hyacinth.]

jack (jăk) *n.* **1.** Often **Jack.** A man; fellow; chap. **2.** Someone who does odd or heavy jobs; a laborer. Usu. used in combination: *lumberjack.* **3.** A sailor; a tar. **4.** A playing card showing the figure of a knave and ranking below a queen. **5.** A usu. portable device for raising heavy objects by means of force applied with a lever, screw, or hydraulic press. **6.** A male donkey; jackass. **7. a. jacks.** (*used with a sing. verb*). A game played with a set of small six-pointed metal pieces and a small ball, the object being to pick up

the pieces in various combinations. **b.** One of the metal pieces used. **8.** A socket that accepts a plug at one end and attaches to another circuit at the other. **9.** A small flag flown at the bow of a ship, usu. to indicate nationality. **10.** *Slang.* Money. —*tr.v.* **1.** To hoist with or as if with a jack: *jack up the car.* **2.** To raise: *She jacked the rent.* [From the name *Jack.*]

jack·al (jăk′əl, -ôl′) *n.* **1.** Any of several doglike carnivorous mammals of the genus *Canis,* of Africa and Asia. **2.** Someone who does menial tasks for another. [Turkish *chakāl,* from Persian *shagāl.*]

jack·a·napes (jăk′ə-nāps′) *n.* A conceited or impudent person. [From *Jack Napes,* nickname of William de la Pole, first Duke of Suffolk (d. 1450).]

jack·ass (jăk′ăs′) *n.* **1.** A male ass or donkey. **2.** A foolish or stupid person; blockhead. [JACK (male) + ASS.]

jack·daw (jăk′dô′) *n.* A Eurasian bird, *Corvus monedula,* related to the crow. Also called **daw.**

jack·et (jăk′ĭt) *n.* **1.** A short coat, usu. extending to the hip: *a sport jacket.* **2.** A protective cover for a book, phonograph record, etc. **3.** An outer covering or casing, as of an electric wire, a machine or machine part, or a bullet. [Middle English *jaket,* from Old French *jaquet,* dim. of *jaque,* short jacket.]

jack·ham·mer (jăk′hăm′ər) *n.* A hand-held pneumatic machine for drilling rock.

jack-in-the-box (jăk′ĭn-thə-bŏks′) *n.* A toy consisting of a usu. grotesque puppet that springs up out of a box when the lid is opened.

jack-in-the-pul·pit (jăk′ĭn-thə-pŏŏl′pĭt, -pŭl′-) *n.* A plant, *Arisaema triphyllum,* of eastern North America, with a leaflike spathe enclosing a clublike flower stalk.

jack·knife (jăk′nīf′) *n.* **1.** A large clasp pocketknife. **2.** A dive in which one bends over, touches the toes, and then straightens out before entering the water hands first. —*v.* **-knifed, -knif·ing.** —*tr.v.* To fold or double like a jackknife. —*intr.v.* To bend or fold up like a jackknife.

jack-of-all-trades (jăk′əv-ôl′trādz′) *n.,* pl. **jacks-of-all-trades.** A person who can do many kinds of work.

jack-o'-lan·tern (jăk′ə-lăn′tərn) *n.* **1.** A lantern made from a hollowed pumpkin with a carved face. **2.** An ignis fatuus.

jack·pot (jăk′pŏt′) *n.* The top prize or cumulative stakes in any of various games and contests. [JACK (playing card) + POT.]

---

jack rabbit. Any of several large long-eared, long-legged hares of the genus *Lepus,* of western North America. [JACK(ASS) (from its long ears) + RABBIT.]

jack·screw (jăk′skrōō′) *n.* A jack for lifting, operated by a screw.

jack·straw (jăk′strô′) *n.* **1. jackstraws.** (*used with a sing. verb*). A game played with a pile of straws or thin sticks, with the players attempting in turn to remove a single stick without disturbing the others. **2.** One of the straws or sticks used in this game.

Jac·o·bin (jăk′ə-bĭn) *n.* **1.** A radical republican during the French Revolution. **2.** A political radical or leftist. **3.** A Dominican friar. [French, from Late Latin *Jacōbus,* after the Jacobin friars, in whose convent the French political group was founded (1789).]

Jac·o·bite (jăk′ə-bīt′) *n.* A supporter of James II of England or of the Stuart pretenders following 1688. [From Latin *Jacobus,* James.]

Ja·cob's ladder (jā′kəbz). *Naut.* A rope or chain ladder with rigid rungs. [From the ladder seen by the patriarch *Jacob* in a dream. (Genesis 28:12).]

jade¹ (jād) *n.* Either of two distinct minerals, nephrite and jadeite, that are gen. pale green or white and are used mainly as gemstones or in carving. —**modifier:** *a jade bracelet.* [French *jade,* from Spanish *ijada,* from *(piedra de) ijada,* "(stone of the) flank" (from the belief that it was a cure for renal colic).]

jade² (jād) *n.* **1.** A broken-down or useless horse; a nag. **2.** A disreputable woman. —*v.* **jad·ed, jad·ing.** —*tr.v.* To exhaust or wear out. —*intr.v.* To become weary or spiritless. [Middle English.]

jad·ed (jā′dĭd) *adj.* **1.** Wearied; worn out. **2.** Dulled, as by overindulgence; sated: *jaded appetites.* **3.** Insensitive; callous. —**jad′ed·ly** *adv.* —**jad′ed·ness** *n.*

jae·ger (yā′gər, jā′-) *n.* Any of several sea birds of the genus *Stercorarius,* that snatch food from other birds. [German *Jäger,* hunter.]

jaeger
George Miksch Sutton

jag¹ (jăg) *n.* A sharp projecting point; barb. —*tr.v.* **jagged, jag·ging. 1.** To cut jags in; to notch. **2.** To cut unevenly. [Middle English *jagge.*]

jag² (jăg) *n. Slang.* A binge; spree. [Orig. unknown.]

jag·ged (jăg′ĭd) *adj.* Notched or rough; uneven: *a jagged edge.* —**jag′ged·ly** *adv.* —**jag′ged·ness** *n.*

jag·uar (jăg′wär′, -yōō-är′) *n.* A large feline mammal, *Panthera onca,* of tropical America, with a tawny coat spotted with black rosettelike markings. [Spanish and Portuguese, from Tupi *jaguara.*]

jai a·lai (hī′ lī′, hī′ ə-lī′, hī′ ə-lī′). An extremely fast court game popular in Spain and Latin America, in which players use a hand-shaped basket to propel the ball against a wall. Also called **pelota.** [Spanish, from Basque : *jai,* festival + *alai,* joyous.]

jail (jāl). Also *Brit.* **gaol.** —*n.* A place for the confinement of persons in lawful detention; prison. —*tr.v.* To put in jail; imprison. [Middle English *jaiole,* from Old French, ult. from Latin *cavea,* a hollow, den, coop.]

jail·bird (jāl′bûrd′) *n. Informal.* A prisoner or ex-convict.

jail·break (jāl′brāk′) *n.* An escape from jail.

jail·er (jā′lər) *n.* Also **jail·or.** The keeper of a jail.

Jain (jīn). Also **Jai·na** (jī′nə). —*n.* A follower of Jainism. —*adj.* Of or pertaining to Jainism or the Jains. [Hindi *jaina,* from Sanskrit *jainas,* saintly, from *jinas,* saint, from *jayati,* to conquer.]

Jain·ism (jī′nĭz′əm) *n.* An ascetic religion of India, founded in the sixth cent. B.C., that teaches the immortality and transmigration of the soul and denies the existence of a perfect or supreme being.

jal·ap (jăl′əp) *n.* **1.** A Mexican plant, *Exogonium purga.* **2.** A cathartic drug made from the dried rootstock of this plant. [French, from Mexican Spanish *jalapa,* from *(purga de) Jalapa,* (purgative of) *Jalapa,* a city in Mexico.]

ja·lop·y (jə-lŏp′ē) *n., pl.* **-ies.** *Informal.* An old, dilapidated automobile or airplane. [Orig. unknown.]

ja·lou·sie (jăl′ə-sē) *n.* A blind or shutter with overlapping horizontal slats that can be adjusted to regulate the passage of air and light. [French, jealousy.]

jam¹ (jăm) *v.* **jammed, jam·ming.** —*tr.v.* **1.** To drive or squeeze into a tight space: *jam a cork into a bottle.* **2.** To activate or apply suddenly: *jam the brakes on.* **3.** To cause to lock in an unworkable position: *jam the typewriter keys.* **4.** To fill or pack to excess; cram. **5.** To block, congest, or clog: *The drain was jammed by debris.* **6.** To crush or bruise: *jam a finger.* **7.** To interfere with or prevent the clear reception of (broadcast signals) by electronic means. —*intr.v.* **1.** To become wedged; stick. **2.** To become inoperable because of jammed parts. **3.** To force into or through a limited space. **4.** To play jazz improvisations. —*n.* **1.** The act of jamming or the condition of being jammed. **2.** A congestion of people or things in a limited space: *a traffic jam.* **3.** *Informal.* A difficult situation; a predicament. [Perh. imit.]

jam² (jăm) *n.* A preserve made from whole fruit boiled to a pulp with sugar. [Perh. from JAM.]

jamb (jăm) *n.* One of the vertical posts or pieces of a door or window frame. [Middle English *jambe,* from Old French, leg, jamb, from Late Latin *gamba,* hoof, from Greek *kampē,* joint.]

jam·bo·ree (jăm′bə-rē′) *n.* **1.** A noisy celebration or gathering. **2.** A large assembly, often international, as of Boy Scouts. [Orig. unknown.]

jam session. A gathering at which a group of jazz musicians improvise together.

jan·gle (jăng′gəl) *v.* **-gled, -gling.** —*intr.v.* To make a harsh, metallic sound. —*tr.v.* **1.** To cause to make a harsh, discordant sound. **2.** To grate on: *jangle one's nerves.* —*n.* A harsh, metallic sound. [Middle English *janglen,* from Old French *jangler.*] —**jan′gler** *n.*

jan·is·sar·y (jăn′ĭ-sĕr′ē) *n., pl.* **-ies.** Also **jan·i·zar·y** (-zĕr′ē) A soldier in an elite guard of Turkish troops organized in the 14th cent. and abolished in 1826. [French *janissaire,* from Turkish *yeniçeri* : *yeni,* new + *çeri,* militia.]

jan·i·tor (jăn′ĭ-tər) *n.* A person employed to maintain and clean a building. [Latin *jānitor,* from *jānua,* door, from *jānus,* arched passage.] —**jan′i·to′ri·al** (-tôr′ē-əl, -tōr′-) *adj.*

jan·i·zar·y (jăn′ĭ-zĕr′ē) *n.* Var. of **janissary.**

Jan·u·ar·y (jăn′yōō-ĕr′ē) *n., pl.* **-ies.** The first month of the year. January has 31 days. [Middle English *Januarie,* from Latin *Jānuārius (mensis),* (month) of Janus.]

Ja·nus (jā′nəs) *n. Rom. Myth.* The ancient god of gates and doorways, depicted with two opposite faces.

ja·pan (jə-păn′) *n.* A black enamel or lacquer used to produce a durable glossy finish. —*tr.v.* **-panned, -pan·ning.** To varnish with japan. [From *Japan.*]

Jap·a·nese (jăp′ə-nēz′, -nēs′) *adj.* Of or pertaining to Japan, or its people, language, or culture. —*n., pl.* **-nese. 1.** A native or inhabitant of Japan. **2.** The native language of the Japanese people.

Japanese beetle. A metallic-green and brownish beetle, *Popillia japonica,* native to eastern Asia, that is a serious plant pest in North America.

Japanese quince. A shrub, the japonica.

jape (jāp) *v.* **japed, jap·ing.** *Archaic.* —*intr.v.* To joke or quip. —*tr.v.* To joke about. —*n.* A joke or quip. —See Syns at **joke.** [Middle English *japen,* to trick, from Old French *japper,* to yap.] —**jap′er** *n.* —**jap′er·y** *n.*

ja·pon·i·ca (jə-pŏn′ĭ-kə) *n.* **1.** A shrub, the camellia. **2.** A shrub, *Chaenomeles japonica,* native to Japan, cultivated for its red flowers; Japanese quince. [New Latin, Japanese, from *Japonia,* Japan.]

| ă pat | ā pay | â care | ä father | ĕ pet | ē be | hw which | ĭ pit | ī tie | î pier | ŏ pot | ō toe | ô paw, for | oi noise |
| ōō took | ōō boot | ou out | th thin | th this | ŭ cut | | û urge | zh vision | ə about, item, edible, gallop, circus | | | | |

jar¹ (jär) *n.* **1.** A cylindrical glass or earthenware vessel with a wide mouth and usu. without handles. **2.** The amount contained in a jar. [French *jarre,* from Provençal *jarra,* from Arabic *jarrah,* large earthen vase.]

jar² (jär) *v.* **jarred, jar·ring.** —*intr.v.* **1.** To make or utter a harsh sound. **2.** To disturb or irritate; grate. **3.** To shake or vibrate from impact. **4.** To clash or conflict. —*tr.v.* **1.** To bump or cause to move or shake from impact. **2.** To startle or unsettle. —*n.* **1.** A jolt or sudden movement; a shock. **2.** A harsh or grating sound. [Prob. imit.]

jar·di·nière (jär'dn-îr', zhär'dən-yâr') *n.* A large, decorative stand or pot for plants. [French, from *jardin,* garden, from Old French.]

jar·gon (jär'gən) *n.* **1.** Nonsensical, incoherent, or meaningless talk; gibberish. **2.** A hybrid language or dialect, used esp. for communication between peoples of different languages. **3.** The specialized or technical language of a profession, class, etc: *medical jargon.* —See Syns at **language.** [Middle English *iargoun,* meaningless chatter, from Old French *jargoun,* twittering.]

jas·mine (jăz'mĭn) *n.* Also **jes·sa·mine** (jĕs'ə-mĭn). **1.** Any of several vines or shrubs of the genus *Jasminum,* with fragrant white or yellow flowers used in making perfume. **2.** Any of several woody vines of the genus *Gelsemium,* with fragrant yellow flowers. **3.** Any of several other plants or shrubs with fragrant flowers. [French *jasmin,* from Arabic *yās(a)mīn,* from Persian *yasmīn.*]

jasmine

Ja·son (jā'sən) *n. Gk. Myth.* The leader of the Argonauts in quest of the Golden Fleece.

jas·per (jăs'pər) *n.* **1.** An opaque variety of quartz, reddish, brown, or yellow in color. **2.** Chalcedony, esp. green chalcedony. [Middle English *jaspre,* from Old French, from Latin *jaspis,* from Greek *iaspis.*]

ja·to (jā'tō) *n.* An auxiliary rocket engine used as an aid to an aircraft in taking off. [J(ET) A(SSISTED) T(AKE)O(FF).]

jaun·dice (jôn'dĭs, jän'-) *n.* **1.** *Path.* Yellowish discoloration of tissues and bodily fluids with bile pigment caused by any of several conditions in which normal processing of bile is interrupted. **2.** An attitude or feeling that prejudices outlook or judgment. [Middle English *jaun(d)is,* from Old French *jaunice,* from *jaune,* yellow, from Latin *galbinus,* greenish yellow, from *galbus.*]

jaunt (jônt, jänt) *n.* A short, usu. pleasurable trip or excursion; an outing. —*intr.v.* To make such a trip. [Orig. unknown.]

jaun·ty (jôn'tē, jän'-) *adj.* **-ti·er, -ti·est. 1.** Having a carefree or self-confident air; lively. **2.** Stylish; dapper. [Earlier *jantee,* elegant, genteel, from French *gentil.*] —**jaun'ti·ly** *adv.* —**jaun'ti·ness** *n.*

ja·va (jăv'ə, jä'və) *n. Informal.* Coffee. [From *Java.*]

Java man. Pithecanthropus.

Jav·a·nese (jăv'ə-nēz', -nēs') *adj.* Of or pertaining to Java, or its people, language, or culture. —*n., pl.* **-nese. 1.** A native or inhabitant of Java. **2.** The Indonesian language in Java.

jave·lin (jăv'lən, jăv'ə-) *n.* **1.** A light spear, used as a weapon. **2.** A lightweight metal or metal-tipped spear, gen. not less than 8 1/2 feet in length for men, used in contests of distance throwing. **3.** The athletic contest in which it is thrown. Also called **javelin throw.** [French *javeline,* from Old French.]

jaw (jô) *n.* **1.** Either of two bony or cartilaginous structures

in most vertebrates forming the framework of the mouth and holding the teeth. **2.** The parts of the body forming the wall of the mouth and serving to open and close it. **3.** Either of two hinged parts in a mechanical device: *the jaws of a wrench.* **4. jaws.** The walls of a pass, canyon, or cavern. **5. jaws.** A dangerous situation. **6.** *Slang.* **a.** Back talk. **b.** Chatter. —*intr.v. Slang.* To talk; jabber. [Middle English *iawe.*]

jaw·bone (jô'bōn') *n.* Any bone of the jaw, esp. the bone of the lower jaw.

jaw·break·er (jô'brā'kər) *n.* **1.** A kind of hard, round candy. **2.** *Slang.* A word that is difficult to pronounce.

jay (jā) *n.* **1.** Any of various, usu. crested birds within the family Corvidae, that often have a loud, harsh call. **2.** *Slang.* A newcomer or inexperienced person. [Middle English, from Old French, from Late Latin *gāia.*]

jay·walk (jā'wôk') *intr.v.* To cross a street recklessly or in violation of traffic regulations. —**jay'walk'er** *n.*

jazz (jăz) *n.* **1.** A kind of native American music marked by a strong but flexible rhythmic understructure with solo and ensemble improvisations on basic tunes and chord patterns, and, recently, a highly sophisticated harmonic idiom. **2.** *Slang.* Extreme exaggeration; stuff. —*tr.v.* **1.** To play in a jazz style. **2.** *Slang.* To lie or exaggerate to: *Don't jazz me.* —*phrasal verb.* **jazz up.** *Informal.* To make more interesting; enliven. [Orig. unknown.]

jeal·ous (jĕl'əs) *adj.* **1.** Fearful or wary of losing what one has to another, esp. someone's love or affection. **2.** Resentful of another's success, advantages, etc.; envious: *jealous of his wealth.* **3.** Careful in guarding something; vigilant: *jealous of his good name.* **4.** Concerning or arising from feelings of envy, apprehension, or bitterness: *jealous thoughts; jealous rage.* **5.** Intolerant of disloyalty or infidelity; autocratic: *a jealous God.* [Middle English *ielus,* jealous, zealous for, from Old French *jelous,* from Medieval Latin *zēlōsus,* from Late Latin *zēlus,* from Greek *zēlos,* zeal.] —**jeal'ous·ly** *adv.* —**jeal'ous·ness** *n.*

jeal·ous·y (jĕl'ə-sē) *n., pl.* **-ies.** A jealous attitude or disposition, esp. toward a rival.

jean (jēn) *n.* **1.** A heavy, strong, twilled cotton, used chiefly in making uniforms and work clothes. **2. jeans.** Clothes, esp. pants, made of such fabric. [Middle English *Jene, Gene,* Genoa, where it was first made.]

jeep (jēp) *n.* A small, durable motor vehicle with four-wheel drive and quarter-ton capacity, used as an all-purpose vehicle, esp. by the armed forces. [From *G.P.,* "general purpose."]

jeer (jîr) *intr.v.* To speak or shout derisively; to mock. —*tr.v.* To abuse openly; to taunt. —*n.* A scoffing or taunting remark. [Orig. unknown.] —**jeer'er** *n.*

Je·ho·vah (jĭ-hō'və) *n.* In the Old Testament, God.

Jehovah's Witnesses. A religious sect founded in the United States during the late 19th cent. whose followers preach the imminent approach of the millennium and are strongly opposed to war and to the authority of government in matters of conscience.

je·june (jĭ-jōōn') *adj.* **1.** Lacking in nutrition; insubstantial. **2.** Not interesting; dull. **3.** Childish; immature. [From Latin *jējūnus,* hungry, fasting.] —**je·june'ly** *adv.* —**je·june'ness** *n.*

je·ju·num (jĭ-jōō'nəm) *n., pl.* **-na** (-nə). The section of the small intestine between the duodenum and the ileum. [Medieval Latin *jējūnum (intestīnum),* "the fasting (intestine)," from *jējūnus,* fasting (so named because in dissection it was always found empty).]

jell (jĕl) *intr.v.* **1.** To become firm or gelatinous; congeal. **2.** To take shape; crystallize: *My ideas on the subject haven't jelled yet.* —*tr.v.* **1.** To cause to become firm or gelatinous. **2.** To give shape to. —*n.* Jelly. [Back-formation from JELLY.]

Jell-O (jĕl'ō) *n.* A trademark for a gelatin dessert.

jel·ly (jĕl'ē) *n., pl.* **-lies. 1.** A soft, semisolid food substance with a springy consistency, made by causing a liquid containing pectin or gelatin to set, esp. such a substance made of fruit juice containing pectin boiled with sugar. **2.** Any substance with the consistency of jelly, such as a petroleum ointment. —*v.* **-lied, -ly·ing.** —*tr.v.* **1.** To make or cause to become jelly. **2.** To spread or prepare with jelly. —*intr.v.* To become jelly; to set. [Middle English *geli,* from Old French *gelee*, frost, jelly, ult. from Latin *gelāre*, to freeze.]

jel·ly·bean (jĕl'ē-bēn') *n.* A small, chewy candy with a hardened sugar coating.

jel·ly·fish (jĕl'ē-fĭsh') *n., pl.* **-fish** or **-fish·es.** Any of numerous usu. free-swimming saltwater animals of the class Scyphozoa, with a gelatinous, often bell-shaped body and stinging tentacles.

jellyfish

jen·net (jĕn'ĭt) *n.* A small Spanish saddle horse. [Middle English *jennett, genett,* from Old French *genet,* from Spanish *jinete,* light horseman, from Arabic *Zenetī,* a Berber tribe famed for horsemanship.]

jen·ny (jĕn'ē) *n., pl.* **-nies.** 1. A female donkey. 2. A female wren. 3. A spinning jenny. [From *Jenny,* pet form of the name *Jane.*]

jeop·ard·ize (jĕp'ər-dīz') *tr.v.* **-ized, -iz·ing.** To expose to loss or injury; endanger; imperil.

jeop·ard·y (jĕp'ər-dē) *n.* 1. Danger or risk of loss or injury; peril. 2. *Law.* The defendant's risk or danger of conviction when put on trial. —See Syns at **danger.** [Middle English *jeopartie,* even chance, from Old French *jeu parti: jeu,* game, from Latin *jocus* + *parti,* past part. of *partir,* to divide, from Latin *partīre,* from *pars,* part.]

jer·bo·a (jər-bō'ə) *n.* Any of various small, mouselike, leaping rodents of the family Dipodidae, of Asia and northern Africa, with long hind legs and a long, tufted tail. [From Medieval Latin *jerbōa,* from Arabic *yerbō',* flesh of the loins (from the animal's highly developed thighs).]

jer·e·mi·ad (jĕr'ə-mī'əd) *n.* A prolonged lamentation or a tale of woe. [French *jérémiade,* after *Jérémie,* Jeremiah, a Hebrew prophet of the 7th and 6th cent. B.C.]

jerk¹ (jûrk) *tr.v.* 1. To give an abrupt thrust, push, pull, or twist to. 2. To throw or toss with a quick abrupt motion. —*intr.v.* 1. To move in sudden abrupt motions; to jolt. 2. To make spasmodic motions: *His legs jerked from fatigue.* —*n.* 1. A sudden yank, tug, or twist. 2. A jolting or lurching motion. 3. A sudden spasmodic, muscular movement. 4. *Slang.* A dull, stupid, or foolish person. [Orig. unknown.]

   Syns: jerk, snap, tug, wrench, yank (Informal) *v.* Core meaning: To move (something) with a sudden, abrupt motion *(jerked the window open).*

jerk² (jûrk) *tr.v.* To cut (meat) into long strips and dry in the sun or cure by exposing to smoke. [Back-formation from JERKY (cured meat).]

jer·kin (jûr'kĭn) *n.* 1. A sleeveless waistcoat; vest. 2. A short, close-fitting coat or jacket, usu. sleeveless and often made of leather. [Orig. unknown.]

jerk·wa·ter (jûrk'wô'tər, -wŏt'ər) *adj.* *Informal.* Remote and insignificant: *a jerkwater town.* [From an early railroad term for a remote place where water had to be "jerked" or drawn and carried to trains.]

jerk·y¹ (jûr'kē) *adj.* **-i·er, -i·est.** Moving by sudden starts or stops. —**jerk'i·ly** *adv.* —**jerk'i·ness** *n.*

jerk·y² (jûr'kē) *n., pl* **-ies.** Meat, esp. beef, cured by jerking. [Earlier *jerkin beef,* from Spanish *charqui,* cured meat, from Quechua *ch'arki.*]

jer·ry-built (jĕr'ē-bĭlt') *adj.* Built hastily, cheaply and poorly. [Orig. unknown.]

jer·sey (jûr'zē) *n., pl.* **-seys.** 1. A soft, elastic, knitted fabric of wool, cotton, rayon, etc., used for clothing. 2. A garment, such as a sport shirt, made of this fabric. 3. *Jersey.*

One of a breed of light-brown cattle raised for milk and milk products. [After *Jersey,* one of the Channel Islands, famous for its knitted garment.]

Je·ru·sa·lem artichoke (jə-rōō'sə-ləm, -zə-). 1. A North American sunflower, *Helianthus tuberosus,* with yellow, rayed flowers and edible tuberous roots. 2. The tuber of this plant, eaten as a vegetable. [By folk ety. from Italian *girasole,* sunflower.]

jess (jĕs) *n.* A short strap fastened around the leg of a hawk or other bird used in falconry, and to which a leash may be fastened. —*tr.v.* To put jesses on (a hawk). [Middle English *gesse,* from Old French *ges,* ult. from Latin *jacere,* to throw.]

jes·sa·mine (jĕs'ə-mĭn) *n.* Var. of **jasmine.**

jest (jĕst) *n.* 1. Something said or done to provoke amusement and laughter. 2. A playful or frivolous mood or manner: *spoken in jest.* 3. A jeering remark; a taunt. 4. An object of laughter or ridicule; laughingstock. —See Syns at **joke.** —*intr.v.* 1. To act or speak playfully; to joke. 2. To make witty or amusing remarks. 3. To utter scoffs or jeers; to gibe. —*tr.v.* To make fun of; ridicule. [Middle English *geste,* deed, tale, from Old French, from Latin *gesta,* exploits, from *gerere,* to do.]

jest·er (jĕs'tər) *n.* A person who jests, esp. a paid fool or clown at medieval courts.

Je·su (jē'zōō; *Latin* yā'sōō) *n.* *Archaic & Poet.* Jesus. [Late Latin *Jēsū,* vocative of *Jēsus,* Jesus.]

Jes·u·it (jĕzh'ōō-ĭt, jĕz'yōō-) *n.* *Rom. Cath. Ch.* A member of the Society of Jesus, an order founded by Saint Ignatius Loyola in 1534. [French *Jésuite.*] —**Jes'u·it'i·cal** (-ĭ-kəl) *adj.*

Je·sus (jē'zəs) *n.* The founder of Christianity, regarded by Christians as the son of God and the Messiah.

jet¹ (jĕt) *n.* 1. A dense black coal that takes a high polish and is used for jewelry. 2. A deep black. —*modifier: a jet necklace.* —*adj.* Deep black. [Middle English *jeet,* from Old French *jayet,* from Latin *gagātēs,* from Greek, "stone of Gagai" (town in Lycia).] —**jet'ty** *adj.*

jet² (jĕt) *n.* 1. A high-velocity stream of liquid or gas forced through a narrow opening or nozzle under pressure. 2. Something emitted in or as if in such a stream: *a jet of steam.* 3. An outlet, as a nozzle, for emitting such a stream. 4. **a.** A jet-propelled aircraft or other vehicle. **b.** A jet engine. —*v.* **jet·ted, jet·ting.** —*intr.v.* 1. To move quickly. 2. To travel by jet plane. —*tr.v.* To propel outward. [Old French, from *jeter,* to spout forth, from Latin *jactāre,* freq. of Latin *jacere,* to throw.]

jet engine. 1. Any engine that develops thrust by ejecting a jet of fluid, esp. a jet of gaseous combustion products. 2. Such an engine equipped to consume a mixture of fuel and atmospheric oxygen, used esp. in aircraft.

jet-pro·pelled (jĕt'prə-pĕld') *adj.* Propelled by one or more jet engines: *a jet-propelled airplane.*

jet propulsion. Propulsion derived from the expulsion of matter in a jet of fluid, esp. by jet engines.

jet·sam (jĕt'səm) *n.* 1. Cargo or equipment thrown overboard to lighten a ship in distress. 2. Discarded cargo or equipment found washed ashore, used esp. in the phrase: *flotsam and jetsam.* 3. Discarded odds and ends. [From JETTISON.]

jet stream. 1. A high-speed wind near the base of the stratosphere, gen. moving from a westerly direction at speeds often exceeding 250 miles an hour. 2. A high-speed stream; a jet.

jet·ti·son (jĕt'ĭ-sən, -zən) *tr.v.* 1. To cast off or overboard. 2. To discard (something): *jettison a strategy.* —*n.* 1. The act of jettisoning. 2. Jetsam. [From Middle English *jetteson,* a throwing overboard, from Norman French *getteson,* from Latin *jactātiō,* from *jactāre,* to throw.]

jet·ty (jĕt'ē) *n., pl.* **-ties.** 1. A pier or other structure projecting into a body of water to influence the current or tide or protect a harbor or shoreline. 2. A wharf; pier. [Middle English *jette,* from Old French *jetee,* a jutting, projection, from *jeter,* to throw, project.]

Jew (jōō) *n.* 1. An adherent of Judaism. 2. A descendant of the Hebrew people.

jew·el (jōō'əl) *n.* 1. A precious stone; gem. 2. An ornament, such as a ring or necklace, esp. one of precious metal set with gems. 3. A small gem or gem substitute used as a bearing, as in a watch. **4.** A person or thing that is greatly admired or valued. —*tr.v.* **-eled** or **-elled, -el·ing** or **-el·ling.** To adorn or set with jewels. [Middle English *iuel,* from Norman French *juel.*]

jew·el·er (jōō′ə-lər) *n.* Also *Brit.* **jew·el·ler.** A person who makes, repairs, or deals in jewelry.

jew·el·ry (jōō′əl-rē) *n.* Ornaments to be worn, made of precious metals set with gems or from imitation materials; jewels in general.

jew·el·weed (jōō′əl-wēd′) *n.* Any of several plants of the genus *Impatiens.* Also called **touch-me-not.**

Jew·ess (jōō′ĭs) *n.* A Jewish woman or girl.

jew·fish (jōō′fĭsh′) *n., pl.* **jewfish** or **-fish·es.** Any of several large, dark green or black, rough-scaled saltwater fishes of the family Serranidae, of tropical waters.

Jew·ish (jōō′ĭsh) *adj.* Of, concerning, or characteristic of the Jews, their customs, or their religion.

Jewish calendar. A calendar used by the Jewish people that dates the creation of the world at 3761 B.C.

Jew·ry (jōō′rē) *n.* **1.** The Jewish people. **2.** A section of a medieval city inhabited by Jews; ghetto.

jew's-harp (jōōz′härp′) *n.* Also **jews'-harp.** A small musical instrument with a lyre-shaped metal frame and a projecting, flexible steel tongue that is held between the teeth when played.

jez·e·bel (jĕz′ə-bĕl′, -bəl) *n.* A scheming, wicked woman. [After *Jezebel,* an idolatrous queen of Israel (I Kings 16).]

jib[1] (jĭb) *n.* A triangular sail set forward of the mast and stretching to the bowsprit or the bow. [Orig. unknown.]

jib[2] (jĭb) *n.* **1.** The arm of a mechanical crane. **2.** The boom of a derrick. [Prob. from GIBBET.]

jib[3] (jĭb) *intr.v.* **jibbed, jib·bing.** To jibe. [Orig. unknown.]

jib[4] (jĭb) *intr.v.* **jibbed, jib·bing.** To draw back, balk, or shy, as a horse. [Orig. unknown.]

jib boom. A spar that forms an extension of the bowsprit.

jibe[1] (jĭb) *v.* **jibed, jib·ing.** —*intr.v.* To shift a fore-and-aft sail from one side of a vessel to the other while sailing before the wind. —*tr.v.* To cause to jibe. [From obs. Dutch *gijben.*]

jibe[2] (jĭb) *v. & n.* Var. of **gibe.**

jibe[3] (jĭb) *intr.v.* *Informal.* To be in accord; harmonize; agree. —See Usage note at **gibe.** [Orig. unknown.]

jif·fy (jĭf′ē) *n., pl.* **-fies.** Also **jiff** (jĭf). *Informal.* A moment; an instant; no time at all. —See Syns at **moment.** [Orig. unknown.]

jig (jĭg) *n.* **1. a.** Any of various lively dances in triple time. **b.** The music for such a dance. **2.** A metal fishing lure with one or more hooks, usu. fished on near the bottom and jerked up and down. **3.** A device for guiding a tool or for holding work as it is fed to a tool. —*v.* **jigged, jig·ging.** —*intr.v.* **1.** To dance or play a jig. **2.** To move or bob up and down jerkily and rapidly. **3.** To operate a jig, as in fishing or machine work. —*tr.v.* **1.** To bob or jerk up and down or to and fro. **2.** To machine with the aid of a jig. [Orig. unknown.]

jig·ger[1] (jĭg′ər) *n.* **1.** A person who jigs or operates a jig. **2. a.** A small measure for liquor, usu. holding 1 1/2 ounces. **b.** This amount of liquor. **3.** Any of various devices that operate with a jerking or jolting motion, as a drill. **4.** *Naut.* **a.** A light all-purpose tackle. **b.** A small sail set in the stern of a yawl or similar boat. **c.** A **jigger mast.**

jig·ger[2] (jĭg′ər) *n.* A mite, the chigger. [Var. of CHIGOE.]

jig·gle (jĭg′əl) *v.* **-gled, -gling.** —*intr.v.* To move or rock lightly up and down or to and fro in an unsteady, jerky manner. —*tr.v.* To cause to move in this manner. —*n.* A jiggling motion. [Freq. of JIG (to move).]

jig·saw (jĭg′sô′) *n.* A saw with a narrow blade fixed vertically in a frame, used to cut curved or wavy lines.

jigsaw puzzle. A game consisting of a mass of irregularly shaped pieces of cardboard or wood that are fitted together to form a picture.

jilt (jĭlt) *tr.v.* To deceive or cast aside (a lover). —*n.* A person who discards a lover. [Prob. from earlier *jillet,* a flirtatious woman, from *jill,* girl.]

Jim Crow. *Slang.* The practice of discriminating against and segregating black people. [After *Jim Crow,* a character in an act by Thomas D. Rice (1808–60), American entertainer.] —**jim′-crow** or **Jim′-Crow** *adj.*

jim·my (jĭm′ē) *n., pl.* **-mies.** A short crowbar with curved ends, often regarded as a burglar's tool. —*tr.v.* **-mied, -my·ing.** To pry open with or as if with a jimmy. [*Jimmy,* pet form of the name *James.*]

jim·son·weed (jĭm′sən-wēd′) *n.* A coarse, poisonous plant, *Datura stramonium,* with large, trumpet-shaped white or purplish flowers and prickly fruit. Also called **stramonium.** [From earlier *Jamestown weed,* after *Jamestown,* Virginia.]

jin·gle (jĭng′gəl) *v.* **-gled, -gling.** —*intr.v.* **1.** To make a tinkling or ringing metallic sound. **2.** To have the catchy sound of a poetic jingle. —*tr.v.* To cause to jingle. —*n.* **1.** The sound produced by bits of metal striking together. **2.** A simple, repetitious, catchy rhyme or doggerel. [Middle English *ginglen.*]

jin·go (jĭng′gō) *n., pl.* **-goes.** A person who is characterized by jingoism. —*adj.* **1.** Of or pertaining to a jingo. **2.** Characterized by jingoism. [From the phrase *by Jingo,* used in a belligerently chauvinistic song.] —**jin′go·is′tic** *adj.* —**jin′go·ist** *n. & adj.*

jin·go·ism (jĭng′gō-ĭz′əm) *n.* Extreme chauvinism or patriotism, esp. the advocacy of a belligerent and aggressive foreign policy.

jin·ni (jĭn′ē, jĭ-nē′) *n., pl.* **jinn** (jĭn). In Moslem legend, a spirit capable of assuming various forms and exercising supernatural power over men. [Arabic *jinnīy.*]

jin·rik·sha or **jin·rick·sha** (jĭn-rĭk′shô′) *n.* Also **jin·rik·i·sha** (-rĭk′shō′). A small, two-wheeled, oriental carriage drawn by one man. Also called **rickshaw.** [Japanese *jinrikisha* : *jin,* man + *riki,* strength + *sha,* vehicle.]

jinx (jĭngks) *n.* *Informal.* **1.** Something or someone believed to bring bad luck. **2.** A condition or spell of bad luck caused by such an object or person. —*tr.v.* To bring bad luck or misfortune to. [Poss. from Greek *iunx,* a bird used in magic.]

jit·ney (jĭt′nē) *n.* *Informal.* A small bus or automobile that transports passengers on a route for a small fare. [Orig. unknown.]

jit·ter·bug (jĭt′ər-bŭg′) *n.* *Slang.* **1.** A lively dance consisting of various two-step patterns often with twirls and acrobatic maneuvers, esp. popular in the 1940's. **2.** A person who does such a dance. —*intr.v.* **-bugged, -bug·ging.** To dance the jitterbug.

jit·ters (jĭt′ərz) *pl.n.* *Informal.* A fit of nervousness. [Orig. unknown.]

jit·ter·y (jĭt′ə-rē) *adj.* **-i·er, -i·est.** Nervous and fidgety. —See Syns at **edgy.**

jiu·jit·su or **jiu·jut·su** (jōō-jĭt′sōō) *n.* Vars. of **jujitsu.**

jive (jīv) *n.* *Slang.* **1.** Jazz or swing music. **2.** The jargon of jazz musicians and enthusiasts. **3.** Deceptive, nonsensical, or glib talk. [Orig. unknown.]

job (jŏb) *n.* **1.** An action or piece of work that needs to be done; a task. **2.** A regular activity performed in exchange for payment, esp. a trade, occupation, or profession. **3.** A specific piece of work to be done for a set fee: *an expensive repair job.* **4.** An object or task to be worked on. **5.** Anything resulting from or produced by work. **6.** A position of employment. **7.** A duty or responsibility. **8.** *Informal.* A difficult or strenuous task: *Trucking is a tough job.* **9.** *Informal.* A bad or unsatisfactory piece of work: *Boy, he did a job on her hair.* **10.** *Informal.* A criminal act, esp. a robbery. —See Syns at **work.** —*v.* **jobbed, job·bing.** —*intr.v.* **1.** To work by the piece or at odd jobs. **2.** To act

jigsaw   jinriksha

ă pat   ā pay   â care   ä father   ĕ pet   ē be   hw which   ĭ pit   ī tie   î pier   ŏ pot   ō toe   ô paw, for   oi noise
ōō took   ōō boot   ou out   th thin   *th* this   ŭ cut   û urge   zh vision   ə about, item, edible, gallop, circus

as a middleman or jobber. —*tr.v.* **1.** To purchase (merchandise) from manufacturers and sell it to retailers. **2.** To arrange for (work) to be done in portions by others; to subcontract. —*idiom.* **on the job.** *Informal.* Paying close attention to one's work or responsibilities. [Perh. from obs. *job,* piece.] —**job′less** *adj.* —**job′less·ness** *n.*

job action. A temporary action (as a strike or slowdown) by workers to exact demands or as a protest against a company decision.

job·ber (jŏb′ər) *n.* **1.** A person who buys merchandise from manufacturers and sells it to retailers. **2.** A person who works by the piece or at odd jobs.

job·hold·er (jŏb′hōl′dər) *n.* One who has a regular job.

job lot. **1.** Miscellaneous merchandise sold in one lot. **2.** Any collection of cheap items.

jock·ey (jŏk′ē) *n., pl.* **-eys.** A person who rides horses in races, esp. as a profession. —*v.* **-eyed, -ey·ing.** —*tr.v.* **1.** To ride (a horse) as jockey. **2.** To direct or maneuver by cleverness or skill: *jockey a car into a tight space.* **3.** To trick; to cheat. —*intr.v.* **1.** To ride a horse in a race. **2.** To maneuver in order to gain an advantage: *jockey for power.* [Dim. of Scottish *Jock,* pet form of the name *Jack.*]

jock·strap (jŏk′străp′) *n.* Also **jock strap.** An athletic supporter. [Slang *jock,* penis, + STRAP.]

jo·cose (jō-kōs′) *adj.* **1.** Given to joking; merry. **2.** Characterized by joking; humorous. [Latin *jocōsus,* from *jocus,* jest, joke.] —**jo·cose′ness** or **jo·cos′i·ty** (jō-kŏs′ĭ-tē) *n.* —**jo·cose′ly** *adv.*

joc·u·lar (jŏk′yə-lər) *adj.* **1.** Given to or characterized by joking; fun-loving. **2.** Meant in jest; facetious. [Latin *joculāris,* from *joculus,* dim. of *jocus,* jest, joke.] —**joc′u·lar′i·ty** (jŏk′yə-lăr′ĭ-tē) *n.* —**joc′u·lar·ly** *adv.*

joc·und (jŏk′ənd, jō′kənd) *adj.* Cheerful; merry; gay. [Middle English, from Old French, from Late Latin *jōcundus,* from Latin *jūcundus,* pleasant, from *juvāre,* to delight.] —**jo·cun′di·ty** (jō-kŭn′dĭ-tē) *n.* —**joc′und·ly** *adv.*

jodh·purs (jŏd′pərz) *pl.n.* Breeches worn for horseback riding that fit loosely above the knees and tightly from the knees to the ankles. [After *Jodhpur,* India.]

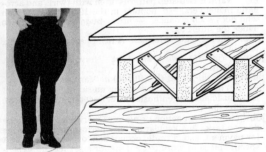

jodhpurs　　　　　　　　　　joist

jog¹ (jŏg) *v.* **jogged, jog·ging.** —*tr.v.* **1.** To jar or move by shoving, bumping, or jerking. **2.** To give a slight push or shake; to nudge. **3.** To stimulate, esp. one's memory. —*intr.v.* **1.** To run or ride at a steady slow trot. **2.** To run in such a way for exercise or sport. **3.** To proceed leisurely with or as if with occasional bumps. —*n.* **1.** A slight jolt or nudge. **2.** A slow steady pace; a trot. [Orig. unknown.] —**jog′ger** *n.*

jog² (jŏg) *n.* **1.** A protruding or receding part in a surface or line. **2.** An abrupt change in direction. [Perh. var. of JAG.]

jog·gle (jŏg′əl) *v.* **-gled, -gling.** —*tr.v.* To shake slightly. —*intr.v.* To move with a shaking motion. —*n.* A shaking or jolting motion. [Freq. of JOG.]

John Bull (jŏn bool′). **1.** A personification of England or the English. **2.** A typical Englishman. [From a character in *Law is a Bottomless Pit* (1712), a satire by John Arbuthnot (1667-1735), Scottish writer.]

John Doe (jŏn dō′). **1.** A name used in legal proceedings to designate a fictitious or unidentified person. **2.** The average, everyday man.

John Han·cock (jŏn hăn′kŏk′). *Informal.* A person's signature. [After John *Hancock* (1737-93), American statesman, whose signature appears prominently on the

Declaration of Independence.]

john·ny·cake (jŏn′ē-kāk′) *n.* A thin, flat cornmeal bread, often baked on a griddle.

John·ny-jump-up (jŏn′ē-jŭmp′ŭp′) *n.* A plant, the heartsease. [From its quick growth.]

John·ny-on-the-spot (jŏn′ē-ŏn′thə-spŏt′,-ôn′-) *n. Informal.* A person who is ready to act when necessary.

John·ny Reb (jŏn′ē rĕb′). *Informal.* A confederate soldier.

joie de vi·vre (zhwä də vē′vrə) *French.* Carefree enjoyment of life.

join (join) *tr.v.* **1.** To put or bring together; unite or make continuous: *A bridge joins the two islands.* **2.** To put or bring into close association or relationship. **3.** To meet and unite with: *The stream joins the river up ahead.* **4.** To unite or combine: *join forces.* **5.** To become a part or member of: *join the party.* **6.** To take a place among, in, or with; enter into the company of: *I shall join you later.* **7.** To become associated with: *If you can't lick 'em, join 'em.* **8.** To take part; participate: *joined the argument.* **9.** *Informal.* To adjoin. **10.** *Geom.* To connect (points), as with a straight line. —*intr.v.* **1.** To come or act together; form a connection, junction, or alliance: *Neighbors joined in looking for the missing child.* **2.** To take part; participate: *He joined in the singing.* —*n.* A joint; junction. —*idiom.* **join up.** To enlist, esp. in the armed forces. [Middle English *joinen,* from Old French *joindre,* from Latin *jungere.*]

Syns: join, connect, link, unite *v. Core meaning:* To bring or come together (*join hands; join the links of a chain; join in wedlock*). Join has the widest application, in both literal and figurative use. CONNECT and LINK imply a looser relationship in which individual units retain their identity while coming together at some point (*capillaries connecting the arteries and the veins; the Panama Canal that links the Atlantic and the Pacific*). UNITE stresses the oneness that results from joining (*a plan to unite the thirteen colonies under one government; uniting all nations for peace*).

join·er (joi′nər) *n.* **1.** Someone or something that joins. **2.** A skilled carpenter or craftsman who makes indoor woodwork and furniture, esp. one who builds objects fastened together with wooden fittings. **3.** *Informal.* A person given to joining groups, causes, etc.

join·er·y (joi′nə-rē) *n.* **1.** The skill or craft of a joiner. **2.** Woodwork and other objects made by a joiner.

joint (joint) *n.* **1.** *Anat.* A point at which movable body parts are connected or come together, as between bones or between segments in the leg of an arthropod. **2.** A point at which or a structure by which two or more things come or are fitted together. **3.** Something used to join two parts or hold them together: *a ball-and-socket joint.* **4.** *Bot.* A point on a stem from which a leaf or branch may grow; a node. **5.** *Geol.* A fracture or crack in a rock mass along which no appreciable movement has occurred. **6.** A large cut of meat, such as the shoulder or leg, used for roasting. **7.** *Slang.* **a.** A cheap or disreputable gathering place, such as a restaurant or bar. **b.** Any public establishment or dwelling. **8.** *Slang.* A marijuana cigarette. —*adj.* **1.** Shared by or common to two or more. **2.** Sharing with another or others: *joint ownership* **3.** Formed or characterized by cooperation or united action: *a joint effort.* **4.** Involving both houses of a legislature: *a joint effort.* —*tr.v.* **1.** To provide with a joint or joints. **2.** To cut (meat) into joints. —*idiom.* **out of joint.** **1.** Dislocated, as a bone. **2.** Not harmonious; inconsistent. **3.** Out of order; unsatisfactory. [Middle English, from Old French, from the past part. of *joindre,* to join.] —**joint′ed** *adj.*

Joint Chiefs of Staff. The principal military advisory group to the President of the United States, composed of the chiefs of the Army, Navy, and Air Force.

joint·ly (joint′lē) *adv.* Together; in common.

joint-stock company (joint′stŏk′). A business whose capital is held in transferable shares of stock by its joint owners.

join·ture (join′chər) *n.* Property set aside by a husband to be used for the support of his wife after his death. [Middle English, from Old French, from Latin *junctūra,* a joining.]

joist (joist) *n.* Any of the parallel horizontal beams set from wall to wall to support the boards of a floor or ceiling. [Middle English *giste,* from Old French, beam supporting a bridge, from Latin *jacitum*, from the past part. of *jacēre*, to lie down.]

joke (jōk) *n*. **1.** A short story, esp. one with a punch line, designed to cause laughter. **2.** An amusing or jesting remark. **3.** A mischievous trick; prank. **4.** An amusing or ludicrous incident or situation. **5.** Something not to be taken seriously: *His accident was no joke.* **6.** An object of amusement or laughter; a laughingstock. —*intr.v.* **joked, jok·ing. 1.** To tell or play jokes: *She's always joking about something.* **2.** To speak in fun; be facetious: *Don't joke, this is serious.* [Latin *jocus*, jest, joke.] —**jok'ing·ly** *adv.*
Syns: joke, gag (*Informal*), **jape, jest, quip, witticism** *n.* Core meaning: Words or actions intended to cause laughter or amusement (*opened the show with a joke*).

jok·er (jō'kər) *n*. **1. a.** A person who tells jokes or is inclined to joking. **b.** A prankster or practical joker; smart aleck. **2.** A playing card, used in certain games as the highest ranking card or as a wild card. **3.** A minor clause in a document such as a legislative bill that voids or changes its original or intended purpose.

jol·li·fi·ca·tion (jŏl'ə-fĭ-kā'shən) *n.* Festivity; merrymaking. [From JOLLY.]

jol·li·ty (jŏl'ĭ-tē) *n.* The condition or quality of being jolly; gaiety; merriment. —See Syns at **gaiety.**

jol·ly (jŏl'ē) *adj*. **-li·er, -li·est. 1.** Full of merriment and good spirits; fun-loving. **2.** Showing or causing happiness or mirth; cheerful: *jolly laughter.* **3.** *Brit. Informal.* Greatly pleasing; enjoyable: *It was jolly to see her.* —*adv. Brit. Informal.* Very; extremely: *a jolly good cook.* —*tr.v.* **-lied, -ly·ing.** To keep amused or diverted for one's own purposes; to humor. [Middle English *jolif, joli*, from Old French, gay, pleasant.] —**jol'li·ly** *adv.* —**jol'li·ness** *n.*

jol·ly·boat (jŏl'ē-bōt') *n.* A small boat carried aboard a larger ship. [Orig. unknown.]

Jolly Rog·er (rŏj'ər). A black flag bearing the emblematic white skull and crossbones of a pirate ship.

jolt (jōlt) *tr.v*. **1.** To shake violently with a sudden, sharp blow. **2.** To put into a specified condition by or as if by a blow: *The tragedy jolted us out of our complacency.* —*intr.v.* To move in a bumpy or jerky fashion: *a bus jolting to a stop.* —*n.* **1.** A sudden jerk or bump. **2.** An abrupt or unexpected shock or reversal: *The news came as a jolt.* [Orig. unknown.]

Jo·nah (jō'nə) *n.* Someone thought to bring bad luck. [After *Jonah*, an Old Testament prophet who brought danger to the ship in which he was journeying.]

jon·gleur (jŏng'glər; French zhôN-glœr') *n.* A wandering minstrel and storyteller in Medieval Europe. [French, from Old French, var. of *joglere*, juggler.]

jon·quil (jŏng'kwĭl, jŏn'-) *n.* A widely cultivated plant, *Narcissus jonquilla*, with long, narrow leaves and short-tubed, fragrant yellow flowers. [From Spanish *junquillo*, dim. of *junco*, rush, reed, from Latin *juncus*.]

jonquil

Joshua tree

jor·dan almond (jôr'dn). **1.** A large variety of almond from Spain, used widely in confections. **2.** An almond with a sugar coating. [By folk ety. from Middle English *jardyne almaunde*, "garden almond."]

josh (jŏsh) *tr.v.* To tease (someone) good-humoredly. —*intr.v.* To banter; to joke. [Orig. unknown.]

Josh·u·a tree (jŏsh'ŏŏ-ə) A treelike plant, *Yucca brevifolia*, of the southwestern United States, with swordshaped leaves and greenish-white flowers. [From its

greatly extended branches, recalling the outstretched arm of the prophet Joshua as he pointed with his spear to the city of Ai. (Joshua 8:18).]

joss (jŏs) *n.* A Chinese idol or image. [Pidgin English, from Portuguese *deos*, god, from Latin *deus*.]

joss house. A Chinese temple or shrine.

jos·tle (jŏs'əl). Also **jus·tle** (jŭs'-). —*v.* **-tled, -tling.** —*intr.v.* **1.** To move against by pushing or elbowing: *a crowd jostling in the square.* **2.** To vie for an advantage or favorable position. —*tr.v.* To bump or knock into: *couples jostled each other on the dance floor.* —*n.* A rough shove or push. [Middle English *justlen*, to come against in combat, freq. of *justen*, from Old French *juster*, to joust.]

jot (jŏt) *n.* The smallest bit or particle; iota. —*tr.v.* **jot·ted, jot·ting.** To write down briefly and hastily. [Earlier *iote*, from Latin *iōta*, from Greek, iota.]

joule (jōōl, joul) *n. Abbr.* **J** A unit of energy, equal to the work done when the point of application of a force of 1 newton is displaced 1 meter in the direction of the force. [After James Prescott Joule (1818–89), British physicist.]

jounce (jouns) *v.* **jounced, jounc·ing.** —*intr.v.* To move with bumps and jolts. —*tr.v.* To cause to jounce. —*n.* A rough, jolting bounce. [Middle English *jouncen*.]

jour·nal (jûr'nəl) *n.* **1.** A daily record of occurrences, experiences, or observations. **2.** An official record of daily proceedings or transactions, as of a legislative body. **3.** A newspaper. **4.** A periodical presenting news in a particular area: *a medical journal.* **5.** The part of a shaft or axle supported by a bearing. [Middle English, from Old French *jornal*, from *journal*, daily, from Late Latin *diurnālis*, from Latin *diēs*, day.]

jour·nal·ese (jûr'nə-lēz', -lēs') *n.* The slick, superficial style of writing often held to be characteristic of newspapers and magazines.

jour·nal·ism (jûr'nə-lĭz'əm) *n.* **1.** The collecting, writing, editing, and publishing of news or news articles through newspapers or magazines. **2.** The profession of or academic training in journalism. **3.** Written material of current interest or wide popular appeal.

jour·nal·ist (jûr'nə-lĭst) *n.* A person whose occupation is journalism, esp. a reporter or editor.

jour·nal·is·tic (jûr'nə-lĭs'tĭk) *adj.* Of or pertaining to, or characteristic of journalism or journalists.

jour·ney (jûr'nē) *n., pl.* **-neys. 1.** Travel from one place to another. **2.** The distance to be traveled or the time required for such a trip. —*intr.v.* To travel. —*tr.v.* To travel over or through. [Middle English, a day's traveling, from Old French *jornee*, from Latin *diurnum*, daily portion, from *diēs*, day.] —**jour'ney·er** *n.*

jour·ney·man (jûr'nē-mən) *n.* **1.** A person who has mastered a trade or craft and works in another's employ. **2.** Any competent worker.

joust (joust, jŭst, jōōst) *n.* **1.** A combat with lances between two mounted knights. **2. jousts.** A series of these matches; a tournament. **3.** Any combat or struggle suggestive of a joust. —*intr.v.* To engage in such combat; to tilt. [Middle English, from Old French *jouste*, from *juster*, to join battle, joust, ult. from Latin *juxtā*, close together.]

Jove (jōv) *n.* **1.** *Rom. Myth.* The god Jupiter. **2.** *Poet.* The planet Jupiter.

jo·vi·al (jō'vē-əl) *adj.* Marked by good humor and hearty conviviality; jolly. [Orig. "born under the influence of (the planet) Jupiter," from French *jovial*, from Italian *gioviale*, from *Giove*, Jove.] —**jo'vi·al'i·ty** (-ǎl'ĭ-tē) *n.* —**jo'vi·al·ly** *adv.*

jowl¹ (joul) *n.* **1.** The jaw, esp. the lower jaw. **2.** The cheek. [Middle English *chawle*, from Old English *ceafl*.]

jowl² (joul) *n.* **1.** The flesh under the lower jaw, esp. when plump or flabby. **2.** A similar fleshy part, as a dewlap or a wattle. [Middle English *cholle*.]

joy (joi) *n.* **1.** A condition or feeling of great pleasure or happiness. **2.** The expression or manifestation of such feeling. **3.** A source of pleasure or satisfaction. —*intr.v.* To take pleasure; rejoice. [Middle English, from Old French *joye*, from Latin *gaudium*, gladness, from *gaudēre*, to rejoice.]

joy·ful (joi'fəl) *adj.* **1.** Full of joy: *a joyful occasion.* **2.** Showing or expressing joy: *a joyful song.* —See Syns at **glad** and **merry.** —**joy'ful·ly** *adv.* —**joy'ful·ness** *n.*

joy·less (joi′lĭs) *adj.* Cheerless; dismal. —See Syns at **gloomy.** —**joy′less·ly** *adv.* —**joy′less·ness** *n.*

joy·ous (joi′əs) *adj.* Feeling or causing joy. —See Syns at **glad and merry.** —**joy′ous·ly** *adv.* —**joy′ous·ness** *n.*

joy·ride (joi′rīd′) *n.* An often reckless automobile ride taken for fun and thrills.

ju·bi·lant (jōō′bə-lənt) *adj.* Feeling or expressing great joy; rejoicing. [Latin *jūbilāns*, pres. part. of *jūbilāre*, to shout for joy.] —**ju′bi·lance** *n.* —**ju′bi·lant·ly** *adv.*

ju·bi·la·tion (jōō′bə-lā′shən) *n.* **1.** The condition of being jubilant; exultation. **2.** A celebration or other expression of joy.

ju·bi·lee (jōō′bə-lē′) *n.* **1. a.** A special anniversary, esp. a 25th or 50th anniversary. **b.** The celebration of such an anniversary. **2.** A season or occasion of joyful celebration. **3.** Jubilation; rejoicing. **4.** *Rom. Cath. Ch.* A year during which plenary indulgence may be obtained by the performance of certain pious acts. [Middle English, from Old French *jubilé*, from Late Latin *jūbilaeus (annus)*, "(year) of jubilee," from Late Greek *iōbēlaios*, ult. from Hebrew *yōbhēl*, ram's horn (used to proclaim the jubilee).]

Ju·da·ic (jōō-dā′ĭk) or **Ju·da·i·cal** (-ĭ-kəl) *adj.* Of or pertaining to Jews or Judaism.

Ju·da·ism (jōō′dē-ĭz′əm) *n.* **1.** The monotheistic religion of the Jewish people, that has its spiritual and ethical principles embodied chiefly in the Bible and the Talmud. **2.** Observation of the traditional ceremonies and rites of the Jewish religion. **3.** The cultural, spiritual, and social way of life of the Jewish people.

Ju·da·ize (jōō′dē-īz′) *v.* **-ized, -iz·ing.** —*tr.v.* To bring into conformity with Judaism. —*intr.v.* To adopt Jewish customs and beliefs.

Ju·das (jōō′dəs) *n.* A person who betrays under the appearance of friendship. [From *Judas* Iscariot, a disciple who betrayed Jesus.]

Judas tree. The redbud. [After *Judas* Iscariot, who was believed to have hanged himself on such a tree.]

judge (jŭj) *v.* **judged, judg·ing.** —*tr.v.* **1.** To hear and pass judgment upon in a court of law. **2.** To determine or settle authoritatively after deliberation. **3.** To form an opinion about; assess; appraise: *judge character; judge distances.* **4.** To criticize; to censure. **5.** *Informal.* To think; consider; suppose: *I judge him a good father.* —*intr.v.* **1.** To act or decide as a judge; pass judgment. **2.** To form an opinion or estimation: *You must judge for yourself in this matter.* —*n.* **1.** A public official who hears and decides cases brought before a court of law. **2.** An appointed arbiter in a contest or competition. **3.** One whose critical judgment or opinion is sought; a connoisseur: *a judge of fine wines.* **4.** *Judges.* See table at **Bible.** [Middle English *jugen*, from Old French *jugier*, from Latin *jūdicāre*, from *jūdex*, judge.]

Syns: judge, arbitrate, decide, decree, determine, referee, rule, umpire *v.* **Core meaning:** To make a decision about (a controversy or dispute) after deliberating about it (*a jury judging the merits of the case*).

judge·ment (jŭj′mənt) *n.* Var. of **judgment.**

judge·ship (jŭj′shĭp′) *n.* The office or jurisdiction of a judge or the length of a judge's term in office.

judg·ment (jŭj′mənt) *n.* Also **judge·ment.** **1.** The capacity to perceive, discern, or make reasonable decisions. **2.** The act of or an instance of judging. **3.** A decision, opinion, or conclusion reached after due consideration. **4.** A formal decision, as of an arbiter in a contest. **5.** An estimation or guess: *make a judgment of the distance.* **6.** *Law.* **a.** A determination or decree of a court of law; a judicial decision. **b.** A court act creating or affirming an obligation, such as a debt. **c.** A writ in witness of such an act.

Judgment Day. In the teleology of Judaism, Christianity, and Islam, the day of God's final judgment.

ju·di·ca·ture (jōō′dĭ-kə-choor′, -chər) *n.* **1.** The administering of justice. **2.** The position, function, or authority of a judge. **3.** The jurisdiction of a law court or a judge. **4.** A court of law. **5.** A system of law courts and their judges. [Old French, from Medieval Latin *jūdicātūra*, from Latin *jūdicāre*, to judge.]

ju·di·cial (jōō-dĭsh′əl) *adj.* **1.** Of, pertaining to, or proper to courts of law or to the administration of justice. **2.** Decreed by or proceeding from a court of justice: *judicial decision.* **3.** Characterized by or expressing judgment; critical. [Middle English, from Old French, from Latin *jūdiciālis*, from *jūdicium*, judgment, from *jūdex*, judge.] —**ju·di′cial·ly** *adv.*

Usage: judicial, judicious. *Judicial* refers broadly to courts of law and the administration of justice: *judicial branch of government; the judicial process;* whereas *judicious* indicates the exercise of sound judgment: *a judicious executive; judicious measures.*

ju·di·ci·ar·y (jōō-dĭsh′ē-ĕr′ē) *adj.* Of or pertaining to courts, judges, or the administration of justice. —*n., pl.* **-ar·ies.** **1.** The judicial branch of government. **2.** A system of courts of justice. **3.** Judges in general. [Latin *jūdiciārius*, from *jūdicium*, judgment.]

ju·di·cious (jōō-dĭsh′əs) *adj.* Having or exhibiting forethought and sound judgment; sensible: *a judicious use of resources.* —See Usage note at **judicial.** [Old French *judicieux*, from Latin *jūdicium*, judgment.] —**ju·di′cious·ly** *adv.* —**ju·di′cious·ness** *n.*

ju·do (jōō′dō) *n.* A modern form of jujitsu applying principles of balance and leverage, often used as a method of physical and mental training. [Japanese *jūdō* : *jū*, soft + *dō*, way.]

judo

jug (jŭg) *n.* **1.** A small pitcher. **2. a.** A tall, often rounded vessel of earthenware, glass, or metal with a small mouth and handle, made for holding liquids. **b.** The contents of a jug. **c.** The amount of liquid a jug will hold. **3.** *Slang.* A jail. —*tr.v.* **jugged, jug·ging. 1.** To stew or cook in an earthenware jug or jar. **2.** *Slang.* To put in jail. [Orig. unknown.]

jug·ger·naut (jŭg′ər-nôt′) *n.* A massive advancing force or object that crushes anything in its path. [From JUGGERNAUT.]

Jug·ger·naut (jŭg′ər-nôt′) *n.* An idol of the Hindu deity Krishna, drawn in an annual procession on a huge car or wagon under whose wheels worshipers are said to have thrown themselves to be crushed. [Hindi *Jagannath*, from Sanskrit *Jaganātha*, "Lord of the world."]

jug·gle (jŭg′əl) *v.* **-gled, -gling.** —*tr.v.* **1.** To keep (two or more balls, plates, etc.) in the air at one time by alternately tossing and catching them. **2.** To keep (more than one activity) in motion or progress at one time: *juggling two jobs.* **3.** To attempt to balance or otherwise cope with: *juggle a handbag and glass at a cocktail party.* **4.** To manipulate in order to deceive: *juggle figures in a ledger.* —*intr.v.* **1.** To perform tricks with sleight of hand. **2.** To use trickery or deceive. —*n.* **1.** An act of juggling. **2.** A deception or trick. [Middle English *jogelen*, from Old French *jogler*, from Latin *joculārī*, to jest, from *jocus*, jest, joke.]

jug·gler (jŭg′lər) *n.* **1.** An entertainer who juggles balls or other objects. **2.** Someone who uses tricks, deception, or fraud.

jug·u·lar (jŭg′yə-lər) *adj.* Of, pertaining to, or located in the neck or throat. —*n.* A jugular vein. [Late Latin *jugulāris*, from Latin *jugulum*, collarbone, dim. of *jugum*, yoke.]

jugular vein. Any of several large veins of the neck.

juice (jōōs) *n.* **1.** Any fluid naturally contained in plant or animal tissue, esp. that from a fruit or vegetable used as a beverage. **2.** Any bodily secretion. **3.** *Slang.* Vigorous life and vitality. **4.** *Slang.* **a.** Electric current. **b.** Fuel for an engine. —*tr.v.* **juiced, juic·ing.** To extract the juice from. [Middle English *jus*, from Old French, from Latin *jūs*, broth, sauce, juice.]

juic·er (jōō′sər) *n.* A kitchen appliance for extracting juice from fruits and vegetables.

ă pat　ā pay　â care　ä father　ĕ pet　ē be　hw which　ĭ pit　ī tie　î pier　ŏ pot　ō toe　ô paw, for　oi noise
ōō took　ōō boot　ou out　th thin　th this　ŭ cut　û urge　zh vision　ə about, item, edible, gallop, circus

juic·y (jōō'sē) *adj.* **-i·er, -i·est. 1.** Full of juice; succulent. **2.** Interesting, colorful, or racy. **—juic'i·ness** *n.*

ju·jit·su (jōō-jĭt'sōō) *n.* Also **ju·jut·su, jiu·jit·su, jiu·jut·su.** A Japanese art of self-defense or hand-to-hand combat based on set maneuvers that force an opponent to use his weight and strength against himself. [Japanese *jūjitsu* : *jū,* soft, yielding + *jitsu,* art.]

ju·jube (jōō'jōōb) *n.* **1.** A spiny, Old World tree, *Ziziphus jujuba,* with small yellowish flowers and dark-red fruit. **2.** The fleshy, edible fruit of the jujube. **3.** (*also* jōō'jōō-bē). A fruit-flavored, usu. chewy candy. [Middle English *iuiube,* from Medieval Latin *jujuba,* from Latin *zizy-phum,* from Greek *zizuphon.*]

ju·jut·su (jōō-jĭt'sōō) *n.* Var. of **jujitsu.**

juke box (jōōk). A coin-operated phonograph, usu. with push buttons for the selection of records. [From earlier *juke-house,* a brothel, from Gullah *juke,* disorderly.]

ju·lep (jōō'lǝp) *n.* **1.** A mint julep. **2.** A sweet syrupy drink, esp. one to which medicine may be added. [Middle English *iulep,* from Old French *julep,* from Arabic *julāb,* from Persian *gulāb,* rose water : *gul,* rose + *āb,* water.]

Jul·ian calendar (jōōl'yǝn). The calendar introduced by Julius Caesar in Rome in 46 B.C., eventually replaced by the Gregorian calendar.

ju·li·enne (jōō'lē-ĕn'; *French* zhl-yĕn') *adj.* Cut into long thin strips: *julienne potatoes.* [From French *à la julienne,* prob. from the name *Julien* or *Jules.*]

Ju·ly (jōō-lī', jǝ-) *n.* The seventh month of the year. July has 31 days. [Middle English *Julie,* from Norman French, from Latin *Jūlius (mēnsis),* (month of) Julius Caesar.]

jum·ble (jŭm'bǝl) *tr.v.* **-bled, -bling. 1.** To stir or mix in a disordered mass: *jumbled the shoes together.* **2.** To muddle; confuse: *The rapid-fire questioning jumbled his thoughts.* —See Syns at **confuse.** *—n.* **1.** A confused or disordered mass. **2.** A disordered state; a muddle. [Orig. unknown.]

jum·bo (jŭm'bō) *n., pl.* **-bos.** An unusually large person, animal, or thing. *—adj.* Much larger than average. —See Syns at **giant.** [After *Jumbo,* a large elephant exhibited by P.T. Barnum in the 1880's.]

jump (jŭmp) *intr.v.* **1.** To spring off the ground or other base by a muscular effort of the legs and feet. **2.** To move suddenly and in one motion: *jumped out of bed.* **3.** To start involuntarily, as in fear or surprise: *jump at a loud noise.* **4.** To move or be displaced with a sudden jerk or jerks: *The phonograph needle jumped.* **5.** To throw oneself down, off, out, or into something: *jumped out the window. He jumped into the political fray.* **6.** To rise suddenly and pronouncedly: *Prices jumped.* **7.** To pass quickly from one thing to another further on, as if by skipping intermediate or unnecessary points: *Her lecture kept jumping from one subject to another.* **8.** To spring at with the intent to assail or criticize: *He jumped at me as soon as I began to speak.* **9.** To arrive at hastily or haphazardly: *jump to conclusions.* **10.** To grab at eagerly: *jump at a bargain.* **11.** *Informal.* To respond or act quickly: *Jump when I give you an order.* **12.** *Slang.* To have a lively, pulsating quality: *a nightclub that jumps.* **13.** *Checkers.* To move over an opponent's playing piece. **14.** *Bridge.* To make a jump bid. *—tr.v.* **1.** To leap over or across: *jump the rope.* **2.** To leap upon: *jump a bus.* **3.** To cause to leap: *jump a horse over a hurdle.* **4.** To spring upon in sudden attack: *The muggers jumped him.* **5.** To move or start prematurely: *jumped the traffic light.* **6.** To leave (a course or track) abruptly through mishap: *The train jumped the rail.* **7.** To cause to increase suddenly and markedly: *The embargo jumped gas prices.* **8.** To pass over or skip: *The typewriter jumped a space.* **9.** To promote, esp. by more than one level: *He was jumped to head foreman.* **10.** *Checkers.* To take (an opponent's piece) by moving over it with one's own checker. **11.** *Bridge.* To raise (a partner's bid) by more than is necessary. *—n.* **1.** The act of jumping; a leap. **2.** The space or distance covered by a leap. **3.** A hurdle, barrier, or span to be jumped. **4.** A track sport featuring skill in jumping. **5.** A sudden, involuntary movement, as when startled. **6.** A sudden, pronounced rise, as in price or salary. **7.** A step or level: *a jump ahead of the others.* **8.** A major or sudden transition, as from one career, subject, etc. to another. **9.** A short trip. **10.** *Checkers.* A move made by jumping.

—idioms. get (or **have**) **a jump on one.** *Informal.* To have a head start over another. **jump a claim.** To take land or rights from another by violence or fraud. **jump down one's throat.** To answer sharply or angrily. **jump ship.** To desert. **jump the gun.** To start something too soon. [Prob. imit.]

Syns: jump, hurdle, leap, vault *v.* **Core meaning:** To spring into the air *(jumped over the fence).*

jump ball. *Basketball.* A method of starting play or determining possession in which an official tosses the ball up between two opposing players who must then jump and try to tap the ball to a teammate.

jump·er¹ (jŭm'pǝr) *n.* **1.** Someone or something that jumps. **2.** A short length of wire used temporarily to complete or by-pass a circuit.

jum·per² (jŭm'pǝr) *n.* **1.** A sleeveless dress worn over a blouse or sweater. **2.** A loose smock, blouse, or jacket worn over other clothes to protect them. **3. jumpers.** A child's overalls. [Prob. from British dial. *jump,* man's jacket, woman's bodice, from French *juppe,* var. of *jupe,* skirt, from Arabic *jubbah.*]

jump·ing bean. A seed, as of certain Mexican shrubs or plants of the genera *Sebastiana* and *Sapium,* containing the larva of a moth, *Laspeyresia saltitans,* the movements of which cause the seed to jerk or roll.

jumping jack. A toy figure with jointed limbs that can be made to dance by pulling an attached string.

jump·ing-off place (jŭm'pĭng-ôf', -ŏf'). **1.** A very remote spot or outpost. **2.** A beginning point.

jump shot. *Basketball.* A shot made by a player at the highest point of his jump.

jump-start (jŭmp'stärt) *tr.v.* **1.** To start (an automobile engine) by rolling and suddenly releasing the clutch. **2.** To start (an automobile engine) using a booster cable connected to the battery of another automobile.

jump·y (jŭm'pē) *adj.* **-i·er, -i·est. 1.** Moving by fitful, jerky movements. **2.** Easily unsettled or alarmed; on edge; nervous. —See Syns at **edgy.** **—jump'i·ness** *n.*

jun·co (jŭng'kō) *n., pl.* **-cos.** Any of various North American birds of the genus *Junco,* with predominantly gray plumage. [Spanish, reed.]

junc·tion (jŭngk'shǝn) *n.* **1.** The act of joining or the condition of being joined. **2.** The place where two things join or meet. **3.** The place where two roads or railway routes join or cross paths. [Latin *junctiō,* from *junctus,* past part. of *jungere,* to join.]

junc·ture (jŭngk'chǝr) *n.* **1.** The act of joining or the condition of being joined. **2.** The line, point, or seam at which two things join; joint. **3.** A point in time, esp. a crisis or turning point caused by a concurrence of circumstances. [Middle English, from Latin *junctūra,* from *junctus,* past part. of *jungere,* to join.]

June (jōōn) *n.* The sixth month of the year. June has 30 days. [Middle English, from Old French *juin,* from Latin *Jūnius (mēnsis),* (month) of Juno.]

June beetle. Any of various large North American beetles of the subfamily Melolonthinae, with larva that are often destructive to crops. Also called **June bug.**

jun·gle (jŭng'gǝl) *n.* **1.** Land densely overgrown with tropical vegetation and trees. **2.** Any dense, confused, or uncontrolled overgrowth: *a bureaucratic jungle.* **3.** A scene or place of ruthless competition or struggle for survival. **4.** *Slang.* A rendezvous for hoboes. [Hindi *jaṅgal,* wasteland, forest, from Sanskrit *jāṅgala,* desert.]

jungle fowl. Any of several birds of the genus *Gallus,* of southeastern Asia, esp. one considered to be the ancestor of the common domestic fowl.

jun·ior (jōōn'yǝr) *adj.* **1.** Younger, esp. when used to distinguish the son from the father of the same name, and written after the full name: *William Jones, Jr.* **2.** Of or for younger persons: *junior dresses.* **3.** Of lower rank or shorter length of service. **4.** Of or pertaining to the third year of a U.S. high school or college. **5.** Lesser in scale than the usual. *—n.* **1.** A person who is younger than another: *He was four years my junior.* **2.** A person lower in rank or length of service; subordinate. **3.** A third-year student in a U.S. high school or college. —See Syns at **subordinate.** [Latin *jūnior,* ult. from *juvenis,* young.]

junior college. A school offering a two-year course that is the equivalent of the first two years of a four-year college.

| ă pat | ā pay | â care | ä father | ĕ pet | ē be | hw which | ĭ pit | ī tie | î pier | ŏ pot | ō toe | ô paw, for | oi noise |
| ōō took | ōō boot | ou out | th thin | th this | ŭ cut | | û urge | zh vision | ǝ about, item, edible, gallop, circus |

junior high school. A school intermediate between grammar school and high school, including the seventh, eighth, and sometimes ninth grades.

ju·ni·per (jōō'nə-pər) *n.* Any of various evergreen trees or shrubs of the genus *Juniperus,* with scalelike, often prickly foliage and aromatic, bluish-gray, berrylike fruit. [Middle English *junipere,* from Latin *jūniperus.*]

junk[1] (jŭngk) *n.* **1.** Scrap materials such as glass, rags, or metals that can be converted into something usable. **2.** *Informal.* **a.** Anything worn-out or fit to be discarded. **b.** Anything useless, cumbersome, or fatuous: *a lot of fancy dials and other junk.* **3.** *Slang.* Heroin. **4.** *Naut.* **a.** Hard salt beef, used as food on a sea journey. **b.** Old cordage, reused for gaskets, caulking, and mats. *—tr.v.* To throw away or discard as useless; to scrap. [From earlier *junk,* old, worn-out pieces of nautical rope or cable, from Middle English *jonke.*]

junk[2] (jŭngk) *n.* A Chinese flat-bottomed ship with a high poop and battened sails. [Ult. from Malay *jong,* sea-going ship.]

junk[2]

jun·ket (jŭng'kĭt) *n.* **1.** A sweet custardlike food made from flavored milk and rennet. **2.** A party, banquet, or outing. **3.** A trip taken by a public official or businessperson and paid for with public or corporate funds. **4.** An excursion or tour, esp. a trip covering some professional circuit. *—intr.v.* **1.** To hold a party or banquet. **2.** To make an excursion using public funds. [Middle English *jonket,* a kind of egg custard served on rushes or made in a rush mat, from *junket,* rush basket, from Old North French *jonquette,* from *jonc,* rush, from Latin *juncus.*] *—jun'ket·er n.*

junk·ie (jŭng'kē) *n.* Also **junk·y** *pl.* **-ies.** *Slang.* A narcotics addict, esp. one using heroin.

Ju·no (jōō'nō) *n. Rom. Myth.* The principal goddess of the Pantheon, wife and sister of Jupiter, patroness of marriage and the well-being of women, identified with the Greek goddess Hera.

Ju·no·esque (jōō'nō-ĕsk') *adj.* Having the stately bearing and imposing beauty of the goddess Juno.

jun·ta (hōōn'tə, hōōn'-, jŭn'-) *n.* **1.** A group of military officers who govern a country after a coup d'état. **2.** A council or small legislative body in a government, esp. in Latin America. [Spanish and Portuguese, from Latin *juncta,* joined, past part. of *jungere,* to join.]

Ju·pi·ter (jōō'pĭ-tər) *n.* **1.** *Rom. Myth.* The supreme god, patron of the Roman state, brother and husband of Juno, identified with the Greek god Zeus. Also called **Jove.**

Jupiter

2. The fifth planet from the sun, the largest and most massive in the solar system, that has a diameter of approximately 86,000 miles and a mass approximately 318 times that of Earth, and which orbits the sun once every 11.86 years at a mean distance of 483 million miles.

Ju·ras·sic (jōō-răs'ĭk) *n.* Also **Jurassic period.** A geologic period that began 180 million years ago and ended 135 million years ago, characterized by the existence of dinosaurs and the appearance of primitive birds and mammals. *—modifier: a Jurassic fossil.* [French *jurassique,* after the Jura Mountains, a mountain range on the French-Swiss border.]

ju·rid·i·cal (jōō-rĭd'ĭ-kəl) or **ju·rid·ic** (-ĭk) *adj.* Of or pertaining to the law and its administration. [From Latin *jūridicus : jūs,* law + *dīcere,* to say.]

ju·ris·dic·tion (jōōr-ĭs-dĭk'shən) *n.* **1.** The authority to interpret and apply the law. **2.** The power of authority or control. **3.** The limits within which an authority or control may operate. **4.** The territory under a given authority or control. [Middle English *jurisdiccioun,* from Old French *juridiction,* from Latin *jūrisdictiō : jūs,* law + *dictiō,* declaration.] *—ju'ris·dic'tion·al adj.*

ju·ris·pru·dence (jōōr-ĭs-prōōd'ns) *n.* **1.** The science or philosophy of law. **2.** A system of laws: *17th cent. jurisprudence.* **3.** A division or department of law: *corporate jurisprudence.* [Latin *jūrisprūdentia,* skill in law: *jūs,* law + *prūdentia,* knowledge, from *prūdēns,* knowing.]

ju·rist (jōōr'ĭst) *n.* A person skilled in the law, esp. an eminent judge, lawyer, or scholar. [Old French, from Medieval Latin *jūrista,* from Latin *jūs,* law.]

ju·ris·tic (jōō-rĭs'tĭk) or **ju·ris·ti·cal** (-tĭ-kəl) *adj.* **1.** Of or pertaining to a jurist or to jurisprudence. **2.** Of or pertaining to law or legality.

ju·ror (jōōr'ər, -ôr') *n.* A member of or a person called to serve on a jury. [Middle English *juroure,* from Norman French *jurour,* from Latin *jūrātor,* swearer, from *jūrātus,* past part. of *jūrāre,* to swear.]

ju·ry[1] (jōōr'ē) *n., pl.* **-ries. 1.** A body of persons summoned by law and sworn to hear and hand down a verdict upon a case presented in court. **2.** A committee to select winners and award prizes, as in a contest, competition, etc. [Middle English *jurie,* from Norman French *juree,* from Old French *juree,* oath, inquest, from Latin *jūrāta,* thing sworn, from *jūrāre,* to swear. From Latin *jūs,* law.]

ju·ry[2] (jōōr'ē) *adj. Naut.* For emergency or temporary use; makeshift: *a jury rig.* [Orig. unknown.]

ju·ry·man (jōōr'ē-mən) *n.* A juror.

just (jŭst) *adj.* **1.** Honest and impartial in one's dealings and actions; honorable; fair: *a just ruler.* **2.** Consistent with standards of what is moral and proper; right; equitable: *a just cause; a just resentment.* **3.** Properly due or merited: *just deserts.* **4.** Valid within the law; legitimate. **5.** Suitable or proper; fitting: *a just touch of solemnity.* **6.** Sound or reasonable; well-founded: *a just appraisal.* **7.** Conforming with fact or truth; exact; accurate: *a just account.* —See Syns at **fair**[1] and **suitable.** *—adv.* (jŭst; unstressed jəst, jĭst). **1.** Precisely; exactly: *That's just what I was going to say.* **2.** At that instant: *It's just six.* **3.** Quite recently: *He just came.* **4.** Barely; shortly: *You just missed her.* **5.** Only a little distance; immediately: *just down the road.* **6.** Merely; simply: *I just meant that I agree.* **7.** Really; certainly: *It's just beautiful.* [Middle English, from Old French *juste,* from Latin *jūstus.*] *—just'ly adv. —just'ness n.*

    Syns: just, due, right *adj.* Core meaning: Consistent with accepted standards and circumstances *(just punishment).* See also Syns at **fair**[1].

jus·tice (jŭs'tĭs) *n.* **1.** Moral or absolute rightness; morality; equity: *One does not always see justice in the ways of the world.* **2.** The upholding of what is just; fair treatment and due reward in accordance with honor, standards, or law: *ruled with justice.* **3.** That which is just or due: *Justice was served by his downfall.* **4.** The quality of being just, fair, or impartial; honorableness: *An ardent sense of justice informed her appeal.* **5.** Good reason or sound basis; validity: *He's very angry, and with justice.* **6.** The administration and procedure of law: *the Department of Justice.* **7.** A judge. *—idiom.* **do justice to. 1.** To approach with proper appreciation; enjoy fully. **2.** To show to full advantage. [Middle English, from Old French, from Latin *jūstitia,* from *jūstus,* just.]

justice of the peace. A local magistrate with the authority to act upon minor offenses, perform marriages, and administer oaths.

jus·ti·fi·a·ble (jŭs′tə-fī′ə-bəl, jŭs′tə-fī′-) *adj.* Capable of being justified; excusable. —**jus′ti·fi′a·bly** *adv.*

jus·ti·fi·ca·tion (jŭs′tə-fĭ-kā′shən) *n.* **1.** The act of justifying or the condition of being justified. **2.** A fact or circumstance that justifies; a good reason.

jus·ti·fy (jŭs′tə-fī′) *v.* **-fied, -fy·ing.** —*tr.v.* **1.** To demonstrate or prove to be just, right, or valid; vindicate: *His excuses could not justify what he did.* **2.** To provide sufficient or sound reasons for; to warrant: *The accident justified the need for better safety measures.* **3.** To declare free of blame; absolve. **4.** *Law.* To demonstrate good reason for (an action taken). **5.** *Printing.* To adjust or space (lines) to the proper length. —*intr.v.* To be or become properly spaced and of the correct length. Said of a line of type. —See Syns at **defend.** [Middle English *justifien,* to judge, punish, from Old French *justifier,* from Late Latin *jūstificāre,* to do justice toward, to forgive, pardon : *jūstus,* just + *facere,* to do.]

jus·tle (jŭs′əl) *v.* Var. of **jostle.**

jut (jŭt) *intr.v.* **jut·ted, jut·ting.** To project upward or outward; stick out; protrude. —*n.* Something that protrudes; a projection. [Var. of JET.]

jute (jo͞ot) *n.* **1.** Either of two Asian plants, *Corchorus cap-* *sularis* or *C. olitorius,* that yield a fiber used to make rope, twine, and burlap. **2.** The fiber obtained from the jute. [Bengali *jhuṭo,* from Sanskrit *jūṭa.*]

Jute (jo͞ot) *n.* A member of a Germanic people who invaded Britain in the 5th cent. A.D. and became part of the Anglo-Saxon people.

ju·ve·nes·cent (jo͞o′və-nĕs′ənt) *adj.* Becoming or growing young or youthful. [From Latin *juvenis,* young + -ESCENT.] —**ju′ve·nes′cence** *n.*

ju·ve·nile (jo͞o′və-nəl, -nīl′) *adj.* **1.** Young; youthful. **2.** Characteristic of youth or children; immature; childish. **3.** Intended for or appropriate to children or youths: *juvenile shoes.* —See Syns at **young.** —*n.* **1. a.** A young person; youth. **b.** A young animal that has not reached sexual maturity. **2.** An actor or actress who plays children or young persons. **3.** A children's book. [Latin *juvenīlis,* from *juvenis,* young, a youth.] —**ju′ve·nile·ness** *n.*

juvenile delinquency. Antisocial or criminal behavior by children or adolescents —**juvenile delinquent.**

ju·ve·nil·i·ty (jo͞o′və-nĭl′ə-tē) *n., pl.* **-ties. 1.** The quality or condition of being foolishly juvenile; immaturity. **2.** The quality or condition of being young or youthful.

jux·ta·pose (jŭk′stə-pōz′) *tr.v.* **-posed, -pos·ing.** To place side by side, esp. for comparison or contrast.

jux·ta·po·si·tion (jŭk′stə-pə-zĭsh′ən) *n.* The act of juxtaposing or the condition of being juxtaposed. [French : Latin *juxtā,* close together + French *position,* position.] —**jux′-ta·po·si′tion·al** *adj.*

jute

Kk

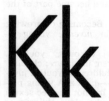

Phoenician – About 3,000 years ago the Phoenicians and other Semitic peoples began to use graphic signs to represent individual speech sounds instead of syllables or whole words. They used this symbol to represent the sound of the consonant "k" and gave it the name kaph, the Phoenician word for "hollow of the hand."

Greek – The Greeks borrowed the Phoenician alphabet with some modifications. They reversed the orientation of kaph and altered its name to kappa. They used kappa to represent the sound of the consonant "k," as kaph did in Phoenician.

Roman – The Romans borrowed the alphabet from the Greeks via the Etruscans and adapted it for carving Latin in stone. This monumental script, as it is called, became the basis for modern printed capital letters.

Medieval – By medieval times – around 1,200 years ago – the Roman monumental capitals had become adapted to being relatively quickly written on paper, parchment, or vellum. The cursive minuscule alphabet became the basis for modern printed lower-case letters.

Modern – Since the invention of printing about 500 years ago modifications have been made in the shape and style of the letter K, but its basic form has remained unchanged.

---

k, K (kā) n., pl. **k's** or **K's.** The 11th letter of the modern English alphabet.

K The symbol for the element potassium. [New Latin *kalium*.]

Ka·a·ba (kä′ə-bə, kä′bə) n. Also **Ca·a·ba.** A Moslem shrine in Mecca, the goal of pilgrims and the point toward which Moslems turn to pray. [Arabic *ka′bah*, "square building," from *ka′b*, cube.]

kab·a·la or **kab·ba·la** (kăb′ə-lə, kə-bä′lə) n. Var. of **cabala.**

ka·bob (kə-bŏb′) n. **Shish kebab.**

ka·bu·ki (kä-bōō′kē, kə-) n. A Japanese popular drama in which gestures, dances, and songs are performed in a formal and stylized manner. [Japanese, "art of singing and dancing."]

Kad·dish (kä′dĭsh) n. *Judaism.* A prayer recited in the daily synagogue services and by mourners after the death of a close relative. [Aramaic *qaddîsh*.]

kaf·fir (kăf′ər) n. Also **kaf·ir.** A variety of sorghum, *Sorghum vulgare caffrorum*, of Africa, cultivated in dry regions for its grain and as fodder. Also called **kaffir corn.**

kaf·tan (kăf′tən, kăf-tăn′) n. Var. of **caftan.**

kai·ak (kī′ăk′) n. Var. of **kyak.**

Kai·ser (kī′zər) n. An emperor of the Holy Roman Empire (A.D. 962–1806), of Austria (1804–1918), or of Germany (1871–1918). [German *Kaiser*, from Old High German *Keisar*, from Latin *Caesar*, Caesar.]

kale (kāl) n. Also **kail.** A variety of cabbage, *Brassica oleracea acephala*, with ruffled or crinkled leaves that do not form a tight head. [Middle English *cal(e)*, cole, cabbage, from Old English *cāl*.]

ka·lei·do·scope (kə-lī′də-skōp′) n. **1.** A tube-shaped optical instrument that is rotated to produce a succession of symmetrical designs by means of mirrors reflecting the constantly changing patterns made by bits of colored glass at one end of the tube. **2.** A constantly changing set of colors. **3.** A series of changing phases or events. [Greek *kalos*, beautiful + *eidos*, form + -SCOPE.] **—ka·lei′do·scop′ic** (-skŏp′ĭk) or **ka·lei′do·scop′i·cal** adj. **—ka·lei′do·scop′i·cal·ly** adv.

kal·ends (kăl′əndz, kā′ləndz) n. Var. of **calends.**

kal·so·mine (kăl′sə-mīn′). n. *Brit.* Var. of **calcimine.**

ka·mi·ka·ze (kä′mĭ-kä′zē) n. **1.** *WWII.* A Japanese pilot trained to make a suicidal crash attack. **2.** An airplane loaded with explosives to be piloted in a suicide attack. [Japanese, "divine wind."]

kan·ga·roo (kăng′gə-rōō′) n., pl. **-roos.** Any of various herbivorous marsupials of the family Macropodidae, of Australia and adjacent areas, with short forelimbs, large hind limbs adapted for leaping, and a long, tapered tail. [Prob. from a native name in Australia.]

kangaroo court. 1. A court set up in violation of established legal procedure. **2.** A court characterized by dishonesty or incompetence.

kangaroo rat. Any of various long-tailed North American rodents of the genera *Dipodomys* and *Microdipodops*, with long hind legs adapted for jumping.

ka·o·lin (kā′ə-lĭn) n. Also **ka·o·line.** A fine clay used in ceramics and refractories and as a filler or coating for paper and textiles. [French, from Mandarin Chinese *kao¹ ling³*, "high mountain" a hill in Kiangsi Province.]

ka·pok (kā′pŏk′) n. A silky fiber obtained from the fruit of the silk-cotton tree, and used for insulation and as padding in pillows, mattresses, and life preservers. [Malay.]

kap·pa (kăp′ə) n. The tenth letter in the Greek alphabet, written K, κ. [Greek.]

ka·put (kä-pōōt′) adj. *Informal.* **1.** Destroyed; ruined. **2.** Not in working order. [German *kaputt*, from French *(être) capot*, to have lost all tricks at cards.]

kar·a·kul (kăr′ə-kəl) n. Also **car·a·cul. 1.** One of a breed of central Asian sheep, with wool that is curled and glossy in the young but wiry and coarse in the adult. **2.** Fur made from the pelt of a karakul lamb. Also called **broadtail.** [After *Kara Kul*, a lake in Tadzhik S.S.R.]

kar·at (kăr′ət) n. Also **car·at. Abbr. k, kt.** A measure of the proportion of gold in an alloy equal to ¹/₂₄ part of pure gold. For example, 12 karat gold is 50 per cent pure gold. [Old French *carat*, unit of weight for precious stones.]

ka·ra·te (kə-rä′tē, kä-rä′tā) n. A Japanese art of unarmed

kangaroo

karate   kayak   kepi

self-defense that stresses efficiently struck blows. [Japanese, "empty-handed."]

kar·ma (kär′mə, kûr′mə) n. **1.** *Hinduism & Buddhism.* The total effect of a person's actions and conduct during the successive phases of his existence, regarded as determining his destiny. **2.** Fate; destiny. [Sanskrit, deed, work.] —**kar′mic** (-mĭk) adj.

kar·roo (kə-rōō′, kä-) n., pl. **-roos.** Also **ka·roo.** An arid plateau of southern Africa. [Afrikaans *karo.*]

karst (kärst) n. A limestone region characterized by sinkholes, underground streams, caverns, and the absence of surface streams and lakes. [German *Karst.*]

kash·mir (kăzh′mĭr′, kăsh′-) n. Var. of **cashmere.**

ka·ty·did (kā′tē-dĭd′) n. Any of various green insects related to the grasshoppers and the crickets, with specialized organs on the wings of the male that produce a shrill sound when rubbed together. [Imit.]

kay·ak (kī′ăk′) n. Also **kai·ak. 1.** An Eskimo canoe made of skins stretched over a light wooden frame, with a deck covering that closes around the waist of the paddler. **2.** A lightweight covered canoe similar to a kayak. [Eskimo *qajaq.*]

kay·o (kā′ō, kā′ō′) n. & v. Var. of **KO.** [Pronunciation of the initial letters of *knock out.*]

ka·zoo (kə-zōō′) n., pl. **-zoos.** A toy musical instrument with a membrane that vibrates and produces a sound when a player hums or sings into the mouthpiece. [Imit.]

ke·a (kē′ə, kā′ə) n. A brownish-green New Zealand parrot, *Nestor notabilis,* that normally eats insects but sometimes kills sheep by slashing them and eating their fat and flesh. [Maori.]

ke·bab or **ke·bob** (kə-bŏb′) n. **Shish kebab.**

kedge (kĕj) n. A light anchor used for warping a vessel. —v. **kedged, kedg·ing.** —tr.v. To warp (a vessel) by means of a kedge. —intr.v. To move by means of a kedge. [From earlier *cadge,* to warp a ship, perh. from Middle English *caggen,* to tie, bind.]

keel (kēl) n. **1. a.** The principal structure of a ship, running lengthwise along the center line, from bow to stern, to which the frames are attached. **b.** A corresponding structure in an aircraft. **2.** *Poet.* A ship. **3.** A structure similar to a ship's keel in form or function, such as the breastbone of a flying bird. **4.** A pair of united petals in certain flowers, as those of the pea. —intr.v. To roll or turn over; capsize. —**idiom. keel over.** To collapse or fall: *keeled over from the shock.* [Middle English *keole,* from Old Norse *kjölr.*]

keel·boat (kēl′bōt′) n. A shallow river boat with a keel, used esp. for carrying freight.

keel·haul (kēl′hôl′) tr.v. **1.** To punish by dragging under the keel of a ship. **2.** To rebuke harshly. [Dutch *kielhalen* : *kiel,* keel of a ship + *halen,* to pull, haul.]

keel·son (kēl′sən, kĕl′-) n. Also **kel·son** (kĕl′-). *Naut.* A timber or girder fastened above and parallel to the keel for additional strength. [Prob. from Low German *kielswin.*]

keen¹ (kēn) adj. **-er, -est. 1.** Having a fine, sharp edge or point. **2.** Intellectually acute. **3.** Acutely sensitive. **4.** Sharp; vivid; strong: *"His entire body hungered for keen sensation, something exciting"* (Richard Wright). **5.** Intense; piercing: *a keen wind.* **6.** Pungent; acrid. **7. a.** Ardent; enthusiastic. **b.** Eagerly desirous: *keen on going.* **8.** *Slang.* Great; splendid; fine. —See Syns at **sharp.** [Middle English *kene,* from Old English *cēne,* wise, bold, powerful.] —**keen′ly** adv. —**keen′ness** n.

keen² (kēn) n. A loud wailing lament for the dead. —intr.v. To wail over the dead. [Irish Gaelic *caoine,* lamentation.] —**keen′er** n.

keep (kēp) v. **kept** (kĕpt), **keep·ing.** —tr.v. **1.** To retain possession of. **2.** To have as a supply. **3.** To provide with maintenance; support: *kept a wife and a brood of children on a meager salary.* **4.** To maintain for use or service. **5.** To manage, tend, or have charge of. **6.** To raise: *keep chickens.* **7.** To cause to continue in a state, condition, or course of action: *struggled to keep his head above water.* **8.** To maintain by making entries in: *keep records.* **9.** To preserve and protect. **10.** To prevent or deter: *keep ice from melting.* **11.** To refrain from revealing: *keep a secret; keep counsel.* **12.** To maintain: *keep late hours.* **13.** To adhere to; fulfill: *keep one's word.* **14.** To celebrate; observe. —intr.v. **1.** To remain in a state or condition: *keep quiet.* **2.** To continue to do: *keep guessing; kept on working industriously.* **3.** To remain fresh or unspoiled: *The dessert won't keep.* —See Syns at **save.** —**phrasal verbs. keep down.** To prevent from accomplishing or succeeding. **keep up. 1.** To maintain. **2.** To persevere in; carry on. **3.** To continue at the same level or pace. —n. **1.** Care; charge. **2.** A means of support: *earned his keep by helping in the kitchen.* **3.** The stronghold of a castle. **4.** A jail. —See Syns at **living.** —**idioms. keep at it.** To persevere in a course of action. **for keeps. 1.** Forever: *He gave it to me for keeps.* **2.** Seriously and permanently: *We're separating for keeps.* [Middle English *kepen,* from Old English *cēpan,* to seize, hold, guard.]

keep·er (kē′pər) n. A person who keeps, guards, or has charge of something.

keep·ing (kē′pĭng) n. **1.** The action of holding, guarding, supporting, etc. **2.** Custody; care; guardianship. **3.** Harmony; conformity.

keep·sake (kēp′sāk′) n. Something given or kept as a reminder; a memento.

keg (kĕg) n. A small barrel, usu. with a capacity of five to ten gallons. [Middle English *kag,* from Old Norse *kaggi.*]

kelp (kĕlp) n. **1.** Any of various large brown seaweeds of the order Laminariales. **2.** The ashes of kelp, used as fertilizer and as a source of potash and iodine. [Middle English *cülpe.*]

kel·son (kĕl′sən) n. Var. of **keelson.**

Kelt (kĕlt) n. Var. of **Celt.**

Kelt·ic (kĕl′tĭk) n. & adj. Var. of **Celtic.**

kel·vin (kĕl′vĭn) n. Symbol **k** The unit of thermodynamic temperature, equal to $1/_{273.16}$ of the thermodynamic temperature of the triple point of water.

Kel·vin (kĕl′vĭn) adj. Abbr. **K** Of or pertaining to a temperature scale, the zero point of which is equivalent to −273.16°C. [After William Thomson, Lord *Kelvin* (1824–1907), British physicist.]

ken (kĕn) tr.v. **kenned, ken·ning.** *Scot.* To know. —n. **1.** Range; understanding; comprehension. **2.** Range of vision. [Middle English *kennen,* from Old English *cennan,* to make known.]

ken·nel (kĕn′əl) n. **1.** A shelter for a dog. **2.** An establishment where dogs are bred, trained, or boarded. —v. **-neled** or **-nelled, -nel·ing** or **-nel·ling. —**tr.v. To keep or place in or as in a kennel. —intr.v. To shelter in or as in a kennel. [Middle English *kenel,* ult. from Latin *canis,* dog.]

kep·i (kā′pē, kĕp′ē) n., pl. **-is.** A French military cap with a flat, circular top and a visor. [French *képi,* from Swiss

German *käppi*, dim. of German *Kappe*, cap, from Old High German *kappa*, cloak, from Late Latin *cappa*, hood, cloak.]

kept (kĕpt) v. Past tense and past participle of **keep.**

ker·a·tin (kĕr′ə-tən) n. A tough, fibrous protein that forms the outer layer of epidermal structures such as hair, nails, horns, and hoofs. [Greek *keras*, horn + -IN.] **—ke·rat′i·nous** (kə-răt′n-əs) adj.

kerb (kûrb) n. Brit. Var. of **curb.**

ker·chief (kûr′chĭf) n. 1. A square scarf, often worn by a woman as a head covering. 2. A handkerchief. [Middle English *kercheffe*, from Old French *couvrechef*, head covering : *couvrir*, to cover + *ch(i)ef*, head, from Latin *caput*.]

kerf (kûrf) n. A groove or notch made by a saw or ax. [Middle English, from Old English *cyrf*, act of cutting.]

ker·mis (kûr′məs) n. Also **ker·mess** or **kir·mess.** An outdoor fair in the Low Countries. [Dutch, from Middle Dutch *kercmisse* : *kerc*, church + *misse*, Mass, church festival, from Late Latin *missa*.]

ker·nel (kûr′nəl) n. 1. A grain or seed of a cereal plant. 2. The inner, usu. edible part of a nut or fruit stone. 3. The most material and central part; core. —See Syns at **heart.** [Middle English *kernell*, from Old English *cyrnel*, seed, kernel, dim. of *corn*, seed.]

ker·o·sene (kĕr′ə-sēn′, kĕr′ə-sēn′) n. Also **ker·o·sine.** A thin oil distilled from petroleum or shale oil, used as a fuel and alcohol denaturant. [Greek *kēros*, wax + -ENE.]

Kerry blue terrier. One of an Irish breed of terriers, with a dense, wavy bluish-gray coat.

kes·trel (kĕs′trəl) n. 1. A small Old World falcon, *Falco tinnunculus*, that has brown and gray plumage and hovers in the air against the wind. 2. Any of several similar birds. [Middle English *castrell*, from Old French *cresserelle*.]

ketch (kĕch) n. A two-masted fore-and-aft-rigged sailing vessel with a mizzen or jigger mast aft. [Middle English *cache*.]

ketch·up (kĕch′əp, kăch′-) n. Also **catch·up** (kăch′əp, kĕch′-) or **cat·sup** (kăt′səp, kăch′əp, kĕch′-). A condiment consisting of a thick, smooth, spicy sauce usu. made from tomatoes. [Malay *kechap*, from Chinese *kētsiap*, fish sauce.]

ket·tle (kĕt′l) n. 1. A metal pot for boiling or stewing. 2. A teakettle. [Middle English *ketel*, from Old Norse *ketill*, from Latin *catillus*, small bowl from *catīnus*, pot.]

ket·tle·drum (kĕt′l-drŭm′) n. A large copper or brass hemispherical drum with a parchment head that may be tuned by adjusting the tension.

kettledrum

key¹ (kē) n., pl. **keys.** 1. a. A usu. metal implement that is turned to open or close a lock. b. A device that functions like a key: *the key of a clock.* 2. Something that is a means of, access, control, or possession. 3. a. A vital or crucial element. b. A set of answers to a test. c. A table, gloss, or cipher for decoding or interpreting. 4. A device, as a wedge or pin, inserted to lock together mechanical or structural parts. 5. A button or lever that is pressed with the finger to operate a machine or play a musical instrument. 6. *Mus.* a. A tonal system consisting of seven tones in fixed relationship to a tonic; tonality. b. The principal tonality of a musical work: *the key of E.* 7. The pitch of a voice or other sound: *She spoke in a high key.* 8. A characteristic tone or level of intensity, as of a speech, theatrical performance, or sales campaign. 9. *Bot.* A samara. —*tr.v.* 1. To lock with or as if with a key. 2. To furnish (an arch)

with a keystone. 3. To regulate the musical pitch of. 4. To bring into harmony; adjust; adapt. 5. To supply an explanatory key for. **—phrasal verb. key up.** To make tense or nervous. [Middle English, from Old English *cæg(e)*.]

key² (kē) n., pl. **keys.** A low offshore island or reef, esp. in the Gulf of Mexico. [Spanish *cayo*, island, reef.]

key·board (kē′bôrd′, -bōrd′) n. A set of keys, as on a piano, an organ, or a typewriter. —*tr.v.* To set (copy) by means of a typesetting machine with a keyboard.

key fruit. A samara.

key·hole (kē′hōl′) n. The hole in a lock into which a key fits.

key·note (kē′nōt′) n. 1. The tonic of a musical key. 2. A prime or dominant element, theme, or tone: *the keynote of his work is liveliness.* —*tr.v.* **-not·ed, -not·ing.** To give or set the keynote of.

keynote address. An opening address, as at a political convention, that outlines the issues to be considered. Also called **keynote speech.**

key punch. A keyboard machine that is used to punch holes in cards or tapes for data-processing systems.

key signature. The sharps or flats at the right of the clef on a musical staff to identify the key.

key·stone (kē′stōn′) n. *Archit.* 1. The central wedge-shaped stone at the top of an arch that locks its parts together. 2. Something that supports the associated elements of a whole.

khak·i (kăk′ē, kä′kē) n., pl. **khakis. 1.** A yellowish brown. **2. a.** A sturdy wool or cotton cloth of khaki color. **b. khakis.** A uniform of this cloth. **—modifier:** *khaki trousers.* —*adj.* Yellowish brown. [Urdu *khākī*, dusty, dust-colored, from *khāk*, dust, from Persian *khāk*.]

khan (kän, kăn) n. 1. A ruler, official, or man of rank in some central Asian countries. 2. Formerly, an emperor of China or a ruler of a Mongol, Tartar, or Turkish tribe. [Middle English *caan*, from Old French, from Turkish *khān*, prince.]

khi (kī) n. Var. of **chi.**

kib·butz (kĭ-bōōts′) n., pl. **-but·zim** (-bōōt′sēm′). A collective farm or settlement in modern Israel. [Hebrew *qibbūtz*, from *qibbētz*, he gathered.]

kib·itz (kĭb′ĭts) *intr.v. Informal.* To look on and offer unwanted and usu. meddlesome advice to others. [Yiddish *kibitsen*, from German *kiebitzen*, to look on.] **—kib′itz·er** n.

ki·bosh (kī′bŏsh) n. Something that checks or stops. [Orig. unknown.]

kick (kĭk) *intr.v.* 1. To strike out with the foot. 2. To score or gain ground by kicking a ball. 3. To recoil, as a gun when fired. 4. *Informal.* To object vigorously; complain; protest. —*tr.v.* 1. To strike or propel with the foot. 2. To score (a goal or point) by kicking a ball. **—phrasal verbs. kick around.** *Informal.* 1. To treat badly. 2. To give consideration or thought to. **kick back.** To pay a kickback. **kick in.** *Slang.* To contribute (a share). **kick off.** 1. To begin or resume play with a kickoff. 2. To begin. **kick out.** *Slang.* To throw out; dismiss. **kick up.** *Informal.* To raise trouble: *The motor began to kick up.* —*n.* 1. a. A blow with the foot. b. The motion or thrust of the legs in swimming. 2. The recoil of a gun. 3. a. *Slang.* A complaint or objection. b. The grounds or reason for a complaint or objection. 4. *Slang.* Power, impact, or force: *still a lot of kick in that engine.* 5. *Slang.* A feeling of pleasurable stimulation. 6. *Slang.* A temporary enthusiasm for something: *He's on a science-fiction kick.* 7. a. An act or instance of kicking a ball. b. The kicked ball. c. The distance covered by a kicked ball: *a 47-yard kick.* **—idiom. kick the bucket.** *Slang.* To die. [Middle English *kiken*.]

kick·back (kĭk′băk′) n. 1. A sharp response or reaction. 2. *Slang.* A secret or illicit payment to another, made from income or money received.

kick·off (kĭk′ôf′, -ŏf′) n. 1. A place kick in football or soccer with which play begins. 2. A beginning.

kid (kĭd) n. 1. A young goat. 2. Leather made from the skin of a young goat. 3. *Slang.* a. A child. b. A young person. —*v.* **kid·ded, kid·ding.** *Informal.* —*tr.v.* 1. To make fun of; tease. 2. To deceive in fun; fool. —*intr.v.* To engage in teasing or good-humored fooling. [Middle English *kide*, from Old Norse *kidh*.] **—kid′der** n.

Kid·dush (kĭd′əsh, kĭ-dōōsh′) n. *Judaism.* A prayer recited over wine or bread on the eve of the Sabbath or a festival. [Hebrew *qiddūsh*, sanctification, from *qiddesh*, he sanctified.]

kid glove. A glove made of kidskin. —*idiom.* **with kid gloves.** With tact and caution.

kid·nap (kĭd′năp′) *tr.v.* **-naped** or **-napped, -naping** or **-nap·ping.** To seize and detain unlawfully. [Back-formation from KIDNAPER : KID (child) + *napper*, thief.] —**kid′nap′er** or **kid′nap′per** *n.*

kid·ney (kĭd′nē) *n., pl.* **-neys. 1.** *Anat.* Either of a pair of organs that are located in the dorsal region of the vertebrate abdominal cavity and function to maintain proper water balance, regulate acid-base concentration, and excrete metabolic wastes as urine. **2.** An excretory organ of certain invertebrates. **3.** The kidney of certain animals, eaten as food. **4.** Disposition; temperament. [Middle English *kydney.*]

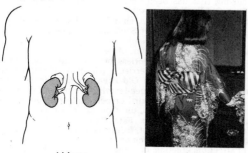

kidney   kimono

kidney bean. 1. A bean, *Phaseolus vulgaris*, cultivated in many forms for its edible seeds. **2.** The reddish seed of the kidney bean.

kid·skin (kĭd′skĭn′) *n.* Soft leather made from the skin of a young goat.

kill (kĭl) *tr.v.* **1.** To cause the death of; deprive of life: *Famine killed thousands.* **2.** To put an end to; extinguish. **3.** To harm greatly; to ruin: *killed the taste.* **4.** To pass (time) idly or unproductively. **5.** To consume entirely; finish off: *kill a bottle of champagne.* **6.** To cause extreme pain to: *My shoes are killing me.* **7.** To delete or cancel. **8.** To defeat; veto: *kill a congressional bill.* **9.** To cause to stop; turn off. **10.** To hit with such force as to make a return impossible. —*intr.v.* **1.** To be fatal; cause death or extinction. **2.** To commit murder. —*n.* **1.** The act of killing. **2.** The animal or animals killed, esp. in hunting. [Middle English *killen.*]
    Syns: kill, destroy, dispatch, finish, slay, zap (Slang) *v.* Core meaning: To cause the death of *(a plague that killed thousands).* See also Syns at **murder.**

kill·deer (kĭl′dîr′) *n., pl.* **-deers** or **killdeer.** A New World wading bird, *Charadrius vociferus*, with a distinctive wailing cry. [Imit. of its cry.]

kill·er (kĭl′ər) *n.* Someone or something that kills.

killer whale. A black and white predatory whale, *Orcinus orca*, of cold seas.

kill·ing (kĭl′ĭng) *n.* **1.** The act of someone or something that kills. **2.** A sudden large profit. —*adj.* **1.** Designed or likely to kill; fatal. **2.** Exhausting.

kill·joy (kĭl′joi′) *n.* A person who spoils the enjoyment of others.

kiln (kĭl, kĭln) *n.* An oven for hardening, firing, or drying. [Middle English *kylne*, from Old English *cyline*, from Latin *culīna*, kitchen, ult. from *coquere*, to cook.]

ki·lo (kē′lō, kĭl′ō) *n., pl.* **-los. 1.** A kilogram. **2.** A kilometer.

kilo-. *Symbol* **k** A prefix meaning 1,000 (10³): **kilowatt, kilocalorie.** [From Greek *khilioi*, thousand.]

kil·o·cy·cle (kĭl′ə-sī′kəl) *n. Abbr.* **kc** A unit equal to 1,000 cycles.

kil·o·gram (kĭl′ə-grăm′) *n. Abbr.* **kg** The basic unit of mass in the metric system, equal to 1,000 grams or about 2.2046 pounds.

kil·o·me·ter (kĭl′ə-mē′tər, kĭ-lŏm′ə-tər) *n. Abbr.* **km** One thousand meters, approx. 0.62137 of a mile. —**kil′o·met′ric** (-mĕt′rĭk) *adj.*

kil·o·ton (kĭl′ə-tŭn′) *n.* **1.** One thousand tons. **2.** An explosive force equivalent to that of 1,000 tons of TNT.

kil·o·watt (kĭl′ə-wŏt′) *n. Abbr.* **kW** One thousand watts.

kil·o·watt-hour (kĭl′ə-wŏt′our′) *n.* A unit of energy equal to the power of one kilowatt acting for one hour.

kilt (kĭlt) *n.* A knee-length, pleated skirt, usu. of tartan, worn by men in Scotland. [From dial. *kilt*, to fasten up, tuck up, from Middle English *kilten*, of Scandinavian orig.]

kil·ter (kĭl′tər) *n.* Good condition; proper form: *The radio was out of kilter.* [Orig. unknown.]

ki·mo·no (kə-mō′nə, -nō) *n., pl.* **-nos. 1.** A long, loose, wide-sleeved Japanese robe, worn by men and women as an outer garment. **2.** A bathrobe or dressing gown similar to a kimono. [Japanese, "thing for wearing."]

kin (kĭn) *n.* A person's relatives. —*adj.* Related; akin. [Middle English, from Old English *cynn*.]

–kin. A suffix meaning small or diminutive: **pipkin.** [Middle English, from Middle Dutch.]

kind¹ (kīnd) *adj.* **-er, -est. 1.** Of a friendly and generous nature. **2.** Possessing or showing sympathy or warmheartedness: *a kind word.* [Middle English, from Old English *gecynde*, natural, innate.]
    Syns: **kind, benign, kindhearted, kindly** *adj.* Core meaning: Having or showing a tender, considerate, and helping nature *(a kind person; a kind gesture).*

kind² (kīnd) *n.* **1.** Variety; sort; type: *the kind of people who are cheerful in the morning.* **2.** A class or category of similar or related individuals: *What kind of dog is that?* —*idioms.* **in kind. 1.** With produce or commodities rather than with money. **2.** With something equivalent. **kind of.** *Informal.* Somewhat: *I'm kind of hungry.* [Middle English, from Old English *cynd, gecynde*, birth, nature, race.]
    Syns: **kind, breed, feather, ilk, sort, species, stripe, type, variety** *n.* Core meaning: A class that is defined by the common attribute or attributes possessed by all its members *(the kind of person who gets angry easily; flowers of all kinds).*
    Usage: **kind.** *Kind* is a singular classifying noun. These patterns are always acceptable: **1.** singular modifier + *kind* + *of* + singular noun + singular verb, if only one class or type is meant: *This kind of book has little value.* **2.** plural modifier + *kinds* + *of* + plural noun + plural verb, if more than one class or type is meant: *All kinds of people make a world.* **3.** interrogative adjective + *kind/ kinds* + *of* + singular/plural noun + singular/plural verb, with the number of the nouns and the verb agreeing with one another and depending on whether a single class or multiple classes is meant: *What kind of person does that? What kinds of people make a world?* Criticism may arise if you combine the singular *kind* with a plural element and vice versa. Although constructions like the following have a long and distinguished history in English, some editors and writers still avoid them: *These kind of men are untrustworthy. These kind of apples were hard to find.* When writing formal compositions, you should try to make all the elements in your sentences agree in number, as shown in the first three examples.

kin·der·gar·ten (kĭn′dər-gärt′n) *n.* A program or class for four- to six-year-old children. [German *Kindergarten*, "children's garden."]

kin·der·gart·ner (kĭn′dər-gärt′nər) *n.* Also **kin·der·gar·ten·er** (-gärt′n-ər). A child who attends kindergarten.

kind·heart·ed (kīnd′här′tĭd) *adj.* Kind and sympathetic in nature. —See Syns at **kind.** —**kind′heart′ed·ly** *adv.* —**kind′heart′ed·ness** *n.*

kin·dle (kĭn′dl) *v.* **-dled, -dling.** —*tr.v.* **1.** To set fire to; ignite. **2.** To cause to glow; light up. **3.** To arouse; excite: *kindled rebellion.* —*intr.v.* **1.** To catch fire. **2.** To become bright; glow. —See Syns at **ignite** and **provoke.** [Middle English *kindelen*, from Old Norse *kynda*, to catch fire.]

kin·dling (kĭnd′lĭng) *n.* Material that burns easily, used to start a fire.

kind·ly (kīnd′lē) *adj.* **-li·er, -li·est. 1.** Of a sympathetic or benevolent nature. **2.** Agreeable; pleasant. —See Syns at **kind.** —*adv.* **1.** Out of kindness: *kindly overlooked the mistake.* **2.** In a kind manner: *She spoke kindly to him.* **3.** Pleasantly; agreeably. **4.** As a kindness; please: *would you kindly close the door?*

ă pat   ā pay   â care   ä father   ĕ pet   ē be   hw which   ĭ pit   ī tie   î pier   ŏ pot   ō toe   ô paw, for   oi noise
ōō took   ōō boot   ou out   th thin   *th* this   ŭ cut   û urge   zh vision   ə about, item, edible, gallop, circus

kind·ness (kīnd′nĭs) *n.* **1.** The quality or state of being kind. **2.** A kind act.

kin·dred (kĭn′drĭd) *n.* **1.** A group of related persons, such as a family, clan, or tribe. **2.** A person's relatives; one's family. —*adj.* Having a similar or related origin or nature. [Middle English *kinrede,* : *kin,* family + -*rede,* from Old English *rædan,* to advise, rule.] —**kin′dred·ness** *n.*

kine (kīn) *n. Archaic.* Plural of **cow.**

kin·e·mat·ics (kĭn′ə-măt′ĭks) *n.* (*used with a sing. verb*). *Physics.* The study of motion exclusive of the influences of mass and force. [From Greek *kinēma,* motion, from *kinein,* to move.]

kin·e·scope (kĭn′ə-skōp′) *n.* **1.** The cathode-ray tube of a television receiver on which the picture appears. **2.** A film of a transmitted television program. [KINE(TIC) + -SCOPE.]

kin·es·the·sia (kĭn′əs-thē′zhə) *n.* The sensation of bodily position, presence, or movement resulting chiefly from stimulation of sensory nerve endings in muscles, tendons, and joints. [Greek *kinēma,* motion + ESTHESIA.]

ki·net·ic (kĭ-nĕt′ĭk) *adj.* Of, relating to, or produced by motion. [Greek *kinētikos,* from *kinētos,* moving, from *kinein,* to move.]

kinetic energy. Energy associated with motion.

ki·net·ics (kĭ-nĕt′ĭks) *n.* (*used with a sing. verb*). *Physics.* The science that deals with the effects of forces upon the motions of material bodies.

kin·folk (kĭn′fōk′) or **kin·folks** (-fōks′) *pl.n.* Vars. of **kins·folk.**

king (kĭng) *n.* **1.** A male sovereign. **2.** Someone or something that is the most powerful or eminent in a particular sphere. **3. King.** God or Christ. **4.** A playing card bearing a picture of a king. **5.** The principal piece in chess, capable of moving one square in any direction. **6.** A checker that has been crowned. [Middle English, from Old English *cyning.*]

king·bird (kĭng′bûrd′) *n.* Any of several American birds of the family Tyrannidae.

king·bolt (kĭng′bōlt′) *n.* A vertical bolt used for such purposes as joining the body of a wagon to the front axle, and usu. serving as a pivot. Also called **kingpin.**

king cobra. A large venomous snake, *Ophiophagus hannah,* of tropical Asia.

king crab. 1. A large, edible crab, *Paralithodes camtschatica,* found in the coastal waters of Alaska, Japan, and Siberia. **2.** The **horseshoe crab.**

king·dom (kĭng′dəm) *n.* **1.** A country ruled by a king or queen. **2.** An area in which one person or thing is dominant: *the kingdom of the imagination.* **3.** One of the three categories into which all organisms and natural substances are divided: *the mineral kingdom.* [Middle English, from Old English *cyningdōm.*]

king·fish·er (kĭng′fĭsh′ər) *n.* Any of various birds of the family Alcedinidae, usu. with a crested head and a long, pointed bill. [From Middle English *kyngys fischare.*]

King James Bible. An Anglican translation of the Bible from Hebrew and Greek into English published in 1611 under the auspices of James I. See table at **Bible.**

king·ly (kĭng′lē) *adj.* **-li·er, -li·est. 1.** Of the status or rank of king. **2.** Relating to or suitable for a king; regal. —**king′li·ness** *n.* —**king′ly** *adv.*

king·pin (kĭng′pĭn′) *n.* **1.** The foremost or central pin in an arrangement of bowling pins. **2.** The most important or essential person or thing. **3.** A kingbolt.

King's English. A style of speaking or writing English that is held up as standard and accepted.

king·ship (kĭng′shĭp′) *n.* **1.** The position, power, or dignity of a king. **2.** Government by a king; monarchy.

king snake. Any of various nonvenomous New World snakes of the genus *Lampropeltis,* with yellow or reddish markings.

kink (kĭngk) *n.* **1.** A tight curl or twist, as in a wire, rope, or hair. **2.** A painful muscle spasm; a crick. **3.** A slight difficulty or flaw, as in a plan or system. **4.** A quirk of personality. —*tr.v.* To cause to have a kink. —*intr.v.* To form a kink. [Low German *kinke,* a twist in a rope, from Middle Low German.]

kink·a·jou (kĭng′kə-jōō′) *n.* An arboreal mammal, *Potos flavus,* native to tropical America, with brownish fur and a

long, prehensile tail. [French *quincajou,* of Algonquian orig.]

kink·y (kĭng′kē) *adj.* **-i·er, -i·est. 1.** Tightly curled; frizzy: *kinky hair.* **2.** Deviant; perverse.

kins·folk (kĭnz′fōk′) *pl.n.* Also *informal* **kin·folk** (kĭn′-), **kin·folks** (kĭn′fōks). Members of one's family; kindred.

kin·ship (kĭn′shĭp′) *n.* The quality or condition of being kin.

kins·man (kĭnz′mən) *n.* **1.** A male blood relation or, loosely, a relation by marriage. **2.** Someone of the same racial, cultural, or national background. —**kins′wom′an** *n.*

ki·osk (kē-ŏsk′, kē′ŏsk′) *n.* **1.** An open summerhouse or pavilion. **2.** A small structure used esp. as a newsstand, refreshment booth, or telephone booth. [French *kiosque,* from Turkish *kŏshk,* pavilion, from Persian *kūshk,* palace.]

kip·per (kĭp′ər) *tr.v.* To cure by salting and smoking. —*n.* **1.** A male salmon or sea trout in the spawning season. **2.** A herring that has been kippered. [Middle English *kypre,* from Old English *cypera.*]

kirk (kûrk) *n.* **1.** *Scot.* A church. **2. Kirk.** The established Presbyterian Church of Scotland. [Middle English, from Old English *circe,* church.]

kir·mess (kûr′məs) *n.* Var. of **kermis.**

kirsch (kîrsh) *n.* A colorless brandy made from the fermented juice of cherries. [German *Kirsch(wasser),* "cherry (water)," from Old High German *kirsa,* cherry.]

kir·tle (kûr′tl) *n.* **1.** A knee-length tunic or coat for a man. **2.** A woman's dress, skirt, or petticoat. [Middle English, from Old English *cyrtel,* ult. from Latin *curtus,* cut short.]

kis·met (kĭz′mĭt, -mĕt′-) *n.* Fate; fortune. [Turkish *kiusmet,* from Arabic *qismah,* lot, from *qasama,* he allotted.]

kiss (kĭs) *tr.v.* **1.** To touch or caress with the lips as a sign of affection, greeting, or respect. **2.** To touch lightly; brush against. —*intr.v.* To touch or caress another with the lips. —*n.* **1.** A caress or touch with the lips. **2.** A slight or gentle touch. **3.** A small piece of candy, esp. of chocolate. **4.** A small cookie made of meringue. [Middle English *kissen,* from Old English *cyssan.*]

kiss·er (kĭs′ər) *n.* **1.** A person who kisses. **2.** *Slang.* The mouth. **3.** *Slang.* The face.

kiss of death. Something that brings about ultimate ruin or disaster. [From Judas' betrayal of Jesus with a kiss.]

kit (kĭt) *n.* **1.** A set of instruments or tools. **2.** A set of parts or materials to be assembled: *a model airplane kit.* **3.** A collection of items for personal use, esp. for travel. **4.** A container, such as a box or case, for a kit. —*idiom.* **the whole kit and caboodle.** *Informal.* The entire collection. [Middle English *kitt,* wooden tub, from Middle Dutch *kitte,* jug, tankard.]

kitch·en (kĭch′ən) *n.* **1.** A room or area with the facilities and equipment for preparing and serving food. **2.** A department that prepares, cooks, and serves food. [Middle English *kichene,* from Old English *cycene,* from Late Latin *coquīna,* ult. from Latin *coquere,* to cook.]

kitch·en·ette (kĭch′ə-nĕt′) *n.* A small kitchen.

kitchen midden. A refuse heap on the site of a prehistoric human dwelling place or settlement.

kitchen police. *Mil.* **1.** The kitchen tasks connected with preparing and serving meals. **2.** The persons assigned to perform kitchen tasks.

kitch·en·ware (kĭch′ən-wâr′) *n.* Utensils, such as pots and pans, for use in the kitchen.

kite (kīt) *n.* **1.** A light frame covered with paper or cloth

kinkajou

and often with a tail for balance, designed to be flown in the air at the end of a long string. **2.** Any of various predatory birds of the subfamilies Milvinae and Elaninae, with a long, often forked tail. [Middle English *kyte,* kite (bird), from Old English *cȳta.*]

kith (kĭth) *n.* Friends, relatives, and neighbors: *kith and kin.* [Middle English, from Old English *cȳth,* knowledge, relationship, home.]

kit·ten (kĭt′n) *n.* A young cat. [Middle English *kitoun.*]

kit·ten·ish (kĭt′n-ĭsh) *adj.* Playful; coy. **—kit′ten·ish·ly** *adv.*

kit·ty[1] (kĭt′ē) *n., pl.* **-ties. 1.** *Cards.* A fund made up of a contribution from each player's winnings. **2.** Any pool, as of money, made up of small contributions. [Orig. "small bowl," dim. of KIT (tub).]

kit·ty[2] (kĭt′ē) *n., pl.* **-ties.** A kitten or cat. [From KITTEN.]

ki·wi (kē′wē) *n.* Any of several flightless New Zealand birds of the genus *Apteryx,* with vestigial wings, a long, slender bill, and brownish hairlike feathers. [Maori.]

kiwi
George Miksch Sutton

Klan (klăn) *n.* The Ku Klux Klan.

Kleen·ex (klē′nĕks′) *n.* A trademark for a soft cleansing tissue.

klep·to·ma·ni·a (klĕp′tə-mā′nē-ə) *n.* Also **clep·to·ma·ni·a.** An obsessive impulse to steal, esp. in the absence of economic need. [Greek *kleptein,* to steal + MANIA.] **—klep′to·ma′ni·ac′** *n.*

klieg light (klēg). A powerful carbon-arc lamp, used esp. in making movies. [Invented by the brothers John H. *Kliegl* (1869–1959) and Anton T. *Kliegl* (1872–1927), American lighting experts.]

knack (năk) *n.* **1.** A clever method of doing something. **2.** A specific talent or skill. —See Syns at **ability.** [Middle English *knakke.*]

knap·sack (năp′săk′) *n.* A case or bag, usu. strapped to the back, for carrying supplies and equipment, as on a hike. [Low German *knappsack: knappen,* to eat + *sack,* bag, sack.]

knap·weed (năp′wēd′) *n.* Any of various plants of the genus *Centaurea,* with purplish, thistlelike flowers. [Middle English *knopwed : knop,* knob + *wed,* weed.]

knave (nāv) *n.* **1.** A dishonest, crafty man. **2.** *Archaic.* A male servant. **3.** *Cards.* The jack. [Middle English, from Old English *cnafa,* boy, lad.] **—knav′ish** *adj.*

knav·er·y (nā′və-rē) *n., pl.* **-ies. 1.** The behavior of a knave. **2.** A tricky or deceitful act.

knead (nēd) *tr.v.* **1.** To mix, fold, and press with the hands: *knead bread dough.* **2.** To shape or form by kneading. **3.** To squeeze, press, or roll with the hands, as if by kneading. [Middle English *kneden,* from Old English *cnedan.*] **—knead′er** *n.*

knee (nē) *n.* **1. a.** *Anat.* The joint of the human leg at which the tibia, fibula, and patella come together. **b.** The region of the leg near and around this joint. **2.** A joint that corresponds to the knee, as in the forelimb of a hoofed animal. **3.** Something that resembles a knee, as a point where something bends sharply. **4.** The part of a garment that covers the knee. **—tr.v. kneed, knee·ing.** To push or strike with the knee. [Middle English, from Old English *cnēo.*]

knee·cap (nē′kăp′) *n.* The patella.

knee-deep (nē′dēp′) *adj.* **1.** Reaching to the knees; knee-high. **2.** Submerged to the knees. **3.** Deeply involved.

kneel (nēl) *intr.v.* **knelt** (nĕlt) or **kneeled, kneel·ing.** To fall or rest on the knees. [Middle English *knewlen,* from Old English *cnēowlian.*]

knee·pad (nē′păd′) *n.* A protective covering for the knee.

knell (nĕl) *intr.v.* **1.** To ring a bell, esp. for a funeral. **2.** To sound mournfully or ominously. **—tr.v.** To announce or summon by or as if by tolling. **—n. 1.** A stroke or toll of a bell esp. for a funeral. **2.** An omen of death, disaster, or failure. [Middle English *knellen,* from Old English *cnyllan.*]

knew (nōō) *v.* Past tense of **know.** [Middle English, from Old English *cnēow.*]

Knick·er·bock·er (nĭk′ər-bŏk′ər) *n.* **1.** A descendant of the Dutch settlers of New York. **2.** A New Yorker. **3. knickerbockers.** Knickers. [After Diedrich *Knickerbocker,* a character in Washington Irving's *History of New York.*]

knick·ers (nĭk′ərz) *pl.n.* Loose pants gathered in with a band just below the knee.

knick·knack (nĭk′năk′) *n.* Also **nick·nack.** A small, ornamental article. [From KNACK (device).]

knife (nīf) *n., pl.* **knives** (nīvz). **1.** A cutting instrument consisting of a sharp blade with a handle. **2.** Any cutting edge or blade. **—tr.v. 1.** To cut or stab with a knife. **2.** *Informal.* To betray by underhand means. **—intr.v.** To move through like a knife. [Middle English *knif,* from Old English *cnif.*]

knife-edge (nīf′ĕj′) *n.* **1.** The cutting edge of a blade. **2.** Any sharp, knifelike edge. **3.** A wedge of metal used as a low-friction fulcrum for a balancing beam or lever.

knight (nīt) *n.* **1.** In feudal times, mounted man-at-arms in military service to a king or lord. **2.** A medieval gentleman-soldier, often of high birth, raised to privileged military status after service as a page and squire. **3.** In Great Britain, a man who has been honored by a sovereign for personal merit or service to the country. **4.** A member of any of several orders or brotherhoods. **5.** A defender or champion, esp. of a lady. **6.** A chess piece that can move two squares horizontally and one vertically, or two vertically and one horizontally. **—tr.v.** To raise (a person) to knighthood. [Middle English *knyght,* from Old English *cniht,* boy, servant.]

knight errant *pl.* **knights errant.** A medieval knight who wandered in search of adventure in order to prove his chivalry and military skill. **—knight′-er′rant·ry** *n.*

knight·hood (nīt′hŏŏd′) *n.* **1.** The rank, profession, or dignity of a knight. **2.** The behavior or qualities appropriate to a knight. **3.** Knights as a body or class.

knight·ly (nīt′lē) *adj.* Of, pertaining to, or appropriate to a knight. **—knight′li·ness** *n.*

Knight Templar *pl.* **Knights Templar.** A member of an order of knights founded to protect pilgrims in the Holy Land. Also called **Templar.**

knish (knĭsh) *n.* A piece of dough stuffed with filling, as of meat or cheese, and baked or fried. [Yiddish, from Russian.]

knit (nĭt) *v.* **knit** or **knit·ted, knit·ting. —tr.v. 1.** To make (a fabric or garment) by intertwining yarn or thread in a series of connected loops with special needles, either by hand or by machine. **2.** To join or bend together closely; unite firmly. **3.** To draw together in wrinkles. **—intr.v. 1.** To make a fabric or garment by intertwining yarn or thread in connected loops. **2.** To come or grow together securely. **3.** To come together in wrinkles or furrows. **—n.** A fabric or garment made by knitting. [Middle English *knitten,* from Old English *cnyttan,* to tie in a knot.] **—knit′ter** *n.*

knit·ting (nĭt′ĭng) *n.* **1.** The action of a knitter. **2.** Knitted work.

knitting needle. A long, thin, pointed rod used in knitting.

knives (nīvz) *n.* Plural of **knife.**

knob (nŏb) *n.* **1. a.** A rounded lump or protuberance. **b.** A rounded handle. **2.** A rounded hill or mountain. [Middle English *knobbe,* from Middle Low German.] **—knobbed** *adj.* **—knob′by** *adj.*

knock (nŏk) *tr.v.* **1.** To strike with a hard blow; hit. **2.** To make, effect, or bring about by or as if by knocking: *She knocked a hole in the wall. Try to knock some sense into his head.* **3.** To cause to collide. **4.** *Slang.* To find fault with; criticize. **—intr.v. 1.** To strike a blow; to rap; to pound. **2.** To collide; to bump. **3.** To make the pounding or clanking noise of a laboring or defective engine. —See Syns at **hit. —phrasal verbs. knock about** (or **around**). *Informal.* To wander aimlessly from place to place. **knock**

down. **1.** To sell to the highest bidder at an auction. **2.** To take apart. **knock off. 1.** *Informal.* To stop or cease. **2.** *Informal.* To make or do hastily. **3.** *Informal.* To deduct: *knocked a few dollars off the bill.* **4.** *Slang.* To take the life of (another). **5.** To hold up; nob. —See Syns at **murder** and **rob. knock out. 1.** In boxing, to knock (an opponent) unconscious. **2.** To put out of commission; make inoperative or useless. **knock over.** *Slang.* To hold up; rob. —See Syns at **rob. knock together.** To make or assemble quickly or roughly. —*n.* **1. a.** A sharp top or blow. **b.** The sound of such a blow; a rap. **2.** A pounding, clanking noise made by an engine, esp. one in poor operating condition. **3.** A misfortune. **4.** *Slang.* A harsh criticism. [Middle English *knokken,* from Old English *cnocian.*]

knock·a·bout (nŏk'ə-bout') *n. Naut.* A small sloop with a mainsail, a jib, and a keel, but no bowsprit. —*adj.* **1.** Rough; boisterous; rowdy. **2.** Appropriate for rough wear or use.

knock·down (nŏk'doun') *adj.* **1.** Strong enough to knock down or overwhelm. **2.** Quickly and easily assembled or disassembled: *knockdown furniture.*

knock·er (nŏk'ər) *n.* Something that knocks, esp. a hinged device attached to a door, used for knocking.

knock-knee (nŏk'nē') *n.* An abnormal condition in which one or both legs turn inward at the knee. —**knock'-kneed'** *adj.*

knock·out (nŏk'out') *n.* **1.** A blow that causes unconsciousness. **2.** The act of knocking out an opponent. **3.** *Slang.* A person or a thing that is extraordinarily impressive or attractive.

knoll (nōl) *n.* A small rounded hill; a hillock. [Middle English *knolle,* from Old English *cnoll.*]

knot (nŏt) *n.* **1.** A fastening made by intertwining or tying together lengths, as of rope or string. **2.** A bow of ribbon, fabric, or braid. **3.** Any tie or bond, esp. a marriage bond. **4.** A dense, compact intersection as of interlaced cord or ribbon. **5.** A tight cluster of persons or things. **6.** A difficulty; problem. **7. a.** A lump or node at the point from which a woody branch grows out from a stem. **b.** The circular cross section of such a node on a piece of cut lumber. **8.** A lump or swelling as in a gland or muscle. **9.** *Naut.* **a.** *Abbr.* **kn.** A unit of speed, one nautical mile per hour, about 1.15 statute miles per hour. **b.** One nautical mile. —*v.* **knot·ted, knot·ting.** —*tr.v.* **1.** To tie in or with a knot; make a knot in. **2.** To combine firmly or intricately; entangle. —*intr.v.* To become snarled or entangled. —*idiom.* **tie the knot.** *Slang.* To get married. [Middle English, from Old English *cnotta.*]

Usage: **knot.** In nautical measure, *knot* is a unit of speed, with a built-in sense of "per hour." A ship is said to travel at ten *knots* (not *knots per hour*) and to cover ten *nautical miles in an hour.*

knot·grass (nŏt'grăs', -gräs') *n.* **1.** A low-growing, weedy plant *Polygonum aviculare,* with very small greenish flowers. **2.** Any of several similar plants.

knot·hole (nŏt'hōl') *n.* A hole in a piece of lumber where a knot has come out.

knot·ted (nŏt'ĭd) *adj.* **1.** Tied or fastened in or with a knot. **2.** Intricate; knotty. **3.** Full of knots; gnarled: *a knotted branch.* **4.** Decorated with knots or knobs.

knot·ty (nŏt'ē) *adj.* **-ti·er, -ti·est. 1.** Tied or snarled in knots: *a knotty cord.* **2.** Having many knots or knobs; gnarled: *a knotty board.* **3.** Difficult to understand; intricate; puzzling. —See Syns at **complex** and **difficult.** —**knot'ti·ness** *n.*

knout (nout) *n.* A leather scourge formerly used for flogging criminals. [French, from Russian *knut,* from Old Norse *knūtr,* knot.]

know (nō) *v.* **knew** (nōo, nyōo), **known, know·ing.** —*tr.v.* **1. a.** To perceive directly. **b.** To have an understanding of. **2.** To be certain of; regard or accept as true. **3.** To be skilled in or have a practical grasp of as a result of experience, study, or practice: *knew how to swim; knows several languages.* **4.** To have firmly secured in the mind or memory. **5.** To be able to identify; recognize: *doesn't know one tune from another.* **6.** To be acquainted or familiar with. —*intr.v.* **1.** To possess knowledge. **2.** To be aware. —*idiom.* **in the know.** Possessing special or confidential information. [Middle English *knowen,* from Old English *cnāwan.*] —**know'a·ble** *adj.* —**know'er** *n.*

Usage: **know.** In affirmative sentences, *know* is followed by *that: I know that I can come.* In negative and interrogative sentences, *know* can be followed by *that, whether,* or *if: I don't know that* (or *whether* or *if) I am right.* Avoid substitution of *as* for *that, whether,* and *if* in such sentences.

know-how (nō'hou') *n. Informal.* Knowledge of how to do something easily and well; skill. —See Syns at **ability.**

know·ing (nō'ĭng) *adj.* **1.** Possessing or indicating knowledge, information, or understanding: *a knowing glance.* **2.** Shrewd. **3.** Done intentionally; deliberate. —See Syns at **aware** and **wise.** —**know'ing·ly** *adv.* —**know'ing·ness** *n.*

knowl·edge (nŏl'ĭj) *n.* **1.** The state or fact of knowing. **2.** Information, ideas, or understanding gained through experience, observation, or study. **3.** The sum or range of what has been perceived, discovered, or learned. **4.** Learning; erudition: *a person who valued knowledge for its own sake.* [Middle English *knowlege,* from *knowelechen,* to confess, recognize, ult. from Old English *cnāwan,* to know.]

Syns: **1. knowledge, information, lore, wisdom** *n. Core meaning:* That which is known *(new additions to our knowledge of the universe).* **2. knowledge, education, erudition, instruction, learning, scholarship** *n. Core meaning:* Known facts, ideas, and skill that have been imparted *(knowledge gained in the classroom).*

knowl·edge·a·ble (nŏl'ĭ-jə-bəl) *adj.* Possessing or showing knowledge.

known (nōn) *v.* Past participle of **know.**

know-noth·ing (nō'nŭth'ĭng) *n.* **1.** A completely ignorant person. **2.** A member of an American political group of the 1850's that was antagonistic toward immigrants and Roman Catholics.

knuck·le (nŭk'əl) *n.* **1.** *Anat.* **a.** A joint where the ends of two bones come together esp. one of the finger joints. **b.** Any of the rounded protuberances at such a joint. **2.** A cut of meat centering on a knuckle joint. **3. knuckles.** Brass knuckles. —*tr.v.* **-led, -ling.** To press, rub, or hit with the knuckles. —*phrasal verbs.* **knuckle down.** To apply oneself earnestly to a task. **knuckle under.** To yield to pressure; give in. [Middle English *knokel,* from Middle Low German *knökel.*]

knurl (nûrl) *n.* **1.** A protuberance such as a knob or knot. **2.** One of a series of small ridges or beads placed along the edge of a metal object such as a thumbscrew or coin as an aid in gripping. —*tr.v.* To provide with knurls; to mill. [Perh. from *knur,* knob, knot.] —**knurl'y** *adj.*

KO (kā'ō'). *Slang.* —*tr.v.* **KO'd, KO'ing.** Also **kay·o.** To knock out. —*n. Boxing.* A knockout.

ko·a·la (kō-ä'lə) *n.* A furry Australian marsupial, *Phascolarctos cinereus,* that lives in eucalyptus trees and feeds chiefly on their leaves and bark. [Earlier *koola,* from native Australian name *kūlla.*]

koala

kohl (kōl) *n.* A cosmetic preparation used to darken the skin around the eyes. [Arabic *kohl,* powder of antimony.]

kohl·ra·bi (kōl-rä'bē, kōl'rä'-) *n., pl.* **-bies.** A plant, *Brassica caulorapa,* with a thickened basal part that is eaten as a vegetable. [German *Kohlrabi,* from Italian *cavoli rape,* pl. of *cavolo rapa : cavolo,* cole, cabbage + *rapa,* turnip.]

ko·la (kō'lə) *n.* Also **co·la.** Either of two African trees, *Cola nitida* or *C. acuminata,* bearing nuts used in the manufacture of beverages and medicines. [From a native West African name.]

kola nut. Also **cola nut.** The nut of a kola tree, containing caffeine and theobromine, and yielding an extract used in beverages and in medicines.

Kol Ni·dre (kōl' nĭd'rä, -rē, -rə). *Judaism.* A prayer recited in the synagogue on the eve of Yom Kippur. [Aramaic *kol nidhrē*, "all vows," from the opening words of the prayer.]

kook·a·bur·ra (kōōk'ə-bûr'ə) *n.* A large Australian kingfisher, *Dacelo novaeguineae* (or *D. gigas),* whose call sounds like raucous laughter. [Native Australian name.]

ko·peck (kō'pĕk') *n.* Also **co·peck** or **ko·pek.** A coin equal to ¹/₁₀₀ of the rouble of the Union of Soviet Socialist Republics. [Russian *kopeĭka*, from *kop'e*, lance (from the figure of the czar with a lance in his hand orig. stamped on the coin).]

Ko·ran (kô-rǎn', -rän', kō-) *n.* The sacred text of Islam, believed to contain the revelations made by Allah to Mohammed. [Arabic *qur'ān*, reading, recitation, from *qara'a*, to read, recite.] **—Ko·ran'ic** *adj.*

ko·ru·na (kôr'ōō-nä') *n., pl.* **-ny** (-nē) or **-nas.** The basic monetary unit of Czechoslovakia. [Czech, crown, from Latin *corōna*, crown.]

ko·sher (kō'shər) *adj.* **1.** *Judaism.* Conforming to or prepared in accordance with laws, esp. the dietary laws; ritually pure: *kosher meat.* **2.** Preparing or selling kosher food: *a kosher delicatessen.* **3.** *Slang.* Proper; legitimate. **—***tr.v.* To make kosher. [Yiddish, from Hebrew *kāshēr*, proper.]

kow·tow (kou'tou', kō'-) *n.* Also **ko·tow** (kō'-). **1.** A salutation in which one kneels and touches the forehead to the ground as an expression of respect or submission. **2.** An act or gesture of exaggerated respect or obedience. **—***intr.v.* To show respect or submission by or as if by kowtowing. [Mandarin *k'o¹ t'ou²* : *k'o¹*, to knock, bump + *t'ou²*, head.]

Kr The symbol for the element krypton.

kraal (kräl) *n.* **1.** A village of southern African natives, typically consisting of huts surrounded by a stockade. **2.** An enclosure for livestock in southern Africa. **—***tr.v.* To put in a kraal. [Afrikaans, enclosure for cattle, from Portuguese *curral*.]

krait (krīt) *n.* Any of several Southeast Asian venomous snakes of the genus *Bungarus.* [Hindi *karait*.]

K ration. A lightweight, emergency field ration developed for the use of the U.S. armies in World War II.

Krem·lin (krĕm'lən) *n.* **1.** The citadel of Moscow, housing the major offices of the Soviet government. **2.** The Soviet government. [French, from Russian *kreml'*, citadel.]

krim·mer (krĭm'ər) *n.* Gray, curly fur made from the pelts of lambs of the Crimean region. [German *Krimmer*, from *Krim*, the Crimean peninsula.]

kris (krēs) *n.* A dagger or short sword of Malayan origin with a wavy double-edged blade. [Malay *kĕris*.]

Krish·na (krĭsh'nə). *Hinduism.* The chief hero of Hindu mythology, worshiped as an incarnation of the god Vishnu. **—Krish'na·ism'** *n.*

kro·na¹ (krō'nə) *n., pl.* **-nur** (-nər). The basic monetary unit of Iceland. [Icelandic *krōna*, from Old Norse *krūna*, crown, from Latin *corōna*.]

kro·na² (krō'nə) *n., pl.* **-nor** (-nôr'). The basic monetary unit of Sweden. [Swedish, from Latin *corōna*, crown.]

kro·ne (krō'nə) *n., pl.* **-ner** (-nər). The basic monetary unit of Denmark and Norway. [Danish *krone* and Norwegian *krune*, crown, from Old Norse *krūna*, from Latin *corōna*.]

krul·ler (krŭl'ər) *n.* Var. of **cruller.**

kryp·ton (krĭp'tŏn') *n.* Symbol **Kr** A whitish, inert, gaseous element used chiefly in gas-discharge lamps, fluorescent lamps, and electronic flash tubes. Atomic number 36, atomic weight 83.80, melting point –156.6°C, boiling point –152.30°C, density 3.73 grams per liter (0°C). [New Latin, "hidden (element)," from Greek *krupton*, hidden, from *kruptein*, to hide.]

ku·dos (kyōō'dŏs', -dōs') *n.* Acclaim or prestige as a result of achievement or position: *"all the kudos of the Presidency of the United States"* (Eric F. Goldman). [From Greek *kudos*, glory, fame.]

    ***Usage:* kudos.** This term is a singular noun: *Kudos was due him.* The singular back-formation ("kudo") which is sometimes seen is nonstandard and should be avoided.

ku·du (kōō'dōō) *n.* Also **koo·doo.** Either of two African antelopes, *Tragelaphus strepsiceros* or *T. imberbis,* with long spirally curved horns and a coat marked with narrow white vertical stripes. [Afrikaans *koedoe*, from Bantu *iqudu*.]

Ku Klux Klan (kōō' klŭks' klǎn', kyōō'). **1.** A secret society organized in the South after the Civil War to assert white supremacy with terroristic methods. **2.** A secret, fraternal organization founded in Georgia in 1915 and modeled upon the earlier Ku Klux Klan. [Orig. unknown.] **—Ku Kluxer** or **Ku Klux Klanner. —Ku Kluxism.**

ku·lak (kōō-lǎk', -läk') *n.* A prosperous or landed peasant in Czarist Russia and during the October Revolution. [Russian, "fist," "tight-fisted person."]

küm·mel (kĭm'əl; German kü'məl) *n.* A colorless liqueur flavored with caraway, anise, or cumin. [German *Kümmel*, cumin seed, from Old High German *kumil*, from Latin *cumīnum*, cumin.]

kum·quat (kŭm'kwŏt') *n.* Also **cum·quat. 1.** A small citrus fruit similar to an orange, with an acid pulp and a thin, edible rind. **2.** A tree that bears kumquats. [Cantonese *kam kwat*, "golden orange."]

kung fu (kōōng' fōō', gōōng'-). A Chinese system of self-defense similar to karate. [Mandarin *ch¹üan² fa³*, "boxing principles."]

Kuo·min·tang (kwō'mǐn'tǎng') *n.* The nationalist party of the Republic of China, orig. founded by Sun Yat-sen. [Mandarin *kuo² min² tang³*, "Nationalist Party."]

Kurd (kûrd, kōōrd) *n.* One of a nomadic Moslem people living chiefly in Kurdistan.

kwash·i·or·kor (kwǎsh'ē-ôr'kôr, kwä'shē-) *n.* A disease of infants and young children, caused by a protein deficiency. [Native word in Ghana.]

ky·mo·graph (kī'mə-grǎf', -gräf') *n.* Also **cy·mo·graph** (sī'-). An instrument for recording variations in pressure, esp. of the blood. [From Greek *kūma*, wave + -GRAPH.]

Kyr·i·e e·le·i·son (kĭr'ē-ā' ĭ-lā'ə-sən). A liturgical prayer that begins with or consists of the words "Lord, have mercy." [Late Latin, from Greek *Kurie eleēson*, "Lord, have mercy."]

kookaburra
George Miksch Sutton

kumquat

ă pat   ā pay   â care   ä father   ĕ pet   ē be   hw which   ĭ pit   ī tie   î pier   ŏ pot   ō toe   ô paw, for   oi noise
ōō took   ōō boot   ou out   th thin   th this   ŭ cut   û urge   zh vision   ə about, item, edible, gallop, circus

L l

| Phoenician | Greek | Roman | Medieval | Modern |

Phoenician – About 3,000 years ago the Phoenicians and other Semitic peoples began to use graphic signs to represent individual speech sounds instead of syllables or whole words. They used this symbol to represent the sound of the consonant "l" and gave it the name lāmedh.
Greek – The Greeks borrowed the Phoenician alphabet with some modifications. They changed the orientation of lāmedh and altered its name to lambda. They used lambda to represent the sound of the consonant "l," as lāmedh did in Phoenician.
Roman – The Romans borrowed the alphabet from the Greeks via the Etruscans and adapted it for carving Latin in stone. This monumental script, as it is called, became the basis for modern printed capital letters.
Medieval – By medieval times – around 1,200 years ago – the Roman monumental capitals had become adapted to being relatively quickly written on paper, parchment, or vellum. The cursive minuscule alphabet became the basis of modern printed lower-case letters.
Modern – Since the invention of printing about 500 years ago modifications have been made in the shape and style of the letter L, but its basic form has remained unchanged.

---

l, L (ĕl) n., pl. **l's** or **L's. 1.** The 12th letter of the English alphabet. **2.** Anything shaped like the letter L.
la (lä) n. Mus. The syllable used to represent the sixth tone of the diatonic scale. [Middle English, from Medieval Latin.]
La The symbol for the element lanthanum.
lab (lăb) n. Informal. A laboratory.
la·bel (lā′bəl) n. **1.** Something , such as a small piece of paper or cloth, attached to an article to identify its origin, owner, contents, use, or destination. **2.** A descriptive term; an epithet: quickly received the label "troublemaker." —tr.v. **-beled** or **-belled, -bel·ing** or **-bel·ling. 1.** To attach a label to. **2.** To identify or designate with a number, letter, word, etc.: Label one side of the triangle A. **3.** To describe or classify as: labeled his opponent a reactionary. [Middle English, from Old French, ribbon, strip.] —**la·bel·er** or **la′bel·ler** n.
la·bel·lum (lə-bĕl′əm) n., pl. **-bel·la** (-bĕl′ə). The often enlarged lip of an orchid. [From Latin, small lip, dim. of labrum, lip.]
la·bi·a (lā′bē-ə) n. Plural of **labium.**
la·bi·al (lā′bē-əl) adj. **1.** Of or pertaining to the lips or labia. **2.** Phonet. Formed mainly by closing or partly closing the lips, as b, m, v, and w. —n. A labial sound. [Medieval Latin labiālis, from Latin labium, lip.]
la·bi·ate (lā′bē-ĭt, -āt′) adj. Having lips or liplike parts.
la·bi·o·den·tal (lā′bē-ō-dĕn′tl). Phonet. —adj. Formed with the lips and teeth. —n. A labiodental sound.
la·bi·um (lā′bē-əm) n., pl. **-bi·a** (-bē-ə). **1.** A lip or liplike structure. **2.** Any of four folds of tissue of the female external genitalia. [From Latin, lip.]
la·bor (lā′bər). Also Brit. **la·bour.** —n. **1.** Physical or mental exertion. **2.** A specific task. **3.** A particular form of work or method of working: manual labor. **4.** Work for wages as distinguished from work for profits. **5. a.** Workers in general; the laboring class. **b.** The trade-union movement, esp. its officials: Labor supported the President's policies. **6.** A political party representing the interests of workers, esp. in Great Britain. **7.** Something produced by labor. **8.** The physical efforts of childbirth; parturition. —intr.v. **1.** To work; toil: They labored long hours in the factory. **2.** To strive painstakingly: She labored to make her meaning clear. **3.** To proceed slowly; plod: The train labored up the mountain. **4.** To suffer from a burden or disadvantage: labor under a misconception. —tr.v. To deal with in excessive detail: labor a point. [Middle English, from Old French, from Latin.]
Syns: labor, drudgery, toil, travail, work n. Core meaning: Physical exertion that is usu. difficult and exhausting (a life of labor and little rest).
lab·o·ra·to·ry (lăb′rə-tôr′ē, -tōr′ē) n., pl. **-ries. 1.** A room or building equipped for scientific experimentation, research, or testing. **2.** A place where drugs and chemicals are manufactured. **3.** Any place for practice, observation, or testing: a language laboratory. [Medieval Latin labōrātōrium, workshop, from Latin labōrāre, to labor, from labor, labor.]
Labor Day. The first Monday in Sept., a legal holiday observed in the United States and Canada in honor of working people.
la·bored (lā′bərd) adj. **1.** Done or produced with effort: labored breathing. **2.** Lacking natural ease; strained: a labored reply to the question.
la·bor·er (lā′bər-ər) n. A worker, esp. one who does unskilled manual labor.
la·bo·ri·ous (lə-bôr′ē-əs, -bōr′-) adj. **1.** Requiring much hard or tedious work: a laborious task. **2.** Hard-working; industrious: laborious workers for the public good. —See Syns at **burdensome.** —**la·bo′ri·ous·ly** adv. —**la·bo′ri·ous·ness** n.
la·bor·ite (lā′bə-rīt′) n. **1.** A member or supporter of a labor movement or union. **2.** A member of a political party representing labor, esp. in Great Britain.
la·bor·sav·ing (lā′bər-sā′vĭng) adj. Designed to conserve or decrease the amount of human labor needed: laborsaving devices.
labor union. An organization of wage earners formed to protect and further their collective interests with respect to wages and working conditions.
la·bour (lā′bər) n. & v. Brit. Var. of labor.
Lab·ra·dor retriever (lăb′rə-dôr′). A dog of a breed that originated in Newfoundland, with a short, dense coat and a tapering tail.
la·bur·num (lə-bûr′nəm) n. Any of several trees or shrubs of the genus Laburnum, with drooping clusters of yellow flowers. [Latin.]
lab·y·rinth (lăb′ə-rĭnth′) n. **1. a.** A network of winding, interconnected passages through which it is difficult to find one's way without help; maze. **b. Labyrinth.** Gk. Myth. The maze in which the Minotaur was confined. **2.** Something extremely intricate or confused, as a subject or situation. **3.** Anat. The semicircular canals, vestibule, and cochlea of the inner ear. [Middle English laborintus, from Latin labyrinthus, from Greek laburinthos.]
lab·y·rin·thine (lăb′ə-rĭn′thĭn, -thēn′) adj. **1.** Of or constituting a labyrinth. **2.** Intricate. —See Syns at **complex.**

ă pat   ā pay   â care   ä father   ĕ pet   ē be   hw which   ĭ pit   ī tie   î pier   ŏ pot   ō toe   ô paw, for   oi noise
ŏŏ took   ōō boot   ou out   th thin   th this   ŭ cut   û urge   zh vision   ə about, item, edible, gallop, circus

lac (lăk) *n.* A resinous secretion of the lac insect, used in making shellac. [Dutch *lak* or French *laque*, from Hindi *lākh*, from Sanskrit *lākshā*.]

lace (lās) *n.* **1.** A cord or string threaded through eyelets or around hooks to pull and tie opposite edges together. **2.** A delicate fabric of silk, cotton, nylon, or other thread woven in an open weblike pattern with fancy designs. **3.** Gold or silver braid ornamenting an officer's uniform. —*v.* **laced, lac·ing.** —*tr.v.* **1.** To thread a cord through the eyelets or around the hooks of. **2.** To draw together and tie the laces of: *Lace your shoes tight.* **3.** To intertwine: *lace strands into a braid.* **4.** To apply lace to. **5.** To add a small amount of liquor to (a beverage). **6.** To streak with color. **7.** To give a beating to; thrash. —*intr.v.* To be fastened with lace or laces. —*phrasal verb.* **lace into.** To attack; assail. [Middle English, cord, from Old French *las*, from Latin *laqueus*, noose, trap.] —**lac'er** *n.*

lac·er·ate (lăs'ə-rāt') *tr.v.* **-at·ed, -at·ing.** **1.** To rip, cut, or tear: *lacerate an elbow.* **2.** To distress deeply; hurt: *harsh words that lacerate feelings.* [From Latin *lacerāre*, from *lacer*, torn.]

lac·er·a·tion (lăs'ə-rā'shən) *n.* **1.** The act or an example of lacerating. **2.** A jagged wound or tear.

lace·wing (lās'wĭng') *n.* Any of various greenish or brownish insects of the families Chrysopidae and Hemerobiidae, with four gauzy wings and larvae that feed on aphids and other insect pests.

Lach·e·sis (lăk'ĭ-sĭs) *n. Gk. Myth.* One of the three Fates.

lach·ry·mal (lăk'rə-məl) or **lac·ri·mal** *adj.* Of or pertaining to tears or the glands that produce tears. —*n.* **lachrymals.** The lachrymal glands. [Medieval Latin *lachrymālis*, from Latin *lacrima*, tear.]

lach·ry·mose (lăk'rə-mōs') *adj.* **1.** Weeping or inclined to weep; tearful. **2.** Causing tears; sorrowful: *a sentimental, lachrymose story.* [Latin *lacrimōsus*, from *lacrima*, tear.] —**lach'ry·mose'ly** *adv.*

lac·ing (lā'sĭng) *n.* **1.** Something that laces; a lace. **2.** A beating or thrashing.

lac insect. An Asian insect, *Laccifer lacca*, the female of which secretes the resinous substance lac.

lack (lăk) *n.* **1.** A condition of being in short supply or totally absent: *a lack of money.* **2.** Something that is needed: *water is a real lack during a drought.* —See Syns at **deficiency.** —*tr.v.* **1.** To be entirely without or have very little of: *lacks will power to diet.* **2.** To need: *a house that lacks closet space.* —*intr.v.* To be wanting or deficient: *What she lacks in beauty she has in charm.* [Middle English *lacke.*]

lack·a·dai·si·cal (lăk'ə-dā'zĭ-kəl) *adj.* Lacking spirit, liveliness, or interest. [From earlier *lackadaisy*, from *(a)lackaday*, an exclamation of regret or surprise.] —**lack'a·dai'si·cal·ly** *adv.*

lack·ey (lăk'ē) *n., pl.* **-eys. 1.** A male servant in uniform; footman. **2.** A servile follower; toady. —*intr.v.* To act in a servile manner; fawn. [French *laquais*, from Old French.]

lack·lus·ter (lăk'lŭs'tər) *adj.* Lacking luster, brightness, or vitality; dull: *a lackluster conversation.*

la·con·ic (lə-kŏn'ĭk) *adj.* Using few words to express something fully or pointedly; terse; succinct. —See Syns at **concise.** [Latin *laconicus*, from Greek *Lakōnikos*, Spartan (from the Spartans' proverbial brevity of speech).] —**la·con'i·cal·ly** *adv.*

lac·quer (lăk'ər) *n.* **1.** Any of various clear or colored synthetic coatings made by dissolving cellulose derivatives in a mixture of volatile solvents and used to give wood and metal surfaces a high gloss. **2.** Any glossy, often resinous material used as a surface coating, esp. one from an Asian sumac tree. —*tr.v.* To coat with or as if with lacquer: *lacquer a table; lacquer fingernails.* [From obs. French *lacre*, sealing wax, from Spanish *laca*, resin, from Hindi *lākh*, lac.]

lac·ri·mal (lăk'rə-məl) *adj. & n.* Var. of **lachrymal.**

la·crosse (lə-krôs', -krŏs') *n.* A game, played on a field by two teams of ten players each, in which participants use a long-handled stick with a webbed pouch to maneuver a ball into the opposing team's goal. [Canadian French, from French *(le jeu de) la crosse*, (the game of) the hooked stick, from Old French *crosse*, crosier.]

lact-. Var. of **lacto-.**

lac·tase (lăk'tās') *n.* An enzyme, found in some yeasts and in the intestinal juices of mammals, that acts in the conversion of lactose into glucose and galactose.

lac·tate (lăk'tāt') *intr.v.* **-tat·ed, -tat·ing.** To secrete or produce milk. —*n.* A salt or ester of lactic acid. —**lac·ta'tion** *n.*

lac·te·al (lăk'tē-əl) *n.* Any of numerous minute lymph-carrying vessels that convey chyle from the intestine to the thoracic duct. —*adj.* **1.** Of or like milk; milky. **2.** *Anat.* Of or pertaining to the lacteals. [From Latin *lacteus*, of milk, from *lac*, milk.]

lac·tic (lăk'tĭk) *adj.* Of or derived from milk.

lactic acid. An organic acid, $C_3H_6O_3$, found in muscles, sour milk, molasses, wines, and various fruits, and used as a flavoring and preservative for foods.

lac·tif·er·ous (lăk-tĭf'ər-əs) *adj.* **1.** Producing, secreting, or conveying milk. **2.** *Bot.* Yielding a milky juice. [Late Latin *lactifer : lacti-*, milk + *-fer*, bearing.]

lacto- or **lact-.** A prefix meaning milk: *lactate.* [From Latin *lac*, milk.]

lac·tose (lăk'tōs') *n.* A white crystalline sugar, $C_{12}H_{22}O_{11}$, found in milk and used in pharmaceuticals, infant foods, bakery products, and confections. Also called **milk sugar.**

la·cu·na (lə-koō'nə, -kyoō'-) *n., pl.* **-nae** (-nē) or **-nas. 1.** An empty space or missing part; a gap: *a lacuna in a manuscript.* **2.** *Anat.* A cavity or depression. [Latin *lacūna*, pool.]

la·cus·trine (lə-kŭs'trĭn) *adj.* **1.** Of or pertaining to a lake. **2.** Living or growing in or near lakes. [From French *lacustre*, of a lake, from Latin *lacus*, lake.]

lac·y (lā'sē) *adj.* **-i·er, -i·est.** Of or resembling lace. —**lac'i·ness** *n.*

lad (lăd) *n.* A boy or young man. [Middle English *ladde.*]

lad·der (lăd'ər) *n.* **1.** A device for climbing, consisting usu. of two long, parallel side pieces or ropes crossed by equally spaced rungs. **2.** Any means of ascent or series of ascending stages or levels: *climbing the social ladder.* [Middle English, from Old English *hlædder.*]

lad·die (lăd'ē) *n.* A young lad.

lade (lād) *v.* **lad·ed, lad·en** (lād'n) or **lad·ed, lad·ing.** —*tr.v.* **1.** To load with or as if with cargo: *lade a ship.* **2.** To weigh down; to burden; oppress: *She's laden with troubles.* **3.** To ladle. —*intr.v.* **1.** To take on cargo. **2.** To ladle a liquid. [Middle English *laden*, from Old English *hladan.*]

lad·en (lād'n) *v.* A past participle of **lade.** —*adj.* **1.** Weighed down with a load; heavy: *a rescue ship laden with food and medical supplies.* **2.** Oppressed; burdened: *laden with grief.*

lad·ing (lā'dĭng) *n.* Cargo; freight: *a bill of lading.*

la·dle (lād'l) *n.* A long-handled spoon with a deep bowl for serving liquids. —*tr.v.* **-dled, -dling.** To lift out and pour with a ladle. [Middle English *ladel*, from Old English *hlædel*, from *hladan*, to draw out, lade.]

la·dy (lā'dē) *n., pl.* **-dies. 1.** A woman of breeding, culture, or high station. **2. a.** A woman regarded as proper and virtuous. **b.** A well-behaved young girl: *She's a perfect little lady.* **3.** Any woman, esp. when spoken of in a polite way: *the lady who lives next door.* **4. ladies.** A word used in speaking of or to or in writing to women as members of a group: *Ladies and gentlemen, I bid you welcome.* **5.** The female head of a household. **6. Lady.** *Brit.* The general female title of nobility or other rank. [Middle English *ladi*, from Old English *hlæfdige.*]

la·dy·bug (lā'dē-bŭg') *n.* Any of numerous small beetles of the family Coccinellidae, often reddish with black spots, that feed on insect pests such as aphids and scale insects. Also called **ladybird.**

la·dy·fin·ger (lā'dē-fĭng'gər) *n.* A small, finger-shaped sponge cake.

lady in waiting *pl.* **ladies in waiting.** A lady of a court appointed to attend a queen or princess.

la·dy·like (lā'dē-līk') *adj.* Characteristic of, appropriate for, or becoming a lady.

la·dy·love (lā'dē-lŭv') *n.* A beloved woman; sweetheart.

La·dy·ship (lā'dē-shĭp') *n.* A word used in speaking or referring to a woman who holds the rank of lady.

la·dy's-slip·per (lā'dēz-slĭp'ər) *n.* Any of various orchids of the genus *Cypripedium*, having variously colored flowers with an inflated, pouchlike lip.

| ă pat | ā pay | â care | ä father | ĕ pet | ē be | hw which | ĭ pit | ī tie | î pier | ŏ pot | ō toe | ô paw, for | oi noise |
| oō took | oō boot | ou out | th thin | th this | ŭ cut | û urge | zh vision | ə about, item, edible, gallop, circus |

lag (lăg) *intr.v.* **lagged, lag·ging. 1.** To fail to keep up a pace; straggle: *lagged behind the other riders.* **2.** To weaken or diminish; to flag: *Our spirits began to lag. Sales lagged in the summer.* —See Syns at **delay.** —*n.* **1.** The act or condition of lagging. **2.** An extent or duration of lagging: *"He wondered darkly at how great a lag there was between his thinking and his actions"* (Thomas Wolfe). [Orig. unknown.]

la·ger (lä'gər) *n.* A type of beer brewed by slow fermentation and aged from six weeks to six months to allow sedimentation. [Short for German *Lager(bier),* (beer) for storing, from *lager,* store, lair.]

lag·gard (lăg'ərd) *n.* Someone or something that lags behind. —*adj.* Lagging behind; backward: *a laggard runner.* —See Syns at **slow.**

la·gniappe (lăn-yăp', lăn'yăp') *n.* **1.** A small gift that comes or is given with a purchase. **2.** *Informal.* An extra or unexpected gift; a gratuity or bonus. [Louisiana French, from American Spanish *la ñapa.*]

lag·o·morph (lăg'ə-môrf') *n.* Any of various gnawing mammals of the order Lagomorpha, which includes the rabbits and hares. [Greek *lagōs,* hare + -MORPH.] —**lag'o·mor'phic** *adj.*

la·goon (lə-goon') *n.* A shallow body of water, esp. one separated from the sea by sandbars or coral reefs. [French *lagune,* from Latin *lacūna,* pool, cavity, from *lacus,* lake.]

la·ic (lā'ĭk) or **la·i·cal** (-ĭ-kəl) *adj.* Of or relating to the laity; secular. [Late Latin *lāicus,* lay.]

laid (lād) *v.* Past tense and past participle of **lay** (to put). [Middle English *leide, leyed,* from Old English *legde, gelegd.*]

lain (lān) *v.* Past participle of **lie** (to rest). [Middle English *leyen,* from Old English *gelegen.*]

lair (lâr) *n.* **1.** The den or dwelling of a wild animal. **2.** A den or hideaway. [Middle English, from Old English *leger.*]

laird (lârd) *n. Scot.* The owner of a landed estate. [Scottish, var. of LORD.]

lais·sez faire (lĕs'ā fâr'). **1.** An economic doctrine, developed in the 18th cent., that opposes any governmental regulation or interference in commerce beyond the minimum necessary for a free-enterprise system to operate according to its own economic laws. **2.** *Informal.* Noninterference in the affairs of others. [French, "allow (them) to do."]

la·i·ty (lā'ĭ-tē) *n., pl.* **-ties. 1.** The lay people of a religious group as distinguished from the clergy. **2.** All those persons who are not members of a given profession, art, or other specialization; nonprofessionals.

La·ius (lā'əs) *n. Gk. Myth.* The king of Thebes who was mistakenly killed by his own son, Oedipus.

lake¹ (lāk) *n.* **1.** A large inland body of fresh or salt water. **2.** A large pool of any liquid. [Middle English *lac,* from Old French, from Latin *lacus.*]

lake² (lāk) *n.* **1.** A pigment consisting of organic coloring matter with an inorganic base or carrier. **2.** A deep red. [Var. of LAC.]

lake dwelling. A dwelling, esp. a prehistoric dwelling, built on piles in a shallow lake.

lake herring. A food fish, *Coregonus artedii* (or *Leucichthys artedi*), of the Great Lakes region, related to the whitefishes.

lake trout. A freshwater food fish, *Salvelinus namaycush,* of North American lakes.

lam (lăm) *n.* —**on the lam.** In flight, esp. from the law. [Orig. unknown.]

la·ma (lä'mə) *n.* A Buddhist monk of Tibet or Mongolia. [Tibetan *blama.*]

La·ma·ism (lä'mə-ĭz'əm) *n.* The religion of Tibet and Mongolia and neighboring areas, a form of Buddhism combined with native animism, stressing the dominance of monks. —**La'ma·ist** *n.* —**La'ma·is'tic** *adj.*

La·marck·i·an (lə-mär'kē-ən) *adj.* Of or relating to Lamarckism. —*n.* A supporter of Lamarckism.

La·marck·ism (lə-mär'kĭz'əm) *n.* The evolutionary theory that adaptive changes to environment cause structural changes in plants and animals that are then genetically transmitted to offspring. [After Jean B. P. A. de Monet

(1744–1829), Chevalier de *Lamarck,* French naturalist, its developer.]

la·ma·ser·y (lä'mə-sĕr'ē) *n., pl.* **-ies.** A monastery of lamas.

lamb (lăm) *n.* **1. a.** A young sheep. **b.** The flesh of a young sheep used as meat. **2.** Lambskin. **3.** A sweet, mild-mannered person; a dear. —**modifier:** *lamb* chops. —*intr.v.* To give birth to a lamb. [Middle English, from Old English.]

lam·baste (lăm-bāst') *tr.v.* **-bast·ed, -bast·ing.** *Slang.* **1.** To thrash; beat. **2.** To find fault with sharply. —See Syns at **scold.** [Perh. *lam,* to beat + *baste,* to beat.]

lamb·da (lăm'də) *n.* The 11th letter in the Greek alphabet, written Λ, λ. [Greek.]

lam·bent (lăm'bənt) *adj.* **1.** Flickering lightly over a surface. **2.** Having a gentle glow; luminous: *"His eyes soft and lambent but wild, like a stag's"* (Katherine Anne Porter). **3.** Characterized by effortless brilliance or lightness: *a lambent wit.* [From Latin *lambens,* pres. part. of *lambere,* to lick, tap.] —**lam'ben·cy** *n.* —**lam'bent·ly** *adv.*

lam·bre·quin (lăm'brə-kĭn, -brĭ-) *n.* A short, ornamental drapery hanging from the top of a window or door or the edge of a shelf. [French, from Dutch *lamper,* veil.]

lamb·skin (lăm'skĭn') *n.* **1.** The skin of a lamb, esp. when dressed without removing the fleece. **2.** Leather made from the dressed hide of a lamb.

lame (lām) *adj.* **lam·er, lam·est. 1.** Disabled in one or more limbs, esp. in a leg or foot so that walking is impaired. **2.** Limping, as from disability or exhaustion. **3.** Weak and ineffectual; unsatisfactory: *a lame excuse.* —*tr.v.* **lamed, lam·ing.** To make lame. [Middle English, from Old English *lama.*] —**lame'ly** *adv.* —**lame'ness** *n.*

la·mé (lă-mā', lä-) *n.* A fabric in which metal threads of or resembling gold or silver are woven with threads of fiber such as silk. —**modifier:** *a lamé dress.* [French, from adj., spangled, from Old French *lame,* thin metal plate.]

lame duck. An elected officeholder who has not been re-elected but continues in office during the period between the election and the inauguration of a successor.

la·mel·la (lə-mĕl'ə) *n., pl.* **-mel·lae** (-mĕl'ē) or **-mel·las.** A thin scale, plate, or layer, as in the gills of a bivalve mollusk or forming one of the gills of a mushroom. [From Latin *lāmella,* dim. of *lāmina,* thin plate.] —**la·mel'lar** *adj.*

lam·el·late (lăm'ə-lāt', lə-mĕl'āt') *adj.* Having, resembling, composed of, or arranged in thin layers or lamellae. —**lam'el·la'tion** *n.*

la·mel·li·branch (lə-mĕl'ə-brăngk') *n.* Any of the mollusks of the class Pelecypoda (or Lamellibranchia), having a hinged bivalve shell and including the clams, mussels, and oysters. [New Latin *Lamellibranchia,* "plate-gilled."]

la·ment (lə-mĕnt') *tr.v.* **1.** To express grief for or about; mourn over: *lament a death.* **2.** To regret deeply; deplore: *She lamented her decision.* —*intr.v.* To grieve. —*n.* **1.** An expression of sorrow or grief; a lamentation. **2.** A song or poem expressing grief. [French *lamenter,* from Old French, from Latin *lāmentārī,* from *lāmentum,* expression of sorrow.] —**la·ment'er** *n.*

lam·en·ta·ble (lăm'ən-tə-bəl, lə-mĕn'-) *adj.* **1.** That is to be lamented; regrettable: *a lamentable mistake.* **2.** Exhibiting sorrow or grief; mournful: *a lamentable ballad of lost love.* —**lam'en·ta·bly** *adv.*

lam·en·ta·tion (lăm'ən-tā'shən) *n.* **1.** The act of lamenting; an expression of sorrow, grief, etc. **2. Lamentations.** See table at **Bible.**

lam·i·na (lăm'ə-nə) *n., pl.* **-nae** (-nē') or **-nas. 1.** A thin plate, sheet, or layer. **2.** *Bot.* The blade of a leaf. [From Latin *lāmina,* thin plate.]

lam·i·nate (lăm'ə-nāt') *tr.v.* **-nat·ed, -nat·ing. 1.** To beat or compress (metal) into a thin plate or sheet. **2.** To divide into thin layers. **3.** To make by uniting several layers: *laminate plywood.* **4.** To cover with thin sheets: *laminate a driver's license.* —*adj.* (lăm'ə-nĭt, -nāt'). Consisting of, arranged in, or covered with a lamina or laminae. —*n.* A laminated product, as plywood. —**lam'i·na'tor** *n.*

lam·i·nat·ed (lăm'ə-nā'tĭd) *adj.* Composed of layers bonded together.

lam·i·na·tion (lăm'ə-nā'shən) *n.* **1.** The process of laminating or the condition of being laminated. **2.** Something laminated. **3.** A lamina.

Lam·mas (lăm'əs) n. A harvest festival formerly held in England on August 1. [Middle English *Lammasse,* from Old English *hlāfmæsse* : *hlāf,* loaf + *mæsse,* Mass.]

lamp (lămp) n. **1.** Any device that uses gas, oil, electricity, etc., to generate light, heat, or therapeutic radiation. **2.** A vessel containing oil or alcohol burned through a wick for illumination. **3.** An electric bulb and its housing. [Middle English *lampe,* from Old French, from Latin *lampas,* from Greek, torch, from *lampein,* to shine.]

lamp·black (lămp'blăk') n. A gray or black pigment made from the finely powdered soot collected from incompletely burned carbon materials.

lamp·light·er (lămp'lī'tər) n. A person employed to light street lamps.

lam·poon (lăm-pōōn') n. **1.** A piece of writing or acting that uses ridicule to attack a person, institution, etc. **2.** A light, good-humored satire. —*tr.v.* To ridicule or satirize with a lampoon. [French.] —**lam·poon'er** or **lam·poon'ist** n. —**lam·poon'er·y** n.

lam·prey (lăm'prē) n., pl. **-preys.** Any of various primitive elongated freshwater or anadromous fishes of the family Petromyzontidae, with a jawless sucking mouth and a raspy tongue. [Middle English *lamprei,* from Old French *lampreie,* from Medieval Latin *lamprēda.*]

la·nai (lə-nī', lä-) n., pl. **-nais.** A verandah or roofed patio. [Hawaiian.]

lance (lăns) n. **1.** A thrusting weapon with a long wooden shaft and a sharp metal head. **2.** A similar implement, as one for spearing fish. **3.** A cavalryman armed with a lance. **4.** A lancet. —*tr.v.* **lanced, lanc·ing. 1.** To pierce with a lance. **2.** To make an incision in with or as if with a lancet: *lance a boil.* [Middle English, from Old French, from Latin *lancea.*]

lance corporal. 1. In the U.S. Marine Corps, an enlisted man ranking above a private first class and below a corporal. **2.** In the British Army, a private acting as a corporal.

lance·let (lăns'lĭt) n. Any of various small, flattened saltwater organisms of the subphylum Cephalochordata, allied to the vertebrates but having a notochord rather than a true vertebral column.

Lan·ce·lot (lăn'sə-lət, -lŏt', län'-). Also **Laun·ce·lot.** *Arthurian Legend.* The bravest knight of the Round Table whose love affair with Queen Guinevere resulted in a war with King Arthur.

lan·ce·o·late (lăn'sē-ə-lāt') adj. *Bot.* Narrow and tapering at each end: *lanceolate leaves.* [Late Latin *lanceolātus,* from Latin *lanceola,* dim. of *lancea,* lance.]

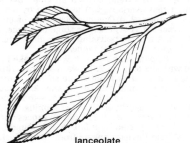

lanceolate

lanc·er (lăn'sər) n. A cavalryman armed with a lance or a cavalry regiment orig. so armed.

lanc·ers (lăn'sərz) n. (*used with a sing. verb*). **1.** A form of quadrille. **2.** The music for this dance.

lan·cet (lăn'sĭt) n. A surgical knife with a short, wide, pointed double-edged blade.

land (lănd) n. **1.** The solid ground of the earth, esp. as distinguished from the sea. **2.** The ground or soil; the earth: *till the land.* **3.** A distinct region or area: *desert land.* **4. a.** A nation; a country: *the highest office in the land.* **b.** The people of a nation, district, or region: *anger and suspicion sweeping the land.* **5. lands.** Territorial possessions or property. **6.** An area or realm: *the land of make-believe.* —See Syns at **nation.** —*tr.v.* **1. a.** To set down on land or other surface: *land an airplane.* **b.** To bring to and unload on land: *land cargo.* **2.** To cause to arrive in a place or condition: *His pranks landed him in*

jail. **3. a.** To catch and pull in (a fish). **b.** To win; to secure: *land a big contract.* **4.** To deliver: *land a blow on the head.* —*intr.v.* **1. a.** To come to shore. **b.** To disembark. **2.** To descend toward and settle on the ground or other surface. **3.** To come to rest in a certain way or place: *land on one's feet.* **4.** To arrive in a place or condition: *land up in jail.* [Middle English, from Old English.]

lan·dau (lăn'dou', -dô') n. **1.** A four-wheeled closed carriage with front and back passenger seats that face each other and a roof made in two sections for lowering or detachment. **2.** A style of automobile with a roof similar to this. [After *Landau,* Germany.]

land·ed (lăn'dĭd) adj. **1.** Owning land: *landed gentry.* **2.** Consisting of land or real estate: *a landed estate.*

land·fall (lănd'fôl') n. **1.** The sighting or reaching of land on a voyage or flight. **2.** The land sighted or reached.

land grant. A government grant of public land for a railroad, highway, or state college.

land·hold·er (lănd'hōl'dər) n. A person who owns land. —**land'hold'ing** n.

land·ing (lăn'dĭng) n. **1.** The act or process of coming to land or rest. **2.** A site for landing or unloading cargo. **3.** A level platform in the middle or at the end of a flight of stairs.

landing craft. A flat-bottomed naval craft specifically designed to convey troops and equipment from ship to shore.

landing field. An area of level land used by aircraft for landing and taking off.

landing gear. The undercarriage of an aircraft, including wheels or pontoons, designed to support an aircraft on the ground or in the water.

landing net. A net attached to a handle, used to remove a hooked fish from the water.

landing strip. An aircraft runway without airport facilities.

land·la·dy (lănd'lā'dē) n. **1.** A woman who owns and rents real estate, buildings, or dwelling units. **2.** A woman who runs a rooming house or inn; innkeeper.

land·locked (lănd'lŏkt') adj. **1.** Entirely or almost entirely surrounded by land. **2.** Confined to inland waters, as certain salmon.

land·lord (lănd'lôrd') n. **1.** A man who owns and rents real estate, buildings, or dwelling units. **2.** A man who runs a rooming house or inn; innkeeper.

land·lub·ber (lănd'lŭb'ər) n. A person unfamiliar with the sea or seamanship.

land·mark (lănd'märk') n. **1.** A fixed marker indicating a boundary line. **2.** A prominent and identifying feature of a landscape. **3.** An event marking an important stage of development or a turning point in history. **4.** A building or site that has historical significance.

land·mass (lănd'măs') n. A large area of land.

land mine. An explosive mine laid usu. just below the surface of the ground, often set to go off when stepped on or driven over.

land-of·fice business (lănd'ô'fĭs, -ŏf'ĭs). Thriving, extensive, or rapidly moving volume of trade.

land·own·er (lănd'ō'nər) n. A person who owns land. —**land'own'ing** adj.

land-poor (lănd'pōōr') adj. Owning much land but lacking capital.

land·scape (lănd'skāp') n. **1. a.** A view or vista of scenery on land. **b.** A painting, photograph, etc., depicting such a scene. **2.** The branch of art dealing with the representation of natural scenery. —*v.* **-scaped, -scap·ing.** —*tr.v.* To adorn or improve (a section of ground), as by planting flowers, shrubs, or trees. —*intr.v.* To arrange grounds artistically as a profession. [Dutch *landschap,* from Middle Dutch, landscape, region.]

landscape architect. A person whose profession is the decorative and functional alteration and planting of grounds, esp. at or around a building or recreational site. —**landscape architecture.**

landscape gardener. A person whose job is the decoration of land by planting trees and shrubs and designing gardens. —**landscape gardening.**

land·scap·ist (lănd'skā'pĭst) n. A painter or photographer of landscapes.

land·slide (lănd′slīd′) *n.* **1.** Also *Brit.* **land·slip** (-slĭp′). **a.** The fall or slide of a mass of earth and rock down a slope. **b.** The mass that slides. **2.** An overwhelming victory, esp. in an election.

lands·man (lăndz′mən) *n.* Someone who lives and works on land.

land·ward (lănd′wərd) *adv.* Also **land·wards.** To or toward land. —**land′ward** *adj.*

lane (lān) *n.* **1. a.** A narrow way or passage between walls, hedges, or fences. **b.** A narrow country road. **2.** A set course or way over water or through the air, used by ships or aircraft. **3.** A lengthwise division of a street, highway, racecourse, etc. **4.** A wood-surfaced passageway along which a bowling ball is rolled. [Middle English, from Old English.]

lang·syne (lăng-zīn′) Also **lang syne.** *Scot.* —*adv.* Long ago; long since. —*n.* Time long past; times past. [Middle English *lang sine* : *lang,* long + *sine,* since.]

lan·guage (lăng′gwĭj) *n.* **1. a.** The use by human beings of voice sounds, and often of written symbols that represent these sounds, in organized combinations and patterns to express and communicate thoughts and feelings. **b.** A system of words formed from such combinations and patterns, used by the people of a particular country or by a group of people with a shared history or set of traditions: *Many languages are spoken in Africa.* **2.** Any method of communicating ideas, as by a system of signs, symbols or gestures: *the language of algebra.* **3.** The special vocabulary and usages of a scientific, professional, or other group: *medical language.* **4.** A characteristic style of speech or writing: *ribald language.* **5.** The manner or means of communication between living creatures other than humans: *the language of dolphins.* **6.** Language as a subject of study. **7.** *Law.* The wording of a document or statute as distinct from the spirit. —*idiom.* **speak the same language.** To have the same background, experience, or understanding as another person. [Middle English, from Old French *langage,* from Latin *lingua,* tongue, language.]

Syns: 1. language, dialect, speech, tongue, vernacular *n. Core meaning:* A system of terms used by a people sharing a history and culture (*Polish and Russian—two Slavic languages*). **2. language, cant, idiom, jargon, lexicon, terminology, vocabulary** *n. Core meaning:* Specialized expressions characteristic of a field, subject, trade, or subculture (*the language of electrical engineering; street language*).

lan·guid (lăng′gwĭd) *adj.* **1.** Lazily slow or relaxed. **2.** Lacking spirit or energy; sluggish; weak. **3.** Causing a feeling of laziness or listlessness: *languid weather.* [Old French *languide,* from Latin *languidus,* from *languēre,* to languish.] —**lan′guid·ly** *adv.*

lan·guish (lăng′gwĭsh) *intr.v.* **1.** To become weak or feeble; lose strength or vigor; decline: *languished under the tropical sun.* **2.** To remain under miserable or disheartening conditions: *languish in a dungeon.* **3.** To become listless and depressed; pine: *languish for a lost love.* **4.** To assume a wistful or languid air, esp. to gain sympathy. [Middle English *languishen,* from Old French *languir,* from Latin *languēre,* to be faint or weak.] —**lan′guish·er** *n.* —**lan′guish·ment** *n.*

lan·guish·ing (lăng′gwĭ-shĭng) *adj.* **1.** Becoming weak; fading. **2.** Slow; lingering. **3.** Expressing languor; full of sentimentality.

lan·guor (lăng′gər, lăng′ər) *n.* **1.** Lack of energy; fatigue; listlessness. **2.** A dreamy, lazy mood or quality: *the languor of a warm summer afternoon.* **3.** Oppressive quiet or stillness. [Middle English, from Old French, from Latin, from *languēre,* to languish.] —**lan′guor·ous** *adj.* —**lan′guor·ous·ly** *adv.*

lan·gur (lăng-gŏŏr′) *n.* Any of various slender, long-tailed Asian monkeys of the genus *Presbytis.* [Hindi *langūr.*]

lan·iard (lăn′yərd) *n.* Var. of **lanyard.**

lank (lăngk) *adj.* **-er, -est. 1.** Long and lean; gaunt. **2.** Long, straight, and limp: *lank hair.* [Ult. from Old English *hlanc.*] —**lank′ness** *n.*

lank·y (lăng′kē) *adj.* **-i·er, -i·est.** Tall, thin, and ungainly. —**lank′i·ly** *adv.* —**lank′i·ness** *n.*

lan·o·lin (lăn′ə-lĭn) *n.* A yellowish-white fatty substance obtained from wool and used in soaps, cosmetics, and ointments. [German *Lanolin,* from Latin *lāna,* wool.]

lan·tern (lăn′tərn) *n.* **1. a.** A usu. portable case that has transparent or translucent sides for holding and protecting a light. **b.** A decorative casing for a light, usu. of paper. **2.** The room at the top of a lighthouse where the light is located. **3.** *Archit.* A structure built on top of a roof with open or windowed walls to let in light and air. **4.** A slide projector. [Middle English *lanterne,* from Old French, from Latin *lanterna,* from Greek *lamptēr,* lantern, torch, from *lampein,* to shine.]

lantern jaw. 1. A long thin jaw. **2.** A lower jaw that protrudes beyond the upper jaw. —**lan′tern-jawed′** *adj.*

lan·tha·nide (lăn′thə-nīd′) *n.* **Rare-earth element.** [LANTHA-N(UM) + -IDE.]

lanthanide series. The set of chemically related elements with atomic numbers from 57 to 71; the rare-earth elements.

lan·tha·num (lăn′thə-nəm) *n.* Symbol **La** A soft, silvery-white, malleable, ductile, metallic rare-earth element, obtained chiefly from monazite and bastnaesite, used in glass manufacture and in carbon lights for motion-picture and television studio lighting. Atomic number 57; atomic weight 138.91; melting point 920°C; boiling point 3,469°C; specific gravity 5.98 to 6.186; valence 3. [From Greek *lanthanein,* to hide (from the finding of lanthanum in cerium oxide).]

lan·yard (lăn′yərd) *n.* Also **lan·iard. 1.** A short rope used on ships to secure the rigging. **2.** A braided cord worn around the neck for carrying a knife, whistle, keys, etc. **3.** A cord with a hook at one end used to fire a cannon. [Middle English *lanyer,* from Old French *laniere,* from *lasne,* thong, strap.]

La·oc·o·on (lā-ŏk′ō-ŏn′) *n. Gk. Myth.* A Trojan priest of Apollo who, with his two sons, was killed by two serpents for having warned his people against the Trojan horse.

lap¹ (lăp) *n.* **1.** The level place formed by the front part of the legs above the knees of a seated person. **2.** The part of a person's clothing that covers the lap. **3.** Someone's care or responsibility: *always dumps his troubles in my lap.* **4.** A secure place or environment. [Middle English *lappe,* from Old English *læppa,* flap of a garment.]

lap² (lăp) *v.* **lapped, lap·ping.** —*tr.v.* **1.** To fold, wrap, or wind (something) over or around: *lap pie crust over a filling.* **2.** To envelop in something; enwrap; swathe: *lapped in sables.* **3.** To place or lay (a thing) so as to cover part of another: *lap shingles.* **4.** To get ahead of (an opponent) in a race by one or more complete circuits of the course. **5.** To polish until smooth. —*intr.v.* **1.** To fold or wind around something. **2.** To extend beyond an edge; overlap. —*n.* **1. a.** A part that overlaps. **b.** The amount by which a part overlaps another. **2. a.** One complete turn or circuit, esp. of a racetrack. **b.** A segment or stage of a race, trip, process, etc. **3.** A tool for polishing stone, glass, etc. [Middle English *lappen,* prob. from *lappe,* lap.]

lap³ (lăp) *v.* **lapped, lap·ping.** —*tr.v.* **1.** To take in (a liquid or food) with the tongue. **2.** To wash against with a gentle slapping sound: *waves lapping the shore.* —*intr.v.* **1.** To drink by lifting a liquid with the tongue. **2.** To dash or slap softly against a shore or other surface. —*phrasal verb.* **lap up.** To receive eagerly or greedily: *lapping up the attention and acclaim.* —*n.* **1.** The act or process of lapping. **2.** The amount ingested by a lap. **3.** The sound of lapping water. [Middle English *lappen,* from Old English *lapian.*]

lap·board (lăp′bôrd′, -bōrd′) *n.* A board held on the lap and used as a table or desk.

lap dog. A small, easily held dog kept as a pet.

la·pel (lə-pĕl′) *n.* Either of two flaps that extend down from the collar of a coat, jacket, etc., and fold back against the chest. [From LAP (flap of a garment).]

lap·ful (lăp′fŏŏl′) *n., pl.* **-fuls.** As much as the lap can support or hold.

lap·i·dar·y (lăp′ĭ-dĕr′ē) *n., pl.* **-ies. 1.** A person who works at cutting, polishing, or engraving gems. **2.** A dealer in precious or semiprecious stones. —*adj.* **1.** Of or relating to precious stones or the art of working with them. **2. a.** Engraved in stone. **b.** Suitable for engraving in stone: *lapidary prose.* [Latin *lapidārius,* stoneworker, from *lapis,* stone.]

lap·in (lăp′ĭn) *n.* Rabbit fur, esp. when sheared and dyed. [French, rabbit.]

lap·is laz·u·li (lăp'ĭs lăz'yŏŏ-lē, lăzh'ŏŏ-). An opaque, azure-blue to deep-blue mineral that is used as a gemstone. **—modifier:** *lapis lazuli beads.* [Middle English, from Medieval Latin : *lapis,* stone + *lazulum,* lapis lazuli, from Arabic *lāzaward,* from Persian *lāzhuward.*]

lap joint. A joint in which ends or edges are overlapped and fastened together. **—lap'-joint'ed** (lăp'join'tĭd) *adj.*

Lapp (lăp) *n.* **1.** A member of a nomadic people that inhabits Lapland. **2.** The Finno-Ugric language of the Lapps.

lapse (lăps) *n.* **1.** A slip, error, or failure, esp. a slight or unimportant one: *a lapse of memory.* **2.** A return or change to an earlier or different, often less desirable, condition: *a lapse into barbarism.* **3.** An interval or period of passing time: *a lapse of three months.* **4.** The termination of an agreement, right, privilege, custom, etc., through neglect, disuse, or the passage of time: *the lapse of a lease.* **—See Syns at error. —intr.v. lapsed, laps·ing. 1. a.** To fall away by degrees; decline; vanish: *My enthusiasm soon lapsed.* **b.** To subside gradually; drift: *lapse into dreaminess.* **2.** To elapse: *Years had lapsed since we last met.* **3.** To be no longer in force because of neglect, disuse, the passage of time, etc.: *He allowed his insurance policy to lapse.* [Latin *lapsus,* error, a sliding, from *lābī,* to slide.] **—laps'er** *n.*

lap·wing (lăp'wĭng') *n.* Any of several Old World birds of the genus *Vanellus,* related to the plovers, esp. *V. vanellus,* with a narrow crest. Also called **pewit.** [Middle English *lappewinke,* from Old English *hlēapewince.*]

lar·board (lär'bərd) *n.* The port side of a ship or boat. **—adj.** On the port side. [From Middle English *laddborde.*]

lar·ce·ny (lär'sə-nē) *n., pl.* **-nies.** The crime of taking and removing another's personal property with the intent of permanently depriving the owner; theft. [Middle English, from Old French *larcin,* from Latin *latrōcinium,* military service for pay, freebooting, from *latrō,* mercenary soldier, from Greek *latron,* pay.] **—lar'ce·nous** (-nəs) *adj.*

larch (lärch) *n.* **1.** Any of several coniferous trees of the genus *Larix,* with deciduous needles and heavy, durable wood. **2.** The wood of a larch. [German *Lärche,* from Middle High German *larche,* ult. from Latin *larix.*]

lard (lärd) *n.* The white solid or semisolid rendered fat of a hog. **—tr.v. 1.** To cover or coat with lard or a similar fat. **2.** To insert strips of bacon or fat in (lean meat or poultry) before cooking. **3.** To enrich or try to enrich (speech, writing, etc.) with additions; embellish: *He larded his report with quotations.* [Middle English, from Old French, from Latin *lārdum.*] **—lard'y** *adj.*

lar·der (lär'dər) *n.* **1.** A room, cupboard, etc., where meat and other foods are kept. **2.** A supply of food.

lar·es and pe·na·tes (lâr'ēz; pə-nā'tēz). **1.** The household gods and spirits in ancient Rome. **2.** Esteemed household possessions. [Latin.]

large (lärj) *adj.* **larg·er, larg·est. 1.** Of a size or amount greater than average; not small: *large animals such as whales and elephants; a large sum of money.* **2.** Great; considerable: *Scientific discoveries have increased our knowledge to a large extent.* **3.** Understanding; tolerant; liberal: *a large and generous spirit.* **—See Syns at big. —idioms. at large. 1.** Not in confinement or captivity; at liberty; free: *a convict still at large.* **2.** As a whole; in general: *the country at large.* **3.** Representing a nation, state, or district as a whole. **4.** Not assigned to any particular country: *an ambassador at large.* **by and large.** For the most part; on the whole. [Middle English, from Old French, from Latin *largus,* generous, bountiful.] **—large'ness** *n.*

large-heart·ed (lärj'här'tĭd) *adj.* Having a generous disposition; sympathetic. **—large'-heart'ed·ness** *n.*

large intestine. The portion of the intestine that extends from the end of the small intestine to the anus, forms an arch around the convolutions of the small intestine, and includes the cecum, colon, rectum, and anal canal. It serves to absorb water from the waste matter left after food is digested.

large·ly (lärj'lē) *adv.* **1.** For the most part; mainly: *largely responsible for the accident.* **2.** On a large scale; amply: *contributed largely to the pension fund.*

large·mouth bass (lärj'mouth'). A North American freshwater food and game fish, *Micropterus salmoides.*

large-scale (lärj'skāl') *adj.* **1.** Of large scope; extensive: *large-scale farming.* **2.** Drawn or made large to show detail: *a large-scale map.*

lar·gess (lär-zhĕs', -jĕs', lär'jĕs') *n.* Also **lar·gesse. 1.** Liberality in giving. **2.** Money or gifts bestowed. [Middle English *largesse,* from Old French, from *large,* generous, large.]

lar·ghet·to (lär-gĕt'ō). *Mus.* **—adv.** Moderately slow in tempo; somewhat faster than largo. **—adj.** Moderately slow. **—n., pl. -tos.** A moderately slow section of a composition. [Italian, dim. of *largo,* slow.]

larg·ish (lär'jĭsh) *adj.* Fairly large.

lar·go (lär'gō). *Mus.* **—adv.** In a slow, solemn manner. **—adj.** Very slow. **—n., pl. -gos.** A very slow section of a composition. [Italian, slow, from Latin *largus,* large.]

lar·i·at (lăr'ē-ət) *n.* **1.** A long rope with an adjustable noose at one end, used esp. for catching horses and cattle; a lasso. **2.** A rope for tying grazing horses or mules. [Spanish *la reata,* "the lasso."]

lark¹ (lärk) *n.* **1.** Any of various chiefly Old World birds of the family Alaudidae, with a sustained, melodious song. **2.** Any of several similar birds, as the meadowlark. [Middle English *larke,* from Old English *lāwerce.*]

lark² (lärk) *n.* A carefree adventure or harmless prank. **—intr.v.** To engage in fun or merry pranks. [Prob. var. of dial. *lake,* to play, from Middle English *leiken,* from Old Norse *leika.*]

lark·spur (lärk'spûr') *n.* Any of various plants of the genus *Delphinium,* with spurred, variously colored flowers.

lar·rup (lăr'əp). *Regional.* **—tr.v.** To beat; flog; thrash. **—n.** A blow. [Orig. unknown.]

lar·va (lär'və) *n., pl.* **-vae** (-vē). **1.** The wingless, often wormlike form, such as a caterpillar, of a newly hatched insect before undergoing metamorphosis. **2.** The newly hatched, earliest stage of any of various animals that undergo metamorphosis, differing markedly in form and appearance from the adult. [Latin *lārva,* disembodied spirit, mask.] **—lar'val** *adj.*

laryng-. Var. of **laryngo-.**

la·ryn·ge·al (lə-rĭn'jē-əl, -jəl, lăr'ən-jē'əl) *adj.* Also **la·ryn·gal** (lə-rĭng'gəl). Of, pertaining to, affecting, or near the larynx. **—n.** A part of the larynx. [From New Latin *laryngeus,* from *larynx,* larynx.]

la·ryn·ges (lə-rĭn'jēz) *n.* A plural of **larynx.**

lar·yn·gi·tis (lăr'ən-jī'tĭs) *n.* Inflammation of the larynx. [LARYNG(O)- + -ITIS.] **—lar'yn·git'ic** (-jĭt'ĭk) *adj.*

laryngo- or **laryng-.** A prefix meaning larynx: *laryngoscope.* [Greek *laryngo-,* from *larynx,* larynx.]

la·ryn·go·scope (lə-rĭng'gə-skōp') *n.* A tubular instrument or apparatus used to observe the interior of the larynx. **—la·ryn'go·scop'ic** (-skōp'ĭk) or **la·ryn'go·scop'i·cal** *adj.* **—la·ryn'go·scop'i·cal·ly** *adv.* **—lar'yn·gos'co·py** (lăr'ĭng-gŏs'kə-pē) *n.*

lar·ynx (lăr'ĭngks) *n., pl.* **la·ryn·ges** (lə-rĭn'jēz) or **-ynx·es.** The upper part of the respiratory tract between the pharynx and the trachea, having cartilaginous walls and containing the vocal cords, which are enveloped in folds of mucous membrane attached to the sides [Greek *larunx.*]

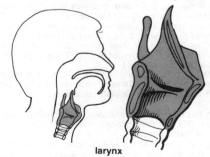

larynx

la·sa·gna (lə-zän'yə) *pl.n.* Also **la·sa·gne. 1.** Pasta cut into flat wide strips. **2.** A dish made by baking lasagna with layers of ground meat, tomato sauce, and cheese. [Italian, from Latin *lasanum,* cooking pot.]

ă **pat**   ā **pay**   â **care**   ä **father**   ĕ **pet**   ē **be**   hw **which**   ĭ **pit**   ī **tie**   î **pier**   ŏ **pot**   ō **toe**   ô **paw, for**   oi **noise**
ŏŏ **took**   ŏŏ **boot**   ou **out**   th **thin**   th **this**   ŭ **cut**   û **urge**   zh **vision**   ə **about, item, edible, gallop, circus**

las·civ·i·ous (lə-sĭv′ē-əs) adj. 1. Of or characterized by lust; lewd; lecherous: lascivious novels. 2. Exciting sexual desires. [Late Latin lascīviōsus, from Latin lascīvia, lewedness, from lascīvus, lustful.] —**las·civ′i·ous·ly** adv. —**las·civ′i·ous·ness** n.

la·ser (lā′zər) n. Any of a number of devices that use the radiating properties of systems of atoms or molecules to generate light that is of one or more discrete wavelengths, with all of the waves polarized, exactly aligned, and matching each other in their phases. —modifier: a laser beam. [L(IGHT) A(MPLIFICATION BY) S(TIMULATED) E(MISSION OF) R(ADIATION).]

lash[1] (lăsh) n. 1. A stroke or blow with or as if with a whip. 2. A whip or its thongs. 3. A remark that insults, reprimands, or ridicules. 4. An eyelash. —tr.v. 1. To strike with or as if with a whip. 2. To strike against with force or violence. 3. To move or wave rapidly to and fro: like an angry lion lashing his tail. 4. To make a violent verbal or written attack against. 5. To incite or goad: His words lashed them into into action. —intr.v. 1. To produce a whipping motion: The thorny brambles lashed across his body. 2. To move rapidly or violently; to dash: The wind lashed at the trees. 3. To make a verbal or written attack: The senator lashed back at the reporters. —phrasal verb. **lash out.** To attack with sudden violence. [Middle English lashe.]

lash[2] (lăsh) tr.v. To secure or bind, as with a rope, cord, or chain. [Middle English lasshen, from Old French lac(h)ier, from Latin laqueāre, to ensnare, from laqueus, snare.]

lash·ing (lăsh′ĭng) n. Something used for securing or binding, as a rope or cord.

lass (lăs) n. 1. A girl or young woman. 2. A sweetheart. [Middle English lasse.]

lass·ie (lăs′ē) n. A lass.

las·si·tude (lăs′ĭ-tōōd′, -tyōōd′) n. A state of listless weakness, exhaustion, or torpor. [Latin lassitūdō, from lassus, tired, weary.]

las·so (lăs′ō, lă-sōō′) n., pl. **-sos** or **-soes.** A long rope or leather thong with an adjustable noose at one end, used esp. to catch horses and cattle; lariat. —tr.v. To catch with or as if with a lasso; to rope. [Spanish lazo, from Latin laqueus, snare.]

last[1] (lăst) adj. 1. Coming, being, or placed after all others; final: the last game of the season. 2. Being the only one or ones left; remaining: We shot off the last Roman candle. 3. Just past: last night. 4. Being the latest possible: waited until the last minute. 5. Least likely or expected: the last person we would have suspected. —adv. 1. After all others: Grandpa arrived last. 2. At the end; finally: Beat the eggs, stir in the sugar, and last add the flour. 3. Most recently: when I last saw her. —n. 1. Someone or something that is last: ate all the chocolates but the last. 2. The end: He held out to the last. —idioms. **at last.** Finally. **at long last.** After a long time or wait. [Middle English, from Old English latost.]

    Syns: 1. last, final, terminal adj. Core meaning: Coming after all others (the last act). **2. last, final, ultimate** adj. Core meaning: Of or relating to a terminative condition, stage, or point (the last stages of cancer; the last rites). **3. last, foregoing, preceding, previous** adj. Core meaning: Next before the present one (last night).

last[2] (lăst) intr.v. 1. To continue in existence; go on: The war lasted four years. 2. To remain in good condition; endure: Clay lasts longer than paper. 3. To remain in adequate supply: Will our water last? [Middle English lasten, from Old English lǣstan.]

last[3] (lăst) n. A foot-shaped block or form used in making or repairing shoes. —tr.v. To mold or shape on a last. [Middle English laste, from Old English lǣste, from lāst, sole, footprint.]

last·ing (lăs′tĭng) adj. Continuing or remaining for a long time; durable: a lasting peace between nations. —**last′ing·ly** adv. —**last′ing·ness** n.

last·ly (lăst′lē) adv. At the end; in conclusion; finally.

last straw. The last of a series of annoyances or disappointments that leads one to a final loss of patience, temper, trust, etc.

Last Supper. Christ's supper with his disciples on the night before his Crucifixion. Also called **Lord's Supper.**

last word. 1. The final statement in a verbal argument. 2. The power or authority of ultimate decision. 3. Informal. The newest in fashion.

latch (lăch) n. A fastening or lock, usu. consisting of a movable bar that fits into a notch or slot. —tr.v. To close or lock with a latch. —intr.v. To be capable of being fastened with a latch. —phrasal verb. **latch on to** (or **onto**). Informal. 1. To attach oneself to; cling to. 2. To get possession of; obtain. [Middle English lache, from lachen, to latch, seize, from Old English lǣccan, to grasp.]

latch·string (lăch′strĭng′) n. A cord attached to a latch and often passed through a hole in the door to allow lifting of the latch from the outside.

late (lāt) adj. **lat·er, lat·est. 1.** Coming, happening, or doing something after the expected, usual, or proper time; not on time or early; tardy: late for his appointment; a late supper. 2. Past or beyond the usual or accustomed time: The road was dark and lonely, and it was very late. 3. Near or toward the end or more advanced part of a time period, series, etc.: the late afternoon; the late 19th century. 4. Of a time just past; recent: This tractor is a late model. 5. Dead for a comparatively short time; recently deceased: the late President. —adv. **lat·er, lat·est. 1.** After or beyond the expected, usual, or proper time: The train arrived late. 2. At an advanced stage, place, etc.: scored a run late in the game. 3. Recently: as late as last week. —idiom. **of late.** In the near past; lately. [Middle English, late, from Old English lǣt.] —**late′ness** n.

    Syns: late, belated, overdue, tardy, adj. Core meaning: Not on time (late thanks for the gift; was late for the meeting).

late·com·er (lāt′kŭm′ər) n. Someone or something that arrives late.

la·teen sail (lə-tēn′, lă-). A triangular sail hung on a long pole attached at an angle to a short mast. [French (voile) latine, "Latin (sail)."]

Late Greek. Greek from the 4th to the 9th cent. A.D.

Late Latin. Latin from the 3rd to the 7th cent. A.D.

late·ly (lāt′lē) adv. Not long ago; recently.

la·tent (lāt′nt) adj. Present or potential but not evident or active: latent talent; latent energy. [Latin latēns, pres. part. of latēre, to lie hidden.] —**la′ten·cy** n. —**la′tent·ly** adv.

latent heat. The quantity of heat absorbed or released by a substance undergoing a change of state, as by ice changing to water or water to steam.

latent period. The time interval between the introduction of a cause and the moment when the effects become apparent, esp. the incubation period of an infectious disease.

lat·er·al (lăt′ər-əl) adj. On, of, toward, or from the side or sides: a lateral motion of a machine; a lateral branch of a tree. —n. 1. A lateral part, projection, passage, or appendage. 2. Football. A lateral pass. [Latin laterālis, from latus, side.] —**lat′er·al·ly** adv.

lateral line. A linear series of sensory pores and tubes that extends along the side of a fish or certain other aquatic animals.

lateral pass. Football. A pass thrown sideways, parallel to the line of scrimmage. Also called **lateral.**

lat·er·ite (lăt′ə-rīt′) n. A red residual soil in humid tropical and subtropical regions that contains concentrations of iron and aluminum hydroxides and is sometimes used as an ore of iron, aluminum, manganese, or nickel. [Latin later, brick, tile + -ITE.]

la·tex (lā′tĕks′) n. 1. The usu. milky, sticky sap of certain trees and plants, such as the rubber tree, that coagulates on exposure to air. 2. A synthetic emulsion of rubber or plastic globules in water, used in paints, adhesives, and various synthetic rubber products. 3. A paint made with a synthetic latex base. [From Latin latex, fluid.]

lath (lăth) n., pl. **laths** (lăthz, lăths). 1. A narrow, thin strip of wood or metal, used esp. in making a supporting structure for plaster, shingles, or tiles. 2. Any other building material, such as a sheet of metal mesh, used for similar purposes. 3. Work made of or using laths; lathing. —tr.v. To build, cover, or line with laths. [Middle English lathe, from Old English lætt.]

lathe (lāth) n. A machine on which a piece of wood, metal, etc., is spun and shaped by a tool. —tr.v. **lathed, lath·ing.**

To cut or shape on a lathe. [Perh. from Middle English *lath*, supporting stand.]

lath·er (lăth′ər) *n.* **1.** A light foam formed by soap or detergent agitated in water. **2.** Froth formed by profuse sweating, as on a horse. **3.** *Informal.* A condition of impatient or troubled excitement. —*tr.v.* **1.** To coat with lather. **2.** *Informal.* To give a beating to; to whip. —*intr.v.* **1.** To produce lather; to foam. **2.** To become coated with lather, as a horse. [Ult. from Old English *lēathor*.] —**lath′er·er** *n.* —**lath′er·y** *adj.*

lath·ing (lăth′ĭng, lăth′-) *n.* **1.** The act or process of building with laths. **2.** Work made of or using laths.

Lat·in (lăt′n) *adj.* **1.** Of or relating to Latium, its people, or its culture. **2.** Of or relating to ancient Rome, its people, or its culture. **3.** Of or relating to the language of ancient Rome and Latium. **4.** Of or relating to the countries or peoples using Romance languages, esp. the countries of Latin America. **5.** Of or relating to the Roman Catholic Church as distinguished from the Eastern Orthodox Church. —*n.* **1.** The Italic language of ancient Rome that became dominant in western Europe and until early modern times remained the official language of church and state. **2.** A native of ancient Latium. **3.** A member of a Latin people, esp. of Latin America. **4.** A Roman Catholic.

Latin cross. A cross with the lower limb longest.

Lat·in·ism (lăt′n-ĭz′əm) *n.* An idiom, structure, or word derived from or imitative of Latin.

Lat·in·ist (lăt′n-ĭst) *n.* A scholar of Latin.

Lat·in·ize (lăt′n-īz′) *tr.v.* **-ized, -iz·ing. 1.** To transliterate into the characters of the Latin alphabet. **2.** To cause to adopt or acquire Latin characteristics or customs. —**Lat′in·i·za′tion** *n.*

lat·ish (lā′tĭsh) *adj. & adv. Informal.* Fairly late.

lat·i·tude (lăt′ĭ-tōōd′, -tyōōd′) *n.* **1.** Extent; breadth; range. **2.** Freedom from normal restraints, limitations, or regulations. **3.** *Geog.* The angular distance north or south of the equator, measured in degrees along a meridian, as on a map or globe. **4.** A region of the earth considered in relation to its distance from the equator: *temperate latitudes.* **5.** *Astron.* The angular distance of a celestial body north or south of the ecliptic. [Middle English *latitūdo,* from *lātus,* wide, broad.] —**lat′i·tu′di·nal** *adj.* —**lat′i·tu′di·nal·ly** *adv.*

lat·i·tu·di·nar·i·an (lăt′ĭ-tōōd′n-âr′ē-ən, -tyōōd′-) *adj.* Favoring freedom of thought and behavior, esp. in religion. —*n.* A latitudinarian person. —**lat′i·tu′di·nar′i·an·ism** *n.*

la·trine (lə-trēn′) *n.* A communal toilet of the type often used in a barracks, esp. one without plumbing. [French, from Latin *latrīna,* from *lavātrīna,* bath.]

lat·ter (lăt′ər) *adj.* **1.** Being the second or second mentioned of two: *The latter place was easier to reach than the former.* **2.** Closer to the end: *the latter part of the book.* [Middle English, from Old English *lætra.*] —**lat′ter·ly** *adv.*

lat·ter-day (lăt′ər-dā′) *adj.* Belonging to present or recent time; modern.

Latter-day Saint. A Mormon.

lat·tice (lăt′ĭs) *n.* **1. a.** An open framework made of interwoven strips of metal, wood, etc., crossing at regular intervals to form patterned spaces. **b.** A screen, window, gate, etc., made of a lattice. **2.** Something that resembles a lattice. **3.** *Physics.* A regular, periodic configuration of points, particles, or objects throughout an area or space, esp. the arrangement of ions or molecules in a crystalline solid. —*tr.v.* **-ticed, -tic·ing.** To construct or furnish with a lattice or latticework. [Middle English *latis,* from Old French *lattis,* from *latte,* lath.] —**lat′ticed** *adj.*

lat·tice·work (lăt′ĭs-wûrk′) *n.* **1.** A lattice or something resembling a lattice. **2.** A structure made of lattices.

laud (lôd) *tr.v.* To praise highly. —See Syns at **praise.** —*n.* **1.** Praise; glorification. **2. Lauds** or **lauds.** *Eccles.* **a.** An early-morning church service at which psalms of praise are sung. **b.** The service of prayers following the matins and constituting with them the first of the seven canonical hours. [Latin *laudāre,* to praise, from *laus,* praise.]

laud·a·ble (lô′də-bəl) *adj.* Deserving praise; commendable; praiseworthy. —**laud′a·bil′i·ty** or **laud′a·ble·ness** *n.* —**laud′a·bly** *adv.*

lau·da·num (lôd′n-əm) *n.* A tincture of opium. [New Latin.]

lau·da·tion (lô-dā′shən) *n.* The act of lauding; praise.

lau·da·to·ry (lô′də-tôr′ē, -tōr′ē) *adj.* Expressing, including, or giving praise; eulogistic.

laugh (lăf, läf) *intr.v.* **1. a.** To express happiness, mirth, scorn, nervousness, etc., by a series of inarticulate sounds, usu. with a smile. **b.** To say while making such sounds: *"You're so funny!" laughed Joel.* **2.** To produce sounds or cries resembling laughter: *Hyenas laughed in the distance.* —*tr.v.* To drive, induce, or effect with or by laughter: *They laughed him from the stage.* —**phrasal verb. laugh at. 1.** To exhibit amusement at. **2.** To poke fun at; ridicule; deride. **3.** To refuse to consider seriously. —*n.* **1.** The act of laughing or a sound made in laughing. **2.** *Informal.* A cause or reason for laughing. —**idiom. laugh up** (or **in**) **(one's) sleeve.** To be secretly amused, esp. over the difficulties of another. [Middle English *laughen,* from Old English *hlæhhan.*] —**laugh′er** *n.*

laugh·a·ble (lăf′ə-bəl, läf′ə-) *adj.* **1.** Causing laughter. **2.** Deserving laughter. —**laugh′a·ble·ness** *n.* —**laugh′a·bly** *adv.*

> **Syns: laughable, comic, comical, funny, laughing, ludicrous, ridiculous, risible** *adj.* **Core meaning:** Deserving laughter (*a laughable matter*).

laugh·ing (lăf′ĭng, läf′ĭng) *adj.* **1.** Not serious in intent; laughable. **2.** Producing or seeming to produce laughter. —See Syns at **laughable.** —**laugh′ing·ly** *adv.*

laughing gas. An anesthetic, **nitrous oxide.**

laugh·ing·stock (lăf′ĭng-stŏk′, läf′ĭng-) *n.* An object of jokes, laughter, or ridicule; a butt.

laugh·ter (lăf′tər, läf′-) *n.* The act or sound of laughing. [Middle English, from Old English *hleahtor.*]

Laun·ce·lot (lăn′sə-lət, -lŏt′, län′-) *n.* Var. of **Lancelot.**

launch[1] (lônch, länch) *tr.v.* **1.** To move or set in motion with force; propel: *launch a missile.* **2.** To slide or lower (a boat) into the water, esp. for the first time. **3.** To put into action; inaugurate; initiate: *launch a new research project.* **4.** To set or start (someone) on a particular course of action: *The invention launched him on a new career.* —*intr.v.* **1.** To begin a new project or venture; start out on a new course of action: *launched forth on a new career.* **2.** To make a beginning: *launch into a new subject.* **3. a.** To move out to sea. **b.** To move into air or space. —See Syns at **introduce.** —*n.* The action or process of launching something, esp. a rocket or spacecraft. [Middle English *launchen,* to hurl, pierce, from Old North French *lancher,* from *lance,* lance.]

launch[2] (lônch, länch) *n.* **1.** A large ship's boat, formerly sloop-rigged but now powered. **2.** Any large, open motorboat. [Portuguese *lancha,* from Malay.]

launch·er (lôn′chər, län′-) *n.* Someone or something that launches, as a device for firing rockets.

launch pad. Also **launching pad.** The base or platform from which a rocket or space vehicle is launched.

launch vehicle. A booster for launching a spacecraft.

laun·der (lôn′dər, län′-) *tr.v.* **1.** To wash or wash and iron (clothes or linens). **2.** To conceal the source of (money), as by channeling it through an intermediary. —*intr.v.* **1.** To be capable of being washed. **2.** To wash or wash and iron clothes or linens. [From Middle English *launder,* launderer, from Old French *lavandier,* from Latin *lavanda,* things that need washing, from *lavāre,* to wash.] —**laun′der·er** *n.*

laun·dress (lôn′drĭs, län′-) *n.* A woman employed to wash or wash and iron clothes or linens.

Laun·dro·mat (lôn′drə-măt′, län′-) *n.* A trademark for a commercial establishment equipped with washing machines and dryers, usu. coin-operated.

laun·dry (lôn′drē, län′-) *n., pl.* **-dries. 1.** Clothes, linens, etc., that are to be washed or that have just been washed. **2.** A place where laundering is done.

lau·re·ate (lôr′ē-ĭt, lŏr′-) *n.* **1.** A poet laureate. **2.** A person honored for outstanding achievement. —*adj.* Worthy of honor for one's achievements; pre-eminent. [Latin *laureātus,* crowned with laurel, from *laurus,* laurel.] —**lau′re·ate·ship′** *n.*

lau·rel (lôr′əl, lŏr′-) *n.* **1.** A shrub or tree, *Laurus nobilis,* native to the Mediterranean region, with aromatic evergreen leaves and small blackish berries. Also called **bay. 2.** Any of several similar or related shrubs or trees, such as

---

ă pat　ā pay　â care　ä father　ĕ pet　ē be　hw which　ĭ pit　ī tie　î pier　ŏ pot　ō toe　ô paw, for　oi noise
ōō took　ōō boot　ou out　th thin　*th* this　ŭ cut　û urge　zh vision　ə about, item, edible, gallop, circus

the mountain laurel. **3.** Often **laurels.** A laurel wreath or crown conferred as a mark of honor. **4.** Often **laurels.** Honor won for achievement. **—idioms. look to (one's) laurels.** To protect one's position of eminence against rivals. **rest on (one's) laurels.** To be content with past achievements. [Middle English *laurer*, from Old French *lorier*, from *lor*, from Latin *laurus*.]

la·va (lä′və, lăv′ə) *n.* **1.** Molten rock that issues from a volcano or a crack in the earth's surface. **2.** The rock formed by the cooling and hardening of lava. [Italian, lava stream, stream caused by rain, from *lavare*, to wash, from Latin *lavāre*.]

la·vage (lə-väzh′) *n.* A washing out, esp. of a hollow organ, such as the stomach or lower bowel, with repeated injections of water. [French, a washing, from Old French, from *laver*, to wash, from Latin *lavāre*.]

lav·a·liere (lăv′ə-lîr′) *n.* Also **lav·a·lier.** A pendant worn on a chain around the neck. [French *lavallière*, after Louise de La Vallière (1644–1710), a mistress of Louis XIV.]

lav·a·to·ry (lăv′ə-tôr′ē, -tōr′ē) *n., pl.* **-ries. 1.** A room equipped with washing and toilet facilities, esp. in a public building, institution, etc. **2.** A sink or washbowl for washing the face and hands. [Middle English *lavatorie*, from Late Latin *lavātorium*, washing place, from Latin *lavāre*, to wash.]

lave (lāv) *v.* **laved, lav·ing. —tr.v. 1.** To wash or bathe. **2.** To lap or wash against: *The stream laved the rocks.* **—intr.v.** To bathe oneself. [Middle English *laven*, from Old French *laver*, from Latin *lavāre*.]

lav·en·der (lăv′ən-dər) *n.* **1. a.** Any of various aromatic Old World plants of the genus *Lavandula*, esp. *L. officinalis* (or *L. spica* or *L. vera*) that have clusters of small purplish flowers and yields an oil used in perfumery. **b.** The fragrant dried leaves, stems, and flowers of such a plant. **2.** A pale or light purple. **—adj.** Pale or light purple. [Middle English *lavendre*, from Norman French, from Medieval Latin *lavendula*.]

lavender

la·ver¹ (lā′vər) *n.* A large basin used in ancient Judaism by the priest for ablutions before making a sacrificial offering. [Middle English *laver, lavor*, from Old French *lavoir*.]

la·ver² (lā′vər) *n.* Any of several edible seaweeds of the genus *Porphyra*. [From Latin *laver*.]

lav·ish (lăv′ish) *adj.* **1.** Given or provided very plentifully: *a party with lavish refreshments.* **2.** Very generous or free in giving or using: *lavish with praise.* **3.** Luxurious: *a lavish hotel.* **—See Syns at luxurious. —tr.v.** To give or pour forth unstintingly: *lavished affection on her grandchildren.* [Middle English, from *lavas*, an outpouring, from Old French *lavasse*, torrent of rain, from *laver*, to wash, from Latin *lavāre*.] **—lav′ish·ly** *adv.* **—lav′ish·ness** *n.*

law (lô) *n.* **1. a.** A rule established by authority, society, or custom. **b.** A set or system of such rules. **c.** The force or authority of such a system of rules: *respect for law and order.* **2.** The system of courts, judicial processes, and legal officers giving effect to the laws of a society: *resort to the law in defense of one's interests.* **3. a.** The science and study of law; jurisprudence. **b.** The profession of a lawyer or judge. **4.** A statement or ruling that must be obeyed: *His word was law.* **5.** An accepted rule, principle, or practice: *the laws of grammar.* **6.** A scientific or mathematical

statement that is true under particular circumstances: *the law of gravity.* **7. Law.** A code of behavior of divine origin: *Mosaic Law.* **8.** Often **laws.** Principles of conduct: *the laws of decency.* **9. the law.** Someone or something that represents the force or authority of the law, as the police or a policeman. **—idiom. lay down the law. 1.** To make firm and authoritative statements that command obedience. **2.** To scold vehemently. [Middle English, binding custom or practice, from Old English *lagu*, code of rules.]

law-a·bid·ing (lô′ə-bī′dĭng) *adj.* Obeying or acting in accordance with the law.

law·break·er (lô′brā′kər) *n.* A person who breaks the law. **—law′break′ing** *n.*

law·ful (lô′fəl) *adj.* **1.** Allowed or established by law: *lawful entry.* **2.** Recognized by the law; legally acknowledged: *the lawful heir.* **—See Syns at legal. —law′ful·ly** *adv.* **—law′ful·ness** *n.*

law·giv·er (lô′gĭv′ər) *n.* **1.** A person who establishes a code of laws for a people. **2.** A lawmaker; legislator.

law·less (lô′lĭs) *adj.* **1.** Disregarding or violating the law: *a lawless mob; a lawless act.* **2.** Unrestrained by law; disobedient: *a lawless person.* **—See Syns at criminal. —law′less·ly** *adv.* **—law′less·ness** *n.*

law·mak·er (lô′mā′kər) *n.* A person who drafts or helps enact laws; a legislator. **—law′mak′ing** *n.*

lawn¹ (lôn) *n.* A piece of ground planted with grass or similar plants that is mowed regularly. [Middle English *launde*, from Old French, heath, of Germanic orig.] **—lawn′y** *adj.*

lawn² (lôn) *n.* A very fine, thin fabric of cotton or linen. [Middle English, prob. after *Laon*, France.]

lawn·mow·er (lôn′mō′ər) *n.* Also **lawn mower.** A rotary-blade machine for cutting grass.

lawn tennis. The game of tennis.

law·ren·ci·um (lô-rĕn′sē-əm, lō-) *n. Symbol* **Lw** An element, a metal first produced by bombarding californium isotopes with boron isotopes. It has a single isotope with mass number 257 and a half-life of 8 seconds. Atomic number 103. [After Ernest O. *Lawrence* (1901–58), American physicist.]

law·suit (lô′sōōt′) *n.* A question, claim, etc., brought before a court of law for settlement.

law·yer (lô′yər, loi′ər) *n.* A person whose profession is to give legal advice to clients and represent them in court; attorney. [Middle English *lawyere*, from *lawe*, law.]

lax (lăks) *adj.* **-er, -est. 1. a.** Remiss; negligent: *lax about paying bills.* **b.** Not strict; too lenient: *lax rules.* **2. a.** Not taut, firm, or compact; slack. **b.** Loose: *lax bowels.* **4.** *Phonet.* Pronounced with the muscles of the tongue and jaw partially relaxed, as *e* in *let.* **—See Syns at loose.** [Middle English, from Latin *laxus*, slack, loose.] **—lax′ly** *adv.* **—lax′ness** *n.*

lax·a·tive (lăk′sə-tĭv) *n.* A medicine that stimulates bowel movements. **—adj.** Having the effect of a laxative: *a laxative food.* [Middle English, from Old French *laxatif*, loosening, relaxing, from Latin *laxātīvus*, from *laxus*, loose.]

lax·i·ty (lăk′sĭ-tē) *n.* The condition or quality of being lax.

lay¹ (lā) *v.* **laid** (lād), **lay·ing. —tr.v. 1. a.** To cause to lie; put in a horizontal position: *lay a child in a crib.* **b.** To place or rest in a particular state or position. **2.** To produce inside the body and bring forth (an egg or eggs). **3.** To cause to settle, subside, or stop being troublesome: *lay a rumor.* **4.** To assign or attribute; charge: *laid the blame on him.* **5.** To impose as a burden or punishment: *lay a penalty upon him.* **6.** To put in a setting; locate: *The story was laid in Italy.* **7.** To place in the proper position or install: *lay a carpet.* **8.** To arrange in a required order for use; put in readiness: *lay a trap.* **9.** To devise; make: *lay plans.* **10.** To place or give (importance): *lay stress on clarity of expression.* **11.** To put forth for examination; present; submit: *lay a case before a committee.* **12. a.** To place (a bet or wager): *lay bets on the fight.* **b.** To bet; wager: *lay ten dollars on a horse.* **13.** To bring down forcefully: *laid him on the ground with a single punch.* **—intr.v. 1.** To produce and deposit eggs. **2.** *Nonstandard.* To lie; recline. **—phrasal verbs. lay aside. 1.** To give up; abandon: *lay aside old prejudices.* **2.** To put aside for the future; save. **lay away. 1.** To reserve for the future; save. **2.** To hold

(merchandise) for delivery after paid for in full. —See Syns at **save**. **lay by**. To keep on hand for future needs; save. **lay down**. **1.** To set forth; establish: *lay down the rules.* **2.** To give up or be willing to give up: *lay down one's weapons.* **lay in**. To obtain and stock (provisions, supplies, etc.); to store. **lay into**. **1.** To thrash. **2.** To scold sharply. **lay low**. **1.** To bring (someone) to a condition of weakness, helplessness, or destruction. **2.** *Slang.* To stay out of sight; to hide. **lay off**. **1.** To dismiss or suspend from a job, esp. during a slow period. **2.** *Slang.* **a.** To stop teasing, criticizing, or picking on. **b.** To stop using or doing something. **c.** To cease trying to do or continue. —See Syns at **abandon** and **stop**. **lay open**. **1.** To cut open; to slash. **2.** To expose; reveal. **lay out**. **1.** To arrange according to a plan: *lay out the day's work.* **2.** To spend or supply, sometimes with the expectation of being reimbursed. **lay up**. **1.** To stock (supplies) for future needs. **2.** *Informal.* To keep in bed or out of action as a result of illness or injury. —*n.* General manner, surface, position, or appearance. —*idiom.* **lay of the land**. **1.** The nature, surface, or form of an area of land. **2.** *Informal.* The overall situation or outlook. [Middle English *leggen*, from Old English *lecgan*.]
Usage: lay, lie. These verbs are commonly confused and misused, mainly because their meanings are complementary and their principal parts overlap. The principal parts of *lay* (to put, place, or prepare) are *laid*, *laying*. The principal parts of *lie* (to recline, to be situated) are *lay*, *lain*, *lying*. *Lie* is not typically transitive. On the other hand, *lay* is more often transitive than intransitive, and its intransitive sense "to recline" is nonstandard. In these examples *lay* is the correct choice: *laid the letter on the desk; lay the cards on the table; laid the blame on me; laid plans; the hen that had laid the eggs.* In these examples *lie* is the correct choice: *wanted to lie on the bed for a while; had lain there for an hour when the phone rang; lying half asleep; a dispute that lies unresolved; property that lay on the border; property that lies on the border; a choice that lay with them alone.*

lay² (lā) *adj.* **1.** Not of or belonging to the ordained religious clergy; of the laity; secular: *a lay preacher.* **2.** Not of or belonging to a particular profession: *a lay observer on a scientific expedition.* [Middle English *laie*, from Old French *lai*, from Late Latin *lāicus*, from Greek *laikos*, from *laos*, the people.]

lay³ (lā) *n.* A simple poem or song that tells a story; ballad. [Middle English, from Old French *lai*.]

lay⁴ (lā) *v.* Past tense of **lie** (to recline). [Middle English *laie*, from Old English *læg*.]

lay·a·way (lā′ə-wā′) *n.* A method of buying and selling whereby a store holds merchandise until the purchaser has paid the full price.

lay·er (lā′ər) *n.* **1.** A single thickness, coating, or sheet of material spread out or covering a surface: *a cake with three layers.* **2.** Someone or something that lays: *a carpet layer.* **3.** *Hort.* A stem that is covered with soil for rooting while still part of a living plant. —*tr.v.* *Hort.* To propagate (a plant) by layering. [Middle English *leyer*, from *leggen*, to lay.]

lay·er·ing (lā′ər-ĭng) *n.* The process of rooting branches, twigs, or stems that are still attached to a parent plant, as by placing a specially treated part in moist soil.

lay·ette (lā-ĕt′) *n.* A complete set of clothing and other supplies for a newborn child. [French, from Old French, dim. of *laie*, box, from Middle Dutch *laege*.]

lay·man (lā′mən) *n.* **1.** Someone who is not a member of the religious clergy. **2.** Someone who is not a member of a particular profession.

lay·off (lā′ôf′, -ŏf′) *n.* **1.** A temporary dismissal of employees. **2.** Any period of temporary inactivity or rest.

lay·out (lā′out′) *n.* **1.** The laying out of something. **2.** The arrangement, plan, or structure of something laid out: *the layout of an apartment.* **3.** The plan that shows the arrangement of printed matter and pictures to go on a page of a newspaper, magazine, advertisement, etc. **4.** A set of tools or implements.

lay reader. A layman in the Anglican and Episcopal churches authorized to read some parts of the service.

lay-up (lā′ŭp′) *n.* Also **lay-up shot.** *Basketball.* A usu. one-handed, banked shot made close to the basket.

la·zar (lā′zər, lăz′ər) *n.* *Archaic.* A beggar afflicted with some loathsome disease, esp. leprosy; a leper. [Middle English, from Medieval Latin *Lazarus*, after the beggar in Luke 16:20.]

laze (lāz) *v.* **lazed, laz·ing.** —*intr.v.* To be lazy; to loaf. —*tr.v.* To spend (time) in loafing: *laze the day away.*

la·zy (lā′zē) *adj.* **-zi·er, -zi·est. 1.** Not willing to work or be energetic; disposed to idleness; slothful. **2.** Slow-moving; sluggish: *a lazy river; lazy clouds.* **3.** Causing, expressing, or suggesting idleness or lack of energy: *a lazy summer day; a lazy yawn.* [Orig. unknown.] —**la′zi·ly** *adv.* —**la′zi·ness** *n.*
Syns: lazy, idle, indolent, shiftless, slothful, trifling (Chiefly Regional) *adj.* *Core meaning:* Resisting exertion, work, or other activity (*a lazy student*).

la·zy·bones (lā′zē-bōnz′) *n., pl.* **lazybones.** *Slang.* A lazy person.

lazy Su·san (soo′zən). A revolving tray for condiments or food.

lea (lē, lā) *n.* A meadow. [Middle English *leye*, from Old English *lēa*.]

leach (lēch) *tr.v.* **1.** To remove (soluble materials) from a substance by causing or allowing a liquid to wash through or over it: *Heavy rains leached minerals from the soil.* **2.** To cause or allow a liquid to wash through (a substance) and remove the soluble materials in it: *Heavy rains have leached the soil of minerals.* **3.** To pass (a liquid) through a substance so as to remove soluble materials. —*intr.v.* To be dissolved and washed out by leaching: *Minerals leached through the soil.* [Prob. ult. from Old English *leccan*, to moisten.] —**leach′er** *n.*

lead¹ (lēd) *v.* **led** (lĕd), **lead·ing.** —*tr.v.* **1. a.** To show or guide along the way: *The ranger will lead us to the top of the mountain.* **b.** To show (the way) in this manner: *He led the way.* **2.** To guide by taking by the hand or by a rope: *lead a horse.* **3.** To serve as a route for; conduct on a particular course: *The path led him to a stream.* **4.** To cause to follow some course of action or line of thought; induce: *led him to believe otherwise.* **5.** To direct the performance or activities of: *lead an orchestra.* **6.** To assume leadership in; guide: *lead a discussion.* **7.** To be at the head of: *His name led the list.* **8.** To be ahead of: *led the runner-up by three strides.* **9.** To pursue; to live: *leading a hectic life.* **10.** *Cards.* To begin a round of play by putting down a (card): *led an ace.* —*intr.v.* **1.** To be first; be ahead: *Who leads in batting averages?* **2.** To go first as a guide: *You lead, we'll follow.* **3.** To act as commander, director, or conductor: *born to lead.* **4.** To maneuver a partner in dance steps. **5.** To afford a passage, course, or route. **6.** To tend toward a certain goal or result. **7. a.** To make the beginning motion: *Lead with your right foot.* **b.** To make the initial play, as in a card game. —*phrasal verbs.* **lead off. 1.** To make the initial play, move, or speech; to start. **2.** *Baseball.* To be the first batter in an inning or line-up. **lead on.** To tempt or lure (someone) into doing something unwise or believing something untrue. **lead up to.** To proceed toward (one's true purpose or subject), as by a long series of hints or remarks. —*n.* **1.** The front, foremost, or winning position: *Our team took the lead.* **2.** The margin by which one is ahead: *a five-point lead.* **3.** A piece of information of possible use in a search; a clue: *several good leads for a job.* **4.** Command; leadership: *take the lead.* **5.** An example; precedent: *follow her lead in becoming a doctor.* **6. a.** The principal role in a dramatic production. **b.** The person playing such a part. **7. a.** The opening line or paragraph of a news story. **b.** A prominently displayed news story. **8.** *Cards.* The first play. **b.** The right or turn to make the first play. **c.** The card played in such a turn. **9.** *Baseball.* A position taken by a base runner away from his base toward the next. **10.** A leash, rope, or strap for leading an animal. **11.** *Elect.* A conductor by which one circuit element is electrically connected to another or to the circuit. —*modifier:* *the lead dog of a team; a lead rope.* [Middle English *leden*, from Old English *lǣdan*.]

lead² (lĕd) *n.* **1.** *Symbol* **Pb** A soft, malleable, ductile, bluish-white, dense metallic element, extracted chiefly from galena and used in containers and pipes for corrosives, in solder and type metal, bullets, radiation shielding, paints, and antiknock compounds. Atomic number 82;

atomic weight 207.19; melting point 327.5°C; boiling point 1,744°C; specific gravity 11.35; valences 2, 4. **2.** A piece of lead or other metal attached to a length of line, used in measuring depths. **3.** Bullets from or for firearms; shot. **4. leads.** Strips of lead used in fitting windows with panes. **5.** *Printing.* A thin strip of metal used to separate lines of type or keep them in place. **6. a.** A material, often basically graphite, used as the writing substance in pencils. **b.** A thin stick of such material. —*tr.v.* **1.** To cover, line, weight, fill, or treat with lead. **2.** To add lead to: *lead gasoline.* **3.** *Printing.* To provide space between (lines of type) with leads. **4.** To secure (window glass) with leads. [Middle English, from Old English *lead.*]

lead acetate (lĕd). A poisonous white crystalline compound, $Pb(C_2H_3O_2)_2 \cdot 3H_2O$, used in dyes, waterproofing compounds, and varnishes.

lead arsenate (lĕd). A poisonous white crystalline compound, $Pb_3(AsO_4)_2$, used in insecticides and herbicides.

lead·en (lĕd'n) *adj.* **1.** Made of or containing lead. **2.** Dull, dark gray: *a leaden sky.* **3.** Heavy like lead. **4.** Burdened; weighted down; depressed: *a leaden heart.* —**lead'en·ly** *adv.* —**lead'en·ness** *n.*

lead·er (lē'dər) *n.* **1.** A person who leads others along a way; a guide. **2.** A person in charge or in command of others. **3. a.** The head of a political party or organization. **b.** A person who has an influential voice in politics. **4. a.** The conductor of an orchestra, band, or choral group. **b.** The principal performer of an orchestral section, as the first violinist. **5.** The foremost horse or other draft animal in a harnessed team. **6.** A **loss leader. 7. leaders.** *Printing.* Dots or dashes in a row leading the eye across a page. **8.** A pipe for carrying rainwater from a roof to the ground. **9.** A short length of gut, wire, etc., by which a hook is attached to a fishing line. **10.** *Bot.* The growing apex or main shoot of a shrub or tree. —**lead'er·less** *adj.* —**lead'er·ship'** *n.*

lead glass (lĕd). **Flint glass.**

lead-in (lēd'ĭn') *n.* **1.** An introduction. **2.** A program, as on television, that precedes another. **3.** The part of an antenna or aerial that leads to an electronic transmitter or receiver. —**modifier:** *lead-in* wires.

lead·ing¹ (lē'dĭng) *adj.* **1.** In the first or front position: *the leading horse in a race.* **2.** Most important; main; foremost: *the leading countries in car production.* **3.** Designed to encourage a desired response: *a leading question.* —**lead'ing·ly** *adv.*

lead·ing² (lĕd'ĭng) *n.* **1.** A border or rim of lead, as around a windowpane. **2.** *Printing.* The strips of lead used to separate lines of type or keep them in place.

lead monoxide. Litharge.

lead·off (lēd'ôf', -ŏf') *n.* **1.** An opening play or move. **2.** A player who starts the action of a game, esp. the first batter in a baseball line-up or in an inning.

lead pencil (lĕd). A pencil that contains a thin stick of graphite as its marking substance.

lead poisoning (lĕd). Acute or chronic poisoning by lead or any of its salts, the acute form causing severe gastroenteritis and the chronic form causing anemia, abdominal pain, constipation, partial paralysis, and convulsions.

lead-time (lĕd'tīm') *n.* The time needed or available between the decision to start a project and the completion of the work.

leaf (lēf) *n., pl.* **leaves** (lēvz). **1.** A usu. thin, flat, green plant part attached to a stem or stalk that functions as a principal organ in photosynthesis and transpiration. **2.** A leaflike part, such as a petal. **3.** The condition of having leaves: *trees bursting into leaf.* **4.** The leaves of a plant used or processed for a specific purpose: *tobacco leaf.* **5.** One of the sheets of paper forming the pages of a book, magazine, notebook, etc. **6.** A very thin sheet of metal: *gold leaf.* **7.** A flat, movable part, as one put into a table to make it larger. **8.** One of several metal strips forming a leaf spring. —*intr.v.* **1.** To produce leaves; put forth foliage. **2.** To turn pages rapidly; glance: *leafed through the magazine.* —**idioms. take a leaf from (someone's) book.** To follow someone's example. **turn over a new leaf.** To make a fresh start by deciding to improve one's ways. [Middle English *leef,* from Old English *leaf.*] —**leaf'less** *adj.*

leaf·age (lē'fĭj) *n.* Leaves; foliage.

leaf·hop·per (lēf'hŏp'ər) *n.* Any of numerous insects of the family Cicadellidae that suck juices from plants.

leaf·let (lēf'lĭt) *n.* **1.** One of the segments of a compound leaf. **2.** A small leaf or leaflike part. **3. a.** A printed, usu. folded handbill or flier, such as an advertising circular. **b.** A small booklet; pamphlet.

leaf miner. Any of numerous small flies and moths that in the larval state dig into and feed on leaf tissue.

leaf mold. Humus or compost consisting of decomposed leaves and other organic material.

leaf spring. A composite spring, used esp. in automotive suspensions, that consists of several layers of flexible metallic strips joined to act as a single unit.

leaf·stalk (lēf'stôk') *n.* The stalk by which a leaf is attached to a stem; a petiole.

leaf·y (lē'fē) *adj.* **-i·er, -i·est. 1.** Having or covered with leaves: *leafy branches.* **2.** Consisting of leaves: *leafy vegetables.* **3.** Of or like leaves: *a leafy green.*

league¹ (lēg) *n.* **1.** An association of states, organizations, or individuals working together for common action; alliance. **2.** An association of sports teams or clubs that compete chiefly among themselves. **3.** *Informal.* A level of competition, ability, or quality; a class: *out of his league.* —*v.* **leagued, leagu·ing.** —*intr.v.* To come together for a common purpose; unite. —*tr.v.* To bring together under a common agreement; join. [Middle English *ligg,* from Old French *ligue,* from Italian *liga,* from *legare,* to bind, from Latin *ligāre.*]

league² (lēg) *n.* Any of several approx. equal units of distance, esp. one equal to 3 miles. [Middle English *leghe,* from Late Latin *leuga.*]

leagu·er (lē'gər) *n.* A person who belongs to a sports league.

leak (lēk) *n.* **1.** A hole, crack, or similar opening through which something can escape or pass: *a leak in the gas pipe.* **2.** An escape or passage of something through or as if through such an opening: *can't stop the leak.* **3. a.** A disclosure of confidential information. **b.** The information disclosed. **c.** The source of such information. —*intr.v.* **1.** To permit the escape of something through a breach or flaw: *The water pipes leaked.* **2.** To escape through a breach or flaw: *Gas leaked through the sealed windows.* **3.** To become publicly known through a breach of secrecy: *The news leaked out.* —*tr.v.* **1.** To permit (a substance) to escape through a breach or flaw: *The barrel leaked oil.* **2.** To disclose (information) without authorization or official sanction: *He leaked the secret to the newspapers.* [Middle English *leken,* prob. from Old Norse *leka.*]

leak·age (lē'kĭj) *n.* **1.** The process of leaking. **2. a.** Something that escapes or enters by leaking. **b.** The amount that leaks in or out.

leak·y (lē'kē) *adj.* **-i·er, -i·est.** Having, allowing, or tending to allow a leak or leaks: *a leaky valve.*

lean¹ (lēn) *v.* **leaned** or **leant** (lĕnt), **lean·ing.** —*intr.v.* **1.** To bend or slant away from the vertical: *Lean down so I can whisper to you.* **2.** To incline the weight of the body so as to be supported: *leaning against the railing.* **3.** To rely for assistance or support: *Lean on me for help.* **4.** To have a tendency or preference: *She leans toward the group approach.* —*tr.v.* **1.** To set or place so as to be resting or supported. **2.** To cause to incline: *Lean your head back.* —*n.* A slant or inclination away from the vertical. [Middle English *lenen,* from Old English *hleonian.*]

lean² (lēn) *adj.* **-er, -est. 1.** Not fleshy or fat; thin. **2.** Containing little or no fat: *a lean steak.* **3.** Not productive or abundant: *the lean years of the Depression.* **4.** Having little or no ornamentation or elaboration: *a lean style of architecture.* —*n.* Meat with little or no fat. [Middle English *lene,* from Old English *hlæne.*] —**lean'ly** *adv.* —**lean'ness** *n.*

lean·ing (lē'nĭng) *n.* A tendency; preference.

leant (lĕnt) *v.* A past tense and past participle of **lean** (to bend or incline).

lean-to (lēn'tōō') *n., pl.* **-tos. 1.** A shed with a sloping roof, built against a wall or the side of a building. **2.** A simple shelter, often having a sloping roof resting on the ground at one side and raised on poles at the other.

leap (lēp) *v.* **leaped** or **leapt** (lĕpt, lēpt), **leap·ing.** —*intr.v.*

1. To jump off the ground with a spring of the legs. **2.** To move quickly, abruptly, or impulsively: *leaps from loyalty to loyalty.* —*tr.v.* **1.** To jump over; to hurdle: *leap the brook.* **2.** To cause to jump: *leap a horse.* —See Syns at **jump.** —*phrasal verb.* **leap at.** To accept eagerly: *He leaped at the film offer.* —*n.* **1.** The act of springing up or forward; vault; bound. **2.** The distance cleared in a forward spring: *a ten-foot leap.* **3.** An abrupt or precipitous passage, shift, or transition: *a nation's leap into the atomic age.* —*idiom.* **by leaps and bounds.** Very quickly and by large degrees. [Middle English *leapen,* from Old English *hlēapan.*] —**leap'er** *n.*

leap·frog (lēp'frôg', -frŏg') *n.* A game in which players take turns bending over and then leaping with the legs astraddle the next player. —*v.* **-frogged, -frog·ging.** —*tr.v.* To jump over in or as if in leapfrog. —*intr.v.* To move forward or progress by or as if by alternating leaps.

leapt (lĕpt, lēpt) *v.* A past tense and past participle of **leap.**

leap year. A year in the Gregorian calendar having 366 days, with the extra day, February 29, added to compensate for the quarter-day difference between an ordinary year and the astronomical year.

learn (lûrn) *v.* **learned** or **learnt** (lûrnt), **learn·ing.** —*tr.v.* **1.** To gain knowledge, comprehension, or mastery of through experience or study: *He learned French.* **2.** To fix in the mind; memorize: *learned the poem by heart.* **3.** To acquire through experience: *learned humility.* **4.** To become informed of; find out: *learn the true story.* —*intr.v.* **1.** To gain knowledge, comprehension, or mastery: *learns easily.* **2.** To become informed; find out: *learned about it in the newspaper.* [Middle English *lernen,* from Old English *leornian.*] —**learn'er** *n.*
   Usage: **learn, teach.** In modern usage these are carefully distinguished. *Learn* is confined to the act of gaining knowledge. It is not acceptably used to express the act of instructing or imparting knowledge, a sense expressed only by *teach.*

learn·ed (lûr'nĭd) *adj.* Having or demonstrating profound knowledge or scholarship; erudite; scholarly. —**learn'ed·ly** *adv.* —**learn'ed·ness** *n.*

learn·ing (lûr'nĭng) *n.* **1.** Instruction; education: *a real hunger for learning.* **2.** Acquired knowledge or skill, esp. thorough knowledge gained by study: *men of learning.* —See Syns at **knowledge.**

learnt (lûrnt) *v.* A past tense and past participle of **learn.**

lear·y (lîr'ē) *adj.* Var. of **leery.**

lease (lēs) *n.* **1.** A contract by which an owner of property grants the use of it to someone else for a certain time in exchange for rent. **2.** The period of time specified in a lease. —*tr.v.* **leased, leas·ing.** **1.** To grant use or occupation of under contract in exchange for rent: *lease tractors.* **2.** To use or occupy by contract in exchange for rent: *lease a house.* [Middle English *les,* from Norman French, from *lesser,* to lease, from Old French *laissier,* to let go, from Latin *laxāre,* to loosen, from *laxus,* lax.]

lease·hold (lēs'hōld') *n.* **1.** Possession by lease. **2.** Property held by lease. —**lease'hold'er** *n.*

leash (lēsh) *n.* **1.** A chain, rope, or strap attached to the collar or harness of an animal and used to hold it in check. **2.** Control; check: *kept in leash.* **3.** A set of three hounds or other animals. —*tr.v.* To restrain with or as if with a leash. [Middle English *leshe,* from Old French *laisse,* from *laissier,* to loosen.]

least (lēst). A superlative of **little.** —*adj.* **1.** Lowest in importance or rank. **2.** Smallest in magnitude or degree. —*adv.* Superlative of **little.** To or in the smallest degree: *the least skilled carpenter.* —*n.* **1.** The smallest in size or importance: *The least of them spoke up boldly when encouraged.* **2.** The smallest appropriate thing: *The least you could do would be to apologize.* —*idioms.* **at least. 1.** According to the lowest possible assessment; no less than: *eat out at least three times a week.* **2.** In any event; anyway: *You might at least answer.* **in the least.** At all: *I don't mind in the least.* [Middle English, from Old English *lǣst.*]

least common denominator. *Math.* The **lowest common denominator.**

least common multiple. *Abbr.* **l.c.m.** *Math.* The smallest number that is exactly divisible by each of two or more designated quantities.

least·wise (lēst'wīz') *adv.* Also **least·ways** (-wāz'). *Informal.* Anyway; at least.

leath·er (lĕth'ər) *n.* **1.** The dressed or tanned hide of an animal, usu. with the hair removed. **2.** Any of various articles or parts made of leather, as a strap or boot. —*modifier: leather shoes.* —*tr.v.* **1.** To cover with leather. **2.** *Informal.* To beat with a leather strap. [Middle English *lether,* from Old English.]

leath·er·back (lĕth'ər-băk') *n.* A large, chiefly tropical saltwater turtle, *Dermochelys coriacea,* with a leathery, longitudinally ridged carapace.

Leath·er·ette (lĕth'ə-rĕt') *n.* A trademark for an imitation leather.

leath·ern (lĕth'ərn) *adj. Archaic.* **1.** Made of or covered with leather. **2.** Resembling leather.

leath·er·neck (lĕth'ər-nĕk') *n. Slang.* A U.S. marine. [From the leather neckband that was once part of the uniform.]

leath·er·y (lĕth'ə-rē) *adj.* Having the texture or appearance of leather; tough or weathered: *leathery skin.*

leave¹ (lēv) *v.* **left** (lĕft), **leav·ing.** —*tr.v.* **1.** To go out of or away from. **2.** To go without taking or removing: *left his book on the subway.* **3.** To have as a result or aftermath: *left a trail of smoke.* **4.** To allow to remain in a certain condition or place: *Leave the dishes in the sink.* **5.** To have remaining after death: *He leaves a son.* **6.** To give after one's death, as in a will; bequeath: *leaves his estate to his wife.* **7.** To submit to another to be done, acted upon, or accomplished: *Leave the hard work for Jones to do.* **8.** To cause to remain after a loss or reduction: *Ten minus two leaves eight.* —*intr.v.* To depart; set out; go. —See Syns at **abandon.** —*phrasal verbs.* **leave alone.** To stop annoying or troubling. **leave off. 1.** To stop; cease. **2.** To stop doing or using: *leave off alcohol.* **leave out.** To fail to include; omit. —See Syns at **stop.** [Middle English *leven,* from Old English *lǣfan.*]
   Usage: **leave, let. 1.** These verbs are interchangeable when followed by a noun or pronoun and *alone: leave* (or *let*) *me alone.* The meaning is to refrain from disturbing. Be sure that your use of *let* in such a locution is clear, though. Some writers prefer *let alone* when the meaning is to refrain from disturbing, and they confine *leave alone* to contexts in which the meaning is to depart and allow one to remain in solitude (a sense that *let alone* cannot convey). **2.** *Leave* is no longer used in place of *let* in formal English when the desired meaning is to allow or permit. Only *let* is acceptable in the following: *Let me be. Let go of the rail. Let us not argue. Let it lie.* Note also that *let* is followed by the objective case in the preceding examples and in *Let George and me* (not *I*) *help.*

leave² (lēv) *n.* **1.** Permission: *leave to stay out until midnight.* **2. a.** Official permission to be absent from work or duty, esp. that granted to military personnel. **b.** An absence of this kind: *on leave.* **3.** A formal farewell: *took leave of her friends.* [Middle English *leve,* from Old English *lēaf.*]

leaved (lēvd) *adj.* **1.** Having or bearing a leaf or leaves. **2.** Having a specified number or kind of leaves: *three-leaved; wide-leaved.*

leav·en (lĕv'ən) *n.* Also **leav·en·ing** (lĕv'ə-nĭng). **1.** A substance, such as yeast, used as an ingredient in batters and doughs to cause them to rise. **2.** Any element or influence that works to lighten or enliven the whole. —*tr.v.* **1.** To add yeast or another fermenting agent to. **2.** To pervade with a lightening or enlivening influence. [Middle English *levain,* from Old French, from Latin *levāre,* to raise.] —**leav'ened** *n.*

leaves (lēvz) *n.* Plural of **leaf.**

leave-tak·ing (lēv'tā'kĭng) *n.* A departure or farewell.

leav·ings (lē'vĭngz) *pl.n.* Scraps or remains; leftovers.

Le·bens·raum (lā'bəns-roum') *n.* Additional territory considered necessary for a nation's economic well-being. [German, "living space."]

lech·er (lĕch'ər) *n.* A man given to excessive sexual activity. [Middle English *lechour,* from Old French *lecheor,* from *lechier,* to live in debauchery.]

lech·er·ous (lĕch'ər-əs) *adj.* Preoccupied with thoughts of sexual activity. —**lech'er·ous·ly** *adv.* —**lech'er·ous·ness** *n.*

lech·er·y (lĕch'ə-rē) *n.* Excessive sexual activity.

ă pat	ā pay	â care	ä father	ĕ pet	ē be	hw which	ĭ pit	ī tie	î pier	ŏ pot	ō toe	ô paw, for	oi noise
ōō took	ōō boot	ou out	th thin	th this	ŭ cut	û urge	zh vision	ə about, item, edible, gallop, circus

lec·i·thin (lĕs′ə-thĭn) *n.* Any of a group of phosphatides found in all plant and animal tissues, produced commercially from egg yolks, soybeans, and corn, and used in the processing of foods, pharmaceuticals, cosmetics, paints and inks, and rubber and plastics. [Greek *lekithos*, egg yolk + -IN.]

lec·tern (lĕk′tərn) *n.* A reading desk, often with a slanted top, that serves as a support for the notes or books of a speaker. [Middle English *lectorn*, from Old French *lettrun*, from Medieval Latin *lectrum*, from Latin *legere*, to read.]

lec·ture (lĕk′chər) *n.* 1. A speech providing information about a given subject, delivered before an audience or class. 2. A serious, lengthy warning or reproof. —See Syns at **speech.** —*v.* **-tured, -tur·ing.** —*intr.v.* To deliver a lecture or lectures. —*tr.v.* 1. To give a lecture to (a class or audience). 2. To scold soberly and at length. [Middle English, a reading, from Old French, from Medieval Latin *lectūra*, from Latin *legere*, to read.] —**lec′tur·er** *n.*

led (lĕd) *v.* Past tense and past participle of **lead** (to guide).

Le·da (lē′də) *n. Gk. Myth.* A queen of Sparta and mother of Castor and Pollux, Clytemnestra, and Helen of Troy, fathered by Zeus in the form of a swan.

ledge (lĕj) *n.* 1. A narrow shelf that projects from a wall. 2. A cut or projection that forms a shelf on a cliff or rock wall. 3. A ridge or rock shelf under water. 4. A level of rock bearing ore; a vein. [Middle English *legge*, a raised strip or bar.]

ledg·er (lĕj′ər) *n.* An account book in which sums of money received and paid out are recorded. [Middle English *legger*, book remaining in one place, perh. from *leggen*, to lay.]

ledger line. *Mus.* A short line placed above or below a staff for notes above or below the staff's range.

lee (lē) *n.* 1. The side or quarter away from the direction from which the wind blows; the sheltered side: *in the lee of the island.* 2. Cover; shelter. —*adj.* 1. Away from the wind; sheltered: *a fire built on the lee side.* 2. Lying on the side of a ship toward which the ship is being driven by the wind: *a dangerous lee shore.* [Middle English, from Old English *hlēo*, shelter.]

leech[1] (lēch) *n.* 1. Any of various chiefly aquatic bloodsucking or carnivorous annelid worms of the class Hirudinea, of which one species, *Hirudo medicinalis,* was formerly used by physicians to bleed their patients. 2. A person who preys on or constantly clings to another; a parasite. —*tr.v. Med.* To bleed (someone) with leeches. —*intr.v.* To attach oneself to another in the manner of a leech. [Middle English *leche*, physician, from Old English *læce.*]

leech[2] (lēch) *n. Naut.* 1. Either vertical edge of a square sail. 2. The after edge of a fore-and-aft sail. [Middle English *leche.*]

leek (lēk) *n.* A plant, *Allium porrum,* that is related to the onion and has a white, slender bulb and dark-green leaves. [Middle English, from Old English *lēac.*]

leek

leer (lîr) *n.* An insulting, lustful, or nasty look; an arrogant or contemptuous glance. —*intr.v.* To look with a leer. [Prob. from obs. *leer*, cheek, from Middle English *lere*, from Old English *hlēor.*]

leer·y (lîr′ē) *adj.* **-i·er, -i·est.** Also **lear·y.** *Informal.* Suspicious; wary. —**leer′i·ly** *adv.* —**leer′i·ness** *n.*

lees (lēz) *pl.n.* Dregs that settle during fermentation, esp.

in wine. [Pl. of obs. *lee*, sediment, from Middle English *lie*, from Old French, from Medieval Latin *lia.*]

lee·ward (lē′wərd, lōō′ərd) *adj.* Facing away from the wind: *the leeward quarter.* —*n.* The lee side or quarter: *a whale to the leeward of us.* —*adv.* Downwind: *passing leeward of the reef.*

lee·way (lē′wā′) *n.* 1. The drift of a ship or plane to leeward of true course. 2. A margin of time, space, or expenditure that offers freedom or variation of activity; latitude.

left[1] (lĕft) *adj.* 1. Of, at, or on the side of the body that is toward the west when an individual faces north. 2. Directed or situated toward the left side: *a left turn.* 3. Often **Left.** Of, relating to, or holding radical or liberal political beliefs. —*n.* 1. The left hand. 2. The direction or location of the left hand or side. 3. Often **Left.** Those who advocate the adoption of sometimes extreme measures in order to achieve the equality, economic freedom, and well-being of the citizens of a state. —*adv.* Toward or on the left. [Middle English, from Old English *lyft.*]

left[2] (lĕft) *v.* Past tense and past participle of **leave** (to go away).

left field. *Baseball.* 1. The third of the outfield that is to the left, looking from home plate. 2. The position played by the left fielder. —*idiom.* **out in left field.** Very far from being correct, probable, or logical.

left fielder. *Baseball.* The player who defends left field.

left-hand (lĕft′hănd′) *adj.* 1. Of, pertaining to, or located on the left. 2. Turning from right to left: *a screw with left-hand threads.*

left-hand·ed (lĕft′hăn′dĭd) *adj.* 1. Using the left hand more naturally and easily than the right. 2. Executed with the left hand. 3. Designed for wear on or use by the left hand: *left-handed scissors.* 4. Awkward; clumsy: *a left-handed apology.* 5. Doubtful in meaning or sincerity: *left-handed flattery.* 6. Turning or spiraling from right to left; counterclockwise: *a left-handed conch shell.* —*adv.* With the left hand. —**left′-hand′ed·ly** *adv.* —**left′-hand′ed·ness** *n.*

left-hand·er (lĕft′hăn′dər) *n.* A person who is left-handed or uses the left hand.

left·ist (lĕf′tĭst) *n.* A person with political views associated with the left; a liberal or radical. —*adj.* Of the political left: *leftist publications.* —**left′ism** *n.*

left·o·ver (lĕft′ō′vər) *adj.* Remaining unused or uneaten. —*n.* Often **leftovers.** Something that is leftover.

left wing. The leftist faction of a group. —*modifier* (left-wing): *a left-wing journal.* —**left′-wing′er** *n.*

left·y (lĕf′tē) *n., pl.* **-ies.** *Slang.* A left-handed person.

leg (lĕg) *n.* 1. A limb or appendage of an animal used for locomotion and support. 2. The lower or hind limb in a human being, monkey, ape, etc. 3. Any supporting part resembling a leg in shape or function: *a table leg.* 4. One of the branches of a forked or jointed object: *a leg of a compass.* 5. Any part of a garment, esp. of a pair of trousers, that covers the leg. 6. *Geom.* Either side of a right triangle that is not the hypotenuse. 7. A stage of a journey or course, esp.: **a.** The distance traveled by a sailing vessel on a single tack. **b.** That part of an air route that is between two successive stops. —*idioms.* **give a leg up.** To assist or aid by boosting or providing support. **not have a leg to stand on.** To have no justifiable or logical basis for a defense or proposition. **on (one's) last legs.** At the end of one's strength or health; ready to collapse, fail, or die. **pull (someone's) leg.** *Informal.* To deceive in fun; tease; kid. **shake a leg.** *Slang.* 1. To hasten; hurry. 2. To dance. **stretch (one's) legs.** To stand or walk, esp. after sitting for a long time. —*intr.v.* **legged, leg·ging.** To go on foot; walk or run. [Middle English, from Old Norse *leggr.*]

leg·a·cy (lĕg′ə-sē) *n., pl.* **-cies.** 1. Money or property bequeathed to someone by will. 2. Something handed on from those who have come before: *a legacy of religious freedom.* [Middle English *legacie*, from Old French, from Medieval Latin *lēgantia*, from Latin *lēgāre*, to depute, commission, bequeath.]

le·gal (lē′gəl) *adj.* 1. Of, relating to, or concerned with law or lawyers: *legal papers.* 2. **a.** Authorized by or based on law: *a legal right.* **b.** Established by law; statutory: *the legal owner.* 3. In conformity with or permitted by law: *legal steps to recover property.* 4. Recognized or enforced by law rather than by equity. [Old French, from Latin *lēgālis,*

ă pat   ā pay   â care   ä father   ĕ pet   ē be   hw which
ōō took   ōō boot   ou out   th thin   th this   ŭ cut
ĭ pit   ī tie   î pier   ŏ pot   ō toe   ô paw, for   oi noise
û urge   zh vision   ə about, item, edible, gallop, circus

from *lĕx,* law.] —**le′gal·ly** *adv.*

  Syns: legal, lawful, legit (*Slang*), **legitimate** *adj.* Core meaning: Within, allowed by, or sanctioned by the law (*legal entry; a legal marriage*).

legal age. The age at which a person may by law assume the rights and responsibilities of an adult.

legal holiday. Any holiday authorized by law and characterized by a limit or ban on work or official business.

le·gal·ism (lē′gə-lĭz′əm) *n.* Strict, literal adherence to the law. —**le′gal·ist** *n.* —**le′gal·is′tic** *adj.* —**le′gal·is′ti·cal·ly** *adv.*

le·gal·i·ty (lē-găl′ĭ-tē) *n., pl.* **-ties.** The condition or quality of being legal; lawfulness.

le·gal·ize (lē′gə-līz′) *tr.v.* **-ized, -iz·ing.** To make legal or lawful. —**le′gal·i·za′tion** *n.*

legal tender. Currency that may legally be offered in payment of a debt and that a creditor must accept.

leg·ate (lĕg′ĭt) *n.* An official emissary, esp. an official representative of the pope. [Middle English, from Old French, from Latin *lēgātus,* from the past part. of *lēgāre,* to commission.] —**leg′ate·ship′** *n.*

leg·a·tee (lĕg′ə-tē′) *n.* Someone to whom a legacy is bequeathed.

le·ga·tion (lĭ-gā′shən) *n.* **1.** A diplomatic mission in a foreign country that ranks below an embassy. **2.** The legate and staff of such a mission. **3.** The premises occupied by a legation.

le·ga·to (lĭ-gä′tō) *Mus.* —*adv.* In a smooth, even style. —*adj.* Smooth and even. —*n., pl.* **-tos.** A smooth, even style, performance, or passage. [Italian, connected from *legare,* to bind, from Latin *ligāre.*]

leg·end (lĕj′ənd) *n.* **1.** An unverified popular story handed down from earlier times. **2.** A romanticized or popularized story of modern times. **3.** A person who achieves legendary fame. **4.** An inscription on a banner, coat of arms, coin, etc. **5.** An explanatory caption or note accompanying a map, chart, illustration, etc. [Middle English *legende,* saint's life, from Old French, from Medieval Latin *legenda,* things for reading, from Latin *legere,* to read.]

leg·en·dar·y (lĕj′ən-dĕr′ē) *adj.* **1.** Based on or told of in legends: *legendary heroes.* **2.** Talked about frequently; famous: *His rages were legendary.*

leg·er·de·main (lĕj′ər-də-mān′) *n.* **1.** Tricks performed with the hands, as by a magician. **2.** Any deception or trickery. [Middle English *legerdemayn,* from Old French *leger de main,* "light of hand."]

leg·ged (lĕg′ĭd, lĕgd) *adj.* Having a specified number or kind of legs: *a bony-legged boy; six-legged creatures.*

leg·gings (lĕg′ĭngz) *n.* A leg covering of cloth or leather, usu. extending from the knee to the foot.

leg·gy (lĕg′ē) *adj.* **-gi·er, -gi·est. 1.** Having long, awkward legs: *a leggy colt.* **2.** *Informal.* Having attractively long and slender legs. **3.** Having long, spindly, often leafless stems. —**leg′gi·ness** *n.*

leg·horn (lĕg′hôrn′, -ərn) *n.* **1.** Often **Leghorn.** One of a breed of domestic fowl raised esp. for production of eggs. **2. a.** The dried and bleached straw of an Italian variety of wheat. **b.** A hat made from this straw. [After *Leghorn* (Livorno), Italy.]

leg·i·ble (lĕj′ə-bəl) *adj.* Capable of being read or deciphered: *legible handwriting.* [Middle English *legibille,* from Late Latin *legibilis,* from Latin *legere,* to read.] —**leg′i·bil′i·ty** or **leg′i·ble·ness** *n.* —**leg′i·bly** *adv.*

le·gion (lē′jən) *n.* **1.** The major unit of the Roman army consisting of 3,000 to 6,000 infantrymen and more than 100 cavalrymen. **2.** Any large number; a multitude: *legions of insects.* [Middle English *legioun,* from Old French *legion,* from Latin *legiō,* from *legere,* to gather.]

le·gion·ar·y (lē′jə-nĕr′ē) *adj.* Of, relating to, or constituting a legion. —*n., pl.* **-ies.** A soldier of a legion.

legionary ant. An army ant.

le·gion·naire (lē′jə-nâr′) *n.* A member of a legion. [French *légionnaire,* from Old French *legion,* legion.]

leg·is·late (lĕj′ĭ-slāt′) *v.* **-lat·ed, -lat·ing.** —*intr.v.* To pass a law or laws. —*tr.v.* To create or bring about by legislation; enact into law.

leg·is·la·tion (lĕj′ĭ-slā′shən) *n.* **1.** The act or process of legislating; lawmaking. **2.** A proposed or enacted law or group of laws: *legislation now before Congress.*

leg·is·la·tive (lĕj′ĭ-slā′tĭv) *adj.* **1.** Of or relating to legislation or a legislature. **3.** Having the power to create laws: *the legislative branch of government.* —*n.* The legislative body of a government.

leg·is·la·tor (lĕj′ĭ-slā′tər) *n.* A member of a body that enacts laws. [Latin *lēgis lātor,* "proposer of law."]

leg·is·la·ture (lĕj′ĭ-slā′chər) *n.* A body of persons empowered to make the laws of a nation or state.

le·git (lə-jĭt′) —*adj. Slang.* Legitimate; lawful. —See Syns at **legal.**

le·git·i·ma·cy (lə-jĭt′ə-mə-sē) *n.* The fact of being legitimate.

le·git·i·mate (lə-jĭt′ə-mĭt) *adj.* **1.** In compliance with the law; lawful: *a legitimate business.* **2.** Based on logical reasoning or common sense; reasonable: *a legitimate solution.* **3.** Born of legally married parents. **4.** Of or pertaining to drama performed on a stage as opposed to other media, such as motion pictures. —See Syns at **legal.** —*tr.v.* (lə-jĭt′ə-māt′) **-mat·ed, -mat·ing.** To make, establish, or declare legitimate. [Middle English, born in wedlock, from Medieval Latin *legitimātus,* past part. of *legitimāre,* to make lawful, from Latin *legitimus,* lawful, from *lĕx,* law.] —**le·git′i·mate·ly** *adv.*

leg-of-mut·ton (lĕg′ə-mŭt′n, lĕg′əv-) *adj.* Resembling a leg of mutton in shape, as a sleeve.

leg·ume (lĕg′yoōm′, lə-gyoōm′) *n.* **1.** A pod, such as that of a pea or bean, that splits into two valves with the seeds attached to the lower edge of one of the valves. **2.** Such a pod or its seed, used as food. **3.** Any plant of the family Leguminosae that characteristically bear such pods. [French *légume,* from Latin *legūmen,* bean.] —**le·gu′mi·nous** (lə-gyoō′mə-nəs) *adj.*

leg·work (lĕg′wûrk′) *n. Informal.* Work, such as collecting information, that involves walking or traveling about.

le·hu·a (lā-hoō′ə) *n.* A tree, *Metrosideros collina,* of Hawaii and other Pacific islands, with showy red flowers. [Hawaiian.]

lei (lā, lā′ē) *n.* A garland of flowers, esp. one worn around the neck. [Hawaiian.]

lei

lemon

lei·sure (lē′zhər, lĕzh′ər) *n.* Freedom from work or time-consuming duties, responsibilities, or activities; time to do as one pleases. —*idioms.* **at leisure. 1.** Having free time. **2.** Not employed, occupied, or engaged. **at (one's) leisure.** At one's convenience; when one has free time. [Middle English *leisour,* freedom, opportunity, from Old French *leisir,* to be permitted, from Latin *licēre.*]

lei·sure·ly (lē′zhər-lē, lĕzh′ər-) *adj.* Without haste or exertion; unhurried: *a leisurely meal.* —**lei′sure·li·ness** *n.* —**lei′sure·ly** *adv.*

leit·mo·tif (līt′mō-tēf′) *n.* Also **leit·mo·tiv.** A dominant and recurring theme, as in an opera or a novel. [German *Leitmotiv,* "leading motif."]

lem·ming (lĕm′ĭng) *n.* Any of various rodents of the genus *Lemmus* and related genera, of northern regions, esp. the European species *L. lemmus,* noted for its mass migrations into the sea. [Norwegian.]

lem·on (lĕm′ən) *n.* **1. a.** A spiny evergreen tree, *Citrus limonia,* native to Asia, widely cultivated for its yellow, egg-shaped fruit. **b.** The fruit of this tree, with an aromatic rind and acid, juicy pulp. **2.** A bright, clear yellow. **3.** *Informal.*

ă pat   ā pay   â care   ä father   ĕ pet   ē be   hw which   ĭ pit   ī tie   î pier   ŏ pot   ō toe   ô paw, for   oi noise
oō took   oō boot   ou out   th thin   th this   ŭ cut   û urge   zh vision   ə about, item, edible, gallop, circus

Something or someone that is defective, unsuitable, or disappointing. —**modifier:** *lemon juice.* —*adj.* Bright, clear yellow. [Middle English *lymon,* from Old French *limon,* from Arabic *laymūn,* from Persian *līmūn.*]

lem·on·ade (lĕm′ə-nād′) *n.* A drink made of lemon juice, water, and sugar.

lem·pi·ra (lĕm-pîr′ə) *n.* The basic monetary unit of Honduras. [After *Lempira,* Indian leader who resisted the Spanish.]

le·mur (lē′mər) *n.* Any of several small, tree-living monkeylike animals chiefly of the family Lemuridae, with large eyes and a long tail. [From Latin *lemurēs,* ghosts (from its ghostly appearance and nocturnal habits).]

lend (lĕnd) *tr.v.* **lent** (lĕnt), **lend·ing.** **1.** To give or allow the use of (something) temporarily on the condition that it is to be returned. **2.** To provide (money) temporarily, usu. at a certain rate of interest. **3.** To contribute; impart: *Books lent a feeling of warmth to the room.* **4.** To put at another's service or use: *lend a helping hand.* —**idiom. lend (oneself) to.** To be suitable for: *laws that lend themselves to various interpretations.* [Middle English *lenden,* from Old English *lænan,* to lend, give.] —**lend′er** *n.*
   Syns: lend, advance, loan *v.* **Core meaning:** To supply (money), esp. on credit (*refused to lend us any more cash*).

lending library. A library from which books may be borrowed for a fee.

length (lĕngkth, lĕngth) *n.* **1.** The measurement of the extent of something along its greatest dimension: *the length of a boat.* **2.** A piece, usu. measured to a certain size, cut from a larger piece: *a length of silk.* **3.** A measure of something used as a unit to estimate distances: *an arm's length.* **4.** The full extent of something from beginning to end: *the length of a story.* **5.** The amount of time between specified moments; duration: *the length of a club meeting.* **6.** An extent to which an action or policy is carried; an extreme: *went to great lengths to prove him wrong.* —**idiom. at length. 1.** After some time; eventually. **2.** For a considerable time; fully. [Middle English *lengthe,* from Old English *lengthu.*]

length·en (lĕngk′thən, lĕng′-) *tr.v.* To make longer. —*intr.v.* To become longer.

length·wise (lĕngkth′wīz′, lĕngth′-) *adv.* Also **length·ways** (-wāz′). Along the direction of the length; longitudinally. —*adj.* Longitudinal.

length·y (lĕngk′thē, lĕng′-) *adj.* **-i·er, -i·est.** Of considerable length. —See Syns at **long.** —**length′i·ly** *adv.* —**length′i·ness** *n.*

le·ni·en·cy (lē′nē-ən-sē, lēn′yən-) *n., pl.* **-cies.** Also **le·ni·ence** (lē′nē-əns, lēn′yəns). **1.** The condition or quality of being lenient. **2.** A lenient action.

le·ni·ent (lē′nē-ənt, lēn′yənt) *adj.* **1.** Inclined not to be harsh; merciful: *a lenient judge.* **2.** Not austere or strict; generous: *lenient rules.* [Latin *lēniēns,* pres. part. of *lēnīre,* to soothe, make soft, from *lēnis,* soft.] —**le′ni·ent·ly** *adv.*

Len·in·ism (lĕn′ə-nĭz′əm) *n.* The theory and practice of proletarian revolution as developed by Lenin, an expansion of Marxism to include the theory of imperialism as the final form of capitalism and the shifting of the communist struggle from the developed to the underdeveloped countries. —**Len′in·ist** *n.*

lens (lĕnz) *n.* **1.** A carefully ground or molded piece of glass, plastic, or other transparent material that has opposite surfaces either or both of which are curved, by means of which light rays are refracted so that they converge or diverge to form an image. **2.** A combination of two or more such lenses, sometimes with other optical devices such as prisms, used to form an image for viewing or photographing. **3.** A transparent, biconvex body of the vertebrate eye between the iris and the vitreous humor that focuses light rays entering through the pupil to form an image on the retina. Also called **crystalline lens. 4.** Any device that causes radiation other than light to converge or diverge by an action analogous to that of an optical lens: *an electron lens.* [From Latin *lēns,* lentil (from the resemblance of an optical lens to a lentil seed).]

lent (lĕnt) *v.* Past tense and past participle of **lend.**

Lent (lĕnt) *n.* The 40 weekdays from Ash Wednesday until Easter observed by Christians as a season of fasting and penitence. [Middle English *lente,* spring, Lent, from Old English *lengten.*] —**Lent′en** *adj.*

len·ti·cel (lĕn′tĭ-sĕl′) *n. Bot.* One of the small pores on the surface of the stems of woody plants, that allows the passage of gases to and from the interior tissue. [From Latin *lēns,* lentil.]

len·til (lĕn′təl) *n.* **1.** A leguminous plant, *Lens esculenta* (or *L. culinaris*), native to the Old World, with pods that contain edible seeds. **2.** The round, flattened seed of this plant. [Middle English, from Old French *lentille,* from Latin *lenticula,* dim. of *lēns,* lentil.]

len·to (lĕn′tō) *Mus.* —*adv.* Slowly. —*adj.* Slow. [Italian, from Latin *lentus,* slow.]

Le·o (lē′ō) *n.* **1.** A constellation in the Northern Hemisphere near Cancer and Virgo. **2.** The fifth sign of the zodiac.

le·o·nine (lē′ə-nīn′) *adj.* Of, pertaining to, or characteristic of a lion. [Middle English, from Old French, from Latin *leōnīnus,* from *leō,* lion.]

leop·ard (lĕp′ərd) *n.* **1.** A large feline mammal, *Panthera pardus,* of Africa and Asia, that has a tawny coat with dark rosettelike markings and also a black color phase. **2.** Any of several similar felines, such as the cheetah or the snow leopard. —**modifier:** *a leopard coat.* [Middle English, from Old French, from Late Latin *leopardus,* from Late Greek *leopardos* : *leōn,* lion + *pardos,* pard.]

leop·ard·ess (lĕp′ər-dĭs) *n.* A female leopard.

le·o·tard (lē′ə-tärd′) *n.* Often **leotards.** A snugly fitting, stretchable one-piece garment that covers the torso, orig. worn by dancers and acrobats. [After Jules *Léotard,* 19th-cent. French aerialist.]

lep·er (lĕp′ər) *n.* **1.** A person afflicted with leprosy. **2.** A person avoided by others. [Middle English, from *leper,* leprosy, from Old French *lepre,* from Late Latin *lepra,* from Greek, from *lepros,* scaly.]

lep·i·dop·ter·an (lĕp′ĭ-dŏp′tər-ən) *n.* Also **lep·i·dop·ter·on** (-tə-rŏn′, -tər-ən) *pl.* **-ter·a** (-tə-rə). A lepidopterous insect. [From New Latin *Lepidoptera,* "scale-winged ones."]

lep·i·dop·ter·ist (lĕp′ĭ-dŏp′tər-ĭst) *n.* An entomologist who specializes in the study of butterflies and moths.

lep·i·dop·ter·ous (lĕp′ĭ-dŏp′tər-əs) *adj.* Of or belonging to the order Lepidoptera, which includes insects, such as the butterflies and moths, that have four wings covered with small scales.

lep·re·chaun (lĕp′rĭ-kôn′, -kŏn′) *n.* In Irish folklore, an elf who can reveal hidden treasure to someone who catches him. [Irish *leipracán.*]

lep·ro·sy (lĕp′rə-sē) *n.* An infectious bacterial disease that causes ulcers and sores on the body and in its severe forms causes progressive destruction of tissue, with paralysis and loss of sensation. Also called **Hansen's disease.**

lep·rous (lĕp′rəs) *adj.* **1.** Having leprosy. **2.** Of or suggesting leprosy. **3.** *Biol.* Having or consisting of loose, flaky scales. [Middle English, from Late Latin *leprōsus,* from *lepra,* leprosy.]

lep·ton (lĕp′tŏn′) *n.* Any of a family of subatomic particles that include the electron, the muon, and their associated neutrinos, all having spin equal to $1/2$ and masses less than those of the mesons. [Greek *leptos,* thin, small, + -ON.]

les·bi·an (lĕz′bē-ən) *n.* A female homosexual. —*adj.* Of or characteristic of female homosexuals. [After *Lesbos,* an island of Greece and the residence of Sappho and her supposedly homosexual followers.]

lese majesty (lēz′) *pl.* **lese majesties. 1.** An offense or crime committed against the ruler or supreme power of a state. **2.** An affront to another's dignity. [From Old French *lese-majeste,* from Latin *laesa mājestās,* "injured majesty."]

le·sion (lē′zhən) *n.* **1.** A wound or injury. **2.** A small, well-defined area of the body in which tissue has changed in a way that is characteristic of some disease. [Middle English *lesioun,* from Old French *lesion,* from Latin *laesiō,* from *laedere,* to injure, damage.]

les·pe·de·za (lĕs′pĭ-dē′zə) *n.* Any plant of the genus *Lespedeza,* which includes the bush clovers. [After Vincente Manuel de *Céspedes* (d. 1785), Spanish governor of East Florida.]

less (lĕs) *adj.* **1.** A comparative of **little.** Not as great in amount or quantity: *less time to spare.* **2.** Fewer: *less than ten.* **3.** Lower in rank or importance: *The guest was no less a person than the First Lady.* —See Usage note at **few.**

ă pat	ā pay	â care	ä father	ĕ pet	ē be	hw which
ŏŏ took	ōō boot	ou out	th thin	*th* this	ŭ cut	
			û urge	zh vision	ə about, item, edible, gallop, circus	

ĭ pit   ī tie   î pier   ŏ pot   ō toe   ô paw, for   oi noise

—*adv.* Comparative of **little.** To a smaller extent, degree, or frequency: *less frightened.* —*prep.* Minus; subtracting: *Six less 1 is 5.* —*n.* A smaller amount or share: *He got less than he asked for.* —*pron.* Fewer things or persons: *Many things begin badly; less end well.* —**idioms. less than.** Not at all: *a less than satisfactory reply.* **much** (**or still**) **less.** Certainly not: *I'm not accusing anybody, much less you.* [Middle English, from Old English *lǣssa.*]

-less. A suffix meaning lacking or without: **toothless, sleepless, blameless.** [Middle English *-lesse,* from Old English *-lēas,* from *lēas,* lacking, free from.]

les·see (lĕ-sē′) *n.* A tenant holding a lease. [Middle English, from Norman French, from Old French *lesser,* to lease.]

less·en (lĕs′ən) *tr.v.* To cause to decrease; make less. —*intr.v.* To decrease; become less. —See Syns at **decrease.**

less·er (lĕs′ər) *adj.* **1.** Smaller in size, importance, etc.: *a lesser evil.* **2.** Of a smaller size than other similar forms: *the lesser anteater.*

les·son (lĕs′ən) *n.* **1.** Something to be learned. **2.** A period of time devoted to teaching or learning a certain subject: *three piano lessons a week.* **3.** An assignment or exercise in which something is to be learned: *an algebra textbook divided into 40 lessons.* **4.** An experience, example, or observation from which beneficial new knowledge or wisdom may be learned. **5.** A reprimand or punishment. **6.** A reading from the Bible given as part of a religious service. [Middle English, a reading, from Old French *lecon,* from Latin *lectiō.*]

les·sor (lĕs-ôr′, lĕ-sôr′) *n.* A person who rents property to another by a lease. [Middle English *lessour,* from Norman French, from *lesser,* to lease.]

lest (lĕst) *conj.* For fear that; so as to prevent the possibility that: *tried to discourage her lest she be hurt.* [Middle English *leste,* from Old English *thȳ lǣs the,* whereby less.]

let¹ (lĕt) *tr.v.* **let, let·ting. 1.** To grant permission to; allow to: *She let him continue.* **2.** To cause; make: *Let me know what happened.* **3.** To allow as an assumption; suppose: *Let x equal 4.* **4.** To permit to move: *Let me in. Let the cat out.* **5.** To rent or lease: *lets his rooms to students.* **6.** To assign or grant (work) to another: *letting a construction job to the lowest bidder.* **7.** —Used as an auxiliary verb in the imperative to indicate: **a.** Request, proposal, or command: *Let's get going.* **b.** Warning or threat: *Just let him try to lay his hands on me!* **c.** Acceptance of or resignation to the inevitable: *Let things fall as they may.* —See Syns at **permit** and Usage note at **leave.** —*phrasal verbs.* **let down. 1.** To slow down; ease up: *We've nearly finished, so don't let down now!* **2.** To fail to support or satisfy; disappoint: *I trust you; please don't let me down.* **let off. 1.** To emit or release: *let off steam.* **2.** To excuse or dismiss: *let the workmen off early.* **3.** To release with little or no punishment: *He was let off with a year on probation.* **let on.** To allow it to be known: *Don't let on that you know me.* **let out. 1.** To give forth; emit: *let out a yelp.* **2.** To loosen or widen by releasing material from a seam: *let out a tight dress.* **let up.** To become slower or less intense; diminish: *The rain has begun to let up a bit.* [Middle English *leten,* from Old English *lǣtan,* to leave behind, leave undone.]

let² (lĕt) *n.* **1.** Obstacle; obstruction: *free to investigate without let or hindrance.* **2.** *Sports.* A served ball in tennis and other net games that must be replayed because it has touched the net before falling into the proper court. —*tr.v.* **let·ted** or **let, let·ting.** *Archaic.* To obstruct or hinder. [Middle English, a hindrance, from *letten,* to prevent, from Old English *lettan.*]

-let. A suffix meaning: **1.** Small: **booklet. 2.** An article worn on: **anklet.** [Middle English *-lette,* from Old French *-elet.*]

let·down (lĕt′doun′) *n.* **1.** A decrease or decline, as of effort or energy. **2.** A disappointment.

le·thal (lē′thəl) *adj.* Causing or capable of causing death: *a lethal dose of a drug; a lethal weapon.* —See Syns at **fatal.** [Latin *lethālis,* from *lēthum,* death.] —**le′thal·ly** *adv.* —**le′thal·ness** *n.*

lethal gene. A gene that does not permit an organism to develop and often kills it before it matures.

le·thar·gic (lə-thär′jĭk) *adj.* Of, causing, or in a condition of lethargy. —**le·thar′gi·cal·ly** *adv.*

leth·ar·gy (lĕth′ər-jē) *n., pl.* **-gies. 1.** Drowsy or sluggish indifference; apathy. **2.** An unconscious state resembling deep sleep. [Middle English *letargie,* from Old French *litargie,* from Latin *lēthargia,* drowsiness, from Greek, from *lēthē,* forgetfulness.]

Le·the (lē′thē) *n. Gk. Myth.* **1.** The river of forgetfulness in Hades. **2.** Often **lethe.** Loss of memory.

Le·to (lē′tō) *n. Gk. Myth.* A consort of Zeus and the mother of Apollo and Artemis.

let's (lĕts). Contraction of let us.

let·ter (lĕt′ər) *n.* **1.** A written symbol or mark that represents a speech sound and is used to spell words; one of the characters of an alphabet. **2.** A written or printed communication directed to an individual or organization. **3.** The literal meaning of something: *the letter of the law.* **4. letters.** Literary culture or learning: *a man of letters.* **5.** *Printing.* **a.** A piece of type that prints a single character. **b.** A specific style of type. —*tr.v.* **1.** To write letters on: *letter a poster.* **2.** To write in letters. —*intr.v.* To write or form letters. [Middle English, from Old French *lettre,* from Latin *littera,* letter of the alphabet.] —**let′ter·er** *n.*

let·ter·box (lĕt′ər-bŏks′) *n. Brit.* A mailbox.

letter carrier. A mailman.

let·tered (lĕt′ərd) *adj.* **1.** Educated to read and write; literate. **2.** Of or relating to literacy or learning. **3.** Inscribed or marked with letters.

let·ter·head (lĕt′ər-hĕd′) *n.* **1.** A printed heading at the top of a sheet of letter paper, usu. including a name and address. **2.** Stationery with such a heading.

let·ter·ing (lĕt′ər-ĭng) *n.* **1.** The act, process, or art of forming letters. **2.** Letters inscribed, as on a sign.

let·ter-per·fect (lĕt′ər-pûr′fĭkt) *adj.* Correct to the last detail.

let·ter·press (lĕt′ər-prĕs′) *n.* The process of printing from a raised inked surface.

letters of marque (märk). Also **letter of marque. 1.** A document issued by a nation allowing a private citizen to seize citizens or goods of another nation. **2.** A document issued by a nation allowing a private citizen to act as a privateer, by equipping a ship with arms in order to attack enemy ships. [Middle English, from Old French *marque,* reprisal.]

letters patent. *Law.* A document issued by a sovereign or government granting an exclusive right or title, esp. the right to manufacture, sell, or franchise an invention for a specified number of years.

let·tuce (lĕt′əs) *n.* **1. a.** Any of various plants of the genus *Lactuca,* esp. *L. sativa,* cultivated for its edible leaves. **b.** The leaves of *L. sativa,* eaten as salad. **2.** *Slang.* Paper money. [Middle English *letuse,* from Old French *laituës,* from Latin *lactūca,* from *lac,* milk (from its milky juice).]

let·up (lĕt′ŭp′) *n.* **1.** A reduction in pace, force, or intensity; a slowdown. **2.** A temporary stop; a pause.

leu·cine (loo′sēn′) *n.* An essential amino acid $C_6H_{13}O_2$, derived from the hydrolysis of protein. [LEUC(O)- + -INE.]

leuco-. Var. of **leuko-.**

leu·co·plast (loo′kə-plăst′) *n.* Also **leu·co·plas·tid** (-plăs′tĭd). A colorless plastid in the cytoplasm of plant cells, around which starch collects. [LEUCO- + PLAST(ID).]

leuk-. Var. of **leuko-.**

leu·ke·mi·a (loo-kē′mē-ə) *n.* Any of a group of diseases in which the leukocytes increase in uncontrolled numbers; cancer of the blood. [LEUK(O)- + -EMIA.]

leuko- or **leuk-** or **leuco-.** A prefix meaning: **1.** White or colorless: **leucoplast. 2.** Leukocyte: **leukemia.** [From Greek *leukos,* clear, white.]

leu·ko·cyte (loo′kə-sīt′) *n.* Also **leu·co·cyte.** Any of the white or colorless nucleated cells that appear in blood, many of which function as a defense against infection. Also called **white blood cell.** [LEUKO- + -CYTE.] —**leu′ko·cyt′ic** (-sĭt′ĭk) *adj.*

leu·ko·cy·to·sis (loo′kō-sī-tō′sĭs) *n., pl.* **-ses** (-sēz′). Also **leu·co·cy·to·sis.** A large increase in the number of leukocytes in the blood. [LEUKOCYT(E) + -OSIS.] —**leu′ko·cy·tot′ic** (-tŏt′ĭk) *adj.*

leu·ko·pe·ni·a (loo′kə-pē′nē-ə) *n.* Also **leu·co·pe·ni·a.** An abnormally low number of leukocytes in the circulating blood. [LEUKO- + Greek *penia*, lack.]

le·va·tor (lə-vā′tər) *n., pl.* **lev·a·to·res** (lĕv′ə-tôr′ēz, -tōr′-) or **-tors.** *Anat.* A muscle that raises a part. [From Latin *levāre,* to raise.]

lev·ee¹ (lĕv′ē) *n.* **1.** A bank of earth, concrete, or other material raised along a river to keep it from flooding. **2.** A landing place on a river; pier. [French, from Old French, "raising," from *lever,* to raise.]

lev·ee² (lĕv′ē, lə-vē′) *n.* **1.** A reception orig. held by a monarch or other high-ranking person upon arising from bed. **2.** A formal reception, as at a court. [French *levé,* var. of *lever,* rising, from *lever,* to rise.]

lev·el (lĕv′əl) *n.* **1.** A height or depth: *a platform at knee level.* **2.** A standard elevation from which other heights and depths are measured: *below sea level.* **3.** A relative position, rank, or class: *people of all levels of society; a high level of education.* **4.** Also **spirit level.** A liquid-filled tube containing an air bubble that moves to a center window when the tube is set on a perfectly horizontal surface. **5.** A flat, smooth surface. —*adj.* **1.** Having a flat, smooth surface: *level farmland.* **2.** Horizontal: *at an angle, not level.* **3.** Steady; uniform; unwavering: *a level tone.* **4.** Being at the same height, rank, or position; even: *a night table level with the bed.* —*tr.v.* **-eled** or **-elled, -el·ing** or **-el·ling.** **1.** To make horizontal, flat, or even: *leveled the lawn with a roller.* **2.** To tear down; raze: *The tornado leveled buildings.* **3.** To knock down with or as if with a blow: *The boxer leveled his opponent.* **4.** To place on the same level; equalize. **5.** To aim along a horizontal plane: *level a gun at her head.* **6.** To direct emphatically or forcefully toward someone: *level charges of dishonesty at her.* —*intr.v.* **1.** To render persons or things equal; equalize. **2.** To aim a weapon horizontally. **3.** *Informal.* To be frank and open: *The negotiators began by leveling with each other.* —See Syns at **destroy.** —*phrasal verb.* **level off.** **1.** To move toward stability or consistency. **2.** To maneuver an aircraft into flight that is horizontal after gaining or losing altitude. —*idioms.* **(one's) level best.** The best one can do in an earnest attempt. **on the level.** *Informal.* Without deception or dishonesty. [Middle English, from Old French *livel,* from Latin *lībella,* dim. of *lībra,* balance, level.] —**lev′el·er** *n.* —**lev′el·ly** *adv.* —**lev′el·ness** *n.*
 Syns: **level, flat, flush, plane, smooth, straight** *adj. Core meaning:* Having no irregularities, roughness, or indentations (*level boards*).

lev·el·head·ed (lĕv′əl-hĕd′ĭd) *adj.* Self-composed and sensible. —**lev′el·head′ed·ness** *n.*

lev·er (lĕv′ər, lē′vər) *n.* **1.** A simple machine consisting of a rigid bar or rod that turns on a fixed pivot or fulcrum. **2.** A projecting handle used to control, adjust, or operate a device or machine.. **3.** A means of accomplishment: *used his friendship as a lever to a career.* —*tr.v.* To move or lift with a lever. [Middle English, from Old French *leveor,* from *lever,* to raise, from Latin *levāre,* from *levis,* light.]

lev·er·age (lĕv′ər-ĭj, lē′vər-) *n.* **1.** The action or mechanical advantage of a lever. **2.** Power to act effectively: *Being on two committees gave him leverage.*

lev·er·et (lĕv′ər-ĭt) *n.* A young hare, esp. one less than a year old. [Middle English, from Norman French *leveret,* dim. of *levre,* hare, from Latin *lepus.*]

le·vi·a·than (lə-vī′ə-thən) *n.* **1.** In the Old Testament, a monstrous sea creature. **2.** Any very large animal. **3.** Anything unusually large for its kind. [Middle English, from Late Latin, from Hebrew *libhyāthān.*]

Le·vi's (lē′vīz′) *n.* A trademark for close-fitting trousers of heavy denim.

lev·i·tate (lĕv′ĭ-tāt′) *v.* **-tat·ed, -tat·ing.** —*intr.v.* To rise into the air and float, in apparent defiance of gravity. —*tr.v.* To cause to rise into the air and float. [From LEVITY.] —**lev′i·ta′tion** *n.* —**lev′i·ta′tor** *n.*

Le·vit·i·cus (lə-vĭt′ĭ-kəs) *n.* See table at **Bible.**

lev·i·ty (lĕv′ĭ-tē) *n., pl.* **-ties.** A light manner or attitude, esp. when inappropriate; frivolity. [Latin *levitās,* from *levis,* light.]

lev·u·lose (lĕv′yə-lōs′) *n.* Fructose. [Latin *laevus,* left (from the counterclockwise polarization of light by its solution) + -OSE.]

lev·y (lĕv′ē) *v.* **-ied, -y·ing.** —*tr.v.* **1.** To impose or collect (a tax, fine, etc.). **2.** To draft into military service. **3.** To declare and carry on: *the power to levy war.* —*intr.v.* To confiscate property, esp. in accordance with a legal judgment. —*n., pl.* **-ies.** **1.** The act or process of levying. **2.** Money, property, or troops levied. [Middle English *levee,* from Old French, a raising, from *lever,* to raise.] —**lev′i·er** *n.*

lewd (lōōd) *adj.* **-er, -est.** **1.** Depicting or referring to sex in a coarse or insulting way; obscene; indecent. **2.** Preoccupied with sexual desire; lustful. [Middle English, ignorant, vulgar, from Old English *lǣwede,* lay, nonclerical.] —**lewd′ly** *adv.* —**lewd′ness** *n.*

lex·i·cal (lĕk′sĭ-kəl) *adj.* **1.** Of or relating to the vocabulary or words of a language. **2.** Of lexicography or a lexicon. [From LEXICON.] —**lex′i·cal·ly** *adv.*

lex·i·cog·ra·phy (lĕk′sĭ-kŏg′rə-fē) *n.* The process or work of writing or compiling a dictionary or dictionaries. [LEXICO(N) + -GRAPHY.] —**lex′i·cog′ra·pher** *n.* —**lex′i·co·graph′ic** (-kə-grăf′ĭk) or **lex′i·co·graph′i·cal** *adj.* —**lex′i·co·graph′i·cal·ly** *adv.*

lex·i·con (lĕk′sĭ-kŏn′) *n.* **1.** A dictionary, esp. one that gives translations of words from an ancient language. **2.** A stock of terms used in a particular subject or profession; vocabulary: *the lexicon of sports.* —See Syns at **language.** [From Greek *lexikon (biblion),* (book) pertaining to words, from *lexis,* word, from *legein,* to speak.]

Ley·den jar (līd′n). An early form of capacitor consisting of a glass jar covered inside and out with metal foil and having a conductor that contacts the inner foil lining and passes out of the jar through an insulated stopper. [After *Leyden,* a city in the Netherlands.]

Lha·sa ap·so (lä′sə äp′sō, läs′ə äp′sō). A small dog of a Tibetan breed, with a long, straight coat. [*Lhasa,* a city in Tibet + Tibetan *apso,* Lhasa apso.]

Lhasa apso

Li The symbol for the element lithium.

li·a·bil·i·ty (lī′ə-bĭl′ĭ-tē) *n., pl.* **-ties.** **1.** Something that one owes; an obligation; debt. **2.** Legal responsibility to fulfill some contract or obligation. **3.** Something that holds one back; a hindrance; handicap. **4.** A tendency; susceptibility.

li·a·ble (lī′ə-bəl) *adj.* **1.** Legally obligated; responsible: *liable for the damages.* **2.** Susceptible; subject: *delicate skin, liable to sunburn.* **3.** Likely; apt: *liable to make mistakes.* [From Old French *lier,* to bind, from Latin *ligāre.*]

li·ai·son (lē′ā-zŏn′, lē-ā′zŏn′, lē′ə-) *n.* **1.** Communication between different offices or units of an organization. **2.** A channel or means of communication: *He served as the President's liaison with Congress.* **3.** A love affair. **4.** In French and some other languages, the pronunciation of the usu. silent final consonant of a word when followed by a word beginning with a vowel. [French, from Old French, "binding," from *lier,* to bind.]

li·an·a (lē-än′ə, -ăn′ə) *n.* Also **li·ane** (-än′). Any of various high-climbing, usu. woody vines common in the tropics. [French *liane,* perh. from *lier,* to bind.]

li·ar (lī′ər) *n.* A person who tells lies.

li·ba·tion (lī-bā′shən) *n.* **1. a.** The pouring of a liquid offering as a religious ritual. **b.** The liquid poured. **2.** *Informal.* A drink, esp. an alcoholic beverage. [Middle English *libacioun,* from Latin *lībātiō,* from *lībāre,* to taste, pour out as an offering.]

li·bel (lī′bəl) *n.* **1.** Any written, printed, or pictorial statement that damages a person's reputation or exposes a person to ridicule. **2.** The act of presenting a libel to the public. —*tr.v.* **-beled** or **-belled, -bel·ing** or **-bel·ling.** To make or publish a libel about. [Middle English, formal written claim of a plaintiff, from Old French, from Latin

ă pat	ā pay	â care	ä father	ĕ pet	ē be	hw which	ĭ pit	ī tie	î pier	ŏ pot	ō toe	ô paw, for	oi noise
ōō took	ōō boot	ou out		th thin	*th* this	ŭ cut		û urge	zh vision	ə about, item, edible, gallop, circus			

libellus, petition, dim. of *liber*, book.] —**li'bel·er** or **li'bel·ist** *n.* —**li'bel·ous** *adj.*

lib·er·al (lĭb′ər-əl, lĭb′rəl) *adj.* **1.** Tending to give generously: *a liberal benefactor.* **2.** Generous in amount; ample: *a liberal tip.* **3.** Loose; approximate: *a liberal adaptation of the novel for the screen.* **4.** Of or relating to the liberal arts. **5.** Respectful of different people and ideas; tolerant. **6.** Having or expressing political views that favor civil liberties, democratic reforms, and the use of governmental power to promote social progress. **7. Liberal.** Of or belonging to a political party that advocates liberal social or political views, esp. in Great Britain, the United States, and Canada. —See Syns at **generous.** —*n.* **1.** A person with liberal ideas or opinions. **2. Liberal.** A member of a Liberal political party. [Middle English, from Old French, from Latin *liberālis*, from *liber*, free.] —**lib'er·al·ly** *adv.* —**lib'er·al·ness** *n.*

liberal arts. College studies such as languages, history, and philosophy as distinguished from the sciences or technical studies.

lib·er·al·ism (lĭb′ər-ə-lĭz′əm, lĭb′rə-) *n.* **1.** Liberal views and policies, esp. in regard to social or political questions. **2.** Often **Liberalism.** A liberalizing movement within Protestantism.

lib·er·al·i·ty (lĭb′ə-răl′ĭ-tē) *n.*, *pl.* **-ties. 1.** Generosity. **2.** Openness of mind or attitude; tolerance.

lib·er·al·ize (lĭb′ər-ə-līz′, lĭb′rə-) *v.* **-ized, -iz·ing.** —*tr.v.* To make liberal or more liberal. —*intr.v.* To become liberal or more liberal. —**lib'er·al·i·za'tion** *n.*

lib·er·ate (lĭb′ə-rāt′) *tr.v.* **-at·ed, -at·ing. 1.** To set free, as from oppression, confinement or foreign control. **2.** *Chem.* To release from combination, as a gas. **3.** *Slang.* To obtain by looting: *some fine brandy we had liberated from the Germans.* —See Syns at **free.** [From Latin *liberāre*, from *liber*, free.] —**lib'er·a'tion** *n.* —**lib'er·a'tion·ist** *n.* —**lib'er·a'tor** *n.*

lib·er·tar·i·an (lĭb′ər-târ′ē-ən) *n.* **1.** A person who believes in freedom of action and thought. **2.** A person who believes in free will. [From LIBERTY.] —**lib'er·tar'i·an·ism** *n.*

lib·er·tine (lĭb′ər-tēn′) *n.* Someone who acts irresponsibly and immorally; a dissolute person. —*adj.* Morally unrestrained; dissolute. [Middle English *libertyn*, freed slave, from Latin *libertīnus*, from *liber*, free.] —**lib'er·tin·ism** *n.*

lib·er·ty (lĭb′ər-tē) *n.*, *pl.* **-ties. 1. a.** Freedom from restriction or control. **b.** Freedom of action, belief, or expression. **c.** Freedom from confinement, servitude, or forced labor. **2.** Political freedom from unjust or undue government control. **3.** A legal right to engage in certain actions without control or interference: *the liberties protected by the Bill of Rights.* **4.** Often **liberties. a.** A social action regarded as more familiar than polite convention permits: *Is it a liberty to use your first name?* **b.** A statement, attitude, or action not warranted by conditions or actualities: *a historical novel that takes liberties with chronology.* **5.** A period during which a sailor is authorized to go ashore. —See Syns at **freedom.** —*idiom.* **at liberty. 1.** Not in confinement or under constraint; free. **2.** Allowed: *at liberty to leave.* **3.** Not employed, occupied, or in use. [Middle English *liberte*, from Old French, from Latin *libertās*, from *liber*, free.]

li·bid·i·nous (lĭ-bĭd′n-əs) *adj.* **1.** Characterized by or having lustful desires; licentious; lascivious. **2.** Of or pertaining to the libido. [Middle English *lybydynous*, from Latin *libidinōsus*, from *libīdō*, desire.]

li·bi·do (lĭ-bē′dō, -bī′-) *n.*, *pl.* **-dos. 1.** The psychic and emotional energy associated with basic biological urges or drives. **2.** Sexual desire. [Latin *libīdō*, desire, lust.] —**li·bid'i·nal** (lĭ-bĭd′n-əl) *adj.*

Li·bra (lī′brə, lē′-) *n.* **1.** A constellation in the Southern Hemisphere near Scorpio and Virgo. **2.** The seventh sign of the zodiac.

li·brar·i·an (lī-brâr′ē-ən) *n.* A person who is a specialist in library work. —**li·brar'i·an·ship'** *n.*

li·brar·y (lī′brĕr′ē) *n.*, *pl.* **-ies. 1.** A place to keep literary and artistic materials, such as books, periodicals, newspapers, pamphlets, and prints, for reading, reference, or borrowing. **2.** A collection of such literary and artistic materials. [Middle English *librarie*, from Old French *librairie*, from Latin *librāria (taberna)*, book (shop), from *liber*, book.]

li·bret·tist (lĭ-brĕt′ĭst) *n.* The author of a libretto.

li·bret·to (lĭ-brĕt′ō) *n.*, *pl.* **-tos** or **-bret·ti** (-brĕt′ē). **1.** The text of an opera, musical comedy, or other dramatic musical work. **2.** A book that contains such a text. [Italian, dim. of *libro*, book, from Latin *liber.*]

lice (līs) *n.* A plural of **louse.**

li·cense (lī′səns). Also *Brit.* **li·cence.** —*n.* **1. a.** Official or legal permission to do or own a specified thing. **b.** Proof of permission granted, usu. in the form of a document, card, plate, or tag. **3.** Deviation from normal rules, practices, or methods in order to achieve a certain end or effect: *poetic license.* **4.** Latitude of action, esp. in behavior or speech. **5.** Lack of due restraint; excessive freedom. —*tr.v.* **-censed, -cens·ing. 1.** To give or yield permission to or for. **2.** To grant a license to or for; authorize. [Middle English, from Old French, from Latin *licentia*, freedom, from *licēre*, to be lawful, be permitted.] —**li'cens·a·ble** *adj.* —**li'cens·er** *n.*

li·cens·ee (lī′sən-sē′) *n.* A person to whom a license has been granted.

li·cen·tious (lī-sĕn′shəs) *adj.* Defying all rules of conduct; unrestrained; immoral. [Latin *licentiōsus*, from *licentia*, freedom, license.] —**li·cen'tious·ly** *adv.* —**li·cen'tious·ness** *n.*

li·chee (lē′chē) *n.* Var. of **litchi.**

li·chen (lī′kən) *n.* Any of numerous plants that consist of a fungus, usu. of the class Ascomycetes, in close combination with certain of the green or blue-green algae and that characteristically form a crustlike, scaly, or branching growth on rocks or tree trunks. [Latin *līchēn*, from Greek *leikhēn*.] —**li'chen·ous** *adj.*

lich gate (lĭch). Also **lych gate.** A roofed gateway to a churchyard, used orig. as a resting place for a bier before burial. [Middle English *lycheyate* : *lich*, body, corpse, from Old English *līc* + *yate*, gate.]

lic·it (lĭs′ĭt) *adj.* Within the law; legal. —See Syns at **legal.** [Middle English, from Latin *licitus*, from *licēre*, to be permitted.] —**lic'it·ly** *adv.* —**lic'it·ness** *n.*

lick (lĭk) *tr.v.* **1.** To pass the tongue over or along. **2.** To lap up. **3.** To move over or flicker at like a tongue: *The waves licked the rocks lining the shore.* **4.** *Slang.* To punish with a beating; thrash. **5.** *Slang.* To get the better of; defeat: *licked her weight problem.* —*intr.v.* To pass or move quickly and rapidly: *The flames licked at our feet.* —See Syns at **defeat.** —*n.* **1.** A movement of the tongue over something. **2.** A small amount. **3.** A deposit of exposed natural salt that is licked by passing animals. **4.** A blow. —*idioms.* **lick and a promise.** A superficial effort made without care or enthusiasm. **lick (one's) chops.** To anticipate delightedly. **lick (one's) wounds.** To recuperate after a defeat. [Middle English *licken*, from Old English *liccian*.] —**lick'er** *n.*

lick·e·ty-split (lĭk′ĭ-tē-splĭt′) *adv.* *Informal.* With great speed. [From LICK and SPLIT.]

lick·ing (lĭk′ĭng) *n.* **1.** *Slang.* A beating; thrashing. **2.** *Slang.* A severe loss or defeat.

lick·spit·tle (lĭk′spĭt′l) *n.* Someone who flatters others for personal gain; a toady.

lic·o·rice (lĭk′ər-ĭs, -ĭsh) *n.* Also *Brit.* **liqu·o·rice. 1.** A plant, *Glycyrrhiza glabra*, of the Mediterranean region, with blue flowers and a sweet, distinctively flavored root. **2.** The root of licorice, used as a flavoring in candy, liquors, tobacco, and medicines. **3.** A chewy, often black candy flavored with an extract from licorice root. [Middle English, from Old French *licoresse*, from Late Latin *liquirītia*, from Greek *glukurrhiza* : *glukus*, sweet + *rhiza*, root.]

lic·tor (lĭk′tər) *n.* A Roman functionary who carried fasces in attendance on a magistrate. [Latin.]

lid (lĭd) *n.* **1.** A removable cover for a hollow receptacle: *the lid of a jar.* **2.** An eyelid. **3.** A curb or restraint: *put a lid on crime.* **4.** *Slang.* A hat. —*tr.v.* **lid·ded, lid·ding.** To cover with or as if with a lid. —*idiom.* **flip (one's) lid.** *Slang.* To lose one's composure or sanity. [Middle English, from Old English *hlid*, covering, gate, opening.] —**lid'less** *adj.*

lie¹ (lī) *intr.v.* **lay** (lā), **lain** (lān), **ly·ing. 1.** To be in or place oneself in a flat, horizontal, or recumbent position; recline: *He lay down under an elm to sleep.* **2.** To be placed on or supported by a surface that is usu. horizontal: *Dirty dishes lay on the table.* **3.** To be or remain in a specific condition: *The dust has lain undisturbed for years.* **4.** To exist; be inherent: *The answer lies in further research.* **5.** To occupy a place: *The spring lies beyond this hill.* **6.** To extend: *Our land lies between these trees and the river.* —See Usage note at **lay.** —*phrasal verbs.* **lie in.** To be in confinement for childbirth. **lie to.** *Naut.* To remain stationary while facing the wind. **lie with. 1.** To be decided by, dependent upon, or up to: *The choice lies with you.* **2.** *Archaic.* To have sexual intercourse with. —*n.* **1.** The manner or position in which something is situated: *the uneven lie of the hillside.* **2.** A haunt or hiding place of an animal. —*idioms.* **lie down on the job.** To do less than one can or should. **lie in wait. 1.** To remain alert or in readiness. **2.** To prepare an ambush. **lie low.** To keep oneself or one's plans hidden. [Middle English *lien,* from Old English *licgan.*]

lie² (lī) *intr.v.* **lied, ly·ing. 1.** To present false information with the intention of deceiving: *lied about his prison record.* **2.** To convey a false image or impression: *Appearances often lie.* —*n.* **1.** A false statement deliberately presented as being true; a falsehood. **2.** Anything meant to deceive or give a wrong impression. —*idiom.* **give the lie to. 1.** To accuse of lying. **2.** To prove to be untrue. [Middle English *lien,* from Old English *lēogan.*]

   Syns: lie, **faslehood, falsity, fib, fiction, story, tale, untruth** *n.* *Core meaning:* An untrue declaration (*spread lies about the star's personal life*).

lied (lēd, lēt) *n., pl.* **lie·der** (lē'dər). A German lyric song. [German *Lied,* song.]

lie detector. A machine that records changes in heartbeat, blood pressure, and other physiological functions for the purpose of determining whether an individual is lying; polygraph.

lief (lēf) *adv.* Readily; willingly: *I would as lief go now as later.* [Middle English *leef,* from *leef,* beloved, from Old English *lēof.*]

liege (lēj) *n.* **1.** A lord or sovereign in feudal times. **2.** A vassal or subject owing allegiance and services to a liege. —*adj.* **1.** Entitled to the loyalty and services of vassals or subjects: *a liege lord.* **2.** Bound to give allegiance and services to a lord or monarch: *a liege subject.* **3.** Loyal. —See Syns at **faithful.** [Middle English, from Old French, from Late Latin *laetus,* serf.]

liege·man (lēj'mən) *n.* **1.** A feudal vassal or subject. **2.** A loyal supporter or follower.

lien (lēn, lē'ən) *n.* The legal right to take or hold the property of someone who owes one money until the debt has been repaid. [Old French *loien,* bond, tie, from Latin *ligāmen,* from *ligāre,* to bind.]

lieu (lōō) *n.* **1.** *Archaic.* Place; stead. **2. in lieu of.** In place of; instead of. [Middle English *liue,* from Old French *lieu,* from Latin *locus,* place.]

lieu·ten·ant (lōō-tēn'ənt) *n.* **1.** An officer in the U.S. Army, Air Force, or Marine Corps ranking below a captain. A **first lieutenant** ranks above a **second lieutenant. 2.** An officer in the U.S. Navy ranking above an ensign and below a lieutenant commander. **3.** An officer in a police or fire department ranking below a captain. **4.** One who can act in place of his superior; a deputy. [Middle English *lieutenaunt,* vice regent, from Old French *lieutenant* : *lieu,* place + *tenant,* pres. part. of *tenir,* to hold, from Latin *tenēre.*] —**lieu·ten'an·cy** *n.*

lieutenant colonel. An officer in the U.S. Army, Air Force, or Marine Corps ranking above a major and below a colonel.

lieutenant commander. An officer in the U.S. Navy or Coast Guard ranking above a lieutenant and below a commander.

lieutenant general. An officer in the U.S. Army, Air Force, or Marine Corps ranking above a major general and below a general.

lieutenant governor. 1. An elected state official ranking just below the governor. **2.** The nonelective chief of government of a Canadian province.

life (līf) *n., pl.* **lives** (līvz). **1.** The property or quality that distinguishes living organisms from dead organisms and nonliving matter, shown in the ability to grow, carry on metabolism, respond to stimuli, and reproduce. **2.** The period of time between birth and death; lifetime: *He lived there for the rest of his life.* **3.** The time for which something exists or works: *the useful life of a car.* **4.** Living organisms in general: *plant life; marine life.* **5.** A living

being: *The earthquake claimed hundreds of lives.* **6.** Human existence or activity in general: *city life; real life.* **7.** A manner of living: *the outdoor life.* **8.** Liveliness or vitality; animation: *His face was eager, bright, and full of life.* **9.** A source of vitality; animating force: *She's the life of the show.* **10.** An account of a person's life; a biography. **11.** Actual environment or reality; nature. —*modifier:* *life imprisonment; a life story.* —*idioms.* **come to life.** To become animated; grow lively. **for dear life.** Desperately or urgently. **for the life of (one).** *Informal.* Though trying hard: *For the life of me I couldn't remember his name.* **not on your life.** *Informal.* Not for any reason; definitely not. [Middle English, from Old English *līf.*]

life belt. A life preserver worn like a belt.

life·blood (līf'blŭd') *n.* The indispensable vital part of a thing: *Capable workers are the lifeblood of a business.*

life·boat (līf'bōt') *n.* **1.** A boat carried on a ship for use if the ship has to be abandoned. **2.** A boat used for rescue service.

life buoy. A ring made of cork or other buoyant material for keeping a person afloat.

life cycle. The series of changes through which a living thing passes from the time it begins to exist to the mature stage in which it can take part in the process of reproduction that will again start the series for a new organism or organisms.

life expectancy. The number of years that an individual is expected to live as determined by statistics.

life·guard (līf'gärd') *n.* An expert swimmer employed to safeguard swimmers or bathers.

life history. 1. The history of changes undergone by an organism from the beginning of its existence to its present state or its death. **2.** The developmental history of an individual or group in society.

life insurance. Insurance on a person's life, guaranteeing a certain sum of money to an individual upon the death of the insured.

life jacket. A personal flotation device in the form of a jacket or vest.

life·less (līf'lĭs) *adj.* **1.** Having no life; inanimate: *lifeless puppets.* **2.** Not inhabited by living beings: *a lifeless planet.* **3.** Having lost life; dead. **4.** Lacking vitality or animation: *lifeless colors.* —See Syns at **dead.** —**life'less·ly** *adv.* —**life'less·ness** *n.*

life·like (līf'līk') *adj.* **1.** Resembling a living thing: *a lifelike statue of the actress.* **2.** Accurately representing real life: *a lifelike description.* —**life'like'ness** *n.*

life·line (līf'līn') *n.* **1.** An anchored line thrown as a support to someone falling or drowning. **2.** A line shot to a ship in distress. **3.** A line used to raise and lower deep-sea divers. **4.** Any means or route by which necessary supplies are transported.

life·long (līf'lông', -lŏng') *adj.* Continuing for a lifetime.

life preserver. A buoyant device, usu. in the shape of a ring, belt, or jacket, designed to keep a person afloat in the water; personal flotation device.

lif·er (lī'fər) *n.* *Slang.* A prisoner serving a life sentence.

life raft. A raft or flat-bottomed boat usu. made of wood or inflatable material and used to rescue people who have abandoned a ship or airplane.

life·sav·er (līf'sā'vər) *n.* **1.** Someone or something that saves another's life. **2.** A lifeguard. **3.** A person or thing that provides help in a crisis or emergency. **4.** A life preserver shaped like a ring.

life·sav·ing (līf'sā'vĭng) *n.* The techniques or skills used to save lives and rescue people, esp. in water emergencies. —*modifier:* *lifesaving equipment.*

life·size (līf'sīz') *adj.* Also **life-sized** (-sīzd'). Being of the same size as the original: *a life-size statue.*

life span. The period of time during which an organism remains alive.

life·style or **life-style** (līf'stīl') *n.* Also **life style.** A way of life or style of living that reflects the attitudes and values of an individual or a group.

life-sup·port system (līf'sə-pôrt', -pōrt'). **1.** The equipment that keeps conditions in a spacecraft such that the crew can live. **2.** Equipment in a hospital that allows a patient who might not be able to survive independently to continue to live.

ă pat	ā pay	â care	ä father	ĕ pet	ē be	hw which	ĭ pit	ī tie	î pier	ŏ pot	ō toe	ô paw, for	oi noise
ŏŏ took	ōō boot	ou out	th thin	*th* this	ŭ cut		û urge	zh vision	ə about, item, edible, gallop, circus				

life·time (līf'tīm') *n.* **1.** The period of time during which an individual is alive. **2.** The period of time during which an object, property, process, or phenomenon exists or functions.

life·work (līf'wûrk') *n.* The chief or entire work of a person's lifetime.

lift (lĭft) *tr.v.* **1.** To direct or carry from a lower to a higher position; raise; elevate. **2.** To take back or remove; revoke; rescind: *lift a ban.* **3.** To project or sound in loud, clear tones: *They lifted their voices in song.* **4.** *Informal.* To steal; pilfer. **5.** *Informal.* To copy from something already published; plagiarize. —*intr.v.* **1.** To rise; ascend. **2.** To disappear or disperse by or as if by rising: *By afternoon the clouds had lifted.* **3.** To improve in condition or mood: *Their spirits lifted when help arrived.* —See Syns at **raise.** —*phrasal verb.* **lift off.** To begin flight, as a rocket or spacecraft. —*n.* **1.** An example of lifting or being lifted. **2.** A short ride in a vehicle. **3.** The extent, height, or distance something is raised. **4.** An elevation of the spirit: *The news gave us a big lift.* **5. a.** A machine or device designed to pick up, raise, or carry something. **b.** A cable used for carrying people up a slope. **6.** One of the layers of leather, rubber, or other material making up the heel of a shoe. **7.** Any kind of assistance or help. **8.** *Brit.* An elevator. **9.** *Aviation.* The component of the total aerodynamic force acting on an airfoil, or on an entire aircraft or winged missile, perpendicular to the relative wind and normally exerted in an upward direction, opposing the pull of gravity. [Middle English *liften,* from Old Norse *lypta.*] —**lift'er** *n.*

lift-off (lĭft'ôf', -ŏf') *n.* The initial movement by which or instant in which a rocket or other craft begins flight.

lig·a·ment (lĭg'ə-mənt) *n.* A sheet or band of tough, fibrous tissue that connects two or more bones or cartilages or supports an organ, fascia, or muscle. [Middle English, from Latin *ligāmentum,* bond, bandage, from *ligāre,* to bind.] —**lig'a·men'tous** (-mĕn'təs) *adj.*

li·gate (lī'gāt') *tr.v.* **-gat·ed, -gat·ing.** To tie up with a ligature. [From Latin *ligāre.*] —**li·ga'tion** *n.*

lig·a·ture (lĭg'ə-choŏr', -chər) *n.* **1.** The act of tying together or binding. **2.** A cord, wire, or bandage used for tying, binding, or constricting. **3.** A surgical thread, wire, cord, etc., applied in a tight loop, as to close vessels or tie off ducts. **4.** *Printing.* A character or type combining two or more letters, as æ.

light¹ (līt) *n.* **1. a.** Any electromagnetic radiation that can be perceived by the normal, unaided human eye, having wavelengths between about 3,900 angstroms and about 7,700 angstroms. **b.** Electromagnetic radiation with wavelengths just beyond those of visible light: *infrared light; ultraviolet light.* **2. a.** A source of either of these types of radiation, esp. an electric lamp: *Leave a light burning in the hallway.* **b.** Any mechanical object that uses such radiation as a signal or warning, esp. a traffic signal or beacon. **3.** The illumination derived from such a source. **4.** The sensation of perceiving such radiation: *The sudden light made him blink.* **5. a.** Daylight. **b.** Dawn; daybreak. **6.** Visible light considered necessary for seeing: *enough light to read by.* **7.** Something that admits light, as a window. **8.** A source of fire, as a match or cigarette lighter: *Mister, have you got a light?* **9.** Public attention; general knowledge: *They brought the scandal to light.* **10.** A way of looking at or considering a certain matter: *This puts the whole thing in a different light.* **11. lights.** One's individual opinions, choices, or life philosophy: *They acted according to their own lights.* **12.** A prominent or distinguished person: *one of the leading lights of the theater.* **13.** An expression of the eyes or face. **14.** A bright or pale shade of color: *the lights and darks in a painting.* —*modifier:* a light bulb; light rays. —*adj.* **-er, -est. 1.** Not dark; bright: *a light room with the curtains opened.* **2.** Not dark in color; fair: *light hair and skin.* **3.** Being mixed with white: *a light pink.* —*v.* **light·ed** or **lit** (lĭt), **light·ing.** —*tr.v.* **1.** To set on fire; ignite; kindle: *light the oven.* **2.** To cause to give out light; make luminous: *light a lamp.* **3.** To provide, cover, or fill with light; illuminate: *light the room.* —*intr.v.* To start to burn; be ignited or kindled: *Green wood will not light easily.* —See Syns at **ignite.** —*idioms.* **come to light.** To come to public attention; be revealed: *New information has re-*

cently come to light. **in (the) light of.** In consideration of; in relationship to. **see the light.** To comprehend or perceive the meaning of something for the first time. **shed (or throw) light on.** To make more comprehensible. [Middle English, from Old English *lēoht.*]

light² (līt) *adj.* **-er, -est. 1.** Of relatively low weight; not heavy: *a light suitcase.* **2.** Of relatively low density; having a low weight for its size or bulk: *Titanium is a light metal.* **3.** Exerting little pressure; having less force or impact than normal: *a light kick.* **4. a.** Having less quantity, intensity, length, or volume: *a light snow; a light murmur.* **b.** Consuming relatively moderate amounts: *a light eater.* **5.** Having little importance or value; insignificant: *light chatter.* **6.** Intended as entertainment; not serious or profound: *a light comedy.* **7.** Free from worries or troubles; blithe: *a light heart.* **8.** Moving easily and quickly; nimble: *light and graceful on her feet.* **9.** Designed for ease and quickness of movement: *a light vehicle.* **10.** Requiring relatively little equipment and relatively simple processes: *light manufacturing.* **11.** *Mil.* Carrying little equipment or arms: *a light brigade.* **12.** Easily awakened or disturbed: *a light sleeper.* **13. a.** Having a spongy or flaky texture; airy: *light pastries.* **b.** Having a loose, porous consistency; easily crumbled: *light earth.* **14.** Containing a relatively small amount of alcohol: *a light wine.* **15.** Pronounced with little or no stress. —*adv.* **1.** Lightly. **2.** With little weight or few burdens: *traveling light.* —*intr.v.* **light·ed** or **lit** (lĭt), **light·ing. 1.** To get down, as from a mount or vehicle; dismount; alight. **2.** To descend to the ground after flight; perch; land. —*phrasal verb.* To attack verbally or physically; assail: *He lit into his opponent.* —*idiom.* **make light of.** To regard or treat as unimportant; minimize. [Middle English, from Old English *lēoht.*]

light·en¹ (līt'n) *tr.v.* To make light or lighter; brighten. —*intr.v.* To become light or lighter; brighten.

light·en² (līt'n) *tr.v.* **1.** To make less heavy, as by a reduction in weight or load. **2. a.** To lessen the oppressiveness, trouble, or severity of: *Appliances lighten household work.* **b.** To relieve of cares or worries; to cheer; gladden: *The good news lightened our hearts.* —*intr.v.* **1.** To become lighter. **2.** To become less oppressive, troublesome, or severe.

light·er¹ (lī'tər) *n.* **1.** Someone or something that ignites. **2.** A device for lighting a cigarette, cigar, or pipe.

light·er² (lī'tər) *n. Naut.* A large barge used for loading and unloading ships moored outside a harbor too shallow for them to enter. —*tr.v.* To convey (cargo) in a lighter. [Middle English.]

light·er-than-air (lī'tər-thən-âr') *adj.* Having a weight less than that of the air displaced, as certain aircraft.

light·face (līt'fās') *n. Printing.* A typeface or font of characters with relatively thin, light lines. This definition is printed in lightface. —**light'faced'** *adj.*

light-fin·gered (līt'fĭng'gərd) *adj.* **1.** Skilled at petty thievery. **2.** Having quick and nimble fingers. —**light'-fin'gered·ness** *n.*

light-foot·ed (līt'foŏt'ĭd) *adj.* Treading with light and nimble ease. —**light'-foot'ed·ness** *n.*

light-head·ed (līt'hĕd'ĭd) *adj.* **1.** Dizzy, giddy, or faint. **2.** Given to frivolity; fanciful; silly. —**light'head'ed·ly** *adv.* —**light'head'ed·ness** *n.*

light-heart·ed (līt'här'tĭd) *adj.* Blithe; carefree; gay. —**light'heart'ed·ly** *adv.* —**light'heart'ed·ness** *n.*

light heavyweight. *Boxing & Wrestling.* A fighter weighing between 161 and 175 pounds, or 73 to 79 kilograms.

light·house (līt'hous') *n.* A tall structure topped by a powerful light used to guide ships.

light·ing (lī'tĭng) *n.* **1.** Light supplied, as for a room or area; illumination. **2. a.** The means or equipment used to provide artificial illumination: *electric lighting.* **b.** The illumination so provided: *stage lighting.* **3.** The act or process of igniting.

light·ly (līt'lē) *adv.* **1.** With little pressure or force; gently: *Tread lightly.* **2.** With a small or light amount; sparingly: *dress lightly.* **3.** With buoyancy or ease; quickly and gracefully. **4.** In a carefree manner; blithely: *take the news lightly.* **5.** Without enough care or serious consideration; indifferently: *Don't treat his work lightly.* **6.** Without serious punishment or penalty: *The judge let him off lightly.*

| ă pat | ā pay | â care | ä father | ĕ pet | ē be | hw which | ĭ pit | ī tie | î pier | ŏ pot | ō toe | ô paw, for | oi noise |
| oō took | oō boot | ou out | th thin | th this | ŭ cut | | û urge | zh vision | ə about, item, edible, gallop, circus | | | | |

light meter. *Photog.* An instrument that indicates the intensity of light from a source, usu. equipped with scales to help compute the correct adjustment for a camera and film to be used in photographing that source. Also called **exposure meter.**

light meter

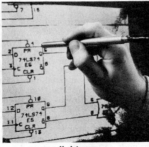

light pen

light·mind·ed (līt'mīn'dĭd) *adj.* Frivolous, silly, or inanely giddy. —**light'-mind'ed·ly** *adv.*

light·ness¹ (līt'nĭs) *n.* A property or quality of a color measured as the degree to which an object of that color reflects light or allows light to pass through; brightness or paleness.

light·ness² (līt'nĭs) *n.* **1.** The property or quality of having little weight or force. **2.** Ease or quickness of movement; agility; nimbleness; buoyancy. **3.** Freedom from worry or trouble; blitheness; gaiety. **4.** Lack of appropriate seriousness; levity.

light·ning (līt'nĭng) *n.* **1.** A large-scale high-tension natural electric discharge in the atmosphere. **2.** The visible flash of light accompanying such a discharge. —*adj.* Moving with great speed; appearing to be very fast or sudden, like a flash of lightning. [Middle English *lightening,* from *lightenen,* to illuminate, from *light,* illumination.]

lightning arrester. A protective device for electrical equipment that reduces excessive voltage resulting from lightning to a safe level.

lightning bug. A firefly.

lightning rod. A metal rod placed high on a structure to prevent damage by conducting lightning to ground.

light opera. A dramatic musical work on a light subject with vocalists and orchestra; operetta.

light pen. An electronic device shaped somewhat like a pen that emits a light and may be used to make corrections and changes on a cathode-ray tube connected to a computer.

light·proof (līt'proof') *adj.* Not capable of being penetrated by light radiation.

lights (līts) *pl.n.* The lungs of an animal, esp. one used for food. [Middle English *lighte,* from *light,* light, not heavy.]

light·ship (līt'shĭp') *n.* A ship with a powerful light or warning signals that is anchored in dangerous waters to alert other vessels.

light·some¹ (līt'səm) *adj.* **1.** Providing light; illuminating; luminous. **2.** Covered with or full of light; bright. —**light'some·ly** *adv.* —**light'some·ness** *n.*

light·some² (līt'səm) *adj.* **1.** Light, nimble, or graceful in movement; buoyant. **2.** Carefree; blithe; cheerful. **3.** Frivolous; silly. —**light'some·ly** *adv.* —**light'some·ness** *n.*

light·weight (līt'wāt') *n.* **1.** Someone or something that weighs relatively little. **2.** *Boxing & Wrestling.* A fighter weighing between 127 and 135 pounds, or 58 and 61 kilograms. **3.** A person of little ability, intelligence, influence, or importance. —*adj.* Weighing relatively little.

light-year (līt'yîr') *n.* Also **light year.** A measure of the distance that light travels through empty space in one year, approx. 5.878 trillion miles, or 9.458 trillion kilometers.

lig·ne·ous (lĭg'nē-əs) *adj.* Consisting of or having the texture or appearance of wood; woody. [Latin *ligneus,* from *lignum,* wood.]

lig·nin (lĭg'nĭn) *n.* The chief noncarbohydrate constituent of wood, a polymer that functions as a natural binder and support for the cellulose fibers of woody plants. [Latin *lignum,* wood + -IN.]

lig·nite (lĭg'nīt) *n.* A low-grade, brownish-black coal. Also called **brown coal.** [French.]

lig·num vi·tae (lĭg'nəm vī'tē) *pl.* **lignum vi·taes.** **1.** Either of two tropical American trees, *Guaiacum officinale* or *G. sanctum,* that have evergreen leaves and heavy, durable, resinous wood. **2.** The very hard, heavy wood of either of these trees. **3.** Any of several similar or related trees. [New Latin, "wood of life."]

lig·ro·in (lĭg'rō-ĭn) *n.* A volatile, flammable fraction of petroleum, obtained by distillation and used as a solvent. Also called **benzine.** [Orig. unknown.]

lik·a·ble (lī'kə-bəl) *adj.* Also **like·a·ble.** Easy to like; pleasing. —**lik'a·ble·ness** *n.*

like¹ (līk) *v.* **liked, lik·ing.** —*tr.v.* **1.** To be fond of: *She likes Jim but not enough to go steady.* **2.** To find pleasant; enjoy: *like the place enough to stay longer.* **3.** To want, wish, or prefer: *Which jacket do you like best?* **4.** To feel toward or respond to; to view; to regard: *How do you like your math course?* —*intr.v.* To have an inclination or preference; choose: *If you like, we can meet you there.* —*n.* **likes.** The things one enjoys; preferences; predilections: *likes and dislikes.* [Middle English *likien,* from Old English *līcian,* to please, be sufficient.] —**lik'er** *n.*

Syns: like, dig (*Slang*), **enjoy, relish, savor** *v.* Core meaning: To receive pleasure from (*likes a good meal*). See also Syns at **choose.**

Usage: like. This verb is followed by infinitives (*likes to read*), by gerunds (*likes reading*), and by *for* + a noun/pronoun + infinitive (*likes for her children to read books*). The last contruction, though controversial in recent years, has been current in educated speech and literary English since the fifteenth century. It is standard idiom throughout the United States and esp. in the South. An alternative way of wording the last example is: *likes her children to read books.*

like² (līk) *prep.* **1. a.** The same as or similar to, as in nature or characteristics: *Habits are like measles; they can be catching.* **b.** Similar to, as in appearance or sound: *There was a crash like thunder.* **2.** In the same or a similar manner as: *act like a man.* **3.** In character with: *It's not like him to fall down on the job.* **4.** Such as: *great peaks like Mt. Rainier.* —*adj.* **1.** Similar or nearly similar: *My uncle left $100 to me and a like sum to my sister.* **2.** Equivalent; equal: *like sides of an isosceles triangle.* —*n.* Persons or things similar to the one or ones named: *denim, gabardine, and the like.* —*idiom.* **(as) like as not.** *Informal.* Probably: *Like as not, we'll never hear from him again.* [Middle English *lik,* from Old English *gelīc.*]

Syns: like, alike, analogous, comparable, corresponding, equivalent, parallel, uniform *adj.* Core meaning: Having the same or almost the same characteristics (*two sisters of like opinions*).

Usage: like. 1. As prepositions *like* and *as* express different things. *Like* most often indicates a resemblance to the object mentioned: *run like a greyhound; a boy like him; not at all like her to give up.* As indicates a role, capacity, or function: *serve as chairperson.* In these usages the two words are not synonymous and are not interchangeable. The distinction is illustrated by *act like a leader* and *serve as leader.* **2.** *Like* can also occur as a conjunction in standard spoken and written English, though it is often avoided in formal written compositions except when it introduces an elliptical clause containing an unexpressed verb. This last construction is not controversial: *The car looked like new. She took to skating like a fish to water. It looks like a good spring for gardening.* In the following examples *as* or *as if* is preferred by some writers, although *like* is not incorrect: *He talks like his late father did. The car looked like it was new.* Formal: *He talks as his late father did. The car looked as if it were new.*

-like. A suffix meaning: **1.** Similar to: **lifelike. 2.** Characteristic of: **childlike, ladylike.**

like·a·ble (lī'kə-bəl) *adj.* Var. of likable.

like·li·hood (līk'lē-hŏŏd') *n.* **1.** The chance of a certain thing happening; probability. **2.** Something that is probable.

like·ly (līk'lē) *adj.* **-li·er, -li·est. 1.** Having, expressing, or showing a strong probability; apt: *They are likely to be-*

come angry with him. **2.** Probable: *He's a likely choice.* **3.** Seeming to be true; credible; plausible: *a likely excuse.* **4.** Apparently capable of doing well or becoming successful; promising. **5.** Attractive; pleasant; enjoyable. —*adv.* Probably: *Most likely it's just a passing fad.* [Middle English, from Old Norse *līkligr,* from *līkr,* like.]

    Syns: likely, probable *adj. Core meaning:* Showing a strong probability of happening or of being true (*likely to rain at any moment; carelessness—the probable cause of the accident*). Both also describe what seems to be true but is not certain (*a likely excuse; a probable explanation*).

like·mind·ed (līk'mīn'dĭd) *adj.* Of the same way of thinking or bent of mind. —**like'-mind'ed·ly** *adv.* —**like'-mind'ed·ness** *n.*

lik·en (lī'kən) *tr.v.* To see, mention, or show as like or similar; compare.

like·ness (līk'nĭs) *n.* **1.** Similarity or resemblance: *a strong likeness between Edward and his father.* **2.** An imitative appearance; a semblance or guise. **3.** A copy or picture of something; an image: *The painting is a perfect likeness of you.*

like·wise (līk'wīz') *adv.* **1.** In the same way; similarly: *"Some have little power to do good, and have likewise little strength to resist evil"* (Samuel Johnson). **2.** Moreover; also; too: *sings and likewise plays guitar.*

lik·ing (lī'kĭng) *n.* **1.** A feeling of fondness or affection: *a liking for her friend.* **2.** Preference or taste: *I'll choose a name more to your liking.*

li·lac (lī'lək, -lŏk', -lăk') *n.* **1.** Any of various shrubs of the genus *Syringa,* esp. *S. vulgaris,* widely cultivated for its clusters of fragrant purplish or white flowers. **2.** A pale purple. —*adj.* Pale purple. [Obs. French, from Spanish, from Arabic *līlak,* from Persian, *nīlak,* from *nīl,* indigo, blue.]

Lil·ith (lĭl'ĭth) *n.* **1.** In ancient Semitic legend, an evil female spirit or demon believed to haunt lonely, deserted places. **2.** In Hebrew folklore, the first wife of Adam, believed to have been in existence before the creation of Eve.

Lil·li·pu·tian (lĭl'ə-pyōō'shən) *n.* **1.** One of the six-inch-high inhabitants of the imaginary country of Lilliput in Jonathan Swift's *Gulliver's Travels* (1726). **2.** Often **lilliputian.** A tiny person. —*adj.* Often **lilliputian. 1.** Very small; tiny. **2.** Trivial; petty.

lilt (lĭlt) *n.* **1.** A light, happy tune or song. **2.** A cheerful, rhythmic, or lively manner of speaking or moving. —*intr.v.* To speak, sing, play, or move with liveliness or rhythm. [Middle English *lulten,* to sound, sing.]

lil·y (lĭl'ē) *n., pl.* **-ies. 1.** Any of various plants of the genus *Lilium,* with showy, variously colored, often trumpet-shaped flowers. **2.** Any of various similar or related plants, such as the day lily or the water lily. **3.** The flower of such a plant. [Middle English *lilie,* from Old English, from Latin *lilium.*]

lil·y-liv·ered (lĭl'ē-lĭv'ərd) *adj.* Cowardly; timid.

lily of the valley *pl.* **lilies of the valley.** A widely cultivated plant, *Convallaria majalis,* with a cluster of fragrant, bell-shaped white flowers.

lily of the valley

lily pad. One of the floating leaves of a water lily.

lil·y-white (lĭl'ē-hwīt', -wīt') *adj.* **1.** White as a lily. **2.** Beyond reproach; blameless; pure.

li·ma bean (lī'mə). **1.** Any of several varieties of a tropical American plant, *Phaseolus limensis,* with flat pods that contain large, light-green, edible seeds. **2.** The seed of such a plant. [After *Lima,* Peru.]

limb¹ (lĭm) *n.* **1.** One of the larger branches of a tree. **2.** One of the jointed appendages of an animal, as an arm, leg, wing, or flipper. —*idiom.* **out on a limb.** *Informal.* In a difficult, dangerous, or vulnerable position. [Middle English *lim,* from Old English.]

limb² (lĭm) *n.* **1.** The outer edge of the apparent disk of a celestial object. **2.** *Bot.* The expanded tip of a petal or the expanded upper part of a united corolla. [French *limbe,* from Latin *limbus,* border.]

lim·ber¹ (lĭm'bər) *adj.* **1.** Bending or flexing readily; pliable: *a dancer's limber muscles.* **2.** Capable of moving, bending, or contorting easily; agile; supple: *a limber gymnast.* —*tr.v.* To make limber. —*intr.v.* To become limber. [Orig. unknown.] —**lim'ber·ness** *n.*

lim·ber² (lĭm'bər) *n.* A two-wheeled attachment for a field gun, used to move the gun and to carry ammunition. [Middle English *lymour,* shaft of a carriage, poss. from Medieval Latin *limō,* shaft.]

lim·bo (lĭm'bō) *n., pl.* **-bos. 1.** Often **Limbo.** In some Christian theologies, the abode of souls kept from heaven by circumstance, such as lack of baptism. **2.** A place or condition of neglect or stagnation. **3.** A state or place of confinement. **4.** An intermediate place or condition. [Middle English, from Medieval Latin *in limbō,* "(region) on the border (of hell)."]

Lim·burg·er (lĭm'bûr'gər) *n.* A soft white cheese with a very strong odor and flavor, orig. produced in Limburg, Belgium.

lime¹ (līm) *n.* **1.** A spiny tree, *Citrus aurantifolia,* that has evergreen leaves, fragrant white flowers, and edible, egg-shaped fruit with a green rind and acid juice. **2.** The fruit of this tree. —*modifier:* lime juice. [French, from Provençal *limo,* from Arabic *līmah.*]

lime² (līm) *n.* Any of several Old World linden trees. [Var. of *line,* from obs. *lind,* linden.]

lime³ (līm) *n.* **1.** *Chem.* **Calcium oxide. 2.** A sticky substance smeared on twigs and used to catch small birds; birdlime. —*tr.v.* **limed, lim·ing. 1.** To treat with lime. **2.** To smear with birdlime. [Middle English *lim,* from Old English *līm,* shaft.]

lime·ade (lī-mād') *n.* A drink made of lime juice, sugar, and water.

lime·kiln (līm'kĭl', -kĭln') *n.* A furnace used to reduce naturally occurring calcium carbonate to lime.

lime·light (līm'līt') *n.* **1.** A stage light in which lime is heated to incandescence, producing brilliant illumination. **2. the limelight.** A focus of public attention.

lim·er·ick (lĭm'ər-ĭk) *n.* A humorous five-line poem in which the first, second, and last lines rhyme with each other and the third line rhymes with the fourth. [After *Limerick,* Ireland.]

lime·stone (līm'stōn') *n.* A form of sedimentary rock that consists mainly of calcium carbonate with varying amounts of magnesium carbonate and quartz, used as a building material and in making lime and cement.

lime·wa·ter (līm'wô'tər, -wŏt'ər) *n.* A clear, colorless alkaline solution of calcium hydroxide in water, used in skin preparations and sometimes as an antacid.

lim·ey (lī'mē) *n., pl.* **-eys.** *Slang.* **1.** A British seaman. **2.** An Englishman. [From *lime-juicer,* from the fact that British sailors were required to be served lime juice while at sea to prevent scurvy.]

lim·it (lĭm'ĭt) *n.* **1.** The point, edge, or line beyond which something cannot or may not proceed. **2.** Often **limits.** The boundary surrounding a specific area; bounds: *within city limits.* **3.** The greatest amount or number allowed: *a speed limit.* **4.** The utmost extent; the breaking point: *press one's luck to the limit.* **5. the limit.** *Informal.* Something that exhausts one's patience. **6.** *Math.* A fixed value or number which a variable function may approach indefinitely but never reach. —*tr.v.* To confine or restrict within a limit or limits. [Middle English *limite,* from Latin *līmes,* boundary.] —**lim'it·a·ble** *adj.* —**lim'it·er** *n.*

lim·i·ta·tion (lĭm'ĭ-tā'shən) *n.* **1.** Something that limits; a restriction: *limitations on the king's powers.* **2.** A shortcoming: *learn to accept one's limitations.*

lim·it·ed (lĭm'ĭ-tĭd) *adj.* **1.** Confined within certain limits: *a* person of limited experience; a limited success. **2.** Having governmental or ruling powers restricted by enforceable limitations, as a constitution or legislative body. **3.** Limiting the liability of each partner in a business to his actual investment. **4.** Making few stops and carrying relatively few passengers: a limited train. —**lim'it·ed·ly** adv.

lim·it·less (lĭm'ĭt-lĭs) adj. Having no bounds or limits. —**lim'it·less·ly** adv. —**lim'it·less·ness** n.

limn (lĭm) tr.v. Archaic. **1.** To depict by painting or drawing. **2.** To describe. [Middle English limnen, to illuminate (manuscript), from Old French luminer, from Latin lūmen, light.] —**limn'er** (lĭm'ər, -nər) n.

lim·nol·o·gy (lĭm-nŏl'ə-jē) n. The scientific study of freshwater life and phenomena. [Greek limnē, pool, lake + -LOGY.] —**lim'no·log'i·cal** (-nə-lŏj'ĭ-kəl) adj. —**lim·nol'o·gist** n.

li·mo·nite (lī'mə-nīt') n. A yellowish-brown to black natural iron oxide, essentially $FeO(OH)·nH_2O$, used as an ore of iron. [German Limonit, from Greek leimōn, meadow.] —**li'mo·nit'ic** (-nĭt'ĭk) adj.

lim·ou·sine (lĭm'ə-zēn', lĭm'ə-zēn') n. **1.** A large, luxurious automobile, often with a glass partition between the driver and the passengers. **2.** A small bus used to carry passengers to airports, hotels, etc. [After Limousin, a region of France.]

limp (lĭmp) intr.v. **1.** To walk lamely, esp. with irregularity, as if favoring one leg. **2.** To move or proceed haltingly or unsteadily: The damaged ship limped back to port. —n. An irregular, jerky, or awkward gait. —adj. -er, -est. **1.** Lacking or having lost stiffness or the ability to support itself; flaccid: a limp leaf; limp rags. **2.** Lacking strength or firmness; weak: a limp excuse. [Prob. from obs. limphalt, lame.] —**limp'ly** adv. —**limp'ness** n.

lim·pet (lĭm'pĭt) n. Any of numerous saltwater gastropod mollusks, as of the families Acmaeidae and Patellidae, that characteristically have a tent-shaped shell and adhere to rocks of tidal areas. [Middle English lempet, from Old English lempedu, from Medieval Latin lamprēda, lamprey.]

lim·pid (lĭm'pĭd) adj. **1.** Characterized by transparent clearness; pellucid: a limpid pool. **2.** Easily intelligible; clear: a limpid explanation. [French limpide, from Latin limpidus.] —**lim·pid'i·ty** or **lim'pid·ness** n. —**lim'pid·ly** adv.

limp·kin (lĭmp'kĭn) n. A brownish wading bird, Aramus guarauna, of warm, swampy regions of the New World, with a distinctive, wailing call. [LIMP + -KIN.]

lim·y (lī'mē) adj. -i·er, -i·est. Of, resembling, or containing lime (calcium oxide). —**lim'i·ness** n.

lin·age (lī'nĭj) n. Also **line·age**. **1.** The number of lines of printed or written material. **2.** Payment for written work according to the number of lines.

linch·pin (lĭnch'pĭn') n. A metal pin inserted in the end of a shaft, as in an axle, to prevent a wheel from slipping off. [Middle English lynspin : lins, linchpin, from Old English lynis + pin, pin.]

lin·den (lĭn'dən) n. Any of various trees of the genus Tilia that have heart-shaped leaves and yellowish, often fragrant flowers. [Perh. from Middle English, made of linden wood, from Old English, from linde, the linden.]

line[1] (līn) n. **1. a.** Any path taken by a point that is free to move: a curved line. **b.** A path of this kind in which there is no change of direction. **2.** A long, thin, continuous mark, as one made on paper by a pen or pencil. **3.** A border or boundary: the county line. **4.** A group of people or things arranged in a row: marched in a line behind him. **5.** Often **lines.** Outline, contour, or styling: the sleek lines of the new car. **6.** A row of words printed or written across a page or column. **7.** Often **lines.** The words recited by an actor in a play: busy memorizing his lines. **8.** A wrinkle or crease on the skin, esp. of the face. **9.** A cable, rope, string, cord, wire, etc.: a fishing line. **10.** A course of progress or movement: the line of flight. **11.** An attitude or policy: His party supported the compromise, but he took a different line. **12.** A sequence of related ideas leading to a certain ending or conclusion: a line of reasoning. **13.** A system of transportation or a company owning such a system: a bus line. **14.** A system of wires or other conductors used to connect electricity, usu. over long distances: a power line. **15.** A pipe or system of pipes used to carry water or other liquid.

16. A brief letter; note: Drop me a line. **17.** A succession of persons or animals descended from a common ancestor. **18.** Football. The seven players stationed at the line of scrimmage as a play begins. **19.** A range of merchandise: a line of cars. **20.** A person's occupation or field of interest: What is your line of work? **21.** Informal. A false or exaggerated story intended to impress or deceive a listener. **22.** Informal. A piece of useful information: See if you can get a line on what he's doing. **23.** Mus. One of the five parallel marks composing a staff. **24.** Mil. **a.** A formation in which elements, such as troops, tanks, or ships, are arranged abreast of each other. **b.** The battle area closest to the enemy. **c.** The troops in this area. **d.** Combatant troops. **25.** The officers in direct command of warships. —v. **lined, lin·ing.** —tr.v. **1.** To mark with a line or lines: line paper. **2.** To form a row or rows along: Thousands of people lined the street. —intr.v. To form a line: The children lined up quickly. —phrasal verb. **line up. 1.** To arrange in a line; align. **2.** To win over to a cause; secure; gain: He has already lined up considerable support for the bill. —idioms. **bring into line.** To persuade to agree or conform. **hold the line.** To maintain a firm position; not yield: holding the line on new expenditures. **in line.** Behaving properly: keeping the children in line. **in line for.** Due for: in line for a promotion. **in line with.** Conforming to; in accordance with: The new proposal is in line with our general policy. **lay it on the line.** Informal. To speak openly, concealing nothing. **on the line. 1.** Immediately available; ready: cash on the line. **2.** At stake: Your reputation is on the line. **out of line.** Improper; uncalled-for: a remark somewhat out of line. **read between the lines.** To seek a hidden meaning. [Middle English, cord, mark, ult. from Latin līnea, thread, line, from līnum, flax.]

line[2] (līn) tr.v. **lined, lin·ing. 1.** To sew or fit a covering to the inside surface of: line a coat with fur. **2.** To cover the inner surface of: Moisture lined the walls. **3.** To fill plentifully, as with money or food: line your pockets with goodies. [Middle English linen, from line, flax, from Old English līn, from Latin līnum, flax.]

lin·e·age[1] (lĭn'ē-ĭj) n. **1.** Direct descent from a particular ancestor; ancestry. **2.** All of the descendants of a particular ancestor. [Middle English linage, from Old French, from ligne, line.]

line·age[2] (lī'nĭj) n. Var. of linage.

lin·e·al (lĭn'ē-əl) adj. **1.** In the direct line of descent from an ancestor. **2.** Derived from or relating to a line of descent: the lineal rights of royalty. **3.** Linear. [Middle English, from Old French, from Late Latin līneālis, from Latin līnea, line.] —**lin'e·al·ly** adv.

lin·e·a·ment (lĭn'ē-ə-mənt) n. A distinctive shape, contour, or feature, esp. of the face. [Middle English liniament, from Latin līneāmentum, from līneāre, to make straight, from līnea, line.]

lin·e·ar (lĭn'ē-ər) adj. **1.** Of, relating to, consisting of, or resembling a line or lines; straight. **2.** Geom. **a.** Of, like, or involving a line, esp. a straight line. **b.** Of or involving a linear equation. **c.** Having only one dimension. **3.** Narrow and elongated like a straight line: a linear leaf. [Latin līneāris, from līnea, line.] —**lin'e·ar·ly** adv.

linear accelerator. An electron, proton, or heavy-ion accelerator in which the paths of the particles accelerated are straight lines rather than circles or spirals.

linear equation. An algebraic equation of the form $ax + by + c = 0$, where a, b, and c are constants and a and b are not both zero.

linear measure. 1. Measurement of length or distance. **2.** A unit or system of units for measuring length or distance.

line·back·er (līn'băk'ər) n. Football. Any of three defensive players that form a second line of defense usu. just behind the ends and tackles.

line breeding. Selective breeding to perpetuate certain qualities or characteristics in a strain of stock.

line drawing. A drawing made with lines only.

line drive. Baseball. A batted ball hit sharply so that its path roughly describes a straight line. Also called **liner.**

line engraving. 1. A metal plate, used in intaglio printing, on the surface of which design lines have been hand-engraved. **2.** The process of making such a plate. **3.** A print made from such a plate.

line·man (līn′mən) n. **1.** A person employed to install or repair telephone, telegraph, or other power lines; linesman. **2.** A person employed to inspect and repair railroad tracks. **3.** Football. A player stationed within one yard of a team's line of scrimmage.

lin·en (lĭn′ən) n. **1. a.** Thread made from fibers of the flax plant. **b.** Cloth woven from this thread. **c.** Garments or articles made from this cloth, or from similar material. **d.** Often **linens.** Cloth household articles, such as sheets and towels, made of this fabric or of other fabrics. **2.** Paper made with a finish that resembles linen cloth. —*modifier:* *a linen table cloth.* [Middle English, from Old English *līnen*, made of flax, from Latin *līnum*, flax.]

line of force. Any of a set of lines imagined to exist in a field of force so that a tangent to a line at any point gives the direction of the field at that point and the number of lines passing through a region represents the strength of the field in that region.

line of scrimmage. An imaginary line across a football field on which the ball rests and at which the teams line up for a new play.

line of sight. 1. An imaginary line from the eye to the object being looked at. **2.** *Electronics.* An unobstructed path between sending and receiving antennas.

lin·er¹ (lī′nər) n. **1.** A commercial ship or airplane, esp. one carrying passengers on a regular route. **2.** Something or someone that draws or makes a line or lines. **3.** Baseball. A **line drive.**

lin·er² (lī′nər) n. **1.** A person who makes or puts in linings. **2.** Something used as a lining.

line segment. The part of a line lying between two points that are chosen to be its ends.

lines·man (līnz′mən) n. **1.** *Sports.* An official who assists a referee in football, ice hockey, tennis, and other sports. **2.** A person who repairs or installs telephone, telegraph, or other power lines; lineman.

line-up or **line·up** (līn′ŭp′) n. **1.** A line of persons formed for inspection or identification: *a police line-up.* **2. a.** The members of a team chosen to start a game: *a football line-up.* **b.** A list of such players. **3.** A group of persons, organizations, or things enlisted or arrayed for a specific purpose.

ling (lĭng) n., pl. **ling** or **lings.** Any of various saltwater food fishes related to or resembling the cod, such as *Molva molva*, of northern European Atlantic waters, or a burbot or hake. [Middle English *leng(e).*]

–ling¹. A suffix meaning: **1.** One who belongs to or is connected with: **worldling, hireling. 2.** Someone or something small: **duckling, nursling, princeling.** [Middle English, from Old English.]

–ling². A suffix meaning: **1.** Direction or position: **sideling. 2.** Condition: **underling.** [Middle English, from Old English.]

ling·cod (lĭng′kŏd′) n., pl. **lingcod** or **-cods.** A food fish, *Ophiodon elongatus*, of northern Pacific waters.

lin·ger (lĭng′gər) intr.v. **1.** To remain in a place longer than usual, as if reluctant to leave: *linger at the dinner table.* **2.** To remain alive even though close to death. **3.** To persist: *The memory still lingers.* **4.** To be tardy in acting; procrastinate: *linger over a decision.* —See Syns at **delay.** [Middle English *lengeren*, freq. of *lengen*, to tarry, from Old Norse *lengja*.] —**lin′ger·er** n. —**lin′ger·ing·ly** adv.

lin·ge·rie (lăn′zhə-rē′, län′zhə-rā′) n. Women's underwear and sleeping garments. [French, from *linge*, linen, from Latin *līneus*, made of linen, from *līnum*, flax.]

lin·go (lĭng′gō) n., pl. **-goes. 1.** Language that contains many specialized or unusual words. **2.** Language that is unintelligible because it is foreign. [Portuguese *lingoa*, tongue, language, from Latin *lingua*.]

lin·gua fran·ca (lĭng′gwə frăng′kə). **1. Lingua franca.** A mixture of Italian with French, Spanish, Arabic, Greek, and Turkish, spoken in the Mediterranean area, esp. in the Levant. **2.** A language used between people who normally speak different languages. [Italian, "the Frankish tongue."]

lin·gual (lĭng′gwəl) adj. **1.** Of, pertaining to, or resembling the tongue. **2.** *Phonet.* Produced with the tongue in conjunction with other organs of speech, as the sounds *t* and *l*.

3. Of or relating to language or linguistics; linguistic. [Middle English, from Medieval Latin *lingualis*, from Latin *lingua*, tongue.] —**lin′gual·ly** adv.

lin·gui·ni (lĭng-gwē′nē) pl.n. (used with a sing. verb). Pasta in long, flat, thin strands. [Italian, pl. of *linguino*, "small tongue," from *lingua*, tongue, from Latin.]

lin·guist (lĭng′gwĭst) n. **1.** A person who speaks several languages fluently. **2.** A specialist in linguistics. [From Latin *lingua*, tongue, language.]

lin·guis·tic (lĭng-gwĭs′tĭk) adj. Of or relating to language or linguistics. —**lin·guis′ti·cal·ly** adv.

linguistic form. Any meaningful unit of speech, such as an affix, word, phrase, or sentence.

lin·guis·tics (lĭng-gwĭs′tĭks) n. (used with a sing. verb). The science of language; the study of the nature and structure of human speech.

lin·i·ment (lĭn′ə-mənt) n. A liquid medicine rubbed on the skin to sooth or relieve pain. [Middle English *lynyment*, from Late Latin *linīmentum*, from Latin *linere*, to anoint.]

li·nin (lī′nĭn) n. The filamentous, achromatic material in the nucleus of a cell that interconnects the chromatin granules. [Latin *līnum*, flax + -IN.]

lin·ing (lī′nĭng) n. **1.** An interior covering or coating: *the lining of the stomach.* **2.** A layer of material used on an inside surface: *a silk lining; a removable lining.*

link (lĭngk) n. **1.** One of the rings or loops that form a chain. **2.** Anything that resembles a chain link in its physical arrangement or its connecting function, as: **a.** One of several sausages strung together. **b.** A bridge or other unit in a transportation or communications system: *a new rail link.* **c.** A single connecting element in a narrative. **2.** A rod or lever transmitting motion in a machine. **3.** Anything that creates a connection in the mind: *a link with the past.* **4.** A cuff link. **5.** A unit of length used in surveying, equal to one hundredth of a chain, 7.92 in., or 20.12 centimeters. —tr.v. To connect or couple with or as if with links. —intr.v. To become connected with or as if with links. — See Syns at **join.** [Middle English.]

link·age (lĭng′kĭj) n. **1.** The act or process of linking or the condition of being linked. **2.** A system of interconnected machine elements, such as rods, springs, and pivots, used to transmit power or motion. **3.** *Elect.* A measure of the induced voltage in a circuit caused by a magnetic flux, equal to the flux times the number of turns in the coil that surrounds it. **4.** A relationship between two or more genes occupying the same chromosome and therefore having closely associated inherited effects.

linking verb. A verb that connects the subject of a sentence with a predicate adjective or predicate nominative; for example, *was* in *She was very happy*, *seemed* in *Arthur seemed uncertain*, and *became* in *He became a truck driver* are linking verbs.

links (lĭngks) pl.n. A golf course. [Middle English, from Old English *hlincas*, pl. of *hlinc*, ridge.]

Lin·nae·an (lĭ-nē′ən, -nā′-) adj. Also **Lin·ne·an.** Of or pertaining to Carolus Linnaeus or to the binomial nomenclature system developed by him for classifying and naming living things.

lin·net (lĭn′ĭt) n. **1.** A small Old World songbird, *Acanthis cannabina*, with brownish plumage. **2.** A similar bird, *Carpodacus mexicanus*, of western North America. [Old French *linette*, from *lin*, flax (from its feeding on linseeds), from Latin *līnum*.]

lin·o·le·ic acid (lĭn′ə-lē′ĭk). A liquid, $C_{18}H_{32}O_2$, an important component of drying oils and an essential fatty acid in the human diet. [Greek *linon*, flax + OLEIC ACID (from its occurrence in flax).]

lin·o·len·ic acid (lĭn′ə-lĕn′ĭk). A colorless liquid, $C_{18}H_{30}O_2$, an important component of natural drying oils and an essential fatty acid in the human diet. [From LINOLEIC ACID.]

li·no·le·um (lĭ-nō′lē-əm) n. A durable, washable material made in sheets by pressing a mixture of hot linseed oil, rosin, powdered cork, and coloring onto a cloth backing and used as a floor and counter-top covering. [Latin *līnum*, flax + *oleum*, oil.]

Li·no·type (lī′nə-tīp′) n. A trademark for a keyboard-operated machine that can set an entire line of type on a single metal slug.

lin·seed (lĭn′sēd′) n. The seeds of the flax plant, esp. when pressed to obtain linseed oil; flaxseed. [Middle English, from Old English *linsǣd : līn,* flax + *sǣd,* seed.]

lin·seed oil. An oil that thickens and hardens when exposed to air, extracted from flaxseeds and used as a drying oil in paints and varnishes, and in linoleum, printing inks, and synthetic resins.

lin·sey-wool·sey (lĭn′zē-wŏŏl′zē) *n., pl.* **-seys.** A coarse fabric of cotton or linen woven with wool. —*modifier: a linsey-woolsey dress.* [Middle English *lynsy-wolsye.*]

lint (lĭnt) *n.* **1.** Bits of fiber and fluff that rub off yarn or cloth. **2.** Downy material obtained by scraping linen cloth, formerly used for dressing wounds. **3.** The mass of soft fibers surrounding the seeds of unginned cotton. [Middle English *lynet,* from Latin *linteum,* linen cloth, from *linteus,* made of linen, from *līnum,* flax.]

lin·tel (lĭn′tl) *n.* The horizontal beam over the top of a door or window that supports the weight of the structure above it. [Middle English, from Old French, from Latin *līmen,* threshold.]

lint·er (lĭn′tər) *n.* **1. linters.** The short fibers that cling to cotton seeds after the first ginning. **2.** A machine that removes linters from cotton seeds.

li·on (lī′ən) *n.* **1. a.** A large, carnivorous feline mammal, *Panthera leo,* of Africa and India, with a short, tawny coat and a long, heavy mane around the neck and shoulders of the male. **b.** Any of several related animals, esp. a mountain lion. **2.** A person of great strength or courage. **3.** A person who is a center of public attention; a celebrity: *a literary lion.* —*idiom.* **the lion's share.** The greatest or best part of the whole. [Middle English *leoun,* from Old French *lion,* from Latin *leō,* from Greek *leōn.*]

lion

li·on·ess (lī′ə-nĭs) *n.* A female lion.

li·on·heart·ed (lī′ən-här′tĭd) *adj.* Extraordinarily courageous.

li·on·ize (lī′ə-nīz′) *tr.v.* **-ized, -iz·ing.** To look upon or treat (a person) as a celebrity.

lip (lĭp) *n.* **1.** Either of the fleshy, muscular folds of tissue that together surround the mouth. **2.** Any structure that similarly encircles an opening, as: **a.** The flesh around a wound. **b.** The open rim of a glass, container, bell, etc. **3.** *Bot.* A protruding part of certain flowers, such as a snapdragon. **4.** The tip of a pouring spout. **5.** *Slang.* Insolent talk. —*tr.v.* **lipped, lip·ping. 1.** To touch the lips to. **2.** To speak, esp. in a whisper or murmur. —*adj.* **1.** *Phonet.* Formed or uttered with the lips; labial. **2.** Uttered insincerely: *lip admiration.* —*idioms.* **button (one's) lip.** *Slang.* To stop talking. **keep a stiff upper lip.** To appear stoical and courageous in the face of danger or great disappointment. [Middle English, from Old English *lippa.*]

lip-. Var. of **lipo-.**

li·pase (lī′pās′, lĭp′ās′) *n.* An enzyme that hydrolyzes fats to form glycerol and fatty acids. [LIP(O)- + -ASE.]

lip·id (lĭp′ĭd, lī′pĭd) *n.* Also **lip·ide** (lĭp′īd′, lī′pīd′). Any of a large number of fats or fatty substances that are insoluble in water and soluble in organic solvents and that are important structural materials of living cells. [French *lipide,* from Greek *lipos,* fat.]

lipo- or **lip-.** A prefix meaning fat: **lipoid.** [From Greek *lipos,* fat.]

lip·oid (lĭp′oid′) *adj.* Also **li·poi·dal** (lĭ-poi′dl). Resembling fat; fatty. [LIP(O)- + -OID.]

li·pol·y·sis (lĭ-pŏl′ĭ-sĭs, lī-) *n.* Hydrolysis of fat. [LIPO- + -LYSIS.]

li·po·ma (lĭ-pō′mə, lī-) *n., pl.* **-ma·ta** (-mə-tə) or **-mas.** A benign tumor of chiefly fatty cells. [LIP(O)- + -oma, tumor.] —**li·po′ma·tous** (-mə-təs) *adj.*

li·po·pro·tein (lĭ′pō-prō′tēn′, -tē-ĭn) *n.* A conjugated protein that consists of a simple protein combined with a lipid group.

lip-read (lĭp′rēd′) *v.* **-read** (-rĕd′), **-read·ing.** —*tr.v.* To interpret (another's utterance) by lip reading. —*intr.v.* To use lip reading.

lip reading. A technique for understanding unheard speech by interpreting lip and facial movements, used esp. by the deaf. —**lip reader.**

lip service. Insincere agreement or payment of respect.

lip·stick (lĭp′stĭk′) *n.* A cosmetic stick of waxy lip coloring enclosed in a small case.

liq·ue·fac·tion (lĭk′wə-făk′shən) *n.* **1.** The act or process of liquefying. **2.** The condition of being liquefied.

liq·ue·fy (lĭk′wə-fī′) *v.* **-fied, -fy·ing.** —*tr.v.* To cause to become liquid, esp.: **a.** To melt (a solid) by heating. **b.** To condense (a gas) by cooling. —*intr.v.* To become liquid. [Old French *liquefier,* from Latin *liquefacere : liquēre,* to be liquid + *facere,* to make.]

li·queur (lĭ-kûr′, -kyŏŏr′) *n.* A sweet alcoholic beverage made with various aromatic ingredients; a cordial. [French, from Old French *licour,* liquid, liquor.]

liq·uid (lĭk′wĭd) *n.* **1. a.** The state of matter in which a substance characteristically flows readily, has little or no tendency to disperse, and is relatively difficult to compress. **b.** Matter or a particular body of matter in this state: *a pool of liquid.* **2.** *Phonet.* The sounds of *l* and *r,* which are nonfrictional and vowellike. —*adj.* **1.** Of or being a liquid. **2.** Liquefied, esp.: **a.** Melted by heating: *liquid wax.* **b.** Condensed by cooling: *liquid oxygen.* **3.** Transparent; shining: *liquid brown eyes.* **4. a.** Flowing; limpid: *liquid prose.* **b.** Vowellike and articulated without friction, as a speech sound. **5.** Flowing gracefully in motion. **6.** Readily converted into cash: *liquid assets.* [From Middle English *liquide* (adj.), from Old French, from Latin *liquidus,* from *liquēre,* to be liquid.] —**li·quid′i·ty** (lĭ-kwĭd′ĭ-tē) *n.*

liquid air. Air in the liquid state, condensed from the gas by cooling and sometimes pressure.

liq·ui·date (lĭk′wĭ-dāt′) *tr.v.* **-dat·ed, -dat·ing. 1.** To pay off or settle (a debt, claim, etc.). **2.** To wind up the affairs of (a business firm, a bankrupt estate, etc.) by determining the liabilities and applying the assets to their discharge. **3.** To convert (assets) into cash. **4.** To put an end to; abolish. **5.** To put to death; kill. —See Syns at **murder.** [From Late Latin *liquidāre,* to make clear, melt, from Latin *liquidus,* liquid.] —**liq′ui·da′tion** *n.*

liquid measure. 1. A unit or system of units for measuring liquid volume or capacity. **2.** A measure for liquids.

liq·uor (lĭk′ər) *n.* **1.** An alcoholic beverage made by distillation rather than by fermentation. **2.** Any broth or juice produced in cooking. **3.** *Pharm.* A water solution of a nonvolatile substance. —*tr.v. Slang.* To cause to become drunk with alcoholic liquor. [Middle English *licour,* liquid, beverage, from Old French, from Latin *liquor,* from *liquēre,* to be liquid.]

liqu·o·rice (lĭk′ər-ĭs, -ĭsh) *n. Brit.* Var. of **licorice.**

li·ra (lîr′ə, lē′rə) *n.* The basic monetary unit of Italy and Turkey. [Italian, from Latin *lībra,* balance, measure.]

lisle (līl) *n.* **1.** A fine, smooth, tightly twisted thread spun from long-stapled cotton, used esp. for hosiery and underwear. **2.** Fabric knitted of lisle. [After *Lisle,* Lille, a city in France.]

lisp (lĭsp) *n.* **1.** A speech defect or mannerism, esp. one in which *s* and *z* are pronounced (th) and (th). **2.** The sound of a lisp. —*intr.v.* **1.** To speak with a lisp. **2.** To speak imperfectly, as a child does. —*tr.v.* To pronounce with a lisp. [Middle English *lispen,* from Old English *wlispian,* from *wlisp,* a lisping.] —**lisp′er** *n.*

lis·some (lĭs′əm) *adj.* Also **lis·som. 1.** Capable of moving or bending with ease; limber. **2.** Moving with agility and grace; nimble; lithe. [Var. of LITHESOME.] —**lis′some·ly** *adv.* —**lis′some·ness** *n.*

list[1] (lĭst) *n.* A series of names of people or things, written or printed one after the other: *a guest list; a shopping list.* —*tr.v.* **1.** To make a list of; itemize: *List your reasons.* **2.** To enter in a list: *not listed in the phone book.* —*intr.v.*

567

list² / litter

To have a stated list price: *The radio lists for $10 more than the sale price.* [Old French *liste*, band, strip of paper, from Old Italian *lista*.]

list² (list) *n.* An inclination to one side, as of a ship; a tilt. —*intr.v.* To lean to the side; to heel. —*tr.v.* To cause to lean to the side. [Orig. unknown.]

list³ (list) *n.* **1. a.** A narrow strip, esp. of wood. **b.** A border, as of cloth. **2.** A stripe or band of color. **3. lists. a.** An arena for tournaments or other contests, esp. one used by knights for jousting. **b.** Any place of combat. **c.** Any controversial issue. [Middle English *liste*, border, edge, strip, from Old English *liste*.]

list⁴ (list) *Poet.* —*tr.v.* To listen to. —*intr.v.* To listen. [Middle English *listen*, from Old English *hlystan*.]

lis·ten (lĭs′ən) *intr.v.* **1.** To make an effort to hear something. **2.** To pay attention; give heed: *They won't listen to the warnings.* —*phrasal verb.* **listen in. 1.** To tune in and listen to a broadcast. **2.** To listen to a conversation between others; eavesdrop. [Middle English *listnen*, from Old English *hlysnan*.] —**lis′ten·er** *n.*

list·er (lĭs′tər) *n.* A plow equipped with a double moldboard that turns up the soil on each side of the furrow. [From LIST (border).]

list·ing (lĭs′tĭng) *n.* **1.** A series of names of people or things. **2.** An entry in a list or directory.

list·less (lĭst′lĭs) *adj.* Marked by a lack of energy or disinclination toward any effort; lethargic. [Middle English *listles* : *list*, desire, from *listen*, to be pleasing + *-les*, without.] —**list′less·ly** *adv.* —**list′less·ness** *n.*

list price. A basic published or advertised price, often subject to discount.

lit (lĭt) *v.* **1.** A past tense and past participle of **light** (to illuminate). **2.** A past tense and past participle of **light** (to descend).

lit·a·ny (lĭt′n-ē) *n., pl.* **-nies. 1.** A liturgical prayer that consists of phrases recited by a leader who alternates with responses by the congregation. **2.** Any repetitive recital: *her daily litany of complaints.* [Middle English *letanie*, from Old French, from Late Latin *litanīa*, from Greek *litaneia*, entreaty.]

li·tchi (lē′chē) *n.* Also **li·chee** or **ly·chee. 1.** A Chinese tree, *Litchi chinensis*, that bears edible fruit. **2.** Also **litchi nut.** The fruit of this tree, with a bumpy covering and juicy white flesh. [Cantonese *lai chi*.]

-lite. A suffix meaning stone: **cryolite.** [French *-lite* and German *-lit*, from Greek *lithos*, stone.]

li·ter (lē′tər) *n.* Also *Brit.* **li·tre.** *Abbr* **l** A unit of volume that is equal to the volume of a cube that is one-tenth of a meter on each edge or about 1.056 liquid quarts or 0.908 dry quart. [French *litre*, from obs. *litron*, a measure of capacity, from Medieval Latin *lītra*, from Greek *litra*, a unit of weight.]

lit·er·a·cy (lĭt′ər-ə-sē) *n.* The condition or quality of being literate, esp. the ability to read and write.

lit·er·al (lĭt′ər-əl) *adj.* **1.** Reflecting or conforming to the exact or primary meaning of a word or words. **2.** Word for word; verbatim: *a literal translation.* **3.** Concerned chiefly with facts; prosaic: *a literal mind.* **4.** Avoiding exaggeration, metaphor, or embellishment; plain: *a literal statement.* **5.** Consisting of, using, or expressed by letters: *literal notation.* [Middle English, of letters, written, from Old French, from Late Latin *litterālis*, from Latin *littera*, letter.] —**lit′er·al·ly** *adv.* —**lit′er·al·ness** *n.*

lit·er·al·ism (lĭt′ər-ə-lĭz′əm) *n.* **1.** Adherence to the literal meaning of a given text or doctrine. **2.** Literal portrayal; realism. —**lit′er·al·ist** *n.* —**lit′er·al·is′tic** *adj.*

lit·er·ar·y (lĭt′ə-rĕr′ē) *adj.* **1.** Of, relating to, or dealing with literature. **2.** Suited to literature rather than to everyday speech or writing. **3.** Versed in or fond of literature or learning: *a literary man.* **4.** Of or relating to writers or the profession of literature: *literary circles.* [French *littéraire*, from Latin *litterārius*, of writing, from *litterae*, epistle, writing, pl. of *littera*, letter.]

lit·er·ate (lĭt′ər-ĭt) *adj.* **1.** Able to read and write. **2.** Skillful in the use of words. **3.** Knowledgeable; well-read. [Middle English *litterate*, from Latin *lit(t)erātus*, acquainted with writings, learned, from *litterae*, epistle, writing, pl. of *littera*, letter.] —**lit′er·ate** *n.*

lit·er·a·ti (lĭt′ə-rä′tē) *pl.n.* Distinguished writers and schol-

ars in general. [Italian, from Latin *litterātī*, pl. of *litterātus*, literate.]

lit·er·a·tim (lĭt′ə-rā′tĭm, -rä′-) *adv.* Letter for letter; literally. [Medieval Latin, from *littera*, letter.]

lit·er·a·ture (lĭt′ər-ə-chŏor′, -chər) *n.* **1.** A body of writing in prose or verse. **2.** Imaginative or creative writing, esp. of recognized artistic value. **3.** The art or occupation of a literary writer. **4.** The body of written work on a given subject: *medical literature.* **5.** Printed material of any kind, as for an advertising campaign. **6.** *Mus.* An entire group of compositions for a particular instrument or ensemble. [Middle English, from Old French, from Latin *litterātūra*, writing, learning, from *litterātus*, learned, literate.]

lith-. Var. of **litho-.**

-lith. A suffix meaning stone or rock: **batholith.** [Greek *lithos*, stone.]

lith·arge (lĭth′ärj′, lĭ-thärj′) *n.* A yellow lead oxide, PbO, used in storage batteries and glass and as a pigment. Also called **lead monoxide.** [Middle English, from Old French, from Latin *lithargyrus*, from Greek *litharguros*, "silver stone."]

lithe (lῑth, lῑth) *adj.* **lith·er, lith·est. 1.** Readily bent; supple: *lithe branches.* **2.** Marked by effortless grace: *a lithe gazelle.* [Middle English, meek, mild, flexible, from Old English *līthe*.] —**lithe′ly** *adv.* —**lithe′ness** *n.*

lithe·some (lῑth′səm, lῑth′-) *adj.* Lithe; lissome.

lith·ic (lĭth′ĭk) *adj.* **1.** Pertaining to stone. **2.** Pertaining to lithium. [Greek *lithikos*, from *lithos*, stone.]

-lithic. A suffix meaning the use of stone: **Neolithic.**

lith·i·um (lĭth′ē-əm) *n. Symbol* **Li** A soft, silvery, highly reactive metallic element that is used as a heat transfer medium, in thermonuclear weapons, and in various alloys, ceramics, and optical forms of glass. Atomic number 3; atomic weight 6.939; melting point 179°C; boiling point 1,317°C; specific gravity 0.534; valence 1. [LITH(O)- (from its mineral origin) + -IUM.]

litho- or **lith-.** A prefix meaning stone: **lithosphere.** [Latin, from Greek, from *lithos*, stone.]

lith·o·graph (lĭth′ə-grăf′) *n.* A print produced by lithography. —*tr.v.* To produce by lithography. —**li·thog′ra·pher** (lĭ-thŏg′rə-fər) *n.* —**lith′o·graph′ic** or **lith′o·graph′i·cal** *adj.* —**lith′o·graph′i·cal·ly** *adv.*

li·thog·ra·phy (lĭ-thŏg′rə-fē) *n.* A printing process in which the printing surface, often a metal plate, is treated so that ink will stick only to those parts that are to be printed.

li·thol·o·gy (lĭ-thŏl′ə-jē) *n.* **1.** The physical characteristics of a rock or a rock formation. **2.** The study, description, and classification of rock. —**lith′o·log′ic** *adj.* —**lith′o·log′i·cal·ly** *adv.* —**li·thol′o·gist** *n.*

lith·o·sphere (lĭth′ə-sfîr′) *n.* **1.** The solid part of the earth as distinguished from the hydrosphere and atmosphere. **2.** The rocky crust of the earth.

Lith·u·a·ni·an (lĭth′ŏo-ā′nē-ən) *adj.* Of or pertaining to Lithuania, its people, or their language. —*n.* **1.** An inhabitant or native of Lithuania. **2.** The Baltic language of the Lithuanians.

lit·i·gant (lĭt′ĭ-gənt) *n.* A person who is engaged in a lawsuit.

lit·i·gate (lĭt′ĭ-gāt′) *v.* **-gat·ed, -gat·ing.** —*tr.v.* To subject to legal proceedings. —*intr.v.* To engage in legal proceedings. [From Latin *lītigāre*, to dispute, quarrel, sue : *līs*, lawsuit + *agere*, to drive, lead, act.] —**lit′i·ga′tion** *n.* —**lit′i·ga′tor** *n.*

li·ti·gious (lĭ-tĭj′əs) *adj.* **1.** Of or pertaining to lawsuits or litigation. **2.** Tending to engage in lawsuits: *a litigious man.* —**li·ti′gious·ly** *adv.* —**li·ti′gious·ness** *n.*

lit·mus (lĭt′məs) *n.* A blue powder, derived from certain lichens, that changes from blue to red in an acid solution and from red to blue in an alkaline solution. [Perh. from Old Norse *litmosi*, "dye moss."]

litmus paper. White paper impregnated with litmus, used to distinguish acid and alkaline solutions.

li·tre (lῑ′tər) *n. Brit.* Var. of **liter.**

lit·ter (lĭt′ər) *n.* **1.** A couch with a canopy mounted on poles, used to carry a person from place to place. **2.** A stretcher for the sick or wounded. **3.** Straw or other material used as bedding for animals. **4.** Young animals produced at one birth by a single mother. **5.** Carelessly scattered scraps of

ă pat ā pay â care ä father ĕ pet ē be hw which ĭ pit ῑ tie î pier ŏ pot ō toe ô paw, for oi noise ŏŏ took ŏŏ boot ou out th thin th this ŭ cut û urge zh vision ə about, item, edible, gallop, circus

paper and other waste material. **6.** The uppermost layer of the forest floor, consisting chiefly of decaying organic matter. —*tr.v.* **1.** To give birth to (a litter). **2.** To make (a place) untidy by discarding rubbish carelessly. **3.** To scatter about. —*intr.v.* **1.** To give birth to a litter. **2.** To scatter litter. [Middle English *litere*, bed, offspring at birth, from Old French *litiere*, from Medieval Latin *lectāria*, from Latin *lectus*, bed.] —**lit′ter·er** *n.*

lit·té·ra·teur (lĭt′ər-ə-tûr′) *n.* Also **lit·ter·a·teur.** A person of letters. [French, from Latin *litterātor*, elementary teacher, grammarian, from *littera*, letter.]

lit·ter·bug (lĭt′ər-bŭg′) *n. Informal.* A person who litters public areas with waste materials.

lit·tle (lĭt′l) *adj.* **lit·tler** or **less** (lĕs), **lit·tlest** or **least** (lēst). **1.** Small in size: *a stout little man.* **2. a.** Young: *All but the littlest of the children had to work hard.* **b.** Younger: *He was close to his little brother all their lives.* **3.** Also comparative **less,** superlative **least. a.** Short in extent or duration; brief: *little time.* **b.** Small in quantity or degree: *little money.* **c.** Unimportant; trivial: *little trouble.* **4.** Narrow; petty: *Ignore his mean little comments.* **5.** Without much power or influence; of minor status: *the little people of the world.* **6.** Appealing; endearing: *the little rascal.* —*adv.* **less, least. 1.** Not much; scarcely: *He sleeps little.* **2.** Not at all; not in the least: *They little expected such trouble.* —*n.* **1.** A small amount or quantity: *Give me a little.* **2.** Something much less than all: *I know little of his history.* **3.** A short distance or time: *a little down the road; a little past four o'clock.* —*idioms.* **a little. 1.** Slightly: *I have to be a little careful about my diet.* **2.** A small amount of: *I wish I had a little flour to put in the pan.* **little by little.** By small degrees or increments; gradually. [Middle English *litel,* from Old English *lȳtel.*] —**lit′tle·ness** *n.*

Syns: 1. little, bantam, petite, small *adj.* Core meaning: Notably below average in amount, size, or scope (*a little dress; a little car*). **2. little, inconsequential, insignificant, trivial, unimportant** *adj.* Core meaning: Not of great importance (*upset by every little thing*).

Little Dipper. A constellation, **Ursa Minor.**

Little League. An organization of baseball teams for boys and girls eight to twelve years old.

lit·tle·neck (lĭt′l-nĕk′) *n.* The quahog clam when small and suitable for eating raw. [After *Littleneck* Bay, Long Island.]

little slam. *Bridge.* A contract of twelve tricks.

lit·to·ral (lĭt′ər-əl) *adj.* Of or existing on a shore, esp. a seashore. —*n.* A shore or coastal region. [Latin *littorālis,* from *lītus,* shore.]

li·tur·gi·cal (lĭ-tûr′jĭ-kəl) or **li·tur·gic** (-jĭk) *adj.* Of, relating to, or used in liturgy. —**li·tur′gi·cal·ly** *adv.*

lit·ur·gy (lĭt′ər-jē) *n., pl.* **-gies. 1.** The rite of the Eucharist. **2.** The prescribed form for a religious service; ritual. [Late Latin *lītūrgia,* from Greek *leitourgia,* public service, from *leitourgos,* public servant, priest.]

liv·a·ble (lĭv′ə-bəl) *adj.* Also **live·a·ble. 1.** Suitable to live in; habitable. **2.** Bearable; endurable.

live¹ (lĭv) *v.* **lived, liv·ing.** —*intr.v.* **1.** To be alive; exist: *Fish cannot live long out of water.* **2.** To continue to be alive: *Long live the king!* **3.** To support oneself; subsist: *living on rice and fish; lived on inherited income.* **4.** To reside; dwell: *He lives on a farm.* **5.** To conduct one's life in a particular manner: *live frugally.* **6.** To enjoy life to the utmost: *He really lived!* **7.** To remain in human memory: *He lives in the minds of us all.* —*tr.v.* **1.** To spend or pass (one's life): *lived his whole life there.* **2.** To embody in one's manner of existence: *He lived his beliefs.* —*phrasal verbs.* **live down.** To overcome or reduce the shame of (a scandal, misdeed, embarrassment, etc.) over a period of time. **live up to. 1.** To live in accordance with: *lived up to their ideals.* **2.** To come up to; not disappoint: *live up to a great reputation.* **3.** To fulfill; carry out: *live up to her end of the bargain.* **live with.** To put up with; resign oneself to: *We'll have to live with the new rules until we can change them.* —*idiom.* **live it up.** *Informal.* To engage in pleasures one usu. denies oneself. [Middle English *liven,* from Old English *libban.*]

live² (līv) *adj.* **1.** Having life; living: *live fishing bait.* **2.** Broadcast while actually being performed; not taped, filmed, or recorded: *a live television program.* **3.** Of cur-

rent interest: *a live topic.* **4.** Glowing; burning: *a live coal.* **5.** Not yet exploded; capable of being fired: *live ammunition.* **6.** Carrying an electric current or energized with electricity: *dangerous live wires.* **7.** Native; not mined or quarried: *live ores.* **8.** Providing or transmitting motion: *a live axle.* **9.** *Sports.* Being or capable of being in play: *a live ball.* —See Syns at **alive.** [Short for ALIVE.]

live·a·ble (līv′ə-bəl) *adj.* Var. of **livable.**

live·li·hood (līv′lē-hood′) *n.* Means of support; way of earning sustenance. —See Syns at **living.** [Var. of Middle English *liv(e)lode,* course of life, sustenance, from Old English *līflād : līf,* life + *lād,* course.]

live·long (līv′lông′, -lŏng′) *adj.* Complete; whole: *the livelong day.* [Middle English *lefe longe : lef* (intensive) + *long,* long.]

live·li·ness (līv′lē-nĭs) *n.* The condition or quality of being lively. —See Syns at **spirit.**

live·ly (līv′lē) *adj.* **-li·er, -li·est. 1.** Full of life, energy, or activity; vigorous: *a lively baby.* **2.** Full of spirit; gay and animated: *a lively tune.* **3.** Keen; brisk: *lively trade between the two countries.* **4.** Bouncing readily upon impact; resilient: *a lively baseball.* —See Syns at **vigorous.** —*adv.* In a vigorous, energetic, or spirited manner: *Step lively!*

liv·en (lī′vən) *tr.v.* To cause to become lively. —*intr.v.* To become lively.

live oak (līv). Any of several evergreen American oaks, such as *Quercus virginiana,* of the southeastern United States, or *Q. agrifolia,* of southwestern North America.

liv·er¹ (lĭv′ər) *n.* **1.** A large glandular organ in the abdomen of vertebrates that secretes bile and acts in the formation of blood and in the metabolism of carbohydrates, fats, proteins, minerals, and vitamins. **2.** A similar organ of invertebrate animals. **3.** The liver of an animal used as food. —*modifier:* *liver pâté.* [Middle English, from Old English *lifer.*]

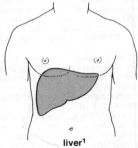

liver¹

liv·er² (lĭv′ər) *n.* Someone who lives in a specified manner: *a high liver.*

liver fluke. Any of several parasitic trematode worms that infest the liver of various animals, including humans.

liv·er·ied (lĭv′ə-rēd, lĭv′rēd) *adj.* Wearing livery, esp. as a servant: *a liveried footman.*

liv·er·ish (lĭv′ər-ĭsh) *adj.* **1.** Having a liver ailment; bilious. **2.** Having a disagreeable disposition; irritable.

liv·er·wort (lĭv′ər-wûrt′, -wôrt′) *n.* The hepatica.

liv·er·wurst (lĭv′ər-wûrst′, -woorst′) *n.* A sausage made of or containing ground liver.

liv·er·y (lĭv′ə-rē, lĭv′rē) *n., pl.* **-ies. 1.** A distinctive uniform worn by the male servants of a household, as by footmen. **2.** The distinctive dress worn by the members of a particular group. **3. a.** The stabling and care of horses for a fee. **b.** The hiring out of horses and carriages. **c.** A **livery stable.** [Middle English *livere,* from Old French *livree,* allowance granted to servants, from *livrer,* to deliver, relieve, from Latin *līber,* free.]

liv·er·y·man (lĭv′ə-rē-mən, lĭv′rē-) *n.* A keeper or employee of a livery stable.

livery stable. A stable that boards horses and keeps horses and carriages for hire. Also called **livery.**

lives (līvz) *n.* Plural of **life.**

live·stock (līv′stŏk′) *n.* Domestic animals, such as cattle or horses, raised for home use or for profit.

live wire (līv). **1.** A wire carrying electric current. **2.** *Slang.* A vivacious, alert, or energetic person.

ă pat	ā pay	â care	ä father	ĕ pet	ē be	hw which	ĭ pit	ī tie	î pier	ŏ pot	ō toe	ô paw, for	oi noise
oo took	oo boot	ou out	th thin	th this	ŭ cut		û urge	zh vision	ə about, item, edible, gallop, circus				

liv·id (lĭv'ĭd) *adj.* **1.** Discolored, as from a bruise; black-and-blue. **2.** Ashen or very pale, as from anger. **3.** Extremely angry; furious. [French *livide,* from Latin *līvidus,* from *līvēre,* to be bluish.] —**li·vid·i·ty** (lĭ-vĭd'ĭ-tē) or **liv·id·ness** *n.* —**liv·id·ly** *adv.*

liv·ing (lĭv'ĭng) *adj.* **1.** Possessing life; alive: *famous living painters.* **2.** In active function or use: *a living language.* **3.** True to life; real: *the living image of her mother.* **4.** *Informal.* Definite; absolute: *a living doll.* —See Syns at **alive.** —*n.* **1.** The condition or action of maintaining life: *the high cost of living.* **2.** A manner or style of life: *plain living.* **3.** A means of maintaining life; livelihood: *made their living by hunting.*

Syns: *living, keep, livelihood, maintenance, subsistence, support, sustenance n. Core meaning:* The means needed to support life (*earn a living*).

living room. A room for general use in a household.

living wage. A wage sufficient to provide minimally satisfactory living conditions.

liz·ard (lĭz'ərd) *n.* **1.** Any of numerous reptiles of the suborder Sauria (or Lacertilia), with an often elongated, scaly body, four legs, and a tapering tail. **2.** Leather made from the skin of a lizard. —*modifier: lizard shoes.* [Middle English *liserd,* from Old French *lesard,* from Latin *lacerta.*]

lla·ma (lä'mə) *n.* A South American mammal, *Lama peruana,* related to the camel and raised for its wool and for carrying loads. [Spanish, from Quechua.]

lla·no (lä'nō, lăn'ō) *n., pl.* **-nos.** A large, grassy, almost treeless plain, esp. one in South America. [Spanish, from Latin *plānum,* a plain, from *plānus,* level.]

lo (lō) *interj.* A word used to call attention to something remarkable or important. [Middle English, from Old English *lā.*]

loach (lōch) *n.* Any of various Old World freshwater fishes of the family Cobitidae, with barbels around the mouth. [Middle English *loche,* from Old French.]

load (lōd) *n.* **1.** A weight or mass that is carried, lifted, or supported. **2. a.** Anything that is carried, as by a vehicle, person, or animal: *a load of firewood.* **b.** The quantity of such material: *a wagon with a full load of hay.* **3. a.** The share of work allocated to or required of an individual, machine, group, or organization. **b.** The demand for services or performance made on a machine or system. **4.** The amount that can be loaded into a machine or device at one time. **5.** A single charge of ammunition for a firearm. **6. a.** Mental stress regarded as a depressing weight or burden: *a load off my mind.* **b.** A responsibility regarded as an oppressive weight. **7.** The external mechanical resistance against which a machine acts. **8. a.** The power output of a generator or power plant. **b.** A device or the resistance of a device to which power is delivered. **9.** Often **loads.** *Informal.* A great number or amount: *loads of parties.* —*tr.v.* **1. a.** To put or place (a load) in or on a structure, device, or conveyance: *load grain onto a train.* **b.** To put or place in or on (a structure, device, or conveyance): *load a ship.* **2.** To provide or fill nearly to overflowing: *load a table with food.* **3.** To weigh down; burden: *Illness loaded him with worries.* **4.** To charge (a firearm) with ammunition. **5. a.** To insert (film, tape, etc.) into a holder or magazine: *load film into a camera.* **b.** To insert film, tape, etc., into: *load a camera.* **6.** To make (dice) heavier on one side by adding weight. **7.** To distort (a question or questions) so as to elicit a desired response. **8.** To dilute, adulterate, or doctor. —*intr.v.* To receive a load. —*idiom.* **get a load of.** *Slang.* To take notice of: *Get a load of that new car.* [Middle English *lode,* from Old English *lād,* way, course, conveyance.] —**load'er** *n.*

load·ed (lō'dĭd) *adj.* **1.** *Slang.* Intoxicated. **2.** *Slang.* Having much money; rich. —See Syns at **rich.**

load·star (lōd'stär') *n.* Var. of **lodestar.**

load·stone (lōd'stōn') *n.* Var. of **lodestone.**

loaf¹ (lōf) *n., pl.* **loaves** (lōvz). **1.** A shaped mass of bread baked in one piece. **2.** Any shaped mass of food: *veal loaf.* —*modifier: a loaf pan.* [Middle English *loof,* from Old English *hlāf,* loaf, bread.]

loaf² (lōf) *intr.v.* To spend time lazily or aimlessly. —*tr.v.* To spend (time) lazily or aimlessly: *loafed the day away.* [Prob. back-formation from LOAFER.]

loaf·er (lō'fər) *n.* **1.** Someone who loafs; an idler. **2.** A ca-

sual or informal moccasinlike shoe without laces. [Orig. unknown.]

loam (lōm) *n.* **1.** Soil consisting mainly of sand, clay, silt, and organic matter. **2.** A mixture of moist clay and sand, together with straw, used esp. in making bricks and foundry molds. [Middle English *lome,* from Old English *lām.*] —**loam'y** *adj.*

loan (lōn) *n.* **1.** A sum of money lent at interest. **2.** Anything lent for temporary use; something borrowed. **3.** The action of lending. —*tr.v.* To lend. —See Syns at **lend.** [Middle English *lone,* from Old Norse *lān.*]

loan shark. *Informal.* A usurer, esp. one who is financed and supported by gangsters.

loan-word (lōn'wûrd') *n.* Also **loan word** or **loan·word.** A word borrowed from another language that has become at least partly naturalized.

loath (lōth, lōth) *adj.* Also **loth.** Unwilling; reluctant; disinclined: *loath to go.* [Middle English *lothe,* from Old English *lāth,* hateful, loathsome.]

loathe (lōth) *tr.v.* **loathed, loath·ing.** To dislike greatly; detest; abhor. —See Syns at **hate.** [Middle English *lothen,* from Old English *lāthian.*]

loath·ing (lō'thĭng) *n.* Extreme dislike; abhorrence.

loath·ly (lōth'lē, lōth'-) *adj.* Loathsome.

loath·some (lōth'səm, lōth'-) *adj.* Abhorrent; detestable; repulsive; disgusting. —**loath'some·ly** *adv.* —**loathe'some·ness** *n.*

loaves (lōvz) *n.* Plural of **loaf** (bread).

lob (lŏb) *v.* **lobbed, lob·bing.** —*tr.v.* To hit, throw, or propel (a ball) in a high arc. —*intr.v.* To hit a ball in a high arc. —*n.* A ball hit or thrown in a high arc. [Prob. of Low German orig.]

lo·bar (lō'bər, -bär') *adj.* Of or relating to a lobe, such as one of those in the lungs: *lobar pneumonia.*

lo·bate (lō'bāt') *adj.* Also **lo·bat·ed** (-bā'tĭd). **1.** Having lobes. **2.** Resembling a lobe.

lob·by (lŏb'ē) *n., pl.* **-bies. 1.** A hall, foyer, or waiting room at or near the entrance to buildings, such as hotels, apartment houses, or theaters. **2.** A public room next to the assembly chamber of a legislative body. **3.** A group of private persons engaged in trying to influence legislators in favor of some special interest. —*v.* **-bied, -by·ing.** —*intr.v.* To seek to influence legislators in favor of some special interest. —*tr.v.* To seek to influence legislators to pass (legislation). [Medieval Latin *lobium,* a monastic cloister.] —**lob'by·ist** *n.*

lobe (lōb) *n.* A rounded projection, esp. a projecting anatomical part such as the fleshy lower part of the external human ear. [Old French, from Late Latin *lobus,* from Greek *lobos,* earlobe.] —**lobed** *adj.*

lo·be·li·a (lō-bē'lē-ə, -bēl'yə) *n.* Any of numerous plants of the genus *Lobelia,* with terminal clusters of variously colored flowers. [After Matthias de Lobel (1538–1616), Flemish botanist.]

lob·lol·ly (lŏb'lŏl'ē) *n., pl.* **-lies.** *Regional.* **1.** A mudhole; a mire. **2.** A lout. [Orig. "a thick gruel."]

loblolly pine. A pine, *Pinus taeda,* of the southeastern United States, with strong wood used as lumber.

lo·bo (lō'bō) *n., pl.* **-bos.** *Western U.S.* The gray or timber wolf, *Canis lupus.* [Spanish, from Latin *lupus,* wolf.]

lo·bot·o·my (lō-bŏt'ə-mē, lə-) *n., pl.* **-mies.** A surgical operation that severs one or more frontal lobes of the brain. [LOB(E) + -TOMY.]

lob·ster (lŏb'stər) *n.* **1.** Any of several relatively large salt-

lobster

water crustaceans of the genus *Homarus* that have five pairs of legs, with the first pair modified into large claws. **2.** Any of several related crustaceans, such as the spiny lobster. **3.** The flesh of any of these crustaceans used as food. [Middle English, from Old English *loppestre,* from Latin *locusta,* locust, lobster.]

lobster pot. A cage for trapping lobsters.

lob·ule (lŏb′yool) *n.* **1.** A small lobe. **2.** A section or subdivision of a lobe. **—lob′u·lar** (-yə-lər) *adj.*

lo·cal (lō′kəl) *adj.* **1.** Of a limited area or place: *local governments.* **2.** Making many stops; not express: *a local train.* **3.** Limited to part of the body rather than the entire system: *a local infection.* **—n.** **1.** A person who lives in a certain region or neighborhood. **2.** A local branch of an organization, esp. of a labor union. **3.** A local train, bus, etc. [Middle English, from Old French, from Late Latin *locālis,* from Latin *locus,* place.] **—lo′cal·ly** *adv.*

local anesthetic. An anesthetic that acts only on and around the point where it is applied or injected.

local color. The interest or flavor of a locality imparted by the customs and sights peculiar to it.

lo·cale (lō-kăl′, -käl′) *n.* **1.** A locality with reference to some event. **2.** The scene or setting as of written work. [French *local,* from Old French, local.]

lo·cal·ism (lō′kə-lĭz′əm) *n.* **1.** An idiom, mannerism, custom, etc., peculiar to a locality. **2.** Provincialism.

lo·cal·i·ty (lō-kăl′ĭ-tē) *n., pl.* **-ties.** **1.** A certain neighborhood, place, or region. **2.** A site, as of an event.

lo·cal·ize (lō′kə-līz′) *v.* **-ized, -iz·ing.** **—tr.v.** **1.** To confine or restrict to a particular area or part: *localize the infection.* **2.** To attribute to a particular locality. **—intr.v.** To become local, esp. to become fixed in one area or part: *The pain localized in her abdomen.* **—lo′cal·i·za′tion** *n.*

local option. Option granted usu. by a state government to a local government in such issues as whether to keep stores open on Sundays.

lo·cate (lō′kāt, lō-kāt′) *v.* **-cat·ed, -cat·ing.** **—tr.v.** **1.** To determine or specify the position and boundaries of: *locate Albany on the map.* **2.** To find by searching, examining, or experimenting: *locate the source of error.* **3.** To situate or place: *locate an agent in Rochester.* **—intr.v.** To become established in some spot; settle: *The family has located in Alaska.* **—**See Syns at **find.** [From Latin *locāre,* to place, from *locus,* place, locus.] **—lo′ca·tor** *n.*

lo·ca·tion (lō-kā′shən) *n.* **1.** The act or process of locating. **2.** The fact of being located or settled. **3.** A place where something is or might be located; a site or position: *the location of the hospital.* **4.** A site away from a motion-picture studio at which a scene is filmed: *shot on location in Spain.* **5.** A tract of land that has been surveyed and marked off.

loc·a·tive (lŏk′ə-tĭv) *adj.* Of a noun case in an inflected language that denotes place or the place where. **—n.** **1.** The locative case. **2.** A word in this case. [French *locatif,* from Old French, from Latin *locāre,* to locate.]

loch (lŏкн, lŏk) *n. Scot.* **1.** A lake. **2.** An arm of the sea similar to a fjord. [Middle English *louch,* from Scottish Gaelic *loch.*]

lo·ci (lō′sī′) *n.* Plural of **locus.**

lock[1] (lŏk) *n.* **1.** A device used to hold, close, or secure, esp. a device operated by a key or combination that holds a door, lid, etc., shut. **2.** A section of a canal, closed off with gates, in which a vessel may be raised or lowered by raising or lowering the water level. **3.** A mechanism in a firearm for exploding the charge. **4.** Any of several holds in wrestling. **5.** An airlock. **—tr.v.** **1. a.** To fasten shut or secure with a lock: *lock a door.* **b.** To shut by fastening all locks: *lock up a house.* **2.** To confine or safeguard by putting behind a lock: *lock the dog in for the night.* **3.** To engage and fasten securely: *The brake locks the wheels.* **4.** To clasp or link firmly; intertwine: *They locked arms and walked off.* **5.** To make and hold (eye contact): *They locked eyes.* **6.** To jam or force together so as to make unmovable: *He shifted too quickly and locked the gears.* **—intr.v.** To become locked. **—phrasal verbs. lock out. 1.** To shut out by or as if by locking a door: *locked him out of their games.* **2.** To prevent (employees) from entering their place of work during a labor dispute. **lock up.** To put in jail or a place of restraint. **—idiom. lock, stock, and**

barrel. Together with everything; completely; entirely: *sold the place lock, stock, and barrel.* [Middle English, from Old English *loc.*]

lock[2] (lŏk) *n.* **1.** A strand or curl of hair; tress; ringlet. **2. locks.** The hair of the head. **3.** A small wisp or tuft, as of wool or cotton. [Middle English, from Old English *locc.*]

lock·age (lŏk′ĭj) *n. Naut.* **1.** The passage of a vessel through a lock. **2.** A system of locks.

lock·er (lŏk′ər) *n.* **1.** An enclosure that can be locked, esp. one at a gymnasium or public place for the safekeeping of clothing and valuables. **2.** A flat trunk for storing things. **3.** A refrigerated cabinet or room for storing frozen foods. **4.** Someone who locks.

locker room. **1.** A room in a gymnasium, school, clubhouse, etc., with metal lockers. **2.** A room for changing one's clothes, as at a public swimming place.

lock·et (lŏk′ĭt) *n.* A small ornamental case for a keepsake, usu. worn on a chain around the neck. [Old French *locquet,* latch, dim. of *loc,* lock.]

lock·jaw (lŏk′jô′) *n.* **1.** Tetanus. **2.** A symptom of tetanus in which the jaw is held tightly closed by a spasm of muscles.

lock·nut (lŏk′nŭt′) *n.* Also **lock nut. 1.** A usu. thin nut screwed down on a primary nut to keep the latter from loosening. **2.** A self-locking nut.

lock·out (lŏk′out′) *n.* The closing down of a plant by an employer to force the workers to meet his terms or modify theirs. Also called **shutout.**

lock·smith (lŏk′smĭth′) *n.* A person who makes or repairs locks.

lock step. A marching technique in which the marchers follow each other as closely as possible.

lock stitch. A stitch made on a sewing machine by the interlocking of the upper thread and the bobbin thread.

lock·up (lŏk′ŭp′) *n. Informal.* A jail, esp. one in which offenders are held while awaiting a court hearing.

lo·co (lō′kō) *n., pl.* **-cos.** Locoweed. **—adj. Slang.** Mad; insane. **—**See Syns at **insane.** [Mexican Spanish, from Spanish, crazy, insane.]

lo·co·mo·tion (lō′kə-mō′shən) *n.* The act or capability of moving from place to place. [Latin *locō,* from *locus,* place + MOTION.]

lo·co·mo·tive (lō′kə-mō′tĭv) *n.* A self-propelled engine, now usu. electric or diesel-powered, that pulls or pushes freight or passenger cars on railroad tracks. **—adj. 1.** Of or involved in locomotion: *locomotive organs.* **2.** Able to move independently from place to place. **3.** Of or relating to travel. [Old French, capable of moving from place to place.]

lo·co·mo·tor (lō′kə-mō′tər) *adj.* Of or relating to locomotion; locomotive.

locomotor ataxia. *Pathol.* A disease in which the dorsal columns of the spinal cord harden and the ability to coordinate voluntary movements is lost.

lo·co·weed (lō′kō-wēd′) *n.* Any of several plants of the genera *Oxytropis* and *Astragalus,* of the western and central United States, that cause severe poisoning when eaten by livestock.

loc·ule (lŏk′yool) *n.* Also **loc·u·lus** (-yə-ləs) *pl.* **-li** (-lī′). A small cavity or compartment within an organ or part such as a plant ovary. [Latin, dim. of *locus,* place.]

lo·cum te·nens (lō′kəm tē′nĕnz′, -nənz) *Brit.* A substitute for another, esp. a physician or clergyman. [Medieval Latin *locum tenēns,* "(one) holding the place."]

lo·cus (lō′kəs) *n., pl.* **-ci** (-sī′). **1.** A place. **2.** *Math.* The set or arrangement of all points that satisfy specified mathematical conditions. **3.** *Genetics.* The position that a gene occupies on a chromosome. [Latin.]

lo·cust[1] (lō′kəst) *n.* **1.** Any of numerous grasshoppers of

locust[1]

the family Locustidae, often traveling in swarms and causing damage to vegetation. **2.** A cicada such as the seventeen-year locust. [Middle English, from Old French *locuste*, from Latin *locusta*.]

lo·cust² (lō′kəst) *n.* **1.** A North American tree, *Robinia pseudo-acacia*, that has compound leaves, drooping clusters of fragrant white flowers, hard, durable wood, and beanlike pods. **2.** Any of several similar or related trees, such as the carob. **3.** The wood of such a tree. [From the locust-shaped pods of some species.]

lo·cu·tion (lō-kyōō′shən) *n.* **1.** A particular word, phrase, or expression considered from the point of view of style. **2.** Style of speaking; phraseology. [Middle English *locucion*, from Latin *locūtiō*, speech, utterance, from *locūtus*, past part. of *loquī*, to speak.]

lode (lōd) *n.* A deposit of a metal-bearing ore, such as a vein clearly bounded by rock that is not ore. [Middle English, course, way, from Old English *lād*.]

lode·star (lōd′stär′) *n.* Also **load·star.** **1.** A star that is used as a point of reference, esp. Polaris, the North Star. **2.** A guiding principle, interest, or ambition. [Middle English *lode sterre* : *lode*, course, guidance + *sterre*, star.]

lode·stone (lōd′stōn′) *n.* Also **load·stone.** **1.** A magnetized piece of magnetite. **2.** Someone or something that attracts strongly. [From obs. *lode*, course + STONE.]

lodge (lŏj) *n.* **1.** A cottage or cabin, often rustic, used as a temporary abode or shelter: *a ski lodge.* **2.** A small house on the grounds of an estate for a caretaker, gatekeeper, etc. **3.** An inn. **4. a.** A North American Indian hogan, wigwam, or long house. **b.** The group who live in such a unit. **5. a.** A local chapter of certain fraternal organizations. **b.** The meeting hall of such a society. **6.** The den of certain animals, as the dome-shaped structure built by beavers. —*v.* **lodged, lodg·ing.** —*tr.v.* **1. a.** To provide with quarters temporarily, esp. for sleeping. **b.** To rent a room or rooms to. **2.** To place or establish in quarters: *lodge children with relatives.* **3.** To serve as a depository for; to harbor: *His cellar lodges the stolen money.* **4.** To place, leave, or deposit, as for safety: *lodge the evidence in the safe.* **5.** To fix, force, or implant: *lodge a bullet in the wall.* **6.** To register (a charge) in court or with an appropriate party: *lodge a complaint.* —*intr.v.* **1. a.** To live in a rented room or rooms. **b.** To rent accommodations, esp. for sleeping. **2.** To be or become embedded: *A splinter lodged in his foot.* [Middle English *loge*, from Old French, shed, small house.]

lodge·pole pine (lŏj′pōl′). A pine, *Pinus contorta*, of western North America, that has light wood used in construction.

lodg·er (lŏj′ər) *n.* A person who rents and lives in a furnished room or rooms; roomer.

lodg·ing (lŏj′ĭng) *n.* **1.** Sleeping accommodations: *a lodging for the night.* **2. lodgings.** Rented rooms.

lo·ess (lō′əs, lĕs, lōōs) *n.* A yellow to gray fine-grained silt or clay, thought to be deposited as dust blown by the wind. [German *Löss*, from dial. German *Lösch*, from *lösch*, loose.]

loft (lôft, lŏft) *n.* **1.** A large, usu. unpartitioned floor in a commercial or industrial building. **2.** An open space under a roof; attic. **3.** A gallery or balcony, as in a church: *a choir loft.* **4.** A hayloft. **5.** *Golf.* **a.** The backward slant of the face of a club head, designed to drive the ball in a high arc. **b.** The upward course of a lofted ball. —*tr.v.* **1.** To put, store, or keep in a loft. **2.** To send (a golfball) in a high arc. [Middle English *lofte*, upper room, sky, from Old English *loft*, sky, air, from Old Norse *lopt*, air, attic.]

loft·y (lôf′tē, lŏf′-) *adj.* **-i·er, -i·est.** **1.** Of imposing height; towering: *lofty mountains.* **2.** Elevated in character; exalted; noble: *lofty thoughts; lofty principles.* **3.** Arrogant; haughty: *lofty treatment of others.* [Middle English, from *lofte*, raised, elevated, from *lofte*, sky, loft.] —**loft′i·ly** *adv.* —**loft′i·ness** *n.*

log¹ (lôg, lŏg) *n.* **1. a.** A trunk of a tree that has fallen or been cut down. **b.** A cut section of such wood, used for building, firewood, or lumber. **2.** *Naut.* A device trailed from a ship to determine its speed through the water. **3. a.** An official record of speed, progress, and important events, kept on a ship or aircraft. **b.** Any journal or record. —*modifier:* *a log cabin.* —*v.* **logged, log·ging.** —*tr.v.*

1. a. To cut down the timber of (a section of land). **b.** To cut (trees) into logs. **2. a.** To enter (something) in a ship's or aircraft's log. **b.** To travel (a specified distance, time, or speed): *She logs 15 miles an hour.* **3.** To chalk up creditably: *He's logged 25 years with his company.* —*intr.v.* To cut down, trim, and haul timber. [Middle English *logge.*]

log² (lôg, lŏg) *n.* Logarithm.

lo·gan·ber·ry (lō′gən-bĕr′ē) *n.* **1.** A prickly plant, *Rubus loganobaccus*, cultivated for its edible fruit. **2.** The red fruit of this plant. [After James H. *Logan* (1841–1928), American judge and horticulturist.]

log·a·rithm (lô′gə-rĭth′əm, lŏg′ə-) *n.* The exponent that indicates the power to which a fixed positive number, called the base, must be raised to produce a given number. For example, if $n^x = a$, the logarithm of a, with n as the base, is x; symbolically, $\log_n a = x$. [Greek *logos*, reckoning, reason, ratio + *arithmos*, number.] —**log′a·rith′mic** (-rĭth′-mĭk) or **log′a·rith′mi·cal** *adj.* —**log′a·rith′mi·cal·ly** *adv.*

log·book (lôg′bŏok′, lŏg′-) *n.* Also **log book.** The official record book of a ship or aircraft; log.

loge (lōzh) *n.* **1.** A small compartment, esp. a box in a theater. **2.** The front rows of a theater's mezzanine. [French, from Old French, shed, small house.]

log·ger (lô′gər, lŏg′ər) *n.* **1.** A lumberjack. **2.** A machine used for hauling or loading logs.

log·ger·head (lô′gər-hĕd′, lŏg′ər-) *n.* **1.** A marine turtle, *Caretta caretta*, with a large, beaked head. **2.** *Informal.* A stupid person; blockhead; dolt. —*idiom.* **at loggerheads.** In a head-on dispute; at odds. [Dial. *logger*, wooden block, from LOG + HEAD.]

log·gi·a (lō′jē-ə, lŏj′ē-ə) *n.* A roofed but open gallery or arcade along the front or side of a building. [Italian, from French *loge*, loge.]

log·ging (lô′gĭng, lŏg′ĭng) *n.* The work of felling and trimming trees and transporting the logs to a mill.

log·ic (lŏj′ĭk) *n.* **1.** The study of the principles of reasoning, esp. of the forms and relationships between statements as distinguished from the content of statements. **2.** A particular system or method of reasoning. **3.** Valid reasoning, esp. as distinguished from invalid or irrational reasoning. **4.** The relationship of element to element to whole in a set of objects, individuals, principles, or events. [Middle English *logik*, from Old French *logique*, from Late Latin *logica*, from Greek *logikē (tekhnē)*, "(art) of reasoning."]

log·i·cal (lŏj′ĭ-kəl) *adj.* **1.** Of, using, or agreeing with logic. **2.** Showing consistency of reasoning: *a logical essay.* **3.** Reasonable: *a logical choice.* **4.** Able to reason clearly: *a logical thinker.* —See Syns at **sensible.** —**log′i·cal·ly** *adv.* —**log′i·cal·ness** *n.*

lo·gi·cian (lō-jĭsh′ən) *n.* A person who practices or is skilled in logic.

lo·gis·tic (lō-jĭs′tĭk) or **lo·gis·ti·cal** (-tĭ-kəl) *adj.* Of or pertaining to logistics. —**lo·gis′ti·cal·ly** *adv.*

lo·gis·tics (lō-jĭs′tĭks) *n.* (*used with a sing. verb*). The problems and methods of obtaining, transporting, distributing, maintaining, and replacing material and personnel, as in a military operation. [French *logistique*, from Greek *logistikē*, the art of arithmetic, from *logos*, reason.]

log·jam (lôg′jăm′, lŏg′-) *n.* Also **log-jam** or **log jam.** **1.** A mass of floating logs crowded immovably together. **2.** A deadlock; impasse.

lo·go·type (lō′gə-tīp′, lŏ′-, lôg′ə-) *n.* **1.** A single piece of type bearing two or more separate elements. **2.** The name, symbol, or trademark of a company or publication. [Greek *logos*, word + TYPE.]

log·roll·ing or **log-roll·ing** (lôg′rō′lĭng, lŏg′-) *n.* **1.** The sport of rolling logs; birling. **2.** The exchanging of political favors, esp. the trading of influence or votes among legislators to achieve passage of projects of interest to one another. —**log′roll′er** *n.*

log·wood (lôg′wŏod′, lŏg′-) *n.* A tropical American tree, *Haematoxylon campechianum*, with dark heartwood from which a dye is obtained.

lo·gy (lō′gē) *adj.* **-gi·er, -gi·est.** Sluggish; lethargic. [Perh. from Dutch *log*, heavy, sluggish.] —**lo′gi·ness** *n.*

-logy A suffix meaning: **1.** Discourse or expression: **phraseology.** **2.** The science, theory, or study of: **geology.** [Middle English *-logie*, from Old French, from Latin *-logia*, from Greek, from *logos*, word, speech.]

ă pat	ā pay	â care	ä father	ĕ pet	ē be	hw which	ĭ pit	ī tie	î pier	ŏ pot	ō toe	ô paw, for	oi noise
ōō took	ōō boot	ou out	th thin	th this	ŭ cut	û urge	zh vision	ə about, item, edible, gallop, circus

loin (loin) n. **1.** Often **loins.** The part of the sides and back of the body between the ribs and the hipbones. **2.** A cut of meat taken from the loin of a four-legged animal. **3. a. loins.** The region of the thighs and groin. **b.** The reproductive organs. [Middle English *loyne*, from Old French *loigne*, ult. from Latin *lumbus*, loin.]

loin·cloth (loin′klôth′, -klŏth′) n. A strip of cloth worn around the loins as a garment.

loi·ter (loi′tər) intr. v. **1.** To stand idly about; linger aimlessly. **2.** To proceed slowly or with many stops. **3.** To dawdle: *loiter over a job.* —See Syns at **delay.** [Middle English *loyteren.*] —**loi′ter·er** n.

Lo·ki (lō′kē) n. Norse Myth. A god who created discord, esp. among his fellow gods.

loll (lŏl) intr.v. **1.** To move, stand, or recline in a lazy or relaxed manner: *lolling about in a robe at home.* **2.** To hang laxly: *The wolf's tongue lolled.* —tr.v. To permit to hang laxly. [Middle English *lollen.*]

lol·li·pop (lŏl′ē-pŏp′) n. Also **lol·ly·pop.** A piece of hard candy on the end of a stick. [Perh. LOLL + POP.]

Lom·bar·dy poplar (lŏm′bər-dē, lŭm′-). A tree, *Populus nigra italica,* with upward-pointing branches that form a slender, columnar outline.

lone (lōn) adj. **1.** Companionless; solitary: *a lone tree.* **2.** Only; sole: *the lone doctor in the county.* **3.** Isolated; unfrequented; remote; lonely: *the lone prairie.* **4.** Unmarried or widowed. —See Syns at **single.** [Short for ALONE.]

lone·li·ness (lōn′lē-nĭs) n. The condition of being alone or lonely. —See Syns at **solitude.**

lone·ly (lōn′lē) adj. **-li·er, -li·est. 1. a.** Sad at being alone: *a lonely boy with no friends.* **b.** Producing such sadness: *the loneliest night of the week.* **2. a.** Without companions; lone: *a lonely traveler.* **b.** Characterized by aloneness; solitary: *a lonely existence.* **3.** Empty of people; unfrequented; remote; desolate: *a lonely crossroads.* —See Syns at **alone.**

lon·er (lō′nər) n. Informal. Someone who avoids other people.

lone·some (lōn′səm) adj. **1.** Sad and depressed at feeling alone: *a lonesome girl away from home for the first time.* **2.** Producing a sense of loneliness: *a lonesome trip.* **3.** Deserted; unfrequented: *a lonesome valley.* **4.** Lone. —See Syns at **alone.** —**lone′some·ly** adv. —**lone′some·ness** n.

long¹ (lông, lŏng) adj. **-er, -est. 1.** Having great length: *a long river; a long book.* **2.** Of the greater or greatest length: *the long wall of the room.* **3.** Of relatively great duration or extent: *a long time; a long journey.* **4.** Of a certain linear extent or duration: *a mile long; an hour long.* **5.** Extending beyond an average or a standard: *a long game.* **6.** Extending far into the future or past; far-reaching: *a long view of the problem.* **7.** Risky; chancy: *long odds.* **8.** Having an abundance or an excess of: *long on hope.* **9.** Phonet. Having a sound that is comparatively drawn out or prolonged: *a long vowel; a long syllable.* —adv. **1.** During or for an extended period of time: *Stay as long as you like.* **2.** For or throughout a specified period: *They talked all night long.* **3.** At a point of time distant from that referred to: *long before we were born.* —n. A long time. —idioms. **as** (or **so**) **long as.** Inasmuch as; since: *As long as you're going, I'll join you.* **no longer.** Not now as formerly; no more: *He no longer smokes.* [Middle English, from Old English.]

Syns: long, elongate, extended, lengthy adj. Core meaning: Having great physical length (*a long distance*).

long² (lông, lŏng) intr.v. To wish earnestly; desire greatly; yearn: *He longed to go home.* [Middle English *longen,* from Old English *langian,* to yearn for.]

long·boat (lông′bōt′, lŏng′-) n. The longest boat carried by a sailing ship.

long·bow (lông′bō′, lŏng′-) n. A wooden, hand-drawn bow 5 to 6 ft. long.

long-dis·tance (lông′dĭs′təns, lŏng′-) adj. Of or involving telephone communications to a distant station. —adv. By long-distance telephone.

long division. A process of division in arithmetic, usu. used when the divisor has more than one digit.

lon·gev·i·ty (lŏn-jĕv′ĭ-tē) n. **1.** Long life. **2.** Long duration, as in an occupation or political office. [Late Latin *longevitās,* from Latin *longaevus,* living to a great age : *longus,* long + *aevum,* age.]

long·hair (lông′hâr′, lŏng′-) n. Informal. **1.** A person dedicated to the arts and esp. to classical music. **2.** A person whose taste in the arts is held to be overrefined. —**long′hair′** or **long′haired′** adj.

long·hand (lông′hănd′, lŏng′-) n. Handwriting in which the letters of each word are joined together; cursive writing.

long·head·ed or **long·head·ed** (lông′hĕd′ĭd, lŏng′-) adj. **1.** Having a head that is considerably longer than it is wide; dolichocephalic. **2.** Foresighted; shrewd.

long·horn (lông′hôrn′, lŏng′-) n. One of a breed of cattle with long, spreading horns, formerly bred in the southwestern United States.

long·house (lông′hous′, lŏng′-) n. Also **long house.** A long wooden dwelling of the Iroquois.

long·ing (lông′ĭng, lŏng′-) n. A persistent yearning or desire. —adj. Affected by longing. —**long′ing·ly** adv.

long·ish (lông′ĭsh, lŏng′-) adj. Fairly long.

lon·gi·tude (lŏn′jĭ-tōōd′, -tyōōd′) n. Distance east and west of the prime meridian at Greenwich, England, measured as the angle between the plane that contains that meridian and the plane that contains the meridian through the point to which the distance is measured. [Middle English, from Latin *longitūdō,* from *longus,* long.]

lon·gi·tu·di·nal (lŏn′jĭ-tōōd′n-əl, -tyōōd′-) adj. **1.** Of or involving length or longitude. **2.** Placed or running lengthwise. —**lon′gi·tu′di·nal·ly** adv.

long johns. Informal. Long, warm underwear.

long jump. A jump made for distance. Also called **broad jump.**

long-leaf pine (lông′lēf′, lŏng′-). An evergreen tree, *Pinus australis* (or *P. palustris*), of the southeastern United States, with long needles and heavy, tough, resinous wood valued as timber.

long-lived (lông′līvd′, -lĭvd′, lŏng′-) adj. Having a long life; existing for a long time.

long-play·ing (lông′plā′ĭng, lŏng′-) adj. Also **LP** (ĕl′pē). Of or relating to a microgroove phonograph record that turns at 33⅓ revolutions per minute.

long-range (lông′rānj′, lŏng′-) adj. **1.** Involving a span of years; not immediate: *long-range planning.* **2.** Of or designed for great distances: *a long-range bomber.*

long·shore·man (lông′shôr′mən, -shōr′-, lŏng′-) n. A dock worker who loads and unloads ships.

long shot. 1. An entry, as in a horse race, with only a slight chance of winning. **2. a.** A bet made at and against great odds. **b.** A risky venture that will pay off handsomely if successful.

long-sight·ed (lông′sī′tĭd, lŏng′-) adj. Farsighted.

long-stand·ing (lông′stăn′dĭng, lŏng′-) adj. Of long duration: *a long-standing feud.*

long-suf·fer·ing (lông′sŭf′ər-ĭng, lŏng′-) adj. Patiently enduring pain or difficulties. —**long′-suf′fer·ing·ly** adv.

long suit. 1. Cards. A suit containing more cards than any of the other suits in a hand. **2.** The personal quality or talent that is one's strongest asset; a forte.

long-term (lông′tûrm′, lŏng′-) adj. In effect for or involving a number of years: *a long-term relationship.*

long-time (lông′tīm′, lŏng′-) adj. Having existed or persisted for a long time: *a long-time acquaintance.*

long ton. A ton weighing 2,240 pounds, or approx. 1,016 kilograms.

long-wind·ed (lông′wĭn′dĭd, lŏng′-) adj. **1.** Wearisomely talkative. **2.** Not subject to quick loss of breath. —**long′-wind′ed·ly** adv. —**long′-wind′ed·ness** n.

look (lŏŏk) intr.v. **1.** To use the eyes to see: *He looked carefully around him.* **2.** To focus one's gaze or attention: *She looked toward the river.* **3.** To seem or appear to be: *These bananas look ripe.* **4.** To face in a specified direction: *The cottage looks on the river.* —tr.v. **1.** To convey by one's expression: *She looked her joy.* **2.** To have an appearance in conformity with: *look one's age.* —See Syns at **appear.** —phrasal verbs. **look after.** To take care of: *looked after the baby.* **look at.** To regard; consider: *a good way to look at the problem.* **look down on** (or **upon**). To regard with contempt or condescension: *He looks down on women.* **look for. 1.** To search, using one's eyes: *looked everywhere for the book.* **2.** To expect: *I'll look for news soon.* **look forward to.** To anticipate eagerly. **look into.** To investigate:

looking into the theft. **look on. 1.** To be a spectator: *The boys fought while a crowd looked on.* **2.** To consider; regard: *We look on her as a great artist.* **look out.** To be on guard: *Look out for snakes in the hills.* **look over.** To inspect, esp. in a casual way. **look to. 1.** To expect: *He looks to great things from his son.* **2.** To attend to; take care of: *Look to the chickens while I'm gone.* **3.** To rely upon: *We look to farmers for our food.* **look up. 1.** To search for and find, as in a reference book. **2.** To locate and call upon; to visit. **3.** *Informal.* To improve: *Business is looking up.* **look up to.** To admire. —*n.* **1.** The action of looking; a gaze or glance. **2.** Appearance or aspect. **3. looks.** Physical appearance, esp. when pleasing. [Middle English *loken,* from Old English *lōcian.*]

look·er (lŏŏk′ər) *n.* **1.** One who looks. **2.** *Slang.* A very pretty woman or a very handsome man.

look·er-on (lŏŏk′ər-ŏn′, -ôn′) *n., pl.* **look·ers-on.** A spectator.

looking glass. A mirror.

look·out (lŏŏk′out′) *n.* **1.** The act of observing or keeping watch. **2.** A high place that commands a wide view for observation. **3.** A person assigned to keep watch. **4.** A particular concern or worry; a problem: *His health is his own lookout.*

loom[1] (lŏŏm) *intr.v.* **1.** To come into view as a massive, distorted, or indistinct image: *Clouds loomed behind the mountain.* **2.** To seem close at hand; appear imminent: *Danger loomed.* [Prob. of Low German orig.]

loom[2] (lŏŏm) *n.* A machine or device on which cloth is produced by interweaving thread or yarn at right angles. [Middle English *lome,* from Old English *gelōma,* utensil, tool.]

loon[1] (lŏŏn) *n.* Any of several diving birds of the genus *Gavia,* of northern regions, with a laughlike cry. Also called **diver.** [Prob. from Old Norse *lomr.*]

loon[1]
George Miksch Sutton

loon[2] (lŏŏn) *n.* A simple-minded or mad person. [Middle English *loun.*]

loon·y (lŏŏ′nē). *Informal.* —*adj.* **-i·er, -i·est.** Crazy; insane. —See Syns at **insane.** —*n., pl.* **-ies.** A loony person.

loop (lŏŏp) *n.* **1.** A roughly circular or oval length of rope, thread, or wire joined at the ends. **2.** Any roughly circular or oval pattern or path that closes or nearly closes on itself: *The car made a loop around the town.* **3.** A closed path in an electric circuit. **4.** A maneuver in which an aircraft flies in a circle that lies in a vertical plane without changing the direction in which its wings point. —*tr.v.* **1.** To form into a loop or loops. **2.** To fasten, join, or encircle with a loop or loops. —*intr.v.* **1.** To form a loop or loops. **2.** To fly a loop or loops in an airplane. [Middle English *loupe.*]

loop·er (lŏŏ′pər). An **inchworm.**

loop·hole (lŏŏp′hōl′) *n.* **1.** A small hole or slit in a wall for looking or shooting through. **2.** A means of escape, esp. an omission or unclear provision in a contract or a law that provides a means of evasion.

loose (lŏŏs) *adj.* **loos·er, loos·est. 1.** Not tightly fastened or secured: *a loose shoelace.* **2.** Free from confinement, bonds, fetters, etc.: *The stallion was loose.* **3.** Not tightly stretched; slack: *the loose skin of a bulldog's cheeks.* **4.** Not tight-fitting or tightly fitted: *a loose robe.* **5.** Not bound, bundled, packaged, stapled, or gathered together: *a* crate of loose peanuts. **6.** Not compact or dense: *loose sand.* **7.** Not strict or exact: *a loose translation.* **8.** Lacking a sense of restraint or responsibility: *loose talk.* **9.** Licentious; immoral: *loose behavior.* —*adv.* In a loose manner: *The cows ran loose.* —*tr.v.* **loosed, loos·ing. 1.** To set free; release. **2.** To undo, untie, or unwrap. **3.** To make less tight, firm, or compact; loosen. **4.** To relax (rules or regulations); make less strict. **5.** To let fly (a missile): *loose an arrow.* —*idioms.* **at loose ends.** Without plans or direction. **cut loose.** To behave in an uninhibited manner. **on the loose.** At large; unconfined; free: *a criminal on the loose.* [Middle English *loos,* from Old Norse *louss.*] —**loose′ly** *adv.* —**loose′ness** *n.*

Syns: loose, lax, relaxed, slack *adj.* Core meaning: Not tautly bound to something else (*a loose anchor line*).

loose-joint·ed (lŏŏs′join′tĭd) *adj.* Having joints that are or seem to be connected to allow unusually free movement. —**loose′-joint′ed·ness** *n.*

loose-leaf (lŏŏs′lēf′) *adj.* Designed to hold easily removed pages: *a loose-leaf notebook.*

loos·en (lŏŏ′sən) *tr.v.* **1.** To untie or make less tight. **2.** To free from restraint, pressure, or strictness. **3.** To break into small pieces: *loosen the soil with a hoe.* —*intr.v.* To become loose or looser.

loose·strife (lŏŏs′strīf′) *n.* **1.** Any of various plants of the genus *Lysimachia,* usu. with yellow flowers. **2.** Any of various plants of the genus *Lythrum.*

loot (lŏŏt) *n.* **1.** Valuables pillaged in time of war; spoils. **2.** Stolen goods. **3.** *Informal.* Desirable items obtained by fair means: *Halloween loot.* **4.** *Slang.* Money. —*tr.v.* **1.** To plunder; pillage, esp. in time of war. **2.** To steal. —*intr.v.* To engage in looting. —See Syns at **sack.** [Hindi *lūt,* from Sanskrit *lō(p)tra,* booty.] —**loot′er** *n.*

lop (lŏp) *tr.v.* **lopped, lop·ping. 1.** To cut off branches or twigs from; trim: *lopped the shrub.* **2.** To cut off from a tree or shrub: *lop superfluous branches.* **3.** To cut (a part) from, esp. with a single swift blow: *lopped off the dead blossoms.* **4.** To eliminate or excise: *lopped money from the budget.* [Orig. unknown.] —**lop′per** *n.*

lope (lōp) *intr.v.* **loped, lop·ing.** To run or ride with a steady, easy gait. —*n.* A steady, easy gait. [Middle English *lopen,* from Old Norse *hlaupa,* to leap.] —**lop′er** *n.*

lop-eared (lŏp′îrd′) *adj.* Having drooping ears. [Earlier *lop,* to droop + EARED.]

lop·sid·ed (lŏp′sī′dĭd) *adj.* **1.** Heavier, larger, or higher on one side than on the other; not symmetrical. **2.** Sagging, slanting, or leaning to one side: *a lopsided old barn.* —**lop′sid′ed·ly** *adv.* —**lop′sid′ed·ness** *n.*

lo·qua·cious (lō-kwā′shəs) *adj.* Very talkative. [From Latin *loquāx,* from *loquī,* to speak.] —**lo·qua′cious·ly** *adv.* —**lo·qua′cious·ness** or **lo·quac′i·ty** (-kwăs′ĭ-tē) *n.*

lo·quat (lō′kwŏt′) *n.* **1.** A small tree, *Eriobotrya japonica,* native to eastern Asia, that bears yellow, pear-shaped fruit. **2.** The edible fruit of the loquat. [Cantonese *lō kwat,* "rush orange."]

lo·ran (lôr′ăn′, lōr′-) *n.* A long-range navigational system based on pulsed radio signals from ground stations by which a navigator can establish his position. [LO(NG)·RA(NGE) N(AVIGATION).]

lord (lôrd) *n.* **1.** A man of high rank in a feudal society, as a king or the owner of a manor. **2. Lord.** *Brit.* The general masculine title of nobility and other rank. **3. Lord. a.** God. **b.** Christ. **4.** Anyone with great authority or power: *lords of industry.* **5. Lords.** *Brit.* The House of Lords. —*intr.v.* To behave in a domineering, haughty, or patronizing manner: *a matron who lorded over the club members.* [Middle English, from Old English *hlāford : hlāf,* loaf + *weard,* guardian.]

lord·ly (lôrd′lē) *adj.* **-li·er, -li·est. 1.** Of, pertaining to, or suitable for a lord: *the lordly pursuit of hunting; a lordly mansion.* **2.** Arrogant; overbearing; haughty: *a lordly manner.* —See Syns at **arrogant** and **grand.** —*adv.* In a lordly fashion. —**lord′li·ness** *n.*

lor·do·sis (lôr-dō′sĭs) *n.* An abnormal forward curvature of the spine in the lumbar region. [Greek *lordōsis,* from *lordos,* bent backward.]

lord·ship (lôrd′shĭp′) *n.* **1.** A form of address for a British nobleman, judge, or bishop. **2.** The rank or domain of a lord.

Lord's Prayer. The prayer taught by Christ to his disciples; the paternoster.

Lord's Supper. The **Last Supper.**

lore (lôr, lōr) *n.* **1.** Accumulated fact, tradition, or belief about a particular subject: *sea lore.* **2.** Knowledge acquired by experience, tradition, or education. —See Syns at **knowledge.** [Middle English, from Old English *lār.*]

Lo·re·lei (lôr′ə-lī′, lōr′-) *n. Germanic Myth.* A siren of the Rhine whose singing lured sailors to shipwreck.

lor·gnette (lôrn-yĕt′) *n.* Eyeglasses or opera glasses with a short handle. [French, from *lorgner,* to leer at, from Old French, from *lorgne,* squinting.]

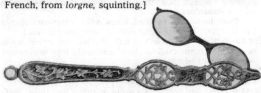

lorgnette

lo·ris (lôr′ĭs, lōr′-) *n.* Any of several small, nocturnal, arboreal primates of the genera *Loris* and *Nycticebus,* of tropical Asia, with dense, woolly fur, large eyes, and a vestigial tail. [French.]

lorn (lôrn) *adj. Poet.* Bereft of; forlorn. [Middle English, lost, from Old English *(ge)loren,* past part. of *lēosan,* to lose.]

lor·ry (lôr′ē, lōr′ē) *n., pl.* **-ries. 1.** A low, horse-drawn, four-wheeled wagon. **2.** *Brit.* A motor truck. **3.** A flatbed freight car that runs on rails. [Orig. unknown.]

lose (lōōz) *v.* **lost** (lôst, lŏst), **los·ing.** *—tr.v.* **1.** To be unable to find. **2.** To be unable to maintain, sustain, or keep: *lose one's balance.* **3. a.** To be deprived of by accident, death, etc.: *lose an arm in a crash.* **b.** To part with or shed through natural causes: *The trees lost their leaves.* **4.** To fail to win: *lose the game.* **5.** To fail to use or take advantage of: *lose precious minutes.* **6.** To fail to hear, see, or understand: *lose the point of the story.* **7.** To remove (oneself), as from everyday reality into a fantasy world: *She lost herself in her dreams.* **8.** To rid oneself of: *lose ten pounds.* **9. a.** To give away as a result of unsuccessful gambling: *lost his money in a poker game.* **b.** To invest more (money) than one receives or is likely to receive: *He lost money on the sale of his business.* **10.** To stray or wander from and be unable to find again: *lose one's way.* **11.** To make (oneself) disappear or fade from view: *He lost himself in the crowd.* **12.** To avoid, escape from, or outdistance: *lose one's pursuers.* **13.** To cause or result in the loss of: *Failure to reply lost her a friend.* **14.** To cause to die or be destroyed: *Both planes were lost in the crash.* *—intr.v.* **1.** To suffer loss. **2.** To be defeated: *We'll fight and we won't lose!* *—phrasal verbs.* **lose out.** To be defeated. **lose out.** To miss: *He lost out on a chance at the big prize.* [Middle English *losen,* from Old English *lōsian,* from *los,* loss, destruction.] **—los′er** *n.*

Syns: lose, mislay, misplace *v. Core meaning:* To be unable to find (*lost her keys*).

loss (lôs, lŏs) *n.* **1.** The act or fact of losing or having lost something. **2.** Something or someone that is lost. **3.** The harm or suffering caused by losing or by being lost: *His death was a loss to the town.* **4. losses.** People who are killed, wounded, or captured in battle. **5.** The difference between a larger amount of money that has been invested and a smaller amount that the investment has returned. *—idioms.* **at a loss.** Perplexed; puzzled; bewildered: *at a loss to know what to do.* **at a loss for.** Unable to produce or come up with: *never at a loss for words.*

loss leader. A commodity offered at cost or less than cost to attract customers. Also called **leader.**

lost (lôst, lŏst) *v.* Past tense and past participle of **lose.** *—adj.* **1.** Strayed or misplaced; missing. **2.** Not won or likely to be won: *a lost cause.* **3.** No longer possessed; gone or passed away: *lost youth.* **4.** Beyond rescue; ruined: *All seemed lost.* **5.** Uncertain; bewildered: *felt lost in the new school.* **6.** Not used; wasted: *a lost opportunity.* **7.** Absorbed; involved: *lost in daydreams.* **8.** No longer practiced: *a lost art.*

lot (lŏt) *n.* **1.** A large amount or number: *a lot of work.* **2.** A number of people or things of a kind: *the runt of the lot.* **3.** A kind, type, or sort: *a bad lot of men.* **4. a.** A piece of land: *a lot behind the house.* **b.** A piece of land having a specific purpose: *a parking lot.* **c.** A movie studio. **5. a.** An object, such as a straw or numbered paper, used to determine or choose something by chance: *drew lots to see who would go.* **b.** The selection made by choosing this way. **6.** Fortune in life; fate; luck. **7.** Miscellaneous goods bought or sold as a group; job lot. *—tr.v.* **lot·ted, lot·ting. 1.** To give out portions of; allot. **2.** To divide (land) into lots. [Middle English, lot, fortune, share, from Old English *hlot.*]

loth (lōth, lŏth) *adj.* Var. of **loath.**

Lo·thar·i·o or **lo·thar·i·o** (lō-thâr′ē-ō′, -thä′rē-ō′) *n., pl.* **-os.** An amoral seducer of women. [From the name of a seducer in *The Fair Penitent,* by Nicholas Rowe.]

lo·tion (lō′shən) *n.* **1.** A liquid medicine applied to the skin. **2.** A cosmetic liquid applied to the body. [Middle English *loscion,* from Old French *lotion,* from Latin *lōtiō,* washing, from *lavere,* to wash.]

lo·tos (lō′təs) *n.* Var. of **lotus.**

lot·ter·y (lŏt′ə-rē) *n., pl.* **-ies.** A contest in which winners are selected in a drawing of lots. *—modifier:* a *lottery* ticket. [Old French *loterie,* from Middle Dutch *loterije,* from *lot,* lot.]

lot·to (lŏt′ō) *n.* A game of chance played with numbered counters selected by lot to be placed upon the corresponding numbers on the players' boards. [French *loto,* from Italian *lotto,* from Old French *lot,* lot.]

lo·tus (lō′təs) *n.* Also **lo·tos. 1. a.** An aquatic plant, *Nelumbo nucifera,* with large leaves, fragrant, pinkish flowers, and a broad, rounded, perforated seed pod. **b.** Any of several similar or related plants, such as certain water lilies. **c.** A representation of such a plant in classical, usu. Egyptian art. **2.** Any of several leguminous plants of the genus *Lotus.* **3. a.** A small tree or shrub, *Zizyphus lotus,* of the Mediterranean region. **b.** The fruit of this tree, said to be that eaten by the lotus-eaters. [Latin *lōtus,* from Greek *lōtos,* a kind of plant.]

lo·tus-eat·er (lō′təs-ē′tər) *n.* **1.** One of a North African people described in the *Odyssey* who fed on the lotus and lived in a drugged, indolent state. **2.** A person devoted to pleasure and luxury.

loud (loud) *adj.* **-er, -est. 1.** Marked by high volume and intensity of sound. **2.** Producing or capable of producing a sound of high volume and intensity. **3.** Noisy and insistent: *loud denials.* **4.** Having offensively bright colors or design; gaudy; flashy: *a loud necktie.* *—adv.* **-er, -est.** In a loud manner. [Middle English, from Old English *hlūd.*] **—loud′ly** *adv.* **—loud′ness** *n.*

loud·mouth (loud′mouth′) *n.* A person whose speech is loud, irritating, and often indiscreet. **—loud′mouthed′** (-mouthd′, -moutht′) *adj.*

loud·speak·er or **loud-speak·er** (loud′spē′kər) *n.* A device that converts electric signals to sound and projects the sound into the surrounding space. Also called **speaker.**

lou·is d'or (lōō′ē dôr′). **1.** A gold coin of France from 1640 until the Revolution. **2.** A 20-franc gold coin of post-Revolutionary France. [French, "gold Louis," after King Louis XIII of France.]

Lou·i·si·an·a French (lōō-ē′zē-ăn′ə) *n.* French as spoken by the descendants of the original French settlers of Louisiana.

lounge (lounj) *v.* **lounged, loung·ing.** *—intr.v.* **1.** To stand, sit, or lie in a lazy, relaxed way. **2.** To pass time idly: *They lounged around the house.* *—tr.v.* To pass (time) in lounging: *lounging the day away.* *—n.* **1. a.** A waiting room or bar in a hotel, theater, or air terminal. **b.** Any room for informal gathering. **c.** A bathroom. **2.** A long couch, esp. one without a back. [Orig. unknown.] **—loung′er** *n.*

lour (lou′ər) *v. & n.* Var. of **lower** (scowl).

louse (lous) *n.* **1.** *pl.* **lice** (līs) Any of numerous small, flat-bodied, wingless, biting or sucking insects of the order Anoplura, many of which are external parasites on various animals, including humans. **2.** *pl.* **lous·es.** *Slang.* A mean or contemptible person. *—tr.v.* **loused, lous·ing.** *Slang.* To make a bad job of; bungle: *louse up a contract.* —See Syns at **botch.** [Middle English *lous,* from Old English *lūs.*]

lous·y (lou′zē) *adj.* **-i·er, -i·est. 1.** Infested with lice. **2.** *Slang.* **a.** Mean; nasty; contemptible: *a lousy trick.* **b.** Painful; unpleasant: *a lousy headache.* **c.** Inferior; worthless: *a lousy paint job.* —See Syns at **cheap.** —**lous′i·ly** *adv.* —**lous′i·ness** *n.*

lout (lout) *n.* An awkward, stupid person. [Perh. ult. from Old Norse *lūtr,* bent low.] —**lout′ish** *adj.*

lou·ver (lo͞o′vər) *n.* Also **lou·vre. 1.** A framed opening in a wall, door, or window fitted with fixed or movable slats. **2.** One of the slanted slats used in a louver. **3.** Any slatted ventilating opening. [Middle English *luver,* from Old French *lov(i)er.*] —**lou′vered** *adj.*

lov·a·ble (lŭv′ə-bəl) *adj.* Also **love·a·ble.** Having characteristics that attract love or affection; adorable; endearing. —**lov′a·ble·ness** *n.* —**lov′a·bly** *adv.*

lov·age (lŭv′ĭj) *n.* An herb, *Levisticum officinale,* whose small aromatic seeds are used as seasoning.

love (lŭv) *n.* **1.** Intense affection and warm feeling for another. **2.** Strong sexual desire for another person. **3.** A strong fondness or enthusiasm for something: *a love of the woods.* **4. a.** A beloved person. **b.** An object of absorbing interest and enthusiasm: *Music is the love of his life.* **5. a.** God's benevolence and mercy toward humans. **b.** Human beings' devotion to or adoration of God. **c.** The benevolence or brotherhood that humans feel toward one another. **6.** A zero score in tennis. —*v.* **loved, lov·ing.** —*tr.v.* **1.** To feel love for. **2.** To desire (another person) sexually; feel deep passion for. **3.** To embrace or caress. **4.** To like or desire enthusiastically; delight in: *Jim loves hockey.* —*intr.v.* To experience loving tenderness or sexual desire for another; be in love. —*idioms.* **in love.** Feeling love for someone or something; enamored. **make love. 1.** To copulate. **2.** To embrace and caress. [Middle English, from Old English *lufu.*]

  Syns: *love, adore, cherish v. Core meaning:* To feel love or strong affection for (*loved her husband; loved his grandchildren*). Love is the most neutral. Adore stresses devotion (*adored her mother*); used in an informal sense, it merely means "to like very much" (*adore skiing*). Cherish emphasizes tender care (*cherished the foundling as if she were his own; a collector who cherishes his paintings*).

love·a·ble (lŭv′ə-bəl) *adj.* Var. of **lovable.**

love·bird (lŭv′bûrd′) *n.* Any of various small Old World parrots, chiefly of the genus *Agapornis.*

love feast. 1. Among early Christians, a meal eaten with others as a symbol of love. **2.** A gathering intended to promote good will among the participants.

love-in-a-mist (lŭv′ĭn-ə-mĭst′) *n.* A plant, *Nigella damascena,* native to Europe, with flowers that are surrounded by numerous threadlike bracts.

love-in-a-mist

love knot. A stylized knot regarded as a symbol of the constancy of two lovers.

love·less (lŭv′lĭs) *adj.* **1.** Characterized by an absence of love. **2.** Feeling no love; unloving. **3.** Receiving no love; unloved. —**love′less·ly** *adv.* —**love′less·ness** *n.*

love·lorn (lŭv′lôrn′) *adj.* Deprived of love or one's lover.

love·ly (lŭv′lē) *adj.* **-li·er, -li·est. 1.** Inspiring love or affection; a lovely, kind person. **2.** Having pleasing or attractive qualities; beautiful: *a lovely girl.* **3.** Enjoyable; delightful: *a lovely party.* —See Syns at **beautiful.** —**love′li·ness** *n.*

love·mak·ing (lŭv′mā′kĭng) *n.* **1.** Courtship. **2.** Sexual activity between lovers.

lov·er (lŭv′ər) *n.* **1.** Someone who loves another, esp. a man in love with a woman. **2.** Someone who is fond of or devoted to something: *a nature lover.* **3. lovers.** A couple in love with each other. **4.** A sexual partner.

love seat. A small sofa that seats two people.

love·sick (lŭv′sĭk′) *adj.* **1.** Pining with love. **2.** Expressing a lover's yearning. —**love′sick′ness** *n.*

lov·ing (lŭv′ĭng) *adj.* Feeling or showing love; devoted.

loving cup. 1. A large, ornamental wine vessel with two or more handles. **2.** A similar cup given as an award in sporting events and contests.

lov·ing-kind·ness (lŭv′ĭng-kīnd′nĭs) *n.* Benevolent affection or tenderness.

low¹ (lō) *adj.* **-er, -est. 1.** Having little relative height: *a low stool; a low sea cliff.* **2.** Of less than usual depth; shallow: *The river is low.* **3.** Near or at the horizon: *The moon is low in the sky.* **4.** Nearest to the equator: *the low latitudes.* **5.** Below average, as in amount, degree, or intensity: *low wages; low cost.* **6. a.** Having a musical pitch that corresponds to a relatively small number of cycles per second. **b.** Not loud; hushed. **7.** Having or denoting inferior social or cultural status: *a man of low birth.* **8.** Of relatively simple structure in the scale of living things: *lower forms of animal life.* **9.** Dejected or depressed: *in low spirits.* **10.** Of small value or quality: *a low opinion of her cousin's friends.* **11. a.** Morally base: *in low company of thieves.* **b.** Vulgar; crude: *low jokes.* **12.** Cut to show the wearer's chest, back, and neck; décolleté. **13.** *Phonet.* Sounded with all or part of the tongue depressed, as the vowel in *large.* —See Syns at **cheap** and **gloomy.** —*adv.* **1.** At, in, or to a low position, level, etc.: *Fly low over the field.* **2.** Softly; quietly: *speak low.* **3.** With or at a low pitch. —*n.* **1.** A low level, position, or degree: *The stock market fell to a new low.* **2.** A mass of atmospheric air that exerts less pressure than the air around it. **3.** The gear configuration or setting that produces the lowest range of output speeds, as in an automotive transmission. [Middle English, from Old Norse *lāgr.*] —**low′ness** *n.*

low² (lō) *n.* The characteristic sound uttered by cattle; a moo. —*intr.v.* To utter a low; to moo. [Middle English *loowen,* from Old English *hlōwan.*]

low-born (lō′bôrn′) *adj.* Of humble birth; lowbred.

low·boy (lō′boi′) *n.* A low, tablelike chest of drawers.

low-bred (lō′brĕd′) *adj.* **1.** Lowborn. **2.** Coarse; vulgar.

low·brow (lō′brou′) *n. Informal.* A person with uncultivated tastes. —*adj.* Uncultivated; vulgar.

Low-Church (lō′chûrch′) *adj.* Of a faction in a Protestant Church that favors widespread preaching of the Gospel and simple ceremony. —**Low′-Church′man** *n.*

low comedy. Comedy characterized by slapstick, burlesque, and horseplay.

low-down (lō′doun′) *n. Slang.* All the facts; the whole truth.

low-down (lō′doun′) *adj.* Mean; despicable.

low·er¹ (lou′ər) *adj.* Also **lour.** —*intr.v.* **1.** To look angry, sullen, or threatening; to scowl. **2.** To appear dark or threatening, as the sky. —*n.* An angry, sullen, or threatening look. [Middle English *louren.*]

low·er² (lō′ər) *adj.* Comparative of **low.** —*adj.* **1.** Below someone or something in rank, position, or authority. **2.** Below a similar or comparable thing: *a lower shelf.* **3.** Designating the larger and usu. more representative house of a legislature with two houses. **4. Lower.** *Geol. & Archaeol.* Being an earlier division of the period named. —*tr.v.* **1.** To let, bring, or move down to a lower level: *lower the flag.* **2.** To reduce in value, degree, or quality. **3.** To reduce the volume of: *Please lower your voices.* **4.** To reduce in standing or respect: *behavior that lowers him in our eyes.* —*intr.v.* To diminish; lessen.

  Syns: 1. lower, drop *v. Core meaning:* To cause to descend (*lowered the shade; lowered her eyes*). **2. lower, cheapen, downgrade, mark down, reduce** *v. Core meaning:* To make or become less in price or value (*lowered the price of the clothes; lowered property values*).

lower case. Small letters as distinguished from capital letters. —*modifier* (**lower-case**): *lower-case letters.*

lower class. The group in society of low social and economic status, ranking below the middle class.

low·er·ing (lou′ər-ĭng) *adj.* Threatening or seeming to threaten; menacing; ominous: *a lowering look.*

low·er·most (lō′ər-mōst′) *adj.* Lowest.

lowest common denominator. *Abbr.* **l.c.d.** The least common multiple of the denominators of a set of fractions. Also called **least common denominator.**

low frequency. A radio-wave frequency in the range from 30 to 300 kilohertz per second.

Low German. **1.** Any of the German dialects spoken in northern Germany. **2.** Any of the Germanic languages of continental Europe except Scandinavian and High German.

low-grade (lō′grād′) *adj.* **1.** Of inferior quality: *low-grade merchandise.* **2.** Not strong or severe: *a low-grade infection.*

low-key (lō′kē′) *adj.* Of low intensity.

low-keyed (lō′kēd′) *adj.* Also **low-key** (lō′kē′). Restrained, as in style or quality: *a low-keyed approach to arbitration.*

low·land (lō′lənd) *n.* An area of land that is low in relation to the surrounding country. —*adj.* Pertaining to or characteristic of lowlands: *lowland crops.*

low·land·er (lō′lən-dər, -lăn′-) *n.* A native or inhabitant of a lowland.

low·ly (lō′lē) *adj.* **-li·er, -li·est.** **1.** Having or suited for a low rank or position. **2.** Humble; meek: *a lowly manner.* —See Syns at **humble.** —*adv.* **1.** In a low manner, condition, or position. **2.** Humbly; meekly. **3.** In a low tone. —**low′li·ness** *n.*

low-mind·ed (lō′mīn′dĭd) *adj.* Exhibiting coarsenss and vulgarity of mind. —**low′-mind′ed·ly** *adv.* —**low′-mind′ed·ness** *n.*

low-pitched (lō′pĭcht′) *adj.* **1.** Low in tone or tonal range. **2.** Having a moderate slope: *a low-pitched roof.*

low-pres·sure (lō′prĕsh′ər) *adj.* **1.** Relaxed; calm; easygoing. **2.** Having atmospheric air that exerts less pressure than the air around it.

low profile. Unobtrusive, restrained behavior or stance, esp. a manner of behavior that does not attract attention.

low relief. Sculptural relief that projects very little from the background. Also called **bas-relief.**

low-spir·it·ed (lō′spĭr′ĭ-tĭd) *adj.* In an unhappy frame of mind; depressed. —**low′-spir′it·ed·ness** *n.*

low tide. **1.** The tide as it reaches its lowest ebb. **2.** The time of this ebb.

lox[1] (lŏks) *n.* Smoked salmon. [Yiddish *laks,* from Middle High German *lahs,* salmon, from Old High German.]

lox[2] (lŏks) *n.* Liquid oxygen, esp. as a rocket fuel oxidizer. [L(IQUID) OX(YGEN).]

loy·al (loi′əl) *adj.* **1.** Steadfast in allegiance to one's homeland, government, or sovereign. **2.** Faithful to a person, ideal, or custom. —See Syns at **faithful.** [Old French, faithful to obligations, legal, from Latin *lēgālis,* legal, from *lēx,* law.] —**loy′al·ly** *adv.*

loy·al·ist (loi′ə-lĭst) *n.* **1.** A person who maintains loyalty to a lawful government, political party, or sovereign, esp. during war or revolutionary change. **2. Loyalist.** A Tory.

loy·al·ty (loi′əl-tē) *n., pl.* **-ties.** The condition or quality of being loyal.

loz·enge (lŏz′ənj) *n.* **1.** A flat, diamond-shaped figure. **2.** A small piece of medicated candy often having this shape. [Middle English *losenge,* from Old French, a diamond-shaped figure in heraldic design.]

LP (ĕl′pē′) *adj.* Long-playing. —*n., pl.* **LP's** or **LPs.** A trademark for a long-playing phonograph record.

LSD A powerful drug, lysergic acid diethylamide, $C_{20}H_{25}N_3O_2$, that induces hallucinations and other usu. temporary psychotic symptoms. Also *slang* **acid.**

Lu The symbol for the element lutetium.

lu·au (lōō-ou′) *n.* A Hawaiian feast. [Hawaiian *lu'au.*]

lub·ber (lŭb′ər) *n.* **1.** A clumsy fellow. **2.** An inexperienced sailor; landlubber. [Middle English *lobur.*]

lube (lōōb) *n. & adj.* Lubricant.

lu·bri·cant (lōō′brĭ-kənt) *n.* Any of a number of slippery substances, such as oil, grease, or graphite, used as a coating for the surfaces of moving parts to reduce friction, wear, etc. —*adj.* Serving as a lubricant.

lu·bri·cate (lōō′brĭ-kāt′) *v.* **-cat·ed, -cat·ing.** —*tr.v.* **1.** To apply a lubricant to. **2.** To make smoother or softer: *lotion to lubricate your hands.* —*intr.v.* To act as a lubricant.

[From Latin *lūbricāre,* from *lūbricus,* slippery.] —**lu′bri·ca′tion** *n.* —**lu′bri·ca′tor** *n.*

lu·bri·cious (lōō-brĭsh′əs) *adj.* Var. of **lubricous.**

lu·bric·i·ty (lōō-brĭs′ĭ-tē) *n.* **1.** Lewdness; salaciousness. **2.** Shiftiness; trickiness. **3.** Slipperiness.

lu·bri·cous (lōō′brĭ-kəs) *adj.* Also **lu·bri·cious** (lōō-brĭsh′əs). **1.** Characterized by lewdness. **2.** Elusive. **3.** Slippery. [From Latin *lūbricus,* slippery.]

lu·cent (lōō′sənt) *adj.* **1.** Giving off light; luminous. **2.** Translucent. [Latin *lūcēns,* pres. part. of *lūcēre,* to shine.] —**lu′cen·cy** *n.* —**lu′cent·ly** *adv.*

lu·cerne (lōō-sûrn′) *n. Brit.* Alfalfa. [French *luzerne,* from Provençal *luzerno.*]

lu·cid (lōō′sĭd) *adj.* **1.** Easily understood; clear: *a lucid speech.* **2.** Mentally sound; sane; rational. **3.** Clear enough to see through; translucent. [French *lucide,* from Latin *lūcidus,* from *lūcēre,* to shine.] —**lu·cid′i·ty** or **lu′cid·ness** *n.* —**lu′cid·ly** *adv.*

Lu·ci·fer (lōō′sə-fər) *n.* **1.** In Christian tradition, the archangel cast from Heaven for leading a revolt of the angels; Satan. **2.** The planet Venus in its appearance as the morning star. **3. lucifer.** A match for striking a light. [Middle English, from Old English, from Latin *Lūcifer,* "light-bearer."]

lu·cif·er·in (lōō-sĭf′ər-ĭn) *n.* A pigment in bioluminescent animals, such as fireflies, that produces an almost heatless, bluish-green light when oxidized.

Lu·cite (lōō′sīt′) *n.* A trademark for a transparent, thermoplastic acrylic resin.

luck (lŭk) *n.* **1.** The chance happening of good or bad events; fate; fortune. **2.** Good fortune; success: *beginner's luck.* —**idioms. down on (one's) luck.** Undergoing misfortune. **in luck.** Fortunate; lucky. **out of luck.** Unfortunate; unlucky. [Middle English *lucke.*]

luck·less (lŭk′lĭs) *adj.* Having no luck; unfortunate. —See Syns at **unfortunate.**

luck·y (lŭk′ē) *adj.* **-i·er, -i·est.** **1.** Having good luck. **2.** Occurring by chance: *a lucky guess.* **3.** Believed to bring good luck: *a lucky penny.* —See Syns at **fortunate.** —**luck′i·ly** *adv.* —**luck′i·ness** *n.*

lu·cra·tive (lōō′krə-tĭv) *adj.* Producing wealth; profitable. [Middle English *lucratif,* from Old French, from Latin *lucrātīvus,* from *lucrārī,* to profit, from *lucrum,* gain.] —**lu′cra·tive·ly** *adv.* —**lu′cra·tive·ness** *n.*

lu·cre (lōō′kər) *n.* Money; gain; profits. [Middle English, from Latin *lucrum,* gain, profit.]

lu·cu·brate (lōō′kyə-brāt′) *intr.v.* **-brat·ed, -brat·ing.** **1.** To stay up late to study. **2.** To write in a scholarly or pretentious fashion. [From Latin *lūcubrāre,* to work at night by lamplight.] —**lu′cu·bra′tion** *n.*

lu·di·crous (lōō′dĭ-krəs) *adj.* Laughable; hilarious. —See Syns at **laughable.** [Latin *lūdicrus,* done playfully, from *lūdus,* game.] —**lu′di·crous·ly** *adv.* —**lu′di·crous·ness** *n.*

luff (lŭf) *n.* **1.** The act of sailing closer into the wind. **2.** The forward side of a fore-and-aft sail. —*intr.v.* To steer a sailing vessel into the wind. [Middle English, from Old French *lof.*]

lug[1] (lŭg) *v.* **lugged, lug·ging.** —*tr.v.* To drag or haul with great difficulty: *lug supplies.* —*intr.v.* To pull with difficulty; tug. —*n.* **1.** The act or task of lugging. **2.** A lugsail. [Middle English *luggen,* to pull.]

lug[2] (lŭg) *n.* **1.** An earlike handle or projection, as on a machine, used to hold or support. **2.** Also **lug nut.** A nut to fit over a bolt, esp. one that is closed at one end to serve as a cap. **3.** *Slang.* A clumsy fool; blockhead. [Middle English *lugge,* flap, ear.]

lug·gage (lŭg′ĭj) *n.* The bags, suitcases, boxes, etc., that can be taken on a trip; baggage. [Prob. LUG (to drag) + (BAG)GAGE.]

lug·ger (lŭg′ər) *n.* A small boat used for fishing or sailing and having two or three masts, each with a lugsail.]

lug nut. A nut for fitting over a bolt; a lug.

lug·sail (lŭg′səl, -sāl′) *n.* A four-sided sail lacking a boom and having the foot larger than the head, bent to a yard that hangs obliquely on the mast. Also called **lug.** [Perh. from obs. *lug,* ear.]

lu·gu·bri·ous (lōō-gōō′brē-əs, -gyōō′-) *adj.* Mournful or sad, esp. to a ridiculous degree. [Latin *lūgubris,* mournful, from *lūgēre,* to mourn.] **—lu·gu'bri·ous·ly** *adv.* **—lu·gu'bri·ous·ness** *n.*

lug·worm (lŭg'wûrm') *n.* A segmented, burrowing saltwater worm, *Arenicola marina,* often used as fishing bait. [Orig. unknown.]

luke·warm (lŏok'wôrm') *adj.* **1.** Mildly warm; tepid: *lukewarm water.* **2.** Lacking in enthusiasm: *a lukewarm welcome.* [Middle English : *luke,* perh. from *lew,* tepid, from Old English *hlēow* + *warm,* warm.] **—luke'warm'ly** *adv.* **—luke'warm'ness** *n.*

lull (lŭl) *tr.v.* **1.** To cause to sleep or rest; soothe. **2.** To deceive into trustfulness: *He used charm to lull his victims.* *—n.* **1.** A relatively calm interval in a storm or other turbulence. **2.** An interval of lessened activity: *a lull in sales.* [Middle English *lullen.*]

lul·la·by (lŭl'ə-bī') *n., pl.* **-bies.** A soothing song with which to lull a child to sleep. [From LULL.]

lum·ba·go (lŭm-bā'gō) *n.* A painful form of rheumatism that affects the muscles and tendons of the lower back. [Latin *lumbāgo,* from *lumbus,* loin.]

lum·bar (lŭm'bər, -bär') *adj.* Of or located in the part of the back and sides between the lowest ribs and the hips. [From Latin *lumbus,* loin.]

lum·ber[1] (lŭm'bər) *n.* **1.** Timber sawed into boards and planks. **2.** Miscellaneous stored articles. *—modifier: a lumber mill.* *—tr.v.* **1. a.** To cut down (trees) and prepare as marketable timber. **b.** To cut down the timber of. **2.** To clutter with or as if with unused articles. *—intr.v.* To cut and prepare timber for the market. [Perh. from LUMBER (to move clumsily).] **—lum'ber·er** *n.*

lum·ber[2] (lŭm'bər) *intr.v.* **1.** To walk or move with heavy clumsiness: *"Lennie lumbered to his feet and disappeared in the bush"* (John Steinbeck). **2.** To move with a rumbling noise: *The trucks lumbered up the hill.* [Middle English *lomeren.*]

lum·ber·jack (lŭm'bər-jăk') *n.* A person who chops down trees and transports the timber to a mill; a logger. [LUMBER (wood) + JACK (man).]

lum·ber·yard (lŭm'bər-yärd') *n.* An establishment that sells lumber and other building materials.

lu·men (lŏo'mən) *n., pl.* **-mens** or **-mi·na** (-mə-nə). **1.** *Anat.* The inner open space of a tubular organ, as of a blood vessel or an intestine. **2.** *Abbr.* **lm** *Physics.* The unit of luminous flux in the International System, equal to the luminous flux emitted in a solid angle of one steradian by a uniform point source that has an intensity of one candela. [From Latin *lūmen,* light, eye, opening.] **—lu'me·nal** or **lu'·mi·nal** *adj.*

lu·mi·nar·y (lŏo'mə-nĕr'ē) *n., pl.* **-ies.** **1.** An object, as a celestial body, that gives light. **2.** A notable person in a specific field. *—adj.* **1.** Giving or shedding light. **2.** Notable; outstanding. [Middle English *luminarye,* from Old French *luminarie,* from Late Latin *lūmināre,* lamp, heavenly body, from Latin *lūmen,* light.]

lu·mi·nes·cence (lŏo'mə-nĕs'əns) *n.* **1.** The production of light by a process that does not use or produce any significant amount of heat, as in fluorescence. **2.** Light that is produced in this way. [Latin *lūmen,* light + -ESCENCE.] **—lu'mi·nes'cent** *adj.*

lu·mi·nif·er·ous (lŏo'mə-nĭf'ər-əs) *adj.* Generating, yielding, or transmitting light. [Latin *lūmen,* light + -FEROUS.]

lu·mi·nos·i·ty (lŏo'mə-nŏs'ĭ-tē) *n.* **1.** The condition or property of being luminous. **2.** Something luminous.

lu·mi·nous (lŏo'mə-nəs) *adj.* **1.** Emitting light. **2.** Full of light; illuminated. **3.** Intelligible; clear: *simple, luminous prose.* *—See Syns at* **bright.** [Middle English, from Old French *lumineux,* from Latin *lūminōsus,* full of light, from *lūmen,* light.] **—lu'mi·nous·ly** *adv.* **—lu'mi·nous·ness** *n.*

luminous energy. The radiant energy of electromagnetic waves in the visible portion of the electromagnetic spectrum.

luminous flux. The rate of flow of light per unit time, esp. the flux of visible light expressed in lumens.

lum·mox (lŭm'əks) *n.* An oaf; lout. [Orig. unknown.]

lump[1] (lŭmp) *n.* **1.** An irregularly shaped mass or piece: *a lump of coal.* **2.** An abnormal swelling or bump in a part of the body. **3.** An ungainly or dull-witted person. **4. lumps.** Punishment that is deserved. *—adj.* **1.** Formed into lumps: *lump sugar.* **2.** Not divided into parts: *a lump sum.* *—tr.v.* **1.** To put together or amass in a single group or pile: *We lumped our money together.* **2.** To make lumpy. *—intr.v.* To become lumpy. [Middle English.]

lump[2] (lŭmp) *tr.v.* To endure or put up with; tolerate: *like it or lump it.* [Orig. unknown.]

lump·ish (lŭm'pĭsh) *adj.* **1.** Stupid; dull. **2.** Clumsy; cumbersome. *—See Syns at* **awkward.** **—lump'ish·ly** *adv.* **—lump'ish·ness** *n.*

lump·y (lŭm'pē) *adj.* **-i·er, -i·est.** **1.** Full of or covered with lumps. **2.** Thickset or cumbersome in appearance. **—lump'i·ness** *n.*

Lu·na (lŏo'nə) *n. Rom. Myth.* The goddess of the moon.

lu·na·cy (lŏo'nə-sē) *n., pl.* **-cies.** **1.** Mental illness; insanity. **2.** Foolish and irresponsible conduct: *It's lunacy to go out in this storm.* *—See Syns at* **insanity.** [From LUNATIC.]

luna moth. A large, pale-green North American moth, *Actias luna,* with a long projection on each hind wing. [From Latin *lūna,* moon (from the yellow rings on its wings).]

lu·nar (lŏo'nər) *adj.* **1.** Of, involving, caused by, or affecting the moon. **2.** Measured by the revolution of the moon. [Latin *lūnāris,* from *lūna,* moon.]

lunar eclipse. A total or partial eclipse of the moon that occurs when the shadow of the earth comes between the sun and moon.

lunar excursion module. Also **lunar module.** A section of a spacecraft designed for a moon mission that can be detached from the main craft, landed on the moon, and finally rejoined with the main craft.

lunar month. The average time between successive full moons, equal to 29 days, 12 hours, 44 minutes, and 2.8 seconds. Also called **lunation.**

lunar year. An interval of 12 lunar months.

lu·nate (lŏo'nāt') *adj.* Crescent-shaped.

lu·na·tic (lŏo'nə-tĭk) *n.* An insane person; madman. *—adj.* **1.** Suffering from lunacy; insane. **2.** Of or for the insane: *a lunatic asylum.* **3.** Wildly or giddily foolish. *—See Syns at* **insane.** [Middle English *lunatik,* from Old French *lunatique,* from Latin *lūnāticus,* moonstruck, crazy, from *lūna,* moon.]

lunatic fringe. The fanatic or irrational members of a society or group.

lu·na·tion (lŏo-nā'shən) *n.* A **lunar month.** [Middle English *lunacioun,* from Medieval Latin *lūnātiō,* from Latin *lūna,* moon.]

lunch (lŭnch) *n.* **1.** A meal eaten at midday. **2.** The food provided for this meal. *—intr.v.* To eat lunch. [Perh. from Spanish *lonja,* slice.] **—lunch'er** *n.*

lunch·eon (lŭn'chən) *n.* **1.** A noonday meal; a lunch. **2.** An early afternoon party at which a light meal is served. [Prob. from LUNCH.]

lunch·eon·ette (lŭn'chə-nĕt') *n.* A small restaurant that serves simple, easily prepared meals.

lune (lŏon) *n.* **1.** A solid crescent-shaped figure that is a portion of a sphere enclosed between two semicircles that have their common end points at opposite poles. **2.** A plane crescent-shaped figure. [From Latin *lūna,* moon.]

lung (lŭng) *n.* **1. a.** Either of two spongy, saclike respiratory organs in most vertebrates that occupy the chest cavity together with the heart and function to remove carbon dioxide from the blood and provide it with oxygen. **b.** A comparable invertebrate structure. **2.** A machine, as an iron lung, to assist breathing. [Middle English *lunge,* from Old English *lungen.*]

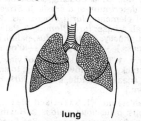

lung

lunge (lŭnj) *n.* **1.** A sudden thrust or pass, as with a sword or rapier. **2.** Any sudden forward movement or plunge.

—*intr.v.* **lunged, lung·ing.** To move with a lunge. [Earlier *allonge*, from French *allonger*, to lengthen, extend : Latin *ad-*, toward + *longus*, long.] —**lung′er** *n.*

lung·fish (lŭng′fĭsh′) *n., pl.* **lungfish** or **-fish·es.** Any of several tropical freshwater fishes of the order Dipnoi (or Dipneusti) that have lungs as well as gills.

lung·wort (lŭng′wûrt′, -wôrt′) *n.* **1.** Any of various plants of the genus *Mertensia*, with drooping clusters of tubular, usu. blue flowers. **2.** Any of several plants of the genus *Pulmonaria*, with long-stalked leaves and coiled clusters of blue or purple flowers. [From its having been used to treat lung diseases.]

lu·nu·la (lōōn′yə-lə) *n., pl.* **-lae** (-lē′). Also **lu·nule** (-yōōl). A small crescent-shaped body structure or marking. [Latin *lūnula*, from *lūna*, moon.]

lu·nu·late (lōōn′yə-lāt′, -lĭt) *adj.* **1.** Small and crescent-shaped. **2.** Having crescent-shaped markings.

lu·nule (lōōn′yōōl) *n.* Var. of **lunula.**

lu·pine¹ (lōō′pĭn) *n.* Also **lu·pin.** Any of various plants of the genus *Lupinus*, with clusters of variously colored flowers. [Middle English, from Latin *lupīnum*, from *lupīnus*, wolflike.]

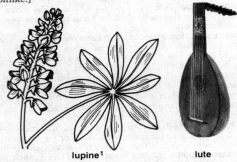

lupine¹　　　　**lute**

lu·pine² (lōō′pĭn) *adj.* **1.** Of or like a wolf: *lupine features.* **2.** Fierce and greedy; rapacious; ravenous. [Latin *lupīnus*, from *lupus*, wolf.]

lu·pus (lōō′pəs) *n.* Any of several diseases of the skin and mucous membranes, many of which cause disfiguring lesions. [From Latin, wolf.]

lurch¹ (lûrch) *intr.v.* **1.** To stagger. **2.** To roll or pitch suddenly or erratically, as a ship during a storm. —*n.* **1.** A staggering or tottering movement or gait. **2.** An abrupt rolling or pitching. [Orig. unknown.]

lurch² (lûrch) *n.* In cribbage and some other games, a severe defeat. —**idiom. in the lurch.** In a difficult or embarrassing position. [From French *lourche*, a game resembling backgammon, defeat, prob. from Middle High German *lurz*, left, wrong, defeat.]

lurch·er (lûr′chər) *n. Brit.* A crossbred dog used by poachers. [From obs. *lurch*, to lurk, from Middle English *lorchen*, var. of *lurken.*]

lure (lōōr) *n.* **1. a.** Anything that entices, tempts, or attracts with the promise of gaining a pleasure or reward. **b.** An attraction or appeal: *the lure of the sea.* **2.** Any decoy used in catching animals, esp. an artificial bait used in catching fish. —*tr.v.* **lured, lur·ing.** To attract by wiles or temptation; entice. —See Syns at **attract.** [Middle English, from Old French *loirre*, bait.]

lu·rid (lōōr′ĭd) *adj.* **1. a.** Causing shock or horror; gruesome: *a lurid description of a crash.* **b.** Stressing violence or sensational elements: *lurid magazines.* **2.** Glowing or glaring through a haze: *lurid flames.* **3.** Pale and ghostly. —See Syns at **ghastly.** [Latin *lūridus*, pallid, ghastly, from *lūror*, ghastliness.] —**lu′rid·ly** *adv.* —**lu′rid·ness** *n.*

lurk (lûrk) *intr.v.* **1.** To be or keep out of view, lying in wait or ready to attack. **2.** To move furtively; to sneak; slink. —See Syns at **sneak.** [Middle English *lurken*, prob. from *luren*, to frown.]

lus·cious (lŭsh′əs) *adj.* **1.** Sweet and pleasant to taste or smell; delicious: *a luscious melon.* **2.** Having strong sensory appeal: *rich, luscious tones.* —See Syns at **delicious.** [Middle English *lucius.*] —**lus′cious·ly** *adv.* —**lus′cious·ness** *n.*

lush¹ (lŭsh) *adj.* **-er, -est. 1.** Having or characterized by luxuriant growth or vegetation: *lush tropical forests.* **2.** Luxurious; sumptuous; opulent: *lush carpets.* **3.** Overelaborate or extravagant: *lush rhetoric.* —See Syns at **luxurious.** [Middle English *lusch*, lax, soft, perh. var. of *lasche*, soft, watery, from Old French, lax, slack, from Latin *laxus*, spacious, loose.] —**lush′ly** *adv.* —**lush′ness** *n.*

lush² (lŭsh) *n. Slang.* **1.** A person who habitually drinks too much; a drunkard. **2.** Intoxicating liquor. [Orig. unknown.]

lust (lŭst) *n.* **1.** Intense, excessive, or unrestrained sexual desire. **2.** Any overwhelming desire or craving: *a lust for power.* —*intr.v.* To have an inordinate or obsessive desire, esp. sexual desire. [Middle English, from Old English, pleasure, desire.] —**lust′ful** *adj.*

lus·ter (lŭs′tər) *n.* Also *Brit.* **lus·tre. 1.** Soft reflected light; sheen; gloss: *the luster of pearls.* **2.** Brilliance or radiance; brightness: *the luster of her dewy eyes.* **3.** Glorious or radiant quality; splendor: *Heroic deeds added luster to his name.* **4.** The appearance of a mineral surface judged by its brilliance and ability to reflect light. [French *lustre*, from Italian *lustro*, from *lustrare*, to brighten, from Latin *lūstrāre*, from *lūstrum*, purification.]

lus·ter·ware (lŭs′tər-wâr′) *n.* Pottery with a metallic sheen.

lus·tre (lŭs′tər) *n. Brit.* Var. of **luster.**

lus·trous (lŭs′trəs) *adj.* **1.** Having a sheen: *lustrous satins.* **2.** Radiant: *lustrous eyes.* —See Syns at **bright.** —**lus′trous·ly** *adv.* —**lus′trous·ness** *n.*

lus·trum (lŭs′trəm) *n.* **1.** A ceremonial purification of the entire ancient Roman population after the census every five years. **2.** A period of five years. [Latin.]

lust·y (lŭs′tē) *adj.* **-i·er, -i·est.** Full of vigor; robust. —**lust′i·ly** *adv.* —**lust′i·ness** *n.*

lu·ta·nist (lōōt′n-ĭst) *n.* A lute player. [From Medieval Latin *lūtānista*, from *lūtāna*, from Old French *lut*, lute.]

lute (lōōt) *n.* A stringed instrument that has a body shaped like half a pear and usu. a bent neck with a fretted fingerboard with pegs for tuning. [Middle English, from Old French *lut*, from Arabic *al-ʿūd*, "the wood."]

lu·te·ti·um (lōō-tē′shē-əm, -shəm) *n.* Also **lu·te·ci·um.** *Symbol* **Lu** A silvery-white rare-earth element that is exceptionally difficult to separate from the other rare-earth elements, used in nuclear technology. Atomic number 71; atomic weight 174.97; melting point 1,652°C; boiling point 3,327°C; specific gravity 9.872; valence 3. [From *Lūtētia*, Latin name for Paris, native city of its discoverer, Georges Urbains (1872–1938), French chemist.]

Lu·ther·an (lōō′thər-ən) *adj.* Of Martin Luther or the branch of the Protestant Church founded on his belief that Christ is all-forgiving and that salvation can be attained through faith in the power of God. —*n.* A member of the Lutheran Church. —**Lu′ther·an·ism** *n.*

lut·ist (lōō′tĭst) *n.* **1.** A maker of lutes. **2.** A lute player.

lux·u·ri·ant (lŭg-zhŏŏr′ē-ənt, lŭk-shŏŏr′-) *adj.* **1.** Growing abundantly, vigorously, or lushly: *luxuriant vegetation.* **2.** Exuberantly elaborate; ornate; florid. **3.** Abundantly fertile or productive. —See Syns at **luxurious.** [Latin *luxuriāns*, pres. part. of *luxuriāre*, to grow profusely.] —**lux·u′ri·ance** *n.* —**lux·u′ri·ant·ly** *adv.*

lux·u·ri·ate (lŭg-zhŏŏr′ē-āt′, lŭk-shŏŏr′-) *intr.v.* **-at·ed, -at·ing. 1.** To take luxurious pleasure; indulge oneself: *luxuriate in the warm summer sun.* **2.** To grow profusely; proliferate: *Weeds luxuriated in the neglected garden.* [From Latin *luxuriāre*, to grow profusely, from *luxuria*, excess, luxury.]

lux·u·ri·ous (lŭg-zhŏŏr′ē-əs, lŭk-shŏŏr′-) *adj.* **1.** Marked by luxury; sumptuous. **2.** Fond of or accustomed to luxury. —**lux·u′ri·ous·ly** *adv.*

Syns: luxurious, lavish, lush, luxuriant, opulent, palatial, plush, rich *adj.* Core meaning: Marked by extravagant, ostentatious magnificence (*a luxurious yacht*).

lux·u·ry (lŭg′zhə-rē, lŭk′shə-) *n., pl.* **-ries. 1.** Something that is not considered essential but that gives great pleasure, esp. something expensive, rare, or hard to obtain: *fur coats and other luxuries.* **2.** The enjoyment of sumptuous living. [Middle English *luxurie*, from Old French, from Latin *luxuria*, excess, rankness, from *luxus*, excess, extravagance.]

Lw The symbol for the element lawrencium.

-ly¹. A suffix meaning: **1.** Characteristic of or resembling: **sisterly. 2.** Appearing or occurring at specified intervals: **weekly, monthly.** [Middle English -*li*, -*lich*, from Old English -*lic*, having the form of.]

-ly². A suffix meaning: **1.** In a specified manner: **gradually, partly. 2.** At a specified interval: **hourly, daily.** [Middle English -*li*, -*liche*, from Old English -*lice*, from -*lic*, having the form of.]

ly·can·thrope (lī'kən-thrōp', lī-kăn'-) n. A werewolf. [From Greek *lukanthrōpos* : *lukos*, wolf + *anthrōpos*, human being.]

ly·cée (lē-sā') n. A French public school roughly equivalent to an American high school. [French.]

ly·ce·um (lī-sē'əm) n. **1.** A hall in which lectures, concerts, etc., are presented. **2.** An organization sponsoring such presentations. [Greek *Lukeion*, Aristotle's school outside Athens.]

ly·chee (lē'chē) n. Var. of **litchi.**

lych gate (lĭch). Var. of **lich gate.**

ly·co·po·di·um (lī'kə-pō'dē-əm) n. **1.** Also **ly·co·pod** (lī'kə-pŏd'). Any plant of the genus *Lycopodium*, which includes the club mosses. **2.** The yellowish powdery spores of certain club mosses, used in fireworks and explosives and as a covering for pills. [New Latin *Lycopodium*, "wolf foot" (from its claw-shaped roots).]

lyd·dite (lĭd'īt') n. An explosive consisting chiefly of picric acid. [After *Lydd*, town in England where it was first tested.]

lye (lī) n. **1.** The liquid obtained by leaching wood ashes. **2. Potassium hydroxide. 3. Sodium hydroxide.** [Middle English *lye*, *ley(e)*, from Old English *lēag*.]

ly·ing¹ (lī'ĭng) v. Present participle of **lie** (to tell an untruth). —*adj.* Untruthful.

ly·ing² (lī'ĭng) v. Present participle of **lie** (to recline). —*adj.* Reclining.

lymph (lĭmf) n. A clear, transparent, watery, sometimes faintly yellowish liquid that contains white blood cells and some red blood cells, travels through the lymphatic system to return to the venous blood stream through the thoracic duct, and acts to remove bacteria and certain proteins from the tissues, to transport fat from the intestines, and to supply lymphocytes to the blood. [Latin *lympha*, water.]

lym·phat·ic (lĭm-făt'ĭk) adj. **1.** Of or relating to lymph, a lymph vessel, or a lymph node. **2.** Sluggish; indifferent; phlegmatic. —*n.* A vessel that conveys lymph.

lymphatic system. The connected system of spaces and vessels between tissues and organs of the body through which lymph circulates.

lymph cell. A lymphocyte.

lymph node. Any of numerous oval or round bodies, located along the lymphatic vessels, that supply lymphocytes to the circulatory system and remove bacteria and foreign particles from the lymph. Also called **lymph gland.**

lym·pho·cyte (lĭm'fə-sīt') n. A white blood cell formed in lymphoid tissue, as in the lymph nodes, spleen, thymus, and tonsils. Also called **lymph cell.**

lym·phoid (lĭm'foid') adj. Pertaining to lymph, lymphatic tissue, or the lymphatic system.

lynch (lĭnch) tr.v. To execute, esp. to hang, without due process of law. [After Charles *Lynch* (1736–1796), Virginia planter and justice of the peace.] —**lynch'er** n.

lynch law. The punishment of persons suspected of crime without due process of law.

lynx (lĭngks) n. Any of several wild cats of the genus *Lynx*, esp. *L. canadensis*, of northern North America, or *L. lynx*, of Eurasia, with thick, soft fur, a short tail, and tufted ears. [Latin, from Greek *lunx*.]

lynx-eyed (lĭngks'īd') adj. Keen of vision.

ly·on·naise (lī'ə-nāz') adj. Cooked with onions: *lyonnaise potatoes*. [From French *à la Lyonnaise*, in the manner of *Lyon*, city in France.]

Ly·ra (lī'rə) n. A constellation in the Northern Hemisphere near Cygnus and Hercules, containing the star Vega.

lyre (līr) n. A stringed instrument of the harp family, used to accompany a singer or reader of poetry, esp. in ancient Greece. [Middle English *lire*, from Old French, from Latin *lyra*, from Greek *lura*.]

lyre·bird (līr'bûrd') n. Either of two Australian birds, *Menura superba* (or *M. novaehollandae*) or *M. alberti*, the male of which spreads his long tail during courtship in a lyre-shaped display.

lyr·ic (lĭr'ĭk) or **lyr·i·cal** (-ĭ-kəl) adj. **1.** Of poetry that is a direct, often songlike expression of the poet's thoughts and feelings. **2.** Highly enthusiastic or emotional; exuberant. **3.** Of or pertaining to the lyre or harp. **4.** Having a singing voice of light weight and bright color: *a lyric soprano*. —*n.* **1.** A lyric poem. **2. lyrics.** The words of a song. [Old French *lyrique*, of a lyre, from Latin *lyricus*, from Greek *lurikos*, from *lura*, lyre.] —**lyr'i·cal·ly** adv.

lyr·i·cism (lĭr'ĭ-sĭz'əm) n. **1.** The character or quality of subjectivism and sensuality of expression, esp. in the arts. **2.** An intense outpouring of exuberant emotion.

lyr·i·cist (lĭr'ĭ-sĭst) n. A person who writes lyrics.

ly·ser·gic acid di·eth·yl·am·ide (lī-sûr'jĭk, lī-; dī'ĕth-əl-ăm'īd'). A hallucinogenic drug. Also called LSD.

ly·sin (lī'sĭn) n. A specific antibody that acts to destroy blood cells, tissues, or microorganisms. [Greek *lusis*, a loosening + -IN.]

ly·sine (lī'sēn', -sĭn) n. An essential crystalline amino acid, $C_6H_{14}N_2O_2$, used in nutrition studies, in culture media, and to fortify foods and feeds. [Greek *lusis*, a loosening + -INE.]

ly·sis (lī'sĭs) n. **1.** *Biochem.* The dissolution or destruction of red blood cells, bacteria, or other antigens by a specific lysin. **2.** *Med.* The gradual subsiding of the symptoms of an acute disease. [From Greek *lusis*, a loosening, deliverance, from *luein*, to loosen, unbind.]

-lysis. A suffix meaning dissolving or decomposition: **hydrolysis.** [From Greek *lusis*.]

-lyte. A suffix indicating a substance that can be decomposed by a specific process: **electrolyte.** [From Greek *lutos*, soluble, from *luein*, to loosen.]

lyt·ta (lĭt'ə) n., pl. **lyt·tae** (lĭt'ē'). A thin cartilaginous strip on the underside of the tongue of certain carnivorous mammals, such as dogs. [Latin, "worm under a dog's tongue" (from its supposed ability to cause madness), from Greek *lutta*, madness, frenzy.]

lyre

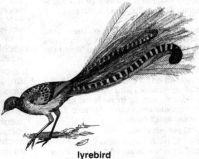

lyrebird
George Miksch Sutton

Mm

ɱ	M	Λ	m	Mm
Phoenician	Greek	Roman	Medieval	Modern

Phoenician – About 3,000 years ago the Phoenicians and other Semitic peoples began to use graphic signs to represent individual speech sounds instead of syllables or whole words. They used this symbol to represent the sound of the consonant "m" and gave it the name mēm, the Phoenician word for "water."

Greek – The Greeks borrowed the Phoenician alphabet with some modifications. They eliminated the tail of mēm and altered its name to mu. They used mu to represent the sound of the consonant "m," as mēm did in Phoenician.

Roman – The Romans borrowed the alphabet from the Greeks via the Etruscans and adapted it for carving Latin in stone. This monumental script, as it is called, became the basis for modern printed capital letters.

Medieval – By medieval times – around 1,200 years ago – the Roman monumental capitals had become adapted to being relatively quickly written on paper, parchment, or vellum. The shape of M became rounded and required fewer pen strokes to write. The cursive minuscule alphabet became the basis for modern printed lower-case letters.

Modern – Since the invention of printing about 500 years ago the basic form of the letter M has remained unchanged.

---

m, M (ĕm) *n., pl.* **m's** or **Ms.** The 13th letter of the modern English alphabet.

Ma'am (măm). A contraction of Madam.

ma·ca·bre (mə-kä′brə, -bər) *adj.* Suggesting the horror of death and decay; gruesome; ghastly: *macabre stories of the unknown.* —See Syns at **ghastly.** [French, ghastly, from Old French *Danse Macabre,* the Dance of Death.]

mac·ad·am (mə-kăd′əm) *n.* A pavement of layers of compacted small stones, usu. bound with tar or asphalt. [After John L. McAdam (1756–1836), Scottish engineer.]

mac·ad·am·ize (mə-kăd′ə-mīz′) *tr.v.* **-ized, -iz·ing.** To construct or pave (a road) with macadam.

ma·caque (mə-kăk′, -kăk′) *n.* Any of several short-tailed monkeys of the genus *Macaca,* of Asia, Gibraltar, and northern Africa. [French, from Portuguese *macaco,* a Congolese monkey.]

mac·a·ro·ni (măk′ə-rō′nē) *n., pl.* **-ni** or **-nies.** A paste of wheat flour pressed into hollow tubes or other shapes, dried, and prepared for eating by boiling. [Obs. Italian *maccaroni,* pl. of *maccarone,* macaroni, macaroon.]

mac·a·roon (măk′ə-rōōn′, măk′ə-rōōn′) *n.* A cookie made with egg whites and almond paste or coconut. [French *macaron,* from Italian *maccarone.*]

ma·caw (mə-kô′) *n.* Any of various tropical American parrots of the genera *Ara* and *Anodorhynchus,* with long saber-shaped tails, curved powerful bills, and usu. brilliant plumage. [Portuguese *macaú.*]

mace[1] (mās) *n.* **1.** A heavy medieval war club with a spiked metal head, used to crush armor. **2.** A ceremonial staff borne or displayed as the symbol of authority of a legislative body. [Middle English, from Old French, from Latin *mateola,* rod, club.]

mace[2] (mās) *n.* An aromatic spice made from the dried, waxy, scarlet or yellowish covering that partly encloses the kernel of the nutmeg. [Middle English, from Medieval Latin *macis,* from Greek *makir,* an Indian spice.]

Mace (mās) *n.* **Chemical Mace.**

mac·er·ate (măs′ə-rāt′) *v.* **-at·ed, -at·ing.** —*tr.v.* **1.** To soften or separate (a solid substance) into constituents by soaking. **2.** To cause to waste away or grow lean, usu. by starvation. —*intr.v.* To become macerated. [From Latin *mācerāre,* to soften.] —**mac′er·a′tion** *n.*

Mach or **mach** (mäk) *n.* **Mach number.**

ma·chet·e (mə-shĕt′ē, -chĕt′ē) *n.* A large, heavy knife used for cutting vegetation and as a weapon. [American Spanish, from Spanish, dim. of *macho,* ax, club, ult. from Latin *mateola,* rod, club.]

Mach·i·a·vel·li·an (măk′ē-ə-vĕl′ē-ən) *adj.* **1.** Of or pertaining to the political doctrine of Niccolò Machiavelli that holds that craft, deceit, and expediency are justified in pursuing and maintaining political power. **2.** Suggestive of or characterized by the principles of expediency, deceit, and cunning attributed to Machiavelli. —*n.* Someone who believes in the theories of Machiavelli. —**Mach′i·a·vel′li·an·ism** *n.*

ma·chic·o·la·tion (mə-chĭk′ə-lā′shən) *n.* A projecting gallery at the top of a castle wall, supported by a row of corbeled arches, with openings in the floor through which stones and boiling liquids could be dropped on attackers. [Medieval Latin *machicolātiō,* from Old French *machicoulis : macher,* to crush + *coulis,* flow.]

mach·i·nate (măk′ĭ-nāt′, măsh′ĭ-) *v.* **-nat·ed, -nat·ing.** —*tr.v.* To devise (a plot). —*intr.v.* To plot. [From Latin *māchinārī,* from *māchina,* machine.] —**mach′i·na′tor** *n.*

mach·i·na·tion (măk′ĭ-nā′shən, măsh′ĭ-) *n.* Often **machinations.** A crafty, intricate, or secret plot, usu. intended to achieve an evil purpose.

ma·chine (mə-shēn′) *n.* **1. a.** A system or device built to use energy to perform a specific task: *a washing machine.* **b.** A simple device, such as a lever, pulley, or inclined plane, used to perform a simple task by altering the magnitude or direction of an applied force. Also called **simple machine. 2.** Any such system or device together with its power source and auxiliary equipment, as an automobile or aircraft. **3.** A person who acts or performs a task mechanically, without thinking or intelligence. **4.** An organized group of persons whose members appear to be under the control of one or more leaders, esp. a local political organization. —*modifier: machine parts; a machine shop.* —*tr.v.* **-chined, -chin·ing.** To cut, shape, or finish by machine. [French, from Old French, from Latin *māchina,* from Greek *mākhos,* contrivance, means.]

machine gun. A gun, often mounted, that fires rapidly and repeatedly.

ma·chine-gun (mə-shēn′gŭn′) *tr.v.* **-gunned, -gun·ning.** To fire at or kill with a machine gun.

ma·chin·er·y (mə-shē′nər-ē, -shēn′rē) *n., pl.* **-ies. 1.** Machines or machine parts in general. **2.** The working parts of a particular machine. **3.** Any system with related elements that operate together: *the machinery of modern society.*

machine tool. A power-driven tool for machining.

ma·chin·ist (mə-shē′nĭst) *n.* Someone who makes, operates, or repairs machines or machine tools.

ma·chis·mo (mä-chēz′mō) *n.* An exaggerated sense of masculinity stressing such attributes as physical courage, viril-

---

ă pat	ā pay	â care	ä father	ĕ pet	ē be	hw which
ŏŏ took	ōō boot	ou out	th thin	*th* this	ŭ cut	

ĭ pit	ī tie	î pier	ŏ pot	ō toe	ô paw, for	oi noise
û urge	zh vision	ə about, item, edible, gallop, circus			

ity, and aggressiveness or violence. [Spanish, from *macho*, masculine, from Latin *masculus*.]

Mach number or **mach number.** The ratio of the speed of an object to the speed of sound in the surrounding medium. [After Ernst *Mach* (1836–1916), Austrian physicist and philosopher.]

ma·cho (mä′chō) *adj.* **1.** Characterized by machismo. **2.** Of or relating to men; manly. —See Syns at **male.** —*n., pl.* **-chos. 1.** Machismo. **2.** A male characterized by machismo. [Spanish, male, virile, from Latin *masculus*.]

mac·in·tosh (măk′ĭn-tŏsh′) *n. Brit.* Var. of **mackintosh.**

mack·er·el (măk′ər-əl, măk′rəl) *n., pl.* **mackerel** or **-els.** Any of several saltwater fishes of the family Scombridae, with dark, wavy bars on the back and a silvery belly, important as game and food fishes. [Middle English *makerel*, from Old French *maquerel*.]

mackerel sky. A formation of clouds resembling the bars on a mackerel's back.

mack·i·naw (măk′ə-nô′) *n.* A short coat of heavy woolen material, usu. plaid. [After *Mackinac* Island, Michigan.]

mack·in·tosh (măk′ĭn-tŏsh′) *n.* Also **mac·in·tosh.** *Brit.* A raincoat. [After Charles *Macintosh* (1766–1843), Scottish chemist, its inventor.]

macr-. Var. of **macro-.**

mac·ra·mé (măk′rə-mā′) *n.* Coarse lacework made by weaving and knotting cords into a pattern. [French, from Italian *macramè*, from Turkish *makrama*, napkin, towel, from Arabic *miqramah*, striped cloth.]

macro- or **macr-.** A prefix meaning: **1.** Large: **macronucleus. 2.** Abnormally large or overdeveloped: **macrencephaly.** [From Greek *makros*, large, long.]

mac·ro·bi·ot·ics (măk′rō-bī-ŏt′ĭks) *pl.n.* (used with a sing. verb). **1.** The theory or practice of promoting longevity. **2.** A method purporting to promote longevity, principally by means of diet. [From Greek *makrobiotos*, long-lived.] —**mac′ro·bi·ot′ic** *adj.*

mac·ro·cosm (măk′rō-kŏz′əm) *n.* **1.** The entire world or universe itself. **2.** A system regarded as an entity containing and reflecting on a large scale subsystems or parts similar to it in structure or character. [French *macrocosme*, from Medieval Latin *macrocosmus*, from Late Greek *makros kosmos*, "great world."] —**mac′ro·cos′mic** *adj.*

mac·ro·ec·o·nom·ics (măk′rō-ĕk′ə-nŏm′ĭks, -ē′kə-) *pl.n.* (used with a sing. verb). The study of the overall aspects and workings of a national economy, such as income and output and the interrelationship among diverse economic sectors.

mac·ro·mol·e·cule (măk′rō-mŏl′ə-kyōōl) *n.* A large complex molecule composed of many smaller molecules linked together, as a polymer.

ma·cron (mā′krŏn′, -krən) *n.* A mark placed over a vowel to indicate a long sound, as the (ā) in *make.* [Greek *makron*, neut. of *makros*, long.]

mac·ro·nu·cle·us (măk′rō-nōō′klē-əs) *n.* A large nonreproductive nucleus in the cells of ciliated protozoans, thought to control nutritional processes.

mac·ro·scop·ic (măk′rə-skŏp′ĭk) or **mac·ro·scop·i·cal** (-ĭ-kəl) *adj.* Large enough to be observed or examined by the naked eye. [MACRO- + -SCOP(E) + -IC.]

mac·u·la (măk′yōō-lə) *n., pl.* **-lae** (-lē) A spot, stain, blemish, or pit, esp. a discoloration of the skin caused by excess or lack of pigment. [Latin *macula*, spot, blemish.] —**mac′u·lar** (-lər) *adj.*

mad (măd) *adj.* **mad·der, mad·dest. 1.** Suffering from a disorder of the mind; insane. **2.** Temporarily or apparently affected or deranged by violent sensations, emotions, or ideas: *"I tell thee I am mad / In Cressid's love."* (Shakespeare). **3.** *Informal.* Feeling or showing strong liking or enthusiasm: *mad about science-fiction movies.* **4.** Feeling anger or resentment. **5.** Lacking restraint, reason, or judgment; wildly foolish; senseless: *He'd have to be mad to take up with her again.* **6.** Marked by extreme excitement, confusion, or agitation; frantic: *a mad scramble for the bus.* **7.** Affected by rabies; rabid. —See Syns at **angry** and **insane.** —*idiom.* **like mad.** *Slang.* Wildly; impetuously: *He drove like mad.* [Middle English *madd*, from Old English *gemǣdd*, past part. of *gemǣdan*, to madden, from *gemǣd*, mad.] —**mad′ly** *adv.*

Mad·am (măd′əm) *n.* **1.** *pl.* **Mes·dames** (mā-däm′). A title of courtesy used alone as a form of address to a woman or used before a surname or a title indicating rank or office: *Madam Ambassador.* **2. madam.** A woman who manages a house of prostitution. [Middle English, from *Madame*, from Old French *ma dame*, my lady.]

Mad·ame (măd′əm, mə-däm′; *Fr.* mä-däm′) *n., pl.* **Mes·dames** (mā-däm′). The French title of courtesy for a married woman. [Middle English, from Old French *ma dame*, "my lady."]

mad·cap (măd′kăp′) *n.* A rash or impulsive person. —*adj.* Rash; impulsive; wild.

mad·den (măd′n) *tr.v.* **1.** To make mad; drive insane. **2.** *Informal.* To make angry; irritate. —**mad′den·ing·ly** *adv.*

mad·der (măd′ər) *n.* **1.** A plant, *Rubia tinctoria*, with small, yellow flowers and a red, fleshy root. **2.** The root of this plant or a red dye obtained from it. [Middle English *mader*, from Old English *mædere*.]

mad·ding (măd′ĭng) *adj. Obs.* Acting as if mad; frenzied.

made (mād) *v.* The past tense and past participle of **make.** —*idiom.* **made for.** Perfectly suited for: *made for each other.*

Ma·dei·ra (mə-dîr′ə) *n.* A fortified white dessert wine from the island of Madeira.

Mad·e·moi·selle (măd′ə-mə-zĕl′; *Fr.* măd-mwä-zĕl′) *n.* **1.** The French title of courtesy for a young girl or unmarried woman, equivalent to the English *Miss.* It may be used separately or prefixed to either a first or last name. **2.** Often **mademoiselle.** A French governess. [French, from Old French *ma demoiselle*, "my young lady."]

made-to-or·der (mād′tōō-ôr′dər) *adj.* **1.** Made in accordance with particular instructions. **2.** Very suitable.

made-up (mād′ŭp′) *adj.* **1.** Not real or true; fictitious; fabricated: *a made-up story.* **2.** Marked by the use of cosmetics or make-up: *a made-up actress.* **3.** Complete or assembled; finished.

mad·house (măd′hous′) *n.* **1.** Formerly, an asylum for the mentally ill. **2.** *Informal.* A place of great disorder.

mad·man (măd′măn′, -mən) *n.* A man who is mad; a maniac.

mad·ness (măd′nĭs) *n.* **1.** Insanity. **2.** Great folly. **3.** Violent rage; fury. **4.** Enthusiasm; excitement. —See Syns at **insanity.**

Ma·don·na (mə-dŏn′ə) *n.* An artistic representation of the Virgin Mary. [Italian, "my lady."]

ma·dras (măd′rəs, mə-drăs′, -dräs′) *n.* A cotton cloth of fine texture, usu. with a plaid, striped, or checked pattern. [After *Madras*, India.]

mad·ri·gal (măd′rĭ-gəl) *n.* **1.** An unaccompanied vocal composition for two or three voices in simple harmony, following a strict poetic form, developed in Italy in the 13th and 14th cent. **2.** A polyphonic part song, usu. unaccompanied, using a secular text, developed in Italy in the 16th cent. **3.** A short lyric poem developed from the lyrics of the 13th-cent. Italian madrigal. **4.** Any part song. [Italian *madrigale*, earlier *madriale*, "(piece) without accompaniment."]

ma·dro·ña (mə-drō′nyə) *n.* A tree, *Arbutus Menziesi*, of western North America, with glossy, evergreen leaves, white flowers, and red-orange fruit. [Spanish *madroño*.]

mad·wom·an (măd′wŏŏm′ən) *n.* A woman who is mad; a maniac.

mael·strom (māl′strəm) *n.* **1.** A large and violent whirlpool. **2.** A situation that resembles such a whirlpool in violence, turbulence, etc.: *caught in the maelstrom of war.* [Dutch : *malen*, to whirl + *stroom*, stream.]

mae·nad (mē′năd′) *n.* **1.** A bacchante. **2.** A frenzied woman. [Latin *maenas*, from Greek *mainas*, madwoman, from *mainesthai*.]

ma·es·to·so (mä′ĕs-tō′sō, -zō) *Mus.* —*adv.* In a majestic and stately manner. Used as a direction. —*adj.* Majestic; stately: *a maestoso march.* [Italian, majestic, from *maestà*, majesty, from Latin *mājestās*.]

maes·tro (mīs′trō; *It.* mä-ĕs′trō) *n., pl.* **-tros** or **-tri** (-trē). A master in an art, esp. a composer, conductor, or music teacher. [Italian, from Latin *magister*, master.]

Mae West (mā′ wĕst′). An inflatable, vestlike life preserver. [After *Mae West*, (1892–1980), U.S. actress.]

Ma·fi·a (mä′fē-ə) *n.* **1.** A secret terrorist organization in Sicily, operating since the early 19th cent. **2.** An alleged international criminal organization believed active since the late 19th cent. [Italian dial. *mafia*, lawlessness, from Arabic *mahyah*, boasting.]

Ma·fi·o·so (mä′fē-ō′sō′) *n., pl.* **-si** (-sē′). A member of the Mafia. [Italian.]

mag·a·zine (măg′ə-zēn′, măg′ə-zēn′) *n.* **1.** A building or room where ammunition is stored. **2.** A periodical containing a collection of articles, stories, pictures, or other features. **3.** A compartment, usu. detachable, in which cartridges are held to be fed into the firing chamber of a firearm. **4.** A compartment in a camera in which rolls or cartridges of film are held for feeding through the exposure mechanism. [Old French *magazin*, storehouse, from Italian *magazzino*, from Arabic *makhāzin*, pl. of *makhzan*, storehouse, from *khazana*, to store up.]

Ma·gen Da·vid (mä′gən dä′vĭd, mŭ′gən dŭ′vĭd). Star of David. [Hebrew *māgēn Dāwid*, "shield of (King) David."]

Magen David

magnetic field

ma·gen·ta (mə-jĕn′tə) *n.* **1.** A coal-tar dye, fuchsin. **2.** A bright purplish red. —*adj.* Bright purplish red. [After *Magenta*, Italy, where a bloody battle was fought (1859).]

mag·got (măg′ət) *n.* **1.** The legless, soft-bodied larva of any of various insects of the order Diptera, esp. of the housefly, usu. found in decaying matter or as a parasite. **2.** An odd or extravagant notion; a whim. [Middle English *magot*.] —**mag′got·y** *adj.*

Ma·gi (mä′jī′) *pl.n.* **1.** The priestly caste of ancient Persia. **2.** In the New Testament, the three wise men of the East who traveled to Bethlehem to pay homage to the infant Jesus. [Middle English, from Latin, pl. of *magus*, sorcerer, from Greek *magos*, from Persian *maguš*.]

mag·ic (măj′ĭk) *n.* **1. a.** The art or alleged art of controlling natural events, effects, or forces by invoking supernatural powers through charms, spells, etc.; witchcraft. **b.** The charms, spells, etc., used to invoke such aid. **2.** The use of sleight of hand and other tricks to produce entertaining and baffling effects. **3.** Any mysterious quality that seems to enchant; a special charm: *the magic of the woods in spring; the magic of Shakespeare's name.* —*adj.* Also **mag·i·cal** (-kəl). **1.** Of, pertaining to, or produced by magic. **2.** Possessing supernatural qualities: *a magic wand.* **3.** Enchanting; bewitching. [Middle English, from Old French *magique*, from Late Latin *magicē*, from Greek *magikē* (*tekhnē*), the sorcerer's art, from *magos*, sorcerer, from Persian *maguš*.] —**mag′i·cal·ly** *adv.*

Syns: magic, sorcery, witchcraft, witchery, wizardry *n.* *Core meaning:* The use of supernatural powers to influence or predict events (*practiced black magic*).

ma·gi·cian (mə-jĭsh′ən) *n.* **1.** A sorcerer; wizard. **2.** A person who performs magic for entertainment or diversion. **3.** One whose skill or art seems to be magical: *a magician with words.*

magic lantern. An early kind of slide projector.

mag·is·te·ri·al (măj′ĭs-tîr′ē-əl) *adj.* **1. a.** Pertaining to or characteristic of a person in a position of authority; commanding. **b.** Dictatorial; dogmatic; overbearing: *offended by his magisterial manner of giving advice.* **2.** Of a magistrate or his official functions. [Latin *magisterius*, from *magister*, master.] —**mag′is·te′ri·al·ly** *adv.*

mag·is·tra·cy (măj′ĭs-trə-sē) *n., pl.* **-cies. 1.** The position, function, or term of office of a magistrate. **2.** A body of

magistrates. **3.** The district under jurisdiction of a magistrate.

mag·is·trate (măj′ĭs-trāt′, -trĭt) *n.* **1.** A civil officer with power to administer and enforce law. **2.** A minor official with limited judicial authority, as a justice of the peace. [Latin *magistrātus*, magistracy, magistrate, from *magister*, master.]

mag·ma (măg′mə, măg′-) *n., pl.* **-ma·ta** (-mä′tə) or **-mas.** The molten matter under the earth's crust, from which igneous rock is formed by cooling and hardening. [Middle English, dregs of a liquid, from Latin, sediment, from Greek *magma*, unguent.]

Mag·na Char·ta or **Mag·na Car·ta** (măg′nə kär′tə). **1.** The great charter of English political and civil liberties granted by King John at Runnymede on June 15, 1215. **2.** Any document or piece of legislation that serves as a guarantee of basic rights. [Medieval Latin, "Great Charter."]

mag·na cum lau·de (măg′nä kōōm lou′dā, măg′nə kōōm lôd′). *Latin.* With great praise. Used to designate a college or university degree, awarded with high honors, or the recipient of such a degree.

mag·na·nim·i·ty (măg′nə-nĭm′ĭ-tē) *n., pl.* **-ties. 1.** The quality of being magnanimous. **2.** A magnanimous act.

mag·nan·i·mous (măg-năn′ə-məs) *adj.* Noble of mind and heart, esp. generous in forgiving; unselfish and gracious. —See Syns at **generous.** [Latin *magnanimus* : *magnus*, great + *animus*, soul.] —**mag·nan′i·mous·ly** *adv.* —**mag·nan′i·mous·ness** *n.*

mag·nate (măg′nāt′) *n.* A powerful or influential person, esp. in business or industry: *a railroad magnate.* [Middle English *magnates*, from Late Latin *magnātēs*, pl. of *magnās*, great man, from Latin *magnus*, great.]

mag·ne·sia (măg-nē′zhə, -shə) *n.* A white, powdery compound, MgO, used in high-temperature refractories, electric insulation, and as a laxative and antacid. [Middle English, from Medieval Latin, from Late Greek *magnēsia*, name of various minerals, after *Magnēsia*, Thessaly.]

mag·ne·si·um (măg-nē′zē-əm, -shəm) *n. Symbol* **Mg** A light, silvery, moderately hard, metallic element that burns with a brilliant white flame, used in lightweight structural alloys. Atomic number 12; atomic weight 24.312; melting point 651°C; boiling point 1,107°C; specific gravity 1.74; valence 2. [From MAGNESIA.]

mag·net (măg′nĭt) *n.* **1.** A body, as of metal, ore, etc., that attracts iron and certain other materials. **2.** An electromagnet. **3.** A person, place, object, or situation that exerts a powerful attraction. [Middle English *magnete*, from Old French, from Latin *magnēs*, from Greek *Magnēs lithos*, "the Magnesian stone," after *Magnēsia*, Thessaly.]

mag·net·ic (măg-nĕt′ĭk) *adj.* **1.** Of or relating to magnetism or magnets. **2.** Having the properties of a magnet; exhibiting magnetism. **3.** Relating to the magnetic poles of the earth: *a magnetic compass bearing.* **4.** Capable of being magnetized or of being attracted by a magnet. **5.** Operating by means of magnetism: *a magnetic recorder.* **6.** Exerting powers of attraction upon persons: *a magnetic personality.* —**mag·net′i·cal·ly** *adv.*

magnetic compass. An instrument in which a magnetic needle is used to determine directions in relation to the earth's magnetic field.

magnetic declination. The angle that a meridian passing through the geographic poles makes with a meridian passing through the magnetic poles at any point on the earth.

magnetic equator. An imaginary line connecting all the points on the earth's surface where a magnetic needle will not dip.

magnetic field. A region of space, as that around a magnet or an electric current, in which a detectable force is exerted on a magnetic body at any point.

magnetic flux. The total number of magnetic lines of force passing through a bounded area in a magnetic field.

magnetic mine. An explosive underwater mine detonated by a mechanism that responds to a mass of magnetic material, such as the steel hull of a ship.

magnetic needle. A light, needle-shaped magnet usu. suspended from a pivot, that aligns itself with any magnetic field around it, used in magnetic compasses.

magnetic north. The direction to which the north-seeking pole of a magnetic needle points.

| ă pat | ā pay | â care | ä father | ĕ pet | ē be | hw which | ĭ pit | ī tie | î pier | ŏ pot | ō toe | ô paw, for | oi noise |
| ōō took | ōō boot | ou out | th thin | th this | ŭ cut | | û urge | zh vision | ə about, item, edible, gallop, circus |

magnetic pickup. A type of phonograph pickup that utilizes a coil in a magnetic field to receive vibrations from the stylus and convert them into electric impulses.

magnetic pole. **1.** Either of two points or regions in a magnet at which the magnet's field is strongest. **2.** Either of two points on the earth, close to but not coinciding with the geographic poles, where the earth's magnetic field is most intense.

magnetic recording. The recording of a signal, such as sound or computer instructions, in the form of a magnetic pattern on a magnetizable surface for storage and subsequent retrieval.

magnetic storm. A severe but temporary disturbance in the earth's magnetic field believed to be produced by sunspots and other solar activity.

mag·net·ism (măg′nə-tĭz′əm) n. **1.** The properties, effects, etc. associated with the presence of magnetic fields. **2.** The study of magnets and their effects. **3.** The force exerted by a magnetic field. **4.** The unusual power to attract, fascinate, or influence: *the magnetism of money.*

mag·net·ite (măg′nə-tīt′) n. The mineral form of black iron oxide, Fe_3O_4, an important ore of iron.

mag·net·ize (măg′nə-tīz′) tr.v. **-ized, -iz·ing. 1.** To make magnetic; give magnetic properties to. **2.** To attract, charm, or influence. —See Syns at **attract.** —**mag′net·i·za′tion** n. —**mag′net·iz′er** n.

mag·ne·to (măg-nē′tō) n., pl. **-tos.** A small generator of alternating current that works by means of permanent magnets, used in the ignition systems of some internal-combustion engines. [Short for *magnetoelectric machine.*]

magneto–. A prefix meaning magnetic: **magnetometer.**

mag·ne·to·e·lec·tric (măg-nē′tō-ĭ-lĕk′trĭk) adj. Of or pertaining to electricity produced by a magnet.

mag·ne·tom·e·ter (măg′nə-tŏm′ə-tər) n. An instrument for measuring the intensity of magnetic fields, esp. of the earth's magnetic field.

mag·ne·to·sphere (măg-nē′tō-sfîr′) n. A region surrounding the earth, extending from about four hundred to several thousand miles above the surface, in which charged atomic particles are trapped by the earth's magnetic field.

Mag·nif·i·cat (măg-nĭf′ĭ-kăt′, -kät′) n. **1.** The canticle of the Virgin Mary beginning *Magnificat anima mea Dominum* ("My soul doth magnify the Lord"). **2.** A musical setting of this text. **3. magnificat.** Any hymn or song of praise.

mag·ni·fi·ca·tion (măg′nə-fĭ-kā′shən) n. **1.** The act of magnifying or the condition of being magnified. **2.** Something that has been magnified; an enlarged representation, image, or model.

mag·nif·i·cent (măg-nĭf′ĭ-sənt) adj. **1.** Splendid in appearance; grand: *a magnificent cathedral; a magnificent view.* **2.** Grand, imposing, or noble in character; exalted: *a magnificent and innovative piece of scholarship.* **3.** Outstanding of its kind; superlative; exceptional: *a magnificent hunting dog.* —See Syns at **grand.** [Old French, from Latin *magnificus,* noble, eminent, from *magnus,* great.] —**magnif′i·cence** n. —**mag·nif′i·cent·ly** adv.

mag·nif·i·co (măg-nĭf′ĭ-kō′) n., pl. **-coes. 1.** Formerly, a nobleman of Venice. **2.** A person of distinguished rank, importance, or appearance. [Italian, from *magnifico,* magnificent, from Latin *magnificus,* noble, eminent, from *magnus,* great.]

mag·ni·fy (măg′nə-fī′) v. **-fied, -fy·ing.** —tr.v. **1.** To make greater in size, extent, or effect; enlarge; amplify: *Success has magnified his influence and power.* **2.** To cause to appear greater or seem more important; exaggerate: *He's always magnifying small problems into large crises.* **3.** To increase the apparent size of, esp. by means of a lens. **4.** To glorify or praise. —intr.v. To increase or have the power to increase the size or volume of an image or sound. —See Syns at **increase.** [Middle English *magnifien,* from Old French *magnifier,* from Latin *magnificāre,* to make great, from *magnificus,* eminent, from *magnus,* great.] —**mag′ni·fi′er** n.

magnifying glass. A lens that enlarges the image of an object seen through it.

mag·nil·o·quent (măg-nĭl′ə-kwənt) adj. Lofty, extravagant, and pompous in speech or manner of expression. [From Latin *magniloquus* : *magnus,* great + *loqui,* to speak.] —**mag·nil′o·quence** n. —**mag·nil′o·quent·ly** adv.

mag·ni·tude (măg′nĭ-tōod′, -tyōod′) n. **1.** Greatness, esp. in size or extent. **2.** Greatness in significance or influence: *a medical breakthrough of great magnitude.* **3.** The relative brightness of a celestial body designated on a numerical scale. —See Syns at **bulk.** [Middle English, from Latin *magnitūdō,* greatness, from *magnus,* great.]

mag·no·lia (măg-nōl′yə) n. **1.** Any of various evergreen or deciduous trees and shrubs of the genus *Magnolia,* often cultivated for their white, pink, purple, or yellow flowers. **2.** The flower of any of these trees or shrubs. [After Pierre *Magnol* (1638–1715), French botanist.]

magnolia

mag·num (măg′nəm) n. **1.** A bottle, holding about two-fifths of a gallon, for wine or liquor. **2.** The amount of liquid contained in such a bottle. [Latin, a big one, neut. of *magnus,* great.]

mag·num o·pus (măg′nəm ō′pəs). A great work, esp. the greatest single work of an artist, writer, or composer. [Latin, "great work."]

mag·pie (măg′pī) n. **1.** Any of various birds of the family Corvidae, found worldwide, that have a long, tapered tail, and black, blue, or green coloring with white markings, and are noted for their chattering call. **2.** A person who chatters constantly. [*Mag* (a dialectal name for a chatterbox) + PIE (magpie).]

ma·guey (mə-gā′, măg′wā) n. **1.** Any of various plants of the genus *Agave,* native to tropical America, esp. any that yield a fiber or beverage. **2.** The fiber obtained from any of these plants. [Spanish, from Taino.]

Mag·yar (măg′yär′, mäg′-; Hungarian mŭd′yär′) n. **1.** A member of the principal ethnic group of Hungary. **2.** Hungarian. —**Mag′yar** adj.

Ma·ha·bha·ra·ta (mə-hä′bä′rə-tə) n. Also **Ma·ha·bha·ra·tam** (-təm). One of the two great epics of ancient India. [Sanskrit *Mahābhārata,* "the great story."]

ma·ha·ra·jah or **ma·ha·ra·ja** (mä′hə-rä′jä, -zhä) n. A king or prince in India, esp. the sovereign of one of the former native states. [Hindi *mahārājā,* from Sanskrit : *mahā,* great + *rājā,* king.]

ma·ha·ra·ni or **ma·ha·ra·nee** (mä′hə-rä′nē) n. **1.** The wife of a maharajah. **2.** A queen or princess in India, esp. the ruler of one of the former native states. [Hindi *mahārānī,* from Sanskrit *mahārājñī* : *mahā,* great + *rājñī,* queen.]

ma·hat·ma (mä-hät′mä, mə-hät′mə) n. A Hindu title of respect for a man renowned for spirituality. [Sanskrit *mahātman* : *mahā,* great + *ātman,* soul.]

Mah·di (mä′dē) n. **1.** The Islamic messiah who, it is believed, will appear at the world's end and establish a reign of peace and righteousness. **2.** A title of various Islamic religious leaders. [Arabic *mahdīy,* "rightly guided (one)."]

mah·jong or **mah·jongg** (mä′zhŏng′, -zhông′) n. A game usu. played by four persons using tiles, bearing various designs. [Cantonese *ma chiung,* from Mandarin *ma²chiang⁴,* "house sparrow" (from the figure of a house sparrow on one of the tiles).]

ma·hog·a·ny (mə-hŏg′ə-nē) n., pl. **-nies. 1. a.** Any of various tropical American trees of the genus *Swietenia,* valued for their hard, reddish-brown wood. **b.** The wood of any of these trees, used for making furniture. **2. a.** Any of several trees having wood resembling true mahogany. **b.** The wood of any of these trees. **3.** A reddish brown. —*modifier: a mahogany table.* —adj. Reddish brown. [Prob. from a native word in Honduras.]

ma·hout (mə-hout′) n. The keeper and driver of an elephant. [Hindi *mahāut*, from Sanskrit *mahāmātra*, "of great measure"(orig. an honorific title).]

maid (mād) *n.* **1.** A girl or an unmarried woman. **2.** A virgin. **3.** A female servant. [Middle English *maide*, short for *maiden*, maiden.]

maid·en (mād'n) *n.* **1.** An unmarried girl or woman. **2.** A virgin. —*adj.* **1.** Of, pertaining to, or befitting a maiden. **2.** Unmarried. **3.** First or earliest: *a maiden voyage.* —See Syns at **first.** [Middle English, from Old English *mægden.*]

maid·en·head (mād'n-hĕd´) *n.* The hymen.

maid·en·hood (mād'n-hŏŏd´) *n.* The condition or time of being a maiden.

maiden name. A woman's family name before marriage.

maid in waiting *pl.* **maids in waiting.** An unmarried woman attendant upon a queen or princess.

maid of honor *pl.* **maids of honor. 1.** An unmarried noblewoman attending a queen or princess. **2.** The chief unmarried female attendant of a bride.

maid·ser·vant (mād'sûr´vənt) *n.* A female servant.

mail[1] (māl) *n.* **1. a.** Materials, such as letters and packages, handled in a postal system. **b.** Postal material for a specific person or organization: *I received my mail today.* **2.** Often **the mails.** A system by which letters, packages, and other postal materials are transported: *sent the documents through the mails.* —*modifier: a mail truck.* —*tr.v.* To send by mail. [Middle English *male*, mailbag, from Old French, pouch, bag, from Old High German *malha*.]

mail[2] (māl) *n.* **1.** Flexible armor made of small overlapping metal rings, loops of chain, or scales. **2.** The protective shell or covering of certain animals, such as the turtle. —*tr.v.* To cover or armor with mail. [Middle English *maille*, from Old French, from Latin *macula*, spot, mesh.]

mail·box (māl'bŏks´) *n.* **1.** A public box for deposit of mail. **2.** A private box for the delivery of mail.

mail·man (māl'măn´, -mən) *n.* Someone who carries and delivers mail. Also called **postman.**

mail order. An order for goods or services that is received, and often filled, through the mail. —*modifier* (**mail-order**): *a mail-order catalogue.*

maim (mām) *tr.v.* **1.** To disable or disfigure, usu. by depriving of the use of a limb; to mutilate or cripple. **2.** To make imperfect or defective; impair: *The bill was maimed by extensive amendments.* [Middle English *maymen*, to wound, from Old French *mahaignier*.]

main (mān) *adj.* **1.** Most important; principal; major: *the main building on the campus.* **2.** Exerted to the utmost; sheer: *by main strength.* **3.** *Naut.* Connected to or located near the mainmast: *a main skysail.* —See Syns at **primary.** —*n.* **1.** The principal pipe or conduit in a system for conveying water, gas, oil, or other utility. **2.** Physical strength. Used chiefly in the phrase *might and main.* **3.** *Poet.* The open ocean: *on the high main.* **4.** *Archaic.* Mainland. —*idiom.* **in the main.** On the whole; mostly. [Middle English, from Old English *mægen*, strength.]

main·land (mān'lănd´, -lənd) *n.* The principal land mass of a country, territory, or continent, as distinguished from an island or peninsula.

main·line (mān'līn´) *intr.v.* **-lined, -lin·ing.** *Slang.* To inject narcotics directly into a vein.

main·ly (mān'lē) *adv.* For the most part; chiefly.

main·mast (mān'məst) *n.* The principal mast of a sailing ship.

main·sail (mān'səl) *n.* The largest sail set on the mainmast of a sailing ship.

main·spring (mān'sprĭng´) *n.* **1.** The principal spring mechanism in a device, esp. in a watch or clock. **2.** A motivating force; an impelling cause.

main·stay (mān'stā´) *n.* **1.** A strong rope that serves to steady and support the mainmast of a sailing ship. **2.** A principal support: *Agriculture is a mainstay of the economy.*

main·stream (mān'strēm´) *n.* The prevailing current or direction of a movement or influence: *writers in the mainstream of 18th-century thought.*

main·tain (mān-tān´) *tr.v.* **1.** To continue; carry on; keep up: *maintain good relations; maintain a custom.* **2.** To preserve or retain: *maintain composure.* **3.** To keep in a condition of good repair or efficiency. **4. a.** To provide for;

bear the expenses of: *maintain a family.* **b.** To keep in existence; sustain: *food to maintain life.* **5.** To defend or sustain; hold against attack: *maintained the position against heavy shelling.* **6.** To declare to be true; defend against dispute: *maintain one's innocence.* **7.** To assert in or as if in an argument; to state; declare. —See Syns at **assert** and **defend.** [Middle English *mainteine*, from Old French *maintenir*, from Medieval Latin *manūtenēre*, from Latin *manū tenēre*, "to hold in the hand," support, know.] —**main·tain·a·ble** *adj.*

main·te·nance (mān'tə-nəns) *n.* **1.** The act of maintaining or the condition of being maintained. **2.** The work of keeping something in proper condition. **3.** Means of support or livelihood. —See Syns at **living.** [Middle English *maintenaunce*, from Old French *maintenance*, from *maintenir*, to maintain.]

main·top (mān'tŏp´) *n.* A platform at the head of the mainmast on a square-rigged vessel.

maî·tre d'hô·tel (mĕ'tr' dō-tĕl´) *pl.* **maî·tres d'hô·tel** (mĕ'tr' dō-tĕl´). **1.** A major-domo. **2.** A headwaiter. Also called **maître d'.** [French, "master of the hotel."]

maize (māz) *n.* **1.** Corn. **2.** A light to strong yellow. —*adj.* Light to strong yellow. [Spanish *maíz*, from Taino *mahiz*.]

ma·jes·tic (mə-jĕs'tĭk) or **ma·jes·ti·cal** (-tĭ-kəl) *adj.* Having or exhibiting stateliness or great dignity; royal; grand. —See Syns at **grand.** —**ma·jes'ti·cal·ly** *adv.*

maj·es·ty (măj'ĭs-tē) *n.*, *pl.* **-ties. 1.** The greatness and dignity of a sovereign. **2.** Supreme authority or power: *the majesty of the law.* **3. Majesty.** A title used in speaking of or to a sovereign monarch: *His Majesty's wish; Your Majesty.* **4. a.** Royal dignity of bearing or aspect; grandeur. **b.** Stateliness, splendor, or magnificence, as of appearance, style, or character; imposing quality. [Middle English *maieste*, from Old French *majeste*, from Latin *mājestās*, authority, grandeur.]

ma·jol·i·ca (mə-jŏl'ĭ-kə, -yŏl'-) *n.* **1.** A richly colored and decorated Italian Renaissance pottery that is enameled and glazed. **2.** A modern pottery made in imitation of this. [Italian *maiolica*, from *Majolica*, Majorca.]

ma·jor (mā'jər) *adj.* **1.** Greater in importance, rank, or stature: *a major writer; a major scientific discovery.* **2.** Serious or dangerous: *major difficulties; a major illness.* **3.** *Law.* Having attained full legal age. **4.** *Mus.* **a.** Designating a scale or mode having half steps between the third and fourth and the seventh and eighth degrees. **b.** Equivalent to the distance between the tonic note and the second or third or sixth or seventh degrees of a major scale or mode: *a major interval.* **c.** Based on a major scale. —*n.* **1.** An officer in the U.S. Army, Air Force, or Marine Corps ranking next above a captain and next below a lieutenant colonel. **2.** *Law.* A person who has reached full legal age. **3. a.** The principal field of academic specialization of a candidate for a degree in a college or university. **b.** A student specializing in such a field: *a history major.* **4.** *Mus.* A major scale, key, interval, or mode. **6.** *Sports.* **the majors.** The major leagues. —*intr.v.* To pursue academic studies in a major field: *major in zoology.* [Middle English, from Latin *mājor*, greater.]

ma·jor-do·mo (mā'jər-dō'mō) *n.*, *pl.* **-mos. 1.** The head steward or butler in the household of a sovereign or great nobleman. **2.** Any steward or butler. [Italian *maggiordomo* and Spanish *mayordomo*, from Medieval Latin *mājor domūs*, "head of the house."]

ma·jor·ette (mā'jər-ĕt´) *n.* A drum majorette.

major general. An officer in the U.S. Army, Air Force, or Marine Corps who ranks next above a brigadier general and next below a lieutenant general.

ma·jor·i·ty (mə-jôr'ĭ-tē, mə-jŏr'-) *n.*, *pl.* **-ties. 1.** A number more than half of the total number of a given group: *the majority of consumers. The majority of these cases prove curable.* **2.** The number of votes cast in any election above the total number of all other votes cast. **3.** *Law.* The status of legal age when full civil and personal rights may be exercised legally. **4.** The political party, group, or faction having the most power by virtue of its larger representation or electoral strength. **5.** The military rank, commission, or office of a major. [Old French *majorite*, from Medieval Latin *mājōritās*, the state of being greater, greater number, from Latin *mājor*, greater.]

ă pat	ā pay	â care	ä father	ĕ pet	ē be	hw which
ĭ pit	ī tie	î pier	ŏ pot	ō toe	ô paw, for	oi noise
ŏŏ took	ōō boot	ou out	th thin	th this	ŭ cut	
û urge	zh vision	ə about, item, edible, gallop, circus				

Usage: **majority.** This word takes a singular verb when the reference is to a specific numerical figure. *Their majority is four votes.* When the meaning is the larger of two groups, the verb may be either singular (if unity or oneness is meant) or plural (if the members are considered as individuals): *The majority is determined to force a vote. The majority are of different minds on this issue.* When the word is followed by *of* + a plural noun referring to it, it takes a plural verb: *The majority of the workers have joined a union.*

majority leader. The leader of the majority party in a legislature, as in the U.S. Senate and House of Representatives.

major league. 1. Either of the two principal groups of professional baseball teams in the United States. 2. Any of the principal leagues in other professional sports, such as basketball, football, or ice hockey. —**ma′jor-league′** *adj.*

make (māk) *v.* **made** (mād), **making.** —*tr.v.* **1. a.** To bring into existence by or as if by shaping, fashioning, or constructing: *make a ladder from scrap lumber.* **b.** To cause to appear or occur; bring about: *make trouble.* **2. a.** To cause to be or become: *The cold air and unaccustomed exercise made him ravenously hungry.* **b.** To appoint to a position or office: *made her treasurer.* **c.** To cause to perform or experience an action: *Heat makes a gas expand.* **d.** To compel: *make him obey.* **3.** To intend for a specified function or purpose: *make Chicago one's home.* **4.** To formulate in the mind: *make plans.* **5. a.** To do, perform, or accomplish: *make a phone call; make war.* **b.** To put into effect; enact; execute: *make a will. make a law.* **6. a.** To gain by effort; earn; acquire: *make money.* **b.** To score; achieve: *make a run in baseball; make two tricks in bridge.* **c.** To manage to reach; catch: *make a train.* **7. a.** To achieve the rank of: *make lieutenant.* **b.** To gain a place or position on: *make the basketball team.* **8. a.** To put into order or proper condition: *make the bed for a guest.* **b.** To make ready; prepare: *make dinner.* **c.** To allow provision for; provide: *make room.* **9.** To guarantee the success of: *That makes my day.* **10.** To calculate or estimate: *We make the distance 20 miles.* **11.** To travel over: *They expect to make 200 miles before sunset.* **12. a.** To possess the qualities necessary for being or becoming: *He will make a fine doctor. Oak makes good building material.* **b.** To amount to; constitute: *Twenty members make a quorum.* —*intr.v.* **1. a.** To give an appearance: *She made as if to shake my hand.* **b.** To behave or act in a specified manner: *make merry.* **2.** To head in the direction; set out: *a ship making for shore.* —*phrasal verbs.* **make out. 1.** To see with difficulty: *He could barely make out the lighthouse through the fog.* **2.** To grasp the meaning of; understand: *I can't make out what he wants.* **3.** To write out or draw up: *He made out the invoices.* **4.** *Slang.* To get along well; succeed: *He has made out in business.* **5.** *Slang.* To neck; pet. **make over. 1.** To change or redo; renovate: *We made over the cellar into a playroom.* **2.** To change or transfer the ownership of, usu. by means of a legal document: *He made over the property to his son.* **make up. 1. a.** To produce or create by assembling. **b.** To think up or imagine; fabricate: *make up an excuse.* **2.** To constitute: *Five members make up a quorum.* **3. a.** To compensate, as for a mistake or omission. **b.** To satisfy a grievance or debt. **4.** To decide: *make up one's mind.* **5.** To resolve a personal quarrel. **6.** To apply cosmetics. —*n.* **1.** The style or manner in which a thing is made: *I dislike the make of this coat.* **2.** A specific line of manufactured goods, identified by the maker's name or the registered trademark: *a famous make of shirt.* —*idioms.* **on the make. 1.** Aggressively seeking social or financial self-improvement. **2.** *Slang.* Eagerly pursuing sexual conquests or encounters. **make away with.** To carry off, esp. to steal. **make do.** To manage or get along with what is available: *made do with the same hat for three years.* **make good. 1.** To carry out successfully; achieve: *He made good his plan.* **2.** To pay back: *make good one's debts.* **3.** To succeed: *make good in the big city.* **make it.** To succeed: *couldn't make it as a professional athlete.* **make time. 1.** To move or travel at a specified rate of speed: *make very good time on the highway.* **2.** To move or travel fast: *We'll have to make time, if we're going to keep the appointment.* **3.** *Slang.* To engage in flirtation. **make way.**

To give room for passage. [Middle English *maken,* from Old English *macian.*]

Syns: make, construct, fabricate, fashion, manufacture, shape *v. Core meaning:* To create by forming, combining, or altering materials (*made a house from logs; make a sandwich*).

make-be·lieve (māk′bĭ-lēv′) *n.* Playful or fanciful pretense. —**make′-be·lieve′** *adj.*

mak·er (mā′kər) *n.* **1.** Someone or something that makes. **2. Maker.** God.

make·shift (māk′shĭft′) *n.* A temporary expedient or substitute. —**make′shift′** *adj.*

make·up (māk′ŭp′) *n.* Also **make-up. 1.** The way in which something is put together or arranged; construction: *the complex make-up of a large corporation.* **2.** The mental, physical, or moral qualities that constitute a personality; disposition. **3.** Cosmetics applied esp. to the face. **4.** The articles, such as cosmetics and wigs, that an actor uses in portraying a role. **5.** A special examination for a student who failed or was absent from a previous examination.

mak·ing (mā′kĭng) *n.* **1.** The act of someone or something that makes. **2.** A means of gaining success: *The job will be the making of him.* **3. makings.** The materials necessary for making or doing something: *We have the makings of a fine organization.*

mal-. A prefix meaning bad, badly, or wrongly: **maladminister.** [Middle English, from Old French, from Latin *mal-, male-,* from *malus,* bad.]

mal·a·chite (măl′ə-kīt′) *n.* A green to nearly black mineral carbonate of copper, $CuCO_3 \cdot Cu(OH)_2$, used as a source of copper and for decorative objects. [French *malachite,* from Old French *melochite,* from Latin *molochitēs,* from Greek *molokhitis,* from *molokhē,* mallow.]

mal·ad·just·ment (măl′ə-jŭst′mənt) *n.* Faulty or poor adjustment. —**mal′ad·just′ed** *adj.*

mal·ad·min·is·ter (măl′əd-mĭn′ĭs-tər) *tr.v.* To administer inefficiently or dishonestly. —**mal′ad·min′is·tra′tion** *n.*

mal·a·droit (măl′ə-droit′) *adj.* Lacking in dexterity; clumsy. [French, from Old French.] —**mal′a·droit′ly** *adv.* —**mal′a·droit′ness** *n.*

mal·a·dy (măl′ə-dē) *n., pl.* **-dies.** A disease, disorder, or ailment: *a malady that could not be healed.* [Middle English *maladie,* from Old French, from *malade,* sick, from Latin *male habitus,* ill-kept, in poor condition.]

Mal·a·gas·y (măl′ə-găs′ē) *n.* **1.** A native of the Malagasy Republic. **2.** The language of the Malagasy Republic. —**Mal′a·gas′y** *adj.*

mal·aise (măl-āz′; *French* mȧ-lĕz′) *n.* A vague feeling of illness or depression. [French, from Old French : *mal-,* bad + *aise,* ease.]

ma·la·mute or **ma·le·mute** (mä′lə-myo͞ot′, măl′ə-) *n.* Also **ma·le·miut.** Any of a powerful breed of dogs developed in Alaska as a sled dog, with a thick coat and a bushy tail. [Eskimo *Mahlemut,* the Alaskan tribe that bred the dog.]

mal·a·prop·ism (măl′ə-prŏp-ĭz′əm) *n.* A ludicrous misuse of a word, for example, Beethoven's *Moonshine* (instead of *Moonlight*) *Sonata.* [After Mrs. *Malaprop,* a character in a play by Richard Brinsley Sheridan.]

mal·a·pro·pos (măl′ăp-rə-pō′) *adj.* Inappropriate; out of place. —See Syns at **unsuitable.** —*adv.* Inappropriately; inopportunely. [French *mal à propos,* "not to the purpose."]

ma·lar·i·a (mə-lâr′ē-ə) *n.* An infectious disease characterized by cycles of chills, fever, and sweating, transmitted by the bite of the infected female anopheles mosquito. [Italian *mal'aria,* foul air, malaria.] —**ma·lar′i·al** *adj.*

mal·ar·key (mə-lär′kē) *n.* Also **ma·lar·ky.** *Slang.* Exaggerated or foolish talk; nonsense. [Orig. unknown.]

mal·a·thi·on (măl′ə-thē′ŏn′) *n.* An organic compound, $I_{10}H_{19}O_6PS_2$, used as an insecticide. [From *Malathion,* orig. a trademark.]

Ma·lay (mā′lā′, mə-lā′) *n.* **1.** A member of a people inhabiting the Malay Peninsula and adjacent areas. **2.** The language of the Malays. —*adj.* **1.** Of, pertaining to, or characteristic of the Malays or their language. **2.** Of or pertaining to Malaya or Malaysia. —**Ma·lay′an** *adj. & n.*

Mal·a·ya·lam (măl′ə-yä′ləm) *n.* A Dravidian language of the Malabar coast in southwestern India.

mal·con·tent (măl′kən-tĕnt′) *adj.* Discontented with exist-

ă pat   ā pay   â care   ä father   ĕ pet   ē be   hw which   ĭ pit   ī tie   î pier   ŏ pot   ō toe   ô paw, for   oi noise
o͞o took   o͞o boot   ou out   th thin   *th* this   ŭ cut   û urge   zh vision   ə about, item, edible, gallop, circus

ing conditions. —*n.* A discontented person.

male (māl) *adj.* **1.** Of, pertaining to, or designating the sex that produces spermatozoa for fertilizing ova. **2.** Of or characteristic of the male sex; masculine. **3.** Virile; manly. **4.** Composed of men or boys, or both: *a male choir.* **5.** *Bot.* **a.** Pertaining to or designating organs, such as stamens or anthers, that are capable of fertilizing female organs. **b.** Bearing stamens but not pistils; staminate: *male flowers.* **6.** Designed for insertion into a hollow bore or socket. —*n.* A male animal or plant. [Middle English, from Old French, from Latin *masculus*, dim. of *mas*, male.] —**male′ness** *n.*

   Syns: *male, macho, manful, manly, masculine, virile adj.* Core meaning: Of, relating to, or suitable to men (*male attire; heard male voices in the hall*).

ma·le·dic·tion (mǎl′ə-dĭk′shən) *n.* A curse. [Middle English, from Late Latin *maledictio*, from Latin *maledīcere*, to curse : *male*, badly + *dīcere*, to speak.]

ma·le·fac·tor (mǎl′ə-fǎk′tər) *n.* **1.** A person who has committed a crime. **2.** An evildoer. [Middle English, from Latin, from *malefacere*, to do wrong : *male*, badly + *facere*, to do.] —**mal′e·fac′tion** (mǎl′ə-fǎk′shən) *n.*

ma·lef·i·cence (mə-lěf′ə-səns) *n.* **1.** An evil or harmful act. **2.** The state or quality of being harmful or evil. [Latin *maleficentia*, from *maleficus*, evil-doing.] —**ma·lef′i·cent** *adj.*

ma·le·mute or **ma·le·miut** (mä′lə-myōōt′, mǎl′ə-) *n.* Vars. of **malamute.**

ma·le·vo·lence (mə-lěv′ə-ləns) *n.* Ill will toward others; spite; malice.

ma·le·vo·lent (mə-lěv′ə-lənt) *adj.* Having or showing ill will; malicious. [Latin *malevolēns* : *male*, ill + *volēns*, pres. part. of *velle*, to will, wish.] —**ma·lev′o·lent·ly** *adv.*

   Syns: *malevolent, evil, malicious, malign, malignant, mean, nasty, poisonous, venomous, vicious, wicked adj.* Core meaning: Marked by ill will and spite (*a malevolent hatred of his rival*).

mal·fea·sance (mǎl-fē′zəns) *n.* *Law.* Misconduct or wrongdoing, esp. by a public official. [From Old French *malfaisant* : *mal-*, ill + *faisant*, pres. part. of *faire*, to do, from Latin *facere*.]

mal·for·ma·tion (mǎl′fôr-mā′shən) *n.* **1.** The condition of being malformed. **2.** An abnormal structure or form.

mal·formed (mǎl-fôrmd′) *adj.* Abnormally or imperfectly formed.

mal·func·tion (mǎl-fŭngk′shən) *intr.v.* **1.** To fail to function. **2.** To function abnormally or imperfectly. —*n.* The process of malfunctioning or an example of malfunctioning.

mal·ice (mǎl′ĭs) *n.* **1.** The desire to harm others or to see others suffer; spite: *"A well-meaning man is one who often does a great deal of mischief without any kind of malice"* (William Hazlitt). **2.** The intent, without just cause or reason, to commit an unlawful act. [Middle English, from Old French, from Latin *malitia*, from *malus*, bad.]

ma·li·cious (mə-lĭsh′əs) *adj.* Resulting from, inclined to, or characterized by malice. —See Syns at **malevolent.** —**ma·li′cious·ly** *adv.* —**ma·li′cious·ness** *n.*

ma·lign (mə-līn′) *tr.v.* To speak evil of; slander; defame. —*adj.* **1.** Characterized by malice; malevolent. **2.** Harmful in influence or effect; injurious. —See Syns at **malevolent.** [Middle English *maligne*, evil, from Old French, from Latin *malignus*, from *malus*, bad.] —**ma·lign′er** *n.* —**ma·lign′ly** *adv.*

ma·lig·nan·cy (mə-lĭg′nən-sē) *n.*, *pl.* **-cies. 1.** The condition or quality of being malignant. **2.** A malignant tumor.

ma·lig·nant (mə-lĭg′nənt) *adj.* **1.** Showing malevolence; actively evil in nature. **2.** Highly injurious; pernicious. **3.** *Pathol.* **a.** Designating an abnormal growth that tends to metastasize. **b.** Threatening to life or health; virulent: *a malignant disease.* —See Syns at **malevolent.** —**ma·lig′nant·ly** *adv.*

ma·lig·ni·ty (mə-lĭg′nə-tē) *n.*, *pl.* **-ties. 1. a.** Intense ill will or hatred; malice. **b.** An act or feeling of great malice. **2.** The condition or quality of being evil or injurious; deadliness.

ma·lin·ger (mə-lĭng′gər) *intr.v.* To pretend to be ill or injured in order to avoid duty or work. [From French *malingre*, sickly, from Old French *malingre*.] —**ma·lin′ger·er** *n.*

mall (môl, mǎl) *n.* **1.** A shady public walk or promenade.

2. A walk lined with stores and closed to vehicles. **3.** A median strip dividing a road or highway. [From The *Mall*, a tree-lined street in London.]

mal·lard (mǎl′ərd) *n.*, *pl.* **-lards** or **mallard.** A wild duck, *Anas platyrhynchos*, of which the male has a green head and neck. [Middle English, from Old French *mallart*.]

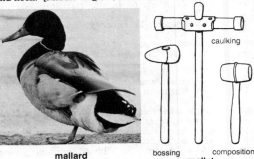

mallard   bossing   composition
        caulking   **mallet**

mal·le·a·ble (mǎl′ē-ə-bəl) *adj.* **1.** Capable of being shaped or formed, as by hammering or pressure: *a malleable metal.* **2.** Capable of being altered or influenced; pliable. [Middle English *malliable*, from Old French *malleable*, from Medieval Latin *malleābilis*, from *malleāre*, to hammer, from *malleus*, a hammer.] —**mal′le·a·bil′i·ty** or **mal′le·a·ble·ness** *n.* —**mal′le·a·bly** *adv.*

mal·let (mǎl′ĭt) *n.* **1.** A short-handled hammer, usu. with a cylindrical head of wood. **2.** A similar long-handled hammer used to strike a ball, as in croquet and polo. [Middle English *maillet*, from Old French, from *mailler*, to hammer, from *mail*, a hammer, from Latin *malleus*, hammer.]

mal·le·us (mǎl′ē-əs) *n.*, *pl.* **mal·le·i** (mǎl′ē-ī′, -ē-ē′). The largest of three small bones in the middle ear. Also called **hammer.** [Latin, hammer.]

mal·low (mǎl′ō) *n.* Any plant of the genus *Malva*, with showy pink or white flowers. [Middle English *malwe*, from Old English *mealwe*, from Latin *malva*.]

malm·sey (mäm′zē) *n.*, *pl.* **-seys.** A fortified sweet white wine. [Middle English, from Medieval Latin *Malmasia*, alteration of Greek *Monembasia*, a Greek seaport.]

mal·nour·ished (mǎl-nûr′ĭsht) *adj.* Inadequately nourished.

mal·nu·tri·tion (mǎl′nōō-trĭsh′ən, mǎl′nyōō-) *n.* Insufficient and poor nutrition.

mal·oc·clu·sion (mǎl′ə-klōō′zhən) *n.* Faulty closure of the teeth of the upper and lower jaws.

mal·o·dor·ous (mǎl-ō′dər-əs) *adj.* Having a bad smell. —**mal·o′dor·ous·ly** *adv.* —**mal·o′dor·ous·ness** *n.*

mal·prac·tice (mǎl-prǎk′tĭs) *n.* **1.** A failure to meet or observe professional standards, as of knowledge, skill, or due care, that results in injury or loss, esp. to a patient or client. **2.** An act or practice that is unethical, injurious, or negligent. —**mal′prac·ti′tion·er** *n.*

malt (môlt) *n.* **1.** Grain, usu. barley, that has been allowed to sprout, and is used chiefly in brewing and distilling. **2.** An alcoholic beverage, such as beer or ale, brewed from malt. **3.** *Informal.* A drink made with malted milk. —*tr.v.* **1.** To process (grain) into malt. **2.** To treat or to mix with malt or a malt extract. —*intr.v.* To become malt. [Middle English, from Old English *mealt*.]

malt·ed milk (môl′tĭd). **1.** A soluble powder made of dried milk, malted barley, and wheat flour. **2.** A beverage made by mixing malted milk usu. with milk and sometimes adding ice cream and flavoring. Also called **malted.**

Maltese cat. A domestic cat with short, silky, bluish-gray hair.

Maltese cross. A cross formed by four arrowheads placed with their points toward the center of a circle.

Mal·thu·sian (mǎl-thōō′zhən, môl-) *adj.* Of or pertaining to the economic theory of Thomas Malthus that population tends to increase faster than food supply unless checked by war, disease, or other disaster. —**Mal·thu′sian** *n.*

mal·tose (môl′tōs′, -tōz′) *n.* A sugar, $C_{12}H_{22}O_{11} \cdot H_2O$.

mal·treat (mǎl-trēt′) *tr.v.* To treat cruelly or roughly. —See Syns at **abuse.** —**mal·treat′ment** *n.*

ma·ma (mä′mə, mə-mä′) *n.* Also **mam·ma.** Mother. [Baby talk.]

mam·ba (mäm′bə) *n.* Any of several venomous African snakes of the genus *Dendraspis.* [Zulu *im-amba.*]

mam·bo (mäm′bō) *n., pl.* **-bos.** A dance of Latin-American origin similar to the rumba. —*intr.v.* To dance the mambo. [American Spanish, from Haitian Creole *mambo,* a voodoo priestess.]

mam·ma (mäm′ə) *n., pl.* **mam·mae** (mäm′ē, mäm′ī). An organ of female mammals that contains milk-producing glands; a breast or udder. [Latin.]

mam·mal (mäm′əl) *n.* A member of the class Mammalia. —**mam·mal′i·an** (mä-mä′lē-ən) *adj. & n.*

Mam·ma·li·a (mä-mä′lē-ə, -mä′yə) *pl.n.* A class of vertebrate animals of more than 15,000 species, including man, distinguished by self-regulating body temperature, hair, and, in the femals, milk-producing mammae. [New Latin, from Latin *mammalis,* of the breast, from *mamma,* breast.]

mam·mal·o·gy (mä-mäl′ə-jē) *n.* The branch of zoology that deals with the study of mammals. [MAMMA(L) + -LOGY.] —**mam·mal′o·gist** *n.*

mam·ma·ry (mäm′ər-ē) *adj.* Of or pertaining to a breast or mamma.

mammary gland. One of the milk-producing glands, such as a breast or udder, in female animals.

Mam·mon (mäm′ən) *n.* **1.** In the New Testament, riches and avarice personified as a false god. **2.** Riches esp. as an object of worship or an evil influence. [Middle English *Mammona,* from Medieval Latin *mammōna,* from Greek *mamōnas,* from Aramaic *māmōnā,* riches.]

mam·moth (mäm′əth) *n.* **1.** An extinct elephant of the genus *Mammuthus,* once found throughout the Northern Hemisphere. **2.** Something of great size. —*adj.* Of enormous size; huge; gigantic. —See Syns at **giant.** [Obs. Russian *mammot′.*]

man (män) *n., pl.* **men** (mĕn). **1.** An adult male human being. **2. a.** A member of the human race. **b.** The human race; mankind: *the accomplishments of man.* **3.** *Zool.* A member of the genus *Homo,* family Hominidae, order Primates, class Mammalia, esp. a member of the species, *Homo sapiens.* **4.** Any person: *Every man for himself!* **5.** A man that possesses the qualities considered characteristic of manhood: *an experience that made a man of him.* **6.** A male employee or worker: *six men on the job.* **7.** *Informal.* Fellow. **8.** Any of the pieces used in games, such as chess, checkers, backgammon. —*tr.v.* **manned, man·ning. 1.** To supply or furnish with men for work: *manning a ship.* **2.** To take one's place for work at: *immigrants who manned the factories.* **3.** To fortify or strengthen: *man oneself for a test of courage.* —*interj.* A word used to emphasize or express intense feeling: *Man, it's a hot day!* —**idioms. as one man.** In unison; unanimously. **one's own man.** Free from outside control; independent. **to a man.** Including everyone; without exceptions. [Middle English, from Old English *mann.*]

man about town A worldly and socially knowledgeable man who frequents fashionable places.

man·a·cle (män′ə-kəl) *n.* Often **manacles. 1.** A device for shackling the hands; handcuff. **2.** Anything that confines or restrains. —*tr.v.* **-cled, -cling.** To restrain with or as if with manacles. [Middle English *manicle,* from Old French, from Latin *manicula,* little hand, handle, dim. of *manus,* hand.]

man·age (män′ĭj) *tr.v.* **-aged, -ag·ing. 1.** To direct the affairs of: *manage a business.* **2.** To make submissive to authority or discipline; control; handle: *She just can't manage him.* **3.** To succeed in doing or accomplishing; contrive or arrange: *I'll manage to come on Friday.* **4.** To control the use of; operate: *manage a tractor.* —*intr.v.* To carry on; get along: *I don't know how they manage without him.* [Italian *maneggiare,* to handle (a horse), from Latin *manus,* hand.]

man·age·a·ble (män′ĭ-jə-bəl) *adj.* Capable of being managed or controlled. —**man′age·a·bil′i·ty** *n.* —**man′age·a·bly** *adv.*

man·age·ment (män′ĭj-mənt) *n.* **1.** The act, manner, or practice of managing. **2.** The person or persons who manage an organization. **3.** Executive ability.

man·ag·er (män′ĭj-ər) *n.* **1.** A person who manages an enterprise. **2.** A person who is in charge of the business affairs of an entertainer. **3.** A person in charge of the training and performance of an athlete or team. —**man′ag·er·ship** *n.*

man·a·ge·ri·al (män′ə-jîr′ē-əl) *adj.* Of, pertaining to, or characteristic of a manager or management. —**man′a·ge′ri·al·ly** *adv.*

ma·ña·na (mä-nyä′nä) *n.* Some indefinite time in the future. —**mañ·a′nä** *adv.* [Spanish, tomorrow.]

man-at-arms (män′ət-ärmz′) *n., pl.* **men-at-arms.** A soldier, esp. a heavily armed mounted soldier in the Middle Ages.

man·a·tee (män′ə-tē′) *n.* An aquatic, primarily tropical mammal of the genus *Trichechus.* [Spanish *manati.*]

man·da·mus (män-dā′məs) *n. Law.* A writ issued by a superior court ordering a public official or body or a lower court to perform a specified duty. [Latin *mandāmus,* "we order," from *mandāre,* to order.]

man·da·rin (män′də-rĭn) *n.* **1.** In imperial China, a member of any one of the nine ranks of high public officials. **2. Mandarin.** The national language of China, based on the dialect spoken in and around Peking. [Portuguese, ult. from Sanskrit *mantrin,* counselor.]

man·da·tar·y (män′də-târ′ē) *n., pl.* **-ies.** The recipient of a mandate.

man·date (män′dāt′) *n.* **1.** An authoritative command or instruction. **2. a.** A commission from the League of Nations authorizing a nation to administer a territory. **b.** Any region under administration. **3.** *Law.* An order issued by a superior court or official to a lower one. —*tr.v.* **-dat·ed, -dat·ing.** To assign or administer under a mandate. [Latin *mandātum,* a command, from *mandāre,* to command.] —**man′da·tor** *n.*

man·da·to·ry (män′də-tôr′ē, -tōr′ē) *adj.* **1.** Of, pertaining to, or holding a mandate. **2.** Required by or as if by mandate; obligatory. —See Syns at **compulsory.**

man·di·ble (män′də-bəl) *n.* A jaw, esp.: **a.** The lower jaw in vertebrates. **b.** Either the upper or lower part of the beak in birds. **c.** Any of various mouth parts in insects. [Old French, from Latin *mandibula,* from *mandere,* to chew.] —**man·dib′u·lar** (män-dĭb′yə-lər) *adj.*

Man·din·go (män-dĭng′gō) *n., pl.* **-gos** or **-goes. 1.** A member of any of various Negroid peoples inhabiting the region of the upper Niger River valley of western Africa. **2.** Any language or dialect of the Mandingos.

man·do·lin (män′də-lĭn′, män′də-lĭn′) *n.* A musical instrument with a pear-shaped body, a fretted neck, and four pairs of metal strings. [French *mandoline,* from Italian *mandolino,* dim. of *mandola, mandora,* lute, from Greek *pandoura.*]

mandolin

man·drake (män′drāk′) *n.* **1.** A Eurasian plant, *Mandragora officinarum,* with purplish flowers and a branched root thought to resemble the human body, once widely believed to have magical powers. **2.** The **May apple.** [Middle English, from Old English *mandragora,* from Latin *mandragoras,* from Greek.]

man·drel or **man·dril** (män′drəl) *n.* **1.** A spindle or axle used to secure or support material being machined. **2.** A metal core around which wood and other materials may be cast or shaped. [Prob. alteration of French *mandrin,* a lathe, from Provençal *mandre,* axle, crank, from Latin *mamphur,* bow-drill.]

man·drill (män′drĭl′) *n.* A large, fierce baboon, *Mandrillus sphinx,* of western Africa, with a beard, a crest, a mane, and brilliant blue, purple, and scarlet facial markings in the adult male. [MAN + DRILL (baboon).]

mane (mān) *n.* **1.** The long hair along the top and sides of the neck of some mammals, such as the horse and the male lion. **2.** A long, thick growth of human hair. [Middle English, from Old English *manu.*]

ă pat   ā pay   â care   ä father   ĕ pet   ē be   hw which   ĭ pit   ī tie   î pier   ŏ pot   ō toe   ô paw, for   oi noise
ŏŏ took   ŏŏ boot   ou out   th thin   *th* this   ŭ cut   û urge   zh vision   ə about, item, edible, gallop, circus

man·eat·er (măn′ē′tər) *n.* An animal that eats or is believed to eat human flesh. —**man′-eat′ing** *adj.*

ma·nège (mă-nĕzh′) *n.* Also **ma·nege.** 1. The art or practice of training or riding horses. 2. A riding academy. [French, from Italian *maneggio,* from *maneggiare,* to manage.]

ma·nes or **Ma·nes** (mā′nēz, mä′nās) *pl.n.* In ancient Rome, the deified spirits of the dead. [Latin *mānēs.*]

ma·neu·ver (mə-nōō′vər, -nyōō′-) *n.* Also *Brit.* **ma·noeu·vre.** 1. a. A strategic or tactical movement of military forces. b. Often **maneuvers.** A large-scale military training exercise that simulates combat. 2. a. A physical movement that usu. requires skill or dexterity. b. A controlled change in the flight path of an aircraft. 3. An adroit and clever move; stratagem: *legal maneuvers that delayed the trial.* Also *Brit.* **ma·noeu·vre, -vred, -vring.** —*intr.v.* 1. To perform or carry out a military maneuver. 2. To use clever tactics or stratagems so as to achieve a desired end. —*tr.v.* To manipulate or guide adroitly to a desired position or goal: *maneuvered the opposition into supporting the bill.* [French *manoeuvre,* from Old French *maneuvre,* from Medieval Latin *manuopera,* manual work, from Latin *manū operāri,* to work by hand.] —**ma·neu′ver·a·bil′i·ty** *n.* —**ma·neu′ver·a·ble** *adj.*

man Friday. A devoted and efficient male servant or employee. [After *Man Friday,* the devoted native servant in Daniel Defoe's novel *Robinson Crusoe.*]

man·ful (măn′fəl) *adj.* 1. Courageous and resolute. 2. Of, relating to, or suitable for men. —See Syns at **male.** —**man′ful·ly** *adv.* —**man′ful·ness** *n.*

man·ga·nese (măng′gə-nēz′, -nēs′) *n. Symbol* **Mn** A gray-white, brittle metallic element. Atomic number 25; atomic weight 54.9380; melting point 1,244°C; boiling point 2,097°C; specific gravity 7.21 to 7.44; valences 1,2,3,4,6,7. [French *manganèse,* from Italian *manganese,* prob. alteration of Medieval Latin *magnēsia,* manganese, magnesia, from Late Greek.]

mange (mānj) *n.* A contagious skin disease esp. of domestic animals, caused by parasitic mites and characterized by itching and loss of hair. [Middle English *maniewe,* from Old French *manjue,* eating, itch, from *mangier,* to eat, from Latin *mandūcāre,* to eat, chew, from *mandūcō,* glutton, from *mandere,* to chew.]

man·gel-wur·zel (măng′gəl-wûr′zəl) *n.* A beet with a large yellowish root, used chiefly as cattle feed. [German, *Mangold-wurzel,* "beet-root."]

man·ger (mān′jər) *n.* A trough or open box in which feed for livestock is placed. [Middle English *maniure,* from Old French *mangeoire,* from Latin *mandūcāre,* to eat, chew.]

man·gle¹ (măng′gəl) *tr.v.* **-gled, -gling.** 1. To batter, hack, or cut. 2. To ruin or spoil; botch: *mangle a speech.* [Middle English *manglen,* from Norman French *mangler,* prob. freq. of Old French *mahaignier,* to wound.] —**man′gler** *n.*

man·gle² (măng′gəl) *n.* A laundry machine for pressing fabrics. —*tr.v.* **-gled, -gling.** To smooth or press with a mangle. [Dutch *mangel,* from German, dim. of Middle High German *mange,* mangle, from Late Latin *manganum,* a military machine, from Greek *manganon.*]

man·go (măng′gō) *n., pl.* **-goes** or **-gos.** 1. A tropical evergreen tree, *Mangifera indica,* that bears edible fruit. 2. The fruit of the mango, with a smooth rind and sweet, juicy, yellow-orange flesh. [Portuguese *manga,* from Malay *mangā,* from Tamil *mānkāy* : *mān,* mango tree + *kāy,* fruit.]

man·go·steen (măng′gə-stēn′) *n.* 1. A tropical tree, *Garcinia Mangostana,* with thick, leathery leaves and edible fruit. 2. The fruit of the mangosteen, with a hard rind and segmented, sweet, juicy pulp. [Malay *manggustan.*]

man·grove (măn′grōv′, măng′grōv′) *n.* Any of various tropical evergreen trees or shrubs of the genus *Rhizophora* that have stiltlike roots and stems and form dense thickets in tidal regions. [From Portuguese *mangue,* from Taino *mangle.*]

man·gy (mān′jē) *adj.* **-gi·er, -gi·est.** 1. Having, resembling, or caused by mange. 2. Having many bare spots; shabby: *a mangy old mink coat.* —**man′gi·ness** *n.*

man·han·dle (măn′hăn′dəl) *tr.v.* **-dled, -dling.** 1. To handle roughly. 2. To move by human strength.

man·hole (măn′hōl′) *n.* A hole or opening in a street, with a removable cover, through which an underground structure, such as a sewer or conduit, can be entered for repair or inspection.

man·hood (măn′hood) *n.* 1. The state or condition of being an adult male human being: *Boys grow to manhood.* 2. The qualities, such as courage, determination, and vigor, ordinarily attributed to a man. 3. Men collectively.

man-hour (măn′our′) An industrial unit of production equal to the work a person can produce in one hour.

man·hunt (măn′hŭnt′) An organized and extensive search for a person, usu. a fugitive criminal.

ma·ni·a (mā′nē-ə, mān′yə) *n.* 1. An intense or unreasonable enthusiasm for something; obsession; craze: *a mania for sailboats.* 2. a. A mental disorder characterized by excessive physical activity and emotional excitement. b. Insanity. —See Syns at **insanity.** [Middle English, madness, from Late Latin, from Greek.]

ma·ni·ac (mā′nē-ăk′) *n.* 1. An insane person; a lunatic. 2. A person with an excessive enthusiasm for something: *a bridge maniac.* [Greek *maniakos,* from *mania,* madness.]

ma·ni·a·cal (mə-nī′ə-kəl) *adj.* 1. Insane: *a maniacal killer.* 2. *Informal.* Characterized by excessive enthusiasm: *a maniacal fondness for gambling.* —See Syns at **insane.** —**ma·ni′a·cal·ly** *adv.*

man·ic (măn′ĭk) *adj.* Of, relating to, or characterized by mania.

man·ic-de·pres·sive (măn′ĭk-dĭ-prĕs′ĭv). *Psychiatry.* —*adj.* Characterized by alternating periods of manic excitement and severe depression. —*n.* A manic-depressive person.

man·i·cot·ti (măn′ĭ-kŏt′ē) *n.* Tubular pasta with a filling, as of chopped ham and ricotta cheese. [Italian, "sleeves" (from the shape of the pasta).]

man·i·cure (măn′ĭ-kyōōr′) *n.* Treatment of the hands and fingernails, esp. shaping, cleaning, and polishing the nails. —*tr.v.* **-cured, -cur·ing.** 1. To give a manicure to. 2. To clip or trim evenly and closely: *He manicured the hedge.* [French: Latin *manus,* hand + *cūra,* care.] —**man′i·cur′ist** *n.*

man·i·fest (măn′ə-fĕst′) *adj.* Clearly apparent to the sight or understanding; obvious: *a manifest hoax.* —*tr.v.* To show plainly; make clear or obvious: *manifest one's greed.* —See Syns at **show.** —*n.* A list of cargo or passengers for a ship or airplane. [Middle English, from Latin *manifestus,* palpable, from *manus,* hand.] —**man′i·fest·ly** *adv.*

man·i·fes·ta·tion (măn′ə-fĕs-tā′shən) *n.* 1. a. The act of manifesting or the state of being manifested. b. The demonstration of the existence, reality, or presence of a person, object, or quality: *a manifestation of ill will.* 2. A public demonstration, usu. of a political nature. —See Syns at **sign.**

man·i·fes·to (măn′ə-fĕs′tō) *n., pl.* **-toes** or **-tos.** A public declaration esp. of political principles or intentions. [Italian, "manifestation."]

man·i·fold (măn′ə-fōld) *adj.* 1. Of many and diverse kinds: *"the manifold exasperations of life"* (Thomas Mann). 2. Having many features or forms. —*n.* 1. A whole composed of many diverse elements. 2. A pipe with several openings for making multiple connections. —*tr.v.* 1. To make several copies of. 2. To make manifold; multiply. [Middle English, from Old English *manig-feald* : *manig,* many + *-feald,* -fold.] —**man′i·fold·ly** *adv.* —**man′i·fold·ness** *n.*

man·i·kin or **man·ni·kin** (măn′ĭ-kĭn) *n.* 1. A little man; a dwarf. 2. An anatomical model of the human body, as used primarily for study. 3. Var. of **mannequin.** [Middle Dutch *mannekin,* dim. of *man,* man.]

ma·nil·a or **ma·nil·la** (mə-nĭl′ə) *n.* Often **Ma·nil·a** or **Ma·nil·la.** 1. Manila hemp. 2. Manila paper. —*modifier: a manila envelope.*

Manila hemp. The fiber of the abaca, used for making rope, cordage, and paper.

Manila paper. Strong paper with usu. buff in color, orig. made from Manila hemp.

man in the street. The common man.

man·i·oc (măn′ē-ŏk′) *n.* The cassava. [French, of Tupian orig.]

man·i·ple (măn′ə-pəl) *n.* 1. A narrow silk band worn as an ecclesiastical vestment over the left arm near the wrist. 2. A subdivision of a Roman legion, containing 60 or 120 men. [Ult. from Latin *manipulus*, handful, from *manus*, hand.]

ma·nip·u·late (mə-nĭp′yə-lāt′) *tr.v.* **-lat·ed, -lat·ing. 1.** To operate or manage by skilled use esp. of the hands. **2.** To influence or manage shrewdly or skillfully: *manipulated public opinion.* **3.** To manage artfully or deceitfully for personal gain or advantage. —See Syns at **handle.** [Back-formation from MANIPULATION.] —**ma·nip′u·la·bil′i·ty** *n.* —**ma·nip′u·lat′ive, ma·nip′u·la·to′ry** (-lə-tôr′ē, -tōr′ē) *adj.* —**ma·nip′u·la′tor** *n.*

ma·nip·u·la·tion (mə-nĭp′yə-lā′shən) *n.* The act of manipulating or of being manipulated. [From Latin *manipulus*, handful.]

man·kind (măn′kīnd′, -kīnd′) *n.* **1.** The human race. **2.** Men as distinguished from women.

man·like (măn′līk′) *adj.* **1.** Resembling man or a man. **2.** Belonging or appropriate to a man.

man·ly (măn′lē) *adj.* **-li·er, -li·est. 1.** Having qualities gen. attributed to a man: *manly courage.* **2.** Belonging to or suitable for a man; masculine: *manly clothes.* —See Syns at **male.** —**man′li·ness** *n.*

man·made (măn′mād′) *adj.* Made by man; synthetic. —See Syns at **artificial.**

man·na (măn′ə) *n.* **1.** In the Old Testament, the food miraculously provided for the Israelites in the wilderness during their flight from Egypt. **2.** Something badly needed that comes unexpectedly. [Aramaic *mannā*, from Hebrew *mān.*]

man·ne·quin (măn′ĭ-kĭn) *n.* Also **man·i·kin. 1.** A life-size representation of the human body, used for fitting or displaying clothes; dummy. **2.** A woman who models clothes. [French, from Middle Dutch *mannekīn,* manikin.]

man·ner (măn′ər) *n.* **1. a.** A way or style of doing something: *proceed in the usual manner.* **b.** The way in which something is done or happens: *shook his fist in a threatening manner.* **2.** A way of acting; a person's characteristic bearing or behavior: *an affectionate, tolerant manner.* **3. manners. a.** Socially proper behavior; etiquette. **b.** The customs of a specific society or period: *a novel of Victorian manners.* **4.** Practice, style, or method in the arts: *This painting is typical of the artist's early manner.* **5.** Kind; sort: *What strange manner of beast is this?* —**idioms. all manners of.** All kinds of. **in a manner of speaking.** In a way; so to speak. [Middle English *manere,* from Norman French *maniere,* from Old French *maniere,* from Latin *manuārius,* of the hand, from *manus,* hand.]

Syns: **manners, decorum, etiquette, proprieties** *n.* Core meaning: Socially correct behavior (*had to mind his manners at the party*). See also Syns at **method.**

man·nered (măn′ərd) *adj.* **1.** Having manners of a particular kind: *ill-mannered.* **2.** Artificial; affected: *mannered speech.*

man·ner·ism (măn′ər-ĭz′əm) *n.* **1.** A peculiarity of behavior or manner. **2.** An exaggerated or affected trait or habit: *speech mannerisms that irritated the listener.*

man·ner·ly (măn′ər-lē) *adj.* Having or displaying good manners; polite. —See Syns at **polite.** —**man′ner·li·ness** *n.* —**man′ner·ly** *adv.*

man·nish (măn′ĭsh) *adj.* Resembling, typical of, or appropriate to a man rather than a woman. —**man′nish·ly** *adv.* —**man′nish·ness** *n.*

ma·noeu·vre (mə-nōō′vər, -nyōō′-) *n. & v. Brit.* Var. of **maneuver.**

man of the world. A sophisticated, worldly man.

man-of-war (măn′ə-wôr′) *n., pl.* **men-of-war. 1.** A warship. **2.** The **Portuguese man-of-war.**

man·or (măn′ər) *n.* **1.** The landed estate of a feudal lord. **2.** Any landed estate. **3.** The main house of an estate; mansion. [Middle English *maner,* from Norman French *manere,* from Old French *maneir,* dwelling place, from *maneir,* to dwell, from Latin *manēre.*] —**ma·no′ri·al** (mă-nôr′ē-əl, mă-nōr′-) *adj.*

man-o′-war bird. The **frigate bird.**

man·pow·er (măn′pou′ər) *n.* Also **man power. 1.** The power of human physical effort. **2.** The total number of people available for work or service.

man·qué (mäN-kā′) *adj.* Unsuccessful. Used after the noun it modifies: *an artist manqué.* [French, from *manquer,* to fail, lack, from Italian *mancare,* from *manco,* lacking, de-

fective, from Latin *mancus,* maimed.]

man·sard (măn′särd) *n.* A roof that has two slopes on all four sides, with the lower slope steeper than the upper. [French *(toit en) mansarde,* "mansard (roof)," after François *Mansart* (1598–1666), French architect, its designer.]

mansard

manse (măns) *n.* The residence of a minister, esp. a Presbyteran minister. [Medieval Latin *mansa,* house, from Latin *manēre,* to dwell.]

man·ser·vant (măn′sûr′vənt) *n., pl.* **men·ser·vants** (mĕn′sûr′vənts). A male servant.

man·sion (măn′shən) *n.* A large, stately house. [Middle English, house, from Old French, from Latin *mānsiō,* dwelling, from *manēre,* to dwell, remain.]

man-sized (măn′sīzd′) *adj. Informal.* Very large: *a man-sized piece of pie: a man-sized job.*

man·slaugh·ter (măn′slô′tər) *n. Law.* The unlawful killing of one human being by another without malice or the intent to do injury.

man·ta (măn′tə) *n.* **1.** Any of several fishes of the family Mobulidae, with large, extremely flattened bodies and winglike pectoral fins. **2.** A coarse cotton fabric or blanket made and used in Spanish America. [Spanish, cape, blanket, from Latin *mantellum,* mantle.]

man·tel (măn′təl) *n.* Also **man·tle. 1.** An ornamental facing around a fireplace. **2.** A mantelpiece. [Middle English, cloak, from Old French, from Latin *mantellum.*]

man·tel·et (măn′təl-ĕt′, mănt′lĭt) *n.* A short cape. [Middle English, from Old French, dim. of *mantel,* mantle, from Latin *mantellum.*]

man·tel·piece (măn′təl-pēs′) *n.* The projecting shelf over a fireplace.

man·til·la (măn-tē′yə, -tĭl′ə) *n.* A scarf, often of lace, worn over the head and shoulders, by Spanish and Latin-American women. [Spanish, dim. of *manta,* cape.]

man·tis (măn′tĭs) *n., pl.* **-tis·es** or **-tes** (-tēz). Any of various insects of the family Mantidae, with powerful forelimbs that are often folded in a praying position. Also called **praying mantis.** [Greek, prophet, diviner, mantis (from its prayerful appearance).]

man·tis·sa (măn-tĭs′ə) *n. Math.* The decimal part of a logarithm. [Latin, makeweight.]

man·tle (măn′təl) *n.* **1.** A loose, sleeveless outer garment. **2.** Anything that covers, envelops, or conceals: *a soft mantle of snow; a mantle of official secrecy.* **3.** A sheath of threads that gives off a strong light when heated by a flame. **4.** *Geol.* The layer of the earth between the crust and the core. **5.** A layer of soft tissue that encloses the internal organs of a mollusk or brachiopod and bears glands that secrete the material that forms the shell. **6.** Var. of **mantel.** —*v.* **-tled, -tling.** —*tr.v.* To cover with or as if with a mantle: *Darkness mantled the earth.* —*intr.v.* **1.** To spread over or cover with or as if with a mantle. **2.** To blush. [Middle English, from Old English *mentel,* cloak, and Old French *mantel,* cloak, both from Latin *mantellum.*]

mant·let (mănt′lĭt) *n.* Var. of **mantelet.**

man·tra (măn′trə) *n. Hinduism.* A sacred formula, often a verse from the Veda, believed to possess magical power and used as an incantation or prayer. [Sanskrit.]

man·tu·a (măn′tōō-ə, -tyōō-ə) *n.* A loose woman's gown worn in the 17th and 18th cent. [From French *manteau,* mantle, from Old French *mantel,* from Latin *mantellum,* cloak.]

man·u·al (măn′yōō-əl) *adj.* **1.** Of or pertaining to the hands: *manual dexterity.* **2.** Used by or operated with the hands:

manual alphabet

maple

maraca

a *manual transmission; manual controls.* **3.** Requiring physical rather than mental effort. —*n.* **1.** A small book of instructions; a guidebook; a handbook. **2.** *Mil.* Prescribed movements in the handling of a weapon, esp. a rifle. Also called **manual of arms.** [Middle English *manuel,* from Old French, from Latin *manuālis,* from *manus,* hand.] —**man'·u·al·ly** *adv.*

manual alphabet. An alphabet of hand signals used for communication by deaf-mutes.

man·u·fac·to·ry (măn'yə-făk'tər-ē) *n., pl.* **-ries.** A factory. [MANUFACT(URE) + (FACT)ORY.]

man·u·fac·ture (măn'yə-făk'chər) *v.* **-tured, -tur·ing.** —*tr.v.* **1. a.** To make or process into a finished product, esp. by means of a large-scale industrial operation: *manufacture flax into linen.* **b.** To make or process from raw materials, esp. with the use of machinery. **2.** To make up; invent; fabricate. —*intr.v.* To make or produce goods. —See Syns at **make.** —*n.* **1.** The act or process of manufacturing. **2.** A product that is manufactured. [Old French, handiwork, from Late Latin *manūfactus,* handmade : Latin *manū,* by hand, + *facere,* to make.] —**man'u·fac'tur·a·ble** *adj.* —**man'u·fac'tur·er** *n.*

man·u·mit (măn'yōō-mĭt') *tr.v.* **-mit·ted, -mit·ting.** To free from slavery; emancipate. [Middle English *manumitten,* from Old French *manumitter,* from Latin *manumittere,* from *manū ēmittere,* "to release from one's hand."]

ma·nure (mə-nōōr', -nyōōr') *n.* Material used to fertilize soil, esp. bodily waste of domestic animals. —*tr.v.* **-nured, -nur·ing.** To apply manure to. [Middle English *manour,* from *manouren,* to till, from Norman French *mainoverer,* from Old French *manoeuvrer,* from Medieval Latin *manuoperārī* : Latin *manū,* by hand, + *operārī,* to work.]

man·u·script (măn'yə-skrĭpt') *n.* **1.** A typewritten or handwritten version of a book, article, document, or other work. **2.** A book, document, or other composition written by hand. —*adj.* Handwritten or typewritten as opposed to printed. [Medieval Latin *manūscrīptus,* handwritten : Latin *manū,* by hand + *scrībere,* to write.]

Manx (măngks) *n., pl.* **Manx. 1.** A native or resident of the Isle of Man. **2.** The Celtic language spoken on the Isle of Man. **3.** A **manx cat.** —**Manx** *adj.*

Manx cat. A domestic breed of cat with short hair and no external tail.

man·y (měn'ē) *adj.* **more** (môr, mōr), **most** (mōst). **1.** Being one of a large, indefinite number; numerous: *many a man. many another day.* **2.** Amounting to or consisting of a large, indefinite number: *many friends.* —*n.* (used with a *pl. verb*). **1.** A large, indefinite number: *Many of the children were ill.* **2. the many.** The majority of the people: *Democracy is the rule of the many.* —*pron.* (used with a *pl. verb*). A large number of persons or things: *"Many are called, but few are chosen"* (Matthew 22:14). [Middle English, from Old English *manig.*]

man·za·ni·ta (măn'zə-nē'tə) *n.* Any of several western North American evergreen shrubs of the genus *Arctostaphylos* that bear clusters of white or pink flowers. [American Spanish, dim. of Spanish *manzana,* apple.]

Mao·ism (mou'ĭzm) *n.* The Communist political philosophy and practice developed in China chiefly by Mao Tsetung.

Ma·o·ri (mou'rē) *n., pl.* **Maori** or **-ris. 1.** A member of the aboriginal people of New Zealand. **2.** The language of the Maori. —**Ma'o·ri** *adj.*

map (măp) *n.* A representation, usu. on a plane surface, of a region, such as the surface of the earth. —*tr.v.* **mapped, map·ping. 1.** To make a map of. **2.** To plan in detail: *mapped out an advertising campaign.* —**idiom. put on the map.** To make famous or known. [Medieval Latin *mappa (mundī),* map (of the world), from *mappa,* napkin, sheet, cloth.] —**map'per** *n.*

ma·ple (mā'pəl) *n.* **1.** Any tree or shrub of the genus *Acer,* with lobed leaves and winged seeds borne in pairs. **2.** The hard, close-grained wood of a maple. [Middle English, from Old English *mapel (treow),* maple (tree).]

maple sugar. A sugar made by boiling down maple syrup.

maple syrup. A sweet syrup made from boiling down the sap of the sugar maple.

map·ping (măp'ĭng) *n. Math.* A rule that establishes a correspondence between each member of a set and usu. a single member of a second set.

mar (mär) *tr.v.* **marred, mar·ring. 1.** To damage or spoil the looks of; deface: *mar the surface of a lacquered table.* **2.** To injure or spoil the quality of. [Middle English *marren,* from Old English *merran.*]

mar·a·bou (măr'ə-bōō') *n.* Also **mar·a·bout. 1.** Any of several large Old World storks of the genus *Leptoptilus.* **2.** The long, downy feathers of the marabou, used esp. as trimming on women's clothing. [French *marabout,* from Portuguese *marabuto,* from Arabic *murābit,* stork.]

ma·ra·ca (mə-rä'kə) *n.* A percussion instrument consisting of a hollow gourd or rattle that contains pebbles or dried beans. [Portuguese, from Tupi.]

mar·a·schi·no (măr'ə-skē'nō, -shē'nō) *n.* A liqueur made from the juice and crushed pits of a bitter cherry. [Italian, from *marasca,* short for *amarasca (ciliego),* bitter (cherry), from *amaro,* bitter, from Latin *amārus.*]

maraschino cherry. A preserved cherry flavored with maraschino.

Ma·ra·thi (mə-rä'tē) *n.* Also **Mah·rat·i** or **Mah·rat·ti** (mə-rä'tē, mə-rät'ē). The major Indic language in the state of Maharashtra, India.

mar·a·thon (măr'ə-thŏn') *n.* **1.** A long-distance race, esp. a footrace of 26 miles, 385 yards or about 42 kilometers. **2.** A test of stamina or endurance: *a dance marathon.* [After *Marathon,* Greece, site of a Greek victory (490 B.C.), the news of which was brought to Athens by a messenger who ran the entire distance.]

ma·raud (mə-rôd') —*intr.v.* To rove in search of plunder. —*tr.v.* To make a raid on. [French *marauder,* from *maraud,* vagabond, rogue.] —**ma·raud'er** *n.*

mar·ble (mär'bəl) *n.* **1.** A sometimes mottled or streaked metamorphic rock, chiefly calcium carbonate, $CaCO_3$, that is used esp. in sculpture and architecture. **2.** A sculpture of marble. **3. a.** A little ball made of a hard substance such as glass, used in children's games. **b. marbles.** (used with a *sing. verb*). A game played with marbles. —*modifier: a marble dome.* —*tr.v.* **-bled, -bling.** To marbleize. —*adj.* **1.** Having irregularly colored markings like marble: *marble ice cream.* **2.** White and smooth: *her marble brow.* [Middle English *marbel,* from Old French *marbre,* from Latin *marmor,* from Greek *marmaros,* marble, hard stone.] —**mar'bly** *adj.*

mar·ble·ize (mär'bəl-īz') *tr.v.* **-ized, -iz·ing.** To give a veined or mottled appearance to.

mar·ca·site (mär'kə-sīt', -zīt') *n.* A pale-colored mineral of iron disulfide, FeS$_2$, similar to pyrite but having a different crystalline structure. [Middle English *marchasite*, from Medieval Latin *marcasīta*, from Arabic *marqashīṭā*.]

mar·cel (mär-sĕl′) *n.* A deep, regular wave made by a heated curling iron. —*tr.v.* **-celled, -cel·ling.** To make or set a marcel in. [After *Marcel* Grateau (d. 1936), French hairdresser.]

march[1] (märch) *intr.v.* **1.** To walk with an even, measured gait, usu. keeping pace with others: *The band marched by the reviewing stand.* **2.** To walk in a purposeful or determined manner; stride: *marched up to the counter and demanded his money back.* **3.** To advance or proceed with steady movement: *The days marched on.* —*tr.v.* To cause to march: *soldiers who were marched into battle.* —*n.* **1.** The act of marching. **2.** The distance or the period of time covered by marching: *a week's march; a fifty-mile march.* **3.** A measured, even step. **4.** Forward movement; progression: *the march of modern medicine.* **5.** *Mus.* A composition in strongly accented, usu. duple rhythm to accompany marching. —**idioms. on the march.** Moving ahead; advancing. **steal a march on.** To get ahead of, esp. by devious or secret methods. [Old French *marcher*, to walk, tramp, trample.]

march[2] (märch) *n.* A border region; frontier. [Middle English *marche*, from Old French, borderland, of Germanic orig.]

March (märch) *n.* The third month of the year, after February and before April. It has 31 days. —*modifier:* *March winds.* [Middle English, from Old French *Marche*, from Latin *Mārtius* (*mēnsis*), (month) of Mars, from *Mārs*, Mars.]

mar·chion·ess (mär′shən-ĭs, mär′shə-nĕs′) *n.* **1.** The wife of a marquis. **2.** A woman who holds the rank of marquis in her own right. Also called **marquise.** [Medieval Latin *marchionissa*, fem. of *marchiō*, marquis, from *marca*, borderland, march.]

march·pane (märch′pān′) *n.* A confection, **marzipan.**

Mar·di gras (mär′dē grä′). Shrove Tuesday, often celebrated by parades of costumed merrymakers. [French, "fat Tuesday."]

mare[1] (mâr) *n.* A female horse, zebra, or related animal. [Middle English, from Old English *mere*.]

ma·re[2] (mä′rā) *n., pl.* **-ri·a** (-rē-ə). *Astron.* Any of the large, dark regions on the moon or Mars. [Latin, sea.]

mare's nest. 1. A seemingly extraordinary discovery that turns out to be a hoax or a mistake. **2.** An extremely complicated or confusing situation.

mare's-tail (mârz′tāl′). **1.** A long, slender cirrus cloud. **2.** An aquatic plant, *Hippuris vulgaris*, native to the North Temperate Zone, with minute flowers and whorls of tapering leaves.

mar·ga·rine (mär′jə-rĭn). Also **mar·ga·rin** *n.* A fatty solid that is used as a butter substitute and consists of a blend of hydrogenated vegetable oils mixed with emulsifiers, vitamins, and coloring matter.

mar·gin (mär′jən) *n.* **1.** An edge and the area that adjoins it; border; verge: *the margin of a pond.* **2.** The space bordering the written or printed area on a page. **3.** An extra amount, as of money or time, allowed beyond what is needed: *a margin of safety.* **4.** A quantity or degree of advantage: *a margin of 500 votes.* **5.** The minimum return that an enterprise may earn and still pay for itself. **6.** The difference between the cost and the selling price. **7.** An amount in money or other collateral deposited by a customer with his broker as a provision against loss on transactions made on account. —*tr.v.* To provide with a margin. [Middle English, from Latin *margō*.]

mar·gin·al (mär′jə-nəl) *adj.* **1.** Written or printed in the margin of a page: *marginal notes.* **2.** Of, relating to, or located at a margin or border. **3.** Barely reaching a lower standard or limit: *marginal writing ability.* **4.** Producing goods whose sale barely covers production costs; yielding little profit: *a marginal industry.* —**mar′gin·al′i·ty** (-năl′ə-tē) *n.* —**mar′gin·al·ly** *adv.*

mar·gi·na·li·a (mär′jə-nā′lē-ə) *pl.n.* Notes in a margin.

mar·grave (mär′grāv′). **1.** The military governor of a medieval German border province. **2.** A prince in the Holy Roman Empire. [Middle Dutch *markgrave* : *mark*, march, border + *grave*, count.]

mar·gra·vine (mär′grə-vēn′) *n.* The wife or widow of a margrave. [Middle Dutch *markgravin*, fem. of *markgrave*, margrave.]

ma·ri·a (mä′rē-ə) *n.* Plural of **mare**[2].

mar·i·gold (mär′ĭ-gōld′, mâr′-) *n.* **1.** Any of several tropical American plants of the genus *Tagetes*, widely cultivated for their showy yellow or orange flowers. **2.** Any of several similar plants, such as the corn marigold and the marsh marigold. [Middle English *marygould* : *Mary*, mother of Jesus + *gold*, gold (from its color).]

mar·i·jua·na or **mar·i·hua·na** (mär′ə-wä′nə) *n.* **1.** The hemp plant. **2.** The dried flower clusters and leaves of the hemp plant smoked for an intoxicating effect. [Mexican Spanish *marihuana*.]

ma·rim·ba (mə-rĭm′bə) *n.* A xylophone with a resonant tube beneath each of the tuned bars. [Of African orig.]

ma·ri·na (mə-rē′nə) *n.* A boat basin that has docks, moorings, supplies, and repair facilities for sailboats and motorboats. [Italian, fem. of *marino*, marine, from Latin *marīnus*.]

mar·i·nade (mär′ə-nād′) *n.* A mixture usu. of vinegar or wine and oil, with various spices and herbs, in which meat and fish are soaked before cooking. —*tr.v.* **-nad·ed, -nad·ing.** To marinate. [French, from Spanish *marinada*, from *marinar*, to marinate, from *marino*, marine, from Latin *marīnus*.]

mar·i·nate (mär′ə-nāt′) *tr.v.* **-nat·ed, -nat·ing.** To soak in a marinade. [Alteration of MARINADE.]

ma·rine (mə-rēn′) *adj.* **1.** Of or relating to the sea: *marine biology.* **2.** Of or pertaining to shipping or trade by sea: *a marine bureau.* **3.** Of or pertaining to sea navigation; nautical: *a marine chart.* —*n.* **1.** A soldier serving on a ship or at a naval installation. **2. Marine.** A member of the U.S. Marine Corps. **3.** A picture of the sea. [Middle English, from Old French *marin*, from Latin *marīnus*, from *mare*, sea.]

Marine Corps. A branch of the U.S. armed forces whose troops are specially trained for amphibious landings and for combat on both land and water.

mar·i·ner (mär′ə-nər) *n.* A sailor. [Middle English, from Old French *marinier*, from *marin*, marine.]

mar·i·o·nette (mär′ē-ə-nĕt′) *n.* A small jointed wooden figure manipulated by strings or wires attached to its limbs. [French, from the name *Marion*.]

mar·i·po·sa lily (mâr′ĭ-pō′zə). Any of several bulbous plants of the genus *Calochortus*, of the southwestern United States and Mexico, with variously colored, tuliplike flowers. [From Spanish *mariposa*, butterfly.]

mar·i·tal (mär′ə-təl) *adj.* Of or relating to marriage. [Latin *marītālis*, from *marītus*, married.] —**mar′i·tal·ly** *adv.*

mar·i·time (mär′ə-tīm′) *adj.* **1.** Located on or near the sea. **2.** Of shipping, commerce or navigation on the sea: *maritime law.* [French, from Latin *maritimus*, from *mare*, sea.]

mar·jo·ram (mär′jər-əm) *n.* An aromatic plant, *Majorana hortensis*, with small flowers and leaves used for seasoning. [Middle English *majorane*, from Old French, from Medieval Latin *majorāna*.]

mark[1] (märk) *n.* **1. a.** A sign, symbol, or token of something. **b.** A visible trace or impression, such as a scratch, dent, or line, on something. **2. a.** Something, as a stamp, label, or seal, placed on an article to indicate ownership, quality, or origin. **b.** A cross made in place of a signature. **c.** A symbol that indicates a level of achievement or merit; grade: *A mark of 95 is excellent.* **d.** A permanent or lasting impression: *made his mark in the world of international commerce.* **3. a.** An indication of a particular quality; distinctive feature. **b.** A standard of quality; norm: *work that is not up to the mark.* **c.** Distinction; importance: *a woman of mark.* **d.** Notice; attention: *a matter worthy of mark.* **4. a.** Something that is aimed at; a target. **b.** Something desired; goal. **c.** An object of abuse, ridicule, or deception. **5. a.** An object that serves to guide or indicate. **b.** Something that is used to register or record. **c.** The starting position for a race or competition. **6.** A border area; frontier. —See Syns at **sign.** —*tr.v.* **1.** To make a mark on: *Dirty fingers marked the woodwork.* **2. a.** To show by means of a mark. **b.** To indicate or set off by or as if by a mark: *marked off a patch of land for a garden.* **3.** To designate or indicate by or as if by making a mark

ă pat   ā pay   â care   ä father   ĕ pet   ē be   hw which
ŏŏ took   ōō boot   ou out   th thin   *th* this   ŭ cut
ĭ pit   ī tie   î pier   ŏ pot   ō toe   ô paw, for   oi noise
û urge   zh vision   ə about, item, edible, gallop, circus

on: *He marked his route on the map in red ink. The company has marked her for promotion.* **4. a.** To be a distinguishing feature of; characterize: *a face that has been marked by despair.* **b.** To make evident; reveal: *A scowl marked her fury.* **5.** To attach a label or tag to. **6.** To evaluate with marks; grade. **7.** To give careful attention to; heed. **8.** To make note of by writing. **—phrasal verbs. mark down.** reduce in price. **—See Syns at lower. mark up.** increase the selling price. **—idioms. beside (or wide of) the mark.** Not to the point; irrelevant. **mark time. 1.** To keep time by moving the feet as in marching, without moving forward. **2.** To make little or no progress. [Middle English, from Old English *mearc,* boundary, landmark, sign.] **—mark'er** *n.*

mark² (märk) *n.* **1.** The Deutsche mark. **2.** The ostmark. [German *Mark.*]

mark·down (märk'doun') *n.* **1.** A reduction of price. **2.** The amount by which an original price has been reduced.

marked (märkt) *adj.* **1.** Having an identifying mark. **2.** Noticeable; distinctive; clearly defined: *A marked difference in the brothers' reactions.* **3.** Singled out, esp. for attack or revenge: *a marked man.* **—mark'ed·ly** (mär'kĭd-lē) *adv.*

mar·ket (mär'kĭt) *n.* **1. a.** A public gathering for buying and selling goods. **b.** The public place in which a market is held. **2.** A retail store that sells a particular type of merchandise: *a meat market.* **3.** A stock market. **4.** Trade or commerce, esp. in a particular commodity: *the international coffee market.* **5. a.** A region or country where goods may be sold: *The South American market.* **b.** A particular group of buyers: *the college market.* **6.** A desire to buy; demand: *Is there a market for this product?* **7.** The extent or degree of demand; level of commercial activity: *a sluggish market.* **8.** The available supply of a particular product or service: *a swollen labor market.* **—modifier:** *a market town; a market price.* **—tr.v. 1.** To sell or offer for sale. **—intr.v. 1.** To buy or sell in a market. **2.** To purchase supplies or provisions: *marketed for Sunday dinner.* **—See Syns at sell. —idioms. in the market.** Interested in buying. **play the market.** To speculate on the stock market. **on the market.** For sale. [Middle English, from Old English, from Latin *mercātus,* from *mercārī,* to trade, from *merx,* merchandise.] **—mark'et·er** *n.*

mar·ket·a·ble (mär'kĭt-ə-bəl) *adj.* **1.** Fit to be offered for sale. **2.** Wanted by buyers: *a very marketable line of clothing.* **—mar'ket·a·bil'i·ty** *n.*

mar·ket·place (mär'kĭt-plās') *n.* Also **market place. 1.** A public square or open place in which a market is set up. **2. a.** An area of commercial activity or trade. **b.** Any area or field in which trade or exchange takes place: *the marketplace of ideas.*

market price. The prevailing price of a commodity in the open market.

market value. The current or market price.

mark·ing (mär'kĭng) *n.* **1.** The act of marking. **2. a.** A mark. **b.** An arrangement or pattern of marks, as on a plant or animal.

mark·ka (mär'kä) *n.,* *pl.* **-kaa** (-kä'). The basic monetary unit of Finland. [Finnish, from Swedish *mark.*]

marks·man (märks'mən) *n.* A person skilled at shooting a weapon, esp. a gun. [From MARK (target).] **—marks'man·ship'** *n.*

mark·up (märk'ŭp') *n.* The amount added to the cost of an item to figure the selling price.

marl (märl) *n.* Clay that contains a large amount of calcium carbonate, sometimes used as fertilizer. [Middle English, from Old English *marle,* from Late Latin *margila,* dim. of *marga,* marl.]

mar·lin (mär'lən) *n.* Any of several large saltwater game fish of the genus *Makaira.* [Short for MARLINESPIKE (from the pointed shape of its snout).]

mar·line (mär'lən) *n.* Also **mar·lin** or **mar·ling** (-lĭng). *Naut.* A light rope made of two loosely twisted strands, used esp. for binding the ends of ropes to prevent fraying. [Middle English *marline,* from Middle Dutch *marlijn* : *marren,* to tie + *lijn,* line, from Latin *līnea.*]

mar·line·spike (mär'lən-spīk') *n.* Also **mar·lin·spike.** *Naut.* A pointed metal spike, used to separate strands of rope in splicing.

mar·ma·lade (mär'mə-lād') *n.* A preserve made with the pulp and rind esp. of citrus fruits. [French, from Portuguese *marmelada,* quince jam, from *marmelo,* quince, from Latin *melimēlum,* from Greek *melimēlon,* "honey-apple" : *meli,* honey + *mēlon,* apple, fruit.]

mar·mo·re·al (mär-môr'ē-əl, -mōr'ē-əl) *adj.* Also **mar·mo·re·an** (mär-môr'ē-ən, -mōr'ē-ən). Of or suggestive of marble: *marmoreal rigidity.* [Latin *marmoreus,* from *marmor,* marble.]

mar·mo·set (mär'mə-sĕt', -zĕt') *n.* Any of various small tropical American monkeys of the genera *Callithrix, Cebuella, Saguinus,* and *Leontideus,* with soft, dense fur, tufted ears, and a long tail. [Middle English, from Old French, grotesque figure.]

mar·mot (mär'mət) *n.* Any of various South and Central American rodents of the genus *Marmota,* with short legs and ears, and a bushy tail. [French *marmotte.*]

ma·roon¹ (mə-rōōn') *tr.v.* **1.** To abandon, as on a deserted island. **2.** To leave (a person) helpless. [French *marron,* from American Spanish *cimarrón,* fugitive slave.]

ma·roon² (mə-rōōn') *n.* A dark purplish red. **—adj.** Dark purplish red. [French *marron.*] **—ma·roon'** *adj.*

mar·quee (mär-kē') *n.* **1.** A large tent with open sides, used chiefly for outdoor entertainment. **2.** A structure that projects over an entrance to a building, such as a theater, often equipped with a signboard. [French *marquise,* a tent pitched on top of an officer's tent to distinguish it from others, from *marquis,* marquis.]

mar·quess (mär'kwĭs) *n. Brit.* Var. of **marquis.**

mar·que·try (mär'kə-trē) *n., pl.* **-tries.** Also **mar·que·terie.** Decoration in which patterns are made by inlaying pieces of material, such as wood or bone, into a veneer applied to the surface usu. of a piece of furniture. [French *marqueterie,* from *marqueter,* to checker, from *marque,* a mark, pattern, from Old French *merc,* from Old Norse *merki.*]

marquetry

mar·quis (mär'kwĭs; *Fr.* mär-kē') *n., pl.* **marquis** or **-quis·es.** Also *Brit.* **mar·quess** (mär'kwĭs). A nobleman who ranks below a duke and above an earl or count. [Middle English *marchis,* from Old French, count of the march (frontier), from *marche,* frontier country.]

mar·quise (mär-kēz') *n.* A marchioness. [French, fem. of *marquis,* marquis.]

mar·qui·sette (mär'kĭ-zĕt', mär'kwĭ-) *n.* A sheer mesh fabric used for clothing, curtains, and mosquito nets. [From MARQUISE (tent).]

mar·riage (mär'ĭj) *n.* **1. a.** The condition of being married; wedlock. **b.** The legal and social union of a man and woman as husband and wife. **2. a.** An act of marrying. **b.** The ceremony of being married; a wedding. **3.** Any close or intimate union: *a true marriage of minds.* **—modifier:** *marriage vows.*

 Syns: marriage, nuptials, wedding *n. Core meaning:* The act or ceremony of being married (*civil and religious marriages*).

mar·riage·a·ble (mär'ĭj-ə-bəl) *adj.* Suitable for marriage. **—mar'riage·a·bil'i·ty** or **mar'riage·a·ble·ness** *n.*

mar·ried (mär'ēd) *adj.* **1.** Joined in marriage. **2.** Of or pertaining to marriage: *married bliss.* **—n.** A married person: *young marrieds.*

mar·row (mär'ō) *n.* **1.** The soft material that fills the cavities inside bones and consists of fat cells and maturing blood cells together with connective tissue and blood vessels. **2.** The nerve tissue that fills the interior of the bones of the spine; the spinal cord. **3.** The essential part; pith: *She was a country girl to the very marrow.* **—See Syns at heart.** [Middle English *marowe,* from Old English *mærh.*]

| ă pat | ā pay | â care | ä father | ĕ pet | ē be | hw which | ĭ pit | ī tie | î pier | ŏ pot | ō toe | ô paw, for | oi noise |
| ōō took | ōō boot | ou out | th thin | th this | ŭ cut | | û urge | zh vision | ə about, item, edible, gallop, circus | | | | |

mar·row·bone (măr′ō-bōn′) *n.* A bone for making soup.

mar·ry[1] (măr′ē) *v.* **-ried, -ry·ing.** —*tr.v.* **1.** To take as a husband or wife: *He married his sweetheart.* **2.** To unite as husband and wife. **3.** To give in marriage: *married off his daughter.* **4.** To obtain by marriage: *marry wealth.* —*intr.v.* **1.** To take a husband or wife; wed: *They married in their twenties.* **2.** To enter into a close relationship; unite. [Middle English *marien,* from Old French *marier,* from Latin *marītāre,* from *marītus,* marital, married.]

mar·ry[2] (măr′ē) *interj.* Archaic. A word used to express surprise or emphasis. [Middle English *Marie,* Mary, the mother of Jesus.]

Mars (märz) *n.* **1.** *Rom. Myth.* The god of war, identified with the Greek god Ares. **2.** The fourth planet of the solar system in order of increasing distance from the sun.

Mars

marsh (märsh) *n.* An area of low-lying, wet land usu. covered with grasses and reeds. [Middle English *mersh,* from Old English *mersc.*]

mar·shal (mär′shəl) *n.* **1.** A Federal or city official who carries out court orders. **2.** The head of a city police or fire department. **3.** A person in charge of a ceremony. **4. a.** A military officer of the highest rank in some countries. **b.** A field marshal. **5.** A high official in a royal household or court. **-shaled** or **-shalled, -shal·ing** or **-shal·ling.** —*tr.v.* **1.** To place in methodical or proper order; organize: *marshal facts for a debate; marshaled the troops for a parade.* **2.** To conduct ceremoniously; usher. [Middle English *mareschal,* marshal, farrier, from Old French *mareschal,* from Old High German *marahscalc,* keeper of the horses.] —**mar′shal·cy** or **mar′shal·ship**′ *n.*

marsh gas. Methane.

marsh mallow. A plant, *Althaea officinalis,* with showy pink flowers and a root used in confectionery and medicine.

marsh·mal·low (märsh′měl′ō, -măl′ō) *n.* A confection made of corn syrup, gelatin, sugar, and starch, and powdered sugar. [From MARSH MALLOW, the root of which was formerly used as an ingredient in the confection.]

marsh marigold. Any plant of the genus *Caltha,* esp. *C. palustris,* that grow in swampy places and bear bright yellow flowers. Also called **cowslip.**

marsh·y (mär′shē) *adj.* **-i·er, -i·est. 1.** Of or like a marsh; swampy. **2.** Growing in or native to a marsh. —**marsh′i·ness** *n.*

mar·su·pi·al (mär-sōō′pē-əl) *n.* Any mammal of the order Marsupialia, such as the kangaroo, opossum, or wombat, of which the female is characterized by an abdominal pouch that contains the mammary glands and serves as a shelter for the young. [From MARSUPIUM.] —**mar·su′pi·al** *adj.*

mar·su·pi·um (mär-sōō′pē-əm) *n., pl.* **-pi·a** (-pē-ə). The external abdominal pouch in a female marsupial. [From Latin *marsupium,* pouch, from Greek *marsupion,* dim. of *marsipos,* purse.]

mart (märt) *n.* A trading center; market. [Middle English, from Old French *market,* market.]

mar·ten (mär′t'n) *n., pl.* **marten** or **-tens. 1.** An animal of the genus *Martes* that is related to the weasel and the mink, and has thick, soft brown fur. **2.** The fur of the marten. [Middle English *martren,* marten, marten's fur, from Old French *martrine,* marten's fur, from *martre,* marten.]

mar·tial (mär′shəl) *adj.* **1.** Of, pertaining to, or suggesting war or a warrior: *martial music.* **2.** Pertaining to or connected with military life. [Middle English, from Latin *mārtiālis,* from *Mārs,* Mars.] —**mar′tial·ly** *adv.*

martial law. Rule by military authorities imposed upon a civilian population during an emergency.

Mar·tian (mär′shən) *adj.* Of or pertaining to the planet Mars. —*n.* A hypothetical inhabitant of the planet Mars. [Middle English, from Latin *mārtius,* from *Mārs,* Mars.]

mar·tin (mär′t'n) *n.* Any of several birds resembling and closely related to the swallows, such as the purple martin. [Middle English, after St. *Martin* (the birds migrate from England near Martinmas).]

mar·ti·net (mär′tə-nět′) *n.* A rigid disciplinarian. [After Jean *Martinet,* 17th-cent. French general.]

mar·tin·gale (mär′tən-gāl′) *n.* The strap of a horse's harness that connects the girth to the noseband and is designed to prevent a horse from throwing its head back. [French, from *(à la) martingale,* (in the manner of a) native of *Martigue,* a village in Provence.]

mar·ti·ni (mär-tē′nē) *n., pl.* **-nis.** A cocktail usu. made of gin or vodka and dry vermouth. [Orig. unknown.]

Mar·tin·mas (mär′tən-məs) *n.* The festival of Saint Martin, celebrated annually on Nov. 11. [Middle English *martynmasse* : Martin + *masse,* mass.]

mar·tyr (mär′tər) *n.* **1.** A person who suffers death rather than renouncing a religious principle or belief. **2.** A person who makes great sacrifices or suffers a great deal for a cause or principle. **3.** A person who endures great suffering. —*tr.v.* **1.** To make a martyr of. **2.** To inflict great pain or suffering upon; torture. [Middle English *martir,* from Old English *martyr,* from Late Latin, from Greek *martus,* witness.]

mar·tyr·dom (mär′tər-dəm) *n.* **1.** The condition of being a martyr. **2.** Extreme suffering.

mar·tyr·ize (mär′tə-rīz′) *tr.v.* **-ized, -iz·ing.** To martyr.

mar·vel (mär′vəl) *n.* A cause of surprise, admiration, or wonder: *the marvels of technology.* —*intr.v.* **-veled** or **-velled, -vel·ing** or **-vel·ling.** To become filled with wonder, surprise, or astonishment. [Middle English *marveile,* from Old French *merveille,* from Latin *mīrābilis,* wonderful, from *mīrārī,* to wonder, from *mīrus,* wonderful.]

mar·vel·ous (mär′vəl-əs) *adj.* Also **mar·vel·lous. 1.** Causing wonder or astonishment: *a marvelous cure.* **2.** Miraculous; supernatural. **3.** Of the highest kind or quality; splendid: *a marvelous vacation.* —See Syns at **fabulous.** —**mar′vel·ous·ly** *adv.* —**mar′vel·ous·ness** *n.*

Marx·ism (märk′sĭz′əm) *n.* The political, social, and economic doctrines of Karl Marx in which the class struggle is held to be the fundamental force that will lead to the establishment of a classless society. —**Marx′ist** *n.*

mar·zi·pan (mär′zə-păn′, märt′sə-pän′) *n.* A confection made of ground almonds, sugar, and egg whites, often molded into decorative forms. Also called **marchpane.** [German *Marzipan,* from Italian *marzapane,* fine box for confections, a coin, from Arabic *mawthabān,* a coin.]

mas·ca·ra (măs-kăr′ə) *n.* A cosmetic applied to color the eyelashes. [Spanish *máscara,* mask, from Italian *maschera.*]

mas·cot (măs′kŏt, -kət) *n.* A person, animal, or object believed to bring good luck: *The team mascot is a donkey.* [French *mascotte,* from Provençal *mascoto,* sorcery, talisman, from *masco,* sorcerer, from Late Latin *masca,* witch.]

mas·cu·line (măs′kyə-lĭn) *adj.* **1.** Of or pertaining to the male sex. **2.** Characteristic of or suitable to a man: *a masculine voice.* **3.** *Gram.* Of, designating, or constituting the gender of words or grammatical forms that usu. denote or refer to males. —See Syns at **male.** —*n.* **1.** The masculine gender. **2.** A word or word form of the masculine gender. [Middle English *masculin,* from Old French, from Latin *masculīnus,* from *masculus,* male, dim. of *mas,* male.] —**mas′cu·line·ly** *adv.* —**mas′cu·lin′i·ty** (măs′kyə-lĭn′ə-tē) or **mas′cu·line·ness** *n.*

ma·ser (mā′zər) *n.* Physics. Any of several devices that convert electromagnetic radiation from a wide range of frequencies to one or more discrete frequencies of highly amplified microwave radiation. [M(ICROWAVE) A(MPLIFICATION BY) S(TIMULATED) E(MISSION OF) R(ADIATION).]

mash (măsh) *n.* **1.** A mixture of crushed malt or grain and hot water used to make an alcoholic beverage, such as beer or whiskey, after fermentation has taken place. **2.** A mixture of ground grain and nutrients for feeding to livestock. **3.** A soft, pulpy mixture or mass. —*tr.v.* **1.** To convert (malt or grain) into mash. **2.** To convert into a soft, pulpy mixture: *mash potatoes*. [Middle English, from Old English *māsc*.]

mash·er (măsh′ər) *n.* **1.** A kitchen utensil for mashing vegetables or fruit. **2.** *Slang.* A man who attempts to force his amorous attentions upon a woman.

mask (măsk, mäsk) *n.* **1.** A covering worn over all or part of the face to disguise or conceal one's identity. **2.** A figure of a head worn by actors in Greek and Roman drama. **3.** A protective covering for the face or head, as in many sports and jobs. **4.** A gas mask. **5.** A sculptured or molded representation of a face or head, often made of papier-mâché or plaster. **6.** The facial markings of certain animals, esp. a dog. **7.** Anything that disguises or conceals. —*tr.v.* **1.** To cover with or as if with a mask. **2.** To disguise or conceal, as a view, ingredient, intention, etc. [French *masque*, from Italian *maschera*.]

mas·o·chism (măs′ə-kĭz′əm) *n.* **1.** An abnormal condition in which sexual satisfaction is largely derived from abuse or physical pain. **2.** The deriving of pleasure from being offended, dominated, or mistreated in some way. **3.** The turning of any sort of destructive tendencies inward or upon oneself. [After Leopold von Sacher-*Masoch* (1836–95), Austrian novelist.] —**mas′o·chist** *n.* —**mas′o·chis′tic** (măs′ə-kĭs′tĭk) *adj.*

ma·son (mā′sən) *n.* **1.** A person who builds or works with stone or brick. **2. Mason.** A Freemason. [Middle English *masoun*, from Norman French *machun*, from Old French *masson*.]

Ma·son·ic (mə-sŏn′ĭk) *adj.* Of or pertaining to Freemasons or Freemasonry.

Mason jar. A wide-mouthed glass jar with a screw top, used for home canning and preserving. [After John L. *Mason* (1832–1902), American inventor, who patented it.]

ma·son·ry (mā′sən-rē) *n., pl.* **-ries. 1.** The trade or work of a mason. **2.** Stonework or brickwork. **3. Masonry.** Freemasonry.

masque (măsk, mäsk) *n.* **1. a.** A dramatic entertainment, usu. based on an allegorical theme, popular in the 16th and early 17th cent. **b.** A dramatic verse composition written for a masque. **2.** A masquerade. [Var. of MASK.]

mas·quer·ade (măs′kə-rād′) *n.* **1.** A costume ball or party at which masks and elaborate costumes are worn. **2.** Any false outward show or pretense: *a masquerade of humility.* —*intr.v.* **-ad·ed, -ad·ing. 1.** To wear a mask or disguise, as at a masquerade. **2.** To have a deceptive appearance: *a sermon masquerading as a novel.* [French *mascarade*, from Italian *mascherata* or Spanish *mascarada*, from Italian *maschera*, mask.] —**mas′quer·ad′er** *n.*

mass (măs) *n.* **1.** A unified body of matter with no specific shape: *a mass of clay.* **2.** A grouping or collection of individual parts or elements that compose a unified body: *a mass of college students.* **3.** Any large but unspecified amount or number: *a mass of bruises.* **4.** The major part of something; majority. **5.** The physical volume or bulk of a solid body. **6.** *Physics. Abbr.* **m, M** The amount of matter contained in a physical body that is the measure of a body's resistance to acceleration, different from but proportional to its weight. **7.** **the masses.** The body of common people; the populace. —See Syns at **bulk.** —*tr.v.* To gather or form into a mass; assemble. —*intr.v.* To assemble in a mass. —*adj.* **1.** Of, pertaining to, or attended by a large number of people: *mass education.* **2.** Done on a large scale: *mass protests.* **3.** Total; complete: *The mass result is impressive.* [Middle English, from Old French *masse*, from Latin *massa*, from Greek *maza*, barley cake, lump, mass.]

Mass or **mass** (măs) *n.* **1. a.** In Roman Catholic and some Protestant churches, the celebration of the Eucharist. **b.** The service including this celebration. **2.** A musical setting of certain parts of the Mass. [Middle English *masse*, from Old English *mæsse*, from Late Latin *missa*, eucharist, dismissal (after a mass), from *mittere*, to send away.]

Mas·sa·chu·set (măs′ə-chōō′sĭt, -zĭt) *n.* Also **Mas·sa·chu·sett. 1.** A large tribe of Algonquian-speaking Indians who lived on or near Massachusetts Bay. **2.** A member of this tribe. **3.** The language of the Massachusets.

mas·sa·cre (măs′ə-kər) *n.* **1.** A savage and indiscriminate wholesale killing. **2.** *Informal.* A severe defeat, as in sports. —*tr.v.* **-cred** (-kərd), **-cring** (-krĭng, -kər-ĭng). **1.** To kill savagely and indiscriminately. **2.** *Informal.* To defeat decisively, as in sports. [French, from Old French *maçacre*, from *massacrer*, to massacre, prob. ult. from Latin *mateola*, a kind of mallet.] —**mas′sa·crer** (-kər-ər, -krər) *n.*

mas·sage (mə-säzh′) *n.* The rubbing or kneading of parts of the body to aid circulation or to relax the muscles. —*tr.v.* **-saged, -sag·ing.** To give a massage to. [French, from *masser*, to massage, prob. from Arabic *mass*, to touch, handle.]

mass-energy equivalence. The physical principle that a measured quantity of energy is equivalent to a measured quantity of mass, the equivalence expressed by Einstein's equation, $E = mc^2$, where E represents energy, m the equivalent mass, and c the speed of light.

mas·seur (mă-sûr′) *n.* A man who gives massages professionally. [French, from *masser*, to massage.]

mas·seuse (mă-sœz′) *n.* A woman who gives massages professionally. [French, fem. of *masseur*, masseur.]

mas·sive (măs′ĭv) *adj.* **1.** Consisting of or making up a large mass; bulky; heavy; solid: *a massive piece of furniture.* **2.** Impressive or imposing in quantity, scope, degree, intensity, or scale: *a massive overhaul.* **3.** Exceedingly large: *a massive palace.* —See Syns at **giant** and **heavy.** —**mas′sive·ly** *adv.* —**mas′sive·ness** *n.*

mass media Any means of public communication reaching a large audience.

mass number. The total number of neutrons and protons in an atomic nucleus.

mass-pro·duce (măs′prə-dōōs′, -dyōōs′, -prō-) *tr.v.* **-duced, -duc·ing.** To manufacture goods in large quantities, esp. by using standardized designs and assembly-line techniques. —**mass production.**

mast¹ (măst, mäst) *n.* **1.** A tall vertical spar that rises from the keel of a sailing vessel to support the sails and running rigging. **2.** Any vertical pole. —*tr.v.* To furnish with a mast. —*idiom.* **before the mast.** Serving as a common sailor. [Middle English *maste*, from Old English *mæst*.]

mast² (măst, mäst) *n.* The nuts of forest trees accumulated on the ground, used esp. as food for swine. [Middle English *maste*, from Old English *mæst*.]

mas·tec·to·my (măs-tĕk′tə-mē) *n., pl.* **-mies.** Surgical removal of a breast. [Greek *mastos*, breast + -ECTOMY.]

mas·ter (măs′tər, mäs′-) *n.* **1. a.** Someone who has power, authority, or control over someone or something: *the master of a plantation; the master of the house.* **b.** A ruler. **2.** The captain of a merchant ship. **3.** The owner of a slave or an animal. **4.** A workman qualified to teach apprentices and to carry on his craft independently. **5.** Someone of great skill or ability; an expert: *a master of design; a master of intrigue.* **6.** Someone who defeats another; a victor. **7.** A skilled or accomplished artist. **8.** A teacher, schoolmaster, or tutor. **9.** A person whose teachings or doctrines are accepted by followers. **10.** A person of great learning; scholar. **11. Master.** A person holding a master's degree. **12.** The title of the head or presiding officer of certain societies, clubs, orders, etc. **13. Master.** A prefix to the name of a boy or youth not considered old enough to be addressed as Mister. **14.** An original from which copies can be made, as a document. —*adj.* **1.** Being the principal or leading force: *a master plan.* **2.** Being a master; expert: *a master plumber; a master thief.* **3.** Being a part of a mechanism that controls all other parts: *a master switch.* **4.** Being the original from which copies are made: *a master recording.* —*tr.v.* **1.** To bring under control; to overcome or defeat: *master one's emotions.* **2.** To become skilled or knowledgeable in: *master German; master toolmaking.* [Middle English, from Old English *magister* and Old French *maistre*, both from Latin *magister*.]

mas·ter-at-arms (măs′tər-ət-ärmz′) *n., pl.* **masters-at-arms.** A naval petty officer assigned to maintain order.

mas·ter·ful (măs′tər-fəl, mäs′-) *adj.* **1.** Given to playing the master; imperious; domineering. **2.** Inclined or fit to command or dominate; powerful. **3.** Having or revealing mastery; expert; skillful. —See Syns at **dictatorial.** —**mas′ter·ful·ly** *adv.*

master key. A key that opens several different locks whose keys are not the same. Also called **passkey.**

mas·ter·ly (măs′tər-lē, mäs′-) *adj.* Like a master, esp. indicating the knowledge or skill of a master. —*adv.* With the skill of a master. —**mas′ter·li·ness** *n.*

mas·ter·mind (măs′tər-mīnd′, mäs′-) *n.* A highly intelligent and ingenious person, esp. one who plans and directs an important project. —*tr.v.* To direct, plan, or supervise (a project or activity).

Master of Arts. 1. A degree granted by a college or university to a person who has completed at least one year of advanced study, esp. in the liberal arts. **2.** A person holding such a degree.

master of ceremonies. A person who introduces the various events and people on the program at a banquet dinner, an entertainment show, etc.

Master of Science. 1. A degree granted by a college or university to a person who has completed at least one year of advanced study in mathematics or the sciences. **2.** A person holding such a degree.

mas·ter·piece (măs′tər-pēs′, mäs′-) *n.* **1.** An outstanding work of art or craft. **2.** Something done with skill or brilliance: *His plan was a masterpiece of ingenuity.*

master sergeant. A noncommissioned officer of the next to highest rating in the U.S. Army, Air Force, and Marine Corps.

mas·ter·ship (măs′tər-shĭp′, mäs′-) *n.* **1.** The office, function, or authority of a master. **2.** The skill or ability of a master. **3.** The condition of being a master.

mas·ter·stroke (măs′tər-strōk′, mäs′-) *n.* A masterly achievement or action.

mas·ter·work (măs′tər-wûrk′, mäs′-) *n.* A masterpiece.

mas·ter·y (măs′tər-ē, mäs′-) *n., pl.* -**ies. 1.** The consummate skill, ability, or knowledge of a master. **2.** The status or condition of being a master; control: *mastery of the seas.* **3.** Full command or control, as of a subject or situation: *a poet's mastery of the language.* —See Syns at **ability.**

mast·head (măst′hĕd′, mäst′-) *n.* **1.** The top of a ship's mast. **2.** The listing in a newspaper, magazine, or other publication of information about its staff and operation.

mas·tic (măs′tĭk) *n.* **1.** The aromatic resin of an evergreen tree, *Pistacia lentiscus,* used in adhesives, varnishes and lacquers, and as an astringent. **2.** The tree from which this resin is obtained. **3.** A pastelike cement, esp. one made with powdered lime or brick and tar. [Middle English *mastyk,* from Old French *mastic,* from Late Latin *masti-chum,* from Greek *mastikhē.*]

mas·ti·cate (măs′tə-kāt′) *tr.v.* -**cat·ed, -cat·ing. 1.** To chew. **2.** To grind and knead to a pulp. [From Late Latin *masti-cāre,* from Greek *mastikhân,* to grind the teeth.] —**mas′ti·ca′tion** *n.* —**mas′ti·ca′tor** *n.*

mas·ti·ca·to·ry (măs′tĭ-kə-tôr′ē, -tōr′ē) *adj.* **1.** Of, pertaining to, or used in mastication. **2.** Being adapted for chewing. —*n., pl.* -**ries.** A substance chewed to increase salivation.

mas·tiff (măs′tĭf) *n.* A large dog with a short brownish coat and short, square jaws. [Middle English *mastif,* from Old French *mastin,* from Latin *mānsuētus,* tamed : *manus,* hand + *suēscere,* to accustom.]

mastiff

mas·to·don (măs′tə-dŏn′) *n.* Any of several extinct mammals of the genus *Mammut,* related to and resembling the elephant. [New Latin, "breast-tooth" (from the nipple-shaped protuberances on the teeth).]

mas·toid (măs′toid′) *n.* The **mastoid process.** —*adj.* Of, pertaining to, or located near the mastoid process. [New Latin *mastoides,* "breast-shaped."]

mas·toid·i·tis (măs′toid-ī′tĭs) *n.* Inflammation of part or all of the mastoid process.

mastoid process. The rear portion of the temporal bone on each side of the head behind the ear. Also called **mastoid.**

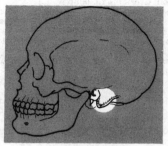

mastoid process

mas·tur·bate (măs′tər-bāt′) *intr.v.* -**bat·ed, -bat·ing.** To perform an act of masturbation. [From Latin *masturbārī.*]

mas·tur·ba·tion (măs′tər-bā′shən) *n.* Excitation of the genital organs, usu. to orgasm, by means other than sexual intercourse.

mat¹ (măt) *n.* **1.** A flat piece of coarse material, such as woven straw, used to wipe one's shoes or feet, or in various other forms as a floor covering. **2.** A small, flat piece of decorated material placed under a lamp, dish, vase, etc. **3.** A thick floor pad to protect athletes, as in wrestling or gymnastics. **4.** Any thickly tangled mass: *a mat of hair.* —*v.* **mat·ted, mat·ting.** —*tr.v.* **1.** To cover, protect, or decorate with a mat. **2.** To interweave or tangle into a thick mass: *A heavy growth of vines matted the bush.* —*intr.v.* To be interwoven into a thick mass; become entangled. [Middle English *matt,* from Old English *matt,* from Late Latin *matta.*]

mat² (măt) *n.* **1.** A decorative usu. cardboard border placed around a picture to serve as a frame or contrast between the picture and a frame. **2.** Matte. —*tr.v.* **mat·ted, mat·ting. 1.** To put a mat around (a picture). **2.** To matte. —*adj.* Matte. [French, dull, from Old French *mattus,* dull, vague.]

mat·a·dor (măt′ə-dôr′) *n.* A person who fights and kills the bull in a bullfight. [Spanish, from *matar,* to kill, from Latin *mactāre,* to sacrifice, from *mactus,* sacred.]

match¹ (măch) *n.* **1. a.** A person or thing that is exactly like another; counterpart. **b.** A person or thing that is like another in one or more specified qualities: *He is John's match for bravery.* **2. a.** A person or thing that closely resembles or harmonizes with another: *The napkins were a nice match for the tablecloth.* **b.** A pair made up of two things or persons that resemble or harmonize with each other: *The colors were a close match.* **3.** A person or thing equal in qualities or able to compete with another of the same class or type: *The boxer had met his match.* **4.** *Sports.* An athletic contest or game in which two or more persons, animals, or teams oppose and compete with each other: *a boxing match.* **5. a.** A marriage or an arrangement of marriage. **b.** A person regarded as a prospective marriage partner. —*tr.v.* **1. a.** To be alike; correspond exactly; to equal: *The color of the chairs doesn't match the color of the couch.* **b.** To be similar to with respect to specified qualities: *The markings on the stamps matched each other.* **2.** To resemble or harmonize with: *The tie matches the suit.* **3.** To adapt or suit so that a balanced or harmonious result is achieved; cause to correspond: *match socks.* **4.** To join in marriage. **5.** To place in opposition or competition with; pit: *They matched wits.* **6.** To provide with an adversary or competitor: *match a contender against the champ.* **7.** To set in comparison; measure; compare: *beauty that could never be matched.* **8. a.** To flip or toss (coins) and compare the sides that land face up. **b.** To toss coins in this manner with (another person). —*intr.v.* To be similar; correspond. [Middle English *macche*, mate, from Old English *gemæcca.*] —**match'a·ble** *adj.*

match² (măch) *n.* **1.** A narrow strip of wood, cardboard, or wax coated on one end with a substance that ignites easily by friction. **2.** An easily ignited cord or wick, formerly used for firing cannons and guns. [Middle English *macche*, lamp wick, candle, from Old French *meiche*, from Medieval Latin *myxa*, lamp wick, from Latin, nozzle of a lamp, from Greek *muxa*, lamp wick.]

match·less (măch'lĭs) *adj.* Having no match or equal; peerless; unsurpassed. —See Syns at **unique.** —**match'-less·ly** *adv.* —**match'less·ness** *n.*

match·lock (măch'lŏk') *n.* An old type of gunlock in which powder is ignited by a match.

match·mak·er (măch'mā'kər) *n.* **1.** Someone who arranges or habitually tries to arrange marriages. **2.** Someone who arranges athletic competitions, esp. in boxing. —**match'-mak'ing** *n. & adj.*

match play. *Golf.* A method of scoring in which the number of holes won by each side are counted rather than the number of strokes taken.

match point. The final point needed to win a sports match.

mate¹ (māt) *n.* **1.** One of a matched pair: *the mate to this glove.* **2.** A spouse. **3.** The male or female of a conjugal pair of animals or birds or one of a pair of animals brought together for breeding. **4.** A close associate; partner. **5.** A deck officer on a merchant ship ranking below the master. **6.** *U.S. Navy.* A petty officer who is an assistant to the warrant officer. —*v.* **mat·ed, mat·ing.** —*tr.v.* **1.** To join closely; pair. **2.** To unite in marriage. **3.** To pair (animals) for breeding. —*intr.v.* **1.** To become joined in marriage. **2.** To become mated; to breed. [Middle English, from Middle Low German, companion.]

mate² (māt). *Chess. n.* A checkmate. —*tr.v.* **mat·ed, mat·ing.** To checkmate. [Middle English *mat*, from Old French, short for *eschec mat*, checkmate.]

ma·té (mä'tā') *n.* **1.** An evergreen tree, *Ilex paraguayensis,* of South America. **2.** A mildly stimulant beverage made from the dried leaves of this tree. [American Spanish, from Quechua, *mate.*]

ma·te·ri·al (mə-tîr'ē-əl) *n.* **1.** The substance or substances from which something is or can be made: *Hemp is often used as a material for ropes.* **2.** Cloth or fabric. **3.** Something, as ideas, information, observations, etc., that may be refined, analyzed, or otherwise reworked and made or incorporated into a finished product: *material for a book; material for a comedy.* **3. materials.** Tools or apparatus for the performance of a given task: *writing materials.* —*adj.* **1.** Of, composed of, or pertaining to matter; physical; corporeal. **2.** Of, pertaining to, or affecting physical well-being: *material comforts.* **3.** Of or concerned with the physical as distinct from the intellectual or spiritual. **4.** Substantial; important; essential: *a material consideration.* **5.** Relevant to the case: *material testimony.* **6.** *Philos.* Of or pertaining to the matter or content, rather than form. —See Syns at **relevant.** [Middle English, from Old French *materiel*, from Late Latin *māteriālis*, from *māteria*, matter.]

ma·te·ri·al·ism (mə-tîr'ē-əl-ĭz'əm) *n.* **1.** The philosophical doctrine that physical matter is the only reality in the universe and that everything else, including thought, feeling, mind, and will, can be explained in terms of physical laws. **2.** The doctrine that physical well-being and worldly possessions make up the greatest good and highest value in life. **3.** Excessive regard for worldly and material concerns. —**ma·te'ri·al·ist** *n.* —**ma·te'ri·al·is'tic** *adj.* —**ma·te'ri·al·is'ti·cal·ly** *adv.*

ma·te·ri·al·ize (mə-tîr'ē-əl-īz') *v.* **-ized, -iz·ing.** —*tr.v.* To cause to become real or actual: *By building the house, he materialized his dream.* —*intr.v.* **1.** To become real or actual; become a fact: *Support for the takeover did not materialize.* **2.** To take on physical or bodily form; appear as if from nowhere: *A heavenly figure materialized before his eyes. The sun materialized above the mountains.* —**ma·te'ri·al·i·za'tion** *n.*

ma·te·ri·al·ly (mə-tîr'ē-əl-ē) *adv.* **1.** With regard to matter as distinguished from form. **2.** To a significant degree;

considerably: *His efforts materially aided the project.* **3.** With regard to what promotes physical well-being: *They are materially comfortable.*

ma·te·ri·a med·i·ca (mə-tîr'ē-ə měd'ĭ-kə). *Med.* **1.** The study of remedies and their sources, preparation, and use. **2.** A substance used in preparing remedies or as a medicine. [Latin, "medical material."]

ma·te·ri·el or **ma·té·ri·el** (mə-tîr'ē-ĕl') *n.* **1.** The equipment, apparatus, and supplies of a military force. **2.** The equipment, apparatus, and supplies of any organization. [French, from *matériel*, material.]

ma·ter·nal (mə-tûr'nəl) *adj.* **1.** Of, relating to, or characteristic of a mother or motherhood; motherly: *maternal instinct.* **2.** Inherited from one's mother: *a maternal trait.* **3.** Related to through one's mother: *my maternal uncle.* [Middle English, from Old French *maternel*, from Latin *māternus*, from *māter*, mother.] —**ma·ter'nal·ly** *adv.*

ma·ter·ni·ty (mə-tûr'nə-tē) *n.* **1.** The condition of being a mother; motherhood. **2.** The feelings or characteristics associated with being a mother; motherliness. —*adj.* Associated with pregnancy and childbirth: *a maternity dress; a maternity ward.* [French *maternité*, from Medieval Latin *māternitās*, from *māternus*, maternal.]

math (măth) *n.* Mathematics.

math·e·mat·i·cal (măth'ə-măt'ĭ-kəl) or **math·e·mat·ic** *adj.* **1.** Of or pertaining to mathematics. **2.** Precise; exact. [Old French *mathematique*, from Latin *mathēmaticus*, from Greek *mathēmatikos*, from *mathēma*, science, from *manthanein*, to learn.] —**math'e·mat'i·cal·ly** *adv.*

mathematical induction. Induction.

math·e·ma·ti·cian (măth'ə-mə-tĭsh'ən) *n.* A specialist in or student of mathematics.

math·e·mat·ics (măth'ə-măt'ĭks) *n.* (used with a sing. verb). The study of numbers, forms, arrangements, and sets, and of their relationships and properties.

mat·i·nee or **mat·i·née** (măt'n-ā') *n.* A dramatic or musical performance given in the afternoon. [French *matinée*, morning, early performance, from Old French *matinee*, from *matin*, morning, from Latin (*tempus*) *mātūtīnum*, morning (time), from *Mātūta*, goddess of dawn.]

mat·ins (măt'ĭnz) *n.* (used with a sing. or pl. verb). Often **Matins.** In the Anglican Church, the service of morning worship. [Middle English *matines*, from Old French, from Medieval Latin (*vigiliae*) *mātūtīnae*, morning (vigils), from Latin *Mātūta*, goddess of dawn.]

matri-. A prefix meaning mother: **matrilineal.** [From Latin *māter*, mother.]

ma·tri·arch (mā'trē-ärk') *n.* **1.** A woman who rules a family, clan, or tribe. **2.** A woman who dominates any group or activity. —**ma'tri·ar'chal** or **ma'tri·ar'chic** *adj.*

ma·tri·ar·chy (mā'trē-är'kē) *n., pl.* **-chies. 1.** A social system in which descent is traced through the mother's side of the family. **2.** A society, tribe, or state in which the dominant authority is held by women.

ma·tri·ces (mā'trə-sēz', măt'rĭ-) *n.* A plural of **matrix.**

mat·ri·cide (măt'rə-sīd') *n.* **1.** The act of killing one's mother. **2.** A person who kills his mother. —**mat'ri·ci'dal** (-sīd'l) *adj.*

ma·tric·u·late (mə-trĭk'yə-lāt') *v.* **-lat·ed, -lat·ing.** —*tr.v.* To enroll in a group, esp. a college or university. —*intr.v.* To become so enrolled. [From Medieval Latin *mātriculāre*, to enroll, from *mātricula*, list, roll, from *mātrīx*, list, womb, source.] —**ma·tric'u·la'tion** *n.*

mat·ri·lin·e·al (măt'rə-lĭn'ē-əl) *adj.* Of, relating to, based upon, or tracing ancestral descent through the maternal line.

mat·ri·mo·ny (măt'rə-mō'nē) *n., pl.* **-nies.** The act or condition of being married. [Middle English, from Norman French *matrimonie*, from Latin *mātrimōnium*, marriage, from *māter*, mother.] —**mat'ri·mo'ni·al** *adj.* —**mat'ri·mo'ni·al·ly** *adv.*

ma·trix (mā'trĭks) *n., pl.* **ma·tri·ces** (mā'trə-sēz', măt'rĭ-) or **-es. 1.** A situation, substance, object, etc., within which something is contained, originates, or develops: *an understanding atmosphere that is the matrix of peace.* **2.** The uterus; womb. **3.** *Anat.* The group of cells from which a fingernail, toenail, or tooth grows. **4.** *Geol.* The solid matter in which a fossil or crystal is embedded. **5.** A mold or die, as for casting or shaping metal. **6.** *Printing.* A metal

---

plate used for casting type faces. **7.** *Math.* A rectangular array of numerical or algebraic quantities treated as an algebraic entity. [Latin *mātrix*, womb, from *māter*, mother.]

ma·tron (mā'trən) *n.* **1.** A married woman, esp. a woman in middle age or older. **2.** A woman who supervises a public institution, such as a school, hospital, or prison. [Middle English, from Old French *matrone*, from Latin *mātrōna*, from *māter*, mother.] —**ma'tron·ly** *adj. & adv.* —**ma'tron·li·ness** *n.*

matron of honor *pl.* **matrons of honor.** A married woman who serves as chief attendant of the bride at a wedding.

matte (măt) Also **mat** or **matt.** —*n.* A dull, often rough finish, as on glass, metal, or paper. —*tr.v.* **mat·ted, mat·ting.** To produce a dull finish on. —*adj.* Having a dull finish. [French *mat*, dull, from Old French, from Latin *mattus.*]

mat·ter (măt'ər) *n.* **1.** Anything that occupies space, has weight, and can be perceived by one or more senses; the substance of which any physical body is constituted. **2.** A specific type of substance: *inorganic matter.* **3.** Discharge or waste from a living organism, as pus or feces. **4.** The actual substance of thought or expression as distinguished from the manner or style in which it is stated or conveyed. **5. a.** Something that is the subject of concern, feeling, or action: *a very serious matter.* **b.** Business, affair, or concern: *This is a personal matter.* **6. the matter.** An unpleasant or disagreeable situation or circumstance; trouble; difficulty: *What's the matter with you?* **7.** An indefinite but approximate quantity, amount, or extent: *a matter of a few cents.* **8.** Something written or printed: *reading matter.* **9.** Something that is sent by mail. —*intr.v.* To be of importance. —*idioms.* **as a matter of fact.** In fact; actually. **for that matter.** So far as that is concerned; as for that. **no matter.** Regardless of: *No matter how hard we try, we cannot achieve our goals.* [Middle English *matere,* from Norman French, from Latin *māteria,* matter.]

matter of course. A natural or logical outcome. —**mat'ter-of-course'** (măt'ər-əv-kôrs', -kōrs') *adj.*

mat·ter-of-fact (măt'ər-əv-făkt') *adj.* **1.** Adhering strictly to facts; prosaic; literal: *a matter-of-fact description.* **2.** Free from emotion, affection, etc.: *a matter-of-fact tone of voice.* —**mat'ter-of-fact'ly** *adv.* —**mat'ter-of-fact'ness** *n.*

mat·ting[1] (măt'ĭng) *n.* **1.** A coarsely woven fabric used for covering floors and similar purposes. **2.** Mats in general.

mat·ting[2] (măt'ĭng) *n.* **1.** Matte. **2.** The process of producing a matte finish. **3.** Mat (border).

mat·tock (măt'ək) *n.* A digging tool with a blade set at right angles to the handle, used for cutting roots or breaking up the soil. [Middle English *mattok,* from Old English *mattuc.*]

mat·tress (măt'rĭs) *n.* A rectangular pad of heavy cloth filled with soft material, and sometimes containing springs, used as or on a bed. [Middle English *materas,* from Old French, from Old Italian *materasso,* from Arabic *matrah,* place where something is thrown, from *taraha,* to throw, fling.]

mat·u·rate (măch'oo-rāt') **-rat·ed, -rat·ing.** —*intr.v.* To mature or ripen. —**mat'u·ra'tive** *adj.*

ma·ture (mə-tyŏŏr', -tŏŏr', -chŏŏr') *adj.* **-er, -est. 1.** Having reached full natural growth or development: *a mature plant.* **2.** Having reached a certain stage of development after a process: *a mature wine.* **3.** Of or having the mental and physical characteristics or qualities of full development; adult: *a mature body; a mature decision.* **4.** Worked out fully by the mind; completed; perfected: *a mature plan of action.* **5.** Having reached the limit of its time; payable; due: *a mature bond.* —*v.* **-tured, -tur·ing.** —*tr.v.* **1.** To bring to full development; ripen. **2.** To work out fully in the mind: *mature one's thoughts on the subject.* —*intr.v.* **1.** To evolve toward full development: *He matured quickly.* **2.** To become due, as a bond. [Middle English, from Latin *mātūrus.*] —**ma·ture'ly** *adv.*

Syns: mature, adult, grown, ripe *adj.* Core meaning: Having reached full growth and development (*mature people; mature oranges*).

ma·tu·ri·ty (mə-tyŏŏr'ə-tē, -tŏŏr'ə-tē, -chŏŏr'ə-tē) *n., pl.* **-ties. 1.** The condition or quality of being mature, esp. having full growth. **2. a.** The time at which a note, bill, or bond is due. **b.** The condition of a note, bill, or bond being due.

mat·zo (mät'sə) *n., pl.* **-zoth** (-sōth', -sōt', -sōs') or **-zos** (-səz, -səs, -sōz'). A brittle, flat piece of unleavened bread, eaten esp. during Passover. [Yiddish *matse,* from Hebrew *maṣṣah.*]

maud·lin (môd'lĭn) *adj.* Excessively sentimental. [From *Maudlin,* Mary Magdalene (from her representation in art as tearfully repentant).]

maul (môl) *n.* A heavy, long-handled hammer used to drive stakes, piles, or wedges. —*tr.v.* **1.** To split (wood) with a maul and wedge. **2.** To injure by or as if by beating, bruising, or tearing. **3.** To handle roughly or clumsily; mishandle. [Middle English *mal,* from Old French *mail,* from Latin *malleus,* hammer.] —**maul'er** *n.*

maun·der (môn'dər, män'-) *intr.v.* **1.** To talk incoherently or aimlessly. **2.** To move or act aimlessly or vaguely; wander. [Orig. "to grumble."]

Maundy Thursday. The Thursday before Easter, commemorating the Last Supper. Also called **Holy Thursday.** [From Middle English *maunde,* ceremony of washing the feet of the poor on Holy Thursday, from Old French *mandé,* from Latin *mandatum,* command.]

mau·so·le·um (mô'sə-lē'əm, mô'zə-) *n., pl.* **-ums** or **-le·a** (-lē'ə). A large, stately tomb, or a building housing such a tomb or tombs. [Latin *mausōlēum,* from Greek *mausōleion,* the tomb of *Mausōlos,* satrap of Caria (d. 353 B.C.).]

mauve (mōv) *n.* A light reddish or grayish purple. —*adj.* Light reddish or grayish purple. [French, "mallow(-colored)," from Latin *malva,* mallow.]

mav·er·ick (măv'ər-ĭk, măv'rĭk) *n.* **1.** An unbranded range calf or colt, traditionally the property of the first person who brands it. **2.** An independent person who refuses to conform to the dictates or stance of his group, esp. in politics. [After Samuel A. *Maverick* (1803–70), Texas cattleman.]

ma·vis (mā'vĭs) *n.* A bird, the **song thrush.** [Middle English *mavys,* from Old French *mauvis.*]

mawk·ish (mô'kĭsh) *adj.* Excessively and obnoxiously sentimental. [From dial. *mawk,* maggot, whim, fastidious person, from Middle English *mathek,* var. of *magot,* maggot.] —**mawk'ish·ly** *adv.* —**mawk'ish·ness** *n.*

max·il·la (măk-sĭl'ə) *n., pl.* **-lae** (-sĭl'ē) or **-las. 1.** *Anat.* One of a pair of bones forming the upper jaw. **2.** *Zool.* Either of two appendages behind the mandibles in insects, usu. functioning as accessory jaws. [Latin, lower jaw.]

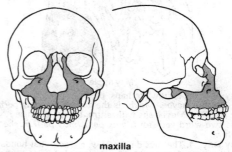

maxilla

max·il·lar·y (măk'sə-lĕr'ē) *n., pl.* **-ies.** A jaw or jawbone. —*adj.* Of or located near the upper jawbone.

max·im (măk'sĭm) *n.* A concise formulation of a basic truth, fundamental principle, or rule of conduct. [Middle English, from Old French *maxime,* from Medieval Latin (*prōpositiō*) *maxima,* greatest (proposition), fundamental axiom, from *maximus,* greatest.]

max·i·ma (măk'sə-mə) *n.* A plural of **maximum.**

max·i·mal (măk'sə-məl) *adj.* Of or being a maximum: *the maximal cost.* —**max'i·mal·ly** *adv.*

max·i·mize (măk'sə-mīz') *tr.v.* **-mized, -miz·ing.** To make as great as possible; increase or utilize to a maximum.

max·i·mum (măk'sə-məm) *n., pl.* **-mums** or **-ma** (-mə). **1.** The greatest possible quantity, degree, or number: *We'll stay a maximum of two weeks.* **2.** An upper limit allowed by law or other authority. —*adj.* The greatest or highest possible: *maximum temperature.* [Latin *maximum,* greatest (quantity), neut. of *maximus,* greatest.]

---

may (mā) *v.* Past **might** (mīt). Used as an auxiliary followed by an infinitive without *to*, or, in reply to a question or suggestion, with the infinitive understood. Used to indicate: **1.** A requesting or granting of permission: *May I take a swim? You may.* **2.** Possibility: *It may rain this afternoon.* **3.** Ability or capacity: *If I may be of service.* **4.** Desire or fervent wish: *Long may he live.* **5.** Contingency, purpose, or result, used in clauses introduced by *that* or *so that:* expressing ideas *so that the average man may understand.* [Middle English, from Old English *maeg* (1st and 3rd person sing.).]
Usage: may, might. *Might* is the past tense of *may.* In modern usage, however, both verb forms are treated as subjunctives capable of expressing present and future time. When they are employed in the senses of possibility and permission, they are basically alike in meaning, and differ in intensity rather than in time. In both senses, *may* is stronger than *might* for *might* connotes conditional possibility: *He may go. He might go.* The example with *may* suggests greater likelihood. The distinction holds with respect to permission: *May he go? Might he go?* The *may* example is more forceful and direct. See also Usage note at **can.**
May (mā) *n.* The fifth month of the year, after April and before June. May has 31 days. **—modifier:** *May flowers.* [Middle English *Mai,* from Latin *Maius* (*mēnsis*), (the month) of *Maia,* a Roman goddess.]
Ma·ya (mä′yə) *n., pl.* **-yas** or **Maya.** A member of a race of Indians in southern Mexico and Central America whose civilization reached its height around A.D. 1000. **—Ma′ya** *adj.*
Ma·yan (mä′yən, mī′ən) *n.* **1.** A Maya. **2.** A family of Indian languages spoken in Central America. **—adj.** **1.** Of Mayan. **2.** Of the Mayas or their language and culture.
May apple. **1.** A plant, *Podophyllum peltatum,* of eastern North America, with a single, nodding white flower, oval yellow fruit, and poisonous roots, leaves, and seeds. Also called **mandrake.** **2.** The fruit of this plant.

May apple

may·be (mā′bē) *adv.* Perhaps; possibly.
Usage: maybe. *Maybe* is the adverb meaning perhaps or possibly: *Maybe she will return.* Do not confuse it with the two-word verb form *may be: It may be that she will return.*
May Day. **1.** The first day of May, a traditional holiday in celebration of spring. **2.** May 1, regarded in a number of places as an international holiday to celebrate labor organizations.
may·day (mā′dā′) *n.* An international radio-telephone signal word used by aircraft and ships in distress. [Alteration of French *m'aider,* help me.]
may·flow·er (mā′flou′ər) *n.* Any of a wide variety of plants that bloom in May, esp. the trailing arbutus.
may·fly (mā′flī′) *n.* Any of various insects of the order Ephemeroptera, with fragile transparent wings and long, hairlike parts that extend from the end of the body.
may·hap (mā′hăp′, mā-hăp′) *adv. Archaic.* Perhaps; perchance. [From the phrase *it may hap.*]
may·hem (mā′hĕm′, mā′əm) *n.* **1.** *Law.* The crime of willfully maiming or crippling a person. **2.** Any willful violent destruction. **3.** A condition of usu. riotous disorder or confusion; havoc. [Middle English, from Norman French *maihem,* injury, from Old French *mahaignier,* to maim.]

may·n't (mā′ənt, mānt). Contraction of may not.
may·on·naise (mā′ə-nāz′) *n.* A creamy dressing made of egg yolks, butter or olive oil, lemon juice or vinegar, and seasonings. [French.]
may·or (mā′ər, mâr) *n.* The chief government official of a city, town, or borough. [Middle English *mair,* from Old French *maire,* from Latin *mājor,* greater.] **—may′or·al** *adj.*
may·or·al·ty (mā′ər-əl-tē, mâr′əl-) *n., pl.* **-ties.** The office or term of office of a mayor.
May·pole or **may·pole** (mā′pōl′) *n.* A pole decorated with streamers, flowers, etc., that May Day celebrants hold while dancing.
maze (māz) *n.* **1.** An intricate, usu. confusing network of walled or hedged pathways; labyrinth. **2.** Any confusing or intricate condition or situation. [Middle English, from *mazen,* to bewilder, from Old English *āmasian.*]
ma·zel tov (mä′zəl tôf′) *interj. Hebrew.* Congratulations.
ma·zur·ka (mə-zûr′kə, -zŏŏr′kə) *n.* Also **ma·zour·ka. 1.** A lively Polish dance that resembles the polka. **2.** A piece of music written for such a dance. [French, from Polish *Mazurka,* from *Mazovia,* a Polish province.]
Mc·In·tosh (măk′ĭn-tŏsh′) *n.* A variety of red eating apple, grown commercially in the northern United States. [First cultivated, in 1796, by John McIntosh, of Ontario, Canada.]
Md The symbol for the element mendelevium.
me (mē) *pron.* The objective case of **I,** used: **1.** As the direct object of a verb: *They blamed me.* **2.** As the indirect object of a verb: *Give me the letter.* **3.** As the object of a preposition: *She addressed it to me.* [Middle English, from Old English *mē.*]
Usage: me, I. *I,* not *me,* is required after the verb *be* in formal writing and in constructions in which relative clauses occur after this first-person pronoun: *It was I who called you.* In informal writing and in speech on all levels, *me* is used acceptably after *be: It's me. The caller was me. It could have been me. The person you forgot to mention was me.*
me·a cul·pa (mā′ə kŭl′pə, mē′ə). *Latin.* My fault; I am at fault.
mead¹ (mēd) *n.* An alcoholic beverage made from fermented honey and water. [Middle English *mede,* from Old English *medu.*]
mead² (mēd) *n. Archaic.* A meadow. [Middle English *mede,* from Old English *mæd.*]
mead·ow (mĕd′ō) *n.* A tract of grassland used as pasture or for growing hay. [Middle English *medwe,* from Old English *mædwe,* from *mæd.*] **—mead′ow·y** *adj.*
mead·ow·lark (mĕd′ō-lärk′) *n.* Any bird of the genus *Sturnella,* with a cone-shaped bill, a brownish back and a yellow breast with a black marking, noted for its song.
mead·ow·sweet (mĕd′ō-swēt′) *n.* Any of several plants of the genus *Spiraea,* esp. *S. alba* or *S. latifolia,* of eastern North America, with pyramidal clusters of flowers.
mea·ger (mē′gər) *adj.* Also **mea·gre. 1.** Thin; lean. **2.** Deficient in quantity, extent, or quality: *a meager allowance.* [Middle English *megre,* from Norman French, from Latin *macer,* thin.] **—mea′ger·ly** *adv.* **—mea′ger·ness** *n.*
meal¹ (mēl) *n.* **1.** The edible seed of any grain, coarsely ground. **2.** Any similar substance produced by grinding. [Middle English *mele,* from Old English *melu,* flour.]
meal² (mēl) *n.* **1.** The food served and eaten in one sitting. **2.** A customary time or occasion for eating. [Middle English *meel,* from Old English *mæl,* mark, fixed time.]
meal·time (mēl′tīm′) *n.* The usual time for eating a meal.
meal·y (mē′lē) *adj.* **-i·er, -i·est. 1.** Resembling meal in texture or consistency; granular: *mealy potatoes.* **2. a.** Made of or containing meal. **b.** Sprinkled or covered with meal or a similar granular substance. **3.** Lacking healthy coloring; pale. **4.** Mealy-mouthed. **—meal′i·ness** *n.*
meal·y-mouthed (mē′lē-mouthd′, -moutht′) *adj.* Unwilling to speak directly or simply.
mean¹ (mēn) *v.* **meant** (mĕnt), **mean·ing. —tr.v. 1.** To serve to signify, indicate, or convey. **2.** To intend to convey or indicate: *What do you mean by that look?* **3.** To have as a purpose or intention: *meant to return early, but missed the bus.* **—intr.v. 1.** To be of a particular degree of importance: *Her approval meant little to him.* **2.** To have intentions of a particular kind: *She means well despite her*

blunders. [Middle English *menen*, from Old English *mænan*, to intend, tell.]

Usage: **mean.** In expressing intention, *mean* is used with *that* or *for: We did not mean that they should leave. We did not mean for them to leave. Mean + that* occurs more often in formal writing.

mean² (mēn) *adj.* **-er, -est. 1.** Low or common in rank, birth, or origin; humble. **2.** Of poor or low quality. **3.** Common or poor in appearance; shabby: *a mean cottage.* **4.** Characterized by petty spite or malice: *a mean remark.* **5.** Miserly; stingy: *a mean, grasping woman who grudged spending a cent.* **6.** *Informal.* Vicious; ill-tempered: *a mean old billy goat.* **7.** *Informal.* In poor health; out of sorts. **8.** *Slang.* Impressive; excellent: *He plays a mean game of poker.* —See Syns at **malevolent** and **stingy.** [Middle English *mene*, from Old English *gemæne*, common.]

mean³ (mēn) *n.* **1.** A middle point between two extremes. **2.** *Math.* **a.** A number that represents a set of numbers, determined from the set in any of several ways; average. **b.** An **arithmetic mean. 3. means.** Something such as a method or course of action by which an end is achieved: *searching for a practical means of capturing the sun's energy.* **4. means.** Resources, such as money or property; wealth: *a woman of means.* —*adj.* **1.** Occupying a middle or intermediate position between two extremes. **2.** Intermediate, as in size, extent, or degree. —*idioms.* **by all means.** Without fail; certainly. **by means of.** With the use of; through. **by no means.** Certainly not. [Middle English *mene*, from Norman French *meen*, from Latin *mediānus*, median, from *medius*, middle.]

Usage: **means.** When *means* is used in the sense of resources such as money and property, it takes a plural verb: *His means are small.* When *means* has the sense of a way of achieving an end, it may be used in either singular or plural constructions. The determination of grammatical number is influenced by the modifying words preceding *means.* For instance, *the means* may be followed by either a singular or a plural verb: But *means, any means, each means, every means,* and *one means* are followed by singular verbs. And *all means, several means,* and *such* (not *such a means*) are followed by plural verbs.

me·an·der (mē-ăn'dər) *intr.v.* **1.** To follow a winding or circuitous course: *Streams tend to meander through level land.* **2.** To wander aimlessly and idly. —*n.* **1.** A circuitous turn or winding, as of a stream or path. **2.** A circuitous path or route. [From Latin *maeander*, a meandering way, from Greek *maiandros*, from *Maiandros*, a river noted for its winding course.]

mean·ing (mē'nĭng) *n.* **1.** The sense conveyed, esp. by language. **2.** That which is intended to be conveyed. **3.** Intent; purpose: *couldn't understand the meaning of his action.*

Syns: **meaning, sense, significance, signification** *n. Core meaning:* What is signified by a term (*synonyms* —words with the same meaning).

mean·ing·ful (mē'nĭng-fəl) *adj.* Having a meaning or function; significant: *meaningful sounds.* —**mean'ing·ful·ly** *adv.*

mean·ing·less (mē'nĭng-lĭs) *adj.* Lacking meaning or significance. —**mean'ing·less·ly** *adv.*

mean·ness (mēn'nĭs) *n.* **1.** The state or quality of being low or inferior, as in rank or origin. **2. a.** The condition of being pettily spiteful. **b.** A spiteful or malicious act.

meant (mĕnt) *v.* Past tense and past participle of **mean.**

mean·time (mēn'tīm') *n.* The time between one occurrence and another; interval. —*adv.* During a period of intervening time; meanwhile.

Usage: **meantime, meanwhile.** Each of these is a noun and an adverb, and are interchangeable: *In the meantime* (or *meanwhile*) *he waited. Meanwhile* (or *meantime*) *we were occupied with other activities.*

mean·while (mēn'hwīl') *adv.* During or in the intervening time: *The jury is deliberating; meanwhile, we must be patient.* —*n.* The intervening time. —See Usage note at **meantime.**

mea·sles (mē'zəlz) *n.* (*used with a sing. verb*). **1.** An acute, contagious viral disease, characterized by coughing, fever, and red spots on the skin. Also called **rubeola. 2.** Any of several milder diseases similar to measles. [Middle English *maseles*, pl. of *masel*, from Middle Dutch *māsel*, blemish.]

mea·sly (mēz'lē) *adj.* **-sli·er, -sli·est. 1.** Infected or spotted with measles. **2.** *Slang.* Contemptibly small: *a measly tip.*

meas·ure (mĕzh'ər) *n.* **1.** The size, amount, capacity, or degree of something determined by comparison with a standard: *Do the line segments have equal measures?* **2. a.** A unit, usu. derived from a standard, used in determining and expressing measures. **b.** A system of such standards and units, such as the metric system. **c.** A device, such as a marked tape or graduated container, used in determining measures. **3.** The extent, amount, or degree of something: *With a good measure of curiosity, you could learn a lot.* **4.** An act of measurement. **5.** A standard or basis of comparison. **6.** An appropriate or fixed amount: *a measure of recognition.* **7.** Rhythmic structure; cadence; meter. **8.** *Mus.* The part of a staff between two successive bars. **9.** A dance, esp. a slow and stately dance. **10. a.** Often **measures.** An action designed to achieve a specified purpose or end. **b.** A legislative bill or act. —*v.* **-ured, -ur·ing.** —*tr.v.* **1.** To ascertain the dimensions, quantity, or capacity of. **2.** To mark or lay out dimensions by means of measurements: *measure off an area.* **3.** To allot or distribute by or as if by measuring: *measured out a pound of sugar.* **4.** To estimate by evaluation or comparison; appraise: *measure the importance of a problem; measure his talent as an actor.* **5.** To bring into opposition or comparison: *She measured her power with that of a dangerous adversary.* **6.** To serve as a measure of: *The meter measures length.* **7.** To consider or choose with care; weigh: *measured his words.* —*intr.v.* **1.** To take a measurement. **2.** To have a specified measurement: *The room measures 10 by 12 feet.* —*phrasal verb.* **measure up to.** To fulfill or meet adequately: *He has not measured up to the demands of his position.* —*idioms.* **for good measure.** In addition to the amount required. **in great** (or **large**) **measure.** To a great extent. [Middle English *mesure*, from Old French *mesure*, from Latin *mēnsūra*, a measure, from *mētīrī*, to measure.] —**meas'ur·a·ble** *adj.* —**meas'ur·er** *n.*

Frère____ Jacques,____

measure

meas·ured (mĕzh'ərd) *adj.* **1.** Determined by measurement: *The measured distance was less than a mile.* **2.** Regular in rhythm and number: *a measured beat.* **3.** Careful; calculated; deliberate: *They took measured steps to finish the projects.* —**meas'ured·ly** *adv.*

meas·ure·less (mĕzh'ər-lĭs) *adj.* Limitless; immeasurable.

meas·ure·ment (mĕzh'ər-mənt) *n.* **1.** The act or process of measuring. **2.** A system of measuring: *measurement in inches, feet, and yards.* **3.** Size or dimensions found by measuring and expressed in units: *The dressmaker took Ann's waist and hip measurements.*

measuring worm. The inchworm.

meat (mēt) *n.* **1.** The edible flesh of an animal, esp. a mammal. **2.** The edible, fleshy, inner part of something: *crab meat; walnut meats.* **3.** Solid food: *meat and drink.* **4.** The principal or essential part; the gist: *the meat of an argument.* —See Syns at **heart.** —*modifier: meat products.* [Middle English *mete*, food, meat, from Old English *mete*, food.]

me·a·tus (mē-ā'təs) *n., pl.* **-es** or **meatus.** A body canal or passage, such as the opening of the ear. [Latin *meātus*, passage, from *meāre*, to pass.]

meat·y (mē'tē) *adj.* **-i·er, -i·est. 1.** Full of meat; fleshy. **2.** Rich in substance: *a meaty book.* —**meat'i·ness** *n.*

mec·ca (mĕk'ə) *n.* A place regarded as a desirable goal: *a museum that was a mecca for connoisseurs.* [From *Mecca,* a holy city of Islam and a place of pilgrimage.]

me·chan·ic (mĭ-kăn'ĭk) *n.* A worker skilled in making, using, or repairing machines. [From **MECHANICAL.**]

me·chan·i·cal (mĭ-kăn'ĭ-kəl) *adj.* **1.** Of or pertaining to machines or tools. **2.** Operated or produced by a machine. **3.** Suggestive of or appropriate for performance by a machine: *routine, mechanical tasks; a mechanical answer.* **4.** Of, pertaining to, or in accordance with the science of mechanics. —*n. Printing.* A layout consisting of type

ă pat   ā pay   â care   ä father   ĕ pet   ē be   hw which
ŏŏ took   ōŏ boot   ou out   th thin   th this   ŭ cut
ĭ pit   ī tie   î pier   ŏ pot   ō toe   ô paw, for   oi noise
û urge   zh vision   ə about, item, edible, gallop, circus

proofs and artwork, positioned and prepared for making a printing plate. [Middle English, pertaining to manual labor, from Latin *mēchanicus*, from Greek *mēkhanikos*, from *mēkhanē*, machine, from *mēkhos*, an expedient.] —**me·chan'i·cal·ly** *adv.* —**me·chan'i·cal·ness** *n.*

mechanical drawing. **1.** A drawing made by the use of instruments, such as compasses or triangles. **2.** The technique or art of making such drawings; drafting.

me·chan·ics (mĭ-kăn'ĭks) *n.* **1.** (*used with a sing. verb*). The scientific study and analysis of the action of forces on matter and systems composed of matter. **2.** (*used with a sing. verb*). The development, production, operation, and use of machines and structures. **3.** (*used with a pl. verb*). The functional and technical aspects of an activity: *The mechanics of football are learned with practice.*

mech·a·nism (měk'ə-nĭz'əm) *n.* **1. a.** A machine or mechanical device. **b.** The arrangement of connected parts in a machine. **2.** Any system of parts that operate or interact like those of a machine: *the mechanism of the solar system.* **3.** A process or means by which something is done or comes into being. **4.** *Philos.* The doctrine that all natural phenomena are subject to and can be explained by natural law.

mech·a·nist (měk'ə-nĭst) *n.* An advocate of philosophical mechanism.

mech·a·nis·tic (měk'ə-nĭs'tĭk) *adj.* **1.** Of or pertaining to mechanics as a branch of physics. **2.** *Philos.* Of or pertaining to mechanism. —**mech'a·nis'ti·cal·ly** *adv.*

mech·a·nize (měk'ə-nīz') *tr.v.* **-nized, -niz·ing.** **1.** To equip with machinery: *mechanize a factory.* **2.** To equip (a military unit) with vehicles, such as tanks and trucks. **3.** To make automatic or mechanical. —**mech'a·ni·za'tion** *n.*

med·al (měd'l) *n.* **1.** A flat piece of metal, often in the form of a coin, issued to commemorate an event or person or to reward bravery or achievement. **2.** A metal disk that bears a religious figure or symbol. [French *médaille*, from Italian *medaglia*, from Latin *metallum*, metal.]

med·al·ist (měd'l-ĭst) *n.* Also *Brit.* **med·al·list.** **1.** Someone who designs or makes medals. **2.** A recipient of a medal.

me·dal·lion (mə-dăl'yən) *n.* **1.** A large medal. **2.** Something that resembles a large medal, such as a decorative tablet or panel in a wall. [French *médaillon*, from Italian *medaglione*, from *medaglia*, medal.]

med·dle (měd'l) *intr.v.* **-dled, -dling.** To intrude in the affairs of others without invitation. —See Syns at **interfere.** [Middle English *medlen*, from Old French *medler*, to mix in, from Latin *miscēre*, to mix.] —**med'dler** (měd'lər, měd'l-ər) *n.*

med·dle·some (měd'l-səm) *adj.* Inclined to meddle or interfere. —**med'dle·some·ly** *adv.* —**med'dle·some·ness** *n.*

Me·de·a (mĭ-dē'ə) *n.* *Gk. Myth.* A sorceress who helped Jason obtain the Golden Fleece.

me·di·a (mē'dē-ə) *n.* A plural of **medium.**
Usage: **media.** This alternate plural form of the noun *medium* is applied in a collective sense to means of mass communication. Each means, considered individually, is a *medium: Television is a highly influential medium* (singular). *Together, television and radio, newspapers, and radio, newspapers, and periodicals make up what we call the media* (plural). When it is used as a subject, *media* (plural) should take a plural verb: *The media are* (not *media is*) *often the target of public criticism.* As a collective plural, *media* expresses the sense of a group of things. Because some writers do not realize this, they sometimes seek to express the group sense by using "medias"—but "medias" is not standard.

me·di·ae·val (mē'dē-ē'vəl, měd-ē'vəl) *adj.* Var. of **medieval.**

me·di·ae·val·ism (mē'dē-ē'vəl-ĭz'əm, měd'ē-) *n.* Var. of **medievalism.**

me·di·al (mē'dē-əl) *adj.* **1.** Of, pertaining to, or situated in the middle. **2.** Average; ordinary. [From Late Latin *mediālis*, from Latin *medius*, middle.] —**me'di·al·ly** *adv.*

me·di·an (mē'dē-ən) *n.* **1.** Something that lies halfway between two extremes; a medium. **2.** *Math.* In a set of numbers, a number that has the property that half of the other numbers are greater than it and half less than it. **3.** *Geom.* **a.** A line joining a vertex of a triangle to the midpoint of the opposite side. **b.** A line that joins the midpoints of the nonparallel sides of a trapezoid. —*adj.* **1.** Located in the middle. **2.** Constituting the median of a set of numbers: *median score.* [Latin *medianus*, from *medius*, middle.]

median strip. A strip that divides the opposing lanes of a highway.

me·di·ate (mē'dē-āt') *v.* **-at·ed, -at·ing.** —*tr.v.* **1.** To bring about by acting as an intermediary between two or more disputing parties: *mediate a settlement.* **2.** To bring agreement out of by action as an intermediary: *mediate a boundary dispute.* **3.** To convey or transmit as an intermediary agent or mechanism. —*intr.v.* **1.** To intervene between two or more disputing parties in order to bring about an agreement or settlement. **2.** To settle or reconcile differences. —*adj.* (mē'dē-ĭt). Acting through an intervening agency. [From Latin *mediāre*, to be in the middle, from *medius*, middle.] —**me'di·ate·ly** *adv.* —**me'di·a'tion** *n.*

me·di·a·tor (mē'dē-ā'tər) *n.* A person or agency that intervenes between two or more disputing parties in order to effect a settlement.

med·ic¹ (měd'ĭk) *n.* Any of several plants of the genus *Medicago*, with clusters of small, usu. yellow flowers and compound leaves with three leaflets. [Middle English *medike*, from Latin *Mēdica*, from Greek *Mēdikē* (*poa*), Median (grass), from *Mēdos*, a Mede.]

med·ic² (měd'ĭk) *n.* *Informal.* A person, such as a physician or medical corpsman, trained to provide medical care. [Latin *medicus*, doctor.]

Med·i·caid or **med·i·caid** (měd'ĭ-kād') *n.* A program that is jointly funded by the states and the federal government, to provide medical care for people whose income is below a certain level. [MEDIC(AL) + AID.]

med·i·cal (měd'ĭ-kəl) *adj.* Of or pertaining to the science or practice of medicine. [French *médical*, from Medieval Latin *medicālis*, from Latin *medicus*, doctor, from *medērī*, to heal.] —**med'i·cal·ly** *adv.*

me·dic·a·ment (mĭ-dĭk'ə-mənt, měd'ĭ-kə-mənt) *n.* A medicine. [Latin *medicāmentum*, from *medicārī*, to medicate.]

Med·i·care (měd'ĭ-kâr') *n.* Also **med·i·care.** A government program that provides medical care for the elderly. [MEDI(CAL) + CARE.]

med·i·cate (měd'ĭ-kāt') *tr.v.* **-cat·ed, -cat·ing.** **1.** To treat with medicine. **2.** To add a medicinal substance to.

med·i·ca·tion (měd'ĭ-kā'shən) *n.* **1.** The act or process of medicating. **2.** A substance that helps to cure a disease or heal an injury.

me·dic·i·nal (mə-dĭs'ə-nəl) *adj.* Of, relating to, or having the properties of medicine; healing; curative. —**me·dic'i·nal·ly** *adv.*

med·i·cine (měd'ə-sən) *n.* **1. a.** The scientific study of diseases and disorders of the body and the methods for diagnosing, treating, and preventing them. **b.** The branch of this science that deals with treatment by means other than surgery. **c.** The practice of this science as a profession. **2.** A substance used to treat disease. **3.** An object believed by the North American Indians to have magical powers; a charm. —*idiom.* **to take (one's) medicine.** To face the consequence's of one's actions. [Middle English, from Old French, from Latin *medicīna*, the art of a physician, from *medicus*, doctor, from *medērī*, to heal.]

medicine ball. A large ball used for exercise.

medicine man. A person believed by North American Indians to possess the power to cure disease.

med·i·co (měd'ĭ-kō') *n., pl.* **-cos.** *Informal.* A doctor or medical student. [Italian and Spanish, from Latin *medicus*, doctor, from *medērī*, to heal.]

me·di·e·val (mē'dē-ē'vəl, měd'ē'vəl) *adj.* Also **me·di·ae·val.** Of, pertaining to, or typical of the Middle Ages. [From New Latin *Medium Aevum*, the Middle Age : Latin *medium*, middle + *aevum*, age.] —**me'di·e'val·ly** *adv.*

me·di·e·val·ism (mē'dē-ē'vəl-ĭz'əm, měd'ē-) *n.* Also **me·di·ae·val·ism.** **1.** The spirit, beliefs, customs, or practices of the Middle Ages. **2.** Devotion to the beliefs, customs, or practices of the Middle Ages. —**me'di·e'val·ist** *n.*

Medieval Latin. Latin as used throughout Europe in the Middle Ages, from about A.D. 700 to 1500.

me·di·o·cre (mē'dē-ō'kər) *adj.* Of poor or only fair quality; ordinary; commonplace. [From Latin *mediocris*, in a middle state, from *medius*, middle.]

me·di·oc·ri·ty (mē'dē-ŏk'rə-tē) *n., pl.* **-ties.** **1.** The condition or quality of being mediocre. **2.** A person who is mediocre.

med·i·tate (měd′ə-tāt′) v. **-tat·ed, -tat·ing.** —tr.v. **1.** To think deeply about; reflect upon; contemplate: *He meditated the sorry state of his affairs.* **2.** To plan or intend. —intr.v. To engage in contemplation. [From Latin *meditārī*.] —**med′i·ta′tor** n.

med·i·ta·tion (měd′ə-tā′shən) n. The act or process of meditating; serious reflection.

med·i·ta·tive (měd′ə-tā′tĭv) adj. Devoted to or characterized by meditation; pensive. —**med′i·ta′tive·ly** adv. —**med′i·ta′tive·ness** n.

me·di·um (mē′dē-əm) n. **1.** pl. **me·di·ums.** A position, choice, or course of action midway between extremes: *a happy medium.* **2.** pl. **me·di·a** (mē′dē-ə) or **mediums.** A substance in which something is kept, preserved, or mixed: *paint in a water medium.* **3.** pl. **media** or **mediums. a.** The substance in which an animal, plant, or other organism normally lives and thrives: *A fish in its medium is almost weightless.* **b.** An artificial substance in which bacteria or other microorganisms are grown for scientific purposes. **4.** pl. **media** or **mediums.** Something through which energy is transmitted, esp. something necessary for transmission to take place: *Air is the medium of sound waves.* **5.** pl. **media** or **mediums.** A means by which something is accomplished or transferred: *money as a medium of exchange; speaking to a friend through the medium of the telephone.* **6.** pl. **mediums.** A person who claims to be able to communicate with the spirits of the dead. **7.** pl. **media** or **mediums. a.** A means for sending information to large numbers of people: *the billboard as an advertising medium.* **b. media.** The various means used to convey information in a society, including magazines, newspapers, radio, and television: *the mass media.* **8.** pl. **media** or **mediums. a.** An art or an art form: *Rodin achieved impressionistic effects through the medium of sculpture.* **b.** One of the techniques or means of expression available to an artist: *A composer has two primary media to choose from, the human voice and instruments.* —See Usage note at **media.** —adj. Occurring midway between extremes; intermediate: *low, medium, and high speeds; of medium height.* [Latin *medium,* the middle, from *medius,* middle.]

med·lar (měd′lər) n. **1.** A Eurasian tree, *Mespilus germanica.* **2.** The fruit of the medlar tree. [Middle English *medler,* from Old French, from Latin *mespila,* from Greek *mespilē.*]

med·ley (měd′lē) n., pl. **-leys. 1.** A confused mixture. **2.** A musical composition that consists of a series of songs or melodies. [Middle English *medlee,* from Old French, from Late Latin *misculāre,* to mix up, freq. of *miscēre,* to mix.]

me·dul·la (mə-dŭl′ə) n., pl. **-las** or **-dul·lae** (-dŭl′ē). **1.** Anat. The inner core of certain body structures of vertebrates, such as the marrow of bone. **2.** The **medulla oblongata.** [Latin, marrow.] —**me·dul′lar** (mə-dŭl′ər) or **med′ul·lar′y** (měd′ə-lěr′ē, mə-dŭl′ə-rē) adj.

medulla ob·lon·ga·ta (ŏb′lông-gä′tə) pl. **medulla ob·lon·ga·tas** or **medullae ob·lon·ga·tae** (-gä′tē). A mass of nerve tissue located at the top of the spinal cord and at the base of the brain. It controls respiration, circulation, and certain other bodily functions. [New Latin, "elongated marrow."]

Me·du·sa (mə-dōō′sə, mə-dyōō′sə, -zə) n. Gk. Myth. **1.** A Gorgon with eyes that had the power to turn an onlooker into stone, who was slain by Perseus. **2. medusa.** A jelly-fish.

meed (mēd) n. Archaic. A well-deserved reward. [Middle English *mede,* from Old English *mēd.*]

meek (mēk) adj. **-er, -est. 1.** Showing patience and humility; gentle; mild. **2.** Lacking spirit or confidence; submissive. —See Syns at **gentle** and **humble.** [Middle English *mēk,* from Old Norse *mjūkr,* soft.] —**meek′ly** adv.

meer·schaum (mîr′shəm, -shôm) n. **1.** A fine, claylike, heat-resistant mineral used esp. to make tobacco pipes. **2.** A tobacco pipe with a meerschaum bowl. [German *Meerschaum : Meer,* sea, + *Schaum,* foam.]

meet[1] (mēt) v. **met** (mět), **meet·ing.** —tr.v. **1.** To come upon or across; encounter: *I met him in the hallway.* **2.** To go to a place so as to be present at the arrival of: *meet a train.* **3.** To make the acquaintance of: *We'd like to meet your sister.* **4.** To come into conjunction with; join: *The Missouri River meets the Mississippi near St. Louis.* **5.** To

come to the notice of: *more here than meets the eye.* **6.** To experience; undergo: *met sorrow stoically.* **7.** To struggle with; oppose; fight: *"We have met the enemy and they are ours"* (Oliver Hazard Perry). **8.** To cope or contend effectively with: *He met his problems in a direct manner.* **9.** To satisfy completely; fulfill: *We met all the conditions of the contract.* **10.** To pay for; settle: *enough money to meet the expenses.* —intr.v. **1.** To come together: *Let's meet tonight.* **2.** To come into contact or conjunction. **3.** To come together as opponents; contend: *The two teams met to decide the championship.* **4.** To be introduced; become acquainted: *We met while on vacation.* **5.** To assemble: *Congress met to pass emergency legislation.* **6.** To experience or undergo: *The housing bill met with approval.* —n. A meeting or contest, esp. an athletic competition. [Middle English *meten,* from Old English *mētan.*]

meet[2] (mēt) adj. **-er, -est.** Archaic. Fitting; proper. [Middle English *mete,* from Old English *gemǣte.*] —**meet′ly** adv.

meet·ing (mē′tĭng) n. **1.** The act or process of coming together; an encounter. **2.** An assembly or gathering of people, as for a business, social, or religious purpose: *a town meeting; a Quaker meeting.* **3.** A place where things join; junction.

mega-. A prefix meaning: **1.** One million (10[6]): **megacycle. 2.** Large: **megalith.** [Greek, from *megas,* great.]

meg·a·cy·cle (měg′ə-sī′kəl) n. Physics. **1. Mc** One million cycles. **2.** Megahertz.

meg·a·hertz (měg′ə-hûrtz) n., pl. **megahertz.** Physics. A unit of frequency of electromagnetic waves equal to one million cycles per second.

meg·a·lith (měg′ə-lĭth′) n. A very large stone, as used in the building of various prehistoric monuments. —**meg′a·lith′ic** adj.

megalo-. A prefix meaning exaggeratedly large or great: **megalomania.** [Greek, from *megas,* great.]

meg·a·lo·ma·ni·a (měg′ə-lō-mā′nē-ə, -mān′yə) n. Psychiat. A mental disorder characterized by feelings of great personal power or omnipotence. —**meg′a·lo·ma′ni·ac′** n. —**meg′a·lo·ma·ni′a·cal** (-mə-nī′ə-kəl) adj.

meg·a·lop·o·lis (měg′ə-lŏp′ə-lĭs) n. A large, thickly populated region, esp. one that contains several large cities in close proximity. [MEGALO- + Greek *polis,* city.] —**meg′a·lo·pol′i·tan** (-lō-pŏl′ə-tən) adj.

meg·a·phone (měg′ə-fōn′) n. A funnel-shaped device used to direct and amplify the voice.

meg·a·ton (měg′ə-tŭn′) n. A unit of explosive force equal to that of one million tons of TNT.

meg·a·watt (měg′ə-wŏt′) n. A unit of electrical power equal to one million watts.

me·grim (mē′grĭm) n. **1.** A migraine. **2.** A caprice or fancy. **3. megrims.** Low spirits; depression. [Middle English *mygreyme,* from Old French *migraine.*]

mei·o·sis (mī-ō′sĭs) n., pl. **-ses** (-sēz′). Biol. The cell division in sexually reproducing organisms that reduces the number of chromosomes of reproductive cells to half the normal number. [From Greek *meiōsis,* diminution, from *meioun,* to diminish, from *meiōn,* less.] —**mei·ot′ic** (mī-ŏt′ĭk) adj. —**mei·ot′i·cal·ly** adv.

Meis·ter·sing·er (mīs′tər-sĭng′ər) n. A member of one of the German guilds organized in the 15th and 16th cent. to encourage the development of music and poetry. [German, from Middle High German, "master singer."]

mel·a·mine resin (měl′ə-mēn′). A synthetic resin, $C_3H_6N_6$,

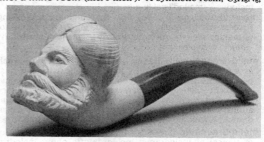

meerschaum
A meerschaum pipe

used for molded products, adhesives, and surface coatings. [From German *Melamin.*]

mel·an-. Var. of **melano-.**

mel·an·cho·li·a (měl'ən-kō'lē-ə) *n.* A mental condition characterized by feelings of severe depression. [From Late Latin *melancholia,* melancholy.]

mel·an·chol·ic (měl'ən-kŏl'ĭk) *adj.* **1.** Inclined or subject to melancholy; gloomy; depressed. **2.** Of, suffering from, or subject to melancholia. —*n.* A person suffering from melancholia.

mel·an·chol·y (měl'ən-kŏl'ē) *n.* **1.** Low spirits; sadness; depression. **2.** An atmosphere of sorrow or sadness; a pervasive gloom. —*adj.* **1.** Marked by or exhibiting melancholy; depressed; sad. **2.** Causing or suggestive of sadness or gloom; depressing: *a melancholy song.* See Syns at **gloomy.** [Middle English *melancholye,* from Old French *melancolie,* from Late Latin *melancholia,* from Greek *melankholia,* sadness (once believed to result from an excess of black bile) : *melas,* black + *kholē,* bile.]

mé·lange (mā-länzн') *n.* Also **me·lange.** A mixture, esp. of incongruous or disparate elements. [French, from Old French, from *mesler,* to mix, from Latin *miscēre,* to mix.]

mel·a·nin (měl'ə-nĭn) *n.* A dark-brown or black pigment of animals and plants.

mel·a·nism (měl'ə-nĭz'əm) *n.* An abnormally dark pigmentation, as of the skin, hair, or eyes. —**mel'a·nis'tic** (-nĭs'tĭk) *adj.*

melano– or **melan-.** A prefix meaning black or dark: **melanoma.** [From Greek, from *melas,* black.]

mel·a·no·ma (měl'ə-nō'mə) *n., pl.* **-mas** or **-ma·ta** (-mə-tə). A colored malignant tumor that contains dark pigment.

Mel·ba toast (měl'bə). Very thinly sliced bread toasted until crisp. [After Dame Nellie *Melba* (1861–1931), Australian soprano.]

meld (měld) *tr.v.* To declare or display (a playing card or combination of cards in a hand) for a score in a card game. —*intr.v.* To present a card or combination of cards for a score. —*n.* A combination of cards to be declared for a score. [German *melden,* to declare, from Old High German *meldōn.*]

me·lee (mā'lā', mā-lā') *n.* Also **mê·lée** (mě-lā'). **1.** A confused fight among a number of people close together. **2.** A confused mingling of people or things. [French *mêlée,* a mixture, from Old French *meslee,* medley.]

mel·io·rate (měl'yə-rāt', mě'lē-ə-) *v.* **-rat·ed, -rat·ing.** —*tr.v.* To make better; improve. —*intr.v.* To grow or become better. [From Latin *meliorāre,* from *melior,* better.] —**mel'io·ra'tion** *n.* —**mel'io·ra'tive** *adj. & n.*

mel·lif·lu·ous (mə-lĭf'lōō-əs) *adj.* Flowing in a smooth or sweet manner. [From Latin *mellifluus,* from *mel,* honey.] —**mel·lif'lu·ous·ly** *adv.* —**mel·lif'lu·ous·ness** *n.*

mel·low (měl'ō) *adj.* **-er, -est.** **1.** Soft, sweet, and full-flavored because of ripeness. **2.** Rich and full in flavor as a result of being properly aged: *a mellow wine.* **3.** Having the gentleness, wisdom, and understanding characteristic of maturity. **4.** Rich, full, and free of harshness or sharp contrast. **5.** Moist, rich, and loamy: *mellow soil.* —*tr.v.* To cause to be mellow. —*intr.v.* To become mellow. [Middle English *mel(o)we.*] —**mel'low·ly** *adv.* —**mel'low·ness** *n.*

me·lo·de·on (mə-lō'dē-ən) *n.* A small reed organ. [Alteration of earlier *melodium,* from MELODY.]

me·lod·ic (mə-lŏd'ĭk) *adj.* Of, pertaining to, or containing melody. —**me·lod'i·cal·ly** *adv.*

me·lo·di·ous (mə-lō'dē-əs) *adj.* **1.** Containing a pleasing succession of sounds: *a melodious aria.* **2.** Of, relating to, or making melody: *melodious birds.* —**me·lo'di·ous·ly** *adv.* —**me·lo'di·ous·ness** *n.*

mel·o·dra·ma (měl'ə-drä'mə, -drăm'ə) *n.* **1. a.** A work, such as a play or motion picture, that relies heavily upon suspense, sensational events, coincidence, and conventional sentiment instead of characterization. **b.** The literary genre that includes such work. **2.** Melodramatic situations, behavior, or events. [French *mélodrame,* musical drama : Greek *melos,* song + French *drame,* drama.]

mel·o·dra·mat·ic (měl'ə-drə-măt'ĭk) *adj.* **1.** Of, relating to, or typical of melodrama: *melodramatic plays; melodramatic events.* **2.** Exaggerated or distorted to heighten sen-

sation: *a melodramatic account.* —**mel'o·dra·mat'i·cal·ly** *adv.*

mel·o·dra·mat·ics (měl'ə-drə-măt'ĭks) *pl.n.* Melodramatic behavior.

mel·o·dy (měl'ə-dē) *n., pl.* **-dies.** **1.** A pleasing succession or arrangement of sounds. **2.** *Mus.* A rhythmic sequence of single tones organized so as to make up a musical phrase. [Middle English *melodie,* from Old French, from Late Latin *melōdia,* from Greek *melōidia,* choral song.]

mel·on (měl'ən) *n.* Any of several large fruits, such as a cantaloupe or watermelon, that grow on a vine and have a hard rind and juicy flesh. [Middle English, from Old French, from Late Latin *mēlo,* from Greek *mēlo(pepōn),* from *mēlon,* apple.]

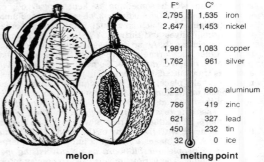

F°	C°	
2,795	1,535	iron
2,647	1,453	nickel
1,981	1,083	copper
1,762	961	silver
1,220	660	aluminum
786	419	zinc
621	327	lead
450	232	tin
32	0	ice

melon   melting point

Mel·pom·e·ne (měl-pŏm'ə-nē') *n. Gk. Myth.* The Muse of tragedy.

melt (mělt) *intr.v.* **1.** To change from a solid to a liquid state usu. as a result of heat or pressure. **2.** To dissolve: *Sugar melts in water.* **3.** To disappear or vanish gradually as if by dissolving: *Their savings melted like snow in the hot sun.* **4.** To pass gradually or imperceptibly; blend: *stripes that melted into the background color.* **5.** To become gentle or mild; soften: *Her heart melted at the child's tears.* —*tr.v.* **1.** To reduce from a solid to a liquid state usu. by the application of heat or pressure. **2.** To dissolve: *melting honey in hot milk.* **3.** To cause to disappear gradually; disperse: *The sun melted the fog.* **4.** To cause to pass gradually or imperceptibly; blend. **5.** To make gentle or tender. —*n.* **1.** A mass of melted material. **2.** The amount melted. [Middle English *melten,* from Old English *meltan.*] —**melt'a·bil'i·ty** *n.* —**melt'a·ble** *adj.* —**melt'er** *n.*

melting point. The temperature at which a solid becomes a liquid at standard atmospheric pressure.

melting pot. 1. A container in which a substance is melted; a crucible. **2.** A place, such as a country or town, where people of different cultures or races live together and create an assimilated community.

mel·ton (měl'tən) *n.* A heavy, smooth woolen cloth used chiefly for making overcoats. [After *Melton* Mowbray, Leicestershire, England.]

mem·ber (měm'bər) *n.* **1.** An individual that makes up a group or category. **2. a.** A part, organ, or limb of a human body or animal body. **b.** An element or part of a whole. **3.** A person who belongs to a group or organization: *a member of Congress; club members.* **4.** *Math.* **a.** An expression on either side of an equation. **b.** An element or part of a set. [Middle English, from Old French *membre,* from Latin *membrum.*]

mem·ber·ship (měm'bər-shĭp') *n.* **1.** The condition of being a member. **2.** All the members of a group or association.

mem·brane (měm'brān') *n.* **1.** *Biol.* A thin, flexible layer of tissue covering surfaces or separating or connecting regions, structures, or organs of an animal or plant. **2.** *Chem.* A thin sheet of natural or synthetic material through which dissolved substances can pass, as in osmosis. [Latin *membrāna,* from *membrum,* member.] —**mem'bra·nous** *adj.*

me·men·to (mə-měn'tō) *n., pl.* **-tos** or **-toes.** A reminder of the past; souvenir. [Middle English, from Latin *mementō,* "remember," imper. of *meminisse,* to remember.]

me·men·to mo·ri (mə-měn'tō môr'ē, môr'ī) Any reminder of death or mortality. [Latin, "remember that you must die."]

---

mem·o (mĕm′ō) *n., pl.* **-os.** A memorandum.

mem·oir (mĕm′wär′, -wôr′) *n.* **1.** An account of the personal experiences of the author. **2. memoirs.** An autobiography. **3.** A biography. **4.** A report, esp. on a scientific or scholarly topic. **5. memoirs.** The report of the proceedings of a learned society. [French *mémoire*, from Old French *memoire*, memory, from Latin *memoria*.]

mem·o·ra·bil·i·a (mĕm′ər-ə-bĭl′ē-ə, -bĭl′yə) *pl.n.* Things worthy of remembrance. [Latin *memorābilia*, from *memorābilis*, memorable.]

mem·o·ra·ble (mĕm′ər-ə-bəl) *adj.* Worth remembering: *a memorable battle.* [Middle English, from Latin *memorābilis*, from *memorāre*, to remember, from *memor*, mindful.] —**mem′o·ra·ble·ness** *n.* —**mem′o·ra·bly** *adv.*

mem·o·ran·dum (mĕm′ə-răn′dəm) *n., pl.* **-dums** or **-da** (-də). **1.** A short note written as a reminder. **2.** An informal record, note, or communication, as in a business office. **3.** *Law.* A short, written statement outlining the terms of a transaction or contract. **4.** A business statement listing goods delivered by a seller to a buyer. **5.** A brief, unsigned diplomatic communication. [Middle English, "let it be remembered," from Latin, from *memorāre*, to remember, from *memor*, mindful.]

me·mo·ri·al (mə-môr′ē-əl, mə-mōr′-) *n.* **1.** Something, such as a monument or a holiday, established to preserve the memory of a person or an event. **2.** A written statement of facts or a petition presented to a government or legislature. —*adj.* Serving as a remembrance of a person or event; commemorative: *a memorial service.*

Memorial Day. May 30, a U.S. holiday officially celebrated on the last Monday in May in honor of servicemen killed in war. Also called **Decoration Day.**

me·mo·ri·al·ize (mə-môr′ē-ə-līz′, mə-mōr′-) *tr.v.* **-ized, -izing. 1.** To commemorate. **2.** To address a memorial to; to petition.

mem·o·rize (mĕm′ə-rīz′) *tr.v.* **-rized, -riz·ing.** To commit to memory; learn by heart. —**mem′o·ri·za′tion** *n.* —**mem′o·riz′er** *n.*

mem·o·ry (mĕm′ər-ē) *n., pl.* **-ries. 1.** The mental capacity to retain and recall past experience. **2.** An act or instance of remembering or the condition of being remembered. **3.** All that a person can remember. **4.** Something or someone remembered: *mixed memories of childhood.* **5.** The cherished thought of a past person, thing, or event: *kept the memory of their grandfather.* **6.** The period of time within which something or someone is or can be remembered: *Nothing like this ever happened in my memory.* **7.** A unit of a computer that stores data for retrieval. [Middle English *memorie*, from Old French, from Latin *memoria*, from *memor*, mindful.]

mem·sa·hib (mĕm′sä′ĭb) *n.* A title of respect applied to a European woman in colonial India. [MA'AM + SAHIB.]

men (mĕn) *n.* Plural of **man.**

men·ace (mĕn′ĭs) *n.* **1.** Someone or something that threatens harm; a threat. **2.** A show of being ready to do harm: *a voice full of menace.* **3.** A troublesome or annoying person. —*v.* **-aced, -ac·ing.** —*tr.v.* To threaten; endanger. —*intr.v.* To be or indicate a threat. [Middle English *manace*, from Old French, from Latin *minācia*, neut. pl. of *mināx* threatening, from *minārī*, to threaten, from *minae*, threats.] —**men′ac·ing·ly** *adv.*

mé·nage (mā-näzh′) *n.* Also **me·nage.** Persons comprising a household. [French, from Old French *menage*, from Latin *mansiō*, house, from *manēre*, to dwell.]

me·nag·er·ie (mə-năj′ə-rē, mə-năzh′-) *n.* **1.** A collection of wild animals kept in cages, pens, etc., esp. for exhibition. **2.** A place where such animals are kept. [French *ménagerie*, the management of domestic animals, from *ménage*, ménage.]

mend (mĕnd) *tr.v.* **1.** To make right; restore; repair: *mend the tear in a jacket.* **2.** To reform, correct, or improve: *mend one's ways.* —*intr.v.* **1.** To improve in health; recover. **2.** To heal: *The bone mended in a month.* **3.** To correct or improve: *a breach that will mend in time.* —See Syns at **correct** and **recover.** —*n.* A mended place: *a mend on the sofa.* —**idiom. on the mend.** Improving, as in health; recuperating. [Middle English *menden*, short for *amenden*, to amend.] —**mend′er** *n.*

men·da·cious (mĕn-dā′shəs) *adj.* **1.** Given to lying; un-

truthful: *a mendacious child.* **2.** False; untrue: *a mendacious statement.* [From Latin *mendāx.*] —**men·da′cious·ly** *adv.*

men·dac·i·ty (mĕn-dăs′ə-tē) *n.* **1.** The condition of being mendacious; untruthfulness. **2.** A lie; falsehood.

men·de·le·vi·um (mĕn′də-lē′vē-əm) *n. Symbol* **Md** An artificially produced radioactive element of the actinide series. Atomic number 101; mass numbers 255 and 256; half-lives approximately 30 minutes (Md255) and 1.5 hours (Md256). [After Dmitri *Mendeleev* (1834–1907), Russian chemist.]

Men·de·li·an (mĕn-dē′lē-ən, -dēl′yən) *adj.* Of or pertaining to Gregor Mendel or his theories of genetics.

Mendel's laws. The principles of heredity of sexually reproducing organisms formulated by Gregor Mendel.

men·di·cant (mĕn′dĭ-kənt) *adj.* Depending on alms for a living; practicing begging. —*n.* **1.** A beggar. **2.** A member of a mendicant order of friars. [Latin *mendīcāns*, pres. part. of *mendicāre*, to beg, from *mendīcus*, beggar, from *mendum*, physical defect.]

Men·e·la·us (mĕn′ə-lā′əs) *n. Gk. Myth.* The king of Sparta, husband of Helen and brother of Agamemnon.

men·folk (mĕn′fōk′) *n., pl.* **-folks.** Men in general, esp. the men of a family, community, or group.

men·ha·den (mĕn-hād′n) *n., pl.* **menhaden** or **-dens.** A fish, *Brevoortia tyrannus*, of the herring family, found in Atlantic waters, and used as a source of fish oil, fish meal, fertilizer, and bait. [Narraganset *munnawhatteaug.*]

men·hir (mĕn′hîr′) *n.* A prehistoric monument consisting of a single tall, upright stone. [French, from Breton *men hir*, "long stone."]

me·ni·al (mē′nē-əl, mēn′yəl) *adj.* **1.** Of, pertaining to, or appropriate for a servant. **2.** Of or pertaining to work or a job regarded as servile: *menial tasks.* —*n.* **1.** A domestic servant. **2.** A person employed to perform simple, routine tasks. [Middle English *meynial*, from Norman French *menial*, from Old French *meinie*, servant, from Latin *mānsiō*, a dwelling.] —**me′ni·al·ly** *adv.*

me·nin·ges (mə-nĭn′jēz) *pl.n. Sing.* **me·ninx** (mē′nĭngks, mĕn′ĭngks). The three membranes that enclose the brain and spinal cord of vertebrates. [Greek *mēninges*, pl. of *mēninx*, membrane.] —**me·nin′ge·al** (-jē-əl) *adj.*

men·in·gi·tis (mĕn′ĭn-jī′tĭs) *n. Pathol.* Inflammation of the meninges, usu. caused by a bacterial infection.

me·ninx (mē′nĭngks, mĕn′ĭngks) *n.* Singular of **meninges.**

me·nis·cus (mə-nĭs′kəs) *n., pl.* **-nis·ci** (-nĭs′ī′) or **-cus·es. 1.** A crescent-shaped body. **2.** A concavo-convex lens. **3.** The curved upper surface of a liquid in a container, concave if the liquid wets the container walls and convex if it does not. [From Greek *mēniskos*, crescent, dim. of *mēnē*, moon.]

Men·non·ite (mĕn′ə-nīt′) *n.* A member of an evangelical Protestant sect noted for its simplicity of living and opposition to taking oaths, holding public office, or performing military service. [German *Mennonit*, after Menno Simons (1492–1559), religious reformer.]

men·o·pause (mĕn′ə-pôz′) *n.* The cessation of menstruation, that occurs usu. between the ages of 45 and 50. [From Greek *meis*, month + PAUSE.]

mensch (mĕnsh) *n. Informal.* A person having admirable characteristics, such as fortitude and firmness of purpose. [Yiddish, from Middle High German, man, from Old High German *mennisco*.]

men·ser·vants (mĕn′sûr′vəntz) *n.* Plural of **manservant.**

men·ses (mĕn′sēz′) *pl.n. Physiol.* The material discharged from the uterus in menstruation. [Latin *mēnsēs*, pl. of *mēnsis*, month.]

men·stru·al (mĕn′strōō-əl) *adj.* Of or relating to menstruation. [Middle English *menstruall*, from Latin *mēnstruālis*, from *mēnstruus*, from *mensis*, month.]

men·stru·ate (mĕn′strōō-āt′) *intr.v.* **-at·ed, -at·ing.** To undergo menstruation.

men·stru·a·tion (mĕn′strōō-ā′shən) *n.* A process occurring at approx. 28-day intervals in women from puberty through middle age, in which blood and cell debris are discharged from the uterus through the reproductive tract if fertilization has not taken place.

men·stru·um (mĕn′strōō-əm) *n., pl.* **-ums** or **-stru·a** (-strōō-ə). A solvent, esp. one used in preparing drugs.

ă **pat**   ā **pay**   â **care**   ä **father**   ĕ **pet**   ē **be**   hw **which**   ĭ **pit**   ī **tie**   î **pier**   ŏ **pot**   ō **toe**   ô **paw, for**   oi **noise**
ōō **took**   ōō **boot**   ou **out**   th **thin**   *th* **this**   ŭ **cut**   û **urge**   zh **vision**   ə **about, item, edible, gallop, circus**

[Middle English, from Medieval Latin mēnstruum, menstrual blood, from Latin mēnstruus, menstrual.]

men·su·ra·ble (mĕn'sər-ə-bəl, -shər-) *adj.* Capable of being measured; measurable. —**men'su·ra·bil'i·ty** *n.*

men·su·ra·tion (mĕn'sə-rā'shən, -shə-) *n.* **1.** The process, act, or technique of measuring. **2.** The branch of mathematics that deals with the measurement of lengths, areas, and volumes.

–ment. A suffix meaning product, means, action, or state: **measurement, environment.** [Middle English, from Old French, from Latin -*mentum,* noun suffix.]

men·tal (mĕn'tl) *adj.* **1.** Of or pertaining to the mind: *mental capacity.* **2.** Carried on or existing in the mind: *a mental image.* **3. a.** Of, relating to, or affected by mental disorder. **b.** Intended for treatment of people affected with mental disorder. [Middle English, from Old French, from Latin *mentālis,* from *mēns,* mind.] —**men'tal·ly** *adv.*

mental age. A measure of mental development, as determined by intelligence tests, gen. restricted to children and expressed as the age at which a given level is average.

men·tal·i·ty (mĕn-tăl'ĭ-tē) *n., pl.* **-ties.** **1.** An individual's intellectual capabilities or endowment; mental capacity; intelligence. **2.** A habitual way of thinking: *a very competitive mentality.*

mental retardation. Mental ability and intelligence that is below normal, reflected in difficulty with learning, that results from genetic causes or brain damage.

men·thol (mĕn'thôl') *n.* A white, crystalline, organic compound, $CH_3C_6H_9(C_3H_7)OH$, obtained from peppermint oil or synthesized, used in perfumes, as a mild anesthetic, and as a flavoring. [German *Menthol,* from Latin *mentha,* mint.]

men·tho·lat·ed (mĕn'thə-lā'tĭd) *adj.* Containing or treated with menthol.

men·tion (mĕn'shən) *tr.v.* To refer to incidentally or briefly. —*n.* An incidental or brief reference or remark: *only got a mention in the newspaper.* [Middle English *mencioun,* from Old French *mention,* from Latin *mentiō,* remembrance, mention.]

men·tor (mĕn'tôr', -tər) *n.* A wise and trusted counselor or teacher. [After *Mentor,* Telemachus' tutor in the *Odyssey.*]

men·u (mĕn'yōō, mān'-) *n.* **1.** A list of the food and drinks available, as at a restaurant. **2. a.** A list of dishes to be served in a meal or a series of meals: *planned a diet menu for the week.* **b.** The dishes served. [French, from *menu,* detailed, small, from Latin *minūtus,* minute, from *minuere,* to diminish.]

me·ow (mē-ou') *n.* The cry of a cat. —*intr.v.* To make such a sound. [Imit.]

Meph·i·stoph·e·les (mĕf'ĭ-stŏf'ə-lēz') *n.* The devil as it appears in versions of the Faust legend as a tempter and buyer of human souls. —**Me·phis'to·phe'le·an** or **Me·phis'to·phe'li·an** (mə-fĭs'tō-fē'lē-ən, -fēl'yən, mĕf'ə-stə-) *adj.*

me·phi·tis (mə-fī'tĭs) *n.* **1.** An offensive smell; stench. **2.** A foul-smelling gas emitted from the earth. [Latin *mefitis,* stench.] —**me·phit'ic** (mə-fĭt'ĭk) *adj.* —**me·phit'i·cal·ly** *adv.*

-mer. Var. of **-mere.**

mer·can·tile (mûr'kən-tēl', -tĭl') *adj.* **1.** Of or pertaining to merchants or trade; commercial. **2.** Of or pertaining to mercantilism. [French, from Italian, from *mercante,* merchant.]

mer·can·til·ism (mûr'kən-tē'lĭz'əm, -tĭ-) *n.* The theory and system of political economy that prevailed in Europe after about 1500 and stressed profit from foreign trade, the founding of colonies and trade monopolies, and the storing of wealth in the form of gold and silver. —**mer'can·til·ist** *n.*

Mer·ca·tor projection (mər-kā'tər). A map projection in which the meridians and parallels of latitude appear as lines crossing at right angles and in which, as the distance from the equator increases, the distance between the lines becomes greater and the land masses depicted become increasingly distorted. [After Gerhardus *Mercator* (1512–94), Flemish cartographer, its inventor.]

mer·ce·nar·y (mûr'sə-nĕr'ē) *adj.* **1.** Concerned with or motivated only by a desire for money or material gain. **2.** Hired for service in a foreign army. —*n., pl.* **-ies.** A professional soldier who is hired by a foreign country. [Middle English *mercenarie,* from Latin *mercēnārius,* from *mercēs,* pay.]

mer·cer (mûr'sər) *n. Brit.* A dealer in textiles. [Middle English, from Old French *mercier,* trader, from Latin *merx,* merchandise.]

mer·cer·ize (mûr'sə-rīz') *tr.v.* **-ized, -iz·ing.** To treat (cotton thread) with sodium hydroxide, so as to shrink the fibers and increase its luster, strength, and ability to hold dyes. [After John *Mercer* (1791–1866), English textile maker, inventor of the process.]

mer·chan·dise (mûr'chən-dīz', -dīs') *n.* Goods that may be bought or sold in commerce; commodities. —*v.* (mûr'chən-dīz') **-dised, -dis·ing.** —*tr.v.* **1.** To buy and sell (goods). **2.** To promote the sale of, as by advertising or display. —*intr.v.* To trade commercially. —See Syns at **sell.** [Middle English *mercheaundise,* from Old French *marcheandise,* from *marcheant,* merchant.] —**mer'chan·dis'er** *n.*

mer·chant (mûr'chənt) *n.* **1.** A person whose occupation is buying and selling goods for profit. **2.** A person who runs a retail business; shopkeeper. —*adj.* **1.** Of or pertaining to a merchant, merchandise, or trade: *a merchant ship.* **2.** Of or pertaining to the merchant marine. [Middle English *marchaund,* from Old French *marcheant,* trader, from Latin *mercārī,* to trade, from *merx,* merchandize.]

mer·chant·a·ble (mûr'chən-tə-bəl) *adj.* Suitable for buying and selling; marketable.

mer·chant·man (mûr'chənt-mən) *n.* A ship used in commerce.

merchant marine. **1.** All of a nation's ships that are engaged in commerce. **2.** The personnel of such ships.

mer·ci·ful (mûr'sĭ-fəl) *adj.* Having, showing, or characterized by mercy; compassionate; lenient. —**mer'ci·ful·ly** *adv.* —**mer'ci·ful·ness** *n.*

mer·ci·less (mûr'sĭ-lĭs) *adj.* Having no mercy; pitiless; cruel. —**mer'ci·less·ly** *adv.* —**mer'ci·less·ness** *n.*

mer·cu·ri·al (mər-kyŏŏr'ē-əl) *adj.* **1.** Having the characteristics of eloquence, shrewdness, swiftness, and thievishness like the mythical Roman Mercury. **2.** Being quick and unpredictably changeable in character: *a mercurial temperament.* **3.** Of, containing, or caused by the action of the element mercury. —See Syns at **capricious.** [Latin *mercuriālis,* from *Mercurius,* the god Mercury.] —**mer·cu'ri·al·ly** *adv.*

mer·cu·ric (mər-kyŏŏr'ĭk) *adj.* Pertaining to or containing bivalent mercury.

Mer·cu·ro·chrome (mər-kyŏŏr'ə-krōm') *n.* A trademark for a red antiseptic and germicidal solution.

mer·cu·rous (mər-kyŏŏr'əs, mûr'kyə-rəs) *adj.* Pertaining to or containing monovalent mercury.

mer·cu·ry (mûr'kyə-rē) *n., pl.* **-ries.** **1.** Symbol **Hg** A silvery-white poisonous metallic element that is liquid at room temperature, used in thermometers, barometers, vapor lamps, and batteries, and in the preparation of chemical pesticides. Atomic number 80; atomic weight 200.59; melting point -38.87°C; boiling point 356.58°C; specific gravity 13.546; valences 1, 2. Also called **quicksilver. 2.** The column of mercury in a thermometer or barometer, used to indicate temperature: *The mercury says it's freezing outside.* **3. Mercury.** *Rom. Myth.* The god of commerce, travel, and thievery, who served as messenger to the other gods, identified with the Greek god Hermes. **4. Mercury.** The smallest of the planets and the one nearest the sun, having a sidereal period of revolution about the sun of 88.0 days at a mean distance of 36.2 million miles, a mean radius of approximately 1,500 miles, and a mass approximately 0.05 that of Earth. [Middle English *mecurie,* from Medieval Latin *Mercurius,* from Latin, the god Mercury.]

mer·cy (mûr'sē) *n., pl.* **-cies.** **1.** Kindness, compassion, and forbearance shown to someone, such as an offender, who expects or rates severe treatment. **2.** A disposition to be kind and forgiving: *I threw myself on his mercy.* **3.** A fortunate occurrence: *It's a mercy he survived.* —*interj.* A word used to express surprise, relief, or fear. —*idiom.* **at the mercy of.** In the power of: *The farmer is at the mercy of the weather.* [Middle English *merci,* from Old French, from Late Latin *mercēs,* reward, God's gratuitous compassion, from Latin *mercēs,* pay, reward.]

mercy killing. Euthanasia.

mere¹ (mîr) *adj.* Superlative **mer·est.** Being nothing more than what is specified: *a mere boy; a mere trifle.* [Latin *merus*, clear, pure, unmixed.] —**mere'ly** *adv.*

mere² (mîr) *n.* A small lake, pond, or marsh. [Middle English, from Old English, sea, lake.]

-mere or **-mer.** A suffix meaning a part or segment: **blastomere.** [French *-mere*, from Greek *meros*, a part.]

mer·e·tri·cious (mĕr'ĭ-trĭsh'əs) *adj.* Attracting attention in a false, cheap, or vulgar manner: *meretricious ornamentation.* [Latin *meritricius*, from *meretrix*, a prostitute, from *merere*, to earn pay.] —**mer'e·tri'cious·ly** *adv.*

mer·gan·ser (mər-găn'sər) *n.* Any fish-eating duck of the genus *Mergus*, with a slim, hooked bill. [New Latin *merganser*, "diver-goose."]

merganser

merge (mûrj) *v.* **merged, merg·ing.** —*tr.v.* To cause to be united or absorbed into so as to lose identity: *merge companies.* —*intr.v.* **1.** To blend together so as to become one: *rivers that run parallel before merging.* **2.** To pass gradually; change without a pause: *Spring merged into sultry summer.* [From Latin *mergere*, to dive, plunge.]

merg·er (mûr'jər) *n.* An act or result of merging, esp. the union of two or more commercial interests or corporations.

me·rid·i·an (mə-rĭd'ē-ən) *n.* **1. a.** An imaginary great circle on the earth's surface that passes through both geographical poles or both of a related set of poles. **b.** Either half of such a circle lying between the poles. **c.** A line drawn on a map to represent either half of such a circle. **2.** A great circle that passes through the two poles of the celestial sphere and the point directly overhead; the celestial meridian. **3.** The highest point or stage; zenith: *reached the meridian of his political power.* [Middle English *meridien*, noon, meridian circle, from Old French, from Latin *merīdiānus*, from *merīdiēs*, midday, var. of *medidiēs* : *medius*, middle + *diēs*, day.]

me·rid·i·o·nal (mə-rĭd'ē-ə-nəl) *adj.* **1.** Of or pertaining to a meridian. **2.** Characteristic of southern areas or people. **3.** Located in the south; southerly. —*n.* An inhabitant of a southern region, esp. of France. [Middle English, from Old French *meridionel*, from Late Latin *merīdiōnālis*.]

me·ringue (mə-răng') *n.* **1.** A topping for pastry or pies made of stiffly beaten and baked egg whites and sugar. **2.** A small pastry shell or cake made of meringue. [French *méringue*.]

me·ri·no (mə-rē'nō) *n., pl.* **-nos. 1. a.** A sheep of a breed ~ig. from Spain. **b.** The fine, soft wool of this sheep. **2.** A ~ft, lightweight fabric made of merino wool. **3.** A fine ~ol and cotton yarn used for knitting underwear, hosiery, ~d other articles of apparel. [Spanish, from Berber *Benī ~rīn*, name of the tribe that developed the breed.]

~it (mĕr'ĭt) *n.* **1.** Value, excellence, or superior quality: *a ~ting of merit.* **2.** A praiseworthy feature or quality: *the ~its of country life.* **3. merits.** The intrinsic right or ~g of any matter: *The case will be decided on its mer-* —*tr.v.* To be worthy of; deserve. [Middle English, ~ Old French *merite*, that which is deserved, from Lat-~eritum*, recompense, from *merēre*, to earn, deserve.]

mer·i·to·ri·ous (mĕr'ĭ-tôr'ē-əs, -tōr-) *adj.* Deserving reward or praise; having merit. [Latin *meritōrius*, earning money, from *meritus*, past part. of *merēre*, to earn, merit.] —**mer'i·to'ri·ous·ly** *adv.*

merit system. A system in which personnel are hired and promoted on the basis of merit, usu. determined by competitive examinations.

merle (mûrl) *n.* Also **merl.** The European blackbird, *Turdus merula.* [Middle English, from Old French, from Latin *merula.*]

mer·lin (mûr'lĭn) *n.* The **pigeon hawk.** [Middle English *meriloun*, from Norman French *merilun*, from Old French *esmerillon*, merlin, from Old High German *smiril.*]

Mer·lin (mûr'lĭn) *n.* In Arthurian legend, the magician and prophet who counseled King Arthur.

mer·lon (mûr'lən) *n.* The solid portion of a battlement between two open spaces. [French, from Italian *merlone*, from *merlo*, blackbird, battlement, from Latin *merula*, blackbird.]

mer·maid (mûr'mād') *n.* A fabled sea creature with the head and upper body of a woman and the tail of a fish. [Middle English *meremaide* : *mer*, sea + *maide*, maid.]

mer·man (mûr'măn', -mən) *n.* A fabled sea creature with the head and upper body of a man and the tail of a fish. [MER(MAID) + MAN.]

-merous. A suffix meaning having (a specified number or kind of) parts: **pentamerous.** [From Greek *-meres*, from *meros*, a part.]

mer·ri·ment (mĕr'ĭ-mənt) *n.* Amusement; gaiety; fun. —See Syns at **gaiety.**

mer·ry (mĕr'ē) *adj.* **-ri·er, -ri·est. 1.** Full of high-spirited gaiety; jolly: *a merry tune.* **2.** Characterized by fun and gaiety; festive: *a merry holiday feast.* **3.** Pleasurable; delightful; entertaining. —*idiom.* **make merry.** To be jolly and gay; have fun. [Middle English *merie*, from Old English *mirige*, pleasant.] —**mer'ri·ly** *adv.* —**mer'ri·ness** *n.*

Syns: **merry, gala, glad, happy, joyful, joyous** *adj.* Core meaning: Marked by celebrations (*had a merry holiday season*).

mer·ry·an·drew (mĕr'ē-ăn'drōō) *n.* A prankster, jester, or clown. [Orig. unknown.]

mer·ry-go-round (mĕr'ē-gō-round') *n.* **1.** A revolving circular platform with seats, usu. in the form of wooden animals, ridden for amusement. **2.** A small circular platform that revolves when pushed or pedaled, used in playgrounds. **3.** Any whirl or swift round of activity: *a merry-go-round of parties.*

mer·ry·mak·ing (mĕr'ē-mā'kĭng) *n.* **1.** Participation in a festive party or celebration. **2.** Fun and gaiety; festivity. —See Syns at **gaiety.** —**mer'ry·mak'er** *n.*

mes-. Var. of **meso-.**

me·sa (mā'sə) *n.* A flat-topped hill or plateau with one or more steep, clifflike sides. [Spanish, from Latin *mēnsa*, table.]

mé·sal·li·ance (mā'zăl-yäNs', mā'zə-lī'əns) *n.* A marriage with a person of inferior social position. [French : *més-*, bad + *alliance*, alliance.]

mes·cal (mĕ-skăl') *n.* **1.** A spineless, globe-shaped cactus, *Lophophora williamsii*, of Mexico and the southwestern United States, with buttonlike tubercles that are dried and chewed as a drug by certain Indian tribes and are the source of the drug mescaline. Also called **peyote. 2.** A usu. colorless Mexican liquor distilled from the fermented juice of certain species of agave. [Spanish, from Nahuatl *mexcalli.*]

mes·ca·line (mĕs'kə-lēn') *n.* An alkaloid drug, $(CH_3O)_3C_6H_2(CH_2CH_2NH_2)$, that produces hallucinations and abnormal mental states.

Mes·dames (mā-dăm') *n.* Plural of **Madame** or **Madam.**

Mes·de·moi·selles (mā'də-mə-zĕl', mād'mwə-) *n.* Plural of **Mademoiselle.**

mes·en·ter·y (mĕs'ən-tĕr'ē) *n., pl.* **-ies.** Any of several folds of tissue in the abdominal cavity that connect the intestines to the rear abdominal wall. [New Latin *mesenterium*, from Greek *mesenterion* : *mes(o)-*, middle + *enteron*, intestine.] —**mes'en·ter'ic** *adj.*

mesh (mĕsh) *n.* **1. a.** Any of the open spaces in a net, sieve, or wire screen. **b.** The size of these open spaces: *a fishnet of medium mesh.* **2. meshes.** The cords, threads, or wires that form a net or network. **3.** A fabric with an open network of interlacing threads. **4. meshes.** Something that snares or entraps: *the meshes of a long legal case.* **5.** The engagement of two sets of gear teeth. —*tr.v.* **1.** To entangle or ensnare. **2.** To cause (gear teeth) to become engaged. —*intr.v.* **1.** To be or become entangled. **2.** To be or become engaged or interlocked, as gear teeth. [Earlier *meash*, from Middle Dutch *masche.*]

mes·mer·ism (mĕz'mə-rĭz'əm, mĕs'-) *n.* Hypnotism. [After Franz Anton *Mesmer* (1734-1815), Austrian physician.]

—**mes·mer'ic** (měz-měr'ĭk, měs-) *adj.*

mes·mer·ize (měz'mə-rīz', měs'-) *tr.v.* **-ized, -iz·ing. 1.** To hypnotize. **2.** To capture and charm; enthrall: *mesmerize an audience.* —**mes'mer·iz'er** *n.*

meso– or **mes–.** A prefix meaning middle: **mesoderm.** [Greek, from *mesos*, middle.]

mes·o·carp (měz'ə-kärp', měs'-) *n.* The middle, usu. fleshy layer of a fruit's pericarp.

mes·o·derm (měz'ə-dûrm', měs'-) *n.* The middle of the three germ layers of an embryo, from which connective, skeletal, and muscular tissue develop. —**mes'o·der'mal** *adj.*

Mes·o·lith·ic (měz'ə-lĭth'ĭk, měs') *n.* The period between the Paleolithic and Neolithic eras, marked by the appearance of the bow and of cutting tools.

mes·o·morph (měz'ə-môrf', měs'-) *n.* A human body characterized by powerfully developed muscles and a predominantly bony framework.

mes·on (měz'ŏn', měs'-, mē'zŏn', -sŏn') *n. Physics.* Any of several subatomic particles with a mass greater than that of an electron and less than that of a proton.

mes·o·sphere (měz'ə-sfîr', měs'-) *n.* The portion of the atmosphere above the stratosphere, from about 20 to 50 miles above the earth.

Mes·o·zo·ic (měz'ə-zō'ĭk, měs'-) *n.* Also **Mesozoic era.** The geologic era that began 230 million years ago and ended 63 million years ago and includes the Triassic, Jurassic, and Cretaceous periods, characterized by the dominance of reptiles. —**modifier:** *a Mesozoic fossil.*

mes·quite (mě-skēt', mə-) *n.* Any of several shrubs or small trees of the genus *Prosopis,* esp. *P. juliflora,* of the southwestern United States and Mexico, with pods that are used as forage. [Spanish *mezquite,* from Nahuatl *mizquitl.*]

mess (měs) *n.* **1.** A disorderly mass or accumulation; a jumble. **2.** A cluttered, untidy, usu. dirty condition. **3.** A disturbing, confusing, or complicated state of affairs; a muddle: *Who got us into this mess?* **4.** A serving of soft, semiliquid food. **5.** A distasteful and unappetizing concoction. **6.** An unspecified amount, usu. of food: *a mess of fish.* **7. a.** A group, usu. in the military, who regularly eat meals together. **b.** A room or hall where such meals are served. **c.** A meal eaten there. —*tr.v.* **1.** To make disorderly or dirty; to clutter: *mess up the kitchen.* **2.** To bungle, mismanage, or botch: *He messed up the test.* —*intr.v.* **1.** To make a mess. **2.** To interfere; meddle: *Don't mess with their plans.* **3.** To take a meal in a military mess. — See Syns at **botch.** [Middle English *mes,* portion of food, from Old French, from Latin *missus,* course of a meal, from *mittere,* to send, place, put.]

mes·sage (měs'ĭj) *n.* **1.** A communication transmitted from one person or group to another. **2.** A statement made before or read before a gathering: *a farewell message.* **3.** A basic theme or meaning: *the message of Buddhism.* [Middle English, from Old French, from Latin *missus,* past part. of *mittere,* to send.]

mes·sen·ger (měs'ən-jər) *n.* **1.** A person responsible for transmitting messages or performing errands. **2.** A person employed to carry telegrams, letters, parcels, etc. **3.** A military or other courier of official dispatches. **4.** *Archaic.* A forerunner; harbinger. [Middle English *messager,* from Old French *messagier,* from *message,* message.]

messenger RNA. An RNA that carries genetic information required for protein synthesis.

Mes·si·ah (mə-sī'ə) *n.* **1.** The expected deliverer and king of the Jews. **2.** Christ, regarded by Christians as the savior of mankind. **3. messiah.** Any expected deliverer or savior. [Aramaic *məshīḥā* or Hebrew *māshiaḥ,* the anointed one, the Messiah.] —**Mes'si·an'ic** *adj.*

Mes·sieurs (mā-syœ') *n.* Plural of **Monsieur.**

mess kit. A compact unit that contains cooking and eating utensils.

mess·mate (měs'māt') *n.* A person with whom one eats regularly, as in a military mess.

mess·y (měs'ē) *adj.* **-i·er, -i·est.** Like, being in, or causing a mess; untidy; dirty; disordered. —See Syns at **disorderly.** —**mess'i·ly** *adv.* —**mess'i·ness** *n.*

met (mět) *v.* Past tense and past participle of **meet.**

met·a·bol·ic (mět'ə-bŏl'ĭk) *adj.* **1.** Of, pertaining to, or involving metabolism. **2.** Of, pertaining to, or undergoing metamorphosis.

me·tab·o·lism (mə-tăb'ə-lĭz'əm) *n. Biol.* **1.** The physical and chemical processes that living things carry on to maintain life; anabolism and catabolism. **2.** The functioning of any specific substance within the living body: *water metabolism; iodine metabolism.* [From Greek *metabolē,* change, from *metaballein,* to change.]

met·a·car·pal (mět'ə-kär'pəl) *adj.* Of or pertaining to the metacarpus. —*n.* Any of the bones of the metacarpus.

met·a·car·pus (mět'ə-kär'pəs) *n. Anat.* The part of the hand between the wrist and fingers or forefoot between the ankle and toes that contains five bones. [Greek *meta-,* behind + CARPUS.]

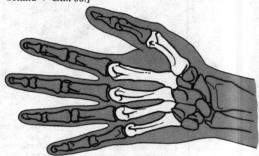

metacarpus

met·al (mět'l) *n.* **1.** Any of a category of chemical elements, as copper, iron, or gold, with certain characteristic properties such as luster, malleability, ductility, and conductivity of electricity and heat. **2.** An alloy of two or more metals, such as bronze. **3.** Basic quality or character of someone or something; mettle. **4.** Molten glass, esp. when used in glassmaking. [Middle English, from Old French, from Latin *metallum,* from Greek *metallon.*]

me·tal·lic (mə-tăl'ĭk) *adj.* **1.** Of, pertaining to, or having the characteristics of a metal. **2.** Containing a metal. **3.** Characteristic or suggestive of metal: *a metallic clanking.*

met·al·lif·er·ous (mět'l-ĭf'ər-əs) *adj.* Containing or yielding metal.

met·al·loid (mět'l-oid') *n.* A nonmetallic element, as arsenic or carbon, that has some of the chemical properties of a metal. —*adj.* **1.** Relating to or having the properties of a metalloid. **2.** Having the appearance of a metal.

met·al·lur·gy (mět'l-ûr'jē) *n.* The science or technology of extracting metals from ores, purifying them, and making useful objects from metals. [From Greek *metallourgos,* a miner : *metallon,* a mine + *ergon,* work.] —**met'al·lur'gic** or **met'al·lur'gi·cal** *adj.* —**met'al·lur'gist** *n.*

met·al·work (mět'l-wûrk') *n.* Artistic work done in metal. —**met'al·work'er** *n.* —**met'al·work'ing** *n.*

met·a·mor·phic (mět'ə-môr'fĭk) *adj.* **1.** Of or relating to metamorphosis. **2.** *Geol.* Of, pertaining to, involving, or changed by metamorphism.

met·a·mor·phism (mět'ə-môr'fĭz'əm) *n.* **1.** *Geol.* Any change in composition, texture, or structure of rock masses, caused by great heat, pressure, or the action of water. **2.** Metamorphosis.

met·a·mor·phose (mět'ə-môr'fōz', -fōs') *v.* **-phosed, -phos·ing.** —*tr.v.* **1.** To transform or alter: *"His eyes turned bloodshot, and he was metamorphosed into a raging fiend"* (Jack London). **2.** To subject to metamorphosis or metamorphism. —*intr.v.* To undergo metamorphosis or metamorphism. [Old French *metamorphoser,* from *metamorphose,* transformation, from Latin *metamorphōsis,* metamorphosis.]

met·a·mor·pho·sis (mět'ə-môr'fə-sĭs) *n., pl.* **-ses** (-sēz'). **1.** A transformation, as by magic or sorcery. **2.** A pronounced change in appearance, character, condition, or function. **3.** *Biol.* Change in the structure, form, or life function of an animal during normal development, usu. in the postembryonic stage, as the emergence of a butterfly from a caterpillar or the transformation of a tadpole into a frog. [Latin *metamorphōsis,* from Greek : *meta-* change + *morphōsis,* formation.]

met·a·phor (mĕt'ə-fôr', -fər) *n.* **1.** A figure of speech in which a term that ordinarily designates an object or idea is used to designate a dissimilar object or idea in order to suggest comparison or analogy, as in the phrase *evening of life.* **2.** Figurative language in general. [Old French *metaphore,* from Latin *metaphora,* from Greek, from *metapherein,* to transfer : *meta-* change + *pherein,* to bear.] —**met·a·phor·ic** (mĕt'ə-fôr'ĭk, -fŏr'-) or **met·a·phor·i·cal** *adj.* —**met·a·phor·i·cal·ly** *adv.*

met·a·phys·i·cal (mĕt'ə-fĭz'ĭ-kəl) *adj.* **1.** Of or pertaining to metaphysics. **2.** Highly abstract; difficult to understand; abstruse. **3.** Often **Metaphysical.** Of or designating a kind of 17th-cent. poetry characterized by complex imagery and elaborate conceits. —**met·a·phys·i·cal·ly** *adv.*

met·a·phy·si·cian (mĕt'ə-fĭ-zĭsh'ən) *n.* A person skilled in metaphysics.

met·a·phys·ics (mĕt'ə-fĭz'ĭks) *n.* *(used with a sing. verb).* **1.** The branch of philosophy that systematically investigates first causes and the nature and problems of ultimate reality. **2.** Speculative or critical philosophy in general. [Medieval Latin *metaphysica,* from Greek *ta meta ta phusika,* "the things after the physics," Aristotle's treatise on transcendental philosophy, so called because it followed his work on physics : *meta-,* after + *phusika,* physics, from *phusikos,* natural.]

me·tas·ta·sis (mə-tăs'tə-sĭs) *n.,* *pl.* **-ses** (-sēz'). The spreading of a disease from its original location to one or more places elsewhere in the body, as in cancer. [From Late Latin, transition, from Greek, from *methistanai,* to change : *meta-* change + *histanai,* cause to stand.] —**met·a·stat·ic** (mĕt'ə-stăt'ĭk) *adj.*

me·tas·ta·size (mə-tăs'tĭ-sīz') *intr.v.* **-sized, -siz·ing.** To spread by metastasis.

met·a·tar·sal (mĕt'ə-tär'səl) *adj.* Of or pertaining to the metatarsus. —*n.* Any of the bones of the metatarsus.

met·a·tar·sus (mĕt'ə-tär'səs) *n.,* *pl.* **-si** (-sī'). **1.** The middle part of the human foot, composed of the five bones between the toes and the tarsus, that forms the instep. **2.** A corresponding part of the hind foot in four-legged animals or of the foot in birds. [Greek *meta-,* behind + TARSUS.]

me·tath·e·sis (mə-tăth'ĭ-sĭs) *n.,* *pl.* **-ses** (-sēz'). Transposition within a word of letters, sounds, or syllables, as in the change from Old English *brid* to modern English *bird.* [Late Latin, from Greek, from *metatithenai,* to transpose : *meta-* change + *tithenai,* to place.]

met·a·zo·an (mĕt'ə-zō'ən) *n.* A member of one of two divisions of the animal kingdom, the Metazoa, which includes all animals more complex than the one-celled protozoan. [Greek *meta-,* later + -ZOAN.] —**met·a·zo'an** or **met·a·zo'ic** *adj.*

mete¹ (mēt) *tr.v.* **met·ed, met·ing.** **1.** To distribute by or as if by measure; allot: *mete out rewards.* **2.** *Archaic.* To measure. [Middle English *meten,* from Old English *metan.*]

mete² (mēt) *n.* A boundary line or limit: *metes and bounds.* [Norman French, from Latin *mēta.*]

me·tem·psy·cho·sis (mə-tĕm'sĭ-kō'sĭs, mĕt'əm-sī-) *n.,* *pl.* **-ses** (-sēz'). The passing of the soul at death into another body, either human or animal; transmigration of souls. [Greek *metempsukhōsis,* from *metempsukhousthai,* to transmigrate : *meta-,* change + *empsukhos,* animate.]

me·te·or (mē'tē-ər, -ôr') *n.* **1.** The luminous trail or streak that appears in the sky when a fragment of solid material from space falls into the earth's atmosphere and is made incandescent by friction. Also called **shooting star. 2.** Such a fragment of solid material from space; meteoroid. [Middle English, from Old French *meteore,* from Medieval Latin *meteōrum,* from Greek *meteōron,* astronomical phenomenon, from *meteōros,* high in the air.]

me·te·or·ic (mē'tē-ôr'ĭk, -ŏr'-) *adj.* **1.** Of, pertaining to, or formed by meteors. **2.** Resembling a meteor in speed, brilliance, or briefness: *a meteoric rise to fame.* **3.** Of or pertaining to the earth's atmosphere: *meteoric phenomenon.*

me·te·or·ite (mē'tē-ə-rīt') *n.* The solid material of a meteoroid that survives passage through the atmosphere and reaches the earth's surface.

me·te·or·oid (mē'tē-ə-roid') *n.* Any of numerous celestial bodies, ranging in size from minute specks to huge asteroids, that appear as meteors when entering the earth's atmosphere.

me·te·or·ol·o·gy (mē'tē-ə-rŏl'ə-jē) *n.* The science dealing with the phenomena of the atmosphere, esp. weather and weather conditions. [Greek *meteōros,* high in the air + -LOGY.] —**me'te·or·o·log'i·cal** (mē'tē-ər-ə-lŏj'ĭ-kəl) or **me'te·or·o·log'ic** *adj.* —**me'te·or·o·log'i·cal·ly** *adv.* —**me'te·or·ol'o·gist** *n.*

me·ter¹ (mē'tər) *n.* Also *Brit.* **me·tre. 1.** A rhythmic pattern used in verse, determined by the number and kinds of metric units in a typical line. **2. a.** The division of music into measures or bars. **b.** Any particular grouping of beats that results from this, as indicated by a time signature. [Middle English, from Old English *mēter* and Old French *metre,* both from Latin *metrum,* measure, from Greek *metron.*]

me·ter² (mē'tər) *n.* Also *Brit.* **me·tre.** *Abbr.* **m** The basic unit of length in the metric system, equal to 39.37 inches. [French *mètre,* from Greek *metron,* measure.]

me·ter³ (mē'tər) *n.* Any device designed to measure time, distance, speed, or intensity, or to record or regulate the amount or volume of something, such as a flow of gas or an electric current. —*tr.v.* To measure or regulate with a metering device. [From -METER.]

-meter. A suffix meaning a measuring device: **barometer, speedometer.** [From Greek *metron,* meter, measure.]

me·ter-kil·o·gram-sec·ond **system** (mē'tər-kĭl'ə-grăm-sĕk'ənd). *Abbr.* **mks** A system of measurement using the meter, the kilogram, and the second as basic units of length, mass, and time.

meth·a·done hydrochloride (mĕth'ə-dōn'). An organic compound, $C_{21}H_{27}NO \cdot HCL$, used as an analgesic and in treating heroin addiction. [From (DI)METH(YL) + A(MINO)- + D(IPHENYL) + (heptan)one, from HEPTANE + -ONE.]

meth·am·phet·a·mine (mĕth'ăm-fĕt'ə-mēn', -mĭn) *n.* An amphetamine derivative, $C_{10}H_{15}N$, used as a stimulant. [METH(YL) + AMPHETAMINE.]

meth·ane (mĕth'ān') *n.* An odorless, colorless, flammable gas, CH_4, that is the major component of natural gas and is used as a fuel and in the production of a wide variety of other organic compounds. [METH(YL) + -ANE.]

meth·a·nol (mĕth'ə-nôl', -nōl') *n.* **Methyl alcohol.** [METHAN(E) + -OL.]

me·thinks (mĭ-thĭngks') *v.* Past tense **me·thought** (mĭ-thôt'). *Archaic.* It seems to me. [Middle English *me thinketh,* from Old English *mē thyncth : mē,* me + *thyncan,* to seem.]

me·thi·o·nine (mə-thī'ə-nēn') *n.* An organic compound, $C_5H_{11}NO_2S$, that is an essential amino acid. [METH(YL) + Greek *theion,* sulfur + -INE.]

meth·od (mĕth'əd) *n.* **1.** A regular and systematic way or manner of accomplishing something. **2.** Orderly and systematic arrangement; regularity. **3.** The established procedures and techniques used in a particular discipline or field of knowledge: *the scientific method.* **4. the Method.** A system of acting in which the actor recalls emotions from his past experience and uses them in the role he is playing. [French *méthode,* from Latin *methodus,* from Greek *methodos,* pursuit : *met(a)-,* after + *hodos,* journey.]

Syns: **method, fashion, manner, mode, system, way** *n.* *Core meaning:* The procedures or plans followed to accomplish a given task (*practical methods of pollution control*). METHOD often suggests regularity of procedure; it emphasizes detailed, logically ordered plans (*three methods of purifying water*). SYSTEM stresses order and regularity affecting all parts and details of a procedure (*a system for improving production*). MANNER, FASHION, and MODE refer more to individual and distinctive procedure, as that dictated by preference, tradition, or custom (*taught in an innovative manner; sings in an interesting fashion; an unusual mode of painting*). WAY is the most neutral and general of these terms and is often an inclusive synonym for them (*a better way of working out accounting problems*).

meth·od·i·cal (mə-thŏd'ĭ-kəl) or **me·thod·ic** (-ĭk) *adj.* **1.** Arranged, performed, or proceeding in regular, systematic manner: *a methodical inspection.* **2.** Characterized by ordered and systematic habits, thoughts, or behavior. —**me·thod'i·cal·ly** *adv.* —**me·thod'i·cal·ness** *n.*

Meth·od·ism (mĕth'ə-dĭz'əm) *n.* The beliefs, worship, and practice of the Methodists.

Meth·od·ist (mĕth'ə-dĭst) *n.* A member of a Protestant denomination founded in 18th-cent. England on the teachings of John and Charles Wesley and characterized by an emphasis on the doctrines of free grace and individual responsibility. **—Meth·od·ist** adj.

meth·od·ize (mĕth′ə-dīz′) tr.v. **-ized, -iz·ing.** To reduce to or organize according to a method; systematize.

meth·od·ol·o·gy (mĕth′ə-dŏl′ə-jē) n., pl. **-gies. 1.** The system of principles, practices, and procedures applied to any specific branch of knowledge. **2.** The branch of logic dealing with the general principles or methods of inquiry as they are applied to any specific branch of knowledge. **—meth′od·o·log′i·cal** (mĕth′ə-də-lŏj′ĭ-kəl) adj.

me·thought (mĭ-thôt′) v. Past tense of **methinks.**

meth·yl (mĕth′əl) n. The univalent organic radical CH_3, derived from methane and occurring in many important organic compounds. [French méthyle, from méthylène, methylene (a bivalent organic radical) : Greek methu, wine + hulē, wood + French -ene, -ene.]

methyl alcohol. A colorless flammable liquid, CH_3OH, used as an antifreeze, solvent, and fuel. Also called **methanol** and **wood alcohol.**

me·tic·u·lous (mə-tĭk′yə-ləs) adj. Extremely or excessively concerned with details: a meticulous worker. —See Syns at **careful.** [Latin meticulōsus, overly concerned, fearful : metus, fear + (per)īculōsus, perilous, from perīculum, peril.] **—me·tic′u·lous·ness** n.

mé·tier (mā-tyā′) n. **1.** An occupation, trade, or profession. **2.** Work or activity for which an individual is particularly well suited; one's specialty. [French, from Old French mestier, from Latin ministerium, mystery, trade.]

met·o·nym (mĕt′ə-nĭm′) n. A word used in metonymy.

me·ton·y·my (mə-tŏn′ə-mē) n., pl. **-mies.** A figure of speech in which an idea or name for one thing is used for another idea or name associated with it; for example, the word sword is a metonym for military career in the sentence "He abandoned the sword forever." [Late Latin metōnymia, from Greek metōnumia : meta-, change + onoma, name.] **—met′o·nym′i·cal** (mĕt′ə-nĭm′ĭ-kəl) adj.

met·o·pe (mĕt′ə-pē) n. One of the spaces between triglyphs on a Doric frieze. [Latin metopa, from Greek metopē : meta, between + opē, opening.]

me·tre (mē′tər) n. Brit. Var. of **meter** (rhythm and measurement).

met·ric (mĕt′rĭk) adj. Of, designating, or pertaining to the metric system.

met·ri·cal (mĕt′rĭ-kəl) adj. **1.** Of, pertaining to, or composed in musical or poetic meter. **2.** Of or pertaining to measurement. [From Latin metricus, from Greek metrikos, from metron, measure, meter.] **—met′ri·cal·ly** adv.

met·ri·ca·tion (mĕt′rĭ-kā′shən) n. Conversion to the metric system of weights and measures.

met·rics (mĕt′rĭks) n. (used with a sing. verb). The branch of prosody dealing with metrical structures.

metric system. A decimal system of weights and measures based on the meter as a standard of length and the kilogram as a standard of mass or weight, with other units, such as the liter for volume and the are for area, being derived from these.

metric ton. Abbr. **m.t., M.T.** A unit of mass equal to 1,000 kilograms.

met·ro or **Mét·ro** (mĕt′rō, mā-trō′) n., pl. **-ros.** The subway system in several cities, esp. Paris. [French, short for (chemin de fer) métropolitain, "metropolitan (railway)."]

met·ro·nome (mĕt′rə-nōm′) n. A device that makes a series of clicks at precise, adjustable intervals of time, used to provide a steady beat for practicing music. [Greek metron, measure + nomos, rule, law.] **—met′ro·nom′ic** (mĕt′-rə-nŏm′ĭk) adj.

me·trop·o·lis (mə-trŏp′ə-lĭs) n. **1.** A major city, esp. the capital or the largest or most important city of a particular country, state, or region. **2.** A large urban center of culture, trade, or other activity. **3.** The chief seat of a metropolitan bishop. [Late Latin mētropolis, from Greek : mētēr, mother + polis, city.]

met·ro·pol·i·tan (mĕt′rə-pŏl′ĭ-tn) adj. **1.** Of, pertaining to, or characteristic of a metropolis: a metropolitan newspaper. **2.** Including a major city and its surrounding suburbs: the metropolitan Los Angeles area. —n. An archbishop who has authority over bishops.

-metry. A suffix meaning the science or process of measuring: photometry. [Middle English -metrie, from Old French, from Latin -metria, from Greek, from metron, meter, measure.]

met·tle (mĕt′l) n. **1.** Courage and fortitude; spirit. **2.** Inherent quality of a person's character and temperament. **—idiom. on (one's) mettle.** Ready to put one's spirit or courage to the test. [Middle English metel, fortitude, metal, var. of metal, metal.]

met·tle·some (mĕt′l-səm) adj. Full of courage; high-spirited. —See Syns at **brave.**

mew¹ (myoo) n. Archaic. A cage for hawks, esp. when they are molting. —tr.v. To confine in or as if in a cage. [Middle English mewe, cage for molting hawks, from Old French mue, a molting, from muer, to molt, from Latin mūtāre, to change.]

mew² (myoo) intr.v. To make the high-pitched, crying sound of a cat; to meow. —n. The high-pitched, crying sound of a cat; a meow. [Middle English mewen (imit.).]

mew³ (myoo) n. A gull, Larus canus, found in northern Europe and western North America. [Middle English, from Old English mæw.]

mewl (myool) intr.v. To cry weakly, as a baby does; to whimper. —n. A weak cry; a whimper. [Imit.]

mews (myooz) n. (used with a sing. verb). A small street behind a residential street, with private stables, now mostly converted into small apartments. [After the Mews at Charing Cross, London, medieval royal stables.]

Mex·i·can (mĕk′sĭ-kən) n. A native or inhabitant of Mexico. —adj. Of or pertaining to Mexico or to its inhabitants, their language, or their culture.

Mexican Spanish. Spanish as spoken in Mexico.

me·zu·zah or **me·zu·za** (mə-zŏŏz′ə, -zŏŏ′zə) n. Judaism. A small piece of parchment inscribed with Biblical passages and marked with the word "Shaddai," a Hebrew name of the Almighty, rolled up in a container and affixed to a door frame as a sign that a Jewish family lives within or worn around the neck as an amulet. [Hebrew məzūzāh, doorpost.]

mez·za·nine (mĕz′ə-nēn′, mĕz′ə-nēn′) n. **1.** A partial story between two main stories of a building. **2.** The lowest balcony in a theater or the first few rows of the balcony. [French, from Italian mezzanino, from mezzano, middle, from Latin mediānus, in the middle, from medius, middle.]

mez·zo (mĕt′sō, mĕd′zō) n., pl. **-zos.** A mezzo-soprano.

mez·zo·so·pran·o (mĕt′sō-sə-prăn′ō, -prä′nō, mĕd′zō-) n., pl. **-os. 1.** A woman's singing voice with a range between soprano and contralto. **2.** A woman with such a voice. **3.** A part written in the range of this voice. [Italian : mezzo, half + soprano, soprano.]

mez·zo·tint (mĕt′sō-tĭnt′, mĕd′zō-) n. **1.** A method of engraving a copper or steel plate by scraping and burnishing areas to produce effects of light and shadow. **2.** A print made from a plate treated in this manner. [Italian mezzotinto : mezzo, half + tinto, tint.]

Mg The symbol for **magnesium.**

mho (mō) n., pl. **mhos.** A unit of electrical conductance, reciprocal to the ohm. [Backward spelling of OHM.]

mi (mē) n. The third tone of the diatonic scale. [Medieval Latin.]

mi·as·ma (mī-ăz′mə, mē-) n., pl. **-mas** or **-ma·ta** (-mə-tə). **1.** A poisonous vapor formerly thought to rise from swamps and rotting matter and to cause disease. **2.** Any harmful or noxious atmosphere or influence: "A miasma of evil suddenly enveloped Profane from behind" (Thomas Pynchon). [From Greek, from miainein, to pollute.] **—mi·as′mal** (-məl) or **mi·as′mic** (-mĭk) adj.

mi·ca (mī′kə) n. Any of a group of silicate minerals, common in igneous and metamorphic rocks, that characteristically can be split into flexible sheets used in electrical insulation. [Latin mīca, grain.]

mice (mīs) n. Plural of **mouse.**

Mich·ael·mas (mĭk′əl-məs) n. A church festival celebrated on Sept. 29 in honor of the archangel Michael. [Middle English mychelmesse, from Old English Michaeles mæsse : Michael, Michael + mæsse, mass.]

Mick·ey Finn (mĭk′ē fĭn′). Slang. An alcoholic beverage that has been secretly drugged so as to make its drinker unconscious. [Orig. unknown.]

ă pat	ā pay	â care	ä father	ĕ pet	ē be	hw which	ĭ pit	ī tie	î pier	ŏ pot	ō toe	ô paw, for	oi noise
ŏŏ took	ŏŏ boot	ou out	th thin	th this	ŭ cut		û urge	zh vision	ə about, item, edible, gallop, circus				

microfilm　　　　　　　　　　micrometer　　　　　　　　　　microscope

Mic·mac (mĭk′măk′) *n., pl.* **Micmac** or **-macs. 1.** An Algonquian tribe of North American Indians formerly inhabiting the areas that are now Nova Scotia and New Brunswick. **2.** A member of this tribe. **3.** The Algonquian language of the Micmac.

mi·cra (mī′krə) *n.* A plural of **micron.**

micro–. A prefix meaning: **1.** Small: **microbe. 2.** Used for or working with small quantities: **microchemistry. 3.** Used or involving a microscope: **microscopy. 4.** One-millionth (10⁻⁶): **microsecond.** [Middle English, from Latin *mīcro-,* from Greek *mikros,* small.]

mi·crobe (mī′krōb′) *n.* A minute life form that can be seen only through a microscope; a microorganism, esp. one that causes disease. —See Usage note at **germ.** [MICRO- + Greek *bios,* life.]

mi·cro·bi·ol·o·gy (mī′krō-bī-ŏl′ə-jē) *n.* The scientific study of microorganisms, esp. their effects on other forms of life. —**mi′cro·bi′o·log′i·cal** (-bī′ə-lŏj′ĭ-kəl) *adj.* —**mi′cro·bi·ol′o·gist** *n.*

mi·cro·coc·cus (mī′krō-kŏk′əs) *n., pl.* **-coc·ci** (-kŏk′sī′, -kŏk′ī′). Any of several species of spherically shaped bacteria.

mi·cro·cosm (mī′krō-kŏz′əm) *n.* **1.** A small or miniature world or universe. **2.** Something regarded as representing a larger entity on a very small scale: *The town meeting is a microcosm of American democracy.* [Middle English *microcosme,* from Medieval Latin *micro(s)cosmus,* from Greek *mikros kosmos,* "small world."] —**mi′cro·cos′mic** or **mi′cro·cos′mi·cal** *adj.*

mi·cro·ec·o·nom·ics (mī′krō-ĕk′ə-nŏm′ĭks, -ē′kə-) *pl.n.* The branch of economics that deals with specific areas of activity.

mi·cro·fiche (mī′krō-fēsh′) *n.* A sheet of microfilm containing rows of pages in reduced form.

mi·cro·film (mī′krə-fĭlm′) *n.* **1.** A film upon which written or printed material can be photographed in greatly reduced size. **2.** A reproduction on microfilm. —*tr.v.* To reproduce on microfilm.

Mi·cro·groove (mī′krō-grōōv′) *n.* A trademark for a long-playing phonograph record.

mi·crom·e·ter (mī-krŏm′ĭ-tər) *n.* A device for measuring minute distances, esp. one based on the rotation of a finely threaded screw.

mi·cron (mī′krŏn′) *n., pl.* **-crons** or **-cra** (-krə). *Symbol* µ A unit of length equal to one-millionth (10⁻⁶) of a meter. [From Greek *mikros,* small.]

Mi·cro·ne·sian (mī′krə-nē′zhən, -shən) *adj.* Of or pertaining to Micronesia, its inhabitants, their languages, or their culture. —*n.* **1.** A native or inhabitant of Micronesia. **2.** A group of related languages spoken in Micronesia.

mi·cro·nu·cle·us (mī′krō-nōō′klē-əs, -nyōō′-) *n.* The smaller nuclear mass in ciliated protozoans, considered to be the center of reproductive functions.

mi·cro·or·gan·ism (mī′krō-ôr′gə-nĭz′əm) *n.* An animal or plant of microscopic size, esp. a bacterium or a protozoan.

mi·cro·phone (mī′krə-fōn′) *n.* A device that converts sound waves into an electric current, usu. fed into an amplifier, recorder, or broadcast transmitter.

mi·cro·scope (mī′krə-skōp′) *n.* An instrument that uses a combination of lenses to produce magnified images of small objects, esp. of objects too small to be seen by the naked eye.

mi·cro·scop·ic (mī′krə-skŏp′ĭk) or **mi·cro·scop·i·cal**
(-ĭ-kəl) *adj.* **1.** Too small to be seen by the naked eye but large enough to be seen under a microscope. **2.** Exceedingly small; minute. **3.** Of, pertaining to, concerned with, or done by a microscope. **4.** Like or resembling a microscope in the ability to observe very small objects. —**mi′cro·scop′i·cal·ly** *adv.*

mi·cros·co·py (mī-krŏs′kə-pē) *n.* **1.** The study or use of microscopes. **2.** Investigation using a microscope. —**mi·cros′co·pist** *n.*

mi·cro·sec·ond (mī′krə-sĕk′ənd) *n.* A unit of time equal to one millionth (10⁻⁶) of a second.

mi·cro·spore (mī′krə-spôr′, -spōr′) *n.* A small plant spore that gives rise to a male gametophyte.

mi·cro·wave (mī′krə-wāv′) *n.* Any electromagnetic wave with a wavelength in the range from approx. 1 centimeter to 1 meter.

microwave oven. An oven in which microwaves are used to heat food by acting on water molecules.

mid¹ (mĭd) *adj.* **1.** Middle; central. **2.** Being the part in the middle or center: *in the mid Pacific.* [Middle English, from Old English *midd.*]

mid² (mĭd) *prep. Poet.* Amid: *mid smoke and flame.*

mid–. A prefix meaning middle: **midship, midway.** [From MID (middle).]

mid·air (mĭd-âr′) *n.* A point or region in the middle of the air.

Mi·das (mī′dəs) *n.* The fabled king of Phrygia to whom Dionysus gave the power of turning to gold all that he touched.

mid·brain (mĭd′brān′) *n.* The middle region of the vertebrate brain; the mesencephalon.

mid·day (mĭd′dā′) *n.* The middle of the day; noon. —*modifier: a midday nap.*

mid·den (mĭd′n) *n.* **1.** A dunghill or refuse heap. **2.** A kitchen midden. [Middle English *myddung.*]

mid·dle (mĭd′l) *n.* **1.** An area or point that is equally distant between extremes or outer limits; the center. **2.** The portion or part that is approx. halfway between a beginning and an end: *stopped in the middle of the story.* **3.** The waist. —*adj.* **1.** Equally distant from extremes or outer limits; central: *the middle point on a line.* **2.** Intermediate in time or age; in-between: *the middle child of three.* **3.** Medium; average; moderate: *a dog of middle size.* **4.** Between earlier and later stages: *Middle English; Middle Mesozoic.* [Middle English *middel,* from Old English.]

middle age. The time of human life between youth and old age, usu. reckoned as the years between 40 and 60.

mid·dle-aged (mĭd′l-ājd′) *adj.* Of, pertaining to, or characterized by middle age.

middle C. *Mus.* The musical tone whose pitch is indicated by the first ledger line below the treble clef and the first ledger line above the bass clef.

middle class. The members of society that occupy a social and economic position intermediate between the laboring classes and those who are wealthy in land or money. —**mid′dle-class′** *adj.*

middle distance. 1. The area between the foreground and background in a painting, drawing, or photograph. **2.** A division of track and field competition in racing with events that range from 440 yards to 1 mile.

Middle Dutch. The Dutch language from the middle of the 12th cent. through the 15th cent. A.D.

middle ear. The space between the tympanic membrane

and the inner ear, containing a chain of 3 small bones that convey sound vibrations to the auditory tube.

Middle English. The English language from the 12th cent. through the 15th cent. A.D.

Middle High German. High German from the 11th cent. through the 15th cent. A.D.

Middle Low German. Low German from the middle of the 13th cent. through the 15th cent. A.D.

mid·dle·man (mĭd′l-măn′) n. **1.** A trader who buys from producers and sells to retailers or consumers. **2.** An intermediary or go-between.

mid·dle·most (mĭd′l-mōst′) adj. Midmost.

mid·dling (mĭd′lĭng) adj. Of medium size, quality, or condition; mediocre; ordinary. —n. **1. middlings.** Products that are intermediate, as in quality, size, or price. **2. middlings.** Coarsely ground wheat mixed with bran. —adv. Informal. Fairly; moderately. [Middle English mydlyn.] —**mid′dling·ly** adv.

mid·dy (mĭd′ē) n., pl. **-dies. 1.** Informal. A midshipman. **2.** A woman's or child's loose blouse with a sailor collar.

midge (mĭj) n. Any of various gnatlike flies of the family Chironomidae, found throughout the world. [Middle English migge, from Old English mycg.]

midg·et (mĭj′ĭt) n. **1.** An extremely small person who is otherwise normally proportioned. **2.** A very small or miniature type or kind. —modifier: a midget automobile; a midget computer. [Dim. of MIDGE.]

mid·land (mĭd′lənd) n. The middle or interior part of a specific country or region. —adj. Of or in a midland.

mid·most (mĭd′mōst′) adj. Located in or near the exact middle; middlemost. —adv. In or near the middle.

mid·night (mĭd′nīt′) n. The middle of the night; twelve o'clock at night. —adj. **1.** Of, pertaining to, or occurring in the middle of the night. **2.** Resembling the middle of the night; dark; gloomy.

midnight sun. The sun as seen at midnight during the summer within the Arctic or Antarctic Circle.

mid·point (mĭd′point′) n. The point at or near the middle of something.

mid·rib (mĭd′rĭb′) n. The central vein of a leaf.

mid·riff (mĭd′rĭf′) n. **1.** The diaphragm. **2.** The part of the human body that extends from approx. the middle of the chest to the waist. [Middle English midrif, from Old English midhrif : midd, mid + hrif, belly.]

mid·ship (mĭd′shĭp′) adj. Of, pertaining to, or located in the middle of a ship.

mid·ship·man (mĭd′shĭp′mən, mĭd-shĭp′mən) n. **1.** A student training to be an officer in the U.S. Navy or Coast Guard. **2.** A student officer ranking below sublieutenant in the British Navy. [From earlier midshipsman : MIDSHIP(S) + MAN.]

mid·ships (mĭd′shĭps′) adv. Amidships.

midst (mĭdst) n. **1.** The middle position or part; the center: a tree in the midst of the garden. **2.** The condition of being surrounded by or enveloped in something: in the midst of a recession. **3.** A position or condition of being among members of a group: rebels in our midst. —prep. Among; amid. [Middle English middest, var. of middes, from midde, mid.]

mid·sum·mer (mĭd′sŭm′ər) n. **1.** The middle of the summer. **2.** The summer solstice, about June 21. —**mid′sum′mer** adj.

mid·term (mĭd′tûrm′) n. **1.** The middle of a school term or a political term of office. **2.** An examination given at the middle of a school term.

mid·way (mĭd′wā′) adv. In the middle of a way, distance, or period of time; halfway. —adj. In the middle of a way, distance, or period of time. —n. (mĭd′wā′). The area of a fair, carnival or circus where side shows and other amusements are located.

mid·week (mĭd′wēk′) n. The middle of the week. —modifier: a midweek appointment. —**mid′week·ly** adj. & adv.

mid·wife (mĭd′wīf′) n. A woman who assists women in childbirth. [Middle English midwif : mid, with, from Old English mid + wif, woman, wife.] —**mid′wife·ry** n.

mid·win·ter (mĭd′wĭn′tər) n. **1.** The middle of the winter. **2.** The winter solstice, about Dec. 22. —modifier: midwinter holidays.

mid·year (mĭd′yĭr′) n. **1.** The middle of a year or school year. **2.** An examination given in the middle of the school year. —modifier: a midyear vacation.

mien (mēn) n. A person's bearing, manner, or appearance, esp. as indicating mood or personality. [Earlier meane, short for demean, behavior.]

miff (mĭf) tr.v. To cause (a person) to become offended or annoyed. [Orig. unknown.]

might¹ (mīt) n. **1.** Tremendous power, force, or influence: the might of the allied armies. **2.** Physical or bodily strength. **3.** The strength or ability to do something: tried with all his might. —See Syns at ability. [Middle English, from Old English miht.]

might² (mīt) v. Past tense of **may.** —Used as an auxiliary to indicate: **1.** Conditional possibility: We might let you go. **2.** Probability: closer than one might think. **3.** Request for permission: Might I trouble you? **4.** Complaint that a specified duty or act of politeness is being omitted: He might at least call. —See Usage note at **may.** [Middle English mighte, from Old English meahte.]

might·i·ly (mī′tə-lē) adv. **1.** In a mighty manner; forcefully; powerfully. **2.** To a great degree; greatly.

might·y (mī′tē) adj. **-i·er, -i·est. 1.** Having or showing great power, strength, or skill: a mighty orator; a mighty blow. **2.** Imposing or awesome in size, degree, or extent: The city stood on a mighty hill. —See Syns at **giant.** —adv. Informal. Very; extremely: a mighty good dinner. —**might′i·ness** n.

mi·gnon·ette (mĭn′yə-nĕt′) n. A plant, Reseda odorata, native to the Mediterranean region but widely cultivated for its clusters of fragrant greenish flowers. [French, dim. of mignon, dainty, small.]

mi·graine (mī′grān′) n. A severe, recurrent headache, usu. affecting only one side of the head. [French, from Old French, from Late Latin hēmicrānia, pain in half of the head, from Greek hēmikrania : hemi-, half + kranion, cranium, head.]

mi·grant (mī′grənt) n. A person, animal, bird, or fish that migrates. —adj. Traveling regularly from one region to another: a migrant worker.

mi·grate (mī′grāt′) intr.v. **-grat·ed, -grat·ing. 1.** To move from one country or region and settle in another. **2.** To move regularly from one region to another, esp. at a particular time of the year. [From Latin migrāre.]

mi·gra·tion (mī-grā′shən) n. **1.** The act of migrating. **2.** A group migrating together. **3.** Chem. The movement of atoms from one position in a molecule to another. —**mi·gra′tion·al** adj.

mi·gra·to·ry (mī′grə-tôr′ē, -tōr′ē) adj. **1.** Migrating regularly: migratory birds. **2.** Of or relating to a migration. **3.** Roving; nomadic.

mi·ka·do (mĭ-kä′dō) n., pl. **-dos.** Often **Mikado.** The emperor of Japan. [Japanese, "exalted gate."]

mike (mīk) n. Informal. A microphone.

mil (mĭl) n. A unit of length equal to one-thousandth (10⁻³) of an inch. [Short for Latin mīllēsimus, thousandth, from mīlle, thousand.]

mi·la·dy (mĭ-lā′dē) n. **1.** My lady. A title of respect used when speaking of or to an English noblewoman or gentlewoman. **2.** A chic or fashionable woman. [French, from English my lady.]

milch (mĭlch) adj. Giving milk: a milch cow. [Middle English milche, from Old English -milce.]

mild (mīld) adj. **-er, -est. 1.** Gentle or kind in disposition, manner, or behavior. **2.** Moderate in type, degree, effect, or force: a mild punishment; a mild fever; a mild climate. **3.** Not sharp, strong, or strong in taste or odor: a mild cheese. —See Syns at **gentle.** [Middle English, from Old English milde.] —**mild′ly** adv. —**mild′ness** n.

mil·dew (mĭl′dōō′, -dyōō′) n. A parasitic fungus that forms a whitish, powdery coating on plant leaves and other organic materials such as paint, cloth, and leather. —tr.v. To affect with mildew. —intr.v. To become affected with mildew. [Middle English, from Old English mildēaw.] —**mil′dew·y** adj.

mile (mīl) n. Abbr. **m., mi. 1.** A unit of length equal to 5,280 feet, 1,760 yards, or 1,609.34 meters. Also called **statute mile. 2.** A nautical mile. [Middle English, from Old English mīl, from Latin mīlia, pl. of mīlle, thousand.]

mile·age (mī′lĭj) *n.* **1.** Total length, extent, or distance measured or expressed in miles. **2.** Total miles covered or traveled in a given time. **3.** The amount of service, use, or wear measured by miles used or traveled: *This tire will give good mileage.* **4.** The number of miles traveled by a motor vehicle on a certain quantity of fuel. **5.** *Informal.* The amount of service something has yielded or may potentially yield; usefulness: *get full mileage out of a typewriter.* **6.** An allowance for travel expenses established at a specified rate per mile. **7.** Expense per mile, as for the use of a rented car.

mile·post (mīl′pōst′) *n.* A post set up to indicate distance in miles, as along a highway.

mil·er (mī′lər) *n.* A person or animal trained to race a mile.

mile·stone (mīl′stōn′) *n.* **1.** A stone marker set up on a roadside to indicate the distance in miles from a given point. **2.** An important event or turning point.

milestone   milkweed

mil·foil (mĭl′foil′) *n.* A yarrow plant. [Middle English, from Old French, from Latin *millefolium*, "thousand-leafed" (from the fine divisions of the leaves).]

mi·lieu (mēl-yœ′) *n.* Environment; surroundings. [French, from Old French, center : *mi*, middle, from Latin *medius* + *lieu*, place, from Latin *locus*.]

mil·i·tant (mĭl′ĭ-tnt) *adj.* **1.** Engaged in combat. **2.** Combative and aggressive, esp. in the service of some cause: *a militant nonsmoker.* —*n.* A militant person. —**mil′i·tan·cy** (mĭl′ĭ-tn-sē) *n.* —**mil′i·tant·ly** *adv.*

mil·i·ta·rism (mĭl′ĭ-tə-rĭz′əm) *n.* **1.** The glorification or exaltation of military sentiments and ideals. **2.** A policy in which military preparedness and efficiency are considered to be of principal importance to the state. —**mil′i·ta·rist** *n.* —**mil′i·ta·ris′tic** *adj.* —**mil′i·ta·ris′ti·cal·ly** *adv.*

mil·i·ta·rize (mĭl′ĭ-tə-rīz′) *tr.v.* **-rized, -riz·ing.** **1.** To equip for or as if for military purposes. **2.** To convert to militarism.

mil·i·tar·y (mĭl′ĭ-tĕr′ē) *adj.* **1.** Of, pertaining to, or characteristic of soldiers, armed forces, or war: *a military bearing.* **2.** Of or pertaining to the army: *military and naval operations.* —*n., pl.* **military** or **-ies.** Armed forces: *ruled by the military.* [French *militaire*, from Latin *mīlitāris*, from *mīles*, soldier.] —**mil′i·tar′i·ly** (-târ′ə-lē) *adv.*

military police. A branch of the armed forces assigned to perform police duties.

mil·i·tate (mĭl′ĭ-tāt′) *intr.v.* **-tat·ed, -tat·ing.** To have force or influence: *evidence that militated against his argument.* [From Latin *mīlitāre*, to serve as a soldier, from *mīles*, soldier.]

mi·li·tia (mĭ-lĭsh′ə) *n.* A military force that is not a part of the regular army and is on call for service in an emergency. [From Latin *mīlitia*, warfare, from *mīles*, soldier.] —**mi·li′tia·man** *n.*

milk (mĭlk) *n.* **1. a.** A whitish liquid that is secreted by the mammary glands of female mammals and is used to nourish their young. **b.** The milk of a domesticated animal, such as a cow, used as food for human beings. **2.** A liquid that resembles milk: *coconut milk.* —**modifier:** *milk glands; milk products.* —*tr.v.* **1.** To draw milk from the breast or udder of. **2.** To draw out or extract from by or as if by milking: *milk a company of its profits.* —*intr.v.* **1.** To yield or supply milk. **2.** To draw milk from a female mammal. [Middle English, from Old English *meolc*.] —**milk′er** *n.*

milk·maid (mĭlk′mād′) *n.* A dairy maid.

milk·man (mĭlk′măn′) *n.* A man who sells or delivers milk to customers.

milk of magnesia. A milky white liquid suspension of magnesium hydroxide, $Mg(OH)_2$, used as an antacid and laxative.

milk shake. A beverage made of milk, flavoring, and usu. ice cream, shaken or whipped until foamy.

milk snake. A nonpoisonous tan or black snake, *Lampropeltis doliata*, of the northeastern United States.

milk·sop (mĭlk′sŏp′) *n.* A boy or man who lacks courage or manliness.

milk sugar. Lactose.

milk tooth. Any of the temporary first teeth of a young mammal.

milk·weed (mĭlk′wēd′) *n.* A plant of the genus *Asclepias*, with milky juice, clusters of fragrant, dull-purple flowers, and pointed pods that split open to release seeds with downy tufts.

milk·y (mĭl′kē) *adj.* **-i·er, -i·est.** **1.** Resembling milk. **2.** Of or containing milk. —**milk′i·ness** *n.*

Milky Way. The galaxy in which the solar system is located, visible as a broad, luminous band that stretches across the night sky.

mill¹ (mĭl) *n.* **1.** A building or establishment equipped with machinery for grinding grain into flour or meal. **2.** A device or mechanism for grinding or crushing. **3.** Any of various machines for treating or processing raw materials. **4.** A building or group of buildings equipped with machinery for processing materials: *a textile mill; a steel mill.* —*tr.v.* **1.** To grind or crush in a mill. **2.** To process in a mill, as by cutting, stamping, or finishing. **3. a.** To produce a raised rim around (a coin). **b.** To groove or flute the rim of (a coin). —*intr.v.* To move around in a confused or disorderly manner: *a crowd milling and pushing to get through the gates.* —**idioms. run of the mill.** Ordinary; commonplace. **through the mill.** Through a difficult experience. [Middle English *mille*, from Old English *mylen*, from Late Latin *molīna*, from Latin *mola*, millstone.]

mill² (mĭl) *n.* A monetary unit equal to $1/1000$ of a U.S. dollar, or one-tenth of a cent. [Short for Latin *mīllēsimus*, thousandth.]

mill·dam (mĭl′dăm′) *n.* **1.** A dam built across a stream to raise the water level so the overflow will have enough force to turn a mill wheel. **2.** A millpond.

mil·len·ni·um (mĭ-lĕn′ē-əm) *n., pl.* **-ums** or **-ni·a** (-ē-ə). **1.** A period of one thousand years. **2.** In the New Testament, the thousand-year reign of Christ on earth. **3.** A period of great joy, prosperity, and peace. [Latin *mīlle*, thousand + *annus*, year.] —**mil·len′ni·al** (-lĕn′ē-əl) *adj.*

mil·le·pede (mĭl′ə-pēd′) *n.* Var. of **millipede.**

mil·le·pore (mĭl′ə-pôr′, -pōr′) *n.* Any of various reef-building corals of the genus *Millepora*, found in tropical waters. [New Latin *Millepora* (genus), "thousand-pored."]

mill·er (mĭl′ər) *n.* **1.** A person who operates or owns a mill, esp. a grain mill. **2.** Any of various moths whose wings are covered with a whitish-gray powder.

mil·let (mĭl′ət) *n.* **1.** Any of several cereal or forage grasses with small seeds. **2.** The seed of a millet. [Middle English *milet*, from Old French, from Latin *milium*.]

milli-. A prefix meaning one-thousandth (10^{-3}): **millimeter.** [French, from Latin *mīlli-*, from *mīlle*, thousand.]

mil·liard (mĭl′yərd, -yärd′, mĭl′ē-ärd′) *n. Brit.* A billion. [French, from Old French *miliart*, from *milion*, million.]

mil·li·bar (mĭl′ə-bär′) *n.* A unit of atmospheric pressure equal to 1000 dynes per square centimeter.

mil·li·gram (mĭl′ĭ-grăm′) *n.* A unit of mass or weight equal to one-thousandth (10^{-3}) of a gram.

mil·li·li·ter (mĭl′ə-lē′tər) *n.* A unit of fluid volume or capacity equal to one-thousandth (10^{-3}) of a liter.

mil·li·me·ter (mĭl′ə-mē′tər) *n. Abbr.* **mm** A unit of length equal to one-thousandth (10^{-3}) of a meter, or 0.0394 inch.

mil·li·ner (mĭl′ə-nər) *n.* A person who makes or sells women's hats. [Alteration of obs. *Milaner*, native of Milan, a seller of fancy goods such as women's finery.]

mil·li·ner·y (mĭl′ə-nĕr′ē) *n.* **1.** Women's hats. **2.** The profession or business of a milliner.

mill·ing (mĭl′ĭng) *n.* **1.** The act or process of grinding, esp.

of grinding grain into flour or meal. **2.** The operation of cutting, shaping, finishing, or working metal, cloth, or any other product manufactured in a mill. **3.** The ridges cut on the edge of a coin.

mil·lion (mĭl′yən) *n., pl.* **million** or **-lions. 1.** The cardinal number, written 1,000,000 or 10⁶, that is equal to the sum of one thousand thousands. **2.** Often **millions.** An indefinitely large number: *She has millions of complaints.* [Middle English *milioun,* from Old French *milion,* from Old Italian *milione,* from *mille,* thousand, from Latin *mīlle.*] **—mil′lion** *adj.*
     Usage: **million.** The plural is either *million* or *millions.* The first is almost invariably found when a specific number precedes: *fifty million Frenchmen. Millions* is used (with *of*) in the sense of an indefinitely large number: *millions of wasted opportunities.*

mil·lion·aire (mĭl′yə-nâr′) *n.* A person whose wealth amounts to a million or more units of currency. [French *millionnaire,* from *million,* million.]

mil·lionth (mĭl′yənth) *n.* **1.** In a set of items arranged to match the natural numbers in a one-to-one correspondence, the item that matches the number one million. **2.** One of one million equal parts of a unit; the fraction writen 1/1,000,000, or .000001, or 10⁻⁶. **—mil′lionth** *adj.*

mil·li·pede or **mil·le·pede** (mĭl′ə-pēd′) *n.* Any crawling, plant-eating arthropod of the class Diplopoda, with long, segmented bodies and legs attached in double pairs to most body segments. [Latin *millepeda,* woodlouse, "thousand-feet."]

mil·li·sec·ond (mĭl′ĭ-sĕk′ənd) *n.* A unit of time equal to one-thousandth (10⁻³) of a second.

mill·race (mĭl′rās′) *n.* **1.** The fast-moving stream of water that drives a mill wheel. **2.** A canal or channel for the water that drives a mill wheel.

mill·stone (mĭl′stōn′) *n.* **1.** One of a pair of large, circular stones used to grind grain. **2.** A heavy burden.

mill·stream (mĭl′strēm′) *n.* **1.** The water in a millrace. **2.** A stream whose flow is used to run a mill.

mi·lord (mĭ-lôrd′) *n.* My Lord. A title of respect used when speaking of or to an English nobleman or gentleman. [French, from English *my lord.*]

milque·toast (mĭlk′tōst′) *n.* A meek, timid person. [After Caspar *Milquetoast,* a character in the newspaper cartoon *The Timid Soul,* by Harold Tucker Webster (1885–1952), from *milk toast,* a bland dish of hot buttered toast in warm milk.]

milt (mĭlt) *n.* The sperm and seminal fluid of fishes. [Prob. from Middle Dutch *milte,* milt, spleen.]

mime (mīm) *n.* **1.** An actor. **2. a.** Acting by means of gestures and movements without speech; pantomime. **b.** An actor in pantomime. *—v.* **mimed, mim·ing.** *—tr.v.* **1.** To imitate; mimic. **2.** To portray or act by means of pantomime. *—intr.v.* To act a part in pantomime. [Latin *mīmus,* from Greek *mimos,* imitator.] **—mim′er** *n.*

mim·e·o·graph (mĭm′ē-ə-grăf′) *n.* A machine that makes copies of written or typed material from a stencil. *—tr.v.* To make (a copy of) on a mimeograph. [From *Mimeograph,* a trademark.]

mi·me·sis (mĭ-mē′sĭs, mī-) *n.* **1.** The imitation or representation of nature, esp. in art and literature. **2.** The appearance, often due to hysteria, of symptoms of a disease not actually present. [Greek *mimēsis,* from *mimeisthai,* to imitate, from *mimos,* imitator.]

mi·met·ic (mĭ-mĕt′ĭk, mī-) *adj.* **1.** Pertaining to, marked by, or showing mimicry. **2.** Of or pertaining to imitation; imitative. [Greek *mimētikos,* from *mimeisthai,* to imitate.] **—mi·met′i·cal·ly** *adv.*

mim·ic (mĭm′ĭk) *tr.v.* **-icked, -ick·ing. 1.** To copy or imitate closely, as in speech, expression, or gesture; to ape. **2.** To ridicule by imitating; mock: *mimicked their Boston accent.* **3.** To take on or assume the appearance of. **4.** To resemble closely: *an insect mimicking a twig.* —See Syns at **imitate.** *—n.* **1.** Someone who mimics, esp. a mime. **2.** Something that copies or imitates. *—adj.* **1.** Characterized by imitation; make-believe; mock: *a mimic quarrel.* **2.** Of, pertaining to, or characteristic of a mimic or mimicry. [Latin *mīmicus,* imitative, from Greek *mimikos,* from *mimos,* imitator.]

mim·ic·ry (mĭm′ĭ-krē) *n., pl.* **-ries. 1. a.** The act, practice, or art of mimicking. **b.** An example of mimicking. **2.** *Biol.* A resemblance of one organism to another or to a natural object, usu. serving to conceal or protect.

mi·mo·sa (mĭ-mō′sə, -zə) *n.* Any of various mostly tropical shrubs or trees of the genus *Mimosa,* with featherlike leaves and ball-like clusters of small flowers. [From Latin *mīmus,* mime, from its imitation of animal sensitivity.]

mi·na¹ (mī′nə) *n., pl.* **-nas** or **-nae** (-nē). An ancient unit of weight or money. [Latin, from Greek *mna.*]

mi·na² (mī′nə) *n.* Var. of **myna.**

min·a·ret (mĭn′ə-rĕt′) *n.* A tall, slender tower on a mosque, with a balcony from which a muezzin summons the people to prayer. [French, from Spanish *minarete,* from Turkish *minâret,* from Arabic *manârat,* lamp.]

min·a·to·ry (mĭn′ə-tôr′ē, -tōr′ē) *adj.* Also **min·a·to·ri·al** (-tôr′-ē-əl, -tōr′-). Of a menacing nature; threatening. [French *minatoire,* from Late Latin *minātōrius,* from Latin *minārī,* to menace.] **—min′a·to′ri·ly** *adv.*

mince (mĭns) *v.* **minced, minc·ing.** *—tr.v.* **1.** To cut or chop into very small pieces. **2.** To say or pronounce in an affected way. **3.** To refrain from the forthright and plain use of: *Let's not mince words; the man is a liar.* *—intr.v.* To walk with very short steps in a prim or affected manner. *—n.* Finely chopped food, esp. mincemeat. [Middle English *mincen,* from Old French *mincier,* to diminish, from Late Latin *minūtia,* minutia, from Latin *minuere,* to diminish.] **—minc′er** *n.*

mince·meat (mĭns′mēt′) *n.* **1.** *Obs.* Finely chopped meat. **2.** A mixture of finely chopped apples, spices, and sometimes meat, used esp. as a pie filling. **—idiom. make mincemeat of.** *Slang.* To ruin or destroy completely.

minc·ing (mĭn′sĭng) *adj.* Affectedly refined or dainty. **—minc′ing·ly** *adv.*

mind (mīnd) *n.* **1.** The element or elements in an individual governing reason, thought, perception, feeling, will, memory, and imagination. **2.** The power to think and reason; intellect; intelligence. **3.** Attention: *keeping his mind on his job.* **4.** The scope of remembrance; memory; recall: *the strangest coincidence within the mind of man.* **5.** Position or point of view; opinion: *change one's mind.* **6.** Desire; purpose: *had half a mind not to go.* **7.** Imagination: *a sickness that was all in the mind.* **8.** A healthy mental condition; sanity: *lose one's mind.* **9.** A person considered with respect to intellect or intelligence: *Newton, one of the greatest minds of science.* *—tr.v.* **1.** To become aware of; perceive; notice. **2.** To obey: *The children minded their mother.* **3.** To make sure: *Mind you drive slowly.* **4.** To attend to; heed: *Mind what I tell you.* **5.** To be careful about; watch out for: *Mind how you swing that ax.* **6.** To object to; dislike: *She didn't mind the noise.* **7.** To take care or take charge of; look after: *said she's mind the baby.* *—intr.v.* **1.** To take notice; give heed: *I'm still going to do it, mind you.* **2.** To behave obediently: *a dog that minds.* **3.** To be concerned; care: *Will she mind if I come?* **4.** To be cautious or careful: *Mind closely or you'll slip.* —See Syns at **obey. —idioms. of one mind.** In agreement. **on (one's) mind.** Troubling one's thoughts. **out of (one's) mind. 1.** Insane. **2.** Frantic; wild. [Middle English *minde,* from Old English *gemynd,* memory, mind.]

mind·ed (mīn′dĭd) *adj.* **1.** Disposed; inclined: *He can be charming when so minded.* **2.** Having a particular kind of mind: *strong-minded.*

mind·ful (mīnd′fəl) *adj.* Aware; heedful. —See Syns at **aware. —mind′ful·ly** *adv.* **—mind′ful·ness** *n.*

mind·less (mīnd′lĭs) *adj.* **1.** Lacking intelligence, sense, or purpose: *mindless humor.* **2.** Giving or showing little attention or care: *They went on, mindless of the dangers.* **—mind′less·ly** *adv.* **—mind′less·ness** *n.*

mind reading. The supposed faculty of perceiving another's thoughts by means other than normal communication; telepathy. **—mind reader.**

mine¹ (mīn) *n.* **1. a.** An excavation or pit in the earth for the purpose of extracting minerals. **b.** The site of such an excavation, with its surface buildings, elevator shafts, and equipment. **2.** A deposit of ore or minerals. **3.** An abundant source: *a mine of information.* **4.** *Mil.* **a.** A tunnel dug under an enemy position or fortification. **b.** An explosive device, either buried in the ground or floating in the water, detonated by contact or by a time fuse. *—v.* **mined,**

min·ing. —*tr.v.* **1. a.** To extract from a mine. **b.** To dig a mine into to get ores or minerals. **2.** To make (a tunnel) by digging; dig under. **3.** *Mil.* To lay explosive mines in: *mine a shipping channel.* **4.** To attack, damage, or destroy by devious or gradual means; undermine; subvert. **5.** To search as if by digging: *mine the archives for detailed information.* —*intr.v.* **1.** To work in a mine. **2.** To dig a tunnel under an enemy position or fortification. **3.** To lay explosive mines. [Middle English, from Old French.] —**min′a·ble** or **mine′a·ble** *adj.*

mine² (mĭn) *pron.* Used to indicate the one or ones belonging to me: *If you can't find your hat, take mine. The green boots are mine.* [Middle English *min,* from Old English *mīn.*]

mine detector. An electromagnetic device used to locate explosive mines.

mine·field (mĭn′fēld′) *n.* An area in which explosive mines have been placed.

min·er (mĭ′nər) *n.* Someone who works in a mine.

min·er·al (mĭn′ər-əl) *n.* **1.** Any natural inorganic substance with a definite chemical composition and characteristic physical structure. **2.** Any substance, such as granite or other rock, composed of a mixture of minerals. **3.** Any substance, such as coal or petroleum, that is obtained usu. from the ground. **4. a.** An element, such as gold or silver, that is found uncombined in nature. **b.** An ore of a metal. **5. a.** Any substance that is neither animal nor vegetable. **b.** Inorganic matter. —*modifier:* *mineral deposits.* [Middle English, from Medieval Latin *minerāle,* from Old French *miniere,* from *mine,* mine.]

min·er·al·ize (mĭn′ər-ə-līz′) *tr.v.* **-ized, -iz·ing. 1.** To convert to a mineral substance; petrify. **2.** To transform a metal into an ore. **3.** To supply or impregnate with minerals. —**min′er·al·i·za′tion** *n.*

min·er·al·o·gist (mĭn′ə-rŏl′ə-jĭst, -răl′-) *n.* An expert or specialist in the study of minerals.

min·er·al·o·gy (mĭn′ə-rŏl′ə-jē, -răl′-) *n.* The scientific study of minerals, their characteristics, and their classification. —**min′er·a·log′i·cal** (mĭn′ər-ə-lŏj′ĭ-kəl) *adj.* —**min′er·a·log′i·cal·ly** *adv.*

mineral oil. 1. Any of various oils of mineral origin. **2.** A refined oil distilled from petroleum, used esp. as a laxative.

mineral water. Water that contains dissolved minerals or gases.

mineral wool. A fibrous material produced from glass, rock, or slag and used as a heat or sound insulator.

Mi·ner·va (mĭ-nûr′və) *n. Rom. Myth.* The goddess of wisdom, the arts, and warfare, identified with the Greek Athena.

min·e·stro·ne (mĭn′ĭ-strō′nē) *n.* A thick soup that contains beans, pasta, and assorted vegetables. [Italian, from *minestrare,* to serve, dish out, from Latin *ministrāre,* to serve, from *minister,* servant, minister.]

mine sweeper. A ship equipped for detecting, removing, or neutralizing explosive mines.

min·gle (mĭng′gəl) *v.* **-gled, -gling.** —*tr.v.* To mix or bring together; combine: *mingle laughter and tears.* —*intr.v.* **1.** To be or become mixed or united. **2.** To join in; associate with others: *mingled with the visitors.* [Middle English *menglen,* freq. of *mengen,* to mix, from Old English *mengan.*] —**min′gler** *n.*

mini-. A prefix meaning miniature: *miniskirt.* [From MINIATURE.]

min·i·a·ture (mĭn′ē-ə-chŏŏr′, mĭn′ə-, -chər) *n.* **1.** A copy or model of something in a greatly reduced size. **2. a.** A very small painting or portrait. **b.** A small portrait, picture, or decorative letter on an illuminated manuscript. **c.** The art of painting miniatures. —*adj.* Very small; greatly reduced in size or scale. [Italian *miniatura,* painting (esp. the miniature illuminations in medieval manuscripts), from *miniare,* to illuminate, from Latin *miniāre,* to color with red lead, from *minium,* red lead.]

min·i·a·tur·ize (mĭn′ē-ə-chə-rīz′, mĭn′ə-chə-rīz′) *tr.v.* **-ized, -iz·ing.** To plan or make in a very small size. —**min′i·a·tur·i·za′tion** *n.*

min·im (mĭn′əm) *n.* **1.** *Abbr.* **M.** A unit of fluid measure equal to ¹⁄₆₀ of a fluid dram. **2.** Something very small. [From Medieval Latin *minimus,* least, from Latin.]

min·i·ma (mĭn′ə-mə) *n.* A plural of **minimum.**

min·i·mal (mĭn′ə-məl) *adj.* Least in amount or degree. —**min′i·mal·ly** *adv.*

min·i·mize (mĭn′ə-mīz′) *tr.v.* **-mized, -miz·ing. 1.** To reduce to the smallest possible amount, extent, size, or degree: *insulation that minimized heat loss.* **2.** To speak or write about as having the least degree of importance or value; depreciate: *The report minimized his achievement.*

min·i·mum (mĭn′ə-məm) *n., pl.* **-mums** or **-ma** (-mə). **1.** The smallest quantity or degree possible or allowable: *kept his expenses to a minimum.* **2.** The lowest quantity, degree, or number reached or recorded: *a temperature minimum of 70°.* —*adj.* **1.** Representing the least possible or allowed: *made a minimum number of mistakes.* **2.** Representing the lowest amount or degree reached or recorded: *the minimum rainfall.* [Latin, from *minimus,* least, superl. of *minor,* minor.]

minimum wage. The lowest wage, set by law or contract, that can be paid for a specified job.

min·ing (mī′nĭng) *n.* The process or business of extracting coal, minerals, or ore from a mine.

min·ion (mĭn′yən) *n.* **1.** A person who is esteemed; a favorite. **2.** A usu. servile follower or dependent. **3.** A subordinate official. [French *mignon,* darling, from Old High German *minna,* love.]

min·i·skirt (mĭn′ē-skûrt′) *n.* An extremely short skirt.

min·is·ter (mĭn′ĭ-stər) *n.* **1.** A person authorized to perform religious functions in a church, esp. a Protestant church; a member of the clergy. **2.** A person at the head of a governmental department. **3.** A person ranking below an ambassador and authorized to represent his government in diplomatic dealings with other governments. **4.** A person who serves as an agent for another. —*intr.v.* To give assistance and attention: *minister to the homeless.* [Middle English *ministre,* from Old French, from Latin *minister,* attendant, servant.]

min·is·te·ri·al (mĭn′ĭ-stîr′ē-əl) *adj.* **1.** Of, pertaining to, or characteristic of a minister or ministry. **2.** Acting or serving as an agent. —**min′is·te′ri·al·ly** *adv.*

min·is·trant (mĭn′ĭ-strənt) *adj.* Serving as a minister. —**min′is·trant** *n.*

min·is·tra·tion (mĭn′ĭ-strā′shən) *n.* **1.** The act of serving or aiding. **2.** The act of performing the duties of a minister of religion. —**min′is·tra′tive** *adj.*

min·is·try (mĭn′ĭ-strē) *n., pl.* **-tries. 1.** The act of serving; ministration. **2. a.** The profession, duties, and services of a minister of religion. **b.** Ministers of religion in general; the clergy. **c.** The term of service of a minister of religion. **3. a.** A governmental department headed by a minister. **b.** The building in which such a department is housed. **c.** The position, duties, or term of office of a government minister. **d.** Often **Ministry.** A body of ministers who govern a nation or state.

min·i·um (mĭn′ē-əm) *n. Chem.* **Red lead.** [Latin.]

min·i·ver (mĭn′ə-vər) *n.* A white or light-gray fur used orig. as a trim on medieval robes and now used as trim on ceremonial robes of state. [Middle English *meniver,* from Old French *menu vair,* small vair (a kind of fur) : *menu,* small, from Latin *minūtus* + *vair,* variegated fur, from Latin *varius,* varied.]

mink (mĭngk) *n., pl.* **mink** or **minks. 1.** Any weasellike semiaquatic mammal of the genus *Mustela,* esp. *M. vison,* with short ears, a pointed snout, short legs, and partly webbed toes. **2.** The soft, thick, lustrous fur of the mink. [Middle English *mynk,* of Scandinavian orig.]

mink

min·ne·sing·er (mĭn′ĭ-sĭng′er) *n.* One of a class of lyric poets and musicians active in Germany in the 12th to 14th cent. [German *Minnesinger* : *Minne*, love + *Singer*, singer.

min·now (mĭn'ō) *n., pl.* **minnow** or **-nows.** Any of several small, freshwater fishes of the family Cyprinidae. [Middle English *menawe*, from Old English *mynwe*.]

Mi·no·an (mĭ-nō'ən) *adj.* Of or pertaining to the Bronze Age culture that flourished in Crete from about 3000 to 1100 B.C. [From Latin *Mīnōus*, of Minos, a city in Crete.]

mi·nor (mī'nər) *adj.* **1.** Smaller in amount, size, or extent: *minor expenses; minor alterations.* **2.** Lesser in importance or rank: *a minor official.* **3.** Lesser in seriousness or danger: *a minor injury.* **4.** Not of legal age: *a minor child.* **5.** *Mus.* **a.** Designating a minor scale. **b.** Less by a half step than the corresponding major interval: *a minor third; a minor sixth.* **c.** Based on a minor scale: *a minor key.* —*n.* **1.** A person who has not yet reached legal age. **2. a.** A secondary area of specialized academic study. **b.** A student studying a minor: *a chemistry minor.* **3.** *Mus.* A minor key, scale, or interval. **4.** *Sports.* **the minors.** The minor leagues of a sport as a group. —*intr.v.* To pursue academic studies in a minor field: *minor in Spanish.* [Middle English, from Latin, less.]

mi·nor·i·ty (mĭ-nôr'ĭ-tē, -nŏr'-, mī-) *n., pl.* **-ties. 1.** The smaller in number of two groups forming a whole. **2.** A group that differs, as in race, religion, or ethnic background, from the larger group of which it is a part. **3.** The condition or period of being under legal age. —*modifier: minority groups; a minority vote.*

minority leader. The leader of the minority party in a legislative body.

minor league. Any league of professional sports clubs other than the major leagues. —*modifier* (**minor-league**): *a minor-league club.*

minor scale. *Mus.* A scale in which the third, sixth, and seventh steps are lower by a semitone than the corresponding steps in a major scale.

min·ster (mĭn'stər) *n. Brit.* A large, important church or cathedral. [Middle English, from Old English *mynster*, from Late Latin *monastērium*, monastery.]

min·strel (mĭn'strəl) *n.* **1.** A medieval traveling musician who sang and recited poetry. **2. a.** A poet. **b.** A musician. **3.** A performer in a minstrel show. [Middle English *ministral*, from Old French *menestral*, entertainer, servant, from Late Latin *ministeriālis*, household officer, from Latin *ministerium*, ministry.]

minstrel show. A variety show, formerly popular in the United States, in which performers, often in blackface, sing, dance, tell jokes, and perform comic skits.

min·strel·sy (mĭn'strəl-sē) *n., pl.* **-sies. 1.** The art or profession of a minstrel. **2.** A group of minstrels. **3.** The ballads and lyrics sung by minstrels.

mint¹ (mĭnt) *n.* **1.** A place where the money of a country is coined by authority of the government. **2.** *Informal.* A large amount, esp. of money: *He is worth a mint.* **3.** Anything that may be used as a source of money or ideas: *a mint of useful thoughts.* —*tr.v.* **1.** To produce (money) by stamping metal; to coin. **2.** To invent or fabricate; make up: *mint phrases.* —*adj.* In original condition; freshly minted or made; unused: *dimes in mint condition.* [Middle English *mynt*, from Old English *mynet*, money, from Latin *monēta*, money, mint, from *Monēta*, epithet of Juno, whose palace housed the mint in ancient Rome.]

mint² (mĭnt) *n.* **1.** Any of various plants, as the peppermint or spearmint, that belong to the genus *Mentha* and are the source of an aromatic oil used for flavoring. **2.** A candy flavored with mint. [Middle English *minte*, from Old English *minte*, from Latin *menta, mentha*, from Greek *minthē*.] —**mint'y** *adj.*

mint·age (mĭn'tĭj) *n.* **1.** The act or process of minting coins. **2.** Money manufactured in a mint.

mint julep. A drink made of bourbon whiskey, sugar, crushed mint leaves, and shaved ice.

min·u·end (mĭn'yo͞o-ĕnd') *n.* A number from which another number is to be subtracted. [Latin *minuendum*, something to be diminished, from *minuendus*, to be diminished, from *minuere*, to lessen.]

min·u·et (mĭn'yo͞o-ĕt') *n.* **1.** A slow, stately dance that originated in 17th-cent. France. **2.** Music for or in the rhythm of a minuet. [French, from obs. *menuet*, dainty, small,

from Old French *menu*, small, from Latin *minūtus*, small, minute.]

mi·nus (mī'nəs) *prep.* **1.** *Math.* Reduced by; less: *Seven minus four equals three.* **2.** *Informal.* Lacking; deprived of; without. —*adj.* **1.** *Math.* Less than zero; negative: *a minus value.* **2.** Slightly lower or less than a specified norm: *a grade of B minus.* —*n.* **1.** The **minus sign.** **2.** A negative number or quantity. **3.** A deficiency; disadvantage. [Middle English *mynus*, from Latin *minus*, less, from *minor*, less, minor.]

min·us·cule (mĭn'ə-sky o͞ol', mĭ-nŭs'ky o͞ol') *adj.* Very small; minute. [French, from Latin *minuscula (littera)*, minuscule (letter), from *minusculus*, less, from *minor*, less.]

minus sign. *Math.* The symbol (−), as in $4 - 2 = 2$, used to indicate subtraction or a negative quantity.

min·ute¹ (mĭn'ĭt) *n.* **1. a.** A unit of time equal to one-sixtieth of an hour, or to 60 seconds. **b.** A unit of angular measurement equal to one-sixtieth of a degree. **2.** Any short interval of time; a moment: *Wait a minute.* **3.** A specific point in time: *leaving this very minute.* **4. minutes.** An official record of the proceedings at a meeting. —See Syns at **moment.** [Middle English, from Old French, from Medieval Latin *minūta*, minute, from Late Latin, from *minūtus*, small.]

mi·nute² (mī-no͞ot', -nyo͞ot', mĭ-) *adj.* **1.** Exceptionally small; tiny. **2.** Insignificant; trifling. **3.** Characterized by close or careful attention to detail: *a minute inspection.* [Latin *minūtus*, small, from *minuere*, to lessen.]

min·ute·man or **Min·ute·man** (mĭn'ĭt-măn') *n.* A Revolutionary War militiaman ready to fight on a minute's notice.

mi·nu·ti·a (mĭ-no͞o'shē-ə, -nyo͞o'-, -shə) *n., pl.* **-ti·ae** (-shē-ē'). A small or trivial detail: *overwhelmed with minutiae.* [Latin *minūtia*, smallness, from *minūtus*, small, minute.]

minx (mĭngks) *n.* An impudent or flirtatious girl. [Low German *minsk*, hussy.]

Mi·o·cene (mī'ə-sēn') *n.* **1.** Also **Miocene epoch.** The fourth epoch of the Tertiary period, characterized by the appearance of whales, grazing animals, and primitive apes. **2.** The rock system of the Miocene epoch. —*modifier: a Miocene fossil.* [Greek *meiōn*, less + -CENE.]

mir·a·cle (mĭr'ə-kəl) *n.* **1.** An extraordinary or unusual event that is considered to be a manifestation of divine or supernatural power. **2.** Someone or something that excites admiration, awe, or wonder: *the miracles of modern science.* **3.** A **miracle play.** [Middle English, from Old French, from Latin *mīrāculum*, from *mīrārī*, to wonder at, from *mīrus*, wonderful.]

miracle play. A religious drama of the Middle Ages based on the lives of saints or martyrs who performed miracles.

mi·rac·u·lous (mĭ-răk'yə-ləs) *adj.* **1.** Of the nature of a miracle. **2.** Caused by or as if by a miracle: *a miraculous cure.* **3.** Having the power to work miracles: *a miraculous drug.* **4.** So unusual as to elicit disbelief: *a miraculous recovery.* —See Syns at **fabulous.** [Old French *miraculeux*, from Medieval Latin *mīrāculōsus*, from Latin *mīrāculum*, miracle.] —**mi·rac'u·lous·ly** *adv.* —**mi·rac'u·lous·ness** *n.*

mi·rage (mĭ-räzh') *n.* **1.** An optical illusion, as nonexistent bodies of water or inverted reflections of distant objects, caused by distortions that occur as light passes between alternate layers of hot and cool air. **2.** Something that is illusory or insubstantial like a mirage. [French, from *mirer*, to look at, from Latin *mīrārī*, to wonder at, from *mīrus*, wonderful.]

mire (mīr) *n.* **1.** An area of wet, soggy, and muddy ground; a bog. **2.** Deep, slimy soil or mud. —*v.* **mired, mir·ing.** —*tr.v.* **1.** To cause to sink or become stuck in mire. **2.** To soil with mud. **3.** To trap or entangle as if in mire. —*intr.v.* To sink or become stuck in mire. [Middle English, from Old Norse *mȳrr*, a bog.]

mir·ror (mĭr'ər) *n.* **1.** Any surface, as a piece of glass backed with silver or highly polished metal, that is capable of reflecting enough light without scattering it so that it forms an image. **2.** Anything that reflects or gives a true picture. —*tr.v.* To reflect in or as if in a mirror. [Middle English *mirour*, from Old French *mirour*, from *mirer*, to look at, from Latin *mīrārī*, to wonder at, from *mīrus*, wonderful.]

mirth (mûrth) *n.* Gaiety; merriment. —See Syns at **gaiety.** [Middle English *mirthe*, from Old English *myrgth*.]

| ă pat | ā pay | â care | ä father | ĕ pet | ē be | hw which | ĭ pit | ī tie | î pier | ŏ pot | ō toe | ô paw, for | oi noise |
| o͞o took | o͞o boot | ou out | th thin | th this | ŭ cut | | û urge | zh vision | ə about, item, edible, gallop, circus | | | | |

mirth·ful (mûrth′fəl) *adj.* Full of mirth; merry; gay. **—mirth′ful·ly** *adv.* **—mirth′ful·ness** *n.*

mis-. A prefix meaning: **1.** Wrong or wrongly: **misspell. 2.** Improper or improperly: **misdeed, misbehave. 3.** Lack of: **mistrust. 4.** Failure: **misfire.** [Middle English, from Old English.]

mis·ad·ven·ture (mĭs′əd-vĕn′chər) *n.* A misfortune; mishap. [Middle English *misaventure*, from Old French *mesaventure*, from *mesavenir*, to result in misfortune : *mes-*, badly + *avenir*, to turn out, from Latin *advenīre*, to come to.]

mis·al·li·ance (mĭs′ə-lī′əns) *n.* An unsuitable alliance, esp. in marriage. [French *mésalliance* : *més-*, improper + *alliance*, alliance.]

mis·an·thrope (mĭs′ən-thrōp′, mĭz′-) *n.* A person who hates or distrusts mankind. [Greek *misanthrōpos*, hating mankind : *misein*, to hate + *anthrōpos*, human being.]

mis·an·thro·py (mĭ-săn′thrə-pē, -zăn′-) *n.* Hatred or distrust of mankind.

mis·ap·ply (mĭs′ə-plī′) *tr.v.* **-plied, -ply·ing.** To use or apply wrongly. **—mis·ap′pli·ca′tion** *n.*

mis·ap·pre·hend (mĭs-ăp′rĭ-hĕnd′) *tr.v.* To misunderstand. **—mis·ap′pre·hen′sion** *n.*

mis·ap·pro·pri·ate (mĭs′ə-prō′prē-āt′) *tr.v.* **-at·ed, -at·ing.** To appropriate or take wrongly for one's own use.

mis·be·got·ten (mĭs′bĭ-gŏt′n) *adj.* Also **mis·be·got** (-bĭ-gŏt′). Illicitly or abnormally begotten; illegitimate.

mis·be·have (mĭs′bĭ-hāv′) *intr.v.* **-haved, -hav·ing.** To behave badly. **—mis′be·hav′ior** *n.*

mis·be·lief (mĭs′bĭ-lēf′) *n.* **1.** A false or erroneous belief. **2.** A false or unorthodox religious belief.

mis·cal·cu·late (mĭs-kăl′kyə-lāt′) *v.* **-lat·ed, -lat·ing.** *—tr.v.* To calculate wrongly; misjudge. *—intr.v.* To make an error in calculation. **—mis·cal′cu·la′tion** *n.*

mis·call (mĭs-kôl′) *tr.v.* To call by a wrong name.

mis·car·riage (mĭs-kăr′ĭj) *n.* **1.** Failure to attain the proper or desired result, usu. because of mismanagement: *a miscarriage of justice.* **2.** The accidental expulsion of a fetus from the uterus before it has developed enough to survive.

mis·car·ry (mĭs-kăr′ē) *intr.v.* **-ried, -ry·ing. 1.** To go astray; be lost in transit: *The letter miscarried.* **2.** To fail to achieve a goal or purpose: *Our plan miscarried because of bad timing.* **3.** To have a miscarriage.

mis·cast (mĭs-kăst′) *tr.v.* **-cast, -cast·ing.** To cast in an unsuitable role.

mis·ce·ge·na·tion (mĭs′ĭ-jə-nā′shən, mĭ-sĕj′ə-) *n.* Marriage, cohabitation, or interbreeding between persons of different races. [Latin *miscēre*, to mix + *genus*, race.]

mis·cel·la·ne·ous (mĭs′ə-lā′nē-əs) *adj.* **1.** Made up of many different parts or elements: *a miscellaneous assortment of chocolates.* **2.** Having a variety of characteristics or traits. **3.** Concerned with many unrelated subjects or topics. [Latin *miscellāneus*, from *miscellus*, mixed, from *miscēre*, to mix.] **—mis′cel·la′ne·ous·ly** *adv.*

mis·cel·la·ny (mĭs′ə-lā′nē; *Brit.* mĭ-sĕl′ə-nē) *n., pl.* **-nies. 1.** A collection of various items, parts, or elements. **2. miscellanies.** A collection of literary works. [Latin *miscellānea*, from *miscellus*, mixed, from *miscere*, to mix.]

mis·chance (mĭs-chăns′) *n.* **1.** Bad luck. **2.** An instance of bad luck.

mis·chief (mĭs′chĭf) *n.* **1.** An action that causes irritation or petty annoyance. **2.** Someone that causes minor trouble or vexation: *The child was a mischief in school.* **3.** Evil or harm caused by a specific person or thing: *His interference caused irremediable mischief.* **4.** The condition or quality of being mischievous: *a child who was full of mischief.* [Middle English *meschief*, from Old French *meschief*, from *meschever*, to meet with misfortune : *mes-*, ill + *chever*, to happen.]

mis·chie·vous (mĭs′chə-vəs) *adj.* **1.** Inclined to or characterized by behavior that causes vexation and annoyance: *a mischievous little imp.* **2.** Showing a tendency to irritating or troublesome behavior: *a mischievous smile.* **3.** Causing petty irritation or trouble: *a mischievous prank.* **4.** Causing harm, injury, or damage: *a mischievous lie.* **—mis′chie·vous·ly** *adv.* **—mis′chie·vous·ness** *n.*

mis·ci·ble (mĭs′ə-bəl) *adj. Chem.* Capable of being mixed in all proportions: *Water and alcohol are miscible.* [Medieval Latin *miscībilis*, from Latin *miscēre*, to mix.] **—mis′ci·bil′i·ty** *n.*

mis·con·ceive (mĭs′kən-sēv′) *tr.v.* **-ceived, -ceiv·ing.** To interpret or judge incorrectly. **—mis′con·ceiv′er** *n.* **—mis′con·cep′tion** *n.*

mis·con·duct (mĭs-kŏn′dŭkt′) *n.* **1.** Improper conduct or behavior. **2.** Dishonest or bad management. *—tr.v.* (mĭs′kən-dŭkt′). **1.** To behave improperly. **2.** To manage poorly or dishonestly.

mis·con·struc·tion (mĭs′kən-strŭk′shən) *n.* An inaccurate or wrong interpretation.

mis·con·strue (mĭs′kən-strōō′) *tr.v.* **-strued, -stru·ing.** To mistake the meaning of; misinterpret.

mis·count (mĭs-kount′) *tr.v.* To count incorrectly. *—intr.v.* To make an error in counting. *—n.* (mĭs′kount′). An inaccurate count.

mis·cre·ant (mĭs′krē-ənt) *n.* A person who behaves badly or criminally. [Middle English *miscreaunt*, heretical, unbelieving, from Old French *mescreant*, pres. part. of *mescroire*, to disbelieve : *mes-*, amiss + *croire*, to believe, from Latin *crēdere*.] **—mis′cre·ant** *adj.*

mis·cue (mĭs-kyōō′) *n.* **1.** In billiards, a stroke that misses or just brushes the ball due to a slip of the cue. **2.** A blunder or mistake. —See Syns at **error.** *—intr.v.* **-cued, -cu·ing. 1.** To make a miscue. **2.** To miss or mistake a stage cue.

mis·deal (mĭs-dēl′) *v.* **-dealt** (-dĕlt′), **-deal·ing.** *—tr.v.* To deal (playing cards) in the wrong order or improperly. *—intr.v.* To deal cards improperly. **—mis′deal′** *n.*

mis·deed (mĭs-dēd′) *n.* An improper, immoral, or illegal act.

mis·de·mean·or (mĭs′dĭ-mē′nər) *n.* **1.** *Archaic.* Misbehavior. **2.** *Law.* An offense of less seriousness than a felony.

mis·di·rect (mĭs′dĭ-rĕkt′, -dī-) *tr.v.* To direct incorrectly.

mis·do (mĭs-dōō′) *tr.v.* **-did** (-dĭd′), **-done** (-dŭn′), **-do·ing.** To do wrongly or improperly. **—mis·do′er** *n.*

mis·doubt (mĭs-dout′) *tr.v.* To suspect; fear; distrust. *—n.* A suspicion or doubt.

mis·em·ploy (mĭs′ĕm-ploi′) *tr.v.* To put to a wrong use; abuse. **—mis′em·ploy′ment** *n.*

mi·ser (mī′zər) *n.* A grasping, avaricious person, esp. one who lives meanly in order to hoard money. [Latin, wretched, unfortunate.]

mis·er·a·ble (mĭz′ər-ə-bəl, mĭz′rə-bəl) *adj.* **1.** Very unhappy; wretched: *He made my life miserable.* **2.** Causing distress or discomfort: *a miserable climate.* **3.** Mean; shameful: *That was a miserable trick to play on her.* **4.** Wretchedly poor; squalid: *raised in a miserable shack.* **5.** Of poor quality; inferior: *a miserable movie.* [Middle English, from Old French, from Latin *miserābilis*, pitiable, from *miserārī*, to have pity, from *miser*, wretched, unfortunate.] **—mis′er·a·ble·ness** *n.* **—mis′er·a·bly** *adv.*

mi·ser·ly (mī′zər-lē) *adj.* Characteristic of a miser; stingy. —See Syns at **stingy.** **—mi′ser·li·ness** *n.*

mis·er·y (mĭz′ə-rē) *n., pl.* **-ies. 1.** A condition of great, often prolonged mental or physical suffering as a result of unhappiness, pain, or extreme poverty. **2.** A cause or source of suffering or pain. —See Syns at **distress.** [Middle English *miserie*, from Norman French, from Latin *miseria*, from *miser*, wretched.]

mis·file (mĭs-fīl′) *tr.v.* **-filed, fil·ing.** To file incorrectly or inappropriately.

mis·fire (mĭs-fīr′) *intr.v.* **-fired, -fir·ing. 1.** To fail to fire, explode, or ignite at the proper time. **2.** To fail to achieve an intended result: *a plan that misfired.* **—mis′fire′** *n.*

mis·fit (mĭs′fĭt′, mĭs-fĭt′) *n.* **1.** Something that does not fit properly. **2.** A person who is poorly adjusted to his environment.

mis·for·tune (mĭs-fôr′chən) *n.* **1.** Bad fortune or ill luck. **2.** An unfortunate occurrence.

mis·give (mĭs-gĭv′) *v.* **-gave** (-gāv′), **-giv·en** (-gĭv′ən), **-giv·ing.** *—tr.v.* To cause fear or suspicion in. *—intr.v.* To be apprehensive or doubtful. [MIS- + *obs. give*, to suggest.]

mis·giv·ing (mĭs-gĭv′ĭng) *n.* A feeling of doubt or suspicion. —See Syns at **qualm.**

mis·gov·ern (mĭs-gŭv′ərn) *tr.v.* To govern or rule badly. **—mis·gov′ern·ment** *n.*

mis·guide (mĭs-gīd′) *tr.v.* **-guid·ed, -guid·ing.** To direct or guide wrongly; lead astray. **—mis·guid′ance** *n.* **—mis·guid′er** *n.*

ă pat	ā pay	â care	ä father	ĕ pet	ē be	hw which	ĭ pit	ī tie	î pier	ŏ pot	ō toe	ô paw, for	oi noise
ōō took	ōō boot	ou out	th thin	th this	ŭ cut		û urge	zh vision	ə about, item, edible, gallop, circus

mis·guid·ed (mĭs-gī'dĭd) *adj.* Characterized or guided by mistaken beliefs or principles. —**mis·guid'ed·ly** *adv.*

mis·han·dle (mĭs-hăn'dl) *tr.v.* **-dled, -dling. 1.** To treat roughly. **2.** To deal with or manage badly. —See Syns at **botch.**

mis·hap (mĭs'hăp', mĭs-hăp') *n.* An unfortunate accident; bad luck.

mis·hear (mĭs-hîr') *tr.v.* **-heard** (-hûrd'), **-hear·ing.** To hear incorrectly.

mish-mash (mĭsh'măsh') *n.* A confused mixture; hodgepodge. [From MASH.]

Mish·nah (mĭsh'nə) *n.* Also **Mish·na.** The first section of the Talmud that is a compilation of Jewish legal traditions and oral interpretations of the scriptures compiled about A.D. 200. [Hebrew *mishnāh,* repetition, instruction, from *shā-nāh,* to repeat.] —**Mish·na'ic** (mĭsh-nā'ĭk) *adj.*

mis·in·form (mĭs'ĭn-fôrm') *tr.v.* To give false or inaccurate information to. —**mis·in·for·ma'tion** *n.*

mis·in·ter·pret (mĭs'ĭn-tûr'prĭt) *tr.v.* To explain or understand incorrectly. —**mis·in·ter'pre·ta'tion** *n.*

mis·judge (mĭs-jŭj') *v.* **-judged, -judg·ing.** —*tr.v.* To judge incorrectly. —*intr.v.* To err in judging. —**mis·judg'ment** *n.*

mis·lay (mĭs-lā') *tr.v.* **-laid** (-lād'), **-lay·ing.** To put in a place that is afterward forgotten; lose. —See Syns at **lose.**

mis·lead (mĭs-lēd') *tr.v.* **-led** (-lĕd'), **-lead·ing. 1.** To lead in the wrong direction. **2.** To lead into a mistaken action, opinion, or conclusion. —See Syns at **deceive.**

mis·like (mĭs-līk') *tr.v.* **-liked, -lik·ing.** To dislike. —*n.* Dislike; disapproval. [Middle English *misliken,* from Old English *mislīcian,* to displease : *mis-,* ill + *līcian,* to please.]

mis·man·age (mĭs-măn'ĭj) *tr.v.* **-aged, -ag·ing.** To manage badly or improperly. —See Syns at **botch.** —**mis·man'age·ment** *n.*

mis·match (mĭs-măch') *tr.v.* To match unsuitably or badly, esp. in marriage. —**mis'match'** *n.*

mis·mate (mĭs-māt') *tr.v.* **-mat·ed, -mat·ing.** To mate unsuitably.

mis·name (mĭs-nām') *tr.v.* **-named, -nam·ing.** To call by a wrong name.

mis·no·mer (mĭs-nō'mər) *n.* A wrong or inappropriate name: *To call a whale a fish is to use a misnomer.* [Middle English, from Norman French, from Old French *mesnommer,* to misname : *mes-,* wrongly + *nommer,* to name, from Latin *nōmināre,* from *nōmen,* name.]

mi·sog·a·my (mĭ-sŏg'ə-mē) *n.* Hatred of marriage. [Greek *misein,* to hate + -GAMY.] —**mi·sog'a·mist** *n.*

mi·sog·y·ny (mĭ-sŏj'ə-nē) *n.* Hatred of women. [Greek *misogunia : misein,* to hate + *gunē,* woman.] —**mi·sog'y·nist** *n.* —**mi·sog'y·nis'tic** or **mi·sog'y·nous** *adj.*

mis·place (mĭs-plās') *tr.v.* **-placed, -plac·ing. 1.** To put in a wrong place. **2.** To mislay. —See Syns at **lose.** —**mis·place'ment** *n.*

mis·play (mĭs'plā') *n.* A wrong or inept play in a game. —*tr.v.* (mĭs-plā'). To make a misplay of.

mis·print (mĭs-prĭnt') *tr.v.* To print incorrectly. —*n.* (mĭs'-prĭnt', mĭs-prĭnt'). An error in printing.

mis·pri·sion (mĭs-prĭzh'ən) *n. Law.* **1.** Maladministration of public office. **2.** Neglect in preventing or reporting a crime. [Middle English, from Norman French *mesprisioun,* from *mesprendre,* to err : *mes-,* wrongly + *prendre,* to take, from Latin *praehendere,* to grasp, seize.]

mis·prize (mĭs-prīz') *tr.v.* **-prized, -priz·ing. 1.** To undervalue. **2.** To despise; scorn.

mis·pro·nounce (mĭs'prə-nouns') *tr.v.* **-nounced, -nounc·ing.** To pronounce incorrectly. —**mis'pro·nun'ci·a'tion** (mĭs'prə-nŭn'sē-ā'shən) *n.*

mis·quote (mĭs-kwōt') *tr.v.* **-quot·ed, -quot·ing.** To quote incorrectly. —**mis'quo·ta'tion** (mĭs'kwō-tā'shən) *n.*

mis·read (mĭs-rēd') *tr.v.* **-read** (-rĕd'), **-read·ing. 1.** To read incorrectly. **2.** To misinterpret.

mis·rep·re·sent (mĭs-rĕp'rĭ-zĕnt') *tr.v.* To represent or describe falsely or misleadingly. —**mis'rep're·sen·ta'tion** *n.*

mis·rule (mĭs-rool') *tr.v.* **-ruled, -rul·ing.** To rule or govern badly. —*n.* **1.** Incompetent or unjust rule. **2.** Disorder or lawless confusion.

miss¹ (mĭs) *tr.v.* **1.** To fail to hit, reach, catch, meet, or obtain: *miss the target.* **2.** To fail to perceive, understand, or grasp: *You're missing my point.* **3.** To fail to accomplish,

achieve, or attain (a goal): *He missed winning the race.* **4.** To fail to attend or be present for: *Don't miss even one day of work.* **5.** To leave out or omit: *He missed a name in typing the list.* **6.** To fail to perceive or notice: *miss an item in the newspaper.* **7.** To let go by; let slip: *miss a chance.* **8.** To escape or avoid: *miss the traffic.* **9.** To discover the absence or loss of: *Only after three days did he miss his wallet.* **10.** To regret the absence or loss of: *He missed his wife.* **11.** To fail to answer correctly; get wrong: *miss questions on a test.* —*intr.v.* **1.** To fail to hit or make contact with something: *fired a final shot and missed again.* **2.** To misfire. **3. a.** To be unsuccessful; fail. **b.** To lose a benefit or opportunity: *miss out on all the fun.* —*n.* A failure to achieve a goal or aim. [Middle English *missen,* from Old English *missan.*]

miss² (mĭs) *n.* **1. a. Miss.** A title of courtesy used before the name of an unmarried woman. **b.** A word used without a name in speaking to an unmarried woman: *I beg your pardon, miss.* **2.** An unmarried woman. [Short for MISTRESS.]

mis·sal (mĭs'əl) *n.* A book containing all the prayers and responses necessary for celebrating the Mass throughout the year. [Middle English *messel,* from Medieval Latin *missāle,* from Late Latin *missa,* Mass.]

mis·shape (mĭs-shāp') *tr.v.* **-shaped, -shap·ing.** To shape badly; deform. —**mis·shap'en** *adj.*

mis·sile (mĭs'əl; *Brit.* mĭs'īl') *n.* **1.** An object, such as a stone, bullet, or shell, that is projected at a target. **2.** A guided missile. **3.** A ballistic missile. [Latin *missilis,* from *missus,* past part. of *mittere,* to let go, send.]

missile

mis·sile·ry (mĭs'əl-rē) *n.* The science of making and using guided or ballistic missiles.

miss·ing (mĭs'ĭng) *adj.* **1.** Absent; lost: *a missing person.* **2.** Lacking: *a book that had twelve pages missing.*

missing link. 1. A hypothetical primate intermediate between the anthropoid apes and man. **2.** Something lacking but needed to complete a series.

mis·sion (mĭsh'ən) *n.* **1. a.** A group of persons sent to a foreign country to conduct negotiations, perform a special task, or provide services. **b.** A permanent diplomatic office; embassy. **2. a.** A group of persons sent esp. to a foreign country to perform religious or charitable work. **b.** An establishment of missionaries. **c.** A missionary headquarters or station. **d. missions.** Missionary duty or work. **3.** A church or parish without its own priest. **4.** A special series of religious services organized to make converts and to strengthen the faith and devotion of believers. **5. a.** A task assigned to an individual or a group. **b.** A combat operation or task. **6.** A strong inclination to a particular task or duty; calling: *Her mission is to reform him.* [French, from Latin *missiō,* from *mittere,* to send.]

mis·sion·ar·y (mĭsh'ə-nĕr'ē) *n., pl.* **-ies. 1.** A person who goes or is sent on a religious or charitable mission among nonbelievers. **2.** A zealous advocate of a belief or cause. —*modifier:* missionary work.

mis·sis or **mis·sus** (mĭs'ĭz, -ĭs) *n. Informal.* **1.** The mistress of a household. **2.** A wife. [Var. of MISTRESS.]

mis·sive (mĭs'ĭv) *n.* A written message. [From Middle English *(letter) missive,* (letter) sent (by superior authority), from Medieval Latin *litterae missīvae* (pl.), from Latin *missus,* past part. of *mittere,* to send.]

mis·spell (mĭs-spĕl') *tr.v.* **-spelled** or **-spelt** (-spĕlt'), **-spell·ing.** To spell incorrectly. —**mis·spell'ing** *n.*

mis·spend (mĭs-spĕnd′) *tr.v.* **-spent** (-spĕnt′), **-spend·ing.** To spend improperly or foolishly; squander.

mis·state (mĭs-stāt′) *tr.v.* **-stat·ed, -stat·ing.** To state wrongly or falsely; give a wrong account of. **—mis·state′ment** *n.*

mis·step (mĭs-stĕp′) *n.* **1.** A wrong step. **2.** A mistake in conduct or behavior. **—See Syns at error.**

mis·sus (mĭs′ĭz, -ĭs) *n.* Var. of **missis.**

miss·y (mĭs′ē) *n.,* pl. **-ies.** Often **Missy.** *Informal.* A familiar form of **miss.**

mist (mĭst) *n.* **1.** A mass of tiny droplets of water in the atmosphere, near or in contact with the ground. **2.** Water vapor condensed on and clouding a surface. **3.** Fine drops of any liquid, such as perfume, sprayed into the air. **4.** Something that dims or obscures sight or judgment, as a haze from tears in the eyes. *—intr.v.* **1.** To be or become obscured or concealed by or as if by a mist. **2.** To rain in a fine shower. *—tr.v.* To conceal or cover with or as if with a mist. [Middle English, from Old English.]

mis·tak·a·ble (mĭ-stā′kə-bəl) *adj.* Capable of being mistaken or misunderstood. **—mis·tak′a·bly** *adv.*

mis·take (mĭ-stāk′) *n.* An error or fault, as in action, judgment, or calculation. **—See Syns at error.** *—v.* **-took** (-tŏŏk′), **-tak·en** (-stā′kən), **-tak·ing.** *—tr.v.* **1.** To understand wrongly; misinterpret: *mistake politeness for friendliness.* **2.** To recognize or identify incorrectly: *He mistook her for her sister.* *—intr.v.* To make a mistake. [Middle English *mistaken,* from Old Norse *mistaka,* to take in error : *mis-,* wrongly + *taka,* to take.]

mis·tak·en (mĭ-stā′kən) *adj.* **1.** Wrong in opinion, understanding, or perception. **2.** Based on error; wrong: *a mistaken view of the situation.* **—mis·tak′en·ly** *adv.*

Mis·ter (mĭs′tər) *n.* **1.** A title of respect used when speaking to or of a man, usu. written in its abbreviated form and placed before a man's surname or title of office: *Mr. Jones; Mr. Secretary.* **2. mister.** *Informal.* A form of address used without a name: *Watch out, mister, or I'll knock your teeth in.* [Alteration of MASTER.]

mis·tle·toe (mĭs′əl-tō′) *n.* **1.** Any of various parasitic shrubs, such as *Phoradendron flavescens,* of eastern North America, that grow on tree branches and have light-green leaves and white berries. **2.** A sprig of mistletoe, often used as a Christmas decoration. [Middle English *mistilto,* from Old English *misteltān* : *mistel,* mistletoe + *tān,* twig.]

mistletoe

mis·took (mĭ-stŏŏk′) *v.* Past tense of **mistake.**

mis·tral (mĭs′trəl, mĭ-strāl′) *n.* A dry, cold, sometimes violent wind that blows from the north of France toward the southern Mediterranean coast. [French, from Provençal, from Latin *magistrālis (ventus),* "master (wind)."]

mis·treat (mĭs-trēt′) *tr.v.* To handle or treat roughly; to abuse. **—See Syns at abuse. —mis·treat′ment** *n.*

mis·tress (mĭs′trĭs) *n.* **1.** A woman in a position of authority, control, or ownership, as the head of a household or estate. **2.** A woman owning an animal or, formerly, a slave. **3.** A woman who has ultimate control over something: *the mistress of his heart.* **4.** Often **Mistress.** Any idea or object personified as a woman having control or authority over something: *Is America mistress of her own fate?* **5.** A woman who has mastered a skill. **6.** A woman who has a continuing sexual relationship with a man to whom she is not married. **7. Mistress.** Formerly, a title of courtesy used when speaking to or of a woman. **8.** *Brit.* A fe-

male schoolteacher. [Middle English *maistresse,* from Old French *maistresse,* from *maistre,* master.]

mis·tri·al (mĭs-trī′əl, -trīl′) *n.* *Law.* **1.** A trial declared invalid because of a procedural problem or error. **2.** A trial in which the jurors fail to reach a verdict.

mis·trust (mĭs-trŭst′) *n.* Lack of trust; suspicion; doubt. **—See Syns at distrust.** *—tr.v.* To regard with suspicion. *—intr.v.* To be wary or doubtful. **—mis·trust′ful** *adj.* **—mis·trust′ing·ly** *adv.*

mist·y (mĭs′tē) *adj.* **-i·er, -i·est.** **1.** Consisting of, filled with, or resembling mist: *a misty rain.* **2.** Obscured or clouded by or as if by mist: *a misty mountain range in the distance.* **3.** On the verge of shedding tears. **4.** Lacking in clarity; vague: *a misty memory of the event.* **—See Syns at vague. —mist′i·ly** *adv.* **—mist′i·ness** *n.*

mis·un·der·stand (mĭs′ŭn-dər-stănd′) *tr.v.* **-stood** (-stŏŏd′), **-stand·ing.** To understand incorrectly.

mis·un·der·stand·ing (mĭs′ŭn-dər-stăn′dĭng) *n.* **1.** A failure to understand correctly. **2.** A disagreement or quarrel.

mis·un·der·stood (mĭs′ŭn-dər-stŏŏd′) *adj.* **1.** Understood wrongly or incorrectly. **2.** Not appreciated or given understanding: *a misunderstood child.* *—v.* Past tense and past participle of **misunderstand.**

mis·use (mĭs-yōōz′) *tr.v.* **-used, -us·ing.** **1.** To use wrongly or incorrectly: *misuse a word in a sentence.* **2.** To mistreat; abuse. **—See Syns at abuse.** *—n.* (mĭs-yōōs′) Wrong or improper use; misapplication.

mis·word (mĭs-wûrd′) *tr.v.* To word improperly or incorrectly.

mite[1] (mīt) *n.* Any of various small, often parasitic arachnids, related to spiders and ticks, that may infest foods and carry disease. [Middle English, from Old English *mīte.*]

mite[2] (mīt) *n.* **1.** A very small amount of money or contribution. **2.** Any very small object, creature, or particle. [Middle English, from Middle Dutch *mīte.*]

mi·ter (mī′tər). Also *Brit.* **mi·tre.** *—n.* **1.** A tall, pointed hat with peaks in front and back, worn by bishops and certain other ecclesiastics. **2.** The ceremonial headdress worn by ancient Jewish high priests. **3. a.** A **miter joint. b.** The edge of a piece of material that has been beveled to form a miter joint. *—tr.v.* **1.** To raise to a rank entitled to wear a miter. **2.** To join with a miter joint. [Middle English *mitre,* from Old French, from Latin *mitra,* from Greek, headband, headdress of the Jewish high priest.]

miter box. A box open at the ends, with sides slotted to guide a saw in cutting miter joints.

miter joint. A joint made by fitting together two beveled edges to form a 90° corner.

miter square. A carpenter's square with a blade that is either adjustable or set at a 45-degree angle.

Mith·ras (mĭth′rəs) *n.* Also **Mith·ra** (mĭth′rə). *Persian Myth.* The god of light and guardian against evil, often identified with the sun.

mit·i·gate (mĭt′ĭ-gāt′) *tr.v.* **-gat·ed, -gat·ing.** To make less severe or intense; moderate: *tried to mitigate her displeasure.* [Middle English *mitigaten,* from Latin *mītigāre,* from *mītis,* gentle, mild.] **—mit′i·ga·ble** (mĭt′ĭ-gə-bəl) *adj.* **—mit′i·ga′tion** *n.* **—mit′i·ga′tor** *n.*

mi·to·chon·dri·a (mī′tə-kŏn′drē-ə) *pl.n.* The less frequently used sing. is **mi·to·chon·dri·on** (-drē-ən). *Biol.* Any of certain microscopic structures found in almost all living cells, containing enzymes responsible for the conversion of food to usable energy. [Greek *mitos,* thread + *khondrion,* small grain.] **—mi′to·chon′dri·al** (-drē-əl) *adj.*

mi·to·sis (mī-tō′sĭs) *n.* *Biol.* **1.** The process in which the chromosomes of a cell duplicate themselves and separate into two identical groups just before the cell divides. **2.** The entire sequence of processes involved in the division of a cell when both of the daughter cells have as many chromosomes as the original cell. [Greek *mitos,* a thread + -OSIS.] **—mi·tot′ic** (-tŏt′ĭk) *adj.* **—mi·tot′i·cal·ly** *adv.*

mi·tral (mī′trəl) *adj.* **1.** Of, pertaining to, or resembling a miter. **2.** Of or pertaining to a mitral valve.

mitral valve. The heart valve that regulates blood flow from the auricle to the ventricle.

mi·tre (mī′tər) *n. & v. Brit.* Var. of **miter.**

mits·vah (mĭts′və) *n.* Var. of **mitzvah.**

mitt (mĭt) *n.* **1.** A woman's glove that extends over the hand but only partially covers the fingers. **2.** A mitten. **3.** A baseball glove, esp. the specialized models used by catchers and first basemen. **4.** Often **mitts.** *Slang.* A hand or fist. [Short for MITTEN.]

mit·ten (mĭt'n) *n.* A covering for the hand that has a separate section for the thumb and one wide section for all four fingers. [Middle English *mytayne,* from Old French *mitaine,* from Latin *medietās,* half, from *medius,* middle.]

mitz·vah (mĭts'və) *n., pl.* **-voth** (-vōt', -vōth', -vōs') or **-vahs.** Also **mits·vah.** *Judaism.* **1.** A command of the Law. **2.** Any worthy deed. [Hebrew *miṣwāh,* "(divine) commandment," from *siwwāh,* to command.]

mix (mĭks) *tr.v.* **1.** To combine or blend (ingredients or elements) into a single mass or mixture so that the constituent parts are indistinguishable: *mix sugar and egg yolks.* **2.** To create or make by combining ingredients: *mix a cake; mix drinks.* **3.** To combine or join: *mix business with pleasure.* **4.** To bring into social contact: *mix boys and girls in the same classes.* **5.** To crossbreed. —*intr.v.* **1.** To become mixed or blended together. **2.** To be capable of being blended together: *Oil does not mix with water.* **3.** To associate socially; mingle: *He does not mix well at parties.* **4.** To be crossbred. —*phrasal verb.* **mix up. 1.** To confuse: *The directions only mixed us up.* **2.** To throw into disorder; jumble: *mix up the pieces.* **3.** To involve: *get mixed up in a robbery.* —See Syns at **confuse.** —*n.* **1.** An act or result of mixing. **2.** A mixture, esp. of ingredients packaged and sold commercially: *a cake mix.* [Back-formation from *mixed, mixt,* from Middle English, from Norman French *mixte,* from Latin *mixtus,* past part. of *miscere,* to mix.] —**mix'a·ble** or **mix'i·ble** *adj.*

mixed (mĭkst) *adj.* **1.** Blended together into one unit or mass. **2.** Composed of various, sometimes conflicting qualities: *mixed emotions.* **3.** Composed of members of both sexes: *a mixed audience.* **4.** Involving different races or religions: *a mixed marriage.*

mixed metaphor. A succession of metaphors whose literal meanings contradict each other, thus producing an absurd effect, as *burning hatreds in a sea of discontent.*

mixed number. A number, such as 7¹/₄, equal to the sum of an integer and a fraction.

mix·er (mĭk'sər) *n.* **1.** Someone or something that mixes, esp. a mechanical device that mixes substances or ingredients. **2.** A sociable person: *He was a good mixer.* **3.** An informal dance or party arranged to give people, usu. members of a group, an opportunity to get acquainted. **4.** A beverage, such as soda water or ginger ale, added to an alcoholic drink.

mixt (mĭkst) *v. Archaic.* Past tense and past participle of **mix.**

mix·ture (mĭks'chər) *n.* **1.** Something produced by mixing. **2.** Anything consisting of different elements: *a mixture of joy and sorrow.* **3.** The act of mixing or the condition of being mixed. **4.** *Chem.* Any composition of two or more substances that are not chemically combined: *Air is a mixture of several gases.* [French, from Latin *mixtūra,* from *mixtus,* past part. of *miscere,* to mix.]

mix-up (mĭks'ŭp') *n.* A confused situation; a muddle.

miz·en (mĭz'ən) *n.* Var. of **mizzen.**

miz·en·mast (mĭz'ən-məst, -măst') *n.* Var. of **mizzenmast.**

miz·zen (mĭz'ən) *n.* Also **miz·en. 1.** A fore-and-aft sail set on the mizzenmast. **2.** A mizzenmast. [Middle English *mesan,* from Old French *misaine,* ult. from Latin *medius,* middle.]

miz·zen·mast (mĭz'ən-məst, -măst') *n.* Also **miz·en·mast** The third mast aft on sailing ships carrying three or more masts.

mne·mon·ic (nĭ-mŏn'ĭk) *adj.* Relating to or designed to assist the memory. —*n.* A device, such as a formula or rhyme, used as an aid in remembering. [Medieval Latin *mnēmonicus,* from Greek *mnēmonikos,* from *mnēmōn,* mindful.] —**mne·mon'i·cal·ly** *adv.*

mne·mon·ics (nĭ-mŏn'ĭks) *n. (used with a sing. verb).* A system to improve or develop the memory.

Mne·mos·y·ne (nĭ-mŏs'ə-nē, -mŏz'-) *n. Gk. Myth.* The goddess of memory, mother of the Muses.

Mo The symbol for the element molybdenum.

mo·a (mō'ə) *n.* Any of various extinct, large, ostrichlike birds of the order Dinorthiformes, native to New Zealand. [Maori.]

moan (mōn) *n.* **1.** A low, drawn-out, mournful sound, usu. indicative of sorrow or pain. **2.** Any similar sound: *the moan of the wind.* —*intr.v.* **1.** To utter a moan. **2.** To make a sound resembling a moan: *The wind moaned through the trees.* —*tr.v.* **1.** To bewail; complain about. **2.** To utter with a moan or moans. [Middle English *mone,* complaint.]

moat (mōt) *n.* A wide, deep ditch, usu. filled with water, surrounding a medieval town, fortress, or castle as a protection against assault. —*tr.v.* To surround with or as if with a moat. [Middle English *mote,* from Old French, clod, hill, mound.]

mob (mŏb) *n.* **1.** A large, disorderly, often violent crowd or throng. **2.** The masses; the common people. **3.** *Informal.* An organized gang of criminals; a crime syndicate. —*tr.v.* **mobbed, mob·bing. 1.** To crowd around and jostle or annoy, esp. in anger or enthusiasm: *an audience mobbing the stage.* **2.** To crowd into: *Crowds mobbed the department store.* **3.** To attack violently, usu. in a crowd or mob. [Shortening of earlier *mobile,* from Latin *mōbile (vulgus),* "the fickle (crowd)."]

mob·cap (mŏb'kăp') *n.* A large, high cap trimmed with frills and ribbons, worn by women in the 18th and early 19th cent. [Obs. *mob,* negligee, informal attire + CAP.]

mo·bile (mō'bəl, -bēl', -bīl') *adj.* **1.** Capable of moving or of being moved from place to place: *a mobile hospital.* **2.** Changing quickly from one condition or expression to another: *"His mouth was wide and mobile, the mouth of an actor or preacher"* (Joyce Cary). **3.** Marked by a relatively easy movement from one social class to another: *a mobile society.* **4.** Flowing freely: *a mobile liquid.* —See Syns at **moving.** —*n.* (mō'bēl'). A type of sculpture consisting of parts that move, esp. in response to air currents. [Old French, from Latin *mōbilis.*] —**mo·bil'i·ty** (mō-bĭl'ī-tē) *n.*

mo·bi·lize (mō'bə-līz') *v.* **-lized, -liz·ing.** —*tr.v.* **1.** To assemble, prepare, or put into operation for war or a similar emergency: *mobilize troops.* **2.** To assemble or coordinate for a particular purpose: *mobilize public opinion.* —*intr.v.* To become prepared for war or a similar emergency. —**mo'bi·li·za'tion** *n.*

Mö·bi·us strip (mœ'bē-əs). *Topology.* A mathematical surface having a single surface and a single edge, represented as a model by taking a strip of paper, twisting one end through 180°, and attaching it to the other end. [After August *Möbius* (1790–1868), German mathematician, its inventor.]

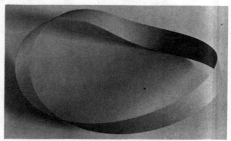

Möbius strip

mob·ster (mŏb'stər) *n. Slang.* A member of a criminal gang.

moc·ca·sin (mŏk'ə-sĭn) *n.* **1.** A soft leather slipper with no heel, orig. worn by American Indians. **2.** A shoe or slipper resembling an Indian moccasin. **3.** A **water moccasin.** [Natick *mohkussin.*]

moccasin flower. A lady's-slipper.

mo·cha (mō'kə) *n.* **1.** A rich, pungent, choice Arabian coffee. **2.** A flavoring made of coffee often mixed with chocolate. **3.** A soft, thin glove leather usu. made from goatskin. [After *Mocha,* a port of Yemen.]

mock (mŏk) *tr.v.* **1.** To treat with scorn or contempt; deride; ridicule. **2.** To imitate, as in sport or derision. —*intr.v.* To express scorn or ridicule: *They mocked at their parents' values.* —See Syns at **imitate** and **ridicule.** —*n.* **1.** An act of mocking or ridicule. **2.** Something deserving of derision. **3.** An imitation or counterfeit. —*adj.* Simulated; false; sham: *a mock battle.* [Middle English *mokken,* from Old French *mocquer,* to deride.] —**mock′er** *n.* —**mock′ing·ly** *adv.*

mock·er·y (mŏk′ə-rē) *n., pl.* **-ies. 1.** Scornful contempt; ridicule; derision. **2.** A specific example of ridicule or derision. **3.** An object of scorn or ridicule. **4.** A false, ridiculous, or impudent imitation; a travesty: *The trial was a mockery of justice. "I leave/no pallid ghost or mockery of a man"* (William B. Yeats).

mock-he·ro·ic (mŏk′hĭ-rō′ĭk) *adj.* Satirizing or burlesquing the heroic manner, style, or character: *a mock-heroic poem.* —*n.* A satirical imitation or burlesque of the heroic manner, style, or character, esp. as a literary work. —**mock′-he·ro′i·cal·ly** *adv.*

mock·ing·bird (mŏk′ĭng-bûrd′) *n.* Any of several species of New World birds of the family Mimidae, with gray and white plumage, noted for the ability to mimic the notes of other birds.

mock orange. Any of several deciduous shrubs of the genus *Philadelphus,* with white, usu. fragrant flowers. Also called **syringa.**

mock·up or **mock-up** (mŏk′ŭp′) *n.* A scale model, often full-sized, of a building, machine, or structure, used for demonstration, study, or testing.

mod (mŏd) *n.* A fashionable style of youthful dress that originated in England in the 1960's. —*adj.* Stylishly up-to-date, esp. in a modern, unconventional way. [Short for MODERN.]

mod·al (mŏd′l) *adj.* **1.** Of, pertaining to, or characteristic of a mode. **2.** *Gram.* Of, pertaining to, or expressing the mood of a verb.

modal auxiliary. One of a set of English verbs, including *can, may, ought, should,* and *will,* that are used with other verbs to express mood or tense.

mo·dal·i·ty (mō-dăl′ĭ-tē) *n., pl.* **-ties.** The fact, condition, or quality of being modal.

mode (mōd) *n.* **1. a.** A manner, way, or method of doing or acting: *a mode of travel.* **b.** A particular form, variety, or manner: *Broadcasting is one mode of communication.* **2.** The current fashion or style, esp. in dress. **3.** *Mus.* **a.** Any of certain arrangements of the diatonic tones of an octave, produced by starting, in turn, on each of the eight tones of a major scale and proceeding through an octave. **b.** Either of the two modes of the modern diatonic scale in Western music, the major and the minor. **4.** *Statistics.* The value or item occurring most frequently in a series of data. —See Syns at **fashion** and **method.** [Middle English *moede,* from Latin *modus,* measure, manner, size, harmony, melody.]

mod·el (mŏd′l) *n.* **1.** A small-scale reproduction of something: *an airplane model.* **2.** A preliminary pattern or figure of an item not yet made, usu. serving as the plan from which the finished work will be produced: *a plaster model for a statue.* **3.** A tentative description of a theory or system that accounts for all of its known properties. **4.** A style or design of an item: *His car is last year's model.* **5.** A person or object serving as an example to be imitated or compared. **6.** A person or object serving as the subject for an artist or photographer. **7.** A person employed to display clothing by wearing it. —See Syns at **ideal.** —*v.* **-eled** or **-elled, -el·ing** or **-el·ling.** —*tr.v.* **1.** To plan or fashion according to a model: *modeled the church after a French cathedral.* **2.** To make or construct a model of: *model animals in clay.* **3.** To make by shaping: *model clay into animals.* **4.** To display by wearing or posing: *model a dress.* **5.** In painting and drawing, to give a three-dimensional appearance to, as by shading. —*intr.v.* **1.** To make or construct a model: *models in bronze.* **2.** To serve as a model: *She models for a living.* —*adj.* **1.** Serving as or used as a model. **2.** Worthy of imitation: *a model child.* [Obs. French *modelle,* from Italian *modello,* from Latin *modulus,* little measure, dim. of *modus,* measure, rhythm, harmony.] —**mod′el·er** *n.*

mod·er·ate (mŏd′ər-ĭt) *adj.* **1.** Within reasonable limits; not excessive or extreme: *a moderate price.* **2.** Not violent; mild; calm: *a moderate climate.* **3.** Medium or average in quantity, quality, or extent: *a moderate income.* **4.** Opposed to radical or extreme views or measures, esp. in

politics or religion. —*n.* Someone who holds moderate views or opinions, esp. in politics or religion. —*v.* (mŏd′ə-rāt′) **-at·ed, -at·ing.** —*tr.v.* **1.** To make less violent, severe, or extreme: *moderate one's demands.* **2.** To preside over: *moderate a debate.* —*intr.v.* **1.** To become less violent, severe, or extreme; abate. **2.** To act as a moderator. [Latin *moderātus,* from *moderāri,* to reduce, regulate, control.] —**mod′er·ate·ly** *adv.*

mod·er·a·tion (mŏd′ə-rā′shən) *n.* **1.** The act of moderating or the condition of being moderated. **2.** The avoidance of extremes; quality of being moderate.

mod·er·a·to (mŏd′ə-rä′tō) *adv. Mus.* In moderate tempo; slower than allegretto but faster than andante. Used as a direction to the performer. —**mod′er·a′to** *adj. & n.* [Italian, from Latin *moderātus,* moderate.]

mod·er·a·tor (mŏd′ə-rā′tər) *n.* **1.** Someone or something that moderates, esp. someone who presides over a meeting or discussion. **2.** *Physics.* A substance, such as water or graphite, that is used in a nuclear reactor to decrease the speed of fast neutrons and consequently increase the likelihood of fission.

mod·ern (mŏd′ərn) *adj.* **1.** Of, pertaining to, or characteristic of recent times or the present: *modern history; modern music.* **2.** Advanced in style, technique, or technology; up-to-date: *the most modern computers.* —See Usage note at **contemporary.** —*n.* **1.** A person who lives in modern times. **2.** A person with modern ideas, tastes, or beliefs. [Old French *moderne,* from Late Latin *modernus,* from *modō,* just now, exactly, to the measure, from *modus,* measure.] —**mod′ern·ly** *adv.*

    Syns: modern, current, present-day *adj.* Core meaning: Of or relating to recent times or the present (*modern history; modern medicine*).

Modern English. The English language since 1500 A.D.

mod·ern·ism (mŏd′ər-nĭz′əm) *n.* **1.** Modern thought, character, behavior, or practice. **2.** Something, as a new style or usage of a word, that is characteristic of modern times. **3.** Often **Modernism.** In Christian Churches, the name given to movements that attempt to define church teachings in the light of modern developments in science and philosophy. **4.** The theory and practice of modern art. —**mod′ern·ist** *n.* —**mod′ern·ist′ic** *adj.*

mo·der·ni·ty (mō-dûr′nĭ-tē, mə-) *n.* The quality or condition of being modern.

mod·ern·ize (mŏd′ər-nīz′) *v.* **-ized, -iz·ing.** —*tr.v.* To make modern in appearance, style, or character. —*intr.v.* To accept or adopt modern ways, ideas, or styles. —**mod′ern·i·za′tion** *n.*

mod·est (mŏd′ĭst) *adj.* **1.** Tending to minimize or play down one's own talents, abilities, or accomplishments. **2.** Having or characteristic of a shy and retiring nature; reserved: *a modest demeanor.* **3.** Having a regard for decorum in behavior or dress. **4.** Humble in appearance; unpretentious: *a modest house.* **5.** Moderate; not extreme: *a modest charge.* [Old French *modeste,* from Latin *modestus,* keeping due measure.] —**mod′est·ly** *adv.*

    Syns: modest, demure, diffident, shy *adj.* Core meaning: Reticent or reserved in manner (*too modest to speak up for herself*). See also Syns at **humble.**

mod·es·ty (mŏd′ĭ-stē) *n., pl.* **-ties. 1.** The quality or condition of being modest. **2.** Reserve or propriety in speech, dress, or behavior.

mod·i·cum (mŏd′ĭ-kəm) *n., pl.* **-cums** or **-ca** (-kə). A small or moderate amount or quantity. [Latin, short way, short time, from *modicus,* moderate, from *modus,* measure.]

mod·i·fi·ca·tion (mŏd′ə-fĭ-kā′shən) *n.* **1.** The act of modifying or the condition of being modified. **2.** The result of modifying: *a modification of his original idea.* **3.** A small alteration or adjustment.

mod·i·fi·er (mŏd′ə-fī′ər) *n.* **1.** Someone or something that modifies. **2.** *Gram.* A word, phrase, or clause that limits or qualifies the sense of another word or group of words.

mod·i·fy (mŏd′ə-fī′) *v.* **-fied, -fy·ing.** —*tr.v.* **1.** To change in form or character; alter: *modify the terms of a contract.* **2.** To make less extreme, severe, or strong: *modify a prison sentence.* **3.** *Gram.* To qualify or limit the meaning of. —*intr.v.* To be or become modified. —See Syns at **change.** [Middle English *modifien,* to limit, moderate, from Old French *modifier,* from Latin *modificāre : modus,* a measure + *facere*, to do, make.] **—mod'i·fi'a·ble** *adj.*

mod·ish (mō'dĭsh) *adj.* Stylish; fashionable. **—mod'ish·ly** *adv.* **—mod'ish·ness** *n.*

mo·diste (mō-dēst') *n.* Someone who produces, designs, or deals in ladies' fashions. [French, from *mode*, fashion.]

mod·u·lar (mŏj'ə-lər, mŏd'yə-) *adj.* Of, pertaining to, or based on a module or modulus.

mod·u·late (mŏj'ə-lāt', mŏd'yə-) *v.* **-lat·ed, -lat·ing.** **—tr.v.** 1. To adjust or adapt; regulate: *modulate the flow of a faucet.* 2. To change or vary the pitch, intensity, or tone of: *modulated her voice.* 3. To sing or intone, as a chant or prayer. 4. *Electronics.* To vary the frequency, amplitude, or other characteristic of (a carrier wave) so that it corresponds to a signal that is to be transmitted. **—intr.v.** *Mus.* To pass from one key or tonality to another by means of a regular melodic or chord progression. [From Latin *modulārī*, to set to a measure, play music, from *modulus*, dim. of *modus*, measure, rhythm.] **—mod'u·la·to·ry** (-lə-tôr'ē, -tōr'ē) *adj.*

mod·u·la·tion (mŏj'ə-lā'shən, mŏd'yə-) *n.* 1. The act or process of modulating or the condition of being modulated. 2. *Mus.* A passing from one tonality to another by means of a regular melodic or chord progression. 3. **a.** A change in pitch or loudness of the voice. **b.** The use of a particular vocal inflection to convey meaning. 4. *Electronics.* The process by which a characteristic of a carrier wave, such as its amplitude or frequency, is changed to make it correspond to a signal that is to be transmitted.

mod·u·la·tor (mŏj'ə-lā'tər, mŏd'yə-) *n.* 1. Someone or something that modulates. 2. *Electronics.* A device or electric circuit used to modulate a carrier wave.

mod·ule (mŏj'ōōl, mŏd'yōōl) *n.* 1. A standard or unit of measurement. 2. *Archit.* A standard structural component used repeatedly in a building or structure. 3. *Electronics.* A self-contained assembly used as a component of a larger system, as a stage in a computer. 4. A self-contained unit of a spacecraft that performs a specific task: *a lunar module.* [Latin *modulus*, small measure, dim. of *modus*, measure.]

mod·u·lus (mŏj'ə-ləs, mŏd'yə-) *n.,* pl. **-li** (-lī'). 1. *Physics.* A number that expresses the degree to which a substance possesses some property. 2. *Math.* **a.** The absolute value of a complex number. **b.** An integer that produces the same remainder when divided into each of two other numbers. [Latin, small measure, dim. of *modus*, measure.]

mo·dus op·er·an·di (mō'dəs ŏp'ə-răn'dē, -dī'). *Latin.* The manner or method in which someone or something operates.

mo·dus vi·ven·di (vī-vĕn'dē, -dī'). *Latin.* 1. A way of living. 2. A temporary agreement between opposing parties pending a final settlement.

Mo·gen Da·vid (mō'gən dä'vĭd, mŭg'ən dŭv'ĭd). Var. of **Magen David.**

Mo·ghul (mō'gəl, mō-gŭl') *n.* Var. of **Mogul.**

mo·gul (mō'gəl) *n.* A small mound on a ski slope. [Prob. of Scandinavian orig.]

Mo·gul (mō'gəl, mō-gŭl') *n.* 1. Also **Mo·ghul.** A follower or a descendant of a follower of the Mongols who conquered India in 1526 and founded an empire that lasted until 1857. 2. A Mongol or Mongolian. 3. **mogul.** A very rich or powerful person: *a movie mogul.*

mo·hair (mō'hâr') *n.* 1. The soft, silky hair of the Angora goat. 2. A woolly fabric made of this hair. [Var. of earlier *mocayare*, from Italian *moccaiaro*, from Arabic *mukhayyar*, cloth of goat's hair.]

Mo·ham·med·an (mō-hăm'ĭ-dən) *adj.* Of Islam, its believers, or its prophet Mohammed. **—n.** A believer in Islam.

Mo·ham·med·an·ism (mō-hăm'ĭ-də-nĭz'əm) *n.* The Mohammedan religion; Islam.

Mo·hawk (mō'hôk') *n.,* pl. **Mohawk** or **-hawks.** 1. A North American Indian tribe of the Iroquois Nation of upper New York State. 2. A member of this tribe. 3. The Iroquoian language of the Mohawk. **—Mo'hawk'** *adj.*

Mo·ho·ro·vi·čić discontinuity (mō'hə-rō'və-chĭch'). The boundary between the earth's crust and the earth's mantle, ranging in depth from 6 to 8 miles under oceans and from 20 to 25 miles under continents. Also called **Moho.** [After Andrija *Mohorovičić* (1857-1936), Yugoslav geologist.]

Mohs scale (mōz). A scale for determining the relative hardness of a mineral according to its resistance to scratching by 15 standard minerals arranged in order of increasing hardness from talc, the softest, to diamond, the hardest. [After Friedrich *Mohs* (1773-1839), German mineralogist.]

moi·e·ty (moi'ĭ-tē) *n.,* pl. **-ties.** 1. A half. 2. A part, portion, or share. [Middle English *moite*, from Old French, from Latin *medietās*, half, from *medius*, middle.]

moil (moil) *intr.v.* To toil; work hard. **—n.** 1. Toil; drudgery. 2. Confusion; turmoil. [Middle English *moillen*, to moisten, smear, from Old French *moillier*, to moisten, paddle in mud, from Latin *mollis*, soft.]

moi·ré (mwä-rā') *n.* 1. Cloth, esp. silk, that has a watered or wavy pattern. 2. A watered pattern pressed on cloth by engraved rollers. [French.] **—moi·ré'** *adj.*

moist (moist) *adj.* **-er, -est.** 1. Slightly wet; damp: *a moist climate.* 2. Filled with moisture. 3. Tearful: *moist eyes.* [Middle English *moiste*, from Old French, from Latin *mūcidus*, from *mūcus*, mucus.] **—moist'ly** *adv.* **—moist'ness** *n.*

moist·en (mois'ən) *tr.v.* To make moist. **—intr.v.** To become moist.

mois·ture (mois'chər) *n.* Diffuse wetness that can be felt as vapor in the air or as condensed liquid on a surface; dampness.

mol (mōl) *n.* Var. of **mole** (gram weight).

mol·al (mō'ləl) *adj. Chem.* Of a solution containing one mole of solute in 1,000 grams of solvent.

mo·lar¹ (mō'lər) *adj.* 1. Containing one mole of a substance. 2. Of a solution that contains one mole of solute per liter of solution.

mo·lar² (mō'lər) *n.* In most mammals, a tooth with a broad crown for grinding food, located behind the bicuspids. **—adj.** 1. Of or pertaining to the molar teeth. 2. Capable of grinding. [Latin *molāris*, from *mola*, millstone.]

mo·las·ses (mə-lăs'ĭz) *n.* A thick, brownish syrup produced as a byproduct in refining sugar. [From Portuguese *melaço*, from Late Latin *mellāceum*, must, from Latin *mel*, honey.]

mold¹ (mōld). Also *Brit.* **mould.** **—n.** 1. A hollow form or container for shaping a liquid or plastic substance. 2. A frame or model around or on which something is formed or shaped. 3. Something that is made or shaped in or on a mold. 4. The pattern of a mold. 5. General shape or form: *the square mold of his chin.* 6. Distinctive shape, character, or type: *a man of serious mold.* **—tr.v.** 1. To shape in or on a mold. 2. To form into a desired shape. 3. To guide or determine the growth or development of; to influence: *mold young minds.* [Middle English *molde*, alteration of Old French *modle*, from Latin *modulus*, a small measure, dim. of *modus*, measure.] **—mold'a·ble** *adj.*

mold² (mōld). Also *Brit.* **mould.** **—n.** 1. Any of various threadlike, fuzzy, fungous growths that form on and often cause disintegration of food and other organic matter. 2. A fungus that causes mold. **—intr.v.** To become moldy; grow musty. [Middle English *mowlde.*]

mold³ (mōld) *n.* Also *Brit.* **mould.** 1. Loose soil that is rich in humus and rich for planting. 2. *Poet.* The earth; the ground. [Middle English *molde*, from Old English.]

mold·board (mōld'bôrd', -bōrd') *n.* The curved plate of a plow that turns over the soil. [MOLD (earth) + BOARD.]

mold·er (mōl'dər) *intr.v.* To turn into dust gradually by natural decay; crumble. **—tr.v.** To cause to decay or crumble. [Prob. from MOLD (fungus).]

mold·ing (mōl'dĭng) *n.* 1. Anything that is molded. 2. The process of shaping in a mold. 3. An ornamental strip used to decorate a surface, esp. an upper wall.

mold·y (mōl'dē) *adj.* **-i·er, -i·est.** 1. Covered with or containing mold: *moldy bread.* 2. Musty or stale, as from age or decay. **—mold'i·ness** *n.*

mole¹ (mōl) *n.* A small congenital growth or spot on the human skin, usu. slightly raised and dark. [Middle English, from Old English *māl.*]

mole² (mōl) *n.* Any of various small, insectivorous, burrowing mammals of the family Talpida, most of which live underground, that have thickset bodies, silky light-brown to dark-gray fur, rudimentary eyes, tough muzzles, and strong forefeet for digging. [Middle English.]

mole³ (mōl) *n.* 1. A massive stone wall used as a breakwater or jetty or to enclose an anchorage or harbor. **2.** The anchorage or harbor enclosed by a mole. [French *môle*, from Medieval Greek *môlos*, from Latin *môlēs*, pier, dam, massive structure, heavy bulk.]

mole⁴ (mōl) *n.* Also **mol** (mōl). *Chem.* The amount of a substance that has a weight in grams numerically equal to the molecular weight of the substance. Also called **gram molecule.** [German *Mol*, short for *Molekulargewicht*, molecular weight.]

mo·lec·u·lar (mə-lĕk′yə-lər) *adj.* Of, pertaining to, consisting of, or caused by molecules.

molecular biology. The branch of biology that deals with the structure and development of biological systems analyzed in terms of the physics and chemistry of their molecular constituents.

molecular weight. *Abbr.* **mol. wt.** *Chem.* The sum of the atomic weights of the atoms in a molecule.

mol·e·cule (mŏl′ĭ-kyōōl′) *n.* **1.** The simplest structural unit that has the characteristic physical and chemical properties of a compound, composed of a stable, electrically neutral configuration of atomic nuclei and electrons bound together by electrostatic and electromagnetic forces. **2.** A small particle; tiny bit. [French *molécule*, dim. of Latin *môlēs*, mass, bulk.]

mole·hill (mōl′hĭl′) *n.* A small mound of loose earth thrown up by a burrowing mole.

mole·skin (mōl′skĭn′) *n.* **1.** The short, soft, silky fur of the mole. **2.** A sturdy cotton fabric with a thick, fine nap on one side.

mo·lest (mə-lĕst′) *tr.v.* **1.** To disturb, interfere with, or annoy. **2.** To harass sexually or force sexual contact on. [Middle English *molesten*, from Old French *molester*, from Latin *molestāre*, to annoy, from *molestus*, troublesome.] —**mo′les·ta′tion** (mō′lĕs-tā′shən, mŏl′ĕs-) *n.* —**mo·lest′er** *n.*

moll (mŏl) *n. Slang.* A female companion of a gangster. [From *Moll*, pet form of the name *Mary*.]

mol·lie (mŏl′ē) *n.* Var. of **molly.**

mol·li·fy (mŏl′ə-fī′) *tr.v.* **-fied, -fy·ing. 1.** To allay the anger of; placate; calm: *tried to mollify her.* **2.** To make less intense; soften or ease: *mollify a child's disappointment.* [Middle English *mollifien*, from Old French *mollifier*, from Latin *mollificāre*, to make soft : *mollis*, soft + *facere*, to make, to do.] —**mol′li·fi·ca′tion** *n.*

mol·lusk (mŏl′əsk) *n.* Also **mol·lusc.** Any of a large group of soft-bodied, primarily saltwater invertebrates of the phylum Mollusca, which includes the edible shellfish and some 100,000 other species. [French *mollusque*, from Latin *mollis*, soft.]

mol·ly (mŏl′ē) *n., pl.* **-lies.** Also **mol·lie.** Any of several brightly colored tropical and subtropical fishes of the genus *Mollinesia*, often raised in aquaria. [After Comte François N. *Mollien* (1758–1850), French statesman.]

mol·ly·cod·dle (mŏl′ē-kŏd′l) *n.* A person who seeks to be pampered and protected. —*tr.v.* **-dled, -dling.** To overprotect; indulge; pamper. —See Syns at **baby.** [Obs. *molly*, "milksop."]

Mol·o·tov cocktail (mŏl′ə-tôf′, mō′lə-). A makeshift incendiary bomb made of a bottle filled with gasoline or other flammable liquid and provided with a rag wick. [After Vyacheslav *Molotov* (b. 1890), Soviet statesman.]

molt (mōlt) Also *Brit.* **moult.** —*intr.v.* To shed an outer covering, such as feathers or skin, for replacement by a new growth. —*tr.v.* To shed or cast off (an outer covering). —*n.* **1.** The act or process of molting. **2.** The material shed during molting. [Middle English *mouten*, from Latin *mūtāre*, to change.]

mol·ten (mōl′tn) *v.* Archaic past participle of **melt.** —*adj.* **1.** Made liquid by heat; melted: *molten iron.* **2.** Made by melting and casting. [Middle English *moltyn*, from Old English (ge)*molten.*]

mol·to (mōl′tō) *adv. Mus.* Very; much. Used with directions to the performer. [Italian, from Latin *multum*, much.]

mo·ly (mō′lē) *n., pl.* **-lies.** In the *Odyssey*, a legendary magic herb with black roots and white flowers, given to Odysseus by Hermes to nullify the spells of Circe. [Latin *môly*, from Greek *môlu.*]

mo·lyb·de·nite (mə-lĭb′də-nīt′) *n.* A mineral form of molybdenum sulfide, MoS₂, the principal ore of molybdenum.

mo·lyb·de·num (mə-lĭb′də-nəm) *n. Symbol* **Mo** A hard, gray metallic element used to toughen steel alloys and soften tungsten alloy. Atomic number 42; atomic weight 95.94; melting point 2,620°C; boiling point 4,800°C; specific gravity 10.2; valences 2, 3, 4, 5. [From Latin *molybdaena*, galena, from Greek *molubdaina*, a lead (of a plumb line), from *molubdos*, lead.]

mom (mŏm) *n. Informal.* Mother. [Short for *momma*, from baby talk.]

mo·ment (mō′mənt) *n.* **1.** A brief, often significant yet indefinite interval of time; an instant. **2.** A specific point in time, esp. the present time: *He is reading at the moment.* **3.** A particular period or stage of importance: *The victory was the greatest moment in the team's history.* **4.** Outstanding significance or value; importance: *a discovery of great moment.* **5.** *Physics. Abbr.* **M** The product of a quantity and its perpendicular distance from a reference point. [Middle English, from Old French, from Latin *mōmentum*, movement, momentum.]

Syns: **moment, flash, instant, jiffy** *(Informal),* **minute, second, trice** *n. Core meaning:* A brief but usu. not insignificant period *(a great moment in history).* MINUTE, used strictly, is specific; it is also interchangeable with moment *(had to wait a minute or moment).* An INSTANT or a FLASH is a period of time almost too brief to detect; each word implies haste and usu. urgency *(must have these papers this instant; gone in a flash).* SECOND may be used specifically or it may be used loosely, as the equivalent of *instant (pulled the lever and held it down for one second; need to see you this second).* TRICE, a literary term, and JIFFY appear in combinations preceded by *in a* (as in *a trice* or *jiffy*); they are imprecise but approximately equal in duration to instant.

mo·men·ta (mō-mĕn′tə) *n.* A plural of **momentum.**

mo·men·tar·i·ly (mō′mən-târ′ə-lē) *adv.* **1.** For only an instant or moment: *momentarily stunned by the blow.* **2.** Very soon: *News is expected momentarily.*

mo·men·tar·y (mō′mən-tĕr′ē) *adj.* **1.** Lasting only a brief time: *a momentary delay.* **2.** Occurring at every moment: *in momentary fear of being exposed.* [Latin *mōmentārius*, from *mōmentum*, movement.] —**mo′men·tar′i·ness** *n.*

mo·ment·ly (mō′mənt-lē) *adv.* **1.** Every moment; from moment to moment. **2.** At any moment. **3.** For a moment.

mo·men·tous (mō-mĕn′təs) *adj.* Of great importance or significance: *a momentous occasion.* —See Syns at **important.** —**mo·men′tous·ly** *adv.* —**mo·men′tous·ness** *n.*

mo·men·tum (mō-mĕn′təm) *n., pl.* **-ta** (-tə) *or* **-tums. 1.** *Symbol* **p** *Physics.* The product of the mass and velocity of a body. **2. a.** The force or speed of motion; impetus. **b.** Impetus in human action or affairs; controlling force or power: *We gained momentum after we turned the other team's fumble into a touchdown.* [Latin *mōmentum*, motion, movement, from *movēre*, to move.]

mon-. Var. of **mono-.**

mo·nad (mō′năd, mŏn′ăd) *n.* **1.** *Biol.* Any single-celled organism. **2.** *Chem.* An atom or radical with a valence of 1. [Late Latin *monas*, unit, from Greek *monas*, from *monos*, single.]

mo·nad·nock (mə-năd′nŏk′) *n.* A mountain or rocky mass that has resisted erosion and stands isolated in a plain. [After Mt. *Monadnock* in New Hampshire.]

mon·arch (mŏn′ərk, -ärk′) *n.* **1.** A sole and absolute ruler of a state. **2.** A hereditary sovereign, such as a king or emperor. **3.** Someone or something that surpasses others in power or significance: *the reigning monarch of professional tennis.* **4.** A large orange and black butterfly, *Danaus plexippus*, with a wingspread of up to four inches.

monarch
A monarch butterfly

—**mo·nar′chal** (mə-när′kəl) or **mo·nar′chi·al** *adj.*

mon·ar·chi·cal (mə-när′kĭ-kəl) or **mo·nar·chic** (-kĭk) *adj.* Of, pertaining to, characteristic of, or ruled by a monarch or monarchy.

mon·ar·chism (mŏn′ər-kĭz′əm) *n.* **1.** The principles of monarchy. **2.** Belief in or advocacy of monarchy. —**mon′ar·chist** (-kĭst) *n. & adj.* —**mon′ar·chis′tic** *adj.*

mon·ar·chy (mŏn′ər-kē) *n., pl.* **-chies. 1.** Government by a monarch. **2.** A country or state ruled by a monarch.

mon·as·ter·y (mŏn′ə-stĕr′ē) *n., pl.* **-ies. 1.** The dwelling place of a community of persons under religious vows, esp. monks. **2.** The community of monks living in a monastery. [Middle English *monasterie,* from Late Latin *monastērium,* from Late Greek *monastērion,* from Greek *monazein,* to live alone, from *monos,* alone.] —**mon′as·te′ri·al** (-stĭr′ē-əl, -stĕr′-) *adj.*

mo·nas·tic (mə-năs′tĭk) or **mo·nas·ti·cal** (-tĭ-kəl) *adj.* Of, pertaining to, or characteristic of monasteries or monks or their way of life: *monastic vows.* —*n.* A monk. —**mo·nas′ti·cism** *n.*

mon·a·tom·ic (mŏn′ə-tŏm′ĭk) *adj.* Occurring as single atoms, as helium.

mon·au·ral (mŏn-ôr′əl, mō-nôr′-) *adj.* **1.** Of, designating, or involving sound reception by one ear. **2.** Using a single channel to transmit or reproduce sound; monophonic.

Mon·day (mŭn′dē, -dā′) *n.* The second day of the week, after Sunday and before Tuesday. [Middle English *monday,* from Old English *mōnan dæg,* "moon's day."]

mo·nel metal (mō-nĕl′). A trademark for a corrosion-resistant alloy of nickel, copper, iron, and manganese.

mon·e·tar·y (mŏn′ĭ-tĕr′ē, mŭn′-) *adj.* **1.** Of or pertaining to money. **2.** Of or pertaining to a nation's currency or coinage: *a monetary system.* [Late Latin *monētārius,* from Latin *monēta,* money.] —**mon′e·tar′i·ly** (-târ′ə-lē) *adv.*

mon·e·tize (mŏn′ĭ-tīz′, mŭn′-) *tr.v.* **-tized, -tiz·ing. 1.** To establish as legal tender. **2.** To coin into money.

mon·ey (mŭn′ē) *n., pl.* **-eys** or **-ies. 1.** A commodity such as gold or silver that is legally declared to have fixed value and is used as an exchangeable equivalent of all other commodities and as a measure of their comparative values. **2.** The official coins and printed bills issued by a government, used as payment for goods and services; currency. **3.** Assets and property considered in terms of their monetary value; wealth: *His family has money.* **4.** Profit or loss measured in money: *make money on a sale.* **5.** Any unspecified amount of currency: *money for groceries.* **6.** Often **moneys.** Sums of money collected or stored; funds: *state tax moneys.* —*idiom.* **put money on.** To place a bet on or have confidence in. [Middle English *moneye,* from Old French *moneie,* from Latin *monēta,* from Monēta, epithet of Juno, whose temple in Rome housed the mint.]

mon·ey·bag (mŭn′ē-băg′) *n.* **1.** A bag for holding money. **2. moneybags** *(used with a sing. verb). Slang.* A rich person.

mon·ey·chang·er (mŭn′ē-chān′jər) *n.* **1.** A person who exchanges money, as from one currency to another. **2.** A machine that holds and dispenses coins.

mon·eyed (mŭn′ēd) *adj.* Also **mon·ied. 1.** Having a great deal of money; wealthy. **2.** Representing or arising from money or wealth: *moneyed interests.* —See Syns at **rich.**

mon·ey·lend·er (mŭn′ē-lĕn′dər) *n.* A person whose business is lending money at interest.

mon·ey·mak·ing (mŭn′ē-mā′kĭng) *n.* The acquisition of money or other wealth. —*adj.* **1.** Engaged in acquiring wealth. **2.** Actually or likely to be profitable: *a money-making venture.* —**mon′ey·mak′er** *n.*

money of account. Any of the various monetary units in which accounts are kept, which may or may not correspond to actual current denominations.

money order. An order for the payment of a specified amount of money, usu. issued and payable at a bank or post office.

-monger. A suffix meaning: **1.** A dealer in a specific commodity: **ironmonger. 2.** A person promoting something undesirable: **scandalmonger, warmonger.** [From *monger,* dealer, from Middle English *mongere,* from Old English *mangere,* from *mangian,* to traffic, from Latin *mangō,* (fraudulent) dealer.]

Mon·gol (mŏng′gəl, -gōl′, mŏn′-) *n.* **1.** A member of the nomadic tribes of Mongolia. **2.** Any Mongolian language.

Mon·go·li·an (mŏng-gō′lē-ən, -gōl′yən, mŏn-) *n.* **1.** A native or inhabitant of Mongolia. **2.** A member of the Mongoloid race. **3.** Any of a group of related languages spoken in Mongolia. —**Mon·go′li·an** *adj.*

mon·gol·ism or **Mon·gol·ism** (mŏng′gə-lĭz′əm, mŏn′-) *n.* Down's Syndrome.

Mon·gol·oid (mŏng′gə-loid′, mŏn′-) *adj.* **1.** Of or pertaining to a major ethnic division of the human species whose members are characterized by yellowish-brown to white skin, coarse, straight black hair, dark eyes with pronounced epicanthic folds, and prominent cheekbones. This division is considered to include most peoples of eastern Asia and Japan, Eskimos, and American Indians. **2.** Characteristic of or like a Mongol. **3. mongoloid.** Of, characterized by, or relating to mongolism. —*n.* A member of the Mongoloid ethnic division of the human species.

mon·goose (mŏng′gōōs′, mŏn′-) *n., pl.* **-goos·es.** Any of various weasellike carnivorous mammals of the genus *Herpestes* and related genera, native to Asia and Africa, that have a slender body and a long tail and are notable for the ability to kill venomous snakes. [Marathi *mangūs.*]

mongoose

mon·grel (mŭng′grəl, mŏng′-) *n.* **1.** An animal, esp. a dog, of mixed breed or unknown ancestry. **2.** A person or thing that is a mixture of different origins or elements. —*adj.* Of mixed origin or character. [Prob. from Middle English *mong,* mixture, from Old English *gemang.*]

mon·ick·er (mŏn′ĭ-kər) *n.* Var. of **moniker.**

mon·ied (mŭn′ēd) *adj.* Var. of **moneyed.**

mon·ies (mŭn′ēz′) *n.* A plural of **money.**

mon·i·ker or **mon·ick·er** (mŏn′ĭ-kər) *n. Slang.* A personal name or nickname. —See Syns at **name.** [Orig. unknown.]

mo·nism (mō′nĭz′əm, mŏn′ĭz′-) *n.* A metaphysical theory that all reality is composed of and reducible to one substance. [German *Monismus,* from Greek *monos,* single.] —**mo′nist** *n. & adj.* —**mo·nis′tic** (mō-nĭs′tĭk, mō-) *adj.*

mo·ni·tion (mō-nĭsh′ən, mə-) *n.* **1.** A warning or admonition of some impending danger. **2.** *Law.* A summons directing the recipient to appear and answer. [Middle English *monicioun,* from Old French *monition,* from Latin *monitiō,* from *monēre,* to warn.]

mon·i·tor (mŏn′ĭ-tər) *n.* **1.** A person who admonishes, cautions, or reminds. **2.** A pupil who assists a teacher in routine duties. **3. a.** Any device used to record or control a process or activity: *a radiation monitor.* **b.** A screen used to watch or check the picture being broadcast or picked up by a camera. **4.** Any of various large, tropical carnivorous lizards of the genus *Varanus,* which range in length from several inches to ten feet. —*tr.v.* **1.** To watch or check (the transmission quality of a signal) by means of a receiver. **2.** To keep track of by means of an electronic device. **3.** To keep watch over; supervise: *monitor an examination.* —*intr.v.* To act as a monitor. [Latin, one who warns, from *monēre,* to warn.] —**mon′i·to′ri·al** (-tôr′ē-əl, -tōr′-) *adj.*

mon·i·to·ry (mŏn′ĭ-tôr′ē, -tōr′ē) *adj.* Giving a warning or reproof: *a monitory glance.* —*n., pl.* **-ries.** A letter of admonition.

monk (mŭngk) *n.* A member of a religious brotherhood living in a monastery and bound by vows to the rules and practices of a religious order. [Middle English *munk,* from Old English *munuc,* from Late Latin *monachus,* from Late Greek *monakhos,* from Greek *monos,* alone.]

mon·key (mŭng′kē) *n., pl.* **-keys. 1.** Any member of the order Primates except man, anthropoid apes, lemurs, lorises, tree shrews, and tarsiers; specif. most long-tailed primates, including the Old and New World monkeys and the marmosets, with hands and feet adapted for climbing and grasping. **2.** A mischievous, playful child or young person. **3.** A person who is made to appear ludicrous or foolish. —*intr.v.* **1.** *Informal.* To tamper or fiddle with something: *monkeying with the broken switch.* **2.** *Informal.* To behave in a silly or careless way: *Don't monkey around during the ceremony.* —*tr.v.* To imitate or mimic; ape. [Prob. of Low German orig.]

monkey bread. The fruit of the baobab.

monkey business. *Slang.* Silly, mischievous, or deceitful acts.

mon·key·shine (mŭng′kē-shīn′) *n.* Often **monkeyshines.** *Slang.* A playful, mischievous trick.

monkey suit. *Slang.* A man's formal dress suit.

monkey wrench. 1. A hand tool with adjustable jaws for turning nuts of varying sizes. **2.** *Informal.* Something that disrupts: *He threw a monkey wrench into the plans.*

monk·ish (mŭng′kĭsh) *adj.* Of, relating to, or characteristic of monks or monasticism.

monks·hood (mŭngks′hŏŏd′) *n.* Any of various often poisonous plants of the genus *Aconitum*, with hooded flowers of various colors. Also called **aconite** and **wolfsbane.**

mono- or **mon-.** A prefix meaning: **1.** One; single; alone: **monophonic. 2.** Containing one atom, radical, or group in a compound: **monobasic.** [Middle English, from Old French, from Latin, from Greek, from *monos*, single.]

mon·o·ba·sic (mŏn′ə-bā′sĭk) *adj. Chem.* Having only one metal ion or positive radical.

mon·o·chord (mŏn′ə-kôrd′) *n.* An acoustical instrument consisting of a sounding box with one string and a movable bridge, used to study musical tones.

mon·o·chro·mat·ic (mŏn′ə-krō-măt′ĭk) *adj.* **1.** Of or having only one color. **2.** Having or producing radiation of only one wavelength.

mon·o·chrome (mŏn′ə-krōm′) *n.* **1.** A painting or drawing done in different shades of one color. **2.** The technique of executing such paintings or drawings. [MONO- + Greek *khrōmā*, color.] —**mon′o·chro′mic** (-krō′mĭk) *adj.*

mon·o·cle (mŏn′ə-kəl) *n.* An eyeglass for one eye. [French, from Late Latin *monoculus*, one-eyed : *mono-*, sole + *oculus*, eye.] —**mon′o·cled** (-kəld) *adj.*

monocle

mon·o·cli·nous (mŏn′ə-klī′nəs) *adj.* Having pistils and stamens in the same flower. [MONO- + Greek *klinē*, couch.]

mon·o·cot·y·le·don (mŏn′ə-kŏt′l-ēd′n) *n.* Also **mon·o·cot** (mŏn′ə-kŏt′). *Bot.* Any plant of the subclass Monocotyledonae, one of the two major divisions of flowering plants, with only a single cotyledon in the embryo. —**mon′o·cot′y·le′don·ous** *adj.*

mo·noc·u·lar (mŏ-nŏk′yə-lər, mə-) *adj.* **1.** Having or pertaining to one eye. **2.** Adapted for use by only one eye.

mon·o·cyte (mŏn′ə-sīt′) *n.* A large white blood corpuscle with a pale, oval nucleus.

mon·o·dy (mŏn′ə-dē) *n., pl.* **-dies. 1.** In ancient Greek poetry, an ode for one voice or actor. **2.** An elegiac poem lamenting someone's death. **3.** *Mus.* **a.** A style of composition in which one vocal part or melodic line predominates. **b.** A composition in this style. [Late Latin *monōdia*, from Greek *monōidia* : *monos*, sole + *ōidē*, song.]

mo·noe·cious (mə-nē′shəs, mŏ-) *adj. Bot.* Having male and female reproductive organs in separate flowers on a single plant. [MON(O)- + Greek *oikia*, dwelling, from *oikos*, house.]

mo·nog·a·mous (mə-nŏg′ə-məs) *adj.* Of, pertaining to, or practicing monogamy. —**mo·nog′a·mous·ly** *adv.*

mo·nog·a·my (mə-nŏg′ə-mē) *n.* **1.** The custom or condition of being married to only one person at a time. **2.** The condition of having one mate for life. —**mo·nog′a·mist** *n.*

mon·o·gram (mŏn′ə-grăm′) *n.* A design composed of one or more letters, usu. the initials of a name. —*tr.v.* **-grammed** or **-gramed, -gram·ming** or **-gram·ing.** To mark with a monogram. —**mon′o·gram·mat′ic** (mŏn′ə-grə-măt′ĭk) *adj.*

mon·o·graph (mŏn′ə-grăf′) *n.* A scholarly book or article on a specific and usu. limited subject.

mon·o·lith (mŏn′ə-lĭth′) *n.* **1.** A large block of stone used in architecture or sculpture. **2.** Anything resembling a monolith in massiveness, solidity, or uniformity, as an organization, institution, or movement. —**mon′o·lith′ic** *adj.*

mon·o·logue or **mon·o·log** (mŏn′ə-lôg′, -lŏg′) *n.* **1.** A long speech or talk made by one person, often monopolizing conversation. **2.** A soliloquy or any literary composition in the form of a soliloquy. **3.** A continuous series of jokes or comic routines delivered by a single comedian. [French, from Greek *monologos* : *monos*, alone + *logos*, speaking.] —**mon′o·log·ist** (mə-nŏl′ə-jĭst, mŏn′ə-lô′gĭst, -lŏg′ĭst) *n.*

mon·o·ma·ni·a (mŏn′ō-mā′nē-ə, -măn′yə) *n.* **1.** A mental disorder characterized by an obsession with one idea. **2.** An intense preoccupation with or exaggerated enthusiasm for one subject or idea. —**mon′o·ma′ni·ac′** (-ăk′) *n.* —**mon′o·ma·ni′a·cal** (-mə-nī′ə-kəl) *adj.*

mon·o·mer (mŏn′ə-mər) *n.* Any molecule that can be chemically bound as a unit of a polymer. [MONO- + Greek *meros*, part.]

mon·o·met·al·lism (mŏn′ō-mĕt′l-ĭz′əm) *n.* The economic theory or practice of using only one metal, usu. gold or silver, as a standard of money. —**mon′o·met′al·list** *n.*

mo·no·mi·al (mŏ-nō′mē-əl, mə-) *n.* **1.** *Alg.* An expression consisting of only one term. **2.** *Biol.* A taxonomic name consisting of a single word. [MON(O)- + (BIN)OMIAL.] —**mo·no′mi·al** *adj.*

mon·o·nu·cle·o·sis (mŏn′ō-nōō′klē-ō′sĭs, -nyōō′-) *n.* An acute, contagious, but rarely serious blood disease in which there is an abnormally large number of single-nuclei white blood cells in the bloodstream and which is characterized by fever, fatigue, and loss of appetite. Also called **infectious mononucleosis** and **glandular fever.** [MONO- + NUCLE(US) + -OSIS.]

mon·o·phon·ic (mŏn′ə-fŏn′ĭk) *adj.* **1.** *Mus.* Having a single melodic line; monodic. **2.** *Electronics.* Using one channel to record, store, or reproduce sound: *a monophonic phonograph.*

Mo·noph·y·site (mə-nŏf′ĭ-sīt′) *n.* An adherent of the doctrine that in the person of Christ there was but a single, divine nature, as opposed to both a human and a divine nature, advocated by Coptic and Syrian Christians. [Medieval Latin *monophysīta*, from Medieval Greek *monophusitēs* : *monos*, single + *phusis*, nature.] —**Mo·noph′y·sit′ism** (mə-nŏf′ĭ-sī′tĭz-əm) *n.*

mon·o·plane (mŏn′ə-plān′) *n.* An airplane with only one pair of wings.

mo·nop·o·lize (mə-nŏp′ə-līz′) *tr.v.* **-lized, -liz·ing. 1.** To acquire or maintain a monopoly of. **2.** To dominate by excluding others: *monopolize a conversation.* —**mo·nop′o·li·za′tion** *n.* —**mo·nop′o·liz′er** *n.*

mo·nop·o·ly (mə-nŏp′ə-lē) *n., pl.* **-lies. 1.** Exclusive control by one group of the means of producing or selling a commodity or service. **2.** *Law.* A right granted by a government to a single party, giving exclusive control over a particular commercial activity. **3. a.** A company or group having exclusive control over a commercial activity. **b.** A commodity or service so controlled. **4.** Exclusive possession of or control over anything. [From Latin *monopōlium*, from Greek *monopōlion*, sole selling rights : *monos*, sole + *pōlein*, to sell.]

mon·o·rail (mŏn′ə-rāl′) *n.* **1.** A single rail on which a car or train of cars travels. **2.** A railway system using a monorail.

mon·o·syl·lab·ic (mŏn′ə-sĭ-lăb′ĭk) *adj.* **1.** Having only one syllable. **2.** Characterized by or consisting of monosyllables: *a monosyllabic language.* —**mon·o·syl·lab′i·cal·ly** *adv.*

mon·o·syl·la·ble (mŏn′ə-sĭl′ə-bəl) *n.* A word of one syllable.

mon·o·the·ism (mŏn′ə-thē-ĭz′əm) *n.* The doctrine or belief that there is only one God. —**mon′o·the′ist** *n. & adj.* —**mon′o·the·is′tic** *adj.*

mon·o·tone (mŏn′ə-tōn′) *n.* **1.** A succession of sounds or words uttered in a single tone of voice: *delivered the speech in a numbing monotone.* **2.** *Mus.* The repeated singing of a single tone with different words and time values, as in chanting. **3.** A tiresome lack of variety in style, manner, or color. —*adj.* **1.** Of, pertaining to, or characteristic of sounds emitted at a single pitch. **2.** Monotonous.

mo·not·o·nous (mə-nŏt′n-əs) *adj.* **1.** Spoken or sounded in an unvarying tone or pitch: *spoke in a monotonous drone.* **2.** Dull or tiresome from a lack of variation or variety: *a monotonous diet; a monotonous life.* —**mo·not′o·nous·ly** *adv.* —**mo·not′o·nous·ness** *n.*

mo·not·o·ny (mə-nŏt′n-ē) *n.* **1.** Lack of variation in pitch, intonation, or inflection. **2.** Tiresome lack of variety; dull sameness.

mon·o·treme (mŏn′ə-trēm′) *n.* A member of the Monotremata, a primitive order of egg-laying mammals, of Australia and New Guinea, which includes the platypus and the echidna. [MONO- + Greek *trēma,* hole.]

mon·o·type (mŏn′ə-tīp′) *n. Biol.* The sole member of a group, as a species that also constitutes a genus. —**mon′o·typ′ic** (-tĭp′ĭk) *adj.*

Mon·o·type (mŏn′ə-tīp′) *n.* A trademark for a typesetting machine operated from a keyboard that casts and assembles type in individual letters.

mon·o·va·lent (mŏn′ə-vā′lənt) *adj.* Univalent. —**mon′o·va′lence** or **mon′o·va′len·cy** *n.*

mon·ox·ide (mə-nŏk′sīd′) *n.* An oxide containing one oxygen atom in each molecule. [MON(O) + OXIDE.]

Mon·sei·gneur (mōn′sān-yœr′) *n., pl.* **Mes·sei·gneurs** (mā′sān-yœr′). A French title of honor or respect given to princes and prelates. [French, "my lord."]

Mon·sieur (mə-syœ′) *n., pl.* **Mes·sieurs** (mā-syœ′). A French title of courtesy prefixed to the name or title of a man. [French, "my lord."]

Mon·si·gnor (mŏn-sēn′yər) *n., pl.* **-gnors** or **-ri** (-rē). Also **mon·si·gnor.** *Rom. Cath. Ch.* **1.** A title given to certain officials or dignitaries. **2.** A person holding the title Monsignor. [Italian, from French *monseigneur,* Monseigneur.]

mon·soon (mŏn-sōōn′) *n.* **1.** A system of winds that influences the climate of a large area and reverses direction seasonally, esp. the wind system that produces the dry and wet seasons in India and southern Asia. **2.** The summer monsoon season in India and southern Asia, characterized by heavy rains. [Obs. Dutch *monssoen,* from Portuguese *monção,* from Arabic *mausim,* season, monsoon season.]

mon·ster (mŏn′stər) *n.* **1.** An imaginary creature composed of elements from various human or animal forms, as a centaur or mermaid. **2.** An animal or plant that is abnormal in form or appearance. **3.** Any very large animal, plant, or object. **4.** A person whose evil or immoral behavior inspires horror or disgust. [Middle English *monstre,* from Old French, from Latin *mōnstrum,* prodigy, portent, from *monēre,* to warn.]

mon·strance (mŏn′strəns) *n. Rom. Cath. Ch.* A vessel in which the Host is held and exposed during the Mass. [Middle English, from Old French, from Medieval Latin *mōnstrantia,* from Latin *mōnstrāre,* to show, from *mōnstrum,* portent, monster.]

mon·stros·i·ty (mŏn-strŏs′ĭ-tē) *n., pl.* **-ties. 1.** Someone or something that is monstrous. **2.** The quality or condition of being monstrous.

mon·strous (mŏn′strəs) *adj.* **1.** Abnormal in appearance, structure, or character; grotesque. **2.** Exceptionally large; enormous: *a monstrous lie.* **3.** Hideously shocking; outrageous: *a monstrous crime.* **4.** Of, pertaining to, or like a fabulous monster. —See Syns at **giant** and **outrageous.** [Middle English *monstrows,* from Old French *monstruex,* from Latin *mōnstruōsus,* from *mōnstrum,* monster.] —**mon′strous·ly** *adv.* —**mon′strous·ness** *n.*

mon·tage (mŏn-tăzh′, môn-) *n.* **1. a.** The art, style, or process of making a picture from many pictures or designs, closely arranged or superimposed upon each other. **b.** A picture so made. **2.** *Motion Pictures & Television.* A rapid sequence of thematically related scenes or images that exhibits different aspects of the same idea or situation. **3.** In other art forms, a composition of different elements arranged in a sequential pattern. [French, "mounting," from *monter,* to mount.]

mon·te (mŏn′tē) *n.* A game of Spanish origin in which each player bets that one of two cards will be matched by the dealer before the other one. Also called **monte bank.** [Spanish, mountain, pile of unplayed cards, from Latin *mōns,* mountain.]

Mon·tes·so·ri method (mŏn′tĭ-sôr′ē, -sōr′ē). A method of instructing young children that stresses development of a child's own initiative. Also called **Montessori system.** [After Maria *Montessori* (1870–1952), Italian physician and educator.]

month (mŭnth) *n.* **1.** One of the 12 divisions of a year. Also called **calendar month. 2.** Any period extending from a date in one calendar month to the corresponding date in the following month. **3.** Any period of about four weeks or 30 days. **4.** The average period of a complete revolution of the moon around the earth. Also called **sidereal month. 5.** The average time between successive new, or full, moons. Also called **synodic month** and **lunar month. 6.** One twelfth of a tropical year. Also called **solar month.** [Middle English *moneth,* from Old English *mōnath.*]

month·ly (mŭnth′lē) *adj.* **1.** Occurring, appearing, or payable every month. **2.** Continuing or lasting for a month. —*adv.* Once a month; every month. —*n., pl.* **-lies.** A publication appearing once each month.

mon·u·ment (mŏn′yə-mənt) *n.* **1.** A structure, such as a tower or statue, erected as a memorial to a person or an event. **2.** An engraved stone or other marker placed at a grave or tomb. **3.** A structure preserved or admired for its historical or aesthetic significance. **4.** Any place or region preserved by a government for its special interest or significance. **5.** An outstanding and enduring achievement viewed as a model for later generations. **6.** An exceptional example of something: *His book is a monument of careful scholarship.* **7.** A stone, post, pillar, etc., serving as a boundary marker. [Middle English, from Latin *monumentum,* from *monēre,* to remind, warn.]

mon·u·men·tal (mŏn′yə-mĕn′tl) *adj.* **1.** Of, resembling, or serving as a monument. **2.** Impressively large: *monumental dams and viaducts.* **3.** Of outstanding significance: *a monumental piece of legislation.* **4.** Enormous and outrageous: *a monumental fraud.* —See Syns at **giant.** —**mon′u·men′tal·ly** *adv.*

moo (mōō) *n.* The deep, throaty sound made by a cow. —*intr.v.* To make a moo. [Imit.]

mooch (mōōch) *v. Slang.* —*tr.v.* To obtain free; beg: *mooch a ride.* —*intr.v.* **1.** To obtain free of charge. **2.** To lurk or skulk about. [Prob. ult. from Old French *muchier,* to hide, skulk.] —**mooch′er** *n.*

mood[1] (mōōd) *n.* **1.** A temporary state of mind or feeling: *a gloomy mood.* **2.** An impression on the feelings of an observer: *the somber mood of the painting.* [Middle English *mod,* from Old English *mōd.*]

mood[2] (mōōd) *n. Gram.* A set of verb forms used to indicate the factuality or likelihood of the action or condition expressed. In English the *indicative mood* is used for definite statements and questions, the *imperative mood* is used in giving commands, and the *subjunctive mood* is used, now only for the verb *be,* to suggest doubt or unlikelihood. [Alteration of MODE.]

mood·y (mōō′dē) *adj.* **-i·er, -i·est. 1.** Given to changeable moods, esp. of anger or depression. **2.** Gloomy; uneasy; glum: *a moody silence.* —**mood′i·ly** *adv.* —**mood′i·ness** *n.*

moon (mōōn) *n.* **1.** The natural satellite of the earth, visible by reflection of sunlight, with a slightly elliptical orbit, approx. 221,600 miles distant at perigee and 252,950 miles at apogee. Its mean diameter is 2,160 miles, its mass approx. one-eightieth that of the earth, and its average period of revolution around the earth 29 days 12 hours 44 minutes calculated with respect to the sun. **2.** Any natural satellite revolving around a planet. **3.** The moon as seen at a particular time in its cycle of phases: *a half moon.* **4.** A month, esp. a lunar month. **5.** Any disk, globe, or crescent resembling the moon. **6.** Moonlight: *There's a strong moon tonight.* —*intr.v.* To wander about or pass time in a dreamy or aimless manner. [Middle English *moone,* from Old English *mōna.*]

moon·beam (mōōn'bēm') *n.* A ray of moonlight.

moon·light (mōōn'līt') *n.* The light reflected from the moon. —*modifier: a moonlight stroll.* —*intr.v. Informal.* To work at a second job, often at night, in addition to one's regular job. —**moon'light'er** *n.*

moon·scape (mōōn'skāp') *n.* A view or picture of the surface of the moon.

moon·shine (mōōn'shīn') *n.* **1.** Moonlight. **2.** *Informal.* Foolish or nonsensical talk or thought; nonsense. **3.** *Slang.* Illegally distilled whiskey. —*v.* **-shined, -shin·ing.** —*tr.v.* To distill (liquor) illegally. —*intr.v.* To operate an illegal still. —**moon'shin'er** *n.*

moon·stone (mōōn'stōn') *n.* A mineral valued as a gem for its pearly translucent luster. It is a variety of feldspar containing either albite or orthoclase.

moon·struck (mōōn'strŭk') *adj.* **1.** Mentally unbalanced. **2.** Dazed or distracted with romantic sentiment; infatuated; lovelorn. [From the belief that moonlight causes insanity.]

moon·y (mōō'nē) *adj.* **-i·er, -i·est. 1.** Resembling the moon or moonlight. **2.** Dreamy in mood or nature; absentminded.

moor[1] (mōōr) *tr.v.* **1.** To secure or make fast (a vessel or aircraft) with cables or anchors. **2.** To fix in place; secure. —*intr.v.* **1.** To secure a vessel or aircraft. **2.** To be secured by or as if by cables or anchors. [Middle English *moren,* from Middle Low German *mōren.*] —**moor'age** (-Ij) *n.*

moor[2] (mōōr) *n.* A broad tract of open, poorly drained land, usu. covered with marshes and peat bogs and often patches of low shrubs such as heather. [Middle English *mor,* from Old English *mōr.*]

Moor (mōōr) *n.* **1.** A member of a Moslem people of mixed Berber and Arab descent, now living chiefly in northern Africa. **2.** One of the Saracens who invaded Spain in the 8th cent. A.D. —**Moor'ish** *adj.*

moor·ing (mōōr'ĭng) *n.* **1.** Equipment, such as anchors, chains, or lines, for securing a vessel or aircraft. **2.** The act of securing a vessel or aircraft. **3.** A place at which a vessel or aircraft can be moored. **4.** Often **moorings.** Elements, such as personal beliefs or routines, that provide stability or security.

moor·land (mōōr'lănd') *n.* A tract of land consisting of moors.

moose (mōōs) *n., pl.* **moose.** A large, hoofed mammal, *Alces alces,* of the deer family, found in forests of northern North America, with a broad, pendulous muzzle and large, flat antlers in the male. [Natick *moos.*]

moose

moot (mōōt) *adj.* **1.** Subject to debate; arguable; unresolved: *a moot question.* **2. a.** *Law.* Without legal significance because of having been previously decided or settled. **b.** Of no practical value or interest; academic. —*tr.v.* **1.** To bring up for discussion or debate. **2.** To discuss or debate. —*n.* An ancient English meeting, esp. one of freemen to administer justice. [Middle English *assembly,* from Old English *mōt.*]

moot court. A mock court where hypothetical cases are tried for the training of law students.

mop (mŏp) *n.* **1.** An implement made of absorbent mate-

rial, such as sponge or yarn, attached to a handle and used for dusting, washing, and drying floors. **2.** Any loosely tangled bunch or mass: *a mop of hair.* —*tr.v.* **mopped, mop·ping.** To wash or wipe with or as if with a mop. —*phrasal verb.* **mop up. 1.** *Mil.* To clear (an area) of remaining enemy troops after a victory. **2.** To complete a task or action. [Middle English *mappe.*]

mope (mōp) *intr.v.* **moped, mop·ing.** To be gloomy, dejected, or resentful; to sulk or brood. —*n.* **1.** A person given to gloomy or dejected moods. **2. mopes.** Low spirits; the blues. [Perh. from obs. *mop,* fool.] —**mop'er** *n.* —**mop'ing·ly** *adv.*

mo·ped (mō'pĕd') *n.* A motor-driven vehicle resembling a motorbike that can be pedaled. [MO(TOR) + PED(AL).]

mop·pet (mŏp'ĭt) *n.* A young child, esp. a little girl. [Dim. of obs. *mop,* child, fool, from Middle English *mop.*]

mop-up (mŏp'ŭp') *n.* The act of clearing away or disposing of small details after the completion of a task or action.

mo·quette (mō-kĕt') *n.* A heavy fabric with a thick nap, used for upholstery or carpets. [French.]

mo·raine (mə-rān') *n.* An accumulation of boulders, stones, or other debris carried and deposited by a glacier. [French.]

mor·al (môr'əl, mŏr'-) *adj.* **1.** Of or concerned with the principles of right and wrong in relation to human action or character; ethical. **2.** Teaching or exhibiting rightness or goodness of character and behavior: *a moral lesson.* **3.** Conforming to standards of what is right or just in behavior; virtuous: *a moral decision.* **4.** Arising from conscience or the sense of right and wrong: *a moral obligation.* **5.** Psychological rather than physical or concrete in effect: *a moral victory.* **6.** Based upon strong probability or conviction rather than actual evidence: *a moral certainty.* —*n.* **1.** The lesson or principle taught by a fable, story, or event. **2.** A concisely expressed precept or general truth; maxim. **3. morals.** Principles or habits of what constitutes right or wrong conduct, esp. sexual conduct. [Middle English, from Old French, from Latin *mōrālis,* from *mōs,* custom.] —**mor'al·ly** *adv.*

mo·rale (mə-răl') *n.* The condition or attitude of an individual or group in regard to the willingness to perform assigned tasks, confidence, cheerfulness, and discipline. [French, fem. of *moral,* moral.]

mor·al·ism (môr'ə-lĭz'əm, mŏr'-) *n.* The practice of or belief in a system of principles that govern conduct.

mor·al·ist (môr'ə-lĭst, mŏr'-) *n.* **1.** A teacher or student of moral principles and questions. **2.** A person who follows a system of moral principles.

mor·al·is·tic (môr'ə-lĭs'tĭk, mŏr'-) *adj.* Characterized by or given to moralizing, esp. in a conventional or self-righteous manner. —**mor'al·is'ti·cal·ly** *adv.*

mo·ral·i·ty (mə-răl'ĭ-tē, mô-) *n., pl.* **-ties. 1.** The quality or condition of being moral. **2.** A system of conduct based on principles of right and wrong: *Christian morality.* **3.** Virtuous conduct; morals. —See Syns at **virtue.**

morality play. An allegorical drama of the 15th and 16th cent. in which characters personify abstract virtues and vices, such as patience and jealousy.

mor·al·ize (môr'ə-līz', mŏr'-) *v.* **-ized, -iz·ing.** —*tr.v.* **1.** To derive or interpret a moral lesson from. **2.** To improve the morals of; reform. —*intr.v.* To think about or discuss moral issues. —**mor'al·iz'er** *n.*

mo·rass (mə-răs', mô-) *n.* **1.** An area of low-lying, soggy ground; a bog or marsh. **2.** Any difficult or perplexing condition or situation. [Dutch *moeras,* var. of Middle Dutch *marasch,* from Old French *marasc.*]

mor·a·to·ri·um (môr'ə-tôr'ē-əm, -tōr'-, mŏr'-) *n., pl.* **-ums** or **-to·ri·a** (-tôr'ē-ə, -tōr'-). **1.** *Law.* An authorization to a debtor permitting temporary suspension of payments. **2.** A temporary suspension or delay: *a moratorium on building nuclear weapons.* [From Late Latin *morātōrius,* delaying, from Latin *mora,* delay.]

Mo·ra·vi·an (mə-rā'vē-ən) *n.* **1.** A native or inhabitant of Moravia. **2.** The Czech dialect spoken in Moravia. **3.** A member of the Moravian Church, a Protestant denomination founded in Saxony in 1722 by Hussite emigrants from Moravia. —**Mo·ra'vi·an** *adj.*

mo·ray (môr'ā, mə-rā') *n.* Any of various often brightly colored, voracious saltwater eels of the family Muraenidae, of tropical coastal waters, feared for their ferocious attacks on swimmers. [Portuguese *moreia,* from Latin *mūrēna,* from Greek *muraina.*]

mor·bid (môr′bĭd) *adj.* **1. a.** Of, relating to, or caused by disease. **b.** Psychologically unhealthy: *a morbid fear of insects.* **2.** Characterized by a preoccupation with gloom, death, decay, etc.; gruesome: *a morbid fascination with torture; a dark, morbid novel.* [Latin *morbidus,* diseased, from *morbus,* disease.] **—mor′bid·ly** *adv.* **—mor′bid·ness** *n.*

mor·bid·i·ty (môr-bĭd′ĭ-tē) *n., pl.* **-ties. 1.** The condition or quality of being morbid. **2.** The rate of occurrence of a disease.

mor·da·cious (môr-dā′shəs) *adj.* **1.** Given to biting. **2.** Caustic; sarcastic. [From Latin *mordāx* , caustic, biting, from *mordēre,* to bite.] **—mor·da′cious·ly** *adv.* **—mor·dac′i·ty** (-dăs′ĭ-tē) *n.*

mor·dant (môr′dnt) *adj.* **1.** Bitingly sarcastic: *mordant criticism.* **2.** Incisive and trenchant: *a mordant wit.* —See Syns at **sarcastic.** **—n. 1.** A substance, such as tannic acid, used to fix coloring matter in textiles, leather, or other materials. **2.** A corrosive substance, such as an acid, used in etching metal. [French, from Old French, from *mordre,* to bite, from Latin *mordēre.*] **—mor′dan·cy** *n.* **—mor′dant·ly** *adv.*

mor·dent (môr′dnt, môr-dĕnt′) *n. Mus.* A melodic ornament in which a principal note is rapidly alternated with a note a half or full step below. [German, from Italian *mordente,* a musical grace, from *mordere,* to bite (from the sharpness of attack with which it is executed), from Latin *mordēre.*]

more (môr, mōr) *adj. Superlative* **most** (mōst). **1. a.** Greater in number. Comparative of **many:** *More people came to the show tonight than ever before.* Often used as a pronoun: *Go ahead and invite everybody you know—the more the merrier.* **b.** Greater in size, amount, extent, or degree. Comparative of **much:** *He does more work than anybody else.* Often used as a pronoun: *There is more than meets the eye in this caper.* **2.** Additional; extra: *We brought more food along just in case.* **—n.** A greater or additional quantity, number, degree, or amount: *More of the same brand is being ordered. More of us are coming, so sit tight.* **—adv. 1.** To or in a greater extent or degree. Used to form the comparative of many adjectives and adverbs: *more difficult; more intelligently.* **2.** In addition; again: *The conspirators stabbed him several times more and then fled.* **—idioms. more or less. 1.** Approximately; about: *The trip takes six hours more or less.* **2.** To some indefinite extent; somewhat: *The book was considered to be more or less a classic.* **all the more.** Even more: *Every delay in the negotiations made him all the more determined to drive a hard bargain.* [Middle English, from Old English *māra.*]

Usage: **more, most.** In comparisons of two persons or things *more* is the usual choice: *She is more talented than her sister. She is the more talented of the two sisters. Most* is used when more than two are present: *She is the most talented pianist in the class.*

mo·reen (mə-rēn′, mō-) *n.* A sturdy ribbed fabric of wool or cotton, used for clothing and upholstery. [Perh. blend of MOIRÉ and VELVETEEN or SATEEN.]

mo·rel (mə-rĕl′, mō-) *n.* Any of various edible mushrooms of the genus *Morchella,* with a brownish, spongelike cap. [French *morille,* from Old French, from Latin *Maurus,* Moor, from Greek *Mauros.*]

more·o·ver (môr-ō′vər, mōr-, môr′ō′vər, mōr′-) *adv.* In addition to what has been said; further; besides.

mo·res (môr′āz, mōr′-, -ēz′) *pl.n.* The customs and rules of a particular social group that are gen. regarded as essential to its survival. [Latin *mōrēs,* pl. of *mōs,* custom.]

Mor·gan (môr′gən) *n.* Any of a breed of light American saddle and trotting horses. [After Justin Morgan, (1747–98), owner of the stallion from which the breed is descended.]

mor·ga·nat·ic (môr′gə-năt′ĭk) *adj.* Of or pertaining to a type of legal marriage between a person of royal or noble birth and a partner of lower rank, in which the person of lower rank and the offspring of the marriage do not share in any titles or estates of the royal or noble partner. [From Medieval Latin *matrimonium ad morganaticam,* "marriage for (no dowry but) the morning-gift" (i.e., the hus-band's token gift to the wife on the morning after the wedding night), from Old High German *morgan,* morning.]

Mor·gan le Fay (môr′gən lə fā′). In Arthurian legend, the sorceress sister and enemy of King Arthur.

morgue (môrg) *n.* **1.** A place in which the bodies of persons found dead are kept until identified. **2.** A file in a newspaper or magazine office for storing old issues and reference material. [French, from *le Morgue,* the mortuary building in Paris.]

mor·i·bund (môr′ə-bŭnd′, mŏr′-) *adj.* In a condition approaching death or an end: *a moribund custom.* [Latin *moribundus,* from *morī,* to die.] **—mor′i·bun′di·ty** *n.*

mo·ri·on (môr′ē-ŏn′, mōr′-) *n.* A metal helmet with a curved peak in front and back, worn by soldiers in the 16th and 17th cent. [French, from Spanish *morrion,* from *morro,* crown of the head.]

Mor·mon (môr′mən) *n.* A member of the Church of Jesus Christ of Latter-day Saints. **—adj.** Of or pertaining to the Mormons, their religion, or their church. **—Mor′mon·ism** *n.*

morn (môrn) *n. Poet.* The morning. [Middle English, from Old English *morgen.*]

morn·ing (môr′nĭng) *n.* **1.** The early part of the day, lasting from midnight to noon or from sunrise to noon. **2.** The hour from daybreak to sunrise; dawn. **3.** The first or early part of anything: *the morning of one's life.* **—modifier:** *the morning sun.*

morn·ing-glo·ry (môr′nĭng-glôr′ē, -glōr′ē) *n., pl.* **-ries.** Any of various usu. twining vines of the genus *Ipomoea,* with funnel-shaped, variously colored flowers that close late in the day.

morning-glory

morning star. A planet, esp. Venus, visible in the eastern sky just before sunrise.

Mo·ro (môr′ō, mōr′ō) *n., pl.* **-ros.** A member of any of the Moslem Malay tribes of the southern Philippines. [Spanish, from Latin *Maurus,* Moor.] **—Mo′ro** *adj.*

mo·roc·co (mə-rŏk′ō) *n., pl.* **-cos. 1.** A soft, fine leather of goatskin tanned with sumac, orig. made in Morocco, used chiefly for bookbindings and shoes. **2.** Any imitation of morocco.

mo·ron (môr′ŏn′, mōr′-) *n.* **1.** A designation for a mentally retarded person with a mental age between 7 and 12 years. **2.** A very stupid or foolish person. [Greek *mōron,* neut. of *mōros,* foolish.] **—mo·ron′ic** (mə-rŏn′ĭk) *adj.*

mo·rose (mə-rōs′, mō-) *adj.* Sullen and gloomy in temperament or mood. [Latin *mōrōsus,* fretful, from *mōs,* custom.] **—mo·rose′ly** *adv.* **—mo·rose′ness** *n.*

morph-. Var. of **morpho-.**

-morph. A suffix meaning: **1.** Form, shape, or structure: **isomorph. 2.** Morpheme: **allomorph.** [From Greek *morphē,* shape, form.]

mor·pheme (môr′fēm′) *n.* A linguistic unit that has meaning and that cannot be divided into smaller meaningful parts, as words such as *man* and *most* or word elements such as *-ly* and *al-* as found in *manly* and *almost.* [French *morphème,* from Greek *morphē,* form.]

mor·phine (môr′fēn′) *n.* A powerfully addictive narcotic drug extracted from opium, used as a light anesthetic and sedative. [French, from *Morpheus,* Greek god of dreams.]

morpho- or **morph-.** A prefix meaning: **1.** Shape, form, or structure: **morphogenesis. 2.** Morpheme: **morphology.** [From Greek *morphē,* shape.]

A .-	Q --.-	1 .----
B -...	R .-.	2 ..---
C -.-.	S ...	3 ...--
D -..	T -	4 ....-
E .	U ..-	5 .....
F ..-.	V ...-	
G --.	W .--	
H	X -..-	, (comma) --..--
I ..	Y -.--	. (period) .-.-.-
J .---	Z --..	; -.-.-.
K -.-	Á .--.-	: ---...
L .-..	Ä .-.-	? ..--..
M --	É ..-..	/ -..-.
N -.	Ñ --.--	- (hyphen) -....-
O ---	Ö ---.	apostrophe .----.
P .--.	Ü ..--	parenthesis -.--.-
		underline ..--.-

Morse code

mor·pho·gen·e·sis (môr′fə-jĕn′ĭ-sĭs) n. Evolutionary or embryological development of the structure of an organism or part. —**mor′pho·ge·net′ic** (-jə-nĕt′ĭk) or **mor′pho·gen′ic** (-jĕn′ĭk) adj.

mor·phol·o·gy (môr-fŏl′ə-jē) n. 1. The biological study of the form and structure of living organisms. 2. The structure and form of an organism, excluding its functions. 3. Ling. The study of word formation, including the origin and function of inflections and derivations. —**mor′pho·log′i·cal** (môr′fə-lŏj′ĭ-kəl) or **mor′pho·log′ic** adj. —**mor′pho·log′i·cal·ly** adv.

mor·ris (môr′ĭs, mŏr′-) n. An English folk dance in which a story is acted by costumed dancers. Also called **morris dance.** [Middle English Moreys, Moorish, from More, Moor.]

Morris chair. A large easy chair with an adjustable back and removable cushions. [After William Morris (1834–96), English artist and writer, its designer.]

mor·row (môr′ō, mŏr′ō) n. 1. The following day. 2. Archaic. The morning. [Middle English morwe, from Old English morgen, morning.]

Morse code (môrs). A code, used esp. in telegraphy, in which letters of the alphabet and numbers are represented by combinations of short and long sounds, light, or written dots and dashes. [After Samuel Morse (1791–1872), American artist, its inventor.]

mor·sel (môr′səl) n. 1. A small piece or bite of food. 2. A small piece or amount of anything. [Middle English, from Old French mors, a bite, from Latin mordēre, to bite.]

mor·tal (môr′tl) adj. 1. Liable or subject to death: mortal creatures. 2. Of or resembling a human being as an imperfect creature; human: a mortal weakness. 3. Of, pertaining to, or accompanying death: mortal throes. 4. Causing death; fatal: a mortal wound. 5. Fought to the death: mortal combat. 6. Unrelentingly antagonistic; implacable: a mortal enemy. 7. Very great or intense; dire: in mortal terror. 8. Capable of being understood; conceivable: There is no mortal reason for us to go. 9. Of this world; earthly: mortal remains. 10. Very long and tedious: "Six mortal hours did I endure her loquacity" (Sir Walter Scott). 11. Rom. Cath. Ch. Causing spiritual death and eternal damnation: Suicide is a mortal sin. —See Syns at fatal. —n. A human being. [Middle English, from Old French, from Latin mortālis, from mors, death.] —**mor′tal·ly** adv.

mor·tal·i·ty (môr-tăl′ĭ-tē) n., pl. -ties. 1. The condition of being subject to death. 2. Frequency of number of deaths in proportion to a population; death rate. 3. Death, esp. of large numbers: a war accompanied by widespread civilian mortality. 4. Mankind; humanity.

mor·tar (môr′tər) n. 1. A receptacle made of a hard material in which substances are crushed or ground with a pestle. 2. A muzzle-loading cannon used to fire shells at short ranges and high trajectories. 3. A mixture of cement or lime with sand and water, used in building to bind bricks, stones, etc. —tr.v. 1. To plaster or join with mortar. 2. To bombard with mortars. [Middle English morter, partly from Old English mortere and partly from Old French mortier, both from Latin mortārium, a mortar and the substance made in it.]

mor·tar·board (môr′tər-bôrd′, -bōrd′) n. 1. A square board with a handle, used to hold and carry mortar. 2. An academic cap with a flat square top and a tassel, worn at graduation and other ceremonies.

mortar
A mortar and pestle

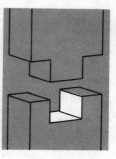

mortise

mort·gage (môr′gĭj) n. 1. A legal pledge of property to a creditor as security for the payment of a loan or other debt. 2. A contract or deed specifying the terms of such a pledge. 3. The claim that the creditor has upon property pledged in this manner. —tr.v. -gaged, -gag·ing. 1. To pledge (property) as security for the payment of a debt. 2. To pledge or stake against future success or failure; risk: mortgage one's future. [Middle English morgage, from Old French mortgage, "dead pledge."]

mort·gag·ee (môr′gə-jē′) n. The holder of a mortgage.

mort·ga·gor (môr′gə-jôr′, môr′gə-jər) n. Also **mort·gag·er** (môr′gə-jər). A person who mortgages his property.

mor·ti·cian (môr-tĭsh′ən) n. An undertaker. [MORT(UARY) + -ICIAN.]

mor·ti·fi·ca·tion (môr′tə-fĭ-kā′shən) n. 1. A feeling of shame, humiliation, or embarrassment. 2. The act or practice of subduing or disciplining bodily appetites and passions by self-denial and austere living. 3. The death or decay of one part of a living body; gangrene.

mor·ti·fy (môr′tə-fī′) v. -fied, -fy·ing. —tr.v. 1. To cause to experience shame, humiliation, or embarrassment. 2. To subdue or discipline (one's bodily appetites and passions) by self-denial and austere living. —intr.v. 1. To practice self-denial or punishment of the body. 2. To become gangrenous. [Middle English mortifien, from Old French mortifier, from Late Latin mortificāre, to cause to die.]

mor·tise (môr′tĭs) n. A usu. rectangular cavity in a piece of wood, stone, or other material, prepared to receive a tenon or similarly shaped projection of another piece so as to join the two together. —tr.v. -tised, -tis·ing. 1. To join or fasten securely with or as if with a mortise and tenon. 2. To cut a mortise in. [Middle English mortays, from Old French mortoise.]

mort·main (môrt′mān′) n. Law. Perpetual ownership of real estate by institutions such as churches that cannot transfer or sell them. [Middle English mortemayne, from Old French mortemain, "dead hand," mortmain.]

mor·tu·ar·y (môr′chōō-ĕr′ē) n., pl. -ies. A place where dead bodies are prepared or kept prior to burial or cremation. [Middle English mortuarie, from Norman French, from Late Latin mortuārium, from Latin mortuus, dead, from mors, death.]

mo·sa·ic (mō-zā′ĭk) n. 1. A picture or decorative design made by setting small colored pieces of glass or tile in cement. 2. The art or process of making such pictures or designs. 3. Anything that resembles a mosaic: Her life was a mosaic of tremendous successes and failures. [Middle English musycke, from Old French mosaique, from Medieval Latin mosaicus, from Greek mouseion, from mouseios, belonging to the Muses.]

Mo·sa·ic (mō-zā′ĭk) adj. Of or pertaining to Moses or the laws ascribed to him.

Mosaic Law. The ancient law of the Hebrews, traditionally attributed to Moses and contained mainly in the Pentateuch.

mo·sey (mō′zē) intr.v. -seyed, -sey·ing. Informal. 1. To amble or shuffle along slowly. 2. To get going; move along. [Orig. unknown.]

Mos·lem (mŏz′ləm, mŏs′-). Also **Mus·lim** or **Mus·lem** (mŭz′-ləm, mōōz′-, mŭs′-, mōōs′-). —n. A believer in or adherent of Islam. —adj. Of Islam. [Arabic muslim.]

ă pat	ā pay	â care	ä father	ĕ pet	ē be	hw which
ōō took	ōō boot	ou out	th thin	th this	ŭ cut
ĭ pit	ī tie	î pier	ŏ pot	ō toe	ô paw, for	oi nois
û urge	zh vision	ə about, item, edible, gallop, circu

Usage: **Moslem, Muslim.** *Moslem* is found largely in journalism and popular usage in general. *Muslim* is preferred by scholars and English-speaking adherents of Islam. *Muslim* is the only form used by the organization of American blacks, Nation of Islam.

mosque (mŏsk) *n.* A Moslem house of worship. [French *mosquée,* from Italian *moschea,* from Arabic *masjid,* a place of worship, from *sajada,* to worship.]

mos·qui·to (mə-skē′tō) *n., pl.* **-toes** or **-tos.** Any of various winged insects of the family Culicidae, in which the female of most species has a long proboscis for sucking blood. Some species transmit diseases such as malaria and yellow fever. [Spanish, from *mosca,* fly, from Latin *musca.*]

mosquito

mosquito net. A fine net used to cover windows and beds to keep out mosquitoes.

moss (môs, mŏs) *n.* **1.** Any of various nonflowering, usu. small green plants of the class Musci, division Bryophyta, that often form a dense, matlike growth on damp ground, rocks, or tree trunks. **2.** Any of various other plants that are similar to moss. [Middle English, from Old English *mos.*]

moss rose. A variety of rose, *Rosa centifolia muscosa,* with fragrant pink flowers and a mossy flower stalk and buds.

moss·y (mô′sē, mŏs′ē) *adj.* **-i·er, -i·est. 1.** Covered with moss or something like moss. **2.** Resembling moss. **—moss′i·ness** *n.*

most (mōst) *adj.* **1. a.** Greatest in number or quantity. Superlative of **many:** *This is the most people I've ever seen in one place.* Often used as a pronoun: *Most came here by special bus.* **b.** Largest in amount, size, or degree. Superlative of **much:** *the most money.* Often used as a pronoun: *Most of the collection was lost in the war.* **2.** In the greatest number of instances: *Most fish have fins.* —See Usage note at **more. —***n.* **1.** The greatest amount, quantity, or degree; the largest part: *Most of this land is good.* **2.** The largest number; the majority: *Most of these stones are worthless.* **3. the most.** *Slang.* Someone or something extremely good or exciting: *That group is really the most.* —*adv.* **1.** In the highest degree, quantity, or extent. Used with many adjectives and adverbs to form the superlative: *most honest; most impatiently.* **2.** Very: *a most impressive piece of work.* **3.** *Informal.* Almost; just about: *Most everybody's here already.* **—idioms. at (the) most.** At the absolute limit: *She's in her late teens, 20 at the most.* **for the most part.** Mostly; mainly: *The settlers were, for the most part, farmers.* **make the most of.** To make the best use of: *making the most of a bad situation.*

-most. A suffix indicating the superlative degree of adverbs and adjectives: *innermost.* [Middle English, from Old English *-mæst, -mest.*]

most·ly (mōst′lē) *adv.* For the most part; almost entirely.

mot (mō) *n.* A short, witty, or clever saying. [French, word, saying, from Old French *muttum,* grunt, from *muttīre,* to mutter.]

mote (mōt) *n.* A speck, esp. of dust. [Middle English *mot,* from Old English.]

mo·tel (mō-tĕl′) *n.* A hotel for motorists, usu. with blocks of rooms opening directly on a parking area. [Blend of MOTOR and HOTEL.]

mo·tet (mō-tĕt′) *n.* A polyphonic musical composition, often based on a religious text and usu. sung without accompaniment. [Middle English, from Old French, from *mot,* phrase, word.]

moth (môth, mŏth) *n., pl.* **moths** (môthz, mŏthz, môths,

moths). Any of numerous insects of the order Lepidoptera, related to the butterflies but distinguished from them by their flying at night, their hairlike or feathery antennae, and their stout bodies. [Middle English *motthe,* from Old English *moththe.*]

moth·ball (môth′bôl′, mŏth′-) *n.* **1.** A marble-sized ball of camphor or naphthalene, stored with clothes to repel moths. **2. mothballs.** A condition of long storage: *warships put into mothballs.*

moth-eat·en (môth′ēt′n, mŏth′-) *adj.* **1.** Eaten away by moths. **2.** Old-fashioned or run-down.

moth·er¹ (mŭth′ər) *n.* **1.** A female that has borne an offspring. **2.** A female who has adopted a child or otherwise acted as a guardian for another person. **3.** A creative or environmental source; origin; cause: *Poverty is the mother of many ills.* **4.** A woman having some of the responsibilities of a mother: *a house mother.* **5.** Qualities attributed to a mother, as the capacity to love: *The baby appealed to the mother in her.* **6.** An elderly woman. **7.** A **mother superior.** —*adj.* **1.** Being or resembling a mother: *a mother hen.* **2.** Characteristic of a mother: *mother love.* **3.** Protecting or nourishing like a mother: *the mother church.* **4.** Native: *one's mother tongue.* —*tr.v.* **1.** To give birth to; be the mother of. **2.** To watch over, nourish, and protect. [Middle English *moder,* from Old English *mōdor.*] **—moth′er·less** *adj.*

moth·er² (mŭth′ər) *n.* A stringy slime composed of yeast cells and bacteria that forms on the surface of fermenting liquid and is added to wine or cider to start production of vinegar. [Prob. from MOTHER.]

Mother Car·ey's chicken (kâr′ēz). Any of various petrels, esp. the storm petrel. [Orig. unknown.]

Mother Goose. The imaginary author of a collection of English nursery rhymes.

moth·er·hood (mŭth′ər-hŏŏd′) *n.* The condition of being a mother.

Mother Hub·bard (hŭb′ərd). **1.** The title of a well-known nursery rhyme. **2.** A woman's long, loose, unbelted dress.

moth·er-in-law (mŭth′ər-ĭn-lô′) *n., pl.* **moth·ers-in-law.** The mother of one's wife or husband.

moth·er·land (mŭth′ər-lănd′) *n.* **1.** The land or country of one's birth. **2.** The native country of one's ancestors.

moth·er·ly (mŭth′ər-lē) *adj.* Of, befitting, resembling, or characteristic of a mother; maternal. **—moth′er·li·ness** *n.*

moth·er-of-pearl (mŭth′ər-əv-pûrl′) *n.* The hard, smooth, pearly layer on the inside of certain oyster shells and other seashells, used to make buttons, jewelry, etc. Also called **nacre.**

Mother's Day. The second Sunday in May set aside in honor of mothers and motherhood.

mother superior. A woman in charge of a female religious community.

mother tongue. 1. A person's native language. **2.** A language from which another is derived.

moth·proof (môth′prŏŏf′, mŏth′-) *adj.* Resistant to damage by moths. —*tr.v.* To make resistant to damage by moths.

moth·y (mô′thē, mŏth′ē) *adj.* **-i·er, -i·est.** Infested or damaged by moths.

mo·tif (mō-tēf′) *n.* **1.** A recurrent thematic element, as an idea, symbol, or incident, in an artistic or literary work. **2.** A short melodic fragment in a musical composition that can be associated with a particular theme. **3.** A repeated figure, shape, color, or design in architecture or decoration: *a necktie with a flower motif.* [French.]

mo·tile (mōt′l, mō′tīl′) *adj.* Moving or having the power to move, as certain spores and microorganisms. [From MOTION.] **—mo·til·i·ty** (mō-tĭl′ĭ-tē) *n.*

mo·tion (mō′shən) *n.* **1.** The act or process of moving or changing position. **2.** A meaningful or expressive change in the position of the body or a part of the body; a movement: *the subtle motions of a dancer.* **3.** A formal proposal made in a court of law or deliberative assembly: *a motion to vote on the issue.* —*tr.v.* To signal to or direct by making a gesture: *The policeman motioned us to cross.* —*intr.v.* To make a gesture signifying something, such as agreement. [Middle English *mocioun,* from Old French *motion,* from Latin *mōtiō,* from *movēre,* to move.] **—mo′tion·less** *adj.*

motion picture. 1. A series of filmed images projected on a screen in rapid succession to create the illusion of motion and continuity. **2.** A series of such pictures designed to depict a particular story or record a set of events.

motion sickness. Nausea, vomiting, and often dizziness caused by motion, as from riding in an automobile, airplane, or ship.

mo·ti·vate (mō'tə-vāt') *tr.v.* **-vat·ed, -vat·ing.** To stir to action; provide with a motive. —See Syns at **provoke.**

mo·ti·va·tion (mō'tə-vā'shən) *n.* **1.** The act or process of motivating. **2.** An incentive or motive, esp. for an act. —See Syns at **stimulus.** **—mo'ti·va'tion·al** *adj.*

mo·tive (mō'tĭv) *n.* **1.** An emotion, desire, bodily need, or similar impulse that causes one to act in a particular manner: *a crime with no apparent motive.* **2.** (also mō-tēv'). A motif. *—adj.* Causing or able to cause motion: *motive power produced by an engine.* [Middle English, from Old French *motif,* from from Late Latin *mōtīvus,* causing to move, from Latin *movēre,* to move.]

mot juste (mō zhüst') *pl.* **mots justes** (mō zhüst'). *French.* The most suitable word or expression.

mot·ley (mŏt'lē) *adj.* **1.** Made up of an odd or varied assortment of different types: *a motley crew.* **2.** Having many colors; multicolored: *the motley suit of a clown.* *—n.* **1.** A costume of many colors, esp. one worn by a clown or jester. **2.** A mixture of incongruous or diverse elements. [Middle English *motteley.*]

mo·to·neu·ron (mō'tə-nŏŏr'ŏn', -nyŏŏr'-) *n.* A neuron that stimulates motion; motor nerve cell. [MOTO(R) + NEURON.]

mo·tor (mō'tər) *n.* **1.** Something that imparts or produces motion, as a machine or engine. **2.** A device that converts any form of energy into mechanical energy, esp. an internal-combustion engine. **3.** A motorized vehicle, esp. an automobile. *—adj.* **1.** Causing or producing motion: *motor power.* **2.** Driven by or having a motor: *a motor scooter.* **3.** Of, pertaining to, or for motor vehicles: *motor oil.* **4.** *Physiol.* **a.** Of, pertaining to, or designating nerves carrying impulses from the nerve centers to the muscles. **b.** Of or relating to movements of the muscles: *motor coordination.* *—intr.v.* To drive or travel in a motor vehicle. [Latin *mōtor,* mover, from *movēre,* to move.]

mo·tor·bike (mō'tər-bīk') *n.* **1.** A lightweight motorcycle. **2.** A bicycle powered by an attached motor.

mo·tor·boat (mō'tər-bōt') *n.* A boat propelled by an internal-combustion engine.

mo·tor·bus (mō'tər-bŭs') *n.* A bus.

mo·tor·cade (mō'tər-kād') *n.* A procession of automobiles. [MOTOR + (CAVAL)CADE.]

mo·tor·car (mō'tər-kär') *n.* An automobile.

motor court. A motel.

mo·tor·cy·cle (mō'tər-sī'kəl) *n.* A vehicle with two wheels, similar to a bicycle but larger and heavier, propelled by an internal-combustion engine. *—intr.v.* **-cled, -cling.** To ride on or drive a motorcycle. **—mo'tor·cy'clist** (-sī'klĭst) *n.*

mo·tor·ist (mō'tər-ĭst) *n.* A person who drives or rides in an automobile.

mo·tor·ize (mō'tə-rīz') *tr.v.* **-ized, -iz·ing.** **1.** To equip with a motor. **2.** To supply with motor-driven vehicles: *motorized infantry divisions.* **—mo'tor·i·za'tion** *n.*

mo·tor·man (mō'tər-mən) *n.* A person who drives a streetcar, locomotive, or subway train.

motor scooter. A small two-wheeled vehicle with a low-powered gasoline engine.

motor vehicle. Any self-propelled motor-powered vehicle that travels on wheels but does not run on rails.

mot·tle (mŏt'l) *tr.v.* **-tled, -tling.** To cover with spots or streaks of different shades or colors. *—n.* A mottled coloration or pattern, as on marble. [Prob. back-formation from MOTLEY.]

mot·to (mŏt'ō) *n., pl.* **-toes** or **-tos.** **1.** A brief sentence, phrase, or word used to express a principle, goal, or ideal: *His motto was "Live and let live."* **2.** A brief statement inscribed on or attached to something to indicate its nature or content. [Italian, word, from Latin *muttum,* grunt, from *muttīre,* to mutter.]

moue (mōō) *n.* A grimace; a pout. [French.]

mou·flon (mōō'flŏn') *n.* Also **mouf·flon.** A wild sheep, *Ovis musimon,* of Sardinia and Corsica, with a dark coat, and large curving horns in the male. [French, from Italian *muflone,* from Late Latin *mufrō,* sheep.]

mould (mōld) *n. & v. Brit.* Var. of **mold.**

moult (mōlt) *v. & n. Brit.* Var. of **molt.**

mound (mound) *n.* **1.** A manmade pile of earth, gravel, sand, etc., as for protection or concealment: *a burial mound.* **2.** A natural elevation, such as a small hill. **3.** Any pile or raised mass, as of hay. **4.** *Baseball.* The slightly elevated pitcher's area in the center of the diamond. *—tr.v.* **1.** To fortify or conceal with a mound. **2.** To heap in a mound. [Orig. unknown.]

mound builder. A member of one of the prehistoric North American Indian tribes who built burial mounds, mainly in the Mississippi valley.

mount¹ (mount) *tr.v.* **1.** To climb or ascend: *mounted the stairs.* **2.** To get up on: *mount a horse.* **3.** To provide with a riding horse. **4. a.** To fix securely by attaching to a support or structure: *mount an antenna on a chimney.* **b.** To place or fix on or in a secure position for display or study: *mount pictures on cardboard.* **5.** To plan and start to carry out: *mount an attack; mount an advertising campaign.* **6.** To provide (a theatrical presentation) with scenery, costumes, and other accessories. **7. a.** To set (guns) in position. **b.** To be furnished with or carry: *The warship mounted ten guns.* **c.** To post (a guard): *mount sentries.* *—intr.v.* **1.** To go or move upward: *a rocket mounting to the heavens.* **2.** To get or climb up on a horse or vehicle. **3.** To increase, as in amount, degree, extent, intensity, or number: *The suspense mounted. The death toll mounted.* —See Syns at **increase** and **rise.** *—n.* **1.** A horse or other animal for riding. **2.** An object or structure that secures and supports something else: *a camera mount.* [Middle English *mounten,* from Old French *monter,* from Latin *mōns,* mountain.]

mount² (mount) *n.* A mountain or hill. [Middle English *mont,* from Old French *mont* and Old English *munt,* both from Latin *mōns,* mountain.]

moun·tain (moun'tən) *n.* **1.** A natural elevation of the earth's surface that has considerable mass, gen. steep sides, and a height greater than that of a hill. **2.** A large heap: *a mountain of ironing.* **3.** A huge quantity: *a mountain of trouble.* [Middle English *mountaine,* from Old French *montaigne,* from Latin *montānus,* mountainous, from *mōns,* mountain.]

mountain ash. Any of various deciduous trees of the genus *Sorbus,* belonging to the rose family, with clusters of small white flowers and bright orange-red berries.

moun·tain·eer (moun'tə-nîr') *n.* **1.** A person who lives in a mountainous area. **2.** A person who climbs mountains for sport.

mountain goat. A hoofed mammal, *Oreamnos americanus,* of northwestern North America, with short, curved black horns and thick yellowish-white hair and beard. Also called **Rocky Mountain goat.**

mountain laurel. An evergreen shrub, *Kalmia latifolia,* of eastern North America, with leathery, poisonous leaves and clusters of pink or white flowers.

mountain laurel

mountain lion. A large, powerful wild cat, *Felis concolor,* of mountainous regions of western North America and South America, with an unmarked tawny body. Also called **cougar, panther,** and **puma.**

moun·tain·ous (moun'tə-nəs) *adj.* **1.** Having many mountains. **2.** Huge; massive: *mountainous snowdrifts.* See Syns at **giant.**

ă pat	ā pay	â care	ä father	ĕ pet	ē be	hw which	ĭ pit	ī tie	î pier	ŏ pot	ō toe	ô paw, for	oi noise
ōō took	ōō boot	ou out	th thin	th this	ŭ cut		û urge	zh vision	ə about, item, edible, gallop, circus				

mountain range. A series of mountain ridges alike in form, direction, and origin.

moun·tain·side (moun'tən-sīd') *n.* Any of the sloping sides of a mountain.

Mountain Standard Time. Standard time as reckoned in the region between the meridians at 97.5° and 112.5° west of Greenwich, England. The Rocky Mountain area of the United States is in this region.

moun·tain·top (moun'tən-tŏp') *n.* The summit of a mountain.

moun·te·bank (moun'tə-băngk') *n.* **1.** A roving peddler of quack medicines who attracts customers with stories, jokes, or tricks. **2.** Any imposter or swindler. [Italian *montambanco : montare,* to mount + *banco, banca,* bench.]

mount·ed (moun'tĭd) *adj.* **1.** Seated or riding on a horse: *a mounted guard.* **2.** Equipped with a horse or horses: *a mounted policeman.* **3.** Fitted into or set in a backing or support: *a mounted photograph; a mounted gemstone.*

mount·ing (moun'tĭng) *n.* **1.** The act of rising or getting up on something. **2.** A supporting structure or frame; a mount: *lift a globe from its mounting.*

mourn (môrn, mōrn) *intr.v.* **1.** To express or feel grief or sorrow, esp. for someone who has died. **2.** To express public grief and honor for. —*tr.v.* To feel or express sorrow for; lament; deplore: *mourn his sad fate.* [Middle English *mournen,* from Old English *murnan.*] —**mourn'er** *n.*

mourn·ful (môrn'fəl, mōrn'-) *adj.* **1.** Feeling or expressing grief. **2.** Arousing or suggesting grief: *a mournful song.* —**mourn'ful·ly** *adv.* —**mourn'ful·ness** *n.*

mourn·ing (môr'nĭng, mōr'-) *n.* **1.** The expression of grief. **2.** The conventional outward signs of grief for the dead, esp. the wearing of black. **3.** The period during which a death is mourned. —**mourn'ing·ly** *adv.*

mourning dove. A wild dove, *Zenaidura macroura,* of North America, noted for its plaintive call.

mouse (mous) *n., pl.* **mice** (mīs). **1.** Any of numerous small rodents of the families Muridae and Cricetidae that characteristically have a pointed snout, proportionately small ears, and a long, narrow, almost hairless tail. **2.** *Informal.* A cowardly or timid person. **3.** *Slang.* A black eye. —*intr.v.* (mouz) **moused, mous·ing. 1.** To hunt, stalk, or catch mice. **2.** To search secretly for something; prowl. [Middle English *mous,* from Old English *mūs.*]

mous·er (mou'zər) *n.* An animal, esp. a cat, that catches mice.

mousse (mōōs) *n.* **1.** A chilled dessert made with whipped cream, gelatin, and flavoring. **2.** A molded dish made from a purée of meat, fish, or shellfish with whipped cream. [French, "froth."]

mousse·line (mōō-slēn') *n.* A fine cotton fabric orig. made in Mosul, Iraq. [French, muslin.]

mous·tache (mŭs'tăsh', mə-stăsh') *n.* Var. of **mustache.**

mous·y (mou'sē, -zē) *adj.* **-i·er, -i·est. 1.** Mouselike in color or appearance: *mousy hair.* **2.** Timid and unnoticeable.

mouth (mouth) *n., pl.* **mouths** (mouthz). **1.** *Anat.* **a.** The opening through which an animal takes in food. **b.** The group of organs associated with this opening and its function, including the lips, teeth, tongue, and associated parts with which food is chewed and swallowed and sounds and speech are articulated. **2.** The part of the lips visible on the human face. **3.** A consumer of food: *hungry mouths to feed.* **4.** A pout, grimace, or similar expression. **5.** A manner of speech: *a foul mouth; a big mouth.* **6.** A natural opening, such as the part of a river that empties into a larger body of water or the entrance to a canyon or cave. **7.** An opening into a container or enclosure: *the mouth of a bottle.* —*tr.v.* **1.** To utter mechanically, without conviction or understanding: *mouthing phrases.* **2.** To put, take, or move around in the mouth. —*intr.v.* To speak in an affected manner; rant. —**idiom. down in (or at) the mouth.** *Informal.* Crestfallen; unhappy; depressed. [Middle English, from Old English *mūth.*]

mouth·ful (mouth'fōōl') *n., pl.* **-fuls. 1.** The amount of food or other material that can be taken into the mouth at one time. **2.** *Informal.* A word or phrase that is complicated or difficult to pronounce. —**idiom. say a mouthful.** *Slang.* To utter an important or esp. perceptive remark or observation.

mouth organ. 1. A harmonica. **2.** A panpipe.

mouth·piece (mouth'pēs') *n.* **1.** A part, as of a musical instrument or a telephone, that is used by placing in or near the mouth. **2.** A protective rubber device worn over the teeth by boxers and certain other athletes. **3.** *Informal.* A spokesman. **4.** *Slang.* A criminal lawyer.

mouth·y (mou'thē, -thē) *adj.* **-i·er, -i·est.** Given to ranting; bombastic.

mov·a·ble (mōō'və-bəl) *adj.* Also **move·a·ble. 1.** Capable of being moved. **2.** Varying in date from year to year: *a movable holiday.* —See Syns at **moving.** —*n.* Often **movables. 1.** Something that can be moved, esp. furniture, as opposed to permanent fixtures. **2.** *Law.* Personal property as distinguished from real property such as land. —**mov'a·bil'i·ty** or **mov'a·ble·ness** *n.* —**mov'a·bly** *adv.*

move (mōōv) *v.* **moved, mov·ing.** —*intr.v.* **1.** To change in position from one place or point to another: *Move away from the window.* **2.** To go forward; advance: *a novel that moves slowly.* **3.** To proceed in a specified direction or course: *The earth moves in orbit.* **4.** To change one's place of residence or business. **5.** To change hands, as by sale: *Furs move slowly in summer.* **6.** To show activity; stir: *was so tired that I couldn't move.* **7.** To take action: *moved quickly to block the strike.* **8.** To live or be active in a particular environment: *move in diplomatic circles.* **9.** To make a formal motion in parliamentary procedure: *move for an adjournment.* —*tr.v.* **1. a.** To change the place or position of. **b.** To change from one position to another in a board game: *moved a pawn.* **2.** To cause to take action: *Patriotism moved him to enlist.* **3. a.** To set or maintain in motion: *wind moving a windmill.* **b.** To cause to function. **4.** To arouse the emotions of: *Her tears moved him deeply.* **5.** To propose in formal parliamentary procedure: *move adjournment.* **6.** To sell: *can't move the big cars.* **7.** To cause (the bowels) to evacuate. —See Syns at **provoke.** —*n.* **1.** The act of moving: *Nobody dared make a move.* **2.** A change of residence or place of business. **3.** *Board Games.* **a.** The act of moving a piece. **b.** A player's turn to move a piece. **4.** A calculated action to achieve an end: *His shrewdest move was to do nothing.* —**idioms. get a move on.** To get started; get going. **on the move. 1.** Traveling about. **2.** Making progress; advancing: *a company on the move.* [Middle English *moven,* from Norman French *mover,* from Latin *movēre,* to move.]

move·a·ble (mōō'və-bəl) *adj.* Var. of **movable.**

move·ment (mōōv'mənt) *n.* **1.** The act, process, or an instance of moving. **2.** A group engaged in actions intended to achieve a specific goal: *the labor movement.* **3.** A tendency or trend: *a movement toward fiscal conservatism.* **4. a.** An evacuation of the bowels. **b.** The matter so evacuated. **5.** *Mus.* **a.** A section of a large composition, as a symphony or sonata. **b.** Rhythm; tempo. **6.** A mechanism that produces motion, as the works of a watch.

mov·er (mōō'vər) *n.* **1.** Someone or something that moves. **2.** A person or company that is hired to move furniture and other belongings from one place to another.

mov·ie (mōō'vē) *n. Informal.* **1.** A motion picture. **2. movies.** A showing of a motion picture. **3. movies.** The motion picture industry. [Short for MOVING PICTURE.]

mov·ing (mōō'vĭng) *adj.* **1.** Capable of or showing movement: *moving parts; a moving train.* **2.** Causing or producing motion or action: *the moving force behind his success.* **3.** Affecting the emotions: *a moving love story.* **4.** Of or related to a change of residence: *a moving van.* —**mov'ing·ly** *adv.*

Syns: 1. moving, mobile, movable *adj.* **Core meaning:** Capable of moving or being moved from place to place (*a moving automobile; moving missile launchers*). **2. moving, poignant, stirring, touching** *adj.* **Core meaning:** Eliciting a deep emotional response (*a moving sermon*).

moving picture. A motion picture.

mow¹ (mō) *v.* **mowed, mowed** or **mown** (mōn), **mow·ing.** —*tr.v.* **1.** To cut down with a scythe, lawn mower, or machine. **2.** To cut esp. grain or grass from: *mow the lawn.* —*phrasal verb.* **mow down.** To destroy in great numbers, as in battle. [Middle English *mowen,* from Old English *māwan.*] —**mow'er** *n.*

mow² (mou) *n.* **1.** A pile of hay or grain, esp. in a barn. **2.** The part of a barn where such a pile is stored. [Middle

English, stack of hay, from Old English *mūwa*.]

Mox·ie (mŏk′sē) *n. Slang.* The ability to face difficulty with spirit; nerve; guts. [From *Moxie*, a trademark for a soft drink.]

moz·za·rel·la (mŏt′sə-rĕl′ə, mŏt′-) *n.* A soft, white Italian cheese with a mild flavor. [Italian, dim. of *mozza*, slice, (sliced) cheese, from *mozzare*, to cut off.]

mu (myōō, mōō) *n.* The 12th letter in the Greek alphabet, written M, μ. [Greek.]

much (mŭch) *adj.* **more, most.** Great in quantity, degree, or extent: *Did much rain fall?* —*n.* **1.** A large quantity or amount: *Did you get much done?* **2.** Something remarkable or important: *As a leader, he is not much.* —*adv.* **more, most. 1.** To a large extent; greatly: *much easier.* **2.** Just about; almost: *much the same.* —**idioms. make much of.** To pay great attention to: *to make much of small error.* [Middle English *muche*, from Old English *mycel*, great, much.]

mu·ci·lage (myōō′sə-lĭj) *n.* **1.** A sticky substance widely used as an adhesive. **2.** A sticky substance made from the natural gum of certain plants. [Middle English *muscilage*, from Old French *mucilage*, from Late Latin *mūcilāgō*, musty juice, from Latin *mūcus*, mucus.] —**mu′ci·lag′i·nous** (-lăj′ə-nəs) *adj.*

muck (mŭk) *n.* **1.** A moist, sticky mixture, esp. of mud and filth. **2.** Moist animal dung; manure. **3.** Dark, fertile soil containing putrid vegetable matter. **4.** Something regarded as filthy or disgusting. —*tr.v. Informal.* To soil or make dirty with or as if with muck. —*phrasal verb.* **muck up.** *Informal.* To mismanage; botch. [Middle English *muk*, from Old Norse *mykr*.] —**muck′y** *adj.*

muck·rake (mŭk′rāk′) *intr.v.* **-raked, -rak·ing.** To search for and expose wrongdoing or corruption. [Back-formation from MUCKRAKER.] —**muck′rak′er** *n.*

mu·cous (myōō′kəs) *adj.* **1.** Producing or secreting mucus. **2.** Of or resembling mucus. [Latin *mūcōsus*, from *mūcus*, mucus.]

mucous membrane. The mucus-secreting membrane that lines bodily passages, such as the respiratory and alimentary tracts, that open to outside air.

mu·cus (myōō′kəs) *n.* The viscous liquid secreted as a protective, lubricant coating by glands in the mucous membrane. [Latin *mūcus*.]

mud (mŭd) *n.* Wet, sticky, soft earth. [Middle English *mudde*.]

mud dauber. Any of several wasps with long hind legs and a slender abdomen. The female lays eggs in a nest of mud provided with paralyzed insects as food for the larva.

mud·dle (mŭd′l) *tr.v.* **-dled, -dling. 1.** To make disorderly or confused; jumble: *The report muddles the issues.* **2.** To confuse with or as if with alcohol; befuddle. **3.** To mismanage; bungle: *muddle a job.* See Syns at **botch** and **confuse.** —*phrasal verb.* **muddle through.** To accomplish in a confused, blundering fashion. —*n.* **1.** A state of confusion. **2.** A jumble; mess. [Perh. from Middle Dutch *moddelen*, to make muddy, from *modde*, mud.] —**mud′dler** *n.*

mud·dle-head·ed (mŭd′l-hĕd′ĭd) *adj.* Mentally confused; stupid; dull.

mud·dy (mŭd′ē) *adj.* **-di·er, -di·est. 1.** Covered, full of, or soiled with mud. **2.** Cloudy or dull with or as if with mud: *a muddy creek.* **3.** Confused or obscure: *a muddy style of writing.* —*tr.v.* **-died, -dy·ing. 1.** To soil with mud. **2.** To make dull or cloudy with or as if with mud. **3.** To confuse or obscure: *muddy an issue.* —**mud′di·ly** *adv.* —**mud′di·ness** *n.*

mud·guard (mŭd′gärd′) *n.* A covering that deflects mud, usu. positioned over a vehicle's wheel.

mud hen. Any of various birds, such as the coot, gallinule, or rail, inhabiting marshy regions.

mud puppy. Any of various aquatic salamanders of the genus *Necturus*, with prominent conspicuous clusters of external gills.

mud·sling·er (mŭd′slĭng′ər) *n.* A person who makes abusive and slanderous charges about an opponent. —**mud′sling′ing** *n.*

mud turtle. Any turtle of the genus *Kinosternon*, found in freshwater ponds and rivers throughout the Western Hemisphere.

mu·ez·zin (myōō-ĕz′ĭn, mōō-) *n.* A Moslem crier who calls the daily hours of prayer. [Arabic *mu'adhdhin*, from *adhana*, to cause to listen, from *adhina*, to listen.]

muff[1] (mŭf) *v.* **muffed, muf·fing.** —*tr.v.* To perform clumsily; bungle: *He muffed his chance for the job.* —See Syns at **botch.** —*n.* A clumsy or bungled act. [Orig. unknown.]

muff[2] (mŭf) *n.* A cylindrical cover open at both ends, used to keep the hands warm. [Dutch *mof*, from Middle Dutch *moffel*, from Old French *moufle*, glove.]

muf·fin (mŭf′ĭn) *n.* A small, cup-shaped bread, usu. served hot. [Prob. from Low German *muffen*, pl. of *muffe*, cake.]

muf·fle (mŭf′əl) *tr.v.* **-fled, -fling. 1.** To wrap up in for warmth, protection, or secrecy. **2.** To wrap or pad in order to deaden a sound: *muffle a drum.* **3.** To deaden the sound of: *a muffled scream.* **4.** To suppress or silence: *muffle political opposition.* [Middle English *muflen*, from Old French *enmoufler*, to put on a muff or mittens, from *moufle*, mitten, from Medieval Latin *muffula*.]

muf·fler (mŭf′lər) *n.* **1.** A heavy scarf worn around the neck for warmth. **2.** A device that absorbs noise, esp. that in an automotive engine.

muf·ti (mŭf′tē) *n.* Civilian dress. [From Arabic *muftī*, judge.]

mug (mŭg) *n.* **1.** A large, heavy drinking cup. **2.** The liquid contained in a mug: *a mug of coffee.* **3.** *Slang.* A person's face. **4.** *Slang.* A hoodlum. —*v.* **mugged, mug·ging.** *Slang.* —*tr.v.* **1.** To take a photograph of for police files. **2.** To assault with intent to rob. —*intr.v.* To grimace, esp. to get attention. [Orig. unknown.]

mug·ger (mŭg′ər) *n.* Someone who assaults with the intent to rob.

mug·gy (mŭg′ē) *adj.* **-gi·er, -gi·est.** Warm and extremely humid. [From English dial. *mug*, fine rain, from Middle English *muggen*, to drizzle, from Old Norse *mugga*.] —**mug′gi·ness** *n.*

mug·wump (mŭg′wŭmp′) *n.* **1.** A Republican who refused to support the party candidate for the U.S. presidency in 1884. **2.** A person who acts independently, esp. in politics. [Natick *mugwomp*, captain.]

Mu·ham·mad·an (mō-hăm′ĭ-dən) *n.* A Mohammedan. —**Mu·ham′mad·an** *adj.* —**Mu·ham′mad·an·ism** *n.*

muk·luk (mŭk′lŭk′) *n.* **1.** A soft Eskimo boot made of reindeer skin or sealskin. **2.** A slipper similar to a mukluk. [Eskimo *muklok*, large seal.]

mu·lat·to (mōō-lăt′ō, -lä′tō, myōō-) *n., pl.* **-tos** or **-toes. 1.** A person having one white and one Negro parent. **2.** Any person of mixed white and Negro ancestry. [Spanish *mulato*, from *mulo*, mule, from Latin *mūlus*.]

mul·ber·ry (mŭl′bĕr′ē, -bə-rē) *n., pl.* **-ries. 1.** Any of several trees of the genus *Morus*, with irregularly shaped leaves and sweet, purplish or white fruit. **2.** The sweet, edible, berry like fruit of any of these trees. **3.** A dull purplish red. —*adj.* Dull purplish red. [Middle English *mulberrie*, from Old English *mōrberie* : Latin *mōrum*, mulberry + Old English *berie*, berry.]

mulch (mŭlch) *n.* A protective covering, as of leaves or hay, placed around plants to prevent evaporation of moisture and to control weeds. —*tr.v.* To cover with a mulch. [Earlier, rotten hay, prob. from Middle English *mulsh*, soft, yielding, from Old English *mylsc*, mild, mellow.]

mulct (mŭlkt) *n.* A fine or similar penalty. —*tr.v.* **1.** To penalize by fining. **2.** To swindle or defraud. [Latin *mulcta*, a fine.]

mule[1] (myōōl) *n.* **1.** A sterile hybrid animal that is the offspring of a donkey and a horse. **2.** *Informal.* A stubborn person. **3.** A type of spinning machine that draws and spins thread or fibers into yarn. [Middle English *mul*, from Old English *mūl* and Old French *mul*, both from Latin *mūlus*, mule.]

mule[2] (myōōl) *n.* An open slipper or shoe that leaves the heel bare. [Old French, slipper, from Latin *mulleus* (*calceus*), "red (shoe)."]

mule deer. A hoofed mammal, *Odocoileus hemionus*, of western North America, with long ears, two-pronged antlers, and a brownish gray coat.

mule·skin·ner (myōōl′skĭn′ər) *n. Informal.* A driver of mules.

mu·le·teer (myōō′lə-tîr′) *n.* A driver of mules. [Old French *muletier*, from *mulet*, dim. of *mul*, mule.]

ă pat   ā pay   â care   ä father   ĕ pet   ē be   hw which   ĭ pit   ī tie   î pier   ŏ pot   ō toe   ô paw, for   oi noise
ōō took   ōō boot   ou out   th thin   th this   ŭ cut   û urge   zh vision   ə about, item, edible, gallop, circus

mull¹ (mŭl) *tr.v.* To heat with spices and sweetening: *mulled cider.* [Perh. from Middle English *mul,* dust, meal, powdered spice, from Middle Dutch.]

mull² (mŭl) *intr.v.* To ponder or ruminate: *mull over a plan.* [From Middle English *mullen,* to pulverize, from *mul,* dust, from Middle Dutch.]

mull³ (mŭl) *n.* A soft, thin kind of muslin used in dresses and for trimmings. [Short for *mulmull,* from Hindi *malmal,* from Persian.]

mul·lah (mŭl'ə, mŏŏl'ə) *n.* A Moslem religious teacher or leader, esp. one trained in law. [Turkish *mulla* and Persian *mullā,* from Arabic *mawlā,* "master."]

mul·lein (mŭl'ən) *n.* Any of various tall plants of the genus *Verbascum,* with closely clustered yellow flowers and leaves covered with dense, woolly down. [Middle English *moleyne,* from Old French *moleine,* prob. from *mol,* soft, from Latin *mollis.*]

mul·let (mŭl'ĭt) *n., pl.* **mullet** or **-lets.** Any of various saltwater and freshwater edible fishes of the family Mugilidae found worldwide in tropical and temperate regions. [Middle English *molet,* from Old French *mulet,* from Latin *mullus,* red mullet, from Greek *mullos.*]

mul·li·gan (mŭl'ĭ-gən) *n.* A stew of various meats and vegetables. Also called **mulligan stew.** [Prob. from the name *Mulligan.*]

mul·lion (mŭl'yən) *n.* A vertical strip dividing the panes of a window. [Var. of obs. *monial,* a mullion, from Middle English *moniel,* from Old French *moynel,* from *moyen,* middle, from Latin *mediānus,* from *medius.*]

multi-. A prefix meaning: **1.** Many or much: **multicolored. 2.** More than one: **multivalent.** [Middle English, from Latin, from *multus,* much.]

mul·ti·cel·lu·lar (mŭl'tĭ-sĕl'yə-lər) *adj.* Containing many cells.

mul·ti·col·ored (mŭl'tĭ-kŭl'ərd) *adj.* Having many colors.

mul·ti·far·i·ous (mŭl'tə-fâr'ē-əs) *adj.* Having great variety; of many parts or kinds. [Latin *multifārius : multi-,* many + *fārius,* doing.] **—mul'ti·far'i·ous·ly** *adv.* **—mul'ti·far'i·ous·ness** *n.*

mul·ti·form (mŭl'tə-fôrm') *adj.* Occurring in or having many forms, shapes, or appearances.

mul·ti·lat·er·al (mŭl'tə-lăt'ər-əl) *adj.* **1.** Having many sides. **2.** Involving more than two governments or parties. **—mul'ti·lat'er·al·ly** *adv.*

mul·ti·mil·lion·aire (mŭl'tə-mĭl'yə-nâr') *n.* A person whose assets equal many millions.

mul·ti·na·tion·al (mŭl'tē-năsh'ən-əl, -năsh'nəl) *adj.* Of, relating to, or involving more than one country: *a multinational corporation.*

mul·tip·a·rous (mŭl-tĭp'ər-əs) *adj.* **1.** Having borne more than one child. **2.** Giving birth to more than one offspring at one time. [MULTI- + -PAROUS.]

mul·ti·ple (mŭl'tə-pəl) *adj.* Having, pertaining to, or consisting of more than one individual, element, or part; manifold: *multiple imperfections.* **—n.** *Math.* A quantity into which another quantity may be divided with zero remainder: *4, 6, and 12 are multiples of 2.* [Old French, from Late Latin *multiplus.*]

mul·ti·ple-choice (mŭl'tə-pəl-chois') *adj.* Offering a number of answers from which the correct one is to be chosen.

multiple sclerosis. A disease in which there is degeneration of the central nervous system, with hard patches of tissue formed throughout the brain or spinal cord.

multiple star. Three or more stars that appear as one to the naked eye.

mul·ti·plex (mŭl'tə-plĕks') *adj.* **1.** Multiple; manifold. **2.** Of or being a communication system that can simultaneously transmit two or more messages on the same circuit or radio channel. [Latin.]

mul·ti·pli·cand (mŭl'tə-plĭ-kănd') *n.* The number that is or is to be multiplied by another. [Latin *multiplicandum,* from *multiplicāre,* to multiply.]

mul·ti·pli·ca·tion (mŭl'tə-plĭ-kā'shən) *n.* **1.** The act or process of multiplying. **2.** The reproduction of plants and animals. **3.** *Math.* The operation of adding a number to itself a designated number of times. **—mul'ti·pli·ca'tive** *adj.*

mul·ti·plic·i·ty (mŭl'tə-plĭs'ə-tē) *n., pl.* **-ties. 1.** The condition of being various or multiple. **2.** A large number: *a*

multiplicity of alternatives. [French *multiplicité,* from Latin *multiplicitās,* from *multiplex,* multiplex.]

mul·ti·pli·er (mŭl'tə-plī'ər) *n.* **1.** Someone or something that multiplies. **2.** *Math.* A number by which another number is multiplied.

mul·ti·ply (mŭl'tə-plī') *v.* **-plied, -ply·ing. —tr.v. 1.** To increase the amount, number, or degree of; make more numerous. **2.** *Math.* To perform multiplication on. **—intr.v. 1.** To become more in number, amount, or degree. **2.** To breed; reproduce. **3.** *Math.* To perform multiplication. [Middle English *multiplien,* from Old French *multiplier,* from Latin *multiplicāre,* from *multiplex,* multiplex.]

mul·ti·stage (mŭl'tə-stāj') *adj.* Having or operating in two or more stages: *a multistage rocket.*

mul·ti·tude (mŭl'tə-tōōd', -tyōōd') *n.* A great, indefinite number: *"There certainly were a dreadful multitude of ugly women in Bath"* (Jane Austen). [Middle English, from Old French, from Latin *multitūdō,* from *multus,* many.]

mul·ti·tu·di·nous (mŭl'tə-tōōd'n-əs, -tyōōd'n-əs) *adj.* Very numerous; existing in great numbers. **—mul'ti·tu'di·nous·ly** *adv.*

mul·ti·va·lent (mŭl'tə-vā'lənt, mŭl-tĭv'ə-lənt) *adj.* Polyvalent. **—mul'ti·va'lence** *n.*

mum¹ (mŭm) *adj.* Not talking; silent. [Middle English, prob. of Low German orig.]

mum² (mŭm) *n. Informal.* A chrysanthemum.

mum·ble (mŭm'bəl) *v.* **-bled, -bling. —tr.v. 1.** To speak or utter indistinctly by lowering the voice or partially closing the mouth. **2.** To chew slowly without or as if without teeth. **—intr.v.** To speak or utter indistinctly. [Middle English *momelen.*] **—mum'ble** *n.* **—mum'bler** *n.*

mum·bo jum·bo (mŭm'bō jŭm'bō). **1.** An object or idol believed to have supernatural powers. **2.** An obscure ritual or incantation. **3.** Confusing or meaningless activity or language. [Mandingo *mā-mā-gyo-mbō,* "magician who makes the troubled spirits of ancestors go away."]

mum·mer (mŭm'ər) *n.* **1.** A person who wears a mask or costume, as for a festival. **2.** An actor. [Middle English *mummar,* from Middle Dutch *mommer,* from Old French *mommeur,* from *momer,* to act as a mummer.]

mum·mer·y (mŭm'ə-rē) *n., pl.* **-ies. 1.** A performance by mummers. **2.** A ridiculous show or ceremony.

mum·mi·fy (mŭm'ə-fī') *tr.v.* **-fied, -fy·ing.** To make into a mummy by embalming and drying. **—intr.v.** To dry up like a mummy. **—mum'mi·fi·ca'tion** *n.*

mum·my (mŭm'ē) *n., pl.* **-ies.** A body embalmed after death according to the practice of the ancient Egyptians. [Middle English *mummie,* from Old French *momie,* from Medieval Latin *mumia,* from Arabic *mūmiyā,* from *mūm,* wax.]

mummy

mumps (mŭmps) *n. (used with a sing. verb).* A contagious viral disease, marked by a painful swelling esp. of the salivary glands. [Pl. of dial. *mump,* grimace, from *mump,* to mumble, grimace.]

munch (mŭnch) *tr.v.* To chew noisily. [Middle English *monchen* (imit.).]

mun·dane (mŭn-dān', mŭn'dān') *adj.* **1.** Of this world; worldly. **2.** Typical of or concerned with the practical, ordinary, or usual: *the mundane affairs of the workaday world.* [Middle English *mondeyne,* from Old French *mondain,* from Late Latin *mundānus,* from Latin *mundus,* the world.] **—mun·dane'ly** *adv.*

mu·nic·i·pal (myōō-nĭs'ə-pəl) *adj.* **1.** Of or pertaining to a municipality. **2.** Having local self-government. [Latin *mūnicipālis*, from *mūnicipium*, a franchised city, from *mūniceps*, citizen : *mūnus*, public office + *capere*, to take.] —**mu·nic′i·pal·ly** *adv.*

mu·nic·i·pal·i·ty (myōō-nĭs′ə-păl′ĭ-tē) *n., pl.* **-ties.** A political unit, as a city or town, that is incorporated for self-government.

mu·nif·i·cent (myōō-nĭf′ĭ-sənt) *adj.* **1.** Extremely liberal in giving; generous. **2.** Showing great generosity: *a munificent gift.* —See Syns at **generous.** [Latin *mūnificens,* from *mūnificus,* generous, bountiful, from *mūnus,* office, duty, gift.] —**mu·nif′i·cence** *n.* —**mu·nif′i·cent·ly** *adv.*

mu·ni·ments (myōō′nə-mənts) *pl. n.* Documents such as deeds by which a person defends his ownership of property. [Middle English, from Old French, from Medieval Latin *mūnīmentum,* from Latin, defense, from *mūnīre,* to defend, fortify.]

mu·ni·tions (myōō-nĭsh′əns) *pl.n.* Supplies or provisions for war, esp. weapons and ammunition. [Old French, fortification from Latin *mūnītiō,* from *mūnīre,* to defend, fortify.]

mu·on (myōō′ŏn′) *n. Symbol* μ *Physics.* A negatively charged subatomic particle with a mass greater than that of an electron.

mu·ral (myŏōr′əl) *n.* A painting applied directly to a wall or ceiling. [Old French, from Latin *mūrālis,* from *mūrus,* a wall.] —**mu′ral·ist** *n.*

mur·der (mûr′dər) *n.* **1.** The unlawful and deliberate killing of a human being. —*tr.v.* **1.** To kill (a human being) unlawfully. **2.** To mar or spoil by ineptness: *The actor murdered the role.* **3.** *Slang.* To defeat decisively. —*intr.v.* To commit murder. [Middle English *mordre,* from Old English *morthor.*] —**mur′der·er** *n.*

 Syns: murder, do in (Slang), **hit** (Slang), **kill, knock off** (Slang), **liquidate, off** (Slang), **rub out** (Slang), **slay, waste** (Slang), **wipe out** (Informal), **zap** (Slang) *v. Core meaning:* To take the life of (a person or persons) unlawfully and deliberately (*murdered his parents*).

mur·der·ous (mûr′dər-əs) *adj.* **1.** Capable of, causing, or intent upon murder: *a murderous mob.* **2.** Characteristic of murder; deadly: *a murderous ambush.* **3.** Very severe or dangerous: *a murderous ordeal.* —**mur′der·ous·ly** *adv.*

mu·rex (myŏōr′ĕks′) *n., pl.* **-ric·es** (myŏōr′ĭ-sēz′) or **-rex·es.** Any of various saltwater gastropods of the genus *Murex,* that yield a purple dye. [From Latin *mūrex,* a kind of fish.]

mu·ri·at·ic acid (myŏōr′ē-ăt′ĭk). Hydrochloric acid.

murk (mûrk) *n.* Darkness; gloom. —*adj. Archaic.* Dark; gloomy. [Middle English *mirke,* from Old English *mirce,* darkness.]

murk·y (mûr′kē) *adj.* **-i·er, -i·est. 1.** Cloudy and dark; foggy: *murky water.* **2.** Dark or gloomy. **3.** Difficult to understand; obscure. —See Syns at **dark.** —**murk′i·ness** *n.*

mur·mur (mûr′mər) *n.* **1.** A low, indistinct, and continuous sound: *the murmur of the wind.* **2.** A grumbled complaint; a mutter. **3.** *Med.* An abnormal sound in the heart, lungs, or blood vessels. —*intr.v.* **1.** To make a low, continuous sound. **2.** To complain; to grumble. —*tr.v.* To say in a low indistinct voice. [Middle English *murmure,* from Old French, from Latin *murmur.*] —**mur′mur·er** *n.* —**mur′mur·ing·ly** *adv.*

mur·rain (mûr′ən) *n.* A highly infectious, usu. fatal disease of domestic plants or animals, such as potato blight or anthrax. [Middle English *moreyne,* from Old French *morine,* from *morir,* to die, from Latin *morī,* to die.]

mus·ca·dine (mŭs′kə-dīn′) *n.* A purple grape cultivated in the southeastern United States. [Var. of MUSCATEL.]

mus·cat (mŭs′kăt′, -kət) *n.* Any of various sweet white grapes used for making wine or raisins. [Old French, from Old Provençal *muscat,* musky, from *musc,* musk, from Late Latin *muscus.*]

mus·ca·tel (mŭs′kə-tĕl′) *n.* A rich, sweet wine made from muscat grapes. [Middle English *muscadelle,* from Old French *muscadel,* from Old Provençal *muscadel,* dim. of *muscat,* muscat.]

mus·cle (mŭs′əl) *n.* **1.** A body tissue composed of fibers that are capable of contracting and relaxing to produce movement or exert force. **2.** An organ composed of such tissue, esp. one attached to a bone and functioning to move part of the body. **3.** Muscular strength; brawn. **4.** Power; force. —*intr.v.* **-cled, -cling.** To force one's way:

muscle in on someone else's job. [Old French, from Latin *mūsculus,* little mouse, muscle (from the shape of certain muscles), from *mūs,* mouse.]

mus·cle-bound (mŭs′əl-bound′) *adj.* Having stiff, overdeveloped muscles, usu. as a result of excessive exercise.

mus·co·vite (mŭs′kə-vīt′) *n.* A mineral that is a colorless to pale brown mica. [From *Muscovy* glass, from *Muscovy,* Moscow.]

Mus·co·vite (mŭs′kə-vīt′) *n.* A native or resident of Moscow. —**Mus′co·vite′** *adj.*

mus·cu·lar (mŭs′kyə-lər) *adj.* **1.** Of, pertaining to, or consisting of muscles. **2.** Performed by muscles. **3.** Having well-developed muscles. [From Latin *mūsculus,* muscle.] —**mus′cu·lar′i·ty** (-lăr′ĭ-tē) *n.* —**mus′cu·lar·ly** *adv.*

muscular dystrophy. A chronic, noncontagious disease of unknown cause in which gradual but irreversible muscular deterioration results in complete incapacitation.

mus·cu·la·ture (mŭs′kyə-lə-chōōr′, -chər) *n.* The system of muscles of an animal or a body part. [French, from Latin *mūsculus,* muscle.]

muse (myōōz) *intr.v.* **mused, mus·ing.** To ponder, consider, or deliberate at length. [Middle English *musen,* from Old French *muser,* from *mus,* snout, from Medieval Latin *mūsum.*]

Muse (myōōz) *n.* **1.** *Gk. Myth.* Any of the nine goddesses, daughters of Mnemosyne and Zeus, each of whom presided over a different art or science. **2. muse.** A source of inspiration.

mu·se·um (myōō-zē′əm) *n.* A place in which works of artistic, historical, and scientific value are cared for and exhibited. [Latin *mūsēum,* library, museum, from Greek *mouseion,* place of the Muses, from *Mousa,* Muse.]

mush¹ (mŭsh) *n.* **1.** A porridge made of cornmeal boiled in water or milk. **2.** Something thick, soft, and pulpy in texture. **3.** *Informal.* Excessive or maudlin sentimentality. [Prob. alteration of MASH.]

mush² (mŭsh) *interj.* A word used as a command to a team of sled dogs to start or go faster. —*intr.v.* To travel with a dog sled. [Canadian French *mouche,* "run!" from *moucher,* to fly, hasten, from French *mouche,* a fly, from Latin *musca.*]

mush·room (mŭsh′rōōm′, -rōōm′) *n.* Any of various fungus plants of the class Basidiomycetes, with a stalk topped by an umbrella-shaped cap, esp. an edible fungus. —*intr.v.* To grow or spread rapidly. [Middle English *muscheron,* from Old French *mousseron.*]

mush·y (mŭsh′ē) *adj.* **-i·er, -i·est. 1.** Soft and pulpy like mush. **2.** *Informal.* Excessively sentimental or romantic. —**mush′i·ness** *n.*

mu·sic (myōō′zĭk) *n.* **1.** The art of producing expressive or pleasing combinations or sequences of sounds. **2.** Vocal or instrumental sounds that have rhythm, melody, and harmony. **3. a.** A musical composition. **b.** The score for a musical composition. **4.** A pleasing or harmonious sound or combination of sounds: *the music of her voice.* —**idiom. face the music.** *Informal.* To meet an unpleasant situation bravely. [Middle English *musik,* from Old French *musique,* from Latin *mūsica,* from Greek *mousikē (tekhnē),* (art) of the Muses, from *Mousa,* Muse.]

mu·si·cal (myōō′zĭ-kəl) *adj.* **1.** Of, pertaining to, or producing music: *a musical instrument.* **2.** Pleasing to the ear; melodious: *a musical speaking voice.* **3.** Set to or accompanied by music. **4.** Devoted to or skilled in music. —*n.* A musical comedy. —**mu′si·cal·ly** *adv.*

musical chairs. A game in which the players walk to music around a row of chairs containing one chair fewer than the number of players, and rush to sit down when the music stops.

musical comedy. A play in which dialogue is interspersed with songs and dances.

mu·si·cale (myōō′zĭ-kăl′) *n.* A program of music performed at a private social gathering. [French *(soirée) musicale,* "musical (evening)."]

music box. A box containing a mechanical device that produces music.

music hall. A vaudeville theater.

mu·si·cian (myōō-zĭsh′ən) *n.* A person skilled in composing or performing music, esp. professionally. —**mu·si′cian·ly** *adj.* —**mu·si′cian·ship′** *n.*

ă pat   ā pay   â care   ä father   ĕ pet   ē be   hw which
ŏŏ took   ōō boot   ou out   th thin   th this   ŭ cut
ĭ pit   ī tie   î pier   ŏ pot   ō toe   ô paw, for   oi noise
û urge   zh vision   ə about, item, edible, gallop, circus

musk ox

muskrat

mustard

mu·si·col·o·gy (myōō′zĭ-kŏl′ə-jē) *n.* The historical and scientific study of music. **—mu′si·col′o·gist** *n.*

mus·ing (myōō′zĭng) *n.* Contemplation; meditation. **—mus′ing·ly** *adv.*

musk (mŭsk) *n.* **1. a.** A greasy secretion with a powerful odor, produced by certain abdominal glands of the male musk deer and used in making perfumes. **b.** A similar secretion produced by certain other animals, such as the otter or musk ox. **2.** The odor of musk. [Middle English *muske,* from Old French *musc,* from Late Latin *muscus,* from Greek *moskhos,* from Persian *mushk.*]

musk deer. A small, hornless deer, *Moschus moschiferus,* that is native to central and northeastern Asia.

mus·kel·lunge (mŭs′kə-lŭnj′) *n., pl.* **muskellunge** or **-lung·es.** A large, North American, freshwater game fish, *Esox masquinongy.* [Of Algonquian orig.]

mus·ket (mŭs′kĭt) *n.* A smoothbore, long-barreled shoulder gun. [French *mousquet,* from Italian *moschetto,* dim. of *mosca,* a fly, from Latin *musca.*]

mus·ket·eer (mŭs′kĭ-tîr′) *n.* A soldier armed with a musket. [French *mousquetaire,* from *mousquet,* musket.]

mus·ket·ry (mŭs′kĭ-trē) *n.* **1.** Muskets in general. **2.** Musketeers. **3.** The technique of using small arms.

musk·mel·on (mŭsk′mĕl′ən) *n.* Any of several varieties of edible melon, such as the cantaloupe, with a rough rind and juicy flesh.

musk ox. A large, hoofed mammal, *Ovibos moschatus,* of northern Canada and Greenland, that has a long, shaggy, dark coat and curved horns.

musk·rat (mŭsk′răt′) *n., pl.* **muskrat** or **-rats.** **1.** An aquatic rodent, *Ondatra zibethica,* of North America, with a brown coat, partly webbed hind feet, and a broad, flat tail. **2.** The fur of the muskrat.

musk·y (mŭs′kē) *adj.* **-i·er, -i·est.** Of, pertaining to, or having an odor resembling musk.

Mus·lim or **Mus·lem** (mŭz′ləm, mŏŏs′-, mŏŏz′-) *n.* Vars. of **Moslem.** —See Usage note at **Moslem.**

mus·lin (mŭz′lĭn) *n.* A sturdy, plain-weave cotton fabric. [French *mousseline,* from Italian *mussolina,* "cloth of Mosul," a city in Iraq.]

muss (mŭs) *tr.v.* To make messy or untidy; rumple: *mussed up her hair.* —*n.* Disorder; mess. [Perh. alteration of MESS.]

mus·sel (mŭs′əl) *n.* **1.** Any of several saltwater bivalve mollusks, esp. the edible *Mytilus edulis,* with a narrow blue-black shell. **2.** Any of several similar freshwater bivalve mollusks of the genera *Anodonta* and *Unio,* found in the central United States. [Middle English *muscle,* from Old English, from Latin *mūsculus,* little mouse, mussel (from its mouselike shape), from *mūs,* mouse.]

muss·y (mŭs′ē) *adj.* **-i·er, -i·est.** Messy; untidy; disarranged. **—muss′i·ly** *adv.* **—muss′i·ness** *n.*

must¹ (mŭst) *v.* Used as an auxiliary to indicate: **1.** Necessity or obligation: *If you want to get good grades in school, you must read all your assignments.* **2.** Probability: *It must be about time for supper.* **3.** Certainty or inevitability: *All good things must come to an end.* **4.** Insistence: *I must repeat, there is an excellent swimmer and has earned her badge.* —*n. Informal.* Something that is essential, required, or indispensable: *Catch that new movie; it's a must.* [Middle English *moste,* from Old English *mōste,* past tense of *mōtan,* to be allowed.]

must² (mŭst) *n.* Staleness. [Back-formation from MUSTY.]

must³ (mŭst) *n.* Unfermented or fermenting fruit juice. [Middle English, from Old English, from Latin *mustum,* new wine, from *mustus,* new, newborn.]

mus·tache (mŭs′tăsh′, mə-stăsh′) *n.* Also **mous·tache.** **1.** The hair growing on the upper lip of a human being. **2.** Bristles or hair about the mouth of an animal. [Old French *moustache,* from Italian *mustaccio,* from Medieval Greek *moustaki,* from Greek *mustax,* the upper lip, mustache.]

mus·ta·chio (mə-stăsh′ō, -stăsh′ē-ō′, -stä′shō, stä′shē-ō′) *n., pl.* **-chios.** Often **mustachios.** A mustache, esp. one that is large and full. [Spanish *mostaccho* and Italian *mustaccio.*]

mus·tang (mŭs′tăng′) *n.* A small, wild horse of the North American plains, descended from stock brought by Spanish explorers. [Mexican Spanish *mestengo,* from Spanish, stray (animal), from *mesta,* meeting of owners of stray animals, from Medieval Latin *(animalia) mixta,* wild or stray animals that mixed with and became attached to a grazier's herd, from Latin *miscēre,* to mix.]

mus·tard (mŭs′tərd) *n.* **1.** Any of various plants of the genus *Brassica,* with four-petaled yellow flowers and slender pods, esp. certain species cultivated for their pungent seeds. **2.** A pungent powder or paste made from mustard seeds mixed with various other spices. **3.** A dark brownish yellow. —*adj.* Dark brownish yellow. [Middle English *mustarde,* from Old French *moustarde,* from Latin *mustum,* must, new wine.]

mustard gas. A deadly poisonous, oily liquid, $(ClCH_2CH_2)_2S$, that has a blistering effect on the skin, eyes, and lungs. [From its mustardlike odor.]

mustard plaster. A pastelike mixture of powdered mustard, flour, and water, spread on cloth or paper, and applied as a poultice.

mus·ter (mŭs′tər) *tr.v.* **1.** To summon or assemble (troops). **2.** To collect or gather: *Muster up your courage.* —*intr.v.* To assemble or gather: *mustering for inspection.* —See Syns at **gather.** —*phrasal verbs.* **muster in.** To enlist (someone) in military service. **muster out.** To discharge (someone) from military service. —*n.* **1.** A gathering, esp. of troops, for inspection, roll call, etc. **2.** The official roll of men in a military or naval unit. **3.** Any gathering or collection. [Middle English *mustren,* from Old French *moustrer,* from Latin *monstrāre,* to show, indicate (by an omen), from *mōnstrum,* an omen, prob. from *monēre,* to warn.]

must·n't (mŭs′ənt). Contraction of must not.

must·y (mŭs′tē) *adj.* **-i·er, -i·est.** **1.** Having a stale or moldy odor or taste. **2.** Antiquated; old-fashioned. **3.** Stale. [Var. of obs. *moisty,* from MOIST.] **—must′i·ness** *n.*

mu·ta·ble (myōō′tə-bəl) *adj.* **1.** Subject to or capable of change. **2.** Prone to change; inconstant. **—mu′ta·bil′i·ty** or **mu′ta·ble·ness** *n.* **—mu′ta·bly** *adv.*

mu·tant (myōōt′nt) *n.* An individual or organism differing from the parental strain as a result of mutation. —*adj.* Of, relating to, or resulting from mutation.

mu·tate (myōō′tāt′, myōō-tāt′) *v.* **-ta·ted, -tat·ing.** —*tr.v.* To cause to undergo change or alteration by or as if by mutation. —*intr.v.* To undergo change or alteration by or as if by mutation. —See Syns at **change.** [From Latin *mūtāre.*]

mu·ta·tion (myōō-tā′shən) *n.* **1.** The act or process of being changed or altered. **2.** A change or alteration, as in nature or form. **3.** *Biol.* **a.** Any change in the genes or chromosomes of an organism that can be inherited by its off-spring. **b.** A mutant.

mute (myōōt) *adj.* **mut·er, mut·est. 1.** Not having the power of speech. **2.** Refraining from speech; silent: *remained mute under questioning.* **3.** Expressed without speech; unspoken: *The scorched forest bore mute testimony to the savagery of the fire.* **4.** *Phonet.* Not pronounced; silent, as the *e* in *house.* —*n.* **1.** A person who cannot speak. **2.** *Mus.* Any of various devices used to muffle or soften the tone of an instrument. **3.** *Phonet.* A silent or unpronounced letter. —*tr.v.* **mut·ed, mut·ing. 1.** To muffle or soften the sound of. **2.** To soften the tone, color, or shade of. [Middle English *muet,* from Old French, dim. of *mu,* mute, from Latin *mūtus,* silent.] —**mute′ly** *adv.* —**mute′-ness** *n.*

mute

mu·ti·late (myōōt′l-āt′) *tr.v.* **-lat·ed, -lat·ing. 1.** To cut off an essential part. **2.** To cut or change radically: *mutilate a script.* [From Latin *mutilāre,* to cut off, from *mutilus,* maimed.] —**mu′ti·la′tion** *n.* —**mu′ti·la′tor** *n.* —**mu′ti·la′tive** *adj.*

mu·ti·neer (myōōt′n-îr′) *n.* A person who mutinies.

mu·ti·nous (myōōt′n-əs) *adj.* **1.** Engaged in, or disposed toward mutiny: *a mutinous crew.* **2.** Of, pertaining to, or constituting mutiny. —**mu′ti·nous·ly** *adv.* —**mu′ti·nous-ness** *n.*

mu·ti·ny (myōōt′n-ē) *n., pl.* **-nies.** Open rebellion against constituted authority, esp. rebellion of military personnel against their superior officers. —*intr.v.* **-nied, -ny·ing.** To commit mutiny. —See Syns at **rebellion.** [Obs. *mutine,* from Old French *mutin,* rebellion, from *muete,* revolt, from Latin *movēre,* to move.]

mutt (mŭt) *n. Slang.* A mongrel dog. [Short for *mutton-head,* a fool.]

mut·ter (mŭt′ər) *intr.v.* **1.** To speak indistinctly and in a low voice. **2.** To complain or grumble. —*tr.v.* To utter or say in low, indistinct tones. —*n.* A low, indistinct utterance, often of complaint. [Middle English *muteren.*] —**mut′ter-er** *n.*

mut·ton (mŭt′n) *n.* The flesh of a full-grown sheep. [Middle English *motoun,* from Old French *moton,* sheep, from Medieval Latin *multō.*]

mutton chops. Side whiskers that are narrow at the temples and wide and rounded at the bottom.

mu·tu·al (myōō′chōō-əl) *adj.* **1.** Having the same feelings each for the other: *mutual friends.* **2.** Given and received in equal amounts: *mutual concern.* **3.** Possessed or shared in common: *mutual interests.* [Middle English *mutuall,* from Old French *mutuel,* from Latin *mūtuus,* reciprocal.] —**mu′tu·al′i·ty** (-ăl′ĭ-tē) *n.* —**mu′tu·al·ly** *adv.*

mutual fund. An investment company that by the sale of its shares acquires funds which it invests in a variety of securities.

mu·tu·al·ism (myōō′chōō-ə-lĭz′əm) *n. Biol.* A mutually beneficial association between different kinds of organisms.

muu·muu (mōō′mōō′) *n.* A loose dress. [Hawaiian *mu′u mu′u.*]

mu·zhik (mōō-zhĕk′, -zhĭk′) *n.* Also **mou·jik, mu·jik,** or **mu·zjik.** A peasant in czarist Russia. [Russian, a peasant, dim. of *muzh,* man.]

muz·zle (mŭz′əl) *n.* **1.** The projecting part of an animal's head, including the jaws and nose; snout. **2.** A leather or wire device placed over the mouth of an animal to prevent biting or eating. **3.** The front end of the barrel of a firearm. —*tr.v.* **-zled, -zling. 1.** To put a muzzle on. **2.** To restrain

from speech or expression. [Middle English *musell,* from Old French *musel,* from Late Latin *mūsum,* snout.] —**muz′zler** *n.*

muz·zle-load·er (mŭz′əl-lō′dər) *n.* A firearm loaded through the muzzle. —**muz′zle-load′ing** *adj.*

my (mī). The possessive case of I, used as a modifier before a noun: *my past failure; my work; my first defeat.* —*Note:* As a modifier, *my* is used in certain forms of polite address: *my lord; my dear Mrs. Fulton.* It is also used in expressions of surprise or dismay: *My word! My goodness! My!* —*interj.* A word used to express surprise or dismay: *Oh, my!* [Middle English *mīn.*]

my·as·the·ni·a gra·vis (mī′ăs-thē′nē-ə grăv′ĭs). An inherited disease characterized by progressive muscular weakness and fatigue caused by degeneration of muscle fibers. [Greek *mus,* muscle + *asthenia,* weakness + Latin *gravis,* grave.]

myc-. Var. of **myco-.**

my·ce·li·um (mī-sē′lē-əm) *n., pl.* **-li·a** (-lē-ə). The vegetative part of a fungus, consisting of a mass of branching, thread-like filaments that form its main growing structure. [MYC(O)- + Greek *hēlos,* nail, wart.] —**my·ce′li·al** *adj.*

-mycete. A suffix meaning a member of a specified class of fungi: **phycomycete.** [From Greek *mukētes,* pl. of *mukēs,* fungus.]

-mycin. A suffix meaning a substance derived from bacteria or fungi: **streptomycin.** [MYC(O)- + -IN.]

myco- or **myc-.** A prefix meaning fungus: **mycology.** [From Greek *mukēs,* fungus.]

my·col·o·gy (mī-kŏl′ə-jē) *n.* The branch of botany that deals with fungi. —**my′co·log′i·cal** (mī′kə-lŏj′ĭ-kəl) or **my′co·log′ic** *adj.* —**my·col′o·gist** *n.*

my·co·sis (mī-kō′sĭs) *n., pl.* **-ses** (-sēz′). A disease or infection caused by a fungus.

my·e·lin (mī′ə-lĭn) *n.* Also **my·e·line** (mī′ə-lĭn, -lēn′). A white, fatty material that sheathes certain nerve fibers. [Greek *muelos,* marrow + -IN.]

my·e·lo·ma (mī′ə-lō′mə) *n., pl.* **-mas** or **-ma·ta** (-mə-tə). A malignant tumor of the bone marrow. [From Greek *muelos,* marrow.]

my·na (mī′nə) *n.* Also **my·nah** or **mi·na.** Any of several Asian birds of the family Sturnidae, that are related to the starlings, and have blue-black to dark-brown plumage with yellow bills. [Hindi *mainā,* from Sanskrit *madana.*]

my·o·car·di·um (mī′ō-kär′dē-əm) *n.* The muscle tissue of the heart. [Greek *mus,* muscle + *kardia,* the heart.] —**my′o·car′di·al** *adj.*

my·o·pi·a (mī-ō′pē-ə) *n.* The condition of being near-sighted. [Greek *muōpia,* from *muōps,* myopic : *muein,* to close + *ōps,* eye.] —**my·op′ic** (mī-ŏp′ĭk, -ō′pĭk) *adj.* —**my·op′i·cal·ly** *adv.*

myria-. A prefix meaning: **1.** A very large number: **myria-pod. 2.** Ten thousand (10⁴): **myriameter.** [From Greek *murioi,* ten thousand, pl. of *murios,* countless.]

myr·i·ad (mîr′ē-əd) *adj.* Constituting a very large, indefinite number: *the myriad stars of the galaxy.* —*n.* A vast number. [Late Latin *mȳrias,* from Greek *murias,* from *murios,* countless.]

myr·i·a·me·ter (mîr′ē-ə-mē′tər) *n.* A unit of length equal to 10,000 meters.

myr·i·a·pod (mîr′ē-ə-pŏd′) *n.* Any of several arthropods, such as the centipede.

Myr·mi·don (mûr′mĭ-dŏn′, -dən) *n.* **1.** *Gk. Myth.* One of a legendary people of ancient Thessaly who were followers of Achilles in the Trojan War. **2. myrmidon.** Any faithful

muzzle

follower or subordinate who carries out orders without question.

myrrh (mûr) *n.* A bitter-tasting, aromatic gum resin obtained from several trees and shrubs of the genus *Commiphora*, used in perfume and incense. [Middle English *myrre*, from Old English *myrrha*, from Latin *myrrha*, from Greek *murrha*.]

myr·tle (mûr′tl) *n.* **1.** Any of several evergreen shrubs or trees of the genus *Myrtus*, that bear pink or white flowers and blue-black berries. **2.** The periwinkle. [Middle English *mirtille*, from Old French, from Medieval Latin *myrtillus*, dim. of Latin *myrtus*, from Greek *murtos*.]

my·self (mī-sĕlf′) *pron.* **1.** That one identical with me. Used: **a.** Reflexively as the direct or indirect object of a verb or as the object of a preposition: *I bought myself a new pair of shoes.* **b.** For emphasis: *I myself was responsible for the mistake.* **2.** My normal, healthy condition or state: *I'm just not myself these days.*

Usage: **myself.** The pronoun *myself* is most commonly used as a reflexive (*I hurt myself skating.*) and as an intensive (*I myself am not to blame.*), but it also occurs in several other constructions. For example, *myself* occurs as a predicate nominative after the verb *to be: I am not myself today. The team members are Brenda, John, Donna, and myself.* This construction is standard. *Myself* also occurs in comparisons on all usage levels: *It was not easy for as inexperienced a person as myself to undertake the task.* It occurs less often in absolute constructions, but the usage is acceptable: *A number of editors, myself included, attended the meeting. Myself* is also used as an element of a compound subject or object: *My wife and myself attended the party. The sermon impressed my family and myself.* Although this construction has a distinguished literary history dating to Middle English, it is now considered somewhat old-fashioned and awkward by many grammarians. Alternative, and more modern, wordings are: *My wife and I attended . . . and . . . impressed my family and me. Myself* is now rarely used to replace *I* as the sole subject of a sentence; this usage is poetic.

mys·te·ri·ous (mī-stîr′ē-əs) *adj.* Of, containing, or implying a mystery: *a mysterious light in the deserted house.* **—mys·te′ri·ous·ly** *adv.* **—mys·te′ri·ous·ness** *n.*

mys·ter·y (mĭs′tə-rē) *n., pl.* **-ies. 1.** Something that cannot be explained or understood: *the mysteries of nature.* **2.** The quality associated with the unexplained, secret, or unknown: *the wizard's aura of magic and mystery.* **3.** A piece of fiction dealing usu. with a mysterious crime. **4.** A religious truth incomprehensible to the reason and known only through divine revelation. **5.** One of 15 occurrences, such as the Nativity or the Ascension, commemorated in the 15 divisions of the rosary. [Middle English *mysterie*, from Latin *mystērium*, from Greek *mustērion*, secret rites, from *mustēs*, one initiated into secret rites, from *muein*, to

initiate, from *muein*, to close the eyes or mouth, to keep secret.]

mystery play. A form of medieval drama based on scriptural events or episodes.

mys·tic (mĭs′tĭk) *adj.* **1.** Of or pertaining to sacred mysteries, rites, or practices; occult. **2.** Mysterious; enigmatic. **3.** Mystical. **4.** Of or pertaining to mystics or mysticism. *—n.* Someone who believes in or practices mysticism. [Middle English *mistik*, from Latin *mysticus*, from Greek *mustikos*, from *mustēs*, an initiated person.]

mys·ti·cal (mĭs′tĭ-kəl) *adj.* **1.** Of, pertaining to, or characteristic of mystics, mysticism, or sacred mysteries. **2.** Of a nature or meaning that can neither be grasped by the intellect nor perceived by the senses: *"The mystical vision of God cannot be passed on from father to son"* (Thomas Merton). **3.** Spiritually symbolic: *a mystical emblem of the Trinity.* **—mys′ti·cal·ly** *adv.* **—mys′ti·cal·ness** *n.*

mys·ti·cism (mĭs′tĭ-sĭz′əm) *n.* **1. a.** A reliance on subjective means, such as intuition or visionary experience, rather than on the perceptions of the senses or the intellect, in order to achieve a direct knowledge of and communion with absolute or ultimate reality. **b.** The practices or habits by which this direct communion is achieved. **2.** Confused or vague speculation.

mys·ti·fy (mĭs′tə-fī′) *tr.v.* **-fied, -fy·ing. 1.** To perplex; bewilder: *a crime that mystified the police.* **2.** To make obscure or difficult to understand. [French *mystifier*, from *mystère*, mystery, from Latin *mystērium*.] **—mys′ti·fi·ca′tion** *n.*

mys·tique (mĭ-stēk′) *n.* A body of attributes or qualities associated with a particular person, group, or thing. [French, from adjective, "mystic."]

myth (mĭth) *n.* **1.** A traditional account that often deals with supernatural beings and events in explanation of a cultural belief or practice or a natural phenomenon. **2.** A fictitious or imaginary being or object: *The unicorn is only a myth.* **3.** A false belief: *the myth of racial supremacy.* [From Late Latin *mythos*, tale, myth, from Greek *muthos*.]

myth·i·cal (mĭth′ĭ-kəl) or **myth·ic** (-ĭk) *adj.* **1.** Of, existing in, or constituting a myth: *the mythical exploits of the Argonauts.* **2.** Imaginary; fictitious; fancied: *a mythical account of what happened.* **—myth′i·cal·ly** *adv.*

myth·o·log·i·cal (mĭth′ə-lŏj′ĭ-kəl) *adj.* Of, pertaining to, or existing in mythology: *a mythological beast.* **—myth′o·log′i·cal·ly** *adv.*

my·thol·o·gy (mĭ-thŏl′ə-jē) *n., pl.* **-gies. 1.** A body of myths esp. of a particular culture or people. **2.** The field of study that deals with myths. **—my·thol′o·gist** *n.*

myx·e·de·ma (mĭk′sĭ-dē′mə) *n.* A condition caused by decreased activity of the thyroid gland and characterized by dry skin, swellings around the lips and nose, and subnormal mental and physical activity. Also called **cretinism.** [Greek *muxa*, mucus + EDEMA.]

Phoenician – *About 3,000 years ago the Phoenicians and other Semitic peoples began to use graphic signs to represent individual speech sounds instead of syllables or whole words. They used this symbol to represent the sound of the consonant "n" and gave it the name* nūn, *the Phoenician word for "fish."*

Greek – *The Greeks borrowed the Phoenician alphabet with some modifications. They changed the orientation of* nūn *and altered its name to* nū. *They used* nū *to represent the sound of the consonant "n," as* nūn *did in Phoenician.*

Roman – *The Romans borrowed the alphabet from the*

Greeks via the Etruscans and adapted it for carving Latin in stone. This monumental script, as it is called, became the basis for modern printed capital letters.

Medieval – *By medieval times – around 1,200 years ago – the Roman monumental capitals had become adapted to being relatively quickly written on paper, parchment, or vellum. The shape of N became rounded and required fewer pen strokes to write. The cursive minuscule alphabet became the basis for modern printed lower-case letters.*

Modern – *Since the invention of printing about 500 years ago the basic form of the letter N has remained unchanged.*

n, N (ĕn) *n., pl.* **n's** or **N's.** The 14th letter of the modern English alphabet.

Na The symbol for the element sodium. [Latin *natrium.*]

nab (năb) *tr.v.* **nabbed, nab·bing.** *Slang.* **1.** To seize and arrest: *The policeman nabbed the muggers.* **2.** To grab; snatch. —See Syns at **arrest.** [Var. of dial. *nap,* to seize.]

na·celle (nə-sĕl′) *n.* A streamlined enclosure on an aircraft for housing an engine, cargo, or the crew. [French, "small boat," from Latin *nāvicella,* dim. of *nāvis,* ship.]

na·cre (nā′kər) *n.* Mother-of-pearl. [French, from Italian *naccara,* mother-of-pearl, from Arabic *naggāra,* shell.] —**na′cre·ous** (-krē′əs) *adj.*

na·dir (nā′dər, -dîr′) *n.* **1.** A point on the celestial sphere diametrically opposite the zenith. **2.** The lowest point: *the nadir of our fortunes.* [Middle English, from Old French, from Arabic *nazīr as-samt,* opposite the zenith.]

nae (nā). *Scot.* **1.** No. **2.** Not.

nag¹ (năg) *v.* **nagged, nag·ging.** —*tr.v.* **1.** To annoy by constant scolding, complaining, or urging. **2.** To irritate or harass persistently. —*intr.v.* **1.** To scold, complain, or find fault constantly: *nagged at the child.* **2.** To be a source of anxiety or annoyance. —*n.* A person who nags. [Brit. dial., to bite, worry at, nag, from Old Norse *gnaga,* to bite.] —**nag′ger** *n.* —**nag′ging·ly** *adv.*

nag² (năg) *n.* A horse, esp. an old or worn-out horse. [Middle English *nagge,* from Middle Dutch *negghe,* horse.]

Na·hua·tl (nä′wät′l) *n., pl.* **Nahuatl** or **-tls. 1.** A group of Mexican and Central American Indian tribes, including the Aztecs. **2.** The Uto-Aztecan language of the Nahuatl.

nai·ad (nā′əd, -ăd′, nī′-) *n., pl.* **-ads** or **-a·des** (-ə-dēz′). **1.** *Gk. Myth.* One of the nymphs living in and presiding over brooks, springs, streams, and fountains. **2.** The aquatic nymph of certain insects, such as the mayfly.

nail (nāl) *n.* **1.** A slim, pointed piece of metal, often with a head, hammered into a material as a fastener. **2. a.** A fingernail or toenail. **b.** A claw or talon. —*tr.v.* **1.** To fasten, join, or attach with or as if with nails: *nailed the boards together.* **2.** To cover, enclose, or shut by fastening with nails: *nail up a window.* **3.** To keep fixed, motionless, or intent: *Fear nailed him to his seat.* **4.** *Slang.* To seize; catch: *The police nailed the thief.* —*phrasal verb.* **nail down.** To settle clearly and definitely. [Middle English, from Old English *nægl.*] —**nail′er** *n.*

nail file. A small, flat file for shaping the fingernails.

nail polish. A cosmetic lacquer for the nails.

nain·sook (nān′sŏŏk′) *n.* A soft, light cotton material. [Hindi *nainsukh,* "pleasure to the eye."]

na·ive or **na·ïve** (nä-ēv′) *adj.* **1.** Simple and unaffected; artless. **2.** Showing a lack of experience or judgment; unsophisticated. [French, fem. of *naif,* from Old French, ingenuous, natural, from Latin *nātīvus,* native, from *nāscī,* to be born.] —**na·ive′ly** *adv.* —**na·ive′ness** *n.*

na·ive·té or **na·ive·te** (nä-ēv-tā′) *n.* Also **na·ive·ty** or **na·ive·ty** (nä-ēv′ĭ-tē) *pl.* **-ties. 1.** The condition or quality of being naive. **2.** A naive statement or action. [French, ingenuousness, from *naif,* naive.]

na·ked (nā′kĭd) *adj.* **1. a.** Without clothing; nude. **b.** Without the usual covering: *a naked sword.* **c.** Devoid of vegetation, trees, or foliage; stripped or bare: *trees with naked branches.* **2.** Without addition, disguise, or embellishment: *the naked facts.* **3.** Lacking protective covering such as scales or shell: *naked seeds.* **4.** Without artificial aids: *the naked eye.* —See Syns at **bare.** [Middle English, from Old English *nacod.*] —**na′ked·ly** *adv.* —**na′ked·ness** *n.*

nam·by-pam·by (năm′bē-păm′bē) *adj.* **1.** Insipid and sentimental. **2.** Lacking vigor or decisiveness. —**nam′by-pam′by** *n.* [From *Namby-Pamby,* a satire on Ambrose Philips (1675?-1749).]

name (nām) *n.* **1.** A word or words by which a person or thing is called or known. **2.** A descriptive and often disparaging expression: *Names will never hurt me.* **3.** Appearance rather than reality: *a democracy in name only.* **4. a.** General reputation: *a bad name.* **b.** A distinguished reputation; renown: *made a name for herself.* **5.** *Informal.* Someone or something that is famous: *a big name in the movies.* —*modifier:* *name brands.* —*tr.v.* **named, nam·ing. 1.** To give a name to. **2.** To identify by name. **3.** To mention or specify by name. **4.** To nominate or appoint to a specific duty, office, or honor. **5.** To specify or fix: *name the time of our meeting.* —*idioms.* **in the name of. 1.** For the sake of: *Let him answer the charges in the name of justice.* **2.** By the authority of: *in the name of the law.* **to**

box
finishing
common
masonry, fluted
dual-head
flooring
wood-shingle
roofing, smooth
roofing, barbed
brick-siding

nail

(one's) name. Among one's possessions: *not a book to his name.* [Middle English, from Old English *nama.*] —**nam′a·ble** or **name′a·ble** *adj.* —**nam′er** *n.*

Syns: name, appellation, cognomen, denomination, designation, handle (Slang), **moniker** (Slang), *n. Core meaning:* The word or words by which one is called and identified (*gave his son two names; the name of a book*).

name·less (nām′lĭs) *adj.* **1.** Having or bearing no name: *nameless stars.* **2.** Not known by name; anonymous: *a nameless donor.* **3.** Too difficult to describe: *a nameless longing.* —**name′less·ly** *adv.* —**name′less·ness** *n.*

name·ly (nām′lē) *adv.* That is to say; specifically: *exempted two groups, namely students and the clergy.*

name·sake (nām′sāk′) *n.* Someone or something named after another. [From *for the name's sake.*]

nan·keen (năn-kēn′) *n.* Also **nan·kin** (năn-kēn′, -kĭn′). A sturdy yellow or buff cotton cloth. [After *Nanking,* China.]

nan·ny (năn′ē) *n., pl.* **-nies.** A children's nurse. [From baby talk.]

nanny goat. A female goat. [From *Nanny,* pet form for Ann.]

nap[1] (năp) *n.* A brief sleep, usu. during the day. —*intr.v.* **napped, nap·ping. 1.** To doze or sleep for a brief period. **2.** To be unprepared. [Middle English *nappen,* to doze, from Old English *hnappian.*]

nap[2] (năp) *n.* A fuzzy surface on cloth or leather. [Middle English *noppe,* from Middle Dutch.]

na·palm (nā′päm′) *n.* **1.** An aluminum soap of various fatty acids that is mixed with gasoline to make a firm jelly. **2.** A jelly that consists of gasoline mixed with napalm and is used in flame throwers and fire bombs. [*Na(phthenate)* + *palm(itate),* two substances used in its composition.]

nape (nāp) *n.* The back of the neck. [Middle English.]

na·per·y (nā′pə-rē) *n.* Household linen, esp. table linen. [Middle English *naperie,* from Old French, from *nappe,* tablecloth, from Latin *mappa,* napkin, towel.]

naph·tha (năf′thə, năp′-) *n.* **1.** A colorless flammable liquid, obtained from crude petroleum and used as a solvent and cleaning fluid and as a raw material for gasoline. **2.** Any of several volatile hydrocarbon liquids derived from coal tar and other materials and used as solvents. [Greek.]

naph·tha·lene (năf′thə-lēn′) *n.* Also **naph·tha·line, naph·tha·lin** (năf′thə-lĭn, năp′-). A white crystalline compound, $C_{10}H_8$, derived from coal tar or petroleum, and used to manufacture dyes, moth repellents, explosives, and solvents. [NAPHTH(A) + AL(COHOL) + -ENE.]

naph·thol (năf′thôl′, -thŏl′, năp′-) *n.* Also **naph·tol** (năf′tôl′, -tŏl′, năp′-). An organic compound, $C_{10}H_7OH$, occurring in two isomeric forms and used in making dyes. [NAPHTH(A-LENE) + -OL (hydroxyl group).]

nap·kin (năp′kĭn) *n.* **1.** A piece of cloth or absorbent paper, used while eating to protect one's clothes or wipe one's lips and fingers. **2.** A cloth or towel. [Middle English *nappekin,* dim. of *nappe,* tablecloth, from Old French.]

na·po·le·on (nə-pō′lē-ən, -pōl′yən) *n.* **1.** A rectangular piece of pastry, made with crisp, flaky layers filled with custard cream. **2.** A former 20-franc gold coin of France. [After NAPOLEON I.]

narc (närk) *n. Slang.* A narcotics agent.

nar·cis·sism (när′sĭ-sĭz′əm) *n.* Excessive love or admiration of oneself. [After NARCISSUS.] —**nar′cis·sist** *n.* —**nar′cis·sis′tic** *adj.*

nar·cis·sus (när-sĭs′əs) *n., pl.* **-sus·es** or **-cis·si** (-sĭs′ī′, -sĭs′-ē). Any of several widely cultivated plants of the genus *Narcissus,* having narrow, grasslike leaves and usu. white or yellow flowers with a cup-shaped or trumpet-shaped central crown. [Latin, from Greek *narkissos.*]

Nar·cis·sus (när-sĭs′əs) *n. Gk. Myth.* A youth who fell in love with his own image in a pool of water and was transformed into the flower that bears his name.

nar·co·sis (när-kō′sĭs) *n., pl.* **-ses** (-sēz′). Deep unconsciousness produced by a drug. [Greek *narkōsis,* a numbing, from *narkoun,* to make numb, from *narkē,* numbness.]

nar·cot·ic (när-kŏt′ĭk) *n.* **1.** A drug that dulls the senses, induces sleep, and becomes addictive with prolonged use. **2.** Something that numbs, soothes, or induces a dreamlike state. —*adj.* **1.** Inducing sleep or stupor. **2.** Of or relating

to narcotics, their effects, or their use. **3.** Of or relating to narcotic addicts. —**nar·cot′i·cal·ly** *adv.*

nar·co·tize (när′kə-tīz′) *tr.v.* **-tized, -tiz·ing. 1.** To place under the influence of a narcotic. **2.** To put to sleep; lull. **3.** To make unconscious.

nard (närd) *n.* Spikenard. [Middle English *narde,* from Old French, from Latin *nardus,* from Greek *nardos.*]

nar·is (nâr′ĭs) *n., pl.* **-es** (-ēz). An opening in the nasal cavity of a vertebrate; nostril. [Latin *nārēs,* pl. of *nāris,* nostril.]

Nar·ra·gan·set (năr′ə-găn′sĭt) *n., pl.* **Narraganset** or **-sets.** Also **Nar·ra·gan·sett** *pl.* **Narragansett** or **-setts. 1.** A member of a tribe of Algonquian-speaking Indians that formerly inhabited the area of Rhode Island. **2.** The language of the Narraganset. —**Nar′ra·gan′set** *adj.*

nar·rate (năr′āt′, nă-rāt′) *tr.v.* **-rat·ed, -rat·ing.** To give or relate an account of. [From Latin *narrāre,* from *gnārus,* knowing.] —**nar′ra·tor** *n.*

nar·ra·tion (nă-rā′shən) *n.* **1.** The act or an example of narrating. **2.** A narrative.

nar·ra·tive (năr′ə-tĭv) *n.* **1.** A narrated account. **2.** The act, technique, or process of narrating. —**nar′ra·tive** *adj.* —**nar′ra·tive·ly** *adv.*

nar·row (năr′ō) *adj.* **-er, -est. 1.** Of small or slender width. **2.** Limited in area or scope; cramped. **3.** Lacking flexibility; rigid: *a man of narrow beliefs.* **4.** Barely sufficient: *a narrow margin of victory.* —*tr.v.* **1.** To make narrow or narrower. **2.** To limit or restrict: *He narrowed down the possibilities.* —*intr.v.* **1.** To become narrower; contract. —*n.* **1.** A narrow part, such as a narrow pass through mountains or the narrow part of a valley. **2. narrows.** A narrow body of water connecting two larger ones. [Middle English *nearwe,* from Old English *nearu.*] —**nar′row·ly** *adv.* —**nar′row·ness** *n.*

narrow gauge. Also **narrow gage. 1.** A distance between the rails of a railroad track that is less than the standard width of 56$\frac{1}{2}$ inches. **2.** A locomotive, car, or railway of a narrow gauge. —*modifier* (narrow-gauge): *a narrow-gauge track.* —**nar′row-gauged′** *adj.*

nar·row-mind·ed (năr′ō-mīn′dĭd) *adj.* Lacking breadth of view, tolerance, or sympathy; bigoted. —**nar′row-mind′ed·ly** *adv.* —**nar′row-mind′ed·ness** *n.*

nar·thex (när′thĕks′) *n. Archit.* **1.** A portico or lobby of an early Christian or Byzantine church or basilica. **2.** A church entrance hall leading to the nave. [Medieval Greek *narthēx,* enclosure, from Greek, giant fennel, from Sanskrit *narda.*]

nar·whal (när′wəl) *n.* An arctic aquatic mammal, *Monodon monoceros,* with a spotted pelt and characterized in the male by a single long, spirally twisted tusk. [Norwegian or Danish *narhval,* perh. from Old Norse *nāhvalr,* "corpse-whale," from its whitish color.]

nar·y (nâr′ē) *adj. Regional.* Not one; no. [From *ne'er a,* "never a."]

na·sal (nā′zəl) *adj.* **1.** Of or relating to the nose. **2.** *Phonet.* Uttered so that most of the air is exhaled through the nose rather than the mouth, as in sounding *m, n,* and *ng.* **3.** Characterized by or resembling a resonant sound produced through the nose: *a nasal twang.* —*n.* **1.** *Phonet.* A nasal sound. **2.** A nasal part. [French, ult. from Latin *nāsus,* nose.] —**na·sal′i·ty** (nā-zăl′ĭ-tē) *n.* —**na′sal·ly** *adv.*

nas·cent (năs′ənt, nā′sənt) *adj.* Coming into existence; in

narcissus

the process of emerging. [Latin *nāscēns*, pres. part. of *nāscī*, to be born.] —**nas'cence** *n.*

nas·tic (năs'tĭk) *adj.* Of, designating, or characterized by plant growth in response to internal cell pressures, as distinguished from growth due to environmental influences. [From Greek *nastos*, pressed down, from *nassein*, to press.]

na·stur·tium (nə-stûr'shəm, nă-) *n.* Any of various plants of the genus *Tropaeolum*, having showy orange, yellow, or red flowers and rounded, pungent leaves. [Latin *nāsturtium*, a kind of cress.]

nasturtium

nas·ty (năs'tē) *adj.* **-ti·er, -ti·est. 1.** Disgustingly dirty; filthy; foul. **2.** Morally offensive; indecent. **3.** Malicious; spiteful; mean. **4.** Having or displaying an ill temper. **5.** Causing discomfort or trouble; unpleasant; annoying: *nasty weather.* **6.** Painful and dangerous: *a nasty accident.* — See Syns at **irritable** and **malevolent.** [Middle English.] —**nas'ti·ly** *adv.* —**nas'ti·ness** *n.*

na·tal (nāt'l) *adj.* Of, relating to, or accompanying birth. [Middle English, from Latin *nātālis*, from *nātus*, past part. of *nāscī*, to be born.]

na·tal·i·ty (nā-tăl'ĭ-tē, nə-) *n., pl.* **-ties.** Birth rate.

na·ta·tion (nā-tā'shən, nă-) *n.* The action or skill of swimming.

na·ta·to·ri·al (nā'tə-tôr'ē-əl, -tōr'-, năt'ə-) *adj.* Also **na·ta·to·ry** (-tôr'ē, -tōr'ē). Of, relating to, or adapted for swimming.

na·ta·to·ri·um (nā'tə-tôr'ē-əm, -tōr', năt'ə-) *n., pl.* **-to·ri·ums** or **-to·ri·a** (-tôr'ē-ə, -tōr'-). An indoor swimming pool. [Late Latin *natātōrium*, from *natāre*, to swim.]

Natch·ez (năch'ĭz) *n., pl.* **Natchez. 1.** A member of a tribe of Muskhogean-speaking Indians, formerly living in the area of Mississippi. **2.** The language of the Natchez. —**Natch'ez** *adj.*

Na·tick (nā'tĭk) *n.* A dialect of Massachuset.

na·tion (nā'shən) *n.* **1.** A people who share common customs, origins, and history. **2.** A group of people who inhabit a specific territory and are organized under a single government. **3.** A federation of tribes, esp. of North American Indians. **4.** The territory of a nation. [Middle English *nacioun*, from Old French *nacion*, from Latin *nātiō*, race, from *nāscī*, to be born.]

Syns: **nation, country, land, state** *n. Core meaning:* An organized geopolitical unit (*nations of the free world*). NATION primarily signifies a political body—a group of human beings organized under a single government, without close regard for their origins (*the new nations of Africa*); it also denotes the territory occupied by a political body (*all across the nation*). STATE even more specifically indicates governmental organization, gen. on a sovereign basis and in a well-defined area (*the state of Israel*). COUNTRY signifies the territory of one nation (*the country of France*) and is also used in the sense of *nation* (*all the countries of the free world*). LAND is a term for a region (*the land of the bison and beaver*); it also can be used to mean *nation* (*the highest elective office in the land*).

na·tion·al (năsh'ə-nəl, năsh'nəl) *adj.* **1.** Of, relating to, or belonging to a nation as a whole. **2.** Characteristic of or peculiar to the people of a nation. —See Syns at **public.** —*n.* A citizen of a particular nation. —**na'tion·al·ly** *adv.*

national bank. In the United States, a bank chartered and supervised by the Federal government.

National Guard. In the United States, the military reserve unit of each state, equipped by the Federal government and subject to the call of either the Federal or state government.

national income. The total income of a nation over a specified period of time, usu. including wages, profits, rents, and interest.

na·tion·al·ism (năsh'ə-nə-lĭz'əm, năsh'nə-) *n.* Devotion to the interests or culture of a particular nation and the promotion of its interests above those of all other nations. —**na'tion·al·ist** *n.* —**na'tion·al·is'tic** *adj.* —**na'tion·al·is'ti·cal·ly** *adv.*

na·tion·al·i·ty (năsh'ə-năl'ĭ-tē) *n., pl.* **-ties. 1.** The condition or fact of belonging to a particular nation by origin, birth, or naturalization. **2.** A people having common origins or traditions and often constituting a nation.

na·tion·al·ize (năsh'ə-nə-līz', năsh'nə-) *tr.v.* **-ized, -iz·ing. 1.** To change from private to governmental ownership and control: *nationalize an industry.* **2.** To make national in character. —**na'tion·al·i·za'tion** *n.*

National League. One of the two major professional leagues in baseball.

national monument. A landmark, structure, or site of historic interest set aside by a national government and maintained for enjoyment or study by the public.

national park. An area of land maintained by a national government for the recreational and cultural use of the public.

National Socialism. Nazism

na·tion·hood (nā'shən-hood') *n.* The condition of being a nation.

na·tion·wide (nā'shən-wīd') *adj.* Throughout a whole nation.

na·tive (nā'tĭv) *adj.* **1.** Belonging to one by nature; inborn; innate: *native ability.* **2.** Being such by birth or origin: *a native Englishman.* **3.** One's own by birth: *one's native language.* **4.** Originally living, growing, or produced in a certain place: *a plant native to Asia.* **5.** Of, belonging to, or characteristic of the original inhabitants of a place: *native customs.* **6.** Occurring in nature pure or uncombined with other substances: *native copper.* **7.** Natural and unaffected: *native grace.* —*n.* **1.** Someone born in or connected with a place by birth. **2. a.** An original inhabitant. **b.** A lifelong resident. **3.** Something, esp. an animal or a plant, that is native to a particular place. [Middle English *natif*, from Old French, from Latin *nātīvus*, born, native, from *nātus*, past part. of *nāscī*, to be born.] —**na'tive·ly** *adv.* —**na'tive·ness** *n.*

Syns: **native, endemic, indigenous** *adj. Core meaning:* Belonging to one esp. because of the place of one's birth (*our native land*). NATIVE indicates birth or immediate origin in a specific place (*a native Englishman*). ENDEMIC stresses restriction to a localized area (*revolutionary activity and guerrilla fighters endemic to the mountains*). INDIGENOUS, similar to ENDEMIC, specifies that something or someone is of a kind orig. living or growing in a region rather than coming or being brought from another part of the world (*the bison—indigenous to North America; the Ainu—indigenous to the northernmost islands of Japan*).

na·tive-born (nā'tĭv-bôrn') *adj.* Belonging to a place by birth.

na·tiv·i·ty (nə-tĭv'ĭ-tē, nā-) *n., pl.* **-ties. 1.** Birth, esp. the process, conditions, or circumstances of being born. **2. Nativity. a.** The birth of Jesus. **b.** Christmas. [Middle English *nativite*, from Old French, from Latin *nātīvitās*, from *nātīvus*, born, native.]

nat·ty (năt'ē) *adj.* **-ti·er, -ti·est.** *Informal.* Neat, trim, and smart. [Orig. unknown.]

nat·u·ral (năch'ər-əl, năch'rəl) *adj.* **1.** Present in or produced by nature: *natural satellite of the earth.* **2.** Of, relating to, or concerning nature: *natural science.* **3.** Conforming to the usual or ordinary course of nature: *a natural death.* **4. a.** Inherent; not acquired. **b.** Having a particular character by nature: *a natural leader.* **5.** Free from affectation or artificiality. **6.** Not altered, treated, or disguised: *natural coloring.* **7.** Usually or essentially associated with a person or a thing. **8.** Born of unwed parents; illegitimate. **9.** *Mus.* **a.** Not sharped or flatted: *a B natural.* **b.** Having no sharps or flats. —*n.* **1.** *Informal.* Someone obviously suited or qualified: *a natural for the job.* **2.** *Mus.* **a.** The sign (♮) placed before a note to cancel a preceding sharp or flat. **b.** A note so affected. —**nat′u·ral·ness** *n.*

natural gas. A mixture of hydrocarbon gases, principally methane, occurring with petroleum deposits and used as a fuel and in the manufacture of organic compounds.

natural history. The study of natural objects and organisms, their origins, evolution, interrelationships, and description.

nat·u·ral·ism (năch′ər-ə-līz′əm, năch′rə-) *n.* **1.** Factual or realistic representation, esp. in art and literature. **2.** The view that all phenomena can be explained in terms of natural causes and laws.

nat·u·ral·ist (năch′ər-ə-lĭst, năch′rə-) *n.* **1.** Someone who specializes in natural history, esp. in the study of plants and animals in their natural environments. **2.** Someone who believes in naturalism.

nat·u·ral·is·tic (năch′ər-ə-lĭs′tĭk, năch′rə-) *adj.* Of, characterized by, or in accordance with naturalism.

nat·u·ral·ize (năch′ər-ə-līz′, năch′rə-) *v.* **-ized, -iz·ing.** —*tr.v.* **1.** To grant full citizenship to. **2.** To adopt into general use. **3.** To adapt or accustom to a new environment. **4.** To make natural or lifelike. —*intr.v.* To become naturalized or acclimated; adapt. —**nat′u·ral·i·za′tion** *n.*

natural logarithm. *Symbol* **ln** *Math.* A logarithm using the base *e* (=2.71828. . .). For example, ln 10 = log₍e₎10 = 2.30258.

nat·u·ral·ly (năch′ər-ə-lē, năch′rə-) *adv.* **1.** In a natural manner. **2.** By nature; inherently: *naturally blond hair.* **3.** Without a doubt; surely; of course.

natural number. *Math.* One of the set of positive whole numbers.

natural science. A science, such as biology, chemistry, or physics, based chiefly on observations and measureable phenomena.

natural selection. The principle that in a given environment some members of a species have characteristics that aid survival, and that these individuals tend to produce more offspring than the others, so that the proportion of the species having these characteristics increases with each generation.

na·ture (nā′chər) *n.* **1.** The material world and its phenomena. **2.** Often **Nature.** The forces and processes that produce and control all the phenomena of the material world: *the laws of nature.* **3.** The world of living things and the outdoors: *the beauties of nature.* **4.** A primitive state of existence, untouched and uninfluenced by civilization or artificiality. **5.** *Theol.* Man's natural state, as distinguished from the state of grace. **6.** The essential characteristics and qualities of a person or a thing: *the nature of the problem.* **7.** The fundamental character or disposition of an individual: *had a sweet nature.* **8.** Kind; type. **9.** The processes and functions of the body. —See Syns at **disposition.** —*modifier: nature study.* [Middle English, from Old French, from Latin *nātūra,* nature, birth, from *nātus,* past part. of *nāscī,* to be born.] —**na′tured** *adj.*

na·tur·op·a·thy (nā′chə-rŏp′ə-thē) *n.* A system of medical treatment that relies wholly on natural remedies such as sunlight, diet, and massage.

naught (nôt) *n.* Also **nought.** **1.** Nothing. **2.** A cipher; zero; the figure 0. —*adj.* Also **nought.** Of no value or significance. [Middle English *nauht,* from Old English *nāwiht : nā,* no + *wiht,* creature, thing.]

naugh·ty (nô′tē) *adj.* **-ti·er, -ti·est.** **1.** Disobedient; mischievous: *a naughty child.* **2.** Improper. [Middle English *nauhty,* from *nauht,* worthless, naught.] —**naugh′ti·ly** *adv.* —**naugh′ti·ness** *n.*

nau·se·a (nô′zē-ə, -zhə, -sē-ə, -shə) *n.* **1.** A stomach disturbance characterized by a feeling of the need to vomit. **2.** Extreme or intense disgust. [Latin, from Greek *nausia,* seasickness, from *naus,* ship.]

nau·se·ate (nô′zē-āt′, -zhē-, -sē-, -shē-) *v.* **-at·ed, -at·ing.** —*tr.v.* To cause to feel nausea. —*intr.v.* To feel nausea or queasiness. —See Syns at **repel.** —**nau′se·at′ing·ly** *adv.* —**nau′se·a′tion** *n.*

nau·seous (nô′shəs, -zē-əs) *adj.* **1.** Causing nausea; sickening. **2.** Feeling nausea. —**nau′seous·ly** *adv.*

nau·ti·cal (nô′tĭ-kəl) *adj.* Of, relating to, or characteristic of ships, shipping, seamen, or navigation on a body of water.

[From Latin *nauticus,* from Greek *nautikos,* from *nautēs,* seaman, from *naus,* ship.] —**nau′ti·cal·ly** *adv.*

nautical mile. A unit of length used in sea and air navigation equal to 1,852 meters or about 6,076 feet.

nau·ti·lus (nôt′l-əs) *n., pl.* **-lus·es** or **-li** (-lī′). **1.** Any mollusk of the genus *Nautilus,* that is found in the Indian and Pacific oceans and has a spiral shell with a series of air-filled chambers. **2.** The chambered nautilus. [Latin, from Greek *nautilos,* sailor, from *naus,* ship.]

Nav·a·ho (năv′ə-hō′, nä′və-) *n., pl.* **Navaho** or **-hos** or **-hoes.** Also **Nav·a·jo** (năv′ə-hō′, nä′və-). **1.** A member of a group of Athapascan-speaking Indians occupying an extensive reservation in parts of New Mexico, Arizona, and Utah. **2.** The language of the Navaho. —**Nav′a·ho′** *adj.*

na·val (nā′vəl) *adj.* **1.** Of or relating to a navy or to the equipment, installations, personnel, or customs of a navy. **2.** Having a navy: *a great naval power.*

nave¹ (nāv) *n.* The central part of a church, extending from the entrance to the chancel and flanked by aisles. [Medieval Latin *nāvis,* ship, from Latin.]

nave¹

nave² (nāv) *n.* The hub of a wheel. [Middle English, from Old English *nafu.*]

na·vel (nā′vəl) *n.* **1.** The mark on the abdomen of mammals where the umbilical cord was attached before birth. **2.** A central point; middle. [Middle English *navel,* from Old English *nafela.*]

navel orange. A sweet, usu. seedless orange having a navel-like formation opposite the stem end.

nav·i·ga·ble (năv′ĭ-gə-bəl) *adj.* **1.** Deep or wide enough to provide passage for vessels. **2.** Capable of being steered. —**nav′i·ga·bil′i·ty** or **nav′i·ga·ble·ness** *n.* —**nav′i·ga·bly** *adv.*

nav·i·gate (năv′ĭ-gāt′) *v.* **-gat·ed, -gat·ing.** —*tr.v.* **1.** To plan, record, and control the course and position of (a ship or aircraft). **2.** To follow a course on, across, or through: *navigate a stream.* —*intr.v.* **1.** To control the course of a ship or aircraft. **2.** To voyage over water in a boat or ship; sail. **3.** *Informal.* **a.** To make one's way. **b.** To walk. [From Latin *nāvigāre,* to manage a ship : *nāvis,* ship + *agere,* to drive, conduct.]

nav·i·ga·tion (năv′ĭ-gā′shən) *n.* **1.** The theory and practice of navigating esp. a ship or aircraft. **2.** Travel or traffic by vessels, esp. commercial shipping. —*modifier: navigation charts.* —**nav′i·ga′tion·al** *adj.*

nav·i·ga·tor (năv′ĭ-gā′tər) *n.* Someone who navigates.

nav·vy (năv′ē) *n., pl.* **-vies.** *Brit.* A laborer. [Short for obs. *navigator,* a laborer who builds canals.]

na·vy (nā′vē) *n., pl.* **-vies.** **1.** All of a nation's warships. **2.** Often **Navy.** A nation's entire military organization for sea warfare and defense, including vessels, personnel, and shore establishments. **3.** A group of ships; a fleet. **4.** Navy blue. [Middle English *navie,* from Old French, from Latin *nāvis,* ship.]

navy bean. A kidney bean, cultivated for its nutritious white seeds.

navy blue. Dark blue. [From the color of the British naval uniform.] —**na′vy-blue′** *adj.*

navy yard. A dockyard for the construction, repair, equipping, or docking of naval ships.

na·wab (nə-wŏb′) *n.* A governor or ruler in India under the Mogul empire. [Hindi *nawwāb,* from Arabic *nuwwāb,* orig. pl. of *nā′ib,* deputy.]

nay (nā) *adv.* **1.** No: *All but four Democrats voted nay.*

---

2. And moreover: *He was ill-favored, nay, hideous.* —*n.* **1.** A denial or refusal. **2.** A negative vote or voter. [Middle English, from Old Norse *nei* : *ne*, not + *ei*, ever.]

Na·zi (nät'sē, nắt'-) *n., pl.* **-zis.** **1.** A member of a facist party founded in Germany in 1919 and brought to power in 1933 under Adolf Hitler. **2.** Often **nazi.** Someone who believes in or advocates policies characteristic of a Nazi. [German, short for *Nationalsozialist,* National Socialist.] —**Na'zi** *adj.*

Na·zism (nät'sĭz'əm, nắt'-) *n.* Also **Na·zi·ism** (nät'sē-ĭz'əm, nắt'-). The doctrine and policy of the Nazis, including state control of the economy, racist nationalism, and national expansion.

Nb The symbol for the element niobium.

Nd The symbol for the element neodymium.

Ne The symbol for the element neon.

Ne·an·der·thal (nē-ăn'dər-thôl', -tôl', nä-ăn'dər-täl') *adj.* Of, relating to, or characteristic of Neanderthal man. —**Ne·an'der·thal'** *n.*

Neanderthal man. An extinct species of man, *Homo neanderthalensis,* living during the late Pleistocene age in the Old World, and associated with Middle Paleolithic tools. [After *Neanderthal,* a valley near Düsseldorf, West Germany, where human remains were found.]

neap tide (nēp). A tide of lowest range, occurring at the first and third quarters of the moon. [Middle English *neep,* from Old English *nēpflōd,* neap tide.]

near (nîr) *adv.* **-er, -est.** **1.** To, at, or within a short distance or interval in space or time. **2.** Almost; nearly: *near exhausted by the heat.* **3.** With or in a close relationship. —*adj.* **-er, -est.** **1.** Close in time, space, position, or degree: *near equals.* **2.** Closely related by kinship or association: intimate: *near and dear friends.* **3.** Failing or succeeding by a very small margin: *a near miss.* **4.** Closely corresponding to or resembling an original: *a near likeness.* **5. a.** Closer of two or more. **b.** Being on the left side. **6.** Short and direct: *the nearest route to town.* **7.** Stingy; parsimonious. —*prep.* Close to: *an inn near London.* —*tr.v.* To come close or closer to. —*intr.v.* To draw near or nearer; approach. [Middle English *nere,* from Old English *nēah,* comp. adv. of *nēah,* near.] —**near'ness** *n.*

   Syns: near, close, immediate, nearby, nigh *adj.* Core meaning: Not far from another in space, time, or relation (*an airport that was near to the town; was near to me in age*).

near·by (nîr'bī') *adj.* Located a short distance away; close at hand. —See Syns at **convenient** and **near.** —*adv.* Not far away.

near·ly (nîr'lē) *adv.* Almost but not quite.

near·sight·ed (nîr'sī'tĭd) *adj.* Unable to see distant objects clearly; myopic. —**near'sight'ed·ly** *adv.* —**near'sight'ed·ness** *n.*

neat[1] (nēt) *adj.* **-er, -est.** **1.** Orderly and clean; tidy. **2.** Marked by ingenuity and skill; adroit: *a neat turn of phrase.* **3.** Not diluted or mixed with other substances: *neat whiskey.* **4.** Left after all deductions; net: *neat profit.* **5.** *Slang.* Wonderful; terrific; fine: *That was a neat party.* [Old French *net,* from Latin *nitidus,* elegant, shiny, from *nitēre,* to shine.] —**neat'ly** *adv.* —**neat'ness** *n.*

   Syns: neat, orderly, shipshape, tidy, trim *adj.* Core meaning: In good order or clean condition (*kept a neat yard*).

neat[2] (nēt) *n., pl.* **neat.** *Archaic.* A domestic bovine such as a cow. [Middle English *nete,* from Old English *nēat.*]

neath or **'neath** (nēth) *prep. Poet.* Beneath.

neat's-foot oil (nēts'fŏŏt'). A light, yellow oil obtained from the feet and shinbones of cattle, used chiefly to process leather.

neb (nĕb) *n.* **1. a.** A beak of a bird. **b.** A nose; snout. **2.** A nib. [Middle English, from Old English *nebb.*]

neb·u·la (nĕb'yə-lə) *n., pl.* **-lae** (-lē', -lī') or **-las.** *Astron.* An enormous mass of interstellar gas or dust. [Latin, cloud.] —**neb'u·lar** *adj.*

nebular hypothesis. The theory that the solar system evolved as a result of the processes of cooling and contraction undergone by a rotating nebula.

neb·u·lize (nĕb'yə-līz') *tr.v.* **-lized, -liz·ing.** To convert (a liquid) to a fine spray; atomize. —**neb'u·li·za'tion** *n.* —**neb'u·liz'er** *n.*

neb·u·los·i·ty (nĕb'yə-lŏs'ĭ-tē) *n., pl.* **-ties.** **1.** The condition or quality of being nebulous. **2.** A mass of nebular material; nebula.

neb·u·lous (nĕb'yə-ləs) *adj.* **1.** Lacking definite form or limits; vague. **2.** Of, relating to, or characteristic of a nebula. —**neb'u·lous·ly** *adv.* —**neb'u·lous·ness** *n.*

nec·es·sar·i·ly (nĕs'ĭ-sâr'ə-lē) *adv.* Of necessity; inevitably.

nec·es·sar·y (nĕs'ĭ-sĕr'ē) *adj.* **1.** Absolutely essential; indispensable. **2.** Inevitably or unavoidably determined. **3.** Logically inevitable. **4.** Required, as by obligation, compulsion, or convention. —*n., pl.* **-ies.** Something that is indispensable or necessary. [Middle English *necessarie,* from Latin *necessārius,* from *necesse,* necessary.]

   ***Syns:* necessary, essential, indispensable, vital** *adj.* Core meaning: Needed to achieve a result or fulfill a requirement (*fresh vegetables necessary to good nutrition*). NECESSARY implies that which fills an urgent but not invariably an all-compelling need (*fill out the necessary forms*). VITAL refers to what is basic and therefore of crucial importance (*irrigation being vital to early civilization*). INDISPENSABLE even more strongly applies to what cannot be left out or done without (*oxygen—indispensable for human life*). See also Syns at **compulsory.**

ne·ces·si·tate (nə-sĕs'ĭ-tāt') *tr.v.* **-tat·ed, -tat·ing.** **1.** To make necessary or unavoidable: *The emergency necessitated a change in plans.* **2.** To require or compel: *a situation that necessitated immediate action.* —**ne·ces'si·ta'tion** *n.*

ne·ces·si·tous (nə-sĕs'ĭ-təs) *adj.* **1.** Needy; destitute; indigent. **2.** Compelling; pressing; urgent. —**ne·ces'si·tous·ly** *adv.*

ne·ces·si·ty (nə-sĕs'ĭ-tē) *n., pl.* **-ties.** **1. a.** The condition or quality of being necessary. **b.** Something that is necessary. **2.** The force exerted by circumstance. **3.** The fact of being in need. —See Syns at **need.** —**idiom. of necessity.** As an inevitable consequence; necessarily. [Middle English *necessite,* from Old French, from Latin *necessitās,* from *necesse,* necessary.]

neck (nĕk) *n.* **1.** The part of the body joining the head to the trunk. **2.** The part of a garment around or near the neck. **3.** A relatively narrow part that resembles or functions like a neck: *the neck of a bottle.* **4.** *Mus.* The narrow part of a stringed instrument along which the strings extend to the pegs. **5.** *Slang.* A narrow margin by which a competition is won or lost. —**modifier:** *neck muscles.* —**idioms. neck and neck.** Even in a race or contest. **stick one's neck out.** *Slang.* To risk criticism, trouble, or danger by acting. —*intr.v. Slang.* To kiss and caress. [Middle English *necke,* from Old English *hnecca.*]

neck·er·chief (nĕk'ər-chĭf) *n.* A kerchief worn around the neck.

neck·lace (nĕk'lĭs) *n.* An ornament worn around the neck.

neck·line (nĕk'līn') *n.* The line formed by the edge of a garment at or near the neck.

neck·tie (nĕk'tī') *n.* A long, narrow band of fabric worn around the neck and tied in a knot or bow close to the throat.

neck·wear (nĕk'wâr') *n.* Articles, such as neckties or scarfs, worn around the neck.

necro- or **necr-.** A prefix meaning death or the dead: *necrology.* [From Greek *nekros,* corpse.]

ne·crol·o·gy (nə-krŏl'ə-jē, nĕ-) *n., pl.* **-gies.** **1.** A list or record of people who have died, esp. in the recent past. **2.** An obituary. —**nec'ro·log'ic** (nĕk'rə-lŏj'ĭk) or **nec'ro·log'i·cal** *adj.* —**ne·crol'o·gist** *n.*

nec·ro·man·cy (nĕk'rə-măn'sē) *n.* **1.** The practice of communicating with the spirits of the dead in order to predict the future. **2.** Black magic; sorcery. [NECRO- + Greek *manteia,* divination, from *mantis,* prophet.] —**nec'ro·man'cer** *n.* —**nec'ro·man'tic** *adj.*

ne·crop·o·lis (nə-krŏp'ə-lĭs, nĕ-) *n., pl.* **-lis·es** or **-leis** (-lās'). A cemetery, esp. a large and elaborate cemetery of an ancient city. [Greek *nekropolis* : *nekros,* corpse + *polis,* city.]

ne·cro·sis (nə-krō'sĭs, nĕ-) *n., pl.* **-ses** (-sēz'). The pathologic death of living tissue in a plant or animal. —**ne·crot'ic** (-krŏt'ĭk) *adj.*

nec·tar (nĕk'tər) *n.* **1.** *Gk. & Rom. Myth.* The drink of the gods. **2.** A delicious drink. **3.** A sweet liquid secreted by

---

ă pat	ā pay	â care	ä father	ĕ pet	ē be	hw which
ŏŏ took	ōō boot	ou out	th thin	*th* this	ŭ cut	

ĭ pit	ī tie	î pier	ŏ pot	ō toe	ô paw, for	oi noise
û urge	zh vision	ə about, item, edible, gallop, circus				

flowers of various plants and gathered by bees for making honey. [Greek *nektar*.] —**nec·tar·ous** *adj.*

nec·tar·ine (nĕk′tə-rēn′) *n.* A variety of peach with a smooth, waxy skin. [Short for *nectarine peach*, from obs. *nectarine*, "sweet as nectar."]

nec·ta·ry (nĕk′tə-rē) *n., pl.* **-ries.** A plant organ that secretes nectar. —**nec·tar′i·al** (nĕk-târ′ē-əl) *adj.*

née or **nee** (nā) *adj.* Born. Used to indicate the maiden name of a married woman: *Mary Smith, née Jones.* [French, fem. past part. of *naître*, to be born, from Latin *nāscī*.]

need (nēd) *n.* **1.** A lack of something required or desirable: *crops in need of water; a need for affection.* **2.** Necessity; obligation: *There is no need for you to go.* **3.** Something required or wanted; requisite: *Our needs are modest.* **4.** A condition of poverty or misfortune: *He is in dire need.* —*tr.v.* To have need of; require: *a wall that needs paint; needing more money.* —*intr.v.* **1.** To be under a necessity; be obliged: *She need not come. He needs to study.* **2.** To be in need or want. —**idiom. if need be.** If necessary. [Middle English *nede*, from Old English *nēod*, necessity, distress.]

Syns: **need, exigency, necessity** *n. Core meaning:* A condition in which something necessary is required or wanted (*patients in need of nursing*).

Usage: **need.** *Need* is often employed as an auxiliary verb meaning be obliged or have to. As such it has several peculiarities. It is regularly followed by an infinitive (*need to sleep*), but in varying ways. When the example is a negative statement or a question, the infinitive that follows is sometimes expressed with *to*, and sometimes not: *You need not leave. Need we leave?* But: *You do not need to leave. Do we need to leave?* In examples in which the verb *need* is active, *to* is always expressed when the infinitive follows the inflected forms *needs* and *needed: She needs to rest. They needed to stop.* In examples in which the verb *need* is passive and a gerund occurs, *to* is omitted: *She needs counseling. He needs talking to about his behavior.* In negative statements and questions, *need* as an auxiliary is not inflected in the third person singular, present tense, as it is in positive statements: *He need not try. He needs to try. Need it have occurred?*

need·ful (nēd′fəl) *adj.* Necessary; required. —**need′ful·ly** *adv.* —**need′ful·ness** *n.*

need·i·ness (nē′dē-nĭs) *n.* The condition of being in need; poverty.

nee·dle (nēd′l) *n.* **1.** A slender, sewing implement, usu. made of polished steel with a point at one end and an eye at the other through which a length of thread is passed and held. **2. a.** A slender, pointed rod used in knitting. **b.** A similar implement, usu. shorter, and with a hook at one end, used in crocheting. **3.** A stylus used to transmit vibrations from the grooves of a phonograph record. **4.** A slender pointer or indicator, as on a dial. **5.** A hypodermic needle. **6.** A stiff, narrow leaf, as on a pine tree. **7.** A sharp, pointed object, as a spine of a sea urchin. —*v.* **-dled, -dling.** —*tr.v.* **1.** To prick, pierce, or stitch with or as if with a needle. **2.** *Informal.* To goad, provoke, or tease. [Middle English *nedle*, from Old English *nǣdl*.]

nee·dle·point (nēd′l-point′) *n.* **1.** Embroidery on canvas done with even stitches to resemble a woven tapestry. **2.** A type of lace worked on paper patterns with a needle. —*modifier: a needlepoint cushion.*

need·less (nēd′lĭs) *adj.* Not needed or wished for; unnecessary. —**need′less·ly** *adv.* —**need′less·ness** *n.*

nee·dle·wom·an (nēd′l-wŏŏm′ən) *n.* A woman who does needlework, esp. a seamstress.

nee·dle·work (nēd′l-wûrk′) *n.* Work done with a needle, such as embroidery. —**nee′dle·work′er** *n.*

need·n't (nēd′nt). Need not.

needs (nēdz) *adv.* Of necessity; necessarily: *He must needs go.* [Middle English *nedes*, from Old English *nēdes*, genitive of *nēd*, need.]

need·y (nē′dē) *adj.* **-i·er, -i·est.** Being in need; impoverished. —See Syns at **poor.**

ne′er (nâr). *Poet.* Never.

ne′er-do-well (nâr′dŏŏ-wĕl′) *n.* A worthless, irresponsible person. —**ne′er′-do-well′** *adj.*

ne·far·i·ous (nə-fâr′ē-əs) *adj.* Evil; wicked. [Latin *nefārius*,

from *nefās*, sin.] —**ne·far′i·ous·ly** *adv.* —**ne·far′i·ous·ness** *n.*

ne·gate (nə-gāt′) *tr.v.* **-gat·ed, -gat·ing.** **1.** To make ineffective or invalid: *a new ruling that negates previous ones.* **2.** To deny. [From Latin *negāre*, to deny.]

ne·ga·tion (nə-gā′shən) *n.* **1.** The act or process of negating. **2.** A negative statement. **3.** The opposite of something regarded as positive or affirmative.

neg·a·tive (nĕg′ə-tĭv) *adj.* **1.** Expressing, containing, or consisting of a negation, refusal, or denial: *a negative answer.* **2.** Not positive or constructive: *negative criticism.* **3.** *Med.* Indicating that a suspected disease, disorder, or microorganism is not present: *x rays that proved negative.* **4.** *Math.* Relating to or denoting: **a.** A quantity less than zero. **b.** A quantity to be subtracted from another. **5.** *Physics.* Relating to or denoting: **a.** Electric charge of the same sign as that of an electron, designated by the symbol (-). **b.** Any body having an excess of electrons. **6.** *Biol.* Indicating resistance to, opposition to, or motion away from a stimulus: *a negative tropism.* —*n.* **1.** A denial or refusal. **2.** Something that is the opposite of something positive. **3.** *Gram.* A word or part of a word, such as *no, not,* or *non-,* that indicates negation. **4.** The side in a debate that contradicts or opposes the question being debated. **5. a.** An image in which the light areas of the object rendered appear dark and the dark areas appear light. **b.** A film, plate, or other photographic material containing such an image. **6.** *Math.* A negative quantity. —*tr.v.* **-tived, -tiv·ing.** **1.** To refuse to approve; veto. **2.** To deny; contradict. **3.** To counteract or neutralize. —**neg′a·tive·ly** *adv.* —**neg′a·tive·ness** or **neg′a·tiv′i·ty** *n.*

negative electrode. A negatively charged electrode; cathode.

neg·a·tiv·ism (nĕg′ə-tĭ-vĭz′əm) *n.* A habitual attitude of skepticism or resistance to the beliefs, suggestions, or instructions of others. —**neg′a·tiv·ist** *n.* —**neg′a·tiv·is′tic** *adj.*

ne·glect (nĭ-glĕkt′) *tr.v.* **1.** To ignore or pay no attention to; disregard: *They neglected his warning.* **2.** To fail to care for or give proper attention to: *She neglected her appearance.* **3.** To fail to do, as through carelessness or oversight: *He neglected to make his point.* —*n.* **1.** The act or an example of neglecting. **2.** The condition of being neglected. [From Latin *neglígere*, not to heed : *neg-,* not + *legere,* to choose.] —**ne·glect′er** or **ne·glec′tor** *n.*

ne·glect·ful (nĭ-glĕkt′fəl) *adj.* Characterized by neglect; careless; heedless: *neglectful of responsibilities.* —**ne·glect′ful·ly** *adv.* —**ne·glect′ful·ness** *n.*

neg·li·gee (nĕg′lĭ-zhā′, nĕg′lĭ-zhā′) *n.* Also **neg·li·gée,** **neg·li·gé.** **1.** A woman's long, loose dressing gown. **2.** Informal or incomplete attire. [French, from *négliger,* to neglect, from Latin *negligere.*]

neg·li·gence (nĕg′lĭ-jəns) *n.* **1.** The condition or quality of being negligent. **2.** A negligent act. **3.** *Law.* The omission or neglect of any reasonable precaution, care, or action.

neg·li·gent (nĕg′lĭ-jənt) *adj.* **1.** Habitually guilty of neglect; lacking in proper care or concern. **2.** Extremely careless or casual. [Middle English, from Old French, from Latin *negligens,* pres. part. of *negligere,* to neglect.] —**neg′li·gent·ly** *adv.*

neg·li·gi·ble (nĕg′lĭ-jə-bəl) *adj.* Worthy of neglect; trifling. —**neg′li·gi·bil′i·ty** or **neg′li·gi·ble·ness** *n.* —**neg′li·gi·bly** *adv.*

ne·go·tia·ble (nĭ-gō′shə-bəl, -shē-ə-) *adj.* **1.** Capable of being negotiated. **2.** Capable of being legally transferred from one person to another, either by delivery or by delivery and endorsement. —**ne·go′tia·bil′i·ty** *n.*

ne·go·ti·ate (nĭ-gō′shē-āt′) *intr.v.* **-at·ed, -at·ing.** To confer with another in order to come to terms or reach an agreement. —*tr.v.* **1.** To arrange or settle by conferring or discussing: *negotiate a contract.* **2.** To transfer title to or ownership of (notes, funds, documents, or similar property) to another person or party in return for value received. **3.** To succeed in going over, accomplishing, or coping with: *negotiate a sharp curve.* [Latin *negōtiārī,* to transact business, from *negōtium,* business : *neg-,* not + *ōtium,* leisure.] —**ne·go′ti·a′tor** *n.*

ne·go·ti·a·tion (nĭ-gō′shē-ā′shən) *n.* **1.** The act or process of negotiating. **2.** Often **negotiations.** Discussions for the purpose of reaching an agreement or settlement.

Ne·gril·lo (nĭ-grĭl′ō, -grē′yō) *n., pl.* **-los** or **-loes.** Any member of a group of Negroid peoples of Africa, including the Bushmen and the Pygmies, who are short in stature.

Ne·gri·to (nĭ-grē'tō) *n.*, *pl.* **-tos** or **-toes.** Any member of various groups of Negroid people of short stature inhabiting parts of Malaysia, the Philippines, and southeastern Asia.

ne·gri·tude (nĕg'rĭ-tood', -tyood', nēg'rĭ-) *n.* Awareness of and pride in the culture and history of blacks. [French *négritude*, from *nègre*, Negro.]

Ne·gro (nē'grō) *n.*, *pl.* **-groes. 1.** A member of the Negroid ethnic division of the human species. **2.** A person of Negro descent. **—Ne'gro** *adj.*

Ne·groid (nē'groid') *adj.* *Anthropol.* Of, relating to, or designating a major ethnic division of the human species whose members are characterized by brown to black pigmentation and often by tightly curled hair. **—Ne'groid** *n.*

ne·gus (nē'gəs) *n.* A beverage made of wine, hot water, lemon juice, sugar, and nutmeg. [After Colonel Francis Negus (d. 1732), English soldier.]

neigh (nā) *n.* The long, high-pitched sound made by a horse. *—intr.v.* To utter a neigh. [Middle English *neien*, from Old English *hnǣgan.*]

neigh·bor (nā'bər). Also *chiefly Brit.* **neigh·bour.** *—n.* **1.** A person who lives or is located near another. **2.** A fellow human. *—tr.v.* To lie close to; border upon; adjoin. *—intr.v.* To live or be situated close by. [Middle English, from Old English *nēahgebūr* : *nēah*, near + *gebūr*, dweller.]

neigh·bor·hood (nā'bər-hood') *n.* **1.** A district or area with distinctive characteristics: *one of the older neighborhoods in the city.* **2.** The people who live in a particular area or district: *The shot disturbed the whole neighborhood.* **—modifier:** *the neighborhood children.* **—idiom. in the neighborhood of. 1.** Near: *We left him in the neighborhood of that village.* **2.** Approximately: *inflation in the neighborhood of three per cent a year.*

neigh·bor·ly (nā'bər-lē) *adj.* Appropriate to or showing the feelings of a friendly neighbor. **—neigh'bor·li·ness** *n.*

nei·ther (nē'thər, nī'-) *adj.* Not either; not one nor the other: *Neither shoe fits comfortably.* *—pron.* **1.** Not either one; not the one nor the other: *Neither of them fits.* **2.** Not any one of more than two: *Neither of the men stood up.* *—conj.* **1.** —Used with *nor* to mark two negative alternatives; not either: *They had neither seen nor heard of us.* **2.** Nor: *So you don't have a job? Neither do I.* [Middle English, from Old English *nāhwæther* : *nā*, no, not + *hwæther*, which of two.]

nek·ton (nĕk'tən, -tŏn') *n.* Saltwater animal organisms that swim independently of currents, ranging in size from microscopic organisms to whales. [German, from Greek *nēkton*, "swimming thing," from *nēkhein*, to swim.] **—nek·ton'ic** (nĕk-tŏn'ĭk) *adj.*

nel·son (nĕl'sən) *n.* A hold in wrestling in which the user places an arm under the opponent's arm and applies pressure with the palm of the hand against the opponent's neck. [Orig. unknown.]

nemato-. A prefix meaning threadlike: *nematocyst.* [From Greek *nēma*, thread.]

nem·a·to·cyst (nĕm'ə-tə-sĭst', nĭ-măt'ə-) *n.* *Zool.* One of the stinging cells in the tentacles of various coelenterates, such as a jellyfish or hydra. **—nem'a·to·cys'tic** *adj.*

nem·a·tode (nĕm'ə-tōd') *n.* Any worm of the phylum Nematoda, that have unsegmented, threadlike bodies and are often parasitic in animals and plants.

Nem·bu·tal (nĕm'byə-tôl') *n.* A trademark for the drug pentobarbital sodium.

nem·e·sis (nĕm'ĭ-sĭs) *n.*, *pl.* **-ses** (-sēz'). **1. Nemesis.** *Gk. Myth.* The goddess of retributive justice or vengeance. **2.** Someone or something that is the cause of just punishment or retribution; avenger. **3.** Just punishment; retributive justice. **4.** An unbeatable rival: *She met her nemesis in the tennis match.*

neo-. A prefix meaning new or recent: *neoplasm.* [Greek, from *neos*, new.]

ne·o·clas·si·cism (nē'ō-klăs'ĭ-sĭz'əm) *n.* A revival of classical forms in art, music, and literature. **—ne'o·clas'sic** or **ne'o·clas'si·cal** *adj.*

ne·o·dym·i·um (nē'ō-dĭm'ē-əm) *n.* *Symbol* **Nd** A bright, metallic rare-earth element. Atomic number 60; atomic

weight 144.24; melting point 1,024°C; boiling point 3,027°C; specific gravity 6.80 or 7.004 (depending on allotropic form); valence 3. [NEO- + *(di)dymium*, a mixture of rare-earth elements, from Greek *didumos*, twin.]

Ne·o·lith·ic (nē'ə-lĭth'ĭk) *adj.* *Archaeol.* Of or denoting the period of human culture that began around 10,000 B.C. in the Middle East, and was characterized by the introduction of farming and the making and use of fairly advanced stone tools and implements. **—modifier:** *A Neolithic weapon.*

ne·ol·o·gism (nē-ŏl'ə-jĭz'əm) *n.* A newly coined word or expression. [French *néologisme*.] **—ne·ol'o·gist** *n.* **—ne·ol'o·gis'tic** or **ne·ol'o·gis'ti·cal** *adj.*

ne·o·my·cin (nē'ō-mī'sĭn) *n.* An antibiotic drug that consists of a group of organic complexes produced by the metabolism of bacteria.

ne·on (nē'ŏn) *n.* *Symbol* **Ne** A rare, inert, gaseous element that occurs in the atmosphere to the extent of 18 parts per million, and is used in display and television tubes. Atomic number 10; atomic weight 20.183; melting point -248.67°C; boiling point -245.95°C; valence 0. [From Greek *neon*, new.]

ne·o·phyte (nē'ə-fīt') *n.* **1.** A recent convert. **2.** A beginner; novice. [Late Latin *neophytus*, from Greek *neophutos*, "newly planted."]

ne·o·plasm (nē'ə-plăz'əm) *n.* An abnormal new growth of tissue in animals or plants; tumor. **—ne'o·plas'tic** *adj.*

ne·o·prene (nē'ə-prēn') *n.* A tough synthetic rubber that is resistant to the effects of oils, solvents, heat, and weather. [NEO- + PR(OPYL) + -ENE.]

Nep·al·ese (nĕp'ə-lēz', -lēs') *n.*, *pl.* **Nepalese. 1.** A native or resident of Nepal. **2.** The Indic language of Nepal. **—Nep'al·ese'** *adj.*

ne·pen·the (nĭ-pĕn'thē) *n.* **1.** A legendary drug of ancient times, used as a remedy for grief. **2.** Something that brings forgetfulness of sorrow or eases pain. [Greek *nēpenthes (pharmakon)*, "grief-banishing (drug)."]

neph·ew (nĕf'yoo) *n.* A son of one's brother or sister or of one's brother-in-law or sister-in-law. [Middle English *neveu*, nephew, grandson, from Old French *neveu*, from Latin *nepōs*.]

ne·phrid·i·um (nə-frĭd'ē-əm) *n.*, *pl.* **-i·a** (-ē-ə). An excretory organ in many invertebrates. [From Greek *nephros*, kidney.] **—ne·phrid'i·al** *adj.*

neph·rite (nĕf'rīt') *n.* A white to dark green variety of jade. [German *Nephrit*, "kidney mineral" (from its supposed power to cure kidney diseases).]

ne·phrit·ic (nə-frĭt'ĭk) *adj.* **1.** Of or pertaining to the kidneys. **2.** *Path.* Of, pertaining to, or affected with nephritis.

ne·phri·tis (nə-frī'tĭs) *n.* Inflammation of the kidneys.

nephro- or **nephr-.** A prefix meaning kidney: *nephrogenous.* [Greek, from *nephros*, kidney.]

ne plus ul·tra (nē' plŭs ŭl'trə, nā' ploos ool'trä). The highest point of excellence or achievement. [Latin, "(sail) no more beyond (this point)," a warning to mariners allegedly inscribed on the Pillars of Hercules.]

nep·o·tism (nĕp'ə-tĭz'əm) *n.* Preference or patronage given to relatives. [French *népotisme*, from Italian *nepotismo*, from *nepote*, nephew, from Latin *nepōs*.] **—nep'o·tist** *n.*

Nep·tune (nĕp'toon', -tyoon') *n.* **1.** *Rom. Myth.* The god of the sea, corresponding to the Greek Poseidon. **2.** The eighth planet of the solar system in order of increasing

neoclassicism

distance from the sun. —**Nep·tu′ni·an** *adj.*

nep·tu·ni·um (nĕp-tōō′nē-əm, -tyōō′-) *n. Symbol* **Np** A silvery, metallic, naturally radioactive element, produced synthetically by nuclear reactions. [After NEPTUNE.]

Ne·re·id (nîr′ē-ĭd) *n. Gk. Myth.* A sea nymph. [Latin *Nereis*, from Greek *Nēreis*, from *Nēreus*, a sea-god.]

ne·re·is (nîr′ē-ĭs) *n., pl.* **ne·re·i·des** (nə-rē′ĭ-dēz′). Any of several saltwater worms of the genus *Nereis*, with a long, flat, segmented body and a pair of paddles on each segment. [From Latin *Nēreis*, Nereid.]

ne·rit·ic (nə-rĭt′ĭk) *adj.* Pertaining to the shallow waters of a shoreline. [Prob. from Latin *nērīta*, sea snail, from Greek *nērītēs*, from *Nēreus*, Nereus.]

ner·o·li (nĕr′ə-lē) *n.* An essential oil distilled from orange flowers and used in making perfume. [French, after Anna Maria de la Trémoille, princess of *Neroli*.]

ner·va·tion (nûr-vā′shən) *n.* A pattern of veins or nerves; venation.

nerve (nûrv) *n.* **1.** Any of the bundles of fibers interconnecting the central nervous system and the organs or parts of the body, capable of transmitting both sensory stimuli and motor impulses from one part of the body to another. **2.** Patience; endurance. **3.** **nerves.** Hysteria, caused by fear, anxiety, or stress: *an attack of nerves.* **4.** Strong will; courage. **5.** *Informal.* Impudent boldness; audacity: *He has more nerve than brains.* —*tr.v.* **nerved, nerv·ing.** To give strength or courage to: *She nerved herself for the encounter.* —See Syns at **encourage.** —*idiom.* **get on (one's) nerves.** To exasperate or irritate. [Latin *nervus*, sinew, nerve.]

nerve cell. A neuron.

nerve center. 1. A group of nerve cells that perform a specific function. **2.** A source or focus of power or control.

nerve fiber. An axon or dendrite.

nerve gas. Any of several poisonous gases used in warfare that attack the respiratory and central nervous systems.

nerve impulse. The electrical and chemical disturbance that moves along a stimulated nerve fiber.

nerve·less (nûrv′lĭs) *adj.* **1.** Lacking strength or energy: *The pipe dropped from his nerveless fingers.* **2.** Calm; poised: *nerveless in the face of competition.* —**nerve′less·ly** *adv.* —**nerve′less·ness** *n.*

nerve-rack·ing (nûrv′răk′ĭng) *adj.* Also **nerve-wrack·ing.** Intensely distressing or irritating to the nerves.

nerv·ous (nûr′vəs) *adj.* **1.** Of, affecting, or having to do with the nerves or the nervous system: *a nervous disorder.* **2.** High-strung; jittery: *a nervous person.* **3.** Uneasy; fearful; anxious: *nervous about staying home alone.* **4.** Spirited in style, feeling, or thought: *a nervous, vibrant prose.* —See Syns at **edgy.** —**nerv′ous·ly** *adv.* —**nerv′ous·ness** *n.*

nervous breakdown. A severe mental or emotional disorder.

nervous system. *Anat.* A coordinating mechanism in most multicellular animals that serves to regulate internal functions and responses to stimuli, and in vertebrates includes the brain, spinal cord, nerves, and structures that are parts of the sense organs and the organs that perform the various actions of the organism.

nerv·y (nûr′vē) *adj.* **-i·er, -i·est. 1.** *Informal.* Impudently bold or confident; rude. **2.** Marked by strength, energy, or endurance. **3.** Jumpy; nervous.

nes·cience (nĕsh′əns, nĕsh′ē-, nĕs′ē-) *n.* Lack of knowledge or awareness; ignorance. [Late Latin *nesciēntia*, from *nesciens*, ignorant, pres. part. of *nescīre*, to be ignorant : *ne-*, not + *scīre*, to know.] —**nes′cient** *adj. & n.*

-ness. A suffix meaning state, quality, or condition of being: *quietness.* [Middle English, from Old English.]

Nes·sel·rode (nĕs′əl-rōd′) *n.* A mixture of chestnuts, cherries, candied fruits, and liqueur, used in puddings, ice cream, or pies. [After Count Karl Robert *Nesselrode* (1780–1862), Russian diplomat.]

nest (nĕst) *n.* **1. a.** A container or shelter made by a bird for holding its eggs and young. **b.** A similar shelter, as of insect, fish, or animal. **2.** A snug, cozy place or shelter. **3.** The occupants of a nest. **4.** A set of objects of different sizes made so that each one fits into or under the one next above it in size: *a nest of tables.* —*intr.v.* To build or occupy a nest: *Robins nested in the willow tree.* —*tr.v.* **1.** To place in or as if in a nest. **2.** To put snugly together or inside one another. [Middle English, from Old English.]

nest egg. 1. An artificial or natural egg placed in a nest to induce a bird to lay. **2.** A sum of money saved for future use.

nes·tle (nĕs′əl) *v.* **-tled, -tling.** —*intr.v.* **1. a.** To settle snugly and comfortably: *The children were nestled in their beds.* **b.** To lie in a sheltered location: *The cottage nestled in the wood.* **2.** To draw or press close: *The child nestled up to his mother.* —*tr.v.* To rest, snuggle, or press contentedly: *The kitten nestled its chin on my lap.* [Middle English *nestlen*, from Old English *nestlian*, to make a nest.] —**nes′tler** *n.*

nest·ling (nĕst′lĭng) *n.* **1.** A bird too young to leave its nest. **2.** A young child.

net¹ (nĕt) *n.* **1.** An open fabric made of threads, cords, or ropes that are woven or knotted together with holes between them. **2. a.** A device used to catch fish, birds, butterflies, or other animals. **b.** A screen, shield, or covering used to protect from insects such as mosquitoes. **3.** *Sports.* A barrier strung between two posts to divide a tennis, badminton, or volleyball court in half. **4.** Something that entraps. —*tr.v.* **net·ted, net·ting. 1.** To catch in or as if in a net: *He netted a rare butterfly.* **2.** To cover with or as if with a net. **3.** To hit (a ball) into a net. [Middle English, from Old English *nett*.]

net² (nĕt) *adj.* **1.** Remaining after all necessary additions, subtractions, or adjustments have been made: *net profit.* **2.** Final; ultimate: *What was the net result?* —*n.* A net amount. —*tr.v.* **net·ted, net·ting. 1.** To bring in or yield as profit. **2.** To clear as profit. [Middle English, neat, clear, plain, from Old French, from Latin *nitidus*, bright, clear, from *nitēre*, to shine.]

neth·er (nĕth′ər) *adj.* Located beneath or below; lower or under: *the nether regions of the earth.* [Middle English, from Old English *nithera*, from *nither*, down, downward.]

neth·er·most (nĕth′ər-mōst′) *adj.* Lowest.

net·ting (nĕt′ĭng) *n.* A network.

net·tle (nĕt′l) *n.* Any plant of the genus *Urtica*, with toothed leaves covered with stinging hairs. —*tr.v.* **-tled, -tling.** To annoy; irritate. —See Syns at **annoy.** [Middle English, from Old English *netle*.]

net·work (nĕt′wûrk′) *n.* **1.** An open fabric or structure in which cords, threads, or wires cross at regular intervals. **2.** A system or pattern made up of a number of parts, passages, lines, or routes that cross, branch out, or interconnect: *a network of roads and railways; a network of veins.* **3.** A chain of interconnected radio or television broadcasting stations, usu. sharing a large proportion of their programs. **4.** A group or system of electric components designed to function in a specific manner.

neur-. Var. of **neuro-.**

neu·ral (nōōr′əl, nyōōr′-) *adj.* Of or pertaining to the nerves or nervous system: *a neural cavity.*

neu·ral·gia (nōō-răl′jə, nyōō-) *n.* Intense pain that occurs along a nerve. [NEUR(O)- + Greek *algos*, pain.] —**neu·ral′gic** *adj.*

neu·ri·lem·ma (nōōr′ə-lĕm′ə, nyōōr′-) *n.* Also **neu·ri·lem·a** or **neu·ro·lem·ma.** The outer covering of a nerve fiber. [NEUR(O)- + Greek *eilēma*, veil, covering, from *eilein*, to wind.] —**neu′ri·lem′mal** or **neu′ri·lem·mat′ic** (-lə-măt′ĭk) or **neu′ri·lem′ma·tous** (-lĕm′ə-təs) *adj.*

neu·ri·tis (nōō-rī′tĭs, nyōō-) *n.* Inflammation of a nerve. —**neu·rit′ic** (-rĭt′ĭk) *adj.*

neuro- or **neur-.** A prefix meaning nerve or nervous system: *neuralgia.* [From Greek *neuron*, tendon, nerve.]

neu·rog·li·a (nōō-rŏg′lē-ə, nyōō-) *n.* The network of branched cells and fibers that supports the tissue of the central nervous system. [NEURO- + Greek *glia*, glue, tissue.] —**neu·rog′li·al** *adj.*

neu·rol·o·gy (nōō-rŏl′ə-jē, nyōō-) *n.* The medical science of the nervous system and its diseases and disorders. —**neu′ro·log′i·cal** *adj.* —**neu·rol′o·gist** *n.*

neu·ron (nōōr′ŏn′, nyōōr′-) *n.* Also **neu·rone** (-ōn′). Any of the cells that make up the tissue of nerves and of the nervous system, consisting typically of a main portion that contains the nucleus and threadlike structures that extend from this portion, carrying impulses to and away from the cell. [Greek *neuron*, sinew, nerve.] —**neu·ron′ic** (-rŏn′ĭk) *adj.*

neu·rop·ter·an (nŏo-rŏp'tər-ən, nyŏo-) *n.* Any insect of the order Neuroptera, with four net-veined wings, such as the **ant lion, dobson fly,** or **lacewing.** [New Latin *Neuroptera,* "nerve-winged."] —**neu·rop'ter·ous** *adj.*

neu·ro·sis (nŏo-rō'sĭs, nyŏo-) *n., pl.* **-ses** (-sēz'). A disorder in which the function of the mind or emotions is disturbed with no apparent physical cause.

neu·rot·ic (nŏo-rŏt'ĭk, nyŏo-) *adj.* **1.** Of, involving, or caused by a neurosis. **2.** Suffering from or affected by neurosis. —**neu·rot·ic** *n.* —**neu·rot'i·cal·ly** *adv.*

neu·ro·tox·in (nŏor'ō-tŏk'sĭn) *n.* A protein complex poisonous to the nervous system. —**neu·ro·tox·ic** *adj.*

neu·ter (nŏo'tər, nyŏo'-) *adj.* **1.** *Gram.* Neither masculine nor feminine in gender. **2.** Lacking sex glands or sex organs. —*n.* **1.** *Gram.* **a.** The neuter gender. **b.** A neuter word. **2.** An animal or plant with undeveloped sex glands or organs, esp. an undeveloped female insect, such as a worker in a colony of ants or bees. [Middle English *neutre,* from Old French, from Latin *neuter,* neither.]

neu·tral (nŏo'trəl, nyŏo'-) *adj.* **1.** Not allied with, supporting, or favoring any side in a war, dispute, or contest: *a neutral nation.* **2.** Belonging to neither side nor party: *on neutral ground.* **3.** Of or indicating a color, such as gray, black, or white, that lacks hue; achromatic. **4.** *Chem.* Neither acid nor alkaline. **5.** *Physics.* Having positive electric charges exactly balanced by negative electric charges; having a net electric charge of zero. —*n.* **1.** A person or thing that is neutral. **2.** A neutral color. **3.** A position in which a set of gears is disengaged. [Latin *neutrālis,* neuter, from *neuter.*] —**neu'tral·ly** *adv.*

neu·tral·ism (nŏo'trə-lĭz'əm, nyŏo'-) *n.* Neutrality, esp. in a war or dispute. —**neu'tral·ist** *n.*

neu·tral·i·ty (nŏo-trăl'ĭ-tē, nyŏo'-) *n.* The quality or condition of being neutral.

neu·tral·ize (nŏo'trə-līz', nyŏo'-) *tr.v.* **-ized, -iz·ing. 1.** To cancel or counteract the effect of. **2.** To counterbalance and reduce to zero: *neutralize an electric charge.* **3.** To make neutral and immune from invasion, use, or control by any warring nation. **4.** *Chem.* To cause to be neither acid nor alkaline. —**neu'tral·i·za'tion** *n.* —**neu'tral·iz'er** *n.*

neutral spirits. Ethyl alcohol distilled at or above 190 proof and used frequently in alcoholic beverage blends.

neu·tri·no (nŏo-trē'nō, nyŏo-) *n., pl.* **-nos.** *Physics.* Either of two electrically neutral subatomic particles that interact weakly with matter. [Italian, dim. of *neutrone,* neutron, from English NEUTRON.]

neu·tron (nŏo'trŏn, nyŏo-) *n.* *Physics.* An electrically neutral subatomic particle having about the mass of a proton. It is stable when bound in an atomic nucleus, contributing to the mass of the nucleus without affecting atomic number or electric charge: *"These strange effects were due to a neutral particle . . . the neutron postulated by Rutherford in 1920 had at last revealed itself"* (Sir James Chadwick). [NEUTR(AL) + -ON.]

neutron star. A celestial body hypothesized to occur in a final stage of stellar evolution, consisting of a superdense mass essentially of neutrons, and having a powerful gravitational attraction from which only neutrinos and high-energy photons can escape.

né·vé (nā-vā') *n.* **1.** The upper part of a glacier, where the snow turns into ice. **2.** A field of granular snow. [Dial. French, from Latin *nix,* snow.]

nev·er (nĕv'ər) *adv.* **1.** At no time; on no occasion; not ever: *I have never been here before.* **2.** Not at all; in no way: *Never fear. Never mind.* [Middle English, from Old English *næfre* : *ne,* not + *æfre,* ever.]

nev·er·more (nĕv'ər-môr', -mōr') *adv.* Never again.

nev·er·the·less (nĕv'ər-thə-lĕs') *adv.* None the less; however: *The plan may fail, but we must try it nevertheless.*

ne·vus (nē'vəs) *n., pl.* **-vi** (-vī'). Also **nae·vus.** A congenital growth or mark on the skin, such as a birthmark. [Latin *naevus.*] —**ne'void** (nē'void') *adj.*

new (nŏo, nyŏo) *adj.* **-er, -est. 1.** Recently made, built, established, created, or formed: *a new skyscraper.* **2.** Just found, discovered, or learned: *new information.* **3.** Recently obtained or acquired: *new political power.* **4.** Never used or worn; not old or secondhand: *a new bicycle.* **5.** Fresh: *a new coat of paint.* **6.** Recent; modern: *new techniques.* **7.** Additional: *Industry needed new sources of*

energy. **8.** Coming after or taking the place of a previous one or ones: *a new edition.* **9.** Starting over again in a cycle: *the new moon.* **10.** Unfamiliar; novel; strange: *words that are new to you.* **11.** Recently arrived or established in a place, position, or relationship: *new neighbors; the new salesgirl.* **12.** Inexperienced or untrained: *He is new at this work.* **13.** Not encountered before; novel: *new ideas.* —See Syns at **fresh** and **strange.** —*adv.* Freshly; recently: *the smell of new-mown hay.* [Middle English *newe,* from Old English *nīwe.*] —**new'ness** *n.*

new·born (nŏo'bôrn', nyŏo'-) *adj.* **1.** Just born; very recently born: *a newborn baby.* **2.** Reborn or renewed: *newborn courage.*

new·com·er (nŏo'kŭm'ər, nyŏo'-) *n.* Someone who has only recently arrived.

New Deal. The programs and policies for economic recovery and reform, relief, and social security, introduced during the 1930's by President Franklin D. Roosevelt and his administration. —**New Dealer.**

new·el (nŏo'əl, nyŏo'-) *n.* **1.** The upright support at the center of a circular staircase. **2.** A post that supports a handrail at the bottom or at the landing of a staircase. [Middle English *nowell,* from Old French *nouel,* from Latin *nucālis,* nut-shaped, from *nux,* nut.]

newel   Newfoundland

new·fan·gled (nŏo'făng'gəld, nyŏo'-) *adj.* New; novel: *newfangled ideas.* —See Syns at **fresh.** [Middle English *newe fangled,* alteration of *newefangel,* fond of new things.]

New·found·land (nŏo'fən-lənd, nyŏo'-) *n.* A large breed of dog with a broad head, a powerful body, and a dense, usu. black coat. [After *Newfoundland,* Canada.]

New Latin. Latin as used from 1500 to the present.

new·ly (nŏo'lē, nyŏo'-) *adv.* **1.** Lately; recently; just: *newly baked bread.* **2.** In a new or different way; freshly: *an old idea newly phrased.*

new·ly·wed (nŏo'lē-wĕd', nyŏo'-) *n.* A person recently married.

new math. Mathematics based on set theory.

new moon. 1. The phase of the moon that occurs as it passes between the earth and the sun and is invisible, or visible only as a thin crescent at sunset. **2.** The crescent moon.

news (nŏoz, nyŏoz) *n. (used with a sing. verb).* **1.** Recent events and happenings, esp. those that are unusual or notable. **2. a.** Information about recent events of general interest, esp. as reported by newspapers, periodicals, radio, or television. **b.** A broadcast of such information; newscast. **3.** Newsworthy material.

news agency. An organization that provides news coverage to subscribers, as newspapers or periodicals.

news·boy (nŏoz'boi', nyŏoz'-) *n.* A boy who sells newspapers.

news·cast (nŏoz'kăst', nyŏoz'-) *n.* A radio or television broadcast of events in the news. [NEWS + (BROAD)CAST.] —**news'cast'er** *n.*

news·let·ter (nŏoz'lĕt'ər, nyŏoz'-) *n.* A report, usu. giving news or information of interest to a special group.

news·man (nŏoz'măn', -mən, nyŏoz'-) *n.* A person who gathers, reports, or edits news.

news·pa·per (nŏoz'pā'pər, nyŏoz'-) *n.* A publication that is usu. issued daily or weekly and contains current news, editorials, feature articles, and advertisements. —*modifier: a newspaper reporter.*

news·pa·per·man (nōōz′pā′pər-măn′, nyōōz′-) *n.* Someone who owns or is employed on a newspaper.

news·print (nōōz′prĭnt′, nyōōz′-) *n.* A cheap, thin paper, made from wood pulp, on which newspapers are printed.

news·reel (nōōz′rēl′, nyōōz′-) *n.* A short motion picture dealing with recent news events.

news·stand (nōōz′stănd′, nyōōz′-) *n.* A stand where newspapers and periodicals are sold.

New Style. The current method of calculating the months and days of the year, according to the Gregorian calendar, as distinct from the former method which followed the Julian calendar.

news·wor·thy (nōōz′wûr′thē, nyōōz′-) *adj.* Interesting or significant enough to be included in a news report. —**news′wor′thi·ness** *n.*

news·y (nōō′zē, nyōō′-) *adj.* **-i·er, -i·est.** *Informal.* Full of news; informative.

newt (nōōt, nyōōt) *n.* Any of several small salamanders of the genus *Triturus* and related genera that live both on the land and in the water. [Middle English, from the phrase *a newte,* orig. *an ewte.*]

New Testament. The second of the two main divisions of the Christian Bible, recording the life, acts, and teachings of Christ and his followers.

new·ton (nōōt′n, nyōōt′n) *n.* *Abbr.* **N** *Physics.* A unit of force equal to the force needed to accelerate a mass of one kilogram one meter per second per second. [After Sir Isaac *Newton,* (1642–1727), English scientist.]

New·to·ni·an (nōō-tō′nē-ən, nyōō-) *adj.* Of, pertaining to, or in accordance with the work of Newton, esp. in mechanics and gravitation.

New World. The Western Hemisphere; North and South America and adjacent islands.

New Year. **1.** The first day or days of a calendar year. **2.** Rosh Hashanah.

New Year's Day. The first day of the year, January 1.

New Year's Eve. The night before New Year's Day, December 31.

next (někst) *adj.* **1.** Immediately preceding or following in time, order, or sequence: *next year; the next President.* **2. a.** Closest or nearest in space or position. **b.** Adjacent or adjoining: *the next room.* —*adv.* **1.** In the time, position, or order nearest or immediately after: *What comes next?* **2.** On the first occasion that is to come: *When will the hands of the clock be together next?* —*prep.* Close to; nearest. [Middle English *nexte,* from Old English *nēhst,* superl. of *nēah,* near.]

next of kin. The person or persons most nearly related to one.

next to. **1.** Beside or alongside: *someone sitting next to you.* **2.** Coming immediately before or after: *next to the last.* **3.** Nearly; practically; almost: *That's next to impossible.*

nex·us (něk′səs) *n.,* *pl.* **nexus** or **-us·es.** **1.** A means of connection between members of a group or series; bond; link. **2.** A connected series or group. [Latin, from *nectere,* to bind, connect.]

Nez Percé (něz′ pûrs′). *pl.* **Nez Perce** or **Nez Perces** (pûr′sĭz). **1. a.** A tribe of Indians, formerly occupying much of the Pacific Northwest. **b.** A member of this tribe. **2.** The language of the Nez Percé.

Ni The symbol for the element nickel.

ni·a·cin (nī′ə-sĭn) *n.* Nicotinic acid. [NI(COTINIC) AC(ID) + -IN.]

nib (nĭb) *n.* **1.** The point of a pen. **2.** Any sharp point or tip. **3.** A bird's beak or bill. [Prob. alteration of *neb,* beak.]

nib·ble (nĭb′əl) *v.* **-bled, -bling.** —*tr.v.* **1.** To bite at gently and repeatedly. **2.** To eat with small, quick bites or in small morsels: *nibble a cracker.* —*intr.v.* To take small or hesitant bites: *The fish nibbled at the bait.* —*n.* **1.** An act of nibbling. **2.** A small morsel, as of food. [Prob. from Low German *nibbeln,* to gnaw, nibble.] —**nib′bler** *n.*

Ni·be·lung (nē′bə-lŏōng′) *n.* *Germanic Myth.* **1.** Any of a race of subterranean dwarfs whose riches and magic ring were taken from them by Siegfried. **2.** Any of the followers of Siegfried.

nice (nīs) *adj.* **nic·er, nic·est.** **1.** Good; pleasant; agreeable: *a nice time.* **2.** Executed with skill: *a nice piece of work.*

3. Courteous and polite; considerate: *a nice gesture.* **4.** Respectable; well-bred: *a nice family.* **5.** Also **nice and.** Used as an intensive: *nice and warm.* **6.** Showing or marked by great precision and sensitive discernment; subtle: *a nice distinction.* **7.** Characterized by sometimes excessive delicacy or fastidiousness; fussy. [Middle English, foolish, wanton, shy, from Old French, silly, from Latin *nescius,* ignorant.] —**nice′ly** *adv.* —**nice′ness** *n.*

Ni·cene Creed (nī′sēn′, nī-sēn′). A formal statement of doctrine of the Christian faith adopted at the Council of Nicaea in A.D. 325 and expanded in later councils.

ni·ce·ty (nī′sĭ-tē) *n.,* *pl.* **-ties.** **1.** The quality of showing or requiring careful and precise treatment. **2.** A fine point, small detail, or subtle distinction. **3.** An elegant or refined feature: *the niceties of civilized life.*

niche (nĭch, nēsh) *n.* **1.** A recess in a wall, as for holding a statue. **2.** A cranny, hollow, or crevice, as in rock. **3.** A situation or activity specially suited to a person's abilities or character. —*tr.v.* **niched, nich·ing.** To place in a niche. [French, from Old French, nest, from *nichier,* to nest, ult. from Latin *nīdus,* nest.]

niche

nick (nĭk) *n.* A shallow cut, notch, or chip on a surface: *nicks in the table; razor nicks on one's face.* —*tr.v.* To cut a nick or notch in. —*idiom.* **in the nick of time.** Just at the critical moment. [Middle English *nyke,* var. of *nocke,* nock.]

nick·el (nĭk′əl) *n.* **1.** *Symbol* **Ni** A silvery, hard, ductile, ferromagnetic metallic element used in alloys, in corrosion-resistant surfaces and batteries, and for electroplating. Atomic number 28; atomic weight 58.71; melting point 1,453°C; boiling point 2,732°C; specific gravity 8.902; principal valence 2. **2.** A U.S. coin worth five cents, made of a nickel and copper alloy. [Swedish, short for *kopparnickel,* from German *Kupfernickel,* "copper-demon" : *Kupfer,* copper + *nickel,* demon (from the deceptive resemblance of some nickel ores to copper).]

nick·el·o·de·on (nĭk′ə-lō′dē-ən) *n.* **1.** A movie house that charges an admission price of five cents. **2. a.** A player piano. **b.** A juke box. [NICKEL + (MEL)ODEON.]

nickel silver. A silvery alloy of copper, zinc, and nickel.

nick·nack (nĭk′năk′) *n.* Var. of **knickknack.**

nick·name (nĭk′nām′) *n.* **1.** A descriptive name used instead of or along with the real name of a person, place, or thing. **2.** A familiar or shortened form of a proper name. —*tr.v.* **-named, -nam·ing.** To give a nickname to. [Middle English *a nekename,* orig. *an ekename,* an additional name.]

nic·o·tine (nĭk′ə-tēn′) *n.* A poisonous alkaloid, $C_5H_4NC_4H_7NCH_3$, derived from the tobacco plant, used in medicine and as an insecticide. [French, earlier *nicotiane,* from *nicotiana,* the tobacco plant.]

nic·o·tin·ic (nĭk′ə-tĭn′ĭk) *adj.* **1.** Of or pertaining to nicotine. **2.** Of or pertaining to nicotinic acid.

nicotinic acid. A member of the vitamin B complex, C_5H_4NCOOH, that occurs in living cells as an essential substance for growth and is synthesized for use in treating pellagra.

niece (nēs) *n.* A daughter of one's brother or brother-in-law, or sister or sister-in-law. [Middle English *nece,* from Norman French, from Old French *niece,* from Latin *neptis,* granddaughter, niece.]

nif·ty (nĭf′tē) *adj.* **-ti·er, -ti·est.** *Slang.* Very good; first-rate. [Orig. unknown.]

nig·gard (nĭg′ərd) *n.* A stingy person; miser. —*adj.* Stingy; miserly. [Middle English, from *nig*, a miser, of Scandinavian orig.]

nig·gard·ly (nĭg′ərd-lē) *adj.* **1.** Unwilling to give, spend, or share; stingy; grudging. **2.** Scanty; meager. —See Syns at **stingy.** —*adv.* Stingily. —**nig′gard·li·ness** *n.*

nig·gling (nĭg′lĭng) *adj.* **1.** Excessively concerned with details; fussy. **2.** Showing or requiring close attention to details; exacting: *niggling paperwork.* [From *niggle*, to fret, carp.] —**nig′gling·ly** *adv.*

nigh (nī) *adv.* **-er, -est.** Near in time, space, or relationship: *I'd perch by her window as evening drew nigh.* —*adj.* Being near in time, place, or relationship; close. —See Syns at **near.** —*prep.* Near. [Middle English *neigh*, from Old English *nēah.*]

night (nīt) *n.* **1.** The period between sunset and sunrise, esp. the hours of darkness. **2.** Nightfall: *They worked from morning to night.* **3.** Darkness. —*modifier: a night game.* [Middle English *night*, from Old English *niht.*]

night blindness. Subnormal vision in poor light. —**night′-blind′** *adj.*

night-bloom·ing cereus (nīt′bloo′mĭng). Any of several flowering cacti having large, fragrant flowers that open at night.

night·cap (nīt′kăp′) *n.* **1.** A cloth cap worn esp. in bed. **2.** *Informal.* A usu. alcoholic drink taken just before bedtime. **3.** *Slang.* The last event in a day's competition, esp. the final game in a baseball double-header.

night-clothes (nīt′klōz′, -klōthz′) *pl.n.* Clothes worn in bed.

night·club (nīt′klŭb′) *n.* An establishment that stays open late at night and provides food, drink, and entertainment.

night crawler. An earthworm that crawls out from the ground at night.

night·dress (nīt′drĕs′) *n.* **1.** A nightgown. **2.** Nightclothes.

night·fall (nīt′fôl′) *n.* The coming of darkness.

night·gown (nīt′goun′) *n.* A loose garment worn to bed.

night·hawk (nīt′hôk′) *n.* **1.** Any of several mainly nocturnal birds of the genus *Chordeiles*, with buff to black mottled feathers, esp. *C. minor*, of North America. Also called **mosquito hawk. 2.** The European nightjar. **3.** *Informal.* A night owl.

night·in·gale (nīt′n-gāl′, nī′tĭng-) *n.* A European songbird, *Luscinia megarhynchos*, with brownish plumage, noted for its melodious nocturnal song. [Middle English *nihtyngale*, from Old English *nihtegale*, "night-singer."]

night·jar (nīt′jär′) *n.* Any of various nocturnal birds of the family Caprimulgidae, esp. the common European nightjar, *Caprimulgus europaeus*. [NIGHT + JAR (to make a harsh sound).]

nightjar
George Miksch Sutton

Nike

night latch. A spring lock that may be opened from the inside by turning a knob and from the outside with a key.

night letter. A telegram sent at night at a reduced rate for delivery the next morning.

night·long (nīt′lông′, -lŏng′) *adj.* Lasting through the whole night. —*adv.* Through the night; all night.

night·ly (nīt′lē) *adj.* Occurring, done, or used at night or every night: *a watchman's nightly rounds.* —**night′ly** *adv.*

night·mare (nīt′mâr′) *n.* **1.** An extremely frightening dream. **2.** Something, as an event or experience, that is as intensely distressing as a nightmare. [Middle English *nihtmare*, female incubus : *niht*, night + *mare*, incubus, from

Old English, goblin.] —**night′mar′ish** *adj.*

night owl. A person who habitually stays up late.

night school. A school that holds classes in the evening.

night·shade (nīt′shād′) *n.* Any of several plants of the genus *Solanum*, such as the potato, morning glory, and belladonna. [Middle English *nighteschede*, from Old English *nihtscada.*]

night·shirt (nīt′shûrt′) *n.* A long shirt worn in bed.

night·stick (nīt′stĭk′) *n.* A club carried by a policeman.

night·time (nīt′tīm′) *n.* The time between sunset and sunrise.

night·y (nī′tē) *n., pl.* **-ies.** *Informal.* A nightgown.

ni·hil·ism (nī′ə-lĭz′əm, nĭ′hə-, nē′-) *n.* **1.** The belief that destruction of existing political or social institutions is necessary for future improvement. **2.** Also **Nihilism.** The doctrine of a Russian movement of the 19th cent. that advocated assassination and terrorism. [From Latin *nihil*, nothing.] —**ni′hil·ist** *n.* —**ni′hil·is′tic** *adj.*

ni·hil·i·ty (nī-hĭl′ĭ-tē, nē-) *n.* Nonexistence; nothingness. [French *nihilité*, from Old French, from Medieval Latin *nihilitās*, from *nihil*, nothing.]

Ni·ke (nī′kē) *n. Gk. Myth.* The winged goddess of victory.

nil (nĭl) *n.* Nothing; zero. [Latin, from *nihil*, nothing.]

nim·bi (nĭm′bī′) *n.* A plural of **nimbus.**

nim·ble (nĭm′bəl) *adj.* **-bler, -blest. 1.** Quick, light, or easy in movement or action; deft: *nimble fingers.* **2.** Quick and clever in thinking, understanding, or responding: *nimble wit.* [Middle English *nymbyl*, agile, from Old English *numol*, capacious, from *niman*, to take.] —**nim′ble·ness** *n.* —**nim′bly** *adv.*

nim·bo·stra·tus (nĭm′bō-strā′təs, -străt′əs) *n.* A gray, often dark cloud usu. producing rain, sleet, or snow. [From NIMB(US) + STRATUS.]

nim·bus (nĭm′bəs) *n., pl.* **-bi** (bī′) or **-bus·es. 1.** A cloudy radiance said to surround a god or goddess when on earth. **2.** A radiant light that appears usu. in the form of a circle about the head in the representation of a deity or saint. **3.** A uniformly gray rain cloud that extends over the sky. [Latin *nimbus*, heavy rain, rain cloud.]

nim·rod (nĭm′rŏd′) *n.* A hunter. [After Nimrod, a hunter and king in the Old Testament.]

nin·com·poop (nĭn′kəm-poop′, nĭng′-) *n.* A silly or stupid person; blockhead. [Orig. unknown.]

nine (nīn) *n.* **1.** A number, written 9 in Arabic numerals, that is equal to the sum of 8 + 1. **2. a.** A set of nine persons or things. **b.** A baseball team. —*idiom.* **(up) to the nines.** To the highest degree: *dressed to the nines.* [Middle English *nyne*, from Old English *nigon.*] —**nine** *adj. & pron.*

nine days' wonder. Something that creates a brief sensation.

nine·pin (nīn′pĭn′) *n.* **1.** A wooden pin used in the game of ninepins. **2. ninepins.** (used with a sing. verb). A bowling game played with nine wooden pins.

nine·teen (nīn′tēn′) *n.* A number, written 19 in Arabic numerals, that is equal to the sum of 18 + 1. [Middle English *nynetene*, from Old English *nigontīne.*] —**nine′teen′** *adj. & pron.*

nine·teenth (nīn′tēnth′) *n.* **1.** The ordinal number that matches the number 19 in a series. **2.** One of nineteen equal parts of a unit, written 1/19. —**nine′teenth′** *adj. & adv.*

nine·ti·eth (nīn′tē-ĭth) *n.* **1.** The ordinal number that matches the number 90 in a series. **2.** One of ninety equal parts of a unit, written 1/90. —**nine′ti·eth** *adj. & adv.*

nine·ty (nīn′tē) *n., pl.* **-ties.** A number, written 90 in Arabic numerals, that is equal to the product of 9 × 10. —**nine′ty** *adj. & pron.*

nin·ny (nĭn′ē) *n., pl.* **-nies.** A fool; simpleton. [From INNOCENT (simple, foolish).]

ninth (nīnth) *n.* **1.** The ordinal number that matches the number 9 in a series. **2.** One of nine equal parts of a unit, written 1/9. **3.** *Mus.* An interval equal to an octave plus a whole step or a half step. —**ninth** *adj. & adv.*

ni·o·bi·um (nī-ō′bē-əm) *n. Symbol* **Nb** A silvery, soft, ductile, metallic element that occurs chiefly in columbite-tantalite, and is used in steel alloys, arc welding, and superconductivity research. Atomic number 41; atomic weight 92.906; melting point 2,468°C; boiling point 4,927°C; specific gravity 8.57; valences 2, 3, 5. [After

Niobe, the daugher of Tantalus (from its being obtained from tantalite).]

nip¹ (nĭp) *v.* **nipped, nip·ping.** —*tr.v.* **1.** To seize and pinch or bite: *The lobster nipped my toe.* **2.** To remove by or as if by nipping: *The rabbit nipped off the plant leaf.* **3.** To sting with the cold; chill. **4.** To stop the further growth or development of; blight: *nip a scandal in the bud.* **5.** *Slang.* **a.** To snatch up hastily. **b.** To steal. —*intr.v. Brit. Slang.* To move quickly; dart. —*n.* **1.** A small, sharp bite or pinch. **2.** A small bit or portion. **3.** Sharp, stinging cold. **4.** A sharp, biting flavor; tang. —*idiom.* **nip and tuck.** Very close; neck and neck. [Middle English *nippen*, prob. from Old Norse *hnippa*.]

nip² (nĭp) *n.* A small amount of liquor. —*v.* **nipped, nip·ping.** —*tr.v.* To drink (liquor) in small amounts. —*intr.v.* To take a nip or nips of alcoholic liquor: *He nips all day.* [Short for *nipperkin*, prob. from Dutch *nippertje*, a dram, from *nippen*, to sip.] —**nip′per** *n.*

nip·per (nĭp′ər) *n.* **1. nippers.** A tool, such as pliers or pincers, used for grasping or nipping. **2.** A pincerlike part, such as the large claw of a lobster. **3.** *Brit.* A small boy.

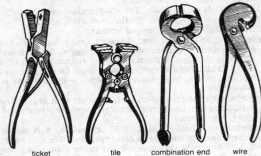

ticket   tile   combination end   wire
nipper

nip·ple (nĭp′əl) *n.* **1.** A small projection of a mammary gland containing the outlets of the milk ducts. **2.** A soft rubber cap made in imitation of this and used on a bottle from which a baby nurses. [From earlier *nible*, dim. of *neb, nib*, a point, beak.]

Nip·pon·ese (nĭp′ə-nēz′, -nēs′) *adj.* Japanese.

nip·py (nĭp′ē) *adj.* **-pi·er, -pi·est. 1.** Sharp or biting: *nippy cheese.* **2.** Bitingly cold: *a nippy fall day.* —See Syns at **cold.** —**nip′pi·ly** *adv.*

nir·va·na (nîr-vä′nə, nûr-) *n.* **1.** Often **Nirvana.** *Buddhism.* The state of absolute blessedness, characterized by release from the cycle of reincarnations and attained through the extinction of the self. **2.** An ideal condition of rest, harmony, stability, or joy. [Sanskrit *nirvāna*, "extinction (of individual existence)," from *nirvā*, to be extinguished.]

Ni·sei (nē-sā′, nē′sā′) *n., pl.* **Nisei** or **-seis.** A person born in America of parents who emigrated from Japan. [Japanese, "second generation."]

nit (nĭt) *n.* The egg or young of a parasitic insect, such as a louse. [Middle English *nite*, from Old English *hnitu*, louse egg.] —**nit′ty** *adj.*

ni·ter (nī′tər) *n.* Also *Brit.* **ni·tre. 1.** Potassium nitrate. **2.** Sodium nitrate. [Middle English *nitre*, from Old French, from Latin *nitrum*, from Greek *nitron*, soda.]

nit-pick (nĭt′pĭk′) *intr.v. Informal.* To be concerned with or find fault with petty details. —**nit′-pick′er** *n.*

ni·trate (nī′trāt) *n.* **1.** A salt or ester of nitric acid. **2.** Fertilizer consisting of sodium nitrate or potassium nitrate. —*tr.v.* **-trat·ed, -trat·ing.** To treat with nitric acid or with a nitrate, usu. to change an organic compound into a nitrate. —**ni·tra′tion** *n.* —**ni′tra′tor** *n.*

ni·tric (nī′trĭk) *adj.* Of, derived from, or containing nitrogen, esp. in one of its higher valences.

nitric acid. A transparent, colorless to yellowish, corrosive liquid, HNO_3, used as an oxidizing agent and in the production of fertilizers, explosives, and rocket fuels.

nitric oxide. A colorless, poisonous gas, NO, produced during the manufacture of nitric acid from ammonia or atmospheric nitrogen.

ni·tride (nī′trīd′) *n.* A compound containing nitrogen with another, more electropositive element.

ni·tri·fi·ca·tion (nī′trə-fĭ-kā′shən) *n.* A process in which ammonia present in soil, as from the decomposition of protein matter, is oxidized by bacteria to form nitrites that are oxidized by other bacteria to form nitrates.

ni·tri·fy (nī′trə-fī′) *tr.v.* **-fied, -fy·ing. 1.** To treat or combine with nitrogen or compounds containing nitrogen. **2.** To carry on nitrification. —**ni′tri·fi′er** *n.*

ni·trite (nī′trīt′) *n.* Any salt or ester of nitrous acid.

nitro- or **nitr-.** A prefix indicating a compound containing the univalent group NO_2: **nitride.** [From Latin *nitrum*, soda, from Greek *nitron*.]

ni·tro·bac·te·ri·a (nī′trō-băk-tîr′ē-ə) *pl.n.* Soil bacteria that produce nitrification.

ni·tro·ben·zene (nī′trō-bĕn′zēn′, -bĕn-zēn′) *n.* A poisonous oily liquid, $C_6H_5NO_2$, that has the odor of almonds, and is used in the manufacture of aniline, insulating compounds, and polishes.

ni·tro·cel·lu·lose (nī′trō-sĕl′yə-lōs′) *n.* A pulpy or cotton-like substance derived from cellulose treated with sulfuric and nitric acids, used in the manufacture of explosives, plastics, and rocket fuels.

ni·tro·gen (nī′trə-jən) *n. Symbol* **N** A nonmetallic element that constitutes nearly four-fifths of the air by volume, occurring as a colorless, odorless, almost inert diatomic gas, N_2, in various minerals and in all proteins and is used in a wide variety of important manufactures, including ammonia, nitric acid, TNT, and fertilizers. Atomic number 7; atomic weight 14.0067; melting point –209.86°C; boiling point –195°C; valence 3, 5. —**ni·trog′e·nous** (nī-trŏj′ə-nəs) *adj.*

nitrogen balance. The difference between the amounts of nitrogen taken into and lost by the body or the soil.

nitrogen cycle. The continuous cycle of chemical reactions by which nitrogen in the atmosphere forms compounds that are dissolved in rain, deposited in the soil, transformed and assimilated by bacteria and living plants that are in turn eaten by animals, and is returned to the atmosphere by the decomposition and metabolism of organic substances.

nitrogen dioxide. A poisonous brown gas, NO_2, often found in smog and automobile exhaust fumes, and synthesized for use as a nitrating agent, catalyst, and oxidizing agent.

nitrogen fixation. The conversion by certain algae and soil bacteria of inorganic nitrogen compounds into organic compounds that plants can assimilate. —**ni′tro·gen-fix′ing** *adj.*

ni·tro·glyc·er·in (nī′trō-glĭs′ər-ĭn) or **ni·tro·glyc·er·ine** *n.* A thick, pale-yellow, explosive liquid, $CH_2NO_3CHNO_3CH_2NO_3$, used in the production of dynamite and blasting gelatin, and in medicine as a drug that dilates blood vessels.

ni·trous (nī′trəs) *adj.* Of, relating to, or containing nitrogen, esp. in a valence state lower than that in a comparable nitric compound. [From Latin *nitrōsus*, full of soda, from *nitrum*, soda, from Greek *nitron*.]

nitrous acid. A weak, unstable acid, HNO_2.

nitrous oxide. A colorless, sweet inorganic gas, N_2O, used as a mild anesthetic.

nit·ty-grit·ty (nĭt′ē-grĭt′ē, nĭt′ē-grĭt′ē) *n. Slang.* The specific or practical details. [Orig. unknown.]

nit·wit (nĭt′wĭt′) *n. Informal.* A stupid or silly person. [Perh. NIT + WIT.]

nix¹ (nĭks) *n.* A water sprite, usu. in human form or half-human and half-fish. [German.]

nix² (nĭks). *Slang.* —*n.* Nothing. —*adv.* No. —*tr.v.* To forbid; veto. [German, from *nichts*, nothing.]

no¹ (nō) *adv.* **1.** Not so. Used to express refusal, denial, or disagreement: *No, I'm not going.* **2.** Not at all. Used with the comparative: *no better; no more.* **3.** Not: *whether or no.* —*n., pl.* **noes. 1.** A negative response; a denial or refusal: *The proposal produced only noes.* **2.** A negative vote or voter. [Middle English, from Old English *nā* : *ne*, no + *ā*, ever.]

no² (nō) *adj.* **1.** Not any; not one: *No cookies are left.* **2.** Not at all; not close to being: *He is no child.* [Middle English, from Old English *nā*, from *nān*, none.]

No The symbol for the element nobelium.

no·bel·i·um (nō-běl′ē-əm, -bēl′ē-) *n.* Symbol **No** An element produced by bombarding an isotope of curium with carbon nuclei. Atomic number 102. [After the *Nobel* Institute at Stockholm, Sweden.]

No·bel Prize (nō-běl′). Any of six international prizes awarded annually by the Nobel Foundation for outstanding achievements in the fields of physics, chemistry, physiology or medicine, literature, economics, and the promotion of peace.

no·bil·i·ty (nō-bǐl′ĭ-tē) *n., pl.* **-ties.** **1.** A class of persons distinguished by high birth or rank. **2.** Noble rank or status: *Congress may not grant titles of nobility.* **3.** The quality or condition of being noble. [Middle English *nobilite,* from Old French, from Latin *nōbilitās,* from *nōbilis,* noble.]

no·ble (nō′bəl) *adj.* **-bler, -blest.** **1.** Of, in, or belonging to the nobility. **2.** Having or showing qualities of high moral character, as courage, generosity, or honor: *a noble spirit.* **3. a.** Superior in nature or character; exalted: *a noble ideal.* **b.** Grand and stately in appearance; majestic: *noble mountain peaks.* **4.** Chemically inactive or inert: *noble gases.* —*n.* A member of the nobility. [Middle English, from Old French, from Latin *nōbilis,* known, famous, noble.] —**no′ble·ness** *n.* —**no′bly** *adv.*

no·ble·man (nō′bəl-mən) *n.* A man who belongs to the nobility.

no·blesse o·blige (nō-blěs′ ō-blēzh′). Kind and generous behavior considered to be the responsibility of persons of high birth or rank. [French, "nobility obligates."]

no·ble·wom·an (nō′bəl-wŏŏm′ən) *n.* A woman who belongs to the nobility.

no·bod·y (nō′bŏd′ē, -bə-dē) *pron.* No person; no one. —See Usage note at **none.** —*n., pl.* **-ies.** A person of no importance.

nock (nŏk) *n.* **1.** The groove at either end of a bow for holding the bowstring. **2.** The notch in the end of an arrow that fits on the bowstring. —*tr.v.* **1.** To put a nock in (a bow or arrow). **2.** To fit (an arrow) to a bowstring. [Middle English *nocke,* from Middle Dutch.]

noc·tur·nal (nŏk-tûr′nəl) *adj.* **1.** Of, relating to, or occurring in the night: *nocturnal stillness.* **2.** Active at night rather than by day: *Owls are nocturnal birds.* [Late Latin *nocturnālis,* from Latin *nocturnus,* of night, at night, from *nox,* night.] —**noc·tur′nal·ly** *adv.*

noc·turne (nŏk′tûrn′) *n.* **1.** A painting of a night scene. **2.** *Mus.* A romantic composition intended to suggest or call forth thoughts and feelings of night. [French, *nocturnal.*]

nod (nŏd) *v.* **nod·ded, nod·ding.** —*intr.v.* **1.** To lower the head quickly, as in agreement or drowsiness. **2.** To be careless or momentarily inattentive. **3.** To sway, droop, or bend downward: *flowers nodding on long stems.* —*tr.v.* **1.** To lower and raise (the head) quickly in agreement or acknowledgment. **2.** To express by lowering and raising the head: *He nodded his acceptance.* [Middle English *nodden,* perh. of Low German orig.] —**nod** *n.* —**nod′der** *n.*

node (nōd) *n.* **1. a.** A protuberance or swelling. **b.** A mass of body tissue that has a clear outer boundary but few or no internal divisions or distinctions: *a lymph node.* **2.** *Bot.* An often knoblike marking on a plant stem where a leaf, bud, or stem is attached. **3.** *Physics.* A point or region of minimum or zero amplitude in a periodic system. **4.** *Astron.* Either of the two points at which the orbit of a planet intersects the ecliptic. [Latin *nōdus,* knob, knot.] —**nod′al** *adj.*

nod·ule (nŏj′ōol) *n.* **1.** A small node, as of body tissue. **2.** *Anat.* A localized swelling. **3.** *Bot.* A small, knoblike lump or outgrowth, such as those found on the roots of clover, alfalfa, soybeans, etc. **4.** A small lump of a mineral or a mixture of minerals. —**nod′u·lar** (nŏj′ə-lər) *adj.*

No·ël or **No·el** (nō-ĕl′) *n.* **1.** Christmas. **2. noël** or **noel.** A Christmas carol. [French, from Old French *nouel,* from Latin *nātālis (dies),* "birth(day of Christ)," from *nātālis,* of birth, from *nātus,* past part. of *nāscī,* to be born.]

nog (nŏg) *n.* Eggnog. [Orig. unknown.]

nog·gin (nŏg′ĭn) *n.* **1.** A small mug or cup. **2.** A small drink of liquor equal to one-quarter of a pint. **3.** *Slang.* The head. [Orig. unknown.]

no-hit·ter (nō′hĭt′ər) *n.* A baseball game in which one pitcher allows the opposing team no hits.

no·how (nō′hou′) *adv. Nonstandard.* In no way; not at all.

noise (noiz) *n.* **1.** Sound or a sound that is loud, unpleasant, unexpected, or undesired: *fire sirens and other street noises.* **2.** Sound or a sound of any kind: *The only noise was the wind in the pines.* **3.** A loud outcry or commotion. **4.** *Physics.* Persistent interference in an electronic signal. —*tr.v.* **noised, nois·ing.** To spread the rumor or report of. [Middle English, from Old French, from Latin *nausea,* seasickness, from Greek *nausia,* from *naus,* ship.]

noise·less (noiz′lĭs) *adj.* Creating no noise; silent; quiet. —**noise′less·ly** *adv.* —**noise′less·ness** *n.*

noise·mak·er (noiz′mā′kər) *n.* Someone or something that makes noise, esp. a device such as a horn or a rattle used to make noise at a party. —**noise′mak′ing** *n.*

noi·some (noi′səm) *adj.* **1.** Offensive; foul; disgusting: *a noisome odor.* **2.** Harmful or dangerous: *noisome fumes.* [Middle English *noyesum.*] —**noi′some·ly** *adv.* —**noi′some·ness** *n.*

Usage: **noisome, noisy.** These have no relationship in meaning. *Noisome* refers to what is extremely offensive or harmful: *a noisome odor.* *Noisy* refers only to noise: *a noisy party.*

nois·y (noi′zē) *adj.* **-i·er, -i·est.** **1.** Making noise. **2.** Full of, characterized by, or accompanied by noise. —See Usage note at **noisome.** —**nois′i·ly** *adv.* —**nois′i·ness** *n.*

nol·le pros·e·qui (nŏl′ē prŏs′ə-kwī′). *Law.* A formal notice that the prosecutor or plaintiff will not pursue an action or suit. [Latin, "to be unwilling to pursue."]

no·lo con·ten·de·re (nō′lō kən-těn′də-rē). *Law.* A plea made by the defendant in a criminal action that is equivalent to an admission of guilt but allows the defendant to deny the charges in other proceedings. [Latin, "I do not wish to contend."]

no·mad (nō′măd′) *n.* **1.** A member of a group of people who have no permanent home and move about from place to place seeking food, water, and grazing land. **2.** A wanderer who roams about instead of settling in one place. [Old French *nomade,* from Latin *nomas,* from Greek, one that wanders about for pasture.]

no·mad·ic (nō-măd′ĭk) or **no·mad·i·cal** (-ĭ-kəl) *adj.* Leading the life of a nomad; wandering; roving: *nomadic herdsmen.* —**no·mad′i·cal·ly** *adv.*

no man's land. **1.** An unclaimed or unowned piece of land. **2.** Land under dispute by two opposing parties, esp. the field of battle between two opposing entrenched armies. **3.** An area of uncertainty or ambiguity.

nom de guerre (nŏm′ də gâr′). A fictitious name; pseudonym. [French, "war name."]

nom de plume (nŏm′ də ploom′). A pen name. [French, "pen name."]

no·men·cla·ture (nō′mən-klā′chər, nō-měn′klə-) *n.* A system of names used in an art or science. [Latin *nōmenclātūra,* from *nōmenclātor,* namer : *nomen,* name + *calāre,* to call.]

nom·i·nal (nŏm′ə-nəl) *adj.* **1. a.** Of, like, or consisting of a name or names. **b.** Bearing a person's name: *nominal shares.* **2.** Existing in name only and not in actuality. **3.** Insignificantly small; trifling: *a nominal sum.* **4.** *Gram.* Of or relating to a noun or a word group that functions as a noun. [Latin *nōminālis,* from *nōmen,* name.] —**nom′i·nal·ly** *adv.*

nom·i·nate (nŏm′ə-nāt′) *tr.v.* **-nat·ed, -nat·ing.** To propose as a candidate, as for election or office. —**nom′i·na′tor** *n.*

nom·i·na·tion (nŏm′ə-nā′shən) *n.* **1.** The act or process of nominating. **2.** The condition of being nominated for a position, office, or honor. —*modifier:* *a nomination speech.*

nom·i·na·tive (nŏm′ə-nə-tĭv) *adj.* Of, relating to, or belonging to a grammatical case that usu. indicates the subject of a verb. —*n.* The nominative case.

nom·i·nee (nŏm′ə-nē′) *n.* Someone who has been nominated. [NOMIN(ATE) + -EE.]

-nomy. A suffix meaning the system of laws governing a specified field: **astronomy.** [From Greek *nomos,* from *nemein,* to distribute, manage, law.]

non-. A prefix meaning not: **nonconductor.** [Middle English, from Old French, from Latin *nōn,* not.]

non·age (nŏn′ĭj, nō′nĭj) *n.* **1.** The period during which one is legally underage. **2.** A period of immaturity. [Middle English, from Old French.]

ă pat	ā pay	â care	ä father	ĕ pet	ē be	hw which
ŏŏ took	ōō boot	ou out	th thin	*th* this	ŭ cut	

ĭ pit	ī tie	î pier	ŏ pot	ō toe	ô paw, for	oi noise
û urge	zh vision	ə about, item, edible, gallop, circus				

non·a·ge·nar·i·an (nŏn′ə-jə-nâr′ē-ən, nō′nə-) *adj.* Being ninety years old or between ninety and one hundred years old. [From Latin *nōnāgēnārius,* from *nōnāgēnī,* ninety each, from *nōnāginta,* ninety : *novem,* nine + *-gintā,* ten times.] **—non′a·ge·nar′i·an** *n.*

non·a·gon (nŏn′ə-gŏn′, nō′nə-) *n.* A plane geometric figure bounded by nine line segments and containing nine angles. [Latin *nonus,* nine + -GON.]

non·a·ligned (nŏn′ə-līnd′) *adj.* Not in alliance with any other nations; neutral. **—non′a·lign′ment** *n.*

nonce (nŏns) *n.* —**for the nonce.** For the present or particular occasion. [Middle English *for the nones,* from *for then anes,* "for the one (purpose or occasion)."]

nonce word. A word occurring, invented, or used just for a particular occasion.

non·cha·lant (nŏn′shə-länt′) *adj.* Cool, carefree, and casually unconcerned. [French, from Old French, from *nonchaloir,* to be unconcerned.] **—non′cha·lance′** *n.* **—non′-cha·lant′ly** *adv.*

non·com (nŏn′kŏm′) *n. Informal.* A noncommissioned officer.

non·com·bat·ant (nŏn′kəm-băt′nt, nŏn-kŏm′bə-tənt) *n.* **1.** A member of the armed forces, as a chaplain, whose duties exclude fighting. **2.** A civilian in wartime.

non·com·mis·sioned officer (nŏn′kə-mĭsh′ənd). An enlisted member of the armed forces appointed to a subordinate rank, such as sergeant or corporal.

non·com·mit·tal (nŏn′kə-mĭt′l) *adj.* Not indicating or revealing what one feels or thinks: *a noncommittal reply.* **—non′com·mit′tal·ly** *adv.*

non·com·pli·ance (nŏn′kəm-plī′əns) *n.* Failure or refusal to comply with something. **—non′com·pli′ant** *adj. & n.*

non com·pos men·tis (nŏn kŏm′pəs mĕn′tĭs). *Law.* Not of sound mind and hence not legally responsible. [Latin, "not having control of the mind."]

non·con·duc·tor (nŏn′kən-dŭk′tər) *n.* A substance that conducts little or no electricity or heat. **—non′con·duct′ing** *adj.*

non·con·form·ist (nŏn′kən-fôr′mĭst) *n.* **1.** Someone who does not conform to accepted customs, beliefs, or practices. **2.** Often **Nonconformist.** A person who does not belong to a national or established church, esp. to the Church of England.

non·con·form·i·ty (nŏn′kən-fôr′mĭ-tē) *n.* **1.** Refusal or failure to conform to accepted customs, beliefs, or practices. **2.** Often **Nonconformity.** Refusal to accept or conform to the doctrines of the Church of England.

non·de·nom·i·na·tion·al (nŏn′dĭ-nŏm′ə-nā′shə-nəl) *adj.* Not restricted to or associated with a particular religious denomination.

non·de·script (nŏn′dĭ-skrĭpt′) *adj.* Lacking in distinctive qualities. [NON- + Latin *dēscrīptus,* past part. of *dēscrībere,* to describe.] **—non′de·script′** *n.*

none (nŭn) *pron.* **1.** No one; not one; nobody: *None dared to do it.* **2.** Not any: *None of my classmates survived the war.* **3.** No part; not any: *none of his business.* *—adv.* In no way; not at all: *He is none too happy.* [Middle English, from Old English *nān : ne,* no + *ān,* one.]

Usage: **none.** The indefinite pronoun *none* can be construed as a singular or a plural, depending on the intended meaning. If the writer means "not one," "no one," or "nobody," a singular verb is used: *None is without blemish. None is to blame. None of our scholars has written about him.* But if the writer means "not any," a plural verb is used: *None of them were there. None were more deserving of pity than the survivors who returned hopelessly injured.* Whatever the choice, the singular or plural nature of the construction should be consistent throughout: *None has completed his work; none have completed their work.*

non·en·ti·ty (nŏn-ĕn′tĭ-tē) *n., pl.* **-ties. 1.** A person of no importance or significance. **2.** Something that does not exist, or that exists only in the imagination.

nones (nōnz) *pl.n.* In the ancient Roman calendar, the seventh day of March, May, July, or October, and the fifth day of the other months. [From Latin *nonus,* ninth.]

none·such (nŭn′sŭch′) *n.* Also **non·such** (nŭn′sŭch′, nŏn′-). A person or thing without equal. **—none′such′** *adj.*

none·the·less (nŭn′thə-lĕs′) *adv.* Also **none the less.** Nevertheless; however.

non-Eu·clid·e·an (nŏn′yōō-klĭd′ē-ən) *adj.* Not in accordance with or based on postulates of Euclidean geometry.

non·ex·ist·ent (nŏn′ĭg-zĭs′tənt) *adj.* Not existing. **—non′ex·ist′ence** *n.*

non·fat (nŏn′făt′) *adj.* Lacking fat solids or having the fat content removed.

non·fea·sance (nŏn-fē′zəns) *n. Law.* Failure to perform some act that is either an official duty or a legal requirement. [NON- + obs. *feasance,* a doing, from Old French *faisance.*]

non·fer·rous (nŏn-fĕr′əs) *adj.* **1.** Not composed of or containing iron. **2.** Of or designating metals other than iron.

non·fic·tion (nŏn-fĭk′shən) *n.* Literary works other than fiction. **—non·fic′tion·al** *adj.*

non·flam·ma·ble (nŏn-flăm′ə-bəl) *adj.* Not flammable; not tending to catch fire easily. **—non·flam′ma·bil′i·ty** *n.*

non·hu·man (nŏn-hyōō′mən) *adj.* Not human. —See Usage note at **inhuman.**

no·nil·lion (nō-nĭl′yən) *n.* **1.** In the United States and France, the cardinal number represented by the figure 1 followed by 30 zeros; usu. written 10^{30}. **2.** In Great Britain and Germany, the cardinal number represented by the figure 1 followed by 54 zeros; usu. written 10^{54}. [French, "the ninth power of a million."] **—no·nil′lion** *adj.*

no·nil·lionth (nō-nĭl′yənth) *n.* The ordinal number that matches the number nonillion in a series. **—no·nil′lionth** *adj.*

non·in·ter·ven·tion (nŏn′ĭn-tər-vĕn′shən) *n.* Failure or refusal to intervene, esp. in the affairs of another nation. **—non′in·ter·ven′tion·ist** *n. & adj.*

non·ju·ror (nŏn-jōōr′ər, -ôr′) *n.* **1.** A person who refuses to take an oath, as of allegiance. **2. Nonjuror.** An Anglican clergyman who refused to swear allegiance to William and Mary in 1689. [NON- + Latin *jurāre,* to swear.]

non·met·al (nŏn-mĕt′l) *n.* Any of the elements, such as oxygen or sulfur, that usu. become more electrically negative in forming a compound, that have oxides which form acids, and that conduct heat and electricity poorly when in a solid state. **—non′me·tal′lic** (nŏn′mə-tăl′ĭk) *adj.*

no·non·sense (nō-nŏn′sĕns′, -səns) *adj.* Practical; businesslike: *a no-nonsense approach.*

non·pa·reil (nŏn′pə-rĕl′) *adj.* Having no equal; matchless; peerless. *—n.* **1.** Someone or something that has no equal; a paragon. **2.** A small, flat chocolate drop covered with white pellets of sugar. [Middle English *nonparaille,* from Old French *nonpareil : non-,* not + *pareil,* equal, from Latin *pār.*]

non·par·ti·san (nŏn-pär′tĭ-zən) *adj.* Not based or influenced by party membership: *a nonpartisan investigation.* **—non·par′ti·san·ship′** *n.*

non·plus (nŏn-plŭs′) *n.* A condition of perplexity, confusion, or bewilderment. *—tr.v.* **-plused** or **-plussed, -plusing** or **-plussing.** To put at a loss so that one does not know what to think, say, or do; bewilder. [Latin *nōn plūs,* "no more (can be said)."]

non·pro·duc·tive (nŏn′prə-dŭk′tĭv) *adj.* **1.** Not yielding or producing. **2.** Not engaged in the direct production of goods: *nonproductive clerical personnel.* **—non′pro·duc′tive·ly** *adv.*

non·pro·fes·sion·al (nŏn′prə-fĕsh′ə-nəl) *n.* One who is not a professional. —See Syns at **amateur.**

non·prof·it (nŏn-prŏf′ĭt) *adj.* Not seeking profit.

non·rep·re·sen·ta·tion·al (nŏn-rĕp′rĭ-zən-tā′shə-nəl) *adj.* Not representing objects as they are recognized in nature.

non·res·i·dent (nŏn-rĕz′ĭ-dənt) *adj.* Not living in a particular place. **—non·res′i·dent** *n.*

non·re·stric·tive (nŏn′rĭ-strĭk′tĭv) *adj. Gram.* Of or designating a descriptive word, clause, or phrase that may be left out without changing the basic meaning of the sentence and that is set off from the rest of the sentence by commas. For example, in the sentence *Mary, who has brown hair, is younger than Helen,* the clause *who has brown hair* is nonrestrictive.

non·sched·uled (nŏn-skĕj′ōōld) *adj.* Not having a regular schedule of passenger or cargo flights: *a nonscheduled airline.*

non·sec·tar·i·an (nŏn′sĕk-târ′ē-ən) *adj.* Not limited to or associated with a particular religious denomination.

non·sense (nŏn′sĕns′, -səns) n. **1.** Behavior or language that is foolish or absurd. **2.** Something of little or no importance or usefulness.

non·sen·si·cal (nŏn-sĕn′sĭ-kəl) adj. Foolish; silly; absurd. —See Syns at **foolish**. —**non·sen′si·cal·ly** adv.

non se·qui·tur (nŏn sĕk′wĭ-tər, -toor′) n. A statement that does not follow logically from what preceded it. [Latin, "it does not follow."]

non·skid (nŏn′skĭd′) adj. Designed to prevent skidding.

non·stan·dard (nŏn-stăn′dərd) adj. **1.** Varying from or not adhering to the standard. **2.** Of, relating to, or indicating a level of language usage that is usu. avoided by educated speakers and writers.

non·stop (nŏn′stŏp′) adv. Performed or accomplished without a stop. —adj. Not making any stops: a nonstop flight. —See Syns at **continuous**.

non·such (nŭn′sŭch′, nŏn′-) n. Var. of **nonesuch**.

non·suit (nŏn-sōōt′) n. Law. A judgment given against a plaintiff when he fails to prosecute his case or to present sufficient evidence. —tr.v. To dismiss the lawsuit of. [Middle English, from Norman French nounsuyte.]

non·sup·port (nŏn′sə-pôrt′, -pōrt′) n. Law. Failure to provide financial support to a dependent.

non trop·po (nŏn trô′pō, nôn). Mus. Moderately. Used to modify a direction. [Italian, "not too much."]

non·un·ion (nŏn-yōōn′yən) adj. **1.** Not belonging to a labor union: nonunion workers. **2.** Not recognizing or dealing with a labor union or employing union members: a nonunion shop.

non·vi·o·lence (nŏn-vī′ə-ləns) n. The doctrine, policy, or practice of rejecting violence in favor of peaceful tactics as a means of gaining esp. political ends. —**non·vi′o·lent** adj. —**non·vi′o·lent·ly** adv.

noo·dle[1] (nōōd′l) n. **1.** Slang. The head. **2.** A stupid person; fool. [Poss. alteration of NODDLE (head).]

noo·dle[2] (nōōd′l) n. A narrow, ribbonlike strip of dried dough, usu. made of flour, eggs, and water. [German Nudel.]

nook (nŏŏk) n. **1.** A small corner, alcove, or recess, esp. one that is part of a larger room: a kitchen with a breakfast nook. **2.** A hidden or secluded spot: a cozy nook. [Middle English noke, perh. of Scandinavian orig.]

noon (nōōn) n. Twelve o'clock in the daytime; midday. —modifier: a noon meal. [Middle English, midday, the hour of the nones, from Old English nōn, "the ninth hour (after sunrise)," from Late Latin nōna (hōra), from Latin nōnus, ninth.]

noon·day (nōōn′dā′) n. Noon.

no one. Also **no-one** (nō′wŭn′). No person; nobody. —See Usage note at **none**.

noon·tide (nōōn′tīd′) n. Noon; noontime. [Middle English nonetyde, Old English nōntīd.]

noon·time (nōōn′tīm′) n. Noon.

noose (nōōs) n. **1.** A loop formed in a rope by means of a slipknot so that it binds tighter as the rope is pulled. **2.** A snare or trap. —tr.v. **noosed, noos·ing.** To capture or hold by or as if by a noose. [Middle English nose, from Old French nous, from Latin nōdus, knot.]

nor (nôr, nər when unstressed) conj. And not; or not; not either: He has no experience, nor does he want any. He is neither able nor willing to do anything. [Middle English, contraction of nother, neither.]

Usage: nor. This conjunction is used primarily to express the sense of continuing negation. In varying examples it stands for and not, or not, likewise not, or not either. It is often paired with neither: She insisted that she was neither for it nor opposed. Nor, not or, is always the choice to signify continuing negation in sentences having successive independent clauses: She said she was neither for the proposal nor was she opposed. He had no experience in cost accounting, nor did the subject interest him. But when such examples are expressed within a single independent clause, or, rather than nor, is used following the opening negative statement, when it is clear that the negative sense carries over to the element introduced by or: She was not strongly for or against the proposal. He had no experience or interest in cost accounting. He would not accept the explanation or even consider it. See also Usage note **3** at **neither.**

Nor·dic (nôr′dĭk) adj. **1.** Of or belonging to the division of the Caucasoid group of the human species that is most predominant in Scandinavia. **2.** Of or relating to a class consisting of people who typically are tall, longheaded, blond, and blue-eyed. [French nordique, from Old French nord, north, from Old English north.] —**Nor′dic** n.

Nor·folk jacket (nôr′fək). A belted jacket with two box pleats in front and back. [After Norfolk, England.]

norm (nôrm) n. **1.** A standard, model, or pattern regarded as typical for a specific group. **2.** An average or a statistical mode. [Latin norma, carpenter's square, pattern.]

nor·mal (nôr′məl) adj. **1.** Conforming to a usual or typical standard: normal room temperature; one's normal weight. **2. a.** Relating to or marked by average intelligence and development. **b.** Free from physical or emotional disorder. **3.** Chem. **a.** Having one gram equivalent weight of solute per liter. **b.** Having a straight chain of carbon atoms. **4.** Geom. Being perpendicular; at right angles. —See Syns at **ordinary**. —n. **1.** Anything that is normal; the standard. **2.** The usual or expected state, form, amount, or degree. **3.** An average. **4.** Geom. A perpendicular, esp. a perpendicular to a line tangent to a plane curve or to a plane tangent to a curved surface. —**nor′mal·cy** n. —**nor′mal·i·ty** n. —**nor′mal·ly** adv.

nor·mal·ize (nôr′mə-līz′) tr.v. **-ized, -iz·ing.** To make normal. —**nor′mal·i·za′tion** n. —**nor′mal·iz′er** n.

normal school. A school that trains teachers, chiefly for the elementary grades.

Nor·man (nôr′mən) n. **1.** A member of a Scandinavian people who conquered Normandy in the tenth cent. **2.** A member of a people of Norman and French blood who conquered England in 1066. **3.** A native of Normandy. **4.** Norman French. —**Nor′man** adj.

Norman French. The dialect of French used in medieval Normandy.

nor·ma·tive (nôr′mə-tĭv) adj. Of, relating to, or prescribing a norm or standard. —**nor′ma·tive·ly** adv. —**nor′ma·tive·ness** n.

Norse (nôrs) adj. **1.** Of or relating to ancient Scandinavia, its people, or its language. **2. a.** Of or relating to West Scandinavia or the languages of its inhabitants. **b.** Of or relating to Norway, its people, or its language. —n. **1. a.** The people of Scandinavia. **b.** The Norwegians. **2. a.** The Scandinavian branch of the Germanic languages. **b.** Any of the West Scandinavian languages or dialects, esp. Norwegian.

Norse·man (nôrs′mən) n. A member of one of the peoples of ancient Scandinavia.

north (nôrth) n. **1. a.** The direction along a meridian 90 degrees counterclockwise from east; the direction to the left of sunrise. **b.** The cardinal point on the mariner's compass located at 0 degrees. **2.** Often **North.** An area or region lying to the north of a particular point. —adj. **1.** To, toward, of, facing, or in the north. **2.** Coming from or originating in the north. —adv. In, from, or toward the north. [Middle English from Old English.]

north·bound (nôrth′bound′) adj. Going toward the north.

north·east (nôrth-ēst′) n. **1.** The direction that is 45 degrees counterclockwise from east and 45 degrees clockwise from north. **2.** An area or region lying to the northeast of a particular point. —adj. **1.** Situated toward, facing, or in the northeast. **2.** Coming from or originating in the northeast. —adv. In, from, or toward the northeast. —**north·east′ern** adj.

north·east·er (nôrth-ē′stər; nôr-ē′stər) n. A storm or gale from the northeast.

north·east·er·ly (nôrth-ē′stər-lē) adj. **1.** Toward or in the northeast. **2.** From the northeast. —adv.: a gale blowing northeasterly.

north·east·ward (nôrth-ēst′wərd) adv. Also **north·east·wards** (-wərdz). Toward the northeast. —adj.: a northeastward view. —n. A direction or region to the northeast. —**north·east′ward·ly** adj. & adv.

north·er (nôr′thər) n. A sudden cold gale from the north.

north·er·ly (nôr′thər-lē) adj. **1.** In or toward the north. **2.** From the north. —n., pl. **-lies.** A storm or wind from the north. —**north′er·ly** adv.

north·ern (nôr′thərn) adj. **1.** Of, in, or toward the north. **2.** From the north. **3.** Characteristic of or found in northern regions. [Middle English *northerne*, from Old English.]

Northern Cross. A cross formed by six stars in the constellation Cygnus.

north·ern·er (nôr'thər-nər) *n.* Often **Northerner.** A native or inhabitant of a northern region, esp. of the northern region of the United States.

Northern Hemisphere. The half of the earth north of the equator.

northern lights. The aurora borealis.

north·ern·most (nôr'thərn-mōst') *adj.* Farthest north.

north·land (nôrth'lănd', -lənd) *n.* Often **Northland.** A region in the north, of a country or territory. —**north'land·er** *n.*

North·man (nôrth'mən) *n.* A Norseman.

north-north·east (nôrth'nôrth-ēst') *n.* The direction, or point on a compass, halfway between north and northeast. —**north'north·east'** *adj. & adv.*

north-north·west (nôrth'nôrth-wĕst') *n.* The direction, or point on a mariner's compass, halfway between north and northwest. —**north'north·west'** *adj. & adv.*

North Pole. **1.** The northernmost point of the earth at which the earth's axis of rotation intersects the surface of the earth. **2.** The point, about one degree from the star Polaris, at which the earth's axis of rotation intersects the celestial sphere. **3. north pole.** The pole of a magnet that tends to point north when the magnet is free to move.

North Star. Polaris.

north·ward (nôrth'wərd) *adv.* Also **north·wards** (-wərdz). To or toward the north. —*adj.:* *northward expansion.* —*n.* **1.** A direction or point toward the north. **2.** A region situated in or toward the north.

north·west (nôrth-wĕst') *n.* **1.** The direction that is 45 degrees counterclockwise from north and 45 degrees clockwise from west. **2.** An area or region lying to the northwest of a particular point. —**north·west** *adj. & adv.* —**north·west'ern** *adj.*

north·west·er (nôrth-wĕs'tər; nôr-wĕs'tər) *n.* A storm or gale from the northwest.

north·west·er·ly (nôrth-wĕs'tər-lē) *adj.* **1.** Toward or in the northwest. **2.** From the northwest: *northwesterly breezes.*

north·west·ward (nôrth-wĕst'wərd) *adv.* Also **north·west·wards** (-wərdz). To or toward the northwest. —**north·west'ward** *adj. & n.*

Nor·way maple (nôr'wā'). A tall Eurasian tree, *Acer platanoides,* widely used in North America as a shade tree.

Nor·we·gian (nôr-wē'jən) *n.* **1.** A native or inhabitant of Norway. **2.** The Germanic language of the Norwegians. —**Nor·we'gian** *adj.*

nose (nōz) *n.* **1.** In human beings and other animals, the structure on the face or the forward part of the head that contains the nostrils and organs of smell and forms the beginning of the respiratory tract. **2.** The sense of smell. **3.** The ability to detect things, as if by smell: *a nose for gossip.* **4.** The forward end of an airplane, rocket, submarine, or other pointed structure. **5.** *Informal.* The nose considered as a symbol of prying: *Keep your nose out of my business.* **6.** A narrow margin: *won by a nose.* —*v.* **nosed, nos·ing.** —*tr.v.* **1.** To find out by or as if by smell. **2.** To touch or examine with the nose; nuzzle. **3.** To cause to move or advance cautiously: *nosed the car into the traffic flow.* —*intr.v.* **1.** To smell or sniff. **2.** *Informal.* To pry curiously or in a meddlesome way: *nose around in someone else's business.* **3.** To push forward with caution: *The liner nosed into its berth.* —**idioms. on the nose.** Exactly; precisely: *predicted the amount on the nose.* **under (someone's) nose.** In plain view of: *took the jewels from right under the noses of the guards.* [Middle English, from Old English *nosu.*]

nose·band (nōz'bănd') *n.* The part of a bridle or halter that passes over the animal's nose.

nose·bleed (nōz'blēd') *n.* Bleeding from the nostrils.

nose cone. The forward, usu. separable end of a rocket or guided missile.

nose dive. **1.** A very steep dive made by an airplane. **2.** A sudden, swift drop or plunge. —**nose'-dive** *intr.v.*

nose·gay (nōz'gā') *n.* A small bunch of flowers. [Middle English : *nose,* nose + *gay,* toy, ornament.]

nose·piece (nōz'pēs') *n.* **1.** A piece of armor that forms part of a helmet and protects the nose. **2.** The part of a pair

of eyeglasses that fits across the nose. **3.** A noseband. **4.** The part of a microscope to which one or more lenses are attached.

nos·ey (nō'zē) *adj.* Var. of **nosy.**

nosh (nŏsh) *n. Informal.* A tidbit; snack. —*intr.v. Informal.* To eat snacks between meals. [Short for Yiddish *nosherai,* tidbits, from Old High German *(h)nascōn,* to gnaw, nibble.]

nos·tal·gia (nŏ-stăl'jə, nə-) *n.* A bittersweet longing for the things of the past. [Greek *nostos,* a return + *algos,* pain.] —**nos·tal'gic** *adj.* —**nos·tal'gi·cal·ly** *adv.*

nos·tril (nŏs'trəl) *n.* Either of the external openings of the nose. [Middle English *nostrill,* from Old English *nosthyrl* : *nosu,* nose + *thyrl,* hole.]

nos·trum (nŏs'trəm) *n.* **1.** A medicine, esp. a quack remedy, whose ingredients are usu. secret. **2.** A favorite but untested remedy for problems or evils. [Latin *nostrum,* ours.]

nos·y (nō'zē) *adj.* **-i·er, -i·est.** Also **nos·ey.** Prying; inquisitive. —See Syns at **curious.** [From NOSE.] —**nos'i·ly** *adv.* —**nos'i·ness** *n.*

not (nŏt) *adv.* In no way; to no degree. Used to express negation, denial, refusal, or prohibition: *I will not go. You may not have any.* [Middle English, from Old English *nōwiht* : *nā,* no + *wiht,* creature.]

no·ta be·ne (nō'tə bĕn'ē). *Latin.* Note well.

no·ta·bil·i·ty (nō'tə-bĭl'ĭ-tē) *n., pl.* **-ties.** **1.** The condition of being notable. **2.** A notable or prominent person.

no·ta·ble (nō'tə-bəl) *adj.* Worthy of notice; striking: *notable beauty.* —*n.* A person of distinction or of great reputation. —**no'ta·ble·ness** *n.* —**no'ta·bly** *adv.*

no·ta·rize (nō'tə-rīz') *tr.v.* **-rized, -riz·ing.** To witness and authenticate (a document) as a notary public. —**no'ta·ri·za'tion** *n.*

no·ta·ry (nō'tə-rē) *n., pl.* **-ries.** A notary public. [Middle English *notarie,* clerk, from Latin *notārius,* stenographer, from *notārius,* cipher, from *nota,* mark, note.]

notary public *pl.* **notaries public.** A person legally empowered to witness and certify documents and to take affidavits and depositions.

no·ta·tion (nō-tā'shən) *n.* **1. a.** The use of standard symbols or figures to represent quantities, tones, or values briefly and clearly: *musical notation.* **b.** A system of such symbols or figures. **2.** A brief note or record. —**no·ta'tion·al** *adj.*

notch (nŏch) *n.* **1.** A V-shaped cut. **2.** A narrow pass between mountains. **3.** A level or degree: *He is a notch better than his brother.* —*tr.v.* **1.** To cut a notch in. **2.** To record by or as if by making notches. [From *a notch,* orig. *an otch,* from Old French *o(s)che,* from *o(s)chier,* to notch, from Latin *absecāre,* to cut off.]

note (nōt) *n. Abbr.* **n.** **1.** A brief record, esp. as an aid to the memory. **2.** A short, informal letter or message. **3.** A formal diplomatic or official communication. **4.** A comment or explanation, as on a passage in a text. **5. a.** A piece of paper currency. **b.** A promissory note. **6.** *Mus.* **a.** A symbol for a musical tone, indicating pitch by its position on a staff and relative length by its shape. **b.** A musical tone. **7.** A characteristic animal call or cry: *the clear note of a cardinal.* **8.** A sign of a certain quality: *ended his plea on a note of despair.* **9.** Importance; consequence: *gentlemen of note.* **10.** Notice; observation: *He took note of what had happened.* —*tr.v.* **not·ed, not·ing.** **1.** To observe carefully;

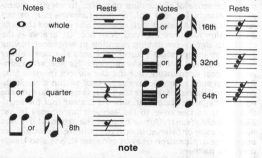

Notes		Rests		Notes			Rests	
o	whole			or		16th		
or	half			or		32nd		
or	quarter			or		64th		
or	8th							

note

notice; perceive. **2.** To write down; make a note of. **3.** To make mention of; remark. —*idiom.* **compare notes.** To exchange views or observations. [Middle English, from Old French, from Latin *nota,* mark, sign.] —**not′er** *n.*

note·book (nōt′bŏok′) *n.* A book of blank pages for notes.

not·ed (nō′tĭd) *adj.* Well-known; famous: *a noted author.*

note·wor·thy (nōt′wûr′thē) *adj.* Deserving notice or attention; remarkable. —**note′wor′thi·ly** *adv.* —**note′wor′thi·ness** *n.*

noth·ing (nŭth′ĭng) *n.* **1.** No thing; not anything. **2.** No part; no portion: *Nothing remains of its former glory.* **3.** Someone or something of no interest or importance. **4.** Absence of anything perceptible; nonexistence: *The sound faded into nothing.* **5.** That which has no value; zero. —*adv.* Not at all: *He looks nothing like me.* —*idiom.* **nothing doing.** *Informal.* Certainly not. [Middle English, from Old English *nāthing* : *nān,* none + *thing,* thing.]

noth·ing·ness (nŭth′ĭng-nĭs) *n.* **1.** The condition or quality of being nothing; nonexistence. **2.** Empty space; void. **3.** Something of little or no value.

no·tice (nō′tĭs) *n.* **1.** Attention; observation: *That detail escaped my notice.* **2.** Respectful attention or consideration. **3.** An announcement. **4.** A written or printed announcement. **5.** A critical review, as of a play or book. —*tr.v.* **-ticed, -tic·ing. 1.** To observe. **2.** To comment on; mention. [Middle English *notyce,* from Old French *notice,* from Latin *nōtitia,* knowledge, from *nōtus,* known, past part. of *nōscere,* to get acquainted with.]

no·tice·a·ble (nō′tĭ-sə-bəl) *adj.* **1.** Readily observed; evident. **2.** Deserving of notice. —See Syns at **perceptible.** —**no′tice·a·bly** *adv.*

no·ti·fi·ca·tion (nō′tə-fĭ-kā′shən) *n.* **1.** The act or an example of notifying. **2.** Something, as a letter, that notifies.

no·ti·fy (nō′tə-fī′) *tr.v.* **-fied, -fy·ing.** To give notice to; inform: *notify the police of the theft.* [Middle English *notifien,* from Old French *notifier,* from Latin *nōtificāre,* to make known.] —**no′ti·fi′er** *n.*

no·tion (nō′shən) *n.* **1.** A mental image or representation; idea. **2.** A belief; opinion. **3.** A fanciful impulse; whim: *had a notion to take the day off.* **4. notions.** Small useful items, such as needles, buttons, or thread. —See Syns at **belief.** [Latin *nōtiō,* from *nōtus,* past part. of *nōscere,* to get acquainted.] —**no′tion·al** *adj.*

no·to·chord (nō′tə-kôrd′) *n.* A cordlike strip of cartilage that occurs along the back of lower vertebrates, such as the lancelet, and in the embryos of higher vertebrates from which the spine develops. —**no′to·chord′al** *adj.* [Greek *nōtos,* back + CHORD (cord).]

no·to·ri·e·ty (nō′tə-rī′ĭ-tē) *n.* The quality or condition of being notorious.

no·to·ri·ous (nō-tôr′ē-əs, -tōr′-) *adj.* Known widely and usu. unfavorably. [Medieval Latin *nōtōrius,* from Late Latin, causing to be known, from *nōtus,* known, past part. of *nōscere,* to get acquainted.] —**no·to′ri·ous·ly** *adv.* —**no·to′ri·ous·ness** *n.*

no-trump (nō′trŭmp′) *n.* **1.** In bridge and other card games, a declaration to play a hand without a trump suit. **2.** A hand played without a trump suit. —**no′-trump′** *adj.*

not·with·stand·ing (nŏt′wĭth-stăn′dĭng, -wĭth-) *prep.* In spite of. —*adv.* All the same; nevertheless. —*conj.* In spite of the fact that; although. [Middle English *notwithstonding.*]

ou·gat (nōo′gət) *n.* A candy made from nuts and honey or ugar. [French, from Provençal *no·ʌt,* confection of nuts, from Latin *nux,* nut.]

ʌght (nôt) *n. & adj.* Var. of **naught.**

ʌn (noun) *n. Abbr.* **n.** *Gram.* A word that is used to name ʌrson, place, thing, quality, or action and that can funcʌas the subject or object of a verb or the object of a ʌosition. [Middle English *nowne,* from French *noun,* a ʌne, noun, from Old French *non,* from Latin *nōmen,* ʌe.]

ʌ·ish (nûr′ĭsh, nŭr′-) *tr.v.* **1.** To provide with food. **2.** To foster the development of; promote. **3.** To keep alive; maintain. [Middle English *norishen,* from Old French *norrir,* from Latin *nūtrīre,* to feed.] —**nour′ish·er** *n.*

nour·ish·ment (nûr′ĭsh-mənt, nŭr′-) *n.* **1. a.** The act of nourishing. **b.** The condition of being nourished. **2.** Something that nourishes.

nou·veau riche (nōo′vō rēsh′) *pl.* **nou·veaux riches** (nōo′vō rēsh′). A person who has recently become rich, esp. one who flaunts his wealth. [French, "new rich."]

no·va (nō′və) *n., pl.* **-vae** (-vē) or **-vas.** *Astron.* A star that suddenly increases greatly in brightness and then returns to its original appearance over a period of time. [New Latin *(stella) nova,* "new (star)," from Latin *novus,* new.]

nov·el[1] (nŏv′əl) *n.* A fictional prose narrative of considerable length, typically having a plot that is unfolded by the actions, speech, and thoughts of the characters. [Italian *(storia) novella,* "new (story)."]

nov·el[2] (nŏv′əl) *adj.* Strikingly new or unusual. —See Syns at **fresh.** [Middle English, from Old French, from Latin *novellus,* from *novus,* new.] —**nov′el·ly** *adv.*

nov·el·ette (nŏv′ə-lĕt′) *n.* A short novel.

nov·el·ist (nŏv′ə-lĭst) *n.* A writer of novels.

nov·el·is·tic (nŏv′ə-lĭs′tĭk) *adj.* Of, relating to, or characteristic of novels. —**nov′el·is′ti·cal·ly** *adv.*

nov·el·la (nō-vĕl′ə) *n., pl.* **-las** or **-le** (-vĕl′ē). **1.** A short prose tale characterized by wit, terseness, or satire. **2.** A short novel. [Italian.]

nov·el·ty (nŏv′əl-tē) *n., pl.* **-ties. 1.** The quality of being novel. **2.** Something new and unusual; an innovation. **3. novelties.** Small mass-produced articles, as toys or trinkets.

No·vem·ber (nō-vĕm′bər) *n.* The 11th month of the year. [Middle English *Novembre,* from Old French, from Latin *Novembris (mensis),* "ninth (month)," from *novem,* nine.]

no·ve·na (nō-vē′nə) *n., pl.* **-nas** or **-nae** (-nē). *Rom. Cath. Ch.* Prayers and devotions for a special purpose, repeated for nine consecutive days. [Medieval Latin *novēna,* from Latin *novēnus,* nine each, from *novem,* nine.]

nov·ice (nŏv′ĭs) *n.* **1.** A person new to any field or activity; beginner. **2.** A person who has entered a religious order, but has not yet taken the final vows. [Middle English *novyce,* from Old French *novice,* from Medieval Latin *novīcius,* from Latin *novus,* new.]

no·vi·ti·ate (nō-vĭsh′ē-ĭt, -āt′) *n.* Also **no·vi·ci·ate. 1.** The period of being a novice. **2.** A place where novices live. **3.** A novice. [French *noviciat,* from Medieval Latin *novīciātus,* from *novīcius,* novice.]

No·vo·cain (nō′və-kān′) *n.* A trademark for a local anesthetic used in medicine and dentistry.

now (nou) *adv.* **1.** At the present time: *I can't leave now.* **2.** In the immediate past; very recently: *He left just now.* **3.** In the immediate future; very soon: *They are going just now.* **4.** At this point in the series of events; then: *The ship was now listing to port.* **5.** In these circumstances; as things are: *Now we won't be able to stay.* **6.** Used esp. to introduce a command, reproof, or request: *Now pay attention.* —*conj.* Since; seeing that: *Now that we have eaten, let's go.* —*n.* The present time or moment: *wouldn't work up to now.* —*adj. Informal.* Of the present time; current. —*idiom.* **now and again** (or **then**). Occasionally. [Middle English, from Old English *nū.*]

now·a·days (nou′ə-dāz′) *adv.* In these days; during the present time. [Middle English *now a dayes,* "on this day."]

no·way (nō′wā′) *adv.* Also **no·ways** (-wāz′). *Informal.* In no way; not at all.

no·where (nō′hwâr′, -wâr′) *adv.* **1.** Not anywhere. **2.** To no place or result: *You'll get nowhere doing it that way.* —*n.* A remote or unknown place: *a cabin in the middle of nowhere.*

no·wise (nō′wīz′) *adv.* In no way, manner or degree; not at all.

nox·ious (nŏk′shəs) *adj.* Injurious or harmful to health or morals. [Latin *noxius,* from *noxa,* injury, damage.] —**nox′ious·ly** *adv.* —**nox′ious·ness** *n.*

noz·zle (nŏz′əl) *n.* A projecting part with an opening through which something is discharged. [Earlier *nosle,* dim. of NOSE.]

Np The symbol for the element neptunium.

nth (ĕnth) *adj.* **1.** Corresponding in order to an indefinitely large whole number. **2.** Highest; utmost: *delighted to the nth degree.*

nu (nōo, nyōo) *n.* The thirteenth letter of the Greek alphabet. [Greek.]

nu·ance (nōo-äns′, nyōo-, nōo′äns′, nyōo′-) *n.* A subtle or slight degree of difference, as in meaning, color, or tone.

ă pat	ā pay	â care	ä father	ĕ pet	ē be	hw which	ĭ pit	ī tie	î pier	ŏ pot	ō toe	ô paw, for	oi noise
ōo took	ōo boot	ou out	th thin	th this	ŭ cut		û urge	zh vision	ə about, item, edible, gallop, circus				

[French *nuance*, from Old French, from *nuer*, to show shades of color (as in clouds), from *nue*, cloud, from Latin *nūbēs*.]

nub (nŭb) *n.* **1.** A lump or knob. **2.** The essence; core. — See Syns at **heart**. [Var. of *knub*, from Middle Low German *knubbe*, knot on a tree, var. of *knobbe*, knob.]

nub·bin (nŭb′ĭn) *n.* Something, as an ear of corn, that is stunted or imperfectly developed. [Dim. of NUB.]

nub·ble (nŭb′əl) *n.* A small lump or knob. [Dim. of NUB.] —**nub′bly** *adj.*

nu·bile (nōō′bəl, -bīl′) *adj.* Ready for marriage; of a marriageable age. [French, from Latin *nūbilis*, marriageable, from *nūbere*, to take a husband.] —**nu·bil′i·ty** (nōō-bĭl′ĭ-tē, nyōō-) *n.*

nu·cel·lus (nōō-sĕl′əs, nyōō-) *n., pl.* **-cel·li** (-sĕl′ī′). The center of the seed of a plant, containing the embryo sac. [From Latin *nucella*, dim. of *nux*, nut.] —**nu·cel′lar** *adj.*

nucle-. Var. of **nucleo-.**

nu·cle·ar (nōō′klē-ər, nyōō′-) *adj.* **1.** *Biol.* Of, relating to, or forming a nucleus. **2.** *Physics.* Of or concerning atomic nuclei. **3.** Of or using nuclear energy. **4.** Having or using nuclear weapons. [From NUCLEUS.]

nuclear energy. Energy that is released from an atomic nucleus, esp. by fission, fusion, or radioactive decay.

nuclear fission. Fission.

nuclear fusion. Fusion.

nuclear reaction. Any reaction that alters the energy, composition, or structure of an atomic nucleus.

nuclear reactor. A device in which a nuclear chain reaction is started and controlled.

nu·cle·ase (nōō′klē-ās′, -āz′, nyōō′-) *n.* Any of several enzymes that hydrolyze nucleic acids. [NUCLE(O)- + -ASE.]

nu·cle·ate (nōō′klē-ĭt, nyōō′-) *adj.* Having a nucleus or nuclei. —*v.* (nōō′klē-āt′, nyōō′-) **-at·ed, -at·ing.** —*tr.v.* **1.** To bring together into a nucleus. **2.** To act as a nucleus for. —*intr.v.* To form a nucleus. [NUCLE(US) + -ATE.] —**nu′cle·a′tion** *n.*

nu·cle·i (nōō′klē-ī′, nyōō′-) *n.* A plural of **nucleus.**

nu·cle·ic acid (nōō-klē′ĭk, nyōō-). Any member of either of two groups of complex chemical compounds found in all living cells. [From NUCLE(O)- + -IC.]

nucleo- or **nucle-.** A prefix meaning: **1.** Nucleus: **nucle-on. 2.** Nucleic acid: **nucleoside.** [From NUCLEUS.]

nu·cle·o·lus (nōō-klē′ə-ləs, nyōō-) *n., pl.* **-li** (-lī′). Also **nu·cle·ole** (nōō′klē-ōl′, nyōō′-). *Biol.* A small, usu. round body composed of protein and ribonucleic acid in the nucleus of a cell. Also called **plasmosome.** [From Latin, dim. of *nucleus*, a kernel, nucleus.] —**nu·cle′o·lar** (-lər) *adj.*

nu·cle·on (nōō′klē-ŏn′, nyōō′-) *n.* A proton or a neutron, esp. as part of an atomic nucleus. [NUCLE(O)- + -ON.] —**nu′cle·on′ic** *adj.*

nu·cle·on·ics (nōō′klē-ŏn′ĭks, nyōō′-) *n. (used with a sing. verb).* The branch of science and engineering that deals with the practical application of nuclear energy.

nu·cle·o·pro·tein (nōō′klē-ō-prō′tēn′, -prō′tē-ĭn, nyōō′-) *n.* Any of a group of substances found in all living cells and viruses, composed of a protein and a nucleic acid.

nu·cle·o·side (nōō′klē-ə-sīd′, nyōō′-) *n.* Any compound made of a sugar and a purine or pyrimidine base, esp. one obtained by hydrolysis of a nucleic acid, such as adenosine. [NUCLE(O) + -OS(E) + -IDE.]

nu·cle·o·tide (nōō′klē-ə-tīd′, nyōō′-) *n.* Any of various organic compounds consisting of a nucleoside combined with phosphoric acid. [From NUCLEO- + -IDE.]

nu·cle·us (nōō′klē-əs, nyōō′-) *n., pl.* **-cle·i** (-klē-ī′) or **-us·es.** **1.** A central or essential part around which other parts are grouped or collected; core: *the nucleus of a city.* **2.** *Biol.* A complex, usu. spherical structure within a living cell that contains the cell's hereditary material and that controls its metabolism, growth, and reproduction. **3.** *Bot.* **a.** The **nucellus. b.** The central kernel of a nut or seed. **c.** The central point of a starch granule. **4.** *Anat.* A group of nerve cells in the brain where nerve fibers interconnect. **5.** *Physics.* The central, positively charged core of an atom, composed of protons and neutrons, and containing almost all of the mass of the atom. **6.** *Astron.* **a.** The central portion of the head of a comet. **b.** The central or brightest part of a nebula or of a galaxy. [Latin, a nut, kernel, from *nux*, nut.]

nu·clide (nōō′klīd, nyōō′-) *n.* An atomic nucleus specified by its atomic number, atomic mass, and energy state. [NUCLE(O)- + -IDE.] —**nu·clid′ic** (nōō-klĭd′ĭk, nyōō-) *adj.*

nude (nōōd, nyōōd) *adj.* Without clothing; naked. — See Syns at **bare.** —*n.* **1.** The unclothed human figure, esp. in artistic representation. **2.** The condition of being unclothed: *in the nude.* [Latin *nūdus.*] —**nude′ly** *adv.* —**nude′ness** or **nu′di·ty** *n.*

nudge (nŭj) *tr.v.* **nudged, nudg·ing.** To push against gently, esp. in order to gain attention or give a signal. —*n.* A gentle push. [Prob. of Scandinavian orig.]

nud·ism (nōō′dĭz′əm, nyōō′-) *n.* The belief in or practice of going nude. —**nu′dist** *n.*

nug·get (nŭg′ĭt) *n.* A small, solid lump, esp. of gold. [Brit. dial. *nugget*, lump, dim. of *nug.*]

nui·sance (nōō′səns, nyōō′-) *n.* Something that is inconvenient, annoying, or unpleasant. [Middle English *nusaunce*, injury, from Old French *nuisance*, from *nuire*, to harm, from Latin *nocēre.*]

null (nŭl) *adj.* **1.** Having no legal force; invalid. **2.** Of no consequence, effect, or value; insignificant. **3.** Amounting to nothing; absent; nonexistent. **4.** *Math.* Of or designating a set having no members. —*n.* Zero; nothing. [Old French *nul*, none, from Latin *nūllus* : *ne*, not + *ullus*, any.]

nul·li·fi·ca·tion (nŭl′ə-fĭ-kā′shən) *n.* **1.** The action of nullifying or the condition of being nullified. **2.** The refusal or failure of a state to recognize or enforce a U.S. law within its boundaries. —**nul′li·fi·ca′tion·ist** *n.*

nul·li·fy (nŭl′ə-fī′) *tr.v.* **-fied, -fy·ing. 1.** To make null; invalidate. **2.** To counteract the force or effectiveness of. —**nul′li·fi′er** *n.*

nul·li·ty (nŭl′ĭ-tē) *n., pl.* **-ties. 1.** The condition of being null. **2.** Something that is null.

numb (nŭm) *adj.* **numb·er, numb·est. 1.** Deprived of the power to feel or move normally: *toes numb with cold.* **2.** Stunned or paralyzed, as from shock or strong emotion: *too numb with fear to cry out.* [Middle English *nome(n)*, seized with palsy, past part. of *nimen*, to take, seize, from Old English *niman.*] —**numb** *tr.v.* —**numb′ly** *adv.* —**numb′ness** *n.*

num·ber (nŭm′bər) *n.* **1.** *Math.* **a.** Any member of the set of positive whole numbers or integers that have unique meaning and that can be derived in a fixed order by counting. **b.** Any of the further set of mathematical objects, such as the negative integers and real numbers, that can be derived from the positive integers by various mathematical operations. **2. numbers.** Arithmetic: *good at numbers.* **3.** One of a numerically ordered series. **4. a.** A symbol used to represent a number. **b.** A numeral or series of numerals for reference or identification: *a telephone number.* **5.** A total; sum: *the number of feet in a mile.* **6.** Quantity: *The crowd was small in number.* **7. numbers.** Verses in meter; metrical poetry. **8.** *Gram.* The indication of whether a word refers to one or more than one: *The verb must agree in number with its subject.* **9. numbers.** A kind of lottery in which bets are made on an unpredictable number, such as a daily stock-exchange figure. **11. Numbers.** See table at **Bible.** —*tr.v.* **1.** To total in number or amount; add up to. **2.** To count or determine the number

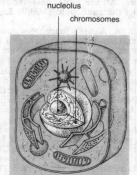

nucleolus
chromosomes

nucleus

or amount of. **3.** To include in a group or category: *He was numbered among the lost.* **4.** To mention one by one; enumerate. **5.** To assign a number to. **6.** To limit or restrict in number: *The days of his life are numbered.* —*intr.v.* **1.** To count or call off numbers: *numbering to ten.* **2.** To constitute a group or number: *The applicants numbered in the thousands.* —*idiom.* **without** (or **beyond**) **number.** Too many to be counted; countless. [Middle English *noumbre,* from Old French *nombre,* from Latin *numerus.*] —**num'ber·er** *n.*

num·ber·less (nŭm'bər-lĭs) *adj.* Innumerable; countless.

numb·skull (nŭm'skŭl') *n.* Var. of **numskull.**

nu·mer·a·ble (nōō'mər-ə-bəl, nyōō'-) *adj.* Capable of being counted; countable.

nu·mer·al (nōō'mər-əl, nyōō'-) *n.* **1.** A symbol or mark used to represent a number. **2. numerals.** The last two digits of a student's year of graduation, used as a name or emblem of his class. —*adj.* Of or expressing numbers. —**nu'mer·al·ly** *adv.*

nu·mer·ate (nōō'mə-rāt', nyōō'-) *tr.v.* **-at·ed, -at·ing.** To count; number. [From Latin *numerāre,* to number, count, from *numerus,* number.]

nu·mer·a·tion (nōō'mə-rā'shən, nyōō'-) *n.* **1.** The act or process of counting or numbering. **2.** A system of enumeration.

nu·mer·a·tor (nōō'mə-rā'tər, nyōō'-) *n.* The number that is written above the line in a common fraction and tells how many of the number of the denominator are taken.

nu·mer·i·cal (nōō-mĕr'ĭ-kəl, nyōō-) or **nu·mer·ic** (-ĭk) *adj.* Of, relating to, represented by, or representing a number. —**nu·mer'i·cal·ly** *adv.*

nu·mer·ol·o·gy (nōō'mə-rŏl'ə-jē, nyōō-) *n.* The study of the occult meanings of numbers. [Latin *numerus,* number + -LOGY.] —**nu'mer·ol'o·gist** *n.*

nu·mer·ous (nōō'mər-əs, nyōō'-) *adj.* Consisting of many persons or items. —**nu'mer·ous·ly** *adv.* —**nu'mer·ous·ness** *n.*

nu·mis·mat·ic (nōō'mĭz-măt'ĭk, -mĭs-, nyōō'-) *adj.* **1.** Of or relating to coins. **2.** Of or relating to numismatics. [French *numismatique,* from Latin *numisma,* a coin, from Greek *nomisma,* from *nomizein,* to have in use, from *nomos,* custom.]

nu·mis·mat·ics (nōō'mĭz-măt'ĭks, -mĭs-, nyōō'-) *n.* *(used with a sing. verb).* The collection or study of coins, currency, and medals. —**nu·mis'ma·tist** (nōō-mĭz'mə-tĭst, -mĭs'-, nyōō-) *n.*

num·skull (nŭm'skŭl') *n.* Also **numb·skull.** A stupid person; blockhead. [NUMB + SKULL.]

nun (nŭn) *n.* A woman who belongs to a religious order. [Middle English, from Old English *nunne* and Old French *nonne,* both from Medieval Latin *nonna.*]

nun·ci·o (nŭn'sē-ō', nŏn'-) *n., pl.* **-os.** A papal ambassador or representative. [Italian, from Latin *nūntius,* messenger.]

nun·ner·y (nŭn'ə-rē) *n., pl.* **-ies.** A convent.

nup·tial (nŭp'shəl, -chəl) *adj.* Of or relating to marriage or the wedding ceremony. —*n.* **nuptials.** A wedding ceremony. —See Syns at **marriage.** [Latin *nuptiālis,* from *nuptiae,* wedding, from *nuptus,* past part. of *nūbere,* to take a husband.]

nurse (nûrs) *n.* **1.** A person trained to care for the sick or disabled under the supervision of a physician. **2.** A person employed to take care of a child; nursemaid. **3.** A worker ant or bee that cares for the young. —*v.* **nursed, nurs·ing.** —*tr.v.* **1.** To feed at the breast; suckle. **2.** To serve as a nurse for. **3.** To try to cure or treat: *nurse a cough.* **4.** To take special care of; foster; cultivate: *He nursed his business through the depression.* **5.** To bear in the mind: *nursing a grudge.* **6.** To treat carefully. —*intr.v.* **1.** To take nourishment from the breast; suckle. **2.** To serve as a nurse. [Middle English, from Old French *norrice,* from Late Latin *nūtrīcia,* from *nūtrīcius,* nourishing, from *nūtrix,* a nurse.] —**nurs'er** *n.*

nurse·maid (nûrs'mād') *n.* Also **nurs·er·y·maid** (nûr'sə-rē-mād', nûrs'rē-). A girl or woman employed to take care of children.

nurs·er·y (nûr'sə-rē, nûrs'rē) *n., pl.* **-ies.** **1.** A room or area set apart for the children. **2. a.** A nursery school. **b.** A place for the temporary care of children. **3.** A place where

plants are grown for sale, transplanting, or experimentation.

nurs·er·y·man (nûr'sə-rē-mən, nûrs'rē-) *n.* A person who owns or works in a nursery for plants.

nursery rhyme. A short, rhymed poem for children.

nursery school. A school for children who are not old enough to attend kindergarten.

nurs·ling (nûrs'lĭng) *n.* **1.** A nursing infant or young animal. **2.** A carefully nurtured person or thing.

nur·ture (nûr'chər) *n.* **1.** Anything that nourishes; sustenance; food. **2.** Training; rearing. —*tr.v.* **-tured, -tur·ing.** **1.** To nourish. **2.** To educate; train. **3.** To help grow or develop; cultivate. [Middle English, from Old French *noureture,* from Late Latin *nūtrītūra,* a feeding, from Latin *nūtrīre,* to feed, suckle.] —**nur'tur·er** *n.*

nut (nŭt) *n.* **1. a.** A fruit or seed with a hard shell and an inner kernel. **b.** The often edible kernel of such a fruit. **2.** *Slang.* **a.** A crazy or eccentric person. **b.** An enthusiast: *a movie nut.* **3.** A small block of metal or wood that has a threaded hole in its center and is designed to screw onto and hold a matching bolt or screw. **4.** *Mus.* **a.** A device at the lower end of the bow of a stringed instrument, used to tighten or loosen the hairs. **b.** A ridge of wood at the top of the finger board or neck of stringed instruments, over which the strings pass. —*intr.v.* **nut·ted, nut·ting.** To gather or hunt for nuts. [Middle English *nute,* from Old English *hnutu.*] —**nut'ter** *n.*

nut·crack·er (nŭt'krăk'ər) *n.* **1.** An implement used to crack nuts, usu. consisting of two hinged metal levers between which the nut is squeezed. **2. a.** A bird, *Nucifraga caryocatactes,* of northern Eurasia. **b.** A bird, *N. columbianus,* of western North America.

nut·gall (nŭt'gôl') *n.* A nutlike swelling produced on an oak or other tree by certain parasitic wasps.

nut·meg (nŭt'mĕg') *n.* **1.** An evergreen tree, *Myristica fragrans,* orig. native to the East Indies. **2.** The hard, aromatic seed of this tree used as a spice when grated or ground. [Middle English *nutemuge,* from Old French *nois muscade* : Latin *nux,* nut + *muscus,* musk.]

nu·tri·a (nōō'trē-ə, nyōō'-) *n.* **1.** The coypu. **2.** The fur of the coypu. [Spanish, var. of *lutra,* otter, from Latin.]

nu·tri·ent (nōō'trē-ənt, nyōō'-) —*adj.* Providing nourishment. [Latin *nūtriēns,* pres. part. of *nūtrīre,* to feed, nourish.] —**nu'tri·ent** *n.*

nu·tri·ment (nōō'trə-mənt, nyōō'-) *n.* Something that nourishes. —**nu'tri·men'tal** (-mĕn'tl) *adj.*

nu·tri·tion (nōō-trĭsh'ən, nyōō-) *n.* The process of nourishing or being nourished, esp. the process by which a living organism assimilates and uses food. —**nu·tri'tion·al** *adj.*

nu·tri·tion·ist (nōō-trĭsh'ə-nĭst, nyōō-) *n.* A person who specializes in the study of nutrition.

nu·tri·tious (nōō-trĭsh'əs, nyōō-) *adj.* Providing nourishment. —**nu·tri'tious·ly** *adv.* —**nu·tri'tious·ness** *n.*

nu·tri·tive (nōō'trĭ-tĭv, nyōō'-) *adj.* **1.** Nourishing. **2.** Of or relating to nutrition. —**nu'tri·tive·ly** *adv.*

nuts (nŭts) *adj.* *Slang.* **1.** Crazy; insane. **2.** Extremely enthusiastic: *He's nuts about opera.* —See Syns at **insane.** —*interj.* *Slang.* A word used to express disappointment, contempt, or refusal. [From NUT.]

nut·shell (nŭt'shĕl') *n.* The shell enclosing the meat of a nut. —*idiom.* **in a nutshell.** In a few words; concisely.

nut·ty (nŭt'ē) *adj.* **-ti·er, -ti·est.** **1.** Full of or tasting like nuts. **2.** *Slang.* Crazy. —**nut'ti·ly** *adv.* —**nut'ti·ness** *n.*

nux vom·i·ca (nŭks vŏm'ĭ-kə) *n.* The toxic seed of a tree, *Strychnos nux-vomica,* containing strychnine.

nuz·zle (nŭz'əl) *v.* **-zled, -zling.** —*tr.v.* To rub or push against gently with the nose or snout. —*intr.v.* To nestle together. [Middle English *noselen,* from *nose,* nose.]

ny·lon (nī'lŏn') *n.* **1.** Any of various very strong, elastic synthetic resins. **2.** Cloth or yarn made from nylon. **3. nylons.** Stockings made of nylon. —*modifier:* *nylon cord; nylon bristles.* [Coined by the inventors, E. I. duPont de Nemours & Co., Inc.]

nymph (nĭmf) *n.* **1.** *Gk. & Rom. Myth.* One of the female spirits dwelling in woodlands and waters. **2.** A young, incompletely developed form of certain insects, such as the grasshopper or dragonfly, that goes through a series of gradual changes before reaching the adult stage.

ă pat   ā pay   â care   ä father   ĕ pet   ē be   hw which   ĭ pit   ī tie   î pier   ŏ pot   ō toe   ô paw, for   oi noise
ŏŏ took   ōŏ boot   ou out   th thin   th this   ŭ cut   û urge   zh vision   ə about, item, edible, gallop, circus

Phoenician	Greek	Roman	Medieval	Modern

Phoenician – About 3,000 years ago the Phoenicians and other Semitic peoples began to use graphic signs to represent individual speech sounds instead of syllables or whole words. They used this symbol to represent a laryngeal consonant that is not found in English or any other Indo-European language. They gave it the name ayin, the Phoenician word for "eye."

Greek – The Greeks borrowed the Phoenician alphabet with some modifications. Since they did not have laryngeal consonants in their language they used ayin to represent the sound of the short vowel "o." They gave it the name omikron, which means "small 'o,'" to distinguish it from omega, or "long 'o.'"

Roman – The Romans borrowed the alphabet from the Greeks via the Etruscans They used omikron to represent both long and short "o" and adapted the shape for carving Latin in stone. This monumental script, as it is called, became the basis for modern printed capital letters.

Medieval – By medieval times – around 1,200 years ago – the Roman monumental capitals had become adapted to being relatively quickly written on paper, parchment, or vellum. The cursive minuscule alphabet became the basis of modern printed lower-case letters.

Modern – Since the invention of printing about 500 years ago few modifications have been made in the shape and style of the letter o, which throughout its history has remained relatively unchanged.

---

o or **O** (ō) n., pl. **o's** or **O's.** **1.** The 15th letter of the English alphabet. **2.** A zero.

O (ō) interj. **1.** A word used before the name of a person or thing being formally addressed: Hear us, O Lord. **2.** A word used to express surprise or strong emotion: O my goodness!

 Usage: O, oh. The interjections O and oh have separate functions and they are gen. not interchangeable. O is used most often in literature and in religious contexts to express earnestness or solemnity: O God on high! In this usage, O depends on the words following it and does not stand alone. O is rarely used in exclamations (O dear!) where oh is the usual choice (Oh, dear!). O is always capitalized, it is usu. the first word of a sentence, and it is never followed by punctuation. Oh, on the other hand, can express emotion (Oh, no! Not you again!) but also a reflective pause: Oh, yes...Let me see, now. Oh is capitalized only when it begins a sentence: Oh, you are wrong. I think two, oh, maybe three inches will do. It can be followed by a comma (Oh, I see), by an exclamation point (Oh! What a shame.), or by a question mark (Oh?), depending on the strength of emphasis and the type of sentence.

o' (ə, ō) prep. Of.

oaf (ōf) n. A stupid or clumsy person. [Earlier aufe, changeling, idiot child, from Old Norse alfr, elf.] —**oaf'ish** adj. —**oaf'ish·ly** adv. —**oaf'ish·ness** n.

oak (ōk) n. **1.** Any of various deciduous or evergreen trees or shrubs of the genus Quercus, bearing acorns as fruit. **2.** The durable wood of any of these trees. —modifier: an oak table. [Middle English ook, from Old English āc.] —**oak'en** adj.

oak apple. A harmless gall on oak trees, caused by the larva of a wasp.

oa·kum (ō'kəm) n. Hemp or jute fiber, sometimes treated with tar, creosote, or asphalt, and used for caulking seams and packing pipe joints. [Middle English okum, from Old English ācumba, "off-combings" : ā-, off + cemban, to comb.]

oar (ōr, ôr) n. **1.** A long pole with a blade at one end, used to row or steer a boat. **2.** An oarsman. [Middle English oor, from Old English ār.]

oar·lock (ōr'lŏk', ôr'-) n. A U-shaped device used to hold an oar in place while rowing.

oars·man (ōrz'mən, ôrz'-) n. A person who rows a boat, esp. in a racing crew.

o·a·sis (ō-ā'sĭs) n., pl. -ses (-sēz'). A fertile spot or area in a desert. —modifier: an oasis village. [Late Latin, from Greek.]

oat (ōt) n. **1.** Any of several grasses of the genus Avena, esp., A. sativa, widely cultivated for its edible seeds. **2. oats.** The seeds of the oat, used as food and fodder. [Middle English ote, from Old English āte.] —**oat'en** adj.

oath (ōth) n., pl. **oaths** (ō<u>th</u>z, ōths). **1.** A declaration or promise to act in a certain way, made with God or a deity as witness. **2.** A profane or irreverent use of the name of God or a deity. —idiom. **under** (or **on**) **oath.** Bound by an oath, as in a court of law. [Middle English ooth, from Old English āth.]

oat·meal (ōt'mēl') n. **1.** Meal made from ground or rolled oats. **2.** A porridge made from rolled or ground oats. —modifier: oatmeal cookies.

ob·bli·ga·to (ŏb'lĭ-gä'tō) n., pl. -tos or -ti (-tē). Also **ob·li·ga·to.** Mus. An accompaniment to a solo, usu. played on a single instrument. [Italian, past part. of obbligare, to obligate, from Latin obligāre, to oblige.]

ob·du·ra·cy (ŏb'dyə-rə-sē, ŏb-dŏŏr'ə-, -dyŏŏr'-) n. The condition or quality of being obdurate.

ob·du·rate (ŏb'dŏŏ-rĭt, -dyŏŏ-) adj. **1.** Hardened in wickedness or wrongdoing. **2.** Unmoved by persuasion; unyielding; stubborn: obdurate in her refusal. [Middle English obdurat, from Latin obdūrātus, past part. of obdūrāre, to harden : ob (intensive) + dūrus, hard.] —**ob'du·rate·ly** adv. —**ob'du·rate·ness** n.

o·be·di·ence (ō-bē'dē-əns) n. **1.** The quality or condition of being obedient. **2.** An act or example of obeying.

o·be·di·ent (ō-bē'dē-ənt) adj. Obeying willingly or inclined to obey. [Middle English, from Old French, from Latin oboediēns, pres. part. of oboedīre, to obey.] —**o·be'di·ent·ly** adv.

o·bei·sance (ō-bā'səns, ō-bē'-) n. **1.** A gesture or movement of the body expressing reverence or respect, such as a bow or curtsy. **2.** Great deference; homage. —See Syns at **honor.** [Middle English obeisaunce, from Old French obeissance, from obeir, to obey.] —**o·bei'sant** adj.

ob·e·lisk (ŏb'ə-lĭsk') n. A tall, four-sided shaft of stone, usu. tapering to a pyramidal point. [Old French obelisque, from Latin obeliscus, from Greek obeliskos, dim. of obelos, spit.]

o·bese (ō-bēs') adj. Fat; corpulent. —See Syns at **fat.** [Latin obēsus, past part. of obedere, to devour : ob, away + edere, to eat.] —**o·be'si·ty** (ō-bē'sĭ-tē) n. or **o·bese'ness** n.

ă pat   ā pay   â care   ä father   ĕ pet   ē be   hw which   ĭ pit   ī tie   î pier   ŏ pot   ō toe   ô paw, for   oi noise

ŏŏ took   ŏŏ boot   ou out   th thin   <u>th</u> this   ŭ cut   û urge   zh vision   ə about, item, edible, gallop, circus

o·bey (ō-bā′) *tr.v.* **1.** To carry out or fulfill the command, order, or instruction of. **2.** To follow or comply with: *obey the law.* —*intr.v.* To behave obediently. [Middle English *obeien*, from Old French *obeir*, from Latin *oboedire* : *ob*, to, toward + *audire*, to hear.] —**o·bey′er** *n.*

Syns: obey, comply, follow, mind *v. Core meaning:* To act in conformity with a request, rule, order, or the like. OBEY suggests an accepting of authority (*obeying traffic regulations*): COMPLY, the inclination to yield without protest (*a singer who complied with the audience's request by singing an encore*). FOLLOW suggests adhering to a prescribed course of action (*followed the doctor's orders*). MIND applies esp. to good behavior (*minds his mother*).

ob·fus·cate (ŏb′fə-skāt′, ŏb-fŭs′kāt′, əb-) *tr.v.* **-cat·ed, -cat·ing.** **1.** To make indistinct or dark. **2.** To confuse or becloud: *His emotions obfuscated his judgment.* [From Late Latin *obfuscare*, to darken : *ob* (intensive) + Latin *fuscus*, dark.] —**ob·fus·ca′tion** *n.* —**ob·fus′ca·to·ry** (ŏb-fŭs′kə-tôr′ē, -tōr′ē, əb-) *adj.*

o·bi (ō′bē) *n.* A wide sash worn with a Japanese kimono. [Japanese.]

obi

oboe

o·bit (ō′bĭt, ō-bĭt′) *n. Informal.* An obituary.

o·bit·u·ar·y (ō-bĭch′ōō-ĕr′ē) *n., pl.* **-ies.** A notice of a person's death, usu. with a brief biography. [Medieval Latin *obituarius*, (report) of death, from Latin *obitus*, death, from *obire*, to die : *ob*, down + *ire*, to go.] —**o·bit′u·ar′y** *adj.*

ob·ject¹ (əb-jĕkt′) *intr.v.* **1.** To present or raise an objection: *object to the testimony of a witness.* **2.** To feel or express disapproval. —*tr.v.* To put forward as an objection. [Middle English *objecten*, from Latin *objectus*, past part. of *objicere*, to oppose : *ob*, toward + *jacere*, to throw.] —**ob·jec′tor** *n.*

ob·ject² (ŏb′jĭkt, -jĕkt′) *n.* **1.** Something perceptible esp. to the sense of vision or touch. **2.** A focus for thought or action: *an object of investigation.* **3.** Someone or something that excites emotion: *an object of scorn.* **4.** A purpose; goal. **5.** *Gram.* **a.** A word or phrase that receives or is affected by the action of a verb. **b.** A noun, pronoun, or noun phrase that follows a preposition. [Middle English, from Latin *objectus*, from *objicere*, to throw before, object.]

ob·jec·tion (əb-jĕk′shən) *n.* **1.** An act of objecting. **2. a.** A feeling of disapproval: *had no objection to the boy as his son-in-law.* **b.** A reason or cause for disapproving.

ob·jec·tion·a·ble (əb-jĕk′shə-nə-bəl) *adj.* Arousing disapproval; offensive: *objectionable conduct.* —**ob·jec′tion·a·bil′i·ty** *n.* —**ob·jec′tion·a·bly** *adv.*

ob·jec·tive (əb-jĕk′tĭv) *adj.* **1. a.** Existing in a concrete or observable form; material: *objective phenomena.* **b.** Having existence outside of the mind; actual: *objective facts.* **2.** Of or relating to an object or goal. **3.** Not influenced by emotion or prejudice; impartial: *an objective account.* **4.** *Gram.* Of or designating the case of a noun or pronoun serving as the object of a verb or preposition. —See Syns at **fair.** —*n.* **1.** Something worked toward or striven for; a goal. **2.** *Gram.* **a.** The objective case. **b.** A word in the objective case. **3. a.** The lens or lens system in a microscope or telescope that is closest to the object. **b.** A lens or lens system in a camera or projector that forms the image of the object. [Medieval Latin *objectivus*, from Latin *objectus*, an object.] —**ob·jec′tive·ly** *adv.* —**ob·jec′tive·ness** *n.*

ob·jec·tiv·i·ty (ŏb′jĕk-tĭv′ĭ-tē) *n.* **1.** The condition or quality of being objective. **2.** External or material reality.

object lesson. A lesson taught by concrete examples.

ob·jet d'art (ôb′zhĕ där′, -zhä) *pl.* **ob·jets d'art** (ôb′zhĕ där′, -zhä). An object of artistic merit. [French, "object of art."]

ob·jur·gate (ŏb′jər-gāt′, ŏb-jûr′gāt′) *tr.v.* **-gat·ed, -gat·ing.** To scold or rebuke sharply; berate. [From Latin *objurgare* : *ob*, against + *jurgare*, rebuke, from *jus*, law.] —**ob′jur·ga′tion** *n.*

ob·late (ŏb′lāt′, ŏb-lāt′) *adj.* Compressed along or flattened at the poles: *The earth is an oblate spheroid.* [New Latin *oblatus*, stretched, from Latin *oblatus*, past part. of *offerre*, to bring to, offer.] —**ob′late·ly** *adv.* —**ob′late·ness** *n.*

ob·la·tion (ə-blā′shən, ŏ-blā′-) *n.* **1.** An offering to a god. **2.** Oblation. The bread and wine of the Eucharist. [Middle English *oblacioun*, from Old French *oblation*, from Medieval Latin *oblatio*, from *oblatus*, something offered.]

ob·li·gate (ŏb′lĭ-gāt′) *tr.v.* **-gat·ed, -gat·ing.** To bind, compel, or constrain by a legal or moral tie: *was obligated by contract to work there for two years.* —*adj.* (ŏb′lĭ-gĭt, -gāt′). *Biol.* Able to survive in only one environment. —**ob′li·ga′tor** *n.*

ob·li·ga·tion (ŏb′lĭ-gā′shən) *n.* **1.** The act of binding oneself by a social, legal, or moral tie. **2.** Something, as a contract or promise, that constrains one to a certain course of action. **3.** The constraining power of a law, promise, contract, or sense of duty. **4.** The fact or condition of being indebted to another for a service or favor.

ob·li·ga·to (ŏb′lĭ-gä′tō) *n., pl.* **-tos** or **-ti** (-tē). Var. of **obbligato.**

o·blig·a·to·ry (ə-blĭg′ə-tôr′ē, -tōr′ē, ŏb′lĭ-gə-) *adj.* Legally or morally required; compulsory: *obligatory attendance.* —See Syns at **compulsory.** —**o·blig′a·to′ri·ly** *adv.*

o·blige (ə-blīj′) *tr.v.* **o·bliged, o·blig·ing.** **1.** To bind or constrain; compel. **2.** To make indebted or grateful: *They were obliged to him for his hospitality.* **3.** To do a service or favor for. [Middle English *obligen*, from Old French *obliger*, from Latin *obligare* : *ob*, to + *ligare*, to bind.] —**o·blig′er** *n.*

o·blig·ing (ə-blī′jĭng) *adj.* Ready to do favors for others; accommodating. —**o·blig′ing·ly** *adv.* —**o·blig′ing·ness** *n.*

o·blique (ō-blēk′, ə-blēk′) *adj.* **1. a.** Having a slanting or sloping direction, course, or position; inclined. **b.** *Geom.* Designating lines or planes that are neither parallel nor perpendicular. **2.** Indirect or evasive; not straightforward. —*n.* Something oblique. [Middle English *oblike*, from Latin *obliquus*.] —**o·blique′ly** *adv.* —**o·blique′ness** *n.* —**o·bliq′ui·ty** *n.*

oblique angle. An acute or obtuse angle.

o·blit·er·ate (ə-blĭt′ə-rāt′) *tr.v.* **-at·ed, -at·ing.** To do away with completely; wipe out. [From Latin *obliterare*, to erase : *ob*, away from + *littera*, letter.] —**o·blit′er·a′tion** *n.* —**o·blit′er·a·tive** (ə-blĭt′ə-rā′tĭv, -ər-ə-tĭv) *adj.* —**o·blit′er·a·tor** *n.*

o·bliv·i·on (ə-blĭv′ē-ən) *n.* **1.** The condition of being completely forgotten. **2.** The act or an example of forgetting. [Middle English, from Old French, from Latin *oblivio*, from *oblivisci*, to forget.]

o·bliv·i·ous (ə-blĭv′ē-əs) *adj.* **1.** Lacking all memory or attentiveness; forgetful. **2.** Unaware or unmindful: *He sped along, oblivious to danger.* —See Syns at **ignorant.** —**o·bliv′i·ous·ly** *adv.* —**o·bliv′i·ous·ness** *n.*

ob·long (ŏb′lông′, -lŏng′) *adj.* **1.** Having greater length in one direction than in the other and the opposite sides parallel to each other; rectangular. **2.** *Bot.* Having a somewhat elongated form with approximately parallel sides. [Middle English *oblonge*, from Latin *oblongus* : *ob* (intensive) + *longus*, long.] —**ob′long** *n.*

ob·lo·quy (ŏb′lə-kwē) *n., pl.* **-quies.** **1.** Abusive or slanderous language. **2.** Ill repute; disgrace. [Middle English *obloqui*, from Late Latin *obloquium*, from Latin *obloqui*, to speak against : *ob*, against + *loqui*, to speak.]

ob·nox·ious (ŏb-nŏk′shəs, əb-) *adj.* Highly disagreeable or offensive; odious. [Latin *obnoxiosus*, injurious, from *obnoxius*, subject to harm : *ob*, to + *noxa*, a hurt.] —**ob·nox′ious·ly** *adv.* —**ob·nox′ious·ness** *n.*

o·boe (ō′bō) *n.* A slender woodwind instrument with a conical bore and a double-reed mouthpiece. [Italian, from French *hautbois*.] —**o′bo·ist** *n.*

ă pat   ā pay   â care   ä father   ĕ pet   ē be   hw which
ōō took   ōō boot   ou out   th thin   th this   ŭ cut

I pit   ī tie   î pier   ŏ pot   ō toe   ô paw, for   oi noise
û urge   zh vision   ə about, item, edible, gallop, circus

ob·scene (ŏb-sēn', əb-) *adj.* **1.** Offensive to decency or modesty. **2.** Inciting lustful feelings; lewd. **3.** Repulsive to the senses. [Old French, from Latin *obscēnus*, inauspicious, repulsive.] —**ob·scene'ly** *adv.*

ob·scen·i·ty (ŏb-sĕn'ĭ-tē, əb-) *n.*, *pl.* **-ties. 1.** The quality or condition of being obscene. **2.** Something that is obscene.

ob·scur·ant·ism (ŏb-skyōŏr'ən-tĭz'əm, əb-, ŏb'skyōŏ-răn'-tĭz'əm) *n.* Opposition to free inquiry or the advancement of knowledge. —**ob·scur'ant·ist** *n. & adj.*

ob·scure (ŏb-skyōŏr', əb-) *adj.* **-scur·er, -scur·est. 1.** Lacking in light; dark; gloomy. **2.** Not easily perceived; indistinct; faint. **3.** Not easily discovered; remote; hidden: *an obscure retreat.* **4.** Not famous or well-known; humble: *an obscure country priest.* **5.** Not clearly expressed or understood: *the obscure workings of nature.* —See Syns at **dark.** —*tr.v.* **-scured, -scur·ing. 1.** To darken. **2.** To conceal from view; hide. **3.** To make less clear or distinct. [Middle English, from Old French *obscur*, from Latin *obscūrus*.] —**ob·scure'ly** *adv.* —**ob·scure'ness** *n.*

ob·scu·ri·ty (ŏb-skyōŏr'ə-tē, əb-) *n.*, *pl.* **-ties.** The quality or condition of being obscure.

ob·se·qui·ous (ŏb-sē'kwē-əs, əb-) *adj.* Excessively eager to serve, obey, or ingratiate oneself; fawning. [Middle English, from Latin *obsequiōsus*, from *obsequium*, compliance, from *obsequī*, to comply with : *ob*, to + *sequī*, to follow.] —**ob·se'qui·ous·ly** *adv.* —**ob·se'qui·ous·ness** *n.*

ob·se·quy (ŏb'sĭ-kwē) *n.*, *pl.* **-quies.** A funeral rite or ceremony. [Middle English *obseque*, from Old French, from Medieval Latin *obsequiae*, from Latin *obsequium*, compliance, service.]

ob·serv·ance (əb-zûr'vəns) *n.* **1.** A customary act, ceremony, or practice. **2.** The act or custom of keeping or following a custom, ritual, or practice. **3.** The action of watching attentively; observation.

ob·serv·ant (əb-zûr'vənt) *adj.* **1.** Quick to observe or take notice; alert. **2.** Diligent in observing a law, custom, duty, or principle. —See Syns at **alert.** —**ob·serv'ant·ly** *adv.*

ob·ser·va·tion (ŏb'zər-vā'shən) *n.* **1. a.** The act of observing. **b.** The condition of being observed. **2.** Something that has been observed. **3.** A comment; remark. —*modifier: an observation deck.* —**ob'ser·va'tion·al** *adj.* —**ob'ser·va'tion·al·ly** *adv.*

ob·ser·va·to·ry (əb-zûr'və-tôr'ē, -tōr'ē) *n.*, *pl.* **-ries. 1.** A building designed and equipped for making observations of astronomical, meteorological, or other natural phenomena. **2.** A structure overlooking an extensive view.

ob·serve (əb-zûrv') *v.* **-served, -serv·ing.** —*tr.v.* **1.** To perceive; notice. **2.** To watch attentively. **3.** To make a systematic or scientific observation of. **4.** To say by way of comment or remark. **5.** To adhere to or abide by: *observe the terms of a contract.* **6.** To keep or celebrate according to custom: *observe an anniversary.* —*intr.v.* **1.** To take notice. **2.** To make a comment or remark. —See Syns at **watch.** [Middle English *observen*, from Old French *observer*, from Latin *observāre*, to pay attention to : *ob*, to + *servāre*, to watch.] —**ob·serv'a·ble** *adj.* —**ob·serv'a·ble·ness** *n.* —**ob·serv'a·bly** *adv.*

ob·serv·er (əb-zûr'vər) *n.* **1.** Someone who observes. **2.** A delegate who observes but does not participate.

ob·sess (əb-sĕs') *tr.v.* To preoccupy the mind of excessively: *obsessed by his quest for the white whale.* [Latin *obsessus*, past part. of *obsidēre*, to beset : *ob*, on + *sedēre*, to sit.]

ob·ses·sion (əb-sĕsh'ən, ŏb-) *n.* **1.** An excessive preoccupation with an idea or emotion. **2.** An often unreasonable idea or emotion that is the cause of an obsession. —**ob·ses'sion·al** *adj.* —**ob·ses'sive** *adj.* —**ob·ses'sive·ly** *adv.*

ob·sid·i·an (ŏb-sĭd'ē-ən) *n.* An acid-resistant, lustrous volcanic glass, usu. black or banded and displaying curved, shiny surfaces when fractured. [Latin *obsidiānus (lapis)*, alteration of *obsiānus (lapis)*, stone of Obsius, its supposed discoverer.]

ob·so·les·cent (ŏb'sə-lĕs'ənt) *adj.* Passing out of use or usefulness; becoming obsolete. [Latin *obsolēscēns*, pres. part. of *obsolēscere*, to grow old.] —**ob'so·les'cence** *n.* —**ob'so·les'cent·ly** *adv.*

ob·so·lete (ŏb'sə-lēt', ŏb'sə-lēt') *adj.* **1.** No longer in use: *an obsolete word.* **2.** No longer useful; outmoded; worn out. [Latin *obsolētus*, from *obsolescere*, to wear out, grow old.]

—**ob'so·lete'ly** *adv.* —**ob'so·lete'ness** *n.*

ob·sta·cle (ŏb'stə-kəl) *n.* Something that stands in the way of or holds up progress toward a goal. [Middle English, from Old French, from Latin *obstāculum*, from *obstāre*, to hinder : *ob*, against + *stāre*, to stand.]

ob·stet·ric (ŏb-stĕt'rĭk, əb-) or **ob·stet·ri·cal** (ŏb-stĕt'rĭ-kəl, əb-) *adj.* Of or relating to obstetrics. [Latin *obstetrīcius*, from *obstetrīx*, midwife, from *obstāre*, to stand before : *ob*, before + *stāre*, to stand.] —**ob·stet'ri·cal·ly** *adv.*

ob·ste·tri·cian (ŏb'stĭ-trĭsh'ən) *n.* A physician specializing in obstetrics.

ob·stet·rics (ŏb-stĕt'rĭks, əb-) *n.* *(used with a sing. verb).* The branch of medicine concerned with childbirth and the care of women during and after pregnancy.

ob·sti·na·cy (ŏb'stə-nə-sē) *n.*, *pl.* **-cies. 1.** The condition or quality of being obstinate. **2.** An instance of stubbornness.

ob·sti·nate (ŏb'stə-nĭt) *adj.* **1.** Firmly adhering to an attitude, opinion, or course of action in spite of argument or entreaty. **2.** Difficult to manage, control, or subdue. [Middle English *obstinat*, from Latin *obstinātus*, past part. of *obstināre*, to persist.] —**ob'sti·nate·ly** *adv.* —**ob'sti·nate·ness** *n.*

Syns: obstinate, bullheaded, dogged, hardheaded, headstrong, intractable, perverse, pigheaded, refractory, stubborn, tough, willful *adj.* *Core meaning:* Tenaciously unwilling to yield (*an obstinate person who never apologized*).

ob·strep·er·ous (əb-strĕp'ər-əs, ŏb-) *adj.* **1.** Defiant; unruly. **2.** Noisy; boisterous. [Latin *obstreperus*, from *obstrepere*, to make noise against : *ob*, against + *strepere*, to make noise.] —**ob·strep'er·ous·ly** *adv.* —**ob·strep'er·ous·ness** *n.*

ob·struct (əb-strŭkt', ŏb-) *tr.v.* **1.** To block or fill with obstacles; make impassable. **2.** To interfere with; impede. **3.** To block or cut off from view. —See Syns at **hinder.** [Latin *obstructus*, past part. of *obstruere* : *ob*, against + *struere*, to pile up.] —**ob·struct'er** or **ob·struc'tor** *n.* —**ob·struc'tive** *adj.*

ob·struc·tion (əb-strŭk'shən, ŏb-) *n.* **1.** Something or someone that gets in the way; obstacle. **2.** The act or an instance of impeding or obstructing.

ob·struc·tion·ist (əb-strŭk'shə-nĭst, ŏb-) *n.* Someone who systematically obstructs or interrupts progress or normal procedure. —**ob·struc'tion·ism** *n.*

ob·tain (əb-tān', ŏb-) *tr.v.* To get or acquire as the result of planning or endeavor. —*intr.v.* To be established, accepted, or customary. [Middle English *obteinen*, from Old French *obtenir*, from Latin *obtinēre* : *ob* (intensive) + *tenēre*, to hold.] —**ob·tain'a·ble** *adj.* —**ob·tain'er** *n.*

ob·trude (əb-trood', ŏb-) *v.* **-trud·ed, -trud·ing.** —*tr.v.* **1.** To force upon others with undue insistence or without invitation. **2.** To thrust out; push forward. —*intr.v.* To force oneself upon others or upon their attention. [Latin *obtrudere* : *ob*, against + *trūdere*, to thrust.] —**ob·trud'er** *n.* —**ob·tru'sion** (əb-troo'zhən, ŏb-) *n.*

ob·tru·sive (əb-troo'sĭv, -zĭv, ŏb-) *adj.* Tending to obtrude; intrusive. [From Latin *obtrūdere*, to obtrude.] —**ob·tru'sive·ly** *adv.* —**ob·tru'sive·ness** *n.*

ob·tuse (ŏb-toos', -tyoos', əb-) *adj.* **1. a.** Not sharp or pointed; blunt. **b.** Not acute or intense; dull. **2.** Lacking astuteness or discernment; slow to apprehend or perceive. —See Syns at **stupid.** [Latin *obtūsus*, past part. of *obtundere*, to blunt.] —**ob·tuse'ly** *adv.* —**ob·tuse'ness** *n.*

obtuse angle. An angle greater than 90 degrees and less than 180 degrees.

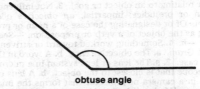

obtuse angle

ob·verse (ŏb-vûrs', əb-, ŏb'vûrs') *adj.* **1.** Facing or turned toward the observer. **2.** Serving as a counterpart or complement. —*n.* (ŏb'vûrs', ŏb-vûrs', əb-). **1.** The side, as of a coin or medal, that bears the principal stamp or design.

2. A counterpart or complement. [Latin *obversus*, past part. of *obvertere*, to turn toward, obvert.] —**ob·verse′ly** *adv.*

ob·vi·ate (ŏb′vē-āt′) *tr.v.* **-at·ed, -at·ing.** To prevent by making unnecessary. [Late Latin *obviāre*, to prevent, from Latin *obviam*, in the way.] —**ob′vi·a′tion** *n.* —**ob′vi·a′tor** *n.*

ob·vi·ous (ŏb′vē-əs) *adj.* Easily perceived or understood; quite apparent: *an obvious lie.* [Latin *obvius*, from *obviam*, in the way : *ob*, against + *via*, way.] —**ob′vi·ous·ly** *adv.* —**ob′vi·ous·ness** *n.*

oc·a·ri·na (ŏk′ə-rē′nə) *n.* A small wind instrument having a flutelike tone, with a mouthpiece, finger holes, and an ovoid shape. [Italian, "little goose" (from its shape).]

oc·ca·sion (ə-kā′zhən) *n.* **1. a.** An event or happening. **b.** The time at which something occurs. **2.** A significant or special event. **3.** An appropriate or favorable time; opportunity. **4.** That which brings on an action or event; immediate cause: *His entrance was the occasion for hearty laughter.* **5.** Ground; reason. —See Syns at **opportunity.** —*tr.v.* To provide occasion for; cause. —*idiom.* **on occasion.** From time to time. [Middle English *occasioun*, from Old French *occasion*, from Latin *occāsiō*, from *occidere*, to fall down : *ob*, down + *cadere*, to fall.]

oc·ca·sion·al (ə-kā′zhə-nəl) *adj.* **1.** Occurring from time to time: *occasional showers.* **2.** Occurring on or created for a special occasion: *occasional verse.* —**oc·ca′sion·al·ly** *adv.*

Oc·ci·dent (ŏk′sĭ-dənt, -dĕnt′) *n.* The countries of Europe and the Western Hemisphere. [Middle English, from Old French, from Latin *occīdēns*, from *occidere*, to fall down, set.]

oc·ci·den·tal (ŏk′sĭ-dĕn′tl) *adj.* Often **Occidental.** Of or relating to the countries of the Occident, their peoples, or their culture; western. —*n.* Often **Occidental.** A member of a people of the Occident.

oc·cip·i·tal (ŏk-sĭp′ĭ-tl) *adj.* Of the occiput or the occipital bone. —*n.* The occipital bone.

occipital bone. A curved, trapezoidal, compound bone that forms the lower posterior part of the skull.

oc·ci·put (ŏk′sə-pət) *n., pl.* **oc·cip·i·ta** (ŏk-sĭp′ĭ-tə) or **-puts.** The back of the skull, esp. the occipital area. [Latin : *ob*, in back of + *caput*, head.]

oc·clude (ə-klōōd′) *v.* **-clud·ed, -clud·ing.** —*tr.v.* **1.** To cause to become closed; obstruct. **2.** To shut in, out, or off. **3.** *Chem.* To absorb or adsorb in great quantity. —*intr.v.* To close so that the opposing tooth surfaces meet. [Latin *occlūdere* : *ob* (intensive) + *claudere*, to close.]

occluded front. *Meteorol.* The air front established when a cold front overtakes a warm front and forces the warm air upward.

oc·clu·sion (ə-klōō′zhən) *n.* **1. a.** The action of occluding or being occluded. **b.** Something that occludes or blocks. **2.** *Meteorol.* An occluded front.

oc·cult (ə-kŭlt′, ŏ-kŭlt′, ŏk′ŭlt′) *adj.* **1.** Of or relating to supernatural influences, phenomena, or knowledge. **2.** Beyond human understanding; mysterious. **3.** Not divulged; secret. [Latin *occultus*, past part. of *occulere*, to conceal.] —**oc·cult′ly** *adv.* —**oc·cult′ness** *n.*

oc·cul·ta·tion (ŏk′əl-tā′shən) *n.* **1.** *Astron.* A process in which a celestial body blocks a second celestial body from view. **2.** The condition of being hidden from sight.

oc·cult·ism (ə-kŭl′tĭz′əm, ŏ-kŭl′-, ŏk′əl-tĭz′əm) *n.* **1.** The study of the supernatural. **2.** A belief in supernatural or occult powers. —**oc·cult′ist** *n.*

oc·cu·pan·cy (ŏk′yə-pən-sē) *n., pl.* **-cies. 1.** The act of occupying or the condition of being occupied. **2.** The period during which something is occupied.

oc·cu·pant (ŏk′yə-pənt) *n.* Someone that occupies a position or place.

oc·cu·pa·tion (ŏk′yə-pā′shən) *n.* **1. a.** An activity that is one's business or profession; vocation. **b.** An activity that keeps one busy: *Gardening was one of her summertime occupations.* **2. a.** The act or process of occupying. **b.** The condition of being occupied. **3.** The seizing, holding, and control of a nation or territory by a foreign military force. —See Syns at **work.** —*modifier:* occupation forces. —**oc′cu·pa′tion·al** *adj.* —**oc′cu·pa′tion·al·ly** *adv.*

occupational therapy. Therapy in which the principal element is some form of productive or creative activity.

oc·cu·py (ŏk′yə-pī′) *tr.v.* **-pied, -py·ing. 1.** To seize or hold

possession of. **2.** To fill up (time or space): *a lecture that occupied three hours.* **3.** To dwell or reside in; be a tenant of. **4.** To engage or employ the efforts or attention of: *occupied himself with a mystery story.* [Middle English *occupien*, from Old French *occuper*, from Latin *occupāre*, to seize : *ob* (intensive) + *capere*, to take.] —**oc′cu·pi′er** *n.*

oc·cur (ə-kûr′) *intr.v.* **-curred, -cur·ring. 1.** To take place; come about. **2.** To be found; appear. **3.** To come to mind; suggest itself. [Latin *occurrere*, to run to meet : *ob*, toward + *currere*, to run.]

oc·cur·rence (ə-kûr′əns, ə-kŭr′-) *n.* **1.** An act of occurring. **2.** Something that takes place.

o·cean (ō′shən) *n.* **1.** The entire body of salt water that covers about 72 per cent of the earth's surface. **2.** Any of the principal divisions of this body of water: *the Atlantic Ocean.* **3.** Any great expanse or amount: *oceans of money.* —*modifier:* ocean currents. [Middle English *ocean*, from Old French, from Latin *ōceanus*, from Greek *ōkeanos*, *Oceanus*.] —**o′ce·an′ic** *adj.*

o·cean·ar·i·um (ō′shə-nâr′ē-əm) *n., pl.* **-i·ums** or **-i·a** (-ē-ə). A large aquarium for the study or display of saltwater life.

o·cean·og·ra·phy (ō′shə-nŏg′rə-fē) *n.* The exploration and scientific study of the ocean and its phenomena. —**o′cean·og′ra·pher** *n.* —**o′cean·o·graph′ic** (ō′shə-nə-grăf′ĭk) or **o′cean·o·graph′i·cal** *adj.*

o·cel·lus (ō-sĕl′əs) *n., pl.* **o·cel·li** (ō-sĕl′ī′). **1.** A small simple eye, found in many invertebrates. **2.** A marking that resembles an eye. [From Latin, dim. of *oculus*, eye.] —**o·cel′lar** (ō-sĕl′ər) *adj.*

oc·e·lot (ŏs′ə-lŏt′, ō′sə-) *n.* A brush- and forest-dwelling cat, *Felis pardalis*, of the southwestern United States and Central and South America, with a tawny-grayish or yellow coat with black spots. [French, from Nahuatl *ocelotl*.]

ocelot

o·cher (ō′kər) *n.* Also **o·chre. 1.** Any of several earthy mineral oxides of iron occurring in yellow, brown, or red, used as pigments. **2.** A yellowish or brownish orange. —*adj.* Yellowish or brownish orange. [Middle English *oker*, from Old French *ocre*, from Latin *ōchra*, from Greek *ōkhra*, from *ōkhros*, yellow.] —**o′cher·ous** (ō′kər-əs) or **o′cher·y** (ō′krē) *adj.*

o′clock (ə-klŏk′) *adv.* **1.** Of or according to the clock: *three o'clock.* **2.** According to an imaginary clock dial with the observer at the center and 12 o'clock considered as straight ahead in horizontal position or straight up in vertical position: *enemy planes approaching at 10 o'clock.* [Short for *of the clock.*]

o·co·ti·llo (ō′kə-tē′yō, -tēl′-) *n., pl.* **-llos.** A cactuslike tree, *Fouquieria splendens*, of Mexico and the southwestern United States, having clusters of scarlet tubular flowers. Also called **candlewood.** [Mexican Spanish, dim. of *ocote*, a Mexican pine, from Nahuatl *ocotl*, torch.]

oct-. Var. of **octo-.**

octa-. Var. of **octo-.**

oc·ta·gon (ŏk′tə-gŏn′) *n.* A polygon with eight sides and angles. —**oc·tag′o·nal** *adj.* —**oc·tag′o·nal·ly** *adv.*

oc·ta·he·dron (ŏk′tə-hē′drən) *n., pl.* **-drons** or **-dra** (-drə). A solid geometric figure bounded by eight planes.

oc·tane (ŏk′tān′) *n.* **1.** Any of various isomeric paraffin hydrocarbons with the formula C_8H_{18}. **2.** A colorless, inflammable hydrocarbon, $CH_3(CH_2)_6CH_3$, found in petroleum, and used as a solvent. **3.** Octane number.

octane number. A number that measures the antiknock rating of gasoline, based on the percentage of a particular

---

form of octane that is contained in a reference standard to which the sample of gasoline is comparable.

oc·tant (ŏk′tənt) *n.* **1. a.** One-eighth of the arc of a circle; an arc of 45 degrees. **b.** One-eighth of the area of a circle; the area bounded by a pair of radii and an arc of 45 degrees that they intercept. **2.** A navigation instrument similar to a sextant but based on an arc of 45 degrees rather than 60 degrees. [Latin *octans*, half-quadrant, from *octō*, eight.]

oc·tave (ŏk′tĭv, -tāv′) *n.* **1.** *Mus.* **a.** The interval of eight diatonic degrees between two tones, one of which has twice as many vibrations per second as the other. **b.** A tone that is eight full tones above or below another given tone. **c.** A series of tones included within this interval. **2.** *Eccles.* The entire period between a feast day and the eighth day following it. **3.** Any group or series of eight. **4.** *Pros.* **a.** A stanza of eight lines. **b.** An **octet.** [Middle English, the eighth day (after a festival), from Medieval Latin *octāva (diēs)*, from Latin *octō*, eight.]

oc·ta·vo (ŏk-tā′vō, -tä′-) *n., pl.* **-vos. 1.** The page size (from 5 × 8 inches to 6 × 9¹⁄₂ inches) of a book composed of printer's sheets folded into eight leaves. **2.** A book composed of pages of this size. —*modifier: an octavo edition.* [Latin *(in) octāvō,* "in an eighth," from *octāvus,* eighth.]

oc·ten·ni·al (ŏk-tĕn′ē-əl) *adj.* **1.** Happening or recurring every eight years. **2.** Lasting eight years. [From Late Latin *octennium,* period of eight years.] —**oc·ten′ni·al·ly** *adv.*

oc·tet (ŏk-tĕt′) *n.* Also **oc·tette. 1.** A musical composition written for eight voices or eight instruments. **2.** A group of eight singers or eight instrumentalists. **3.** Any group of eight. **4.** *Pros.* The first eight lines of an Italian sonnet; octave. [Italian *ottetto,* from *otto,* eight, from Latin *octō.*]

oc·til·lion (ŏk-tĭl′yən) *n.* **1.** The cardinal number represented by the figure 1 followed by 27 zeros; usu. written 10²⁷. **2.** *Brit.* The cardinal number represented by the figure 1 followed by 48 zeros; usu. written 10⁴⁸. [OCT(O)- + (M)ILLION.]

octo- or **octa-** or **oct-.** A prefix meaning eight: **octane.** [From Latin *octō,* eight, and Greek *oktō.*]

Oc·to·ber (ŏk-tō′bər) *n. Abbr.* **Oct.** The tenth month of the year. [Middle English *octobre,* from Old French, from Latin *Octōber,* "eighth month," from *octō,* eight.]

oc·to·ge·nar·i·an (ŏk′tə-jə-nâr′ē-ən) *n.* A person between eighty and ninety years of age. [From Latin *octōgēnārius,* containing eighty, from *octōgintā,* eighty.]

oc·to·pus (ŏk′tə-pəs) *n., pl.* **-pus·es** or **oc·to·pi** (ŏk′tə-pī′). **1.** Any of numerous carnivorous, nocturnal, marine mollusks of the genus *Octopus,* or related genera, with a rounded, saclike body, eight tentacles, each bearing two rows of suckers, a large distinct head, and a strong beaklike mouth. Also called **devilfish. 2.** Any powerful and far-reaching organization, such as a large corporation. [From Greek *oktōpous,* eight-footed.]

octopus

oc·u·lar (ŏk′yə-lər) *adj.* **1.** Of or having to do with the eye or the vision. **2.** Seen by the eye; visual: *ocular evidence.* —*n.* The eyepiece of a microscope, telescope, etc. [Late Latin *oculāris,* from Latin *oculus,* eye.]

oc·u·list (ŏk′yə-lĭst) *n.* **1.** An ophthalmologist. **2.** An optometrist. [French *oculiste,* from Latin *oculus,* eye.]

odd (ŏd) *adj.* **odd·er, odd·est. 1. a.** Strange, unusual, or peculiar: *an odd name.* **b.** Eccentric in conduct. **2.** Not fitting into a recognized class or category; miscellaneous. **3.** Irregular; occasional: *at odd moments.* **4.** Being one of

an incomplete pair or set: *an odd shoe.* **5.** *Math.* Designating an integer not divisible by two: *1, 3,* and *5 are odd numbers.* —See Syns at **strange.** —*n.* Anything odd. [Middle English *odde,* from Old Norse *oddi,* triangle, odd number.] —**odd′ly** *adv.* —**odd′ness** *n.*

odd·ball (ŏd′bôl′) *n. Informal.* An eccentric person.

odd·i·ty (ŏd′ĭ-tē) *n., pl.* **-ties. 1.** Someone or something that is odd or strange. **2.** The condition of being odd; strangeness: *the oddity of human behavior.*

odd·ment (ŏd′mənt) *n.* Something left over; remnant.

odds (ŏdz) *pl.n.* **1.** An advantage given beforehand to a weaker side in a contest to equalize the chances of all participants. **2.** A ratio expressing the probability of an event or outcome. **3.** A ratio between the amount of a bet and the amount to be paid for winning the bet: *odds of ten to one.* **4.** The likelihood that one thing will occur rather than another: *The odds are that he will win on the first ballot.* **5.** Difference. —*idiom.* **at odds.** In disagreement; in conflict. [Pl. of ODD.]

odds and ends. Miscellaneous items.

ode (ōd) *n.* A usu. rhymed lyric poem characterized by exalted style and complex form. [French, from Old French, from Late Latin *ōdē,* from Greek *aoidē,* song.]

-ode¹. A suffix meaning a way or path: **electrode.** [Greek *-odos,* from *hodos,* a way.]

-ode². A suffix meaning resemblance or characteristic nature: **nematode.** [Greek *-ōdēs,* from *eidos,* form, shape.]

O·din (ō′dĭn) *n. Norse Myth.* The ruler of the gods and creator of the universe and man.

o·di·ous (ō′dē-əs) *adj.* Exciting hatred or repugnance. —**o′di·ous·ly** *adv.* —**o′di·ous·ness** *n.*

o·di·um (ō′dē-əm) *n.* **1.** The condition or quality of being odious. **2.** Strong dislike; contempt or aversion. **3.** The disgrace resulting from hateful conduct. [Latin, hatred, from *odisse,* to hate.]

o·dom·e·ter (ō-dŏm′ĭ-tər) *n.* An instrument that measures and indicates distance traveled by a vehicle. [French *odomètre,* from Greek *hodometron* : *hodos,* road, journey + *metron,* measure.]

o·don·tol·o·gy (ō′dŏn-tŏl′ə-jē) *n.* The study of the anatomy, growth, and diseases of the teeth. [Greek *odous,* tooth + -LOGY.] —**o·don′to·log′i·cal** (ō-dŏn′tə-lŏj′ĭ-kəl) *adj.* —**o·don′to·log′i·cal·ly** *adv.* —**o′don·tol′o·gist** *n.*

o·dor (ō′dər) *n.* Also *Brit.* **o·dour. 1.** The property or quality of a thing that is perceived by the sense of smell; scent. **2.** Any sensation, stimulation, or perception of the sense of smell. **3.** A strong, pervasive quality. **4.** Esteem; repute: *a doctrine that is not currently in good odor.* [Middle English *odour,* from Old French, from Latin *odor.*]

o·dor·if·er·ous (ō′də-rĭf′ər-əs) *adj.* Having or giving off an odor. [From Latin *odōrifer* : *odor,* odor + *ferre,* to bear.] —**o′dor·if′er·ous·ly** *adv.* —**o′dor·if′er·ous·ness** *n.*

o·dor·less (ō′dər-lĭs) *adj.* Having no odor. —**o′dor·less·ly** *adv.*

o·dor·ous (ō′dər-əs) *adj.* Having a distinctive odor. —**o′dor·ous·ly** *adv.* —**o′dor·ous·ness** *n.*

o·dour (ō′dər) *n. Brit.* Var. of **odor.**

O·dys·seus (ō-dĭs′yōōs′, ō-dĭs′ē-əs) *n.* Latin name, **U·lys·ses** (yōō-lĭs′ēz). *Gk. Myth.* The cunning king of Ithaca, a leader of the Greeks in the Trojan War, whose return home after the war was for ten years frustrated by the enmity of Poseidon.

od·ys·sey (ŏd′ĭ-sē) *n.* A long, adventurous wandering. [After ODYSSEUS.]

Oed·i·pus (ĕd′ə-pəs, ē′də-) *n. Gk. Myth.* A son of Laius and Jocasta, who was abandoned at birth and who unwittingly killed his father and married his mother.

Oedipus complex. *Psychoanal.* Libidinal feelings in a child, esp. a male child, for the parent of the opposite sex. —**oed′i·pal** *adj.*

o'er (ôr, ōr) *prep. & adv. Poet.* Over.

oer·sted (ûr′stəd) *n. Abbr.* **Oe** The centimeter-gram-second electromagnetic unit of magnetic intensity, equal to the magnetic intensity one centimeter from a unit magnetic pole. [After Hans Christian *Oersted* (1777–1851), Danish physicist.]

oe·soph·a·gus (ĭ-sŏf′ə-gəs) *n.* Var. of **esophagus.**

of (ŭv, ŏv; əv *when unstressed*) *prep.* **1.** Derived or coming from; originating at or from: *men of the north.* **2.** Caused by; resulting from: *his death of tuberculosis.* **3.** Away from; at a distance from: *a mile east of here.* **4.** So as to be separated or relieved from: *robbed of his dignity; cured of distemper.* **5.** From the total or group comprising: *give of one's time; two of his friends; most of the cases.* **6.** Composed or made from: *a dress of silk.* **7.** Associated with or adhering to: *a man of your religion.* **8.** Belonging or connected to: *the rungs of a ladder.* **9.** Possessing; having: *a man of honor.* **10.** Containing or carrying: *a basket of groceries.* **11.** Specified as; named or called: *a depth of ten feet; the Garden of Eden.* **12.** Centering upon; directed toward: *a love of horses.* **13.** Produced by; issuing from: *products of the vine.* **14.** Characterized or identified by: *a year of famine.* **15.** Concerning; with reference to; about: *think highly of his proposals; speak of it later.* **16.** Set aside for; taken up by: *a day of rest.* **17.** Before; until: *five minutes of ten.* **18.** During or on: *of recent years.* **19.** By: *beloved of his family.* [Middle English, from Old English.]

 Usage: **of.** When it indicates possession or association, *of* is followed by either an uninflected noun (*friend of my brother; parts of a machine*) or by a noun or pronoun in the possessive case (*friend of my brother's; a son of hers*).

off (ôf, ŏf) *adv.* **1.** At or to a distance from a nearer place; away: *drive off.* **2.** Distant in space or time: *a mile off; a week off.* **3.** So as to be no longer on, attached, or connected: *shaved off his mustache.* **4.** So as to be no longer continuing, operating, or functioning: *turn off the radio.* **5.** So as to be done completely and finally: *kill off the mice.* **6.** So as to be smaller, fewer, or less: *Sales dropped off.* **7.** Away from work or duty: *They took a day off.* —*adj.* **1.** Distant or removed; remote; farther: *the off side of the barn.* **2.** Not on, attached, or connected: *with his shoes off.* **3.** Not continuing, operating, or functioning. **4.** No longer existing or effective; canceled: *The wedding is off.* **5.** Not up to standard; below a normal or satisfactory level: *Your pitching is off today.* **6.** Inconsistent with accuracy or truth; in error: *My guess was slightly off.* **7.** Absent or away from work or duty. **8.** On the right side of a vehicle or draft team: *The off horse is lame.* **9.** *Naut.* Seaward; farthest from the shore. —*prep.* **1.** So as to be removed or distant from (a position of rest or support): *The bird hopped off the branch.* **2.** Away or relieved from: *off duty.* **3. a.** By consuming: *living off locusts and honey.* **b.** With the means provided by: *living off his pension.* **4.** Extending or branching out from: *an artery off the heart.* **5.** Deviating from; not up to the standard of: *off his game.* **6.** Abstaining from: *He went off narcotics.* **7.** Seaward of: *a mile off Sandy Hook.* —*tr.v.* Slang. To take the life of. —See Syns at **murder.** —*idiom.* **off and on.** Intermittently: *She slept off and on.* [Middle English, from Old English *of.*]

 Usage: **off.** **1.** *off* + *of* occurs in informal English and was once standard in earlier American writing and speech: *took the book off of the shelf.* While the expression is still not wrong, a more concise wording esp. in formal composition is: *took the book off the shelf.* **2.** *off* + *from* also occurs in American English but more often in British English: *got off from work at five o'clock.* This expression is acceptable, as is the more concise alternative: *got off work at five o'clock.* **3.** American grammarians gen. disapprove the use of *off* in expressions indicating a source: *got a loan from* (not *off*) *him.*

of·fal (ô'fəl, ŏf'əl) *n.* **1.** Waste parts, esp. of a butchered animal. **2.** Refuse; rubbish. [Middle English, from Middle Dutch *afval*, refuse : *af*, off + *vallen*, to fall.]

off·beat (ôf'bēt', ŏf'-) *n.* An unaccented beat in a musical measure. —*adj.* (ôf'bēt', ŏf'-). *Slang.* Unconventional.

off chance. A remote or slight chance.

off-col·or (ôf'kŭl'ər, ŏf'-) *adj.* **1.** Varying from the usual, expected, or required color. **2.** Improper; in bad taste.

of·fence (ə-fĕns') *n. Brit.* Var. of **offense.**

of·fend (ə-fĕnd') *tr.v.* **1.** To create or excite anger, resentment, or annoyance in; affront. **2.** To be displeasing or disagreeable to. —*intr.v.* **1.** To cause displeasure or annoyance. **2.** To violate a moral or divine law; to sin. —See Syns at **insult.** [Middle English *offenden*, from Old French *offendre*, from Latin *offendere*, to strike against.]

of·fense (ə-fĕns') *n.* Also *Brit.* **of·fence. 1.** The act of offend-

ing. **2.** Any violation of a legal, moral, or social code; sin. **3.** Something that offends. **4.** (ŏf'ĕns'). The act of attacking or assaulting. **5.** (ŏf'ĕns'). The attacker, as in a game or contest. [Middle English, from Old French, from Latin *offensa*, from *offendere*, to offend.]

of·fen·sive (ə-fĕn'sĭv) *adj.* **1.** Disagreeable to the senses: *an offensive odor.* **2.** Causing anger, displeasure, or resentment; giving offense. **3.** Of, constituting, or characteristic of an attack; aggressive: *an offensive maneuver.* —See Syns at **unpleasant.** —*n.* **1.** An attitude of attack. **2.** An attack; assault. —**of·fen'sive·ly** *adv.* —**of·fen'sive·ness** *n.*

of·fer (ô'fər, ŏf'ər) *tr.v.* **1.** To present for acceptance or rejection: *offered him a drink.* **2.** To put forward for consideration; propose: *offer an opinion.* **3.** To present for sale. **4.** To propose as payment; to bid. **5.** To present as an act of worship: *offer up prayers.* **6.** To exhibit readiness or desire to do: *offered to escort her.* **7.** To provide; furnish. —*intr.v.* **1.** To present an offering in worship or devotion. **2.** To present itself; appear. —*n.* **1.** The act of offering: *an offer of assistance.* **2.** Something offered, such as a suggestion, proposal, bid, or recommendation. [Middle English *offeren*, ult. from Latin *offerre* : *ob*, to + *ferre*, to bring, carry.] —**of'fer·er** or **of'fer·or** *n.*

 Syns: **offer, extend, present, proffer, tender, volunteer** *v.* Core meaning: To put before another for acceptance or rejection (*offered us cookies; offer sympathy to a widow; offered her help*).

of·fer·ing (ô'fər-ĭng, ŏf'ər-) *n.* **1.** The act of making an offer. **2.** Something that is offered. **3.** A presentation made to a deity as an act of religious worship or sacrifice.

of·fer·to·ry (ô'fər-tôr'ē, -tōr'ē, ŏf'ər-) *n., pl.* **-ries. 1.** Often **Offertory. a.** The part of the Eucharist at which bread and wine are offered to God. **b.** A musical setting of the Offertory. **2.** A collection of offerings at a religious service. [Old French *offertoire*, from Medieval Latin *offertōrium*, from Latin *offerre*, to offer.]

off·hand (ôf'hănd', ŏf'-) *adv.* Without preparation or forethought. —*adj.* Also **off·hand·ed** (-hăn'dĭd). Said or done offhand. —**off'hand'ed·ly** *adv.* —**off'hand'ed·ness** *n.*

of·fice (ô'fĭs, ŏf'ĭs) *n.* **1. a.** A place in which business, clerical, or professional activities are conducted. **b.** The staff working in such a place. **2.** An assigned duty or function. **3.** A position of authority, duty, or trust, esp. in government: *the office of vice president.* **4. a.** A branch of the U.S. government ranking just below the departments. **b.** A major executive division of some governments, often headed by a cabinet minister. **5.** Often **offices.** A usu. beneficial act performed for another. **6.** A prescribed religious ceremony. —*modifier:* *office buildings; office work.* [Middle English, from Old French, from Latin *officium*, duty.]

of·fice·hold·er (ô'fĭs-hōl'dər, ŏf'ĭs-) *n.* A person who holds a public office.

of·fi·cer (ô'fĭ-sər, ŏf'ĭ-) *n.* **1.** A person who holds an office of authority or trust. **2.** A person holding a commission in the armed forces. **3.** A person licensed in the merchant marine as master, mate, chief engineer, or assistant engineer. **4.** A policeman.

of·fi·cial (ə-fĭsh'əl) *adj.* **1.** Of or relating to an office or post of authority. **2.** Authorized by a proper authority; authoritative: *official permission.* **3.** Holding office or serving in some public capacity; authorized to perform some special duty: *an official representative.* **4.** Characteristic of or befitting a person of authority. —*n.* **1.** A person who holds an office or position. **2.** A referee, as at a sports contest. —**of·fi'cial·dom** *n.* —**of·fi'cial·ly** *adv.*

of·fi·cial·ism (ə-fĭsh'ə-lĭz'əm) *n.* Rigid adherence to official regulations, procedures, and formalities.

of·fi·ci·ate (ə-fĭsh'ē-āt') *intr.v.* **-at·ed, -at·ing. 1.** To perform the duties and functions of an office or position of authority. **2.** To serve as a priest, minister, or rabbi at a religious service. **3.** To serve as referee or umpire in any of various sports. —**of·fi'ci·a'tion** *n.* —**of·fi'ci·a'tor** *n.*

of·fic·i·nal (ə-fĭs'ə-nəl) *adj.* Available without prescription. —*n.* An officinal drug. [Medieval Latin *officīnālis*, used or kept in a workshop, from Latin *officīna*, workshop, from *opifex*, workman : *opus*, work + *facere*, to do.]

of·fi·cious (ə-fĭsh'əs) *adj.* Excessively forward in offering one's services or advice to others. [Latin *officiōsus*, from

---

ă pat   ā pay   â care   ä father   ĕ pet   ē be   hw which
ŏŏ took   ōō boot   ou out   th thin   *th* this   ŭ cut

ĭ pit   ī tie   î pier   ŏ pot   ō toe   ô paw, for   oi noise
û urge   zh vision   ə about, item, edible, gallop, circus

officium, duty, service.] **—of·fi′cious·ly** *adv.* **—of·fi′cious·ness** *n.*

off·ing (ô′fĭng, ŏf′ĭng) *n.* **1.** The part of the sea that is distant yet visible from the shore. **2.** The near or immediate future. [From OFF.]

off·ish (ô′fĭsh, ŏf′ĭsh) *adj.* Inclined to be distant and reserved in manner; aloof. **—off′ish·ly** *adv.* **—off′ish·ness** *n.*

off·set (ôf′sĕt′, ŏf′-) *n.* **1.** Something that balances, counteracts, or compensates. **2.** Something deriving or originating but set off from something else. **3.** *Archit.* A ledge or recess in a wall, formed by a reduction in thickness above. **4.** *Bot.* A shoot that develops laterally at the base of a plant, often rooting to form a new plant. **5.** *Geol.* A spur of a range of mountains or hills. **6.** A bend, as in a pipe or bar, made so as to pass around an obstruction. **7.** *Printing.* **a. Offset** printing. **b.** The unintentional or faulty transfer of wet ink from a printed sheet. **—***tr.v.* (ôf-sĕt′, ŏf-) **-set,** **-set·ting.** **1.** To counterbalance or compensate for: *strengths that offset our weaknesses.* **2.** To make or form an offset in.

offset printing. A printing process in which the image to be printed is transferred first to the surface of a rotating cylinder and then onto the surface to be printed. Also called **offset.**

off·shoot (ôf′shoot′, ŏf′-) *n.* **1.** Something that branches out or derives its existence or origin from a particular source. **2.** A branch, descendant, or member of a family or social group. **3.** A lateral shoot from the main stem of a plant.

off·shore (ôf′shôr′, -shōr′, ŏf′-) *adj. & adv.* **1.** Away from the shore. **2.** At a distance from the shore.

off·side (ôf′sīd′, ŏf′-) *adj.* Also **off side. 1.** In front of the ball before the play in football has properly begun. **2.** Illegally ahead of the ball or puck in an attacking zone.

off·spring (ôf′sprĭng′, ŏf′-) *n., pl.* **offspring** or **-springs.** **1.** The young of an animal. **2.** Something that results from something else. **—See Syns at descendant.** [Middle English *ofspring,* from Old English *ofspring : of,* off + *springan,* to spring.]

off·stage (ôf′stāj′, ŏf′-) *adj. & adv.* Away from the area of a stage visible to the audience.

off-the-rec·ord (ôf′thə-rĕk′ərd, ŏf′-) *adj. & adv.* Not for publication or attribution.

off-white (ôf′hwīt′, -wīt′, ŏf′-) *n.* Grayish or yellowish white. **—off′-white′** *adj.*

oft (ôft, ŏft) *adv. Poet.* Often. [Middle English, from Old English.]

of·ten (ô′fən, ŏf′ən, ôf′tən, ŏf′-) *adv.* Frequently; many times. [Middle English, from *oft,* oft.]

of·ten·times (ô′fən-tīmz′, ŏf′ən-, ôf′tən-, ŏf′-) *adv.* Also **oft·times** (ôf′tīmz′, ŏf′, ŏft′tīmz′, ŏf′-) *adv.* Frequently; repeatedly.

o·gee (ō′jē′) *n. Archit.* **1.** A molding having in profile an S-shaped curve. **2.** An arch of two reversed curves meeting at a point. [Alteration of *ogive,* the diagonal rib of a vault, from French.]

o·gle (ō′gəl, ŏ′gəl) *tr.v.* **o·gled, o·gling.** To stare at impertinently, flirtatiously, or amorously. **—See Syns at gaze.** **—***n.* An impertinent or flirtatious stare. [Prob. from Low German *oegeln,* from *oegen,* to eye, from *oog,* eye.] **—o′gler** *n.*

o·gre (ō′gər) *n.* **1.** A fabled, man-eating giant or monster. **2.** A cruel, brutish, or hideous person. [French.] **—o′gre·ish** (ō′gər-ĭsh, ō′grĭsh) *adj.*

oh (ō) *interj.* Also rare **O. 1.** A word used to express strong emotion, such as surprise, fear, anger, or pain. **2.** A word used to indicate understanding or acknowledgment: *"Oh, I see,"* he replied. **—See Usage note at O.** [Middle English *o.*]

ohm (ōm) *n. Symbol* Ω A unit of electrical resistance equal to that of a conductor in which a current of one ampere is produced by a potential of one volt across its terminals. [After Georg Simon *Ohm* (1787–1854), German physicist.]

ohm·me·ter (ōm′mē′tər) *n. Elect.* An instrument for direct measurement of the resistance of a conductor in ohms.

-oid. A suffix meaning likeness or similarity to: **anthropoid.** [Latin *-oīdēs,* from Greek *-oeidēs,* of or having the shape or nature of, from *eidos,* form, shape.]

oil (oil) *n.* **1.** Any of numerous mineral, vegetable, and syn-thetic substances and animal and vegetable fats that are gen. slippery, combustible, viscous, liquid or liquefiable at room temperatures, soluble in various organic solvents, such as ether, but not in water, and used in a great variety of products, esp. lubricants and fuels. **2. a.** Petroleum. **b.** A petroleum derivative, such as a machine oil or lubricant. **3.** Any substance with an oily consistency. **4.** An **oil color. 5.** An **oil painting. —***modifier: an oil lamp; oil companies.* **—***tr.v.* To lubricate, supply, cover, or polish with oil. [Middle English *oil(e),* (olive) oil, from Old French, from Latin *oleum,* from Greek *elaion,* from *elaia,* olive.]

oil·cloth (oil′klôth′, -klŏth′) *n.* A fabric treated with clay, oil, and pigments and used as a cover for tables or shelving.

oil color. A pigment for making oil paint.

oil·er (oi′lər) *n.* Something used to apply oil.

oil field. An area containing underground deposits of petroleum.

oil gland. A gland that secretes oil.

oil of vitriol. *Chem.* **Sulfuric acid.**

oil paint. A paint in which the vehicle is a drying oil.

oil painting. **1.** A painting done in oil colors. **2.** The art or practice of painting with oil colors.

oil·skin (oil′skĭn′) *n.* **1.** Cloth treated with oil so that it is waterproof. **2.** A garment made of this material. **—***modifier: an oilskin raincoat.*

oil slick. A thin film of oil on water.

oil·stone (oil′stōn′) *n.* A smooth whetstone lubricated with oil, used for fine sharpening.

oil well. A well from which petroleum flows or is pumped.

oil·y (oi′lē) *adj.* **-i·er, -i·est.** **1.** Of or like oil. **2.** Impregnated or smeared with oil; greasy. **3.** Excessively suave in action or behavior; unctuous. **—oil′i·ly** *adv.* **—oil′i·ness** *n.*

oint·ment (oint′mənt) *n.* A thick, often oily substance made to be rubbed on the skin. [Middle English, from Old French *oignement,* from Latin *unguentum,* from *unguere,* to anoint.]

O·jib·wa (ō-jĭb′wä′, -wə) *n., pl.* **Ojibwa** or **-was.** Also **O·jib·way** (ō-jĭb′wä′) *pl.* **Ojibway** or **-ways. 1.** A tribe of North American Indians inhabiting regions of the United States and Canada around Lake Superior. **2.** A member of this tribe. **3.** The language of the Ojibwa.

O.K. or **OK** or **o·kay** (ō-kā′, ō-kā′) *n., pl.* **O.K.'s** or **OK's** or **o·kays.** *Informal.* Approval; agreement: *Get your parents' O.K. before we start on the trip.* **—***tr.v.* **O.K.'d** or **OK'd** or **o·kayed, O.K.'ing** or **OK'ing** or **o·kay·ing.** *Informal.* To approve or endorse; agree to: *The governor O.K.'d the plans for the new highway.* **—***interj. Informal.* All right; very well. **—***adj. Informal.* All right; acceptable; fine: *That's O.K. with me.* **—***adv. Informal.* Well enough; acceptably: *She's doing O.K.* [Abbr. of obs. slang spelling *oll korrect* for *all correct.*]

Usage: **O.K.** or **OK** or **okay.** This most popular of American coinages is used and understood throughout the world, but is best kept for informal writing and business correspondence: *got the treasurer's O.K. Please O.K. this policy.*

o·ka·pi (ō-kä′pē) *n., pl.* **okapi** or **-pis.** A ruminant African mammal, *Okapia johnstoni,* that is related to the giraffe, but is smaller and has a short neck. [Native Central African name.]

okapi   okra

o·kay (ō′kā′, ō-kā′) *n., pl.* **o·kays.** *tr.v.* **o·kayed, o·kay·ing.** *interj., adj., & adv.* Var. of **O.K.**

o·kra (ō′krə) *n.* **1.** A tall tropical and semitropical plant, *Hi-*

biscus esculentus, having edible, mucilaginous green pods. **2.** The edible pods of the okra. [West African native name *nkruma.*]

–ol. *Chem.* A suffix meaning alcohol or phenol: **glycerol.** [From ALCOHOL.]

old (ōld) *adj.* **old·er** or **eld·er** (ĕl'dər), **old·est** or **eld·est** (ĕl'dĭst). **1. a.** Having lived or existed for a long time; far advanced in years or life. **b.** Relatively advanced in age. **2.** Made long ago; not new: *an old book.* **3.** Of a long life or persons who have had a long life: *a ripe old age.* **4.** Having or exhibiting the physical characteristics of age: *a prematurely old face.* **5.** Having or exhibiting the wisdom of age; mature; sensible: *That child is old for her years.* **6.** Having a specified age: *She was twelve years old.* **7. a.** Belonging to a remote or former period in history; ancient: *old manuscripts.* **b.** Belonging to or being of an earlier time: *his old classmates.* **8.** Often **Old.** Being the earlier or earliest of two or more related objects, stages, versions, or periods: *the Old Testament; Old High German.* **9.** Worn or dilapidated through age or use: *an old coat.* **10.** Known through long acquaintance or use; long familiar: *an old friend.* **11.** Skilled or able through long experience; practiced: *He was an old hand at shipbuilding.* **12.** *Informal.* Fine; excellent; great: *We had a high old time.* —*n.* Former times; yore: *in days of old.* [Middle English, from Old English *eald.*] —**old'ness** *n.*

   Syns: 1. old, aged, elderly, senior *adj. Core meaning:* Far along in life or time (*an old lady in her nineties*). **2. old, olden, ancient, aged, antique, venerable** *adj. Core meaning:* Belonging to, existing in, or occurring in times long past (*an old castle; an old tale*).
old country. The native country of an immigrant.
Old Danish. The Danish language from the 12th to the 14th cent. A.D.
old·en (ōl'dən) *adj.* Of an earlier time; ancient. —See Syns at **old.** [Middle English, from *old,* old.]
Old English. The English language from the middle of the 5th to the beginning of the 12th cent. A.D.
old-fash·ioned (ōld'făsh'ənd) *adj.* **1.** Belonging to or typical of an earlier time and no longer in style. **2.** Following or preferring the ways or ideas of an earlier time.
Old French. The French language from the 9th to the 16th cent. A.D.
Old Glory. The flag of the United States.
old guard. The conservative, often reactionary element of a class, society, or political group.
old hat. *Informal.* Old-fashioned.
Old High German. The southern dialects of German from the 9th to the end of the 11th cent. A.D.
Old Irish. The Irish language from the 8th through the 10th cent. A.D.
Old Italian. The Italian language before the middle of the 16th cent. A.D.
old-line (ōld'līn') *adj.* **1.** Adhering to conservative or reactionary principles. **2.** Long established; traditional.
old man. A man in authority.
old master. 1. A distinguished European artist, esp. a painter, of the period from around 1500 to the early 1700's. **2.** A work by an old master.
Old Nick. The devil; Satan.
Old Norse. The Germanic language of the Scandinavian peoples from the 9th to the 13th cent. A.D.
Old North French. The northern dialects of Old French, esp. Norman French.
Old Provençal. The Provençal language before the middle of the 16th cent. A.D.
old school. A group committed to traditional ideas or practices. —**old'-school'** *adj.*
Old Spanish. The Spanish language before the 16th cent. A.D.
old·ster (ōld'stər) *n. Informal.* An old or elderly person.
Old Style. According to the Julian calendar.
Old Testament. The first of the two main divisions of the Christian Bible, containing the Hebrew Scriptures.
old-time (ōld'tīm') *adj.* Of a time in the past.
old-tim·er (ōld'tī'mər) *n. Informal.* **1. a.** An old person. **b.** Someone who has served in or belonged to an organization for a long time. **2.** Something that is very old.

old wives' tale. A bit of superstitious folklore.
old-world (ōld'wûrld') *adj.* **1.** Antique; old-fashioned; quaint. **2. Old-World.** Of or belonging to the Old World.
Old World. The Eastern Hemisphere, esp. Europe.
ole-. Var. of **oleo-.**
–ole. A suffix meaning small: **centriole.** [From Latin *-olus.*]
o·le·ag·i·nous (ō'lē-ăj'ə-nəs) *adj.* **1.** Containing or consisting of oil. **2.** Oily; unctuous. [Latin *oleāginus,* belonging to the olive tree, from *olea,* olive, from Greek *elaia.*] —**o'le·ag'i·nous·ly** *adv.* —**o'le·ag'i·nous·ness** *n.*
o·le·an·der (ō'lē-ăn'dər, ō'lē-ăn'-) *n.* Any poisonous evergreen shrub of the genus *Nerium,* found in warm climates, esp. *N. oleander,* with fragrant white, rose, or purple flowers. [Medieval Latin.]
o·le·as·ter (ō'lē-ăs'tər, ō'lē-ăs'-) *n.* A small Eurasian tree, *Elaeagnus angustifolia,* with oblong silvery leaves and olivelike fruit. [Latin, wild olive tree.]
o·le·ate (ō'lē-āt') *n.* An ester or salt of oleic acid.
o·le·fin (ō'lə-fĭn) *n.* Also **o·le·fine** (ō'lə-fĭn, -fēn'). Any of a class of unsaturated hydrocarbons, such as ethylene, having the general formula C_nH_{2n} and characterized by relatively great chemical activity. [French *(gaz) oléfiant,* "oil-forming (gas)," ethylene.] —**o'le·fin'ic** (-fĭn'ĭk) *adj.*
o·le·ic (ō-lē'ĭk) *adj. Chem.* Of, pertaining to, or derived from oil.
oleic acid. An oily liquid, $CH_3(CH_2)_7CH:CH(CH_2)_7COOH,$ occurring in animal and vegetable oils.
o·le·in (ō'lē-ĭn) *n.* Also **o·le·ine** (ō'lē-ĭn, -ēn'). A yellow oily liquid, $(C_{17}H_{33}COO)_3C_3H_5,$ occurring naturally in most fats and oils.
o·le·o (ō'lē-ō') *n.* Oleomargarine.
oleo- or **ole-.** A prefix meaning oil: **oleic.** [French *oléo-,* from Latin *oleo-,* from *oleum,* (olive) oil, from Greek *elaion,* from *elaia,* olive.]
o·le·o·mar·ga·rine (ō'lē-ō-mär'jər-ĭn, -jə-rēn') *n.* Margarine. [French *oléomargarine.*]
o·le·o·res·in (ō'lē-ō-rĕz'ĭn) *n.* A naturally occurring mixture of an oil and a resin, such as the exudate from pine trees. —**o'le·o·res'in·ous** (-rĕz'ĭ-nəs) *adj.*
ol·fac·tion (ŏl-făk'shən, ōl-) *n.* **1.** The sense of smell. **2.** The action of smelling. [From Latin *olfacere,* to smell.]
ol·fac·to·ry (ŏl-făk'tə-rē, -trē, ōl-) *adj.* Of or relating to the sense of smell. [Latin *olfactōrius,* from *olfacere,* to smell : *olēre,* to smell + *facere,* to make.]
olfactory nerve. Either of two bundles of nerve fibers, one on each side of the nasal cavity, that conduct chemical indications of smell.
ol·i·garch (ŏl'ĭ-gärk') *n.* A member of an oligarchy. [Greek *oligarkhēs* : *oligo-,* few + *-archēs,* ruler.]
ol·i·gar·chy (ŏl'ĭ-gär'kē) *n., pl.* **-chies. 1. a.** Government by the few. **b.** Those making up such a faction. **2.** A state governed by oligarchy. —**ol'i·gar'chic** or **ol'i·gar'chi·cal** or **ol'i·gar'chal** *adj.*
oligo-. A prefix meaning few: **Oligocene.** [Greek, from *oligos,* few, little.]
Ol·i·go·cene (ŏl'ĭ-gō-sēn') *n.* Also **Ol·i·go·cene epoch.** The geologic epoch of the Cenozoic era that began about 36 million years ago and ended about 25 million years ago.
o·li·o (ō'lē-ō') *n., pl.* **-os.** A mixture or medley; hodgepodge. [Modification of Spanish *olla,* pot.]
ol·ive (ŏl'ĭv) *n.* **1.** An Old World semitropical evergreen tree, *Olea europaea,* having an edible fruit, yellow flowers, and leathery leaves. **2.** The small fruit of the olive, important as a food and a source of oil. **3.** A dull yellowish green. —*adj.* **1.** Dull yellowish green. **2.** Slightly tinged with olive: *an olive complexion.* [Middle English, from Old French, from Latin *olīva,* from Greek *elaia.*]
olive branch. 1. A branch of an olive tree, esp. as an emblem of peace. **2.** An offer of peace.
olive drab. 1. A dull brownish or grayish green. **2.** Cloth of this color, often used for military uniforms.
olive oil. Oil pressed from olives, used in salad dressings, for cooking, as an ingredient of soaps, and as an emollient.
ol·iv·ine (ŏl'ĭ-vēn') *n.* A mineral silicate of iron and magnesium, principally Fe_2SiO_4 and $Mg_2SiO_4,$ found in igneous and metamorphic rocks and used as a structural material in refractories and in cements. [German *Olivin,* chrysolite.]

ă pat   ā pay   â care   ä father   ĕ pet   ē be   hw which   ĭ pit   ī tie   î pier   ŏ pot   ō toe   ô paw, for   oi noise
ōō took   ōō boot   ou out   th thin   *th* this   ŭ cut   û urge   zh vision   ə about, item, edible, gallop, circus

O·lym·pi·ad (ō-lǐm′pē-ăd′) *n.* **1.** The interval of four years between celebrations of the Olympic games, by which the ancient Greeks reckoned dates. **2.** A celebration of the modern Olympic games. [Middle English *Olympiade*, from Latin *Olympias*, from Greek *Olympias*, from *Olumpia*, the site of the Olympic games.]

O·lym·pi·an (ō-lǐm′pē-ən) *adj.* **1.** Of or relating to the greater gods of the ancient Greek pantheon, whose abode was Olympus. **2.** Majestic; lofty. —*n.* **1.** One of the major Greek gods that inhabited Olympus. **2.** A contestant in the Olympic games.

Olympic games. **1.** An ancient Greek festival of athletic competitions and contests in poetry and dancing, held every four years in Olympia in honor of the god Zeus. **2.** A modern international athletic competition held every four years in a different part of the world.

O·lym·pics (ō-lǐm′pǐks) *n.* The modern Olympic games.

O·ma·ha (ō′mə-hô′, -hä′) *n., pl.* **O·ma·ha** or **-has.** A member of a tribe of Siouan Indians of northeastern Nebraska.

o·ma·sum (ō-mā′səm) *n., pl.* **-sa** (-sə). The third stomach of a ruminant animal, located between the abomasum and the reticulum. [Latin *omāsum*, pouch, bullock's tripe.]

om·buds·man (ŏm′bŭdz′mən, -bōōdz′-) *n.* A government official who investigates citizens' complaints against the government or its functionaries. [Norwegian, from Old Norse *umbodhsmadhr*, steward, manager : *um*, about + *bodh*, command + *madhr*, man.]

o·me·ga (ō-mĕg′ə, ō-mē′gə, ō-mā′-) *n.* **1.** The 24th and final letter in the Greek alphabet, written Ω, ω. **2.** The end or last of anything. **3.** *Symbol* Ω⁻ *Physics.* A subatomic particle in the baryon family, having a mass 3,276 times that of the electron, a negative electric charge, and a mean lifetime of 1.5×10^{-10} second. [Greek *ō mega*, "large ō."]

om·e·let (ŏm′ə-lǐt, ŏm′lǐt) *n.* Also **om·e·lette.** A dish consisting of beaten eggs cooked and folded, often around a filling. [French *omelette*, from Old French *amelette*, "thin plate," from Latin *lāmella*, thin metal plate, dim. of *lāmina*, plate, layer.]

o·men (ō′mən) *n.* Something regarded as a sign of future good or evil. [Latin *ōmen*.]

om·i·cron (ŏm′ĭ-krŏn′, ō′mĭ-) *n.* The 15th letter in the Greek alphabet, written O, o. [Greek *o mikron*, "small o."]

om·i·nous (ŏm′ə-nəs) *adj.* Of or being an omen, esp. of evil. [Latin *ōminōsus*, from *ōmen*, omen.] —**om′i·nous·ly** *adv.* —**om′i·nous·ness** *n.*

o·mis·si·ble (ō-mĭs′ə-bəl) *adj.* Capable of or fit for omission. [From Latin *omittere*, to omit.]

o·mis·sion (ō-mĭsh′ən) *n.* **1.** The act or an instance of omitting. **2.** The condition of being omitted. **3.** Something that is omitted or neglected. [Middle English *omissioun*, from Late Latin *omissiō*, from Latin *omissus*, past part. of *omittere*, to omit.]

o·mit (ō-mĭt′) *tr.v.* **o·mit·ted, o·mit·ting.** **1.** To leave out; fail to include. **2.** To pass over; neglect. [Middle English *omitten*, from Latin *omittere* : *ob*, away + *mittere*, to send.]

omni-. A prefix meaning all: *omnidirectional.* [Latin, from *omnis*, all.]

om·ni·bus (ŏm′nĭ-bŭs′) *n., pl.* **-bus·es.** **1.** A bus. **2.** A printed anthology of the works of one author or of writings on related subjects. —*adj.* Including many things or classes; covering many things or situations at once: *an omnibus law.* [French *(voiture) omnibus* "(vehicle) for all," from Latin *omnis*, all.]

omnibus

om·ni·di·rec·tion·al (ŏm′nĭ-dĭ-rĕk′shə-nəl, -dī-) *adj.* Capable of transmitting or receiving signals in all directions.

om·ni·far·i·ous (ŏm′nĭ-fâr′ē-əs) *adj.* Of all kinds. [Late Latin *omnifarius* : *omni*, all + *fārius*, "doing."] —**om′ni·far′i·ous·ness** *n.*

om·nip·o·tent (ŏm-nĭp′ə-tənt) *adj.* Having unlimited or universal power, authority, or force. —*n.* **Omnipotent.** God. [Middle English, from Old French, from Latin *omnipotēns* : *omni-*, all + *potēns*, powerful.] —**om·nip′o·tence** *n.* —**om·nip′o·tent·ly** *adv.*

om·ni·pres·ent (ŏm′nĭ-prĕz′ənt) *adj.* Present everywhere. —**om′ni·pres′ence** *n.*

om·ni·range (ŏm′nĭ-rānj′) *n.* A radio network that provides complete bearing information for aircraft.

om·nis·cient (ŏm-nĭsh′ənt) *adj.* Having total knowledge; knowing everything. [Medieval Latin *omnisciēns* : *omni-*, all + *sciēns*, pres. part. of *scīre*, to know.] —**om·nis′cience** *n.* —**om·nis′cient·ly** *adv.*

om·ni·um-gath·er·um (ŏm′nē-əm-găth′ər-əm) *n.* A miscellany; hodgepodge. [From Latin *omnium*, all + GATHER.]

om·niv·o·rous (ŏm-nĭv′ər-əs) *adj.* **1.** *Zool.* Eating both animal and vegetable substances; consuming all kinds of food. **2.** Taking in everything available: *an omnivorous reader.* —**om·niv′o·rous·ly** *adv.* —**om·niv′o·rous·ness** *n.*

on (ŏn, ôn) *prep.* **1.** Used to indicate: **a.** Position above and in contact with: *The vase is on the table.* **b.** Contact with any surface, regardless of position: *a picture on the wall.* **c.** Location at or along: *a house on the beach.* **d.** Proximity: *a town on the border.* **2.** Used to indicate: **a.** Motion or direction toward a position: *He threw the books on the floor.* **b.** Motion toward, against, or onto: *jump on the table; the march on Washington.* **3.** Used to indicate: **a.** Occurrence during: *on July third.* **b.** The particular occasion or circumstance: *On entering the room, she saw him.* **c.** The exact time: *on the hour.* **4.** Used to indicate: **a.** The object affected by an action: *The spotlight fell on the actress.* **b.** The agent or agency of a specified action: *He cut his foot on the broken glass; talk on the telephone.* **5.** Used to indicate a source or basis: *live on bread and water; make a profit on gambling.* **6.** Used to indicate: **a.** The state, condition, or process of: *on leave; on fire.* **b.** The purpose of: *travel on business.* **c.** A means of conveyance: *ride on a train.* **d.** Availability by means of: *beer on tap; a nurse on call.* **e.** Association with: *a doctor on the hospital staff.* **f.** Addition or repetition: *error on error.* **7.** Concerning; about: *a book on astronomy.* **8.** In the possession of; with: *I haven't a cent on me.* **9.** At the expense of: *drinks on the house.* —See Usage note at **upon.** —*adv.* **1.** In or into a position of being attached to or covering something: *Put your clothes on.* **2.** In or into a position or condition of being supported by or in contact with something. **3.** In the direction of a specified event or activity: *He looked on while the ship docked.* **4.** Forward or ahead in space or time: *The army moved on to the next town; later on.* **5.** In a continuous course: *He worked on quietly.* **6.** In or into performance or operation: *Turn on the radio.* —*idioms.* **and so on.** And others like the preceding. **on and off.** Intermittently. **on and on.** Without stopping; continuously. **on to.** *Informal.* Aware of; informed about. [Middle English, from Old English.]

Usage: on, onto, on to. Both *on* and *onto* indicate motion to a position, and in many examples they are interchangeable. But *onto* more clearly expresses movement toward the object specified, while *on* stresses the physical state of having contact with a surface: *leaped onto the platform; leaped on the platform.* In constructions in which *on* is an adverb and *to* a preposition, they are not joined as one word: *move on to* (not *onto*) *other problems; hold on to* (not *onto*) *what we have.* In such usage, *on* may be considered part of the verb.

-on. A suffix meaning subatomic unit: **baryon.** [From ION.]

on·a·ger (ŏn′ə-jər) *n., pl.* **-gers.** **1.** An Asian wild ass, *Equus hemionus onager.* **2.** An ancient and medieval catapult used to propel large stones. [Middle English, from Latin, from Greek *onagros* : *onos*, ass + *agros*, field.]

once (wŭns) *adv.* **1.** One time only: *once a day.* **2.** At one time in the past; formerly. **3.** At any time; ever: *Once known, never forgotten.* —*n.* A single occurrence; one time: *You can go this once.* —*conj.* As soon as: *Once he* goes, we can clean up. —adj. Former: the once capital of the nation. —idioms. all at once. 1. All at the same time. 2. Suddenly. at once. 1. All together; simultaneously. 2. Immediately. once and for all. Finally; conclusively. once in a while. Now and then. [Middle English ones, from on, one, from Old English ān.]

once-o·ver (wŭns'ō'vər) n. Informal. A quick but thorough look or examination.

on·col·o·gy (ŏn-kŏl'ə-jē) n. The scientific study of tumors. [Greek onkos, mass, tumor + -LOGY.]

on·com·ing (ŏn'kŭm'ĭng, ôn'-) adj. Coming nearer; approaching: the oncoming storm.

one (wŭn) adj. 1. Being a single entity, unit, or object: one dog. 2. Characterized by unity; undivided: They spoke with one voice. 3. Designating one in particular as contrasted with another or others: from one end to the other. 4. Not designated or established; indefinite: He will come one day. 5. Informal. Used as an intensifier of the quality specified: That is one fine dog. —See Syns at single. —n. 1. The cardinal number written 1 or roman numeral I. 2. A single person or thing; unit. —pron. 1. Any person; anyone: One should do one's best. 2. An individual member of a specified class: one of the players. —idioms. all one. Of equal importance; all the same: Maybe she's coming and maybe not—it's all one to me. at one. In accord or agreement: We found ourselves at one on the whole treaty issue. one and all. Everyone. one another. Each other. —See Usage note at each other. one by one. Individually and in succession. [Middle English on, from Old English ān.]

Usage: The indefinite pronoun one is singular and as such, it takes a singular verb: I am one (singular) who (relative pronoun) likes (singular verb) to ice skate. Confusion arises in constructions beginning with relative pronouns whose antecedents are plural: I am one of those people (plural antecedent of who) who like/likes to ice skate. The choice of the number of the verb in the who clause is up to the writer. If the writer feels that the verb is governed by the singular one regardless of any intervening plural word or words, then the writer can use a singular verb (likes, in this example). But if the writer feels that the verb in the who clause should agree in number with the plural antecedent (people) of the relative pronoun (who), the writer can use a plural verb (like). Both constructions are standard, but whatever the choice, the elements should be written consistently singular or plural throughout.

-one. A suffix meaning a ketone or an analogous oxygen-containing compound: acetone. [From Greek -ōnē, fem. suffix.]

one-horse (wŭn'hôrs') adj. 1. Drawn by or using only one horse. 2. Contemptibly small or insignificant: a one-horse town.

one·ness (wŭn'nĭs) n. 1. The quality or condition of being one. 2. Unison; agreement: oneness of purpose.

on·er·ous (ŏn'ər-əs, ō'nər-) adj. Troublesome or oppressive; burdensome. —See Syns at burdensome. [Middle English, from Old French onereus, from Latin onerōsus, from onus, burden.] —on'er·ous·ly adv. —on'er·ous·ness n.

one·self (wŭn-sĕlf') pron. Also one's self (wŭn sĕlf', wŭnz sĕlf'). 1. A person's own self. Used: a. Reflexively as the direct or indirect object of a verb or the object of a preposition: forget oneself; faith in oneself. b. For emphasis: One must take a certain amount of initiative oneself. 2. One's normal, healthy condition.

one-sid·ed (wŭn'sī'dĭd) adj. 1. Favoring one side or group; biased: a one-sided view. 2. Unequal: a one-sided contest. —one'-sid'ed·ly adv. —one'-sid'ed·ness n.

one-step (wŭn'stĕp') n. A ballroom dance consisting of a series of rapid steps in 2/4 time. —one-step v.

one-time (wŭn'tīm') adj. Also one·time. At or in some past time; former: a one-time champion.

one-to-one (wŭn'tə-wŭn') adj. Pairing each member of a set uniquely with a member of another.

one-track (wŭn'trăk') adj. Obsessed by a single idea or purpose: a one-track mind.

one-way (wŭn'wā') adj. 1. Moving or permitting movement in one direction only: a one-way street. 2. Providing for travel in one direction only: a one-way ticket.

on·go·ing (ŏn'gō'ĭng, ôn'-) adj. 1. Currently going on: ongoing research. 2. Progressing.

on·ion (ŭn'yən) n. 1. A bulbous plant, Allium cepa, cultivated as a vegetable. 2. The rounded, edible bulb of the onion plant, composed of tight, concentric layers, and having a pungent odor and taste. [Middle English unyon, from Old French oignon, from Latin uniō, a kind of onion.] —modifier: onion soup.

on·ion·skin (ŭn'yən-skĭn') n. A thin, strong, translucent paper.

on·look·er (ŏn'lŏŏk'ər, ôn'-) n. Someone who looks on; spectator. —on'look'ing adj.

on·ly (ōn'lē) adj. 1. Alone in its kind or class; sole: an only child. 2. Standing alone by reason of superiority or excellence: She's the only one for me. —See Syns at single. —adv. 1. Nothing more or different; just: If you would only come home. 2. Merely: I only work here. 3. Exclusively; solely: I work only here. —conj. But; except: She could win easily, only she doesn't realize it. [Middle English, from Old English ānlīc.]

Usage: only. 1. The position of the adverb only with regard to the word it modifies is not rigidly fixed in standard English usage. In fact, a study has shown that at least eight different meanings can result from placing only in eight different slots within a single test sentence. Two simple examples of meanings changed by varying the position of only in a single locution are: Only I work here. I only work here. In written English, the word only is typically placed just before the word or words it modifies: She had only a few minutes. They arrived only an hour ago. Only if you cooperate can a cure be effected. 2. The conjunction only meaning but or except has been used over 600 years by respected writers. Examples: We would have come to the party, only our mother became ill.

on·o·mat·o·poe·ia (ŏn'ə-măt'ə-pē'ə) n. The formation or use of words, as buzz or cuckoo, that imitate what they denote. [Late Latin, from Greek onomatopoiia, from onomatopoiein, to coin names : onoma, name + poiein, to make.] —on'o·mat'o·poe'ic (-pē'ĭk) or on'o·mat'o·po·et'ic (-pō-ĕt'ĭk) adj. —on'o·mat'o·po·et'i·cal·ly adv.

on·rush (ŏn'rŭsh', ôn'-) n. 1. A forward rush or flow: the onrush of events. 2. An assault. —on'rush'ing adj.

on·set (ŏn'sĕt', ôn'-) n. 1. An onslaught. 2. A beginning.

on·shore (ŏn'shôr', -shōr', ôn'-) adj. & adv. Toward the shore.

on·slaught (ŏn'slôt', ôn'-) n. A violent attack. [Earlier anslaight, from Dutch aanslag, from Middle Dutch aenslag : aan, on + slag, a striking.]

on·to (ŏn'tōō', ôn'-, ŏn'tə, ôn'-) prep. 1. On top of; to a position on; upon: The dog jumped onto the chair. 2. Informal. Aware or cognizant of; informed about: I'm onto your schemes. —See Usage note at on.

onto-. A prefix meaning being or existence: ontogeny. [Late Greek, from ōn, pres. part. of einai, to be.]

on·tog·e·ny (ŏn-tŏj'ə-nē) n., pl. -nies. The course of development of an individual organism. —on'to·ge·net'ic (ŏn'-tə-jə-nĕt'ĭk) adj.

o·nus (ō'nəs) n. 1. Something that is burdensome. 2. Blame: bore the onus for his team's defeat. [Latin, burden.]

on·ward (ŏn'wərd, ôn'-) adv. Also on·wards (-wərdz). At or toward a position that is ahead in space or time; forward: plodding onward through the storm. —on'ward adj.

Usage: onward, onwards. The adjective is only onward: an onward movement. The adverb is either onward or onwards: moving steadily onward (or onwards).

-onym. A suffix meaning word or name: antonym. [From Greek onuma, name.]

on·yx (ŏn'ĭks) n. A chalcedony that occurs in bands of different colors. [Middle English onix, from Old French, from Latin onyx, from Greek onux, claw, fingernail, onyx.]

oo-. A prefix meaning egg or ovum: oogenesis. [Greek ōio-, from ōion, egg.]

o·o·cyte (ō'ə-sīt') n. 1. A cell, derived from an oogonium, that undergoes meiosis and produces an ovum. 2. A female gamete in certain protozoa.

oo·dles (ōōd'lz) pl.n. Informal. A great amount; a lot. [Perh. alteration of HUDDLE.]

o·o·gen·e·sis (ō'ə-jĕn'ĭ-sĭs) n. Biol. The enlargement and meiotic division of an oogonium that produces an ovum.

o·o·go·ni·um (ō'ə-gō'nē-əm) n., pl. -ni·a (-nē-ə) or -ums. 1.

ă pat	ā pay	â care	ä father	ĕ pet	ē be	hw which	ĭ pit	ī tie	î pier	ŏ pot	ō toe	ô paw, for	oi noise
ŏŏ took	ōō boot	ou out	th thin	th this	ŭ cut		û urge	zh vision	ə about, item, edible, gallop, circus				

Biol. One of the cells that form the bulk of ovarian tissue. **2.** *Bot.* A female reproductive structure in certain fungi. [oo- + Greek *gonos,* seed.]

o·o·lite (ō′ə-līt′) *n.* Also **o·o·lith** (ō′ə-līth′). **1.** A small, round, calcareous grain found in such rocks as limestones and dolomites. **2.** Rock, usu. limestone, composed of such grains. —**o′o·lit′ic** (ō′ə-lĭt′ĭk) *adj.*

o·ol·o·gy (ō-ŏl′ə-jē) *n.* The branch of ornithology that deals with birds' eggs. —**o′o·log′ic** (ō′ə-lŏj′ĭk) or **o′o·log′i·cal** *adj.* —**o′o·log′i·cal·ly** *adv.* —**o·ol′o·gist** *n.*

oo·long (oo′lông′, -lŏng′) *n.* A dark Chinese tea that is partly fermented before drying. [Mandarin *wu¹ lung²,* "black dragon."]

oomph (oomf) *n. Slang.* **1.** Spirit; vigor. **2.** Sex appeal.

ooze¹ (ooz) *v.* **oozed, ooz·ing.** —*intr.v.* **1.** To flow or leak out slowly, as through small openings. **2.** To disappear or ebb slowly: *His courage oozed away.* **3.** To progress slowly but steadily. —*tr.v.* To give off; exude. —*n.* **1.** The act of oozing; a gradual flow or leak. **2.** Something that oozes. [Middle English *wosen,* from *wose,* juice, from Old English *wōs.*] —**ooz′y** *adj.* —**ooz′i·ness** *n.*

ooze² (ooz) *n.* **1.** The layer of mudlike sediment covering the floor of oceans and lakes, composed chiefly of remains of microscopic sea animals. **2.** Muddy ground; bog. [Middle English *wose,* from Old English *wāse.*] —**ooz′y** *adj.* —**ooz′i·ness** *n.*

o·pac·i·ty (ō-păs′ĭ-tē) *n., pl.* **-ties. 1.** The quality or condition of being opaque. **2.** Something that is opaque. **3.** Obscurity; impenetrability. [French *opacité,* from Latin *opācitās,* from *opācus,* opaque.]

o·pal (ō′pəl) *n.* A translucent mineral of hydrated silicon dioxide, often used as a gem. [Latin *opalus,* from Greek *opallios,* from Sanskrit *úpala,* (precious) stone.] —**o′pal·ine′** (ō′pə-līn′, -lēn′) *adj.*

o·pal·esce (ō′pə-lĕs′) *intr.v.* **-esced, -esc·ing.** To emit or show an iridescent shimmer of colors. [Back-formation from OPALESCENCE.]

o·pal·es·cence (ō′pə-lĕs′əns) *n.* A rainbowlike shimmer of colors like that of an opal. —**o′pal·es′cent** *adj.*

o·paque (ō-pāk′) *adj.* **1.** Not transmitting light; neither transparent nor translucent. **2. a.** Obtuse; dense. **b.** Obscure or unintelligible: *"The opaque allusion . . . accomplishes nothing."* (Marianne Moore). —*n.* Something that is opaque. [Partly from Middle English *opake,* partly from Old French *opaque,* both from Latin *opācus,* dark.] —**o·paque′ly** *adv.* —**o·paque′ness** *n.*

ope (ōp) *v.* **oped, op·ing.** *Poet.* To open.

OPEC (ō′pĕk′) Organization of Petroleum Exporting Countries.

o·pen (ō′pən) *adj.* **1. a.** Allowing unobstructed entrance and exit; not shut or closed. **b.** Permitting unobstructed passage or view; spacious and unenclosed. **2.** Having no protective or concealing cover: *an open fire.* **3.** Not sealed, tied, or folded: *an open package.* **4.** Having gaps, spaces, or intervals: *a coarse, open weave.* **5. a.** Accessible to all; unrestricted: *an open meeting.* **b.** Free from limitations, boundaries, or restrictions. **6. a.** Accessible; responsive: *open to persuasion.* **b.** Susceptible; vulnerable: *open to attack.* **7. a.** Available: *The job is still open.* **b.** Available for use: *an open account.* **8.** Ready to transact business. **9.** Unengaged; unoccupied: *an hour open for emergency cases.* **10.** Frank; candid: *an open nature.* —*tr.v.* **1.** To cause to become open; release from a closed or fastened position. **2.** To remove obstructions from; clear. **3.** To make an opening in: *open an old wound.* **4.** To remove the cover or wrapping from; undo. **5.** To unfold; spread out: *open a magazine.* **6.** To begin; commence: *open a meeting.* **7.** To make more responsive or understanding: *opened her heart to their pleas.* —*intr.v.* **1.** To become open. **2.** To draw apart; separate. **3.** To spread apart; unfold. **4.** To come into view; become revealed. **5.** To begin; commence. **6.** To give access or view: *a large window that opens onto the lake.* —See Syns at **spread.** —*phrasal verb.* **open up.** *Informal.* To speak or act freely and unrestrainedly. —*n.* **1. a.** An unobstructed area of land or water. **b.** The outdoors. **2.** A tournament or contest in which both professional and amateur players may participate. [Middle English, from Old English.] —**o′pen·ly** *adv.* —**o′pen·ness** *n.*

o·pen-air (ō′pən-âr′) *adj.* Outdoor: *an open-air concert.*

o·pen-and-shut (ō′pən-ən-shŭt′) *adj.* Presenting no difficulties; simple: *an open-and-shut case.*

open chain. *Chem.* A linear arrangement of atoms that is the basic form of various carbon and silicon compounds.

open door. A policy that permits trade between a nation and all other nations on equal terms. —*modifier* (**open-door**): *an open-door policy.*

o·pen-end (ō′pən-ĕnd′) *adj.* Having no definite limit of duration or amount: *an open-end contract.*

o·pen-eyed (ō′pən-īd′) *adj.* **1.** Having the eyes wide open. **2.** Watchful and alert. —See Syns at **alert.**

o·pen-hand·ed (ō′pən-hăn′dĭd) *adj.* Giving freely; generous.

o·pen-heart·ed (ō′pən-här′tĭd) *adj.* **1.** Frank. **2.** Kindly.

o·pen-hearth (ō′pən-härth′) *adj.* Of, used in, or designating a process for producing high-quality steel in a furnace with a heat-reflecting roof.

open house. An occasion on which hospitality is extended to all.

o·pen·ing (ō′pə-nĭng) *n.* **1.** The act of becoming open or making open. **2.** An open space. **3.** A hole. **4.** The first period or stage. **5.** A first performance. **6.** A series of beginning moves, as in chess. **7.** An opportunity; chance. **8.** An unfilled job or position; vacancy. —See Syns at **opportunity.**

open letter. A letter on a subject of general interest, addressed to an individual but intended for all to read.

o·pen-mind·ed (ō′pən-mīn′dĭd) *adj.* Having a mind receptive to new ideas or to reason; free from prejudice or bias. —**o′pen-mind′ed·ly** *adv.* —**o′pen-mind′ed·ness** *n.*

o·pen-mouthed (ō′pən-mouthd′, -moutht′) *adj.* Having the mouth wide open, esp. in astonishment.

open shop. A business establishment or factory in which workers are employed without regard to union membership.

o·pen·work (ō′pən-wûrk′) *n.* Ornamental work containing numerous openings, usu. in set patterns.

op·er·a¹ (ŏp′ər-ə, ŏp′rə) *n.* **1.** A musical and dramatic work consisting of a play with stage action and the words sung to music, usu. with orchestral accompaniment. **2.** An opera performance. **3.** A theater designed primarily for operas. [Italian, from Latin *opera,* work.] —**op′er·at′ic** *adj.*

op·er·a² (ŏp′ər-ə, ŏp′rə) *n.* A plural of **opus.**

op·er·a·ble (ŏp′ər-ə-bəl, ŏp′rə-) *adj.* **1.** Capable of or suitable for use. **2.** Capable of being treated surgically: *an operable stage of cancer.* —**op′er·a·bil′i·ty** *n.*

op·er·a buf·fa (ŏp′rə boo′fə, ŏp′ər-ə). Also French **o·pé·ra bouffe** (ō-pā-rä boof′). A comic opera. [Italian, "comic opera."]

o·pé·ra co·mique (ŏp′rə kō-mēk′, kō-, ŏp′ər-ə). Opera with spoken dialogue. [French, "comic opera."]

opera glasses. Small, low-powered binoculars for use esp. at a theatrical performance.

opera hat. A collapsible top hat.

opera house. A theater designed chiefly for operas.

op·er·ate (ŏp′ə-rāt′) *v.* **-at·ed, -at·ing.** —*intr.v.* **1.** To function effectively; work. **2.** To have an effect; act: *poisons that operate on the nervous system.* **3.** To perform surgery. **4.** To carry on a military or naval action. —*tr.v.* **1.** To run or control the functioning of. **2.** To conduct the affairs of; manage. **3.** To bring about or effect. [From Latin *operārī,* to work, labor, from *opus,* a work.]

op·er·a·tion (ŏp′ə-rā′shən) *n.* **1.** A method or way of operating. **2.** The condition of being operative. **3.** *Med.* A surgical procedure for remedying an injury, ailment, or dysfunction in a living body. **4.** *Math.* A process or action, such as addition, performed in a specified sequence and in accordance with specific rules of procedure. **5.** A military or naval action, campaign, or project. —**op′er·a′tion·al** *adj.* —**op′er·a′tion·al·ly** *adv.*

op·er·a·tive (ŏp′ər-ə-tĭv, ŏp′rə-, -ə-rā′tĭv) *adj.* **1.** Exerting influence or force. **2.** Functioning effectively. **3.** Being in force, in effect, or in operation: *operative regulations.* **4.** Of, relating to, or involving a surgical operation. —*n.* **1.** A skilled worker, esp. in industry. **2. a.** A secret agent. **b.** A detective. —**op′er·a·tive·ly** *adv.*

op·er·a·tor (ŏp′ə-rā′tər) *n.* **1.** A person who operates a mechanical device. **2.** A person who operates a business. **3.** A dealer in stocks or commodities. **4.** A symbol, such as a plus sign, that denotes a mathematical operation. **5.** *Informal.* A shrewd and sometimes unscrupulous person who gets what he wants.

o·per·cu·late (ō-pûr′kyə-lĭt) *adj.* Also **o·per·cu·lat·ed** (ō-pûr′kyə-lā′tĭd). Having an operculum.

o·per·cu·lum (ō-pûr′kyə-ləm) *n., pl.* **-la** (-lə) or **-lums.** **1.** *Biol.* A lid or flap covering an aperture, such as the gill cover in some fishes or the horny shell cover in snails or other mollusks. **2.** *Anat.* Any flap or lid, such as the layer of tissue over an erupting tooth. [Latin, a lid, cover, from *operīre,* to cover.]

op·er·et·ta (ŏp′ə-rĕt′ə) *n.* An opera, of a light subject and style, sometimes comic. [Italian, dim. of *opera,* opera.]

o·phid·i·an (ō-fĭd′ē-ən) *adj.* Of or relating to snakes. —*n.* Any member of the suborder Ophidia or Serpentes; snake. [From Greek *ophis,* snake.]

oph·thal·mi·a (ŏf-thăl′mē-ə, ŏp-) *n.* Inflammation of the eye, esp. of the conjunctiva. [Middle English *obtalmia,* from Late Latin *ophthalmia,* from Greek, from *ophthalmos,* eye.]

oph·thal·mic (ŏf-thăl′mĭk, ŏp-) *adj.* Of or relating to the eye.

ophthalmo-. A prefix meaning the eye or eyeball: **ophthalmology.** [Greek, from *ophthalmos,* eye.]

oph·thal·mol·o·gist (ŏf′thăl-mŏl′ə-jĭst, ŏp′-, -thəl-) *n.* A physician specializing in the treatment of diseases of the eye.

oph·thal·mol·o·gy (ŏf′thăl-mŏl′ə-jē, ŏp′-, -thəl-) *n.* The medical specialty that deals with the anatomy, functions, pathology, and treatment of the eye. —**oph′thal·mo·log′ic** (-mə-lŏj′ĭk) or **oph′thal·mo·log′i·cal** *adj.* —**oph′thal·mo·log′i·cal·ly** *adv.*

oph·thal·mo·scope (ŏf-thăl′mə-skōp′, ŏp-) *n.* An instrument for examining the interior of the eye. —**oph′thal·mo·scop′ic** (-skŏp′ĭk) or **oph′thal·mo·scop′i·cal** *adj.*

-opia. A suffix meaning a specific visual condition or defect; **amblyopia.** [Greek *-ōpia,* from *ōps,* eye.]

o·pi·ate (ō′pē-ĭt, -āt′) *n.* **1.** A derivative of opium. **2.** A narcotic. **3.** Something that relaxes or that induces sleep. —*adj.* (ō′pē-ĭt, -āt′). **1.** Consisting of or containing opium. **2.** Causing or producing sleep or sedation. [Medieval Latin *opiātum,* an opiate, from *opiātus,* treated with opium, soporific, from Latin *opium,* opium.]

o·pine (ō-pīn′) *tr.v.* **o·pined, o·pin·ing.** To hold or state as an opinion. [Old French *opiner,* from Latin *opīnārī,* to think.]

o·pin·ion (ə-pĭn′yən) *n.* **1.** A belief held often without positive knowledge or proof. **2.** An evaluation or judgment based on special knowledge and given by an expert. **3.** A judgment or estimation of a person or thing: *stood low in his opinion.* —See Syns at **belief.** —*modifier:* an *opinion* poll. [Middle English, from Old French, from Latin *opīniō,* from *opīnārī,* to think.]

o·pin·ion·at·ed (ə-pĭn′yə-nā′tĭd) *adj.* Holding stubbornly and often unreasonably to one's own opinions. —**o·pin′ion·at′ed·ly** *adv.* —**o·pin′ion·at′ed·ness** *n.*

o·pin·ion·a·tive (ə-pĭn′yə-nā′tĭv) *adj.* **1.** Of, consisting of, or based on opinion. **2.** Opinionated. —**o·pin′ion·a′tive·ly** *adv.*

o·pi·um (ō′pē-əm) *n.* **1.** A bitter, yellowish-brown, narcotic drug prepared from the dried juice of unripe pods of the opium poppy, containing alkaloids such as morphine, narcotine, codeine, and papaverine. **2.** Something that numbs or stupefies. [Middle English, from Latin, from Greek *opion,* poppy juice, opium, dim. of *opos,* juice.]

opium poppy. A plant, *Papaver somniferum,* orig. of Asia Minor, that has grayish-green leaves and variously colored flowers and is a source of opium.

o·pos·sum (ə-pŏs′əm, pŏs′əm) *n., pl.* **opossum** or **-sums.** Any of various nocturnal, arboreal marsupials of the family Didelphidae, esp. *Didelphis marsupialis,* of the Western Hemisphere. [Algonquian *aposoum.*]

op·po·nent (ə-pō′nənt) *n.* A person or group that opposes another or others. —*adj.* **1.** Opposing; antagonistic. **2.** Opposite. [Latin *oppōnēns,* pres. part. of *oppōnere,* to oppose.]

    Syns: opponent, adversary, antagonist *n.* Core meaning: One that opposes another in a battle, contest, or controversy (*Congressional opponents of the legislation*).

op·por·tune (ŏp′ər-tōōn′, -tyōōn′) *adj.* Occurring at a fit-

ting or appropriate time: *Wait for the opportune moment.* [Middle English, from Old French *opportun,* from Latin *opportūnus,* seasonable : *ob,* to + *portus,* harbor.] —**op′por·tune′ly** *adv.* —**op′por·tune′ness** *n.*

op·por·tun·ism (ŏp′ər-tōō′nĭz′əm, -tyōō′-) *n.* The practice of taking advantage of any opportunity to achieve an end, usu. with little or no regard for moral principles. —**op′por·tun′ist** *n.* —**op′por·tun·is′tic** *adj.*

op·por·tu·ni·ty (ŏp′ər-tōō′nĭ-tē, -tyōō′-) *n., pl.* **-ties.** A favorable time or occasion for a certain purpose: *seized the opportunity afforded by the open window and escaped.*

    Syns: opportunity, break (*Informal*)**, chance, occasion, opening** *n.* Core meaning: A favorable time or circumstance (*waited for a good opportunity to attack*).

op·pos·a·ble (ə-pō′zə-bəl) *adj.* **1.** Capable of being opposed. **2.** Capable of being placed opposite something. —**op·pos′a·bil′i·ty** *n.*

op·pose (ə-pōz′) *v.* **-posed, -pos·ing.** —*tr.v.* **1.** To be in contention or conflict with; combat; resist: *oppose the enemy force.* **2.** To be against; be hostile to: *oppose new ideas.* **3.** To place in opposition or be in opposition to; contrast or counterbalance. **4.** To move so as to be opposite something else; place in contraposition. —See Syns at **resist.** [French *opposer,* from Old French, from Latin *oppositus,* past part. of *oppōnere,* to set against : *ob,* against + *pōnere,* to put.] —**op·pos′er** *n.*

op·po·site (ŏp′ə-zĭt, -sĭt) *adj.* **1.** Placed or located directly across from something else or from each other: *opposite sides of a building.* **2.** Facing or moving away from each other: *opposite directions.* **3.** Contrary in nature or tendency; diametrically opposed: *opposite views.* **4.** *Bot.* Growing in pairs on either side of a stem: *opposite leaves.* —*n.* A person or thing that is opposite or contrary to another. —*adv.* In an opposite position. —*prep.* Across from or facing: *Park your car opposite the bank.* [Middle English, from Old French, from Latin *oppositus,* past part. of *oppōnere,* to oppose.] —**op′po·site·ly** *adv.* —**op′po·site·ness** *n.*

op·po·si·tion (ŏp′ə-zĭsh′ən) *n.* **1.** The act or condition of opposing or resisting: *opposition to the proposed law.* **2.** A position or location opposite to or facing another: *the weak tides when the sun and moon are in opposition.* **3.** Something that opposes. **4.** Often **Opposition.** A political party or group opposed to the party in power. **5.** *Astron.* **a.** A geometric configuration in which the earth lies on a straight line between the sun and a planet. **b.** The position of the exterior planet in this configuration. —*modifier:* opposition *parties.* —**op′po·si′tion·al** *adj.*

op·press (ə-prĕs′) *tr.v.* **1.** To burden harshly, unjustly, or tyrannically. **2.** To weigh heavily upon the mind or spirit. [Middle English *oppressen,* from Old French *oppresser,* from Medieval Latin *oppressāre,* from Latin *oppressus,* past part. of *opprimere,* to press against : *ob,* against + *premere,* to press.] —**op·pres′sor** *n.*

op·pres·sion (ə-prĕsh′ən) *n.* **1.** The act of oppressing or the condition of being oppressed. **2.** Something that oppresses harshly or unjustly. **3.** A feeling of being mentally or physically burdened; depression.

op·pres·sive (ə-prĕs′ĭv) *adj.* **1. a.** Difficult to bear; harsh. **b.** Tyrannical. **2.** Weighing heavily on the senses or spirits; over-powering: *an oppressive silence.* —See Syns at **burdensome.** —**op·pres′sive·ly** *adv.* —**op·pres′sive·ness** *n.*

op·pro·bri·ous (ə-prō′brē-əs) *adj.* **1.** Expressing or carrying

opossum

contemptuous scorn. **2.** Shameful; infamous: *opprobrious conduct.* **—op·pro′bri·ous·ly** *adv.*

op·pro·bri·um (ə-prō′brē-əm) *n.* **1.** Disgrace arising from shameful conduct. **2.** Scorn; contempt. **3.** A cause of shame or disgrace. [Latin, dishonor : *ob*, against + *probrum*, reproach, infamy.]

op·so·nin (ŏp′sə-nĭn) *n.* A substance naturally present in the blood that renders foreign cells more susceptible to destruction by phagocytes. [From Latin *opsōnium*, a relish, ult. from Greek *opson*, relish, delicacy.]

-opsy. A suffix meaning examination: **biopsy.** [From Greek *opsis*, sight.]

opt (ŏpt) *intr.v.* To make a choice or decision: *opted for an early retirement.* [French *opter*, from Latin *optāre.*]

op·tic (ŏp′tĭk) *adj.* Of or relating to the eye or to vision. [Old French *optique*, from Medieval Latin *opticus*, from Greek *optikos*, from *optos*, visible.]

op·ti·cal (ŏp′tĭ-kəl) *adj.* **1.** Of or relating to sight. **2.** Of or relating to optics. **—op′ti·cal·ly** *adv.*

op·ti·cian (ŏp-tĭsh′ən) *n.* A person who makes or sells lenses, eyeglasses, and other optical instruments.

optic nerve. Either of two sensory nerves that connect the retinas of the eyes with the brain.

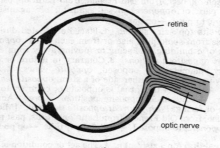

retina

optic nerve

optic nerve

op·tics (ŏp′tĭks) *n.* *(used with a sing. verb).* The scientific study of light and vision.

op·ti·ma (ŏp′tə-mə) *n.* A plural of **optimum.**

op·ti·mal (ŏp′tə-məl) *adj.* Most desirable or favorable. **—op′ti·mal·ly** *adv.* [OPTIM(UM) + -AL.]

op·ti·mism (ŏp′tə-mĭz′əm) *n.* **1.** A tendency to expect the best possible outcome, or to dwell upon the most hopeful aspects of a situation: *"The incurable optimism of childhood"* (Frank O'Connor). **2.** The doctrine that this world is the best of all possible worlds. [French *optimisme*, from Latin *optimum*, best.] **—op′ti·mist** *n.* **—op′ti·mis′tic** *adj.* **—op′ti·mis′ti·cal·ly** *adv.*

op·ti·mum (ŏp′tə-məm) *n.*, *pl.* **-ma** (-mə) or **-mums.** The best or most favorable condition, degree, or amount for a particular situation. [Latin, best.] **—op′ti·mum** *adj.*

op·tion (ŏp′shən) *n.* **1.** The power or right of choosing. **2. a.** A right to buy or sell something at a specified price within a specified time. **b.** A clause in an insurance policy permitting the policyholder to specify the manner in which payments are to be made or credited to him. **3.** Something available as a choice. **—See Syns at choice.** [French, from Latin *optiō*, choice.]

op·tion·al (ŏp′shə-nəl) *adj.* Allowing a choice; not compulsory or automatic. **—op′tion·al·ly** *adv.*

op·tom·e·trist (ŏp-tŏm′ĭ-trĭst) *n.* A person who specializes in optometry.

op·tom·e·try (ŏp-tŏm′ĭ-trē) *n.* The profession of examining, measuring, and treating visual defects by means of corrective lenses. [Greek *optos*, visible + -METRY.] **—op′to·met′ric** (ŏp′tə-mĕt′rĭk) *adj.*

op·u·lent (ŏp′yə-lənt) *adj.* **1.** Having or displaying great wealth and luxury; luxurious. **2.** Abundant; plentiful; lavish. **—See Syns at luxurious.** [Latin *opulentus.*] **—op′u·lent·ly** *adv.* **—op′u·lence** *n.*

o·pun·ti·a (ō-pŭn′shē-ə, -shə) *n.* A prickly pear. [After *Opus*, an ancient city of Greece, where it grew abundantly.]

o·pus (ō′pəs) *n.*, *pl.* **o·per·a** (ō′pər-ə, ŏp′ər-ə) or **o·pus·es.** A

creative work, esp. a musical composition or set of musical compositions. [Latin, work.]

or¹ (ôr; ər *when unstressed*) *conj.* Used to indicate: **1. a.** An alternative, usu. only before the last term of a series: *hot or cold; this, that, or the other.* **b.** The second of two alternatives, the first being preceded by either or whether: *Your answer is either ingenious or wrong. She didn't know whether to laugh or cry.* **c.** *Archaic.* The first of two alternatives, with the force of *either* or *whether: "Tell me where is fancy bred/ Or in the heart or in the head?"* (Shakespeare). **2.** A synonymous or equivalent expression: *acrophobia,* or *fear of great heights.* **3.** Uncertainty or indefiniteness: *two or three.* [Middle English, contraction of *other*, from Old English *oththe.*]

Usage: **or.** When all elements of a sentence connected by **or** are singular, the verb they govern is singular: *This version or the other has to be correct. A tax increase or a subsidy or a reduction in services is indicated.* When the elements are all plural, the verb is correspondingly plural: *The newspaper publishers or the television stations are responsible for this coverage.* When the elements do not agree in grammatical number, or when one or more is a personal pronoun, the verb agrees in number with the element to which it is nearer or nearest: *Cold symptoms or headache is the usual first sign. Nausea or fainting spells are often early indications. Baseball or football or similar games have little place in their program. He or I am most likely to be chosen.* See also Usage note at **and/or.**

or² (ôr) *n.* *Heraldry.* Gold or yellow. [Old French, from Latin *aurum.*]

-or. A suffix indicating the performer of an action: **percolator, investor.** [Middle English, from Old French *-eor, -eur*, from Latin *-or.*]

o·ra (ôr′ə, ōr′ə) *n.* Plural of **os** (mouth).

or·a·cle (ôr′ə-kəl, ŏr′-) *n.* **1. a.** A shrine at which a god revealed knowledge or disclosed the future. **b.** The person through whom the prophecies or messages from the god were made. **c.** A revelation from an oracle. **2.** A person considered to be a source of wise counsel or opinion. [Middle English, from Old French, from Latin *ōrāculum*, from *ōrāre*, to speak.]

o·rac·u·lar (ô-răk′yə-lər, ō-răk′-) *adj.* **1.** Of, relating to, or being an oracle. **2.** Resembling or characteristic of an oracle, in mystery or solemnity. **—o·rac′u·lar·ly** *adv.*

o·ral (ôr′əl, ōr′-) *adj.* **1.** Spoken rather than written. **2.** Of the mouth: *oral hygiene.* **3.** Used in or taken through the mouth: *an oral thermometer; oral vaccine.* [From Latin *ōs*, the mouth.] **—o′ral·ly** *adv.*

Usage: **oral, verbal.** *Oral* is the more precise term for specifying that something is conveyed by word or mouth. *Oral* refers only to what is spoken (*oral objections*), whereas *verbal* can also apply to what is written (*a verbal description*). Nevertheless, the phrases *verbal agreement* and *verbal contract* gen. signify something unwritten and are understood accordingly.

or·ange (ôr′ĭnj, ŏr′-) *n.* **1.** Any of several evergreen trees of the genus *Citrus*, that bear fragrant white flowers and round fruit. **2.** The fruit of the orange tree, with a yellowish-red rind and a sectioned, edible pulp. **3.** A color between red and yellow in hue. **—modifier:** *orange juice.* [Middle English, from Old French, from Arabic *nāranj*, from Persian *nārang*, from Sanskrit *nāranga*, orange, orange tree.] **—or′ange** *adj.*

or·ange·ade (ôr′ĭn-jād′, ŏr′-) *n.* A beverage of orange juice, sugar, and water.

Or·ange·man (ôr′ĭnj-mən, ŏr′-) *n.* **1.** A member of a Protestant secret society founded in Northern Ireland in 1795. **2.** A Protestant Irishman. [After William, Prince of *Orange* (King William III of England).]

or·ange·wood (ôr′ĭnj-wŏŏd′, ŏr′-) *n.* The fine-grained wood of the orange tree.

o·rang·u·tan (ō-răng′ə-tăn′, ə-răng′-) *n.* Also **o·rang·ou·tan,** **o·rang·u·tang** (ō-răng′ə-tăng′, ə-răng′-). An arboreal anthropoid ape, *Pongo pygmaeus*, of Borneo and Sumatra, having a shaggy reddish-brown coat, very long arms, and no tail. [Malay *orang hutan* : *ōrang*, man + *hūtan*, forest.]

o·rate (ō-rāt′, ō-rāt′, ôr′āt′, ōr′āt′) *intr.v.* **o·rat·ed, o·rat·ing.** To speak in a dignified and often pompous manner. [Back-formation from ORATION.]

ă pat ā pay â care ä father ĕ pet ē be hw which ĭ pit ī tie î pier ŏ pot ō toe ô paw, for oi noise
ŏŏ took ōō boot ou out th thin th this ŭ cut û urge zh vision ə about, item, edible, gallop, circus

o·ra·tion (ô-rā′shən, ō-rā′-) *n.* A formal address or speech. —See Syns at **speech.** [Latin *ōrātiō,* from *ōrāre,* to speak.]

or·a·tor (ôr′ə-tər, ŏr′-) *n.* **1.** A person who delivers an oration. **2.** A person skilled in the art of public speaking.

or·a·to·ri·o (ôr′ə-tôr′ē-ō′, -tōr′-, ŏr′-) *n., pl.* **-os.** A musical composition for voices and orchestra, which usu. tells a sacred story without costumes, scenery, or dramatic action. [Italian, from *Oratorio,* the Oratory of St. Philip Neri at Rome, where famous musical services were held in the 16th cent.]

or·a·to·ry[1] (ôr′ə-tôr′ē, -tōr′ē, ŏr′-) *n.* **1.** The art of public speaking; rhetoric. **2.** Skill or style in public speaking. [Old French *(art)* oratoire, from Latin *(ars) ōrātōria,* (the art) of public speaking, from *ōrātōrius,* of an orator, oratorical, from *ōrātor,* orator.]

or·a·to·ry[2] (ôr′ə-tôr′ē, -tōr′ē, ŏr′-) *n., pl.* **-ries.** A place for prayer, such as a small private chapel. [Middle English *oratorie,* from Late Latin *ōrātōrium (templum),* (place) of prayer, from *ōrātōrius,* of praying, from Latin *ōrāre,* to pray, speak.]

orb (ôrb) *n.* **1.** A sphere. **2.** A celestial body. **3.** A sphere surmounted by a cross, symbolizing the power of a sovereign. —*tr.v.* **1.** To shape into a circle or sphere. **2.** *Archaic.* To encircle; enclose. [Old French *orbe,* from Latin *orbis,* orb, disk.]

or·bic·u·lar (ôr-bĭk′yə-lər) *adj.* Circular; spherical. [Middle English *orbiculer,* from Old French *orbiculaire,* from Late Latin *orbiculāris,* from Latin *orbiculus,* dim. of *orbis,* orb.] —**or·bic′u·lar′i·ty** (ôr-bĭk′yə-lăr′ĭ-tē) *n.* —**or·bic′u·lar·ly** *adv.*

or·bit (ôr′bĭt) *n.* **1.** The path of one celestial body as it revolves around another. **2.** The path of a body in a field of force surrounding another body. **3.** A range of activity or influence. **4.** Either of the two bony cavities that contain an eye; eye socket. —See Syns at **range.** —*tr.v.* **1.** To put into or cause to move in an orbit: *The first man-made satellite was orbited in 1957.* **2.** To revolve around (a center of attraction): *The moon orbits the earth.* —*intr.v.* To revolve or move in orbit. [Latin *orbita,* from *orbitus,* circular, from *orbis,* orb.] —**or′bit·al** *adj.* —**or′bit·al·ly** *adv.*

or·chard (ôr′chərd) *n.* **1.** An area of land devoted to the cultivation of fruit or nut trees. **2.** The trees cultivated in an orchard. [Middle English *orchard,* from Old English *ortgeard* : Latin *hortus,* a garden + Old English *geard,* yard.]

or·ches·tra (ôr′kĭ-strə, ôr′kĕs′trə) *n.* **1.** A group of musicians who play together on various musical instruments, usu. including strings, woodwinds, brass instruments, and percussion instruments. **2.** The area immediately in front of and below a stage. **3. a.** The front section of seats on the main floor of a theater. **b.** The entire main floor of a theater. [Latin *orchēstra,* from Greek *orkhēstra,* from *orkheisthai,* to dance.]

or·ches·tral (ôr-kĕs′trəl) *adj.* Of, like, or composed for an orchestra. —**or·ches′tral·ly** *adv.*

or·ches·trate (ôr′kĭ-strāt′) *tr.v.* **-trat·ed, -trat·ing. 1.** To compose or arrange (music) for performance by an orchestra. **2.** To arrange or organize so as to achieve a desired or effective combination: *orchestrate a campaign.* —**or′ches·tra′tion** *n.*

or·chid (ôr′kĭd) *n.* **1. a.** Any of numerous epiphytic or terrestrial plants of the family Orchidaceae, often having brightly colored flowers of irregular and unusual shapes. **b.** The flower of one of these plants. **2.** A light reddish purple. —*adj.* Light reddish purple. [Latin *orchis,* from Greek *orkhis.*]

or·chis (ôr′kĭs) *n.* Any orchid of the genus *Orchis,* having magenta, white, or magenta-spotted flowers. [Latin.]

or·dain (ôr-dān′) *tr.v.* **1.** To install as a minister, priest, or rabbi. **2.** To order by or as if by decree. **3.** To predestine. [Middle English *ordeinen,* from Anglo-French *ordeiner,* from Late Latin *ōrdināre,* from Latin, to arrange, from *ōrdō,* order.] —**or·dain′er** *n.* —**or·dain′ment** *n.*

or·deal (ôr-dēl′, ôr′dēl′) *n.* **1.** An extremely difficult or painful experience. **2.** A former method of determining guilt or innocence in which the accused was subjected to physically painful or dangerous tests, whose results were regarded as a divine judgment. [Ult. from Old English *ordēl.*]

or·der (ôr′dər) *n.* **1.** A logical or harmonious arrangement among the separate elements of a group. **2.** Condition in regard to proper function or appearance. **3.** The existing structure or method of social organization: *"Every revolution exaggerates the evils of the old order."* (C. Wright Mills). **4.** The rule of law and custom or the observance of prescribed procedure. **5.** A sequential arrangement of events or objects. **6.** The established customary procedure: *the order of worship.* **7.** A command or direction. **8. a.** A commission or instruction to buy, sell, or supply goods or services. **b.** That which is supplied, bought, or sold. **9.** A portion of food requested by a customer at a restaurant. **10.** *Eccles.* **a.** Any of several grades of the Christian ministry: *the order of priesthood.* **b. orders.** The ceremony of ordination. **11.** A group sharing a religious rule. **12.** A social or fraternal organization. **13. a.** A group of persons who have won honors for unusual service or merit. **b.** The insignia of an order. **14.** A social class. **15.** Kind; rank. **16.** *Archit.* **a.** A style of classical architecture characterized by the type of column employed: *the Doric order.* **b.** A specific style of architecture. **17.** *Biol.* A taxonomic category of plants and animals ranking above the family and below the class. —*tr.v.* **1.** To issue a command or instruction to. **2.** To give a command or instruction for: *The judge ordered a recount of the ballots.* **3.** To give an order for: *order groceries.* **4.** To put in order. —*intr.v.* To place or give an order. —See Syns at **command.** —*idioms.* **in order to.** For the purpose of; so that. **on order.** Requested or purchased but not yet delivered. **on the order of.** Similar to; like; resembling. **out of order.** Not according to rule. **to order.** According to the buyer's specifications: *a suit made to order.* [Middle English *ordre,* from Old French, from Latin *ōrdō.*] —**or′der·er** *n.*

or·der·ly (ôr′dər-lē) *adj.* **1.** Having a methodical and systematic arrangement; tidy. **2.** Without violence or disruption; peaceful. —See Syns at **neat.** —*n., pl.* **-lies. 1.** An attendant in a hospital. **2.** A soldier assigned to attend upon a superior officer and carry orders or messages. —**or′der·li·ness** *n.*

or·di·nal (ôr′dn-əl) *adj.* Being of a specified position in a numbered series. —*n.* **1.** An ordinal number. **2.** A book of forms for ordination. [Late Latin *ōrdinālis,* from Latin *ōrdō,* order.]

ordinal number. A number indicating position in a series or order.

or·di·nance (ôr′dn-əns) *n.* **1.** An authoritative command or order. **2.** A custom or practice established by long usage. **3.** A statute or regulation esp. by a city government. [Middle English *ordinaunce,* from Old French *ordenance,* the art of arranging, from Medieval Latin *ōrdinantia,* from Latin *ōrdināre,* to put in order, from *ōrdō,* order.]

or·di·nar·i·ly (ôr′dn-âr′ə-lē, ôr′dn-ĕr′-) *adv.* **1.** As a general rule; usually. **2.** In the regular or usual manner: *ordinarily dressed.* **3.** To the usual extent or degree: *ordinarily large profits.*

or·di·nar·y (ôr′dn-ĕr′ē) *adj.* **1.** Commonly encountered; usual. **2.** Occurring regularly or routinely; normal. **3.** Average in rank, ability, or merit; commonplace. —*n., pl.* **-ies. 1.** The usual, normal, or average condition. **2.** *Eccles.* The part of the Mass that remains unchanged from day to day. [Middle English *ordinarie,* from Latin *ōrdinārius,* from *ōrdō,* order.] —**or′di·nar′i·ness** *n.*

    Syns: 1. ordinary, average, common, commonplace, plain, unexceptional *adj. Core meaning:* Of no special quality or type *(an ordinary rodent; an ordinary response).* **2. ordinary, common, normal, typical, usual** *adj. Core meaning:* To be expected *(ordinary problems of city life).*

ordinary seaman. A seaman of the lowest grade in the merchant marine.

or·di·nate (ôr′dn-ĭt, -āt′) *adj.* Arranged in regular rows, as spots on an insect's wings. —*n. Symbol* **y** *Math.* The plane Cartesian coordinate representing the distance from a specified point to the *x*-axis, measured parallel to the *y*-axis. [From Latin *ōrdināre,* to arrange, from *ōrdō,* order.]

or·di·na·tion (ôr′dn-ā′shən) *n.* The act or ceremony of ordaining a person to the ministry.

ord·nance (ôrd′nəns) *n.* **1.** Military weapons, along with ammunition and the equipment to keep them in good repair. **2.** Heavy guns; artillery. [Middle English *ordinaunce,* ordinance.]

Or·do·vi·cian (ôr′də-vĭsh′ən) *adj. Geol.* Of, pertaining to, or designating the geologic time, system of rocks, and sedimentary deposits of the second period of the Paleozoic era, characterized by the appearance of primitive fishes. —*n.* The Ordovician period. [After the *Ordovices,* an ancient Celtic tribe of North Wales.]

or·dure (ôr′jər) *n.* **1.** Excrement; dung. **2.** Something morally offensive; filth. [Middle English, from Old French, from *ord,* dirty, from Latin *horridus,* horrid, from *horrēre,* to shudder.]

ore (ôr, ōr) *n.* A mineral or rock from which a valuable constituent, esp. a metal, can be mined or extracted. [Middle English *oor,* from Old English *ār,* brass.]

ö·re (œ′rə) *n., pl.* **ö·re.** A coin equal to ¹/₁₀₀ of the krona of Sweden and the krone of Denmark and Norway. [Ult. from Latin *aureus,* gold coin, from *aurum,* gold.]

o·re·ad (ôr′ē-ăd′, ōr′-) *n. Gk. Myth.* A mountain nymph. [Greek *oreias,* from *oros,* mountain.]

o·reg·a·no (ə-rĕg′ə-nō′, ô-rĕg′-) *n.* An herb seasoning made from the dried leaves of a species of marjoram, *Origanum vulgare.* [American Spanish *orégano,* from Spanish, marjoram, from Latin *origanum,* from Greek *origanon.*]

O·res·tes (ô-rĕs′tēz) *n. Gk. Myth.* The son of Agamemnon and Clytemnestra, who, with his sister Electra, avenged his father by killing his mother and her lover Aegisthus.

or·gan (ôr′gən) *n.* **1.** A musical instrument consisting of a number of pipes that sound the tones of a musical scale when supplied with air, and a keyboard that operates a mechanism controlling the flow of air to the pipes. **2.** An instrument designed to imitate the organ electronically. **3.** A differentiated part, such as the stomach or the heart, of a living thing, adapted for a specific function. **4.** A body or agency that is part of a larger organization. **5.** A periodical. —*modifier: organ music.* [Middle English, from Old French *organe,* from Late Latin *organum,* church organ, from Latin, implement, instrument, from Greek *organon.*]

organ

or·gan·dy (ôr′gən-dē) *n., pl.* **-dies.** Also **or·gan·die.** A fine fabric, as of cotton or silk, usu. with a crisp finish. [French *organdi.*]

or·gan·elle (ôr′gə-nĕl′) *n. Biol.* A specialized part of a cell that resembles and functions as an organ. [Dim. of Latin *organum,* organ.]

organ grinder. A street musician who plays a hurdy-gurdy.

or·gan·ic (ôr-găn′ĭk) *adj.* **1.** Of, relating to, or affecting an organ of the body. **2.** Of, relating to, or derived from living organisms. **3.** Using or grown with fertilizers consisting only of animal or vegetable matter, with no use of chemical fertilizers or pesticides: *organic gardening; organic foods.* **4.** Having properties associated with living organisms: *the organic growth and decay of an empire.* **5.** Likened to an organism in organization or development: *an organic whole.* **6. a.** Of or constituting an integral part of something; fundamental. **b.** *Law.* Designating or pertaining to the fundamental laws and precepts of a government or organization. **7.** *Chem.* Of or relating to carbon compounds. [Old French *organique,* from Late Latin *organicus,* from Greek *organikos,* serving as an instrument, from *organon,* implement.] —**or·gan′i·cal·ly** *adv.*

organic chemistry. The chemistry of carbon compounds.

or·gan·ism (ôr′gə-nĭz′əm) *n.* **1.** A living being. **2.** A system likened to a living body: *the social organism.* —**or′gan·is′-**

mal (ôr′gə-nĭz′məl) or **or′gan·is′mic** *adj.*

or·gan·ist (ôr′gə-nĭst) *n.* A person who plays the organ.

or·gan·i·za·tion (ôr′gə-nĭ-zā′shən) *n.* **1.** The act of organizing or the process of being organized. **2.** The condition or manner of being organized: *a high degree of organization.* **3.** Something that has been organized and functions as a whole. **4.** A group united by a common interest or goal. —**or′gan·i·za′tion·al** *adj.* —**or′gan·i·za′tion·al·ly** *adv.*

or·gan·ize (ôr′gə-nīz′) *v.* **-ized, -iz·ing.** —*tr.v.* **1.** To put together into an orderly, functional, structured whole. **2.** To arrange or systematize: *organize one's thoughts before speaking.* **3.** To arrange or bring about by planning and coordinating: *organize a party.* **4.** To persuade to form or join a labor union. —*intr.v.* **1.** To develop into or assume an organic structure. **2.** To join or form an organization, esp. a labor union. [Middle English *organysen,* from Old French *organiser,* from Medieval Latin *organizāre,* from Latin *organum,* instrument.] —**or′gan·iz′er** *n.*

or·gan·za (ôr-găn′zə) *n.* A sheer, stiff fabric of silk or synthetic material. [Orig. unknown.]

or·gasm (ôr′găz′əm) *n.* The climax of sexual excitement. [French *orgasme,* from Greek *orgasmos,* from *organ,* to swell, be excited.] —**or·gas′mic** (ôr-găz′mĭk) *adj.*

or·gi·as·tic (ôr′jē-ăs′tĭk) *adj.* Of, relating to, or characteristic of an orgy. [Greek *orgiastikos,* from *orgiazein,* to hold secret rites, from *orgia,* secret rites.]

or·gy (ôr′jē) *n., pl.* **-gies. 1.** Often **orgies.** A secret rite in the cults of cetain Greek or Mediterranean deities, typically involving frenzied singing, dancing, drinking, and sexual activity. **2.** A wild revel or celebration, often marked by unrestrained sexual activity. **3.** Excessive indulgence in anything. [From Old French *orgies,* from Latin *orgia,* from Greek.]

o·ri·el (ôr′ē-əl, ōr′-) *n.* A projecting bay window supported by corbels or brackets. [Middle English, from Old French *oriol,* from Medieval Latin *oriolum,* upper chamber.]

o·ri·ent (ôr′ē-ənt, -ĕnt′, ōr′-) *adj. Poet.* Eastern; oriental. **2.** Sparkling and lustrous. —*n.* **Orient.** The countries of Asia, esp. of eastern Asia. —*v.* (ôr′ē-ĕnt′, ōr′-). Also **o·ri·en·tate** (-ĕn-tāt′, -ən-), **-tat·ed, -tat·ing.** —*tr.v.* **1.** To locate or place in a particular relation to the points of the compass. **2.** To place so as to face the east. **3.** To ascertain the position of: *He oriented himself by finding a familiar landmark.* **4.** To make familiar or acquainted with a situation. [Middle English, from Old French, from Latin *oriēns,* from *orīrī,* to rise.]

o·ri·en·tal (ôr′ē-ĕn′tl, ōr′-) *adj.* **1.** Eastern. **2.** Often **Oriental.** Of or characteristic of the Orient. —*n.* Often **Oriental.** A member of one of the peoples native to the Orient. —**o′ri·en′tal·ly** *adv.*

O·ri·en·tal·ism (ôr′ē-ĕn′tl-ĭz′əm, ōr′-) *n.* Also **o·ri·en·tal·ism. 1.** A quality, mannerism, or custom peculiar to or characteristic of the Orient. **2.** Scholarly study of eastern cultures, languages, and peoples. —**O′ri·en′tal·ist** *n.*

Oriental poppy. A plant, *Papaver orientale,* widely cultivated for its brilliant scarlet and black flowers.

Oriental rug. A rug made by hand in the Orient.

o·ri·en·ta·tion (ôr′ē-ĕn-tā′shən, -ən-, ōr′-) *n.* **1.** The act of orienting or the condition of being oriented. **2.** Location or position relative to the points of the compass. **3.** General position or tendency: *a Marxist orientation.*

or·i·fice (ôr′ə-fĭs, ŏr′-) *n.* A mouth or vent; opening. [Old French, from Late Latin *ōrificium* : Latin *ōs,* mouth + *facere,* to make.]

o·ri·flamme (ôr′ə-flăm′, ŏr′-) *n.* Also **au·ri·flamme.** An inspiring standard or symbol. [Middle English *oriflamble,* from Old French *oriflambe,* from Medieval Latin *auriflamma* : Latin *aurum,* gold + *flamma,* flame.]

o·ri·ga·mi (ôr′ĭ-gä′mē) *n.* The Japanese art or process of folding paper. [Japanese : *ori,* a folding + *kami,* paper.]

or·i·gin (ôr′ə-jĭn, ŏr′-) *n.* **1.** The primary source or cause of something. **2.** Parentage; ancestry. **3.** A coming into being. **4.** *Math.* The point of intersection of coordinate axes, as in the Cartesian coordinate system. [Middle English *origyne,* from Latin *orīgō,* from *orīrī,* to rise.]

Syns: origin, derivation root source *n. Core meaning:* A point of origination (*"vodka"—a word of Russian origin*).

o·rig·i·nal (ə-rĭj′ə-ənl) *adj.* **1.** Of or existing from the beginning; initial; first: *the original thirteen states of the Union.*

2. Fresh and unusual; not copied; new. **3.** Able to produce new things or present new ideas; creative; inventive. **4.** Designating the one from which a copy, reproduction, or translation is made. —See Syns at **first** and **fresh.** —*n.* **1.** The primary form of anything from which varieties arise. **2.** An authentic work, as of art or literature, as distinguished from a copy or reproduction. **3.** A unique or eccentric person. [Middle English, from Old French, from Latin *orīginālis,* from *orīgō,* origin.] —**o·rig'i·nal·ly** *adv.*

o·rig·i·nal·i·ty (ə-rĭj'ə-năl'ĭ-tē) *n., pl.* **-ties. 1.** The quality of being original. **2.** The capacity to act or think independently.

original sin. *Theol.* The state of deprivation from grace resulting from Adam's sinful disobedience.

o·rig·i·nate (ə-rĭj'ə-nāt') *v.* **-nat·ed, -nat·ing.** —*tr.v.* To bring into being; create; invent. —*intr.v.* To come into being; start; spring. —See Syns at **begin** and **introduce.** —**o·rig'i·na'tion** *n.* —**o·rig'i·na'tor** *n.*

o·ri·ole (ôr'ē-ōl', ōr'-) *n.* **1.** Any of various Old World birds of the family Oriolidae, of which the males are characteristically bright-yellow and black. **2.** Any of various New World birds of the family Icteridae, of which the males are black and orange or yellow. [French *oriol,* from Old French, from Medieval Latin *oriolus,* "golden (bird)," from Latin *aurum,* gold.]

oriole
A golden oriole
George Miksch Sutton

O·ri·on (ō-rī'ən) *n.* A constellation in the celestial equator near Gemini and Taurus.

or·i·son (ôr'ĭ-sən, -zən, ŏr'-) *n.* A prayer. [Middle English, from Old French, from Latin *ōrātiō,* oration.]

Or·lon (ôr'lŏn') *n.* A trademark for a synthetic acrylic fiber.

or·mo·lu (ôr'mə-lōō') *n.* An alloy, sometimes gilded, that resembles gold in appearance and is used esp. to decorate furniture. [French *or moulu,* "ground gold."]

or·na·ment (ôr'nə-mənt) *n.* **1.** Something that decorates or adorns. **2.** A person considered as a source of pride, honor, or credit. **3.** *Mus.* A note or group of notes that embellishes a melody. —*tr.v.* (ôr'nə-mĕnt'). **1.** To furnish with ornaments. **2.** To be an ornament to. [Middle English, from Old French *ornement,* from Latin *ōrnāmentum,* from *ōrnāre,* to adorn.] —**or'na·ment'er** *n.*

or·na·men·tal (ôr'nə-mĕn'tl) *adj.* Of or serving as an ornament. —*n.* A plant grown for its beauty. —**or'na·men'tal·ly** *adv.*

or·na·men·ta·tion (ôr'nə-mĕn-tā'shən) *n.* **1. a.** The act, process, or result of ornamenting. **b.** The condition of being ornamented. **2.** Something that ornaments. **3.** A group of ornaments.

or·nate (ôr-nāt') *adj.* **1.** Elaborately and heavily ornamented; excessively decorated. **2.** Marked by flowery language or rhetoric. [Middle English *ornat,* from Latin *ōrnātus,* past part. of *ōrnāre,* to adorn.] —**or·nate'ly** *adv.* —**or·nate'ness** *n.*

or·ner·y (ôr'nə-rē) *adj.* **-i·er, -i·est.** Mean and stubborn: *an ornery child.* —See Syns at **contrary.**

or·ni·thol·o·gy (ôr'nə-thŏl'ə-jē) *n.* The scientific study of birds as a branch of zoology. [From Greek *ornithologia.*] —**or'ni·tho·log'i·cal** (ôr'nə-thə-lŏj'ĭ-kəl) or **or'ni·tho·log'ic** (-ĭk) *adj.* —**or'ni·tho·log'i·cal·ly** *adv.* —**or'ni·thol'o·gist** *n.*

o·ro·tund (ôr'ə-tŭnd', ōr'-, ŏr'-) *adj.* **1.** Full in sound; sonorous. **2.** Pompous and bombastic. [Latin *ōre rotundō,* "with round mouth."] —**o'ro·tun'di·ty** (ôr'ə-tŭn'dĭ-tē, ōr'-, ŏr'-) *n.*

or·phan (ôr'fən) *n.* A child whose parents are dead. —*tr.v.* To deprive of one or both parents. [Late Latin *orphanus,* from Greek *orphanos,* orphaned.] —**or'phan·hood'** *n.*

or·phan·age (ôr'fə-nĭj) *n.* An institution for the care of orphans.

Or·phe·us (ôr'fē-əs, -fyōōs') *n. Gk. Myth.* A musician and poet whose music had the power to charm wild beasts.

or·pi·ment (ôr'pə-mənt) *n.* Arsenic trisulfide, As_2S_3, a lemon-yellow pigment, used in tanning and in linoleum manufacture. [Middle English, from Old French, from Latin *auripigmentum : aurum,* gold + *pigmentum,* pigment.]

or·pine (ôr'pĭn) *n.* Any of several plants of the genus *Sedum,* esp. *S. telephium,* with clusters of reddish-purple flowers. [Middle English *orpin,* from Old French *orpine,* short for *orpiment,* orpiment (after the yellow flowers of one species).]

or·ris (ôr'ĭs, ŏr'-) *n.* **1.** Any of several species of iris having a fragrant rootstock. **2.** Orrisroot. [Var. of IRIS.]

or·ris·root (ôr'ĭs-rōōt', -rŏŏt', ŏr'-) *n.* The fragrant rootstock of the orris, used in perfumes and cosmetics.

orth-. Var. of **ortho-.**

ortho- or **orth-.** A prefix meaning: **1.** Straight or upright: *orthopteran.* **2.** *Math.* Perpendicular to or at right angles: *orthorhombic.* **3.** Correct or correcting: *orthodontia.* [Middle English, from Old French, from Latin, from Greek, from *orthos,* straight, correct, upright.]

or·tho·clase (ôr'thə-klās', -klāz') *n.* A feldspar, potassium aluminum silicate, $KAlSi_3O_8$, characterized by a monoclinic crystalline structure and found in igneous or granitic rock. [German *Orthoklas.*]

or·tho·don·tics (ôr'thə-dŏn'tĭks) *n.* The dental specialty and practice of correcting abnormally aligned or positioned teeth. [ORTHO- + Greek *odous,* tooth.] —**or'tho·don'tic** *adj.* —**or'tho·don'tist** *n.*

or·tho·dox (ôr'thə-dŏks') *adj.* **1.** Adhering to traditional or established beliefs, esp. in religion. **2.** Adhering to what is commonly accepted, customary, or traditional. **3. Orthodox. a.** Of or relating to the Eastern Orthodox Church. **b.** Of or relating to Orthodox Judaism. [Old French *orthodoxe,* from Late Latin *orthodoxus,* from Greek *orthodoxos,* having the right opinion.] —**or'tho·dox'ly** *adv.*

Orthodox Church. The Eastern Orthodox Church.

Orthodox Judaism. Judaism that adheres to the Mosaic Law as interpreted in the Talmud and considers it binding in modern as well as ancient times.

or·tho·dox·y (ôr'thə-dŏk'sē) *n., pl.* **-ies. 1.** The quality or condition of being orthodox. **2.** An orthodox practice, custom, or belief.

or·thog·o·nal (ôr-thŏg'ə-nəl) *adj.* Forming or composed of right angles. [Greek *orthogōnios : orthos,* straight + *gōnia,* angle.] —**or·thog'o·nal·ly** *adv.*

or·tho·graph·ic (ôr'thə-grăf'ĭk) or **or·tho·graph·i·cal** (ôr'thə-grăf'ĭ-kəl) *adj.* **1.** Of orthography. **2.** Spelled correctly. **3.** *Math.* Having perpendicular lines. —**or'tho·graph'i·cal·ly** *adv.*

or·thog·ra·phy (ôr-thŏg'rə-fē) *n., pl.* **-phies. 1.** The study of correct spelling according to established usage. **2.** A method of representing the sounds of language by written or printed symbols. —**or·thog'ra·pher** *n.*

or·tho·pe·dics (ôr'thə-pē'dĭks) *n. (used with a sing. verb).* The branch of medicine that deals with disorders or injuries of the bones, joints, and associated muscles. [From French *orthopédie : Greek orthos,* straight + *pais,* child.] —**or'tho·pe'dic** *adj.* —**or'tho·pe'di·cal·ly** *adv.* —**or'tho·pe'dist** *n.*

or·thop·ter·an (ôr-thŏp'tər-ən) *n.* Also **or·thop·ter·on** (ôr-thŏp'tə-rŏn', -tər-ən). Any insect of the order Orthoptera, characterized by membranous, folded hind wings covered by leathery, narrow fore wings, and including the locusts, cockroaches, crickets, and grasshoppers. [New Latin *Orthoptera* (order), "straight-wings."] —**or·thop'ter·an** or **or·thop'ter·ous** or **or·thop'ter·al** *adj.*

or·tho·rhom·bic (ôr'thə-rŏm'bĭk) *adj.* Of or having a crystalline structure of three mutually perpendicular axes of different length.

or·to·lan (ôr'tə-lən) *n.* **1.** A small, brownish bird, *Emberiza hortulana,* of the Old World, eaten as a delicacy. **2.** Any of several New World birds, such as the bobolink and the sora. [French, from Provençal, gardener, from Latin *hortolānus,* from *hortus,* garden.]

ă pat	ā pay	â care	ä father	ĕ pet	ē be	hw which	ĭ pit	ī tie	î pier	ŏ pot	ō toe	ô paw, for	oi noise
ŏŏ took	ōō boot	ou out	th thin	th this	ŭ cut		û urge	zh vision	ə about, item, edible, gallop, circus				

-o·ry¹. A suffix meaning: **1.** A place for: **crematory. 2.** An instrument for: **directory.** [Middle English -*orie*, from Old French, from Latin -*orium*.]

-o·ry². A suffix meaning: **1.** Of, relating to, or characterized by: **transitory. 2.** Serving as or possessing the nature of: **compensatory.** [Middle English -*orie*, from Old French, from Latin -*orius*.]

o·ryx (ôr′ĭks, ōr′-, ŏr′-) *n.*, *pl.* **o·ryx·es** or **oryx.** Any of several antelopes of the genus *Oryx*, of Africa and southwest Asia, with long, straight horns. [Latin, from Greek *orux*, pickax, spike, gazelle (from its sharp horns).]

os¹ (ŏs) *n.*, *pl.* **o·ra** (ôr′ə, ōr′ə). *Anat.* A mouth or opening. [Latin *ōs*, mouth.]

os² (ŏs) *n.*, *pl.* **os·sa** (ŏs′ə). *Anat.* A bone. [Latin.]

Os The symbol for the element osmium.

Os·car (ŏs′kər) *n.* A golden statuette awarded annually by the Academy of Motion Picture Arts and Sciences for achievement in motion pictures. [Orig. unknown.]

os·cil·late (ŏs′ə-lāt′) *intr.v.* **-lat·ed, -lat·ing. 1.** To swing back and forth with a steady uninterrupted rhythm. **2.** To waver between two or more thoughts or courses of action; vacillate. **3.** *Physics.* To vary between alternate extremes, usu. with a definable period. [From Latin *ōscillāre*, from *ōscillum*, a swing, a mask of Bacchus hung from a tree as a charm, dim. of *ōs*, face, mouth.] **—os′cil·la·to·ry** (-lə-tôr′ē, -tōr′ē) *adj.*

os·cil·la·tion (ŏs′ə-lā′shən) *n.* **1.** The act, process, or condition of oscillating. **2.** A single cycle of motion or variation about a central position. **3.** A wave, esp. an electromagnetic wave.

os·cil·la·tor (ŏs′ə-lā′tər) *n.* Something that oscillates, esp. a device that produces electromagnetic waves or an alternating current.

os·cil·lo·scope (ŏ-sĭl′ə-skōp′, ə-sĭl′-) *n.* An electronic instrument that produces an instantaneous visual display or trace of electron motion on the screen of a cathode-ray tube corresponding to external oscillatory motion. [OSCILL(ATION) + -SCOPE.] **—os·cil′lo·scop′ic** (-skŏp′ĭk) *adj.*

os·cine (ŏs′īn′) *adj.* Of or pertaining to the Oscines, a large suborder of the passerine birds that includes most songbirds. [From Latin *oscinēs*, pl. of *oscen*, a singing bird used for augury.] **—os′cine′** *n.*

os·cu·lum (ŏs′kyə-ləm) *n.*, *pl.* **-la** (-lə). Also **os·cule** (ŏs′-kyōōl′). *Zool.* An opening in a sponge for expelling water. [From Latin *ōsculum*, little mouth, dim. of *ōs*, mouth.] **—os′cu·lar** *adj.*

-ose¹. A suffix meaning possession of or similarity to: **grandiose.** [Middle English, from Latin -*ōsus.*]

-ose². A suffix meaning: **1.** A carbohydrate: **lactose. 2.** A product of protein hydrolysis: **proteose.** [From GLUCOSE.]

o·sier (ō′zhər) *n.* **1. a.** Any of several willows with long, rodlike twigs used in basketry. **b.** A twig of such a willow. **2.** Any of several varieties of American dogwood. [Middle English, from Old French, from Medieval Latin *ausēria*, willow bed.]

-osis. A suffix meaning: **1.** A condition or process: **hypnosis. 2.** A diseased or abnormal condition: **cirrhosis.** [Middle English, from Latin, from Greek -*ōsis*, noun suffix.]

os·mi·um (ŏz′mē-əm) *n. Symbol* **Os** A bluish-white, hard, metallic element, found in small amounts in osmiridium, nickel, and platinum ores, used as a platinum hardener, and also as a catalyst in cortisone synthesis. Atomic number 76; atomic weight 190.2; melting point 3,000° C; boiling point 5,000° C; specific gravity 22.57; valences 2, 3, 4, 8. [From Greek *osmē*, odor (from the odor of osmium tetroxide).]

os·mose (ŏz′mōs′, ŏs′-) *v.* **-mosed, -mos·ing.** *—intr.v.* To diffuse by osmosis. [From OSMOSIS.]

os·mo·sis (ŏz-mō′sĭs, ŏs-) *n.* **1.** The diffusion of fluid through a semipermeable membrane until there is an equal concentration of fluid on either side of the membrane. **2.** The tendency of fluids to diffuse in such a manner. **3.** Any gradual process of assimilation or absorption that resembles osmosis: *learn a language by osmosis.* [From Greek *ōsmos*, action of pushing, from *ōthein*, to push.] **—os·mot′ic** (ŏz-mŏt′ĭk, ŏs-) *adj.* **—os·mot′i·cal·ly** *adv.*

os·prey (ŏs′prē, -prā′) *n.*, *pl.* **-preys.** A fish-eating hawk, *Pandion haliaetus*, having plumage that is dark on the back and white below. [Middle English *ospray*, prob. ult. from Latin *avis praedae*, "bird of prey."]

os·sa (ŏs′ə) *n.* Plural of **os** (bone).

os·se·ous (ŏs′ē-əs) *adj.* Composed of, containing, or resembling bone; bony. [Latin *osseus*, from *os*, bone.] **—os′-se·ous·ly** *adv.*

os·si·cle (ŏs′ĭ-kəl) *n. Anat.* A small bone, esp. one of the three bones of the inner ear. [Latin *ossiculum*, dim. of *os*, bone.]

os·si·fi·ca·tion (ŏs′ə-fĭ-kā′shən) *n.* **1.** The natural process of bone formation. **2. a.** The abnormal hardening or calcification of soft tissue into a bonelike material. **b.** A mass or deposit of such material.

os·si·fy (ŏs′ə-fī′) *v.* **-fied, -fy·ing.** *—intr.v.* **1.** To convert into bone; become bony. **2.** To become rigid or inflexible. *—tr.v.* **1.** To make or form bone in or of; convert into bone. **2.** To make rigid; harden. [Latin *os*, bone + -FY.]

oste-. Var. of **osteo-.**

os·ten·si·ble (ŏ-stĕn′sə-bəl, ə-stĕn′-) *adj.* Represented or appearing as such; seeming; professed: *His ostensible purpose was charity, his real goal popularity.* [French, from Medieval Latin *ostensibilis*, from Latin *ostendere*, to show.] **—os·ten′si·bly** *adv.*

os·ten·sive (ŏ-stĕn′sĭv) *adj.* **1.** Ostensible; apparent. **2.** Clearly pointing out or showing; demonstrative. [Late Latin *ostensivus*, from Latin *ostensus*, past part. of *ostendere*, to show.] **—os·ten′sive·ly** *adv.*

os·ten·ta·tion (ŏs′tĕn-tā′shən, -tən-) *n.* Pretentious or excessive display. [Middle English *ostentacioun*, from Old French *ostentation*, from Latin *ostentātiō*, from *ostentāre*, freq. of *ostendere*, to show.]

os·ten·ta·tious (ŏs′tĕn-tā′shəs, -tən-) *adj.* Characterized by or given to ostentation. **—os′ten·ta′tious·ly** *adv.*

osteo- or **oste-.** A prefix meaning bone: **osteomyelitis.** [Greek, from *osteon*, bone.]

os·te·ol·o·gy (ŏs′tē-ŏl′ə-jē) *n.* The anatomical study of bones. [Greek *osteologia*.] **—os′te·o·log′i·cal** (ŏs′tē-ə-lŏj′-ĭ-kəl) *adj.* **—os′te·ol′o·gist** *n.*

os·te·o·my·e·li·tis (ŏs′tē-ō-mī′ə-lī′tĭs) *n.* Inflammation of the bone marrow. [OSTEO- + MYELITIS.]

os·te·o·path (ŏs′tē-ə-păth′) *n.* Also **os·te·op·a·thist** (ŏs′-tē-ŏp′ə-thĭst). A person who practices osteopathy.

os·te·op·a·thy (ŏs′tē-ŏp′ə-thē) *n.* A system that emphasizes manipulation esp. of the bones for treating disease. [OSTEO- + -PATHY.] **—os′te·o·path′ic** (ŏs′tē-ə-păth′ĭk) *adj.* **—os′te·o·path′i·cal·ly** *adv.*

os·tler (ŏs′lər) *n.* Var. of **hostler.**

ost·mark (ôst′märk′, ŏst′-) *n.* The basic monetary unit of East Germany. [German *Ostmark*, "east mark."]

os·tra·cism (ŏs′trə-sĭz′əm) *n.* **1.** Banishment or exclusion from a group. **2.** In Athens and other cities of ancient Greece, the temporary banishment by popular vote of a citizen considered dangerous to the state.

os·tra·cize (ŏs′trə-sīz′) *tr.v.* **-cized, -ciz·ing. 1.** To banish or exclude from a group. **2.** To exile by ostracism, as in ancient Greece. [Greek *ostrakizein*, from *ostrakon*, shell, shard (from the shard with which the Athenian citizen voted for ostracism).]

os·trich (ŏs′trĭch, ôs′trĭch) *n.* Any of several large, flightless African birds of the genus *Struthio*, with long, bare necks and legs, two-toed feet, and plumage valuable for decoration and brushes. [Middle English *ostriche*, from Old French *ostrusce* : Latin *avis*, bird + Late Latin *strūthiō*, ostrich, from Greek *struthiōn*.]

Os·tro·goth (ŏs′trə-gŏth′) *n.* One of a tribe of eastern Goths that conquered and ruled Italy from A.D. 493 to 555. **—Os′-tro·goth′ic** *adj.*

ot-. Var. of **oto-.**

oth·er (ŭth′ər) *adj.* **1. a.** Being the remaining one of two or more: *Let me look at the other shoe.* **b.** Being the remaining one of several: *My other friends are away on vacation.* **2.** Different or distinct from what has been mentioned: *some other time.* **3.** Just recent or past: *the other day.* **4.** Additional; extra: *I have no other clothes than what I'm wearing.* **5.** Alternate; second: *We play tennis every other day.* *—n.* **1. a.** The remaining one of two or more: *One took a taxi and the other walked home.* **b. oth·ers.** The remaining ones of several: *How are the others doing now that I'm gone?* **2. a.** A different one: *one hurri-*

cane after the other. **b.** An additional one: *Where are the others?* —*pron.* Another person or thing: *The mayor's out at the airport welcoming some V.I.P. or other.* —*adv.* Otherwise: *He soon found that he would never succeed other than by work.* [Middle English, from Old English *ōther.*]

Usage: other than, otherwise. The phrase *other than* is used both adjectivally and adverbially to express difference or opposition: *firearms other* (i.e., different) *than pistols; acted other than* (or *otherwise than*) *perfectly. Other than* used as the equivalent of apart from or aside from is idiomatic American English; it is used so widely as to be considered standard now: *Other than what I've just said, I can't think of anything else that must be discussed. She has a bad headache, but other than that, her condition is good.*

oth·er·wise (ŭth′ər-wīz′) *adv.* **1.** In another way; differently: *She thought otherwise.* **2.** Under other circumstances: *Otherwise I might have helped.* **3.** In other respects: *an otherwise logical mind.* —See Usage note at **other.** —*adj.* **1.** Other than supposed; different: *The evidence is otherwise.* **2.** Other: *be otherwise than happy.* [Middle English, from Old English (*on*) *ōthre wīsan,* (in) another manner.]

oth·er·world·ly (ŭth′ər-wûrld′lē) *adj.* **1.** Of or characteristic of another world, esp. a mystical or transcendental world. **2.** Devoted to the world of the mind; concerned with intellectual or imaginative things. —**oth′er·world′li·ness** *n.*

-otic. A suffix meaning: **1.** Of, pertaining to, or characterized by a specified process, state, or condition: **epizootic, narcotic. 2.** Having a specified disease or abnormal condition: **sclerotic.** [From Greek *-ōticos,* adj. suffix.]

o·ti·ose (ō′shē-ōs′, ō′tē-) *adj.* **1.** Having a lazy nature; indolent. **2.** Having no use, purpose, or effect; futile. [Latin *ōtiōsus,* from *ōtium,* leisure.] —**o′ti·ose′ly** *adv.*

oto- or **ot-.** A prefix meaning the ear: **otology.** [From Greek *ous,* ear.]

o·to·lar·yn·gol·o·gy (ō′tō-lăr′ĭng-gŏl′ə-jē) *n.* The branch of medicine that deals with the ear, nose, and throat. —**o′to·la·ryn′go·log′i·cal** (-lə-rĭng′gə-lŏj′ĭ-kəl) *adj.* —**o′to·lar′yn·gol′o·gist** *n.*

Ot·ta·wa (ŏt′ə-wə, -wä′, -wō′) *n.* **1. a.** A group of Algonquian-speaking Indians, orig. inhabiting the region of the Ottawa River in Ontario, Canada. **b.** A member of this group. **2.** The language of the Ottawa.

ot·ter (ŏt′ər) *n., pl.* **otter** or **-ters. 1.** Any of various aquatic, carnivorous mammals of the genus *Lutra* and allied genera, with webbed feet and dark-brown fur. **2.** The fur of an otter. [Middle English *oter,* from Old English *otor.*]

otter

Ot·to·man (ŏt′ə-mən) *n., pl.* **-mans. 1.** A Turk. **2. ottoman. a.** An upholstered sofa or divan without arms or a back. **b.** An upholstered footstool. —*adj.* Turkish.

ou·bli·ette (ōō′blē-ĕt′) *n.* A dungeon with a trap door in the ceiling as its only means of entrance or exit. [French, from *oublier,* to forget, from Old French *oblider,* ult. from Latin *oblīviscī,* to forget.]

ouch (ouch) *interj.* A word used to express sudden pain.

ought¹ (ôt) *v.* Used as an auxiliary verb followed by an infinitive with *to.* Indicates: **1.** Obligation or duty: *You ought to work harder than that.* **2.** Expediency or prudence: *You ought to wear a raincoat.* **3.** Desirability: *You ought to have been there; it was great fun.* **4.** Probability or likelihood: *She ought to finish by next week.* [Middle English *oughten,* to be obliged to, owe, from *oughte,*

owned, from Old English *āhte,* p.t. of *āgan,* to possess.]

Usage: ought. *Ought* is an auxiliary verb and is not inflected. It is often used with an infinitive, the choice of which is important in indicating time. Present time is expressed by a present infinitive: *They ought to comply.* Past time is expressed by a perfect infinitive: *They ought to have complied.* A negative sense is indicated by using *not* right after *ought: ought not to have complied.* Other auxiliary verb forms, such as *did, could, had,* and *should,* are never used with *ought: She ought to go* (not *had ought*). *They ought not to complain* (not *hadn't ought* or *shouldn't ought*). Sometimes the infinitive following *ought* is omitted and only *to* is expressed, if the sense is clear from the context: *Shall we try again? We ought to.* But sometimes the reverse holds true; the infinitive without *to* is used in negative sentences: *ought not complain; ought not have complied.* However, the writer must not omit *to* in combinations such as these: *She ought and can call. She ought and could have called.* The word *to* is necessary in these positive sentences, and structural revision is also in order. Make them: *She can and ought to call. She could and ought to have called.* The corrected last example permits *could* and *ought* in a single sentence.

ought² (ôt) *pron. & adv.* Var. of **aught.**

ounce¹ (ouns) *n. Abbr.* **oz 1. a.** A unit of weight in the U.S. Customary System, an avoirdupois unit equal to 16 drams or 437.5 grains. **b.** A unit of apothecary weight, equal to 480 grains or 1.097 avoirdupois ounces. **2. a.** A unit of volume or capacity in the U.S. Customary System, used in liquid measure, equal to 8 fluid drams or 1.804 cubic inches. **b.** A unit of volume or capacity in the British Imperial System, used in dry and liquid measure, equal to 1.734 cubic inches. **3.** A tiny bit. [Middle English *unce,* from Old French *unce,* from Latin *uncia,* a twelfth, an ounce, from *ūnus,* unit, one.]

ounce² (ouns) *n.* The snow leopard. [Middle English *once,* from Old French, var. of *lonce,* from Latin *lynx,* lynx, from Greek *lunx.*]

our (our) *pron.* The possessive form of **we,** used as a modifier before a noun: *our homework; our greatest setback.* [Middle English *oure,* from Old English *ūre.*]

ours (ourz) *pron.* Used to indicate the one or ones belonging to us: *The house is ours. He is a friend of ours.* [Middle English *oures,* from *oure,* our.]

our·self (our-sĕlf′, är-) *pron.* Myself. Used in royal proclamations or editorial commentaries.

Usage: ourself, ourselves. 1. *Ourself* is a singular form approximately equivalent in meaning to *myself.* It is used only when *we* is employed in the sense of *I*—when a monarch employs *we* or an editor uses the same term in speaking for a publication. Thus an editor might write: *We ourself favor the incumbent mayor for reelection, but we shall also present other opinions.* Though the average writer has little use for *ourself,* it is important to understand that the word cannot be substituted for *ourselves.* The latter term is the usual form of the first person plural pronoun, used in sentences such as the following: *We should not permit ourselves such liberties. We ourselves are not directly involved. We have not been ourselves since the accident.* (In none of the examples can *ourself* replace *ourselves.*) **2.** *Ourselves* should not replace *us* and *we* in compound object and subjects, as in the following: *They have invited the Smiths and us* (not *ourselves*). *We* (not *ourselves*) *and the Smiths are invited.*

our·selves (our-sĕlvz′, är-) *pron.* **1.** Those identical with us. Used: **a.** Reflexively as the direct object of a verb or the object of a preposition: *We injured ourselves.* **b.** For emphasis: *We ourselves are excluded from the contract.* **2.** Our normal or healthy condition: *We have not been ourselves since he left.* —See Usage note at **ourself.** —*idiom.* **by ourselves. 1.** Alone: *We're going by ourselves.* **2.** Without help: *We'll make that decision by ourselves.*

-ous. A suffix meaning: **1.** Possessing: **joyous. 2.** Occurring with a valence that is lower than that in a comparable *-ic* system: **ferrous.** [Middle English from Old French *-os, -eus,* from Latin *-ōsus, -us.*]

ou·sel (ōō′zəl) *n.* Var. of **ouzel.**

oust (oust) *tr.v.* To eject from a position or place; force out: *"the American Revolution, which ousted the English"*

(Virginia S. Eifert). [Anglo-French *ouster*, from Latin *ob-stāre*, to hinder.]

oust·er (ou'stər) *n.* The act or an example of ousting. [Anglo-French, from *ouster*, to oust.]

out (out) *adv.* **1.** Away or forth from inside: *go out of the office.* **2.** Away from the center or middle: *The troops fanned out.* **3.** Away or absent from a normal or usual place: *stepped out for a minute.* **4.** From inside a building or shelter into the open air; outside: *The boy went out to play.* **5. a.** To exhaustion or depletion: *The supplies have run out.* **b.** To extinction: *The fire has gone out.* **c.** To a finish or conclusion: *Play the game out.* **6.** Into the open: *The moon came out.* **7.** Into circulation: *giving out free passes.* **8.** Into disuse or disfavor: *Knee-length hems have gone out.* **9.** Used to intensify the action of a verb: *pick out a number; speak out.* **10.** *Baseball.* So as to be retired: *He grounded out to the shortstop.* —*adj.* **1.** Exterior; external. **2.** Unable to be used; in disrepair: *The road is out beyond this point.* **3.** *Informal.* Without an amount possessed previously: *I am out ten dollars.* **4.** Not available for use or consideration: *A taxi is out, because we haven't the money.* —*prep.* Through; forth from: *He fell out the window.* —*n.* **1.** A person or party that is out of power. **2.** A means of escape: *The window was my only out.* **3.** *Baseball.* A play in which a batter or base runner is retired. **4.** A serve or return that falls out of bounds in a court game, such as tennis. —*intr.v.* To be disclosed or revealed; come out: *Truth will out.* —*idioms.* **on the outs.** *Informal.* Not on friendly terms; disagreeing. **out for.** Trying to get or have: *She's out for the committee chairmanship.* **out from under.** *Informal.* Relieved from danger or distress: *He's finally out from under financially.* **out of. 1.** From among: *one out of thousands.* **2.** Past the boundaries, limits, or usual position of: *The eagle soared out of sight.* **3.** From: *made out of wood.* **4.** Because of; owing to: *He did it out of malice.* [Middle English, from Old English *ūt.*]

out-. A prefix meaning: **1.** To a surpassing or superior degree: **outshoot. 2.** Outside or external: **outboard, outhouse.** [From OUT.]

out-and-out (out'n-out') *adj.* Complete; thoroughgoing. —See Syns at **utter.**

out·back (out'băk') *n.* The wild, remote part esp. of Australia or New Zealand.

out·bid (out-bĭd') *tr.v.* **-bid, -bid·den** (-bĭd'n) or **-bid, -bid·ding.** To bid higher than.

out·board (out'bôrd', -bōrd') *adj.* **1.** *Naut.* **a.** Situated outside the hull of a vessel. **b.** Being away from the center line of the hull of a ship. **2.** *Aviation.* Situated toward or nearer the end of a wing. —**out'board'** *adv.*

outboard motor. A detachable engine mounted on the stern of a boat or on outboard brackets.

out·bound (out'bound') *adj.* Outward bound.

out·break (out'brāk') *n.* A sudden eruption.

out·build·ing (out'bĭl'dĭng) *n.* A building separate from but associated with a main building.

out·burst (out'bûrst') *n.* A sudden, often violent display, as of activity or emotion.

out·cast (out'kăst') *n.* Someone who has been excluded from a society. —**out'cast'** —*adj.*

out·class (out-klăs') *tr.v.* To surpass decisively so as to appear of a higher class.

out·come (out'kŭm') *n.* A result; consequence.

out·crop (out'krŏp') *n.* *Geol.* A portion of bedrock or other rock from a lower stratum that extends up above the level of the soil. —*intr.v.* (out'krŏp', out-krŏp') **-cropped, -crop·ping.** *Geol.* To protrude above the surface.

out·cry (out'krī') *n., pl.* **-cries. 1.** A loud cry or clamor. **2.** A strong protest or objection.

out·dat·ed (out-dā'tĭd) *adj.* Out-of-date; antiquated.

out·dis·tance (out-dĭs'təns) *tr.v.* **-tanced, -tanc·ing.** To go ahead of by a wide margin.

out·do (out-do͞o') *tr.v.* **-did** (-dĭd'), **-done** (-dŭn'), **-do·ing.** To do better than. —See Syns at **surpass.**

out·door (out'dôr', -dōr') *adj.* Also **out-of-door** (out'əv-dôr', -dōr'). Located in, done in, or suited to the open air: *outdoor clothing; an outdoor fireplace.*

Usage: **outdoor, outdoors.** *Outdoor* is an adjective: *outdoor lighting.* *Outdoors* is an adverb: *went outdoors,*

and a noun: *enjoying the great outdoors.*

out·doors (out-dôrz', -dōrz') *adv.* Also **out-of-doors** (out'-əv-dôrz', -dōrz'). In or into the open; outside of a house or shelter. —*n.* Also **out-of-doors.** The open air; the area outside buildings. —See Usage note at **outdoor.**

out·er (ou'tər) *adj.* **1.** Located on the outside; external. **2.** Farther from the center or middle.

outer ear. The external ear.

out·er·most (ou'tər-mōst') *adj.* Most distant from the center or inside.

outer space. Space beyond the limits of a celestial body or system.

out·face (out-fās') *tr.v.* **-faced, -fac·ing. 1.** To overcome with a bold or self-assured look; stare down. **2.** To defy; resist.

out·field (out'fēld') *n.* The grass-covered playing area extending outward from a baseball diamond, divided into right, center, and left field. —**out'field'er** *n.*

out·fit (out'fĭt') *n.* **1.** Clothing or equipment for a special purpose: *a welder's outfit.* **2.** *Informal.* A group or association of persons who work together. —*tr.v.* **-fit·ted, -fit·ting.** To provide with an outfit. —**out'fit'ter** *n.*

out·flank (out-flăngk') *tr.v.* **1.** To maneuver around the flank of (an opposing force). **2.** To gain a tactical advantage over.

out·flow (out'flō') *n.* **1.** The act of flowing out. **2.** Something that flows out.

out·fox (out-fŏks') *tr.v.* To outsmart.

out·go (out'gō') *n., pl.* **-goes.** Something, esp. money, that goes out.

out·go·ing (out'gō'ĭng) *adj.* **1.** Departing; going out; *an outgoing steamship.* **2.** Friendly; sociable.

out·grow (out-grō') *tr.v.* **-grew** (-gro͞o'), **-grown** (-grōn'), **-grow·ing. 1.** To grow too large for: *He outgrew his new suit.* **2.** To grow too mature for: *outgrew childish games.* **3.** To surpass in growth.

out·growth (out'grōth') *n.* **1.** Something that grows out of something else: *an outgrowth of new shoots on a branch.* **2.** A result or consequence: *Inflation is an outgrowth of war.*

out·guess (out-gĕs') *tr.v.* To anticipate correctly the plans or actions of.

out·house (out'hous') *n.* **1.** A toilet housed in a small outdoor structure. **2.** An outbuilding.

out·ing (ou'tĭng) *n.* **1.** An excursion or pleasure trip, often including a picnic. **2.** A walk outdoors; an airing.

outing flannel. A soft, lightweight cotton fabric, usu. with a short nap on both sides.

out·land (out'lănd', -lənd) *n.* **1.** A foreign land. **2. outlands.** The outlying areas of a country. [Middle English, from Old English *ūtland* : *ūt,* out + *land,* land.] —**out'land'er** *n.*

out·land·ish (out-lăn'dĭsh) *adj.* **1.** Strikingly foreign; unfamiliar. **2.** *Archaic.* Of foreign origin; not native. **3.** Geographically remote from the familiar world. **4.** Conspicuously unconventional; bizarre; absurd. —**out·land'ish·ly** *adv.* —**out·land'ish·ness** *n.*

out·last (out-lăst') *tr.v.* To last longer than.

out·law (out'lô') *n.* **1.** A person excluded from normal legal protection and rights. **2.** A person who is a fugitive from the law. —*tr.v.* **1.** To declare illegal. **2.** To ban. **3.** To deprive of the protection of law. —See Syns at **forbid.** [Middle English *outlawe,* from Old English *ūtlaga,* from Old Norse *ūtlagi,* from *ūtlagr,* outlawed.] —**out'law'ry** *n.*

out·lay (out'lā') *n.* **1.** The spending or disbursing of money. **2.** The amount spent.

out·let (out'lĕt', -lĭt) *n.* **1.** A passage for escape or exit; vent. **2.** A means of release or expression, as for energy or talent. **3. a.** A commercial market for goods or services. **b.** A store that sells the goods esp. of a particular manufacturer or wholesaler. **4.** A receptacle, esp. one mounted in a wall, that is connected to a power supply and equipped with a socket for a plug.

out·line (out'līn') *n.* **1. a.** A line forming the outer boundary of any object or figure. **b.** Contour; shape. **2.** A style of drawing in which objects are represented by their outer edges, without shading. **3.** A short summary, description, or account, usu. arranged point by point: *an outline for a composition.* —*modifier:* *an outline map.* —*tr.v.* **-lined,**

-lin·ing. **1.** To draw the outline of. **2.** To give the main points of; summarize.

out·live (out-lĭv′) *tr.v.* **-lived, -liv·ing.** To live longer than; outlast.

out·look (out′lŏŏk′) *n.* **1. a.** A place where something can be viewed. **b.** The view seen from such a place. **2.** A point of view or attitude. **3.** Prospect; expectation: *The outlook is for continued inflation.*

out·ly·ing (out′lī′ĭng) *adj.* Distant or remote from a center.

out·mod·ed (out-mō′dĭd) *adj.* **1.** Not in fashion. **2.** No longer usable or practical; obsolete: *outmoded machinery.*

out·most (out′mōst′) *adj.* Farthest out; outermost.

out·num·ber (out-nŭm′bər) *tr.v.* To be more numerous than.

out-of-date (out′əv-dāt′) *adj.* Outmoded; old-fashioned.

out-of-door (out′əv-dôr′, -dōr′) *adj.* Var. of **outdoor.**

out-of-doors (out′əv-dôrz′, -dōrz′) *adv. &. n.* Var. of **outdoors.**

out-of-the-way (out′əv-thə-wā′) *adj.* **1.** Distant; remote; secluded. **2.** Out of the ordinary; unusual.

out·pa·tient (out′pā′shənt) *n.* A patient who receives treatment at a hospital or clinic without being hospitalized. **—modifier:** *an outpatient clinic.*

out·play (out-plā′) *tr.v.* To play better than.

out·post (out′pōst′) *n.* **1.** A detachment of troops stationed at a distance from a main unit of forces. **2.** The station occupied by an outpost. **3.** An outlying settlement.

out·pour·ing (out′pôr′ĭng, -pōr′-) *n.* **1.** The act of pouring out. **2.** Something that pours out or is poured out; outflow.

out·put (out′pŏŏt′) *n.* **1.** The act of producing; production. **2.** The amount of something produced or manufactured esp. during a given time. **3. a.** The energy, power, or work produced by a system. **b.** The information produced by a computer from a specific input.

out·rage (out′rāj′) *n.* **1.** An act of extreme violence or viciousness. **2.** Any act grossly offensive to decency, morality, or good taste. **3.** Resentful anger aroused by a violent or offensive act: *public outrage over the scandal.* —See Syns at **harm.** *—tr.v.* **-raged, -rag·ing.** **1.** To inflict violence upon. **2.** To rape. **3.** To produce anger or resentment in. — See Syns at **insult.** [Middle English, excess, from Old French, excess, atrocity, from *outre,* beyond.]

out·ra·geous (out-rā′jəs) *adj.* **1. a.** Being an outrage; grossly offensive. **b.** Disgraceful; shameful. **2.** Extravagant; immoderate; extreme: *an outrageous liar.* **—out·ra′geous·ly** *adv.* **—out·ra′geous·ness** *n.*

    Syns: 1. outrageous, atrocious, crying, flagrant, heinous, monstrous, scandalous, shocking *adj.* **Core meaning:** Disgracefully and grossly offensive (*an outrageous violation of their civil rights*). **2. outrageous, preposterous, ridiculous, unreasonable** *adj.* **Core meaning:** Beyond all reason (*charged an outrageous sum to fix the car*).

ou·tré (ŏŏ-trā′) *adj.* Eccentric; bizarre. [French, past part. of *outrer,* to go to excess, from *outre,* beyond, from Old French, from Latin *ultrā.*]

out·reach (out-rēch′) *tr.v.* **1.** To surpass in reach. **2.** To go beyond. *—intr.v.* To reach out.

out·rid·er (out′rī′dər) *n.* A mounted attendant or escort.

out·rig·ger (out′rĭg′ər) *n.* **1. a.** A long, thin float attached parallel to a seagoing canoe by projecting spars as a means of preventing it from capsizing. **b.** Any vessel fitted with such a float. **2.** Any projecting frame extending laterally beyond the main structure of a vessel, vehicle, aircraft, or machine, to stabilize the structure or to support an extending part.

out·right (out′rīt′, -rīt′) *adv.* **1.** Without reservation or qualification: *gave him the property outright.* **2.** Entirely; utterly; wholly. **3.** Without delay; straightway. *—adj.* (out′rīt′). **1.** Without reservation; unqualified: *an outright gift.* **2.** Thoroughgoing; out-and-out: *outright viciousness.* —See Syns at **utter.**

out·run (out-rŭn′) *tr.v.* **-ran** (-răn′), **-run, -run·ning.** **1.** To run faster than. **2.** To go beyond or exceed.

out·sell (out-sĕl′) *tr.v.* **-sold** (-sōld′), **-sell·ing.** **1.** To surpass in amount sold. **2.** To outdo in selling.

out·set (out′sĕt′) *n.* Beginning; start; commencement.

out·shine (out-shīn′) *v.* **-shone** (-shōn′), **-shin·ing.** *—tr.v.* **1.** To shine brighter than. **2.** To exceed (another). *—intr.v.*

To shine forth. —See Syns at **surpass.**

out·shoot (out-shŏŏt′) *tr.v.* **-shot** (-shŏt′), **-shoot·ing.** **1.** To shoot better than. **2.** To go or extend beyond.

out·side (out-sīd′, out′sīd′) *n.* **1.** An outer surface or side; exterior. **2.** The space beyond a boundary or limit. **3.** The utmost limit; maximum: *We'll be leaving in ten days at the outside.* *—adj.* **1.** Acting, occurring, originating, or existing at a place beyond certain limits; outer; foreign: *outside assistance.* **2.** Of, restricted to, or situated on the outside of an enclosure or boundary; external: *an outside door lock.* **3.** Extreme; uttermost: *The cost exceeded even my outside estimate.* **4.** Slight; remote: *an outside chance.* *—adv.* On or into the outside; outdoors: *Let's go outside for some fresh air.* *—prep.* **1.** On or to the outer side of: *outside the playing field.* **2.** Beyond the limits of: *outside the rules.* **3.** With the exception of; except: *no information outside the figures given.* **—idiom. outside of. 1.** Beyond the confines of. **2.** To the outer side of. **3.** Apart from; except.

    Usage: **outside, outside of.** Both *outside* and *outside of* are standard and can be used interchangeably to mean *beyond the limits or confines of,* to the outer side of, or *except: There is a yard outside* (of) *the house. He ran outside* (of) *his yard. No one knew the whole story outside* (of) *a select few.*

out·sid·er (out-sī′dər) *n.* A person who is not part of a certain group or community.

out·size (out′sīz′) *n.* An unusual size; esp., a very large size. *—adj.* Also **out·sized** (out′sīzd′). Unusually large.

out·skirts (out′skûrts′) *pl.n.* The parts or regions remote from a central district.

out·smart (out-smärt′) *tr.v.* To gain the advantage over by cunning; outwit.

out·spo·ken (out-spō′kən) *adj.* Marked by frankness and lack of reserve: *outspoken opposition; an outspoken critic.* **—out·spo′ken·ness** *n.*

out·spread (out-sprĕd′) *v.* **-spread, -spread·ing.** *—intr.v.* To spread out; stretch. *—tr.v.* To cause to spread out. **—out′spread′** *adj.*

out·stand·ing (out-stăn′dĭng, out′stăn′-) *adj.* **1.** Standing out; projecting upward or outward. **2.** Standing out among others of its kind; prominent. **3.** Superior to others of its kind; distinguished; excellent. **4. a.** Still in existence. **b.** Not settled or resolved: *outstanding debts.*

out·stay (out-stā′) *tr.v.* To stay longer than; overstay.

out·stretch (out-strĕch′) *tr.v.* To stretch out; extend. **—out′stretched′** *adj.* —See Syns at **spread.**

out·strip (out-strĭp′) *tr.v.* **-stripped, -strip·ping.** **1.** To outrun. **2.** To exceed; surpass: *"Material development outstripped human development"* (Edith Hamilton).

out·ward (out′wərd) *adj.* **1.** Of or moving toward the outside or exterior: *an outward flow of cash.* **2.** Visible on the surface; superficial: *His outward manner remained composed.* *—adv.* Also **out·wards** (-wərdz). Toward the outside; away from a center: *extending outward.* **—out′ward·ly** *adv.* **—out′ward·ness** *n.*

out·wear (out-wâr′) *tr.v.* **-wore** (-wôr′, -wōr′), **-worn** (-wôrn′, -wōrn′), **-wear·ing.** To wear or last longer than; outlast.

out·weigh (out-wā′) *tr.v.* **1.** To weigh more than. **2.** To be more significant than: *fear that outweighed love.*

out·wit (out-wĭt′) *tr.v.* **-wit·ted, -wit·ting.** To gain an advantage over by cleverness or cunning; outsmart.

out·work¹ (out-wûrk′) *tr.v.* To work better or faster than.

out·work² (out′wûrk′) *n.* A trench or other defensive position that is outside a fortification.

ou·zel (ŏŏ′zəl) *n.* Also **ou·sel. 1.** Any of various European birds of the genus *Turdus.* **2.** The water ouzel. [Middle English *ousel,* from Old English *ōsle.*]

o·va (ō′və) *n.* Plural of **ovum.**

o·val (ō′vəl) *adj.* **1.** Resembling an egg in shape. **2.** Resembling an ellipse; elliptical. *—n.* **1.** An oval form or figure. **2.** An oval track, as for horse racing or athletic events. [Medieval Latin *ōvālis,* from Latin *ōvum,* egg.] **—o′val·ly** *adv.* **—o′val·ness** *n.*

o·va·ry (ō′və-rē) *n., pl.* **-ries. 1.** *Zool.* One of a pair of female reproductive glands that produce ova. **2.** *Bot.* The part of a pistil containing the ovules. [New Latin *ovarium,* from Latin *ōvum,* egg.] **—o·var′i·an** (ō-vâr′ē-ən) *adj.*

ă pat   ā pay   â care   ä father   ĕ pet   ē be   hw which   ĭ pit   ī tie   î pier   ŏ pot   ō toe   ô paw, for   oi noise
ŏŏ took   ŏŏ boot   ou out   th thin   th this   ŭ cut   û urge   zh vision   ə about, item, edible, gallop, circus

o·vate (ō′vāt′) *adj.* **1.** Oval; egg-shaped. **2.** *Bot.* Broad and rounded at the base and tapering toward the end: *an ovate leaf.* [Latin *ōvātus,* egg-shaped, from *ōvum,* egg.] —**o′vate·ly** *adv.*

o·va·tion (ō-vā′shən) *n.* **1.** An ancient Roman victory ceremony less important than a triumph. **2.** Enthusiastic and prolonged applause. [Latin *ovātiō,* from *ovāre,* to rejoice.]

ov·en (ŭv′ən) *n.* A chamber or enclosed compartment, as in a stove, for baking, heating, or drying. [Middle English, from Old English *ofen.*]

ov·en·bird (ŭv′ən-bûrd′) *n.* A thrushlike North American warbler, *Seiurus aurocapillus,* that has a shrill call, and characteristically builds a domed nest on the ground. [From its oven-shaped nests.]

o·ver (ō′vər) *prep.* **1.** In or at a position above or higher than: *a sign over the door.* **2.** Above and across from one end or side to the other: *a jump over the fence.* **3.** On the other side of: *a village over the border.* **4.** Through the extent of: *traveled all over Europe and Asia.* **5.** So as to cover: *a mulch of salt hay over the flower beds.* **6.** Through the period or duration of: *records maintained over two years.* **7.** Until or beyond the end of: *stay over the holidays.* **8.** More than, in degree, quantity, or extent: *over ten miles.* **9.** In a position of preeminence, influence, or control: *preside over a meeting.* **10.** Upon; directed toward: *poured the bucket of water over his head.* **11.** While occupied with or engaged in: *a chat over coffee.* **12.** With reference to; concerning: *an argument over methods.* —*adv.* **1.** Above the top or surface. **2. a.** Across to another or opposite side: *flying over to Europe.* **b.** Across the edge or brim: *The coffee spilled over.* **3.** Across a distance or space: *over at police headquarters.* **4.** Throughout an area or region: *wander all over.* **5.** To a different opinion or allegiance: *win someone over.* **6.** To a different person, condition, or title: *sign over land.* **7.** Completely; thoroughly: *The river froze over.* **8. a.** From an upright position: *The book fell over.* **b.** From an upward position to an inverted or reversed position: *turn the book over.* **9.** Another time; again: *Count your cards over.* **10.** In repetition: *ten times over.* **11.** In addition or excess; in surplus: *three pennies left over.* **12.** Beyond or until a specified time: *stay a day over.* —*adj.* **1.** Finished; done; past: *The war is over.* **2.** Having gone across or to the other side: *A quick leap and she was over.* **3. a.** Upper; higher. **b.** External; outer. **4.** In excess: *His estimate was fifty dollars over.* —*idioms.* **over against.** As opposed to; contrasted with. **over and above.** In addition to; besides. [Middle English, from Old English *ofer.*]
    Usage: **over.** As a preposition meaning more than (a specified amount), *over* is well established on all levels of usage: *cost over three dollars; over age sixty-five.* It is clearly out of place in an example having a sense of decrease: *attendance figures down five per cent over last year's* (better: *down...from*).

over-. A prefix meaning: **1.** Above: **overhead, overlord. 2.** Beyond: **overshoot. 3.** Excessive or excessively: **overheat.** [Middle English, from Old English *ofer-,* from *ofer,* over.]

o·ver·a·bun·dance (ō′vər-ə-bŭn′dəns) *n.* Lavish excess. —**o′ver·a·bun′dant** *adj.*

o·ver·a·chieve (ō′vər-ə-chēv′) *intr.v.* **-chieved, -chiev·ing.** To perform better than expected. —**o′ver·a·chiev′er** *n.* —**o′ver·a·chieve′ment** *n.*

o·ver·act (ō′vər-ăkt′) *tr.v.* To act with unnecessary exaggeration. —*intr.v.* To act in an exaggerated manner.

o·ver·age¹ (ō′vər-ĭj) *n.* An excess or surplus. —See Syns at **excess.**

o·ver·age² (ō′vər-āj′) *adj.* Older than the proper or required age.

o·ver·all (ō′vər-ôl′, ō′vər-ôl′) *adj.* **1.** From one end to the other. **2.** Including everything; comprehensive. —See Syns at **general.** —*adv.* (ō′vər-ôl′). As a whole; generally.

o·ver·alls (ō′vər-ôlz′) *pl.n.* Loose-fitting trousers with a bib front and shoulder straps.

o·ver·arm (ō′vər-ärm′) *adj.* Executed with the arm raised above the shoulder.

o·ver·awe (ō′vər-ô′) *tr.v.* **-awed, -aw·ing.** To subdue or overcome with awe.

o·ver·bal·ance (ō′vər-băl′əns) *v.* **-anced, -anc·ing.** —*tr.v.* **1.** To have greater weight or importance than: *virtues that overbalance his defects.* **2.** To throw off balance. —*intr.v.* To lose balance.

o·ver·bear (ō′vər-bâr′) *v.* **-bore** (-bôr′), **-borne** (bôrn′), **-bear·ing.** —*tr.v.* **1.** To crush or press down upon with physical force. **2.** To prevail over, as if by superior weight or force; dominate.

o·ver·bear·ing (ō′vər-bâr′ĭng) *adj.* Domineering and arrogant in manner. —See Syns at **arrogant** and **dictatorial.** —**o′ver·bear′ing·ly** *adv.*

o·ver·bid (ō′vər-bĭd′) *v.* **-bid, -bid·den** (-bĭd′n) or **-bid, -bid·ding.** —*tr.v.* To bid higher than the actual value of. —*intr.v.* To bid higher than the actual value of something.

o·ver·blown (ō′vər-blōn′) *adj.* **1.** Extremely fat. **2.** Blown up; inflated: pretentious. **3.** Past the stage of full bloom.

o·ver·board (ō′vər-bôrd′, -bōrd′) *adv.* Over the side of a boat or ship. —**idiom. go overboard.** *Informal.* To show wild enthusiasm.

o·ver·build (ō′vər-bĭld′) *tr.v.* **-built** (-bĭlt′), **-build·ing.** To build beyond the demand or need of.

o·ver·bur·den (ō′vər-bûr′dn) *tr.v.* To burden with or as if with too much weight. —*n.* (ō′vər-bûrd′n). *Geol.* Material overlying a useful mineral deposit.

o·ver·buy (ō′vər-bī′) *v.* **-bought** (-bôt′), **-buy·ing.** —*tr.v.* To buy in excessive amounts or beyond one's ability to pay. —*intr.v.* To buy goods beyond one's means.

o·ver·call (ō′vər-kôl′) *tr.v.* **1.** To overbid. **2.** *Bridge.* To bid higher than. —*intr.v.* (ō′vər-kôl′). **1.** An overbid. **2.** *Bridge.* An instance of overcalling.

o·ver·cap·i·tal·ize (ō′vər-kăp′ĭ-tl-īz′) *tr.v.* **-ized, -iz·ing.** To estimate the value of (property) too highly. —**o′ver·cap′i·tal·i·za′tion** *n.*

o·ver·cast (ō′vər-kăst′, ō′vər-kăst′) *adj.* **1.** Covered or obscured, as with clouds or mist. **2.** Gloomy; dark. —*n.* (ō′vər-kăst′). A covering, as of mist or clouds. —*tr.v.* (ō′vər-kăst′, ō′vər-kăst′). **-cast·ed** or **-cast, -cast·ing. 1.** To make cloudy or gloomy. **2.** To sew with long, overlying stitches to prevent raveling.

o·ver·charge (ō′vər-chärj′) *tr.v.* **-charged, -charg·ing. 1.** To charge too much. **2.** To fill too full; overload. —*n.* (ō′vər-chärj′). An excessive charge or price.

o·ver·cloud (ō′vər-kloud′) *tr.v.* To cover or spread over with clouds. —*intr.v.* To become cloudy.

o·ver·coat (ō′vər-kōt′) *n.* A heavy coat worn over the ordinary clothing in cold weather.

o·ver·come (ō′vər-kŭm′) *v.* **-came** (-kām′), **-come, -com·ing.** —*tr.v.* **1.** To defeat; conquer. **2.** To surmount; prevail over: *overcome the obstacles of poverty.* **3.** To overpower, as with emotion; affect deeply. —*intr.v.* To be victorious. —See Syns at **defeat.** [Middle English *overcomen,* from Old English *ofercuman.*]

o·ver·com·pen·sate (ō′vər-kŏm′pən-sāt′) *v.* **-sat·ed, -sat·ing.** —*intr.v.* **1.** To make a greater effort than required to achieve compensation. **2.** To engage in overcompensation. —*tr.v.* To compensate excessively. —**o′ver·com·pen·sa·to′ry** (-kəm-pĕn′sə-tôr′ē, -tōr′ē) *adj.*

o·ver·com·pen·sa·tion (ō′vər-kŏm′pən-sā′shən) *n.* The exertion of effort in excess of that needed to compensate for a physical or psychological characteristic or defect.

o·ver·de·vel·op (ō′vər-dĭ-vĕl′əp) *tr.v.* **1.** To develop to excess. **2.** To process (a photographic plate or film) too long. —**o′ver·de·vel′op·ment** *n.*

o·ver·do (ō′vər-dōō′) *tr.v.* **-did** (-dĭd′), **-done** (-dŭn′), **-do·ing. 1.** To do too much: *She overdid her diet and suffered from malnutrition.* **2.** To cook too much or too long.

o·ver·dose (ō′vər-dōs′) *tr.v.* **-dosed, -dos·ing.** To give too large a dose to. —*n.* (ō′vər-dōs′). An excessive dose.

o·ver·draft (ō′vər-drăft′) *n.* **1.** The act of overdrawing an account. **2.** The amount overdrawn.

o·ver·draw (ō′vər-drô′) *tr.v.* **-drew** (-drōō′), **-drawn** (-drôn′), **-draw·ing. 1.** To withdraw more from (an account) than one has credit for. **2.** To exaggerate in telling or describing.

o·ver·dress (ō′vər-drĕs′) *intr.v.* To dress too formally or elaborately for an occasion. —*n.* (ō′vər-drĕs′). A dress worn over another.

o·ver·drive (ō′vər-drīv′) *n.* A gearing mechanism of an automotive engine that reduces the power output required to

---

| ă pat | ā pay | â care | ä father | ĕ pet | ē be | hw which | ĭ pit | ī tie | î pier | ŏ pot | ō toe | ô paw, for | oi noise |
| ōō took | ōō boot | ou out | th thin | *th* this | ŭ cut | û urge | zh vision | ə about, item, edible, gallop, circus |

maintain driving speed in a specific range by increasing the ratio of drive shaft to engine speed.

o·ver·due (ō′vər-dōō′, -dyōō′) *adj.* **1.** Being unpaid after becoming due. **2.** Past due; late. —See Syns at **late.**

o·ver·es·ti·mate (ō′vər-ĕs′tə-māt′) *tr.v.* **-mat·ed, -mat·ing.** To estimate or value too highly. —**o·ver·es·ti·mate** (-mĭt) *n.* —**o′ver·es′ti·ma′tion** *n.*

o·ver·ex·pose (ō′vər-ĭk-spōz′) *tr.v.* **-posed, -pos·ing.** To expose too long or too much. —**o′ver·ex·po′sure** *n.*

o·ver·ex·tend (ō′vər-ĭk-stĕnd′) *tr.v.* To extend beyond a safe or reasonable limit. —**o′ver·ex·ten′sion** *n.*

o·ver·flow (ō′vər-flō′) *intr.v.* To flow or run over the top, brim, or bounds. —*tr.v.* **1.** To flow over the top, brim, or bounds of . **2.** To spread or cover over. —*n.* (ō′-vər-flō′). **1.** The act of overflowing. **2.** The amount that is more than needed or required. **3.** An outlet or vent through which excess liquid may escape. —See Syns at **excess.**

o·ver·grow (ō′vər-grō′) *v.* **-grew** (-grōō′), **-grown** (-grōn′), **-grow·ing.** —*tr.v.* **1.** To spread over with growth: *The weeds overgrew the disused pathway.* **2.** To grow too large for. —*intr.v.* To grow beyond normal size. —**o′ver·growth′** *n.*

o·ver·hand (ō′vər-hănd′) *adj.* Also **o·ver·hand·ed** (ō′-vər-hăn′dĭd). Executed with the hand above the level of the shoulder: *an overhand pitch.* —*adv.* In an overhand manner. —*n.* An overhand throw, stroke, or delivery.

overhand knot. A knot formed by making a loop in a piece of cord and pulling the end through it.

o·ver·hang (ō′vər-hăng′) *v.* **-hung** (-hŭng′), **-hang·ing.** —*tr.v.* **1.** To project or extend beyond. **2.** To threaten or menace; loom over. —**o′ver·hang′** *n.*

o·ver·haul (ō′vər-hôl′, ō′vər-hôl′) *tr.v.* **1.** To examine carefully and make repairs. **2.** To catch up with; overtake. —**o′ver·haul′** *n.*

o·ver·head (ō′vər-hĕd′) *adj.* **1.** Located or functioning above the level of the head: *an overhead light.* **2.** Made with the racket swung over the head: *an overhead smash in tennis.* **3.** Of or relating to the operating expenses of a business concern. —*n.* (ō′vər-hĕd′). **1.** A stroke, as in tennis, made with the racket swung over the head. **2.** The operating expenses of a business, such as rent, utilities, and taxes. —**o′ver·head′** *adv.*

o·ver·hear (ō′vər-hîr′) *tr.v.* **-heard** (-hûrd′), **-hear·ing.** To hear without being addressed and without the knowledge of the speaker. —**o′ver·hear′er** *n.*

o·ver·heat (ō′vər-hēt′) *tr.v.* To heat too much. —*intr.v.* To become too hot.

o·ver·in·dulge (ō′vər-ĭn-dŭlj′) *v.* **-dulged, -dulg·ing.** —*tr.v.* To indulge excessively; gratify too much or unwisely. —*intr.v.* To indulge in something to excess. —**o′ver·in·dul′gence** *n.* —**o′ver·in·dul′gent** *adj.*

o·ver·joyed (ō′vər-joid′) *adj.* Filled with joy; delighted.

o·ver·kill (ō′vər-kĭl′) *n.* **1.** Nuclear destructive capacity exceeding the amount needed to destroy an enemy. **2.** An excessive action or response.

o·ver·land (ō′vər-lănd′, -lənd) *adj.* Over or across land. —**o′ver·land′** *adv.*

o·ver·lap (ō′vər-lăp′) *v.* **-lapped, -lap·ping.** —*tr.v.* **1.** To lie or extend over and cover part of. **2.** To have an area or range in common with. —*intr.v.* **1.** To lie over and partly cover something. **2.** To share or have in common. —**o′ver·lap′** *n.*

o·ver·lay (ō′vər-lā′) *tr.v.* **-laid** (-lād′), **-lay·ing.** To lay or spread over or upon. —**o′ver·lay′** *n.*

Usage: **overlay, overlie.** Though both verbs are transitive, and are related in meaning, they are carefully distinguished in usage. *Overlay* expresses the sense of superimposing one thing over another: *a carpenter who overlays plywood with veneer.* On the other hand, *overlie* refers to lying over or resting upon (something else): *a layer of rock that overlies another.* Both verbs are often used in the passive voice: *wood that was overlaid with silver; bedrock overlain with sand.*

o·ver·leap (ō′vər-lēp′) *tr.v.* **-leaped** or **-leapt** (-lĕpt′), **-leap·ing.** To leap across or over.

o·ver·lie (ō′vər-lī′) *tr.v.* **-lay** (-lā′), **-lain** (-lān′), **-ly·ing.** **1.** To lie over or upon. **2.** To kill by lying upon. —See Usage note at **overlay.**

o·ver·load (ō′vər-lōd′) *tr.v.* To load too heavily: *overload a circuit.* —**o′ver·load′** *n.*

o·ver·long (ō′vər-lông′, -lŏng′) *adj.* Excessively long. —**o′ver·long′** *adv.*

o·ver·look (ō′vər-lōōk′) *tr.v.* **1.** To look over or at from above. **2.** To afford a view over. **3.** To fail to notice or consider. **4.** To ignore deliberately or indulgently; disregard: *Try to overlook the boy's faults.* **5.** To look over; examine. **6.** To watch over; supervise.

o·ver·lord (ō′vər-lôrd′) *n.* **1.** A lord having power or supremacy over another or other lords. **2.** Someone who is in a position of supremacy or domination over others. —**o′ver·lord′ship** *n.*

o·ver·ly (ō′vər-lē) *adv.* To an excessive degree.

o·ver·mas·ter (ō′vər-măs′tər) *tr.v.* To overcome.

o·ver·match (ō′vər-măch′) *tr.v.* **1.** To be more than the match of. **2.** To match with a superior opponent: *Our team was overmatched in the finals.*

o·ver·much (ō′vər-mŭch′) *adj.* Too much; excessive. —*adv.* In too great a degree. —*n.* (ō′vər-mŭch′, ō′-vər-mŭch′). An excessive amount.

o·ver·night (ō′vər-nīt′) *adj.* **1.** Of, lasting for, extending over, or remaining during a night: *an overnight guest.* **2.** Happening as if in a single night; sudden: *an overnight success.* —*adv.* (ō′vər-nīt′). **1.** During or for the length of the night. **2.** In or as if in the course of one night; suddenly: *The situation changed overnight.*

o·ver·pass (ō′vər-păs′) *n.* A passage, roadway, or bridge that crosses above another roadway or thoroughfare. —*tr.v.* (ō′vər-păs′). **1.** To pass over or across; traverse. **2.** To go beyond; exceed; surpass. **3.** To overlook; disregard.

o·ver·pay (ō′vər-pā′) *v.* **-paid** (-pād′), **-pay·ing.** —*tr.v.* **1.** To pay too much. **2.** To pay an amount in excess of (a sum due). —**o′ver·pay′ment** *n.*

o·ver·play (ō′vər-plā′) *tr.v.* **1.** To overact. **2.** To depend on too much: *overplayed his hand.*

o·ver·pow·er (ō′vər-pou′ər) *tr.v.* **1.** To overcome by superior force. **2.** To affect so strongly as to make helpless or ineffective; overwhelm.

o·ver·pro·duce (ō′vər-prə-dōōs′, -dyōōs′) *tr.v.* **-duced, -duc·ing.** To produce too much of. —**o′ver·pro·duc′tion** (ō′-vər-prə-dŭk′shən) *n.*

o·ver·rate (ō′vər-rāt′) *tr.v.* **-rat·ed, -rat·ing.** To rate too highly; overestimate the merits of.

o·ver·reach (ō′vər-rēch′) *tr.v.* **1.** To reach or extend over or beyond. **2.** To miss by reaching too far or attempting too much: *overreach a goal.* **3.** To defeat (oneself) by going too far or by doing or trying to gain too much. **4.** To get the better of; trick; outwit. —*intr.v.* **1.** To reach or go too far. **2.** To outwit others; cheat. —**o′ver·reach′er** *n.*

o·ver·ride (ō′vər-rīd′) *tr.v.* **-rode** (-rōd′), **-rid·den** (-rĭd′n), **-rid·ing.** **1.** To ride across. **2.** To trample upon. **3.** To ride (a horse) too hard. **4.** To prevail over; conquer. **5.** To declare null and void; set aside: *a veto that was overridden by Congress.* —*n.* (ō′vər-rīd′). An act of overriding.

o·ver·ripe (ō′vər-rīp′) *adj.* Too ripe. —**o′ver·ripe′ness** *n.*

o·ver·rule (ō′vər-rōōl′) *tr.v.* **-ruled, -rul·ing.** **1.** To rule against. **2.** To declare null and void; invalidate.

o·ver·run (ō′vər-rŭn′) *v.* **-ran** (-răn′), **-run, -run·ning.** —*tr.v.* **1.** To spread or swarm over in great numbers: *Weeds overran the garden.* **2.** To run or extend beyond; exceed: *The plane overran the runway.* **3.** To defeat and spread out over or through. **4.** To overflow: *The river overran its banks.* —*intr.v.* **1.** To run over; overflow. **2.** To go beyond the normal or desired limit. —*n.* (ō′vər-rŭn′). **1.** An act of overrunning. **2.** The amount by which something overruns.

o·ver·seas (ō′vər-sēz′, ō′vər-sēz′) *adv.* Also **o·ver·sea** (ō′-vər-sē′, ō′vər-sē′). Beyond the sea; abroad. —*adj.* Also **o·ver·sea.** Of, originating in, or situated in areas across the sea: *an overseas flight; an overseas representative.*

o·ver·see (ō′vər-sē′) *tr.v.* **-saw** (-sô′), **-seen** (-sēn′), **-see·ing.** **1.** To watch over and direct; supervise. **2.** To examine; inspect. **3.** To look down upon.

o·ver·se·er (ō′vər-sē′ər) *n.* A person who oversees; superintendent.

o·ver·sell (ō′vər-sĕl′) *tr.v.* **-sold** (-sōld′), **-sell·ing.** **1.** To sell too much of. **2.** To be too eager or insistent in attempting to sell something to (someone). **3.** To make excessive or unwarranted claims for.

o·ver·set (ō′vər-sĕt′) *tr.v.* **-set, -set·ting.** To tip or push over; overturn.

o·ver·shad·ow (ō′vər-shăd′ō) *tr.v.* **1.** To cast a shadow over. **2.** To surpass in importance; outweigh.

o·ver·shoe (ō′vər-shoo′) *n.* An outer shoe worn as protection from water, snow, or cold.

o·ver·shoot (ō′vər-shoot′) *tr.v.* **-shot** (-shŏt′), **-shoot·ing. 1.** To shoot or pass over or beyond: *The arrow overshot the target.* **2.** To miss by or as if by shooting: *overshot his goal.*

o·ver·shot (ō′vər-shŏt′) *adj.* **1.** Having an upper part projecting beyond the lower: *an overshot jaw.* **2.** Operated or turned by a stream of water that passes over the top: *an overshot water wheel.*

o·ver·sight (ō′vər-sīt′) *n.* **1.** An unintentional omission or mistake. **2.** Watchful care or management; supervision.

o·ver·sim·pli·fy (ō′vər-sĭm′plə-fī′) *tr.v.* **-fied, -fy·ing.** To distort by presenting in too simple a form. **—o′ver·sim′pli·fi·ca′tion** *n.*

o·ver·size (ō′vər-sīz′) *adj.* Also **o·ver·sized** (ō′vər-sīzd′). Larger than usual.

o·ver·skirt (ō′vər-skûrt′) *n.* A skirt worn over another.

o·ver·sleep (ō′vər-slēp′) *v.* **-slept** (-slĕpt′), **-sleep·ing.** **—intr.v.** To sleep beyond usual or appointed time for waking.

o·ver·spend (ō′vər-spĕnd′) *v.* **-spent** (-spĕnt′), **-spend·ing.** **—intr.v.** To spend too much. **—tr.v.** To spend in excess of.

o·ver·state (ō′vər-stāt′) *tr.v.* **-stat·ed, -stat·ing.** To state in exaggerated terms. **—o′ver·state′ment** *n.*

o·ver·stay (ō′vər-stā′) *tr.v.* To stay beyond the limits or duration of: *He overstayed his welcome.*

o·ver·step (ō′vər-stĕp′) *tr.v.* **-stepped, -step·ping.** To go beyond.

o·ver·stock (ō′vər-stŏk′) *tr.v.* To stock too much of. **—n.** (ō′vər-stŏk′). An excessive supply. **—See Syns at excess.**

o·ver·stuffed (ō′vər-stŭft′) *adj.* **1.** Filled or stuffed too much. **2.** Thickly upholstered: *overstuffed furniture.*

o·ver·sub·scribe (ō′vər-səb-skrīb′) *tr.v.* **-scribed, -scrib·ing.** To subscribe for in excess of the available supply. **—o′ver·sub·scrip′tion** (-səb-skrĭp′shən) *n.*

o·vert (ō-vûrt′, ō′vûrt′) *adj.* Open and observable; not concealed or hidden. [Middle English, from Old French, from *ovrir*, to open, from Latin *aperīre*.] **—o·vert′ly** *adv.*

o·ver·take (ō′vər-tāk′) *tr.v.* **-took** (-tŏŏk′), **-tak·en** (-tā′kən), **-tak·ing. 1.** To catch up with. **2.** To pass after catching up with. **3.** To come upon unexpectedly; take by surprise.

o·ver·tax (ō′vər-tăks′) *tr.v.* **1.** To tax excessively. **2.** To place an excessive burden or strain on. **—o′ver·tax·a′tion** *n.*

o·ver-the-count·er (ō′vər-thə-koun′tər) *adj.* **1.** Not listed or available on an officially recognized stock exchange. **2.** Sold legally without a prescription: *over-the-counter drugs.*

o·ver·throw (ō′vər-thrō′) *tr.v.* **-threw** (-throo′), **-thrown** (-thrōn′), **-throw·ing. 1.** To throw over; overturn. **2.** To bring about the downfall of: *a plot to overthrow the government.* **—o′ver·throw′** *n.*

o·ver·time (ō′vər-tīm′) *n.* **1. a.** Working hours in addition to those of the regular schedule. **b.** The wage or payment for such work. **2.** Playing time beyond the set time limit of an athletic contest. **—o′ver·time′** *adv.*

o·ver·tone (ō′vər-tōn′) *n.* **1.** *Mus. & Acoustics.* A harmonic. **2.** A suggestion; hint: *praise with overtones of envy.*

o·ver·top (ō′vər-tŏp′) *tr.v.* **-topped, -top·ping. 1.** To extend or rise over or beyond the top of; tower above. **2.** To surpass in importance; override.

o·ver·trick (ō′vər-trĭk′) *n. Cards.* A trick won in excess of the number bid.

o·ver·trump (ō′vər-trŭmp′) *tr.v. Cards.* To trump with a higher trump card than any played on the same trick.

o·ver·ture (ō′vər-chŏŏr′, -chər) *n.* **1. a.** An instrumental composition of moderate length written as an introduction to an opera, oratorio, or suite. **b.** An independent instrumental composition of similar form. **2.** A first offer or proposal: *made overtures of friendship.* [Middle English,

from Old French, from Latin *apertūra*, an opening, from *aperīre*, to open.]

o·ver·turn (ō′vər-tûrn′) *tr.v.* **1.** To cause to turn over or capsize; upset. **2.** To overthrow; defeat. **—intr.v.** To turn over; become upset. **—o′ver·turn′** *n.*

o·ver·use (ō′vər-yooz′) *tr.v.* **-used, -us·ing.** To use to excess. **—o′ver·use′** *n.*

o·ver·val·ue (ō′vər-văl′yoo) *tr.v.* **-ued, -u·ing.** To set too high a value on.

o·ver·view (ō′vər-vyoo′) *n.* A comprehensive view; survey.

o·ver·ween·ing (ō′vər-wē′nĭng) *adj.* **1.** Presumptuously arrogant; overbearing. **2.** Excessive; immoderate: *overweening ambition.*

o·ver·weigh (ō′vər-wā′) *tr.v.* **1.** To have more weight than; outweigh. **2.** To weigh down excessively; overburden.

o·ver·weight (ō′vər-wāt′) *adj.* Weighing more than is normal, allowed, or healthy. **—See Syns at fat. —o′ver·weight′** *n.*

o·ver·whelm (ō′vər-hwĕlm′, -wĕlm′) *tr.v.* **1.** To surge over and submerge; engulf: *waves overwhelming the rocky shoreline.* **2.** To overcome completely, either physically or emotionally; overpower: *overwhelmed with remorse.* **3.** To turn over; upset; overthrow. **—o′ver·whelm′ing·ly** *adv.*

o·ver·work (ō′vər-wûrk′) *v.* **—tr.v. 1.** To work too hard or too long. **2.** To use too often or to excess: *overwork a metaphor.* **—intr.v.** To work too long or too hard. **—o′ver·work′** *n.*

o·ver·write (ō′vər-rīt′) *v.* **-wrote** (-rōt′), **-writ·ten** (-rĭt′n), **-writ·ing. —tr.v. 1.** To write over the top or surface of. **2.** To write about in a mannered or wordy style. **—intr.v.** To write too much.

o·ver·wrought (ō′vər-rôt′) *adj.* Nervous or excited; agitated: *"The Queen was so overwrought that she became physically ill"* (Philip Magnus). [Obs. past part. of OVERWORK.]

ovi– or **ovo–.** A prefix meaning egg or ovum: *oviduct.* [Latin, from *ōvum*, egg.]

o·vi·duct (ō′vĭ-dŭkt′) *n. Zool.* A tube through which ova travel from an ovary. **—o′vi·duc′tal** *adj.*

o·vine (ō′vīn′) *adj.* Of or relating to sheep. [Late Latin *ovīnus*, from Latin *ovis*, sheep.] **—o′vine** *n.*

o·vip·a·rous (ō-vĭp′ər-əs) *adj.* Producing eggs that hatch outside the body. **—o·vip′a·rous·ly** *adv.*

o·vi·pos·i·tor (ō′və-pŏz′ĭ-tər) *n.* A tubular structure, sometimes extending outside the abdomen, with which certain insects lay eggs.

o·void (ō′void′) *adj.* Also **o·voi·dal** (ō-void′l). Egg-shaped. **—n.** Something egg-shaped.

o·vo·vi·vip·a·rous (ō′vō-vī-vĭp′ər-əs) *adj.* Producing eggs that hatch within the female's body, as do some fishes and reptiles. **—o′vo·vi·vip′a·rous·ly** *adv.* **—o′vo·vi·vip′a·rous·ness** *n.*

o·vu·late (ō′vyə-lāt′, ŏv′yə-) *intr.v.* **-lat·ed, -lat·ing.** *Biol.* **1.** To produce ova. **2.** To discharge ova. [From New Latin *ovulum*, ovule.] **—o′vu·la′tion** *n.*

o·vule (ō′vyool, ŏv′yool) *n.* **1.** *Zool.* An immature ovum. **2.** *Bot.* A minute structure which after fertilization becomes a plant seed. [French, from New Latin *ovulum*, dim. of Latin *ōvum*, egg.] **—o′vu·lar** (ō′vyə-lər, ŏv′yə-) *adj.*

o·vum (ō′vəm) *n., pl.* **o·va** (ō′və). The female reproductive cell of animals. [From Latin, egg.]

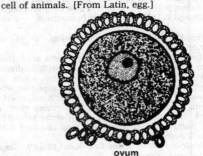

ovum

owe (ō) *v.* **owed, ow·ing. —tr.v. 1.** To be indebted to the amount of; have to pay or repay: *He owes me five dollars.* **2.** To be morally obligated to give or offer: *I owe him an* apology. **3.** To be in debt to: *owes local tradesmen for his supplies.* **4.** To be indebted for: *He owes his success to his father.* **5.** To bear (a certain feeling) toward a person: *He owes them a grudge.* **6.** *Obs.* To own; have. —*intr.v.* To be in debt: *He owes for everything.* [Middle English *owen,* to possess, owe, from Old English *āgan,* to possess.]

owing to. Because of; on account of.

owl (oul) *n.* Any of various often nocturnal birds of prey of the order Strigiformes, with hooked and feathered talons, large heads with short, hooked beaks, and eyes set in a frontal facial plane. [Middle English *owle,* from Old English *ūle.*]

owl
A great horned owl

oxbow

owl·et (ou'lĭt) *n.* A young owl.

owl·ish (ou'lĭsh) *adj.* Resembling an owl. —**owl'ish·ly** *adv.* —**owl'ish·ness** *n.*

own (ōn) *adj.* Of or belonging to oneself or itself: *my own room.* —*n.* That which belongs to one: *Those books are my own.* —*tr.v.* **1.** To have or possess. **2.** To acknowledge or admit: *he owned his mistake.* —*phrasal verb.* **own up.** To admit fully and openly. —See Syns at **acknowledge.** —*idioms.* **come into (one's) own.** To obtain deserved recognition and prosperity: *Jazz really came into its own after World War II.* **on (one's) own.** Completely independent: *He's been on his own since he was sixteen.* [Middle English *owen,* from Old English *āgen.*] —**own'er** *n.*

own·er·ship (ō'nər-shĭp') *n.* The condition or fact of being an owner.

ox (ŏks) *n., pl.* **ox·en** (ŏk'sən). **1.** An adult castrated bull of the genus *Bos.* **2.** A bovine mammal. [Middle English, from Old English *oxa.*]

oxa- or **ox-.** A prefix meaning the presence of oxygen atoms: *oxide.*

ox·a·late (ŏk'sə-lāt') *n.* Any salt or ester of oxalic acid. —*tr.v.* **-lat·ed, -lat·ing.** To treat (a specimen) with an oxalate or oxalic acid. [OXALIC ACID + -ATE.]

ox·al·ic acid (ŏk-săl'ĭk). A poisonous, crystalline organic acid, HOOCCOOH·2H₂O, used as a cleansing agent for metals, as a laundry bleach, and in textile finishing and cleaning. [French *oxalique,* from Latin *oxalis,* oxalis.]

ox·al·is (ŏk-săl'ĭs, ŏk'sə-lĭs) *n.* Any plant of the genus *Oxalis,* having pink, yellow, or white flowers. [From Latin, from Greek, from *oxus,* sharp, sour.]

ox·blood (ŏks'blŭd') *n.* A deep red or reddish brown. —*adj.* Deep red or reddish brown.

ox·bow (ŏks'bō') *n.* **1.** A U-shaped piece of wood that fits under and around the neck of an ox, with its upper ends attached to the bar of the yoke. **2.** A U-shaped bend in a river.

ox·en (ŏk'sən) *n.* Plural of **ox.**

ox·eye (ŏks'ī') *n.* Any of various plants of the genera *Buphthalmum* or *Heliopsis,* with daisylike flowers with yellow rays and dark centers.

ox·ford (ŏks'fərd) *n.* A low shoe that laces over the instep. [After *Oxford,* England.]

ox·heart (ŏks'härt') *n.* A sweet, juicy, cultivated cherry.

ox·i·dant (ŏk'sĭ-dənt) *n.* A chemical reagent that oxidizes.

ox·i·dase (ŏk'sĭ-dās') *n.* Any of various plant or animal enzymes that act as oxidants. [OXID(ATION) + -ASE.]

ox·i·da·tion (ŏk'sĭ-dā'shən) *n.* **1.** The combination of a substance with oxygen. **2.** A reaction in which the atoms in an element lose electrons and its valence is correspondingly increased.

ox·ide (ŏk'sīd) *n.* A binary compound of an element or radical with oxygen. —**ox·id'ic** (ŏk-sĭd'ĭk) *adj.*

ox·i·dize (ŏk'sĭ-dīz') *v.* **-dized, -diz·ing.** —*tr.v.* **1.** To combine with oxygen; make into an oxide. **2.** To increase the positive charge or valence of (an element) by removing electrons. **3.** To coat with oxide. —*intr.v.* To become oxidized. —**ox'i·diz'er** *n.*

ox·lip (ŏks'lĭp') *n.* A Eurasian primrose, *Primula elatior,* having clusters of yellow flowers. [Old English *oxanslyppe : oxan,* ox's + *slyppe,* dung.]

Ox·o·ni·an (ŏk-sō'nē-ən) *n.* A student or graduate of Oxford University. [From Medieval Latin *Oxōnia,* Oxford.] —**ox·o'ni·an** *adj.*

oxy-. A prefix menaing the presence of combined or additional oxygen: *oxyhemoglobin.* [From OXYGEN.]

ox·y·a·cet·y·lene (ŏk'sē-ə-sĕt'l-ĭn, -ēn') *adj.* Containing a mixture of acetylene and oxygen, as commonly used in metal welding and cutting torches.

ox·y·gen (ŏk'sĭ-jən) *n. Symbol* **O** A colorless, odorless, tasteless gaseous element that constitutes 21 per cent of the atmosphere by volume, combines with most elements, is essential for plant and animal respiration, and is required for nearly all combustion and combustive processes. Atomic number 8; atomic weight 15.9994; melting point −218.4°C; boiling point −183.0°C; gas density at 0°C 1.429 grams per liter; valence 2. [French *oxygéne,* "acid-former."] —**ox'y·gen'ic** (ŏk'sĭ-jĕn'ĭk) *adj.*

ox·y·gen·ate (ŏk'sĭ-jə-nāt') *tr.v.* **-at·ed, -at·ing.** To treat, combine, or infuse with oxygen. —**ox'y·gen·a'tion** *n.*

oxygen mask. A masklike device covering the mouth and nose through which oxygen is supplied from a tank.

oxygen tent. A canopy placed over the head and shoulders of a patient to provide a continuous flow of oxygen.

ox·y·he·mo·glo·bin (ŏk'sĭ-hē'mə-glō'bĭn, -hĕm'ə-) *n.* A bright-red chemical complex of hemoglobin and oxygen, that transports oxygen from the lungs to the tissues via the blood.

ox·y·hy·dro·gen blowpipe (ŏk'sĭ-hī'drə-jən). A torch that burns a mixture of hydrogen and oxygen for welding.

ox·y·mo·ron (ŏk'sĭ-môr'ŏn', -mōr'-) *n., pl.* **-mo·ra** (-môr'ə, -mōr'ə). A figure of speech in which incongruous or contradictory terms, such as "a deafening silence," are combined. [Greek *oxumōron,* a clever remark, from *oxumōros,* "sharp-foolish" : *oxus,* sharp + *mōros,* dull, foolish.] —**ox'y·mo·ron'ic** *adj.*

o·yez (ō'yĕs', ō'yĕz', ō-yā') *interj.* A word used to announce the opening of a court of law. [Middle English *oyes!* from Old French *oyez!,* hear ye!, imper. pl. of *oyer,* to hear, from Latin *audīre.*]

oys·ter (oi'stər) *n.* **1.** Any of several edible bivalve mollusks of the genus *Ostrea,* chiefly of shallow marine waters, having an irregularly shaped shell. **2.** Any of various similar or related bivalve mollusks, such as the pearl oyster. [Middle English *oistre,* from Old French, from Latin *ostrea,* from Greek *ostreon.*]

oyster bed. A place where oysters breed or are raised.

oys·ter·catch·er (oi'stər-kăch'ər, -kĕch'-) *n.* Any of several shore birds of the genus *Haematopus,* having black and white plumage and a long orange-red bill.

oyster cracker. A small, dry soda cracker.

oys·ter·man (oi'stər-mən) *n.* Someone who cultivates or sells oysters.

oyster plant. Salsify.

o·zone (ō'zōn') *n.* **1.** A blue, gaseous allotrope of oxygen, O₃, derived or formed naturally from diatomic oxygen by electric discharge or exposure to ultraviolet radiation. It is an unstable, powerfully bleaching, poisonous, oxidizing agent, with a pungent, irritating odor, used to purify and deodorize air, to sterilize water, and as a bleach. **2.** *Informal.* Fresh, pure air. [German *Ozon,* from Greek *ozōn,* pres. part. of *ozein,* to smell, reek.] —**o·zo'nic** (ō-zō'nĭk, ō-zŏn'ĭk) *adj.*

o·zo·no·sphere (ō-zō'nə-sfîr') *n.* A region of the upper atmosphere, between ten and twenty miles in altitude, containing a relatively high concentration of ozone that absorbs solar ultraviolet radiation in a wavelength range not screened by other atmospheric components. [OZON(E) + -SPHERE.] —**o·zo'no·spher'ic** (ō-zō'nə-sfîr'ĭk, -sfĕr'-) or **o·zo'no·spher'i·cal** *adj.*

Pp

Phoenician – About 3,000 years ago the Phoenicians and other Semitic peoples began to use graphic signs to represent individual speech sounds instead of syllables or whole words. They used this symbol to represent the sound of the consonant "p" and gave it the name pē, the Phoenician word for "mouth."

Greek – The Greeks borrowed the Phoenician alphabet with some modifications. They reversed the orientation of pē, gave it a symmetrical angular shape, and altered its name to pi. They used pi to represent the sound of the consonant "p," as in Phoenician.

Roman – The Romans borrowed the alphabet from the Greeks via the Etruscans, who had adopted the earlier, rounded shape of P. The Romans closed the curve into a loop and adapted the shape for carving Latin in stone. This monumental script, as it is called, became the basis for modern printed capital letters.

Medieval – By medieval times – around 1,200 years ago – the Roman monumental capitals had become adapted to being relatively quickly written on paper, parchment, or vellum. The cursive minuscule alphabet became the basis for modern printed lower-case letters.

Modern – Since the invention of printing about 500 years ago the basic form of the letter P has remained unchanged.

---

p, P (pē) n., pl. **p's** or **P's.** The sixteenth letter of the English alphabet.

P The symbol for the element phosphorus.

Pa The symbol for the element protactinium.

pab·u·lum (păb′yə-ləm) n. **1.** Any substance that gives nourishment; food. **2.** Commonplace, uninspired ideas or writings. [Latin food, fodder.]

pace (pās) n. **1. a.** A step made in walking; a stride. **b.** The distance spanned by such a step, esp. a unit of length equal to 30 in. **2. a.** The rate of speed at which a person, animal, or group walks or runs. **b.** The speed at which any activity proceeds: the fast pace of Manhattan living. **3.** A gait of a horse in which both feet on one side leave and return to the ground together; rack. —v. **paced, pac·ing.** —tr.v. **1.** To walk or stride back and forth across: He paced the room impatiently. **2.** To measure by counting the number of steps needed to cover a distance. **3.** To set or regulate the rate of speed for. **4.** To train (a horse) in a particular gait, esp. the pace. —intr.v. **1.** To walk with long, deliberate steps. **2.** To move or proceed. —idioms. **keep pace with.** To match the progress of. **put (one) through (one's) paces.** To test one's abilities or skills. **set the pace.** To set an example for others to follow. [Middle English pas, from Old French, from Latin passus, a step, from pandere, to stretch.] —pac′er n.

pace·mak·er (pās′mā′kər) n. **1.** A person or animal that sets the pace in a race. **2.** A leader in any competition or field. **3.** Any of several usu. miniaturized and surgically implanted electronic devices used to regulate, or to aid in the regulation of, the heartbeat.

pach·y·derm (păk′ĭ-dûrm′) n. Any of various large, thick-skinned, hoofed mammals, as the elephant or hippopotamus. [French pachyderme, from Greek pakhudermos, thick-skinned : pakhus, thick + derma, skin.]

pach·y·san·dra (păk′ĭ-săn′drə) n. Any of several trailing plants of the genus Pachysandra, frequently cultivated as a ground cover. [New Latin, "with thick stamens" : Greek pakhus, thick + aner, man.]

pa·cif·ic (pə-sĭf′ĭk) adj. **1.** Promoting peace; peaceful: pacific statements. **2.** Of a peaceful nature; tranquil; serene: pacific skies. [Old French pacifique, from Latin pācificus, peaceable.] —pa·cif′i·cal·ly adv.

pac·i·fi·ca·tion (păs′ə-fĭ-kā′shən) n. The act of pacifying or the condition of being pacified.

Pacific Standard Time. Standard time as reckoned in the region between the meridians at 112.5° and 127.5° west of Greenwich, England.

pac·i·fi·er (păs′ə-fī′ər) n. **1.** Someone or something that pacifies. **2.** A rubber or plastic nipple or teething ring for a baby to suck or chew on.

pac·i·fism (păs′ə-fĭz′əm) n. Opposition to war or violence, esp. such opposition demonstrated by refusal to participate in military service. —pac′i·fist n. —pac′i·fis′tic adj.

pac·i·fy (păs′ə-fī′) tr.v. **-fied, -fy·ing. 1.** To ease the anger or agitation of; to calm. **2.** To establish peace in; end fighting or violence in. [Middle English pacifien, from Old French pacifier, from Latin pācificāre : pax, peace + facere, to make.]

pack (păk) n. **1. a.** A collection of items tied up or wrapped; a bundle. **b.** A container made to be carried on the back. **2.** A set or package of related items, as playing cards or matches. **3.** A large amount; heap. **4. a.** A group of animals, such as dogs or wolves, that run and hunt together. **b.** A gang or band of people: a pack of hoodlums. **5.** An absorbent material, such as gauze, inserted into a body cavity or wound as a dressing or treatment. **6.** A folded cloth filled with crushed ice and applied to sore or swollen parts of the body; ice pack. **7.** A cosmetic paste applied to the skin and allowed to dry. —modifier: a pack animal. —tr.v. **1.** To fold, roll, or combine into a bundle; wrap up. **2. a.** To put into a container for transporting or storing: pack one's belongings. **b.** To fill up with items: pack one's trunk. **3.** To process and put into containers in order to preserve, transport, or sell: pack meat. **4.** To crowd together; fill up tight; cram: people packed the auditorium. **5.** To treat medically with a pack. **6.** To wrap tightly for protection or to prevent leakage: pack a valve stem. **7.** To press together; compact firmly: clay and straw packed into bricks. **8.** Informal. To have available for action: pack a pistol. **9.** To send abruptly or without ceremony: They packed him off to camp. **10.** To rig (a voting panel) to be fraudulently favorable: pack the jury. —intr.v. **1.** To place one's belongings in boxes or luggage for transporting or storing. **2.** To be capable of being stored compactly. **3.** To become compacted: Rain caused the loose dirt to pack. —idiom. **send packing.** To dismiss abruptly. [Middle English.]

pack·age (păk′ĭj) n. **1.** A parcel or bundle containing one or more objects. **2.** A container in which something is packed for storage or transporting. **3.** A proposition or offer made up of several items. —modifier: a package deal. —tr.v. **-aged, -ag·ing.** To place in a package.

package store. A store that sells sealed bottles of alcoholic beverages for consumption away from its premises.

pack·er (păk′ər) n. A person who packs goods, esp. meat products, for transportation and sale.

pack·et (păk′ĭt) n. **1.** A small package or bundle. **2.** Slang.

ă pat   ā pay   â care   ä father   ĕ pet   ē be   hw which   ĭ pit   ī tie   î pier   ŏ pot   ō toe   ô paw, for   oi noise
ŏŏ took   ŏŏ boot   ou out   th thin   th this   ŭ cut   û urge   zh vision   ə about, item, edible, gallop, circus

A sizable sum of money. **3.** A ship that sails on a regular route, carrying passengers or freight.

pack·ing (păk′ĭng) *n.* **1.** The processing and packaging of food products. **2.** A material used to prevent leakage or seepage, as around a pipe joint.

pack rat. 1. Any of various small North American rodents of the genus *Neotoma*, that collect and store in their nests a great variety of small objects. **2.** *Slang.* An eccentric collector of miscellaneous objects.

pack·sad·dle (păk′săd′l) *n.* A saddle for a pack animal on which loads can be secured.

pact (păkt) *n.* **1.** A formal agreement, as between nations; treaty. **2.** A compact; bargain. [Middle English, from Old French, from Latin *pactum,* past part. of *pasciscī,* to agree.]

pad¹ (păd) *n.* **1.** A thin, cushionlike mass of soft material used as filling or for protection. **2.** An ink-soaked cushion used to ink a rubber stamp. **3.** A number of sheets of paper of the same size stacked one on top of the other and glued together at one end; tablet. **4.** The broad, floating leaf of an aquatic plant, such as the water lily. **5. a.** The cushion-like flesh on the underpart of the toes and feet of many animals. **b.** The foot of such an animal. **6.** A **launch pad. 7.** *Slang.* A person's apartment or room. —*tr.v.* **pad·ded, pad·ding. 1.** To line or stuff with soft material. **2.** To lengthen (something written or spoken) with unnecessary material. **3.** To add fictitious expenses or costs to: *pad an expense account.* [Orig. unknown.]

pad² (păd) *intr.v.* **pad·ded, pad·ding.** To go about on foot, esp. with soft steps: *"But Doris, towelled from the bath, enters padding on broad feet"* (T.S. Eliot). —*n.* A muffled sound resembling that of soft footsteps. [Prob. from Middle Dutch *paden,* to walk along a path, from *pad,* path, road.]

pad·ding (păd′ĭng) *n.* **1.** Soft material used to stuff, line, or cushion. **2.** Matter added to a speech or written work to make it longer.

pad·dle¹ (păd′l) *n.* **1.** A wooden implement with a blade at one or sometimes at both ends, used without an oarlock to propel a canoe or small boat. **2.** Any of various flat-bladed implements used for stirring, mixing, or turning. **3.** A flattened board used to administer physical punishment. **4.** *Sports.* A light wooden racket used in playing table tennis and several other games. —*v.* **-dled, -dling.** —*intr.v.* **1.** To propel a watercraft with a paddle: *paddling against the current.* **2.** To move through water by means of repeated short strokes of the limbs. —*tr.v.* **1.** To propel (a watercraft) with a paddle or paddles. **2.** To beat with a paddle, esp. to punish by spanking. [Middle English *padell.*] —**pad′dler** *n.*

pad·dle² (păd′l) *intr.v.* **-dled, -dling. 1.** To dabble the hands or feet about in shallow water. **2.** To move with a waddling motion; toddle. [Orig. unknown.]

paddle boat. A steamship propelled by paddle wheels on each side or by one paddle wheel astern.

pad·dle·fish (păd′l-fĭsh′) *n., pl.* **-fish** or **-fish·es.** A large fish, *Polyodon spathula,* of the Mississippi River basin, with a long, paddle-shaped snout.

paddle wheel. A steam-driven wheel with boards or paddles attached around its rim, used to propel a ship.

pad·dock (păd′ək) *n.* **1.** A fenced area in which horses are kept for grazing or exercising. **2.** An enclosure at a racetrack where the horses are assembled and paraded. [Var.

of dial. *parrock,* from Middle English *parrok,* from Old English *pearroc.*]

pad·dy (păd′ē) *n., pl.* **-dies. 1.** Rice, esp. in the husk. **2.** A flooded field where rice is grown. [Malay *padi.*]

paddy wagon. *Slang.* A police van for taking suspects into custody. [From PADDY.]

pad·lock (păd′lŏk′) *n.* A detachable lock with a U-shaped bar hinged at one end, designed to be passed through the staple of a hasp or a link in a chain, and then snapped shut. —*tr.v.* To lock up with or as if with a padlock. [Middle English *padlok.*]

pa·dre (pä′drā, -drē) *n.* **1.** A priest in Italy, Spain, Portugal, and Latin America. **2.** A title used for a priest in those countries. **3.** *Informal.* A military chaplain. [Spanish and Italian, father, from Latin *pater.*]

pae·an (pē′ən) *n.* Also **pe·an.** A song of joyful praise, thanksgiving, or exultation. [Latin *paeān,* from Greek *paiōn,* war cry, hymn of praise to Apollo, from *Paiōn,* title of Apollo as physician of the gods.]

pa·el·la (pä-āl′yə, -ä′yə) *n.* A saffron-flavored Spanish dish made with a combination of rice, vegetables, meat, chicken, and seafood. [Catalan, "frying pan."]

pa·gan (pā′gən) *n.* **1.** A person who is not a Christian, Moslem, or Jew. **2.** A person who has no religion. —*adj.* Of pagans or paganism. [Middle English, from Latin *pāgānus,* country-dweller, from *pāgus,* village, country.]

pa·gan·ism (pā′gə-nĭz′əm) *n.* **1.** Pagan beliefs or practices. **2.** The condition of being a pagan.

page¹ (pāj) *n.* **1.** A boy who attended a medieval knight as a first stage of training for knighthood. **2.** Someone employed to run errands or carry messages, as in a hotel. —*tr.v.* **paged, pag·ing.** To summon or call (a person) by name. [Middle English, from Old French, from Italian *paggio,* prob. from Greek *paidion,* child, dim. of *pais,* child, boy.]

page² (pāj) *n.* **1.** One side of a leaf of a book, letter, newspaper, etc. **2.** The printing on one side of a leaf. **3.** A noteworthy or memorable event: *a new page in history.* —*tr.v.* **paged, pag·ing.** To number the pages of; paginate. [Old French, from Latin *pāgina.*]

pag·eant (păj′ənt) *n.* **1.** An elaborate public play in which scenes from history or legend are represented: *an Easter pageant.* **2.** A spectacular procession or celebration. **3.** Colorful display; pageantry. **4.** Showy display; pomp. [Middle English *pagyn,* from Medieval Latin *pāgina,* scene of a play, from Latin, page.]

pag·eant·ry (păj′ən-trē) *n., pl.* **-ries. 1.** Pageants and their presentation. **2.** Grand or showy display.

page·boy (pāj′boi′) *n.* A kind of shoulder-length haircut with the ends evenly curled inward.

pag·i·nate (păj′ə-nāt′) *tr.v.* **-nat·ed, -nat·ing.** To number the pages of.

pag·i·na·tion (păj′ə-nā′shən) *n.* **1.** The system with which pages are numbered. **2.** The arrangement and number of pages in a book.

pa·go·da (pə-gō′də) *n.* **1.** A religious building of the Far East, typically: **a.** An ornamented, pyramid-shaped Hindu temple. **b.** A many-storied Buddhist tower, erected as a memorial or shrine. **2.** A structure built in imitation of this. [Portuguese *pagode.*]

paid (pād) *v.* Past tense and past participle of **pay.**

pail (pāl) *n.* **1.** A usu. watertight cylindrical container, open at the top and fitted with a handle; bucket. **2.** The amount contained in such a vessel. [Middle English *payle,* from Old English *pægel,* small measure, from Medieval Latin *pagella,* a measure, from Latin, dim. of *pagina,* page.]

pain (pān) *n.* **1.** An unpleasant physical sensation that occurs as a consequence of injury, disease, or emotional disorder. **2.** Suffering or distress. **3. pains.** The pangs of childbirth. **4. pains.** Great care or effort: *take pains with one's work.* **5.** *Informal.* A nuisance. —See Syns at **distress** and **effort.** —*tr.v.* To hurt; cause pain to: *It pained her to see him unhappy.* —*intr.v.* To be the cause of pain. —*idiom.* **on** (or **upon** or **under) pain of.** Subject to the penalty of. [Middle English *paine,* from Old French *peine,* from Latin *poena,* penalty, from Greek *poinē.*]

pain·ful (pān′fəl) *adj.* **1.** Causing pain; hurtful: *a painful injury.* **2.** Full of pain; distressing: *a painful moment.* **3.** Requiring care and labor; irksome: *a painful task.*

paddock

pagoda

—**pain′ful·ly** adv. —**pain′ful·ness** n.

pain·kill·er (pān′kĭl′ər) n. Something, such as a drug, that relieves pain. —**pain′kill′ing** adj.

pain·less (pān′lĭs) adj. Free from or causing no pain. —**pain′less·ly** adv. —**pain′less·ness** n.

pains·tak·ing (pānz′tā′kĭng) adj. Characterized by or requiring great care and effort. —**pains′tak′ing·ly** adv.

paint (pānt) n. 1. a. A liquid mixture, usu. of a solid pigment in a liquid, applied to surfaces as a decorative or protective coating. b. The thin dry film formed by such a mixture applied to a surface. c. The solid pigment before it is mixed with a liquid. 2. A cosmetic that colors, such as rouge. 3. A spotted horse; a pinto. —tr.v. 1. To make (a picture) with paints. 2. a. To represent in a picture with paints. b. To depict vividly in words. 3. To coat or decorate with paint: paint a house. 4. To apply cosmetics to. —intr.v. To practice the art of painting pictures. [From Middle English peynten, to paint, from Old French peint, past part. of peindre, from Latin pingere.]

paint·brush (pānt′brŭsh′) n. A brush for applying paint.

paint·er¹ (pān′tər) n. A person who paints, either as an artist or as a workman.

paint·er² (pān′tər) n. A rope attached to the bow of a boat, used for tying up. [Middle English paynter, perh. from Old French pentoir, clothesline, from pendre, to hang, from Latin pendēre.]

paint·ing (pān′tĭng) n. 1. The process, art, or occupation of working with paints. 2. A picture or design in paint.

pair (pâr) n., pl. **pairs** or informal **pair. 1.** Two corresponding persons or items, similar in form or function and matched or associated: a pair of shoes. 2. One object composed of two joined, similar parts, dependent upon each other: a pair of pliers. 3. a. Two persons joined together in marriage or engagement. b. Two persons, animals, or things having something in common and considered together: a pair of hunters. c. Two mated animals. 4. Two playing cards of the same denomination. 5. Gov. Two members of a deliberative body with opposing opinions on a given issue who agree to abstain from voting on the issue, thereby offsetting each other. —See Syns at **couple.** —tr.v. To arrange in sets of two; to couple. 2. To provide a partner for. —intr.v. To form a pair or pairs. [Middle English paire, from Old French, from Latin paria, equal things, from pār, equal.]

Usage: pair. In formal usage, the plural is pairs: three pairs of shoes. In informal and business English, the plural can also be pair: three pair. When pair is used as a subject it always takes a singular verb when the meaning stresses oneness or unity: This pair (of socks) is not mine. A plural construction occurs when the members are considered individually: The pair were seldom in agreement on anything.

pais·ley (pāz′lē) adj. Also **Pais·ley. 1.** Made of a soft wool fabric with a colorful pattern of abstract, curved shapes. 2. Having such a pattern. —n., pl. **-leys.** A shawl or other article of clothing made of paisley fabric. [After Paisley, a city in Scotland.]

pa·ja·mas (pə-jä′məz, -jăm′əz) pl.n. Also Brit. **py·ja·mas.** A loose-fitting outfit of trousers and a jacket, for sleeping or lounging. [Hindi pāejāma : Persian pāī, leg, foot, + jāmah, garment.]

pal (păl) n. Informal. A friend; chum. —intr.v. **palled, pal·ling.** Informal. To associate as pals: pal around together. [Romany, from Sanskrit bhrātar-, brother.]

pal·ace (păl′ĭs) n. 1. The official residence of a royal person. 2. Any large or splendid residence. 3. Any large, often gaudy and ornate building used for entertainment, exhibitions, etc. [Middle English palais, from Old French, from Latin palātium, from Palātium, the Palatine Hill in Rome, where the palaces of the emperors were built.]

pal·a·din (păl′ə-dĭn) n. 1. Any of the 12 peers of Charlemagne's court. 2. A heroic champion or supporter. [French, from Italian paladino, from Latin palātīnus, officer of the palace.]

pal·an·quin (păl′ən-kēn′) n. Also **pal·an·keen.** An east Asian covered couch for transporting a passenger, carried on poles on the shoulders of two or four men. [Portuguese palanquim, from Javanese pĕlangki, from Sanskrit palyaṇka, bed.]

pal·at·a·ble (păl′ə-tə-bəl) adj. 1. Agreeable to the taste. 2. Agreeable to the mind or sensibilities: a palatable solution to the problem. [From PALATE.] —**pal′at·a·bil′i·ty** or **pal′at·a·ble·ness** n. —**pal′at·a·bly** adv.

pal·a·tal (păl′ə-tl) adj. 1. Of or relating to the palate. 2. Produced with the front or blade of the tongue against or near the hard palate, as the y in young or the ch in chin. —n. A palatal sound. —**pal′a·tal·ize** (păl′ə-tl-īz′) tr.v. **-ized, -iz·ing.** To pronounce as a palatal sound or with a palatal quality. —**pal′a·tal·i·za′tion** n.

pal·ate (păl′ĭt) n. 1. Anat. The roof of the mouth in vertebrates, separating the mouth cavity and nasal passage, and consisting of a hard, bony front backed by the soft, fleshy palate. 2. The sense of taste. [Middle English, from Latin palātum.]

pa·la·tial (pə-lā′shəl) adj. 1. Of or suitable for a palace: palatial gardens. 2. Of the nature of a palace; spacious and ornate. —See Syns at **luxurious.** [From Latin palātium, palace.] —**pa·la′tial·ly** adv.

pa·lat·i·nate (pə-lăt′n-āt′, -ĭt) n. 1. The office or powers of a palatine. 2. The territory of a palatine.

pal·a·tine (păl′ə-tīn) n. 1. A soldier of the palace guard of the Roman emperors formed in the time of Diocletian. 2. A title of various administrative officials of the late Roman and Byzantine empires. 3. A count delegated with royal powers. 4. A lord having royal powers within his own domain. —adj. 1. Belonging to or fit for a palace. 2. Pertaining to or designating a palatine or palatinate. 3. Having royal powers or privileges. [Latin palātīnus, from palātium, a palace.]

pa·lav·er (pə-lăv′ər, -lä′vər) n. 1. a. Idle chatter. b. Talk intended to charm or beguile. 2. A parley, esp. one between explorers and representatives of local populations. —intr.v. To chatter idly. [Portuguese palavra, word, speech, from Late Latin parabola, speech, parable.]

pale¹ (pāl) n. 1. A stake or pointed stick; picket. 2. The area enclosed by a fence or boundary. —tr.v. **paled, pal·ing.** To enclose with pales; fence in. —idiom. **beyond the pale.** Beyond the limits of what is safe, accepted, or protected. [Middle English, pointed stake, boundary, from Old French pal, stake, from Latin pālus.]

pale² (pāl) adj. **pal·er, pal·est. 1.** Whitish or lighter than normal in complexion, often because of illness or weakness. 2. Of a low intensity of color; light: pale blue. 3. Of a low intensity of light; dim; faint: a pale moon. 4. Feeble; weak; inferior: a pale imitation. —v. **paled, pal·ing.** —tr.v. To cause to turn pale. —intr.v. 1. To become pale; blanch. 2. To decrease in relative importance; be outshone; diminish. [Middle English, from Old French, from Latin pallidus, from pallēre, to be pale.] —**pale′ly** adv. —**pale′ness** n.

pale-. Var. of **paleo-.**

paleo- or **pale-.** A prefix meaning ancient or prehistoric: paleography. [Greek palaio-, from palaios, ancient, from palai, long ago.]

Pa·le·o·cene (pā′lē-ə-sēn′) n. Also **Paleocene epoch.** A geologic epoch that began about 63 million years ago and ended about 58 million years ago, characterized by the appearance of more advanced mammals. —modifier: a Paleocene fossil.

pa·le·og·ra·phy (pā′lē-ŏg′rə-fē) n. 1. The study of ancient written documents. 2. Ancient written documents. —**pa′le·og′ra·pher** n. —**pa′le·o·graph′ic** (-ə-grăf′ĭk) or **pa′le·o·graph′i·cal** adj.

palanquin

Pa·le·o·lith·ic (pā′lē-ə-lĭth′ĭk) *n.* The period of human culture that began about 750,000 years ago and ended about 15,000 years ago, marked by the earliest use of tools made of chipped stone. —*modifier: a* Paleolithic *tool.*

pa·le·on·tol·o·gy (pā′lē-ŏn-tŏl′ə-jē, -ən-) *n.* The study of fossils and ancient life forms. [PALE(O)- + ONTOLOGY.] —**pa′le·on′to·log′ic** (-ŏn′tə-lŏj′ĭk) or **pa′le·on′to·log′i·cal** *adj.* —**pa′le·on·tol′o·gist** *n.*

Pa·le·o·zo·ic (pā′lē-ə-zō′ĭk) *n.* Also **Paleozoic era.** A geologic era that began about 600 million years ago and ended about 230 million years ago, characterized by the appearance of invertebrate sea life, primitive fishes and reptiles, and land plants. —*modifier: a* Paleozoic *rock.*

pal·ette (păl′ĭt) *n.* **1.** A board, typically with a hole for the thumb, upon which an artist mixes colors. **2.** The range of colors used, as by a particular artist: *a limited* palette. [French, from Old French, flat board, dim. of *pale,* shovel, from Latin *pāla,* spade, shovel.]

pal·frey (pôl′frē) *n., pl.* **-freys.** *Archaic.* A woman's saddle horse. [Middle English, from Old French *palefrei,* from Medieval Latin *palafrēdus,* from Late Latin *paraverēdus,* extra post horse : Greek *para,* beside + Latin *verēdus,* post horse.]

pal·imp·sest (păl′ĭmp-sĕst′) *n.* A document that has been written upon several times, often with remnants of earlier, imperfectly erased writing still visible. [Latin *palimpsēstus,* from Greek *palimpsēstos* : *palin,* again + *psēn,* to rub, scrape.]

pal·in·drome (păl′ĭn-drōm′) *n.* A word, phrase, sentence, or number that reads the same backward or forward, as *A man, a plan, a canal, Panama!* [Greek *palindromos,* running back again : *palin,* again + *dromos,* a running.] —**pal′in·drom′ic** (păl′ĭn-drŏm′ĭk, -drō′mĭk) *adj.*

pal·ing (pā′lĭng) *n.* **1.** A pale; picket. **2.** Pointed sticks used in making fences; pales. **3.** A fence made of pales.

pal·i·sade (păl′ĭ-sād′) *n.* **1.** A fence of stakes forming a defensive barrier. **2.** One of the stakes of such a fence. **3. palisades.** A line of lofty, steep cliffs, usu. along a river. —*tr.v.* **-sad·ed, -sad·ing.** To fortify or surround with a palisade. [French *palissade,* from Provençal *palissada,* from *palissa,* a pale, from Latin *pālus.*]

pall¹ (pôl) *n.* **1.** A cover for a coffin, bier, or tomb. **2.** A coffin being borne to a grave or tomb. **3.** Anything that covers, darkens, obscures or produces a gloomy effect or atmosphere: *a* pall *of smoke.* —*tr.v.* To cover with or as with a pall. [Middle English *pal,* from Old English *pæll,* from Latin *pallium,* a cover, cloak.]

pall² (pôl) *intr.v.* To grow dull or tiresome. To cloy; satiate. [Middle English *pallen,* short for *appallen,* to appall.]

pal·la·di·um¹ (pə-lā′dē-əm) *n. Symbol* **Pd** A soft, ductile, steel-white, tarnish-resistant metallic element occurring naturally with platinum, esp. in gold, nickel, and copper ores, and used as a catalyst in the hydrogenation process, as a purification filter for hydrogen, and is alloyed for use in electric contacts, jewelry, nonmagnetic watch parts, and surgical instruments. Atomic number 46; atomic weight 106.4; melting point 1552°C; boiling point 2927°C; specific gravity 12.02 (20°C); valence 2, 3, 4. [After the asteroid *Pallas.*]

pal·la·di·um² (pə-lā′dē-əm) *n., pl.* **-di·a** (-dē-ə) or **di·ums.** An object having the power to preserve or protect; a safeguard. [Latin, from Greek *Palladion,* the statue of Pallas Athena that assured the safety of Troy, from *Pallas,* Pallas Athena.]

Pal·las Athena. (păl′əs). The goddess **Athena.**

pall·bear·er (pôl′bâr′ər) *n.* One of the persons who carry or attend the coffin at a funeral. [Orig. one who held the corners of the pall.]

pal·let¹ (păl′ĭt) *n.* **1.** A projection on a pawl that engages the teeth of a ratchet wheel in a watch or other machine. **2.** A flat-bladed, wooden tool for mixing and shaping clay. **3.** A portable platform for storing or moving cargo or freight. **4.** A painter's palette. [Old French *palette,* dim. of *pale,* blade, shovel.]

pal·let² (păl′ĭt) *n.* A narrow, hard bed or straw-filled mattress. [Middle English *pailet,* from Norman French *paillete,* bundle of straw, from *paille,* straw, from Latin *palea,* chaff.]

pal·li·ate (păl′ē-āt′) *tr.v.* **-at·ed, -at·ing. 1.** To make (an offense or crime) seem less serious; help to excuse. **2.** To make (as a disease) less severe without curing. [From Late Latin *palliāre,* to cloak, from Latin *pallium,* cloak.] —**pal′li·a′tion** *n.*

pal·li·a·tive (păl′ē-ā′tĭv, -ə-tĭv) *adj.* Reducing pain or severity but not curing. —*n.* Something that palliates.

pal·lid (păl′ĭd) *adj.* **1.** Having an abnormally pale or wan complexion or color. **2.** Lacking in radiance or vitality; dull; lifeless: *"Consider . . . how pallid, and faint and dilute · a thing, all the honors of this world are"* (John Donne). [Latin *pallidus,* from *pallēre,* to be pale.] —**pal′lid·ly** *adv.* —**pal′lid·ness** *n.*

pal·lor (păl′ər) *n.* Extreme or unnatural paleness, esp. of the face. [Latin, from *pallēre,* to be pale.]

palm¹ (päm) *n.* **1.** The inner surface of the hand, from the wrist to the fingers. **2.** A unit of length equal to either the width or the length of the hand. **3.** The part of a glove or mitten that covers the palm of the hand. —*tr.v.* To conceal (something) in the palm of the hand, as in cheating at dice or cards or in a sleight-of-hand trick. —*phrasal verb.* **palm off.** To get rid of by deception: *palming off shoddy goods on unsuspecting customers.* [Middle English *paume,* from Old French, from Latin *palma,* palm of the hand, palm tree.]

palm² (päm) *n.* **1.** Any of various chiefly tropical evergreen trees or shrubs of the family Palmaceae, that characteristically have unbranched trunks with a crown of large pinnate or palmate leaves. **2.** A leaf or frond of a palm tree, carried as a symbol of victory, success, or joy. **3.** Triumph; victory. [Middle English *palme,* from Old English *palm,* from Latin *palma,* palm of the hand, palm tree (from the resemblance of its leaves to the outspread human hand).]

pal·mate (păl′māt′, päl′-, pä′māt′) *adj.* Also **pal·mat·ed** (păl′mā′tĭd, päl′-, pä′mā′-). **1.** Resembling a hand with the fingers extended: *palmate antlers; palmate coral.* **2.** *Bot.* Having leaflets or lobes radiating or diverging from one point. **3.** *Zool.* Having webbed toes, as the feet of many water birds. —**pal′mate′ly** *adv.*

pal·met·to (păl-mĕt′ō) *n., pl.* **-tos** or **-toes.** Any of several small, mostly tropical palms with fan-shaped leaves, esp. *Sabal Palmetto* of the southeastern United States. [Spanish *palmito,* dim. of *palma,* palm, from Latin.]

pal·mist·ry (pä′mĭ-strē) *n.* The practice or art of telling fortunes from the lines, marks, and patterns on the palms of the hands. —**palm′ist** *n.*

pal·mit·ic acid (păl-mĭt′ĭk, päl-, pä-mĭt′-). A common fatty acid, $CH_3(CH_2)_{14}COOH$, that occurs in many natural oils and fats, and is used in making soaps. [From *palmitin,* a substance found in palm oil.]

palm oil. 1. A yellowish fatty oil obtained from the crushed nuts of the West African palm, *Elaeis guineensis,* and used to manufacture soaps, chocolates, cosmetics, and candles. **2.** A reddish-yellow fatty oil with a butterlike consistency obtained from the fermented pulp of this palm and used as a lubricant and in the manufacture of soaps and candles.

Palm Sunday. The Sunday before Easter, commemorating Christ's entry into Jerusalem, when palm branches were strewn before him.

palm·y (pä′mē) *adj.* **-i·er, -i·est. 1.** Of or pertaining to palm trees. **2.** Prosperous; flourishing.

pal·o·mi·no (păl′ə-mē′nō) *n., pl.* **-nos.** A horse with a golden or tan coat and a lighter mane and tail. [American Spanish, from Spanish, dove-colored.]

palp (pălp) *n.* A palpus.

pal·pa·ble (păl′pə-bəl) *adj.* **1.** Capable of being touched or felt; tangible: *a palpable rise in temperature.* **2.** Easily perceived; obvious: *a palpable error.* **3.** Perceptible by palpation: *a palpable tumor.* —See Syns at **perceptible.** [Middle English, from Late Latin *palpābilis,* from Latin *palpāre,* to touch.] —**pal′pa·bil′i·ty** *n.* —**pal′pa·bly** *adv.*

pal·pate (păl′pāt′) *tr.v.* **-pat·ed, -pat·ing.** To examine or explore medically by touching (an organ or area of the body). [From Latin *palpāre,* to touch.] —**pal·pa′tion** *n.*

pal·pi (păl′pī) *n.* Plural of **palpus.**

pal·pi·tate (păl′pĭ-tāt′) *intr.v.* **-tat·ed, -tat·ing. 1.** To shake; quiver; flutter. **2.** To beat rapidly and loudly; throb. [From Latin *palpitāre,* freq. of *palpāre,* to touch.]

pal·pi·ta·tion (păl′pĭ-tā′shən) *n.* **1.** A trembling or shaking.

| ă pat | ā pay | â care | ä father | ĕ pet | ē be | hw which | | ĭ pit | ī tie | î pier | ŏ pot | ō toe | ô paw, for | oi noise |
| ōō took | ōō boot | ou out | th thin | *th* this | ŭ cut | | û urge | zh vision | ə about, item, edible, gallop, circus |

2. Irregular, rapid beating of the heart.

pal·pus (păl′pəs) n., pl. **-pi** (-pī′). A long, segmented sensory organ located near the mouth in invertebrate organisms such as mollusks and insects. [French palpe, from Latin palpus, a touching.]

pal·sied (pôl′zēd) adj. 1. Med. Afflicted with palsy. 2. Trembling; shaking.

pal·sy (pôl′zē) n., pl. **-sies.** 1. Paralysis. 2. A condition marked by loss of power to feel or to control movement in any part of the body. —tr.v. **-sied, -sy·ing.** 1. To paralyze. 2. To make helpless, as with fear. [Middle English palesie, from Old French paralisie, from Latin paralysis.]

pal·ter (pôl′tər) intr.v. 1. To talk or act insincerely; equivocate. 2. To be capricious; trifle. 3. To quibble, esp. in bargaining. [Orig. unknown.]

pal·try (pôl′trē) adj. **-tri·er, -tri·est.** 1. Petty; trifling; insignificant. 2. Worthless; contemptible. —See Syns at **cheap.** [Dial. English paltry, feeble, from palt, rags, rubbish.] —**pal′tri·ly** adv.

pam·pas (păm′pəz, -pəs) pl.n. The less frequently used singular is **pam·pa** (păm′pə) n. A nearly treeless grassland area of South America. [Pl. of American Spanish pampa, from Aymara and Quechua, plain.]

pam·per (păm′pər) tr.v. To treat with excessive care and indulgence; coddle: pamper a favorite child. —See Syns at **baby.** [Middle English pamperen.] —**pam′per·er** n.

pam·phlet (păm′flĭt) n. A short book or printed essay with a paper cover and no binding. [Middle English pamflet, from Pamphilus, a popular short amatory Latin poem of the 12th cent.]

pam·phlet·eer (păm′flĭ-tîr′) n. A writer of pamphlets or other short works, esp. on current issues or causes. —intr.v. To write and publish pamphlets.

pan[1] (păn) n. 1. A wide, shallow, open container for household purposes. 2. Any similar flat shallow container, such as one used to separate gold from earth or gravel by washing. 3. Informal. A harsh critical review, as of a book, film, or performance. —v. **panned, pan·ning.** —tr.v. 1. To wash (gravel, sand, or other sediments) in a pan for precious metal. 2. Informal. To review unfavorably or harshly. —intr.v. 1. To wash gravel, sand, or other sediments in a pan. 2. To yield gold as a result of washing in a pan. —See Syns at **blame.** —phrasal verb. **pan out.** Informal. To turn out well; be successful. [Middle English panne, from Old English.]

pan[2] (păn) v. **panned, pan·ning.** —intr.v. To move a motion-picture or television camera to follow a moving object or scan a scene. —tr.v. To move (a camera) in such a manner. [Short for PANORAMA.]

Pan (păn) n. Gk. Myth. The god of woods, fields, and flocks, having a human torso with goat's legs, horns, and ears.

pan-. A prefix meaning all: panchromatic. [Greek, from pās, all.]

pan·a·ce·a (păn′ə-sē′ə) n. A remedy for all diseases, evils, or difficulties; cure-all. [Latin panacēa, from Greek panakeia, from panakēs, all-healing : pan-, all + akos, cure.]

pa·nache (pə-năsh′, -näsh′) n. 1. A bunch of feathers or a plume, esp. on a helmet. 2. Dash; swagger; verve. [French, from Italian pennachio, from Late Latin pinnāculum, dim. of Latin pinna, feather.]

Pan·a·ma hat (păn′ə-mä′). A natural-colored, hand-plaited hat made from the leaves of a palmlike tropical American plant.

Pan-A·mer·i·can (păn′ə-měr′ĭ-kən) adj. Of or including the countries of North, South, and Central America.

pan-broil (păn′broil′) tr.v. To cook over direct heat in an uncovered, usu. ungreased skillet.

pan·cake (păn′kāk′) n. 1. A thin cake made of batter, poured on a hot, greased skillet and cooked on both sides until brown. 2. A landing in which an airplane levels off in the air and drops almost horizontally to the ground. —v. **-caked, -cak·ing.** —intr.v. To make a pancake landing.

pan·chro·mat·ic (păn′krō-măt′ĭk) adj. Sensitive to all colors: panchromatic film.

pan·cre·as (păng′krē-əs, păn′-) n. Anat. A long, soft, irregularly shaped gland lying behind the stomach. It secretes pancreatic juice into the duodenum and produces insulin which is taken up by the bloodstream. [Greek pankreas : pan-, all + kreas, flesh.] —**pan′cre·at′ic** (-ăt′ĭk) adj.

pancreatic juice. A clear, alkaline secretion of the pancreas containing enzymes that aid in the digestion of proteins, carbohydrates, and fats.

pan·da (păn′də) n. 1. A carnivorous, bearlike mammal, Ailuropoda melanoleuca, related to the raccoon, of China and Tibet, that has woolly fur with distinctive black and white markings. 2. A small, raccoonlike mammal, Ailurus fulgens, of northeastern Asia, with reddish fur and a long, ringed tail. [French, perh. from a native word in Nepal.]

pan·da·nus (păn-dā′nəs, -dăn′əs) n. Any of various palmlike trees and shrubs of the genus Pandanus, of southeastern Asia, with large prop roots and narrow leaves that yield a fiber used in weaving mats and similar articles. Also called **screw pine.** [From Malay pandan.] —**pan′da·na′ceous** (păn′də-nā′shəs) adj

pan·dect (păn′děkt′) n. 1. A comprehensive digest. 2. **pandects.** A complete body of laws; a legal code. 3. **Pandects.** A digest of Roman civil law, compiled in the sixth cent. A.D. [Late Latin Pandectēs, the Corpus Juris Civilis, from Latin, from Greek pandektēs, all-receiving : pan-, all + dektēs, receiver, from dekheisthai, to receive.]

pan·dem·ic (păn-děm′ĭk) adj. 1. Widespread; general; universal. 2. Epidemic over a wide geographic area. Used of a disease. —n. A pandemic disease. [From Late Latin pandēmus, from Greek pandēmos, of all the people : pan-, all + dēmos, people.]

pan·de·mo·ni·um (păn′də-mō′nē-əm) n. Also **pan·dae·mo·ni·um.** 1. Wild uproar or noise; tumult. 2. Any place characterized by uproar and noise. [From Pandæmonium, capital of Hell in Milton's Paradise Lost : PAN- + Greek daimōn, demon.] —**pan′de·mo′ni·ac′** (-ăk′) adj.

pan·der (păn′dər) n. 1. A person who arranges meetings between lovers. 2. A person who seeks clients for a prostitute; pimp. 3. A person who profits by appealing to the lower tastes of others or exploiting their weaknesses. —intr.v. To act as a pander: tabloid newspapers that pander to the public craving for scandal. [From Middle English Pandare, Pandarus, from Latin.] —**pan′der·er** n.

Pan·do·ra (păn-dôr′ə, -dōr′ə) n. Gk. Myth. The first woman, bestowed upon mankind as a punishment for Prometheus' theft of fire. Entrusted with a box containing all the ills that could plague mankind, she opened it.

Pandora's box. A source of many unforseen troubles.

pan·dow·dy (păn-dou′dē) n., pl. **-dies.** Sliced apples baked with sugar and spices in a deep dish, with a thick top crust. [Orig. unknown.]

pane (pān) n. 1. A sheet of glass, esp. one in a window or door. 2. One of the divisions of a window or door, including the glass and its frame. 3. One of the flat surfaces or facets of a many-sided object, as a diamond or bolt. [Middle English, piece of cloth, section, from Old French pan, from Latin pannus, rag.]

pan·e·gyr·ic (păn′ə-jîr′ĭk, -jî′rĭk) n. 1. A formal speech or written work in praise of someone or something. 2. Elaborate praise; laudation. [French panégyrique, from Latin panēgyricus, from Greek (logos) panēgurikos, "(speech) for a public festival" : pan-, all + aguris, agora, assembly.] —**pan′e·gyr′i·cal** adj. —**pan′e·gyr′i·cal·ly** adv. —**pan′e·gyr′ist** n.

pan·el (păn′əl) n. 1. A flat piece, such as a wooden board, forming part of a surface or overlaying it. 2. A piece of cloth sewn lengthwise into or onto a skirt or dress. 3. A

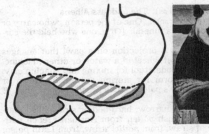

pancreas   panda

framed section in a wall or other surface: *a large fish tank with viewing panels on the side.* **4.** A sliding door, hatch, or partition. **5.** A board with instruments or controls. **6.** A thin wooden board used as a surface for oil painting. **7.** A picture in a rectangular frame or boundary. **8. a.** A list or group of persons chosen for jury duty. **b.** A jury. **9.** A group of persons gathered together to discuss or decide something or to participate in a television game show or other entertainment. —*tr.v.* **-eled** or **elled, -el·ing** or **el·ling.** **1.** To cover, furnish, or decorate with panels. **2.** To select or impanel (a jury). [Middle English, from Old French, piece of parchment on which names of a jury were written, from Latin *pannus*, rag, cloth.]

pan·el·ing (păn'ə-lĭng) *n.* A section of panels or paneled wall.

pan·el·ist (păn'ə-lĭst) *n.* A member of a panel.

panel truck. A small delivery truck with a fully enclosed body.

pan fish. A small fish that can be fried whole.

pang (păng) *n.* A sudden, sharp sensation, as of pain or emotional distress. [Orig. unknown.]

pan·go·lin (păng-gō'lĭn) *n.* Any of several scale-covered mammals of the genus *Manis*, of tropical Africa and Asia, that have a long snout and a sticky tongue with which it catches and eats ants. [Malay *pĕngguling*, from *guling*, to roll.]

pan·han·dle¹ (păn'hăn'dl) *intr.v.* **-dled, -dling.** *Informal.* To beg, esp. on the streets. [Orig. obscure.] —**pan'han'dler** *n.*

pan·han·dle² (păn'hăn'dl) *n.* **1.** The handle of a pan. **2.** Often **Panhandle.** A narrow strip of territory projecting from a larger area: *the Florida Panhandle.*

pan·ic (păn'ĭk) *n.* A sudden, overpowering terror, often affecting many people at once. —*adj.* Of or resulting from such terror: *a panic reaction.* —*v.* **-icked, -ick·ing.** —*tr.v.* To affect with panic. —*intr.v.* To be affected with panic. —See Syns at **frighten.** [From *panic*, of Pan, from French *panique*, from Greek *panikos*, from *Pan*, Pan.] —**pan'ick·y** *adj.*

pan·i·cle (păn'ĭ-kəl) *n.* A flower cluster that is loosely and irregularly branched. [Latin *pānicula*, dim. of *pānus*, tuft, from Greek *pēnos*, web.] —**pan'i·cled** *adj.*

pan·ic-strick·en (păn'ĭk-strĭk'ən) *adj.* Also **pan·ic-struck** (-strŭk'). Overcome by panic; terrified.

pan·jan·drum (păn-jăn'drəm) *n.* A person of importance. [From the *Grand Panjandrum*, character in a story by Samuel Foote (1720–77), English playwright.]

pan·nier (păn'yər, păn'ē-ər) *n.* **1.** A large wicker basket, esp. one of a pair carried on either side of a pack animal. **2. a.** A hoop framework formerly used to expand a woman's skirt at the hips. **b.** A skirt or overskirt puffed out at the hips. [Middle English *panier*, from Old French, from Latin *pānārium*, breadbasket, from *pānis*, bread.]

pan·o·ply (păn'ə-plē) *n., pl.* **-plies.** **1.** The complete arms and armor of a warrior. **2.** An array that covers or protects. **3.** Magnificent display. [Greek *panoplia*, full suit of armor : *pan-*, all + *hoplon*, weapon.]

pan·o·ram·a (păn'ə-răm'ə, -rä'mə) *n.* **1.** An unlimited view of all visible objects over a wide area. **2.** A comprehensive picture of a specific subject: *a panorama of ancient history.* **3.** A picture representing a continuous scene exhibited a part at a time by being unrolled and passed before the spectator. [PAN- + Greek *horāma*, sight, from *horān*, to see.] —**pan'o·ram'ic** *adj.* —**pan'o·ram'i·cal·ly** *adv.*

pan·pipe (păn'pīp') *n.* Often **panpipes.** A primitive wind instrument consisting of a series of pipes or reeds of graduated length bound together, and played by blowing across the top open ends. [PAN + PIPE.]

pan·sy (păn'zē) *n., pl.* **-sies.** A garden plant hybridized from *Viola tricolor hortensis*, with rounded, velvety petals of various colors. [French *pensée*, thought, pansy, from *penser*, to think, from Latin *pendere*, to weigh.]

pant (pănt) *intr.v.* **1.** To breathe rapidly in short gasps, as after exertion. **2.** To make loud puffing sounds. **3.** To yearn impatiently. —*tr.v.* To utter hurriedly or breathlessly. —*n.* **1.** A short, labored breath; gasp. **2.** A short, loud puff. [Middle English *panten*, from Old French *pantaisier*, from Latin *phantasia*, an apparition, fantasy, from Greek *phainein*, to show.] —**pant'ing·ly** *adv.*

pan·ta·lets (păn'tl-ĕts') *pl.n.* Also **pan·ta·lettes.** Long ruf-

fled underdrawers worn by women in the mid-19th cent. [From PANTALOON.]

pan·ta·loon (păn'tl-oon') *n.* **1. pantaloons.** Tight trousers extending from waist to ankle, formerly worn by men. **2. Pantaloon.** A character in the commedia dell'arte, portrayed as a foolish old man with slippers and tight trousers. **3.** A stock character, the butt of a clown's jokes in modern pantomime. [French *Pantalon*, a character in Italian comedy, from Old Italian *Pantalone*, from *Pantaleone*, a saint once popular in Venice.]

pan·the·ism (păn'thē-ĭz'əm) *n.* The belief that God and nature are one. —**pan'the·ist** *n.* —**pan'the·is'tic** or **pan'the·is'ti·cal** *adj.*

pan·the·on (păn'thē-ŏn', -ən) *n.* **1. Pantheon.** A circular temple in Rome dedicated to all the gods. **2.** Any temple dedicated to all gods. **3.** All the gods of a people. **4.** All the most outstanding members in a sphere or activity: *belongs in the pantheon of composers.* **5.** A public building commemorating and dedicated to the great persons of a nation. [Middle English *Panteon*, from Latin *Panthēon*, from Greek *pantheion* : *pan-*, all + *theos*, god.]

pan·ther (păn'thər) *n.* **1.** The leopard, *Panthera pardus*, esp. one with a black coat. **2.** Any of several similar or related animals, such as the mountain lion. [Middle English *panter*, from Old French *pantere*, from Latin *panthēra*, from Greek *panthēr*.]

panther

pant·ies (păn'tēz) *pl.n.* Short underpants for women or children. [From PANTS.]

pan·to·graph (păn'tə-grăf') *n.* An instrument for copying a plane figure to any desired scale. [French *pantographe* : *panto-*, all + *-graphe*, writing instrument.]

pan·to·mime (păn'tə-mīm') *n.* **1.** A technique for the expression of a message or meaning that consists of facial gestures and body movement. **2.** A play or entertainment presented in this way. —*v.* **-mimed, -mim·ing.** —*tr.v.* To represent by pantomime. —*intr.v.* To express oneself in pantomime. [Latin *pantomīmus*, "the complete mime" : Greek *pan-*, all + *mimos*, mime.] —**pan'to·mim'ic** (păn'tə-mĭm'ĭk) *adj.* —**pan'to·mim'ist** (păn'tə-mī'mĭst, -mĭm'ĭst) *n.*

pan·to·then·ic acid (păn'tə-thĕn'ĭk). A component of the vitamin B complex, $C_9H_{17}NO_5$, common in liver but found in all living tissue. [From Greek *pantothen*, from all sides, from *pan*, all.]

pan·try (păn'trē) *n., pl.* **-tries.** A small room or closet, usu. off a kitchen, where food, dishes, etc., are stored. [Middle English *pantrie*, from Old French *paneterie*, bread closet, from *panetier*, servant in charge of the bread, from *pan*, bread, from Latin *pānis*.]

pants (pănts) *pl.n.* **1.** Trousers. **2.** Underpants. [From PANTALOON.]

pant·y·hose (păn'tē-hōz') *pl.n.* A woman's undergarment consisting of stockings and underpants in one piece.

pant·y·waist (păn'tē-wāst') *n.* **1.** A child's undergarment consisting of a shirt and pants buttoned together at the waist. **2.** *Slang.* A weak, effeminate man.

pan·zer (păn'zər, păn'sər, pänt'sər) *adj.* Of or relating to an armored military unit. [German *Panzer*, armor, from Old French *pancier*, body-armor, from *panse*, body, from Latin *pantex*, paunch.]

pap¹ (păp) *n.* **1.** *Archaic.* A teat or nipple. **2.** Something resembling a nipple. [Middle English *pappe*.]

pap² (păp) *n.* Soft, easily digested food, as for infants. [Middle English *pape*, prob. from Latin *pappa*, baby talk for food.]

pa·pa (pä'pə, pə-pä') *n.* Father. [French.]

pa·pa·cy (pä'pə-sē) *n., pl.* **-cies.** **1.** The office of a pope.

2. The period of time during which a pope is in office. **3. Papacy.** The system of church government headed by the pope. [Middle English *papacie*, from Medieval Latin *pāpātia*, from Late Latin *pāpa*, pope.]

pa·pal (pā′pəl) *adj.* Of or relating to the pope or his office. [Middle English, from Old French, from Medieval Latin *pāpālis*, from Late Latin *pāpa*, pope.]

pa·paw (pô′pô′) *n.* Also **paw·paw.** **1.** A tree, *Asimina triloba*, of central North America. **2.** The edible fruit of this tree. Also called **custard apple.** [Prob. from Spanish *papaya*, papaya.]

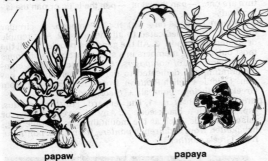

papaw   papaya

pa·pa·ya (pə-pä′yə) *n.* **1.** An evergreen tropical American tree, *Carica Papaya*, bearing large, yellow, edible fruit. **2.** The fruit of this tree. [Spanish, from Cariban.]

pa·per (pā′pər) *n.* **1. a.** A material produced, usu. in thin sheets, from cellulose pulp derived mainly from wood, rags, and certain grasses, and used for writing, printing, drawing, wrapping, and covering walls. **b.** A single sheet of this material. **c.** A sheet of this material with writing or printing on it. **2. a.** A document. **b. papers.** Documents that establish identity or give other information about the bearer. **3. papers.** A collection of letters, memoranda, and other personal writings. **4.** A newspaper. **5.** A report or essay, esp. an academic composition. —*modifier: a paper cup; paper clips; a paper mill.* —*tr.v.* **1.** To wrap or cover in paper. **2.** To cover with wallpaper. —*idiom.* **on paper. 1.** In writing or print. **2.** In theory rather than in reality. [Middle English *papir*, from Old French *papier*, from Latin *papȳrus*, from Greek *papuros*, papyrus.] —**pa′per·y** *adj.*

pa·per·back (pā′pər-băk′) *n.* A book with a flexible paper binding. —*modifier: a paperback edition.*

pa·per·board (pā′pər-bôrd′, -bōrd′) *n.* Cardboard; pasteboard.

pa·per·hang·er (pā′pər-hăng′ər) *n.* A person who applies wallpaper, esp. as a job. —**pa′per·hang′ing** *n.*

pa·per·knife (pā′pər-nīf′) *n.* A thin, dull knife used for opening sealed envelopes.

paper money. Currency in the form of government notes and bank notes.

paper nautilus. An eight-armed saltwater mollusk, *Argonauta argo*, with a paper-thin spiral shell.

pa·per·weight (pā′pər-wāt′) *n.* A small heavy object for holding down loose papers.

pa·per·work (pā′pər-wûrk′) *n.* Routine office work, esp. when it is secondary to a more important task.

pa·pier-mâ·ché (pā′pər-mə-shā′, păp′yā–) *n.* A material made from paper shreds mixed with glue or paste that can be molded when wet and that becomes hard when dry. [French, "chewed paper."]

pa·pil·la (pə-pĭl′ə) *n., pl.* **-pil·lae** (-pĭl′ē). *Biol.* Any small, bodily projection, such as a protuberance on the top of the tongue. [From Latin *papilla*, dim. of *papula*, pimple.] —**pap′il·lar′y** (păp′ə-lĕr′ē, pə-pĭl′ə-rē) *adj.*

pa·pist (pā′pĭst) *n.* A Roman Catholic. Usu. used disparagingly. [French *papiste*, from *pape*, pope, from Late Latin *pāpa*.] —**pa·pis′ti·cal** *adj.* —**pa′pist·ry** *n.*

pa·poose (pă-pōōs′, pə–) *n.* Also **pap·poose.** A North American Indian infant. [Of Algonquian orig.]

pa·pri·ka (pă-prē′kə, pə–, păp′rĭ-kə) *n.* A mild, powdered seasoning made from sweet red peppers. [Hungarian, from Serbian, from *papar*, pepper, from Greek *peperi*.]

Pap test (păp). A test in which a smear of a bodily secretion is immediately fixed and examined to detect cancer in an early stage. Also called **Pap smear.** [Invented by George Papanicolaou (1883–1962), American scientist.]

pa·py·rus (pə-pī′rəs) *n., pl.* **-rus·es** or **-ri** (-rī′). **1.** A tall aquatic sedge, *Cyperus papyrus*, of southern Europe and northern Africa. **2.** A kind of paper made by the ancient Egyptians from the pith stems of this plant. **3.** A document written on this paper. [Middle English *papirus*, paper, from Latin *papȳrus*, from Greek *papuros*, papyrus.]

par (pär) *n.* **1.** An accepted or normal average: *below par in physical condition.* **2.** A level of equality; equal footing: *good wine, but not on a par with imported kinds.* **3.** The number of golf strokes regarded as necessary to complete a given hole or course in expert play. **4.** The value printed on the face of a stock or bond as distinguished from the current market value. —*modifier: the par value.* —*adj.* Equal to the standard; normal: *a par performance.* [Latin, equal.]

para- or **par-.** A prefix meaning: **1.** Near or beside: **parathyroid gland.** **2.** Outside or beyond: **parapsychology. 3.** Resembling or similar to: **paratyphoid fever. 4.** Isomeric to or polymeric to: **paraldehyde.** [From Greek *para*, beside, for.]

par·a·ble (păr′ə-bəl) *n.* A simple story illustrating a moral or religious lesson. [Middle English, from Old French *parabole*, from Late Latin *parabola*, from Greek *parabolē*: *para*, beside + *ballein*, to throw.]

pa·rab·o·la (pə-răb′ə-lə) *n. Geom.* A plane curve formed by: **a.** A conic section taken parallel to an element of the intersected cone. **b.** The locus of points equidistant from a fixed line and a fixed point not on the line. [From Greek *parabolē*.]

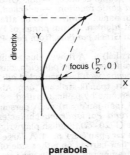

parabola

par·a·bol·ic (păr′ə-bŏl′ĭk) or **par·a·bol·i·cal** (-ĭ-kəl) *adj.* **1.** Of or like a parable. **2.** Of or having the form of a parabola. —**par′a·bol′i·cal·ly** *adv.*

par·a·chute (păr′ə-shōōt′) *n.* **1.** A foldable umbrella-shaped device used to slow the fall of persons or objects from great heights. **2.** A similar device used to slow speeding vehicles. —*v.* **-chut·ed, -chut·ing.** —*tr.v.* To drop (supplies, troops, etc.) by parachute. —*intr.v.* To descend by parachute. [French : *parasol*, parasol + *chute*, fall.] —**par′a·chut′ist** *n.*

pa·rade (pə-rād′) *n.* **1.** A festive public event in which assembled people or vehicles pass by spectators. **2.** A formal review of marching soldiers or sailors. **3.** The group participating in such a public event or military review. **4.** Any large number of people walking by: *the parade of Sunday strollers.* **5.** A long line or succession: *a parade of applicants.* **6.** An elaborate or vulgar display: *making a parade of his wealth.* —*v.* **-rad·ed, -rad·ing.** —*tr.v.* **1.** To assemble (troops) for a formal display or review. **2.** To walk through or around. **3.** To exhibit ostentatiously; flaunt. —*intr.v.* **1.** To assemble for a formal review. **2.** To take part in a parade. **3.** To promenade in a public place. [French, from Italian *parata*, from Latin *parāre*, to prepare.] —**pa·rad′er** *n.*

par·a·digm (păr′ə-dīm′, -dĭm′) *n.* **1.** An example or model: *He is a paradigm of the perfect host.* **2.** A list of all the inflectional forms of a word. [Late Latin *paradīgma*, from Greek *paradeigma*, model : *para*, alongside + *deiknunai*, to show.] —**par′a·dig·mat′ic** (păr′ə-dĭg-măt′ĭk) *adj.*

par·a·dise (păr′ə-dīs′, -dīz′) *n.* **1.** Often **Paradise.** The Garden of Eden. **2.** Heaven. **3.** Any place or condition of perfect happiness or beauty. **4.** An ideal place. [Middle English *paradis*, from Old French, from Late Latin *paradīsus*, from Greek *paradeisos*, garden, park, paradise, from Persian *pairi-daēza*, walled-in park : *pairi*, around + *daēza*, wall.] **—par·a·dis'i·ac'** (păr'ə-dĭz'ē-ăk') or **par·a·di·si'a·cal** (păr'ə-dĭ-sī'ə-kəl, -zī'-) *adj.* **—par'a·di·si'a·cal·ly** *adv.*

par·a·dox (păr'ə-dŏks') *n.* **1.** A statement that contains or implies its own contradiction and therefore has an uncertain meaning or no meaning. **2.** A statement that appears to contradict itself or to be contrary to common sense but that may be true. **3.** Someone or something with apparently contradictory or inconsistent qualities or facets. [Latin *paradoxum*, from Greek *paradoxon* : *para*, beyond + *doxa*, opinion, from *dokein*, to think.] **—par'a·dox'i·cal** *adj.* **—par'a·dox'i·cal·ly** *adv.* **—par'a·dox'i·cal·ness** *n.*

par·af·fin (păr'ə-fĭn) *n.* **1.** *Chem.* A waxy, white or colorless, solid hydrocarbon mixture used to make candles, wax paper, lubricants, and sealing materials. **2.** *Chem.* Any member of the **paraffin series. 3.** *Brit.* Kerosene. *—tr.v.* To saturate, impregnate, or coat with paraffin. [German *Paraffin* : Latin *parum*, too little + *affīnis*, neighboring (from its lack of affinity for other materials).]

paraffin series. *Chem.* A homologous group of saturated aliphatic hydrocarbons having the general formula C_nH_{2n+2}, the simplest and most abundant of which is methane. Also called **methane series.**

par·a·gon (păr'ə-gŏn', -gən) *n.* A model of excellence or perfection: *She is a paragon of honesty.* [Obs. French, from Italian *paragone*, comparison, touchstone, from Greek *parakonan*, to sharpen : *para*, alongside + *akonē*, whetstone, from *akē*, point.]

par·a·graph (păr'ə-grăf') *n.* **1.** A division of a piece of writing that begins on a new, usu. indented line and that consists of one or more sentences on a single idea or aspect of the subject. **2.** A brief article, as in a newspaper. **3.** A mark, ¶, used to indicate where a new paragraph should begin. *—tr.v.* To divide or arrange in paragraphs. [Medieval Latin *paragraphus*, sign marking a new section of writing, from Greek *paragraphos*, line to mark exchange in dialogue : *para*, beside + *graphein*, to write.] **—par'a·graph'ic** *adj.*

par·a·keet (păr'ə-kēt') *n.* Any of various small parrots with long, tapering tails. [Old French *paroquet*.]

par·al·de·hyde (pə-răl'də-hīd') *n.* A colorless aromatic liquid polymer, $C_6H_{12}O_3$, of acetaldehyde, used as a solvent and as a sedative. [PAR(A)- + (ACET)ALDEHYDE.]

par·al·lax (păr'ə-lăks') *n.* An apparent change in the direction of an object, caused by a change in observational position that provides a new line of sight. [French *parallaxe*, from Greek *parallaxis* : *para*, among + *allassein*, to exchange, from *allos*, other.] **—par'al·lac'tic** (păr'ə-lăk'tĭk) *adj.*

par·al·lel (păr'ə-lĕl', -ləl) *adj.* **1.** Lying in the same plane and not intersecting: *parallel lines.* **2.** Not intersecting: *parallel planes.* **3.** Having corresponding points always separated by the same distance: *parallel curves.* **4.** Matching feature for feature; corresponding: *parallel predicaments.* **5.** Of, consisting of, or containing electric devices connected so that the same source of voltage appears across each. —See Syns at **like.** *—adv.* In a parallel course or direction: *a reef running parallel to the shore.* *—n.* **1.** Any of a set of parallel geometric figures, esp. lines. **2.** Something closely resembling something else. **3.** A comparison showing close resemblance; an analogy. **4.** Any of the lines considered to encircle the earth parallel to the plane of the equator, used to represent degrees of latitude. *—tr.v.* **1.** To make or place parallel. **2.** To be or extend parallel to: *The town's main street paralleled a ship canal.* **3.** To correspond to; follow closely. [Latin *parallēlus*, from Greek *parallēlos* : *para*, beside + *allēlōn*, of one another, from *allos*, other.]

parallel bars. Two horizontal poles set parallel to each other in adjustable upright supports and used in gymnastic exercises.

par·al·lel·e·pi·ped (păr'ə-lĕl'ə-pī'pĭd, -pĭp'ĭd) *n.* Also **par·al·lel·o·pi·ped.** A solid with six faces, each a parallelogram. [Greek *parallēlepipedon* : *parallēlos*, parallel + *epipedon*, plane surface.]

par·al·lel·ism (păr'ə-lĕl-ĭz'əm) *n.* **1.** The condition or posi-

tion of being parallel. **2.** Likeness, correspondence, or similarity. **3.** *Gram.* The use of corresponding syntactical forms in adjacent phrases or clauses.

par·al·lel·o·gram (păr'ə-lĕl'ə-grăm') *n.* A four-sided plane figure with opposite sides parallel. [Late Latin *parallēlogrammum*, from Greek *parallēlogrammon* : *parallēlos*, parallel + *grammē*, line.]

parallelogram   parapet

pa·ral·y·sis (pə-răl'ĭ-sĭs) *n.*, *pl.* **-ses** (-sēz'). **1.** Partial or complete loss of the ability to feel sensations in or move a part of the body. **2.** An inability to act or move normally, as from fear or indecision. [Latin, from Greek *paralusis* : *para*, wrongly + *luein*, to release.]

par·a·lyt·ic (păr'ə-lĭt'ĭk) *adj.* **1.** Of, relating to, or causing paralysis: *a paralytic stroke.* **2.** Suffering from paralysis. *—n.* A person who suffers from paralysis.

par·a·lyze (păr'ə-līz') *tr.v.* **-lyzed, -lyz·ing. 1.** To affect with paralysis. **2.** To make helpless or unable to move, as from fear or indecision. **3.** To block the normal functioning of: *The blizzard paralyzed the city.* [French *paralyser*, from *paralysie*, paralysis, from Latin *paralysis*, paralysis.] **—par'a·ly·za'tion** *n.*

par·a·mag·net·ic (păr'ə-măg-nĕt'ĭk) *adj. Physics.* Pertaining to or denoting a substance in which an induced magnetic field is in the same direction as, and greater in strength than, the magnetizing field, but much weaker than in ferromagnetic materials. **—par'a·mag'net·ism** (-măg'nĭ-tĭz'əm) *n.*

par·a·me·ci·um (păr'ə-mē'shē-əm, -sē-) *n.*, *pl.* **-ci·a** (-shē-ə, -sē-ə) or **-ums.** Any of various ciliate protozoans of the genus *Paramecium*, usu. oval and with an oral groove for feeding. [From Greek *paramēkēs*, oblong.]

par·a·med·ic (păr'ə-mĕd'ĭk) *n.* A person who assists a trained medical professional, as a corpsman, nurse, etc. **—par'a·med'i·cal** *adj.*

pa·ram·e·ter (pə-răm'ĭ-tər) *n.* **1.** A variable or an arbitrary constant appearing in a mathematical expression, each value of which restricts or determines the specific form of the expression. **2.** *Informal.* **a.** A fixed limit or boundary. **b.** A characteristic element.

par·a·mount (păr'ə-mount') *adj.* **1.** Of greatest concern or importance. **2.** Supreme in rank, power, or authority. —See Syns at **primary.** [Norman French *paramont*, superior.]

par·a·mour (păr'ə-mŏor') *n.* A lover, esp. a secret one. [Middle English *paramour*, "by way of love," from Old French *par amour*.]

par·a·noi·a (păr'ə-noi'ə) *n.* **1.** A serious mental disorder in which a person imagines himself to be persecuted and often has an exaggerated idea of his own importance. **2.** Irrational fear for one's security. [Greek, madness, from *paranoos*, demented : *para*, beyond + *nous*, mind.] **—par'a·noi'ac'** (păr'ə-noi'ăk', -noi'ĭk) *adj. & n.*

par·a·noid (păr'ə-noid') *adj.* Of, affected with, or characteristic of paranoia. *—n.* Someone affected with paranoia.

par·a·pet (păr'ə-pĭt, -pĕt') *n.* **1.** A low, protective wall or railing along the edge of a roof, balcony, or similar structure. **2.** An embankment protecting soldiers from enemy fire. [French, from Italian *parapetto*, chest-high wall : *para*, protecting, + *petto*, chest, from Latin *pectus*.]

par·a·pher·na·lia (păr'ə-fə-nāl'yə, -fər-) *n.* (used with a sing. or pl. verb). **1.** Personal belongings. **2.** The articles used in some activity; equipment; gear. [Medieval Latin *paraphernália,* a married woman's property exclusive of her dowry, from Greek *parapherna* : *para,* beyond + *phernē,* dowry.]

par·a·phrase (păr′ə-frāz′) *n.* A restatement of a text or passage in other words, often to clarify meaning. —*v.* **-phrased, -phras·ing.** —*tr.v.* To express the meaning of in other words. —*intr.v.* To compose a paraphrase. [French, from Latin *paraphrasis,* from Greek : *para,* alongside + *phrazein,* to show.] —**par′a·phras′er** *n.*

par·a·ple·gi·a (păr′ə-plē′jē-ə, -jə) *n.* Complete paralysis of the lower half of the body, including both legs. [From Greek *paraplēgia,* a stroke on one side : *para,* beside + *plēssein,* to strike.] —**par·a·ple′gic** (-jĭk) *adj. & n.*

par·a·pro·fes·sion·al (păr′ə-prə-fĕsh′ə-nəl) *n.* A nonprofessional worker who assists a professional.

par·a·psy·chol·o·gy (păr′ə-sī-kŏl′ə-jē) *n.* The study of phenomena, such as telepathy, clairvoyance, and psychokinesis, that are not explainable by known natural laws.

par·a·site (păr′ə-sīt′) *n.* **1.** *Biol.* Any organism that grows, feeds, and is sheltered on or in a different organism while contributing nothing to the survival of its host. **2.** A person who exploits or takes advantage of the generosity of another. [Old French, from Latin *parasītus,* from Greek *parasitos* : *para,* beside + *sitos,* grain, food.] —**par′a·sit′ic** (păr′ə-sĭt′ĭk) or **par·a·sit′i·cal** (-ĭ-kəl) *adj.*

par·a·sit·ism (păr′ə-sĭ-tĭz′əm, -sī-) *n.* **1.** The characteristic behavior or mode of existence of a parasite. **2.** A diseased condition resulting from parasitic infestation.

par·a·sit·ize (păr′ə-sĭ-tīz′, -sī-) *tr.v.* **-ized, -iz·ing.** To live on (a host) as a parasite.

par·a·si·tol·o·gy (păr′ə-sĭ-tŏl′ə-jē, -sī-) *n.* The scientific study of parasitism. —**par′a·si′to·log′i·cal** (-sīt′ə-lŏj′ĭ-kəl, -sī′tə) *adj.* —**par′a·si·tol′o·gist** *n.*

par·a·sol (păr′ə-sôl′, -sŏl′) *n.* A light, small umbrella carried, esp. by women, as protection from the sun. [French, from Old Italian *parasole* : *parare,* to shield, from Latin *parāre,* to prepare + *sole,* sun, from Latin *sōl.*]

par·a·sym·pa·thet·ic nervous system (păr′ə-sĭm′pə-thĕt′ĭk). *Anat.* The part of the autonomic nervous system that originates in the central and back parts of the brain and in the lower part of the spinal cord and that, in general, inhibits or opposes the physiological effects of the sympathetic nervous system, as by tending to stimulate digestive secretions, slowing the heart, and dilating blood vessels.

par·a·thy·roid gland (păr′ə-thī′roid′). Any of four small kidney-shaped glands that lie in pairs at the sides of the thyroid gland and secretes a hormone that controls the metabolism of calcium and phosphorus.

par·a·troops (păr′ə-trōops′) *pl.n.* Troops trained and equipped to parachute. [PARA(CHUTE) + TROOPS.] —**par′a·troop·er** *n.*

par·a·ty·phoid fever (păr′ə-tī′foid′). An acute intestinal disease, similar to but less severe than typhoid fever, caused by *Salmonella* bacteria and manifesting itself as food poisoning.

par·boil (pär′boil′) *tr.v.* To cook partially by boiling for a brief period. [Middle English *parboilen,* to boil thoroughly, from Old French *parbouillir,* from Late Latin *perbullīre* : Latin *per,* thoroughly + *bullīre,* to boil.]

Par·cae (pär′sē′, pär′kī′) *pl.n. Rom. Myth.* The three Fates.

par·cel (pär′səl) *n.* **1.** Something wrapped up or packaged; bundle; package. **2.** A portion or plot of land, usu. a division of a larger area. **3.** A group of people or things; a bunch: *a parcel of idiots.* **4.** A distinct, often essential part of something. —*tr.v.* **-celed** or **celled, -cel·ing** or **-cel·ling.** **1.** To divide into parts and distribute. **2.** To make into a parcel; to package. [Middle English *parcelle,* from Old French, from Latin *particula,* portion, particle, dim. of *pars,* part.]

parcel post. The branch of the postal service that handles and delivers parcels.

parch (pärch) *tr.v.* **1.** To make very dry, esp. with intense heat. **2.** To make thirsty. —*intr.v.* **1.** To become very dry. **2.** To become thirsty. [Middle English *parchen.*]

parch·ment (pärch′mənt) *n.* **1.** The skin of a sheep or goat, prepared as a material to write on. **2.** Something written on a sheet of this material. **3.** A diploma. **4.** Paper made in imitation of this material. [Middle English blend of Latin *parchemin,* from Old French *Parthica (pellis),* "Parthian

(leather)," and *pergamīna,* parchment, from Greek *pergamēnē,* from *Pergamon,* Pergamum, a city in Asia Minor (where it was first used as a substitute for papyrus).]

pard¹ (pärd) *n. Archaic.* A leopard or other large cat. [Middle English *parde,* from Old French, from Latin *pardus,* from Greek *pardos.*]

pard² (pärd) *n. Chiefly Western U.S.* A close friend or companion. [Short for *pardner,* var. of *partner.*]

par·don (pär′dn) *tr.v.* **1.** To release (a person) from punishment; forgive. **2.** To pass over (an offense) without punishment. **3.** To forgive or excuse: *Will you pardon a few more questions?* —*n.* **1.** Exemption from punishment granted by an official with authority over a legal case. **2.** Release from the penalties of an offense. **3.** Polite forgiveness, as for a discourtesy, interruption, or failure to hear: *begged her pardon for being late.* **4.** *Rom. Cath. Ch.* An indulgence. [Middle English *pardonen,* from Old French *pardoner,* from Late Latin *perdōnāre,* to grant : *per,* thoroughly + *dōnum,* gift.] —**par′don·a·ble** *adj.* —**par′don·a·bly** *adv.*

Syns: pardon, excuse, forgive *v. Core meaning:* To withhold punishment or blame for an offense or fault (*a criminal pardoned by the governor*). To PARDON is to pass over an offense without demanding punishment or subjecting to disfavor. FORGIVE implies giving up all resentment as well as all claim to retribution (*forgave him for stealing the family silver*). EXCUSE suggests making allowance for or overlooking an offense (*asked them to excuse me for what I said yesterday*).

par·don·er (pär′d'n-ər) *n.* **1.** Someone who pardons. **2.** A medieval ecclesiastic authorized to raise money by granting papal indulgences to contributors.

pare (pâr) *tr.v.* **pared, par·ing.** **1.** To remove the outer covering or skin of by peeling with a knife or similar instrument. **2.** To remove by or as if by cutting, clipping, or shaving: *pare a dead tree limb.* **3.** To make smaller by or as if by cutting: *pared the budget to a bare minimum.* [Middle English *paren,* from Old French *parer,* to prepare, from Latin *parāre.*]

par·e·gor·ic (păr′ĭ-gôr′ĭk, -gŏr′-) *n.* Camphorated tincture of opium, taken internally for the relief of diarrhea and intestinal pain. [Late Latin *parēgoricus,* alleviating, from Greek *parēgorikos,* from *parēgoros,* soothing : *para,* beside + *agora,* assembly.]

pa·ren·chy·ma (pə-rĕng′kə-mə) *n.* **1.** *Anat.* The tissue characteristic of an organ, as distinguished from connective tissue. **2.** *Bot.* Tissue composed of soft, unspecialized, thin-walled cells. [From Greek *parenkhuma,* from *parenkhein,* to pour in beside : *para,* beside + *en,* in + *khein,* to pour.] —**pa·ren′chy·mal** or **par′en·chym′a·tous** (păr′ən-kĭm′ə-təs) *adj.* —**par′en·chym′a·tous·ly** *adv.*

par·ent (pâr′ənt, păr′-) *n.* **1.** A father or mother. **2.** A forefather; ancestor. **3.** Any organism that produces or generates another. **4.** A guardian; protector. **5.** The source or cause of something; origin. [Middle English, from Old French, from Latin *parēns,* pres. part. of *parere,* to give birth.] —**par′ent·hood′** *n.*

par·ent·age (pâr′ən-tĭj, păr′-) *n.* Descent from parents or ancestors; lineage; origin.

pa·ren·tal (pə-rĕn′tl) *adj.* Of, relating to, or characteristic of a parent: *parental guidance.* —**pa·ren′tal·ly** *adv.*

pa·ren·the·sis (pə-rĕn′thĭ-sĭs) *n., pl.* **-ses** (-sēz′). **1.** Either or both of the upright curved lines, ( ), used to mark off explanatory or qualifying remarks in writing or printing. **2.** An additional phrase, explanation, etc., enclosed within such marks. **3.** A qualifying phrase placed within a sentence in such a way that the sentence is grammatically complete without it. **4.** Any comment departing from the main topic. **5.** An interruption of continuity; interval; interlude. [Late Latin, from Greek, insertion : *para,* beside + *en,* in + *tithenai,* to put.]

par·en·thet·i·cal (păr′ən-thĕt′ĭ-kəl) or **par·en·thet·ic** (-thĕt′ĭk) *adj.* **1.** Contained or grammatically capable of being contained within parentheses; qualifying or explanatory: *a parenthetical remark.* **2.** Using or containing parentheses. —**par′en·thet′i·cal·ly** *adv.*

pa·re·sis (pə-rē′sĭs, păr′ĭ-sĭs) *n.* Slight or partial paralysis. [From Greek, act of letting go, from *parienai,* to let fall : *para,* beside + *hienai,* to throw.] —**pa·ret′ic** (pə-rĕt′ĭk) *n. & adj.* —**pa·ret′i·cal·ly** *adv.*

ă pat   ā pay   â care   ä father   ĕ pet   ē be   hw which   ĭ pit   ī tie   î pier   ŏ pot   ō toe   ô paw, for   oi noise
ŏŏ took   ōō boot   ou out   th thin   th this   ŭ cut   û urge   zh vision   ə about, item, edible, gallop, circus

par ex·cel·lence (pär ĕk-sə-läNs'). In the highest degree; pre-eminently: *a craftsman par excellence*. [French, "by (way of) pre-eminence."]

par·fait (pär-fā') *n.* **1.** A dessert made of cream, eggs, sugar, and flavoring frozen together and served in a tall glass. **2.** A dessert of layers, often of ice cream with various toppings, served in a tall glass. [French, from *parfait*, perfect, from Latin *perfectus*.]

par·he·lion (pär-hēl'yən, -hē'lē-ən) *n.*, *pl.* **-he·lia** (-hēl'yə, -hē'lē-ə). A bright spot sometimes appearing to either side of the sun, often on a luminous ring or halo. [Latin *parēlion*, from Greek : *para*, beside, beyond + *hēlios*, sun.]

pa·ri·ah (pə-rī'ə) *n.* **1.** A member of a low caste of workers in southern India and Burma. **2.** A person who has been excluded from society; an outcast. [Tamil *paṛaiyan*, drummer, from *paṛai*, drum.]

pa·ri·e·tal (pə-rī'ĭ-təl) *adj.* Of, pertaining to, or forming the wall of a hollow structure or body cavity. —*n.* Either of two large, irregularly quadrilateral bones, between the frontal and occipital bones, that together form the sides and top of the skull. [French *pariétal*, from Late Latin *parietālis*, from Latin *pariēs*, a wall.]

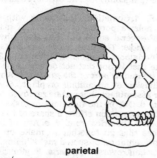

parietal

par·i·mu·tu·el (pär'ĭ-myōo'chōō-əl) *n.* **1.** A system of betting on races in which the winners divide the total amount bet, after deducting management expenses, in proportion to the sums they have wagered individually. **2.** The machine that records bets placed under this system. [French *pari mutuel*, "mutual stake."]

par·ing (pâr'ĭng) *n.* **1.** The act of removing the outer covering or skin. **2.** Something pared off: *cucumber parings*.

par·i pas·su (pär'ē päs'ōō). *Latin*. At the same pace or rate; side by side: *proceed pari passu*.

Par·is (pär'ĭs) *n. Gk. Myth.* The prince of Troy whose abduction of Helen provoked the Trojan War.

par·ish (pär'ĭsh) *n.* **1.** In the Anglican, Roman Catholic, and some other churches, a division of a diocese consisting of an area with its own church. **2.** In Great Britain, a political division of a county. **3.** An administrative district in Louisiana, corresponding to a county in other states. **4.** The members of a parish. [Middle English *parisshe*, from Old French *paroisse*, from Late Latin *parochia*, from Late Greek *paroikia*, from *paroikos*, Christian, from Greek, neighbor : *para*, near + *oikos*, house.]

pa·rish·ion·er (pə-rĭsh'ə-nər) *n.* A member or resident of a parish. [Middle English *parisshoner*, ult. from Old French *paroisse*, parish.]

par·i·ty (pär'ĭ-tē) *n.*, *pl.* **-ties. 1.** Equality, as in amount, status, or value: *firemen striking for parity of pay with policemen*. **2.** A fixed relative value between two different kinds of money. **3.** A level of prices paid to farmers for their products that gives the farmers the same purchasing power they had during a chosen earlier period. [Latin *paritās*, from *pār*, equal.]

park (pärk) *n.* **1.** An area of land set aside for public use, as: **a.** An expanse of enclosed grounds for recreational use within or adjoining a town. **b.** A tract of land kept in its natural state. **2.** A stadium or enclosed playing field. **3.** A country estate, esp. when including extensive grounds. **4.** A place for storing or leaving vehicles: *a trailer park; a car park*. —*tr.v.* **1.** To put or leave (a vehicle) for a time in a certain place. **2.** *Informal*. To place or leave at a certain location: *parked himself on the sofa*. —*intr.v.* To put or

leave a vehicle for a time in a place away from traffic. [Middle English, from Old French *parc*, enclosure, from Medieval Latin *parricus*.]

par·ka (pär'kə) *n.* A warm fur or cloth jacket with a hood. [Aleutian, skin, from Russian, reindeer pelt.]

park·ing lot. An area for parking motor vehicles.

parking meter. A coin-operated timer device to regulate car parking.

Par·kin·son's disease (pär'kĭn-sənz). A progressive nervous disease of the later years, characterized by muscular tremor, slowing of movement, partial facial paralysis, peculiarity of gait and posture, and weakness. [After James Parkinson (1755–1824), English surgeon.]

park·way (pärk'wā') *n.* A broad landscaped highway.

par·lance (pär'ləns) *n.* Particular manner of speaking; language, style, or idiom: *the parlance of lawyers*. [Old French, from *parler*, to speak.]

par·lay (pär'lā', -lē) *n.* A bet on two or more successive events at once, with the winnings of one, plus the original stake, to be automatically risked on the next. —*tr.v.* **1.** To bet (money) in a parlay. **2.** To increase (money) to a much larger amount by repeated investments. **3.** To use to great advantage or profit: *parlayed a knack for mimicry into a career as an entertainer*. [French *paroli*, from Italian, pl. of *parolo*, a set of dice, from *paro*, a pair, from Latin *pār*, equal.]

par·ley (pär'lē) *n.*, *pl.* **-leys.** A discussion or conference, esp. between opponents. —*intr.v.* To hold a parley; confer. [French *parlée*, from *parler*, to talk.]

par·lia·ment (pär'lə-mənt) *n.* **1.** An assembly of persons that makes the laws for a nation. **2. Parliament.** The national legislature of the United Kingdom, made up of the House of Commons and the House of Lords. [Middle English, from Old French *parlement*, from *parler*, to talk.]

par·lia·men·tar·i·an (pär'lə-mĕn-târ'ē-ən) *n.* An expert in parliamentary procedures, rules, or debate.

par·lia·men·ta·ry (pär'lə-mĕn'tə-rē, -mĕn'trē) *adj.* **1.** Of or like a parliament. **2.** Proceeding from, passed, or decreed by parliament. **3.** In accordance with the rules and customs of a parliament: *parliamentary procedure*. **4.** Having a parliament.

par·lor (pär'lər) *n.* Also *Brit.* **par·lour. 1.** A room in a private home set apart for the entertainment of visitors. **2.** A small lounge or sitting room in an inn, tavern, etc. **3.** A business establishment equipped for some special function, and often with an intimate or personalized decor: *a funeral parlor*. [Middle English *parlour*, from Old French *parleur*, room used for conversation, from *parler*, to talk.]

parlor car. A railroad car for day travel fitted with individual reserved seats.

par·lour (pär'lər) *n. Brit.* Var. of **parlor.**

par·lous (pär'ləs) *adj. Archaic.* Perilous; dangerous. [Middle English, var. of PERILOUS.] —**par'lous·ly** *adv.*

pa·ro·chi·al (pə-rō'kē-əl) *adj.* **1.** Of, supported by, or located in a church parish. **2.** Restricted to a narrow scope; provincial: *parochial attitudes*. [Middle English *parochiel*, from Old French *parochial*, from Late Latin *parochiālis*, from *parochia*, parish.] —**pa·ro'chi·al·ly** *adv.* —**pa·ro'chi·al·ism** *n.*

parochial school. A school supported by a church parish.

par·o·dy (pär'ə-dē) *n.*, *pl.* **-dies. 1.** A comic imitation, as of a person, literary work, style, etc., that exaggerates the characteristics of the original to make it seem ridiculous. **2.** A performance so bad as to be equivalent to intentional mockery; travesty: *The trial was a parody of justice.* —*tr.v.* **-died, -dy·ing.** To make, present, or be a parody of. —See Syns at **imitate.** [Latin *parōdia*, from Greek *parōidia*, burlesque poem : *para*, beside + *ōidē*, song.] —**par'o·dist** *n.*

pa·role (pə-rōl') *n.* **1.** The release of a prisoner before his term has expired on condition of continued good behavior. **2.** Word of honor; a promise. **3.** The promise of a prisoner of war to fulfill certain conditions in return for release or favorable treatment. —*tr.v.* **-roled, -rol·ing.** To release (a prisoner) on parole. [French, word, promise.]

pa·rol·ee (pə-rō'lē') *n.* A person who is released from prison on parole.

pa·rot·id gland (pə-rŏt'ĭd). Either of the largest of the paired salivary glands, located below and in front of each ear. Also called **parotid**. [From Greek *parōtis*, tumor near the ear : *para*, beside + *ous*, ear.]

-parous. A suffix meaning giving birth to or bearing: **gemmiparous.** [Latin *-parus*, from *parere*, to give birth to.]

par·ox·ysm (păr′ək-sĭz′əm) *n.* **1.** A sudden outburst of emotion or action: *a paroxysm of laughter.* **2.** A spasm or fit; convulsion. [French *paroxysme*, from Greek *paroxusmos*, from *paroxunein*, to irritate : *para*, beside + *oxus*, sharp.] —**par·ox·ys′mal** (păr′ək-sĭz′məl) *adj.*

par·quet (pär-kā′) *n.* **1. a.** The part of the main floor of a theater in front of the balcony. **b.** The entire main floor of a theater; orchestra. **2.** A floor made of inlaid pieces of wood that are fitted together into a design. —*modifier: a parquet floor.* —*tr.v.* **-queted** (-kād′), **-quet·ing** (-kā′ĭng). To make or furnish with parquet. [French, from Old French, small enclosure, dim. of *parc*, enclosure, park.]

par·quet·ry (pär′kĭ-trē) *n., pl.* **-ries.** Wood, often of contrasting colors, worked into an inlaid pattern, used esp. for floors.

parr (pär) *n., pl.* **parr** or **parrs.** A young salmon during the first two years of its life when it lives in fresh water. [Orig. unknown.]

par·ri·cide (păr′ĭ-sīd′) *n.* **1.** Someone who murders his father or mother or other near relative. **2.** The act of committing such a murder. [Latin *parricidium* : *parri-*, "kin" + *-cidum*, -cide.] —**par′ri·cid′al** (păr′ĭ-sīd′l) *adj.*

par·rot (păr′ət) *n.* **1.** Any of numerous tropical and semitropical birds of the order Psittaciformes, characterized by short, hooked bills, brightly colored plumage, and, in some species, the ability to mimic human speech or other sounds. **2.** A person who repeats or imitates something without understanding it. —*tr.v.* To repeat or imitate without meaning or understanding. [Dial. French *perrot*, from Old French *perroquet*, parakeet.] —**par′rot·er** *n.*

parrot   parsnip

parrot fever. Psittacosis.

par·rot·fish (păr′ət-fĭsh′) *n., pl.* **-fish** or **-fish·es.** Any of various brightly colored tropical saltwater fishes of the family Scaridae, with jaws resembling a parrot's beak.

par·ry (păr′ē) *v.* **-ried, -ry·ing.** —*tr.v.* **1.** To turn aside; deflect: *parry a thrust in fencing.* **2.** To avoid skillfully; evade: *parried questions of the reporters.* —*intr.v.* To deflect or ward off a blow. —*n., pl.* **-ries. 1.** The act of deflecting or warding off a blow, esp. in fencing. **2.** An evasive answer or action. [From French *Parez*, "Parry!" (fencing expression), imper. of *parer*, to defend, parry, from Italian *parare*, from Latin *parāre*, to prepare.]

parse (pärs) *v.* **parsed, pars·ing.** —*tr.v.* **1.** To break (a sentence) down into its parts of speech with an explanation of the form and function of each word. **2.** To describe (a word) by stating its part of speech, form, and function in a sentence. —*intr.v.* To be clearly divisible into parts of speech. [From Latin *pars (ōrātiōnis)*, part (of speech).] —**pars′er** *n.*

par·sec (pär′sĕk′) *n.* A unit of astronomical length based on the distance from earth at which stellar parallax is one second of arc and equal to 3.258 light years or 1.918×10^{13} miles, or 3.086×10^{13} kilometers. [PAR(ALLAX) + SEC(OND).]

Par·see (pär′sē, pär-sē′) *n.* Also **Par·si.** A member of a Zoroastrian religious sect in India, descended from Persians. —**Par′see·ism** *n.*

par·si·mo·ni·ous (pär′sə-mō′nē-əs) *adj.* Marked by parsi-

mony. —See Syns at **stingy.** —**par′si·mo′ni·ous·ly** *adv.* —**par′si·mo′ni·ous·ness** *n.*

par·si·mo·ny (pär′sə-mō′nē) *n.* Extreme or excessive reluctance to spend money or use resources; stinginess; frugality. [Middle English *parcimony*, from Latin *parsimōnia*, from *parcere*, to spare.]

pars·ley (pär′slē) *n.* A widely cultivated herb, *Petroselinum crispum*, with finely-divided, curled leaves that are used as a garnish and for seasoning. [Middle English *persely*, from Old English *petersilie* and Old French *persil*, both from Late Latin *petrosīlium*, from Latin *petroselīnum*, from Greek *petroselinon* : *petra*, rock + *selinon*, celery.]

pars·nip (pär′snĭp′) *n.* **1.** A strong-scented plant, *Pastinaca sativa*, cultivated for its long, white, edible root. **2.** The root of this plant. [Middle English *pasnepe*, from Old French *pasnaie*, from Latin *pastināca*, from *pastinum*, a two-pronged dibble.]

par·son (pär′sən) *n.* **1.** A clergyman in charge of a parish, esp. in the Anglican Church. **2.** Any clergyman. [Middle English *persone*, parish priest, from Old French, from Medieval Latin *persōna (ecclēsiae)*, "person (of the church)."]

par·son·age (pär′sə-nĭj) *n.* The official residence of a parson.

part (pärt) *n.* **1.** Something that along with other things makes a whole; a portion or division of a larger thing. **2. a.** One of several equal portions that when combined make up a whole: *The dressing is two parts of olive oil mixed with one part vinegar.* **b.** A fraction. **3.** Something or someone that is not distinct or separable from something else: *treated as part of the family.* **4.** An organ, limb, or other division of an animal or plant. **5.** A piece in a machine or assemblage that can be removed or replaced; a component. **6.** One of the functions or tasks that must be performed in a common effort; a share of the work: *doing one's part.* **7.** A theatrical role. **8. a.** Any of the individual melodic lines that go together to make up music. **b.** A written representation of such a melodic line. **9.** A side in a dispute or controversy. **10. parts.** Regions; lands; areas: *scattered in remote parts.* **11. parts.** Natural abilities; talents: *"Though his parts were not brilliant, he made up for his lack of talent by meritorious industry"* (William M. Thackeray). **12.** A line on either side of which one combs one's hair in different directions. —*tr.v.* **1.** To divide into two or more parts. **2.** To separate by or as if by coming between; put or keep apart: *had to part them before they throttled each other.* **3.** To comb (the hair) away from a dividing line on the scalp. —*intr.v.* **1.** To divide or break; come apart: *The curtain parted in the middle.* **2.** To go away from one another; separate: *They parted as friends.* **3.** To separate into ways going in different directions, as a road. **4.** To leave; depart. —See Syns at **separate.** —*phrasal verb.* **part with.** To give up; yield: *The old miser hated to part with a penny.* —*adj.* Not full or complete; partial: *a part owner.* —*adv.* In part; partially: *Her dog is part collie, part German Shepherd.* —*idioms.* **for (one's) part.** As far as one is concerned. **for the most part.** In most cases; chiefly. **in large part.** Largely; chiefly. **in part.** To a certain extent; partly. **part and parcel.** An inseparable part. **take part.** To be active; participate. [Middle English, from Old French, from Latin *pars*.]

par·take (pär-tāk′) *intr.v.* **-took** (-tŏŏk′), **-tak·en** (-tā′kən), **-tak·ing. 1.** To take part; participate. **2.** To take a portion: *invited to partake of their dinner.* **3.** To have some quality or characteristic; show evidence: *a nature that partook of the ferocity of the lion.* [Back-formation from *partaker*, from *part taker*.] —**par·tak′er** *n.*

par·terre (pär-târ′) *n.* **1.** The part of the main floor of a theater that is underneath the balcony. **2.** A flower garden having the beds and paths arranged to form a pattern. [French, from Old French, from *par terre*, "on the ground."]

par·the·no·gen·e·sis (pär′thə-nō-jĕn′ĭ-sĭs) *n.* Reproduction of organisms without conjunction of gametes of opposite sexes. [Greek *parthenos*, virgin + -GENESIS.] —**par′the·no·ge·net′ic** (-jə-nĕt′ĭk) *adj.* —**par′the·no·ge·net′i·cal·ly** *adv.*

par·tial (pär′shəl) *adj.* **1.** Of or affecting only part; not total; incomplete: *a partial success.* **2.** Favoring one person or side over another; biased: *too partial to judge fairly.* **3.** Having a particular liking; esp. for a kind of food: *partial*

ă pat	ā pay	â care	ä father	ĕ pet	ē be	hw which		ĭ pit	ī tie	î pier	ŏ pot	ō toe	ô paw, for	oi noise
ŏŏ took	ŏŏ boot	ou out	th thin	th this	ŭ cut			û urge	zh vision	ə about, item, edible, gallop, circus				

to Chinese cooking. [Middle English *parcial*, from Old French *partial*, from Late Latin *partiālis*, from Latin *pars*, part.] **—par'tial·ly** *adv.*

par·ti·al·i·ty (pär'shē-ăl'ĭ-tē, pär-shǎl'-) *n.*, *pl.* **-ties. 1.** The condition of being partial. **2.** Favorable prejudice or bias. **3.** A special fondness; preference.

par·tic·i·pant (pär-tĭs'ə-pənt) *n.* Someone who participates in something. —*adj.* Participating; taking part.

par·tic·i·pate (pär-tĭs'ə-pāt') *intr.v.* **-pat·ed, -pat·ing.** To take part; join or share with others. [From Latin *participāre*, from *particeps*, a partaker.] **—par·tic'i·pa'tion** (-tĭs'-ə-pā'shən) *n.* **—par·tic'i·pa'tor** *n.*

par·tic·i·pi·al (pär'tĭ-sĭp'ē-əl) *adj.* Based on, forming, or formed from a participle: *a participial phrase.* **—par'ti·cip'i·al·ly** *adv.*

par·ti·ci·ple (pär'tĭ-sĭp'əl) *n.* Either of two verb forms, the **past participle** and the **present participle**, that are used with auxiliary verbs to indicate certain tenses and that can also function in certain cases as adjectives or nouns. [Middle English, from Old French, from Latin *participium*, from *particeps*, partaker.]

par·ti·cle (pär'tĭ-kəl) *n.* **1.** A very small piece or part; speck. **2.** A very small amount, trace, or degree: *not a particle of doubt.* **3.** *Physics.* A subatomic particle. **4.** Any of a class of words, including many prepositions and conjunctions, that have little meaning by themselves but help to specify, connect, or limit the meanings of other words. [Middle English, from Latin *particula*, dim. of *pars*, part.]

par·ti-col·ored (pär'tē-kŭl'ərd) *adj.* Having different parts or sections colored differently. [From Middle English *party*, parti-colored, from Old French *parti*, striped, from *partir*, to divide, from Latin *partīre*, from *pars*, part.]

par·tic·u·lar (pər-tĭk'yə-lər) *adj.* **1.** Of, belonging to, or associated with a single person, group, thing, or category. **2.** Separate and distinct from others; specific. **3.** Exceptional; special: *of particular interest.* **4.** Providing full details: *a particular account.* **5.** Giving or demanding close attention to details; fussy: *She's particular about how her meat is cooked.* —See Syns at **single.** —*n.* An individual item, fact, or detail. **—idiom. in particular.** Specifically; particularly. [Middle English *particuler*, concerned with details; from Old French, from Late Latin *particulāris*, from Latin *particula*, detail, particle.]

par·tic·u·lar·i·ty (pər-tĭk'yə-lăr'ĭ-tē) *n.*, *pl.* **-ties. 1.** The quality or condition of being particular or distinct; individuality. **2.** The quality of including or providing details: *the particularity of a newspaper story.* **3.** A detail; a particular. **4.** A distinct characteristic or quality. **5.** Close attention to details; fastidiousness; care.

par·tic·u·lar·ize (pər-tĭk'yə-lə-rīz') *v.* **-ized, -iz·ing.** —*tr.v.* To state in detail; go into details. —*intr.v.* To give details or particulars. **—par·tic'u·lar·i·za'tion** *n.* **—par·tic'u·lar·iz'er** *n.*

par·tic·u·lar·ly (pər-tĭk'yə-lər-lē) *adv.* **1.** As one specific case; specifically. **2.** To a great degree. **3.** With attention to particulars; in detail.

part·ing (pär'tĭng) *n.* **1.** A separation into two or more parts: *a parting in the trail.* **2.** A departure or leave-taking. **3.** Someone's death. —*adj.* Leaving; departing: *a parting friend.*

par·ti·san (pär'tĭ-zən) *n.* **1.** A strong supporter, as of a party, cause, team, or person. **2.** A member of a loosely organized body of fighters who attack an enemy within occupied territory. —*adj.* **1.** Having or showing a strong preference or bias. **2.** Of or marked by conflicting parties or factions: *partisan politics.* [French, from dial. Italian *partigiano*, from *parte*, part, party, from Latin *pars*, part.] **—par'ti·san·ship'** *n.*

par·tite (pär'tīt') *adj.* Divided into parts. [Latin *partītus*, past part. of *partīre*, to divide, from *pars*, part.]

par·ti·tion (pär-tĭsh'ən) *n.* **1.** A usu. thin structure, such as a panel or screen, that divides up a room or other enclosure. **2.** Any structure that divides a space. **3. a.** The division of something into parts, esp. the division of territory by governments. **b.** The condition of being divided into parts. —*tr.v.* **1.** To divide into parts, pieces, or sections. **2.** To divide or separate by means of a partition. —See Syns at **separate.** [Middle English *particioun*, from Old French *partition*, from Latin *partītiō*, from *partīre*, to divide, from *pars*, part.]

part·ly (pärt'lē) *adv.* In part; to some extent.

part·ner (pärt'nər) *n.* **1.** One of two or more persons associated in some common activity: **a.** A member of a business partnership. **b.** A friend with whom one lives, travels, or works. **c.** A spouse or mate. **d.** Either of two persons dancing together. **e.** Either of two persons playing a game together, usu. on the same side. **2.** An ally. —*tr.v.* **1.** To make a partner of. **2.** To be the partner of. [Middle English *partener*, from Anglo-French, *parcener*, from Latin *partītiō*, partition, from *partēre*, to divide, from *pars*, part.]

Syns: **partner, ally, associate, colleague, confederate** *n. Core meaning.* One who cooperates with another in a venture, occupation, or challenge (*partner in business*). *Partner* implies a relationship, frequently between two people, in which each person has equal status and a certain independence but also has unspoken or formal obligation to the other or others. A COLLEAGUE is a fellow member of a profession, staff, or organization (*a doctor and her colleagues*). An ALLY is one who, out of a common cause, has taken one's side and can be relied on (*were allies in the argument; the western Allies*). CONFEDERATE is negative and usu. applied to alleged criminals and suggests guilt by association (*the embezzler and his confederates*). An ASSOCIATE is anyone who works in the same place as another, usu. in direct contact with him (*one of my associates in the office*).

part·ner·ship (pärt'nər-shĭp') *n.* **1.** The condition of being partners. **2.** A business relationship in which two or more persons agree to furnish a part of the capital and labor for an enterprise and to share the profits or losses.

part of speech. Any of the grammatical classes into which words are placed according to how they function in a given context. Traditionally, the parts of speech in English are *noun, pronoun, verb, adjective, adverb, preposition, conjunction,* and *interjection.* Sometimes *article* is considered a part of speech.

par·took (pär-tōōk') *v.* Past tense of **partake.**

par·tridge (pär'trĭj) *n.*, *pl.* **-tridg·es** or **-tridge. 1.** Any of several plump-bodied Old World game birds, esp. of the genera *Perdix* and *Alectoris.* **2.** Any of several similar or related birds, such as the bobwhite. [Middle English *partrich*, from Old French *perdriz*, from Latin *perdix*, from Greek.]

part-time (pärt'tīm') *adj.* For or during less than the usual or standard time: *a part-time job.* **—part'-time'** *adv.*

par·tu·ri·ent (pär-tōōr'ē-ənt, -tyōōr'-) *adj.* **1.** About to bring forth young; being in labor. **2.** Of or relating to childbirth. **—par·tu'ri·en·cy** *n.*

par·tu·ri·tion (pär'chōō-rĭsh'ən, -chə-) *n.* The act of giving birth; childbirth. [Late Latin *parturītiō*, from Latin *parturīre*, to be in labor, from *parere*, to bear.]

par·ty (pär'tē) *n.*, *pl.* **-ties. 1.** A social gathering. **2.** A group of persons assembled for a specific activity or task: *a sailing party; a hunting party.* **3.** A permanent political group organized to promote and support its principles and, usu., to name candidates for public office. **4.** A person or group involved in a legal proceeding. **5.** A participant: *She refused to be a party to the dispute.* **6.** A person. —*modifier:* *a party dress; a party convention.* —*intr.v.* **-tied, -ty·ing.** *Informal.* **1.** To have or attend a party. **2.** To carouse. [Middle English *partie*, part, party, from Old French, from *partir*, to divide, from Latin *partīre*, from *pars*, part.] **—par'ty·er** *n.*

party line. 1. A telephone circuit connecting two or more subscribers with the exchange. **2.** The official policies and principles of a political party or other organization.

par·ve·nu (pär'və-nōō', -nyōō') *n.* A person who has suddenly become wealthy without the background or culture appropriate to his new status. [French, from *parvenir*, to arrive, from Latin *parvenīre*, to come through : *per*, through + *venīre*, to come.]

pas·chal (pǎs'kəl) *adj.* Of or relating to the Passover or to Easter. [Middle English *paskal*, from Old French *pascal*, from Late Latin *paschālis*, from *pascha*, Passover, Easter, from Late Greek *paska*, from Hebrew *pesah*, a passing over.]

paschal lamb. 1. A lamb eaten at the feast of the Passover. **2. Paschal Lamb.** *Christ.* **3. Agnus Dei.**

pa·sha (pä'shə, păsh'ə) n. A high-ranking Turkish military or civil official. [Turkish paṣa.]

Pash·to (pŭsh'tō) or **Push·to** (pŭsh'tōō) n. An Iranian language, one of two official languages of Afghanistan.

pasque·flow·er (păsk'flou'ər) n. Any of several plants of the genus *Anemone*, with large blue, purple, or white flowers and conspicuously plumed fruit. [From earlier *passeflower*, from Old French *passefleur* : *passer*, to surpass + *fleur*, flower.]

pass (păs) intr.v. 1. To move on or ahead; proceed: *people passing from shop to shop on the busy streets.* 2. To run; extend: *The river passes through town.* 3. To gain passage despite obstacles: *pass through a net.* 4. To catch up with and move past another vehicle. 5. To move past in time; elapse: *The days passed quickly.* 6. To be transferred from one to another; circulate: *The wine passed around the table.* 7. To be communicated or exchanged between persons: *Loud words passed.* 8. To be transferred or conveyed to another: *The title passed to the older son.* 9. To change from one condition, form, quality, or characteristic to another: *Daylight passed into darkness.* 10. To come to an end; be terminated: *His anger passed suddenly.* 11. To cease to exist; die. 12. To happen; take place: *What passed during the morning?* 13. To go without notice or challenge: *Let their rude remarks pass.* 14. To get through a test, trial, course, etc., with favorable results. 15. To be accepted as something different: *"would have his Noise and Laughter pass for Wit"* (William Wycherly). 16. To be approved or adopted, as a motion. 17. To express an opinion, judgment, or sentence: *The jury passed on each count of the indictment.* 18. *Sports.* To transfer a ball or puck to a teammate. 19. *Card Games.* To let one's turn to play or bid go by. —tr.v. 1. To go by without stopping; leave behind: *pass a hitchhiker on the road.* 2. To go beyond; exceed: *The returns passed all expectations.* 3. To go across; go through: *pass enemy lines.* 4. a. To undergo (a trial, test, etc.) with favorable results. b. To cause or allow to go through a trial, test, etc., successfully: *The instructor passed all the candidates.* 5. a. To cause to move, esp. into a certain position: *pass a cable around a cylinder.* b. To cause to move as part of a process: *pass liquid through a filter.* 6. To allow to go by or elapse; spend: *He passed his winter in Vermont.* 7. a. To cause to go across or over; transfer: *took the tray and passed it to the next person.* b. To circulate: *They passed the news quickly.* c. To hand over: *pass the bread.* 8. *Sports.* To throw or propel (a ball or puck) to a teammate. 9. *Baseball.* To walk (a batter) intentionally. 10. To cross over; issue from: *No secrets pass her lips.* 11. To discharge from the bowels or bladder; excrete. 12. a. To approve; adopt: *The legislature passed the bill.* b. To be approved by: *The bill passed the legislature.* 13. To pronounce; utter: *pass judgment.* 14. To go past without noticing: *He passed them by without even a nod.* —See Syns at **surpass.** —*phrasal verbs.* **pass away.** 1. To recede or cease. 2. To die. —See Syns at **die. pass off.** To offer, sell, or circulate fraudulently. **pass out.** To faint. **pass over.** To treat lightly or briefly. **pass up.** *Informal.* To turn down; refuse. —n. 1. An act of passing, esp. a transfer of something into another's hands. 2. A motion with the hand or something held in the hand: *made a quick pass with the sponge over the tablecloth.* 3. A route of travel through land that presents an obstacle, esp. a gap in a mountain range or ridge. 4. a. A permit granting the bearer the right to go through a restricted area. b. Any document that grants special rights of movement or access. c. A written leave of absence from a military post or assignment for a brief period. d. A ticket granting free entrance or transportation. 5. *Sports.* An act of passing a ball or puck to a teammate. b. The ball or puck passed. 6. *Baseball.* An intentional walk. 7. A run by a military aircraft over a target area. 8. An attempt; effort. 9. A situation, esp. a difficult or threatening one: *His own folly had brought him to this pass.* —*idioms.* **bring to pass.** To cause to happen; bring about. **come to pass.** To happen. [Middle English *passen*, to proceed, from Old French *passer*, from Latin *passus*, step, from *pandere*, to stretch out.] —**pass'er** n.

pass·a·ble (păs'ə-bəl) adj. 1. Capable of being passed or crossed: *a passable road.* 2. Satisfactory but not outstanding: *a passable performance.* —**pass'a·ble·ness** n. —**pass'a·bly** adv.

pas·sa·ca·glia (pä'sə-käl'yə, päs'ə-käl'yə) n. A 17th- and 18th-cent. musical form consisting of variations on one theme played in the bass. [Italian, from Spanish *passacalle* : *pasar*, to pass + *calle*, street.]

pas·sage (păs'ĭj) n. 1. The act or process of passing. 2. A journey, esp. by water. 3. The right to travel on something, esp. a ship. 4. A narrow path or way between two points: *an underground passage.* 5. A channel, duct, path, etc., through or along which something may pass: *the nasal passages.* 6. Approval of a legislative measure. 7. A sentence or paragraph from a literary work. 8. A section of a musical composition: *a passage for solo violin.*

pas·sage·way (păs'ĭj-wā') n. A corridor.

pass·book (păs'bŏŏk') n. A bankbook.

pas·sé (pă-sā') adj. Out-of-date; no longer current or in fashion. [French, past part. of *passer*, to pass.]

passed ball. *Baseball.* A pitch missed by the catcher, though close enough to him to be fielded cleanly, allowing a base runner to advance.

pas·sen·ger (păs'ən-jər) n. 1. A person riding in, but not driving, a vehicle or conveyance. 2. A wayfarer or traveler. [Middle English *passyngere*, from Old French *passager*, from *passage*, passage.]

passenger pigeon. An extinct migratory bird, *Ectopistes migratorius*, once abundant in North America.

passe par·tout (pås' pär-tōō'). 1. Something enabling one to pass or go everywhere, esp. a master key. 2. a. A mounting for a picture in which gummed colored tape forms the frame. b. The tape so used. 3. A mat used in mounting a picture. [French, "pass everywhere."]

pass·er·by (păs'ər-bī', păs'ər-bī') n., pl. **pass·ers·by.** A person who happens to be passing by.

pas·ser·ine (păs'ə-rīn') adj. Pertaining to or designating birds of the order Passeriformes, which includes more than half of all known birds and consists chiefly of perching birds and songbirds. —n. A bird of the order Passeriformes. [Latin *passerīnus*, from *passer*, sparrow.]

pas·sim (păs'ĭm) adv. Throughout; frequently. A word used in reference notes to indicate that the word or passage occurs frequently in the work cited. [Latin, here and there, from *pandere*, to scatter.]

pass·ing (păs'ĭng) adj. 1. Going by: *a passing car.* 2. Not lasting long; temporary: *a passing fad.* 3. Superficial; casual: *a passing glance.* 4. Satisfactory: *a passing grade.* 5. *Archaic.* Great; surpassing: *" 'Tis a passing shame"* (Shakespeare). —See Syns at **transitory.** —adv. *Archaic.* Very; surpassingly. —n. 1. The act of going by or past. 2. The end of something; death. —*idiom.* **in passing.** By the way; incidentally.

pas·sion (păsh'ən) n. 1. Any powerful emotion or appetite. 2. a. Ardent adoring love. b. Strong sexual desire; lust. c. The object of such love or desire. 3. a. Great enthusiasm for a certain activity, subject, etc. b. The object of such enthusiasm. 4. **Passion.** a. The sufferings of Christ on the cross. b. A narrative of this, as in the Gospels. c. A musical setting of such a narrative. [Middle English, from Old French, from Late Latin *passiō*, suffering, from Latin *patī*, to suffer.] —**pas'sion·less** adj.

Syns: passion, ardor, enthusiasm, fervor, fire, zeal n. **Core meaning:** Strong feeling for or about someone or something (*loved her with great passion; delivered the sermon with passion*). PASSION is a deep, overwhelming feeling or emotion; when directed toward a person, it usu. indicates love and sexual desire, although it can also refer to hostile emotions (*loathed them with passion*). Used lightly, it suggests an avid interest (*a passion for fast cars*). ARDOR can suggest great devotion to a cause but commonly means a warm, loving feeling directed toward persons (*embraced with ardor*). ENTHUSIASM reflects excitement and responsiveness to specific things (*supported the hockey team with enthusiasm*). FERVOR and FIRE indicate a highly intense, sustained emotional condition frequently (like *passion*) with a potential loss of control implied (*fought with fervor; the fire of a true revolutionary*). ZEAL, which sometimes reflects strong, forceful devotion to a cause, expresses a driving motivation or attitude (*the religious zeal of the Puritans*).

| ă pat | ā pay | â care | ä father | ĕ pet | ē be | hw which | ĭ pit | ī tie | î pier | ŏ pot | ō toe | ô paw, for | oi noise |
| ŏŏ took | ōō boot | ou out | th thin | th this | ŭ cut | û urge | zh vision | ə about, item, edible, gallop, circus | | | | | |

pas·sion·ate (păsh′ə-nĭt) *adj.* **1.** Capable of or having intense feelings. **2.** Wrathful by temperament. **3.** Amorous; lustful. **4.** Showing or expressing strong emotion; ardent: *a passionate plea.* —**pas′sion·ate·ly** *adv.*

pas·sion·flow·er (păsh′ən-flou′ər) *n.* Any of various tropical American vines of the genus *Passiflora,* usu. with showy flowers and edible fruit.

passionflower

Passion play. A play representing the Passion of Christ.

pas·sive (păs′ĭv) *adj.* **1.** Receiving or subjected to an action without responding or acting in return. **2.** Accepting without objection or resistance; submissive; compliant. **3.** Not participating, acting, or operating: *a passive role.* **4.** *Gram.* Denoting a verb form or voice used to indicate that the grammatical subject is the object of the action represented by the verb. For example, in the sentence *They were impressed by his manner, were impressed* is in the passive voice. —*n. Gram.* **1.** The passive voice. **2.** A verb or construction in this voice. [Middle English, from Latin *passīvus,* capable of suffering, from *patī,* to suffer.] —**pas′sive·ly** *adv.* —**pas′sive·ness** *n.*

passive resistance. Resistance to authority or law by nonviolent methods, as refusal to comply or fasting.

pas·siv·i·ty (pă-sĭv′ĭ-tē) *n.* The condition or quality of being passive; submissiveness.

pass·key (păs′kē′) *n.* Any of various kinds of keys, such as a master key or skeleton key.

Pass·o·ver (păs′ō′vər) *n.* A Jewish festival celebrated for eight days in the spring commemorating the escape of the Jews from Egypt.

pass·port (păs′pôrt′, -pōrt′) *n.* **1.** An official document that certifies the identity and citizenship of an individual and grants him permission to travel abroad. **2.** A permit issued by a foreign country allowing one to transport goods or to travel through that country. **3.** Anything that enables one to be admitted or accepted: *His wit was his passport to social success.* [French *passeport,* permission to pass through a port.]

pass·word (păs′wûrd′) *n.* A secret word or phrase spoken to a guard to gain admission.

past (păst) *adj.* **1.** No longer current; over: *His youth is past.* **2.** Having existed or occurred in an earlier time; bygone: *past events.* **3. a.** Earlier than the present time; ago: *forty years past.* **b.** Just gone by: *in the past month.* **4.** *Gram.* Of or denoting a verb tense or form used to express an action or condition prior to the time it is expressed. —*n.* **1. the past.** The time before the present. **2.** A person's history, background, or former activities: *a man with a distinguished past.* **3.** *Gram.* **a.** The past tense. **b.** A verb form in the past tense. —*adv.* So as to pass by or go beyond: *He walked past.* —*prep.* **1.** Alongside and then beyond: *The Mississippi flows past St. Louis.* **2.** Beyond in time; after: *It is past midnight.* **3.** Beyond in position: *the lake past the meadow.* **4.** Beyond the power, extent, or influence of: *The problem is past understanding.* **5.** Beyond the number or amount of: *The child couldn't count past 20.* [Middle English, from the past part. of *passen,* to pass.]

pas·ta (pä′stə) *n.* **1.** Dough made of flour and water, used dried, as in macaroni, or fresh, as in ravioli. **2.** A prepared dish of pasta. [Italian, from Late Latin, paste.]

paste (pāst) *n.* **1.** A smooth, sticky substance, as that made of flour and water or starch and water, used to fasten things together. **2.** A dough of flour and water, and shorten-

ing, used in making pastry. **3.** A food that has been made soft and creamy by pounding or grinding: *almond paste.* **4.** A sweet, doughy candy or confection. **5.** Moistened clay used in making porcelain or pottery. **6.** A hard, brilliant glass used in making artificial gems. —*tr.v.* **past·ed, past·ing.** **1.** To fasten or attach with paste. **2.** To cover with something to which paste has been applied: *He pasted the wall with burlap.* **3.** *Slang.* To punch; hit. —See Syns at **hit.** [Middle English, from Old French, from Late Latin *pasta,* from Greek *pastē,* barley porridge, from *passein,* to sprinkle.]

paste·board (pāst′bôrd′, -bōrd′) *n.* A thin, firm board made of sheets of paper pasted together or of pressed paper pulp. —*modifier: a pasteboard placard.*

pas·tel (pă-stĕl′) *n.* **1. a.** A dried paste made of ground and mixed pigment, chalk, water, and gum, used to make crayons. **b.** A crayon of this material. **2.** A picture or sketch drawn with this type of crayon. **3.** A soft, delicate color; a light tint. —*modifier: a pastel drawing.* [French, from Italian *pastello,* from Late Latin *pastellus,* woad dye, dim. of *pasta,* paste.]

pas·tern (păs′tərn) *n.* **1.** The part of a horse's foot between the fetlock and hoof. **2.** A comparable part of the leg of other quadrupeds. [Middle English *pastron,* a horse's hobble, from Old French *pasturon,* a hobble, from Late Latin *pāstōria,* a sheep's hobble, from *pāstor,* shepherd.]

pas·teur·i·za·tion (păs′chə-rĭ-zā′shən) *n.* A process in which milk, beer, and other liquids are heated to about 155°F for about 30 minutes and then chilled to 50°F in order to kill harmful germs or prevent further fermentation. [After Louis *Pasteur* (1822–95), French chemist, its inventor.]

pas·teur·ize (păs′chə-rīz′) *tr.v.* **-ized, -iz·ing.** To subject (a liquid) to pasteurization. —**pas′teur·iz′er** *n.*

pas·tiche (pă-stēsh′, pä-) *n.* **1.** A dramatic, literary, or musical piece openly imitating the previous work of another artist, often with satirical intent. **2.** A selection of excerpts from various sources; hodgepodge. [French, from Italian *pasticcio,* pie, hodgepodge, from Late Latin *pasta,* paste.]

pas·tille (pă-stēl′) *n.* Also **pas·til** (păs′tĭl). **1.** A small medicated or flavored tablet; lozenge; troche. **2.** A tablet containing aromatic substances, burned to fumigate or deodorize the air. [French, from Latin *pāstillus.*]

pas·time (păs′tīm′) *n.* An activity that occupies one's time pleasantly.

past master. 1. A person who has formerly held the position of master in an organization such as a lodge or club. **2.** An expert in a particular craft.

pas·tor (păs′tər) *n.* A Christian minister who is the leader of a congregation. [Middle English *pastour,* from Old French, from Latin *pāstor,* shepherd, from *pascere,* to graze, feed.]

pas·tor·al (păs′tər-əl) *adj.* **1.** Of or relating to shepherds, herdsmen, or their lifestyle. **2.** Of or relating to rural life, esp. the simplicity of idealized rural life: *a pastoral scene; pastoral poetry.* **3.** Of a pastor or his duties. —*n.* **1.** A literary or other artistic work that portrays rural life, usu. in an idealized manner. **2.** *Mus.* A pastorale. [Middle English, from Latin *pāstōrālis,* from *pāstor,* shepherd.]

pas·to·rale (păs′tə-räl′, -răl′, päs′-) *n.* **1.** A vocal composition based on a rural theme or subject. **2.** An instrumental composition with a tender melody suggestive of idealized rural life. [Italian, from *pastorale,* pastoral, from Latin *pāstōrālis.*]

pas·tor·ate (păs′tər-ĭt) *n.* **1.** The office or term of office of a pastor. **2.** Pastors as a group.

past participle. A participle that indicates completed action and that is used in English as an adjective, as in the phrase *guided missile,* and also to form the passive voice and the perfect tenses. Also called **perfect participle.**

past perfect. A verb tense, the pluperfect.

pas·tra·mi (pə-strä′mē) *n.* A highly seasoned smoked cut of beef, usu. from the breast or shoulder. [Yiddish, from Rumanian *pastramă,* from *păstra,* to preserve.]

pas·try (pā′strē) *n., pl.* **-tries. 1.** A baked paste of flour, water, and shortening, used for the crusts of pies, tarts, etc. **2.** Baked foods, such as pies, tarts, or turnovers, made with this paste.

past tense. A verb tense used to express an action or condition that occurred in or during the past.

pas·tur·age (păs′chər-ĭj) n. **1.** The grass or other plants eaten by grazing animals. **2.** Grazing land.

pas·ture (păs′chər) n. **1.** Grass or other plants eaten by grazing animals. **2.** A piece of land on which animals graze. —v. **-tured, -tur·ing.** —tr.v. To herd (animals) into a pasture to graze. —intr.v. To graze in a pasture. [Middle English, from Old French, from Late Latin *pāstūra*, from Latin *pascere*, to feed.]

past·y¹ (pā′stē) adj. **-i·er, -i·est. 1.** Resembling paste in color or texture. **2.** Pale and lifeless-looking.

pas·ty² (păs′tē) n., pl. **-ties.** Brit. A pie with a filling of seasoned meat or fish. [Middle English *pastee*, from Old French *paste*, dough, paste.]

PA system. A public-address system.

pat¹ (păt) v. **pat·ted, pat·ting.** —tr.v. **1. a.** To tap gently with the open hand or with something flat. **b.** To stroke lightly as a gesture of affection. **2.** To mold by tapping gently with the hands or a flat implement. —intr.v. To run or walk with a tapping sound. —n. **1.** A light stroke or tap. **2.** The sound made by such a stroke or tap, or by light footsteps. **3.** A small mass of something: *a pat of butter.* [Middle English *patte*.]

pat² (păt) adj. **1.** Timely; opportune; fitting. **2.** Needing no change; exactly right. **3.** Prepared and ready for use: *a pat answer.* **4.** Facile; glib. —adv. **1.** Without changing position; steadfastly: *standing pat.* **2.** Perfectly; precisely; aptly: *He had the instructions down pat.* [From PAT.] —**pat′ly** adv. —**pat′ness** n.

pa·ta·gi·um (pə-tā′jē-əm) n., pl. **-gi·a** (-jē-ə). An expandable, membranous fold of skin between the wing and body of a bird. [From Latin, gold edging on a woman's tunic.]

patch (păch) n. **1.** A small piece of material attached to another, larger piece to conceal or reinforce a weakened or worn area. **2. a.** Any small piece of cloth used for patchwork. **b.** A small cloth badge affixed to a sleeve to indicate the military unit to which one belongs. **3.** A dressing or bandage applied to protect a wound or sore. **4.** A small pad or shield of cloth worn over an injured eye. **5.** A **beauty spot. 6.** A small piece of land, usu. with plants growing on it: *a berry patch.* **7.** A small part of a surface that differs from or contrasts with the whole: *The flowers made white patches against the grass.* —tr.v. **1.** To put a patch or patches on. **2.** To make by sewing scraps of material together: *patch a quilt.* **3.** To mend, repair, or put together, esp. hastily: *patching old clothes; patched together a treaty.* —phrasal verb. **patch up.** To settle; make up: *patched up a quarrel.* [Middle English *pacche*.] —**patch′a·ble** adj. —**patch′er** n.

patch·ou·li (păch′ə-lē, pə-chōō′lē) n., pl. **-lis.** Also **patch·ou·ly** pl. **-lies. 1.** Any of several Asiatic trees of the genus *Pogostemon*, with leaves that yield a fragrant oil used in perfumes. **2.** A perfume made from this oil. [Tamil *pacci-lai* : *paccu*, green + *ilai*, leaf.]

patch test. A test for allergic sensitivity made by applying a suspected allergen to the skin.

patch·work (păch′wûrk′) n. **1.** Pieces of cloth of various colors, shapes, and sizes sewn together in a pattern to make a covering. **2.** A mixture of many diverse elements; a jumble. —modifier: *a patchwork quilt.*

patch·y (păch′ē) adj. **-i·er, -i·est. 1.** Made up of or marked by patches. **2.** Uneven in quality or performance: *patchy work.*

pate (pāt) n. The head, esp. the top of the head. [Middle English.]

pâ·té (pä-tā′, pă-) n. A meat paste. [French, from Old French *pasté*, from *paste*, paste.]

pâ·té de foie gras (pä-tā′ də fwä grä′, pă-tā′). A paste made from goose liver, usu. with truffles. [French, "pâté of fat liver."]

pa·tel·la (pə-tĕl′ə) n., pl. **-tel·lae** (-tĕl′ē). A flat, triangular bone located at the front of the knee joint; the kneecap. [Latin, dim. of *patina*, plate.] —**pa·tel′lar** or **pa·tel′late** (pə-tĕl′ĭt, -āt′) adj.

pat·en (păt′n) n. **1.** A plate used to hold the Eucharistic bread. **2.** Any plate. **3.** A thin disk of metal. [Middle English, from Old French *patene*, from Latin *patina*, dish, pan, from Greek *patanē*.]

pa·ten·cy (păt′n-sē, pāt′-) n. The quality of being obvious.

pat·ent (păt′nt) n. **1.** A grant made by a government to an inventor, assuring him the sole right to make, use, and sell his invention for a certain period of time. **2.** Something that is protected by such a grant. **3. a.** A grant of public land made by a government to an individual. **b.** The land so granted. **4.** Any exclusive right or title. —adj. **1.** (păt′nt). Open to general inspection; unsealed: *letters patent.* **2.** (păt′nt, pāt′-). Obvious; plain: *patent insincerity.* **3.** (păt′nt). Protected by a patent. —tr.v. (păt′nt). **1.** To obtain a patent on. **2.** To grant a patent to. [Middle English, from Old French, from Latin *patēns*, open, from *patēre*, to be open.] —**pat′ent·a·bil′i·ty** n. —**pat′ent·a·ble** adj.

pat·ent·ee (păt′n-tē′) n. Someone who has been granted a patent.

patent leather. Leather with a smooth, hard, shiny surface. [From its being made by a once-patented process.]

pat·ent·ly (păt′nt-lē, pāt′-) adv. Obviously; clearly; plainly.

patent medicine. A drug or other medical preparation that is protected by a patent and can be bought without a prescription.

patent office. A government bureau which studies claims for and grants patents.

pat·en·tor (păt′n-tər, păt′n-tôr′) n. A person or authority that grants a patent.

patent right. The right granted by a patent, esp. the exclusive right to manufacture and sell an invention.

pa·ter (pā′tər) n. Brit. Obs. Father.

pa·ter·fa·mil·i·as (pā′tər-fə-mĭl′ē-əs, pä′tər-) n., pl. **pa·tres·fa·mil·i·as** (pä′trēz-fə-mĭl′ē-əs, pä′träs-). The father of a family in his capacity as head of the household. [Latin.]

pa·ter·nal (pə-tûr′nəl) adj. **1.** Of or characteristic of a father; fatherly. **2.** Received or inherited from a father. **3.** Of the father's side of a family. [Medieval Latin *paternālis*, from Latin *paternus*, fatherly, from *pater*, father.] —**pa·ter′nal·ly** adv.

pa·ter·nal·ism (pə-tûr′nə-lĭz′əm) n. A policy or practice of treating or governing people in a fatherly manner, esp. by providing for their needs without giving them responsibility. —**pa·ter′nal·is′tic** adj. —**pa·ter′nal·is′ti·cal·ly** adv.

pa·ter·ni·ty (pə-tûr′nĭ-tē) n. **1.** The fact or condition of being a father; fatherhood. **2.** Descent on a father's side. [Old French *paternite*, from Late Latin *paternitās*, from Latin *paternus*, fatherly.]

pa·ter·nos·ter (pā′tər-nŏs′tər, pä′tər-nŏs′tər) n. **1.** Often **Paternoster.** The **Lord's Prayer. 2.** One of the large beads on a rosary, on which the Lord's Prayer is said. [Latin *pater noster*, "our father," first two words in the prayer.]

path (păth, päth) n., pl. **paths** (păthz, päthz, păths, päths). **1.** A track or way made by footsteps. **2.** A way made for walking or other activity, as bicycling. **3.** The route or course along which something moves. **4.** A manner of conduct: *the path of righteousness.* [Middle English, from Old English *pæth*.] —**path′less** adj.

pa·thet·ic (pə-thĕt′ĭk) adj. **1.** Expressing or arousing pity, sympathy, or tenderness; full of pathos: *a pathetic story.* **2.** Distressing and inadequate: *a pathetic attempt to appear worldly.* [French *pathétique*, from Late Latin *pathēticus*, from Greek *pathētikos*, from *pathos*, passion, suffering.] —**pa·thet′i·cal·ly** adv.

pathetic fallacy. The attribution of human emotions or characteristics to things, as in *angry clouds.*

path·find·er (păth′fīn′dər, päth′-) n. A person who discovers a way through or into unexplored regions.

patho-. A prefix meaning disease or suffering: **pathogenesis.** [From Greek *pathos*, emotion, suffering.]

path·o·gen (păth′ə-jən) n. Also **path·o·gene** (păth′ə-jēn′). Any agent that causes disease, esp. a microorganism such as a bacterium. [PATHO- + -GEN.]

path·o·gen·e·sis (păth′ə-jĕn′ĭ-sĭs) n. The development of a diseased or morbid condition.

path·o·gen·ic (păth′ə-jĕn′ĭk) adj. Also **path·o·ge·net·ic** (-jə-nĕt′ĭk). Capable of causing disease.

path·o·log·i·cal (păth′ə-lŏj′ĭ-kəl) or **path·o·log·ic** (-lŏj′ĭk) adj. **1.** Of or pertaining to pathology. **2.** Pertaining to or caused by disease. **3.** So extreme as to indicate a mental disorder: *a pathological liar.* —**path′o·log′i·cal·ly** adv.

pa·thol·o·gy (pə-thŏl′ə-jē, pă-) n., pl. **-gies. 1.** The scientific study of the nature of disease, its causes, processes, development, and consequences. **2.** The anatomic or functional

ă pat	ā pay	â care	ä father	ĕ pet	ē be	hw which	ĭ pit	ī tie	î pier	ŏ pot	ō toe	ô paw, for	oi noise
ōō took	ōō boot	ou out	th thin	th this	ŭ cut	û urge	zh vision	ə about, item, edible, gallop, circus					

manifestations of disease. **—pa·thol'o·gist** n.

pa·thos (pā'thŏs') n. A quality in something or someone that arouses feelings of pity, sympathy, tenderness, or sorrow in another. [Greek, passion, suffering.]

path·way (păth'wā', păth'-) n. A path.

-pathy. A suffix meaning: **1.** Feeling; perception: **telepathy. 2. a.** Disease; a diseased condition: **neuropathy. b.** A system of treating disease: **homeopathy.** [Latin -pathia, from Greek -patheia, from pathos, passion, suffering.]

pa·tience (pā'shəns) n. **1.** The quality of being patient; the capacity of calm endurance. **2.** A game of solitaire.

pa·tient (pā'shənt) adj. **1.** Enduring trouble, hardship, annoyance, delay, etc., without complaint or anger. **2.** Tolerant; understanding. **3.** Persevering; constant: a patient worker. **4.** Capable of bearing delay; not hasty. —n. A person under medical treatment. [Middle English pacient, from Old French patient, from Latin patiēns, from patī, to suffer.] **—pa'tient·ly** adv.

pat·i·na (păt'n-ə, pə-tē'nə) n. **1.** A thin layer of corrosion, usu. brown or green, that appears on copper or copper alloys as a result of oxidation. **2.** The sheen produced by age and use on any antique surface. [Italian, from Latin, shallow dish, plate.]

pat·i·o (păt'ē-ō') n., pl. **-os. 1.** An inner, roofless courtyard. **2.** A recreation area, usu. paved, next to a residence. [Spanish, from Old Spanish, untilled land, courtyard.]

pat·ois (păt'wä', pä'twä, pă-twä') n., pl. **-ois** (-wäz', -twäz', -twäz'). **1.** A regional dialect. **2.** Illiterate or substandard speech. **3.** Jargon; cant. [French, from Old French.]

pat·res·fa·mil·i·as (pä'trēz-fə-mĭl'ē-əs, pä'träs-) n. Plural of **paterfamilias.**

patri-. A prefix meaning father: **patricide.** [From Latin pater, father, and Greek patēr, father.]

pa·tri·arch (pā'trē-ärk') n. **1.** The male leader of a family or tribe. **2. a.** Any of the Old Testament fathers of the human race. **b.** Abraham, Isaac, Jacob, or any of the founders of the 12 tribes of Israel. **3.** A former title for the bishops of Rome, Constantinople, Jerusalem, Antioch, and Alexandria. **4.** Rom. Cath. Ch. A bishop who holds the highest episcopal rank after the pope. **5.** The bishop of various Eastern Orthodox and Greek orthodox churches. **6.** Someone regarded as the founder or head of an enterprise, organization, or tradition. **7.** A very old and venerable man; an elder. [Middle English patriarke, from Old French patriarche, from Late Latin patriarcha, from Greek patriarkhēs : patria, lineage, from patēr, father + archē, ruler.] **—pa'tri·ar'chal** (pā'trē-är'kəl) or **pa'tri·ar'chic** (-kĭk) adj.

pa·tri·ar·chate (pā'trē-är'kĭt, -kāt') n. **1.** The territory, rule, or rank of a patriarch. **2.** A patriarchy.

pa·tri·ar·chy (pā'trē-är'kē) n., pl. **-chies. 1.** A social organization in which the father is the head of the family and descent and succession are traced through the male line. **2.** Rule of a tribe or family by men.

pa·tri·cian (pə-trĭsh'ən) n. **1.** A member of one of the noble families of the ancient Roman Republic. **2.** An aristocrat. **3.** A person of refined manners and tastes. —adj. **1.** Of, belonging to, or characteristic of the aristocracy. **2.** Noble; refined. [Middle English patricion, from Old French patricien, from Latin patricius, (nobleman) of senatorial rank, from patres, senators, from pater, father.] **—pa·tri'cian·ly** adv.

pat·ri·cide (păt'rĭ-sīd') n. **1.** The act of murdering one's father. **2.** Someone who murders his father. **—pat'ri·cid'al** (păt'rĭ-sīd'l) adj.

pat·ri·mo·ny (păt'rə-mō'nē) n., pl. **-nies. 1.** An inheritance from a father or other ancestor. **2.** Legacy; heritage. **3.** An endowment or estate belonging to a church. [Middle English patrimoine, from Old French, from Latin patrimōnium, from pater, father.] **—pat'ri·mo'ni·al** (păt'rə-mō'nē-əl) adj. **—pat'ri·mo'ni·al·ly** adv.

pa·tri·ot (pā'trē-ət, -ŏt') n. A person who loves, supports, and defends his country. [Old French patriote, compatriot, from Late Latin patriōta, from Greek patriōtēs, from patris, fatherland, from patēr, father.]

pa·tri·ot·ic (pā'trē-ŏt'ĭk) adj. Feeling, expressing, or inspired by love of one's country. **—pa'tri·ot'i·cal·ly** adv.

pa·tri·ot·ism (pā'trē-ə-tĭz'əm) n. Love of and devotion to one's country.

pa·tris·tic (pə-trĭs'tĭk) or **pa·tris·ti·cal** (-tĭ-kəl) adj. Of or

relating to the early Christian church fathers or their writings. [PATR(I)- + -IST + -IC.] **—pa·tris'ti·cal·ly** adv.

pa·trol (pə-trōl') n. **1.** The action of moving about an area, keeping watch and checking for possible trouble. **2.** A person or group who carry out such an action. **3.** A unit of soldiers sent out on a reconnaissance or guarding mission. **4.** A group of eight Boy Scouts, a division of a troop. —v. **-trolled, -trol·ling.** —tr.v. To engage in a patrol of. —intr.v. To engage in a patrol. [French patrouiller, from Old French patouiller, to paddle around in mud.] **—pa·trol'er** n.

patrol car. A squad car.

pa·trol·man (pə-trōl'mən) n. A policeman or guard who patrols an assigned area.

pa·tron (pā'trən) n. **1.** Anyone who supports, protects, or champions; benefactor: a patron of the arts. **2.** A regular customer. [Middle English patroun, from Old French patron, from Medieval Latin patrōnus, from Latin, advocate, from pater, father.]

pa·tron·age (pā'trə-nĭj, păt'rə-) n. **1.** Support or encouragement from a patron. **2.** The trade given to a store or restaurant by its customers. **3.** Customers; clientele. **4.** The power of appointing people to governmental or political positions.

pa·tron·ize (pā'trə-nīz', păt'rə-) tr.v. **-ized, -iz·ing. 1.** To act as a patron to; support: patronize the arts. **2.** To go to regularly as a customer. **3.** To treat in an offensively condescending way; talk down to. **—pa'tron·iz'er** n. **—pa'tron·iz'ing·ly** adv.

pa·tro·nym·ic (păt'rə-nĭm'ĭk) n. A name received from one's father or another paternal ancestor, esp. one formed by an affix, as in Johnson, the son of John. [Late Latin patronymicum, from Greek patrōnymikos, "derived from the name of a father" : patro-, father, from patēr + onuma, name.] **—pat'ro·nym'ic** adj.

pa·troon (pə-trōōn') n. Under Dutch colonial rule, a landholder in New York and New Jersey who was granted certain feudal powers. [Dutch, from French patron, patron.]

pat·sy (păt'sē) n., pl. **-sies.** Slang. A person who is cheated, victimized, or made the butt of a joke. [Orig. unknown.]

pat·ten (păt'n) n. A wooden sandal, shoe, or clog. [Middle English patin, from Old French, from patte, a paw, hoof.]

pat·ter¹ (păt'ər) intr.v. **1.** To make a series of quick, light, soft taps: Rain pattered on the roof. **2.** To move with quick, light steps. —n. A series of quick, light, tapping sounds. [Freq. of PAT (tap lightly).]

pat·ter² (păt'ər) intr.v. To chatter glibly and rapidly. —tr.v. To utter in a glib, rapid, or mechanical manner. —n. **1.** The jargon of a particular group; cant. **2.** Glib, rapid speech, as of an auctioneer or comedian. **3.** Meaningless talk; chatter. [Middle English, from Latin pater(noster), pater(noster), from the mechanical recitation of the prayer.] **—pat'ter·er** n.

pat·tern (păt'ərn) n. **1.** An artistic or decorative design. **2.** A diagram used in cutting out garments to be made, consisting of separate pieces, usu. of paper, cut to a certain size and style. **3.** A combination of elements, qualities, actions, or events that form a gen. regular or consistent arrangement: sentence patterns; weather patterns. **4.** An ideal worthy of imitation; a model. **5.** A representative sample; specimen. —tr.v. **1.** To make, mold, or design by following a pattern. **2.** To cover or ornament with a design or pattern. [Alteration of Middle English patron, from Old French, from Medieval Latin patrōnus, patron, model.]

pat·ty (păt'ē) n., pl. **-ties. 1.** A small, oval, flattened cake of chopped food. **2.** A similarly shaped small candy. [French pâté, small pie, from Old French paste, from paste, paste.]

pau·ci·ty (pô'sĭ-tē) n. **1.** Smallness of number; fewness: a paucity of trained workers. **2.** Smallness of quantity; scarcity: the paucity of rainfall. [Middle English paucite, from Old French, from Latin paucitās, from paucus, little, few.]

paunch (pônch, pänch) n. The belly, esp. a potbelly. [Middle English paunche, from Norman French, from Old French pance, from Latin pantex.] **—paunch'i·ness** n. **—paunch'y** adj.

pau·per (pô'pər) n. **1.** Someone who is extremely poor. **2.** Someone living on public charity. [Latin, poor.] **—pau'per·ism** n.

pau·per·ize (pô'pə-rīz') tr.v. **-ized, -iz·ing.** To make a pauper of; impoverish. —**pau·per·i·za'tion** n.

pause (pôz) intr.v. **paused, paus·ing. 1.** To cease or suspend an action for a time. **2.** To linger; tarry: pausing at the café. **3.** To hesitate: paused before replying. —See Syns at **hesitate.** —n. **1.** A brief stop or break in action or speech. **2.** A delay or suspended reaction, as from uncertainty; hesitation. **3.** Mus. A sign indicating that a note or rest is to be held. **4.** A reason for hesitation: The size of the task gives one pause. [Middle English, a pause, from Old French, from Latin pausa, from Greek pausis, a stopping, from pauein, to stop.]

pa·van (pə-văn', -văn') n. Also **pa·vane. 1.** A slow, stately court dance of the 16th cent. **2.** Music for this dance. [Old French pavane, from Old Spanish pavana, from Old Italian (danza) pavanna, "(dance) of Padua."]

pave (pāv) tr.v. **paved, pav·ing. 1.** To cover with a hard, smooth surface for travel. **2.** To cover uniformly, as if with pavement. —idiom. **pave the way.** To make progress or development easier: experiments that paved the way for future research. [Middle English paven, from Old French paver, from Latin pavīre, to strike, stamp.] —**pav'er** n.

pave·ment (pāv'mənt) n. **1.** A hard, paved surface. **2.** The material of which such a surface is made.

pa·vil·ion (pə-vĭl'yən) n. **1.** An ornate tent. **2. a.** A temporary, ornamental, and often open structure, used at parks or fairs for amusement or shelter. **b.** A summerhouse. **3.** A building or other structure connected to a larger building; an annex. **4.** One of a group of related buildings forming a complex, as of a hospital. [Middle English pavilon, from Old French paveillon, from Latin pāpiliō, butterfly, tent (from its resemblance to a butterfly's wings).]

pav·ing (pā'vĭng) n. **1.** The laying of pavement. **2.** A pavement. **3.** Material used for pavement.

paw (pô) n. **1.** The nailed or clawed foot of an animal. **2.** Informal. A human hand, esp. a large, clumsy one. —tr.v. **1.** To strike or scrape with a paw or forefoot. **2.** To handle clumsily, rudely, or with too much familiarity. —intr.v. **1.** To scrape the ground with the forefeet. **2.** To make clumsy, grasping motions with the hands. [Middle English pawe, from Old French poue.] —**paw'er** n.

pawl (pôl) n. A hinged or pivoted device adapted to fit into a notch of a ratchet wheel, either to drive it forward or to prevent backward motion. [Dutch pal, poss. from Latin pālus, stake.]

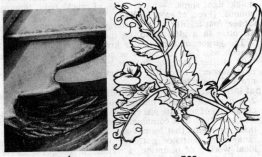

pawl   pea

pawn¹ (pôn) n. **1.** Something given as security for a loan; a pledge. **2.** The condition of being held as a pledge against the payment of a loan: jewels at pawn. —tr.v. **1.** To give or deposit as security for the payment of money borrowed. **2.** To risk; stake: pawn one's honor. [Middle English paun, from Old French pan.] —**pawn'a·ble** adj. —**pawn'er** or **pawn'or** n.

pawn² (pôn) n. **1.** A chessman of the lowest value, able to move forward one square at a time (or two squares on its first move) and capture on either of the two squares diagonally forward. **2.** A person or thing used to further the purposes of another. [Middle English pawne, from Old French peon, from Medieval Latin pedō, a foot soldier, from Latin pēs, foot.]

pawn·bro·ker (pôn'brō'kər) n. A person who lends money at interest in exchange for personal property left as security. —**pawn'bro'king** n.

Paw·nee (pô-nē') n., pl. **-nee** or **-nees. 1.** A confederation of four North American Plains Indian tribes of Caddoan linguistic stock in the region of Kansas and Nebraska, now living on a reservation in Oklahoma. **2.** A member of this confederation. **3.** The language of this confederation.

pawn·shop (pôn'shŏp') n. The shop of a pawnbroker.

paw·paw (pô'pô') n. Var. of **papaw.**

pay (pā) v. **paid** (pād), **pay·ing.** —tr.v. **1.** To give money to in return for goods or services rendered: pay the cashier. **2.** To give (money) in exchange for goods or services: pay five dollars for a book. **3.** To give the indicated amount of: pay taxes. **4.** To gain revenge upon; requite; punish: paid him harshly for his insolence. **5.** To yield as return: This job pays $200 a week. **6.** To bear the cost of: He paid my way through school. **7.** To afford an advantage to; profit: It paid him to be generous. **8.** To give or bestow: pay compliments. **9.** To make (a visit or call). —intr.v. **1.** To make payment. **2.** To discharge a debt or obligation. **3.** To be profitable or worthwhile: It pays to save old receipts. —phrasal verbs. **pay back.** To retaliate upon; get even with. **pay for.** To suffer the consequences of. **pay off. 1.** To pay the full amount of (a debt). **2.** Informal. To bribe. **pay out.** Past tense **payed out.** Naut. To let out (a line or cable) by slackening. **pay up.** To pay the full amount demanded. —adj. Yielding valuable metal in mining: pay streak. —n. **1.** The act of paying or the fact of being paid; payment. **2.** Salary; wages: working for pay. **3.** Recompense or reward: His thanks were pay enough. **4.** Paid employment: the men in our pay. —modifier: a pay raise; a pay telephone. [Middle English payen, from Old French paier, from Medieval Latin pācāre, from Latin, to pacify, from pāx, peace.]

pay·a·ble (pā'ə-bəl) adj. **1.** Requiring payment on a certain date; due. **2.** Specifying payment to a particular person.

pay·check (pā'chĕk') n. **1.** A check issued to an employee in payment of salary or wages. **2.** Salary.

pay dirt. 1. Earth, ore, or gravel with a rich enough metal content to make mining profitable. **2.** Slang. A useful or profitable discovery.

pay·ee (pā-ē') n. A person to whom money is paid.

pay·load (pā'lōd') n. **1.** The revenue-producing part of a cargo, as distinguished from the weight of the vehicle. **2. a.** The total weight of passengers and cargo that an aircraft carries or can carry. **b.** The total weight of the warhead or instruments, crew, and life-support systems that a rocket can carry.

pay·mas·ter (pā'măs'tər) n. A person in charge of paying wages and salaries.

pay·ment (pā'mənt) n. **1.** The act of paying or the condition of being paid. **2.** An amount that is paid: received a large payment. **3.** Reward; recompense.

pay·off (pā'ôf', -ŏf') n. **1.** Full payment of a salary or wages. **2.** Informal. Final settlement or reckoning; climax: the payoff of a mystery movie. **3.** Final retribution or revenge. **4.** Informal. A bribe.

pay·o·la (pā-ō'lə) n. Slang. Bribery, esp. the bribing of disc jockeys to promote records. [PAY + (VICTR)OLA (a trademark for a phonograph).]

pay·roll (pā'rōl') n. **1.** A list of employees receiving wages, with the amounts due to each. **2.** The total sum of money to be paid out to employees at a given time.

Pb The symbol for the element lead. [Latin plumbum.]

Pd The symbol for the element palladium.

pea (pē) n. **1.** A climbing annual vine, Pisum sativum, grown in all temperate zones, that has compound leaves, small white flowers, and edible seeds in a green, elongated pod. **2.** One of the rounded green seeds of the pea, used as a vegetable. **3.** peas. The unopened pods of the pea plant. **4.** Any of several plants of the genus Lathyrus, such as the **sweet pea.** [Back-formation from Middle English pese (taken as pl.), from Old English pise, from Late Latin pīsa, ult. from Greek pison, a pea.]

peace (pēs) n. **1.** The absence of war or other hostilities. **2.** An agreement or treaty to end hostilities. **3.** Freedom from quarrels and disagreement; harmonious relations. **4.** Public security; law and order: disturbing the peace. **5.** Calm; serenity: peace of mind. [Middle English pais, from Old French, from Latin pāx.]

peace·a·ble (pē'sə-bəl) adj. **1.** Inclined or disposed to peace; promoting calm. **2.** Peaceful; without war.

—**peace′a·ble·ness** n. —**peace′a·bly** adv.
peace·ful (pēs′fəl) adj. **1.** Not disposed to, marked by, or involving war: a peaceful nation; peaceful uses of atomic energy. **2.** Calm; serene; tranquil. —See Syns at **calm.** —**peace′ful·ly** adv. —**peace′ful·ness** n.
peace·mak·er (pēs′mā′kər) n. Someone who makes peace, esp. by settling the disputes of others. —**peace′mak′ing** n. & adj.
peace officer. A law officer, such as a policeman or sheriff, responsible for maintaining civil peace.
peace pipe. A long ornamented pipe used in American Indian ceremonies; calumet.
peace·time (pēs′tīm′) n. A time of absence of war.
peach¹ (pēch) n. **1.** A small tree, Prunus persica, native to China but widely cultivated throughout the temperate zones, with pink flowers and edible fruit. **2.** The soft, juicy, single-seeded fruit of this tree, with yellow flesh and downy, red-tinted, yellow skin. **3.** A light yellowish pink. **4.** Slang. Any esp. admirable or pleasing person or thing. —**modifier:** peach blossoms. —adj. Light yellowish pink. [Middle English peche, from Old French, from Late Latin persica, from Latin, pl. of persicum (mālum), "Persian (apple)."]
peach² (pēch) intr.v. Slang. To turn informer. [Middle English pechen, var. of impechen, to impeach.]
peach·y (pē′chē) adj. **-i·er, -i·est. 1.** Resembling a peach. **2.** Slang. Splendid; fine. —**peach′i·ness** n.
pea·cock (pē′kŏk′) n. **1.** The male peafowl, distinguished by its crested head, brilliant blue or green feathers, and long tail feathers that are marked with eyelike, iridescent spots, and that can be spread in a fanlike form. **2.** A vain person given to self-display; a dandy. [Middle English pecok : Old English pēa, peafowl, from Latin pāvō, peacock + cok, cock.]

peacock

peacock blue. A greenish blue. —**pea′cock-blue′** adj.
pea·fowl (pē′foul′) n., pl. **-fowl** or **-fowls.** Either of two large pheasants, Pavo cristatus, of India and Ceylon, or P. muticus, of southeastern Asia. [PEA(COCK) + FOWL.]
pea·hen (pē′hĕn′) n. The female peafowl.
pea jacket. A short, warm, usu. double-breasted coat of heavy wool, worn by sailors. [Prob. from Dutch pijjekker : pij, a kind of coarse cloth + jekker, a jacket.]
peak (pēk) n. **1. a.** The pointed or narrow top of a mountain. **b.** The mountain itself. **2.** Any tapering point that projects upward. **3.** The visor of a cap. **4.** The point of greatest development, value, height, or intensity. —intr.v. **1.** To be formed into a peak or peaks: Beat the egg whites until they peak. **2.** To achieve a maximum of development, performance, value, or intensity. —tr.v. To bring to a peak. —adj. Approaching or constituting the maximum: peak efficiency. [Prob. alteration of PIKE (summit).]
peaked¹ (pēkt, pē′kĭd) adj. Ending in a peak; pointed.
peak·ed² (pē′kĭd) adj. Having a sickly appearance.
peal (pēl) n. **1.** A ringing of a set of bells. **2.** A set of bells tuned to each other; carillon. **3.** A loud burst of noise or series of noises: peals of laughter. —intr.v. To sound in a peal; ring. —tr.v. To cause to ring or sound loudly. [Middle English pele, summons to church by bell, short for appel, an appeal, from appelen, to appeal.]
pe·an (pē′ən) n. Var. of **paean.**
pea·nut (pē′nŭt′, -nət) n. **1.** A vine, Arachis hypogaea, native to tropical America and widely cultivated in semitrop-

ical regions, with yellow flowers on stalks that bend over so that the seed pods ripen underground. **2.** The edible, nutlike, oily seed of this vine. Also called **goober. 3.** Slang. A small or insignificant person. **4. peanuts.** Slang. A very small amount of money; trifling sum. [PEA + NUT.]
peanut brittle. A hard candy containing peanuts.
peanut butter. A food made by grinding roasted peanuts.
peanut oil. The oil pressed from peanuts, used for cooking, in salad oil and margarine, and in soaps.
pear (pâr) n. **1.** A widely cultivated tree, Pyrus communis, with glossy leaves, white flowers, and edible fruit. **2.** The fruit of this tree, spherical at the base and tapering toward the top. [Middle English pere, from Old English pere, from Latin pirum.]
pearl¹ (pûrl) n. **1.** A smooth, lustrous, variously colored deposit, chiefly calcium carbonate, formed around a grain of sand or other foreign matter in the shells of certain mollusks and valued as a gem. **2.** Mother-of-pearl. **3.** A person or object likened to a pearl in beauty or value. **4.** A yellowish white. —**modifier:** pearl earrings. —adj. Yellowish white. —tr.v. **1.** To decorate or cover with or as if with pearls. **2.** To make into the shape or color of pearls. —intr.v. **1.** To dive or fish for pearls or pearl-bearing mollusks. **2.** To form beads resembling pearls. [Middle English perle, from Old French, from Latin perna, sea-mussel.]
pearl² (pûrl) v. & n. Var. of **purl** (stitch).
pearl·y (pûr′lē) adj. **-i·er, -i·est. 1.** Resembling pearls. **2.** Covered or decorated with pearls.
peas·ant (pĕz′ənt) n. **1.** A member of the class of small farmers and tenants, sharecroppers, and laborers on the land where these constitute the main labor force in agriculture. **2.** A countryman; a rustic. **3.** An uncouth, crude, or ill-bred person; a boor. [Middle English paissaunt, from Old French païsant, from païs, country, from Medieval Latin pāgēnsis, a rustic, from Latin pāgus, a district, the country.]
peas·ant·ry (pĕz′ən-trē) n. **1.** The social class made up of peasants. **2.** The condition of a peasant.
pease (pēz) n., pl. **pease** or **peas·en** (pē′zən). Archaic. A pea.
pea·shoot·er (pē′shōō′tər) n. A toy consisting of a tube through which dried peas or other pellets are blown.
peat (pēt) n. Partially carbonized vegetable matter, usu. mosses, found in bogs, and used as fertilizer and fuel. [Middle English pete, from Medieval Latin peta.] —**peat′y** adj.
peat moss. 1. Any moss of the genus Sphagnum, growing in very wet places. **2.** The partly carbonized remains of such mosses, used as a mulch and plant food.
peb·ble (pĕb′əl) n. **1.** A small stone worn smooth by erosion. **2.** A crinkled surface, as on leather or paper. —tr.v. **-bled, -bling. 1.** To pave or pelt with pebbles. **2.** To impart an irregularly rough, grainy surface to (leather or paper). [Middle English pibbil, from Old English papol(stān).] —**peb′bly** adj.
pe·can (pĭ-kän′, -kăn′, pē′kän′) n. **1.** A tree, Carya illinoensis, of the southern United States, with deeply furrowed bark and edible nuts. **2.** The smooth, thin-shelled, oval nut of the pecan. [Earlier paccan, of Algonquian orig.]
pec·ca·dil·lo (pĕk′ə-dĭl′ō) n., pl. **-loes** or **-los.** A small sin or fault. [Spanish pecadillo, dim. of pecado, sin, from Latin peccātum, from peccāre, to sin.]
pec·cant (pĕk′ənt) adj. **1.** Sinful; guilty. **2.** Violating a rule or accepted practice; erring; faulty. [Latin peccāns, pres. part. of peccāre, to sin, stumble.] —**pec′can·cy** n. —**pec′cant·ly** adv.
peck¹ (pĕk) tr.v. **1.** To strike with a beak or some sharp-pointed instrument. **2.** To make (as a hole) by striking repeatedly with the beak or a pointed instrument. **3.** To pick up with the beak: The bird pecked insects from the log. **4.** Informal. To kiss briefly and casually. —intr.v. **1.** To make strokes with the beak or something pointed like a beak: heard birds pecking outside. **2.** To eat in small, sparing bits; to nibble. —n. **1.** A stroke or light blow with the beak. **2.** A mark or hole made by such a stroke. **3.** Informal. A light, quick kiss. [Middle English pecken, prob. var. of piken, to prick.]
peck² (pĕk) n. **1. a.** A unit of volume or capacity in the U.S. system, used in dry measure, equal to 8 quarts or 537.605

ă pat ā pay â care ä father ĕ pet ē be hw which ĭ pit ī tie î pier ŏ pot ō toe ô paw, for oi noise
ōō took ōō boot ou out th thin th this ŭ cut û urge zh vision ə about, item, edible, gallop, circus

cubic inches. **b.** A unit of volume or capacity in the British Imperial System, used in dry and liquid measure, equal to 554.84 cubic inches. **2.** A container holding or measuring this amount. **3.** *Informal.* A great deal: *a peck of troubles.* [Middle English, from Norman French *pek.*]

pecking order. 1. A social ranking within flocks of poultry, according to which each member submits to pecking and domination by the stronger or more aggressive members, and has the privilege of pecking and dominating the weaker members. **2.** Any supposedly similar hierarchy in a human group.

pec·ten (pĕk′tən) *n., pl.* **-ti·nes** (-tə-nēz′). *Zool.* **1.** A comb-like body structure or organ, as the ridged part of the eyelid of reptiles and birds. **2.** A scallop of the genus *Pecten.* [From Latin, comb.]

pec·tin (pĕk′tĭn) *n.* Any of a group of complex colloidal substances of high molecular weight found in ripe fruits, such as apples, and used to jell various foods, drugs, and cosmetics. [French *pectine*, from *pectique*, from Greek *pēktikos*, coagulating, from *pēgnunai*, to coagulate.] **—pec′tic** or **pec′tin·ous** *adj.*

pec·ti·nate (pĕk′tə-nāt′) *adj.* Also **pec·ti·nat·ed** (-nā′tĭd). Having teeth or projections like a comb. [Latin *pecten*, comb + -ATE.] **—pec′ti·na′tion** *n.*

pec·to·ral (pĕk′tər-əl) *adj.* **1.** *Anat.* Of or located in the breast or chest: *a pectoral muscle.* **2.** Worn on the chest or breast: *a pectoral cross.* *—n.* **1.** A chest muscle or organ. **2.** A pectoral fin. [Middle English, something worn on the chest, from Old French, of or worn on the chest, from Latin *pectorālis*, from *pectus*, breast.]

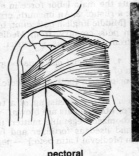

pectoral   pedestal

pectoral fin. Either of the anterior pair of fins attached to the pectoral girdle of fishes.

pectoral girdle. A skeletal structure in vertebrates, attached to and supporting the forelimbs or fins.

pec·u·late (pĕk′yə-lāt′) *v.* **-lat·ed, -lat·ing.** *—tr.v.* To take wrongfully for one's own use; embezzle. *—intr.v.* To steal money or goods entrusted to one. [From Latin *pecūlārī*, to embezzle, from *pecūlium*, "wealth in cattle," private property.] **—pec′u·la′tion** *n.* **—pec′u·la′tor** *n.*

pe·cu·liar (pĭ-kyōōl′yər) *adj.* **1.** Unusual or eccentric; strange; odd: *peculiar behavior.* **2.** Standing apart from others; distinct and particular: *a problem of peculiar complexity.* **3.** Belonging exclusively to one person, group, place, etc. *—See Syns at* **characteristic** and **strange.** [Middle English *peculier*, from Latin *pecūliāris*, one's own, from *pecūlium*, private property, from *pecus*, cattle.] **—pe·cu′liar·ly** *adv.*

pe·cu·li·ar·i·ty (pĭ-kyōō′lē-ăr′ĭ-tē) *n., pl.* **-ties. 1.** The quality or condition of being peculiar. **2.** A notable or distinctive feature or characteristic. **3.** An eccentricity; quirk. *—See Syns at* **eccentricity.**

pe·cu·ni·ar·y (pĭ-kyōō′nē-ĕr′ē) *adj.* **1.** Consisting of or relating to money: *a pecuniary loss; pecuniary motives.* **2.** Requiring the payment of money: *a pecuniary offense.* [Latin *pecūniārius*, from *pecūnia*, wealth, from *pecus*, cattle.]

ped-. Var. of **pedo-.**

-ped or **-pede.** A suffix meaning foot or feet: **biped.** [Latin *pēs*, foot.]

ped·a·gog·ic (pĕd′ə-gŏj′ĭk, -gō′jĭk) or **ped·a·gog·i·cal** (-gŏj′ĭ-kəl, -gō′jĭ-kəl) *adj.* **1.** Of or relating to teaching. **2.** Characterized by pedantic formality: *a pedagogic man-*

ner. **—ped′a·gog′i·cal·ly** *adv.*

ped·a·gog·ics (pĕd′ə-gŏj′ĭks, -gō′jĭks) *n. (used with a sing. verb).* The art of teaching; pedagogy.

ped·a·gogue (pĕd′ə-gŏg′) *n.* **1.** A schoolteacher; educator. **2.** Someone who instructs in a pedantic or dogmatic manner. [Middle English *pedagoge*, from Old French *pedagogue*, from Latin *paedagōgus*, from Greek *paidagōgos*, teacher : *pais*, child, boy + *agein*, to lead.]

ped·a·go·gy (pĕd′ə-gō′jē, -gŏj′ē) *n.* The art or profession of teaching.

ped·al (pĕd′l) *n.* **1.** A lever operated by the foot on various musical instruments. **2.** A lever worked by the foot in a machine, such as a bicycle or sewing machine. *—adj.* Of or relating to a foot or pedal: *the pedal extremities.* *—v.* **-aled** or **-alled, -al·ing** or **-al·ling.** *—intr.v.* **1.** To use or operate a pedal or pedals. **2.** To ride a bicycle. *—tr.v.* To operate the pedals of. [French *pédale*, from Italian *pedale*, (organ) pedal, from Latin *pedālis*, of the foot, from *pēs*, foot.]

ped·ant (pĕd′nt) *n.* **1.** A person who pays too much attention to book learning and formal rules without having an understanding or experience of practical affairs. **2.** A person who shows off his learning or scholarship. [Old French, from Italian *pedante*.] **—pe·dan′tic** (pə-dăn′tĭk) or **pe·dan′ti·cal** *adj.* **—pe·dan′ti·cal·ly** *adv.*

ped·ant·ry (pĕd′n-trē) *n., pl.* **-ries. 1.** Pedantic attention to detail or rules. **2.** An example of pedantic behavior.

ped·ate (pĕd′āt′) *adj.* **1.** *Zool.* Having feet. **2.** Resembling or functioning as a foot. **3.** *Bot.* Having radiating lobes or divisions, with the lateral lobes cleft or divided: *a pedate leaf.* [Latin *pedātus*, from *pēs*, foot.]

ped·dle (pĕd′l) *v.* **-dled, -dling.** *—tr.v.* **1.** To travel about selling: *peddling goods from door to door.* **2.** To give out; dispense: *peddling lies.* *—intr.v.* To travel about selling goods. [Back-formation from PEDDLER.] **—ped′dler** or **ped′lar** *n.*

-pede. Var. of **-ped.**

ped·es·tal (pĕd′ĭ-stəl) *n.* **1.** A support or base, as for a column or statue. **2.** A position of high regard or adoration. [Old French *piedestal*, from Old Italian *piedestallo*, from *pie di stallo*, "foot of a stall."]

pe·des·tri·an (pĭ-dĕs′trē-ən) *n.* A person traveling on foot. *—adj.* **1.** Of or for pedestrians. **2.** Going or performed on foot. **3.** Commonplace; undistinguished; ordinary. [From Latin *pedester*, going on foot, from *pēs*, a foot.]

pe·di·a·tri·cian (pē′dē-ə-trĭsh′ən) *n.* Also **pe·di·a·trist** (pē′dē-ăt′rĭst). A physician who specializes in pediatrics.

pe·di·at·rics (pē′dē-ăt′rĭks) *n. (used with a sing. verb).* The branch of medicine that deals with the care of infants and children and the treatment of their diseases. [PED(O)- + -IATRICS.] **—pe′di·at′ric** *adj.*

pe·di·a·trist (pē′dē-ăt′rĭst) *n.* Var. of **pediatrician.**

ped·i·cel (pĕd′ĭ-səl, -sĕl′) *n.* Also **ped·i·cle** (pĕd′ĭ-kəl). A small stalk, esp. one that bears a single flower in an inflorescence. [New Latin *pedicellus*, dim. of Latin *pediculus*, little foot, from *pēs*, a foot.]

pe·dic·u·lo·sis (pĭ-dĭk′yə-lō′sĭs) *n.* Infestation with lice. [Latin *pediculus*, louse + -*osis*, condition.]

ped·i·cure (pĕd′ĭ-kyōōr′) *n.* **1. a.** Podiatry. **b.** A podiatrist. **2. a.** Cosmetic care of the feet and toenails. **b.** A single cosmetic treatment of the feet and toenails. *—tr.v.* **-cured, -cur·ing.** To give a pedicure to. [French *pédicure* : *ped-*, foot + Latin *cūrāre*, to take care of, from *cūra*, care.] **—ped′i·cur′ist** *n.*

ped·i·gree (pĕd′ĭ-grē′) *n.* **1.** A line of ancestors; ancestry. **2.** A list of ancestors; family tree. **3.** A list of the ancestors of a purebred animal. [Middle English *pedegru*, from Old French *pie de grue*, "crane's foot," from the shape of a family tree.] **—ped′i·greed′** *adj.*

ped·i·ment (pĕd′ə-mənt) *n.* A wide, low-pitched triangular space over the façade of a building in the Greek architectural style. [Var. of earlier *perement*.]

pedo- or **ped-.** A prefix meaning child: **pediatrics.** [Greek *paido-*, from *pais*, child.]

pe·dol·o·gy (pĭ-dŏl′ə-jē, pĕ-dŏl′-) *n.* The scientific study of soils, their origins, characteristics, and uses. [From Greek *pedon*, soil, earth + -LOGY.] **—ped′o·log′ic** or **ped′o·log′i·cal** *adj.* **—ped′o·log′i·cal·ly** *adv.* **—pe·dol′o·gist** *n.*

pe·dom·e·ter (pĭ-dŏm′ĭ-tər) *n.* An instrument that measures and indicates the approximate distance a person travels on foot by keeping track of the number of steps taken. [French *pédomètre* : *pedo-*, foot + *mètre*, meter.]

pe·dun·cle (pē'dŭng'kəl, pĭ-dŭng'-) *n.* **1.** *Bot.* The main stalk of an inflorescence, or a stalk or stem bearing a solitary flower. **2.** *Zool.* A stalklike structure in invertebrate animals. **3.** *Anat.* A stalklike bundle of fibers, esp. of nerve fibers, connecting different parts of the central nervous system. [New Latin *pedunculus*, dim. of Latin *pēs*, foot.]

pe·dun·cu·late (pĭ-dŭng'kyə-lĭt, -lāt') *adj.* Also **pe·dun·cu·lat·ed** (-lā'tĭd). Having or supported on a peduncle.

peek (pēk) *intr.v.* **1.** To glance quickly. **2.** To look or peer secretly, as from a place of concealment. **3.** To become visible briefly or gradually; to peep. —*n.* A secret or brief look. [Middle English *piken*.]

peel¹ (pēl) *n.* The skin or rind of certain fruits. —*tr.v.* **1.** To strip or cut away the skin, rind, or bark from; pare. **2.** To remove by or as if by stripping away: *peeled his coat off.* —*intr.v.* **1.** To lose or shed skin, bark, or other covering. **2.** To come off in thin strips or pieces: *Her sunburned skin began to peel.* —*phrasal verb.* **peel off.** To leave flight formation in order to land or make a dive. [Middle English *pelen*, to peel, from Old French *peler*, from Latin *pilāre*, to remove, plunder.]

peel² (pēl) *n.* A long-handled, shovellike tool used by bakers to move bread or pastries into and out of an oven. [Middle English *pele*, from Old French, shovel, from Latin *pāla*, spade.]

peel·er (pē'lər) *n.* A person or device that peels, esp. a kitchen implement for peeling the rind or skin from a fruit or vegetable.

peen (pēn) *n.* The end of a hammerhead opposite the flat striking surface, often wedge-shaped or ball-shaped and used for chipping, indenting, and metalworking. —*tr.v.* To hammer, bend, or shape with a peen. [Prob. of Scandinavian orig.]

peep¹ (pēp) *intr.v.* **1.** To utter short, soft, high-pitched sounds, like those of a baby bird. **2.** To speak in a hesitant, thin, high-pitched voice. —*n.* **1.** A weak, shrill sound or utterance. **2.** Any slight sound or utterance: *I don't want to hear a peep out of you.* [Middle English *pepen* (imit.).]

peep² (pēp) *intr.v.* **1.** To steal a quick glance. **2.** To peer through a small aperture or from behind something. **3.** To become visible gradually, as though emerging from a hiding place. —*tr.v.* To cause to emerge or become partly visible: *peeped his head over the fence.* —*n.* **1.** A quick or secret look; a glance. **2.** A first glimpse or first appearance: *the peep of dawn.* [Middle English *pepen*, alteration of *piken*, to peek.]

peep·er¹ (pē'pər) *n.* A creature that peeps, esp. a frog.

peep·er² (pē'pər) *n.* **1.** Someone who peeps secretly or from a hiding place. **2.** *Slang.* An eye.

peep·hole (pēp'hōl') *n.* A small hole or crevice through which one may peep.

peeping Tom (tŏm). A person who gets pleasure, esp. sexual pleasure, from secretly watching the actions of others; voyeur. [From the legendary *Peeping Tom* of Coventry, who looked at the naked Lady Godiva and was struck blind.]

peep·show (pēp'shō') *n.* Also **peep show.** An exhibition of pictures or objects viewed through a small hole or magnifying glass.

peer¹ (pîr) *intr.v.* **1.** To look intently, searchingly, or with difficulty. **2.** To be partially visible; show: *The moon peered from behind a cloud.* —See Syns at **gaze.** [Orig. unknown.]

peer² (pîr) *n.* **1.** A person who has equal standing with another, as in rank, class, or age. **2. a.** A nobleman. **b.** A member of the British peerage; a duke, marquis, earl, viscount, or baron. [Middle English, from Old French *per*, equal, one's equal, nobleman, from Latin *pār*, equal.]

peer·age (pîr'ĭj) *n.* **1.** The rank or title of a peer. **2.** Peers as a group. **3.** A book listing peers and their families.

peer·ess (pîr'ĭs) *n.* **1.** The wife or widow of a peer. **2.** A woman who holds a peerage by descent or appointment.

peer·less (pîr'lĭs) *adj.* Without peer; unmatched. —See Syns at **unique.** —**peer'less·ly** *adv.* —**peer'less·ness** *n.*

peeve (pēv) *tr.v.* **peeved, peev·ing.** To annoy or make resentful; vex. —See Syns at **annoy.** —*n.* **1.** A vexation;

grievance. **2.** A resentful mood: *be in a peeve.* [Back-formation from PEEVISH.]

pee·vish (pē'vĭsh) *adj.* **1.** Discontented; fretful. **2.** Ill-tempered. —See Syns at **irritable.** [Middle English *pevish.*] —**pee'vish·ly** *adv.* —**pee'vish·ness** *n.*

pee·wee (pē'wē) *n.* *Informal.* Any relatively or unusually small person or thing. [Var. of *pewee*, a small bird.] —**pee'wee** *adj.*

peg (pĕg) *n.* **1.** A small cylindrical or tapered pin, as of wood, used to fasten things or to plug a hole. **2.** A similar pin forming a projection that may be used as a support or as a boundary marker. **3.** One of the pins of a stringed musical instrument that is turned to tighten or loosen the strings so as to regulate their pitch. **4.** An implement fitted with a pointed prong or claw for tearing or catching. **5.** A degree or notch, esp. in estimation. **6.** *Brit.* A shot of liquor. **7.** *Informal.* A throw, as of a baseball. —*v.* **pegged, peg·ging.** —*tr.v.* **1.** To fasten or plug with a peg. **2.** To designate or mark by means of pegs. **3.** To fix (a price) at a certain level or within a certain range. **4.** *Informal.* To classify; categorize. **5.** *Informal.* To throw. —*intr.v.* To work steadily; hammer away: *"The only thing to do is . . . to keep pegging steadily away until the luck turns"* (T. Roosevelt). [Middle English *pegge.*]

Peg·a·sus (pĕg'ə-səs) *n.* **1.** *Gk. Myth.* The winged steed that caused Hippocrene, the fountain of the Muses on Helicon, to well forth with a stroke of his hoof. **2.** A constellation in the Northern Hemisphere near Aquarius and Andromeda.

peg·board (pĕg'bôrd', -bōrd') *n.* A board with holes into which pegs or hooks can be inserted for hanging up articles or keeping score.

peg leg. *Informal.* An artificial leg, esp. a wooden one.

peg·ma·tite (pĕg'mə-tīt') *n.* A coarse-grained igneous rock, largely granite, sometimes rich in rare elements such as uranium, tungsten, and tantalum. [Greek *pēgma*, framework + -ITE.] —**peg'ma·tit'ic** (-tĭt'ĭk) *adj.*

pei·gnoir (pān-wär', pĕn-) *n.* A woman's loose-fitting dressing gown. [French, from Old French *peigner*, to comb the hair, from Latin *pectināre*, from *pecten*, comb.]

pe·jo·ra·tive (pĭ-jôr'ə-tĭv, -jŏr-, pĕj'ə-rā'tĭv, pē'jə-) *adj.* Expressing or implying a low opinion; disparaging; downgrading: *The word "proper" has come to have the pejorative sense of "prudish."* —*n.* A pejorative word. —**pe·jo'ra·tive·ly** *adv.*

Pe·king·ese (pē'kĭ-nēz', -nēs', -kĭng-ēz', -kĭng-ēs') *n., pl.* **Pekingese.** Also **Pe·kin·ese** (-kĭ-nēz', -nēs'). **1.** A resident or native of Peking, China. **2.** The Chinese dialect of Peking. **3.** (pē'kĭ-nēz', -nēs') A toy dog of a breed developed in China, with a flat nose, a long-haired coat, and short, bowed forelegs.

Peking man (pē'kĭng'). An extinct hominid primate of the genus *Sinanthropus*, known from fossil remains of the Pleistocene epoch. [After *Peking*, China, near which the remains were found.]

pe·koe (pē'kō) *n.* A grade of black tea consisting of the leaves around the buds. [Dial. Chinese *peh ho* : *peh*, white + *ho*, down.]

pe·lag·ic (pə-lăj'ĭk) *adj.* Of or living in open oceans or seas rather than coastal or inland waters. [Latin *pelagicus*, from Greek *pelagikos*, from *pelagos*, sea.]

pelf (pĕlf) *n.* Wealth or riches, esp. when dishonestly acquired. [Middle English, booty, property, from Old French *pelfre.*]

pel·i·can (pĕl'ĭ-kən) *n.* Any of various large, web-footed birds of the genus *Pelecanus*, of tropical and warm regions, with a large pouch under the lower bill used for catching and holding fish. [Middle English, from Old English *pellican*, from Late Latin *pelicānus*, from Greek *pelekan*, from *pelekus*, an ax (prob. from the shape of its bill).]

pe·lisse (pə-lēs') *n.* **1.** A long cloak or outer robe, usu. of fur or with a fur lining. **2.** A woman's loose, light cloak, often with openings for the arms. [French, from Medieval Latin *pellicia*, cloak, from Latin *pellicius*, made of skin, from *pellis*, skin.]

pel·la·gra (pə-lăg'rə, -lā'grə) *n.* A chronic disease caused by niacin deficiency, and characterized by skin eruptions, digestive and nervous disturbances, and eventual mental deterioration. [Italian : *pelle*, skin, from Latin *pellis* + Greek

---

ă pat	ā pay	â care	ä father	ĕ pet	ē be	hw which	ĭ pit	ī tie	î pier	ŏ pot	ō toe	ô paw, for	oi noise
ŏŏ took	ōō boot	ou out	th thin	th this	ŭ cut		û urge	zh vision	ə about, item, edible, gallop, circus				

agra, seizure.] —**pel·lag′rous** *adj.*

pel·let (pĕl′ĭt) *n.* **1.** A small, solid or densely packed ball or mass, as of bread, wax, or medicine. **2.** A bullet or piece of small shot. —*tr.v.* **1.** To make or form into pellets. **2.** To strike with pellets. [Middle English, from Old French *pelote,* from Latin *pila,* ball.]

pel·li·cle (pĕl′ĭ-kəl) *n.* A thin skin or film. [Old French *pellicule,* from Medieval Latin *pellicula,* from Latin, dim. of *pellis,* skin.] —**pel·lic′u·lar** (pə-lĭk′yə-lər) *adj.*

pell-mell (pĕl′mĕl′) *adv.* Also **pell·mell. 1.** In a jumbled, confused manner; helter-skelter. **2.** In frantic, disorderly haste; headlong. [French *pêle-mêle,* from Old French *pesle mesle,* from *mesler,* to mix, from Latin *miscēre.*] —**pell′-mell′** *adj.*

pel·lu·cid (pə-lōō′sĭd) *adj.* **1.** Admitting the maximum passage of light; transparent. **2.** Transparently clear in style or meaning: *pellucid prose.* [Latin *pellūcidus,* from *pellū- cēre,* to shine through : *per,* through + *lūcēre,* to shine.] —**pel·lu·cid′i·ty** (pĕl′yōō-sĭd′ĭ-tē) or **pel·lu·cid·ness** *n.* —**pel·lu′cid·ly** *adv.*

Pe·lops (pē′lŏps) *n. Gk. Myth.* The son of Tantalus and father of Atreus.

pe·lo·rus (pə-lôr′əs, -lōr′-) *n., pl.* **-rus·es.** A navigator's instrument consisting of a fixed compass card and, instead of a magnetic needle, a pair of sight vanes for taking bearings. [Orig. unknown.]

pe·lo·ta (pə-lō′tə) *n.* Jai alai. [Spanish, ball, from French *pelote,* pellet.]

pelt[1] (pĕlt) *n.* **1.** The skin of an animal with the fur or hair still on it. **2.** A stripped animal skin ready for tanning. [Middle English.]

pelt[2] (pĕlt) *tr.v.* **1.** To strike repeatedly with or as if with blows or missiles; bombard: *pelting each other with snowballs.* **2.** To cast, hurl, or throw (missiles): *pelting stones at windows.* —*intr.v.* **1.** To beat or strike heavily and repeatedly: *The rain pelted down for an hour.* **2.** To move at a vigorous gait. —*n.* **1.** A sharp blow; whack. **2.** A rapid pace; speed: *galloped away at full pelt.* [Middle English *pelten.*] —**pelt′er** *n.*

pel·try (pĕl′trē) *n.* Undressed animal pelts.

pel·vic (pĕl′vĭk) *adj.* Of, in, or near the pelvis.

pelvic fin. Either of a pair of lateral hind fins of fishes, attached to the pelvic girdle.

pelvic girdle. The skeletal structure of bone or cartilage by which the hind limbs or analogous parts are supported and joined to the vertebral column.

pel·vis (pĕl′vĭs) *n., pl.* **-vis·es** or **-ves** (-vēz′). *Anat.* **1.** A basin-shaped skeletal structure, composed of the innominate bones on the sides, the pubis in front, and the sacrum and coccyx behind, that rests on the lower limbs and supports the spinal column. **2.** The hollow funnel in the outlet of the kidney into which urine is discharged. In this sense, also called **renal pelvis.** [From Latin *pēlvis,* basin.]

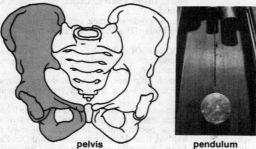

pelvis   pendulum

pem·mi·can (pĕm′ĭ-kən) *n.* Also **pem·i·can.** A food prepared by North American Indians from lean, dried strips of meat pounded into paste, mixed with fat and berries, and pressed into small cakes. [Cree *pimikân,* from *pimii,* grease, fat.]

pen[1] (pĕn) *n.* **1.** An instrument for writing or drawing with ink, formerly made from a large quill, now typically having a metal point and a holder containing a supply of ink. **2.** The practice of writing. **3.** A writer or author. —*tr.v.* **penned, pen·ning.** To write or compose with a pen. [Mid-

dle English *penne,* from Old French, from Latin *penna,* feather.] —**pen′ner** *n.*

pen[2] (pĕn) *n.* **1.** A small, fenced enclosure for animals. **2.** The animals kept in such an enclosure. **3.** Any of various other enclosures, such as a bullpen or a playpen. —*tr.v.* **penned** or **pent** (pĕnt), **pen·ning.** To confine in or as if in a pen. [Middle English, from Old English *penn.*]

pen[3] (pĕn) *n.* A female swan. [Orig. unknown.]

pen[4] (pĕn) *n. Slang.* A penitentiary.

pe·nal (pē′nəl) *adj.* **1.** Of or prescribing punishment, as for breaking the law: *a penal code.* **2.** Subject to punishment: *a penal offense.* **3.** Serving as a means or place of punishment: *penal servitude.* [Middle English, from Old French, from Latin *poenālis,* from *poena,* penalty.] —**pe′nal·ly** *adv.*

pe·na·lize (pē′nə-līz′, pĕn′ə-) *tr.v.* **-ized, -iz·ing. 1.** To subject to a penalty. **2.** To impose a handicap on; to disadvantage: *The educational system penalizes students for whom English is a second language.* —**pe′nal·i·za′tion** *n.*

pen·al·ty (pĕn′əl-tē) *n., pl.* **-ties. 1.** A punishment established by law or authority for a crime or offense. **2.** Something, esp. a sum of money, that must be given up or deducted when a person fails to meet the terms of an agreement. **3.** The disadvantage or painful consequences resulting from an action or condition: *neglected his teeth, and paid the penalty.* **4.** A punishment, handicap, or loss of advantage imposed on a team or competitor for infraction of a rule. [From Medieval Latin *poenālitās,* from Latin *poenālis,* penal.]

pen·ance (pĕn′əns) *n.* **1.** An act of self-mortification or devotion performed voluntarily to show sorrow for a sin or other wrongdoing. **2.** In some Christian churches, a sacrament that includes contrition, confession to a priest, acceptance of punishment, and absolution. [Middle English *penaunce,* from Old French *penance,* from Latin *paeniten- tia,* penitence, from *paenitēns,* penitent.]

pe·na·tes (pĭ-nā′tēz′, -nä-) *pl.n.* The Roman gods of the household. [Latin.]

pence (pĕns) *n. Brit.* A plural of **penny.**

pen·chant (pĕn′chənt) *n.* A strong inclination; a liking: *a penchant for winter sports.* [French, from *pencher,* to incline, from Latin *pendēre,* to hang.]

pen·cil (pĕn′səl) *n.* **1.** A thin stick of graphite encased in wood, used for writing. **2.** Something shaped or used like a pencil: *a styptic pencil; an eyebrow pencil.* —*tr.v.* **-ciled** or **-cilled, -cil·ing** or **-cil·ling. 1.** To write or draw with a pencil. **2.** To mark or color with or as if with a pencil. [Middle English *pencel,* from Old French *pincel,* from Latin *pēni- cillus,* a brush, pencil, dim. of *pēnis,* tail.] —**pen′cil·er** *n.*

pen·dant (pĕn′dənt) *n.* Also **pen·dent. 1.** Something hanging from something else, esp. an ornament or piece of jewelry attached to a necklace or bracelet. **2.** A sculptured ornament suspended from a vaulted Gothic roof or ceiling. **3.** One of a matched pair; a parallel or companion piece. —*adj.* Var. of **pendent.** [Middle English *pendaunt,* from Old French *pendant,* from *pendre,* to hang, from Latin *pen- dēre.*]

pen·dent (pĕn′dənt) *adj.* Also **pen·dant. 1.** Hanging down; dangling; suspended. **2.** Projecting; jutting; overhanging. **3.** Awaiting settlement; undecided; pending. —*n.* Var. of **pendant.** —**pen′dent·ly** *adv.*

pend·ing (pĕn′dĭng) *adj.* Not yet decided or settled; awaiting action: *legislation pending before Congress.* —*prep.* **1.** While in process of; during. **2.** While awaiting; until: *He was suspended pending an investigation of the charges.* [French *pend(ant)* + -ING.]

pen·drag·on (pĕn-drăg′ən) *n.* The title of the supreme war leader of the post-Roman Celts of southern Britain. [Middle English, from Welsh : *pen,* chief, head + *dragon,* standard, from Latin *dracō.*]

pen·du·lar (pĕn′jə-lər, pĕnd′yə-) *adj.* Swinging back and forth like a pendulum.

pen·du·lous (pĕn′jə-ləs, pĕd′yə-) *adj.* **1.** Hanging loosely; suspended so as to swing or sway. **2.** Wavering; undecided. [Latin *pendulus,* from *pendēre,* to hang.] —**pen′du- lous·ly** *adv.* —**pen′du·lous·ness** *n.*

pen·du·lum (pĕn′jə-ləm, pĕnd′yə-) *n.* **1.** A mass hung by a relatively light cord so that it is able to swing freely. **2.** An apparatus of this kind used to regulate the action of some device, esp. a clock. **3.** Something that swings back and forth from one course, opinion, or condition to another: *the pendulum of public opinion.*

Pe·nel·o·pe (pə-nĕl′ə-pē) *n.* In the *Odyssey*, the wife of Odysseus, celebrated for her faithfulness.

pe·ne·plain (pē′nə-plān′, pĕn′ə-) *n.* Also **pe·ne·plane.** A nearly flat land surface representing an advanced stage of erosion. [Latin *paene, pĕne,* almost + PLAIN.]

pe·nes (pē′nēz′) *n.* A plural of **penis.**

pen·e·tra·ble (pĕn′ĭ-trə-bəl) *adj.* Capable of being penetrated. —**pen′e·tra·bil′i·ty** *n.* —**pen′e·tra·bly** *adv.*

pen·e·trate (pĕn′ĭ-trāt′) *v.* **-trat·ed, -trat·ing.** —*tr.v.* **1.** To enter or force a way into; pierce: *Little light penetrated the dense forest.* **2. a.** To enter into and permeate: *The cold penetrated my bones.* **b.** To cause to be permeated or diffused; steep. **3.** To grasp the inner significance of; understand. **4.** To see through. **5.** To affect deeply. —*intr.v.* **1.** To make a way in or through something; get through. **2.** To gain admittance or access. **3.** To gain insight: *penetrating deeper into the mysteries of the atom.* [Latin *penetrāre,* from *penitus,* deeply, from *penus,* the interior of a house.]

pen·e·trat·ing (pĕn′ĭ-trā′tĭng) *adj.* **1.** Piercing; biting; sharp: *a penetrating chill.* **2.** Acute; discerning; incisive: *a penetrating mind.* —**pen′e·trat′ing·ly** *adv.*

pen·e·tra·tion (pĕn′ĭ-trā′shən) *n.* **1.** The act or process of penetrating. **2.** The extent or depth to which something penetrates. **3.** The ability to understand; insight.

pen·e·tra·tive (pĕn′ĭ-trā′tĭv) *adj.* Tending to penetrate.

pen·guin (pĕng′gwĭn) *n.* Any of various flightless saltwater birds of the family Spheniscidae, of cool regions of the Southern Hemisphere, with scalelike, barbless feathers, flipperlike wings, and webbed feet. [Orig. unknown.]

penguin   pennon

pen·i·cil·lin (pĕn′ĭ-sĭl′ĭn) *n.* Any of several isomeric antibiotic compounds obtained from penicillium molds, esp. *Penicillium notatum* and *P. chrysogenum,* or produced biosynthetically, and used to prevent or treat a wide variety of diseases and infections. [From PENICILLIUM.]

pen·i·cil·li·um (pĕn′ĭ-sĭl′ē-əm) *n., pl.* **-ums** or **-cil·li·a** (-sĭl′ē-ə). Any of various molds of the genus *Penicillium,* with a characteristic blue-green color and tufts of fine filaments, that grow on decaying fruits and ripening cheese and are used in the production of penicillin and in making cheese. [From Latin *pēnicillus,* brush, pencil.]

pen·in·su·la (pə-nĭn′sə-lə, -nĭns′yə-) *n.* A long projection of land into water. [Latin *pēninsula : pēne,* almost + *īnsula,* island.] —**pen·in′su·lar** *adj.*

pe·nis (pē′nĭs) *n., pl.* **-nis·es** or **-nes** (-nēz′). The male organ of copulation and urination. [Latin *pēnis,* tail, penis.]

pen·i·tent (pĕn′ĭ-tənt) *adj.* Feeling or expressing sorrow and regret for one's misdeeds or sins. —*n.* **1.** Someone who is penitent. **2.** A person performing penance under the direction of a confessor. [Middle English, from Old French, from Latin *paenitēns,* pres. part. of *paenitēre,* to repent.] —**pen′i·tent·ly** *adv.* —**pen′i·tence** *n.*

pen·i·ten·tial (pĕn′ĭ-tĕn′shəl) *adj.* **1.** Of or expressing penitence. **2.** Relating to or of the nature of penance. —**pen′i·ten′tial·ly** *adv.*

pen·i·ten·tia·ry (pĕn′ĭ-tĕn′shə-rē) *n., pl.* **-ries.** A prison for those convicted of major crimes. —*adj.* **1.** Relating to or used for punishment or reform of criminals or wrongdoers. **2.** Resulting in or punishable by imprisonment in a penitentiary. [Middle English *penitenciary,* penance officer,

from Medieval Latin *penitentiārius,* from Latin *paenitentia,* repentance, from *paenitēns,* penitent.]

pen·knife (pĕn′nīf′) *n.* A small pocketknife, orig. used to make or sharpen quill pens.

pen·man (pĕn′mən) *n.* **1.** A copyist; a scribe. **2.** An expert in penmanship. **3.** An author; writer.

pen·man·ship (pĕn′mən-shĭp′) *n.* The art, skill, style, or manner of handwriting.

pen name. Also **pen-name** (pĕn′nām′). A fictitious name assumed by an author.

pen·nant (pĕn′ənt) *n.* **1.** A long, tapering flag, often triangular, used on ships for signaling or for identification. **2.** Any similar flag or emblem. **3.** *Baseball.* **a.** A flag that serves as the emblem of the championship in a professional league. **b.** The yearly championship in a professional league. [Blend of PENDANT and PENNON.]

pen·nate (pĕn′āt′) *adj.* Feathered or winged. [Latin *pennātus,* winged, from *penna,* feather, wing.]

pen·ni·less (pĕn′ĭ-lĭs) *adj.* Entirely without money. —See Syns at **poor.** —**pen′ni·less·ly** *adv.* —**pen′ni·less·ness** *n.*

pen·non (pĕn′ən) *n.* **1.** A long, narrow banner borne upon a lance. **2.** Any banner, flag, or pennant. [Middle English, from Old French *penon,* from *penne,* feather, wing, from Latin *penna.*] —**pen′noned** *adj.*

Penn·syl·va·nia Dutch (pĕn′səl-vān′yə, -vā′nē-ə). **1.** The descendants of German and Swiss immigrants who settled in Pennsylvania in the 17th and 18th cent. **2.** The dialect of German spoken by this group.

Penn·syl·va·nian (pĕn′səl-vān′yən, -vā′nē-ən) *n.* Also **Pennsylvanian period.** A geologic period that began about 310 million years ago and ended about 280 million years ago, characterized by the development of coal-bearing rocks. —*modifier: a Pennsylvanian rock.*

pen·ny (pĕn′ē) *n.* **1.** *pl.* **-nies.** A U.S. or Canadian coin worth 1/100 of a dollar; a cent. **2.** *pl.* **pence** (pĕns) or **-nies.** A British coin worth 1/100 of a pound. **3.** A small sum of money. [Middle English, from Old English, *penning.*]

penny ante. 1. Poker in which the highest bet is limited to a penny or some other small sum. **2.** *Informal.* Small-scale business or commerce.

penny pincher. *Informal.* A person who is very stingy with money. —**pen′ny-pinch′ing** *adj. & n.*

pen·ny·roy·al (pĕn′ē-roi′əl) *n.* **1.** A Eurasian plant of the mint family, *Mentha pulegium,* that yields a useful aromatic oil. **2.** A similiar aromatic plant, *Hedeoma pulegioides,* of eastern North America. [By folk ety. from Anglo-French *puliol real :* Old French *poliol,* thyme, from Latin *pulegium* + *real,* royal.]

pen·ny·weight (pĕn′ē-wāt′) *n.* A unit of troy weight equal to 24 grains, 1/20 of a troy ounce or approx. 1.555 grams.

pen·ny-wise (pĕn′ē-wīz′) *adj.* Careful in dealing with small sums of money or small matters.

pen·ny·worth (pĕn′ē-wûrth′) *n.* **1.** As much as a penny will buy. **2.** A small amount. **3.** A bargain.

pe·nol·o·gy (pĭ-nŏl′ə-jē) *n.* The theory and practice of prison management and the treatment of convicted criminals. [Latin *poena,* penalty, from Greek *poinē* + -LOGY.] —**pe′no·log′i·cal** (pē′nə-lŏj′ĭ-kəl) *adj.* —**pe′no·log′i·cal·ly** *adv.* —**pe·nol′o·gist** *n.*

pen·sile (pĕn′sĭl) *adj.* **1.** Hanging down loosely; suspended. **2.** Building a hanging nest: *pensile birds.* [Latin *pēnsilis,* from *pēnsus,* past part. of *pendere,* to hang.]

pen·sion¹ (pĕn′shən) *n.* A sum of money paid regularly to a person, esp. as a retirement benefit. —*tr.v.* **1.** To grant a pension to. **2.** To retire or dismiss with a pension. [Middle English, from Old French, from Medieval Latin *pēnsiō,* from Latin, payment, from *pendere,* to weigh, pay.]

pen·sion² (pän-syôn′) *n.* A small boarding house or hotel in Europe. [French, from Old French *pension,* payment, ult. from Latin *pendere,* to weigh, pay.]

pen·sion·er (pĕn′shə-nər) *n.* Someone who receives or lives on a pension.

pen·sive (pĕn′sĭv) *adj.* Engaged in or showing deep thoughtfulness. [Middle English *pensif,* from Old French, from *penser,* to think, from Latin *pēnsāre,* freq. of *pendere,* to weigh.] —**pen′sive·ly** *adv.* —**pen′sive·ness** *n.*

pent (pĕnt) *v.* A past tense and past participle of **pen** (to confine). —*adj.* Penned or shut up; closely confined.

---

pen·ta– or **pent–**. A prefix meaning five: **pentameter**. [Greek, from *pente*, five.]

pen·ta·cle (pĕn′tə-kəl) *n.* A five-pointed star formed by five straight lines. Also called **pentagram**. [Medieval Latin *pentaculum* : Greek *penta-*, five + Latin *-culum*, dim. suffix.]

pen·ta·gon (pĕn′tə-gŏn′) *n.* **1.** A polygon having five sides and five interior angles. **2. the Pentagon. a.** A five-sided building near Washington, D.C., that is the headquarters of the U.S. Department of Defense and the offices of the U.S. Armed Forces. **b.** The U.S. Department of Defense. —**pen·tag′o·nal** (pĕn-tăg′ə-nəl) *adj.* —**pen·tag′o·nal·ly** *adv.*

pen·ta·gram (pĕn′tə-grăm′) *n.* A pentacle.

pen·ta·he·dron (pĕn′tə-hē′drən) *n., pl.* **-drons** or **-dra** (-drə) A solid having five plane faces. —**pen′ta·he′dral** (-hē′drəl) *adj.*

pen·tam·er·ous (pĕn-tăm′ər-əs) *adj.* **1.** Having or separated into five similar parts. **2.** *Bot.* Having flower parts, such as petals, in sets of five.

pen·tam·e·ter (pĕn-tăm′ĭ-tər) *n.* **1.** A line of verse composed of five metrical feet. **2.** English verse composed in iambic pentameter; heroic verse.

pen·tane (pĕn′tān′) *n.* Any of three isomeric hydrocarbons, C_5H_{12}, of the methane series: **a.** *Normal pentane.* A colorless flammable liquid used as an anesthetic and a general solvent. **b.** *Isopentane.* A colorless flammable liquid used as a solvent and in the manufacture of polystyrene foam. **c.** *Neopentane.* A colorless gas used in the manufacture of synthetic rubber.

Pen·ta·teuch (pĕn′tə-tōōk′, -tyōōk′) *n.* The first five books of the Old Testament. [Late Latin *Pentateuchus*, from Greek *Pentateukhos* : *penta-*, five + *teukhos*, scroll.]

pen·tath·lon (pĕn-tăth′lən, -lŏn′) *n.* An athletic contest that consists of five events for each participant, usu. running, horseback riding, swimming, fencing, and pistol shooting. [Greek : *pent(a)-*, five + *athlon*, contest.]

Pen·te·cost (pĕn′tĭ-kôst′, -kŏst′) *n.* **1.** A Christian festival celebrated on the seventh Sunday after Easter in memory of the descent of the Holy Ghost upon the disciples; Whitsunday. **2.** A Jewish festival, Shavuot. [Middle English, from Old English *Pentecosten*, from Late Latin *Pentēcostē*, from Greek *pentēkostē (hēmera)*, the fiftieth (day after the Resurrection).]

Pen·te·cos·tal (pĕn′tĭ-kŏs′təl, -kôs′-) *adj.* **1.** Of, relating to, or occurring at Pentecost. **2.** Of, relating to, or being any of various Christian religious congregations that seek to be filled with the Holy Ghost, after the example of the disciples at Pentecost. —*n.* A member of a Pentecostal congregation. —**Pen′te·cos′tal·ism** *n.*

pent·house (pĕnt′hous′) *n.* **1. a.** An apartment or dwelling on the roof of a building. **b.** A residence, often with a terrace, that forms the top floor of an apartment house. **2.** A shed or sloping roof attached to the side of a building or wall. [Alteration of Middle English *pentis*, from Old French *appentis*, from Medieval Latin *appendicium*, appendage, from Latin *appendix*, from *appendēre*, to append, attach.]

pen·to·bar·bi·tal sodium (pĕn′tə-bär′bĭ-tôl′). A white crystalline or powdery barbiturate, $C_{11}H_{17}N_2O_3Na$, used as a sedative. [From PENT(A)- + BARBITAL.]

pent-up (pĕnt′ŭp′) *adj.* Not given expression; repressed: *pent-up anger.*

pe·nult (pē′nŭlt′, pĭ-nŭlt′) *n.* Also **pe·nul·ti·ma** (pĭ-nŭl′tə-mə). The next to the last syllable in a word. [Latin *paenultimus*, last but one : *paene*, almost + *ultimus*, last, from *uls*, beyond.]

pe·nul·ti·mate (pĭ-nŭl′tə-mĭt) *adj.* **1.** Next to last. **2.** Of or relating to the penult of a word. —*n.* The next to the last. [From Latin *paenultimus*, penult.]

pe·num·bra (pĭ-nŭm′brə) *n., pl.* **-brae** (-brē) or **-bras. 1.** A partial shadow between regions of complete shadow and complete illumination. **2.** The partly darkened fringe around a sunspot. [Latin *paene*, *pēne*, almost + *umbra*, shadow.] —**pe·num′bral** or **pe·num′brous** *adj.*

pe·nu·ri·ous (pĭ-nōōr′ē-əs, -nyōōr′-) *adj.* **1.** Miserly; stingy. **2.** Yielding little; barren: *a penurious land.* **3.** Lacking money or wealth; needy. —See Syns at **poor** and **stingy**. —**pe·nu′ri·ous·ly** *adv.* —**pe·nu′ri·ous·ness** *n.*

pen·u·ry (pĕn′yə-rē) *n.* **1.** Extreme poverty; destitution. **2.** Extreme dearth; barrenness; insufficiency. [Middle English, from Latin *pēnūria*, want, scarcity.]

pe·on (pē′ŏn′) or (-ən) *n.* **1.** An unskilled laborer or farm worker in Latin America. **2.** A person once held in a state of servitude to a creditor in Mexico and the southwestern United States. **3.** Any menial worker; a drudge. [Spanish *peón*, Portuguese *peão*, and French *pion*, all from Medieval Latin *pedo*, foot soldier, from Latin *pēs*, foot.]

pe·on·age (pē′ə-nĭj) *n.* **1.** The condition of being a peon. **2.** A system by which debtors are bound in servitude to their creditors until the debts are paid.

pe·o·ny (pē′ə-nē) *n., pl.* **-nies.** Any of various garden plants of the genus *Paeonia*, with large pink, red, white, or creamy flowers. [Middle English *pione*, from Old English *peonie*, from Latin *peōnia*, from Greek *paiōniā*, after *Paiōn*, physician of the gods.]

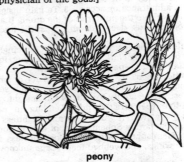

peony

peo·ple (pē′pəl) *n., pl.* **-ple. 1.** Human beings as distinct from other creatures. **2.** A body of persons living in the same country under one national government: *the American people.* **3.** *pl.* **-ples.** An ethnic group sharing a common religion, culture, language, etc.: *primitive peoples.* **4. the people. a.** The mass of ordinary persons; the populace. **b.** The citizens of a nation, state, or other political unit; electorate. **5.** Persons subordinate to or loyal to a ruler, superior, or employer. **6.** Family, relatives, or ancestors. —*tr.v.* **-pled, -pling.** To furnish with a population; populate. [Middle English *peple*, from Old French *pueple*, from Latin *populus.*] —**peo′pler** *n.*

pep (pĕp) *n. Informal.* Energy; high spirits; vim. —See Syns at **spirit**. —*tr.v.* **pepped, pep·ping.** *Informal.* To bring energy or liveliness to: *A good hot meal will pep you up.* [Short for PEPPER.]

pep·lum (pĕp′ləm) *n., pl.* **-lums.** A short overskirt or ruffle attached at the waistline. [Latin, from *peplus, peplos,* from Greek *peplos.*]

pep·per (pĕp′ər) *n.* **1.** A woody vine, *Piper nigrum,* of the East Indies, with small, berrylike fruit. **2.** The dried, blackish fruit of this plant, used as a pungent condiment. When ground whole, it is called *black pepper,* and with the shell removed, *white pepper.* **3.** Any of several other plants of the genus *Piper,* such as cubeb, betel, and kava. **4.** Any of several varieties of a woody plant, *Capsicum frutescens* (or *C. annuum*), of tropical origin. **5.** The podlike fruit of any of these plants, varying in size, shape, and degree of pungency. **6.** Any of various condiments made from the more pungent varieties of *C. frutescens.* —*tr.v.* **1.** To season or sprinkle with pepper. **2.** To sprinkle or shower with many small objects. **3.** To make lively and vivid: *a speech peppered with sharp remarks.* [Middle English *peper,* from Old English *pipor,* from Latin *piper,* from Greek *peperi,* from Sanskrit *pippalī,* berry.]

pep·per-and-salt (pĕp′ər-ən-sôlt′) *adj.* Having a close mixture of black and white: *"A pepper-and-salt matted beard hung almost into his lap"* (Joseph Conrad).

pep·per·corn (pĕp′ər-kôrn′) *n.* A dried berry of the pepper vine *Piper nigrum.*

pepper mill. A utensil for grinding peppercorns.

pep·per·mint (pĕp′ər-mĭnt′) *n.* **1.** A plant, *Mentha piperita,* with small purple or white flowers and downy leaves that yield a pungent oil. **2.** The oil from this plant, or a preparation made from it, used as flavoring. **3.** A candy with this flavoring.

pep·per·o·ni (pĕp′ə-rō′nē) n. A highly spiced pork and beef sausage. [Italian *peperoni*, hot peppers, from *pepe*, pepper, from Latin *piper*.]

pep·per·y (pĕp′ə-rē) adj. 1. Of, like, or containing pepper; hot and spicy. 2. Sharp-tempered; irascible; feisty. 3. Sharp and stinging in style or content: *a peppery speech.* —**pep′per·i·ness** n.

pep pill. Any of various stimulant drugs in the form of a capsule or tablet, esp. amphetamine.

pep·py (pĕp′ē) adj. -**pi·er**, -**pi·est.** Full of energy and vim; lively. —**pep′i·ness** n.

pep·sin (pĕp′sĭn) n. 1. A digestive enzyme found in gastric juice that catalyzes the breakdown of protein to peptides. 2. A substance containing this enzyme, obtained from the stomachs of hogs and used as a digestive aid. [German *Pepsin*, from Greek *pepsis*, digestion, from *peptein*, to digest.]

pep talk. A speech of encouragement, as by a coach to his team.

pep·tic (pĕp′tĭk) adj. 1. a. Of, relating to, or assisting digestion: *peptic secretion.* b. Induced by or associated with the action of digestive secretions: *peptic ulcer.* 2. Of or involving pepsin. —n. A digestive agent. [Latin *pepticus*, from Greek *peptikos*, from *peptein*, to digest.]

pep·tide (pĕp′tīd) n. Any of various natural or synthetic compounds containing two or more amino acids linked by the carboxyl group of one amino acid and the amino group of another. [PEPT(ONE) + -IDE.]

pep·tone (pĕp′tōn) n. Any of various protein compounds obtained by acid or enzyme hydrolysis of natural protein and used as nutrients and culture media. [German *Pepton*, from Greek *peptein*, to digest, cook.] —**pep·ton′ic** (pĕp-tŏn′ĭk) adj.

per (pûr) prep. 1. Through; by means of: *per bearer.* 2. To, for, or by each; for every: *40 cents per gallon.* 3. According to: *per instructions.* [Latin.]

per-. A prefix meaning: 1. Thoroughly or intensely: **perfervid.** 2. a. Containing an element in a high oxidation state: **perchloric acid.** b. Containing a large or the largest possible proportion of an element: **peroxide.** [Latin, from *per*, through.]

per·am·bu·late (pə-răm′byə-lāt′) v. -**lat·ed**, -**lat·ing.** —tr.v. To walk through, esp. so as to inspect; traverse. —intr.v. To walk about; roam; stroll. [From Latin *perambulāre* : *per-*, through + *ambulāre*, to walk.] —**per·am′bu·la·to·ry** (-lə-tôr′ē, -tōr′ē) adj. —**per·am′bu·la′tion** n.

per·am·bu·la·tor (pə-răm′byə-lā′tər) n. Brit. A baby carriage. Also called **pram.**

per an·num (pər ăn′əm). Latin. By the year; annually.

per·cale (pər-kāl′) n. A strong, smooth, closely woven cotton cloth used to make sheets and clothing. —**modifier:** *a percale pillowcase.* [French, from Persian *pargālah*.]

per cap·i·ta (pər kăp′ĭ-tə). Per person: *income per capita.* [Latin, "by heads."]

per·ceive (pər-sēv′) tr.v. -**ceived**, -**ceiv·ing.** 1. To become aware of directly through any of the senses, esp. to see or hear. 2. To take notice of; observe; detect. 3. To become aware of in one's mind; achieve understanding of. [Middle English *perceiven*, from Old French *perceivre*, from Latin *percipere* : *per-*, completely + *capere*, to seize.] —**per·ceiv′a·ble** adj. —**per·ceiv′a·bly** adv.

per cent. Also **per·cent** (pər-sĕnt′). Per hundred; for or out of each hundred: *Sixty per cent of the members approved.* [Short for Latin *per centum*, by the hundred.]

per·cent·age (pər-sĕn′tĭj) n. 1. A fraction or ratio with 100 fixed and understood as the denominator, formed by multiplying a decimal equivalent of a fraction by 100. For example, 0.98 equals a percentage of 98. 2. A proportion or share in relation to the whole: *received a percentage of the profit.* 3. **percentages.** Odds; probability. 4. Informal. Advantage; gain.

per·cen·tile (pər-sĕn′tīl′) n. Any of the smaller numerical ranges formed by dividing the total range of a variable into 100 equal parts that do not overlap. The percentile into which a value of this variable falls is determined by the percentage of the other values that it exceeds. For example, an examination score that exceeds 95 per cent of the other scores is in the 95th percentile.

per cen·tum (pər sĕn′təm). **Per cent.**

per·cep·ti·ble (pər-sĕp′tə-bəl) adj. Capable of being perceived; noticeable. —**per·cep′ti·bil′i·ty** n. —**per·cep′ti·bly** adv.

Syns: perceptible, appreciable, discernible, noticeable, palpable adj. Core meaning: Capable of being noticed or detected (*a perceptible improvement in the patient*).

per·cep·tion (pər-sĕp′shən) n. 1. The process, act, or faculty of perceiving. 2. Something perceived; an observation. 3. An insight; understanding. 4. Perceptiveness. [Latin *perceptiō*, from *perceptus*, past part. of *percipere*, to perceive.] —**per·cep′tion·al** adj.

per·cep·tive (pər-sĕp′tĭv) adj. 1. Of or relating to perception: *perceptive faculties.* 2. a. Having or showing skill at perceiving; observant; keen. b. Marked by discernment and understanding; sensitive. —See Syns at **sharp.** —**per·cep′tive·ly** adv. —**per·cep·tiv′i·ty** (pûr′sĕp-tĭv′ĭ-tē) n.

per·cep·tu·al (pər-sĕp′chōō-əl) adj. Of, based on, or involving perception. —**per·cep′tu·al·ly** adv.

perch¹ (pûrch) n. 1. A rod or branch serving as a place for a bird to rest. 2. A place for resting or sitting. 3. A pole used in acrobatics. 4. a. A unit of length, the rod. b. One square rod of land. —intr.v. 1. To alight or rest on a perch; roost. 2. To stand, sit, or rest on some elevated place or position: *The child perched on the window sill.* —tr.v. To place on or as if on a perch: *"The long thin nose near the end of which a pair of spectacles was perched"* (George Orwell). [Middle English *perche*, from Old French, from Latin *pertica*, stick.]

perch² (pûrch) n., pl. **perch** or **perch·es.** 1. Any of various freshwater fishes of the genus *Perca*, esp. either of two edible species, *P. flavescens*, of North America, and *P. fluviatilis*, of Europe. 2. Any of various related or similar fishes. [Middle English *perche*, from Old French, from Latin *perca*, from Greek *perkē*.]

per·chance (pər-chăns′) adv. Perhaps; possibly. [Middle English *perchaunce*, from Old French *par chance*, "by chance."]

Per·che·ron (pûr′chə-rŏn′, -shə-) n. A large draft horse of a breed developed in France, with a dark, often dappled coat. [French, from *Percheron*, a native of *le Perche*, a district south of Normandy.]

per·cip·i·ent (pər-sĭp′ē-ənt) adj. Having the power of perceiving, esp. perceiving keenly and readily. [Latin *percipiēns*, pres. part. of *percipere*, to perceive.] —**per·cip′i·ence** or **per·cip′i·en·cy** n.

per·co·late (pûr′kə-lāt′) v. -**lat·ed**, -**lat·ing.** —tr.v. 1. To cause (liquid, powder, or small particles) to pass through a porous substance or small holes. 2. To pass or ooze through: *Water percolated the sand.* 3. To make (coffee) in a percolator. —intr.v. 1. To drain or seep through a porous substance or filter. 2. Informal. To become lively or active. [From Latin *percōlāre* : *per-*, through + *cōlum*, sieve.] —**per′co·la′tion** n.

per·co·la·tor (pûr′kə-lā′tər) n. A type of coffeepot in which boiling water is forced repeatedly up through a center tube to filter through a basket of ground coffee.

per·cuss (pər-kŭs′) tr.v. To strike or tap firmly, as in medical percussion. [Latin *percussus*, past part. of *percutere*, to strike hard : *per-* (intensive) + *quatere*, to strike.]

per·cus·sion (pər-kŭsh′ən) n. 1. The striking together of two bodies, esp. when noise is produced. 2. The sound, vibration, or shock caused by such a striking together. 3. The act of detonating a percussion cap in a firearm. 4. A method of medical examination in which a physician taps areas of the body and draws conclusions about internal conditions on the basis of the sounds produced. 5. Percussion instruments as a group. —**modifier:** *the percussion section of the band.*

percussion cap. A thin metal cap containing a detonator that explodes on being struck.

percussion instrument. A musical instrument in which sound is produced by striking, as a drum or piano.

per·cus·sion·ist (pər-kŭsh′ə-nĭst) n. A person who plays percussion instruments.

per·cus·sive (pər-kŭs′ĭv) adj. Of, relating to, or characterized by percussion. —**per·cus′sive·ly** adv. —**per·cus′sive·ness** n.

per di·em (pər dē′əm). 1. Per day. 2. An allowance for daily expenses. [Latin, "by the day."]

per·di·tion (pər-dĭsh′ən) *n.* **1. a.** The loss of the soul; eternal damnation. **b.** Hell. **2.** *Archaic.* Utter loss or ruin. [Middle English *perdicioun,* from Late Latin *perditiō,* from Latin *perdere,* to destroy, lose : *per-,* away + *dare,* to give.]

per·e·gri·nate (pĕr′ə-grə-nāt′) *v.* **-nat·ed, -nat·ing.** *—intr.v.* To journey or travel from place to place. *—tr.v.* To travel through or over. **—per′e·gri·na′tion** *n.* **—per′e·gri·na′tor** *n.*

per·e·grine (pĕr′ĭ-grĭn, -grēn′) *adj.* **1.** Foreign; alien. **2.** Roving or wandering; migratory. *—n.* The peregrine falcon. [Medieval Latin *peregrīnus,* from Latin, foreigner, stranger, from *pereger,* being abroad : *per-,* through + *ager,* land, field.]

peregrine falcon. A widely distributed bird of prey, *Falco peregrinus,* with gray and white plumage, formerly much used in falconry.

peregrine falcon

perfoliate

per·emp·to·ry (pə-rĕmp′tə-rē) *adj.* **1.** Putting an end to all debate or action: *a peremptory decree.* **2.** Not allowing contradiction or refusal; imperative: *peremptory commands.* **3.** Having the nature of or expressing a command; urgent: *spoke with a peremptory tone.* **4.** Offensively self-assured; dictatorial: *a peremptory manner.* [Late Latin *peremptōrius,* from *peremptus,* past part. of *perimere,* to take away completely : *per-,* completely + *emere,* to obtain.] **—per·emp′to·ri·ly** *adv.* **—per·emp′to·ri·ness** *n.*

per·en·ni·al (pə-rĕn′ē-əl) *adj.* **1.** Living, growing, and flowering and producing seeds for several or many years. **2.** Lasting indefinitely; perpetual: *perennial happiness.* **3.** Repeated regularly; appearing again and again: *perennial fiscal problems.* *—n.* A plant that continues to live, grow, flower, and produce seeds for several or many years. [From Latin *perennis* : *per-,* throughout + *annus,* year.] **—per·en′ni·al·ly** *adv.*

per·fect (pûr′fĭkt) *adj.* **1.** Lacking nothing essential to the whole; complete of its nature or kind: *a perfect circle; a perfect dozen.* **2.** Being completely without defect; flawless: *a perfect specimen.* **3.** Completely skilled or talented in a certain field or area: *a perfect artist.* **4.** Completely reproducing or corresponding to a type or original; accurate; exact: *a perfect reproduction of a painting.* **5.** Complete; thorough; utter: *a perfect fool.* **6.** Pure; undiluted; unmixed: *perfect red.* **7.** Excellent and delightful in all respects: *a perfect day.* **8.** *Bot.* Having both stamens and pistils in the same flower; monoclinous. **9.** *Gram.* Of or being a verb form expressing action completed prior to a fixed point of reference in time. **10.** *Math.* Having a root that is a whole number; formed by raising an integer to an integral power. For example, 25 is a perfect square, and 27 is a perfect cube. **11.** *Mus.* Designating the three basic intervals of the octave, fourth, and fifth. *—n.* **1.** The perfect tense. **2.** A verb or verb form in this tense. *—tr.v.* (pər-fĕkt′). To bring to perfection or completion. [Middle English *parfit,* from Old French, from Latin *perfectus,* complete, excellent, past part. of *perficere,* to complete : *per-,* completely + *facere,* to do.] **—per·fect′er** *n.* **—per′fect·ness** *n.*

Syns: perfect, faultless, impeccable *adj.* Core meaning: Supremely excellent (*a perfect diamond; a perfect performance*). See also Syns at **pure.**

per·fect·i·ble (pər-fĕk′tə-bəl) *adj.* Capable of becoming or being made perfect. **—per·fect′i·bil′i·ty** *n.*

per·fec·tion (pər-fĕk′shən) *n.* **1.** The quality or condition of being perfect. **2.** The process or act of perfecting. **3.** A per-

son or thing considered to be perfect. **4.** An instance or quality of excellence.

per·fec·tion·ism (pər-fĕk′shə-nĭz′əm) *n.* A tendency to set extremely high standards and to be dissatisfied with anything less. **—per·fec′tion·ist** *n.*

per·fect·ly (pûr′fĭkt-lē) *adv.* **1.** In a perfect manner: *performed the piece perfectly.* **2.** Completely; fully: *perfectly content.*

perfect participle. A past participle.

per·fer·vid (pər-fûr′vĭd) *adj.* Very eager or ardent; impassioned. [New Latin *perfervidus* : *per-,* completely + Latin *fervidus,* fiery, eager.] **—per·fer′vid·ly** *adv.*

per·fid·i·ous (pər-fĭd′ē-əs) *adj.* Disloyal; treacherous. **—per·fid′i·ous·ly** *adv.*

per·fi·dy (pûr′fĭ-dē) *n., pl.* **-dies.** Deliberate breach of faith; treachery. [Latin *perfidia,* from *perfidus,* treacherous : *per-,* thoroughly away + *fidēs,* faith.]

per·fo·li·ate (pər-fō′lē-ĭt) *adj.* *Bot.* Designating a leaf that completely clasps the stem and is apparently pierced by it. [New Latin *perfoliatus,* "pierced through the leaf" : Latin *per-,* through + *folium,* leaf.] **—per·fo′li·a′tion** *n.*

per·fo·rate (pûr′fə-rāt′) *tr.v.* **-rat·ed, -rat·ing. 1.** To pierce, punch, or bore a hole: *a perforated spoon.* **2.** To pierce or stamp with rows of holes to allow easy separation: *perforate postage stamps.* *—adj.* (pûr′fə-rĭt, -rāt′). Perforated. [From Latin *perforāre* : *per-,* through + *forāre,* to bore.] **—per′fo·ra′tor** *n.*

per·fo·ra·tion (pûr′fə-rā′shən) *n.* **1.** The act of perforating or the condition of being perforated. **2.** A hole or series of holes punched or bored through something, esp. the series of holes separating sections in a sheet or roll, as of postage stamps.

per·force (pər-fôrs′, -fōrs′) *adv.* By necessity: "*There is no whiskey either at tavern or store, and the people are perforce sober*" (Anne Langton). [Middle English *par force,* from Old French, "by force."]

per·form (pər-fôrm′) *tr.v.* **1.** To begin and carry through to completion; do: *perform surgery.* **2.** To carry out in accordance with prescribed terms; fulfill: *perform contractual obligations.* **3. a.** To enact (a feat or role) before an audience. **b.** To give a public presentation of. *—intr.v.* **1.** To carry on; function: *The car performs well on curves.* **2.** To accomplish something as promised or expected. **3.** To portray a role or demonstrate some skill before an audience. **4.** To present a dramatic or musical work or other entertainment before an audience. [Middle English *performen,* from Norman French *parformer,* Old French *parfornir* : *par-* (intensifier), *fornir,* to execute, accomplish.] **—per·form′a·ble** *adj.* **—per·form′er** *n.*

per·form·ance (pər-fôr′məns) *n.* **1.** The act of performing or the condition of being performed. **2.** The act or style of performing a work or role before an audience. **3.** The way in which someone or something functions: *rating a machine's performance.* **4.** A presentation, esp. a theatrical one, before an audience. **5.** Something performed; an accomplishment; a deed.

per·fume (pûr′fyōōm′, pər-fyōōm′) *n.* **1.** A fragrant liquid distilled from flowers or prepared by synthetic means. **2.** A pleasing scent or odor. *—tr.v.* (pər-fyōōm′). **-fumed, -fum·ing.** To fill with fragrance. [Old French *parfum,* prob. from Old Italian *parfumare,* to perfume : *par-,* through, from Latin *per-* + *fumare,* to smoke, from Latin *fūmus,* smoke.]

per·fum·er·y (pər-fyōō′mə-rē) *n., pl.* **-ies. 1.** Perfumes in general. **2.** The art or process of making perfume.

per·func·to·ry (pər-fŭngk′tə-rē) *adj.* Done or acting routinely and with little interest or care: *a perfunctory inspection.* [Late Latin *perfunctōrius,* from Latin *perfungī,* perform : *per-,* completely + *fungī,* to perform.] **—per·func′to·ri·ly** *adv.* **—per·func′to·ri·ness** *n.*

per·fuse (pər-fyōōz′) *tr.v.* **-fused, -fus·ing. 1.** To coat or fill with liquid, color, or light; suffuse. **2.** To pour or diffuse (a liquid) over or through something. [Latin *perfusus,* past part. of *perfundere,* to wet : *per-,* through + *fundere,* to pour.] **—per·fu′sion** (fyōō′zhən) *n.* **—per·fu′sive** (pər-fyōō′sĭv, -zĭv) *adj.*

per·go·la (pûr′gə-lə) *n.* An arbor or passageway with a roof of trelliswork on which climbing plants are trained to grow. [Italian, from Latin *pergula.*]

per·haps (pər-hăps′) *adv.* Maybe; possibly. [PER (by) + HAP.]

peri-. A prefix meaning: **1.** About, around, encircling, or enclosing: **periscope. 2.** Close at hand, adjacent, or near: **perihelion.** [Latin, from Greek, from *peri*, about, near, around.]

per·i·anth (pĕr′ē-ănth′) *n.* The outer envelope of a flower, consisting of the calyx and corolla. [PERI- + Greek *anthos*, flower.]

per·i·car·di·um (pĕr′ĭ-kär′dē-əm) *n.*, *pl.* **-di·a** (-dē-ə). The membranous sac enclosing the heart. [New Latin, from Greek *perikardios*, around the heart : *peri-*, around + *kardia*, heart.] **—per′i·car′di·al** or **per′i·car′di·ac′** (-ăk′) *adj.*

per·i·carp (pĕr′ĭ-kärp′) *n. Bot.* The wall of a ripened ovary or fruit. [From Greek *perikarpion*, pod, shell : *peri-*, around + *karpos*, fruit.] **—per′i·car′pi·al** (-kär′pē-əl) *adj.*

per·i·cra·ni·um (pĕr′ĭ-krā′nē-əm) *n.*, *pl.* **-ni·a** (-nē-ə). *Anat.* The external **periosteum** that covers the outer surface of the skull. [From Greek *perikranios*, around the skull : *peri-*, around + *kranion*, cranium.] **—per′i·cra′ni·al** *adj.*

per·i·gee (pĕr′ə-jē) *n.* The point nearest the earth in the orbit of the moon or an artificial satellite. [French *périgée*, from Greek *perigeios*, near the earth.]

per·i·he·lion (pĕr′ə-hēl′yən) *n.*, *pl.* **-he·lia** (-hēl′yə). The point nearest the sun in the orbit of a planet or other body. [PERI- + Greek *hēlios*, sun.]

per·il (pĕr′əl) *n.* **1.** Exposure to the risk of harm or loss. **2.** Something that endangers; serious risk: *the perils of the open sea.* —See Syns at **danger.** —*tr.v.* **-iled** or **-illed, -il·ing** or **-il·ling.** To expose to danger; imperil. [Middle English, from Old French, from Latin *perīculum*, trial, danger.]

per·il·ous (pĕr′ə-ləs) *adj.* Full of peril; hazardous. **—per′il·ous·ly** *adv.*

pe·rim·e·ter (pə-rĭm′ĭ-tər) *n.* **1. a.** The sum of the lengths of the segments that form the sides of a polygon. **b.** The total length of any closed curve, such as a circle or elipse. **2.** A fortified strip or boundary protecting a military position. [French *périmètre*, from Latin *perimetros*, from Greek : *peri-*, around + *metron*, measure.]

per·i·ne·um (pĕr′ə-nē′əm) *n.*, *pl.* **-ne·a** (-nē′ə). The portion of the body in the pelvis occupied by urogenital passages and the rectum, bounded in front by the pubic arch, in the back by the coccyx, and laterally by part of the hipbone. [New Latin, from Late Latin *perinaion*, from Greek : *peri-*, around + *inan*, to excrete.] **—per′i·ne′al** *adj.*

pe·ri·od (pîr′ē-əd) *n.* **1.** An interval of time characterized by the occurrence of certain conditions or events: *a period of 12 months; a waiting period.* **2.** An interval of time characterized by the prevalence of a specified culture, ideology, or technology: *the pre-Columbian period.* **3.** A unit of geologic time, longer than an epoch and shorter than an era. **4.** Any of various intervals of time, as the divisions of the academic day or of playing time in a game. **5.** The interval of time between corresponding points in successive occurrences of an action or event that repeats; a cycle. **6.** An instance or occurrence of menstruation. **7.** A point at which something is ended; completion; stop. **8.** The full pause at the end of a spoken sentence. **9.** A punctuation mark (.) indicating a full stop, placed at the end of declarative sentences and after many abbreviations. **10.** In formal writing, a sentence of several carefully balanced clauses. —*adj.* Of, belonging to, or representing a certain historical age or time: *a period piece; period furniture.* [Middle English *paryode*, from Old French *periode*, from Late Latin *periodus*, from Latin, rhetorical period, from Greek *periodos* : *peri-*, around + *hodos*, way.]

pe·ri·od·ic (pîr′ē-ŏd′ĭk) *adj.* **1.** Having periods or repeated cycles: *the periodic motion of a pendulum.* **2.** Happening or appearing at regular intervals. **3.** Taking place now and then; intermittent. **—pe′ri·od′i·cal·ly** *adv.*

pe·ri·od·i·cal (pîr′ē-ŏd′ĭ-kəl) *adj.* **1.** Periodic. **2. a.** Published at regular intervals of more than one day. **b.** Of a publication issued at such intervals. —*n.* A publication issued at regular intervals of more than one day.

pe·ri·o·dic·i·ty (pîr′ē-ə-dĭs′ĭ-tē) *n.* The quality of being periodic; recurrence at regular intervals.

periodic law. *Chem.* The principle that the properties of the elements recur periodically with increasing atomic number.

periodic table. *Chem.* A tabular arrangement of the elements according to their atomic number.

per·i·o·don·tal (pĕr′ē-ō-dŏn′tl) *adj.* Of or designating tissue and structures surrounding and supporting the teeth. [PERI- + Greek *odous*, tooth.]

per·i·os·te·um (pĕr′ē-ŏs′tē-əm) *n.*, *pl.* **-te·a** (-tē-ə). A fibrous membrane covering all bones, except at points of articulation. [From Late Latin *periosteon*, from Greek : *peri-*, around + *osteon*, bone.]

per·i·pa·tet·ic (pĕr′ə-pə-tĕt′ĭk) *adj.* **1.** Walking about from place to place; traveling on foot. **2.** Carried on while walking or moving from place to place: *a peripatetic lesson.* [From French *péripatétique*, from Latin *peripatēticus*, belonging to the Aristotelian philosophy, ult. from Greek *peripatein*, to walk about, from Aristotle's habit of teaching while walking in the Lyceum at Athens.]

pe·riph·er·al (pə-rĭf′ər-əl) *adj.* **1.** Of, relating to, located on, or forming a periphery: *peripheral vision; the peripheral regions of the state.* **2.** Of or relating to the peripheral nervous system. **—pe·riph′er·al·ly** *adv.*

peripheral nervous system. The part of the nervous system that comprises the cranial nerves, the spinal nerves, and the sympathetic nervous system.

pe·riph·er·y (pə-rĭf′ə-rē) *n.*, *pl.* **-ies. 1. a.** The outermost part within a boundary: *the periphery of one's vision.* **b.** The region or area immediately beyond a boundary. **2.** *Math.* **a.** A perimeter. **b.** The surface of a solid. **3.** *Anat.* A region in which nerves end. [Middle English *peripherie*, from Late Latin *peripheria*, from Greek *periphereia* : *peri-*, around + *pherein*, to carry.]

pe·riph·ra·sis (pə-rĭf′rə-sĭs) *n.*, *pl.* **-ses** (-sēz′). Also **per·i·phrase** (pĕr′ə-frāz′). Unnecessarily wordy or roundabout expression; circumlocution. [Latin, from Greek : *peri-*, around + *phrazein*, to say.]

per·i·phras·tic (pĕr′ə-frăs′tĭk) *adj.* **1.** Of or characterized by periphrasis. **2.** *Gram.* Constructed by using an auxiliary word rather than an inflected form. For example, the phrases *the word of his father* and *his father did say* are periphrastic, while *his father's word* and *his father said* are inflected. **—per′i·phras′ti·cal·ly** *adv.*

per·i·scope (pĕr′ĭ-skōp′) *n.* Any of several instruments in which mirrors or prisms allow observation of objects that are not in a direct line of sight.

per·ish (pĕr′ĭsh) *intr.v.* **1.** To die, esp. in a violent or untimely manner. **2.** To pass from existence; disappear gradually. —See Syns at **die.** [Middle English *perisshen*, from Old French *perir*, from Latin *perīre* : *per-*, away + *īre*, to go.]

per·ish·a·ble (pĕr′ĭ-shə-bəl) *adj.* Liable to decay or spoil easily: *perishable fruits.* —*n.* Often **perishables.** Things, such as foods, that spoil or decay easily. **—per′ish·a·bil′i·ty** *n.* **—per′ish·a·bly** *adv.*

per·i·stal·sis (pĕr′ĭ-stôl′sĭs, -stăl′-) *n.*, *pl.* **-ses** (-sēz′). Wavelike muscular contractions that propel contained matter along tubular organs, as in the alimentary canal. [From Greek *peristaltikos*, compressing around : *peri-*, around + *stellein*, to place, set.] **—per′i·stal′tic** (-stôl′tĭk, -stăl′-) *adj.*

per·i·style (pĕr′ĭ-stīl′) *n.* **1.** A series of columns surrounding a building or enclosing a court. **2.** A court enclosed by such columns. [French *péristyle*, from Latin *peristylum*, from Greek *peristulon* : *peri-*, around + *stulos*, pillar.]

per·i·to·ne·um (pĕr′ĭ-tə-nē′əm) *n.*, *pl.* **-ne·a** (-nē′ə). Also **per·i·to·nae·um.** The membrane lining the walls of the abdominal cavity and enclosing the viscera. [Late Latin *peritonēum*, from Greek *peritonaion*, stretched across : *peri-*, around + *tenein*, to stretch.] **—per′i·to·ne′al** *adj.*

per·i·to·ni·tis (pĕr′ĭ-tə-nī′tĭs) *n.* Inflammation of the peritoneum. [PERITON(EUM) + -ITIS.]

per·i·wig (pĕr′ĭ-wĭg′) *n.* A wig, esp. a large powdered wig worn by men in the 17th and 18th cent. [Earlier *perwyke*, from Old French *perruque*, peruke.]

per·i·win·kle¹ (pĕr′ĭ-wĭng′kəl) *n.* **1.** Any of several small, edible saltwater snails, esp. of the genus *Littorina*, with thick, cone-shaped, whorled shells. **2.** The shell of any of these snails. [From Old English *pīnewincle*.]

per·i·win·kle² (pĕr′ĭ-wĭng′kəl) *n.* Any of several trailing, evergreen plants of the genus *Vinca*, esp. one with glossy, dark-green leaves and blue flowers. Also called **myrtle.**

| ă pat | ā pay | â care | ä father | ĕ pet | ē be | hw which | | ĭ pit | ī tie | î pier | ŏ pot | ō toe | ô paw, for | oi noise |
| ōō took | ōō boot | ou out | th thin | *th* this | ŭ cut | | | û urge | zh vision | ə about, item, edible, gallop, circus | | | | |

[Middle English *pervenke*, from Old French *pervenche*, from Latin *pervinca*.]

per·jure (pûr'jər) *tr.v.* **-jured, -jur·ing.** To make (oneself) guilty of perjury by deliberately testifying falsely under oath. [Middle English *perjuren*, from Old French *perjurer*, from Latin *perjūrāre* : *per-*, thoroughly away + *jūrāre*, to swear.] **—per'jur·er** *n.*

per·ju·ry (pûr'jə-rē) *n.*, pl. **-ries.** The deliberate, willful giving of false testimony while under oath. **—per·ju'ri·ous** (pər-jŏŏr'ē-əs) *adj.* **—per·ju'ri·ous·ly** *adv.*

perk (pûrk) *tr.v.* To cause to stick up or jut out: *The cat perked its ears at the noise.* **—phrasal verb. perk up. 1.** To regain or cause to regain one's good spirits or liveliness. **2.** To add to the appearance of; spruce up. [Middle English *perken.*]

perk·y (pûr'kē) *adj.* **-i·er, -i·est.** Cheerful and brisk; animated; lively. **—perk'i·ly** *adv.* **—perk'i·ness** *n.*

perm (pûrm) *n. Informal.* A permanent.

per·ma·frost (pûr'mə-frôst', -frŏst') *n.* Permanently frozen soil below the ground in polar and neighboring frigid regions. [PERMA(NENT) + FROST.]

per·ma·nence (pûr'mə-nəns) *n.* Also **per·ma·nen·cy** (-nən-sē), pl. **-cies.** The condition or quality of being permanent.

per·ma·nent (pûr'mə-nənt) *adj.* **1.** Lasting or meant to last indefinitely; enduring. **2.** Not expected to change in status, condition, or place: *a permanent address.* **—n.** Waves or curls that are set in the hair by chemicals and last for several months. [Middle English, from Old French, from Latin *permanēns*, pres. part. of *permanēre*, to endure : *per-*, throughout + *manēre*, to remain.] **—per'ma·nent·ly** *adv.*

permanent press. Of, pertaining to, or made from a fabric that is chemically treated so that it will dry without wrinkles.

per·me·a·bil·i·ty (pûr'mē-ə-bĭl'ĭ-tē) *n.* **1.** The property or condition of being permeable. **2.** *Physics.* **Magnetic permeability. 3.** The rate of diffusion of a pressurized gas through a porous material.

per·me·a·ble (pûr'mē-ə-bəl) *adj.* Having openings or small gaps that allow liquids or gases to pass through: *a permeable membrane.* **—per'me·a·bly** *adv.*

per·me·ate (pûr'mē-āt') *v.* **-at·ed, -at·ing. —tr.v. 1.** To spread or flow throughout; pervade. **2.** To pass through openings or small gaps in. **—intr.v.** To spread; diffuse. [From Latin *permeāre* : *per-*, through + *meāre*, to go, pass.] **—per'me·a'tion** *n.* **—per'me·a'tive** *adj.*

Per·mi·an (pûr'mē-ən) *n.* Also **Permian period.** A geologic period that began about 280 million years ago and ended about 230 million years ago; the final period of the Paleozoic era. **—modifier:** *a Permian fossil.* [After Perm, former Russian province, where the rock strata were first identified.]

per·mis·si·ble (pər-mĭs'ə-bəl) *adj.* Capable of being permitted; allowable. **—per·mis'si·bil'i·ty** or **per·mis'si·ble·ness** *n.* **—per·mis'si·bly** *adv.*

per·mis·sion (pər-mĭsh'ən) *n.* **1.** The act of permitting. **2.** Consent, esp. formal consent; authorization. [Middle English, from Old French, from Latin *permissiō*, from *permittere*, to permit.]

per·mis·sive (pər-mĭs'ĭv) *adj.* **1.** Granting permission; allowing. **2.** Not forbidden; permitted; allowed. **3.** Allowing freedom of behavior; indulgent; tolerant. **—per·mis'sive·ly** *adv.* **—per·mis'sive·ness** *n.*

per·mit (pər-mĭt') *v.* **-mit·ted, -mit·ting. —tr.v. 1.** To allow (something); consent to; tolerate. **2.** To allow (someone) to do something; authorize: *Permit me to ask you a question.* **3.** To afford opportunity to; make possible: *new regulations that permit greater latitude.* **—intr.v.** To afford opportunity; allow: *if time permits.* **—n.** (pûr'mĭt, pər-mĭt'). **1.** Permission, esp. in written form. **2.** A document or certificate giving permission to do something; license. [Latin *permittere* : *per-*, through + *mittere*, to let go, send.] **—per·mit'ter** *n.*

Syns: 1. permit, allow, have, let, tolerate *v.* Core meaning: To neither forbid nor prevent (*permitted the children to run wild*). **2. permit, allow, authorize, let, sanction** *v.* Core meaning: To give consent to (*permitted five days of sick leave*).

per·mu·ta·tion (pûr'myŏŏ-tā'shən) *n.* **1.** A complete change; transformation. **2.** The act of altering a given set of objects in a group. **3. a.** Any of the ordered subsets that can be formed from the elements of a set. **b.** The act or process of forming such a subset of another set. [Middle English *permutacion*, exchange, from Old French, from Latin *permūtātiō* : *per-*, thoroughly + *mūtāre*, to change.] **—per'mu·ta'tion·al** *adj.*

per·ni·cious (pər-nĭsh'əs) *adj.* **1.** Tending to cause death or serious injury; deadly: *a pernicious disease.* **2.** Causing great harm; destructive; evil: *a pernicious doctrine.* [Latin *perniciōsus*, from *perniciēs*, destruction : *per-*, completely + *nex*, death.] **—per·ni'cious·ly** *adv.* **—per·ni'cious·ness** *n.*

pernicious anemia. A severe anemia associated with failure to absorb vitamin B_{12} and characterized by the presence of abnormally large red blood cells, gastrointestinal disturbances, and lesions of the spinal cord.

per·nick·e·ty (pər-nĭk'ĭ-tē) *adj.* Var. of **persnickety.**

per·o·rate (pĕr'ə-rāt') *intr.v.* **-rat·ed, -rat·ing. 1.** To conclude a speech, esp. with a formal summing up. **2.** To speak at great length; declaim. [From Latin *perōrāre*, to harangue at length : *per-*, thoroughly + *ōrāre*, to speak.]

per·o·ra·tion (pĕr'ə-rā'shən) *n.* **1.** A formal speech; oration. **2.** The concluding part of a speech, summing up or bringing to a climax what has been said.

per·ox·ide (pə-rŏk'sīd') *n. Chem.* **1. Hydrogen peroxide. 2.** Any compound containing oxygen that yields hydrogen peroxide with an acid, such as sodium peroxide, Na_2O_2. **—tr.v. -id·ed, -id·ing. 1.** To treat with peroxide. **2.** To bleach (hair) with hydrogen peroxide. [PER- + OXIDE.]

per·pen·dic·u·lar (pûr'pən-dĭk'yə-lər) *adj.* **1.** Intersecting at or forming right angles. **2.** At right angles to the horizontal; vertical. **—See Syns at vertical. —n. 1.** A line or plane perpendicular to a given line or plane. **2.** A perpendicular position. **3.** A vertical or nearly vertical line or plane. [Middle English *perpendiculer*, from Old French, from Latin *perpendiculārius*, from *perpendiculum*, plumb line.] **—per'pen·dic'u·lar'i·ty** (-lăr'ĭ-tē) *n.*

per·pe·trate (pûr'pĭ-trāt') *tr.v.* **-trat·ed, -trat·ing.** To be guilty of doing or performing; commit: *perpetrate a crime.* [From Latin *perpetrāre*, to accomplish : *per-*, completely + *patrāre*, to do, bring about.] **—per'pe·tra'tion** *n.* **—per'pe·tra'tor** *n.*

per·pet·u·al (pər-pĕch'ŏŏ-əl) *adj.* **1.** Lasting forever; everlasting. **2.** Lasting for an indefinitely long time. **3.** Valid, in effect, or intended for an indefinitely long time: *a treaty of perpetual friendship.* **4.** Ceaselessly repeated or continuing without interruption: *perpetual nagging.* **5.** Flowering throughout the growing season. **—See Syns at continuous.** [Middle English *perpetuel*, from Old French, from Latin *perpetuālis*, from *perpetuus*, continuous : *per-*, thoroughly + *petere*, to go toward.] **—per·pet'u·al·ly** *adv.* **—per·pet'u·al·ness** *n.*

perpetual motion. The hypothetical continuous operation of an isolated mechanical device or other closed system without a sustaining energy source.

per·pet·u·ate (pər-pĕch'ŏŏ-āt') *tr.v.* **-at·ed, -at·ing. 1.** To make perpetual. **2.** To prolong the existence of: *perpetuate a custom.* **—per·pet'u·a'tion** *n.* **—per·pet'u·a'tor** *n.*

per·pe·tu·i·ty (pûr'pĭ-tōō'ĭ-tē, -tyōō'-) *n.*, pl. **-ties. 1.** The quality or condition of being perpetual. **2.** Time without end; eternity. **3.** *Law.* **a.** The condition of an estate that is limited so as to be intransferable either perpetually or longer than the period determined by law. **b.** An estate so limited.

per·plex (pər-plĕks') *tr.v.* **1.** To confuse or puzzle; bewilder. **2.** To make confusedly intricate. **—See Syns at confuse.** [From Latin *perplexus*, intricate : *per-*, thoroughly + *plectere*, to weave.]

per·plex·i·ty (pər-plĕk'sĭ-tē) *n.*, pl. **-ties. 1.** The condition of being perplexed; puzzlement. **2.** The condition of being intricate. **3.** Something that perplexes.

per·qui·site (pûr'kwĭ-zĭt) *n.* **1.** A payment or profit received in addition to a regular wage or salary, esp. a benefit expected as one's due. **2.** A tip; gratuity. **3.** Something claimed as an exclusive right. [Middle English, from Medieval Latin *perquīsītum*, acquisition, from *perquīrere*, to search for : *per-*, thoroughly + *quaerere*, to seek.]

per se (pər sā', sē'). In or by itself; as such. [Latin.]

per·se·cute (pûr'sĭ-kyōōt') *tr.v.* **-cut·ed, -cut·ing. 1.** To

ă pat	ā pay	â care	ä father	ĕ pet	ē be	hw which	ĭ pit	ī tie	î pier	ŏ pot	ō toe	ô paw, for	oi noise
ŏŏ took	ōō boot	ou out	th thin	th this	ŭ cut		û urge	zh vision	ə about, item, edible, gallop, circus				

cause to suffer, esp. on account of politics, religion, etc.; oppress. **2.** To annoy persistently; to bother. [Old French *persecuter*, from Latin *persecútus*, past part. of *persequi*, to pursue : *per-*, throughout + *sequī*, to follow.] —**per'se·cu'tor** *n.*

per·se·cu·tion (pûr'sĭ-kyōō'shən) *n.* **1.** The act or practice of persecuting. **2.** The condition of being persecuted. —**per·se·cu'tion·al** *adj.*

Per·seph·o·ne (pər-sĕf'ə-nē) *n. Gk. Myth.* The wife of Hades and queen of the underworld; identified with Proserpina.

Per·se·us (pûr'sē-əs, -sōōs') *n.* **1.** *Gk. Myth.* The son of Zeus and Danae who slew Medusa and rescued Andromeda. **2.** A constellation in the Northern Hemisphere near Andromeda and Auriga.

per·se·ver·ance (pûr'sə-vîr'əns) *n.* The holding to a course of action, belief, or purpose without giving way.

per·se·vere (pûr'sə-vîr') *intr.v.* **-vered, -ver·ing.** To persist in or remain constant to a purpose, idea, or task in spite of obstacles or discouragement. [Middle English *perseveren*, from Old French *persevrer*, from Latin *persevērāre* : *per-*, thoroughly + *sevērus*, serious, severe.] —**per'se·ver'ing·ly** *adv.*

Per·sian (pûr'zhən) *adj.* Of or pertaining to Persia or Iran, its people, language, or culture. —*n.* **1.** A native or inhabitant of ancient Persia or modern Iran. **2.** The Iranian language of the Persians.

Persian cat. A type of domestic cat with long silky fur.

Persian lamb. The glossy, tightly curled fur obtained from a young lamb of the karakul sheep.

per·si·flage (pûr'sə-fläzh') *n.* Light, jesting or teasing talk or writing; banter. [French, from *persifler*, to banter.]

per·sim·mon (pər-sĭm'ən) *n.* **1.** Any of various chiefly tropical trees of the genus *Diospyros*, with hard wood and orange-red fruit that is edible only when completely ripe. **2.** The fruit of any of these trees. [Of Algonquian orig.]

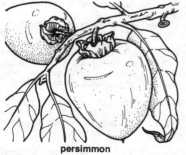

persimmon   perspective

per·sist (pər-sĭst') *intr.v.* **1.** To go on or maintain firmly or stubbornly, in spite of opposition or difficulty; persevere. **2.** To continue in existence; last: *poor management that persisted for years.* [Latin *persistere* : *per-*, exceedingly + *sistere*, to stand firm.]

per·sis·tence (pər-sĭs'təns) *n.* Also **per·sis·ten·cy** (-tən-sē) *pl.* **-cies.** **1.** The act of persisting. **2.** The quality of being persistent; perseverance; tenacity.

per·sis·tent (pər-sĭs'tənt) *adj.* **1.** Refusing to give up or let go; tenacious: *a persistent salesperson.* **2.** Lasting for a long time or longer than usual; constant; enduring: *a persistent headache; persistent delays.* —**per·sis'tent·ly** *adv.*

per·snick·e·ty (pər-snĭk'ĭ-tē) *adj.* Also **per·nick·e·ty** (pər-nĭk'ĭ-tē). *Informal.* Excessively attentive to detail; fastidious. [Orig. *pernickety*, perh. var. of PARTICULAR.]

per·son (pûr'sən) *n.* **1.** A living human being; an individual. **2.** The living body of a human being: *He had two guns on his person.* **3.** Guise; character: *"Well, in her person, I say I will not have you"* (Shakespeare). **4.** Physique and general appearance. **5.** *Law.* A human being or organization with legal rights and duties. **6.** *Gram.* Any of three groups of pronoun forms with corresponding verb inflections that distinguish between the speaker (first person), the individual addressed (second person), and the individual or thing spoken of (third person). —*idiom.* **in person.** Physically present. [Middle English, from Old French *persone*, from

Latin *persōna*, mask, the character played by an actor.]

per·so·na (pər-sō'nə) *n.* **1.** *pl.* **-nae** (-nē). A character in a dramatic or literary work. **2.** *pl.* **-nas.** *Psychol.* The role that a person assumes in order to display his conscious intentions to himself and to others. [Latin *persōna*, mask, person.]

per·son·a·ble (pûr'sə-nə-bəl) *adj.* Pleasing in appearance or personality; attractive. —**per'son·a·ble·ness** *n.*

per·son·age (pûr'sə-nĭj) *n.* **1.** A character in a literary work. **2. a.** A person. **b.** A person of distinction.

per·son·al (pûr'sə-nəl) *adj.* **1.** Of a particular person: *personal identification.* **2. a.** Done, made, or performed in person: *a personal appearance.* **b.** Done to or for or directed toward a particular person: *a personal favor.* **3.** Private; intimate. **4.** Tending to be overly concerned or curious about another's affairs. **5.** Of the body or physical being: *personal cleanliness.* **6.** Indicating grammatical person. —*n.* A personal item or notice in a newspaper.

per·son·al·i·ty (pûr'sə-nǎl'ĭ-tē) *n., pl.* **-ties. 1.** The condition or quality of being a person. **2. a.** The totality of qualities and traits, as of character or behavior, that are peculiar to each person. **b.** A person regarded as having distinctive traits: *a dynamic political personality.* **3.** The distinctive qualities that make someone socially appealing: *won the election more on personality than on capability.* **4.** A person of importance or renown: *television personalities.* **5.** The characteristics of a place or situation that give it distinctive character: *Colors give a room personality.*

per·son·al·ize (pûr'sə-nə-līz') *tr.v.* **-ized, -iz·ing. 1.** To personify. **2.** To have printed, engraved, or monogrammed with one's name or initials.

per·son·al·ly (pûr'sə-nə-lē) *adv.* **1.** In person; without the agency of another: *I thanked him personally.* **2.** As far as oneself is concerned: *Personally, I don't care.* **3.** As a person: *I admire his skill but dislike him personally.*

personal pronoun. *Gram.* A pronoun that indicates the person speaking (*I, me, we, us*), the person spoken to (*you*), or the person or thing spoken about (*he, she, it, they, him, her, them*).

personal property. *Law.* Temporary or movable property as distinguished from real property.

per·son·al·ty (pûr'sə-nəl-tē) *n., pl.* **-ties.** *Law.* Personal property.

per·so·na non gra·ta (pər-sō'nə nŏn grä'tə, grăt'ə). A person who is not acceptable or welcome, esp. a diplomat who is not fully acceptable to a foreign government. [Latin, "unacceptable person."]

per·son·ate (pûr'sə-nāt') *tr.v.* **-at·ed, -at·ing. 1.** To impersonate (a character); assume the identity or role of. **2.** To endow with personal qualities; personify. —**per'son·a'tion** *n.* —**per'son·a'tor** *n.*

per·son·i·fi·ca·tion (pər-sŏn'ə-fĭ-kā'shən) *n.* **1.** The act of personifying. **2.** Someone or something that typifies a certain quality or idea; an embodiment: *He is the personification of evil.* **3.** A figure of speech in which lifeless objects or abstractions are endowed with human qualities or form.

per·son·i·fy (pər-sŏn'ə-fī') *tr.v.* **-fied, -fy·ing. 1.** To think of or represent (a lifeless object or abstraction) as having human qualities or human form: *personifying justice as a blindfolded woman.* **2.** To be the embodiment or perfect example of: *She personifies kindness.* —See Syns at **represent.** —**per·son'i·fi'er** *n.*

per·son·nel (pûr'sə-nĕl') *n.* **1.** The body of persons employed by or active in an organization, business, or service. **2.** An administrative division of an organization concerned with this body of persons. —*modifier:* *a personnel manager.* [French, from Old French *personal*, personal, from Late Latin *personālis*, from Latin *persōna*, mask, person.]

per·spec·tive (pər-spĕk'tĭv) *n.* **1.** The technique of representing objects on a flat surface so that they have the three-dimensional quality they have when seen with the eye. **2.** A view or vista: *the perspective of the city as seen from the rooftops.* **3.** A mental view of the relationships of the aspects of a subject to each other and to a whole: *a narrow perspective of the situation.* **4.** An idea of the relative importance of something; proper relation: *seeing life and death in perspective.* —*adj.* Of, seen, or represented in perspective. [Middle English, from Medieval Latin *pers-*

pectīva, optics, from Late Latin *perspectīvus*, of a view, from Latin *perspicere*, to inspect : *per-*, thoroughly + *specere*, to look.] —**per·spec'tive·ly** *adv.*

per·spi·ca·cious (pûr'spĭ-kā'shəs) *adj.* Able to perceive or understand keenly; mentally perceptive. [From Latin *perspicāx*, clear-sighted, from *perspicere*, to see through.] —**per·spi·ca'cious·ly** *adv.* —**per·spi·ca'cious·ness** *n.*

per·spi·cac·i·ty (pûr'spĭ-kăs'ĭ-tē) *n.* The ability to perceive or understand keenly; mental perceptiveness.

per·spic·u·ous (pər-spĭk'yōō-əs) *adj.* Clearly expressed or presented; lucid. [Latin *perspicuus*, from *perspicere*, to see through.] —**per·spi·cu'i·ty** (-kyōō'ĭ-tē) *n.* —**per·spic'u·ous·ly** *adv.* —**per·spic'u·ous·ness** *n.*

per·spi·ra·tion (pûr'spə-rā'shən) *n.* **1.** The saline moisture excreted through the pores of the skin by the sweat glands; sweat. **2.** The act or process of perspiring.

per·spire (pər-spīr') *intr.v.* -**spired,** -**spir·ing.** To excrete perspiration through the pores of the skin. [French *perspirer*, from Old French, from Latin *perspīrāre*, to breathe through : *per-*, through + *spīrāre*, to blow, breathe.]

per·suade (pər-swād') *tr.v.* -**suad·ed,** -**suad·ing.** To cause (someone) to do or believe something by means of argument, reasoning, or entreaty. [Latin *persuādēre* : *per-*, thoroughly + *suādēre*, to urge.] —**per·suad'a·ble** *adj.* —**per·suad'er** *n.*

per·sua·si·ble (pər-swā'zə-bəl, -sə-) *adj.* Open-minded enough to be persuaded; persuadable.

per·sua·sion (pər-swā'zhən) *n.* **1.** The act of persuading or the condition of being persuaded. **2.** The ability or power to persuade. **3.** A strong conviction or belief. **4.** A body of religious beliefs; religion: *worshipers of various persuasions.*

per·sua·sive (pər-swā'sĭv, -zĭv) *adj.* Tending or having the power to persuade: *a persuasive argument.* —**per·sua'sive·ly** *adv.* —**per·sua'sive·ness** *n.*

pert (pûrt) *adj.* -**er,** -**est.** **1.** Impudently bold; saucy. **2.** High-spirited; lively. **3.** Trim and stylish; jaunty. [Middle English, short for Old French *apert*, straightforward, open, from Latin *apertus*, past part. of *aperīre*, to open.] —**pert'ly** *adv.* —**pert'ness** *n.*

per·tain (pər-tān') *intr.v.* **1.** To have reference; relate: *evidence pertaining to the accident.* **2.** To belong as a part or related thing; be connected: *the farm and all the lands which pertain to it.* **3.** To be fitting or suitable. [Middle English *partenen*, from Old French *partenir*, from Latin *pertinēre* : *per-*, thoroughly + *tenēre*, to hold.]

per·ti·na·cious (pûr'tn-ā'shəs) *adj.* **1.** Holding firmly to some purpose, belief, or opinion. **2.** Stubbornly or perversely persistent. [From Latin *pertināx* : *per-*, thoroughly + *tenāx*, tenacious, from *tenēre*, to hold.] —**per'ti·na'cious·ly** *adv.* —**per'ti·na'cious·ness** *n.* —**per'ti·nac'i·ty** (-ăs'ĭ-tē) *n.*

per·ti·nent (pûr'tn-ənt) *adj.* Of, relating to, or connected with a specific matter. —See Syns at **relevant.** [Middle English, from Old French, from Latin *pertinēns,* pres. part. of *pertinēre,* to pertain.] —**per'ti·nence** or **per'ti·nen·cy** *n.* —**per'ti·nent·ly** *adv.*

per·turb (pər-tûrb') *tr.v.* **1.** To disturb greatly; make uneasy or anxious. **2.** To throw into great confusion. [Middle English *perturben,* from Old French *perturber,* from Latin *perturbāre* : *per-*, thoroughly + *turba,* confusion.]

per·tur·ba·tion (pûr'tər-bā'shən) *n.* **1. a.** The act of perturbing. **b.** The condition of being perturbed; agitation. **2.** Variation in a regular orbit, as of an electron or planet, that results from the influence of one or more external bodies.

per·tus·sis (pər-tŭs'ĭs) *n.* A disease, **whooping cough.** [Latin *per-,* very much + *tussis,* a cough.] —**per·tus'sal** *adj.*

pe·ruke (pə-rōōk') *n.* A wig, esp. one worn by men in the 17th and 18th cent. [French *perruque,* from Italian *perrucca,* head of hair, wig.]

pe·rus·al (pə-rōō'zəl) *n.* The action of perusing; a careful reading.

pe·ruse (pə-rōōz') *tr.v.* -**rused,** -**rus·ing.** To read or examine, esp. with great care. [Middle English *perusen,* to use up : Latin *per-,* completely + Middle English *usen,* to use.] —**pe·rus'er** *n.*

Pe·ru·vi·an bark (pə-rōō'vē-ən). A medicinal bark, cinchona.

per·vade (pər-vād') *tr.v.* -**vad·ed,** -**vad·ing.** To spread through; be present throughout; permeate: *"A marvellous stillness pervaded the world"* (Joseph Conrad). [Latin *pervādere* : *per-,* through + *vādere,* to go.] —**per·va'sion** (pər-vā'zhən) *n.*

per·va·sive (pər-vā'sĭv, -zĭv) *adj.* Tending to pervade; spreading throughout: *a pervasive aroma.* —**per·va'sive·ly** *adv.* —**per·va'sive·ness** *n.*

per·verse (pər-vûrs') *adj.* **1.** Directed away from what is right or good; perverted: *perverse behavior.* **2.** Persisting in an error or fault; wrongly self-willed or stubborn. **3.** Marked by or arising from a disposition to oppose and contradict. **4.** Cranky; peevish. —See Syns at **contrary** and **obstinate.** [Middle English *pervers,* from Old French, from Latin *perversus,* past part. of *pervertere,* to pervert.] —**per·verse'ly** *adv.* —**per·verse'ness** *n.*

per·ver·sion (pər-vûr'zhən) *n.* **1.** The act of perverting or the condition of being perverted. **2.** A sexual practice or act considered abnormal or unnatural.

per·ver·si·ty (pər-vûr'sĭ-tē) *n., pl.* -**ties. 1.** The quality or condition of being perverse. **2.** An instance of being perverse.

per·vert (pər-vûrt') *tr.v.* **1.** To cause to turn from what is considered the right or moral course; to corrupt. **2.** To employ wrongly or incorrectly; misuse: *perverted the law to suit his own ends.* **3.** To interpret incorrectly: *an analysis that perverts the meaning of the poem.* —*n.* (pûr'vûrt'). Someone whose sexual behavior is considered abnormal or unnatural. [Middle English *perverten,* from Old French *pervertir,* from Latin *pervertere* : *per-,* completely + *vertere,* to turn.] —**per·vert'er** *n.*

per·vi·ous (pûr'vē-əs) *adj.* **1.** Open to passage or entrance; permeable. **2.** Open to arguments, ideas, or change. [Latin *pervius* : *per-,* through + *via,* way, road.] —**per'vi·ous·ly** *adv.* —**per'vi·ous·ness** *n.*

pe·se·ta (pə-sā'tə) *n.* The basic monetary unit of Spain. [Spanish, dim. of *peso,* peso.]

pes·ky (pĕs'kē) *adj.* -**ki·er,** -**ki·est.** *Informal.* Troublesome; annoying. [Prob. from PEST.] —**pes'ki·ly** *adv.* —**pes'ki·ness** *n.*

pe·so (pā'sō, pĕs'ō) *n., pl.* -**sos. 1.** The basic monetary unit of Mexico, the Republic of the Philippines, and certain Latin American countries. **2.** A coin or note worth one peso. [Spanish, from Latin *pēnsum,* weight, from *pendere,* to weigh.]

pes·si·mism (pĕs'ə-mĭz'əm) *n.* **1.** A tendency to take the gloomiest possible view of a situation. **2.** The doctrine or belief that the evil in the world outweighs the good. [French *pessimisme,* from Latin *pessimus,* worst.] —**pes'si·mist** *n.*

pes·si·mis·tic (pĕs'ə-mĭs'tĭk) *adj.* Of or marked by pessimism: *a pessimistic outlook.* —See Syns at **gloomy.** —**pes'si·mis'ti·cal·ly** *adv.*

pest (pĕst) *n.* **1.** An annoying person or thing; nuisance. **2.** An injurious plant or animal, esp. one harmful to man: *locusts, weevils, gophers, and other pests.* **3.** A pestilence. [French *peste,* plague, from Latin *pestis.*]

pes·ter (pĕs'tər) *tr.v.* To harass with petty annoyances; to bother. [Prob. from Old French *empestrer,* to tie up (an animal), impede.] —**pes'ter·er** *n.*

pes·ti·cide (pĕs'tĭ-sīd') *n.* Any chemical that is used to kill pests, esp. insects and rodents. —**pes'ti·cid'al** *adj.*

pes·tif·er·ous (pĕ-stĭf'ər-əs) *adj.* **1.** Producing, causing, or contaminated with an infectious disease. **2.** Morally evil or deadly; pernicious. **3.** Bothersome; annoying. —**pes·tif'er·ous·ly** *adv.*

pes·ti·lence (pĕs'tə-ləns) *n.* **1.** Any usu. fatal epidemic disease, esp. bubonic plague. **2.** An epidemic of such a disease. **3.** A pernicious, evil influence or agent.

pes·ti·lent (pĕs'tə-lənt) *adj.* Also **pes·ti·len·tial** (pĕs'tə-lĕn'shəl). **1.** Tending to cause death; deadly; fatal. **2.** Likely to cause an epidemic disease. **3.** Morally, socially, or politically harmful; pernicious. [Middle English, from Latin *pestilēns,* from *pestis,* plague.]

pes·tle (pĕs'əl, pĕs'təl) *n.* A club-shaped hand tool for grinding or mashing substances in a mortar. —*tr.v.* -**tled,** -**tling.** To pound, grind, or mash with a pestle. [Middle

English *pestel*, from Old French, from Latin *pistillum*.]

pet¹ (pĕt) *n.* **1.** An animal kept for amusement or companionship. **2.** A person or thing esp. loved or indulged; a favorite. **—modifier:** *a pet bird; the scientist's pet project.* **—v. pet·ted, pet·ting. —tr.v.** To stroke or caress gently. **—intr.v. Informal.** To engage in amorous fondling and caressing. [Orig. unknown.] **—pet'ter** *n.*

pet² (pĕt) *n.* A fit of bad temper or pique. **—intr.v. pet·ted, pet·ting.** To be sulky and peevish. [Orig. unknown.]

pet·al (pĕt'l) *n.* A separate, often brightly colored segment of a corolla. [From Greek *petalon,* leaf.] **—pet'aled** or **pet'alled** *adj.*

pe·tard (pə-tärd') *n.* A small bell-shaped bomb formerly used to blow apart a gate or wall. **—idiom. hoist with (or by) (one's) own petard.** Harmed or foiled by one's own cleverness; caught in one's own trap. [French *pétard,* from *péter,* to break wind, from Latin *pēdere.*]

pet·cock (pĕt'kŏk') *n.* A small valve or faucet used to drain or reduce pressure from pipes, radiators, and boilers. [Perh. PET(TY) + COCK.]

pe·ter (pē'tər) *intr.v.* **—peter out. 1.** To come to an end slowly; diminish; dwindle: *The mine petered out.* **2.** To become exhausted. [Orig. unknown.]

pet·i·ole (pĕt'ē-ōl') *n.* **1.** *Bot.* The stalk by which a leaf is attached to a stem; a leafstalk. **2.** *Zool.* The slender, stalklike connection between the thorax and abdomen in certain insects. [From Late Latin *petiolus,* fruit stalk, from Latin *pediculus,* dim. of *pēs,* foot.] **—pet'i·o·late** (-ə-lāt', -ē-ō'lĭt) *adj.*

pet·it (pĕt'ē) *adj.* Also **pet·ty.** *Law.* Lesser; minor: *petit larceny.* [Middle English, from Old French, small.]

pe·tite (pə-tēt') *adj.* Small, slender, and trim. **—See Syns at little.** [French, fem. of *petit,* small.]

pet·it four (pĕt'ē fôr', fōr, fōōr, pə-tē') *pl.* **pet·its fours** or **pet·it fours** (pĕt'ē fôrz', fōrz', fōōrz', pə-tē') A small, rich tea cake, frosted and decorated. [French, "small oven."]

pe·ti·tion (pə-tĭsh'ən) *n.* **1.** A solemn request to a superior authority; an entreaty. **2.** A formal written document requesting a right or a benefit from a person or group in authority. **3.** *Law.* **a.** A formal written application requesting a court for a specific judicial action: *a petition for appeal.* **b.** That which is asked for in any such request. **—tr.v. 1.** To address a petition to. **2.** To ask for by petition; request formally. **—intr.v.** To make a formal request: *petition for retrial.* [Middle English *peticioun,* from Old French *petition,* from Latin *petītiō,* solicitation, from *petere,* to seek, demand.] **—pe·ti'tion·ar'y** (pə-tĭsh'ə-nĕr'ē) *adj.* **—pe·ti'tion·er** *n.*

pet·it jury (pĕt'ē). Also **pet·ty jury.** A jury of 12 persons that sits at civil and criminal trials.

pet·it mal (pĕt'ē mäl', măl') *n.* A mild form of epilepsy characterized by frequent but transient lapses of consciousness and only rare spasms or falling. [French, "small illness."]

pet·it point (pĕt'ē point') **1.** A small stitch used in needlepoint. **2.** Needlepoint done with such a stitch. [French, "small point."]

Pe·trar·chan sonnet (pĭ-trär'kən). A sonnet form of Italian origin that consists of an octave with the rhyme pattern *abbaabba,* and a sestet of various rhyme patterns such as *cdccdc* or *cdecde.* [After *Petrarch* (1304–74), Italian poet.]

pet·rel (pĕt'rəl) *n.* Any of various sea birds of the order Procellariiformes, esp. the **storm petrel.** Also called **Mother Carey's chicken.** [Var. of earlier *pitteral.*]

pet·ri·fac·tion (pĕt'rə-făk'shən) *n.* Also **pet·ri·fi·ca·tion** (-fĭ-kā'shən). **1.** The process of petrifying; the conversion of organic matter into stone or a stony substance. **2.** The condition of being petrified, as by fear.

pet·ri·fy (pĕt'rə-fī') *v.* **-fied, -fy·ing. —tr.v. 1.** To convert (wood or other organic matter) into a stony mass by causing minerals to fill and finally replace its internal structure. **2.** To cause to become stiff or stonelike; deaden. **3.** To stun or paralyze with terror. **—intr.v.** To become stony, esp. by mineral replacement of organic matter. [Old French *petrifier* : Latin *petra,* stone, from Greek + *facere,* to make.]

petro-. A prefix meaning: **1.** Rock or stone: *petrology.* **2.** Petroleum: *petrochemical.* [From Greek *petros,* stone and *petra,* rock.]

pet·ro·chem·i·cal (pĕt'rō-kĕm'ĭ-kəl) *n.* Any chemical de-

rived from petroleum or natural gas.

pet·ro·dol·lar (pĕt'rō-dŏl'ər) *n.* A unit of hard currency, as a dollar, held by oil-exporting countries as a result of the sharp increases in oil prices since 1973.

pe·trog·ra·phy (pə-trŏg'rə-fē) *n.* The description and classification of rocks. **—pe·trog'ra·pher** *n.* **—pet'ro·graph'ic** (pĕt'rə-grăf'ĭk) or **pet'ro·graph'i·cal** *adj.* **—pet'ro·graph'i·cal·ly** *adv.*

pet·rol (pĕt'rəl) *n. Brit.* Gasoline. [From French (*essence de*) *pétrole,* "(essence of) petroleum," gasoline.]

pet·ro·la·tum (pĕt'rə-lā'təm) *n.* A jellylike, usu. colorless mixture of hydrocarbons obtained from petroleum, used in making ointments and lubricants. Also called **petroleum jelly.** [New Latin, from Medieval Latin *petroleum,* mineral oil.]

pe·tro·le·um (pə-trō'lē-əm) *n.* A thick, yellowish-black, flammable liquid mixture of hydrocarbons that occurs naturally, mainly below the surface of the earth. It is processed to make natural gas, gasoline, naphtha, kerosene, fuel and lubricating oils, paraffin wax, asphalt, and a wide variety of derivative products. Also called **crude oil.** [Medieval Latin *petroleum,* mineral oil.]

petroleum jelly. Petrolatum.

pe·trol·o·gy (pə-trŏl'ə-jē) *n.* The study of the origin, composition, structure, and alteration of rocks. **—pet'ro·log'ic** (pĕt'rə-lŏj'ĭk) or **pet'ro·log'i·cal** *adj.* **—pet'ro·log'i·cal·ly** *adv.* **—pe·trol'o·gist** *n.*

pet·ti·coat (pĕt'ē-kōt') *n.* A skirt, esp. a woman's slip or underskirt. [Middle English *petycote* : *pety,* small, + *cote,* a garment.]

pet·ti·fog·ger (pĕt'ē-fŏ'gər, -fŏg'ər) *n.* A petty, quibbling, unscrupulous lawyer. [Orig. unknown.]

pet·tish (pĕt'ĭsh) *adj.* Ill-tempered; peevish; petulant. [Prob. from PET (ill temper).] **—pet'tish·ly** *adv.*

pet·ty (pĕt'ē) *adj.* **-ti·er, -ti·est. 1.** Small or insignificant in quantity or quality; trivial: *petty grievances.* **2.** Of contemptibly narrow mind or views: *a petty outlook.* **3.** Spiteful; mean. **4.** Of subordinate or inferior rank: *a petty nobleman.* **5.** *Law.* Var. of **petit.** [Middle English *pety,* small, from French *petit.*] **—pet'ti·ly** *adv.* **—pet'ti·ness** *n.*

petty cash. A small fund of money for incidental expenses, as in an office.

petty jury. Var. of **petit jury.**

petty officer. A noncommissioned naval officer.

pet·u·lant (pĕch'ōō-lənt) *adj.* Unreasonably ill-tempered; peevish. **—See Syns at irritable.** [Old French, hot-tempered, from Latin *petulāns,* impudent, from *petere,* to attack.] **—pet'u·lance** or **pet'u·lan·cy** *n.* **—pet'u·lant·ly** *adv.*

pe·tu·nia (pə-tōōn'yə, -tyōōn') *n.* Any of various widely cultivated plants of the genus *Petunia,* native to South America, with funnel-shaped flowers in colors from white to purple. [From obs. French *petun,* tobacco, from Tupi *petyn.*]

pew (pyōō) *n.* A bench for the congregation in a church. [Middle English *pewe,* from Old French *puie,* raised seat, from Latin *podium,* podium, from Greek *podion,* base, dim. of *pous,* foot.]

pe·wee (pē'wē) *n.* Any of various small, olive-brown North American woodland birds of the genus *Contopus.* [Imit.]

pe·wit (pē'wĭt, pyōō'ĭt) *n.* A bird, the lapwing. [Imit.]

pew·ter (pyōō'tər) *n.* **1.** Any of numerous silver-gray alloys of tin with various amounts of antimony, copper, and lead, formerly used for kitchen utensils. **2.** Articles made of pewter. **—modifier:** *a pewter dish.* [Middle English *pewtre,* from Old French *peutre,* var. of *peltre,* tin.]

pe·yo·te (pā-ō'tē) *n.* Also **pe·yo·tl** (pā-ōt'l). **1.** A cactus, mescal. **2.** A hallucinatory drug derived from this cactus. [Mexican Spanish, from Nahuatl.]

pH *Chem.* A measure of the acidity or alkalinity of a solution, numerically equal to 7 for neutral solutions, increasing with increasing alkalinity and decreasing with increasing acidity. [P(OTENTIAL OF) H(YDROGEN).]

pha·e·ton (fā'ĭ-tn) *n.* A light, open, four-wheeled carriage, usu. drawn by a pair of horses. [French *phaéton,* after *Phaeton,* the son of Helios, who attempted to drive the chariot of the sun.]

phag·o·cyte (făg'ə-sīt') *n. Physiol.* A cell such as a leukocyte that engulfs and digests cells, microorganisms, or other foreign bodies in the bloodstream and tissues. [From Greek *phagein*, to eat + -CYTE.] —**phag′o·cyt′ic** (făg′ə-sĭt′ĭk) *adj.*

pha·lanx (fā′lăngks′; *Brit.* făl′ăngks′) *n., pl.* **-lanx·es** or **-lan·ges** (fə-lăn′jēz, fā-). **1.** A formation of infantry carrying overlapping shields and long spears, developed by Philip II of Macedonia in the 4th cent. B.C. **2.** Any close-knit or compact group or team: *a solid phalanx of riot police.* **3.** *pl.* **phalanges.** Any bone of a finger or toe. [Latin, from Greek, wooden beam, finger bone, line of battle.]

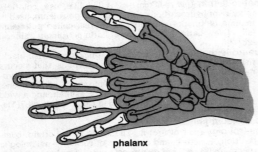

phalanx

phal·lus (făl′əs) *n., pl.* **phal·li** (făl′ī′) or **-lus·es.** **1.** The penis. **2.** A symbol or representation of the penis. [Late Latin, from Greek *phallos*.] —**phal′lic** (-ĭk) *adj.*

phan·tasm (făn′tăz′əm) *n.* **1.** Something apparently seen but having no physical reality; an illusion. **2.** An unreal mental image. **3.** A ghost. [Middle English *fantasme*, from Old French, from Latin *phantasma*, from Greek, from *phantazein*, to make visible, from *phainein*, to show.] —**phan·tas′mal** (făn-tăz′məl) or **phan·tas′mic** (-mĭk) *adj.*

phan·tas·ma·go·ri·a (făn-tăz′mə-gôr′ē-ə, -gōr′-) *n.* **1.** A fantastic sequence of many images passing before the eyes, as in dreams or fever. **2.** Such imagery as represented in art. [From the name of an early 19th-cent. magic-lantern show producing optical illusions.] —**phan·tas′ma·go′ric** or **phan·tas′ma·go′ri·cal** *adj.*

phan·ta·sy (făn′tə-sē) *n.* Var. of **fantasy.**

phan·tom (făn′təm) *n.* **1.** Something apparently seen, heard, or sensed, but having no physical reality. **2.** A ghost; specter. **3.** An image that appears only in the mind. —*adj.* **1.** Unreal; ghostlike. **2.** Phoney; fictitious: *a phantom caller.* [Middle English *fantome*, from Old French, from Latin *phantasma*, phantasm.]

Phar·aoh (fâr′ō, fā′rō) *n.* Also **phar·aoh.** A king of ancient Egypt. [Late Latin *Pharaō*, from Greek *Pharaō*, from Hebrew *par′ōh*, from Egyptian *pr′o*, "great house."] —**Phar′a·on′ic** (fêr′ā-ŏn′ĭk) *adj.*

phar·i·sa·ic (făr′ĭ-sā′ĭk) or **phar·i·sa·i·cal** (-ĭ-kəl) *adj.* **1.** Pharisaic. Of, relating to, or characteristic of the Pharisees. **2.** Hypocritically self-righteous and condemnatory. —**phar′i·sa′i·cal·ly** *adv.* —**phar′i·sa′i·cal·ness** *n.*

Phar·i·sa·ism (făr′ĭ-sā-ĭz′əm) *n.* Also **phar·i·see·ism** (făr′ĭ-sē-ĭz′əm). **1.** Pharisaism. The doctrines and practices of the Pharisees. **2.** Hypocritical observance of the letter of religious or moral law without regard for the spirit; sanctimoniousness.

phar·i·see (făr′ĭ-sē) *n.* **1.** Pharisee. A member of an ancient Jewish sect that emphasized strict interpretation and observance of the Mosaic law. **2.** A hypocritically self-righteous person. [Middle English *pharise*, from Old English *farise*, from Late Latin *pharisaeus*, from Greek *pharisaios*, from Aramaic *perīshayyā*, pl. of *perīsh*, "separated."]

phar·ma·ceu·ti·cal (fär′mə-sōō′tĭ-kəl) or **phar·ma·ceu·tic** (-tĭk) *adj.* Of pharmacy or pharmacists. —*n.* A pharmaceutical product or preparation. [From Late Latin *pharmaceuticus*, from Greek *pharmakeutikos*, from *pharmakeutēs*, druggist, from *pharmakon*, drug.] —**phar′ma·ceu′ti·cal·ly** *adv.*

phar·ma·ceu·tics (fär′mə-sōō′tĭks) *n.* (*used with a sing. verb*). The science of preparing and dispensing drugs.

phar·ma·cist (fär′mə-sĭst) *n.* A person trained in pharmacy; druggist.

pharmaco-. A prefix meaning drugs: **pharmacology.** [From Greek *pharmakon*, drug, poison, potion.]

phar·ma·col·o·gy (fär′mə-kŏl′ə-jē) *n.* The science of drugs, including their composition, uses, and effects. —**phar′ma·co·log′ic** (-kə-lŏj′ĭk) or **phar′ma·co·log′i·cal** *adj.* —**phar′ma·co·log′i·cal·ly** *adv.* —**phar′ma·col′o·gist** *n.*

phar·ma·co·poe·ia (fär′mə-kə-pē′ə) *n., pl.* **-ias.** **1.** A book that contains an official list of medicinal drugs together with information on their preparation and use. **2.** A collection or stock of drugs. [PHARMACO- + Greek *poiein*, to make.] —**phar′ma·co·poe′ial** (-pē′əl) *adj.*

phar·ma·cy (fär′mə-sē) *n., pl.* **-cies.** **1.** The art of preparing and dispensing drugs. **2.** A place where drugs are sold; drugstore. [Middle English *farmacie*, from Old French, from Late Latin *pharmacia*, from Greek *pharmakeia*, from *pharmakon*, drug.]

pharyng-. Var. of **pharyngo-.**

pha·ryn·ge·al (fə-rĭn′jē-əl, -jəl, făr′ĭn-jē′əl) *adj.* Of, in, or from the pharynx. —*n.* A speech sound produced in the pharynx.

phar·yn·gi·tis (făr′ĭn-jī′tĭs) *n.* Inflammation of the pharynx.

pharyngo- or **pharyng-.** A prefix meaning pharynx: **pharyngitis.** [From Greek *pharungo-*, from *pharunx*, pharynx.]

phar·ynx (făr′ĭngks) *n., pl.* **pha·ryn·ges** (fə-rĭn′jēz) or **phar·ynx·es.** The section of the digestive tract that extends from the nasal cavities to the larynx, there becoming continuous with the esophagus. [Greek *pharunx*, throat.]

phase (fāz) *n.* **1.** A distinct stage of development. **2.** A temporary way of behaving. **3.** An aspect; part: *every phase of the operation.* **4.** Any of the forms, recurring in cycles, in which the moon or a planet appears. **5.** A uniform part of a physical system that is distinct and separable from the rest: *Steam and ice are phases of water.* **6.** *Biol.* A characteristic form or appearance that occurs in a cycle or that distinguishes some individuals of a group. —*tr.v.* **phased, phas·ing.** To plan or carry out so as to progress in distinct stages. —*phrasal verbs.* **phase in.** To introduce in stages. **phase out.** To eliminate in stages. [From Greek *phasis*, appearance, phase of the moon, from *phainein*, to show.]

pheas·ant (fĕz′ənt) *n., pl.* **-ants** or **-ant.** Any of various birds of the family Phasianidae, native to the Old World, with long tails and, in the males of many species, brilliantly colored plumage. [Middle English *fesant*, from Old French *fesan*, from Latin *phasiānus*, from Greek *phasianos*, "the Phasian (bird)," after the *Phasis* River in the Caucasus.]

pheasant

pheno- or **phen-.** *Chem.* A prefix meaning: **1.** Showing or displaying: **phenotype.** **2.** A compound derived from, containing, or related to benzene: **phenol.** [From Greek *phainein*, to show.]

phe·no·bar·bi·tal (fē′nō-bär′bĭ-tôl′) *n.* A white, shiny, crystalline compound, $C_{12}H_{12}N_2O_3$, used in medicine as a sedative and hypnotic. [PHENO- + BARBITAL.]

phe·nol (fē′nôl′, -nŏl′) *n.* **1.** A caustic, poisonous, white, crystalline compound, C_6H_5OH, derived from benzene and used in various resins, plastics, disinfectants, and pharmaceuticals. Also called **carbolic acid.** **2.** Any of a class of aromatic organic compounds with at least one hydroxyl group attached directly to the benzene ring. [PHEN(O)- + -OL.]

phe·nol·phthal·ein (fē′nəl-thăl′ēn′, -thăl′ē-ĭn, -thā′lēn′, -thā′lē-ĭn) *n.* A pale-yellow crystalline powder, $(C_6H_4OH)_2C_2O_2C_6H_4$, used as an acid-base indicator and as a cathartic. [PHENOL + *phthalein*, a dye.]

phe·nom·e·nal (fĭ-nŏm′ə-nəl) *adj.* **1.** Of or constituting a phenomenon. **2.** Extraordinary; outstanding; remarkable. —See Syns at **fabulous.** —**phe·nom′e·nal·ly** *adv.*

phe·nom·e·non (fĭ-nŏm′ə-nŏn′) *n., pl.* **-na** (nə) or **-nons.** **1.** Any occurrence or fact that can be perceived by the senses. **2. a.** An unusual, significant, or unaccountable fact or occurrence; a marvel. **b.** A person outstanding for some extreme quality or achievement; paragon. **3.** That which appears real to the senses, regardless of whether its underlying existence is proved or its nature understood. [Late Latin *phaenomenon*, from Greek *phainomenon*, pres. part. of *phainesthai*, to appear, from *phainein*, to show.]

phe·no·type (fē′nə-tīp′) *n.* The observable characteristics of an organism that result from the interaction of genetic and environmental factors. [PHENO- + TYPE.] —**phe′no·typ′ic** (-tĭp′ĭk) or **phe′no·typ′i·cal** *adj.* —**phe′no·typ′i·cal·ly** *adv.*

phen·yl (fĕn′əl, fē′nəl) *n.* The organic radical C₆H₅, derived from benzene by the removal of one hydrogen atom. [PHEN(O)- + -YL.] —**phe·nyl′ic** (fə-nĭl′ĭk) *adj.*

phen·yl·al·a·nine (fĕn′əl-ăl′ə-nēn′, fē′nəl-) *n.* A natural amino acid, C₆H₅CH₂CH(NH₂)COOH, that occurs as a constituent of many proteins and is extracted for use as a dietary supplement.

phe·nix (fē′nĭks) *n.* Var. of **phoenix.**

pher·o·mone (fĕr′ə-mōn′) *n.* A chemical secreted by an animal, as an insect, that serves to communicate to another of the same species and elicit a specific response. [Greek *pherein*, to carry + (HOR)MONE.]

phi (fī) *n.* The 21st letter in the Greek alphabet, written Φ, φ. [From Greek *phei*.]

phi·al (fī′əl) *n.* A small bottle, a vial. [Middle English *fiole*, from Old French, from Old Provençal *fiola*, from Latin *phiala*, vessel, from Greek *phialē*, broad.]

Phi Be·ta Kap·pa (fī′ bā′tə kăp′ə). An honorary fraternity of college students and graduates whose members are chosen on the basis of high academic standing. [From the initials of the Greek phrase *philosophia biou kubernētēs*, "philosophy the guide of life" (motto of the society).]

-phila. A suffix for a biological taxon meaning having an affinity or preference for: **gypsophila.** [Latin, from *-philus*, loving, from Greek *philos*.]

phi·lan·der (fĭ-lăn′dər) *intr.v.* To engage in love affairs frivolously or casually. [From *Philander*, a traditional literary name for a lover.] —**phi·lan′der·er** *n.*

phil·an·throp·ic (fĭl′ən-thrŏp′ĭk) or **phil·an·throp·i·cal** (-ĭ-kəl) *adj.* Of or engaged in philanthropy; charitable.

phi·lan·thro·pist (fĭ-lăn′thrə-pĭst) *n.* A person who practices philanthropy.

phi·lan·thro·py (fĭ-lăn′thrə-pē) *n., pl.* **-pies.** **1.** The effort or desire to increase the well-being of mankind, as by charitable aid or donations. **2.** Love of mankind in general. **3.** An action or institution designed to promote human welfare. [Late Latin *philanthrōpia*, from Greek *philanthrōpia*, benevolence : *philos*, loving + *anthrōpos*, mankind.]

phi·lat·e·ly (fĭ-lăt′l-ē) *n.* The collection and study of postage stamps, postmarks, and related materials; stamp collecting. [French *philatélie* : Greek *philos*, loving + *atelēs*, tax-free (a stamped letter is tax-free to the recipient).] —**phil′a·tel′ic** (fĭl′ə-tĕl′ĭk) *adj.* —**phi·lat′e·list** *n.*

-phile or **-phil.** A suffix indicating someone having love, affinity, or preference for: **Anglophile.** [From Greek *philos*, beloved, dear, loving.]

phil·har·mon·ic (fĭl′här-mŏn′ĭk, fĭl′ər-) *adj.* **1.** Devoted to or appreciative of music. **2.** Of or relating to a symphony orchestra. —*n.* Also **Philharmonic.** A symphony orchestra or the group that supports it. [French *philharmonique*, from Italian *filarmonico* : Greek *philos*, loving + *harmonikos*, harmonic.]

-philia. A suffix meaning: **1.** Tendency toward: **hemophilia. 2.** An abnormal attraction to: **necrophilia.** [From Greek *philia*, friendship, from *philos*, loving.]

-philic. Var. of **-philous.**

Phi·lip·pi·ans (fĭ-lĭp′ē-ənz) *n.* See table at **Bible.**

phi·lip·pic (fĭ-lĭp′ĭk) *n.* Any passionate speech intended to arouse opposition; tirade.

Phil·is·tine (fĭl′ĭ-stēn′, fĭ-lĭs′tĭn, -tēn′) *n.* **1.** A member of an ancient people in Palestine who were enemies of the He-

brews. **2.** Also **philistine.** A conventional or narrow-minded person who is antagonistic to art and culture. —*adj.* **1.** Of the ancient Philistines. **2.** Also **philistine.** Conventional and narrow-minded.

phil·o·den·dron (fĭl′ə-dĕn′drən) *n., pl.* **-drons** or **-dra** (-drə). Any of various climbing tropical American plants of the genus *Philodendron*, many of which are cultivated as house plants. [From Greek : *philos*, loving + *dendron*, tree.]

phi·lol·o·gy (fĭ-lŏl′ə-jē) *n.* **1.** The study of linguistics, esp. as they have developed through time. **2.** Literary study or classical scholarship. [French *philologie*, from Old French, from Latin *philologia*, love of learning, from Greek : *philos*, loving + *logos*, word, reason.] —**phil′o·log′ic** (fĭl′ə-lŏj′ĭk) or **phil′o·log′i·cal** *adj.* —**phil′o·log′i·cal·ly** *adv.* —**phi·lol′o·gist** *n.*

phi·o·mel (fĭl′ə-mĕl′) *n.* Also **phil·o·me·la** (fĭl′ə-mā′lə, -mē′-). *Poet.* A nightingale. [From PHILOMELA.]

Phil·o·me·la (fĭl′ə-mā′lə, -mē′-) *n. Gk. Myth.* A princess of Athens who, after being raped and having had her tongue cut out by Tereus, was turned into a bird.

phi·los·o·pher (fĭ-lŏs′ə-fər) *n.* **1. a.** A person who loves and seeks wisdom. **b.** A student of or specialist in philosophy. **2.** A calm, patient person. [Middle English *philosophre*, from Old French *philosophe*, from Latin *philosophus*, from Greek *philosophos* : *philos*, loving + *sophos*, wise.]

philosophers' stone. An imaginary substance sought by medieval alchemists because of its supposed power of transmuting base metals into gold.

phil·o·soph·i·cal (fĭl′ə-sŏf′ĭ-kəl) or **phil·o·soph·ic** (-ĭk) *adj.* **1.** Of, relating to, or based on a system of philosophy. **2.** Calm; serene: *He accepted his fate with philosophical resignation.* —**phil′o·soph′i·cal·ly** *adv.*

phi·los·o·phize (fĭ-lŏs′ə-fīz′) *intr.v.* **-phized, -phiz·ing. 1.** To reason or think as a philosopher. **2.** To develop and express one's opinions, ideas, etc., as a philosophy. —**phi·los′o·phiz′er** *n.*

phi·los·o·phy (fĭ-lŏs′ə-fē) *n., pl.* **-phies. 1.** The study by logical reasoning of the basic truths and laws governing the universe, nature, life, morals, etc. **2.** A formal system of ideas based upon such study: *Aristotelian philosophy.* **3.** A set of rules or principles of a specific field or study or other activity: *the philosophy of science.* **4.** A personal set of opinions about life, the world, etc.

-philous or **-philic.** A suffix meaning a love of or attraction for something: **xerophilous.** [From Greek *philos*, beloved, dear, loving.]

phil·ter (fĭl′tər) *n.* Also **phil·tre. 1.** A love potion. **2.** Any magic potion or charm. [Old French *philtre*, potion, from Latin *philtrum*, from Greek *philtron*, love charm, from *philos*, dear, loving.]

phleb-. Var. of **phlebo-.**

phle·bi·tis (flĭ-bī′tĭs) *n.* Inflammation of a vein. —**phle·bit′ic** (-bĭt′ĭk) *adj.*

phlebo- or **phleb-.** A prefix meaning vein: **phlebitis.** [Greek, from *phleps*, blood vessel, vein.]

phlegm (flĕm) *n.* **1.** Stringy, thick mucus secreted in the respiratory tract. **2.** One of the four humors of ancient physiology. **3.** Sluggishness of temperament; apathy. **4.** Calm self-possession; equanimity. [Middle English *fleume*, from Old French, from Late Latin *phlegma*, body moisture, from Greek, flame, inflammation, phlegm, from *phlegein*, to burn.] —**phlegm′y** (flĕm′ē) *adj.*

phleg·mat·ic (flĕg-măt′ĭk) or **phleg·mat·i·cal** (-ĭ-kəl) *adj.* **1.** Of or like phlegm; phlegmy. **2.** Having or suggesting a calm, stolid temperament; unemotional. [Middle English *flaumatike*, from Old French *flaumatique*, from Late Latin *phlegmaticus*, like phlegm, from Greek *phlegmatikos*, having phlegm, from *phlegma*, phlegm.]

phlo·em (flō′ĕm′) *n. Bot.* The food-conducting tissue of vascular plants, consisting of sieve tubes and other cellular material. [German *Phloem*, from Greek *phloos*, bark.]

phlox (flŏks) *n., pl.* **phlox** or **phlox·es.** Any plant of the genus *Phlox*, chiefly of North America, with lance-shaped leaves and clusters of white, red, or purple flowers. [Latin, a flower, from Greek, wallflower, flame.]

pho·bi·a (fō′bē-ə) *n.* A persistent, abnormal, or illogical fear of something. [From -PHOBIA.] —**pho′bic** (-bĭk) *adj.*

-phobia. A suffix meaning persistent, illogical, abnormal,

| ă pat | ā pay | â care | ä father | ĕ pet | ē be | hw which | ĭ pit | ī tie | î pier | ŏ pot | ō toe | ô paw, for | oi noise |
| ōō took | ōō boot | ou out | th thin | th this | ŭ cut | | û urge | zh vision | ə about, item, edible, gallop, circus | | | | |

or intense fear: **acrophobia.** [From Late Latin, from Greek, from *phobos,* fear, flight.]

phoe·be (fē′bē) *n.* Any of several small dull-colored North American birds of the genus *Sayornis.* [Imit.]

Phoe·be (fē′bē) *n. Gk. Myth.* Artemis.

Phoe·bus (fē′bəs) *n. Gk. Myth.* Apollo.

Phoe·ni·cian (fə-nĭsh′ən, -nē′shən) *n.* **1.** A native, inhabitant, or subject of ancient Phoenicia. **2.** The Semitic language of ancient Phoenicia. —**Phoe·ni′cian** *adj.*

phoe·nix (fē′nĭks) *n.* Also **phe·nix.** A fabled bird of Arabia said to consume itself by fire every 500 years and to rise renewed from its own ashes. [Middle English *fenix,* from Old French, from Latin *phoenix,* from Greek *phoinix.*]

phon-. Var. of **phono-.**

phone¹ (fōn) *n. Ling.* Any individual speech sound. [From Greek *phōnē,* sound, voice.]

phone² (fōn) *n. Informal.* A telephone. —*v.* **phoned, phon·ing.** *Informal.* —*intr.v.* To telephone. —*tr.v.* **1.** To telephone (someone). **2.** To transmit by telephone: *phone in a report.* [Short for TELEPHONE.]

-phone. A suffix meaning a sound or sound-emitting device: **radiophone.** [From Greek *phōnē,* sound, voice.]

pho·neme (fō′nēm′) *n. Ling.* One of the set of the smallest units of speech that distinguish one utterance or word from another in a given language. The *m* of *mat* and the *b* of *bat* are two English phonemes. [French *phonème,* from Greek *phōnēma,* an utterance, from *phōnē,* sound, voice.] —**pho·ne′mic** (fə-nē′mĭk, fō-) *adj.* —**pho·ne′mi·cal·ly** *adv.*

pho·net·ic (fə-nĕt′ĭk) *adj.* **1.** Of or pertaining to phonetics. **2.** Representing the sounds of speech with a set of distinct symbols, each denoting a single sound. [Greek *phōnētikos,* from *phōnē,* sound, voice.] —**pho·net′i·cal·ly** *adv.*

pho·ne·ti·cian (fō′nĭ-tĭsh′ən) *n.* A student of or expert in phonetics.

pho·net·ics (fə-nĕt′ĭks) *n. (used with a sing. verb).* **1.** The branch of linguistics that deals with the study of the sounds of speech and their representation by written symbols. **2.** The system of sounds of a particular language.

pho·ney (fō′nē) *adj. & n.* Var. of **phony.**

phon·ic (fŏn′ĭk) *adj.* Of or involving sound, esp. speech sound. —**phon′i·cal·ly** *adv.*

phon·ics (fŏn′ĭks) *n. (used with a sing. verb).* **1.** The study of sound; acoustics. **2.** The use of elementary phonetics in the teaching of reading.

phono- or **phon-.** A prefix meaning sound or voice: **phonograph.** [Greek *phōnē,* sound, voice.]

pho·no·gram (fō′nə-grăm′) *n.* A character or symbol, as in a phonetic alphabet, that represents a word or phoneme in speech.

pho·no·graph (fō′nə-grăf′) *n.* A machine that reproduces sound recorded on a grooved disc. —**pho′no·graph′ic** *adj.*

pho·nog·ra·phy (fə-nŏg′rə-fē, fō-) *n.* The science or practice of transcribing speech by means of symbols that represent sounds; phonetic transcription.

pho·nol·o·gy (fə-nŏl′ə-jē, fō-) *n.* The science of speech sounds, including phonetics and phonemics. —**pho′no·log′ic** (fō′nə-lŏj′ĭk) or **pho′no·log′i·cal** *adj.* —**pho′no·log′i·cal·ly** *adv.* —**pho·nol′o·gist** *n.*

pho·non (fō′nŏn′) *n. Physics.* The quantum of acoustic or vibrational energy, considered a discrete particle and used esp. in mathematical models to calculate thermal and vibrational properties of solids. [PHON(O)- + -ON.]

pho·ny (fō′nē) *adj.* **-ni·er, -ni·est.** Also **pho·ney, -ni·er, -ni·est.** *Informal.* Not genuine or real; fake. —*n., pl.* **-nies.** Also **pho·ney,** *pl.* **-neys** or **-nies.** *Informal.* **1.** Something not genuine; a fake. **2.** An insincere or hypocritical person; a fake. —See Syns at **impostor.** [Orig. unknown.] —**pho′ni·ly** *adv.* —**pho′ni·ness** *n.*

-phony. A suffix meaning sound: **telephony.** [Greek *-phōnia,* from *phōnē,* sound.]

-phore. A suffix meaning a bearer or producer of: **semaphore.** [From Greek *-phoros,* bearing, from *pherein,* to bear.]

-phorous. A suffix meaning bearing or producing: **electrophorous.** [Greek *-phoros,* from *pherein,* to bear.]

phos-. A prefix meaning light: **phosgene.** [Greek *phōs,* light.]

phos·gene (fŏs′jēn′, fŏz′-) *n.* A colorless volatile liquid or gas, COCl₂, used as a poison gas and in making glass, dyes, resins, and plastics. [PHOS- (from the former method of obtaining the compound by exposure to sunlight) + -GENE.]

phos·phate (fŏs′fāt′) *n.* **1.** *Chem.* Any salt or ester of phosphoric acid. **2.** A fertilizer containing phosphorus compounds. **3.** A carbonated beverage of water, flavoring, and a small amount of phosphoric acid. [French *phosphat,* from *phosphore,* phosphorous.] —**phos·phat′ic** (fŏs-făt′ĭk) *adj.*

phos·phide (fŏs′fīd′) *n.* Also **phos·phid** (fŏs′fĭd). A compound of phosphorus and a more electropositive element. [PHOSPH(ORUS) + -IDE.]

phos·phite (fŏs′fīt′) *n.* Any salt of phosphorous acid. [PHOSPH(ORUS) + -ITE.]

phos·phor (fŏs′fər, -fôr′) *n.* **1.** Any substance that can be stimulated to emit light by incident radiation. **2.** Something exhibiting phosphorescence. [French *phosphore,* from New Latin *phosphorus,* phosphorus.]

phos·pho·resce (fŏs′fə-rĕs′) *intr.v.* **-resced, -resc·ing.** To persist in emitting light, with little or no heat, after exposure to and removal of a source of radiation. [Prob. a back-formation from PHOSPHORESCENE.]

phos·pho·res·cence (fŏs′fə-rĕs′əns) *n.* **1.** The process or phenomenon by which a body emits light as a result of and for some time after being exposed to radiation. **2.** The generation of light by a living thing; bioluminescence. **3.** The light that results from either of these. [PHOSPHOR + -ESCENCE.]

phos·pho·res·cent (fŏs′fə-rĕs′ənt) *adj.* Having or showing the property of phosphorescence. —**phos′pho·res′cent·ly** *adv.*

phos·phor·ic (fŏs-fôr′ĭk, -fŏr′-) *adj.* Of, pertaining to, or containing phosphorus, esp. in a higher valence state than that of a phosphorous compound.

phosphoric acid. A clear colorless liquid, H₃PO₄, used in fertilizers, soaps and detergents, food flavoring, pharmaceuticals, and animal feed.

phos·pho·rous (fŏs′fər-əs, fŏs-fôr′əs, -fŏr′-) *adj.* Of, pertaining to, or containing phosphorus, esp. with valence 3.

phosphorous acid. A white or yellowish hygroscopic crystalline solid, H₃PO₃, used as a reducing agent and to produce phosphite salts.

phos·pho·rus (fŏs′fər-əs) *n.* **1.** *Symbol* **P** A highly reactive, poisonous, nonmetallic element occurring naturally in phosphates, esp. apatite, and existing in three allotropic forms, white (sometimes yellow), red, and black, that is an essential constituent of protoplasm and, depending on the allotropic form, is used in safety matches, pyrotechnics, incendiary shells, fertilizers, glass, and steel. Atomic number 15; atomic weight 30.9738; melting point (white) 44.1°C; boiling point 280°C; specific gravity (white) 1.82; valences 3, 5. **2.** Any phosphorescent substance. [From Greek *phōsphoros,* "light-bearing" (so named from the fact that white phosphorus is phosphorescent in air) : *phōs,* light + *phoros,* bearing.]

phot-. Var. of **photo-.**

pho·tic (fō′tĭk) *adj.* **1.** Of or relating to light. **2.** *Biol.* Pertaining to the production of light by organisms. **3.** Penetrated by sunlight: *the photic zone of the ocean.*

pho·to (fō′tō) *n., pl.* **-tos.** *Informal.* A photograph.

photo- or **phot-.** A prefix meaning: **1.** Light: **photic. 2.** Photographic: **photomontage.** [Greek *phōs,* light.]

pho·to·chem·is·try (fō′tō-kĕm′ĭ-strē) *n.* The chemistry of the interactions of radiant energy and chemical systems. —**pho′to·chem′i·cal** *adj.*

pho·to·com·po·si·tion (fō′tō-kŏm′pə-zĭsh′ən) *n.* The preparation of manuscript for printing by the projection of images of type characters on photographic film.

pho·to·cop·y (fō′tō-kŏp′ē) *tr.v.* **-cop·ied, -cop·y·ing.** To make a photographic reproduction of (printed or pictorial material). —*n., pl.* **-cop·ies.** A photographic reproduction of graphic material. —**pho′to·cop′i·er** (-ē-ər) *n.*

pho·to·e·lec·tric (fō′tō-ĭ-lĕk′trĭk) or **pho·to·e·lec·tri·cal** (-trĭ-kəl) *adj.* Of or having to do with electrical effects that result from or depend on the presence of light.

photoelectric cell. An electronic device with an electrical output that varies in response to the intensity of the light striking it. Also called **electric eye.**

ă pat   ā pay   â care   ä father   ĕ pet   ē be   hw which
ŏŏ took   ōŏ boot   ou out   th thin   *th* this   ŭ cut
ĭ pit   ī tie   î pier   ŏ pot   ō toe   ô paw, for   oi noise
û urge   zh vision   ə about, item, edible, gallop, circus

pho·to·e·lec·tron (fō'tō-ĭ-lĕk'trŏn') *n.* An electron released or ejected from a substance struck by visible light or other electromagnetic radiation.

pho·to·en·grave (fō'tō-ĕn-grāv') *tr.v.* **-graved, -grav·ing.** To reproduce by photoengraving. **—pho'to·en·grav'er** *n.*

pho·to·en·grav·ing (fō'tō-ĕn-grā'vĭng) *n.* **1.** The process of reproducing graphic material by photographing it on a metal plate and then etching the plate for printing. **2.** A plate prepared by this method. **3.** A reproduction made by this method.

photo finish. 1. A race in which the leading contestants cross the finish line so close together that the winner must be determined by a photograph taken at the moment of crossing. **2.** Any close contest.

pho·to·gen·ic (fō'tə-jĕn'ĭk) *adj.* **1.** Attractive as a subject for photography. **2.** *Biol.* Producing or emitting light; phosphorescent. **—pho'to·gen'i·cal·ly** *adv.*

pho·to·gram·me·try (fō'tə-grăm'ĭ-trē) *n.* The science of making maps, scale drawings, or precise measurements by aerial or other photography. [PHOTO + -GRAM + -METRY.]

pho·to·graph (fō'tə-grăf') *n.* An image formed on a light-sensitive surface by a camera and developed by chemical means to produce a positive print. *—tr.v.* To take a photograph of. *—intr.v.* **1.** To practice photography. **2.** To be the subject for photographs.

pho·tog·ra·pher (fə-tŏg'rə-fər) A person who takes photographs, esp. as a profession.

pho·to·graph·ic (fō'tə-grăf'ĭk) or **pho·to·graph·i·cal** (-ĭ-kəl) *adj.* **1.** Of, relating to, or consisting of photography or a photograph. **2.** Used in photography: *a photographic lens.* **3.** Resembling a photograph, as in accuracy and detail. **4.** Capable of forming accurate and lasting impressions: *a photographic memory.* **—pho'to·graph'i·cal·ly** *adv.*

pho·tog·ra·phy (fə-tŏg'rə-fē) *n.* **1.** The process or technique of creating images on light-sensitive surfaces. **2.** The art, practice, or profession of making photographs.

pho·to·gra·vure (fō'tə-grə-vyŏor') *n.* The process of printing from an intaglio plate, etched according to a photographic image. [PHOTO- + GRAVURE.]

pho·tom·e·ter (fō-tŏm'ĭ-tər) *n.* An instrument for measuring a property of light, esp. its intensity.

pho·tom·e·try (fō-tŏm'ĭ-trē) *n.* The measurement of the intensity, brightness, or other properties of light. **—pho'to·met'ric** (-mĕt'rĭk) or **pho'to·met'ri·cal** *adj.*

pho·to·mi·cro·graph (fō'tō-mī'krə-grăf') *n.* A photograph made through a microscope. *—tr.v.* To make (a photograph) through a microscope. **—pho'to·mi'cro·graph'ic** *adj.* **—pho'to·mi·crog'ra·phy** *n.*

pho·to·mon·tage (fō'tō-mŏn-täzh', -môn-) *n.* **1.** The technique of making a picture by assembling pieces of photographs, often in combination with other types of graphic material. **2.** A composite picture produced by this technique.

pho·ton (fō'tŏn') *n.* The quantum of electromagnetic energy, gen. regarded as a discrete particle with zero mass, no electric charge, and an indefinitely long lifetime. [PHOT(O)- + -ON.]

pho·to·sen·si·tive (fō'tō-sĕn'sĭ-tĭv) *adj.* Sensitive to light. **—pho'to·sen'si·tiv'i·ty** *n.*

pho·to·sphere (fō'tə-sfîr') *n.* The surface of a star, esp. of the sun. **—pho'to·spher'ic** (-sfîr'ĭk, -sfĕr'-) *adj.*

Pho·to·stat (fō'tə-stăt') *n.* A trademark for a device used to make quick copies of written or printed material. **2.** A copy made by Photostat. *—v.* **-stat·ed** or **-stat·ted, -stat·ing** or **-stat·ting.** *—tr.v.* To make a copy of by Photostat. *—intr.v.* To make a copy by Photostat.

pho·to·syn·the·sis (fō'tō-sĭn'thĭ-sĭs) *n.* The process by which chlorophyll-containing cells in green plants convert incident light to chemical energy and synthesize organic compounds from inorganic compounds, esp. carbohydrates from carbon dioxide and water, with the simultaneous release of oxygen. **—pho'to·syn·thet'ic** (-sĭn-thĕt'ĭk) *adj.* **—pho'to·syn·thet'i·cal·ly** *adv.*

pho·to·tro·pism (fō-tŏt'rə-pĭz'əm) *n. Biol.* Growth or movement in response to a source of light. **—pho'to·trop'ic** (fō'tə-trŏp'ĭk) *adj.* **—pho'to·trop'i·cal·ly** *adv.*

phrase (frāz) *n.* **1.** Any sequence of words intended to have meaning. **2.** A brief and cogent expression, esp. one in common usage. **3.** *Gram.* A group of words that is mean-

ingful but lacks the subject and predicate of a complete sentence. For example, *on the table* is a phrase. **4.** *Mus.* A short segment of a composition, usu. consisting of from four to eight measures. *—tr.v.* **phrased, phras·ing. 1.** To express in spoken or written words: *He phrased his answer carefully.* **2.** To pace or mark off (something read aloud or spoken) by pauses. **3.** *Mus.* **a.** To divide (a passage) into phrases. **b.** To combine (notes) in a phrase. [Latin *phrasis,* from Greek, speech, style of speech, from *phrazein,* to show, explain.] **—phras'al** *adj.* **—phras'al·ly** *adv.*

phra·se·ol·o·gy (frā'zē-ŏl'ə-jē) *n., pl.* **-gies. 1.** The manner in which words and phrases are used in speech or writing; style. **2.** A set of expressions used by a particular person or group: *nautical phraseology.* **—phra'se·o·log'i·cal** (-ə-lŏj'ĭ-kəl) *adj.*

phras·ing (frā'zĭng) *n.* **1.** Phraseology. **2.** *Mus.* The manner in which a phrase is rendered or interpreted.

phre·net·ic (frə-nĕt'ĭk) or **phre·net·i·cal** (-ĭ-kəl) *adj.* Var. of frenetic.

phre·nol·o·gy (frĭ-nŏl'ə-jē) *n.* The practice of trying to determine character and mental capacity from the shape and irregularities of a person's skull. [Greek *phrēn,* mind + -LOGY.] **—phren'o·log'ic** (frĕn'ə-lŏj'ĭk, frē'nə-) or **phren'o·log'i·cal** *adj.* **—phre·nol'o·gist** *n.*

phthi·sis (thī'sĭs, thĭs'ĭs) *n.* **1.** Tuberculosis of the lungs. **2.** Wasting away or emaciation and atrophy of the body or part of the body. [Latin, from Greek, from *phthinein,* to decay, waste away.]

phy·co·my·cete (fī'kō-mī'sēt', -mī-sēt') *n.* Any of various fungi that resemble algae, including certain molds and mildews. [From Greek *phukos,* seaweed + -MYCETE.] **—phy'co·my·ce'tous** *adj.*

phy·la (fī'lə) *n.* Plural of phylum.

phy·lac·ter·y (fĭ-lăk'tə-rē) *n., pl.* **-ies. 1.** *Judaism.* Either of two small leather boxes that contain strips of parchment inscribed with quotations from the Hebrew Scriptures, with one strapped to the forehead and the other to the left arm by Jewish men during morning worship. **2.** An amulet; charm. [Middle English *filakterie,* from Late Latin *phylactērium,* from Greek *phulaktērion,* safeguard, from *phulax,* guard.]

phy·le (fī'lē) *n., pl.* **-lae** (-lē'). A citizens' organization constituting the largest political subdivision of an ancient Greek city-state. [Greek *phulē,* tribe.]

-phyll. A suffix meaning leaf: **chlorophyll.** [From Greek *phullon,* leaf.]

phyllo- or **phyll-.** A prefix meaning leaf: **phyllotaxy.** [From Greek *phullon,* leaf.]

phyl·lo·tax·y (fĭl'ə-tăk'sē) *n.* Also **phyl·lo·tax·is** (fĭl'ə-tăk'sĭs). *Bot.* **1.** The arrangement of leaves on a stem. **2.** The principles governing leaf arrangement. [PHYLLO- + -TAXIS.]

phy·log·e·ny (fī-lŏj'ə-nē) *n., pl.* **-nies.** Also **phy·lo·gen·e·sis** (fī'lō-jĕn'ĭ-sĭs) *pl.* **-ses** (-sēz'). The evolutionary development of any species of plant or animal. [From Greek *phulon,* tribe, race + -GENY.] **—phy'lo·ge·net'ic** (fī'lō-jə-nĕt'ĭk) or **phy'lo·gen'ic** (-jĕn'ĭk) *adj.* **—phy'lo·ge·net'i·cal·ly** *adv.*

phy·lum (fī'ləm) *n., pl.* **-la** (-lə). *Biol.* A taxonomic division of the animal kingdom or, less commonly, the plant kingdom, next above a class in size. [From Greek *phulon,* tribe, class, race.]

physi-. Var. of physio-.

phys·ic (fĭz'ĭk) *n.* **1.** Any medicine or drug. **2.** A cathartic. **3.** *Archaic.* The profession of medicine. *—tr.v.* **-icked, -ick·ing. 1.** *Archaic.* To treat with or as if with medicine. **2.** To act upon as a cathartic. [Middle English *fisike,* from Old French *fisique,* from Latin *physica,* natural medicine or science, from Greek *phusikē,* from *phusikos,* natural, from *phusis,* nature, from *phuein,* to make grow.]

phys·i·cal (fĭz'ĭ-kəl) *adj.* **1.** Of or pertaining to the body: *physical strength.* **2.** Of material things: *physical environment.* **3.** Of non-living matter and energy as distinguished from living phenomena: *the physical sciences.* **4.** Of or pertaining to physics. *—n.* A **physical examination.** [Middle English *phisycal,* from Medieval Latin *physicālis,* medicinal, from Latin *physica,* physics.] **—phys'i·cal·ly** *adv.*

physical education. Instruction in the care and development of the human body, stressing athletics and hygiene.

physical geography. The study of the physical features of the earth's surface, including land formation, climate, currents, and distribution of flora and fauna. Also called **phys-iography**.

physical science. Any of the sciences, such as physics, chemistry, and geology, that analyzes the nature and properties of energy and nonliving matter.

physical therapy. The treatment of disease and injury by mechanical means such as exercise, heat, light, and massage. Also called **physiotherapy.** —**physical therapist.**

phy·si·cian (fĭ-zĭsh'ən) n. A person licensed to practice medicine; medical doctor.

phys·i·cist (fĭz'ĭ-sĭst) n. A scientist who specializes in physics.

phys·ics (fĭz'ĭks) n. (used with a sing. verb). **1.** The science of matter and energy and of the interactions between the two, grouped in traditional fields such as acoustics, optics, mechanics, thermodynamics, and electromagnetism, as well as in modern extensions including atomic and nuclear physics, cryogenics, solid-state physics, particle physics, and plasma physics. **2.** Physical properties, interactions, processes, or laws: *the physics of supersonic flight.*

physio- or **physi-**. A prefix meaning: **1.** Natural or nature: **physiography. 2.** Physical: **physiotherapy.** [Greek *phusio-*, from *phusis*, nature, from *phuein*, to make grow.]

phys·i·og·no·my (fĭz'ē-ŏg'nə-mē, -ŏn'ə-mē) n., pl. **-mies.** **1.** The art of judging human character from facial features. **2.** Facial features, esp. when regarded as revealing character. **3.** The external aspect or physical features of a geographical region. [From Middle English *phisnomye*, from Old French *phizonomie*, from Medieval Latin *physiono-mia*, from Late Greek *phusiognōmia*, from Greek *phusiog-nōmonia*.] —**phys'i·og·nom'ic** (fĭz'ē-ŏg-nŏm'ĭk, -ə-nŏm'ĭk) or **phys'i·og·nom'i·cal** adj. —**phys'i·og·nom'i·cal·ly** adv.

phys·i·og·ra·phy (fĭz'ē-ŏg'rə-fē) n. Physical geography. —**phys'i·og'ra·pher** n. —**phys'i·o·graph'ic** (-ə-grăf'ĭk) or **phys'i·o·graph'i·cal** adj. —**phys'i·o·graph'i·cal·ly** adv.

phys·i·o·log·i·cal (fĭz'ē-ə-lŏj'ĭ-kəl) or **phys·i·o·log·ic** (-lŏj'-ĭk) adj. **1.** Of physiology. **2.** In accord with or characteristic of the normal functioning of a living organism. —**phys'i·o·log'i·cal·ly** adv.

phys·i·ol·o·gy (fĭz'ē-ŏl'ə-jē) n. **1.** The biological science of essential and characteristic life processes, activities, and functions. **2.** All the vital processes of an organism. —**phys'i·ol'o·gist** n.

phys·i·o·ther·a·py (fĭz'ē-ō-thĕr'ə-pē) n. Physical therapy. —**phys'i·o·ther'a·peu'tic** (-thĕr'ə-pyōō'tĭk) adj.

phy·sique (fĭ-zēk') n. The body, considered with reference to its proportions, muscular development, and appearance. [French, from adj. *physical.*]

phyt-. Var. of **phyto-**.

-phyte. A suffix indicating a plant with a specified character or habitat: **bryophyte.** [From Greek *phuton*, plant, from *phuein*, to make grow.]

phyto- or **phyt-**. A prefix meaning plant or plant life: **phy-tology.** [Greek *phuto-*, from *phuton*, plant, from *phuein*, to make grow.]

pi¹ (pī) n., pl. **pis.** **1.** The 16th letter in the Greek alphabet, written Π, π. **2.** *Symbol* π *Math.* A transcendental number, approx. 3.14159, representing the ratio of the circumference to the diameter of a circle and appearing as a constant in a wide range of mathematical problems. [Greek *pei.*]

pi² (pī) Also **pie.** —n., pl. **pis.** Any amount of type that has been jumbled or thrown together at random. —tr.v. **pied, pi·ing.** Also **pie, pied, pie·ing.** *Printing.* To jumble or mix up (type). [Orig. unknown.]

pi·a ma·ter (pī'ə mā'tər, pē'ə mä'tər). *Anat.* The fine vascular membrane that is the innermost of the three coverings of the brain and spinal cord. [Middle English, from Medieval Latin.]

pi·an·ism (pē-ăn'ĭz'əm, pē'ə-nĭz'əm) n. The technique or execution of piano playing.

pi·a·nis·si·mo (pē'ə-nĭs'ə-mō'). *Mus.* —adv. Very softly or quietly. —n., pl. **-mos.** A passage to be played very softly. [Italian, superl. of *piano*, soft.] —**pi'a·nis'si·mo'** adj.

pi·an·ist (pē-ăn'ĭst, pē'ə-nĭst) n. A person who plays the piano.

pi·an·o¹ (pē-ăn'ō, -ä'nō) n., pl. **-os.** A musical instrument with a manual keyboard actuating hammers that strike wire strings, producing sounds that may be softened or

sustained by means of pedals. [Italian, short for PIANO-FORTE.]

pi·a·no² (pē-ä'nō) *Mus.* —adv. Softly; quietly. —n., pl. **-nos.** A passage to be played softly. [Italian, soft, from Late Latin *plānus*, smooth, from Latin, even, level, flat.] —**pi·a'no** adj.

pi·an·o·for·te (pē-ăn'ō-fôr'tā, -tē, -fôrt', -ä'nō-) n. A piano. [Italian, from *piano e forte*, "soft and loud."]

pi·az·za (pē-ăz'ə, -ä'zə) n. **1.** A public square in an Italian town. **2.** A verandah; porch. [Italian, from Latin *platea*, broad street, courtyard, from Greek *plateia*, from *platus*, broad, flat.]

pi·broch (pē'brŏKH') n. A series of variations on a traditional dirge or martial theme for the highland bagpipe. [Scottish Gaelic *piobaireachd*, pipe music.]

pi·ca (pī'kə) n. **1. a.** A printer's unit of type size, equal to 12 points. **b.** The height of this type, about ⅙ inch, used as a unit of measure esp. in page and book designing. **2.** A type size for typewriters, providing 10 characters to the inch. [Orig. unknown.]

pic·a·dor (pĭk'ə-dôr') n., pl. **-dors** or **-do·res** (pĭk'ə-dôr'ēz). A horseman in a bullfight who lances the bull's neck muscles so that it will tend to keep its head low for the subsequent stages. [Spanish, from *picar*, to prick, pierce.]

pic·a·resque (pĭk'ə-rĕsk' pē'kə-) adj. **1.** Of or involving clever rogues or adventurers. **2.** Of, belonging to, or characteristic of a type of prose fiction in which the rogue-hero and his escapades are depicted with broad realism and satire. [French, from Spanish *picaresco*, from *picaro*, rogue.]

pic·a·yune (pĭk'ē-yōōn') adj. **1.** Of little value or importance; paltry. **2.** Petty; mean. —n. **1.** A Spanish coin of little value formerly used in the southern United States. **2.** Something of very small value; a trifle: *not worth a pica-yune.* [French *picaillon*, small copper coin, from Provençal *picaioun*.]

pic·ca·lil·li (pĭk'ə-lĭl'ē, pĭk'ə-lĭl'ē) n., pl. **-lis.** A pickled relish made of various chopped vegetables. [Perh. blend of PICKLE and CHILI.]

pic·co·lo (pĭk'ə-lō') n., pl. **-los.** A small flute pitched an octave above a regular flute. [Italian, small.]

pick¹ (pĭk) tr.v. **1.** To select from a group: *pick a restaurant; pick an all-star team.* **2.** To gather in; harvest: *pick cotton.* **3. a.** To make bare or clean by removing an outer covering or clinging matter: *pick a chicken clean of feathers.* **b.** To tear off bit by bit: *pick meat from the bones.* **4.** To dig and pull at with the fingers or a tool: *pick one's teeth.* **5.** To break up, separate, or detach by means of a sharp, pointed instrument. **6.** To pierce or make (a hole) with a sharp instrument. **7.** To seek and discover (a flaw): *He picked holes in their argument.* **8.** To steal the contents of: *My pocket has been picked.* **9.** To gain the knowledge contained in: *picked her brains.* **10.** To open (a lock) without the use of the key. **11.** To make (one's way) carefully: *picked his way through the crowd.* **12.** To provoke: *pick a fight.* **13.** To play a musical instrument by plucking. —intr.v. To work with a pointed instrument: *picked away at the rock.* —See Syns at **choose.** —**phrasal verbs. pick apart.** To find flaws in by close examination. **pick at. 1.** To pluck or pull at with the fingers. **2.** To eat sparingly or without appetite: *He picked at his meal.* **3.** *Informal.* To nag. **pick off. 1.** To shoot after singling out: *I picked the ducks off one by one.* **2.** *Baseball.* To tag out (a base runner) after he has taken a premature lead off a base. **pick on.** *Informal.* To tease or bully. **pick out. 1.** To choose or

piano¹

select. **2.** To discern from the surroundings; distinguish. **3.** To play (music) slowly by ear: *pick out a tune.* **pick up. 1.** To take on (passengers, freight, etc.): *pick up a hitchhiker.* **2.** To accelerate: *picked up speed.* **3.** To change for the better; improve. **4.** To take into custody; arrest. **5.** To receive or intercept: *He picked up radio signals from a ship in distress.* **6.** To learn without great effort: *He picked up several foreign languages during his years abroad.* —See Syns at **arrest.** —*n.* **1.** The act of picking, esp. with a pointed instrument. **2.** The act of selecting or choosing; choice. **3. a.** That which is selected. **b.** The best or choicest part: *the pick of the crop.* —*idiom.* **pick and choose.** To decide with great care. [Middle English *piken,* to pierce, prob. from Old French *piquer,* to prick, pick.] —**pick′er** *n.*

pick² (pĭk) *n.* **1.** A tool for breaking hard surfaces, that consists of a curved bar sharpened at both ends and fitted to a long handle. **2.** Anything used for picking, as an ice pick or a toothpick. **3.** A small flat piece of plastic, bone, etc., used to pluck the strings of an instrument; a plectrum. [Middle English *pik.*]

pick·a·back (pĭk′ə-băk′) *adv.* Var. of **piggyback.**

pick·ax or **pick·axe** (pĭk′ăks′) *n.* A pick in which one end of the head is pointed and the other is fashioned with a chisellike edge. —*v.* **-axed, -ax·ing.** —*intr.v.* To use a pickax. —*tr.v.* To use a pickax on. [Alteration of Middle English *pikeis,* from Old French *picois,* from *pic,* perh. from *piquer,* to prick.]

pick·er·el (pĭk′ər-əl, pĭk′rəl) *n., pl.* **-el** or **-els. 1.** Any of several North American freshwater game and food fishes of the genus *Esox.* **2.** Any of various similar or related fishes, such as the walleye. [Middle English *pikerel,* dim. of *pik,* pike.]

pick·et (pĭk′ĭt) *n.* **1.** A pointed stake, as one driven into the ground to support a fence or secure a tent. **2.** *Mil.* A detachment of one or more soldiers positioned to give warning of enemy approach. **3.** A person or persons stationed outside a building, as during a strike or boycott, to express grievance or protest. —*tr.v.* **1.** To enclose, secure, tether, mark out, or fortify with pickets. **2.** *Mil.* To post as or guard with a picket. **3.** To post or act as a picket at a strike or demonstration. —*intr.v.* To act or serve as a picket. [French *piquet,* from Old French, from *piquer,* to prick, pierce.] —**pick′et·er** *n.*

picket fence. A fence of pointed, upright pickets.

picket line. A line or procession of people picketing a place of business or otherwise staging a public protest.

pick·ings (pĭk′ĭngz) *pl.n.* **1.** Something that is or may be picked. **2.** Leftovers. **3.** A share of spoils.

pick·le (pĭk′əl) *n.* **1.** Any edible product, as a cucumber, that has been preserved and flavored in a solution of brine or vinegar. **2.** A solution of brine or vinegar, often spiced, for preserving and flavoring food. **3.** An acid or other chemical solution used as a bath to remove scale and oxides from the surface of metals before plating or finishing. **4.** *Informal.* A troublesome or difficult situation. —*tr.v.* **-led, -ling. 1.** To preserve or flavor in a solution of brine or vinegar. **2.** To treat (metal) in a chemical bath. [Middle English *pekille.*]

pick·pock·et (pĭk′pŏk′ĭt) *n.* A thief who steals from his victims' pockets or purses.

pick·up (pĭk′ŭp′) *n.* **1.** The action or process of picking up. **2.** Someone or something that is picked up. **3.** *Informal.* An improvement: *a pickup in attendance.* **4.** Ability to accelerate rapidly. **5.** *Electronics.* **a.** The part of a phonograph that changes the variations of the record groove into an electrical signal to be amplified as it is fed to a loudspeaker. **b.** The tone arm of a record player. **6.** *Radio & TV.* **a.** The reception of light or sound waves for conversion to electrical impulses. **b.** The apparatus used for such reception. **c.** A telecast originating outside of a studio. **d.** The apparatus for transmitting a broadcast from some outside place to the broadcasting station. **7.** A **pickup truck.**

pickup truck. A light truck with an open body and low sides.

pick·y (pĭk′ē) *adj.* **-i·er, -i·est.** *Informal.* Excessively hard to please or reluctant to choose; fussy.

pic·nic (pĭk′nĭk) *n.* **1.** A meal eaten outdoors on an excursion. **2.** *Slang.* An easy task or pleasant experience.

—*intr.v.* **-nicked, -nick·ing.** To have a picnic. [French *piquenique.*] —**pic′nick·er** *n.*

pi·cot (pē′kō, pē-kō′) *n.* A small embroidered loop forming an ornamental edging on some ribbon and lace. —*tr.v.* **pi·coted** (pē′kōd, pē-kōd′), **-cot·ing** (pē′kō-ĭng, pē-kō′ĭng). To trim with edging. [French, from Old French, from *pic,* point, from *piquer,* to prick.]

pic·ric acid (pĭk′rĭk). A poisonous, explosive yellow crystalline solid, $C_6H_2(NO_2)_3OH$, used in explosives, dyes, and antiseptics. [From Greek *pikros,* bitter.]

Pict (pĭkt) *n.* One of the ancient people of North Britain, absorbed by the invading Scots between the 6th and 9th cent. A.D. —**Pict′ish** (pĭk′tĭsh) *adj. & n.*

pic·to·gram (pĭk′tə-grăm′) *n.* A pictograph. [PICTO(GRAPH) + -GRAM.]

pic·to·graph (pĭk′tə-grăf′) *n.* **1.** A picture or series of pictures representing a word, idea, or message. **2.** A graph or diagram representing data; pictogram. [Latin *pictus,* past part. of *pingere,* to paint + -GRAPH.] —**pic′to·graph′ic** *adj.* —**pic′to·graph′i·cal·ly** *adv.* —**pic·tog′ra·phy** (pĭk-tŏg′rə-fē) *n.*

pic·to·ri·al (pĭk-tôr′ē-əl, -tōr′-) *adj.* **1.** Characterized by or composed of pictures. **2.** Having the descriptive quality of a picture; vivid; graphic: *pictorial prose.* **3.** Illustrated by pictures. —*n.* An illustrated periodical. [Latin *pictorius,* from Latin *pictor,* painter.] —**pic·to′ri·al·ly** *adv.*

pic·ture (pĭk′chər) *n.* **1.** A visual representation or image painted, drawn, photographed, or otherwise rendered on a flat surface. **2.** A vivid or realistic verbal description. **3.** A person or object that bears a striking resemblance to another: *She's the picture of her mother.* **4.** A person, object, or scene that typifies or embodies an emotion, state of mind, or mood: *"Edna's face was a blank picture of bewilderment"* (Kate Chopin). **5.** The chief circumstances of an event or time; situation: *His arrival changes the whole picture.* **6.** A motion picture. **7.** An image or series of images on a television or movie screen. —*tr.v.* **-tured, -tur·ing. 1.** To make a visible representation or picture of. **2.** To form a mental image of; visualize. **3.** To describe vividly in words. [Middle English, from Latin *pictūra,* from *pictus,* past part. of *pingere,* to paint.]

pic·tur·esque (pĭk′chə-rĕsk′) *adj.* **1.** Of or suggesting a picture; visually striking or interesting. **2.** Irregularly or quaintly attractive; charming: *picturesque customs.* **3.** Strikingly expressive or vivid: *picturesque language.* [Alteration of French *pittoresque,* from Italian *pittoresco,* from *pittore,* painter, from Latin *pictor.*] —**pic′tur·esque′ly** *adv.* —**pic′tur·esque′ness** *n.*

picture writing. 1. The use of pictures depicting actions to transmit messages or record events. **2.** An instance of this.

pid·dle (pĭd′l) *v.* **-dled, -dling.** —*tr.v.* To use triflingly; squander: *piddle away one's time.* —*intr.v.* To spend time aimlessly; diddle. [Orig. unknown.]

pid·dling (pĭd′lĭng) *adj.* Beneath consideration; trifling; trivial.

pidg·in (pĭj′ĭn) *n.* A simplified speech that is used for communication between groups speaking different languages. [From PIDGIN ENGLISH.] —**pidg′in** *adj.*

Pidgin English. Also **pidgin English.** A pidgin based on English and used as a trade language in Far Eastern ports. [Alteration of *business English.*]

pie¹ (pī) *n.* **1.** A baked food composed of a shell of pastry that is filled with fruit, meat, cheese, or other ingredients and usu. covered with a pastry crust. **2.** A layer cake having cream, custard, or jelly filling. —*modifier: a pie filling.* [Middle English *pie.*]

pie² (pī) *n.* A bird, the **magpie.** [Middle English, from Old French, from Latin *pīca.*]

pie³ (pī) *n. & v.* Var. of **pi** (jumbled type).

pie·bald (pī′bôld′) *adj.* Spotted or patched, esp. in black and white: *a piebald horse.* —*n.* A piebald animal, esp. a horse. [PIE (magpie) + *bald,* streaked with white.]

piece (pēs) *n.* **1.** A thing considered as a part of a larger quantity or class; portion. **2.** A portion or part that has been separated from a whole: *a piece of cake.* **3.** An object that is one member of a group or class: *a piece of furniture.* **4.** An artistic, musical, or literary work or composition. **5.** An instance; specimen: *a piece of good luck.* **6.** One's fully expressed opinion; one's mind: *speak one's piece.* **7.** A coin or counter: *a ten-cent piece.* **8.** One of the counters or men used in playing various board games. **9.** A firearm. —*tr.v.* **pieced, piec·ing. 1.** To mend by adding a piece to. **2.** To join or unite the pieces of: *He pieced together the vase.* —*idioms.* **a piece of (one's) mind.** *Informal.* Vehement, frank criticism or censure, often based on one's own attitude or opinions. **go to pieces.** *Informal.* To lose self-control; break down. **of a piece.** Of the same kind, type, or group. [Middle English, from Old French *pece,* from Medieval Latin *pecia.*]

pièce de ré·sis·tance (pē-ĕs′ də rā′zē-stäns′). *French.* **1.** The principal dish of a meal. **2.** An outstanding item or event in a series; climax.

piece goods. Fabrics made and sold in standard lengths.

piece·meal (pēs′mēl′) *adv.* **1.** Piece by piece; gradually: *built her collection piecemeal.* **2.** In pieces; apart. —*adj.* Accomplished or made piece by piece: *the piecemeal destruction of the landscape.* [Middle English *pecemele* : *pece,* piece + *-mele,* by a certain measure, from Old English *mǣl,* time, measure.]

piece of eight. An obsolete Spanish silver coin.

piece·work (pēs′wûrk′) *n.* Work paid for according to the number of products turned out. —**piece′work′er** *n.*

pied (pīd) *adj.* Patchy in color; splotched; piebald. [Middle English, from *pie,* magpie, from its piebald coloring.]

pied·mont (pēd′mŏnt′) *adj.* Formed or lying at the foot of a mountain or mountain range. —*n.* A piedmont area or region. [French : *pied,* foot + *mont,* mountain.]

pie·plant (pī′plănt′) *n.* A plant, **rhubarb.**

pier (pîr) *n.* **1.** A platform extending from a shore over water and supported by piles or pillars, used to secure, protect, and provide access to ships or boats. **2.** A supporting structure at the junction of connecting spans of a bridge. **3.** Any of various vertical supporting structures, esp. a pillar supporting an arch or roof or portion of a wall between windows. [Middle English *pere,* from Norman French, from Old French *puier,* to support, ult. from Latin *podium,* raised platform.]

pierce (pîrs) *v.* **pierced, pierc·ing.** —*tr.v.* **1.** To cut or pass through with or as if with a sharp instrument; stab; penetrate. **2.** To make a hole or opening in; perforate. **3.** To make a way through: *The path pierced the wilderness.* **4.** To sound sharply through: *His shout pierced the air.* **5.** To succeed in discerning or understanding: *He pierced the heart of the mystery.* **6.** To affect penetratingly; move deeply: *pierced by anguish.* —*intr.v.* To penetrate into or through something. [Middle English *percen,* from Old French *percer,* from Latin *pertūsus,* past part. of *pertundere,* to pierce through : *per,* through + *tundere,* to thrust.] —**pierc′er** *n.* —**pierc′ing·ly** *adv.*

pi·e·tism (pī′ĭ-tĭz′əm) *n.* **1.** Piety. **2.** Affected or exaggerated piety. **3. Pietism.** A reform movement in the German Lutheran Church during the 17th and 18th cent.—**pi′e·tis′tic** or **pi′e·tis′ti·cal** *adj.* —**pi′e·tis′ti·cal·ly** *adv.*

pi·e·ty (pī′ĭ-tē) *n., pl.* **-ties. 1.** Religious devotion and reverence to God. **2.** Devotion and reverence to parents and family. **3.** A pious act or thought. **4.** The condition or quality of being pious. [French *piété,* from Latin *pietās,* from *pius,* dutiful, devout.]

pi·e·zo·e·lec·tric·i·ty (pē-ā′zō-ĭ-lĕk-trĭs′ĭ-tē, pē-āt′sō-) *n.* The generation of electricity or of electric polarity in dielectric crystals subjected to mechanical stress and, conversely, the generation of stress in such crystals subjected to an applied voltage. [From Greek *piezein,* to squeeze + ELECTRICITY.] —**pi·e′zo·e·lec′tric** or **pi·e′zo·e·lec′tri·cal** *adj.*

pif·fle (pĭf′əl) *intr.v.* **-fled, -fling.** To talk or act in a feeble or futile way. —*n.* Nonsense. [Orig. unknown.]

pig (pĭg) *n.* **1.** Any of several mammals of the family Suidae, with short legs, cloven hoofs, bristly hair, and a cartilaginous snout used for digging, esp. the domesticated hog, *Sus scrofa,* when young or of comparatively small size. **2.** The edible parts of a pig. **3.** *Informal.* A greedy, messy, or dirty person. **4. a.** An oblong block of metal, usu. iron or lead, poured from a smelting furnace. **b.** A mold in which such metal is cast. —*intr.v.* **pigged, pig·ging.** To give birth to pigs; farrow. —*idiom.* **pig it.** To live in a slovenly fashion. [Middle English *pigge.*]

pi·geon (pĭj′ən) *n.* **1.** Any of various birds of the widely distributed family Columbidae, with deepchested bodies, small heads, and short legs, esp. any of the domesticated

varieties. **2.** *Slang.* Someone who is easily swindled; a dupe. [Middle English *pijon,* from Old French, young bird, from Latin *pīpiō,* from *pīpīre,* to chirp.]

pigeon hawk. A small falcon, *Falco columbarius.* Also called **merlin.**

pi·geon·hole (pĭj′ən-hōl′) *n.* **1.** A small hole for nesting in a pigeon loft. **2.** A small compartment or recess, as in a desk, for holding papers; cubbyhole. —*tr.v.* **-holed, -hol·ing. 1.** To place or file in a pigeonhole. **2.** To classify mentally; categorize. **3.** To put aside and ignore.

pi·geon-toed (pĭj′ən-tōd′) *adj.* Having the toes turned inward.

pig·gish (pĭg′ĭsh) *adj.* Like a pig; greedy or dirty. —**pig′gish·ly** *adv.* —**pig′gish·ness** *n.*

pig·gy·back (pĭg′ē-băk′) *adv.* Also **pick·a·back** (pĭk′ə-băk′). **1.** On the shoulders or back. **2.** By a method of transportation in which truck trailers are carried on trains, or cars on specially designed trucks. [Orig. unknown.] —**pig′gy·back′** *adj.*

piggy bank. A child's coin bank shaped like a pig.

pig·head·ed (pĭg′hĕd′ĭd) *adj.* Stubborn. —See Syns at **obstinate.** —**pig′head′ed·ly** *adv.* —**pig′head′ed·ness** *n.*

pig iron. Crude iron cast in blocks or pigs.

pig·let (pĭg′lĭt) *n.* A young pig.

pig·ment (pĭg′mənt) *n.* **1.** Any substance or matter used as coloring. **2.** Dry coloring matter, usu. an insoluble powder, to be mixed with water, oil, or another base to produce paint and similar products. **3.** *Biol.* A substance, such as chlorophyll or hemoglobin, that produces a characteristic color in plant or animal tissue. —*tr.v.* To color with pigment. [Latin *pigmentum,* from *pingere,* to paint.] —**pig′men·tar′y** (-mən-tĕr′ē) *adj.*

pig·men·ta·tion (pĭg′mən-tā′shən) *n.* Coloration of animal or plant tissues by pigment.

pig·my (pĭg′mē) *n. & adj.* Var. of **pygmy.**

Pig·my (pĭg′mē) *n. & adj.* Var. of **Pygmy.**

pig·pen (pĭg′pĕn′) *n.* **1.** A pen for pigs. **2.** A dirty or messy place.

pig·skin (pĭg′skĭn′) *n.* **1.** The skin of a pig. **2.** Leather made from this. **3.** *Informal.* A football.

pig·sty (pĭg′stī′) *n., pl.* **-sties.** A pigpen.

pig·tail (pĭg′tāl′) *n.* **1.** A braid of hair that hangs down the back or side. **2.** A twisted roll of tobacco. —**pig′tailed′** *adj.*

pi·ka (pē′kə, pī′-) *n.* Any of several small, tailless harelike mammals of the genus *Ochotona,* of the mountains of North America and Eurasia. [Tungus *piika.*]

pike[1] (pīk) *n.* A long spear formerly used by infantry. [Old French *pique,* from *piquer,* to prick, pierce.]

pike[2] (pīk) *n., pl.* **pike** or **pikes. 1.** A freshwater game and food fish, *Esox lucius,* of the Northern Hemisphere, that has a long snout and attains a length of over four feet. **2.** Any of various similar or related fishes. [Middle English.]

pike[3] (pīk) *n.* A turnpike. [Short for TURNPIKE.]

pike[4] (pīk) *n.* Any spike or sharp point, such as the tip of a spear. [Middle English, from Old English *pīc.*]

pike perch. Any of various fishes related to the perches and resembling the pike, such as the walleye.

pik·er (pī′kər) *n. Slang.* A stingy, petty person, esp. one who gambles cautiously. [Orig. unknown.]

pike·staff (pīk′stăf′) *n.* **1.** The shaft of a pike. **2.** A walking stick tipped with a metal spike.

pig

pi·laf or **pi·laff** (pǐ-läf′, pē-) *n.* A steamed rice dish cooked with bits of meat, shellfish, or vegetables. [Turkish *pilâw*, from Persian.]

pi·las·ter (pǐ-lǎs′tər, pǐ-lǎs′-) *n.* A rectangular column, usu. ornamental, that is set into and projects slightly from a wall. [Old French *pilastre*, from Italian *pilastro*, from Medieval Latin *pilastrum*, from Latin *pīla*, pillar.]

pilaster

pile¹ (pīl) *n.* **1.** A quantity of objects stacked or thrown together; a heap. **2.** *Informal.* A large accumulation or quantity: *a pile of trouble.* **3.** *Slang.* A large sum of money; fortune. **4.** A funeral pyre. **5.** A **nuclear reactor.** **6.** *Elect.* **Voltaic pile.** —*v.* **piled, pil·ing.** —*tr.v.* **1.** To set or stack in a pile or heap. **2.** To load with a pile: *He piled the table with books.* **3.** To place or assign in abundance: *They piled honors on him.* —*intr.v.* **1.** To form a heap or pile. **2.** To move in a disorderly mass or group: *pile out of a car in a great hurry.* [Middle English, from Old French, from Latin *pīla*, pillar.]

pile² (pīl) *n.* A heavy beam of timber, concrete, or steel driven into the earth as a foundation or support for a structure. —*tr.v.* **piled, pil·ing.** **1.** To drive piles into. **2.** To support with piles. [Middle English *pile*, pointed shaft, stake, Old English *pīl*, ult. from Latin *pīlum*, heavy javelin, pestle.]

pile³ (pīl) *n.* **1.** Cut or uncut loops of yarn forming the surface of certain fabrics, such as carpeting. **2.** Soft, fine hair, fur, or wool. [Middle English, from Norman French *pyle*, from Latin *pilus*, hair.] —**piled** *adj.*

pi·le·at·ed woodpecker (pī′lē-ā′tĭd, pĭl′ē-). A large North American woodpecker, *Dryocopus pileatus*, with black and white plumage and a bright red crest.

pile driver. A machine that drives piles into the ground by raising a weight between guideposts and dropping it on the head of the pile.

piles (pīlz) *pl.n.* Hemorrhoids. [Pl. of *pile*, from Latin *pila*, ball.]

pil·fer (pĭl′fər) *tr.v.* To steal (a small amount or item); filch. —*intr.v.* To engage in small thefts. [Old French *pelfrer*, to rob, despoil, from *pelfre*, booty.] —**pil′fer·age** *n.* —**pil′fer·er** *n.*

pil·grim (pĭl′grĭm, -grəm) *n.* **1.** A religious devotee who journeys to a shrine or sacred place. **2.** Someone who makes a long journey in quest of a sacred or otherwise important end. **3. Pilgrim.** One of the English Puritans who founded the colony of Plymouth in New England (1620). [Middle English *pelegrim*, from Old French *peligrin*, from Late Latin *pelegrīnus*, alteration of Latin *peregrīnus*, stranger, foreigner.]

pil·grim·age (pĭl′grə-mĭj) *n.* **1.** A journey to a sacred place or shrine. **2.** Any long journey or search. —*intr.v.* **-aged, -ag·ing.** To go on a pilgrimage.

pil·ing (pī′lĭng) *n.* Piles, or a structure composed of piles.

pill (pĭl) *n.* **1.** A small pellet or tablet of medicine, often coated, taken by swallowing whole or chewing. **2. the pill.** *Informal.* An oral contraceptive. **3.** Anything distasteful or unpleasant but necessary: *swallow the bitter pill of failure.* **4.** *Slang.* A boring or disagreeable person. [Latin *pilula*, dim. of *pila*, ball.]

pil·lage (pĭl′ĭj) *v.* **-laged, -lag·ing.** —*tr.v.* **1.** To rob of goods by violent seizure; to plunder. **2.** To take as spoils: *pillaging the grain reserves.* —*intr.v.* To take spoils by robbery and violence. —See Syns at **sack.** —*n.* **1.** The act of pillag-

ing. **2.** Something pillaged; spoils. [Middle English, from Old French, from *piller*, to plunder, from *pille*, rag, cloth, prob. from Latin *pilleus*, felt cap.] —**pil′lag·er** *n.*

pil·lar (pĭl′ər) *n.* **1.** A slender, freestanding, vertical support; column. **2.** Any similar structure used for decoration or as a monument. **3.** Someone who occupies a central or responsible position: *a pillar of the state.* —*idiom.* **from pillar to post.** From one place or situation to another. [Middle English *piller*, from Old French *pilier*, from Latin *pīla*, pillar.]

pill·box (pĭl′bŏks′) *n.* **1.** A small box for pills. **2.** A woman's small, round, brimless hat. **3.** A roofed concrete emplacement for a machine gun or other weapon.

pill bug. Any of various small, terrestrial crustaceans of the genus *Armadillidium* or related genera, with convex, segmented bodies capable of being curled into a ball.

pil·lion (pĭl′yən) *n.* A pad or cushion for an extra rider behind the saddle on a horse or motorcycle. —*adv.* On a pillion: *riding pillion.* [Scottish Gaelic *pillean*, dim. of *peall*, covering, from Latin *pellis*, skin.]

pil·lo·ry (pĭl′ə-rē) *n., pl.* **-ries.** A wooden framework on a post, with holes for the head and hands, in which offenders were formerly locked to be exposed to public scorn as punishment. —*tr.v.* **-ried, -ry·ing.** **1.** To put in a pillory as punishment. **2.** To expose to ridicule and abuse. [Middle English, from Old French *pilori*, from Medieval Latin *pilōrium*, prob. from Latin *pīla*, pillar.]

pil·low (pĭl′ō) *n.* **1.** A cloth case stuffed with something soft, such as down, feathers, or foam rubber, used to cushion the head during sleep. **2.** A decorative cushion. —*tr.v.* **1.** To rest (one's head) on or as if on a pillow. **2.** To serve as a pillow for. [Middle English *pilwe*, from Old English, *pylu*, from Latin *pulvīnus*, pillow.] —**pil′low·y** *adj.*

pil·low·case (pĭl′ō-kās′) *n.* A removable covering for a pillow.

pi·lose (pī′lōs′) *adj.* Covered with fine, soft hair. [Latin *pilōsus*, from *pilus*, a hair.]

pi·lot (pī′lət) *n.* **1.** A person who flies or is licensed to fly an aircraft in flight. **2.** A licensed specialist who steers large ships in and out of port or through dangerous waters. **3.** A ship's helmsman. **4.** A guide or leader. **5.** A pilot light. **6.** A cowcatcher. **7.** A television program produced as a prototype of a series being considered for adoption by a network. **8.** Any small-scale experimental model. —*modifier:* *a pilot project.* —*tr.v.* **1.** To serve as the pilot of. **2.** To steer or control the course of. [French *pilote*, from Italian *pilota*, ult. from Greek *pēdon*, rudder.]

pi·lot·age (pī′lə-tĭj) *n.* **1.** The technique or act of piloting. **2.** The fee paid to a pilot.

pilot balloon. A small balloon used to determine wind velocity.

pilot fish. A saltwater fish, *Naucrates ductor*, that often swims in company with larger fishes, esp. sharks.

pi·lot·house (pī′lət-hous′) *n.* An enclosed area on the deck or bridge of a vessel from which the vessel is controlled when under way. Also called **wheel house.**

pilot light. **1.** A small jet of gas that is kept burning in order to ignite a gas burner, as in a stove. **2.** A pilot lamp.

Pilt·down man (pĭlt′doun′). A supposed early genus and species of man, *Eoanthropus dawsoni*, postulated from bones allegedly found in an early Pleistocene gravel bed between 1909 and 1915 and proved in 1953 to have been a forgery. [From the site near *Piltdown* Common, Sussex, England.]

pi·ma (pē′mə) *n.* Also **Pi·ma.** A very strong high-grade cotton of medium fiber developed from selected Egyptian cottons in the southwestern United States. —*modifier:* *pima cotton.* [After *Pima* County, Arizona.]

pi·men·to (pǐ-měn′tō) *n., pl.* **-tos.** **1.** A tree, the allspice, or its berries. **2.** The pimiento. [Spanish *pimienta*, pepper, allspice, from Late Latin *pigmenta*, pl. of *pigmentum*, plant juice, pigment.]

pi mes·on (pī′ měz′ŏn′, mē′zŏn′, měs′ŏn′, mē′sŏn′). *Physics.* A subatomic particle, the pion.

pi·mien·to (pǐ-měn′tō, pǐm-yěn′-) *n., pl.* **-tos.** A garden pepper, *Capsicum anuum*, or its mild, ripe, red fruit, used in salads, cookery, and as stuffing for green olives. [Spanish, from *pimienta*, pepper.]

pimp (pĭmp) *n.* Someone who manages and procures cus-

pimpernel

pince-nez

pincers

tomers for a prostitute. —*intr.v.* To serve as a pimp. [Orig. unknown.]

pim·per·nel (pĭm′pər-nĕl′, -nəl) *n.* Any plant of the genus *Anagallis,* esp. the scarlet pimpernel, *A. arvensis,* whose red, purple, or white flowers close in bad weather. [Middle English *pympernele,* from Old French *pimpernelle,* ult. from Latin *piper,* pepper.]

pim·ple (pĭm′pəl) *n.* A small swelling of the skin, sometimes containing pus; pustule. [Middle English *pinple.*] —**pim′pled** or **pim′ply** *adj.*

pin (pĭn) *n.* **1.** A short, straight, stiff piece of wire with a blunt head and a sharp point, used esp. for fastening. **2.** Anything resembling a pin in shape or use, as a hairpin. **3.** An ornament fastened to the clothing by means of a clasp. **4.** A bar or rod for holding or fastening parts together, or serving as a support for suspending one thing from another. **5.** *Mus.* One of the pegs securing the strings and regulating their tension on a stringed instrument. **6.** The part of a key stem entering a lock. **7.** One of the wooden clubs at which the ball is aimed in bowling. **8.** *Golf.* The pole bearing a pennant to mark a hole. **9. pins.** *Slang.* The legs. **10.** Something of little or no value: "*I would not care a pin*" (Shakespeare). —*tr.v.* **pinned, pinning.** **1.** To fasten or secure with or as if with a pin. **2.** To make completely dependent: *pinned all our hopes on his coming through.* **3.** To win a fall from in wrestling. **4.** To hold fast; immobilize: *He was pinned under the wreckage.* **5.** To attribute (a wrongdoing or crime): *pinned the murder on the victim's wife.* —*phrasal verb.* **pin down.** To fix or establish clearly. —*idiom.* **on pins and needles.** In a state of suspense or anxiety. [Middle English, peg, from Old English *pinn.*]

pin·a·fore (pĭn′ə-fôr′, -fōr′) *n.* A sleeveless, apronlike garment, worn esp. by small girls. [PIN (to fasten) + AFORE.]

pi·ña·ta (pĭn-yä′tə, pēn-) *n.* A decorated container filled with candy and toys and suspended from the ceiling to be broken by a blindfolded child with a stick, used as part of the Christmas celebration in certain Latin American countries. [Spanish, pot.]

pin·ball (pĭn′bôl′) *n.* A game played on a machine in which a ball propelled by a plunger rolls down a slanted surface, reaching pins or holes that record the score electronically. —*modifier:* a *pinball machine.*

pince-nez (păns-nā′, păns-) *n., pl.* **pince-nez** (-nāz′, -nā′). Eyeglasses that are clipped to the bridge of the nose. [French, "pinch-nose."]

pin·cers (pĭn′sərz) *pl.n.* Also **pin·chers** (pĭn′chərz). **1.** A grasping tool with a pair of jaws and handles that are pivoted together to work in opposition. **2.** The jointed, prehensile claws of certain arthropods, such as the lobster. **3.** *Mil.* A maneuver in which the enemy is attacked from two flanks and the front. [Middle English *pynsour,* ult. from Old French *pincier,* to pinch.]

pinch (pĭnch) *tr.v.* **1.** To squeeze between the thumb and a finger, the jaws of a tool, or other edges. **2.** To squeeze or bind (a part of the body) so as to cause discomfort or pain. **3.** To wither or shrivel: *buds pinched by the frost.* **4.** To force strict economy on; straiten. **5.** *Slang.* To steal. **6.** *Slang.* To arrest. —*intr.v.* **1.** To press, squeeze, or bind painfully. **2.** To be miserly. —See Syns at **arrest.** —*n.* **1.** The act of pinching. **2.** An amount that can be held between thumb and forefinger: *a pinch of rosemary.* **3.** The pressure of reduced resources or finances; hardship. **4.** An

emergency. **5.** *Informal.* A theft or robbery. **6.** *Slang.* An arrest. —*idiom.* **pinch pennies.** To be thrifty or frugal. [Middle English *pinchen,* from Old French *pincier.*] —**pinch′er** *n.*

pinch·beck (pĭnch′bĕk′) *n.* **1.** An alloy of zinc and copper used as imitation gold. **2.** A cheap imitation. —*adj.* **1.** Made of pinchbeck. **2.** Imitation; spurious. [After Christopher *Pinchbeck* (1670?–1732), English watchmaker, its inventor.]

pinch·cock (pĭnch′kŏk′) *n.* A clamp used to regulate or close a flexible tube, esp. in laboratory apparatus.

pinch·ers (pĭn′chərz) *pl.n.* Var. of **pincers.**

pinch-hit (pĭnch′hĭt′) *intr.v.* **-hit, -hit·ting.** **1.** *Baseball.* To bat in place of a player scheduled to bat. **2.** *Informal.* To substitute for another in an emergency. —**pinch hitter.**

pin·cush·ion (pĭn′kŏosh′ən) *n.* A small, firm cushion in which pins are stuck when not in use.

Pindaric ode. An ode in the form developed by Pindar, consisting of a series of triads formed by the strophe, antistrophe, and epode.

pine¹ (pīn) *n.* **1.** Any of various cone-bearing evergreen trees of the genus *Pinus,* with needle-shaped leaves in clusters, valued for shade and ornament and for its wood and resinous sap, which yields turpentine and pine tar. **2.** Any coniferous tree, esp. of the family Pinaceae, such as the cedar, spruce, or fir. **3.** The wood of any of these trees. [Middle English, from Old English *pīn,* from Latin *pīnus.*]

pine² (pīn) *intr.v.* **pined, pin·ing.** **1.** To suffer longing; yearn: *pining for a lost love.* **2.** To wither or waste from longing or grief: *pine away.* [Middle English *pinen,* from Old English *pīnian,* from Latin *poena,* penalty, from Greek *poinē.*]

pin·e·al (pĭn′ē-əl, pī′nē-) *adj.* **1.** Having the form of a pine cone. **2.** Relating to the pineal body. [French *pinéal,* from Latin *pīnea,* pine cone, from *pīnus,* pine.]

pineal body. A small mass of poorly developed glandular tissue found in the brain whose function is unknown.

pine·ap·ple (pīn′ăp′əl) *n.* **1.** A tropical American plant, *Ananas comosus,* with large, swordlike leaves and a large, fleshy, edible fruit that consists of the flowers fused into a compound whole with a terminal tuft of leaves. **2.** The fruit of this plant. [Middle English *pinappel,* pinecone (from its shape).]

pine needle. The needle-shaped leaf of a pine tree.

pine nut. The edible seed of certain pines, as the piñon.

pine tar. A thick liquid or semisolid brown to black substance produced by the destructive distillation of pine wood and used in roofing compositions, paints and varnishes, expectorants, and as an antiseptic.

pin·ey (pī′nē) *adj.* Var. of **piny.**

ping (pĭng) *n.* A brief, high-pitched sound, such as that made by a bullet striking metal. —*intr.v.* To produce a ping. [Imit.]

Ping-Pong (pĭng′pông′, -pŏng′) *n.* A trademark for table-tennis equipment, often applied to the game of table tennis.

pin·head (pĭn′hĕd′) *n.* **1.** The head of a pin. **2.** Anything small, trifling, or insignificant. **3.** *Slang.* A stupid person. —**pin′head′ed** *adj.*

pin·hole (pĭn′hōl′) *n.* A tiny puncture made by or as if by a pin.

pin·ion¹ (pĭn′yən) *n.* **1.** A bird's wing. **2.** The outer rear edge of a bird's wing, containing the primary feathers.

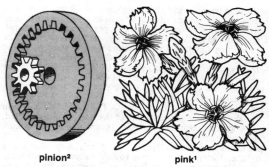

pinion²   **pink¹**

3. A primary feather of a bird. —*tr.v.* **1. a.** To clip or tie the wing feathers of (a bird) to prevent flight. **b.** To clip or tie (the wings of a bird). **2.** To hold or bind to prevent movement. [Middle English *pynyon,* from Old French *pignon,* from Latin *pinna,* a feather, wing.]

pin·ion² (pĭn'yən) *n.* A small cogwheel that engages or is engaged by a larger cogwheel or a rack. [French *pignon,* from Old French, from *peigne,* a comb, from Latin *pecten.*]

pink¹ (pĭngk) *n.* **1.** Any of various plants of the genus *Dianthus,* often cultivated for their fragrant flowers. **2.** A flower of any of these plants. **3.** The highest degree of excellence or perfection: *in the pink of health.* **4.** A light or pale red. —*adj.* **-er, -est.** Light or pale red. [Orig. unknown.] —**pink'ness** *n.*

pink² (pĭngk) *tr.v.* **1.** To stab lightly with a pointed weapon; to prick. **2.** To decorate with a pattern of small holes. **3.** To cut with pinking shears. [Middle English *pynken.*]

pink·eye (pĭngk'ī') *n.* Also **pink eye.** Acute contagious conjunctivitis, characterized by inflamed eyelids and eyeballs.

pink·ie (pĭng'kē) *n.* Also **pink·y,** *pl.* **-ies.** The fifth or little finger. [Orig. unknown.]

pinking shears. Sewing scissors with notched or serrated blades, used to finish edges of cloth with a scalloped or zigzag pattern for decoration or to prevent raveling.

pink·ish (pĭng'kĭsh) *adj.* Somewhat pink.

pink·y (pĭng'kē) *n.* Var. of **pinkie.**

pin money. Money for incidental expenses.

pin·na (pĭn'ə) *n., pl.* **pin·nae** (pĭn'ē') or **-nas. 1.** *Bot.* Any of the leaflets of a pinnate leaf. **2.** *Anat.* The external part of the ear; auricle. [Latin, wing, feather.] —**pin'nal** *adj.*

pin·nace (pĭn'əs) *n.* **1.** A small sailing boat formerly used as a tender for merchant and war vessels. **2.** Any small ship or ship's boat. [French *pinace,* ult. from Latin *pīnus,* pine tree.]

pin·na·cle (pĭn'ə-kəl) *n.* **1.** A small turret or spire on a roof or buttress. **2.** Any tall, pointed formation, such as a mountain peak. **3.** The highest point; summit; acme. [Middle English, from Old French, from Late Latin *pinnāculum,* "little wing," from dim. of Latin *pinna,* wing.]

pin·nate (pĭn'āt') *adj.* **1.** Resembling a feather; pennate. **2.** *Bot.* Having leaflets, lobes, or divisions in a featherlike arrangement on each side of a common axis, as do many compound leaves. [Latin *pinnātus,* feathered, from *pinna,* feather.] —**pin'nate·ly** *adv.*

pi·noch·le (pē'nŭk'əl, -nŏk'-) *n.* Also **pi·noc·le. 1.** A game of cards for two to four persons, played with a special deck of 48 cards, with points being scored by taking tricks and forming certain combinations. **2.** The combination of the queen of spades and jack of diamonds in this game. [Orig. unknown.]

pi·ñon (pĭn'yən, -yōn') *n., pl.* **pi·ñons** or **pi·ño·nes** (pĭn-yō'nĕz) Any of several pine trees that bear edible, nutlike seeds, esp. *Pinus cembroides edulis,* of the western United States and Mexico. [American Spanish, from Spanish, pine nut, pine cone, ult. from Latin *pīnus,* pine.]

pin·point (pĭn'point') *tr.v.* **1.** To locate and identify precisely. **2.** To take precise aim at: *pinpoint a target.* —See Syns at **find.** —*adj.* **1.** Characterized by extreme precision: *pinpoint accuracy.* **2.** Very small; minute.

pin·prick (pĭn'prĭk') *n.* **1.** A slight puncture made by a pin. **2.** An insignificant wound. **3.** A minor annoyance. —*tr.v.* To puncture with a pin.

pins and needles. A tingling felt in a part of the body that has been numbed from lack of circulation.

pin·stripe (pĭn'strīp') *n.* **1.** A thin stripe on a fabric. **2.** A kind of fabric with thin stripes.

pint (pīnt) *n.* **1. a.** A unit of volume or capacity in the U.S. Customary System, used in liquid measure, equal to 16 fluid ounces or 28.875 cubic inches. **b.** A unit of volume or capacity in the U.S. Customary System, used in dry measure, equal to ½ quart or 33.6 cubic inches. **2.** A container with such a capacity or the amount of a substance that can be contained in it: *drank a pint of milk.* —*modifier:* a pint bottle. [Middle English *pinte,* from Old French, prob. from Medieval Latin *pincta,* "painted mark (on a measuring container)."]

pin·tail (pĭn'tāl') *n., pl.* **-tails** or **-tail.** A duck, *Anas acuta,* of the Northern Hemisphere, with gray, brown, and white plumage and a sharply pointed tail.

pin·to (pĭn'tō) *n., pl.* **-tos** or **-toes.** Any horse with irregular spots or markings. —*adj.* Irregularly marked: *a pinto horse.* [American Spanish, from obs. Spanish, "painted," "spotted."]

pinto bean. A form of the common string bean that has mottled seeds and is grown chiefly in the southwestern United States.

pint-size (pīnt'sīz') *adj.* Also **pint-sized** (-sīzd'). *Informal.* Of small dimensions; diminutive.

pin·up (pĭn'ŭp') *n.* **1.** A picture to be pinned up on a wall, esp. a photograph of an attractive person or a celebrity. **2.** A person considered a suitable model for such a picture. —*adj.* Designed to be attached to a wall: *a pinup lamp.*

pin·wheel (pĭn'hwēl', -wēl') *n.* **1.** A toy consisting of vanes of colored paper or plastic pinned to the end of a stick so as to revolve in the wind. **2.** A firework that forms a rotating wheel of colored flames.

pin·y (pī'nē) *adj.* **-i·er, -i·est.** Also **pine·y. 1.** Consisting of or covered with pines. **2.** Of or like pines, esp. in odor: *a fresh piny smell.*

pi·on (pī'ŏn) *n. Symbol* π *Physics.* Either of two subatomic particles in the meson family: **a.** pi zero, having a mass 264 times that of the electron, zero electric charge, and a mean lifetime of 0.9×10^{-16} second. **b.** pi plus, having a mass 273 times that of the electron, a positive electric charge, and a mean lifetime of 2.6×10^{-8} second. Also called **pi meson.** [PI + (MES)ON.]

pi·o·neer (pī'ə-nîr') *n.* **1.** A person who first enters or settles a region, opening it up for others. **2.** A person who leads the way in a field of science, research, etc. **3.** A plant or animal that is the first kind to grow or live in an environment where there have been no living things. —*tr.v.* **1.** To explore or settle. **2.** To participate in the origin or early development of. —*intr.v.* **1.** To act as an explorer or early settler. **2.** To lead the way; innovate: *He pioneered in the use of antiseptics in surgery.* [Old French *pionier,* from *pion,* foot soldier, from Medieval Latin *pedō,* from Late Latin, pedestrian, from Latin *pēs,* foot.]

pi·ous (pī'əs) *adj.* **1.** Having or exhibiting reverence and earnest devotion in the performance of religious duties; devout. **2.** Marked by false devoutness; solemnly hypocritical: *a pious speech to impress his elders.* **3.** Devotional: *pious readings.* [From Latin *pius,* dutiful.] —**pi'ous·ly** *adv.* —**pi'ous·ness** *n.*

pip¹ (pĭp) *n.* **1.** The small seed of a fruit, as of an apple or orange. **2.** *Informal.* Something remarkable of its kind: *a pip of a plan.* [Short for PIPPIN.]

pip² (pĭp) *n.* **1.** A dot on dice or dominoes. **2.** A rootstock of certain flowering plants, esp. the lily of the valley. [Earlier *peepe.*]

pip³ (pĭp) *v.* **pipped, pip·ping.** —*tr.v.* To break through (an eggshell) in hatching. —*intr.v.* To peep or chirp, as a chick or young bird does. —*n.* A short, high-pitched radio signal. [Perh. imit.]

pip⁴ (pĭp) *n.* **1.** A disease of birds, characterized by a thick mucous discharge that forms a crust in the mouth and throat. **2.** The crust symptomatic of this disease. [Middle English *pippe,* from Middle Dutch, phlegm, mucus, ult. from Latin *pītuīta,* phlegm.]

pipe (pīp) *n.* **1. a.** A tube or hollow cylinder through which a liquid or gas can be made to flow. **b.** A section of such a tube. **2. a.** An object used for smoking that consists of a hollow tube with a mouthpiece at one end and a small bowl at the other. **b.** The amount of tobacco needed to fill the bowl of such a pipe. **3.** A tubelike part or organ of the body. **4. pipes.** *Informal.* The human respiratory system. **5. a.** A tubular musical instrument, esp. a simple or primitive one, similar to a flute, clarinet, or oboe. **b.** Any of the tubes used in an organ to produce musical tones. **c. pipes.** A small wind instrument consisting of a number of tuned tubes bound together. **d.** Often **pipes.** A bagpipe. **6.** A kind of whistle used for signaling a ship's crew. **7.** Often **pipes.** The sound of the voice. **8.** *Mining.* A vertical, cylindrical vein of ore. **9.** A large wine cask. —*v.* **piped, piping.** —*tr.v.* **1.** To convey (liquid or gas) by means of pipes. **2.** To provide or connect with pipes. **3.** To play on a pipe or pipes: *"Piper, pipe that song again"* (William Blake). **4.** To call (a ship's crew) by sounding the boatswain's pipe. **5.** To utter in a shrill, reedy tone. **6.** To furnish (a garment or fabric) with piping. —*intr.v.* **1.** To play on a pipe. **2.** To speak shrilly; make a shrill sound. —*phrasal verbs.* **pipe down.** *Slang.* To stop talking; be quiet. **pipe up.** To speak up, esp. in a small, shrill voice. [Middle English, from Old English *pīpe*, ult. from Latin *pīpāre*, to chirp.]

pipe dream. A wishful, fantastic notion or hope. [From the fantasies induced by smoking opium.]

pipe·fit·ting (pīp'fīt'ĭng) *n.* **1.** The act or work of installing and repairing pipes. **2.** A section of pipe used to join two or more pipes together. —**pipe fitter.**

pipe·line (pīp'līn') *n.* **1.** A line of pipe used to carry water, petroleum, natural gas, etc., over great distances. **2.** A line of communication or route of supply.

pipe organ. A musical instrument, the organ.

pip·er (pī'pər) *n.* A person who plays on a pipe. —*idiom.* **pay the piper.** To bear the consequences of one's actions.

pi·pette (pī-pĕt') *n.* Also **pi·pet.** Any of variously shaped glass tubes, open at both ends and often graduated, used for transferring liquids in a laboratory.

pip·ing (pī'pĭng) *n.* **1.** A system of pipes. **2.** The act of playing music on a pipe. **3.** A shrill, high-pitched sound, such as that of music played on a pipe. **4.** A narrow band or fold of material, used as a trimming on edges or seams. —*adj.* Thin, clear, and shrill: *the high, piping notes of the flute.* —*adv.* Extremely: *piping hot biscuits.*

pip·it (pĭp'ĭt) *n.* Any of various widely distributed songbirds of the genus *Anthus*, with brownish upper plumage and a streaked breast. Also called **titlark.** [Imit.]

pip·kin (pĭp'kĭn) *n.* A small earthenware or metal cooking pot. [Prob. PIPE (cask) + -KIN.]

pip·pin (pĭp'ĭn) *n.* Any of several varieties of apple. [Middle English *pipin*, seed, from Old French *pepin*.]

pip-squeak (pĭp'skwēk') *n.* A small or insignificant person.

pi·quant (pē'kənt, -känt', pē-känt') *adj.* **1.** Pleasantly pungent in taste or odor; spicy. **2.** Appealingly provocative: *touched by the piquant faces of children.* [Old French, pres. part. of *piquer*, to pierce, prick.] —**pi'quan·cy** or **pi'quant·ness** *n.* —**pi'quant·ly** *adv.*

pique (pēk) *n.* A feeling of resentment or vexation arising from wounded pride or vanity. —*tr.v.* **piqued, piqu·ing.** **1.** To cause to feel resentment; hurt the pride of. **2.** To provoke; arouse; spur: *The portrait piqued my curiosity.* [Old French, from *piquer*, to pierce, prick.]

pi·qué (pĭ-kā', pē'kā') *n.* A firm cloth, usu. cotton, woven with lengthwise ribs or with a diamond, honeycomb, or waffle pattern. [French, quilting, from *piquer*, to pierce.]

pi·quet (pĭ-kā') *n.* A card game for two people, played with a 32-card deck. [French, dim. of *pic*, a score of 30 points at cards, from *piquer*, to prick.]

pi·ra·cy (pī'rə-sē) *n., pl.* **-cies.** The act or practice of pirating.

pi·ra·gua (pĭ-räg'wə) *n.* **1.** A canoe made by hollowing out a tree trunk. **2.** A flat-bottomed sailing boat with two masts. [Spanish, from Carib *piraguas*.]

pi·ra·nha (pĭ-rän'yə, -rän') *n.* Also **pi·ra·ña.** Any of several tropical American freshwater fishes of the genus *Serrasalmus*. They are voraciously carnivorous and often attack and destroy living animals. Also called **caribe.** [Portuguese, from Tupi, "toothed fish" : *pirá*, fish + *sainha*, tooth.]

pi·rate (pī'rĭt) *n.* **1.** A person who robs at sea or plunders

the land from the sea. **2.** A ship used for this purpose. **3.** A person who makes use of or reproduces the work, esp. literary work, of another, without permission. —*tr.v.* **-rated, -rat·ing.** **1.** To seize by piracy. **2.** To make use of or reproduce (another's work) without permission. [Middle English, from Latin *pīrāta*, from Greek *peiratēs*, attacker, from *peiran*, to attempt, attack, from *peira*, an attempt.] —**pi·rat'ic** (pī-răt'ĭk) or **pi·rat'i·cal** *adj.* —**pi·rat'i·cal·ly** *adv.*

pi·rogue (pē'rōg', pĭ-rōg') *n.* A piragua. [French, from Spanish *piragua*, piragua.]

pir·ou·ette (pĭr'oo-ĕt') *n. Ballet.* A full turn of the body on the tip of the toe or on the ball of the foot. —*intr.v.* **-et·ted, -et·ting.** To perform a pirouette. [French, from Old French *pirouet*, a spinning top.]

pis·ca·to·ri·al (pĭs'kə-tôr'ē-əl, -tōr'-) *adj.* Also **pis·ca·to·ry** (-tôr'ē, -tōr'ē). Of or relating to fish, fishermen, or fishing. [Latin *piscātōrius*, from *piscātor*, fisherman, from *piscis*, fish.] —**pis'ca·to'ri·al·ly** *adv.*

Pi·sces (pī'sēz) *n.* **1.** A constellation in the equatorial region of the Northern Hemisphere near Aries and Pegasus. **2.** The 12th sign of the zodiac.

pi·scine (pī'sēn', pĭs'īn') *adj.* Of, relating to, or typical of fish. [Medieval Latin *piscīnus*, from *piscis*, fish.]

pis·mire (pĭs'mīr', pĭz'-) *n.* An ant. [Middle English *pissemyre* : *pisse*, urine (from the urinelike smell of an anthill) + *mire*, ant.]

pis·ta·chi·o (pĭ-stăsh'ē-ō', -stä'shē-ō') *n., pl.* **-os.** **1.** A tree, *Pistacia vera*, of the Mediterranean region and western Asia, that bears small hard-shelled nuts. **2.** The nut of this tree, with an edible, oily, green kernel. Also called **pistachio nut.** **3.** The flavor of these nuts. [Italian *pistacchio*, from Latin *pistācium*, from Greek *pistakion*, pistachio nut, from *pistakē*, pistachio tree, from Persian *pistah*.]

pis·til (pĭs'təl) *n.* The seed-bearing organ of a flower, including the stigma, style, and ovary. [French *pistil*, from Latin *pistillum*, pestle.]

pis·til·late (pĭs'tə-lāt', -lĭt) *adj. Bot.* **1.** Having pistils. **2.** Bearing pistils but no stamens: *pistillate flowers.*

pis·tol (pĭs'təl) *n.* A firearm designed to be held and fired with one hand. [French *pistole*, from German *Pistole*, from Czech *pištala*, pipe.]

pis·tole (pĭ-stōl') *n.* An obsolete gold coin, used in various European countries until the late 19th cent. [French, var. of *pistolet*, small pistol.]

pis·ton (pĭs'tən) *n.* **1.** A cylinder or disk that fits snugly into a hollow cylinder and moves back and forth under the pressure of a fluid, as in many engines, or moves or compresses a fluid, as in a pump or compressor. **2.** A valve mechanism in brass instruments, used for changing pitch. [French, from Old French, from Old Italian *pistone*, a large pestle, from *pistare*, to pound, from Latin *pinsāre*.]

piston ring. An adjustable metal ring that fits around a piston and closes the gap between the piston and cylinder wall.

piston rod. A connecting rod that transmits power to or is powered by a piston.

pit¹ (pĭt) *n.* **1.** A relatively deep hole in the ground, either natural or man-made. **2.** A trap consisting of a concealed hole in the ground; pitfall. **3.** Any hidden danger or unexpected trouble. **4.** An enclosed space, often one dug in the ground, in which animals, such as dogs or gamecocks, are placed for fighting. **5. a.** A natural depression in the surface of a body, organ, or part. **b.** A small indentation in the skin left by disease or injury; pockmark. **6.** The section directly in front of the stage of a theater, in which the musicians sit. **7.** The section of an exchange where trading in a specific commodity is carried on. **8.** A sunken area in a garage where mechanics can work underneath automobiles. **9.** Often **pits.** *Informal.* A despairing condition. —*v.* **pit·ted, pit·ting.** —*tr.v.* **1.** To make pits or similar depressions in. **2.** To put in opposition or competition; match: *"a man pitted in conflict against the sea"* (D.H. Lawrence). —*intr.v.* To become marked with small pits. [Middle English *pitt*, from Old English *pytt*, from Latin *puteus*, a pit, well.]

pit² (pĭt) *n.* The single, hard-shelled seed of certain fruits, such as a peach or cherry; stone. —*tr.v.* **pit·ted, pit·ting.** To extract pits from (fruit). [Dutch, from Middle Dutch *pitte*.]

ă pat	ā pay	â care	ä father	ĕ pet	ē be	hw which	ĭ pit	ī tie	î pier	ŏ pot	ō toe	ô paw, for	oi noise
ŏŏ took	ōō boot	ou out	th thin	*th* this	ŭ cut		û urge	zh vision	ə about, item, edible, gallop, circus				

pit·a·pat (pĭt′ə-păt′) *intr.v.* **-pat·ted, -pat·ting. 1.** To move with a series of quick, tapping steps. **2.** To make a repeated tapping sound. —*n.* A series of quick steps, taps, or beats. —*adv.* With a rapid tapping sound. [Imit.]

pitch¹ (pĭch) *n.* **1.** Any of various thick, dark, sticky substances obtained from the distillation residue of coal tar, wood tar, or petroleum, and used for waterproofing, roofing, and paving. **2.** Any of various natural bitumens, such as mineral pitch or asphalt, with similar uses. **3.** A resin derived from the sap of various coniferous trees, such as the pines. —*tr.v.* To cover with or as if with pitch. [Middle English *pich,* from Old English *pic,* from Latin *pix.*]

pitch² (pĭch) *tr.v.* **1.** To throw, usu. in a specific direction; to hurl or toss: *pitching horseshoes.* **2.** *Baseball.* **a.** To throw (the ball) from the mound to the batter. **b.** To play (a game) in the position of pitcher. **3.** To put up or in position: *pitching a tent.* **4.** To set firmly; implant; embed: *pitch stakes.* **5. a.** To fix the level of: *pitch one's expectations high.* **b.** To set the character and course of: *He pitched his speech to the party line.* **6.** To set at a specified pitch or level. —*intr.v.* **1.** To throw or toss something. **2.** *Baseball.* To play in the position of pitcher. **3.** To fall forward; plunge. **4.** To stumble around; lurch. **5. a.** To dip bow and stern alternately. **b.** To buck, as a horse. **6.** To slope downward. **7.** To set up living quarters; encamp. — See Syns at **fall.** —*phrasal verb.* **pitch in.** To set to work vigorously, esp. in cooperation with others. —*n.* **1.** An act of pitching. **2.** *Baseball.* **a.** A throw of the ball by the pitcher to the batter. **b.** A ball so thrown: *The pitch was fouled off.* **3.** An up-and-down movement, as of a ship's bow. **4. a.** Any steep downward slant. **b.** The degree of such a slant. **5.** A point or stage of development or intensity: *The dispute reached a feverish pitch.* **6. a.** The quality of a musical tone or other complex sound by which someone can judge it to be high or low, determined mostly by the frequency of the sound. **b.** The relative position of a tone in a scale, as determined by this property. **c.** Any of several standards that establish the frequency of each musical tone. **7.** *Machinery.* **a.** The distance traveled by a screw in a single revolution. **b.** The distance between two corresponding points on adjacent screw threads or gear teeth. **8.** The distance a propeller would travel in an ideal medium during one complete revolution. **9.** *Slang.* A talk designed to persuade; sales talk. [Middle English *picchen,* to pierce, fix, set, throw.]

pitch-black (pĭch′blăk′) *adj.* Extremely black.

pitch·blende (pĭch′blĕnd′) *n.* The principal ore of uranium, a brownish-black mineral of uraninite and uranium trioxide with small amounts of water and uranium decay products. [German *Pechblende* : *Pech,* pitch (from its black color) + *Blende,* a shiny mineral.]

pitch-dark (pĭch′därk′) *adj.* Extremely dark.

pitched battle. 1. A battle fought in close contact by troops whose formation and tactics have been carefully planned. **2.** Any fierce combat or dispute.

pitch·er¹ (pĭch′ər) *n.* **1.** Someone or something that pitches. **2.** *Baseball.* The player who throws the ball from the mound to the batter.

pitch·er² (pĭch′ər) *n.* A vessel for liquids, with a handle and a lip or spout for pouring. [Middle English *picher,* from Old French *pichier,* from Medieval Latin *bicārius,* goblet, from Greek *bikos,* jar.]

pitcher plant. Any of various insectivorous plants of the

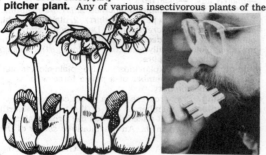

pitcher plant   **pitch pipe**

genera *Sarracenia, Nepenthes,* or *Darlingtonia,* with leaves modified to form pitcherlike organs that attract and trap insects.

pitch·fork (pĭch′fôrk′) *n.* A large fork with sharp, widely spaced prongs for pitching hay and breaking ground. —*tr.v.* To lift or toss with a pitchfork. [Middle English *pychforke,* alteration of *pikforke.*]

pitch·out (pĭch′out′) *n.* **1.** *Baseball.* A pitch deliberately thrown high and away from the batter to make it easier for the catcher to throw out a base runner attempting to steal. **2.** *Football.* A lateral pass from one back to another back behind the line of scrimmage.

pitch pipe. A small pipe sounded to give the pitch for a piece of music or for tuning an instrument.

pitch·y (pĭch′ē) *adj.* **-i·er, -i·est. 1.** Full of or covered with pitch. **2.** Resembling pitch. **3.** Extremely dark; black.

pit·e·ous (pĭt′ē-əs) *adj.* Arousing pity; pathetic. [Middle English *piteus,* from Old French, from *pite,* pity.] —**pit′e·ous·ly** *adv.* —**pit′e·ous·ness** *n.*

pit·fall (pĭt′fôl′) *n.* **1.** A trap made by digging a hole in the ground and concealing its opening. **2.** Any danger or difficulty that is not easily anticipated or avoided.

pith (pĭth) *n.* **1.** *Bot.* The soft, spongelike substance in the center of stems and branches of most vascular plants. **2.** The essential or central part; essence; gist. **3.** Force; strength; vigor. —See Syns at **heart.** [Middle English *pithe,* from Old English *pitha.*]

pith·e·can·thro·pus (pĭth′ĭ-kăn′thrə-pəs, -kăn-thrō′-) *n.* A member of a genus formerly designated *Pithecanthropus,* based on bone fragments found in Java and thought to indicate the existence of a primate between man and ape. Also called **Java man.** [Greek *pithēkos,* ape + *anthrōpos,* human being.]

pith·y (pĭth′ē) *adj.* **-i·er, -i·est. 1.** Consisting of or resembling pith. **2.** Pointed and meaningful. —See Syns at **concise.** —**pith′i·ly** *adv.* —**pith′i·ness** *n.*

pit·i·a·ble (pĭt′ē-ə-bəl) *adj.* **1.** Arousing or deserving pity or compassion; lamentable. **2.** Arousing disdainful pity; despicable. —**pit′i·a·ble·ness** *n.* —**pit′i·a·bly** *adv.*

pit·i·ful (pĭt′ĭ-fəl) *adj.* **1.** Arousing pity; pathetic. **2.** So inferior or insignificant as to be contemptible; paltry: *a pitiful excuse.* —**pit′i·ful·ly** *adv.* —**pit′i·ful·ness** *n.*

pit·i·less (pĭt′ĭ-lĭs) *adj.* Having no pity; without mercy. —**pit′i·less·ly** *adv.* —**pit′i·less·ness** *n.*

pi·ton (pē′tŏn′) *n.* A metal spike with an eye or ring through which to pass a rope, used in mountain climbing as a hold. [French, from Old French, nail.]

pit·tance (pĭt′ns) *n.* A small amount or portion, esp. of money. [Middle English *pitaunce,* from Old French *pitance,* from Medieval Latin *pittantia,* from *pietārī,* to be charitable, from Latin *pietās,* piety.]

pit·ter-pat·ter (pĭt′ər-păt′ər) *n.* A rapid series of light, tapping sounds. [Imit.] —**pit′ter-pat′ter** *adv.*

pi·tu·i·tar·y (pĭ-tōō′ĭ-tĕr′ē, -tyōō′-) *n., pl.* **-ies. 1.** *Anat.* The pituitary gland. **2.** *Med.* An extract from the anterior or posterior lobes of the pituitary gland, prepared for therapeutic use. —*adj.* Of the pituitary gland. [Latin *pītuītārius,* from *pītuīta,* phlegm.]

pituitary gland. A small, oval endocrine gland attached to the base of the vertebrate brain, the secretions of which control the other endocrine glands and influence growth, metabolism, and maturation. Also called **hypophysis** and **pituitary body.**

pit viper. Any of various venomous snakes of the family Crotalidae, such as a copperhead or rattlesnake, characterized by a small pit on each side of the head.

pit·y (pĭt′ē) *n., pl.* **-ies. 1.** Sorrow aroused by the misfortune of another; compassion for suffering. **2.** A regrettable or disagreeable fact or necessity. —*v.* **-ied, -y·ing.** —*tr.v.* To feel pity for. —*intr.v.* To feel pity. [Middle English *pite,* from Old French, from Late Latin *pietās,* compassion, from *pius,* pious, dutiful.]

piv·ot (pĭv′ət) *n.* **1.** A short rod or shaft about which a related part rotates or swings. **2.** A person or thing that chiefly determines the direction or effect of something. **3.** A wheeling movement made as if on a pivot. —*tr.v.* **1.** To mount on, attach by, or furnish with a pivot. **2.** To cause to turn on a pivot, esp. to place under the control of a determining factor. —*intr.v.* To turn on or as if on a pivot; wheel: *The shortstop pivoted and threw to first.* [French, from Old French.]

piv·ot·al (pĭv′ə-təl) *adj.* **1.** Of or used as a pivot. **2.** Of central importance: *pivotal decisions.* —**piv′ot·al·ly** *adv.*

pix·y (pĭk′sē) *n., pl.* **-ies.** Also **pix·ie.** A fairylike or elfin creature. [Orig. unknown.]

piz·za (pēt′sə) *n.* An Italian baked dish consisting of a shallow pielike crust covered usu. with a spiced mixture of tomatoes and cheese. [Italian.]

piz·ze·ri·a (pēt′sə-rē′ə) *n.* A place where pizzas are made and sold.

piz·zi·ca·to (pĭt′sĭ-kä′tō) *adj. Mus.* Played by plucking rather than bowing the strings of an instrument. —*n., pl.* **-tos.** A passage or note played in this way. [Italian, past part. of *pizzicare,* to pluck, pinch.] —**piz′zi·ca′to** *adv.*

plac·a·ble (plăk′ə-bəl, plā′kə-) *adj.* Easily calmed or pacified; tolerant; tractable. [Middle English, agreeable, from Old French, placable, from Latin *plācābilis,* from *plācāre,* to calm, appease.] —**plac′a·bil′i·ty** *n.* —**plac′a·bly** *adv.*

plac·ard (plăk′ärd, -ərd) *n.* A printed or written announcement for display in a public place; poster. —*tr.v.* **1.** To announce or advertise on a placard. **2.** To post placards on or in. [Middle English *placquart,* plate, breastplate, from Old French *plaquart,* from *plaquier,* to plaster, from Middle Dutch *placken,* to patch, paste.] —**plac′ard·er** *n.*

pla·cate (plā′kāt′, plăk′āt′) *tr.v.* **-cat·ed, -cat·ing.** To calm the anger of, esp. by yielding concessions; appease. [From Latin *plācāre,* to calm, appease.] —**pla′cat′er** *n.* —**pla·ca′tion** (plā-kā′shən, plă-) *n.* —**pla′ca·to·ry** (-kə-tôr′ē, -tōr′ē) or **pla′ca′tive** *adj.*

place (plās) *n.* **1.** A portion of space; an area with definite or indefinite boundaries. **2.** An area occupied by or set aside for someone or something: *a place to relax and be alone.* **3.** A definite location, esp.: **a.** A house, apartment, or other abode. **b.** A business establishment or office. **c.** A particular town or city. **4.** Often **Place.** A public square or a short street in a town. **5.** A space for one person to sit or stand. **6.** A job. **7.** A position regarded as possessed by someone or something else; stead: *I was chosen in his place.* **8.** A point up to which one has read in a book: *I lost my place.* **9.** Existing function; role: *behavior that has no place in a classroom.* **10.** Proper or customary location or order: *Everything is in place.* **11.** A social station entailing a certain mode of behavior: *He overstepped his place.* **12.** Any high rank or office: *"By any means get wealth and place"* (Alexander Pope). **13.** A relative position in a series; standing: *fourth place.* —*v.* **placed, plac·ing.** —*tr.v.* **1.** To put in some particular position: *place cups on the table.* **2.** To put in a relation or order: *Place the words in alphabetical order.* **3.** To find a job or living quarters for (someone). **4.** To appoint to a post. **5.** To rank in an order or sequence. **6.** To date or identify. **7.** To recollect clearly the circumstances or context of: *I can't place his face.* **8.** To make: *place a telephone call.* **9.** To apply for; request formally: *place an order.* —*intr.v.* **1.** To arrive among the first three finishers in a race. **2.** To finish in second place in a race. —**idioms. go places.** *Informal.* To become successful. **in place of.** Instead of. **take place.** To be set in (a particular time, region, etc.). [Middle English, space, locality, from Old French, from Latin *platea,* street, open space, from Greek *plateia (hodos),* "broad (street)," from *platus,* broad.]

pla·ce·bo (plə-sē′bō) *n., pl.* **-bos** or **-boes.** A substance containing no medication, given to humor a patient, to activate self-curing processes, or as a control in an experiment. [Latin, "I shall please."]

place kick. *Football.* A kick, as for a field goal, for which the ball is held or propped up in a fixed position. —**place′-kick** *v.*

place mat. A decorative and protective mat for a single setting of dishes and silver at mealtime.

place·ment (plās′mənt) *n.* **1. a.** The act of placing or arranging. **b.** The condition of being placed or arranged. **2.** The act or business of finding jobs, lodgings, or other positions for applicants.

pla·cen·ta (plə-sĕn′tə) *n., pl.* **-tas** or **-tae** (-tē) **1.** *Anat.* A vascular, membranous organ that develops in female mammals during pregnancy, lining the uterine wall and partially enveloping the fetus, to which it is attached by the umbilical cord. **2.** A similar organ in certain other animals, including certain sharks and reptiles. **3.** *Bot.* **a.** The part of the ovary to which the ovules are attached. **b.** In nonflowering plants, the tissue that bears the spore cases. [Latin, flat cake, from Greek *plakoenta,* from *plax,* flat surface.] —**pla·cen′tal** *adj.*

plac·er (plăs′ər) *n.* A deposit of sand or gravel left by a river or glacier, containing particles of valuable minerals. [Spanish, sandbank, from *plaza,* place.]

plac·id (plăs′ĭd) *adj.* Having an undisturbed surface or aspect; outwardly composed. —See Syns at **calm.** [French, from Latin *placidus,* pleasing, gentle, from *placēre,* to please.] —**pla·cid′i·ty** (plə-sĭd′ĭ-tē) or **plac′id·ness** *n.* —**plac′id·ly** *adv.*

plack·et (plăk′ĭt) *n.* A slit, often zippered, in a garment to make it easy to put on or take off. [Orig. unknown.]

plac·oid (plăk′oid′) *adj. Zool.* Platelike, as are the hard, toothlike scales of sharks, skates, and rays. [From Greek *plax,* flat surface, plate.]

pla·gia·rism (plā′jə-rĭz′əm) *n.* **1.** The act of plagiarizing. **2.** Something that is plagiarized. [From Latin *plagiarius,* kidnapper, from *plagium,* kidnapping.] —**pla′gia·rist** *n.*

pla·gia·rize (plā′jə-rīz′) *v.* **-rized, -riz·ing.** —*tr.v.* **1.** To steal and use (the ideas or writings of another) as one's own. **2.** To take passages or ideas from (another) and use them as one's own. —*intr.v.* To take and use as one's own the writings or ideas of another. —**pla′gia·riz′er** *n.*

plague (plāg) *n.* **1.** A great calamity. **2.** A very contagious, usu. fatal, epidemic disease, esp. bubonic plague or a closely related disease. **3.** *Informal.* A cause of annoyance; a nuisance. —*tr.v.* **plagued, plagu·ing. 1.** To harass, pester, or annoy. **2.** To cause misery or persistent trouble in or for. [Middle English, from Old French, from Late Latin *plāga,* from Latin, a stroke, wound.] —**plagu′er** *n.*

plagu·y (plā′gē) *adj.* Also **plagu·ey.** *Informal.* Irritating; bothersome. —**plagu′i·ly** (-gə-lē) *adv.*

plaice (plās) *n., pl.* **plaice** or **plaic·es. 1.** An edible saltwater flatfish, *Pleuronectes platessa,* of western European waters. **2.** Any of related flatfishes, such as *Hippoglossoides platessoides,* of North American Atlantic waters. [Middle English, from Old French *plais, plaïz,* from Late Latin *platessa,* ult. from Greek *platus,* broad, flat.]

plaid (plăd) *n.* **1.** A rectangular woolen scarf of a checked or tartan pattern worn over one shoulder by Scottish Highlanders. **2.** Cloth with a tartan or checked pattern. **3.** A tartan or checked pattern. —*adj.* Having a tartan or checked pattern. [Scottish Gaelic *plaide.*] —**plaid′ed** *adj.*

plain (plān) *adj.* **-er, -est. 1.** Free from obstructions; open to view. **2.** Easily understood; clearly evident; obvious. **3.** Uncomplicated; simple: *plain cooking.* **4.** Straightforward; frank; candid: *plain dealing.* **5.** Not mixed with other substances; pure. **6.** Common in rank or station; average; ordinary: *a plain man.* **7.** Not pretentious; unaffected; unsophisticated. **8.** With little ornamentation or decoration: *a plain dress.* **9.** Not beautiful or handsome; unattractive: *a plain face.* **10.** Sheer; utter; unqualified: *plain hard work.* —*n.* An extensive, level, treeless area of land. —*adv.* **1.** Clearly; without obstruction: *He could see the target plain.* **2.** Bluntly and honestly: *He spoke plain to me.* **3.** Utterly; completely: *It was just plain silly.* [Middle English, from Old French, from Latin *plānus,* flat, clear.] —**plain′ly** *adv.* —**plain′ness** *n.*

Syns: 1. plain, simple, unadorned *adj. Core meaning:* Without decoration (*a plain gray skirt*). **2. plain, forthright, straightforward** *adj. Core meaning:* Done openly and without pretense (*plain dealing*). **3. plain, homely** *adj. Core meaning:* Not physically attractive (*a plain girl*). See also Syns at **ordinary** and **pure.**

plain·clothes man (plān′klōz′). Also **plain·clothes·man** (plān′klōz′mən). A member of a police force who wears civilian clothes on duty.

plain sailing. Easy progress over a direct course.

Plains Indian. A member of any of the tribes of North American Indians that once inhabited the Great Plains.

plains·man (plānz′mən) *n.* An inhabitant or settler of the prairie regions.

plain·song (plān′sông′, -sŏng′) *n.* **1.** A Gregorian chant. **2.** Any medieval church music without strict meter and sung without accompaniment.

ă pat   ā pay   â care   ä father   ĕ pet   ē be   hw which   ĭ pit   ī tie   î pier   ŏ pot   ō toe   ô paw, for   oi noise
ōō took   ōō boot   ou out   th thin   th this   ŭ cut   û urge   zh vision   ə about, item, edible, gallop, circus

plain·spo·ken (plān'spō'kən) *adj.* Frank; straightforward: *a plain-spoken critic.* —**plain'spo'ken·ness** *n.*

plaint (plānt) *n.* **1.** A complaint. **2.** An utterance of grief or sorrow; lamentation. [Middle English, from Old French *plainte,* from Latin *planctus,* past part. of *plangere,* to strike (one's breast), lament.]

plain·tiff (plān'tǐf) *n. Law.* The party that institutes a suit in a court. [Middle English *plaintif,* from Old French, complaint, from *plaintif,* plaintive.]

plain·tive (plān'tǐv) *adj.* Expressing sorrow; mournful; melancholy: *"a fragile, plaintive fluting of woodwind notes"* (J.R. Salamanca). —**plain'tive·ly** *adv.* —**plain'tive·ness** *n.*

plait (plāt, plăt) *n.* **1.** A braid, esp. of hair. **2.** A pleat. —*tr.v.* **1.** To braid. **2.** To pleat. **3.** To make by braiding or pleating. [Middle English, fold, crease, from Old French *pleit,* from Latin *plicitus,* from *plicāre,* to fold.]

plan (plăn) *n.* **1.** An idea of what to do or how to do it, thought out ahead of time. **2.** A drawing or diagram showing how to build or assemble something. —*v.* **planned, plan·ning.** —*tr.v.* **1.** To think out ahead of time: *plan a vacation.* **2.** To have as a specific aim or purpose; intend. **3.** To draw or design (something to be built). —*intr.v.* To make plans. [French, plane, ground-plan, from Latin *plānus,* flat.] —**plan'ner** *n.*

pla·nar (plā'nər) *adj.* **1.** Of or situated in a plane. **2.** Flat: *a planar surface.* —**pla·nar'i·ty** (plə-năr'ĭ-tē) *n.*

pla·nar·i·an (plə-nâr'ē-ən) *n.* Any of various flatworms of the order Tricladida, with broad, ciliated bodies and a three-branched digestive cavity. [From Latin *plānus,* flat.]

plane¹ (plān) *n.* **1.** A geometric surface that contains all the straight lines required to connect every pair of points lying on the surface. **2.** Any flat or level surface. **3.** A level or stage of existence or development. **4.** An airplane or hydroplane. **5.** A supporting surface of an airplane; an airfoil or wing. —*adj.* Lying in a plane: *a plane curve.* —See Syns at **level.** [Latin *plānum,* a flat surface.] —**plane'ness** *n.*

plane² (plān) *n.* **1.** A carpenter's tool with an adjustable blade for smoothing and leveling wood. **2.** A trowel-shaped tool for smoothing the surface of clay, sand, or plaster in a mold. —*tr.v.* **planed, plan·ing.** **1.** To smooth or finish with or as if with a plane. **2.** To remove with a plane. [French, from Old French, from Late Latin *plāna,* from *plānāre,* to plane, from *plānus,* level.] —**plan'er** *n.*

plane²

plane³ (plān) *intr.v.* **planed, plan·ing.** **1.** To rise partly out of the water, as a hydroplane does at high speeds. **2.** To soar or glide. **3.** To travel by airplane. [French *planer,* to soar, from *plan,* a level surface, from Latin *plānus,* flat.]

plane⁴ (plān) *n.* A sycamore or related tree, with leaves resembling those of the maple and ball-shaped seed clusters. [French, from Latin *platanus,* from Greek *platanos,* from *platus,* broad (from its broad leaves).]

plane angle. An angle formed by two straight lines.

plane geometry. The geometry of planar figures.

plan·et (plăn'ĭt) *n.* **1.** A nonluminous celestial body illuminated by light from a star, such as the sun, around which it revolves. In the solar system there are nine known major planets: Mercury, Venus, Earth, Mars, Jupiter, Saturn, Uranus, Neptune, and Pluto. **2.** *Astrol.* A heavenly body that supposedly influences human beings and events. [Middle English *planete,* from Old French, from Late Latin *planēta,* from Greek *(astra) planēta,* wandering (stars), from *planasthai,* to wander.]

plan·e·tar·i·um (plăn'ĭ-târ'ē-əm) *n., pl.* **-i·ums** or **-i·a** (-ē-ə). **1.** An apparatus or model representing the solar system. **2.** A device for projecting images of celestial bodies on the inner surface of a dome. **3.** A building or room containing such a device.

plan·e·tar·y (plăn'ĭ-tĕr'ē) *adj.* **1.** Of or resembling a planet. **2.** Worldwide; global: *changing planetary weather patterns.* **3.** Denoting a gear train consisting of a central gear with an internal ring gear and one or more pinions.

plan·e·tes·i·mal (plăn'ĭ-tĕs'ə-məl, -tĕz'-) *n.* Any of innumerable small bodies thought to have orbited the sun during the formation of the planets. [PLANET + (INFINIT)ESIMAL.] —**plan'e·tes'i·mal** *adj.*

plan·e·toid (plăn'ĭ-toid') *n.* An asteroid.

plan·gent (plăn'jənt) *adj.* **1.** Striking with a deep, reverberating sound, as waves against the shore. **2.** Expressing sadness; plaintive: *a plangent melody.* [Latin *plangens,* pres. part. of *plangere,* to strike (one's breast).] —**plan'gen·cy** *n.* —**plan'gent·ly** *adv.*

plani-. Var. of **plano-.**

plank (plăngk) *n.* **1.** A piece of lumber cut thicker than a board. **2.** A foundation; support. **3.** One of the articles of a political platform. —*tr.v.* **1.** To furnish, lay, or cover with planks. **2.** To bake or broil and serve (fish or meat) on a plank. **3.** To put or set down emphatically or with force. [Middle English, from Old North French *planke,* from Latin *planca.*]

plank·ing (plăng'kĭng) *n.* A number or covering of planks.

plank·ton (plăngk'tən) *n.* Plant and animal organisms, gen. microscopic, that float or drift in great numbers in fresh or salt water. [German, from Greek, wandering, from *plazesthai,* to wander, drift.] —**plank·ton'ic** (plăngk-tŏn'ĭk) *adj.*

plano- or **plani-.** A prefix meaning flat: **planography.** [From Latin *plānus,* flat.]

pla·no·con·cave (plā'nō-kŏn-kāv', -kŏn'kāv') *adj.* Flat on one side and concave on the other.

pla·no·con·vex (plā'nō-kŏn-vĕks', -kŏn'vĕks') *adj.* Flat on one side and convex on the other.

pla·nog·ra·phy (plə-nŏg'rə-fē, plā-) *n.* A process for printing from a smooth surface, as lithography or offset. —**pla'no·graph'ic** (plā'nə-grăf'ĭk) *adj.* —**pla'no·graph'i·cal·ly** *adv.*

plant (plănt) *n.* **1.** Any organism of the vegetable kingdom that has cellulose cell walls, grows by synthesis of inorganic substances, and lacks the power of locomotion. **2.** A plant that has no permanent woody stem; an herb, as distinguished from a tree or shrub. **3.** An industrial or manufacturing establishment; factory. **4.** The buildings and equipment belonging to a factory, school, or other establishment. **5.** The act of planting. **6.** Someone or something placed secretly in order to mislead. —*tr.v.* **1.** To place or set in the ground to grow. **2. a.** To furnish or supply (a plot of land) with plants or seeds. **b.** To stock (water) with fish or spawn. **c.** To introduce (an animal) into an area. **3.** To fix or set firmly in position: *He planted both feet on the ground.* **4.** To establish or set up; to found: *plant a colony.* **5.** To implant in the mind; introduce and establish firmly: *plant a sense of justice.* **6.** To place secretly or quietly for the purposes of spying, misleading, or trapping: *Detectives planted all over the grounds.* **7.** *Slang.* To deliver (a blow or punch). [Middle English *plante,* from Old French and Old English, from Latin *planta,* shoot, from *plantāre,* to plant, from *planta,* sole of the foot.] —**plant'a·ble** *adj.*

plan·tain¹ (plăn'tən) *n.* Any of various plants of the genus *Plantago,* a common weed with broad leaves and a spike of small, greenish flowers. [Middle English, from Old French, from Latin *plantāgō,* from *planta,* sole of the foot (from its broad leaves).]

plan·tain² (plăn'tən) *n.* **1.** A large tropical plant, *Musa paradisiaca,* that resembles the banana and bears similar fruit. **2.** The fruit of this plant, used as a staple food in tropical regions. [Spanish *plantano,* plane tree, from Medieval Latin *plantanus,* from Latin *platanus.*]

plan·tar (plăn'tər, -tär') *adj.* Of or occurring on the sole of the foot: *plantar warts.* [Latin *plantāris,* from *planta,* sole of the foot.]

plan·ta·tion (plăn-tā'shən) *n.* **1.** A group of cultivated trees or plants. **2.** A large estate or farm on which crops are grown and harvested, usu. by resident workers. **3.** A newly established colony or settlement.

plant·er (plăn'tər) n. **1.** Someone or something that plants, esp. a machine or tool for planting or sowing seeds. **2.** The owner or manager of a plantation. **3.** An early settler or colonist. **4.** A decorative container for house plants.

plan·ti·grade (plăn'tĭ-grād') adj. Zool. Walking with the entire lower surface of the foot on the ground, as human beings do. —n. A plantigrade animal. [French, from New Latin plantigradus : Latin planta, sole of the foot + gradus, step.]

plant louse. An aphid.

plaque (plăk) n. **1.** A flat plate, slab, or disk that is ornamented or engraved for mounting, as on a wall for decoration or on a monument for information. **2.** A small pin or brooch worn as an ornament or a badge of membership. **3.** A deposit of matter that builds up on a tooth or on the inner wall of a blood vessel. [French, from Old French, metal plate, coin, from Middle Dutch placke, from placken, to patch, paste.]

plash (plăsh) n. A light splash. —tr.v. To spatter (liquid) about; splash. —intr.v. To splash lightly. [Perh. from Dutch plassen.]

plasm-. Var. of plasmo-.

-plasm. A suffix meaning the material characteristically forming cells: cytoplasm. [From PLASMA.]

plas·ma (plăz'mə) n. **1. a.** The clear, yellowish fluid portion of blood, lymph, or intramuscular fluid, in which cells are suspended. **b.** Cell-free, sterilized blood plasma, used in transfusions. **2.** Protoplasm or cytoplasm. **3.** The fluid portion of milk from which the curd has been separated by coagulation; whey. **4.** Physics. An electrically neutral, highly ionized gas composed of ions, electrons, and neutral particles. [From Late Latin plasma, a form, mold, from Greek, from plassein, to mold.] —plas·mat·ic (plăz-măt'ĭk) or plas'mic adj.

plasmo- or **plasm-.** A prefix meaning plasma or resemblance to plasma: plasmolysis. [From PLASMA.]

plas·mo·di·um (plăz-mō'dē-əm) n., pl. -di·a (-dē-ə). **1.** Any protozoan of the genus Plasmodium, which includes the parasites that cause malaria. **2.** A naked, multinucleate mass of protoplasm such as that characteristic of the vegetative phase of the slime molds. [PLASMO- + -ODE + -IUM.]

plas·mol·y·sis (plăz-mŏl'ĭ-sĭs) n. Shrinkage or contraction of the protoplasm in a cell, esp. a plant cell, caused by loss of water through osmosis. —plas'mo·lyt'ic (plăz'mə-lĭt'ĭk) adj. —plas'mo·lyt'i·cal·ly adv.

-plast. A suffix indicating an organized unit of living matter: chloroplast. [From Greek plastos, from plassein, to mold.]

plas·ter (plăs'tər) n. **1.** A mixture of lime, sand, and water, sometimes with hair or other fiber added, that hardens to a smooth solid and is used for coating walls and ceilings. **2.** Plaster of Paris. **3.** A pastelike mixture applied to a part of the body for healing or cosmetic purposes. **4.** Mustard plaster. —tr.v. **1.** To cover, coat, or repair with plaster. **2.** To cover thoroughly or excessively: plastered the walls with campaign posters. **3.** To apply a healing or cosmetic plaster to. **4.** To press or stick tightly. —intr.v. To apply plaster. [Middle English, from Old English, from Medieval Latin plastrum, from Latin emplastrum, from Greek emplastron, salve, from emplassein, to daub on.] —plas'ter·er n.

plas·ter·board (plăs'tər-bôrd', -bōrd') n. A thin, rigid board composed of layers of fiberboard or paper, bonded to a plaster core and used to cover walls and ceilings.

plaster cast. **1.** A mold or cast of a piece of sculpture or other object made with plaster of Paris. **2.** A cast.

plaster of Paris. Any of a group of gypsum cements, essentially hemihydrated calcium sulfate, $CaSO_4 \cdot 1/2H_2O$, a white powder that forms a paste when mixed with water and hardens into a solid, used in making casts, molds, and sculpture.

plas·tic (plăs'tĭk) adj. **1.** Capable of being shaped or formed; pliable: Clay is a plastic material. **2.** Relating to or dealing with shaping or modeling: Sculpture is a plastic art. **3.** Giving form or shape to a substance; formative: plastic forces. **4.** Easily influenced; impressionable. **5.** Having the qualities of a piece of sculpture; well-formed. **6.** Made of plastic. **7.** Physics. Capable of undergoing con-

tinuous deformation without rupture or relaxation. —See Syns at flexible. —n. Any of various complex organic compounds produced by polymerization, capable of being molded, extruded, or cast into various shapes and films, or drawn into filaments used as textile fibers. [French plastique, from Latin plasticus, from Greek plastikos, fit for molding, from plastos, molded, from plassein, to mold.] —plas'ti·cal·ly adv. —plas·tic'i·ty n.

plastic surgery. Surgery to remodel, repair, or restore injured or defective tissue or body parts. —plastic surgeon.

plas·tid (plăs'tĭd) n. Any of several specialized cytoplasmic structures occurring in plant cells and in some plantlike organisms. [German Plastid, from Greek plastos, molded, from plassein, to mold.] —plas·tid'i·al (plă-stĭd'ē-əl) adj.

plas·tron (plăs'trən) n. **1.** A breastplate worn as part of a suit of armor. **2.** A protective breastplate worn by fencers. **3.** A trimming on the front of a bodice. **4.** The ventral surface of the shell of a turtle or tortoise. [Old French, from Old Italian piastrone, from piastra, metal plate, from Latin emplastra, plaster.]

plat (plăt) tr.v. plat·ted, plat·ting. To plait or braid. —n. A braid. [Middle English platen, var. of plaiten.]

plate (plāt) n. **1.** A shallow dish, usu. circular, from which food is eaten. **2.** The contents of a dish. **3.** Food and service for one person at a meal: supper at a dollar a plate. **4.** A thin, flat sheet or piece of metal or other rigid material. **5.** A piece of flat metal on which something is engraved, as a license plate, name plate, etc. **6.** Armor or a piece of armor. **7.** A print of a woodcut or lithograph, esp. when reproduced in a book. **8.** A full-page book illustration, often printed on special paper. **9.** A sheet of light-sensitive glass or metal upon which a photographic image can be recorded. **10.** A piece of metal or plastic fitted to the gums to hold false teeth in place. **11. the plate.** Baseball. Home plate. **12.** Dishes and other household articles made of or coated with gold or silver. **13.** A thin cut of beef from the brisket. **14. a.** An electrode, as in a storage battery or capacitor. **b.** The positive electrode of an electron tube. —tr.v. plat·ed, plat·ing. **1.** To coat or cover with a thin layer of metal. **2.** To armor. **3.** Printing. To make a stereotype or electrotype from. [Middle English, from Old French, from plat, flat, ult. from Greek platus, broad, flat.]

pla·teau (plă-tō') n., pl. -teaus or -teaux (-tōz'). **1.** A relatively level area that is at a higher elevation than the land around it. **2. a.** A level or stage of growth or development. **b.** A period of little progress following a period of rapid progress. [French, from Old French platel, a flat piece, from plat, flat, ult. from Greek platus.]

plate glass. A strong rolled and polished glass containing few impurities.

plate·let (plāt'lĭt) n. A protoplasmic disk, smaller than a red blood cell, found in the blood of vertebrates and important in promoting coagulation. [Dim. of PLATE.]

plat·en (plăt'n) n. **1.** A flat metal plate that serves to position the paper and hold it against the inked type in a printing press. **2.** The roller on a typewriter. [Earlier plattin, from Old French platine, from plate, plate.]

plat·form (plăt'fôrm') n. **1.** Any floor or horizontal surface higher than an adjoining area: a speakers' platform. **2.** A formal declaration of principles, as by a political party or candidate. [Old French plate-forme, "flat form."]

plat·ing (plā'tĭng) n. **1.** A thin layer or coating of metal, such as gold or silver. **2.** A covering of metal sheets or plates.

plat·i·num (plăt'n-əm) n. **1.** Symbol Pt A silver-white metallic element found worldwide that is ductile and malleable, does not oxidize in air, and is used in electrical components, jewelry, dentistry, electroplating, and as a catalyst. Atomic number 78; atomic weight 195.09; melting point 1769°C; boiling point 3827°C; specific gravity 21.45; valences 1, 2, 3, 4. **2.** A medium to light gray color. [From Spanish platina, dim. of plata, silver, plate.]

plat·i·tude (plăt'ĭ-tōōd', -tyōōd') n. **1.** A commonplace and shallow idea or remark. **2.** Lack of originality; triteness. [French, from plat, flat.]

plat·i·tu·di·nous (plăt'ĭ-tōōd'n-əs, -tyōōd'-) adj. **1.** Commonplace; trite: a platitudinous remark. **2.** Full of or inclined to use platitudes: a platitudinous sermon.

Pla·ton·ic (plə-tŏn'ĭk, plā-) adj. **1.** Of or characteristic of

Plato or his philosophy. **2.** Often **platonic.** Transcending physical desire and tending toward the purely ideal: *platonic love.* **—Pla·ton′i·cal·ly** *adv.*

Pla·to·nism (plāt′n-ĭz′əm) *n.* The philosophy of Plato, esp. the idea that the world is a shadow or reflection of a higher reality. **—Pla′to·nist** *n.*

pla·toon (plə-tōōn′) *n.* **1.** A unit of soldiers smaller than a company but larger than a squad, normally commanded by a lieutenant. **2.** A similar unit, as of police or firemen. **3.** A group of football players that are specially trained for offense or defense and that play as a unit. [French *peloton,* group of soldiers, from Old French *pelote,* ball, from Latin *pila.*]

plat·ter (plăt′ər) *n.* **1.** A large, shallow dish or plate, used esp. for serving food. **2.** A phonograph record. [Middle English *plater,* from Norman French, from Old French *plate,* plate.]

plat·y·pus (plăt′ə-pəs) *n., pl.* **-pus·es.** A semiaquatic, egg-laying mammal, *Ornithorhynchus anatinus,* of Australia and Tasmania, with a broad, flat tail, webbed feet, and a snout resembling a duck's bill. Also called **duckbill** and **duck-billed platypus.** [From Greek *platupous,* "flat-footed" : *platus,* flat + *pous,* foot.]

plau·dit (plô′dĭt) *n.* An enthusiastic expression of praise, as enthusiastic reviews or applause. [Orig. "an appeal for applause," from Latin *plaudite,* imper. pl. of *plaudere,* to applaud.]

plau·si·ble (plô′zə-bəl) *adj.* **1.** Seemingly or apparently valid, likely, or acceptable: *a plausible forecast.* **2.** Giving a deceptive impression of trustworthiness; specious: *a plausible sales pitch.* [Orig. "deserving applause," acceptable, from Latin *plausibilis,* from *plausus,* past part. of *plaudere,* to applaud, acclaim.] **—plau′si·bil′i·ty** or **plau′si·ble·ness** *n.* **—plau′si·bly** *adv.*

play (plā) *intr.v.* **1.** To occupy oneself in amusement, sport, or other recreation. **2. a.** To take part in a game. **b.** To gamble. **3.** To act in jest or sport: *only playing around.* **4.** To deal or behave carelessly or indifferently; to toy or trifle: *She played with men's feelings.* **5.** To make love in a sportive or playful way. **6.** To act or behave in a specified way: *play fair.* **7.** To act or perform, esp. in a dramatic production. **8.** To perform on a musical instrument. **9.** To emit sound or be sounded in performance: *The band is playing.* **10.** To be performed, as in a theater or on television. **11.** To move or seem to move quickly, lightly, or irregularly: *The breeze played on the water.* **12.** To function or operate uninterruptedly; esp., to discharge a steady stream: *The fountains played in the courtyard.* **13.** To move or operate freely within a bounded space, as machine parts do. *—tr.v.* **1. a.** To perform or act (a role or part) in a dramatic performance. **b.** To assume the role of; act as: *play the villain.* **2.** To put on or present (a theatrical work) on or as if on the stage. **3.** To put on or produce a theatrical performance in: *They played Boston last week.* **4.** To pretend to be: *The boys played cowboy.* **5.** To participate in (a game or sport). **6.** To compete against in a game or sport. **7. a.** To occupy or work at (a position) in a game: *He plays first base.* **b.** To employ (a player) in a game or position: *play him at first base.* **c.** To use or move (a card, piece, or ball) in a game or sport: *play the queen of hearts.* **8.** To perform or put into effect, esp. as a jest or deception: *play a joke.* **9.** To use or manipulate, esp. for one's own interests: *He played his two opponents against each other.* **10. a.** To bet or wager. **b.** To make a wager on: *play the horses.* **11. a.** To perform on (a musical instrument). **b.** To perform (music) on an instrument. **12.** To cause (a record or phonograph, for example) to emit recorded sounds. **13.** To discharge, set off, or cause to operate in or as if in a continuous stream: *play a hose on a fire.* **14.** To cause to move rapidly, lightly, or irregularly: *play lights over the dance floor.* **—phrasal verbs. play along.** To cooperate or pretend to cooperate. **play down.** To minimize the importance of. **play off.** To determine the winner of (a tie) by playing an additional game or games. **play on** (or **upon**). To take advantage of (another's feelings or hopes) for one's own purposes. **play up.** To emphasize or publicize, often with some exaggeration. **play up to.** To try to win the favor of (someone) by flattery. *—n.* **1. a.** A literary work written for performance on the stage; drama. **b.** The performance of such a work: *attending a play.* **2.** Activity en-

gaged in for enjoyment or recreation. **3.** Fun or jesting. **4. a.** The act of carrying on or engaging in a game or sport: *After a delay, play was resumed.* **b.** The manner or way of playing a game or sport. **5.** A general manner or method of dealing with people: *fair play.* **6.** A move or action in a game: *It's your play.* **7.** Participation in betting; gambling. **8.** The condition of a ball, puck, or similar object in active or legitimate use or motion: *in play; out of play.* **9.** Action, motion, or use: *the play of the imagination.* **10.** Quick, often irregular movement or action, esp. of light or color. **11.** Movement or space for movement: *He loosened his jacket to give his arms more play.* **—idioms. play back.** To replay (a newly made record or tape). **play ball.** *Slang.* To cooperate. **play both ends against the middle.** To maneuver between two antagonists to get what one wants. **play into the hands of.** To act or react so as to give an advantage to an opponent. **play on words.** A pun. [Middle English *playen,* from Old English *plegan.*] **—play′a·ble** *adj.*

pla·ya (plī′ə) *n.* A nearly level area at the bottom of a desert basin, sometimes temporarily covered with water. [Spanish, shore, from Medieval Latin *plagia,* from Greek *plagos,* side.]

play·act (plā′ăkt′) *intr.v.* **1.** To play a role in a dramatic performance. **2.** To make believe. **3.** To behave in an over-dramatic or artificial manner.

play·back (plā′băk′) *n.* The act or process of replaying a newly made record or tape.

play·bill (plā′bĭl′) *n.* **1.** A program for a theatrical performance. **2.** A poster announcing a theatrical performance.

play·boy (plā′boi′) *n.* A carefree man devoted to pleasure.

play-by-play (plā′bī-plā′) *adj.* Consisting of a detailed running commentary or account, as of the action of a sports event.

play·er (plā′ər) *n.* **1.** Someone who participates in a game or sport. **2.** Someone who performs in theatrical roles. **3.** Someone who plays a musical instrument. **4.** The mechanism that runs a player piano.

player piano. A mechanically operated piano that uses a perforated paper roll to control the keys.

play·ful (plā′fəl) *adj.* **1.** Full of fun; frolicsome; sportive. **2.** Humorous; jesting: *a playful gibe.* **—play′ful·ly** *adv.* **—play′ful·ness** *n.*

play·go·er (plā′gō′ər) *n.* A person who attends the theater.

play·ground (plā′ground′) *n.* **1.** An outdoor area for recreation and play, often with swings, seesaws, etc. **2.** A field or sphere of unrestricted activity.

play·house (plā′hous′) *n.* **1.** A theater. **2.** A small house for children to play in.

playing card. Any of the cards, usu. in a deck of 52, used to play a wide variety of games. Each card is in one of 4 suits and has one of 13 ranks.

playing field. A marked-off field for various games.

play·mate (plā′māt′) *n.* A companion in play.

play·off (plā′ôf′, -ŏf′) *n.* **1.** A final game or series of games played to break a tie. **2.** A series of games played to determine a championship.

play·pen (plā′pĕn′) *n.* A portable enclosure in which a baby or young child can be left to play.

play·room (plā′rōōm′, -rŏŏm′) *n.* A room designed or set aside for recreation or playing.

play·thing (plā′thĭng′) *n.* Something to play with; a toy.

play·wright (plā′rīt′) *n.* A person who writes plays; dramatist.

pla·za (plä′zə, plăz′ə) *n.* **1.** A public square or similar open area in a town or city. **2.** A broad paved area for automobiles. **3.** A shopping center with parking space. [Spanish, from Latin *platea,* broad street, courtyard, from Greek *plateia (hodos),* broad (street), from *platus,* broad, flat.]

plea (plē) *n.* **1.** An appeal or entreaty. **2.** An excuse; pretext. **3.** *Law.* The answer of the defendant to a criminal charge or lawsuit. [Middle English *plai,* a lawsuit, pleading, from Norman French, from Medieval Latin *placitum,* opinion, decision, ult. from Latin *placēre,* to please.]

plead (plēd) *v.* **plead·ed** or **pled** (plĕd), **plead·ing.** *—intr.v.* **1.** To appeal earnestly; implore; beg. **2.** To argue or offer persuasive reasons: *pleading for the passage of the bill.* **3.** *Law.* **a.** To put forward a plea in a court of law. **b.** To address a court as a lawyer or advocate. *—tr.v.* **1.** To assert or urge as defense, vindication, or excuse: *plead illness.* **2.** To present as an answer to a charge, indictment, or declaration made against one. **3.** To argue or present (a case) in a court or to an authorized person. [Middle English *pleden,* from Old French *plaidier,* from Medieval Latin *placitāre,* from *placitum,* legal action, plea.] **—plead'a·ble** *adj.* **—plead'er** *n.* **—plead'ing·ly** *adv.*

plead·ing (plē'dĭng) *n.* **1. a.** The act of entreating or making a plea. **b.** A plea or entreaty. **2.** *Law.* **a.** The act or technique of presenting pleas in legal cases. **b. pleadings.** The consecutive statements made in turn by plaintiff and defendant, or prosecutor and accused, until a single issue is reached upon which the trial may be held.

pleas·ant (plĕz'ənt) *adj.* **-er, -est. 1.** Pleasing; agreeable; delightful. **2.** Pleasing or favorable in manner; amiable: *a pleasant disposition.* **—pleas'ant·ly** *adv.* **—pleas'ant·ness** *n.*
    Syns: **pleasant, enjoyable, pleasing, pleasurable** *adj.* *Core meaning:* Providing enjoyment (*a pleasant way to spend an evening*).

pleas·ant·ry (plĕz'ən-trē) *n.,* *pl.* **-ries. 1.** A pleasant, entertaining, or humorous remark or action. **2.** Pleasingly humorous style or manner in conversation or social situations.

please (plēz) *v.* **pleased, pleas·ing. —tr.v. 1.** To give enjoyment, pleasure, or satisfaction to. **2.** To be the will or desire of: *if it please the court.* **3.** To be willing to; be so kind as to. Used in the imperative to introduce a polite request: *Please close the door. —intr.v.* **1.** To give satisfaction or pleasure; be agreeable: *eager to please.* **2.** To have the will or desire; wish: *Do whatever you please.* [Middle English *plesen,* from Old French *plaisir,* from Latin *placēre.*]
    Syns: **please, satisfy, suit** *v. Core meaning:* To be satisfactory to (*an arrangement that pleases everyone*). See also Syns at **choose.**

pleas·ing (plē'zĭng) *adj.* Giving pleasure or enjoyment. See Syns at **pleasant.** **—pleas'ing·ly** *adv.*

pleas·ur·a·ble (plĕzh'ər-ə-bəl) *adj.* Agreeable; gratifying. See Syns at **pleasant.** **—pleas'ur·a·ble·ness** *n.* **—pleas'ur·a·bly** *adv.*

pleas·ure (plĕzh'ər) *n.* **1.** An enjoyable sensation or emotion; satisfaction; delight. **2.** A source of enjoyment, gratification, or delight. **3.** Sensual gratification or indulgence. **4.** A person's preference, wish, or choice: *What is your pleasure?*

pleat (plēt) *n.* A fold in cloth or other material, made by doubling the material upon itself and then pressing or stitching into place. **—tr.v.** To press or arrange in pleats. [Var. of PLAIT.]

pleb (plĕb) *n.* A plebeian. [Short for PLEBEIAN.]

plebe (plēb) *n.* A freshman at the U.S. Military or Naval Academy. [French *plèbe,* the common people, from Latin *plēbs.*]

ple·be·ian (plĭ-bē'ən) *adj.* **1.** Of or relating to the Roman plebs. **2.** Of, belonging to, or characteristic of common people. **3.** Crude; vulgar; low: *plebeian tastes. —n.* **1.** One of the Roman plebs. **2.** One of the common people. **3.** Someone who is vulgar or coarse. [Latin *plēbēius,* from *plēbs,* the common people.] **—ple·be'ian·ism** *n.*

pleb·i·scite (plĕb'ĭ-sīt') *n.* A direct vote by an entire people on an important issue. [French *plébiscite,* from Latin *plēbiscītum,* people's decree : *plēbs,* the common people + *scītum,* decree, from *scīre,* to know.]

plebs (plĕbz) *n.,* *pl.* **ple·bes** (plē'bēz'). **1.** The common people of ancient Rome. **2.** The common people; the populace. [Latin *plēbs.*]

plec·trum (plĕk'trəm) *n.,* *pl.* **-trums** or **-tra** (-trə). Also **plectron** (plĕk'trŏn'). A small, thin, flexible piece of metal, plastic, bone, or other material, used to pluck the strings of a musical instrument; a pick. [Latin, from Greek *plēktron,* from *plēssein,* to strike.]

pled (plĕd) *v.* A past tense and past participle of **plead.**

pledge (plĕj) *n.* **1.** A formal vow; a solemn promise. **2.** The words or text of a formal vow, oath, or promise. **3. a.** Something considered as security to guarantee payment of a debt or an obligation. **b.** The condition of something considered as such security: *jewels left in pledge.* **4.** A token or sign: *exchanged rings as a pledge of devotion.* **5.** A toast. **6.** Someone who has been accepted for membership in a fraternity or similar organization but has not yet been initiated. **—v. pledged, pledg·ing. —tr.v. 1.** To offer or guarantee by a solemn promise: *pledged their support.* **2.** To bind or secure by or as if by a pledge: *pledged to secrecy.* **3.** To deposit as security; to pawn. **4.** To drink a toast to. **5. a.** To promise to join (a fraternity or similar organization). **b.** To accept as a prospective member of such an organization. **—intr.v. 1.** To make a solemn promise. **2.** To drink a toast: *"Drink to me only with thine eyes, and I will pledge with mine"* (Ben Jonson). [Middle English *plegge,* from Old French *plege.*]

Plei·a·des (plē'ə-dēz') *pl. n.* **1.** *Gk. Myth.* The seven daughters of Atlas who were turned into stars. **2.** *Astron.* An open star cluster in the constellation Taurus, consisting of several hundred stars, of which six are visible to the naked eye.

Pleis·to·cene (plī'stə-sēn') *n.* Also **Pleistocene epoch.** The epoch of geologic time that began between 500,000 and 2,000,000 years ago and ended about 11,000 years ago, characterized by the alternate appearance and recession of glaciers in the Northern Hemisphere and by the appearance of the ancestors of modern man. **—modifier:** *a Pleistocene fossil.* [Greek *pleistos,* most + -CENE.]

ple·na·ry (plē'nə-rē, plĕn'ə-) *adj.* **1.** Complete in all aspects or essentials; full; absolute: *a diplomat with plenary powers.* **2.** Fully attended by all qualified members: *a plenary session of the council.* [Late Latin *plēnārius,* from Latin *plēnus,* full.] **—ple'na·ri·ly** *adv.*

plen·i·po·ten·ti·ar·y (plĕn'ə-pə-tĕn'shē-ĕr'ē, -shə-rē) *adj.* Invested with or conferring full powers. **—n.,** *pl.* **-ies.** A diplomatic agent, as an ambassador, fully authorized to represent his government. [Medieval Latin *plēnipotentiārius,* from Late Latin *plēnipotens* : Latin *plēnus,* full + *potens,* powerful.]

plen·i·tude (plĕn'ĭ-tood', -tyood') *n.* Abundance; fullness. [Middle English, from Old French, from Latin *plēnitūdō,* from *plēnus,* full.]

plen·te·ous (plĕn'tē-əs) *adj.* **1.** Abundant; plentiful. **2.** Producing or yielding in abundance. [Middle English *plentivous,* from Old French *plentiveus,* from *plentif,* abundant.] **—plen'te·ous·ly** *adv.* **—plen'te·ous·ness** *n.*

plen·ti·ful (plĕn'tĭ-fəl) *adj.* **1.** Existing in great quantity or ample supply; abundant. **2.** Providing or producing an abundance. **—See** Syns at **generous.** **—plen'ti·ful·ly** *adv.* **—plen'ti·ful·ness** *n.*

plen·ty (plĕn'tē) *n.* **1.** An ample amount or supply; as much as is needed: *plenty of exercise; plenty of time.* **2.** A large amount or number; a lot: *plenty of work to do.* **3.** General abundance or prosperity: *a time of plenty. —adj.* Ample; more than enough: *There's plenty room here. —adv. Informal.* Excessively; very: *The wound hurt plenty.* [Middle English *plentie,* from Old French *plente,* from Latin *plēnitās,* from *plēnus,* full.]

ple·o·nasm (plē'ə-năz'əm) *n.* **1.** The use of more words than are required to express an idea; redundancy. **2.** An example of this. [Late Latin *pleonasmus,* from Greek *pleonasmos,* from *ple(i)ōn,* more.] **—ple'o·nas'tic** *adj.* **—ple'o·nas'ti·cal·ly** *adv.*

ple·si·o·sau·rus (plē'sē-ə-sôr'əs, -zē-) *n.,* *pl.* **-sau·ri** (-sôr'ī'). Also **ple·si·o·saur** (plē'sē-ə-sôr', -zē-). A large saltwater reptile of the extinct suborder Plesiosauria, common in Europe and North America during the Mesozoic era. [Greek *plēsios,* near + -SAURUS.]

pleth·o·ra (plĕth'ər-ə) *n.* **1.** Superabundance; excess. **2.** *Med.* An excess of blood in the circulatory system or in one organ or area. [Medieval Latin *plēthōra,* from Greek, fullness, from *plēthein,* to be full.]

ple·tho·ric (plə-thôr'ĭk, -thŏr'-, plĕ-, plĕth'ə-rĭk) *adj.* **1. a.** Excessive in quantity; superabundant. **b.** Excessive in style; turgid: *plethoric prose.* **2.** *Med.* Characterized by an overabundance of blood. **—ple·tho'ri·cal·ly** *adv.*

pleu·ra (ploor'ə) *n.,* *pl.* **-rae** (-ē'). Either of two membranous sacs, each of which lines one side of the thoracic cavity and envelops the lung on that side. [Medieval Latin, from Greek, side, rib.] **—pleu'ral** *adj.*

pleu·ri·sy (ploor'ĭ-sē) *n.* Inflammation of the pleura, characterized by fever, difficult breathing, and coughing. [Middle English *pleresye,* from Old French *pleuresie,* from Medieval Latin *pleuresis,* from Late Latin *pleurisis,* ult.

from Greek *pleura,* side, rib.] **—pleu·rit'ic** (-rĭt'ĭk) *adj.*

Plex·i·glas (plĕk'sĭ-glăs', -gläs') *n.* A trademark for a light, transparent, weather-resistant thermoplastic.

plex·us (plĕk'səs) *n., pl.* **plexus** or **-us·es. 1.** *Anat.* A structure in the form of a network, esp. of nerves, blood vessels, or lymphatics: *the solar plexus.* **2.** Any interlacing of parts. [Latin, network, from *plectere,* to plait.]

pli·a·ble (plī'ə-bəl) *adj.* **1.** Easily bent or shaped; flexible. **2. a.** Receptive to change; adaptable. **b.** Easily influenced, persuaded, or swayed. [Middle English, from Old French, from *plier,* to bend, from Latin *plicāre,* to fold.] **—pli·a·bil'i·ty** or **pli'a·ble·ness** *n.* **—pli'a·bly** *adv.*

pli·an·cy (plī'ən-sē) *n.* The quality or condition of being pliant or flexible.

pli·ant (plī'ənt) *adj.* **1.** Easily bent or flexed; supple; limber: *a birch tree's pliant limbs.* **2.** Readily changing to fit conditions; adaptable. **3.** Yielding readily to influence or domination; docile; compliant. [Middle English *plyante,* from Old French *pliant,* pres. part. of *plier,* to bend, from Latin *plicāre,* to fold.] **—pli'ant·ly** *adv.*

pli·cate (plī'kāt') *adj.* Arranged in folds like those of a fan; pleated. [Latin *plicātus,* past part. of *plicāre,* to fold.]

pli·er (plī'ər) *n.* Someone who plies a trade.

pli·ers (plī'ərz) *n. (used with a pl. verb)* A tool with a pair of pivoted jaws, used for gripping objects tightly and for bending and cutting.

plies (plīz) *n.* Plural of the noun **ply. —v.** Third person singular present tense of the verb **ply.**

plight¹ (plīt) *n.* A condition or situation of difficulty or adversity: *the plight of the rural poor.* [Middle English *plit,* from Old French *pleit,* situation, from Latin *plicitus,* past part. of *plicāre,* to fold.]

plight² (plīt) *tr.v.* To promise or bind by a solemn pledge, esp. to betroth. **—idiom. plight one's troth.** To become engaged to marry. [Middle English *plighten,* from Old English *plihtan,* to imperil, compromise, from *pliht,* peril.] **—plight'er** *n.*

plinth (plĭnth) *n.* **1.** A block or slab upon which a pedestal, column, or statue is placed. **2.** A continuous course of stones supporting a wall. **3.** A square base, as of a vase. [French *plinthe,* from Latin *plinthus,* from Greek *plinthos,* brick, square stone block.]

plinth   plow

Pli·o·cene (plī'ə-sēn') *n.* Also **Pliocene epoch.** The epoch of geologic time that began about 13 million years ago and ended about 2 million years ago, characterized by the appearance of distinctly modern plants and animals. **—modifier:** *a Pliocene rock.* [Greek *pleiōn,* more + -CENE.]

Pli·o·film (plī'ə-fĭlm') *n.* A trademark for a pliant, transparent rubber compound used for raincoats, umbrellas, and other waterproof items.

plod (plŏd) *v.* **plod·ded, plod·ding. —intr.v. 1.** To move or walk heavily or laboriously; to trudge. **2.** To work or act slowly and wearily. **—tr.v.** To trudge heavily and slowly along or over. **—n. 1.** The act of moving or walking heavily and slowly. **2.** The sound made by a heavy step. [Imit.] **—plod'der** *n.* **—plod'ding·ly** *adv.*

plop (plŏp) *v.* **plopped, plop·ping. —intr.v. 1.** To fall with a sound like that of an object falling into water. **2.** To drop or sink heavily: *plop into a chair.* **—tr.v.** To drop or set down so as to make a heavy thud: *She plopped the tomatoes onto the plate.* **—n.** A plopping sound or movement. [Imit.]

plo·sive (plō'sĭv, -zĭv) *adj. Phonet.* Pronounced with a complete closure and abrupt opening of the oral passage: *the plosive sound of (p) in top.* **—n.** *Phonet.* A plosive speech sound. [French, from *explosif,* explosive.]

plot (plŏt) *n.* **1. a.** A small piece of ground. **b.** A measured area of land; lot. **2.** A ground plan, as for a building. **3.** The series of events that constitute the action of a narrative or drama. **4.** A secret plan to accomplish a hostile or illegal purpose; a scheme. **—v. plot·ted, plot·ting. —tr.v. 1.** To represent graphically, as on a chart: *plot a ship's course.* **2.** To form a plot for: *plot an assassination.* **3.** To conceive and arrange the action and incidents of: *plot a novel.* **4.** *Math.* **a.** To locate (points or other figures) on a graph by means of coordinates. **b.** To draw (a curve) connecting points on a graph. **—intr.v.** To devise secretly; conspire. [Middle English] **—plot'ter** *n.*

Syns: 1. plot, intrigue, story *n.* Core meaning: The series of events and relationships that form the basis of a composition (*a novel with a complex plot*). **2. plot, collusion, conspiracy, intrigue, scheme** *n.* Core meaning: A secret plan to achieve an evil or illegal goal (*a plot to hijack an airliner*).

plough (plou) *n. & v. Brit.* Var. of **plow.**

plov·er (plŭv'ər, plō'vər) *n., pl.* **-ers** or **-er. 1.** Any of various widely distributed wading birds of the family Charadriidae, with rounded bodies, short tails, and short bills. **2.** Any of various similar or related birds. [Middle English, from Old French, from Latin *pluvia,* rain, from *pluere,* to rain.]

plow (plou). Also *Brit.* **plough. —n. 1.** A farm implement that consists of a heavy blade at the end of a beam, usu. hitched to a draft team or motor vehicle, and used to break up soil and cut furrows in preparation for sowing. **2.** Any implement of similar function, as a snowplow. **—tr.v. 1.** To break and turn over (earth) with a plow. **2. a.** To form with a plow: *plowing deep furrows.* **b.** To make with driving force: *plowed his way through the crowd.* **3.** To cut through (water): *plow the high seas.* **—intr.v. 1.** To break and turn up earth with a plow. **2.** To be capable of being plowed. **3.** To move or progress with driving force: *plowing through the line for a gain of six yards.* **4.** To proceed laboriously; to plod. **—phrasal verbs. plow back.** To reinvest (earnings or profits) in one's business. **plow into.** *Informal.* To undertake with enthusiasm or energy. [Middle English *plogh,* from Old English *plōh,* plowland.] **—plow'er** *n.*

plow·boy (plou'boi') *n.* **1.** A boy who leads or guides a team of animals in plowing. **2.** A country boy.

plow·man (plou'mən) *n.* **1.** A person who plows. **2.** A farmer or rustic.

plow·share (plou'shâr') *n.* The cutting blade of a plow.

ploy (ploi) *n.* A carefully planned action or move, as in a conversation or game, to obtain an advantage over an opponent; stratagem. [Scottish.]

pluck (plŭk) *tr.v.* **1.** To detach by pulling with the fingers; to pick: *pluck a flower.* **2.** To pull out the hair or feathers of: *pluck a chicken.* **3.** To give an abrupt pull to; tug at: *pluck a sleeve.* **4.** To sound (the strings of a musical instrument) by pulling and releasing them with the fingers or a plectrum. **—intr.v.** To give an abrupt pull. **—n. 1.** The act of plucking; a tug or pull. **2.** Resourceful courage and daring in the face of difficulties; spirit. **3.** The heart, liver, windpipe, and lungs of a slaughtered animal. [Middle English *plukken,* from Old English *pluccian.*] **—pluck'er** *n.*

pluck·y (plŭk'ē) *adj.* **-i·er, -i·est.** Having or showing courage or spirited resourcefulness.—See Syns at **brave.** **—pluck'i·ly** *adv.* **—pluck'i·ness** *n.*

plug (plŭg) *n.* **1.** An object, such as a cork or wad of cloth, used to stop a hole or gap. **2.** *Elect.* **a.** A fitting, usu. with two metal prongs for insertion in a fixed socket, used to connect an appliance to a power supply. **b.** A spark plug. **3.** A fireplug. **4. a.** A flat cake of pressed or twisted tobacco. **b.** A portion of chewing tobacco. **5.** *Geol.* A mass of igneous rock filling the opening or vent of a volcano. **6.** *Informal.* A favorable public mention of a commercial product, business, etc., esp. when inserted in noncommercial material. **7.** *Slang.* Anything inferior, useless, or defective, esp. an old, worn-out horse. **8.** *Slang.* A gunshot or bullet. **—v. plugged, plug·ging. —tr.v. 1.** To fill (a hole) tightly with or as if with a plug; stop up. **2.** To use as a plug: *plugged a cork in a bottle.* **3.** *Slang.* **a.** To hit with a bullet; shoot. **b.** To hit with the fist; to punch. **4.** *Informal.* **a.** To make favorable public mention of (a product or business). **b.** To publicize repeatedly. —*intr.v.* **1.** *Informal.* To work doggedly and persistently: *keep plugging away.* **2.** *Informal.* To work for a particular cause or person: *plug for a promotion.* [Middle Dutch *plugge.*] —**plug′ger** *n.*

plum (plŭm) *n.* **1.** Any of several shrubs or small trees of the genus *Prunus,* that bear smooth-skinned, fleshy, edible fruit with a single hard-shelled seed. **2.** The fruit of any of these trees. **3. a.** Any of several trees that bear plumlike fruit. **b.** The fruit of such a tree. **4.** A raisin, when added to a pudding or cake. **5.** A sugarplum. **6.** A dark reddish purple. **7.** Something esp. desirable or envied, such as a job or high honor. —*modifier: plum jam.* —*adj.* Dark reddish purple. [Middle English, from Old English *plūme,* from Latin *prūnum.*]

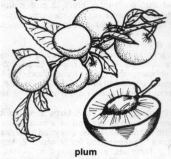

plum   plume

plum·age (plōō′mĭj) *n.* **1.** The feathers of a bird. **2.** Ornamental feathers. **3.** Elaborate dress; finery.

plu·mate (plōō′māt′) *adj.* Resembling a plume or feather.

plumb (plŭm) *n.* **1.** A weight suspended from the end of a line, used to determine water depth. **2.** Such a device used to test vertical alignment. —*adj.* **1.** Exactly vertical. **2.** *Informal.* Utter; absolute; sheer: *a plumb fool.* —See Syns at **vertical.** —*adv.* **1.** In a vertical or perpendicular line. **2.** *Informal.* Utterly; completely; entirely: *plumb tired.* —*tr.v.* **1.** To test the alignment or angle of with a plumb. **2.** To straighten or make perpendicular: *plumb up a post.* **3.** To determine the depth of; to sound. **4.** To examine closely; probe into. **5.** To seal with lead. —*intr.v.* To work as a plumber. [Middle English *plumbe,* from Old French *plombe,* from Latin *plumbum,* lead.] —**plumb′a·ble** *adj.*

plum·ba·go (plŭm-bā′gō) *n., pl.* **-gos.** Graphite. [Latin *plumbāgō,* lead ore, from *plumbum,* lead.]

plumb bob. A usu. conical piece of metal attached to the end of a plumb line; plummet.

plumb·er (plŭm′ər) *n.* A worker who installs and repairs pipes and plumbing.

plumb·ing (plŭm′ĭng) *n.* **1.** The pipes, fixtures, and other apparatus of a water, gas, or sewage system. **2.** The work or trade of a plumber.

plumb line. **1.** A line from which a weight is suspended to determine verticality or depth. **2.** A line regarded as directed exactly toward the earth's center of gravity.

plume (plōōm) *n.* **1.** A feather, esp. one that is large and showy. **2.** A large feather or cluster of feathers worn as an ornament or symbol of rank. **3.** A token of honor or achievement. **4.** Anything resembling a feather: *a plume of smoke.* —*tr.v.* **plumed, plum·ing.** **1.** To decorate with or as if with plumes. **2.** To preen; smooth with the beak: *The parrot plumed its feathers.* **3.** To pride or congratulate (oneself). [Middle English, from Old French, from Latin *plūma.*] —**plum′y** *adj.*

plum·met (plŭm′ĭt) *n.* A plumb bob. —*intr.v.* To drop straight down; to plunge. [Middle English *plomet,* from Old French *plombet,* ball of lead, dim. of *plomb,* lead, from Latin *plumbum.*]

plu·mose (plōō′mōs′) *adj.* **1.** Having plumes or feathers; feathered. **2.** Resembling a feather or plume; feathery.

plump¹ (plŭmp) *adj.* **-er, -est.** Well-rounded and full in form. —*tr.v.* To make plump: *plump up a pillow.* —*intr.v.* To become plump. [Middle Low German, thick, blunt,

dull.] —**plump′ly** *adv.* —**plump′ness** *n.*

plump² (plŭmp) *intr.v.* **1.** To drop abruptly or heavily: *plump into a chair.* **2.** To give full support or praise: *plumping for her candidate.* —*tr.v.* To drop or throw down heavily or abruptly: *plump an ice cube into a glass.* —*n.* **1.** A heavy or abrupt fall or collision. **2.** The sound of this. —*adv.* **1.** With a heavy or abrupt impact: *ran plump into a tree trunk.* **2.** Straight down. [Middle Low German *plumpen,* to fall or plunge into water.]

plum pudding. A rich boiled or steamed pudding made with flour, suet, raisins, currants, and spices.

plu·mule (plōōm′yōōl) *n.* **1.** A down feather. **2.** *Bot.* The rudimentary bud of a plant embryo.

plun·der (plŭn′dər) *tr.v.* **1.** To rob of goods by force, esp. in time of war; to pillage. **2.** To seize wrongfully or by force; to steal. —*intr.v.* To take booty; rob; pillage. —See Syns at **sack.** —*n.* **1.** Property stolen by fraud or force; booty. **2.** The act or practice of plundering. [German *plünder,* from Middle High German, from *plunder,* household goods.] —**plun′der·er** *n.*

plunge (plŭnj) *tr.v.* **plunged, plung·ing.** **1.** To thrust or throw forcefully into a substance or place: *plunged the lobster into the pot of boiling water.* **2.** To cast suddenly or violently into a given condition or situation: *"The street was plunged in cool shadow"* (Richard Wright). —*intr.v.* **1.** To throw oneself into a substance or place, esp. into water. **2.** To throw oneself energetically into a given condition or activity: *He plunged into his work.* **3.** To enter violently or speedily. **4.** To descend steeply: *The cliff plunges to the rocky shoreline.* **5.** To move forward and downward violently. **6.** *Informal.* To take a chance; to gamble. —See Syns at **fall.** —*n.* **1.** An act of plunging. **2.** A swim; dip. **3.** *Informal.* A gamble. [Middle English *plungen,* from Old French *plonger,* ult. from Latin *plumbum,* lead.]

plung·er (plŭn′jər) *n.* **1.** Someone or something that plunges, esp. a machine part that operates with a repeated thrusting or plunging movement. **2.** A device consisting of a rubber suction cup attached to the end of a stick, used to clean out clogged drains and pipes.

plunk (plŭngk) *Informal.* —*tr.v.* **1.** To strum or pluck (the strings of a musical instrument). **2.** To throw or place heavily or abruptly: *plunk one's money down.* —*intr.v.* **1.** To emit a hollow, twanging sound. **2.** To drop or fall abruptly or heavily; plump. —*n.* *Informal.* **1.** A short, hollow, twanging sound. **2.** A heavy blow or stroke. —*adv.* **1.** With a short, hollow thud. **2.** Exactly; precisely: *The dart landed plunk in the center of the target.* [Imit.] —**plunk′er** *n.*

plu·per·fect (plōō-pûr′fĭkt) *adj.* Of or designating a verb tense used to express action completed prior to a specified or implied past time. —*n.* **1.** The pluperfect tense, formed in English with the past participle of a verb and one or more auxiliaries. For example, in the sentence *He had been gone an hour when we arrived, had been gone* is in the pluperfect. **2.** A verb or form in this tense. Also called **past perfect.** [New Latin *plūsperfectum,* from Latin *(tempus praeteritum) plūs quam perfectum,* "(past tense) more than perfect."]

plu·ral (plŏŏr′əl) *adj.* **1.** Of or composed of more than one. **2.** Of or relating to a grammatical form that designates more than one of the things specified: *a plural noun.* —*n.* **1.** The plural grammatical number or form. **2.** A word or term in the plural form. [Middle English, from Old French *plurel,* from Latin *plūrālis,* from *plūs,* more.] —**plu′ral·ly** *adv.*

plu·ral·ism (plŏŏr′ə-lĭz′əm) *n.* **1.** The condition of being plural. **2.** A condition of society in which numerous distinct ethnic, religious, or cultural groups coexist within one nation. **3.** *Philos.* The doctrine that reality is composed of many ultimate substances.

plu·ral·i·ty (plŏŏ-răl′ĭ-tē) *n., pl.* **-ties.** **1.** The condition or fact of being plural. **2. a.** In a contest of more than two candidates, the number of votes cast for the winner if this number is less than half of the total votes cast. **b.** The number by which the vote of a winning candidate is more than that of his closest opponent. **3.** The larger or greater part of anything.

plus (plŭs) *prep.* **1.** Added to: *Two plus three is five.* **2.** Increased by; along with: *wages plus bonuses.* —*adj.* **1.** Of addition: *a plus button on a calculator.* **2.** Greater than zero; positive. **3.** Of or indicating an electric charge that is like that of a proton and unlike that of an electron. **4.** Added or extra: *a plus benefit.* **5.** Slightly more than: *a grade of B plus.* —*n.* **1.** The plus sign (+). **2.** A positive quantity. **3.** A favorable factor. [Latin *plūs,* more.]

plush (plŭsh) *n.* A fabric of silk, rayon, cotton, or other material, with a thick, deep pile. —*adj.* **-er, -est.** Lavish and rich: *a plush restaurant.* —See Syns at **luxurious.** [Old French *p(e)luche,* from *peluch(i)er,* to pluck.] —**plush′ly** *adv.*

Plu·to (plōō′tō) *n.* **1.** *Rom. Myth.* The god of the dead and the ruler of the underworld, identified with the Greek god Hades. **2.** The ninth and farthest planet from the sun, with a sidereal period of revolution about the sun of 248.4 years, 2.8 billion miles distance at perihelion and 4.6 billion miles at aphelion, and a diameter approximately half that of the earth.

plu·toc·ra·cy (plōō-tŏk′rə-sē) *n., pl.* **-cies. 1.** Government by the wealthy. **2.** A wealthy class that controls a government. [Greek *ploutokratia* : *ploutos,* wealth + *kratos,* power.]

plu·to·crat (plōō′tə-krăt′) *n.* **1.** A member of a wealthy governing class. **2.** Anyone having political influence or control because of wealth. [From PLUTOCRACY.]

plu·to·crat·ic (plōō′tə-krăt′ĭk) or **plu·to·crat·i·cal** (-ĭ-kəl) *adj.* Of, relating to, or resembling a plutocrat or plutocracy. —**plu′to·crat′i·cal·ly** *adv.*

plu·ton·ic (plōō-tŏn′ĭk) *adj. Geol.* Of deep igneous or magmatic origin: *plutonic water.* [From PLUTO (god).]

plu·to·ni·um (plōō-tō′nē-əm) *n. Symbol* **Pu** A naturally radioactive, silvery, metallic transuranic element that is found in uranium ores and artificially produced by neutron bombardment of uranium, having fifteen isotopes with masses ranging from 232 to 246 and half-lives from 20 minutes to 76 million years, used as a reactor fuel and in nuclear weapons. Atomic number 94; melting point 639.5°C; boiling point 3,235°C; specific gravity 19.8; valence 3, 4, 5, 6. [After the planet PLUTO.]

plu·vi·al (plōō′vē-əl) *adj.* **1.** Of or relating to rain. **2.** *Geol.* Caused by rain. [Latin *pluviālis,* from *pluvia,* rain, from *pluere,* to rain.]

ply¹ (plī) *tr.v.* **plied, ply·ing. 1.** To join together, as by molding or twisting. **2.** To double over (cloth, paper, etc.). —*n., pl.* **plies. 1.** A layer, as cloth, paperboard, wood. **2.** One of the strands twisted together to make yarn, rope, or thread. —*modifier: three-ply yarn.* [Middle English *plien,* from Old French *plier,* from Latin *plicāre,* to fold.]

ply² (plī) *v.* **plied, ply·ing.** —*tr.v.* **1.** To use or wield diligently: *ply an axe; ply a sword.* **2.** To engage in; practice: *ply a trade.* **3.** To traverse or sail over regularly: *Trading ships plied the routes between coastal ports.* **4.** To continue supplying or offering: *plying her guests with food.* **5.** To assail vigorously: *plied them with questions.* —*intr.v.* **1.** To traverse a route or course regularly. **2.** To perform or work diligently or regularly. —See Syns at **handle.** [Middle English *(ap)plien,* to employ.]

Plymouth Rock. An American breed of fowl raised for both meat and eggs.

ply·wood (plī′wōŏd′) *n.* A building material made of layers of wood glued tightly together, usu. with the grains of adjoining layers at right angles to each other. [PLY (layer) + WOOD.]

Pm The symbol for the element promethium.

pneu·mat·ic (nōō-măt′ĭk, nyōō-) or **pneu·mat·i·cal** (-ĭ-kəl) *adj.* **1.** Of or relating to air or other gases. **2.** Of or relating to pneumatics. **3.** Run by or using compressed air: *a pneumatic drill.* **4.** Filled with air, esp. compressed air: *a pneumatic tire.* [French *pneumatique,* from Latin *pneumaticus,* from Greek *pneumatikos,* from *pneuma,* wind.] —**pneu·mat′i·cal·ly** *adv.*

pneu·mat·ics (nōō-măt′ĭks, nyōō-) *n. (used with a sing. verb).* The study of the mechanical properties of air and other gases.

pneu·mo·coc·cus (nōō′mə-kŏk′əs, nyōō′-) *n., pl.* **-coc·ci** (-kŏk′sī′, kŏk′ī′). A bacterium, *Diplococcus pneumoniae,* that causes pneumonia. [Greek *pneuma,* breath + -COC-CUS.] —**pneu′mo·coc′cal** (-kŏk′əl) *adj.*

pneu·mo·nia (nōō-mōn′yə, nyōō-) *n.* An acute or chronic disease marked by inflammation of the lungs, and caused by viruses, bacteria, and physical and chemical agents. [From Greek *pneumonia,* alteration of *pleumonia,* disease of the lungs, from *pleumōn,* lung.]

pneu·mon·ic (nōō-mŏn′ĭk, nyōō-) *adj.* **1.** Of, affected by, or similar to pneumonia. **2.** Of or affecting the lungs; pulmonary. [Greek *pneumonikos,* of the lungs, from *pneumōn,* alteration of *pleumōn,* lung.]

Po The symbol for the element polonium.

poach¹ (pōch) *tr.v.* To cook in a gently boiling or simmering liquid: *fish poached in wine.* [Middle English *pochen,* from Old French *poch(i)er (des œufs),* to put (eggs) into a pocket.] —**poach′er** *n.*

poach² (pōch) *intr.v.* **1.** To trespass on another's property in order to take fish or game. **2.** To take fish or game in a forbidden area. —*tr.v.* **1.** To trespass on (another's property) for fishing or hunting. **2.** To take (fish or game) illegally. [Old French *pochier,* to thrust, poke.] —**poach′er** *n.*

pock (pŏk) *n.* **1.** A pus-filled swelling of the skin caused by smallpox or a similar disease. **2.** A mark or scar left in the skin by such a pustule; a pockmark. [Middle English *pokke,* from Old English *pocc.*]

pock·et (pŏk′ĭt) *n.* **1.** A small, flat pouch sewed into or onto the outside of a garment and used to carry small articles. **2.** Any receptacle, cavity, or opening that resembles a pocket. **3.** Supply of money; financial means. **4.** One of the pouchlike receptacles at the corners and sides of a pool table. **5.** A small, isolated or protected area or group: *pockets of civilization.* **6.** A mass or accumulation of a substance surrounded by another substance from which it is more or less distinct: *a pocket of ore.* —*adj.* **1.** Suitable for carrying in one's pocket: *a pocket edition.* **2.** Tiny; miniature. —*tr.v.* **1.** To place in or as if in one's pocket. **2.** To take possession of for oneself, esp. dishonestly. **3.** To accept quietly: *pocket an insult.* **4.** To suppress or conceal: *He pocketed his pride.* **5.** To hit (a ball) into a pocket of a pool table. [Middle English *poket,* from Old North French, dim. of *poke, poque,* bag.] —**pock′et·er** *n.*

pocket billiards. The game of pool.

pock·et·book (pŏk′ĭt-bōŏk′) *n.* **1.** A pocket-sized folder or case used to hold money and papers; wallet; billfold. **2.** A bag used to carry money, papers, and other small articles; purse. **3.** Supply of money; financial resources. **4.** A pocket-sized, usu. paperbound book.

pock·et·ful (pŏk′ĭt-fōŏl′) *n., pl.* **-fuls** or **pock·ets·ful.** As much as a pocket will hold.

pocket gopher. A mammal, the **gopher.**

pock·et·knife (pŏk′ĭt-nīf′) *n.* A small knife with a blade or blades that folds into the handle.

pocket veto. The indirect veto of a bill by an executive by his retaining the bill unsigned until the legislature adjourns.

pock·mark (pŏk′märk′) *n.* A pitlike scar left on the skin by smallpox or another eruptive disease. —**pock′marked′** *adj.*

po·co (pō′kō) *adv. Mus.* Somewhat. Used as a direction. [Italian, little, from Latin *paucus.*]

pod (pŏd) *n. Bot.* **a.** A dehiscent seed vessel or fruit of a leguminous plant, such as the pea. **b.** A fruit that contains several seeds, and that usu. dries and splits open. **2.** A podlike protective covering. **3.** An external streamlined compartment on aircraft that encloses engines, machine guns, or fuel. —*v.* **pod·ded, pod·ding.** —*intr.v.* **1.** To bear or produce pods. **2.** To expand or swell like a pod. —*tr.v.* To remove (seeds) from a pod. [Prob. alteration of COD.]

-pod or **-pode.** A suffix meaning foot or feet: **gastropod.** [From Greek *pous,* foot.]

po·di·a·try (pə-dī′ə-trē) *n.* The study and treatment of foot ailments. Also called **chiropody.** [Greek *pous,* foot + *iatros,* healer.] —**po·di′a·trist** *n.*

po·di·um (pō′dē-əm) *n., pl.* **-di·a** (-dē-ə) or **-ums. 1.** An elevated platform for an orchestra conductor, lecturer, etc.; dais. **2.** A low wall serving as a foundation. **3.** A wall circling the arena of an ancient amphitheater. [Latin, raised platform, balcony, from Greek *podion,* base, from *pous,* foot.]

po·em (pō′əm) *n.* **1.** A verse composition designed to convey an imaginative sense of experience, characterized by condensed language that is used for its sound and sugges-

---

â pat	ā pay	â care	ä father	ĕ pet	ē be	hw which	ĭ pit	ī tie	î pier	ŏ pot	ō toe	ô paw, for	oi noise
ōō took	ōō boot	ou out	th thin	th this	ŭ cut		û urge	zh vision	ə about, item, edible, gallop, circus				

tive power as well as its meaning. **2.** Any composition in verse rather than in prose. **3.** Any literary composition written with an intensity or beauty of language more characteristic of poetry than of prose: *a prose poem.* **4.** Any creation, object, or experience thought to have the beauty or perfection of form of poetry. [Old French *poeme,* from Latin *poēma,* from Greek *poiēma,* from *poiein,* to make, create.]

po·e·sy (pō′ĭ-zē, -sē) *n., pl.* **-sies.** *Archaic.* **1.** Poetry. **2.** The art or practice of composing poems. [Middle English *poesie,* from Old French, from Latin *poēsis,* from Greek, from *poiein,* to make, create.]

po·et (pō′ĭt) *n.* **1.** A writer of poems. **2.** A person who is esp. gifted in the perception and expression of the beautiful or lyrical. [Middle English *poete,* from Old French, from Latin *poēta,* from Greek *poiētēs,* from *poiein,* to make, create.]

po·et·as·ter (pō′ĭ-tăs′tər) *n.* An inferior poet. [Medieval Latin.]

po·et·ess (pō′ĭ-tĭs) *n.* A woman poet.

po·et·ic (pō-ĕt′ĭk) or **po·et·i·cal** (-ĭ-kəl) *adj.* **1.** Of or relating to poetry: *poetic works.* **2.** Having a quality or style characteristic of poetry: *poetic diction.* **3.** Suitable as a subject for poetry: *a poetic love affair.* **4.** Of or befitting a poet: *poetic insight.* —**po·et′i·cal·ly** *adv.*

poetic justice. The rewarding of virtue and the punishing of vice in a manner that is particularly and often ironically fitting.

poetic license. The liberty taken, esp. by an artist or writer, in deviating from conventional form or fact to achieve a desired effect.

po·et·ics (pō-ĕt′ĭks) *n. (used with a sing. verb).* **1.** Literary criticism that deals with the nature, forms, and laws of poetry. **2.** A treatise on poetry or aesthetics.

poet laureate *pl.* **poets laureate** or **poet laureates.** **1.** A poet appointed by the British sovereign to a lifetime position as chief poet of the kingdom. **2.** A poet acclaimed as the most excellent or representative of a locality or group. **3.** Any poet honored for excellence.

po·et·ry (pō′ĭ-trē) *n.* **1.** The art or work of a poet. **2. a.** Poems regarded as a division of literature. **b.** The poetic works of a given author, group, nation, or kind. **3.** Any piece of literature written in meter; verse. **4.** Prose that resembles a poem, as in sound or language. **5.** The quality of a poem, as possessed by an object, act, or experience: *the poetry of her dance movements.*

po·go stick (pō′gō). A strong stick with a heavy spring set into the bottom end and two footrests on which a person stands and hops. [From *Pogo,* a former trademark.]

po·grom (pə-grŭm′, -grŏm′, pō′grəm) *n.* An organized and often officially encouraged massacre or persecution of a minority group, esp. one conducted against the Jews. [Russian, devastation.]

poi (poi, pō′ē) *n.* A Hawaiian food made from cooked taro root that is pounded to a paste and often fermented. [Hawaiian.]

poign·ant (poin′yənt) *adj.* **1.** Keenly distressing or painful: *poignant anxiety.* **2.** Affecting the emotions sharply; touching: *poignant memories.* **3.** Piercing; incisive: *poignant criticism.* **4.** Agreeably intense or stimulating: *poignant delight.* —See Syns at **moving.** [Middle English *poynaunt,* pointed, sharp, from Old French *puignant,* from Latin *pungens,* pres. part. of *pungere,* to prick, pierce.] —**poign′ance** or **poign′an·cy** *n.* —**poign′ant·ly** *adv.*

poi·ki·lo·therm (poi-kē′lə-thûrm′, -kĭl′ə-) *n. Zool.* A cold-blooded organism, such as a fish or reptile. [Greek *poikilos,* various + -THERM.]

poin·ci·an·a (poin′sē-ăn′ə, -ä′nə) *n.* Any of various tropical trees of the genus *Poinciana,* with large orange or red flowers. [After M. de Poinci, 17th-cent. governor of the French Antilles.]

poin·set·ti·a (poin-sĕt′ē-ə, -sĕt′ə) *n.* A tropical American shrub, *Euphorbia pulcherrima,* with showy, usu. scarlet bracts beneath the small yellow flowers. [After Joe Roberts Poinsett (1799–1851), U.S. minister to Mexico.]

point (point) *n.* **1.** The sharp or tapered end of something: *the point of a knife.* **2.** Something that has a sharp or tapered end, as a knife or needle. **3.** A tapering extension of land projecting into water; promontory; cape. **4.** A mark formed by or as if by the sharp end of something. **5.** A mark or dot used in printing or writing. **6.** A mark used in punctuation, esp. a period. **7.** A decimal point. **8.** *Geom.* A dimensionless geometric object having no property but location. **9.** A position, place, or locality; spot: *a good point to begin.* **10.** A specified degree, condition, or limit: *the boiling point; the point of no return.* **11. a.** Any of the 32 directions indicated on a mariner's compass. **b.** The distance or interval of 11 degrees, 15 minutes between any two adjacent markings on a mariner's compass. **12.** A specific moment in time. **13.** An important, essential, or primary part: *the point of the story.* **14.** A purpose, goal, or reason: *the point of his visit.* **15.** A significant, outstanding, or effective idea, argument, or suggestion: *the major points in a speech.* **16.** A separate or individual item or element; detail. **17.** A striking or distinctive characteristic or quality: *made the most of their good points.* **18.** A single unit, as in counting, rating, scoring, or measuring. **19.** A unit of academic credit usu. equal to one hour of class work per week during one semester. **20.** The stiff and attentive stance taken by a hunting dog. **21.** An electrical contact, esp. one in the distributor of an automobile engine. **22.** *Finance.* A unit equal to one dollar and used to quote or state the current prices of stocks, commodities, etc. **23.** *Mus.* A phrase, such as a fugue subject, in contrapuntal music. **24.** *Printing.* A unit of type size equal to 0.01384 inch, or approximately $^1/_{72}$ of an inch. **25.** A jeweler's unit of mass equal to 2 milligrams or 0.01 carat. **26. a.** Needlepoint. **b.** Bobbin lace. **27.** A branch of a deer's antler. —*tr.v.* **1.** To direct or aim: *point a weapon.* **2.** To indicate the position or direction of: *point the way.* **3.** To provide with a point; sharpen. **4.** To mark with a point or period; punctuate. **5.** To give emphasis to; to stress. **6.** To indicate the presence and position of (game) by standing immobile and directing the muzzle toward it. —*intr.v.* **1.** To direct attention or indicate position with or as if with the finger. **2.** To turn the mind or thought in a particular direction: *Mathematical probability points to life existing elsewhere in the universe.* **3.** To be turned or faced in a given direction; to aim. **4.** To show the location of animals hunted as game by standing still and facing in that direction, as a hunting dog does. —**idioms. in point.** Being considered: *three cases in point.* **in point of.** With reference to; in the matter of. **make a point of.** To attach great importance to; insist upon. [Middle English, from Old French, a prick, dot, small particle, and *pointe,* pointed end or tip, both from Latin *punctus,* past part. of *pungere,* to pierce, prick.]

point-blank (point′blăngk′) *adj.* **1.** Aimed straight at the mark or target. **2.** Very close to a target: *pointblank range.* **3.** Straightforward; blunt. —*adv.* **1.** With a straight aim at a close target: *fired pointblank.* **2.** Without hesitation; bluntly: *answer pointblank.* [Prob. from Old French *de pointe en blanc,* "(straight) from the aiming into the target."]

point·ed (poin′tĭd) *adj.* **1.** Having an end coming to a point. **2.** Sharp; cutting; incisive: *a pointed question.* **3.** Directed at or referring to a particular person: *a pointed comment.* **4.** Conspicuous; marked: *a pointed lack of interest.* —**point′ed·ly** *adv.* —**point′ed·ness** *n.*

point·er (poin′tər) *n.* **1.** Someone or something that points, esp. a long stick for indicating objects or items, as on a chart. **2.** A marker that indicates numbers, as in a clock or

poinsettia

meter. **3.** One of a breed of hunting dogs with a short-haired coat. **4.** A piece of advice; helpful hint.

poin·til·lism (point'tl-ĭz'əm, pwăn'-) *n.* A painting technique associated with Seurat and his followers in late 19th cent. France and characterized by the application of paint in small dots and brush strokes that blend together when seen from a distance. [French *pointillisme*, from *pointiller*, to paint small dots, from *pointille*, small point or dot.] —**poin·til·list** *n. & adj.* —**poin·til·lis·tic** *adj.*

point·less (point'lĭs) *adj.* **1.** Meaningless; irrelevant. **2.** Ineffectual. —**point·less·ly** *adv.* —**point·less·ness** *n.*

point of honor. A matter that affects one's honor.

point of order. A question as to whether what is being discussed or done is allowed by parliamentary rules.

point of view. 1. The position from which something is observed or considered; standpoint. **2.** A person's manner of viewing things; attitude.

poise (poiz) *v.* **poised, pois·ing.** —*tr.v.* To carry or hold in equilibrium; to balance: *poised the spinning ball on the tip of his finger.* —*intr.v.* To be balanced or held in suspension; hover: *poise on the brink.* —*n.* **1.** The condition of being balanced; stability; balance. **2.** Freedom from affectation or embarrassment; dignity of manner; composure. [Middle English *poisen*, to weigh, from Old French *poiser*, ult. from Latin *pendere*, to weigh.]

poi·son (poi'zən) *n.* **1.** Any substance that causes injury, illness, or death, esp. by chemical means. **2.** Anything that is destructive or fatal. **3.** *Chem.* A substance that inhibits or retards a chemical reaction. —*tr.v.* **1.** To kill or harm with poison. **2.** To put poison on or into: *poison a cup.* **3. a.** To pollute: *Noxious fumes poison the air.* **b.** To have a harmful influence on; to corrupt: *Jealousy poisoned their friendship.* **4.** *Chem.* To inhibit or retard (a chemical reaction). —*adj.* Poisonous. [Middle English *poysoun*, potion, poisonous drink, from Old French *poison*, from Latin *pō-tiō*, from *pōtāre*, to drink.] —**poi'son·er** *n.*

poison gas. Any lethal or crippling vapor used in warfare.

poison ivy. A North American shrub or vine, *Rhus radicans*, with leaflets in groups of three, small green flowers, and whitish berries, whose foliage causes a rash on contact.

poison oak. Either of two shrubs, *Rhus toxicodendron* of the southeastern United States, or *R. diversiloba* of western North America, that is related to poison ivy and causes a similar rash.

poi·son·ous (poi'zə-nəs) *adj.* **1.** Capable of harming or killing by or as if by poison. **2.** Containing a poison. **3.** Full of hatred or ill will: *a poisonous glance.* —See Syns at **malevolent.** —**poi'son·ous·ly** *adv.*

poison sumac. A swamp shrub, *Rhus vernix*, of the southeastern United States, with compound leaves and greenish-white berries, whose foliage causes an itching rash on contact.

poke[1] (pōk) *v.* **poked, pok·ing.** —*tr.v.* **1.** To push or jab, as with a finger or arm; to prod. **2.** To make by or as if by prodding or thrusting: *He poked his way to the front of the crowd.* **3.** To push; thrust: *A seal poked its head out of the water.* **4.** To stir (a fire) by prodding the wood or coal with a poker or stick. **5.** To strike; punch. —*intr.v.* **1.** To make thrusts or jabs. **2.** To pry or meddle; intrude. **3.** To search or look in a leisurely manner: *poking around the attic.* **4.** To proceed in a slow or lazy manner; to putter. **5.** To thrust forward; appear suddenly: *His head poked from under the blankets.* —See Syns at **delay.** —*n.* **1.** A push, thrust, or jab. **2.** A punch or blow with the fist. —*idiom.* **poke fun at.** To make fun of; to kid. [Middle English *poken*, from Middle Dutch and Middle Low German, to strike, thrust.]

poke[2] (pōk) *n.* A sack or bag. —*idiom.* **a pig in a poke.** Something offered for sale sight unseen. [Middle English, from Old North French *poque*, var. of Old French *poche*, pocket.]

poke·ber·ry (pōk'bĕr'ē) *n.* **1.** The blackish-red berry of the pokeweed. **2.** The plant itself, pokeweed.

po·ker[1] (pō'kər) *n.* A metal rod used to stir a fire.

pok·er[2] (pō'kər) *n.* Any of various card games played by two or more players who bet on the value of their hands. [Orig. unknown.]

poker face. A face lacking any interpretable expression.

—pok·er·faced' (pō'kər-fāst') *adj.*

poke·weed (pōk'wēd') *n.* A tall North American plant, *Phytolacca americana*, with small white flowers, blackish-red berries, and a poisonous root. The young shoots are sometimes eaten as greens.

po·key (pō'kē) *n., pl.* **-keys.** *Slang.* Jail. [Orig. unknown.]

pok·y or **pok·ey** (pō'kē) *adj.* **-i·er, -i·est.** *Informal.* **1.** Dawdling; slow. **2.** Small and cramped. —See Syns at **slow.** [From POKE (to thrust).]

po·lar (pō'lər) *adj.* **1. a.** Of or indicating a pole. **b.** Measured from or referred to a pole: *polar diameter.* **2.** Of, connected with, or located near the North Pole or South Pole. **3.** Very cold. **4.** Directly opposite; diametrically opposed. **5.** Serving as a guide, as a pole of the earth. **6.** Central; pivotal: *polar influence.* —See Syns at **frigid.**

polar bear. A large, white-furred bear, *Thalarctos maritimus*, of Arctic regions.

polar bear

polar body. *Genetics.* A minute cell that forms and is discarded in the development of an oocyte, and contains little or no cytoplasm but has one of the nuclei derived from the first or second meiotic division.

polar circle. 1. The **Arctic Circle. 2.** The **Antarctic Circle.**

polar coordinate. Either of two coordinates, the radius vector or the polar angle, that together specify the position of any point in a plane.

Po·lar·is (pō-lăr'ĭs, -lâr'-) *n.* A star of the second magnitude, at the end of the handle of the Little Dipper and almost at the North Celestial Pole. Also called **North Star** and **polestar.**

po·lar·i·scope (pō-lăr'ĭ-skōp', -lâr'-) *n.* An instrument for measuring or displaying the properties of polarized light, or for studying the interactions of polarized light with optically transparent media.

po·lar·i·ty (pō-lăr'ĭ-tē, -lâr'-) *n., pl.* **-ties. 1.** A basic division or separation into opposing or contrary types, as of a physical property: *electric polarity; magnetic polarity.* **2.** Either of a pair of opposite or contrary types or natures: *a negative electric polarity.* **3.** The possession of two opposing attributes, tendencies, or principles: *political polarity.*

po·lar·i·za·tion (pō'lər-ĭ-zā'shən, -ī-zā'-) *n.* **1.** The production or condition of polarity, as: **a.** *Optics.* The uniform and nonrandom elliptical, circular, or linear variation of a wave characteristic, esp. of vibrational orientation, in light or other radiation. **b.** *Physics & Chem.* The partial or complete polar separation of positive and negative electric charge in a nuclear, atomic, molecular, or chemical system. **2.** A concentration, as of groups, forces, or interests, about two conflicting or contrasting positions: *The polarization of opinion made compromise difficult.*

po·lar·ize (pō'lə-rīz') *v.* **-ized, -iz·ing.** —*tr.v.* **1.** To cause polarization in. **2.** To set at opposite extremes, leaving no middle ground. —*intr.v.* To acquire polarity. —**po'lar·iz'a·ble** *adj.* —**po'lar·iz'er** *n.*

Po·lar·oid (pō'lə-roid') *n.* A trademark for a light-polarizing plastic, used in glare-reducing optical devices.

pole[1] (pōl) *n.* **1.** Either of the points at which an axis that passes through the center of a sphere intersects the surface of the sphere. **2.** Either of the points at which the earth's axis of rotation intersects the earth's surface; the North Pole or South Pole. **3.** A **celestial pole. 4.** A **magnetic pole. 5.** Either of a pair of oppositely charged electric terminals. **6.** A region at either extreme of a nucleus, cell, or organism that is distinct in form, structure, or function from the regions around it. **7.** The fixed point used as a reference in a system of polar coordinates. **8.** Either of two opposite ideas, forces, or positions. [Middle English, from Latin *polus*, from Greek *polos*, axis of a sphere.]

pole² (pōl) *n.* **1.** A long, slender, and usu. rounded piece of wood or other material. **2. a.** A unit of length, a rod. **b.** A unit of area equal to a square rod (30¹/₄ square yards). —*v.* **poled, pol·ing.** —*tr.v.* **1.** To propel with a pole, as a boat. **2.** To support (plants) with a pole. **3.** To strike, poke, or stir with a pole. —*intr.v.* **1.** To propel a boat or other craft with a pole. **2.** To use ski poles to gain speed. [Middle English, from Old English *pāl*, ult. from Latin *pālus*, stake.]

pole·ax or **pole·axe** (pōl'ăks') *n.* A long-handled battle ax, esp. one with hammer and pick combination opposite the blade. [Middle English *pollax* : *poll*, head + *ax*.]

pole bean. Any of various cultivated climbing beans trained to grow on poles or supports.

pole·cat (pōl'kăt') *n.* **1.** A carnivorous mammal, *Mustela putorius,* of Eurasia and northern Africa, with dark-brown or black fur. **2.** Any of several similar animals, esp. the skunk. [Middle English *polcat.*]

po·lem·ic (pə-lĕm'ĭk) *n.* **1.** A controversial argument, esp. an attack on an accepted doctrine or belief. **2.** polemics (*used with a sing. verb*). The art or practice of arguing or debating controversial subjects. —*adj.* Also **po·lem·i·cal** (pə-lĕm'ĭ-kəl). Of, pertaining to, or likely to cause public debate; controversial. [Medieval Latin *polemicus,* controversialist, from Greek *polemikos,* hostile, from *polemos,* war.] —**po·lem'i·cal·ly** *adv.*

po·lem·i·cist (pə-lĕm'ĭ-sĭst) *n.* A person skilled or involved in polemics.

pole·star (pōl'stär') *n.* **1.** The star Polaris. **2.** A guiding principle.

pole vault. An athletic field event in which the contestant jumps or vaults over a high crossbar with the aid of a long pole.

pole-vault (pōl'vôlt') *intr.v.* To perform or complete a pole vault. —**pole'-vault'er** *n.*

po·lice (pə-lēs') *n.,* *pl.* **police. 1.** The department of government established to maintain order, enforce the law, and prevent and detect crime. **2.** (*used with a pl. verb*). The members of this department. **3.** (*used with a pl. verb*). Any group resembling a police force: *campus police.* —*tr.v.* **-liced, -lic·ing. 1.** To guard or patrol so as to maintain order. **2.** To make (an area) neat; clean up. [French, from Late Latin *polītia,* administration of the commonwealth, from Latin *polītīa,* the state, from Greek *politeia,* polity, citizenship, from *politēs,* citizen, from *polis,* city.]

police dog. A dog trained to aid the police, esp. the German shepherd.

police force. A body of persons trained in methods of law enforcement and crime prevention and detection, and given authority to maintain the peace, safety, and order of the community.

po·lice·man (pə-lēs'mən) *n.* A male member of a police force.

police state. A country or other political unit in which the government exercises rigid control over the social, economic, and political life, esp. by means of a secret police force.

police station. The headquarters of a unit of a police force.

po·lice·wom·an (pə-lēs'wŏŏm'ən) *n.* A female member of a police force.

pol·i·cy¹ (pŏl'ĭ-sē) *n.,* *pl.* **-cies. 1.** A general principle or plan that guides the actions taken by a person or group. **2.** Care and skill in managing one's affairs or advancing one's interests; prudence; shrewdness. [Middle English *policye,* from Old French *policie,* from Latin *polītīa,* state, from Greek *politeia,* citizenship, from *politēs,* citizen, from *polis,* city.]

pol·i·cy² (pŏl'ĭ-sē) *n.,* *pl.* **-cies. 1.** A written contract or certificate of insurance. **2.** A form of gambling; numbers. [Old French *police,* from Italian *polizza,* from Medieval Latin *apodixa,* from Latin *apodīxis,* from Greek *apodeixis,* proof, from *apodeiknunai,* to make known.]

pol·i·cy·hold·er (pŏl'ĭ-sē-hōl'dər) *n.* A person who holds an insurance contract or policy.

po·li·o (pō'lē-ō') *n.* Poliomyelitis.

po·li·o·my·e·li·tis (pō'lē-ō-mī'ə-lī'tĭs) *n.* An infectious viral disease that occurs mainly in children and in its acute forms attacks the central nervous system and produces paralysis, muscular atrophy, and often deformity. Also called **infantile paralysis.** [Greek *polios,* gray + MYELITIS.]

pol·is (pŏl'ĭs) *n.,* *pl.* **pol·eis** (pŏl'ās'). A city-state of ancient Greece. [Greek.]

pol·ish (pŏl'ĭsh) *tr.v.* **1.** To make smooth and shiny by rubbing or chemical action. **2.** To free from coarseness; refine: *polished her writing style.* —*intr.v.* To become smooth or shiny by or as if by rubbing. —*phrasal verb.* **polish off.** *Informal.* To finish or dispose of quickly and easily. —*n.* **1.** A substance containing chemicals or an abrasive material for smoothing or shining a surface. **2.** Smoothness and shininess of a surface or finish. **3.** A high degree of refinement: *His performance lacks polish.* [Middle English *polisshen,* from Old French *polir,* from Latin *polīre.*] —**pol'ish·er** *n.*

Po·lish (pō'lĭsh) *adj.* Of Poland, its inhabitants, or their language or culture. —*n.* The Slavic language of the Poles.

pol·it·bu·ro (pŏl'ĭt-byŏŏr'ō, pə-lĭt'-) *n.* The chief political and executive committee of a Communist party. [From Russian *Polit(icheskoe) Buro,* political bureau.]

po·lite (pə-līt') *adj.* **-lit·er, -lit·est. 1.** Marked by consideration for others; tactful; courteous. **2.** Refined; elegant; cultivated: *polite society.* [Middle English *polyt,* polished, smoothed, from Latin *polītus,* past part. of Latin *polīre,* to polish.] —**po·lite'ly** *adv.* —**po·lite'ness** *n.*

Syns: **polite, civil, courteous, genteel, mannerly** *adj.* *Core meaning:* Having good manners (*a polite person*).

pol·i·tic (pŏl'ĭ-tĭk) *adj.* **1.** Artful; ingenious; shrewd: *a politic negotiator.* **2.** Using, displaying, or proceeding from policy; prudent; judicious: *a politic decision.* **3.** Crafty; unscrupulous; cunning. [Middle English *polytyk,* pursuing a policy, prudent, from Old French *politique,* from Latin *politicus,* from Greek *politikos,* political, from *politēs,* citizen, from *polis,* city.] —**pol'i·tic·ly** *adv.*

po·lit·i·cal (pə-lĭt'ĭ-kəl) *adj.* **1.** Of or dealing with the structure or affairs of government. **2.** Having an organized policy or structure of government. **3.** Of or having to do with politics. —**po·lit'i·cal·ly** *adv.*

political science. The study of the processes and principles of government and of political institutions.

pol·i·ti·cian (pŏl'ĭ-tĭsh'ən) *n.* **1. a.** A person who is actively involved in politics, esp. party politics. **b.** A person who holds or seeks a political office. **2.** A person who seeks personal or partisan gain, often with cunning or dishonest means.

po·lit·i·cize (pə-lĭt'ĭ-sīz') *tr.v.* **-cized, -ciz·ing.** To make political.

pol·i·tick (pŏl'ĭ-tĭk') *intr.v.* To engage in or talk politics.

po·lit·i·co (pə-lĭt'ĭ-kō') *n.,* *pl.* **-cos.** A politician. [Italian and Spanish, political, from Latin *politicus,* politic.]

pol·i·tics (pŏl'ĭ-tĭks) *n.* **1.** (*used with a sing. verb*). The art or science of government; political science. **2.** (*used with a sing. verb*). The activities or affairs of a government, politician, or political party. **3.** (*used with a pl. verb*). Intrigue or maneuvering within a group: *office politics.* **4.** (*used with a pl. verb*). A person's general position or attitude on political subjects.

pol·i·ty (pŏl'ĭ-tē) *n.,* *pl.* **-ties.** The form of government of a nation, state, church, or organization. [Old French *politie,* from Latin *polītīa,* from Greek *politeia,* government, from *politēs,* citizen, from *polis,* city.]

pol·ka (pōl'kə, pō'kə) *n.* **1.** A lively round dance of central European origin, performed by couples in duple meter. **2.** Music for this dance. —*intr.v.* **-kaed, -ka·ing.** To dance the polka. [French and German, from Czech, from Polish, Polish woman.]

pol·ka dot (pō'kə). **1.** One of a number of dots or round spots forming a pattern on cloth. **2.** A pattern or fabric with such dots.

poll (pōl) *n.* **1.** The casting and registering of votes in an election. **2.** The number of votes cast or recorded. **3.** Often **polls.** The place where votes are cast and registered. **4.** A survey of the public or of a sample of the public to acquire information or record opinion. **5.** The head, esp. the top of the head where hair grows. **6.** The blunt or broad end of a hammer, ax, or similar tool. —*tr.v.* **1.** To receive (a given

ă pat   ā pay   â care   ä father   ĕ pet   ē be   hw which   ĭ pit   ī tie   î pier   ŏ pot   ō toe   ô paw, for   oi noise
ŏŏ took   ōō boot   ou out   th thin   th this   ŭ cut   û urge   zh vision   ə about, item, edible, gallop, circus

number of votes). **2.** To receive or record the votes of: *poll a jury.* **3.** To cast (a vote or ballot). **4.** To question in a survey; to canvass. **5.** To cut off or trim; to clip: *poll wool.* **6.** To trim or cut off the hair, wool, branches, or horns of; shear: *poll sheep.* —*intr.v.* To vote at the polls or in an election. [Middle English *polle,* head.] —**poll'er** *n.*

pol·lack (pŏl'ək) *n.* Var. of **pollock.**

pol·len (pŏl'ən) *n.* The fine, powderlike material produced by the anthers of flowering plants, and functioning as the male element in fertilization. [Latin, flour, dust.]

pol·li·nate (pŏl'ə-nāt') *tr.v.* **-nat·ed, -nat·ing.** To convey or transfer pollen from an anther to a stigma of (a plant or flower) in the process of fertilization. —**pol'li·na'tion** *n.* —**pol'li·na'tor** *n.*

pol·li·wog (pŏl'ē-wŏg', -wôg') *n.* Also **pol·ly·wog.** A tadpole. [Middle English *polwygle.*]

pol·lock (pŏl'ək) *n., pl.* **-lock** or **-locks.** Also **pol·lack.** A saltwater food fish, *Pollachius virens,* of northern Atlantic waters. [Scottish *podlok.*]

poll·ster (pōl'stər) *n.* A person who takes public-opinion surveys.

poll tax. A tax levied on persons rather than on property, often as a requirement for voting.

pol·lut·ant (pə-lōōt'nt) *n.* Anything that pollutes, esp. a waste material that contaminates air, soil, or water.

pol·lute (pə-lōōt') *tr.v.* **-lut·ed, -lut·ing.** **1.** To make unfit for or harmful to living things, esp. by the addition of waste matter. **2.** To corrupt. [Middle English *polluten,* from Latin *polluere.*] —**pol·lut'er** *n.*

pol·lu·tion (pə-lōō'shən) *n.* **1.** The act or process of polluting or the condition of being polluted. **2.** The contamination of soil, water, or the atmosphere by the discharge of harmful substances.

Pol·lux (pŏl'əks) *n.* **1.** *Gk. Myth.* **Castor** and **Pollux.** **2.** *Astron.* A bright star in the constellation Gemini.

Pol·ly·an·na (pŏl'ē-ăn'ə) *n.* A foolishly or blindly optimistic person. [After the title character in *Pollyanna* (1913), a novel by Eleanor Porter (1868–1920).]

pol·ly·wog (pŏl'ē-wŏg', -wôg') *n.* Var. of **polliwog.**

po·lo (pō'lō) *n.* **1.** A game played by two teams of three or four players on horseback, equipped with long-handled mallets for driving a small wooden ball through the opponents' goal. **2.** Water polo. [Of Tibetan orig.] —**po'lo·ist** *n.*

pol·o·naise (pŏl'ə-nāz', pō'lə-) *n.* **1.** A stately, marchlike Polish dance in triple time. **2.** Music for or in the style of this dance. **3.** A woman's dress of the 18th cent., having a fitted bodice and draped cutaway skirt, worn over an elaborate underskirt. [French, Polish, from Medieval Latin *Polōnia,* Poland, from Polish *Polanie.*]

po·lo·ni·um (pə-lō'nē-əm) *n. Symbol* **Po** A naturally radioactive metallic element that occurs in minute quantities as a product of radium disintegration and is produced by bombarding bismuth or lead with neutrons. It has 27 isotopes ranging in mass number from 192 to 218, of which Po 210, with a half-life of 138.39 days, is the most readily available. Atomic number 84; melting point 254°C; boiling point 962°C; specific gravity 9.32; valence 2, 4, 6. [From Latin *Polōnia,* Poland.]

polo shirt. A pullover sport shirt of knitted cotton.

pol·ter·geist (pōl'tər-gīst') *n.* A noisy, usu. playful ghost. [German *Poltergeist : poltern,* to make noises, rattle + *Geist,* ghost.]

pol·troon (pŏl-trōōn') *n. Archaic.* A base coward. [Old French *poultron,* from Old Italian *poltrone,* foal from *poltro,* from Latin *pullus,* young animal.] —**pol·troon'er·y** *n.*

poly-. A prefix meaning more than one, many, or much: *polyclinic.* [From Greek *polus,* much, many.]

pol·y·an·drous (pŏl'ē-ăn'drəs) *adj.* **1.** Of or relating to polyandry. **2.** *Bot.* Having an indefinite number of stamens.

pol·y·an·dry (pŏl'ē-ăn'drē) *n.* **1.** The condition or practice of having more than one husband at a time. **2.** *Bot.* The condition of being polyandrous.

pol·y·an·thus (pŏl'ē-ăn'thəs) *n.* Any of a group of hybrid garden primroses with clusters of variously colored flowers. [From Greek *poluanthos,* "having many flowers."]

pol·y·chro·mat·ic (pŏl'ē-krō-măt'ĭk). *adj.* Also **pol·y·chro·mic** (-krō'mĭk) Having many colors or changes of color.

pol·y·chrome (pŏl'ē-krōm') *adj.* **1.** Having many colors.

2. Made or decorated in many or various colors. —*n.* An object having or decorated in many colors. [Greek *polukhrōmos,* many-colored.]

pol·y·chro·mic (pŏl'ē-krō'mĭk) *adj.* Var. of **polychromatic.**

pol·y·clin·ic (pŏl'ē-klĭn'ĭk) *n.* A clinic or hospital that treats all types of diseases and injuries.

pol·y·es·ter (pŏl'ē-ĕs'tər) *n.* Any of numerous synthetic resins, used in boat hulls, swimming pools, waterproof fibers, adhesives, and molded parts. [POLY(MER) + ESTER.]

pol·y·eth·yl·ene (pŏl'ē-ĕth'ə-lēn') *n.* A polymerized ethylene resin, used for packaging materials or molded for a wide variety of containers, kitchenware, and tubing. [POLY(MER) + ETHYLENE.]

po·lyg·a·mist (pə-lĭg'ə-mĭst) *n.* A person who practices polygamy.

po·lyg·a·mous (pə-lĭg'ə-məs) *adj.* **1.** Of, relating to, engaged in, or characterized by polygamy. **2.** *Bot.* Having both hermaphroditic and unisexual flowers on the same plant. —**po·lyg'a·mous·ly** *adv.*

po·lyg·a·my (pə-lĭg'ə-mē) *n.* The condition or practice of having more than one wife or husband at a time.

pol·y·glot (pŏl'ē-glŏt') *adj.* Speaking, writing, written in, or composed of several languages. —*n.* **1.** A person who speaks many languages. **2.** A book, esp. a Bible, containing several versions of the same text in different languages. **3.** A mixture or confusion of languages. [French *polyglotte,* from Greek *poluglōttos : polus,* many + *glōtta,* tongue.]

pol·y·gon (pŏl'ē-gŏn') *n.* A closed geometric plane figure bounded by three or more line segments. —**po·lyg'o·nal** (pə-lĭg'ə-nəl) *adj.* —**po·lyg'o·nal·ly** *adv.*

pol·y·graph (pŏl'ē-grăf') *n.* An instrument that simultaneously records changes in such bodily processes as heartbeat, blood pressure, and respiration, often used as a lie detector. —**pol'y·graph'ic** *adj.*

po·lyg·y·ny (pə-lĭj'ə-nē) *n.* The condition or practice of having more than one wife at a time. —**po·lyg'y·nous** *adj.*

pol·y·he·dron (pŏl'ē-hē'drən) *n., pl.* **-drons** or **-dra** (-drə). A solid geometric figure bounded by polygons. —**pol'y·he'dral** *adj.*

Pol·y·hym·ni·a (pŏl'ē-hĭm'nē-ə). *n. Gk. Myth.* The Muse of singing, rhetoric, and mime.

pol·y·math (pŏl'ē-măth') *n.* A person of great or varied learning. [From Greek *polumathēs,* knowing much.] —**pol'y·math'** or **pol'y·math'ic** *adj.*

pol·y·mer (pŏl'ə-mər) *n.* Any of numerous natural and synthetic compounds of usu. high molecular weight consisting of up to millions of repeated linked units, each a relatively light and simple molecule. [From POLYMERIC.] —**pol'y·mer'ic** (pŏl'ə-mĕr'ĭk) *adj.*

po·lym·er·i·za·tion (pə-lĭm'ər-ĭ-zā'shən, pŏl'ə-mər-) *n.* **1.** The uniting of two or more monomers to form a polymer. **2.** Any chemical process that effects such a union.

po·lym·er·ize (pə-lĭm'ə-rīz', pŏl'ə-mə-) *v.* **-ized, -iz·ing.** —*tr.v.* To subject to polymerization. —*intr.v.* To undergo polymerization.

pol·y·mor·phic (pŏl'ē-môr'fĭk) *adj.* Also **pol·y·mor·phous** (-fəs). Having or occurring in various forms or shapes.

pol·y·mor·phism (pŏl'ē-môr'fĭz'əm) *n.* **1.** *Biol.* The occurrence of different forms, stages, or color types in individual organisms or in organisms of the same species. **2.** *Chem.* Crystallization of a compound in at least two distinct forms.

pol·y·mor·phous (pŏl'ē-môr'fəs) *adj.* Var. of **polymorphic.**

Pol·y·ne·sian (pŏl'ə-nē'zhən, -shən) *adj.* Of Polynesia, its inhabitants, culture, or languages. —*n.* **1.** A native of Polynesia. **2.** Any Austronesian language spoken in Polynesia.

pol·y·no·mi·al (pŏl'ē-nō'mē-əl) *adj.* Of or consisting of more than two names or terms. —*n. Math.* An algebraic function of two or more summed terms, each term consisting of a constant multiplier and one or more variables raised, in general, to integral powers. [POLY- + (BI)-NOMIAL.]

pol·yp (pŏl'ĭp) *n.* **1.** *Zool.* A coelenterate having a cylindrical body and an oral opening usu. surrounded by tentacles, as a hydra or coral. **2.** *Pathol.* A growth protruding from the mucous lining of an organ. [French *polype,* octopus, from Latin *polypus,* from Greek *polupous,* "many-footed."] —**pol'yp·oid'** *adj.*

Pol·y·phe·mus (pŏl'ə-fē'məs) *n. Gk. Myth.* The Cyclops who confined Odysseus and his companions in a cave until Odysseus blinded him and escaped.

pol·y·phon·ic (pŏl'ĭ-fŏn'ĭk) *adj.* Of, relating to, or characteristic of polyphony. —**pol'y·phon'i·cal·ly** *adv.*

po·lyph·o·ny (pə-lĭf'ə-nē) *n., pl.* **-nies.** Music with two or more independent melodic parts sounded together. [Greek *poluphōnia,* variety of tones : *polus,* many + *phonē,* sound.]

pol·y·ploid (pŏl'ĭ-ploid') *adj.* Having more than twice the normal haploid chromosome number. —*n.* An organism with more than two sets of chromosomes. [POLY- + (HA)PLOID.] —**pol'y·ploi'dic** *adj.*

pol·y·sac·cha·ride (pŏl'ĭ-săk'ə-rīd') *n.* A group of nine or more monosaccharides joined by glycosidic bonds, such as starch and cellulose.

pol·y·sty·rene (pŏl'ĭ-stī'rēn') *n.* A hard, rigid, thermoplastic polymer that is an excellent thermal and electrical insulator.

pol·y·syl·lab·ic (pŏl'ĭ-sĭ-lăb'ĭk) *adj.* **1.** Having more than three syllables. **2.** Characterized by words having more than three syllables: *a polysyllabic style..* —**pol'y·syl·lab'i·cal·ly** *adv.*

pol·y·syl·la·ble (pŏl'ĭ-sĭl'ə-bəl) *n.* A word of more than three syllables.

pol·y·tech·nic (pŏl'ĭ-tĕk'nĭk) *adj.* Of or dealing with many arts or sciences. —*n.* A school specializing in the teaching of industrial arts and applied sciences. [French *polytechnique,* from Greek *polutekhnos,* skilled in many arts.]

pol·y·the·ism (pŏl'ĭ-thē-ĭz'əm) *n.* The worship of or belief in more than one god. —**pol'y·the'ist** *n.* —**pol'y·the·is'tic** *adj.*

pol·y·un·sat·u·rat·ed (pŏl'ē-ŭn-săch'ə-rā'tĭd) *adj.* Pertaining to long-chain carbon compounds, esp. fats, with many unsaturated bonds.

pol·y·u·re·thane (pŏl'ē-yoor'ə-thān') *n.* Any of various thermoplastic or thermosetting resins used in coatings and in adhesives, foams, and electrical insulation.

pol·y·va·lent (pŏl'ĭ-vā'lənt) *adj.* **1.** Containing, sensitive to, or interacting with more than one kind of antigen, antibody, toxin, or microorganism. **2.** *Chem.* **a.** Having more than one valence. **b.** Having a valence of 3 or higher. —**pol'y·va'lence** or **pol'y·va'len·cy** *n.*

po·made (pə-mād', -mäd', pō-) *n.* A perfumed ointment for the hair. —*tr.v.* **-mad·ed, -mad·ing.** To apply pomade to. [French *pommade,* from Italian *pomata,* from *pomo,* apple, from Latin *pōmum.*]

po·man·der (pō'măn'dər, pō-măn'-) *n.* **1.** A mixture of aromatic substances, formerly worn enclosed in a bag or box as a protection against odor and infection. **2.** A case, box, or bag for holding this mixture. [Middle English, from Old French *pome d'embre,* "ball of amber."]

pome·gran·ate (pŏm'grăn'ĭt, pŭm'-) *n.* **1.** A semitropical shrub or small tree, *Punica granatum,* native to Asia, and widely cultivated for its edible fruit. **2.** The fruit of this tree, that has a tough, reddish rind, and many seeds enclosed in a juicy red pulp with a mildly acid flavor. [Middle English *pomegranard,* from Old French *pome grenate* : *pome,* apple + *grenate,* having many seeds.]

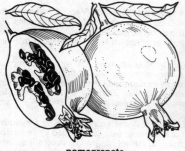

pomegranate

poncho

pom·mel (pŭm'əl, pŏm'-) *n.* **1.** A knob on the hilt of a sword or other weapon. **2.** The knob at the front of a saddle. —*tr.v.* **-meled** or **-melled, -mel·ing** or **-mel·ling.** To beat; pummel. [Middle English *pomel,* from Old French, from Latin *pōmum,* apple.]

po·mol·o·gy (pō-mŏl'ə-jē) *n.* The scientific study of the cultivation of fruit. [Latin *pōmum,* fruit + -LOGY.] —**po'mo·log'i·cal** (pō'mə-lŏj'ĭ-kəl) *adj.* —**po'mo·log'i·cal·ly** *adv.* —**po·mol'o·gist** *n.*

pomp (pŏmp) *n.* **1.** Dignified or magnificent display; splendor. **2.** Vain or showy display. [Middle English, from Old French *pompe,* from Latin *pompa,* from Greek *pompē,* solemn procession, from *pempein,* to send.]

pom·pa·dour (pŏm'pə-dôr', -dōr') *n.* A hair style formed by sweeping the hair straight up from the forehead. [After the Marquise de *Pompadour* (1721–64), mistress of Louis XV of France.]

pom·pa·no (pŏm'pə-nō', pŭm'-) *n., pl.* **-no** or **-nos.** Any of several saltwater food fishes of the genus *Trachinotus,* found in tropical and temperate Atlantic waters. [Spanish *pámpano.*]

pom-pom (pŏm'pŏm') *n.* **1.** In World War I a variety of large machine gun using one-pound shells. **2.** In World War II an automatic rapid-fire antiaircraft cannon. [Imit.]

pom·pon (pŏm'pŏn') *n.* Also **pom-pom** (-pŏm'). **1.** A tuft or ball of wool, feathers, or other material worn as decoration. **2.** A small, buttonlike flower of some chrysanthemums and dahlias. [French.]

pom·pous (pŏm'pəs) *adj.* **1.** Characterized by an exaggerated show of dignity or self-importance; pretentious. **2.** Full of high-sounding words and phrases: *a pompous speech.* **3.** Characterized by pomp or stately display; ceremonious. —**pom·pos'i·ty** (pŏm-pŏs'ĭ-tē) *n.* —**pom'pous·ly** *adv.* —**pom'pous·ness** *n.*

pon·cho (pŏn'chō) *n., pl.* **-chos. 1.** A blanketlike cloak with a hole in the center for the head, worn orig. in South America. **2.** A similar garment used as a raincoat. [American Spanish, from Araucanian *pontho,* woolen fabric.]

pond (pŏnd) *n.* A still body of water, smaller than a lake. [Middle English *ponde,* enclosure.]

pon·der (pŏn'dər) *tr.v.* To weigh mentally; consider carefully: *ponder the alternatives.* —*intr.v.* To think carefully; reflect: *ponder over a decision.* [Middle English *ponderen,* from Old French *ponderer,* from Latin *ponderāre,* to weigh, ponder, from *pondus,* weight.] —**pon'der·er** *n.*

pon·der·a·ble (pŏn'dər-ə-bəl) *adj.* Capable of being weighed or assessed; appreciable. —**pon'der·a·bil'i·ty** *n.*

pon·der·o·sa pine (pŏn'də-rō'sə). A tall timber tree, *Pinus ponderosa,* of western North America, with long, dark-green needles. [From Latin *ponderōsus,* ponderous + PINE.]

pon·der·ous (pŏn'dər-əs) *adj.* **1.** Extremely heavy; massive; huge. **2.** Graceless or clumsy from weight. **3.** Lacking fluency or brevity; labored; dull: *a ponderous speech.* —See Syns at **heavy.** [Middle English, from Old French *pondereux,* from Latin *ponderōsus,* from *pondus,* weight.] —**pon'der·ous·ly** *adv.* —**pon·der·os'i·ty** (pŏn'də-rŏs'ĭ-tē) or **pon'der·ous·ness** *n.*

pond lily. The water lily.

pone (pōn) *n.* **Corn pone.** [Of Algonquian orig.]

pon·gee (pŏn-jē', pŏn'jē') *n.* A soft, thin cloth of Chinese or Indian silk with a knotty weave. [Mandarin *pen³chi¹,* "(made by) one's own loom" : *pen³,* own + *chi¹,* loom.]

pon·iard (pŏn'yərd) *n.* A dagger. —*tr.v.* To stab with a poniard. [French *poignard,* from *poing,* fist, from Old French, from Latin *pugnus.*]

pons (pŏnz) *n., pl.* **pon·tes** (pŏn'tēz). *Anat.* Any slender tissue joining two parts of an organ. [Latin *pōns,* bridge.]

pon·ti·fex (pŏn'tə-fĕks') *n., pl.* **pon·tif·i·ces** (pŏn-tĭf'ĭ-sēz'). A member of the highest body of priests in ancient Rome. [Latin.]

pon·tiff (pŏn'tĭf) *n.* **1.** The pope. **2.** A bishop. [French *pontif,* from Latin *pontifex,* pontifex.]

pon·tif·i·cal (pŏn-tĭf'ĭ-kəl) *adj.* **1.** Of, characteristic of, or suitable for a pope or bishop: *pontifical robes.* **2.** Pompously authoritative. —*n.* **pontificals.** The vestments and insignia of a pontiff. —**pon·tif'i·cal·ly** *adv.*

pon·tif·i·cate (pŏn-tĭf'ĭ-kĭt, -kāt') *n.* The office or term of office of a pontiff. —*intr.v.* (pŏn-tĭf'ĭ-kāt') **-cat·ed, -cat·ing.**

ă pat	ā pay	â care	ä father	ĕ pet	ē be	hw which	ĭ pit	ī tie	î pier	ŏ pot	ō toe	ô paw, for	oi noise
ōō took	ōō boot	ou out	th thin	*th* this	ŭ cut		û urge	zh vision	ə about, item, edible, gallop, circus				

1. To administer the office of a pontiff. **2.** To speak or behave with pompous authority. **—pon·tif'i·ca'tion** n. **—pon·tif'i·ca'tor** n.

pon·toon (pŏn-tōon') n. **1.** A flat-bottomed boat or other structure used to support a floating bridge. **2.** A float on a seaplane. [French *ponton*, floating bridge, from Old French, from Latin *pontō*, from *pōns*, bridge.]

pontoon bridge. A temporary floating bridge using pontoons for support.

po·ny (pŏ'nē) n., pl. **-nies. 1.** Any of several types or breeds of horses that are small in size when full-grown. **2.** Any small horse. **3.** *Informal.* A translation used in preparing foreign-language lessons. [Earlier *powny*, prob. ult. from Latin *pullus*, foal.]

pony express. A system of mail transportation by relays of ponies, specif. the system in operation from St. Joseph, Missouri, to Sacramento, California (1860–61).

po·ny·tail (pŏ'nē-tāl') n. A hair style in which the hair is drawn back and fastened with a clip or band so that it hangs down like a horse's tail.

pooch (pōoch) n. *Slang.* A dog. [Orig. unknown.]

poo·dle (pōod'l) n. Any of a breed of dogs orig. developed in Europe as hunting dogs, that have thick, curly hair, and range in size from the fairly large standard poodle to the very small toy poodle. [German *Pudel(hund)*, "poodle (dog)."]

poodle

pooh (pōo) *interj.* A word used to express disdain.

pooh-pooh (pōo'pōo, pōo-pōo') tr.v. *Informal.* To dimiss as having no value: *He pooh-poohed the idea.*

pool¹ (pōol) n. **1.** A small body of still water. **2.** A puddle of any liquid. **3.** A deep place in a river or stream. **4.** A **swimming pool.** [Middle English, from Old English *pōl.*]

pool² (pōol) n. **1.** A game played on a table that has pockets on the sides and corners, the object being to make a white ball strike one or more variously colored balls so they drop into the pockets. Also called **pocket billiards. 2. a.** A game of chance, resembling a lottery, in which the contestants put money into a common fund that is later paid to the winner or winners. **b.** The fund containing the bets made in a game of chance or on a horse race. **3.** A common fund for buying and selling securities. **4.** An agreement between competing business companies to establish controls over production, marketing, and price for common profit. **5.** An arrangement for sharing the use of a number of persons, vehicles, etc.: *a car pool.* —tr.v. To put into a common fund for use by all: *pool resources.* —intr.v. To join or form a pool. [French *poule*, stakes, target hen, from Late Latin *pullus*, hen, from Latin, young of an animal.]

pool·room (pōol'rōom', -rōom') n. A business or room for the playing of pool or billiards.

pool table. A six-pocket billiard table on which pool is played.

poop¹ (pōop) n. *Naut.* **1.** A raised structure at the stern of a ship. **2.** The poop deck. —tr.v. To break over the stern of. [Old French *poupe*, from Latin *puppis.*]

poop² (pōop) tr.v. *Slang.* To exhaust; tire out. **—phrasal verb. poop out.** To quit because of exhaustion: *poop out of the race.* [Orig. unknown.]

poop deck. The aftermost deck of a ship.

poor (pōor) adj. **-er, -est. 1.** Having little or no money. **2.** Lacking in resources or in something specified: *an area poor in timber and coal.* **3.** Lacking in mental or moral quality: *a poor spirit.* **4.** Inferior; inadequate: *a poor*

choice. **5.** Lacking fertility: *poor soil.* **6.** Lacking in quantity: *poor attendance.* **7.** Deserving pity; unfortunate: *the poor fellow.* [Middle English *povere*, from Old French *povre*, from Latin *pauper.*] **—poor'ness** n.

Syns: poor, broke (Informal), **destitute, indigent, needy, penniless, penurious, strapped** (Informal) adj. *Core meaning:* Having little or no money (*too poor to eat well*). See also Syns at **cheap.**

poor box. A box, esp. in a church, for collecting alms.

poor·house (pōor'hous') n. Formerly a place where poor people were maintained at public expense.

poor·ly (pōor'lē) adv. In a poor manner; badly. —adj. *Regional.* In poor health; ill: *feeling poorly.*

pop¹ (pŏp) v. **popped, pop·ping.** —intr.v. **1.** To make a short, sharp, explosive sound. **2.** To burst with such a sound: *The flash bulb popped.* **3.** To move or appear quickly or unexpectedly; appear abruptly: *popped into view.* **4.** To open wide suddenly: *Her eyes popped open with disbelief.* **5.** *Baseball.* To hit a short high fly ball. —tr.v. **1.** To cause to make a sharp bursting sound: *pop open a soda bottle.* **2.** To cause to explode with such a sound: *pop a balloon.* **3.** To put or thrust suddenly or unexpectedly. —n. **1.** A sudden sharp, explosive sound. **2.** A shot with a firearm. **3.** A nonalcoholic, flavored, carbonated beverage. —adv. **1.** With a popping sound. **2.** Abruptly or unexpectedly. [Middle English *poppen.*]

pop² (pŏp) n. *Informal.* Father. [Short for *poppa*, var. of PAPA.]

pop³ (pŏp) adj. *Informal.* Of or specializing in popular music: *a pop singer.* [Short for POPULAR.]

pop art. A form of art that depicts objects of everyday life and adapts techniques of commercial art, such as comic strips.

pop·corn (pŏp'kôrn') n. A variety of corn, *Zea mays everta*, with hard kernels that burst to form white, irregularly shaped puffs when heated.

pope (pōp) n. Often **Pope.** The bishop of Rome and head of the Roman Catholic Church. [Middle English, from Old English *pāpa*, from Late Latin, from Greek *pappas*, title of bishops, papa.]

pop·er·y (pō'pə-rē) n. The doctrines and rituals of the Roman Catholic Church. Used disparagingly.

pop·eyed (pŏp'īd') adj. Having bulging eyes.

pop fly. *Baseball.* A short high fly ball.

pop·gun (pŏp'gŭn') n. A toy gun that uses compressed air to fire corks or pellets and makes a popping noise.

pop·in·jay (pŏp'ĭn-jā') n. A vain, talkative, conceited person. [Middle English *papejay*, parrot, from Old French *papegai*, from Arabic *babaghā.*]

pop·ish (pō'pĭsh) adj. Of the popes or the Roman Catholic Church. Used disparagingly. **—pop'ish·ly** adv. **—pop'ish·ness** n.

pop·lar (pŏp'lər) n. **1.** Any of several fast-growing deciduous trees of the genus *Populus.* **2.** The wood of these trees. [Middle English *poplere*, from Old French *poplier*, from Latin *pōpulus.*]

pop·lin (pŏp'lĭn) n. A strong fabric of silk, rayon, wool, or cotton, with fine crosswise ridges. [Obs. French *papeline*, from Italian *papalina* (from its manufacture in the papal town of Avignon).]

pop·o·ver (pŏp'ō'vər) n. A very light, puffy, hollow muffin made with eggs, milk, and flour.

pop·per (pŏp'ər) n. **1.** Someone or something that pops. **2.** A container or pan for making popcorn.

pop·pet (pŏp'ĭt) n. An intake or exhaust valve that plugs and unplugs its opening by moving up and down. [Middle English *popet*, child, doll.]

pop·py (pŏp'ē) n., pl. **-pies. 1.** Any of numerous plants of the genus *Papaver*, of temperate regions, with showy red, orange, or white flowers, and a milky white juice. **2.** Any of several similar or related plants. **3.** The narcotic extracted from the opium poppy. [Middle English *popi*, from Old English *popig*, ult. from Latin *papāver.*]

pop·py·cock (pŏp'ē-kŏk') n. Senseless talk; nonsense. [Dial. Dutch *pappekak*, "soft dung."]

pop·u·lace (pŏp'yə-ləs) n. **1.** The common people; masses. **2.** A population. [French, from Italian *popolaccio*, rabble, from *popolo*, the people, from Latin *populus.*]

pop·u·lar (pŏp′yə-lər) *adj.* **1.** Widely liked or appreciated: *a popular resort.* **2.** Of, representing, or carried on by the people at large: *the popular vote.* **3.** Fit for or reflecting the taste and intelligence of the people at large: *popular entertainment.* **4.** Accepted by or prevalent among the people in general: *a popular misunderstanding.* **5.** Suited to or within the means of ordinary people: *popular prices.* —See Syns at **public.** [Latin *populāris,* of the people, from *populus,* people.] —**pop′u·lar·ly** *adv.*

pop·u·lar·i·ty (pŏp′yə-lăr′ĭ-tē) *n.* The quality of being popular.

pop·u·lar·ize (pŏp′yə-lə-rīz′) *tr.v.* **-ized, -iz·ing.** To make popular; esp., to make known to the general public. —**pop′u·lar·i·za′tion** *n.* —**pop′u·lar·iz′er** *n.*

pop·u·late (pŏp′yə-lāt′) *tr.v.* **-lat·ed, -lat·ing.** **1.** To supply with inhabitants, as by colonization: *populate a remote region.* **2.** To inhabit; live in. [From Medieval Latin *populāre,* to people, from Latin *populus,* people.]

pop·u·la·tion (pŏp′yə-lā′shən) *n.* **1.** The total number of people inhabiting a specified area. **2.** The total number of inhabitants of a particular race, class, or group in a specified area. **3.** The act or process of furnishing with inhabitants. **4.** The set of individuals, items, or data from which a statistical sample is taken. **5.** All the plants or animals of the same kind living in a particular region.

Pop·u·lism (pŏp′yə-lĭz′əm) *n.* **1.** The philosophy of the Populist Party. **2. populism.** A political philosophy directed to the needs of the common people and opposing the concentration of power in the hands of corporations, government bureaucracies, and the rich.

Pop·u·list (pŏp′yə-lĭst) *n.* **1.** A member or supporter of the Populist Party. **2. populist.** An advocate of populism. —*adj.* **1.** Of the Populist Party. **2. populist.** Of or characteristic of populism or its advocates.

Populist Party. An American political party that sought to represent the interests of farmers and laborers in the 1890's, advocating increased currency issue, free coinage of gold and silver, public ownership of railroads, and a graduated federal income tax.

pop·u·lous (pŏp′yə-ləs) *adj.* Containing many people or inhabitants; thickly settled or populated. —**pop′u·lous·ly** *adv.* —**pop′u·lous·ness** *n.*

por·ce·lain (pôr′sə-lĭn, pôr′-, pôrs′lĭn, pōrs′-) *n.* **1.** A hard, white, translucent ceramic made by firing a pure clay and glazing with variously colored materials; china. **2.** An object made of this material. [French *porcelaine,* from Old French *pourcelaine,* from Italian *porcellana,* cowry shell, porcelain.]

porch (pôrch, pōrch) *n.* **1.** A covered platform, usu. with a separate roof, at an entrance to a house. **2.** An open or enclosed gallery or room attached to the outside of a building; verandah. [Middle English *porche,* from Old French, from Latin *porticus,* portico.]

por·cine (pôr′sīn′) *adj.* Of or resembling swine or a pig. [Latin *porcīnus,* from *porcus,* pig.]

por·cu·pine (pôr′kyə-pīn′) *n.* Any of various rodents of the genera *Hystrix* and *Erethizon,* characteristically covered with long, sharp quills or spines. [Middle English *porkepin,* from Old French *porc espin,* "spiny pig."]

porcupine

pore¹ (pôr, pōr) *intr.v.* **pored, por·ing.** **1.** To gaze steadily or earnestly. **2.** To read or study carefully and attentively. **3.** To meditate deeply; ponder. [Middle English *pouren.*]

pore² (pôr, pōr) *n.* A tiny opening, as in an animal's skin, through which perspiration passes, or on the surface of a leaf, through which water vapor, carbon dioxide, and oxygen pass. [Middle English, from Old French, from Latin *porus,* from Greek *poros,* passage.]

por·gy (pôr′gē) *n., pl.* **-gies** or **-gy.** **1.** Any of various deep-bodied saltwater fishes of the family Sparidae. **2.** Any of several similar or related fishes. [Spanish *pargo,* from Latin *phagrus,* sea bream, from Greek *phagros.*]

pork (pôrk, pōrk) *n.* The flesh of a pig or hog used as food. [Middle English, from Old French *porc,* pig, from Latin *porcus.*]

pork barrel. *Slang.* A government project or appropriation benefiting a specific locale and a legislator's constituents.

pork·er (pôr′kər) *n.* A fattened young pig.

pork·pie (pôrk′pī′, pōrk′-) *n.* A man's hat with a low, flat crown and a snap brim.

por·no (pôr′nō) *n.* Also **porn** (pôrn). *Slang.* Pornography.

por·nog·ra·phy (pôr-nŏg′rə-fē) *n.* Written or pictorial matter intended to arouse sexual feelings. [From Greek *pornographos,* writing about prostitutes : *pornē,* prostitute + *graphē,* writing.] —**por·nog′ra·pher** *n.* —**por′no·graph′ic** (pôr′nə-grăf′ĭk) *adj.*

po·ros·i·ty (pə-rŏs′ĭ-tē, pô-, pō-) *n., pl.* **-ties.** The condition, property, or degree of being porous.

po·rous (pôr′əs, pōr′-) *adj.* **1.** Having or full of pores. **2.** Admitting the passage of gas or liquid through pores or interstices. —**po′rous·ly** *adv.* —**po′rous·ness** *n.*

por·phy·ry (pôr′fə-rē) *n., pl.* **-ries.** A fine-grained igneous rock containing relatively large crystals, esp. of feldspar or quartz. [Middle English *porfurie,* red or purple stone, from Medieval Latin *porphyrium,* from Latin *porphyrītēs,* from Greek *porphurītēs,* from *porphura,* purple.]

por·poise (pôr′pəs) *n., pl.* **-pois·es** or **-poise.** **1.** Any of several gregarious aquatic mammals of the genus *Phocaena* and related genera, of oceanic waters, with a blunt snout and a triangular dorsal fin. **2.** Any of several related aquatic mammals, as the dolphin. [Middle English *porpoys,* from Old French *porpois* : Latin *porcus,* pig + *piscis,* fish.]

por·ridge (pôr′ĭj, pŏr′-) *n.* Boiled oatmeal, usu. eaten with milk at breakfast. [Var. of POTTAGE.]

por·rin·ger (pôr′ĭn-jər, pŏr′-) *n.* A shallow cup or bowl with a handle. [Alteration of *pottinger,* Middle English *potinger,* from Old French *potager,* from *potage,* pottage.]

port¹ (pôrt, pōrt) *n.* **1. a.** A town that has a harbor for ships to take on or discharge cargoes. **b.** A place on a waterway that provides a harbor for a nearby city. **2.** A place of anchorage or shelter for ships; haven. [Middle English, from Old English and Old French, both from Latin *portus,* house door, port.]

port² (pôrt, pōrt) *n.* The left-hand side of a ship or aircraft facing forward. —*adj.* Of or on this side of a ship or aircraft: *a port cabin.* —*tr.v.* To turn or shift (the helm of a vessel) to the left. [Orig. unknown.]

port³ (pôrt, pōrt) *n.* **1.** *Naut.* **a.** A porthole. **b.** A covering for this. **2.** An opening, as in a cylinder or valve face, for the passage of steam or fluid. [Middle English, opening, from Old French *porte,* gate, door, from Latin *porta.*]

port⁴ (pôrt, pōrt) *n.* A rich sweet wine. [After *Oporto,* a city in Portugal.]

port⁵ (pôrt, pōrt) *tr.v.* To carry (a rifle, sword, or other weapon) diagonally across the body, with the muzzle or blade near the left shoulder. —*n.* **1.** The position of a rifle or other weapon when ported. **2.** The manner in which a person carries himself; bearing. [Middle English, deportment from Old French, from *porter,* to bear, from Latin *portāre.*]

port·a·ble (pôr′tə-bəl, pōr′-) *adj.* **1.** Capable of being carried. **2.** Easily carried or moved. —*n.* Something that is portable, such as a light typewriter. [Middle English, from Old French, from Late Latin *portābilis,* from Latin *portāre,* to carry.] —**port′a·bil′i·ty** or **port′a·ble·ness** *n.* —**port′a·bly** *adv.*

port·age (pôr′tĭj, pōr′-, pôr-täzh′) *n.* **1.** The carrying of boats and supplies overland between two waterways. **2.** A track or route by which this is done. —*v.* **-aged, -ag·ing.** —*tr.v.* To transport by portage. —*intr.v.* To make a portage: *We portaged around the rapids.* [Middle English, from Old French, from Medieval Latin *portāgium,* from Latin *portāre,* to carry.]

por·tal (pôr′tl, pōr′-) *n.* **1.** A large, imposing doorway or entrance. **2.** Any entrance or means of entrance: *a portal of knowledge.* —*adj.* Of or relating to the portal vein. [Middle English, from Old French, from Medieval Latin *portāle*, a city gate, porch, from Latin *porta*, a gate.]

portal vein. A vein that conducts blood from the digestive organs, spleen, pancreas, and gall bladder to the liver.

por·cul·lis (pôr-kŭl′ĭs, pōr-) *n.* A sliding grating suspended in the gateway of a fortified place in such a way that it can be quickly lowered in case of attack. [Middle English *porculis,* from Old French *porte coleïce*, "sliding gate."]

porte-co·chère or **porte-co·chere** (pôrt′kō-shâr′, pōrt′-) *n.* **1.** A carriage entrance leading into the courtyard of a town house. **2.** A porch roof projecting over a driveway at the entrance to a building. [French *porte cochère*, "coach-door."]

por·tend (pôr-tĕnd′, pōr-) *tr.v.* To serve as an advance indication or warning of; presage: *economic declines that portend trouble.* [Middle English *portenden*, from Latin *portendere.*]

por·tent (pôr′tĕnt′, pōr′-) *n.* An indication of something momentous, calamitous, or evil about to occur; an omen. [Latin *portentum,* from *portendere,* to portend.]

por·ten·tous (pôr-tĕn′təs, pōr-) *adj.* **1.** Of the nature of or constituting a portent; foreboding; ominous: *portentious indications.* **2.** Full of unspecifiable significance; exciting wonder and awe; prodigious: *"Such a portentous and mysterious monster roused all my curiosity"* (Herman Melville). **3.** Pretentiously weighty; pompous. —**por·ten′tous·ly** *adv.* —**por·ten′tous·ness** *n.*

por·ter¹ (pôr′tər, pōr′-) *n.* **1.** A person employed to carry travelers' luggage. **2.** A railroad employee who waits on passengers in a sleeping car or parlor car. [Middle English *portour,* from Old French *porteur,* from Late Latin *portātor,* from Latin *portāre,* to carry.]

por·ter² (pôr′tər, pōr′-) *n. Brit.* A gatekeeper; doorman. [Middle English, from Old French *portier,* from Late Latin *portārius,* from Latin *porta,* a gate.]

por·ter³ (pôr′tər, pōr′-) *n.* A dark beer made from browned or charred malt. [Short for *porter's beer* or *porter's ale.*]

por·ter·house (pôr′tər-hous′, pōr′-) *n.* A cut of beef taken from the thick end of the short loin, with a T-bone and a sizable piece of tenderloin.

port·fo·li·o (pôrt-fō′lē-ō′, pōrt-) *n., pl.* **-os.** **1. a.** A portable case for holding loose papers, drawings, etc. **b.** The materials collected in such a case, esp. when representative of a person's work: *an illustrator's portfolio.* **2.** The office or post of a cabinet member or minister of state. **3.** A list of the investments, securities, and commercial paper owned, as by a bank or individual investor. [Italian *portafoglio :portare,* to carry, from Latin *portāre* + *foglio,* leaf, sheet, from Latin *folium.*]

port·hole (pôrt′hōl′, pōrt′-) *n.* **1.** A small, usu. circular window in a ship's side. **2.** An embrasure.

por·ti·co (pôr′tĭ-kō′, pōr′-) *n., pl.* **-coes** or **-cos.** A porch or walkway with a roof supported by columns, often leading to the entrance of a building. [Italian, from Latin *porticus,* porch, from *porta,* a gate.]

por·tière or **por·tiere** (pôrt-yâr′, pōrt-) *n.* A heavy curtain hung across a doorway. [French, from *porte,* door, from Old French, gate.]

por·tion (pôr′shən, pōr′-) *n.* **1.** A section or quantity within a larger thing; a part of a whole. **2.** A part separated from a whole. **3.** A part allotted to a person or group, esp. an amount of food served to one person. **4.** A woman's dowry. **5.** A person's lot or fate. —*tr.v.* **1.** To distribute in portions; parcel out. **2.** To provide with a share, inheritance, or dowry. [Middle English, from Old French, from Latin *portiō.*]

Port·land cement (pôrt′lənd, pōrt′-). A cement made by heating a mixture of limestone and clay in a kiln and pulverizing the resultant mass. [From its resemblance to *Portland stone,* limestone quarried at *Portland,* England.]

port·ly (pôrt′lē, pōrt′-) *adj.* **-li·er, -li·est.** Stout; corpulent. —See Syns at **fat.** [From PORT (bearing).] —**port′li·ness** *n.*

port·man·teau (pôrt-măn′tō, pōrt-, pôrt′măn-tō′) *n., pl.* **-teaus** or **-teaux** (-tōz). A large leather suitcase that opens into two hinged compartments. [French *porteman-*

teau, from Old French, "coat-carrier."]

port of call. A port where ships dock in the course of voyages to load or unload cargo, obtain supplies, or undergo repairs.

port of entry. A place where travelers or goods may enter or leave a country under official supervision.

por·trait (pôr′trĭt, -trāt′, pōr′-) *n.* **1.** A painting, photograph, or other likeness of a person, esp. one showing the face. **2.** A verbal picture or description, esp. of a person. [French, from Old French, from *portraire,* to portray.]

por·trait·ist (pôr′trə-tĭst, pōr-) *n.* A person who makes portraits, esp. a painter or photographer.

por·trai·ture (pôr′trĭ-chŏor′, -chər, pōr′-) *n.* **1.** The practice or art of making portraits. **2.** A portrait or group of portraits.

por·tray (pôr-trā′, pōr-) *tr.v.* **1.** To show by means of a picture. **2.** To picture through the use of words; depict. **3.** To play on stage or on the screen: *portray Lincoln.* [Middle English *portraien,* from Old French *portraire,* from Latin *prōtrahere,* to reveal : *prō,* forth + *trahere,* to draw.] —**por·tray′er** *n.*

por·tray·al (pôr-trā′əl, pōr-) *n.* **1.** The act or process of portraying. **2.** A representation or description.

Por·tu·guese (pôr′chə-gēz′, -gēs′, pōr′-, pôr′chə-gēz′, -gēs′, pōr′-) *adj.* Of Portugal, its people, or their language. —*n., pl.* **Portuguese. 1.** A native or inhabitant of Portugal. **2.** The Romance language of Portugal and Brazil.

Portuguese man-of-war. A complex colonial organism of the genus *Physalia,* of warm seas, with a bluish, bladderlike float from which are suspended numerous long stinging tentacles capable of inflicting severe injury.

Portuguese man-of-war   **portulaca**

por·tu·lac·a (pôr′chə-lăk′ə, pōr′-) *n.* Any plant of the genus *Portulaca,* with fleshy stems and leaves, esp. one species cultivated for its showy flowers that open only in sunlight. [From Latin *portulāca,* from *portula,* dim. of *porta,* gate (from the gatelike covering on its capsule).]

pose (pōz) *v.* **posed, pos·ing.** —*intr.v.* **1.** To assume or hold a particular position or posture, as in sitting for a portrait. **2.** To represent oneself falsely; pretend to be other than what one is. —*tr.v.* **1.** To place in a specific position: *posing a group for a photograph.* **2.** To present or put forward: *pose a threat; pose a question.* —*n.* **1.** A bodily attitude or position. **2.** A false appearance or attitude; a pretense. [Middle English *posen,* from Old French *poser,* from Late Latin *pausāre,* to cease, from Latin *pausa,* a pause, from Greek *pausis,* from *pauein,* to pause.]

Po·sei·don (pō-sīd′n) *n. Gk. Myth.* The god of the waters, earthquakes, and horses, and brother of Zeus, identified with the Roman god Neptune.

po·seur (pō-zûr′) *n.* A person who assumes a false attitude, character, or manner to impress others. [French, from Old French *poser,* to pose.]

posh (pŏsh) *adj. Informal.* Smart and fashionable; exclusive. [Orig. unknown.]

pos·it (pŏz′ĭt) *tr.v.* **1.** To place in position. **2.** To put forward as a fact or assumption; to postulate. [Latin *positus,* past part. of *pōnere,* to place.]

po·si·tion (pə-zĭsh′ən) *n.* **1.** A place or location. **2.** The right or appropriate place: *The guns were in position.* **3. a.** The way in which something or someone is placed: *in a conspicuous position.* **b.** The arrangement of bodily parts; posture: *a standing position.* **4.** An advantageous place or location: *jockeys maneuvering for position.* **5.** A situation as it relates to the surrounding circumstances: *You've put me in an awkward position.* **6.** A point of view or attitude on a certain question. **7.** A post of employment; a job. **8.** *Sports.* The area or station assigned to a member of a team. —*tr.v.* To place in proper position. [Old French, from Latin *positiō,* from *positus,* past part. of *pōnere,* to place.] —**po·si'tion·al** *adj.* —**po·si'tion·er** *n.*

pos·i·tive (pŏz'ĭ-tĭv) *adj.* **1.** Characterized by or displaying approval, acceptance, or affirmation: *a positive answer.* **2.** Measured or moving in a direction of increase, progress, or forward motion. **3.** Explicitly expressed: *a positive demand.* **4.** Admitting of no doubt; certain. **5.** Determined or settled in opinion or assertion; confident: *a positive manner; positive that he's right.* **6.** Formally or arbitrarily determined; prescribed. **7.** Concerned with practical rather than theoretical matters. **8.** Composed of or characterized by the presence of particular qualities or attributes; real. **9.** *Informal.* Utter; absolute: *She's a positive angel.* **10.** *Math.* Pertaining to or designating: **a.** A quantity greater than zero. **b.** The sign (+). **c.** A quantity, number, angle, or direction opposite to another designated as negative. **11.** *Physics.* Pertaining to or designating electric charge of a sign opposite to that of an electron. **12.** Indicating the presence of something sought or suspected: *a positive Wassermann test.* **13.** Indicating or characterized by response or motion toward the source of a stimulus: *positive tropism.* **14.** *Photog.* Having the areas of light and dark in their original and normal relationship, as in a print made from a negative. **15.** *Gram.* Of or denoting the simple uncompared degree of an adjective or adverb, as opposed to either the comparative or superlative. —See Syns at **explicit** and **utter.** —*n.* **1.** *Photog.* An image in which the lights and darks appear as they do in nature. **2.** *Gram.* The uncompared degree of an adjective or adverb. [Middle English, from Old French *positif,* from Latin *positīvus,* dogmatic, from *pōnere* to place.] —**pos'i·tive·ly** *adv.* —**pos'i·tive·ness** *n.*

pos·i·tiv·ism (pŏz'ĭ-tĭ-vĭz'əm) *n.* **1.** A philosophical doctrine contending that sense perceptions are the only admissible basis of human knowledge and precise thought. **2.** Dogmatic certainty, as in speculation and argument. —**pos'i·tiv·ist** *n.* —**pos'i·tiv·is'tic** *adj.*

pos·i·tron (pŏz'ĭ-trŏn') *n.* The antiparticle of the electron. [POSI(TIVE) + (ELEC)TRON.]

pos·se (pŏs'ē) *n.* **1.** A group of people summoned by a sheriff to aid in law enforcement. **2.** A search party. [Short for Medieval Latin *posse comitātūs,* "force of the county."]

pos·sess (pə-zĕs') *tr.v.* **1.** To have as property; to own. **2.** To have as a quality, ability, or other attribute: *possessed great tact.* **3.** To gain or exert influence or control over; dominate: *Fury possessed him.* **4.** To cause to own, hold, or master something, such as property or knowledge: *possessed herself of the unclaimed goods.* [Middle English *possessen,* from Old French *possesser,* from Latin *possīdere,* to take possession of, and *possidēre,* to own, possess.] —**pos·ses'sor** *n.*

pos·sessed (pə-zĕst') *adj.* **1.** Owning or having: *possessed of superhuman strength.* **2.** Controlled by or as if by a spirit or other force; obsessed.

pos·ses·sion (pə-zĕsh'ən) *n.* **1.** The act or fact of possessing. **2.** The condition of being possessed. **3.** Something or someone that is owned or possessed. **4. possessions.** Wealth or property. **5.** *Law.* Actual holding or occupancy, with or without rightful ownership. **6.** A territory subject to foreign control. **7.** Self-control. **8.** Domination by or as if by evil spirits or by an obsession.

pos·ses·sive (pə-zĕs'ĭv) *adj.* **1.** Of or relating to ownership or possession. **2.** Having or showing a desire to control or dominate: *a possessive mother.* **3.** *Gram.* Of or designating a noun or pronoun case that indicates possession. —*n. Gram.* **1.** The possessive case. **2.** A possessive form or construction. —**pos·ses'sive·ly** *adv.* —**pos·ses'sive·ness** *n.*

possessive adjective. *Gram.* A pronominal adjective expressing possession. In the sentence *This is my duty,* the possessive adjective is *my.*

possessive pronoun. *Gram.* One of several pronouns denoting possession and capable of substituting for noun phrases. The possessive pronouns are *mine, his, hers, its, ours, yours, theirs,* and *whose.*

pos·set (pŏs'ĭt) *n.* A spiced drink of hot sweetened milk curdled with wine or ale. [Middle English *possot.*]

pos·si·bil·i·ty (pŏs'ə-bĭl'ĭ-tē) *n., pl.* **-ties. 1.** The fact or condition of being possible. **2.** Something that is possible. **3. possibilities.** Potentially favorable results: *The idea has tremendous possibilities.*

pos·si·ble (pŏs'ə-bəl) *adj.* **1.** Capable of happening, existing, or being true without contradicting proven facts, laws, or circumstances: *prepared for all possible accidents.* **2.** Capable of favorable development; potential: *a possible site for the new capital.* **3.** That may or may not occur; of uncertain likelihood. [Middle English, from Old French, from Latin *possibilis,* from *posse,* to be able.] —**pos'si·bly** *adv.*

pos·sum (pŏs'əm) *n.* Var. of **opossum.** —*idiom.* **play possum.** To pretend to be dead, asleep, or unaware in order to deceive someone.

post¹ (pōst) *n.* **1.** A stake of wood or other material set upright into the ground to serve as a marker or support. **2.** Anything resembling this. **3.** The starting gate at a racetrack. —*tr.v.* **1.** To put up in a place of public view. **2.** To announce by or as if by posters: *post banns.* **3.** To put up signs on (property) warning against trespassing. **4.** To publish on a list. [Middle English, from Old English, from Latin *postis.*]

post² (pōst) *n.* **1. a.** A military base where troops are stationed. **b.** The grounds and buildings of a military base. **2.** A local organization of military veterans. **3.** An assigned position or station. **4.** A position of employment. **5.** A place to which anyone is assigned for duty. **6.** A trading post. —*tr.v.* **1.** To assign to a specific position or station: *post a sentry.* **2.** To appoint to a naval or military command. **3.** To put forward; present: *post bail.* [French *poste,* from Old Italian *posto,* from Latin *positum,* past part. of *pōnere,* to place.]

post³ (pōst) *n.* **1. a.** One of a series of relay stations along a fixed route, furnishing fresh riders and horses for the delivery of mail on horseback. **b.** A rider on such a mail route; courier. **2.** *Brit.* **a.** A governmental system for transporting and delivering the mail. **b.** A post office. **3. a.** A delivery of mail. **b.** The mail delivered. —*tr.v.* **1.** To send by mail in a system of relays on horseback. **2.** To mail (a letter). **3.** To inform of the latest news. **4.** *Bookkeeping.* **a.** To transfer (an item or items) to a ledger. **b.** To make the necessary entries in (a ledger). —*intr.v.* To travel quickly; hasten. —*adv.* **1.** By mail. **2.** With great speed; rapidly. [French *poste,* from Italian *posta,* from Latin *posita,* past part. of *pōnere,* to place.]

post-. A prefix meaning: **1.** After in time; later; subsequent to: **postgraduate. 2.** After in position; behind; posterior to: **postorbital.** [Latin, from *post,* behind, after.]

post·age (pō'stĭj) *n.* The charge for mailing an item.

postage meter. A machine used in bulk mailing to print the correct amount of postage on mail.

postage stamp. A small engraved piece of paper issued by a government and affixed to items of mail as evidence of the payment of postage.

post·al (pō'stəl) *adj.* Of the post office or mail service.

postal card. A postcard, esp. a government-issued postcard with an imprinted postage stamp.

post·bel·lum (pōst-bĕl'əm) *adj.* Happening after a war, esp. the American Civil War. [Latin *post,* after + *bellum,* war.]

post·card (pōst'kärd') *n.* Also **post card.** A card used for sending short messages through the mail, usu. containing a picture on one side, with space on the other side for a postage stamp, an address, and a message.

post chaise. A closed, four-wheeled, horse-drawn carriage, formerly used to transport mail and passengers. [POST (mail) + CHAISE.]

post·date (pōst-dāt') *tr.v.* **-dat·ed, -dat·ing. 1.** To put a date on (a check, letter, or document) that is later than the actual date. **2.** To occur later than; follow in time.

post·er (pō'stər) *n.* A large printed notice or announcement, often illustrated, posted to advertise or publicize something.

pos·te·ri·or (pŏ-stîr'ē-ər, pō-) *adj.* **1.** Located behind a part or toward the rear of a structure. **2.** *Anat.* **a.** Of, in, or near the side of the human body in which the spine is located. **b.** Of, in, or near the part of an animal body that is close to the tail. **3.** *Bot.* Next to or nearest the main stem or axis. **4.** Following in time; later; subsequent. —*n.* The buttocks. [Latin, comp. of *posterus*, next, from *post*, after.] —**pos·te'ri·or·ly** *adv.*

pos·te·ri·or·i·ty (pŏ-stîr'ē-ôr'ĭ-tē, -ôr'-, pō-) *n.* The condition of being posterior in location or time.

pos·ter·i·ty (pŏ-stĕr'ĭ-tē) *n.* **1.** Future generations. **2.** All of a person's descendants. [Middle English *posterite*, from Old French *posterite*, from Latin *posteritās*, from *posterus*, next.]

pos·tern (pō'stərn, pŏs'tərn) *n.* A small rear gate, esp. one in a fort or castle. —*adj.* Situated in back or at the side. [Middle English *posterne*, from Old French *posterle*, from Late Latin *posterula*, dim. of *postera*, back door.]

post exchange. A store on a military base that sells to military personnel and their families.

post·grad·u·ate (pōst-grăj'ōō-ĭt, -āt') *adj.* Of or pursuing advanced study beyond the level of a bachelor's degree. —*n.* A person engaged in such study.

post·haste (pōst'hāst') *adv.* With great speed; hastily; rapidly. [Orig. *post, haste*, a direction on letters.]

post·hu·mous (pŏs'chə-məs, -choo-) *adj.* **1.** Occurring or continuing after one's death: *a posthumous award.* **2.** Published after the author's death. **3.** Born after the death of the father. [Latin *posthumus*, alteration of *postumus*, superl. of *posterus*, coming after, next.] —**post'hu·mous·ly** *adv.* —**post'hu·mous·ness** *n.*

post·hyp·not·ic suggestion (pōst'hĭp-nŏt'ĭk). A suggestion made to a hypnotized person specifying an action to be performed in a subsequent waking state.

pos·til·ion (pō-stĭl'yən, pə-) *n.* Also **pos·til·lion.** A person who rides the left-hand lead horse to guide the team drawing a coach. [French *postillon*, from Italian *postiglione*, from *posta*, post, mail.]

post·im·pres·sion·ism (pōst'ĭm-prĕsh'ə-nĭz'əm) *n.* A school of painting in France in the late 19th cent. that rejected the objective naturalism of impressionism and used form and color in more personally expressive ways. —**post'im·pres'sion·ist** *n. & adj.* —**post'im·pres'sion·is'tic** *adj.*

post·lude (pōst'lood') *n.* **1.** An organ voluntary played at the end of a church service. **2.** A concluding piece of music. [POST- + (PRE)LUDE.]

post·man (pōst'mən) *n.* A mailman.

post·mark (pōst'märk') *n.* An official mark printed over the stamp on a piece of mail, esp. one that cancels the stamp and records the date and place of mailing. —*tr.v.* To stamp with a postmark.

post·mas·ter (pōst'măs'tər) *n.* A government official in charge of the operations of a local post office. —**post'mas'ter·ship'** *n.*

postmaster general *pl.* **postmasters general.** The executive head of a national postal service.

post·me·rid·i·an (pōst'mə-rĭd'ē-ən) *adj.* Of or taking place in the afternoon.

post me·rid·i·em (pōst' mə-rĭd'ē-əm). After noon. Used chiefly in the abbreviated form to specify the hour: *10:30 P.M.* [Latin *post merīdiem*, after midday.]

post·mor·tem (pōst-môr'təm) *adj.* **1.** Occurring or done after death. **2.** Of a post-mortem examination. —*n.* **1.** A post-mortem examination. **2.** *Informal.* An analysis or review of some completed event. [Latin *post mortem*, after death.]

post-mortem examination. A medical or scientific investigation of a corpse, esp. an autopsy.

post·na·sal (pōst-nā'zəl) *adj.* Of, in, or from the area in back of the nose.

post·na·tal (pōst-nāt'l) *adj.* Of or occurring during the period immediately after birth. —**post·na'tal·ly** *adv.*

post office. 1. The public department responsible for the transportation and delivery of the mails. **2.** Any local office where mail is received, sorted, and delivered, and stamps and other postal matter are sold.

post·op·er·a·tive (pōst-ŏp'ər-ə-tĭv, -ŏp'rə-, -ŏp'ə-rā'-) *adj.* Happening or done after surgery: *postoperative care.*

post·paid (pōst'pād') *adj.* With the postage paid in advance.

post·par·tum (pōst-pär'təm) *adj.* Of or occurring in the period shortly after childbirth. [Latin *post partum*, after birth.]

post·pone (pōst-pōn', pōs-pōn') *tr.v.* **-poned, -pon·ing.** To delay until a future time; put off. [Latin *postpōnere* : *post*, after + *pōnere*, to put, place.] —**post·pon'a·ble** *adj.* —**post·pone'ment** *n.*

post·script (pōst'skrĭpt', pōs'skrĭpt') *n.* **1.** A message added at the end of a letter after the writer's signature. **2.** Additional information added at the end of a book, article, etc. [Latin *postscriptum* : *post*, after + *scrībere*, to write.]

pos·tu·lant (pŏs'chə-lənt) *n.* **1.** A person submitting a request or application; petitioner. **2.** A candidate for admission into a religious order. [French, from Latin *postulāns*, pres. part. of *postulāre*, to demand.] —**pos'tu·lan·cy** or **pos'tu·lant·ship** *n.*

pos·tu·late (pŏs'chə-lāt') *tr.v.* **-lat·ed, -lat·ing.** To assume or claim as true with no proof, esp. as a basis of an argument. —*n.* (pŏs'chə-lĭt, -lāt'). **1.** Something assumed without proof as being self-evident or gen. accepted. **2.** A fundamental element; basic principle. **3.** *Geom.* An axiom. **4.** A requirement; prerequisite. [From Latin *postulāre*, to request, demand.] —**pos'tu·la'tion** *n.*

pos·ture (pŏs'chər) *n.* **1.** A position or attitude of the body or of bodily parts: *a sitting posture.* **2.** A characteristic way of bearing one's body, esp. the trunk and head: *learning good posture.* **3.** The present condition or tendency of something: *the military posture of a nation.* **4.** A frame of mind; overall attitude. —*v.* **-tured, -tur·ing.** —*intr.v.* To assume an exaggerated or unnatural pose or mental attitude. —*tr.v.* To put in a posture; to pose. [French, from Italian *postura*, from Latin *positūra*, position, from *positus*, past part. of *pōnere*, to place.] —**pos'tur·er** *n.*

post·war (pōst'wôr') *adj.* Occurring after a war.

po·sy (pō'zē) *n., pl.* **-sies. 1.** A flower or bunch of flowers; nosegay. **2.** *Archaic.* A brief verse or sentimental phrase. [Var. of POESY.]

pot (pŏt) *n.* **1. a.** A round, fairly deep cooking vessel with a handle. **b.** Such a vessel and its contents: *a pot of soup.* **c.** The amount that such a vessel will hold; potful. **2.** A decorative ceramic vessel of any size or shape. **3.** Something resembling a round cooking vessel in appearance or function, as a chimney pot or chamber pot. **4.** A trap for fish, crustaceans, or eels, consisting of a wicker or wire basket. **5.** *Card Games.* The total amount staked by all the players in one hand. **6.** *Informal.* A common fund to which the members of a group contribute. **7.** *Slang.* Marijuana. —*tr.v.* **pot·ted, pot·ting. 1.** To place or plant in a pot: *pot a plant.* **2.** To preserve (food) in a pot. **3.** To cook in a pot. **4.** *Informal.* To shoot with a pot shot. —*idiom.* **go to pot.** To go to ruin; deteriorate. [Middle English, from Old English *pott*.]

po·ta·ble (pō'tə-bəl) *adj.* Fit to drink. —*n.* **potables.** Drinks; beverages. [French, from Late Latin *pōtābilis*, from Latin *pōtāre*, to drink.] —**po·ta·bil'i·ty** or **po'ta·ble·ness** *n.*

pot·ash (pŏt'ăsh') *n.* **1.** Potassium carbonate. **2.** Potassium hydroxide. **3.** Any of several compounds containing potassium, esp. soluble compounds, used chiefly in fertilizers. [Sing. of earlier *pot ashes*.]

po·tas·si·um (pə-tăs'ē-əm) *n.* Symbol **K** A soft, silver-white, light, highly or explosively reactive metallic element obtained by electrolysis of its common hydroxide and found in, or converted to, a wide variety of salts used esp. in fertilizers and soaps. Atomic number 19; atomic weight 39.102; melting point 63.65°C; boiling point 774°C; specific gravity 0.862; valence 1. [New Latin, from *potassa*, potassium monoxide, from English *potash*, potash.] —**po·tas'sic** *adj.*

potassium bi·tar·trate (bī-tär'trāt'). A white powder $KHC_4H_4O_6$, used in baking powder and in laxatives.

potassium bromide. A white crystalline solid or powder, KBr, used as a sedative, in photographic emulsion, and in spectroscopy. Also called **bromide.**

potassium carbonate. A transparent, white, granular powder, K_2CO_3, used in making glass, pigments, ceramics,

---

ă pat   ā pay   â care   ä father   ĕ pet   ē be   hw which   ĭ pit   ī tie   î pier   ŏ pot   ō toe   ô paw, for   oi noise
ōō took   ōō boot   ou out   th thin   *th* this   ŭ cut   û urge   zh vision   ə about, item, edible, gallop, circus

and soaps. Also called **pearl ash.**

potassium chloride. A colorless crystalline solid or powder, KCl, used widely in fertilizers.

potassium cyanide. An extremely poisonous white compound, KCN, used in electroplating and in the extraction of gold and silver from ores.

potassium hydroxide. A caustic white solid, KOH, used as a bleach and in the manufacture of liquid detergents and soaps.

potassium nitrate. A transparent white crystalline compound, KNO_3, used to pickle meat and in the manufacture of explosives, matches, rocket propellants, and fertilizers. Also called **niter** and **saltpeter.**

potassium permanganate. A dark-purple crystalline compound, $KMnO_4$, used as an oxidizing agent, disinfectant, and in deodorizers and dyes.

po·ta·tion (pō-tā'shən) n. **1.** The act of drinking. **2.** A drink, esp. an alcoholic beverage. [Middle English *potacioun*, from Old French *potation*, from Latin *pōtātiō*, drinking, from *pōtāre*, to drink.]

po·ta·to (pə-tā'tō) n., pl. **-toes. 1.** A plant, *Solanum tuberosum*, native to South America and widely cultivated for its starchy, edible tubers. **2.** A tuber of this plant. [Spanish *patata*, from Taino *batata*.]

potato beetle. A small yellow-and-black striped beetle, *Leptinotarsa decemlineata*, that is a major agricultural pest. Also called **Colorado potato beetle.**

potato chip. A thin slice of potato fried in deep fat until crisp and then salted.

pot·bel·ly (pŏt'bĕl'ē) n. A protruding belly. **—pot'bel'lied** *adj.*

potbelly stove. Also **potbellied stove.** A short rounded stove in which wood or coal is burned.

pot·boil·er (pŏt'boi'lər) n. A literary or artistic work of poor quality, produced quickly for profit.

pot cheese. Cottage cheese.

po·ten·cy (pōt'n-sē) n., pl. **-cies. 1.** The quality or condition of being potent. **2.** Capacity for growth and development; potentiality.

po·tent (pōt'nt) *adj.* **1.** Possessing strength; powerful. **2.** Having a strong effect or influence; cogent: *potent arguments.* **3.** Having great control or authority: *"The police were potent only so long as they were feared"* (Thomas Burke). **4.** Capable of causing strong physiological or chemical effects: *a potent medicine; potent liquors.* **5.** Able to perform sexually. Said of a male. [Middle English, from Latin *potēns.*] **—po'tent·ly** *adv.*

po·ten·tate (pōt'n-tāt') n. **1.** A person who has the power and position to rule over others; monarch. **2.** Someone who dominates or leads any group or endeavor: *an industrial potentate.* [Middle English *potentat*, from Old French, from Late Latin *potentātus*, from Latin, power, rule, from *potēns*, potent.]

po·ten·tial (pə-tĕn'shəl) *adj.* Capable of being but not yet realized; latent: *potential customers; a potential problem.* **—n. 1.** Capacity for further growth, development, or progress; promise. **2.** *Elect.* The potential energy of a unit charge at any point in an electric circuit measured with respect to a specified reference point in the circuit or to ground; voltage. **—po·ten'tial·ly** *adv.*

potential difference. The work required to bring a unit electric charge from one point to another.

potential energy. The energy of a particle or system of particles derived from position, rather than motion, with respect to a specified datum in a field of force.

po·ten·ti·al·i·ty (pə-tĕn'shē-ăl'ĭ-tē) n., pl. **-ties. 1.** Capacity for growth, development, or progress. **2.** An ability, quality, tendency, or talent that can be developed.

po·ten·ti·om·e·ter (pə-tĕn'shē-ŏm'ə-tər) n. An instrument for measuring an unknown voltage or potential difference by comparison to a standard voltage.

poth·er (pŏth'ər) n. **1.** A commotion; disturbance. **2.** A condition of nervous activity or anxiety. **3.** A cloud of smoke or dust that chokes or smothers. **—tr.v.** To make confused; trouble; worry. **—intr.v.** To take too much concern with trifles; fuss. [Orig. unknown.]

pot·hole (pŏt'hōl') n. **1.** A large hole, esp. in a road surface. **2.** A deep, round hole worn in rock by whirling loose stones in strong rapids or waterfalls.

pot·hook (pŏt'hook') n. **1.** A hooked piece of iron for hanging a pot over a fire. **2.** A curved iron rod with a hooked end used for lifting hot pots, irons, or stove lids. **3.** A curved, S-shaped stroke in writing.

po·tion (pō'shən) n. A liquid dose, esp. of medicinal, magic, or poisonous content: *a sleeping potion; a love potion.* [Middle English *pocioun*, from Old French *potion*, from Latin *pōtiō*, from *pōtāre*, to drink.]

pot·latch (pŏt'lăch') n. A ceremonial feast among Indian tribes living on the northwest Pacific coast, in which the host distributes gifts. [Chinook Jargon.]

pot·luck (pŏt'lŭk') n. Whatever food happens to be available for a meal, esp. when offered to a guest.

pot·pie (pŏt'pī') n. **1.** A mixture of meat or poultry and vegetables covered with a pastry crust and baked in a deep dish. **2.** A meat or poultry stew with dumplings.

pot·pour·ri (pō'poo-rē') n., pl. **-ris. 1.** A combination of diverse elements. **2.** A miscellaneous anthology or collection. **3.** A mixture of dried flower petals and spices, kept in a jar and used to scent the air. [French *pot pourri*, "rotten pot."]

pot roast. A cut of beef that is browned and then cooked until tender in a covered pot.

pot·sherd (pŏt'shûrd') n. Also **pot·shard** (-shärd'). A fragment of broken pottery, esp. one found in an archaeological excavation. [Middle English *pot-schoord* : *pot*, pot + *schoord*, shard.]

pot shot. 1. A shot fired without taking careful aim or fired at a target within easy range. **2.** A criticism made without careful thought and aimed at a handy target for attack: *reporters taking pot shots at the mayor.*

pot·tage (pŏt'ĭj) n. A thick soup or stew of vegetables and sometimes meat. [Middle English *potage*, from Old French.]

pot·ted (pŏt'ĭd) *adj.* **1.** Placed or grown in a pot: *potted plants.* **2.** Preserved in a pot, can, or jar: *potted beef.* **3.** *Slang.* Intoxicated.

pot·ter¹ (pŏt'ər) n. A person who makes earthenware pots, dishes, etc.

pot·ter² (pŏt'ər) v. *Brit.* Var. of **putter** (to occupy oneself aimlessly).

potter's field. A place for the burial of poor or unknown persons. [From the potter's field mentioned in Matthew 27:7.]

potter's wheel. A revolving, treadle-operated horizontal disk upon which clay is shaped manually.

pot·ter·y (pŏt'ə-rē) n., pl. **-ies. 1.** Objects, such as vases, pots, bowls, or plates, shaped from moist clay and hardened by heat. **2.** The craft or occupation of a potter. **3.** The place where a potter works.

pot·ty (pŏt'ē) n., pl. **-ties.** A small pot for use as a toilet by an infant or young child.

pouch (pouch) n. **1.** A small or medium-sized bag of flexible material used for holding or carrying various things. **2.** A baglike or pocketlike body part, such as the one in which a kangaroo, opossum, or other marsupial carries its young. **3.** A baglike or puffy part, such as a fold of flesh: *pouches under the eyes.* **—tr.v. 1.** To place in or as if in a pouch; to pocket. **2.** To cause to resemble a pouch in shape. **—intr.v.** To assume the form of a pouch or pouchlike cavity. [Middle English *pouche*, from Old French.] **—pouch'y** *adj.*

poul·tice (pōl'tĭs) n. A moist, soft mass of bread, meal, clay, or other adhesive substance, usu. heated, spread on cloth, and applied to warm, moisten, or stimulate an aching or inflamed part of the body. **—tr.v. -ticed, -tic·ing.** To apply a poultice to. [Earlier *pultes*, from Medieval Latin *pultēs*, pulp, thick paste.]

poul·try (pōl'trē) n. Domestic fowls, such as chickens, turkeys, ducks, or geese, raised for meat or eggs. [Middle English *pultrie*, from Old French *pouleterie*, from *pouletier*, poulterer.]

pounce¹ (pouns) *intr.v.* **pounced, pounc·ing.** To spring or swoop suddenly so as to seize something, as a cat or hawk does in catching prey. **—n.** The action of pouncing. [Orig. unknown.] **—pounc'er** n.

pounce² (pouns) n. **1.** A fine powder formerly used to smooth and finish writing paper and to soak up ink. **2.** A fine powder, such as pulverized charcoal, dusted over a

ă pat   ā pay   â care   ä father   ĕ pet   ē be   hw which
ŏŏ took   ōŏ boot   ou out   th thin   th this   ŭ cut
ī pit   ī tie   î pier   ŏ pot   ō toe   ô paw, for   oi noise
û urge   zh vision   ə about, item, edible, gallop, circus

stencil to transfer a design to an underlying surface. —*tr.v.* **pounced, pounc·ing.** **1.** To sprinkle, smooth, or treat with pounce. **2.** To transfer (a stenciled design) with pounce. [French *ponce,* from Latin *pūmex,* pumice.] —**pounc'er** *n.*

pound¹ (pound) *n., pl.* **pounds** or **pound.** **1. a.** A unit of avoirdupois weight equal to 16 ounces or 7,000 grains. **b.** A unit of apothecary weight equal to 5,760 grains or 0.823 avoirdupois pound. **2.** A unit of weight differing in various countries and times. **3.** A British unit of force equal to the weight of a standard one-pound mass where the local acceleration of gravity is 32.174 feet per second per second. **4.** *Brit.* The basic monetary unit of the United Kingdom. Also called **pound sterling.** **5.** The basic monetary unit of various other countries. [Middle English, from Old English *pund,* from Latin *pondō,* a unit of weight.]

pound² (pound) *tr.v.* **1.** To strike or hammer with a heavy blow or blows. **2.** To drive (something) in or out with repeated blows; hammer. **3.** To beat to a powder or pulp; pulverize. **4.** To instill by persistent and emphatic repetition: *pound knowledge into their heads.* —*intr.v.* **1.** To strike vigorous, repeated blows: *He pounded on the table.* **2.** To move along heavily and noisily. **3.** To pulsate rapidly and heavily: *Her heart pounded.* **4.** To work or move laboriously: *a ship pounding through heavy seas.* —*n.* **1.** A heavy blow. **2.** The sound of a heavy blow; a thump. [Middle English *pounen,* from Old English *pūnian.*]

pound³ (pound) *n.* **1.** A public enclosure for the confinement of stray dogs or livestock. **2.** An enclosure in which animals or fish are trapped or kept. **3.** A place of confinement for lawbreakers. [Middle English.]

pound·age (poun'dĭj) *n.* **1.** A tax, commission, or rate based on value per pound (sterling). **2.** Weight measured in pounds.

pound·al (poun'dl) *n.* A unit of force in the foot-pound-second system of measurement, equal to the force required to accelerate a standard one-pound mass one foot per second per second. [POUND + (QUINT)AL.]

pound cake. A rich cake containing eggs and orig. made with a pound each of flour, butter, and sugar.

pound sterling. *Brit.* Pound (monetary unit).

pour (pôr, pōr) *tr.v.* **1.** To cause (a liquid or granular solid) to flow in a steady stream. **2.** To send forth, produce, express, or utter abundantly, as if in a stream or flood: *pouring money into the project.* —*intr.v.* **1.** To stream or flow continuously or profusely. **2.** To rain hard or heavily. **3.** To go forth or stream in large numbers or quantity: *The army poured into enemy territory.* **4.** To serve drinks by letting liquid flow from a larger container into glasses, cups, etc. —*n.* A pouring or flowing forth, esp. a downpour of rain. [Middle English *pouren.*] —**pour'er** *n.*

pout¹ (pout) *intr.v.* **1.** To protrude the lips in an expression of displeasure or sulkiness. **2.** To show displeasure or disappointment; to sulk. **3.** To project or protrude. —*tr.v.* To push out or protrude (the lips). —*n.* **1.** A protrusion of the lips, esp. as an expression of sullen discontent. **2.** Often **pouts.** A fit of petulant sulkiness. [Middle English *pouten.*]

pout² (pout) *n., pl.* **pout** or **pouts.** Any of various freshwater or saltwater fishes, esp. an eelpout. [From Old English *-pūte* (as in *aele-pūte,* eelpout).]

pout·er (pou'tər) *n.* One of a breed of pigeons capable of distending the crop until the breast puffs out.

pov·er·ty (pŏv'ər-tē) *n.* **1.** The condition of being poor; lack of the means of providing material needs or comforts. **2.** Deficiency in amount; scantiness: *the poverty of his vocabulary.* **3.** Unproductiveness; infertility: *the poverty of the soil.* [Middle English *poverte,* from Old French, from Latin *paupertās,* from *pauper,* poor.]

pow·der (pou'dər) *n.* **1.** A substance consisting of ground, pulverized, or otherwise finely dispersed solid particles. **2.** Any of various preparations in this form, as certain cosmetics and medicines. **3.** Gunpowder or a similar explosive mixture. **4.** Light, dry snow. —*tr.v.* **1.** To reduce to powder; pulverize. **2.** To dust or cover with or as if with powder. —*intr.v.* **1.** To become pulverized; turn to powder. **2.** To use powder as a cosmetic. —*idiom.* **take a powder.** *Slang.* To run away. [Middle English *poudre,* from Old French, from Latin *pulvis.*] —**pow'der·er** *n.*

powder blue. A pale blue. —**pow'der-blue'** *adj.*

powder horn. A container made of an animal's horn capped at the open end, formerly used to carry gunpowder.

powder puff. A soft pad for applying skin powder.

powder room. A lavatory for women.

pow·der·y (pou'də-rē) *adj.* **1.** Composed of or similar to powder. **2.** Dusted or covered with or as if with powder. **3.** Easily made into powder; friable.

pow·er (pou'ər) *n.* **1.** The ability or capacity to do something: *the power of movement.* **2.** Often **powers.** A specific capacity, faculty, or aptitude: *powers of concentration.* **3.** Strength or force exerted or capable of being exerted; might. **4.** The ability or official capacity to exercise control; authority. **5.** A person, group, or nation having great influence or control over others. **6.** The might of a nation, political organization, or similar group. **7.** Forcefulness; effectiveness: *a novel of unusual power.* **8.** *Physics.* The rate at which work is done, commonly measured in units such as the watt and horsepower. **9.** Electricity: *The power failed during the storm.* **10.** *Math.* **a.** An **exponent.** **b.** The number of elements in a finite set. **11.** *Optics.* A measure of the magnification of an optical instrument, as a microscope or telescope. —*tr.v.* To supply with power, esp. mechanical power. [Middle English *pouer,* from Old French *poeir,* from *poeir,* to be able.]

Syns: power, authority, clout (*Informal*), **control** *n.* Core meaning: The right or ability to dominate or rule others (*the power of an emperor*). POWER is the most general; it applies whether it is based on rank, position, character, or other advantages (*a general with the power to send troops into action*). AUTHORITY suggests legitimate and recognized power (*the mayor's authority to dismiss dishonest commissioners*). CONTROL stresses the right to regulate or direct as well as dominate (*the conductor's control over the orchestra*). CLOUT stresses the existence of strong influence over others (*a politician with a lot of clout on Capitol Hill*).

pow·er·boat (pou'ər-bōt') *n.* A motorboat.

pow·er·ful (pou'ər-fəl) *adj.* **1.** Having or capable of exerting power: *powerful muscles; a powerful nation.* **2.** Effective or potent: *a powerful drug.* —*adv.* Very: *It was powerful hot.* —**pow'er·ful·ly** *adv.* —**pow'er·ful·ness** *n.*

pow·er·house (pou'ər-hous') *n.* **1.** A station for the generating of electricity. **2.** A person who possesses great force or energy.

pow·er·less (pou'ər-lĭs) *adj.* **1.** Lacking strength or power; helpless; ineffectual. **2.** Lacking legal or other authority. —**pow'er·less·ly** *adv.* —**pow'er·less·ness** *n.*

Syns: 1. powerless, helpless, impotent, incapable *adj.* Core meaning: Unable to manage for oneself (*a dying patient powerless to speak*). **2. powerless, defenseless, helpless** *adj.* Core meaning: Lacking help or protection (*powerless hostages at the mercy of their captors*).

power of attorney. A legal instrument authorizing one to act as another's attorney or agent.

power pack. A usu. compact, portable device that converts supply current to direct or alternating current as required by specific equipment.

power plant. **1.** All the equipment, including structural members, that constitutes a unit power source: *the power plant of a truck.* **2.** A complex of structures, machinery, and associated equipment for generating power, esp. electric power.

power play. **1.** A play in ice hockey in which the active players on one team, temporarily outnumbering those on the other because of a penalty, seek to press their advantage and score a goal. **2.** A maneuver using superior strength, as in politics or business.

power shovel. A large, usu. mobile machine with a boom, a dipper stick, and a bucket for excavating.

pow·wow (pou'wou') *n.* **1.** Among North American Indians, a ceremony in which charms, spells, and dances are used to call down divine help in hunting, fighting, or healing. **2.** A conference or meeting with or of North American Indians. **3.** *Informal.* Any gathering, meeting, or conference. —*intr.v.* To hold a conference or powwow. [Of Algonquian orig.]

pox (pŏks) *n.* **1.** Any disease characterized by purulent skin

---

eruptions, such as chicken pox or smallpox. **2.** Syphilis. [Pl. of POCK (mark).]

Pr The symbol for the element praseodymium.

prac·ti·ca·ble (prăk′tĭ-kə-bəl) *adj.* **1.** Capable of being effected, done, or executed; feasible: *a practicable solution.* **2.** Capable of being used for a specified purpose: *a practicable way of entry.* —**prac′ti·ca·bil′i·ty** *n.* —**prac′ti·ca·bly** *adv.*

prac·ti·cal (prăk′tĭ-kəl) *adj.* **1.** Serving or capable of serving a useful purpose; useful; effective. **2.** Coming from or involving experience, practice, or use rather than theory, study, or speculation: *practical knowledge.* **3.** Concerned with useful, down-to-earth matters; realistic. **4.** Having or showing good judgment; sensible. **5.** Being actually so, though not officially or admittedly so; virtual: *a practical disaster.* —**prac′ti·cal′i·ty** (prăk′tĭ-kăl′ĭ-tē) or **prac′ti·cal·ness** *n.*

Syns: **practical, functional, handy, serviceable, useful, utilitarian** *adj. Core meaning:* Serving or capable of serving a useful purpose (*a practical kitchen device—not a useless gadget*).

practical joke. A mischievous trick or prank played on a person to make him look or feel foolish.

practical nurse. A professional nurse who is not a nursing-school graduate.

prac·tice (prăk′tĭs) Also *Brit.* **prac·tise.** —*n.* **1.** A habitual or customary action or way of doing something. **2. a.** Repeated performance of an activity in order to learn or perfect a skill. **b.** The condition of being skilled through repeated exercise: *out of practice.* **3.** The act or process of doing something; performance: *Put into practice what you have learned.* **4.** The exercise of an occupation or profession: *the practice of law.* **5.** The business of a professional person. **6. practices.** Habitual actions or acts that are objectionable, questionable, or unacceptable. **7.** The methods of procedure used in a court of law. —*v.* **–ticed, –tic·ing.** —*tr.v.* **1.** To do or perform habitually or customarily; make a habit of: *practice restraint.* **2.** To exercise or perform repeatedly in order to acquire or polish a skill. **3.** To give lessons or repeated instructions to; to drill: *practice students in handwriting.* **4.** To work at, esp. as a profession: *practice law.* **5.** To carry out in action; observe: *practice one's religion.* —*intr.v.* **1.** To do something repeatedly in order to acquire or polish a skill. **2.** To work at a profession. [Middle English *practisen,* from Old French *practiser,* from Medieval Latin *practicāre,* from Late Latin *practicus,* practical, from Greek *praktikos,* from *prassein,* to accomplish.] —**prac′tic·er** *n.*

prac·ticed (prăk′tĭst) *adj.* **1.** Proficient; skilled; expert: *a practiced archer.* **2.** Acquired by practice.

prac·tise (prăk′tĭs) *n. & v. Brit.* Var. of **practice.**

prac·ti·tio·ner (prăk-tĭsh′ə-nər) *n.* **1.** A person who practices an occupation, profession, or technique. **2.** *Christian Science.* A person engaged in the public ministry of spiritual healing. [From earlier *practician,* from obs. French *practicien,* from *practique,* practice, from Late Latin *practicus,* practical.]

prae·fect (prē′fĕkt′) *n.* Var. of **prefect.**

prae·no·men (prē-nō′mən) *n., pl.* **–nom·i·na** (-nŏm′ə-nə, -nō′mə-) or **–no·mens.** Any first or given name. [Latin *praenōmen :* prae, before + *nōmen,* name.] —**prae·nom′i·nal** (-nŏm′ə-nəl) *adj.*

prae·tor (prē′tər) *n.* A high elected magistrate of the ancient Roman Republic, ranking below the consuls and serving as a judge. [Latin.] —**prae′tor·ship′** *n.*

prae·to·ri·an (prē-tôr′ē-ən, -tōr-) *adj.* **1.** Of or relating to a praetor. **2. Praetorian.** Of, making up, or belonging to the elite bodyguard of the Roman emperors. —*n.* **1.** A praetor. **2. Praetorian.** A member of the bodyguard of the Roman emperors.

prag·mat·ic (prăg-măt′ĭk) or **prag·mat·i·cal** (-ĭ-kəl) *adj.* **1.** Concerned with causes and effects or with needs and results rather than with ideas or theories; practical. **2.** Of or following the theory or methods of pragmatism. [Latin *pragmaticus,* skilled in affairs, from Greek *pragmatikos,* from *pragma* deed, affair, from *prassein,* to do, accomplish.] —**prag·mat′i·cal·ly** *adv.*

prag·ma·tism (prăg′mə-tĭz′əm) *n.* **1.** The philosophical theory that an idea, belief, or course of action is to be judged solely by its practical results. **2.** A method of conducting political affairs by using practical means to meet immediate needs. —**prag′ma·tist** *n.* —**prag′ma·tis′tic** *adj.*

prai·rie (prâr′ē) *n.* An extensive area of flat or rolling grassland, as in central North America. [French, from Old French *praerie,* from Latin *prātum,* meadow.]

prairie chicken. Either of two birds, *Tympanuchus cupido* or *T. pallidicinctus,* of western North America, with deep-chested bodies and mottled brownish plumage.

prairie dog. Any of several burrowing rodents of the genus *Cynomys,* of west-central North America, with yellowish fur and a barklike call.

prairie dog

prairie schooner. A canvas-covered wagon used by pioneers crossing the North American prairies.

praise (prāz) *n.* **1.** An expression of warm approval or admiration; strong commendation. **2.** The extolling of a deity, ruler, or hero. —*tr.v.* **praised, prais·ing.** **1.** To express warm approval of or admiration for; commend. **2.** To extol or exalt; worship. [Middle English *preisen,* from Old French *presier,* to prize, praise, from Late Latin *pretiāre,* from Latin *pretium,* price.] —**prais′er** *n.*

Syns: **praise, acclaim, applaud, commend, laud** *v. Core meaning:* To express approval (*praise the restaurant's food*). To praise is to express one's esteem or admiration (*praised her good sense and learning*). ACCLAIM and APPLAUD are often—but not always—used literally to indicate actual applause or cheering (*the audience acclaimed the artist's performance; critics applauding her new novel*). COMMEND implies speaking well of and is usu. more formal and official (*commended the commission for its thorough report*). LAUD is also a formal term meaning to give the highest praise to; to extol (*a hero lauded for his exploits*).

praise·wor·thy (prāz′wûr′thē) *adj.* Meriting praise; commendable. —**praise′wor′thi·ly** *adv.* —**praise′wor′thi·ness** *n.*

Pra·krit (prä′krĭt) *n.* Any of the ancient or modern vernacular Indic languages of India, as opposed to the literary language, Sanskrit. —**Pra·krit′ic** *adj.*

pra·line (prä′lēn′, prā′-) *n.* A crisp candy made of nut kernels stirred in boiling sugar syrup until brown. [French, after Count du Plessis-Praslin (1598–1675), French field marshal.]

pram (prăm) *n. Brit.* A perambulator.

prance (prăns) *v.* **pranced, pranc·ing.** —*intr.v.* **1.** To spring forward on the hind legs, as a spirited horse does. **2.** To ride on a prancing horse. **3.** To move about in a lively manner; to caper; strut. —*tr.v.* To cause (a horse) to prance. —*n.* An act of prancing; a caper. [Middle English *prauncen.*] —**pranc′er** *n.* —**pranc′ing·ly** *adv.*

pran·di·al (prăn′dē-əl) *adj.* Of or relating to a meal, esp. dinner. [From Latin *prandium,* late breakfast.] —**pran′di·al·ly** *adv.*

prank¹ (prăngk) *n.* A mischievous trick; practical joke. [Orig. unknown.]

prank² (prăngk) *tr.v.* To decorate or dress gaily or gaudily. [Perh. from Dutch *pronken,* to strut.]

prank·ster (prăngk′stər) *n.* Someone who plays pranks.

pra·se·o·dym·i·um (prā′zē-ō-dĭm′ē-əm, -sē-) *n.* Symbol **Pr** A soft, silvery, malleable, ductile rare-earth element, used to color glass yellow, as a core material for carbon arcs, and in metallic alloys. Atomic number 59; atomic weight 140.907; melting point 935°C; boiling point 3,127°C; spe-

---

ă pat | ā pay | â care | ä father | ĕ pet | ē be | hw which | ĭ pit | ī tie | î pier | ŏ pot | ō toe | ô paw, for | oi noise
ŏŏ took | ōō boot | ou out | th thin | th this | ŭ cut | û urge | zh vision | ə about, item, edible, gallop, circus

cific gravity 6.8; valence 3, 4. [New Latin : Greek *prasios*, leek-green, from *prason*, leek + *didymium*, a metal mixture.]

prate (prāt) *v.* **prat·ed**, **prat·ing**. —*intr.v.* To talk idly and at great length; to chatter. —*tr.v.* To utter idly: *prating nonsense.* —*n.* Empty, foolish, or trivial talk. [Middle English *praten*.] —**prat'er** *n.*

prat·fall (prăt'fôl') *n.* A fall on the buttocks. [*Prat*, buttocks + FALL.]

prat·tle (prăt'l) *v.* **-tled**, **-tling.** —*intr.v.* To talk idly or meaninglessly; to babble. —*tr.v.* To utter in a childish or silly way. —*n.* Childish or meaningless sounds; babble. [Freq. of PRATE.] —**prat'tler** *n.*

prawn (prôn) *n.* Any of various edible shrimplike crustaceans of the genus *Palaemonetes* and related genera. [Middle English *prayne*.]

pray (prā) *intr.v.* **1.** To utter or address a prayer to God. **2.** To make a fervent request; plead; beg. —*tr.v.* **1.** To say a prayer to. **2.** To ask imploringly; beseech: *Give me water, I pray you.* **3.** To make a devout or earnest request for: *I pray your indulgence.* **4.** To move or bring by prayer or entreaty. [Middle English *preyen*, from Old French *preier*, from Latin *precārī*, to entreat, from *prex*, prayer.]

pray·er[1] (prā'ər) *n.* Someone who prays.

prayer[2] (prâr) *n.* **1.** An expression of human thoughts, hopes, or needs directed to God. **2.** A special formula of words used in speaking or appealing to God: *the Lord's Prayer.* **3.** The act of praying. **4.** Often **prayers.** A worship service for the saying of prayers: *morning prayer; family prayers.* **5.** An earnest appeal, request, or plea. **6.** The slightest chance or hope, as for survival or success: *don't have a prayer of finishing on time.* [Middle English *preyere*, from Old French *preiere*, from Medieval Latin *precāria*, from Latin *precārī*, to entreat, pray.]

prayer book. A book that contains prayers and other forms of worship.

prayer·ful (prâr'fəl) *adj.* **1.** Inclined to pray frequently; devout. **2.** Solemnly sincere; earnest. —**prayer'ful·ly** *adv.* —**prayer'ful·ness** *n.*

praying mantis. A green or brownish predatory insect, *Mantis religiosa*, that, while at rest, folds its front legs as if in prayer.

pre-. A prefix meaning: **1.** An earlier or prior time: **pre-Columbian. 2.** Preliminary or preparatory: **preschool. 3.** A location in front or anterior: **prefix.** [Middle English, from Old French, from Latin *prae-*, from *prae*, before, in front.]

preach (prēch) *tr.v.* **1.** To expound upon, esp. to urge acceptance of or compliance with: *preach tolerance.* **2.** To deliver or put forth as religious or moral instruction. —*intr.v.* **1.** To deliver a sermon. **2.** To give religious or moral instruction, esp. in a drawn-out, tiresome manner. [Middle English *prechen*, from Old French *prechier*, from Late Latin *praedīcāre*, from Latin, to proclaim : *prae*, before + *dicāre*, to say.]

preach·er (prē'chər) *n.* **1.** A Protestant clergyman; minister. **2.** A person who preaches.

pre·am·ble (prē'ăm'bəl) *n.* **1.** A preliminary statement, esp. the introduction to a formal document that explains its purpose. **2.** An introductory occurrence or fact; preliminary. [Middle English, from Old French *preambule*, from Medieval Latin *praeambulum*, from Late Latin *praeambulus*, walking in front : *prae*, in front + *ambulāre*, to walk.]

pre·am·pli·fi·er (prē-ăm'plə-fī'ər) *n.* Also **pre·amp** (prē-ămp'). An electronic circuit or device that detects and sufficiently amplifies weak signals, esp. from a radio receiver, for subsequent amplification stages.

pre·ar·range (prē'ə-rānj') *tr.v.* **-ranged**, **-rang·ing.** To arrange in advance. —**pre'ar·range'ment** *n.*

preb·end (prĕb'ənd) *n.* **1.** A clergyman's stipend, drawn from a special endowment belonging to his cathedral or church. **2.** The property or tithe providing the endowment for such a stipend. **3.** The clergyman who receives such a stipend; a prebendary. [Middle English *prebende*, from Old French, from Medieval Latin *praebenda*, from Late Latin, from Latin *praebēre*, to grant : *prae*, forth + *habēre*, to hold, offer.] —**pre·ben'dal** (prə-běn'dl, prĕb'ən-dəl) *adj.*

preb·en·dar·y (prĕb'ən-dĕr'ē) *n., pl.* **-ies.** A clergyman who receives a prebend.

Pre·cam·bri·an or **Pre-Cam·bri·an** (prē-kăm'brē-ən) *n.*

Also **Precambrian era** or **Pre-Cambrian era.** The era that represents the oldest and largest division of geologic time, ending about 600 million years ago and characterized by the appearance of primitive forms of life. —*modifier:* Precambrian rocks.

pre·car·i·ous (prĭ-kăr'ē-əs) *adj.* **1.** Dangerously lacking in security or stability; unsafe: *a precarious position.* **2.** Subject to chance or unknown conditions: *a precarious financial venture.* **3.** Based upon uncertain or unproved premises. [From Latin *precārius*, dependent on prayer, from *precārī*, to entreat, from *prex*, entreaty.] —**pre·car'i·ous·ly** *adv.* —**pre·car'i·ous·ness** *n.*

pre·cau·tion (prĭ-kô'shən) *n.* **1.** An action taken in advance to protect against possible failure or danger; a safeguard. **2.** Caution practiced in advance; forethought: *a need for precaution.* —See Syns at **prudence.** [French *précaution*, from Late Latin *praecautiō*, ult. from Latin *praecavēre*, to beware : *prae*, before + *cavēre*, to guard against.]

pre·cau·tion·ar·y (prĭ-kô'shə-nĕr'ē) *adj.* **1.** Of or constituting a precaution. **2.** Advising or exercising precaution.

pre·cau·tious (prĭ-kô'shəs) *adj.* Exercising precaution. —**pre·cau'tious·ly** *adv.* —**pre·cau'tious·ness** *n.*

pre·cede (prĭ-sēd') *v.* **-ced·ed**, **-ced·ing.** —*tr.v.* **1.** To come before in time; exist or occur prior to. **2.** To come before in order or rank; outrank. **3.** To be in a position in front of; go in advance of. **4.** To preface; introduce: *precede a speech with an anecdote.* —*intr.v.* To exist or go before. [Middle English *preceden*, from Old French *preceder*, from Latin *praecēdere* : *prae*, before + *cēdere*, to go.]

prec·e·dence (prĕs'ĭ-dəns, prĭ-sēd'ns) *n.* Also **prec·e·den·cy** (prĕs'ĭ-dən-sē, prĭ-sēd'n-sē). **1.** The right to go before or to be considered before, as because of rank or importance; priority. **2.** The act of preceding, as in time or position.

prec·e·dent (prĕs'ĭ-dnt) *n.* **1.** An act or instance that may be used as an example in dealing with subsequent similar cases: *a judicial precedent.* **2.** An earlier occurrence of the same or a comparable thing. **3.** Convention or custom. —*adj.* **pre·ce·dent** (prĭ-sēd'nt, prĕs'ĭ-dnt). Preceding; prior.

pre·ced·ing (prĭ-sē'dĭng) *adj.* **1.** Existing or coming before in time, place, rank, or sequence; previous. **2.** Next before the present one. —See Syns at **last.**

pre·cen·tor (prĭ-sĕn'tər) *n.* A person who directs the singing of a church choir. [Late Latin, from Latin *praecinere*, to sing before : *prae*, before + *canere*, to sing.]

pre·cept (prē'sĕpt') *n.* A rule or principle imposing a particular standard of action or conduct. [Middle English, from Latin *praeceptum*, from *praecipere*, to warn, teach : *prae*, before + *capere*, to take.]

pre·cep·tor (prĭ-sĕp'tər, prē'sĕp'-) *n.* A teacher; instructor. —**pre·cep·to·ri·al** (prē'sĕp-tôr'ē-əl, -tōr'-) *adj.* —**pre·cep·to'ri·al·ly** *adv.*

pre·ces·sion (prĭ-sĕsh'ən) *n.* *Physics.* A complex motion that changes the axis of rotation of a spinning body when that body is subjected to a torque, characterized by a conical locus of the axis. [New Latin *praecessio*, from Medieval Latin *praecessiō*, a going forward, from Latin *praecessus*, past part. of *praecēdere*, to precede.] —**pre·ces'sion·al** *adj.*

precession of the equinoxes. *Astron.* A slow westward shift of the equinoctial points along the plane of the ecliptic at a rate of 50.27 seconds of arc per year, resulting from precession of the earth's axis of rotation.

pre·cinct (prē'sĭngkt') *n.* **1. a.** A subdivision or district of a city patrolled by a unit of the police force. **b.** The police station in such a district. **2.** An election district of a city or town. **3.** Often **precincts. a.** A place or enclosure marked off by definite limits. **b.** A boundary. **4. precincts.** Neighborhood; environs. **5. precincts.** An area of thought or action; province; sphere. [Middle English *precincte*, from Medieval Latin *praecinctum*, enclosure, from Latin *praecingere*, to gird about : *prae*, around + *cingere*, to gird.]

pre·ci·os·i·ty (prĕsh'ē-ŏs'ĭ-tē) *n., pl.* **-ties.** Extreme meticulousness or overrefinement, as in language.

pre·cious (prĕsh'əs) *adj.* **1.** Of high cost or worth; valuable. **2.** Highly esteemed; cherished. **3.** Dear; beloved. **4.** Affectedly dainty or overrefined. —See Syns at **valuable.** —*n.* Someone who is precious; a darling. —*adv.* Very; extremely: *"He had precious little right to complain"* (James Agee). [Middle English, from Old French *precieus*, from

Latin *pretiōsus,* from *pretium,* price.] —**pre′cious·ly** *adv.*
—**pre′cious·ness** *n.*

precious stone. Any of various minerals, as a diamond or ruby, valued as a gem.

prec·i·pice (prĕs′ə-pĭs) *n.* **1.** An extremely steep or overhanging mass of rock. **2.** The brink of a dangerous situation. [Old French, from Latin *praecipitium,* from *praecipitāre,* to throw headlong.]

pre·cip·i·tance (prĭ-sĭp′ĭ-tns) *n.* Also **pre·cip·i·tan·cy** (-tn-sē) *pl.* **-cies.** The quality of being precipitant.

pre·cip·i·tant (prĭ-sĭp′ĭ-tnt) *adj.* **1.** Rushing or falling headlong. **2.** Impulsive in thought or action; rash. **3.** Abrupt or unexpected; sudden. —**pre·cip′i·tant·ly** *adv.*

pre·cip·i·tate (prĭ-sĭp′ĭ-tāt′) *v.* **-tat·ed, -tat·ing.** —*tr.v.* **1.** To throw from or as if from a great height; hurl downward. **2.** To cause to happen before anticipated or required: *precipitate a crisis.* **3.** To cause (water vapor) to condense and fall as rain or snow. **4.** *Chem.* To chemically cause (a solid substance) to be separated from a solution. —*intr.v.* **1.** To condense and fall as rain or snow. **2.** *Chem.* To be chemically separated from a solution as a precipitate. **3.** To fall headlong. —*adj.* (prĭ-sĭp′ĭ-tĭt, -tāt′). **1.** Speeding headlong; moving rapidly and heedlessly. **2.** Acting with excessive haste or impulse; lacking due deliberation. **3.** Occurring suddenly or unexpectedly. —*n.* (prĭ-sĭp′ə-tāt′, -tĭt). *Chem.* A solid or solid phase chemically separated from a solution. [From Latin *praecipitāre,* to throw headlong, from *praeceps,* headlong : *prae,* in front + *caput,* head.] —**pre·cip′i·tate·ly** *adv.* —**pre·cip′i·tate·ness** *n.* —**pre·cip′i·ta·tive** *adj.* —**pre·cip′i·ta·tor** *n.*

pre·cip·i·ta·tion (prĭ-sĭp′ĭ-tā′shən) *n.* **1.** A headlong fall or rush. **2.** Abrupt or impulsive haste. **3. a.** Water droplets or ice particles condensed from atmospheric water vapor and sufficiently massive to fall to the earth's surface; any form of rain or snow. **b.** The amount of this falling in a specific area within a specific period. **4.** *Chem.* The production of a precipitate.

pre·cip·i·tous (prĭ-sĭp′ĭ-təs) *adj.* **1.** Like a precipice; extremely steep. **2.** Having precipices: *a precipitous bluff.* **3.** Abrupt and ill-considered; precipitate. —**pre·cip′i·tous·ly** *adv.* —**pre·cip′i·tous·ness** *n.*

pré·cis (prā-sē′, prā′sē) *n., pl.* **précis** (prā-sēz′, prā′sēz). A concise summary of the essential facts or statements of a book, article, or other text. —*tr.v.* **pré·cised, -cis·ing.** To make a précis of. [French *précis,* from Old French *precis,* precise.]

pre·cise (prĭ-sīs′) *adj.* **1.** Clearly expressed or delineated; definite: *a precise description.* **2.** Capable of, resulting from, or designating an action, performance, or process executed or successively repeated within close specified limits: *a precise measurement with precise instruments.* **3.** Exactly corresponding to what is indicated; correct: *the precise amount of seasoning.* **4.** Strictly distinguished from others; very: *at that precise moment.* **5.** Distinct and correct in sound or statement: *precise articulation.* **6.** Conforming strictly to rule or proper form: *precise etiquette.* —See Syns at **accurate** and **explicit.** [Old French *precis,* from Latin *praecīsus,* shortened, from *praecīdere,* to shorten : *prae,* in front + *caedere,* to cut.] —**pre·cise′ly** *adv.* —**pre·cise′ness** *n.*

pre·ci·sion (prĭ-sĭzh′ən) *n.* The quality of being precise. —*adj.* **1.** Used or intended for precise measurement: *a precision tool.* **2.** Of or characterized by precise action: *a precision maneuver.* —**pre·ci′sion·ism** *n.*

pre·clude (prĭ-klōōd′) *tr.v.* **-clud·ed, -clud·ing.** To make impossible or impracticable by previous action; prevent. [Latin *praeclūdere* : *prae,* in front + *claudere,* to close.] —**pre·clu′sion** (-klōō′zhən) *n.* —**pre·clu′sive** (-klōō′sĭv, -zĭv) *adj.* —**pre·clu′sive·ly** *adv.*

pre·co·cious (prĭ-kō′shəs) *adj.* **1.** Characterized by unusually early development or maturity, esp. in mental aptitude. **2.** *Bot.* Blossoming before the leaves sprout. [From Latin *praecox,* from *praecoquere,* to cook before : *prae,* before + *coquere,* to cook.] —**pre·co′cious·ly** *adv.* —**pre·co′cious·ness** or **pre·coc′i·ty** (-kŏs′ĭ-tē) *n.*

pre·cog·ni·tion (prē′kŏg-nĭsh′ən) *n.* Knowledge of something in advance of its occurrence. —**pre·cog′ni·tive** (prē-kŏg′nĭ-tĭv) *adj.*

pre·Co·lum·bi·an (prē′kə-lŭm′bē-ən) *adj.* Of, relating to,

or originating in the Americas before Columbus's voyage in 1492: *pre-Columbian artifacts.*

pre·con·ceive (prē′kən-sēv′) *tr.v.* **-ceived, -ceiv·ing.** To form an opinion or conception of beforehand.

pre·con·cep·tion (prē′kən-sĕp′shən) *n.* **1.** An opinion or conception formed in advance of actual knowledge. **2.** A prejudice.

pre·cook (prē-kōōk′) *tr.v.* To cook in advance, or cook partially before final cooking.

pre·cur·sor (prĭ-kûr′sər, prē′kûr′-) *n.* **1.** Someone or something that precedes and indicates or announces someone or something to come; forerunner; harbinger: *"The crafty smile, which was the precursor of the little joke"* (Nathaniel Hawthorne). **2.** An ancestor; predecessor. [Latin *praecursor,* from *praecurrere,* to run before : *prae,* before + *currere,* to run.]

pre·cur·so·ry (prĭ-kûr′sə-rē) *adj.* Also **pre·cur·sive** (-sĭv). **1.** Preceding in the manner of a precursor; preliminary; introductory. **2.** Suggesting or indicating something to follow; premonitory.

pre·da·cious or **pre·da·ceous** (prĭ-dā′shəs) *adj.* Living by seizing or taking prey; predatory. [From Latin *praedāri,* to plunder.] —**pre·da′cious·ness** or **pre·dac′i·ty** (-dăs′ĭ-tē) *n.*

pre·date (prē-dāt′) *tr.v.* **-dat·ed, -dat·ing.** **1.** To mark or designate with an earlier date than the actual one. **2.** To precede in time; antedate.

pred·a·tor (prĕd′ə-tər, -tôr′) *n.* **1.** An animal that lives by preying upon others. **2.** Someone who plunders or abuses other people for his own profit. [Latin *praedātor,* from *praedāri,* to plunder.]

pred·a·to·ry (prĕd′ə-tôr′ē, -tōr′ē) *adj.* **1.** Of, relating to, or characterized by plundering, pillaging, or marauding: *a predatory war.* **2.** Preying on other animals; predacious. —**pred′a·to′ri·ly** *adv.* —**pred′a·to′ri·ness** *n.*

pred·e·ces·sor (prĕd′ĭ-sĕs′ər, prē′dĭ-) *n.* **1.** Someone or something that precedes another in time, esp. in an office or position. **2.** Something that has been succeeded by another. **3.** An ancestor or forefather. [Middle English *predecessour,* from Old French *predecesseur,* from Late Latin *praedecessor* : Latin *prae,* before + *dēcēdere,* to die, go away.]

pre·des·ti·nate (prē-dĕs′tə-nāt′) *tr.v.* **-nat·ed, -nat·ing.** **1.** To destine or determine in advance; foreordain. **2.** *Theol.* To predestine. —*adj.* (prē-dĕs′tə-nĭt, -nāt′). Foreordained; predestined.

pre·des·ti·na·tion (prē-dĕs′tə-nā′shən) *n.* **1.** The act of predestining or the condition of being predestined. **2.** *Theol.* **a.** The act whereby God is believed to have foreordained all things. **b.** The assignment of all souls to either salvation or damnation by this act. **c.** The doctrine that God has foreordained all things, esp. the salvation of individual souls. **3.** Destiny; fate.

pre·des·tine (prē-dĕs′tĭn) *tr.v.* **-tined, -tin·ing.** **1.** To fix upon, decide, or decree in advance; foreordain. **2.** *Theol.* To foreordain by divine will or decree.

pre·de·ter·mine (prē′dĭ-tûr′mĭn) *tr.v.* **-mined, -min·ing.** **1.** To determine, decide, or establish in advance: *called at a predetermined time.* **2.** To give a tendency to beforehand; to predispose or bias. —**pre′de·ter′mi·na′tion** *n.* —**pre′de·ter′min·er** *n.*

pred·i·ca·ble (prĕd′ĭ-kə-bəl) *adj.* Capable of being stated or

pre-Columbian
A pendant

predicated. —*n.* Something that can be predicated; a quality or attribute. —**pred'i·ca·bil'i·ty** or **pred'i·ca·ble·ness** *n.*

pre·dic·a·ment (prĭ-dĭk'ə-mənt) *n.* A troublesome or embarrassing situation. [Middle English, from Late Latin *praedicāmentum,* from *praedicāre,* to proclaim, predicate.] —**pre·dic'a·men'tal** (-mĕn'tl) *adj.*

pred·i·cate (prĕd'ĭ-kāt') *tr.v.* **-cat·ed, -cat·ing. 1.** To base or establish: *He predicates his argument on these facts.* **2.** To state or affirm as an attribute or quality of something: *predicate perfectibility of mankind.* **3.** To proclaim; assert; declare. —*n.* (prĕd'ĭ-kĭt). **1.** *Gram.* The part of a sentence or clause that expresses something about the subject, consisting of a verb and often including objects, modifiers, or complements of the verb. In the sentence *The messenger rode faster and faster,* the predicate is *rode faster and faster.* **2.** *Logic.* Whatever is stated about the subject of a proposition. —*adj.* (prĕd'ĭ-kĭt). **1.** *Gram.* Of or belonging to the predicate of a sentence or clause. **2.** Predicated; stated. [From Late Latin *praedicāre,* to proclaim, from Latin : *prae,* in front of + *dicāre,* to say.] —**pred'i·ca'tive** *adj.* —**pred'i·ca'tive·ly** *adv.*

predicate adjective. An adjective that follows a linking verb and modifies the subject of the sentence.

predicate nominative. A noun or pronoun that follows a linking verb and refers to the same person or thing as the subject.

pred·i·ca·tion (prĕd'ĭ-kā'shən) *n.* **1.** The act or procedure of predicating, esp. a logical assertion or affirmation. **2.** Something predicated. —**pred'i·ca'tion·al** *adj.*

pre·dict (prĭ-dĭkt') *tr.v.* To state, tell about, or make known in advance, esp. on the basis of special knowledge; foretell: *predict the weather.* —*intr.v.* To foretell what will happen; prophesy. [From Latin *praedīcere,* to foretell : *prae,* before + *dīcere,* to tell, say.] —**pre·dict'a·bil'i·ty** *n.* —**pre·dict'a·ble** *adj.* —**pre·dict'a·bly** *adv.*

pre·dic·tion (prĭ-dĭk'shən) *n.* **1.** The act of predicting. **2.** Something foretold or predicted. —**pre·dic'tive** *adj.* —**pre·dic'tive·ly** *adv.* —**pre·dic'tive·ness** *n.*

pre·di·lec·tion (prĕd'l-ĕk'shən, prēd'l-) *n.* A partiality or disposition in favor of something; preference. [French *prédilection,* from Medieval Latin *praedīligere,* to prefer : Latin *prae,* before + *dīligere,* to love, choose.]

pre·dis·pose (prē'dĭ-spōz') *tr.v.* **-posed, -pos·ing. 1.** To make (someone) inclined in advance: *His good manners predispose people to like him.* **2.** To make susceptible or liable: *conditions that predispose miners to lung disease.* —**pre'dis·pos'al** *n.*

pre·dis·po·si·tion (prē'dĭs-pə-zĭsh'ən) *n.* The condition of being predisposed; tendency or inclination.

pre·dom·i·nance (prĭ-dŏm'ə-nəns) *n.* Also **pre·dom·i·nan·cy** (-nən-sē). The condition or quality of being predominant; preponderance.

pre·dom·i·nant (prĭ-dŏm'ə-nənt) *adj.* **1.** Greater than all others in strength, authority, or importance; dominant: *the predominant nation of the Middle East.* **2.** Most common, numerous, or noticeable: *the predominant color in a design.* —**pre·dom'i·nant·ly** *adv.*

pre·dom·i·nate (prĭ-dŏm'ə-nāt') *intr.v.* **-nat·ed, -nat·ing. 1.** To be of greater power, importance, or quantity: *Red and yellow predominate in this plaid.* **2.** To have authority, power, or controlling influence; prevail. [From Latin *praedominārī,* to subdue beforehand : *prae,* before + *dominārī,* to dominate.] —**pre·dom'i·nate·ly** (-nĭt-lē) *adv.* —**pre·dom'i·na'tion** *n.*

pre·em·i·nent or **pre·em·i·nent** (prē-ĕm'ə-nənt) *adj.* Superior to or notable above all others; outstanding. —See Syns at **primary.** [Late Latin *praeēminēns,* from Latin, *praeēminēre,* to excel : *prae,* in front of + *ēminēre,* to stand out.] —**pre·em'i·nence** *n.* —**pre·em'i·nent·ly** *adv.*

pre·empt or **pre·empt** (prē-ĕmpt') *tr.v.* **1.** To gain possession of by prior right or opportunity, esp. to settle on (public land) so as to obtain the right to buy before others. **2.** To appropriate or seize for oneself before anyone else can. **3.** To be presented in place of; displace: *The special news program pre-empted the scheduled shows.* [Back-formation from PRE-EMPTION.] —**pre·emp'tor** *n.* —**pre·emp'to·ry** *adj.*

pre·emp·tion or **pre·emp·tion** (prē-ĕmp'shən) *n.* **1.** The act or right of purchasing something, esp. government-owned land, before others. **2.** Acquisition or seizure of something beforehand. [Medieval Latin *praeemptiō,* from *praeemere,* to buy beforehand : *prae,* before + *emere,* to buy.]

pre·emp·tive or **pre·emp·tive** (prē-ĕmp'tĭv) *adj.* **1.** Of or characteristic of pre-emption: *pre-emptive rights.* **2.** Having or granted by the right of pre-emption. —**pre·emp'tive·ly** *adv.*

preen (prēn) *tr.v.* **1.** To smooth or clean (feathers) with the beak or bill. **2.** To dress or groom (oneself) with elaborate care or vanity; primp. **3.** To take pride or satisfaction in (oneself); to gloat. —*intr.v.* To dress or groom oneself carefully or vainly; primp: *preening in front of a mirror.* [Middle English *preinen.*] —**preen'er** *n.*

pre·es·tab·lish or **pre·es·tab·lish** (prē'ĭ-stăb'lĭsh) *tr.v.* To establish beforehand.

pre·ex·ist or **pre·ex·ist** (prē'ĭg-zĭst') *intr.v.* To exist before. —*tr.v.* To exist before (something): *dinosaurs that pre-existed mammals.* —**pre'·ex·ist'ence** *n.* —**pre'·ex·ist'ent** *adj.*

pre·fab' (prē'făb') *n.* A prefabricated part or structure. —*adj.* Prefabricated.

pre·fab·ri·cate (prē-făb'rĭ-kāt') *tr.v.* **-cat·ed, -cat·ing. 1.** To construct or manufacture in advance. **2.** To construct in standard sections that can be easily shipped and assembled. —**pre·fab'ri·ca'tion** *n.* —**pre·fab'ri·ca'tor** *n.*

pref·ace (prĕf'ĭs) *n.* **1. a.** A introductory statement or essay to a speech, book, etc., explaining its scope, intention, or background. **2.** Anything introductory or preliminary. —*tr.v.* **-aced, -ac·ing. 1.** To introduce by or provide with a preface. **2.** To serve as an introduction to: *the ceremony that prefaced the game.* [Middle English, from Old French, from Medieval Latin *prefātia,* from Latin *praefātiō* : *prae,* before + *fārī,* to speak.] —**pref'ac·er** *n.*

pref·a·to·ry (prĕf'ə-tôr'ē, -tōr'ē) *adj.* Also **pref·a·to·ri·al** (prĕf'ə-tôr'ē-əl, -tōr'-). Of, pertaining to, or serving as a preface; introductory: *prefatory remarks.* [From Latin *prefātiō,* preface.] —**pref'a·to'ri·ly** *adv.*

pre·fect (prē'fĕkt') *n.* Also **prae·fect. 1.** Any of several ancient Roman officials of high rank. **2.** Any high administrative official, esp. the chief of police of Paris. **3.** A student officer, esp. in a private school. [Middle English, from Old French, from Latin *praefectus* : *prae,* before + *facere,* to do.]

pre·fec·ture (prē'fĕk'chər) *n.* **1.** The district, office, or authority of a prefect. **2.** The residence of a prefect. —**pre·fec'tur·al** (prĭ-fĕk'chər-əl, prē'fĕk'-) *adj.*

pre·fer (prĭ-fûr') *tr.v.* **-ferred, -fer·ring. 1.** To choose as more desirable; like better: *prefers classical to popular music.* **2.** To file or present for consideration before a legal authority: *prefer charges.* **3.** To recommend for advancement or appointment before someone. [Middle English *preferren,* from Old French *preferer,* from Latin *praeferre* : *prae,* before + *ferre,* to bear.] —**pre·fer'rer** *n.*

pref·er·a·ble (prĕf'ər-ə-bəl) *adj.* More desirable or worthy; preferred. —**pref'er·a·bil'i·ty** or **pref'er·a·ble·ness** *n.* —**pref'er·a·bly** *adv.*

pref·er·ence (prĕf'ər-əns) *n.* **1.** The act of preferring; the exercise of choice. **2.** A liking for someone or something over another or others: *expressed a preference for old shoes.* **3.** Someone or something preferred: *a window seat was his preference.* **4.** The granting of precedence or advantage to one over all others. —See Syns at **choice.**

pref·er·en·tial (prĕf'ə-rĕn'shəl) *adj.* **1.** Of, having, providing, or obtaining advantage or preference: *preferential treatment.* **2.** Demonstrating or originating from partiality or preference: *preferential tariff rates.* —**pref'er·en'tial·ly** *adv.*

preferential shop. A union shop whose management gives priority or advantage to union members.

pre·fer·ment (prĭ-fûr'mənt) *n.* **1. a.** The act of singling someone out for promotion or favored treatment. **b.** The condition of being thus singled out. **2.** The action of filing or presenting: *the preferment of a legal suit.*

preferred stock. The portion of a corporation's stock that has a priority over the common stock in the distribution of dividends and assets.

pre·fig·u·ra·tion (prē-fĭg'yə-rā'shən) *n.* **1.** The act of representing, suggesting, or imagining in advance; foreshadow-

---

ing. **2.** Something that prefigures. —**pre·fig′u·ra·tive** *adj.* —**pre·fig′u·ra·tive·ly** *adv.* —**pre·fig′ure·ment** *n.*

pre·fig·ure (prē-fĭg′yər) *tr.v.* **-ured, -ur·ing. 1.** To suggest, indicate, or represent by an earlier form or model; presage: *The popular assemblies of ancient Athens prefigured the modern town meetings.* **2.** To imagine or picture to oneself in advance. —**pre·fig′ure·ment** *n.*

pre·fix (prē-fĭks′) *tr.v.* **1.** (*also* prē′fĭks′) To add at the beginning or front: *prefixed the title "Dr." to his name.* **2.** To settle or arrange in advance. —*n.* (prē′fĭks′). **1.** An affix put before a word, changing or modifying the meaning. **2.** A title placed before a person's name. [From Latin *praefīxus,* past part. of *praefīgere,* to fix before : *prae,* before + *fīgere,* to fix.] —**pre′fix′al** *adj.* —**pre′fix′al·ly** *adv.*

preg·na·ble (prĕg′nə-bəl) *adj.* Vulnerable to seizure or capture: *a pregnable fort.* [Middle English *prenable,* from Old French, from *prendre,* to take, capture, from Latin *prehendere.*] —**preg′na·bil′i·ty** *n.*

preg·nan·cy (prĕg′nən-sē) *n., pl.* **-cies. 1.** The condition of being pregnant. **2.** The period during which a developing fetus is carried within the uterus.

preg·nant (prĕg′nənt) *adj.* **1.** Carrying a developing fetus within the uterus. **2.** Creative; inventive. **3.** Heavy with significance or implication: *a pregnant silence.* **4. a.** Abounding; profuse. **b.** Filled; charged; fraught: *pregnant with fate.* **5.** Producing results; fruitful: *a pregnant decision.* [Middle English, from Latin *praegnāns.*] —**preg′nant·ly** *adv.*

pre·heat (prē-hēt′) *tr.v.* To heat beforehand.

pre·hen·sile (prĭ-hĕn′sĭl, -sīl′) *adj.* Adapted for seizing or holding, esp. by wrapping around an object: *a prehensile tail.* [French *préhensile,* from Latin *prehensus,* past part. of *prehendere,* to seize.] —**pre′hen·sil′i·ty** *n.*

pre·his·tor·ic (prē′hĭ-stôr′ĭk, -stŏr′-) or **pre·his·tor·i·cal** (-ĭ-kəl) *adj.* Of or belonging to the era before recorded history. —**pre′his·tor′i·cal·ly** *adv.*

pre·his·to·ry (prē-hĭs′tə-rē) *n.* The history of mankind in the period before written or recorded history, investigated by archaeology. —**pre′his·to′ri·an** (-hĭ-stôr′ē-ən, -stŏr′-) *n.*

pre·judge (prē-jŭj′) *tr.v.* **-judged, -judg·ing.** To judge beforehand without having adequate evidence. —**pre·judg′er** *n.* —**pre·judg′ment** or **pre·judge′ment** *n.*

prej·u·dice (prĕj′ə-dĭs) *n.* **1.** A strong feeling about some subject, formed unfairly or before one knows the facts; a bias: *a prejudice in favor of his home town; a prejudice against unfamiliar foods.* **2.** Hostility toward members of races, religions, or nationalities other than one's own. **3.** Harm or injury, esp. when unfairly caused: *settled the matter without prejudice to anyone's rights or interests.* —*tr.v.* **-diced, -dic·ing. 1.** To cause (someone) to judge prematurely and irrationally; to bias. **2.** To do harm to; injure: *prejudiced his own cause.* [Middle English, from Old French, from Latin *praejūdicium : prae,* before + *jūdicium,* judgment, from *jūdex,* judge.]

prej·u·di·cial (prĕj′ə-dĭsh′əl) *adj.* Harmful; detrimental. —**prej′u·di′cial·ly** *adv.*

prel·a·cy (prĕl′ə-sē) *n., pl.* **-cies. 1. a.** The office or station of a prelate. **b.** Prelates as a group. **2.** Church government administered by prelates.

prel·ate (prĕl′ĭt) *n.* A high-ranking clergyman, such as a bishop or an abbot. [Middle English *prelat,* from Old French, from Medieval Latin *praelātus,* from Latin, past part. of *praeferre,* to prefer : *prae,* before + *ferre,* to carry.]

pre·lim·i·nar·y (prĭ-lĭm′ə-nĕr′ē) *adj.* Prior to or preparing for the main matter, action, or business; introductory; prefatory. —*n., pl.* **-ies.** Something that leads to or serves as preparation for a main event, action, or business. [French *préliminaire,* from Medieval Latin *praelīmināris : prae,* before + *līmen,* threshold, lintel.] —**pre·lim′i·nar′i·ly** (-nâr′ə-lē) *adv.*

pre·lit·er·ate (prē-lĭt′ər-ĭt) *adj.* Of or relating to any culture not having a written language.

prel·ude (prāl′yōōd′, prē′lōōd′) *n.* **1.** An introductory performance, event, or action preceding a more important one; a preliminary. **2.** *Mus.* **a.** A piece or movement that acts as introduction to a larger work. **b.** A fairly short composition in a free style, usu. for piano. —*v.* **-lud·ed, -lud·ing.** —*tr.v.* **1.** To serve as a prelude to. **2.** To intro-

duce with or as if with a prelude. —*intr.v.* To serve as a prelude or introduction. [Old French, from Medieval Latin *praelūdium,* from Latin *praelūdere,* to play beforehand : *prae,* before + *lūdus,* game.] —**prel·ud′er** *n.* —**pre·lu′di·al** (prĭ-lōō′dē-əl) *adj.*

pre·ma·ture (prē′mə-tōōr′, -tyōōr′, -chōōr′) *adj.* **1.** Occurring, growing, or existing prior to the customary, correct, or assigned time; early: *a premature death.* **2.** Too hurried or impulsive. **3.** Born after a gestation period of less than the normal time: *a premature baby.* —See Syns at **early.** —**pre′ma·ture′ly** *adv.* —**pre′ma·tu′ri·ty** *n.*

pre·med (prē′mĕd′) *adj. Informal.* Premedical. —*n. Informal.* A premedical student.

pre·med·i·cal (prē-mĕd′ĭ-kəl) *adj.* Preparing for or leading to the study of medicine: *premedical courses.*

pre·med·i·tate (prē-mĕd′ĭ-tāt′) *v.* **-tat·ed, -tat·ing.** —*tr.v.* To plan, arrange, or plot in advance. —*intr.v.* To meditate or deliberate beforehand. —**pre·med′i·tat′ed·ly** *adv.* —**pre·med′i·ta′tive** *adj.* —**pre·med′i·ta′tion** *n.*

pre·mier (prē-mē′ər, prĭ-mîr′; *Brit.* prĕm′yər) *adj.* **1.** First in status or importance; chief; supreme. **2.** First to occur or exist; earliest. —See Syns at **primary.** —*n.* (prĭ-mîr′). **1.** A prime minister. **2.** The chief executive of a Canadian province. [Middle English *primier,* from Old French *premier,* from Latin *prīmus,* first.]

pre·mière (prĭ-mîr′, -myâr′) *n.* A first public presentation, as of a play or exhibition. —*v.* **-mièred, -mièr·ing.** —*tr.v.* To present the first public performance of. —*intr.v.* To have the first public presentation. —*adj.* Premier; paramount; outstanding. [French, first, chief.]

prem·ise (prĕm′ĭs) *n.* **1. a.** A proposition upon which an argument is based or from which a conclusion is drawn. **b.** *Logic.* One of the first two propositions (major or minor) of a syllogism, from which the conclusion is drawn. **2. premises.** *Law.* The preliminary or explanatory statements or facts of a document, as in an equity bill or deed. **3. premises. a.** Land and the buildings upon it. **b.** A building or part of a building. —*v.* **-ised, -is·ing.** —*tr.v.* **1.** To state in advance as introduction or explanation. **2.** To state or assume as a proposition in an argument. —*intr.v.* To make a premise. [Middle English *premisse,* from Old French, from Medieval Latin *praemissa (prōpositiō),* "(proposition) put before," from Latin : *prae,* before + *mittere,* to send.]

pre·mi·um (prē′mē-əm) *n.* **1.** A prize awarded for quality or performance. **2.** An extra or unexpected benefit; a bonus. **3. a.** An amount charged in addition to the standard or usual price. **b.** An amount added to the face value of a security, stock, etc. **4.** An unusually high value: *placed an undue premium on profits.* **5.** An amount paid for an insurance policy, esp. one of a series of payments that fall due at specified times. —*modifier:* premium gifts. —*adj.* Of esp. high quality or price: *premium gasoline.* —*idiom.* **at a premium.** Esp. valuable or hard to obtain. [Latin *praemium,* profit derived from booty : *prae,* before + *emere,* to take.]

pre·mo·lar (prē-mō′lər) *n.* One of the bicuspid teeth in human beings located in pairs on each side of the upper and lower jaws, behind the canines and in front of the molars.

pre·mo·ni·tion (prē′mə-nĭsh′ən, prĕm′ə-) *n.* **1.** A warning in advance; forewarning. **2.** A feeling that something is going to happen; a presentiment. [Old French, from Late Latin *praemonitiō,* from Latin *praemonēre,* to forewarn : *prae,* before + *monēre,* to warn.] —**pre·mon′i·to′ri·ly** (prē-mŏn′ĭ-tôr′ə-lē, -tōr′-) *adv.* —**pre·mon′i·to′ry** *adj.*

pre·na·tal (prē-nāt′l) *adj.* Existing or taking place prior to birth; preceding birth. —**pre·na′tal·ly** *adv.*

pre·oc·cu·pa·tion (prē-ŏk′yə-pā′shən) *n.* **1.** The condition of being preoccupied. **2.** Something that preoccupies or engrosses the mind: *Chess was his main preoccupation.*

pre·oc·cu·pied (prē-ŏk′yə-pīd′) *adj.* **1.** Deep in thought; engrossed: *sat quietly all through dinner, frowning and preoccupied.* **2.** Already occupied.

pre·oc·cu·py (prē-ŏk′yə-pī′) *tr.v.* **-pied, -py·ing. 1.** To occupy completely the mind or attention of; engross. **2.** To occupy or take possession of in advance or before another.

pre·or·dain (prē′ôr-dān′) *tr.v.* To decree, order, or ordain in advance; foreordain. —**pre·or′di·na′tion** (-ôr′dn-ā′shən) *n.*

prep (prĕp). *Informal.* —*adj.* Preparatory: *a prep course.*

ă pat	ā pay	â care	ä father	ĕ pet	ē be	hw which	ĭ pit	ī tie	î pier	ŏ pot	ō toe	ô paw, for	oi noise
ōō took	ōō boot	ou out	th thin	th this	ŭ cut		û urge	zh vision	ə about, item, edible, gallop, circus				

—*n.* **1.** A **preparatory school. 2.** *Brit.* The preparing of lessons; homework. —*v.* **prepped, prep·ping.** —*intr.v.* To study or train in preparation: *prepping for law school.* —*tr.v.* To prepare: *prep a patient for surgery.*

pre·pack·age (prē-păk'ĭj) *tr.v.* **-aged, -ag·ing.** To wrap or package (products) before marketing them.

prep·a·ra·tion (prĕp'ə-rā'shən) *n.* **1.** The act or process of preparing. **2.** The condition of being made ready beforehand; readiness. **3.** Often **preparations.** Preliminary measures that serve to make ready for something: *preparations for the party.* **4.** A substance, such as a medicine, prepared for a particular purpose.

pre·par·a·to·ry (prĭ-păr'ə-tôr'ē, -tōr'ē,-păr'-) *adj.* **1.** Serving to make ready or prepare; preliminary: *preparatory exercises before a race.* **2.** Occupied in or relating to preparation, esp. for admission to college. —**pre·par'a·to'ri·ly** *adv.*

preparatory school. A secondary school, usu. private, preparing students for college or, in Great Britain, for public school.

pre·pare (prĭ-pâr') *v.* **-pared, -par·ing.** —*tr.v.* **1.** To make ready for some purpose, task, or event: *Prepare yourself for a shock. Prepare the wood by sanding.* **2.** To put together and make from various ingredients: *foods that are easy to prepare.* —*intr.v.* To put things or oneself in readiness; get ready: *preparing to leave town.* [Middle English *preparen,* from Old French *preparer,* from Latin *praeparāre,* to prepare in advance : *prae,* before + *parāre,* to prepare.] —**pre·par'er** *n.*

pre·par·ed·ness (prĭ-pâr'ĭd-nĭs) *n.* The condition of being prepared, esp. military readiness for war.

pre·pay (prē-pā') *tr.v.* **-paid** (-pād'), **-pay·ing.** To pay or pay for beforehand. —**pre·pay'ment** *n.*

pre·pon·der·ance (prĭ-pŏn'dər-əns) *n.* Also **pre·pon·der·an·cy** (-ən-sē). A clear superiority in weight, quantity, power, importance, etc.

pre·pon·der·ant (prĭ-pŏn'dər-ənt) *adj.* Greater in weight, number, importance, etc. —**pre·pon'der·ant·ly** *adv.*

pre·pon·der·ate (prĭ-pŏn'də-rāt') *intr.v.* **-at·ed, -at·ing. 1.** To exceed something else in weight. **2.** To be greater in power, force, quantity, importance, etc.; predominate: *"In balancing his faults with his perfections, the latter seemed rather to preponderate"* (Henry Fielding). [From Latin *praeponderāre* : *prae,* in front of, exceeding + *ponderāre,* to weigh, from *pondus,* weight.] —**pre·pon'der·at'ing·ly** *adv.* —**pre·pon'der·a'tion** *n.*

prep·o·si·tion (prĕp'ə-zĭsh'ən) *n. Gram.* A word used with a noun, pronoun, or noun equivalent to indicate the relationship between that object and something or someone else. [Middle English *preposicioun,* from Latin *praepositiō,* from *praepositus,* past part. of *praepōnere,* to place in front : *prae,* in front + *pōnere,* to place.] —**prep'o·si'tion·al** *adj.* —**prep'o·si'tion·al·ly** *adv.*

pre·pos·sess (prē'pə-zĕs') *tr.v.* **1.** To preoccupy the mind of to the exclusion of other thoughts or feelings. **2.** To influence beforehand against or esp. in favor.

pre·pos·sess·ing (prē'pə-zĕs'ĭng) *adj.* Impressing favorably; pleasing: *a prepossessing manner.* —**pre'pos·sess'ing·ly** *adv.* —**pre'pos·sess'ing·ness** *n.*

pre·pos·ses·sion (prē'pə-zĕsh'ən) *n.* **1.** A preconception or prejudice. **2.** The condition of being preoccupied with thoughts, opinions, or feelings.

pre·pos·ter·ous (prĭ-pŏs'tər-əs) *adj.* Contrary to nature, reason, or common sense; absurd. —See Syns at **foolish** and **outrageous.** [Latin *praeposterus* : *prae-,* before + *posterus,* coming after, next, from *post,* after.] —**pre·pos'ter·ous·ly** *adv.* —**pre·pos'ter·ous·ness** *n.*

pre·puce (prē'pyōōs') *n.* **1.** The foreskin. **2.** A similar structure covering the tip of the clitoris. [Middle English, from Old French, from Latin *praepūtium.*]

pre-Raph·a·el·ite (prē-răf'ē-ə-līt', -rā'fē-, -rä'fē-) *n.* A painter or writer belonging to or influenced by a group founded in 1848 by Dante Gabriel Rossetti and others to advance the style and spirit of Italian painting since Raphael. —*adj.* Of or characteristic of the pre-Raphaelites.

pre·req·ui·site (prē-rĕk'wĭ-zĭt) *adj.* Required as a prior condition: *courses prerequisite to graduation.* —*n.* Something that is prerequisite.

pre·rog·a·tive (prĭ-rŏg'ə-tĭv) *n.* An exclusive right or privilege, esp. one that accompanies one's rank or position.

—*adj.* Of, arising from, or exercising a prerogative. [Middle English, from Old French, from Latin *praerogātīva* : *prae-,* before + *rogāre,* to ask.]

pres·age (prĕs'ĭj) *n.* **1.** An indication or warning of a future occurrence; omen. **2.** A feeling or intuition of what is going to occur; presentiment. **3.** Prophetic significance or meaning. —*v.* **pre·sage** (prĭ-sāj', prĕs'ĭj) **-saged, -sag·ing.** —*tr.v.* **1.** To indicate or warn of in advance; to portend. **2.** To have a presentiment of. **3.** To foretell or predict: *gloomy writers who always presage doom.* —*intr.v.* **1.** To make or utter a prediction. [Middle English, from Latin *praesāgium,* foreboding, from *praesāgīre,* to forebode : *prae-,* before + *sāgīre,* to perceive.]

pres·by·ter (prĕz'bĭ-tər, prĕs'-) *n.* **1.** An officer of a Presbyterian Church congregation; an elder. **2.** An official in various other churches, as a priest in the Anglican Church. [Late Latin, an elder, from Greek *presbuteros,* a priest, comp. of *presbus,* old man.]

pres·by·te·ri·an (prĕz'bĭ-tîr'ē-ən, prĕs'-) *adj.* **1.** Of ecclesiastical government by presbyters. **2.** Of a Presbyterian Church. —*n.* A member or adherent of a Presbyterian Church. —**pres'by·te'ri·an·ism** *n.*

Presbyterian Church. Any of various Protestant churches governed by presbyters and traditionally Calvinist in doctrine.

pres·by·ter·y (prĕz'bĭ-tĕr'ē, prĕs'-) *n., pl.* **-ies. 1.** *Presbyterian Ch.* **a.** A court composed of the ministers and representative elders of a particular locality. **b.** The district represented by this court. **2.** Presbyters as a group. **3.** Government of a church by presbyters. **4.** The section of the church reserved for the clergy.

pre·school (prē'skōōl') *adj.* Of or relating to a child of nursery-school age. —**pre'school'er** *n.*

pre·science (prē'shəns, prē'shē-əns, prĕsh'əns, prĕsh'ē-əns) *n.* Knowledge of actions or events before they occur; foreknowledge; foresight.

pre·scient (prē'shənt, prē'shē-ənt, prĕsh'ənt, prĕsh'ē-ənt) *adj.* Possessing prescience. [Latin *praesciēns,* pres. part. of *praescīre,* to know beforehand : *prae-,* before + *scīre,* to know.] —**pre'scient·ly** *adv.*

pre·scribe (prĭ-skrīb') *v.* **-scribed, -scrib·ing.** —*tr.v.* **1.** To set down as a rule or guide; ordain. **2.** To order or recommend the use of (a drug or other therapy). —*intr.v.* **1.** To establish rules, laws, or directions. **2.** To order or recommend a remedy or treatment. [From Latin *praescrībere,* to appoint : *prae-,* before, in front + *scrībere,* to write.] —**pre·scrib'er** *n.*

pre·script (prē'skrĭpt') *n.* Something prescribed, esp. a rule or regulation of conduct. —*adj.* (prē'skrĭpt', prĭ-skrĭpt'). Established as a rule; set down. [Latin *praescriptum,* past part. of *praescrībere,* to prescribe.]

pre·scrip·tion (prĭ-skrĭp'shən) *n.* **1. a.** The act of prescribing. **b.** Something that is prescribed. **2. a.** A written instruction by a physician for the preparation and administration of a medicine. **b.** A prescribed medicine. **c.** An ophthalmologist's or optometrist's written instruction for the grinding of corrective lenses. **3.** A formula directing the preparation of anything.

pre·scrip·tive (prĭ-skrĭp'tĭv) *adj.* **1.** Sanctioned or authorized by long-standing custom or usage. **2.** Making or giving directions, laws, or rules: *a prescriptive grammar.* —**pre·scrip'tive·ly** *adv.*

pres·ence (prĕz'əns) *n.* **1.** The condition or fact of being present. **2.** Immediate nearness in time or space. **3.** The area immediately surrounding someone, esp. a great personage. **4.** A person who is present. **5.** A person's manner of carrying himself; bearing. **6.** The power of creating a strong impression simply by being present: *an actress with great stage presence.* **7.** A supernatural influence felt to be nearby.

presence of mind. Ability to think and act efficiently, esp. in an emergency.

pres·ent¹ (prĕz'ənt) *n.* **1.** A moment or period in time perceptible as intermediate between past and future; now. **2.** *Gram.* **a.** The **present tense. b.** A verb form in the present tense. **3.** *Law.* The document or instrument in question: *be it known by these presents.* —*adj.* **1.** Being or occurring at a moment or period in time considered as the present: *his present difficulties.* **2.** Being at hand: *The* people present broke into loud applause. **3.** *Gram.* Denoting a verb tense or form that expresses current time. **—idioms. at present.** At the present time; right now. **for the present.** For the time being; temporarily. [Middle English, from Old French, from Latin *praesēns,* pres. part. of *praeesse,* to be present : *prae-,* in front of + *esse,* to be.]

pre·sent² (prĭ-zĕnt′) *tr.v.* **1.** To introduce, esp. formally. **2.** To bring before the public: *present a play.* **3. a.** To make a gift or award of: *present a medal.* **b.** To make a gift to: *present an endowment to the college.* **4.** To offer for inspection; display: *present one's credentials.* **5.** To offer for consideration. **6.** To aim or direct (a weapon) in a particular direction. **7.** *Law.* To bring (a charge or indictment) against someone. —See Syns at **offer.** —*n.* **pres·ent** (prĕz′ənt). Something presented; a gift. [Middle English *presenten,* from Old French *presenter,* from Latin *praesentāre,* from *praesēns,* present.] —**pre·sent′er** *n.*

pre·sent·a·ble (prĭ-zĕn′tə-bəl) *adj.* **1.** Capable of being given, displayed, or offered. **2.** Fit for introduction to others. —**pre·sent′a·bil′i·ty** or **pre·sent′a·ble·ness** *n.* —**pre·sent′a·bly** *adv.*

pres·en·ta·tion (prĕz′ən-tā′shən, prē′zən-) *n.* **1. a.** The act of presenting. **b.** The condition of being presented. **2.** A performance, as of a drama. **3.** Something that is presented. **4.** A formal introduction. —**pres′en·ta′tion·al** *adj.*

pres·ent-day (prĕz′ənt-dā′) *adj.* Current. —See Syns at **modern.**

pre·sen·ti·ment (prĭ-zĕn′tə-mənt) *n.* A sense of something about to occur; premonition. [Obs. French, from Old French *presentir,* to have a presentiment, from Latin *praesentīre,* to presage : *prae-,* before + *sentīre,* to perceive.]

pres·ent·ly (prĕz′ənt-lē) *adv.* **1.** In a short time; soon; directly: *She will arrive presently.* **2.** At this time or period; now: *He is presently staying with us.*

pre·sent·ment (prĭ-zĕnt′mənt) *n.* **1.** The act of presenting; presentation. **2.** Something presented, such as a picture or exhibition. **3.** *Law.* The report written by a grand jury concerning an offense, based on the jury's own knowledge and observation. **4.** The presenting of a bill or note for payment.

present participle. *Gram.* A participle that expresses present action or condition, formed in English by adding *-ing* to the infinitive, and sometimes used as an adjective.

present perfect. *Gram.* **1.** The verb tense expressing action completed at the present time, formed in English by combining the present tense of *have* with a past participle. **2.** A verb in this tense.

present tense. *Gram.* The verb tense expressing action in the present time.

pre·serv·a·tive (prĭ-zûr′və-tĭv) *adj.* Tending or able to preserve. —*n.* Something used to preserve, esp. a chemical used in foods to inhibit spoilage.

pre·serve (prĭ-zûrv′) *tr.v.* **-served, -serv·ing. 1.** To protect from injury or peril; maintain in safety: *preserve the peace.* **2.** To keep or maintain intact: *preserve one's looks; preserve one's dignity.* **3.** To prepare (food) for future use, as by canning or salting. **4.** To prevent (organic bodies) from decaying or spoiling: *preserved the specimen in alcohol.* —*n.* **1.** Something that acts to preserve; a preservative. **2.** Often **preserves.** Fruit cooked with sugar to protect against decay or fermentation. **3.** An area maintained for the protection of wildlife or natural resources. **4.** Something considered restricted to the use of certain persons: *Ancient Greek is the preserve of scholars.* [Middle English *preserven,* from Old French *preserver,* from Medieval Latin *praeservāre* : Latin *prae-,* before + *servāre,* to keep, guard.] —**pre·serv′a·bil′i·ty** or **pre·serv′a·ble·ness** *adj.* —**pres′er·va′tion** (prĕz′ər-vā′shən) *n.* —**pre·serv′er** *n.*

pre·side (prĭ-zīd′) *intr.v.* **-sid·ed, -sid·ing. 1.** To hold the position of authority; act as chairperson. **2.** To possess or exercise authority or control. **3.** *Mus.* To be the featured instrumental performer. [French *presider,* from Latin *praesidēre,* to superintend : *prae-,* before + *sedēre,* to sit.]

pres·i·den·cy (prĕz′ĭ-dən-sē, -dĕn′-) *n., pl.* **-cies. 1.** The office, function, or term of a president. **2.** Often **Presidency.** The office of president of a republic, esp. of President of the United States. **3.** A governing body of the Mormon Church.

pres·i·dent (prĕz′ĭ-dənt, -dĕnt′) *n.* **1.** A person appointed or elected to preside over an organized body of people, as an assembly or meeting. **2.** Often **President.** The chief executive of a republic, esp. of the United States. **3.** The chief officer of a branch of government, a corporation, a board of trustees, a university, or any similar body. [Middle English, from Old French, from Latin *praesidens,* pres. part. of *praesidēre,* to preside.] —**pres′i·den′tial** (prĕz′ĭ-dĕn′shəl) *adj.*

pres·i·dent-e·lect (prĕz′ĭ-dənt-ĭ-lĕkt′) *n.* A person who has been elected president but has not yet begun his term of office.

pre·sid·i·um (prĭ-sĭd′ē-əm) *n., pl.* **-i·a** (-ē-ə) or **-ums. 1.** Any of various permanent executive committees in Communist countries with the power to act for a larger governing body. **2. Presidium.** A committee of the Supreme Soviet, headed by the premier, and constituting the highest policy-making body of the Soviet Union. [Russian *prezidium,* from Latin *praesidium,* guard, protection.]

press¹ (prĕs) *tr.v.* **1.** To exert steady weight or force against; bear down on: *Press the button.* **2. a.** To squeeze the juice or other contents from: *press apples.* **b.** To extract by squeezing or compressing: *to press cider.* **3. a.** To make compact or reshape by applying steady force: *pressing wrecked cars into blocks.* **b.** To iron: *press a suit.* **4.** To clasp or embrace closely. **5.** To try hard to persuade; ask or entreat persistently. **6.** To attempt to force to action; urge on; spur. **7.** To occupy or burden heavily: *pressed by a heavy workload.* **8.** To lay stress upon; emphasize: *press a point.* **9.** To advance or carry on vigorously: *pressed the attack.* —*intr.v.* **1.** To exert force or pressure: *We pressed against the door.* **2.** To weigh heavily, as on the mind. **3.** To advance eagerly; push forward: *pressed onward.* **4.** To require haste; be urgent: *Time presses.* **5.** To iron clothes or other material. **6.** To assemble closely and in large numbers; crowd. **7.** To employ urgent persuasion or entreaty; ask earnestly or persistently. —See Syns at **urge.** —*n.* **1.** Any of various machines or devices that apply pressure. **2.** A printing press. **3.** A place or establishment where matter is printed. **4.** The method, art, or business of printing. **5. a.** Printed matter as a whole, esp. newspapers and magazines. **b.** The people involved with the collection, editing, and presentation of news. **c.** The matter dealt with by the news media. **6.** A large gathering; throng: *"A great, slow-moving press of men and women in evening dress filled the vestibule"* (Frank Norris). **7.** The act of applying pressure. **8.** The haste or urgency of business or affairs. **9.** The set of proper creases in a garment or fabric, formed by ironing. **10.** An upright closet or case used for storing clothing, books, or other articles. —**idioms. be (hard) pressed for.** To be lacking in. **press (one's) luck.** To push for something in spite of odds against it. [Middle English *pressen,* from Old French *presser,* from Latin *pressāre,* freq. of *premere,* to press.] —**press′er** *n.*

press² (prĕs) *tr.v.* **1.** To force into service in the army or navy; impress. **2.** To use in a manner different from the usual or intended: *press a scarf into service as a tourniquet.* —*n.* Conscription or impressment into service, esp. into the navy. [Alteration of earlier *prest,* to have by partially paying in advance, from Middle English *prest,* wages paid in advance, from Old French, loan, from *prester,* to lend, from Medieval Latin *praestāre,* from Latin, to offer, from *praestō,* at hand.]

press agent. A person employed to arrange advertising and publicity for an actor, theater, business, etc.

press box. A section for reporters, as in a stadium.

press conference. An interview held for newsmen by a political figure or celebrity.

press·ing (prĕs′ĭng) *adj.* **1.** Demanding immediate attention; urgent: *a pressing need.* **2.** Importunate; insistent: *a pressing invitation.* —**press′ing·ly** *adv.*

press·man (prĕs′mən, -măn′) *n.* **1.** A printing press operator. **2.** *Brit.* A newspaperman.

press release. A notice of an event, performance, or other news or publicity item issued to the press.

press·run (prĕs′rŭn′) *n.* The specific number of copies printed during a continuous operation of a printing press.

pres·sure (prĕsh′ər) *n.* **1. a.** The act of pressing. **b.** The condition of being pressed. **2.** The application of continuous force by one body upon another that it is touching. **3.** *Physics.* Force applied over a surface, measured as force per unit of area. **4.** A constraining influence upon the mind or will: *under pressure to resign.* **5.** Urgent claim or demand: *under the pressure of business.* —*tr.v.* **-sured, -suring.** To force, as by overpowering influence or persuasion. [From Latin *pressūra,* from *premere,* to press.]

pressure cooker. An airtight metal pot that uses steam under pressure to cook food quickly.

pressure group. Any group that exerts pressure on legislators and public opinion to advance or protect its interests.

pressure suit. A garment that is worn in high-altitude aircraft or in spacecraft to compensate for low-pressure conditions.

pressure suit

pres·sur·ize (prĕsh′ə-rīz′) *tr.v.* **-ized, -iz·ing. 1.** To maintain normal air pressure in (an enclosure, as an aircraft or submarine). **2.** To put (gas or liquid) under a greater than normal pressure. —**pres′sur·i·za′tion** *n.*

pres·ti·dig·i·ta·tion (prĕs′tĭ-dĭj′ĭ-tā′shən) *n.* Manual skill and dexterity in the execution of tricks; sleight of hand. [French, from *prestidigitateur,* juggler : *preste,* nimble, + Latin *digitus,* finger.] —**pres′ti·dig′i·ta′tor** *n.*

pres·tige (prĕ-stēzh′, -stēj′) *n.* **1.** Prominence or influential status in the eyes of others; repute. **2.** The power to command admiration in a group: *a position with great prestige.* —See Syns at **honor.** [French, orig. illusion brought on by magic, from Latin *praestigiae,* juggler's tricks, illusions.] —**pres·tig′ious** (prĕ-stĭj′əs, -stē′jəs) *adj.* —**pres·tig′ious·ly** *adv.* —**pres·tig′ious·ness** *n.*

pres·tis·si·mo (prĕ-stĭs′ə-mō′) *adv. Mus.* At as fast a tempo as possible. Used as a direction. —*n. Mus.* A section or passage to be played prestissimo. [Italian, superl. of *presto,* fast.] —**pres·tis′si·mo′** *adj.*

pres·to (prĕs′tō) *adv.* **1.** *Mus.* In rapid tempo. Used as a direction. **2.** Suddenly; at once. —*n. Mus.* A section or passage to be played presto. [Italian, from Latin *praestus,* ready, from *praestō,* at hand.] —**pres′to** *adj.*

pre·sume (prĭ-zo͞om′) *v.* **-sumed, -sum·ing.** —*tr.v.* **1.** To take for granted; assume to be true in the absence of proof to the contrary: *I presume the bus will be on time.* **2.** To give reasonable evidence for assuming; appear to prove. **3.** To venture; dare: *Children should not presume to contradict their elders.* —*intr.v.* **1.** To act overconfidently; take liberties. —*phrasal verb.* **presume on** (or **upon**). To take uncalled-for advantage of: *She presumed on his good nature.* [Middle English *presumen,* from Old French *presumer,* from Late Latin *praesūmere,* to venture, from Latin, to assume : *prae-,* before + *sūmere,* to take.] —**pre·sum′a·ble** (-zo͞o′mə-bəl) *adj.* —**pre·sum′a·bly** *adv.* —**pre·sum′er** *n.*

pre·sump·tion (prĭ-zŭmp′shən) *n.* **1.** Behavior or language that is boldly arrogant or offensive; effrontery. **2.** The act of presuming or accepting as true: *the presumption of a defendant's innocence.* **3.** A belief based on reasonable evidence; an assumption or supposition. **4.** A condition or basis for accepting or presuming. —See Syns at **temerity.**

pre·sump·tive (prĭ-zŭmp′tĭv) *adj.* **1.** Providing a reasonable basis for belief or acceptance. **2.** Based on probability or presumption; presumed: *an heir presumptive.* —**pre·sump′tive·ly** *adv.*

pre·sump·tu·ous (prĭ-zŭmp′cho͞o-əs) *adj.* Impertinently presuming too much; overconfident; arrogant. —See Syns at **arrogant** and **impudent.** —**pre·sump′tu·ous·ly** *adv.* —**pre·sump′tu·ous·ness** *n.*

pre·sup·pose (prē′sə-pōz′) *tr.v.* **-posed, -pos·ing. 1.** To assume or suppose in advance; take for granted. **2.** To require or involve necessarily as an antecedent condition: *Construction will begin next month presupposing receipt of the building permit.* —**pre′sup·po·si′tion** (-sŭp-ə-zĭsh′ən) *n.*

pre·tence (prē′tĕns′, prĭ-tĕns′) *n. Brit.* Var. of **pretense.**

pre·tend (prĭ-tĕnd′) *tr.v.* **1.** To put on a false show of; feign: *pretend illness.* **2.** To claim or allege insincerely or falsely; profess: *pretended ignorance of the problem.* **3.** To represent fictitiously in play; make believe. **4.** To take upon oneself; venture: *"Whether my bullets did any execution or not I cannot pretend to say"* (W.H. Hudson). —*intr.v.* **1.** To give a false appearance, as in deceiving or playing: *He's only pretending.* **2.** To put forward a claim: *a nobleman who pretends to the throne.* [Middle English *pretenden,* from Latin *praetendere,* to assert : *prae-,* before + *tendere,* to stretch.] —**pre·tend′ed·ly** *adv.*

pre·tend·er (prĭ-tĕn′dər) *n.* **1.** Someone who pretends or alleges falsely; a hypocrite or dissembler. **2. a.** Someone who sets forth a claim. **b.** A claimant to a throne. —See Syns at **imposter.**

pre·tense (prē′tĕns′, prĭ-tĕns′) *n.* Also *Brit.* **pre·tence. 1.** A false appearance or action intended to deceive: *a pretense of respect.* **2.** A false reason or excuse; pretext. **3.** Something imagined or pretended; make-believe. **4.** A mere show without reality; an outward appearance: *not even a pretense of a fair trial.* **5.** A right asserted with or without foundation; a claim. **6.** Ostentation; pretentiousness. [Middle English, from Norman French *pretensse,* from Latin *praetendere,* to pretend.]

pre·ten·sion (prĭ-tĕn′shən) *n.* **1.** An allegation, esp. when false or groundless. **2.** A lofty claim or purpose, esp. when unrealistic or immodest. **3.** Pretentiousness; ostentation.

pre·ten·tious (prĭ-tĕn′shəs) *adj.* **1.** Claiming or demanding a position of distinction or merit, esp. when unjustified. **2.** Making an extravagant show; ostentatious. —**pre·ten′tious·ly** *adv.* —**pre·ten′tious·ness** *n.*

pret·er·it or **pret·er·ite** (prĕt′ər-ĭt) *adj. Gram.* Denoting the verb tense that expresses or describes a past or completed action or condition. —*n. Gram.* **1.** The past tense. **2.** A verb form in this tense. [Middle English, past tense, from Old French, from Latin *praeteritus,* past, past part. of *praeterīre,* to pass : *praeter,* beyond, comp. of *prae,* before + *īre,* to go.]

pre·ter·nat·u·ral (prē′tər-năch′ər-əl) *adj.* **1.** Out of or beyond the normal course of nature; abnormal; exceptional: *preternatural sensitivity to noise.* **2.** Supernatural. [Medieval Latin *praeternātūrālis,* from Latin *praeter nātūram,* "beyond nature."] —**pre′ter·nat′u·ral·ly** *adv.* —**pre′ter·nat′u·ral·ness** *n.*

pre·test (prē′tĕst′) *n.* **1.** A test given to determine whether a class is sufficiently prepared for a new course. **2.** The advance testing of something, such as a questionnaire, product, or idea. —*tr.v.* (prē-tĕst′). To subject to a pretest.

pre·text (prē′tĕkst′) *n.* A purpose or excuse given to hide the real reason for something. [Latin *praetextus,* outward show, pretense, from past part. of *praetexere,* to disguise, pretend : *prae-,* before + *texere,* to weave.]

pret·ti·fy (prĭt′ĭ-fī′) *tr.v.* **-fied, -fy·ing.** To make pretty. —**pret′ti·fi·ca′tion** *n.*

pret·ty (prĭt′ē) *adj.* **-ti·er, -ti·est. 1.** Pleasing or attractive in a graceful or delicate way. **2.** Excellent; fine; good. Often used ironically: *a pretty mess you've made of everything.* **3.** *Informal.* Considerable in size or extent: *a pretty fortune.* —*adv.* To a fair degree; somewhat; moderately: *He is a pretty good student.* —*n., pl.* **-ties.** Someone or something that is pleasing or pretty. —*tr.v.* **-tied, -ty·ing.** *Informal.* To make pretty. —*idiom:* **sitting pretty.** *Informal.* In a favorable condition or position. [Middle English *prety,* clever, skillfully made, fine, from Old English *prættig,* cunning, tricky, from *prætt,* trick, craft.] —**pret′ti·ly** *adv.* —**pret′ti·ness** *n.*

pret·zel (prĕt′səl) *n.* A glazed biscuit, salted on the outside, usu. baked in the form of a loose knot or stick. [German *Pretzel,* from Old High German *brezitella,* from Latin *bracchium,* arm, (from its shape either as an armlet or as folded arms).]

pre·vail (prĭ-vāl′) *intr.v.* **1.** To triumph or win a victory. **2.** To succeed; win out: *Goodness shall prevail in the end.*

3. To be most common or frequent; be predominant. **4.** To be in force, use, or effect; be current: *a style that prevailed in the 1920's.* —*phrasal verb.* **prevail on** (or **upon**). To persuade successfully. [Middle English *prevayllen,* from Latin *praevalēre* : *prae-,* beyond + *valēre,* to be strong.] —**pre·vail'er** *n.* —**pre·vail'ing·ly** *adv.*

prev·a·lent (prĕv'ə-lənt) *adj.* Widely or commonly occurring or existing; gen. accepted or practiced. —**prev'a·lence** *n.* —**prev'a·lent·ly** *adv.*

pre·var·i·cate (prĭ-vār'ĭ-kāt') *intr.v.* **-cat·ed, -cat·ing.** To stray from or evade the truth; equivocate. [Latin *praevāricāri,* to deviate from one's course or duty : *prae-,* before, beyond + *vāricāre,* to straddle, from *vārus,* stretched, bent.] —**pre·var'i·ca'tion** *n.* —**pre·var'i·ca'tor** *n.*

pre·vent (prĭ-vĕnt') *tr.v.* **1.** To keep from happening, as by some prior action; avert: *prevent spoilage.* **2.** To keep from doing something; hinder; impede: *prevent him from making a mistake.* [Middle English *preventen,* to anticipate, from Latin *praevenīre* : *prae-,* before + *venīre,* to come.] —**pre·vent'a·ble** or **pre·vent'i·ble** *adj.* —**pre·vent'er** *n.*

pre·ven·ta·tive (prĭ-vĕn'tə-tĭv) *adj. & n.* Var. of **preventive.**

pre·ven·tion (prĭ-vĕn'shən) *n.* **1.** The act of preventing. **2.** A hindrance; obstacle.

pre·ven·tive (prĭ-vĕn'tĭv). Also **pre·ven·ta·tive** (-tə-tĭv). —*adj.* **1.** Designed or used to prevent or hinder; acting as an obstacle: *preventive measures against accidents.* **2.** Thwarting or warding off illness or disease: *preventive medicine.* —*n.* **1.** Something that prevents; an obstacle. **2.** Something used to ward off illness. —**pre·ven'tive·ly** *adv.* —**pre·ven'tive·ness** *n.*

pre·view (prē'vyōō) *n.* Also **pre·vue. 1.** A private advance showing of a motion picture, an art exhibition, or some other event prior to public presentation. **2.** Any advance viewing or exhibition, esp. the presentation of several scenes advertising a forthcoming motion picture. —*tr.v.* Also **pre·vue, -vued, -vu·ing.** To view or exhibit in advance.

pre·vi·ous (prē'vē-əs) *adj.* Existing or occurring prior to something else in time or order; antecedent. —See Syns at **last.** [Latin *praevius,* going before : *prae-,* before + *via,* way.] —**pre'vi·ous·ly** *adv.* —**pre'vi·ous·ness** *n.*

previous question. The parliamentary motion, adopted by a two-thirds vote, to end debate and take an immediate vote on the main question being considered.

pre·vi·sion (prĭ-vĭzh'ən) *n.* **1.** Foresight or anticipation. **2.** Foreknowledge; prescience.

pre·vue (prē'vyōō) *n. & v.* Var. of **preview.**

prey (prā) *n.* **1.** Any creature hunted or caught for food; quarry. **2.** A victim. **3.** The act or habit of living by hunting and seizing other animals for food. —*intr.v.* —**prey on** or **upon. 1.** To hunt, catch, or eat as prey. **2.** To take unfair advantage of; victimize. **3.** To plunder or pillage. **4.** To have a persistent, harmful effect on; trouble: *Remorse preyed upon his mind.* [Middle English *preye,* from Old French *preie,* from Latin *praeda.*] —**prey'er** *n.*

Pri·am (prī'əm) *n. Gk. Myth.* King of Troy, the father of Paris and Hector, killed during the Trojan War.

price (prīs) *n.* **1.** The sum of money or goods asked or given for something. **2.** The cost at which something is obtained: *Poverty was the price of his independence.* **3.** The cost of bribing someone: *Every man has his price.* **4.** A reward offered for the capture or killing of a person. **5.** Value or worth: *"She is a pearl / Whose price hath launched above a thousand ships"* (Shakespeare). —*tr.v.* **priced, pric·ing. 1.** To fix or establish a price for. **2.** To find out the price of: *spent the day pricing cars.* [Middle English *pris,* from Old French, from Latin *pretium,* value, reward.]

price index. A number relating prices of a group of commodities to their prices at a chosen past time.

price·less (prīs'lĭs) *adj.* **1.** Having great worth; invaluable. **2.** Highly amusing, absurd, or odd: *a priceless remark.* —See Syns at **valuable.**

prick (prĭk) *n.* **1. a.** The act of piercing or pricking. **b.** The sensation of being pierced or pricked. **2.** Any painful or stinging feeling or reflection: *prick of remorse.* **3.** A small mark or puncture made by a pointed object. **4.** A pointed object, as an ice pick or bee sting. —*tr.v.* **1.** To stab or puncture lightly. **2.** To affect sharply with a mental or emotional pang. **3.** To incite; impel: *"My duty pricks me on"* (Shakespeare). **4.** To mark or delineate on a surface by means of small punctures: *prick a pattern.* —*intr.v.* **1.** To pierce or puncture something. **2.** To feel a stinging or pricking sensation. —*idiom.* **prick up (one's) ears. 1.** To raise one's ears erect, as do certain animals. **2.** To listen with attentive interest. [Middle English *prikke,* from Old English *prica,* pricked mark, puncture.]

prick·er (prĭk'ər) *n.* **1.** A pricking tool. **2.** A prickle or thorn.

prick·ly (prĭk'lē) *adj.* **-li·er, -li·est. 1.** Having prickles. **2.** Tingling; smarting. —**prick'li·ness** *n.*

prickly heat. A noncontagious skin disease.

prickly pear. 1. Any of various cacti of the genus *Opuntia,* with bristly flattened or cylindrical joints, showy, usu. yellow flowers, and ovoid, sometimes edible fruit. **2.** The fruit of any of these plants.

prickly pear   priedieu

pride (prīd) *n.* **1.** A sense of one's own proper dignity or value; self-respect. **2.** Pleasure or satisfaction taken in one's work, achievements, or possessions. **3.** A cause or source of pride: *These men were their country's pride.* **4.** An excessively high opinion of oneself; conceit; arrogance. **5.** A group of lions. —*tr.v.* **prid·ed, prid·ing.** To esteem (oneself): *I pride myself on this garden.* [Middle English, from Old English *prȳde,* from *prūd,* proud, from Old French.] —**pride'ful** *adj.* —**pride'ful·ly** *adv.*

prie·dieu (prē-dyœ') *n., pl.* **-dieus** or **-dieux** (-dyœz'). A low desk with space for a book above and with a foot piece below for kneeling in prayer. [French *prie-Dieu,* "pray God."]

priest (prēst) *n.* **1.** In the Roman Catholic, Eastern Orthodox, Anglican, and certain other Christian churches, a member of the second grade of clergy who rank below a bishop but above a deacon and have authority to pronounce absolution and administer all sacraments save that of ordination. **2.** A person empowered to conduct ceremonies and supervise religious practice in a non-Christian religion. [Middle English *preost,* from Old English *prēost,* from Late Latin *presbyter,* from Greek *presbuteros,* comp. of *presbus,* old man.]

priest·ess (prē'stĭs) *n.* A female priest.

priest·hood (prēst'hŏod') *n.* **1.** The character, office, or vocation of a priest. **2.** The clergy.

priest·ly (prēst'lē) *adj.* **-li·er, -li·est.** Of or befitting a priest or priests. —**priest'li·ness** *n.*

prig (prĭg) *n.* A person regarded as overprecise, arrogant, or smug. [Orig. unknown.] —**prig'ger·y** (-ə-rē) *n.* —**prig'gish** *adj.* —**prig'gish·ly** *adv.*

prim (prĭm) *adj.* **prim·mer, prim·mest.** Excessively precise, neat, or formal; proper. [Orig. unknown.] —**prim'ly** *adv.* —**prim'ness** *n.*

pri·ma ballerina (prē'mə) *pl.* **prima ballerinas.** The leading female dancer in a ballet company. [Italian, "first ballerina."]

pri·ma·cy (prī'mə-sē) *n., pl.* **-cies. 1.** The condition of being first or foremost. **2.** The office or province of an ecclesiastical primate.

pri·ma don·na (prē'mə dŏn'ə, prĭm'ə) *pl.* **pri·ma don·nas. 1.** The leading female soloist in an opera company. **2.** A temperamental and conceited performer. [Italian, "first lady."]

pri·ma fa·cie (prī'mə fā'shē, fā'shə). At first sight; before closer inspection. [Latin *prīmā faciē,* "on first appearance."] —**pri'ma·fa'cie** *adj.*

---

prima-facie evidence. *Law.* Evidence that would, if un-contested, establish or raise a presumption of a fact.

pri·mal (prī′məl) *adj.* **1.** Being first in time; original: *the primal innocence of Adam and Eve.* **2.** Of first importance; primary.

pri·mar·i·ly (prī-mĕr′ə-lē, -mâr′-) *adv.* **1.** At first; originally. **2.** Chiefly; principally.

pri·ma·ry (prī′mĕr′ē, -mə-rē) *adj.* **1.** Occurring first in time or sequence; earliest; original; primitive: *still in the primary stages of development.* **2.** Coming before and usu. preparatory to something, esp. as part of a sequence: *the primary school grades.* **3.** Of the first or greatest degree, quality, or importance; primary: *his primary function.* **4.** Not derived from something else: *primary sources of information.* **5.** Immediate; direct: *the primary result.* **6.** Fundamental; basic: *primary instincts.* **7.** Of or being a primary color. **8.** *Elect.* Of or designating an inducting current, circuit, or coil. **9.** Of or designating the main flight feathers projecting along the outer edge of a bird's wing. **10.** Of or referring to present or future time: *primary tenses.* —*n., pl.* **-ries.** **1.** Someone or something that is primary. **2.** A primary election. **3.** One of the main flight feathers projecting along the outer edge of a bird's wing. **4.** A celestial body, esp. a star, to which the orbit of a satellite, or secondary, is referred.

Syns: primary, capital[1], cardinal, chief, dominant, first, foremost, main, paramount, pre-eminent, premier, prime, principal, top *adj.* Core meaning: Most important, influential, or significant (*primary responsibilities to the family; a primary leader of the opposition*).

primary accent. **1.** The strongest degree of stress placed on a syllable in the pronunciation of a word. **2.** The mark (′) used to indicate this degree of stress.

primary color. **1.** Any of the three colors of light, red, green, and blue, from which light of any color can be made by mixing. **2.** Any of the three colors of pigment, purplish red, greenish blue, and yellow, from which pigment of any color can be made by mixing. **3.** Any of the colors, red, yellow, green, and blue, and black and white, into which any color can be potentially broken down.

primary election. A preliminary election in which voters nominate party candidates for office.

primary school. A school including the first three or four grades and sometimes kindergarten.

pri·mate (prī′māt′) *n.* **1.** (*also* prī′mĭt). A bishop of highest rank in a province or country. **2.** Any member of the order Primates, which includes the monkeys, apes, and man. [Middle English *primat*, from Old French, from Medieval Latin *prīmās*, archbishop, from Latin, chief, leader, from *prīmus*, first.]

prime (prīm) *adj.* **1.** First in excellence, quality, importance or value: *prime television time: her prime concern.* **2.** First in degree or rank; chief: *"Have I not made you/The prime man of the state?"* (Shakespeare). **3.** First or early in time, order, or sequence. **4.** Of the highest U.S. Government grade of meat: *a prime cut.* **5.** *Math.* Designating a prime number. —See Syns at **excellent, fine,** and **primary.** —*n.* **1.** The earliest or beginning part; the first stage. **2.** The first season of the year; spring. **3.** The age of ideal physical perfection and intellectual vigor: *a woman in her prime.* **4.** The period or phase of ideal or peak condition: *apples in their early-season prime.* **5.** The best or most choice part: *the prime of the lot.* **6.** A mark (′) used to represent feet, minutes of arc, or minutes of time: *a 10′ board; an angle of 27°13′.* **6.** *Math.* A prime number. —*tr.v.* **primed, prim·ing.** **1.** To prepare (a gun or mine) for firing by inserting a charge of gunpowder or a primer. **2.** To prepare for operation, as by pouring water into a pump or gasoline into a carburetor. **3.** To prepare (a surface) for painting by covering with size, primer, or an undercoat. **4.** To prepare with information; to coach. [Middle English, from Old French, from Latin *prīmus*.] —**prime′ly** *adv.* —**prime′ness** *n.*

prime meridian. The meridian whose position is indicated as 0°, used as a reference line from which longitude is measured. It passes through Greenwich, England.

prime minister. **1.** A chief minister appointed by a ruler. **2.** The head of the cabinet and usu. also the chief executive of a parliamentary democracy. —**prime ministership.** —**prime ministry.**

prime number. A number that has itself and unity as its only factors.

prim·er[1] (prĭm′ər) *n.* **1.** An elementary textbook. **2.** A book that covers the basic elements of any subject. [Middle English, from Norman French, from Medieval Latin *prīmārium (manuāle)*, "basic (handbook)," from Latin *prīmārius*, basic, primary.]

prim·er[2] (prī′mər) *n.* **1.** A coat of paint or similar material applied to a surface to prepare it for further painting or finishing. **2.** A device for setting off an explosive charge.

prime rate. The lowest rate of interest on bank loans at any given time and place, offered to preferred borrowers.

pri·me·val (prī-mē′vəl) *adj.* Belonging to the first or earliest age or ages; original. [From Latin *prīmaevus*, young : *prīmus*, first + *aevum*, age.] —**pri·me′val·ly** *adv.*

prim·ing (prī′mĭng) *n.* **1.** The explosive used to ignite a charge. **2.** A preliminary coat of paint or size applied to a surface.

prim·i·tive (prĭm′ĭ-tĭv) *adj.* **1.** Of or relating to the earliest or original stage or condition: *primitive Christianity; primitive rain forests.* **2.** Not derived; original. **3.** Characterized by simplicity or crudity; unsophisticated: *primitive weapons.* **4.** Of or relating to early stages in the evolution of human culture: *primitive societies.* **5. a.** Having the style of an early or unsophisticated culture. **b.** Self-taught: *primitive art.* —See Syns at **early.** —*n.* **1.** A person belonging to a primitive society. **2.** Someone or something at a low or early stage of development. **3.** An artist that has or affects a primitive style. **4.** *Ling.* A word or word element from which another word or inflected form of the word is derived. [Middle English *primitif*, from Old French, from Latin *prīmitīvus*, first of its kind, from *prīmus*, first.] —**prim′i·tive·ly** *adv.* —**prim′i·tive·ness** *n.*

primitive

prim·i·tiv·ism (prĭm′ĭ-tĭ-vĭz′əm) *n.* **1.** The condition or quality of being primitive. **2.** The style of primitive art, esp. in painting. —**prim′i·tiv·ist** *adj. & n.* —**prim′i·tiv·is′tic** *adj.*

pri·mo·gen·i·tor (prī′mō-jĕn′ĭ-tər) *n.* The earliest ancestor or forefather. [Medieval Latin : Latin *prīmus*, first + *genitor*, father.]

pri·mo·gen·i·ture (prī′mō-jĕn′ĭ-chŏŏr′, -chər) *n.* **1.** The condition of being the first-born child of the same parents. **2.** *Law.* The right of the eldest child, esp. the eldest son, to inherit the entire estate of one or both of his parents. [Medieval Latin *prīmōgenitūra* : Latin *prīmus*, first + *genitūra*, birth, from *gignere*, to beget.]

pri·mor·di·al (prī-môr′dē-əl) *adj.* **1.** Being or happening first; primeval; original. **2.** Primary; fundamental: *play a primordial role.* [Middle English, from Late Latin *prīmōrdiālis*, from Latin *prīmōrdium*, origin, from *prīmōrdius*, original : *prīmus*, first + *ordīrī*, to begin.] —**pri·mor′di·al·ly** *adv.*

primp (prĭmp) *tr.v.* To neaten (one's appearance) with considerable attention to detail. —*intr.v.* To preen. [Prob. from PRIM.]

prim·rose (prĭm′rōz′) *n.* Any of various plants of the genus *Primula*, that have tubular, variously colored flowers with five lobes. [Middle English *primerose*, from Old French, from Medieval Latin *prīma rosa*, "first rose."]

primrose path. A way of life of worldly ease or pleasure.

prince (prĭns) *n.* **1.** *Archaic.* A hereditary ruler; king. **2.** The ruler of a principality. **3.** A male member of a royal family other than the monarch. **4.** A nobleman of varying

ă pat   ā pay   â care   ä father   ĕ pet   ē be   hw which
ŏŏ took   ōō boot   ou out   th thin   *th* this   ŭ cut
ĭ pit   ī tie   î pier   ŏ pot   ō toe   ô paw, for   oi noise
û urge   zh vision   ə about, item, edible, gallop, circus

rank in different countries. **5.** An outstanding man in any group or class: *a merchant prince.* [Middle English, from Old French, from Latin *princeps*, first in rank, sovereign, ruler.]

prince consort. The husband of a sovereign queen.

prince·dom (prĭns′dəm) *n.* **1.** The territory ruled by a prince; principality. **2.** The rank or status of a prince.

prince·ly (prĭns′lē) *adj.* **-li·er, -li·est.** Of or befitting a prince: *his princely generosity; a princely estate.* —See Syns at **grand.** —**prince′li·ness** *n.* —**prince′ly** *adv.*

Prince of Wales (wālz). A title given to the eldest son of a British sovereign.

prin·cess (prĭn′sĭs, -sĕs′, prĭn-sĕs′) *n.* **1.** *Archaic.* A hereditary female ruler; queen. **2.** The female ruler of a principality. **3.** A female member of a royal family other than the monarch. **4.** A noblewoman of varying rank in different countries. **5.** The wife of a prince. **6.** Any woman thought of as having the qualities of a princess. —*adj.* Also **prin·cesse** (prĭn-sĕs′). Designed to hang in smooth, close-fitting, unbroken lines from shoulder to flared hem: *a dress cut princess style.*

prin·ci·pal (prĭn′sə-pəl) *adj.* First, highest, or foremost in importance, rank, worth, or degree; chief. —See Syns at **primary.** —*n.* **1.** A person who holds a position of presiding rank, esp. the head of an elementary or high school. **2.** A main participant in a given situation. **3.** A person having a leading or starring role. **4.** *Finance.* **a.** The capital or main body of an estate or financial holding. **b.** A sum of money owed as a debt, upon which interest is calculated. **5.** *Law.* **a.** A person who empowers another to act as his representative. **b.** The person having prime responsibility for an obligation. **c.** Someone who commits or is an accomplice to a crime. [Middle English, from Old French, from Latin *principālis*, first, ruler, from *princeps*, first one in rank.] —**prin′ci·pal·ly** *adv.*

prin·ci·pal·i·ty (prĭn′sə-păl′ĭ-tē) *n., pl.* **-ties. 1.** A territory ruled by a prince or from which a prince derives his title. **2.** The position or jurisdiction of a prince.

principal parts. In inflected languages, the main forms of the verb from which all other forms are derived. In English, the principal parts are considered to be the present infinitive, the past tense, the past participle, and the present participle.

prin·cip·i·um (prĭn-sĭp′ē-əm) *n., pl.* **-i·a** (-ē-ə). A principle, esp. one that is basic. [Latin, basis, origin.]

prin·ci·ple (prĭn′sə-pəl) *n.* **1.** A basic truth, law, or assumption. **2. a.** A rule or standard of personal conduct: *a rascal without principles.* **b.** Moral or ethical standards or judgments: *a decision based on principle rather than expediency.* **3.** A fixed or predetermined rule guiding behavior; policy: *acting on the principle of every man for himself.* **4.** A rule or law concerning the functioning of natural phenomena or mechanical processes: *the principle of jet propulsion.* [Middle English, fundamental truth, from Old French *principe*, from Latin *principium*, from *princeps*, first.]

prin·ci·pled (prĭn′sə-pəld) *adj.* Motivated by or based on moral or ethical principles.

prink (prĭngk) *tr.v.* To adorn or groom (oneself) in a showy manner. —*intr.v.* To primp. [Prob. alteration of PRANK (adorn).] —**prink′er** *n.*

print (prĭnt) *n.* **1.** A mark or impression made in or upon a surface by pressure. **2. a.** A device or implement, such as a stamp, die, or seal, used to press markings on or into a surface. **b.** Something formed or marked by such a device: *a print of butter.* **3. a.** Lettering or other impressions produced by a printing press or other means. **b.** Printed matter, such as newsprint. **c.** The condition or form of matter so produced. **4.** A design or picture transferred from an engraved plate, lithographic stone, or other medium. **5.** A photographic image transferred to paper or a similar surface, usu. from a negative. **6. a.** A fabric or garment with a dyed pattern that has been pressed onto it, usu. by engraved rollers. **b.** The pattern itself. —*tr.v.* **1.** To press (a mark, design, etc.) onto or into a surface. **2.** To make an impression on or in (a surface) with a stamp, seal, die, or similar device. **3.** To press (a stamp or similar device) onto or into a surface to leave a marking. **4.** To produce by means of pressed type on a paper surface or as if with

a printing press. **5.** To publish in printed form: *print books.* **6.** To write (something) in characters similar to those commonly used in print. **7.** To produce (a positive photograph) by passing light through a negative onto sensitized paper. —*intr.v.* **1.** To work as a printer. **2.** To write characters similar to those commonly used in print. **3.** To produce or receive an impression, marking, or image. —*phrasal verb.* **print out.** To print (a message, statement, instruction, etc.) automatically, as a computer or teletypewriter does. —*idioms.* **in print.** Still offered for sale by a publisher. **out of print.** No longer offered for sale by a publisher. [Middle English *preinte*, from Old French, from *preindre*, to press, from Latin *premere*.]

print·a·ble (prĭn′tə-bəl) *adj.* **1.** Capable of being printed or of producing a print. **2.** Regarded as fit for publication.

printed circuit. An electric circuit in which the conducting connections are formed by depositing a conducting metal, such as copper, in predetermined patterns on an insulating substrate, while other materials, esp. semiconductors, are deposited to form various electronic components.

print·er (prĭn′tər) *n.* **1.** A person whose occupation is printing. **2.** Someone or something that prints. **3.** The part of a computer that produces printed matter.

printer's devil. An apprentice in a printing establishment.

print·ing (prĭn′tĭng) *n.* **1.** The process, art, or business of producing printed material, esp. by means of a printing press. **2.** Matter that is printed. **3.** All the copies of a book or other publication that are printed at one time.

printing press. A machine that transfers images onto paper or similar material by contact with an inked surface.

print-out (prĭnt′out′) *n.* The printed output of a computer.

pri·or¹ (prī′ər) *adj.* **1.** Earlier in time or order: *a prior commitment.* **2.** Preceding in importance or value: *a prior consideration.* —*idiom.* **prior to.** Before. [Latin.]

pri·or² (prī′ər) *n.* A monk in charge of a priory or ranking next under the abbot of an abbey. [Middle English *priour*, from Old English and Old French *prior*, both from Medieval Latin, from Latin, former, superior.]

pri·or·ess (prī′ər-ĭs) *n.* A nun at the head of a priory or ranking next below an abbess in an abbey.

pri·or·i·ty (prī-ôr′ĭ-tē, -ŏr′-) *n., pl.* **-ties. 1.** The right to be considered before others because of importance or urgency; precedence. **2.** Order of importance or urgency: *Safety is given the highest priority.* **3.** One of a number of items ranked according to importance or urgency: *Energy conservation is high on our list of national priorities.* **4.** The condition or fact of coming earlier in time.

pri·or·y (prī′ə-rē) *n., pl.* **-ies.** A monastery or convent governed by a prior or prioress.

prise (prīz) *v. & n.* Var. of **prize** (pry).

prism (prĭz′əm) *n.* **1.** *Geom.* A polyhedron with parallel, congruent polygons as bases and parallelograms as sides. **2.** *Optics.* A homogeneous transparent solid, usu. with triangular bases and rectangular sides, used to produce or analyze a continuous spectrum. **3.** A cut-glass object, such as a pendant of a chandelier. **4.** A crystalline solid having three or more similar faces parallel to a single axis. [Late Latin *prisma*, from Greek, from *priein*, to saw.]

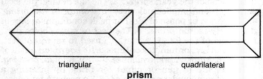

triangular   quadrilateral

prism

pris·mat·ic (prĭz-măt′ĭk) or **pris·mat·i·cal** (-ĭ-kəl) *adj.* **1.** Of or resembling a prism. **2.** Refracting light as a prism does. **3.** Multicolored; iridescent. —**pris·mat′i·cal·ly** *adv.*

pris·on (prĭz′ən) *n.* **1.** A place where persons convicted or accused of crimes are confined; a penitentiary. **2.** Any place or condition of confinement or forcible restraint: *in the prison of his own rigid beliefs.* [Middle English, from Old French, capture, from Latin, *prehensiō*, from *prehendere*, to seize.]

pris·on·er (prĭz′ə-nər, prĭz′nər) *n.* **1.** A person held in custody or captivity, esp. in a prison. **2.** A person deprived of freedom of action or expression: *a prisoner of fate.*

prisoner of war. A person captured by or surrendering to enemy forces during wartime.

pris·sy (prĭs′ē) *adj.* **-si·er, -si·est.** Finicky, fussy, and prudish. [Blend of PRIM and SISSY.] **—pris′si·ly** *adv.* **—pris′si·ness** *n.*

pris·tine (prĭs′tēn′, prĭ-stēn′) *adj.* **1.** Of the earliest time or condition; primitive; original. **2.** Remaining in a pure state; uncorrupted: *the pristine beauty of the wilderness.* [Latin *prīstīnus*, original.]

prith·ee (prĭth′ē, prĭth′ē) *interj. Archaic.* Please; I pray thee. [Earlier *preythe*, from (I) *pray thee.*]

pri·va·cy (prī′və-sē) *n., pl.* **-cies. 1.** The condition of being secluded or isolated from contact with others. **2.** Concealment; secrecy.

pri·vate (prī′vĭt) *adj.* **1.** Secluded from the sight, presence, or intrusion of others: *a private place to work without interruption.* **2.** Of or confined to one person; personal: *private opinions.* **3.** Not available for public use, control, or participation: *a private club.* **4.** Belonging to a particular person or persons: *private property.* **5.** Not holding an official or public position: *a private person.* **6.** Not public; intimate; secret: *a private matter.* —*n.* **1. a.** An enlisted person ranking below private first class in the Army or Marine Corps. **b.** A person having a similar rank in other armies or organizations. **2. privates.** The genitals. —*idiom.* **in private.** Secretly; confidentially. [Middle English *privat*, from Latin *prīvātus*, deprived of office, from *prīvāre*, to deprive, from *prīvus*, single, deprived of.] **—pri′vate·ly** *adv.* **—pri′vate·ness** *n.*

private enterprise. Free enterprise.

pri·va·teer (prī′və-tîr′) *n.* **1.** A ship privately owned and manned but authorized by a government during wartime to attack and capture enemy vessels. **2.** The commander or one of the crew of such a ship. —*intr.v.* To sail as a privateer.

private first class. An enlisted person ranking below corporal and above private in the Army or Marine Corps.

pri·va·tion (prī-vā′shən) *n.* **1.** Lack of the basic necessities or comforts of life. **2.** An act or result of depriving; deprivation. [Middle English *privacion*, from Old French *privation*, from Latin *prīvātiō*, from *prīvāre*, to deprive.]

priv·a·tive (prĭv′ə-tĭv) *adj.* **1.** Causing deprivation, lack, or loss. **2.** *Gram.* Altering the meaning of a term from positive to negative. —*n. Gram.* A privative prefix or suffix. [Latin *prīvātīvus*, from *prīvāre*, to deprive.] **—priv′a·tive·ly** *adv.*

priv·et (prĭv′ĭt) *n.* Either of two shrubs, *Ligustrum vulgare* or *L. ovalifolium*, with pointed leaves and white flowers, widely used for hedges. [Orig. unknown.]

priv·i·lege (prĭv′ə-lĭj) *n.* A special advantage, right, or benefit granted to or enjoyed by an individual or group. —*tr.v.* **-leged, -leg·ing.** To grant a privilege to. [Middle English, from Old French, from Latin *prīvilēgium*, prerogative : *prīvus*, individual + *lēx*, law.]

priv·i·leged (prĭv′ə-lĭjd) *adj.* **1.** Enjoying or having a privilege. **2.** Legally exempt from disclosure; confidential: *the privileged communication between lawyer and client.*

priv·i·ly (prĭv′ə-lē) *adv.* Privately; secretly.

priv·y (prĭv′ē) *adj.* **1.** Made a participant in knowledge of something private or secret: *"If a man thinks at all . . . he must be privy to his own thoughts and desires"* (Laurence Sterne). **2.** Belonging to a person, such as a sovereign, in his private rather than his official capacity. **3.** *Archaic.* Concealed; secret. —*n., pl.* **-ies. 1.** A latrine. **2.** An outhouse. [Middle English *prive*, secret, private, from Old French *prive*, from Latin *prīvātus*, private.]

Privy Council. 1. An advisory council of the British sovereign, now having chiefly ceremonial functions. **2.** An advisory council of the chief executive in certain other countries. **—Privy Councillor.**

prize¹ (prīz) *n.* **1.** Something offered or won as an award for achieving superiority or excellence in competition with others. **2.** Something offered for winning in a game of chance. **3.** Anything worth striving for or aspiring to. —*modifier: prize money.* —*adj.* Given or worthy of a prize: *a prize cow.* —*tr.v.* **prized, priz·ing. 1.** To value highly; esteem. **2.** To estimate the worth of; appraise; evaluate. —See Syns at **appreciate.** [Middle English *pris*, value, from Old French *pris*, from Latin *pretium*, reward.]

prize² (prīz) *n.* **1.** Something seized by force or taken as booty, esp. an enemy ship and cargo captured at sea during wartime. **2.** The act of seizing; capture. [Middle English *prise*, from Old French, from Latin *prehendere*, to seize.]

prize³ (prīz) *n.* Also **prise** (prīz). —*tr.v.* **prized, priz·ing.** To move or force with or as if with a lever; to pry. —*n.* **1.** Leverage. **2.** Something used as a lever or for prying. [Middle English *prise*, a lever.]

prize·fight (prīz′fīt′) *n.* A match fought between professional boxers for money. **—prize′fight′er** *n.* **—prize′fight′ing** *n.*

prize ring. 1. The platform enclosed by ropes in which contending boxers meet. **2.** Professional boxing.

pro¹ (prō) *n., pl.* **pros.** An argument in favor of something; affirmative consideration or vote: *weighing the pros and cons.* —*adv.* In favor; affirmatively. —*adj.* Favoring; supporting. [Middle English, from Latin *prō*, for.]

pro² (prō) *n., pl.* **pros.** *Informal.* **1.** A professional, esp. in sports. **2.** An expert in any field. —*adj. Informal.* Professional: *pro football.*

pro-¹. A prefix meaning acting in the place of: **progesterone.** [Latin *prō-*, from *prō*, for.]

pro-². A prefix meaning: **1.** Prior to: **prothrombin. 2.** In front of: **procambium.** [From Greek *pro*, before, in front of.]

prob·a·bil·i·ty (prŏb′ə-bĭl′ĭ-tē) *n., pl.* **-ties. 1.** The quality or condition of being probable; likelihood: *a good probability of rain.* **2.** A probable situation, condition, or event. **3.** *Math.* A number expressing the likelihood of occurrence of a specific event, such as the ratio of the number of experimental results that would produce the event to the total number of results considered possible.

prob·a·ble (prŏb′ə-bəl) *adj.* **1.** Likely to happen or to be true: *estimated the probable cost.* **2.** Relatively likely but not certain; plausible: *a probable explanation.* —See Syns at **likely.** [Middle English, from Old French, from Latin *probābilis*, provable, from *probāre*, to approve, test.]

probable cause. *Law.* Reasonable grounds for belief that an accused person is guilty as charged.

prob·a·bly (prŏb′ə-blē) *adv.* Most likely; presumably.

pro·bate (prō′bāt′) *adj.* Having to do with a probate court or its action. —*n.* **1.** Legal establishment of the validity of a will. **2.** The right to validate wills. —*tr.v.* **-bat·ed, -bat·ing.** To establish the validity of (a will). [Middle English *probat*, from Latin *probātum*, something proved, from *probāre*, to examine, test.]

probate court. A court limited to the jurisdiction of probating wills and administering estates.

pro·ba·tion (prō-bā′shən) *n.* **1.** A trial period in which a person's fitness for membership in a working or social group is tested. **2.** A trial period in which a student is permitted to redeem failing grades or bad conduct. **3. a.** The release of a convicted offender on condition of good behavior. **b.** The period during which an offender is released on condition of good behavior. [Middle English *probacioun*, from Old French *probation*, from Latin *probātiō*, from *probāre*, to test.] **—pro·ba′tion·al** or **pro·ba′tion·ar′y** (-shə-nĕr′ē) *adj.* **—pro·ba′tion·al·ly** *adv.*

pro·ba·tion·er (prō-bā′shə-nər) *n.* A person on probation.

pro·ba·tive (prō′bə-tĭv) *adj.* Also **pro·ba·to·ry** (-tôr′ē, -tōr′ē). **1.** Serving to test or try. **2.** Furnishing evidence or proof. [Middle English *probatiffe*, from Latin *probātīvus*, of proof, from *probāre*, to try, test.]

probe (prōb) *n.* **1.** An object introduced into a place, region, etc., for purposes of research or investigation: *a space probe.* **2.** A long, slender tool used to examine a cavity, esp. an instrument used to explore a wound or body cavity. **3.** Any thorough examination or investigation. —*v.* **probed, prob·ing.** —*tr.v.* **1.** To explore with a probe. **2.** To examine or investigate penetratingly; delve into: *a Congressional committee probing unfair hiring practices.* —*intr.v.* To conduct an exploratory investigation. [Medieval Latin *proba*, examination, from Late Latin, proof, test, from Latin *probāre*, to test, prove.] **—prob′er** *n.*

pro·bi·ty (prō′bĭ-tē) *n.* Complete and confirmed integrity; uprightness. [Old French *probité*, from Latin *probitās*, honesty, from *probus*, good, honest.]

prob·lem (prŏb′ləm) *n.* **1.** A question or situation that presents uncertainty, perplexity, or difficulty. **2.** A person who is difficult to deal with. **3.** A question put forward for consideration, discussion, or solution. —*adj.* **1.** Difficult to deal with or handle: *a problem child.* **2.** Dealing with a social or moral problem: *a problem play.* [Middle English *probleme*, from Old French, from Latin *problēma*, from Greek, obstacle, problem : *pro-*, forward + *ballein*, to throw.]

prob·lem·at·i·cal (prŏb'lə-măt'ĭ-kəl) or **prob·lem·at·ic** (-ĭk) *adj.* Having the puzzling, uncertain, or debatable character of a problem. —**prob'lem·at'i·cal·ly** *adv.*

pro·bos·cis (prō-bŏs'ĭs) *n., pl.* **-cis·es** or **-bos·ci·des** (-bŏs'ĭ-dēz'). **1.** A long, flexible snout or trunk, as of an elephant. **2.** A slender, tubular feeding and sucking structure of some insects and worms. [Latin, from Greek *proboskis* : *pro-*, in front + *boskein*, to feed.]

pro·caine (prō'kān') *n.* A white crystalline powder, $C_{13}H_{20}O_2N_2$. HCl, used as a local anesthetic. Also called **procaine hydrochloride.** [PRO- (in place of) + (CO)CAINE.]

pro·cam·bi·um (prō-kăm'bē-əm) *n. Bot.* A layer of undifferentiated plant cells from which the vascular tissue is formed. —**pro·cam'bi·al** *adj.*

pro·ce·dure (prə-sē'jər) *n.* **1.** A manner of proceeding; way of performing or effecting something. **2.** An act composed of steps; course of action: *the tedious procedure of registering for classes.* **3.** A set of established forms or methods for conducting the affairs of a business, legislative body, or court of law. [French *procédure*, from Old French, from *proceder*, to proceed.] —**pro·ce'dur·al** (-jər-əl) *adj.* —**pro·ce'dur·al·ly** *adv.*

pro·ceed (prō-sēd', prə-) *intr.v.* **1.** To continue, esp. after an interruption. **2.** To undertake and carry on some action or process: *proceeded with her reorganization plans.* **3.** To move on in an orderly manner. **4.** To issue forth; originate. **5.** To institute and conduct legal action. —See Syns at **advance.** [Middle English *proceden*, from Old French *proceder*, from Latin *prōcēdere* : *prō-*, forward + *cēdere*, to go.] —**pro·ceed'er** *n.*

pro·ceed·ing (prō-sē'dĭng, prə-) *n.* **1.** A course of action; procedure. **2. proceedings.** A sequence of events occurring at a particular place or occasion. **3. proceedings.** A record of business carried on by an organization. **4.** *Law.* **a. proceedings.** Legal action; litigation. **b.** The instituting or conducting of litigation.

pro·ceeds (prō'sēdz') *pl.n.* The amount of money derived from a commercial or fund-raising venture.

proc·ess (prŏs'ĕs', prō'sĕs') *n.* **1.** A series of steps, actions, or operations used in making something or bringing about a desired result: *a manufacturing process.* **2.** A series of actions, changes, etc., by which something passes from one condition to another: *a lake in the process of drying up.* **3.** Course of events or passage of time: *he started working out and lost ten pounds in the process.* **4.** *Law.* **a.** A summons or writ to appear in court. **b.** The entire course of a legal action. **5.** A part that extends or projects from the body; outgrowth: *a bony process.* —*tr.v.* **1.** To put through the steps of a prescribed procedure: *process an application.* **2.** To prepare, treat, or convert by subjecting to some special process: *processing crude oil into plastic.* **3.** *Law.* **a.** To serve with a summons or writ. **b.** To institute legal proceedings against; prosecute. —*adj.* Prepared or converted by a special treatment: *process cheese.* [Middle English *proces*, from Old French, from Latin *prōcessus*, past part. of *prōcēdere*, to proceed.] —**proc'es'sor** or **proc'ess'er** *n.*

pro·ces·sion (prə-sĕsh'ən) *n.* **1.** The act of proceeding, moving along, or issuing forth. **2. a.** A group of persons, vehicles, or objects moving along in an orderly and formal manner, usu. in a long line: *a wedding procession.* **b.** The movement of such a group. **3.** Any continuous and orderly course: *the procession of the seasons.* [Middle English, from Old French, from Late Latin *prōcessiō*, religious procession, from Latin, a marching forward, from *prōcēdere*, to proceed.]

pro·ces·sion·al (prə-sĕsh'ə-nəl) *adj.* Of or suitable for a procession: *a processional march.* —*n.* **1.** A book containing the ritual observed during a religious procession. **2.** Any music intended to be played or sung during a procession. —**pro·ces'sion·al·ly** *adv.*

pro·claim (prō-klām', prə-) *tr.v.* **1.** To announce officially and publicly; declare: *proclaim a holiday.* **2.** To make plain; reveal: *His tears proclaimed his regret.* [Middle English *proclaymen*, from Old French *proclamer*, from Latin *prōclāmāre* : *prō-*, forth + *clāmāre*, to cry out.] —**pro·claim'er** *n.*

proc·la·ma·tion (prŏk'lə-mā'shən) *n.* **1.** The act of proclaiming. **2.** Something proclaimed, esp. an official public announcement.

pro·cliv·i·ty (prō-klĭv'ĭ-tē) *n., pl.* **-ties.** A natural inclination; predisposition: *a proclivity for the arts.* [Latin *prōclīvitās* : *prō-*, forward + *clīvus*, slope, hill.]

pro·con·sul (prō-kŏn'səl) *n.* **1.** An ancient Roman governor of a province. **2.** A high administrator in one of the European colonial empires. [Middle English, from Latin *prō consule*, (one acting) for a consul.] —**pro·con'su·lar** (-sə-lər) *adj.* —**pro·con'su·late** (-sə-lĭt) *n.*

pro·cras·ti·nate (prə-krăs'tə-nāt', prō-) *v.* **-nat·ed, -nat·ing.** —*intr.v.* To put off doing something until a future time. —*tr.v.* To postpone or delay needlessly. —See Syns at **delay.** [From Latin *prōcrāstināre* : *prō-*, forward + *crās*, tomorrow.] —**pro·cras'ti·na'tion** *n.* —**pro·cras'ti·na'tor** *n.*

pro·cre·ate (prō'krē-āt') *v.* **-at·ed, -at·ing.** —*tr.v.* To produce (offspring); beget. —*intr.v.* To beget offspring; reproduce. [Latin *prōcreāre* : *prō-*, forth + *creāre*, to create.] —**pro'cre·a'tion** *n.* —**pro'cre·a'tive** *adj.* —**pro'cre·a'tor** *n.*

pro·crus·te·an (prō-krŭs'tē-ən) *adj.* Also **Pro·crus·te·an.** Producing or designed to produce conformity by ruthless or arbitrary means. [After *Procrustes*, a fabulous Greek giant who stretched or shortened captives to fit one of his iron beds.]

proc·tol·o·gy (prŏk-tŏl'ə-jē) *n.* The physiology and pathology of the rectum and anus. [Greek *prōktos*, anus + -LOGY.] —**proc·tol'o·gist** *n.*

proc·tor (prŏk'tər) *n.* A person appointed to supervise students during examinations. —*tr.v.* To serve as proctor at (an examination). [Middle English *procutour*, agent, deputy, contraction of *procuratour*, procurator.] —**proc·to'ri·al** (prŏk-tôr'ē-əl, -tōr'-) *adj.*

pro·cum·bent (prō-kŭm'bənt) *adj.* **1.** *Bot.* Trailing along the ground: *a procumbent vine.* **2.** Lying face down; prone. [Latin *prōcumbens*, pres. part. of *prōcumbere*, to fall forward, bend down.]

proc·u·ra·tor (prŏk'yə-rā'tər) *n.* **1.** An agent having power of attorney. **2.** An official of the Roman Empire acting as a financial agent of the emperor or as the administrator of a minor province. [Middle English *procuratour*, from Old French, from Latin *prōcūrātor*, from *prōcūrāre*, to take care of, procure.] —**proc'u·ra·to'ri·al** (prŏk'yər-ə-tôr'ē-əl, -tōr'-) *adj.*

pro·cure (prō-kyŏŏr', prə-) *v.* **-cured, -cur·ing.** —*tr.v.* **1.** To obtain; acquire. **2.** To bring about; effect: *procure a solution.* **3.** To obtain (a woman) to serve as a prostitute. —*intr.v.* To work as a procurer of women. [Middle English *procuren*, from Old French *procurer*, from Late Latin *prōcūrāre*, from Latin, to manage for someone else : *prō-*, for, on behalf of + *cūrāre*, to take care of.] —**pro·cure'ment** *n.*

Pro·cy·on (prō'sē-ŏn', prŏs'ē-) *n.* A double star in the constellation Canis Minor.

prod (prŏd) *tr.v.* **prod·ded, prod·ding. 1.** To jab or poke, as with a pointed instrument. **2.** To rouse to action; stir. —See Syns at **urge.** —*n.* **1.** Anything pointed used to prod; a goad. **2.** An incitement or stimulus. [Orig. unknown.] —**prod'der** *n.*

prod·i·gal (prŏd'ĭ-gəl) *adj.* **1.** Recklessly wasteful; extravagant. **2.** Profuse; lavish: *prodigal praise.* —*n.* A person given to luxury or extravagance; a spendthrift. [Latin *prōdigus*, from *prōdigere*, to squander : *prōd-*, var. of *prō-*, forth + *agere*, to drive.] —**prod'i·gal'i·ty** (-găl'ĭ-ē) *n.* —**prod'i·gal·ly** *adv.*

pro·di·gious (prə-dĭj'əs) *adj.* **1.** Impressively great in size, force, or extent; enormous. **2.** Extraordinary; marvelous: *a prodigious appetite.* [Latin *prōdigiōsus*, from *prōdigium*, omen, portent.] —**pro·di'gious·ly** *adv.* —**pro·di'gious·ness** *n.*

prod·i·gy (prŏd'ĭ-jē) *n., pl.* **-gies. 1.** A person with exceptional talents or powers, esp. a child. **2.** An act or event so extraordinary or rare as to inspire wonder; a marvel. **3.** *Archaic.* An omen or portent. [Latin *prōdigium*, prophetic sign, marvel.]

pro·duce (prə-dōos', -dyōos', prō-) v. **-duced**, **-duc·ing.** —tr.v. **1.** To bring forth; to yield: *Seeds produce plants.* **2.** To create by mental or physical effort. **3.** To manufacture. **4.** To cause to occur or exist; give rise to. **5.** To bring forward; exhibit: *produced identification.* **6.** To sponsor and present to the public: *produce a play.* **7.** *Geom.* To extend (an area or volume) or lengthen (a line). —intr.v. To make or yield the expected product or products. —See Syns at **create.** —n. (prŏd'ōos, -yōos, prō'dōos, -dyōos). Something produced, esp. farm products raised for selling. [Latin *prōdūcere* : *prō-*, forward + *dūcere*, to lead.] —**pro·duc'i·ble** *adj.*

pro·duc·er (prə-dōo'sər, -dyōo'-, prō-) n. **1.** Someone or something that produces. **2.** A person who finances and supervises the production of a play or other public entertainment.

prod·uct (prŏd'əkt) n. **1.** Anything produced by human or mechanical effort or by a natural process. **2.** A direct result; consequence. **3.** *Chem.* A substance produced by a chemical change. **4.** *Math.* The result obtained by performing multiplication. [Latin *prōductum*, from the past part. of *prōdūcere*, to produce.]

pro·duc·tion (prə-dŭk'shən, prō-) n. **1.** The act or process of producing. **2.** Something produced; a product. **3.** The total number of products; output. **4.** A public presentation of a play or other form of entertainment. —**pro·duc'tion·al** *adj.*

pro·duc·tive (prə-dŭk'tĭv, prō-) adj. **1.** Producing or capable of producing: *a productive worker.* **2.** Producing abundantly; fertile; prolific. **3.** Yielding favorable or useful results; constructive: *productive talks.* —See Syns at **fertile.** —**pro·duc'tive·ly** adv. —**pro·duc·tiv'i·ty** (prō'dŭk-tĭv'ĭ-tē, prŏd'ək-) or **pro·duc'tive·ness** n.

pro·em (prō'ĕm') n. A short introduction; a preface. [Middle English *proheme*, from Old French, from Latin *prooemium*, from Greek *prooimion* : *pro-*, before + *oimē*, song, lay.]

prof (prŏf) n. *Informal.* A professor.

prof·a·na·tion (prŏf'ə-nā'shən) n. The act or an instance of profaning; desecration.

pro·fane (prō-fān', prə-) adj. **1.** Showing contempt or irreverence toward sacred things; blasphemous. **2.** Nonreligious in subject matter, form, or use; secular. **3.** Vulgar; coarse. —tr.v. **-faned**, **-fan·ing.** **1.** To treat with irreverence; blaspheme. **2.** To put to an improper, unworthy, or degrading use; to abuse. [Middle English *prophane*, from Old French, from Latin *profānus*, not sacred, secular, impious : *prō-*, before + *fānum*, temple.] —**pro·fane'ly** adv. —**pro·fane'ness** n. —**pro·fan'er** n.

pro·fan·i·ty (prō-făn'ĭ-tē, prə-) n., pl. **-ties. 1.** The condition or quality of being profane. **2. a.** Abusive, vulgar, or irreverent language. **b.** The use of such language.

pro·fess (prə-fĕs', prō-) tr.v. **1.** To affirm openly; declare. **2.** To claim; pretend: *professing a sympathy that he did not feel.* **3.** To claim skill in or knowledge of: *profess medicine.* **4.** To affirm belief in: *profess Catholicism.* **5.** To receive into a religious order. —intr.v. To make an open affirmation. [Latin *professus*, past part. of *profitērī*, to declare publicly : *prō-*, forth, in public + *fatērī*, to acknowledge.]

pro·fessed (prə-fĕst', prō-) adj. **1.** Openly declared; avowed: *a professed liberal.* **2.** Declared with the purpose of deceiving; pretended: *his professed honesty.* —**pro·fess'ed·ly** (-fĕs'ĭd-lē) adv.

pro·fes·sion (prə-fĕsh'ən) n. **1.** An occupation, esp. one requiring training and specialized study. **2.** The body of persons engaged in an occupation or field. **3.** The act or an instance of professing; declaration; claim. **4.** An avowal of faith in a religion.

pro·fes·sion·al (prə-fĕsh'ə-nəl) adj. **1.** Of, pertaining to, characteristic of, or engaged in a profession: *professional schools; professional training.* **2.** Engaged in a specific activity as a source of livelihood: *a professional actor.* **3.** Performed by persons receiving pay: *professional football.* **4.** Engaged in an activity as though it were a profession: *a professional student.* —n. A person following a profession. —**pro·fes'sion·al·ly** adv.

pro·fes·sion·al·ism (prə-fĕsh'ə-nə-lĭz'əm) n. Professional status, methods, character, or standards.

pro·fes·sor (prə-fĕs'ər) n. **1. a.** A teacher of the highest rank in an institution of higher learning. **b.** A teacher or instructor. **2.** Someone who professes. —**pro·fes·so·ri·al** (prō'fĭ-sôr'ē-əl, -sōr'-, prŏf'ĭ-) adj. —**pro·fes·so'ri·al·ly** adv.

pro·fes·sor·ship (prə-fĕs'ər-shĭp') n. The rank or office of a professor.

prof·fer (prŏf'ər) tr.v. To present for acceptance; offer. —See Syns at **offer.** —n. The act of proffering; an offer. [Middle English *profren*, from Old French *poroffrir* : *por-*, from Latin *prō-*, forth + *offrir*, to offer, from Latin *offerre.*] —**prof'fer·er** n.

pro·fi·cien·cy (prə-fĭsh'ən-sē) n., pl. **-cies.** The condition or quality of being proficient; skill; competence.

pro·fi·cient (prə-fĭsh'ənt) adj. Performing in a given art, skill, or branch of learning with expert correctness and facility; adept: *proficient at the piano.* —n. An adept; expert. [Latin *prōficiens*, pres. part. of *prōficere*, to make progress.] —**pro·fi'cient·ly** adv.

pro·file (prō'fīl') n. **1. a.** A side view of an object or structure, esp. of a human head. **b.** A representation of an object or structure seen from the side. **2.** An outline of any object. **3.** A biographical essay presenting the subject's most noteworthy characteristics and achievements. **4.** A graph or table representing numerically the extent to which a person or thing shows various tested characteristics: *an organizational profile.* —tr.v. **-filed**, **-fil·ing. 1.** To draw or shape a profile of. **2.** To write a profile of. [Italian *profilo*, from *profilare*, to draw in outline : *pro-*, forward + *filare*, to spin, draw a line, from Latin *filum*, thread, string.]

prof·it (prŏf'ĭt) n. **1.** An advantage gained from doing something; a benefit. **2.** The money made in a business venture, sale, or investment after all expenses have been met. **3. profits. a.** The return received on an investment after all charges have been paid. **b.** The rate of increase in the net worth of a business enterprise in a given accounting period. —intr.v. **1.** To make a gain or profit: *profited from the sale.* **2.** To be advantageous; benefit: *It profits little to complain.* —tr.v. To be beneficial to. [Middle English, from Old French, from Latin *prōfectus*, from *prōficere*, to make progress, accomplish.]

prof·it·a·ble (prŏf'ĭ-tə-bəl) adj. **1.** Yielding a profit; moneymaking. **2.** Yielding benefits; worthwhile. —**prof'it·a·bil'i·ty** or **prof'it·a·ble·ness** n. —**prof'it·a·bly** adv.

prof·i·teer (prŏf'ĭ-tîr') n. Someone who makes excessive profits on commodities in short supply. —intr.v. To act as a profiteer.

profit sharing. A system by which employees receive a share of the profits of a business enterprise.

prof·li·gate (prŏf'lĭ-gĭt, -gāt') adj. **1.** Recklessly wasteful or extravagant. **2.** Completely given over to self-indulgence and vice; dissolute. —n. A very wasteful or dissolute person. [Latin *prōflīgātus*, from *prōflīgāre*, to ruin : *prō-*, forward, down + *flīgere*, to strike.] —**prof'li·ga·cy** (-gə-sē) n.

pro for·ma (prō fôr'mə). *Latin.* As a matter of, or according to, form.

pro·found (prə-found', prō-) adj. **-er**, **-est. 1.** Extending to or coming from a great depth; deep. **2.** Coming as if from the depths of one's being: *profound contempt.* **3.** Thoroughgoing; far-reaching: *a profound influence.* **4.** Penetrating beyond what is superficial or obvious: *a profound mind.* **5.** Unqualified; absolute; complete: *a profound silence.* —See Syns at **deep.** [Middle English *profounde*, from Old French *profund*, from Latin *profundus* : *prō-*, before + *fundus*, bottom.] —**pro·found'ly** adv. —**pro·found'ness** n.

pro·fun·di·ty (prə-fŭn'dĭ-tē, prō-) n., pl. **-ties. 1.** Great depth. **2.** Depth of intellect, feeling, or meaning. **3.** Something profound or abstruse.

pro·fuse (prə-fyōos', prō-) adj. **1.** Plentiful; overflowing: *profuse vegetation.* **2.** Given freely and abundantly; extravagant: *profuse regrets.* [Middle English, from Latin *prōfūsus*, past part. of *prōfundere*, to pour forth : *prō-*, forth + *fundere*, to pour.] —**pro·fuse'ly** adv. —**pro·fuse'ness** n.

pro·fu·sion (prə-fyōo'zhən, prō-) n. **1.** The condition of being profuse; abundance. **2.** Lavish or unrestrained expense; extravagance. **3.** A profuse outpouring or display: *a profusion of butterflies.*

pro·gen·i·tor (prō-jĕn'ĭ-tər) n. **1.** A direct ancestor. **2.** An originator of a line of descent. —See Syns at **ancestor.** [Middle English *progenitour,* from Old French *progeniteur,* from Latin *prōgenitor* : *prō-,* forth + *gignere,* to beget.]

prog·e·ny (prŏj′ə-nē) *n., pl.* **-nies. 1.** Children or descendants; offspring. **2.** A result of creative effort; product. [Middle English *progenie,* from Old French, from Latin *prōgeniēs,* from *prōgignere,* to beget.]

pro·ges·ter·one (prō-jĕs′tə-rōn′) *n.* A female hormone, $C_{21}H_{30}O_2$, secreted by the corpus luteum of the ovary prior to implantation of the fertilized ovum. [PRO- (acting for) + GES(TATION) + STER(OL) + -ONE.]

prog·na·thous (prŏg′nə-thəs, prŏg-nā′-) *adj.* Also **prog·nath·ic** (prŏg-năth′ĭk). Having jaws that project beyond the upper part of the face. [PRO- (in front of) + Greek *gnathos,* jaw.] **—prog′na·thism′** (-thĭz′əm) *n.*

prog·no·sis (prŏg-nō′sĭs) *n., pl.* **-ses** (-sēz′). **1. a.** A prediction of the probable course of a disease. **b.** The likelihood of recovery from a disease. **2.** Any forecast or prediction. [Late Latin, from Greek *prognōsis,* from *progignōskein* : *pro-,* before + *gignōskein,* to know.]

prog·nos·tic (prŏg-nŏs′tĭk) *adj.* **1.** Of, relating to, or acting as a prognosis. **2.** Predicting; foretelling. —*n.* **1.** A sign or omen of some future happening. **2.** A prediction; prophecy. [Medieval Latin *prognōsticus,* from Greek *prognōstikos,* from *progignōskein,* to know beforehand.]

prog·nos·ti·cate (prŏg-nŏs′tĭ-kāt′) *tr.v.* **-cat·ed, -cat·ing. 1.** To predict, using present indications as a guide. **2.** To foreshadow; portend. **—prog·nos′ti·ca′tor** *n.* **—prog·nos′ti·ca′tion** *n.*

pro·gram (prō′grăm′, -grəm) *n.* Also *Brit.* **pro·gramme. 1.** A listing of the order of events and other information for some public presentation: *a concert program.* **2.** The presentation itself; performance. **3.** A radio or television show. **4.** Any organized list of activities, courses, or procedures; schedule. **5.** An organized series of activities, courses, or events: *the school athletic program.* **6.** An organized, usu. large-scale effort to achieve a goal by stages; a project: *the space program.* **7. a.** A procedure for solving a problem, including collection of data, processing, and presentation of results. **b.** Such a procedure coded for a computer. —*tr.v.* **-grammed** or **-gramed, -gram·ming** or **-gram·ing. 1.** To include in a program. **2.** To design or schedule programs. **3.** To provide (a computer) with a set of instructions for solving a problem. **4.** To train or regulate (the mind, senses, etc.) to perform in a certain way. [French *programme,* from Late Latin *programma,* public notice, from Greek : *pro-,* before + *graphein,* to write.] **—pro′gram·mat′ic** (prō′grə-măt′ĭk) *adj.*

pro·gram·mer (prō′grăm′ər) *n.* Also **pro·gram·er.** A person who prepares a computer program.

prog·ress (prŏg′rĕs′, -rĭs; *Brit.* prō′grĕs′) *n.* **1.** Movement toward a goal. **2.** Development; unfolding: *the progress of the plot.* **3.** Steady improvement, as of a society or civilization. **4.** A journey or tour made by a sovereign or other royalty. —*intr.v.* **pro·gress** (prə-grĕs′). **1.** To advance; proceed. **2.** To advance toward a more desirable form. —See Syns at **advance.** —*idiom.* **in progress.** Taking place; going on. [Middle English *progresse,* from Latin *prōgressus,* from *prōgredī,* to go forward : *prō-,* forward + *gradī,* to step, go.]

pro·gres·sion (prə-grĕsh′ən) *n.* **1.** Progress; forward movement. **2.** Advancement or development to a higher or different stage. **3.** A series of things or events; sequence: *the formal dinner with its progression of great dishes and fine wines.* **4.** *Math.* A sequence of numbers, each derived from the one before by some regular rule. **5.** *Mus.* **a.** A succession of tones or chords. **b.** A series of repetitions of a phrase, each in a new position on the scale. **—pro·gres′sion·al** *adj.*

pro·gres·sive (prə-grĕs′ĭv) *adj.* **1.** Moving forward; ongoing; advancing. **2.** Proceeding in steps; continuing steadily. **3.** Promoting or favoring political reform; liberal. **4. Progressive.** Of or belonging to a Progressive Party. **5.** Of, relating to, or influenced by a theory of education characterized by emphasis on the individual needs and capacities of each child and informality of curriculum. **6.** Of or denoting a tax system in which the rate of taxation increases as the taxable amount increases. **7.** *Pathol.* Continuously spreading or increasing in severity. **8.** *Gram.*

Designating a verb tense or form that expresses an action or condition in progress. —*n.* **1.** A person who favors or strives for reform in politics, education, or other fields. **2. Progressive.** Someone who belongs to a Progressive Party. **3.** *Gram.* A progressive verb form. **—pro·gres′sive·ly** *adv.* **—pro·gres′sive·ness** *n.*

Progressive Party. 1. An American political party organized under the leadership of Theodore Roosevelt in 1912. **2.** A party with similar goals organized in 1924 and led by Robert M. La Follette. **3.** A party formed in 1948, orig. led by Henry A. Wallace.

pro·gres·siv·ism (prə-grĕs′ĭ-vĭz′əm) *n.* The doctrines and practice of political or educational progressives.

pro·hib·it (prō-hĭb′ĭt, prə-) *tr.v.* **1.** To forbid, esp. by authority; make unlawful. **2.** To prevent or debar. —See Syns at **forbid.** [Middle English *prohibiten,* from Latin *prōhibēre,* to hinder : *prō-,* in front + *habēre,* to hold.]

pro·hi·bi·tion (prō′ə-bĭsh′ən) *n.* **1.** The act of prohibiting or the condition of being prohibited. **2.** A law, order, or decree that forbids something. **3. a.** The forbidding by law of the manufacture, transportation, and sale of alcoholic beverages. **b. Prohibition.** The period (1920–33) during which such a law was in force in the United States.

pro·hi·bi·tion·ist (prō′ə-bĭsh′ən-ĭst) *n.* A person in favor of outlawing the manufacture and sale of alcoholic beverages.

pro·hib·i·tive (prō-hĭb′ĭ-tĭv, prə-) *adj.* Also **pro·hib·i·to·ry** (-tôr′ē, -tōr′ē). **1.** Prohibiting; forbidding. **2.** Preventing or discouraging purchase or use: *prohibitive prices.* **—pro·hib′i·tive·ly** *adv.*

proj·ect (prŏj′ĕkt′, -ĭkt) *n.* **1.** A plan or proposal; a scheme. **2.** An undertaking requiring concerted effort. **3.** A research undertaking. **4.** A complex of houses or apartment buildings. —*v.* **pro·ject** (prə-jĕkt′). —*tr.v.* **1.** To thrust outward or forward: *projected his jaw defiantly.* **2.** To throw forward; hurl; impel: *project a missile.* **3.** To transport in one's imagination. **4.** To convey; transmit: *songs that project a romantic mood.* **5.** To externalize and attribute to someone or something else: *projecting her emotions to her friend.* **6.** To direct (one's voice) so as to be heard clearly at a distance. **7.** To form a plan or intention for. **8.** To cause (an image) to appear upon a surface. **9.** *Math.* To produce a projection. **10.** To predict by extending present trends or figures. —*intr.v.* **1.** To extend forward or out; protrude. **2.** To direct one's voice so as to be heard clearly at a distance. **3.** To make predictions by extending present trends or figures. [Middle English *proiecte,* from Latin *prōjectum,* a projecting, projection, from the past part. of *prō(j)icere,* to throw forth : *prō-,* forth + *jacere,* to throw.]

pro·jec·tile (prə-jĕk′təl, -tīl′) *n.* **1.** An object that is projected by an external force, esp. one used as a weapon, as a bullet. **2.** A self-propelling missile, such as a rocket. —*adj.* **1.** Capable of being impelled or hurled forward. **2.** Driving forward; impelling. [New Latin *prōjectilis,* from Latin *prō(j)icere,* to throw forth, project.] **—pro·jec′tive** *adj.*

pro·jec·tion (prə-jĕk′shən) *n.* **1.** The act of projecting. **2.** Something that thrusts outward; a protuberance. **3.** A plan for an anticipated course of action. **4. a.** The process of projecting a filmed image onto a screen or other surface. **b.** The image so projected. **5.** The image of a geometric figure produced by a coordinate mapping. **6.** A system of intersecting lines, such as the grid of a map, on which part or all of the globe or the celestial sphere may be represented as a plane surface. **7.** *Psychol.* The naive or unconscious attribution of one's own feelings, attitudes, or desires to others. **8.** An estimate of what something will be in the future, based on the present trend or rate of change.

pro·jec·tion·ist (prə-jĕk′shə-nĭst) *n.* **1.** Someone who operates a motion-picture projector. **2.** A map-maker.

projective geometry. The study of geometric properties that do not vary under projection.

pro·jec·tor (prə-jĕk′tər) *n.* **1.** A machine for projecting an image onto a screen. **2.** A device for projecting a beam of light. **3.** A person who devises plans or projects.

pro·lac·tin (prō-lăk′tĭn) *n.* A pituitary hormone that stimulates the secretion of milk.

pro·late (prō′lāt′) *adj.* Designating the shape of a solid, esp. of a spheroid, with its polar axis longer than its equatorial diameter; cigar-shaped. [Latin *prōlātus*, stretched out, past part. of *prōferre*, to bring forward, stretch out.] —**pro'late'ly** *adv.* —**pro'late'ness** *n.*

pro·leg (prō'lĕg') *n.* One of the stubby limbs on the abdominal segments of caterpillars and some other insect larvae.

pro·le·tar·i·an (prō'lĭ-târ'ē-ən) *adj.* Of, relating to, or characteristic of the proletariat. —*n.* A member of the proletariat. [From Latin *prōlētārius*, Roman citizen of the lowest class (who served the state only by producing offspring), from *prōlēs*, offspring.]

pro·le·tar·i·at (prō'lĭ-târ'ē-ət) *n.* **1. a.** The class of industrial wage earners who must earn their living from their labor power. **b.** The poorest class of working people of a society. **2.** In ancient Rome, the lowest class of citizens. [French *prolétariat*, from Latin *prōlētārius*, proletarian.]

pro·lif·er·ate (prə-lĭf'ə-rāt') *v.* -**at·ed, -at·ing.** —*intr.v.* **1.** To reproduce or produce new growth or parts rapidly and repeatedly, as cells. **2.** To increase or spread at a rapid rate: *acts of civil disobedience proliferating across the country.* —See Syns at **fertile.** —*tr.v.* To cause to grow or increase rapidly. [From French *prolifère*, proliferous, from Medieval Latin *prōlifer*, producing offspring, from Latin *prōlēs*, offspring.] —**pro·lif'er·a'tion** *n.* —**pro·lif'er·a'tive** *adj.*

pro·lif·ic (prə-lĭf'ĭk) *adj.* **1.** Producing offspring or fruit in great abundance; fertile. **2.** Producing abundant works or results: *a prolific writer.* [French *prolifique*, from Medieval Latin *prōlificus*, from Latin *prōlēs*, offspring.] —**pro·lif'i·ca·cy** (-lĭf'ĭ-kə-sē) or —**pro·lif'ic·ness** *n.* —**pro·lif'i·cal·ly** *adv.*

pro·lix (prō-lĭks', prō'lĭks) *adj.* **1.** Wordy and tedious. **2.** Tending to speak or write at great length. [Middle English, from Old French *prolixe*, from Latin *prōlixus*, abundant.] —**pro·lix'i·ty** *n.* —**pro·lix'ly** *adv.*

pro·logue (prō'lôg', -lŏg') *n.* **1.** A preface to a play, opera, or literary work. **2.** An introductory act or event. [Middle English *prolog*, from Old French *prologue*, from Latin *prologus* : *pro-*, before + *legein*, to speak.]

pro·long (prə-lông', -lŏng') *tr.v.* Also **pro·lon·gate** (prə-lông'gāt', -lŏng'-), -**gat·ed, -gat·ing. 1.** To lengthen in duration; protract: *prolong a vacation.* **2.** To lengthen in extent. [Middle English *prolongen*, from Old French *prolonguer*, from Late Latin *prōlongāre* : Latin *prō-*, out, extending + *longus*, long.] —**pro'lon·ga'tion** *n.*

prom (prŏm) *n.* A ball or formal dance held for a high-school or college class. [Short for PROMENADE.]

prom·e·nade (prŏm'ə-nād', -näd') *n.* **1.** A leisurely walk, esp. one taken in a public place as a social activity. **2.** A public place for such walking. **3. a.** A formal ball. **b.** A formal march by the guests at the opening of a ball. **4.** A march performed by square dancers. —*modifier: promenade deck.* —*v.* -**nad·ed, -nad·ing.** —*intr.v.* **1.** To go on a leisurely walk. **2.** To execute a promenade in square dancing. —*tr.v.* **1.** To take a promenade along or through. **2.** To take or display on or as if on a promenade. [French, from *se promener*, to take a walk, from Late Latin *prōmināre*, to drive forward : *prō-*, forward + *mināre*, to drive, from Latin *minae*, threats.] —**prom'e·nad'er** *n.*

Pro·me·the·an (prə-mē'thē-ən) *adj.* **1.** Of or suggestive of Prometheus. **2.** Boldly creative; life-bringing. —*n.* Someone who is Promethean in manner or actions.

Pro·me·the·us (prə-mē'thē-əs, -thyōōs') *n. Gk. Myth.* A Titan who stole fire from Olympus and gave it to man.

pro·me·thi·um (prə-mē'thē-əm) *n. Symbol* **Pm** A radioactive rare-earth element prepared by fission of uranium or by neutron bombardment of neodymium, with 14 isotopes with mass numbers ranging from 141 to 154, and used as a source of beta rays. Atomic number 61; melting point 1,035°C; boiling point 2,730°C; valence 3. [After PROMETHEUS.]

prom·i·nence (prŏm'ə-nəns) *n.* **1.** The condition or quality of being prominent. **2.** Something that is prominent; a projection. **3.** A tonguelike cloud of flaming gas rising from the sun's surface.

prom·i·nent (prŏm'ə-nənt) *adj.* **1.** Projecting outward; bulging or jutting. **2.** Highly noticeable; readily evident; conspicuous. **3.** Well-known; leading; eminent: *a prominent politician.* [Latin *prōminēns*, pres. part. of *prōminēre*, to jut out, project.] —**prom'i·nent·ly** *adv.*

prom·is·cu·i·ty (prŏm'ĭ-skyōō'ĭ-tē, prō'mĭ-) *n., pl.* -**ties. 1.** The quality of being promiscuous. **2.** Promiscuous sexual intercourse. **3.** An indiscriminate mixture.

pro·mis·cu·ous (prə-mĭs'kyōō-əs) *adj.* **1.** Consisting of diverse and unrelated parts or individuals: *promiscuous tangles of weeds and flowers.* **2.** Lacking standards of selection, esp. engaging in sexual intercourse indiscriminately with many partners. **3.** Casual; random. [Latin *prōmiscuus*, mixed : *prō-*, thoroughly + *miscēre*, to mix.] —**pro·mis'cu·ous·ly** *adv.* —**pro·mis'cu·ous·ness** *n.*

prom·ise (prŏm'ĭs) *n.* **1.** A declaration assuring that one will or will not do something; a vow. **2.** Something that one undertakes to do or not do. **3.** Indication of something forthcoming: *the promise of snow in the chill wind.* **4.** Indication of future excellence or success: *a rookie pitcher who shows promise.* —*v.* -**ised, -is·ing.** —*tr.v.* **1.** To pledge or offer assurance of. **2.** To afford a basis for expecting: *clouds that promised rain.* —*intr.v.* **1.** To make a promise. **2.** To afford a basis for expectation: *Early election returns promised well for the governor.* [Middle English *promys*, from Latin *prōmissum*, past part. of *prōmittere*, to promise : *prō-*, forth + *mittere*, to send.] —**prom'is·er** *n.*

Promised Land. 1. In the Old Testament, the land of Canaan, promised to Abraham and his descendants. **2. promised land.** Any place of anticipated happiness.

prom·is·ing (prŏm'ĭ-sĭng) *adj.* Likely to develop in a desirable manner: *a promising beginning; a promising child.* —**prom'is·ing·ly** *adv.*

prom·is·so·ry (prŏm'ĭ-sôr'ē, -sōr'ē) *adj.* Containing, involving, or having the nature of a promise.

promissory note. A written promise to pay or repay a specified sum of money at a stated time or on demand.

prom·on·to·ry (prŏm'ən-tôr'ē, -tōr'ē) *n., pl.* -**ries.** A high ridge of land or rock jutting out into a body of water. [Medieval Latin *prōmontōrium*, alteration of Latin *prōmuntu-rium*, mountain ridge.]

pro·mote (prə-mōt') *tr.v.* -**mot·ed, -mot·ing. 1. a.** To raise to a more important or responsible job or rank. **b.** To advance (a student) to the next higher grade. **2.** To contribute to the progress or growth of; to further. **3.** To urge the adoption of; to advocate. **4.** To attempt to sell or popularize by advertising or by securing financial support: *promote a new product.* —See Syns at **advance.** [Middle English *promoten*, from Latin *prōmōtus*, past part. of *prōmovēre*, to advance : *prō-*, forward + *movēre*, to move.]

pro·mot·er (prə-mō'tər) *n.* **1.** An active supporter; an advocate. **2.** A finance and publicity organizer, as of a boxing match.

pro·mo·tion (prə-mō'shən) *n.* **1.** The act of promoting. **2.** An advancement in rank or responsibility. **3.** Encouragement; furtherance. **4.** Advertising or other publicity. —**pro·mo'tion·al** *adj.*

prompt (prŏmpt) *adj.* -**er, -est. 1.** On time; punctual. **2.** Done without delay: *a prompt reply.* —*tr.v.* **1.** To urge to some action; incite: *The threat of violence prompted the police to cordon off the area.* **2.** To give rise to; inspire: *The issue prompted a heated debate.* **3.** To assist with a reminder; remind: *prompt an actor.* —See Syns at **urge.** —*n.* **1.** The act of prompting or giving a cue. **2.** The information suggested; a reminder or cue. [Middle English, from Old French, from Latin *promptus*, at hand, ready, past part. of *prōmere*, to bring forth : *prō-*, forth + *emere*, to take.] —**prompt'ly** *adv.* —**promp'ti·tude** (prŏmp'tĭ-tōōd', -tyōōd') or **prompt'ness** *n.*

prompt·er (prŏmp'tər) *n.* Someone who prompts, esp. someone who reminds actors of their lines on stage.

prom·ul·gate (prŏm'əl-gāt', prō-mŭl'-) *tr.v.* -**gat·ed, -gat·ing. 1.** To make known (a decree, law, or doctrine) by public declaration; announce officially. **2.** To put (a law) into effect by formal public announcement. [From Latin *prōmul-gāre*.] —**prom'ul·ga'tion** *n.* —**prom'ul·ga'tor** *n.*

prone (prōn) *adj.* **1.** Lying with the front or face downward; prostrate. **2.** Tending; inclined: *prone to mischief.* [Middle English, from Latin *prōnus*, bending.] —**prone'ness** *n.*

prong (prông, prŏng) *n.* **1.** A sharply pointed part of a tool or instrument, such as a tine of a fork. **2.** Any sharply pointed projection. —*tr.v.* To pierce with a prong. [Middle English *pronge*, forked instrument.]

pronged (prôngd, prŏngd) *adj.* Having prongs.

prong·horn (prông′hôrn′, prŏng′-) *n., pl.* **-horns** or **-horn.** A small deer, *Antilocapra americana*, that resembles an antelope and has small forked horns, found on western North American plains.

pronghorn

pro·nom·i·nal (prō-nŏm′ə-nəl) *adj.* Of, resembling, or functioning as a pronoun. *His* in *his choice* is a pronominal adjective. **—pro·nom′i·nal·ly** *adv.*

pro·noun (prō′noun′) *n.* One of a class of words that function as substitutes for nouns or noun phrases and denote persons or things asked for, previously specified, or understood from the context.

pro·nounce (prə-nouns′) *v.* **-nounced, -nounc·ing.** —*tr.v.* **1.** To produce (a word or speech sound); articulate. **2.** To transcribe (a word) in phonetic symbols. **3.** To state officially and formally; declare: *pronounced them man and wife.* **4.** To declare to be in a specified condition: *tasted the dish and pronounced it good.* —*intr.v.* **1.** To declare one's opinion. **2.** To articulate words. [Middle English *pronouncen*, from Old French *prononcier*, from Latin *prōnuntiāre*, to declare : *prō-*, forth, in public + *nuntiāre*, to declare, from *nuntius*, message.] **—pro·nounce′a·ble** *adj.* **—pro·nounc′er** *n.*

pro·nounced (prə-nounst′) *adj.* Distinct; strongly marked: *a pronounced limp.* **—pro·nounc′ed·ly** (-noun′sĭd-lē) *adv.*

pro·nounce·ment (prə-nouns′mənt) *n.* **1.** A formal declaration. **2.** An authoritative statement.

pron·to (prŏn′tō) *adv. Informal.* Without delay; quickly. [Spanish, from Latin *promptus*, prompt.]

pro·nun·ci·a·men·to (prō-nŭn′sē-ə-měn′tō) *n., pl.* **-tos.** An authoritative declaration; proclamation. [Spanish, *pronunciamiento*, pronouncement.]

pro·nun·ci·a·tion (prə-nŭn′sē-ā′shən) *n.* **1.** The act or manner of pronouncing words. **2.** A phonetic representation of a given word.

proof (prōōf) *n.* **1.** The evidence establishing the truth or validity of something: *offered proof of his identity.* **2.** Conclusive demonstration of something. **3.** The act of testing the truth or validity of something by experiment or trial: *put one's beliefs to the proof.* **4.** *Law.* The whole body of evidence that determines the verdict or judgment in a case. **5. a.** A trial sheet of printed material, checked against the original manuscript for errors. **b.** A trial impression of an engraved plate, stone, or block. **c.** A trial print of a photograph. **6.** The alcoholic content of a liquor, expressed as a given number of parts of alcohol per 200 parts of liquor. Liquor marked 100 proof is 50 per cent alcohol. —*adj.* **1.** Fully or successfully resistant; impervious: *building materials that are proof against fire.* **2.** Of standard alcoholic strength. **3.** Used in proving or making corrections. —*tr.v.* **1.** To proofread (copy). **2.** To make resistant or impervious: *chambers that have been proofed against light and noise.* —*intr.v.* To proofread. [Middle English *prove*, from Old French *preove*, from Late Latin *proba*, from Latin *probāre*, to test.]

–proof. A suffix meaning impervious to or able to resist or withstand: **waterproof.** [From PROOF (adj.).]

proof·read (prōōf′rēd′) *v.* **-read** (-rĕd′), **-read·ing.** —*tr.v.* To read and mark corrections in (printed material). —*intr.v.* To correct a printer's proof while reading against the original manuscript. **—proof′read′er** *n.*

prop[1] (prŏp) *n.* **1.** A vertical support used to keep something from falling. **2.** Someone or something depended on for support or assistance. —*tr.v.* **propped, prop·ping.** **1.** To keep from falling or failing. **2.** To place in a leaning or resting position: *She propped her chin in her hands.* [Middle English *proppe.*]

prop[2] (prŏp) *n.* A stage property.

prop[3] (prŏp) *n. Informal.* A propeller.

prop·a·gan·da (prŏp′ə-găn′də) *n.* **1.** The communication of a given doctrine to large numbers of people, esp. by constant repetition. **2.** Ideas, information, or other material distributed for the purpose of winning people over to a given doctrine, often without regard to truth or fairness. [From *Sacra Congregatio de Propaganda Fide,* Sacred Congregation for Propagating the Faith, an organization of the Roman Catholic Church responsible for missions.] **—prop′a·gan′dist** *n.* **—prop′a·gan·dis′tic** *adj.*

prop·a·gan·dize (prŏp′ə-găn′dīz′) *v.* **-dized, -diz·ing.** —*tr.v.* **1.** To spread (a doctrine or opinion) by means of propaganda. **2.** To subject (a person or group of persons) to propaganda. —*intr.v.* To spread propaganda.

prop·a·gate (prŏp′ə-gāt′) *v.* **-gat·ed, -gat·ing.** —*tr.v.* **1.** To cause (animals or plants) to multiply or breed. **2.** To breed (offspring). **3.** To transmit (characteristics) from one generation to another. **4.** To make known; publicize. **5.** *Physics.* To cause (light waves, heat, etc.) to move through a medium; to transmit. —*intr.v.* To breed or multiply. [From Latin *prōpāgāre*, from *prōpāgo*, shoot, offspring.] **—prop′a·ga′tive** *adj.* **—prop′a·ga′tor** *n.*

prop·a·ga·tion (prŏp′ə-gā′shən) *n.* **1.** Increase or spread, as by natural reproduction. **2.** Dissemination, as of a belief: *propagation of the Gospel.* **—prop′a·ga′tion·al** *adj.*

pro·pane (prō′pān′) *n.* A colorless gas, C_3H_8, found in natural gas and petroleum, and widely used as a fuel. [PROP(I-ONIC ACID) + -ANE.]

pro·pel (prə-pěl′) *tr.v.* **-pelled, -pel·ling.** **1.** To cause to move or continue in motion: *the engines that propel a jet airplane.* **2.** To urge ahead; impel. [Middle English *propellen*, from Latin *prōpellere* : *prō-*, forward + *pellere*, to drive.]

pro·pel·lant (prə-pěl′ənt) Also **pro·pel·lent.** —*n.* Something that propels or provides thrust, as an explosive charge or a rocket fuel. —*adj.* Serving to propel.

pro·pel·ler (prə-pěl′ər) *n.* Also **pro·pel·lor.** A device for propelling aircraft or boats, esp. one with radiating blades mounted on a revolving power-driven shaft. Also called **screw** and **screw propeller.**

pro·pen·si·ty (prə-pěn′sĭ-tē) *n., pl.* **-ties.** An innate inclination; tendency; bent. [From obs. *propense,* inclined, from Latin *prōpensus,* past part. of *prōpendēre,* to be inclined.]

prop·er (prŏp′ər) *adj.* **1.** Suitable; appropriate: *the proper tools for the job.* **2.** Normally or characteristically belonging to the person or thing in question: *regained his proper frame of mind.* **3.** Called for by rules or conventions; correct. **4.** Strictly following rules or conventions, esp. in social behavior; seemly. **5.** In the strict sense of the term. **6.** Out-and-out; thorough: *a proper whipping.* [Middle English *propre,* one's own, correct, from Old French, from Latin *proprius,* one's own, particular.] **—prop′er·ly** *adv.*

proper fraction. A fraction in which the numerator is less or of lower degree than the denominator.

proper noun. A noun that is the name of a particular person, place, or thing. Also called **proper name.**

prop·er·tied (prŏp′ər-tēd) *adj.* Owning land or securities, esp. as a principal source of income.

prop·er·ty (prŏp′ər-tē) *n., pl.* **-ties.** **1.** Something or a number of things owned by someone. **2.** Land owned by someone. **3.** Something that one has the right to use: *A contribution of one scientist becomes the property of scientists to follow.* **4.** A quality or attribute, esp. one that serves to define or describe something: *the chemical properties of a metal.* **5.** Any movable object, except costumes and scenery, that appears on the stage during a dramatic performance. [Middle English *proprete,* from Old French *propriete,* from Latin *proprietās,* ownership, peculiarity, from *proprius,* own, particular, proper.]

pro·phase (prō′fāz′) *n.* The first stage in cell division by mitosis, during which chromosomes form from the chromatin of the nucleus. [Pro-, before + PHASE.]

proph·e·cy (prŏf′ĭ-sē) *n., pl.* **-cies.** **1.** A declaration or warning of something to come; a vivid, pointed, or solemn prediction. **2.** The inspired utterance of a prophet, viewed as a declaration of divine will. [Middle English *prophecie*, from Old French *prophecie*, from Latin *prophētīa*, from Greek *prophēteia*, from *prophētēs*, prophet.]

proph·e·sy (prŏf'ĭ-sī') *v.* **-sied, -sy·ing.** —*tr.v.* **1.** To reveal by divine inspiration. **2.** To predict. **3.** To prefigure; foreshow. —*intr.v.* **1.** To reveal the will or message of God. **2.** To predict the future. [Middle English *prophecien*, from Old French *prophecier*, from *prophecie*, prophecy.] —**proph'e·si'er** *n.*

proph·et (prŏf'ĭt) *n.* **1.** A person who speaks by divine inspiration or as the interpreter through whom a divinity expresses his will. **2.** A predictor or soothsayer. **3.** The chief spokesman of some movement or cause. **4. the Prophet.** *Islam.* Mohammed. **5. the Prophets.** The prophetic writings of the Hebrew Scriptures. [Middle English, from Old French, from Latin *prophēta*, from Greek *prophētēs*, interpreter for the gods or oracles : *pro-*, before + *phanai*, to say.]

proph·et·ess (prŏf'ĭ-tĭs) *n.* A female prophet.

pro·phet·ic (prə-fĕt'ĭk) or **pro·phet·i·cal** (-ĭ-kəl) *adj.* **1.** Of or belonging to a prophet or prophecy: *phophetic writings.* **2.** Of the nature of prophecy: *a warning that proved prophetic.* —**pro·phet'i·cal·ly** *adv.*

pro·phy·lac·tic (prō'fə-lăk'tĭk, prŏf'ə-) *adj.* Acting to defend against or prevent something, esp. disease; protective. —*n.* A prophylactic medicine, device, or measure, esp. a condom. [Greek *prophulaktikos* : *pro-*, before + *phulax*, a guard.] —**pro'phy·lac'ti·cal·ly** *adv.*

pro·phy·lax·is (prō'fə-lăk'sĭs, prŏf'ə-) *n.*, *pl.* **-lax·es** (-lăk'sēz'). The prevention of or protective treatment for disease. [New Latin, from Greek *prophulaktikos*, prophylactic.]

pro·pin·qui·ty (prə-pĭng'kwĭ-tē) *n.* **1.** Nearness; proximity. **2.** Kinship. **3.** Similarity in nature. [Middle English *propinquite*, from Latin *propinquitās*, from *propinquus*, near.]

pro·pi·ti·ate (prō-pĭsh'ē-āt') *tr.v.* **-at·ed, -at·ing.** To soothe and win over; appease: *"Rain had to be prayed for and gods and priests propitiated"* (Lesley B. Simpson). [From Latin *propitiāre*, from *propitius*, propitious.] —**pro·pi'ti·a'tion** (-pĭsh'ē-ā'shən) *n.* —**pro·pi'ti·a'tor** *n.*

pro·pi·ti·a·to·ry (prō-pĭsh'ē-ə-tôr'ē, -tōr'ē) *adj.* Of or offered in propitiation; conciliatory.

pro·pi·tious (prō-pĭsh'əs) *adj.* **1.** Favorable; auspicious: *a propitious time to apply for a loan.* **2.** Kindly; gracious. —See Syns at **favorable.** [Middle English *propycyous*, from Old French *propicius*, from Latin *propitius*, favorable, kind.] —**pro·pi'tious·ly** *adv.* —**pro·pi'tious·ness** *n.*

pro·po·nent (prə-pō'nənt) *n.* A supporter; an advocate. [Latin *prōpōnēns*, pres. part. of *prōpōnere*, to propose.]

pro·por·tion (prə-pôr'shən, -pōr'-) *n.* **1.** A part considered in relation to the whole. **2.** A relationship between things or parts of things with respect to comparative magnitude, quantity, or degree. **3.** A relationship between quantities, such that if one varies, another varies in a manner dependent on the first; ratio: *"We do not always find visible happiness in proportion to visible virtue"* (Samuel Johnson). **4.** Harmonious relation; balance; symmetry: *a face swollen out of proportion.* **5.** Often **proportions.** Dimensions; size. **6.** *Math.* A relation of equality between two ratios. —*tr.v.* **1.** To adjust so that proper relations between parts are attained. **2.** To form with symmetry. [Middle English *proporcioun*, from Old French *proportion*, from Latin *prō portiōne*, "for (its) share," proportionally.]

pro·por·tion·al (prə-pôr'shə-nəl, -pōr'-) *adj.* **1.** Corresponding in size, amount, or degree; in proportion. **2.** *Math.* Related by a constant factor. **3.** Determined or calculated by means of fixed proportions: *a proportional share of the profits.* —*n.* *Math.* A term in a proportion. —**pro·por'tion·al'i·ty** (-năl'ĭ-tē) *n.* —**pro·por'tion·al·ly** *adv.*

proportional representation. Representation of all parties in a legislature in proportion to their popular vote.

pro·por·tion·ate (prə-pôr'shə-nĭt, -pōr'-) *adj.* Being in due proportion; proportional. —*tr.v.* (prə-pôr'shə-nāt', -pōr'-) **-at·ed, -at·ing.** To make proportionate. —**pro·por'tion·ate·ly** *adv.* —**pro·por'tion·ate·ness** *n.*

pro·pos·al (prə-pō'zəl) *n.* **1.** The act of proposing. **2.** A plan or scheme that is proposed; suggestion. **3.** An offer of marriage.

pro·pose (prə-pōz') *v.* **-posed, -pos·ing.** —*tr.v.* **1.** To put forward for consideration, discussion, or adoption; suggest: *propose new methods.* **2.** To present or nominate (a person) for a position, office, or membership. **3.** To offer (a toast to be drunk). —*intr.v.* To form or make a proposal, esp. of marriage. [Middle English *proposen*, from Old French *proposer*, from Latin *prōpositus*, past part. of *prōpōnere*, to put forth : *prō*, forward + *pōnere*, to place.] —**pro·pos'er** *n.*

prop·o·si·tion (prŏp'ə-zĭsh'ən) *n.* **1.** An offer; proposal. **2.** A plan or scheme offered for consideration. **3.** A statement or idea advanced tentatively or against opposition; a hypothesis. **4. a.** A mathematical statement, as the statement of a theorem. **b.** A statement in logic, esp. one that satisfies certain rules or is constructed in a certain form. **5.** A matter to be handled or dealt with; an undertaking. —*tr.v.* *Informal.* To make a proposal to, esp. a sexual proposal. [Middle English *proposicioun*, from Old French *proposition*, from Latin *prōpositiō*, from *prōpōnere*, to propose.] —**prop'o·si'tion·al** *adj.* —**prop'o·si'tion·al·ly** *adv.*

pro·pound (prə-pound') *tr.v.* To put forward for consideration; set forth. [Middle English *proponen*, from Latin *prōpōnere*, to propose.] —**pro·pound'er** *n.*

pro·pri·e·tar·y (prə-prī'ĭ-tĕr'ē) *adj.* **1.** Of or belonging to a proprietor: *proprietary rights.* **2.** Exclusively owned; private. **3.** Exclusively made and sold by a private individual or corporation under a trademark or patent. —*n.*, *pl.* **-ies.** **1.** A proprietor. **2.** A group of proprietors. **3.** Ownership; proprietorship. **4.** *U.S. History.* The governor of a proprietary colony. **5.** A proprietary medicine. [Late Latin *proprietārius*, from Latin *proprietās*, property, propriety.]

proprietary colony. Any of certain early North American colonies organized in the 17th cent. in territories granted by the English Crown to one or more Lords Proprietary, who had full governing rights.

pro·pri·e·tor (prə-prī'ĭ-tər) *n.* **1.** A person who has legal title to something; an owner. **2.** The owner or owner-manager of a business or other institution. [Alteration of PROPRIETARY (noun).] —**pro·pri'e·tor·ship'** *n.*

pro·pri·e·ty (prə-prī'ĭ-tē) *n.*, *pl.* **-ties. 1.** The quality or condition of being proper. **2.** Conformity to prevailing rules and conventions, esp. in social conduct; seemliness. **3. the proprieties.** The rules and conventions of polite social behavior. —See Syns at **manner(s).** [Middle English *propriete*, ownership, one's own nature, from Old French, from Latin *proprietās*, from *proprius*, proper.]

pro·pri·o·cep·tor (prō'prē-ə-sĕp'tər) *n.* A sensory receptor, chiefly in muscles, tendons, and joints, that responds to stimuli arising within the organism. [Latin *proprius*, one's own + (RE)CEPTOR.] —**pro'pri·o·cep'tive** *adj.*

pro·pul·sion (prə-pŭl'shən) *n.* **1.** The process of driving or propelling. **2.** A driving or propelling force. [Medieval Latin *prōpulsiō*, from Latin *prōpulsus*, past part. of *propellere*, to drive forward, propel.] —**pro·pul'sive** or **pro·pul'so·ry** *adj.*

pro·pyl (prō'pəl) *n.* *Chem.* A univalent organic radical with composition C_3H_7, derived from propane. [PROP(IONIC ACID) + -YL.]

pro·pyl·ene (prō'pə-lēn') *n.* A flammable gas, $CH_3CH{:}CH_2$, derived from petroleum hydrocarbon cracking and used in organic synthesis. Also called **propene.** [PROPYL + -ENE.]

propylene glycol. A colorless viscous hygroscopic liquid, $CH_3CHOHCH_2OH$, used in antifreeze solutions, in hydraulic fluids, and as a solvent.

pro ra·ta (prō rā'tə, răt'ə, rä'tə). In proportion. [Latin *pro rata (parte)*, "according to the calculated (share).")]

pro·rate (prō-rāt', prō'rāt') *v.* **-rat·ed, -rat·ing.** —*tr.v.* To divide, distribute, or assess proportionately: *prorating the phone bills among the roommates.* —*intr.v.* To settle affairs on the basis of proportional distribution. [From PRO RATA.] —**pro·rat'a·ble** *adj.* —**pro·ra'tion** *n.*

pro·rogue (prō-rōg') *tr.v.* **-rogued, -rogu·ing.** To discontinue a session of (a parliament or similar body). [Middle English *prorogen*, from Old French *proroguer*, from Latin *prōrogāre*, to prolong : *prō-*, forward, in public + *rogāre*, to ask.] —**pro'ro·ga'tion** *n.*

pro·sa·ic (prō-zā'ĭk) *adj.* **1. a.** Of or like prose; not poetic. **b.** Matter-of-fact; straightforward. **2.** Lacking in imagination or interest; dull; ordinary: *a prosaic film; a prosaic*

---

mind. [Late Latin *prōsaicus,* from Latin *prōsa,* prose.]
—**pro·sa'i·cal·ly** *adv.*

pro·sce·ni·um (prō-sē'nē-əm) *n., pl.* **-ni·a** (-nē-ə). **1.** In the modern theater, the area located between the curtain and the orchestra. **2.** In the ancient theater, the stage, located between the background and the orchestra. [Latin, from Greek *proskēnion* : *pro-,* before + *skēnē,* tent.]

pro·scribe (prō-skrīb') *tr.v.* **-scribed, -scrib·ing. 1.** To denounce or condemn. **2.** To prohibit; forbid. **3.** To banish; outlaw. —See Syns at **forbid.** [Latin *prōscrībere* : *prō-,* in front, publicly + *scrībere,* to write.] —**pro·scrib'er** *n.*

pro·scrip·tion (prō-skrĭp'shən) *n.* **1.** The act of proscribing; prohibition. **2.** The condition of being proscribed; outlawry. —**pro·scrip'tive** *adj.* —**pro·scrip'tive·ly** *adv.*

prose (prōz) *n.* **1.** Ordinary speech or writing as distinguished from verse. **2.** Commonplace expression or quality. —*adj.* **1.** Written in or charactistic of prose: *a prose narrative; prose rhythms.* **2.** Commonplace; dry. —*intr.v.* **prosed, pros·ing.** To speak or write in a dull, tiresome style. [Middle English, from Old French, from Latin *(ōrātiō),* "straightforward discourse," from *prōsus,* straightforward, direct, from *prōversus,* past part. of *prōvertere,* to turn forward : *prō-,* forward + *vertere,* to turn.]

pros·e·cute (prŏs'ĭ-kyōōt') *v.* **-cut·ed, -cut·ing.** —*tr.v.* **1. a.** To initiate or conduct a legal action against (someone). **b.** To present (a case, crime, suit, etc.) before a court of law for punishment or settlement. **2.** To press to completion; pursue determinedly: *prosecuting a war.* **3.** To engage in; perform or practice: *prosecuting his occupation.* —*intr.v.* **1.** To initiate and conduct legal proceedings. **2.** To act as prosecutor. [Middle English *prosecuten,* to follow, from Latin *prōsecūtus,* past part. of *prōsequī,* to follow : *prō-,* forward + *sequī,* to follow.]

prosecuting attorney. An attorney empowered to prosecute cases on behalf of a government.

pros·e·cu·tion (prŏs'ĭ-kyōō'shən) *n.* **1.** The act of prosecuting or the condition of being prosecuted, esp. the institution and conduct of a legal proceeding. **3. the prosecution.** The party, usu. a government, that brings legal action against a person accused of a crime.

pros·e·cu·tor (prŏs'ĭ-kyōō'tər) *n.* **1.** Someone who initiates and carries out a legal action, esp. criminal proceedings. **2.** A prosecuting attorney.

pros·e·lyte (prŏs'ə-līt') *n.* A new convert to a religion or doctrine. —*v.* Var. of **proselytize.** [Middle English *proselite,* from Late Latin *prosēlytus,* from Greek *prosēlutos,* stranger, religious convert.]

pros·e·ly·tism (prŏs'ə-lə-tĭz'əm, -lĭ-tĭz'əm) *n.* **1.** The practice of proselytizing. **2.** The condition of being a proselyte; conversion.

pros·e·ly·tize (prŏs'ə-lə-tīz') *v.* **-tized, -tiz·ing.** Also **pros·e·lyte.** —*intr.v.* To make proselytes. —*tr.v.* To convert from one belief or faith to another. —**pros'e·ly·tiz'er** *n.*

Pro·ser·pi·na (prə-sûr'pə-nə) *n.* Also **Pros·er·pi·ne** (prŏs'ər-pīn', prə-sûr'pə-nē). *Rom. Myth.* The wife of Pluto and daughter of Ceres; the goddess of the underworld, corresponding to the Greek Persephone.

pro·sit (prō'sĭt, prōst) *interj.* To your health. Used as a drinking toast. [German, from Latin, "may it be advantageous."]

pros·o·dy (prŏs'ə-dē) *n.* **1.** The study of the metrical structures of verse. **2.** A particular system of versification. [Middle English *prosodye,* from Latin *prosōdia,* tone or accent of a syllable, from Greek *prosōidia,* modulation of voice : *pros-,* to, in addition to + *ōidē,* song.] —**pro·sod'ic** (prə-sŏd'ĭk) *adj.* —**pro·sod'i·cal·ly** *adv.*

pros·pect (prŏs'pĕkt') *n.* **1.** Something expected or forseen; expectation. **2. prospects.** Chances for success. **3. a.** A potential customer or purchaser. **b.** A candidate deemed likely to succeed. **4.** The direction in which an object, such as a building, faces; an outlook. **5.** Something presented to the eye; a scene; view: *a pleasant prospect.* —*tr.v.* To search for or explore (a region) for gold or other mineral deposits. —*intr.v.* To explore or search about, esp. for mineral deposits. [Middle English *prospecte,* from Latin *prōspectus,* distant view, vista, from *prōspicere,* to look forward : *prō-,* forward + *specere,* to look.]

pro·spec·tive (prə-spĕk'tĭv) *adj.* **1.** Looking forward in time; characterized by foresight: *a prospective view of the*

nation's needs. **2.** Likely to occur; expected: *prospective budget cuts.* —**pro·spec'tive·ly** *adv.*

pros·pec·tor (prŏs'pĕk'tər) *n.* Someone who explores an area for natural deposits, such as gold or oil.

pro·spec·tus (prə-spĕk'təs) *n.* A printed description of a proposed business or other venture, sent out to gain interest or support for the venture. [Latin, prospect.]

pros·per (prŏs'pər) *intr.v.* To be fortunate or successful; thrive. —*tr.v. Archaic.* To cause to thrive. [Middle English *prosperen,* from Old French *prosperer,* from Latin *prosperāre,* to make fortunate, from *prosperus,* fortunate.]
   Syns: **prosper, boom, flourish, thrive** *v. Core meaning:* To fare well (*a prospering industry*).

pros·per·i·ty (prŏ-spĕr'ĭ-tē) *n., pl.* **-ties.** The condition of being prosperous, esp. having financial success.

pros·per·ous (prŏs'pər-əs) *adj.* **1.** Having success; flourishing. **2.** Well-to-do; well-off. **3.** Propitious; favorable. —**pros'per·ous·ly** *adv.* —**pros'per·ous·ness** *n.*

pros·ta·glan·din (prŏs'tə-glăn'dĭn) *n.* Any of numerous fatty acids that are produced in animals, are considered to be hormones, and are implicated in various physiological activities, as regulation of blood pressure. [PROSTA(TE) GLAND + -IN.]

pros·tate (prŏs'tāt') *n.* A gland in male mammals composed of muscular and glandular tissue that surrounds the urethra at the bladder. Also called **prostate gland.** [New Latin *prostata,* from Greek *prostatēs* : *pro-,* in front + *histanai,* to cause to stand.] —**pros'tate'** or **pro·stat'ic** (prō-stăt'ĭk) *adj.*

pros·the·sis (prŏs-thē'sĭs) *n., pl.* **-ses** (-sēz'). **1.** The artificial replacement of a limb or other part of the body. **2.** An artificial device used in such replacement. [Late Latin, addition of a letter or syllable, from Greek, addition : *pros-,* in addition + *tithenai,* to place, put.] —**pros·thet'ic** (-thĕt'ĭk) *adj.* —**pros·thet'i·cal·ly** *adv.*

pros·ti·tute (prŏs'tĭ-tōōt', -tyōōt') *n.* **1.** Someone who performs sexual acts with others for pay. **2.** Someone who debases himself or his abilities for money or an unworthy motive. —*tr.v.* **-tut·ed, -tut·ing. 1.** To offer (oneself or another) for sexual acts in return for pay. **2.** To sell (oneself or one's talents) to an unworthy cause. [Latin *prōstitūta,* from *prōstituere,* to prostitute : *prō-,* forth, in public + *statuere,* to set, place, from *stare,* to stand.]

pros·ti·tu·tion (prŏs'tĭ-tōō'shən, -tyōō'-) *n.* **1.** The practice or work of a prostitute. **2.** The act of prostituting; debasement: *the prostitution of an artist's talents.*

pros·trate (prŏs'trāt') *tr.v.* **-trat·ed, -trat·ing. 1.** To make (oneself) bow or kneel down in humility or adoration. **2.** To throw down flat. **3.** To weaken or render helpless; overcome: *a disease that prostrates its victims.* —*adj.* **1.** Lying face down, as in submission or adoration. **2.** Lying down full-length: *a sleeper prostrate on the floor.* **3.** Physically or emotionally incapacitated; helpless: *prostrate with fear.* **4.** *Bot.* Growing flat along the ground. [Middle English *prostrat,* lying face down, from Latin *prōstrātus,* past part. of *prōsternere,* to prostrate : *prō-,* down before + *sternere,* to stretch out.] —**pros'tra'tor** *n.*

pros·tra·tion (prŏ-strā'shən) *n.* **1. a.** The act of prostrating oneself. **b.** The condition of being prostrate. **2.** Total exhaustion.

pros·y (prō'zē) *adj.* **-i·er, -i·est. 1.** Matter-of-fact; dry; prosaic. **2.** Dull; commonplace. —**pros'i·ness** *n.*

prot-. Var. of **proto-.**

pro·tac·tin·i·um (prō'tăk-tĭn'ē-əm) *n. Symbol* **Pa** A rare radioactive element chemically similar to uranium, having 12 known isotopes, the most common of which is Pa 231 with a half-life of 32,480 years. Atomic number 91; melting point 1,230°C; specific gravity 15.37; valence 4 or 5. [PROT(O)- + ACTINIUM .]

pro·tag·o·nist (prō-tăg'ə-nĭst) *n.* **1.** The leading character in a drama or other literary work. **2.** Any leading or principal figure. [Greek *prōtagōnistēs* : *prot(o)-,* foremost, first + *agōnistēs,* actor, from *agōnia,* a contest, from *agein,* to lead.]

pro·te·an (prō'tē-ən, prō-tē'-) *adj.* Readily taking on different shapes or forms; variable: *a protean talent.* [From PROTEUS.]

pro·te·ase (prō'tē-ās', -āz') *n.* An enzyme that catalyzes the hydrolytic breakdown of proteins. [PROTE(IN) + -ASE.]

pro·tect (prə-tĕkt´) *tr.v.* **1.** To keep from harm, attack, or injury; to guard. **2.** To help (domestic industry) with tariffs on imported goods. —See Syns at **defend.** [Latin *prōtectus,* past part. of *prōtegere,* to protect : *prō-,* in front + *tegere,* to cover.]

pro·tec·tion (prə-tĕk´shən) *n.* **1.** The act of protecting. **2.** The condition of being protected. **3.** Someone or something that protects. **4.** A tariff system protecting domestic industries from foreign competition. **5.** Money extorted by racketeers in exchange for a promise of freedom from molestation.

pro·tec·tion·ism (prə-tĕk´shə-nĭz´əm) *n.* The theory or system of protecting domestic industries from foreign competition by means of tariffs. —**pro·tec´tion·ist** *n.*

pro·tec·tive (prə-tĕk´tĭv) *adj.* Adapted or intended to protect: *a protective coat of paint.* —*n.* Something that protects. —**pro·tec´tive·ly** *adv.* —**pro·tec´tive·ness** *n.*

pro·tec·tor (prə-tĕk´tər) *n.* **1.** A person who protects; guardian. **2.** A title given to a person ruling during the absence, minority, or illness of a monarch. —**pro·tec´tor·ship´** *n.*

pro·tec·tor·ate (prə-tĕk´tər-ĭt) *n.* **1. a.** A relationship of protection and partial control assumed by a nation over a dependent foreign country. **b.** A dependent country or region in such a relationship. **2.** The rule, office, or period of rule of a protector.

pro·té·gé (prō´tə-zhā´) *n.* A person guided in his career by another, more influential or experienced person. [French, from *protéger,* to protect, from Latin *prōtegere.*]

pro·tein (prō´tēn´, -tē-ĭn) *n.* Any of a group of complex nitrogenous organic compounds of high molecular weight that contain amino acids as their basic structural units and that occur in all living matter and are essential for the growth and repair of animal tissue. [French *protéine,* "primary substance (to the body)," from Late Greek *proteios,* primary, from Greek *prōtos,* first.] —**pro´tein·a·ceous** (prōt´n-ā´shəs, prō´tē-ə-nā´-) *adj.*

pro tem (prō tĕm´). Pro tempore.

pro tem·po·re (prō tĕm´pə-rē). *Latin.* For the time being; temporarily.

proteo-. A prefix meaning protein: **proteolysis.** [From PROTEIN.]

pro·te·ol·y·sis (prō´tē-ŏl´ĭ-sĭs) *n.* The breaking down of proteins into simpler, soluble substances, as in digestion. —**pro´te·o·lyt´ic** (-ə-lĭt´ĭk) *adj.*

pro·te·ose (prō´tē-ōs´, -ōz´) *n.* Any of several water-soluble proteins produced during digestion.

Prot·er·o·zo·ic (prŏt´ər-ə-zō´ĭk, prō´tər-) *n.* Also **Proterozoic era.** A geologic era extending from the middle of the Precambrian era to the beginning of the Paleozoic era, ending about 600 million years ago. —*modifier: a Proterozoic fossil.* [Greek *proteros,* earlier, anterior + -ZOIC.]

pro·test (prə-tĕst´, prō-, prō´tĕst´) *tr.v.* **1.** To express strong objection to, esp. in a formal statement or public demonstration. **2.** To promise or affirm earnestly: *protested her innocence.* **3.** *Law.* To declare (a bill) dishonored or refused. —*intr.v.* **1.** To express strong objection. **2.** To make an earnest avowal or affirmation. —*n.* (prō´tĕst´). **1.** A formal expression of disapproval or objection. **2.** Any individual or collective gesture or display of disapproval. **3.** *Law.* A formal statement declaring that the debtor has refused to accept or honor a bill. [Middle English *protesten,* from Old French *protester,* from Latin *prōtestārī* : *prō-,* forth, in public + *testis,* a witness, will.] —**pro·test´er** *n.* —**pro·test´ing·ly** *adv.*

Prot·es·tant (prŏt´ĭ-stənt) *n.* **1.** Any Christian belonging to a sect descending from those that broke away from the Roman Catholic Church in the 16th cent. **2. protestant.** A person who protests. —*adj.* Of Protestants or Protestantism.

Prot·es·tant·ism (prŏt´ĭ-stən-tĭz´əm) *n.* **1.** The beliefs and practices of Protestants. **2.** Protestant churches or their membership in general.

prot·es·ta·tion (prŏt´ĭ-stā´shən, prō´tĭ-) *n.* **1.** An emphatic declaration. **2.** A strong or formal dissent.

Pro·te·us (prō´tē-əs, -tyōōs´) *n.* *Gk. Myth.* A sea god who could change his shape at will.

pro·thal·lus (prō-thăl´əs) *n., pl.* **-thal·li** (-thăl´ī´). Also **pro·thal·li·um** (-thăl´ē-əm) *pl.* **-li·a** (-ē-ə). *Bot.* A small, flat mass of tissue produced by a germinating spore of ferns and related plants that bears sexual organs and eventually develops into a mature plant. [PRO- (in front of) + *thallos,* a shoot.] —**pro·thal´li·al** *adj.*

pro·throm·bin (prō-thrŏm´bĭn) *n.* A plasma protein that is converted into thrombin during blood coagulation. [PRO- (before) + THROMBIN.]

pro·tist (prō´tĭst) *n.* *Biol.* Any of the unicellular organisms of the kingdom Protista, which includes protozoans, bacteria, some algae, and other forms not readily classified as either plants or animals. [From Greek *prōtista,* from *prōtos,* first.]

proto- or **prot-.** A prefix meaning first in rank or time: **protoplasm, prototype.** [From Greek *prōtos,* first.]

pro·to·col (prō´tə-kôl´, -kōl´, -kŏl´) *n.* **1.** The forms of ceremony and etiquette observed by diplomats and heads of state. **2.** The first copy of a treaty or other document prior to its ratification. **3.** Any preliminary draft or record of a transaction. [Old French *prothocole,* from Medieval Latin *protocollum,* from Late Greek *prōtokollon,* first sheet glued to a papyrus roll, bearing a table of contents : *prōtos-,* first + *kolla,* glue.]

pro·ton (prō´tŏn´) *n.* A stable, positively charged subatomic particle in the baryon family with a mass 1,836 times that of the electron. [Greek *prōton,* first.] —**pro·ton´ic** *adj.*

pro·to·plasm (prō´tə-plăz´əm) *n.* A complex, jellylike colloidal substance conceived of as constituting the living matter of plant and animal cells, and performing the basic life functions. —**pro´to·plas´mic** (-plăz´mĭk) or **pro´to·plas´mal** (-məl) or **pro´to·plas·mat´ic** (-plăz-măt´ĭk) *adj.*

pro·to·type (prō´tə-tīp´) *n.* **1.** A first or early example of something, on which later examples are based or judged. **2.** The first full-scale model to be constructed of a new type of vehicle, machine, device, etc. —**pro´to·typ´al** (-tī´pəl) or **pro´to·typ´ic** (-tĭp´ĭk) or **pro´to·typ´i·cal** *adj.*

pro·to·zo·an (prō´tə-zō´ən) *n., pl.* **-ans** or **-zo·a** (-zō´ə). Any of the single-celled, usu. microscopic organisms of the phylum or subkingdom Protozoa, which includes the most primitive forms of animal life. [PROTO- + -ZOAN.] —**pro´to·zo´an** or **pro´to·zo´ic** (-zō´ĭk) *adj.*

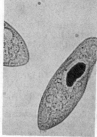

protozoan   protractor

pro·tract (prō-trăkt´, prə-) *tr.v.* **1.** To draw out or lengthen in time; prolong. **2.** To draw to scale by means of a scale and protractor; to plot. **3.** *Anat.* To extend or protrude. [Latin *prōtractus,* past part. of *prōtrahere,* to lengthen : *prō-,* out, extending + *trahere,* to drag, pull.] —**pro·tract´ed·ly** (-trăk´tĭd-lē) *adv.* —**pro·tract´ed·ness** *n.* —**pro·trac´tion** *n.*

pro·trac·tile (prō-trăk´tĭl, -tīl´) *adj.* Capable of being extended: *protractile claws.* —**pro´trac·til´i·ty** *n.*

pro·trac·tor (prō-trăk´tər) *n.* **1.** A semicircular instrument for measuring and constructing angles. **2.** An adjustable pattern used by tailors.

pro·trude (prō-trōōd´) *v.* **-trud·ed, -trud·ing.** —*tr.v.* To push or thrust outward. —*intr.v.* To jut out; project. [Latin *prōtrūdere* : *prō-,* forth + *trūdere,* to thrust.]

pro·tru·sion (prō-trōō´zhən) *n.* **1. a.** The act of protruding. **b.** The condition of being protruded. **2.** Something that protrudes.

pro·tru·sive (prō-trōō´sĭv, -zĭv) *adj.* Tending to protrude; protruding. —**pro·tru´sive·ly** *adv.*

pro·tu·ber·ance (prō-tōō´bər-əns, -tyōō´-) *n.* **1.** Something that protrudes; a bulge or knob. **2.** The condition of being protuberant.

pro·tu·ber·ant (prō-tōō′bər-ənt, -tyōō′-) *adj.* Swelling outward; bulging. [Late Latin *prōtūberāns,* pres. part. of *prōtūberāre,* to swell out.] **—pro·tu′ber·ant·ly** *adv.*

proud (proud) *adj.* **-er, -est. 1. a.** Feeling pleasure and satisfaction over something one owns, makes, does, or is a part of. **b.** Arousing or marked by such a feeling; gratifying: *a proud moment.* **2.** Full of self-respect and independence of spirit: *too proud to ask for help.* **3.** Highly respected; honored: *a proud name.* **4.** Dignified; stately; majestic: *the proud carriage of a queen.* **5.** Haughty; arrogant. —See Syns at **arrogant.** [Middle English, from Old English *prūd,* from Old French *prud,* gallant, brave, from Late Latin *prōde,* advantageous, from Latin *prōdesse,* to be beneficial : *prōd-,* var. of *prō-,* for + *esse,* to be.] **—proud′ly** *adv.* **—proud′ness** *n.*

prove (prōōv) *v.* **proved, proved** or **prov·en** (prōō′vən), **prov·ing.** —*tr.v.* **1.** To establish the truth or validity of; demonstrate convincingly. **2.** *Law.* To establish the authenticity of (a will). **3.** To determine the quality of by testing; try out. **4.** *Math.* **a.** To validate (a hypothesis or proposition) by a proof. **b.** To verify (the result of a calculation). **5.** *Printing.* To make a sample impression of (type). **6.** *Archaic.* To experience; undergo. —*intr.v.* To be shown to be; turn out. [Middle English *proven,* to put to test, prove, from Old French *prover,* from Latin *probāre,* to test, from *probus,* good, virtuous.] **—prov′a·ble** *adj.* **—prov′a·bly** *adv.* **—prov′er** *n.*

    Syns: **prove, authenticate, confirm, demonstrate, show, substantiate, validate, verify** *v. Core meaning:* To establish as true or genuine (*proved my identity with a passport*).

prov·e·nance (prŏv′ə-nəns, -näns′) *n.* The place of origin; derivation. [French, from *provenant,* pres. part. of *provenir,* to originate, from Latin *prōvenīre* : *prō-,* forth + *venīre,* to come.]

Pro·ven·çal (prō′vən-säl′, prŏv′ən-) *n.* **1.** A native or inhabitant of Provence, France. **2.** The Romance language of Provence, esp. the literary language of the troubadours. **—Pro′ven·çal′** *adj.*

prov·erb (prŏv′ûrb′) *n.* A short, popular saying expressing a well-known truth or fact. [Middle English *proverbe,* from Old French, from Latin *prōverbium* : *prō-,* forth + *verbum,* word.]

pro·ver·bi·al (prə-vûr′bē-əl) *adj.* **1.** Of the nature of a proverb. **2.** Expressed in a proverb or proverbs: *the proverbial word to the wise.* **3.** Widely referred to, as if the subject of a proverb; famous. **—pro·ver′bi·al·ly** *adv.*

Prov·erbs (prŏv′ûrbz′) *n.* See table at **Bible.**

pro·vide (prə-vīd′) *v.* **-vid·ed, -vid·ing.** —*tr.v.* **1.** To furnish; supply. **2.** To yield; afford: *a job that will provide valuable experience.* **3.** To make available. **4.** To set down as a stipulation. —*intr.v.* **1.** To take measures in preparation: *provide against emergencies.* **2.** To supply means of subsistence: *provide for one's family.* **3.** To set down an instruction, rule, or conditions: *The Constitution provides for a bicameral legislature.* [Middle English *providen,* to foresee, make provision, from Latin *prōvidēre* : *prō-,* beforehand, + *vidēre,* to see.] **—pro·vid′er** *n.*

pro·vid·ed (prə-vī′dĭd) *conj.* On the condition; if.

prov·i·dence (prŏv′ĭ-dəns, -dĕns′) *n.* **1.** Care or preparation in advance; foresight. **2.** Prudent management; economy. **3.** The care, guardianship, and control exercised by a deity. **4. Providence.** God.

prov·i·dent (prŏv′ĭ-dənt, -dĕnt′) *adj.* **1.** Providing for future needs or events. **2.** Frugal; economical. **—prov′i·dent·ly** *adv.*

prov·i·den·tial (prŏv′ĭ-dĕn′shəl) *adj.* **1.** Of or resulting from divine providence. **2.** Happening as if through divine intervention; fortunate; opportune. —See Syns at **fortunate. —prov′i·den′tial·ly** *adv.*

pro·vid·ing (prə-vī′dĭng) *conj.* On the condition; provided.

prov·ince (prŏv′ĭns) *n.* **1.** Any of various lands outside Italy conquered and ruled by the ancient Romans. **2.** A territory governed as an administrative or political unit of a country or empire. **3.** A division of territory under the jurisdiction of an archbishop. **4. the provinces.** Areas of a country situated away from the capital or population center. **5.** An area of knowledge, activity, or interest. **6.** The range of one's proper duties and functions; scope. [Middle English

provynce, from Old French *province,* from Latin *prōvincia.*]

pro·vin·cial (prə-vĭn′shəl) *adj.* **1.** Of or relating to a province. **2.** Of or characteristic of people from the provinces; not fashionable or sophisticated. **3.** Limited in perspective; narrow and self-centered: *provincial attitudes.* —*n.* **1.** A native or inhabitant of the provinces. **2.** A person who has provincial ideas or habits. **—pro·vin′cial·ism′** or **pro·vin′ci·al′i·ty** (-vĭn′shē-ăl′ĭ-tē) *n.* **—pro·vin′cial·ly** *adv.*

proving ground. A place for testing new devices or theories.

pro·vi·sion (prə-vĭzh′ən) *n.* **1.** The act of supplying or fitting out. **2.** Something that is provided for one's benefit: *a safety provision.* **3. provisions.** Stocks of food and other necessary supplies. **4.** A measure taken in preparation: *making provisions for her wedding.* **5.** A section of a contract, will, or other document that covers a certain subject; a stipulation. —*tr.v.* To supply with provisions. [Middle English, foresight, precaution, from Old French, from Latin *prōvīsiō,* from *prōvīsus,* past part. of *prōvidēre,* to provide.] **—pro·vi′sion·er** *n.*

pro·vi·sion·al (prə-vĭzh′ə-nəl) *adj.* Provided for the time being; temporary. **—pro·vi′sion·al·ly** *adv.*

pro·vi·so (prə-vī′zō) *n.,* pl. **-sos** or **-soes.** A clause in a document making a qualification, condition, or restriction. [Middle English, from Medieval Latin *prōvīsō (quod),* "provided (that)".]

pro·vi·so·ry (prə-vī′zə-rē) *adj.* Depending on a proviso; conditional. **—pro·vi′so·ri·ly** *adv.*

pro·vi·ta·min (prō-vī′tə-mĭn) *n.* A substance converted to a vitamin within the body, as carotene into vitamin A. [PRO-(before) + VITAMIN.]

prov·o·ca·tion (prŏv′ə-kā′shən) *n.* **1.** The act of provoking. **2.** An action that provokes anger or aggression.

pro·voc·a·tive (prə-vŏk′ə-tĭv) *adj.* **1.** Tending to arouse curiosity or interest. **2.** Tending to irritate or arouse resentment. **—pro·voc′a·tive·ly** *adv.* **—pro·voc′a·tive·ness** *n.*

pro·voke (prə-vōk′) *tr.v.* **-voked, -vok·ing. 1.** To incite to anger or resentment. **2.** To stir or incite to action; arouse. **3.** To bring on by inciting: *provoke a fight.* [Middle English *provoken,* from Old French *provoquer,* from Latin *prōvocāre,* to challenge : *prō-,* forth + *vocāre,* to call.] **—pro·vok′ing·ly** *adv.*

    Syns: **provoke, arouse, excite, galvanize, goad, impel, incite, inflame, inspire, instigate, kindle, motivate, move, rouse, spur, stimulate** *v. Core meaning:* To stir to action or feeling (*carelessness that provoked anger*). See also Syns at **annoy.**

pro·vost (prō′vōst′, -vəst, prŏv′əst) *n.* **1.** The chief magistrate of certain Scottish cities. **2.** The chief administrative officer of some colleges. **3.** The highest official in certain cathedrals or collegiate churches. [Middle English, from Old English *profost* and Old French *provost,* both from Medieval Latin *prōpositus,* from Latin *praepositus,* superintendent, from *praepōnere,* to place over : *prae-,* before + *pōnere,* to place.]

pro·vost marshal (prō′vō). The head of military police in a U.S. Army command.

prow (prou) *n.* **1.** The forward part of a ship's hull; the bow. **2.** A similar projecting part, such as the forward end of a ski. [French *proue,* from Latin *prōra,* from Greek *prōira.*]

prow·ess (prou′ĭs) *n.* **1.** Bravery and resourcefulness, esp. in battle. **2.** Exceptional skill; excellence. [Middle English *prowesse,* from Old French *proesse,* from *prou,* var. of *prud,* gallant, brave, proud.]

prowl (proul) *tr.v.* To roam through stealthily, as in search of prey or plunder. —*intr.v.* To roam stealthily. —See Syns at **sneak.** —*n.* An act of prowling: *on the prowl.* [Middle English *prollen.*] **—prowl′er** *n.*

prowl car. A police patrol car; squad car.

prox·i·mal (prŏk′sə-məl) *adj.* **1.** Nearest; proximate. **2.** *Biol.* Near the central part of the body or a point of attachment or origin: *the proximal end of a bone.* **—prox′i·mal·ly** *adv.*

prox·i·mate (prŏk′sə-mĭt) *adj.* **1.** Nearest; next. **2.** Approximate. [Latin *proximātus,* past part. of *proximāre,* to come near, from *proximus,* nearest.] **—prox′i·mate·ly** *adv.*

prox·im·i·ty (prŏk-sĭm′ĭ-tē) *n.* The condition, quality, or fact of being near or next; closeness.

ă pat	ā pay	â care	ä father	ĕ pet	ē be	hw which	ĭ pit	ī tie	î pier	ŏ pot	ō toe	ô paw, for	oi noise
ōō took	ōō boot	ou out	th thin	th this	ŭ cut	û urge	zh vision	ə about, item, edible, gallop, circus

prox·i·mo (prŏk'sə-mō') *adv. Archaic.* Of or in the following month. [From Latin *proximō (mense),* "in the next (month)".]

prox·y (prŏk'sē) *n., pl.* **-ies.** **1.** A person authorized to act for another. **2. a.** The authority to act for another. **b.** The written authorization for such action. **c.** The act of granting such authorization. [Middle English *proxcy,* from Norman French *procuracie,* from Medieval Latin *prōcūrātia,* from Latin *prōcūrāre,* to take care of.]

prude (prōod) *n.* A person who is too concerned with being proper and virtuous and who is easily offended by sexual references. [French, short for Old French *pr(e)udefemme,* virtuous woman.]

pru·dence (prōod'ns) *n.* **1.** The condition, quality, or fact of being prudent; discretion. **2.** Careful management; economy.

> **Syns:** prudence, caution, circumspection, precaution *n.* Core meaning: The use of good judgment and common sense (*the prudence of good investors*).

pru·dent (prōod'nt) *adj.* **1.** Wise in handling practical matters. **2.** Careful in regard to one's own interests; frugal. **3.** Careful about one's conduct; circumspect; discreet. — See Syns at **careful.** [Middle English, from Old French, from Latin *prūdēns,* foreseeing, wise, from *prōvidēns,* provident.] **—pru'dent·ly** *adv.*

pru·den·tial (prōo-děn'shəl) *adj.* **1.** Arising from or characterized by prudence. **2.** Exercising prudence. **—pru·den'tial·ly** *adv.*

prud·er·y (prōo'də-rē) *n., pl.* **-ies.** **1.** The condition or quality of being prudish; excessive regard for propriety, modesty, or morality. **2.** An instance of prudish behavior or talk.

prud·ish (prōo'dĭsh) *adj.* Marked by or exhibiting prudery. **—prud'ish·ly** *adv.* **—prud'ish·ness** *n.*

prune¹ (prōon) *n.* The partially dried fruit of any of several varieties of plum. [Middle English, from Old French, from Latin *prūnum,* plum.]

prune² (prōon) *v.* **pruned, prun·ing.** *—tr.v.* **1.** To cut off parts or branches of (a plant, shrub, or tree) to improve shape or growth. **2.** To remove or cut out as superfluous. **3.** To reduce: *prune the budget.* *—intr.v.* To remove branches or parts from a plant. [Middle English *prouynen,* from Old French *pro(o)ignier.*] **—prun'er** *n.*

pru·ri·ent (prōor'ē-ənt) *adj.* Characterized by or arousing an obsessive interest in private or improper matters, esp. of a sexual nature. [Latin *prūriēns,* pres. part. of *prūrīre,* to itch.] **—pru'ri·ence** *n.* **—pru'ri·ent·ly** *adv.*

Prus·sian (prŭsh'ən) *adj.* **1.** Of Prussia, its people, or their language and culture. **2.** Like or suggestive of the Junkers and the military class of Prussia. *—n.* **1.** One of the western Balts anciently inhabiting the region between the Vistula and Neman. **2.** A Baltic inhabitant of Prussia. **3.** A German inhabitant of Prussia.

prus·sic acid (prŭs'ĭk). **Hydrocyanic acid.** [French *acide prussique.*]

pry¹ (prī) *intr.v.* **pried, pry·ing.** To look or inquire closely or curiously, often in a furtive manner; to snoop. [Middle English *prien.*] **—pry'ing·ly** *adv.*

pry² (prī) *tr.v.* **pried, pry·ing.** **1.** To raise, move, or force open with a lever. **2.** To obtain with difficulty: *pry a confession out of a suspect.* *—n., pl.* **pries.** Something used to apply leverage, as a crowbar. [Alteration of PRIZE (to force open).]

psalm (säm) *n.* **1.** A sacred song; hymn. **2.** Often **Psalm.** Any of the sacred songs or hymns collected in the Old Testament Book of Psalms. [Middle English, from Old English *psealm,* from Late Latin *psalmus,* from Greek *psalmos,* from *psallein,* to play the harp.]

psalm·ist (sä'mĭst) *n.* A writer or composer of psalms.

psalm·o·dy (sä'mə-dē) *n., pl.* **-dies.** **1.** The singing of psalms in divine worship. **2.** A collection of psalms. [Middle English *psalmodie,* from Late Latin *psalmōdia,* from Greek, singing to the harp : *psalmos,* psalm + *ōidē,* song, ode.]

Psalms (sämz) *n.* See table at **Bible.**

Psal·ter (sôl'tər) *n.* Also **psal·ter.** A book containing the Book of Psalms or a particular version of, musical setting for, or selection from it. [Middle English, from Old English *psaltere* and Old French *psautier,* both from Late Latin

psaltērium, from Greek *psaltērion,* psalm, song.]

psal·ter·y (sôl'tə-rē) *n., pl.* **-ies.** Also **psal·try** (sôl'trē), *pl.* **-tries.** An ancient, stringed musical instrument played by plucking the strings with the fingers or a plectrum.

pseu·do (sōo'dō) *adj.* False or counterfeit; fake. [From PSEUDO-.]

pseudo- or **pseud-.** A prefix meaning false; deceptive: **pseudoscience.** [Middle English, from Late Latin, from Greek *pseudos,* falseness.]

pseu·do·nym (sōod'n-ĭm') *n.* A fictitious name, esp. one assumed by an author; pen name. **—pseu·don'y·mous** (sōo-dŏn'ə-məs) *adj.*

pseu·do·po·di·um (sōo'də-pō'dē-əm) *n., pl.* **-di·a** (-dē-ə). Also **pseu·do·pod** (sōo'də-pŏd'). A temporary protrusion of the cytoplasm of a cell that serves as a means of locomotion and of surrounding and ingesting food in certain organisms, as the amoeba. [PSEUDO- + Greek *podion,* foot, dim. of *pous,* foot.]

pshaw (shô) *interj.* A word used to indicate impatience, irritation, disapproval or disbelief.

psi (sī, psī) *n.* The 23rd letter in the Greek alphabet, written Ψ, ψ. [From Greek *psei.*]

psit·ta·co·sis (sĭt'ə-kō'sĭs) *n.* A virus disease of parrots and related birds, communicable to man, in whom it produces high fever and complications similar to pneumonia. [Latin *psittacus,* parrot + -OSIS.]

pso·ri·a·sis (sə-rī'ə-sĭs) *n.* A chronic, noncontagious skin disease characterized by inflammation and white, scaly patches. [From Greek *psōriasis,* from *psōra,* an itch, from *psēn,* to rub, scratch.] **—pso·ri·at'ic** (sôr'ē-ăt'ĭk, sōr'-) *adj.*

psy·che (sī'kē) *n.* **1.** The soul or spirit, as distinguished from the body. **2.** The mind functioning as the center of thought, feeling, and behavior, and consciously or unconsciously adjusting and relating the body to its social and physical environment. [Latin, from Greek *psukhē,* breath, life, soul.]

Psy·che (sī'kē) *n. Gk. & Rom. Class. Myth.* A maiden loved by Eros and united with him after Aphrodite's jealousy was overcome. She became the personification of the soul.

psy·che·del·ic (sī'kĭ-dĕl'ĭk) *adj.* Of, inducing, or marked by hallucinations, distortions of perception, or altered states of consciousness. *—n.* A psychedelic drug, esp. LSD. [From PSYCHE (mind) + Greek *dēlos,* clear, visible.]

psy·chi·a·trist (sĭ-kī'ə-trĭst, sī-) *n.* A physician specially trained to practice psychiatry.

psy·chi·a·try (sĭ-kī'ə-trē, sī-) *n.* The medical study, diagnosis, treatment, and prevention of mental illness. **—psy·chi·at'ric** (sī'kē-ăt'rĭk) or **psy·chi·at'ri·cal** *adj.* **—psy·chi·at'ri·cal·ly** *adv.*

psy·chic (sī'kĭk) or **psy·chi·cal** (-kĭ-kəl) *adj.* **1.** Of the human mind or psyche. **2.** Of, relating to, or caused by alleged mental phenomena, such as extrasensory perception and mental telepathy, which are not explainable by known natural laws. *—n.* **1.** A person apparently responsive to psychic forces. **2.** A medium. **—psy'chi·cal·ly** *adv.*

psycho-. A prefix meaning the mind: **psychology.** [From Greek *psukhē,* breath, life, psyche.]

psy·cho·a·nal·y·sis (sī'kō-ə-năl'ĭ-sĭs) *n.* **1.** The analytic technique originated by Sigmund Freud that uses free association, dream interpretation, and analysis of the patient's feelings and behavior to investigate mental processes. **2.** The theory of human psychology founded by Freud that stresses the importance of the unconscious mind, early childhood experience, and the repression or diversion of sexual impulses. **—psy·cho·an·a·lyst** (-ăn'ə-lĭst) *n.* **—psy·cho·an·a·lyt'ic** (-ăn'ə-lĭt'ĭk) or **psy·cho·an·a·lyt'i·cal** *adj.* **—psy·cho·an·a·lyt'i·cal·ly** *adv.*

psy·cho·an·a·lyze (sī'kō-ăn'ə-līz') *tr.v.* **-lyzed, -lyz·ing.** To analyze and treat by psychoanalysis.

psy·cho·dra·ma (sī'kō-drä'mə, -drăm'ə) *n.* A psychotherapeutic and analytic technique in which individuals are assigned roles to be spontaneously enacted.

psy·cho·log·i·cal (sī'kə-lŏj'ĭ-kəl) or **psy·cho·log·ic** (-ĭk) *adj.* **1.** Of psychology. **2.** Of or derived from the mind or emotions: *a psychological advantage.* **3.** Influencing, affecting, or aimed at the mind or emotions: *psychological torture.* **—psy·cho·log'i·cal·ly** *adv.*

psy·chol·o·gist (sī-kŏl'ə-jĭst) *n.* A person trained to perform psychological analysis, therapy, or research.

psy·chol·o·gy (sī-kŏl'ə-jē) *n., pl.* **-gies. 1.** The science of mental processes and behavior. **2.** The emotional and behavioral characteristics of an individual, group, or activity: *the psychology of war.*

psy·cho·met·rics (sī'kə-mĕt'rĭks) *n. (used with a sing. verb).* The measurement of psychological variables, such as intelligence, aptitude, and emotional disturbance.

psy·cho·neu·ro·sis (sī'kō-nŏō-rō'sĭs, -nyŏo-) *n., pl.* **-ses** (-sēz'). A neurosis. **—psy'cho·neu·rot'ic** (-rŏt'ĭk) *adj. & n.*

psy·cho·path (sī'kə-păth') *n.* A person with a severe personality disorder, esp. one manifested in aggressively antisocial behavior. **—psy'cho·path'ic** *adj.*

psy·chop·a·thy (sī-kŏp'ə-thē) *n.* Mental disorder.

psy·cho·phys·ics (sī'kō-fĭz'ĭks) *n. (used with a sing. verb).* The psychological study of relationships between physical stimuli and sensory response. **—psy'cho·phys'i·cal** *adj.* **—psy'cho·phys'i·cal·ly** *adv.*

psy·cho·sis (sī-kō'sĭs) *n., pl.* **-ses** (-sēz'). Any of a class of serious mental disorders in which the mind cannot function normally and the ability to deal with reality is impaired or lost.

psy·cho·so·mat·ic (sī'kō-sə-măt'ĭk) *adj.* **1.** Of or relating to phenomena that involve both the mind and the body. **2.** Of or related to physical symptoms or disorders that are caused or aggravated by mental conditions.

psy·cho·ther·a·py (sī'kō-thĕr'ə-pē) *n.* The psychological treatment of mental, emotional, and nervous disorders. **—psy'cho·ther'a·peu'tic** (-pyŏo'tĭk) *adj.* **—psy'cho·ther'a·pist** *n.*

psy·chot·ic (sī-kŏt'ĭk) *n.* A person afflicted with a psychosis. **—adj.** Of or caused by psychosis. [From PSYCHOSIS.] **—psy·chot'i·cal·ly** *adv.*

psy·chrom·e·ter (sī-krŏm'ĭ-tər) *n.* An instrument that measures atmospheric moisture by using the difference in readings between two thermometers, one with a wet bulb ventilated to cause evaporation and the other with a dry bulb. [Greek *psuchros*, cold + -METER.]

Pt The symbol for the element platinum.

ptar·mi·gan (tär'mĭ-gən) *n., pl.* **-gan** or **-gans.** Any bird of the genus *Lagopus*, of the arctic and subarctic regions of the Northern Hemisphere, with feathered feet and plumage that is brownish in summer and white in winter. [Alteration of Scottish Gaelic *tarmachan*.]

PT boat (pē-tē). A fast, maneuverable, lightly armed vessel used to torpedo enemy shipping. [From *Patrol Torpedo boat*.]

pte·rid·o·phyte (tə-rĭd'ə-fīt', tĕr'ĭ-dō-) *n.* Any plant of the division Pteridophyta, including the ferns and club mosses. [Greek *pteris*, fern + -PHYTE.] **—pte·rid'o·phyt'ic** (-fĭt'ĭk) or **pter'i·doph'y·tous** (tĕr'ĭ-dŏf'ĭ-təs) *adj.*

ptero-. A prefix meaning feather, wing, or winglike part: **pterodactyl.** [From Greek *pteron*, feather, wing.]

pter·o·dac·tyl (tĕr'ə-dăk'təl) *n.* Any of various extinct flying reptiles of the family Pterodactylidae.

pter·o·saur (tĕr'ə-sôr') *n.* Any of various extinct flying reptiles of the order Pterosauria, including the pterodactyls, of the Jurassic and Cretaceous periods, characterized by wings consisting of a flap of skin supported by the very long fourth digit on each front leg.

Ptol·e·ma·ic (tŏl'ə-mā'ĭk) *adj.* **1.** Of or relating to the astronomer Ptolemy. **2.** Of or relating to the Ptolemies or to Egypt during their rule (323–30 B.C.).

Ptolemaic system. The astronomical system of Ptolemy,

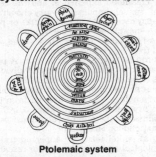

Ptolemaic system

with the earth at the center of the universe, with the sun, moon, planets, and the stars revolving about it.

pto·maine (tō'mān', tō-mān') *n.* Also **pto·main.** Any of various basic nitrogenous materials, some poisonous, that form when proteins decompose. [French *ptomaïne*, from Italian *ptomaina*, from Greek *ptōma*, corpse, from *piptein*, to fall.]

ptomaine poisoning. Food poisoning caused by bacteria or bacterial toxins.

pty·a·lin (tī'ə-lĭn) *n.* A salivary enzyme in man and some lower animals that hydrolyzes starch into maltose and various dextrins. [From Greek *ptualon*, saliva, from *ptuein*, to spit.]

Pu The symbol for the element plutonium.

pub (pŭb) *n.* A tavern; bar. [Short for PUBLIC HOUSE.]

pu·ber·ty (pyŏo'bər-tē) *n.* The stage of maturation in which the individual becomes physiologically capable of sexual reproduction. [Middle English *puberte*, from Latin *pubertās*, from *pūber*, adult.]

pu·bes (pyŏo'bēz') *n.* Plural of **pubis.**

pu·bes·cence (pyŏo-bĕs'əns) *n.* **1. a.** A covering of soft down or short hairs, as on certain plants and insects. **b.** The condition of being pubescent. **2.** The attainment or onset of puberty.

pu·bes·cent (pyŏo-bĕs'ənt) *adj.* **1.** Covered with short hairs or soft down. **2.** Reaching or having reached puberty. [French, from Latin *pūbēscens*, pres. part. of *pūbēscere*, to reach puberty, from *pūber*, adult.]

pu·bic (pyŏo'bĭk) *adj.* Of or in the region of the lower part of the abdomen, the pubis, or the pubes.

pu·bis (pyŏo'bĭs) *n., pl.* **-bes** (-bēz'). The forward portion of either of the hipbones, at the juncture forming the front arch of the pelvis. [New Latin *(os) pubis*, (bone) of the groin, from Latin *pūbis*, pubes.]

pub·lic (pŭb'lĭk) *adj.* **1.** Of, concerning, or affecting the community or the people: *the public good.* **2.** Maintained for or used by the people or community: *a public park.* **3.** Participated in or attended by the people or community: *public worship.* **4.** Connected with or acting on behalf of the people, community, or government, rather than private matters or interests: *public office.* **5.** Open to the knowledge or judgment of all: *made the testimony public.* **—n. 1.** The community or the people as a whole. **2.** A group of people sharing a common interest: *the reading public.* **3.** Admirers or followers, esp. of a celebrity. **—idiom. in public.** In the presence of people at large; openly. [Middle English *publyk*, from Old French *public*, from Latin *pūblicus*, from *populus*, people.] **—pub'lic·ness** *n.*

   Syns: 1. public, civic, civil, national *adj.* Core meaning: Of, concerning, or affecting the people (*done for the public good*). **2. public, democratic, general, popular** *adj.* Core meaning: Of, representing, or carried on by the people (*public elections*).

pub·lic-ad·dress system (pŭb'lĭk-ə-drĕs'). An electronic amplification apparatus installed and used for broadcasting in public areas.

pub·li·can (pŭb'lĭ-kən) *n.* **1.** *Brit.* The keeper of a public house; tavernkeeper. **2.** A collector of public taxes or tolls in the ancient Roman Empire. [Middle English, tax collector, from Old French *publicain*, from Latin *pūblicānus*, contractor for public revenues, from *pūblicum*, public revenue, from *pūblicus*, public.]

pub·li·ca·tion (pŭb'lĭ-kā'shən) *n.* **1.** The act or process of publishing printed matter. **2.** An issue of any printed material offered for sale or distribution. **3.** The communication of information to the public. [Middle English *publicacioun*, from Old French, from Late Latin *pūblicātiō*, from *pūblicāre*, to make public, from *pūblicus*, public.]

public defender. An attorney or staff of attorneys, usu. appointed, with responsibility for the legal defense of those unable to afford or obtain legal assistance.

public domain. 1. Land owned and controlled by the state or federal government. **2.** The status of publications, products, and processes that are not protected under patent or copyright.

public house. *Brit.* An inn, tavern, bar, or similar place licensed to sell alcoholic beverages.

pub·li·cist (pŭb'lĭ-sĭst) *n.* A person who publicizes something or someone, esp. a press or publicity agent.

pub·lic·i·ty (pŭ-blĭs′ĭ-tē) n. **1.** Information given out, as to the press, as a means of attracting public notice to a person or thing. **2.** Public notice directed toward someone or something. **3.** The work of a person hired to bring someone or something to public notice.

pub·li·cize (pŭb′lĭ-sīz′) tr.v. **-cized, -ciz·ing.** To give publicity to; bring to public attention; advertise.

pub·lic·ly (pŭb′lĭk-lē) adv. **1.** In a public manner; not privately; openly. **2.** By or with the public or its representatives: a publicly owned electric utility.

public relations. 1. (used with a sing. or pl. verb). The methods and activities employed by an individual, organization, or government to promote a favorable relationship with the public. **2.** (used with a sing. verb). The art or science of establishing such a relationship.

public school. 1. In the United States, an elementary or secondary school supported by public funds and providing free education for children of the community or district. **2.** In Great Britain, a private boarding school for pupils of from thirteen to eighteen years of age for entry into a university or the public services.

public servant. A person who holds a government position by election or by appointment.

public speaking. The art or process of making speeches before an audience. **—public speaker.**

pub·lic-spir·i·ted (pŭb′lĭk-spĭr′ĭ-tĭd) adj. Motivated by or showing active devotion to the good of the general public. **—pub′lic-spir′it·ed·ness** n.

public utility. A private company that is subject to governmental regulation because it provides an essential service or commodity, such as water, electricity, or communication, to the public.

public works. Construction projects financed by public funds and constructed by a government for the benefit or use of the general public.

pub·lish (pŭb′lĭsh) tr.v. **1.** To prepare and issue (printed material) for public distribution or sale. **2.** To prepare and issue the work of (an author) in printed form. **3.** To bring to the public attention; announce. **—intr.v. 1.** To issue a publication. **2.** To be the author of a published work. [Middle English publishen, from Old French publier, from Latin pūblicāre, to make public, from pūblicus, public.] **—pub′lish·a·ble** adj.

pub·lish·er (pŭb′lĭ-shər) n. A person or company engaged in publishing printed material.

puce (pyōōs) n. A deep, grayish red or purple. **—adj.** Deep, grayish red or purple. [French (couleur) puce, "flea (color)," from Latin pūlex, flea.]

puck (pŭk) n. A hard rubber disk used in ice hockey. [From Brit. dial. puck, to strike, poke.]

Puck (pŭk) n. A mischievous sprite of English folklore.

puck·er (pŭk′ər) tr.v. To draw up into small wrinkles or folds: puckered the cloth. **—intr.v.** To become contracted and wrinkled. **—n.** A wrinkle or wrinkled part, as in tightly stitched cloth. [Prob. from POKE (bag).]

puck·ish (pŭk′ĭsh) adj. Mischievous; impish: a puckish grin. **—puck′ish·ly** adv. **—puck′ish·ness** n.

pud·ding (pŏŏd′ĭng) n. **1. a.** A sweet dessert, usu. containing flour or a cereal product, that has been boiled, steamed, or baked. **b.** Any mixture with a soft, smooth consistency. **2.** A sausagelike preparation made with minced meat or various other ingredients stuffed into a bag or skin and boiled. [Middle English, from Old French boudin, from Latin botulus, sausage.]

pud·dle (pŭd′l) n. **1.** A small pool of dirty, stagnant water. **2.** A small pool of any liquid. **3.** A paste of wet clay and sand used as waterproofing. **—v. -dled, -dling. —tr.v. 1.** To make muddy. **2.** To work (clay or sand) into a thick, watertight paste. **3.** To process (impure metal) by puddling. **—intr.v.** To splash or dabble in or as if in a puddle. [Middle English podel, dim. of Old English pudd, ditch.] **—pud′dly** adj.

pud·dling (pŭd′lĭng) n. **1.** The purification of impure metal, esp. pig iron, by melting and stirring in an oxidizing atmosphere. **2.** Compaction of wet clay or a similar material to make a watertight paste.

pu·den·cy (pyōōd′n-sē) n. Modesty; shame; prudishness.

[Late Latin pudentia, shame, from Latin pudēns, pres. part. of pudēre, to feel shame.]

pu·den·dum (pyōō-dĕn′dəm) n., pl. **-da** (-də). The external genital organs, esp. of a woman. [From Late Latin pudenda, from Latin pudendus, shameful, from pudēre, to be ashamed.]

pudg·y (pŭj′ē) adj. **-i·er, -i·est.** Short and fat; chubby: pudgy fingers. [Orig. unknown.] **—pudg′i·ness** n.

pueb·lo (pwĕb′lō) n., pl. **-los. 1.** A community dwelling, up to five stories high, built of stone or adobe by Indian tribes of the southwestern United States. **2. Pueblo.** A member of a tribe, such as the Hopi or Zuñi, inhabiting such dwellings. **3.** An Indian village of the southwestern United States. [Spanish, people, from Latin populus.]

pu·er·ile (pyōō′ər-əl, pyōōr′əl, -īl′) adj. **1.** Belonging to childhood; juvenile. **2.** Immature; childish. [French puéril, from Latin puerīlis, from puer, child, boy.] **—pu′er·ile·ly** adv. **—pu′er·il′i·ty** or **pu′er·ile·ness** n.

pu·er·per·al (pyōō-ûr′pər-əl) adj. Connected with, resulting from, or following childbirth. [Latin puerperus, bearing young : puer, child + parere, to give birth to.]

puff (pŭf) n. **1. a.** A short, forceful discharge or gust, as or air, smoke, or vapor. **b.** A short, abrupt sound produced by such a discharge or gust. **2.** An act of drawing in and breathing out, as in smoking tobacco. **3.** Something that looks light and fluffy. **4.** A soft pad for applying cosmetic powder. **5.** A light, flaky pastry, often filled with custard or cream. **6.** A soft roll of hair forming part of a hairdo. **7.** A section of full, gathered fabric that balloons out as though filled with air. **8.** Informal. An expression of exaggerated or ·deliberately flattering praise. **—intr.v. 1.** To blow in puffs. **2.** To come forth in a puff or puffs: Smoke puffed from the steamboat. **3.** To breathe forcefully and rapidly. **4.** To emit puffs of smoke, vapor, etc. **5.** To take puffs on a cigarette, pipe, or cigar. **6.** To swell or seem to swell, as with air or pride: Her feet puffed up from the long walk. **—tr.v. 1.** To emit or give forth in a puff or puffs. **2.** To impel with puffs. **3.** To smoke (a cigar, pipe, etc.). **4.** To fill with or as if with air or padding; inflate. **5.** To fill with pride or conceit. **6.** Informal. To praise or publicize exaggeratedly. [Middle English puffen, from Old English pyffan.] **—puff′i·ly** adv. **—puff′i·ness** n. **—puff′y** adj.

puff adder. 1. A venomous African viper, Bitis arietans, with crescent-shaped yellowish markings. **2.** The hognose snake.

puff·ball (pŭf′bôl′) n. Any of various fungi of the genus Lycoperdon and related genera, with a ball-shaped fruiting body that, when broken open, releases the enclosed spores in puffs of dust.

puff·er (pŭf′ər) n. **1.** Someone or something that puffs. **2.** Any of various saltwater fishes of the family Tetraodontidae, that are capable of swelling up. Also called **blowfish** and **swellfish.**

puf·fin (pŭf′ĭn) n. Any of several sea birds of the genera Fratercula and Lunda, of northern regions, characteristically with black and white plumage and a vertically flattened, brightly colored bill. [Middle English poffoun.]

puffin   **pug¹**

puff pastry. Dough that is rolled and folded in layers and that expands in baking to form light, flaky pastry.

pug¹ (pŭg) n. **1.** A small dog of a breed originating in China, with a snub nose, wrinkled face, square body, short smooth hair, and a curled tail. **2.** A pug nose. [Orig. unknown.]

pug² (pŭg) *n. Slang.* A boxer. [Short for PUGILIST.]

pu·gi·lism (pyōō'jə-lĭz'əm) *n.* The skill or practice of fighting with the fists; boxing. [From Latin *pugil,* fighter, from *pugnus,* fist.]

pu·gi·list (pyōō'jə-lĭst) *n.* A professional boxer. **—pu'gi·lis'tic** *adj.*

pug·na·cious (pŭg-nā'shəs) *adj.* Eager to fight; having a quarrelsome disposition. [From Latin *pugnāx,* fond of fighting, from *pugnāre,* to fight, from *pugnus,* fist.] **—pug·na'cious·ly** *adv.* **—pug·na'cious·ness** or **pug·nac'i·ty** (-năs'ĭ-tē) *n.*

pug nose. A short nose that is somewhat flattened and turned up at the end. [Prob. from PUG (dog).] **—pug'-nosed'** *adj.*

puis·sance (pwĭs'əns, pyōō'ĭ-səns, pyōō-ĭs'əns) *n.* Power; potency; might.

puis·sant (pwĭs'ənt, pyōō'ĭ-sənt, pyōō-ĭs'ənt) *adj.* Mighty; powerful; potent. [Middle English *puissaunt,* from Old French, from Latin *posse,* to be powerful.] **—puis'sant·ly** *adv.*

puke (pyōōk) *v.* **puked, puk·ing.** *—intr.v.* To vomit. *—tr.v.* To vomit (something) up. *—n.* Vomit. [Prob. imit.]

pul·chri·tude (pŭl'krĭ-tōōd', -tyōōd') *n.* Physical beauty and appeal. [Middle English *pulcritude,* from Latin *pulchritūdō,* from *pulcher,* beautiful.] **—pul'chri·tu'di·nous** (pŭl'krĭ-tōōd'n-əs, -tyōōd'-) *adj.*

pule (pyōōl) *intr.v.* **puled, pul·ing.** To whine; whimper; fret. [Earlier *pewle.*] **—pul'er** *n.*

pull (pŏŏl) *tr.v.* **1.** To apply force to so as to cause or tend to cause motion toward the source of the force: *pull a chair closer; pull a sled.* **2.** To remove from a fixed position; extract: *pull teeth.* **3.** To tug at; jerk or tweak. **4.** To rip or tear; rend. **5.** To stretch repeatedly: *pull taffy.* **6.** To strain injuriously: *pull a muscle.* **7.** To attract; draw: *a performer who pulls large crowds.* **8.** *Informal.* To perform; bring about: *pull a stunt.* **9.** *Slang.* To draw out (a knife or gun) in readiness for use. **10.** *Informal.* To use less than full force in delivering (a punch). **11.** *Baseball.* To hit (a ball) in the direction one is facing when the swing is carried through. **12.** To operate (an oar) in rowing. **13.** *Printing.* To produce (a print or impression) from type. *—intr.v.* **1.** To exert force in pulling something. **2.** To move: *The bus pulled away from the curb.* **3.** To drink or inhale deeply. **4.** To row a boat. *—See Syns at* **attract.** *—phrasal verbs.* **pull down. 1.** To tear down; raze. **2.** To earn: *pull down a hefty salary.* **pull for.** To work or hope for the success of: *We are pulling for you.* **pull in.** To arrive. **pull off.** To do or accomplish in spite of difficulties. **pull out. 1.** To leave; depart. **2.** To withdraw from a situation or commitment. **pull over.** To stop a vehicle on the side of a road. **pull through.** To come or bring successfully through difficulty. **pull up.** To come to a stop: *The truck pulled up in front of the building.* *—n.* **1.** The action or process of pulling. **2.** Force exerted in pulling, or required to overcome resistance in pulling. **3.** A force that attracts or draws; attraction: *magnetic pull.* **4.** Any sustained effort: *a long pull across the mountains.* **5.** Something used for pulling, such as a knob on a drawer. **6.** A deep inhalation or draft, as on a cigar. **7.** *Slang.* A means of gaining special advantage; influence. **8.** *Informal.* Ability to draw or attract; appeal: *a star with pull at the box office.* *—idioms:* **pull (oneself) together.** To regain one's composure or self-control. **pull together.** To cooperate. [Middle English *pullen,* to pull, pluck, from Old English *pullian.*] **—pull'er** *n.*

pull·back (pŏŏl'băk') *n.* The act or process of pulling something back, esp. an orderly troop withdrawal.

pul·let (pŏŏl'ĭt) *n.* A young hen, esp. of the common domestic fowl. [Middle English *pulet,* from Old French *poulet,* dim. of *poul,* cock, and *poule,* hen, from Latin *pullus,* young of an animal, chicken.]

pul·ley (pŏŏl'ē) *n., pl.* **-leys. 1.** A simple machine used to change the direction and point of application of a pulling force, consisting essentially of a wheel with a grooved rim in which a pulled rope or chain is run. **2.** A wheel turned by or driving a belt. [Middle English *pouley,* from Old French *poulie.*]

Pull·man (pŏŏl'mən) *n.* A railroad parlor car or sleeping car. Also called **Pullman car.** [Designed by George M. *Pullman* (1831–97), American industrialist.]

pull·out (pŏŏl'out') *n.* **1.** A withdrawal, esp. of troops. **2.** An aircraft's change from a dive into level flight. **3.** Something designed to be pulled out.

pull·o·ver (pŏŏl'ō'vər) *n.* A garment, such as a sweater, that is put on by being drawn over the head. **—modifier:** *a pullover shirt.*

pul·lu·late (pŭl'yə-lāt') *intr.v.* **-lat·ed, -lat·ing. 1.** To put forth sprouts; germinate. **2.** To breed rapidly or abundantly. **3.** To teem; swarm. [From Latin *pullulāre,* to grow, sprout, from *pullulus,* sprout, dim. of *pullus,* chicken.] **—pul'lu·la'tion** *n.*

pul·mo·nar·y (pŏŏl'mə-nĕr'ē, pŭl'-) *adj.* **1.** Of or affecting the lungs. **2.** Having lungs or lunglike organs. [Latin *pulmōnārius,* from *pulmō,* lung.]

pulmonary artery. An artery in which blood travels directly from the heart to the lungs.

pulmonary vein. One of four veins in which blood travels directly from the lungs to the heart.

pul·mo·nate (pŏŏl'mə-nāt', pŭl'-) *adj.* Having lungs or lunglike organs.

pulp (pŭlp) *n.* **1.** A soft, moist, shapeless mass of matter. **2.** The soft, moist part of fruit. **3.** A mass of pressed vegetable matter; *apple pulp.* **4.** The soft pith forming the contents of the stem of a plant. **5.** A mixture of cellulose material, such as wood, paper, and rags, ground up and moistened to make paper. **6.** The soft inner structure of a tooth, containing nerve tissue and blood vessels. **7.** A magazine or book containing sensational subject matter and usu. printed on rough, coarse paper. *—tr.v.* **1.** To reduce to pulp. **2.** To remove the pulp from. *—intr.v.* To become reduced to a pulpy consistency. [Latin *pulpa,* solid flesh, pulp.] **—pulp'i·ness** *n.* **—pulp'y** *adj.*

pul·pit (pŏŏl'pĭt, pŭl'-) *n.* **1.** An elevated platform, lectern, or stand used in preaching or conducting a religious service. **2.** Any similar raised platform, such as one used by harpooners in a whaling boat. **3. the pulpit. a.** Clergymen as a group. **b.** The ministry as a profession. [Middle English, from Latin *pulpitum,* scaffold, platform.]

pulp·wood (pŭlp'wŏŏd') *n.* Soft wood, such as spruce, aspen, or pine, used in making paper.

pul·que (pŏŏl'kā', -kē, pŏŏl'-) *n.* A fermented, milky beverage made in Mexico from various species of agave. [Mexican Spanish.]

pul·sar (pŭl'sär') *n.* Any of several very short-period variable galactic radio sources believed to be a rotating neutron star. [PULSE + (QUAS)AR.]

pul·sate (pŭl'sāt') *intr.v.* **-sat·ed, -sat·ing. 1.** To expand and contract rhythmically; to throb. **2.** To quiver. **3.** To move or recur rhythmically: *electricity pulsating through a wire.* [From Latin *pulsāre,* freq. of *pellere,* to push, beat, strike.]

pul·sa·tion (pŭl-sā'shən) *n.* **1.** The act of pulsating. **2.** A single beat, throb, or vibration.

pulse¹ (pŭls) *n.* **1.** The rhythmical expansion and contraction of the arteries as blood is pushed through them by the beating of the heart. **2.** Any regular or rhythmical beating: *the pulse of the drums.* **3.** A single beat or throb; pulsation. **4.** A short, sudden, and temporary change in some characteristic of a physical system, esp. a short burst of electrical energy or wave energy. **5.** The perceptible emotions or sentiments of a group of people: *the pulse of the electorate.* *—intr.v.* **pulsed, puls·ing.** To pulsate. [Middle English *puls,* from Old French *pols,* from Latin *pulsus,* beating, striking, from *pellere,* to push, beat, strike.]

pulley   **pulmonary artery**

pulse² (pŭls) *n.* **1.** The edible seeds of certain pod-bearing plants, such as peas and beans. **2.** A plant yielding such seeds. [Middle English *puls*, from Old French *pouls*, porridge, from Latin *puls*, from Greek *poltos*.]

pulse-jet (pŭls'jĕt') *n.* A jet engine in which air intake and combustion occur intermittently, producing rapid periodic bursts of thrusts.

pul·ver·ize (pŭl'və-rīz') *v.* **-ized, -iz·ing.** —*tr.v.* **1.** To pound, crush, or grind to a powder or dust. **2.** To demolish. —*intr.v.* To be ground or reduced to powder or dust. [Old French *pulveriser*, from Late Latin *pulverizāre*, from Latin *pulvis*, dust.] —**pul'ver·iz'a·ble** *adj.* —**pul'ver·i·za'tion** *n.* —**pul'ver·iz'er** *n.*

pu·ma (pyōō'mə) *n.* The **mountain lion.** [Spanish, from Quechua.]

pum·ice (pŭm'ĭs) *n.* A porous, lightweight volcanic rock used as an abrasive. —*tr.v.* **-iced, -ic·ing.** To clean, polish, or smooth with pumice. [Middle English *pomys*, from Old French *pomis*, from Latin *pūmex*.]

pum·mel (pŭm'əl) *tr.v.* **-meled** or **-melled, -mel·ing** or **-mel·ling.** To strike repeatedly; pound; pommel. —*n.* A pommel.

pump¹ (pŭmp) *n.* **1.** A device for transferring a fluid from a source or container to another container or receiver. **2.** An act of moving up and down: *He gave my hand a quick pump.* —*tr.v.* **1.** To raise or cause to flow by means of a pump. **2.** To inflate with gas by means of a pump. **3.** To remove the water from. **4.** To cause to operate with the up-and-down motion of a pump handle. **5.** To propel, eject, or insert with or as if with a pump: *pump bullets into a target.* **6.** To question closely or persistently: *pump a witness.* **7.** To move up and down like a pump handle: *pumped the guests' hands.* —*intr.v.* **1.** To operate a pump. **2.** To raise or move gas or liquid with a pump. **3.** To gush or spurt rhythmically. [Middle English *pumpe.*] —**pump'er** *n.*

pump¹   pumpkin

pump² (pŭmp) *n.* A low-cut shoe without fastenings. [Orig. unknown.]

pum·per·nick·el (pŭm'pər-nĭk'əl) *n.* A dark bread made from whole, coarsely ground rye. [German.]

pump·kin (pŭmp'kĭn, pŭm'-, pŭng'-) *n.* **1.** A coarse, trailing vine, *Cucurbita pepo,* widely cultivated for its fruit. **2.** The large, pulpy round fruit of this vine, with a thick, orange-yellow rind and numerous seeds. **3.** Either of two similar vines, *C. maxima* or *C. moschata* that bear large, pumpkinlike squashes. [Var. of earlier *pumpion,* from Old French *pompon,* from Latin *pepō,* from Greek *pepōn,* a large melon, from *pepōn,* ripe, from *peptein,* to cook, ripen.]

pump·kin·seed (pŭmp'kĭn-sēd', pŭm'-, pŭng'-) *n.* **1.** The seed of the pumpkin. **2.** A North American sunfish, *Lepomis gibbosus,* with brightly colored markings.

pun (pŭn) *n.* A play on words, sometimes on different senses of the same word and sometimes on the similar sense or sound of different words. —*intr.v.* **punned, punning.** To make a pun. [Orig. unknown.]

punch¹ (pŭnch) *n.* **1.** A tool for piercing or perforating: *a leather punch.* **2.** A tool for forcing a pin, bolt, or rivet in or out of a hole. **3.** A tool for stamping a design on a surface. —*tr.v.* To use a punch on; perforate: *punch a ticket.* —*intr.v.* To use a punch. [Short for PUNCHEON (punching tool).]

punch² (pŭnch) *tr.v.* **1.** To hit with a sharp blow of the fist. **2.** To press the operating mechanism of: *punch a time clock.* **3.** To poke or prod with a stick. **4.** *Western U.S.* To herd (cattle). —*phrasal verb.* **punch in** (or **out**). To check in (or out) formally at a job before (or after) a day's work. —*n.* **1.** A blow with the fist. **2.** Vigor or drive. [Middle English *punchen.*]

punch³ (pŭnch) *n.* A sweetened beverage of fruit juices, often spiced, usu. with wine or liquor. [Perh. short for PUNCHEON (cask).]

punch-drunk (pŭnch'drŭngk') *adj.* **1.** Suffering from the effects of repeated blows on the head. **2.** Acting in a dazed manner.

punch card. Also **punched card.** A card punched with a pattern of holes or notches to represent data, for use in a computer.

pun·cheon¹ (pŭn'chən) *n.* **1.** A short, wooden upright used in structural framing. **2.** A piece of broad, heavy timber, roughly dressed, with one face finished flat. **3.** A punching, perforating, or stamping tool. [Middle English *ponchon,* a sharp tool, from Old French *poinchon,* ult. from Latin *pungere,* to prick.]

pun·cheon² (pŭn'chən) *n.* **1.** A cask with a capacity of 84 U.S. gallons or approx. 318 liters. **2.** This amount of liquid. [Old French *poinchon.*]

punching bag. A stuffed or inflated leather bag, usu. suspended, punched with the fists for exercise.

punch line. The climax of a joke or humorous story.

punch tape. Paper tape in which holes have been punched to represent data to be processed by computer.

punch·y (pŭn'chē) *adj.* **-i·er, -i·est.** Punch-drunk. —**punch'i·ly** *adv.* —**punch'i·ness** *n.*

punc·til·i·o (pŭngk-tĭl'ē-ō') *n., pl.* **-os.** **1.** A fine point of etiquette. **2.** Precise observance of formalities. [Italian *punctiglio.*]

punc·til·i·ous (pŭngk-tĭl'ē-əs) *adj.* **1.** Attentive to the finer points of etiquette and formal conduct. **2.** Precise; scrupulous. —**punc·til'i·ous·ly** *adv.* —**punc·til'i·ous·ness** *n.*

punc·tu·al (pŭngk'chōō-əl) *adj.* **1.** Acting or arriving at the time appointed; prompt. **2.** Precise; punctilious. [Medieval Latin *punctuālis,* "to the point," from Latin *punctum,* point.] —**punc·tu·al'i·ty** (-ăl'ĭ-tē) or **punc'tu·al·ness** *n.* —**punc'tu·al·ly** *adv.*

punc·tu·ate (pŭngk'chōō-āt') *v.* **-at·ed, -at·ing.** —*tr.v.* **1.** To provide (a text) with punctuation marks. **2.** To interrupt periodically: *a speech punctuated by hecklers.* **3.** To stress; emphasize. —*intr.v.* To use punctuation. [From Medieval Latin *punctuāre,* from Latin *punctum,* point, from *pungere,* to prick, pierce.] —**punc'tu·a'tor** *n.*

punc·tu·a·tion (pŭngk'chōō-ā'shən) *n.* **1.** The use of standard marks and signs in writing and printing to separate words into sentences, clauses, and phrases in order to clarify meaning. **2.** The marks so used. **3.** An act of punctuating.

punctuation mark. Any of the marks used in punctuating written or printed material.

punc·ture (pŭngk'chər) *v.* **-tured, -tur·ing.** —*tr.v.* **1.** To pierce with a pointed object. **2.** To make (a hole) by piercing. **3.** To cause to collapse by piercing. **4.** To depreciate; deflate: *She punctured his ego.* —*intr.v.* To be pierced or punctured. —*n.* **1.** An act of puncturing. **2.** A hole or depression made by a sharp object, esp. a hole in a pneumatic tire. [Latin *punctūra,* a pricking, from *punctus,* past part. of *pungere,* to prick.]

pun·dit (pŭn'dĭt) *n.* A learned or authoritative person. [Hindi *paṇḍit,* from Sanskrit *paṇḍita,* a learned man.]

pun·gent (pŭn'jənt) *adj.* **1.** Affecting the organs of taste or smell with a sharp, acrid sensation: *a pungent sauce; pungent smoke.* **2.** Penetrating; biting; caustic: *pungent satire.* [Latin *pungēns,* pres. part. of *pungere,* to prick, sting.] —**pun'gen·cy** (-jən-sē) *n.* —**pun'gent·ly** *adv.*

Pu·nic (pyōō'nĭk) *adj.* Of ancient Carthage or its people. —*n.* The Semitic language of ancient Carthage.

pun·ish (pŭn'ĭsh) *tr.v.* **1.** To subject to penalty for a crime, fault, or misbehavior. **2.** To inflict a penalty on a criminal or wrongdoer for (an offense). **3.** To handle roughly; injure; hurt: *Heavy rains punished the coastal towns.* —*intr.v.* To give punishment. [Middle English *punissen,* from Old French *punir,* from Latin *poenīre,* from *poena,*

penalty, punishment, from Greek *poinē*.] —**pun'ish·er** *n*.
　Syns: punish, correct, discipline *v. Core meaning:* To subject (someone) to a penalty for a wrong (*punished them for playing hooky*).

pun·ish·a·ble (pŭn'ĭ-shə-bəl) *adj.* Liable to punishment: *a crime punishable by imprisonment.*

pun·ish·ment (pŭn'ĭsh-mənt) *n.* **1. a.** An act of punishing. **b.** The condition of being punished. **2.** A penalty imposed for wrongdoing. **3.** Rough handling.

pu·ni·tive (pyoo'nĭ-tĭv) *adj.* Inflicting or designed to inflict punishment; punishing: *took punitive action against the offenders.* [French *punitif,* from Medieval Latin *pūnītīvus,* from Latin *pūnītus,* past part. of *pūnīre,* to punish.] —**pu'ni·tive·ly** *adv.* —**pu'ni·tive·ness** *n.*

punk[1] (pŭngk) *n.* **1.** Dry, decayed wood, used as tinder. **2.** Any of various substances that smolder when ignited, used to light fireworks. **3.** Chinese incense. [Orig. unknown.]

punk[2] (pŭngk) *n. Slang.* **1.** An inexperienced or callow youth. **2.** A young tough; hoodlum. —*adj. Slang.* **1.** Of poor quality; worthless. **2.** Weak in spirits or health. [Orig. unknown.]

pun·ster (pŭn'stər) *n.* A person given to making puns.

punt[1] (pŭnt) *n.* An open, flat-bottomed boat with squared ends, propelled by a long pole and used in shallow waters. —*tr.v.* **1.** To propel (a boat) with a pole. **2.** To carry in a punt. —*intr.v.* To go in a punt. [Middle Low German *punte,* ferryboat, from Latin *pontō,* floating bridge, from *pōns,* bridge.] —**punt'er** *n.*

punt[1]

punt[2] (pŭnt) *n. Football.* A kick in which the ball is dropped from the hands and kicked before it touches the ground. —*tr.v.* To propel (a football) by means of a punt. —*intr.v.* To execute a punt. [Poss. from English dial. *bunt,* to push, butt.]

punt[3] (pŭnt) *intr.v.* **1.** To lay a bet against the bank in a gambling game such as roulette. **2.** To gamble. [French *ponter,* from *ponte,* bet against the banker, from Spanish *punto,* ace, from Latin *punctum,* point.] —**punt'er** *n.*

pu·ny (pyoo'nē) *adj.* **-ni·er, -ni·est.** Of inferior size, strength, or significance; weak. [Old French *puisne,* born afterward : *puis,* afterward, from Latin *post,* after + *ne,* born, from Latin *nātus,* past part. of *nāscī,* to be born.] —**pu'ni·ly** *adv.*

pup (pŭp) *n.* **1.** A young dog; puppy. **2.** The young of certain other animals, as the seal. [Back-formation from PUPPY.]

pu·pa (pyoo'pə) *n., pl.* **-pae** (-pē') or **-pas.** The inactive stage in the metamorphosis of many insects, following the larval stage and preceding the adult form. [From Latin *pūpa,* girl, doll, fem. of *pūpus,* boy.] —**pu'pal** *adj.*

pu·pate (pyoo'pāt') *intr.v.* **-pat·ed, -pat·ing.** To become a pupa. —**pu·pa'tion** (pyoo-pā'shən) *n.*

pu·pil[1] (pyoo'pəl) *n.* A student under the direct supervision of a teacher. [Middle English *pupille,* orphan, pupil, from Old French, from Latin *pūpillus,* dim. of *pūpus,* boy.]

pu·pil[2] (pyoo'pəl) *n.* The apparently black circular aperture in the center of the iris by which light enters the eye. [Middle English *pupilla* and Old French *pupille,* both from Latin *pupilla,* orphan girl, pupil of the eye (from the miniature reflection of oneself seen by looking closely at another's eye), dim. of *pupa,* girl.]

pup·pet (pŭp'ĭt) *n.* **1.** A small figure of a person or animal, with jointed parts manipulated from above by strings or wires; marionette. **2.** A similar figure having a cloth body and hollow head, designed to be fitted over and manipulated by the hand. **3.** A toy representing a human figure;

doll. **4.** A person, group, or government whose behavior is determined by the will of others. [Middle English *popette,* small child, doll, from Old French *poupette,* ult. from Latin *pūpa,* girl, doll.]

pup·pet·eer (pŭp'ĭ-tîr') *n.* A person who operates and entertains with puppets or marionettes.

pup·pet·ry (pŭp'ĭ-trē) *n., pl.* **-ries.** The art of making puppets and presenting puppet shows.

pup·py (pŭp'ē) *n., pl.* **-pies.** **1.** A young dog; pup. **2.** A conceited or inexperienced youth. [Middle English *popi,* from Old French *poupee,* doll, toy, plaything.] —**pup'py·ish** *adj.*

pup tent. A shelter tent.

pur·blind (pûr'blīnd') *adj.* **1.** Nearly or partly blind. **2.** Slow in understanding or discernment; dull. [Middle English, totally blind : *pur,* completely + *blind,* blind.] —**pur'blind'ly** *adv.* —**pur'blind'ness** *n.*

pur·chas·a·ble (pûr'chĭ-sə-bəl) *adj.* **1.** Capable of being bought. **2.** Capable of being bribed; venal.

pur·chase (pûr'chĭs) *tr.v.* **-chased, -chas·ing.** **1.** To obtain in exchange for money or its equivalent; to buy. **2.** To acquire by effort; earn. **3.** To move or hold with a mechanical device, as a lever or wrench. —*n.* **1.** Something that is bought. **2.** The act of buying. **3.** A grip applied manually or mechanically to move something or prevent it from slipping. **4.** A tackle, lever, or other device used to obtain mechanical advantage. **5.** A position, as of a lever or one's feet, affording means to move or secure a weight. [Middle English *pourchasen,* from Old French *purchacier,* to pursue, seek to obtain : *pour-,* for, from Latin *prō* + *chacier,* to chase.] —**pur'chas·er** *n.*

pur·dah (pûr'də) *n.* **1.** A curtain used to screen women from men or strangers in Hindu and Moslem countries. **2.** The practice, observed by Hindus and some Moslems, of secluding women. [Hindi *parda,* screen, veil, from Persian *pardah.*]

pure (pyoor) *adj.* **pur·er, pur·est.** **1.** Having a homogeneous or uniform composition; not mixed: *pure oxygen.* **2.** Free from adulterants or impurities; full-strength: *pure chocolate.* **3.** Free from dirt, defilement, or pollution. **4.** Free from foreign elements. **5.** Containing nothing inappropriate or extraneous: *a pure literary style.* **6.** Complete; utter: *pure folly.* **7.** Without faults; perfect; sinless. **8.** Chaste; virgin. **9.** Of unmixed blood or ancestry. **10.** *Genetics.* Breeding true to parental type; homozygous. **11.** Theoretical rather than applied: *pure science.* See Syns at **utter.** [Middle English, from Old French *pur,* from Latin *pūrus,* clean.] —**pure'ness** *n.*
　Syns: pure, perfect, plain, sheer, unadulterated *adj. Core meaning:* Free from extra, unneeded elements (*pure gold; pure brilliance*).

pure·bred (pyoor'brĕd') *adj.* Of a strain established through breeding many generations of unmixed stock. —*n.* (pyoor'brĕd'). A purebred animal.

pu·rée (pyoo-rā', pyoor'ā) *tr.v.* **-réed, -rée·ing.** To rub (food) through a strainer so that it becomes a fine pulp or thick liquid. —*n.* Food prepared by puréeing. [French, from Old French *purer,* to purify, from Latin *pūrāre,* from *pūrus,* pure.]

pure·ly (pyoor'lē) *adv.* **1.** In a pure manner. **2.** Innocently; chastely. **3.** Totally; entirely: *purely by chance.*

pur·ga·tion (pûr-gā'shən) *n.* The act of purging or purifying.

pur·ga·tive (pûr'gə-tĭv) *adj.* Tending to cleanse or purge, esp. tending to cause evacuation of the bowels. —*n.* A purgative agent or medicine; a strong laxative.

pur·ga·to·ri·al (pûr'gə-tôr'ē-əl, -tōr'-) *adj.* **1.** Serving to purify of sin; expiatory. **2.** Of or resembling purgatory.

pur·ga·to·ry (pûr'gə-tôr'ē, -tōr'ē) *n., pl.* **-ries.** **1.** *Rom. Cath. Ch.* A place or condition of temporary punishment in which the souls of those who have died in grace must expiate their sins. **2.** Any place or condition of expiation, suffering, or remorse.

purge (pûrj) *v.* **purged, purg·ing.** —*tr.v.* **1.** To free from impurities; purify. **2.** To rid of sin, guilt, or defilement. **3.** To rid of persons considered to be undesirable, esp. by harsh methods: *purge a political party.* **4. a.** To cause evacuation of (the bowels). **b.** To induce evacuation of the bowels in (a patient). —*intr.v.* **1.** To become pure or clean. **2.** To undergo or cause an emptying of the bowels.

—*n.* **1.** The act or an instance of purging. **2.** Something that purges, esp. a medicinal purgative. [Middle English *purgen,* from Old French *purger,* from Latin *purgāre,* to cleanse.] —**purg'er** *n.*

pu·ri·fi·ca·tion (pyōōr'ə-fĭ-kā'shən) *n.* The act or process of purifying or the condition of being purified.

pu·ri·fy (pyōōr'ə-fī') *v.* **-fied, -fy·ing.** —*tr.v.* **1.** To rid of impurities; cleanse. **2.** To rid of foreign or objectionable elements. **3.** To free from sin, guilt, or other defilement. —*intr.v.* To become clean or pure. [Middle English *purifien,* from Old French *purifier,* from Latin *pūrificāre :* *pūrus,* pure + *facere,* to make.] —**pu'ri·fi'er** *n.*

pu·rine (pyōōr'ēn') *n.* **1.** A colorless crystalline compound, $C_5H_4N_4$, used in organic synthesis and metabolism studies. **2.** Any of a group of naturally occurring organic compounds derived from or having molecular structures related to purine, including uric acid, adenine, guanine, and caffeine. [German *Purin :* Latin *pūrus,* pure + New Latin *uricus,* uric acid (in which it is found) + German *-in,* -ine.]

pur·ism (pyōōr'ĭz'əm) *n.* Strict observance of or insistence upon traditional correctness, esp. of language.

pur·ist (pyōōr'ĭst) *n.* Someone who practices or urges strict correctness, esp. in the use of language. —**pu·ris'tic** (pyōō-rĭs'tĭk) *adj.* —**pu·ris'ti·cal·ly** *adv.*

Pu·ri·tan (pyōōr'ĭ-tn) *n.* **1.** A member of a group of English Protestants who, in the 16th and 17th cent., advocated simplification of the ceremonies and creeds of the Church of England and strict religious discipline. **2. puritan.** A person who strictly practices a moral code and who regards luxury or pleasure as sinful. —*adj.* **1.** Of the Puritans or Puritanism. **2. puritan.** Characteristic of a puritan; puritanical. [From Late Latin *pūritās,* purity, from *pūrus,* pure.]

pu·ri·tan·i·cal (pyōōr'ĭ-tăn'ĭ-kəl) *adj.* **1.** Rigorous in matters of religion or morality. **2. Puritanical.** Of or characteristic of the Puritans. —**pu'ri·tan'i·cal·ly** *adv.* —**pu'ri·tan'i·cal·ness** *n.*

Pu·ri·tan·ism (pyōōr'ĭ-tn-ĭz'əm) *n.* **1.** The practices and doctrines of the Puritans. **2. puritanism.** Moral strictness; esp., hostility to pleasures and indulgences.

pu·ri·ty (pyōōr'ĭ-tē) *n.* **1.** The quality or condition of being pure. **2.** The degree to which something is pure: *gold of high purity.* **3.** Freedom from sin or guilt; innocence; chastity. **4.** The absence in speech or writing of foreign words, slang, or other elements deemed inappropriate to good style.

purl[1] (pûrl) *intr.v.* To flow or ripple with a murmuring sound. —*n.* The sound made by rippling water. [Norwegian *purla.*]

purl[2] (pûrl) *v.* Also **pearl.** —*tr.v.* **1.** To knit with a purl stitch. **2.** To edge or finish with lace or embroidery. —*intr.v.* **1.** To do knitting with a purl stitch. **2.** To edge or finish with lace or embroidery. —*n.* Also **pearl. 1.** The inversion of a knit stitch; a purl stitch. **2.** A decorative edging of lace or embroidery. **3.** Gold or silver wire used in embroidery. [Orig. unknown.]

pur·lieu (pûrl'yōō, pûr'lōō) *n.* **1.** Any outlying or neighboring area. **2. purlieus.** Outskirts; environs. **3.** A place that one frequents. [Middle English *purlewe,* from Norman French *puralée,* perambulation, from Old French *puraler,* to traverse : *por,* through, from Latin *prō,* forth + *aler,* to go, from Latin *ambulāre,* to walk.]

pur·lin (pûr'lĭn) *n.* Also **pur·line.** One of several horizontal timbers supporting the rafters of a roof. [Middle English *purlyon.*]

pur·loin (pər-loin', pûr'loin') *tr.v.* To steal. —*intr.v.* To commit theft. [Middle English *purloynen,* to remove, from Norman French *purloigner,* to put far away : Old French *pur-,* away, from Latin *prō-* + *loign,* far, from Latin *longus,* long.] —**pur·loin'er** *n.*

purl stitch. An inverted knitting stitch, often alternated with the plain stitch to produce a ribbed effect. Also called **purl.**

pur·ple (pûr'pəl) *n.* **1.** Any of a group of colors produced by mixing red and blue pigments or dyes. **2.** Cloth of this color, formerly worn as a symbol of royalty or high office. —*adj.* **1.** Of the color purple. **2.** Royal or imperial; regal. **3.** Elaborate and ornate: *purple prose.* —*v.* **-pled, -pling.** —*tr.v.* To make purple. —*intr.v.* To become purple. [Middle English *purpel,* from Old English *purple,* from

purpura, purple cloth, from Latin, purple, from Greek *porphura,* purple dye.]

Purple Heart. The U.S. Armed Forces medal of the Order of the Purple Heart, awarded to servicemen wounded in action.

pur·plish (pûr'plĭsh) *adj.* Somewhat purple.

pur·port (pər-pôrt', -pōrt') *tr.v.* To contain the claim (to be or do something), often deceptively; profess: *The book purports to be a factual account, but is really fictitious.* —*n.* (pûr'pôrt', -pōrt'). The apparent meaning or purpose; import; significance. [Middle English *purporten,* to imply, from Old French *porporter,* to contain, from Medieval Latin *prōportāre,* to carry forth : Latin *prō,* forth + *portāre,* to carry.] —**pur·port'ed·ly** (-pôr'tĭd-lē, -pōr'-) *adv.*

pur·pose (pûr'pəs) *n.* **1.** The object toward which one strives or for which something exists; goal; aim. **2.** A result or effect that is intended or desired; intention. **3.** Determination; resolution: *a man of firm purpose.* **4.** The matter at hand; point at issue: *raised questions that were not to the purpose.* —*tr.v.* **-posed, -pos·ing.** To resolve on; intend to do: *"I was purposing to travel over the north this summer"* (John Keats). —**idioms. for all practical purposes.** Effectively; in fact if not in name: *For all practical purposes, Russia has gone capitalist again.* **on purpose.** Intentionally; deliberately. **to good purpose.** With good results. **to little** (or **no**) **purpose.** With few (or no) results. [Middle English *purpos,* from Old French, from *purposer,* to intend, from Latin *prōpositus,* past part. of *proponere,* to propose.]

pur·pose·ful (pûr'pəs-fəl) *adj.* **1.** Having a purpose; intentional. **2.** Having or manifesting purpose; determined: *a sure and purposeful stride.* —**pur'pose·ful·ly** *adv.* —**pur'pose·ful·ness** *n.*

pur·pose·less (pûr'pəs-lĭs) *adj.* Without purpose; pointless. —**pur'pose·less·ly** *adv.* —**pur'pose·less·ness** *n.*

pur·pose·ly (pûr'pəs-lē) *adv.* With a specific purpose; deliberately.

pur·po·sive (pûr'pə-sĭv) *adj.* **1.** Having or serving a purpose. **2.** Purposeful as opposed to aimless or random: *purposive behavior.* —**pur'po·sive·ly** *adv.*

purr (pûr) *n.* **1.** The softly vibrant sound made by a cat to express pleasure or contentment. **2.** Any similar sound. —*intr.v.* To make or emit a purr. —*tr.v.* To express by a purr. [Imit.]

purse (pûrs) *n.* **1.** A small bag or pouch for carrying money. **2.** A woman's pocketbook or handbag. **3.** Anything that resembles a bag or pouch. **4.** Available wealth or resources; money. **5.** A sum of money collected as a present or offered as a prize. —*tr.v.* **pursed, purs·ing.** To gather or contract (the lips or brow) into wrinkles or folds. [Middle English *purs,* from Old English, from Late Latin *bursa,* bag, oxhide, from Greek *bursa,* leather, hide.]

purs·er (pûr'sər) *n.* The officer in charge of money matters on board a ship.

purs·lane (pûr'slĭn, -slān') *n.* A trailing weed, *Portulaca oleracea,* with small yellow flowers, reddish stems, and fleshy leaves that are sometimes used in salads. [Middle English, from Old French *porcelaine,* cowrie shell, from Late Latin *porcillāgo,* from Latin *portulāca.*]

pur·su·ance (pər-sōō'əns) *n.* The carrying out or putting into effect of something; pursuit; prosecution.

pur·su·ant (pər-sōō'ənt) *adj.* **1.** Pursuing; following. **2.** Resultant; consequent. —**idiom. pursuant to.** In accordance with; in carrying out. —**pur·su'ant·ly** *adv.*

pur·sue (pər-sōō') *v.* **-sued, -su·ing.** —*tr.v.* **1.** To follow in an effort to overtake or capture; to chase. **2.** To strive to gain or accomplish: *pursue an ambition.* **3.** To proceed along; follow: *pursue a winding course.* **4.** To carry further; advance. **5.** To be engaged in: *pursue a hobby.* **6.** To harass; persecute: *pursued by doubts.* —*intr.v.* **1.** To chase; follow. **2.** To continue; carry on. [Middle English *pursuen,* from Norman French *pursuer,* from Latin *prōsequī :* *prō-,* forth, onward + *sequī,* to follow.] —**pur·su'er** *n.*

pur·suit (pər-sōōt') *n.* **1.** The act or an instance of chasing or pursuing. **2.** The act of striving: *the pursuit of success.* **3.** A vocation, hobby, or other regular activity of work or play. [Middle English *pursuite,* from Old French *poursuite,* from *poursuivre,* to pursue.]

pur·sui·vant (pûr'swə-vənt) *n.* **1.** In the British Colleges of

Heralds, an officer ranking below a herald. **2.** *Archaic.* A follower or attendant. [Middle English *pursevant,* from Old French *poursuivant,* follower, from *poursuivre,* to pursue.]

pu·ru·lence (pyŏŏr'ə-ləns, pyŏŏr'yə-) *n.* **1.** The condition of secreting or containing pus. **2.** Pus.

pu·ru·lent (pyŏŏr'ə-lənt, pyŏŏr'yə-) *adj.* Containing or secreting pus. [Latin *pūrulentus,* from *pūs,* pus.] —**pu'ru·lent·ly** *adv.*

pur·vey (pər-vā', pûr'vā') *tr.v.* To supply; furnish: *purvey provisions for an army.* [Middle English *purveien,* from Old French *porveoir,* from Latin *prōvidēre,* to foresee, provide.] —**pur·vey'ance** *n.*

pur·vey·or (pər-vā'ər) *n.* A person who furnishes provisions, esp. food.

pur·view (pûr'vyŏŏ') *n.* **1.** The extent or range of function, power, or competence; scope: *matters within the purview of the local government.* **2.** Range of vision, comprehension, or experience; outlook. [Middle English *purveu,* proviso, from Norman French *purveu,* "(it is) provided" (word used to introduce a proviso), from Old French *porveeir,* to provide.]

pus (pŭs) *n.* A thick, yellowish-white fluid formed in infected tissue, consisting chiefly of leucocytes, cellular debris, and liquefied tissue elements. [Latin *pūs.*]

push (pŏŏsh) *tr.v.* **1.** To exert force against (an object) to move it away: *He pushed the door, but it wouldn't budge.* **2.** To move (an object) by exerting force in this manner; thrust; shove: *push a stalled car out of an intersection.* **3.** To force (one's way). **4.** To promote; urge forward: *push a cause.* **5.** To urge insistently to do something; to pressure. **6.** To bear hard upon; press. **7.** To extend or enlarge: *push civilization past the frontier.* **8.** *Slang.* **a.** To promote or sell (a product). **b.** To sell (a narcotic) illegally. —*intr.v.* **1.** To exert outward force against something. **2.** To advance despite difficulty or opposition; press forward: *push on into the jungle.* **3.** To expend great or vigorous effort. —**phrasal verbs. push around.** *Informal.* To treat or threaten to treat roughly; intimidate. **push off.** *Informal.* To depart; set out. —*n.* **1.** The act of pushing; a thrust. **2.** A vigorous or insistent effort; a drive. **3.** A provocation to action; a stimulus. **4.** *Informal.* Persevering energy; enterprise. [Middle English *pusshen,* from Old French *poulser,* to push, beat, from Latin *pulsāre,* freq. of *pellere,* to push, beat.]

push button. A small button that activates an electric circuit.

push-but·ton (pŏŏsh'bŭt'n) *adj.* Operated by or as if by push buttons: *push-button warfare.*

push·cart (pŏŏsh'kärt') *n.* A light cart pushed by hand.

push·er (pŏŏsh'ər) *n.* **1.** Someone or something that pushes. **2.** *Slang.* A person who sells drugs illegally.

push·ing (pŏŏsh'ĭng) *adj.* **1.** Energetic; enterprising. **2.** Aggressive; forward.

push·o·ver (pŏŏsh'ō'vər) *n. Slang.* **1.** Anything easily accomplished. **2.** A person or group easily defeated or taken advantage of.

Push·tu (pŭsh'tŏŏ) *n.* Var. of **Pashto.**

push·up (pŏŏsh'ŭp') *n.* An exercise for strengthening arm muscles, performed by lying with the face and palms to the floor and by pushing the body up and down with the arms.

push·y (pŏŏsh'ē) *adj.* **-i·er, -i·est.** *Informal.* Offensively forward or aggressive. —**push'i·ly** *adv.* —**push'i·ness** *n.*

pu·sil·la·nim·i·ty (pyŏŏ'sə-lə-nĭm'ĭ-tē) *n.* The condition or quality of being pusillanimous; cowardice.

pu·sil·lan·i·mous (pyŏŏ'sə-lăn'ə-məs) *adj.* Lacking courage; cowardly. [From Late Latin *pūsillanimis* : Latin *pūsillus,* very small, weak, from *pūsus,* boy + *animus,* mind, soul.]

puss[1] (pŏŏs) *n. Informal.* A cat. [Orig. unknown.]

puss[2] (pŏŏs) *n. Slang.* **1.** The mouth. **2.** The face. [Irish *bus,* lip, mouth, from Old Irish, lip.]

puss·y[1] (pŏŏs'ē) *n.,* pl. **-ies.** *Informal.* **1.** A cat. **2.** A fuzzy catkin, esp. of the pussy willow.

pus·sy[2] (pŭs'ē) *adj.* **-si·er, -si·est.** Resembling or containing pus.

puss·y·foot (pŏŏs'ē-fŏŏt') *intr.v.* **1.** To move stealthily or

cautiously. **2.** *Slang.* To act or proceed too cautiously or timidly.

pussy willow. **1.** A North American shrub or small tree, *Salix discolor,* with silky catkins. **2.** Any of several similar willows.

pussy willow

pus·tu·lant (pŭs'chə-lənt, pŭs'tyə-) *adj.* Causing pustules to form. —*n.* An agent that produces pustules.

pus·tu·lar (pŭs'chə-lər, pŭs'tyə-) *adj.* Of, characterized by, or having pustules.

pus·tu·late (pŭs'chə-lāt', pŭs'tyə-) *v.* **-lat·ed, -lat·ing.** —*tr.v.* To cause (tissue) to form pustules. —*intr.v.* To form pustules. —*adj.* Covered with pustules or pustulelike blisters.

pus·tu·la·tion (pŭs'chə-lā'shən, pŭs'tyə-) *n.* **1.** The formation or appearance of pustules. **2.** A pustule.

pus·tule (pŭs'chŏŏl', -tyŏŏl') *n.* **1.** A slight, inflamed elevation of the skin filled with pus. **2.** Any small swelling similar to a blister or pimple. [Middle English, from Old French, from Latin *pustula,* a blister.]

put (pŏŏt) *v.* **put, put·ting.** —*tr.v.* **1.** To place in a specified position; to set. **2.** To cause to be in a specified condition: *put one's room in order.* **3.** To cause to undergo something; to subject: *put him to a lot of trouble.* **4.** To assign; to attribute: *put a false interpretation on events.* **5.** To estimate: *He put the time at five o'clock.* **6.** To impose or levy: *put a tax on cigarettes.* **7.** To bet: *put all his money on a long shot.* **8.** To hurl with an overhand pushing motion: *put the shot.* **9.** To bring up for consideration or judgment: *He put the question up for debate.* **10.** To express; to state: *putting it bluntly.* **11.** To render in a specified language or literary form: *put prose into verse.* **12.** To adapt: *lyrics put to music.* **13.** To urge or force to some action: *put an outlaw to flight.* **14.** To apply: *We must put our minds to it.* —*intr.v.* To proceed: *The ship put into the harbor.* —**phrasal verbs. put about.** *Naut.* To change direction; go from one tack to another. **put across. 1.** To state so as to be understood or accepted. **2.** To carry out by deception. **put aside.** To save for later use; reserve. **put away. 1.** To put in prison or in an asylum. **2.** To abandon; renounce: *put away childish things.* **3.** To kill. **4.** To eat or drink: *He really puts it away.* **put down. 1.** To suppress: *put down an uprising.* **2.** *Slang.* To criticize or reject. **put forth. 1.** To sprout: *branches putting forth buds.* **2.** To exert: *Put forth all the strength you've got.* **3.** To advance or propose. **4.** To set forth or embark: *putting forth to sea.* **put in. 1.** To enter: *putting in an insurance claim.* **2.** To do: *putting in a hard day's work.* **3.** *Naut.* To make a stop at a port. **4.** To say; insert. **put off. 1.** *Informal.* To repel: *Her behavior puts me off.* **2.** *Informal.* To evade: *keeps putting me off with promises.* **3.** To postpone. **put on. 1.** To clothe oneself with; don. **2.** To set on the stove or fire: *put on the kettle for tea.* **3.** To apply or activate: *put on the brake.* **4.** To assume or pretend to have: *putting on an air of kindliness.* **5.** *Slang.* To mock or fool: *He's always putting somebody on.* **6.** To present (a play). **7.** To add: *putting on weight.* **put out. 1.** To extinguish. **2.** *Informal.* To worry, annoy, or anger: *put out by her lateness.* **3.** To put (oneself) to some trouble or inconvenience for another. **4.** To publish. **5.** *Baseball.* To cause (a batter or runner) to be out. **put over.** *Informal.* To achieve. **2.** To win acceptance for deceitfully. **put through. 1.** To complete successfully. **2.** To connect by phone. **put up. 1.** To raise: *put up your hands.* **2.** To build. **3.** To provide or contribute: *putting up $10 apiece.* **4.** To offer, as for sale.

5. To prepare: *putting up plum jelly.* **6.** To accommodate: *He put us up for the night.* **put upon.** To impose on; take advantage of: *He was put upon by his friends.* —*n.* An act of putting the shot. —*adj. Informal.* Fixed; stationary: *stay put.* —**idioms. be hard put.** To have difficulty doing, finding, or getting something: *She was hard put for an excuse.* **put in for.** To apply for: *putting in for a different job.* **put up with.** To endure; tolerate. [Middle English *putten.*]

pu·ta·tive (pyōō′tə-tĭv) *adj.* Generally regarded as such; supposed; reputed: *testing the putative excellence of the region's wines.* [Middle English, from Old French *putatif,* from Late Latin *putātīvus,* from Latin *putāre,* to compute, consider.] —**pu·ta·tive·ly** *adv.*

put-down (pōōt′doun′) *n. Slang.* A dismissal or rejection, esp. in the form of a critical or slighting remark.

put-on (pōōt′ŏn′, -ôn′) *adj.* Pretended; feigned. —*n. Slang.* **1.** The act of teasing or misleading someone, esp. for amusement. **2.** Something intended as a hoax or joke, as an ironic or absurd assertion.

put-out (pōōt′out′) *n. Baseball.* A play that causes a batter or base runner to be out.

pu·tre·fac·tion (pyōō′trə-făk′shən) *n.* **1.** The partial decomposition of organic matter by microorganisms, producing foul-smelling matter. **2.** Putrefied matter. **3.** The condition of being putrefied. [Middle English *putrefaccioun,* from Late Latin *putrefactiō,* from Latin *putrefacere,* to putrefy.]

pu·tre·fac·tive (pyōō′trə-făk′tĭv) *adj.* **1.** Bringing about putrefaction. **2.** Of or characterized by putrefaction.

pu·tre·fy (pyōō′trə-fī′) *v.* **-fied, -fy·ing.** —*tr.v.* To decompose (something); cause to decay. —*intr.v.* To decompose. [Middle English *putrefien,* from Old French *putrefier,* from Latin *putrefacere* : *puter,* rotten + *facere,* to make.]

pu·tres·cent (pyōō-trĕs′ənt) *adj.* **1.** Becoming putrid; putrefying. **2.** Of putrefaction. [Latin *putrēscens,* pres. part. of *putrēscere,* to grow rotten, from *putrēre,* to be rotten, from *puter,* rotten.] —**pu·tres′cence** (-əns) *n.*

pu·trid (pyōō′trĭd) *adj.* **1.** In a decomposed, foul-smelling condition; rotten. **2.** Proceeding from or displaying putrefaction: *a putrid smell.* **3.** Corrupt; morally rotten. **4.** Extremely objectionable; vile. [Latin *putridus,* from *putrēre,* to be rotten.] —**pu·trid′i·ty** (-trĭd′ĭ-tē) or **pu′trid·ness** *n.* —**pu′trid·ly** *adv.*

putsch (pōōch) *n.* Also **Putsch.** A sudden attempt by a group to overthrow a government. [German *Putsch,* from Swiss German, a thrust.]

putt (pŭt) *Golf.* —*n.* A light stroke made on the putting green in an effort to place the ball into the hole. —*tr.v.* To hit (a ball) with such a stroke on the green. —*intr.v.* To execute a putt. [Var. of PUT.]

put·tee (pŭ-tē′, pŭt′ē) *n.* **1.** A strip of cloth wound spirally around the leg from ankle to knee, worn by soldiers and sportsmen. **2.** A leather covering for the lower leg. [Hindi *paṭṭī,* from Sanskrit *paṭṭikā,* from *paṭṭa,* cloth band.]

put·ter¹ (pŭt′ər) *Golf. n.* **1.** A short, stiff-shafted club used for putting. **2.** A golfer who is putting.

put·ter² (pŭt′ər) *v.* Also *Brit.* **pot·ter** (pŏt′ər). —*intr.v.* To occupy oneself in an active but aimless or ineffectual way: *just puttering around the garden.* —*tr.v.* To waste (time) in idling: *puttered the day away.* [Prob. from dial. *pote,* to push, kick.] —**put′ter·er** *n.*

putt·ing green (pŭt′ĭng). *Golf.* The area of smooth, closely cut grass at the end of a fairway in which the hole is placed.

put·ty (pŭt′ē) *n., pl.* **-ties.** **1.** A doughlike cement made by mixing whiting and linseed oil, used to fill holes in woodwork and to secure panes of glass. **2.** Any substance with a similar consistency or function. —*tr.v.* **-tied, -ty·ing.** To fill, cover, or secure with putty. [French *potée,* from Old French, a potful, from *pot,* a pot.]

put-up (pōōt′ŭp′) *adj. Informal.* Planned or prearranged secretly: *a put-up job.*

puz·zle (pŭz′əl) *v.* **-zled, -zling.** —*tr.v.* To cause uncertainty and indecision in; perplex. —*intr.v.* **1.** To be perplexed. **2.** To ponder over a problem in an effort to solve or understand it. —*phrasal verb.* **puzzle out.** To solve by lengthy reasoning or study. —*n.* **1.** Something that puzzles. **2.** A toy, game, or testing device that tests ingenuity.

3. The condition of being perplexed; bewilderment. [Orig. unknown.] —**puz′zler** *n.*

puz·zle·ment (pŭz′əl-mənt) *n.* The condition of being confused or baffled; perplexity.

pyc·nom·e·ter (pĭk-nŏm′ĭ-tər) *n.* A standard vessel used in measuring the density or specific gravity of materials. [Greek *puknos,* thick, dense + -METER.]

py·e·mi·a (pī-ē′mē-ə) *n.* The presence of pus in the blood. [Greek *puon,* pus + -EMIA.] —**py·e′mic** *adj.*

Pyg·ma·lion (pĭg-māl′yən, -mā′lē-ən) *n. Gk. Myth.* A king of Cyprus who carved and then fell in love with a statue of a woman, which Aphrodite brought to life as Galatea.

pyg·my (pĭg′mē). Also **pig·my** *n., pl.* **-mies.** An individual of unusually small size or significance. —*adj.* **1.** Unusually or atypically small: *a pygmy hippopotamus.* **2.** Unimportant; trivial. [Middle English *pigmie,* from Latin *pygmaeus,* dwarfish, from Greek *pugmaios,* from *pugmē,* fist.]

Pyg·my (pĭg′mē). Also **Pig·my** —*n., pl.* **-mies. 1.** A member of any of several African and Asian peoples with a hereditary stature of from four to five feet. **2.** *Gk. Myth.* A member of a race of dwarfs. —*adj.* Of or relating to the Pygmies.

py·ja·mas (pə-jä′məz, -jăm′əz) *pl.n. Brit.* Var. of **pajamas.**

py·lon (pī′lŏn′) *n.* **1.** A monumental gateway in the form of a pair of flat-topped pyramids that serves as the entrance to an ancient Egyptian temple. **2.** Any large structure or structures that marks an entrance or approach. **3.** A tower that marks a turning point in an air race. **4.** A steel tower that supports high-tension wires. [Greek *pulōn,* gateway, from *pulē,* a gate.]

py·lo·rus (pī-lôr′əs, -lōr′-, pĭ-) *n.* The passage that connects the stomach and the beginning of the small intestine. [Late Latin *pylōrus,* from Greek *pulōros* : *pulē,* gate + *ouros,* watcher, from *horan,* to see.] —**py·lo′ric** (-ĭk) *adj.*

py·or·rhe·a or **py·or·rhoe·a** (pī′ə-rē′ə) *n.* Inflammation of the gum and tooth sockets leading to loosening of the teeth. [Greek *puon,* pus + -RRHEA.] —**py′or·rhe′al** *adj.*

pyr·a·mid (pĭr′ə-mĭd) *n.* **1.** *Geom.* A polyhedron with a polygonal base and triangular faces that meet in a common vertex. **2.** Anything pyramidal in shape. **3.** A massive monument found esp. in Egypt, that has a rectangular base and four triangular faces that culminate in a single apex, and serves as a tomb or temple. —*tr.v.* To place or build in or as if in the shape of a pyramid. —*intr.v.* **1.** To assume the shape of a pyramid. **2.** To increase rapidly and on a widening base: *housing costs pyramiding at an alarming rate.* [Latin *pyramis,* from Greek *puramis.*]

pyramid

pyr·a·mi·dal (pĭ-răm′ĭ-dəl) *adj.* Also **pyr·a·mid·ic** (pĭr′ə-mĭd′-ĭk) or **pyr·a·mid·i·cal** (-ĭ-kəl). Of or having the shape of a pyramid. —**pyr·am′i·dal·ly** *adv.*

pyre (pīr) *n.* **1.** A pile of wood for burning a corpse as a funeral rite. **2.** Any pile of combustibles. [Latin *pyra,* from Greek *pura,* from *pur,* fire.]

pyr·e·thrin (pī-rē′thrĭn) *n.* Either of two viscous liquid esters, $C_{21}H_{28}O_3$ or $C_{21}H_{28}O_5$, that are extracted from pyrethrum flowers and are used as insecticides. [PYRETHR(UM) + -IN.]

py·re·thrum (pī-rē′thrəm, -rĕth′rəm) *n.* **1.** Any of several Old World plants of the genus *Chrysanthemum* and related genera, cultivated for its showy flowers. **2.** The dried flowers of certain of these plants used as an insecticide. [From Latin *pyrethrum,* Spanish chamomile, from Greek *purethron,* feverfew.]

py·ret·ic (pī-rĕt′ĭk) *adj.* Characterized or affected by fever; feverish. [From Greek *puretikos*, from *puretos*, fever, from *pur*, fire.]

Py·rex (pī′rĕks′) *n.* A trademark for any of various types of heat-resistant and chemical-resistant glass.

pyr·i·dine (pĭr′ĭ-dēn′) *n.* A flammable, colorless or yellowish liquid base, C_5H_5N, used to synthesize vitamins and drugs, as a solvent, and as a denaturant for alcohol. [PYR(O)- + -ID + -INE.] **—py·rid·ic** (pī-rĭd′ĭk) *adj.*

pyr·i·dox·ine (pĭr′ĭ-dŏk′sēn′, -sĭn) *n.* Also **pyr·i·dox·in** (-sĭn). A pyridine derivative, $C_8H_{11}O_3N$, occurring in plant and animal tissues and active in various metabolic processes. Also called **vitamin B$_6$**. [PYRID(INE) + OX- + -INE.]

py·rim·i·dine (pī-rĭm′ĭ-dēn′, pĭ-) *n.* **1.** A liquid and crystalline organic base, $C_4H_4N_2$. **2.** Any of several basic compounds, such as uracil, that has a molecular structure similar to pyrimidine and is found in living matter as a nucleotide component. [Var. of PYRIDINE.]

py·rite (pī′rīt′) *n.* A yellow to brown, widely occurring mineral sulfide, FeS_2, used as an iron ore and to produce sulfur dioxide for sulfuric acid. Also called **fool's gold**. [Latin *pyrītēs*, pyrites.] **—py·rit·ic** (pī-rĭt′ĭk) or **py·rit′i·cal** *adj.*

py·ri·tes (pī-rī′tēz, pĭ-) *n., pl.* **pyrites.** Any of various natural metallic sulfides, esp. of iron. [Latin *pyrītēs*, flint, pyrite, from Greek *puritēs (lithos)*, "fire (stone)," from *pur*, fire.]

pyro-. A prefix meaning fire or heat: **pyrotechnic.** [From Greek *pur*, fire.]

py·rog·ra·phy (pī-rŏg′rə-fē) *n.* **1.** The art or process of producing designs on wood, leather, or other material by using heated tools or a fine flame. **2.** A design made by this process. **—py′ro·graph′** (pī′rə-grăf′) *n.* **—py·rog′ra·pher** *n.* **—py′ro·graph′ic** *adj.*

py·rol·y·sis (pī-rŏl′ĭ-sĭs) *n.* Chemical change caused by heat. **—py′ro·lyt′ic** (pī′rə-lĭt′ĭk) *adj.*

py·ro·ma·ni·a (pī′rō-mā′nē-ə, -mān′yə) *n.* The uncontrollable impulse to start fires. **—py′ro·ma′ni·ac′** (-mā′nē-ăk′) *n.* **—py′ro·ma·ni′a·cal** (-mə-nī′ə-kəl) *adj.*

py·rom·e·ter (pī-rŏm′ĭ-tər) *n.* An electrical thermometer for measuring high temperatures.

py·ro·tech·nic (pī′rə-tĕk′nĭk) or **py·ro·tech·ni·cal** (-nĭ-kəl) *adj.* **1.** Of or relating to fireworks. **2.** Resembling fireworks; brilliant: *a pyrotechnic wit.* **—py′ro·tech′ni·cal·ly** *adv.*

py·ro·tech·nics (pī′rə-tĕk′nĭks) *n.* **1.** *(used with a sing. verb).* Also **py·ro·tech·ny** (-nē). The art of manufacturing or setting off fireworks. **2.** *(used with a sing. or pl. verb).* A fireworks display. **3.** *(used with a sing. or pl. verb).* A brilliant display, as of eloquence or artistic talent. **—py′ro·tech′nist** *n.*

py·rox·y·lin (pī-rŏk′sə-lĭn, pĭ-) *n.* Also **py·rox·y·line** (-lēn′, -lĭn). A highly flammable nitrocellulose used in the manufacture of plastics and lacquers. [PYRO- + XYL(O)- + -IN.]

Pyr·rhic victory (pĭr′ĭk). A victory won with staggering losses, such as that of Pyrrhus (319–272 B.C.), king of Epirus, over the Romans at Asculum in 279 B.C.

py·ru·vic acid (pī-rōō′vĭk, pĭ-). A colorless liquid, CH_3CO-COOH, formed as a fundamental intermediate in protein and carbohydrate metabolism. [PYR(O)- + Latin *ūva*, grape.]

Py·thag·o·re·an theorem (pī-thăg′ə-rē′ən). The theorem that the sum of the squares of the lengths of the sides of a right triangle is equal to the square of the length of the hypotenuse. [After *Pythagoras*, Greek philosopher of the 6th cent. B.C.]

Pyth·i·an (pĭth′ē-ən) *adj.* Of or relating to ancient Delphi, the temple of Apollo at Delphi, or its oracle. [From Latin *Pythius*, from Greek *Puthios*, from *Puthō, Puthōn*, an ancient name for Delphi.]

Py·thon (pī′thŏn′, -thən) *n. Gk. Myth.* **1.** A dragon or serpent that guarded the oracular cult at Delphi until killed by Apollo. **2.** Any of various large, nonvenomous Old World snakes of the family Pythonidae, that coil around and crush their prey.

py·tho·ness (pī′thə-nĭs, pĭth′ə-) *n.* **1.** The priestess of Apollo at Delphi. **2.** A prophetess. [Middle English *phitonesse*, from Old French *pithonise*, from Late Latin *pȳthōnissa*, from Greek *Puthōn*, Python.]

pyx (pĭks) *n.* **1. a.** A container in which supplies of wafers for the Eucharist are kept. **b.** A container in which the Eucharist is carried to the sick. **2.** A chest in a mint in which specimen coins are placed to await testing. [Middle English *pyxe*, from Latin *pyxis*, box, from Greek *puxis*.]

pyx·id·i·um (pĭk-sĭd′ē-əm) *n., pl.* **-i·a** (-ē-ə). A seed capsule having a circular lid that falls off to release the seeds. Also called **pyxidium.** [Greek *puxis*, box.]

ă pat   ā pay   â care   ä father   ĕ pet   ē be   hw which   ĭ pit   ī tie   î pier   ŏ pot   ō toe   ô paw, for   oi noise
ōō took   ōō boot   ou out   th thin   *th* this   ŭ cut   û urge   zh vision   ə about, item, edible, gallop, circus

| Phoenician | Greek | Roman | Medieval | Modern |

q, Q (kyōō) *n., pl.* **q's** or **Q's.** The 17th letter of the modern English alphabet.

quack[1] (kwăk) *n.* The characteristic sound of a duck. —*intr.v.* To make a quack. [Imit.]

quack[2] (kwăk) *n.* **1.** A person who pretends to have medical knowledge. **2.** A charlatan. —See Syns at **imposter.** —*modifier: a quack cure.* [Short for *quacksalver,* from Dutch.] —**quack'er·y** *n.*

quack grass. A weedy, rapidly spreading grass, *Agropyron repens.* [Var. of QUITCH GRASS.]

quad[1] (kwŏd) *n. Informal.* A quadrangle.

quad[2] (kwŏd) *n. Printing.* A quadrat.

quad[3] (kwŏd) *n.* Quadruplet.

quadr-. Var. of quadri-.

quad·ran·gle (kwŏd'răng'gəl) *n.* **1.** *Geom.* A quadrilateral. **2. a.** A rectangular area surrounded on all four sides by buildings. **b.** The buildings bordering this area. [Middle English, from Old French, from Late Latin *quadriangulum,* from Latin, having four angles.]

quad·rant (kwŏd'rənt) *n.* **1.** *Geom.* **a.** A quarter of a circle; an arc of 90°. **b.** The area bounded by a quarter circle and two perpendicular radii. **c.** Any of the four areas into which a plane is divided by perpendicular axes in a Cartesian coordinate system. **2.** A navigational and astronomical instrument, used to measure altitude and the angular distance between an object and the horizon. [Middle English, quarter of a day, from Latin *quadrāns,* fourth part, quarter.]

quad·ra·phon·ic (kwŏd'rə-fŏn'ĭk) *adj.* Of or used in a sound-reproduction system with four transmission channels. [QUADR(I)- + PHONIC.]

quad·rat (kwŏd'rət, -răt') *n.* A piece of type metal lower than the raised typeface, used for filling spaces and blank lines. [Var. of QUADRATE.]

quad·rate (kwŏd'rāt', -rĭt) *n.* An approx. square or rectangular area or object. —*adj.* Square or rectangular.

quad·rat·ic (kwŏ-drăt'ĭk) *adj.* Of, pertaining to, or containing mathematical quantities of the second degree and no higher.

quadratic equation. An equation of the second degree, with the general form $ax^2 + bx + c = 0.$

quad·ra·ture (kwŏd'rə-chōōr', -chər) *n.* **1.** *Math.* The process of constructing a square equal in area to a given surface. **2.** A configuration in which there is an angular separation of 90° between two celestial bodies, as measured from a third.

quad·ren·ni·al (kwŏ-drĕn'ē-əl) *adj.* **1.** Happening once in four years. **2.** Lasting for four years. [From Latin *quadrennium,* a period of four years : *quadr-,* four + *annus,* year.] —**quad·ren'ni·al·ly** *adv.*

quadri– or **quadru–** or **quadr–.** A prefix meaning four: quadriceps. [Latin.]

quad·ri·ceps (kwŏd'rĭ-sĕps') *n.* The large four-part extensor muscle at the front of the thigh. [QUADRI- + (BI)CEPS.]

quad·ri·lat·er·al (kwŏd'rə-lăt'ər-əl) *n.* A polygon that has four sides and four angles. —*adj.* Having four sides.

qua·drille (kwŏ-drĭl', kwə-, kwŏ-) *n.* **1.** A square dance performed by four couples. **2.** Music for a quadrille. [French, orig. "one of the four divisions of an army," from Spanish *cuadrilla,* from Latin *quadra.*]

quad·ril·lion (kwŏ-drĭl'yən) *n.* **1.** In the United States, the cardinal number represented by 1 followed by 15 zeros. **2.** In Great Britain, the cardinal number represented by 1 followed by 24 zeros. [French : *quadr(i)-,* four + *(m)illion,* million.] —**quad·ril'lion** *adj.*

quad·ri·par·tite (kwŏd'rə-pär'tīt') *adj.* **1.** Consisting of or divided into four parts. **2.** Involving four participants.

quad·roon (kwŏ-drōōn') *n.* A person with one quarter Negro ancestry. [From Spanish *cuarteron,* from *cuarto,* quarter, from Latin *quārtus.*]

quadru-. Var. of quadri-.

quad·ru·ped (kwŏd'rə-pĕd') *n.* A four-footed animal. —*adj.* Four-footed.

quad·ru·ple (kwŏ-drōō'pəl, -drŭp'əl, kwŏd'rə-pəl) *adj.* **1.** Having four parts. **2.** Multiplied by four; fourfold. **3.** *Mus.* Having four beats to the measure. —*n.* A number or amount four times as many or as much as another. —*v.* **-pled, -pling.** —*tr.v.* To multiply or increase by four. —*intr.v.* To become four times as great. [French, from Latin *quadruplus.*]

quad·ru·plet (kwŏ-drŭp'lĭt, -drōō'plĭt, kwŏd'rə-plĭt) *n.* **1.** A group or combination of four. **2.** One of four offspring born in a single birth.

quad·ru·pli·cate (kwŏ-drōō'plĭ-kĭt) *adj.* Multiplied by four; quadruple. —*n.* One of a set or group of four. —*v.* (-kāt') **-cat·ed, -cat·ing.** —*tr.v.* To quadruple. [Latin *quadruplicātus,* past part. of *quadruplicāre,* to multiply by four, from *quadruplex,* fourfold.] —**quad·ru'pli·ca'tion** *n.*

quaes·tor (kwĕs'stər, kwē'stər) *n.* Any of various public officials in ancient Rome responsible for finance and administration. [Middle English *questor,* from Latin *quaestor,* from *quaerere,* to seek, to ask.]

---

quaff (kwŏf, kwăf, kwôf) *tr.v.* To drink heartily. —*intr.v.* To drink something heartily. [Orig. unknown.] —**quaff** *n.*

quag (kwăg, kwŏg) *n.* A bog; marsh. [Orig. unknown.]

quag·ga (kwăg'ə, kwŏg'ə) *n.* An extinct zebralike mammal, *Equus quagga*, of southern Africa. [Afrikaans.]

quag·gy (kwăg'ē, kwŏg'ē) *adj.* **-gi·er, -gi·est.** Marshy; soggy.

quag·mire (kwăg'mīr', kwŏg'-) *n.* **1.** Land with a soft, muddy surface that yields when stepped on. **2.** A difficult or precarious situation.

qua·hog (kwô'hôg', -hŏg', kwō'-, kō'-) *n.* An edible, hard-shelled clam, *Venus mercenaria*, of the Atlantic coast of North America. [Narraganset *poquaûhock*.]

quail[1] (kwāl) *n., pl.* **quail** or **quails.** Any of various chickenlike game birds of the genus *Coturnix*, usu. with mottled brown plumage and a short tail. [Middle English *quaille*, from Old French, from Medieval Latin *quaccula*.]

quail[1]
George Miksch Sutton

quail[2] (kwāl) *intr.v.* To shrink back in fear; cower. [Middle English *quailen*, to decline, fail.]

quaint (kwānt) *adj.* **-er, -est. 1.** Charmingly old-fashioned: *a quaint old inn.* **2.** Unfamiliar or unusual in character. — See Syns at **strange.** [Middle English *queinte*, clever, skillfully made, from Old French *cointe*, expert, elegant, from Latin *cognitus*, past part. of *cognōscere*, to be acquainted with.] —**quaint'ly** *adv.* —**quaint'ness** *n.*

quake (kwāk) *intr.v.* **quaked, quak·ing. 1.** To shake or tremble, as from instability or shock. **2.** To shiver or tremble, as from cold or fear. —See Syns at **shake.** —*n.* **1.** An instance of quaking. **2.** An earthquake. [Middle English *quaken*, from Old English *cwacian*.] —**quak'y** *adj.*

Quak·er (kwā'kər) *n.* A member of the Society of Friends. —**Quak'er·ism'** *n.*

qual·i·fi·ca·tion (kwŏl'ə-fĭ-kā'shən) *n.* **1.** The act of qualifying or the condition of being qualified. **2.** A quality or ability that suits a person for a particular position or task. **3.** A condition that must be met or complied with. **4.** A restriction or limitation: *accept without qualification.*

qual·i·fied (kwŏl'ə-fīd') *adj.* **1.** Possessing the qualifications for a specific position or task. **2.** Limited, restricted, or modified: *qualified optimism.* —See Syns at **able.**

qual·i·fi·er (kwŏl'ə-fī'ər) *n.* **1.** Someone or something that qualifies. **2.** *Gram.* A word or phrase that qualifies, limits, or modifies the meaning of another word or phrase.

qual·i·fy (kwŏl'ə-fī') *v.* **-fied, -fy·ing.** —*tr.v.* **1.** To describe by naming the characteristics of; characterize. **2.** To make competent or eligible for an office, position, or task. **3.** To declare competent or capable; certify. **4.** To modify, limit, or restrict. **5.** To make less harsh or severe; moderate. **6.** *Gram.* To modify the meaning of (a word or phrase). —*intr.v.* To be or to become qualified. [Old French *qualifier*, from Medieval Latin *quālificāre*, to attribute a quality to : Latin *quālis*, of what kind + *facere*, to make.]

qual·i·ta·tive (kwŏl'ĭ-tā'tĭv) *adj.* Of, pertaining to, or concerning quality. —**qual'i·ta'tive·ly** *adv.*

qualitative analysis. A chemical analysis that identifies the constituents of a substance.

qual·i·ty (kwŏl'ĭ-tē) *n., pl.* **-ties. 1.** The essential character of something; nature. **2. a.** An inherent or distinguishing characteristic; property. **b.** A personal trait, esp. a character trait: *He has many redeeming qualities.* **3.** Degree or grade of excellence: *yard goods of low quality.* **4.** High social position: *a lady of quality.* **6.** *Mus.* Timbre, as of a tone or an instrument. [Middle English *qualite*, from Old French, from Latin *quālitās*, from *quālis*, of what kind.]

qualm (kwŏm, kwôm) *n.* **1.** A sudden, brief feeling of sickness, faintness, or nausea. **2.** A sudden feeling of doubt or misgiving. **3.** A pang of conscience. [Orig. unknown.] —**qualm'ish** *adj.*

Syns: **qualm, compunction, misgiving, reservation, scruple** *n.* *Core meaning:* A feeling of uncertainty about the fitness or correctness of an action (*had qualms about printing that kind of story*).

quan·da·ry (kwŏn'də-rē, kwŏn'drē) *n., pl.* **-ries.** A condition of uncertainty or doubt; dilemma. [Origin unknown.]

quan·ta (kwŏn'tə) *n.* Plural of **quantum.**

quan·ti·fy (kwŏn'tə-fī') *tr.v.* **-fied, -fy·ing.** To determine or express the quantity of. [Medieval Latin *quantificāre* : *quantus*, how great + *facere*, to make.]

quan·ti·ta·tive (kwŏn'tĭ-tā'tĭv) *adj.* Of, pertaining to, or expressed as the measurement of quantity.

quantitative analysis. A chemical analysis that determines amounts or proportions of constituents in a substance.

quan·ti·ty (kwŏn'tĭ-tē) *n., pl.* **-ties. 1.** A specified or indefinite number or amount. **2.** A large amount or number: *produce oil in quantity.* **3.** The property of a thing that can be determined by measurement. **4.** *Math.* Something, as a number or symbol, that serves as the object of a mathematical operation. **5.** *Ling.* The duration of a speech sound. [Middle English *quantite*, from Old French, from Latin *quantitās*, from *quantus*, how great.]

quan·tum (kwŏn'təm) *n., pl.* **-ta** (-tə). **1.** A quantity or amount. **2.** *Physics.* A very small indivisible unit of energy. [Latin, neuter of *quantus*, how great.]

quantum mechanics. *Physics.* Quantum theory, esp. of the structure and behavior of atoms and molecules.

quantum theory. *Physics.* A theory of atomic and subatomic interaction based on the behavior of the photon as both a wave and a particle.

quar·an·tine (kwôr'ən-tēn', kwŏr'-) *n.* **1. a.** A period of time during which a person, animal, or object suspected of carrying a contagious disease is detained at a port of entry to prevent disease from entering a country. **b.** A place for such detention. **2.** A condition of enforced isolation. —*tr.v.* **-tined, -tin·ing.** To isolate in or as if in quarantine. [Italian *quarantina (giorni)*, forty(days), from *quaranta*, forty, from Latin *quadrāgintā*.]

quark (kwôrk) *n.* *Physics.* One of a group of hypothetical subatomic particles that have electric charges of a magnitude one-third or two-thirds that of the electron, proposed as the fundamental units of matter. [Coined by Murray Gell-Mann (b. 1929), American physicist, perh. after a word in James Joyce's *Finnegans Wake*.]

quar·rel (kwôr'əl, kwŏr'-) *n.* **1.** An angry dispute; argument. **2.** A cause for a dispute or argument. —*intr.v.* **-reled** or **-relled, -rel·ing** or **-rel·ling. 1.** To engage in a quarrel. **2.** To find fault with something; complain: *quarrel with a panel's conclusions.* —See Syns at **argue.** [Middle English, (cause for) complaint, from Old French, from Latin *querēla*, from *querī*, to complain.]

quar·rel·some (kwôr'əl-səm, kwŏr'-) *adj.* Tending to quarrel. —**quar'rel·some·ly** *adv.* —**quar'rel·some·ness** *n.*

quar·ry[1] (kwôr'ē, kwŏr'ē) *n., pl.* **-ries. 1.** A hunted animal; prey. **2.** The object of a hunt or pursuit. [Middle English *querre*, entrails of a beast given to the hounds, from Old French *cuiree*, from Late Latin *corāta*, viscera, from Latin *cor*, heart.]

quar·ry[2] (kwôr'ē, kwŏr'ē) *n., pl.* **-ries.** An open excavation or pit from which stone is obtained by digging, cutting, or blasting. —*tr.v.* **-ried, -ry·ing. 1.** To dig or obtain from or as if from a quarry. **2.** To make a quarry in. [Middle English *quarey*, from Old French *quarriere*, from Latin *quadrus*, square.] —**quar'ri·er** *n.*

quart (kwôrt) *n. Abbr.* **q., qt, qt. 1. a.** A unit of liquid volume or capacity equal to two pints or 57.75 cubic inches. **b.** A unit of dry volume or capacity equal to two pints or 67.2 cubic inches. **2.** A container with a capacity of one quart. [Middle English, from Old French *quarte*, fourth part (of a gallon), from Latin *quārtus*, fourth.]

quar·tan (kwôr'tn) *adj.* Occurring every fourth day, count-

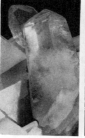

quarter-deck	quarter horse	quartz	quatrefoil

ing inclusively, or every 72 hours. —*n.* A recurrent malarial fever, occurring every 72 hours. [Middle English *quarteyne,* from Old French *quartaine,* from Latin *quārtāna (fēbris),* from *quārtus,* fourth.]

quar·ter (kwôr′tər) *n. Abbr.* **q., qr., quar. 1.** One of four equal parts of something. **2.** A U.S. or Canadian coin equal to one-fourth of the dollar, or 25 cents. **3.** A quarter-hour. **4.** One-fourth of a year; three months. **5.** An academic term lasting for approx. three months. **6.** *Astron.* One-fourth of the period of the moon's revolution around the earth. **7.** *Sports.* One of four equal periods of playing time in which some games are divided. **8.** A unit that equals one-fourth of a larger unit, esp. of length or weight. **9. a.** One of the four major divisions of the compass. **b.** One of the four major divisions of the horizon. **10.** *Naut.* The rear side of a ship. **11.** *Heraldry.* Any of four equal divisions of a shield. **12.** One leg of a carcass of a four-legged animal, usu. including the adjoining parts. **13.** The part of the side of a shoe between the heel and the vamp. **14. quarters.** A place of residence. **15.** Often **quarters.** A proper or assigned station or place, as on a warship. **16.** A specific district or section, as of a city: *the Latin quarter.* **17.** An unspecified direction, person, or group of persons: *information from the highest quarters.* **18.** Mercy, esp. to a defeated enemy. —*tr.v.* **1.** To divide into four equal or equivalent parts. **2.** To divide or separate into a number of parts. **3.** To dismember. **4.** To furnish with housing. —*intr.v.* To occupy or be assigned lodgings. —*adj.* Equal to or being a quarter. —*idiom.* **at close quarters.** At close range. [Middle English, from Old French *quartier,* from Latin *quārtārius,* from *quārtus,* fourth.]

quar·ter·back (kwôr′tər-băk′) *n. Football.* **1.** An offensive backfield player whose position is behind the center of scrimmage and who usu. calls the signals for the plays. —*tr.v.* Football. To play quarterback.

quar·ter·deck (kwôr′tər-děk′) *n.* The rear area of the upper deck of a sailing ship, usu. reserved for officers.

quarter horse. A strong, muscular saddle horse able to run short distances at high speed. [From its being trained for quarter-mile races.]

quar·ter·hour (kwôr′tər-our′) *n.* Also **quarter hour. 1.** Fifteen minutes. **2.** A quarter point of an hour, as marked on a clock.

quar·ter·ly (kwôr′tər-lē) *adj.* Occurring at regular three-month intervals. —*adv.* At three-month intervals. —*n., pl.* **-lies.** A publication issued regularly every three months.

quar·ter·mas·ter (kwôr′tər-măs′tər) *n.* **1.** A military officer responsible for the food, clothing, and equipment of troops. **2.** A naval petty officer responsible for the navigation of a ship. [From QUARTER (residence).]

quar·tern (kwôr′tərn) *n.* A quarter; one-fourth. [Middle English *quarteron,* from Old French, from *quartier,* quarter.]

quarter note. A musical note equal to one-fourth the time value of a whole note.

quar·ter·saw (kwôr′tər-sô′) *tr.v.* **-sawed, -sawed** or **-sawn** (-sôn′), **-saw·ing.** To saw (a log) into quarters lengthwise.

quarter section. A quarter of a square mile of land.

quar·ter·staff (kwôr′tər-stăf′) *n., pl.* **-staves** (-stāvz′). A long wooden staff, formerly used as a weapon.

quar·tet (kwôr-tĕt′) *n.* Also **quar·tette. 1.** A musical composition for four voices or instruments. **2.** A group of four.

[Italian *quartetto,* dim. of *quarto,* fourth, from Latin *quārto.*]

quar·to (kwôr′tō) *n., pl.* **-tos. 1.** The page size obtained by folding a whole sheet into four leaves. **2.** A book composed of quarto pages. [Latin *(in) quārto,* in quarter, from *quārtus,* fourth.]

quartz (kwôrts) *n.* A hard, crystalline mineral composed of silicon dioxide, SiO_2, that is colorless and transparent in its pure state, and sometimes brightly colored in certain impure varieties, such as agate, chalcedony, and opal. [German *Quarz.*]

quartz·ite (kwôrt′sīt′) *n.* A metamorphic rock that results from the compression of quartz sandstone.

qua·sar (kwā′zär′, -sär′) *n.* Any of several classes of starlike objects that emit radio waves and visible radiation. Also called **quasi-stellar object.** [QUAS(I) + (STELL)AR.]

quash (kwŏsh, kwôsh) *tr.v.* **1.** *Law.* To set aside or annul: *quash an indictment.* **2.** To put down or suppress forcibly and completely: *quashed the rebellion.* [Middle English *quassen,* from Old French *quasser,* from Late Latin *cassāre,* from Latin *cassus,* empty, void.]

qua·si (kwā′zī′, -sī′, kwä′zē, -sē) *adj.* Having a resemblance or likeness to something. [From QUASI-.]

quasi-. A prefix meaning almost or somewhat: **quasi-stellar object.** [Latin *quasi,* as if : *quam,* than, how + *sī,* if.]

qua·si-stel·lar object (kwā′zī-stĕl′ər, -sī-, kwä′zē-, -sē-). A quasar.

quas·sia (kwŏsh′ə) *n.* **1.** A tree, *Quassia amara,* of tropical America, with bright scarlet flowers. **2.** A bitter tonic substance obtained from the wood and bark of the quassia, used in medicine and as an insecticide. [After Graman Quassi, discoverer of its medicinal properties.]

Qua·ter·nar·y (kwŏt′ər-nĕr′ē, kwə-tûr′nə-rē) *n.* Also **Quaternary period.** A geologic period that began 2,000,000 to 500,000 years ago and extends to the present time. [Latin *quaternārius,* consisting of four each, from *quater,* four times.]

quat·rain (kwŏt′rān′, kwŏ-trān′) *n.* A poem or stanza of four lines. [French, from Old French, from *quatre,* four, from Latin *quattuor.*]

quat·re·foil (kăt′ər-foil′, kăt′rə-) *n.* **1.** A figure of a flower with four petals or a leaf with four leaflets. **2.** *Archit.* An ornament or design with four foils or lobes. [Middle English *quaterfoile,* set of four leaves : *quater-,* four, from Old French *quatre* + *foile,* leaf.]

qua·ver (kwā′vər) *intr.v.* **1.** To shake or tremble, as from weakness. **2.** To speak tremulously or shakily. **3.** To produce a trill on a musical instrument or with the voice. —*tr.v.* To utter or sing in a trilling voice. —See Syns at **shake.** —*n.* **1.** A quavering sound. **2.** A trill. [Middle English *quaveren,* freq. of *quaven,* to tremble.] —**qua′ver·ing·ly** *adv.* —**qua′ver·y** *adj.*

quay (kē) *n.* A wharf or reinforced bank where ships are loaded or unloaded. [Middle English *kay,* from Old French *cay.*]

quean (kwēn) *n.* A disreputable woman. [Middle English *quene,* from Old English *cwene,* woman.]

quea·sy (kwē′zē) *adj.* **-si·er, -si·est.** Also **quea·zy. 1. a.** Nauseated. **b.** Causing nausea. **2.** Easily nauseated. **3. a.** Causing uneasiness: *a queasy situation.* **b.** Uneasy; troubled: *feeling queasy about the situation.* **4.** Easily troubled; squeamish or fastidious. [Middle English qwesye, unsettled.] —**quea'si·ly** adv. —**quea'si·ness** n.

que·bra·cho (kā-brä'chō, kǐ-) n., pl. **-chos.** 1. Any of several South American trees of the sumac family with very hard wood, esp. *Schinopsis lorentzii,* whose wood yields tannin. 2. The bark or wood of a quebracho.[American Spanish, var. of *quiebrahacha,* "ax-breaker."]

Quech·ua (kěch'wə) n, pl. **Quechua** or **-uas.** 1. A member of a tribe of South American Indians of central Peru. 2. The language of the Quechua. —**Quech'uan** adj.

queen (kwēn) n. 1. The wife or widow of a king. 2. A female monarch or ruler. 3. A woman, a goddess, or a personification as a woman, considered to be eminent or supreme in a given domain: *Paris is the queen of European cities.* 4. *Chess.* The most powerful piece, with the ability to move in any direction in a straight line. 5. A playing card bearing the figure of a queen, ranking above the jack and below the king in each suit. 6. The fertile, fully developed female in a colony of social bees, ants, or termites. —*tr.v.* 1. To make (a woman) a queen. 2. *Chess.* To raise (a pawn) to queen. [Middle English *queene,* from Old English *cwēn,* woman.] —**queen'li·ness** n. —**queen'ly** adj.

queen
Queen Elizabeth II

Queen Anne's lace

Queen Anne's lace (ănz). A widely distributed plant, *Daucus carota,* with finely divided leaves and flat clusters of small white flowers. Also called **wild carrot.**

queen consort. The wife of a reigning king.

queen mother. A dowager queen who is the mother of the reigning monarch.

queen post. One of two vertical supporting posts set between the rafters and the tie beam at the truss of a roof.

queer (kwîr) adj. 1. Differing from the expected or normal; strange: *a queer spring snowfall.* 2. Odd or unconventional in behavior; eccentric. 3. Arousing suspicion; questionable. 4. Not feeling well physically; queasy. 5. *Slang.* Fake; counterfeit: *a queer dollar bill.* —See Syns at **strange.** —*tr.v. Slang.* 1. To ruin or thwart. 2. To put into a bad or embarrassing position. [Orig. unknown.] —**queer'ly** adv. —**queer'ness** n.

quell (kwěl) tr.v. 1. To put down forcibly; suppress: *quell a revolt.* 2. To pacify; quiet: *quell one's fears.* [Middle English *quellen,* to kill, destroy, from Old English *cwellan.*]

quench (kwěnch) tr.v. 1. To put out; extinguish: *quench a candle.* 2. To suppress; squelch: *quench one's jealousy.* 3. To put an end to; destroy. 4. To slake; satisfy. 5. To cool (hot metal) by thrusting in water or other liquid. —See Syns at **extinguish.** [Middle English *quenchen,* Old English *ācwencan.* —**quench'a·ble** adj.

quern (kwûrn) n. A hand-turned mill for grinding grain. [Middle English *querne,* from Old English *cweorn.*]

quer·u·lous (kwěr'ə-ləs, kwěr'yə-) adj. 1. Given to complaining or fretting; peevish. 2. Expressing or showing a complaint; fretful: *a querulous voice.* —See Syns at **irritable.** [Latin *querulus,* from *queri,* to complain.] —**quer'u·lous·ly** adv. —**quer'u·lous·ness** n.

que·ry (kwîr'ē) n., pl. **-ries.** 1. A question; an inquiry. 2. A doubt in the mind; reservation. 3. A question mark. —*tr.v.* **-ried, -ry·ing.** 1. To express doubt about. 2. To put in the form of a question. 3. To put a question to (a person). 4. To mark with a question mark. [From Latin *quaere,* imper. of *quaerere,* to seek, ask.]

quest (kwěst) n. 1. A search; pursuit. 2. In medieval romance, a chivalrous expedition undertaken by a knight.

—*intr.v.* To go on a quest. [Middle English *queste,* from Old French, from the past part. of Latin *quaerere,* to seek.]

ques·tion (kwěs'chən) n. 1. An expression of inquiry made to elicit information. 2. A subject open to doubt or controversy. 3. A matter; issue: *a question of ethics.* 4. A subject under discussion or being considered: *debating the question of how to implement the new regulations.* 5. A proposition brought up for consideration by an assembly. 6. Uncertainty; doubt: *no question about its importance.* —See Syns at **doubt.** —*tr.v.* 1. To put a question to. 2. To interrogate, as a witness or suspect. 3. To express doubt about. —*intr.v.* To ask questions. —**idioms. in question.** Under discussion: *the individual in question.* **out of the question.** Not to be considered; unthinkable. [Middle English, from Old French, from Latin *quaestiō,* from *quaestus,* past part. of *quaerere,* to seek, ask.] —**ques'tion·er** n. —**ques'tion·ing·ly** adv.

ques·tion·a·ble (kwěs'chə-nə-bəl) adj. 1. Open to doubt; uncertain. 2. Of dubious morality or respectability; suspicious: *questionable behavior.* —**ques'tion·a·bly** adv.

question mark. A punctuation symbol (?) written at the end of a sentence or phrase to indicate a direct question.

ques·tion·naire (kwěs'chə-nâr') n. A set of questions asked of a number of people as a means of gathering statistical information. [French, from *questionner,* to question, from *question,* question.]

quet·zal (kět-säl') n., pl. **-zals** or **-za·les** (-sä'läs). A Central American bird, *Pharomacrus mocino,* with brilliant bronze-green and red plumage and, in the male, long, flowing tail feathers. [American Spanish, from Nahuatl *quetzalli,* large brilliant tail feather.]

queue (kyōō) n. 1. A line of people or vehicles. 2. A long braid of hair worn hanging down the back of the neck. —*intr.v.* **queued, queu·ing.** To form or wait in a line: *We queued up for tickets.* [French, tail, line, from Old French *cue,* tail, braid, from Latin *cauda,* tail.]

quib·ble (kwĭb'əl) intr.v. **-bled, -bling.** To make trivial distinctions or objections, esp. in order to evade an issue. —See Syns at **argue.** —n. A trivial distinction, objection, or criticism. [Perh. from obs. *quib,* an equivocation.] —**quib'bler** n.

quick (kwĭk) adj. **-er, -est.** 1. Moving or acting rapidly and energetically; speedy: *quick on one's feet.* 2. Occurring or achieved in a brief space of time: *a quick recovery.* 3. Understanding, thinking, or learning with speed; bright. 4. Perceiving or responding with speed and sensitivity; keen: *a quick wit.* 5. Easily stirred or aroused: *a quick temper.* 6. *Archaic.* Alive. —n. Sensitive flesh, as under the fingernails. —**idiom. cut to the quick.** To wound or offend deeply. [Middle English *quicke,* swift, lively, alive, from Old English *cwicu,* living, alive.] —**quick'ly** adv. —**quick'ness** n.

quick·en (kwĭk'ən) tr.v. 1. To make more rapid; accelerate. 2. To make alive. 3. To excite and stimulate; arouse: *quicken the emotions.* —*intr.v.* 1. To become more rapid. 2. To come or return to life. —See Syns at **expedite.**

quick-freeze (kwĭk'frēz') tr.v. **-froze** (-frōz'), **-fro·zen** (-frō'zən), **-freez·ing.** To freeze (food) so rapidly that natural flavor and nutritional value are preserved.

quick·ie (kwĭk'ē) n. *Informal.* Something made or done rapidly.

quick·lime (kwĭk'līm') n. Calcium oxide.

quick·sand (kwĭk'sănd') n. A soft, shifting mass of loose sand mixed with water which yields easily to pressure and in which a heavy object tends to sink.

quick·sil·ver (kwĭk'sĭl'vər) n. The element mercury. [Middle English *quicksilver,* from Old English *cwicseolfor* : *cwic,* alive + *seolfor,* silver.]

quick·step (kwĭk'stěp') n. *Mus.* A quick-tempo march tune for accompanying a military march.

quick-tem·pered (kwĭk'těm'pərd) adj. Easily angered.

quick time. A military marching pace of 120 steps per minute.

quick-wit·ted (kwĭk'wĭt'ĭd) adj. Mentally alert and sharp.

quid[1] (kwĭd) n. A piece of something chewable. [Middle English *quide,* cud, from Old English *cwidu.*]

quid[2] (kwĭd) n., pl. **quid** or **quids.** *Brit. Slang.* A pound sterling. [Orig. unknown.]

quid pro quo (kwĭd' prō kwō'). Something given in exchange for something else. [Latin, "something for something."]

qui·es·cent (kwī-ĕs′ənt, kwē-) *adj.* In a condition of inactivity or rest. [Latin *quiēscēns*, pres. part. of *quiēscere*, to be quiet.] —**qui·es′cence** *n.* —**qui·es′cent·ly** *adv.*

qui·et (kwī′ĭt) *adj.* **-er, -est. 1.** Making little or no noise; silent. **2.** Free of noise; hushed: *quiet street.* **3.** Calm and unmoving; still. **4.** Free of turmoil and agitation; untroubled. **5.** Characterized by tranquillity; serene; peaceful. **6.** Not showy; unobtrusive: *quiet clothing.* —*n.* The quality or condition of being quiet. —*tr.v.* To cause to become quiet. —*intr.v.* To become quiet. [Middle English, from Old French, from Latin *quiētus*, from *quiēscere*, to be quiet, to be at rest, from *quiēs*, quiet.] —**qui′et·ly** *adv.* —**qui′et·ness** *n.*

qui·e·tude (kwī′ĭ-tōōd′, -tyōōd′) *n.* A condition of tranquillity or repose.

qui·e·tus (kwī-ē′təs) *n.* **1.** Something that suppresses or quiets. **2.** Release from life; death. **3.** A final discharge, as of a duty or debt. [Medieval Latin *quiētus (est),* "(he is) discharged," from Latin *quiētus,* at rest, quiet.]

quill (kwĭl) *n.* **1.** The hollow, stemlike main shaft of a feather. **2.** Any of the larger wing or tail feathers of a bird. **3.** Anything made from or resembling the hollow stem of a feather, as a writing pen. **4.** One of the sharp hollow spines of a porcupine or hedgehog. **5.** A spindle or bobbin around which yarn is wound in weaving. **6.** A small roll of dried bark, esp. cinnamon. **7.** A hollow shaft that rotates on a solid shaft when gears are engaged. [Middle English *quille.*]

quilt (kwĭlt) *n.* **1.** A bed cover made of two layers of fabric filled with stuffing, as feathers or down, all held together by stitches that form a design. **2.** Something that is quilted or that resembles a quilt. —*tr.v.* To make by stitching together (layers of fabric). **2.** To make like a quilt: *quilt a skirt.* —*intr.v.* To make a quilt or quilted work. [Middle English *quilte,* from Old French *cuilte,* from Latin *culcita,* sack filled with feathers, mattress.]

quilt·ing (kwĭl′tĭng) *n.* **1.** The act or process of doing quilted work. **2.** Material that is quilted or used to make quilts.

quince (kwĭns) *n.* **1.** A tree, *Cydonia oblonga,* native to western Asia, with white flowers and applelike fruit. **2.** The aromatic, many-seeded fruit of this tree, edible only when cooked. [Middle English *quynce,* pl. of *quyn,* quince, from Old French *cooin,* from Latin *cydōneum (mālum),* "Cydonian (apple)."]

quince

qui·nine (kwī′nīn′) *n.* A bitter, colorless, crystalline powder, $C_{20}H_{24}N_2O_2 \cdot 3H_2O$, derived from certain cinchona barks and used in medicine to treat malaria. [From Spanish *quina,* cinchona bark.]

quinine water. A carbonated beverage flavored with quinine.

Quin·qua·ges·i·ma (kwĭng′kwə-jĕs′ə-mə) *n.* The Sunday before Lent, about 50 days before Easter. [Medieval Latin *quinquāgēsima,* from Latin, fiftieth, from *quinquāginta,* fifty.]

quin·quen·ni·al (kwĭn-kwĕn′ē-əl, kwĭng′-) *adj.* **1.** Happening once every five years. **2.** Lasting for five years. [From Latin *quinquennis,* every fifth year : *quinque,* five + *annus,* year.] —**quin·quen′ni·al** *n.* —**quin·quen′ni·al·ly** *adv.*

quin·sy (kwĭn′zē) *n.* An acute inflammation of the tonsils

and the surrounding tissue, often leading to the formation of an abscess. [Middle English *quinesye,* from Old French *quinencie,* from Medieval Latin *quinancia,* from Greek *kunanchē,* sore throat.]

quint (kwĭnt) *n.* A quintuplet.

quin·tal (kwĭn′tl) *n.* **1.** A unit of mass in the metric system equal to 100 kilograms. **2.** A hundredweight. [Middle English, from Old French, from Medieval Latin *quintāle,* from Arabic *qintār,* a unit of weight, ult. from Latin *centum,* hundred.]

quin·tes·sence (kwĭn-tĕs′əns) *n.* **1.** The purest, most essential element of something: *Freedom of choice is the quintessence of democracy.* **2.** The most perfect or typical example of something: *"thou fiery-faced quintessence of all that is abominable"* (Poe). [Middle English, from Old French *quinte essence,* from Medieval Latin *quinta essentia,* "fifth essence."] —**quin′tes·sen′tial** (kwĭn′tĭ-sĕn′shəl) *adj.*

quin·tet (kwĭn-tĕt′) *n.* Also **quin·tette. 1.** A group of five persons or things. **2.** A musical composition for five voices or instruments. [Italian *quintetto,* from *quinto,* fifth, from Latin *quintus.*]

quin·til·lion (kwĭn-tĭl′yən) *n.* **1.** In the United States, the cardinal number represented by 1 followed by 18 zeros. **2.** In Great Britain, the cardinal number represented by 1 followed by 30 zeros. [Latin *quintus,* fifth + (M)ILLION.] —**quin·til′lion** *adj.* —**quin·til′lionth** *n. & adj.*

quin·tu·ple (kwĭn-tōō′pəl, -tyōō′-, -tŭp′əl, kwĭn′tə-pəl) *adj.* **1.** Consisting of five parts. **2.** Multiplied by five. —*n.* A fivefold amount or number. —*v.* **-pled, -pling.** —*tr.v.* To multiply by five. —*intr.v.* To be multiplied by five. [Old French, from Late Latin *quintuplex.*]

quin·tu·plet (kwĭn-tŭp′lĭt, -tōō′plĭt, -tyōō′plĭt, kwĭn′tə-plĭt) *n.* **1.** A group or combination of five of a kind. **2.** One of five offspring born in a single birth. [From QUINTUPLE.]

quin·tu·pli·cate (kwĭn-tōō′plĭ-kĭt, -tyōō′-) *adj.* **1.** Consisting of a set of five. **2.** Being the fifth of a set of copies. —*n.* **1.** One of a set of five. **2.** A set of five copies. —*tr.v.* (-kāt′) **-cat·ed, -cat·ing.** To make five copies of. [Late Latin *quintuplicātus,* from *quintuplicāre,* to make fivefold, from *quintuplex,* quintuple.]

quip (kwĭp) *n.* **1.** A brief, witty, usu. spontaneous remark. **2.** A cleverly sarcastic remark; gibe. —See Syns at **joke.** —*intr.v.* **quipped, quip·ping.** To make quips. [Short for obs. *quippy,* perh. from Latin *quippe,* indeed, certainly.]

quire (kwīr) *n.* A set of 24 or sometimes 25 sheets of paper of the same size and stock. [Middle English, from Old French *quaer,* set of four sheets, from Latin *quaternī,* set of four, from *quater,* four.]

quirk (kwûrk) *n.* **1.** A sudden sharp turn or twist: *a quirk of fate.* **2.** A peculiarity of behavior; idiosyncracy. —See Syns at **eccentricity.** [Orig. unknown.] —**quirk′i·ly** *adv.* —**quirk′i·ness** *n.* —**quirk′y** *adj.*

quirt (kwûrt) *n.* A short-handled riding whip with a lash of braided rawhide. [Perh. from Spanish *cuerda,* whip, cord, from Latin *chorda,* cord.]

quis·ling (kwĭz′lĭng) *n.* A traitor who collaborates with an invading enemy, esp. as a member of a puppet government. [After Vidkun *Quisling* (1887–1945), head of the State Council of Norway during the German occupation (1940–45).]

quit (kwĭt) *v.* **quit** or **quit·ted, quit·ting.** —*tr.v.* **1.** To depart from; leave: *quit the country.* **2.** To give up; relinquish or abandon: *quit a job.* **3.** To discontinue; cease; stop: *quit smoking.* **4.** To conduct (oneself) in a specified way: *Quit yourselves like gentlemen.* —*intr.v.* **1.** To stop doing something. **2.** To give up or stop, as in defeat; surrender. **3.** To leave a job. —See Syns at **abandon** and **stop.** —*adj.* Absolved of a duty or obligation; free; released: *quit of all worries.* [Middle English *quiten,* to set free, release, deliver from, from Old French *quiter,* from Medieval Latin *quiētāre,* to set free, quit, discharge, from Latin *quiētus,* freed, quiet.]

quitch grass (kwĭch). Quack grass. [Ult. from Old English *cwice.*]

quit·claim (kwĭt′klām′) *n. Law.* The transfer of a title, right, or claim to another. —*tr.v.* To renounce all claim to. [Middle English *quiteclaimen,* from Old French *quiteclamer,* "to declare free."]

quite (kwīt) adv. 1. Completely; altogether: *not quite finished.* 2. Actually; really: *quite a story.* 3. Somewhat; rather: *quite angry.* [Middle English, free, rid of, from Old French, from Latin *quiētus,* freed, quiet.]
　Usage: quite. In its primary senses the adverb means completely or altogether (*quite alone*), and actually or truly (*quite happy*). But it is also used acceptably in the less rigid sense of somewhat or rather: *quite cool for August.*

quit·rent (kwīt′rĕnt′) n. A rent paid by a freeman instead of services to a feudal lord. [Middle English *quiterent* : *quite,* free + *rent,* rent.]

quits (kwĭts) adj. Even with someone by payment or revenge. —*idiom.* **call it quits.** To call a halt to something. [Middle English, discharged, paid up, from Medieval Latin *quittus,* var. of *quiētus,* freed.]

quit·tance (kwĭt′ns) n. 1. a. Release from a debt, obligation, or penalty. b. A document or receipt certifying such a release. 2. Something given as recompense; repayment. [Middle English *quitance,* from Old French, from *quiter,* to free, discharge a debt, quit.]

quit·ted (kwĭt′ĭd) v. A past tense and past participle of **quit.**

quit·ter (kwĭt′ər) n. Someone who gives up easily.

quiv·er[1] (kwĭv′ər) intr.v. To shake with a trembling motion. —*tr.v.* To cause to quiver. —See Syns at **shake.** —*n.* The act or motion of quivering. [Middle English *quiveren,* perh. from *quiver,* nimble.]

quiv·er[2] (kwĭv′ər) n. A case for holding arrows. [Middle English, from Old French *cuivre.*]

quiver [2]　　　　　Quonset hut

qui vive (kē vēv′). French. A sentinel's challenge. —*idiom.* **on the qui vive.** On the alert; vigilant; watchful.

quix·ot·ic (kwĭk-sŏt′ĭk) adj. Impractically romantic or idealistic. [After Don *Quixote,* hero of a satirical chivalric romance (1605–15) by Miguel de Cervantes (1547–1616), Spanish author.] —**quix·ot′i·cal·ly** adv.

quiz (kwĭz) n., pl. **quiz·zes.** A short oral or written examination. —*tr.v.* **quizzed, quiz·zing.** To question closely; interrogate. [Orig. unknown.] —**quiz′zer** n.

quiz·zi·cal (kwĭz′ĭ-kəl) adj. 1. Suggesting puzzlement; questioning: *a quizzical look.* 2. Teasing; mocking. 3. Unusual; odd. —**quiz′zi·cal·ly** adv.

quoin (koin, kwoin) n. 1. An exterior angle of a wall or building. 2. A block forming a quoin. [Var. of earlier *coin,* corner, coin.]

quoit (kwoit, koit) n. 1. **quoits** (used with a sing. verb). A game in which flat rings of iron or rope are pitched at a peg. 2. One of the rings used in quoits. [Middle English *coite.*]

quon·dam (kwŏn′dəm, -dăm′) adj. That once was; former. [Latin, formerly, from *quom,* when.]

Quon·set hut (kwŏn′sĭt). A trademark for a prefabricated portable hut with a semicircular roof of corrugated metal that curves down to form walls.

quo·rum (kwôr′əm, kwōr′-) n. The minimum number of members of a committee or organization who must be present for the valid transaction of business. [Middle English, a quorum of justices of the peace, from Latin *quorum,* "of whom," from the wording of a commission naming certain persons as members of a body (as a bench).]

quo·ta (kwō′tə) n. 1. A proportional share, as of goods, assigned to a group or to each member of a group; allotment. 2. The maximum number or proportion, esp. of persons that may be admitted, as to a nation, group, or institution. [Medieval Latin, from Latin, of what number.]

quot·a·ble (kwō′tə-bəl) adj. Suitable for or worth quoting.

quo·ta·tion (kwō-tā′shən) n. 1. The act of quoting. 2. A passage that is quoted. 3. *Comm.* The quoting of current prices and bids for securities and goods.

quotation mark. Either of a pair of punctuation marks (" " or ' ') used to mark the beginning and end of a passage attributed to another and repeated word for word.

quote (kwōt) v. **quot·ed, quot·ing.** —*tr.v.* 1. To repeat the words of (another), usu. with acknowledgment of the source. 2. To cite as illustration or proof: *quoted statistics from a research project.* 3. To state (a price) for securities, goods, or services. —*intr.v.* To give a quotation, as from a book. —*n. Informal.* 1. A quotation. 2. A quotation mark. [Middle English *coten,* to mark (as chapters or references) with numbers, from Medieval Latin *quotāre,* from Latin *quotus,* of what number, from *quot,* how many.]

quoth (kwōth) tr.v. *Archaic.* Uttered; said. Used with the first and third persons and in a position before the subject. [Middle English *quoth,* Old English *cwæth,* he said, from *cwethan,* to say.]

quo·tid·i·an (kwō-tĭd′ē-ən) adj. 1. Occurring or recurring daily. 2. Everyday; commonplace. [Middle English *cotidien,* from Old French, from Latin *quotīdiānus,* from *quotīdiē,* each day : *quot,* how many, as many as + *diēs,* day.]

quo·tient (kwō′shənt) n. The number that results from the division of one number by another. [Middle English *quocient,* from Latin *quotiēns,* how many times, from *quot,* how many.]

Phoenician – *About 3,000 years ago the Phoenicians and other Semitic peoples began to use graphic signs to represent individual speech sounds instead of syllables or whole words. They used this symbol to represent the sound of the consonant "r" and gave it the name* rēsh, *the Phoenician word for "head."*

Greek – *The Greeks borrowed the Phoenician alphabet with some modifications. They changed the shape of* rēsh *slightly, reversed its orientation, and altered its name to* rho. *They used* rhō *to represent the sound of the consonant "r" as* rēsh *did in Phoenician.*

Roman – *The Romans borrowed the alphabet from the Greeks via the Etruscans. They added a tail to* rhō *in order to distinguish it from their letter P. They also adapted the alphabet for carving Latin in stone, and this monumental script, as it is called, became the basis for modern printed capital letters.*

Medieval – *By medieval times – around 1,200 years ago – the Roman monumental capitals had become adapted to being relatively quickly written on paper, parchment, or vellum. The cursive minuscule alphabet became the basis for modern printed lower-case letters.*

Modern – *Since the invention of printing about 500 years ago the basic form of the letter R has remained unchanged.*

---

r or **R** (är) *n., pl.* **r's** or **R's.** The 18th letter of the modern English alphabet.

Ra The symbol for the element radium.

rab·bet (răb'ĭt) *n.* A cut or groove along or near the edge of a piece of wood that allows another piece to fit into it to form a joint. —*tr.v.* **1.** To cut a rabbet in. **2.** To join by a rabbet. [Middle English *rabet,* from Old French *rabat,* a beating down, from *rabattre,* to beat down, reduce.]

rab·bi (răb'ī) *n., pl.* **-bis. 1.** The ordained spiritual leader of a Jewish congregation. **2.** Formerly, a person authorized to interpret Jewish law. [Hebrew *rabbī,* my master.] —**rab·bin·i·cal** (rə-bĭn'ī-kəl) or **rab·bin'ic** *adj.*

rab·bit (răb'ĭt) *n., pl.* **-bits** or **rabbit. 1.** Any of various burrowing mammals of the family Leporidae, with long ears, soft fur, and a short tail. **2.** A hare. **3.** The fur of a rabbit or hare. [Middle English *rabet.*]

rabbit

raccoon

rab·ble (răb'əl) *n.* **1.** A noisy, unruly mob. **2.** Common people, often regarded with contempt. [Orig. unknown.]

rab·ble-rous·er (răb'əl-rou'zər) *n.* A person who appeals to the emotions and prejudices of the public; a demagogue.

rab·id (răb'ĭd) *adj.* **1.** Of or afflicted with rabies. **2.** Overzealous; fanatical: *a rabid baseball fan.* **3.** Raging; furious. [Latin *rabidus,* raving, from *rabere,* to rave.] —**rab'id·ly** *adv.* —**rab'id·ness** *n.*

ra·bies (rā'bēz) *n.* An infectious, often fatal viral disease of most mammals that attacks the central nervous system and is transmitted by the bite of an infected animal. Also called **hydrophobia.** [Latin *rabiēs,* rage, from *rabere,* to rave.] —**ra'bi·et'ic** (-ĕt'ĭk) *adj.*

rac·coon (ră-kōōn') *n., pl.* **-coons** or **raccoon.** Also **ra·coon. 1.** A carnivorous North American mammal, *Procyon lotor,* with grayish-brown fur, black, masklike facial markings, and a bushy, black-ringed tail. Also called **coon. 2.** The fur of this animal. [Algonquian *aroughcoune.*]

race[1] (rās) *n.* **1.** A group of people considered to be more or less distinct on the basis of physical characteristics that are genetically transmitted. **2.** Mankind as a whole. **3.** Any group of people united on the basis of common history, nationality, or region of origin: *the Italian race.* **4.** Ancestry; lineage; family. **5.** *Biol.* A group of plants or animals that have inherited similar characteristics and form a distinct type within a species or breed. [French, group of people, generation.]

race[2] (rās) *n.* **1. a.** A contest of speed, as in running or riding. **b. races.** A series of such contests, esp. horse races: *win at the races.* **2.** Any contest of supremacy: *the Presidential race.* **3.** Steady or rapid onward movement: *the race of time.* **4. a.** A strong or swift current of water. **b.** The channel of such a current. **c.** An artificial channel built to transport water and utilize its energy. **5.** A groove-like part of a machine in which a moving part slides or rolls. —*v.* **raced, rac·ing.** —*intr.v.* **1.** To compete in a contest of speed. **2.** To move rapidly or at top speed: *raced home.* **3.** *Machinery.* To run too rapidly, as an automobile engine, because of a lighter load or disengaged transmission. —*tr.v.* **1.** To compete against in a contest of speed. **2.** To cause to compete in a race. —See Syns at **rush.** [Middle English *raas,* from Old Norse *rās.*] —**rac'er** *n.*

ra·ceme (rā-sēm', rə-) *n. Bot.* A flower cluster with stalked flowers arranged singly along a common main stem, as in the lily of the valley. [Latin *racēmus,* cluster of grapes.]

rac·e·mose (răs'ə-mōs', rā-sē'-) *adj.* **1.** *Bot.* Growing in a raceme. **2.** *Anat.* Having a structure of clustered parts: *racemose glands.* —**rac'e·mose'ly** *adv.*

ra·chis (rā'kĭs) *n., pl.* **-chis·es** or **-chi·des** (-kĭ-dēz'). *Biol.* A main axis or shaft, such as the main stem of a flower cluster. [From Greek *rhakhis,* backbone.] —**ra'chi·al** *adj.*

ra·chi·tis (rə-kī'tĭs) *n.* Rickets. [From Greek *rhakhitis,* disease of the spine, from *rhakhis,* backbone.]

ra·cial (rā'shəl) *adj.* **1.** Of, pertaining to, or based on race: *racial characteristics.* **2.** Arising from or based on relations between races: *racial unrest.* —**ra'cial·ly** *adv.*

rac·ism (rā'sĭz'əm) *n.* Racial prejudice or discrimination. —**rac'ist** *n.*

rack[1] (răk) *n.* **1.** A framework, stand, or bar in which to hold, display, or hang various articles: *a coat rack.* **2.** A receptacle for livestock feed; a hayrack. **3.** A metal bar with teeth that mesh with those of a pinion or gearwheel. **4.** An instrument of torture on which the victim's body was

---

ă pat ā pay â care ä father ĕ pet ē be hw which ĭ pit ī tie î pier ŏ pot ō toe ô paw, for oi noise
ōō took ōō boot ou out th thin *th* this ŭ cut û urge zh vision ə about, item, edible, gallop, circus

stretched. —*tr.v.* **1.** To torture by means of the rack. **2.** To torment or afflict: *Pain racked his entire body.* **3.** To strain with great effort: *rack one's brain.* **—phrasal verb. rack up.** *Slang.* To accumulate or score: *rack up points.* [Middle English *rakke*, prob. from Middle Dutch *rec*, framework.]

rack² (răk) *n.* Either of two gaits of horses, the single-foot or the pace. —*intr.v.* To go at a rack. [Orig. unknown.]

rack³ (răk) *n.* Destruction. **—idiom. go to rack and ruin.** To fall apart. [Var. of WRACK (ruin).]

rack·et¹ (răk′ĭt) *n.* Also **rac·quet. 1.** A device, used to strike a ball or shuttlecock, that consists of an oval frame with a tight interlaced network of strings and a handle. **2.** A wooden paddle, as used in table tennis. [Old French *raquette*, from Arabic *ráhet*, palm of the hand.]

rack·et² (răk′ĭt) *n.* **1.** A loud noise; clamor. **2.** A dishonest business, esp. one that obtains money through fraud or extortion. **3.** *Slang.* A job. [Orig. unknown.]

rack·et·eer (răk′ĭ-tîr′) *n.* A person engaged in an illegal business. —*intr.v.* To engage in a racket.

rac·on·teur (răk′ŏn-tûr′, -ən-) *n.* A person who tells stories and anecdotes with skill and wit. [French, from Old French, from *raconter*, to tell.]

rac·quet (răk′ĭt) *n.* Var. of **racket** (paddle).

rac·quet·ball (răk′ĭt-bôl′) *n.* A court game that is identical to handball but utilizes a short strung racquet and a larger, softer ball.

rac·quets (răk′ĭts) *n.* *(used with a sing. verb).* A game similar to tennis but played on a court with no net and enclosed by four walls.

ra·coon (ră-kōōn′) *n.* Var. of **raccoon.**

rac·y (rā′sē) *adj.* **-i·er, -i·est. 1.** Having a distinctive quality or taste. **2.** Vigorous; lively. **3.** Slightly improper; risqué. [From *race*, liveliness, piquancy.]

ra·dar (rā′där′) *n.* **1.** A method of detecting distant objects and determining their position, velocity, size, etc., by analysis of radio waves reflected from their surfaces. **2.** The equipment used in such detection. **—modifier:** *a radar station.* [RA(DIO) D(ETECTING) A(ND) R(ANGING).]

radar

ra·dar·scope (rā′där-skōp′) *n.* The viewing screen of a radar receiver. [RADAR + (OSCILLO)SCOPE.]

ra·di·al (rā′dē-əl) *adj.* **1.** Of, pertaining to, or arranged like rays or radii. **2.** Having or characterized by parts radiating from a common center. **3.** Moving or directed along a radius. —*n.* A radial part, such as a ray, spoke, or radius. [Medieval Latin *radiālis*, from Latin *radius*, rod, ray.] **—ra′di·al·ly** *adv.*

radial engine. An internal-combustion engine, as used in propeller-driven aircraft, with radially arrayed cylinders.

radial symmetry. A pattern in which forms or features that are opposite each other at equal distances from a central point are identical.

ra·di·an (rā′dē-ən) *n.* *Math.* A unit of angular measure equal to the angle subtended at the center of a circle by an arc of length equal to the radius of the circle. It is equal to $360/_{2\pi}$ degrees, or approximately 57°17′44.6″. [From RADIUS.]

ra·di·ance (rā′dē-əns) *n.* Also **ra·di·an·cy** (-ən-sē). The condition or quality of being radiant.

ra·di·ant (rā′dē-ənt) *adj.* **1.** Sending forth light, heat, or other radiation: *a radiant star.* **2.** Consisting of or transmitted as radiation: *radiant energy.* **3.** Filled with happiness, joy, love, etc.: *a radiant smile.* **4.** Glowing; bright: *a radiant diamond.* —See Syns at **bright. —ra′di·ant·ly** *adv.*

radiant energy. *Physics.* Energy transferred by radiation, esp. by an electromagnetic wave.

ra·di·ate (rā′dē-āt′) *v.* **-at·ed, -at·ing.** —*intr.v.* **1.** To be sent forth as radiation. **2.** To issue in rays. **3.** To spread out from a center, as the spokes of a wheel. —*tr.v.* **1.** To send forth (heat, light, or other energy). **2.** To spread out from or as if from a center. **3.** To illuminate (an object). **4.** To exude; project: *radiate confidence.* —See Syns at **spread.** —*adj.* (rā′dē-ĭt). *Bot.* Having rays or raylike parts. [From Latin *radiāre*, to emit beams, from *radius*, ray.] **—ra′di·a′tive** *adj.*

ra·di·a·tion (rā′dē-ā′shən) *n.* **1.** The act or process of radiating. **2.** *Physics.* **a.** The emission and movement of waves, atomic particles, etc., through space or other media. **b.** The waves or particles that are emitted.

radiation sickness. An often fatal illness caused by overexposure to x-rays, radioactive material, etc., characterized by nausea, diarrhea and changes in blood chemistry.

ra·di·a·tor (rā′dē-ā′tər) *n.* **1.** A heating device that consists of a series of connected pipes for the circulation of steam or hot water. **2.** A cooling device, as in automotive engines, through which water or other fluids circulate.

rad·i·cal (răd′ĭ-kəl) *adj.* **1.** Arising from or going to a root or origin; fundamental; basic. **2.** Carried to the farthest limit; extreme. **3.** Advocating extreme or revolutionary changes, esp. in politics or government. —*n.* **1.** A person who advocates political and social revolution. **2.** *Math.* The root of a quantity as indicated by the radical sign. **3.** *Chem.* A group of atoms that behaves as a unit in chemical reactions and is only stable as a part of a compound. **4.** *Ling.* A root. [Middle English, from Late Latin *rādicālis*, having roots, from Latin *rādix*, root.] **—rad′i·cal·ly** *adv.* **—rad′i·cal·ness** *n.*

rad·i·cal·ism (răd′ĭ-kə-lĭz′əm) *n.* The doctrines or practices of political radicals.

radical sign. The sign $\sqrt{}$ placed before a quantity to indicate that its root is to be extracted.

rad·i·cand (răd′ĭ-kănd′) *n.* The quantity under a radical sign. [Latin *rādicandum*, from *rādix*, root.]

rad·i·ces (răd′ĭ-sēz′, rā′dĭ-) *n.* A plural of **radix.**

rad·i·cle (răd′ĭ-kəl) *n.* *Bot.* The part of the plant embryo that develops into the primary root. [Latin *rādicula*, dim. of *rādix*, root.]

ra·di·i (rā′dē-ī′) *n.* A plural of **radius.**

ra·di·o (rā′dē-ō′) *n., pl.* **-os. 1.** The use of electromagnetic waves lying between about 10 kilohertz and 300,000 megahertz to carry messages or information between points without the use of wires. **2. a.** The equipment used to generate such electromagnetic waves and alter them so that they carry information; a transmitter. **b.** The equipment used to receive such waves; a receiver. **3.** The sending forth of programs of entertainment, news, information, etc., in this way, esp. as a business; broadcasting. **4.** A message sent by radio. **—modifier:** *a radio wave; a radio broadcast.* —*tr.v.* To transmit a message to or communicate with by radio. —*intr.v.* To transmit a message by radio. [Short for RADIOTELEGRAPHY.]

radio-. A prefix meaning radiation: *radioactive.* [From RADIATION.]

ra·di·o·ac·tive (rā′dē-ō-ăk′tĭv) *adj. Physics.* Of or exhibiting radioactivity. **—ra′di·o·ac′tive·ly** *adv.*

ra·di·o·ac·tiv·i·ty (rā′dē-ō-ăk-tĭv′ĭ-tē) *n.* **1.** The spontaneous emission of radiation, either directly from unstable atomic nuclei or as a consequence of a nuclear reaction. **2.** The radiation emitted.

radio astronomy. The scientific study of celestial objects and phenomena by observation and analysis of radio waves that reach the earth.

radio beacon. A radio transmitter that broadcasts specific signals as a navigational aid to ships and aircraft.

ra·di·o·car·bon (rā′dē-ō-kär′bən) *n.* Any radioactive isotope of carbon, esp. carbon 14.

radio frequency. 1. The frequency of the waves transmitted by a specific radio station. **2.** Any frequency in the range within which radio waves may be transmitted, from about 10 kilohertz to about 300,000 megahertz.

---

ra·di·o·gram (rā′dē-ō-grăm′) *n.* A message transmitted by radiotelegraphy.

ra·di·o·graph (rā′dē-ō-grăf′) *n.* An image produced by radiation other than visible light, esp. by x-rays. —*tr.v.* To make a radiograph of. —**ra′di·o·graph′ic** *adj.* —**ra′di·o·graph′i·cal·ly** *adv.* —**ra′di·og′ra·phy** (-ŏg′rə-fē) *n.*

ra·di·o·i·so·tope (rā′dē-ō-ī′sə-tōp′) *n.* A naturally or artificially produced radioactive isotope of an element.

ra·di·o·lar·i·an (rā′dē-ō-lâr′ē-ən) *n.* Any of various saltwater protozoans of the order Radiolaria, with siliceous skeletons and small radiating spines. [From Late Latin *radiolus,* small sunbeam, dim. of Latin *radius,* ray.]

ra·di·ol·o·gy (rā′dē-ŏl′ə-jē) *n.* The use of ionizing radiation, esp. of x-rays, in medical diagnosis and treatment. —**ra′di·o·log′i·cal** (-ə-lŏj′ĭ-kəl) *adj.* —**ra′di·ol′o·gist** *n.*

ra·di·om·e·ter (rā′dē-ŏm′ĭ-tər) *n.* A device used to detect and measure radiation. —**ra′di·o·met′ric** (-ō-mĕt′rĭk) *adj.* —**ra′di·om′e·try** *n.*

ra·di·o·phone (rā′dē-ō-fōn′) *n.* A radiotelephone.

ra·di·o·pho·to·graph (rā′dē-ō-fō′tə-grăf′) *n.* A photograph transmitted by radio waves.

ra·di·o·sonde (rā′dē-ō-sŏnd′) *n.* An instrument carried aloft, chiefly by balloon, to gather and transmit meteorological data. [RADIO- + French *sonde,* sounding line.]

ra·di·o·te·leg·ra·phy (rā′dē-ō-tə-lĕg′rə-fē) *n.* Wireless telegraphy in which messages are sent by radio. [RADI(ATE) + TELEGRAPHY.] —**ra′di·o·tel′e·graph′** (-tĕl′ĭ-grăf′) *n.*

ra·di·o·tel·e·phone (rā′dē-ō-tĕl′ə-fōn′) *n.* A telephone system in which messages are sent by radio waves instead of wires. —**ra′di·o·te·leph′o·ny** (-tə-lĕf′ə-nē) *n.*

radio telescope. A very sensitive radio receiver, typically equipped with a large, dishlike reflecting antenna, used to detect radio waves that reach the earth from space.

ra·di·o·ther·a·py (rā′dē-ō-thĕr′ə-pē) *n.* The treatment of disease with radioactive substances or x-rays.

radio wave. A radio-frequency electromagnetic wave.

rad·ish (răd′ĭsh) *n.* 1. Any of various related plants of the genus *Raphanus,* esp. *R. sativus,* with a thickened, edible root. 2. The pungent root of this plant. [Middle English *radiche,* from Old English *rædic,* from Latin *radix,* root.]

ra·di·um (rā′dē-əm) *n. Symbol* Ra One of the elements, a rare, white, highly radioactive metal. It has 13 isotopes with mass numbers ranging from 213 to 230, of which Ra 226, with a half-life of 1,622 years, is the most common. It is used in cancer radiotherapy, as a neutron source for some research purposes, and as a constituent of luminescent paints. Atomic number 88; melting point 700°C; boiling point 1,737°C; valence 2. [From Latin *radius,* ray.]

ra·di·us (rā′dē-əs) *n., pl.* **-di·i** (-dē-ī′) or **-us·es.** 1. **a.** A line segment that joins the center of a circle with any point on its circumference. **b.** A line segment that joins the center of a sphere with any point on its surface. **c.** The length of such a line segment. **d.** Such a line segment used as a measure of circular area: *every family within a radius of 25 miles.* 2. *Anat.* **a.** The shorter and thicker of the two bones that make up the forearm. **b.** A similar bone in many vertebrates. [Latin *radius,* spoke of a wheel, ray.]

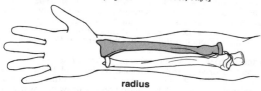

radius

ra·dix (rā′dĭks) *n., pl.* **rad·i·ces** (răd′ĭ-sēz′, rā′dĭ-) or **-dix·es.** 1. *Biol.* A plant root. 2. *Math.* The base of a system of numbers. [Latin *radix,* root.]

ra·dome (rā′dōm′) *n.* A domelike protective housing for a radar antenna. [RA(DAR) + DOME.]

ra·don (rā′dŏn′) *n. Symbol* Rn A colorless, radioactive, inert gaseous element formed by disintegration of radium. It is used as a radiation source in radiotherapy and to produce neutrons for research. Atomic number 86; atomic weight 222; melting point –71°C; boiling point –61.8°C; specific gravity (solid) 4; valence 0; half-life 3.823 days. [From RADIUM.]

rad·u·la (răj′ə-lə) *n., pl.* **-lae** (-lē′) or **-las.** *Zool.* In mollusks, a flexible, tonguelike organ with rows of horny teeth on the surface. [From Latin *rādula,* scraper, from *rādere,* to scrape.] —**rad′u·lar** *adj.*

raf·fi·a (răf′ē-ə) *n.* 1. An African palm tree, *Raphia ruffia,* with large leaves that yield a useful fiber. 2. The fiber of these leaves, used for mats, baskets, etc. [Malagasy *rafia.*]

raf·fi·nose (răf′ə-nōs′) *n.* A white crystalline sugar, $C_{18}H_{32}O_{16} \cdot 5H_2O$, obtained from cottonseed meal and sugar beets. [French, from *raffiner,* to refine.]

raff·ish (răf′ĭsh) *adj.* 1. Vulgar; showy. 2. Rakish. [Prob. from dial. *raff,* trash.] —**raff′ish·ly** *adv.* —**raff′ish·ness** *n.*

raf·fle (răf′əl) *n.* A lottery in which a number of persons buy chances on a prize. —*tr.v.* **-fled, -fling.** To offer as a prize in a raffle: *raffle off a car.* [Middle English *rafle,* from Old French *rafle,* a game of chance.]

raft¹ (răft) *n.* A floating platform used for conveying or traveling over water. —*tr.v.* 1. To convey on a raft. 2. To make a raft from. —*intr.v.* To travel by raft. [Middle English *rafte,* from Old Norse *raptr,* beam, rafter.]

raft² (răft) *n. Informal.* A great number or amount. [Var. of *raff,* trash.]

raf·ter (răf′tər) *n.* One of the sloping beams that support a roof. [Middle English, from Old English *ræfter.*]

rag¹ (răg) *n.* 1. A scrap of worn or leftover cloth. 2. Cloth converted to pulp for papermaking. 3. A scrap or fragment. 4. **rags.** Shabby, worn, or tattered clothing. [Middle English *ragge,* ult. from Old Norse *rögg,* tuft.]

rag² (răg) *tr.v.* **ragged, rag·ging.** *Slang.* 1. To tease; taunt. 2. To scold. [Orig. unknown.]

rag·a·muf·fin (răg′ə-mŭf′ĭn) *n.* A dirty or unkempt child. [Ult. from RAG (scrap of cloth).]

rage (rāj) *n.* 1. **a.** Violent anger. **b.** A fit of anger. 2. Furious intensity, as of a storm. 3. A fad; craze: *Short skirts were all the rage.* —See Syns at **fashion.** —*intr.v.* **raged, rag·ing.** 1. To speak or act furiously. 2. To continue with great violence: *The storm raged.* 3. To spread or prevail uncontrolled. [Middle English, from Old French, from Latin *rabiēs,* madness, from *rabere,* to rave.]

rag·ged (răg′ĭd) *adj.* 1. Tattered, frayed, or torn. 2. Dressed in tattered or shabby clothes. 3. Unkempt or shaggy: *a ragged beard.* 4. Having a rough surface or edges; jagged. 5. Imperfect; sloppy: *a ragged performance.* [Middle English, prob. from *ragge,* rag.] —**rag′ged·ly** *adv.* —**rag′ged·ness** *n.*

rag·lan (răg′lən) *n.* A loose coat, jacket, or sweater with slanted shoulder seams and with the sleeves extending in one piece to the neckline. [After the 1st Baron *Raglan* (1788–1855), British soldier.]

rag·man (răg′măn′) *n.* A person who gathers and sells rags and trash.

ra·gout (ră-gōo′) *n.* A meat and vegetable stew. [French *ragoût,* from *ragoûter,* to renew the appetite.]

rag·time (răg′tīm′) *n.* A style of jazz in which a highly syncopated melody is played against a steadily accented accompaniment. [Perh. from *ragged time,* syncopated beat.]

rag·weed (răg′wēd′) *n.* Any of several weeds of the genus *Ambrosia,* esp. *A. artemisiifolia* or *A. trifida,* whose profuse pollen is one of the chief causes of hay fever.

rag·wort (răg′wûrt′, -wôrt′) *n.* Any of several plants of the genus *Senecio,* with yellow flowers.

rah (rä) *interj.* A word used to express approval, pleasure, or victory. [Short for HURRAH.]

raid (rād) *n.* 1. A surprise attack, as one made by a commando force. 2. A sudden and forcible entry of a place by police. —*tr.v.* To carry out a raid on. [Scottish dial., foray, from Middle English *rade,* from Old English *rād,* ride, road.] —**raid′er** *n.*

rail¹ (rāl) *n.* 1. A horizontal bar or timber supported at both ends or at close intervals, as in a fence. 2. A railing or fence. 3. A steel bar used, usu. as one of a pair, to form a track for railroad cars, engines, etc. 4. Railroads: *goods transported by rail.* —*tr.v.* To enclose or supply with a rail or rails. [Middle English *raile,* from Old French *reille,* bar, from Latin *regula,* rod, straight piece of wood.]

rail² (rāl) *intr.v.* To use strong or emphatic language. [Middle English *railen,* from Old French *railler,* to mock, from Old Provençal *ralhar,* to scold, from Late Latin *ragere,* to neigh, roar.] —**rail′er** *n.*

ă pat   ā pay   â care   ä father   ĕ pet   ē be   hw which
oo took   ōo boot   ou out   th thin   *th* this   ŭ cut
ĭ pit   ī tie   î pier   ŏ pot   ō toe   ô paw, for   oi noise
û urge   zh vision   ə about, item, edible, gallop, circus

rail³ (rāl) *n.* A brownish, short-winged marsh bird of the family Rallidae. [Middle English *raile*, from Old French *raale*, from Old Provençal *rasclar*, to scrape, from Latin *rāsus*, past part. of *radere*, to scrape.]

rail³
George Miksch Sutton

rail·ing (rā'lĭng) *n.* **1. a.** A fence made of rails. **b.** A banister or handrail. **2.** Material for making rails.

rail·ler·y (rā'lə-rē) *n., pl.* **-ies.** Good-natured teasing or ridicule. [French *raillerie*, from Old French *railler*, to rail.]

rail·road (rāl'rōd') *n.* **1.** A road composed of parallel steel rails supported by ties and providing a track for locomotives, trains, and other rolling stock. **2.** The entire system of such track, together with the land, stations, trains, and other property needed for its operation. —*tr.v.* **1.** To transport by railroad. **2.** *Informal.* **a.** To rush or push through quickly in order to prevent careful consideration: *railroad a law through Congress.* **b.** To cause (someone) to be imprisoned without a fair trial or on false charges. —*intr.v.* To work for a railroad company.

rail·road·ing (rāl'rō'dĭng) *n.* The operation or construction of railroads.

rail·way (rāl'wā') *n.* **1.** A railroad, esp. one operated over a limited area. **2.** A track providing a pathway for wheeled equipment.

rai·ment (rā'mənt) *n.* Clothing; garments. [Middle English *rayment*, short for *arrayment*, from Old French *araiement*, an array, from *arayer*, to array.]

rain (rān) *n.* **1. a.** Water that condenses from atmospheric vapor and falls to the earth as drops. **b.** A fall of such water; a rainstorm. **2.** A rapid or heavy fall of anything. **3.** Often **rains.** A season or time of rainy weather. —*intr.v.* **1.** To fall in drops of water from the clouds. **2.** To fall like rain: *Ticker tape rained down on the motorcade.* —*tr.v.* **1.** To send or pour down like rain. **2.** To offer or give abundantly. [Middle English, from Old English *regn.*]

rain·bow (rān'bō') *n.* **1.** An arc-shaped spectrum of color seen in the sky opposite the sun, esp. after rain, caused by sunlight refracted by droplets of water. **2.** Any similar spectrum, as one seen in the mist of a waterfall.

rain·coat (rān'kōt') *n.* A waterproof or water-resistant coat.

rain·drop (rān'drŏp') *n.* A drop of rain.

rain·fall (rān'fôl') *n.* **1.** A fall of rain; a shower. **2.** *Meteorol.* The amount of water, usu. measured in inches, that falls over a given area during a given time.

rain forest. A dense evergreen forest in a tropical region with an annual rainfall of at least 100 inches.

rain gauge. A device for measuring rainfall.

rain·mak·ing (rān'mā'kĭng) *n.* *Informal.* Cloud seeding. —**rain'mak'er** *n.*

rain·storm (rān'stôrm') *n.* A storm accompanied by rain.

rain·wa·ter (rān'wô'tər, -wŏt'ər) *n.* Water that falls as rain.

rain·y (rā'nē) *adj.* **-i·er, -i·est.** Marked by much rain.

rainy day. A time of need or trouble.

raise (rāz) *tr.v.* **raised, rais·ing.** **1.** To cause to move upward or to a higher position; lift: *raise the window.* **2.** To place or set upright. **3.** To erect or build. **4.** To cause to arise or appear: *a swelling raised by a blow.* **5.** To increase in amount, size, or worth: *raise prices.* **6.** To increase in intensity, degree, strength, or volume: *raised his voice.* **7.** To improve in rank or dignity; promote. **8. a.** To grow or breed: *raise flowers.* **b.** To bring up; rear: *raise children.*

9. To put forward for consideration; bring up: *raise a question.* **10.** To express or utter (a cry, shout, etc.). **11.** To bring about; cause; provoke: *raise a smile.* **12.** To arouse or stir up: *raise a revolt.* **13.** To gather together; collect: *raise money.* **14.** To cause (dough) to puff up. **15.** To end (a siege) by withdrawing troops or forcing the enemy troops to withdraw. **16.** To make contact with by radio. **17. a.** To indicate, as by an exponent, that a number or mathematical quantity is to be used a given number of times as a factor. **b.** To calculate the value of (a number to which an exponent has been applied). **c.** To write (an algebraic expression affected by an exponent) in expanded form. —*n.* **1.** An act of raising or increasing. **2.** An increase in salary. [Middle English *raisen*, from Old Norse *reisa.*] —**rais'er** *n.*

    Syns: **raise, boost, elevate, hoist, lift, uplift** *v. Core meaning:* To move (something) to a higher position (*raised the window; raise a drawbridge*).

    Usage: **raise, rise.** In the sense of moving upward or to a higher position *raise* is transitive and *rise* intransitive: *Raise the window. The window rises easily.* As nouns both words mean an increase in salary; *raise* is the more common in American English and *rise* in British.

rai·sin (rā'zĭn) *n.* A sweet dried grape. [Middle English, from Old French, grape, from Latin *racēmus*, raceme.]

rai·son d'ê·tre (rā'zôN dĕt'rə). *French.* Reason for being.

ra·jah or **ra·ja** (rä'jə) *n.* A prince, chief, or ruler in India or the East Indies. [Hindi *rājā*, from Sanskrit *rājan*, king.]

rake¹ (rāk) *n.* **1.** A long-handled garden tool with a row of projecting teeth at its head. **2.** Any similarly shaped tool. —*v.* **raked, rak·ing.** —*tr.v.* **1.** To gather, smooth, loosen, or scrape with or as if with a rake. **2.** To gain rapidly and in abundance: *rake in profits.* **3.** To revive or bring to light: *rake up old gossip.* **4.** To search or examine thoroughly: *rake through a drawer.* **5.** To aim heavy gunfire along the length of. —*intr.v.* To use a rake. [Middle English, from Old English *raca.*] —**rak'er** *n.*

rake² (rāk) *n.* A dissolute person; libertine; roué. [Short for *rakehell*, scoundrel.] —**rak'ish** *adj.*

rake³ (rāk) *intr.v.* **raked, rak·ing.** To slant or incline from the vertical, as a ship's mast. [Orig. unknown.]

rake-off (rāk'ôf', -ŏf') *n.* *Slang.* A percentage or share of the profits of an enterprise given or accepted as a bribe.

rak·ish (rā'kĭsh) *adj.* Gay and jaunty in appearance. [From RAKE (to incline).] —**rak'ish·ly** *adv.* —**rak'ish·ness** *n.*

ral·len·tan·do (räl'ən-tän'dō). *Mus.* —*adj.* Gradually slowing in tempo. —*n., pl.* **-dos.** A passage or movement performed with a gradual reduction in tempo. [Italian, slowing down.] —**ral'len·tan'do** *adv.*

ral·ly (răl'ē) *v.* **-lied, -ly·ing.** —*tr.v.* **1.** To call together for a common purpose; assemble. **2.** To reassemble and restore to order: *rally retreating troops.* **3.** To rouse or revive from inactivity or decline: *rally the team's confidence.* —*intr.v.* **1.** To meet for or join in an effort for a common cause. **2.** To recover abruptly from a setback: *The stock market rallied.* **3.** To show improvement in health or spirits: *rallied after four days of fever.* **4.** *Tennis.* To exchange several strokes. —See Syns at **recover.** —*n., pl.* **-lies.** **1.** The act of rallying. **2.** A mass meeting or assembly intended to generate enthusiasm for a cause: *a political rally.* **3.** *Tennis.* An exchange of several strokes before one side scores a point. [French *rallier*, from Old French *ralier* : *re-*, again + *alier*, to unite.]

ram (răm) *n.* **1.** A male sheep. **2.** Any of several devices used to drive, batter, or crush by forceful impact, as a battering-ram. **3.** The plunger or piston of a force pump or hydraulic press. **4.** A projection on the prow of a warship, used to batter an enemy vessel. **5.** A hydraulic ram. —*tr.v.* **rammed, ram·ming.** **1.** To strike or drive against with a heavy impact; to butt. **2.** To force or press into place. [Middle English, from Old English *ramm.*]

Ra·ma (rä'mə) *n.* *Hinduism.* Any of three of the incarnations of Vishnu, regarded as heroes.

Ram·a·dan (răm'ə-dän', -dän') *n.* The ninth month of the Moslem year, spent in fasting from sunrise to sunset. [Arabic *Ramaḍān*, the hot month, from *ramaḍ*, dryness.]

ram·ble (răm'bəl) *intr.v.* **-bled, -bling.** **1.** To walk or wander aimlessly; stroll or roam. **2.** To follow a winding course; meander. **3.** To speak or write with many digressions.

ă pat	ā pay	â care	ä father	ĕ pet	ē be	hw which	ĭ pit	ī tie	î pier	ŏ pot	ō toe	ô paw, for	oi noise
ŏŏ took	ōō boot	ou out	th thin	th this	ŭ cut		û urge	zh vision	ə about, item, edible, gallop, circus				

—*n.* A leisurely stroll. [Middle English *romblen,* freq. of *romen,* to roam.]

ram·bler (răm′blər) *n.* **1.** Someone or something that rambles. **2.** A type of climbing rose with numerous red, pink, or white flowers.

ram·bling (răm′blĭng) *adj.* **1.** Roaming; roving; wandering. **2.** Following a winding or irregular course. **3.** Extending out in an irregular pattern; sprawling: *a rambling house.* **4.** Lengthy and aimless: *a rambling speech.*

ram·bunc·tious (răm-bŭngk′shəs) *adj. Informal.* Wild; boisterous; unruly. [Prob. ult. from ROBUST.]

ram·e·kin (răm′ĭ-kĭn) *n.* Also **ram·e·quin.** A small individual baking dish. [French *ramequin,* from Middle Dutch *rameken,* dim. of *ram,* cream.]

ram·ie (răm′ē) *n.* **1.** A woody Asian plant, *Boehmeria nivea,* with broad leaves. **2.** The flaxlike fiber from the stem of the ramie, used in making fabrics. [Malay *rami.*]

ram·i·fi·ca·tion (răm′ə-fĭ-kā′shən) *n.* **1.** The process of branching. **2.** A branch or branching parts that extend from a main body. **3.** A development or consequence that grows out of a problem, plan, or statement.

ram·i·fy (răm′ə-fī′) *intr.v.* **-fied, -fy·ing.** To extend in branches or divisions. [Old French *ramifier,* from Medieval Latin *rāmificāre,* from Latin *rāmus,* branch.]

ram·jet (răm′jĕt′) *n.* A jet engine that propels by igniting fuel with air taken in and compressed by the engine.

ramp (rămp) *n.* A sloping passage or roadway that connects different levels, as of a building or road. [French *rampe,* from *ramper,* to slope, creep.]

ram·page (răm′pāj′) *n.* A course of violent, frenzied action or behavior. —*intr.v.* **-paged, -pag·ing.** To move about wildly or violently; to rage. [Scottish, perh. from *ramp,* to rage.] —**ram·pag′er** *n.*

ram·pant (răm′pənt) *adj.* **1.** Growing or extending unchecked; unrestrained; widespreading: *a rampant growth of weeds.* **2.** Characterized by uncontrolled violence, extravagance, or lack of restraint: *rampant corruption.* **3.** Rearing up on the hind legs. [Middle English *rampaunt,* from Old French *rampant,* pres. part. of *ramper,* to climb.] —**ram′pan·cy** *n.* —**ram′pant·ly** *adv.*

ram·part (răm′pärt′, -pərt) *n.* A wall or embankment raised around a fort, city, or other area for protection against attack. [French, from *ramparer,* to fortify : *re-* (intensifier) + *emparer,* to defend, fortify.]

ram·rod (răm′rŏd′) *n.* **1.** A metal rod used to force the charge into a muzzleloading firearm. **2.** A rod used to clean the barrel of a firearm. —*adj.* **1.** Like a rod in stiffness; inflexible. **2.** Severe; harsh.

ram·shack·le (răm′shăk′əl) *adj.* Likely to fall apart because of shoddy construction; rickety; dilapidated. [Back-formation from *ramshackled, ransackled,* from *ransackle,* freq. of Middle English *ransaken,* to ransack.]

ran (răn) *v.* Past tense of **run.** [Middle English, from Old English.]

ranch (rănch) *n.* **1.** A large farm, esp. one on which cattle, sheep, or horses are raised. **2.** Any large farm on which a particular crop or kind of animal is raised. —*intr.v.* To work on or manage a ranch. [Mexican Spanish *rancho,* from Spanish, mess room, from Old Spanish *rancher,* be billeted, from Old French *ranger,* to put in a line, from *renc,* line, row.]

ranch·er (răn′chər) *n.* A person who owns, manages, or works on a ranch.

ranch house. A rectangular, one-story house with a low-pitched roof.

ranch·man (rănch′mən) *n.* A rancher.

ran·cho (răn′chō) *n., pl.* **-chos.** *Southwestern U.S.* A ranch. [Mexican Spanish, ranch.]

ran·cid (răn′sĭd) *adj.* Having the unpleasant odor or taste of decomposed oils or fats: *rancid butter.* [Latin *rancidus,* from *rancēre,* to stink.] —**ran·cid′i·ty** *n.* or **ran′cid·ness** *n.*

ran·cor (răng′kər) *n.* Also *Brit.* **ran·cour.** Bitter, long-lasting resentment; deep-seated ill will. [Middle English *rancour,* from Old French, from Latin *rancor,* rancidity, from *rancēre,* to stink.] —**ran′cor·ous** *adj.* —**ran′cor·ous·ly** *adv.*

ran·dom (răn′dəm) *adj.* **1.** Having no particular pattern, purpose, or objective; haphazard. **2.** *Statistics.* **a.** Of or designating a phenomenon that does not produce the same outcome or consequences every time it occurs under identical circumstances. **b.** Of or designating an event having a relative frequency of occurrence that approaches a stable limit as the number of observations of the event increases to infinity. —*idiom.* **at random.** Without a definite method or purpose. [Middle English *randoun,* from Old French *randon,* haphazard, from *randir,* to run.] —**ran′dom·ly** *adv.*

ran·dom·ize (răn′də-mīz′) *tr.v.* **-ized, -iz·ing.** To make random, esp. for scientific experimentation. —**ran′dom·i·za′tion** *n.*

ra·nee (rä′nē) *n.* Var. of **rani.**

rang (răng) *v.* Past tense of **ring** (sound a bell). [Middle English; formed on the model of such verbs as *sing, sang.*]

range (rānj) *n.* **1.** An extent or region within which something can vary: *a wide range of prices.* **2.** An extent of perception, knowledge, or understanding: *within viewing range; a mind of limited range.* **3.** An area treated or considered; scope: *The contents suggest the range of the book.* **4.** The set of values that the dependent variable of a mathematical function can take. **5.** The maximum or effective distance that a sound, radio signal, missile, etc., can travel. **6.** *Mus.* The gamut of tones within the capacity of a voice or instrument. **7.** The maximum distance that a ship, aircraft, or other vehicle can travel before using up its fuel. **8.** A place for shooting at targets. **9.** A number or extent of various things; variety: *A wide range of courses is offered.* **10.** The area in which a kind of animal or plant normally lives or grows. **11.** A large expanse of open land on which livestock wander and graze. **12.** A large stove with spaces for cooking a number of things at the same time. **13.** An extended group or series, esp. of mountains. **ranged, rang·ing.** —*tr.v.* **1.** To arrange or place in a particular order, esp. in a row or line. **2.** To place in a group or category; classify. **3.** To align (a gun, telescope, etc.) with a target; to sight. **4.** To determine the distance of (a target). **5.** To move or travel over or through (a region), as in exploration. **6.** To wander and graze over (an area). —*intr.v.* **1.** To vary within specified limits: *ages ranging from two to ten.* **2.** To extend in a particular direction: *a river ranging to the east.* **3.** To move over or through a given area, as in exploration. **4.** To roam or wander; rove. **5.** To live or grow over a particular region. [Middle English, series, line, from Old French, range, rank, *reng,* line, row.]

Syns: **range, extent, orbit, reach, realm, scope, sphere, sweep** *n. Core meaning:* An area within which something or someone exists, acts, or has influence or power (*the range of a missile; the range of the human intellect*).

range finder. Any of various instruments used to determine the distance of an object.

rang·er (rān′jər) *n.* **1.** One of an armed troop employed in patrolling a specific region. **2.** **Ranger.** A member of a group of U.S. soldiers specially trained for making raids. **3.** A person employed to patrol and guard a forest.

rang·y (rān′jē) *adj.* **-i·er, -i·est.** **1.** Inclined to rove. **2.** Long-legged and slender. **3.** Providing ample range; roomy.

ra·ni (rä′nē) *n., pl.* **-nis.** Also **ra·nee.** **1.** The wife of a rajah. **2.** A reigning Hindu princess or queen. [Hindi *rānī,* from Sanskrit *rājñī,* fem. of *rājan,* king.]

rank¹ (răngk) *n.* **1.** A relative position on a scale of performance, production, value, quality, etc.: *in the middle rank of his class.* **2.** High position in society; eminence: *gentlemen of rank.* **3.** An official position or grade: *an adviser with cabinet rank.* **4.** A row or line, esp. of people or things side by side: *The soldiers formed ranks for inspection.* **5. ranks.** The enlisted men of a military force. **6. ranks.** A body of people classed together; numbers: *joined the ranks of the unemployed.* —*tr.v.* **1.** To arrange in a row or on a scale: *ranked the children by height.* **2.** To give a particular order or position to; evaluate; classify: *ranked the team second.* **3.** To outrank or take precedence over. —*intr.v.* To hold a particular rank: *rank first.* [Old French *renc.*]

rank² (răngk) *adj.* **-er, -est.** **1.** Growing profusely and without control: *rank weeds.* **2.** Strong and unpleasant in odor or taste: *rank meat.* **3.** Indecent; disgusting. **4.** Absolute; complete: *a rank amateur.* [Middle English, from Old

English *ranc*, haughty, full-grown, overbearing.] —**rank′ly**
adv. —**rank′ness** *n.*

rank and file. **1.** The common soldiers of an army.
2. Those who form the major portion of any group or organization, excluding the leaders and officers.

rank·ing (răng′kĭng) *adj.* Having a high or the highest rank.

ran·kle (răng′kəl) *v.* **-kled, -kling.** —*intr.v.* To cause persistent irritation or resentment; annoy. —*tr.v.* To fill (someone) with a nagging resentment; embitter; irritate. [Middle English *ranclen*, from Old French *rancler*, from *rancle*, ulcer, festering sore, ult. from Latin *dracō*, serpent.]

ran·sack (răn′săk′) *tr.v.* **1.** To search or examine thoroughly. **2.** To pillage. [Middle English *ransaken*, from Old Norse *rannsaka*, to search a house : *rann*, house + *-saka*, search.] —**ran′sack·er** *n.*

ran·som (răn′səm) *n.* **1.** The release of a person or property held captive in return for the payment of a demanded price. **2.** The price or payment demanded or paid. —*tr.v.* To obtain the release of (a person or property held captive) by paying a demanded price. [Middle English *ransoun*, from Old French *rançon*, from Latin *redemptiō*, redemption.] —**ran′som·er** *n.*

rant (rănt) *intr.v.* To speak violently, loudly, and at length; rave: *ranted against high taxes.* —*n.* A loud, violent speech; a tirade. [Prob. from Dutch *ranten*.] —**rant′er** *n.*

rap¹ (răp) *v.* **rapped, rap·ping.** —*tr.v.* **1.** To hit (a surface) sharply; to strike: *rapped the table with his fist.* **2.** To utter sharply: *rap out a complaint.* **3.** *Slang.* To criticize or blame. —*intr.v.* **1.** To strike a quick, light blow or blows; to knock: *rapped on the door.* **2.** *Slang.* To discuss freely and at length. —See Syns at **blame.** —*n.* **1.** A quick, light blow or knock. **2.** *Slang.* A talk, conversation, or discussion. **3.** *Slang.* **a.** A criminal charge. **b.** A prison sentence. **c.** Blame or responsibility: *took the rap for his friends.* [Middle English *rappen*.]

rap² (răp) *n. Informal.* The least bit: *I don't care a rap.* [Short for Irish-Gaelic *rapaire*, pike.]

ra·pa·cious (rə-pā′shəs) *adj.* **1.** Greedy; avaricious. **2.** Existing by feeding on live prey. [From Latin *rapax*, from *rapere*, to seize.] —**ra·pa′cious·ly** *adv.* —**ra·pa′cious·ness** or **ra·pac′i·ty** (rə-păs′ĭ-tē) *n.*

rape¹ (rāp) *n.* **1.** The crime of forcing a female to submit to sexual intercourse. **2.** *Archaic.* The act of seizing and carrying off by force; abduction. —*tr.v.* **raped, rap·ing.** **1.** To force (a female) to submit to sexual intercourse. **2.** *Archaic.* To seize and carry off by force. [Middle English, from *rapen*, to rape, from Anglo-French *raper*, to seize, from Latin *rapere*.] —**rap′ist** *n.*

rape² (rāp) *n.* A Eurasian plant, *Brassica napus*, cultivated for its seed, which yields a useful oil, and as fodder. [Middle English, from Latin *rāpa*, turnip.]

ra·phe (rā′fē) *n., pl.* **-phae** (-fē). *Biol.* A seamlike line or ridge, as in the coat of certain seeds. [From Greek *rhaphē*, seam, from *rhaptein*, to sew.]

rap·id (răp′ĭd) *adj.* **-er, -est.** Moving, acting, or occurring with great speed; swift. —See Syns at **fast.** —*n.* Often **rapids.** An extremely fast-moving part of a river, caused by a steep descent in the riverbed. [Latin *rapidus*, hurrying, seizing, from *rapere*, to seize.] —**rap′id·ly** *adv.* —**ra·pid′i·ty** (rə-pĭd′ĭ-tē) or **rap′id·ness** *n.*

rap·id-fire (răp′ĭd-fīr′) *adj.* **1.** Designed to fire shots in rapid succession. **2.** Marked by continuous, rapid occurrence: *rapid-fire questions.*

rapid transit. An urban passenger transportation system using elevated or underground trains or both.

ra·pi·er (rā′pē-ər, răp′yər) *n.* A sword with a double-edged blade, used for thrusting. [French (*espée*) *rapière*, rapier (sword).]

rap·ine (răp′ĭn) *n.* The seizure of property by force; plunder. [Middle English *rapyne*, from Old French *rapine*, from Latin *rapīna*, from *rapere*, to seize.]

rap·port (ră-pôr′, -pōr′, rə-) *n.* The condition of mutual trust and understanding. —See Syns at **harmony.** [French, from *rapporter*, to bring back, to yield, from Old French *raporter*.]

rap·proche·ment (ră′prôsh-mäN′) *n.* A re-establishment of cordial relations between two countries. [French, from *rapprocher*, to bring together.]

rap·scal·lion (răp-skăl′yən) *n.* A rascal; scamp. [Var. of obs. *rascallion*, from RASCAL.]

rapt (răpt) *adj.* **1.** Deeply moved or delighted; enraptured: *listening with rapt admiration.* **2.** Deeply absorbed; engrossed: *rapt in thought.* [Middle English, from Latin *raptus*, seized, from *rapere*, to seize.]

rap·to·ri·al (răp-tôr′ē-əl, -tōr′-) *adj.* **1.** Adapted for seizing prey; predatory. **2.** Of or characteristic of birds of prey. [From Latin *raptor*, robber, from *rapere*, to seize.]

rap·ture (răp′chər) *n.* The condition of being carried away by overwhelming joy; bliss; ecstasy. [Medieval Latin *raptūra*, from Latin *raptus*, rapt.]

rap·tur·ous (răp′chər-əs) *adj.* Filled with great joy or rapture; ecstatic. —**rap′tur·ous·ly** *adv.* —**rap′tur·ous·ness** *n.*

ra·ra a·vis (râr′ə ā′vĭs) *pl.* **rara a·vis·es** or **ra·rae a·ves** (râr′ē ā′vēz). A rare person or thing. [Latin, "rare bird."]

rare¹ (râr) *adj.* **rar·er, rar·est.** **1.** Infrequently occurring; uncommon; unusual: *a rare disease.* **2.** Highly valued because of uncommonness; special: *a rare gift for writing.* **3.** Thin in density; rarefied: *a rare gas.* —See Syns at **uncommon.** [Middle English, from Latin *rārus*, loose, thin, scarce, remarkable.] —**rare′ness** *n.*

rare² (râr) *adj.* **rar·er, rar·est.** Cooked a short time: *rare meat.* [Middle English *rere*, slightly cooked, from Old English *hrēr*.] —**rare′ness** *n.*

rare-earth element (râr′ûrth′). Any of the metallic elements with atomic numbers ranging from 57 through 71. Also called **lanthanide.**

rar·e·fac·tion (râr′ə-făk′shən, răr′-) *n.* Also **rar·e·fi·ca·tion** (-fĭ-kā′shən). The act or process of rarefying or the condition of being rarefied. —**rar′e·fac′tive** *adj.*

rar·e·fy (râr′ə-fī′, răr′-) *v.* **-fied, -fy·ing.** —*tr.v.* **1.** To make thin, less compact, or less dense. **2.** To purify or refine. —*intr.v.* To become thin, less dense, or purer. [Middle English *rarefien*, from Old French *rarefier*, from Latin *rārēfacere* : *rārus*, rare + *facere*, to make.]

rare·ly (râr′lē) *adv.* **1.** Not often; seldom; infrequently: *"The truth is rarely pure and never simple."* (Oscar Wilde). **2.** To an unusual degree; exceptionally: *a rarely charming woman.* **3.** With uncommon excellence.

rar·i·ty (râr′ĭ-tē, răr′-) *n., pl.* **-ties.** **1.** The quality or condition of being rare. **2.** Something that is rare: *Snow is a rarity in Florida.*

ras·cal (răs′kəl) *n.* **1.** A dishonest person; a scoundrel. **2.** A mischievous person; a scamp. [Middle English *rascaille*, from Old French, rabble.] —**ras′cal·ly** *adj.*

ras·cal·i·ty (ră-skăl′ĭ-tē) *n., pl.* **-ties.** **1.** The behavior or character of a rascal. **2.** A dishonest or mischievous act.

rash¹ (răsh) *adj.* **-er, -est.** **1.** Reckless; impetuous. **2.** Too hasty; careless: *a rash action.* [Middle English *rasch*, nimble, quick, eager.] —**rash′ly** *adv.* —**rash′ness** *n.*

rash² (răsh) *n.* **1.** An eruption of the skin. **2.** An outbreak of many occurrences within a brief period: *a rash of burglaries.* [Poss. from Old French *rasche*, scurf.]

rash·er (răsh′ər) *n.* **1.** A thin slice of bacon to be fried or broiled. **2.** A dish of such slices. [Orig. unknown.]

rasp (răsp) *n.* **1.** A coarse file with sharp, raised, pointed projections. **2.** The act of filing with a rasp. **3.** A grating sound. —*tr.v.* **1.** To file or scrape with a rasp. **2.** To utter in a grating voice. **3.** To irritate; grate upon (nerves, feelings, etc.). —*intr.v.* **1.** To grate; scrape harshly. **2.** To make a grating sound. [Middle English *raspen*, from Old French *rasper*, to scrape.] —**rasp′er** *n.*

rasp·ber·ry (răz′bĕr′ē) *n.* **1. a.** Any of various shrubby, usu.

raspberry

rat

ratchet

rattlesnake

prickly plants of the genus *Rubus*. **b.** The sweet, many-seeded, edible fruit of any of these plants, consisting of a mass of small, fleshy, usu. red drupelets. **2.** Also **razz·ber·ry.** *Slang.* A jeering or contemptuous sound made by vibrating the tongue between the lips. [From earlier *rasp*, raspberry + BERRY.]

rat (răt) *n.* **1.** Any of various long-tailed rodents related to and resembling the mouse but larger, esp. one of the genus *Rattus*. **2.** *Slang.* A despicable, sneaky person, esp. one who betrays or informs on his associates. —*intr.v.* **rat·ted, rat·ting. 1.** To hunt for or catch rats. **2.** *Slang.* To betray one's comrades by giving information. [Middle English, from Old English *ræt.*]

ratch·et (răch′ĭt) *n.* **1.** A mechanism consisting of a pawl, or hinged catch, that fits into the sloping teeth of a wheel or bar and permits motion in one direction only. **2.** The pawl, wheel, or bar of such a mechanism. [French *rochet*, from Old French *rocquet*, head of a lance.]

rate¹ (răt) *n.* **1.** A quantity measured with respect to another measured quantity: *a rate of speed of 60 miles an hour.* **2.** A measure of a part with respect to a whole; proportion: *the birth rate.* **3.** The cost or price charged per unit of a commodity or service: *postal rates.* **4.** A charge or payment calculated with respect to another sum or quantity: *interest rates.* **5.** A level of quality: *a jewel of no common rate.* **6.** *Brit.* A property tax assessed locally. —*v.* **rat·ed, rat·ing.** —*tr.v.* **1.** To calculate the value of; appraise: *rate a building for tax purposes.* **2.** To place in a particular grade or rank on a scale; rank: *rate cuts of meat.* **3.** To regard or consider: *rated the musical a great success.* **4.** To set a rate for (goods to be shipped). **5.** *Informal.* To merit or deserve: *rate special treatment.* —*intr.v.* **1.** To be ranked in a particular class. **2.** *Informal.* To have status, importance, or influence. —*idiom.* **at any rate. 1.** Whatever happens; in any case. **2.** At least. [Middle English, from Old French, from Medieval Latin *rata*, calculated, fixed, past part. of Latin *rērī*, to calculate.]

rate² (răt) *tr.v.* **rat·ed, rat·ing.** To berate; scold. [Middle English *raten.*]

rate of exchange. The ratio at which the unit of currency of one country may be exchanged for the unit of currency of another country.

rath·er (răth′ər, rä′thər) *adv.* **1.** To a certain extent; somewhat: *feeling rather sleepy.* **2.** Preferably; more willingly: *I'd rather stay home tonight.* **3.** More exactly; more accurately: *He is a businessman or, rather, a banker.* **4.** Instead; to the contrary: *The photograph did not show the whole family but rather all the boys.* [Middle English, from Old English *hrathor*, comp. of *hrathe*, early.]

rat·i·fy (răt′ə-fī′) *tr.v.* **-fied, -fy·ing.** To give formal approval to; make officially valid; confirm. [Middle English *ratifien*, from Old French *ratifier*, from Medieval Latin *ratificāre* : Latin *ratus*, fixed + *facere*, to make.] —**rat′i·fi·ca′tion** *n.*

rat·ing (rā′tĭng) *n.* **1.** A classification assigned according to quality, performance, skill, etc. **2.** An estimate of someone's financial status and ability to pay back debts: *a high credit rating.* **3.** A specified performance limit, as of capacity, range, or operational capability.

ra·tio (rā′shō, -shē-ō′) *n., pl.* **-tios. 1.** *Math.* An indicated quotient of a pair of numbers, often used as a means of comparing them: *The ratio of 7 to 4 is written 7:4 or 7/4.* **2.** A relationship between the amounts or sizes of two things, expressed as a ratio; proportion: *mixed flour and water in the ratio of five to two.* [Latin *ratiō*, computation,

from *ratus*, past part. of *rērī*, to consider.]

ra·ti·oc·i·nate (răsh′ē-ŏs′ə-nāt′) *intr.v.* **-nat·ed, -nat·ing.** To reason methodically and logically. [From Latin *ratiōcināre*, from *ratiō*, computation.] —**ra·ti·oc′i·na′tion** *n.*

ra·tion (răsh′ən, rā′shən) *n.* **1.** A fixed amount, esp. of food, allotted periodically. **2. rations.** Food issued or available to members of a group. —*tr.v.* **1.** To distribute or make available in fixed, limited amounts during periods of scarcity: *ration gasoline.* **2.** To supply with allotments of food; give rations to. **3.** To restrict to limited amounts: *ration salt in a diet.* [French, from Latin *ratiō*, computation.]

ra·tio·nal (răsh′ə-nəl) *adj.* **1.** Having or using the ability to reason: *man, the rational animal.* **2.** Consistent with or based on reason; logical: *rational behavior.* **3.** Of sound mind; sane. **4.** *Math.* Of a rational number. —See Syns at **sensible.** —*n.* A rational number. [Latin *ratiōnālis*, from *ratiō*, reason, computation.] —**ra′tio·nal·ly** *adv.*

ra·tio·nale (răsh′ə-năl′) *n.* The fundamental reasons for something; a logical basis. [Latin *ratiōnāle*, rational.]

ra·tio·nal·ism (răsh′ə-nə-lĭz′əm) *n.* The theory that reason is the prime source of knowledge and the basis for human action and beliefs. —**ra′tio·nal·ist** *n.* —**ra′tio·nal·is′tic** *adj.* —**ra′tio·nal·is′ti·cal·ly** *adv.*

ra·tio·nal·i·ty (răsh′ə-năl′ĭ-tē) *n., pl.* **-ties. 1.** The quality or condition of being rational. **2.** A rational belief or practice.

ra·tio·nal·ize (răsh′ə-nə-līz′) *v.* **-ized, -iz·ing.** —*tr.v.* **1.** To interpret or explain from a rational standpoint. **2.** To devise reasonable explanations for (one's behavior) that are different from the true motivation. **3.** *Math.* To remove radicals without changing the value of (an equation). —*intr.v. Psychol.* To devise self-satisfying but usu. incorrect reasons or explanations for one's behavior. —**ra′tio·nal·i·za′tion** *n.*

rational number. Any number that can be expressed as an integer or a quotient of integers.

rat·line (răt′lĭn) *n.* Also **rat·lin.** Any of the small ropes that are fastened horizontally to the shrouds of a ship and form a ladder for going aloft. [Orig. unknown.]

rat·tan (ră-tăn′, rə-) *n.* **1.** Any of various climbing palms of the genera *Calamus, Daemonorops,* or *Plectomia,* of tropical Asia, with long, tough, slender stems. **2.** The stems of any of these palms, used to make wickerwork. **3.** A switch or cane made from a rattan stem. [Malay *rotan.*]

rat·tle (răt′l) *v.* **-tled, -tling.** —*intr.v.* **1.** To make or emit a quick succession of short, sharp sounds: *so frightened his teeth rattled.* **2.** To talk rapidly and at length, usu. without much thought: *rattled on about his problems.* —*tr.v.* **1.** To cause to make a quick succession of short, sharp sounds: *a gale that rattled the windows.* **2.** To utter or perform rapidly or effortlessly: *rattle off a list of names.* **3.** *Informal.* To disturb the composure or confidence of; fluster; unnerve. —*n.* **1.** Short, sharp sounds produced in rapid succession. **2.** A device that rattles when shaken, as a baby's toy. **3.** A rattling sound in the throat caused by obstructed breathing, esp. at the time of death. **4.** A dry, horny ring at the end of a rattlesnake's tail that makes a rattling sound when shaken. [Middle English *ratelen,* from Middle Low German *rattelen.*]

rat·tler (răt′lər) *n.* **1.** Someone or something that rattles. **2.** A rattlesnake.

rat·tle·snake (răt′l-snāk′) *n.* Any of various poisonous New World snakes having at the end of the tail a series of dry, horny rings that can be shaken rapidly to make a rattling or buzzing sound.

ă pat	ā pay	â care	ä father	ĕ pet	ē be	hw which	ĭ pit	ī tie	î pier	ŏ pot	ō toe	ô paw, for	oi noise
ōō took	ōō boot	ou out	th thin	th this	ŭ cut		û urge		zh vision	ə about, item, edible, gallop, circus			

rat·tling (răt′lĭng) *adj. Informal.* **1.** Animated; brisk: *a rattling conversation.* **2.** Very good.

rat·ty (răt′ē) *adj.* **-ti·er, -ti·est. 1.** Characteristic of or infested by rats. **2.** *Slang.* Disreputable; shabby.

rau·cous (rô′kəs) *adj.* **1.** Rough-sounding and harsh: *raucous laughter.* **2.** Boisterous; disorderly: *a raucous party.* [Latin *raucus,* hoarse, harsh.] **—rau′cous·ly** *adv.* **—rau′cous·ness** *n.*

rav·age (răv′ĭj) *v.* **-aged, -ag·ing. —tr.v. 1.** To bring heavy destruction upon; devastate: *A tornado ravaged the countryside.* **2.** To pillage; sack. **—intr.v.** To wreak destruction. —See Syns at **sack. —n. 1.** The act of ravaging. **2.** Severe damage; destructive effect: *the ravages of smallpox.* [French, from Old French, from *ravir,* to ravish.] **—rav′ag·er** *n.*

rave (rāv) *intr.v.* **raved, rav·ing. 1.** To speak wildly or irrationally. **2.** To roar; rage: *The storm raved in the forest.* **3.** To speak with wild enthusiasm: *He raved about her looks.* **—n. 1.** The act or an example of raving. **2.** *Informal.* An extravagantly enthusiastic opinion, description, or review. **—modifier:** *rave reviews.* [Middle English *raven,* to be delirious, to wander, from Old North French *raver.*]

rav·el (răv′əl) *v.* **-eled** or **-elled, -el·ing** or **-el·ling. —tr.v. 1.** To separate the fibers or threads of (cloth, rope, etc.); unravel; fray. **2.** To clarify by separating the elements or aspects of. **3.** To tangle, complicate, or confuse. **—intr.v.** To become separated into loose fibers or threads. **—n. 1.** A raveling. **2.** A broken or loose thread. [From Dutch *rafelen,* to fray.] **—rav′el·er** *n.*

rav·el·ing (răv′ə-lĭng) *n.* A thread or fiber that has become separated from a woven material.

ra·ven¹ (rā′vən) *n.* A large black bird, *Corvus corax,* with black plumage and a croaking cry. *—adj.* Black and shiny: *raven hair.* [Middle English, from Old English *hræfn.*]

rav·en² (răv′ən) *tr.v.* **1.** To devour greedily. **2.** To seek or seize as prey or plunder. **—intr.v. 1.** To seek or seize prey or plunder. **2.** To eat ravenously. [Old French *raviner,* to ravage, from Latin *rapīna,* rapine, from *rapere,* to seize.]

rav·en·ous (răv′ə-nəs) *adj.* **1.** Greedily eager for food; extremely hungry. **2.** Predatory; rapacious. **3.** Greedily seeking satisfaction or gratification. **—rav′en·ous·ly** *adv.* **—rav′en·ous·ness** *n.*

ra·vine (rə-vēn′) *n.* A deep, narrow cut in the earth's surface, esp. one worn by the flow of water. [French, mountain torrent, from Old French, rapine.]

rav·i·o·li (răv′ē-ō′lē, rä′vē-) *pl.n.* Small casings of pasta with various fillings, as chopped meat or cheese. [Italian, pl. of *raviolo,* dim. of *rava,* turnip, from Latin *rapa.*]

rav·ish (răv′ĭsh) *tr.v.* **1.** To seize and take by force. **2.** To rape. **3.** To ruin; despoil. **4.** To carry away with delight or other strong emotion; enrapture. [Middle English *ravisshen,* from Old French *ravir,* from Latin *rapere,* to seize.] **—rav′ish·er** *n.* **—rav′ish·ment** *n.*

rav·ish·ing (răv′ĭ-shĭng) *adj.* **1.** Delightful; enchanting. **2.** Gorgeous; beautiful. —See Syns at **beautiful.**

raw (rô) *adj.* **-er, -est. 1. a.** In a natural condition; not processed or refined: *raw wool.* **b.** To be further processed or refined: *raw metal.* **2.** Uncooked: *raw meat.* **3.** Not finished, covered, or coated: *furniture sanded down to raw wood.* **4.** Inexperienced; unskilled: *raw recruits.* **5.** Having tissue below the skin exposed: *a raw wound.* **6.** Badly irritated; inflamed; sore: *a raw throat.* **7.** Unpleasantly damp and chilly: *raw weather.* **8.** Cruel and unfair: *a raw deal.* [Middle English, from Old English *hrēaw.*] **—raw′ly** *adv.* **—raw′ness** *n.*

raw·boned (rô′bōnd′) *adj.* Having a lean, gaunt frame with prominent bones.

raw·hide (rô′hīd′) *n.* **1.** The untanned hide of cattle or other animals. **2.** A whip or rope made of rawhide. **—tr.v. -hid·ed, -hid·ing.** To beat with a rawhide whip.

raw material. 1. Any product or material that is converted into another by processing or manufacturing. **2.** Any material from which something is made or built.

ray¹ (rā) *n.* **1. a.** A thin line or narrow beam of light or other radiation. **b.** A stream of particles, as in radioactive material, flowing in the same line. **2.** A small amount; a trace. **3.** *Geom.* **a.** A straight line extending from a point. **b.** One of several lines or parts extending from a common center. **4.** *Bot.* A **ray flower. 5.** *Zool.* **a.** One of the bony spines sup-

porting the membrane of a fish's fin. **b.** A radiating limb of an animal, such as a starfish, characterized by radial symmetry. **—tr.v.** To send out as rays; emit. [Middle English, from Old French *rai,* from Latin *radius.*]

ray² (rā) *n.* Any of various saltwater fishes of the order Rajiformes (or Batoidei), with cartilaginous skeletons, horizontally flattened bodies, and narrow tails. [Middle English *raye,* from Old French *raie,* from Latin *raia.*]

ray flower. Any of the narrow, petallike flowers surrounding the disklike central head of certain flowers, such as the daisy. Also called **ray floret.**

ray·on (rā′ŏn) *n.* **1.** Any of several synthetic textile fibers produced by forcing a cellulose solution through fine holes and solidifying the resulting filaments. **2.** Any fabric woven or knit from rayon. [From RAY (light).]

raze (rāz) *tr.v.* **razed, raz·ing.** To tear down or demolish; level to the ground. —See Syns at **destroy.** [Middle English *rasen,* from Old French *raser,* from Latin *rāsus,* past part. of *radere,* to scrape.]

ra·zor (rā′zər) *n.* A sharp-edged cutting instrument used esp. for shaving the face. [Middle English *rasour,* from Old French *rasor,* from *raser,* to scrape.]

ra·zor·back (rā′zər-băk′) *n.* **1.** A semiwild hog of the southeastern United States that has a narrow body with a ridged back. **2.** A whale, the rorqual.

razz (răz). *Slang. —n.* A derisive sound; a raspberry. **—tr.v.** To ridicule; heckle. [Short for RAZZBERRY.]

razz·ber·ry (răz′bĕr′ē) *n.* Var. of **raspberry** (derisive sound).

Rb The symbol for the element rubidium.

re¹ (rā) *n. Mus.* A syllable used to represent the second tone of a major scale or sometimes the tone D. [Middle English, from Medieval Latin.]

re² (rē, rā) *prep.* Concerning; in reference to; in the case of. [Latin *rē,* from *rēs,* thing.]

Re The symbol for the element rhenium.

Re (rā) *n.* Var. of **Ra.**

re-. A prefix meaning: **1.** Back: **repay, replace. 2.** Again: **reactivate. 3.** Against: **react.** *—Note:* When re- is followed by *e,* it may appear with a hyphen: **re-entry** or **reentry.** [Middle English *re-,* from Old French, from Latin *re-, red-,* back, backward, against, again.]

reach (rēch) *tr.v.* **1.** To stretch out; extend: *reach out one's arms.* **2.** To touch or grasp by stretching out or extending, esp. the hand: *couldn't reach the ceiling.* **3. a.** To get to; arrive at; attain: *reach a conclusion; reach the speed of sound.* **b.** To extend as far as: *His property reached the shore.* **c.** To succeed in doing. **4.** To succeed in communicating with: *They reached him by wire.* **5.** To make an impression on; affect: *Neither threats nor tears reached him.* **6.** *Informal.* To hand over; pass: *Reach me the sugar.* **—intr.v. 1.** To extend or stretch out with or as if with the hand. **2.** To stretch out in order to grasp or touch something: *reach for a gun.* —See Syns at **accomplish. —n. 1.** The action or an act of reaching. **2.** The distance a person can extend an arm: *a boxer with a short reach.* **3. a.** The extent to which one exists, acts, or exerts influence; range. **b.** The range of a person's understanding; comprehension: *a topic beyond his reach.* **4.** An unbroken expanse. —See Syns at **range.** [Middle English *rechen,* from Old English *ræcan.*] **—reach′er** *n.*

re·act (rē-ăkt′) *intr.v.* **1.** To act in response to a stimulus or prompting: *The eye reacts to light. She reacted angrily to the teasing.* **2.** To act in opposition to some former condition or act: *composers who reacted against romanticism.* **3.** To take part in or undergo chemical change.

re·ac·tance (rē-ăk′təns) *n.* Opposition to the flow of alternating electric current caused by the inductance and capacitance in a circuit.

re·ac·tant (rē-ăk′tənt) *n.* A substance that participates in a chemical reaction.

re·ac·tion (rē-ăk′shən) *n.* **1.** The act or process of reacting. **2.** An action, feeling, or attitude aroused as a response to something: *Her first reaction was to cry.* **3.** The response of a living thing to a stimulus: *the body's reaction to a drug.* **4. a.** The process or condition of taking part in a chemical change. **b.** A chemical change. **5. a.** Opposition to something new or proposed. **b.** Political opposition to progress, reform, or change. **6.** A **nuclear reaction. —re·**

ac·tion·al *adj.* —**re·ac'tion·al·ly** *adv.*

re·ac·tion·ar·y (rē-ăk'shə-nĕr'ē) *adj.* Opposing progress, reform, or change: *a reactionary politician.* —*n., pl.* **-ies.** An opponent of progress or liberalism.

reaction time. The time interval between the application of a stimulus and the occurrence of a response.

re·ac·ti·vate (rē-ăk'tə-vāt') *tr.v.* **-vat·ed, -vat·ing.** To make active again. —**re·ac'ti·va'tion** *n.*

re·ac·tive (rē-ăk'tĭv) *adj.* **1.** Tending to be responsive or to react. **2.** Of or marked by reaction.

re·ac·tor (rē-ăk'tər) *n.* **1.** Someone or something that reacts. **2.** A **nuclear reactor.**

read (rēd) *v.* **read** (rĕd), **read·ing.** —*tr.v.* **1.** To understand or take in the meaning of (written or printed words or symbols): *reading books.* **2.** To speak aloud the words of (something written or printed): *She read the poem while we listened.* **3.** To know (a language) well enough to understand written and printed material. **4.** To interpret the true nature or meaning of (someone or something) through close observation: *read disappointment in her eyes.* **5.** To determine the intent or mood of: *He read her mind.* **6.** To derive a special meaning from or give a special significance to (something read, experienced, or observed): *read hostility into her silence.* **7.** To foretell or predict (the future). **8.** To perceive, receive, or comprehend (a signal, message, etc.): *I read you fine.* **9.** To study or make a study of: *read law.* **10.** To take in the meaning of (something symbolic, graphic, hidden, or in code); interpret: *reading a blueprint.* **11.** To learn or get knowledge from (something written or printed): *He read that crime was rife.* **12.** To have or use as a preferred reading in a particular passage: *For "colour" read "color."* **13.** To indicate or register: *The dial reads 0°.* —*intr.v.* **1.** To read printed or written characters, as of words or music. **2.** To speak aloud written or printed material: *read to his children every night.* **3.** To become informed or learn through written or printed matter: *He read about the Seneca Indians.* **4.** To have a particular wording: *The line reads thus.* —*idioms.* **read between the lines.** To find an implicit or hidden meaning that is not actually expressed. **read up on.** To gain information about by reading. [Middle English *reden,* from Old English *rǣdan,* to advise, explain, read.] —**read'·a·bil'i·ty** or **read'a·ble·ness** *n.* —**read'a·ble** *adj.*

read·er (rē'dər) *n.* **1.** A person who reads. **2.** A textbook of reading exercises.

read·i·ly (rĕd'l-ē) *adv.* **1.** Without hesitation; willingly: *advice that was readily accepted.* **2.** Without difficulty; easily: *paints that are readily available.*

read·i·ness (rĕd'ē-nĭs) *n.* **1.** The condition of being ready. **2.** Favorable disposition; willingness. **3.** Ease and promptness; facility. —See Syns at **ease.**

read·ing (rē'dĭng) *n.* **1.** Books and other material read or to be read. **2.** The act of speaking aloud written material, esp., an official or public recitation, as of a document. **3.** An interpretation of a word or passage in a text. **4.** The data or information indicated by an instrument, gauge, etc.

re·ad·just (rē'ə-jŭst') *tr.v.* To adjust or arrange again. —**re'ad·just'ment** *n.*

read-out (rēd'out') *n.* Presentation of computer data from calculations or storage.

read·y (rĕd'ē) *adj.* **-i·er, -i·est. 1.** Prepared or available for action or use: *ground ready for planting.* **2.** Inclined; willing: *ready to believe them.* **3.** About to do something; liable: *seemed ready to cry.* **4.** Quick in understanding or responding; alert and prompt: *a ready intelligence.* **5.** Conveniently available; close at hand: *ready cash.* **6.** Presenting no difficulty: *a ready solution.* —See Syns at **easy** and **glad.** —*tr.v.* **-ied, -y·ing.** To make ready; prepare. [Middle English *redy,* from Old English *rǣde.*]

read·y-made (rĕd'ē-mād') *adj.* **1.** Already made, prepared, or available: *ready-made clothes.* **2.** Thought up by someone else; preconceived: *ready-made opinions.*

re·af·firm (rē'ə-fûrm') *tr.v.* To affirm or state again. —**re·af'fir·ma'tion** (rē-ăf'ər-mā'shən) *n.*

re·a·gent (rē-ā'jənt) *n.* Any substance used in a chemical reaction to detect, measure, examine, or produce other substances.

re·al (rē'əl, rēl) *adj.* **1.** Not imaginary, fictional, or pretended; actual: *concealed his real purpose.* **2.** Not artifi-

cial; authentic or genuine: *a real ruby.* **3.** Essential; basic: *The real subject is people.* **4.** Being no less than what is stated; worthy of the name: *a real friend.* **5.** Serious; not to be taken lightly: *in real trouble.* **6.** Of or being real property. **7.** *Math.* Of a real number. —*adv. Informal.* Very: *real sorry.* [Middle English, relating to things, from Old French, from Late Latin *reālis,* actual, real, from Latin *rēs,* thing.] —**real'ness** *n.*

> **Syns: real, substantial, substantive, tangible** *adj.* Core meaning: Having actual reality (*real evidence; real, not imagined pain*).

real estate. Land, including all the natural resources and permanent buildings on it.

re·al·ism (rē'ə-lĭz'əm) *n.* **1.** Conformity to reality; authenticity. **2.** Concern with facts and things as they actually are. **3.** The depiction of reality, as in painting, sculpture, or literature. **4.** *Philos.* The doctrine that the objects of human perception exist independently of the ability to perceive them. —**re'al·ist** *n.* —**re'al·is'tic** *adj.* —**re'al·is'ti·cal·ly** *adv.*

re·al·i·ty (rē-ăl'ĭ-tē) *n., pl.* **-ties. 1.** The condition or quality of being real or true; actual existence. **2.** A person, thing, or event that is real.

re·al·ize (rē'ə-līz') *tr.v.* **-ized, -iz·ing. 1.** To comprehend completely or correctly: *realized his mistake.* **2.** To make real or actual; achieve: *realized his ambition to succeed.* **3.** To obtain or bring in as profit: *realize a large sum on an investment.* —See Syns at **accomplish.** —**re'al·iz'a·ble** *adj.* —**re'al·i·za'tion** *n.* —**re'al·iz'er** *n.*

re·al·ly (rē'ə-lē, rē'lē) *adv.* **1.** In actual truth or fact: *The horseshoe crab isn't really a crab at all.* **2.** Truly: *a really enjoyable evening.*

realm (rĕlm) *n.* **1.** A kingdom. **2.** Any field, sphere, or province: *the realm of science.* **3.** Range; extent. —See Syns at **range.** [Middle English *reaume,* from Old French, from Latin *regimen,* system of government, from *regere,* to rule.]

real number. Any member of the set of rational or irrational numbers.

Re·al·tor (rē'əl-tər, -tôr') *n.* **1.** A real-estate agent affiliated with the National Association of Real Estate Boards. **2. re·altor.** A person whose occupation is buying and selling real estate.

real property. Property that is fixed or permanent and cannot be moved by the owner, as land or buildings.

re·al·ty (rē'əl-tē) *n., pl.* **-ties.** Real estate.

ream¹ (rēm) *n.* **1.** A quantity of paper of the same size and stock, formerly 480 sheets, now 500 or 516 sheets. **2. reams.** A large amount. [Middle English *reme,* from Old French *remme,* from Arabic *rizmah,* bundle.]

ream² (rēm) *tr.v.* **1.** To shape, enlarge, or clean out (a hole, tube, gun barrel, etc.) with or as if with a reamer. **2.** To remove (material) by reaming. [Prob. from Middle English *remen,* to make room, from Old English *rȳman,* to widen.]

ream·er (rē'mər) *n.* **1.** A tool used to shape, enlarge, or clean out holes. **2.** A kitchen utensil used for extracting juice from citrus fruits.

reamer

reaper

reap (rēp) *tr.v.* **1.** To cut and gather (grain or a similar crop): *reap wheat.* **2.** To gather a crop from; harvest: *reap a field.* **3.** To gain as a reward, esp. as a result of effort: *reap profits from an invention.* —*intr.v.* To cut or harvest grain or a similar crop. [Middle English *repen,* from Old English *rīpan.*]

reap·er (rē'pər) *n.* **1.** A person who reaps. **2.** A machine for harvesting grain or similar crops.

re·ap·pear (rē′ə-pîr′) intr.v. To appear again.

re·ap·por·tion (rē′ə-pôr′shən) tr.v. To distribute again, esp. with the goal of equally dividing the population within legislative districts. —**re′ap·por′tion·ment** n.

rear¹ (rîr) n. **1.** The part of something that is at or closest to the back. **2.** The area or direction behind or at the back of something: *the rear of the house.* **3.** The part of a military deployment farthest from the fighting front. **4.** *Informal.* The buttocks. —adj. Of, at, or located in the rear. [Short for *arrear*, behind.]

rear² (rîr) tr.v. **1.** To care for (a child or children) during the early years of life; bring up. **2.** To lift upright; raise. **3.** To build; erect: *rear a skyscraper.* **4.** To raise; breed: *reared sheep.* —intr.v. **1.** To rise on the hind legs, as a horse. **2.** To rise high in the air; tower. [Middle English *reren*, to lift up, raise, from Old English *ræran*.]

rear admiral. A naval officer ranking below a vice admiral and above a captain.

rear guard. A detachment of troops that protects the rear of a military force.

re·arm (rē-ärm′) tr.v. To arm or equip again, esp. with better weapons. —**re·ar′ma·ment** (rē-är′mə-mənt) n.

rear·most (rîr′mōst′) adj. Farthest in the rear; last.

re·ar·range (rē′ə-rānj′) tr.v. **-ranged, -rang·ing.** To arrange in a different way or order. —**re′ar·range′ment** n.

rear·ward (rîr′wərd) adv. Also **rear·wards** (-wərdz). Toward, to, or at the rear.

rea·son (rē′zən) n. **1.** The basis or motive for an action, decision, feeling, or belief: *a reason for being late.* **2.** A statement made to explain or justify: *asked her reason for staying.* **3.** An underlying fact or cause that justifies the rationale for a statement or conclusion: *I have reason to believe she's alive.* **4.** The ability or faculty of thinking logically, comprehending, or making inferences; intelligence. **5.** A normal mental state; sanity: *lost his reason.* —intr.v. **1.** To use the faculty of reason; think logically. **2.** To talk or argue logically and persuasively: *could not reason with her.* —tr.v. To determine or conclude by logical thinking. —idioms. **by reason of.** Because of. **within reason.** Within the bounds of good sense or practicality. **with reason.** With good reasons; justifiably: *angry, and with reason.* [Middle English *reisun*, from Old French, from Latin *ratiō*, calculation, reasoning, from *ratus*, past part. of *rērī*, to think, reason.] —**rea′son·er** n.

Usage: reason. Since *because* and *why* are inherent in the noun *reason*, the expressions *the reason is because* and *the reason why* are better avoided in formal writing.

rea·son·a·ble (rē′zə-nə-bəl) adj. **1.** Using or capable of using reasoning; rational. **2.** In accordance with reason; logical: *a reasonable solution.* **3.** Not excessive or extreme; moderate: *reasonable prices.* —See Syns at **sensible.** —**rea′son·a·ble·ness** n. —**rea′son·a·bly** adv.

rea·son·ing (rē′zə-nĭng) n. **1.** The use of reason, esp. to form conclusions, judgments, etc. **2.** The evidence or arguments used in reasoning.

re·as·sure (rē′ə-shoor′) tr.v. **-sured, -sur·ing. 1.** To restore confidence to. **2.** To assure again. **3.** To reinsure.

re·bate (rē′bāt′) n. A deduction from an amount to be paid or a return of part of an amount given in payment; a refund or discount. —tr.v. (rē′bāt, rĭ-bāt′) **-bat·ed, -bat·ing.** To deduct or return (an amount) from a payment or bill. [Middle English *rebaten*, to deduct, from Old French *rabattre*, to reduce : *re-*, again + *abattre*, to beat down.]

re·bel (rĭ-bĕl′) intr.v. **-belled, -bel·ling. 1.** To refuse loyalty to or oppose by force an established government or ruling authority. **2.** To resist or oppose any authority. **3.** To feel or express strong unwillingness or repugnance: *rebelled at the suggestion.* —n. **reb·el** (rĕb′əl). A person who rebels or is in rebellion. —modifier: *a rebel attack.* [Middle English *rebellen*, from Old French *rebeller*, from Latin *rebellāre*, to make war again : *re-*, again + *bellum*, war.]

re·bel·lion (rĭ-bĕl′yən) n. **1.** An uprising or organized armed resistance intended to change or overthrow an existing government or ruling authority. **2.** An act or show of defiance toward any authority.

Syns: rebellion, insurgence, insurrection, mutiny, revolt, uprising n. **Core meaning:** Organized opposition intended to change or overthrow existing authority (*a left-wing re-*

bellion against the dictator).

re·bel·lious (rĭ-bĕl′yəs) adj. **1.** Participating in or inclined toward a rebellion. **2.** Resisting management or control; unruly. —**re·bel′lious·ly** adv. —**re·bel′lious·ness** n.

re·birth (rē-bûrth′, rē′bûrth′) n. **1.** A second or new birth; reincarnation. **2.** A renaissance; revival.

re·born (rē-bôrn′) adj. Born again.

re·bound (rĭ-bound′) intr.v. **1.** To spring or bounce back after hitting or colliding with something. **2.** To recover, as from depression or disappointment. —n. (rē′bound′, rĭ-bound′). **1.** A springing or bounding back; recoil. **2.** *Sports.* A rebounding hockey puck or basketball. **3.** A quick reaction to disappointment or depression: *marriage on the rebound.*

re·broad·cast (rē-brôd′kăst′) tr.v. **-cast** or **-cast·ed, -cast·ing. 1.** To repeat the broadcast of (a program). **2.** To repeat (a broadcast). —**re·broad′cast′** n.

re·buff (rĭ-bŭf′) n. A blunt or abrupt refusal, as of an offer; a snub. —tr.v. To refuse bluntly or abruptly; to snub. [Old French *rebuffer*, from Italian *ribuffare*, to scold, from *ribuffo*, reprimand.]

re·build (rē-bĭld′) tr.v. **-built** (-bĭlt′), **-build·ing. 1.** To build again. **2.** To make extensive structural repairs on; remodel. —See Syns at **restore.**

re·buke (rĭ-byōōk′) tr.v. **-buked, -buk·ing.** To criticize or scold sharply; reprimand. —See Syns at **admonish** and **scold.** —n. Words or actions expressing strong disapproval; severe criticism. [Middle English *rebuken*, from Old North French *rebuker*.]

re·bus (rē′bəs) n. A puzzle composed of words or syllables that appear in the form of pictures. [Latin *rēbus*, by things, from *rēs*, thing.]

re·but (rĭ-bŭt′) tr.v. **-but·ted, -but·ting.** To refute, esp. by offering opposing evidence or arguments, as in a legal case.—See Syns at **disprove.** [Middle English *rebuten*, from Old French *rebuter*.] —**re·but′ter** n.

re·but·tal (rĭ-bŭt′l) n. **1.** The act of rebutting. **2.** The statement made in rebutting.

re·cal·ci·trant (rĭ-kăl′sĭ-trənt) adj. Stubbornly resistant to authority or guidance; refractory; obstinate. —n. A recalcitrant person. [Latin *recalcitrāns*, pres. part. of *recalcitrāre*, to kick back.] —**re·cal′ci·trance** or **re·cal′ci·tran·cy** n.

re·call (rĭ-kôl′) tr.v. **1.** To call back; ask or order to return. **2.** To remember or recollect. **3.** To cancel, take back, or revoke. **4.** To bring back; restore. —See Syns at **remember.** —n. (rĭ-kôl′, rē′kôl′). **1.** The act of recalling or summoning back, esp. an official order to return. **2.** The ability to remember; recollection. **3.** The act of revoking. **4.** The act of removing a public official from office by popular vote. —**re·call′a·ble** adj.

re·cant (rĭ-kănt′) tr.v. To deny formally; disavow. —intr.v. To make a formal denial or disavowal of a previously held belief. [Latin *recantāre* : *re-*, back + *cantāre*, to sing, chant, freq. of *canere*, to sing.] —**re′can·ta′tion** n.

re·cap¹ (rē-kăp′) tr.v. **-capped, -cap·ping.** To restore (a used automobile tire) by vulcanizing and cementing new rubber onto the worn tread. —n. (rē′kăp′). A recapped tire.

re·cap² (rē′kăp′, rĭ-kăp′) tr.v. **-capped, -cap·ping.** To summarize by recapitulating. —n. A summary or recapitulation, as of a news report. [Short for RECAPITULATE.]

re·ca·pit·u·late (rē′kə-pĭch′ə-lāt′) v. **-lat·ed, -lat·ing.** —tr.v. To repeat in concise form. —intr.v. To summarize. [From Late Latin *recapitulāre* : *re-*, back, again + *capitulāre*, to put under headings, from Latin *caput*, head.] —**re′ca·pit′u·la′tion** n.

re·cap·ture (rē-kăp′chər) tr.v. **-tured, -tur·ing. 1.** To capture again; retake or recover. **2.** To recall: *an attempt to recapture the past.* —n. The act of taking or discovering again.

re·cede (rĭ-sēd′) intr.v. **-ced·ed, -ced·ing. 1.** To move back or away from a limit, point, or mark: *The flood waters receded.* **2.** To slope backward: *His hairline receded.* **3.** To become or seem to become more distant. [Latin *recēdere*, to go back.]

re·ceipt (rĭ-sēt′) n. **1.** The fact of receiving something. **2. receipts.** The quantity or amount of something received. **3.** A written acknowledgment that a specified article, sum of money, or delivery has been received. **4.** *Regional.* A recipe. —tr.v. **1.** To mark (a bill) as having been paid.

ă pat	ā pay	â care	ä father	ĕ pet	ē be	hw which	ĭ pit	ī tie	î pier	ŏ pot	ō toe	ô paw, for	oi noise
ŏŏ took	ōō boot	ou out	th thin	th this	ŭ cut		û urge	zh vision	ə about, item, edible, gallop, circus				

2. To give or write a receipt for (money paid or goods delivered). [Middle English *receite*, from Old North French, from Medieval Latin *recepta*, from Latin *receptus*, past part. of *recipere*, to take.]

re·ceiv·a·ble (rĭ-sē'və-bəl) *adj.* **1.** Capable of being received. **2.** Awaiting or requiring payment; due.

re·ceive (rĭ-sēv') *v.* **-ceived, -ceiv·ing.** —*tr.v.* **1.** To take or acquire (something given, offered, or transmitted); get: *receive payment.* **2.** To acquire knowledge of or information about: *receive bad news.* **3.** To meet with; experience: *receive sympathetic treatment.* **4.** To take the force or impact of: *receive a blow.* **5.** To greet or welcome: *receive guests.* —*intr.v.* **1.** To admit or welcome guests or visitors; entertain. **2.** *Electronics.* To convert incoming electromagnetic waves into pictures or sounds. [Middle English *receiven*, from Old North French *receivre*, from Latin *recipere*, to accept, receive.]

re·ceiv·er (rĭ-sē'vər) *n.* **1.** Someone or something that receives. **2.** *Law.* A person appointed by a court to hold and administer the property of others pending litigation. **3.** *Electronics.* A device, such as a part of a radio, television set, or telephone, that receives incoming electromagnetic signals and converts them into the form, as sounds or pictures, in which they are to be used.

re·ceiv·er·ship (rĭ-sē'vər-shĭp') *n. Law.* **1.** The office or functions of a receiver. **2.** The condition of being held by a receiver.

re·cent (rē'sənt) *adj.* **1.** Of, belonging to, or occurring at a time immediately prior to the present. **2.** Modern; new. **3.** Recent. *Geol.* Of, relating to, or being the geologic epoch of the Cenozoic era that began about 11,000 years ago at the end of the Pleistocene era and extends to the present. [Latin *recēns*, fresh, new.] —**re'cent·ly** *adv.* —**re'cent·ness** *n.*

re·cep·ta·cle (rĭ-sĕp'tə-kəl) *n.* **1.** Something that holds or contains; a container. **2.** *Bot.* The part of a flower stalk that bears and supports the floral organs. **3.** *Elect.* A fitting connected to a power supply and equipped to receive a plug. [Latin *receptāculum*, from *receptāre*, to take again, freq. of *recipere*, to receive.]

re·cep·tion (rĭ-sĕp'shən) *n.* **1.** The act or process of receiving. **2.** A welcome, greeting, or acceptance: *a favorable reception.* **3.** A social function: *a wedding reception.* **4.** *Electronics.* **a.** The process of receiving electromagnetic signals. **b.** The quality of the signals received. [Latin *receptiō*, from *receptus*, past part. of *recipere*, to receive.]

re·cep·tion·ist (rĭ-sĕp'shə-nĭst) *n.* A person employed chiefly to receive callers and answer the telephone.

re·cep·tive (rĭ-sĕp'tĭv) *adj.* **1.** Capable of receiving. **2.** Ready or willing to receive something favorably: *a receptive audience.* —**re·cep'tive·ly** *adv.* —**re·cep'tive·ness** *n.* or **re·cep'tive·ness** *n.*

re·cep·tor (rĭ-sĕp'tər) *n.* A nerve ending specialized to sense or to receive stimuli.

re·cess (rē'sĕs', rĭ-sĕs') *n.* **1. a.** A temporary cessation or suspension of a customary activity. **b.** The period of such cessation. **2.** A remote, secret, or hidden place: *the recesses of his mind.* **3.** An indentation or small hollow; an alcove. —*tr.v.* **1.** To place in a recess. **2.** To make a recess in. **3.** To suspend for a recess. —*intr.v.* To take a recess. [Latin *recessus*, from *recēdere*, to recede.]

re·ces·sion (rĭ-sĕsh'ən) *n.* **1.** The act of withdrawing or going back. **2.** The filing out of clergy and choir members after a church service. **3.** A moderate and temporary decline in economic activity.

re·ces·sion·al (rĭ-sĕsh'ə-nəl) *n.* A hymn that accompanies the exit of the clergy and choir after a service.

re·ces·sive (rĭ-sĕs'ĭv) *adj.* **1.** Tending to go backward or recede. **2.** *Genetics.* Of or indicating a gene whose action is not apparent in the physical characteristics of an organism when it is paired with an unlike gene for the same characteristic. —*n. Genetics.* **1.** A recessive trait. **2.** An organism with a recessive trait. —**re·ces'sive·ly** *adv.*

re·cher·ché (rə-shĕr-shā') *adj.* **1.** Intensely sought after; uncommon; rare. **2.** Exquisite or refined. **3.** Overrefined; forced. [French, past part. of *rechercher*, to search for.]

re·cid·i·vism (rĭ-sĭd'ə-vĭz'əm) *n.* A tendency to relapse into a former pattern of behavior, esp. a tendency to return to criminal habits. [From *recidivist*, from French *récidiviste*,

relapser, from *récidiver*, to relapse, from Medieval Latin *recidīvāre*, from Latin *recidīvus*, a falling back, from *recidere*, to fall back.] —**re·cid'i·vist** *n.* —**re·cid'i·vis'tic** *adj.*

rec·i·pe (rĕs'ə-pē) *n.* **1.** A set of directions with a list of ingredients for making or preparing something, esp. food. **2.** *Symbol* ℞ A medical prescription. **3.** A formula for accomplishing a certain thing: *a recipe for a happy marriage.* [Latin, "take," imper. of *recipere*, to take, receive.]

re·cip·i·ent (rĭ-sĭp'ē-ənt) *n.* Someone or something that receives. —*adj.* Functioning as a receiver. [Latin *recipiēns*, pres. part. of *recipere*, to receive.]

re·cip·ro·cal (rĭ-sĭp'rə-kəl) *adj.* **1.** Given or shown in return: *reciprocal trade concessions.* **2.** Experienced, felt, or done by both sides; mutual: *reciprocal respect; reciprocal hatred.* **3.** *Math.* Of or pertaining to a quantity divided into 1. —*n.* **1.** Something that is reciprocal to something else. **2.** *Math.* Either of a pair of numbers, as 7 and $^1/_7$, whose product is 1. [Latin *reciprocus*, alternating, returning.] —**re·cip'ro·cal·ly** *adv.* —**re·cip'ro·cal·ness** *n.*

re·cip·ro·cate (rĭ-sĭp'rə-kāt') *v.* **-cat·ed, -cat·ing.** —*tr.v.* **1.** To give or take mutually; to change. **2.** To show or feel in return: *reciprocated her love.* —*intr.v.* **1.** To move back and forth alternately, as a machine part. **2.** To make a return for something given or done. —**re·cip'ro·ca'tion** *n.* —**re·cip'ro·ca'tive** *adj.* —**re·cip'ro·ca'tor** *n.*

reciprocating engine. An engine having a crankshaft turned by the back and forth motion of pistons.

rec·i·proc·i·ty (rĕs'ə-prŏs'ĭ-tē) *n.* **1.** A reciprocal condition or relationship. **2.** A mutual exchange or interchange of favors, esp. the exchange of rights or privileges of trade between nations.

re·cit·al (rĭ-sīt'l) *n.* **1.** The act of reading or reciting in a public performance. **2.** A very detailed account or report of something; a narration. **3.** A performance of music or dance, esp. by a solo performer.

rec·i·ta·tion (rĕs'ĭ-tā'shən) *n.* **1.** The act of reading or reciting in a public performance. **2.** The oral delivery of prepared lessons by a pupil during a class period.

rec·i·ta·tive (rĕs'ĭ-tə-tēv') *n.* **1.** A musical style, used in opera and oratorio, in which the text is declaimed in the rhythm of natural speech with slight melodic variation. **2.** A passage in the style of recitative. [Italian *recitativo*, from *recitare*, to recite, from Latin *recitāre*.]

re·cite (rĭ-sīt') *v.* **-cit·ed, -cit·ing.** —*tr.v.* **1.** To repeat (something rehearsed or memorized), esp. before an audience. **2.** To tell in detail: *recite one's problems.* —*intr.v.* **1.** To deliver a recitation. **2.** To repeat lessons prepared or memorized. [Middle English *reciten*, from Old French *reciter*, from Latin *recitāre*, to read out, cite again.] —**re·cit'er** *n.*

reck·less (rĕk'lĭs) *adj.* **1.** Without care or caution; careless: *reckless driving.* **2.** Headstrong; rash: *a reckless lover.* [Middle English *reckeles*, from Old English *rēcelēas.*] —**reck'less·ly** *adv.* —**reck'less·ness** *n.*

reck·on (rĕk'ən) *tr.v.* **1.** To count or calculate; figure: *reckon the cost.* **2.** To consider as being; regard as: *reckoned him a stranger.* **3.** *Informal.* To think or assume: *Do you reckon we'll finish on time?* —*intr.v.* **1.** To make a calculation. **2.** To depend: *reckon on aid.* —**phrasal verb. reckon with.** To come to terms or settle accounts with. [Middle English *reknen*, from Old English *gerecenian*, to enumerate.]

reck·on·ing (rĕk'ə-nĭng) *n.* **1.** The act or process of counting or computing. **2.** A statement of an amount due. **3.** The calculation of the position of a ship, aircraft, etc.

re·claim (rĭ-klām') *tr.v.* **1.** To make (land, soil, etc.) usable for growing crops or living on, as by irrigating. **2.** To extract (useful substances) from waste products. **3.** To turn (a person) from error or evil; reform. [Middle English *reclamen*, to call back, from Old French *reclamer*, from Latin *reclāmāre*, to exclaim against: *re*, against + *clāmāre*, to call.] —**re·claim'a·ble** *adj.* —**re·claim'er** *n.*

rec·la·ma·tion (rĕk'lə-mā'shən) *n.* The act or process of reclaiming or the condition of being reclaimed.

re·cline (rĭ-klīn') *v.* **-clined, -clin·ing.** —*tr.v.* To cause to assume a leaning or prone position. —*intr.v.* To lie back or down. [Middle English *reclinen*, from Old French *recliner*, from Latin *reclīnāre*: *re-*, back, again + *-clīnāre*, to bend.]

rec·luse (rĕk'lōōs', rĭ-klōōs') *n.* A person who withdraws from the world to live in solitude and seclusion. —*adj.* Withdrawn from the world; solitary. [Middle English, from Old French, past part. of *reclure,* to shut up, from Latin *reclūdere,* to close off.] —**re·clu'sive** (-sĭv, -zĭv) *adj.*

rec·og·ni·tion (rĕk'əg-nĭsh'ən) *n.* **1.** The act of recognizing or the condition of being recognized. **2.** An acknowledgment, as of a claim: *a recognition of his civil rights.* **3.** Attention or favorable notice: *recognition for his achievements.* **4.** A formal acknowledgment or acceptance of the sovereignty of a government or nation by another.

re·cog·ni·zance (rĭ-kŏg'nĭ-zəns, -kŏn'ĭ-) *n. Law.* **1.** An obligation of record or bond committing a person to perform a particular act, as to appear in court. **2.** A sum of money that is forfeited if the legal obligation is not met.

rec·og·nize (rĕk'əg-nīz') *tr.v.* **-nized, -niz·ing.** **1.** To know or identify from past experience or knowledge: *recognize an owl by its call.* **2.** To acknowledge or accept: *recognize the truth.* **3.** To acknowledge or accept the status or position of: *recognize a new government.* **4.** To acknowledge the acquaintance of; greet: *hardly recognized her.* **5.** To acknowledge, approve of, or appreciate: *recognize services rendered.* **6.** To acknowledge as a speaker in a formally conducted meeting. [Old French *reconoistre,* from Latin *recognōscere,* to know again.] —**rec'og·niz'a·ble** *adj.* —**rec'og·niz'a·bly** *adv.*

re·coil (rĭ-koil') *intr.v.* **1.** To move or jerk back, as a gun upon firing. **2.** To shrink back in fear or dislike. —*n.* (rē'-koil', rĭ-koil'). **1.** The backward action of a firearm upon firing. **2.** The act or condition of recoiling. [Middle English *recoilen,* from Old French *reculer* : *re-,* back, again + *cul,* backside, from Latin *cūlus.*] —**re·coil'er** *n.*

rec·ol·lect (rĕk'ə-lĕkt') *tr.v.* To recall to mind; remember. —*intr.v.* To have a recollection; remember. —See Syns at **remember.** [Medieval Latin *recollectus,* past part. of *recolligere,* to recall, from Latin, to gather again : *re-,* again + *colligere,* to gather.] —**rec'ol·lec'tion** *n.*

re·com·bi·nant DNA (rē-kŏm'bĭ-nənt). DNA that has been artificially prepared by combining DNA fragments taken from different species.

re·com·bi·na·tion (rē-kŏm'bĭ-nā'shən) *n.* The formation in offspring of genetic combinations not present in parents.

rec·om·mend (rĕk'ə-mĕnd') *tr.v.* **1.** To praise or commend to another or others as being worthy or desirable; endorse: *recommended him for the job.* **2.** To advise or counsel (a course of action). **3.** To make attractive or acceptable: *lack of discipline that did not recommend him.* [Middle English *recommenden,* from Medieval Latin *recommendāre.*] —**rec'om·mend'a·ble** *adj.*

rec·om·men·da·tion (rĕk'ə-mĕn-dā'shən) *n.* **1.** The act of recommending. **2.** Something that recommends, as a letter or favorable statement.

re·com·mit (rē'kə-mĭt') *tr.v.* **-mit·ted, -mit·ting.** **1.** To commit again. **2.** To refer to a committee again, as proposed legislation. —**re'com·mit'ment** or **re'com·mit'tal** *n.*

rec·om·pense (rĕk'əm-pĕns') *tr.v.* **-pensed, -pens·ing.** **1.** To pay or reward: *recompensed him for his services.* **2.** To give as compensation for; make up for: *recompense losses.* —*n.* **1.** Amends made for something, such as damage, loss, or injury. **2.** Payment in return for something given or done. [Middle English *recompensen,* from Old French *recompenser,* from Late Latin *recompensāre.*]

rec·on·cil·a·ble (rĕk'ən-sī'lə-bəl, rĕk'ən-sī'-) *adj.* Capable of being reconciled. —**rec'on·cil'a·bil'i·ty** *n.*

rec·on·cile (rĕk'ən-sīl') *tr.v.* **-ciled, -cil·ing.** **1.** To restore friendship between: *reconcile feuding friends.* **2.** To settle or resolve, as a dispute. **3.** To bring (oneself) to accept: *reconciled herself to her loss.* **4.** To make compatible or consistent: *reconcile different points of view.* [Middle English *reconcilen,* from Old French *reconcilier,* from Latin *reconciliāre* : *re-,* again + *conciliāre,* to conciliate.] —**rec'on·cile'ment** or **rec'on·cil'i·a'tion** (-sĭl'ē-ā'shən) *n.* —**rec'on·cil'er** *n.* —**rec'on·cil'i·a·to'ry** (-sĭl'ē-ə-tôr'ē, -tōr'ē) *adj.*

rec·on·dite (rĕk'ən-dīt', rĭ-kŏn'dīt') *adj.* **1.** Not easily understood; abstruse. **2.** Dealing with abstruse concerns. **3.** Concealed; hidden. [Latin *reconditus,* past part. of *recondere,* to hide : *re-,* again + *condere,* to bring together.] —**rec'on·dite'ly** *adv.* —**rec'on·dite'ness** *n.*

re·con·di·tion (rē'kən-dĭsh'ən) *tr.v.* To restore by repairing, renovating, or rebuilding. —See Syns at **restore.**

re·con·nais·sance (rĭ-kŏn'ə-səns, -zəns) *n.* An inspection or exploration of an area, esp. one made to gather military information. [French, from Old French *reconoissance,* recognizance.]

re·con·noi·ter (rē'kə-noi'tər, rĕk'ə-) *tr.v.* To make a preliminary survey or inspection of. —*intr.v.* To make a reconnaissance. [Obs. French *reconnoître,* from Old French *reconoistre,* to recognize.] —**re'con·noi'ter·er** *n.*

re·con·sid·er (rē'kən-sĭd'ər) *tr.v.* To consider again, esp. with intent to change or modify a previous decision. —*intr.v.* To consider again. —**re'con·sid'er·a'tion** *n.*

re·con·sti·tute (rē-kŏn'stĭ-tōōt', -tyōōt') *tr.v.* **-tut·ed, tut·ing.** To restore to a former condition, esp. by adding water.

re·con·struct (rē'kən-strŭkt') *tr.v.* To construct again; restore. —See Syns at **restore.**

re·con·struc·tion (rē'kən-strŭk'shən) *n.* **1.** The act or result of reconstructing. **2. Reconstruction.** The period (1865–77) during which the states of the Southern Confederacy were controlled by the Federal government before being readmitted to the Union.

rec·ord (rĕk'ərd) *n.* **1.** Information, facts, etc., usu. set down in writing as a means of preserving knowledge: *a police record.* **2.** The known history of performance or achievement: *your high-school record.* **3. a.** The best performance known, as in a sport: *the world record in the mile run.* **b.** The highest or lowest statistical mark known, as in weather readings: *the record for least rainfall in a year.* **4.** A disk designed to be played on a phonograph. —*modifier:* *a record altitude.* —*tr.v.* **re·cord** (rĭ-kôrd'). —*tr.v.* **1.** To set down for preservation in writing or other permanent form. **2.** To register or indicate: *A thermometer records temperatures.* **3.** To store (sound) in some permanent form, such as a trace cut in a surface of a disk or a series of variations in the magnetization of a tape. —*idioms.* **off the record.** Not for publication, as in a news report. **on record.** Known to have taken or stated a certain position. [Middle English *recorde,* from Old French *record,* from *recorder,* to record, from Latin *recordārī,* to remember, think over : *re-,* again + *cor,* mind, heart.]

re·cord·er (rĭ-kôr'dər) *n.* **1.** Someone or something that records: *a tape recorder.* **2.** A judge who has criminal jurisdiction in certain cities. **3.** A flute with eight finger holes and a whistlelike mouthpiece.

recorder

re·cord·ing (rĭ-kôr'dĭng) *n.* Something on which sound is recorded, as a magnetic tape or a phonograph record.

re·count (rĭ-kount') *tr.v.* To narrate the facts or particulars of; tell in detail. [Middle English *recounten,* from Old French *reconter* : *re-,* again, back + *conter,* to relate, count.]

re·count (rē-kount') *tr.v.* To count again. —*n.* (rē'kount', rē-kount'). A second count, as of votes.

re·coup (rĭ-kōōp') *tr.v.* **1. a.** To receive the equivalent of (something lost); make up for: *recoup the loss.* **b.** To regain. **2.** To pay back; compensate: *recouped his tenants for damages.* —See Syns at **recover.** [Middle English *recoupen,* from Old French *recouper,* to cut back, retrench : *re-,* back + *couper,* to cut, strike, from *coup,* blow.]

re·course (rē'kôrs', -kōrs', rĭ-kôrs', -kōrs') *n.* **1.** A turning or applying to a person or thing for aid, support, or protection: *have recourse to the courts.* **2.** Someone or something that is turned to for help or as a solution. [Middle English *recours,* from Old French, from Latin *recursus,* a running back, from *recurrere*, to run back.]

re·cov·er (rĭ-kŭv′ər) *tr.v.* **1.** To get back; regain: *recovered his watch.* **2.** To restore (oneself) to a normal condition, as of physical or mental health. **3.** To gain or regain by legal process: *recover damages.* **4.** To reclaim: *recover iron from scrap.* —*intr.v.* **1.** To return to a normal or usual condition, as of health: *recover after a long illness.* **2.** To receive a favorable judgment in a lawsuit. [Middle English *recoveren*, from Old French *recoverer*, from Latin *reciperāre*, to obtain again.] —**re·cov′er·a·ble** *adj.*

Syns: 1. recover, recoup, regain, retrieve *v. Core meaning:* To get back (*hoped to recover her stolen car*). **2. recover, mend, rally, recuperate** *v. Core meaning:* To regain one's health (*recovering after illness*).

re·cov·er·y (rĭ-kŭv′ə-rē) *n., pl.* **-ies. 1.** A return to a normal condition, as of health. **2.** The act of getting back.

rec·re·ant (rĕk′rē-ənt) *adj.* **1.** Unfaithful or disloyal to belief, promise, or cause. **2.** Craven or cowardly. —*n.* **1.** A faithless or disloyal person. **2.** A coward. [Middle English, from Old French, pres. part. of *recroire*, to yield, surrender, from Medieval Latin *recrēdere*: Latin *re-*, back, opposite + *crēdere*, to believe.]

rec·re·ate (rĕk′rē-āt′) *tr.v.* **-at·ed, -at·ing.** To refresh mentally or physically. [From Latin *recreāre*, to create anew.]

re·cre·ate (rē′krē-āt′) *tr.v.* **-at·ed, -at·ing.** To create again or anew. —**re′cre·a′tion** *n.*

rec·re·a·tion (rĕk′rē-ā′shən) *n.* Refreshment of a person's mind or body after work through some activity that amuses or stimulates; play. —**rec′re·a′tion·al** *adj.*

Syns: recreation, diversion, entertainment *n. Core meaning:* Activity that refreshes the mind or body after work (*jogging and other forms of recreation*). RECREATION implies something that restores one's strength, spirits, or vitality (*played tennis for recreation*). DIVERSION suggests something to take one's attention off customary affairs (*went shopping for diversion*). ENTERTAINMENT shares these meanings but esp. suggests a performance or show that is designed to amuse or divert (*sought entertainment in night clubs*).

re·crim·i·nate (rĭ-krĭm′ə-nāt′) *v.* **-nat·ed, -nat·ing.** —*tr.v.* To accuse (a person) in return. —*intr.v.* To counter one accusation with another. [From Medieval Latin *recrīmināre*: Latin *re-*, again, back + *crīmināre*, to accuse, from *crīmen*, accusation.] —**re·crim′i·na′tion** *n.*

re·cru·desce (rē′krōō-dĕs′) *intr.v.* **-desced, -desc·ing.** To break out anew after a dormant or inactive period, as a disease. [Latin *recrūdēscere*: *re-*, again + *crūdēscere*, to get worse, from *crūdus*, harsh, raw.] —**re′cru·des′cence** *n.* —**re′cru·des′cent** *adj.*

re·cruit (rĭ-krōōt′) *tr.v.* **1.** To seek out and engage (persons) for work or service. **2.** To strengthen or raise (an armed force) by enlistment. **3.** To renew or restore (health or vitality). —*intr.v.* To raise a military force. —*n.* **1.** A newly engaged member of a military force. **2.** A new member of any organization or body. [Old French *recruter*, from *recrute*, new growth, from *recroître*, to grow again, from Latin *recrēscere*.] —**re·cruit′er** *n.* —**re·cruit′ment** *n.*

rec·tan·gle (rĕk′tăng′gəl) *n. Geom.* A parallelogram containing an angle of 90 degrees. [Medieval Latin *rēctangulum*: Latin *rēctus*, upright, straight + *angulus*, angle.]

rec·tan·gu·lar (rĕk-tăng′gyə-lər) *adj.* **1.** Having the shape of a rectangle. **2.** Having right angles. **3.** Designating a geometric coordinate system with axes that meet at right angles. —**rec·tan′gu·lar′i·ty** (-lăr′ĭ-tē) *n.* —**rec·tan′gu·lar·ly** *adv.*

rec·ti·fi·er (rĕk′tə-fī′ər) *n.* **1.** A person or thing that rectifies. **2.** *Elect.* A device, such as a diode, that converts alternating current to direct current.

rec·ti·fy (rĕk′tə-fī′) *tr.v.* **-fied, -fy·ing. 1.** To set right; correct. **2.** To correct by calculation or adjustment. **3.** *Chem.* To refine or purify, esp. by distillation. **4.** *Elect.* To convert (alternating current) into direct current. —See Syns at **correct.** [Middle English *rectifien*, from Old French *rectifier*, from Medieval Latin *rēctificāre*: Latin *rēctus*, straight + *facere*, to make.] —**rec′ti·fi·ca′tion** *n.*

rec·ti·lin·e·ar (rĕk′tə-lĭn′ē-ər) *adj.* Moving in, bounded by, or characterized by a straight line or lines. [From Late Latin *rēctilīneus*: *rēctus*, straight + *līnea*, line.]

rec·ti·tude (rĕk′tĭ-tōōd′, -tyōōd′) *n.* **1.** Moral uprightness.

2. Straightness. —See Syns at **honesty.** [Middle English, from Old French, from Late Latin *rēctitūdō*, from Latin *rēctus*, straight.]

rec·to (rĕk′tō) *n., pl.* **-tos.** A right-hand page. [Latin *rēctō (foliō)*, on the right side of (a page).]

rec·tor (rĕk′tər) *n.* **1.** A clergyman in charge of a parish. **2.** *Rom. Cath. Ch.* A priest appointed to be head of an institution such as a seminary. **3.** The principal of certain schools, colleges, and universities. [Latin *rēctor*, governor, from *rēctus*, past part. of *regere*, to rule.]

rec·to·ry (rĕk′tə-rē) *n., pl.* **-ries.** A rector's dwelling.

rec·tum (rĕk′təm) *n., pl.* **-tums** or **-ta** (-tə). The lower end of the alimentary canal, extending from the colon to the anus. [New Latin *rectum (intestinum)*, straight (intestine), from Latin *rēctus*, straight.] —**rec′tal** *adj.*

re·cum·bent (rĭ-kŭm′bənt) *adj.* **1.** Lying down; reclining. **2.** Resting; idle. [Latin *recumbēns*, pres. part. of *recumbere*, to lie down.] —**re·cum′bent·ly** *adv.*

re·cu·per·ate (rĭ-kōō′pə-rāt′, -kyōō′-) *intr.v.* **-at·ed, -at·ing. 1.** To return to health or strength; recover. **2.** To recover from a loss. —See Syns at **recover.** [From Latin *recuperāre*, to recover.] —**re·cu′per·a′tion** *n.* —**re·cu′per·a′tive** *adj.*

re·cur (rĭ-kûr′) *intr.v.* **-curred, -cur·ring. 1.** To happen, come up, or show up again or repeatedly. **2.** To return in thought or discourse. —See Syns at **return.** [Latin *recurrere*, to run back.] —**re·cur′rence** *n.*

re·cur·rent (rĭ-kûr′ənt, -kŭr′-) *adj.* **1.** Occurring or appearing repeatedly or regularly. **2.** *Anat.* Reversing direction: *a recurrent artery.* —**re·cur′rent·ly** *adv.*

re·curve (rē-kûrv′) *v.* **-curved, -curv·ing.** —*tr.v.* To bend or curve backward or downward. —*intr.v.* To become bent or curved backward or downward.

re·cy·cle (rē-sī′kəl) *tr.v.* **-cled, -cling.** To put or pass through a cycle again, as to extract useful materials.

red (rĕd) *n.* **1.** Any of a group of colors whose hue resembles that of blood. **2.** A red pigment or dye. **3.** Often **Red.** A revolutionary, esp. a Communist. —*adj.* **red·der, red·dest. 1.** Of the color red. **2.** Being or having distinctive parts that are reddish in color: *a red fox.* **3.** Ruddy or flushed in complexion: *red with embarrassment.* **4.** Often **Red.** Of, directed by, or favoring Communists. —*idiom.* **in the red.** Operating at a loss; in debt. [Middle English, from Old English *rēad*.] —**red′ly** *adv.* —**red′ness** *n.*

re·dact (rĭ-dăkt′) *tr.v.* **1.** To draw up or frame: *redact a proclamation.* **2.** To make ready for publication; edit or revise. [Latin *redactus*, past part. of *redigere*, to collect, drive back: *re-*, back + *agere*, to drive, do.] —**re·dac′tor** *n.*

red·bird (rĕd′bûrd′) *n.* Any of various birds with red plumage, as the cardinal.

red blood cell. Any of the cells in the blood, disk-shaped and lacking nuclei, that contain hemoglobin and give the blood its red color.

red-blood·ed (rĕd′blŭd′ĭd) *adj.* Strong or virile.

red·breast (rĕd′brĕst′) *n.* A bird with a red breast, esp. the robin.

red·bud (rĕd′bŭd′) *n.* Any of several shrubs or small trees of the genus *Cercis*, with pinkish flowers that bloom before the leaves appear. Also called **Judas tree.**

red·cap (rĕd′kăp′) *n.* A porter, usu. in a railroad station.

red cedar. 1. An evergreen tree, *Juniperus virginiana*, of eastern North America. **2.** A tall evergreen tree, *Thuja plicata*, of western North America. **3.** The reddish, aromatic, durable wood of either of these trees.

red cent. *Informal.* Something of insignificant value.

red clover. A Eurasian plant, *Trifolium pratense*, with globular heads of fragrant rose-purple flowers, frequently planted as a forage or cover crop.

red-coat (rĕd′kōt′) *n.* A British soldier during the American Revolution and the War of 1812.

red deer. A common European deer, *Cervus elaphus*, with a reddish-brown coat and many-branched antlers.

red·den (rĕd′n) *tr.v.* To make red. —*intr.v.* To grow red.

red·dish (rĕd′ĭsh) *adj.* Mixed or tinged with red; somewhat red. —**red′dish·ness** *n.*

re·dec·o·rate (rē-dĕk′ə-rāt′) *v.* **-rat·ed, -rat·ing.** —*tr.v.* To change the décor of, as by painting. —*intr.v.* To change the décor of a room, building, etc. —**re·dec′o·ra′tion** *n.*

---

re·deem (rĭ-dēm′) *tr.v.* **1.** To recover ownership of by paying a specified sum. **2.** To pay off, as a promissory note. **3.** To turn in (coupons, trading stamps, etc.) and receive something in exchange. **4. a.** To set free; rescue. **b.** To save from sin and its consequences. **5.** To make up for: *a deed that redeemed his earlier mistake.* [Middle English *redemen,* from Latin *redimere,* to buy back.] —**re·deem′a·ble** *adj.*

re·deem·er (rĭ-dē′mər) *n.* **1.** A person who redeems; a savior. **2. the Redeemer.** Christ.

re·demp·tion (rĭ-dĕmp′shən) *n.* **1.** The act of redeeming or the condition of being redeemed. **2.** A recovery of something pawned or mortgaged. [Middle English *redempcioun,* from Old French *redemption,* from Latin *redemptiō,* from *redemptus,* past part. of *redimere,* to redeem.] —**re·demp′tion·al** or **re·demp′tive** *adj.*

re·de·vel·op (rē′dĭ-vĕl′əp) *tr.v.* **1.** To develop (something) again. **2.** To restore to a better condition; renew or reclaim: *redevelop a slum area.* —**re′de·vel′op·er** *n.* —**re′de·vel′op·ment** *n.*

red fox. Any of several foxes of the genus *Vulpes,* characteristically with reddish fur.

red giant. A very large, relatively cool star.

red-hand·ed (rĕd′hăn′dĭd) *adv. & adj.* In the act of doing, or having just done something wrong: *caught red-handed.*

red·head (rĕd′hĕd′) *n.* **1.** A person with red hair. **2.** A North American duck, *Aythya americana,* of which the male has black and gray plumage and a reddish head.

red heat. 1. The temperature of a red-hot substance. **2.** The physical condition of a red-hot substance.

red herring. 1. A smoked herring with a reddish color. **2.** Something that draws attention away from the subject under notice or discussion. [From the use of red herring to distract hunting dogs from the scent.]

red-hot (rĕd′hŏt′) *adj.* **1.** Glowing hot; very hot. **2.** Heated, as with excitement: *a red-hot speech.* **3.** *Informal.* New; recent: *red-hot information.* —See Syns at **hot.**

red·in·gote (rĕd′ĭng-gōt′) *n.* A woman's full-length unlined coat or dress open down the front to show a dress or underdress. [French, from English *riding coat.*]

re·dis·count (rē-dĭs′kount′) *tr.v.* To discount again. —*n.* **1.** The act of rediscounting. **2.** Often **rediscounts.** Commercial paper that is discounted a second time.

re·dis·trib·ute (rē′dĭ-strĭb′yōōt) *tr.v.* **-ut·ed, -ut·ing.** To distribute again; reallocate. —**re′dis·tri·bu′tion** *n.*

re·dis·trict (rē-dĭs′trĭkt) *tr.v.* To give new boundaries to; divide again, as into administrative or election districts.

red lead. A bright-red powder, Pb_3O_4, used in paints, glass, pottery, and pipe-joint packing. Also called **minium.**

red-let·ter (rĕd′lĕt′ər) *adj.* Memorably happy or important: *a red-letter day.* [From the use of red letters to mark feast days in church calendars.]

red maple. A medium-sized American maple, *Acer rubrum,* with reddish twigs and buds.

red·neck (rĕd′nĕk′) *n. Slang.* A member of the white rural laboring class in the southern United States.

re·do (rē-dōō′) *tr.v.* **-did** (-dĭd′), **-done** (-dŭn′), **-do·ing. 1.** To do over again. **2.** To redecorate.

red ocher. 1. A natural red mixture of clay and iron oxide. **2.** A refined form of red ocher used as pigment.

red·o·lent (rĕd′l-ənt) *adj.* **1.** Having or emitting a pleasant odor; scented: *redolent bouquets.* **2.** Suggestive; reminiscent: *a campaign redolent of machine politics.* [Middle English, from Old French, from Latin *redolēns,* pres. part. of *redolēre,* to emit an odor.] —**red′o·lence** *n.*

re·dou·ble (rē-dŭb′əl) *v.* **-bled, -bling.** —*tr.v.* **1.** To double. **2.** To increase greatly; intensify: *redoubled their efforts.* —*intr.v.* To become doubled.

re·doubt (rĭ-dout′) *n.* A small, often temporary defensive fortification. [Old French *redoute,* from Old Italian *ridotto,* from Medieval Latin *reductus,* concealed place, from Latin, withdrawn, past part. of *redūcere,* to withdraw : *re-,* back + *dūcere,* to lead.]

re·doubt·a·ble (rĭ-dou′tə-bəl) *adj.* **1.** Awesome; formidable; fearsome. **2.** Worthy of respect or honor. [Middle English, from Old French *redoutable,* from *redouter,* to dread : *re-* (intensive) + *douter,* to fear.] —**re·doubt′a·bly** *adv.*

re·dound (rĭ-dound′) *intr.v.* To have an effect, esp. by bringing or reflecting credit or discredit. [Middle English *redounden,* to abound, from Old French *redonder,* from Latin *redundāre,* to overflow.]

red pepper. 1. The pungent, red fruit of any of several varieties of the pepper plant. **2. Cayenne pepper.**

red·poll (rĕd′pōl′) *n.* Any of several finches of the genus *Acanthis,* with brownish plumage and a red crown.

re·dress (rĭ-drĕs′) *tr.v.* **1.** To set right; remedy or rectify: *redress wrongs.* **2.** To make amends for. **3.** To adjust: *redress a balance.* —*n.* (rĕ′drĕs′, rĭ-drĕs′). **1.** Satisfaction or amends for wrong done; reparation. **2.** Correction or reformation. [Middle English *redressen,* from Old French *redresser* : *re-,* back + *dresser,* to make straight.]

red shift. An increase in the wavelength of radiation emitted by a receding celestial body.

red snapper. Any of several saltwater food fishes of the genus *Lutjanus,* of tropical and semitropical waters, with a red or reddish body.

red squirrel. A North American squirrel, *Tamiasciurus hudsonicus,* with reddish or tawny fur.

red·start (rĕd′stärt′) *n.* **1.** A small North American bird, *Setophaga ruticilla,* the male of which has black plumage with orange patches on the wings and tail. **2.** A European bird, *Phoenicurus phoenicurus,* with grayish plumage and a rust-red breast and tail. [RED + obs. *start,* tail, from Middle English *stert,* from Old English *steort.*]

red tape. Official forms and procedures, esp. when needlessly complex and time-consuming. [From the tape used to tie English governmental documents.]

red tide. Ocean waters colored by masses of red, one-celled, plantlike animals in sufficient numbers to kill fish.

red·top (rĕd′tŏp′) *n.* A widely cultivated grass, *Agrostis alba,* native to Europe, with reddish flower clusters.

re·duce (rĭ-dōōs′, -dyōōs′) *v.* **-duced, -duc·ing.** —*tr.v.* **1.** To lessen in extent, amount, number, degree, price, or other quality; diminish. **2.** To gain control of; conquer. **3.** To put in order or arrange systematically. **4.** To separate into orderly components by analysis. **5.** To bring to a certain condition: *reduce marble to dust.* **6.** *Chem.* **a.** To decrease the valence of (an atom) by adding electrons. **b.** To deoxidize. **c.** To add hydrogen to. **d.** To change to a metallic state; smelt. **7.** *Math.* To change the form of (an expression) without changing the value. **8.** *Surgery.* To restore (a fractured or displaced body part) to a normal condition. —*intr.v.* **1.** To become diminished. **2.** To lose weight, as by dieting. —See Syns at **decrease** and **lower.** [Middle English *reducen,* to bring back, from Latin *redūcere* : *re-,* back, again + *dūcere,* to lead.] —**re·duc′er** *n.* —**re·duc′i·bil′i·ty** *n.* —**re·duc′i·ble** *adj.* —**re·duc′i·bly** *adv.*

reducing agent. A substance that chemically reduces other substances. Also called **reductant.**

re·duc·ti·o ad ab·sur·dum (rĭ-dŭk′tē-ō′ ăd əb-sûr′dəm). Disproof of a proposition by showing the absurdity of its inevitable conclusion. [Latin, "reduction to absurdity."]

re·duc·tion (rĭ-dŭk′shən) *n.* **1.** The act or process of reducing. **2.** The result of reducing. **3.** The amount by which something is reduced. **4.** *Biol.* The first cell division in meiosis, in which the chromosome number is reduced. Also called **reduction division. 5.** *Chem.* A decrease in positive valence or an increase in negative valence by the gaining of electrons. **6.** *Math.* **a.** The canceling of common factors in the numerator and denominator of a fraction, changing it into a simpler form. **b.** The converting of a fraction to its decimal equivalent. —**re·duc′tion·al** or **re·duc′tive** *adj.*

re·dun·dan·cy (rĭ-dŭn′dən-sē) *n., pl.* **-cies. 1.** The condition of being redundant. **2.** Superfluity or excess. **3.** Unnecessary repetition, esp. of words or expressions.

re·dun·dant (rĭ-dŭn′dənt) *adj.* **1.** Exceeding what is necessary or natural; superfluous. **2.** Needlessly repetitive; verbose. [Latin *redundāns,* pres. part. of *redundāre,* to overflow, run back.] —**re·dun′dant·ly** *adv.*

re·du·pli·cate (rĭ-dōō′plĭ-kāt′, -dyōō′-) *v.* **-cat·ed, -cat·ing.** —*tr.v.* **1.** To make again; copy. **2.** *Ling.* **a.** To double (the initial syllable or all of a root word) to produce an inflectional or derivative form. **b.** To form (a new word) by doubling all or part of a word. —*intr.v.* (rĭ-dōō′plĭ-kĭt, -dyōō′-). Doubled. [From Late Latin *reduplicāre* : Latin *re-,* again + *duplicāre,* to duplicate.] —**re·du·pli·ca′tion** *n.* —**re·du′pli·ca′tive** *adj.*

red-winged blackbird (rĕd′wĭngd′). A North American blackbird, *Agelaius phoeniceus*, the male of which has scarlet patches on the wings.

red·wood (rĕd′wŏŏd′) *n.* **1.** A very tall evergreen tree, *Sequoia sempervirens*, of coastal and northern California, that sometimes grows to a height of over 300 feet. **2.** The soft, reddish wood of this tree.

re·ech·o (rē-ĕk′ō) *intr.v.* To echo back; sound back or reverberate. —*tr.v.* To resound with.

reed (rĕd) *n.* **1.** Any of several tall, hollow-stemmed grasses or similar plants that grow in wet places. **2. a.** A springy strip of cane or metal, used in the mouthpiece of certain wind instruments, that vibrates when air passes over it and causes the air in the instrument to vibrate. **b.** A similar strip of metal that causes the air in an organ pipe to vibrate. **c.** A woodwind instrument, such as an oboe, played with a reed. [Middle English *rede*, from Old English *hrēod*.]

reed·bird (rĕd′bûrd′) *n.* The bobolink.

reed organ. A keyboard instrument in which free-beating reeds produce tones when acted upon by currents of air.

re·ed·u·cate (rē-ĕj′ŏŏ-kāt′) *tr.v.* **-cat·ed, -cat·ing. 1.** To instruct again. **2.** To retrain (a person) to function effectively; rehabilitate. —**re·ed′u·ca′tion** *n.*

reed·y (rē′dē) *adj.* **-i·er, -i·est. 1.** Full of reeds: *a reedy swamp.* **2.** Resembling a reed: *a slim, reedy girl.* **3.** Having the high, shrill, or breathy sound of a reed instrument: *the oboe's reedy tone.* —**reed′i·ness** *n.*

reef[1] (rēf) *n.* **1.** A strip or ridge of rocks, sand, or coral at or near the surface of water. **2.** *Mining.* A vein. [Middle Dutch *rif*, ridge, ult. from Old Norse, rib, ridge.]

reef[2] (rēf) *n.* A portion of a sail rolled and tied down to lessen the area exposed to the wind. —*tr.v.* To reduce the size of (a sail) by tucking in a part and tying it to or rolling it around a yard. [Middle English *riff*, from Old Norse *rif*, ridge, rib.]

reef·er[1] (rē′fər) *n.* **1.** A person who reefs. **2.** A short, heavy, close-fitting, double-breasted jacket.

reef·er[2] (rē′fər) *n. Slang.* A marijuana cigarette. [Perhaps from REEF (to shorten a sail).]

reef knot. A square knot.

reek (rēk) *intr.v.* **1.** To smoke, steam, or fume. **2.** To be pervaded by something unpleasant: *The letter reeked of pride.* **3.** To give off a strong and unpleasant odor: *The salad reeked of garlic.* —*n.* **1.** A strong and offensive odor; stench. **2.** Vapor; steam. [Middle English *reken*, from Old English *rēocan*.]

reel[1] (rēl) *n.* **1.** A cylinder, spool, or frame that turns on an axis and is used for winding rope, tape, film, fishing line, etc. **2.** The quantity of material wound on one reel. —*tr.v.* **1.** To wind upon a reel. **2.** To recover by winding on a reel: *reel in a marlin.* [Middle English, from Old English *hrēol*.] —**reel′a·ble** *adj.*

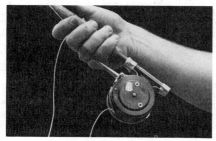

reel[1]

reel[2] (rēl) *intr.v.* **1.** To be thrown off balance or fall back. **2.** To stagger or lurch, as from drunkenness. **3.** To be in a confused condition. —*n.* A reeling movement. [Middle English *relen.*]

reel[3] (rēl) *n.* **1.** A fast dance of Scottish origin. **2.** The music for a reel. [From REEL (whirl).]

re·e·lect or **re·e·lect** (rē′ĭ-lĕkt′) *tr.v.* To elect again. —**re′e·lec′tion** or **re′e·lec′tion** *n.*

re·en·force or **re·en·force** (rē′ĕn-fôrs′, -fōrs′) *v.* Vars. of reinforce.

re·en·ter or **re·en·ter** (rē-ĕn′tər) *intr.v.* To come in or enter again. —*tr.v.* **1.** To enter (a room, place, etc.) again. **2.** To record again on a list or ledger.

re·en·try or **re·en·try** (rē-ĕn′trē) *n., pl.* **-tries. 1.** The act of re-entering; a second or subsequent entry. **2.** *Law.* The recovery of possession under a right reserved in a previous property transaction. **3.** *Aerospace.* The return of a missile or spacecraft into the earth's atmosphere.

re·es·tab·lish or **re·es·tab·lish** (rē′ĭ-stăb′lĭsh) *tr.v.* To establish again; restore. —See Syns at **restore.** —**re′·es·tab′-lish·ment** or **re′es·tab′lish·ment** *n.*

reeve[1] (rēv) *n.* **1.** A high officer of local administration appointed by the Anglo-Saxon kings. **2.** In the later medieval period, a bailiff or steward of a manor. [Middle English, Old English (*ge*)*rēfa.*]

reeve[2] (rēv) *tr.v.* **reeved** or **rove** (rōv), **reev·ing.** *Naut.* **1.** To pass (a rope or rod) through a hole, ring, pulley, or block. **2.** To fasten by passing through. [Orig. unknown.]

reeve[3] (rēv) *n.* A bird, the female ruff. [Poss. var. of RUFF.]

re·fec·tion (rĭ-fĕk′shən) *n.* **1.** Refreshment with food and drink. **2.** A light meal. [Middle English *refeccioun*, from Old French *refection*, from Latin *refectiō*, a restoring, from *reficere*, to refresh.]

re·fec·to·ry (rĭ-fĕk′tə-rē) *n., pl.* **-ries.** A room where meals are served. [Late Latin *refectōrium*, from Latin *reficere*, to refresh.]

re·fer (rĭ-fûr′) *v.* **-ferred, -fer·ring.** —*tr.v.* **1.** To direct to a source for help or information: *refer her to a heart specialist.* **2.** To assign or attribute: *referring things to their right causes.* **3.** To direct the attention of: *refer him to his duties.* —*intr.v.* **1.** To pertain; apply: *exercises that refer to today's lecture.* **2.** To allude to or make reference: *referring to Connecticut as the Nutmeg State.* **3.** To turn to, as for information or authority: *refer to his text.* [Middle English *referren*, from Old French *referer*, from Latin *referre* : *re-*, back, again + *ferre*, to carry.] —**re·fer′ral** *n.*

ref·er·ee (rĕf′ə-rē′) *n.* **1.** A person to whom something is referred for settlement; an arbitrator. **2.** *Sports.* An official who supervises play and enforces the rules. —*v.* **-eed, -ee·ing.** —*tr.v.* To supervise as referee. —*intr.v.* To act as referee. —See Syns at **judge.**

ref·er·ence (rĕf′ər-əns, rĕf′rəns) *n.* **1.** The act of referring. **2.** Relation; regard; respect: *a reply in reference to your query.* **3.** An allusion or mention: *frequent references to his trip to Europe.* **4.** A note in a book or other publication that directs the reader to another part of the book or to another source of information. **5. a.** A person who is in a position to recommend another or to vouch for his fitness, as for a job. **b.** A statement about a person's character or qualifications.

reference book. A book, such as a dictionary, that provides useful information systematically arranged.

ref·er·en·dum (rĕf′ə-rĕn′dəm) *n., pl.* **-dums** or **-da** (-də). **1.** The submission of a proposed public measure or actual statute to a direct popular vote. **2.** Such a vote. [Latin, from *referre*, to refer.]

re·fill (rē-fĭl′) *tr.v.* To fill again. —*n.* (rē′fĭl′). **1.** A product packaged to replace the used contents of a container. **2.** A second or subsequent filling. —**re·fill′a·ble** *adj.*

re·fine (rĭ-fīn′) *v.* **-fined, -fin·ing.** —*tr.v.* **1.** To reduce to a pure state; purify. **2.** To free from coarse characteristics: *refined his manners.* —*intr.v.* **1.** To become free of impurities. **2.** To acquire polish or elegance. **3.** To use subtlety and precise distinctions in thought or speech. [RE- + *fine*, to make pure.] —**re·fin′er** *n.*

re·fined (rĭ-fīnd′) *adj.* **1.** Free from coarseness or vulgarity; polite; genteel: *refined manners.* **2.** Free of impurities; purified: *refined oil.* **3.** Precise to a fine degree; exact.
    Syns: **refined, cultivated, cultured, urbane, well-bred** *adj.* Core meaning: Marked by good taste and broad knowledge as a result of development and education (*a refined man of the world*).

re·fine·ment (rĭ-fīn′mənt) *n.* **1. a.** An act of refining. **b.** The condition of being refined. **2.** The result of refining; an improvement. **3.** Fineness of thought or expression; polish. **4.** A keen or precise phrasing; subtle distinction.

re·fin·er·y (rĭ-fī′nə-rē) *n., pl.* **-ies.** An industrial plant for purifying a crude substance, such as petroleum.

re·fin·ish (rē-fĭn'ĭsh) *tr.v.* To put a new finish on (furniture). **—re·fin'ish·er** *n.*

re·fit (rē-fĭt') *v.* **-fit·ted, -fit·ting.** **—tr.v.** To prepare and equip for additional use: *refit a ship for service in the Arctic.* **—intr.v.** To be made ready for additional use.

re·flect (rĭ-flĕkt') *tr.v.* **1.** To cast or turn back (heat, light, sound, etc.) after impact with a surface. **2.** To form an image of (an object); to mirror. **3.** To reveal as if through a mirror; manifest: *His work reflects intelligence.* **—intr.v.** **1.** To be cast or turned back after impact with a surface. **2.** To give back a likeness. **3.** To think or consider seriously. **4.** To bring blame or discredit: *The misconduct of diplomats reflects on their country.* [Middle English *reflecten,* from Old French *reflecter,* from Latin *reflectere,* to bend back.]

re·flec·tance (rĭ-flĕk'təns) *n.* The ratio of the total radiation, as of light, reflected by a surface to the total incident on the surface.

reflecting telescope. An optical telescope in which the principal image-forming element is a parabolic or spherical mirror. Also called **reflector.**

re·flec·tion (rĭ-flĕk'shən) *n.* Also *Brit.* **re·flex·ion.** **1.** The act or process of reflecting. **2.** Something reflected, as light or sound. **3. a.** Serious thought; meditation. **b.** An idea, remark, or piece of writing resulting from this. **4.** An imputation of censure or discredit. **—re·flec'tion·al** *adj.*

re·flec·tive (rĭ-flĕk'tĭv) *adj.* **1. a.** Of, produced by, or resulting from reflection. **b.** Tending to reflect. **2.** Thoughtful; pensive. **—re·flec'tive·ly** *adv.* **—re'flec·tiv'i·ty** *n.*

re·flec·tor (rĭ-flĕk'tər) *n.* **1.** Something or someone that reflects, esp. a surface that reflects radiation. **2.** A **reflecting telescope.**

re·flex (rē'flĕks') *adj.* **1.** Turned, thrown, or bent backward. **2.** *Physiol.* Involuntary: *a reflex neural response.* **—n.** **1.** Reflection or an image produced by reflection. **2.** *Physiol.* An involuntary response to a stimulus. **3.** *Psychol.* An unlearned or instinctive response to a stimulus. [Latin *reflexus,* past part. of *reflectere,* to reflect.]

reflex arc. *Physiology.* The neural path of a simple reflex.

re·flex·ion (rĭ-flĕk'shən) *n. Brit.* Var. of **reflection.**

re·flex·ive (rĭ-flĕk'sĭv) *adj.* **1.** *Gram.* **a.** Designating a verb having an identical subject and direct object, as *dressed* in the sentence *She dressed herself.* **b.** Designating the pronoun used as the direct object of a reflexive verb, as *herself* in the preceding example. **2.** Of or constituting a reflex; involuntary. **—n.** A reflexive verb or pronoun. **—re·flex'ive·ly** *adv.* **—re·flex'ive·ness** or **re'flex·iv'i·ty** *n.*

re·flux (rē'flŭks') *n.* A flowing back; ebb. [Middle English, from Medieval Latin *refluxus* : Latin *re-,* back + *fluxus,* a flow, from *fluere,* to flow.]

re·for·est (rē-fôr'ĭst, -fŏr'-) *tr.v.* To replant (an area) with trees. **—re·for'es·ta'tion** *n.*

re·form (rĭ-fôrm') *tr.v.* **1.** To improve by correction of error or removal of defects: *reform society.* **2.** To abolish abuse or malpractice in: *reform the government.* **—intr.v.** To give up irresponsible or immoral practices. **—n.** **1.** An act, process, or example of reforming; an improvement: *prison reform.* **2.** A movement that attempts to institute reform. **3.** Moral improvement. [Middle English *reformen,* from Old French *reformer,* from Latin *reformāre,* to change : *re-,* again + *fôrma,* form.] **—re·form'a·ble** *adj.* **—re·for'ma·tive** *adj.* **—re·form'er** *n.*

ref·or·ma·tion (rĕf'ər-mā'shən) *n.* **1.** The act of reforming or the condition of being reformed. **2. Reformation.** The political and religious rebellion in 16th-cent. Europe that resulted in the separation of the Protestant churches from the Roman Catholic Church. **—ref'or·ma'tion·al** *adj.*

re·for·ma·to·ry (rĭ-fôr'mə-tôr'ē, -tōr'ē) *n., pl.* **-ries.** An institution, partly a prison and partly a school, for young lawbreakers. **—adj.** Serving or intending to reform.

re·formed (rĭ-fôrmd') *adj.* **1.** Improved in conduct or character. **2. Reformed.** Of, relating to, or denoting the Protestant churches that follow the teachings of the 16th-cent. religious reformers John Calvin and Ulrich Zwingli.

Reform Judaism. A branch of Judaism introduced in the 19th cent. that seeks to reconcile historical Judaism with present-day life without requiring strict observance of traditional law.

re·fract (rĭ-frăkt') *tr.v.* To cause the path of (light or other

radiation) to bend or deflect by refraction. [Latin *refractus,* past part. of *refringere,* to break off.]

refracting telescope. A telescope in which the final image is produced entirely by lenses. Also called **refractor.**

re·frac·tion (rĭ-frăk'shən) *n. Physics.* The bending or deflection of the path of a wave, as of light or sound, as it passes between mediums in which its velocity is different, with its original path meeting the boundary between the mediums at an oblique angle. **—re·frac'tion·al** or **re·frac'tive** *adj.* **—re·frac'tive·ly** *adv.* **—re·frac'tive·ness** or **re'frac·tiv'i·ty** (rē'frăk-tĭv'ĭ-tē) *n.*

refractive index. Index of refraction.

re·frac·tor (rĭ-frăk'tər) *n.* A **refracting telescope.**

re·frac·to·ry (rĭ-frăk'tə-rē) *adj.* **1.** Obstinate; unmanageable: *a refractory child.* **2.** Difficult to melt, refine, shape, or work: *a refractory ore.* **3.** Not responsive to treatment: *a refractory disease.* **—See Syns at obstinate.** **—n.,** *pl.* **-ries.** Any of various heat-resistant materials, such as alumina, silica, or magnesite. [From Latin *refractārius,* from *refractus,* past part. of *refringere,* to break off.] **—re·frac'to·ri·ly** *adv.* **—re·frac'to·ri·ness** *n.*

re·frain¹ (rĭ-frān') *intr.v.* To hold oneself back; forbear: *refrain from singing.* [Middle English *refreynen,* from Old French *refrener,* from Latin *refrēnāre,* to restrain : *re-,* back + *frēnum,* bridle.] **—re·frain'ment** *n.*

re·frain² (rĭ-frān') *n.* **1.** A phrase or verse repeated at intervals throughout a song or poem, esp. at the end of each stanza. **2.** Music for a refrain. [Middle English *refreyn,* from Old French *refrain,* from *refraindre,* to echo, break off, ult. from Latin *refringere,* to break off.]

re·fran·gi·ble (rĭ-frăn'jə-bəl) *adj.* Capable of being refracted. [RE- + FRANGIBLE.] **—re·fran'gi·bil'i·ty** *n.*

re·fresh (rĭ-frĕsh') *v.* Also **re·fresh·en.** **—tr.v.** **1.** To revive (a person) with or as if with rest, food, or drink. **2.** To make cool, clean, or damp; freshen: *towels for refreshing the face.* **3.** To rouse; stimulate: *refresh one's memory.* **—intr.v.** To take refreshment. [Middle English *refresshen,* from Old French *refreschier* : *re-,* again + *fresche,* fresh.]

re·fresh·er (rĭ-frĕsh'ər) *n.* **1.** Someone or something that refreshes. **2.** Study or review designed to reacquaint one with material previously studied.

re·fresh·ing (rĭ-frĕsh'ĭng) *adj.* **1.** Serving to refresh. **2.** Pleasantly new and different: *a refreshing interpretation of an old song.* **—re·fresh'ing·ly** *adv.*

re·fresh·ment (rĭ-frĕsh'mənt) *n.* **1.** The act of refreshing or the condition of being refreshed. **2.** Something that refreshes. **3. refreshments.** A light meal or snack.

re·frig·er·ant (rĭ-frĭj'ər-ənt) *n.* A substance, such as air, ammonia, water, or carbon dioxide, used to produce refrigeration.

re·frig·er·ate (rĭ-frĭj'ə-rāt') *tr.v.* **-at·ed, -at·ing.** **1.** To cool or chill (a substance). **2.** To preserve (food) by chilling. [From Latin *refrigerāre* : *re-,* again + *frigerāre,* to make cool, from *frigus,* cool.] **—re·frig'er·a'tion** *n.*

re·frig·er·a·tor (rĭ-frĭj'ə-rā'tər) *n.* A box or cabinet used to store substances, such as food, at a low temperature.

re·fu·el (rē-fyōō'əl) *tr.v.* To supply again with fuel. **—intr.v.** To take on a fresh supply of fuel.

ref·uge (rĕf'yōōj) *n.* **1.** Protection or shelter, as from danger or hardship. **2.** A place providing protection or shelter; haven or sanctuary. [Middle English, from Old French, from Latin *refugium,* from *refugere,* to escape : *re-,* away, back + *fugere,* to flee.]

ref·u·gee (rĕf'yōō-jē') *n.* A person who flees, esp. from his own country, to find refuge from oppression or persecution. [French *refugié,* from *refugier,* to put in a refuge, from *refuge,* refuge.]

re·ful·gent (rĭ-fōol'jənt, -fŭl'-) *adj.* Shining radiantly; brilliant; resplendent. [Latin *refulgēns,* pres. part. of *refulgēre,* to shine : *re-,* back + *fulgēre,* to flash.] **—re·ful'gence** *n.*

re·fund¹ (rĭ-fŭnd', rē'fŭnd') *v.* **1.** To return or repay; give back: *refund their money.* **—n.** (rē'fŭnd'). **1.** A repayment of funds. **2.** The amount repaid. [Middle English *refunden,* to pour back, from Old French *refunder,* from Latin *refundere* : *re-,* back + *fundere,* to pour.] **—re·fund'a·ble** *adj.*

re·fund² (rē-fŭnd') *tr.v.* **1.** To fund anew. **2.** *Finance.* To pay back (a debt) with new borrowing.

re·fur·bish (rē-fûr'bĭsh) *tr.v.* To make clean, bright, or

ă pat   ā pay   â care   ä father   ĕ pet   ē be   hw which   ĭ pit   ī tie   î pier   ŏ pot   ō toe   ô paw, for   oi noise
ōō took   ōō boot   ou out   th thin   th this   ŭ cut   û urge   zh vision   ə about, item, edible, gallop, circus

fresh again; renovate. —**re·fur'bish·ment** n.

re·fus·al (rĭ-fyōō'zəl) n. **1.** The act of refusing. **2.** The opportunity to accept or reject; option.

re·fuse¹ (rĭ-fyōōz') v. **-fused, -fus·ing.** —tr.v. To decline to do, accept, allow, or give: refuse permission. —intr.v. To decline to do, accept, allow, or give something. —See Syns at **reject.** [Middle English refusen, from Old French refuser, ult. from Latin refundere, to pour back.]

ref·use² (rĕf'yōōs) n. Anything discarded or rejected as useless or worthless; trash; rubbish. [Middle English, something rejected, from Old French refus, refusal, from refuser, to refuse.]

re·fute (rĭ-fyōōt') tr.v. **-fut·ed, -fut·ing.** To prove to be false or erroneous; disprove. —See Syns at **disprove.** [Latin refutāre, to rebut, drive back.] —**re·fut'a·ble** adj. —**re·fut'a·bly** adv. —**re·fut'er** n.

re·gain (rē-gān') tr.v. **1.** To recover possession of; get back again. **2.** To reach again. —See Syns at **recover.**

re·gal (rē'gəl) adj. **1.** Of a king; royal. **2.** Belonging to or befitting a king: regal attire. —See Syns at **grand.** [Middle English, from Old French, from Latin rēgālis, from rēx, king.] —**re'gal·ly** adv.

re·gale (rĭ-gāl') v. **-galed, -gal·ing.** —tr.v. **1.** To delight or entertain: He regaled his friends with amusing stories. **2.** To entertain sumptuously with food and drink; provide a feast for. —intr.v. To feast. [French régaler, from Old French regaler, from regal, regal.]

re·ga·lia (rĭ-gāl'yə) n. (used with a sing. or pl. verb). **1.** The emblems and symbols of royalty, as the crown and scepter. **2.** The distinguishing symbols of any rank, office, order, or society. **3.** Magnificent or fancy attire; finery.

re·gard (rĭ-gärd') tr.v. **1.** To look at attentively; watch: regarded us suspiciously. **2.** To look upon or consider: I regard him as a fool. **3.** To have great affection or admiration for: She regards her father highly. **4.** To have reference to; concern: This item regards your question. —n. **1.** A look or gaze. **2.** Careful thought or attention; concern; heed: He gives little regard to his appearance. **3.** Respect, favor, or esteem: He has won the regard of all. **4. regards.** Sentiments of respect or affection; good wishes: send one's regards. **5.** Reference or relation: in regard to this case. **6.** A particular point or respect: I agree in this regard. —See Syns at **favor.** [Middle English regarden, from Old French regarder.]

re·gard·ful (rĭ-gärd'fəl) adj. **1.** Showing regard; observant; heedful. **2.** Showing deference; respectful; considerate. —**re·gard'ful·ly** adv.

re·gard·ing (rĭ-gär'dĭng) prep. In reference to; concerning.

re·gard·less (rĭ-gärd'lĭs) adj. Heedless; unmindful: regardless of the consequences. —adv. In spite of everything; anyway: She loved him regardless. —**re·gard'less·ly** adv.
    Usage: regardless, irregardless. Only regardless is correct; the double negative irregardless is not acceptable.

re·gat·ta (rĭ-gä'tə, -gǎt'ə) n. A boat race or an organized series of boat races. [Italian, gondola race.]

re·gen·cy (rē'jən-sē) n., pl. **-cies. 1.** The office, area of jurisdiction, or government of a regent or regents. **2.** The period during which a regent governs.

re·gen·er·a·cy (rĭ-jĕn'ər-ə-sē) n. The condition of being regenerated.

re·gen·er·ate (rĭ-jĕn'ə-rāt') v. **-at·ed, -at·ing.** —tr.v. **1.** To reform spiritually or morally. **2.** To form, construct, or create anew. **3.** To replace (a lost or damaged organ or part) by formation of new tissue. —intr.v. **1.** To become formed or constructed again. **2.** To undergo spiritual conversion or rebirth. **3.** To grow back after loss or damage. —adj. (rĭ-jĕn'ər-ĭt). **1.** Spiritually or morally revitalized. **2.** Restored; refreshed; renewed. —**re·gen'er·a'tion** n. —**re·gen'er·a'tive** —**re·gen'er·a'tor** n.

re·gent (rē'jənt) n. **1.** A person who rules during the minority, absence, or disability of a sovereign. **2.** A person serving on a governing board, as of a state university. —adj. Ruling as a regent. [Middle English, from Old French, ruling, from Medieval Latin regēns, from Latin, pres. part. of regere, to rule.]

reg·i·cide (rĕj'ĭ-sīd') n. **1.** The killing of a king. **2.** A person who kills or helps to kill a king. [Latin rēx, king + -CIDE.] —**reg'i·cid'al** (-sīd'l) adj.

re·gime (rā-zhēm', rĭ-). Also **ré·gime. 1.** A government in power; an administration. **2.** A system or form of government: a Communist regime. **3.** A regimen. [French régime, from Latin regimen, rule, from regere, to rule.]

reg·i·men (rĕj'ə-mən, -mĕn') n. **1.** Governmental rule or control. **2.** A system of therapy; course of treatment. [Middle English, from Latin, rule.]

reg·i·ment (rĕj'ə-mənt) n. A military unit of ground troops consisting of at least two battalions. —tr.v. (rĕj'ə-mĕnt'). **1.** To put into order; systematize. **2.** To force uniformity and discipline upon. [Middle English, from Old French, from Late Latin regimentum, rule, from Latin regere, to rule.] —**reg'i·men·ta'tion** n.

reg·i·men·tal (rĕj'ə-mĕn'tl) adj. Of or belonging to a regiment. —n. **regimentals.** The uniform of a regiment.

re·gion (rē'jən) n. **1.** Any large, usu. continuous segment of a surface or space; an area: uncharted regions of outer space. **2.** A large and indefinite portion of the earth's surface: polar regions. **3.** A specified district or territory. **4.** A field of interest or activity; sphere. **5.** A section or area of the body: the abdominal region. [Middle English regioun, kingdom, from Old French region, from Latin regiō, direction, boundary, from regere, to direct.]

re·gion·al (rē'jə-nəl) adj. **1.** Of, relating to, or characteristic of an entire region rather than a locality: regional playoffs. **2.** Of, relating to, or characteristic of a particular region: a regional accent. —**re'gion·al·ly** adv.

reg·is·ter (rĕj'ĭ-stər) n. **1. a.** A formal or official recording of items, names, or actions. **b.** A book for such entries. **2.** A device that automatically records or displays a quantity or number: a cash register. **3.** A grill-like device through which heated or cooled air is released into a room. **4.** Mus. **a.** The range of an instrument or voice. **b.** A part of such a range: the low register of a contralto. **c.** A group of matched organ pipes; a stop. —tr.v. **1.** To enter in a register; record officially: register a birth. **2.** To indicate, as on an instrument or scale. **3.** To show; reveal: His face registered no emotion. **4.** To cause (mail) to be officially recorded by payment of a fee. —intr.v. **1.** To place or cause placement of one's name in a register: registered for classes. **2.** To have one's name officially placed on a list of eligible voters. **3.** To create an impression: Her name registered in my memory. [Middle English registre, from Old French, from Medieval Latin registrum, from Late Latin regesta, list, from Latin regerere, to bring back.] —**reg'is·tra·ble** (-strə-bəl) adj.

reg·is·tered (rĕj'ĭ-stərd) adj. **1.** Having the owner's name listed in a register: registered bonds. **2.** Having the pedigree recorded in a breed association studbook.

registered nurse. A graduate trained nurse who has passed a state registration examination.

reg·is·trar (rĕj'ĭ-strär', rĕj'ĭ-strär') n. An official of a college or corporation who is responsible for keeping records.

reg·is·tra·tion (rĕj'ĭ-strā'shən) n. **1.** The act or process of registering. **2.** The number of persons or things registered; enrollment. **3.** An entry in a register. **4.** A card, paper, etc., carried as proof of having registered.

reg·is·try (rĕj'ĭ-strē) n., pl. **-tries. 1.** Registration. **2.** A ship's registered nationality; flag. **3.** An official record of births, deaths, etc. **4.** A place where registers are kept.

reg·nant (rĕg'nənt) adj. **1.** Reigning; ruling. **2.** Predominant. **3.** Widespread; prevalent. [Latin regnāns, pres. part. of regnāre, to reign, from regnum, reign.]

reg·o·lith (rĕg'ə-lĭth') n. The layer of loose rock material resting on bedrock that constitutes the surface of most land. [Greek rhēgos, blanket + -LITH.]

re·gress (rĭ-grĕs') intr.v. To go back; return, esp. to a previous condition: Under hypnosis the patient regressed to early childhood. —n. (rē'grĕs'). **1.** Return or withdrawal. **2.** Backward movement; systematize. [Latin regressus, past part. of regredī, to go back : re-, back + gradī, to step, go.]

re·gres·sion (rĭ-grĕsh'ən) n. **1.** Backward movement. **2.** Relapse to a less perfect or developed state. **3.** Psychoanal. Reversion to a less mature behavior pattern.

re·gres·sive (rĭ-grĕs'ĭv) adj. **1.** Tending to return or revert. **2.** Lessening in rate as an amount taxed increases: a regressive tax. —**re·gres'sive·ly** adv. —**re·gres'sive·ness** n.

re·gret (rĭ-grĕt') tr.v. **-gret·ted, -gret·ting. 1.** To feel sorry, disappointed, or distressed about. **2.** To feel sorrow or grief over; mourn. —n. **1.** Distress over a desire unfulfilled or an action performed or not performed. **2.** An expression of grief or disappointment. **3. regrets.** A polite reply turning down an invitation. [Middle English *regretten,* from Old French *regreter,* to lament.] —**re·gret′ta·ble** *adj.* —**re·gret′ta·bly** *adv.*

re·gret·ful (rĭ-grĕt′fəl) *adj.* Full of regret or sorrow. —**re·gret′ful·ly** *adv.* —**re·gret′ful·ness** *n.*

re·group (rē-grōōp′) *tr.v.* To form into a new group or groups. —*intr.v.* To assemble in a new group or groups.

reg·u·lar (rĕg′yə-lər) *adj.* **1.** Customary, usual, or normal: *Our regular newspaper is on strike.* **2.** Orderly or symmetrical: *Her face has regular features.* **3.** Conforming to set procedure, principle, or discipline: *regular meals.* **4.** Methodical; well-ordered. **5.** Evenly spaced; periodic: *at regular intervals.* **6.** Constant; not varying. **7.** Formally correct; proper. **8.** Perfect; complete; thorough: *a regular villain.* **9.** *Informal.* Good; nice: *a regular guy.* **10.** *Gram.* Belonging to a standard mode of inflection or conjugation: *a regular verb.* **11.** Belonging to a religious order and bound by its rules: *the regular clergy.* **12.** *Geom.* **a.** Having equal sides and equal angles: *regular polygons.* **b.** Having faces that are congruent regular polygons and congruent polyhedral angles: *regular polyhedrons.* **13.** Belonging to or constituting the army of a nation. —See Syns at **common.** —*n.* **1.** A clergyman or other member of a religious order. **2.** A soldier belonging to a regular army. [Middle English *reguler,* under religious rule, from Old French, from Latin *rēgulāris,* containing rules, from *rēgula,* rule.] —**reg′u·lar′i·ty** (rĕg′yə-lăr′ĭ-tē) *n.* —**reg′u·lar·ly** *adv.*

reg·u·lar·ize (rĕg′yə-lə-rīz′) *tr.v.* -**ized,** -**iz·ing.** To make regular or cause to conform. —**reg′u·lar·i·za′tion** *n.*

reg·u·late (rĕg′yə-lāt′) *tr.v.* -**lat·ed,** -**lat·ing.** **1.** To control or direct according to a rule: *power to regulate commerce.* **2.** To adjust or control (a flow, rate, output, etc.) so that it remains within certain limits: *regulate traffic.* **3.** To adjust (a mechanism) for accurate and proper functioning. [From Late Latin *rēgulāre,* from Latin *rēgula,* a rule.] —**reg′u·la·tor** *n.* —**reg′u·la·to′ry** (-lə-tôr′ē, -tōr′ē) *adj.*

reg·u·la·tion (rĕg′yə-lā′shən) *n.* **1.** The act of regulating. **2.** A principle, rule, or law designed to control or govern behavior. **3.** A governmental order having the force of law. —*adj.* Conforming with a rule: *a regulation uniform.*

re·gur·gi·tate (rē-gûr′jĭ-tāt′) *v.* -**tat·ed,** -**tat·ing.** —*intr.v.* To rush or surge back. —*tr.v.* **1.** To cast up (partially digested food) from the stomach through the mouth. **2.** To give forth as if by vomiting. [From Medieval Latin *regurgitāre* : *re-,* back + Late Latin *gurgitāre,* to engulf, flood, from Latin *gurges,* a whirlpool.] —**re·gur′gi·ta′tion** *n.*

re·ha·bil·i·tate (rē′hə-bĭl′ĭ-tāt′) *tr.v.* -**tat·ed,** -**tat·ing.** **1. a.** To restore to useful life through education and therapy: *rehabilitate disabled veterans.* **b.** To restore to a previous normal condition; rebuild: *rehabilitated dwellings.* **2.** To reinstate the good name or former rank of. —See Syns at **restore.** [From Medieval Latin *rehabilitāre* : Late Latin *re-,* again + Latin *habilitas,* ability.] —**re′ha·bil′i·ta′tion** *n.* —**re′ha·bil′i·ta′tive** *adj.*

re·hash (rē-hăsh′) *tr.v.* To repeat, rework, or rewrite, often without anything new resulting: *rehashed their old disagreement.* —*n.* (rē′hăsh′). **1.** The act of rehashing. **2.** Something rehashed. [RE- + HASH (to chop over).]

re·hears·al (rĭ-hûr′səl) *n.* **1.** The act or process of rehearsing, esp. in preparation for a public performance. **2.** A session devoted to rehearsing.

re·hearse (rĭ-hûrs′) *v.* -**hearsed,** -**hears·ing.** —*tr.v.* **1.** To practice (all or part of a program) in preparation for a public performance. **2.** To train and prepare by means of rehearsals. **3.** To retell or recite. —*intr.v.* To rehearse all or part of a program. [Middle English *rehercen,* from Old French *rehercer,* to repeat : *re-,* again + *hercer,* to harrow, from *herce,* a harrow, from Latin *hirpex.*]

reign (rān) *n.* **1. a.** The exercise of political power by a monarch. **b.** The term during which a monarch rules. **2.** Dominance or prevalence: *the reign of reason.* —*intr.v.* **1.** To exercise the power of a monarch. **2.** To be predominant or prevalent: *A stillness reigned throughout the room.* [Middle English *reingne,* from Old French, from Latin *rēgnum,* from *rēx,* a king.]

re·im·burse (rē′ĭm-bûrs′) *tr.v.* -**bursed,** -**burs·ing.** To pay back. [RE- + obs. *imburse,* to pay, from Old French

embourser : *en-,* in + *borse,* a purse, from Late Latin *bursa,* oxhide, from Greek, hide, skin.] —**re′im·burse′ment** *n.*

rein (rān) *n.* **1.** Often **reins.** A long, narrow leather strap attached to the bit of a bridle and used by a rider or driver to control a horse or other animal. **2.** Often **reins.** Means of guidance or control: *the reins of government.* **3.** A means of restraint; a check or brake: *kept a tight rein on the budget.* —*tr.v.* **1.** To check or hold back: *reined in his anger.* **2.** To guide or control. —**idiom. give (free) rein to.** To release from restraints. [Middle English *reine,* from Old French *resne,* from Latin *retinēre,* to retain.]

re·in·car·nate (rē′ĭn-kär′nāt′) *tr.v.* -**nat·ed,** -**nat·ing.** To cause to be reborn in another body; to incarnate again. —**re·in′car·na′tion** *n.*

rein·deer (rān′dîr′) *n., pl.* **reindeer** or -**deers.** A large deer, *Rangifer tarandus,* of arctic regions of the Old World and Greenland, with branched antlers in both sexes. [Middle English *reyndere,* from Old Norse *hreindȳri* : *hreinn,* reindeer + *dȳr,* animal.]

reindeer moss. An erect, grayish, branching lichen, *Cladonia rangiferina,* of arctic regions, that is the chief source of food for reindeer.

re·in·force (rē′ĭn-fôrs′, -fōrs′) *tr.v.* -**forced,** -**forc·ing.** Also **re·en·force** or **re·en·force.** **1.** To give more force or effectiveness to; strengthen; support. **2.** *Mil.* To strengthen with additional manpower or equipment. [RE- + *inforce,* var. of ENFORCE.]

reinforced concrete. Poured concrete containing steel bars or metal netting to increase its tensile strength. Also called **ferroconcrete.**

re·in·force·ment (rē′ĭn-fôrs′mənt, -fōrs′-) *n.* **1. a.** The act or process of reinforcing. **b.** The condition of being reinforced. **2.** Something that reinforces. **3. reinforcements.** Additional manpower or equipment sent to support a military action.

re·in·state (rē′ĭn-stāt′) *tr.v.* -**stat·ed,** -**stat·ing.** **1.** To bring back into use or existence. **2.** To restore to a previous condition or position. —See Syns at **restore.** —**re′in·state′ment** *n.*

re·in·vest (rē′ĭn-vĕst′) *tr.v.* To invest (capital or earnings) again. —**re′in·vest′ment** *n.*

re·is·sue (rē-ĭsh′ōō) *tr.v.* -**sued,** -**su·ing.** To issue again. —**re·is′sue** *n.*

re·it·er·ate (rē-ĭt′ə-rāt′) *tr.v.* -**at·ed,** -**at·ing.** To say over again; repeat. —**re·it′er·a′tion** *n.* —**re·it′er·a′tive** *adj.*

re·ject (rĭ-jĕkt′) *tr.v.* **1.** To be unwilling to accept, recognize, or make use of; repudiate. **2.** To be unwilling to consider or grant; deny. **3.** To refuse affection or recognition to (a person). **4.** To throw out; discard. **5.** *Med.* To subject to attack by the immunological system. —*n.* (rē′jĕkt′). Something or someone that has been rejected. [Middle English *rejecten,* from Latin *rejectus,* past part. of *rejicere,* to throw back : *re-,* back, away + *jacere,* to throw.] —**re·jec′tion** *n.*

    Syns: reject, decline, dismiss, refuse, spurn, turn down *v.* Core meaning: To be unwilling to accept, consider, or receive (*rejected all offers of help*).

re·joice (rĭ-jois′) *v.* -**joiced,** -**joic·ing.** —*intr.v.* To feel or be joyful. —*tr.v.* To fill with joy; gladden. [Middle English *rejoicen,* from Old French *rejoir* : *re-* (intensifier), again + *joir,* to be joyful, from Latin *gaudēre.*] —**re·joic′er** *n.*

re·join¹ (rē-join′) *tr.v.* **1.** To come together again in company with. **2.** To join or put together again; reunite.

re·join² (rĭ-join′) *intr.v.* To respond; answer. —See Syns at **answer.** [Middle English *rejoinen,* from Old French *rejoindre* : *re-,* back, again + *joindre,* to join.]

re·join·der (rĭ-join′dər) *n.* An answer, esp. in response to a reply. [Middle English *rejoyner,* from Old French *rejoindre,* to rejoin, answer.]

re·ju·ve·nate (rĭ-jōō′və-nāt′) *tr.v.* -**nat·ed,** -**nat·ing.** To restore the youthful vigor or appearance of. [RE- + Latin *juvenis,* a youth.] —**re·ju′ve·na′tion** *n.*

re·lapse (rĭ-lăps′) *intr.v.* -**lapsed,** -**laps·ing.** **1.** To fall back or revert to a former, often worse state. **2.** To become sick again after a partial recovery. —*n.* (rē′lăps′, rĭ-lăps′). The act or result of relapsing. [Latin *relapsus,* past part. of *relābī,* to slide back.] —**re·laps′er** *n.*

re·late (rĭ-lāt′) *v.* -**lat·ed,** -**lat·ing.** —*tr.v.* **1.** To narrate or tell. **2.** To bring into logical or natural association: *trying* *to relate the various clues.* —*intr.v.* **1.** To have connection, relation, or reference. **2.** *Informal.* To interact with others in a meaningful way. [From Latin *relātus*, past part. of *referre*, to carry back, refer.]

re·lat·ed (rĭ-lā'tĭd) *adj.* **1.** Connected; associated. **2.** Connected by kinship, marriage, or common origin.

re·la·tion (rĭ-lā'shən) *n.* **1.** A logical or natural association between two or more things; the bearing of one thing on another. **2.** The connection of people by blood or marriage; kinship. **3.** A person akin to another by blood or marriage; a relative. **4. relations.** Dealings or associations with others: *social relations; diplomatic relations.* **5.** Reference; regard. **6.** The act of telling or narrating.

re·la·tion·ship (rĭ-lā'shən-shĭp') *n.* **1.** A connection between things, processes, facts, etc.: *the relationship between the moon and the tides.* **2.** Connection by blood or marriage; kinship. **3.** A connection or tie between persons or groups: *a business relationship.*

rel·a·tive (rĕl'ə-tĭv) *adj.* **1.** Having pertinence or relevance; connected; related. **2.** Considered in comparison to or dependent on something else; not absolute: *relative luxury.* **3.** *Gram.* Referring to or qualifying an antecedent. —*n.* **1. a.** A person related by kinship. **b.** A thing related to or connected with another. **2.** *Gram.* A relative term. —**rel'a·tive·ly** *adv.* —**rel'a·tive·ness** *n.*

relative clause. A dependent clause introduced by a relative pronoun.

relative humidity. The ratio of the amount of water vapor in the air at a specific temperature to the maximum capacity of the air at that temperature.

relative pronoun. A pronoun that introduces a relative clause and refers to an antecedent.

rel·a·tiv·i·ty (rĕl'ə-tĭv'ĭ-tē) *n.* **1.** The condition or quality of being relative. **2.** *Physics.* **General relativity.**

re·lax (rĭ-lăks') *tr.v.* **1.** To make less tight or tense: *relax one's grip.* **2.** To make less severe or strict: *relax school rules.* **3.** To relieve from effort or strain: *Music relaxes me.* —*intr.v.* **1.** To take one's ease; rest. **2.** To become lax or loose. **3.** To become less severe or strict. **4.** To become less formal, aloof, or tense: *relaxed at the party.* [Middle English *relaxen*, from Latin *relaxāre* : *re*-, back + *laxus*, lax, loose.] —**re·lax'er** *n.*

re·lax·ant (rĭ-lăk'sənt) *n.* A drug or therapeutic treatment that relaxes or relieves muscular or nervous tension.

re·lax·a·tion (rē'lăk-sā'shən) *n.* **1. a.** The act of relaxing. **b.** The condition of being relaxed. **2.** Refreshment of body or mind; recreation: *play golf for relaxation.*

re·laxed (rĭ-lăkst') *adj.* **1.** Not tightly bound to something else. **2.** Not constrained by rigid standards. —See Syns at **informal** and **loose.**

re·lay (rē'lā', rĭ-lā') *n.* **1.** A fresh animal or team of animals, as for a stagecoach. **2.** A crew of laborers who relieve another crew; a shift. **3.** The act of passing something along from one person, group, or station to another. **4. a.** A **relay race.** **b.** A length or lap of a relay race. **5.** *Elect.* An automatic electromagnetic or electromechanical device that responds to a small current or voltage change by activating switches or other devices in an electric circuit. —*tr.v.* **1.** To pass or send along by or as if by relay: *relay a message.* **2.** *Elect.* To control or retransmit by means of a relay. [Middle English *relai*, from Old French, from *relaier*, to relay, leave behind : *re*-, back + *laier*, to leave.]

relay race. A race between two or more teams in which each team member runs only part of the race and then is relieved by another teammate.

re·lease (rĭ-lēs') *tr.v.* **-leased, -leas·ing.** **1.** To set free from confinement, restraint, or bondage; liberate. **2.** To free, unfasten, or let go of. **3.** To relieve from debt or obligation. **4.** To allow performance, sale, publication, or circulation of: *release a film.* **5.** To relinquish (a right, claim, etc.). —See Syns at **free.** —*n.* **1.** The act of releasing; liberation. **2.** An authoritative discharge from an obligation or from prison. **3.** An unfastening or letting go of something caught or held fast. **4.** A device or catch for locking or releasing a mechanism. **5. a.** A freeing of something for general publication, use, or circulation. **b.** Something thus released: *a press release.* **6.** *Law.* The relinquishment of a right, title, or claim to another. [Middle English *relesen*, from Old French *relaissier*, from Latin *relaxāre*, to relax.]

—**re·leas'a·ble** *adj.* —**re·leas'er** *n.*

rel·e·gate (rĕl'ĭ-gāt') *tr.v.* **-gat·ed, -gat·ing.** **1.** To send or consign, esp. to a place or position of less importance or lower status. **2.** To refer or assign to another for decision or performance. [From Latin *relēgāre*, to send away : *re*-, back, away + *lēgāre*, to send.] —**rel'e·ga'tion** *n.*

re·lent (rĭ-lĕnt') *intr.v.* To become softened or gentler in attitude, temper, or determination. [Middle English *relenten* : Latin *re*- (intensifier) + *lentus*, pliable.]

re·lent·less (rĭ-lĕnt'lĭs) *adj.* **1.** Unyielding; pitiless: *relentless persecution.* **2.** Continuing steadily and persistently; unremitting: *relentless heat.* —See Syns at **continuous.** —**re·lent'less·ly** *adv.* —**re·lent'less·ness** *n.*

rel·e·vant (rĕl'ə-vənt) *adj.* Having to do with the matter at hand; to the point: *relevant testimony.* [Medieval Latin *relevāns*, from Latin, pres. part. of *relevāre*, to lift up, relieve.] —**rel'e·vance** or **rel'e·van·cy** *n.* —**rel'e·vant·ly** *adv.*

> **Syns: relevant, germane, material, pertinent** *adj.* Core meaning: Related to the matter at hand (*relevant issues; relevant questions*).

re·li·a·ble (rĭ-lī'ə-bəl) *adj.* Capable of being relied upon; dependable: *a reliable employee.* —**re·li'a·bil'i·ty** or **re·li'a·ble·ness** *n.* —**re·li'a·bly** *adv.*

re·li·ance (rĭ-lī'əns) *n.* **1.** The act of relying; dependence. **2.** Confidence; trust. **3.** Something or someone depended on; a mainstay. —See Syns at **confidence.**

re·li·ant (rĭ-lī'ənt) *adj.* Having or demonstrating reliance. —**re·li'ant·ly** *adv.*

rel·ic (rĕl'ĭk) *n.* **1.** An object or custom surviving from a culture or period that has disappeared: *relics of an ancient civilization.* **2.** Something treasured for its age or for its association with a person, place, or event: *Civil War relics.* **3.** An object of religious significance, esp. something thought to be associated with a saint or martyr. [Middle English *relike*, from Old French *relique*, from Late Latin *reliquiae*, remains, from Latin, from *relinquere*, to leave behind.]

relic   relief
From ancient Greece

re·lief (rĭ-lēf') *n.* **1.** Ease from or lessening of pain or discomfort. **2.** Anything that lessens pain, discomfort, fear, boredom, etc. **3.** Assistance, in the form of money or food, given to the needy, the aged, or to disaster victims. **4. a.** A release from a job, post, or duty. **b.** The person or persons taking over the duties of another. **5.** *Art & Architecture.* **a.** The apparent projection of figures or forms from a flat background in a painting or drawing. **b.** The projection of a sculpted figure from a flat background. **6.** *Geog.* The variations in elevation of the earth's surface: *a map that shows relief.* **7.** Distinction or prominence resulting from contrast: *"The light brought the white church . . . into relief from the flat ledges"* (Willa Cather). [Middle English, from Old French, from *relever*, to relieve.]

relief map. A map that shows the physical features of land, as with contour lines, shading, or colors.

re·lieve (rĭ-lēv') *tr.v.* **-lieved, -liev·ing.** **1.** To lessen or alleviate (anything that is painful, oppressive, or distressing); ease. **2.** To free from pain, anxiety, fear, etc.: *relieve them of worries.* **3.** To furnish assistance or aid to: *relieve the victims of a flood.* **4.** To take something from the possession of: *relieved him of his gun.* **5.** To free from a specified duty by providing or acting as a replacement: *relieved the guard at midnight.* **6.** To make less unpleasant, monotonous, or tiresome: "*An explosive little laugh relieved the tension*" (F. Scott Fitzgerald). [Middle English *releven*, from Old French *relever*, from Latin *relevāre* : *re-*, again + *levāre*, to raise.] —**re·liev′er** *n.*

re·lig·ion (rĭ-lĭj′ən) *n.* **1. a.** The expression of belief in and reverence for a superhuman power or powers. **b.** Any particular system of this expression: *the Hindu religion.* **2.** Any objective attended to or pursued with zeal or conscientious devotion: *Politics is her religion.* [Middle English *religioun*, from Old French *religion*, from Latin *religiō*, reverence for the gods, perh. from *religāre*, to bind back · *re-*, back + *ligāre*, to bind, fasten.]

re·lig·ious (rĭ-lĭj′əs) *adj.* **1.** Of or relating to religion. **2.** Adhering to or manifesting religion; pious; godly. **3.** Extremely faithful; scrupulous. **4.** Of or belonging to a monastic order. —*n., pl.* **religious.** A person belonging to a monastic order, as a monk or nun. —**re·lig′ious·ly** *adv.* —**re·lig′ious·ness** *n.*

re·lin·quish (rĭ-lĭng′kwĭsh) *tr.v.* **1.** To leave; abandon. **2.** To put aside or desist from (something practiced, professed, or intended). **3.** To surrender; renounce. **4.** To let go; release. [Middle English *relinquysshen*, from Old French *relinquir*, from Latin *relinquere*, to leave behind : *re-*, behind + *linquere*, to leave.] —**re·lin′quish·ment** *n.*

rel·i·quar·y (rĕl′ĭ-kwĕr′ē) *n., pl.* **-ies.** A receptacle, such as a coffer or shrine, for keeping or displaying sacred relics. [French *reliquaire*, from Medieval Latin *reliquiārium*, from Late Latin *reliquiae*, remains.]

rel·ish (rĕl′ĭsh) *n.* **1.** An appetite for something; an appreciation or liking: *a relish for luxury.* **2. a.** Pleasure; zest. **b.** Anything that lends pleasure or zest. **3.** A spicy or savory condiment served with other food. —See Syns at **zest.** —*tr.v.* **1.** To take pleasure in; enjoy: *She relishes a close tennis match.* **2.** To give flavor to; to spice. —See Syns at **like.** [Middle English *reles*, a taste, from Old French *relais*, something remaining, from *relaissier*, to release, from Latin *relaxāre*, to relax.] —**rel′ish·a·ble** *adj.*

re·live (rē-lĭv′) *v.* **-lived, -liv·ing.** —*tr.v.* To undergo again; live through another time. —*intr.v.* To live again.

re·lo·cate (rē-lō′kāt′) *v.* **-cat·ed, -cat·ing.** —*tr.v.* To establish in a new place. —*intr.v.* To become established in a new place. —**re′lo·ca′tion** *n.*

re·luc·tance (rĭ-lŭk′təns) *n.* Also **re·luc·tan·cy** (-tən-sē). The condition of being reluctant; unwillingness; disinclination.

re·luc·tant (rĭ-lŭk′tənt) *adj.* **1.** Unwilling; averse: *reluctant to help.* **2.** Marked by unwillingness: *a reluctant admission.* [Latin *reluctāns*, pres. part. of *reluctārī*, to struggle against.] —**re·luc′tant·ly** *adv.*

re·ly (rĭ-lī′) *intr.v.* **-lied, -ly·ing.** —**rely on** (or **upon**). **1.** To depend on: *relied on the rope to hold him.* **2.** To trust confidently: *rely on the children to behave.* [Middle English *relien*, to gather, rally, from Old French *relier*, from Latin *religāre*, to bind back : *re-*, back + *ligāre*, to fasten, tie.]

REM (rĕm). The rapid, jerky movement of the eyes during certain stages of the sleep cycle when dreaming takes place. [R(APID) + E(YE) + M(OVEMENT).]

re·main (rĭ-mān′) *intr.v.* **1.** To continue without change. *She remained unsympathetic.* **2.** To stay or be left over after the removal, departure, loss, or destruction of others: *A few columns remained.* **3.** To be left as still to be dealt with: *A cure remains to be found.* **4.** To stay in the same place or behind: *The children remained after she left.* [Middle English *remaynen*, from Old French *remanoir*, *remaindre*, from Latin *remanēre*, to stay behind.]

re·main·der (rĭ-mān′dər) *n.* **1.** The remaining part; the rest. **2.** *Math.* **a.** In division, the dividend minus the product of the divisor and quotient. **b.** In subtraction, the difference. **3.** The copy or copies of a book remaining with a publisher after sales have fallen off. —*tr.v.* To sell (books) as remainders, usu. at a reduced price. [Middle English *remaynder*, from Old French *remainder*, from *remaindre*, to remain.]

re·mains (rĭ-mānz′) *pl.n.* **1.** All that is left after other parts have been taken away, used up, or destroyed. **2.** A corpse.

re·make (rē-māk′) *tr.v.* **-made** (-mād′), **-mak·ing.** To make anew; reconstruct. —**re′make′** (-mād′).

re·mand (rĭ-mănd′) *tr.v.* **1.** *Law.* To send back (a person in

custody) to prison, to another court, or to another agency for further proceedings. **2.** *Law.* To send back (a case) to a lower court with instructions about further proceedings. —*n.* **1.** The condition of being remanded. **2.** The act of remanding. [Middle English *remaunden*, from Old French *remander*, from Late Latin *remandāre*, to send back word : Latin *re-*, back + *mandāre*, to send word.]

re·mark (rĭ-märk′) *n.* **1.** A casual statement; a comment. **2.** The act of noticing or observing. —*intr.v.* To make a remark; to comment: "*Chilly today,*" *he remarked.* —*tr.v.* To notice; observe: *remarked several changes in the town.* [French *remarque*, from *remarquer*, to notice : *re-* (intensive) + *marquer*, to note, mark.]

re·mark·a·ble (rĭ-mär′kə-bəl) *adj.* **1.** Worthy of notice. **2.** Extraordinary; conspicuous: *a remarkable achievement.* —See Syns at **uncommon.** —**re·mark′a·ble·ness** *n.* —**re·mark′a·bly** *adv.*

re·me·di·a·ble (rĭ-mē′dē-ə-bəl) *adj.* Capable of being remedied. —**re·me′di·a·ble·ness** *n.* —**re·me′di·a·bly** *adv.*

re·me·di·al (rĭ-mē′dē-əl) *adj.* Intended to correct something, esp. a deficiency: *a remedial reading course.* —**re·me′di·al·ly** *adv.*

rem·e·dy (rĕm′ĭ-dē) *n., pl.* **-dies. 1.** A medicine or therapy that relieves pain or cures disease. **2.** Something that corrects an evil, fault, or error. —*tr.v.* **-died, -dy·ing. 1.** To relieve or cure (a disease or disorder). **2.** To counteract or rectify (an error or defect). —See Syns at **correct.** [Middle English *remedie*, from Anglo-French, from Latin *remedium*, medicine : *re-*, again + *medērī*, to heal.]

re·mem·ber (rĭ-mĕm′bər) *tr.v.* **1.** To renew (an image or thought) through an act of memory; think of again. **2.** To retain in the mind; keep in memory. **3.** To keep (someone) in mind as worthy of affection or recognition. **4.** To give a gift, tip, etc. to: *remembered her nieces on their birthdays.* **5.** To mention (someone) to another as sending greetings. —*intr.v.* To have or use the faculty of memory. [Middle English *remembren*, from Old French *remembrer*, from Late Latin *rememorārī* : *re-*, again + Latin *memor*, mindful.]

Syns: remember, recall, recollect *v. Core meaning:* To bring to mind (*remembered her name*).

re·mem·brance (rĭ-mĕm′brəns) *n.* **1.** The act of remembering. **2.** The condition of being remembered. **3.** Something that serves to remind; a memento or souvenir.

re·mind (rĭ-mīnd′) *tr.v.* To cause (someone) to remember or think of something. —**re·mind′er** *n.*

rem·i·nisce (rĕm′ə-nĭs′) *intr.v.* **-nisced, -nisc·ing.** To remember and tell of past experiences or events. [Backformation from REMINISCENT.]

rem·i·nis·cence (rĕm′ə-nĭs′əns) *n.* **1.** The act or process of recalling the past. **2.** Something remembered; a memory. **3.** Often **reminiscences.** A narration of past experiences.

rem·i·nis·cent (rĕm′ə-nĭs′ənt) *adj.* **1.** Of or containing reminiscence. **2.** Recalling to the mind; suggestive: *a melody reminiscent of a folk song.* [Latin *reminiscens*, pres. part. of *reminiscī*, to recollect.] —**rem′i·nis′cent·ly** *adv.*

re·miss (rĭ-mĭs′) *adj.* Lax in attending to duty; negligent: *remiss in answering her letters.* [Middle English, from Latin *remissus*, slack, past part. of *remittere*, to remit.] —**re·miss′ly** *adv.* —**re·miss′ness** *n.*

re·mis·si·ble (rĭ-mĭs′ə-bəl) *adj.* Capable of being remitted or forgiven. —**re·mis′si·bil′i·ty** *n.* —**re·mis′si·bly** *adv.*

re·mis·sion (rĭ-mĭsh′ən) *n.* **1. a.** The act of remitting. **b.** The condition of being remitted. **2.** A lessening of intensity or seriousness, as of a disease. **3.** Pardon or forgiveness: *the remission of sin.*

re·mit (rĭ-mĭt′) *v.* **-mit·ted, -mit·ting.** —*tr.v.* **1.** To send (money); transmit. **2. a.** To cancel (a penalty or punishment). **b.** To pardon; forgive. **3.** To restore to an original condition; put back. **4.** *Law.* To refer (a case) back to a lower court for further consideration. **5.** To relax; slacken. **6.** To defer; postpone. —*intr.v.* **1.** To transmit money. **2.** To diminish; abate: *The symptoms remitted.* [Middle English *remitten*, from Latin *remittere*, to release : *re-*, back + *mittere*, to send.] —**re·mit′ta·ble** *adj.* —**re·mit′ter** *n.*

re·mit·tal (rĭ-mĭt′l) *n.* Remission.

re·mit·tance (rĭ-mĭt′ns) *n.* **1.** A sum of money or credit sent to someone. **2.** The act of sending money or credit.

re·mit·tent (rĭ-mĭt′nt) *adj.* Characterized by temporary

ă pat	ā pay	â care	ä father	ĕ pet	ē be	hw which	ĭ pit	ī tie	î pier	ŏ pot	ō toe	ô paw, for	oi noise
ŏŏ took	ōō boot	ou out	th thin	th this	ŭ cut		û urge	zh vision	ə about, item, edible, gallop, circus				

abatements in severity: *a remittent fever.*

rem·nant (rĕm′nənt) *n.* **1.** Something left over; a remainder: *remnants of fabric.* **2.** A surviving trace or vestige: *a remnant of an ancient empire.* [Middle English *remenant,* from Old French, pres. part. of *remaindre,* to remain.]

re·mod·el (rē-mŏd′l) *tr.v.* **-eled** or **-elled, -el·ing** or **-el·ling.** To rebuild or redesign in order to improve; renovate: *remodel a house.* —**re·mod′el·er** *n.*

re·mon·strance (rĭ-mŏn′strəns) *n.* **1.** The act of remonstrating. **2.** An expression of remonstration.

re·mon·strant (rĭ-mŏn′strənt) *adj.* Characterized by remonstrance; objecting or protesting.

re·mon·strate (rĭ-mŏn′strāt′, rĕm′ən-) *v.* **-strat·ed, -strat·ing.** —*tr.v.* To say or plead in protest, objection, or reproof. —*intr.v.* To make objections; argue against some action. [From Medieval Latin *remōnstrāre,* to demonstrate : Latin *re-,* completely + *monstrum,* an omen, from *monēre,* to warn.] —**re·mon′stra′tion** (rĭ-mŏn′strā′shən, rĕm′ən-) *n.* —**re·mon′stra·tive** (rĭ-mŏn′strə-tĭv) *adj.*

rem·o·ra (rĕm′ər-ə) *n.* Any of several saltwater fishes of the family Echeneidae that have a sucking disk on the head with which they attach themselves to sharks, whales, sea turtles, or the hulls of ships. [Latin, delay.]

re·morse (rĭ-môrs′) *n.* Bitter regret or guilt for past misdeeds. [Middle English, from Old French *remors,* from Medieval Latin *remorsus,* from Latin, a biting back, from *remordēre,* to bite again : *re-,* again + *mordēre,* to bite.] —**re·morse′ful** *adj.* —**re·morse′ful·ly** *adv.*

re·morse·less (rĭ-môrs′lĭs) *adj.* Having no pity or compassion; merciless. —**re·morse′less·ly** *adv.* —**re·morse′less·ness** *n.*

re·mote (rĭ-mōt′) *adj.* **-mot·er, -mot·est.** **1.** Located far away; relatively distant in space: *a remote Arctic island.* **2.** Distant in time: *the remote past.* **3.** Barely discernible; slight: *a remote interest.* **4.** Being distantly related by blood or marriage: *a remote cousin.* **5.** Distant in manner; aloof. —See Syns at **far.** [Latin *remōtus,* past part. of *removēre,* to move away.] —**re·mote′ly** *adv.* —**re·mote′ness** *n.*

remote control. Control of an activity, process, or machine from a distance, esp. by radio or electricity.

re·mov·al (rĭ-mōō′vəl) *n.* **1.** The act of removing. **2.** The fact of being removed.

re·move (rĭ-mōōv′) *v.* **-moved, -mov·ing.** —*tr.v.* **1.** To move from a position occupied: *Remove the pie from the oven.* **2.** To change the location or residence of. **3.** To take off or away: *remove one's hat; remove stains.* **4.** To dismiss, as from political office. —*intr.v.* To change one's place of residence or business; move. —*n.* **1.** The act of removing; removal. **2.** The distance or degree of space, time, or status that separates persons or things: *at a safe remove from the fire.* —**re·mov′a·ble** *adj.* —**re·mov′a·bly** *adv.* —**re·mov′er** *n.*

re·moved (rĭ-mōōvd′) *adj.* **1.** Distant in space, time, or nature; remote. **2.** Separated in relationship by a given degree of descent: *My first cousin's child is my first cousin once removed.* —See Syns at **far.**

re·mu·ner·ate (rĭ-myōō′nə-rāt′) *tr.v.* **-at·ed, -at·ing.** To pay for goods provided, services rendered, or losses incurred. [From Latin *remūnerāre* : *re-* (intensive) + *mūnerāre,* to give, from *mūnus,* a gift.] —**re·mu′ner·a′tion** *n.* —**re·mu′ner·a′tor** *n.*

re·mu·ner·a·tive (rĭ-myōō′nə-rā′tĭv) *adj.* **1.** Likely to be remunerated; profitable. **2.** Serving to remunerate. —**re·mu′ner·a′tive·ly** *adv.* —**re·mu′ner·a′tive·ness** *n.*

ren·ais·sance (rĕn′ĭ-säns′, -zäns′, rĭ-nā′səns) *n.* **1.** A rebirth or revival, esp. of intellectual or cultural activity. **2. Renaissance. a.** The humanistic revival of classical art, literature, and learning in Europe. **b.** The period of this revival, roughly from the 14th through the 16th cent. [French, a rebirth, from Old French, from *renaistre,* to be born again, from Latin *renascī* : *re-,* again + *nascī,* to be born.]

re·nal (rē′nəl) *adj.* Of or near the kidneys. [French *rénal,* from Late Latin *rēnālis,* from Latin *rēnes,* kidneys.]

re·nas·cent (rĭ-năs′ənt, -nās′ənt) *adj.* Showing renewed growth or vigor. [Latin *renascēns,* pres. part of *renascī,* to be born again.] —**re·nas′cence** *n.*

rend (rĕnd) *tr.v.* **rent** (rĕnt) or **rend·ed, rend·ing.** **1.** To tear apart or into pieces violently; to split. **2.** To remove forc-

ibly; wrest. **3.** To penetrate and disturb as if by tearing: *screams that rend the silence.* **4.** To distress painfully. [Middle English *renden,* from Old English *rendan.*]

ren·der (rĕn′dər) *tr.v.* **1.** To submit or present for consideration or payment: *render a bill.* **2.** To give or make available: *render assistance.* **3.** To give in return: *render an apology for his rudeness.* **4.** To surrender or relinquish; yield. **5.** To represent in a verbal or artistic form; depict: *render a leaf in detail.* **6.** To perform an interpretation of: *render a song artfully.* **7.** To express in another language or form; translate. **8.** To pronounce formally; hand down: *render a verdict.* **9.** To cause to become; make: *The hailstorm rendered the crops worthless.* **10.** To melt down (fat) by heating. [Middle English *rendren,* to relinquish, from Old French *rendre,* to give back, ult. from Latin *reddere* : *re-,* back + *dare,* to give.] —**ren′der·er** *n.*

ren·dez·vous (rän′dā-vōō′, -də-) *n., pl.* **-vous** (-vōōz′). **1.** A prearranged meeting place. **2.** A prearranged meeting. **3.** A popular gathering place. —*v.* **-voused** (-vōōd′), **-vous·ing** (-vōō′ĭng), **-vous** (-vōōz′). —*tr.v.* To bring together at a specified time and place. —*intr.v.* To meet together at a specified time and place. [Old French, from *rendez vous,* "present yourselves."]

ren·di·tion (rĕn-dĭsh′ən) *n.* **1.** The act of rendering. **2.** An interpretation of a musical or dramatic work. **3.** A performance of a musical or dramatic work. **4.** A translation. [Obs. French, from Old French *rendre,* to give back, render.]

ren·e·gade (rĕn′ĭ-gād′) *n.* **1.** A person who rejects his religion, cause, allegiance, or group for another; a traitor. **2.** An outlaw. —*adj.* Of or like a renegade; traitorous. [Spanish *renegado,* from Medieval Latin *renegātus,* from *renegāre,* to deny.]

re·nege (rĭ-nĭg′, -nĕg′) *intr.v.* **-neged, -neg·ing.** **1.** To fail to carry out a promise or commitment. **2.** *Card Games.* To fail to follow suit when able and required by the rules to do so. [Medieval Latin *renegāre,* to deny.] —**re·neg′er** *n.*

re·new (rĭ-nōō′, -nyōō′) *tr.v.* **1.** To make new or as if new again; restore. **2.** To take up again; resume: *renewing an old acquaintance.* **3.** To repeat so as to reaffirm: *renew their marriage vows.* **4.** To regain (spiritual or physical vigor); revive. **5.** To arrange for the extension of: *renew a contract.* **6.** To replenish. **7.** To bring into being again; reestablish. —See Syns at **restore.** —**re·new′al** *n.*

ren·in (rĕn′ĭn) *n.* A protein-digesting enzyme released by the kidneys that acts to raise blood pressure. [Latin *rēnes,* kidneys + -IN.]

ren·net (rĕn′ĭt) *n.* **1.** The inner lining of the fourth stomach of calves and other young ruminants. **2.** A dried extract of this lining, used to curdle milk. **3.** Rennin. [Middle English.]

ren·nin (rĕn′ĭn) *n.* A milk-coagulating enzyme produced from rennet and used in making cheeses and junkets. [RENN(ET) + -IN.]

re·nounce (rĭ-nouns′) *tr.v.* **-nounced, -nounc·ing.** **1.** To give up, esp. by formal announcement: *renounced his title.* **2.** To reject; repudiate: *renounce their children.* —See Syns at **abandon.** [Middle English *renouncen,* from Old French *renoncer,* from Latin *renūntiāre,* to announce, renounce : *re-,* back, against + *nūntiāre,* to inform, from *nūntium,* message.] —**re·nounce′ment** *n.*

ren·o·vate (rĕn′ə-vāt′) *tr.v.* **-vat·ed, -vat·ing.** To restore to an earlier condition; improve by repairing or remodeling: *renovate the old cottage.* [From Latin *renovāre* : *re-,* again + *novus,* new.] —**ren′o·va′tion** *n.* —**ren′o·va′tor** *n.*

re·nown (rĭ-noun′) *n.* Widespread honor and fame; celebrity. [Middle English *renoune,* from Old French *renom,* from *renomer,* to name again, make famous.]

re·nowned (rĭ-nound′) *adj.* Having renown; famous. —See Syns at **famous.**

rent¹ (rĕnt) *n.* A contracted payment made at specified intervals in return for the right to occupy or use the property of another. —*tr.v.* **1.** To obtain occupancy or use of (another's property) in return for regular payments. **2.** To grant temporary occupancy or use of (one's own property) in return for regular payments. —*intr.v.* To be for rent. —*idiom.* **for rent.** Available to be rented. [Middle English *rente,* income from property, from Old French.] —**rent′a·ble** *adj.* —**rent′er** *n.*

| ă pat | ā pay | â care | ä father | ĕ pet | ē be | hw which | ĭ pit | ī tie | î pier | ŏ pot | ō toe | ô paw, for | oi noise |
| ōō took | ōō boot | ou out | th thin | th this | ŭ cut | | û urge | zh vision | ə about, item, edible, gallop, circus | | | | |

rent² (rĕnt) v. A past tense and past participle of **rend.** —n. An opening made by rending; a rip or gap.

rent·al (rĕn'tl) n. 1. An amount paid out or taken in as rent. 2. Property available for renting. 3. The act of renting. —*modifier:* rental money.

re·nun·ci·a·tion (rĭ-nŭn'sē-ā'shən) n. The act or practice of renouncing. [Middle English, from Latin *renūntiātiō*, from *renūntiāre*, to renounce.] —**re·nun'ci·a'tive** or **re·nun'ci·a·to'ry** (-ə-tôr'ē, -tōr'ē) adj.

re·o·pen (rē-ō'pən) tr.v. To open or take up again. —intr.v. To start over; resume.

re·or·der (rē-ôr'dər) tr.v. 1. To order again. 2. To straighten out or put in order again. 3. To rearrange. —intr.v. To order the same goods again. —**re·or'der** n.

re·or·gan·i·za·tion (rē-ôr'gə-nĭ-zā'shən) n. 1. The act or process of reorganizing. 2. A thorough restructuring of a business corporation, esp. after a bankruptcy.

re·or·gan·ize (rē-ôr'gə-nīz') v. -**ized, -iz·ing.** —tr.v. To organize again or anew. —intr.v. To undergo or effect changes in organization. —**re·or'gan·iz'er** n.

rep¹ (rĕp) n. Also **repp.** A ribbed or corded fabric of various materials, such as cotton, wool, or silk. [French *reps.*]

rep² (rĕp) n. Informal. A representative.

re·pack·age (rē-păk'ĭj) tr.v. -**aged, -ag·ing.** To package again or differently.

re·pair¹ (rĭ-pâr') tr.v. 1. To restore to proper or useful condition after damage or injury; fix. 2. To set right; remedy. 3. To renew or refresh. 4. To make up for; compensate for. —n. 1. The work, act, or process of repairing. 2. General condition after use or repairing: in good repair. 3. An example of repairing: a ship in drydock for repair. [Middle English repairen, from Old French reparer, from Latin reparāre : re-, back + parāre, to put in order, prepare.] —**re·pair'a·ble** adj. —**re·pair'er** n.

re·pair² (rĭ-pâr') intr.v. To go: The guests repaired to the parlor. [Middle English reparen, to return, from Old French repairer, from Late Latin repatriāre, to repatriate.]

re·pair·man (rĭ-pâr'măn', -mən) n. A person whose occupation is making repairs.

rep·a·ra·ble (rĕp'ər-ə-bəl) adj. Capable of being repaired.

rep·a·ra·tion (rĕp'ə-rā'shən) n. 1. a. The act or process of repairing. b. The condition of being repaired. 2. The act or process of making amends. 3. Something done or paid to make amends; compensation, esp. that required from a nation for damage inflicted during a war. [Middle English reparacioun, from Old French reparation, from Late Latin reparātiō, from Latin reparāre, to repair.]

re·par·a·tive (rĭ-păr'ə-tĭv) adj. 1. Tending to repair. 2. Of or of the nature of a reparation.

rep·ar·tee (rĕp'ər-tē', -tā', -är-) n. 1. A swift, witty reply. 2. Witty and spirited conversation characterized by repartee. [French repartie, from repartir, to reply readily, from Old French, to depart back again : re-, again + partir, to part, from Latin partīre, from pars, a part.]

re·past (rĭ-păst') n. 1. A meal. 2. The food eaten or served at a meal. [Middle English, from Old French, from repaistre, to feed, from Late Latin repascere, to feed again : Latin re-, again + pascere, to feed.]

re·pa·tri·ate (rē-pā'trē-āt') tr.v. -**at·ed, -at·ing.** To return to the country of birth or citizenship: repatriate war refugees. —n. (rē-pā'trē-ət, -āt'). Someone who has been repatriated. [From Late Latin repatriāre : Latin re-, back + patria, native country.] —**re·pa'tri·a'tion** n.

re·pay (rĭ-pā') v. -**paid** (-pād'), -**pay·ing.** —tr.v. 1. To pay back (money); refund. 2. To return; requite: repaid his anger with indignation. —intr.v. To make repayment. —**re·pay'a·ble** adj. —**re·pay'ment** n.

re·peal (rĭ-pēl') tr.v. To withdraw or annul officially; revoke: repeal a law. —n. The act or process of repealing. [Middle English repelen, from Anglo-French repeler : re-, back, contrary + apeler, to appeal.]

re·peat (rĭ-pēt') tr.v. 1. To utter or state again: repeat a question. 2. To utter in duplication of what another has said: repeat the phrase after the teacher. 3. To recite from memory: repeat a poem. 4. To tell to someone else: repeat gossip. 5. To do, experience, or produce again: repeat an error. —n. 1. The act of repeating. 2. Something repeated. 3. Mus. a. A passage or section that is repeated.

b. A sign consisting of two vertical dots, indicating a passage to be repeated. [Middle English repeten, from Old French repeter, from Latin repetere, to return : re-, again + petere, to go, to seek.]

re·peat·ed (rĭ-pē'tĭd) adj. Said, done, or occurring again and again: repeated mistakes. —**re·peat'ed·ly** adv.

re·peat·er (rĭ-pē'tər) n. 1. Someone or something that repeats. 2. A watch or clock with a pressure-activated mechanism that strikes the hour. 3. A firearm capable of firing several times without reloading. 4. A student who repeats a course.

repeating decimal. A decimal that contains a pattern of one or more digits that repeats endlessly.

re·pel (rĭ-pĕl') v. -**pelled, -pel·ling.** 1. To drive back; ward off or keep away. 2. To offer resistance to; fight against: repel an invasion. 3. To turn away from; spurn: repel a suitor. 4. To cause aversion or distaste in. 5. To be resistant to; be incapable of absorbing or mixing with: a fabric that repels water. —intr.v. To cause aversion or distaste. [Middle English repellen, from Latin repellere : re-, back + pellere, to drive.] —**re·pel'ler** n.

Syns: 1. repel, combat, fend, repulse, ward off v. Core meaning: To turn or drive away (repel advances; repel an opponent). **2. repel, disgust, nauseate, repulse, revolt, sicken** v. Core meaning: To cause aversion in (behavior that repelled all his friends).

re·pel·lent (rĭ-pĕl'ənt) adj. 1. Serving or tending to repel. 2. Inspiring aversion or distaste; repulsive. —**re·pel'lence** or **re·pel'len·cy** n.

re·pent (rĭ-pĕnt') intr.v. 1. To feel remorse or self-reproach for what one has done or failed to do; be contrite. 2. To regret and change one's mind about past conduct. —tr.v. 1. To feel regret or self-reproach for. 2. To change one's mind regarding (past conduct). [Middle English repenten, from Old French repentir : re-, in response to + pentir, to be sorry, from Latin paenitēre.] —**re·pent'er** n.

re·pen·tance (rĭ-pĕn'tns) n. 1. Remorse or contrition for past conduct or sin. 2. The act or process of repenting.

re·pen·tant (rĭ-pĕn'tnt) adj. Feeling or demonstrating repentance; penitent. —**re·pen'tant·ly** adv.

re·per·cus·sion (rē'pər-kŭsh'ən, rĕp'ər-) n. 1. An indirect effect or result produced by an event or action. 2. A reflection or echo. [Latin repercussiō, from repercussus, past part. of repercutere, to cause to rebound.] —**re·per·cus'sive** adj.

rep·er·toire (rĕp'ər-twär') n. Also **rep·er·to·ry** (-tôr'ē, -tōr'ē). 1. The stock of songs, plays, operas, or other works that a person or company is prepared to perform. 2. The range or number of skills, aptitudes, or special accomplishments of a person or group. [French répertoire, from Late Latin repertōrium, repertory.]

rep·er·to·ry (rĕp'ər-tôr'ē, -tōr'ē) n., pl. -**ries.** 1. A repertoire. 2. A collection, as of information. [Late Latin repertōrium, from Latin repertus, past part. of reperīre, to find out : re-, again + parīre, to produce, invent.]

rep·e·ti·tion (rĕp'ĭ-tĭsh'ən) n. 1. The act or process of repeating. 2. Something repeated or produced by repeating. [Latin repetītiō, from repetere, to repeat.]

rep·e·ti·tious (rĕp'ĭ-tĭsh'əs) adj. Characterized by or filled with repetition, esp. needless or tedious repetition. —**rep'e·ti'tious·ly** adv. —**rep'e·ti'tious·ness** n.

re·pet·i·tive (rĭ-pĕt'ĭ-tĭv) adj. Marked by repetition; repetitious. —**re·pet'i·tive·ly** adv. —**re·pet'i·tive·ness** n.

re·phrase (rē-frāz') tr.v. -**phrased, -phras·ing.** To phrase again, esp. in a clearer way.

re·pine (rĭ-pīn') intr.v. -**pined, -pin·ing.** 1. To be discontented. 2. To complain or fret. [RE- + PINE (to yearn).]

re·place (rĭ-plās') tr.v. -**placed, -plac·ing.** 1. To put back in place: replace the key on the hook. 2. To take or fill the place of; supplant or supersede: Automobiles replaced horses as a common form of transportation. 3. To be or provide a substitute for: replace a broken window. —**re·place'a·ble** adj. —**re·plac'er** n.

re·place·ment (rĭ-plās'mənt) n. 1. The act or process of replacing or of being replaced. 2. Someone or something that replaces another, esp. a substitute.

re·plant (rē-plănt') tr.v. 1. To plant again, or in a new place. 2. To supply with new plants: replant a window box.

re·plen·ish (rĭ-plĕn'ĭsh) tr.v. To fill again; add a new stock or supply to. [Middle English *replenisshen,* from Old French *replenir* : *re-,* again + *plenir,* to fill, from *plein,* full, from Latin *plēnus.*] —**re·plen′ish·ment** *n.*

re·plete (rĭ-plēt′) *adj.* **1.** Plentifully supplied; abounding. **2.** Filled to satiation; gorged. [Middle English *replet,* from Old French, from Latin *replētus,* past part. of *replēre,* to refill.] —**re·ple′tion** or **re·plete′ness** *n.*

rep·li·ca (rĕp′lĭ-kə) *n.* **1.** A copy or reproduction of a work of art. **2.** Any copy or close reproduction. [Italian, from *replicare,* to repeat, from Latin *replicāre.*]

rep·li·cate (rĕp′lĭ-kāt′) *tr.v.* **-cat·ed, -cat·ing.** **1.** To make a replica of; duplicate. **2.** To fold over or bend back upon itself. [From Late Latin *replicāre,* to repeat, from Latin *re-,* back + *plicāre,* to fold.]

rep·li·ca·tion (rĕp′lĭ-kā′shən) *n.* **1.** A reply; response. **2.** A copy or reproduction. **3.** The act or process of duplicating or reproducing.

re·ply (rĭ-plī′) *v.* **-plied, -ply·ing.** —*intr.v.* **1.** To give an answer in speech or writing. **2.** To respond by some action or gesture. —*tr.v.* To say or give as an answer. —See Syns at **answer.** —*n., pl.* **-plies.** An answer in speech, writing, action, or gesture. [Middle English *replien,* from Old French *replier,* to fold back, reply, from Latin *replicāre,* to repeat.] —**re·pli′er** *n.*

re·port (rĭ-pôrt′, -pōrt′) *n.* **1.** An oral or written account containing information, often prepared or delivered in organized form. **2.** Rumor or gossip; common talk: *According to report they eloped.* **3.** Reputation; repute: *a man of bad report.* **4.** An explosive sound, as of a firearm being discharged. —*tr.v.* **1.** To make or present an account of, often formally or in organized form: *reported the incident to his superiors.* **2.** To relate or tell about; to present: *report one's findings.* **3.** To provide (an account or summation) for publication or broadcast: *report the news.* **4.** To submit or relate the result of considerations concerning: *The committee reported the bill.* **5.** To carry back and repeat to another: *report a message.* **6.** To complain about or denounce: *Report him to the police.* —*intr.v.* **1.** To make a report. **2.** To present oneself: *report for duty.* [Middle English, from Old French, from *reporter,* to carry back, from Latin *reportāre* : *re-,* back + *portāre,* to carry.]

report card. A report of a student's achievement presented at regular intervals to a parent or guardian.

re·port·ed·ly (rĭ-pôr′tĭd-lē, -pōr′-) *adv.* By report.

re·port·er (rĭ-pôr′tər, -pōr′-) *n.* **1.** A person who reports. **2.** A writer or broadcaster of news. **3.** A person authorized to make official reports of judicial or legislative proceedings. —**re·por′to·ri·al** (rĕp′ər-tôr′ē-əl, -tōr′-, rē′pər-) *adj.*

re·pose¹ (rĭ-pōz′) *n.* **1. a.** The act of resting; a rest. **b.** The condition of being at rest; relaxation. **2.** Peace of mind; freedom from anxiety; composure. **3.** Calmness; tranquillity. —*v.* **-posed, -pos·ing.** —*tr.v.* To lay to rest. —*intr.v.* To lie at rest. [Middle English *reposen,* from Old French *reposer,* from Late Latin *repausāre* : *re-,* again + *pausāre,* to rest, from Latin *pausa,* a pause, from Greek *pausis,* from *pauein,* to stop.]

re·pose² (rĭ-pōz′) *tr.v.* **-posed, -pos·ing.** To place (faith, trust, etc.): *They repose their hopes in him.* [Middle English *reposen,* to replace, from Latin *reponere.*]

re·pose·ful (rĭ-pōz′fəl) *adj.* Expressing repose; calm. —**re·pose′ful·ly** *adv.* —**re·pose′ful·ness** *n.*

re·pos·i·to·ry (rĭ-pŏz′ĭ-tôr′ē, -tōr′ē) *n., pl.* **-ries.** **1. a.** A place where things may be put for safekeeping. **b.** A warehouse. **c.** A museum. **2.** A burial vault; tomb. **3.** A person to whom a secret is told.

re·pos·sess (rē′pə-zĕs′) *tr.v.* **1.** To take back possession of. **2.** To give back possession to. —**re′pos·ses′sion** *n.*

repp (rĕp) *n.* Var. of **rep** (fabric).

rep·re·hend (rĕp′rĭ-hĕnd′) *tr.v.* To reprove; censure. [Middle English *reprehenden,* from Latin *reprehendere,* to rebuke, hold back : *re-,* back + *prehendere,* to seize.]

rep·re·hen·si·ble (rĕp′rĭ-hĕn′sə-bəl) *adj.* Worthy of censure or blame. [Late Latin *reprehēnsibilis,* from Latin *reprehēnsus,* past part. of *reprehendere,* to reprehend.] —**rep′re·hen′si·bil′i·ty** or **rep′re·hen′si·ble·ness** *n.* —**rep′re·hen′si·bly** *adv.*

rep·re·hen·sion (rĕp′rĭ-hĕn′shən) *n.* Reproof; censure.

rep·re·sent (rĕp′rĭ-zĕnt′) *tr.v.* **1.** To stand for; symbolize. **2.** To depict, as in a painting; portray. **3.** To serve as an

example of. **4.** To describe as having a certain identity or character: *represented himself as a salesman.* **5.** To serve as a delegate for, as in a legislature. [Middle English *representen,* from Latin *repraesentāre,* to show : *re-,* again + *praesentāre,* to present.] —**rep′re·sent′a·bil′i·ty** *n.* —**rep′re·sent′a·ble** *adj.*

    Syns: represent, embody, epitomize, exemplify, personify, symbolize, typify *v. Core meaning:* To serve as the image of (*a sword that represented valor in the painting*).

rep·re·sen·ta·tion (rĕp′rĭ-zĕn-tā′shən, -zən-) *n.* **1.** The act of representing or the condition of being represented, esp. in a legislative body. **2.** Something that represents, such as a picture or symbol. **3.** A statement, as of facts or arguments. —**rep′re·sen·ta′tion·al** *adj.*

rep·re·sen·ta·tive (rĕp′rĭ-zĕn′tə-tĭv) *n.* **1.** A typical example, esp. of a class. **2.** A delegate or agent acting on behalf of another or others. **3. Representative.** A member of the U.S. House of Representatives or of a state legislature. —*adj.* **1.** Representing a group or class. **2.** Of, relating to, or based on political representation: *representative government.* **3.** Serving as a typical example. —**rep′re·sen′ta·tive·ly** *adv.* —**rep′re·sen′ta·tive·ness** *n.*

re·press (rĭ-prĕs′) *tr.v.* **1.** To hold back; restrain: *repress a laugh.* **2.** To suppress; quell: *repress a rebellion.* **3.** To keep out of the conscious mind. [Middle English *repressen,* from Latin *repressus,* restrained, past part. of *reprimere,* to check : *re-,* back + *premere,* to press.] —**re·press′i·ble** *adj.* —**re·press′or** *n.*

re·pres·sion (rĭ-prĕsh′ən) *n.* **1. a.** The action of repressing. **b.** The condition of being repressed. **2.** *Psychoanal.* The exclusion of disturbing wishes or fears from the conscious mind.

re·pres·sive (rĭ-prĕs′ĭv) *adj.* Of or tending to cause repression. —**re·pres′sive·ly** *adv.* —**re·pres′sive·ness** *n.*

re·prieve (rĭ-prēv′) *n.* **1.** The postponement of a punishment. **2.** Temporary relief, as from pain. —*tr.v.* **-prieved, -priev·ing.** To postpone the punishment of. [Middle English *repryen,* from Old French *reprendre,* to take back, from Latin *reprehendere,* to hold back.] —**re·priev′a·ble** *adj.*

rep·ri·mand (rĕp′rĭ-mănd′) *n.* A severe or formal rebuke. —*tr.v.* To rebuke or censure severely; criticize. —See Syns at **admonish** and **scold.** [Old French *reprimender,* from *reprimende,* a reprimand, from Latin *reprimenda,* from *reprimere,* to repress.]

re·print (rē′prĭnt′) *n.* **1.** A new or additional printing of a book. **2.** A separately printed excerpt. —*tr.v.* (rē-prĭnt′). To print again. —**re·print′er** *n.*

re·pri·sal (rĭ-prī′zəl) *n.* Retaliation for an injury with the intent of inflicting at least as much injury in return. [Middle English *reprisail,* from Old French *reprisaille,* from Medieval Latin *repraesālia,* from Latin *reprehensus,* past part. of *reprehendere,* to reprehend.]

re·prise (rĭ-prēz′) *n. Mus.* A repetition of an original theme. [Middle English, from Old French, from *reprendre,* to take back, from Latin *reprehendere,* to reprehend.]

re·proach (rĭ-prōch′) *tr.v.* To rebuke severely or sternly; blame. —See Syns at **admonish** and **scold.** —*n.* **1.** Blame; disapproval. **2.** A rebuke. **3.** A source of shame. [Middle English *reprochen,* from Old French *reprochier* : Latin *re-,* back + *prope,* near.] —**re·proach′ful** *adj.* —**re·proach′ful·ly** *adv.*

rep·ro·bate (rĕp′rə-bāt′) *n.* A wicked, immoral person. —*adj.* Immoral; depraved; corrupt. —*tr.v.* **-bat·ed, -bat·ing.** To disapprove of; condemn. [Late Latin *reprobātus,* past part. of *reprobāre,* to condemn : Latin *re-,* against + *probāre,* to test.] —**rep′ro·ba′tion** *n.*

re·pro·duce (rē′prə-dōōs′, -dyōōs′) *v.* **-duced, -duc·ing.** —*tr.v.* **1.** To produce a copy of. **2.** *Biol.* To generate (offspring) by sexual or asexual means. **3.** To produce again or anew. —*intr.v.* **1.** To generate offspring. **2.** To undergo copying: *a color that reproduces poorly.* —**re′pro·duc′er** *n.* —**re′pro·duc′i·ble** *adj.*

re·pro·duc·tion (rē′prə-dŭk′shən) *n.* **1.** The act of reproducing or the fact of being reproduced. **2.** Something that is reproduced; copy. **3.** *Biol.* The process by which organisms generate others of the same kind.

re·pro·duc·tive (rē′prə-dŭk′tĭv) *adj.* **1.** Of or relating to reproduction. —**re′pro·duc′tive·ly** *adv.*

ă pat	ā pay	â care	ä father	ĕ pet	ē be	hw which	ĭ pit	ī tie	î pier	ŏ pot	ō toe	ô paw, for	oi noise
ōō took	ōō boot	ou out	th thin	*th* this	ŭ cut		û urge	zh vision	ə about, item, edible, gallop, circus				

re·proof (rĭ-proof′) *n.* Blame for a fault; rebuke.

re·prove (rĭ-proov′) *tr.v.* **-proved, -prov·ing. 1.** To rebuke for a fault or misdeed; scold. **2.** To find fault with. —See Syns at **admonish** and **scold.** [Middle English *reproven,* from Old French *reprover,* from Late Latin *reprobāre,* to condemn.] —**re·prov′a·ble** *adj.* —**re·prov′er** *n.* —**re·prov′ing·ly** *adv.*

rep·tile (rĕp′tĭl, -tīl′) *n.* **1.** Any of various cold-blooded, usu. egg-laying vertebrates of the class Reptilia, as a snake or crocodile, that are covered with scales or horny plates and breathe by means of lungs. **2.** A sly or treacherous person. —*adj.* Reptilian. [Middle English *reptil,* from Old French *reptile,* from Late Latin *reptile,* creeping, from Latin *repere,* to creep.]

rep·til·i·an (rĕp-tĭl′ē-ən, -tĭl′yən) *adj.* Of, relating to, or resembling a reptile. —*n.* A reptile.

re·pub·lic (rĭ-pŭb′lĭk) *n.* **1.** A government in which the head of state is usu. a president. **2.** A country governed by the elected representatives of its people. [Old French *republique,* from Latin *rēspūblica* : *rēs,* matter + *pūblica,* public.]

re·pub·li·can (rĭ-pŭb′lĭ-kən) *adj.* **1.** Of, relating to, or advocating a republic. **2. Republican.** Of or belonging to the Republican Party. —*n.* **1.** An advocate of a republican form of government. **2. Republican.** A member or a supporter of the Republican Party. —**re·pub′li·can·ism** *n.*

Republican Party. One of the two major U.S. political parties.

re·pu·di·ate (rĭ-pyoo′dē-āt′) *tr.v.* **-at·ed, -at·ing. 1.** To reject the truth or validity of. **2.** To refuse to recognize or pay: *repudiate a debt.* **3.** To disown. [From Latin *repudiāre,* from *repudium,* a casting off.] —**re·pu′di·a′tion** *n.* —**re·pu′di·a′tive** *adj.* —**re·pu′di·a′tor** *n.*

re·pug·nance (rĭ-pŭg′nəns) *n.* Also **re·pug·nan·cy** (-nən-sē). Extreme dislike or aversion.

re·pug·nant (rĭ-pŭg′nənt) *adj.* **1.** Offensive; distasteful. **2.** Contrary; antagonistic. [Middle English, from Old French, from Latin *repugnāns,* pres. part. of *repugnāre,* to oppose.] —**re·pug′nant·ly** *adv.*

re·pulse (rĭ-pŭls′) *tr.v.* **-pulsed, -puls·ing. 1.** To drive back; repel. **2.** To repel with rudeness, coldness, or denial. —See Syns at **repel.** —*n.* **1.** The act of repulsing or the condition of being repulsed. **2.** A rejection. [Latin *repulsus,* past part. of *repellere,* to repel.]

re·pul·sion (rĭ-pŭl′shən) *n.* **1.** The act or process of repulsing or repelling. **2.** Extreme aversion or dislike; revulsion.

re·pul·sive (rĭ-pŭl′sĭv) *adj.* **1.** Causing repugnance or disgust. **2.** Tending to repel or drive off. —**re·pul′sive·ly** *adv.* —**re·pul′sive·ness** *n.*

rep·u·ta·ble (rĕp′yə-tə-bəl) *adj.* Having a good reputation. —**rep′u·ta·bil′i·ty** *n.* —**rep′u·ta·bly** *adv.*

rep·u·ta·tion (rĕp′yə-tā′shən) *n.* **1.** The general opinion of a person or thing held by others or the public. **2.** The condition of being held in high esteem. **3.** A specific character or trait for which a person or thing is noted: *a reputation for courtesy.* —See Syns at **honor.**

re·pute (rĭ-pyoot′) *n.* Reputation or esteem. —See Syns at **honor.** —*tr.v.* **-put·ed, -put·ing.** To believe; regard. [Middle English *reputen,* from Old French *reputer,* from Latin *reputāre,* to consider : *re-,* again + *putāre,* to compute, consider.]

re·put·ed (rĭ-pyoo′tĭd) *adj.* Generally supposed. —**re·put′ed·ly** *adv.*

re·quest (rĭ-kwĕst′) *tr.v.* **1.** To ask for; express a desire for. **2.** To ask of: *requested him to leave.* —*n.* **1.** An act or example of asking. **2.** Something requested. **3.** The condition of being requested or sought after; demand: *in great request as a home decorator.* [Old French *requester,* from *requeste,* a request, from Latin *requīrere,* to seek again, require.]

req·ui·em (rĕk′wē-əm, rē′kwē-) *n.* **1. Requiem. a.** A mass sung for the dead. **b.** A musical composition for such a mass. **2.** A hymn, composition, or service for the dead. [Middle English, from Latin (first word of the introit of the requiem mass), accusative of *requiēs* : *re-,* after, + *quiēs,* rest.]

req·ui·es·cat (rĕk′wē-ĕs′kăt′, -kät′) *n.* A prayer for the repose of the souls of the dead. [Latin, "may he (or she) rest," from *requiescere,* to rest.]

re·quire (rĭ-kwīr′) *tr.v.* **-quired, -quir·ing. 1.** To need: *Most plants require sunlight.* **2.** To demand; insist upon: *The college requires all students to take a science course.* —See Syns at **command.** [Middle English *requiren,* from Old French *requere,* from Latin *requīrere,* to search for : *re-,* again + *quaerere,* to seek, ask.] —**re·quir′er** *n.*

re·quire·ment (rĭ-kwīr′mənt) *n.* Something that is required: *a person's daily food requirement.*

req·ui·site (rĕk′wĭ-zĭt) *adj.* Required; necessary. —*n.* A necessity; something needed. [Middle English, from Latin *requīsītus,* past part. of *requīrere,* to require.] —**req′ui·site·ly** *adv.* —**req′ui·site·ness** *n.*

req·ui·si·tion (rĕk′wĭ-zĭsh′ən) *n.* **1.** A formal request for something that is needed. **2.** The condition of being needed or taken for use. —*tr.v.* To acquire or take with a requisition.

re·quit·al (rĭ-kwīt′l) *n.* **1.** The act of requiting. **2.** Something given in return.

re·quite (rĭ-kwīt′) *tr.v.* **-quit·ed, -quit·ing. 1.** To make repayment or return for. **2.** To avenge. [RE- + obs. *quite,* to repay, var. of QUIT.] —**re·quit′er** *n.*

re·run (rē′rŭn′) *n.* A repetition, esp. of a recorded performance. —*tr.v.* (rē-rŭn′) **-ran** (-răn′), **-run, -run·ning.** To run again.

re·sale (rē′sāl′, rē-sāl′) *n.* The act of selling again.

re·scind (rĭ-sĭnd′) *tr.v.* To void; repeal. [Latin *rēscindere,* to abolish : *re-,* + *scindere,* to cut.] —**re·scind′er** *n.*

re·scis·sion (rĭ-sĭzh′ən) *n.* The act of rescinding. [Late Latin *rescissiō,* from *rēcissus,* past part. of *rēscindere,* to rescind.]

res·cue (rĕs′kyoo) *tr.v.* **-cued, -cu·ing.** To save, as from danger or imprisonment. —See Syns at **save.** —*n.* An act of rescuing. [Middle English *rescuen,* from Old French *rescourre : re-,* + *excutere,* to shake out or off.] —**res′cu·er** *n.*

re·search (rĭ-sûrch′, rē′sûrch′) *n.* Scholarly or scientific study of a given subject, field, or problem. —*tr.v.* To investigate or study thoroughly. [Old French *recherche,* from *recercher,* to seek out : *re-,* again + *cerch(i)er,* to search.] —**re·search′er** *n.*

re·sec·tion (rĭ-sĕk′shən) *n.* The surgical removal of part of an organ or structure. [Latin *resectiō,* a cutting away, from *resectus,* past part. of *resecāre,* to cut off.]

re·sem·blance (rĭ-zĕm′bləns) *n.* **1.** A similarity, esp. in appearance. **2.** Something that resembles another.

re·sem·ble (rĭ-zĕm′bəl) *tr.v.* **-bled, -bling.** To have a similarity to. [Middle English *resemblen,* from Old French *resembler : re-* + *sembler,* to be like, from Latin *simulāre,* similāre, to imitate, from *similis,* like.]

re·sent (rĭ-zĕnt′) *tr.v.* To feel angry or bitter about. [Obs. French *resentir,* to feel strongly : *re-* + *sentir,* to feel, from Latin *sentīre.*]

re·sent·ful (rĭ-zĕnt′fəl) *adj.* Feeling or showing resentment. —**re·sent′ful·ly** *adv.* —**re·sent′ful·ness** *n.*

re·sent·ment (rĭ-zĕnt′mənt) *n.* Anger or indignation over something held to be wrong or unfair.

res·er·va·tion (rĕz′ər-vā′shən) *n.* **1.** The act of reserving. **2.** A limiting qualification or condition. **3.** A tract of land set apart for a special purpose, as for the use of an American Indian people or tribe. **4.** An arrangement by which accommodations, as in a hotel or on an airplane, are held for one. —See Syns at **qualm.**

re·serve (rĭ-zûrv′) *tr.v.* **-served, -serv·ing. 1.** To set aside for future use or a special purpose. **2.** To set apart for a particular person or use: *reserve a table.* **3.** To keep for the future; defer: *reserve judgment.* —*n.* **1.** Something saved for future use or special purpose: *a cash reserve.* **2.** The condition of being reserved: *funds held in reserve.* **3.** The act of reserving; exception. **4.** Self-restraint in expression; reticence. **5.** A reservation of public land. **6.** Often **reserves.** The part of a country's armed forces that is not part of the regular military force. [Middle English *reserven,* from Old French *reserver,* from Latin *reservāre,* to keep back.] —**re·serv′er** *n.*

re·served (rĭ-zûrvd′) *adj.* **1.** Held for a particular person or persons: *a reserved seat.* **2.** Quiet and restrained in manner. —**re·serv′ed·ly** (rĭ-zûr′vĭd-lē) *adv.* —**re·serv′ed·ness** *n.*

re·serv·ist (rĭ-zûr′vĭst) *n.* A member of a military reserve.

res·er·voir (rĕz′ər-vwär′, -vwôr′, -vôr′) *n.* **1.** A body of wa-

---

ă pat	ā pay	â care	ä father	ĕ pet	ē be	hw which	ĭ pit	ī tie	î pier	ŏ pot	ō toe	ô paw, for	oi noise
oo̅o̅ took	oo̅o̅ boot	ou out	th thin	*th* this	ŭ cut		û urge	zh vision	ə about, item, edible, gallop, circus				

ter collected and stored in a natural or artificial lake. **2.** A reserve supply. [French *réservoir*, from *réserver*, to reserve.]

re·shape (rē-shāp′) *tr.v.* **-shaped, -shap·ing.** To form into a new shape.

re·side (rĭ-zīd′) *intr.v.* **-sid·ed, -sid·ing. 1.** To live in a place for an extended or permanent period; dwell: *He resides in Boston.* **2.** To be inherently present: *the power that resides in the electorate.* [Middle English *residen*, from Old French *resider*, from Latin *residēre*, to sit down : *re-*, back, + *sedēre*, to sit.] **—re·sid′er** *n.*

res·i·dence (rĕz′ĭ-dəns) *n.* **1.** The place in which one lives; a dwelling; abode. **2.** The act or a period of residing somewhere. **3.** Medical residency.

res·i·den·cy (rĕz′ĭ-dən-sē, -dĕn′-) *n., pl.* **-cies.** A period of specialized training for a physician.

res·i·dent (rĕz′ĭ-dənt, -dĕnt′) *n.* **1.** A person that makes his home in a particular place. **2.** A physician serving a period of residency. —*adj.* **1.** Dwelling in a particular place. **2.** Living somewhere in connection with duty or work: *a resident poet.* **3.** Inherently present.

res·i·den·tial (rĕz′ĭ-dĕn′shəl) *adj.* **1.** Relating to or having residence: *a residential voting requirement.* **2.** Containing or suitable for homes: *a residential neighborhood.*

re·sid·u·al (rĭ-zĭj′ōō-əl) *adj.* Of, characteristic of, or remaining as a residue. —*n.* **1.** A part or fraction left over at the end of a process; remainder. **2.** Payment made to a performer for a rerun. **—re·sid′u·al·ly** *adv.*

re·sid·u·ar·y (rĭ-zĭj′ōō-ĕr′ē) *adj.* Of, relating to, or constituting a residue.

res·i·due (rĕz′ĭ-dōō′, -dyōō′) *n.* **1.** The part left after something is removed; remainder. **2.** *Law.* The remainder of an estate after all claims, debts, and bequests are satisfied. [Middle English, from Old French *residu*, from Latin *residuum*, from *residuus*, remaining, from *residēre*, to reside.]

re·sid·u·um (rĭ-zĭj′ōō-əm) *n., pl.* **-u·a** (-ōō-ə). Remainder; residue. [Latin, residue.]

re·sign (rĭ-zīn′) *tr.v.* **1.** To force to accept something; submit: *We must resign ourselves to growing old.* **2.** To give up (a position); quit. **3.** To relinquish formally. —*intr.v.* **1.** To give up a position, esp. by formal notice: *resign from the army.* **2.** To concede defeat. [Middle English *resignen*, from Old French *resigner*, from Latin *resignāre*, to invalidate : *re-*, back + *signum*, a mark, sign.] **—re·sign′er** *n.*

res·ig·na·tion (rĕz′ĭg-nā′shən) *n.* **1.** The act of resigning. **2.** A formal statement that one is resigning. **3.** Unresisting acceptance; submission.

re·signed (rĭ-zīnd′) *adj.* Feeling or marked by resignation; acquiescent. **—re·sign′ed·ly** (rĭ-zī′nĭd-lē) *adv.*

re·sil·ient (rĭ-zĭl′yənt) *adj.* **1.** Capable of returning to an original shape after being bent, stretched, or compressed; elastic. **2.** Recovering quickly from disruption, misfortune, or illness. —See Syns at **flexible.** [Latin *resiliens*, pres. part. of *resilīre*, to spring back : *re-*, back + *salīre*, to leap.] **—re·sil′ience** or **re·sil′ien·cy** *n.*

res·in (rĕz′ĭn) *n.* **1.** Any of numerous clear or translucent, yellow or brown, viscous substances of plant origin, such as copal, rosin, and amber, used principally in lacquers, varnishes, inks, adhesives, synthetic plastics, and pharmaceuticals. **2.** Any of various artificial substances that have properties similar to natural resins. [Middle English *resyn*, from Old French *resine*, from Latin *rēsīna*, from Greek *rhētinē*.] **—res′in·ous** (rĕz′ə-nəs) *adj.*

re·sist (rĭ-zĭst′) *tr.v.* **1.** To strive or work against; oppose. **2.** To remain firm against the action or effect of: *Diamonds resist melting.* —*intr.v.* To act in opposition. —*n.* A substance that can cover and protect a surface, as from corrosion. [Middle English *resisten*, from Latin *resistere* : *re-*, against + *sistere*, to set, place.] **—re·sist′er** *n.*

Syns: 1. resist, fight, withstand *v.* **Core meaning:** To oppose actively and with force (*rebels who resisted the invading armies*). **2. resist, dispute, oppose** *v.* **Core meaning:** To take a stand against (*resisted the court ruling*).

re·sis·tance (rĭ-zĭs′təns) *n.* **1.** The act, process, or capacity of resisting. **2.** A force that opposes or retards. **3.** *Elect.* **a.** The opposition that a material body offers to the passage of an electric current. **b.** An electric circuit element that is a source of resistance. **4.** Often **Resistance.** An un-

derground organization engaged in the struggle for national liberation in a country under military occupation. **—re·sis′tant** *adj.*

re·sist·i·ble (rĭ-zĭs′tə-bəl) *adj.* Capable of being resisted. **—re·sist′i·bil′i·ty** *n.* **—re·sist′i·bly** *adv.*

re·sist·less (rĭ-zĭst′lĭs) *adj.* **1.** Irresistible. **2.** Unresisting. **—re·sist′less·ly** *adv.*

re·sis·tor (rĭ-zĭs′tər) *n.* An electric circuit element used to provide resistance.

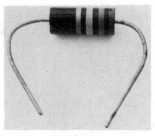

resistor

res·o·lute (rĕz′ə-lōōt′) *adj.* Characterized by firmness, determination, and often loyalty. —See Syns at **faithful.** [Latin *resolūtus*, past part. of *resolvere*, to resolve.] **—res′o·lute′ly** *adv.* **—res′o·lute′ness** *n.*

res·o·lu·tion (rĕz′ə-lōō′shən) *n.* **1.** The quality of being resolute. **2. a.** Something that has been resolved: *made a resolution to stop smoking.* **b.** A formal statement of a decision voted, as by a legislature or assembly. **3.** The action or process of reducing to a simpler form. **4.** A solving, as of a problem or puzzle. **5.** *Mus.* The progression of a dissonant tone or chord to a usu. consonant tone or chord.

re·solve (rĭ-zŏlv′) *v.* **-solved, -solv·ing.** —*tr.v.* **1.** To make a firm decision about: *He resolved to work harder.* **2.** To decide or express by formal vote. **3.** To separate (something) into constituent or simpler parts. **4.** To find a solution to. **5.** To dispel: *resolve a conflict.* **6.** *Mus.* To cause (a tone or chord) to progress from dissonance to consonance. —*intr.v.* **1.** To reach a decision; make a determination: *resolve on a change of plans.* **2.** To become separated or reduced to constituents. **3.** *Mus.* To undergo resolution. —See Syns at **decide.** —*n.* **1.** Firmness of purpose; resolution. **2.** A determination or decision. [Middle English *resolven*, to solve, from Latin *resolvere*, to release : *re-*, again + *solvere*, to release.] **—re·solv′er** *n.*

re·solved (rĭ-zŏlvd′) *adj.* Fixed in purpose; determined. **—re·solv′ed·ly** (rĭ-zŏl′vĭd-lē) *adv.*

res·o·nance (rĕz′ə-nəns) *n.* **1.** The quality or condition of being resonant. **2.** *Physics.* **a.** The increased response of an electric or mechanical system to a periodic driving force oscillating at the frequency at which the system tends to oscillate naturally. **b.** A frequency at which such a system tends to oscillate naturally. **3.** The intensification esp. of musical tones by sympathetic vibrations. **4.** *Chem.* The phenomenon of interrelated alternative bond structures in certain molecules, produced by redistribution of valence electrons without change in the relative positions of bound atoms and resulting in highly stable compounds.

res·o·nant (rĕz′ə-nənt) *adj.* **1.** Continuing to sound; echoing. **2.** Of or exhibiting resonance. **3.** Having a full, pleasing sound. **—res′o·nant·ly** *adv.*

res·o·nate (rĕz′ə-nāt′) *intr.v.* **-nat·ed, -nat·ing. 1.** To exhibit resonance. **2.** To resound. [From Latin *resonāre*, to resound.]

res·o·na·tor (rĕz′ə-nā′tər) *n.* **1.** A resonating system. **2.** A hollow chamber or cavity with dimensions chosen to permit internal resonant oscillation of electromagnetic or acoustical waves of specific frequencies.

res·or·cin·ol (rĭ-zôr′sə-nôl′, -nōl′) *n.* Also **res·or·cin** (rĭ-zôr′sĭn). A white crystalline compound, $C_6H_4(OH)_2$, used to treat certain skin diseases and in dyes, resin adhesives, and pharmaceuticals. [RES(IN) + *orc(hil)*, a kind of lichen + -IN + -OL.]

re·sort (rĭ-zôrt′) *intr.v.* **1.** To have recourse: *resorted to force.* **2.** To go customarily or frequently. —*n.* **1.** A place where people go for relaxation or recreation. **2.** Customary or frequent visiting. **3.** Recourse. **4.** A person or thing turned to for aid or relief. **—modifier:** *a resort hotel.* [Middle English *resorten,* to return, from Old French *resortir,* to retire : *re-,* again + *sortir,* to go out.]

re·sound (rĭ-zound′) *intr.v.* **1.** To be filled with sound; reverberate. **2.** To make a loud, long, or reverberating sound. **3.** To sound loudly. **4.** To become famous or celebrated. **—tr.v. 1.** To utter or sound loudly. **3.** To celebrate; extol. [Middle English *resounen,* from Old French *resoner,* from Latin *resonāre,* to echo : *re-,* again + *sonāre,* to sound.] **—re·sound′ing·ly** *adv.*

re·source (rē′sôrs′, -sōrs′, -zôrs′, -zōrs′, rĭ-) *n.* **1.** A source of support or help. **2.** The ability to deal with a situation effectively. **3. resources. a.** Means; assets. **b.** A natural source of wealth. [French *ressource,* from Old French *ressourse,* relief, recovery, from *resourdre* from Latin *resurgere* : *re-,* again + *surgere,* to rise.]

re·source·ful (rĭ-sôrs′fəl, -sōrs′-, -zôrs′-, -zōrs′-) *adj.* Clever and imaginative, esp. in dealing with a difficult situation. **—re·source′ful·ly** *adv.* **—re·source′ful·ness** *n.*

re·spect (rĭ-spĕkt′) *n.* **1.** Deferential or high regard; esteem. **2.** The condition of being esteemed. **3.** An act of showing consideration. **4. respects.** Expressions of consideration or deference: *pay one's respects.* **5.** A particular aspect; detail: *differ in one respect.* **6.** Relation; reference: *with respect to his request.* **—See Syns at favor. —tr.v. 1.** To have esteem for. **2.** To avoid violation of. **3.** To concern. **—See** Syns at **appreciate.** [Latin *respectus,* past part. of *respicere,* to look back : *re-,* back + *specere,* to look.] **—re·spect′er** *n.*

re·spect·a·ble (rĭ-spĕk′tə-bəl) *adj.* **1.** Worthy of respect or esteem. **2.** Correct or proper in behavior or conduct. **3.** Moderately good. **4.** Considerable in amount, number, or size: *a respectable sum.* **5.** Acceptable in appearance; presentable: *a respectable suit.* **—re·spect′a·bil′i·ty** or **re·spect′a·ble·ness** *n.* **—re·spect′a·bly** *adv.*

re·spect·ful (rĭ-spĕkt′fəl) *adj.* Showing respect. **—re·spect′ful·ly** *adv.* **—re·spect′ful·ness** *n.*

re·spect·ing (rĭ-spĕk′tĭng) *prep.* In relation to; concerning.

re·spec·tive (rĭ-spĕk′tĭv) *adj.* Individual; particular: *"The two women stood by their respective telephones"* (Doris Lessing). **—re·spec′tive·ness** *n.*

re·spec·tive·ly (rĭ-spĕk′tĭv-lē) *adv.* Each in the order named: *Albany, Augusta, and Atlanta are respectively the capitals of New York, Maine, and Georgia.*

res·pi·ra·tion (rĕs′pə-rā′shən) *n.* **1.** The act or process of inhaling and exhaling; breathing. **2.** The metabolic process by which an organism takes in oxygen and oxidizes nutrients to produce energy, usu. releasing carbon dioxide and other products of oxidation.

res·pi·ra·tor (rĕs′pə-rā′tər) *n.* **1.** An apparatus used in administering artificial respiration. **2.** A device worn over the mouth or nose to protect the respiratory tract.

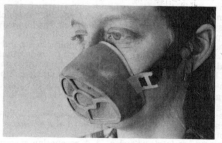

respirator

res·pi·ra·to·ry (rĕs′pər-ə-tôr′ē, -tōr′ē, rĭ-spīr′-) *adj.* Of, relating to, or used in respiration.

re·spire (rĭ-spīr′) *v.* **-spired, -spir·ing. —intr.v.** To engage in respiration. **—tr.v.** To breathe. [Middle English *respyren,* from Latin *respīrāre* : *re-,* again + *spīrāre,* to breathe.]

res·pite (rĕs′pĭt) *n.* **1.** A short interval of rest or relief. **2.** A postponement; a reprieve. [Middle English *respit,* from Old French, from Latin *respectus,* a refuge, from *respicere,* to look back.]

re·splen·dent (rĭ-splĕn′dənt) *adj.* Shining with splendor.

[Middle English, from Latin *resplendēns,* pres. part. of *resplendēre,* to shine brightly : *re-* + *splendēre,* to shine.] **—re·splen′dence** or **re·splen′den·cy** *n.* **—re·splen′dent·ly** *adv.*

re·spond (rĭ-spŏnd′) *intr.v.* **1.** To make a reply; to answer. **2.** To react positively: *"Every individual responds to confidence"* (Booker T. Washington). **—tr.v.** To say in reply; to answer. **—See Syns at answer.** [Latin *respondēre,* to promise in return : *re-,* back + *spondēre,* to promise.] **—re·spond′er** *n.*

re·spon·dent (rĭ-spŏn′dənt) *adj.* **1.** Responsive. **2.** *Law.* Being a respondent. **—n. 1.** A person who responds. **2.** *Law.* A defendant, esp. in divorce or equity cases.

re·sponse (rĭ-spŏns′) *n.* **1.** The act of responding; answer. **2.** A reaction, as that of an organism or mechanism, to a specific stimulus. **3.** Something that is spoken or sung by a congregation or choir in answer to the officiating minister or priest. [Middle English *respons,* from Old French, from Latin *responsum,* from *respondēre,* to respond.]

re·spon·si·bil·i·ty (rĭ-spŏn′sə-bĭl′ĭ-tē) *n., pl.* **-ties. 1.** The condition, quality, or fact of being responsible. **2.** A thing or person that one is responsible for.

re·spon·si·ble (rĭ-spŏn′sə-bəl) *adj.* **1.** Liable to be called to account for something. **2.** Being the cause or source of something: *Viruses are responsible for many diseases.* **3.** Dependable; reliable; trustworthy. **4.** Involving important duties or obligations: *a responsible job.* [Obs. French, correspondent to, from Latin *respondēre,* to respond.] **—re·spon′si·bly** *adv.*

re·spon·sive (rĭ-spŏn′sĭv) *adj.* **1.** Readily reacting. **2.** Marked by responses between leader and group. **—re·spon′sive·ly** *adv.* **—re·spon′sive·ness** *n.*

rest¹ (rĕst) *n.* **1.** A period of inactivity, relaxation, or sleep. **2.** Death. **3.** Absence of or freedom from activity or motion: *The ball came to rest.* **4.** *Mus.* **a.** An interval of silence equal to a note of the same time value. **b.** The symbol indicating a rest. **5.** *Pros.* A short pause in a line of verse; caesura. **—intr.v. 1.** To refresh oneself by ceasing work or activity or esp. by sleeping. **2.** To be at peace or ease: *couldn't rest until they were safe.* **3.** To be, become, or remain temporarily quiet or inactive: *Let the matter rest.* **4.** To be supported: *a clock resting on the shelf.* **5.** To be imposed or placed, esp. as a responsibility: *Final authority rests on the president's shoulders.* **6.** To depend or rely: *We rested on his experience and judgment.* **7.** *Law.* To cease voluntarily the presentation of evidence in a case: *The defense rests.* **—tr.v. 1.** To give rest or repose to; refresh by rest. **2.** To place, as for support or repose: *rested his cane against the chair.* **3.** To base or ground. **4.** To fix or direct. **5.** To bring to rest; halt. **6.** *Law.* To cease voluntarily the introduction of evidence in (a case). [Middle English *reste,* from Old English *reste,* rest, resting place.] **—rest′er** *n.*

rest² (rĕst) *n.* **1.** Something that is left over; remainder. **2.** (used with a pl. verb). The others remaining: *The rest are coming later.* [Middle English, from Old French *reste,* from *rester,* to remain, from Latin *restāre,* to keep back : *re-,* back + *stāre,* to stand.]

re·state (rē-stāt′) *tr.v.* **-stat·ed, -stat·ing.** To state again or in a new form. **—re·state′ment** *n.*

res·tau·rant (rĕs′tər-ənt, -tə-ränt′) *n.* An establishment where meals are served to the public. [French, from *restaurer,* from Old French *restorer,* to restore.]

res·tau·ra·teur (rĕs′tər-ə-tûr′) *n.* The manager of a restaurant. [French.]

rest·ful (rĕst′fəl) *adj.* **1.** Offering rest. **2.** Pleasant and soothing: *restful colors.* **—rest′ful·ly** *adv.* **—rest′ful·ness** *n.*

rest home. An establishment where elderly or sick people are housed and cared for.

res·ti·tu·tion (rĕs′tĭ-tōō′shən, -tyōō′-) *n.* **1.** The act of restoring something to the rightful owner. **2.** The act of making good for loss, damage, or injury. [Middle English, from Old French, from Latin *restitūtio,* from *restituere,* to restore : *re-,* back + *statuere,* to set up.]

res·tive (rĕs′tĭv) *adj.* **1.** Impatiently restless; uneasy. **2.** Difficult to control; unruly. **—See Syns at edgy.** [Middle English *restyffe,* unwilling to move, stationary, from Old French *restif,* from Latin *restāre,* to keep back : *re-,* back + *stāre,* to stand.] **—res′tive·ly** *adv.* **—res′tive·ness** *n.*

ă pat	ā pay	â care	ä father	ĕ pet	ē be	hw which	ĭ pit	ī tie	î pier	ŏ pot	ō toe	ô paw, for	oi noise
ōō took	ōō boot	ou out	th thin	*th* this	ŭ cut		û urge	zh vision	ə about, item, edible, gallop, circus				

rest·less (rĕst′lĭs) *adj.* **1.** Without rest or sleep: *a restless night.* **2. a.** Unable or reluctant to rest or be still. **b.** Feeling or manifesting nervous tension. **3.** Never still or motionless. —See Syns at **edgy.** —**rest′less·ly** *adv.* —**rest′less·ness** *n.*

rest mass. The physical mass of a body as observed in a reference system with respect to which the body is at rest.

res·to·ra·tion (rĕs′tə-rā′shən) *n.* **1.** The act of restoring or the condition of being restored. **2.** Something that has been restored, as a renovated building. **3. Restoration. a.** The return of Charles II to the British throne in 1660. **b.** The period between the return of Charles II and the Revolution of 1688.

re·stor·a·tive (rĭ-stôr′ə-tĭv, -stōr′-) *adj.* **1.** Of renewal or restoration. **2.** Tending to renew or restore something. —*n.* Something that restores health or strength.

re·store (rĭ-stôr′, -stōr′) *tr.v.* **-stored, -stor·ing. 1.** To bring back into existence; re-establish: *restore order.* **2.** To bring back to a previous or original condition. **3.** To give back; make restitution of: *restore the stolen funds.* [Middle English *restoren,* from Old French *restorer,* from Latin *restaurāre,* to renew.] —**re·stor′er** *n.*

Syns: **1. restore, reestablish, reinstate, renew, revive** *v.* *Core meaning:* To bring back into existence or use (*restore law and order*). **2. restore, rebuild, recondition, reconstruct, rehabilitate** *v.* *Core meaning:* To bring back to a previous condition (*restored a Victorian mansion*). **3. restore, reinstate, return** *v.* *Core meaning:* To give (something) back to its owner or possessor (*an emperor's throne restored to him*).

re·strain (rĭ-strān′) *tr.v.* **1.** To check; hold back. **2.** To deprive of freedom. **3.** To limit or restrict. [Middle English *restreynen,* from Old French *restraindre,* from Latin *restringere,* to restrict.] —**re·strain′a·ble** *adj.* —**re·strain′er** *n.*

re·strained (rĭ-strānd′) *adj.* Using or characterized by restraint. —**re·strain′ed·ly** *adv.*

re·straint (rĭ-strānt′) *n.* **1.** The act of restraining. **2.** The condition of being restrained. **3.** Something that holds back or restrains. **4.** Reserve or moderation in action or expression. [Middle English *restreinte,* from Old French *restrainte,* from *restraindre,* to restrain.]

re·strict (rĭ-strĭkt′) *tr.v.* To keep within limits; confine. [Latin *restrictus,* past part. of *restringere,* to restrain : *re-,* back + *stringere,* to bind.] —**re·strict′ed** *adj.* —**re·strict′ed·ly** *adv.*

re·stric·tion (rĭ-strĭk′shən) *n.* **1.** The act of restricting or the condition of being restricted. **2.** Something that restricts.

re·stric·tive (rĭ-strĭk′tĭv) *adj.* **1.** Tending or serving to restrict. **2.** *Gram.* Limiting the meaning or scope of a modified word or phrase. —**re·stric′tive·ly** *adv.*

rest room. A public lavatory.

re·sult (rĭ-zŭlt′) *intr.v.* **1.** To come about as a consequence: *Nothing resulted from her efforts.* **2.** To have a particular outcome: *Bad grammar can result in misunderstanding.* —*n.* A consequence; outcome. [Middle English *resulten,* from Medieval Latin *resultāre,* from Latin, to rebound : *re-,* back + *saltāre,* to leap, freq. of *salīre,* to leap.]

re·sul·tant (rĭ-zŭl′tənt) *adj.* Following as a result. —*n.* **1.** A result. **2.** *Math.* The sum of two or more vectors.

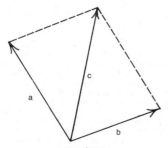

resultant
c is the resultant of vectors a and b

re·sume (rĭ-zōōm′) *v.* **-sumed, -sum·ing.** —*tr.v.* **1.** To begin again or continue after interruption. **2.** To occupy or take again: *resume power.* —*intr.v.* To begin again or continue after interruption. [Middle English *resumen,* from Old French *resumer,* from Latin *resūmere* : *re-,* again + *sūmere,* to take up.]

rés·u·mé (rĕz′ōō-mā′, rĕz′ōō-mā′) *n.* A summary, esp. of a person's history and work experience, submitted when applying for a job. [French, from *résumer,* to sum up, from Old French *resumer,* to resume.]

re·sump·tion (rĭ-zŭmp′shən) *n.* The act of resuming. [Middle English, from Old French, from Late Latin *resūmptiō,* from Latin *resūmere,* to resume.]

re·sur·gent (rĭ-sûr′jənt) *adj.* Rising again. [From Latin *resurgens,* pres. part. of *resurgere* : *re-,* again + *surgere,* to rise.] —**re·sur′gence** *n.*

res·ur·rect (rĕz′ə-rĕkt′) *tr.v.* **1.** To raise from the dead. **2.** To bring back into notice or use: *resurrect an old custom.* [Back-formation from RESURRECTION.]

res·ur·rec·tion (rĕz′ə-rĕk′shən) *n.* **1.** A revival; rebirth. **2. Resurrection. a.** The rising again of Christ on the third day after the Crucifixion. **b.** The rising again of the dead at the Last Judgment. [Middle English *resurreccion,* from Old French *resurrection,* from Late Latin *resurrēctiō,* from Latin *resurgere* : *re-,* again + *surgere,* to rise.] —**res′ur·rec′tion·al** *adj.*

re·sus·ci·tate (rĭ-sŭs′ĭ-tāt′) *v.* **-tat·ed, -tat·ing.** —*tr.v.* To restore consciousness, vigor, or life to. —*intr.v.* To return to life or consciousness; revive. [From Latin *resuscitāre,* to revive : *re-,* again + *suscitāre,* to raise, stir up.] —**re·sus′ci·ta′tion** *n.* —**re·sus′ci·ta′tive** *adj.* —**re·sus′ci·ta′tor** *n.*

ret (rĕt) *tr.v.* **ret·ted, ret·ting.** To moisten or soak so as to soften and separate the fibers by partial rotting. [Middle English *reten.*]

re·tail (rē′tāl′) *n.* The sale of commodities to the general public. —*adv.* At a retail price. —*tr.v.* **1.** To sell at retail. **2.** (*also* rĭ-tāl′). To tell; repeat. —*intr.v.* To make retail sales. —See Syns at **sell.** [Middle English *retaile,* division, from Old French *retaille,* from *retailler,* to cut up.] —**re′tail′er** *n.*

re·tain (rĭ-tān′) *tr.v.* **1.** To keep or hold in possession or use: *retained his post.* **2.** To keep in one's service or pay, esp. by paying a fee. [Middle English *reteinen,* from Old French *retenir,* from Latin *retinēre* : *re-,* back + *tenēre,* to hold.] —**re·tain′ment** *n.*

re·tain·er[1] (rĭ-tā′nər) *n.* **1.** A person or thing that retains. **2. a.** An attendant in a feudal household. **b.** A servant.

re·tain·er[2] (rĭ-tā′nər) *n.* A fee paid to engage the services of a professional, such as a lawyer. [Middle English *reteyner,* the act of withholding.]

re·take (rē-tāk′) *tr.v.* **-took** (-tōōk′), **-tak·en** (-tā′kən), **-tak·ing. 1.** To take again. **2.** To photograph again. —*n.* (rē′tāk′). A rephotographed scene. —**re·tak′er** *n.*

re·tal·i·ate (rĭ-tăl′ē-āt′) *v.* **-at·ed, -at·ing.** —*intr.v.* To return like for like: *retaliate against an attack.* —*tr.v.* To pay back (an injury) in kind. [From Latin *retaliāre* : *re-,* back + *tāliō,* punishment in kind.] —**re·tal′i·a′tion** *n.* —**re·tal′i·a·to′ry** (-ə-tôr′ē, -tōr′ē) *adj.*

re·tard (rĭ-tärd′) *tr.v.* **1.** To slow the progress of; impede or delay. **2.** To obstruct the progress of; hinder. —See Syns at **delay** and **hinder.** —*n.* *Mus.* A slackening of tempo. [Middle English *retarden,* from Old French *retarder,* from Latin *retardāre* : *re-,* back, + *tardāre,* to delay, from *tardus,* slow.]

re·tar·da·tion (rē′tär-dā′shən) *n.* **1.** The act or the condition of being retarded. **2.** The amount or time of delay or hindrance. **3.** Mental deficiency.

re·tard·ed (rĭ-tär′dĭd) *adj.* Slow or backward in mental or emotional development.

retch (rĕch) *intr.v.* To try to vomit. [Ult. from Old English *hræcan,* to cough up phlegm.]

re·ten·tion (rĭ-tĕn′shən) *n.* **1.** The act of retaining or the condition of being retained. **2.** The capacity or ability to retain. [Middle English *retencion,* from Old French, from Latin *retentiō,* from *retinēre,* to retain.]

re·ten·tive (rĭ-tĕn′tĭv) *adj.* Having the ability or capacity to retain. —**re·ten′tive·ly** *adv.* —**re·ten′tive·ness** *n.*

ret·i·cent (rĕt′ĭ-sənt) *adj.* **1.** Disinclined to speak out; quiet. **2.** Restrained or reserved in style. [Latin *reticēns,* pres. part. of *reticēre,* to keep silent : *re-* + *tacēre,* to be silent.] —**ret′i·cence** *n.* —**ret′i·cent·ly** *adv.*

re·tic·u·lar (rĭ-tĭk′yə-lər) *adj.* **1.** Netlike. **2.** Intricate.
re·tic·u·late (rĭ-tĭk′yə-lĭt, -lāt′) *adj.* Resembling or forming a network. —*v.* (-lāt′) **-lat·ed, -lat·ing.** —*tr.v.* To make a network. —*intr.v.* To form a network. —**re·tic′u·la′tion** *n.*
ret·i·cule (rĕt′ĭ-kyōōl′) *n.* A woman's drawstring handbag or purse. [French *réticule*, from Latin *rēticulum*, net.]
re·tic·u·lum (rĭ-tĭk′yə-ləm) *n., pl.* **-la** (-lə). **1.** A netlike formation or structure. **2.** *Zool.* The second compartment of the stomach of ruminant mammals. [Latin *rēticulum*, net.]
ret·i·na (rĕt′n-ə) *n., pl.* **-nas** or **ret·i·nae** (rĕt′n-ē′). A delicate multilayer light-sensitive membrane that lines the inside of the eyeball and is connected to the brain by the optic nerve. [Middle English *rethina*, from Medieval Latin *retina*, poss. from Latin *rēte*, net.] —**ret′i·nal** *adj.*
ret·i·nue (rĕt′n-ōō′, -yōō′) *n.* A group of attendants that accompany a person of rank. [Middle English *retenue*, from Old French, from *retenir*, to retain.]
re·tire (rĭ-tīr′) *intr.v.* **-tired, -tir·ing.** **1.** To withdraw from one's business or occupation. **2.** To go to bed. **3.** To go away, as for seclusion. **4.** To go back or away; retreat. —*tr.v.* **1.** To cause to withdraw from service or from a position or occupation. **2.** To withdraw from action. **3.** To take out of circulation. **4.** *Baseball.* To put out (a batter). [Old French *retirer* : *re-*, back + *tirer*, to draw.]
re·tire·ment (rĭ-tīr′mənt) *n.* **1.** The act of retiring. **2.** The condition of being retired, esp. from an occupation.
re·tir·ing (rĭ-tīr′ĭng) *adj.* Seeking to avoid attention or notice; shy. —**re·tir′ing·ly** *adv.* —**re·tir′ing·ness** *n.*
re·tool (rē-tōōl′) *tr.v.* To provide with new tools, machinery, or equipment.
re·tort¹ (rĭ-tôrt′) *tr.v.* **1.** To reply to, esp. in a quick, direct manner. **2.** To return in kind; pay back. —*intr.v.* To make an often quick, clever reply. —See Syns at **answer.** —*n.* A quick, clever reply, esp. one that turns the first speaker's words to his own disadvantage. [Latin *retortus*, past part. of *retorquēre*, to bend back : *re-*, back + *torquēre*, to bend.]
re·tort² (rĭ-tôrt′, rē′tôrt′) *n.* A laboratory vessel used for distilling or decomposing substances by heat. [Old French *retorte*, from Medieval Latin *retorta*, "bent back" (from the shape of the vessel), from *retorquēre*, to bend back.]

retort²

re·touch (rē-tŭch′) *tr.v.* **1.** To touch up. **2.** *Photog.* To change, esp. by removing flaws. —**re′touch′** *n.* —**re·touch′er** *n.*
re·trace (rē-trās′) *tr.v.* **-traced, -trac·ing.** To trace again.
re·tract (rĭ-trăkt′) *tr.v.* **1.** To take back; recant: *retract an accusation.* **2.** To draw back or in. [Middle English *retracten*, from Old French *retracter*, from Latin *retractāre*, to handle again, freq. of *retrahere*, to draw back : *re-*, back, again + *trahere*, to draw.] —**re·tract′a·ble** or **re·tract′i·ble** *adj.*
re·trac·tile (rĭ-trăk′tĭl, -tīl′) *adj.* Capable of being drawn back or in.
re·trac·tion (rĭ-trăk′shən) *n.* **1.** Something that retracts a previous statement. **2.** The act of retracting. **3.** The condition of being retracted.
re·trac·tor (rĭ-trăk′tər) *n.* **1.** Someone or something that retracts. **2.** *Anat.* A muscle that retracts an organ or part.
re·tread (rē-trĕd′) *tr.v.* **-tread·ed, -tread·ing.** To fit a new tread on. —*n.* (rē′trĕd′). A retreaded tire.
re·treat (rĭ-trēt′) *n.* **1.** The act of withdrawing, esp. from danger or difficulty. **2.** A safe, secluded place; refuge. **3.** A

period of retirement, esp. for religious meditation. **4. a.** The withdrawal of a military force from a dangerous position or from an enemy attack. **b.** The signal for such a withdrawal. **5.** *Mil.* A trumpet call that signals the lowering of the flag. —*intr.v.* To make a retreat; withdraw. [Middle English *retret*, from Old French *retrait*, from *retraire*, to draw back, from Latin *retrahere*, to retract.]
re·trench (rĭ-trĕnch′) *tr.v.* To cut down; reduce: *retrench expenses.* —*intr.v.* To reduce expenses; economize. [Obs. French *retrencher*, from Old French *retrenchier* : *re-* + *trenchier*, to cut off.] —**re·trench′ment** *n.*
re·tri·al (rē-trī′əl) *n.* A second trial.
ret·ri·bu·tion (rĕt′rə-byōō′shən) *n.* Something given, esp. as punishment. [Middle English *retribucion*, from Old French *retribution*, from Late Latin *retribūtiō*, from Latin *retribuere*, to pay back : *re-*, back + *tribuere*, to pay.]
re·trib·u·tive (rĭ-trĭb′yə-tĭv) *adj.* Also **re·trib·u·to·ry** (-tôr′ē, -tōr′ē). Of, relating to, or characterized by retribution.
re·triev·al (rĭ-trē′vəl) *n.* **1.** The act or process of retrieving. **2.** The possibility of retrieving: *beyond retrieval.*
re·trieve (rĭ-trēv′) *tr.v.* **-trieved, -triev·ing.** **1.** To get or bring back, as to a former location or condition; regain: *retrieve a ball; retrieve a position of power.* **2.** To make good; remedy: *retrieve an error.* **3.** To find and carry back (game that has been shot), as a hunting dog does. —See Syns at **recover.** [Middle English *retreven*, to find again, from Old French *retrover* : *re-*, again + *trover*, to find.] —**re·triev′a·ble** *adj.* —**re·triev′a·bly** *adv.*
re·triev·er (rĭ-trē′vər) *n.* **1.** Someone or something that retrieves. **2.** Any of several breeds of dog developed and trained to retrieve game.
retro-. A prefix meaning backward or back: *retrorocket.* [From Latin *retrō*, backward, behind.]
ret·ro·ac·tive (rĕt′rō-ăk′tĭv) *adj.* Effective on or applying to an earlier date: *a retroactive pay increase.* —**ret′ro·ac′tive·ly** *adv.* —**ret′ro·ac·tiv′i·ty** *n.*
ret·ro·cede (rĕt′rō-sēd′) *intr.v.* **-ced·ed, -ced·ing.** To go back; recede. [Latin *retrōcēdere*, to go back.] —**ret′ro·ces′sion** (-sĕsh′ən) *n.*
ret·ro·flex (rĕt′rə-flĕks′) *adj.* Also **ret·ro·flexed** (-flĕkst′). **1.** Bent, curved, or turned backward. **2.** *Phonet.* Pronounced with the tip of the tongue turned back against the roof of the mouth. [New Latin *retroflexus*, from Late Latin *retrōflectere*, to bend back.] —**ret′ro·flex′ion** or **ret′ro·flec′tion** *n.*
ret·ro·grade (rĕt′rə-grād′) *adj.* **1.** Moving or tending backward; reversed. **2.** Reverting to an inferior condition. —*intr.v.* **-grad·ed, -grad·ing.** **1.** To move or seem to move backward. **2.** To decline to an inferior condition. [Middle English, from Latin *retrōgradus*.]
ret·ro·gress (rĕt′rə-grĕs′, rĕt′rə-grĕs′) *intr.v.* To return or move backward, esp. to an earlier or less complex condition. [Latin *retrōgressus*, past part. of *retrogradī*, to go backward.] —**ret′ro·gres′sion** *n.* —**ret′ro·gres′sive** *adj.* —**ret′ro·gres′sive·ly** *adv.*
ret·ro·rock·et (rĕt′rō-rŏk′ĭt) *n.* A rocket engine used to slow, stop, or reverse the motion of an aircraft, missile or spacecraft.
ret·ro·spect (rĕt′rə-spĕkt′) *n.* A contemplation of things in the past. [Latin *retrōspectus*, past part. of *retrōspicere*, to look back at.] —**ret′ro·spec′tion** *n.* —**ret′ro·spec′tive** *adj.* —**ret′ro·spec′tive·ly** *adv.*
re·turn (rĭ-tûrn′) *intr.v.* To go or come back. —*tr.v.* **1.** To send, put, or carry back; restore. **2.** To give or send back, as in payment, exchange, or response. **3.** To bring in (profit); yield: *stocks that returned ten percent.* **4.** To send back or reflect. **5.** To deliver (a verdict). **6.** To re-elect to an office or position. —*n.* **1.** The act of returning. **2.** Something that is returned. **3.** A periodic recurrence. **4.** A reply; response; answer. **5.** A profit or yield. **6.** An official report: *a tax return.* **7.** Of, relating to, or involving a return: *return trip.* **8.** Given, sent, or done in return: *a return visit.* [Middle English *retournen*, from Old French *retorner* : Latin *re-*, back + *tornāre*, to turn in a lathe, from *tornus*, lathe, from Greek *tornos*.] —**re·turn′er** *n.*
Syns: return, recur, revert *v.* **Core meaning:** To come back to a former condition (*a disease that returned*). See also Syns at **answer** and **restore.**
re·turn·a·ble (rĭ-tûr′nə-bəl) *adj.* **1.** Capable of return. **2.** Re-

quired to be returned: *a writ returnable in five days.*

re·turn·ee (rĭ-tûr'nē') *n.* Someone who has returned, as from a voyage or military service.

re·un·ion (rē-yōōn'yən) *n.* **1.** The act or an example of re-uniting. **2.** A reuniting of the members of a group: *a family reunion.*

re·u·nite (rē'yōō-nīt') *v.* **-nit·ed, -nit·ing.** *—tr.v.* To bring together again. *—intr.v.* To come together again.

rev (rĕv) *n. Informal.* A revolution, as of an engine or motor. *—v.* **revved, rev·ving.** *Informal.* *—tr.v.* To increase the speed of: *rev up the motor.*

re·val·u·ate (rē-văl'yōō-āt') *tr.v.* To make a new valuation of. *—re·val'u·a'tion* *n.*

re·vamp (rē-vămp') *tr.v.* To make over; revise.

re·veal (rĭ-vēl') *tr.v.* **1.** To make known: *reveal a secret.* **2.** To display or show clearly. [Middle English *revelen,* from Old French *reveler,* from Latin *revēlāre* : *re-,* back, + *vēlum,* a veil.] *—re·veal'a·ble* *adj.* *—re·veal'er* *n.*

rev·eil·le (rĕv'ə-lē) *n.* A signal, as on a drum or bugle, given early in the morning to awaken and summon persons in a camp or garrison. [French *réveillez,* imper. of *réveiller,* to rouse, awaken, from Old French *reveiller.*]

rev·el (rĕv'əl) *intr.v.* **-eled** or **-elled, -el·ing** or **-el·ling.** **1.** To take part in unrestrained festivities. **2.** To take great pleasure or satisfaction: *He reveled in his new freedom.* *—n.* An unrestrained party or celebration. [Middle English *revelen,* from Old French *reveler,* to make noise, to rebel, from Latin *rebellāre,* to rebel.] *—rev'el·er* or *rev'el·ler* *n.*

rev·e·la·tion (rĕv'ə-lā'shən) *n.* **1.** Something that is revealed, esp. something surprising. **2.** An act of revealing. **3.** An act of revealing divine truth. **4. Revelation.** See table at **Bible.** [Middle English, from Old French, from Late Latin *revēlātiō,* from Latin *revēlāre,* to reveal.]

rev·el·ry (rĕv'əl-rē) *n., pl.* **-ries.** Unrestrained, sometimes boisterous, merrymaking. —See Syns at **gaiety.**

re·venge (rĭ-vĕnj') *tr.v.* **-venged, -veng·ing. 1.** To inflict punishment in return for: *revenge a murder.* **2.** To take vengeance on behalf of: *They revenged themselves by making his crimes public.* *—n.* **1.** The act of revenging. **2.** A desire for revenge. **3.** An opportunity to get even. —See Usage note at **avenge.** [Middle English *revengen,* from Old French *revenger,* from Late Latin *revindicāre,* to avenge : Latin *re-* + *vindicāre,* to vindicate.]

re·venge·ful (rĭ-vĕnj'fəl) *adj.* Full of revenge; seeking revenge. *—re·venge'ful·ly* *adv.* *—re·venge'ful·ness* *n.*

rev·e·nue (rĕv'ə-nōō', -nyōō') *n.* **1.** The income of a government collected for the payment of public expenses. **2.** Income from property or investments. [Middle English, a return, from Old French, from *revenir,* to return, from Latin *revenīre* : *re-,* back + *venīre,* to come.]

re·ver·ber·ate (rĭ-vûr'bə-rāt') *v.* **-at·ed, -at·ing.** *—intr.v.* To echo; resound. [From Latin *reverberāre,* to repel : *re-,* back + *verberāre,* to whip, from *verbera,* whips, rods.] *—re·ver'ber·a'tion* *n.* *—re·ver'ber·a·to·ry* (-rə-tôr'ē, -tōr'ē) or *re·ver'ber·ant* or *re·ver'ber·a'tive* *adj.*

re·vere[1] (rĭ-vîr') *tr.v.* **-vered, -ver·ing.** To regard with great respect or devotion. [Latin *reverērī* : *re-* + *verērī,* to respect.] *—re·ver'er* *n.*

re·vere[2] (rĭ-vîr', -vâr') *n.* Var. of **revers.**

rev·er·ence (rĕv'ər-əns) *n.* **1.** Profound honor and respect. **2.** An act of respect, such as a bow or curtsy. **3. Reverence.** A title of respect for a clergyman. *—tr.v.* **-enced, -enc·ing.** To feel reverence for.

rev·er·end (rĕv'ər-ənd) *adj.* **1.** Worthy of reverence. **2.** Often **Reverend.** Designating a member of the clergy. *—n. Informal.* A member of the clergy. [Middle English, from Old French, from Latin *reverendus,* from *reverērī,* to revere.]

rev·er·ent (rĕv'ər-ənt) *adj.* Feeling or showing reverence. *—rev'er·ent·ly* *adv.*

rev·er·en·tial (rĕv'ə-rĕn'shəl) *adj.* Expressing or feeling reverence; reverent. *—rev'er·en'tial·ly* *adv.*

rev·er·ie (rĕv'ə-rē) Also **rev·er·y.** *n.* **1.** Abstracted thought. **2.** A daydream. [Middle English, from Old French, from *rever,* to dream.]

re·vers (rĭ-vîr', -vâr') *n., pl.* **revers.** Also **re·vere.** A lapel, esp. on a woman's garment. [French, from Old French, reverse.]

re·ver·sal (rĭ-vûr'səl) *n.* **1.** An act or instance of reversing. **2.** A change from better to worse.

re·verse (rĭ-vûrs') *adj.* **1.** Turned backward in position, direction, or order; opposite; contrary. **2.** Causing backward movement: *a reverse gear.* *—n.* **1.** The opposite or contrary of something. **2.** The back or rear of something, esp. a coin. **3.** A change to an opposite position, condition, or direction. **4.** A change in fortune from better to worse; setback. **5.** A mechanism for reversing movement, as a gear in an automobile. *—v.* **-versed, -vers·ing.** *—tr.v.* **1.** To turn to the opposite direction or position. **2.** To turn inside out or upside down. **3.** To exchange the positions of; transpose. **4.** *Law.* To revoke or annul: *reverse a decision.* **5.** To cause to move or go in an opposite direction. *—intr.v.* **1.** To turn or move in the opposite direction. **2.** To reverse the action of an engine. [Middle English *revers,* from Old French, from Latin *reversus,* past part. of *revertere,* to revert.] *—re·vers'er* *n.* *—re·verse'ly* *adv.*

Syns: *reverse, invert, transpose* *v.* Core meaning: To change to the opposite position, course, or direction (*reversed the order of the pictures in the album*).

re·vers·i·ble (rĭ-vûr'sə-bəl) *adj.* **1.** Capable of being reversed. **2.** Capable of being worn or used with either side out: *a reversible jacket.* **3.** *Chem. & Physics.* Capable of successively assuming or producing either of two states. *—n.* A reversible garment. *—re·vers'i·bil'i·ty* *n.* *—re·vers'i·bly* *adv.*

re·ver·sion (rĭ-vûr'zhən) *n.* **1.** A return, as to a former condition or belief. **2.** A turning away or in the opposite direction; reversal. **3. a.** The reappearance of a trait after several generations of absence. **b.** An organism in which such a reappearance occurs. **4.** The right to succeed to an estate.

re·ver·sion·ar·y (rĭ-vûr'zhə-nĕr'ē) *adj.* Of, relating to, or involving the reversion of an estate.

re·vert (rĭ-vûrt') *intr.v.* **1.** To return to a former condition, practice, or belief. **2.** *Law.* To go back to the possession of a former owner or his heirs. —See Syns at **return.** [Middle English *reverten,* from Old French *revertir,* from Latin *revertere,* to turn back : *re-,* back + *vertere,* to turn.] *—re·vert'er* *n.* *—re·vert'i·ble* *adj.*

rev·er·y (rĕv'ə-rē) *n., pl.* **-ries.** Var. of **reverie.**

re·vet (rĭ-vĕt') *tr.v.* **-vet·ted, -vet·ting.** To provide with a facing, as of stone or masonry. [French *revêtir,* from Old French *revestir,* to clothe again.]

re·vet·ment (rĭ-vĕt'mənt) *n.* **1.** A facing, as of masonry, used to support an embankment. **2.** A barricade for protection against explosives.

revetment

re·view (rĭ-vyōō') *tr.v.* **1.** To look over; examine again. **2.** To consider retrospectively; look back on. **3.** To give a critical report on: *review a movie.* **4.** *Law.* To examine (an action or determination) again, esp. in a higher court. **5.** To conduct a formal inspection of: *reviewed the squadron.* *—intr.v.* **1.** To go over or restudy material. **2.** To act as a reviewer, as for a newspaper. *—n.* **1.** A reexamination or reconsideration. **2.** A summary or survey. **3.** The act of restudying. **4.** An inspection or examination for the purpose of evaluation. **5. a.** A critical estimate of a work or performance. **b.** A periodical devoted primarily to critical reviews. **6.** A formal military inspection. **7.** *Law.* A reexamination of an action or determination, usu. conducted by a higher court. [From Old French *revoir* : *re-,*

ă pat	ā pay	â care	ä father	ĕ pet	ē be	hw which
ŏŏ took	ōō boot	ou out	th thin	th this	ŭ cut	

ĭ pit   ī tie   î pier   ŏ pot   ō toe   ô paw, for   oi noise
û urge   zh vision   ə about, item, edible, gallop, circus

again + *voir*, to see, from Latin *vidēre*.] —**re·view′a·ble** *adj.*

re·view·er (rĭ-vyoō′ər) *n.* A person who reviews, esp. a newspaper or magazine critic.

re·vile (rĭ-vīl′) *v.* **-viled, -vil·ing.** —*tr.v.* To subject to abusive language. —*intr.v.* To use abusive language. [Middle English *revilen,* from Old French *reviler* : *re-* (intensifier) + *vil,* vile.] —**re·vile′ment** *n.* —**re·vil′er** *n.*

re·vise (rĭ-vīz′) *tr.v.* **-vised, -vis·ing.** **1.** To review in order to improve or bring up to date. **2.** To change or modify. [French *réviser,* from Latin *revīsere,* to look back.] —**re·vis′er** or **re·vi′sor** *n.*

re·vi·sion (rĭ-vĭzh′ən) *n.* **1.** The act or procedure of revising. **2.** A revised version. —**re·vi′sion·ar·y** (-ə-nĕr′ē) *adj.*

re·vi·sion·ism (rĭ-vĭzh′ə-nĭz′əm) *n.* A revision of Marxist doctrine, in which evolutionary rather than revolutionary methods are advocated. —**re·vi′sion·ist** *n. & adj.*

re·vi·tal·ize (rē-vīt′l-īz′) *tr.v.* **-ized, -iz·ing.** To give new life or vigor to. —**re·vi′tal·i·za′tion** *n.*

re·viv·al (rĭ-vī′vəl) *n.* **1. a.** The act or process of reviving. **b.** The condition of being revived. **2.** A new presentation, as of a play or motion picture. **3.** A meeting or series of meetings for the purpose of reawakening religious faith or for gaining converts.

re·viv·al·ism (rĭ-vī′və-lĭz′əm) *n.* The spirit or activities characteristic of religious revivals.

re·viv·al·ist (rĭ-vī′və-lĭst) *n.* A person who conducts religious revivals.

re·vive (rĭ-vīv′) *v.* **-vived, -viv·ing.** —*tr.v.* **1.** To bring back to life or consciousness. **2.** To impart new health or vigor to. **3.** To restore to use, currency or activity, or notice. —*intr.v.* **1.** To return to life or consciousness. **2.** To regain health, vigor, or good spirits. **3.** To return to use, currency, or notice. —See Syns at **restore.** [Middle English *reviven,* from Old French *revivre,* from Late Latin *revīvere* : Latin *re-,* again + *vīvere,* to live.] —**re·viv′er** *n.*

re·viv·i·fy (rĭ-vĭv′ə-fī′) *tr.v.* **-fied, -fy·ing.** To give new life to. —**re·viv′i·fi·ca′tion** *n.*

rev·o·ca·ble (rĕv′ə-kə-bəl) *adj.* Capable of being revoked.

re·voke (rĭ-vōk′) *v.* **-voked, -vok·ing.** —*tr.v.* To make void by withdrawing or canceling; annul: *revoke a license.* [Middle English *revoken,* from Old French *revoquer,* from Latin *revocāre,* to call back : *re-,* back + *vocāre,* to call.] —**rev′o·ca′tion** *n.* —**re·vok′er** *n.*

re·volt (rĭ-vōlt′) *intr.v.* **1.** To attempt to overthrow the authority of the state; rebel. **2.** To oppose or refuse to accept something: *revolt against high taxes.* —*tr.v.* To fill with disgust; repel. —See Syns at **repel.** —*n.* **1.** An uprising, esp. against state authority; rebellion. **2.** An act of opposition or rejection. **3.** The condition of opposition or rebellion: *be in revolt.* —See Syns at **rebellion.** [Old French *revolter,* from Italian *rivoltare,* from Latin *revolvere,* to roll back, revolve.] —**re·volt′er** *n.*

re·volt·ing (rĭ-vōl′tĭng) *adj.* Extremely disgusting; repulsive; abhorrent. —See Syns at **unspeakable.** —**re·volt′ing·ly** *adv.*

rev·o·lu·tion (rĕv′ə-loō′shən) *n.* **1. a.** Movement in an orbit around a point, esp. as distinguished from rotation on an axis. **b.** A spinning or rotation about an axis. **c.** A single complete cycle of motion about a point in a closed path. **2.** A sudden or momentous change in any situation: *the revolution in physics.* **3.** A sudden political overthrow or seizure of power brought about from within a given system. [Middle English *revolucioun,* from Old French *revolution,* from Late Latin *revolūtiō,* from Latin *revolūtus,* past part. of *revolvere,* to revolve.]

rev·o·lu·tion·ar·y (rĕv′ə-loō′shə-nĕr′ē) *adj.* **1.** Pertaining to revolution: *revolutionary slogans.* **2.** Promoting revolution; radical. —*n., pl.* **-ies.** A person who is engaged in or promotes revolution.

Revolutionary War. The American Revolution.

rev·o·lu·tion·ist (rĕv′ə-loō′shə-nĭst) *n.* A revolutionary.

rev·o·lu·tion·ize (rĕv′ə-loō′shə-nīz′) *tr.v.* **-ized, -iz·ing.** **1.** To change radically or drastically. **2.** To cause to undergo a political or social revolution. **3.** To fill with revolutionary principles.

re·volve (rĭ-vŏlv′) *v.* **-volved, -volving.** —*intr.v.* **1.** To orbit a central point. **2.** To turn on an axis; rotate. **3.** To have as a center: *His life revolves around his job.* **4.** To recur period-

ically. —*tr.v.* **1.** To cause to revolve. **2.** To think over; ponder: *revolve a question in one's mind.* [Middle English *revolven,* from Latin *revolvere,* to roll back : *re-,* back + *volvere,* to roll.] —**re·volv′a·ble** *adj.*

re·volv·er (rĭ-vŏl′vər) *n.* A pistol with a revolving cylinder that places the cartridges one at a time in a position to be fired.

re·vue (rĭ-vyoō′) *n.* A musical show consisting of satirical skits, songs, and dances. [French, from Old French, past part. of *revoir,* to review.]

re·vul·sion (rĭ-vŭl′shən) *n.* **1.** A sudden, strong feeling of disgust or loathing. **2.** A withdrawing or turning away from something. [Latin *revulsiō,* from *revulsus,* past part. of *revellere,* to pull back : *re-,* back + *vellere,* to pull.] —**re·vul′sive** *adj.*

re·ward (rĭ-wôrd′) *n.* Something, such as money, given or offered for some special service, such as the return of a lost article or the capture of a criminal. —*tr.v.* **1.** To give a reward to. **2.** To give a reward in return for: *rewarded his deed with a medal.* [Middle English *rewarden,* from Norman French *rewarder,* to regard : *re-* + *warder,* to watch over.] —**re·ward′a·ble** *adj.* —**re·ward′er** *n.*

re·word (rē-wûrd′) *tr.v.* To state in different words.

re·work (rē-wûrk′) *tr.v.* **1.** To work over again; revise. **2.** To subject to a repeated or new process. —*n.* (rē′wûrk′). Something that has been reworked: *That is just a rework of an old design.*

re·write (rē-rīt′) *tr.v.* **-wrote** (-rōt′), **-writ·ten** (-rĭt′n), **-writ·ing.** **1.** To write again, esp. in a different or improved form. **2.** To write (an account given by a reporter) in a form suitable for publishing. —**re·writ′er** *n.*

re·zone (rē-zōn′) *tr.v.* **-zoned, -zon·ing.** To change the zoning of.

Rh The symbol for the element rhodium.

rhap·so·dize (răp′sə-dīz′) *v.* **-dized, -diz·ing.** —*intr.v.* To express oneself rhapsodically.

rhap·so·dy (răp′sə-dē) *n., pl.* **-dies.** **1.** Excessively enthusiastic expression of feeling in speech or writing. **2.** *Mus.* A composition of irregular form and an often improvisatory character. [Latin *rhapsōdia,* epic poem, from Greek *rhapsōidia,* from *rhapsōidos,* a reciter of poems : *rhaptein,* to string together + *ōidē,* ode, song.] —**rhap·sod·ic** (răp-sŏd′ĭk) *adj.* —**rhap·sod′i·cal·ly** *adv.*

rhe·a (rē′ə) *n.* Any of several flightless, three-toed South American birds of the genus *Rhea,* resembling the ostrich but somewhat smaller. [After *Rhea,* a Greek goddess.]

rhea
George Miksch Sutton

rhesus monkey

rhe·ni·um (rē′nē-əm) *n. Symbol* **Re** A rare dense silvery-white metallic element used for electrical contacts and with tungsten for high-temperature thermocouples. Atomic number 75; atomic weight 186.2; melting point 3,180°C; boiling point 5,627°C; specific gravity 21.02; valences 1, 2, 3, 4, 5, 6, 7. [From Latin *Rhēnus,* Rhine.]

rhe·o·stat (rē′ə-stăt′) *n.* A resistor whose value can be continuously varied between two extremes, used to control the flow of current in an electric current. [Greek *rheos,* current + -STAT.] —**rhe·o·stat′ic** *adj.*

Rh·e·sus factor (rē′səs). **Rh factor.**

rhe·sus monkey (rē′səs). A brownish Indian monkey, *Macaca mulatta,* often used in biological research. [From Latin *Rhēsus,* a mythological king of Thrace.]

rhet·o·ric (rĕt′ər-ĭk) *n.* **1.** The study of the elements, as structure or style, used in writing and speaking. **2.** The art of effective expression and the persuasive use of language. **3.** Affected or pretentious language. [Middle English *rethorik*, from Old French *rethorique*, from Latin *rhētorica*, from Greek *rhētorikē (tekhnē)*, "rhetorical (art)," from *rhētōr*, public speaker, orator.]

rhe·tor·i·cal (rĭ-tôr′ĭ-kəl, -tŏr′-) *adj.* **1.** Given to or using rhetoric. **2.** Of, relating to, or involving rhetoric. —**rhe·tor′i·cal·ly** *adv.*

rhetorical question. A question to which no answer is expected.

rhet·o·ri·cian (rĕt′ə-rĭsh′ən) *n.* **1.** An expert in or teacher of rhetoric. **2.** An orator. **3.** A person given to affected or pretentious language.

rheum (rōōm) *n.* A watery mucous discharge esp. from the eyes or nose. [Middle English *reume*, from Old French, from Latin *rheuma*, from Greek.] —**rheum′y** *adj.*

rheu·mat·ic (rōō-măt′ĭk) *adj.* Of, pertaining to, or afflicted with rheumatism. —*n.* A person afflicted with rheumatism. [Middle English *rewmatyk*, from Latin *rheumaticus*, troubled with rheum, from Greek *rheumatikos*, subject to rheum, from *rheuma*, rheum.]

rheumatic fever. A severe infectious disease occurring chiefly in children, characterized by fever and painful inflammation of the joints, and frequently resulting in permanent damage to the heart.

rheu·ma·tism (rōō′mə-tĭz′əm) *n.* Any of several diseased conditions of the muscles, tendons, joints, bones, or nerves, that cause pain and disability. [Latin *rheumatismus*, rheum, from Greek *rheumatismos*, from *rheuma*, rheum.]

rheu·ma·toid arthritis (rōō′mə-toid′). A chronic disease marked by stiffness and inflammation of the joints, weakness, loss of mobility, and deformity.

Rh factor. Any of several substances that are present in the red blood cells and are capable of causing a severe antigenic reaction. [From its occurrence in the blood of *rhesus monkeys*.]

rhine·stone (rīn′stōn′) *n.* An imitation diamond made of paste or glass. [After the *Rhine* river.]

Rhine wine (rīn). **1.** Any of several dry, white wines produced in the Rhine valley. **2.** Any of various light, dry wines.

rhi·ni·tis (rī-nī′tĭs) *n.* Inflammation of the nasal mucous membranes. [Greek *rhins*, nose + -ITIS.]

rhi·no (rī′nō) *n., pl.* **-nos.** *Informal.* A rhinoceros.

rhi·noc·er·os (rī-nŏs′ər-əs) *n., pl.* **rhinoceros** or **-os·es.** Any of several large, thick-skinned, herbivorous mammals of the family Rhinocerotidae, of Africa and Asia, with one or two upright horns on the snout. [Middle English *rinoceros*, from Latin *rhīnocerōs*, from Greek *rhinokerōs* : *rhis*, nose + *keras*, horn.]

rhinoceros

rhizo- or **rhiz-.** A prefix meaning a root: *rhizoid.* [From Greek *rhiza*, root.]

rhi·zo·bi·um (rī-zō′bē-əm) *n., pl.* **-bi·a** (-bē-ə). Any of various nitrogen-fixing bacteria of the genus *Rhizobium* that form nodules on the roots of leguminous plants such as clover and beans. [RHIZO- + Greek *bios*, life.]

rhi·zoid (rī′zoid′) *adj.* Rootlike. —*n.* A slender, rootlike filament by which mosses, lichens, liverworts, and ferns absorb nourishment and are attached to the soil or a rock surface. —**rhi·zoi′dal** *adj.*

rhi·zome (rī′zōm′) *n.* A rootlike plant stem that grows under or along the ground and sends out roots below and leaves or shoots above, from *rhiza*, root.]

rhi·zo·pod (rī′zə-pŏd′) *n.* Any protozoan of the class or subclass Rhizopoda, such as an amoeba or radiolarian, characteristically moving and taking in food by means of pseudopodia.

rhi·zo·pus (rī′zə-pəs) *n.* Any of various often destructive fungi of the genus *Rhizopus*, such as *R. nigricans*, the common bread mold. [RHIZO- + Greek *pous*, foot.]

Rh negative. Lacking an Rh factor.

rho (rō) *n.* The 17th letter in the Greek alphabet written P, ρ. [Greek *rhō*.]

Rhode Island Red (rōd). An American breed of domestic fowls with dark reddish-brown feathers.

Rho·de·sian man (rō-dē′zhən). A fossil man found in south-central Africa, with a large, low skull, massive brow ridges, and skeletal bones similar to modern man.

rho·di·um (rō′dē-əm) *n. Symbol* **Rh** A hard, durable, silvery-white metallic element that is used to form high-temperature alloys with platinum. Atomic number 45; atomic weight 102.905; melting point 1,966°C; boiling point 3,727°C; specific gravity 12.41; valences 2, 3, 4, 5. [New Latin, "rose red" (from the color of its compounds), from Greek *rhodon*, rose.]

rho·do·den·dron (rō′də-dĕn′drən) *n.* Any evergreen shrub of the genus *Rhododendron* with clusters of pink, white, or purplish flowers. [Latin, from Greek : *rhodon*, rose + *dendron*, tree.]

rhom·bic (rŏm′bĭk) *adj.* **1.** Having the shape of a rhombus. **2.** *Crystallog.* Orthorhombic.

rhom·bo·he·dron (rŏm′bō-hē′drən) *n., pl.* **-drons** or **-dra** (-drə). A prism with six faces, each of which is a rhombus. [RHOMBUS + -HEDRON.] —**rhom′bo·he′dral** (-drəl) *adj.*

rhom·boid (rŏm′boid′) *n.* A parallelogram with oblique angles and unequal adjacent sides. —**rhom·boi′dal** (rŏm-boid′l) *adj.*

rhom·bus (rŏm′bəs) *n., pl.* **-bus·es** or **-bi** (-bī′). A parallelogram with usu. oblique angles and four equal sides. [Latin, from Greek *rhombos*.]

Rh positive. Containing an Rh factor.

rhu·barb (rōō′bärb′) *n.* **1.** Any of several plants of the genus *Rheum*, esp. *R. rhaponticum*, with long, green or reddish, acid leafstalks that are edible when sweetened and cooked. **2.** *Slang.* A noisy argument or fight. [Middle English *rubarbe*, from Old French, prob. from Medieval Latin *reubarbarum*, prob. alteration of *rha barbarum*, "foreign rhubarb".]

rhum·ba (rŭm′bə, rōōm′-) *n. & v.* Var. of **rumba.**

rhyme (rīm). Also **rime.** —*n.* **1.** Correspondence or repetition of sounds of two or more words, syllables, or the ends of lines of verse. **2.** Poetry or verse in rhyme. **3.** A word that corresponds with another in terminal sound. —*intr.v.* **rhymed, rhym·ing. 1.** To form a rhyme. **2.** To compose rhymes or verse. —*tr.v.* **1.** To put into rhyme. **2.** To use as a rhyme. [Middle English *rime*, from Medieval Latin *rithmus*, var. of Latin *rhythmus*, rhythm, from Greek *rhuthmos*.] —**rhym′er** *n.*

rhyme·ster (rīm′stər) *n.* Also **rime·ster.** A maker of light verse.

rhythm (rĭth′əm) *n.* **1.** A movement, action, or condition characterized by a regularly recurring element: *the rhythm of the tides.* **2.** *Mus.* **a.** A pattern formed by a series of notes or beats of different lengths and stresses. **b.** A particular pattern of this type: *a waltz rhythm.* **3.** *Poetry.* **a.** Metrical movement as regulated by the alternation of long and short or accented and unaccented syllables. **b.** A specific kind of metrical rhythm. [Old French *rhythme*, from Latin *rhythmus*, from Greek *rhuthmos*.]

rhyth·mic (rĭth′mĭk) or **rhyth·mi·cal** (-mĭ-kəl) *adj.* Pertaining to or having rhythm; recurring with measured regularity. —**rhyth′mi·cal·ly** *adv.*

ri·al·to (rē-ăl′tō) *n.* **1.** A theatrical district. **2.** A marketplace. [After *Rialto*, an island in Venice, Italy.]

ri·a·ta (rē-ä′tə, -ăt′ə) *n.* Also **re·a·ta.** A lasso. [Spanish *reata*.]

rib (rĭb) *n.* **1.** One of the paired, curved bones that are found in most vertebrates, extend from the spine to or toward the breastbone, and enclose the chest cavity. **2.** Something similar to a rib that shapes or supports: *the ribs of a ship's hull.* **3.** A cut of meat containing a rib. **4.** A raised ridge or wale in knitted material or in cloth. **5.** *Bot.* A major vein, as of a leaf. —*tr.v.* **ribbed, rib·bing. 1.** To shape, support, or provide with a rib or ribs. **2.** To make with ridges. **3.** *Slang.* To tease or make fun of. [Middle English, from Old English *ribb.*] —**ribbed** *adj.*

rib·ald (rĭb'əld) *adj.* Vulgar and indecent. [From Middle English *ribaud*, retainer of low rank, rascal, from Old French *ribauld*, from *riber*, to be wanton.] —**rib'ald·ry** *n.*

rib·and (rĭb'ənd) *n. Archaic.* A ribbon used esp. as a decoration. [Middle English *ryband*, var. of *riban.*]

rib·bing (rĭb'ĭng) *n.* **1.** Ribs in general. **2.** An arrangement of ribs, as in a boat. **3.** A ridged, knitted pattern as is often found on cuffs, necklines, and the lower edge of sweaters and knitwear shirts. **4.** *Slang.* An example of joking or teasing.

rib·bon (rĭb'ən) *n.* **1.** A narrow strip of fabric, finished at the edges and used for trimming or tying. **2.** Anything resembling a ribbon; a strip or stripe: *a ribbon of highway.* **3. ribbons.** Tatters; rags. **4.** An inked strip of cloth in a typewriter. **5. a.** A band of colored cloth given as a prize in a competition. **b.** A colored ribbon worn to indicate the award of a medal or decoration. [Middle English *riban*, from Old French.]

rib·bon·fish (rĭb'ən-fĭsh') *n., pl.* **ribbonfish** or **-fish·es.** Any of several saltwater fishes, chiefly of the genus *Trachipterus*, with long, narrow, compressed bodies.

ribbon worm. A nemertean.

rib cage. The enclosing structure formed by the ribs and the bones to which they are attached.

ri·bo·fla·vin (rī'bō-flā'vĭn) *n.* A crystalline orange-yellow pigment, $C_{17}H_{20}O_6N_4$, the principal growth-promoting factor in the vitamin B_2 complex. [RIBO(SE) + Latin *flāvus*, yellow.]

ri·bo·nu·cle·ic acid (rī'bō-nōō-klē'ĭk, -nyōō-). RNA. [RI-BO(SE) + NUCLEIC ACID.]

ri·bose (rī'bōs') *n.* A pentose sugar, $C_5H_{10}O_5$, that occurs as a component of nucleic acids. [From German *Ribonsäure*, an acid from which ribose is obtained.]

ri·bo·some (rī'bə-sōm') *n.* A spherical cytoplasmic RNA-containing particle active in the synthesis of protein. [RI-BO(SE) + -SOME.] —**ri'bo·som'al** *adj.*

rice (rīs) *n.* **1.** A cereal grass, *Oryza sativa*, that is cultivated extensively in warm climates for its edible seed. **2.** The starchy seed of the rice plant, used as a food. [Middle English *rys*, from Old French *ris*, from Italian *riso*, from Latin *orȳza*, from Greek *oruza.*]

rice·bird (rīs'bûrd') *n.* **1.** *Southern U.S.* The bobolink. **2.** Any of various birds that frequent rice fields.

rice paper. 1. A thin paper made chiefly from the pith of the rice-paper tree, a small tree of Eastern Asia of the ginseng family. **2.** A thin paper made from the straw of rice plants.

ric·er (rī'sər) *n.* A kitchen utensil in which soft foods are forced through small holes.

rich (rĭch) *adj.* **-er, -est. 1.** Possessing great material wealth. **2.** Having great worth or value: *a rich harvest.* **3.** Magnificent; sumptuous: *a rich brocade.* **4. a.** Having an abundant supply of something: *rich in tradition.* **b.** Abounding, esp. in natural resources: *a rich land.* **5.** Extremely productive. **6.** Containing a large amount of choice ingredients, as butter, sugar, or eggs: *a rich dessert.* **7. a.** Pleasantly full and mellow: *a rich tenor voice.* **b.** Warm and strong in color. **8.** Containing a large proportion of fuel to air: *a rich mixture.* **9.** *Informal.* Highly amusing. [Middle English *riche*, powerful, wealthy, from Old English *rīce.*] —**rich'ness** *n.*

Syns: rich, affluent, loaded (*Slang*), **moneyed, wealthy** *adj.* Core meaning: Having a large amount of money, land, or other material possessions (*a rich aristocrat*). See also Syns at **fertile** and **luxurious.**

rich·en (rĭch'ən) *tr.v.* To make rich or richer.

rich·es (rĭch'ĭz) *pl.n.* Valuable or precious possessions. [Middle English *richesse*, wealth, from Old French, from *riche*, powerful, rich, of Germanic orig.]

rich·ly (rĭch'lē) *adv.* **1.** In a rich manner. **2.** Fully; thoroughly: *richly satisfying.*

Rich·ter scale (rĭk'tər). A logarithmic scale ranging from 1 to 10, used to express the magnitude or total energy of an earthquake. [After Charles F. *Richter* (b. 1900), American seismologist.]

rick (rĭk) *n.* A stack, as of hay, esp. when covered or thatched for protection from the weather. —*tr.v.* To pile in ricks. [Middle English *reke*, from Old English *hrēac.*]

rick·ets (rĭk'ĭts) *n.* A disease of the young that results from a lack of vitamin D in the diet and is characterized by defective bone growth. [Var. of RACHITIS.]

rick·ett·si·a (rĭ-kĕt'sē-ə) *n., pl.* **-si·ae** (-sē-ē'). Any of various microorganisms of the genus *Rickettsia*, that cause various diseases, such as typhus. [After Howard T. *Ricketts* (1871–1910), American pathologist.] —**rick·ett'si·al** *adj.*

rick·et·y (rĭk'ĭ-tē) *adj.* **-i·er, -i·est. 1.** Likely to break or fall apart; shaky: *a rickety chair.* **2.** Feeble with age; infirm. **3.** Of or having rickets. [From RICKETS.]

rick·ey (rĭk'ē) *n., pl.* **-eys.** A drink of soda water, lime juice, sugar and usu. gin. [Prob. from the name *Rickey.*]

rick·rack (rĭk'răk') or **ric·rac** (rĭk'răk') *n.* A flat, narrow braid in zig-zag form, used as a trimming. [From RACK (to torture).]

rick·shaw or **rick·sha** (rĭk'shô') *n.* A jinriksha. [Short for JINRIKSHA.]

ric·o·chet (rĭk'ə-shā') *intr.v.* **-cheted** (-shād') or **-chet·ted** (-shĕt'ĭd), **-chet·ing** (-shā'ĭng) or **-chet·ting** (-shĕt'ĭng). To rebound from a surface. —*n.* A rebound from a surface. [French.]

ri·cot·ta (rĭ-kŏt'ə) *n.* An Italian soft cheese that resembles cottage cheese. [Italian, from Latin *recocta*, past part. of *recoquere*, to cook again : *re-*, again + *coquere*, to cook.]

ric·tus (rĭk'təs) *n.* A grimace. [Latin, from *ringī*, to gape.]

rid (rĭd) *tr.v.* **rid** or **rid·ded, rid·ding.** To make free: *rid the streets of litter.* [Middle English *ridden*, from Old Norse *rythja.*]

rid·dance (rĭd'ns) *n.* **1.** An act of ridding. **2.** A deliverance.

rid·den (rĭd'n) *v.* Past participle of **ride.** [Middle English *riden*, from Old English.]

rid·dle¹ (rĭd'l) *tr.v.* **-dled, -dling. 1.** To pierce with numerous holes; perforate: *riddle with bullets.* **2.** To put through a coarse sieve. **3.** To spread throughout: *a theory riddled with flaws.* —*n.* A coarse sieve, as for gravel. [Middle English *riddlen*, to sift, from *riddil*, sieve, from Old English *hriddel.*] —**rid'dler** *n.*

rid·dle² (rĭd'l) *n.* **1.** A puzzling question or statement requiring thought to answer or understand; conundrum. **2.** Someone or something perplexing. —*v.* **-dled, -dling.** —*tr.v.* To solve or explain. —*intr.v.* To speak in riddles. [Middle English *ridil*, from Old English *rǣdelse.*] —**rid'dler** *n.*

ride (rīd) *v.* **rode** (rōd), **rid·den** (rĭd'n), **rid·ing.** —*intr.v.* **1.** To be carried or conveyed, as in a vehicle or on horseback. **2. a.** To travel over a surface: *This car rides well.* **b.** To move or proceed. **3.** To float or move on or as if on water. **4.** To lie at anchor. **5.** To seem to float: *a star riding in the sky.* **6. a.** To be sustained or supported. **b.** To depend: *the outcome rides on the election.* **7.** To continue without interference: *We let the problem ride.* —*tr.v.* **1.** To sit on and drive or control: *ride a bike; ride a horse.* **2.** To move upon: *rode the waves.* **3.** To travel over, along, or through: *ride the highways.* **4.** To rest upon by overlapping; overlie. **5.** To take part in or do by riding: *He rode his last race.* **6.** To control or dominate. **7.** *Informal.* To tease or ridicule. —*phrasal verb.* **ride out.** To survive: *ride out a storm.* —*n.* **1.** An act of riding, as on an animal or in a vehicle. **2.** A path or way made for riding. **3.** Something, as at a fair or in an amusement park, that one rides for pleasure or excitement. [Middle English *riden*, from Old English *rīdan.*]

rid·er (rī'dər) *n.* **1.** Someone or something that rides. **2.** A clause added to a legislative bill. **3.** An amendment or addition to a document or record.

ridge (rĭj) *n.* **1.** The line formed by the junction of two sloping surfaces: *the ridge of a roof.* **2.** A long, narrow formation of hills or mountains. **3.** A long, narrow, or crested part, esp. of the body: *the ridge of the nose.* **4.** A raised strip of plowed ground. —*tr.v.* **ridged, ridg·ing.** To mark with, form into, or provide with ridges. [Middle English

---

ă pat   ā pay   â care   ä father   ĕ pet   ē be   hw which   ĭ pit   ī tie   î pier   ŏ pot   ō toe   ô paw, for   oi noise
ōō took   ōō boot   ou out   th thin   *th* this   ŭ cut   û urge   zh vision   ə about, item, edible, gallop, circus

rigge, back, ridge, from Old English *hrycg*.]

ridge·pole (rĭj′pōl′) *n.* **1.** A horizontal beam at the ridge of a roof, to which the upper ends of the rafters are attached. **2.** The horizontal pole at the top of a tent.

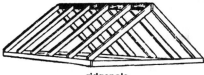

ridgepole

ridg·y (rĭj′ē) *adj.* **-i·er, -i·est.** Having or forming ridges.

rid·i·cule (rĭd′ĭ-kyōōl′) *n.* Words or actions intended to mock or deride. —*tr.v.* **-culed, -cul·ing.** To make fun of. [French, from Latin *rīdiculum*, joke, jest, from *rīdiculus*, laughable, from *rīdēre*, to laugh.] —**rid′i·cul′er** *n.*

> **Syns: ridicule, deride, gibe, mock, taunt, twit** *v. Core meaning:* To make fun of (*angry fans ridiculing the losing quarterback*).

ri·dic·u·lous (rĭ-dĭk′yə-ləs) *adj.* Deserving or inspiring ridicule; absurd or preposterous; silly or laughable. —See Syns at **laughable** and **outrageous.** —**ri·dic′u·lous·ly** *adv.* —**ri·dic′u·lous·ness** *n.*

rid·ing (rī′dĭng) *n.* **1.** The action of riding. **2.** Horseback riding.

riding habit. The costume worn by a horseback rider.

rife (rīf) *adj.* **rif·er, rif·est. 1.** Common or frequent in occurrence; widespread: *Disease was rife in the village.* **2.** Abounding; full: *rife with corruption.* [Middle English *rif*, from Old English *rȳfe*.]

riff (rĭf) *n. Mus.* A constantly repeated rhythmic phrase in jazz. [Perh. short for REFRAIN.]

rif·fle (rĭf′əl) *n.* **1.** A rocky shoal or sandbar lying just below the surface of a waterway. **2.** A ripple. —*tr.v.* **-fled, -fling. 1.** To stir up ripples on. **2.** To leaf or thumb through: *riffled the pages.* [Perh. blend of RUFFLE and RIPPLE.]

riff·raff (rĭf′răf′) *n.* **1.** Worthless or disreputable persons. **2.** Rubbish; trash. [Middle English *rif and raf,* "one and all," from Old French *rif et raf.*]

ri·fle¹ (rī′fəl) *n.* **1.** A firearm with a long barrel containing spiral grooves. **2.** An artillery piece with spiral grooves in the bore. —*tr.v.* **-fled, -fling.** To cut spiral grooves within. [From *rifle,* to cut spiral grooves, from Old French *rifler,* to file.]

ri·fle² (rī′fəl) *tr.v.* **-fled, -fling. 1.** To search with intent to steal. **2.** To ransack and steal. [Middle English *riflen,* from Old French *rifler,* to scratch, file, plunder.] —**ri′fler** *n.*

ri·fling (rī′flĭng) *n.* **1.** The process or operation of cutting spiral grooves, as in a rifle barrel. **2.** Spiral grooves cut in the bore of a gun.

rift (rĭft) *n.* **1. a.** A fault, as in a system of rock. **b.** A narrow break or crack in a rock. **c.** A narrow opening. **2.** A break in friendly relations. —*intr.v.* To split open. —*tr.v.* To cause to split open. [Middle English, of Scandinavian orig.]

rig (rĭg) *tr.v.* **rigged, rig·ging. 1.** To fit out; equip. **2.** To equip (a ship) with rigging. **3.** *Informal.* To dress, clothe, or adorn: *rigged out in her best dress.* **4.** To make or equip in a makeshift manner: *rig up a tent for the night.* **5.** To manipulate dishonestly: *rig a prize fight.* —*n.* **1.** The arrangement of masts, spars, and sails on a sailing vessel. **2.** Equipment, machinery, or gear for a particular purpose. **3.** A vehicle with its horses. **4.** *Informal.* An outfit. [Middle English *riggen.*]

rig·a·ma·role (rĭg′ə-mə-rōl′) *n.* Var. of **rigmarole.**

rig·ger (rĭg′ər) *n.* **1.** A person who rigs. **2.** A ship with a specific kind of rigging: *a square rigger.*

rig·ging (rĭg′ĭng) *n.* **1.** The system of ropes, chains, and tackle used to support and control the masts, sails, and yards of a vessel. **2.** The supporting material for construction work.

right (rīt) *n.* **1. a.** The side opposite the left: *On the face of a clock, the number 3 is on the right.* **b.** The direction of this side. **2.** Often **Right.** The persons who adhere to traditional attitudes and beliefs and hold conservative political views. **3.** That which is morally and ethically proper, just, or good. **4.** A just moral or legal claim: *the right to vote.*

—*adj.* **1. a.** Of or located on the side opposite the left. **b.** Toward this side: *a right turn.* **2.** Often **Right.** Of or relating to the political right. **3.** Intended to be worn facing outward: *the right side of the dress.* **4.** In accordance with fact, reason, or truth; correct: *the right answer.* **5.** Morally correct or justifiable: *the right thing to do.* **6.** Advantageous, desirable, or suitable: *in the right place at the right time.* **7.** Fitting; proper: *just right for the part.* —See Syns at **accurate, just,** and **suitable.** —*adv.* **1.** To or on the right. **2.** In a straight line; directly: *came right by the door.* **3.** In a correct manner; properly: *doing it right.* **4.** Exactly; just: *right where he was standing.* **5.** Immediately: *right after breakfast.* **6.** Very: *the Right Reverend Mr. Smith.* **7.** Used as an intensive: *Keep right on going.* —*tr.v.* **1.** To put in or restore to an upright position: *They righted their boat.* **2.** To put in or restore to a proper state. **3.** To make reparation or amends for; redress: *right a wrong.* —*intr.v.* To regain an upright or proper position: *The car rolled over twice and then righted.* —See Syns at **correct.** —**idioms. by right** (or **rights**). Justly; properly. **right away.** Immediately. **to rights.** In a satisfactory or orderly condition: *set the place to rights.* [Middle English, from Old English *riht, straight.*] —**right′ness** *n.*

> **Usage: right, rightly.** Both are adverbs, but *right* has the wider application. They are often interchangeable when correctly is the sense: *answered her right* (or *rightly*). *Rightly* is used most often when the desired sense is either properly or uprightly: *quite rightly refused the request; can rightly claim title to the land.* In the last example, *rightfully* could also be used; *right* would be impossible in either one.

right angle. An angle of 90 degrees, formed by two lines perpendicular to each other. —**right′-an′gled** *adj.*

right·eous (rī′chəs) *adj.* Morally right; just. [Middle English *rightwise,* from Old English *rihtwīs* : *riht,* right + *wīs,* manner.] —**right′eous·ly** *adv.* —**right′eous·ness** *n.*

right field. *Baseball.* **1.** The part of the outfield that is to the right as viewed from home plate. **2.** The position played by the right fielder.

right fielder. *Baseball.* The player who defends right field.

right·ful (rīt′fəl) *adj.* **1.** Morally right. **2.** Right or proper; just: *a rightful position of honor.* **3. a.** Having a just or proper claim: *the car's rightful owner.* **b.** Held or owned by just or proper claim: *a rightful share of the inheritance.* —**right′ful·ly** *adv.* —**right′ful·ness** *n.*

right-hand (rīt′hănd′) *adj.* **1.** Located on the right side. **2.** Directed toward the right side. **3.** Of or done by the right hand. **4.** Indispensable; reliable: *my right-hand man.*

right-hand·ed (rīt′hăn′dĭd) *adj.* **1.** Using the right hand more skillfully than the left. **2.** Done with the right hand: *a right-handed throw.* **3.** Made for the right hand. **4.** Turning from left to right; clockwise. —**right′-hand′ed** or **right′-hand′ed·ly** *adv.* —**right′-hand′ed·ness** *n.*

right·ist (rī′tĭst) *n.* A political conservative or reactionary.

right·ly (rīt′lē) *adv.* **1.** In a correct manner; properly: *act rightly.* **2.** With honesty; justly: *Rightly or wrongly, I think he should be punished.* **3.** *Informal.* Really: *I don't rightly know.* —See Usage note at **right.**

right of way. Also **right-of-way** (rīt′əv-wā′). **1.** *Law.* **a.** The right to pass over property owned by another. **b.** The path or thoroughfare on which such passage is made. **2.** The strip of land over which facilities such as highways, railroads, or power lines are built. **3.** The customary or legal right of a person, vessel, or vehicle to pass before another.

right-on (rīt′ŏn′, -ôn′) *adj. Slang.* Up-to-date and sophisticated; trendy.

right triangle. A triangle containing a right angle.

right whale. Any of several whales of the family Balaenidae, with a large head, whalebone plates in the mouth, and no dorsal fin.

right wing. A division holding conservative views within a larger political group. —**right′-wing′er** *n.*

rig·id (rĭj′ĭd) *adj.* **1.** Not bending; stiff; inflexible. **2.** Not moving; fixed; unyielding: *rigid rules.* **3.** Harsh and exacting; rigorous: *a rigid examination.* **4.** Scrupulously strict; undeviating: *a rigid social structure.* [Old French *rigide,* from Latin *rigidus,* from *rigēre,* to be stiff.] —**rig′id·ly** *adv.* —**ri·gid′i·ty** or **rig′id·ness** *n.*

ă pat	ā pay	â care	ä father	ĕ pet	ē be	hw which
ŏŏ took	ōō boot	ou out	th thin	*th* this	ŭ cut	

ĭ pit	ī tie	î pier	ŏ pot	ō toe	ô paw, for	oi noise
û urge	zh vision	ə about, item, edible, gallop, circus				

Syns: **rigid, inelastic, inflexible, stiff, unbending, unyielding** *adj. Core meaning:* Not changing shape or bending (*rigid iron bars*).

rig·ma·role (rĭg′mə-rōl′) *n.* Also **rig·a·ma·role** (-ə-mə-rōl′). **1.** Meaningless speech; nonsense. **2.** A complicated procedure. [Alteration of obs. *ragman roll,* list, catalog.]

rig·or (rĭg′ər) *n.* Also *Brit.* **rig·our. 1.** Strictness; severity. **2.** A trying condition; hardship. **3.** A severe or cruel act. **4.** A shivering or trembling, as from a chill. [Middle English *rigour,* from Old French, from Latin *rigor,* stiffness, severity, from *rigēre,* to be stiff.]

rig·or mor·tis (rĭg′ər môr′tĭs). Muscular stiffening following death. [Latin, "the stiffness of death."]

rig·or·ous (rĭg′ər-əs) *adj.* **1.** Characterized by or acting with rigor; rigid and severe: *rigorous physical training of the astronauts.* **2.** Full of rigors; trying; burdensome: *a rigorous climate.* **3.** Precisely accurate tasks. —See Syns at **burdensome.** —**rig′or·ous·ly** *adv.* —**rig′or·ous·ness** *n.*

rile (rīl) *tr.v.* **riled, ril·ing. 1.** To anger or irritate. **2.** To stir up (liquid); roil. [Var. of ROIL.]

rill (rĭl) *n.* A small brook. [Perh. of Low German orig.]

rim (rĭm) *n.* **1.** The border, edge, or margin of something: *the rim of a cup.* **2.** The outer part of a wheel around which the tire is fitted. —*tr.v.* **rimmed, rim·ming. 1.** To furnish with a rim; border. **2.** *Sports.* To roll around the rim of (a hole, basket, or cup) without falling in. [Middle English *rym,* from Old English *rima.*]

rime¹ (rīm) *n.* A frost or granular ice coating, as on grass and trees; hoarfrost. —*tr.v.* **rimed, rim·ing.** To cover with or as if with rime. [Middle English *rim,* from Old English *hrīma.*] —**rim′y** *adj.*

rime² (rīm) *n. & v.* Var. of **rhyme.**

rime·ster (rīm′stər) *n.* Var. of **rhymester.**

rind (rīnd) *n.* A tough outer covering, such as the bark of a tree or the skin of a fruit. [Middle English *rinde,* from Old English.]

rin·der·pest (rĭn′dər-pĕst′) *n.* An acute, often fatal, contagious virus disease, chiefly of cattle, and sometimes of goats and sheep. [German *Rinderpest* : *Rinder,* cows + *Pest,* pestilence, plague, from Latin *pestis.*]

ring¹ (rĭng) *n.* **1. a.** A circle with a vacant center. **b.** Something circular used to carry, pull, or hold: *a napkin ring.* **c.** Any circular part, marking, etc. **2.** A small circular band, often of precious metal, worn on a finger. **3.** An enclosed, usu. circular, area in which exhibitions, sports, or contests take place: *the circus ring.* **4. a.** A rectangular area in which boxing matches are held. **b.** Boxing. **5.** A group of persons acting illegally for their own gain. **6.** A group of atoms in an arrangement that can be represented as a ring. **7.** *Bot.* An **annual ring.** —*tr.v.* **1.** To surround with or as if with a ring; encircle. **2.** To supply with a ring. **3.** *Games.* To toss a ring over (a peg). —*intr.v.* To form a ring. —See Syns at **surround.** [Middle English, from Old English *hring.*]

ring² (rĭng) *v.* **rang** (răng), **rung** (rŭng), **ring·ing.** —*intr.v.* **1.** To give forth a clear, resonant sound: *The doorbell rang.* **2.** To sound a bell in order to summon someone. **3.** To hear a persistent humming or buzzing: *ears ringing from the blast.* **4.** To be filled with sound; resound: *The room rang with laughter.* **5.** To have a sound or character suggestive of a particular quality: *a story that rings true.* **6.** To be filled with talk or rumor: *the country rang with the news.* —*tr.v.* **1.** To cause to ring. **2.** To produce by or as if by ringing. **3.** To announce, proclaim, or signal by or as if by ringing: *a clock that rings the hour.* **4.** To call on the telephone: *ring up a friend.* —*phrasal verb.* **ring up.** To record: *ring up a sale.* —*n.* **1.** The sound created by or as if by a bell. **2.** A loud sound that is continued or repeated. **3.** A telephone call. **4.** A suggestion of a particular quality: *His offer has a suspicious ring.* [Middle English *ringen,* from Old English *hringan.*]

Usage: **ring, rung.** When the verb pertains to sound, the past tense is *rang,* not *rung,* particularly in written usage: *when the telephone rang.* The past participle is *rung: when it had rung several times.*

ring·bolt (rĭng′bōlt′) *n.* A bolt having a ring fitted through an eye at its head.

ring·er¹ (rĭng′ər) *n.* **1.** Someone or something that rings. **2.** A horseshoe or quoit thrown so that it encircles the peg.

ring·er² (rĭng′ər) *n.* **1.** Someone or something that sounds a bell or chime. **2.** *Slang.* A contestant entered dishonestly in a competition. **3.** *Slang.* A person who bears a striking resemblance to another.

ring·lead·er (rĭng′lē′dər) *n.* A leader of a ring engaged, esp. in unlawful or improper activities.

ring·let (rĭng′lĭt) *n.* **1.** A long, spirally curled lock of hair. **2.** A small circle or ring. —**ring′let·ed** *adj.*

ring-necked pheasant (rĭng′nĕkt′). A pheasant, *Phasianus colchicus,* native to the Old World, characterized by a white ring around the neck.

ring·side (rĭng′sīd′) *n.* A place providing a close view, esp. the area immediately outside the ring at a prize fight.

ring·worm (rĭng′wûrm′) *n.* A contagious skin disease caused by a fungus and resulting in ring-shaped, scaly, itching patches on the skin.

rink (rĭngk) *n.* **1.** An area surfaced with smooth ice for skating: *a hockey rink.* **2.** A smooth floor suited for roller-skating. **3.** A building that houses a surface prepared for skating. [Middle English *rinc,* race course, from Old French *renc,* row, rank.]

rinse (rĭns) *tr.v.* **rinsed, rins·ing. 1.** To wash lightly with water. **2.** To remove with water or another solution. —*n.* **1.** The act or an example of rinsing. **2.** The liquid used in rinsing. **3.** A solution used in coloring the hair. [Middle English *ryncen,* from Old French *rincer.*] —**rins′er** *n.*

ri·ot (rī′ət) *n.* **1.** Public uproar or disturbance. **2.** A disturbance of the peace by three or more persons assembled together. **3.** A profuse display. **4. a.** Unrestrained merrymaking; revelry. **b.** *Arch.* Debauchery. **5.** *Slang.* An extremely funny person or thing. —*intr.v.* **1.** To take part in a riot. **2.** To live wildly or engage in uncontrolled revelry. —*tr.v.* To waste recklessly. [Middle English, from Old French *rihote.*] —**ri′ot·er** *n.*

riot act. An energetic or forceful warning or reprimand. [After the Riot Act, 18th-cent. English law.]

ri·ot·ous (rī′ə-təs) *adj.* **1.** Of or participating in a riot. **2.** Boisterous or unrestrained. **3.** Dissolute; wanton. **4.** Abundant or luxuriant: *a riotous growth.* —See Syns at **disorderly.** —**ri′ot·ous·ly** *adv.* —**ri′ot·ous·ness** *n.*

rip¹ (rĭp) *v.* **ripped, rip·ping. 1.** To tear or split open or apart. **2.** To split or saw (wood) along the grain. —*intr.v.* To become torn or split apart. —*phrasal verb.* **rip off.** *Slang.* **1.** To steal from: *rip off a store.* **2.** To steal: *rip off a coat.* —See Syns at **rob.** —*n.* A torn or split place; tear. [Middle English *rippen.*] —**rip′per** *n.*

rip² (rĭp) *n.* A stretch of rough water in a river, channel, or estuary. [Perh. from RIP (to tear).]

rip³ (rĭp) *n.* **1.** A dissolute person. **2.** An old or worthless horse. [Perh. short for REPROBATE.]

ri·par·i·an (rĭ-pâr′ē-ən) *adj.* Of, on, or pertaining to the bank of a natural course of water. [From Latin *rīpārius,* from *rīpa,* bank, shore.]

rip·cord (rĭp′kôrd′) *n.* A cord pulled to release a parachute from its pack.

rip current. A current of water disturbed by an opposing current or by passage over an irregular bottom, esp. in tidal waters.

ripe (rīp) *adj.* **rip·er, rip·est. 1.** Fully grown and developed. **2.** Resembling matured fruit, as in health, color, or fullness: *a ripe figure.* **3.** Aged and ready for use. **4.** Advanced in years: *the ripe age of 85.* **5.** Fully prepared; ready: *a team ripe for its first victory.* **6.** Fully matured; seasoned: *ripe judgment.* **7.** Suitable; opportune: *The time is ripe.* —See Syns at **mature.** [Middle English, from Old English *rīpe.*] —**ripe′ly** *adv.* —**ripe′ness** *n.*

rip·en (rī′pən) *tr.v.* To make ripe. —*intr.v.* To become ripe. —**rip′en·er** *n.*

rip-off (rĭp′ôf′, -ŏf′) *n. Slang.* **1.** A theft. **2.** An act of exploitation.

ri·poste (rĭ-pōst′) *n.* Also **ri·post. 1.** *Fencing.* A quick thrust given after parrying an opponent's lunge. **2. a.** A retaliatory maneuver. **b.** A retort. —*intr.v.* **-posted, -post·ing.** To make a riposte. [French, from Old French *risposte,* from Italian *risposta,* answer, past part. of *rispondere,* to answer, from Latin *respondēre,* to respond.]

rip·ple (rĭp′əl) *n.* **1.** A small wave. **2.** A wavelike motion; undulation: *the ripple of muscles.* **3.** A sound like rippling water: *a ripple of laughter.* —*v.* **-pled, -pling.** —*intr.v.*

1. To become covered with small waves on the surface. **2.** To flow with small waves on the surface. **3.** To rise and fall gently in tone or volume. —*tr.v.* To cause to form small waves. [Orig. unknown.] —**rip′pler** *n.* —**rip′pling·ly** *adv.*

rip·rap (rĭp′răp′) *n.* **1.** A loose pile or layer of broken stones erected in water or on soft ground as a guard against erosion. **2.** The stone used for a riprap. —*tr.v.* **-rapped, -rapping.** To construct a riprap in or upon. [From RAP (to strike).]

rip-roar·ing (rĭp′rôr′ĭng, -rōr′) *adj.* Noisy, lively, and exciting. [From RIP + ROAR.]

rip·saw (rĭp′sô′) *n.* A coarse-toothed saw used for cutting wood along the grain.

ripsaw

rip·tide (rĭp′tīd′) *n.* A **rip current.**

rise (rīz) *intr.v.* **rose** (rōz), **ris·en** (rĭz′ən), **ris·ing.** **1.** To move from a lower to a higher position; ascend: *Hot air rises.* **2.** To get up from a sitting or lying position. **3.** To exert oneself to deal with a matter: *The boy was willing to rise to the challenge of an adventure.* **4.** To get out of bed. **5.** To increase in size, volume, or level: *The Mississippi rises every spring.* **6.** To increase in number, amount, or value: *a temperature that rose to 101° F.* **7.** To increase in intensity, force, or speed: *The wind has risen.* **8.** To increase in pitch or volume. **9.** To advance in status, rank, or condition: *wanted to rise in the world.* **10.** To slope or extend upward: *Mt. McKinley rises to 20,320 feet.* **11.** To become visible above the horizon: *The sun rises a little later each morning in the fall.* **12.** To come back to life: *The phoenix is said to rise from its own ashes.* **13.** To come into existence: *Many streams rise in the Andes.* **14.** To rebel: *"the right to rise up, and shake off the existing government"* (Abraham Lincoln). —*n.* **1.** An act of rising; upward movement; an ascent. **2.** An upward slope. **3.** The appearance, as of the sun, above the horizon. **4.** An increase in volume, size, or height. **5.** An increase, as in amount, value, or intensity: *a rise in prices.* **6.** An improvement in status, rank, or condition. **7.** An origin; beginning. **8.** *Informal.* An angry or irritated reaction. —See Usage note at **raise.** [Middle English *risen,* from Old English *rīsan.*]

Syns: rise, ascend, climb, mount, soar *v.* Core meaning: To move upward (*hot air that rises*). RISE is applied to a great range of events, chiefly involving steady or customary upward movement (*the sun rising over the eastern horizon; prices that rise and fall*). ASCEND means rising step by step, literally or figuratively (*ascend a staircase; ascend through the ranks*). CLIMB suggests steady progress against gravity or other resistance (*a rocket climbing rapidly; climbed to the top of her profession*). MOUNT often implies reaching a level or limit (*a death toll that mounted; mounting to the top of the hill*). SOAR suggests the effortless attainment of great height (*eagles soaring in the sky*); often it refers to what rises rapidly and suddenly, esp. above what is normal (*soaring cost of living*).

ris·er (rī′zər) *n.* **1.** A person who rises, esp. from sleep. **2.** The vertical part of a stair step.

ris·i·bil·i·ty (rĭz′ə-bĭl′ĭ-tē) *n., pl.* **-ties. 1.** Often **risibilities.** The ability or tendency to laugh. **2.** Laughter; hilarity.

ris·i·ble (rĭz′ə-bəl) *adj.* **1.** Capable of or inclined to laugh. **2.** Likely to cause laughter; funny. —See Syns at **laughable.** [Late Latin *rīsibilis,* from Latin *rīsus,* past part. of *rīdēre,* to laugh.] —**ris′i·bly** *adv.*

risk (rĭsk) *n.* **1.** The possibility of harm or loss; danger. **2.** A

factor, situation, or course of action exposing one to danger; a hazard. **3. a.** The danger or probability of loss to the insurer. **b.** A person or thing considered with respect to the possibility of loss to an insurer: *a poor risk.* —See Syns at **danger.** —*tr.v.* **1.** To expose to a chance of loss or damage: *risked her life.* **2.** To incur the risk of: *risk an accident.* [French *risque,* from Italian *risico,* from Latin *resecāre,* to cut off.] —**risk′er** *n.*

risk·y (rĭs′kē) *adj.* **-i·er, -i·est.** Involving risk or danger. —**risk′i·ness** *n.*

ris·qué (rĭ-skā′) *adj.* Tinged with indelicacy or indecency. [French, from *risquer,* to risk, from *risque,* risk.]

ri·tar·dan·do (rē′tär-dän′dō) *adj. Mus.* Gradually slowing in tempo. [Italian, from Latin *retardandum,* from *retardāre,* to retard.]

rite (rīt) *n.* **1.** An established form for a ceremony. **2.** The prescribed form for conducting a religious ceremony. **3.** Often **Rite.** A branch of the Christian church distinguished by its own liturgy. **4.** A ceremonial act. [Middle English *ryte,* from Latin *rītus.*]

rit·u·al (rĭch′ōō-əl) *n.* **1.** The form for a ceremony. **2.** A system or set of ceremonies. **3.** Often **rituals.** A ceremonial act or a series of such acts. **4.** A procedure faithfully and regularly followed: *a daily ritual.* [Latin *rītuālis,* from *rītus,* rite.] —**rit′u·al·ly** *adv.*

rit·u·al·ism (rĭch′ōō-ə-lĭz′əm) *n.* **1.** The observance of ritual. **2.** Rigid adherence to ritual. —**rit′u·al·ist** *n.* —**rit′u·al·is′tic** *adj.* —**rit′u·al·is′ti·cal·ly** *adv.*

ritz·y (rĭt′sē) *adj.* **-i·er, -i·est.** *Slang.* Elegant; fancy; fashionable. [After the *Ritz* hotels, founded by César Ritz (1850–1918), Swiss hotelier.]

ri·val (rī′vəl) *n.* **1.** A person who competes with or attempts to outdo another. **2.** Someone or something that equals another: *a performance without rival.* —*tr.v.* **-valed** or **-valled, -val·ing** or **val·ling. 1.** To attempt to equal or surpass: *"His ambition led him to rival the career of Edmund Burke."* (Henry Adams). **2.** To be a match for: *Her talents rivaled her beauty.* [Old French, from Latin *rīvālis,* neighbor, from *rīvālis,* of a brook, from *rīvus,* brook.]

ri·val·ry (rī′vəl-rē) *n., pl.* **-ries. 1.** The act of rivaling **2.** The condition of being a rival.

rive (rīv) *v.* **rived, rived** or **riv·en** (rĭv′ən), **riv·ing.** —*tr.v.* **1.** To tear apart; rend. **2.** To break into pieces, as by a blow. —*intr.v.* To be or become split. [Middle English *riven,* from Old Norse *rīfa.*]

riv·er (rĭv′ər) *n.* **1.** A relatively large natural stream of water. **2.** A stream or flow of liquid resembling a river: *a river of tears.* [Middle English *rivere,* from Old French, riverbank, river, from Latin *rīpārius,* on a bank, from *rīpa,* bank.]

riv·er·bed (rĭv′ər-bĕd′) *n.* The area covered by a river.

riv·er·boat (rĭv′ər-bōt′) *n.* A boat for river travel.

riv·er·ine (rĭv′ə-rīn′, -rēn′) *adj.* **1.** Pertaining to or resembling a river. **2.** Located on or inhabiting the banks of a river.

riv·er·side (rĭv′ər-sīd′) *n.* The bank or side of a river.

riv·et (rĭv′ĭt) *n.* A metal bolt or pin, with a head on one end, that is used to join two or more objects by passing through a hole in each piece and whose headless end is then hammered to form another head. —*tr.v.* **1.** To fasten with or as if with a rivet. **2.** To hammer so as to form a head and fasten something. **3.** To fix firmly: *stood riveted to the spot.* **4.** To hold unwaveringly: *a play that riveted their attention.* [Middle English *ryvette,* from Old French *river,* to fix.] —**riv′et·er** *n.*

riv·u·let (rĭv′yə-lĭt) *n.* A small brook or stream. [Prob. from Italian *rivoletto,* dim. of *rivolo,* small stream, from Latin *rīvulus,* dim. of *rīvus,* brook, stream.]

Rn The symbol for the element radon.

RNA A universal polymeric constituent of all living cells, consisting of a single-stranded chain of alternating phosphate and ribose units with the bases adenine, guanine, cytosine, and uracil bonded to the ribose, the structure and base sequence of which are determinants of protein synthesis; ribonucleic acid. [R(IBO)N(UCLEIC) A(CID).]

roach¹ (rōch) *n., pl.* **roach** or **roach·es. 1.** A freshwater fish, *Rutilus rutilus,* of northern Europe, related to the carp. **2.** Any of various fishes similar or related to the roach. [Middle English *roche,* from Old French.]

---

roach² (rōch) *n.* A cockroach.

road (rōd) *n.* **1.** An open way for the passage of vehicles, persons, and animals. **2.** A path; course. **3.** A railroad. **4. roads.** A roadstead. —*idiom.* **on the road. 1.** On tour. **2.** Traveling, esp. as a salesman. [Middle English *rode,* riding, journey, from Old English *rād.*]

road·bed (rōd'bĕd') *n.* **1.** The foundation upon which the ties, rails, and ballast of a railroad are laid. **2.** The foundation and surface of a road.

road·block (rōd'blŏk') *n.* An obstruction in a road, esp. a barricade.

road hog. A driver whose vehicle overlaps another's traffic lane.

road·house (rōd'hous') *n.* An inn, restaurant, or night club located on a road outside a city.

road metal. Crushed stone or cinders used in the construction and repair of roads and roadbeds.

road·run·ner (rōd'rŭn'ər) *n.* A swift-running, crested bird, *Geococcyx californianus,* of southwestern North America, with streaked, brownish plumage and a long tail.

roadrunner
George Miksch Sutton

road·side (rōd'sīd') *n.* The area bordering a road.

road·stead (rōd'stĕd') *n.* A sheltered, offshore anchorage area for ships.

road·ster (rōd'stər) *n.* An open automobile for two people, with a rumble seat or luggage compartment in the back.

road·way (rōd'wā') *n.* A road, esp. the part over which vehicles travel.

road·work (rōd'wûrk') *n.* Long runs as a form of exercise or conditioning.

roam (rōm) *intr.v.* To move or travel purposelessly; wander. —*tr.v.* To wander over or through: *roam the streets.* [Middle English *romen.*] —**roam'er** *n.*

roan (rōn) *adj.* Brownish or blackish and thickly sprinkled with white or gray hairs: *a roan horse.* —*n.* **1.** The coloring of a roan animal. **2.** A roan animal. [Old French, from Old Spanish *roano.*]

roar (rôr) *intr.v.* **1.** To utter a loud, deep, prolonged sound, esp. in distress, rage, or excitement. **2.** To laugh loudly or excitedly. **3.** To make or produce a loud, deep sound or noise: *The engines roared.* —*tr.v.* To utter or express with a deep, loud, and prolonged sound: *The audience roared its approval.* **2.** To cause to roar: *roar an engine.* —*n.* **1.** A loud, deep sound or cry, as of pain or rage. **2.** The loud, deep cry of a wild animal. **3.** A loud, prolonged noise. [Middle English *roren,* from Old English *rārian.*] —**roar'er** *n.*

roar·ing (rôr'ĭng) *adj.* Very lively and successful.

roast (rōst) *tr.v.* **1.** To cook with dry heat, as in an oven or in hot ashes. **2.** To dry, brown, or parch by exposing to heat: *roast coffee beans.* **3.** To expose to great or excessive heat. **4.** To heat (ore) in a furnace in order to dehydrate, purify, or oxidize. **5.** *Informal.* To criticize or ridicule harshly. —*intr.v.* To undergo roasting. —*n.* **1.** A cut of meat roasted or suitable for roasting. **2.** A picnic outing at which food is cooked by roasting. [Middle English *rosten,* from Old French *rostir,* of Germanic orig.]

rob (rŏb) *v.* **robbed, rob·bing.** —*tr.v.* **1.** To take property from illegally, by using force or the threat of force: *rob a bank.* **2.** To take unlawfully; steal. **3.** To deprive of illegally, harmfully, or unfairly: *rob a person of his reputation.* —*intr.v.* To commit or engage in robbery. [Middle

English *robben,* from Old French *rober,* of Germanic orig.] —**rob'ber** *n.*

Syns: rob, heist (*Slang*), **hit** (*Slang*), **hold up, knock off** (*Slang*), **knock over** (*Slang*), **rip off** (*Slang*), **stick up** (*Informal*) *v.* **Core meaning:** To take property or possessions from (another) unlawfully and forcibly (*robbed a pedestrian; robbing banks*).

robber fly. Any of various predatory flies of the family Asilidae, characteristically with long, bristly legs.

rob·ber·y (rŏb'ə-rē) *n., pl.* **-ies.** The act or crime of robbing.

robe (rōb) *n.* **1.** A long, loose, flowing garment. **2.** Often **robes.** A garment worn, as by a judge, to show office or rank. **3.** A bathrobe or dressing gown. **4.** A blanket or covering, esp. one for the lap and legs. —*v.* **robed, rob·ing.** —*tr.v.* To dress in a robe. —*intr.v.* To put on a robe. [Middle English, from Old French, of Germanic orig.]

rob·in (rŏb'ĭn) *n.* **1.** A North American songbird, *Turdus migratorius,* with a rust-red breast and gray and black upper plumage. **2.** A small Old World bird, *Erithacus rubecula,* with an orange breast and a brown back. [Short for *Robin redbreast,* from the name *Robin.*]

ro·bot (rō'bət, -bŏt') *n.* **1.** A machine with the appearance of a human being and the ability to perform human tasks or to imitate human actions. **2.** A person who works or follows orders mechanically. **3.** A machine or device that works automatically or by remote control. [Czech, from *robota,* compulsory labor, drudgery.]

ro·bust (rō-bŭst', rō'bŭst') *adj.* **1.** Full of health and vigor. **2.** Requiring or suited to physical strength or endurance. **3.** Boisterous; rough: *robust humor.* **4.** Marked by richness and fullness. [Latin *rōbustus,* oaken, from *rōbur,* oak, strength.] —**ro·bust'ly** *adv.* —**ro·bust'ness** *n.*

roc (rŏk) *n.* A legendary bird of prey of enormous size and strength. [Arabic *rukhkh,* from Persian *rukh.*]

Ro·chelle salt (rō-shĕl') A colorless, efflorescent, crystalline compound, $KNaC_4H_4O_6·4H_2O$, used as a laxative. [After *La Rochelle,* a city in France.]

roch·et (rŏch'ĭt) *n.* A ceremonial vestment made of linen or lawn, worn by bishops and other church dignitaries. [Middle English, from Old French.]

rock¹ (rŏk) *n.* **1. a.** A relatively hard naturally occurring material of mineral origin. **b.** A small piece or fragment of such material; a stone. **2.** A relatively large mass of stony material, as a cliff or peak. **3.** *Geol.* A naturally formed mineral mass that constitutes a significant part of the earth's crust. **3.** Someone or something that is very firm, stable, or dependable. **4.** *Slang.* A large gem, esp. a diamond. —*idiom.* **on the rocks. 1.** In or into ruin. **2.** Served over ice cubes. [Middle English *rokke,* from Old North French *roque,* var. of Old French *roche.*]

rock² (rŏk) *intr.v.* **1.** To move back and forth or from side to side in a rhythmic motion. **2.** To shake violently, as from a shock or blow. —*tr.v.* **1.** To cause to sway back and forth. **2.** To cause to shake or sway: *The earthquake rocked the village.* **3.** To shock; stun. —*n.* **1.** A rhythmic, swaying motion. **2. Rock 'n' roll.** —*idiom.* **rock the boat.** *Slang.* To disturb the balance of a situation. [Middle English *rokken,* from Old English *roccian.*]

rock-and-roll (rŏk'ən-rōl') *n.* Var. of **rock 'n' roll.**

rock bottom. The lowest level. —**rock'-bot'tom** *adj.*

rock-bound (rŏk'bound') *adj.* Hemmed in by or bordered with rocks: *a rock-bound lake.*

rock crystal. Transparent quartz, esp. when colorless.

rock·er (rŏk'ər) *n.* **1.** Something, as a rocking chair, that rocks. **2.** A curved piece upon which something, as a cradle, rocks. **3.** A machine part that has a rocking motion. —*idiom.* **off one's rocker.** *Slang.* Out of one's mind; crazy.

rock·et (rŏk'ĭt) *n.* **1. a.** A device propelled by a force or thrust that is developed by ejecting, esp. a high-velocity stream of gas produced by burning fuel with oxygen or an oxidizer carried in the device. **b.** An engine that produces a thrust in this way. **2.** A weapon, as a bomb, consisting of an explosive charge and propelled by a rocket. **3.** A firework that is shot up into the sky. —*intr.v.* **1.** To travel with great speed in or as if in a rocket. **2.** To rise rapidly or unexpectedly. —*tr.v.* To carry by means of a rocket. [Italian *rocchetta,* dim. of *rocca,* distaff.]

rock·et·eer (rŏk'ĭ-tîr') *n.* A person who designs, launches, studies, or pilots rockets.

rock·et·ry (rŏk′ĭ-trē) *n.* The science and technology of rocket design, construction, and flight.

rock·fish (rŏk′fĭsh′) *n., pl.* **rockfish** or **-fish·es.** Any of various food or sport fishes, chiefly of the genus *Sebastodes,* that live among rocks.

rocking chair. A chair mounted on rockers or springs.

rocking horse. A toy horse mounted upon rockers. Also called **hobbyhorse.**

rock lobster. The **spiny lobster.**

rock 'n' roll (rŏk′ ən rōl′). Also **rock-and-roll** (rŏk′ən-rōl′). A form of popular music characterized by a strongly accented beat and combining elements of blues, country, and folk music. Also called **rock.**

rock-ribbed (rŏk′rĭbd′) *adj.* **1.** Rocky. **2.** Stern and unyielding.

rock salt. Common salt in large masses.

rock wool. Fireproof fibers, made by shooting steam through molten rock and used as insulation.

rock·y[1] (rŏk′ē) *adj.* **-i·er, -i·est. 1.** Consisting of, containing, or full of rocks. **2.** Resembling or suggesting rock; unyielding. —**rock′i·ness** *n.*

rock·y[2] (rŏk′ē) *adj.* **-i·er, -i·est. 1.** Inclined to sway or totter; shaky. **2.** Weak, dizzy, or nauseated. —**rock′i·ness** *n.*

Rocky Mountain goat. A mountain goat.

Rocky Mountain sheep. The **bighorn.**

Rocky Mountain spotted fever. An acute infectious disease caused by a microorganism, *Rickettsia rickettsii,* and characterized by muscular pains, high fever, and skin rashes.

ro·co·co (rə-kō′kō, rō′kə-kō′) *adj.* **1.** Of an artistic style characterized by fanciful, asymmetric ornamentation. **2.** Overly elaborate; ornate. [French, alteration of *rocaille,* rockwork, from Old French *roche,* rock.] —**ro·co′co** *n.*

rod (rŏd) *n.* **1.** A straight, thin stick or bar. **2. a.** A stick used to punish by whipping. **b.** Punishment. **3.** A fishing rod. **4.** A measuring stick. **5. a.** A linear measure equal to 5.5 yards, 16.5 feet, or 5.03 meters. **b.** A square rod equal to 30.25 square yards. **6.** *Anat.* Any of the elongated cells in the retina of the eye that are sensitive to dim light and incapable of distinguishing colors. **7.** *Slang.* A pistol or revolver. [Middle English *rodd,* from Old English.]

rode (rōd) *v.* Past tense of **ride.** [Middle English, from Old English *rād.*]

ro·dent (rōd′nt) *n.* Any of various mammals of the order Rodentia, such as a mouse or beaver, that have large incisors adapted for gnawing or nibbling. [From Latin *rōdens,* pres. part. of *rōdere,* to gnaw.]

ro·de·o (rō′dē-ō′, rō-dā′ō) *n., pl.* **-os. 1.** A cattle roundup. **2.** A competition in which cowboys display skills such as riding broncos or lassoing. [Spanish, from *rodear,* to surround, from Latin *rotāre,* to rotate.]

roe[1] (rō) *n.* The eggs of a fish, often with the membranes in which they are held. [Middle English *row.*]

roe[2] (rō) *n.* The **roe deer.**

roe deer. A rather small, delicately formed Eurasian deer, *Capreolus capreolus,* with a brownish coat and short, branched antlers in the male. Also called **roe.** [Middle English *ro,* from Old English *rā.*]

roent·gen (rĕnt′gən, rŭnt′-) *n.* Also **rönt·gen.** *Symbol* **R** *Physics.* A unit used to measure the intensity of exposure to x-rays, gamma rays, and similar ionizing radiation. [After Wilhelm Konrad *Roentgen* (1845–1923), German physicist, who discovered x-rays.] —**roent′gen** *adj.*

Roentgen ray. An x-ray.

Rogation Days. *Eccles.* The three days preceding Ascension Day, designated as days of special prayer.

Rog·er (rŏj′ər) or **rog·er** *interj.* A word used in radio to indicate a message has been received. [From the name *Roger,* code word for the letter *R* meaning *received.*]

rogue (rōg) *n.* **1.** An unprincipled person; scoundrel. **2.** A mischievous person; scamp. **3.** A vicious and solitary animal. [Orig. unknown.]

ro·guer·y (rō′gə-rē) *n., pl.* **-ies. 1.** Behavior characteristic of a rogue; trickery. **2.** Mischief.

rogues' gallery. A collection of photographs of criminals maintained in police files.

ro·guish (rō′gĭsh) *adj.* **1.** Dishonest; unprincipled. **2.** Playfully mischievous. —**rog′uish·ly** *adv.* —**rog′uish·ness** *n.*

roil (roil) *tr.v.* **1.** To make muddy or cloudy by stirring up sediment. **2.** To irritate; vex. [Orig. unknown.]

roil·y (roi′lē) *adj.* **-i·er, -i·est. 1.** Muddy; cloudy. **2.** Agitated.

rois·ter (roi′stər) *intr.v.* To engage in boisterous merrymaking. [Prob. from Old French *rustre,* boor, alteration of *ruste,* rude, from Latin *rūsticus,* rural, rustic.] —**rois′ter·er** *n.* —**rois′ter·ous** *adj.*

role or **rôle** (rōl) *n.* **1.** A character played esp. by an actor or singer. **2.** A function. [French *rôle,* from Old French *rolle,* roll (on which a part is written), from Medieval Latin *rotulus,* roll of parchment, from Latin, small wheel.]

roll (rōl) *intr.v.* **1.** To move forward along a surface by revolving on an axis or by repeatedly turning over: *The coin rolled across the sidewalk.* **2.** To travel or be moved on or as if on wheels or rollers. **3.** To gain momentum: *The campaign began to roll.* **4.** To go by; elapse: *The hours rolled on.* **5.** To rotate: *His eyes rolled with fright.* **6.** To move with a steady motion. **7.** To have an uneven, wavy surface: *The hills roll to the sea.* **8.** To move or rock from side to side. **9.** To make a deep, prolonged sound, as thunder. —*tr.v.* **1.** To cause to move forward along a surface by revolving on an axis, or by repeatedly turning over: *roll a tire.* **2.** To move or push along on wheels or rollers. **3.** To impel and send forth in a steady, swelling motion. **4.** To cause to sway or rock: *Heavy seas rolled the ship.* **5.** To rotate: *roll one's eyes.* **6.** To pronounce with a trill: *rolls her "r's."* **7.** To beat (a drum) with a continuous series of short blows. **8.** To wrap into the shape of a tube: *roll a cigarette.* **9.** To spread, compress, or flatten by applying pressure with a roller: *roll dough.* —*n.* **1.** An act or the action of rolling. **2.** Something rolled up in the form of a cylinder or tube: *a roll of tape.* **3.** A quantity of something, as cloth or wallpaper, rolled into a cylinder, often considered as a unit of measure. **4.** A piece of parchment or paper suitable for rolling up; scroll. **5.** A list, esp. of the names of the members of a group. **6. a.** A small, rounded portion of bread. **b.** A portion of food shaped like a tube with a filling. **7.** *Slang.* Money, esp. a wad of paper money. —**idioms. roll in. 1.** To arrive in large numbers; pour in: *Contributions are rolling in.* **2.** *Informal.* To enjoy ample amounts of; abound in: *rolling in money.* **roll up.** *Informal.* To acquire; amass: *rolled up a fortune.* [Middle English *rollen,* to roll, from Old French *roller,* from Latin *rotulus,* small wheel, from *rota,* wheel.]

roll call. The procedure of reading aloud of a list of names to determine who is present.

roll·er (rō′lər) *n.* **1.** A small wheel, as on a roller skate or caster. **2.** A cylinder around which something is wound, as a window shade or towel. **3.** A heavy cylinder used to level or crush. **4.** A cylinder, often of hard rubber, for applying paint, ink, etc., onto a surface. **5.** A heavy, swelling wave that breaks on the coast.

roller bearing. A bearing using rollers to reduce friction between machine parts.

roller coaster. A steep, sharply banked, elevated railway in an amusement park with small open passenger cars.

roller coaster

roll·er-skate (rō′lər-skāt′) *intr.v.* **-skat·ed, -skat·ing.** To skate on roller skates. —**roller skater.**

rol·lick (rŏl′ĭk) *intr.v.* To behave or move in a carefree, joyous manner; to romp. [Orig. unknown.]

rol·lick·ing (rŏl′ĭ-kĭng) *adj.* Carefree and high-spirited.

rolling mill. 1. A factory in which metal is rolled into sheets, bars, etc. **2.** A machine used for rolling metal.

rolling pin. A smooth cylinder for rolling out dough.

ro·ly-po·ly (rō′lē-pō′lē) *adj.* Short and plump. —*n., pl.* **-lies.** A roly-poly creature. [From ROLL.]

ro·maine (rō-mān′) *n.* A variety of lettuce, *Lactuca sativa longifolia,* with long crisp leaves that form a slender head. Also called **cos.** [French, Roman.]

Ro·man (rō′mən) *n.* **1.** A native, inhabitant or citizen of Rome, esp. ancient Rome. **2.** The Latin language. **3. ro·man.** *Printing.* The most common style of type, characterized by upright letters. —*adj.* **1.** Of or pertaining to Rome and its people, esp. ancient Rome. **2.** Latin. **3.** Of or pertaining to the Roman Catholic Church. **4. roman.** *Printing.* Of, set, or printed in roman.

ro·man à clef (rō-mäN′ ä klā′) *pl.* **ro·mans a clef** (rō-mäN′ ä klā′). A novel in which actual persons or places are depicted in fictional form. [French, "novel with a key."]

Roman candle. A firework consisting of a tube from which balls of fire are ejected.

Roman Catholic. 1. Of or pertaining to the Roman Catholic Church. **2.** A member of the Roman Catholic Church.

Roman Catholic Church. The Christian church that is organized in a hierarchical structure of bishops and priests with the pope in Rome at its head.

ro·mance (rō-mǎns′, rō′mǎns′) *n.* **1. a.** A long verse or prose story about the adventures of heroes, often with exotic settings and extraordinary events. **b.** The class of literature composed of such stories. **2.** A quality that suggests the adventure and heroic deeds found in such stories. **3.** A spirit or quality favorable to love. **4.** A love affair. **5.** A fanciful notion or explanation. **6. Romance.** The Romance languages. —*v.* (rō-mǎns′) **-manced, -manc·ing.** —*intr.v.* **1.** To invent, write, or tell fanciful stories. **2.** To think or behave in a romantic manner. —*tr.v. Informal.* To carry on a love affair or courtship with; woo. —*adj.* **Romance.** Of or relating to the Romance languages. [Middle English *romaunce,* French, work written in French, from Old French *romant,* from Latin *Rōmānicus,* Roman, made in Rome, from *Rōmānus,* Roman.]

Romance languages. A group of vernacular languages that developed from Latin, including French, Italian, Portuguese, Rumanian, and Spanish.

Ro·man·esque (rō′mə-něsk′) *adj.* Of, pertaining to, or designating a style of European architecture prevalent from the 9th to the 12th cent. —*n.* The Romanesque style of architecture.

Ro·ma·ni·an (rō-mā′nē-ən, -mān′yən) *adj. & n.* Var. of **Rumanian.**

Roman nose. A nose with a high, prominent bridge.

Roman numeral. Any of the numerals formed with the characters I, V, X, L, C, D, and M in the ancient Roman system of numeration.

ro·man·tic (rō-mǎn′tĭk) *adj.* **1.** Of or characteristic of the stories of romance. **2.** Full of the quality or spirit of romance. **3.** Inclined to dream of adventure, heroism, or love. **4.** Imaginative but impractical: *romantic notions.* **5.** Of love or a love affair. **6.** Of romanticism in the arts or literature. —*n.* **1.** A romantic person. **2.** A romanticist. [French *romantique,* from Old French *romant,* romance.] —**ro·man′ti·cal·ly** *adv.*

ro·man·ti·cism (rō-mǎn′tĭ-sĭz′əm) *n.* **1.** An artistic and intellectual movement that originated in the late 18th cent., and stressed strong emotion, imagination, freedom from classical correctness in art forms, and rebellion against social conventions. **2.** The spirit and attitudes characteristic of romantic thought. —**ro·man′ti·cist** *n.*

ro·man·ti·cize (rō-mǎn′tĭ-sīz′) *v.* **-cized, -ciz·ing.** —*tr.v.* To interpret romantically. —*intr.v.* To think in a romantic way. —**ro·man′ti·ci·za′tion** *n.*

Rom·a·ny (rŏm′ə-nē, rō′mə-) *n., pl.* **Romany** or **-nies. 1.** A Gypsy. **2.** The Indic language of the Gypsies; Gypsy. —*adj.* Of or pertaining to the Gypsies, their culture, or their language.

romp (rŏmp) *intr.v.* To play in a boisterous manner. —*n.* Lively, merry play; frolic. [Var. of *ramp,* to rage.]

romp·er (rŏm′pər) *n.* **1.** A person who romps. **2. rompers.** A child's loose-fitting one-piece play suit.

ron·do (rŏn′dō, rŏn-dō′) *n., pl.* **-dos.** *Mus.* A composition in which a refrain occurs at least three times in its original

key between contrasting themes. [Italian *rondò,* from French *rondeau,* rondeau.]

rood (rōod) *n.* **1.** A cross or crucifix. **2.** A measure of land equal to ¼ acre or 40 square rods. [Middle English, from Old English *rōd,* rod, cross.]

roof (rōof, rŏof) *n.* **1.** The exterior covering on the top of a building. **2.** The top covering of anything. **3.** The upper part of the mouth. —*tr.v.* To furnish or cover with a roof. [Middle English, from Old English *hrōf.*]

roof·er (rōo′fər, rŏof′ər) *n.* A person who lays or repairs roofs.

roof·ing (rōo′fĭng, rŏof′ĭng) *n.* Materials used in constructing a roof.

roof·less (rōof′lĭs, rŏof′-) *adj.* Homeless; destitute.

roof·tree (rōof′trē′, rŏof′-) *n.* A long horizontal beam extending along the ridge of a roof; ridgepole.

rook¹ (rŏok) *n.* An Old World bird, *Corvus frugilegus,* related to the American crow. —*tr.v. Slang.* To cheat; swindle. [Middle English *rok,* from Old English *hrōc.*]

rook² (rŏok) *n.* A chess piece that may move horizontally or vertically across any number of unoccupied squares. Also called **castle.** [Middle English *roke,* from Old French *rock,* from Arabic *rukh,* from Persian *rukh.*]

rook·er·y (rŏok′ə-rē) *n., pl.* **-ies. 1.** A place where rooks nest and breed. **2.** The breeding ground of certain other birds and animals. **3.** *Informal.* A crowded tenement.

rook·ie (rŏok′ē) *n. Slang.* **1.** An untrained recruit. **2.** *Sports.* A player in his first year. **3.** A beginner; novice. [Alteration of RECRUIT.]

room (rōom, rŏom) *n.* **1.** Open space. **2. a.** An area of a building set off by walls or partitions. **b.** The people present in such an area. **3. rooms.** Living quarters. **4.** The capacity to receive, accept, or allow something: *no room for error.* —*intr.v.* To occupy a room; to live or lodge. [Middle English *roum,* from Old English *rūm.*]

room·er (rōo′mər, rŏom′ər) *n.* A lodger.

room·ette (rōo-mět′, rŏom-) *n.* A small private compartment in a railroad sleeping car.

room·ful (rōom′fŏol′, rŏom′-) *n., pl.* **-fuls. 1.** As much or as many as a room will hold. **2.** The number of people in a room.

rooming house. A house where lodgers can rent rooms.

room·mate (rōom′māt′, rŏom′-) *n.* A person with whom one shares a room or apartment.

room·y (rōo′mē, rŏom′ē) *adj.* **-i·er, -i·est.** Having plenty of room; spacious; large. —**room′i·ness** *n.*

roost (rōost) *n.* **1.** A branch, rod, or similar resting place on which birds perch or sleep. **2.** A place where birds perch or settle for the night. —*intr.v.* To perch for the night, as a bird. [Middle English *rooste,* from Old English *hrōst.*]

roost   rooster

roost·er (rōo′stər) *n.* **1.** The adult male of the common domestic fowl. **2.** The adult male of other birds.

root¹ (rōot, rŏot) *n.* **1. a.** The usu. underground portion of a plant that serves as support, draws food and water from the soil, and stores food. **b.** Any similar underground plant part, such as a rhizome or tuber. **c.** One of many small, hairlike growths that serve to attach and support plants such as the ivy and other vines. **2.** The part of an organ or body structure, as a hair, tooth, or nerve, that is embedded in other tissue. **3.** Any base or support. **4.** A source; origin. **5.** The essential part; core; heart: *the root of the matter.*

6. roots. Relationships and feelings of loyalty that make one belong to a place, group, tradition, etc. **7.** *Ling.* **a.** In etymology, a word or word element from which other words are formed. **b.** In morphology, a base to which prefixes and suffixes may be added. Also called **radical.** **8.** *Math.* **a.** A number that when used as a factor in multiplication a given number of times produces a specified product. **b.** A number that changes an equation to an identity if it is substituted for a variable in that equation; a solution. **9.** *Mus.* **a.** The note from which a chord is built. **b.** The first or lowest note of a triad or chord. —See Syns at **heart** and **origin.** —*intr.v.* **1.** To send forth or grow a root or roots. **2.** To become firmly established, settled, or entrenched. —*tr.v.* **1.** To cause to put out roots and grow. **2.** To implant by or as if by the roots: *Fear rooted us to the ground.* **3.** To pull up or remove by or as if by the roots. [Middle English *rote,* from Old English *rōt,* from Old Norse.] —**root′less** *adj.* —**root′less·ness** *n.*

root² (rŏot, rŏŏt) *tr.v.* To dig or dig up (something) with or as with the snout or nose. —*intr.v.* **1.** To dig in the earth with or as with the snout or nose. **2.** To rummage for something. [Alteration of earlier *wroot,* from Middle English *wroten,* from Old English *wrōtan.*] —**root′er** *n.*

root³ (rŏot, rŏŏt) *intr.v.* **1.** To give encouragement to; to cheer. **2.** To lend support to someone or something: *root for her success.* [Orig. unknown.] —**root′er** *n.*

root beer. A carbonated soft drink made from extracts of certain plant roots.

root canal. A pulp-filled cavity in a root of a tooth.

root hair. A thin, hairlike outgrowth of a plant root that absorbs water and minerals from the soil.

root·let (rŏot′lĭt, rŏŏt′-) *n.* A small root or division of a root.

root·stock (rŏot′stŏk′, rŏŏt′-) *n.* **1.** A rootlike plant stem, a rhizome. **2.** A source or origin.

rope (rōp) *n.* **1.** A heavy, strong cord made of twisted strands of fiber, wire, or other material. **2.** A cord with a noose at one end for hanging a person. **3.** Death by hanging. **4.** A lasso or lariat. **5.** Any string of items attached in one line by or as if by twisting or braiding: *a rope of onions.* **6. ropes.** *Informal.* Any specialized techniques or procedures: *learning the ropes.* —*tr.v.* **roped, rop·ing.** **1.** To tie or fasten with or as with a rope. **2.** To enclose with a rope: *rope off an area.* **3.** To catch with a rope or lasso. —*intr.v.* To become ropy and sticky. —*idiom.* **on the ropes.** Nearing total collapse or ruin. [Middle English, from Old English *rāp.*]

rope·walk (rōp′wôk′) *n.* A long, usu. covered path or alley where ropes are made.

rop·y (rō′pē) *adj.* **-i·er, -i·est.** **1.** Resembling a rope. **2.** Forming sticky strings or threads, as some liquids. —**rop′i·ly** *adv.* —**rop′i·ness** *n.*

Roque·fort cheese (rōk′fərt). A tangy cheese made from goat's and ewe's milk that contains a blue mold.

ror·qual (rôr′kwəl) *n.* Any of several whalebone-bearing whales of the genus *Balaenoptera,* with longitudinal grooves on the throat and a small, pointed dorsal fin. Also called **finback** and **razorback.** [French, from Norwegian, ult. from Old Norse *reytharhvalr.*]

Ror·schach test (rôr′shäk′, -shäКн). A psychological personality test in which a subject's interpretations of ten standard inkblot designs are analyzed as a measure of emotional health and intellectual functioning. [After Hermann *Rorschach* (1884–1922), Swiss psychiatrist.]

ro·sa·ry (rō′zə-rē) *n., pl.* **-ries.** *Rom. Cath. Ch.* **1.** A series of prayers. **2.** A string of beads on which these prayers are counted. [Medieval Latin *rosārium,* rosary beads, from Latin, rose garden, from *rosa,* rose.]

rose¹ (rōz) *n.* **1.** Any of numerous shrubs or vines of the genus *Rosa,* usu. with prickly stems, compound leaves, and variously colored, often fragrant flowers. **2.** The flower of any of these plants. **3.** A deep pink. **4.** A **compass card.** —*modifier:* *rose petals.* —*adj.* Deep pink. [Middle English, from Old English *rōse,* from Latin *rosa.*]

rose² (rōz) *v.* Past tense of **rise.** [Middle English, from Old English *rās.*]

ro·sé (rō-zā′) *n.* A pink, light wine made from red grapes from which the skins are removed during fermentation. [French, from Old French *rose,* rosy, from Latin *rosa,* rose.]

ro·se·ate (rō′zē-ĭt, -āt′) *adj.* **1.** Rose-colored. **2.** Cheerful; optimistic; rosy. —**ro′se·ate·ly** *adv.*

rose·bud (rōz′bŭd′) *n.* The bud of a rose.

rose·bush (rōz′bŏŏsh′) *n.* A shrub or vine that bears roses.

rose·col·ored (rōz′kŭl′ərd) *adj.* **1.** Having a rose color. **2.** Optimistic or overoptimistic: *rose-colored expectations.*

rose fever. A spring or early summer hay fever.

rose·fish (rōz′fĭsh′) *n., pl.* **rosefish** or **-fish·es.** A bright-red saltwater food fish, *Sebastes marinus,* of North Atlantic waters.

rose geranium. A woody plant, *Pelargonium graveolens,* with rose-pink flowers and fragrant leaves that are used for flavoring and in perfumery.

rose mallow. A tall plant, *Hibiscus moscheutos,* that grows in brackish marshes of eastern North America and has white or pink flowers.

rose·mar·y (rōz′mâr′ē) *n., pl.* **-ies.** **1.** An aromatic evergreen shrub, *Rosmarinus officinalis,* of southern Europe, with light-blue flowers and grayish-green leaves. **2.** The leaves of this plant, used as a seasoning in cooking and in manufacturing perfume. [Middle English, alteration of *rosmarine,* from Latin *rōs marīnus,* "sea dew."]

rose of Sharon. A tall shrub, *Hibiscus syriacus,* with large reddish, purple, or white bell-shaped flowers.

ro·se·o·la (rō-zē′ə-lə, rō′zē-ō′lə) *n.* A rose-colored skin rash. [New Latin, dim. of Latin *roseus,* from *rosa,* rose.]

ro·sette (rō-zĕt′) *n.* **1.** An ornament, as of ribbon or silk, that resembles a rose. **2.** *Bot.* A circular cluster of leaves or other plant parts.

rose water. A fragrant preparation made by steeping or distilling rose petals in water, used in cosmetics.

rose window. A circular window usu. of stained glass with radiating ornamentation in the form of a rose.

rose·wood (rōz′wŏŏd′) *n.* **1.** Any of various tropical trees, chiefly of the genus *Dalbergia,* that have hard reddish or dark wood with a strongly marked grain. **2.** The wood of any of these trees, used in cabinetwork.

Rosh Ha·sha·nah (rōsh′ hə-shä′nə, rōsh′). The Jewish New Year, celebrated in late September or early October. [Hebrew *rōsh hashshānāh,* "beginning of the year."]

Ro·si·cru·cian (rō′zĭ-krŏŏ′shən, rŏz′ĭ-) *n.* **1.** A member of an international fraternity of religious mysticism devoted to the application of esoteric religious doctrine to modern life. **2.** A member of any of several similar secret religious organizations active in the 17th and 18th cent. —*adj.* Of or pertaining to Rosicrucians or their philosophy. [After

Rorschach test   rose¹   rose window

| ă pat | ā pay | â care | ä father | ĕ pet | ē be | hw which | ĭ pit | ī tie | î pier | ŏ pot | ō toe | ô paw, for | oi noise |
| ŏŏ took | ŏŏ boot | ou out | th thin | th this | ŭ cut | | û urge | zh vision | ə about, item, edible, gallop, circus | | | | |

(*Frater*) *Rosae Crucis,* supposed founder of the society.] **—Ro'si·cru'cian·ism** *n.*

ros·in (rŏz'ĭn) *n.* A translucent yellowish to dark-brown resin derived from the sap of various pine trees, applied to the bows of certain stringed instruments and dancers' shoes to prevent slipping and also used in a wide variety of manufactured products. —*tr.v.* To coat or rub with rosin. [Middle English *rosyn,* var. of *resyn,* resin.] **—ros'in·ous** *adj.*

ros·ter (rŏs'tər, rô'stər) *n.* A list of the members of a group, esp. one ordered by duty assignments. [Dutch *rooster,* gridiron, list (on a ruled sheet), from Middle Dutch, gridiron, from *roosten,* to roast.]

ros·trum (rŏs'trəm, rô'strəm) *n., pl.* **-trums** or **-tra** (-trə). **1.** A raised platform for public speaking. **2.** *Biol.* A beaklike projection. [Latin, beak, ship's prow.] **—ros'tral** (-trəl) *adj.*

ros·y (rō'zē) *adj.* **-i·er, -i·est. 1.** Having a rose or deep pink color: *rosy cheeks.* **2.** Bright; promising: *The future looks rosy.* **—ros'i·ly** *adv.* **—ros'i·ness** *n.*

rot (rŏt) *v.* **rot·ted, rot·ting.** —*intr.v.* **1.** To undergo decomposition as a result of the action of bacteria or fungi. **2.** To become damaged or useless because of decay: *beams which had rotted away.* **3.** To undergo moral corruption; degenerate. —*tr.v.* To cause to decompose. —*n.* **1. a.** The process of rotting or the condition of being rotten. **b.** Something that is rotting or has rotted. **2.** Any of several plant or animal diseases characterized by the breakdown of tissue. **3.** Something, as words or an opinion, that is foolish, meaningless, or worthless. [Middle English *roten,* from Old English *rotian.*]

Ro·tar·i·an (rō-târ'ē-ən) *n.* A member of a Rotary Club.

ro·ta·ry (rō'tə-rē) *adj.* **1.** Of, pertaining to, or characterized by rotation about an axis. **2.** Having a part that rotates on an axis. —*n., pl.* **-ries. 1.** A rotary machine. **2.** A traffic circle. [Medieval Latin *rotārius,* from Latin *rota,* wheel.]

Rotary Club. An international service organization.

rotary engine. An engine, such as a turbine, in which power is supplied directly to vanes or other rotary parts.

ro·tate (rō'tāt') *v.* **-tat·ed, -tat·ing.** —*intr.v.* **1.** To turn about or as if about an axis. **2.** To perform a task or operation in successive turns; alternate. —*tr.v.* **1.** To cause to undergo rotation. **2.** To plant or grow (crops) in a fixed order of succession. **3.** To pass (a job or task) from one person to another in a recurring order. [From Latin *rotāre,* to revolve, from *rota,* wheel.] **—ro'tat'a·ble** *adj.* **—ro'ta'tor** *n.*

ro·ta·tion (rō-tā'shən) *n.* **1. a.** The act or process of rotating, esp. on an axis. **b.** A single complete cycle of such motion. **2.** Passage from one person, task, or position to another in a recurring order. **3.** Variation of the crops planted in a field to keep the soil from being depleted. **—ro·ta'tion·al** *adj.*

rote (rōt) *n.* **1.** Memorization usu. achieved by repetition without understanding. **2.** Mechanical routine or repetition. [Middle English, custom, rote, poss. from Latin *rota,* wheel.]

ro·ti·fer (rō'tə-fər) *n.* Any of various minute, multicellular aquatic organisms of the phylum Rotifera, with a wheellike ring of cilia at one end. [Latin *rota,* wheel + -FER.]

ro·tis·ser·ie (rō-tĭs'ə-rē) *n.* An appliance with a rotating spit for cooking food. [French *rôtisserie,* from Old French *rostisserie,* from *rostir,* to roast.]

ro·to·gra·vure (rō'tə-grə-vyŏŏr') *n.* **1.** A printing process in which an image or impression is produced on a surface from an etched copper cylinder in a rotary press. **2.** A picture or printed material produced by rotogravure. [Latin *rota,* wheel + GRAVURE.]

ro·tor (rō'tər) *n.* **1.** A rotating part of a machine or device, as an electric motor. **2.** An assembly of airfoils that rotates, as in a helicopter.

rot·ten (rŏt'n) *adj.* **-ten·er, -ten·est. 1.** Marked by rot or decay; putrid. **2.** Made weak or unsound by rot: *rotten floor boards.* **3.** Morally corrupt; despicable. **4.** Very bad; wretched: *rotten weather.* [Middle English *roten, rotin,* from Old Norse *rotinn.*] **—rot'ten·ly** *adv.* **—rot'ten·ness** *n.*

ro·tund (rō-tŭnd') *adj.* **1.** Rounded in shape; plump. **2.** Full and sonorous: *a rotund voice.* [Latin *rotundus,* round.] **—ro·tun'di·ty** or **ro·tund'ness** *n.* **—ro·tund'ly** *adv.*

ro·tun·da (rō-tŭn'də) *n.* **1.** A round building or hall, esp. one

with a dome. **2.** A large central room with a high ceiling. [Italian *rotonda,* from Latin *rotunda,* round.]

rou·ble (rōō'bəl) *n.* Var. of **ruble.**

rou·é (rōō-ā') *n.* A lecherous, dissipated man; rake. [French, *rouer,* to break on the wheel, from Medieval Latin *rotāre,* to turn, from Latin, to rotate.]

rouge (rōōzh) *n.* **1.** A red or pink cosmetic used to color the cheeks or lips. **2.** A fine reddish powder, chiefly ferric oxide, used as a polish, as for gems or metal. —*v.* **rouged, roug·ing.** —*tr.v.* To put rouge on. —*intr.v.* To use rouge. [French, from Old French, red, from Latin *rubeus.*]

rough (rŭf) *adj.* **-er, -est. 1. a.** Having a bumpy, irregular surface; not smooth or even. **b.** Coarse or shaggy to the touch: *a rough, scratchy blanket.* **2.** Stormy; turbulent: *rough waters.* **3.** Marked by violence or force; harsh: *rough handling.* **4.** *Informal.* Difficult to endure or do; taxing: *a rough time.* **5.** Harsh to the ear. **6.** Crude and unmannerly; uncouth. **7.** Not polished or refined; crude. **8.** Not complete, exact, or fully detailed: *a rough drawing.* —See Syns at **burdensome, coarse,** and **harsh.** —*n.* **1. a.** Rugged, overgrown ground. **b.** *Golf.* The uncleared part of a course that borders the open fairway and the greens. **2.** A crude, unmannerly person; rowdy. —*tr.v.* **1.** To make rough; roughen. **2.** To treat roughly or with physical violence. **3.** To make or do in a rough or incomplete form: *rough out a house plan.* **—idioms. in the rough.** In a crude or unpolished condition. **rough it.** To live without comforts or conveniences. [Middle English *rowgh,* from Old English *rūh.*] **—rough'ly** *adv.* **—rough'ness** *n.*

rough·age (rŭf'ĭj) *n.* Coarse, indigestible food, such as bran, that contains cellulose and stimulates intestinal peristalsis.

rough-and-read·y (rŭf'ən-rĕd'ē) *adj.* Rough or crude in character but effective or usable.

rough-and-tum·ble (rŭf'ən-tŭm'bəl) *adj.* Characterized by roughness and disregard for order or rules.

rough·cast (rŭf'kăst') *n.* **1.** A coarse plaster used for outside wall surfaces. **2.** A rough model. —*tr.v.* **-cast, -cast·ing. 1.** To plaster with roughcast. **2.** To shape roughly.

rough-dry (rŭf'drī') *tr.v.* **-dried, -dry·ing.** To dry (laundry) without ironing or smoothing out.

rough·en (rŭf'ən) *tr.v.* To make rough. —*intr.v.* To become rough.

rough·hew (rŭf'hyōō') *tr.v.* **-hewed** or **-hewn** (-hyōōn'), **-hew·ing. 1.** To hew or shape roughly, without finishing or smoothing. **2.** To fashion crudely.

rough·house (rŭf'hous') *n.* Rowdy, rough play or behavior. —*v.* **-housed, -hous·ing.** —*intr.v.* To engage in roughhouse. —*tr.v.* To handle or treat roughly.

rough·neck (rŭf'nĕk') *n.* A rough, unruly person; rowdy.

rough·rid·er (rŭf'rī'dər) *n.* **1.** A person who breaks in wild horses or rides horses with little training. **2. Roughrider.** A member of the 1st U.S. Volunteer Cavalry regiment under Theodore Roosevelt in the Spanish-American War.

roughrider
Teddy Roosevelt and the Roughriders

rough·shod (rŭf'shŏd') *adj.* Shod with heavy horseshoes that have projecting nails or points to prevent slipping. **—idiom. ride roughshod over.** To treat in a rough or violent manner.

rou·lade (rōō-läd') *n.* A slice of meat rolled around a filling and cooked. [French, from *rouler,* to roll, from Old French *roller.*]

rou·lette (rōō-lĕt') *n.* **1.** A gambling game in which players bet on which numbered slot on a rotating wheel a ball will come to rest in. **2.** A tool with a rotating toothed disk for making rows of dots, as in engraving, or rows of perforations, as on a sheet of postage stamps. **3.** Short consecutive perforations or slits made between stamps in a sheet as an aid to separation. [French, dim. of *rouelle,* wheel, from Old French *roele,* from Late Latin *rotella,* dim. of Latin *rota,* a wheel.]

Rou·ma·ni·an (rōo-mā′nē-ən, -mān′yən) *adj. & n.* Var. of **Rumanian.**

round (round) *adj.* **-er, -est. 1. a.** Having a shape that is spherical. **b.** Having a cross section that is circular, as a cylinder or cone. **c.** Having a curved edge or surface. **2.** Whole or complete; full; entire: *a round dozen.* **3.** Approximate; not exact: *a round number.* **4.** Large; considerable: *a round sum.* **5.** Brought to perfection; finished: *a round, polished writing style.* **6.** Full in resonance or tone; sonorous. **7.** *Phonet.* Outspoken; candid; blunt: *a round scolding.* **8.** Made with full force; unrestrained. **9.** *Phonet.* Formed or articulated with rounded lips. —*n.* **1.** The condition or property of being round. **2.** Something round, as a circle or ring: *a round of bread.* **3.** A rung, as on a ladder or chair. **4.** Movement in a curved or circular path. **5. a.** A series of similar actions or events. **b.** Often **rounds.** A customary or assigned course. **6.** One drink for each person in a gathering or group. **7.** An outburst, as of applause or cheers. **8. a.** A single shot or volley from a weapon. **b.** Ammunition for a single shot. **9.** A round dance. **10.** A cut of beef from the hind leg between the rump and shank. **11.** A unit of play in a game or contest that occupies a specified time, includes a specific number of plays, covers a stated distance, or allows each player a turn. **12.** *Mus.* A composition for two or more voices in which each voice enters at a different time with the same melody. —*tr.v.* **1.** To make round. **2.** To move in a circle or curved path around. **3.** To bring to completion. **4.** To adjust to or express as a round number. **5.** To encompass; encircle. —*intr.v.* **1.** To become round, full, or plump. **2.** To take a circular or curved course. **3.** To come to completion. —*phrasal verb.* **round up. 1.** To collect together in a roundup. **2.** To gather or bring together. —*adv.* Around. —*prep.* Around. **2.** From the beginning to the end of; throughout: *a plant that grows round the year.* —*idiom.* **in the round. 1.** With the stage in the center of the audience. **2.** Fully shaped so as to stand free of a background. [Middle English, from Old French *ronde,* from Latin *rotundus.*] —**round′ness** *n.*

round·a·bout (round′ə-bout′) *adj.* Not direct. —See Syns at **indirect.** —*n.* **1.** *Brit.* A merry-go-round. **2.** *Brit.* A traffic circle.

round dance. 1. A folk dance in which the dancers are arranged in a circle. **2.** A ballroom dance in which the couples move around the room.

roun·del (roun′dl) *n.* A round form, such as a circular panel, window, or recess. [Middle English, from Old French *rondel,* small circle.]

roun·de·lay (roun′də-lā′) *n.* **1.** A poem or song with a regularly recurring refrain. **2.** A dance performed in a circle. [From Old French *rondelet,* dim. of *rondel,* rondeau.]

round·er (roun′dər) *n.* **1.** Something that rounds, esp. a tool for rounding corners and edges. **2.** *Informal.* A dissolute or dishonest person. **3. rounders.** (used with a sing. verb). An English ball game similar to baseball.

Round·head (round′hĕd′) *n.* A member or supporter of the Parliamentary party in England during the 17th cent. [From the Puritans' practice of cutting their hair relatively short.]

round·house (round′hous′) *n.* **1.** A circular building for housing and switching locomotives. **2.** *Naut.* A cabin on the after part of a quarter-deck. **3.** *Slang.* A punch or swing delivered with a sweeping movement.

round·ish (roun′dĭsh) *adj.* Rather round.

round·ly (round′lē) *adv.* **1.** In the form of a circle or sphere. **2.** With full force or vigor; severely or thoroughly: *roundly applauded.* **3.** Bluntly; frankly: *speaking roundly.*

round robin. 1. A tournament in which each contestant is matched in turn against every other contestant. **2.** A petition or protest with the signatures in a circle in order to conceal the order of signing. **3.** A letter sent in turn to the members of a group, often with comments added by each.

round-shoul·dered (round′shōl′dərd) *adj.* Having the shoulders and upper back bent forward; stooped.

Round Table. 1. a. King Arthur and his knights as a group. **b.** The circular table around which King Arthur and his knights gathered. **2. round table.** A conference at which a number of people discuss a given topic.

round-the-clock (round′thə-klŏk′) *adj.* Throughout the entire day. —See Syns at **continuous.**

round trip. A trip to a place and back.

round·up (round′ŭp′) *n.* **1.** The bringing or gathering together of cattle on the range. **2.** A gathering together of persons or things. **3.** A summary: *a news roundup.*

round·worm (round′wûrm′) *n.* A nematode.

rouse (rouz) *v.* **roused, rous·ing.** —*tr.v.* **1.** To arouse from sleep, unconsciousness, or inactivity. **2.** To stir up, as to anger or action; excite. —*intr.v.* **1.** To awaken. **2.** To become active. —See Syns at **provoke.** [Orig. unknown.] —**rous′er** *n.*

rous·ing (rou′zĭng) *adj.* **1.** Inducing enthusiasm or excitement; stirring. **2.** Lively; vigorous.

roust·a·bout (rou′stə-bout′) *n.* An unskilled laborer, esp. on a dock or ship, in a circus, or in an oil field.

rout¹ (rout) *n.* **1.** A disorderly retreat or flight. **2.** An overwhelming defeat. —*tr.v.* **1.** To put to disorderly flight or retreat. **2.** To defeat overwhelmingly. —See Syns at **defeat.** [Middle English *route,* troop, disorderly crowd, from Old French, dispersed group, troop, from Latin *ruptus,* past part. of *rumpere,* to break.] —**rout′er** *n.*

rout² (rout) *intr.v.* **1.** To dig for food with the snout. **2.** To search; rummage. —*tr.v.* **1.** To bring to light; uncover. **2.** To hollow or gouge out; cut away. **3.** To drive or force out; eject. [Var. of ROOT (to dig up).] —**rout′er** *n.*

route (rōot, rout) *n.* **1. a.** A road or course for traveling from one place to another. **b.** A highway. **c.** A means of reaching a goal. **2.** A customary or fixed course of travel. —*tr.v.* **rout·ed, rout·ing. 1.** To send by a particular route. **2.** To schedule or sequence a series of procedures. —See Syns at **send.** [Middle English, from Old French.]

rou·tine (rōo-tēn′) *n.* **1.** A prescribed and detailed course of action to be followed regularly. **2.** A set of customary and often mechanically performed procedures or activities. **3.** A program or piece of entertainment, esp. in a nightclub or theater. —*adj.* **1.** In accordance with established procedure: *a routine check of passports.* **2.** Habitual; regular. **3.** Not special; ordinary: *a routine day.* —See Syns at **common.** [French, from Old French, from *route,* beaten path.] —**rou·tine′ly** *adv.*

rove¹ (rōv) *v.* **roved, rov·ing.** —*intr.v.* To wander about at random; roam. —*tr.v.* To roam or wander around, over, or through. [Middle English *roven,* to shoot (an arrow) at a random mark.]

rove² (rōv) *v.* Alternate past tense and past participle of **reeve.** [From REEVE, formed on the model of such verbs as *heave, hove, hove.*]

rov·er (rō′vər) *n.* A person who roves; wanderer; nomad. [Middle English *rover,* to shoot at a random mark.]

ro·ver² (rō′vər) *n.* A pirate. [Middle English *rover,* from Middle Dutch *rōver,* robber, from *rōven,* to rob.]

row¹ (rō) *n.* **1.** A series of persons or things placed next to each other, usu. in a straight line. **2.** A succession without a break or gap in time: *won the title for three years in a row.* **3.** A continuous line of buildings along a street. [Mid-

roundhouse

dle English, from Old English *rāw*.]

row² (rō) *intr.v.* To propel a boat with or as if with oars. —*tr.v.* **1.** To propel (a boat) with or as if with oars. **2.** To carry in or on a boat propelled by oars. **3.** To propel or convey in a manner resembling rowing. **4.** To pull (an oar) as part of a racing crew. **5.** To race against by rowing. —*n.* An act of rowing. [Middle English *rowen*, from Old English *rōwan*.] —**row'er** *n.*

row³ (rou) *n.* **1.** A noisy quarrel or fight. **2.** Noise; uproar. —*intr.v.* To take part in a row. [Orig. unknown.]

row·an (rou'ən) *n.* A small, deciduous tree, *Sorbus aucuparia*, native to Europe, with clusters of white flowers and orange-red berries. [Of Scandinavian orig.]

row·boat (rō'bōt') *n.* A small boat propelled by oars.

row·dy (rou'dē) *n., pl.* **-dies.** A rough, disorderly person. —*adj.* **-di·er, -di·est.** Noisy and disorderly; rough. —See Syns at **disorderly.** [Prob. from ROW (quarrel).] —**row'di·ness** or **row'dy·ism** *n.* —**row'dy·ish** *adj.*

row·el (rou'əl) *n.* A sharp-toothed wheel inserted into the end of the shank of a spur. —*tr.v.* **-eled** or **-elled, -el·ing** or **-el·ling.** To spur; urge with a rowel. [Middle English *rowelle*, from Old French *roele*, wheel, from Late Latin *rotella*, dim. of Latin *rota*, a wheel.]

row·en (rou'ən) *n.* A second crop in a season. [Middle English *rewayn*, from Norman French, from Old French *regain* : *re-*, again + *gain*, rowen, from *gaaignier*, to till.]

row·lock (rō'lŏk') *n. Brit.* An oarlock.

roy·al (roi'əl) *adj.* **1.** Of or pertaining to a king, queen, or other monarch. **2.** Of, pertaining to, or in the service of a kingdom. **3.** Like or fit for a king; stately: *a royal banquet.* **4.** Founded or authorized by a king or queen: *the Royal Society.* —**idiom. the royal road.** A smooth way that poses

rowan   rubbing
                               Brass rubbing from crypt

no difficulties: *the royal road to success.* —See Syns at **easy** and **grand.** [Middle English *roial*, from Old French, from Latin *rēgālis*, from *rēx*, king.] —**roy'al·ly** *adv.*

royal blue. A deep to vivid blue.

roy·al·ist (roi'ə-lĭst) *n.* **1.** A supporter of government by a king or queen; a monarchist. **2. Royalist. a.** A Cavalier. **b.** An American loyal to British rule during the American Revolution; Tory.

royal jelly. A nutritious substance, secreted in the pharyngeal glands of worker bees, that serves as food for the young larvae and as the only food for queen larvae.

royal palm. Any of several palm trees of the genus *Roystonea*, mostly from the West Indies, that have a tall, naked trunk surmounted by a large tuft of pinnate leaves.

royal poinciana. A tropical and semitropical tree, *Delonix regia*, native to Madagascar, with clusters of large scarlet and yellow flowers and long pods.

roy·al·ty (roi'əl-tē) *n., pl.* **-ties. 1. a.** A king, queen, or other person of royal lineage. **b.** Monarchs and their families in general. **2.** The lineage or rank of a monarch. **3.** The status or authority of monarchs. **4.** Royal quality or bearing; kingliness. **5.** A right or prerogative of the crown, as that of receiving a percentage of the proceeds from mines in the royal domain. **6. a.** Often **royalties.** A share paid to an author or composer out of the profits from the sale or performance of his work. **b.** A share in the proceeds paid to an inventor or proprietor for the right to use his invention or services.

-rrhea or **-rrhoea.** A suffix meaning flow or discharge: *pyorrhea.* [Middle English *-ria*, from Late Latin *-rrhoea*, from Greek *-rrhoia*, from *rhoia*, a flowing, flux, from *rhein*, to flow.]

Ru The symbol for the element ruthenium.

rub (rŭb) *tr.v.* **rubbed, rub·bing. 1.** To press something against (a surface) and move it back and forth. **2.** To press (something) against a surface and move it back and forth. **3.** To clean, polish, shape, or remove by rubbing. **4.** To apply firmly and with friction upon a surface. **5.** To move (an object or objects) against another or each other repeatedly and with friction; scrape. **6.** To remove or erase: *rub out the mistake.* —*intr.v.* **1.** To exert pressure and friction on something: *She rubbed hard till the spot came out.* **2.** To move along in contact with a surface; scrape. **3.** To become worn or chafed from friction. **4.** To be removed by pressure and friction. —*phrasal verbs.* **rub down.** To massage. **rub off.** To be transferred by contact or proximity: *I wish her luck would rub off on me.* **rub out.** *Slang.* To murder. —See Syns at **murder.** —*n.* **1.** An act or gesture of rubbing. **2.** An act or remark that wounds the feelings. **3.** A difficulty; a catch. [Middle English *rubben.*]

ru·ba·to (rōō-bä'tō). *Mus.* —*n., pl.* **-tos.** Rhythmic flexibility within a phrase or measure. [Italian, *(tempo) rubato,* "stolen (time)."]

rub·ber¹ (rŭb'ər) *n.* **1.** An amorphous, elastic, solid substance, prepared by coagulation and drying of the milky sap of various tropical plants, and then modified for finishing as any of a wide variety of manufactured products. **2.** Any of numerous synthetic elastic materials with properties similar to those of natural rubber. **3.** Often **rubbers.** A low overshoe made of rubber. **4.** *Baseball.* The oblong piece of hard rubber on which the pitcher must stand when he pitches the ball. [From RUB (from the use of rubber in erasers).]

rub·ber² (rŭb'ər) *n.* **1.** In bridge, whist, and other games and sports, a series of games of which two out of three or three out of five must be won to terminate the play. **2.** Also **rubber game.** The game that breaks a tie and ends such a series. [Orig. unknown.]

rubber band. An elastic loop of rubber, used to hold objects together.

rub·ber·ize (rŭb'ə-rīz') *tr.v.* **-ized, -iz·ing.** To coat, treat, or impregnate with rubber.

rub·ber·neck (rŭb'ər-nĕk'). *Slang.* —*n.* A person who gawks at tourist attractions, traffic accidents, or other sights. —*intr.v.* To gawk or stare.

rubber plant. 1. Any of several tropical plants that yield sap that can be coagulated to form crude rubber. **2.** A small tree, *Ficus elastica*, that has large, glossy, leathery leaves, and is popular as a house plant.

rubber stamp. 1. A piece of rubber affixed to a handle and bearing raised characters, used to make ink impressions of names, dates, messages, etc. **2.** A person or group that gives quick approval or endorsement of a policy without assessing its merit.

rub·ber-stamp (rŭb'ər-stămp') *tr.v.* **1.** To mark with the imprint of a rubber stamp. **2.** To endorse, vote for, or approve without question or deliberation.

rubber tree. A tree, *Hevea brasiliensis*, native to tropical America but widely cultivated throughout the tropics, yielding a milky juice, or latex, that is a major source of commercial rubber.

rub·ber·y (rŭb'ə-rē) *adj.* **-i·er, -i·est.** Of or like rubber; elastic or pliable: *rubbery legs; rubbery dough.*

rub·bing (rŭb'ĭng) *n.* An image of a raised or indented surface made by placing paper over the surface and rubbing the paper with a marking agent such as charcoal.

rub·bish (rŭb'ĭsh) *n.* **1.** Something discarded as refuse; trash. **2.** Foolish talk; nonsense. [Middle English *robishe.*]

rub·ble (rŭb'əl) *n.* **1.** Fragments of rock or masonry. **2. a.** Irregular fragments or pieces of rock used in masonry. **b.** The masonry made with such rocks. Also called **rubblework.** [Middle English *robyl.*] —**rub'bly** *adj.*

rub·down (rŭb'doun') *n.* An energetic body massage.

rube (rōōb) *n. Slang.* An unsophisticated country person. [Prob. from *Rube,* nickname of *Reuben.*]

ru·bel·la (rōō-bĕl'ə) *n.* A disease, German measles. [From

Latin *rubellus,* reddish, from *rubeus,* red.]

ru·be·o·la (rōō-bē'ə-lə, rōō'bē-ō'lə) *n.* A disease, measles. [From Latin *rubeus,* red.] —**ru·be'o·lar** *adj.*

Ru·bi·con (rōō'bĭ-kŏn') *n.* Any irrevocable step or action. —*idiom.* **cross** (or **pass**) **the Rubicon.** To embark on an undertaking from which one cannot turn back. [After the *Rubicon,* a river in Italy, the crossing of which by Julius Caesar in 49 B.C. started a civil war.]

ru·bi·cund (rōō'bĭ-kənd) *adj.* Reddish in complexion; ruddy. [Latin *rubicundus.*] —**ru'bi·cun'di·ty** (-kŭn'dĭ-tē) *n.*

ru·bid·i·um (rōō-bĭd'ē-əm) *n. Symbol* **Rb** A soft silvery alkali element that ignites spontaneously in air and reacts violently with water, used in photocells and in the manufacture of vacuum tubes. Atomic number 37; atomic weight 85.47; melting point 38.89°C; boiling point 688°C; specific gravity (solid) 1.532; valences 1, 2, 3, 4. [From Latin *rubidus,* red (from the red lines in its spectrum).]

ru·ble (rōō'bəl) *n.* Also **rou·ble.** The basic monetary unit of the Soviet Union. [Russian *rubl',* silver bar, from Old Russian, bar, block, from *rubiti,* to cut up, build.]

ru·bric (rōō'brĭk) *n.* **1.** A part of a manuscript or book, a title or heading, or initial letter, that appears in decorative red lettering, or is otherwise distinguished from the rest of the text. **2.** A title or heading of a statute or chapter in a code of law. **3.** A class or category; title. **4.** A direction for a conduct of a religious service or ceremony in a missal, hymnal, or other liturgical book. **5.** Any brief, established rule or direction. [Middle English *rubrike,* from Old French *rubriche,* from Latin *rubrīca (terra),* "red earth," from *ruber,* red.] —**ru'bri·cal** *adj.*

ru·by (rōō'bē) *n., pl.* **-bies. 1.** A deep-red, translucent corundum, highly valued as a precious stone. **2.** A deep red. —*modifier:* *ruby earrings; ruby lipstick.* —*adj.* Deep red. [Middle English, from Old French *rubi,* from Medieval Latin *rubīnus (lapis),* "red stone," from Latin *rubeus,* red.]

ruck (rŭk) *n.* The multitude of ordinary people or things. [Middle English *ruke,* heap, stack.]

ruck·sack (rŭk'săk', rŏŏk'-) *n.* A knapsack. [German *Rucksack* : *Rücken,* back + *Sack,* sack.]

ruck·us (rŭk'əs) *n. Informal.* A noisy disturbance; commotion. [Prob. RUC(TION) + (RUMP)US.]

ruc·tion (rŭk'shən) *n. Informal.* A riotous disturbance. [Prob. shortened alteration of INSURRECTION.]

rud·der (rŭd'ər) *n.* **1.** A vertically hinged plate of metal or wood mounted at the stern of a vessel for steering. **2.** A similar structure at the tail of an aircraft. [Middle English *rodyr,* from Old English *rōther,* steering oar.]

rud·dy (rŭd'ē) *adj.* **-di·er, -di·est. 1.** Having a healthy, reddish color. **2.** Reddish; rosy. [Middle English *rudie,* from Old English *rudig,* from *rudu,* red color.] —**rud'di·ness** *n.*

rude (rōōd) *adj.* **rud·er, rud·est. 1.** Primitive; not civilized; unrefined: *a rude and savage nation.* **2.** Ill-mannered; uncivil; discourteous. **3.** Formed without skill or precision; makeshift; crude: *The log formed a rude footbridge.* **4.** Sudden and jarring: *a rude shock.* [Middle English, from Old French, from Latin *rudis,* rough, raw.] —**rude'ly** *adv.* —**rude'ness** *n.*

   Syns: **rude, discourteous, ill-mannered, impolite, unmannerly** *adj. Core meaning:* Lacking good manners (*rude children; rude behavior*). See also Syns at **coarse.**

ru·di·ment (rōō'də-mənt) *n.* **1.** A fundamental element, principle, or skill, as of a field of learning. **2.** Often **rudiments.** Something in an incipient or undeveloped form; beginnings: *the rudiments of social behavior in children.* [Old French, from Latin *rudīmentum,* beginning, from *rudis,* rude.] —**ru'di·men'ta·ry** (rōō'də-mĕn'tə-rē) *adj.*

rue¹ (rōō) *tr.v.* **rued, ru·ing.** To feel remorse or sorrow for. —*n. Archaic.* Sorrow; regret. [Middle English *ruen,* from Old English *hrēowan,* to make penitent, distress.]

rue² (rōō) *n.* An aromatic Eurasian plant of the genus *Ruta,* esp. *R. graveolens,* with evergreen leaves that yield an acrid, volatile oil formerly used in medicine. [Middle English, from Old French, from Latin *rūta,* from Greek *rhutē.*]

rue anemone. A small North American woodland plant, *Anemonella thalictroides,* with white or pinkish flowers.

rue·ful (rōō'fəl) *adj.* **1.** Full of sorrow or remorse: *a rueful admission of guilt.* **2.** Inspiring pity or compassion: *cutting a rueful figure.* —**rue'ful·ly** *adv.* —**rue'ful·ness** *n.*

ruff¹ (rŭf) *n.* **1.** A stiffly starched circular collar of fine fab-

ric, worn by men and women in the 16th and 17th cent. **2.** A distinctive collarlike projection around the neck, as of feathers on a bird. Also called **ruffle. 3.** The male of a Eurasian sandpiper, *Philomachus pugnax,* that has collarlike, erectile feathers around the neck during the breeding season. [Short for RUFFLE (frill).] —**ruffed** *adj.*

ruff² (rŭf). *Card Games.* —*n.* The playing of a trump card when one cannot follow suit. —*tr.v.* To trump. —*intr.v.* To play a trump. [From Old French *roffle.*]

ruffed grouse. A chickenlike North American game bird, *Bonasa umbellus,* with mottled brownish plumage.

ruf·fi·an (rŭf'ē-ən, rŭf'yən) *n.* A tough or rowdy fellow. [Old French.] —**ruf'fi·an·ism** *n.* —**ruf'fi·an** *adj.*

ruf·fle¹ (rŭf'əl) *n.* **1.** A strip of frilled or closely pleated fabric used for trimming or decoration. **2.** A ruff. **3.** A slight discomposure; an agitation. **4.** An irregularity in smoothness; a ripple. —*tr.v.* **-fled, -fling. 1. a.** To disturb the smoothness or regularity of: *ruffled his hair affectionately.* **b.** To annoy (another); vex. **2.** To pleat or gather (fabric) into a ruffle. **3.** To erect (the feathers). **4.** To discompose; fluster: *ruffled his dignity.* **5.** To shuffle (cards). —*intr.v.* **1.** To become irregular or rough. **2.** To stand up in tufts or projections. **3.** To flutter. **4.** To become flustered. —See Syns at **annoy.** [Middle English *ruffelen,* to roughen, disarrange.]

ruf·fle² (rŭf'əl) *n.* A low continuous beating of a drum that is not as loud as a roll. [Freq. of earlier *ruff,* to ruffle.]

ru·fous (rōō'fəs) *adj.* Reddish or reddish brown. [Latin *rūfus,* red, reddish.]

rug (rŭg) *n.* **1.** A piece of heavy fabric used to cover a floor. **2.** An animal skin used as a floor covering. **3.** *Brit.* A lap robe. [Prob. of Scandinavian orig.]

rug·by (rŭg'bē) *n.* Also **Rugby football.** A form of football in which players on two competing teams may kick, dribble, or run with the ball, and forward passing, substitution of players, and time-outs are not permitted. [After the *Rugby School,* Warwickshire, England.]

rug·ged (rŭg'ĭd) *adj.* **1.** Having a rough, irregular surface: *rugged terrain.* **2.** Tempestuous; stormy: *rugged weather.* **3.** Demanding great effort, ability, or endurance: *a rugged test.* **4.** Lacking culture or polish. **5.** Vigorously healthy; strong; hardy. [Middle English, shaggy, of Scandinavian orig.] —**rug'ged·ly** *adv.* —**rug'ged·ness** *n.*

rug·ger (rŭg'ər) *n. Brit.* Rugby.

ru·in (rōō'ĭn) *n.* **1.** Severe destruction or disintegration, rendering something formless, useless, or valueless. **2.** The cause of such destruction. **3.** A condition of total destruction or collapse: *The city lay in ruin.* **4.** Often **ruins.** The remains of a structure or group of structures that has been destroyed, disintegrated, or decayed. **5. a.** Total loss of one's health, fortune, position, or honor. **b.** The cause of such loss: *Gambling was his ruin.* —*tr.v.* **1.** To reduce to ruin or disintegration. **2.** To harm irreparably. **3.** To reduce to poverty or bankruptcy. —See Syns at **destroy.** [Middle English *ruine,* from Old French, from Latin *ruīna,* fall, from *ruere,* to fall, crumble.]

ru·in·a·tion (rōō'ĭ-nā'shən) *n.* Destruction.

ru·in·ous (rōō'ĭ-nəs) *adj.* **1.** Causing or likely to cause ruin; disastrous. **2.** In ruins. —**ru'in·ous·ly** *adv.*

rule (rōōl) *n.* **1. a.** Governing power, or its possession or use; authority. **b.** The duration of such power. **2.** An authoritative direction for conduct or procedure, esp. one of the regulations governing procedure in a legislative body or a regulation observed by the players in a game, sport, or

ruff¹

contest. **3.** A usual or customary course of action or behavior: *Violence is the rule in that area.* **4.** A statement that describes what is true in most or all cases. **5.** A standard method or procedure for solving a class of mathematical problems. **6.** *Law.* **a.** A court order limited in application to a specific case. **b.** A subordinate regulation governing a particular matter. **7.** A straightedge; ruler. **8.** *Printing.* A thin metal strip, used to print borders or lines, as between columns. —*v.* **ruled, rul·ing.** —*tr.v.* **1.** To exercise control over; govern. **2.** To dominate by powerful influence; hold sway over. **3.** To keep within proper limits; restrain. **4.** *Law.* To decide or declare judicially; decree. **5.** To mark with straight parallel lines. —*intr.v.* **1.** To exercise authority: *She was born to rule.* **2.** To formulate and issue a decree or judgment. —See Syns at **judge.** —*phrasal verb.* **rule out.** To remove from consideration; exclude. [Middle English *reule*, from Old French, from Latin *rēgula*, straight stick, ruler, rule, pattern.] —**rul′a·ble** *adj.*

rule of thumb. A useful principle with wide application, not intended to be strictly accurate.

rul·er (rōō′lər) *n.* **1.** A person or thing that rules or governs, as a sovereign. **2.** A straightedge.

rul·ing (rōō′lĭng) *adj.* Exercising control or dominion; predominant. —*n.* An official decision, esp. the decision of a court of law.

rum (rŭm) *n.* **1.** An alcoholic liquor distilled from fermented molasses or sugar cane. **2.** Intoxicating beverages. [Perh. short for earlier *rumbullion.*]

Ru·ma·ni·an (rōō-mā′nē-ən, -mān′yən). Also **Ro·ma·ni·an** (rō-mā′nē-ən, -mān′yən) or **Rou·ma·ni·an** (rōō-mā′nē-ən, -mān′yən). —*adj.* Pertaining to Rumania, its people, or their language. —*n.* **1.** An inhabitant or native of Rumania. **2.** The Romance language of the Rumanian people.

rum·ba or **rhum·ba** (rŭm′bə, rōōm′-) *n.* **1.** A complex rhythmical dance that originated in Cuba. **2.** A modern ballroom adaptation of this dance. —*intr.v.* To dance the rumba. [American Spanish, from *rumbo*, carousal, from Spanish, pomp.]

rum·ble (rŭm′bəl) *v.* **-bled, -bling.** —*intr.v.* **1.** To make a deep, long, rolling sound. **2.** To move or proceed with such a sound. —*tr.v.* To utter with a rumbling sound. —*n.* **1.** A deep, long, rolling sound. **2.** A widespread murmur of discontent. **3.** *Slang.* A gang fight. [Middle English *romblen,* prob. from Middle Dutch *rommelen.*]

rumble seat. An open passenger seat, usu. one that unfolds, in the rear of an automobile.

ru·men (rōō′mĕn) *n., pl.* **-mi·na** (-mə-nə) or **-mens.** The first division of the stomach of a ruminant animal, in which food is partly digested. [Latin *rūmen,* throat, gullet.]

ru·mi·nant (rōō′mə-nənt) *n.* Any of various hoofed, eventoed mammals of the suborder Ruminantia, as cattle, sheep, goats, and deer, that characteristically have a stomach divided into four compartments, and chew a cud consisting of regurgitated, partially digested food. —*adj.* **1.** Characterized by the chewing of cud. **2.** Of or belonging to the Ruminantia. **3.** Meditative; contemplative.

ru·mi·nate (rōō′mə-nāt′) *v.* **-nat·ed, -nat·ing.** —*intr.v.* **1.** To chew cud. **2.** To meditate at length; muse. —*tr.v.* **1.** To chew (food) again. **2.** To meditate or reflect on. [From Latin *rūmināre,* from *rūmen,* rumen.] —**ru′mi·na′tive·ly** *adv.* —**ru′mi·na′tion** *n.* —**ru′mi·na′tive** *adj.*

rum·mage (rŭm′ĭj) *v.* **-maged, -mag·ing.** —*tr.v.* **1.** To search thoroughly by handling, turning over, or disarranging the contents of. **2.** To discover by searching thoroughly. —*intr.v.* To make an energetic, usu. hasty search. —*n.* A thorough search among a number of things. [From earlier *romage,* arrangement of cargo in a ship's hold, odds and ends, from Old French *arrumage,* from *arrumer,* to put in a ship's hold.]

rummage sale. **1.** A sale of assorted secondhand objects, contributed by donors to raise money for a charity. **2.** A sale of unclaimed or excess goods, as at a warehouse.

rum·my (rŭm′ē) *n.* A card game in which the object is to obtain sets of three or more cards of the same rank or suit. [Orig. unknown.]

ru·mor (rōō′mər) *n.* **1.** A report of uncertain origin and truthfulness, spread by word of mouth. **2.** Information by word of mouth; hearsay. —*tr.v.* To suggest or report by rumor. [Middle English, from Old French, from Latin *rūmor.*]

ru·mor·mon·ger (rōō′mər-mŭng′gər, -mŏng′-) *n.* A person who spreads rumors.

rump (rŭmp) *n.* **1. a.** The fleshy hindquarters of an animal. **b.** A cut of meat from this part. **2.** The human buttocks. **3.** The last or inferior part of something. **4.** A legislature that has only a small part of its original membership and hence is unrepresentative or lacks authority. [Middle English *rumpe,* of Scandinavian orig.]

rum·ple (rŭm′pəl) *v.* **-pled, -pling.** —*tr.v.* **1.** To wrinkle or form into folds or creases. **2.** To muss up; ruffle; tousle. —*intr.v.* To become wrinkled or creased. [Dutch *rompelen,* from Middle Dutch.]

rum·pus (rŭm′pəs) *n.* A noisy disturbance or dispute. [Orig. unknown.]

rumpus room. A room for play and parties.

run (rŭn) *v.* **ran** (răn), **run, run·ning.** —*intr.v.* **1. a.** To move swiftly on foot so that both feet leave the ground during each stride. **b.** To gallop. **2.** To retreat; flee: *turn and run.* **3.** To move freely: *We let the dog run in the yard.* **4.** To make a quick trip or visit: *run down to the shore.* **5.** To go regularly; ply: *The ferry runs every hour.* **6.** To migrate or swim in a school, esp. in order to spawn. **7. a.** To move quickly; hurry: *She ran through her mail.* **b.** To go when in difficulty: *always run to his lawyer.* **8. a.** To take part in a race or contest: *His horse ran in the Derby.* **b.** To compete for elected office: *run for mayor.* **9.** To move or travel quickly: *The car ran downhill.* **10.** To be in operation: *The engine is running.* **11.** *Naut.* To sail before the wind. **12. a.** To flow in a stream. **b.** To melt and flow: *Tin must be hot for the solder to run.* **c.** To spread; dissolve: *Fast colors do not run.* **13.** To discharge a liquid: *Smog made our eyes run.* **14.** To extend or stretch through space or time: *a road that runs to the next town; a lease with two years to run.* **15.** To spread rapidly: *Rumors ran through the town.* **16.** To unravel along a lengthwise line: *Her stocking ran.* **17.** To persist or recur: *Gout runs in the family.* **18.** To take a given form: *His reasoning ran thus.* **19.** To tend or incline: *His tastes run to the sensational.* **20.** To vary or range: *prices ran from medium to high.* **21.** To pass to a specified condition: *We ran into debt.* —*tr.v.* **1.** To traverse by running: *run the entire distance.* **2.** To do or accomplish by or as if by running: *run errands.* **3.** To bring to a given condition by or as if by running: *She ran him ragged.* **4.** To cause to move quickly: *He ran his fingers over the keyboard.* **5. a.** To enter in or as if in a race: *He ran two horses in the Derby.* **b.** To enter as a candidate for office: *They ran him for mayor.* **6.** To cause to move freely. **7.** To cause to function; operate: *run a machine.* **8.** To convey or transport: *Run me into town.* **9.** To cause to ply: *They don't run the ferries in winter.* **10. a.** To smuggle: *run rifles.* **b.** To evade and pass through: *run the blockade.* **11.** To pass over or through: *run the rapids.* **12.** To cause to flow: *run water into a tub.* **13.** To melt and cast (metal). **14.** To cause to extend: *run a road into the hills.* **15.** To stitch: *run a seam.* **16.** To cause to unravel along a line: *She ran her stocking on a splinter.* **17.** To cause to penetrate: *She ran a pin into her thumb.* **18.** To cause to continue: *They ran the film for a month.* **19.** To make oneself subject to: *run a risk.* **20. a.** To conduct or perform: *run an experiment.* **b.** To control, manage, or direct. —See Syns at **rush.** —*phrasal verbs.* **run across.** To find by chance; come upon. **run after.** To pursue; chase. **run along.** To go away; leave. **run away. 1.** To flee; escape. **2.** To stampede. **run away with. 1.** To make off with. **2.** To win by a large margin. **run down. 1.** To stop because of lack of force or power. **2.** To become tired. **3.** To collide with and knock down. **4.** To chase and capture. **5.** To disparage. **6.** To trace to a source. **run in.** To take into legal custody. —See Syns at **arrest. run into. 1.** To meet or find by chance: *ran into an old friend.* **2.** To encounter: *ran into trouble.* **3.** To collide with. **run off.** To print or duplicate: *run off 20 copies.* **run out.** To become used up; be exhausted: *My money has run out.* **run out of.** To exhaust the supply: *run out of gas.* **run over. 1.** To collide with, knock down, and ride over in a vehicle. **2.** To read or review quickly. **run through. 1.** To pierce. **2.** To use up: *run through money.* **3.** To examine or rehearse quickly. —*n.* **1. a.** A pace faster than a walk. **b.** A gait faster than a canter. **2.** An act of running. **3. a.** A distance covered by or as if by running: *a half-mile run.* **b.** The time taken to cover it: *a two minutes' run from the subway.* **4.** A quick trip or visit: *a run into town.* **5. a.** A regular trip. **b.** The distance covered during such a journey. **6.** *Baseball.* A point scored by advancing around the bases and reaching home plate safely. **7.** A large migration of fish, esp. to spawn. **8.** Unrestricted freedom or movement in a place: *I had the run of their library.* **9.** A trail or way used by wild animals. **10.** An enclosure in which domestic animals feed and exercise. **11.** A track or slope along or down which something can travel. **12. a.** A continuous period of operation, as by a machine or factory. **b.** The amount produced during such a period: *a run of 5,000 copies of the book.* **13.** A continuous length: *a ten-foot run of tubing.* **14.** A small, fast-flowing stream or brook. **15.** The direction, trend, or tendency. **16.** A length of unraveled stitches in a knitted fabric: *a run in her stocking.* **17. a.** An unbroken series or sequence: *a run of dry summers.* **b.** A number of consecutive performances: *a long run on Broadway.* **18.** *Mus.* A rapid sequence of notes; roulade. **19.** A series of unexpected and urgent demands by depositors, customers, or creditors: *a run on a bank.* **20.** The common or average kind: *The broad run of voters want him to win.* —*idioms.* **a run for (one's) money.** Strong competition. **in the long run.** Eventually; ultimately. [Middle English *runnen*, from Old English *rinnan*, and Old Norse *rinna*.]

run·a·bout (rŭn'ə-bout') *n.* **1. a.** A small, open automobile or carriage. **b.** A small motorboat. **2.** A wanderer.

run·a·round (rŭn'ə-round') *n.* Deception, usu. in the form of evasive excuses.

run·a·way (rŭn'ə-wā') *n.* **1.** A person who has run away, as a fugitive. **2.** Something that has escaped from control or proper confinement. **3.** *Informal.* An easy victory. —*adj.* **1.** Escaping or having escaped from captivity. **2.** Out of control or proper confinement: *a runaway car.* **3.** Easily won: *runaway victory.* **4.** Of or pertaining to a rapid price rise: *runaway costs.*

run·back (rŭn'băk') *n.* *Football.* **1.** The act of returning a kickoff, punt, or intercepted forward pass. **2.** The distance so covered.

run-down (rŭn'doun') *n.* **1.** A summary or résumé. **2.** *Baseball.* A play in which a runner is put out when he is trapped between bases. —*adj.* **1.** Old and decayed. **2.** Tired or listless: *feeling run-down.* **3.** Unwound and not running: *a run-down clock.*

rune[1] (rōōn) *n.* **1.** One of the letters of an alphabet used by ancient Germanic peoples. **2.** Any poem, riddle, etc., written in runic characters. **3.** Any occult characters or marks. [From Old English and Old Norse *rūn*, secret, runic character.] —**ru'nic** *adj.*

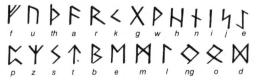

f u th a r k g w h n i j e

p z s t b e m l ng o d

basic Germanic runic alphabet

ð ʒ

edh   yogh

two later runes used in English

rune[1]

rune[2] (rōōn) *n.* A Finnish poem or canto. [Finnish *runo*, of Germanic orig.]

rung[1] (rŭng) *n.* **1.** A rod or bar forming a step of a ladder. **2.** A crosspiece supporting the legs or back of a chair. **3.** The spoke in a wheel. [Middle English, from Old English *hrung*.]

rung[2] (rŭng) *v.* Past participle of **ring** (sound a bell). —See Usage note at **ring**. [Middle English *rungen*.]

run-in (rŭn'ĭn') *n.* A quarrel; an argument; a fight.

run·let (rŭn'lĭt') *n.* A little stream; rivulet. [Dim. of RUN (stream).]

run·nel (rŭn'əl) *n.* **1.** A rivulet; a brook. **2.** A narrow channel or course, as for water. [Middle English *rynel*, from Old English, from *rinnan*, to run, flow.]

run·ner (rŭn'ər) *n.* **1.** Someone who runs: **a.** A person who competes in a race. **b.** *Baseball.* A person who runs the bases. **c.** *Football.* A person who carries the ball. **d.** A messenger. **2.** An agent or collector, as for a bank or brokerage house. **3.** A smuggler. **4.** A vessel engaged in smuggling. **5.** A device in or on which a mechanism slides or moves, as the blade of a skate or the support of a drawer. **6.** A long narrow carpet. **7.** *Bot.* **a.** A slender, creeping stem that puts forth roots from nodes spaced at intervals along its length. **b.** A plant, such as the strawberry, that has such a stem. **c.** A twining vine. **8.** Any of several saltwater fishes of the family Carangidae, such as the blue runner, *Caranx crysos*, of temperate waters of the American Atlantic coast.

run·ner-up (rŭn'ər-ŭp', rŭn'ər-ŭp') *n.* Someone or something that takes second place.

run·ning (rŭn'ĭng) *n.* **1.** The act of someone or something that runs. **2.** The sport or exercise of someone who runs. **3.** The possibility of winning or placing well in a competition: *in the running.* —*adj.* Continuous: *a running commentary.* —*adv.* Consecutively: *for four years running.*

running board. A narrow footboard extending under and beside the doors of some automotive vehicles.

running board

running knot. A slipknot.

running light. One of several lights on a ship or aircraft.

running mate. The candidate or nominee for the less important of two closely associated political offices.

run·ny (rŭn'ē) *adj.* **-ni·er, -ni·est.** Inclined to run or flow.

run-off (rŭn'ôf', -ŏf') *n.* **1.** Rainfall that is not absorbed by the soil. **2.** An extra competition held to break a tie or decide a winner.

run-of-the-mill (rŭn'əv-thə-mĭl') *adj.* Not special; average.

run-on (rŭn'ŏn', -ôn') *n.* Printed matter that is added to the main body of print without beginning a new paragraph, item, or section, as in a dictionary entry. —*adj.* Running on without a break or pause.

runt (rŭnt) *n.* **1.** An undersized animal, esp. the smallest animal of a litter. **2.** An unusually small person. [Orig. unknown.] —**runt'y** *adj.*

run-through (rŭn'thrōō') *n.* A complete but rapid review or rehearsal of something, such as of a theatrical work.

run·way (rŭn'wā') *n.* **1.** A path, channel, or track over which something runs or passes. **2.** A narrow walkway extending from a stage into an auditorium. **3.** A strip of level ground, usu. paved, on which aircraft take off and land.

ru·pee (rōō-pē', rōō'pē) *n.* The basic monetary unit of India, Pakistan, and certain other nations. [Hindi *rupaīyā*, from Sanskrit *rūpya*, wrought silver, from *rūpa*, shape, image.]

rup·ture (rŭp'chər) *n.* **1.** The act or process of breaking open or bursting. **2.** A break in friendly relations between individuals or nations. **3.** A crack; fissure. **4.** *Pathol.* **a.** A hernia, esp. of the groin or intestines. **b.** A tear in bodily tissue. —*v.* **-tured, -tur·ing.** —*tr.v.* **1.** To break open; burst. **2.** To break off; cause a breach in: *ruptured the alliance.* —*intr.v.* To undergo or suffer a rupture. [Middle English *ruptur*, from Old French *rupture*, from Latin *ruptūra*, from *rumpere*, to break.] —**rup'tur·a·ble** *adj.*

ru·ral (rŏŏr'əl) *adj.* **1.** Of, in, or pertaining to the country as opposed to the city; rustic: *rural areas; a rural accent.* **2.** Of or relating to agriculture. [Middle English, from Old French, from Latin *rūrālis*, from *rūs*, country.] **—ru'ral·ly** *adv.*

rural free delivery. Also **rural delivery.** Free government delivery of mail in rural areas.

ruse (rōōs, rōōz) *n.* An action or device meant to confuse or mislead; a deception. [Middle English, detour of a hunted animal, from Old French, from *ruser*, to repulse, detour.]

rush¹ (rŭsh) *intr.v.* **1.** To move or act swiftly; to hurry. **2.** To make a sudden or swift attack or charge. **3.** To flow or surge rapidly, often with noise: *Tons of water rushed over the falls.* **4.** *Football.* To move the ball by running. *—tr.v.* **1.** To cause to move or act with unusual haste: *Don't rush me.* **2.** To perform or do with great haste. **3.** To carry or transport hastily. **4.** To attack swiftly and suddenly. **5.** To entertain or pay great attention to for a purpose: *They rushed him for their fraternity.* *—n.* **1.** The act of rushing; a swift movement. **2.** An anxious and eager movement to get to or from a place: *a rush westward.* **3.** A great flurry of activity or press of business. **4.** A sudden attack; an onslaught. **5.** A rapid, often noisy, flow or passage. **6.** *Football.* An attempt to move the ball by running with it. **7.** Often **rushes.** The first, unedited print of a motion-picture scene. *—adj.* Requiring or marked by haste or urgency: *a rush job.* [Middle English *russhen*, from Norman French *russher*, to repulse, from Latin *recusāre*, to object to.] **—rush'er** *n.*

Syns: **rush, dart, dash, hasten, hurry, hustle** (*Informal*), **race, run, scoot, scurry, speed, tear, whiz, zip, zoom** *v. Core meaning:* To move swiftly (*rushed to the hospital*).

rush² (rŭsh) *n.* **1.** Any of various grasslike marsh plants of the family Juncaceae, with pliant, hollow, or pithy stems. **2.** The stem of a rush, used in making baskets, mats, etc. [Middle English, from Old English *rysc.*]

rusk (rŭsk) *n.* **1.** A light, soft-textured sweetened biscuit. **2.** Sweet raised bread dried and browned in an oven. [Spanish and Portuguese *rosca*, a coil, twisted roll.]

rus·set (rŭs'ĭt) *n.* **1.** A reddish brown. **2.** A coarse reddish-brown to brown homespun cloth. **3.** A winter apple with a rough reddish-brown skin. *—adj.* Reddish brown. [Middle English, from Old French *rousset*, from *rous*, red, from Latin *russus.*]

Rus·sian (rŭsh'ən) *n.* **1.** A native or inhabitant of Russia. **2.** The Slavic language of the Russian people. *—adj.* Of Russia, the Russians, or their language.

Russian Orthodox Church. An independent branch of the Eastern Orthodox Church in the Soviet Union.

Russian thistle. A red-stemmed, prickly plant, *Salsola kali tenuifolia*, a troublesome weed in North America.

Russian wolfhound. A dog, the borzoi.

rust (rŭst) *n.* **1.** Any of various powdery or scaly reddish-brown hydrated ferric oxides formed on iron and iron-containing materials by low-temperature oxidation in the presence of water. **2.** Any of various metallic coatings formed by corrosion. **3.** Any deterioration of ability or character that results from inactivity or neglect. **4. a.** Any of various parasitic fungi of the order Uredinales that are injurious to a wide variety of plants. **b.** A plant disease caused by such fungi, characterized by reddish or brownish spots on leaves, stems, and other parts. **5.** A reddish brown. *—intr.v.* **1.** To become corroded. **2.** To deteriorate or degenerate through inactivity or neglect. **3.** To develop a disease caused by a rust fungus. *—tr.v.* **1.** To corrode or subject (a metal) to rust formation. **2.** To impair or spoil by misuse, inactivity, and the like. *—adj.* Reddish brown. [Middle English, from Old English *rūst.*] **—rust'a·ble** *adj.*

rus·tic (rŭs'tĭk) *adj.* **1.** Typical of country life. **2.** Plain and unsophisticated; simple. **3.** Made of rough tree branches: *rustic furniture.* *—n.* **1.** A rural person. **2.** A crude, coarse or simple person. [Middle English *rustyk*, from Old French *rustique*, from Latin *rūsticus*, from *rūs*, country.] **—rus'ti·cal·ly** *adv.* **—rus·tic'i·ty** (rŭs-tĭs'ə-tē) *n.*

rus·ti·cate (rŭs'tĭ-kāt') *v.* **-cat·ed, -cat·ing.** *—intr.v.* To go to or live in the country. *—tr.v.* **1.** To send to the country. **2.** *Brit.* To suspend (a student) from a university. **—rus'ti·ca'tion** *n.* **—rus'ti·ca'tor** *n.*

rus·tle (rŭs'əl) *v.* **-tled, -tling.** *—intr.v.* To move with soft fluttering or crackling sounds. *—tr.v.* **1.** To cause to make such sounds. **2.** *Informal.* To make, prepare, or get quickly or briskly: *rustle up a dinner.* **3.** To steal (cattle). *—n.* A soft fluttering or crackling sound. [Middle English *rustlen.*] **—rus'tling·ly** *adv.*

rus·tler (rŭs'lər) *n.* A person who steals cattle.

rust·proof (rŭst'prŏŏf') *adj.* Incapable of rusting. *—tr.v.* To make rustproof by treating with a special paint or other substance.

rust·y (rŭs'tē) *adj.* **-i·er, -i·est.** **1.** Covered with rust; corroded. **2.** Consisting of or produced by rust. **3.** Reddish brown. **4.** Weakened or impaired by neglect, disuse, or lack of practice. **—rust'i·ly** *adv.* **—rust'i·ness** *n.*

rut¹ (rŭt) *n.* **1.** A sunken track or groove made by the passage of vehicles. **2.** A habitual, unvaried way of living or acting. *—tr.v.* **rut·ted, rut·ting.** To make ruts in. [Old French *route*, way, route.] **—rut'ty** *adj.*

rut² (rŭt) *n.* A cyclically recurring sexually active condition of a male deer or other male animal ready to mate during the breeding season. [Middle English *rutte*, from Old French *rut*, roar, from Late Latin *rūgitus*, from Latin *rūgīre*, to roar.]

ru·ta·ba·ga (rōō'tə-bā'gə) *n.* **1.** A plant, *Brassica napobrassica*, native to Eurasia with a thick, bulbous root. **2.** The edible root of this plant. [Dial. Swedish *rotabagge.*]

ruth (rōōth) *n.* *Archaic.* **1.** Compassion or pity. **2.** Sorrow; misery; grief. [Middle English *ruthe*, from *rewen*, to rue, from Old English *hrēowan.*]

ru·the·ni·um (rōō-thē'nē-əm) *n.* *Symbol* **Ru** A hard white acid-resistant metallic element found in platinum ores, used to harden platinum and palladium for jewelry and in alloys for electrical contacts. Atomic number 44; atomic weight 101.07; melting point 2,250°C; boiling point 3,900°C; specific gravity 12.41; valences 0, 1, 2, 3, 4, 5, 6, 7, 8. [From Medieval Latin *Ruthenia*, Russia.]

ruth·less (rōōth'lĭs) *adj.* Having no compassion or pity; merciless; cruel. **—ruth'less·ly** *adv.* **—ruth'less·ness** *n.*

-ry. Var. of **-ery.**

rye (rī) *n.* **1.** A widely cultivated cereal grass, *Secale cereale.* **2.** The grain of this plant, used in making flour and whiskey and for livestock feed. **3.** Whiskey made from rye. [Middle English, from Old English *ryge.*]

rye grass. Any of several pasture or meadow grasses of the genus *Lolium*, native to Eurasia.

Ss

Phoenician – *About 3,000 years ago the Phoenicians and other Semitic peoples began to use graphic signs to represent individual speech sounds instead of syllables or whole words. They used this symbol to represent the sound of the consonant represented in English orthography by "sh" and gave it the name* shin, *the Phoenician word for "tooth."*

Greek – *The Greeks borrowed the Phoenician alphabet with some modifications. They changed the orientation of* shin *and altered its name to* sigma. *They used* sigma *to represent the sound of the consonant "s."*

Roman – *The Romans borrowed the alphabet from the*

Greeks via the Etruscans. They gave sigma *a more rounded form and adapted it for carving Latin in stone. This monumental script, as it is called, became the basis for modern printed capital letters.*

Medieval – *By medieval times – around 1,200 years ago – the Roman monumental capitals had become adapted to being relatively quickly written on paper, parchment, or vellum. The cursive minuscule alphabet became the basis of modern printed lower-case letters.*

Modern – *Since the invention of printing about 500 years ago the basic form of the letter S has remained unchanged.*

---

s or **S** (ĕs) *n., pl.* **s's** or **S's. 1.** The 19th letter of the modern English alphabet. **2.** Anything shaped like the letter **S.**

-s¹ or **-es¹.** A suffix indicating the plural of nouns: **charms, toys.** [Middle English *-es, -s,* from Old English *-as.*]

-s² or **-es².** A suffix indicating the third person singular present indicative form of verbs: *He walks.* [Middle English *-es,* from Old English *-es, -as.*]

-s³. A suffix forming adverbs from nouns and adjectives: *They work nights.* [Middle English *-es,* from Old English *-es* (genitive sing. suffix).]

-'s. A suffix indicating the possessive case of singular nouns and irregularly formed plural nouns: **nation's, men's.** [Middle English *-es,* genitive sing. ending, from Old English *-es.*]

Sab·bath (săb'əth) *n.* **1.** The seventh day of the week, Saturday, observed as a day of rest and worship by the Jews and some Christian sects. **2.** The first day of the week, Sunday, observed as the day of rest and worship by most Christians. [Middle English *sabath,* ult. from Latin *sabbatum,* from Greek *sabbaton,* from Hebrew *shabbāth,* from *shābhath,* to rest.]

sab·bat·i·cal (sə-băt'ĭ-kəl) or **sab·bat·ic** (-ĭk) *adj.* **1. Sabbatical.** Pertaining or appropriate to the Sabbath. **2.** Pertaining to a sabbatical year. *—n.* A leave of absence granted every seventh year. [From Late Latin *sabbaticus,* from Greek *sabbatikos,* from *sabbaton,* Sabbath.]

sa·ber (sā'bər) *n.* Also *Brit.* **sa·bre. 1.** A heavy cavalry sword with a one-edged, slightly curved blade. **2.** A kind of fencing sword. *—tr.v.* To strike, injure, or kill with a saber. [French *sabre,* var. of German *Säbel,* from Middle High German *sabel,* of Slavic orig.]

sa·ber-toothed tiger (sā'bər-tootht'). Any of various large prehistoric cats characterized by long upper canine teeth.

Sa·bine (sā'bīn') *n.* A member of an ancient tribe of central Italy, conquered by the Romans in 290 B.C.

sa·ble (sā'bəl) *n.* **1. a.** A carnivorous mammal, *Martes zibellina,* of northern Europe and Asia, with soft, dark fur. **b.** The fur of this animal. **2.** The color black. *—adj.* **1.** Black. **2.** Dark; somber. [Middle English, from Old French, from Medieval Latin *sabelum,* of Slavic orig.]

sa·bot (să-bō', săb'ō) *n.* A wooden shoe worn in certain European countries. [French, from Old French.]

sab·o·tage (săb'ə-täzh') *n.* **1.** The destruction of property or the obstruction of normal operations, as by enemy agents in time of war. **2.** Any treacherous action to defeat or hinder a cause. *—tr.v.* **-taged, -tag·ing.** To commit sabotage against. [French, from *saboter,* to work clumsily, from *sabot,* sabot.]

sab·o·teur (săb'ə-tûr') *n.* A person who commits sabotage. [French.]

sa·bra (sä'brə) *n.* A native-born Israeli. [Hebrew *sābrāh.*]

sa·bre (sā'bər) *n. & v. Brit.* Var. of **saber.**

sac (săk) *n.* A pouch in a plant or animal, sometimes filled with fluid. [French, a bag, from Latin *saccus.*]

sac·cha·rin (săk'ə-rĭn) *n.* A very sweet, white crystalline powder, $C_7H_5NO_3S$, used as a calorie-free sweetener. [SACCHAR(O)- + -IN.]

sac·cha·rine (săk'ə-rĭn, -rēn', -rīn') *adj.* **1.** Of, relating to, or of the nature of sugar or saccharin. **2.** Cloyingly sweet: *a saccharine smile.* [SACCHAR(O)- + -INE.]

saccharo– or **sacchar–.** A prefix meaning sugar: **saccharin.** [From Latin *saccharum,* sugar, from Greek *sakkharon,* ult. from Sanskrit *śarkarā.*]

sac·cule (săk'yool) *n.* Also **sac·cu·lus** (săk'yə-ləs) *pl.* **-li** (-lī'). **1.** A small sac. **2.** The smaller of two membranous sacs in the vestibule of the labyrinth of the ear.

sac·er·do·tal (săs'ər-dōt'l, săk'-) *adj.* Of or pertaining to priests or the priesthood. [Middle English, from Old French, from Latin *sacerdōtālis,* from *sacerdōs,* priest.]

sa·chem (sā'chəm) *n.* The chief of a tribe or confederation of North American Indians, esp. an Algonquian chief. [Narraganset *sâchim,* "chief."]

sa·chet (să-shā') *n.* A small packet of perfumed powder used to scent clothes or linens. [French, from Old French, a small bag, dim. of *sac,* bag, from Latin *saccus.*]

sack¹ (săk) *n.* **1. a.** A large bag of strong, coarse material. **b.** A similar container of paper or plastic. **2.** The amount held in a sack. **3.** A short, loose-fitting garment for women and children. **4.** *Slang.* A dismissal from employment. **5.** *Slang.* A bed. *—tr.v.* **1.** To place in a sack. **2.** *Slang.* To

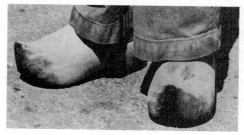

sabot

---

discharge from employment. [Middle English, from Old English *sæcc*, from Latin *saccus*, from Greek *sakkos*, of Semitic orig.]

sack² (săk) *tr.v.* To rob of goods or valuables after capture. —*n.* The looting or pillaging of a captured town. [Old French *(mettre a) sac*, (to put in) a sack, to plunder.]
   Syns: sack, loot, pillage, plunder, ravage *v. Core meaning:* To rob and lay waste esp. in war (*villages sacked by invading Vikings*).

sack³ (săk) *n.* A light, dry, strong wine from Spain or the Canary Islands. [Earlier *seck*, from Old French *(vin) sec*, dry (wine), from Latin *siccus*, dry.]

sack·cloth (săk′klôth′, -klŏth′) *n.* 1. Sacking. 2. A garment made of sackcloth, worn as a symbol of mourning or penitence.

sack·ing (săk′ĭng) *n.* Coarse cloth used for sacks.

sac·ra·ment (săk′rə-mənt) *n.* 1. A formal Christian rite, such as baptism, esp. one considered to have been instituted by Jesus as a means of grace. 2. Often **Sacrament**. **a.** The Eucharist. **b.** The consecrated elements of the Eucharist, esp. the bread or host. [Middle English, from Old French *sacrement*, from Latin *sacrāmentum*, from Latin, oath, solemn obligation, from *sacrāre*, to consecrate, from *sacer*, sacred.] —**sac′ra·men′tal** *adj.*

sa·cred (sā′krĭd) *adj.* 1. Dedicated to or set apart for the worship of a deity. 2. Worthy of religious veneration. 3. Dedicated; consecrated. 4. Worthy of reverence or respect. 5. Of or pertaining to religion. [Middle English, from *sacren*, to consecrate, from Old French *sacrer*, from Latin *sacrāre*, from *sacer*, dedicated, holy, sacred.] —**sa′cred·ly** *adv.* —**sa′cred·ness** *n.*

sacred cow. Someone or something that is immune from criticism.

sac·ri·fice (săk′rə-fīs′) *n.* 1. **a.** The act of offering something to a deity, esp. the ritual slaughter of a victim. **b.** Someone or something offered in this way. 2. The act of giving up something for the sake of another. 3. A loss sustained, esp. by selling something at less than its value. —*v.* **-ficed, -fic·ing.** —*tr.v.* 1. To offer as a sacrifice. 2. To give up for the sake of another. 3. To sell at a loss. —*intr.v.* To make or offer a sacrifice. [Middle English, from Old French, from Latin *sacrificium* : *sacer*, sacred + *facere*, to make.] —**sac′ri·fic′er** *n.*

sac·ri·fi·cial (săk′rə-fĭsh′əl) *adj.* Of or pertaining to sacrifice: *a sacrificial lamb.* —**sac′ri·fi′cial·ly** *adv.*

sac·ri·lege (săk′rə-lĭj) *n.* The profanation of something sacred. [Middle English, from Old French, from Latin *sacrilegium*, from *sacrilegus*, one who steals sacred things.] —**sac′ri·le′gious** (-lĭj′əs, -lē′jəs) *adj.* —**sac′ri·le′gious·ly** *adv.* —**sac′ri·le′gious·ness** *n.*

sac·ris·tan (săk′rĭ-stən) *n.* 1. A person in charge of a sacristy. 2. A sexton. [Middle English, from Medieval Latin *sacristānus*, from *sacrista*, one in charge of sacred vessels, from Latin *sacer*, sacred.]

sac·ris·ty (săk′rĭ-stē) *n., pl.* **-ties.** A room in a church for sacred vessels and vestments. [French *sacristie*, from Medieval Latin *sacristia*, from *sacrista*, sacristan.]

sac·ro·il·i·ac (săk′rō-ĭl′ē-ăk′, să′krō-) *n.* The region of the lower back in which the sacrum and the ilium come together. [From SACRUM + ILIUM.] —**sac′ro·il′i·ac** *adj.*

sac·ro·sanct (săk′rō-săngkt′) *adj.* Sacred and inviolable. [Latin *sacrōsanctus*, consecrated with religious ceremonies.] —**sac′ro·sanc′ti·ty** (săk′rō-săngk′tĭ-tē) *n.*

sa·crum (sā′krəm) *n., pl.* **-cra** (-krə). A triangular bone that forms the posterior section of the pelvis. [From Late Latin *(os) sacrum*, translation of Greek *hieron osteron*, "sacred bone," from its having been used in sacrifices.]

sad (săd) *adj.* **sad·der, sad·dest.** 1. Affected or characterized by sorrow or unhappiness. 2. Expressive of sorrow or unhappiness. 3. Deplorable; sorry. —See Syns at **gloomy**. [Middle English, grave, sad, from Old English *sæd*, sated, weary.] —**sad′ly** *adv.* —**sad′ness** *n.*

sad·den (săd′n) *tr.v.* To make sad. —*intr.v.* To become sad.

sad·dle (săd′l) *n.* 1. A leather seat for a rider, fastened to the back of an animal. 2. A padded seat, as on a bicycle. 3. A cut of meat, consisting of part of the backbone and both loins. 4. A ridge between two peaks. —*tr.v.* **-dled, -dling.** 1. To put a saddle on. 2. To load or burden; encum-

ber: *saddled her with his unpaid bills.* [Middle English *sadel*, from Old English *sadol*.]

sad·dle·bag (săd′l-băg′) *n.* A pouch that hangs from a saddle or over the rear wheel of a motorcycle or bicycle.

sad·dler (săd′lər) *n.* A person who makes, repairs, or sells equipment for horses.

sad·dler·y (săd′lə-rē) *n., pl.* **-ies.** 1. Equipment, such as saddles, for horses. 2. A shop that deals in saddlery.

saddle shoe. A flat-heeled oxford with a band of leather in a contrasting color across the instep.

saddle soap. A mild soap used for cleaning and softening leather.

Sad·du·cee (săj′ə-sē, săd′yə-) *n.* A member of a Jewish sect active from the 2nd cent. B.C. through the 1st cent. A.D., that favored a literal interpretation of the written Mosaic law. [Ult. from Hebrew *Şəddūqī*, prob. from *Şādôq*, Zadok, a high priest of Israel in King David's time and supposedly the founder of the sect.] —**Sad′du·ce′an** (-sē′ən) *adj.* —**Sad′du·cee′ism** *n.*

sa·dism (sā′dĭz′əm, săd′ĭz′-) *n.* 1. *Psychol.* The association of sexual satisfaction with the infliction of pain on others. 2. Delight in cruelty. [After Comte Donatien de *Sade* (1740–1814), French writer.] —**sa′dist** *n.*

sa·dis·tic (sə-dĭs′tĭk) *adj.* Characterized by sadism.

sa·fa·ri (sə-fä′rē) *n., pl.* **-ris.** A hunting expedition, esp. in East Africa. [Arabic *safarīy*, a journey, from *safara*, to travel, set out.]

safe (sāf) *adj.* **saf·er, saf·est.** 1. Secure from danger, harm, or evil. 2. Free from danger or injury. 3. Free from risk: *a safe bet.* 4. Affording protection: *a safe place.* 5. *Baseball.* Reaching a base without being put out. —*n.* A container for storing valuables. [Middle English *sauf*, from Old French, from Latin *salvus*, healthy, uninjured, safe.] —**safe′ly** *adv.* —**safe′ness** *n.*

safe-con·duct (sāf′kŏn′dŭkt) *n.* An official document assuring unmolested passage, as through enemy territory.

safe-crack·er (sāf′krăk′ər) *n.* A person who forces open safes to steal the contents.

safe-de·pos·it box (sāf′dĭ-pŏz′ĭt) *n.* A box, usu. in a bank vault, for the safe storage of valuables.

safe·guard (sāf′gärd′) *n.* Someone or something that serves as a guard or protection. —*tr.v.* To make safe; to guard; protect. —See Syns at **defend**.

safe·keep·ing (sāf′kē′pĭng) *n.* The act of keeping safe or the condition of being kept safe.

safe·ty (sāf′tē) *n., pl.* **-ties.** 1. Freedom from danger, risk, or injury. 2. A device, such as the lock on a firearm, designed to prevent accidents. 3. A football play in which the offensive team downs the ball behind its own goal line, resulting in two points for the defensive team.
   Syns: safety, security *n. Core meaning:* Freedom from danger or harm (*lived in the safety of a fortress*).

safety pin. A pin in the form of a clasp, with a sheath to cover and hold the point.

safety razor. A razor in which the blade is fitted into a holder with guards to prevent cutting of the skin.

safety valve. A valve, as in a steam boiler, that automatically opens when pressure reaches a dangerous level.

saf·flow·er (săf′lou′ər) *n.* A plant, *Carthamus tinctorius*, with orange flowers that yield a dyestuff and seeds that are the source of an oil used in cooking. [Earlier *safflore*, from Dutch *saffloer*, from Old French *saffleur*, from Old

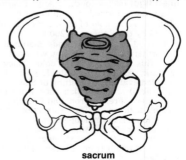

sacrum

Italian *saffiore*, saffron, ult. from Arabic *aṣfar*, yellow, a yellow plant.]

saf·fron (săf′rən) *n.* **1. a.** An Old World plant, *Crocus sativus*, that has flowers with orange stigmas. **b.** The dried stigmas of this plant, used to color foods and as a cooking spice. **2.** A orange-yellow color. —*adj.* Orange-yellow. [Middle English *saffran*, from Old French *safran*, from Medieval Latin *safranum*, from Arabic *za'farān*.]

sag (săg) *intr.v.* **sagged, sag·ging. 1.** To droop, hang downward, or settle from weight or slackness. **2.** To diminish in strength; weaken. **3.** To decline, as in value or price. —*n.* **1.** An instance or extent of sagging. **2.** A sagging area; a depression. [Middle English *saggen*.]

sa·ga (sä′gə) *n.* **1.** A prose narrative about historical and legendary events and figures of Iceland and Norway. **2.** A long narrative. [Old Norse, a story, legend.]

sa·ga·cious (sə-gā′shəs) *adj.* Having or showing sound judgment and keen perception. —See Syns at **wise.** [From Latin *sagāx.*]—**sa·ga·cious·ly** *adv.*—**sa·gac′i·ty** (-găs′ĭ-tē) *n.*

sag·a·more (săg′ə-môr′, -mōr′) *n.* A subordinate chief among the Algonquian Indians. [Abnaki *sákama.*]

sage[1] (sāj) *n.* A person of great wisdom. —*adj.* **sag·er, sag·est.** Judicious; wise. —See Syns at **wise.** [Middle English, from Old French, from Latin *sapere,* to be sensible, be wise.] —**sage′ly** *adv.* —**sage′ness** *n.*

sage[2] (sāj) *n.* **1. a.** Any of various plants and shrubs of the genus *Salvia,* esp. *S. officinalis,* with aromatic grayish-green leaves. **b.** The leaves of this plant used as seasoning. **2.** The sagebrush. [Middle English *sauge,* from Old French *sauge,* from Latin *salvia,* "the healing plant," from *salvus,* healthy, safe.]

sage·brush (sāj′brŭsh′) *n.* Any of several North American shrubby plants of the genus *Artemisia,* with silver-green leaves and clusters of small white flowers.

Sag·it·tar·i·us (săj′ĭ-târ′ē-əs) *n.* **1.** A constellation in the Southern Hemisphere near Scorpius and Capricorn. **2.** The ninth sign of the zodiac.

sag·it·tate (săj′ĭ-tāt′) *adj.* Like an arrowhead in shape: *sagittate leaves.* [From Latin *sagitta,* arrow.]

sa·gua·ro (sə-gwä′rō, sə-wä′rō) *n., pl.* **-ros.** Also **sa·hua·ro** (sə-wä′rō). A large cactus, *Carnegiea gigantea,* of the southwestern United States and northern Mexico, with spiny, sparse branches and edible fruit. [Mexican Spanish.]

saguaro

Saint Bernard

sa·hib (sä′ĭb, sä′hĭb) *n.* Master; sir. Used for Europeans in colonial India. [Hindi *ṣāhib,* master, from Arabic.]

said (sĕd) *v.* Past tense and past participle of **say.** —*adj. Law.* Named or mentioned before. [Middle English *seide,* (y)seyd, from Old English *sægde, gesægd.*]

sail (sāl) *n.* **1. a.** A length of usu. triangular or rectangular fabric, used to catch the wind and propel a vessel. **b.** The sails of a ship or boat. **2.** *pl.* **sail** or **sails.** A sailing vessel. **3.** A trip or voyage in a sailing craft. **4.** Something similar to a sail in function. —*intr.v.* **1.** To move across the surface of water, esp. in a sailing vessel. **2.** To start out on a journey by water. **3.** To operate a sailing craft. **4.** To move swiftly, smoothly, or effortlessly. —*tr.v.* **1.** To navigate or manage (a vessel). **2.** To voyage upon or across: *sail the Pacific.* [Middle English, from Old English *segl.*]

sail·er (sā′lər) *n.* A boat or ship: *a fast sailer.*

sail·fish (sāl′fĭsh′) *n., pl.* **sailfish** or **-fish·es.** Any of various large saltwater fishes of the genus *Istiophorus,* with a

spearlike snout and a large, saillike dorsal fin.

sail·ing (sā′lĭng) *n.* **1.** The skill required to operate a vessel; navigation. **2.** The sport of riding in a sailboat.

sail·or (sā′lər) *n.* **1.** A person who serves in a navy as an ordinary seaman or who works on a ship as a crew member. **2.** A person who travels by water. **3.** A low-crowned straw hat with a flat top and flat brim. —**sail′or·ly** *adj.*

saint (sānt) *n.* **1.** A person considered holy and worthy of public veneration, esp. one who has been canonized. **2.** A very virtuous person. —*tr.v.* To canonize. [Middle English, from Old French, from Latin *sanctus,* sacred, from *sancīre,* to consecrate.]

Saint Ber·nard (bər-närd′). A large, strong dog of a Swiss breed, orig. used in the Swiss Alps to rescue lost travelers. [After the hospice of *Saint Bernard.*]

saint·ed (sān′tĭd) *adj.* **1.** Canonized. **2.** Saintly.

saint·hood (sānt′hŏŏd′) *n.* The status of a saint.

saint·ly (sānt′lē) *adj.* **-li·er, -li·est.** Resembling, pertaining to, or befitting a saint. —**saint′li·ness** *n.*

Saint Nich·o·las (nĭk′ə-ləs). Santa Claus.

Saint Pat·rick's Day (păt′rĭks). March 17, observed in honor of Saint Patrick, the patron saint of Ireland.

Saint Val·en·tine's Day (văl′ən-tīnz′). February 14, the traditional day for sending valentines.

Saint Vi·tus Dance (vī′təs). Chorea. [After *Saint Vitus,* 3rd-cent. Christian child martyr.]

saith (sĭth, sā′əth). *Archaic.* A form of **say.**

sake[1] (sāk) *n.* **1.** Purpose; end: *for the sake of argument.* **2.** Advantage; good: *for your own sake.* [Middle English, lawsuit, from Old English *sacu.*]

sa·ke[2] (sä′kē) *n.* Also **sa·ki.** A Japanese liquor made from fermented rice. [Japanese, liquor.]

sal (săl) *n.* Salt. [Latin *sāl.*]

sa·laam (sə-läm′) *n.* A ceremonious act of deference or obeisance, esp. a low bow performed while placing the right palm on the forehead. —*tr.v.* To greet with a salaam. —*intr.v.* To perform a salaam. [Arabic *salām,* peace.]

sal·a·ble (sā′lə-bəl) *adj.* Capable of being sold. —**sal′a·bil′i·ty** (sā′lə-bĭl′ĭ-tē) *n.* —**sal′a·bly** *adv.*

sa·la·cious (sə-lā′shəs) *adj.* Sexually stimulating. [From Latin *salāx,* leaping, lustful, from *salīre,* to leap.]

sal·ad (săl′əd) *n.* **1.** A dish of mixed, usu. green leafy raw vegetables. **2.** A cold dish of chopped fruit, meat, fish, eggs, or other food. **3.** Any green vegetable used in salad. [Middle English *salade,* from Old French, from Old Provençal *salada,* ult. from Latin *sāl,* salt.]

salad days. The time of youth, innocence, and inexperience. [From *"my salad days when I was green in judgment, cold in blood"* (Shakespeare).]

sal·a·man·der (săl′ə-măn′dər) *n.* **1.** Any of various small, lizardlike amphibians of the order Caudata, with scaleless skin and four usu. weak legs. **2.** A mythical creature, gen. resembling a lizard, believed capable of withstanding fire. [Middle English *salamandre,* from Old French, from Latin *salamandra,* from Greek.]

sa·la·mi (sə-lä′mē) *n.* A highly spiced and salted sausage. —*modifier: a salami sandwich.* [Italian, pl. of *salame,* salted pork, from *salare,* to salt, ult. from Latin *sāl,* salt.]

sal·a·ried (săl′ə-rēd) *adj.* Earning or yielding a salary.

sal·a·ry (săl′ə-rē, săl′rē) *n., pl.* **-ries.** A regular compensation for services or work. [Middle English *salarie,* from Anglo-French, from Latin *salārium,* salt-money, stipend, from *sāl,* salt.]

sale (sāl) *n.* **1.** The exchange of a commodity for money or its equivalent. **2.** A selling of property. **3.** A special disposal of goods at lowered prices. —*idioms.* **for sale.** Offered or available for purchase. **on sale.** Available for purchase, esp. at a lowered price. [Middle English, from Old English *sala,* from Old Norse.]

sales·clerk (sālz′klûrk′) *n.* A person employed to sell goods in a store.

sales·man (sālz′mən) *n.* A man employed to sell merchandise in a store or in a designated territory.

sales·man·ship (sālz′mən-shĭp′) *n.* **1.** The work or occupation of a salesman. **2.** Skill or ability in selling.

sales·per·son (sālz′pûr′sən) *n.* A salesman or saleswoman.

sales tax. A tax levied on the price of goods and services.

---

sales·wom·an (sālz'wŏŏm'ən) *n.* A woman employed to sell merchandise in a store or in a designated territory.

sa·lic·y·late (sə-lĭs'ə-lāt', -lĭt, săl'ə-sĭl'ĭt) *n.* A salt or ester of salicylic acid. [SALICYL(IC ACID) + -ATE.]

sal·i·cyl·ic acid (săl'ĭ-sĭl'ĭk). A white crystalline acid, C₇H₆O₃, used in making aspirin and as a preservative. [From French *salicyle*, the radical of salicylic acid.]

sa·li·ence (sā'lē-əns, sāl'yəns) *n.* Also **sa·li·en·cy** (-ən-sē). 1. The condition of being salient. 2. A striking feature.

sa·li·ent (sā'lē-ənt, sāl'yənt) *adj.* 1. Projecting or jutting beyond a line or surface; protruding up or out. 2. Standing out conspicuously; striking. —*n.* 1. The area of a battle or defense line that projects most toward the enemy. 2. A projecting angle or part. [Latin *saliēns*, pres. part. of *salīre*, to leap, jump.] —**sa'li·ent·ly** *adv.* —**sa'li·ent·ness** *n.*

sa·li·en·tian (sā'lē-ĕn'shən) *n.* An amphibian of the order Salientia, such as the frogs and toads. [From Latin *saliēns*, leaping.] —**sa'li·en·tian** *adj.*

sa·line (sā'lēn', -līn') *adj.* 1. Of, relating to, or resembling salt. 2. Containing or consisting of salt. —*n.* 1. Any salt of magnesium or of the alkalis, used in medicine as a cathartic. 2. A saline solution. [Middle English *salyne*, from Latin *salīnus*, from *sāl*, salt.] —**sa·lin'i·ty** (sə-lĭn'ĭ-tē) *n.*

sa·li·va (sə-lī'və) *n.* The watery, slightly alkaline fluid secreted into the mouth by the salivary glands. [Latin *salīva*.]

sal·i·var·y (săl'ə-vĕr'ē) *adj.* Of or producing saliva.

sal·i·vate (săl'ə-vāt') *intr.v.* **-vat·ed, -vat·ing.** To secrete or produce saliva. —**sal'i·va'tion** *n.*

sal·low¹ (săl'ō) *adj.* **-er, -est.** Of a sickly yellow color. [Middle English *salowe*, from Old English *salo*.]

sal·low² (săl'ō) *n.* Any of several European willows. [Middle English *salwe*, from Old English *sealh*.]

sal·ly (săl'ē) *intr.v.* **-lied, -ly·ing.** 1. To rush out or leap forth suddenly. 2. To set out. —*n., pl.* **-lies.** 1. A sudden rush forward; a leap. 2. An assault from a defensive position; a sortie. 3. A sudden emergence; an outburst. 4. A witticism or clever remark; quip. 5. An excursion. [Old French *saillie*, a sally, from *saillir*, to leap or rush forward, from Latin *salīre*, to leap.]

sal·ma·gun·di (săl'mə-gŭn'dē) *n.* Also **sal·ma·gun·dy.** 1. A salad of chopped meat, anchovies, eggs, and onions. 2. A mixture or assortment. [French *salmigondis*.]

salm·on (săm'ən, sä'mən) *n., pl.* **salmon** or **-ons.** 1. Any of various large food and game fishes of the genera *Salmo* and *Oncorhynchus*, with a pinkish flesh. 2. A yellowish pink or pinkish orange. [Middle English, from Old French *saumon*, from Latin *salmō*.]

sal·mo·nel·la (săl'mə-nĕl'ə) *n., pl.* **salmonella** or **-las** or **-lae** (-lē). Any of various bacteria of the genus *Salmonella*, many of which cause disease in warm-blooded animals. [After Daniel E. *Salmon* (1850–1914), American veterinarian.]

sa·lon (sə-lŏn', sä-lôN') *n.* 1. A large room for receiving and entertaining guests. 2. A periodic gathering of persons usu. of social or intellectual distinction. 3. A hall or gallery for the exhibition of works of art. 4. An exhibition of art works. 5. A stylish commercial establishment: *a beauty salon.* [French, from Italian *salone*, from *sala*, a hall, room, of Germanic orig.]

sa·loon (sə-loon') *n.* 1. A place where alcoholic drinks are sold and drunk; a bar; tavern. 2. A large room or hall for receptions or exhibitions. 3. A large cabin used for social purposes on a ship. [French *salon*, salon.]

sal·si·fy (săl'sə-fē, -fī') *n.* A plant, *Tragopogon porrifolius*, with purple flowers and an edible taproot. [French *salsifis*, from obs. Italian *salsifica*.]

salt (sôlt) *n.* 1. A colorless or white crystalline solid, chiefly sodium chloride, used as a food seasoning and preservative. 2. A chemical compound formed by replacing all or part of the hydrogen ions of an acid with one or more cations of a base. 3. **salts.** Any of various mineral salts used as cathartics. 4. **salts.** Smelling salts. 5. An element that gives flavor or zest. 6. Sharp, lively wit; pungency. 7. *Informal.* A sailor. —*adj.* 1. Tasting of, containing, or filled with salt; salty. 2. Preserved with salt: *salt mackerel.* 3. Flooded with sea water. —*tr.v.* 1. To add salt to; season with salt. 2. To preserve with salt. 3. To add liveliness to: *salt a lecture with anecdotes.* 4. To cause to seem more valuable by adding minerals: *salted the claim with gold dust to hoodwink gullible prospectors.* —*phrasal verbs.* **salt away.** To put aside; save. —See Syns at **save. salt out.** To precipitate (a dissolved substance) by adding salt. —*idioms.* **with a grain of salt.** With skepticism. **worth (one's) salt.** Efficient and capable. [Middle English, from Old English *sealt*.] —**salt'ness** *n.*

salt·box (sôlt'bŏks') *n.* A house with two stories in front and one in back and a roof with a long rear slope.

salt·cel·lar (sôlt'sĕl'ər) *n.* A small container for holding and dispensing salt. [Var. of Middle English *salt saler*.]

sal·tine (sôl-tēn') *n.* A thin, crisp cracker sprinkled with coarse salt. [SALT + -INE.]

salt lick. A block or natural deposit of exposed salt that animals can lick.

salt·pe·ter (sôlt'pē'tər) *n.* 1. Potassium nitrate. 2. Sodium nitrate. [Var. of earlier *salpetre*, from Middle English, from Old French, from Medieval Latin *salpetra*.]

salt·shak·er (sôlt'shā'kər) *n.* A container with a perforated top for sprinkling table salt.

salt·wa·ter (sôlt'wô'tər, -wŏt'ər) *adj.* Pertaining to, consisting of, or inhabiting salt water.

salt·y (sôl'tē) *adj.* **-i·er, -i·est.** 1. Containing or tasting of salt. 2. Suggestive of the sea or sailing life. 3. Sharp; pungent: *salty humor.* —**salt'i·ly** *adv.* —**salt'i·ness** *n.*

sa·lu·bri·ous (sə-loo'brē-əs) *adj.* Favorable to health. [From Latin *salūbris*, from *salūs*, health.] —**sa·lu'bri·ous·ly** *adv.* —**sa·lu'bri·ous·ness** or **sa·lu'bri·ty** (-brĭ-tē) *n.*

sal·u·tar·y (săl'yə-tĕr'ē) *adj.* 1. Beneficial: *salutary advice.* 2. Favorable to health: *a salutary climate.* [Old French *salutaire*, from Latin *salūtāris*, of health, from *salūs*, health.] —**sal'u·tar'i·ly** *adv.* —**sal'u·tar'i·ness** *n.*

sal·u·ta·tion (săl'yə-tā'shən) *n.* 1. A gesture or expression of greeting. 2. The word or phrase of greeting that begins a letter.

sa·lu·ta·to·ri·an (sə-loo'tə-tôr'ē-ən, -tōr-) *n.* The student who delivers the salutatory.

sa·lu·ta·to·ry (sə-loo'tə-tôr'ē, -tōr'ē) *n., pl.* **-ries.** An opening address at a commencement exercise. —*adj.* Expressing a salutation.

sa·lute (sə-loot') *v.* **-lut·ed, -lut·ing.** —*tr.v.* 1. To greet with an expression or gesture of welcome, good will, or respect. 2. To recognize with a prescribed gesture or act of respect. 3. To honor formally. —*intr.v.* To make a gesture of greeting. —*n.* 1. An act or gesture of welcome or greeting. 2. A gesture, sign, or ceremony of honor, recognition, or respect. [Middle English *saluten*, from Latin *salūtāre*, to preserve, salute, wish health to, from *salūs*, health, safety.] —**sa·lut'er** *n.*

sal·va·ble (săl'və-bəl) *adj.* 1. Capable of being saved. 2. Able to be salvaged.

sal·vage (săl'vĭj) *tr.v.* **-vaged, -vag·ing.** To save from loss or destruction. —*n.* 1. **a.** The rescue of a ship, its crew, passengers, or cargo from danger such as shipwreck. **b.** Money paid to those who aid in such a rescue. 2. The act of saving an imperiled property. 3. Rescued property. [French, the act of saving, from Old French, from *salver*, to save, from Late Latin *salvāre*, from Latin *salvus*, safe.] —**sal'vage·a·ble** *adj.* —**sal'vag·er** *n.*

sal·va·tion (săl-vā'shən) *n.* 1. Preservation or deliverance from evil, destruction, danger, or sin. 2. Someone or something that saves or preserves. [Middle English, from Old French, from Late Latin *salvātiō*, from *salvāre*, to save.] —**sal·va'tion·al** *adj.*

salve (săv, säv) *n.* 1. A soothing or healing ointment. 2. Anything that soothes or heals; balm. —*tr.v.* **salved, salv·ing.** To soothe or heal with or as if with salve. [Middle English, from Old English *sealf*.]

sal·ver (săl'vər) *n.* A serving tray. [From French *salve*, from Spanish *salva*, orig. "tasting of food to detect poison," ult. from Late Latin *salvāre*, to save.]

sal·vi·a (săl'vē-ə) *n.* Any of various plants and shrubs of the genus *Salvia*, esp. *S. splendens*, with showy scarlet flowers. [Latin, "the healing plant," sage.]

sal·vo (săl'vō) *n., pl.* **-vos** or **-voes.** 1. **a.** A simultaneous discharge, as of firearms. **b.** The projectiles so released. 2. A sudden outburst. [Italian *salva*, salute, volley, from Latin *salvē*, hail, imper. of *salvēre*, to be in good health, from *salvus*, safe, well.]

ă pat	ā pay	â care	ä father	ĕ pet	ē be	hw which
ŏŏ took	ōō boot	ou out	th thin	th this	ŭ cut	
ĭ pit	ī tie	î pier	ŏ pot	ō toe	ô paw, for	oi noise
û urge	zh vision	ə about, item, edible, gallop, circus				

sam·a·ra (săm′ər-ə, sə-mâr′ə, -măr′ə) *n.* A winged, usu. one-seeded fruit, as of the ash or maple, that does not split open. Also called **key fruit.** [Latin, elm seed.]

Sa·mar·i·tan (sə-măr′ĭ-tən) *n.* A **Good Samaritan.**

sa·mar·i·um (sə-mâr′ē-əm, -măr′-) *n. Symbol* **Sm** A silvery or pale-gray metallic rare-earth element. Atomic number 62; atomic weight 150.35; melting point 1,072°C; boiling point 1,900°C; specific gravity (approximately) 7.50; valences 2, 3. [From *samar(skite),* a mineral oxide, from French, after Colonel von *Samarski,* 19th-cent. Russian mine official.]

sam·ba (săm′bə, säm′-) *n.* A ballroom dance of Brazilian orig. —*intr.v.* To dance the samba. [Portuguese, of African orig.]

same (sām) *adj.* **1.** Being the very one; identical. **2.** Similar in kind, quantity, or degree; equivalent. **3.** Conforming in every detail. **4.** Being the one previously mentioned. —*adv.* In the same way. —*pron.* **1.** Someone or something identical with another. **2.** Someone or something previously mentioned. —*idioms.* **all the same. 1.** Nevertheless. **2.** Of no importance. **just the same.** Nevertheless. [Middle English, from Old Norse *samr.*]

    Syns: **1. same, identical, selfsame, very** *adj. Core meaning:* Being one and not another or others (*the same seat I had yesterday*). **2. same, equal, equivalent, identical** *adj. Core meaning:* Agreeing exactly in value, quantity, or effect (*the same words that the President used*).

same·ness (sām′nĭs) *n.* **1.** The condition of being the same. **2.** A lack of variety or change; monotony.

sam·i·sen (săm′ĭ-sĕn′) *n.* A Japanese musical instrument similar to a banjo. [Japanese, "three-stringed."]

Sa·mo·an (sə-mō′ən) *n.* **1.** A native or inhabitant of Samoa. **2.** The Polynesian language of the Samoans. —**Sa·mo′an** *adj.*

sam·o·var (săm′ə-vär′) *n.* A metal urn with a spigot, used to boil water for tea. [Russian, "self-boiler."]

      samovar   **sampan**

Sam·o·yed (săm′ə-yĕd′) *n.* **1.** A member of a Ural-Altaic nomadic people of the north-central Soviet Union. **2.** Any Uralic language spoken by the Samoyed people. **3.** A working dog of a breed orig. developed in northern Eurasia.

sam·pan (săm′păn′) *n.* A flat-bottomed Chinese skiff. [Mandarin *san¹ pan³.*]

sam·ple (săm′pəl) *n.* **1.** A portion, piece, or single item that is representative of a whole; specimen. **2.** *Statistics.* A set of elements drawn from and analyzed to estimate the characteristics of a population. Also called **sampling.** —*tr.v.* **-pled, -pling.** To take a sample of, esp. in order to test, analyze, or judge the quality of. [Middle English, from Old French *essample,* example.] —**sam′pler** *n.*

sam·pler (săm′plər) *n.* A model piece of needlework.

sam·pling (săm′plĭng) *n. Statistics.* A sample.

sam·u·rai (săm′ōō-rī′) *n., pl.* **samurai** or **-rais.** A professional warrior of feudal Japan. [Japanese.]

san·a·tive (săn′ə-tĭv) *adj.* Capable of curing or healing, as a medicine. [Middle English *sanatif,* from Old French, from Late Latin *sanativus,* ult. from Latin *sanus,* healthy.]

san·a·to·ri·um (săn′ə-tôr′ē-əm, -tōr′-) *n., pl.* **-ums** or **to·ri·a** (-tôr′ē-ə, -tōr′-). **1.** A hospital for patients with chronic diseases. **2.** An institution for the care of convalescents. [From Late Latin *sānātōrius,* from Latin *sānātus,* past part. of *sānāre,* to heal, from *sānus,* healthy.]

sanc·ta (săngk′tə) *n.* A plural of **sanctum.**

sanc·ti·fy (săngk′tə-fī′) *tr.v.* **-fied, -fy·ing. 1.** To set apart or dedicate as holy or sacred; consecrate. **2.** To purify or free from sin; make holy. **3.** To make valid or binding. [Middle English *sanctifien,* from Old French *sanctifier,* from Late Latin *sanctificāre* : Latin *sanctus,* sacred + *facere,* to make.] —**sanc′ti·fi·ca′tion** *n.* —**sanc′ti·fi′er** *n.*

sanc·ti·mo·ni·ous (săngk′tə-mō′nē-əs) *adj.* Hypocritically pious or righteous. —**sanc′ti·mo′ni·ous·ly** *adv.*

sanc·ti·mo·ny (săngk′tə-mō′nē) *n.* Hypocritical piety or righteousness. [Old French *sanctimonie,* from Latin *sanctimōnia,* sacredness, from *sanctus,* sacred.]

sanc·tion (săngk′shən) *n.* **1.** Official permission, consent, or approval. **2.** Support or encouragement, as from public opinion. **3.** A force or influence that determines action. **4.** A coercive measure adopted usu. by several nations against another nation that is in violation of international law. —*tr.v.* **1.** To make valid by official approval; legitimize. **2.** To give support, encouragement, or approval to; permit. —See Syns at **permit.** [Old French, from Latin *sanctiō,* from *sanctus,* sacred.]

sanc·ti·ty (săngk′tĭ-tē) *n., pl.* **-ties. 1.** Holiness of life; saintliness. **2.** The condition or quality of being sacred or inviolable. [Middle English *saunctite,* from Old French *sainctite,* from Latin *sanctus,* sacred.]

sanc·tu·ar·y (săngk′chōō-ĕr′ē) *n., pl.* **-ies. 1. a.** A sacred place, such as a church, temple, or mosque. **b.** The most holy part of such a place. **2.** Any place that provides refuge, asylum, or immunity from arrest. **3.** A refuge in which animals or birds are protected. [Middle English *sanctuarie,* from Old French *sainctuarie,* from Late Latin *sanctuārium,* from Latin *sanctus,* sacred.]

sanc·tum (săngk′təm) *n., pl.* **-tums** or **-ta** (-tə). **1.** A sacred or holy place. **2.** A private retreat in which one is free from intrusion. [Latin, neut. of *sanctus,* sacred.]

sand (sănd) *n.* **1.** Loose, granular, gritty particles of disintegrated rock, finer than gravel and coarser than dust. **2.** Often **sands.** A tract or stretch of land covered with sand such as a beach or desert. **3. sands.** Moments of time or duration: *the sands of life.* —*tr.v.* **1.** To sprinkle or fill with sand. **2.** To polish or smooth, esp. with sandpaper. [Middle English, from Old English.]

san·dal (săn′dəl) *n.* **1.** A shoe consisting of a sole fastened to the foot by thongs or straps. **2.** A low-cut shoe with an ankle strap. [Middle English *sandalie,* from Latin *sandalium,* from Greek *sandalion,* dim. of *sandalon,* sandal.]

san·dal·wood (săn′dəl-wŏŏd′) *n.* **1.** Any of several Asian trees of the genus *Santalum,* esp. *S. album,* with yellowish heartwood used in cabinetmaking and carving and oil used in perfumery. **2.** The wood of the sandalwood tree. [From Middle English *sandal,* sandalwood, from Old French, from Medieval Latin *sandalum,* from Greek *santalon,* prob. from Sanskrit *candana* + WOOD.]

sand·bag (sănd′băg′) *n.* A bag filled with sand, esp. one used in piles to form protective walls. —*tr.v.* **-bagged, -bag·ging. 1.** To put sandbags in or around. **2. a.** To hit with or as if with a sandbag. **b.** To coerce.

sand·bar (sănd′bär′) *n.* An offshore ridge of sand built up by the action of waves or currents.

sand·blast (sănd′blăst′) *n.* A blast of air or steam carrying sand at high velocity, used to etch or to clean stone or glass. —*tr.v.* To engrave or clean with a sandblast. —**sand′blast′er** *n.*

sand·box (sănd′bŏks′) *n.* A box filled with sand for children to play in.

sand·bur (sănd′bûr′) *n.* Any of several grasses of the genus *Cenchrus,* esp. *C. tribuloides,* with burlike seed clusters.

sand dollar. Any of various thin, circular echinoderms of the order Exocycloida (or Clypeasteroidea) of sandy ocean bottoms of the northern Atlantic and Pacific.

sand fly. Any of various small biting tropical flies of the genus *Phlebotomus.*

sand·hog (sănd′hôg′, -hŏg′) *n.* A laborer who works in a caisson in the construction of underwater tunnels.

sand·lot (sănd′lŏt′) *n.* A vacant lot used by children for sports. —*modifier: sandlot baseball.*

sand·man (sănd′măn′) *n.* A character in folklore who puts children to sleep by sprinkling sand in their eyes.

---

sand·pa·per (sănd′pā′pər) *n.* Heavy paper coated on one side with an abrasive material such as sand, used for smoothing or polishing. —*tr.v.* To rub with sandpaper.

sand·pip·er (sănd′pī′pər) *n.* Any of various small, usu. long-billed wading birds of the family Scolopacidae.

sand·stone (sănd′stōn′) *n.* Variously colored sedimentary rock composed chiefly of sandlike quartz grains.

sand·storm (sănd′stôrm′) *n.* A strong wind carrying clouds of sand through the air near the ground.

sand trap. A hazard on a golf course that consists of a depression filled with sand.

sand·wich (sănd′wĭch, săn′-) *n.* **1.** Two slices of bread with a filling placed between them. **2.** Something similar to a sandwich. —*tr.v.* To insert or fit tightly. [After John Montagu, 4th Earl of *Sandwich* (1718–92), English diplomat.]

sandwich board. Two hinged boards bearing advertising placards or notices, hung on a carrier's shoulders.

sandwich man. A man who wears a sandwich board.

sand·wort (sănd′wûrt′, -wôrt′) *n.* Any of numerous low-growing plants of the genus *Arenaria*, with small, usu. white flowers.

sand·y (săn′dē) *adj.* **-i·er, -i·est. 1.** Covered with, full of, or consisting of sand. **2.** Yellowish tan. —**sand′i·ness** *n.*

sane (sān) *adj.* **san·er, san·est. 1.** Mentally healthy. **2.** Rational: *a sane approach.* [Latin *sānus*, sound, whole, healthy.] —**sane′ly** *adv.* —**sane′ness** *n.*

sang (săng) *v.* A past tense of **sing.** [Middle English *sang(e),* from Old English *sang.*]

sang-froid (sän-frwä′) *n.* Composure; imperturbability. [French, "cold blood."]

san·gri·a (săng-grē′ə, săn-) *n.* A cold drink made of red wine mixed with fruit juice and sugar. [Spanish *sangría,* from *sangre,* blood, from Latin *sanguis.*]

san·gui·nar·y (săng′gwə-nĕr′ē) *adj.* **1.** Of or involving bloodshed. **2.** Bloodthirsty. [Latin *sanguinārius,* of blood, from *sanguis,* blood.] —**san′gui·nar′i·ly** *adv.*

san·guine (săng′gwĭn) *adj.* **1. a.** Of the color of blood; red. **b.** Ruddy. **2.** Optimistic; cheerfully confident. [Middle English *sanguin,* from Old French, from Latin *sanguineus,* bloody, from *sanguis,* blood.] —**san′guine·ly** *adv.* —**san′guine·ness** or **san·guin′i·ty** (-gwĭn′ĭ-tē) *n.*

san·guin·e·ous (săng-gwĭn′ē-əs) *adj.* **1.** Of or involving blood or bloodshed. **2.** Red.

san·i·tar·i·an (săn′ĭ-târ′ē-ən) *n.* A public health or sanitation expert.

san·i·tar·i·um (săn′ĭ-târ′ē-əm) *n., pl.* **-ums** or **-i·a** (-ē-ə). A sanatorium. [From Latin *sānitās,* health.]

san·i·tar·y (săn′ĭ-tĕr′ē) *adj.* **1.** Of or relating to health. **2.** Free from elements, as filth or bacteria, that endanger health. [French *sanitaire,* from Latin *sānitās,* health.]

sanitary napkin. A disposable pad of absorbent material worn to absorb menstrual flow.

san·i·ta·tion (săn′ĭ-tā′shən) *n.* **1.** The application of measures, such as the disposal of sewage and the collection of trash, designed to promote or protect public health. **2.** The process or act of sanitizing.

san·i·tize (săn′ĭ-tīz′) *tr.v.* **-tized, -tiz·ing.** To make sanitary.

san·i·ty (săn′ĭ-tē) *n.* The condition of being sane.

San Jo·se scale (săn′ hō-zā′). A scale insect, *Aspidiotus perniciosus,* that damages fruit trees. [After *San Jose,* California.]

sank (săngk) *v.* Past tense of **sink.** —See Usage note at **sink.** [Middle English, from Old English *sanc.*]

sans (sănz) *prep.* Without. [Middle English, from Old French, from Latin *sine.*]

San·sei (săn′sā′) *n., pl.* **Sansei** or **-seis.** Also **san·sei.** The U.S.-born grandchild of Japanese immigrants. [Japanese.]

San·skrit (săn′skrĭt′) *n.* Also **San·scrit.** An ancient Indic language, the classical literary language of India. —**San·skrit·ic** *adj.* —**San′skrit·ist** *n.*

sans serif. A typeface without serifs.

San·ta Claus (săn′tə klôz′). The personification of the spirit of Christmas, usu. represented as a jolly, fat old man with a white beard and a red suit. Also called **Saint Nicholas, Saint Nick.** [Var. of Dutch *Sinterklaas,* from Middle Dutch *Sinterclaes,* from *Sint Nicolaes,* Saint Nicholas.]

sap¹ (săp) *n.* **1.** The watery fluid that circulates through a plant, carrying food and other substances to the tissues. **2.** Health and energy; vitality. **3.** *Slang.* A gullible person; fool. [Middle English, from Old English *sæp.*]

sap² (săp) *n.* A covered trench or tunnel dug to a point beneath an enemy position. —*v.* **sapped, sap·ping.** —*tr.v.* **1.** To undermine. **2.** To weaken gradually. [Earlier *sappe,* trench, from Old French *sappe,* an undermining.]

sa·pi·ent (sā′pē-ənt) *adj.* Wise; discerning. —See Syns at **wise.** [Middle English, from Old French, from Latin *sapiēns,* pres. part. of *sapere,* to be wise.] —**sa′pi·ence** *n.* —**sa′pi·ent·ly** *adv.*

sap·ling (săp′lĭng) *n.* A young tree.

sap·o·dil·la (săp′ə-dĭl′ə) *n.* **1.** A tropical evergreen tree, *Achras zapota,* with a latex that yields chicle. **2.** The edible russet fruit of the sapodilla. [Spanish *zapotillo,* dim. of *zapote,* sapodilla fruit, from Nahuatl *tzapotl.*]

sap·o·na·ceous (săp′ə-nā′shəs) *adj.* Having the qualities of soap.

sa·pon·i·fi·ca·tion (sə-pŏn′ə-fĭ-kā′shən) *n. Chem.* The hydrolysis of an ester by an alkali, producing a free alcohol and an acid salt.

sa·pon·i·fy (sə-pŏn′ə-fī′) *v.* **-fied, -fy·ing.** *Chem.* —*tr.v.* **1.** To convert (an ester) by saponification. **2.** To convert (fats) into soap. —*intr.v.* To undergo saponification. [French *saponifier,* from Latin *sāpō,* soap.] —**sa·pon′i·fi′er** *n.*

sap·per (săp′ər) *n.* A military engineer. [From SAP (trench).]

sap·phire (săf′īr′) *n.* **1.** Any of several relatively pure forms of corundum, esp. a blue form used as a gemstone. **2.** A corundum gem. **3.** The blue color of a sapphire. —*modifier: a sapphire ring.* —*adj.* Deep blue. [Middle English *safir,* from Old French, from Latin *sapphīrus,* from Greek *sappheiros.*]

sap·py (săp′ē) *adj.* **-pi·er, -pi·est. 1.** Full of sap; juicy. **2.** *Slang.* Overly sentimental; mawkish. **3.** *Slang.* Silly.

sap·ro·phyte (săp′rə-fīt′) *n.* A plant that lives on dead or decaying organic matter. [Greek *sapros,* rotten + -PHYTE.] —**sap′ro·phyt′ic** (-fĭt′ĭk) *adj.*

sap·suck·er (săp′sŭk′ər) *n.* Either of two small North American woodpeckers, *Sphyrapicus varius* or *S. thyrsoides,* believed to drink the sap of certain trees.

sap·wood (săp′wŏŏd′) *n.* Newly formed, living outer wood that lies just inside the cambium of a tree or woody plant and is usu. lighter in color than the heartwood.

Sar·a·cen (săr′ə-sən) *n.* **1.** A member of a pre-Islamic nomadic people of the Syrian and northern Arabian deserts. **2.** An Arab. **3.** Any Moslem.

sa·ran (sə-răn′) *n.* Any of various thermoplastic resins used to make packaging films, corrosion-resistant pipes, and fiber for fabrics. [From the trademark *Saran.*]

sa·ra·pe (sə-rä′pē) *n.* Var. of **serape.**

sar·casm (sär′kăz′əm) *n.* **1.** A sharply mocking or ironic remark. **2.** The use of sarcasms. [French *sarcasme,* from Greek *sarkasmos,* from *sarkazein,* to bite the lips in rage, speak bitterly, from *sarx,* flesh.]

sar·cas·tic (sär-kăs′tĭk) *adj.* **1.** Expressing sarcasm. **2.** Given to sarcasm. —**sar·cas′ti·cal·ly** *adv.*

 Syns: sarcastic, caustic, mordant *adj. Core meaning:* Bitter, cutting, and derisive, esp. in expression (*a sarcastic, sneering critic: sarcastic remarks*).

sar·co·ma (sär-kō′mə) *n., pl.* **-ma·ta** (-mə-tə) or **-mas.** A malignant tumor arising from nonepithelial connective tissues. [From Greek *sarkōma,* fleshy excrescence.]

sar·coph·a·gus (sär-kŏf′ə-gəs) *n., pl.* **-gi** (-jī′). A stone cof-

sarcophagus

fin. [Latin *sarcophagus (lapis)*, "flesh-eating (stone)," from Greek *(lithos) sarkophagos*.]

sar·dine (sär-dēn') *n.* **1.** Any of various small edible herrings or related fishes of the family Clupeidae, frequently canned in oil. **2.** Any of numerous fishes similarly processed for eating. [Middle English *sardeyn*, from Old French *sardine*, from Latin *sardīna*, from Greek *sardinos*.]

sar·don·ic (sär-dŏn'ĭk) *adj.* Scornfully mocking. [French *sardonique*, ult. from Greek *sardonios*.] —**sar·don'i·cal·ly** *adv.*

sar·don·yx (sär-dŏn'ĭks, sär'dn-ĭks) *n.* An onyx with alternating brown and white bands. [Middle English *sardonix*, from Latin *sardonyx*, from Greek *sardonux*.]

sar·gas·so (sär-găs'ō) *n.* Gulfweed. [Portuguese *sargaço*.]

sa·ri (sär'ē) *n.*, *pl.* **-ris.** A garment worn by women of India and Pakistan, consisting of a length of cloth with one end wrapped about the waist to form a skirt and the other draped over the shoulder. [Hindi *sārī*, from Sanskrit *śāṭī*, cloth, sari.]

sari   sassafras

sa·rong (sə-rông', -rŏng') *n.* A skirt consisting of a length of brightly colored cloth worn by both men and women in Malaysia, Indonesia, and the Pacific islands. [Malay.]

sar·sa·pa·ril·la (săs'pə-rĭl'ə, sär'sə-pə-) *n.* **1.** The dried roots of an American plant of the genus *Smilax*, used as a flavoring. **2.** A drink so flavored. [Spanish *zarzaparrilla* : *zarza*, bramble, from Arabic *sharaṣ*, thorny plant + *parrilla*, dim. of *parra*, vine.]

sar·to·ri·al (sär-tôr'ē-əl, -tōr'-) *adj.* Of or relating to a tailor or clothing made by a tailor. [From Latin *sartor*, tailor.]

sar·to·ri·us (sär-tôr'ē-əs, -tōr'-) *n.* A flat, narrow thigh muscle that crosses the front of the thigh obliquely from hip to tibia. [New Latin *sartorius (musculus)*, "tailor's (muscle)" (from its enabling one to sit in a cross-legged position like a tailor at work), from Latin *sartor*, a tailor, from *sartus*, past part. of *sarcīre*, to mend.]

sash¹ (săsh) *n.* A band worn about the waist or over the shoulder. [Arabic *shāsh*, muslin.]

sash² (săsh) *n.* A frame in which the panes of a window or door are set. [From French *châssis*, a frame.]

sa·shay (să-shā') *intr.v.* *Informal.* To strut or flounce. [Var. of French *chassé*, a dance step.]

sass (săs) *Informal.* —*n.* Impertinent or disrespectful speech. —*tr.v.* To talk impudently to. [Back-formation from SASSY.]

sas·sa·fras (săs'ə-frăs') *n.* **1.** A North American tree, *Sassafras albidum*, with irregularly lobed leaves and aromatic bark. **2.** The dried root bark of the sassafras tree, used as flavoring. [Spanish *sasafrás*.]

sas·sy (săs'ē) *adj.* **-si·er, -si·est. 1.** Impudent. **2.** Jaunty. —See Syns at **impudent**. [Var. of SAUCY.] —**sas'si·ly** *adv.* —**sas'si·ness** *n.*

sat (săt) *v.* Past tense and past participle of **sit.** [Middle English *satt(e)*, *satte* (past part. from p. t.), from Old English (p. t.) *sæt.*]

Sa·tan (sāt'n) *n.* The Devil. [Middle English, from Old English, from Late Latin *Satān*, from Greek *Satan*, from Hebrew *śāṭān*, from *śāṭan*, to accuse.]

sa·tan·ic (sə-tăn'ĭk) or **sa·tan·i·cal** (-ĭ-kəl) *adj.* **1.** Pertaining to or suggestive of Satan. **2.** Fiendish.

satch·el (săch'əl) *n.* A small valise or bag. [Middle English *sachel*, from Old French, from Latin *saccelus*, dim. of *saccus*, sack.]

sate (sāt) *tr.v.* **sat·ed, sat·ing. 1.** To satisfy completely or fully. **2.** To indulge to excess; surfeit. [Prob. var. of obs. *sade*, from Middle English *sad(d)en*, from Old English *sadian.*]

sat·el·lite (săt'l-īt') *n.* **1.** *Astron.* A relatively small body orbiting a planet; a moon. **2.** A man-made object intended to orbit a celestial body. **3.** A servile attendant or follower. **4.** A nation dominated politically by another. [Old French, from Latin *satelles*, an attendant.]

sa·tia·ble (sā'shə-bəl) *adj.* Capable of being satiated.

sa·ti·ate (sā'shē-āt') *tr.v.* **-at·ed, -at·ing. 1.** To satisfy fully. **2.** To gratify to excess; sate. [From Latin *satiāre*, from *satis*, enough.] —**sa'ti·a'tion** *n.*

sa·ti·e·ty (sə-tī'ĭ-tē) *n.* The condition of being sated. [Old French *satiete*, from Latin *satietās*, sufficiency, from *satis*, sufficient, enough.]

sat·in (săt'n) *n.* A smooth fabric, as of silk or rayon, woven with a glossy face and a dull back. —*adj.* Made of or resembling satin. [Middle English, from Old French.]

sat·in·wood (săt'n-wŏod') *n.* **1.** An East Indian tree, *Chloroxylon swietenia*, with yellowish, close-grained wood. **2.** The wood of a satinwood or similar tree.

sat·in·y (săt'n-ē) *adj.* Lustrous and smooth like satin.

sat·ire (săt'īr') *n.* **1.** An artistic work that attacks human vice or foolishness with irony, derision, or wit. **2.** Irony or caustic wit used to expose or attack human folly. [Old French, from Latin *satira*, satire, mixture, mixed fruits, from *satur*, full of food, sated.]

sa·tir·i·cal (sə-tîr'ĭ-kəl) or **sa·tir·ic** (-tîr'ĭk) *adj.* Of, relating to, or characterized by satire. —**sa·tir'i·cal·ly** *adv.*

sat·i·rist (săt'ə-rĭst) *n.* A writer of satire.

sat·i·rize (săt'ə-rīz') *tr.v.* **-rized, -riz·ing.** To ridicule or attack by means of satire.

sat·is·fac·tion (săt'ĭs-făk'shən) *n.* **1.** Fulfillment or gratification of a desire, need, or appetite. **2.** Pleasure derived from such fulfillment. **3.** Reparation; atonement. **4.** Compensation; amends. **5.** A source of gratification.

sat·is·fac·to·ry (săt'ĭs-făk'tə-rē) *adj.* Giving satisfaction; sufficient to meet a demand or requirement. —**sat'is·fac'to·ri·ly** *adv.* —**sat'is·fac'to·ri·ness** *n.*

sat·is·fy (săt'ĭs-fī') *v.* **-fied, -fy·ing.** —*tr.v.* **1. a.** To gratify the wish or expectation of; make content. **b.** To supply fully the demands of: *satisfy his appetite.* **2. a.** To free from doubt. **b.** To put an end to; dispel. **3.** To pay off. **4.** To meet or conform to the conditions of. **5.** To make reparation for; redress (a wrong). —*intr.v.* To give satisfaction. —See Syns at **please.** [Middle English *satisfien*, from Old French *satisfier*, from Latin *satisfacere* : *satis*, enough + *facere*, to make.] —**sat'is·fi'er** *n.* —**sat'is·fy'ing·ly** *adv.*

sa·trap (sā'trăp', săt'răp') *n.* A governor of a province in ancient Persia. [Middle English *satrape*, from Old French, from Latin *satrapēs*, from Greek, from Persian *khshathra-pāvan*, "protector of the country."]

sat·u·rate (săch'ə-rāt') *tr.v.* **-rat·ed, -rat·ing.** To soak or fill thoroughly. [From Latin *saturāre*, to fill, satiate, from *satur*, full of food, sated.] —**sat'u·ra'tor** *n.*

sat·u·rat·ed (săch'ə-rā'tĭd) *adj.* **1.** Unable to hold or contain more; full. **2.** Soaked with moisture. **3.** *Chem.* **a.** Containing all the solute that can be dissolved: *a saturated solution.* **b.** Having all valence bonds filled.

sat·u·ra·tion (săch'ə-rā'shən) *n.* **1. a.** The act or process of saturating. **b.** The condition of being saturated. **2.** Degree of vividness of a color.

Sat·ur·day (săt'ər-dē, -dā') *n.* The seventh day of the week. [Middle English *Saterday*, from Old English *sæternesdæg*, "Saturn's day."]

Sat·urn (săt'ərn) *n.* **1.** An Italic and Roman deity identified with the Greek god Cronus. **2.** The sixth planet from the sun and the second-largest in the solar system.

sat·ur·na·li·a (săt'ər-nā'lē-ə, -nāl'yə) *pl.n.* **1.** **Saturnalia.** The ancient Roman seven-day festival of Saturn which began on Dec. 17. **2.** *(used with a sing. verb).* Any unrestrained celebration. [Latin *sāturnālia*, from *Sāturnus*, Saturn.]

sat·ur·nine (săt'ər-nīn') *adj.* Gloomy by nature; morose. [Middle English *saturnyne*, born under the influence of (the planet) Saturn, from Medieval Latin *Sāturnīnus*, from *Sāturnus*, Saturn.]

sat·yr (săt′ər, sā′tər) *n.* **1.** *Gk. Myth.* A woodland deity often depicted with the pointed ears, legs, and short horns of a goat. **2.** A lecher. [Middle English, from Latin *satyrus,* from Greek *saturos.*] —**sa·tyr′ic** (sə-tîr′ĭk) or **sa·tyr′i·cal** *adj.*

sauce (sôs) *n.* **1.** A flavorful liquid dressing or relish served with food. **2.** Cooked fruit: *apple sauce.* **3.** Something that adds zest. **4.** *Informal.* Impudence; sauciness. **5.** *Slang.* Alcoholic liquor. —*tr.v.* **sauced, sauc·ing. 1.** To flavor with sauce. **2.** To add zest to. [Middle English, from Old French, from Latin *salsa,* salted, from *sāl,* salt.]

sauce·pan (sôs′păn′) *n.* A deep cooking pan with a handle.

sau·cer (sô′sər) *n.* A small, shallow dish for holding a cup. [Middle English, sauce dish, from Old French *saussier,* from *sausse,* sauce.]

sau·cy (sô′sē) *adj.* **-ci·er, -ci·est. 1.** Disrespectful; impudent. **2.** Pert. —**sau′ci·ly** *adv.* —**sau′ci·ness** *n.*

sau·er·bra·ten (sour′brät′n) *n.* A pot roast of beef marinated in vinegar before cooking. [German *Sauerbraten* : *sauer,* sour + *Braten,* roast meat.]

sau·er·kraut (sour′krout′) *n.* Shredded cabbage salted and fermented in its own juice. [German *Sauerkraut* : *sauer,* sour + *Kraut,* cabbage.]

sau·na (sou′nə, sô′-) *n.* A steambath in which steam is often produced by water thrown on heated rocks. [Finnish.]

saun·ter (sôn′tər) *intr.v.* To walk leisurely. —*n.* A leisurely stroll. [Prob. from Middle English *santeren,* to muse.]

-saur or **-saurus.** A suffix meaning lizard: **brontosaur.** [From New Latin *saurus,* lizard.]

sau·ri·an (sôr′ē-ən) *n.* Any of various reptiles of the suborder Sauria, which includes the true lizards. [From New Latin *saurus,* lizard.] —**sau′ri·an** *adj.*

-saurus. Var. of **-saur.**

sau·sage (sô′sĭj) *n.* Finely chopped and seasoned meat stuffed into a casing. [Middle English *sausige,* from Old North French *saussiche,* from Late Latin *salsīcia,* from *salsīcius,* prepared by salting, from Latin *sāl,* salt.]

sau·té (sō-tā′, sô-) *tr.v.* To fry quickly in a little fat. —*n.* Sautéed food. [French, "tossed (in a pan)," past part. of *sauter,* to leap, from Old French, from Latin *saltāre,* freq. of *salīre,* to leap.]

sau·terne (sō-tûrn′, sô-) *n.* Also **sau·ternes.** A delicate, sweet white wine. [French, after *Sauternes,* France.]

sav·age (săv′ĭj) *adj.* **1.** Produced or growing without human care; not cultivated; wild. **2.** Not civilized: *savage tribes.* **3. a.** Untamed; fierce: *a savage beast.* **b.** Vicious or merciless; brutal. **4.** Lacking polish or manners; rude. —See Syns at **fierce.** —*n.* **1.** A primitive or uncivilized person. **2.** A brutal or fierce person. **3.** A rude person; boor. —*tr.v.* **-aged, -ag·ing.** To attack violently or brutally. [Middle English *sauvage,* from Old French, from Latin *silvāticus,* of the woods, wild, from *silva,* woods, forest.] —**sav′age·ly** *adv.* —**sav′age·ry** *n.*

sa·van·na (sə-văn′ə) *n.* Also **sa·van·nah.** A flat, treeless grassland of tropical or subtropical regions. [Spanish *zavana,* from Taino *zabana.*]

sa·vant (sə-vänt′, -vănt′, săv′ənt, să-vän′) *n.* A learned scholar. [French, from *savoir,* to know, from Latin *sapere,* to be wise.]

save¹ (sāv) *v.* **saved, sav·ing.** —*tr.v.* **1.** To rescue from harm, danger, or loss. **2.** To keep safe; guard from danger or injury. **3.** To prevent the waste or loss of; conserve. **4.** To set aside for future use; store. **5.** To make unnecessary: *This will save you an extra trip.* **6.** To deliver from sin. —*intr.v.* **1.** To avoid waste or expense; economize. **2.** To accumulate money or goods. **3.** To preserve a person or a thing from harm. [Middle English *saven,* from Old French *salver,* from Late Latin *salvāre,* from Latin *salvus,* safe.] —**sav′er** *n.*

Syns: **1. save, deliver, rescue** *v.* Core meaning: To free from danger or confinement (*commandos who saved the hostages*). **2. save, keep, lay away, salt away** *v.* Core meaning: To reserve for the future (*saved some money*).

save² (sāv) *prep.* With the exception of; except: *All arrived on time save one.* —*conj.* **1.** Were it not; except. **2.** *Archaic.* Unless. [Middle English, from Old French, *salf,* from Latin *salvō,* except, from *salvus,* safe, sound, healthy.]

sav·in (săv′ĭn) *n.* Also **sav·ine.** An evergreen Eurasian shrub, *Juniperus sabina,* whose young shoots yield an oil formerly used medicinally. [Middle English, ult. from Latin *(herba) Sabīna,* "Sabine (plant).'']

sav·ing (sā′vĭng) *adj.* **1.** Redeeming; compensating: *saving graces.* **2.** Not wasteful; economical. —*n.* **1.** Preservation or rescue. **2.** Avoidance of excess expenditure; economy. **3. savings.** Money saved. —*prep.* With the exception of. —*conj.* Except; save.

savings account. A bank account that draws interest.

savings bank. A bank that receives, invests, and pays interest on savings accounts.

sav·ior (sāv′yər) *n.* Also *Brit.* **sav·iour. 1.** A person who saves from danger or harm. **2.** Christ. [Middle English *saviour,* from Old French *sauveour,* from Late Latin *salvātor,* from *salvāre,* to save.]

sa·voir-faire (săv′wär-fâr′) *n. French.* The ability to say or do the appropriate thing; tact.

sa·vor (sā′vər) *n.* Also *Brit.* **sa·vour.** —*n.* **1.** The taste or smell of something. **2.** A specific taste or smell. **3.** A distinctive or typical quality. —*intr.v.* To have or show a particular savor or quality: *conduct that savored of arrogance.* —*tr.v.* **1.** To impart a flavor or scent to. **2.** To enjoy with pleasure; to relish. —See Syns at **like.** [Middle English *savour,* from Old French, from Latin *sapor,* from *sapere,* to taste.] —**sa′vor·er** *n.*

sa·vor·y¹ (sā′və-rē) *adj.* **1.** Appetizing to the taste or smell. **2.** Piquant, pungent, or salty to the taste; not sweet. —See Syns at **delicious.** —**sa′vor·i·ness** *n.*

sa·vor·y² (sā′və-rē) *n., pl.* **-ies.** Either of two aromatic herbs, *Satureja hortensis* or *S. montana,* used as a seasoning. [Middle English *saverey,* from Old English *sætherie,* from Latin *satureia.*]

sav·vy (săv′ē). *Slang.* —*intr.v.* **-vied, -vy·ing.** To understand or comprehend. —*n.* Practical understanding or knowledge. [From Spanish *sabe (usted),* "(you) know,'' from *saber,* to know, from Latin *sapere,* to be wise.]

saw¹ (sô) *n.* **1.** A hand or power tool with a sharp-toothed metal blade or disk, used for cutting hard materials. **2.** A machine containing a saw. —*v.* **sawed, sawed** or **sawn** (sôn), **saw·ing.** —*tr.v.* **1.** To cut with or as if with a saw. **2.** To produce or shape with or as if with a saw. —*intr.v.* **1.** To use a saw. **2.** To cut. [Middle English *sawe,* from Old English *sagu.*] —**saw′er** *n.*

saw² (sô) *n.* A familiar and often trite saying. [Middle English *sawe,* from Old English *sagu,* speech, talk.]

saw³ *v.* Past tense of **see** (to perceive with the eyes). [Middle English *sauh,* from Old English *seah.*]

saw·buck (sô′bŭk′) *n.* **1.** A sawhorse, esp. one with X-shaped legs. **2.** *Slang.* A ten-dollar bill (from the resemblance of the legs of a sawhorse to the Roman numeral X).

saw·dust (sô′dŭst′) *n.* The small particles, as of wood, that result from sawing.

sawed-off (sôd′ôf′, -ŏf′) *adj.* **1.** Having one end sawed off: *a sawed-off shotgun.* **2.** *Slang.* Shorter than average height.

saw·fish (sô′fĭsh′) *n., pl.* **sawfish** or **-fish·es.** Any of various marine fishes of the genus *Pristis,* with a bladelike snout bearing teeth along both sides.

saw·fly (sô′flī′) *n.* Any of various destructive insects, chiefly of the family Tenthredinidae, that cut into the leaves and stems of plants.

saw·horse (sô′hôrs′) *n.* A rack or trestle used to support a piece of wood being sawed.

saw·mill (sô′mĭl′) *n.* **1.** A mill where lumber is cut into boards. **2.** A large machine for sawing lumber.

sawn (sôn) *v.* A past participle of **saw** (to cut with a saw). [Earlier *sawen* (perh. after the model of *draw, drawn*).]

saw-toothed (sô′tootht′) *adj.* Having an edge with teeth.

saw·yer (sô′yər) *n.* A person employed to saw wood. [Middle English *sawier,* from *sawen,* to saw, from *sawe,* a saw.]

sax (săks) *n. Informal.* A saxophone.

sax·horn (săks′hôrn′) *n.* A valved, upright brass wind instrument similar to the bugle. [After Adolphe *Sax* (1814-94), Belgian musical instrument maker, its inventor.]

sax·i·frage (săk′sə-frĭj, -frāj′) *n.* Any of numerous plants of the genus *Saxifraga,* with small flowers and leaves that often form a basal rosette. [Middle English, from Old French, from Late Latin *saxifraga (herba),* "rock-breaking (herb).'']

ă pat	ā pay	â care	ä father	ĕ pet	ē be	hw which	ĭ pit	ī tie	î pier	ŏ pot	ō toe	ô paw, for	oi noise
oo took	oo boot	ou out	th thin	th this	ŭ cut		û urge	zh vision	ə about, item, edible, gallop, circus				

Sax·on (săk′sən) *n.* **1.** A member of a Germanic tribal group that inhabited northern Germany and invaded England in the 5th cent. with the Angles and Jutes. **2.** An Englishman. **3.** A native or inhabitant of Saxony. **4.** The Germanic language of the Saxons. —**Sax′on** *adj.*

sax·o·phone (săk′sə-fōn′) *n.* A wind instrument with a single-reed mouthpiece and a usu. curved conical metal tube. [After Adolphe *Sax* (1814–94), Belgian musical instrument maker, its inventor.] —**sax′o·phon′ist** *n.*

saxophone   scallop

say (sā) *v.* **said** (sĕd), **say·ing.** —*tr.v.* **1.** To utter aloud; pronounce; speak. **2.** To express in words. **3.** To state; declare. **4.** To repeat or recite: *say grace.* **5.** To report or maintain; allege. **6.** To indicate; show: *The clock said noon.* **7.** To estimate or suppose; assume: *Let's say that you're right.* —*intr.v.* To make a statement or express an opinion. —*n.* **1.** A turn or chance to express an opinion. **2.** The power to make or influence a decision. —*adv.* **1.** Approximately: *There were, say, 500 people present.* **2.** For instance: *a woodwind, say an oboe.* —*idiom.* **that is to say.** In other words. [Middle English *sayen,* from Old English *secgan.*] —**say′er** *n.*

say·ing (sā′ĭng) *n.* An adage or proverb.

say-so (sā′sō′) *n., pl.* **-sos.** *Informal.* **1.** An unsupported statement or assurance. **2.** An authoritative assertion. **3.** The right or authority to decide.

Sc The symbol for the element scandium.

scab (skăb) *n.* **1.** The crustlike surface that forms on a wound. **2.** Any of various plant diseases caused by fungi or bacteria and resulting in crustlike spots. **3.** *Informal.* A person who takes the place of a worker who is on strike. —*intr.v.* **scabbed, scab·bing. 1.** To form or become covered with a scab. **2.** *Informal.* To take a job held by a worker on strike. [Middle English *scabbe,* from Old Norse *skabb.*]

scab·bard (skăb′ərd) *n.* A sheath or container, as for a dagger or sword. [Middle English *scauberc,* from Anglo-French *escaubers.*]

scab·by (skăb′ē) *adj.* **-bi·er, -bi·est. 1.** Having or covered with scabs. **2.** Afflicted with scabies. —**scab′bi·ly** *adv.* —**scab′bi·ness** *n.*

sca·bies (skā′bēz′) *n. (used with a sing. verb).* A contagious skin disease caused by a mite and characterized by intense itching. [Latin *scabiēs,* roughness, scurf, itch, from *scabere,* to scratch.] —**sca′bi·et′ic** (skā′bē-ĕt′ĭk) *adj.*

scab·rous (skăb′rəs, skā′brəs) *adj.* **1.** Rough to the touch; scaly. **2.** Difficult to handle or solve; knotty. **3.** Improper. [Latin *scabrōsus,* rough, from *scaber,* rough, scurfy.]

scad (skăd) *n., pl.* **scad** or **scads.** Any of several saltwater fishes of the family Carangidae, related to the jacks and pompanos. [Orig. unknown.]

scads (skădz) *pl.n. Informal.* A large number or amount: *scads of people.* [Orig. unknown.]

scaf·fold (skăf′əld, -ōld′) *n.* **1.** A platform, esp. a temporary one used by construction or maintenance workers. **2.** A platform for the execution of condemned prisoners. [Middle English, from Old North French *escafaut,* var. of Old French *eschafaud,* from *chafaud,* scaffold.]

scal·a·wag (skăl′ə-wăg′) *n.* Also **scal·ly·wag** (skăl′ē-wăg′). **1.** *Informal.* A scoundrel. **2.** A white Southerner who was a Republican during Reconstruction. [Orig. unknown.]

scald¹ (skôld) *tr.v.* **1.** To burn with or as if with hot liquid or steam. **2.** To subject to or treat with boiling water or

steam. **3.** To heat almost to the boiling point. —*intr.v.* To be or become scalded. —*n.* A body injury caused by scalding. [Middle English *scalden,* from Old North French *escalder,* from Late Latin *excaldāre,* to wash in hot water.]

scald² (skôld, skäld) *n.* Var. of **skald.**

scale¹ (skāl) *n.* **1. a.** A small, platelike dermal or epidermal structure forming the external covering of fishes, reptiles, and certain mammals. **b.** A similar small, thin, often overlapping part. **2.** A dry, thin flake, as of skin or paint. **3.** A scale insect. **4.** A film, coating, or incrustation that forms esp. on metal. —*v.* **scaled, scal·ing.** —*tr.v.* **1.** To clear or strip of scale or scales. **2.** To remove in layers or scales. —*intr.v.* **1.** To come off in layers or scales; to flake. **2.** To become encrusted. [Middle English, from Old French *escale,* shell, husk.]

scale² (skāl) *n.* **1. a.** A series of marks placed at fixed intervals and used in measurement. **b.** An instrument or device bearing such marks. **2. a.** The proportion between the dimensions of an object represented, as on a map or plan, and the actual dimensions of the object: *a scale of 1 inch to 50 miles.* **b.** A calibrated line, as on a map or architectural plan, that indicates this proportion. **3.** A graduated progression, as of size, amount, or rank. **4.** Relative degree or size: *entertain on a lavish scale.* **5.** *Math.* A basis for a system of numeration: *decimal scale.* **6.** *Mus.* A graduated series of tones ascending or descending in pitch by specified intervals. —*modifier: a scale model; a scale drawing.* —*v.* **scaled, scal·ing.** —*tr.v.* **1.** To climb up or ascend. **2.** To make in accordance with a particular proportion or scale. **3.** To adjust according to a scale. —*intr.v.* To climb; ascend. [Middle English, ladder, from Late Latin *scāla,* from Latin *scālae,* stairs.]

scale³ (skāl) *n.* **1.** An instrument or machine for weighing: *a bathroom scale; a truck scale.* **2. a. scales.** A balance. **b.** Either of the pans or dishes of a balance. —*v.* **scaled, scal·ing.** —*tr.v.* To weigh with scales. —*intr.v.* To have as a weight, as determined by a scales. [Middle English, from Old Norse *skál,* bowl, scale of a balance.]

scale insect. Any of various destructive insects of the family Coccidae, whose young suck plant juices.

sca·lene (skā′lēn′, skā-lēn′) *adj.* Having three unequal sides: *a scalene triangle.* [Late Latin *scalēnus,* from Greek *skalēnos,* uneven.]

scal·lion (skăl′yən) *n.* A young onion with a small bulb. [Middle English *scaloun,* from Norman French, from Latin *Ascalōnia (caepa),* "Ascalonian (onion)," from *Ascalō,* Ascalon, port in southern Palestine.]

scal·lop (skŏl′əp, skăl′-) *n.* Also **scol·lop** (skŏl′əp). **1.** Any of various free-swimming saltwater bivalve mollusks of the family Pectinidae, with a fan-shaped, fluted bivalve shell. **2.** The edible adductor muscle of a scallop. **3.** A scallop shell, or a similarly shaped dish, used for baking. **4.** One of a series of curves in the form of a semicircle making an ornamental border. **5.** Also **es·cal·lop** (ĭ-skŏl′əp, ĭ-skăl′-). A thin, boneless slice of meat. —*tr.v.* **1.** To shape or border with scallops. **2.** To bake in a sauce often covered with a topping of bread crumbs. [Middle English *scalop,* from Old French *escalope,* shell.] —**scal′lop·er** *n.*

scal·ly·wag (skăl′ē-wăg′) *n.* Var. of **scalawag.**

scalp (skălp) *n.* **1.** The skin of the human head. **2.** A part of the human scalp with attached hair cut or torn from an enemy as a battle trophy. **3.** A part corresponding to the scalp of a human, as of a fox. —*tr.v.* **1.** To cut or tear the scalp from. **2.** *Informal.* To buy and resell (tickets) at an excessively high price. [Middle English, prob. of Scandinavian orig.] —**scalp′er** *n.*

scal·pel (skăl′pəl, skăl-pĕl′) *n.* A knife with a thin, sharp blade, used in surgery and dissection. [Latin *scalpellum,* dim. of *scalper,* knife, from *scalpere,* to cut, scratch.]

scal·y (skā′lē) *adj.* **-i·er, -i·est. 1.** Covered with or consisting of scales. **2.** Shedding scales; flaking. —**scal′i·ness** *n.*

scamp¹ (skămp) *n.* **1.** A rogue; rascal. **2.** A mischievous youngster. [From obs. *scamp,* to slip away, bolt.]

scamp² (skămp) *tr.v.* To perform in a hasty, careless, or superficial way. [Prob. a blend of SCANT and SKIMP.]

scam·per (skăm′pər) *intr.v.* To run or go with nimble speed. [Flemish *scamperen,* to decamp, from Old French *escamper* : Latin *ex-,* out of, away + *campus,* field.] —**scam′per** *n.* —**scam′per·er** *n.*

ă pat   ā pay   â care   ä father   ĕ pet   ē be   hw which   ĭ pit   ī tie   î pier   ŏ pot   ō toe   ô paw, for   oi noise
ōō took   ōō boot   ou out   th thin   th this   ŭ cut   û urge   zh vision   ə about, item, edible, gallop, circus

scan (skăn) v. **scanned, scan·ning.** —tr.v. **1.** To examine closely. **2.** To look over or through quickly. **3.** To analyze (verse) into metrical patterns. **4.** Electronics. To move a finely focused beam of light or electrons in a systematic pattern over (a surface) in order to reproduce, or sense and subsequently transmit, an image. —intr.v. **1.** To scan verse. **2.** To conform to a metrical pattern. —n. An act of scanning. [Middle English scannen, from Late Latin scandere, "to analyze the rising and falling rhythm in verses," from Latin, to climb.] —**scan'ner** n.

scan·dal (skăn'dl) n. **1. a.** An act or circumstance that brings disgrace. **b.** The disgrace or damage to the reputation so caused. **2.** A person whose conduct violates standards of decency. **3.** Gossip or malicious talk. [French scandale, from Late Latin scandalum, from Greek skandalon, trap, snare, stumbling block.]

scan·dal·ize (skăn'dl-īz') tr.v. **-ized, -iz·ing.** To offend the moral standards of. —**scan'dal·i·za'tion** n.

scan·dal·ous (skăn'dl-əs) adj. **1.** Offensive to accepted moral standards. **2.** Damaging to the reputation; defamatory. —See Syns at **outrageous.** —**scan'dal·ous·ly** adv.

scan·dal·mon·ger (skăn'dl-mŭng'gər, -mŏng'-) n. A person who spreads scandal.

Scan·di·na·vi·an (skăn'də-nā'vē-ən, -nāv'yən) adj. Pertaining to Scandinavia, its inhabitants, culture, or languages. —n. **1.** A native or inhabitant of Scandinavia. **2.** The group of Germanic languages spoken in Scandinavia.

scan·di·um (skăn'dē-əm) n. Symbol **Sc** A silvery-white, very lightweight metallic element found in various rare minerals and separated as a by-product in the processing of certain uranium ores. Atomic number 21; atomic weight 44.956; melting point 1,539°C; boiling point 2,727°C; specific gravity 2.992; valence 3. [From Latin Scandia, Scandinavia, where it was discovered.]

scan·sion (skăn'shən) n. The analysis of verse into metrical patterns. [Late Latin scansiō, from Latin, a climbing, from scandere, to climb.]

scant (skănt) adj. **-er, -est. 1.** Deficient in quantity or amount; meager. **2.** Being just short of a specific measure: a scant three miles. —tr.v. **1.** To provide with an inadequate share; skimp. **2.** To deal with or treat inadequately. [Middle English, from Old Norse skamt, neut. of skammr, short.] —**scant'ly** adv. —**scant'ness** n.

scant·ling (skănt'lĭng, -lĭn) n. **1.** A very small quantity or amount. **2.** A small piece of timber. [Earlier scantlon, from Middle English scantilon, carpenter's gauge, dimension, from Old French escantillon, ult. from Latin scandere, to climb.]

scant·y (skăn'tē) adj. **-i·er, -i·est. 1.** Barely sufficient. **2.** Deficient; insufficient. —**scant'i·ly** adv. —**scant'i·ness** n.

scape (skāp) n. **1.** Bot. A leafless flower stalk that grows directly from the ground. **2.** A similar stalklike part, such as a feather shaft. [Latin scāpus, stalk.]

–scape. A suffix meaning scene or view: seascape. [From LANDSCAPE.]

scape·goat (skāp'gōt') n. Someone or something that bears the blame for others. [(E)SCAPE + GOAT.]

scap·u·la (skăp'yə-lə) n., pl. **-lae** (-lē') or **-las.** The shoulder blade. [Latin.]

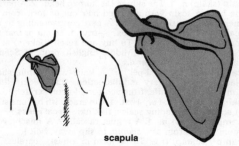

scapula

scap·u·lar (skăp'yə-lər) n. **1.** An ecclesiastical garment that consists of a narrow panel of cloth with a head opening, worn over the shoulders. **2.** Two small pieces of cloth joined by strings and worn over the shoulders as a mark of devotion. **3.** A feather on the shoulder of a bird. —adj. Of

the shoulder or scapula. [Middle English scapulare, from Medieval Latin scapulāre, shoulder cloak, from Latin scapula, shoulder.]

scar (skär) n. **1.** A mark left on the skin after an injury or wound has healed. **2.** Any lingering sign of damage. **3.** Bot. A mark indicating a former point of attachment, as of a leaf to a stem. —v. **scarred, scar·ring.** —tr.v. To mark with a scar. —intr.v. To become marked with a scar. [Middle English scare, from Old French eschare, scab, from Late Latin eschara, from Greek eskhara, hearth, scab caused by burning.]

scar·ab (skăr'əb) n. **1.** A large black beetle, regarded as a symbol of the soul by the ancient Egyptians. **2.** A representation of a scarab beetle. [Old French scarabee, from Latin scarabaeus.]

scarce (skârs) adj. **scarc·er, scarc·est.** Insufficient in quantity; not plentiful. [Middle English scars, from Norman French escars, from Latin excerptus, past part. of excerpere, to pick out, select.] —**scarce'ness** n.

scarce·ly (skârs'lē) adv. **1.** By a small margin; just; barely. **2.** Almost not; hardly. **3.** Certainly not.
　　Usage: **scarcely. 1.** Since this word has senses verging on the negative, it is not used with another negative in the same construction: could scarcely make it out (not couldn't scarcely). **2.** Scarcely is followed by clauses introduced by when (or before) but not by than or until: They had scarcely departed when the storm broke.

scar·ci·ty (skâr'sĭ-tē) n., pl. **-ties.** The condition of being scarce. —See Syns at **deficiency.**

scare (skâr) v. **scared, scar·ing.** —tr.v. To frighten; terrify. —intr.v. To become frightened. —See Syns at **frighten.** —n. **1.** A sudden fear. **2.** A general state of alarm; panic. [Middle English skerren, from Old Norse skirra, from skjarr, shy, timid] —**scar'er** n.

scare·crow (skâr'krō') n. **1.** A crude figure made in the form of a person and set up to scare birds away from growing crops. **2.** A gaunt or ragged person.

scarf¹ (skärf) n., pl. **scarfs** or **scarves** (skärvz). **1.** A rectangular or triangular piece of cloth, worn about the neck, shoulders, or head. **2.** A runner, as for a bureau or table. [Old North French escarpe, from Latin scirpea, basket made of rushes, from scirpus, rush, bulrush.]

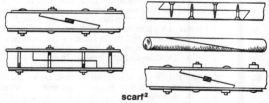

scarf²

scarf² (skärf) n., pl. **scarfs. 1.** A joint made by cutting and notching the ends of two timbers and strapping or bolting them together. Also called **scarf joint. 2.** The end of a timber notched to form a scarf joint. —tr.v. To join by means of a scarf. [Middle English skarf.]

scarf·skin (skärf'skĭn') n. The epidermis or outermost layer of skin, esp. the cuticle.

scar·i·fy (skăr'ə-fī') tr.v. **-fied, -fy·ing. 1.** To make small scratches in. **2.** To criticize severely. [Middle English scarifien, to score the bark of a tree, from Old French scarifier, from Late Latin scarīficāre, from Greek skariphasthai, to scratch an outline, sketch, from skariphos, pencil.] —**scar'i·fi·ca'tion** n.

scar·la·ti·na (skär'lə-tē'nə) n. A usu. mild form of scarlet fever. [From Medieval Latin scarlata, scarlet.]

scar·let (skär'lĭt) n. **1.** A bright red or red-orange. **2.** Scarlet clothing or cloth. —adj. Bright red or red-orange. [Middle English, from Old French escarlate, from Medieval Latin scarlata, scarlet cloth, from Persian sāqirlāt, silk material dyed red.]

scarlet fever. An acute contagious disease caused by a streptococcus, characterized by a rash and high fever.

scarlet pimpernel. A plant, the pimpernel.

scarlet runner. A tropical American bean plant, Phaseolus coccineus, with scarlet flowers and edible seeds.

| ă pat | ā pay | â care | ä father | ĕ pet | ē be | hw which | ĭ pit | ī tie | î pier | ŏ pot | ō toe | ô paw, for | oi noise |
| ŏŏ took | ōō boot | ou out | th thin | th this | ŭ cut | | û urge | zh vision | ə about, item, edible, gallop, circus |

scarlet tanager. A New World bird, *Piranga olivacea*, of which the male has bright scarlet plumage with a black tail and wings.

scarp (skärp) *n.* A steep slope; cliff. —*tr.v.* To cut or make into a steep slope. [Italian *scarpa*.]

scarves (skärvz) *n.* A plural of **scarf** (piece of cloth).

scar·y (skâr′ē) *adj.* **-i·er, -i·est.** *Informal.* **1.** Frightening; alarming. **2.** Easily scared; very timid.

scat¹ (skăt) *intr.v.* **scat·ted, scat·ting.** *Informal.* To go away hastily; leave at once. [Poss. short for SCATTER.]

scat² (skăt) *n.* Jazz singing in which meaningless syllables are sung to a melody. [Perh. imit.]

scathe (skāth) *tr.v.* **scathed, scath·ing.** **1.** To injure esp. by fire. **2.** To criticize severely. [Middle English *scathen*, from Old Norse *skadha*.]

sca·tol·o·gy (skə-tŏl′ə-jē, skă-) *n.* An interest in or obsession with obscenity, esp. in literature. [Greek *skato-*, from *skōr*, excrement + -LOGY.] —**scat′o·log′i·cal** (skăt′ə-lŏj′-ĭ-kəl) *adj.*

scat·ter (skăt′ər) *tr.v.* **1.** To cause to separate and go in various directions; disperse. **2.** To distribute loosely by or as if by sprinkling or strewing. —*intr.v.* **1.** To separate and go in several directions; disperse. **2.** To occur or fall at widely spaced intervals. —See Syns at **spread.** [Middle English *scateren*, poss. var. of *schateren*, to shatter.] —**scat′ter·er** *n.*

Syns: *scatter, dispel, disperse, dissipate v. Core meaning:* To separate or cause to separate and go in various directions (*children scattering on the playground; wind that scattered the leaves*).

scat·ter·brain (skăt′ər-brān′) *n.* A flighty, disorganized, or thoughtless person. —**scat′ter·brained′** *adj.*

scat·ter·ing (skăt′ər-ĭng) *n.* A small quantity or amount scattered irregularly: *a scattering of applause.*

scatter rug. A small rug for carpeting a part of a floor.

scaup (skôp) *n.* Either of two diving ducks, *Aythya marila* or *A. affinis*, with predominantly black and white plumage. [Per. var. of *scalp*, bed of mussels (from its feeding on shellfish).]

scav·enge (skăv′ĭnj) *v.* **-enged, -eng·ing.** —*tr.v.* **1.** To collect and remove refuse from. **2.** To salvage from discarded materials. —*intr.v.* To search through refuse for something useful. [Back-formation from SCAVENGER.]

scav·en·ger (skăv′ĭn-jər) *n.* **1.** An animal that feeds on dead or decaying matter. **2.** A person who scavenges. [Earlier *scavager*, street-cleaner, from Middle English *skawager*, collector of tolls, from Norman French *scawager*, from *scawage*, a toll levied on foreign merchants, ult. from Flemish *scawuen*, to look at.]

sce·nar·i·o (sĭ-nâr′ē-ō′, -när′-) *n., pl.* **-os.** **1.** A plot outline esp. of a literary work. **2.** A screenplay. **3.** An outline of possible future events. [Italian, "scenery."]

sce·nar·ist (sĭ-nâr′ĭst, -när′-) *n.* A writer of scenarios.

scene (sēn) *n.* **1.** A picture presented to a viewer; prospect. **2.** The place where an action or event occurs: *the scene of the wreck.* **3.** A subdivision of an act in which the setting is fixed and the time continuous. **4.** A unit or continuous sequence of action in a film. **5.** The scenery for a dramatic production. **6.** A public display of emotion or temper. **7.** A sphere of activity. [French *scène*, from Old French *scene*, stage, stage performance, from Latin *scaena*, stage, scene, theater, from Greek *skēnē*, tent.] —*idiom.* **behind the scenes. 1.** Backstage. **2.** In private.

scen·er·y (sē′nə-rē) *n.* **1.** A picturesque or striking landscape. **2.** The apparatus, such as curtains or flats, used for a dramatic production. [Italian *scenario*.]

sce·nic (sē′nĭk) *adj.* **1.** Of or relating to the stage or a stage setting. **2.** Of, relating to, or marked by picturesque natural scenery. —**sce′ni·cal·ly** *adv.*

scent (sĕnt) *n.* **1.** A typical and often pleasant odor. **2.** A perfume. **3. a.** An odor left on a surface by an animal. **b.** The trail of a hunted animal or fugitive. **4.** The sense of smell. **5.** A hint of something; suggestion: *a scent of trouble.* —*tr.v.* **1.** To smell. **2.** To detect as if by smelling: *scent danger.* **3.** To fill with a scent; perfume. [Middle English *sent*, from *senten*, to smell, scent, from Old French *sentir*, from Latin *sentīre*, to feel.]

scep·ter (sĕp′tər) *n.* Also *Brit.* **scep·tre. 1.** A staff carried by a sovereign as an emblem of authority. **2.** Royal authority or power. [Middle English *sceptre*, from Old French,

from Latin *sceptrum*, from Greek *skēptron*, staff, stick.]

scep·tic (skĕp′tĭk) *n.* Var. of **skeptic.**

scep·ti·cal (skĕp′tĭ-kəl) *adj.* Var. of **skeptical.**

scep·ti·cism (skĕp′tĭ-sĭz′əm) *n.* Var. of **skepticism.**

sched·ule (skĕj′ōōl, -ōō-əl, skĕj′əl) *n.* **1.** A printed or written list, often in tabular form. **2. a.** A program of forthcoming events or appointments. **b.** A student's program of classes. **3.** A timetable. **4.** A plan of things to be done or dealt with: *a production schedule.* —*tr.v.* **-uled, -ul·ing. 1.** To enter on a schedule. **2.** To plan or appoint for a certain time or date. [Middle English *cedule*, slip of parchment or paper, short note, from Old French, from Late Latin *schedula*, dim. of Latin *scheda*, papyrus leaf, of Greek orig.]

sche·mat·ic (skē-măt′ĭk) *adj.* Pertaining to or in the form of a scheme or diagram. —*n.* A structural diagram.

scheme (skēm) *n.* **1.** A systematic plan of action. **2.** An orderly combination of elements: *a color scheme.* **3.** A plot. **4.** A chart or diagram. —See Syns at **plot.** —*v.* **schemed, schem·ing.** —*tr.v.* To contrive a plan or scheme for. —*intr.v.* To make a scheme. [Latin *schēma*, form, figure, manner, from Greek *skhēma*, form.] —**schem′er** *n.*

scher·zan·do (skĕr-tsän′dō) *adv. Mus.* In a playful manner. [Italian, from *scherzare*, to joke, from *scherzo*, joke.] —**scher·zan′do** *adj.*

scher·zo (skĕr′tsō) *n., pl.* **-zos** or **-zi** (-tsē). *Mus.* A lively movement commonly in triple time. [Italian, joke, from Middle High German *scherz*, from *scherzen*, to joke.]

schil·ling (shĭl′ĭng) *n.* The basic monetary unit of Austria. [German *Schilling*, from Middle High German *schillinc*, from Old High German *skilling*.]

schism (sĭz′əm, skĭz′-) *n.* **1.** A separation or division in a church or religious body. **2.** Any separation or division into factions within a group. [Middle English *scisme*, from Old French, from Late Latin *schisma*, from Greek *skhisma*, a split, division, from *skhizein*, to split.]

schis·mat·ic (sĭz-măt′ĭk, skĭz-) *adj.* Of, relating to, or guilty of schism. —*n.* A person who encourages schism.

schist (shĭst) *n.* Any of various medium- to coarse-grained metamorphic rocks composed of layers of minerals that contain mica. [French *schiste*, from Latin *(lapis) schistos*, "fissile (stone)," from Greek *skhistos (lithos)*, talc, from *skhizein*, to split.] —**schis·tose′** (shĭs′tōs′) *adj.*

schis·to·some (shĭs′tə-sōm′) *n.* Any of several chiefly tropical trematode worms of the genus *Schistosoma*, many of which are parasitic in the blood of mammals. [Greek *skhistos*, cleft, from *skhizein*, to split + -SOME (body).]

schis·to·so·mi·a·sis (shĭs′tə-sō-mī′ə-sĭs) *n.* Any of various gen. tropical diseases caused by infestation with schistosomes. [SCHISTOSOME + -IASIS.]

schizo- or **schiz-.** A prefix meaning division, split, or cleavage: *schizophrenia.* [From Greek *skhizein*, to split.]

schiz·o·carp (skĭz′ə-kärp′, skĭt′sə-) *n.* A dry seed that splits at maturity into two or more closed carpels, each usu. containing one seed, as in the fruit of the carrot or mallow. [SCHIZO- + -CARP.] —**schiz′o·car′pous** (-kär′pəs) *adj.*

schiz·oid (skĭt′soid′) *adj.* Characteristic of or resembling schizophrenia. —*n.* A schizophrenic.

schiz·o·my·cete (skĭz′ō-mī′sēt′, skĭt′sə-) *n.* Any of numerous one-celled microorganisms of the class Schizomycetes, which includes the bacteria. —**schiz′o·my·ce′tous** (-mī-sē′təs) *adj.*

schiz·o·phre·ni·a (skĭt′sə-frē′nē-ə) *n.* A psychosis characterized by withdrawal from reality and by behavioral and intellectual disturbances. [SCHIZO- + Greek *phrēn*, mind.] —**schiz′o·phren′ic** (-frĕn′ĭk) *adj. & n.*

schle·miel (shlə-mēl′) *n. Slang.* A habitual bungler; dolt. [Yiddish.]

schlep (shlĕp) *tr.v.* **schlepped, schlep·ping.** *Slang.* To carry clumsily or with difficulty; to lug. [Yiddish *shleppen*, to drag, from Middle Low German *slēpen*.]

schmaltz (shmälts) *n.* Also **schmalz.** *Slang.* Sentimental art or music. [German *Schmaltz*, melted fat, from Middle High German *smalz*, from Old High German.] —**schmaltz′y** *adj.*

schnapps (shnäps, shnăps) *n.* Any of various distilled liquors. [German *Schnaps*, from Low German *snaps*, mouthful, dram, from *snappen*, to snap, from Middle Low German.]

---

schnau·zer (shnou′zər, shnout′sər) *n.* A dog of a breed developed in Germany, with a wiry gray coat and a blunt muzzle. [German *Schnauzer,* from *Schnauze,* snout.]

schnauzer

schol·ar (skŏl′ər) *n.* **1.** Someone who attends school or studies with a teacher. **2.** A person of great learning, esp. in one of the humanities. **3.** A student who holds or has held a scholarship. [Middle English *scoler,* from Old French *escoler,* from Late Latin *scholāris,* of a school, from Latin *schola,* school, from Greek *skholē.*] —**schol′ar·li·ness** *n.* —**schol′ar·ly** *adv.*

schol·ar·ship (skŏl′ər-shĭp′) *n.* **1.** The methods, discipline, or achievements of a scholar. **2.** Knowledge as a result of study and research in a particular field. **3.** Financial aid to a student, as from a college. —See Syns at **knowledge.**

scho·las·tic (skə-lăs′tĭk) *adj.* **1.** Of school or scholars. **2.** Often **Scholastic.** Of Scholasticism. **3.** Overly concerned with formal rules; pedantic. —*n.* **1.** Often **Scholastic.** A Scholastic philosopher. **2.** A dogmatist. [Latin *scholasticus,* from Greek *skholastikos,* academic, from *skholazein,* to study, from *skholē,* school.] —**scho·las′ti·cal·ly** *adv.*

scho·las·ti·cism or **Scho·las·ti·cism** (skə-lăs′tĭ-sĭz′əm) *n.* A theological and philosophical movement of the Middle Ages, characterized by methods of systematic analysis adapted from the ancient philosophers.

school¹ (skōōl) *n.* **1.** An institution for instruction. **2.** A college or university. **3.** A division of a college or university. **4.** The students of a school. **5.** The process of being instructed: *She finds school easy.* **6.** A session of school. **7.** A group of persons who share common beliefs, methods, or style. —*modifier: a school band.* —*tr.v.* **1.** To instruct in or as if in a school; educate. **2.** To train; drill. [Middle English *scole,* from Old English *scōl,* from Medieval Latin *scōla,* from Latin *schola,* from Greek *skholē.*]

school² (skōōl) *n.* A large group of aquatic animals of the same kind, esp. fish, swimming together. —*intr.v.* To swim in or form into a school. [Middle English *scole,* from Middle Dutch *schōle,* troop, group.]

school·boy (skōōl′boi′) *n.* A boy attending school.

school·girl (skōōl′gûrl′) *n.* A girl attending school.

school·ing (skōō′lĭng) *n.* Instruction or training.

school·marm (skōōl′märm′) *n.* Also **school·ma'am** (-măm, -mäm). *Informal.* **1.** A woman who teaches school. **2.** A prude or pedant. [SCHOOL + dial. *marm,* var. of *ma'am,* madam.]

school·mas·ter (skōōl′măs′tər) *n.* A male schoolteacher.

school·mate (skōōl′māt′) *n.* A school companion.

school·teach·er (skōōl′tē′chər) *n.* A person who teaches in a school below the college level.

schoo·ner (skōō′nər) *n.* **1.** A ship with two or more masts. **2.** A large beer glass. **3.** A **prairie schooner.** [Orig. unknown.]

schot·tische (shŏt′ĭsh) *n.* **1.** A round dance similar to the polka. **2.** Music for a schottische. [German (*der*) *schottische (Tanz),* "(the) Scottish (dance)."]

schuss (shōōs) *intr.v.* To ski a fast, straight, downhill course. —*n.* **1.** A straight, steep skiing course. **2.** The act of schussing. [German *Schuss,* shot, from Middle High German *schuz,* from Old High German *scuz.*]

schwa (shwä) *n.* **1.** A vowel sound that in English often occurs in an unstressed syllable, as the sound of *a* in *alone* or *e* in *linen.* **2.** The symbol ə often used to represent schwa. [German *Schwa,* from Hebrew *shəwā′.*]

sci·at·ic (sī-ăt′ĭk) *adj.* **1.** Pertaining to the ischium. **2.** Per-taining to sciatica. [Old French *sciatique,* from Late Latin *ischiaticus,* var. of Latin *ischiadicus,* from Greek *iskhiadi-kos,* from *iskhion,* hip joint.]

sci·at·i·ca (sī-ăt′ĭ-kə) *n.* **1.** Neuralgia of the sciatic nerve. **2.** Chronic neuralgic pain in the area of the hip or thigh. [Middle English, from Medieval Latin *sciatica (passiō),* "(suffering) in the hip," from Late Latin *sciaticus,* sciatic.]

sciatic nerve. A nerve originating in the sacral plexus and running through the pelvis and upper leg.

sci·ence (sī′əns) *n.* **1.** A domain of systematically organized and classified knowledge: *the social sciences.* **2.** One of the natural sciences. **3.** An activity, discipline, or technique for which systematic methods and principles can be derived. —*modifier: a science project.* [Middle English, knowledge, learning, from Old French, from Latin *scientia,* from *sciēns,* pres. part. of *scīre,* to know.]

science fiction. Fiction in which actual or potential scientific developments form part of the plot. —*modifier* (**science-fiction**): *a science-fiction novel.*

sci·en·tif·ic (sī′ən-tĭf′ĭk) *adj.* Of, relating to, or used in science. [Medieval Latin *scientificus,* "producing knowledge."] —**sci′en·tif′i·cal·ly** *adv.*

sci·en·tist (sī′ən-tĭst) *n.* A person who has expert knowledge of a science, esp. of a natural science.

scim·i·tar (sĭm′ĭ-tər, -tär′) *n.* Also **scim·i·ter** (-tər). A curved sword with a single edge on its convex side. [French *cime-terre,* from Italian *scimitarra,* from Persian *šimšīr.*]

scin·til·la (sĭn-tĭl′ə) *n.* An extremely small amount; trace. [Latin, spark.]

scin·til·late (sĭn′tə-lāt′) *intr.v.* **-lat·ed, -lat·ing.** **1.** To give off sparks or flashes of light; sparkle, twinkle. **2.** To be animated and brilliant. [From Latin *scintillāre,* from *scintilla,* spark.] —**scin′til·la′tion** *n.*

sci·on (sī′ən) *n.* **1.** A descendant or heir. **2.** A detached shoot or twig containing buds from a woody plant and used in grafting. —See Syns at **descendant.** [Middle English, from Old French *cion.*]

scis·sion (sĭzh′ən, sĭsh′-) *n.* The act of cutting or severing; division. [French, from Late Latin *scissiō,* from Latin *scis-sus,* past part. of *scindere,* to cut.]

scis·sor (sĭz′ər) *tr.v.* To cut or clip with scissors or shears. —*n.* Scissors.

scis·sors (sĭz′ərz) *n. (used with a sing. or pl. verb).* **1.** A cutting implement consisting of two blades joined by a swivel pin that allows the cutting edges to be opened and closed. **2.** A wrestling hold in which the legs are locked about the head or body of an opponent. [Middle English *sisoures,* from Old French *cisoires,* from Medieval Latin *cīsōria,* pl. of Late Latin *cīsōrium,* cutting instrument, from Latin *caedere,* to cut.]

scissors kick. A swimming kick used chiefly with the side stroke in which the legs are snapped together like scissors.

scle·ra (sklîr′ə, sklĕr′ə) *n.* The tough, white, fibrous outer envelope of tissue covering all of the eyeball except the cornea. [From Greek *sklēros,* hard.]

scle·ro·sis (sklə-rō′sĭs) *n., pl.* **-ses** (-sēz′). **1.** A thickening or hardening of a body part. **2.** A disease characterized by sclerosis. [Middle English *sclirosis,* from Medieval Latin *sclīrōsis,* from Greek *sklērōsis,* hardening, from *sklēros,* hard.]

scle·rot·ic (sklə-rŏt′ĭk) *adj.* **1.** Affected or characterized by sclerosis. **2.** *Anat.* Of the sclera.

scoff (skŏf, skôf) *tr.v.* To treat with derision; mock. —*intr.v.* To express derision or contempt. —*n.* An expression of derision or scorn; a jeer. [Middle English *scof-fen,* from *scof,* mockery.] —**scoff′er** *n.*

scold (skōld) *tr.v.* To find fault with. —*intr.v.* To find fault. —*n.* A person who scolds habitually. [Middle English *scolden,* from *scold,* ribald or abusive person.] —**scold′er** *n.*

Syns: scold, bawl out (*Informal*), **call down, castigate, chew out** (*Slang*), **rebuke, reprimand, reproach, reprove, upbraid** *v. Core meaning:* To criticize for a fault or offense (*was scolded for repeated tardiness*).

scol·lop (skŏl′əp) *n. & v.* Var. of **scallop.**

sconce (skŏns) *n.* A wall bracket for candles or lights. [Middle English, from Old French *esconse,* lantern, hiding place, from Medieval Latin *asconsa,* from Latin *absconsus,* past part. of *abscondere,* to hide away.]

---

scone (skōn, skŏn) *n.* A small, biscuitlike quick bread sometimes baked on a griddle. [From Dutch *schoonbrood*, fine white bread.]

scoop (skōōp) *n.* **1. a.** A shovellike utensil, usu. having a deep, curved dish and short handle, used with loose or semisoft substances: *a flour scoop.* **b.** The amount a scoop holds. **2.** The bucket or shovel of a steam shovel or dredge. **3.** An act of scooping. **4.** A hole or cavity made by scooping. **5.** *Slang.* **a.** An exclusive news story. **b.** Information. —*tr.v.* **1.** To take up with or as if with a scoop: *scoop out the seeds.* **2.** To hollow out by digging. **3.** *Slang.* To outmaneuver (a competitor) in acquiring and publishing an important news story. [Middle English, from Middle Dutch *schōpe.*] —**scoop'er** *n.*

scoot (skōōt) *intr.v.* To go suddenly and speedily; dart or scurry off. —See Syns at **rush.** [Prob. of Scandinavian orig.]

scoot·er (skōō'tər) *n.* **1.** A child's vehicle consisting of a long footboard mounted on two end wheels controlled by an upright steering handle attached to the front wheel. **2.** A **motor scooter.**

scope (skōp) *n.* **1.** The range or extent of thoughts or actions. **2.** Space or opportunity to function. **3.** The area covered by a given activity or subject: *the scope of the course.* —See Syns at **range.** [Italian *scopo*, aim, purpose, from Greek *skopos*, watcher, goal, aim.]

–scope. A suffix meaning an instrument for observing: **microscope.** [Latin *-scopium*, from Greek *-skopion*, from *skopein*, to see.]

sco·pol·a·mine (skō-pŏl'ə-mēn', -mǐn) *n.* A thick, syrupy, colorless alkaloid, $C_{17}H_{21}NO_4$, extracted from such plants as henbane and used as a sedative and truth serum. [German *Scopolamin*, from New Latin *Scopolia*, genus of plants from which the alkaloid is extracted, after Giovanni Scopoli (1723–88), Italian naturalist.]

scor·bu·tic (skôr-byōō'tǐk) *or* **scor·bu·ti·cal** (-tǐ-kəl) *adj.* Related to, resembling, or afflicted with scurvy. [From Late Latin *scorbūtus*, scurvy.] —**scor·bu'ti·cal·ly** *adv.*

scorch (skôrch) *tr.v.* **1.** To burn slightly so as to alter the color or taste. **2.** To wither or parch with intense heat. **3.** To subject to severe censure. —*intr.v.* To become scorched or singed. —*n.* A slight burn. [Middle English *scorchen.*] —**scorch'er** *n.*

score (skôr, skōr) *n.* **1.** A notch or incision. **2. a.** A record of points made in a game or contest. **b.** The number of points made by each competitor or team in a game or contest. **3.** A ranking or grade, as on a test or examination. **4. a.** An amount due; a debt. **b.** A grievance or grudge kept or held in the mind. **5.** A ground; reason; account: *have no worries on that score.* **6. a.** A group of 20 items. **b. scores.** An indefinitely large number. **7. a.** The written or printed form of a musical composition. **b.** The music for a theatrical production or film. **8.** *Informal.* The realities of a situation: *doesn't know the score.* —*v.* **scored, scor·ing.** —*tr.v.* **1.** To mark with lines or notches. **2.** To make cuts in. **3. a.** To make (a score) in a game or contest. **b.** To count or be worth as points. **4.** *Baseball.* To enable (a runner) to achieve a score. **5.** To achieve (a goal). **6.** To evaluate and assign a grade to. **7.** To orchestrate or write music for. **8.** To criticize harshly. —*intr.v.* **1.** To make a point in a game or contest. **2.** To keep the score of a game or contest. **3.** To achieve an advantage; succeed. —See Syns at **accomplish.** [Middle English *scor*, notch, tally, twenty, from Old Norse *skor.*] —**scor'er** *n.*

score·card (skôr'kärd', skōr'-) *n.* A card used to record the score of a game.

sco·ri·a (skôr'ē-ə, skōr'-) *n., pl.* **-ae** (-ē'). **1.** *Geol.* Rough fragments of burnt, crustlike lava. **2.** The refuse of a smelted ore or metal; slag. [Middle English, slag, from Latin *scōria*, from Greek *skōria*, from *skōr*, excrement.]

scorn (skôrn) *n.* **1.** Contempt or disdain for a person or object considered despicable or inferior. **2.** A person or a thing that is an object of contempt. —*tr.v.* **1.** To consider or treat with scorn; despise. **2.** To refuse with scorn. —See Syns at **despise.** [Middle English *scornen*, to despise.]

scorn·ful (skôrn'fəl) *adj.* Full of scorn; disdainful: *a scornful laugh.* —**scorn'ful·ly** *adv.* —**scorn'ful·ness** *n.*

Scor·pi·o (skôr'pē-ō') *n.* Also **Scor·pi·us.** **1.** A constellation in the Southern Hemisphere near Libra and Sagittarius.

2. The eighth sign of the zodiac.

scor·pi·on (skôr'pē-ən) *n.* Any of various arachnids of the order Scorpionida, with an erectile tail tipped with a venomous sting. [Middle English *scorpioun*, from Old French *scorpion*, from Latin *scorpiō*, from Greek *skorpios.*]

scorpion

Scot (skŏt) *n.* **1.** A native or inhabitant of Scotland. **2.** A member of the ancient Gaelic tribe that migrated to northern Great Britain from Ireland in about A.D. 500.

Usage: **Scot.** *Scot* and *Scotsman* (the preferred terms), together with *Scotchman*, all denote a native or inhabitant of Scotland. The corresponding plural terms are *Scots* and (the) *Scotch.* The adjectives preferred in Scotland are *Scottish* and *Scots; Scotch* is also in common usage. Certain set phrases have been established by idiom, for instance, *Scotch broth, Scotch whiskey,* and *Scots Guards.*

scotch (skŏch) *tr.v.* **1.** To injure so as to render harmless; cripple. **2.** To put an end to; crush. [Middle English *scocchen*, from Norman French *escocher*, to cut a notch.]

Scotch (skŏch) *n.* **1.** *(used with a pl. verb).* The people of Scotland. **2.** A smoky-flavored whiskey distilled in Scotland. —See Usage note at **Scot.** —**Scotch** *adj.*

Scotch-I·rish (skŏch-ī'rĭsh) *adj.* Of or relating to the people of Northern Ireland who are descendants of Scottish settlers.

Scotch·man (skŏch'mən) *n.* A Scot. —See Usage note at **Scot.**

Scotch terrier. A Scottish terrier.

sco·ter (skō'tər) *n.* Any of several dark-colored diving ducks of the genera *Oidemia* and *Melanitta*, of northern Atlantic coasts. [Orig. unknown.]

scot-free (skŏt'frē') *adj.* Free from obligation or penalty. [From Middle English *scot*, tax.]

Scots (skŏts) *adj.* Scottish. —See Usage note at **Scot.** —*n.* The English dialect of Scotland.

Scots·man (skŏts'mən) *n.* A Scot. —See Usage note at **Scot.**

Scot·tie (skŏt'ē) *n.* A Scottish terrier.

Scot·tish (skŏt'ĭsh) *adj.* Of or characteristic of Scotland, its people, or its language. —*n.* **1.** Scots. **2.** The people of Scotland. —See Usage note at **Scot.**

Scottish Gaelic. The Gaelic language of the Scottish Highlanders.

Scottish terrier. A terrier of a breed originating in Scotland, with a heavy-set body, short legs, blunt muzzle, and a dark, wiry coat.

scoun·drel (skoun'drəl) *n.* A villain. [Orig. unknown.]

scour¹ (skour) *tr.v.* **1. a.** To clean, polish, or wash by scrubbing vigorously. **b.** To remove by scrubbing. **2.** To remove dirt or grease from, as by means of a detergent: *scour wool.* **3.** To dig or clear out by or as if by a stream of water. —*intr.v.* To clean or polish something by scrubbing. —*n.* An act of scouring. [Middle English *scouren*, from Middle Dutch *scūren*, from Old French *escurer*, from Late Latin *excūrāre*, to clean out.]

scour² (skour) *tr.v.* To move over or through quickly or thoroughly, as in making a search. —*intr.v.* To move over an area, esp. in a search. [Middle English *scouren*, prob. of Scandinavian orig.]

scourge (skûrj) *n.* **1.** A whip. **2.** Any instrument for inflicting severe punishment. **3.** A cause of great suffering or harm. —*tr.v.* **scourged, scourg·ing.** **1.** To beat or whip severely; flog. **2.** To punish severely. **3.** To afflict severely; devastate. [Middle English, from Old French *escorge*, from *escorgier*, to whip.] —**scourg'er** *n.*

scout¹ (skout) *n.* **1. a.** Someone or something sent out to gather information, esp. in preparation for military action. **b.** The action of reconnoitering. **2.** A person who seeks out persons with talent, as in sports or entertainment. **3. a.** A Boy Scout. **b.** A Girl Scout. —*tr.v.* **1.** To go about and survey in order to obtain information; reconnoiter. **2.** To search: *scout around for food.* —*intr.v.* To search for talented persons. [Middle English *scoute,* from Old French *escoute,* spy, from *escouter,* to listen, from Latin *auscultāre.*] —**scout'er** *n.*

scout² (skout) *tr.v.* To reject with contempt or derision. [Of Scandinavian orig.]

scout·mas·ter (skout'măs'tər) *n.* The adult leader of a troop of Boy Scouts.

scow (skou) *n.* A large flat-bottomed boat with square ends, used chiefly for transporting freight. [Dutch *schouw,* from Middle Dutch *scouwe.*]

scowl (skoul) *intr.v.* To wrinkle or contract the brow, as in anger or disapproval. —*n.* A look of anger or strong disapproval; an angry frown. [Middle English *scoulen,* prob. of Scandinavian orig.] —**scowl'er** *n.*

scrab·ble (skrăb'əl) *v.* **-bled, -bling.** —*intr.v.* **1.** To scrape or grope about frenetically with the hands. **2.** To move or climb with disorderly haste. [Middle Dutch *schrabbelen,* freq. of *schrabben,* to scrape.]

scrag (skrăg) *n.* A bony or scrawny person or animal. [Var. of obs. *crag,* neck, throat, from Middle English, from Middle Dutch *crāghe.*]

scrag·gly (skrăg'lē) *adj.* **-gli·er, -gli·est.** Ragged; unkempt.

scrag·gy (skrăg'ē) *adj.* **-gi·er, -gi·est.** **1.** Jagged; rough. **2.** Bony and lean. —**scrag'gi·ness** *n.*

scram (skrăm) *intr.v.* **scrammed, scram·ming.** *Slang.* To leave at once. [Short for SCRAMBLE.]

scram·ble (skrăm'bəl) *v.* **-bled, -bling.** —*intr.v.* **1.** To move or climb hurriedly, esp. on the hands and knees. **2.** To contend frantically: *scrambled for a place in the front row.* —*tr.v.* **1.** To mix or throw together haphazardly. **2.** To fry (eggs) while mixing and stirring together. —See Syns at **confuse.** —*n.* The act of scrambling. [Blend of obs. *scamble,* to struggle for, and *cramble,* to crawl.] —**scram'bler** *n.*

scrap¹ (skrăp) *n.* **1.** A small bit or fragment. **2. scraps.** Leftover and unwanted bits of food. **3.** Waste or discarded material, such as metal. —*tr.v.* **scrapped, scrap·ping.** **1.** To break down into parts for disposal or salvage. **2.** To discard as useless. —*modifier: a scrap pile.* [Middle English, from Old Norse *skrap,* trifles, remains.]

scrap² (skrăp) *intr.v.* **scrapped, scrap·ping.** *Informal.* To fight or quarrel. —*n. Informal.* A fight; quarrel. [Orig. unknown.] —**scrap'per** *n.*

scrap·book (skrăp'bŏŏk') *n.* A book with blank pages for mounting pictures and other mementos.

scrape (skrāp) *v.* **scraped, scrap·ing.** —*tr.v.* **1.** To rub (a surface) with considerable pressure. **2.** To draw (a hard or abrasive object) forcefully over a surface. **3.** To remove from a surface by or as if by rubbing. **4.** To clear or smooth by rubbing with a sharp or rough instrument. **5.** To injure the surface of by rubbing against something rough or sharp. **6.** To draw over a surface with a harsh, grating sound. **7.** To get together with difficulty: *scrape together enough money to survive.* —*intr.v.* **1.** To come into sliding, abrasive contact. **2.** To rub or move with a harsh grating noise. **3.** To practice petty economies; scrimp. **4.** To succeed or emerge with difficulty: *scraped through by a narrow margin.* —*n.* **1.** The act of scraping. **2.** The sound of scraping. **3.** An abrasion on the skin. **4.** *Slang.* A troublesome predicament. [Middle English *scrapen,* from Old Norse *skrapa.*] —**scrap'er** *n.*

scrap·py¹ (skrăp'ē) *adj.* **-pi·er, -pi·est.** Composed of scraps; fragmentary. —**scrap'pi·ly** *adv.* —**scrap'pi·ness** *n.*

scrap·py² (skrăp'ē) *adj.* **-pi·er, -pi·est.** **1.** Quarrelsome; contentious. **2.** Full of determination and fighting spirit. —**scrap'pi·ly** *adv.* —**scrap'pi·ness** *n.*

scratch (skrăch) *tr.v.* **1.** To make a shallow cut or mark on, as with a sharp instrument. **2.** To scrape or rub (the skin) lightly to relieve itching. **3.** To scrape on a rough surface. **4.** To write or draw. **5.** To strike out or cancel by or as if by drawing a line through. **6.** To withdraw (an entry) from a contest. —*intr.v.* **1.** To use the nails or claws to dig, scrape, or wound. **2.** To rub or scrape the

skin to relieve itching. —*n.* **1.** A mark or wound produced by scratching. **2.** A hasty scribble. **3.** A sound made by scratching. **4.** The starting line for a race. —*adj.* **1.** Done or made by chance. **2.** Assembled at random; haphazard. —*idioms.* **from scratch.** From the beginning. **up to scratch.** *Informal.* Up to standard. [Blend of obs. *scrat,* to scratch, and obs. *cratch,* to scratch.] —**scratch'er** *n.*

scratch·y (skrăch'ē) *adj.* **-i·er, -i·est.** **1.** Marked by or consisting of scratches. **2.** Making a harsh, scratching noise: *a scratchy record.* **3.** Irregular; rough. —**scratch'i·ly** *adv.* —**scratch'i·ness** *n.*

scrawl (skrôl) *tr.v.* To write hastily or illegibly. —*intr.v.* To write in a sprawling, illegible manner. —*n.* Irregular, often illegible handwriting. [Blend of SPRAWL and CRAWL.]

scraw·ny (skrô'nē) *adj.* **-ni·er, -ni·est.** Gaunt and bony; skinny. —See Syns at **thin.** [Orig. unknown.] —**scraw'ni·ness** *n.*

scream (skrēm) *intr.v.* **1.** To utter a long, loud, piercing cry, as of pain or fright. **2.** To make a loud, piercing sound. **3.** To have or produce a startling effect. —*tr.v.* To utter or say in or as if in a screaming voice. —*n.* **1.** A long, loud, piercing cry or sound. **2.** *Slang.* Someone or something hilariously funny. [Middle English *scremen,* from Old Norse *skræma.*] —**scream'er** *n.*

screech (skrēch) *n.* **1.** A high-pitched, harsh, piercing cry; a shriek. **2.** A sound that resembles a screech. —*tr.v.* To say or utter in or as if in a screech. —*intr.v.* **1.** To scream in a high-pitched, strident voice. **2.** To make a prolonged shrill, grating noise. [Earlier *scritch,* from Middle English *scrichen,* from Old Norse *skraekja.*] —**screech'y** *adj.*

screech owl. Any of various small North American owls of the genus *Otus,* esp. *O. asio,* with ear tufts and a quavering, whistlelike call.

screech owl

screed (skrēd) *n.* A long, monotonous discourse. [Middle English *screde,* fragment, strip, from Old English *scrēade.*]

screen (skrēn) *n.* **1.** A movable device, as a panel, designed to divide, conceal, or protect. **2.** Anything that serves to divide, conceal, or protect: *a dense screen of shrubbery.* **3.** A coarse sieve used for sifting out fine particles, as of sand, gravel, and coal. **4.** A frame fitted with mesh, used to keep out insects. **5.** The surface upon which a picture is projected for viewing. **6.** The motion-picture industry. **7.** *Electronics.* The phosphorescent surface in a cathode-ray tube, upon which the image appears. —*modifier: a screen door.* —*tr.v.* **1.** To provide with a screen: *screen a porch.* **2. a.** To conceal from view. **b.** To protect, guard, or shield. **3.** To separate or sift out by or as if by means of a sieve or screen. **4.** To project on a screen. [Middle English *screne,* from Old French *escren,* from Middle Dutch *scherm,* shield.] —**screen'er** *n.*

screen·play (skrēn'plā') *n.* The script for a motion picture.

screen test. A brief motion-picture sequence filmed to test the ability of an aspiring movie actor or actress.

screen·writ·er (skrēn'rī'tər) *n.* A writer of screenplays.

screw (skrōō) *n.* **1.** A simple machine that consists of a solid cylinder bearing a spiral groove. **2.** A device for fastening in the form of a metal pin with an incised spiral thread and a notched head that can be driven with a screwdriver. **3.** A device in the shape of a screw, such as a corkscrew. **4.** A propeller. **5.** A twist or turn of or as if of a screw. —*tr.v.* **1.** To drive or tighten (a screw). **2.** To fasten or attach with or as if with a screw. **3.** To twist out of shape; contort. **4.** To increase or heighten, as in strength

ă pat ā pay â care ä father ĕ pet ē be hw which
ŏŏ took ŏŏ boot ou out th thin th this ŭ cut
ĭ pit ī tie î pier ŏ pot ō toe ô paw, for oi noise
û urge zh vision ə about, item, edible, gallop, circus

or intensity: *screwed up the courage to ask for a raise.* **5.** *Slang.* To take advantage of; to cheat. —*intr.v.* To become attached by or as if by a screw. —*phrasal verb.* **screw up.** *Slang.* To make a mess of; bungle. [Middle English *skrewe,* from Old French *escroue,* nut, from Latin *scrōfa,* sow.] —**screw'er** *n.*

screw·ball (skrōō'bôl') *n.* **1.** *Baseball.* A pitched ball curving in the direction opposite to a normal curve ball. **2.** *Slang.* An odd, eccentric, or crazy person.

screw·driv·er (skrōō'drī'vər) *n.* **1.** A tool used to turn screws. **2.** A cocktail of vodka and orange juice.

screw pine. A tree or shrub, pandanus.

screw propeller. A propeller.

screw thread. The continuous spiral groove on a screw.

screw·y (skrōō'ē) *adj.* **-i·er, -i·est.** *Slang.* **1.** Eccentric; crazy. **2.** Ludicrously odd. —See Syns at **insane.**

scrib·ble (skrĭb'əl) *v.* **-bled, -bling.** —*tr.v.* **1.** To write or draw hastily or carelessly. **2.** To cover with such writing. —*intr.v.* To write or draw in a hurried, careless way. —*n.* Careless, hurried writing or markings. [Middle English *scriblen,* from Medieval Latin *scrībillāre,* freq. of Latin *scrībere,* to write.] —**scrib'bler** *n.*

scribe (skrīb) *n.* **1.** An official copyist of manuscripts and documents. **2.** A public clerk or secretary. **3.** A writer or journalist. **4.** An ancient Hebrew teacher or scholar who interpreted the Mosaic law. —*tr.v.* **scribed, scrib·ing.** To draw, mark, or write with or as if with a scriber: *scribe metal.* [Middle English, from Latin *scrība,* from *scrībere,* to write.]

scrib·er (skrī'bər) *n.* A sharply pointed tool used for marking lines on metal, ceramic, etc., preliminary to cutting.

scrim (skrĭm) *n.* A loosely woven cotton or linen fabric used for curtains and upholstery lining. [Orig. unknown.]

scrim·mage (skrĭm'ĭj) *n.* **1.** A rough-and-tumble struggle; a scuffle. **2.** *Football.* The action from the time the ball is snapped until it is out of play. **3.** A practice game. —*intr.v.* **-maged, -mag·ing.** To engage in a scrimmage. [From obs. *scrimish,* var. of SKIRMISH.]

scrimp (skrĭmp) *intr.v.* To economize severely: *scrimp and save for college.* —*tr.v.* To be excessively sparing with or of. [Perh. of Scandinavian orig.] —**scrimp'i·ly** *adv.* —**scrimp'i·ness** *n.* —**scrimp'y** *adj.*

scrim·shaw (skrĭm'shô') *n.* **1.** The art of carving on ivory, bone, or shells. **2.** An article made in this way. —*tr.v.* To decorate (whale ivory, bone, or shells) with scrimshaw. —*intr.v.* To make scrimshaw. [Orig. unknown.]

scrip¹ (skrĭp) *n.* **1.** A small scrap of paper. **2.** Paper money issued for temporary, emergency use. [Var. of SCRIPT.]

scrip² (skrĭp) *n.* A provisional certificate that entitles the holder to a fractional share of stock or of other jointly owned property. [Short for *subscription receipt.*]

script (skrĭpt) *n.* **1. a.** Letters or characters written by hand; handwriting. **b.** A style of writing with cursive characters. **2.** A particular style of writing. **3.** A printer's type that resembles handwriting. **4.** The text of a play, broadcast, or motion picture. [Middle English *skript,* from Old French *escript,* from Latin *scrīptum,* from *scrībere,* to write.]

scrip·to·ri·um (skrĭp-tôr'ē-əm, -tōr'-) *n., pl.* **-ums** or **-to·ri·a** (-tôr'ē-ə, -tōr'-). A room in a monastery set aside for copying or illuminating manuscripts. [Medieval Latin, from Latin *scrīptus,* past part. of *scrībere,* to write.]

scrip·tur·al (skrĭp'chər-əl) *adj.* **1.** Of or pertaining to writing; written. **2.** **Scriptural.** Of, relating to, based upon, or contained in the Scriptures. —**scrip'tur·al·ly** *adv.*

Scrip·ture (skrĭp'chər) *n.* **1.** Often **Scriptures. a.** A sacred writing, esp. the Old or New Testament. **b.** A passage from such a writing. **2.** **scripture.** A statement regarded as authoritative. [Middle English, from Late English *scrīptūra,* from Latin, act of writing, from *scrībere,* to write.]

script·writ·er (skrĭpt'rī'tər) *n.* A writer of scripts.

scriv·en·er (skrĭv'ə-nər) *n.* *Archaic.* A professional copyist; scribe. [Middle English *scriveiner,* from *scrivein,* scribe, from Old French *escrevein,* from Latin *scrība,* scribe.]

scrod (skrŏd) *n.* A young cod or haddock. [Obs. Dutch *schrood,* slice, shred, from Middle Dutch *schrode.*]

scrof·u·la (skrŏf'yə-lə) *n.* A rare disease characterized by predisposition to tuberculosis, lymphatism, glandular swellings, and respiratory catarrhs. [Middle English *scrophulas,* from Medieval Latin *scrōfulae,* swelling of the glands, "small sows," from Latin *scrōfa,* sow.] —**scrof'u·lous** *adj.*

scroll (skrōl) *n.* **1.** A roll of parchment, papyrus, etc., used esp. for writing a document. **2.** An ornamental object or design, as the curved head on a violin, that resembles a scroll. [Middle English *scrowle,* from Old French *escroue,* strip of parchment.]

scroll·work (skrōl'wûrk') *n.* Ornamental work, esp. in wood or metal, with a scroll or scroll-like pattern.

Scrooge (skrōōj) *n.* A mean-spirited, miserly person; skinflint. [After the miserly character Ebenezer Scrooge in Charles Dickens' *Christmas Carol.*]

scro·tum (skrō'təm) *n., pl.* **-ta** (-tə) or **-tums.** The external sac of skin enclosing the testes in most mammals. [Latin *scrōtum.*] —**scro'tal** (skrōt'l) *adj.*

scrounge (skrounj) *v.* **scrounged, scroung·ing.** *Slang.* —*tr.v.* **1.** To obtain by rummaging or foraging: *scrounge up empty bottles.* **2.** To wheedle; mooch: *scrounge a cigarette.* —*intr.v.* **1.** To forage about. **2.** To wheedle. [Var. of dial. *scrunge,* to steal.] —**scroung'er** *n.*

scrub¹ (skrŭb) *v.* **scrubbed, scrub·bing.** —*tr.v.* **1.** To rub hard, as with a brush, in order to clean. **2.** To remove by such rubbing. **3.** To rid (a gas) of impurities. **4.** *Slang.* To cancel. —*intr.v.* To clean or wash something by hard rubbing. —*n.* An act of scrubbing. [Middle English *scrobben,* from Middle Low German or Middle Dutch *schrobben.*] —**scrub'ber** *n.*

scrub² (skrŭb) *n.* **1.** A straggly, stunted tree or shrub. **2.** A growth or tract of stunted vegetation. **3.** An undersized, poorly developed plant or animal. **4.** A player not on the first team. —*modifier:* *a scrub oak; a scrub team.* [Middle English, var. of *schrubbe,* shrub.]

scrub·by (skrŭb'ē) *adj.* **-bi·er, -bi·est. 1.** Covered with or consisting of scrub or underbrush. **2.** Stunted. **3.** Shabby or inferior.

scrub·wom·an (skrŭb'wŏŏm'ən) *n.* A woman hired to clean; charwoman.

scruff (skrŭf) *n.* The back of the neck or the loose skin there; the nape. [Var. of obs. *scuff.*]

scruf·fy (skrŭf'ē) *adj.* **-fi·er, -fi·est.** Shabby; dirty. [From *scruff,* scurf, Middle English *scrofe,* from Old English *scruf.*]

scrump·tious (skrŭmp'shəs) *adj.* *Slang.* Delicious. —See Syns at **delicious.** [Perh. alteration of SUMPTUOUS.]

scrunch (skrŭnch, skrōōnch) *tr.v.* To crush or squeeze. —*intr.v.* **1.** To hunch. **2.** To make a crunching sound. —*n.* A crunching sound. [Var. of CRUNCH.]

scru·ple (skrōō'pəl) *n.* **1.** Hesitation, or a feeling that produces hesitation, based on ethical objection. **2.** *Abbr.* **sc.** or **scr.** A unit of apothecary weight equal to 20 grains. **3.** A minute part or amount. —See Syns at **qualm.** —*intr.v.* **-pled, -pling.** To hesitate as a result of conscience or principles. [Old French *scrupule,* from Latin *scrūpulus,* small weight, from *scrūpus,* rough stone.]

scru·pu·lous (skrōō'pyə-ləs) *adj.* **1.** Having scruples; principled. **2.** Conscientious; careful. —See Syns at **careful.** [Middle English, from Latin *scrūpulōsus,* from *scrūpulus,* scruple.] —**scru'pu·los·i·ty** (-lŏs'ĭ-tē) or **scru'pu·lous·ness** *n.* —**scru'pu·lous·ly** *adv.*

scru·ti·nize (skrōōt'n-īz') *tr.v.* **-nized, -niz·ing.** To examine with great care. —See Syns at **watch.** —**scru'ti·niz'er** *n.*

scru·ti·ny (skrōōt'n-ē) *n., pl.* **-nies. 1.** A close, careful examination. **2.** Close observation. [Latin *scrūtinium,* from *scrūtārī,* to examine, from *scrūta,* trash.]

scu·ba (skōō'bə) *n.* A tank or tanks of compressed air worn on the back and fitted with a regulator, hose, and mouthpiece, used by divers to breathe underwater. —*modifier:* *a scuba diver.* [S(ELF) C(ONTAINED) U(NDER-WATER) B(REATHING) A(PPARATUS).]

scud (skŭd) *intr.v.* **scud·ded, scud·ding.** To move along swiftly and easily: *A vigorous breeze sent the clouds scudding across the sky.* —*n.* **1.** The act of scudding. **2.** Wind-driven clouds, mist, or rain. [Orig. unknown.]

scuff (skŭf) *tr.v.* **1.** To scrape with the feet. **2.** To scrape and roughen the surface of. —*intr.v.* **1.** To scrape the feet while walking. **2.** To become roughened. —*n.* **1.** The act or result of scuffing. **2.** A flat, backless house slipper. —*modifier:* scuff marks. [Prob. of Scandinavian orig.]

scuf·fle (skŭf′əl) *intr.v.* **-fled, -fling.** **1.** To fight confusedly at close quarters. **2.** To shuffle. —*n.* An act of scuffling. [Prob. of Scandinavian orig.] —**scuf′fler** *n.*

scull (skŭl) *n.* **1.** An oar used for rowing a boat from the stern. **2.** One of a pair of short-handled oars used by a single rower. **3.** A small, light boat for racing. —*tr.v.* To propel with a scull or sculls. —*intr.v.* To use a scull or sculls to propel a boat. [Middle English *sculle.*]

scul·ler·y (skŭl′ə-rē) *n.,* *pl.* **-ies.** A room adjoining the kitchen for dishwashing and other chores. [Middle English, from Norman French *squillerie,* from Old French *escuelerie,* from *escuele,* dish, from Latin *scutella,* dim. of *scutra,* platter.]

scul·lion (skŭl′yən) *n.* A menial kitchen servant. [Middle English *sculyon,* prob. from Old French *escovillon,* dishcloth, dim. of *escouve,* broom, from Latin *scopa.*]

scul·pin (skŭl′pĭn) *n.,* *pl.* **-pins** or **sculpin.** Any of various fishes of the family Cottidae, with a large, flattened head, a broad mouth, and sharp spines. [Perh. var. of obs. *scorpene,* from Latin *scorpaena,* sea scorpion.]

sculpt (skŭlpt) *tr.v.* To sculpture. [French *sculpter,* from Latin *sculpere,* to carve.]

sculp·tor (skŭlp′tər) *n.* A person who sculptures.

sculp·tress (skŭlp′trĭs) *n.* A woman who sculptures.

sculp·ture (skŭlp′chər) *n.* **1.** The art or practice of shaping three-dimensional figures or designs, as by carving wood, chiseling stone, modeling clay, or casting metal. **2. a.** A work of art created in this manner. **b.** Such works in general. —*tr.v.* **-tured, -tur·ing.** **1.** To shape (stone, metal, wood, etc.) into sculpture. **2.** To represent in sculpture. **3.** To ornament with sculpture. **4.** To shape elaborately. [Middle English, from Latin *sculptūra,* from *sculpere,* to carve.] —**sculp′tur·al** *adj.* —**sculp′tur·al·ly** *adv.*

scum (skŭm) *n.* **1.** A filmy, often slimy material on the surface of a liquid. **2.** A similar mass of waste material that rises to the surface of a molten metal. **3.** Refuse. **4.** A person or class of people regarded as vile or worthless. —*v.* **scummed, scum·ming.** —*tr.v.* To remove the scum from. —*intr.v.* To become covered with scum. [Middle English *scume,* from Middle Dutch *schūm.*]

scup (skŭp) *n.,* *pl.* **scup** or **scups.** A food fish, *Stenotomus chrysops,* of western Atlantic waters, related to and resembling the porgies. [From Narraganset *mishcúp.*]

scup·per (skŭp′ər) *n.* An opening in the side of a ship at deck level. [Middle English *skopper.*]

scup·per·nong (skŭp′ər-nông′, -nŏng′) *n.* **1.** A grape, the muscadine. **2.** A wine made from these grapes. [Short for *Scuppernong* grape, after the *Scuppernong* River basin, North Carolina, where it is grown.]

scurf (skûrf) *n.* **1.** Flakes of dry skin, as dandruff. **2.** Any scaly crust. [Middle English, from Old English.] —**scurf′i·ness** *n.* —**scurf′y** *adj.*

scur·ri·lous (skûr′ə-ləs) *adj.* Using coarse or spiteful language; abusive: *a scurrilous attack.* [From Latin *scurrīlis,* buffoonlike, jeering, from *scurra,* buffoon.] —**scur′ri·lous·ly** *adv.* —**scur·ril′i·ty** (skə-rĭl′ĭ-tē) or **scur′ri·lous·ness** *n.*

scur·ry (skûr′ē) *intr.v.* **-ried, -ry·ing.** **1.** To move with or as if with light, rapid steps; to scamper. **2.** To race along hurriedly; to rush. —See Syns at **rush.** —*n.,* *pl.* **-ries.** An act or noise of scurrying. [Prob. short for *hurry-scurry,* from *hurry.*]

scur·vy (skûr′vē) *n.* A disease caused by a deficiency of vitamin C, characterized by soft, bleeding gums and bleeding under the skin. —*adj.* **-vi·er, -vi·est.** Contemptible. [From SCURF.]

scut (skŭt) *n.* A stubby erect tail, as that of a rabbit or deer. [Middle English, hare.]

scu·tate (skyōō′tāt′) *adj.* **1.** *Zool.* Covered with bony plates or scales. **2.** *Bot.* Shaped like a shield. [From Latin *scūtātus,* equipped with a shield, from *scutum,* shield.]

scutch (skŭch) *tr.v.* To separate the valuable fibers of (flax, hemp, etc.) from the woody parts by beating. —*n.* A tool or machine for scutching. [Obs. French *escoucher,* from Old French *escousser,* ult. from Latin *excutere,* to shake out.] —**scutch′er** *n.*

scutch·eon (skŭch′ən) *n.* Var. of **escutcheon.**

scu·tel·lum (skyōō-tĕl′əm) *n.,* *pl.* **-tel·la** (-tĕl′ə). **1.** *Zool.* A

bony plate or scale. **2.** *Bot.* A shield-shaped structure. [Dim. of Latin *scūtum,* shield.]

scut·tle¹ (skŭt′l) *n.* **1.** A small opening in a ship's deck or bulkhead. **2.** The movable cover for such an opening. —*tr.v.* **-tled, -tling.** **1.** To sink (a ship) by boring holes in the bottom. **2.** *Informal.* To discard; abandon. [Middle English *skottell,* from Old French *escoutille,* from Spanish *escotilla,* dim. of *escote,* opening in a garment.]

scut·tle² (skŭt′l) *n.* A metal pail used for carrying coal. [Middle English *scutel,* from Old English, from Latin *scutella,* salver.]

scut·tle³ (skŭt′l) *intr.v.* **-tled, -tling.** To run hastily; scurry. —*n.* A hurried run. [Freq. of SCUD.]

scut·tle·butt (skŭt′l-bŭt′) *n.* **1.** *Archaic.* A cask on a ship used to hold drinking water. **2.** *Slang.* Gossip; rumor. [SCUTTLE (hatch) + BUTT (cask).]

scu·tum (skyōō′təm) *n.,* *pl.* **-ta** (-tə). *Zool.* A bony or horny scale or plate. [Latin *scūtum,* shield.]

Scyl·la (sĭl′ə) *n.* *Gk. Myth.* A sea monster who devoured sailors if they approached too close to it in their attempt to avoid the equally dangerous whirlpool Charybdis. —*idiom.* **between Scylla and Charybdis.** In a spot where avoiding one danger exposes a person to another.

scythe (sīth) *n.* A tool with a long, curved blade and a long, bent handle, used for mowing or reaping. —*tr.v.* **scythed, scyth·ing.** To cut with a scythe. [Middle English *sithe,* from Old English *sīthe.*]

scythe   sea anemone

Se The symbol for the element selenium.

sea (sē) *n.* **1. a.** Often **seas.** The continuous body of salt water that covers most of the surface of the earth. **b.** A region of water within an ocean and partly enclosed by land. **c.** A large lake containing either fresh or salt water, as the Caspian Sea. **2.** Often **seas.** The ocean's surface: *a high sea; choppy seas.* **3.** A mare of the moon. **4.** A vast expanse or extent: *a sea of advancing troops.* —*modifier:* *sea water; sea birds.* —*idioms.* **at sea. 1.** On the open waters of the ocean. **2.** At a loss; perplexed. **go to sea.** To become a sailor. **put to sea.** To leave port. [Middle English *see,* from Old English *sǣ.*]

sea anchor. A drag that floats behind a vessel to prevent drifting or to maintain a heading into the wind. Also called **drag anchor,** and **drogue.**

sea anemone. Any of numerous flowerlike saltwater coelenterates of the class Anthozoa, with a flexible, cylindrical body that remains fastened to a surface and a mouth opening surrounded by many petallike tentacles.

sea bass (băs). Any of various saltwater fishes of the genus *Centropristes* and related genera, esp. *C. striatus,* of coastal Atlantic waters of the United States.

Sea·bee (sē′bē′) *n.* A member of one of the U.S. Navy's construction battalions. [Var. of *cee bee,* from the initials of Construction Battalion.]

sea biscuit. Hardtack.

sea·board (sē′bôrd′, -bōrd′) *n.* Land that borders on or is near the sea; seacoast. [SEA + obs. *board,* border.]

sea·borne (sē′bôrn′, -bōrn′) *adj.* **1.** Transported by ship. **2.** Carried on or over the sea: *a seaborne attack.*

sea bream. Any of various saltwater food fishes of the family Sparidae, esp. *Archosargus rhomboidalis,* of western Atlantic coastal waters.

sea cow. 1. A manatee or dugong. **2.** A walrus.

sea cucumber. Any of various cucumber-shaped echinoderms of the class Holothuroidea that have a flexible body with tentacles surrounding the mouth.

sea·far·er (sē'fâr'ər) *n.* A sailor or mariner.

sea·food (sē'fŏŏd') *n.* Also **sea food.** Edible fish or shellfish from the sea. —*modifier: a seafood dinner.*

sea·girt (sē'gûrt') *adj.* Surrounded by the sea.

sea·go·ing (sē'gō'ĭng) *adj.* **1.** Made or used for ocean voyages: *a seagoing barge.* **2.** Seafaring.

sea gull. A gull, esp. one appearing near coastal areas.

sea horse. 1. Any of several small saltwater fish of the genus *Hippocampus* that have a prehensile tail and a horselike head. **2.** A walrus. **3.** A mythical animal, half fish and half horse.

sea horse   sea lion

seal¹ (sēl) *n.* **1. a.** A device, such as a die or ring with a raised or engraved design, used to stamp an impression upon a soft substance such as wax or lead. **b.** The impression made, esp. such an impression used as an official mark of identification or authority. **c.** A small disk or wafer of wax, lead, or paper bearing such a mark or impression, used to fasten shut or authenticate a document. **2.** Something that serves to authenticate or confirm. **3.** An adhesive agent such as wax used to close or fasten something or to prevent seepage of moisture or air. **4.** An airtight or watertight closure or fitting. **5.** A small decorative paper sticker. —*tr.v.* **1.** To affix a seal to as a mark of genuineness, authority, or legal status: *sign and seal a contract.* **2.** To close with or as if with a seal. **3.** To close so that a liquid or gas cannot enter or escape. **4.** To close tightly so that reopening is difficult or impossible: *seal a tunnel.* **5.** To fix irrevocably: *His fate was sealed.* [Middle English *seel,* from Old French, from Latin *sigillum,* dim. of *signum,* sign.] —**seal'a·ble** *adj.* —**seal'er** *n.*

seal² (sēl) *n.* **1.** Any of various aquatic, carnivorous mammals of the families Phocidae and Otariidae, that have a sleek, streamlined body and paddlelike flippers. **2.** The fur of a seal. **3.** Leather made from the hide of a seal. —*modifier: a seal coat.* —*intr.v.* To hunt seals. [Middle English *seel,* from Old English *seolh.*] —**seal'er** *n.*

sea lavender. Any of several salt-marsh plants of the genus *Limonium,* with clusters of small lavender or pinkish flowers.

sea legs. *Informal.* The ability to walk on board ship with steadiness, esp. in rough seas.

sea level. The level of the ocean's surface, esp., the mean level halfway between high and low tide.

sea lily. Any of various saltwater crinoids with a flowerlike body supported by a long stalk.

sealing wax. A preparation of shellac and turpentine used to seal letters, batteries, jars, etc.

sea lion. Any of several seals of the family Otariidae, mostly of Pacific waters, with small external ears, a sleek body, and brownish hair.

seal·skin (sēl'skĭn') *n.* **1.** The pelt of a fur seal. **2.** A garment made of this skin. —*modifier: a sealskin coat.*

seam (sēm) *n.* **1.** A line, ridge, or groove formed by joining two pieces of material together at their edges, as by sewing or welding. **2.** Any line across any surface. **3.** A thin layer or stratum, as of coal or rock. —*tr.v.* **1.** To join with or as if with a seam. **2.** To mark with a wrinkle or other line: *a face seamed with laugh lines.* [Middle English *seem,* from Old English *sēam.*]

sea·man (sē'mən) *n.* **1.** A mariner or sailor. **2.** An enlisted man of the lowest rank in the U.S. Navy.

sea·man·ship (sē'mən-shĭp') *n.* Skill in handling or navigating a boat or ship.

sea·mark (sē'märk') *n.* A landmark visible from the sea.

seam·stress (sēm'strĭs) *n.* A woman who sews, esp. one who makes her living by sewing.

seam·y (sē'mē) *adj.* **-i·er, -i·est. 1.** Having or showing seams. **2.** Nasty; sordid. —**seam'i·ness** *n.*

sé·ance (sā'äns') *n.* A meeting at which persons attempt to communicate with the dead. [French, "a sitting."]

sea otter. A large, nearly extinct saltwater otter, *Enhydra lutris,* of northern Pacific waters.

sea·plane (sē'plān') *n.* An aircraft equipped with floats for taking off from or landing on water.

sea·port (sē'pôrt', -pōrt') *n.* A harbor or town with facilities for seagoing ships.

sea power. 1. A nation having significant naval strength. **2.** Naval strength.

sear (sîr) *tr.v.* **1.** To make withered; shrivel. **2.** To scorch or burn the surface of. —*adj.* Also **sere.** Withered. —*n.* Also **sere.** A mark caused by searing. [Middle English *seren,* from Old English *sēarian,* from *sēar,* withered.]

search (sûrch) *tr.v.* **1.** To look over carefully in order to find something desired, lost, or hidden: *search the attic; searching suspects for concealed weapons.* **2.** To examine carefully; probe: *search one's conscience.* **3.** To come to know; learn: *search out an enemy's weaknesses.* —*intr.v.* To conduct a thorough investigation; seek. —*n.* The act of searching. [Middle English *serchen,* from Norman French *sercher,* from Late Latin *circāre,* to go around, from Latin *circus,* circle.] —**search'er** *n.*

search·ing (sûr'chĭng) *adj.* **1.** Examining closely or thoroughly: *a searching investigation of stock-market dealings.* **2.** Keen; observant: *searching insights.*

search·light (sûrch'līt') *n.* **1.** A powerful light equipped with a reflector to produce a bright beam. **2.** The beam produced by such a light. **3.** A flashlight.

search warrant. A warrant giving legal authorization to search a specified place, as for unlawful property.

sea robin. Any of various saltwater fishes of the family Triglidae, with a bony head and extremely long pectoral fins with fingerlike feelers.

sea·scape (sē'skāp') *n.* A view of the sea.

sea serpent. A large snakelike marine animal of legend.

sea·shell (sē'shĕl') *n.* The shell of a saltwater mollusk.

sea·shore (sē'shôr', -shōr') *n.* Land by the sea.

sea·sick·ness (sē'sĭk'nĭs) *n.* Nausea and other discomforts resulting from the pitching and rolling motions of a vessel at sea. —**sea'sick'** *adj.*

sea·side (sē'sīd') *n.* The seashore.

sea snake. Any of several venomous tropical saltwater snakes of the family Hydrophidae.

sea·son¹ (sē'zən) *n.* **1. a.** One of the four equal natural divisions of the year, spring, summer, autumn, and winter. **b.** The two divisions of the year, rainy and dry, in tropical climates. **2.** A period of the year devoted to or marked by certain activities or events: *the hunting season; the hurricane season.* **3.** An appropriate, natural, or convenient time. —*idiom.* **in season. 1.** Available or ready for eating or other use. **2.** Legally available to the hunter, fisherman, or trapper. **3.** At the right or proper moment. [Middle English *sesoun,* from Old French *seson,* from Latin *satio,* act of sowing, from *serere,* to sow.]

sea·son² (sē'zən) *tr.v.* **1.** To enhance the flavor of (food) by adding salt, spices, etc. **2.** To add enjoyment or interest to: *seasoned his lecture with anecdotes.* **3.** To dry (lumber) until usable; cure. **4.** To make fit through experience: *hard training to season recruits.* —*intr.v.* To become seasoned. [Middle English *sesounen,* from Old French *saissoner,* to ripen, from *saison,* season of the year.]

sea·son·a·ble (sē'zə-nə-bəl) *adj.* **1.** Suitable for the time or the season: *seasonable weather.* **2.** Occurring at the proper time; timely: *seasonable work.* —**sea'son·a·bly** *adv.*

sea·son·al (sē'zə-nəl) *adj.* Of or dependent upon a particular season: *seasonal employment.* —**sea'son·al·ly** *adv.*

sea·son·ing (sē'zə-nĭng) *n.* Any ingredient that adds to or brings out the flavor of food.

ă pat   ā pay   â care   ä father   ĕ pet   ē be   hw which   ĭ pit   ī tie   î pier   ŏ pot   ō toe   ô paw, for   oi noise
ōō took   ōō boot   ou out   th thin   th this   ŭ cut   û urge   zh vision   ə about, item, edible, gallop, circus

sea squirt. Any of various sedentary saltwater animals of the class Ascidiacea, with a transparent, sac-shaped body with two siphons.

seat (sēt) *n.* **1.** Something that may be sat upon, as a chair or bench. **2.** A place in which one may sit. **3.** A part on which a person rests in sitting: *a bicycle seat.* **4. a.** The buttocks. **b.** That part of a garment covering the buttocks. **5.** A part serving as a base or support. **6. a.** The place where anything is located or based: *the seat of intelligence.* **b.** A center of authority; capital: *the county seat.* **7.** A place of residence. **8.** Membership in a legislature, stock exchange, or other organization. **9.** The manner of sitting on a horse. —*tr.v.* **1. a.** To place in or on a seat. **b.** To cause or assist to sit down: *seat an elderly woman.* **2.** To have or provide seats for: *We can seat 300 in the auditorium.* **3.** To fix firmly in place: *seat a pipe fitting.* [Middle English *sete*, from Old Norse *sæti.*]

seat belt. A safety strap or harness designed to hold a person securely in a seat, as in a car or aircraft.

seat·ing (sē'tĭng) *n.* **1.** The arrangement of seats in a room, auditorium, etc. **2.** Material for upholstering seats.

sea trout. **1.** Any of several saltwater fishes of the genus *Cynoscion,* esp. the weakfish. **2.** Any of several trouts or similar fishes that live in the sea but spawn in fresh water.

sea urchin. Any of various echinoderms of the class Echinoidea, with a soft body enclosed in a round, symmetrical, limy shell covered with long spines.

sea urchin

sea wall. An embankment to prevent erosion of a shore.

sea·ward (sē'wərd) *adv.* Also **sea·wards** (-wərdz). Toward the sea. —**sea'ward** *adj.*

sea·way (sē'wā') *n.* **1.** A sea route. **2.** An inland waterway for ocean shipping. **3.** A ship's headway. **4.** A rough sea.

sea·weed (sē'wēd') *n.* Any of numerous saltwater algae or plants, such as a kelp, rockweed, or gulfweed.

sea·wor·thy (sē'wûr'thē) *adj.* **-thi·er, -thi·est.** Fit or safe for putting to sea. —**sea'wor'thi·ness** *n.*

se·ba·ceous (sĭ-bā'shəs) *adj.* Of, secreting, or resembling fat or oil. [Latin *sēbāceus,* from *sēbum,* tallow.]

sebaceous gland. Any of the tiny glands in the skin that secrete an oily material into the hair follicles.

se·bum (sē'bəm) *n.* The semifluid secretion of the sebaceous glands. [Latin *sēbum,* tallow.]

se·cant (sē'kănt', -kənt) *n. Abbr.* **sec** **1.** *Geom.* **a.** A straight line intersecting a curve at two or more points. **b.** The straight line drawn from the center through one end of a circular arc and intersecting the tangent to the other end of the arc. **2.** *Trig.* **a.** The reciprocal of the cosine of an angle. **b.** For an acute angle, the ratio of the hypotenuse to the side of a right triangle adjacent to the acute angle. [French *(ligne) secante,* "cutting line," from Latin *secāns,* pres. part. of *secāre,* to cut.]

se·cede (sĭ-sēd') *intr.v.* **-ced·ed, -ced·ing.** To withdraw formally from membership in an association or union. [Latin *sēcēdere : sē,* apart + *cēdere,* to go.]

se·ces·sion (sĭ-sĕsh'ən) *n.* The act of seceding. [Latin *sēcessiō,* from *sēcēdere,* to secede.]

se·ces·sion·ist (sĭ-sĕsh'ə-nĭst) *n.* Someone who secedes or believes in secession. —**se·ces'sion·ism** *n.*

se·clude (sĭ-klōōd') *tr.v.* **-clud·ed, -clud·ing.** **1.** To set apart from others; isolate. **2.** To screen from view. [Middle English *secluden,* to shut off, from Latin *sēclūdere : sē,* apart +

claudere, to shut.] —**se·clud'ed·ness** *n.*

se·clu·sion (sĭ-klōō'zhən) *n.* The act of secluding or the condition of being secluded. [Medieval Latin *sēclūsiō,* from Latin *sēclūsus,* past part. of *sēclūdere,* to seclude.]

se·clu·sive (sĭ-klōō'sĭv, -zĭv) *adj.* Fond of seclusion.

sec·ond¹ (sĕk'ənd) *n.* **1.** A unit of time equal to ¹/₆₀ of a minute. **2.** A short period of time. **3.** *Abbr.* **s** or **sec** *Symbol* **'** *Geom.* A unit of angular measure equal to ¹/₆₀ of a minute of arc. —See Syns at **moment.** [Middle English *seconde,* unit in geometry, from Old French, from Medieval Latin *(pars minūta) secunda,* "second (small part)."]

sec·ond² (sĕk'ənd) *adj.* **1.** Corresponding in order to the number two: *the second floor.* **2.** Another: *seeking a second chance.* **3.** Inferior: *cuisine second to none.* **4. a.** Having a lower pitch or range: *the second sopranos of a choir.* **b.** Singing or playing the less important part of a similar pair of parts: *the second violins of an orchestra.* **5.** Producing the next-to-lowest speed in an automobile: *second gear.* —*n.* **1.** In a set of items arranged to match the natural numbers in a one-to-one correspondence, the item that corresponds to the number two. **2.** An imperfect or defective article of merchandise. **3.** An attendant of a contestant in a duel or boxing match. **4. a.** The interval between two adjacent tones of a diatonic musical scale. **b.** A tone separated from another tone by this interval. **5.** The second gear in an automobile transmission. —*tr.v.* **1.** To promote or encourage; give support to. **2.** To endorse (a motion or nomination) as a means of bringing it to a vote. —*adv.* **1.** In the second order, place, or rank: *finished second in the race.* **2.** But for one other; save one: *the second-highest mountain.* [Middle English, from Old French, from Latin *secundus,* following, coming next.]

sec·on·dar·y (sĕk'ən-dĕr'ē) *adj.* **1.** Of the second rank; not primary; lesser: *a secondary cause.* **2.** Derived from what is primary or original: *a secondary source.* **3.** Of or relating to education between the elementary school and college. **4.** *Elect.* Having a current or voltage induced by the magnetic field caused by a current flowing in another coil: *the secondary coil of a transformer.* —*n., pl.* **-ies.** **1.** Someone or something that acts in a subordinate or inferior capacity. **2.** *Elect.* A coil or circuit having an induced current. **3.** *Football.* The defensive backs or the area in which they are stationed. —**sec'on·dar'i·ly** (-dâr'ə-lē) *adv.*

secondary accent. **1.** An accent or stress that is weaker than the primary one; for example, in the word ca'pa·bil'i·ty the secondary accent is on the syllable ca-. **2.** The mark (') used to indicate this accent.

secondary sex characteristic. Any of the genetically transmitted physical or behavioral characteristics, as growth of facial hair or breast development, that serve to distinguish males and females of the same species and do not have a direct relation to reproduction.

second base. *Baseball.* **1.** The base across the diamond from home plate, to be touched second by a runner. **2.** The position played by a second baseman.

second baseman. *Baseball.* The infielder who positions himself near and usu. to the first-base side of second base.

sec·ond-class (sĕk'ənd-klăs') *adj.* **1.** Of the class below the first or best. **2.** Inferior. **3.** Of or pertaining to a class of mail consisting mainly of newspapers and periodicals.

Second Coming. The return of Christ as judge upon the last day.

sec·ond-de·gree burn (sĕk'ənd-dĭ-grē'). A burn that blisters the skin.

second fiddle. A secondary or subordinate role.

second growth. Trees that cover an area after the removal of the original growth, as by cutting or fire.

sec·ond-guess (sĕk'ənd-gĕs') *tr.v.* **1.** To criticize (a decision or decision-maker) after the outcome is known. **2.** To anticipate the moves of; outguess. —*intr.v.* To criticize a decision after its outcome is known. —**sec'ond-guess'er** *n.*

second hand. The hand of a timepiece that marks the seconds.

sec·ond·hand or **sec·ond-hand** (sĕk'ənd-hănd') *adj.* **1.** Previously used by another; not new. **2.** Dealing in previously used merchandise. **3.** Not original; borrowed: *secondhand data.* —*adv.* Indirectly.

second lieutenant. An officer in the U.S. Army and Marine Corps of the lowest commissioned grade.

sec·ond·ly (sĕk′ənd-lē) *adv.* In the second place; second.

second nature. Deeply ingrained habit.

second person. *Gram.* The form of a pronoun or verb used in referring to the person addressed; for example, *you* and *shall* in *you shall not enter.*

sec·ond-rate (sĕk′ənd-rāt′) *adj.* Inferior in quality.

second sight. Clairvoyance.

se·cre·cy (sē′krĭ-sē) *n.* **1.** The condition or quality of being secret. **2.** The ability to keep secrets.

se·cret (sē′krĭt) *adj.* **1.** Concealed from general knowledge or view; kept hidden: *a secret plan.* **2.** Operating in a hidden or confidential manner: *a secret agent.* **3.** Not frequented; secluded. —*n.* **1.** Something kept hidden from others or known only to oneself or to a few. **2.** Something beyond understanding; mystery. **3.** Secrecy: *conferred in secret.* [Middle English, from Old French, from Latin *sēcrētus,* from *sēcernere,* to separate.] —**se′cret·ly** *adv.*

Syns: secret, clandestine, covert, hush-hush *(Informal),* undercover *adj. Core meaning:* Purposely concealed from view or knowledge (*secret intelligence operations*).

sec·re·tar·i·at (sĕk′rĭ-târ′ē-ĭt) *n.* **1.** The department administered by a governmental secretary, esp. for an international organization. **2.** The office or position of a governmental secretary. [French *secrétariat,* from Medieval Latin *sēcrētāriātus,* from *sēcrētārius,* secretary.]

sec·re·tar·y (sĕk′rĭ-tĕr′ē) *n., pl.* **-ies. 1.** A person employed to handle correspondence, keep files, and do clerical work. **2.** An officer of an organization in charge of minutes of meetings, important records, correspondence, etc. **3.** An official presiding over an administrative department of government: *the Secretary of State.* **4.** A desk with a small bookcase on top. [Middle English *secretarie,* from Medieval Latin *sēcrētārius,* confidential officer, from Latin *sēcrētus,* secret.] —**sec′re·tar′i·al** (-târ′ē-əl) *adj.*

secretary bird. A large African bird of prey, *Sagittarius serpentarius,* with long legs and a crest of quills.

secretary bird
George Miksch Sutton

sedan

sec·re·tar·y-gen·er·al (sĕk′rĭ-tĕr′ē-jĕn′ər-əl) *n., pl.* **sec·re·tar·ies-gen·er·al.** A high-ranking executive officer, as in the United Nations.

se·crete[1] (sĭ-krēt′) *tr.v.* **-cret·ed, -cret·ing.** To generate and separate out (a substance) from cells or bodily fluids. [Back-formation from SECRETION.] —**se·cre′tor** *n.*

se·crete[2] (sĭ-krēt′) *tr.v.* **-cret·ed, -cret·ing.** To conceal in a hiding place; hide. —See Syns at **hide.** [From SECRET.]

se·cre·tion (sĭ-krē′shən) *n.* **1.** The act or process of secreting a substance, esp. one that is not a waste, from blood or cells. **2.** The substance so secreted.

se·cre·tive. *adj.* **1.** (sē′krĭ-tĭv). Practicing or inclined to secrecy; close-mouthed. **2.** (sĭ-krē′tĭv). Secretory.

se·cre·to·ry (sĭ-krē′tə-rē) *adj.* Pertaining to or performing the function of secretion.

secret service. 1. The gathering of secret information by a government. **2. Secret Service.** A branch of the U.S. Treasury Department concerned with the suppression of counterfeiters and the protection of the President.

sect (sĕkt) *n.* **1.** A group of people that forms a distinct unit within a larger group by virtue of common beliefs or practices. **2.** A religious body, esp. one which has separated from a larger denomination. [Middle English *secte,* from Old French, from Latin *secta,* following, from *sequī,* to follow.]

-sect. A suffix meaning cut or divide: **bisect.** [From Latin *sectus,* past part. of *secāre,* to cut.]

sec·tar·i·an (sĕk-târ′ē-ən) *adj.* **1.** Of a sect or sects. **2.** Narrow in outlook; partisan or parochial. —*n.* A member of a sect. —**sec·tar′i·an·ism** *n.*

sec·tion (sĕk′shən) *n.* **1.** A part of something; piece; portion. **2. a.** A subdivision of a book or chapter. **b.** A distinct portion of a newspaper. **3.** A distinct area of a town, county, or country: *a residential section.* **4.** *Surveying.* A land unit of 640 acres or 1 sq. mi., equal to $1/_{36}$ of a township. **5.** The act or process of separating or cutting, esp. the surgical separation of tissue. **6.** A thin slice, as of tissue, suitable for microscopic examination. **7.** A segment of a fruit. **8.** The representation of a solid object as it would appear if cut by an intersecting plane. **9.** *Geom.* The set of points formed by the intersection of a solid by a plane. **10.** A part of an orchestra or band playing one class of instruments: *a string section.* **11.** The character (§) used in printing to mark the beginning of a section. —*tr.v.* **1.** To divide into parts. **2.** To separate (tissue) surgically. —See Syns at **separate.** [French, from Latin *sectiō,* a cutting, from *secāre,* to cut.]

sec·tion·al (sĕk′shə-nəl) *adj.* **1.** Of a section. **2.** Of or representing a particular region or district: *a sectional point of view.* **3.** Composed of or divided into component sections: *sectional furniture.* —**sec′tion·al·ly** *adv.*

sec·tion·al·ism (sĕk′shə-nə-lĭz′əm) *n.* Excessive devotion to local interests and customs. —**sec′tion·al·ist** *n.*

sec·tor (sĕk′tər, -tôr′) *n.* **1.** *Geom.* The part of a circle bound by two radii and one of the arcs that they intercept. **2.** A military area or zone of action. **3.** A division of something: *the manufacturing sector of the economy.* · [Late Latin, from Latin, cutter, from *secāre,* to cut.]

sec·u·lar (sĕk′yə-lər) *adj.* **1.** Worldly rather than spiritual. **2.** Not related to religion: *secular music.* **3.** Not living in a religious community: *the secular clergy.* **4.** Occurring or observed once in an age or century. **5.** Long-continuing; age-old. —*n.* A secular clergyman. [Middle English *secular,* from Old French, from Latin *saeculāris,* from *saeculum,* generation, age.] —**sec′u·lar′i·ty** (-lăr′ĭ-tē) *n.*

sec·u·lar·ism (sĕk′yə-lə-rĭz′əm) *n.* Rejection of or indifference to religious considerations or control, as in civil affairs. —**sec′u·lar·ist** *n.* —**sec′u·lar·is′tic** *adj.*

sec·u·lar·ize (sĕk′yə-lə-rīz′) *tr.v.* **-ized, -iz·ing. 1.** To convert from ecclesiastical or religious to civil or lay use, ownership, or control. **2.** To make secular. —**sec′u·lar·i·za′tion** *n.*

se·cure (sĭ-kyŏŏr′) *adj.* **-cur·er, -cur·est. 1.** Free from danger or risk of loss; safe. **2.** Free from fear, anxiety, or doubt; confident. **3.** Not likely to fail or give way; stable: *a secure foothold.* **4.** Assured; certain. —*tr.v.* **-cured, -cur·ing. 1.** To guard from danger or risk of loss: *secured the country against enemies.* **2.** To make firm or tight; to fasten. **3.** To make certain; ensure. **4.** To guarantee with a pledge: *needed collateral to secure a loan.* **5.** To get possession of; acquire: *secure reservations.* **6.** To bring about. —See Syns at **attach, defend,** and **tie.** [Latin *sēcūrus* : *sē,* without + *cūra,* care.] —**se·cure′ly** *adv.* —**se·cure′ment** *n.* —**se·cure′ness** *n.* —**se·cur′er** *n.*

se·cu·ri·ty (sĭ-kyŏŏr′ĭ-tē) *n., pl.* **-ties. 1.** Freedom from danger; safety. **2.** Freedom from doubt or fear; confidence. **3.** Anything that gives or assures safety. **4.** Something deposited or given to guarantee fulfillment of an obligation. **5.** A person who guarantees or assumes the financial obligations of another; surety. **6. securities.** Stocks or bonds. **7.** Measures adopted to guard against attack, theft, or disclosure. —See Syns at **confidence** and **safety.** —*modifier: security guards.*

se·dan (sĭ-dăn′) *n.* **1.** A closed automobile with two or four doors and a front and rear seat. **2.** Also **sedan chair.** An enclosed chair for one person, carried on poles by two men. [Orig. unknown.]

se·date[1] (sĭ-dāt′) *adj.* **-dat·er, -dat·est.** Calm and dignified; composed. [Latin *sēdātus,* past part. of *sēdāre,* to settle, compose.] —**se·date′ly** *adv.* —**se·date′ness** *n.*

se·date[2] (sĭ-dāt′) *tr.v.* **-dat·ed, -dat·ing.** To administer a sedative to (a patient). [Back-formation from SEDATIVE.]

se·da·tion (sĭ-dā′shən) *n.* **1.** The administration of a sedative. **2.** The condition brought on by a sedative.

sed·a·tive (sĕd′ə-tĭv) *adj.* Having a soothing, calming, or quieting effect. —*n.* A sedative medicine or drug.

sed·en·tar·y (sĕd′n-tĕr′ē) *adj.* **1.** Marked by, requiring, or accustomed to much sitting: *sedentary work.* **2.** *Zool.* Attached to a surface and not free-moving. [French *sédentaire,* from Latin *sedentārius,* from *sedēns,* pres. part. of *sedēre,* to sit.] —**sed′en·tar′i·ness** *n.*

Se·der (sā′dər) *n.* The Jewish feast commemorating the exodus of the Israelites from Egypt, usu. celebrated on the first evening of Passover. [Hebrew *sēdher,* order, arrangement.]

sedge (sĕj) *n.* Any of numerous plants of the family Cyperaceae, that resemble grasses but have solid stems. [Middle English *segge,* from Old English *secg.*]

sed·i·ment (sĕd′ə-mənt) *n.* **1.** Finely divided solid matter that is suspended in or falls to the bottom of a liquid or gas. **2.** Material, as rocks, sand, etc., deposited by glaciers, water, or wind. [Old French, from Latin *sedimentum,* a settling, from *sedēre,* to sit, settle.]

sed·i·men·ta·ry (sĕd′ə-mĕn′tə-rē, -mĕn′trē) *adj.* **1.** Of, containing, resembling, or derived from sediment. **2.** *Geol.* Of rocks formed from sediment or from fragments of other rocks deposited in water.

sed·i·men·ta·tion (sĕd′ə-mən-tā′shən, -mĕn-) *n.* The act or process of depositing sediment.

se·di·tion (sĭ-dĭsh′ən) *n.* Conduct or language that incites others to rebel against the state. [Middle English *sedicioun,* from Old French *sedition,* from Latin *sēditiō,* separation : *sē, sēd,* apart + *itiō,* act of going, from *īre,* to go.]

se·di·tious (sĭ-dĭsh′əs) *adj.* Of or engaged in sedition. —**se·di′tious·ly** *adv.* —**se·di′tious·ness** *n.*

se·duce (sĭ-dōōs′, -dyōōs′) *tr.v.* **-duced, -duc·ing.** **1.** To lead (a person) away from duty or proper conduct; to corrupt. **2.** To induce to have sexual intercourse. **3.** To attract, esp. by enticement. [Middle English *seduisen,* from Old French *seduire,* from Latin *sēdūcere,* to mislead : *sē,* apart + *dūcere,* to lead.] —**se·duc′er** *n.*

se·duc·tion (sĭ-dŭk′shən) *n.* Also **se·duce·ment** (sĭ-dōōs′mənt, -dyōōs′-). **1.** The act of seducing or the condition of being seduced. **2.** Something that seduces; enticement.

se·duc·tive (sĭ-dŭk′tĭv) *adj.* Tending to seduce; tempting; alluring. —**se·duc′tive·ly** *adv.* —**se·duc′tive·ness** *n.*

se·duc·tress (sĭ-dŭk′trĭs) *n.* A woman who seduces.

sed·u·lous (sĕj′ə-ləs) *adj.* Diligent; industrious. [Latin *sēdulus.*] —**sed′u·lous·ly** *adv.* —**sed′u·lous·ness** *n.*

se·dum (sē′dəm) *n.* Any of numerous fleshy-leaved plants of the genus *Sedum.* [Latin, a kind of plant.]

see¹ (sē) *v.* **saw** (sô), **seen** (sēn), **see·ing.** —*tr.v.* **1.** To perceive with the eye. **2.** To have a mental image of; visualize: *saw the opportunities.* **3.** To understand; comprehend. **4.** To regard; judge: *see things differently.* **5.** To imagine; believe possible: *I don't see how we can fail.* **6.** To foresee. **7.** To undergo: *I've seen hard times.* **8.** To be characterized by or bring forth: *Our age has seen scientific miracles.* **9.** To find out; ascertain. **10.** To refer to; read: *See the footnote below.* **11.** To prefer to have: *He'd see us dead rather than help.* **12.** To meet regularly, as in dating or courting. **13. a.** To visit or consult. **b.** To receive or admit. **14.** To attend; view. **15.** To escort; attend: *see someone off.* **16.** To ensure: *Please see that it gets done.* **17.** *Card Games.* **a.** To meet (a bet). **b.** To meet the bet of (another player). —*intr.v.* **1.** To have the power of sight. **2.** To understand. **3.** To consider; think over: *Let's see, which should we eat later.* **4.** To wait and decide later. —*phrasal verbs.* **see about. 1.** To attend to. **2.** To investigate. **see through.** To understand the true character of. **see to.** To attend to. [Middle English *seen,* from Old English *sēon.*]

see² (sē) *n.* The position, authority, or jurisdiction of a bishop. [Middle English, from Norman French *se,* from Latin *sēdes,* seat, residence.]

seed (sēd) *n., pl.* **seeds** or **seed. 1.** A usu. small part of a flowering plant that contains an embryo that can grow into a new plant. **2.** Seeds considered together. **3.** Something that can develop or give rise to something else. **4.** Offspring or descendants. **5.** Sperm; semen. —*modifier: a seed bed.* —*tr.v.* **1.** To plant seeds in; sow. **2.** To plant in soil. **3.** To remove the seeds from. **4.** To sprinkle (a cloud) with particles, as of silver iodide, in order to disperse it or produce rain. **5. a.** To arrange (the drawing for positions in a tournament) so that the more skilled contestants meet in

the later rounds. **b.** To rank (a contestant) in this way. —*intr.v.* To sow seed. —*idiom.* **go** (or **run**) **to seed. 1.** To pass into the seed-bearing stage. **2.** To deteriorate. [Middle English, from Old English *sǣd.*]

seed·case (sēd′kās′) *n.* The part of a flowering plant that contains seeds, as a pod.

seed leaf. *Bot.* A cotyledon.

seed·ling (sēd′lĭng) *n.* A young plant that has sprouted from a seed.

seed oyster. A young oyster, esp. one for transplanting.

seed pearl. A very small, often imperfect pearl.

seed plant. A seed-bearing plant; a spermatophyte.

seed·y (sē′dē) *adj.* **-i·er, -i·est. 1.** Having many seeds. **2.** Shabby; run-down. —**seed′i·ly** *adv.* —**seed′i·ness** *n.*

see·ing (sē′ĭng) *conj.* Inasmuch as; considering that. —See Usage note at **being as.**

Seeing Eye. A trademark for a dog trained to lead a blind person.

seek (sēk) *v.* **sought** (sôt), **seek·ing.** —*tr.v.* **1.** To try to locate or discover; search for. **2.** To ask for; request. **3.** To try: *sought to escape.* —*intr.v.* To make a search or investigation. [Middle English *seken,* from Old English *sēcan.*] —**seek′er** *n.*

seem (sēm) *intr.v.* **1.** To give the impression of being; appear: *She seems worried.* **2.** To appear to one's own mind: *I can't seem to stay awake.* —See Syns at **appear.** [Middle English *semen,* to befit, seem, from Old Norse *sœma,* to conform to, honor, from *sœmr,* fitting.]

seem·ing (sē′mĭng) *adj.* Apparent: *his seeming friendliness.* —*n.* Outward appearance. —**seem′ing·ly** *adv.*

seem·ly (sēm′lē) *adj.* **-li·er, -li·est. 1.** Conforming to accepted standards of conduct and good taste; proper: *seemly behavior.* **2.** Of pleasing appearance; handsome. [Middle English *semely,* from Old Norse *sœmiligr,* from *sœmr,* fitting.] —**seem′li·ness** *n.*

seen (sēn) *v.* Past participle of **see** (to perceive with the eyes). [Middle English *seyen,* from Old English *gesewen.*]

seep (sēp) *intr.v.* **1.** To pass slowly through small openings or pores; to ooze: *Gas seeped through the cracked pipe.* **2.** To enter, depart, or spread gradually. [Perh. var. of dial. *sipe,* from Middle English *sipen,* from Old English *sipian.*]

seep·age (sē′pĭj) *n.* **1.** The act or process of seeping; leakage. **2.** The amount of something that has seeped in or out.

seer (sē′ər) *n.* A person supposedly able to visualize, and thus predict, the future; a clairvoyant. [Middle English, from *seen,* to see.]

seer·suck·er (sîr′sŭk′ər) *n.* A light, thin fabric, usu. of cotton or rayon, with a crinkled surface and striped pattern. —*modifier: a seersucker suit.* [Hindi *sirsakar,* from Persian *shīr-o-shakar,* "milk and sugar."]

see·saw (sē′sô′) *n.* **1.** A long plank balanced on a central support so that with a person riding on either end, one end goes up as the other goes down. Also called **teeter-totter. 2.** Any back-and-forth or up-and-down movement. —*intr.v.* **1.** To play on a seesaw. **2.** To fluctuate back and forth or up and down. [From *saw* (to cut).]

seethe (sēth) *intr.v.* **seethed, seeth·ing. 1.** To bubble or churn while or as if while boiling. **2.** To be violently excited or agitated: *seethed with anger.* [Middle English *sethen,* from Old English *sēothan.*]

seg·ment (sĕg′mənt) *n.* **1.** A part into which something is or can be divided; a section. **2.** One of the similar, clearly distinguishable subdivisions of a plant or animal body or structure. **3.** A section of a geometric figure or object that is set off by boundaries, esp.: **a.** A part of a line or curve that is included between any pair of its points. **b.** The region bounded by an arc of a circle and the chord that connects the endpoints of the arc. —*v.* (sĕg-mĕnt′). —*tr.v.* To divide into segments. —*intr.v.* To become divided into segments. —See Syns at **separate.** [Latin *segmentum,* from *secāre,* to cut.] —**seg·ment′al** *adj.*

seg·men·ta·tion (sĕg′mən-tā′shən) *n.* **1.** Division into segments. **2.** *Biol.* The process by which many cells are created from a single cell, as in an egg that has been fertilized.

se·go (sē′gō) *n., pl.* **-gos.** The edible bulb of the sego lily. [Of Ute orig.]

sego lily. A plant, *Calochortus nuttallii,* of western North America, with showy, variously colored flowers.

seg·re·gate (sĕg′rĭ-gāt′) v. **-gat·ed, -gat·ing.** —tr.v. To separate or isolate from others, esp. by race. —intr.v. **1.** To become separated from a main body or mass. **2.** To practice a policy of racial segregation. —adj. Separated; isolated. [From Latin *sēgregāre*, to separate from the flock : *sē*, apart + *grex, flock.*] —**seg′re·ga′tor** n.

seg·re·ga·tion (sĕg′rĭ-gā′shən) n. **1.** The act or process of segregating or the condition of being segregated. **2.** Separation or isolation from others that is imposed esp. by race through the use of discriminatory practices.

seg·re·ga·tion·ist (sĕg′rĭ-gā′shə-nĭst) n. A person who advocates or practices a policy of racial segregation.

seign·ior (sān-yôr′, sān′yôr′) n. A feudal lord. [Middle English *seignour*, from Old French *seigneur*, from Medieval Latin *senior*, from Latin, older, comp. of *senex*, old.]

seine (sān) n. A large fishing net held in a vertical position in the water by means of weights and floats. —v. **seined, sein·ing.** —intr.v. To fish with a seine. —tr.v. To fish for or catch with a seine. [Middle English, from Old English *segne*, from Latin *sagēna*, from Greek *sagēnē*.]

seis·mic (sīz′mĭk) adj. Of, subject to, or caused by an earthquake or earth vibration. [From Greek *seismos*, earthquake, from *seiein*, to shake.] —**seis′mi·cal·ly** adv. —**seis·mic′i·ty** (sīz-mĭs′ĭ-tē) n.

seis·mo·gram (sīz′mə-grăm′) n. The record of an earth tremor made by a seismograph. [Greek *seismos*, earthquake + -GRAM.]

seis·mo·graph (sīz′mə-grăf′) n. An instrument for automatically detecting and measuring earthquakes and other ground vibrations. [Greek *seismos*, earthquake + -GRAPH.] —**seis′mo·graph′ic** adj. —**seis·mog′ra·pher** (sīz-mŏg′rə-fər) n. —**seis·mog′ra·phy** n.

seis·mol·o·gy (sīz-mŏl′ə-jē) n. The geophysical science of earthquakes and of the mechanical properties of the earth. [Greek *seismos*, earthquake + -LOGY.] —**seis′mo·log′ic** (-mə-lŏj′ĭk) or **seis′mo·log′i·cal** adj. —**seis′mo·log′i·cal·ly** adv. —**seis·mol′o·gist** n.

seize (sēz) v. **seized, seiz·ing.** —tr.v. **1. a.** To take hold of suddenly and forcibly; grab. **b.** To take possession of, esp. by force. **2.** To grasp with the mind; comprehend. **3.** To affect suddenly and powerfully; overwhelm. **4.** To take prisoner; arrest. **5.** *Law.* To put in possession of. **6.** *Naut.* To bind with turns of small line. —intr.v. To fix suddenly: *seize on a plan.* —See Syns at **arrest.** [Middle English *seisen*, from Old French *seisir.*]

seiz·ing (sē′zĭng) n. *Naut.* **1.** A binding made with multiple turns of smaller line. **2.** The line used for such bindings.

sei·zure (sē′zhər) n. **1.** The act of seizing or being seized. **2.** A sudden and often acute attack.

se·lah (sē′lə) n. A Hebrew word of unknown meaning that often marks the end of a verse in the Psalms.

sel·dom (sĕl′dəm) adv. Not often; infrequently; rarely. — See Usage note at **rarely.** [Middle English, from Old English *seldan.*]

se·lect (sĭ-lĕkt′) tr.v. To chose from among several; pick out. —intr.v. To make a selection. —See Syns at **choose.** —adj. Also **se·lect·ed** (sĭ-lĕk′tĭd). **1.** Singled out; chosen. **2.** Of special quality; preferred. [Latin *sēlectus*, past part. of *sēligere*, to choose out : *sē*, apart + *legere*, to choose.] —**se·lect′ness** n. —**se·lec′tor** n.

se·lec·tee (sĭ-lĕk-tē′) n. A person who is selected.

se·lec·tion (sĭ-lĕk′shən) n. **1.** The act of selecting or the fact of being selected. **2.** Someone or something that has been selected. **3.** A collection of persons or things. —See Syns at **choice.**

se·lec·tive (sĭ-lĕk′tĭv) adj. **1.** Of or characterized by selection; tending to select. **2.** *Electronics.* Capable of rejecting frequencies other than that selected or tuned. —**se·lec′tive·ly** adv. —**se·lec′tive·ness** or **se·lec·tiv′i·ty** n.

selective service. A system for calling up individuals for compulsory military service.

se·lect·man (sĭ-lĕkt′mən) n. One of a governing board of town officials elected in many New England towns.

sel·e·nite (sĕl′ə-nīt′) n. Gypsum in the form of colorless clear crystals. [Latin *selēnītēs*, from Greek *selēnītēs (lithos)*, "moon (stone)," from *selēnē*, moon.]

se·le·ni·um (sĭ-lē′nē-əm) n. *Symbol* **Se** A nonmetallic element that resembles sulfur chemically, and is obtained pri-

marily as a by-product of electrolytic copper refining. It occurs in allotropic forms including a red powder form, a red crystalline form, a black vitreous form, and a stable, gray, metallike form. Atomic number 34; atomic weight 78.96; melting point (of gray selenium) 217°C; boiling point (gray) 684.9°C; specific gravity (gray) 4.79, (vitreous) 4.28; valence 2, 4, or 6. [From Greek *selēnē*, moon.]

self (sĕlf) n., pl. **selves** (sĕlvz). **1.** The essential qualities that distinguish one individual from another. **2.** The typical character or behavior of an individual. **3.** Private or personal advantage: *one of those concerned only for self.* —pron. Myself, yourself, himself, or herself. —adj. **1.** Of the same character throughout. **2.** Of the same material as the article with which it is used: *a self belt.* [Middle English, from Old English.]

self-. A prefix meaning oneself or itself: **self-control.** [Middle English, from Old English, from *self, self.*]

self-ab·ne·ga·tion (sĕlf′ăb-nĭ-gā′shən) n. The setting aside of self-interest for the sake of others or for a principle.

self-ab·sorbed (sĕlf′ab-sôrbd′, -zôrbd′) adj. Absorbed in oneself or one's concerns. —See Syns at **selfish.** —**self-ab·sorp′tion** n.

self-ad·dressed (sĕlf′ə-drĕst′) adj. Addressed to oneself.

self-ad·vance·ment (sĕlf′əd-văns′mənt) n. The act of advancing oneself or one's interests.

self-ag·gran·dize·ment (sĕlf′ə-grăn′dĭz-mənt) n. The practice of making oneself greater, as in importance.

self-ap·point·ed (sĕlf′ə-poin′tĭd) adj. Appointed by oneself.

self-as·ser·tion (sĕlf′ə-sûr′shən) n. The act of asserting one's own rights, wishes, or views. —**self′-as·ser′tive** adj.

self-as·sured (sĕlf′ə-shoŏrd′) adj. Having or showing confidence in oneself. —**self′-as·sur′ance** n.

self-cen·tered (sĕlf′sĕn′tərd) adj. Selfish; egocentric. — See Syns at **selfish.** —**self′-cen′tered·ness** n.

self-clos·ing (sĕlf-klō′zĭng) adj. Closing automatically.

self-com·posed (sĕlf′kəm-pōzd′) adj. Possessing or displaying control over one's emotions.

self-con·ceit (sĕlf′kən-sēt′) n. An overly high opinion of oneself or one's abilities.

self-con·fessed (sĕlf′kən-fĕst′) adj. By one's own admission.

self-con·fi·dence (sĕlf′-kŏn′fĭ-dəns) n. Confidence in oneself or one's abilities. —See Syns at **confidence.** —**self-con′fi·dent** adj. —**self-con′fi·dent·ly** adv.

self-con·scious (sĕlf′-kŏn′shəs) adj. Uncomfortably conscious of one's appearance or manner; socially ill at ease. —**self-con′scious·ly** adv. —**self-con′scious·ness** n.

self-con·tained (sĕlf′kən-tānd′) adj. **1.** Complete in itself. **2. a.** Possessing or displaying self-control. **b.** Reserved.

self-con·tra·dic·to·ry (sĕlf′-kŏn′trə-dĭk′tə-rē) adj. Containing elements that contradict each other; inconsistent.

self-con·trol (sĕlf′kən-trōl′) n. Control of one's emotions, desires, or actions. —**self′-con·trolled′** adj.

self-de·cep·tion (sĕlf′dĭ-sĕp′shən) n. The act of deceiving oneself or the state of being deceived by oneself.

self-de·feat·ing (sĕlf′dĭ-fē′tĭng) adj. Injurious to one's or its own purposes or welfare.

self-de·fense (sĕlf′dĭ-fĕns′) n. Defense of oneself, esp. from attack or the threat of attack.

self-de·ni·al (sĕlf′dĭ-nī′əl) n. The act or practice of limiting or refraining from the gratification of one's natural desires. —**self′-de·ny′ing** adj. —**self′-de·ny′ing·ly** adv.

self-de·struct (sĕlf′dĭ-strŭkt′) intr.v. To destroy oneself or itself.

self-de·struc·tion (sĕlf′dĭ-strŭk′shən) n. The destruction of oneself, esp. suicide. —**self′-de·struc′tive** adj.

self-de·ter·mi·na·tion (sĕlf′dĭ-tûr′mə-nā′shən) n. **1.** Freedom to decide matters for oneself. **2.** The right of a people to determine its own political status.

self-dis·ci·pline (sĕlf′dĭs′ə-plĭn) n. Training and control of oneself usu. for personal improvement.

self-doubt (sĕlf′dout′) n. Lack of confidence in oneself.

self-ed·u·cat·ed (sĕlf′ĕj′ə-kā′tĭd) adj. Educated by oneself, without formal instruction. —**self′-ed′u·ca′tion** n.

self-ef·fac·ing (sĕlf′ĭ-fā′sĭng) adj. Keeping oneself in the background or out of sight. —**self′-ef·face′ment** n.

self-em·ployed (sĕlf′ĕm-ploid′) adj. Earning an income directly from one's own business or profession rather than as the employee of another. —**self′-em·ploy′ment** n.

self·es·teem (sĕlf′ĭ-stēm′) n. Satisfaction with oneself.

self·ev·i·dent (sĕlf′-ĕv′ĭ-dənt) adj. Requiring no proof or explanation. —**self-ev′i·dence** n. —**self-ev′i·dent·ly** adv.

self·ex·plan·a·to·ry (sĕlf′ĭk-splăn′ə-tôr′ē, -tōr′ē) adj. Needing no explanation.

self·ex·pres·sion (sĕlf′ĭk-sprĕsh′ən) n. Expression of one's own personality, as through a work of art.

self·fer·til·i·za·tion (sĕlf′fûr′tl-ĭ-zā′shən) n. Fertilization of a plant or animal by itself.

self·gov·ern·ment (sĕlf′-gŭv′ərn-mənt) n. 1. Political independence; autonomy. 2. Democracy. —**self-gov′erned** adj. —**self-gov′ern·ing** adj.

self·heal (sĕlf′hēl′) n. Any of several plants believed to have healing powers, esp. *Prunella vulgaris,* a low-growing plant with tightly clustered violet-blue flowers.

self·help (sĕlf′hĕlp′) n. The act or an example of providing for oneself rather than relying on help from others.

self·im·age (sĕlf′-ĭm′ĭj) n. One's conception of oneself.

self·im·por·tance (sĕlf′ĭm-pôr′tns) n. An overly high opinion of one's own importance. —**self′-im·por′tant** adj.

self·im·posed (sĕlf′ĭm-pōzd′) adj. Imposed by oneself.

self·in·crim·i·na·tion (sĕlf′ĭn-krĭm′ə-nā′shən) n. Incrimination of oneself, esp. by furnishing evidence that could make one liable to criminal prosecution.

self·in·duced (sĕlf′ĭn-dōōst′, -dyōōst′) adj. 1. Induced by oneself. 2. *Elect.* Produced by self-induction.

self·in·duc·tion (sĕlf′ĭn-dŭk′shən) n. The generation by a changing current of an electromotive force in the same circuit tending to counteract such change.

self·in·dul·gence (sĕlf′ĭn-dŭl′jəns) n. Excessive indulgence of one's own appetites and desires. —**self′-in·dul′gent** adj. —**self′-in·dul′gent·ly** adv.

self·in·flict·ed (sĕlf′ĭn-flĭk′tĭd) adj. Inflicted on oneself: *a self-inflicted injury.* —**self′-in·flic′tion** n.

self·in·ter·est (sĕlf′-ĭn′trĭst, -ĭn′tər-ĭst) n. 1. Personal advantage or interest; gain. 2. Selfish regard for one's personal advantage or interest. —**self′-in′ter·est·ed** adj.

self·ish (sĕl′fĭsh) adj. Concerned only with oneself or one's personal advantage. —**self′ish·ly** adv. —**self′ish·ness** n.

Syns: selfish, self-absorbed, self-centered, self-seeking *adj. Core meaning:* Concerned only with oneself (*a selfish person who thought only of his own wishes*).

self·knowl·edge (sĕlf′-nŏl′ĭj) n. Knowledge of one's own nature, abilities, and limitations.

self·less (sĕlf′lĭs) adj. Without concern for oneself; unselfish. —**self′less·ly** adv. —**self′less·ness** n.

self·made (sĕlf′mād′) adj. 1. Successful as a result of one's own efforts: *a self-made man.* 2. Made by oneself or itself.

self·pit·y (sĕlf′-pĭt′ē) n. A feeling of often excessive pity for oneself. —**self-pit′y·ing** adj. —**self-pit′y·ing·ly** adv.

self·pol·li·na·tion (sĕlf′-pŏl′ə-nā′shən) n. The transfer of pollen from the anther to the stigma of the same flower.

self·por·trait (sĕlf′-pôr′trĭt, -trāt′, pōr′-) n. A portrait of oneself made by oneself.

self·pos·ses·sion (sĕlf′pə-zĕsh′ən) n. Full command of one's feelings and behavior; presence of mind. —See Syns at **confidence.** —**self′-pos·sessed′** adj.

self·pres·er·va·tion (sĕlf′-prĕz′ər-vā′shən) n. The instinct to preserve oneself from harm or destruction.

self·pro·claimed (sĕlf′prō-klāmd′, -prə-) adj. Proclaimed by oneself: *a self-proclaimed hero.*

self·pro·pelled (sĕlf′prə-pĕld′) adj. Containing its own means of propulsion.

self·re·al·i·za·tion (sĕlf′-rē′ə-lĭ-zā′shən) n. The fulfillment by oneself of one's potential.

self·reg·u·lat·ing (sĕlf′rĕg′yə-lā′tĭng) adj. Regulating oneself or itself without outside control. —**self-reg′u·la′tion** n.

self·re·li·ance (sĕlf′rĭ-lī′əns) n. Reliance upon one's own resources. —**self′-re·li′ant** adj. —**self′-re·li′ant·ly** adv.

self·re·proach (sĕlf′rĭ-prōch′) n. The act of blaming oneself for a fault or mistake. —**self′-re·proach′ful** adj.

self·re·spect (sĕlf′rĭ-spĕkt′) n. Proper respect for oneself and one's value. —**self′-re·spect′ing** adj.

self·re·straint (sĕlf′rĭ-strānt′) n. Restraint imposed on one's emotions, desires, or conduct: self-control.

self·right·eous (sĕlf′-rī′chəs) adj. Smugly sure of one's

righteousness. —**self-right′eous·ly** adv. —**self-right′eous·ness** n.

self·ris·ing (sĕlf′-rī′zĭng) adj. Rising by itself without additional leaven.

self·sac·ri·fice (sĕlf′săk′rə-fīs′) n. Sacrifice of one's personal interests or well-being for the sake of others. —**self-sac′ri·fic′ing** adj.

self·same (sĕlf′sām′) adj. The very same; identical. —See Syns at **same.** —**self′same′ness** n.

self·sat·is·fac·tion (sĕlf′-săt′ĭs-făk′shən) n. Smug satisfaction with oneself or with one's accomplishments.

self·sat·is·fied (sĕlf′-săt′ĭs-fīd′) adj. Feeling or exhibiting self-satisfaction.

self·seek·ing (sĕlf′-sē′kĭng) adj. Concerned or acting only for oneself. —See Syns at **selfish.** —**self′-seek′er** n.

self·serv·ice (sĕlf′-sûr′vĭs) adj. Requiring patrons or users to help themselves: *a self-service elevator.*

self·serv·ing (sĕlf′-sûr′vĭng) adj. Furthering one's own interests: *a self-serving statement.*

self·styled (sĕlf′stīld′) adj. Called or designated by oneself.

self·suf·fi·cient (sĕlf′sə-fĭsh′ənt) adj. Also **self·suf·fic·ing** (-fī′sĭng). Providing for oneself without the help of others; not dependent. —**self′-suf·fi′cien·cy** n.

self·sup·port (sĕlf′sə-pôrt′, -pōrt′) n. Support of oneself without the help of others. —**self′-sup·port′ing** adj.

self·sus·tain·ing (sĕlf′sə-stā′nĭng) adj. Capable of sustaining oneself or itself independently.

self·will (sĕlf′wĭl′) n. Tenacious adherence to one's purposes or views; obstinacy. —**self′-willed′** adj.

self·wind·ing (sĕlf′wīn′dĭng) adj. Not requiring to be wound by hand. —**Sel′juk′** n.

Sel·juk (sĕl′jōōk′, sĕl-jōōk′) adj. Also **Sel·ju·ki·an** (-jōō′kē-ən). 1. Of any one of several Turkish dynasties of the 11th, 12th, and 13th cent. A.D. 2. Of a Turkish people ruled by a Seljuk dynasty. —**Sel′juk′** n.

sell (sĕl) v. **sold** (sōld), **sell·ing.** —tr.v. 1. To exchange or give up for money or its equivalent. 2. To offer for sale: *He sells textiles.* 3. To give up or surrender in exchange for a price or reward. 4. To promote the sale of: *Publicity sold that product.* 5. To gain the acceptance of: *They sold him on the idea.* 6. To promote or gain acceptance for. —intr.v. 1. To engage in selling. 2. To be on sale: *a book that sells for ten dollars.* 3. To be capable of attracting buyers. —phrasal verb. **sell out.** Slang. To betray. [Middle English *sellen,* from Old English *sellan,* to give.]

Syns: sell, handle, market, merchandise, retail, vend v. Core meaning: To offer for sale (*doesn't sell lawnmowers*).

sell·er (sĕl′ər) n. 1. A person who sells; salesman; vender. 2. An item that sells in a particular manner: *a best seller.*

sell·out (sĕl′out′) n. 1. The act of selling out. 2. An event for which all the tickets have been sold.

selt·zer (sĕlt′sər) n. 1. A natural effervescent spring water of high mineral content. 2. Soda water. [German *Selterser (Wasser),* "(water) of Nieder Selters," a district near Wiesbaden, West Germany.]

sel·vage (sĕl′vĭj) n. Also **sel·vedge.** The edge of a fabric so woven so as to prevent raveling. [Middle English : *selve,* self, + *egge,* edge.]

selves (sĕlvz) n. Plural of **self.**

se·man·tic (sə-măn′tĭk) adj. 1. Pertaining to meaning in language. 2. Of or relating to semantics. [Greek *sēmantikos,* significant, from *sēmainein,* to signify, from *sēma,* sign.]

se·man·tics (sə-măn′tĭks) n. (used with a sing. verb). The study of meaning, esp. in language.

sem·a·phore (sĕm′ə-fôr′, -fōr′) n. 1. An apparatus for making visual signals, as with flags, lights, or movable arms. 2. A system for signaling using two flags that are held one in each hand. —v. **-phored, -phor·ing.** —tr.v. To send (a message) by or as if by semaphore. —intr.v. To signal with a semaphore. [Greek *sēma,* sign + -PHORE.]

sem·blance (sĕm′bləns) n. 1. An outward appearance; show. 2. A likeness; resemblance. [Middle English, from Old French, from *semblant,* pres. part. of *sembler,* to resemble, seem.]

se·men (sē′mən) n. A whitish fluid of the male reproductive organs, which carries spermatozoa. [Middle English, from Latin *sēmen,* seed.]

ă pat	ā pay	â care	ä father	ĕ pet	ē be	hw which	ĭ pit	ī tie	î pier	ŏ pot	ō toe	ô paw, for	oi noise
ōō took	ōō boot	ou out	th thin	*th* this	ŭ cut	û urge	zh vision	ə about, item, edible, gallop, circus

se·mes·ter (sə-mĕs'tər) *n.* One of two terms, each from 15 to 18 weeks long, into which an academic year is often divided. [German *Semester,* from Latin *(cursus) sēmēstris,* "(period) of six months" : *sex,* six + *mēnsis,* month.]

semi-. A prefix meaning: **1.** Partly: **semiaquatic. 2.** Half: **semicircle. 3.** Occurring twice within a particular period of time: **semimonthly.** [Latin *sēmi-.*]

sem·i·an·nu·al (sĕm'ē-ăn'yōō-əl) *adj.* Happening twice a year. —See Usage note at **biannual.**

sem·i·a·quat·ic (sĕm'ē-ə-kwăt'ĭk, -kwŏt'-) *adj.* Adapted for living or growing in or near water; not entirely aquatic.

sem·i·au·to·mat·ic (sĕm'ē-ô'tə-măt'ĭk) *adj.* **1.** Partially automatic. **2.** Ejecting the shell and loading the next round of ammunition automatically after each shot has been fired. —*n.* A semiautomatic firearm.

sem·i·ar·id (sĕm'ē-ăr'ĭd) *adj.* Having an annual rainfall from about 20 to 50 centimeters or 10 to 20 inches.

sem·i·cir·cle (sĕm'ē-sûr'kəl) *n.* A half of a circle as divided by a diameter. —**sem'i·cir'cu·lar** (-sûr'kyə-lər) *adj.*

semicircular canal. Any of the three tubular and looped structures in the inner ear, functioning together in the maintenance of a sense of balance and orientation.

sem·i·co·lon (sĕm'ē-kō'lən) *n.* A mark of punctuation (;) indicating a degree of separation intermediate in value between the comma and the period.

sem·i·con·duc·tor (sĕm'ē-kən-dŭk'tər) *n.* Any of various solid crystalline substances, such as germanium or silicon, that have electrical conductivity greater than insulators but less than good conductors.

sem·i·de·tached (sĕm'ē-dĭ-tăcht') *adj.* Attached to another building on one side only: *semidetached houses.*

sem·i·fi·nal (sĕm'ē-fī'nəl) *adj.* Immediately preceding the final, as in a series of competitions. —*n.* A semifinal competition. —**sem'i·fi'nal·ist** *n.*

sem·i·lu·nar valve (sĕm'ē-lōō'nər). Either of two crescent-shaped valves located in the aorta and in the pulmonary artery and preventing blood from flowing back into the heart.

sem·i·month·ly (sĕm'ē-mŭnth'lē) *adj.* Occurring or appearing twice a month. —*n., pl.* **-lies.** A semimonthly publication. —*adv.* Twice monthly; at half-monthly intervals. —See Usage note at **bimonthly.**

sem·i·nal (sĕm'ə-nəl) *adj.* **1.** Of or relating to semen or seed. **2.** Of a creative nature; capable of originating or stimulating growth and development. [Middle English, from Old French, from Latin *sēminālis,* from *sēmen,* seed.]

sem·i·nar (sĕm'ə-när') *n.* **1.** A small group of advanced students engaged in special study or original research. **2.** The course of study of a seminar. [German *Seminar,* from Latin *sēminārium,* seed plot, nursery.]

sem·i·nar·i·an (sĕm'ə-nâr'ē-ən) *n.* A seminary student.

sem·i·nar·y (sĕm'ə-nĕr'ē) *n., pl.* **-ies. 1.** A school for training priests, ministers, or rabbis. **2.** A secondary school, esp. for young women. [Middle English, seed plot, from Latin *sēminārium,* from *sēmen,* seed.]

sem·i·nif·er·ous (sĕm'ə-nĭf'ər-əs) *adj.* Conveying or producing semen or seed. [Latin *sēmen,* semen + *-FEROUS.*]

Sem·i·nole (sĕm'ə-nōl') *n., pl.* **Seminole** or **-noles. 1.** A tribe of North American Indians, orig. from Florida. **2.** A member of this tribe. **3.** The language of the Seminole. —**Sem'i·nole'** *adj.*

sem·i·per·me·a·ble (sĕm'ē-pûr'mē-ə-bəl) *adj.* **1.** Partially permeable. **2.** Permeable to some molecules in a mixture or solution but not to all.

sem·i·pre·cious (sĕm'ē-prĕsh'əs) *adj.* Of somewhat less value than precious: *semiprecious gemstones.*

sem·i·pri·vate (sĕm'ē-prī'vĭt) *adj.* Shared with usu. one to three other hospital patients: *a semiprivate room.*

sem·i·pro (sĕm'ē-prō') *adj. Informal.* Semiprofessional. —**sem'i·pro'** *n.*

sem·i·pro·fes·sion·al (sĕm'ē-prə-fĕsh'ə-nəl) *adj.* **1.** Taking part in a sport for pay but not on a full-time basis. **2.** Composed of or engaged in by semiprofessional players. —*n.* A semiprofessional player.

Sem·ite (sĕm'īt') *n.* One of a group of Middle Eastern peoples that includes chiefly the Jews and Arabs.

Se·mit·ic (sə-mĭt'ĭk) *adj.* **1.** Of the Semites, esp. Jewish or Arabic. **2.** Of or designating a subfamily of the Afro-Asiatic family of languages. —*n.* **1.** The Semitic subfamily of languages. **2.** Any of the Semitic languages.

Sem·i·tism (sĕm'ĭ-tĭz'əm) *n.* **1.** Semitic traits, attributes, or customs. **2.** A predisposition in favor of the Jews.

sem·i·tone (sĕm'ē-tōn') *n. Mus.* An interval equal to half tone in the diatonic scale. —**sem'i·ton'ic** (-tŏn'ĭk) *adj.*

sem·i·trail·er (sĕm'ē-trā'lər) *n.* A trailer with rear wheels only, supported in front by the truck tractor.

sem·i·week·ly (sĕm'ē-wēk'lē) *adj.* Occurring or appearing twice a week. —*n., pl.* **-lies.** A semiweekly publication. —*adv.* Twice weekly. —See Usage note at **biweekly.**

sem·i·year·ly (sĕm'ē-yîr'lē) *adj.* Appearing or occurring twice a year. —*adv.* Twice a year. —See Usage note at **biyearly.**

sem·o·li·na (sĕm'ə-lē'nə) *n.* The gritty, coarse particles of wheat left after the finer flour has been sifted out, used esp. for pasta. [Italian *semolino,* dim. of *semola,* bran, from Latin *simila,* fine flour.]

sem·pi·ter·nal (sĕm'pī-tûr'nəl) *adj.* Eternal; perpetual. [Middle English, from Old French *sempiternel,* from Late Latin *sempiternālis,* from Latin *sempiternus* : *semper,* always + *aeternus,* eternal.] —**sem'pi·ter'ni·ty** *n.*

sen (sĕn) *n., pl.* **sen.** A Japanese coin equal to $1/100$ of a yen. [Japanese.]

sen·ate (sĕn'ĭt) *n.* **1.a.** The upper house in a bicameral legislature. **b.** The highest council of state of the ancient Roman republic and empire. **2.** The building or hall in which a senate meets. **3.** A governing body of some colleges and universities. [Middle English *senat,* from Old French, from Latin *senātus,* from *senex,* old, an elder.]

senate
United States Senate

sen·a·tor (sĕn'ə-tər) *n.* A member of a senate.

sen·a·to·ri·al (sĕn'ə-tôr'ē-əl, -tōr'-) *adj.* Of, concerning, or befitting a senator or a senate. —**sen'a·to'ri·al·ly** *adv.*

send (sĕnd) *v.* **sent,** **send·ing.** —*tr.v.* **1. a.** To cause to be conveyed. **2.** To dispatch, as by mail. **3. a.** To direct or order to go. **b.** To allow or enable to go: *send a son to college.* **c.** To cause to depart. **4.** To give off; emit. **5.** To direct or propel with force; drive. **6. a.** To drive into a particular condition: *sent him into a fury.* **b.** *Slang.* To fill with delight; thrill. —*intr.v.* To dispatch a message, request, or order: *send away for a catalogue.* [Middle English *senden,* from Old English *sendan.*] —**send'er** *n.*

Syns: send, dispatch, forward, route, ship, transmit *v.* Core meaning: To cause (something) to be conveyed to a destination (*sent the package to England*).

send·off (sĕnd'ôf', -ŏf') *n.* A demonstration of affection and good wishes, as for a person about to begin a journey.

se·nes·cent (sĭ-nĕs'ənt) *adj.* Aging; elderly. [Latin *senēscēns,* pres. part. of *senēscere,* to grow old, from *senex,* old.] —**se·nes'cence** *n.*

sen·e·schal (sĕn'ə-shəl) *n.* An official who managed the estate of a feudal lord. [Middle English, from Old French, from Medieval Latin *siniscalcus.*]

se·nile (sē'nīl', sĕn'īl') *adj.* Of or exhibiting old age. [Old French, from Latin *senīlis,* from *senex,* old.] —**se'nile'ly** *adv.*

se·nil·i·ty (sĭ-nĭl'ĭ-tē) *n.* **1.** The condition of being senile. **2.** Mental and physical deterioration of old age.

sen·ior (sēn'yər) *adj.* **1.** Of or designating the older of two persons of the same name. **2.** Above others in age, rank, or length of service. **3.** Of the fourth and last year of high school or college. —See Syns at **old.** —*n.* **1.** A senior per-

ă pat   ā pay   â care   ä father   ĕ pet   ē be   hw which
ōō took   ōō boot   ou out   th thin   th this   ŭ cut
ĭ pit   ī tie   î pier   ŏ pot   ō toe   ô paw, for   oi noise
û urge   zh vision   ə about, item, edible, gallop, circus

son. **2.** A student in the fourth year. [Latin, comp. of *se-nex*, old.]

senior citizen. A person of or over the age of retirement.

senior high school. A high school usu. comprising grades 10, 11, and 12.

sen·ior·i·ty (sēn-yôr′ĭ-tē, -yōr′-) *n.*, *pl.* **-ties. 1.** The condition of being senior. **2.** A position of precedence over others because of length of service.

sen·na (sĕn′ə) *n.* **1.** Any of various plants of the genus *Cassia.* **2.** The dried leaves of these plants, used as a cathartic. [New Latin, from Arabic *sanā′.*]

se·ñor (sān-yôr′, -yōr′) *n.*, *pl.* **se·ñor·es** (sān-yôr′ās, -yōr′-). The Spanish title of courtesy for a man, equivalent to English *Mr.* [Spanish, from Latin *senior*, older, comp. of *senex*, old.]

se·ño·ra (sān-yôr′ə, -yōr′-) *n.*, *pl.* **se·ño·ras** (sān-yôr′əs, -yōr′-). The Spanish title of courtesy for a woman, equivalent to English *Mrs.* [Spanish, fem. of *señor*, señor.]

se·ño·ri·ta (sān′yə-rē′tə) *n.*, *pl.* **-tas.** The Spanish title of courtesy for an unmarried woman or girl, equivalent to English *Miss.* [Spanish dim. of *señora.*]

sen·sa·tion (sĕn-sā′shən, sən-) *n.* **1.** A perception associated with stimulation of a sense organ. **2.** A vague or indefinite feeling. **3. a.** A condition of intense interest and excitement. **b.** A cause of such excitement. [Medieval Latin *sēnsātiō*, from Latin *sensus*, sense.]

sen·sa·tion·al (sĕn-sā′shə-nəl, sən-) *adj.* **1.** Of sensation. **2.** Arousing intense interest, esp. by means of exaggerated or lurid details. **3.** Outstandingly excellent; spectacular. —**sen′sa′tion·al·ly** *adv.*

sen·sa·tion·al·ism (sĕn-sā′shə-nə-līz′əm, sən-) *n.* The use or the effect of sensational matter or methods.

sense (sĕns) *n.* **1.** Any of the animal functions of perception, such as hearing, sight, smell, touch, and taste. **2. senses.** The faculties of sensation. **3.** A capacity to appreciate or understand: *a sense of humor.* **4.** A vague feeling or impression. **5.** Awareness; consciousness: *a sense of guilt.* **6. a.** Often **senses.** The ability to think or reason soundly; judgment. **b.** Reasonableness. **7. a.** The meaning conveyed by language; signification. **b.** One of the meanings of a word. **8.** View; consensus. —See Syns at **meaning.** —*tr.v.* **sensed, sens·ing.** To become aware of through or as if through the senses; perceive. [Latin *sēnsus*, the faculty of perceiving, from the past part. of *sentīre*, to feel.]

sense·less (sĕns′lĭs) *adj.* **1.** Without sense or meaning; purposeless. **2.** Foolish. **3.** Unconscious. —**sense′less·ly** *adv.* —**sense′less·ness** *n.*

sense organ. A specialized organ, such as the eye or ear, that initiates sensory perception when stimulated.

sen·si·bil·i·ty (sĕn′sə-bĭl′ĭ-tē) *n.*, *pl.* **-ties. 1.** The ability to perceive sensations. **2.** Keen intellectual perception. **3.** Acute sensitivity to impressions. **4.** Refined awareness and appreciation in matters of feeling.

sen·si·ble (sĕn′sə-bəl) *adj.* **1.** Capable of being perceived by the senses or the mind. **2.** Easily perceived; considerable. **3.** Having the ability to feel or perceive. **4.** Cognizant; aware. **5.** Possessing or showing good sense. —**sen′si·ble·ness** *n.* —**sen′si·bly** *adv.*

  Syns: **sensible, logical, rational, reasonable** *adj.* Core meaning: Consistent with common sense and reason (*a sensible solution to the problem*).

sen·si·tive (sĕn′sĭ-tĭv) *adj.* **1.** Capable of perceiving. **2.** Responsive to external conditions or stimulation. **3.** Aware of and responsive to the attitudes, feelings, or circumstances of others. **4.** Quick to take offense; touchy. **5.** Easily irritated. **6.** Readily affected by the action of some agent: *sensitive to light.* **7.** Capable of registering very slight differences or changes: *a sensitive barometer.* **8.** Concerned with classified government information. —See Syns at **sharp.** [Middle English, from Old French *sensitif*, from Medieval Latin *sēnsitīvus*, from Latin *sēnsus*, sense.] —**sen′si·tive·ly** *adv.* —**sen′si·tive·ness** *n.*

sensitive plant. A woody tropical American plant, *Mimosa pudica*, with leaflets and stems that fold and droop when touched.

sen·si·tiv·i·ty (sĕn′sĭ-tĭv′ĭ-tē) *n.*, *pl.* **-ties. 1.** The quality or condition of being sensitive. **2.** Responsiveness to stimulation. **3.** *Electronics.* The minimum input signal required to

produce a specified output signal.

sen·si·tize (sĕn′sĭ-tīz′) *v.* **-tized, -tiz·ing.** —*tr.v.* To make sensitive. —*intr.v.* To become sensitive. —**sen′si·ti·za′tion** *n.* —**sen′si·tiz′er** *n.*

sen·sor (sĕn′sər, -sôr′) *n.* A device, such as a photoelectric cell, that detects and responds to a signal or stimulus.

sen·so·ry (sĕn′sə-rē) *adj.* **1.** Of the senses. **2.** Transmitting impulses from sense organs to nerve centers.

sen·su·al (sĕn′shōō-əl) *adj.* **1.** Of or relating to the senses or sensation. **2. a.** Preoccupied with the gratification of the physical appetites, esp. sexual appetites. **b.** Providing pleasure to the senses; voluptuous. —**sen′su·al·ly** *adv.* —**sen′su·al′i·ty** (sĕn′shōō-ăl′ĭ-tē) or **sen′su·al·ness** *n.* —**sen′su·al·ist** *n.* —**sen′su·al·is′tic** *adj.*

sen·su·al·ize (sĕn′shōō-ə-līz′) *tr.v.* **-ized, -iz·ing.** To make sensual. —**sen′su·al·i·za′tion** *n.*

sen·su·ous (sĕn′shōō-əs) *adj.* **1.** Of the senses. **2.** Having qualities that appeal to the senses. **3.** Easily affected by means of the senses. —**sen′su·ous·ly** *adv.* —**sen′su·ous·ness** *n.*

sent (sĕnt) *v.* Past tense and past participle of **send.**

sen·tence (sĕn′təns) *n.* **1.** A grammatical unit consisting of a word or a group of words that is separate from any other grammatical construction, and in writing usu. begins with a capital letter and ends with a period, question mark, or exclamation point. **2. a.** A judgment, esp. a judicial decision as to the punishment of a convicted person. **b.** The penalty imposed. —*tr.v.* **-tenced, -tenc·ing.** To pass sentence upon. [Middle English, opinion, from Old French, from Latin *sententia*, from *sentīre*, to feel.]

sen·ten·tious (sĕn-tĕn′shəs) *adj.* **1.** Terse and forceful in expression; pithy. **2.** Given to pompous moralizing. [Latin *sententiōsus*, full of meaning, from *sententia*, opinion.] —**sen·ten′tious·ly** *adv.* —**sen·ten′tious·ness** *n.*

sen·tience (sĕn′shəns) *n.* Also **sen·tien·cy** (-shən-sē). The condition of being sentient; consciousness.

sen·tient (sĕn′shənt) *adj.* Capable of feeling. [Latin *sentiēns*, pres. part. of *sentīre*, to feel.] —**sen′tient·ly** *adv.*

sen·ti·ment (sĕn′tə-mənt) *n.* **1.** An opinion about a specific matter; a view. **2.** A thought, view, or attitude based on feeling or emotion. **3.** Tender, romantic, or nostalgic feeling. **4.** Delicate and sensitive feeling. —See Syns at **belief.** [Middle English *sentement*, from Old French, from Medieval Latin *sentīmentum*, from Latin *sentīre*, to feel.]

sen·ti·men·tal (sĕn′tə-mĕn′tl) *adj.* **1.** Characterized or swayed by sentiment. **2.** Resulting from or colored by emotion rather than reason. **3.** Affectedly or extravagantly emotional. —**sen′ti·men·tal·ly** *adv.*

sen·ti·men·tal·ism (sĕn′tə-mĕn′tl-ĭz′əm) *n.* A tendency to indulge in sentimentality. —**sen′ti·men·tal·ist** *n.*

sen·ti·men·tal·i·ty (sĕn′tə-mĕn-′tăl′ĭ-tē) *n.*, *pl.* **-ties. 1.** The quality of being excessively or affectedly sentimental. **2.** An example of excessive sentiment.

sen·ti·men·tal·ize (sĕn′tə-mĕn′tl-īz′) *v.* **-ized, -iz·ing.** —*tr.v.* To regard with sentiment; be sentimental about. —*intr.v.* To behave sentimentally. —**sen′ti·men·tal·i·za′tion** *n.*

sen·ti·nel (sĕn′tə-nəl) *n.* A guard; sentry. —*tr.v.* **-neled or -nelled, -nel·ing or -nel·ling.** To watch over as a sentinel. [French *sentinelle*, from Italian *sentinella*, from *sentire*, to perceive, watch, from Latin *sentīre*, to perceive, feel.]

sen·try (sĕn′trē) *n.*, *pl.* **-tries. 1.** A guard, esp. a soldier posted to guard a passageway. **2.** The duty of a sentry. [Perh. short for obs. *centrinell*, var. of **sentinel**.]

se·pal (sē′pəl) *n.* One of the usu. green segments forming the calyx of a flower. [New Latin *sepalum*, ult. from Greek *skepē*, covering.] —**se′paled** or **sep′a·lous** (sĕp′ə-ləs) *adj.*

sep·a·ra·ble (sĕp′ər-ə-bəl, sĕp′rə-) *adj.* Capable of being separated. —**sep′a·ra·bil′i·ty** *n.* —**sep′a·ra·bly** *adv.*

sep·a·rate (sĕp′ə-rāt′) *v.* **-rat·ed, -rat·ing.** —*tr.v.* **1. a.** To set or keep apart; disunite. **b.** To sort. **2.** To discriminate between; distinguish. **3.** To extract from a mixture or combination; isolate. **4.** To part (a married couple) by decree. **5.** To discharge, as from service or employment. —*intr.v.* **1.** To become disconnected or severed. **2.** To withdraw; secede. **3.** To part company; disperse. **4.** To stop living together as husband and wife. —*adj.* (sĕp′ər-ĭt, sĕp′rĭt). **1.** Set apart; detached. **2.** Existing by itself; independent. **3.** Dissimilar; distinct. **4.** Not shared; individual. —See Syns at **single.** —*n.* (sĕp′ər-ĭt, sĕp′rĭt). A garment, such as

a skirt or blouse, that is one of a group designed to be worn in various combinations. [Middle English *separaten,* from Latin *sēparātus,* past part. of *separare : sē,* apart + *parāre,* to make ready, prepare.] **—sep′a·rate·ly** *adv.* **—sep′a·rate·ness** *n.*
  Syns: 1. separate, break up, divide, part, partition, section, segment *v.* *Core meaning:* To make a division into parts (*separated the city into two sectors*). **2. separate, break, disjoin, divide, divorce, split** *v.* *Core meaning:* To become or cause to become apart from the other (*families that separated over the issue of slavery*).
sep·a·ra·tion (sĕp′ə-rā′shən) *n.* **1. a.** The act or process of separating. **b.** The state of being separated. **2.** The place where a division or parting occurs. **3.** A gap. **4.** A formal agreement to live separately.
sep·a·ra·tist (sĕp′ər-ə-tĭst, sĕp′rə-, sĕp′ə-rā′tĭst) *n.* A person who advocates political or religious separation. **—sep′a·ra·tism** *n.* **—sep′a·ra·tis′tic** *adj.*
Se·phar·di (sə-fär′dē) *n., pl.* **-dim** (-dĭm). Also **Se·phar·a·di** (sə-fär′ə-dē). A member of one of the two main divisions of Jews that includes the Spanish and Portuguese Jews. [Hebrew *Səphāradhī,* Spaniard, from *Səphāradh,* Spain.] **—Se·phar′dic** *adj.*
se·pi·a (sē′pē-ə) *n.* **1.** A brown pigment orig. prepared from the ink of the cuttlefish. **2.** A dark brown. **—adj. 1.** Dark brown. **2.** Done in sepia. [Italian *seppia,* from Latin *sēpia,* cuttlefish, dark-brown pigment, from Greek.]
se·poy (sē′poi′) *n.* A native of India serving as a soldier under European command. [Perh. from Portuguese *sipae,* from Hindi *sipāhī,* from Persian *sipāh,* army.]
sep·sis (sĕp′sĭs) *n.* The presence of disease-causing organisms, or their toxins, in the blood or tissues. [Greek *sēpsis,* putrefaction, from *sēpein,* to make rotten.]
sep·ta (sĕp′tə) *n.* Plural of **septum.**
Sep·tem·ber (sĕp-tĕm′bər) *n.* The ninth month of the year. [Middle English *Septembre,* from Old French, from Latin, the seventh month, from *septem,* seven.]
sep·ten·ni·al (sĕp-tĕn′ē-əl) *adj.* **1.** Occurring every seven years. **2.** Consisting of or lasting for seven years. [From Latin *septennium,* period of seven years : *septem,* seven + *annus,* year.] **—sep·ten′ni·al·ly** *adv.*
sep·tet (sĕp-tĕt′) *n.* Also **sep·tette. 1.** A group of seven. **2.** *Mus.* A composition for seven voices or instruments. [German *Septett,* from Latin *septem,* seven.]
sep·tic (sĕp′tĭk) *adj.* **1.** Of or pertaining to sepsis. **2.** Causing putrefaction. [Latin *sēpticus,* putrefying, from Greek *sēptikos,* from *sēptos,* rotten, from *sēpein,* to make rotten.]
sep·ti·ce·mi·a (sĕp′tĭ-sē′mē-ə) *n.* A systemic disease caused by pathogenic organisms or their toxins in the bloodstream. [Latin *sēpticus,* septic + *-EMIA.*]
septic tank. A sewage disposal tank in which solid waste material is decomposed by bacteria.
sep·til·lion (sĕp-tĭl′yən) *n.* **1.** The cardinal number represented by 1 followed by 24 zeros, usu. written 10^{24}. **2.** *Brit.* The cardinal number represented by 1 followed by 42 zeros, usu. written 10^{42}. [French : *septi-* seven + (*mi*)*llion,* million.] **—sep·til′lion** *adj.* **—sep·til′lionth** *adj. & n.*
sep·tu·a·ge·nar·i·an (sĕp′chōō-ə-jə-nâr′ē-ən, sĕp′tōō-) *n.* A person between the ages of seventy and eighty. [From Latin *septuāgēnārius,* from *septuāgēnī,* seventy each, from *septuāgintā,* seventy.] **—sep′tu·a·ge·nar′i·an** *adj.*
Sep·tu·a·gint (sĕp′chōō-ə-jĭnt′, sĕp′tōō-) *n.* A pre-Christian Greek translation of the Old Testament. [Latin *septuāgintā,* seventy, from the number of its translators.]
sep·tum (sĕp′təm) *n., pl.* **-ta** (-tə). A thin partition or membrane. [Latin *sēptum,* partition, from *sēpīre,* to surround with a hedge, from *sēpes,* hedge.]
sep·ul·cher (sĕp′əl-kər) *n.* Also *Brit.* **sep·ul·chre. 1.** A burial vault; tomb. **2.** A receptacle for sacred relics, esp. in an altar. **—tr.v.** To place in or as if in a sepulcher. [Middle English *sepulcre,* from Old French, from Latin *sepulcrum,* from *sepelīre,* past part. of *sepelīre,* to bury.]
se·pul·chral (sə-pŭl′krəl) *adj.* Of or suggestive of the grave. **—se·pul′chral·ly** *adv.*
sep·ul·chre (sĕp′əl-kər) *n. Brit.* Var. of **sepulcher.**
sep·ul·ture (sĕp′əl-chər) *n.* **1.** The act of interment; burial. **2.** A sepulcher. [Middle English, from Old French, from Latin *sepultūra,* from *sepultus,* buried.]
se·quel (sē′kwəl) *n.* **1.** Something that follows or comes

afterward. **2.** A literary work that continues an earlier narrative. **3.** A result or consequence. [Middle English *sequele,* from Old French *sequelle,* from Latin *sequēla,* from *sequī,* to follow.]
se·quel·a (sĭ-kwĕl′ə) *n., pl.* **-quel·ae** (-kwĕl′ē). An aftereffect of a disease or injury. [Latin *sequēla,* sequel.]
se·quence (sē′kwəns) *n.* **1.** A related or continuous series. **2.** A series of scenes in a film. **3.** *Mus.* A melodic phrase or harmonic pattern successively repeated at different pitches. **4.** An order of succession; arrangement. **5.** A consequence. **6.** *Math.* An ordered set of numbers, as x, $2x^2$, $3x^3$, $4x^4$. [Late Latin *sequentia,* from Latin *sequēns,* pres. part. of *sequī,* to follow.]
se·quent (sē′kwənt) *adj.* Following in sequence.
se·quen·tial (sĭ-kwĕn′shəl) *adj.* Sequent. **—se·quen′ti·al·i·ty** (-kwĕn′shē-ăl′ĭ-tē) *n.* **—se·quen′tial·ly** *adv.*
se·ques·ter (sĭ-kwĕs′tər) *tr.v.* To set apart; segregate. [Late Latin *sequestrāre,* to separate, from Latin *sequester,* depository.]
se·ques·trate (sĭ-kwĕs′trāt′) *tr.v.* **-trat·ed, -trat·ing.** To sequester.
se·quin (sē′kwĭn) *n.* A small shiny ornamental disk used on clothing; a spangle. [French, from Italian *zecchino,* from *zecca,* the mint, from Arabic *sikkah,* coin die.]
se·quoi·a (sĭ-kwoi′ə) *n.* Any very large evergreen tree of the genus *Sequoia.* [After *Sequoya,* (1770?–1843), North American Indian leader and scholar.]
se·ra (sîr′ə) *n.* A plural of **serum.**
se·ra·glio (sĭ-răl′yō, -räl′-) *n., pl.* **-glios.** A harem. [Italian *serraglio,* prob. from Turkish *serai,* palace, from Persian.]
se·ra·pe (sə-rä′pē) *n.* Also **sa·ra·pe.** A woolen shawl worn esp. by Mexican men. [Mexican Spanish *sarape.*]
ser·aph (sĕr′əf) *n., pl.* **-aphs** or **-a·phim** (-ə-fĭm) An angel belonging to the highest order. [Back-formation from pl. seraphim, from Late Latin *seraphim,* from Hebrew *sərā-phīm.*] **—se·raph′ic** (sə-răf′ĭk) *adj.*
Serb (sûrb) *n.* A Serbian.
Ser·bi·an (sûr′bē-ən) *n.* **1.** A member of a southern Slavic people of Serbia and Yugoslavia. **2.** A Serbo-Croatian. **3.** Serbo-Croatian as spoken in Serbia. **—Ser′bi·an** *adj.*
Ser·bo-Cro·a·tian (sûr′bō-krō-ā′shən) *n.* **1.** The Slavic language of the Serbs and Croats. **2.** A native speaker of Serbo-Croatian. **—Ser′bo-Cro·a′tian** *adj.*
sere (sîr) *adj. & n.* Var. of **sear.**
ser·e·nade (sĕr′ə-nād′, sĕr′ə-nād′) *n.* A musical performance given to honor or express love for someone. **2.** An instrumental form comprising characteristics of the suite and the sonata. **—v.** (sĕr′ə-nād′) **-nad·ed, -nad·ing.** **—tr.v.** To perform a serenade for. [French *sérénade,* from Italian *serenata,* evening serenade, from *sereno,* serene, from Latin *serēnus.*]
ser·en·dip·i·ty (sĕr′ən-dĭp′ĭ-tē) *n.* The faculty of making valuable discoveries by accident. [After the characters in the fairy tale *The Three Princes of Serendip,* who made such discoveries.] **—ser′en·dip′i·tous** *adj.*
se·rene (sə-rēn′) *adj.* **1.** Unruffled; tranquil; dignified. **2.** Unclouded; fair; bright. **3.** Serene. August. **—See Syns at calm.** [Latin *serēnus.*] **—se·rene′ly** *adv.* **—se·rene′ness** *n.*
se·ren·i·ty (sə-rĕn′ĭ-tē) *n.* The quality of being serene.
serf (sûrf) *n.* A slave, esp. a member of the lowest feudal class in medieval Europe, bound to the land. [Old French, from Latin *servus,* slave.] **—serf′dom** *n.*
serge (sûrj) *n.* A twilled cloth of worsted or worsted and wool. [Middle English *serge,* from Old French, from Latin *sērica,* of Seres (a people), from Greek *sērikos,* from *Sēres,* Seres.]
ser·geant (sär′jənt) *n.* **1. a.** Any of several ranks of non-commissioned officers in the U.S. Army, Air Force, or Marine Corps. **b.** A person holding any of these ranks. **2. a.** The rank of police officer next below a captain, lieutenant, or inspector. **b.** A person holding this rank. **3.** A **sergeant at arms.** [Middle English *sergant,* from Old French *sergent,* from Latin *serviēns,* pres. part. of *servīre,* to serve, from *servus,* slave.] **—ser′gean·cy** *n.*
sergeant at arms *pl.* **sergeants at arms.** An officer appointed to keep order, as at the meetings of a legislature.
sergeant major. 1. A noncommissioned officer serving as

ă pat	ā pay	â care	ä father	ĕ pet	ē be	hw which	ĭ pit	ī tie	î pier	ŏ pot	ō toe	ô paw, for	oi noise
ōō took	ōō boot	ou out	th thin	th this	ŭ cut	û urge	zh vision	ə about, item, edible, gallop, circus

chief administrative assistant of a headquarters unit of the U.S. Army, Air Force, or Marine Corps. **2.** *Brit.* A noncommissioned officer of the highest rank.

se·ri·al (sîr′ē-əl) *adj.* **1.** Of, forming, or arranged in a series: *a serial number.* **2.** Published or produced in installments. —*n.* A literary or dramatic work published or produced in installments. [From SERIES.] —**se′ri·al·ly** *adv.*

se·ri·al·ize (sîr′ē-ə-līz′) *tr.v.* **-ized, -iz·ing.** To write or publish in serial form. —**se′ri·al·i·za′tion** *n.*

se·ri·a·tim (sîr′ē-ā′tĭm, -ăt′ĭm) *adv.* One after another. [Medieval Latin, from Latin *seriēs,* series.]

se·ri·cul·ture (sîr′ĭ-kŭl′chər) *n.* The production of raw silk and the raising of silkworms for this purpose. [French *sériculture* : Latin *sēricus,* silken, + *culture,* culture.] —**se′ri·cul′tur·al** *adj.* —**se′ri·cul′tur·ist** *n.*

se·ries (sîr′ēz) *n., pl.* **series. 1.** A number of similar things or events that occur in a row or follow one another in time. **2. a.** A number of related performances, as of music or drama, that are presented consecutively. **b.** A television or radio show that is presented at regular intervals: *a comedy series.* **c.** A number of games played one after the other by the same opposing teams. **3.** *Math.* The indicated sum of a finite or of a sequentially ordered infinite set of terms. —*idiom.* **in series.** Connected so that electric current passes through each circuit element in turn without branching: *batteries in series.* [Latin *seriēs,* from *serere,* to join.]

ser·if (sĕr′ĭf) *n.* In printing, a fine line finishing off the main strokes, as at the top and bottom of *M,* or ending the cross stroke of *T.* [Perh. from Dutch *schreef,* line, from Middle Dutch *scrēve,* from *scriven,* to write, from Latin *scrībere.*]

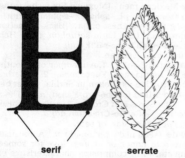

serif   **serrate**

ser·i·graph (sĕr′ĭ-grăf′) *n.* A print made by the silk-screen process. [Latin *sēri(cum),* silk + -GRAPH.]

se·ri·o·com·ic (sîr′ē-ō-kŏm′ĭk) or **se·ri·o·com·i·cal** (-ĭ-kəl) *adj.* Both serious and comic. [SERIO(US) + COMIC.]

se·ri·ous (sîr′ē-əs) *adj.* **1.** Grave in character, quality, or manner; sober. **2.** Said or done in earnest; sincere. **3.** Concerned with important rather than trivial matters. **4.** Marked by considerable effort or devotion. **5.** Causing anxiety; critical. [Middle English *seryous,* from Old French *serieux,* from Late Latin *sēriōsus,* from Latin *sērius.*] —**se′ri·ous·ly** *adv.* —**se′ri·ous·ness** *n.*

se·ri·ous-mind·ed (sîr′ē-əs-mīn′dĭd) *adj.* Displaying or characterized by seriousness of purpose or nature; earnest.

ser·mon (sûr′mən) *n.* **1.** A religious discourse delivered as part of a church service. **2.** Any discourse or speech, esp. a solemn one. [Middle English *sermun,* from Norman French, from Latin *sermō,* a discourse.]

ser·mon·ize (sûr′mə-nīz′) *intr.v.* **-ized, -iz·ing.** To deliver, or speak as though delivering, a sermon. —**ser′mon·iz′er** *n.*

se·rol·o·gy (sĭ-rŏl′ə-jē) *n.* The medical study of serum. [SE-RUM + -LOGY.] —**se·ro·log′ic** (sîr′ə-lŏj′ĭk) or **se′ro·log′i·cal** *adj.* —**se·rol′o·gist** *n.*

se·rous (sîr′əs) *adj.* Containing, secreting, or resembling serum. [From SERUM.]

serous membrane. A thin membrane lining a closed bodily cavity.

ser·pent (sûr′pənt) *n.* **1.** A snake. **2.** A subtle, sly, or treacherous person. [Middle English, from Old French, from Latin *serpēns,* crawling thing, from *serpere,* to crawl, creep.]

ser·pen·tine (sûr′pən-tēn′, -tīn′) *adj.* Of or resembling a

serpent, as in form or movement. —*n.* **1.** Something that winds like a snake. **2.** A greenish, brownish, or spotted mineral, $3MgO \cdot 2SiO_2 \cdot 2H_2O$, used as a source of magnesium and in architecture as a decorative stone.

ser·rate (sĕr′āt′) *adj.* Also **ser·rat·ed** (-ā′tĭd). Edged with notched, toothlike projections: *a serrate leaf.* [Latin *serrātus,* saw-shaped, from Latin *serra,* saw.]

ser·ra·tion (sĕ-rā′shən) *n.* **1.** The condition of being serrate. **2.** A tooth or notch in a serrate edge.

ser·ried (sĕr′ēd) *adj.* Pressed together in rows; in close order. [Perh. from obs. *serry,* to press together, from Old French *serré,* past part. of *serrer,* to crowd.]

se·rum (sîr′əm) *n., pl.* **-rums** or **se·ra** (sîr′ə). **1.** The clear yellowish fluid obtained upon separating whole blood into its solid and liquid components. **2.** The fluid from the tissues of immunized animals, used esp. as an antitoxin. **3.** Any watery bodily fluid. [Latin, whey, serum.]

ser·val (sûr′vəl, sər-văl′) *n.* A long-legged wildcat, *Felis serval,* of Africa, having a yellowish coat with black spots. [French, from Portuguese *(lobo) cerval,* deerlike (wolf), from *cervo,* deer, from Latin *cervus.*]

ser·vant (sûr′vənt) *n.* **1.** A person privately employed to perform services in the household of someone else. **2.** A person publicly employed to perform services, as for a government. **3.** A person expressing submission or debt to another: *your obedient servant.* **4.** Someone or something that serves another: *Art can be a servant to man's needs.*

serve (sûrv) *v.* **served, serv·ing.** —*tr.v.* **1.** To work for; be a servant to. **2. a.** To prepare and offer, as food. **b.** To place food before (someone); wait on. **3. a.** To provide goods and services for (customers). **b.** To supply (goods or services) to customers. **4.** To be of assistance to; promote the interests of; aid. **5.** To spend or complete (time): *serve four terms in Congress.* **6.** To fight or undergo military service for. **7.** To give homage and obedience to. **8.** To requite. **9.** To be used by: *One phone serves the whole office.* **10.** To function for: *His cunning served him well.* **11.** *Law.* **a.** To deliver or present (a legal writ or summons). **b.** To present such a writ to. **12.** To put (the ball) in play, as in tennis, badminton, and jai alai. —*intr.v.* **1.** To be employed as a servant. **2.** To do a term of duty. **3.** To act in a particular capacity: *serve as a clerk.* **4.** To be of service or use; to function: *serve as a reminder.* **5.** To meet requirements or needs; suffice. **6.** To wait on table: *serve at luncheon.* **7.** To put a ball or shuttlecock into play, as in court games. —*n.* The right, manner, or act of serving, as in a court game. [Middle English *serven,* from Old French *servir,* from Latin *servīre,* from *servus,* slave.]

serv·er (sûr′vər) *n.* **1.** Someone or something that serves. **2.** Something used in serving, as a tray. **3.** An attendant to the celebrant at a Mass. **4.** The player who serves.

serv·ice (sûr′vĭs) *n.* **1.** The occupation or duties of a servant. **2.** Employment in duties or work for another: *years of hard service.* **3.** A government branch or department and its employees: *civil service.* **4.** The armed forces of a nation, or any branch thereof. **5.** Work or duties performed for a superior. **6.** Work done for others as an occupation or business: *a shoe-repair service.* **7. a.** Use to or by others: *trying to be of some service.* **b.** A condition in which use is possible; operation: *a telephone out of service.* **c.** Disposal: *I am at your service.* **8.** An act of assistance. **9.** Installation, maintenance, or repairs provided or guaranteed by a dealer or manufacturer. **10.** A facility providing the public with the use of something, such as water or transportation. **11.** Acts of devotion to God; witness. **12.** A religious rite. **13.** The serving of food or the manner in which it is served. **14.** A set of dishes or utensils: *a silver tea service.* **15.** The act, manner, or right of serving, as in tennis, volleyball, and jai alai. —*modifier: a service entrance; a service guarantee.* —*tr.v.* **-iced, -ic·ing. 1.** To maintain and repair: *service a car.* **2.** To provide services to. [Middle English *servise,* from Old French *service,* from Latin *servitium,* servitude, slavery, from *servus,* slave.]

serv·ice·a·ble (sûr′vĭs-ə-bəl) *adj.* **1.** Ready for service; usable. **2.** Wearing well; durable. —See Syns at **practical.** —**serv′ice·a·bil′i·ty** or **serv′ice·a·ble·ness** *n.* —**serv′ice·a·bly** *adv.*

serv·ice·man (sûr′vĭs-măn′, -mən) *n.* **1.** A member of the armed forces. **2.** Also **service man.** A man whose work is the maintenance and repair of equipment.

service station. **1.** A **gas station.** **2.** A place where services can be obtained, as repair of appliances.

service tree. Either of two Old World trees, *Sorbus domestica* or *S. torminalis,* with clusters of white flowers and edible fruit. [From Middle English *serves,* pl. of *serve,* from Old English *syrfe,* from Latin *sorbus.*]

ser·vi·ette (sûr′vē-ĕt′) *n.* A table napkin. [French, from Old French, towel, napkin, from *servir,* to serve.]

ser·vile (sûr′vəl, -vīl′) *adj.* **1.** Submissive; slavish. **2.** Of or suitable to a slave or servant: *servile tasks.* [Middle English, from Latin *servīlis,* from *servus,* slave.] —**ser′vile·ly** *adv.* —**ser′vile·ness** or **ser·vil′i·ty** (sər-vĭl′ĭ-tē) *n.*

serv·ing (sûr′vĭng) *n.* An individual portion or helping of food or drink. —*adj.* Used for serving: *a serving dish.*

ser·vi·tor (sûr′vĭ-tər, -tôr′) *n.* An attendant. [Middle English, from Old French, from Latin *servītor,* from Latin *servīre,* to serve.] —**ser′vi·tor·ship′** *n.*

ser·vi·tude (sûr′vĭ-to͞od′, -tyo͞od′) *n.* **1.** Submission to a master; slavery. **2.** Forced labor imposed as a punishment for crime. —See Syns at **bondage.** [Old French, from Latin *servitūdō,* from *servus,* slave.]

ses·a·me (sĕs′ə-mē) *n.* **1.** A plant, *Sesamum indicum,* of tropical Asia, bearing small, flat seeds used as food and as a source of oil. **2.** The seeds of this plant. [Latin *sēsamum,* from Greek *sēsamon,* of Semitic orig.]

ses·qui·cen·ten·ni·al (sĕs′kwĭ-sĕn-tĕn′ē-əl) *adj.* Pertaining to a period of 150 years. —*n.* A 150th anniversary or its celebration. [Latin *sesqui-,* one and a half + CENTENNIAL.]

ses·qui·pe·da·li·an (sĕs′kwĭ-pə-dā′lē-ĭn, -dāl′yən) *adj.* Also **ses·quip·e·dal** (sĕ-skwĭp′ĭ-dəl). **1.** Long and ponderous; polysyllabic. **2.** Given to using long words. —*n.* A long word. [From Latin *sesquipedalis,* of a foot and a half in length.]

ses·sile (sĕs′ĭl, -īl) *adj.* **1.** *Bot.* Stalkless and attached directly at the base: *sessile leaves.* **2.** *Zool.* Permanently attached or fixed; not free-moving. [Latin *sessilis,* of sitting, low, from *sessus,* past part. of *sedēre,* to sit.]

ses·sion (sĕsh′ən) *n.* **1.** A meeting of a legislative or judicial body. **2.** A series of such meetings. **3.** The part of a year or of a day during which a school holds classes. **4.** A meeting for a purpose; gathering: *a gossip session.* **5.** Any period of time devoted to a specific activity: *a session at the piano.* [Middle English *sessioun,* from Old French *session,* from Latin *sessiō,* from *sessus,* past part. of *sedēre,* to sit.] —**ses′sion·al** *adj.*

ses·terce (sĕs′tûrs′) *n.* A silver or bronze coin of ancient Rome, equivalent to ¼ denarius. [Latin *sestertius.*]

ses·tet (sĕ-stĕt′) *n.* The last six lines of a sonnet. [Italian *sestetto,* from *sesto,* sixth, from Latin *sextus.*]

set¹ (sĕt) *v.* **set, set·ting.** —*tr.v.* **1.** To put in a specified position; to place. **2.** To put into a specified condition: *set him at liberty.* **3.** To put in a stable position; fix. **4. a.** To adjust for proper functioning: *set the alarm.* **b.** To adjust (a saw) by deflecting the teeth. **5.** To adjust according to a standard. **6.** To adjust (an instrument) to a specific point or calibration: *set the dial on "gentle wash."* **7.** To arrange tableware upon (a table) in preparation for a meal. **8.** To apply equipment, as curlers and clips, to (hair) in order to style. **9.** *Printing.* **a.** To arrange (type) into words and sentences preparatory to printing; compose. **b.** To arrange (matter to be printed) into type. **10. a.** To compose (music) to fit a given text. **b.** To write (words) to fit a given melodic line. **11.** To arrange scenery upon (a theater stage). **12.** To prescribe or establish: *set a precedent.* **13.** To prescribe the unfolding of (a scene) in a specific place: *a scene set in Venice.* **14.** To prescribe as a time: *set June 6 as the day of the invasion.* **15.** To detail or assign: *set the boy to cleaning closets.* **16.** To direct. **17. a.** To mount: *set an emerald in a pendant.* **b.** To apply jewels to; to stud. **18.** To cause to sit. **19. a.** To put (a hen) on eggs for the purpose of hatching them. **b.** To put (eggs) beneath a hen or in an incubator. **20.** *Hort.* To produce, as after pollination: *set seed.* —*intr.v.* **1.** To disappear below the horizon: *The sun sets.* **2.** To diminish or decline; wane. **3.** To sit on eggs. **4.** To become fixed; harden or congeal. **5.** To embark upon a journey: *We set out for the beach.* **6.** To become restored to a normal state; knit: *The broken bone set slowly.* **7.** *Hort.* To mature or develop, as after pollination. **8.** *In-*

formal. To sit. —*phrasal verbs.* **set about.** To begin intently: *spread the puzzle out and set about trying to solve it.* **set aside.** **1.** To reserve for a special purpose. **2.** To discard or reject. **3.** To declare invalid; annul or overrule. **set back.** To slow down the progress of; hinder. **set down.** **1.** To put in writing; record. **2.** To assign to a cause; attribute: *set it down to lack of experience.* **set forth.** To present for consideration; express or propose. **set in.** To begin to happen or be apparent. **set off.** **1.** To give rise to; cause to occur: *set off a chemical reaction.* **2.** To cause to explode. **3.** To indicate as being different; distinguish. **4.** To direct attention to by contrast; accentuate. **set on (or upon).** To attack or direct to attack: *setting his dogs upon us.* **set out.** **1.** To begin an earnest attempt or search; undertake: *set out to learn why.* **2.** To plant. **set to.** **1.** To begin working energetically; start in. **2.** To begin fighting. **set up.** **1.** To arrange or assemble. **2.** To found; establish. **3.** To place in a position of authority. **4.** To provide with the necessary means or money. **5.** To prepare to receive or suffer something. —*adj.* **1.** Fixed or established by agreement: *a set time for the launching.* **2.** Established by convention. **3.** Established deliberately; formal; purposeful. **4.** Fixed and rigid. **5. a.** Assembled or formed. **b.** Ready: *get set.* —*n.* **1.** The process of setting, esp. the gradual hardening or stiffening of a substance, as by cooling. **2.** The deflection of the teeth of a saw. **3.** The manner in which something is positioned: *the set of her cap.* **4.** A descent below the horizon. **5.** A direction or course, as of wind or water. [Middle English *setten,* to cause to sit, to place, from Old English *settan.*]

Usage: **set, sit.** The verb *set* has more transitive senses than intransitive ones, whereas *sit* has more intransitive senses than transitive ones. The most common errors involving the pair are uses of *set* for *sit.* In the following, the correct choice is *sit* (not *set*): *Sit with us. The bird sat on a low branch. The town sits in a valley. Her duties and a hostile environment sat heavily on her. Neither the dinner nor the speeches that followed sat well with me.* But either verb is possible in these examples: *The hen sets (or sits) on eggs. The coat sets (or sits) well.*

set² (sĕt) *n.* **1.** A group of persons or things connected by or collected for their similar appearance, interest, importance, etc.: *a chess set; a tool set.* **2.** A social or interest group: *the jet set.* **3.** A group of circumstances, situations, or events treated as a whole: *a set of experiences.* **4. a.** A number of couples required for participation in a square dance. **b.** The movements constituting a square dance. **5. a.** The scenery constructed for a theatrical performance. **b.** The entire enclosure in which a motion picture is being filmed. **6.** The receiving apparatus assembled to operate a radio or television. **7.** *Math.* Any collection of distinct elements: *a set of positive integers.* **8.** A group of games, as in tennis, constituting one division or unit of a match. —See Syns at **circle.** —*modifier: a theatrical set designer.* [Middle English *sette,* from Old French, from Latin *secta,* sect.]

se·ta (sē′tə) *n.,* pl. **se·tae** (sē′tē′). *Biol.* A stiff hair, bristle, or bristlelike process. [Latin *sēta,* bristle.] —**se′tal** *adj.*

set·back (sĕt′băk′) *n.* **1.** An unexpected check in progress; a reverse. **2.** A steplike recession, as in a wall.

set·off (sĕt′ôf′, -ŏf′) *n.* **1.** Anything that sets off something else by contrast. **2.** Anything that offsets or compensates. **3.** A counterclaim. **4.** A ledge; offset.

set·screw (sĕt′skro͞o′) *n.* **1.** A screw used to hold two parts in a position relative to each other without motion. **2.** A screw used to regulate the tension of a spring.

set·tee (sĕ-tē′) *n.* **1.** A long wooden bench with a high back. **2.** A small sofa. [Perh. var. of SETTLE (bench).]

set·ter (sĕt′ər) *n.* **1.** Someone or something that sets. **2.** Any of several breeds of long-haired dogs, orig. trained to indicate game by crouching in a set position.

set theory. The study of the mathematical properties of sets.

set·ting (sĕt′ĭng) *n.* **1. a.** A surrounding area; environment. **b.** The place where something occurs in fact or fiction. **2.** A framework or border in which a jewel is fixed. **3.** A structure on the stage of a theater, designed to represent the place where the action occurs. **4.** Music composed or arranged for a particular text.

set·tle (sĕt′l) *v.* **-tled, -tling.** —*tr.v.* **1.** To put into order;

arrange or fix definitely as desired. **2.** To put firmly in a desired position or place; establish. **3.** To establish as a resident or residents: *settled her family in Iowa.* **4.** To establish residence in: *Pioneers settled the West.* **5.** To establish in a residence, business, profession, etc. **6.** To restore calmness or comfort to. **7. a.** To cause to come to rest, sink, or become compact. **b.** To cause (a liquid) to become clear. **8.** To subdue or make orderly. **9.** To establish on a permanent basis; stabilize; assure. **10. a.** To make compensation for (a claim). **b.** To pay (a debt). **11.** To conclude by coming to an agreement or decision. **12.** To decide (a law suit) by mutual agreement of the involved parties without court action. **13.** To confer or assign by legal means: *He settled the property on his heirs.* —*intr.v.* **1.** To stop moving and come to rest in one place. **2.** To descend or subside gradually. **3.** To sink and become more compact: *The dust settled.* **4. a.** To become clear: *The water settled.* **b.** To be separated from a solution or mixture as a sediment. **5.** To establish one's residence. **6.** To reach a decision; determine. **7.** To compensate for a claim or pay a debt. —See Syns at **decide.** —*phrasal verbs.* **settle down.** **1.** To begin living a more orderly life: *He settled down as a farmer.* **2.** To begin acting in a less nervous, restless, or disorderly way: *settled down when class began.* **settle for.** To accept even though not satisfied. —*n.* A long wooden bench with a high back. [Middle English *setlen,* to place in order, to seat, from Old English *setlan,* from *setl,* seat.]
set·tle·ment (sĕt′l-mənt) *n.* **1.** The act or process of settling. **2. a.** Establishment, as of a person in a business or of people in a new region. **b.** A newly colonized region. **3.** A small community. **4.** An adjustment or other understanding reached. **5. a.** The transfer of property to provide for the future needs of a person. **b.** Property thus transferred. **6.** Also **settlement house.** A welfare center providing community services in an underprivileged area.
set·tler (sĕt′lər, sĕt′l-ər) *n.* **1.** Someone or something that settles. **2.** A person who settles in a new region.
set·tlings (sĕt′lĭngz, sĕt′l-ĭngz) *pl.n.* Sediment; dregs.
set-to (sĕt′tōō′) *n., pl.* **-tos.** A brief but usu. heated contest.
set-up (sĕt′ŭp′) *n.* **1.** *Informal.* The way in which something is arranged or planned. **2.** Often **setups.** *Informal.* The collection of ingredients and mixers necessary for serving a variety of alcoholic drinks. **3.** *Slang.* A contest prearranged to result in an easy or faked victory. **b.** Any endeavor that is intentionally made easy.
sev·en (sĕv′ən) *n.* The cardinal number written 7 or in Roman numerals VII. [Middle English, from Old English *seofon.*] —**sev′en** *adj. & pron.*
seven deadly sins. The sins of pride, lust, envy, anger, covetousness, gluttony, and sloth. Also called **cardinal sins.**
sev·en·fold (sĕv′ən-fōld′) *adj.* **1.** Consisting of seven parts or members. **2.** Having seven times as many or as much. —**sev′en·fold′** *adv.*
seven seas. Also **Seven Seas.** All the oceans of the world.
sev·en·teen (sĕv′ən-tēn′) *n.* The cardinal number written 17 or in Roman numerals XVII. [Middle English *seventene,* from Old English *seofontīne.*] —**sev′en·teen′** *adj. & pron.*
sev·en·teenth (sĕv′ən-tēnth′) *n.* **1.** The ordinal number 17 in a series. Also written 17th. **2.** One of 17 equal parts. —**sev′en·teenth′** *adj. & adv.*
sev·en·teen-year locust (sĕv′ən-tēn-yîr′). A cicada, *Magicicada septendecim,* of the eastern United States, with a nymphal stage in which the northern species remain underground for 17 years and the southern species for 13 years.
sev·enth (sĕv′ənth) *n.* **1.** The ordinal number seven in a series. Also written 7th. **2.** One of seven equal parts. **3.** *Mus.* An interval encompassing seven diatonic degrees. —**sev′enth** *adj. & adv.*
Sev·enth-Day Adventist (sĕv′ənth-dā′). A member of a sect of Adventism distinguished chiefly for its observance of the Sabbath on Saturday.
seventh heaven. A state of great joy and satisfaction.
sev·en·ti·eth (sĕv′ən-tē-ĭth) *n.* **1.** The ordinal number 70 in a series. Also written 70th. **2.** One of 70 equal parts. —**sev′en·ti·eth** *adj. & adv.*
sev·en·ty (sĕv′ən-tē) *n.* The cardinal number written 70 or

in Roman numerals LXX. —**sev′en·ty** *adj. & pron.*
sev·er (sĕv′ər) *tr.v.* **1.** To divide or separate into parts. **2.** To cut or break from a whole: *sever a limb from a tree.* **3.** To break off; dissolve: *sever diplomatic ties.* —*intr.v.* **1.** To become cut or broken apart. **2.** To divide; separate or go apart. [Middle English *severen,* from Norman French *severer,* from Latin *sēparāre,* to separate.]
sev·er·al (sĕv′ər-əl, sĕv′rəl) *adj.* **1.** Being of a number more than two or three, but not many: *several miles away.* **2.** Different; various: *They parted and went their several ways.* —*n.* Several persons or things; a few. [Middle English *severall,* separate, distinct, from Norman French *several,* from Medieval Latin *sēparālis,* from Latin *sēpār,* separate, from *sēparāre,* to separate.] —**sev′er·al·ly** *adv.*
sev·er·ance (sĕv′ər-əns) *n.* **1. a.** The act or process of severing. **b.** The condition of being severed. **2.** Separation; partition. —*modifier: severance pay.*
se·vere (sə-vîr′) *adj.* **-ver·er, -ver·est.** **1.** Unsparing and harsh in treating others; stern; strict. **2.** Corresponding strictly to established rule; maintained rigidly: *severe accuracy.* **3.** Austere or dour; forbidding: *a severe voice.* **4.** Extremely plain: *the severe garb of a Puritan.* **5.** Extreme; intense: *a severe storm.* **6.** Trying; rigorous: *a severe task.* —See Syns at **burdensome.** [Old French, from Latin *sevērus.*] —**se·vere′ly** *adv.* —**se·vere′ness** *n.*
se·ver·i·ty (sə-vĕr′ĭ-tē) *n., pl.* **-ties.** The quality of being severe.
sew (sō) *v.* **sewed, sewn** (sōn) or **sewed, sew·ing.** —*tr.v.* **1.** To make, repair, or fasten with a needle and thread: *sew a dress; sew on a button.* **2.** To close, fasten, or attach with stitches: *sew up a wound.* —*intr.v.* To work with a needle and thread or with a sewing machine. —*phrasal verb.* **sew up.** *Informal.* To complete with success. [Middle English *sewen,* from Old English *seowian.*]
sew·age (sōō′ĭj) *n.* Liquid and solid waste carried off with ground water in sewers or drains. [SEW(ER) + -AGE.]
sew·er¹ (sōō′ər) *n.* An artificial, usu. underground conduit for carrying off sewage or rainwater. —*modifier: sewer pipes.* [Middle English *sewer,* from Norman French *severe* : Latin *ex-,* out of + *aqua,* water.]
sew·er² (sō′ər) *n.* Someone or something that sews.
sew·er·age (sōō′ər-ĭj) *n.* **1.** A system of sewers. **2.** The removal of waste materials by a sewer system. **3.** Sewage.
sew·ing (sō′ĭng) *n.* The article upon which a person is working with needle and thread; needlework.
sewn (sōn) *v.* A past participle of **sew.** [Middle English *sowen.*]
sex (sĕks) *n.* **1.** One of the two divisions, male and female, into which many living things are grouped according to their functions in the process of reproduction. **2.** The combination of characteristics typical of each of these groups. **3.** Activities, feelings, etc., associated with the reproductive functions. **4.** Sexual intercourse. —*modifier: the sex organs.* [Middle English, from Old French *sexe,* from Latin *sexus.*]
sex·a·ge·nar·i·an (sĕk′sə-jə-nâr′ē-ən) *n.* A person between sixty and seventy years old. [From Latin *sexāgēnārius,* from *sexāgēnī,* sixty each, from *sēxāgintā,* sixty.] —**sex′a·ge·nar′i·an** *adj.*
sex chromosome. Either of a pair of chromosomes, usu. designated X or Y, in the germ cells of man, most animals, and some plants, that combine to determine the sex of an individual, XX resulting in a female and XY in a male.
sex hormone. Any of various animal hormones affecting the growth or function of the reproductive organs.
sex·ism (sĕk′sĭz′əm) *n.* **1.** Prejudice against the female sex. **2.** Any arbitrary stereotyping of males and females on the basis of their gender. —**sex′ist** *adj. & n.*
sex·less (sĕks′lĭs) *adj.* **1.** Asexual; neuter. **2.** Arousing or exhibiting no sexual interest or desire.
sex-linked (sĕks′lĭngkt′) *adj.* **1.** Carried by a sex chromosome, esp. an X chromosome: *a sex-linked gene.* **2.** Sexually determined: *a sex-linked trait.* —**sex linkage** *n.*
sex·tant (sĕk′stənt) *n.* A navigational instrument used for measuring the altitudes of celestial bodies. [From Latin *sextāns,* a sixth part (from its having an arc graduated in sixths of a circle), from *sextus,* sixth.]
sex·tet (sĕk-stĕt′) *n.* **1. a.** A group composed of six vocalists or musicians. **b.** A musical composition written for six

ă pat   ā pay   â care   ä father   ĕ pet   ē be   hw which
ŏŏ took   ōō boot   ou out   th thin   th this   ŭ cut
ĭ pit   ī tie   î pier   ŏ pot   ō toe   ô paw, for   oi noise
û urge   zh vision   ə about, item, edible, gallop, circus

performers. **2.** Any group of six persons or things. [From SESTET, influenced by Latin *sex*, six.]

sex·til·lion (sĕk-stĭl′yən) *n.* **1.** The cardinal number represented by 1 followed by 21 zeros, usu. written 10²¹. **2.** *Brit.* The cardinal number represented by 1 followed by 36 zeros, usu. written 10³⁶. [French : *sex-*, six + *(m)illion*, million.] **—sex·til′lion** *adj.* **—sex·til′lionth** *adj. & adv.*

sex·ton (sĕk′stən) *n.* A maintenance man in a church, responsible for the care and upkeep of church property. [Middle English, from Norman French *segerstaine*, from Medieval Latin *sacristānus*, sacristan.]

sex·tu·ple (sĕk-stōō′pəl, -styōō′-, -stŭp′əl, sĕk′stōō-pəl) *v.* **-pled, -pling.** *—tr.v.* To multiply by six. *—intr.v.* To become multiplied by six. *—adj.* **1.** Containing or consisting of six parts; sixfold. **2.** Larger or greater by sixfold. *—n.* A number six times larger than another. [Prob. Latin *sex-*, six + (QUIN)TUPLE.] **—sex′tu·ply** *adv.*

sex·tu·plet (sĕk-stŭp′lĭt, -stōō′plĭt, -styōō′-, sĕk′stōō-plĭt) *n.* **1.** One of six offspring delivered at one birth. **2. sextuplets.** The six offspring of one birth. **3.** A group of six similar persons or things; sextet. [SEXTU(PLE) + (TRI)PLET.]

sex·u·al (sĕk′shōō-əl) *adj.* **1.** Of or involving the union of male and female sex cells: *sexual reproduction.* **2.** Of, affecting, or typical of sex, the sexes, or the sex organs and their functions: *sexual development.* [Late Latin *sexuālis*, from Latin *sexus*, sex.] **—sex′u·al·ly** *adv.*

sexual intercourse. Coitus, esp. between human beings.

sex·u·al·i·ty (sĕk′shōō-ăl′ĭ-tē) *n.* **1.** The condition of being characterized by sex. **2.** Concern with sex. **3.** The quality of possessing a sexual character or potency.

sex·y (sĕk′sē) *adj.* **-i·er, -i·est.** *Informal.* Arousing or intending to arouse sexual desire or interest.

sfer·ics (sfîr′ĭks, sfĕr′-) *n.* (used with a sing. verb). Also **spher·ics.** Atmospherics. [Short for ATMOSPHERICS.]

sfor·zan·do (sfôrt-sän′dō). Also **for·zan·do** (fôrt-). *Mus.* *—adj.* Suddenly and strongly accented. *—n., pl.* **-dos** or **-di** (-dē). A sforzando tone or chord. [Italian, from *sforzare*, to use force.] **—sfor·zan′do** *adv.*

sh (sh) *interj.* Be quiet! Hush!

Shab·bat (shä-bät′, shä′bəs) *n., pl.* **-ba·tim** (-bä′tĭm, -bô′sĭm). The Jewish Sabbath. [Hebrew *shabbāth*, sabbath.]

shab·by (shăb′ē) *adj.* **-bi·er, -bi·est. 1.** Threadbare; worn-out: *shabby clothes.* **2.** Wearing worn garments. **3.** Dilapidated; deteriorated: *shabby houses.* **4.** Despicable; paltry; mean. [From obs. *shab*, a scab, from Middle English *schabbe*, from Old English *sceabb*.] **—shab′bi·ly** *adv.* **—shab′bi·ness** *n.*

Sha·bu·oth (shə-vōō′ōt′, -ōth′, -əs) *n.* Var. of **Shavuot.**

shack (shăk) *n.* A small, crudely built cabin; shanty. [From Mexican Spanish *jacal*, from Aztec *xacalli*, thatched cabin.]

shack·le (shăk′əl) *n.* **1.** A metal fastening, usu. one of a pair, for encircling and confining the ankle or wrist of a prisoner or captive; fetter; manacle. **2.** A hobble for an animal. **3.** Any of several devices used to fasten or couple. **4.** Often **shackles.** Anything that confines or restrains. *—tr.v.* **-led, -ling. 1.** To put shackles on; to fetter. **2.** To fasten or connect with a shackle. **3.** To restrict; confine. [Middle English *schackle*, from Old English *sceacel*, fetter.] **—shack′ler** *n.*

shad (shăd) *n., pl.* **shad** or **shads.** Any of several food fishes of the genus *Alosa*, related to the herrings but atypical in swimming up streams from marine waters to spawn. [Middle English, from Old English *sceadd*.]

shad·ber·ry (shăd′bĕr′ē) *n.* The fruit of the shadbush.

shad·bush (shăd′bōōsh′) *n.* Any of various North American shrubs or trees of the genus *Amelanchier*, with white flowers and edible blue-black or purplish fruit.

shade (shād) *n.* **1.** Light diminished in intensity as a result of the interception of the rays; partial darkness. **2.** An area or space of such partial darkness. **3.** Cover or shelter from the sun. **4.** Any of various devices used to reduce or screen light or heat: *window shades.* **5. shades.** *Slang.* Sunglasses. **6.** Relative obscurity. **7. shades.** Dark shadows gathering at dusk. **8.** The degree to which a color is mixed with black or is decreasingly illuminated. **9.** A slight difference or variation; nuance: *shades of meaning.* **10.** A small amount; trace; jot. **11.** A disembodied spirit; ghost. **12. shades.** *Informal.* Reminders; echoes: *shades of 1776.*

—modifier: a shade tree. *—tr.v.* **shad·ed, shad·ing. 1.** To screen from light or heat. **2.** To obscure or darken. **3.** To cause shade in or on. **4.** To represent or produce degrees of darkness in: *shade a drawing.* **5.** To change or vary by slight degrees: *shade the meaning.* **6.** *Informal.* To make a slight reduction in: *shade prices.* [Middle English *schade*, from Old English *sceadu*.]

shad·ing (shā′dĭng) *n.* Lines or other marks used to fill in outlines to represent gradations of darkness.

shad·ow (shăd′ō) *n.* **1.** An area that is not, or is only partially, illuminated because the light is blocked by an opaque object. **2.** The rough image cast by an object blocking rays of light. **3.** An imperfect imitation or copy of something else. **4. shadows.** The darkness following sunset. **5.** Gloom or unhappiness or an influence that causes such feeling. **6.** A shaded area in a picture or photograph. **7.** A mirrored image or reflection. **8.** A phantom; ghost. **9.** A detective; spy. **10.** A faint indication; premonition. **11.** A vestige; remnant. **12.** An insignificant portion or amount; slight trace. *—tr.v.* **1.** To cast a shadow upon; to shade. **2.** To make gloomy or dark; to cloud. **3.** To represent vaguely, mysteriously, or prophetically. **4.** To darken in a painting or drawing; shade in. **5.** To follow after, esp. in secret; to trail. [Middle English *schadow*, from Old English *sceaduwe*, from *sceadu*, shade.]

shad·ow·box (shăd′ō-bŏks′) *intr.v.* To spar with an imaginary opponent, as for exercise.

shad·ow·y (shăd′ō-ē) *adj.* **-i·er, -i·est. 1.** Of or resembling a shadow. **2.** Full of shadows; shady. **3.** Vague; indistinct.

shad·y (shā′dē) *adj.* **-i·er, -i·est. 1.** Full of shade; shaded. **2.** Casting shade. **3.** Quiet, dark, or concealed; hidden. **4.** Of dubious character or honesty; questionable: *a shady deal.* **—shad′i·ly** *adv.* **—shad′i·ness** *n.*

shaft¹ (shăft) *n.* **1.** The long, narrow stem or body of a spear or arrow. **2.** A spear or arrow. **3.** Something suggestive of a spear in appearance or effect. **4.** A ray or beam of light. **5.** The handle of any of various tools or implements. **6.** The rib of a feather. **7.** A column or obelisk or the section of a column between the capital and base. **8.** One of two parallel poles between which an animal is harnessed. **9.** A long, cylindrical bar, esp. one that rotates and transmits power: *a drive shaft.* [Middle English, from Old English *sceaft*.]

shaft² (shăft) *n.* **1.** A long, narrow passage sunk into the earth; tunnel. **2.** A vertical passage housing an elevator. **3.** A duct or conduit for the passage of air. [Prob. from Middle Low German *schacht*.]

shag (shăg) *n.* **1.** A tangle or mass, esp. of matted hair. **2.** Cloth with a coarse, long nap. **3.** Coarse shredded tobacco. *—modifier: a shag rug.* *—tr.v.* **shagged, shag·ging. 1.** To make shaggy. **2.** *Baseball.* To catch (fly balls) in practice. [Ult. from Old English *sceacga*.]

shag·bark (shăg′bärk′) *n.* A North American hickory tree, *Carya ovata*, that has shaggy bark and edible nuts.

shagbark

shag·gy (shăg′ē) *adj.* **-gi·er, -gi·est. 1.** Having, covered with, or resembling long, rough hair or wool. **2.** Bushy and matted: *shaggy hair.* **3.** Poorly groomed; unkempt.

sha·green (shə-grēn′) *n.* **1.** The rough hide of a shark or ray, used as an abrasive and as leather. **2.** Any grainy-surfaced leather. [French *chagrin*, from Turkish *sağri*, leather.]

shah (shä) *n.* The title of the former hereditary monarchs of Iran. [Persian *shāh*.]

---

shake (shāk) v. **shook** (shŏŏk), **shak·en** (shā'kən), **shak·ing.** —tr.v. **1.** To cause to move to and fro with short jerky movements. **2.** To cause to quiver or tremble. **3.** To cause to stagger or waver. **4.** To remove or dislodge by jerky movements: *shake the dust out.* **5.** To disturb or agitate; unnerve: *shake up the bureaucracy.* **6.** To brandish or wave. **7.** To clasp (hands or another's hand) in greeting or leave-taking or as a sign of agreement. —intr.v. **1.** To move to and fro in short jerky movements. **2.** To tremble, as from cold or in anger. **3.** To totter or waver. **4.** To shake hands. —*phrasal verbs.* **shake down.** *Informal.* **1.** To extort money from. **2.** To make a thorough search of. **shake off.** To free oneself from; get rid of. **shake up.** *Informal.* To rearrange drastically. —n. **1.** An act of shaking. **2.** A trembling or quivering movement. **3.** *Informal.* An earthquake. **4.** A fissure in rock. **5.** A crack in timber caused by wind or frost. **6.** *Slang.* A moment or instant: *I'll do it in a shake.* **7.** A beverage in which the ingredients are mixed by shaking: *a milk shake.* **8. the shakes.** *Informal.* Uncontrollable trembling, as in a sick person. **9.** *Slang.* Bargain; deal: *getting a fair shake.* —*idioms.* **no great shakes.** *Slang.* Ordinary; mediocre. **shake a leg.** *Slang.* To hurry. [Middle English *schaken,* from Old English *sceacan.*]
Syns: **shake, quake, quaver, quiver, shiver, shudder, tremble, tremor** v. *Core meaning:* To move to and fro in short, jerky movements (*was shaking in fear; ground that shook during the earthquake*).

shake·down (shāk'doun') n. **1.** *Informal.* An extortion of money, as by blackmail. **2.** *Informal.* A thorough search of a place or person. **3.** A period of appraisal followed by adjustments to improve efficiency or functioning. **4.** A makeshift bed; pallet. —adj. Designed to test the performance of a ship or airplane: *a shakedown cruise.*

shak·er (shā'kər) n. **1.** Someone or something that shakes. **2.** A container used for shaking something out: *a salt shaker.* **3.** A container used to mix or blend by shaking.

Shake·spear·e·an or **Shake·spear·i·an** (shāk-spîr'ē-ən) adj. Of or like Shakespeare, his works, or his style.

Shakespearean sonnet. The sonnet form perfected by Shakespeare, composed of three quatrains and a terminal couplet with the rhyme pattern *abab cdcd efef gg.*

shake·up (shāk'ŭp') n. A thorough reorganization.

shak·o (shāk'ō, shā'kō, shā'-) n., pl. **-os** or **-oes.** A stiff, cylindrical military dress hat with a short visor and a plume. [French *schako,* from Hungarian *csákó,* from *csákó* (*süveg*), pointed (cap), from *csák,* peak, from German *Zacken,* point, from Middle High German *zacke.*]

shak·y (shā'kē) adj. **-i·er, -i·est. 1.** Trembling or quivering: *a shaky voice.* **2.** Unsteady or unsound; weak: *a shaky table.* —**shak'i·ly** adv. —**shak'i·ness** n.

shale (shāl) n. Any of various easily split sedimentary rocks consisting of layers of fine particles pressed together. [Prob. from Middle English, a dish, shell, from Old English *scealu.*]

shall (shăl) v. past **should** (shŏŏd). Used as an auxiliary followed by a simple infinitive or with the infinitive understood. It can indicate: **1.** In the first person singular or plural, simple futurity: *I shall be twenty-eight tomorrow.* **2.** In the second and third persons: **a.** Determination or promise: *I shall not give in.* **b.** Inevitability: *We shall have to repay those debts. We shall find out in the end.* **c.** Command or compulsion: *Thou shall not kill.* [Middle English *schal,* from Old English *sceal.*]
Usage: **shall, will.** The formal uses of *shall* and *will* are given in their respective definitions. However, distinctions between *shall* and *will* are seldom made today. Their interchangeability is standard, except in the legal senses used in statutes—a sense meaning "must" (*a penalty that shall not exceed thirty days*).

shal·lot (shə-lŏt', shăl'ət) n. **1.** A plant, *Allium ascalonicum,* closely related to the onion, cultivated for its edible bulb. **2.** The mildly flavored bulb. [Obs. French *eschalotte,* from Old French *eschaloigne,* from Latin *Ascalōnia* (*caepa*), (onion) of Ascalon, a city in ancient Palestine.]

shal·low (shăl'ō) adj. **-er, -est. 1.** Measuring little from bottom to top or surface; not deep. **2.** Lacking depth, as in intellect or significance: *a shallow mind.* —n. A shallow part of a body of water; a shoal. —tr.v. To make shallow. —intr.v. To become shallow. [Middle English *schalowe.*]

—**shal'low·ly** adv. —**shal'low·ness** n.

sha·lom (shä-lōm', shə-) *interj. Hebrew.* Peace. Used as a greeting or farewell. [Hebrew *shālōm,* peace.]

shalt (shălt). *Archaic.* A form of **shall,** used with *thou.*

sham (shăm) n. **1.** Something false or empty purporting to be genuine; a spurious imitation. **2.** Empty pretense. **3.** A person who assumes a false character; a pretender or impostor. **4.** A decorative cover made to simulate an article of household linen and used over or in place of it: *a pillow sham.* —adj. Not genuine; fake: *sham modesty.* —v. **shammed, sham·ming.** —tr.v. To put on the false appearance of; feign. —intr.v. To dissemble. [Perh. var. of SHAME.] —**sham'mer** n.

sha·man (shä'mən, shā'-) n. **1.** A priest of shamanism. **2.** A medicine man among certain native North Americans. [German *Schamane,* from Russian *shaman.*]

sha·man·ism (shä'mə-nĭz'əm, shā'-) n. **1.** The religious practices of certain native peoples of northern Asia who believe that good and evil spirits can be summoned through inspired priests acting as mediums. **2.** Any similar form of primitive spiritualism. —**sha'man·ist** n. —**sha'man·is'tic** adj.

sham·ble (shăm'bəl) intr.v. **-bled, -bling.** To walk in an awkward, lazy, or unsteady manner, shuffling the feet. —n. A shambling walk; shuffling gait. [From earlier *shamble,* ungainly.]

sham·bles (shăm'bəlz) n. (used with a sing. verb). **1.** A scene or condition of complete disorder or destruction: *The brawlers left the bar in a shambles.* **2.** A place or scene of bloodshed or carnage. [From pl. of earlier *shamble,* table for display or sale of meat, from Middle English *shamel,* from Old English *sceamel,* table, from Latin *scamellum,* dim. of *scamnum,* bench.]

shame (shām) n. **1.** A painful emotion caused by a strong sense of guilt, embarrassment, unworthiness, or disgrace. **2.** Capacity for such a feeling. **3.** A person or thing that brings dishonor, disgrace, or condemnation. **4.** Disgrace; ignominy. **5.** A great disappointment. —See Syns at **disgrace.** —tr.v. **shamed, sham·ing. 1.** To cause to feel shame. **2.** To bring dishonor or disgrace upon. **3.** To force by making ashamed: *shamed into an apology.* [Middle English *schame,* from Old English *sceamu.*]

shame·faced (shām'fāst') adj. **1.** Feeling or showing shame; ashamed: *a shamefaced explanation.* **2.** Bashful. [Middle English *shamefast,* from Old English *sceamfæst.*] —**shame'fac'ed·ly** (-fā'sĭd-lē) adv. —**shame'fac'ed·ness** n.

shame·ful (shām'fəl) adj. Bringing or deserving shame; disgraceful. —**shame'ful·ly** adv. —**shame'ful·ness** n.

shame·less (shām'lĭs) adj. Being or done without awareness of wrongdoing; impudent; brazen: *a shameless liar.* —**shame'less·ly** adv. —**shame'less·ness** n.

sham·my (shăm'ē) n. Var. of **chamois** (soft leather).

sham·poo (shăm-pōō') n., pl. **-poos. 1.** A preparation of soap or detergent used to wash the hair and scalp. **2.** Any of various cleaning agents for rugs or upholstery. **3.** The act or process of washing or cleaning with shampoo. —tr.v. **-pooed, -poo·ing.** To wash or clean with shampoo. [Hindi *chāmpo,* from *chāmpnā,* massage, mark, from *chāp-nā,* stamp, from *chap-nā,* to be stamped.]

sham·rock (shăm'rŏk') n. Any of several plants, such as a clover or wood sorrel, that have compound leaves with three small leaflets, the national emblem of Ireland. [Irish

shallot   **shamrock**

seamrog, dim. of *seamar,* clover, from Old Irish *semar.*]

sha·mus (shä′məs, shā′-) *n. Slang.* A policeman or private detective. [Perh. from Yiddish *shames,* sexton.]

shang·hai (shăng-hī′) *tr.v.* **1.** To kidnap (a man) for service aboard a ship, esp. after drugging him. **2.** To compel (someone) to do something, esp. by fraud or force. [After *Shanghai,* China, from the former practice of kidnapping sailors to serve on ships going to China.]

shank (shăngk) *n.* **1.** The part of the human leg between the knee and ankle or the corresponding part in other vertebrates. **2.** The whole leg of a human being. **3.** A cut of meat from the leg of an animal. **4.** The long, narrow part of a nail, spoon, or other object. **5.** A stem, stalk, or similar part. **6. a.** The narrow part of a shoe's sole under the instep. **b.** A piece of metal or other material used to reinforce or shape this part. **7. a.** The part of a drill or other tool that connects the functioning end to the handle. **b.** A **tang. 8. a.** The latter or remaining part of anything, esp. of a period of time. **b.** The early or best part of a period of time. [Middle English *shanke,* from Old English *sceanca.*]

shan't or **sha'nt** (shănt, shänt). Contraction of *shall not.*

shan·tey (shăn′tē, chăn′-) *n.* Var. of **chantey.**

shan·tung (shăn-tŭng′) *n.* A heavy silk fabric with a rough, nubby surface. [After *Shantung,* China.]

shan·ty[1] (shăn′tē) *n.,* pl. **-ties.** A roughly built cabin; shack. [Perh. from Irish *sean tig,* "old house."]

shan·ty[2] (shăn′tē, chăn′-) *n.* Var. of **chantey.**

shan·ty·town (shăn′tē-toun′) *n.* A town or section of a town consisting of ramshackle huts or shanties.

shape (shāp) *n.* **1.** Something distinguished from its surroundings by its outline; a form. **2.** The appearance of an object as the eye compares its dimensions and outlines: *the oval shape of an egg.* **3. a.** A definite form. **b.** A desirable form: *a fabric that holds its shape.* **4.** The contours of a person's body; the figure. **5.** Any form or condition in which something may exist or appear: *a god in the shape of a swan.* **6.** Proper condition for action, effectiveness, or use: *an athlete out of shape.* **7.** A device for giving or determining form. *—tr.v.* **shaped, shap·ing. 1.** To give a particular form to. **2.** To modify; adapt. **3.** To plan and supervise. **4.** To make (something). *—See Syns at* **make.** *—phrasal verb.* **shape up.** *Informal.* **1.** To develop; turn out. **2.** To improve so as to meet a standard. [Middle English, from Old English *gesceap.*] *—***shap′er** *n.*

shape·less (shāp′lĭs) *adj.* **1.** Having no distinct shape. **2.** Not shapely. *—***shape′less·ly** *adv.* *—***shape′less·ness** *n.*

shape·ly (shāp′lē) *adj.* **-li·er, -li·est.** Having a pleasing shape; well-proportioned. *—***shape′li·ness** *n.*

shape·up (shāp′ŭp′) *n.* An assembled group of longshoremen from which the day's work crew is chosen.

shard (shärd) *n.* Also **sherd** (shûrd). **1.** A piece of broken pottery; a potsherd. **2.** A fragment of a brittle substance. [Middle English *sherd,* from Old English *sceard.*]

share[1] (shâr) *n.* **1.** A part or portion belonging to, distributed to, contributed by, or owed by a person or group. **2.** A fair or full portion: *doing one's share.* **3.** Any of the equal parts into which the capital stock of a corporation or company is divided. *—v.* **shared, shar·ing.** *—tr.v.* **1.** To divide and parcel out in shares; apportion. **2.** To participate in, use, or experience in common: *sharing the responsibility; share a room.* *—intr.v.* To have or take a part; participate. [Middle English, from Old English *scearu.*] *—***shar′er** *n.*

share[2] (shâr) *n.* A plowshare. [Middle English *shaar,* from Old English *scēar.*]

share·crop·per (shâr′krŏp′ər) *n.* A tenant farmer who gives a share of his crop to the landlord as rent.

share·hold·er (shâr′hōl′dər) *n.* A person who owns or holds a share or shares of stock; a stockholder.

shark (shärk) *n.* **1.** Any of numerous chiefly saltwater fishes of the order Squaliformes (or Selachii), that are often large and voracious and have a cartilaginous skeleton and tough skin covered with small, toothlike scales. **2.** A ruthless, greedy, or dishonest person. **3.** *Slang.* An expert. [Orig. unknown.]

shark·skin (shärk′skĭn) *n.* **1.** A shark's skin. **2.** Leather made from a shark's skin. **3.** A rayon and acetate fabric with a smooth, somewhat shiny surface.

sharp (shärp) *adj.* **-er, -est. 1.** Having a thin edge or a fine point for cutting or piercing: *a sharp knife.* **2.** Pointed: *a*

sharp nose. **3.** Abrupt or acute; sudden: *a sharp drop.* **4.** Clear; distinct. **5.** Shrewd; astute. **6.** Artful; underhand: *sharp practices.* **7.** Vigilant; alert. **8.** Brisk; ardent; vigorous. **9.** Harsh; biting; acrimonious. **10.** Fierce or impetuous; violent. **11.** Intense; severe: *a sharp pain.* **12.** Sudden and shrill. **13.** Composed of hard, angular particles: *sharp sand.* **14.** *Mus.* **a.** Raised in pitch by a semitone from the corresponding natural tone or key: *a C sharp.* **b.** Above the proper pitch: *a sharp note.* **15.** *Phonet.* Voiceless: *a sharp consonant.* **16.** *Slang.* Attractive or stylish. *—adv.* **1.** In a sharp manner. **2.** Punctually; exactly: *at three o'clock sharp.* **3.** *Mus.* Above the true or proper pitch. *—n.* **1.** *Mus.* **a.** A note or tone that is a semitone higher than a corresponding natural note or tone. **b.** A sign (#) indicating this. **2.** *Informal.* A shrewd cheater; a sharper. [Middle English, from Old English *scearp.*] *—***sharp′ly** *adv.* *—***sharp′ness** *n.*

Syns: 1. sharp, keen *adj. Core meaning:* Having a fine, honed edge (*a sharp knife*). **2. sharp, acute, keen, perceptive, sensitive** *adj. Core meaning:* Having or showing great perception (*a sharp observer of the political scene*). See also Syns at **clever.**

sharp·en (shär′pən) *tr.v.* To make sharp or sharper. *—intr.v.* To grow sharp or sharper. *—***sharp′en·er** *n.*

sharp·er (shär′pər) *n.* A person who deals dishonestly with others, esp. a gambler who cheats.

sharp·ie (shär′pē) *n.* **1.** A long, narrow, flat-bottomed fishing boat that has one or two masts, each rigged with a triangular sail. **2.** *Informal.* An alert or quick-witted person. [From SHARP.]

sharp·shoot·er (shärp′shoo′tər) *n.* An expert marksman.

Shas·ta daisy (shăs′tə) A cultivated variety of *Chrysanthemum maximum,* of the Pyrenees, with large, white, daisylike flowers. [After Mt. *Shasta,* an extinct volcano in California.]

shat·ter (shăt′ər) *tr.v.* **1.** To cause to break or burst suddenly into pieces. **2.** To damage irreparably: *shattered his hopes.* *—intr.v.* To break into pieces; smash or burst. *—See Syns at* **destroy.** *—n.* **1.** The act of shattering. **2.** Often **shatters.** A fragmented condition. [Middle English *schateren,* from Old English *sceaterian.*]

shat·ter·proof (shăt′ər-proof′) *adj.* Impervious to shattering.

shave (shāv) *v.* **shaved, shaved** or **shav·en** (shā′vən), **shav·ing.** *—tr.v.* **1.** To remove the beard or other body hair from, as with a razor. **2.** To cut at the surface of the skin with a razor: *shave off a beard.* **3.** To trim or mow closely. **4.** To remove thin slices of or from: *shaving wood from a board.* **5.** To come close to or graze in passing. **6.** *Informal.* To cut (a price) by a slight margin. *—intr.v.* To remove a beard or hair with a razor. *—n.* **1.** The act, process, or result of shaving. **2.** A thin slice or scraping; a shaving. **3.** A tool used for shaving. *—idiom.* **close shave.** *Informal.* A narrow escape. [Middle English *shaven,* to scrape, shave, from Old English *sceafan.*]

shave·ling (shāv′lĭng) *n.* **1.** A monk who has shaved the crown of his head. **2.** A young person.

shav·er (shā′vər) *n.* **1. a.** A person who shaves. **b.** A device for shaving. **2.** *Informal.* A youngster.

shav·ing (shā′vĭng) *n.* A thin strip of material shaved off.

Sha·vu·ot (shə-voo′ōt′, -ōt′, -əs) *n.* Also **Sha·bu·oth.** A Jewish holiday commemorating the revelation of the Law on Mount Sinai. [Hebrew *shābhū′ōth,* from *shābhūa′,* week.]

shawl (shôl) *n.* A square or oblong piece of cloth worn by women as a covering for the head, neck, and shoulders. [Ult. from Persian *shāl.*]

Shaw·nee (shô-nē′) *n.,* pl. **Shawnee** or **-nees. 1.** A tribe of Algonquian-speaking North American Indians, formerly

shark

living in the Tennessee Valley and adjacent areas, now surviving in Oklahoma. **2.** A member of this tribe. **3.** The language of the Shawnee.

shay (shā) *n. Informal.* A chaise. [Back-formation from CHAISE.]

she (shē) *pron.* The third person singular pronoun in the nominative case, feminine gender. **1.** Used to represent the female person or animal most recently mentioned or implied. **2.** Used traditionally of certain objects and institutions regarded as feminine, such as ships and nations. —*n.* A female animal or person. [Middle English *sche*, prob. from Old English *sēo*, fem. of *sē*, that one.]

sheaf (shēf) *n., pl.* **sheaves** (shēvz). **1.** A bound bundle of cut stalks of grain or similar plants. **2.** Any gathering or collection held or bound together. **3.** An archer's quiver. —*tr.v.* To bind into a sheaf. [Middle English *sheef*, from Old English *scēaf*.]

shear (shîr) *v.* **sheared, sheared** or **shorn** (shôrn, shōrn), **shear·ing.** —*tr.v.* **1.** To remove (fleece, hair, etc.) by cutting or clipping with a sharp instrument. **2.** To remove the hair or fleece from. **3.** To cut with or as if with shears: *shearing a hedge.* **4.** To divest or deprive. —*intr.v.* **1.** To use shears or a similar cutting tool. **2.** To move or proceed by or as if by cutting: *shear through the wheat.* —*n.* **1.** The act, process, or result of shearing. **2.** *Physics.* An applied force or system of forces that tends to produce a shearing strain. [Middle English *scheren*, from Old English *sceran*.] —**shear'er** *n.*

shearing strain. A condition in or deformation of an elastic body caused by forces that tend to produce an opposite but parallel sliding motion of the body's planes.

shear legs. An apparatus used to lift heavy weights, consisting of two or more spars joined at the top and spread at the base, the tackle being suspended from the top.

shears (shîrz) *n. (used with a pl. verb).* **1.** A cutting tool resembling scissors but considerably larger. **2.** Also **sheers.** A **shear legs.** [From Middle English *schere*, scissors, from Old English *scēara*.]

shear·wa·ter (shîr'wô'tər, -wŏt'ər) *n.* Any of various hook-billed oceanic birds of the family Procellariidae.

sheath (shēth) *n., pl.* **sheaths** (shēthz, shēths). **1.** A case for the blade of a knife, sword, etc. **2.** Any of various coverings or structures resembling a sheath. **3.** A close-fitting dress. —*tr.v.* To sheathe. [Middle English *schethe*, from Old English *scēath*.]

sheathe (shēth) *tr.v.* **sheathed, sheath·ing. 1.** To insert into or provide with a sheath. **2.** To retract (a claw) into a sheath or sheaths. **3.** To enclose; encase.

sheath·ing (shē'thĭng) *n.* An exterior covering, such as the layer of boards applied to the frame of a building.

sheave¹ (shēv) *tr.v.* **sheaved, sheav·ing.** To bind into a sheaf or sheaves; gather; collect.

sheave² (shĭv, shēv) *n.* A wheel or disk with a grooved rim, esp. one used as a pulley. [Middle English *sheve*.]

sheaves (shēvz) *n.* Plural of **sheaf.**

shed¹ (shĕd) *v.* **shed, shed·ding.** —*tr.v.* **1.** To cause to pour forth: *shed tears.* **2.** To send forth; give off: *shed light.* **3.** To repel without allowing penetration: *A duck's feathers shed water.* **4.** To lose by a natural process: *shed leaves; a snake shedding its skin.* —*intr.v.* **1.** To lose a natural growth or covering by a natural process: *The cat is shedding.* **2.** To pour forth, fall off, or drop out. —*idiom.* **shed blood.** To take life; to kill. [Middle English *sheden*, shed, divide, from Old English *scēadan*.] —**shed'der** *n.*

shed² (shĕd) *n.* **1.** A small structure serving for storage or shelter. **2.** A large low building open on one or more sides. [Earlier *shadde*.]

she'd (shĕd). Contraction of: **1.** She had. **2.** She would.

sheen (shēn) *n.* Glistening brightness; shininess. [From Middle English *shene*, beautiful, bright, from Old English *scīene*.]

sheep (shēp) *n., pl.* **sheep. 1.** Any of various usu. horned, ruminant mammals of the genus *Ovis*, esp. the domesticated species *O. aries*, raised in many breeds for its wool, edible flesh, or skin. **2.** The skin of a sheep or leather made from it. **3.** A person who is meek and submissive. —*modifier: a sheep ranch.* [Middle English, from Old English *scēap*.]

sheep·cote (shēp'kōt, -kŏt') *n.* A sheepfold.

sheep dog. Also **sheep·dog** (shēp'dôg', -dŏg'). A dog trained to guard and herd sheep.

sheep·fold (shēp'fōld') *n.* A fenced-in area for sheep.

sheep·herd·er (shēp'hûr'dər) *n.* A person who herds a large flock of sheep; a shepherd. —**sheep'herd'ing** *n.*

sheep·ish (shē'pĭsh) *adj.* **1.** Embarrassed and apologetic: *confessed with a sheepish grin.* **2.** Like a sheep, as in meekness. —**sheep'ish·ly** *adv.* —**sheep'ish·ness** *n.*

sheeps·head (shēps'hĕd') *n.* A food fish, *Archosargus probatocephalus,* of American Atlantic waters.

sheep·skin (shēp'skĭn') *n.* **1.** The skin of a sheep either tanned with the fleece left on or in the form of leather or parchment. **2.** A diploma. —*modifier: a sheepskin coat.*

sheer¹ (shîr) *intr.v.* To swerve from a course. —*tr.v.* To cause to swerve or deviate. —*n.* **1.** A swerving or deviating course. **2.** *Naut.* The upward curve, or the amount of upward curve, of the fore-and-aft lines of a ship's deck viewed from the side. [Perh. var. of SHEAR.]

sheer² (shîr) *adj.* **-er, -est. 1.** Thin and transparent: *a sheer fabric.* **2.** Undiluted; pure: *sheer delight.* **3.** Perpendicular or nearly so. —See Syns at **pure** and **utter.** —*adv.* Perpendicularly. [Middle English *schir*, bright, pure.] —**sheer'ly** *adv.* —**sheer'ness** *n.*

sheers (shîrz) *n.* A form of the word **shears** (lifting crane).

sheet¹ (shēt) *n.* **1.** A rectangular piece of linen or similar material serving as a basic article of bedding, commonly used in pairs, one above and one below the body of the sleeper. **2.** A broad, thin, usu. rectangular piece of any material. **3.** A broad, flat, continuous surface or expanse: *a sheet of rain.* **4.** A newspaper, esp. a tabloid. **5.** The large block of unseparated postage stamps printed by a single impression of a plate. —*tr.v.* To cover with, wrap in, or provide with a sheet or sheets. [Middle English *schete*, cloth, sheet, towel, from Old English *scēte*.]

sheet² (shēt) *n.* **1.** A rope or chain attached to one or both of the lower corners of a sail, serving to move or extend it. **2. sheets.** The spaces at either end of an open boat, in front of and behind the seats. [Middle English *schete*, from Old English *scēata*, corner of a sail.]

sheet anchor. **1.** A large extra anchor intended for use in emergency. **2.** A person or thing that can be turned to in time of emergency. [Perh. SHEET (rope) + ANCHOR.]

sheet·ing (shē'tĭng) *n.* Material for sheets.

sheet lightning. Lightning that appears as a broad, sheet-like illumination, caused by reflection.

sheet music. Music printed on unbound sheets of paper.

sheik (shēk, shāk) *n.* Also **sheikh. 1.** A Moslem religious official. **2.** An Arab chief. [Arabic *shaikh*, old man, from *shākha*, to be old.] —**sheik'dom** *n.*

shek·el (shĕk'əl) *n.* **1.** Any of several ancient units of weight, esp. a Hebrew unit equal to about half an ounce. **2.** The chief silver coin of the Hebrews, weighing one shekel. [Hebrew *sheqel*, from *shāqal*, to weigh.]

shel·drake (shĕl'drāk') *n.* **1.** Any of various large Old World ducks of the genus *Tadorna*, esp. *T. tadorna*, having predominantly black and white plumage. Also called **shelduck. 2.** A merganser. [Middle English *sheldedrake*.]

shelf (shĕlf) *n., pl.* **shelves** (shĕlvz). **1.** A flat, usu. rectangular structure of a rigid material, as of wood, glass, or metal, fixed at right angles to a wall or other vertical surface and used to hold or store objects. **2.** The contents or capacity of such a structure. **3.** Anything resembling such an object, as a balcony or a ledge of rock. **4.** A reef, sandbar, or shoal. **5.** *Mining.* Bedrock. —*idiom.* **on the shelf.** In a state of disuse; put aside. [Middle English, perh. from Middle Low German *schelf*.]

sheep

shell (shĕl) *n.* **1. a.** The usu. hard outer covering that encases certain organisms. **b.** A similar outer covering on an egg, fruit, or nut. **2.** The material composing such a covering. **3.** Anything resembling such a covering, esp.: **a.** A framework or exterior, as of a building. **b.** A thin layer of pastry. **c.** A long, narrow racing boat propelled by oarsmen. **4. a.** A projectile or piece of ammunition, esp. the hollow tube containing explosives used to propel such a projectile. **b.** A metal or cardboard case, containing the charge, primer, and shot, fired from a shotgun. **5.** *Physics.* **a.** Any of the set of hypothetical spherical surfaces centered on the nucleus of an atom that contain the orbits of electrons having the same principal quantum number. **b.** All the electrons in an atom that have the same principal quantum number. —*modifier:* *shell beads; a shell collection.* —*tr.v.* **1. a.** To remove the shell of; to shuck. **b.** To remove from a shell, pod, etc. **2.** To separate the kernels of (corn) from the cob. **3.** To fire shells at; bombard. —*phrasal verb.* **shell out.** *Informal.* To pay (money). [Middle English, from Old English *scell.*] —**shell′er** *n.*

shell

she'll (shĕl). Contraction of: **1.** She will. **2.** She shall.
shel·lac (shə-lăk′) *n.* **1.** A purified form of a resinous secretion of the lac insect, formed into flakes, and used in varnishes, paints, sealing wax, and phonograph records. **2.** A solution of flakes of this material in alcohol, used as varnish and as a sealer. —*v.* **-lacked, -lack·ing.** —*tr.v.* **1.** To apply shellac to. **2.** *Slang.* To defeat decisively. —*intr.v.* To apply shellac. —See Syns at **defeat.** [SHEL(L) + LAC (lacquer).]
shell bean. Any of various beans cultivated for their edible seeds rather than for their pods.
shell·fire (shĕl′fīr′) *n.* The firing of artillery projectiles.
shell·fish (shĕl′fĭsh′) *n., pl.* **shellfish** or **-fish·es.** Any aquatic animal having a shell or shell-like exoskeleton.
shell game. A swindling game, thimblerig.
shell shock. 1. A nervous disorder resulting in trauma suffered in combat. **2. Combat fatigue.** —**shell′-shocked′** *adj.*
shel·ter (shĕl′tər) *n.* **1. a.** Something that provides cover or protection, as from the weather. **b.** A refuge; haven. **2.** The condition of being covered or protected. —*tr.v.* To provide cover or protection for. —*intr.v.* To take cover; find refuge. [Orig. unknown.] —**shel′ter·er** *n.*
shelter tent. A small tent usu. formed of two or more pieces of waterproof material. Also called **pup tent.**
shel·tie (shĕl′tē) *n.* Also **shel·ty** *pl.* **-ties. 1.** A **Shetland pony. 2.** A **Shetland sheepdog.** [Prob. of Scandinavian orig.]
shelve (shĕlv) *tr.v.* **shelved, shelv·ing. 1.** To place or arrange on a shelf or shelves. **2.** To put aside; postpone: *shelve a proposal.* **3.** To retire from service; dismiss. **4.** To furnish or outfit with shelves. [From SHELF.]
shelves (shĕlvz) *n.* Plural of **shelf.**
she·nan·i·gan (shə-năn′ĭ-gən) *n.* Often **shenanigans.** *Informal.* Playful tricks; mischief. [Orig. unknown.]
she·ol (shē′ōl′) *n.* **1.** Hell. **2. Sheol.** A place described in the Old Testament as the abode of the dead. [Hebrew *shəōl.*]
shep·herd (shĕp′ərd) *n.* **1.** A person who herds, guards, and cares for sheep. **2.** A spiritual guide; minister. **3.** A dog of a breed orig. trained to guard or herd sheep. —*tr.v.* To herd, guard, or care for as or in the manner of a shepherd. [Middle English *sheepherde,* from Old English *scēaphirde* : *scēap,* sheep + *hirde,* herdsman.]
shep·herd·ess (shĕp′ər-dĭs) *n.* A woman shepherd.
shepherd's pie. A casserole consisting of cooked cubes of beef or lamb with gravy, topped by mashed potatoes.

shep·herd's-purse (shĕp′ərdz-pûrs′) *n.* A common weed, *Capsella bursa-pastoris,* with small white flowers and flat, heart-shaped fruit. [From its pouchlike pods.]
sher·bet (shûr′bĭt) *n.* **1.** A sweet, frozen, often fruit-flavored dessert, containing water, milk, and egg whites or gelatin. **2.** *Brit.* A beverage made of sweetened diluted fruit juice. [Turkish *sherbet* and Persian *sharbat,* from Arabic *sharbah,* drink, from *shariba,* to drink.]
sherd (shûrd) *n.* Var. of **shard.**
sher·iff (shĕr′ĭf) *n.* The chief law-enforcement official of a county. [Middle English *shirrif,* from Old English *scīrgerēfa* : *scīr,* shire + *gerēfa,* officer.]
Sher·pa (shûr′pə) *n., pl.* **Sherpa** or **-pas.** A member of a Tibetan people living in northern Nepal.
sher·ry (shĕr′ē) *n., pl.* **-ries.** A fortified, amber-colored wine orig. from Spain, ranging from very dry to sweet. [Earlier *sherris,* "wine of Jerez," a city in Spain.]
Shet·land (shĕt′lənd) *n.* A fine yarn made from the wool of Shetland sheep and used for knitting and weaving.
Shetland pony. A small, compactly built pony of a breed originating in the Shetland Islands. Also called **sheltie.**
Shetland sheepdog. A dog of a breed developed in the Shetland Islands, having a rough coat and resembling a small collie. Also called **sheltie.**
shew (shō) *v. & n. Brit.* Var. of **show.**
shib·bo·leth (shĭb′ə-lĭth, -lĕth′) *n.* **1.** A password, phrase, custom, or usage that reliably distinguishes the members of one group or class from another. **2.** A slogan. [Hebrew *shibbōleth,* an ear of corn (from the use of this word as a password by the Gileadites in the Bible).]
shied (shīd) *v.* **1.** Past tense and past participle of **shy** (to draw back). **2.** Past tense and past participle of **shy** (to throw).
shield (shēld) *n.* **1.** An article of protective armor carried on the forearm to ward off blows or missiles. **2.** A means of defense; protection. **3.** Something resembling a shield. **4.** *Mil.* A steel sheet attached to a gun to protect the gunners from small-arms fire. **5.** *Zool.* A protective plate or similar hard outer covering. **6.** A piece of rubberized or absorbent cloth worn at the armpits of a garment as protection from perspiration. **7.** A layer or mass of material placed around something to keep radiation in or out, esp. a mass of lead or cement used to enclose a nuclear reactor. —*tr.v.* **1.** To protect or defend with or as if with a shield. **2.** To cover up; conceal. —*intr.v.* To act as a shield or safeguard. —See Syns at **defend.** [Middle English *shild,* from Old English *scild.*] —**shield′er** *n.*
shi·er (shī′ər) *adj.* A comparative of **shy** (timid).
shies (shīz) *n.* **1.** Plural of **shy** (a start). **2.** Plural of **shy** (a quick throw).
shi·est (shī′ĭst) *adj.* A superlative of **shy** (timid).
shift (shĭft) *tr.v.* **1.** To move or transfer from one place or position to another. **2.** To change; switch: *shift tactics.* **3.** To change (gears) in an automobile. —*intr.v.* **1.** To change position, direction, form, etc. **2.** To get along; manage: *shifts for himself.* **3.** To change gears, as when driving an automobile. —*n.* **1.** A change from one place or position to another; transfer. **2.** A change of direction or form. **3. a.** A group of workers on duty at the same time, as at a factory. **b.** The working period of such a group: *the night shift.* **4.** A mechanism in a typewriter or similar device for printing two different sets of characters using the same keys. **5.** A mechanism for changing gears, as in an automobile. **6. a.** A loosely fitting dress that hangs straight from the shoulders. **b.** A woman's undergarment; slip; chemise. **7. a.** A means; expedient. **b.** A stratagem; trick. [Middle English *shiften,* to arrange, from Old English *sciftan.*] —**shift′er** *n.*
shift·less (shĭft′lĭs) *adj.* **1.** Lacking ambition; lazy. **2.** Lacking efficiency; not capable. —See Syns at **lazy.** [From *shift,* resourcefulness.] —**shift′less·ly** *adv.* —**shift′less·ness** *n.*
shift·y (shĭf′tē) *adj.* **-i·er, -i·est. 1.** Tricky; crafty. **2.** Full of expedients; resourceful. —**shift′i·ly** *adv.* —**shift′i·ness** *n.*
shill (shĭl) *n. Slang.* A person who works as a secret accomplice to a swindler. [Prob. short for *shillaber,* decoy, impostor.]
shil·le·lagh (shə-lā′lē) *n.* Also **shil·la·lah.** A club or cudgel.

[After *Shillelagh*, a town in County Wicklow, Ireland.]

shil·ling (shĭl′ĭng) *n.* A former British coin worth ¹/₂₀ of a pound. [Middle English, from Old English *scilling*.]

shil·ly-shal·ly (shĭl′ē-shăl′ē) *intr.v.* **-lied, -ly·ing. 1.** To put off acting; hesitate or waver. **2.** To idle or poke; dawdle. —*adj.* Hesitant; vacillating. —*n., pl.* **-lies.** Procrastination; hesitation. [From SHALL I.] —**shil′ly-shal′li·er** *n.*

shim (shĭm) *n.* A thin, often tapered piece of metal, wood, stone, etc., used for leveling or for filling space, as between a chair leg and the floor. —*tr.v.* **shimmed, shim·ming.** To level or fill in with a shim. [Orig. unknown.]

shim·mer (shĭm′ər) *intr.v.* **1.** To shine with a flickering light. **2.** To move with a wavelike or sinuous visual effect. —*n.* A flickering or tremulous light; a glimmer. [Middle English *schimeren*, from Old English *scimerian*.] —**shim′mer·y** *adj.*

shim·my (shĭm′ē) *n., pl.* **-mies. 1.** A dance popular in the 1920's, characterized by rapid shaking of the body. **2.** Abnormal vibration or wobbling, as in the chassis of an automobile. **3.** *Informal.* A chemise. —*intr.v.* **-mied, -my·ing. 1.** To vibrate or wobble. **2.** To dance the shimmy. [Short for *shimmy-shake*, "to shake one's chemise," from *shimmy*, var. of CHEMISE.]

shin (shĭn) *n.* **1.** *Anat.* **a.** The front part of the leg below the knee and above the ankle. **b.** The tibia. **2.** The lower part of the foreleg in beef cattle. —*v.* **shinned, shin·ning.** —*tr.v.* To climb by gripping and pulling alternately with the hands and legs. —*intr.v.* To climb in this way. [Middle English *shine*, from Old English *scinu*.]

shin·bone (shĭn′bōn′) *n.* The tibia.

shin·dig (shĭn′dĭg′) *n. Slang.* A festive party or celebration. Also called **shindy.** [Prob. alteration of *shindy*, uproar.]

shine (shīn) *v.* **shone** (shōn) or **shined, shin·ing.** —*intr.v.* **1.** To emit light; be radiant; beam. **2.** To reflect light; glint or glisten. **3.** To perform conspicuously well; excel. —*tr.v.* **1.** To aim or cast the beam or glow of: *Shine that light over here.* **2.** To make glossy or bright by polishing. —*n.* **1.** Brightness; radiance; luster. **2.** A shoeshine. **3.** Fair weather: *rain or shine.* **4.** **shines.** *Informal.* Foolish pranks or tricks. —*idiom.* **take a shine to.** To like spontaneously. [Middle English *shinen*, from Old English *scīnan*.]

shin·er (shī′nər) *n.* **1.** Someone or something that shines. **2.** *Slang.* A black eye. **3.** A small silvery fish, esp. a North American freshwater fish of the family Cyprinidae.

shin·gle¹ (shĭng′gəl) *n.* **1.** A thin oblong piece of wood or other material laid in overlapping rows to cover the roofs and sides of houses. **2.** *Informal.* A small signboard, as one indicating a doctor's office: *hang out a shingle.* —*modifier: a shingle roof.* —*tr.v.* **-gled, -gling. 1.** To cover (a roof or building) with shingles. **2.** To cut (hair) short and close to the head. [Middle English *scingle*, from Latin *scindula*, var. of *scandula*.] —**shin′gler** *n.*

shin·gle² (shĭng′gəl) *n.* **1.** Beach gravel consisting of large smooth pebbles. **2.** A beach covered with such gravel. [Prob. from Middle Low German *singele, tsingele*, outermost wall, sandbank, ult. from Latin, belt, from *cingere*, to encompass.] —**shin′gly** *adj.*

shin·gles (shĭng′gəlz) *n.* (used with a sing. or pl. verb). A painful virus infection, *herpes zoster*, marked by skin eruption along a nerve path on one side of the body. [Middle English *schingles, cingules*, from Medieval Latin *cingulus*, belt, from Latin, girdle, belt, from *cingere*, to gird.]

shin·ny¹ (shĭn′ē) *n., pl.* **-nies. 1.** A simple form of hockey played by schoolboys. **2.** The curved stick used in this game. [Orig. unknown.]

shin·ny² (shĭn′ē) *intr.v.* **-nied, -ny·ing.** To climb by shinning.

shin·plas·ter (shĭn′plăs′tər) *n.* Paper currency issued privately, esp. when it is devalued by lack of backing or by inflation.

Shin·to (shĭn′tō) *n.* Also **Shin·to·ism** (-ĭz′əm). The traditional religion of Japan, marked by the worship of nature spirits and of ancestors. —*modifier: a Shinto shrine.* [Japanese *shintō*, "the way of the gods."] —**Shin′to·ist** *n.*

shin·y (shī′nē) *adj.* **-i·er, -i·est. 1.** Bright; glistening. **2.** Clear; shining. —**shin′i·ness** *n.*

ship (shĭp) *n.* **1.** Any vessel of considerable size built for deep-water navigation. **2.** A three-masted sailing vessel with square mainsails on all masts. **3.** A ship's company. **4.** An airplane, airship, or spacecraft. —*v.* **shipped, ship·ping.** —*tr.v.* **1.** To place or take on board a ship. **2.** To send or cause to be transported: *shipped the goods by rail.* **3.** To hire for work on a ship: *ship a new crew.* **4.** To take in (water) over the side. **5.** To set in place for use, as the mast or rudder. —*intr.v.* **1.** To go aboard or travel by means of a ship. **2.** To enlist for service on a ship. —See Syns at **send.** [Middle English *schip*, from Old English *scip*.] —**ship′per** *n.*

-ship. A suffix meaning: **1.** Quality or condition: **friendship. 2.** Status, rank, or office: **professorship. 3.** Art or skill: **penmanship.** [Middle English *-schipe*, from Old English *-scipe*.]

ship biscuit. A type of bread, hardtack.

ship·board (shĭp′bôrd′, -bōrd′) *n.* —**on shipboard.** On board a ship. —*modifier: a shipboard romance.*

ship·build·ing (shĭp′bĭl′dĭng) *n.* The business of constructing ships. —**ship′build′er** *n.*

ship·mas·ter (shĭp′măs′tər) *n.* The commander or captain of a merchant ship.

ship·mate (shĭp′māt′) *n.* A fellow sailor.

ship·ment (shĭp′mənt) *n.* **1.** The act of sending or transporting goods. **2.** The goods or cargo transported.

ship·ping (shĭp′ĭng) *n.* **1.** The act or business of transporting goods. **2.** The body of ships belonging to one port, industry, or country. —*modifier: a shipping center.*

shipping clerk. A person employed to manage the shipment or receipt of goods.

ship·shape (shĭp′shāp′) *adj.* Neatly arranged; orderly; tidy. —See Syns at **neat.** —**ship′shape′** *adv.*

ship·worm (shĭp′wûrm′) *n.* Any of various wormlike saltwater mollusks of the genera *Teredo* and *Bankia*, with rudimentary bivalve shells with which they bore into wood.

ship·wreck (shĭp′rĕk′) *n.* **1.** The remains of a wrecked ship. **2.** The destruction of a ship, as by storm or collision. **3.** Complete failure or ruin. —*tr.v.* **1.** To cause to suffer shipwreck. **2.** To ruin utterly. [Middle English *shipwrak*, from Old English *scipwræc*, jetsam.]

ship·wright (shĭp′rīt′) *n.* A carpenter employed in the construction or maintenance of ships.

ship·yard (shĭp′yärd′) *n.* A yard or area where ships are built or repaired.

shire (shīr) *n.* One of the counties of Great Britain. [Middle English, from Old English *scīr*.]

shirk (shûrk) *tr.v.* To put off or avoid discharging. —*intr.v.* To put off or avoid work or duty. [From obs. *shirk*, parasite, rogue.] —**shirk′er** *n.*

shirr (shûr) *tr.v.* **1.** To gather (cloth) into decorative parallel rows. **2.** To cook (eggs) by baking unshelled in molds. —*n.* A decorative gathering of cloth into parallel rows. Also called **shirring.** [Orig. unknown.]

shirt (shûrt) *n.* **1.** A garment for the upper part of the body, typically having a collar, sleeves, and a front opening. **2.** An undershirt. —*modifier: a shirt button.* [Middle English *sherte*, from Old English *scyrte*.]

shirt·waist (shûrt′wāst′) *n.* **1.** A woman's tailored shirt, made to resemble a man's shirt. **2.** A woman's dress with the bodice styled like a tailored shirt.

shish ke·bab (shĭsh′ kə-bŏb′). Also **shish ke·bob** or **shish ka·bob.** A dish consisting of pieces of seasoned meat, often with onions, tomatoes, or green peppers, roasted and served on skewers. [Turkish *şiş kebabıu : şiş*, skewer + *kebap*, roast meat.]

Shi·va (shē′və) *n.* Also **Si·va** (shē′və, sē′-). The Hindu god of destruction and reproduction, a member of the triad along with Brahma and Vishnu.

shiv·er¹ (shĭv′ər) *intr.v.* **1.** To shake from or as if from cold; tremble. **2.** To quiver or vibrate. —See Syns at **shake.** —*n.* **1.** An act of shivering; a tremble. **2.** A quick, cold sensation, as of fear. [Middle English *chiveren*.]

shiv·er² (shĭv′ər) *intr.v.* To break suddenly into fragments or splinters; shatter. —*tr.v.* To cause to break into fragments. —*n.* A thin, sharp fragment; a sliver. [Middle English, from *scivre*, fragment.]

shiv·er·y (shĭv′ə-rē) *adj.* Trembling, as from cold or fear.

shoal¹ (shōl) *n.* **1.** A shallow place in a body of water. **2.** A sandbank or sandbar. —*intr.v.* To become shallow. —*tr.v.* To make shallow. —*adj.* Having little depth; shallow. [Middle English *sholde,* from Old English *sceald,* shallow.]

shoal² (shōl) *n.* **1.** A large group; a crowd. **2.** A school of fish or other water animals. —*intr.v.* To school. [Prob. from Middle Dutch or Middle Low German *schōle.*]

shoat (shōt) *n.* Also **shote.** A young pig just after weaning. [Middle English *shote,* prob. of Low German orig.]

shock¹ (shŏk) *n.* **1.** A violent collision or impact; heavy blow. **2.** Something that jars the mind or emotions as if with a violent, unexpected blow. **3.** The disturbance of mental or emotional condition or functioning caused by such a blow. **4.** A severe offense to a person's sense of propriety or decency; an outrage. **5.** *Pathol.* A gen. temporary state of massive physiological reaction to bodily trauma, usu. characterized by marked loss of blood pressure and the depression of vital processes. **6.** The sensation and muscular spasm caused by an electric current passing through the body or through a bodily part. —*tr.v.* **1.** To strike with great surprise and agitation. **2.** To offend; scandalize. **3.** To induce a state of shock in (a living organism). **4.** To subject (an animal or person) to an electric shock. [Old French *choc,* from *choquer,* to strike with fear.] —**shock'er** *n.*

shock² (shŏk) *n.* **1.** A number of sheaves of grain stacked upright in a field for drying: *a shock of corn.* **2.** A bushy mass: *a shock of fair hair.* —*tr.v.* To gather (grain) into shocks. [Middle English *shokke.*] —**shock'er** *n.*

shock absorber. Any of various devices to absorb mechanical shocks, esp. one used in automobiles.

shock·ing (shŏk'ĭng) *adj.* **1.** Highly disturbing emotionally. **2.** Highly offensive; indecent or distasteful. **3.** Very vivid or intense in tone: *shocking pink.* —See Syns at **outrageous** and **unspeakable.** —**shock'ing·ly** *adv.*

shock therapy. The inducing of shock by electric current or drugs, sometimes with convulsions, as a therapy for mental illness. Also called **shock treatment.**

shock troops. Highly experienced and capable military personnel specially trained to lead attacks.

shock wave. A large-amplitude compression wave caused by supersonic motion of a body in a medium.

shod (shŏd) *v.* Past tense and past participle of **shoe.**

shod·dy (shŏd'ē) *n., pl.* **-dies. 1.** Wool fibers obtained by shredding rags or worn garments. **2.** Yarn, fabric, or garments made from or containing such fibers. **3.** Inferior or imitation goods. —*adj.* **-di·er, -di·est. 1.** Made of or containing shoddy or other inferior material. **2.** Of poor quality or workmanship. **3.** Dishonest: *a shoddy politician.* —See Syns at **cheap.** [Orig. unknown.] —**shod'di·ly** *adv.* —**shod'di·ness** *n.*

shoe (shōō) *n.* **1.** A durable covering for the human foot, esp. one of a matched pair. **2.** A horseshoe. **3.** A part or device placed at an end, foot, or bottom, esp.: **a.** A strip of metal fitted onto the bottom of a sled runner. **b.** A skid placed under the wheel of a vehicle to retard its motion. **c.** The outer covering, casing, or tread of a pneumatic rubber tire. **4.** The part of a brake that presses against the wheel or drum. **5.** The sliding contact plate on an electric train that conducts electricity from the third rail. —*modifier:* *shoe leather.* —*tr.v.* **shod** (shŏd), **shoe·ing.** To furnish or fit with shoes. [Middle English *shoo,* from Old English *scōh.*]

shoe·horn (shōō'hôrn') *n.* A curved tool, often of horn or smooth metal, used at the heel to help slip on a shoe.

shoe·lace (shōō'lās') *n.* A string or cord used for lacing and fastening shoes.

shoe·mak·er (shōō'mā'kər) *n.* A person who makes or repairs shoes and boots as an occupation. —**shoe'mak'ing** *n.*

shoe·string (shōō'strĭng') *n.* A shoelace. —*adj.* Cut long and slender: *shoestring potatoes.* —*idiom.* **on a shoestring.** With very little money.

shoe·tree (shōō'trē') *n.* A foot-shaped form inserted into a shoe to preserve its shape. Also called **boot tree.**

sho·far (shō'fär', -fər) *n., pl.* **-fars** or **sho·froth** (shō-frōt', -frŏth'). A trumpet made of a ram's horn, blown for summoning and ritual purposes by the ancient Hebrews, and now sounded in the synagogue at Rosh Hashanah and Yom Kippur. [Hebrew *shōphār,* ram's horn.]

sho·gun (shō'gən) *n.* Any of a line of military leaders of Japan who, until 1868, exercised absolute rule. [Japanese *shōgun,* general.]

shone (shōn) *v.* A past tense and past participle of **shine.** [Middle English *shon* (p. t.), from Old English *scān;* past part. *shone* from p. t.]

shoo (shōō) *interj.* A word used to scare away animals or birds. —*tr.v.* To drive or scare away, as by crying "shoo." —*intr.v.* To cry "shoo." [Middle English *schowe.*]

shook (shōōk) *v.* Past tense of **shake.** [Middle English *schok,* from Old English *scōc.*]

shoot (shōōt) *v.* **shot** (shŏt), **shoot·ing.** —*tr.v.* **1.** To hit, wound, or kill with a missile fired from a weapon. **2.** To fire or let fly (a missile) from a weapon. **3.** To discharge: *shoot the gun.* **4.** To put forcefully or swiftly. **5.** To send forth swiftly or dartingly: *She shot a retort to the insult.* **6.** To pass over or through swiftly: *shoot the rapids.* **7.** To record on film (a scene, motion picture, etc.). **8.** To pour, empty out, or discharge down or as if down a chute. **9.** To variegate: *a black coat shot with gray.* **10. a.** To propel (a marble or ball) toward its objective. **b.** To score (a point or goal). **c.** To play (golf, craps, or pool). **11.** To slide into or out of a fastening: *shoot a door bolt.* **12.** To measure the altitude of with a sextant or other instrument: *shoot a star.* —*intr.v.* **1.** To discharge a missile from a weapon. **2.** To go off. **3.** To move swiftly; to dart. **4.** To protrude; project. **5.** To hunt with a weapon. **6.** To germinate; sprout: *Plants shoot up in the spring.* **7.** To take pictures; to film. **8.** To propel a ball or other object toward the goal. **9.** To take one's turn at play. —*phrasal verbs.* **shoot for** (or **at**). To strive or aim for. **shoot up. 1.** *Informal.* To grow or get taller rapidly. **2.** *Slang.* To inject (a narcotic drug) directly into a vein. —*n.* **1.** The motion or movement of something that is shot. **2. a.** The young growth arising from a germinating seed; sprout. **b.** A bud or young leaf on a plant. **3.** Any new growing part. **4.** A rapid. **5.** A chute. **6.** A skeet tournament, hunt, or other organized shooting activity. —*idiom.* **shot through with.** Filled with; riddled with. [Middle English *shoten,* from Old English *scēotan.*] —**shoot'er** *n.*

shooting gallery. An enclosed target range for firearms practice or competition.

shooting star. 1. A briefly visible meteor. **2.** Any of several North American plants of the genus *Dodecatheon,* that have nodding flowers with reflexed petals.

shop (shŏp) *n.* **1.** A small retail store or a specialty department in a large store. **2.** A place where goods are manufactured; factory: *a machine shop.* **3. a.** Any commercial or industrial establishment. **b.** A business. **4. a.** A schoolroom fitted with machinery and tools for instruction in the manual arts. **b.** The manual arts as a technical science or course of study. —*modifier:* *a shop window; a shop clerk.* —*v.* **shopped, shop·ping.** —*intr.v.* **1.** To visit stores for the purpose of inspecting and buying merchandise. **2.** To search; hunt. —*tr.v.* To visit or buy from (a particular store). [Middle English *shoppe,* from Old English *sceoppa,* booth, stall.] —**shop'per** *n.*

shop·keep·er (shŏp'kē'pər) *n.* An owner or manager of a shop.

shop·lift·er (shŏp'lĭf'tər) *n.* A person who steals goods on display in a store. —**shop'lift'ing** *n.*

shopping center. A group of stores and shops forming a central retail market, usu. in a rural or suburban area.

shop steward. A union member chosen by his fellow workers to represent them in their dealings with the management.

shop·talk (shŏp'tôk') *n.* Talk or conversation concerning one's business or occupation.

shop·worn (shŏp'wôrn', -wōrn') *adj.* **1.** Tarnished, frayed, faded, or otherwise defective from being on display in a store. **2.** Worn-out; exhausted.

shore¹ (shôr, shōr) *n.* **1.** The land along the edge of an ocean, sea, lake, or river; a coast. **2.** Often **shores.** Land: *native shore.* [Middle English, from Middle Dutch and Middle Low German *schore.*]

shore² (shôr, shōr) *tr.v.* **shored, shor·ing.** To prop up, as with an inclined timber: *shore up the sagging floor.* —*n.* A beam or timber propped against a ship, wall, or other structure as a temporary support. [Middle English, *sho-*

ren, from Middle Dutch *schōren*.]

shore bird. Any of various birds, such as a sandpiper, plover, or snipe, that frequent shores.

shore leave. Permission to go ashore given to members of a ship's crew.

shore·line (shôr'līn', shōr'-) *n.* The line marking the edge of a body of water.

shore·ward (shôr'wərd, shōr'-) *adj. & adv.* In the direction of the shore.

shor·ing (shôr'ĭng, shōr'-) *n.* A system of supporting shores.

shorn (shôrn, shōrn). A past participle of **shear**. [Middle English *shorne*, from Old English *(ge)scoren*.]

short (shôrt) *adj.* **-er, -est. 1.** Having little length; not long. **2.** Having little height; not tall; low. **3.** Having a small extent in time; brief. **4.** Inadequate; insufficient: *water in short supply.* **5.** Lacking in length or amount: *a board short two inches.* **6.** Having an insufficient supply: *short of breath; short on experience.* **7.** Concise; succinct. **8.** Lacking in retentiveness: *a short memory.* **9.** Rudely brief; abrupt; curt. **10.** Containing shortening; crisp: *a short pie crust.* **11.** In English prosody, unstressed. **12.** Pronounced like the (ă) in *pan,* the (ĕ) in *pen,* the (ĭ) in *pin,* the (ŏ) in *pond,* or the (ŭ) in *puck,* as distinguished from the (ā) in *pane,* the (ē) in *penal,* the (ī) in *pine,* the (ō) in *post,* or the (ū) in *pure.* —See Syns at **brief.** —*adv.* **1.** Abruptly; quickly: *stop short.* **2.** Rudely; crossly. **3.** Concisely. **4.** Without reaching a goal or target: *The arrow fell short.* **5.** Unawares: *caught short.* —*n.* **1.** Anything that is short, esp.: **a.** A briefly articulated or unaccented syllable. **b.** A short vowel. **c. shorts.** Short trousers extending to the knee or above. **d. shorts.** Men's undershorts. **e.** A short motion picture. **2. shorts.** A by-product of wheat processing, consisting of bran mixed with coarse meal or flour. **3.** *Elect.* **a.** A short circuit. **b.** A malfunction caused by a short circuit. **4.** *Baseball.* A shortstop. —*tr.v.* **1.** To cause a short circuit in. **2.** *Informal.* To give (a person) less than he is entitled to; shortchange. —*intr.v.* To short-circuit. —*idioms.* **for short.** As an abbreviation: *He's called Ed for short.* **short for.** An abbreviation of: *Ed is short for Edward.* **short of.** Less than: *Taking that risk is nothing short of madness.* [Middle English, from Old English *scort.*] —**short'ness** *n.*

short·age (shôr'tĭj) *n.* A deficiency in amount; deficit; insufficiency. —See Syns at **deficiency.**

short·bread (shôrt'brĕd') *n.* A kneaded dough of flour, sugar, and butter, cut into cookies and baked.

short·cake (shôrt'kāk') *n.* A cake made with rich biscuit dough, split and filled with fruit.

short·change (shôrt'chānj') *tr.v.* **-changed, -chang·ing. 1.** To give (someone) less change than is due. **2.** *Informal.* To swindle, cheat, or trick. —**short'chang'er** *n.*

short circuit. An accidentally established low-resistance connection between two points in an electric circuit, often resulting in an excessive flow of current. Also called **short.**

short-cir·cuit (shôrt'sûr'kĭt) *tr.v.* To cause to have a short circuit. —*intr.v.* To become affected with a short circuit.

short·com·ing (shôrt'kŭm'ĭng) *n.* A deficiency or flaw.

short cut. 1. A more direct route than the customary one. **2.** Any means of saving time or effort.

short division. Arithmetical division performed without writing out the remainders.

short·en (shôr'tn) *tr.v.* **1.** To make short or shorter. **2.** To add shortening to (dough). —*intr.v.* To become short or shorter.

short·en·ing (shôr'tn-ĭng, shôrt'nĭng) *n.* **1.** A fat, such as butter, lard, or vegetable oil, used to make cake or pastry rich and flaky. **2.** A shortened form of something.

short·fall (shôrt'fôl') *n.* **1.** A failure to attain a specified amount or level; shortage; deficiency. **2.** The amount by which a supply falls short. **3.** A monetary deficit.

short·hand (shôrt'hănd') *n.* **1.** A system of rapid handwriting employing symbols to represent words, phrases, and letters; stenography. **2.** Any system of abbreviated reference. —*modifier: a shorthand course.*

short·hand·ed (shôrt'hăn'dĭd) *adj.* Lacking the usual or necessary number of workmen, employees, or assistants.

short·horn (shôrt'hôrn') *n.* One of a breed of beef or dairy cattle originating in northern England and having short,

curved horns. Also called **Durham.**

short-lived (shôrt'līvd', -lĭvd') *adj.* Living or lasting only a short time; ephemeral. —See Syns at **transitory.**

short·ly (shôrt'lē) *adv.* **1.** In a short time; soon; presently. **2.** In a few words; concisely. **3.** Abruptly or curtly.

short order. Food quickly prepared and served, as in a diner. —*modifier* **(short-order):** *a short-order cook.* —*idiom.* **in short order.** Quickly; immediately.

short-range (shôrt'rānj') *adj.* **1.** Extending only briefly into the future: *short-range goals.* **2.** Capable of reaching only a short distance: *short-range weapons.*

short rib. A cut of meat consisting of the area between the rib roast and the plate.

short shrift. 1. A short respite, as from death. **2.** Summary and unsympathetic treatment or dismissal.

short·sight·ed (shôrt'sī'tĭd) *adj.* **1.** Near-sighted; myopic. **2.** Lacking foresight. **3.** Resulting from a lack of foresight. —**short'sight'ed·ly** *adv.* —**short'sight'ed·ness** *n.*

short·stop (shôrt'stŏp') *n. Baseball.* **1.** The field position between second and third bases. **2.** The player who occupies this position.

short story. A relatively brief fictional prose composition that usu. develops a single theme or mood. —*modifier* **(short-story):** *a short-story writer.*

short-tem·pered (shôrt'tĕm'pərd) *adj.* Easily or quickly moved to anger; irascible.

short-term (shôrt'tûrm') *adj.* Payable or reaching maturity within a short time, such as a year: *a short-term loan.*

short ton. A unit of weight, a ton.

short wave. An electromagnetic wave with wavelength in the short-wave region.

short-wave (shôrt'wāv') *adj.* **1.** Having a wavelength of less than approximately 80 meters. **2.** Capable of receiving or transmitting at such wavelengths: *a short-wave radio.*

short-wind·ed (shôrt'wĭn'dĭd) *adj.* Easily winded.

Sho·sho·ne (shō-shō'nē) *n., pl.* **Shoshone** or **-nes.** Also **Sho·sho·ni. 1.** A tribe of Uto-Aztecan-speaking Indians, formerly occupying parts of Nevada, Oregon, Idaho, Utah, Wyoming, and Texas. **2.** A member of this tribe. **3.** The language of the Shoshones.

Sho·sho·ne·an (shō-shō'nē-ən) *n.* A group of Uto-Aztecan languages of western North America. —**Sho·sho'ne·an** *adj.*

shot¹ (shŏt) *n.* **1.** The firing or discharge of a weapon, as of a gun or a bow. **2.** *pl.* **shot.** A bullet or similar missile fired from a weapon. **3.** Something that resembles the directed discharge of a weapon, as a throw, hit, or drive in any of several games. **4.** A person who shoots; marksman. **5.** The distance over which something is shot; range. **6.** An attempt, guess, or opportunity. **7.** The heavy metal ball that is put for distance in the shot-put. **8. a.** A photograph or one in a series of photographs. **b.** A single, continuously photographed scene or view in a motion picture. **9.** A hypodermic injection. **10.** A drink of liquor, esp. a measure of about 1½ ounces. [Middle English, from Old English *scot.*]

shot² (shŏt) *v.* Past tense and past participle of **shoot.** [Middle English *schotte, schotten,* from Old English *(ge)scoten.*]

shote (shōt) *n.* Var. of **shoat.**

shot·gun (shŏt'gŭn') *n.* A shoulder-held firearm that fires multiple pellets through a smooth bore.

shot-put (shŏt'po͝ot') *n.* **1.** An athletic event in which the

shorthorn

shot is thrown for distance. **2.** One such throw. **3.** The ball used in this event. **—shot′-put′ter** n.

should (shŏŏd). Past tense of **shall**, but more often used as an auxiliary verb expressing degrees of the present and future and indicating: **1.** Obligation; duty: *You should send her a note.* **2.** Anticipation of a probable occurrence: *They should arrive at noon.* **3.** Condition: *If he should fall, then so would I.* **4.** Uncertainty in a future event: *I should think he would like to go.* **5.** Moderation of the directness or bluntness of a statement: *I should hate to be late.* [Middle English *sholde*, from Old English *sceolde*, past tense of *sceolon*, to owe, be obliged to.]

    Usage: **should, would.** The various ways in which *should* and *would* can be used are given in their respective definitions. It is, however, worth mentioning here that both *should* and *would* can be used with the first person (singular and plural) in expressions of polite or understated requests, but that only *would* can be used with the second person (singular and plural) in such requests: *We* (first person) *would* (or *should*) *be much obliged if you would help us. Would you* (second person) *please sign here? I wish you would help.* On the other hand, only *should* expresses obligation or duty: *You should study for the test.* And only *would* can be used to mean "wish strongly": *I would that I were young again! Would* is also the choice in constructions expressing simple wish, desire, or intent: *Those who would forbid off-shore oil drilling have forgotten our urgent need for domestic oil.*

shoul·der (shōl′dər) n. **1.** *Anat.* **a.** The part of the human body between the neck and upper arm. **b.** The joint connecting the arm with the trunk. **2.** The corresponding part of an animal. **3. shoulders.** The two shoulders and the area of the back between them. **4.** The forequarter of some animals. **5.** The portion of a garment that covers the shoulder. **6.** The angle between the face and the flank of a bastion in fortifications. **7.** The edge or ridge running on either side of a roadway. **8.** Any shoulderlike projection or slope. **—modifier:** *shoulder muscles; shoulder pads.* **—tr.v. 1.** To place on the shoulder or shoulders for carrying. **2.** To take on; bear; assume: *shouldering the blame.* **3.** To push with or as if with the shoulders. **—intr.v.** To push with the shoulder or shoulders. **—idiom. shoulder to shoulder.** Side by side and close together. [Middle English *shulder*, from Old English *sculdor*.]

shoulder blade. The scapula.

shoulder strap. A strap worn over the shoulder to support the weight of something, such as a knapsack or purse.

should·n't (shŏŏd′nt). Should not.

shouldst (shŏŏdst). Also **should·est** (shŏŏd′ĭst). *Archaic.* A form of **should,** used with *thou.*

shout (shout) n. A loud cry, often expressing strong emotion or a command. **—tr.v.** To say with a shout. **—intr.v.** To utter a shout. [Middle English *shouten.*] **—shout′er** n.

shove (shŭv) v. **shoved, shov·ing. —tr.v.** To push forcefully or rudely. **—intr.v.** To push someone or something with sudden force. **—phrasal verb. shove off. 1.** To set a beached boat afloat. **2.** *Informal.* To leave. **—n.** The act of shoving, esp. a rude push. [Middle English *shouven*, from Old English *scūfan.*] **—shov′er** n.

shov·el (shŭv′əl) n. **1.** A tool with a handle and a somewhat flattened scoop for picking up dirt, snow, etc. **2.** A large mechanical device with a jawed scoop for heavy digging or excavation. **—v. -eled** or **-elled, -el·ing** or **-el·ling. —tr.v. 1.** To dig into or move with a shovel: *shovel snow.* **2.** To clear away or make with a shovel: *shovel the walk.* **3.** To convey or set down in a hasty or careless way; unload. **—intr.v.** To dig or work with a shovel. [Middle English, from Old English *scofl.*]

shov·el·er (shŭv′ə-lər) n. Also **shov·el·ler. 1.** Someone or something that shovels. **2.** A widely ‵distributed duck, *Spatula clypeata* (or *Anas rhynchotis*), having a broad bill.

shov·el·ful (shŭv′əl-fŏŏl′) n. The amount a shovel will hold.

show (shō) v. **showed, shown** (shōn) or **showed, show·ing. —tr.v. 1. a.** To cause or allow to be seen or viewed; to display; make visible. **b.** To present in public exhibition or competition. **2.** To conduct; guide: *Show her around.* **3.** To point out; demonstrate: *show the way out.* **4. a.** To manifest; reveal. **b.** To indicate; to register. **5.** To grant; confer; bestow: *show favor.* **6.** *Law.* To plead; allege: *show cause.*

—intr.v. 1. To be or become visible or evident. **2.** *Informal.* To arrive as expected. **3.** To be exhibited; to run: *The film will show three days.* **4.** To finish third or better in a sports contest. **—phrasal verbs. show off.** To display or behave in an ostentatious or conspicuous manner. **show up. 1.** To expose or reveal (faults, defects, etc.). **2.** To be clearly visible. **3.** To put in an appearance; arrive. **4.** *Informal.* To prove that one is superior to (another); outdo. **—n. 1.** The act of showing or revealing. **2.** A display; demonstration: *a show of power.* **3.** An appearance; semblance. **4.** A striking appearance or display; spectacle. **5.** A pompous or ostentatious display. **6. a.** Any public exhibition or entertainment. **b.** A troupe or company. **7.** A trace; indication. **8.** *Informal.* Any affair or undertaking; a result: *a poor show.* **9.** Third place or better in a sports contest. **—modifier:** *the show ring; a show stopper.* [Middle English *showen*, from Old English *scēawian*, to look at, see.]

    Syns: *show, demonstrate, display, evidence, evince, exhibit, manifest v.* Core meaning: To make apparent (*showed prudence by driving carefully*). See also Syns at **prove.**

show·boat (shō′bōt′) n. A river steamboat having actors and a theater aboard for performances at ports.

show business. The entertainment industry or arts.

show·case (shō′kās′) n. **1.** A display case, as in a store or museum. **2.** A setting for advantageous display.

show·down (shō′doun′) n. An event or circumstance that forces an issue to a conclusion.

show·er (shou′ər) n. **1. a.** A brief fall of rain, hail, or sleet. **b.** A downfall of a group of objects from the sky: *a meteor shower.* **2.** Any brief or sudden downpour. **3.** An abundant flow. **4.** A party held to honor and present gifts to someone: *a bridal shower.* **5.** Also **shower bath. a.** A bath in which water is sprayed on the bather. **b.** A room, booth, or apparatus for such baths. **—modifier:** *a shower curtain.* **—tr.v. 1.** To sprinkle; spray. **2.** To bestow abundantly: *shower praises.* **—intr.v. 1.** To fall or pour down in a shower. **2.** To take a shower. [Middle English *shour*, from Old English *scūr.*]

show·ing (shō′ĭng) n. **1.** A presentation or display. **2.** Performance, as in a competition: *a poor showing.*

show·man (shō′mən) n. **1.** A theatrical producer. **2.** A person with a flair for the dramatic. **—show′man·ship′** n.

shown (shōn) v. A past participle of **show.** [Middle English *shawen.*]

show·off (shō′ôf′, -ŏf′) n. **1.** Ostentatious display or behavior. **2.** Someone who shows off; exhibitionist.

show·piece (shō′pēs′) n. Something exhibited, esp. as an outstanding example of its kind.

show place. A place that is viewed and frequented for its beauty, historical interest, etc.

show room. A room in which merchandise is on display.

show·y (shō′ē) adj. **-i·er, -i·est. 1.** Making a conspicuous display; visually striking: *showy flowers.* **2.** Ostentatious; gaudy; flashy. **—show′i·ly** adv. **—show′i·ness** n.

shrank (shrăngk) v. A past tense of **shrink.** [Middle English *schrank*, from Old English *scranc.*]

shrap·nel (shrăp′nəl) n., pl. **shrapnel. 1.** An artillery shell containing metal balls, fused to explode in the air above enemy troops. **2.** Shell fragments from any high-explosive shell. [After General Henry *Shrapnel* (1761–1842), British artillery officer, its inventor.]

shred (shrĕd) n. **1.** A long, irregular strip cut or torn off from something. **2.** A small amount; particle. **—tr.v. shred·ded** or **shred, shred·ding.** To cut or tear into shreds. [Middle English *shrede*, from Old English *scrēade.*] **—shred′der** n.

shrew (shrōō) n. **1.** Any of various small, chiefly insectivorous mammals of the family Soricidae, having a long, pointed nose and small eyes. Sometimes called **shrewmouse. 2.** A scolding, sharp-tempered woman. [Ult. from Old English *scrēawa.*]

shrewd (shrōōd) adj. **-er, -est. 1.** Discerning; astute. **2.** Artful; cunning. **3.** Sharp; penetrating. [Middle English *shrewede*, wicked, from *shrew*, evil person.] **—shrewd′ly** adv. **—shrewd′ness** n.

    Syns: *shrewd, astute, cagey, slick adj.* Core meaning: Having or showing clever awareness and resourcefulness (*a shrewd operator; a shrewd deal*).

ă pat	ā pay	â care	ä father	ĕ pet	ē be	hw which	ĭ pit	ī tie	î pier	ŏ pot	ō toe	ô paw, for	oi noise
ŏŏ took	ōō boot	ou out	th thin	th this	ŭ cut		û urge		zh vision	ə about,	item, edible, gallop, circus		

shrew·ish (shrōō′ĭsh) *adj.* Ill-tempered; nagging.
—**shrew′ish·ly** *adv.* —**shrew′ish·ness** *n.*

shriek (shrēk) *n.* **1.** A shrill outcry; screech. **2.** Any sound suggestive of a shriek. —*intr.v.* To make a loud, shrill cry. —*tr.v.* To utter with a shriek. [Middle English *shriken.*] —**shriek′er** *n.*

shrift (shrĭft) *n. Archaic.* **1.** The act of shriving. **2.** Confession to a priest. **3.** Absolution given by a priest. [Middle English, from Old English *scrift,* from *scrīfan,* to hear confession, impose penance.]

shrike (shrīk) *n.* Any of various carnivorous birds of the family Laniidae, that has a hooked bill and often impales its prey on thorns or barbs of wire fencing. Also called **butcherbird.** [Prob. ult. from Old English *scrīc,* thrush.]

shrike
George Miksch Sutton

shrill (shrĭl) *adj.* **-er, -est.** High-pitched and piercing: *a shrill whistle.* —*tr.v.* To utter in a shrill manner. —*intr.v.* To produce a shrill sound. [Middle English *shrille,* from *shrillen,* to shriek.] —**shrill′ness** *n.* —**shril′ly** *adv.*

shrimp (shrĭmp) *n., pl.* **shrimp** or **shrimps. 1. a.** Any of various small, slender-bodied, chiefly marine decapod crustaceans of the suborder Natantia, many species of which are edible. **b.** Any of various similar crustaceans. **2.** *Slang.* A small or unimportant person. —*modifier: shrimp salad.* [Middle English *shrimpe.*]

shrine (shrīn) *n.* **1.** A container for sacred relics; reliquary. **2.** The tomb of a saint or other venerated person. **3.** A site or object hallowed or revered for its history or associations. —*tr.v.* **shrined, shrin·ing.** To enshrine. [Middle English, from Old English *scrīn,* from Latin *scrīnium,* box.]

shrink (shrĭngk) *v.* **shrank** (shrăngk) or **shrunk** (shrŭngk), **shrunk** or **shrunk·en** (shrŭng′kən), **shrink·ing.** —*intr.v.* **1.** To draw together or become smaller from heat, moisture, or cold; to contract. **2.** To dwindle: *His savings shrank rapidly.* **3.** To draw back; recoil. —*tr.v.* To cause to shrink. —*n.* **1.** An act of shrinking. **2.** *Slang.* A psychiatrist. [Middle English *shrinken,* from Old English *scrincan.*] —**shrink′a·ble** *adj.* —**shrink′er** *n.*

shrink·age (shrĭng′kĭj) *n.* **1.** The process of shrinking. **2.** The amount or extent of loss by shrinking.

shrinking violet. *Informal.* A shy or retiring person.

shrive (shrīv) *v.* **shrove** (shrōv) or **shrived, shriv·en** (shrĭv′ən) or **shrived, shriv·ing.** —*tr.v.* **1.** To confess and give absolution to (a penitent). **2.** To obtain absolution for (oneself). —*intr.v.* **1.** To make or go to confession. **2.** To hear confessions. [Middle English *shriven,* from Old English *scrīfan,* from Latin *scrībere,* to write.] —**shriv′er** *n.*

shriv·el (shrĭv′əl) *v.* **-eled** or **-elled, -el·ing** or **-el·ling.** —*intr.v.* **1.** To shrink and wrinkle, often in drying. **2.** To lose vitality or intensity. —*tr.v.* To cause to shrivel. [Orig. unknown.]

shriv·en (shrĭv′ən) *v.* A past participle of **shrive.** [Middle English *schriven,* from Old English *(ge)scrifen.*]

shroud (shroud) *n.* **1.** A cloth used to wrap a body for burial. **2.** Something that conceals, protects, or screens. **3.** One of a set of lines stretched from the masthead to a vessel's sides to support the mast. **4.** One of the ropes connecting the harness and canopy of a parachute. —*tr.v.* **1.** To wrap (a corpse) in a cloth for burial. **2.** To screen; hide. —See Syns at **wrap.** [Middle English *schrud,* garment, clothing, from Old English *scrūd.*]

shrove (shrōv) *v.* A past tense of **shrive.** [Middle English, from Old English *scrāf.*]

Shrove·tide (shrōv′tīd′) *n.* The three days, Shrove Sunday,

Shrove Monday, and Shrove Tuesday, preceding Ash Wednesday. [Middle English *schroftyde.*]

shrub (shrŭb) *n.* A low, woody plant with several stems; bush. [Middle English *schrubbe,* from Old English *scrybb.*]

shrub·ber·y (shrŭb′ə-rē) *n., pl.* **-ies. 1.** Shrubs in general. **2.** A group or planting of shrubs.

shrub·by (shrŭb′ē) *adj.* **-bi·er, -bi·est. 1.** Consisting of or covered with shrubs. **2.** Shrublike. —**shrub′bi·ness** *n.*

shrug (shrŭg) *v.* **shrugged, shrug·ging.** —*tr.v.* To raise (the shoulders) as a gesture of doubt, disdain, or indifference. —*intr.v.* To make this gesture. —*phrasal verb.* **shrug off. 1.** To minimize. **2.** To get rid of. **3.** To wriggle out of (clothing). —*n.* **1.** The expressive gesture of raising the shoulders. **2.** A short jacket or sweater, open down the front. [Middle English *shruggen.*]

shrunk (shrŭngk) *v.* A past tense and a past participle of **shrink.** [Middle English *shrunk, shrunken,* from Old English *scruncon, (ge)scruncen.*]

shrunk·en (shrŭng′kən) *v.* A past participle of **shrink.** [Middle English *shrunken,* from Old English *(ge)scruncen.*]

shuck (shŭk) *n.* An outer covering, such as a pea pod, corn husk, or oyster shell. —*tr.v.* **1.** To remove the husk or shell from. **2.** *Informal.* To cast off: *shucked his clothing.* —*interj.* **shucks.** A word used to express disappointment or annoyance. [Orig. unknown.] —**shuck′er** *n.*

shud·der (shŭd′ər) *intr.v.* **1.** To tremble convulsively, as from fear or aversion. **2.** To vibrate; quiver. —See Syns at **shake.** —*n.* A convulsive shiver. [Middle English *shudren,* from Middle Low German *schōderen.*]

shuf·fle (shŭf′əl) *v.* **-fled, -fling.** —*tr.v.* **1.** To drag (the feet) along the floor or ground. **2.** To move (something) from one place to another. **3.** To mix together in a disordered, haphazard fashion. **4.** To put aside or conceal hastily. **5.** To mix together (playing cards, tiles, or dominoes) so that they will later be drawn or dealt in random order. —*intr.v.* **1.** To move with a shambling, idle gait. **2.** To dance the shuffle. **3.** To shift about from place to place. —*n.* **1.** A shuffling gait or movement. **2.** A dance in which the feet scrape along the floor at each step. **3. a.** The act of mixing cards, dominoes, or tiles. **b.** A player's right or turn to do this. [Prob. from Low German *schuffeln,* to walk clumsily, shuffle cards.] —**shuf′fler** *n.*

shuf·fle·board (shŭf′əl-bôrd′, -bōrd′) *n.* **1.** A game in which disks are pushed along a smooth, level surface toward numbered squares. **2.** The surface on which this game is played. [Alteration of earlier *shove-board.*]

shun (shŭn) *tr.v.* **shunned, shun·ning.** To keep away from deliberately: *shun a disgraced person; shun a task.* —See Syns at **avoid.** [Middle English *shunnen,* from Old English *scunian,* to avoid, be afraid, abhor.] —**shun′ner** *n.*

shunt (shŭnt) *n.* **1.** The act of turning aside or moving to an alternate course. **2.** A railroad switch. **3.** *Elect.* A relatively low-resistance connection between two points in an electric circuit that forms an alternative path for a portion of the current. Also called **by-pass.** —*tr.v.* **1.** To turn or move (something) aside or onto another course: *shunting traffic around a bottleneck.* **2.** *Elect.* To provide or divert (current) by means of a shunt. —*intr.v.* To move or turn aside. [Middle English *shunten,* to flinch, shy, run away.]

shush (shŭsh) *interj.* A word used to demand silence. —*tr.v.* To demand silence from by saying "shush."

shut (shŭt) *v.* **shut, shut·ting.** —*tr.v.* **1.** To move (a door, lid, valve, etc.) into closed position over or within an opening. **2.** To block passage or access to. **3.** To prevent or forbid access to: *rooms that were shut off from the public.* **4.** To confine: *shut him in a cage.* **5.** To close (a business establishment). —*intr.v.* To move or be moved to a closed position; close. —*phrasal verbs.* **shut down. 1.** To halt operation of. **2.** To stop operating, esp. automatically. **shut off.** To turn off: *shut off the electricity.* **shut out. 1.** To keep from entering: *shut out noise.* **2.** To prevent (a team) from scoring any runs or points. **shut up. 1.** To cause to be silent. **2.** To be or become silenced. [Middle English *shutten,* from Old English *scyttan.*]

shut·down (shŭt′doun′) *n.* **1.** A temporary closing of an industrial plant. **2.** A cessation of operation.

shut·eye (shŭt′ī′) *n. Slang.* Sleep.

shut-in (shŭt′ĭn′) *n.* A person confined indoors by illness or disability. —*adj.* Confined as by illness.

shut·out (shŭt′out′) *n.* **1.** A lockout. **2.** A game in which one side does not score.

shut·ter (shŭt′ər) *n.* **1.** Someone or something that shuts. **2.** A hinged cover or screen for a window. **3.** A mechanical device that opens and shuts the lens aperture of a camera. —*tr.v.* To furnish or close with a shutter or shutters.

shut·ter·bug (shŭt′ər-bŭg′) *n. Informal.* An amateur photographer.

shut·tle (shŭt′l) *n.* **1.** A device used in weaving to carry the woof thread back and forth between the warp threads. **2.** A device for holding the thread in tatting, in netting, and in a sewing machine. **3.** A train, bus, or plane making short, frequent trips between two points. **4.** The act of traveling back and forth between two points. —*modifier: a shuttle bus.* —*v.* **-tled, -tling.** —*intr.v.* To go, move, or travel back and forth by or as if by a shuttle. —*tr.v.* To move by or as if by a shuttle. [Middle English *schutylle,* from Old English *scytel,* dart, missile.]

shut·tle·cock (shŭt′l-kŏk′) *n.* **1.** A rounded cork or similar material with a crown of feathers, used in the games of badminton and battledore. Also called **bird** and **birdie. 2.** The game of battledore. [SHUTTLE + COCK (bird).]

shy[1] (shī) *adj.* **shi·er** or **shy·er, shi·est** or **shy·est. 1.** Easily startled; timid. **2.** Bashfully reserved; modest. **3.** Distrustful; cautious. **4.** *Informal.* Short; lacking: *Eleven is one shy of a dozen.* —See Syns at **modest.** —*intr.v.* **shied, shy·ing. 1.** To move suddenly, as if startled: *The deer shied at the sound.* **2.** To draw back, as from fear. —*n., pl.* **shies.** A sudden movement; a start. [Middle English *schey,* easily frightened, timid, from Old English *scēoh.*] —**shy′er** *n.* —**shy′ly** *adv.* —**shy′ness** *n.*

shy[2] (shī) *tr.v.* **shied, shy·ing.** To throw with a swift sidewise motion: *shy horseshoes.* —*n., pl.* **shies.** A quick throw; fling. [Prob. from SHY (easily frightened).]

shy·lock (shī′lŏk′) *n.* Also **Shy·lock.** A heartless, exacting creditor. [After *Shylock,* the ruthless usurer in Shakespeare's *Merchant of Venice.*]

shy·ster (shī′stər) *n. Slang.* An unethical or unscrupulous lawyer or politician. [Poss. after *Scheuster,* an unscrupulous 19th-cent. New York lawyer.]

si (sē) *n. Mus.* A syllable formerly used to represent the seventh tone of the diatonic scale; ti. [Italian.]

Si The symbol for the element silicon.

Si·a·mese (sī′ə-mēz′, -mēs′) *adj.* **1.** Thai. **2.** Closely connected or very similar; twin. —*n., pl.* **Siamese.** Thai.

Siamese cat. A short-haired cat of a breed developed in the Orient, having blue eyes and a pale fawn or gray coat with darker ears, face, tail, and feet.

sib (sĭb) *n.* **1. a.** A blood relation. **b.** Relatives; kinfolk. **2.** A brother or sister; sibling. —*adj.* Related by blood. [Middle English, from Old English *sibb.*]

sib·i·lant (sĭb′ə-lənt) *adj.* Producing a hissing sound. —*n.* **1.** A speech sound that suggests hissing, as (s) or (z). **2.** A sibilant consonant. [Latin *sībilāns,* pres. part. of *sībilāre,* to hiss, whistle.] —**sib′i·lance** *n.* —**sib′i·lant·ly** *adv.*

sib·ling (sĭb′lĭng) *n.* One of two or more persons having at least one parent in common; a brother or sister. [Middle English *siblyng,* from Old English *sibling.*]

sib·yl (sĭb′əl) *n.* **1.** One of a number of women regarded as oracles or prophetesses by the ancient Greeks and Romans. **2.** Any female prophet.

sib·yl·line (sĭb′ə-lĭn′, -lēn′) *adj.* Also **si·byl·ic** (sĭ-bĭl′ĭk) or **si·byl·lic. 1.** Of, like, or coming from a sibyl. **2.** Prophetic.

sic[1] (sĭk, sēk) *adv. Latin.* Thus; so. Used in written texts to indicate that a surprising word, phrase, or fact is not a mistake and should be read as it stands. [Latin *sīc.*]

sic[2] (sĭk) *tr.v.* **sicced, sic·cing.** Also **sick. 1.** To urge to attack or chase. **2.** To set upon or chase: *"Sic him," he commanded his dog.* [Dial. var. of SEEK.]

sic·ca·tive (sĭk′ə-tĭv) *n.* A substance added to promote drying; a drier. —*adj.* Drying. [Latin *siccātīvus,* drying, from *siccāre,* to dry, from *siccus,* dry.]

Si·cil·ian (sĭ-sĭl′yən, -sĭl′ē-ən) *adj.* Of Sicily or its inhabitants. —*n.* **1.** A native of Sicily. **2.** The dialect of Italian spoken in Sicily.

sick[1] (sĭk) *adj.* **-er, -est. 1. a.** Ailing; ill; unwell. **b.** Nauseated. **2.** Of or for sick persons: *sick leave.* **3. a.** Mentally ill or disturbed. **b.** Morbid or unwholesome. **c.** Defective; un-

sound: *a sick economy.* **4. a.** Deeply distressed; upset. **b.** Disgusted; revolted. **c.** Weary; tired: *sick of it all.* **d.** Pining; longing: *sick for home.* **5.** Unable to produce a profitable yield of crops. [Middle English *sēk,* from Old English *sēoc.*]

    Syns: **sick, ill, indisposed, unwell** *adj. Core meaning:* Not in good physical or mental condition (*a sick patient*). SICK, ILL, and UNWELL are used interchangeably. INDISPOSED refers to minor sickness (*Although she was indisposed, the singer did not cancel her performance*).

sick[2] (sĭk) *v.* Var. of **sic** (to urge to attack).

sick·bay (sĭk′bā′) *n.* The hospital and dispensary of a ship.

sick·bed (sĭk′bĕd′) *n.* A sick person's bed.

sick call. 1. The daily line-up of military personnel requiring medical attention. **2.** The signal announcing this.

sick·en (sĭk′ən) *tr.v.* To make sick. —*intr.v.* To become sick. —See Syns at **repel.** —**sick′en·er** *n.*

sick·en·ing (sĭk′ə-nĭng) *adj.* **1.** Causing sickness or nausea. **2.** Revolting or disgusting; loathsome. —See Syns at **unspeakable.** —**sick′en·ing·ly** *adv.*

sick·ish (sĭk′ĭsh) *adj.* Somewhat sick. —**sick′ish·ly** *adv.*

sick·le (sĭk′əl) *n.* A tool with a curved blade attached to a short handle, for cutting grain or tall grass. [Middle English *sikel,* from Old English *sicol,* ult. from Latin *sēcula.*]

sickle

sick leave. Time off from work with pay allowed an employee because of sickness.

sickle cell anemia. A hereditary anemia characterized by the presence of oxygen-deficient, abnormally crescent-shaped red blood cells, episodic pain, and leg ulcers.

sick·ly (sĭk′lē) *adj.* **-li·er, -li·est. 1.** Prone to sickness; frail. **2.** Of or associated with sickness: *a sickly pallor.* **3.** Nauseating; sickening. **4.** Feeble; weak: *a sickly smile.* —*adv.* In a sick manner. —**sick′li·ness** *n.*

sick·ness (sĭk′nĭs) *n.* **1.** The condition of being sick; illness. **2.** A disease; malady. **3.** Nausea.

side (sīd) *n.* **1.** *Geom.* **a.** A line segment that forms a part of the boundary of a plane figure. **b.** A segment of a plane that forms a part of the boundary of a three-dimensional figure. **2.** A surface of an object. **3.** Either of two surfaces of a flat object, such as a piece of paper. **4. a.** Either of the two halves into which an object is divided by an axis extending from top to bottom or front to back, or by a plane in which both these axes lie. **b.** Either the right or left half of a human or animal body. **5.** The space immediately next to someone or something: *the side of the road.* **6. a.** An area separated from another by something intervening: *this side of the river.* **b.** A part or area identified by location with respect to a center: *the east side of town.* **7.** One of two or more opposing groups, teams, or opinions. **8.** A distinct aspect or quality of something. **9.** Line of descent. —*adj.* **1.** Located on a side: *a side door.* **2.** From or to one side; oblique: *a side view.* **3.** Minor; incidental: *a side interest.* **4.** Supplementary: *a side benefit.* —*tr.v.* **sid·ed, sid·ing.** To provide sides or siding for: *side a barn.* —*phrasal verb.* **side with** (or **against**). To align oneself with (or against). —*idioms.* **on the side.** In addition to the main portion, occupation, or arrangement. **side by side.** Next to each other; close together. **take sides.** To associate oneself with a faction, contested opinion, or cause. [Middle English, from Old English *sīde.*]

side arm. A small weapon carried at the side or waist.

side·arm (sīd′ärm′) *adj.* Thrown with or marked by a sweep of the arm between shoulder and hip height.

---

side·board (sīd′bôrd′, -bōrd′) *n.* A piece of dining-room furniture with drawers for linens and tableware.

side·burns (sīd′bûrnz′) *pl.n.* Growths of hair down the sides of the face in front of the ears, esp. when worn without a beard. [Alteration of BURNSIDES.]

side·car (sīd′kär′) *n.* A one-wheeled car for a single passenger, attached to the side of a motorcycle.

sid·ed (sī′dĭd) *adj.* Having sides usu. of a specified number or kind: *many-sided; marble-sided.*

side effect. A peripheral or secondary effect, esp. an undesirable secondary effect of a drug or therapy.

side·kick (sīd′kĭk′) *n. Slang.* A close companion; pal.

side·light (sīd′līt′) *n.* **1.** A light coming from the side. **2.** *Naut.* Either of two lights, red to port, green to starboard, shown by ships at night. **3.** Incidental information.

side·line (sīd′līn′) *n.* Also **side line. 1. a.** A line along either of the two sides of a playing court or field, marking its limits. **b. sidelines.** The space outside such limits, occupied by spectators and inactive players. **c. sidelines.** The position or point of view of a spectator. **2.** A line of merchandise carried in addition to regular merchandise. **3.** A secondary job or activity. —*tr.v.* **-lined, -lin·ing.** To remove or keep from active participation.

side·ling (sīd′lĭng) *adj.* **1.** Oblique. **2.** Sloping. —*adv.* Obliquely; sideways. [Middle English *sideling.*]

side·long (sīd′lông′, -lŏng′) *adj.* **1.** Directed to one side; sideways: *a sidelong glance.* **2.** Slanting; sloping. [Alteration of SIDELING.] —**side′long′** *adv.*

side·man (sīd′măn′) *n.* An instrumentalist in a jazz band.

si·de·re·al (sī-dîr′ē-əl) *adj.* Of, concerned with, or measured by the stars: *sidereal time.* [From Latin *sīdereus,* from *sīdus,* constellation.]

sidereal day. The time required for a complete rotation of the earth measured against the vernal equinox, or 23 hours, 56 minutes, 4.09 seconds.

sidereal year. The time required for one complete revolution of the earth about the sun, relative to the fixed stars, or 365 days, 6 hours, 9 minutes, 9.54 seconds.

sid·er·ite (sīd′ə-rīt′) *n.* An impure yellowish-brown iron carbonate mineral. [Greek *sidēros,* iron + -ITE.]

side·sad·dle (sīd′săd′l) *n.* A woman's saddle designed so that a rider may sit with both legs on one side of the horse. —*adv.* On a sidesaddle.

side show. 1. A small show offered in addition to the main attraction. **2.** A diverting spectacle.

side·slip (sīd′slĭp′) *intr.v.* **-slipped, -slip·ping.** To slip or skid to one side. —*n.* A sideways skid or movement.

side·split·ting (sīd′splĭt′ĭng) *adj.* Causing one's sides to ache, as with laughter. —**side′split′ting·ly** *adv.*

side·step (sīd′stĕp′) *v.* **-stepped, -step·ping.** —*intr.v.* **1.** To step aside. **2.** To dodge an issue or responsibility. —*tr.v.* **1.** To step out of the way of. **2.** To evade; skirt.

side stroke. A swimming stroke in which a person swims on one side and thrusts his arms forward alternately while performing a scissors kick.

side·swipe (sīd′swīp′) *tr.v.* **-swiped, -swip·ing.** To strike along the side in passing. —*n.* A glancing blow.

side·track (sīd′trăk′) *tr.v.* **1.** To switch from a main track to a siding. **2.** To divert from a main issue or course. —*intr.v.* To turn aside; digress. —*n.* A railroad siding.

side·walk (sīd′wôk′) *n.* A usu. paved walk or raised path along the side of a road, used by pedestrians.

side·ward (sīd′wərd) *adj.* Moving or directed toward one side. —*adv.* Also **side·wards** (-wərdz) Toward or from one side.

side·ways (sīd′wāz′). Also **side·way** (-wā′) or **side·wise** (-wīz′). —*adv.* **1.** Toward or from one side. **2.** With one side forward. —*adj.* Toward or from one side.

side wheel. One of a pair of paddle wheels on the side of a steamboat. —*modifier* (side-wheel): *a side-wheel steamer.* —**side′-wheel′er** *n.*

side·wind·er (sīd′wīn′dər) *n.* A small rattlesnake, *Crotalus cerastes,* of the southwestern United States and Mexico, that moves by a distinctive lateral looping motion.

side·wise (sīd′wīz′) *adv. & adj.* Var. of **sideways.**

sid·ing (sī′dĭng) *n.* **1.** A short section of railroad track connected by switches with a main track. **2.** Material, such as boards or shingles, used for surfacing a frame building.

si·dle (sīd′l) *intr.v.* **-dled, -dling.** To move sideways or edge along, esp. furtively or unobtrusively. —*n.* A sidelong movement. [Back-formation from SIDELING and SIDELONG.]

siege (sēj) *n.* **1.** The surrounding and blockading of a town or fortress by an army bent on capturing it. **2.** A prolonged period, as of illness or adversity. —*tr.v.* **sieged, sieg·ing.** To lay siege to; besiege. [Middle English *sege,* from Old French, seat, from Latin *sedēre,* to be seated.]

si·en·na (sē-ĕn′ə) *n.* **1.** A special clay containing iron and manganese oxides, used as a pigment for oil and watercolor painting. **2. Raw sienna. 3. Burnt sienna.** [From Italian *terra di Sienna,* "earth of *Siena*", a city in Italy.]

si·er·ra (sē-ĕr′ə) *n.* A rugged range of mountains having a jagged outline. [Spanish, from Latin *serra,* saw.]

si·es·ta (sē-ĕs′tə) *n.* An afternoon rest or nap. [Spanish, from Latin *sexta (hora),* sixth (hour after sunrise), noon.]

sieve (sĭv) *n.* Any meshwork, esp. a utensil of wire mesh or closely perforated metal, used for straining, sifting, or draining. —*v.* **sieved, siev·ing.** —*tr.v.* To pass (something) through a sieve; sift. —*intr.v.* To sift. [Middle English *sive,* from Old English *sife.*]

sift (sĭft) *tr.v.* **1.** To put through a sieve or other straining device in order to separate the fine from the coarse particles. **2.** To distinguish; to screen: *sift the candidates for the job.* **3.** To apply by scattering with or as if with a sieve. **4.** To examine closely and carefully. —*intr.v.* **1.** To sift something. **2.** To pass through or as if through a sieve: *"The troops, sifting through the forest"* (Stephen Crane). **3.** To make a careful examination. [Middle English *siften,* from Old English *siftan.*] —**sift′er** *n.*

sift·ings (sĭf′tĭngz) *pl.n.* Material removed or separated with or as if with a sieve.

sigh (sī) *intr.v.* **1.** To exhale in a long, audible breath, as in sorrow or relief. **2.** To emit a similar sound: *willows sighing in the wind.* **3.** To feel longing or grief; mourn. —*tr.v.* To express with or as if with an audible exhalation. —*n.* The act or sound of sighing. [Middle English *sighen,* prob. from Old English *sīcan.*]

sight (sīt) *n.* **1.** The ability to see. **2.** The act or fact of seeing. **3.** The field of a person's vision. **4.** The foreseeable future; prospect: *no solution in sight.* **5.** A view. **6.** Something worth seeing; a spectacle. **7.** *Informal.* Something unsightly. **8. a.** A device used to assist aim by guiding the eye, as on a firearm. **b.** An aim or observation taken with such a device. **9.** An opportunity to observe. —*tr.v.* **1.** To see or observe within one's field of vision: *sight land.* **2.** To observe or take a sight of with an instrument: *sight a target.* **3.** To adjust the sights of. **4.** To take aim with. —*intr.v.* **1.** To look carefully. **2.** To take aim. —*idiom.* **at** (or **on**) **sight. 1.** When first seen. **2.** On presentation or demand for payment. [Middle English, from Old English *sihth, gesiht, gesiht,* eyesight, vision, thing seen.]

sight·ed (sī′tĭd) *adj.* **1.** Having sight; not blind. **2.** Having eyesight of a specified kind: *keen-sighted.*

sight·ly (sīt′lē) *adj.* **-li·er, -li·est. 1.** Pleasing to see; handsome. **2.** Affording a fine view. —**sight′li·ness** *n.*

sight-read (sīt′rēd′) *v.* **-read** (-rĕd′), **-read·ing.** —*tr.v.* To read or perform without preparation or prior acquaintance: *She sight-read the piano accompaniment.* —*intr.v.* To read or perform something without preparation or prior acquaintance. —**sight′-read′er** *n.*

sight·see·ing (sīt′sē′ĭng) *n.* The act of touring places of interest. —*modifier: a sightseeing bus.* —**sight′se′er** *n.*

side wheel

sig·ma (sĭg′mə) n. **1.** The 18th letter in the Greek alphabet, written Σ,σ, and represented in English as *S, s.* **2.** *Symbol* Σ *Physics.* Any of three subatomic particles in the baryon family. [Greek.]

sig·moid (sĭg′moid′) *adj.* Also **sig·moi·dal** (sĭg-moi′dl). **1.** Having the shape of the letter S. **2.** Pertaining to the sigmoid flexure of the colon.

sigmoid flexure. An S-shaped bend in the colon between the descending section and the rectum.

sign (sīn) n. **1.** Something that suggests the presence or existence of a fact, condition, or quality; an indication: *A fever is a sign of sickness.* **2.** An action or gesture used to convey an idea: *gave the go-ahead sign.* **3.** A board, poster, or placard displayed to convey information or a direction: *a stop sign.* **4.** A conventional figure or device that stands for a word, phrase, or operation. **5.** A presage. **6.** *Astrol.* One of the 12 divisions of the zodiac. —*tr.v.* **1.** To affix one's signature to. **2.** To write: *sign her name.* **3.** To approve or ratify (a document) by affixing a signature, seal, or other mark. **4.** To hire by obtaining a signature on a contract: *sign a new player.* **5.** To relinquish or transfer title to by signature: *sign over the property.* **6.** To express or signify with a sign. —*intr.v.* **1.** To signal. **2.** To write one's signature. —*phrasal verbs.* **sign off.** To stop transmission after identifying the broadcasting station. **sign on. 1.** To agree to work. **2.** To hire to work. **sign up.** To volunteer one's services; enlist. [Middle English *signe,* from Old French, from Latin *signum.*] —**sign′er** n.

 Syns: **sign, evidence, indication, indicator, manifestation, mark, symptom, token** n. *Core meaning:* Something visible or evident that gives grounds for believing in the existence of something else (*intolerance as a sign of bigotry*).

sig·nal (sĭg′nəl) n. **1. a.** A sign, gesture, device, or other indicator serving as a means of communication. **b.** A message communicated by such means. **2.** An occasion; spur: *The execution was the signal for mass protests.* **3.** *Electronics.* An impulse or fluctuating electric quantity, such as voltage or current, the variations of which represent coded information. **4.** The sound, image, or message transmitted or received in telegraphy, telephony, radio, television, or radar. —*modifier: a signal flare.* —*adj.* Remarkable; conspicuous. —v. **-naled** or **-nalled, -nal·ing** or **-nall·ing.** —*tr.v.* **1.** To make a signal or signals to. **2.** To relate or make known by signals. —*intr.v.* To make a signal or signals. [French, from Old French, from Medieval Latin *signāle,* from Latin *signālis,* of a sign, from *signum,* sign.] —**sig′nal·er** or **sig′nal·ler** n. —**sig′nal·ly** adv.

sig·nal·ize (sĭg′nə-līz′) *tr.v.* **-ized, -iz·ing. 1.** To make remarkable or noticeable. **2.** To point out particularly.

sig·nal·man (sĭg′nəl-măn′) n. A person whose responsibility is to send and receive signals, esp. on a ship or train.

sig·na·to·ry (sĭg′nə-tôr′ē, -tōr′ē) n., pl. **-ries.** A person or nation that signs or has signed an agreement. —*adj.* Bound by a signed agreement.

sig·na·ture (sĭg′nə-choŏr′, -chər) n. **1.** The name of a person as written by that person. **2.** A distinctive mark, characteristic, or sound effect. **3.** The act of signing one's name. **4.** *Mus.* **a.** The group of sharps or flats placed at the beginning of a musical staff to indicate key; key signature. **b.** A symbol on a musical staff used to indicate tempo; time signature. **5.** *Printing.* **a.** A section of a book, magazine, etc., that consists of a large sheet printed with four or a multiple of four pages and folded to page size. **b.** A letter, number, or symbol placed at the bottom of the first page of each signature, used as a guide to the proper sequence in binding. [Old French, from *signer,* to sign, from Latin *signāre,* to mark with a sign, from *signum,* sign.]

sign·board (sīn′bôrd′, -bōrd′) n. A board bearing a sign.

sig·net (sĭg′nĭt) n. **1.** A seal, esp. a seal used to stamp official documents. **2.** The impression made with such a seal. —*tr.v.* To mark or officially stamp with a signet. [Middle English, from Old French, dim. of *signe,* sign.]

signet ring. A finger ring bearing a signet.

sig·nif·i·cance (sĭg-nĭf′ĭ-kəns) n. **1.** The condition or quality of being significant. **2.** The sense of something; meaning. **3.** Implied meaning; suggestiveness. —See Syns at **meaning.**

sig·nif·i·cant (sĭg-nĭf′ĭ-kənt) *adj.* **1.** Having or expressing a meaning; meaningful. **2.** Suggestive: *a significant glance.* **3.** Important; notable: *a significant painting.* —See Syns at **important.** [Latin *significāns,* pres. part. of *significāre,* to signify.] —**sig·nif′i·cant·ly** adv.

sig·ni·fi·ca·tion (sĭg′nə-fĭ-kā′shən) n. **1.** The intended meaning; sense. **2.** The act of signifying; communication. —See Syns at **meaning.**

sig·ni·fy (sĭg′nə-fī′) v. **-fied, -fy·ing.** —*tr.v.* **1.** To serve as a sign or symbol of; betoken. **2.** To make known; indicate: *He signified his approval.* —*intr.v.* To have meaning or importance. [Middle English *signifien,* from Old French *signifier,* from Latin *significāre : signum,* sign + *facere,* to make.] —**sig′ni·fi′er** n.

sign language. A system of communication by means of hand gestures, used now esp. by deaf people.

sign of the cross. A gesture of the hand describing a cross from the forehead to the breast and then across the shoulders, made in token of Christian faith.

si·gnor (sēn-yôr′, -yōr′) n., pl. **-gno·ri** (-yō′rē, -yōr′ē) or **-gnors.** The English form of the Italian title *signore.*

si·gno·ra (sēn-yôr′ə, -yōr′ə) n., pl. **-gn·ore** (-yô′rā, -yōr′ā) or **-ras.** The Italian title of courtesy for a married woman, equivalent to the English *Mrs.* or *madam.* [Italian, fem. of *signore,* signor.]

si·gno·re (sēn-yôr′ā, -yōr′ā) n., pl. **-gno·ri** (-yō′rē, -yōr′ē). The Italian title of courtesy for a man, equivalent to the English *Mr.* or *sir.* [Italian, from Latin *senior,* older.]

si·gno·ri·na (sēn′yə-rē′nə) n., pl. **-ne** (-nā) or **-nas.** The Italian title of courtesy for an unmarried woman, equivalent to the English *Miss.* [Italian, dim. of *signora,* signora.]

sign·post (sīn′pōst′) n. **1.** A post with a sign that has information or directions for travelers. **2.** An indicator; guide.

Sikh (sēk) n. A member of a monotheistic religious sect of India founded in the 16th cent. —**Sikh** *adj.* —**Sikh′ism** n.

si·lage (sī′lĭj) n. Green fodder that has been stored and fermented in a silo.

si·lence (sī′ləns) n. **1.** The absence of sound; stillness. **2.** The absence or avoidance of speech or noise, or a period of time marked by this. **3.** Refusal or failure to speak out; secrecy. —*tr.v.* **-lenced, -lenc·ing. 1.** To make silent. **2.** To curtail or stop the expression of; suppress.

si·lenc·er (sī′lən-sər) n. **1.** A device attached to the muzzle of a firearm to muffle the sound it makes when fired. **2.** Someone or something that silences.

si·lent (sī′lənt) *adj.* **1.** Making or having no sound or noise; quiet. **2.** Not disposed to speak; taciturn. **3.** Unable to speak; mute. **4.** Saying or mentioning nothing; secretive. **5.** Not voiced or expressed; tacit: *silent admissions of guilt.* **6.** Inactive. **7.** Unpronounced, as the *b* in *subtle.* [Latin *silēns,* pres. part. of *silēre,* to be silent.] —**si′lent·ly** adv. —**si′lent·ness** n.

silent butler. A small receptacle with a handle and a hinged cover, used for collecting ashes and crumbs.

Si·le·nus (sī-lē′nəs) n. *Gk. Myth.* A satyr, the foster father and teacher of Bacchus.

Si·lex (sī′lĕks′) n. A trademark for a vacuum coffee maker.

sil·hou·ette (sĭl′ŏ͞o-ĕt′) n. **1.** A drawing consisting of the outline of something, esp. a human profile, filled in with a solid color. **2.** An outline of something that appears dark against a light background. —*tr.v.* **-et·ted, -et·ting.** To cause to be seen as a silhouette; to outline. [French, after Étienne de *Silhouette* (1709–67), French author and politician.]

silhouette

sil·i·ca (sĭl′ĭ-kə) *n.* A crystalline compound, SiO_2, that occurs abundantly as quartz, sand, and other minerals, and is used to make glass and concrete. Also called **silicon dioxide**. [New Latin, from Latin *silex*, flint.]

silica gel. Amorphous silica that resembles white sand and is used as a drying and dehumidifying agent.

sil·i·cate (sĭl′ĭ-kāt′, -kĭt) *n.* Any of numerous compounds that contain silicon, oxygen, and a metallic or organic radical, occur in most rocks, and form the basis of common glass and bricks.

si·li·ceous (sĭ-lĭsh′əs) *adj.* Containing or resembling silica. [Latin *siliceus*, of flint or limestone, from *silex*, flint.]

si·lic·ic (sĭ-lĭs′ĭk) *adj.* Of or derived from silica or silicon.

sil·lic·i·fy (sĭ-lĭs′ə-fī′) *v.* **-fied, -fy·ing.** —*tr.v.* To convert into silica. —*intr.v.* To be or become converted into silica. —**si·lic′i·fi·ca′tion** *n.*

sil·i·con (sĭl′ĭ-kən, -kŏn′) *n. Symbol Si* A nonmetallic element that occurs extensively in the earth's crust, has both an amorphous and a crystalline allotrope, and is used in glass, semiconducting devices, concrete, brick, refractories, pottery, and silicones. Atomic number 14; atomic weight 28.086; melting point 1,410°C; boiling point 2,355°C; specific gravity 2.33; valence 4. [From SILICA.]

silicon carbide. A bluish-black crystalline compound, SiC, one of the hardest known substances, used as an abrasive and heat-refractory material.

silicon dioxide. Silica.

sil·i·cone (sĭl′ĭ-kōn′) *n.* Any of a group of semi-inorganic polymers based on the structural unit R_2SiO, where R is an organic group, characterized by wide-range thermal stability and used in adhesives, lubricants, protective coatings, synthetic rubber, and prosthetic replacements. —*modifier: silicone implants.*

sil·i·co·sis (sĭl′ĭ-kō′sĭs) *n.* Fibrosis of the lungs caused by long-term inhalation of silica dust and resulting in a chronic shortness of breath. [SILIC(A) + -OSIS.]

silk (sĭlk) *n.* **1. a.** The fine, glossy fiber produced by a silkworm to form its cocoon. **b.** A similar fine fiber produced by spiders or by certain insect larvae. **2.** Thread or fabric made from the fiber produced by silkworms. **3. a.** A garment or clothing made from this fabric. **b. silks.** The brightly colored garments that identify a jockey or harness driver. **4.** Any silky, soft strands. —*modifier: silk stockings.* [Middle English, from Old English *seoluc*, ult. from Chinese *ssŭ¹*.]

silk cotton. A silky fiber, such as kapok, attached to the seeds of certain trees.

silk-cot·ton tree (sĭlk′kŏt′n). Any of several tropical American trees of the family Bombacaceae, cultivated for their leathery fruit containing a silklike fiber.

silk·en (sĭl′kən) *adj.* **1.** Made of silk: *a silken scarf.* **2.** Smooth and lustrous: *silken tresses.* **3.** Delicately pleasing or caressing: *a silken voice.*

silk screen. **1.** A stencil method in which ink is forced through a design-bearing screen of silk or other fabric onto the printing surface. **2.** A print made by this method.

silk-stock·ing (sĭlk′stŏk′ĭng) *n.* **1.** An aristocratic or wealthy person. **2.** A person who is dressed well or fashionably. —*modifier: the city's silk-stocking area.*

silk·worm (sĭlk′wûrm′) *n.* Any of various caterpillars that produce silk cocoons, esp. the larva of a moth, *Bombyx mori*, native to Asia, that spins a cocoon of fine, lustrous fiber that is the source of commercial silk.

silk·y (sĭl′kē) *adj.* **-i·er, -i·est. 1.** Resembling silk; smooth and lustrous: *silky fur.* **2.** Made of silk. **3.** Having long, silklike hairs. —**silk′i·ly** *adv.* —**silk′i·ness** *n.*

sill (sĭl) *n.* A horizontal support that holds up the upright part of a frame, esp. the base of a window. [Middle English *sille*, from Old English *sylle*, threshold, sill.]

sil·la·bub (sĭl′ə-bŭb′) *n.* Var. of **syllabub.**

sil·ly (sĭl′ē) *adj.* **-li·er, -li·est. 1.** Showing a lack of good sense or clear thinking. **2.** Lacking seriousness or substance; frivolous: *a silly comedy.* **3.** *Informal.* Dazed, as from a blow. —See Syns at **foolish.** —*n., pl.* **-lies.** A silly person. [Middle English, pitiable, from *seely*, happy, blessed, from Old English *gesǣlig*.] —**sil′li·ness** *n.*

si·lo (sī′lō) *n., pl.* **-los. 1. a.** A tall, cylindrical structure in which fodder is stored. **b.** A pit dug for the same purpose. **2.** An underground shelter for a missile. [Spanish, from Latin *sirus*, from Greek *siros*, pit for storing grain.]

silt (sĭlt) *n.* A sedimentary material that consists of mineral particles finer than sand and coarser than clay, often found at the bottom of bodies of water. —*intr.v.* To become filled with silt. —*tr.v.* To fill with silt. [Middle English *cylte*, prob. of Scandinavian orig.]

Si·lu·ri·an (sĭ-lŏŏr′ē-ən, sī-) *n.* The period of geologic time that began about 425 million years ago and ended about 405 million years ago. During this period land plants first appeared. —*modifier: Silurian fossils.* [From *Silures*, a pre-Roman people of Britain.]

sil·van (sĭl′vən) *adj.* Var. of **sylvan.**

sil·ver (sĭl′vər) *n.* **1. Symbol Ag** A lustrous, white, ductile, malleable metallic element, having the highest thermal and electrical conductivity of the metals. It is highly valued for jewelry, tableware, and other ornamental use, and is widely used in coinage, photography, dental and soldering alloys, electrical contacts, and printed circuits. Atomic number 47; atomic weight 107.870; melting point 960.8°C; boiling point 2,212°C; specific gravity 10.50; valences 1, 2. **2.** This metal used as money or as a commodity. **3.** Coins made of this metal. **4. a.** Tableware and other household articles made of or plated with this metal. **b.** Any tableware. **5.** A light, shiny, or metallic gray. —*modifier: a silver bell; a silver salt.* —*adj.* **1.** Of the color silver. **2.** Having a bell-like sound. **3.** Eloquent; persuasive: *a silver tongue.* **4.** Of or designating a 25th anniversary. —*tr.v.* **1.** To cover, plate, or decorate with silver or a similar lustrous substance. **2.** To cause to resemble silver. **3.** To coat (photographic paper) with a film of silver nitrate or other silver salt. —*intr.v.* To become silvery. [Middle English, from Old English *siolfor*.]

sil·ver-bell tree (sĭl′vər-bĕl′). Any of several trees of the genus *Halesia*, esp. *H. carolina*, of the southeastern United States, that has bell-shaped white flowers.

silver bromide. A pale-yellow crystalline compound, AgBr, that turns black on exposure to light, and is used as the light-sensitive component on photographic films.

silver chloride. A white granular powder, AgCl, that turns dark on exposure to light and is used in photography.

sil·ver·fish (sĭl′vər-fĭsh′) *n., pl.* **silverfish** or **-fish·es. 1.** Any of various fishes that have silvery scales, such as a tarpon. **2.** A silvery, wingless insect, *Lepisma saccharina*, that often damages bookbindings and starched clothing.

silver fox. A color phase of the North American red fox, *Vulpes fulva*, having black fur tipped with white.

silver iodide. A pale-yellow powder, AgI, used in artificial rainmaking, photography, and medicine.

silver nitrate. A poisonous, colorless crystalline compound, $AgNO_3$, used in photography, mirror manufacturing, hair dyeing, silver plating, and medicine.

silver plate. Tableware or other articles made of silver or of base metal plated with silver.

sil·ver-plate (sĭl′vər-plāt′) *tr.v.* **-plat·ed, -plat·ing.** To coat with a thin layer of silver by an electrical process.

sil·ver·smith (sĭl′vər-smĭth′) *n.* A person who makes, repairs, or replates articles of silver.

sil·ver·tongued (sĭl′vər-tŭngd′) *adj.* Eloquent.

sil·ver·ware (sĭl′vər-wâr′) *n.* Articles made of or plated with silver, esp. eating and serving utensils.

sil·ver·y (sĭl′və-rē) *adj.* **1.** Containing or coated with silver. **2.** Resembling or suggestive of silver. —**sil′ver·i·ness** *n.*

silo   silversmith

sim·i·an (sĭm′ē-ən) *adj.* Of or like an ape or monkey. —*n.* An ape or monkey. [From Latin *sīmia*, ape.]

sim·i·lar (sĭm′ə-lər) *adj.* **1.** Showing some resemblance; alike though not identical. **2.** *Geom.* Having corresponding angles equal and corresponding sides proportional in length: *similar triangles*. [French *similaire*, from Latin *similis*, like.] —**sim′i·lar·ly** *adv.*
   Usage: **similar.** This is an adjective only. It can follow a linking verb and thus modify the subject: *The mechanism seems similar to ours.* But it cannot acceptably modify a nonlinking verb, a job for an adverb: *The mechanism works similarly* (not *similar*) *to that in our refrigerator.*

sim·i·lar·i·ty (sĭm′ə-lăr′ĭ-tē) *n., pl.* **-ties. 1.** The condition or property of being similar. **2.** A shared feature or property.

sim·i·le (sĭm′ə-lē) *n.* A figure of speech in which two essentially unlike things are compared, often in a phrase introduced by *like* or *as.* For example, *The lighthouse stands like a fort* and *His mind was as vast as an empire* are similes. [Latin, neut. of *similis*, like.]

si·mil·i·tude (sĭ-mĭl′ĭ-tōōd′, -tyōōd′) *n.* **1.** Similarity. **2.** Something closely resembling another. [Middle English, from Old French, from Latin *similitūdo*, from *similis*, like.]

sim·mer (sĭm′ər) *intr.v.* **1.** To cook gently below or just at the boiling point. **2.** To be filled with barely controlled emotion; seethe. —*tr.v.* To cook (food) below or just at the boiling point. —*phrasal verb.* **simmer down.** To become calm after anger or excitement. —*n.* The condition or process of simmering. [Middle English *simperen*.]

si·mon-pure (sī′mən-pyŏŏr′) *adj.* **1.** Genuine; real. **2.** Superficially virtuous; hypocritically good. [After *Simon Pure*, a character who is impersonated by a rival in Susanna Centlivre's play *A Bold Stroke for a Wife* (1718).]

sim·o·ny (sĭm′ə-nē, sī′mə-) *n.* The buying or selling of ecclesiastical pardons, offices, or emoluments. [Middle English *simonie*, from Old French, from Late Latin *sīmōnia*, after *Simon* Magus, a Samaritan who offered money to the Apostles Peter and John for the power of conferring the Holy Ghost on whomever he wished (Acts 8:18–19).]

si·moom (sĭ-mōōm′) *n.* Also **si·moon** (-mōōn′). A strong, hot, sand-laden wind of the Sahara and Arabian deserts. [Arabic *samūm*, poisonous.]

simp (sĭmp) *n. Slang.* A simpleton; a fool.

sim·pa·ti·co (sĭm-pä′tĭ-kō′, -păt′ĭ-) *adj.* **1.** Compatible. **2.** Attractive; pleasing. [Italian *simpatia*, sympathy, from Latin *sympathīa*.]

sim·per (sĭm′pər) *intr.v.* To smile in a silly or self-conscious manner. —*tr.v.* To utter with a silly or self-conscious smile. —*n.* A silly or self-conscious smile. [Of Scandinavian orig.] —**sim′per·er** *n.*

sim·ple (sĭm′pəl) *adj.* **-pler, -plest. 1.** Having or composed of only a single part or unit; not combined or compound. **2.** Not involved or complicated; easy. **3.** Bare; mere: *a simple "yes" or "no."* **4.** Not ornate or adorned: *a simple dress.* **5.** Unassuming or unpretentious. **6.** Humble or lowly in condition or rank. **7.** Not important or significant; trivial. **8.** Having or manifesting little sense or intellect. — See Syns at **dull, easy,** and **plain.** —*n.* **1.** Something uncomplex or unmixed. **2.** A fool; simpleton. **3.** *Archaic.* A medicinal plant or the medicine obtained from it. [Middle English, from Old French, from Latin *simplus*.]

simple fraction. A fraction in which both the numerator and the denominator are whole numbers.

simple machine. Any of six basic mechanical devices, the lever, the pulley, the wheel and axle, the inclined plane, the screw, and the wedge, that vary the ratio of speed to force in doing work.

sim·ple-mind·ed (sĭm′pəl-mīn′dĭd) *adj.* **1.** Not sophisticated; naive. **2.** Stupid or silly. **3.** Mentally defective. —**sim′ple-mind′ed·ly** *adv.* —**sim′ple-mind′ed·ness** *n.*

simple sentence. A sentence having one independent clause and no coordinate or subordinate clauses.

sim·ple·ton (sĭm′pəl-tən) *n.* A silly or stupid person; a fool. [From SIMPLE.]

sim·plic·i·ty (sĭm-plĭs′ĭ-tē) *n., pl.* **-ties. 1.** The property, condition, or quality of being simple. **2.** Absence of luxury or showiness; plainness. **3.** Absence of affectation or pretense. **4.** Lack of good sense or intelligence; foolishness.

[Middle English *symplicite*, from Old French, from Latin *simplicitās*, from *simplex*, simple.]

sim·pli·fy (sĭm′plə-fī′) *tr.v.* **-fied, -fy·ing.** To make simple or simpler; render less complex or intricate. —**sim′pli·fi·ca′tion** *n.* —**sim′pli·fi′er** *n.*

sim·ply (sĭm′plē) *adv.* **1.** In a simple manner; plainly. **2.** Merely; just: *We knew him simply as Joe.* **3.** Absolutely; altogether: *simply delicious.* **4.** Frankly; candidly.

sim·u·la·crum (sĭm′yə-lā′krəm) *n., pl.* **-cra** (-krə). **1.** An image or representation of something. **2.** An unreal or vague semblance. [Latin, from *simulāre*, to simulate.]

sim·u·late (sĭm′yə-lāt′) *tr.v.* **-lat·ed, -lat·ing. 1.** To have, take on, or duplicate the appearance, form, or sound of; imitate: *a device that simulates space flight.* **2.** To pretend; feign: *simulate an interest.* [From Latin *simulāre*, from *similis*, similar.] —**sim′u·la′tive** *adj.* —**sim′u·la′tor** *n.*

sim·u·la·tion (sĭm′yə-lā′shən) *n.* **1.** The act or process of simulating. **2.** An imitation. **3.** A feigning; pretense.

si·mul·cast (sī′məl-kăst′, sĭm′əl-) *tr.v.* To broadcast simultaneously by FM and AM radio or by radio and television. —*n.* A broadcast so transmitted. [SIMUL(TANEOUS) + (BROAD)CAST.]

si·mul·ta·ne·ous (sī′məl-tā′nē-əs, sĭm′əl-) *adj.* Happening, existing, or done at the same time. [Latin *simul*, at the same time + (INSTAN)TANEOUS.] —**si′mul·ta′ne·ous·ly** *adv.* —**si′mul·ta′ne·ous·ness** or **si′mul·ta·ne′i·ty** (-tə-nē′ĭ-tē) *n.*

simultaneous equations. Two or more equations with unknowns that can be satisfied by the same set of values.

sin (sĭn) *n.* **1.** The act or an instance of breaking a religious or moral law. **2.** Any serious offense or fault. —*intr.v.* **sinned, sin·ning. 1.** To violate a religious or moral law. **2.** To commit a serious offense. [Middle English *sinne*, from Old English *synn.*] —**sin′ner** *n.*

since (sĭns) *adv.* **1.** From then until now, or between then and now: *He left town and hasn't been here since.* Also used prepositionally: *Since last month's upset, the team has been winning.* **2.** Before now; ago: *long since forgotten.* —*conj.* **1.** During the time after which: *He hasn't been home since he graduated.* **2.** Continuously from the time when: *He hasn't spoken since he sat down.* **3.** As a result of the fact that: *Since you're not interested, I won't tell you about it.* [Middle English *sinnes*, from *sithenes*, from Old English *siththan*, "after that."]
   Usage: **since.** Though clauses introduced by *since* (referring to time) are in the past tense, the corresponding verb in the clause joined by *since* must be in the perfect tense: *It has been* (not *was*) *two years since I last visited my home. It had been two years since she departed.* See also Usage note at **ago.**

sin·cere (sĭn-sîr′) *adj.* **-cer·er, -cer·est.** Without false appearance or nature; true: *sincere friends; a sincere apology.* [Latin *sincērus*, clean, genuine.] —**sin·cere′ly** *adv.* —**sin·cere′ness** *n.*

sin·cer·i·ty (sĭn-sĕr′ĭ-tē, -sîr′-) *n., pl.* **-ties.** The condition or quality of being sincere; freedom from falseness.

sine (sīn) *n.* In a right triangle, a function of an acute angle equal to the length of the side opposite the angle divided by the length of the hypotenuse. [Medieval Latin *sinus*, from Latin, curve, fold, hollow.]

si·ne·cure (sī′nĭ-kyŏŏr′, sĭn′ĭ-) *n.* A salaried position that requires little or no work. [Medieval Latin *(beneficium) sine cūrā,* "(benefice) without cure (of souls)."]

si·ne di·e (sī′nĭ dī′ē, sĭn′ā dē′ā′). Without a day specified for a future meeting; indefinitely: *Parliament was dismissed sine die.* [Latin, "without a day."]

si·ne qua non (sĭn′ĭ kwä nŏn′, nŏn′, sī′nĭ kwä nŏn′). An indispensable condition or element. [Latin, "without which not."]

sin·ew (sĭn′yōō) *n.* **1. a.** A tendon. **b.** The connective tissue of which tendons are composed. **2.** Vigorous strength; muscular power. [Middle English *sinewe*, from Old English *sinu.*]

sin·ew·y (sĭn′yōō-ē) *adj.* **1.** Of or like sinew: *tough, sinewy meat.* **2.** Lean and muscular. **3.** Strong; vigorous.

sin·ful (sĭn′fəl) *adj.* Marked by or full of sin; wicked. —**sin′ful·ly** *adv.* —**sin′ful·ness** *n.*

sing (sĭng) *v.* **sang** (săng) or **sung** (sŭng), **sung, sing·ing.** —*intr.v.* **1.** To pronounce or utter a series of words or sounds in musical tones. **2.** To perform songs. **3.** To give or have the effect of melody. **4.** To make a high whine or hum: *The machine sang.* **5.** *Slang.* To give information or evidence against someone. —*tr.v.* **1.** To render in tones with musical inflections of the voice: *He sang the message.* **2.** To perform (songs or other vocal selections). **3.** To proclaim or extol, esp. in verse: *sang her praises.* **4.** To bring to a specified state by singing: *sang the baby to sleep.* —*phrasal verb.* **sing out.** To call out loudly. —*n.* A gathering of people for group singing. [Middle English *singen,* from Old English *singan.*]

singe (sĭnj) *tr.v.* **singed, singe-ing. 1.** To burn slightly; scorch. **2.** To burn off the feathers or bristles of. —*n.* A slight burn; a scorch. [Middle English *sengen,* from Old English *sengan.*] —**sing′er** (sĭn′jər) *n.*

sing·er (sĭng′ər) *n.* **1.** A person who sings, esp. a trained or professional vocalist. **2.** A songbird.

Sin·gha·lese (sĭng′gə-lēz′, -lēs′) *n., pl.* **Singhalese.** Also **Sin·ha·lese** (sĭn′hə-). **1.** A people constituting the major portion of the population of Ceylon. **2.** The Indic language of the Singhalese. —**Sin′gha·lese′** *adj.*

sin·gle (sĭng′gəl) *adj.* **1.** Not accompanied by another or others; solitary. **2.** Consisting of one form or part. **3.** Separate; individual: *every single one of them.* **4.** Designed to accommodate one person: *a single bed.* **5.** Unmarried. **6.** Sincere and dedicated. **7.** *Bot.* Having only one rank or row of petals: *a single flower.* **8.** One-against-one: *single combat.* —*n.* **1.** A separate thing or person; individual. **2.** An accommodation for one person. **3.** An unmarried person. **4.** A one-dollar bill. **5.** *Baseball.* A **one-base hit.** **6.** A golf match between two players. **7. singles.** A match between two players in tennis and other games. —*v.* **-gled, -gling.** —*tr.v.* To choose or distinguish from among others: *singled out for praise.* —*intr.v. Baseball.* To make a one-base hit. —See Syns at **choose.** [Middle English *sengle,* from Old French, from Latin *singulus.*] —**sing′gle·ness** *n.*

Syns: 1. single, discrete, individual, separate, singular *adj.* Core meaning: Being a distinct entity (*a sentence made up of single words*). **2. single, lone, one, only, particular, sole, solitary** *adj.* Core meaning: Alone in a given category (*a single prehistoric monument still standing*). **3. single, unmarried, unwed** *adj.* Without a spouse (*single parents*).

sin·gle-breast·ed (sĭng′gəl-brĕs′tĭd) *adj.* Closing with a narrow overlap and fastened down the front with a single row of buttons: *a single-breasted jacket.*

single file. A line of people, animals, or things standing or moving one behind the other.

sin·gle-foot (sĭng′gəl-fŏŏt′) *n.* A rapid gait of a horse in which each foot strikes the ground separately. Also called **rack.** —*intr.v.* To go at a single-foot.

sin·gle-hand·ed (sĭng′gəl-hăn′dĭd) *adj.* **1.** Working or done without help; unassisted. **2.** Having, using, or requiring only one hand. —**sin′gle-hand′ed·ly** *adv.*

sin·gle-mind·ed (sĭng′gəl-mīn′dĭd) *adj.* **1.** Having one overriding purpose or opinion. **2.** Steadfast; not wavering. —**sin′gle-mind′ed·ly** *adv.* —**sin′gle-mind′ed·ness** *n.*

sin·gle-stick (sĭng′gəl-stĭk′) *n.* **1.** A one-handed fencing stick fitted with a hand guard. Also called **backsword. 2.** The art, sport, or exercise of fencing with such a stick.

sin·gle·ton (sĭng′gəl-tən) *n.* A single thing, esp. a playing card that is the only one of its suit in a player's hand. [From SINGLE.]

sin·gle·tree (sĭng′gəl-trē′) *n.* A whiffletree.

sin·gly (sĭng′glē) *adv.* **1.** Without company or help; alone. **2.** One by one; individually.

sing·song (sĭng′sông′, -sŏng′) *n.* **1.** Verse or song having a monotonous regularity of rhythm or rhyme. **2.** A monotonously rising and falling speech cadence. —*adj.* Marked by a singsong.

sin·gu·lar (sĭng′gyə-lər) *adj.* **1.** Naming or standing for a single person or thing or a group considered as one. For example, *I* and *he* are singular pronouns and *army* is a singular noun. **2.** Being only one; single. **3.** Very uncommon; extraordinary; rare: *singular good fortune.* **4.** Very strange; peculiar. —See Syns at **single** and **uncommon.** —*n.* The form taken by a word indicating one person or thing or a group considered as one. [Middle English *singuler,* solitary, single, separate, from Old French, from Latin

singulāris, from *singulus,* single.] —**sin′gu·lar·ly** *adv.* —**sin′gu·lar·ness** *n.*

sin·gu·lar·i·ty (sĭng′gyə-lăr′ĭ-tē) *n., pl.* **-ties. 1.** The condition or quality of being singular. **2.** A distinguishing trait; a peculiarity. **3.** Something uncommon or unusual.

Sin·ha·lese (sĭn′hə-lēz′, -lēs′) *n.* Var. of **Singhalese.**

sin·is·ter (sĭn′ĭ-stər) *adj.* **1.** Suggesting an evil force or motive: *a sinister smile.* **2.** Promising trouble; ominous: *sinister warnings.* **3.** *Heraldry.* On the left of the bearer and hence on the right of the observer. [Middle English *sinistre,* from Old French, from Latin *sinister,* left, on the left, evil, unlucky.] —**sin′is·ter·ly** *adv.* —**sin′is·ter·ness** *n.*

sin·is·tral (sĭn′ĭ-strəl, sĭ-nĭs′-) *adj.* **1.** Of or facing the left side. **2.** Left-handed. —**sin′is·tral·ly** *adv.*

sink (sĭngk) *v.* **sank** (săngk) or **sunk** (sŭngk), **sunk** or **sunk·en** (sŭng′kən), **sink·ing.** —*intr.v.* **1.** To descend beneath the surface or to the bottom of a liquid or soft substance. **2.** To go down slowly or in stages. **3.** To slope downward; to incline. **4.** To pass into a specified condition: *She sank into a deep sleep.* **5.** To pass into a worsened physical condition. **6.** To become weaker, quieter, or less forceful: *His voice sank to a whisper.* **7.** To diminish. **8.** To feel great disappointment or discouragement. **9.** To seep; penetrate. **10.** To make an impression; become understood: *Let the meaning sink in.* **11.** To be hollowed or sunken. —*tr.v.* **1.** To cause to descend beneath the surface. **2.** To drop or lower: *She sank the bucket into the well.* **3.** To force into the ground: *sink a piling.* **4.** To dig or drill (a mine or well) in the earth. **5.** To make weaker, quieter, or less forceful. **6.** To hide; conceal. **7.** *Informal.* To defeat, as in sports. **8.** To invest. **9.** *Sports.* To get (the ball) into the hole or basket, as in golf, pool, or basketball. —*n.* **1.** A water basin fixed to a wall or floor and having a drainpipe and gen. a piped supply of water. **2.** A cesspool. **3.** A sink hole. **4.** Any place regarded as wicked and corrupt. [Middle English *sinken,* from Old English *sincan.*] —**sink′a·ble** *adj.*

sink·er (sĭng′kər) *n.* **1.** Someone or something that sinks. **2.** A weight used for sinking fishing lines, nets, or the like.

sink·hole (sĭngk′hōl′) *n.* A natural depression in a land surface that joins with an underground passage, gen. occurring in limestone regions.

sinking fund. A fund accumulated to pay off a public or corporate debt.

sin·less (sĭn′lĭs) *adj.* Free from or without sin. —**sin′less·ly** *adv.* —**sin′less·ness** *n.*

Sino-. A prefix meaning Chinese: *Sinology.* [French, from Late Latin *Sinae,* the Chinese, from Greek *Sinai,* from Arabic *Sīn,* China, from Mandarin *Ch'in².*]

Si·nol·o·gy (sī-nŏl′ə-jē, sĭ-) *n.* The study of the Chinese language, literature, and people. —**Si·nol′o·gist** *n.*

sin·u·ate (sĭn′yōō-ĭt, -āt′) *adj.* Also **sin·u·at·ed** (-ā′tĭd). Having a wavy indented margin, as a leaf. [Latin *sinuātus,* past part. of *sinuāre,* to bend, wind, from *sinus,* a bend, curve, fold.] —**sin′u·ate·ly** *adv.*

sin·u·os·i·ty (sĭn′yōō-ŏs′ĭ-tē) *n., pl.* **-ties. 1.** The quality of being sinuous. **2.** A curving shape or movement.

sin·u·ous (sĭn′yōō-əs) *adj.* **1.** Having many curves or turns; winding: *a sinuous road.* **2.** Supple and lithe in movement: *a sinuous snake.* [Latin *sinuōsus,* from *sinus,* a bend, curve, fold.] —**sin′u·ous·ly** *adv.* —**sin′u·ous·ness** *n.*

si·nus (sī′nəs) *n.* **1.** A cavity formed by a bending or curving. **2.** *Anat.* **a.** A dilated channel for the passage of chiefly venous blood. **b.** Any of various air-filled cavities in the bones of the skull, esp. one that connects with the nostrils. **3.** *Pathol.* A fistula or channel to a suppurating cavity. **4.** *Bot.* A notch or indentation between lobes of a leaf or corolla. [Latin *sinus,* a bend, curve, fold, hollow.]

si·nus·i·tis (sī′nə-sī′tĭs) *n.* Inflammation of a sinus membrane, esp. in the nasal region.

Si·on (sī′ən) *n.* Var. of **Zion.**

Siou·an (sōō′ən) *n.* A large family of North American Indian languages spoken over an extensive area of the Midwest. —**Siou′an** *adj.*

Sioux (sōō) *n., pl.* **Sioux. 1.** A group of tribes of Plains Indians formerly living in the Dakotas, Minnesota, and Nebraska. **2.** A member of any of these tribes. **3.** Any of the Siouan languages of these tribes. Also called **Dakota.** —**Sioux** *adj.*

sip (sĭp) *v.* **sipped, sip·ping.** —*tr.v.* To drink (something)

ă pat	ā pay	â care	ä father	ĕ pet	ē be	hw which	ĭ pit	ī tie	î pier	ŏ pot	ō toe	ô paw, for	oi noise
ŏŏ took	ōō boot	ou out	th thin	th this	ŭ cut		û urge	zh vision	ə about, item, edible, gallop, circus

delicately and in small quantities: *She sipped the hot tea.* —*intr.v.* To drink in small quantities. —*n.* **1.** The act of sipping. **2.** A small quantity of liquid sipped: *just a sip of water.* [Middle English *sippen,* prob. of Low German orig.]

si·phon (sī'fən). Also **sy·phon.** —*n.* **1.** A pipe or tube in the form of an inverted U, filled with liquid and arranged so that the pressure of the atmosphere forces liquid from a container to flow through the tube, over a barrier, and into a lower container. **2.** A tubelike animal part, as of a clam, through which water is taken in or expelled. —*tr.v.* To draw off or transfer (a liquid) through or as if through a siphon. —*intr.v.* To pass through a siphon. [French, from Latin *sīphōn,* from Greek *siphōn,* pipe, tube.]

siphon

sir (sûr) *n.* **1.** Often **Sir.** A polite form of address used instead of a man's name. **2. Sir.** A title of honor used before the given name or the full name of baronets and knights. [Middle English, var. of *sire,* sire.]

sire (sīr) *n.* **1.** A father or forefather. **2.** The male parent of an animal. **3.** *Archaic.* A title and form of address to a superior. —*tr.v.* **sired, sir·ing.** To be the father or male ancestor of. [Middle English, from Old French, from Latin *senior,* older, comp. of *senex,* old.]

si·ren (sī'rən) *n.* **1.** A device for making a loud whistling or wailing sound as a signal or warning, esp. one using expulsions of compressed air. **2.** Often **Siren.** *Gk. Myth.* One of a group of sea nymphs, part woman and part bird, whose sweet singing lured sailors to their destruction. **3.** A beautiful or captivating woman; temptress. —*modifier: siren singing.* [Middle English, from Old French *sereine,* from Late Latin *sīrēna,* Siren, from Latin *Sīrēn,* from Greek *Seirēn.*]

si·re·ni·an (sī-rē'nē-ən) *n.* Any aquatic mammal of the order Sirenia, which includes the manatee and the dugong. —*adj.* Of the Sirenia. [From Latin *Sīrēn,* Siren.]

Sir·i·us (sîr'ē-əs) *n.* A star in the constellation Canis Major, the brightest star in the night sky, approx. 8.7 light years away from the earth. Also called **Dog Star.**

sir·loin (sûr'loin') *n.* A cut of meat, esp. of beef, from the upper part of the loin. [Old French *surlonge* : *sur,* above, + *longe,* loin.]

si·roc·co (sī-rŏk'ō) *n., pl.* **-cos. 1.** A hot south or southeast wind of southern Europe that originates in the Sahara as a dry, dusty wind but becomes moist as it passes over the Mediterranean. **2.** Any warm southerly wind. [Italian, from Arabic *sharuq,* "east (wind)," from *sharaqa,* (the sun) rose.]

sir·rah (sîr'ə) *n. Obs.* Young man; mister; fellow. Used as a contemptuous form of address. [Perh. alteration of Middle English SIRE (sir).]

sir·up (sîr'əp, sûr'-) *n.* Var. of **syrup.**

sis (sĭs) *n. Informal.* Sister.

si·sal (sī'zəl, -səl) *n.* **1.** A fleshy plant, *Agave sisalana,* native to Mexico, widely cultivated for its large leaves that yield a stiff fiber used for cordage and rope. **2.** The fiber of this plant or related plants. —*modifier: sisal rope.* [Mexican Spanish, after *Sisal,* a town in Yucatán, Mexico.]

sis·sy (sĭs'ē) *n., pl.* **-sies. 1.** An effeminate boy or man. **2.** A timid or cowardly person. [From SIS.]

sis·ter (sĭs'tər) *n.* **1. a.** A girl or woman having the same mother and father as another person. **b.** A girl or woman having one parent in common with another; half sister. **2.** A woman or girl who shares a common ancestry, allegiance, character, or purpose with another or others. **3. Sister.** A nun. **4.** *Brit.* The head nurse in a ward. —*adj.*

Of the same kind or design: *sister ships.* [Middle English, from Old English *sweostor.*]

sis·ter·hood (sĭs'tər-hŏŏd') *n.* **1.** The relationship of being a sister or sisters. **2.** The quality of being sisterly. **3.** A group of women united by a common purpose.

sis·ter-in-law (sĭs'tər-ĭn-lô') *n., pl.* **sis·ters-in-law. 1.** The sister of one's husband or wife. **2.** The wife of one's brother. **3.** The wife of the brother of one's spouse.

sis·ter·ly (sĭs'tər-lē) *adj.* Suitable for a sister or sisters. —*adv.* As a sister. —**sis'ter·li·ness** *n.*

Sis·y·phus (sĭs'ĭ-fəs) *n. Gk. Myth.* A cruel king of Corinth condemned forever to roll a huge stone up a hill in Hades only to have it roll down again when he neared the top.

sit (sĭt) *v.* **sat** (săt), **sit·ting.** —*intr.v.* **1.** To rest with the body supported upon the buttocks and the torso upright; be seated: *He sat on the bench.* **2.** To rest with the hindquarters lowered onto a supporting surface. **3.** To perch. **4.** To cover eggs for hatching; to brood. **5.** To be situated; lie. **6.** To pose for an artist or photographer. **7. a.** To occupy a seat as a member of a body of officials: *the first woman to sit in Congress.* **b.** To be in session. **8.** To lie or rest in a specified manner: *sit idle.* **9.** To weigh: *Official duties sat heavily on him.* **10.** To fit, fall, or drape in a specified manner: *The jacket sits perfectly on you.* **11.** To be agreeable: *The idea didn't sit well with him.* **12.** To baby-sit or keep watch. —*tr.v.* **1.** To cause to sit; to seat: *They sat him at the head of the table.* **2.** To keep one's seat upon (a horse or other animal). —See Usage note at **set.** —*phrasal verbs.* **sit down.** To take a seat; be seated. **sit in on.** To attend or participate in. **sit on** (or **upon**). *Informal.* To suppress or repress: *sit on the evidence.* **sit out. 1.** To stay until the end of. **2.** To remain seated throughout. **sit up. 1.** To sit straight or erect. **2.** To stay up later than the customary bedtime. **3.** To become suddenly alert; to be startled: *sit up and take notice.* —*idiom.* **sit tight.** *Informal.* To be patient and await the next move. [Middle English *sitten,* from Old English *sittan.*]

si·tar (sĭ-tär') *n.* A stringed instrument used in Hindu music, with a long, fretted neck and usu. 6 or 7 playing strings. [Hindi *sitār* : Persian *si,* three + *tār,* string.] —**si·tar'ist** *n.*

sitar

sit·com (sĭt'kŏm') *n. Informal.* Situation comedy.

sit-down strike (sĭt'doun') A work stoppage in which the workers refuse to leave their place of employment until they reach an agreement. Also called **sit-down.**

site (sīt) *n.* **1.** The place or plot of land where something was, is, or is to be located. **2.** The place or setting of an event: *the site of the victory.* —*tr.v.* **sit·ed, sit·ing.** To situate or locate: *siting a power plant.* [Middle English, from Old French, from Latin *situs,* place, locality.]

sit-in (sĭt'ĭn') *n.* A demonstration in which people protesting against certain conditions sit down in an appropriate place and refuse to move until their demands are considered or met.

si·tol·o·gy (sī-tŏl'ə-jē) *n.* The science of foods, nutrition, and diet. [Greek *sitos,* food, grain + -LOGY.]

sit·ter (sĭt'ər) *n.* **1.** Someone or something that sits. **2.** A baby-sitter. **3.** A brooding hen.

sit·ting (sĭt'ĭng) *n.* **1.** A period during which a person is seated and occupied with a single activity. **2.** A term or session, as of a legislature or court. **3. a.** An incubation

---

ă pat   ā pay   â care   ä father   ĕ pet   ē be   hw which
ŏŏ took   ōō boot   ou out   th thin   *th* this   ŭ cut
ĭ pit   ī tie   î pier   ŏ pot   ō toe   ô paw, for   oi noise
û urge   zh vision   ə about, item, edible, gallop, circus

period. **b.** The number of eggs under a brooding bird.

sit·ting duck. *Informal.* An easy target or victim.

sit·ting room. A small living room.

sit·u·ate (sĭch′ōō-āt′) *tr.v.* **-at·ed, -at·ing.** To place in a certain spot; locate. —*adj.* (sĭch′ōō-ĭt, -āt′). Situated. [From Medieval Latin *situāre*, to put, place, from *situs*, place, site.]

sit·u·a·tion (sĭch′ōō-ā′shən) *n.* **1.** The place in which something is situated; location. **2.** A position or status with regard to conditions and attendant circumstances: *his fortunate situation in being near his office.* **3.** A combination of circumstances at a given moment; state of affairs: *the international situation.* **4.** A job. —**sit′u·a′tion·al** *adj.*

situation comedy. A humorous television series with a continuing cast of characters.

sit·up (sĭt′ŭp′) *n.* A form of exercise in which a person lying on his back rises to a sitting position without the support of the arms and usu. without bending the legs.

si·tus (sī′təs) *n., pl.* **situs.** Position, esp. the normal position, as of a bodily organ. [Latin *situs*, place, site.]

Si·va (shē′və, sē′-) *n.* Var. of **Shiva.**

six (sĭks) *n.* A number written 6 in Arabic numerals or in Roman numerals VI, that is equal to the sum of 5 + 1. It is the positive integer that immediately follows 5. —*idiom.* **at sixes and sevens.** In disorder. [Middle English, from Old English *siex*.] —**six** *adj. & pron.*

six-gun (sĭks′gŭn′) *n.* A six-shooter.

six·pence (sĭk′spəns) *n.* A former coin of Great Britain worth six pennies.

six-shoot·er (sĭks′shōō′tər) *n. Informal.* A revolver that can be fired six times before it has to be loaded again.

six·teen (sĭk′stēn′) *n.* A number written 16 in Arabic numerals or in Roman numerals XVI, that is equal to the sum of 15 + 1. It is the positive integer that immediately follows 15. [Middle English *sixtene*, from Old English *sixtȳne.*] —**six′teen′** *adj. & pron.*

six·teenth (sĭk′stēnth′) *n.* **1.** In a set of items arranged to match the natural numbers in a one-to-one correspondence, the item that matches the number sixteen. **2.** One of sixteen equal parts of a unit, written 1/16. —**six′teenth′** *adj. & adv.*

sixteenth note. A musical note that lasts half as long as an eighth note. Also *Brit.* **semiquaver.**

sixth (sĭksth) *n.* **1.** In a set of items arranged to match the natural numbers in a one-to-one correspondence, the item that matches the number six. **2.** One of six equal parts of a unit, written 1/6. **3.** *Mus.* **a.** One of three intervals formed by tones that are six diatonic scale degrees apart. **b.** The sixth tone of a diatonic scale. —**sixth** *adj. & adv.*

sixth sense. Intuition.

six·ti·eth (sĭk′stē-ĭth) *n.* **1.** In a set of items arranged to match the natural numbers in a one-to-one correspondence, the item that matches the number sixty. **2.** One of sixty equal parts of a unit, written 1/60. —**six′ti·eth** *adj. & adv.*

six·ty (sĭk′stē) *n., pl.* **-ties.** A number, written 60 in Arabic numerals or in Roman numerals LX, that is equal to the product of 6 × 10. It is the tenth positive integer after 50. —**six′ty** *adj. & pron.*

siz·a·ble (sī′zə-bəl) *adj.* Also **size·a·ble.** Of considerable size; fairly large. —See Syns at **big.** —**siz′a·ble·ness** *n.* —**siz′a·bly** *adv.*

size¹ (sīz) *n.* **1.** The physical dimensions, proportions, magnitude, or extent of something. **2.** Any of a series of graduated dimensions whereby manufactured articles are classified. **3.** Considerable extent, amount, or dimensions. **4.** Moral or mental qualities, rank, or status with reference to relative importance or capacity. —See Syns at **bulk.** —*tr.v.* **sized, siz·ing.** **1.** To arrange, classify, or distribute according to size. **2.** To make, cut, or shape to a required size. —*phrasal verb.* **size up.** To make an estimate or judgment of: *sized up the situation.* [Middle English *syse,* fixed amount, from Old French *sise,* from *asseoir,* to seat.]

size² (sīz) *n.* A gluey substance used as a glaze or filler for materials such as paper, cloth, or wall surfaces. Also called **sizing.** —*tr.v.* **sized, siz·ing.** To treat or coat with size. [Middle English *syse.*]

size·a·ble (sī′zə-bəl) *adj.* Var. of **sizable.**

sized (sīzd) *adj.* Having a particular or specified size: *a medium-sized crate.*

siz·ing (sī′zĭng) *n.* A glaze or filler; size.

siz·zle (sĭz′əl) *intr.v.* **-zled, -zling. 1.** To make the hissing sound of frying fat. **2.** To seethe with anger. **3.** To be very hot. —*n.* A hissing sound. [Imit.] —**siz′zler** *n.*

skald (skôld, skäld) *n.* Also **scald.** An ancient Scandinavian poet; bard. [Old Norse *skāld.*] —**skald′ic** *adj.*

skat (skät) *n.* A card game for three persons played with 32 cards, sevens through aces. [German *Skat,* from Italian *scarto,* a discard, from *scartare,* to reject, discard.]

skate¹ (skāt) *n.* **1.** A boot, shoe, or metal frame having a bladelike metal runner fixed to its sole, enabling the wearer to glide over ice; ice skate. **2.** A shoe, boot, or frame with four small wheels for rolling along on pavement and hard floors; roller skate. —*intr.v.* **skat·ed, skat·ing.** To glide or move along on or as if on skates. [Dutch *schaats,* a skate, from Old North French *escace,* stilt.] —**skat′er** *n.*

skate² (skāt) *n.* Any of various saltwater fishes of the family Rajidae, with a cartilaginous skeleton and a flattened body with pectoral fins that form winglike lateral extensions. [Middle English *scate,* from Old Norse *skata.*]

skate·board (skāt′bôrd′, -bōrd′) *n.* A short, narrow board having a set of four roller-skate wheels mounted under it.

ske·dad·dle (skĭ-dăd′l) *intr.v.* **-dled, -dling.** *Informal.* To leave hastily; flee.

skeet (skēt) *n.* A form of trapshooting in which clay targets are thrown from traps to simulate birds in flight and are shot at from different stations. [Ult. from Old Norse *skjóta,* to shoot.]

skein (skān) *n.* A length of thread, yarn, etc., wound in a loose, long coil. [Middle English *skeyne,* from Old French *escaigne.*]

skel·e·tal (skěl′ĭ-tl) *adj.* **1.** Of a skeleton. **2.** Meager; emaciated. —**skel′e·tal·ly** *adv.*

skel·e·ton (skěl′ĭ-tn) *n.* **1. a.** The internal supporting structure of a vertebrate, composed of bone and cartilage. **b.** A hard external supporting and protecting structure, as of a crustacean or turtle; exoskeleton. **2.** Any supporting structure or framework: *the skeleton of a building.* **3.** An outline or sketch. **4.** A very thin or emaciated person or animal. —*modifier: a skeleton model.* —*adj.* Having or consisting of minimal or essential elements: *A skeleton staff works weekends.* [Greek, neut. of *skeletos,* dried up, withered.]

skeleton key. A key that can open many different locks. Also called **passkey.**

skep·tic (skěp′tĭk) *n.* Also **scep·tic. 1.** A person who instinctively or habitually doubts, questions, or disagrees. **2.** A person inclined to skepticism in philosophical or religious matters. [Latin *Scepticus,* follower of the Greek philosopher Pyrrho, from Greek *Skepticos,* from *skeptesthai,* to examine, consider.]

skep·ti·cal (skěp′tĭ-kəl) *adj.* Also **scep·ti·cal.** Of or characterized by skepticism; doubting or disbelieving: *a skeptical attitude.* —**skep′ti·cal·ly** *adv.*

skep·ti·cism (skěp′tĭ-sĭz′əm) *n.* Also **scep·ti·cism. 1.** A doubting or questioning attitude or state of mind. **2.** The philosophical doctrine that absolute knowledge or certainty is impossible. **3.** Doubt or disbelief of religious tenets. —See Syns at **doubt.**

sketch (skěch) *n.* **1.** A hasty or undetailed drawing or painting. **2.** A brief composition or outline, as of a book to be completed. **3. a.** A brief, light, or informal short story, essay, or other literary composition. **b.** A short scene or play, often satirical in tone. **c.** *Mus.* A brief composition, esp. for the piano. —*tr.v.* To make a sketch of; to outline. —*intr.v.* To make a sketch or sketches. [Dutch *schets,* from Italian *schizzo,* from *schizzare,* to sketch, from Latin *schedius,* hastily put together, from Greek *skhedios,* impromptu.] —**sketch′er** *n.*

sketch·book (skěch′bŏŏk′) *n.* Also **sketch book. 1.** A pad of paper used for sketching. **2.** A book of sketches.

sketch·y (skěch′ē) *adj.* **-i·er, -i·est.** Lacking in details; incomplete. —**sketch′i·ly** *adv.* —**sketch′i·ness** *n.*

skew (skyōō) *intr.v.* **1.** To take an oblique course or direction. **2.** To look obliquely or sideways. —*tr.v.* **1.** To turn or place at an angle. **2.** To give a bias to; distort. —*adj.*

ă pat　ā pay　â care　ä father　ĕ pet　ē be　hw which　ĭ pit　ī tie　î pier　ŏ pot　ō toe　ô paw, for　oi noise
ŏŏ took　ōō boot　ou out　th thin　*th* this　ŭ cut　û urge　zh vision　ə about, item, edible, gallop, circus

skimmer

skink

1. Turned or placed to one side. **2.** Having a part that diverges from a straight line or a right angle. **3.** Neither parallel nor intersecting: *skew lines.* —*n.* An oblique or slanting movement, position, or direction. [Middle English *skewen,* from Old North French *eskuer,* to avoid.] —**skew′ness** *n.*

skew·er (skyōō′ər) *n.* **1.** A long metal or wooden pin used to secure or suspend food during cooking. **2.** Any of various picks or rods with a similar function. —*tr.v.* To pierce with a skewer. [Var. of dial. *skiver.*]

ski (skē) *n., pl.* **skis** or **ski.** One of a pair of long, flat runners of wood, metal, or plastic that may be attached to a boot for gliding over snow. —*modifier: ski boots.* —*v.* **skied, ski·ing.** —*intr.v.* To travel on skis, esp. as a sport. —*tr.v.* To travel over on skis. [Norwegian, from Old Norse *skíth,* ski, snowshoe.] —**ski′er** *n.*

skid (skĭd) *n.* **1.** The act or process of slipping or sliding over a surface, often sideways. **2. a.** A plank, log, etc. used as a support or track for sliding or rolling heavy objects. **b.** A small platform for stacking merchandise to be moved or temporarily stored. **3.** A runner forming part of the landing gear of some aircraft, such as helicopters. **4.** A wedge that applies pressure to a wheel to brake a vehicle. —*v.* **skidded, skid·ding.** —*intr.v.* **1.** To slip or slide out of control sideways while moving. **2.** To slide without revolving: *The wheel skidded on the ice.* —*tr.v.* **1.** To brake (a wheel) with a skid. **2.** To haul on a skid or skids. —See Syns at **slide.** —*idiom.* **on the skids.** *Slang.* In decline. [Orig. unknown.]

skid row. *Slang.* A squalid district inhabited by derelicts.

skies (skīz) *n.* Plural of **sky.**

skiff (skĭf) *n.* **1.** A flat-bottomed rowboat with a pointed bow and a square stern. **2.** A small, light sailboat or motor boat. [French *esquif,* from Italian *schifo.*]

ski jump. **1.** A jump or leap made by a skier. **2.** A course or chute prepared for such jumping.

ski lift. Any of various power-driven conveyors used to carry skiers to the top of a trail or slope. Also called **ski tow.**

skil·ful (skĭl′fəl) *adj. Brit.* Var. of **skillful.**

skill (skĭl) *n.* **1.** Dexterity; expertness: *her skill at plumbing.* **2.** An art, trade, or technique, esp. one that requires use of the hands or body. —See Syns at **ability.** [Middle English *skile,* reason, skill, from Old Norse *skil.*]

skilled (skĭld) *adj.* **1.** Having or showing skill; expert. **2.** Requiring specialized ability: *a skilled trade.*

skil·let (skĭl′ĭt) *n.* A frying pan. [Middle English *skelet,* prob. from *skele,* pail, of Scandinavian orig.]

skill·ful (skĭl′fəl) *adj. Also Brit.* **skil·ful. 1.** Possessing or exercising skill; expert: *a skillful surgeon.* **2.** Characterized by, showing, or requiring skill: *skillful questioning of the witness.* —**skill′ful·ly** *adv.* —**skill′ful·ness** *n.*

skim (skĭm) *v.* **skimmed, skim·ming.** —*tr.v.* **1.** To remove floating matter from (a liquid). **2.** To remove (floating matter) from a liquid. **3.** To coat or cover with or as with a thin layer. **4. a.** To hurl across the surface of, so as to bounce on water or slide on ice: *skimming stones.* **b.** To glide or pass quickly and lightly over. **5.** To read or glance through quickly or superficially: *skimmed the book.* —*intr.v.* **1.** To glide; to graze. **2.** To give a quick and superficial reading; to glance: *skim through the book.* **3.** To become coated with a thin layer: *The engine skimmed over with grime.* —*n.* **1.** The act of skimming. **2.** Something

that has been skimmed. **3.** A thin layer or film. [Middle English *skymen,* from Old French *escumer,* from *escume,* foam, from Old High German *scūm.*]

skim·mer (skĭm′ər) *n.* **1.** Someone or something that skims. **2.** A wide-brimmed hat with a flat shallow crown. **3.** Any of several chiefly coastal birds of the genus *Rynchops,* with a long lower mandible for skimming the water's surface for food.

skim milk. Milk from which the cream has been removed.

skimp (skĭmp) *tr.v.* **1.** To do carelessly or with poor material. **2.** To be extremely sparing with; scrimp. —*intr.v.* To be very or unduly thrifty. [Poss. a var. of SCRIMP.]

skimp·y (skĭm′pē) *adj.* **-i·er, -i·est. 1.** Inadequate in size or amount; scanty: *a skimpy meal.* **2.** Unduly thrifty; stingy; niggardly. —**skimp′i·ly** *adv.* —**skimp′i·ness** *n.*

skin (skĭn) *n.* **1.** The membranous tissue that forms the outer covering of an animal. **2.** A hide or pelt removed from the body of an animal. **3.** An outer layer, covering, or coating, such as the peel or rind of fruit or the film that forms on the surface of boiled milk. **4.** A container for liquids made from an animal's skin. —*modifier: skin tents; a skin disease.* —*v.* **skinned, skin·ning.** —*tr.v.* **1.** To remove skin from. **2.** To injure by scraping: *fell and skinned her knee.* **3.** To cover with or as if with skin. **4.** *Slang.* To cheat; swindle. —*intr.v.* **1.** To become covered with or as if with skin. **2.** To pass narrowly; squeeze: *skin through the passage.* —*idioms.* **by the skin of (one's) teeth.** By the smallest margin. **get under (one's) skin.** To anger or irritate. [Middle English, from Old Norse *skinn.*]

skin-deep (skĭn′dēp′) *adj.* Superficial or shallow. —*adv.* In a shallow manner; superficially.

skin-dive (skĭn′dīv′) *intr.v.* **-dived** or **-dove** (-dōv′), **-dived, -div·ing.** To participate in skin diving.

skin diving. Underwater swimming, often with flippers, a face mask, and a snorkel or scuba. —**skin diver.**

skin·flint (skĭn′flĭnt′) *n.* A miser.

skink (skĭngk) *n.* Any of numerous smooth, shiny lizards of the family Scincidae. [Latin *scincus,* from Greek *skinkos.*]

skin·ner (skĭn′ər) *n.* **1.** A person who strips, dresses, or sells animal skins. **2.** *Informal.* A mule driver.

skin·ny (skĭn′ē) *adj.* **-ni·er, -ni·est.** Very thin. —See Syns at **thin.** —**skin′ni·ness** *n.*

skin·ny-dip (skĭn′ē-dĭp′) *intr.v.* **-dipped, -dip·ping.** *Informal.* To swim in the nude. —**skin′ny-dip′per** *n.*

skin test. A test for an allergy or infectious disease performed on the skin, as by injection of an allergen.

skin·tight (skĭn′tīt′) *adj.* Fitting or clinging closely.

skip (skĭp) *v.* **skipped, skip·ping.** —*intr.v.* **1.** To move by springing or hopping on one foot and then the other. **2.** To leap lightly about. **3.** To bounce over or be deflected from a surface. **4. a.** To pass from point to point disregarding what intervenes: *skipping over the television channels.* **b.** To be promoted in school beyond the next regular class or grade. **5.** *Informal.* To leave hastily; abscond: *He skipped out just before the police arrived.* —*tr.v.* **1.** To leap or jump lightly over: *skip rope.* **2.** To pass over, omit, or disregard: *skipping the minor details of the episode.* **3.** To cause to ricochet or skim: *skips stones on the pond.* **4.** To be promoted beyond (the next grade or level). **5.** To leave hastily: *He skipped town.* —*n.* **1.** A leaping or jumping movement, esp. one in which hops are taken first on one foot, then on the other. **2.** A passing over or omission. [Middle English *skippen.*]

---

skip·jack (skĭp′jăk′) n., pl. **skipjack** or **-jacks.** 1. Any of several saltwater food fishes of the genus Euthynnus, related to and resembling the tuna. 2. Any of various other fishes, as certain herrings. [SKIP + JACK (fellow).]

ski pole. A thin pointed pole with a disk above the point, used by skiers to help guide them over the snow.

skip·per[1] (skĭp′ər) n. The captain of a ship, esp. of a small one. [Middle English skypper, from Middle Dutch schipper, from schip, ship.]

skip·per[2] (skĭp′ər) n. 1. Someone or something that skips. 2. Any of numerous butterflies of the families Hesperiidae and Megathymidae, with a darting flight pattern.

skirl (skûrl) intr.v. To produce a shrill, piercing tone, as a bagpipe. —tr.v. To play on the bagpipe. —n. The shrill sound made by a bagpipe. [Middle English skirlen, prob. of Scandinavian orig.]

skir·mish (skûr′mĭsh) n. 1. A minor encounter in war between small bodies of troops. 2. Any minor or short conflict. —intr.v. To engage in a skirmish. [Middle English skirmisshe, from Old French eskermir, to fight with the sword.] —skir′mish·er n.

skirt (skûrt) n. 1. The part of a garment, such as a dress or gown, that hangs from the waist down. 2. A separate garment that hangs from the waist down, worn usu. by women and girls. 3. Anything that hangs like a skirt, esp.: **a.** A ruffled or pleated piece of cloth covering the legs of a piece of furniture. **b.** One of the leather flaps hanging from the side of a saddle. 4. A border, margin, or outer edge. 5. **skirts.** The edge or outskirts. 6. Slang. A woman or girl. —tr.v. 1. To run or lie along the edge of: The road skirted the woods. 2. To move or pass around rather than across or through. 3. To evade or avoid: skirt the issue. [Middle English, from Old Norse skyrta, shirt.]

ski run. A hill, slope, or path for skiing.

skit (skĭt) n. 1. A short, usu. comic, theatrical sketch. 2. A short humorous piece of writing. [Orig. unknown.]

ski tow. A ski lift.

skit·ter (skĭt′ər) intr.v. To skip, glide, or move lightly or rapidly along a surface; to dart; flit. —tr.v. To cause to skitter. [Prob. from dial. skite, to run rapidly.]

skit·tish (skĭt′ĭsh) adj. 1. Excitable or nervous. 2. Shy, coy, or timid. 3. Capricious or fickle. —See Syns at **edgy.** [Middle English.] —skit′tish·ly adv. —skit′tish·ness n.

skit·tle (skĭt′l) n. Brit. 1. **skittles.** (used with a sing. verb). The game of ninepins played with a wooden disk or ball. 2. One of the pins used in this game. [Orig. unknown.]

skiv·vy (skĭv′ē) n., pl. **-vies.** Slang. 1. A man's undershirt. 2. **skivvies.** A man's underwear. [Orig. unknown.]

skoal (skōl) interj. A word used as a drinking toast. [Ult. from Old Norse skāl, drinking cup.]

sku·a (skyōō′ə) n. A predatory gull-like sea bird, Catharacta skua, of northern regions, with brownish plumage. [Ult. from Old Norse skūfr.]

skul·dug·ger·y (skŭl-dŭg′ə-rē) n. Var. of skullduggery.

skulk (skŭlk) intr.v. 1. To lurk; lie in hiding. 2. To move about stealthily. —See Syns at **sneak.** —n. A person who skulks. [Middle English skulken, of Scandinavian orig.] —skulk′er n.

skull (skŭl) n. 1. The part of a vertebrate's skeleton that forms the framework of the head. 2. The head regarded as the seat of intelligence. [Middle English skulle.]

skull and crossbones. A representation of a human skull above two long crossed bones, a symbol once used by pirates and now used as a warning label on poisons.

skull·cap (skŭl′kăp′) n. A light, close-fitting, brimless cap sometimes worn indoors.

skull·dug·ger·y (skŭl-dŭg′ə-rē) n. Also **skul·dug·ger·y.** Crafty deception or trickery. [Orig. unknown.]

skunk (skŭngk) n. 1. Any of several small, carnivorous New World mammals of the genus Mephitis and related genera, that have black fur with white markings and eject a bad-smelling secretion. 2. Slang. A mean or despicable person. —tr.v. Slang. To defeat overwhelmingly. [Of Algonquian orig.]

skunk cabbage. 1. An ill-smelling swamp plant, Symplocarpus foetidus, of eastern North America, having minute flowers enclosed in a mottled greenish or purplish spathe. 2. A similar plant, Lysichitum americanum, of western North America. Also called **skunkweed.**

sky (skī) n., pl. **skies.** 1. The upper atmosphere, seen as a hemisphere above the earth. 2. The hemisphere of the celestial sphere that can be seen by an observer on the earth. 3. Often **skies.** The appearance of the upper atmosphere, esp. with respect to weather: threatening skies. [Middle English, cloud, sky, from Old Norse skȳ, cloud.]

sky blue. Light to pale blue; azure. —sky′-blue′ adj.

sky·cap (skī′kăp′) n. A porter at an airport.

sky·dive (skī′dīv′) intr.v. **-dived** or **-dove** (-dōv′), **-dived, -diving.** To jump from an airplane, performing various maneuvers before opening a parachute. —sky′div′er n. —sky′div′ing n.

sky-high (skī′hī′) adv. 1. To a very high level: garbage piled sky-high. 2. To pieces; apart: blew the bridge sky-high. —adj. Extremely high: sky-high prices.

sky·jack (skī′jăk′) tr.v. To hijack (an airplane, esp. one in flight). [SKY + (HI)JACK.] —sky′jack′er n.

sky·lark (skī′lärk′) n. An Old World bird, Alauda arvensis, that has brownish plumage and is noted for its singing while in flight. —intr.v. To romp playfully; to frolic.

sky·light (skī′līt′) n. A window in a roof or ceiling that admits daylight.

sky·line (skī′līn′) n. 1. The line along which the earth and sky appear to meet; the horizon. 2. The outline of mountains, buildings, etc., as seen against the horizon.

sky·rock·et (skī′rŏk′ĭt) n. A firework that ascends high into the air, where it explodes brilliantly. —intr.v. To rise rapidly or suddenly. —tr.v. To cause to rise rapidly.

sky·sail (skī′səl, -sāl′) n. A small sail above the royal in a square-rigged vessel.

sky·scrap·er (skī′skrā′pər) n. A very tall building.

sky·ward (skī′wərd) adv. Also **sky·wards** (-wərdz). Toward the sky: turn skyward. —sky′ward adj.

sky·way (skī′wā′) n. 1. An airline route; air lane. 2. An elevated highway.

sky·writ·ing (skī′rī′tĭng) n. Writing formed in the sky by releasing a visible vapor from a flying airplane. —sky′writ′er n.

slab (slăb) n. 1. A broad, flat, somewhat thick piece, as of stone or metal. 2. An outside piece cut from a log when squaring it for lumber. [Middle English sclabbe.]

slack[1] (slăk) adj. **-er, -est.** 1. Not lively; slow; sluggish. 2. Not busy or active. 3. Not tense, taut, or firm; loose: a slack rope. 4. Careless; negligent: a slack performance. —See Syns at **loose.** —tr.v. 1. To make slack; slacken. 2. To slake (lime). —intr.v. 1. To be or become slack. —phrasal verb. **slack off.** To fall off; abate. —n. 1. A loose or slack part or portion: Take up the slack in the rope. 2. A lack of tension; looseness. 3. A period of little activity; a lull. 4. A cessation of movement in a current of air or water. —adv. In a slack manner. [Middle English slak, from Old English slæc.] —slack′ly adv. —slack′ness n.

slack[2] (slăk) n. A mixture of coal fragments, coal dust, and dirt that remains after screening coal. [Middle English sleck, prob. from Middle Dutch slacke.]

slack·en (slăk′ən) tr.v. 1. To make slower; slow down: The dogs slackened their pace. 2. To make less tense, taut, or firm: He slackened his grip. —intr.v. 1. To slow down: Business slackened. 2. To become less tense, taut, or firm. 3. To let up; ease.

slack·er (slăk′ər) n. A person who avoids work or duty.

skunk   skydive

slacks (slăks) *pl.n.* Long trousers for casual wear.

slack water. The period at high or low tide when there is no visible flow of water.

slag (slăg) *n.* **1.** The glassy mass left by the smelting of metallic ore. Also called **cinder. 2.** Volcanic refuse; scoria. [Middle Low German *slagge.*]

slain (slān) *v.* Past participle of **slay.** [Middle English *sleyn,* from Old English (ge)*slægen.*]

slake (slāk) *v.* **slaked, slak·ing.** —*tr.v.* **1.** To quench; satisfy: *slaked her thirst.* **2.** To lessen the force or activity of; moderate: *slaking his anger.* **3.** To combine (lime) chemically with water or moist air. —*intr.v.* To become slaked, as lime does. [Middle English *slaken,* to lessen, diminish, from Old English *slacian,* from *slæc,* slack.]

slaked lime. *Chem.* **Calcium hydroxide.**

sla·lom (slä'ləm) *n.* **1.** Skiing in a zigzag course. **2.** A race along such a course. [Norwegian, "sloping path."]

slam¹ (slăm) *v.* **slammed, slam·ming.** —*tr.v.* **1.** To shut with force and loud noise: *slam the door.* **2.** To put, throw, or forcefully move so as to produce a loud noise: *slam down the telephone.* **3.** To hit with great force. **4.** *Slang.* To criticize harshly. —*intr.v.* **1.** To close or swing into place with force and a loud noise: *The door slammed shut.* **2.** To crash. —See Syns at **hit.** —*n.* **1. a.** A forceful closing or other movement that produces a loud noise. **b.** The noise so produced. **2.** *Slang.* A harsh criticism. [Perh. of Scandinavian orig.]

slam² (slăm) *n.* In certain card games, such as bridge, the winning of all the tricks, a **grand slam,** or all but one, a **little slam,** during the play of one hand. [Orig. unknown.]

slan·der (slăn'dər) *n.* **1.** *Law.* The uttering of false and malicious statements that damage the reputation or well-being of another. **2.** A malicious statement or report. —*tr.v.* To utter malicious reports about. —*intr.v.* To utter or spread slander. [Middle English *sclaundre,* from Old French *esclandre,* from Latin *scandalum,* scandal.] —**slan'der·er** *n.*

slan·der·ous (slăn'dər-əs) *adj.* Uttering or containing slander: *a slanderous accusation.* —**slan'der·ous·ly** *adv.*

slang (slăng) *n.* **1.** A nonstandard vocabulary of striking and often short-lived coinages, expressions, and figures of speech. **2.** Language peculiar to a certain group: *teen-age slang.* —*modifier: a slang word.* [Orig. unknown.]

slang·y (slăng'ē) *adj.* **-i·er, -i·est.** Like, containing, or using slang. —**slang'i·ly** *adv.* —**slang'i·ness** *n.*

slant (slănt) *intr.v.* To slope or lie at an angle away from horizontal or vertical. —*tr.v.* **1.** To give an oblique direction to. **2.** To present so as to conform with a particular bias: *journalists who slant the news.* —*n.* **1.** A sloping line, plane, direction, or course. **2.** The degree to which something slants. **3.** An attitude or approach. **4.** A bias. [Middle English *slenten.*]

slant·wise (slănt'wīz') *adv.* Also **slant·ways** (-wāz'). At a slant; obliquely. —*adj.* Slanting; oblique.

slap (slăp) *n.* **1. a.** A smacking blow made with the open hand or with any flat thing. **b.** The sound so made. **2.** A sharp rebuke or insult. —*v.* **slapped, slap·ping.** —*tr.v.* **1.** To strike with a flat object, as the palm of the hand. **2.** To criticize or insult sharply. **3.** To put or place with a slapping sound. —*intr.v.* To strike with the force and sound of a slap. —*phrasal verb.* **slap down.** To squelch; suppress. [Low German *slapp.*] —**slap'per** *n.*

slap·dash (slăp'dăsh') *adj.* Hasty or careless: *slapdash work.* —*adv.* In a reckless, haphazard manner.

slap·hap·py (slăp'hăp'ē) *adj.* **-pi·er, -pi·est.** *Slang.* Dazed, silly, or incoherent from or as if from blows to the head.

slap·jack (slăp'jăk') *n.* **1.** A pancake; flapjack. **2.** A simple card game. [SLAP + (FLAP)JACK.]

slap·stick (slăp'stĭk') *n.* **1.** A form of comedy marked by zany chases, collisions, crude practical jokes, and similar boisterous actions. **2.** A paddle designed to produce a loud whacking sound, formerly used by actors in farces.

slash (slăsh) *tr.v.* **1.** To cut with violent sweeping strokes. **2.** To strike with or as if with a whip. **3.** To make a gash or gashes in. **4.** To cut a slit or slits in. **5.** To criticize sharply. **6.** To reduce or curtail drastically: *slash inventory.* —*intr.v.* **1.** To make violent and sweeping strokes with or as with a cutting tool. **2.** To cut one's way with such

strokes: *We slashed through dense jungle.* —*n.* **1.** A sweeping stroke made with a cutting tool. **2.** A cut or other injury made by such a stroke. **3.** An ornamental slit in a garment. **4.** Branches and other residue left on a forest floor after the cutting of timber. **5.** A diagonal mark (/) used in writing and printing. —*modifier: slash sleeves; slash fractions.* [Middle English *slaschen.*] —**slash'er** *n.*

slat (slăt) *n.* A narrow strip of metal or wood, as in a Venetian blind. —*v.* **slat·ted, slat·ting.** To provide or make with slats. [Middle English *sclat,* from Old French *esclat,* splinter, fragment, from *esclater,* to splinter.]

slate (slāt) *n.* **1.** A fine-grained metamorphic rock that splits into thin, smooth-surfaced layers. **2. a.** A piece of this material cut for use as roofing material or a writing surface. **b.** A writing tablet made of a similar material. **3.** A record of past performance or activity: *a clean slate.* **4.** A list of the candidates of a particular political party running for offices. **5.** Dark bluish gray. —*modifier: a slate roof.* —*tr.v.* **slat·ed, slat·ing.** **1.** To cover with slate. **2.** To assign a place to on a list or schedule. **3.** To schedule. [Middle English *sclate,* from Old French *esclate,* fragment, splinter.] —**slat'er** *n.*

slath·er (slăth'ər) *tr.v.* *Informal.* To spread thickly or lavishly. [Orig. unknown.]

slat·tern (slăt'ərn) *n.* A slovenly woman. [Perh. dial. *slattering,* pres. part. of *slatter,* to spill awkwardly.] —**slat'tern·li·ness** *n.* —**slat'tern·ly** *adj. & adv.*

slaugh·ter (slô'tər) *n.* **1.** The killing of animals for food. **2.** The brutal murder of a large number of people or animals; massacre. **3.** *Informal.* A defeat by a wide margin. —*tr.v.* **1.** To butcher (animals) for food. **2.** To kill brutally or in large numbers. **3.** *Informal.* To defeat by a wide margin. [Middle English, prob. from Old Norse *slátr,* butcher's meat.] —**slaugh'ter·er** *n.* —**slaugh'ter·ous** *adj.*

slaugh·ter·house (slô'tər-hous') *n.* **1.** A place where animals are butchered. **2.** A scene of massacre or carnage.

Slav (släv) *n.* A member of one of the Slavic-speaking peoples of eastern Europe.

slave (slāv) *n.* **1.** A person who is owned by and forced to work for someone else. **2.** A person completely controlled by a specified influence, emotion, etc. **3.** Any person who works very hard. —*modifier: slave labor.* —*intr.v.* **slaved, slav·ing.** To work like a slave. [Middle English *sclave,* from Old French *esclave,* from Medieval Latin *sclavus,* from *Sclavus,* Slav.]

slave driver. **1.** A severely exacting employer or supervisor. **2.** An overseer of slaves at work.

slave·hold·er (slāv'hōl'dər) *n.* A person who owns slaves. —**slave'hold'ing** *adj. & n.*

slav·er¹ (slăv'ər, slā'vər) *intr.v.* To let saliva dribble from the mouth; to drool; slobber. —*n.* **1.** Saliva dribbling from the mouth. **2.** Slobbering flattery or drivel. [Middle English *slaveren,* prob. from Old Norse *slafra.*]

slav·er² (slā'vər) *n.* **1.** A ship engaged in transporting slaves. **2.** A person who buys and sells slaves.

slav·er·y (slā'və-rē, slāv'rē) *n.* **1.** The condition of being a slave; bondage. **2.** The practice of owning slaves. **3.** A condition of hard work and subjection. —See Syns at **bondage.**

slave state. Often **Slave State.** Any of the 15 states of the Union in which slavery was legal before the Civil War.

Slav·ic (slä'vĭk, slăv'ĭk) *n.* A branch of the Indo-European language family that includes Bulgarian, Czech, Polish, Russian, Serbo-Croatian, and Slovak. —*adj.* Of the Slavs or their languages.

slav·ish (slā'vĭsh) *adj.* **1.** Like or befitting a slave; servile: *slavish devotion.* **2.** Showing no originality; blindly imitative: *a slavish copy.* —**slav'ish·ly** *adv.* —**slav'ish·ness** *n.*

Sla·von·ic (slə-vŏn'ĭk) *n. & adj.* Slavic.

slaw (slô) *n.* Coleslaw.

slay (slā) *tr.v.* **slew** (slōō), **slain** (slān), **slay·ing.** **1. a.** To kill violently. **b.** To kill deliberately: *slain by an armed robber.* **2.** *Slang.* To overwhelm, as with laughter or love: *Her jokes slay me.* —See Syns at **kill** and **murder.** [Middle English *slen,* from Old English *slēan.*] —**slay'er** *n.*

slea·zy (slē'zē) *adj.* **-zi·er, -zi·est.** **1.** Thin and loosely woven; flimsy: *a coat with a sleazy lining.* **2.** Of poor quality; shoddy. **3.** Vulgar; disreputable: *a sleazy tavern.* [Orig. unknown.] —**slea'zi·ly** *adv.* —**slea'zi·ness** *n.*

ă pat　ā pay　â care　ä father　ĕ pet　ē be　hw which　ĭ pit　ī tie　î pier　ŏ pot　ō toe　ô paw, for　oi noise
ōō took　ōō boot　ou out　th thin　*th* this　ŭ cut　û urge　zh vision　ə about, item, edible, gallop, circus

sled (slĕd) n. 1. A vehicle mounted on runners, used for carrying people or loads over ice and snow; sledge. 2. A light wooden frame mounted on runners, used by children for coasting over snow or ice. —v. **sled·ded, sled·ding.** —tr.v. To carry on or convey by a sled. —intr.v. To ride or use a sled. [Middle English *sledde*, from Middle Low German.] —**sled′der** n.

sledge[1] (slĕj) n. A vehicle on low runners drawn by horses, dogs, or reindeer and used for transporting loads across snow and ice. —v. **sledged, sledg·ing.** —tr.v. To convey on a sledge. —intr.v. To travel on a sledge. [Dutch *sleeds*, from Middle Dutch *sleedse.*]

sledge[2] (slĕj) n. A sledgehammer.

sledge·ham·mer (slĕj′hăm′ər) n. A long, heavy hammer, usu. wielded with both hands. —tr.v. To strike with such a hammer. [From Middle English *slegge*, from Old English *slecg.*]

sledgehammer

sleek (slēk) adj. **-er, -est.** 1. Smooth and lustrous as if polished; glossy. 2. Neat, trim, and graceful. 3. Healthy or well-fed; thriving. 4. Polished or smooth in behavior. —tr.v. To make lustrous or smooth. [Var. of SLICK.] —**sleek′ly** adv. —**sleek′ness** n.

sleep (slēp) n. 1. A natural condition of rest, occurring periodically in many animals, characterized by unconsciousness and lessened responsiveness to external stimuli. 2. A period of this form of rest. 3. Any similar condition of inactivity. —v. **slept** (slĕpt), **sleep·ing.** —intr.v. 1. To be in the state of sleep or to fall asleep. 2. a. To be in a condition resembling sleep. b. To be dead and buried. 3. To be inattentive or negligent: *The question caught me sleeping.* —tr.v. 1. To pass or get rid of by sleeping: *slept the afternoon away.* 2. To provide with accommodations for sleeping: *The cabin sleeps six.* —**idioms. sleep on.** To consider overnight before deciding. **sleep with.** To have sexual intercourse with. [Middle English, from Old English *slǣp.*]

sleep·er (slē′pər) n. 1. A person or animal that sleeps. 2. A sleeping car. 3. Informal. Something that becomes unexpectedly popular or successful. 4. A heavy beam used as a support for rails in a railroad track.

sleeping bag. A large, warmly lined, usu. zippered bag in which a person may sleep, esp. outdoors.

sleeping car. A railroad car with berths or small bedrooms for overnight passengers.

sleeping pill. A sedative, esp. a barbiturate, in the form of a pill or capsule used to relieve insomnia.

sleeping sickness. An often fatal, endemic infectious disease of tropical Africa, caused by either of two protozoans of the genus *Trypanosoma*, transmitted by the tsetse fly, and characterized by fever and lethargy.

sleep·less (slēp′lĭs) adj. 1. Unable to sleep. 2. Without sleep: *a sleepless night.* 3. Always alert or in motion. —**sleep′less·ly** adv. —**sleep′less·ness** n.

sleep·walk·ing (slēp′wô′kĭng) n. A mental or nervous disorder in which the person affected walks about while asleep; somnambulism. —**sleep′walk′er** n.

sleep·y (slē′pē) adj. **-i·er, -i·est.** 1. Ready for sleep; drowsy. 2. Dulled or softened by the nearness of sleep. 3. Quiet; inactive. —**sleep′i·ly** adv. —**sleep′i·ness** n.

sleep·y·head (slē′pē-hĕd′) n. Informal. A sleepy person.

sleet (slēt) n. 1. Frozen or partially frozen raindrops. 2. An icy glaze. —intr.v. To shower sleet. [Middle English *slete.*] —**sleet′y** adj.

sleeve (slēv) n. 1. The part of a garment that covers the arm. 2. A tubular encasement into which a piece of equipment fits. —**idiom. up (one's) sleeve.** Hidden but ready to be used. [Middle English *sleve*, from Old English *slēf.*] —**sleeve′less** adj.

sleigh (slā) n. A light vehicle mounted on runners for use on snow or ice, usu. drawn by a horse. —**modifier:** *a sleigh ride.* —intr.v. To ride in or drive a sleigh. [Dutch *slee*, from Middle Dutch *slēde.*]

sleight (slīt) n. 1. Deftness; dexterity; skill. 2. A clever or skillful trick or deception; an artifice; stratagem. [Middle English, from Old Norse *slœgdh*, from *slœgr*, sly.]

sleight of hand. 1. Tricks or feats performed by jugglers or magicians so quickly that one cannot see how they are done. 2. Skill in performing such feats. —**modifier** (**sleight-of-hand**): *a sleight-of-hand artist.*

slen·der (slĕn′dər) adj. 1. Having little width in proportion to the height or length; thin; slim: *a slender church spire.* 2. Meager; inadequate: *slender wages.* —See Syns at **thin.** [Middle English *sclendre.*] —**slen·der·ly** adv. —**slen·der·ness** n.

slen·der·ize (slĕn′də-rīz′) v. **-ized, -iz·ing.** —intr.v. To become slender or more slender. —tr.v. To make slender.

slept (slĕpt) v. Past tense and past participle of **sleep.**

sleuth (slooth) n. 1. Informal. A detective. 2. A sleuthhound. —tr.v. To track or follow. —intr.v. To act as a detective. [Short for SLEUTHHOUND.]

sleuth·hound (slooth′hound′) n. 1. A bloodhound. 2. A detective. [Middle English : *sleuth*, track of an animal, from Old Norse *slódh* + *hound*, hound.]

slew[1] (sloo) n. Also **slue.** Informal. A large amount or number; a lot: *a whole slew of her friends.* [Irish Gaelic *sluagh*, from Old Irish *slúag, slóg.*]

slew[2] (sloo) v. Past tense of **slay.** [Middle English.]

slew[3] (sloo, slou) n. Var. of **slough** (depression).

slew[4] (sloo) v. & n. Var. of **slue** (twist, turn).

slice (slīs) n. 1. A thin, broad piece cut from a larger object. 2. A portion or share: *a slice of the profits.* 3. A knife with a broad, thin, flexible blade. 4. Sports. a. A stroke that causes a ball to curve off course to the right or, if the player is left-handed, to the left. b. The course followed by such a ball. —v. **sliced, slic·ing.** —tr.v. 1. To cut or divide with or as if with a knife. 2. To cut or remove from a larger piece: *slice off a piece of salami.* 3. Sports. To hit (a ball) with a slice. —intr.v. 1. To move like a knife. 2. Sports. To hit a ball with a slice. [Middle English *sclice*, slice, splinter, from Old French *esclice*, from *esclicer*, to reduce to splinters.] —**slic′er** n.

slick (slĭk) adj. **-er, -est.** 1. Having a smooth, glossy surface. 2. Deftly executed; adroit; facile: *a slick move.* 3. Shrewd; crafty. 4. Superficially attractive or skillful but without depth or quality: *a slick writing style.* —See Syns at **shrewd.** —n. 1. A smooth or slippery surface, esp. a stretch of water covered with a film of oil. 2. Informal. A magazine printed on glossy, high-quality paper. —tr.v. To make smooth, glossy, or oily. [Middle English *slike.*]

slick·er (slĭk′ər) n. 1. A glossy raincoat, esp. one made of oilskin or plastic. 2. Informal. A swindler; crook. 3. Informal. A person with stylish clothing and manners.

slid (slĭd) v. Past tense and a past participle of **slide.** [Middle English *slydde.*]

slide (slīd) v. **slid** (slĭd), **slid, slid·ing.** —intr.v. 1. To move over a surface while maintaining continuous contact. 2. To pass smoothly and quietly; glide: *He slid in unnoticed.* 3. To move downward: *Prices began to slide.* 4. To move accidentally out of place; slip: *The cup slid out of his hand.* 5. To lose one's balance or intended direction on a slippery surface. 6. To go unattended or unacted upon: *They let their business slide.* 7. To go back to a less favorable or less worthy condition. 8. Baseball. To drop down and skid, usu. feet first, into a base to avoid being tagged out.

sleigh

—*tr.v.* To cause to slide or slip: *The movers slid the chair into the room.* —*n.* **1.** A sliding movement or action. **2. a.** A smooth surface or track for sliding, usu. inclined: *a toboggan slide.* **b.** A playground fixture with a slanted surface to slide down. **3.** A part that operates by sliding, as the U-shaped section of tube on a trombone. **4.** An image, usu. photographic, formed on a transparent piece of material for projection on a screen. **5.** A small glass plate for mounting specimens to be examined under a microscope. **6.** The fall of a mass of ice, snow, or rocks down a slope. [Middle English *sliden,* from Old English *slīdan.*] —**slid′er** *n.*
   Syns: slide, coast, drift, glide, slip *v. Core meaning:* To pass smoothly, quietly, and effortlessly on or as if on a slippery surface (*skaters sliding across the ice; sharks sliding through the water*).

slide rule. A device that consists of two rules marked with logarithmic scales and arranged to slide along each other, used in performing mathematical operations.

sliding scale. A scale in which indicated prices, taxes, or wages vary in accordance with some other factor, as wages with the cost-of-living index.

sli·er (slī′ər) *adj.* A comparative of **sly.**

sli·est (slī′ĭst) *adj.* A superlative of **sly.**

slight (slīt) *adj.* **-er, -est. 1.** Small in size, degree, or amount. **2.** Of small importance; trifling. **3.** Slender or frail; delicate. —*tr.v.* **1.** To treat as if of slight importance; underestimate: *He slighted her intelligence.* **2.** To snub or insult. **3.** To neglect. —*n.* An act of pointed disrespect or discourtesy. [Middle English, smooth, slight, from Old Norse *slēttr,* smooth, sleek.] —**slight′ly** *adv.* —**slight′ness** *n.*

slight·ing (slī′tĭng) *adj.* Constituting or conveying a slight; disrespectful; discourteous. —**slight′ing·ly** *adv.*

slim (slĭm) *adj.* **slim·mer, slim·mest. 1.** Small in girth or thickness; thin; slender. **2.** Small in quality or amount; scant; meager. —*v.* **slimmed, slim·ming.** —*tr.v.* To make slim or thin. —*intr.v.* To become slim. [Dutch, small, inferior, from Middle Dutch, bad.] —**slim′ly** *adv.* —**slim′ness** *n.*

slime (slīm) *n.* **1.** A thick, sticky, slippery substance. **2.** A mucous substance secreted by certain animals, such as frogs, fish, or slugs. [Middle English, from Old English *slīm.*]

slime mold. An organism that in one stage of its development forms a slimy, moving mass of protoplasm and in another stage forms a funguslike growth.

slim·y (slī′mē) *adj.* **-i·er, -i·est. 1.** Consisting of or resembling slime. **2.** Covered with or exuding slime. **3.** Vile; filthy. —**slim′i·ly** *adv.* —**slim′i·ness** *n.*

sling (slĭng) *n.* **1.** A looped belt, rope, or chain in which loads are placed to be hoisted. **2.** An adjustable strap for securing and carrying something. **3.** A band of cloth looped around the neck to support an injured arm or hand. **4. a.** A weapon made from a looped strap in which a stone is whirled and then let fly. **b.** A slingshot. **5.** The act of slinging. —*tr.v.* **slung** (slŭng), **sling·ing. 1.** To throw or hurl with a swinging motion of the arm; to fling. **2.** To place, carry, or move in a sling. **3.** To shoot; cast: *sling an arrow.* **4.** To hang loosely or freely; let swing. [Middle English, prob. ult. from Old Norse *slyngva,* to sling.] —**sling′er** *n.*

sling·shot (slĭng′shŏt′) *n.* A Y-shaped stick with an elastic strap attached to the prongs, used for flinging stones.

slink (slĭngk) *intr.v.* **slunk** (slŭngk), **slink·ing.** To move in a quiet, furtive manner. —See Syns at **sneak.** [Middle English *slynken,* from Old English *slincan.*]

slink·y (slĭng′kē) *adj.* **-i·er, -i·est. 1.** Stealthy; furtive. **2.** *Informal.* Graceful, sinuous, and sleek: *a slinky dress.*

slip¹ (slĭp) *v.* **slipped, slip·ping.** —*intr.v.* **1. a.** To move quietly and smoothly; slide or glide. **b.** To move stealthily. **2.** To pass gradually, easily, or unnoticed: *Days slipped by.* **3. a.** To lose one's balance: *slip on the ice.* **b.** To slide out of proper place: *The gear slipped.* **c.** To escape, as from a fastening or grip: *The dog slipped out of its collar.* **4.** To get away: *letting chances slip by.* **5.** To decline; fall off: *His work is slipping.* **6.** To fall behind a scheduled production rate. **7.** To make a mistake or error. —*tr.v.* **1.** To cause to move in a smooth, easy, or sliding motion: *She slipped the bolt into place.* **2.** To place or insert smoothly and quietly. **3.** To insert or give in a sneaky or stealthy way: *The visitor*

slipped *a knife to the prisoner.* **4.** To put on or remove (clothing) easily or quickly: *slip on a sweater; slip off shoes.* **5.** To get loose or free from. **6.** To release; unfasten: *slip the knot.* **7.** To dislocate (a bone). **8.** *Knitting.* To pass (a stitch) from one needle to another without knitting it. —See Syns at **sneak.** —*n.* **1.** The act of slipping or sliding. **2.** A decline, esp. a slight one. **3.** A small mistake: *a slip of the tongue.* **4. a.** A narrow docking place for a ship. **b.** A space for a ship between two docks or wharves. **5.** A woman's undergarment made like a lowcut, sleeveless dress with shoulder straps or like a skirt. **6.** A pillowcase. —See Syns at **error.** —*idioms.* **give (someone) the slip.** *Slang.* To escape the company of. **let slip.** To say unintentionally or thoughtlessly. **slip one over on.** *Informal.* To hoodwink; deceive; dupe. [Middle English *slippen.*]

slip² (slĭp) *n.* **1.** A part of a plant cut or broken off for grafting or planting. **2.** Any long, narrow piece. **3.** A youthful, slender person. **4.** A small piece of paper: *a sales slip.* —*tr.v.* **slipped, slip·ping.** To make a slip from (a plant or plant part). [Middle English *slippe,* a strip.]

slip·case (slĭp′kās′) *n.* A protective box for a book.

slip·cov·er (slĭp′kŭv′ər) *n.* A fitted, removable cover of cloth or other material for a piece of upholstered furniture.

slip·knot (slĭp′nŏt′) *n.* **1.** A knot made with a loop so that it slips easily along the rope or cord around which it is tied. Also called **running knot. 2.** A knot made so that it can readily be untied by pulling one free end.

slip-on (slĭp′ŏn′, -ôn′) *n.* A piece of clothing easily slipped on and off. —*modifier:* slip-on gloves.

slip·page (slĭp′ĭj) *n.* **1.** A slipping. **2.** The amount or extent of slipping. **3.** Loss of motion or power due to slipping.

slipped disk. An injury that results from the shifting out of position of one of the cushioning disks between the spinal vertebrae.

slip·per (slĭp′ər) *n.* A light, low shoe, worn mainly indoors, that may be slipped on and off easily.

slip·per·y (slĭp′ə-rē) *adj.* **-i·er, -i·est. 1.** Causing or tending to cause sliding or slipping. **2.** Tending to slip or slide, as from one's grasp: *a slippery bar of soap.* **3.** Hard to capture or pin down; elusive: *a slippery character.* [Middle English *slipper,* from Old English *slipor.*] —**slip′per·i·ness** *n.*

slippery elm. A tree, *Ulmus rubra,* of eastern North America, that has twigs and leaves with a mucilaginous, aromatic juice formerly used medicinally.

slip ring. A metal ring mounted on a rotating part of a machine to provide a continuous electrical connection through brushes on stationary contacts.

slip·shod (slĭp′shŏd′) *adj.* **1.** Poorly made or done; careless: *a slipshod job.* **2.** Untidy in appearance; shabby; seedy.

slip·stream (slĭp′strēm′) *n.* The turbulent flow of air driven backward by the propeller or propellers of an aircraft. Also called **race.**

slip-up (slĭp′ŭp′) *n. Informal.* An error; oversight; mistake. —See Syns at **error.**

slit (slĭt) *n.* A long, narrow cut, tear, or opening. —*tr.v.* **slit, slit·ting.** To make a slit or slits in. [Middle English *slitte,* perh. from Old English *geslit,* a tearing.]

slith·er (slĭth′ər) *intr.v.* **1.** To slip and slide, as on a loose or uneven surface. **2.** To move along by gliding, as a snake does. —*tr.v.* To cause to slither. —*n.* A slithering movement. [Middle English *slideren,* from Old English *slidorian,* freq. of *slide,* to slide.] —**slith′er·y** *adj.*

sliv·er (slĭv′ər) *n.* **1.** A sharp-ended, thin piece; splinter. **2.** (*also* slī′vər). A continuous strand of loose wool, flax, or cotton. —*tr.v.* To split into splinters. —*intr.v.* To become split into slivers. [Middle English *slivere,* from *slyven,* to cleave, split.]

slob (slŏb) *n. Informal.* A crude, dirty, or slovenly person. [Irish *slab,* mud, prob. of Scandinavian orig.]

slob·ber (slŏb′ər) *intr.v.* **1.** To let saliva or food dribble from the mouth. **2.** To express emotion in an overexcited or exaggerated way; gush. —*tr.v.* To wet or smear with or as if with saliva or food dribbled from the mouth. —*n.* **1.** Saliva or liquid running from the mouth; drivel. **2.** Oversentimental speech or writing. [Middle English *sloberen,* perh. of Low German orig.] —**slob′ber·er** *n.*

sloe (slō) *n.* **1.** A shrub, the blackthorn. **2.** The tart, blue-black, plumlike fruit of this shrub. [Middle English *sloo*, from Old English *slāh*.]

slog (slŏg) *v.* **slogged, slog·ging.** —*tr.v.* To strike with heavy blows, as in boxing. —*intr.v.* **1.** To walk with a slow, plodding gait. **2.** To work diligently for long hours. —See Syns at **hit.** [Orig. unknown.] —**slog'ger** *n.*

slo·gan (slō'gən) *n.* **1.** A phrase expressing the aims or nature of an enterprise, team, or other group; motto. **2.** A battle cry of the Scottish clans. **3.** A catch phrase used in advertising or promotion. [Scottish *slog(g)orne*, from Gaelic *sluagh-ghairm : sluagh*, host + *gairm*, shout, cry, call, from Old Irish.]

sloop (slōōp) *n.* A single-masted, fore-and-aft-rigged sailing boat with a mainsail and a jib. [Dutch *sloep*.]

sloop

slot machine

slop (slŏp) *n.* **1.** Liquid spilled or splashed. **2.** Soft mud or slush. **3.** Unappetizing, watery food or soup. **4.** Often **slops.** Waste food used to feed pigs or other animals; swill. **5.** Often **slops.** Mash remaining after the process of alcohol distillation. **6.** Repulsively effusive writing or speech. —*v.* **slopped, slop·ping.** —*intr.v.* **1.** To spill or splash messily. **2.** To gush with excessive sentimentality. —*tr.v.* **1.** To spill, splash, or spread (liquid) in a messy way: *He slopped the paint on the walls.* **2.** To spill liquid upon. **3.** To dish out or serve unappetizingly or clumsily. [Middle English *sloppe*, a muddy place.]

slope (slōp) *v.* **sloped, slop·ing.** —*intr.v.* To incline upward or downward. —*tr.v.* To cause to slope. —*n.* **1.** Any inclined line, surface, plane, or stretch of ground. **2.** A deviation from the horizontal or the amount of such deviation. **3.** *Math.* The rate at which an ordinate of a point of a line on a coordinate plane changes with respect to a change in its abscissa. [From Middle English *slope*, sloping, short for *aslope*.]

slop·py (slŏp'ē) *adj.* **-pi·er, -pi·est. 1.** Of, like, or covered with slop; muddy: *sloppy ground; sloppy boots.* **2.** Watery and unappetizing: *a sloppy stew.* **3.** Untidy; messy. **4.** Rainy: *sloppy weather.* **5.** Carelessly done. **6.** *Informal.* Oversentimental; gushy. —See Syns at **careless.**

slosh (slŏsh) *tr.v.* To stir or splash in a liquid. —*intr.v.* To splash or flounder in liquid. —*n.* **1.** Slush. **2.** The sound of splashing liquid. [Var. of SLUSH.] —**slosh'y** *adj.*

slot¹ (slŏt) *n.* **1.** A long, narrow groove, opening, or notch, as one in a vending machine for receiving coins. **2.** *Informal.* A suitable position or niche. —*tr.v.* **slot·ted, slot·ting.** To make a slot or slots in. [Middle English, hollow between the breasts, from Old French *esclot.*]

slot² (slŏt) *n.* The track or trail of an animal, esp. a deer. [Old French *esclot*, horse's hoofprint.]

sloth (slôth, slŏth, slōth) *n.* **1.** Laziness; indolence. **2.** Any of various slow-moving, arboreal mammals of the family Bradypodidae, of tropical America. [Middle English *slowthe*, from *slow*, slow.]

sloth bear. A bear, *Melursus ursinus*, of south-central Asia, with a long snout and dark, shaggy hair.

sloth·ful (slôth'fəl, slŏth'-, slōth'-) *adj.* Lazy; indolent. —See Syns at **lazy.** —**sloth'ful·ly** *adv.* —**sloth'ful·ness** *n.*

slot machine. A vending or gambling machine operated by inserting coins through a slot.

slouch (slouch) *intr.v.* **1.** To sit, stand, or walk with an awkward, drooping posture: *slouch over the chair.* **2.** To droop or hang carelessly. —*tr.v.* To cause to droop. —*n.* **1.** An awkward, drooping posture. **2.** A lazy or incompetent person. [Orig. unknown.] —**slouch'er** *n.*

slough¹ (slōō, slou) *n.* **Also slew. 1.** A depression or hollow, usu. filled with deep mud or mire. **2.** **Also slue.** A stagnant swamp, marsh, or bog. **3.** (*also* slōō'). A state of deep despair or moral degradation. [Middle English *slogh*, from Old English *slōh.*]

slough² (slŭf) *n.* **1.** The dead outer skin shed by a snake or amphibian. **2.** *Med.* Dead tissue separated from a living structure. **3.** Any outer layer or covering that is shed. —*intr.v.* **1.** To be cast off or shed. **2.** To shed a slough. —*tr.v.* **1.** To shed or cast off: *The snake sloughed its skin.* **2.** To get rid of; discard. [Middle English *slouh*, poss. of Low German orig.]

Slo·vak (slō'văk', -väk'). **Also Slo·vak·i·an** (slō-vä'kē-ən, -väk'ē-ən). —*n.* **1.** A member of a Slavic people living in Slovakia. **2.** The Slavic language of the Slovaks, which is closely related to Czech. —*adj.* Of or pertaining to Slovakia, the Slovaks, or their language.

slov·en (slŭv'ən) *n.* A person who is careless in his personal appearance or work. [Middle English *sloveyn.*]

slov·en·ly (slŭv'ən-lē) *adj.* **-li·er, -li·est. 1.** Untidy; messy. **2.** Careless; slipshod: *slovenly work.* —See Syns at **careless.** —**slov'en·li·ness** *n.* —**slov'en·ly** *adv.*

slow (slō) *adj.* **-er, -est. 1. a.** Not moving or able to move quickly. **b.** Marked by a low speed or tempo: *a slow waltz.* **2.** Taking or requiring a long time: *the slow job of making bread.* **3. a.** Registering a time or rate behind or below the correct one: *a slow clock.* **b.** Not on time; tardy. **4.** Lacking in promptness or willingness: *slow to accept.* **5.** Sluggish; inactive: *Business was slow.* **6.** *Informal.* Dull; boring: *a slow party.* **7.** Not quick to understand: *a slow student.* —*adv.* **1.** So as to fall behind: *The watch runs slow.* **2.** Slowly: *Go slow!* —*tr.v.* To make slow or slower: *The wind slowed the car.* —*intr.v.* To become slow or slower: *Their pace slowed.* —See Syns at **delay.** [Middle English, from Old English *slāw.*] —**slow'ly** *adv.* —**slow'ness** *n.*

Syns: slow, dilatory, laggard, poky (*Informal*)**, tardy** *adj.* *Core meaning:* Moving at a pace less than usual or desired (*slow traffic in congested streets; slow progress toward peace*). See also Syns at **dull.**

Usage: **slow, slowly.** Both are adverbs. Where they are interchangeable, *slowly* occurs more often in formal writing; *slow* occurs more often in speech, in commands and exhortations, and when emphasis is desired. Established idiom is important in determining a choice. In the following senses, only *slow* conveys the meaning, and it should be used on all levels: *My watch runs slow* (loses time). *The trains are running slow* (behind schedule).

slow·down (slō'doun') *n.* A slackening of pace, esp. an intentional slowing down of production.

slow motion. A motion-picture technique in which the action as projected is slower than the original action. —*modifier* (**slow-motion**): *a slow-motion replay.*

slow·poke (slō'pōk') *n. Informal.* A person who moves, works, or acts slowly.

slow·wit·ted (slō'wĭt'ĭd) *adj.* Slow to comprehend; dull; stupid. —**slow'wit'ted·ly** *adv.* —**slow'wit'ted·ness** *n.*

slow·worm (slō'wûrm') *n.* A snakelike, limbless European lizard, *Anguis fragilis.* Also called **blindworm.**

sludge (slŭj) *n.* **1.** Mud, mire, or ooze covering the ground or forming a deposit, as on a river bed. **2.** Slushy matter or sediment. **3.** Finely broken or half-formed ice on a body of water. [Orig. unknown.] —**sludg'y** *adj.*

slue¹ (slōō) **Also slew.** —*v.* **slued, slu·ing.** —*tr.v.* To turn or twist (something) sideways. —*intr.v.* To turn or twist to the side. —*n.* The act of sluing. [Orig. unknown.]

slue² (slōō) *n.* Var. of **slew** (a large number).

slue³ (slōō, slou) *n.* Var. of **slough** (swamp).

slug¹ (slŭg) *n.* **1.** A round bullet larger than buckshot. **2.** *Informal.* A shot of liquor. **3.** A small metal disk often used illegally in place of a coin. **4.** A lump of metal or glass ready to be processed. **5.** *Printing.* **a.** A strip of type metal, thicker than a lead, used for spacing. **b.** A line of type cast in a single strip of metal. **6.** *Physics.* The unit of mass that is accelerated at the rate of one foot per second per second when acted upon by a force of one pound weight. [Prob. from SLUG (mollusk).]

slug² (slŭg) *n.* **1.** Any of various terrestrial gastropod mollusks of the genus *Limex* and related genera that have an elongated body with no shell. **2.** The smooth, soft larva of certain insects. **3.** *Informal.* A sluggard. [Middle English *slugge,* slow-moving person or animal.]

slug³ (slŭg) *Slang.* —*tr.v.* **slugged, slug·ging.** To strike heavily, esp. with the fist. —See Syns at **hit.** —*n.* A hard, heavy blow, as with the fist. [Perh. from SLUG (bullet).]

slug·fest (slŭg'fĕst') *n. Slang.* **1.** A fight marked by a vicious exchange of blows. **2.** A baseball game in which many hits and runs are scored.

slug·gard (slŭg'ərd) *n.* A lazy person. [Middle English *sluggart,* prob. from *sluggen,* to be lazy.] —**slug'gard·ly** *adj.*

slug·ger (slŭg'ər) *n.* **1.** A person who strikes heavy blows. **2.** *Baseball.* A hardhitting batter.

slug·gish (slŭg'ĭsh) *adj.* **1.** Displaying little movement or activity: *sluggish water.* **2.** Lacking in alertness or energy; dull; lazy: *a sluggish response.* **3.** Slow to perform or respond. [Middle English, perhaps from *sluggen,* to be lazy.] —**slug'gish·ly** *adv.* —**slug'gish·ness** *n.*

sluice (slōōs) *n.* **1.** A man-made channel for water with a valve or gate to regulate the flow. **2.** The water so regulated. **3.** The valve or gate used in a sluice. **4.** A sluiceway. **5.** A long inclined trough, as for floating logs or separating gold ore. *v.* **sluiced, sluic·ing.** —*tr.v.* **1.** To wash with a sudden flow of water; to flush. **2.** To draw off or let out by a sluice. **3.** To send down a sluice. —*intr.v.* To flow out from a sluice. [Middle English *scluse,* from Old French *excluse,* ult. from Latin *exclūdere,* to shut out, exclude.]

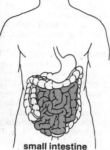

sluice   small intestine

sluice·way (slōōs'wā') *n.* An artificial channel for carrying off excess water; a sluice.

slum (slŭm) *n.* Often **slums.** A heavily populated urban area characterized by poverty, poor housing, and squalor. —*modifier:* **slum** buildings. —*intr.v.* **slummed, slum·ming.** To visit a slum, esp. from curiosity. [Orig. unknown.]

slum·ber (slŭm'bər) *intr.v.* **1.** To sleep or doze. **2.** To be dormant or quiescent. —*n.* **1.** Sleep. **2.** A state of inactivity or dormancy. [Middle English *slumberen,* prob. from *slume,* sleep, from Old English *slūma.*] —**slum'ber·er** *n.*

slum·ber·ous (slŭm'bər-əs) *adj.* Also **slum·brous** (-brəs). **1.** Sleepy; drowsy. **2. a.** Suggestive of sleep. **b.** Quiet; tranquil. **3.** Inducing sleep. —**slum'ber·ous·ly** *adv.* —**slum'ber·ous·ness** *n.*

slum·lord (slŭm'lôrd') *n. Informal.* A landlord of slum property, esp. one who allows the property to deteriorate.

slump (slŭmp) *intr.v.* **1.** To decline or sink suddenly: *Business slumped.* **2.** To slide or drop down suddenly. **3.** To droop; slouch. —*n.* **1.** A sudden falling off or decline, as in interest, activity, prices, or business. **2.** A slouching posture. [Prob. of Scandinavian orig.]

slung (slŭng) *v.* Past tense and past participle of **sling.** [Middle English *slong, slungyn,* prob. from Old Norse *slungu* (pl.), *sluncen.*]

slunk (slŭngk) *v.* Past tense and past participle of **slink.** [Middle English *slonke, slunken,* from Old English *sluncon* (pl.), *sluncen.*]

slur (slûr) *tr.v.* **slurred, slur·ring.** **1.** To pass over lightly or carelessly. **2.** To pronounce indistinctly: *slur words.* **3.** To disparage. **4.** *Mus.* **a.** To glide over (a series of notes) smoothly without a break. **b.** To mark with a curved line to indicate a legato manner of play. —*n.* **1.** A disparaging remark; an aspersion. **2.** *Mus.* **a.** A curved line connecting

notes to indicate that they are to be played or sung legato. **b.** A passage played or sung in this manner. [From Middle English *sloor,* mud.]

slurp (slûrp) *tr.v.* To eat or drink in a noisy manner. —*intr.v.* To eat or drink something noisily. —*n.* The sound made when slurping food. [Dutch *slurpen,* from Middle Dutch *slorpen.*]

slur·ry (slûr'ē, slŭr'ē) *n., pl.* **-ries.** A thin mixture of a liquid, esp. water, and an insoluble substance, such as mud or crushed coal. [Middle English *slory.*]

slush (slŭsh) *n.* **1.** Partially melted snow or ice. **2.** Soft mud; slop; mire. **3.** A greasy compound used as a lubricant for machinery. **4.** Sentimental drivel. [Middle English *sloche.*] —**slush'i·ness** *n.* —**slush'y** *adj.*

slush fund. A fund used to finance corrupt practices, such as bribery or graft. [From *slush,* discarded material sold for the benefit of a ship's crew.]

slut (slŭt) *n.* **1.** A slovenly, dirty woman; slattern. **2.** A woman of loose morals. [Middle English *slutte.*] —**slut'tish** *adj.* —**slut'tish·ly** *adv.* —**slut'tish·ness** *n.*

sly (slī) *adj.* **sli·er** or **sly·er, sli·est** or **sly·est. 1.** Stealthily clever; cunning. **2.** Secretive; underhand; deceitful. **3.** Mischievous; arch: *a sly wink.* —*idiom.* **on the sly.** Secretly. [Middle English *sli,* from Old Norse *slœgr,* cunning, clever.] —**sly'ly** *adv.* —**sly'ness** *n.*

Sm The symbol for the element samarium.

smack¹ (smăk) *tr.v.* **1.** To make a sound by pressing together the lips and pulling them apart quickly. **2.** To kiss noisily. **3.** To strike heartily and noisily. —*intr.v.* To make or give a smack. —See Syns at **hit.** —*n.* **1.** The loud, sharp sound of smacking the lips. **2.** A noisy kiss. **3.** A sharp blow or loud slap. —*adv.* Directly; straight: *hit him smack in the face.* [From Middle Low German or Middle Dutch *smacken.*]

smack² (smăk) *n.* **1.** A distinctive flavor or taste. **2.** A suggestion or trace. —*intr.v.* **smack of.** **1.** To have the flavor or taste of: *cider that smacks of wooden barrels.* **2.** To suggest: *This smacks of foul play.* [Middle English, from Old English *smæc.*]

smack³ (smăk) *n.* A sloop-rigged boat used chiefly in fishing. [Dutch *smak,* from Middle Dutch *smacke.*]

smack-dab (smăk'dăb') *adv. Slang.* Squarely; directly.

smack·er (smăk'ər) *n.* **1.** A loud kiss. **2.** A resounding blow. **3.** *Slang.* A dollar.

smack·ing (smăk'ĭng) *adj.* Brisk; vigorous.

small (smôl) *adj.* **-er, -est. 1.** Measurably less in size, number, quantity, or extent; little. **2.** Limited in importance or significance; trivial: *a small matter.* **3.** Operating on a limited scale: *a small farmer.* **4.** Soft; low: *a small voice.* **5.** Not fully grown; very young. **6.** Petty: *a small mind.* **7.** Belittled; humiliated. —See Syns at **little.** —*adv.* **1.** In small pieces: *Cut it up small.* **2.** Softly. **3.** In a small manner. —*n.* Something smaller than the rest, esp. the narrowest part of the back. [Middle English, from Old English *smæl.*] —**small'ness** *n.*

small arms. Firearms that can be carried in the hand.

small capital. A smaller letter having the form of a capital letter, for example: SMALL CAPITALS.

small change. **1.** Coins of low denomination. **2.** Something of little value or significance.

small·clothes (smôl'klōthz', -klōz') *pl.n.* Men's close-fitting knee breeches worn in the 18th cent.

small fry. **1.** Young or small fish. **2.** Small children. **3.** Unimportant or insignificant persons or things.

small game. Birds and small wild animals hunted for sport or food.

small intestine. The part of the alimentary canal that extends from the outlet of the stomach to the beginning of the large intestine.

small-mind·ed (smôl'mīn'dĭd) *adj.* **1.** Having a narrow or selfish attitude; prejudiced. **2.** Marked by pettiness or selfishness. —**small'-mind'ed·ly** *adv.* —**small'-mind'ed·ness** *n.*

small potatoes. *Informal.* Unimportant persons or things.

small·pox (smôl'pŏks') *n.* An acute, highly infectious disease caused by a virus and characterized by high fever and by pustules that blister and form pockmarks.

small-scale (smôl'skāl') *adj.* **1.** Limited in extent; modest:

a small-scale plan. **2.** Created on a small scale.

small talk. Casual or light conversation.

small·time (smôl′tīm′) *adj. Informal.* Insignificant or unimportant; minor: *a smalltime comedian.* —**small′tim′er** *n.*

smart (smärt) *adj.* **-er, -est. 1. a.** Intelligent; bright. **b.** Amusingly clever; witty. **c.** Impertinent: *a smart answer.* **2.** Quick and energetic: *a smart pace.* **3.** Marked by sharpness in dealings; shrewd: *a smart businessman.* **4.** Fashionable; elegant: *a smart restaurant.* —See Syns at **clever** and **impudent.** —*intr.v.* **1.** To cause a sharp, superficial, stinging pain. **2.** To be the source of such a pain: *The first-aid spray smarts.* **3.** To feel sharp mental pain. —*n.* A stinging physical or mental pain. [Middle English, sharp, from Old English *smeart,* stinging.] —**smart′ly** *adv.* —**smart′ness** *n.*

smart al·eck (ăl′ĭk). *Informal.* A person who is offensively self-assured and assertive [SMART + *Aleck,* pet form of Alexander.] —**smart′-al′eck·y** *adj.*

smart·en (smär′tn) *tr.v.* **1.** To spruce up. **2.** To make brighter or quicker: *smarten the pace.* —*intr.v.* **1.** To make oneself smart or smarter: *They should smarten up.* **2.** To become more brisk or lively: *The wind smartened.*

smash (smăsh) *tr.v.* **1.** To break into pieces suddenly, noisily, and violently; shatter. **2. a.** To throw or dash violently so as to shatter or crush: *The wind smashed the tree into the house.* **b.** To strike with a heavy blow; hit: *smashing rocks with a sledgehammer.* **3.** To hit (a ball or shuttlecock) in a violent overhand stroke. **4.** To crush or destroy completely; ruin: *smash resistance.* —*intr.v.* **1.** To move or be moved suddenly, noisily, and violently. **2.** To break into pieces, as from a violent blow or collision. —See Syns at **destroy** and **hit.** —*n.* **1.** The act or sound of smashing or the condition of having been smashed. **2.** Total defeat or destruction; ruin. **3.** A collision or crash. **4.** A drink made of mint, sugar, soda water, and alcoholic liquor, usu. brandy. **5.** A violent overhand stroke in tennis, badminton, etc. **6.** *Informal.* A resounding success. —*adj. Informal.* Very successful. [Perh. blend of SMACK and CRASH.] —**smash′er** *n.*

smash·ing (smăsh′ĭng) *adj. Informal.* Extraordinarily or unusually impressive or fine; wonderful; admirable.

smash·up (smăsh′ŭp′) *n.* **1.** A total collapse or defeat; a failure. **2.** A serious collision between vehicles; a wreck.

smat·ter (smăt′ər) *tr.v.* **1.** To speak (a language) without fluency. **2.** To study superficially; dabble in. —*n.* A smattering. [Middle English *smateren.*] —**smat′ter·er** *n.*

smat·ter·ing (smăt′ər-ĭng) *n.* Superficial or piecemeal knowledge: *a smattering of Latin.* [From SMATTER.]

smear (smîr) *tr.v.* **1.** To spread, cover, or stain with a sticky or dirty substance. **2.** To stain by or as if by spreading or daubing with a sticky or dirty substance: *smeared her dress with grease.* **3.** To slander; vilify: *smearing his name.* **4.** *Slang.* To defeat utterly; to smash. —*intr.v.* To be or become stained or dirtied. —*n.* **1.** A mark made by smearing; a spot; blot. **2.** A substance to be spread on a surface. **3.** A substance or preparation placed on a slide for microscopic examination. **4.** Vilification; slander. [Middle English *smeren,* to anoint, cover, daub, from Old English *smerian.*] —**smear′y** *adj.*

smell (smĕl) *v.* **smelled** or **smelt** (smĕlt), **smell·ing.** —*tr.v.* **1.** To detect or notice the odor of by means of sense organs located in the nose. **2.** To sense the presence of; detect: *He smelled trouble ahead.* —*intr.v.* **1.** To use the sense of smell. **2.** To have or emit an odor. **3.** To be suggestive: *The cave smells of terror.* **4.** To have or emit an unpleasant odor; stink. **5.** To suggest evil or corruption. —*n.* **1.** The olfactory sense; the ability to smell. **2.** The odor of something; scent. **3.** The act or an example of smelling. **4.** A distinctive quality; an aura: *the smell of success.* [Middle English *smellen.*]

Usage: **smell.** When this verb means to have or emit an odor, it is a linking verb followed by an adjective: *The milk smells good,* or *fresh,* or *sour.* An adverb may occur in constructions such as *smells strongly of vinegar,* where a degree of odor is being shown. When *smell* means to have or emit an unpleasant odor (to stink), it may be modified by an adverb: *The fish smells disgustingly.* Here again, the adverb indicates a degree of foul smell; in contrast, *smells disgusting* merely specifies an odor.

smelling salts. Any of several preparations based on spirits of ammonia, sniffed to relieve faintness or dizziness.

smell·y (smĕl′ē) *adj.* **-i·er, -i·est.** *Informal.* Having an unpleasant or offensive odor.

smelt¹ (smĕlt) *tr.v.* To melt or fuse (ores), separating the metallic constituents. [Dutch or Low German *smelten,* of Low German orig.]

smelt² (smĕlt) *n., pl.* **smelts** or **smelt.** Any of various small silvery saltwater and freshwater food fishes of the family Osmeridae, esp. *Osmerus mordax,* of North America and *O. eperlanus* of Europe. [Middle English, from Old English.]

smelt³ (smĕlt) *v.* A past tense and past participle of **smell.**

smelt·er (smĕl′tər) *n.* **1.** An apparatus or device for smelting ore. **2.** Also **smelt·er·y** (-tə-rē). An establishment for smelting. **3.** A person who works in the smelting industry.

smidg·en (smĭj′ən) *n.* Also **smidg·in.** *Informal.* A very small quantity; a bit. [Prob. var. of dial. *smitch,* particle.]

smi·lax (smī′lăks′) *n.* **1.** Any plant of the genus *Smilax* that includes climbing vines such as the catbrier. **2.** A vine, *Asparagus asparagoides,* that has glossy foliage and is popular as a floral decoration. [Latin *smīlax,* a kind of oak, bindweed, from Greek *smilax.*]

smile (smīl) *n.* **1.** A facial expression formed by an upward curving of the corners of the mouth and indicating pleasure, affection, amusement, etc. **2.** A pleasant or favorable disposition. —*v.* **smiled, smil·ing.** —*intr.v.* **1.** To form a smile. **2.** To express or appear to express approval. —*tr.v.* To express with a smile: *smiled her thanks.* [Middle English *smilen,* perh. of Low German orig.] —**smil′er** *n.* —**smil′ing·ly** *adv.*

Syns: **smile, grin** *v. Core meaning:* To curl the lips upward in amusement, pleasure, or happiness (*smiled and waved good-bye*).

smirch (smûrch) *tr.v.* **1.** To soil, stain, or dirty. **2.** To dishonor or defame. —*n.* A blot, smear, or stain. [Middle English *smorchen.*]

smirk (smûrk) *intr.v.* To smile in an obnoxious, superior, or simpering manner. —*n.* An obnoxious, superior, or simpering smile. [Middle English *smirken,* from Old English *smearcian,* to smile.] —**smirk′er** *n.*

smite (smīt) *v.* **smote** (smōt), **smit·ten** (smĭt′n) or **smote, smit·ing.** —*tr.v.* **1. a.** To inflict a heavy blow on with or as if with the hand or a club. **b.** To drive or strike forcefully onto or into something else. **2.** To attack, damage, kill, or destroy by or as if by blows. **3.** To afflict: *smitten with mumps.* **4.** To affect sharply: *smitten with love.* —*intr.v.* To strike. —See Syns at **hit.** [Middle English *smiten,* from Old English *smītan.*] —**smit′er** *n.*

smith (smĭth) *n.* **1.** A metalworker, esp. one who works metal when it is hot and malleable. **2.** A blacksmith. [Middle English, from Old English.]

smith·er·eens (smĭth′ə-rēnz′) *pl.n. Informal.* Pieces; bits. [Irish *smidirīn,* dim. of *smiodar,* small fragment.]

smith·er·y (smĭth′ə-rē) *n., pl.* **-ies. 1.** The occupation or craft of a smith. **2.** A smithy.

smith·y (smĭth′ē, smĭth′ē) *n., pl.* **-ies.** A blacksmith's shop; a forge. [Middle English *smythy,* from Old Norse *smidhja.*]

smit·ten (smĭt′n) *v.* A past participle of **smite.**

smock (smŏk) *n.* A garment made like a long, loose shirt and worn over other clothes to protect them. —*tr.v.* **1.** To clothe in a smock. **2.** To decorate (fabric) with smocking. [Middle English *smok,* women's undergarment, smock, from Old English *smoc.*]

smock·ing (smŏk′ĭng) *n.* Needlework decoration of stitched gathers in a honeycomb pattern. [From SMOCK.]

smog (smŏg, smôg) *n.* Fog mixed and polluted with smoke. [Blend of SMOKE and FOG.] —**smog′gy** *adj.*

smoke (smōk) *n.* **1.** A mixture of gases with suspended particles of soot or other solids resulting from incomplete burning of materials such as wood, coal, etc. **2.** Any cloud of fine particles. **3.** Anything insubstantial, unreal, or transitory. **4.** The act of smoking any form of tobacco or other plant material. **5.** *Informal.* Tobacco in any form that can be smoked. —*modifier: a smoke shop; a smoke bomb.* —*v.* **smoked, smok·ing.** —*intr.v.* **1.** To emit smoke or a smokelike substance. **2.** To emit smoke excessively. **3.** To draw in and exhale smoke from a cigarette, cigar, pipe, etc. —*tr.v.* **1.** To draw in and exhale the smoke of: *smoked his pipe.* **2.** To preserve (meat or fish) by exposure to smoke. **3.** To fumigate (a house, building, etc.). **4.** To expose (glass) to smoke in order to darken or change its color. —*phrasal verb.* **smoke out. 1.** To force out of a place of hiding or concealment by or as if by the use of smoke. **2.** To expose; reveal. [Middle English, from Old English *smoca.*]

smoke·house (smōk'hous') *n.* A structure in which meat or fish is cured with smoke.

smoke·less (smōk'lĭs) *adj.* Emitting little or no smoke.

smok·er (smō'kər) *n.* **1.** A person who smokes. **2.** A railroad car in which smoking is permitted. Also called **smoking car. 3.** An informal social gathering for men.

smoke screen. 1. A mass of dense artificial smoke used to conceal military areas or operations. **2.** Any action or statement used to conceal plans or intentions.

smoke·stack (smōk'stăk') *n.* A large vertical pipe through which combustion gases and smoke are discharged.

smoke tree. Either of two trees, *Cotinus obovatus,* of the southern United States, or *C. coggygria,* of Eurasia, with yellowish flower clusters like puffs of smoke.

smoking jacket. A man's evening jacket, often made of a fine fabric, elaborately trimmed, and usu. worn at home.

smok·y (smō'kē) *adj.* **-i·er, -i·est. 1.** Producing, giving off, or polluted with smoke. **2.** Tasting of smoke: *smoky meat.* **3.** Having a gray or hazy tone: *a smoky brown.* —**smok'i·ly** *adv.* —**smok'i·ness** *n.*

smol·der (smōl'dər) Also **smoul·der.** —*intr.v.* **1.** To burn with little smoke and no flame. **2.** To exist in a suppressed state: *The rebellious feelings smoldered for years.* —*n.* Thick smoke resulting from a slow fire. [Middle English *smolderen,* from *smolder,* a smolder.]

smolt (smōlt) *n.* A young salmon at the stage at which it migrates from fresh water to the sea. [Middle English.]

smooch (smōōch). *Slang.* —*n.* A kiss. —*intr.v.* To kiss. [Perh. imit.]

smooth (smōōth) *adj.* **-er, -est. 1.** Having a surface free from irregularities, roughness, or projections. **2.** Having a fine texture: *the smooth side of the fabric.* **3.** Having an even consistency; without lumps: *a smooth pudding.* **4.** Having an even or gentle motion or movement: *a smooth ride.* **5.** Having no obstructions or difficulties: *a smooth procedure.* **6.** Flowing easily. **7.** Pleasing to the taste. **8.** Ingratiating: *smooth talk.* —See Syns at **easy** and **level.** —*tr.v.* **1.** To make even, level, unwrinkled, etc. **2.** To rid of obstructions, hindrances, difficulties, etc. **3.** To soothe; make calm. **4.** To make less harsh or crude; refine. —*intr.v.* To become smooth. —*n.* A smooth part of something. [Middle English *smothe,* from Old English *smōth.*] —**smooth'er** *n.* —**smooth'ly** *adv.* —**smooth'ness** *n.*

smooth·bore (smōōth'bôr', -bōr') *adj.* Having no rifling within the barrel: *a smoothbore rifle.* —*n.* Also **smooth bore.** A firearm that has no rifling.

smooth·en (smōō'thən) *tr.v.* To smooth. —*intr.v.* To become smooth.

smooth muscle. The unstriated involuntary muscle of the internal organs, as of the intestine, bladder, and blood vessels, excluding the heart.

smor·gas·bord (smôr'gəs-bôrd', -bōrd') *n.* A buffet meal featuring a varied number of dishes. [Swedish *smörgåsbord* : *smörgas,* (open-faced) sandwich + *bord,* table, from Old Norse *bordh.*]

smote (smōt) *v.* Past tense and a past participle of **smite.** [Middle English *smot,* from Old English *smāt;* past part. from the p.t.]

smoth·er (smŭth'ər) *tr.v.* **1. a.** To deprive of necessary oxygen; suffocate. **b.** To kill by depriving of oxygen. **c.** To deprive (a fire) of the oxygen necessary for combustion. **2.** To conceal, suppress, or hide: *smothered a sob.* **3.** To cover thickly with another foodstuff: *smother the liver with onions.* **4.** To overwhelm with something in excess: *smothering him with affection.* —*intr.v.* **1. a.** To be deprived of necessary oxygen; suffocate. **2.** To die from deprivation of oxygen. **3.** To be extinguished. —*n.* Anything that smothers, as a dense cloud of smoke. [Middle English *smotheren,* from *smorther,* a smother, from Old English *smorian,* to smother.]

smoul·der (smōl'dər) *v. & n.* Var. of **smolder.**

smudge (smŭj) *v.* **smudged, smudg·ing.** —*tr.v.* **1.** To make dirty, esp. in one small area. **2.** To smear or blur: *The rain smudged the paint.* **3.** To fill (an orchard or other planted area) with dense smoke in order to prevent damage from insects or frost. —*intr.v.* To smear, as with dirt, soot, or ink: *Charcoal smudges easily.* —*n.* **1.** A blotch or smear. **2.** A smoky fire used as a protection against insects or frost. [Middle English *smogen.*] —**smudg'i·ly** *adv.* —**smudg'i·ness** *n.* —**smudg'y** *adj.*

smudge pot. A receptacle in which oil or other smoky fuel is burned, usu. to protect an orchard from insects or frost.

smug (smŭg) *adj.* **smug·ger, smug·gest.** Self-satisfied or complacent. [Prob. from Low German *smuck,* neat, smooth, sleek, from Middle Low German, from *smucken,* to adorn.] —**smug'ly** *adv.* —**smug'ness** *n.*

smug·gle (smŭg'əl) *v.* **-gled, -gling.** —*tr.v.* **1.** To convey illicitly or by stealth. **2.** To import or export without paying lawful customs charges or duties. —*intr.v.* To engage in smuggling. [Low German *smuggeln* and Dutch *smokkelen.*] —**smug'gler** *n.*

smut (smŭt) *n.* **1. a.** A particle of dirt. **b.** A smudge. **2.** Obscene speech or writing. **3. a.** Any of various plant diseases caused by fungi that form black, powdery masses of spores. **b.** A fungus that causes such a disease. —*v.* **smut·ted, smut·ting.** —*tr.v.* **1.** To blacken or smudge. **2.** To affect (a plant) with smut. —*intr.v.* To become affected with smut. [Perh. from Low German *smutt.*]

smut·ty (smŭt'ē) *adj.* **-ti·er, -ti·est. 1.** Soiled with smudges. **2.** Obscene. —**smut'ti·ly** *adv.* —**smut'ti·ness** *n.*

Sn The symbol for the element tin (Latin *stannum*).

snack (snăk) *n.* A light meal. —*modifier:* snack foods. —*intr.v.* To eat a light meal. [Middle English *snake,* a bite, from Middle Dutch *snack.*]

snack bar. A food counter where light meals are served.

snaf·fle (snăf'əl) *n.* A jointed bit for a horse. —*tr.v.* **-fled, -fling.** To put a snaffle on. [Orig. unknown.]

sna·fu (snă-fōō'). *Slang.* —*adj.* In a state of complete confusion. —*tr.v.* **1.** To make chaotic or confused. **2.** To make a mess of. —See Syns at **botch** and **confuse.** —*n., pl.* **-fus.** Any chaotic or confused situation. [S(ITUATION) N(ORMAL) A(LL) F(OULED) U(P).]

snag (snăg) *n.* **1.** Any rough, sharp, or jagged protuberance. **2.** A tree or a part of a tree that sticks out above a water surface. **3.** A break, pull, or tear. **4.** An unforeseen or hidden obstacle: *a snag in our plans.* —*v.* **snagged, snag·ging.** —*tr.v.* **1.** To tear or injure on or as if on a snag. **2.** *Informal.* To catch or get unexpectedly. **3.** To hinder; impede. —*intr.v.* To be caught or stopped by a snag. [Prob. of Scandinavian orig.]

snag·gle·tooth (snăg'əl-tōōth') *n.* A tooth that is broken or out of alignment with the others. [Brit. dial. *snaggled,* snaggletoothed, from SNAG.]

snail (snāl) *n.* **1.** Any of numerous aquatic or terrestrial mollusks of the class Gastropoda that characteristically have a spirally coiled shell, a broad retractile foot, and a distinct head. **2.** A slow-moving, lazy, or sluggish person. [Middle English, from Old English *snægel.*]

snail   snake

snake (snāk) *n.* **1.** Any of various scaly, legless, sometimes poisonous reptiles of the suborder Serpentes, with a long, tapering body. **2.** A sneaky, untrustworthy person. **3.** A long, flexible wire used for clearing drains and sewers.

ă pat   ā pay   â care   ä father   ĕ pet   ē be   hw which   ĭ pit   ī tie   î pier   ŏ pot   ō toe   ô paw, for   oi noise
ōō took   ōō boot   ou out   th thin   th this   ŭ cut   û urge   zh vision   ə about, item, edible, gallop, circus

—v. **snaked, snak·ing.** —*tr.v.* To drag or pull lengthwise. —*intr.v.* To move or twist in a snakelike manner. —See Syns at **wind**². [Middle English, from Old English *snaca.*]

snake·bird (snāk'bûrd') *n.* Any of several long-necked, long-billed birds of the genus *Anhinga.* [From its snake-like, elongated neck.]

snake·bite (snāk'bīt') *n.* The bite of a poisonous snake.

snake charmer. A person who utilizes rhythmic music and bodily movements to control snakes.

snake fence. A zigzag fence; worm fence.

snake in the grass. A treacherous person or thing.

snake oil. A worthless preparation fraudulently peddled as a cure for many ills.

snake·root (snāk'rōōt', -rŏot') *n.* Any of various plants with roots that are reputed to cure snakebite.

snake·skin (snāk'skĭn') *n.* The skin of a snake, esp. when prepared as leather. —*modifier: a snakeskin handbag.*

snak·y (snā'kē) *adj.* **-i·er, -i·est.** 1. Of or characteristic of snakes. 2. Having the form or movement of a snake; serpentine. —**snak'i·ly** *adv.* —**snak'i·ness** *n.*

snap (snăp) *v.* **snapped, snap·ping.** —*intr.v.* 1. To make a brisk sharp cracking sound. 2. To break suddenly with a brisk, sharp sound. 3. To give way abruptly under pressure or tension: *The rope snapped.* 4. To bring the jaws briskly together, often with a clicking sound. 5. To snatch or grasp suddenly: *snap at the chance to go abroad.* 6. To speak abruptly or sharply: *She snapped crossly at him.* 7. To move suddenly and abruptly: *snap to attention.* 8. To sparkle. 9. To open or close with a click: *The lock snapped shut.* —*tr.v.* 1. To snatch at with or as if with the teeth. 2. To break suddenly with a snapping sound. 3. To utter abruptly or sharply: *He snapped his commands.* 4. **a.** To cause to emit a snapping sound: *snap a whip.* **b.** To close or latch with a snapping sound: *snap the lid shut.* 5. To cause to move suddenly and abruptly. 6. To take (a photograph). 7. *Football.* To center (the ball). —See Syns at **jerk.** —*phrasal verb.* **snap back.** To recover quickly. —*n.* 1. A sudden, sharp cracking sound or the action producing such a sound. 2. A sudden breaking of something. 3. A fastener that opens and closes with a snapping sound. 4. A sudden attempt to bite, snatch, or grasp. 5. **a.** The sound produced by rapid movement of the second finger from the thumb tip to the base of the thumb. **b.** The act of producing this sound. 6. The sudden release of anything held under pressure or tension. 7. A thin, crisp cooky: *a ginger snap.* 8. *Informal.* Briskness, liveliness, or energy. 9. A brief spell of brisk, cold weather. 10. *Informal.* An effortless task. 11. A snapshot. 12. *Football.* The passing of the ball from the center to a back that starts each play. —*adj.* 1. Made or done on the spur of the moment: *a snap decision.* 2. Fastening with a snap. 3. *Informal.* Simple; easy. —*adv.* With a snap. [Prob. from Middle Low German or Middle Dutch *snappen,* to seize, speak hastily.]

snap bean. A bean, such as the string bean , cultivated for its crisp, edible pods.

snap·drag·on (snăp'drăg'ən) *n.* Any of several plants of the genus *Antirrhinum,* esp. *A. majus,* a widely cultivated species, with clusters of two-lipped flowers.

snapdragon   snare¹

snap·per (snăp'ər) *n.* 1. Someone or something that snaps. 2. *pl.* **snapper** or **-pers.** Any of numerous saltwater fishes of the family Lutjanidae, many of which are prized as food and game fishes. 3. A snapping turtle.

snapping turtle. Any of several New World freshwater turtles of the family Chelydridae, with a rough shell and powerful hooked jaws.

snap·pish (snăp'ĭsh) *adj.* 1. Liable to snap or bite. 2. Irritable; curt. —**snap'pish·ly** *adv.* —**snap'pish·ness** *n.*

snap·py (snăp'ē) *adj.* **-pi·er, -pi·est.** 1. *Informal.* Lively or energetic; brisk. 2. *Informal.* Smart or chic. 3. Snappish. —**snap'pi·ly** *adv.* —**snap'pi·ness** *n.*

snap·shot (snăp'shŏt') *n.* An informal photograph taken with a small hand-held camera.

snare¹ (snâr) *n.* 1. A trap, often consisting of a noose, used for capturing birds and small animals. 2. Anything that serves to entangle the unwary. —*tr.v.* **snared, snar·ing.** 1. To trap with a snare. 2. To entrap: *snaring himself in his own lies.* [Middle English, from Old English *sneare,* from Old Norse *snara.*] —**snar'er** *n.*

snare² (snâr) *n.* 1. Any of the wires or cords stretched across the lower head of a snare drum to increase reverberation. 2. A snare drum. [Probably Dutch *snaar,* string, from Middle Dutch *snare.*]

snare drum. A small double-headed drum having a snare or snares stretched across the lower head.

snarl¹ (snärl) *intr.v.* 1. To growl viciously while baring the teeth. 2. To speak angrily or threateningly. —*tr.v.* To utter with anger or hostility: *He snarled a rude greeting.* —*n.* 1. An angry or threatening growl, often made with bared teeth. 2. Any vicious or hostile utterance. [From obs. *snar,* to snarl, from Middle Low German *snarren.*] —**snarl'er** *n.* —**snarl'ing·ly** *adv.*

snarl² (snärl) *n.* 1. A tangled mass, as of hair or yarn. 2. Any confused or tangled situation. —*intr.v.* To become tangled or confused. —*tr.v.* 1. To tangle or knot. 2. To confuse. —See Syns at **confuse.** [Middle English *snarle,* prob. from *snare,* trap.] —**snarl'er** *n.*

snatch (snăch) *tr.v.* To grasp or seize hastily, eagerly, or illicitly. —*intr.v.* To make grasping or seizing motions. —*n.* 1. The act of snatching; a quick grasp or grab. 2. A brief period of time. 3. A bit or fragment: *a snatch of dialogue.* 4. *Slang.* A kidnaping. [Middle English *snacchen,* to make a sudden gesture, snap at.] —**snatch'er** *n.*

snatch·y (snăch'ē) *adj.* Occurring in snatches; intermittent.

snaz·zy (snăz'ē) *adj.* **-zi·er, -zi·est.** *Slang.* Fashionable and flashy or showy. [Perh. a blend of SNAPPY and JAZZY.]

sneak (snēk) *intr.v.* 1. To go or move in a quiet, stealthy way; slink. 2. To behave in a cowardly or underhanded manner. —*tr.v.* To move, give, take, or put in a quiet, stealthy manner: *sneak candy into his mouth.* —*n.* 1. A stealthy or underhanded person. 2. An instance of sneaking. —*modifier: a sneak attack.* [Orig. unknown.]
  Syns: sneak, creep, glide, lurk, prowl, skulk, slide, slink, slip, steal *v. Core meaning:* To move silently and furtively (*a cat burglar sneaking from room to room*).

sneak·er (snē'kər) *n.* 1. A person who sneaks. 2. A sports shoe made of canvas, nylon, or sometimes leather, with soft rubber soles. Also called **tennis shoe.**

sneak·ing (snē'kĭng) *adj.* 1. Acting in a stealthy, furtive way. 2. Unavowed; secret. 3. Gradually growing or persistent: *a sneaking suspicion.* —**sneak'ing·ly** *adv.*

sneak preview. A single public showing of a motion picture before its general release.

sneak thief. A burglar who enters without breaking in.

sneak·y (snē'kē) *adj.* **-i·er, -i·est.** Furtive; surreptitious. —**sneak'i·ly** *adv.* —**sneak'i·ness** *n.*

sneer (snîr) *n.* 1. A scornful facial expression formed by raising one corner of the upper lip. 2. Any contemptuous facial expression, sound, or statement. —*intr.v.* 1. To assume a sneer. 2. To speak in a scornful, contemptuous, or derisive manner. —*tr.v.* To utter with or as if with a sneer. [Prob. of Low German orig.] —**sneer'er** *n.*

sneeze (snēz) *intr.v.* **sneezed, sneez·ing.** To expel air forcibly from the mouth and nose in an involuntary spasm resulting from irritation of the mucous membranes of the nose. —*n.* An act of sneezing. —*idiom.* **sneeze at.** To treat lightly or with contempt: *His offer is nothing to sneeze at.* [Middle English *snesen,* alteration of *fnesen,* from Old English *fnēosan.*] —**sneez'er** *n.* —**sneez'y** *adj.*

sneeze·weed (snēz'wēd') *n.* Any of several North American plants of the genus *Helenium,* with yellow flowers.

snell (snĕl) *n.* A fine, short line that connects a fishhook to a heavier line; a leader. [Orig. unknown.]

snick (snĭk) *tr.v.* To cut slightly. —*n.* A slight cut; nick. [Orig. unknown.]

snick·er (snĭk′ər). Also **snig·ger** (snĭg′ər). —*n.* A sly, nasty, slightly stifled laugh, often about something improper. —*intr.v.* To utter a snicker. [Imit.]

snide (snīd) *adj.* Slyly disparaging. [Orig. unknown.]

sniff (snĭf) *intr.v.* **1.** To inhale a short, audible breath through the nose, as in smelling. **2.** To indicate ridicule, contempt, or doubt by or as if by sniffing: *sniff at the boy's excuse.* —*tr.v.* **1.** To inhale audibly through the nose. **2.** To perceive or detect by or as if by sniffing: *sniff trouble in the air.* —*n.* **1.** An act or sound of sniffing. **2.** A whiff. [Middle English *sniffen.*]

snif·fle (snĭf′əl) *intr.v.* **-fled, -fling. 1.** To breathe audibly through a congested nose, as when suffering from a cold. **2.** To weep lightly; whimper. —*n.* **1.** An act or sound of sniffling. **2. the sniffles.** *Informal.* A condition, such as a cold, that makes one sniffle. [Freq. of SNIFF.]

sniff·y (snĭf′ē) *adj.* **-i·er, -i·est.** *Informal.* Showing arrogance or contempt; haughty; disdainful.

snif·ter (snĭf′tər) *n.* A goblet that narrows at the top, used esp. in serving brandy. [From dial. *snifter*, to sniff, prob. of Scandinavian orig.]

snig·ger (snĭg′ər) *n. & v.* Var. of **snicker.**

snip (snĭp) *v.* **snipped, snip·ping.** —*tr.v.* To cut, clip, or separate in a short stroke with scissors or shears. —*intr.v.* To cut or clip with short, quick strokes. —*n.* **1.** An act of snipping. **2.** The sound produced by snipping. **3. a.** A small cut made with scissors or shears. **b.** A small piece cut or clipped off. **4.** *Informal.* A small or mischievous person or thing. [Low German or Dutch *snippen*, to snap.]

snipe (snīp) *n., pl.* **snipe** or **snipes. 1.** Any of various long-billed wading birds of the genus *Capella*, esp. the common, widely distributed species *C. gallinago.* **2.** Any of various similar or related birds. **3.** A shot, esp. a gunshot, from a concealed place. —*intr.v.* **sniped, snip·ing. 1.** To shoot at persons from a concealed place. **2.** To make nasty, underhanded remarks or attacks. [Middle English.]

snipe
George Miksch Sutton

snip·er (snī′pər) *n.* **1.** A skilled rifleman detailed to spot and pick off enemy soldiers from a concealed place. **2.** A person who shoots at other people from a concealed place.

snip·pet (snĭp′ĭt) *n.* A tidbit or morsel. [From SNIP.]

snip·py (snĭp′ē) *adj.* **-pi·er, -pi·est.** Also **snip·pet·y** (snĭp′ĭ-tē) **-i·er, -i·est.** *Informal.* **1.** Impertinent; fresh; impudent. **2.** Consisting of snips or bits; fragmentary.

snit (snĭt) *n.* *Slang.* A state of agitation. [Orig. unknown.]

snitch (snĭch) *tr.v.* *Slang.* To steal (something of little value); filch. —*intr.v.* To turn informer: *snitch on his brother.* [Orig. unknown.] —**snitch′er** *n.*

sniv·el (snĭv′əl) *intr.v.* **-eled** or **-elled, -el·ing** or **-el·ling. 1.** To cry with sniffling. **2.** To complain tearfully. **3.** To run at the nose, esp. while crying. **4.** To snuffle or sniffle. —*n.* **1.** The act of sniveling. **2.** Nasal mucus. [Middle English *snevelen.*] —**sniv′el·er** or **sniv′el·ler** *n.*

snob (snŏb) *n.* **1.** A person who is convinced of and flaunts his or her social superiority. **2.** A person who despises those he or she considers inferior in a particular area: *an intellectual snob.* [Obs. *snob*, a lower-class person.]

snob·ber·y (snŏb′ə-rē) *n., pl.* **-ies.** Snobbish behavior.

snob·bish (snŏb′ĭsh) *adj.* Of or characteristic of a snob. —**snob′bish·ly** *adv.* —**snob′bish·ness** *n.*

snob·bism (snŏb′ĭz′əm) *n.* Snobbery; snobbishness.

snood (snood) *n.* **1.** A caplike or baglike net worn over the hair at the back of the head. **2.** A headband or fillet. [Ult. from Old English *snōd.*]

snook (snook, snook) *n., pl.* **snook** or **snooks.** Any of several chiefly saltwater fishes of the family Centropomidae. Also called **robalo.** [Dutch *snoek*, pike, from Middle Dutch *snoec.*]

snook·er (snook′ər) *n.* A pocket billiards game in which 15 red and 6 nonred balls are used. [Orig. unknown.]

snoop (snoop) *Informal.* —*intr.v.* To look or search furtively or pryingly. —*n.* A person who snoops. [Dutch *snoepen*, to eat on the sly.] —**snoop′er** *n.*

snoop·y (snoo′pē) *adj.* **-i·er, -i·est.** *Informal.* Inclined, likely, or known to snoop.

snoot (snoot) *n.* *Slang.* A snout or nose.

snoot·y (snoo′tē) *adj.* **-i·er, -i·est.** *Informal.* Snobbish; haughty. [From Middle English *snute*, snout.]

snooze (snooz). *Informal.* —*intr.v.* **snoozed, snooz·ing.** To take a light nap. —*n.* A light nap. [Orig. unknown.]

snore (snôr, snōr) *intr.v.* **snored, snor·ing.** To breathe with a rough grating noise while sleeping. —*n.* The act or sound of snoring. [Middle English *snoren*, to snort.] —**snor′er** *n.*

snor·kel (snôr′kəl) *n.* **1.** A J-shaped tube used by skin divers for breathing with the face underwater. **2.** A retractable tube that can be extended from a submarine, allowing it to draw in fresh air and expel waste gases while submerged. —*intr.v.* To skin-dive using a snorkel. [German *Schnorchel*, from dial. German, snout, from *schnarchen*, to snore, from Middle High German *snarcheln.*]

snort (snôrt) *n.* **1.** A rough, noisy sound made by breathing forcefully through the nostrils, as a horse or pig does. **2.** A sound resembling this: *the snort of a steam engine.* **3.** *Slang.* A small drink of liquor. —*intr.v.* **1.** To breathe noisily and forcefully through the nostrils. **2.** To make an abrupt noise expressive of scorn or anger. —*tr.v.* To express with a snort. [Middle English *snorten.*] —**snort′er** *n.*

snout (snout) *n.* **1.** The long, pointed or projecting nose, jaws, or facial part of an animal's muzzle. **2.** A similar prolongation of the anterior portion of the head in certain insects, such as weevils. **3.** A spout or nozzle resembling a snout. **4.** *Slang.* The human nose, esp. if large. [Middle English *snoute*, prob. from Middle Dutch *snūte.*]

snout beetle. Any of numerous weevils of the family Curculionidae, with the front of the head elongated.

snow (snō) *n.* **1.** Translucent crystals of ice that form from water vapor in the upper atmosphere and fall to earth. **2.** A falling of snow; a snowstorm. **3. a.** Anything resembling snow. **b.** Specks of white that appear on a television screen as a result of weak reception. —*modifier:* *snow warnings.* —*intr.v.* To fall to the earth as snow. —*tr.v.* **1.** To cover, shut off, isolate, or close off with snow: *The blizzard snowed them in for a week.* **2.** *Slang.* To overwhelm with talk or information, esp. with flattery. [Middle English, from Old English *snāw.*]

snow·ball (snō′bôl′) *n.* **1.** A mass of soft, wet snow packed into a ball. **2.** Any of several cultivated plants or shrubs, esp. *Viburnum opulus*, with rounded clusters of white flowers. —*modifier:* *a snowball fight.* —*intr.v.* **1.** To throw snowballs. **2.** To grow rapidly in significance, importance, or size. —*tr.v.* To throw snowballs at. —See Syns at **increase.**

snow·bank (snō′băngk′) *n.* A large drift or mass of snow.

snow·ber·ry (snō′běr′ē) *n.* A North American shrub, *Symphoricarpos albus*, with pink flowers and white berries.

snow·bird (snō′bûrd′) *n.* Any of several birds, such as the junco, often seen in winter when it is snowy.

snow blindness. Irritation of the eyes and partial or total loss of vision caused by sunlight reflected from snow or ice. —**snow′-blind′** *adj.*

snow·bound (snō′bound′) *adj.* Confined, blocked, or isolated in one place by heavy snow; snowed-in.

snow bunting. A bird, *Plectrophenax nivalis*, of northern regions, with predominantly white winter plumage.

snow·cap (snō′kăp′) *n.* A cap of snow, as on a mountaintop. —**snow′capped′** *adj.*

snow·drift (snō'drĭft') *n.* A large mass of snow that has been banked up by the wind.

snow·drop (snō'drŏp') *n.* Any of several bulbous plants of the genus *Galanthus,* native to Eurasia, with nodding white flowers that bloom early in spring.

snow·fall (snō'fôl') *n.* **1.** A fall of snow. **2.** The amount of snow that falls in a given area over a given time.

snow·flake (snō'flāk') *n.* A single flake of snow.

snow job. *Slang.* An effort to overwhelm with insincere talk, flattery, or information.

snow leopard. A large feline mammal, *Uncia uncia,* of the highlands of central Asia, with long, thick, whitish fur with dark markings. Also called **ounce.**

snow line. The boundary marking the lowest altitude at which a given area is always covered with snow.

snow·man (snō'măn') *n.* A figure made from packed and shaped snow, roughly in the form of a human being.

snow·mo·bile (snō'mō-bēl') *n.* A small vehicle with skilike runners in front and tanklike treads, used for traveling on snow.

snow·plow (snō'plou') *n.* **1.** A device or vehicle used to remove snow. **2.** A stopping maneuver in skiing in which the toe ends of the skis are brought together.

snow·shoe (snō'shōō') *n.* A racket-shaped frame with interlaced strips, attached to the shoe to keep the foot from sinking into deep snow. —*intr.v.* **-shoed, -shoe·ing.** To go on snowshoes. —**snow'sho'er** *n.*

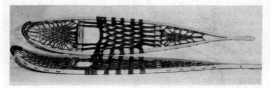

snowshoe

snowshoe rabbit. A hare, *Lepus americanus,* of northern North America, with large feet and fur that is white in winter and brown in summer.

snow·slide (snō'slīd') *n.* An avalanche of snow.

snow·storm (snō'stôrm') *n.* A storm marked by heavy snowfall and high winds; a blizzard.

snow·suit (snō'sōōt') *n.* A warm, one-piece or two-piece outer garment worn in cold weather, esp. by children.

snow tire. A tire with a heavy and deeply grooved tread, used to provide good traction on snow.

snow·y (snō'ē) *adj.* **-i·er, -i·est. 1.** Abounding in or covered with snow. **2.** Resembling or suggestive of snow. —**snow'·i·ly** *adv.* —**snow'i·ness** *n.*

snub (snŭb) *tr.v.* **snubbed, snub·bing. 1.** To slight by ignoring or behaving coldly. **2.** To dismiss or turn down in a decisive way. **3.** To check suddenly the movement of (a rope or cable running out) by turning it about a post. —*n.* **1.** A deliberate slight or affront. **2.** A sudden checking, as of a rope or cable running out. [Middle English *snubben,* to rebuke, from Old Norse *snubba.*] —**snub'ber** *n.*

snub-nosed (snŭb'nōzd') *adj.* Having a short, turned-up nose.

snuff¹ (snŭf) *tr.v.* **1.** To inhale through the nose. **2.** To sniff. —*intr.v.* To sniff; inhale. —*n.* Finely pulverized tobacco that can be drawn up into the nostrils by inhaling. —*idiom.* **up to snuff.** *Informal.* Up to standard. [Prob. from Middle Dutch *snuffen,* to snuffle.]

snuff² (snŭf) *tr.v.* **1.** To cut off the charred portion of (a candlewick). **2.** To extinguish; put out. —*n.* The charred portion of a candlewick. [Middle English *snoffe.*]

snuff·box (snŭf'bŏks') *n.* A small box for carrying snuff.

snuff·er (snŭf'ər) *n.* **1.** Someone or something that snuffs out candles. **2. snuffers.** A scissorslike instrument for cutting the snuff from or for extinguishing a candle.

snuf·fle (snŭf'əl) *v.* **-fled, -fling.** —*intr.v.* **1.** To breathe noisily, as through a blocked nose. **2.** To sniff. **3.** To talk or sing nasally; to whine. —*tr.v.* To utter (something) in a snuffling tone. —*n.* An act or sound of snuffling. [Prob. from Low German or Dutch *snuffelen.*] —**snuf'fler** *n.*

snug (snŭg) *adj.* **snug·ger, snug·gest. 1.** Comfortably sheltered from the cold and the weather; cozy. **2.** Small but well-arranged: *a snug apartment.* **3. a.** Close-fitting: *a snug shirt.* **b.** Close or tight: *a snug fit.* **4.** Closely secured and well-built: *a snug ship.* **5.** Well-hidden: *a snug cove.* —*v.* **snugged, snug·ging.** —*tr.v.* To make snug or secure. —*intr.v.* To nestle or snuggle. [Perh. of Scandinavian orig.] —**snug'ly** *adv.* —**snug'ness** *n.*

snug·ger·y (snŭg'ə-rē) *n., pl.* **-ies.** A snug position or place.

snug·gle (snŭg'əl) *v.* **-gled, -gling.** —*intr.v.* To lie or press close together; nestle or cuddle. —*tr.v.* To hold closely; to hug. [Freq. of SNUG.]

so¹ (sō) *adv.* **1.** In the condition or manner expressed or indicated; thus: *got stuck and remained so.* **2.** To such an extent: *I'm so happy that I could cry.* **3.** To a great extent: *It's so cold.* **4.** Consequently; as a result. **5.** Thereabouts: *The student fare is only $10 or so.* **6.** Too; also; likewise: *She likes the book and so do I.* **7.** Then; apparently. **8.** In truth; indeed. —*adj.* True; factual: *I wouldn't have told you this if it weren't so.* —*conj.* With the result or consequence that: *He failed to show up, so we went without him.* —*interj.* A word used to express surprise or comprehension. —*idioms.* **so as to.** In order to. *Mail your packages early so as to be sure they arrive in time.* **so that.** In order that. [Middle English, from Old English *swā.*]

Usage: **so, so that.** In formal writing, when the conjunction *so* introduces a clause giving the purpose of or reason for an action stated earlier, it is usu. followed by *that: We worked late so that we could complete the shipment.* But in speech, the same thought is very often expressed by *so* alone: *We worked late so we could complete the shipment.* Either is correct. See also Usage note 3 at **as.**

so² (sō) *n.* Var. of **sol** (fifth tone of a musical scale).

soak (sōk) *tr.v.* **1.** To make thoroughly wet by or as if by being immersed. **2.** To absorb (liquid) through pores or interstices: *Sponges soak up water.* **3.** *Informal.* To take in or accept mentally. **4.** *Slang.* To overcharge. —*intr.v.* **1.** To be immersed in a liquid so as to become thoroughly wet. **2.** To penetrate or permeate; seep: *Salt water soaked into the planks.* —*n.* **1.** The act or process of soaking or the condition of being soaked. **2.** *Slang.* A drunkard. [Middle English *soken,* from Old English *socian.*] —**soak'er** *n.*

soak·age (sō'kĭj) *n.* **1.** The process of soaking or the condition of being soaked. **2.** The amount of liquid that soaks into or through an object or seeps out of it.

so-and-so (sō'ən-sō') *n., pl.* **-sos.** An unnamed or unspecified person or thing.

soap (sōp) *n.* **1.** A cleansing agent made from a mixture of the sodium or potassium salts of fatty acids that occur in natural oils and fats. **2.** Any metallic salt of a fatty acid, as of aluminum or iron. **3.** *Slang.* A soap opera. —*modifier: soap powder.* —*tr.v.* To treat or cover with soap. [Middle English *sope,* from Old English *sāpe.*]

soap·ber·ry (sōp'bĕr'ē) *n.* **1.** Any of various chiefly tropical New World trees of the genus *Sapindus,* with pulpy fruit that lathers like soap. **2.** The fruit of any of these trees.

soap·box (sōp'bŏks') *n.* Also **soap box. 1.** A crate in which soap may be packed. **2.** An improvised platform for making an impromptu or nonofficial public speech. —*modifier: a soapbox orator.*

soap opera. A radio or television serial drama, usu. broadcast in the daytime. [So called because many of them were orig. sponsored by soap companies.]

soap plant. 1. A plant, *Chlorogalum pomeridianum,* of California, with small white flowers and a bulbous root formerly used as soap. Also called **amole. 2.** Any of several other plants that have parts used as soap.

soap·stone (sōp'stōn') *n.* Steatite. [From its soapy texture.]

soap·suds (sōp'sŭdz') *pl.n.* Suds from soapy water.

soap·wort (sōp'wûrt', -wôrt') *n.* A plant, the **bouncing Bet.** [So called because the leaves yield a soapy juice.]

soap·y (sō'pē) *adj.* **-i·er, -i·est. 1.** Containing or consisting of soap. **2.** Resembling soap. **3.** *Informal.* Unctuous; oily. —**soap'i·ly** *adv.* —**soap'i·ness** *n.*

soar (sôr, sōr) *intr.v.* **1.** To rise, fly, or glide high and with little apparent effort. **2.** To climb swiftly or powerfully. **3.** *Aviation.* To glide while maintaining altitude. **4.** To ascend to a higher level: *Her spirits soared.* —*n.* The act of soaring. [Middle English *soren,* from Old French *esorer :*

| ă pat | ā pay | â care | ä father | ĕ pet | ē be | hw which | | ĭ pit | ī tie | î pier | ŏ pot | ō toe | ô paw, for | oi noise |
| oō took | ōō boot | ou out | th thin | *th* this | ŭ cut | | | û urge | zh vision | ə about, item, edible, gallop, circus |

Latin *ex-*, out of + *aura*, the air, from Greek, a breeze.] —**soar'er** *n.* —**soar'ing·ly** *adv.*

sob (sŏb) *v.* **sobbed, sob·bing.** —*intr.v.* **1.** To weep aloud with convulsive gasping; cry uncontrollably. **2.** To make a sound resembling that of sobbing. —*tr.v.* **1.** To utter with sobs. **2.** To put or bring by sobbing: *sobbed herself to sleep.* —*n.* The act or sound of sobbing. [Middle English *sobben,* to catch breath, prob. of Low German orig.]

so·ber (sō'bər) *adj.* **-er, -est. 1.** Habitually avoiding the use of alcoholic liquors; temperate. **2.** Not intoxicated. **3.** Serious or grave; sedate: *a sober expression.* **4.** Plain or subdued: *sober garments.* **5.** Without frivolity, excess, or exaggeration. **6.** Marked by self-control or sanity; reasonable. —*tr.v.* To make sober: *The news sobered her.* —*intr.v.* To become sober: *sobered up the next morning.* [Middle English *sobre,* from Old French, from Latin *sōbrius.*] —**so'ber·ly** *adv.* —**so'ber·ness** *n.*

so·bri·e·ty (sō-brī'ĭ-tē) *n.* **1.** Seriousness or gravity; solemnity. **2.** Absence of alcoholic intoxication.

so·bri·quet (sō'brĭ-kā', -kĕt') *n.* Also **sou·bri·quet** (sōō'-). **1.** An affectionate or humorous nickname. **2.** An assumed name. [French.]

sob story. A tale of personal hardship or misfortune intended to arouse pity.

so-called (sō'kôld') *adj.* So named or designated, often incorrectly.

soc·cer (sŏk'ər) *n.* A game, played on a field, in which two teams of 11 members seek to propel the ball into the opposing team's goal by kicking it or by using any part of the body except the arms and hands. —*modifier: a soccer team.* [Shortened and altered from ASSOCIATION (football).]

soccer

so·cia·ble (sō'shə-bəl) *adj.* **1.** Liking the company of others; friendly. **2.** Providing occasion for friendly social relations. —*n.* A social. [Old French, from Latin *sociābilis,* from *sociāre,* to share, from *socius,* partner, sharer.] —**so'cia·bil'i·ty** or **so'cia·ble·ness** *n.* —**so'cia·bly** *adv.*

so·cial (sō'shəl) *adj.* **1. a.** Living together in communities or similar organized groups: *social insects.* **b.** Of or typical of such a way of life: *social activities.* **2.** Of or in society. **3.** Sociable or companionable. **4.** Marked by or promoting friendly social relations: *a social gathering.* **5.** Of or occupied with welfare work. —*n.* An informal social gathering: *a church social.* [Latin *sociālis,* of companionship, from *socius,* partner.]

social climber. A person who strives for acceptance in fashionable society.

social disease. Venereal disease.

so·cial·ism (sō'shə-lĭz'əm) *n.* **1. a.** A doctrine or movement calling for public ownership of factories and other means of production. **b.** A social system that practices this doctrine. **2.** In Marxist-Leninist theory, the stage of society between capitalism and communism.

so·cial·ist (sō'shə-lĭst) *n.* **1.** An advocate of socialism. **2.** Often **Socialist.** A member of a socialist party. —*adj.* **1.** Of, promoting, or practicing socialism. **2. Socialist.** Of, belonging to, or constituting a socialist party.

so·cial·is·tic (sō'shə-lĭs'tĭk) *adj.* Of, advocating, or tending toward socialism. —**so'cial·is'ti·cal·ly** *adv.*

so·cial·ite (sō'shə-līt') *n.* A person who is prominent in fashionable society.

so·ci·al·i·ty (sō'shē-ăl'ĭ-tē) *n., pl.* **-ties. 1.** Sociability. **2.** The tendency to form societies.

so·cial·ize (sō'shə-līz') *v.* **-ized, -iz·ing.** —*tr.v.* **1.** To place under government or group ownership or control. **2.** To fit for companionship with others; make sociable: *Families and schools help socialize children.* **3.** To convert or adapt to the needs of society. —*intr.v.* To take part in social activities. —**so'cial·i·za'tion** *n.* —**so'cial·iz'er** *n.*

socialized medicine. The provision of medical and hospital care for the people at nominal cost through government regulation of health services and tax subsidies.

so·cial·ly (sō'shə-lē) *adv.* **1.** In a social manner. **2.** By or with regard to society: *socially important.*

social science. Any of the sciences, such as sociology, psychology, or anthropology, that study society or the relationships between the individual and society.

Social Security. A government program that provides monthly payments to the elderly and others, financed by payments made both by employers and employees.

social service. Organized efforts to advance the welfare of those who need help; social work.

social studies. A course of study that includes geography, history, government, and sociology, taught in secondary and elementary schools.

social work. Organized efforts by a community or an organization for the betterment of the poor and to counsel those with special problems. —**social worker.**

so·ci·e·tal (sə-sī'ĭ-təl) *adj.* Of or pertaining to the structure, organization, or functioning of society. —**so·ci'e·tal·ly** *adv.*

so·ci·e·ty (sə-sī'ĭ-tē) *n., pl.* **-ties. 1.** Human beings in general. **2.** A group of people with a common culture or way of life. **3.** A group of people who unite to share a common interest: *a stamp-collecting society.* **4.** The rich and fashionable social class: *her introduction into society.* **5.** Companionship; company. **6.** *Biol.* A community of organisms, usu. of the same species. —*modifier: the society page.* [Old French *societe,* from Latin *societās,* from *socius,* a sharing.]

Society of Friends. A Christian sect founded by George Fox in about 1650 in England, opposed to ritual, formal sacraments, a formal creed, a priesthood, and violence. Also called **Quakers.**

socio-. A prefix meaning: **1.** Society: **sociology. 2.** Social: **socioeconomic.** [From Latin *socius,* a sharing.]

so·ci·o·ec·o·nom·ic (sō'sē-ō'-ĕk'ə-nŏm'ĭk, -ē'kə-, -shē-) *adj.* Both social and economic.

so·ci·o·log·i·cal (sō'sē-ə-lŏj'ĭ-kəl, -shē-) or **so·ci·o·log·ic** (-lŏj'ĭk) *adj.* **1.** Of or involving sociology. **2.** Having to do with society. —**so'ci·o·log'i·cal·ly** *adv.*

so·ci·ol·o·gist (sō'sē-ŏl'ə-jĭst, -shē-) *n.* A social scientist who specializes in sociology.

so·ci·ol·o·gy (sō'sē-ŏl'ə-jē, -shē-) *n.* The study of human social behavior, esp. the study of the origins, organization, institutions, and development of human society.

so·ci·o·po·lit·i·cal (sō'sē-ō'pə-lĭt'ĭ-kəl, -shē-) *adj.* Both social and political.

sock¹ (sŏk) *n., pl.* **socks** or **sox** (sŏks). A short stocking reaching at least to the ankle and no higher than the knee. —*tr.v.* To provide with socks. —*phrasal verbs.* **sock away.** *Informal.* To stash (money); save. **sock in.** To close in by bad weather. [Middle English *socke,* from Old English *socc,* a kind of light shoe, from Latin *soccus,* prob. from Greek *sukkhos.*]

sock² (sŏk). *Slang.* —*tr.v.* To strike forcefully; punch. —*intr.v.* To deliver a blow. —See Syns at **hit.** —*n.* A hard blow or punch. [Orig. unknown.]

sock·et (sŏk'ĭt) *n.* **1.** An opening or cavity into which an inserted part is designed to fit: *a light-bulb socket.* **2.** *Anat.* **a.** The hollow part of a joint that receives the end of a bone. **b.** A hollow or concavity into which a part, such as the eye, fits. [Middle English *soket,* spearhead shaped like a plowshare, socket, from Norman French *soket,* dim. of Old French *soc,* plowshare.]

sock·eye salmon (sŏk'ī'). A salmon, *Oncorhynchus nerka,* of northern Pacific coastal waters, that is a commercially valuable food fish. Also called **red salmon.** [By folk ety. from *suk-kegh,* a North American Indian word.]

So·crat·ic (sə-krăt'ĭk, sō-) or **So·crat·i·cal** (-ĭ-kəl) *adj.* Of or pertaining to the Greek philosopher Socrates, his followers, or his method of trying to arrive at the truth by asking questions. —**So·crat'i·cal·ly** *adv.*

ă pat   ā pay   â care   ä father   ĕ pet   ē be   hw which   ĭ pit   ī tie   î pier   ŏ pot   ō toe   ô paw, for   oi noise
ŏŏ took   ōō boot   ou out   th thin   *th* this   ŭ cut   û urge   zh vision   ə about, item, edible, gallop, circus

sod (sŏd) *n.* **1.** A section of grass-covered surface soil held together by matted roots; turf. **2.** The ground, esp. when covered with grass. —*modifier:* a sod roof. —*tr.v.* **sod·ded, sod·ding.** To cover with sod. [Middle English, from Middle Low German or Middle Dutch *sode*.]

so·da (sō′də) *n.* **1. a.** Any of various forms of sodium carbonate. **b.** Chemically combined sodium. **2. a.** Carbonated water. **b.** A flavored, carbonated soft drink; soda pop. **c.** A drink made from carbonated water, ice cream, and usu. flavoring. [Medieval Latin *soda*, barilla, a plant whose ashes are a source of sodium carbonate.]

soda ash. Crude anhydrous sodium carbonate.

soda cracker. A thin, usu. square cracker leavened slightly with baking soda.

soda fountain. A counter equipped for preparing and serving soft drinks and ice-cream dishes.

soda jerk. *Slang.* A person who works at a soda fountain.

soda lime. A mixture of calcium hydroxide and sodium or potassium hydroxide, used as a drying agent and carbon dioxide absorbent.

so·dal·i·ty (sō-dăl′ĭ-tē) *n., pl.* **-ties. 1.** An association, esp. in the Roman Catholic Church, a devotional or charitable society. **2.** Fellowship. [Latin *sodālitās*, fellowship, from *sodālis*, fellow, intimate.]

soda pop. *Informal.* A carbonated soft drink; soda.

soda water. Water that has been charged with carbon dioxide under pressure, used in various drinks.

sod·den (sŏd′n) *adj.* **1.** Thoroughly soaked; saturated. **2.** Soggy and heavy. **3.** Bloated and dull, esp. from drink. [Middle English *soden*, from the past part. of *sethen*, to seethe.] —**sod′den·ly** *adv.* —**sod′den·ness** *n.*

so·di·um (sō′dē-əm) *n. Symbol* **Na** A soft, light, extremely malleable silver-white metallic element that reacts explosively with water, is naturally abundant in combined forms, esp. in common salt, and is used in the production of a wide variety of industrially important compounds. Atomic number 11; atomic weight 22.99; melting point 97.8°C; boiling point 892°C; specific gravity 0.971; valence 1. [SOD(A) + -IUM.]

sodium benzoate. The sodium salt of benzoic acid, C_6H_5COONa, used as a food preservative and antiseptic. Also called **benzoate of soda.**

sodium bicarbonate. A white crystalline compound, $NaHCO_3$, with a slightly alkaline taste, used esp. in making effervescent salts and beverages and baking soda. Also called **baking soda** and **bicarbonate of soda.**

sodium carbonate. 1. A white powdery compound, Na_2CO_3, used in the manufacture of sodium bicarbonate, sodium nitrate, glass, ceramics, detergents, and soap. **2.** Any of various hydrated carbonates of sodium.

sodium chloride. A colorless crystalline compound, NaCl, used in the manufacture of chemicals and as a food preservative and seasoning. Also called **table salt.**

sodium cyanide. A poisonous white crystalline compound, NaCN, used in smelting gold and silver from ores.

sodium glu·ta·mate (glo͞o′tə-māt′). A white crystalline compound used for seasoning food.

sodium hydroxide. An alkaline compound, NaOH, used in chemicals and soaps and in petroleum refining. Also called **caustic soda** and **lye.**

sodium hyposulfite. Sodium thiosulfate.

sodium nitrate. A white crystalline compound, $NaNO_3$, used in explosives and tobacco. Also called **saltpeter.**

sodium thi·o·sul·fate (thī′ə-sŭl′fāt′). A white, translucent crystalline compound, $Na_2S_2O_3 \cdot 5H_2O$, used as a photographic fixing agent and as a bleach. Also called **hyposulfite.**

so·di·um-va·por lamp (sō′dē-əm-vā′pər). An electric lamp that contains a small amount of sodium and neon gas, used in generating yellow light for lighting streets.

Sod·om (sŏd′əm) *n.* **1.** In the Old Testament, a city that God destroyed for wickedness. **2.** A sinful place.

so·fa (sō′fə) *n.* A long upholstered seat with a back and arms. [Ult. from Arabic *suffah*, a dais used for sitting.]

sof·fit (sŏf′ĭt) *n.* The underside of a structural component, such as a beam, arch, staircase, or cornice. [French *soffite*, from Italian *soffita*, from Latin *suffīxus*, "something fastened beneath."]

soft (sôft, sŏft) *adj.* **-er, -est. 1.** Not hard or firm; offering little resistance. **2.** Out of condition; flabby. **3.** Smooth or fine to the touch. **4.** Not loud, harsh, or irritating; low-toned: *a soft voice.* **5.** Not brilliant or glaring; subdued: *soft colors.* **6.** Not sharply drawn or delineated: *soft charcoal shading.* **7.** Mild; balmy: *a soft breeze.* **8. a.** Of a gentle disposition; yielding. **b.** Affectionate. **c.** Not stern; lenient. **9.** *Informal.* Simple; feeble: *soft in the head.* **10.** *Informal.* Easy: *a soft job.* **11.** Apt to change, fluctuate, or devaluate. **12.** Containing relatively little dissolved mineral matter: *soft water.* **13.** Designating the sound of the letters *c* and *g* as they are pronounced in *receive* and *general.* —See Syns at **gentle.** —*adv.* Gently; softly. [Middle English, agreeable, pleasant, from Old English *sōfte*.] —**soft′ly** *adv.* —**soft′ness** *n.*

soft·ball (sôft′bôl′, sŏft′-) *n.* **1.** A variation of baseball played on a smaller diamond with a larger, softer ball that is pitched underhand. **2.** The ball used in this game. —*modifier:* a softball player.

soft-boiled (sôft′boild′, sŏft′-) *adj.* Boiled for a short time so that no part becomes solid: *a soft-boiled egg.*

soft coal. Bituminous coal.

soft drink. A cold beverage that is nonalcoholic.

soft·en (sô′fən, sŏf′ən) *tr.v.* To make less severe or softer. —*intr.v.* To become soft or softer. —**soft′en·er** *n.*

soft-finned (sôft′find′, sŏft′-) *adj.* Having fins supported by flexible cartilaginous rays.

soft·head·ed (sôft′hĕd′ĭd, sŏft′-) *adj.* Lacking judgment, realism, or firmness. —**soft′head′ed·ly** *adv.*

soft·heart·ed (sôft′här′tĭd, sŏft′-) *adj.* Easily moved; tender; merciful. —See Syns at **gentle.** —**soft′heart′ed·ly** *adv.* —**soft′heart′ed·ness** *n.*

soft landing. The landing of a space vehicle at a velocity low enough to prevent damage.

soft palate. The movable fold that hangs from the back of the hard palate and closes off the nasal cavity from the mouth cavity during swallowing or sucking.

soft pedal. A pedal used to mute tone, as on a piano.

soft-ped·al (sôft′pĕd′l, sŏft′-) *tr.v.* **-aled** or **-alled, -al·ing** or **-al·ling. 1.** To soften or mute the tone of by depressing the soft pedal. **2.** *Informal.* To make less emphatic or obvious.

soft sell. *Informal.* A subtly persuasive and low-pressure method of selling or advertising.

soft-shell (sôft′shĕl′, sŏft′-) *adj.* Also **soft-shelled** (-shĕld′). Having a soft shell, esp. as a result of recent molting.

soft-shell clam. A common edible clam, *Mya arenaria*, with a thin, elongated shell.

soft-shoe (sôft′sho͞o′, sŏft′-) *adj.* Of or describing a type of tap dancing performed in tapless, soft-soled shoes.

soft shoulder. A border of soft earth running along the edge of a road.

soft soap. 1. A semifluid soap. **2.** *Informal.* Cajolery.

soft-soap (sôft′sōp′, sŏft′-) *tr.v. Informal.* To flatter in order to gain something; cajole. —**soft′-soap′er** *n.*

soft-spo·ken (sôft′spō′kən, sŏft′-) *adj.* **1.** Speaking with a soft or gentle voice. **2.** Gently persuasive.

soft·ware (sôft′wâr′, sŏft′-) *n.* Written or printed data, such as programs, routines, and symbolic languages, essential to the operation and maintenance of computers.

soft·wood (sôft′wo͝od′, sŏft′-) *n.* **1.** The wood of a cone-bearing tree, such as a pine, fir, or cedar. **2.** A cone-bearing tree. —*modifier:* softwood panels.

soft·y (sôft′tē, sŏf′-) *n., pl.* **-ies.** *Informal.* **1.** A weak or sentimental person. **2.** A person who finds it difficult to punish or be strict.

sog·gy (sŏg′ē, sô′gē) *adj.* **-gi·er, -gi·est. 1.** Saturated or sodden with moisture; soaked. **2.** Lacking spirit; dull. [From dial. *sog*, to soak.] —**sog′gi·ly** *adv.* —**sog′gi·ness** *n.*

soil¹ (soil) *n.* **1.** The top layer of the earth's surface, suitable for the growth of plant life. **2.** A particular kind of earth or ground: *sandy soil.* **3.** Country; territory; region: *native soil.* **4.** A place or condition favorable to growth. [Middle English, from Norman French, from Latin *solium*, seat.]

soil² (soil) *tr.v.* **1.** To make dirty, esp. on the surface; begrime. **2.** To disgrace; tarnish: *soil his reputation.* **3.** To corrupt; defile. **4.** To dirty with excrement. —*intr.v.* To become dirty, stained, or tarnished. —*n.* **1. a.** The condition of being soiled. **b.** A stain. **2.** Manure, esp. human excrement, used as fertilizer. [Middle English *soilen,* from Old French *souiller,* from Latin *suculus,* dim. of *sūs,* pig.]

soil·age (soi′lĭj) *n.* Green crops cut for feeding livestock.

soiled (soild) *adj.* Covered with dirt. —See Syns at **dirty.**

soi·ree or **soi·rée** (swä-rā′) *n.* An evening party or reception. [French *soirée,* from *soir,* evening, from Latin *sērum,* late.]

so·journ (sō′jûrn′, sō-jûrn′) *intr.v.* To stay for a time. —*n.* A temporary stay. [Middle English *sojournen,* from Old French *sojorner* : Latin *sub-,* under + Late Latin *diurnum,* day, from Latin *diurnus,* daily, from *diēs,* day.] —**so′-journ′er** *n.*

sol[1] (sōl) *n.* Also **so** (sō). *Mus.* **1.** The syllable used to represent the fifth tone of a diatonic scale. **2.** The tone G. [Middle English, from Medieval Latin.]

sol[2] (sŏl, sôl) *n.* A liquid colloidal dispersion. [Short for HYDROSOL.]

Sol (sŏl) *n.* The sun. [Middle English, from Latin *sōl.*]

sol·ace (sŏl′əs) *n.* **1.** Comfort in sorrow or distress; consolation. **2.** That which furnishes comfort or consolation. —*tr.v.* **-aced, -ac·ing. 1.** To comfort or console, as in trouble or sorrow. **2.** To allay or assuage. [Middle English *solas,* from Old French, from Latin *sōlācium,* from *sōlārī,* to comfort, console.] —**sol′ac·er** *n.*

so·lar (sō′lər) *adj.* **1.** Of or proceeding from the sun: *solar rays.* **2.** Using or operating by energy derived from the sun: *a solar heating system.* **3.** Determined or measured with respect to the sun: *the solar year.* [Middle English, from Latin *sōlāris,* from *sōl,* sun.]

solar battery. An electrical battery that consists of a number of solar cells connected together.

solar cell. A semiconductor device that converts solar radiation into electrical energy and is often used in space vehicles.

solar flare. A temporary outburst of gases from a small area of the sun's surface.

so·lar·i·um (sō-lâr′ē-əm, -lär′-) *n., pl.* **-i·a** (-ē-ə) or **-i·ums.** A room, gallery, or glassed-in porch exposed to the sun. [Latin *sōlārium,* balcony, from *sōl,* sun.]

solar plexus. 1. The large network of sympathetic nerves and ganglia located in the peritoneal cavity behind the stomach, with branching tracts that supply nerves to the abdominal viscera. **2.** *Informal.* The pit of the stomach. [From the radially branching ganglia.]

solar system. The sun together with the nine planets and all other celestial bodies that orbit the sun.

solar wind. The flow of charged atomic particles that radiates from the sun.

sold (sōld) *v.* Past tense and past participle of **sell.**

sol·der (sŏd′ər, sô′dər) *n.* **1.** Any of various alloys, mainly of tin and lead, applied in the molten state to metal parts in order to join them. **2.** Anything that joins or cements. —*tr.v.* To join, mend, or connect with solder. —*intr.v.* **1.** To unite or repair things with solder. **2.** To be joined by solder. [Middle English *souldour,* from Old French *soldure,* from *solder,* to solder, from Latin *solidāre,* to make solid, from *solidus,* solid.] —**sol′der·er** *n.*

sol·dier (sōl′jər) *n.* **1.** A person who serves in an army. **2.** An enlisted person or a noncommissioned officer as distinguished from a commissioned officer. **3.** An active and loyal follower or worker. **4.** A sexually undeveloped form of certain ants and termites. —*intr.v.* To serve or be as a soldier. [Middle English *souldeour,* mercenary, from Old French *soldier,* from *soulde,* pay, from Latin *solidus,* a Roman coin.]

sol·dier·ly (sōl′jər-lē) *adj.* Befitting a good soldier.

soldier of fortune. A person who will serve in any army for personal gain or love of adventure.

sol·dier·y (sōl′jə-rē) *n., pl.* **-ies. 1.** Soldiers in general. **2.** A body of soldiers. **3.** The military profession.

sole[1] (sōl) *n.* **1.** The undersurface of the foot. **2.** The undersurface of a shoe or boot, often excluding the heel. **3.** The part on which something rests while standing. —*tr.v.* **soled, sol·ing.** To furnish (a shoe or boot) with a sole. [Middle English, from Old French *solea,* sandal, from *solum,* sole of the foot.]

sole[2] (sōl) *adj.* **1.** Being the only one; single; only: *her sole purpose.* **2.** Belonging to only one; exclusive: *The court has the sole right to decide.* —See Syns at **single.** [Middle English, from Old French, from Latin *sōlus.*]

sole[3] (sōl) *n., pl.* **sole** or **soles. 1.** Any of various chiefly saltwater flatfishes of the family Soleidae, esp. *Solea solea,* valued as food. **2.** Any of various other flatfishes. [Middle English, from Old French.]

sol·e·cism (sŏl′ĭ-sĭz′əm, sō′lĭ-) *n.* **1.** A nonstandard usage or grammatical construction. **2.** A violation of etiquette. [Latin *soloecismus,* from Greek *soloikismos,* from *soloikos,* speaking incorrectly.] —**sol′e·cist** *n.*

sole·ly (sōl′lē) *adv.* **1.** Alone; singly: *solely responsible.* **2.** Entirely; exclusively.

sol·emn (sŏl′əm) *adj.* **1.** Deeply earnest; serious; grave. **2.** Performed with full ceremony: *a solemn High Mass.* **3.** Gloomy; somber. [Middle English *solempne,* from Old French, from Latin *sollemnis,* stated, established, appointed.] —**sol′emn·ness** *n.* —**sol′emn·ly** *adv.*

so·lem·ni·ty (sə-lĕm′nĭ-tē) *n., pl.* **-ties. 1.** The condition or quality of being solemn; seriousness. **2.** A solemn event.

sol·em·nize (sŏl′əm-nīz′) *tr.v.* **-nized, -niz·ing. 1.** To celebrate or observe with solemnity. **2.** To perform with formal ceremony. **3.** To make serious or grave. —**sol′em·ni·za′tion** *n.*

so·le·noid (sō′lə-noid′) *n.* A coil of insulated wire in which a magnetic field is established when an electric current is passed through it. [French *solénoïde,* from Greek *sōlēnceidēs,* pipe-shaped.] —**so′le·noid′al** *adj.*

sol-fa (sōl-fä′) *Mus.* *n.* The set of syllables *do, re, mi, fa, sol, la, ti,* used to represent the tones of the scale. **2.** The use of the sol-fa syllables. —*intr.v.* To use the sol-fa syllables. —*tr.v.* To sing with the sol-fa syllables. [SOL (note) + FA.]

sol·feg·gio (sōl-fĕj′ē-ō′, -fĕj′ō) *n.* Also **sol·fège** (sōl-fĕzh′, -fäzh′). A singing exercise in which the sol-fa syllables are used. [Italian, from *solfeggiare,* to sol-fa, from *solfa,* sol-fa.]

so·lic·it (sə-lĭs′ĭt) *tr.v.* **1.** To seek to obtain by persuasion, entreaty, or formal application: *solicit votes.* **2.** To petition persistently; importune: *solicit his neighbors for donations.* **3.** To approach or accost (a person) for immoral purposes. —*intr.v.* To solicit one or more people. [Middle English *soliciten,* to disturb, from Old French *solliciter,* from Latin *sollicitāre,* from *sollicitus,* solicitous.] —**so·lic′i·ta′tion** *n.*

so·lic·i·tor (sə-lĭs′ĭ-tər) *n.* **1.** A person who solicits. **2.** The chief law officer of a city, town, or government department. **3.** *Brit.* A lawyer who is not a member of the bar and who may be heard only in the lower courts.

solicitor general *pl.* **solicitors general. 1.** A law officer who assists an attorney general. **2.** The chief law officer in a state that does not have an attorney general.

so·lic·i·tous (sə-lĭs′ĭ-təs) *adj.* **1.** Concerned; attentive: *a solicitous parent.* **2.** Eager. [Latin *sollicitus,* agitated : *sollus,* whole + *citus,* past part. of *ciēre,* to move.] —**so·lic′i·tous·ly** *adv.* —**so·lic′i·tous·ness** *n.*

so·lic·i·tude (sə-lĭs′ĭ-tōōd′, -tyōōd′) *n.* **1.** Care; concern. **2.** Something or someone that causes anxiety.

sol·id (sŏl′ĭd) *adj.* **-er, -est. 1.** Having a definite shape and volume; not liquid or gaseous. **2.** Not hollowed out. **3.** Being the same substance or color throughout. **4.** Having or dealing with three dimensions: *solid figures.* **5.** Without gaps or breaks; continuous. **6.** Of good quality and substance; well-made. **7.** Substantial; hearty: *a solid breakfast.* **8.** Sound; reliable; concrete: *solid facts.* **9.** Financially sound. **10.** Upstanding and dependable. **11.** Written without a hyphen or space: *solid compounds.* **12.** *Printing.* Without spacing leads between the lines. **13.** Acting together; unanimous. —See Syns at **hard** and **valid.** —*n.* **1.** A substance that has a definite shape and volume. **2.** A geometric figure that has three dimensions. [Middle English *solide,* whole, from Old French, from Latin *solidus.*] —**sol′id·ly** *adv.* —**sol′id·ness** *n.*

sol·i·dar·i·ty (sŏl′ĭ-dăr′ĭ-tē) *n., pl.* **-ties.** A unity of interests, purposes, or sympathies among members of a group.

so·lid·i·fy (sə-lĭd′ə-fī′) *v.* **-fied, -fy·ing.** —*tr.v.* **1.** To make solid, compact, or hard. **2.** To make strong or united. —*intr.v.* To become solid or united. —**so·lid′i·fi·ca′tion** *n.*

so·lid·i·ty (sə-lĭd′ĭ-tē) n., pl. **-ties. 1.** The condition of being solid. **2.** Soundness of mind, character, or financial condition.

sol·id-state (sŏl′ĭd-stāt′) adj. **1.** Of or concerned with the physical properties of crystalline solids. **2.** Based on or using transistors or related semiconductor devices.

so·lil·o·quize (sə-lĭl′ə-kwīz′) intr.v. **-quized, -quiz·ing.** To deliver a soliloquy. **—so·lil′o·quist** or **so·lil′o·quiz′er** n.

so·lil·o·quy (sə-lĭl′ə-kwē) n., pl. **-quies. 1.** A dramatic discourse in which a character reveals his thoughts in the form of a monologue. **2.** The act of speaking to oneself. [Late Latin *sōliloquium* : Latin *sōlus*, alone + *loquī*, to speak.]

sol·ip·sism (sŏl′əp-sĭz′əm, sō′ləp-) n. The philosophical theory that the self is the only thing that can be known and that only the self exists. [Latin *sōlus*, alone + *ipse*, self + -ISM.] **—sol′ip·sist** n.

sol·i·taire (sŏl′ĭ-târ′) n. **1.** A diamond or other gemstone set alone, as in a ring. **2.** Any of a number of card games played by one person. [French, from Old French, solitary, from Latin *sōlitārius*.]

sol·i·tar·y (sŏl′ĭ-tĕr′ē) adj. **1.** Existing, living, or going without others; alone: *a solitary traveler*. **2.** Happening, done, or made alone: *a solitary evening*. **3.** Remote; secluded. **4.** Having no companions; single. **5.** Sole. **—See Syns at alone** and **single. —n.**, pl. **-ies. 1.** A person who lives alone; a recluse. **2.** *Informal.* Solitary confinement. [Middle English, from Latin *sōlitārius*, from *sōlus*, alone.] **—sol′i·tar′i·ly** adv. **—sol′i·tar′i·ness** n.

sol·i·tude (sŏl′ĭ-tōōd′, -tyōōd′) n. **1.** The condition of being alone or remote from others; isolation. **2.** A lonely or secluded place. [Middle English, from Old French, from Latin *sōlitūdo*, from *sōlus*, alone.]

    Syns: solitude, isolation, loneliness n. *Core meaning:* The quality or state of being alone (*solitude causing eccentricity*).

so·lo (sō′lō) n., pl. **-los. 1.** A musical composition or passage for an individual voice or instrument, with or without accompaniment. **2.** Any performance or accomplishment by a single individual. **—adj. 1.** Composed for, arranged for, or performed by a single voice or instrument: *a solo passage.* **2.** Made or done by a single individual: *a solo flight.* **—adv.** Unaccompanied; alone. **—intr.v. 1.** To perform a solo. **2.** To fly an airplane alone. [Italian, from Latin *sōlus*, alone.]

so·lo·ist (sō′lō-ĭst) n. A person who performs a solo.

Sol·o·mon's seal (sŏl′ə-mənz). **1.** A six-pointed star supposed to possess mystical powers. **2.** Any of several plants of the genus *Polygonatum*, with paired, drooping, greenish or yellowish flowers.

Solomon's seal

so·lon (sō′lən) n. A wise lawgiver. [After *Solon* (638?–559 B.C.), Athenian lawgiver.]

so long. *Informal.* Good-by.

sol·stice (sŏl′stĭs, sōl′-) n. Either of the two times of year, approx. June 22, the summer solstice, and December 22, the winter solstice, at which the sun reaches an extreme of its northward or southward motion. [Middle English, from Old French, from Latin *sōlstitium*.] **—sol·sti′tial** (-stĭsh′əl) adj.

sol·u·bil·i·ty (sŏl′yə-bĭl′ĭ-tē) n., pl. **-ties. 1.** The condition or property of being soluble. **2.** The amount of a substance that can be dissolved in a particular liquid, esp. water.

sol·u·ble (sŏl′yə-bəl) adj. **1.** Capable of being dissolved. **2.** Capable of being solved or explained. [Middle English, from Old French, from Late Latin *solūbilis*, from *solvere*, to loosen.] **—sol′u·ble·ness** n. **—sol′u·bly** adv.

sol·ute (sŏl′yōōt′, sō′lōōt′) n. A substance that is dissolved in another substance and is usu. the substance that makes up the smallest proportion of a solution. **—adj.** In solution; dissolved. [Latin *solūtus*, past part. of *solvere*, to loosen.]

so·lu·tion (sə-lōō′shən) n. **1.** A mixture of two or more substances that appears to be uniform throughout except at the molecular level, and that is capable of forming by itself when the substances are in contact. **2.** The act or process of forming such a mixture. **3.** The condition or property of being dissolved. **4.** An answer to a problem. **5.** The method or procedure used in solving an equation, problem, etc.

solution set. The set composed of all the solutions of an equation, inequality, or logic statement.

solv·a·ble (sŏl′və-bəl) adj. Capable of being solved. **—solv′a·bil′i·ty** n.

solve (sŏlv) tr.v. **solved, solv·ing.** To find a solution to; answer; explain. [Middle English *solven*, to loosen, unbind, from Latin *solvere*.] **—solv′er** n.

sol·vent (sŏl′vənt) adj. **1.** Able to meet financial obligations. **2.** Capable of dissolving another substance. **—n. 1.** The substance that makes up the largest proportion of a solution. **2.** A liquid that is capable of dissolving another substance. [Latin *solvēns*, pres. part. of *solvere*, to loosen.] **—sol′ven·cy** n.

so·ma (sō′mə) n., pl. **-ma·ta** (-mə-tə) or **-mas.** The entire physical part of an organism except for the germ cells. [From Greek *sōma*, body.]

So·ma·li (sō-mä′lē) n., pl. **Somali** or **-lis. 1.** A member of one of a group of Hamitic tribes of Somaliland. **2.** The Hamitic language of the Somalis. **—So·ma′li** adj.

so·mat·ic (sō-măt′ĭk, sə-) adj. **1.** Of the body, esp. as distinguished from any of its parts, the mind, or the germ cells. **2.** Of the wall of the body cavity. **3.** Of somatoplasm. [Greek *sōmatikos*, from *sōma*, body.]

somatic cell. Any bodily cell other than a germ cell.

so·ma·to·plasm (sō′mə-tə-plăz′əm, sō-mặt′ə-) n. **1.** The whole specialized protoplasm, other than germ plasm, that constitutes the body. **2.** The protoplasm of a somatic cell. [Greek *sōma*, body + -PLASM.]

so·ma·to·type (sō′mə-tə-tīp′, sō-măt′ə-) n. The form and structural part of a human body; physique. [Greek *sōma*, body + TYPE.]

som·ber or **som·bre** (sŏm′bər) adj. **1.** Dark; gloomy. **2.** Melancholy; dismal: *a somber mood.* **—See Syns at gloomy.** [French *sombre*, from Old French, shade : Latin *sub-*, under + *umbra*, shade.]

som·bre·ro (sŏm-brâr′ō) n., pl. **-ros.** A large straw or felt hat with a broad brim and tall crown, worn in Mexico and the Southwest. [Spanish, hat, from *sombra*, shade.]

some (sŭm) adj. **1.** Being an unspecified number or quantity; a few or a little: *some people; some sugar.* **2.** Unknown or unspecified by name: *Some student was just here and left you this note.* **3.** *Informal.* Considerable; remarkable: *some cook.* **—pron.** An indefinite or unspecified number or quantity. **—adv. 1.** Approximately; about. **2.** *Informal.* Somewhat. [Middle English, from Old English *sum*, one, a certain one.]

    Usage: **some.** The indefinite pronoun *some* is construed as singular when it occurs with a mass noun, and plural when it occurs with a countable noun: *Some of the power* (mass noun) *is held by the king. Some of the land* (mass noun) *lies to the north. Some* is construed as a plural when it occurs with a countable noun: *Some of the children* (countable noun) *are ill. Some of the grapes* (countable noun) *are rotten.*

–some¹. A suffix meaning characterized by a (certain) state, quality, action, or thing: **burdensome, quarrelsome.** [Middle English *-som*, from Old English *-sum.*]

–some². A suffix meaning body: **chromosome.** [From Greek *sōma*, body.]

–some³. A suffix indicating a group of (so many members): **threesome.** [Middle English *-sum*, from *sum*, *som*, some, one.]

ă pat   ā pay   â care   ä father   ĕ pet   ē be   hw which   ĭ pit   ī tie   î pier   ŏ pot   ō toe   ô paw, for   oi noise
ōō took   ōō boot   ou out   th thin   th this   ŭ cut   û urge   zh vision   ə about, item, edible, gallop, circus

some·bod·y (sŭm'bŏd'ē, -bŭd'ē, -bə-dē) *pron.* An unspecified or unknown person; someone. —*n. Informal.* A person of importance: *He thinks he's really somebody.*
Usage: somebody, someone, some one. 1. somebody, someone. In formal usage, *somebody* and *someone* take singular verbs, and accompanying pronouns and pronominal adjectives are also singular: *Someone has lost his way.* **2. someone, some one.** *Some one* (two words) refers specifically to a person or thing singled out of a group: *Some one of them will be called on to explain.* In such an example, *someone* cannot be used.

some·day (sŭm'dā') *adv.* At some time in the future.

some·how (sŭm'hou') *adv.* **1.** In some way or other. **2.** For some reason. —See Usage note at **someway.**

some·one (sŭm'wŭn', -wən) *pron.* Some person; somebody: *Someone called, but didn't leave a name.* —See Usage note at **somebody.** —*n. Informal.* A somebody.

some·place (sŭm'plās') *adv.* Somewhere: *Let's go someplace else.*

som·er·sault (sŭm'ər-sôlt'). Also **sum·mer·sault.** *n.* **1.** An acrobatic stunt in which the body rolls in a complete circle, heels over head. **2.** Any complete reversal. —*intr.v.* To execute a somersault. [Old French *sombresault*, var. of *sobresault*, *sobre-*, over, from Latin *suprā* + *sault*, leap, from Latin *saltus*, from *salīre*, to leap.]

some·thing (sŭm'thĭng) *pron.* An unspecified or not definitely known thing. —*n. Informal.* A remarkable or important thing or person. —*adv.* Somewhat. —*idiom.* **something of.** To some extent.

some·time (sŭm'tīm') *adv.* **1.** At an indefinite or unstated time: *I'll meet you sometime this afternoon.* **2.** At an indefinite time in the future: *Let's get together sometime.* —*adj.* Former.

some·times (sŭm'tīmz') *adv.* Now and then.

some·way (sŭm'wā') *adv.* Also **some·ways** (-wāz'). *Informal.* **1.** In some way or other; somehow. **2.** For some reason or other.
Usage: someway, some way, someways. The adverb *someway* is standard in American usage. Its variant *someways* is informal. An alternative to *someway* is *somehow.*

some·what (sŭm'hwŏt', -wŏt', -hwŭt', -wŭt', sŭm-hwŏt', -wŏt', -hwŭt', -wŭt') *adv.* To some extent or degree; rather. —*pron. Archaic.* Something.

some·where (sŭm'hwâr', -wâr') *adv.* **1.** At, in, or to a place not specified or known: *I found this turtle somewhere near the edge of the swamp.* **2.** To a place or state of further development or progress: *finally getting somewhere.* **3.** Approximately; roughly: *somewhere about halfway through.* —*n.* An unspecified place.

som·me·lier (sŏm'əl-yā') *n.* A wine steward in a restaurant. [French, from Old French, officer in charge of provisions, pack-animal driver, from *somme*, pack, from Late Latin *sagma*, from Greek, packsaddle.]

som·nam·bu·lant (sŏm-năm'byə-lənt) *adj.* Walking or inclined to walk while asleep.

som·nam·bu·late (sŏm-năm'byə-lāt') *intr.v.* **-lat·ed, -lat·ing.** To walk while asleep. [Latin *somnus*, sleep + *ambulātus*, past part. of *ambulare*, to walk.]

som·nam·bu·lism (sŏm-năm'byə-lĭz'əm) *n.* The act of walking while asleep. Also called **sleepwalking.** —**som·nam'bu·list** *n.* —**som·nam'bu·lis'tic** *adj.*

som·nif·er·ous (sŏm-nĭf'ər-əs) *adj.* Inducing or causing sleep. [From Latin *somnifer.*]

som·no·lence (sŏm'nə-ləns) *n.* Drowsiness; sleepiness.

som·no·lent (sŏm'nə-lənt) *adj.* Drowsy; sleepy. [Middle English *sompnolent*, from Old French, from Latin *somnolentus*, from *somnus*, sleep.] —**som'no·lent·ly** *adv.*

son (sŭn) *n.* **1. a.** A boy or man thought of in relation to his parents; male offspring. **b.** An adopted male offspring. **2.** Any male descendant. **3.** A man or boy associated with a place or cause. **4.** Young man. Used as a familiar term of address. **5. the Son.** Christ. [Middle English, from Old English *sunu.*]

so·nant (sō'nənt) *Phonet.* —*adj.* Voiced, as a speech sound. —*n.* A voiced speech sound. [Latin *sonāns*, pres. part. of Latin *sonāre*, to sound.]

so·nar (sō'när') *n.* A system or apparatus similar in principle to radar, that uses reflected sound waves to detect and locate underwater objects. [SO(UND) NA(VIGATION) R(ANGING).]

so·na·ta (sə-nä'tä) *n.* Any of several types of instrumental musical compositions, esp. one written in three or four movements, the first of which is in sonata form. [Italian, from *sonare*, to sound, from Latin *sonāre.*]

sonata form. A form for a musical movement, consisting of the exposition of themes, their development, and their restatement, sometimes followed by a coda.

so·na·ti·na (sō'nə-tē'nə, sŏn'ə-) *n., pl.* **-nas** or **-ne** (-nā). A sonata with short movements. [Italian, dim. of *sonata*, sonata.]

song (sông, sŏng) *n.* **1.** A brief musical composition written or adapted for singing. **2.** The act or art of singing. **3.** A melodious utterance. **4. a.** Poetry; verse. **b.** A lyric poem or ballad. —*idiom.* **for a song.** At a low price. [Middle English, from Old English *sang.*]

song·bird (sông'bûrd', sŏng'-) *n.* A bird, esp. one of the suborder Passeres, that has a melodious song or call.

song·fest (sông'fĕst', sŏng'-) *n.* A casual gathering for group singing.

song·ful (sông'fəl, sŏng'-) *adj.* Melodious; tuneful.

Song of Sol·o·mon (sŏl'ə-mən). See table at **Bible.**

song sparrow. A North American songbird, *Melospiza melodia*, with streaked brownish plumage.

song·ster (sông'stər, sŏng'-) *n.* A singer or songwriter.

song thrush. A European songbird, *Turdus philomelos*, with brown upper plumage and a spotted breast. Also called **mavis.**

song·writ·er (sông'rī'tər, sŏng'-) *n.* A person who writes lyrics or composes tunes for songs.

son·ic (sŏn'ĭk) *adj.* **1.** Of or relating to sound, esp. audible sound: *a sonic wave.* **2.** Having a speed equal to that of sound in air, approx. 738 miles per hour at sea level at normal temperatures. [Latin *son(us)*, sound + -IC.]

sonic barrier. The sudden sharp increase in drag exerted by the atmosphere on an aircraft approaching the speed of sound. Also called **sound barrier.**

sonic boom. The shock wave caused by an aircraft traveling at a supersonic speed, often audible on the ground.

son-in-law (sŭn'ən-lô') *n., pl.* **sons-in-law.** The husband of one's daughter.

son·net (sŏn'ĭt) *n.* A 14-line poetic form, usu. in iambic pentameter, with a fixed rhyme pattern. [French, from Italian *sonetto*, from Old Provençal *sonet*, dim. of *son*, song, from Latin *sonus*, sound.]

son·net·eer (sŏn'ĭ-tîr') *n.* A composer of sonnets.

son·ny (sŭn'ē) *n., pl.* **-nies.** Little boy; young man. Used as a familiar form of address. [Dim. of SON.]

so·nor·i·ty (sə-nôr'ĭ-tē, -nŏr'-) *n., pl.* **-ties. 1.** The quality of being sonorous. **2.** A resonant sound.

so·no·rous (sə-nôr'əs, -nŏr'-, sŏn'ər-) *adj.* **1.** Having or producing sound, esp. full, deep, or rich sound. **2.** Impressive; grandiloquent: *sonorous prose.* [Latin *sonorus*, from *sonor*, sound, from *sonāre*, to sound.] —**so·no'rous·ly** *adv.*

soon (sōōn) *adv.* **-er, -est. 1. a.** In the near future. **b.** Within a short time; quickly. **2.** Early: *not an instant too soon.* **3.** Quickly; fast: *Phone your mother as soon as we get into the house.* **4.** Gladly; willingly: *I'd as soon leave right now.* —*idioms.* **no sooner . . . than.** As soon as: *No sooner was the frost off the ground than the work began.* **sooner or later.** Sometime; eventually. [Middle English, from Old English *sōna.*]

soot (sŏŏt, sōōt, sŭt) *n.* A black powdery substance, chiefly carbon, produced by the incomplete combustion of fuel. —*tr.v.* To cover or smudge with soot. [Middle English, from Old English *sōt.*]

sooth (sōōth). *Archaic.* —*adj.* **1.** Real; true. **2.** Soft; soothing; sweet. —*n.* Truth; reality. [Middle English, from Old English *sōth.*] —**sooth'ly** *adv.*

soothe (sōōth) *v.* **soothed, sooth·ing.** —*tr.v.* **1.** To calm or quiet. **2.** To ease or relieve the pain of. —*intr.v.* To bring calm or comfort. [Middle English *sothen*, to show to be true, from Old English *sōthian*, from *sōth*, truth.] —**sooth'er** *n.* —**sooth'ing·ly** *adv.*

sooth·say·er (sōōth'sā'ər) *n.* A person who claims to be able to foretell events or predict the future; a seer.

soot·y (sŏŏt'ē, sōō'tē, sŭt'ē) *adj.* **-i·er, -i·est. 1.** Of, produced, or covered with soot. **2.** Black or dark like soot.

sop (sŏp) *v.* **sopped, sop·ping.** —*tr.v.* **1.** To dip, soak, or drench in a liquid. **2.** To take up by absorption; soak up: *sop up water with a towel.* —*intr.v.* To be or become thoroughly soaked or saturated. —*n.* **1.** Something, as a bit of bread, soaked in a liquid. **2.** Something thoroughly soaked. **3.** Something yielded to placate or soothe. [From Middle English *soppe*, dipped bread, from Old English *sopp*.]

soph·ism (sŏf′ĭz′əm) *n.* A seemingly reasonable argument that is actually invalid.

soph·ist (sŏf′ĭst) *n.* **1. Sophist.** Any of a class of ancient Greek teachers known for their overly subtle and often misleading arguments. **2.** A scholar or thinker skillful in devious argument. [Latin *sophistēs*, from Greek, expert, deviser, from *sophizesthai*, to play subtle tricks, from *sophos*, skilled, clever.]

so·phis·tic (sə-fĭs′tĭk) or **so·phis·ti·cal** (-tĭ-kəl) *adj.* **1.** Of or characteristic of sophists. **2.** Ingenious and subtle but misleading; specious. —**so·phis′ti·cal·ly** *adv.*

so·phis·ti·cate (sə-fĭs′tĭ-kāt′) *v.* **-cat·ed, -cat·ing.** —*tr.v.* **1.** To cause to become less naive. **2.** To make more complex or advanced. **3.** To corrupt or pervert. —*intr.v.* To use sophistry. —*n.* (sə-fĭs′tĭ-kĭt). A sophisticated person. —**so·phis′ti·ca′tion** *n.*

so·phis·ti·cat·ed (sə-fĭs′tĭ-kā′tĭd) *adj.* **1.** Having acquired worldly knowledge or refinement. **2.** Elaborate, complex or complicated: *a sophisticated machine.* **3.** Suitable for or appealing to the tastes of sophisticates: *a sophisticated play.* —**so·phis′ti·cat·ed·ly** *adv.*

soph·ist·ry (sŏf′ĭ-strē) *n., pl.* **-tries. 1.** A seemingly reasonable but misleading or false argument. **2.** A clever and plausible but faulty method of reasoning or arguing.

soph·o·more (sŏf′ə-môr′, -mōr′) *n.* A second-year student in an American college or high school. —*modifier: the sophomore class.* [Greek *sophos*, wise + *mōros*, foolish.]

soph·o·mor·ic (sŏf′ə-môr′ĭk, -mŏr′-, -mōr′-) *adj.* **1.** Of or characteristic of a sophomore. **2.** Immature and overconfident. —**soph′o·mor′i·cal·ly** *adv.*

sop·o·rif·er·ous (sŏp′ə-rĭf′ər-əs) *adj.* Causing sleep; soporific. [From Latin *soporifer*.] —**sop′o·rif′er·ous·ly** *adv.*

sop·o·rif·ic (sŏp′ə-rĭf′ĭk) *adj.* **1.** Causing or tending to cause sleep. **2.** Drowsy. —*n.* A sleep-inducing drug.

sop·ping (sŏp′ĭng) *adj.* Thoroughly soaked; drenched.

sop·py (sŏp′ē) *adj.* **-pi·er, -pi·est.** Soaked; sopping.

so·pran·o (sə-prăn′ō, -prä′nō) *n., pl.* **-os. 1.** The highest singing voice of a woman or young boy. **2.** A singer having a soprano voice. **3.** A part written in the range of the soprano voice. —*modifier: a soprano aria.* [Italian, from *sopra*, above, from Latin *suprā*.]

so·ra (sôr′ə, sōr′ə) *n.* A North American marsh bird, *Porzana carolina*, with grayish-brown plumage. [Prob. of American Indian orig.]

sorb (sôrb) *tr.v.* To take up and hold, as by absorption or adsorption. [Back-formation from ADSORB and ABSORB.]

sor·cer·er (sôr′sər-ər) *n.* A person who practices sorcery; a wizard.

sor·cer·ess (sôr′sər-ĭs) *n.* A female sorcerer.

sor·cer·y (sôr′sə-rē) *n., pl.* **-ies.** The use of supernatural power; witchcraft; magic. —See Syns at **magic.** [Middle English *sorcerie*, from Old French, from *sorcier*, sorcerer, from Latin *sors*, lot.] —**sor′cer·ous** *adj.* —**sor′cer·ous·ly** *adv.*

sor·did (sôr′dĭd) *adj.* **1.** Filthy or dirty; foul: *a sordid tale.* **2.** Depressingly squalid; wretched. **3.** Morally degraded; vile; base. **4.** Grasping; selfish. [French *sordide*, from Latin *sordidus*, from *sordēre*, to be dirty.] —**sor′did·ly** *adv.* —**sor′did·ness** *n.*

sore (sôr, sōr) *adj.* **sor·er, sor·est. 1.** Painful or tender. **2.** Suffering or feeling pain; hurting: *sore all over.* **3.** Causing misery, sorrow, or distress; grievous: *sore need.* **4.** Causing embarrassment or irritation: *a sore subject.* **5.** *Informal.* Angry; offended. —See Syns at **angry.** —*adv.* *Archaic.* Sorely. —*n.* **1.** An open injury, wound, ulcer, etc. **2.** Any source of pain or distress. [Middle English *sor*, from Old English *sār*.] —**sore′ness** *n.*

sore·head (sôr′hĕd′, sōr′-) *n. Slang.* A person who is easily offended, annoyed, or angered.

sore·ly (sôr′lē, sōr′-) *adv.* **1.** Severely; grievously. **2.** Extremely; greatly: *sorely needed.*

sor·ghum (sôr′gəm) *n.* **1.** An Old World grass, *Sorghum vulgare*, several varieties of which are widely cultivated as grain and forage or as a source of syrup. **2.** Syrup made from the juice of the sorghum. [From Italian *sorgo*.]

so·ri (sôr′ī, sōr′ī) *n.* Plural of **sorus.**

so·ro·ral (sə-rôr′əl, -rōr′-) *adj.* Of or like a sister; sisterly. [From Latin *soror*, sister.]

so·ror·i·ty (sə-rôr′ĭ-tē, -rōr′-, -rŏr′-) *n., pl.* **-ties.** A social or civic club for women, esp. one at a college. [Medieval Latin *sororitās*, from Latin *soror*, sister.]

sor·rel[1] (sôr′əl, sōr′-) *n.* **1.** Any of several plants of the genus *Rumex*, with acid-flavored leaves sometimes used in salads. **2.** Any of various plants of the genus *Oxalis*. [Middle English *sorel*, from Old French *surele*, from *sur*, sour.]

sor·rel[2] (sôr′əl, sōr′-) *n.* **1.** A yellowish brown. **2.** A yellowish-brown horse. —*adj.* Yellowish brown. [From Middle English *sorelle*, sorrel-colored, from Old French *sorel*, from *sor*, red-brown.]

sor·row (sŏr′ō, sôr′ō) *n.* **1.** Mental suffering because of loss or injury; sadness; grief. **2.** Something that causes sadness or grief. —*intr.v.* To feel or display sadness or grief; grieve. [Middle English *sorow*, from Old English *sorh*.]

Syns: **sorrow, grief, heartache, heartbreak, woe** *n. Core meaning:* Mental anguish (*the sorrow of the grieving widow*).

sor·row·ful (sŏr′ō-fəl, sôr′-) *adj.* Causing, feeling, or expressing sorrow; mournful: *a sorrowful event; a sorrowful voice.* —**sor′row·ful·ly** *adv.* —**sor′row·ful·ness** *n.*

sor·ry (sŏr′ē, sôr′ē) *adj.* **-ri·er, -ri·est. 1.** Feeling or expressing sympathy, pity, or regret; sorrowful: *I am sorry to be late.* **2.** Poor; wretched: *a sorry excuse.* **3.** Causing sorrow, grief, or misfortune. [Middle English *sory*, from Old English *sārig*, painful, sad.] —**sor′ri·ly** *adv.* —**sor′ri·ness** *n.*

sort (sôrt) *n.* **1.** A group or collection of similar persons or things; class; kind. **2.** The character or nature of something; type; quality: *an interesting sort of person.* **3.** A manner; style. **4.** Often **sorts.** One of the characters in a font of type. —See Syns at **kind.** —*tr.v.* **1.** To arrange according to class, kind, or size; classify. **2.** To separate from others. —*idioms.* **of sorts.** Of a mediocre or inferior kind. **out of sorts.** *Informal.* **1.** Somewhat ill. **2.** In a bad mood. **sort of.** *Informal.* Somewhat; rather: *sort of silly.* [Middle English, from Old French *sorte*, from Latin *sors*, lot, fortune.] —**sort′a·ble** *adj.* —**sort′er** *n.*

Usage: **sort.** When the noun *sort* means a group or collection, it is a synonym of *kind.* The information provided in the entry for *kind* also applies to *sort.* See also Usage note at **kind.**

sor·tie (sôr′tē, sôr-tē′) *n.* **1.** An armed attack made from a place surrounded by enemy forces. **2.** A flight of a warplane on a combat mission. [French, from Old French, from *sortir*, go out.]

so·rus (sôr′əs, sōr′-) *n., pl.* **so·ri** (sôr′ī, sōr′ī). *Bot.* One of the clusters of spore cases formed on the undersides of fern fronds. [From Greek *sōros*, heap.]

S O S **1.** The letters represented by the signal ···---···, used internationally as a distress signal. **2.** Any call for help.

so-so (sō′sō′) *adj.* Mediocre. —*adv.* Indifferently.

sos·te·nu·to (sō′stə-nōō′tō, sŏs′tə-). *Mus.* —*adv.* In a sustained or prolonged manner. Used as a direction. —*n., pl.* **-tos** or **-ti** (-tē). A passage played or sung in this manner. [Italian, past part. of *sostenere*, to sustain, from Latin *sustinēre*, to sustain.] —**sos′te·nu′to** *adj.*

sot (sŏt) *n.* A drunkard. [Middle English *sot*, a fool, from Old English *sott*, from Medieval Latin *sottus*.]

sot·tish (sŏt′ĭsh) *adj.* **1.** Stupefied from or as if from drink. **2.** Tending to drink excessively; drunken. —**sot′tish·ly** *adv.*

sot·to vo·ce (sŏt′ō vō′chē). Very softly, esp. so as not to be overheard; in an undertone. [Italian, "under the voice."]

sou (sōō) *n.* A former French coin. [French, from Old French *sous*, from Latin *solidus*, a Roman coin.]

sou·brette (sōō-brĕt′) *n.* **1.** A saucy, coquettish lady's maid in comedies or comic opera. **2.** Any flirtatious young woman. [French, from Provençal *soubreto*, fem. of *soubret*, conceited, from *soubra*, to leave aside, from Old Provençal *sobras*, to be excessive, from Latin *superāre*, from *super*, above.]

| ă pat | ā pay | â care | ä father | ĕ pet | ē be | hw which | ĭ pit | ī tie | î pier | ŏ pot | ō toe | ô paw, for | oi noise |
| ōō ɔok | ōō boot | ou out | th thin | *th* this | ŭ cut | û urge | zh vision | ə about, item, edible, gallop, circus |

sou·bri·quet (sōō′brĭ-kā′, -kĕt′) n. Var. of **sobriquet**.

souf·flé (sōō-flā′) n. A light, fluffy baked dish made with egg yolks and beaten egg whites combined with various other ingredients. —*modifier: a soufflé dish.* [French, from *souffler*, to puff up, from Latin *sufflāre* : *sub-*, up from under + *flāre*, to blow.]

sough (sŭf, sou) intr.v. To make a soft murmuring sound. —n. A soft murmuring sound, as of the wind. [Middle English *swoghen*, from Old English *swōgan*.]

sought (sôt) v. Past tense and past participle of **seek**.

soul (sōl) n. **1.** The animating and vital principle in a person credited with the faculties of thought, action, and emotion and often conceived as an immaterial entity that survives death. **2.** A spirit; a ghost. **3.** A human being: *not a soul in sight.* **4.** The central or vital part of something: *the soul of a poem.* **5.** A person considered as the embodiment of an intangible quality: *the soul of discretion.* **6.** A person's emotional or moral nature. **7.** Emotional or expressive intensity. —*adj. Slang.* Of or derived from blacks and their culture: *soul food; soul music.* [Middle English, from Old English *sāwol*.]

soul·ful (sōl′fəl) adj. Full of or expressing a deep feeling: *a soulful sigh.* —**soul′ful·ly** adv. —**soul′ful·ness** n.

soul·less (sōl′lĭs) adj. Lacking sensitivity or the capacity for deep feeling. —**soul′less·ly** adv. —**soul′less·ness** n.

soul-search·ing (sōl′sûr′chĭng) n. The penetrating examination of one's motives, convictions, and attitudes.

sound¹ (sound) n. **1.** A type of wave motion that travels through air and other elastic materials and is detectable by human ears. **2.** Any sensation produced in the organs of hearing. **3.** A distinctive noise: *a hollow sound.* **4.** The distance over which something can be heard; earshot. **5.** An articulation made by the vocal apparatus. **6.** Recorded material, as for a motion picture. **7.** A conveyed impression; tone: *He did not like the sound of the invitation.* —*modifier: sound waves.* —intr.v. **1.** To make or give forth a sound: *The whistle sounded.* **2.** To present a particular impression; seem to be: *sounds reasonable.* —tr.v. **1.** To cause to make a sound: *He sounded the gong.* **2.** To summon, announce, or signal by a sound. **3.** To articulate; pronounce: *sound a vowel.* **4.** To make known; celebrate. **5.** To examine (a bodily organ or part) by causing to emit sound: *sound one's chest.* —*phrasal verb.* **sound off. 1.** To speak loudly. **2.** To express one's views vigorously. [Middle English *soun*, from Old French *son*, from Latin *sonus*.]

sound² (sound) adj. **-er, -est. 1.** Free from defect, decay, or damage; in good condition: *a sound building.* **2.** Having a firm basis; solid: *a sound foundation.* **3.** Secure or safe. **4.** Based on valid reasoning. **5.** Thorough; complete: *a sound thrashing.* **6.** Deep and undisturbed: *a sound sleep.* **7.** *Law.* Valid; legal: *sound title.* —See Syns at **healthy** and **valid**. [Middle English *sund*, from Old English *gesund*.] —**sound′ly** adv. —**sound′ness** n.

sound³ (sound) n. **1.** A long body of water, wider than a strait or a channel, that usu. connects larger bodies of water. **2.** The air bladder of a fish. [Middle English *sound*, from Old English *sund*, swimming, water.]

sound⁴ (sound) tr.v. **1.** To measure the depth of (water), esp. by means of a weighted line; to fathom. **2.** To try to learn the attitudes or opinions of: *sound out her feelings.* **3.** To probe. —intr.v. **1.** To measure depth. **2.** To dive swiftly downward, as a whale. **3.** To investigate. —n. A surgical instrument used to examine body cavities. [Middle English *sounden*, from Old French *sonder*, from *sonde*, a sounding line, prob. from Old English *sund*, sea.]

sound barrier. The **sonic barrier**.

sound·board (sound′bôrd′, -bōrd′) n. *Mus.* A **sounding board**.

sound box. A hollow chamber in the body of a musical instrument that intensifies the resonance of the tone.

sound effects. Imitative sounds, as of thunder or an explosion, produced artificially for theatrical purposes.

sound·er (soun′dər) n. Someone or something that sounds, esp. a device for making soundings of the sea.

sound·ing¹ (soun′dĭng) n. **1.** A measured depth of water. **2.** A scientific examination of atmospheric conditions at a specific altitude. **3.** A sampling of opinion.

sound·ing² (soun′dĭng) adj. **1.** Emitting a full sound; resonant. **2.** Noisy but with little significance; high-sounding.

sounding board. 1. A thin board forming the upper portion of the resonant chamber in a musical instrument. Also called **soundboard. 2.** Any structure suspended behind or over a podium, pulpit, or platform to reflect the speaker's voice to the audience. **3.** Any device or means serving to spread or popularize opinions.

sounding line. A line marked at intervals of fathoms, used to determine the depth of water.

sound·less¹ (sound′lĭs) adj. Having or making no sound; quiet; silent. —**sound′less·ly** adv. —**sound′less·ness** n.

sound·less² (sound′lĭs) adj. Too deep to be measured.

sound·proof (sound′prōōf′) adj. Designed or treated to allow little or no audible sound to pass through or enter: *a soundproof room.* —tr.v. To make soundproof.

sound stage. A usu. soundproof room or studio used for the production of motion pictures.

sound·track (sound′trăk′) n. The narrow strip at one side of a motion-picture film that carries the sound recording.

soup (sōōp) n. A liquid food prepared from meat, fish, or vegetable stock, with various other ingredients added. —*modifier: a soup bowl.* —tr.v. **soup up.** *Slang.* To add horsepower or greater speed potential to (an engine or vehicle). [French *soupe*, from Old English *broth.*]

soup·çon (sōōp-sôn′) n. A very small amount. [French.]

soup kitchen. A place where food is offered to the poor.

soup·spoon (sōōp′spōōn′) n. A spoon somewhat larger than a teaspoon, used for eating soup.

soup·y (sōō′pē) adj. **-i·er, -i·est. 1.** Having the consistency or appearance of soup. **2.** Foggy.

sour (sour) adj. **-er, -est. 1.** Having a sharp or acid taste. **2.** Spoiled; rank; rancid: *a sour odor.* **3.** Bad-tempered. **4.** Unpleasant; disagreeable. **5.** Below standard; bad. **6.** Excessively acid and damaging to crops: *sour soil.* —n. **1.** The sensation of a sharp, acid taste, one of the four primary tastes. **2.** Something that is sour. —tr.v. **1.** To make sour. **2.** To make disagreeable, disillusioned, or disenchanted. —intr.v. **1.** To become sour. **2.** To become disagreeable or disillusioned. [Middle English, from Old English *sūr*.] —**sour′ly** adv. —**sour′ness** n.

sour·ball (sour′bôl′) n. A round piece of hard, tart candy.

source (sôrs, sōrs) n. **1.** A place or thing from which something comes or derives; point of origin. **2.** A spring or other body of water at which a stream or river originates. **3.** A cause, creator, or maker. **4.** A person, place, book, etc. that supplies information. —See Syns at **origin**. [Middle English, from Old French *sourse*, from *sourdre*, to rise, from Latin *surgere*.]

sour cherry. 1. A tree, *Prunus cerasus*, with white flowers and tart red fruit. **2.** The edible fruit of this tree.

sour·dough (sour′dō′) n. **1.** Sour fermented dough used as leaven for bread. **2.** *Slang.* An old-time settler or prospector, esp. in Alaska.

sour grapes. A belittling attitude toward something desired but unattained.

sour gum. A tree, *Nyssa sylvatica*, of eastern North America, with glossy, somewhat leathery leaves and soft wood.

sour·sop (sour′sŏp′) n. **1.** A tropical American tree, *Annona muricata*, that bears spiny fruit with tart, edible pulp. **2.** The fruit of this tree.

sou·sa·phone (sōō′zə-fōn′, -sə-) n. A large brass wind instrument similar to the tuba that has a flaring bell and is used in marching bands. [After John Philip *Sousa* (1854–1932), American bandmaster and composer.]

souse (sous) v. **soused, sous·ing.** —tr.v. **1.** To plunge in a liquid. **2.** To make soaking wet; drench. **3.** To steep. **4.** *Slang.* To make intoxicated. —intr.v. To become immersed or soaking wet. —n. **1.** The act or process of sousing. **2. a.** Food steeped in pickle, esp. pork trimmings. **b.** Brine. **3.** *Slang.* A drunkard. [Middle English *sousen*, to pickle, from *souse*, pickled meat, from Old French *sous*, from Old High German *sulza*, brine.]

sou·tane (sōō-tän′, -tăn′) n. A cassock worn by Roman Catholic priests. [French, from Italian *sottana*, underskirt, from *sotto*, under, from Latin *subtus*, beneath, from *sub*, under.]

south (south) n. **1. a.** The direction along a meridian 90 degrees clockwise from the direction from which the sun rises. **b.** The cardinal point on the compass 180 degrees clockwise from north. **2.** Often **South.** A region or part of the earth that lies in this direction. **3. the South.** The southern part of the United States, esp. the states that fought for the Confederacy during the Civil War. —*adj.* **1.** Of, in, or toward the south. **2.** Often **South.** Forming or belonging to a region, country, etc., toward the south: *South Korea.* **3.** From the south: *a dry south wind.* —*adv.* In a direction to or toward the south. [Middle English, from Old English *sūth.*]

south·bound (south′bound′) *adj.* Going toward the south.

south·east (south-ēst′, sou-ēst′) *n.* **1.** The direction that lies 45 degrees clockwise from east, or halfway between east and south. **2.** An area or region that lies in this direction. **3. the Southeast.** The part of the United States south of Pennsylvania and the Ohio River and east of the Mississippi River. —*adj.* **1.** Of, in, or toward the southeast. **2.** From the southeast: *a southeast wind.* —*adv.* In a direction to or toward the southeast. —**south·east·ern** *adj.*

south·east·er (south-ē′stər, sou-ē′-) *n.* A storm or gale that blows from the southeast.

south·east·er·ly (south-ē′stər-lē, sou-ē′-) *adj.* **1.** In or toward the southeast. **2.** From the southeast.

south·east·ward (south-ēst′wərd, sou-ēst′-). Also **south·east·wards** (-wərdz). —*adv.* To or toward the southeast. —*adj.:* *a southeastward journey.* —*n.* A direction or region to the southeast. —**south·east′ward·ly** *adj. & adv.*

south·er (sou′thər) *n.* A strong wind from the south.

south·er·ly (sŭth′ər-lē) *adj.* **1.** In or toward the south. **2.** From the south. —*n., pl.* **-lies.** A storm or wind from the south. —**south′er·ly** *adv.*

south·ern (sŭth′ərn) *adj.* **1.** Of, in, or toward the south. **2.** From the south. **3.** Characteristic of or found in southern regions: *a southern climate.* **4. Southern.** Of the South of the United States. [Middle English *southerne,* from Old English *sūtherne.*]

Southern Cross. A constellation in the Southern Hemisphere near Centaurus and Musca.

south·ern·er (sŭth′ər-nər) *n.* Often **Southerner. 1.** A person who lives in or comes from the south. **2.** A person from the South of the United States.

south·ern·most (sŭth′ərn-mōst′) *adj.* Farthest south.

south·land (south′lănd′, -lənd) *n.* Often **Southland.** A region in the south, esp. the South of the United States.

south·paw (south′pô′). *Slang.* —*n.* A left-handed person, esp. a left-handed baseball pitcher. —*adj.* Left-handed.

South Pole. 1. The southernmost point of the earth; the point in the south at which the earth's axis of rotation intersects the surface of the earth. **2.** The celestial zenith of the heavens as viewed from the south terrestrial pole. **3. south pole.** The south-pointing pole of a magnet.

south-south·east (south′south-ēst′, sou′sou-ēst′) *n.* The direction, or point on the compass, halfway between due south and southeast. —**south′-south·east′** *adj. & adv.*

south-south·west (south′south-wĕst′, sou′sou-wĕst′) *n.* The direction, or point on the compass, halfway between due south and southwest. —**south′-south·west′** *adj. & adv.*

south·ward (south′wərd, sŭth′ərd) *adv.* Also **south·wards** (south′wərdz, sŭth′ərdz). To or toward the south. —*adj.: a southward hike.* —*n.* A direction or region toward the south. —**south′ward·ly** *adj. & adv.*

south·west (south-wĕst′, sou-wĕst′) *n.* **1.** The direction or point on the compass 45 degrees clockwise from south; the direction halfway between south and west. **2.** An area or region lying in this direction. **3. the Southwest.** A region of the United States gen. considered to include New Mexico, Arizona, Texas, California, Nevada, Utah, and Colorado. —*adj.* **1.** Of, in, or toward the southwest. **2.** From the southwest. —*adv.* To or toward the southwest: *facing southwest.* —**south·west′ern** *adj.*

south·west·er (south-wĕs′tər, sou-wĕs′tər) *n.* Also **sou′-west·er** (sou-wĕs′tər). **1.** A storm or gale from the southwest. **2.** A waterproof hat with a broad brim in back.

south·west·er·ly (south-wĕs′tər-lē, sou-wĕs′-) *adj.* **1.** In or toward the southwest: *a southwesterly march.* **2.** From the southwest.

south·west·ward (south-wĕst′wərd, sou-wĕst′-) *adv.* Also **south·west·wards** (-wərdz). To or toward the southwest. —*n.* A direction or region to the southwest. —**south·west′ward** *adj. & adv.*

sou·ve·nir (sōō′və-nîr′) *n.* Something kept as a remembrance; a memento. —*modifier: a souvenir shop.* [French, from *souvenir,* to remember, from Latin *subvenīre,* to come to mind.]

sou′west·er (sou-wĕs′tər) *n.* Var. of **southwester.**

sov·er·eign (sŏv′ər-ən, sŏv′rən) *n.* **1.** The chief of state in a monarchy; a king or queen. **2.** A former British gold coin worth one pound. —*adj.* **1.** Paramount; supreme. **2.** Having supreme rank or power. **3.** Self-governing; independent. **4.** Unsurpassed; superior: *a sovereign remedy.* [Middle English *souverein,* from Old French, from Latin *super,* above.] —**sov′er·eign·ly** *adv.*

sov·er·eign·ty (sŏv′ər-ən-tē, sŏv′rən-) *n., pl.* **-ties. 1.** Supremacy of authority or rule: *sovereignty over a territory.* **2.** Royal rank, authority, or power. **3.** Complete independence and self-government. **4.** A territory existing as an independent state. —See Syns at **freedom.**

so·vi·et (sō′vē-ĕt′, -ĭt, sŏv′ē-) *n.* **1.** In the Soviet Union, one of the popularly elected legislative assemblies that exist at local, regional, and national levels. **2. the Soviets.** The people and government of the Soviet Union. —*adj.* **1.** Of a soviet. **2. Soviet.** Of the Soviet Union. [Russian *sovet,* council, from Old Russian *suvĕtu.*]

sow[1] (sō) *v.* **sowed, sown** (sōn) or **sowed, sow·ing.** —*tr.v.* **1.** To plant (seeds) to produce a crop. **2.** To plant or scatter seed in or upon. **3.** To spread; propagate; disperse: *sow rumors and dissension.* **4.** To strew or cover. —*intr.v.* To scatter seed for growing. [Middle English *sowen,* from Old English *sāwan.*] —**sow′er** *n.*

sow[2] (sou) *n.* **1.** A full-grown female pig. **2.** The full-grown female of certain other animals. [Middle English, from Old English *sugu.*]

sow bug. Any of various small, oval, terrestrial crustaceans, chiefly of the genera *Oniscus* and *Porcellio,* that are commonly found under logs or stones. Also called **wood louse.**

sown (sōn) *v.* A past participle of **sow** (to plant).

sow thistle. Any of various plants of the genus *Sonchus,* esp. *S. oleraceus,* native to Europe, with prickly leaves.

sox (sŏks) *n.* A plural of **sock** (stocking).

soy (soi) *n.* Also **soy·a** (soi′ə). **1.** Soybeans. **2.** Soy sauce. [Japanese *shō-yu,* soy sauce, from Chinese *shi-yu,* "bean oil."]

soy·a (soi′ə) *n.* Var. of **soy.**

soy·bean (soi′bēn′) *n.* **1.** A leguminous Asiatic plant, *Glycine max,* widely cultivated for forage, soil improvement, and for its nutritious, edible seeds. **2.** The seed of this plant. Also called **soya bean.**

soybean

soy sauce. Also **soya sauce.** A brown, salty liquid made from soybeans and used to flavor food.

spa (spä) *n.* **1.** A spring whose waters contain dissolved mineral salts. **2.** A resort area where such springs exist. [After *Spa,* a resort town in Belgium.]

space (spās) *n.* **1. a.** A set of points or elements that is assumed to satisfy some set of geometric postulates: *non-Euclidean space.* **b.** The familiar three-dimensional field of everyday experience. **2. a.** The expanse in which the solar system, stars, and galaxies exist; the universe. **b.** The distance between a pair of objects, events, etc. **3.** Any blank or empty area: *the spaces between words. Fill in the blank space.* **4.** An area provided for a particular purpose: *a parking space.* **5. a.** A period or interval of time. **b.** A little while: *for a space.* **6.** An interval during a telegraph transmission when the key is not in contact. **7.** A reserved or available accommodation. **—*modifier:*** *space travel.* **—*tr.v.*** **spaced, spac·ing.** To arrange or organize with spaces between. [Middle English, distance, from Old French *espace,* from Latin *spatium.*] **—spac'er** *n.*

space·craft (spās'krăft') *n., pl.* **spacecraft.** A vehicle designed to be launched into space.

space flight. Flight beyond the atmosphere of earth.

space heater. A small, usu. portable device used to heat a limited enclosed area.

space·man (spās'măn') *n.* A person who travels in outer space; an astronaut.

space·port (spās'pôrt', -pōrt') *n.* An installation for testing and launching spacecraft.

space shuttle. A space vehicle designed to transport astronauts between the earth and an orbiting space station.

space station. A large manned satellite placed in permanent orbit around the earth.

space suit. A protective pressurized suit designed to allow the wearer to move about freely in space.

spa·cial (spā'shəl) *adj.* Var. of **spatial.**

spac·ing (spā'sĭng) *n.* The separation between things, usu. according to a specified arrangement.

spa·cious (spā'shəs) *adj.* **1.** Large; extensive. **2.** Wide in range or scope: *a spacious view.* **—See Syns at broad.** **—spa'cious·ly** *adv.* **—spa'cious·ness** *n.*

Spack·le (spăk'əl) *n.* A trademark for a powder to be mixed with water, or a ready-to-use plastic paste, designed to fill cracks and holes in plaster before painting or papering. **—*tr.v.*** **-led, -ling.** To fill or repair with Spackle.

spade[1] (spād) *n.* **1.** A digging tool with a long handle and a flat iron blade that is pressed into the ground with the foot. **2.** Any of various similar tools. **—*tr.v.*** **spad·ed, spad·ing.** To dig or place with a spade. [Middle English, from Old English *spadu.*] **—spad'er** *n.*

spade[2] (spād) *n.* **1.** A black figure, shaped like an inverted heart with a short stalk at the bottom, on a playing card. **2.** A card bearing this figure. **3. spades.** The suit on a deck of cards identified by this figure. [Italian *spada,* "broad sword" (from its shape), from Latin *spatha,* spatula, from Greek *spathē,* broad blade.]

spade·work (spād'wûrk') *n.* **1.** Work requiring a spade. **2.** Any preparatory work necessary to a project or activity.

spa·dix (spā'dĭks) *n., pl.* **spa·di·ces** (-dĭ-sēz'). A clublike stalk bearing tiny flowers, often surrounded by a leaflike or petallike part, as in the jack-in-the-pulpit. [Latin *spādīx,* broken-off palm branch, from Greek *spadix.*]

spa·ghet·ti (spə-gĕt'ē) *n.* Pasta made into long, solid strings and cooked by boiling. **—*modifier:*** *spaghetti sauce.* [Italian, pl. dim. of *spago,* string.]

spake (spāk) *v. Archaic.* Past tense of **speak.** [Middle English *spaak,* from Old English *spæc.*]

span[1] (spăn) *n.* **1.** The distance between two points, lines, objects, etc. **2. a.** The distance that a horizontal structural part extends between vertical supports. **b.** A section of a bridge that extends from one point of vertical support to another. **3.** The distance from the tip of the thumb to the tip of the little finger when the hand is fully extended, formerly used as a unit of measure equal to about 9 in. **4.** A period of time: *a span of four hours.* **—*tr.v.*** **spanned, span·ning. 1.** To stretch the extended hand over or across. **2.** To extend across: *a memory that spans 30 years.* [Middle English, short interval, from Old English *span(n).*]

span[2] (spăn) *n.* A pair of harnessed or matched animals, such as oxen. [Middle Dutch *spannen.*]

span·drel (spăn'drəl) *n.* Also **span·dril.** *Archit.* **1.** The triangular space between the left or right outer curve of an arch and the rectangular framework surrounding it. **2.** The space between two arches and a horizontal molding or cornice above them. [Middle English *spaundrell,* dim. of Norman French *spaundere,* from Old French *espandre,* to expand, from Latin *expandere.*]

span·gle (spăng'gəl) *n.* **1.** A small, often circular disk of shiny metal or plastic sewn esp. on garments for decoration; a sequin. **2.** Any small sparkling object. **—*v.*** **-gled, -gling. —*tr.v.*** To decorate with or as if with spangles. **—*intr.v.*** To sparkle in the manner of spangles. [Middle

English *spangele,* dim. of *spange,* from Middle Dutch, ornament, buckle.]

span·iel (spăn'yəl) *n.* Any of several breeds of small to medium-sized dogs, with drooping ears, short legs, and a silky, wavy coat. [Middle English *spaynel,* from Old French *espaignol,* Spanish, from Latin *Hispāniolus,* from *Hispānia,* Spain.]

Span·ish (spăn'ĭsh) *n.* **1. the Spanish.** The people of Spain. **2.** The Romance language of Spain and those areas of Latin America once under Spanish domination. **—*adj.*** Of Spain, the Spanish, or their language.

Spanish fly. 1. A European blister beetle, *Lytta vesicatoria.* **2.** A preparation produced from these beetles, formerly used as a medicine and as an aphrodisiac.

Spanish moss. An epiphytic plant, *Tillandsia usneoides,* of the southeastern United States and tropical America, that forms drooping clusters of threadlike stems.

Spanish onion. A mild-flavored, yellow-skinned onion.

spank (spăngk) *tr.v.* To slap on the buttocks with a flat object or with the open hand as punishment. **—*n.*** A slap on the buttocks. [Perh. imit.]

spank·er (spăng'kər) *n.* A fore-and-aft sail set abaft the after mast of a square-rigged sailing ship.

spanker

spank·ing (spăng'kĭng) *adj.* **1.** *Informal.* Exceptional of its kind; remarkable. **2.** Quick; lively. **3.** Brisk and fresh: *a spanking breeze.* [Orig. unknown.]

span·ner (spăn'ər) *n. Brit.* A wrench. [Obs. *spanner,* winding tool, from German *Spanner,* from *spannen,* to stretch, tighten, from Old High German *spannan.*]

span·worm (spăn'wûrm') *n.* An inchworm.

spar[1] (spär) *n.* **1.** *Naut.* A wooden or metal pole used as a mast, boom, etc., to support rigging. **2.** A principal longitudinal structural member in an airplane wing. **—*tr.v.*** **sparred, spar·ring.** To supply with spars. [Middle English *sparre,* pole, from Old Norse *sperra,* beam.]

spar[2] (spär) *intr.v.* **sparred, spar·ring. 1.** To box, esp. for practice. **2.** To bandy words about; to dispute. **—*n.*** The act of sparring. [Middle English *sparren,* to strike rapidly, from Old English *sperran,* to strike.]

spar[3] (spär) *n.* Any of various minerals that are nonmetallic, have a glassy luster, and break easily along planes of cleavage. [Low German, from Middle Low German.]

spare (spâr) *v.* **spared, spar·ing. —*tr.v.*** **1. a.** To treat mercifully; deal with leniently. **b.** To refrain from harming or destroying. **2.** To save or relieve from pain, shame, trouble, etc. **3.** To use with restraint: *spare the horses.* **4.** To give or grant out of one's resources: *spare ten minutes.* **—*intr.v.*** **1.** To be frugal. **2.** To be merciful or lenient. **—*adj.*** **spar·er, spar·est. 1. a.** Kept in reserve: *a spare tire.* **b.** Extra: *spare cash.* **c.** Free for other use; unoccupied: *spare time.* **2. a.** Economical; meager: *a spare budget.* **b.** Thin or lean. **—See Syns at thin. —*n.*** **1.** A replacement, such as a tire, reserved for future need. **2.** *Bowling.* **a.** The act of knocking down all ten pins with two successive rolls of the ball. **b.** The score made by doing this. [Middle English *sparen,* to leave unharmed, show mercy, from Old English *sparian.*] **—spare'ly** *adv.* **—spare'ness** *n.*

spare·ribs (spâr'rĭbz') *pl.n.* A cut of pork that consists of the lower ribs with most of the meat trimmed off. [From Low German *ribbespēr,* from Middle Low German : *ribbe,* rib + *spēr,* spit.]

spar·ing (spâr'ĭng) *adj.* **1.** Thrifty; frugal. **2.** Lenient.

3. Scanty. **—spar'ing·ly** *adv.* **—spar'ing·ness** *n.*

spark¹ (spärk) *n.* **1.** A glowing particle, such as one thrown off from a fire. **2.** A glistening particle of something, such as metal. **3. a.** A brief flash of light, esp. one produced by electric discharge. **b.** An electric discharge of this kind, esp. a short one. **c.** The current that flows in such a discharge. **4.** A quality or factor with latent potential; a seed: *the spark of genius.* **5.** A vital or animating factor. **—***intr.v.* To produce or give off sparks. **—***tr.v.* To set in motion or rouse to action: *sparked a desire for freedom.* [Middle English *sparke*, from Old English *spærca.*]

spark² (spärk) *n.* **1.** A young dandy or gallant. **2.** A lover; suitor. **—***tr.v.* To court or woo. **—***intr.v.* To be a suitor. [Perh. ult. from Old Norse *sparkr*, lively.]

spar·kle (spär'kəl) *intr.v.* **-kled, -kling. 1.** To give off or produce sparks. **2.** To give off or reflect flashes of light. **3.** To be brilliant or witty. **4.** To release gas bubbles; effervesce: *Champagne sparkles.* **—***n.* **1.** A small spark or glowing particle. **2.** A glittering quality or appearance. **3.** Effervescence. **4.** Vivacity. [Middle English *sparklen*, freq. of *sparken*, to spark, from *sparke*, spark.]

spar·kler (spär'klər) *n.* **1.** Someone or something that sparkles. **2.** A firework that burns slowly and produces a shower of sparks. **3.** *Informal.* A diamond.

spark plug. 1. A device inserted in the head of an internal-combustion-engine cylinder that ignites the fuel mixture by means of an electric spark. **2.** *Informal.* A person who gives life or energy to an undertaking.

spar·row (spăr'ō) *n.* **1.** Any of various small New World birds of the genera *Spizella, Zonotrichia, Melospiza* and related genera. **2.** Any of several similar or related birds, such as the common house sparrow. [Middle English *sparowe*, from Old English *spearwa.*]

sparrow hawk. 1. A small North American falcon, *Falco sparverius*, that preys on small birds and animals. **2.** A similar European hawk, *Accipiter nisus.*

sparrow hawk   **spat³**

sparse (spärs) *adj.* **spars·er, spars·est.** Growing or settled at widely spaced intervals: *a sparse population.* [Latin *sparsus*, past part. of *spargere*, to scatter.] **—sparse'ly** *adv.* **—sparse'ness** or **spar'si·ty** (spär'sĭ-tē) *n.*

Spar·tan (spär'tn) *adj.* **1.** Of Sparta or its people. **2.** Resembling the Spartans in fortitude or self-discipline; rigorous; austere: *a Spartan diet.* **—***n.* **1.** A citizen of Sparta. **2.** Someone of Spartan character. **—Spar'tan·ism'** *n.*

spasm (spăz'əm) *n.* **1.** A sudden, involuntary contraction of a muscle. **2.** A sudden outburst. [Middle English *spasme*, from Old French, from Latin *spasmus*, from Greek *spasmos*, from *span*, to draw, pull.]

spas·mod·ic (spăz-mŏd'ĭk) *adj.* **1.** Of, like, or affected by a spasm; convulsive. **2.** Happening intermittently; fitful. **3.** Given to sudden outbursts of energy or feeling; excitable. [Greek *spasmodikos*, from *spasmos*, spasm.] **—spas·mod'i·cal·ly** *adv.*

spas·tic (spăs'tĭk) *adj.* Of, affected by, or displaying spasms. **—***n.* **1.** A person suffering from muscular spasms. **2.** A person afflicted with spastic paralysis. [Latin *spasticus*, from Greek *spastikos*, from *span*, to pull, draw.] **—spas'ti·cal·ly** *adv.*

spastic paralysis. A chronic diseased condition involving exaggerated tendon reflexes and muscular spasms accompanying hardening of the spinal cord.

spat¹ (spăt) *v.* A past tense and past participle of **spit** (to eject saliva). [From SPIT, formed on the model of such verbs as *sit, sat, sat.*]

spat² (spăt) *n., pl.* **spat** or **spats.** An oyster or similar bivalve mollusk in the larval stage. [Orig. unknown.]

spat³ (spăt) *n.* Often **spats.** A cloth or leather gaiter covering the shoe upper and the ankle and fastening under the shoe with a strap. [Short for earlier *spatterdash.*]

spat⁴ (spăt) *n.* **1.** A brief, petty quarrel. **2.** *Informal.* A slap or smack. **3.** A spattering sound, as of raindrops. **—***v.* **spat·ted, spat·ting. —***intr.v.* **1.** To engage in a brief, petty quarrel. **2.** To strike with a light spattering sound; to slap. **—***tr.v.* *Informal.* To slap. [Orig. unknown.]

spate (spāt) *n.* A sudden flood, rush, or outpouring: *a spate of words.* [Middle English *spate.*]

spathe (spā*th*) *n.* A leaflike organ that encloses or spreads from the base of the spadix of certain plants, such as the jack-in-the-pulpit or the calla. [Latin *spatha*, broad flat instrument, from Greek *spathē*, broad blade.]

spa·tial (spā'shəl) *adj.* Also **spa·cial.** Of or relating to space. [From Latin *spatium*, space.] **—spa'tial·ly** *adv.*

spat·ter (spăt'ər) *tr.v.* **1.** To scatter (a liquid substance) in drops or small splashes. **2.** To spot, splash, or soil. **3.** To defame. **—***intr.v.* **1.** To spit out small splashes; splatter. **2.** To fall with a splash or a splashing sound. **—***n.* **1.** The act or sound of spattering. **2.** A drop or splash of something spattered. [Prob. of Low German orig.]

spat·ter·dock (spăt'ər-dŏk') *n.* An aquatic plant, *Nuphar advena*, of eastern North America, with broad leaves and yellow flowers. [SPATTER + DOCK (plant).]

spat·u·la (spăch'ə-lə) *n.* A small implement with a broad, flat, flexible blade that is used esp. to spread or mix frosting, plaster, paint, etc. [Latin *spathula*, dim. of *spatha*, broad sword, from Greek *spathē.*]

spat·u·late (spăch'ə-lət) *adj.* Shaped like a spatula.

spav·in (spăv'ĭn) *n.* Either of two diseases affecting the hock joint of horses and causing stiffness and lameness. [Middle English *spaveyne*, from Old French *espavin.*] **—spav'ined** *adj.*

spawn (spôn) *n.* **1.** The eggs of aquatic animals such as bivalve mollusks, fishes, and amphibians. **2.** Offspring produced in large numbers; brood. **3.** The product or outcome of something. **4.** Fragments of mycelia used to start a mushroom culture. **—***intr.v.* **1.** To deposit eggs; produce spawn. **2.** To produce many offspring. **—***tr.v.* **1.** To produce (spawn). **2.** To give rise to; engender. [Middle English *spawne*, from *spawnen*, to spawn, from Norman French *espaundre*, to shed roe, from Old French *espandre*, to shed, from Latin *expandere*, to expand.]

spay (spā) *tr.v.* To remove the ovaries of (a female animal). [Middle English *spayen*, from Old French *espeer*, to cut with a sword, from *espee*, sword, from Latin *spatha*, broad sword, from Greek *spathē.*]

speak (spēk) *v.* **spoke** (spōk), **spo·ken** (spō'kən), **speak·ing. —***intr.v.* **1.** To utter words; talk. **2. a.** To converse. **b.** To be on good terms: *They are no longer speaking.* **3.** To make a speech. **4.** To convey a message: *Actions speak louder than words.* **5.** To emit a report on firing. **—***tr.v.* **1.** To articulate with the voice: *speak words.* **2.** To converse in or be able to converse in: *speak Spanish.* **3.** To express aloud; tell: *spoke the truth.* **—phrasal verbs. speak down.** To speak condescendingly: *speaking down to children.* **speak for. 1.** To speak in behalf of: *spoke for my client.* **2.** To claim: *This ticket is spoken for.* **speak out. 1.** To talk loudly and clearly. **2.** To talk freely and fearlessly. **speak up. 1.** To raise the voice. **2.** To speak without hesitation or fear. **—idioms. so to speak.** In a manner of speaking. **to speak of.** Worthy of mention. [Middle English *speken*, from Old English *sprecan.*]

speak·eas·y (spēk'ē'zē) *n., pl.* **-ies.** *Slang.* A place for the illegal sale of alcoholic drinks, as during U.S. Prohibition.

speak·er (spē'kər) *n.* **1. a.** A person who speaks. **b.** A spokesman. **2.** A person who delivers a public speech. **3.** Often **Speaker.** The presiding officer of a legislative assembly. **4.** A loud-speaker.

speak·er·ship (spē'kər-shĭp') *n.* The position of presiding officer of a legislative assembly.

speak·ing (spē'kĭng) *adj.* **1.** Expressive or telling; eloquent. **2.** Striking; true to life: *a speaking likeness.*

ă pat   ā pay   â care   ä father   ĕ pet   ē be   hw which   ĭ pit   ī tie   î pier   ŏ pot   ō toe   ô paw, for   oi noise
ōō took   ōō boot   ou out   th thin   *th* this   ŭ cut   û urge   zh vision   ə about, item, edible, gallop, circus

spear (spîr) *n.* **1.** A weapon consisting of a long shaft with a sharply pointed head. **2.** A shaft with a sharp point and barbs for spearing fish. **3.** A slender stalk, as of asparagus. —*modifier: spear wounds.* —*tr.v.* **1.** To pierce with or as if with a spear. **2.** To catch with a thrust of the arm: *spear the football.* —*intr.v.* **1.** To stab with or as if with a spear. **2.** To sprout like a spear. [Middle English *spere,* from Old English.] —**spear'er** *n.*

spear

spear·head (spîr'hĕd') *n.* **1.** The sharpened head of a spear. **2. a.** The front forces of a military attack. **b.** A leading force. —*tr.v.* To be the leader of (a drive or an attack).
spear·man (spîr'mən) *n.* A soldier armed with a spear.
spear·mint (spîr'mĭnt') *n.* An aromatic plant, *Mentha spicata,* native to Europe, that has clusters of small purplish flowers and yields an oil widely used as flavoring.
spe·cial (spĕsh'əl) *adj.* **1.** Exceptional: *a special occasion.* **2. a.** Distinct among others of a kind; singular. **b.** Primary: *one's special interest.* **3.** Particular: *his own special chair.* **4. a.** Having a limited or specific function, application, or scope: *a special role in the mission.* **b.** Arranged for a particular occasion or purpose. **5.** Additional; extra. —*n.* **1.** Something arranged or designed for a particular service or occasion: *a television special.* **2.** A featured attraction, such as a reduced price: *a special on lamb chops.* [Middle English, from Old French *especial,* from Latin *speciālis,* from *speciēs,* kind, species.] —**spe'cial·ly** *adv.*
special delivery. The delivery of a piece of mail, for an additional charge, by a special messenger rather than by scheduled delivery. —**spe'cial-de·liv'er·y** *adj.*
spe·cial·ist (spĕsh'ə-lĭst) *n.* **1.** A person who has devoted himself to a particular branch of study or research. **2.** A physician certified to limit his practice to one branch of medicine. —**spe'cial·is'tic** *adj.*
spe·ci·al·i·ty (spĕsh'ē-ăl'ĭ-tē) *n., pl.* **-ties.** **1.** A distinguishing mark or feature. **2. specialities.** Details; particulars. **3.** *Brit.* A specialty.
spe·cial·ize (spĕsh'ə-līz') *v.* **-ized, -iz·ing.** —*intr.v.* **1.** To train or employ oneself in a special study or activity. **2.** *Biol.* To develop so as to become adapted to a specific environment or function. **3.** To concentrate on a particular activity or product: *The shop specializes in large-size clothing.* —*tr.v.* **1.** To make specific mention of; specify. **2.** To give a particular character or function to. **3.** *Biol.* To adapt to a specific environment or function. —**spe'cial·i·za'tion** *n.*
spe·cial·ty (spĕsh'əl-tē) *n., pl.* **-ties.** **1.** A special pursuit, occupation, service, product, etc.: *Her specialty is portrait painting.* **2.** An aspect of medicine to which physicians confine their practice. **3.** A special feature or characteristic; peculiarity. **4.** The condition or quality of being special. —*modifier: a specialty shop.*
spe·cie (spē'shē, -sē) *n.* Coined money; coin. [Latin *(in) specie,* "(in) kind," from *speciēs,* kind, species.]
spe·cies (spē'shēz, -sēz) *n., pl.* **species.** **1.** *Biol.* **a.** A fundamental category of taxonomic classification consisting of organisms capable of interbreeding. **b.** An organism belonging to such a category, identified by a Latin adjective or epithet following a genus name. **2.** A kind, variety, or type. **3.** *Rom. Cath. Ch.* Either of the consecrated elements of the Eucharist. —See Syns at **kind.** [Latin *speciēs,* kind, species, from *specere,* to look at.]
spe·cif·ic (spĭ-sĭf'ĭk) *adj.* **1.** Explicitly set forth; particular; definite. **2.** Of, characterizing, or relating to a plant or animal species. **3.** Special, distinctive, or unique. **4.** Intended for, applying to, or acting upon a particular thing. **5.** Effective in the treatment of a particular disease: *home remedies specific for asthma.* —See Syns at **explicit.** —*n.* **1.** Something specific. **2.** A remedy for some particular ailment or disorder. [Medieval Latin *specificus,* from Latin *speciēs,* kind, species.] —**spe·cif'i·cal·ly** *adv.* —**spec'i·fic'i·ty** (spĕs'ə-fĭs'ĭ-tē) *n.*
spec·i·fi·ca·tion (spĕs'ə-fĭ-kā'shən) *n.* **1.** An act of specifying. **2. a. specifications.** A detailed and exact statement of particulars, esp. a statement fully describing something to be built, installed, printed, etc. **b.** A single item or article in such a statement.
specific gravity. *Abbr.* **sp gr** The ratio of the mass of a solid or liquid to the mass of an equal volume of distilled water at 4°C or of a gas to an equal volume of air or hydrogen under prescribed conditions of temperature and pressure.
specific heat. *Abbr.* **sp ht** **1.** The ratio of the amount of heat required to raise the temperature of a unit mass of a substance by one unit of temperature to the amount of heat required to raise the temperature of a similar mass of water by the same amount. **2.** The amount of heat, measured in calories, required to raise the temperature of one gram of a substance by one degree Celsius.
spec·i·fy (spĕs'ə-fī) *tr.v.* **-fied, -fy·ing.** **1.** To state in a clear, unambiguous way. **2.** To include in a specification. [Middle English *specifien,* from Old French *specifier,* from Medieval Latin *specificāre,* from *specificus,* specific.]
spec·i·men (spĕs'ə-mən) *n.* An element or a part taken as representative of an entire set or whole; a sample. [Latin, mark, token, from *specere,* to look at.]
spe·cious (spē'shəs) *adj.* Attractive but false; deceptive: *a specious argument.* —See Syns at **false.** [Middle English, attractive, fair, from Latin *speciōsus,* good-looking, from *speciēs,* appearance, from *specere,* to look at.] —**spe'cious·ly** *adv.* —**spe'cious·ness** *n.*
speck (spĕk) *n.* **1.** A small spot or mark. **2.** A particle: *a speck of dust.* —*tr.v.* To mark with specks; to speckle. [Middle English *specke,* from Old English *specca.*]
speck·le (spĕk'əl) *n.* A speck or small spot, esp. a natural dot of color on skin, plumage, or foliage. —*tr.v.* **-led, -ling.** To mark or cover with or as if with speckles. [Perh. from Middle Dutch *spekkel.*]
speckled trout. The brook trout.
specs (spĕks) *pl.n. Informal.* **1.** Also **specks.** Eyeglasses; spectacles. **2.** Specifications, as for construction work.
spec·ta·cle (spĕk'tə-kəl) *n.* **1.** A public performance or display. **2. a.** A marvel or curiosity. **b.** An object or scene regrettably exposed to the public gaze. **3.** Something seen or able to be seen. **4. spectacles.** A pair of eyeglasses. [Middle English, from Old French, from Latin *spectāculum,* from *spectāre,* to look at, freq. of *specere.*]
spec·ta·cled (spĕk'tə-kəld) *adj.* Wearing spectacles.
spec·tac·u·lar (spĕk-tăk'yə-lər) *adj.* Of the nature of a spectacle; sensational; marvelous. —*n.* Something that is spectacular. —**spec·tac'u·lar·ly** *adv.*
spec·ta·tor (spĕk'tā'tər) *n.* **1.** A person who attends and views a show, sports event, etc. **2.** An observer of an event; eyewitness; onlooker. —*modifier: a spectator sport.* [Latin *spectātor,* from *spectāre,* to look at.]
spec·ter (spĕk'tər) *n.* Also *Brit.* **spec·tre.** **1.** A ghost; phantom; apparition. **2.** A threatening or haunting possibility: *the specter of nuclear war.* [French *spectre,* from Latin *spectrum,* appearance, image.]
spec·tra (spĕk'trə) *n.* A plural of **spectrum.**
spec·tral (spĕk'trəl) *adj.* **1.** Of or resembling a specter; ghostly. **2.** Of or produced by a spectrum. —See Syns at **ghastly.** —**spec'tral·ly** *adv.* —**spec'tral·ness** *n.*
spec·tre (spĕk'tər) *n. Brit.* Var. of **specter.**
spectro-. A prefix meaning spectrum: *spectrograph.* [From SPECTRUM.]
spec·tro·gram (spĕk'trə-grăm') *n.* A graph or photograph of a spectrum.
spec·tro·graph (spĕk'trə-grăf') *n.* **1.** A spectroscope equipped to photograph spectra. **2.** A spectrogram. —**spec'tro·graph'ic** *adj.* —**spec'tro·graph'i·cal·ly** *adv.* —**spec·trog'ra·phy** (-trŏg'rə-fē) *n.*
spec·trom·e·ter (spĕk-trŏm'ĭ-tər) *n.* **1.** A spectroscope

equipped for measuring the wavelengths of radiation observed by it. **2.** An instrument used to measure indices of refraction. —**spec·tro·met·ric** (-trə-mĕt′rĭk) *adj.* —**spec·trom′e·try** *n.*

spec·tro·scope (spĕk′trə-skōp′) *n.* Any of various instruments used to resolve radiation into spectra. —**spec′tro·scop′ic** (-skŏp′ĭk). —**spec′tro·scop′i·cal·ly** *adv.* —**spec·tros′co·py** (spĕk-trŏs′kə-pē) *n.*

spec·trum (spĕk′trəm) *n.*, *pl.* -**tra** (-trə) or -**trums. 1.** The distribution of a characteristic of a physical system or phenomenon, esp.: **a.** The bands of color seen when white light, esp. light from the sun, is broken up by refraction, as in a rainbow or by a prism. **b.** The distribution of energy emitted by any radiant source, arranged in order of wavelengths. **c.** A graphic or photographic representation of any such distribution. **2. a.** A range of values of a quantity or set of related quantities. **b.** A broad sequence or range: *the whole spectrum of 20th-century thought.* [Latin, appearance, image, form, from *specere*, to look at.]

spec·u·la (spĕk′yə-lə) *n.* A plural of **speculum.**

spec·u·lar (spĕk′yə-lər) *adj.* Of, resembling, or produced by a mirror or speculum.

spec·u·late (spĕk′yə-lāt′) *intr.v.* -**lat·ed, -lat·ing. 1.** To meditate on a given subject; reflect. **2.** To theorize without sufficient evidence for certainty. **3.** To engage in risky business ventures that offer the chance of large profits. [From Latin *speculārī*, to watch, observe, from *specula*, watchtower, from *specere*, to look at.] —**spec′u·la′tion** *n.* —**spec′u·la·tive** *adj.* —**spec′u·la′tor** *n.*

spec·u·lum (spĕk′yə-ləm) *n.*, *pl.* -**la** (-lə) or -**lums. 1.** A mirror or polished metal plate used as a reflector in optical instruments. **2.** An instrument for dilating the opening of a body cavity for medical examination. **3.** A bright spot of color on the wing of a bird or insect. [Latin, mirror, from *specere*, to look at.]

sped (spĕd) *v.* A past tense and past participle of **speed.**

speech (spēch) *n.* **1.** The act of speaking. **2.** The ability to speak. **3.** That which is spoken; an utterance. **4.** The manner in which a person speaks. **5.** A talk or address, esp. one prepared for delivery to an audience. **6.** The language or dialect of a nation or region. —*modifier: a speech defect; speech sounds.* [Middle English *speche*, from Old English *spĕc, sprǽc.*]
  Syns: 1. speech, discourse, talk, utterance, voice *n.* Core meaning: The faculty, act, or product of speaking (*a sore throat that made speech difficult; words occurring often in speech*). **2. speech, lecture, oration, talk** *n.* Core meaning: A formal oral communication to an audience (*a valedictory speech at graduation*). See also Syns at **language.**

speech·i·fy (spē′chə-fī′) *intr.v.* -**fied, -fy·ing.** To orate; harangue. —**speech′i·fi′er** *n.*

speech·less (spēch′lĭs) *adj.* **1.** Lacking the faculty of speech; dumb. **2.** Temporarily unable to speak, as through astonishment. **3.** Refraining from speech; silent. **4.** Unexpressed or inexpressible in words: *speechless admiration.* —**speech′less·ly** *adv.* —**speech′less·ness** *n.*

speed (spēd) *n.* **1.** The rate or a measure of the rate of motion, esp. distance traveled divided by the time of travel. **2.** A rate of action, activity, or performance: *the speed of a chemical reaction.* **3.** Rapidity; swiftness. **4.** A transmission gear or set of gears in a motor vehicle. **5.** *Photog.* **a.** A numerical expression of the sensitivity of a film, plate, or paper to light. **b.** The capacity of a lens to accumulate light at an appropriate aperture. **c.** The length of time required or permitted for a camera shutter to open and admit light. **6.** *Slang.* Any amphetamine drug. **7.** *Archaic.* Prosperity; success; luck. —See Syns at **haste.** —*v.* **sped** (spĕd) or **speed·ed, speed·ing.** —*tr.v.* **1. a.** To hasten. **b.** To send or dispatch with speed or haste. **2. a.** To increase the speed or rate of; accelerate. **b.** To set the speed of (a machine). **3.** To drive (a motor vehicle) at a high or illegal rate of speed. **4. a.** To wish Godspeed to. **b.** *Archaic.* To help to succeed or prosper; to aid. —*intr.v.* **1. a.** To go or move rapidly. **b.** To drive fast; exceed a traffic speed limit. **2.** To pass quickly: *The months sped by.* **3.** To accelerate: *The car speeds up on hills.* —See Syns at **expedite** and **rush.** [Middle English *spede*, success, speed, from Old English *spĕd.*]

speed·boat (spēd′bōt′) *n.* A fast motorboat.

speed·er (spē′dər) *n.* Someone or something that speeds, esp. a driver who exceeds a legal or safe speed.

speed limit. The maximum speed of vehicles that is legally permitted on a given stretch of road.

speed·om·e·ter (spē-dŏm′ĭ-tər, spĭ-) *n.* **1.** An instrument for indicating speed. **2.** An odometer.

speed·ster (spēd′stər) *n.* **1.** A speeder. **2.** A fast car.

speed trap. A stretch of road where traffic speed is secretly checked by police using electronic or other devices.

speed·up (spēd′ŭp′) *n.* An increase in speed, esp. of production without increase in pay.

speed·way (spēd′wā′) *n.* **1.** A course for automobile racing. **2.** A road designed for fast-moving traffic.

speed·well (spēd′wĕl′) *n.* Any of various plants of the genus *Veronica*, with clusters of small, usu. blue flowers.

speed·y (spē′dē) *adj.* -**i·er, -i·est. 1.** Characterized by rapid motion; swift. **2.** Prompt; quick: *a speedy recovery.* —See Syns at **fast.** —**speed′i·ly** *adv.* —**speed′i·ness** *n.*

spe·le·ol·o·gy (spē′lē-ŏl′ə-jē) *n.* **1.** The study of caves. **2.** The exploration of caves. [Latin *spēleum*, cave, from Greek *spēlaion* + -LOGY.] —**spe′le·ol′o·gist** *n.*

spell[1] (spĕl) *v.* **spelled** or **spelt** (spĕlt), **spell·ing.** —*tr.v.* **1.** To name or write in order the letters of (a word or part of a word). **2.** To be the letters of; form (a word). **3.** To mean; signify. —*intr.v.* To form a word or words correctly by means of letters. —*phrasal verb.* **spell out. 1.** To make explicit; specify. **2.** To read slowly, letter by letter. [Middle English *spellen*, to read out, from Old French *espeller*, of Germanic orig.]

spell[2] (spĕl) *n.* **1.** An incantational word or formula. **2.** A bewitched state; trance. **3.** Compelling attraction; fascination. —*tr.v.* To put under a spell. [Middle English, discourse, from Old English, story, fable.]

spell[3] (spĕl) *n.* **1.** A short, indefinite period of time. **2.** *Informal.* A period of weather: *a dry spell.* **3.** A short turn of work; turn; shift. **4.** *Informal.* A period, bout, or fit of illness, indisposition, or irritability. —*tr.v.* To relieve (someone) from work temporarily by taking a turn. [Perh. from Middle English *spelen*, to relieve at work, from Old English *spelian*, to substitute.]

spell·bind (spĕl′bīnd′) *tr.v.* -**bound** (-bound′), -**bind·ing.** To hold under a spell; enthrall. —See Syns at **charm.**

spell·bind·er (spĕl′bīn′dər) *n.* An eloquent orator.

spell·ing (spĕl′ĭng) *n.* **1.** The forming of words with letters in an accepted order; orthography. **2.** The way in which a word is spelled. —*modifier: spelling lessons.*

spelt[1] (spĕlt) *n.* A hardy wheat, *Triticum spelta*, grown mostly in Europe. [Prob. from Middle Dutch *spelte.*]

spelt[2] (spĕlt) *v.* A past tense and past participle of **spell** (to form words).

spel·ter (spĕl′tər) *n.* Zinc, esp. in the form of ingots, slabs, or plates. [Perh. from Middle Dutch *speauter.*]

spe·lunk·er (spĭ-lŭng′kər, spē′lŭng′kər) *n.* A person who explores and studies caves; a speleologist. [From obs. *spelunk*, cave, from Middle English, from Latin *spelunca*, from Greek *spēlunx.*] —**spe·lun′king** *n.*

spend (spĕnd) *v.* **spent** (spĕnt), **spend·ing.** —*tr.v.* **1.** To use up or put out; expend: *spent an hour each day practicing.* **2.** To pay out (money); disburse. **3.** To exhaust; wear out: *spent his creative energies early.* **4.** To pass (time) in a specified manner or place. **5.** To throw away; waste; squander. —*intr.v.* To pay out or expend money. [Middle English *spenden*, partly from Old English *spendan*, from Latin *expendēre*, to expend, and partly from Old French *despendre*, to dispend, from Latin *dispendere*, to weigh out.] —**spend′er** *n.*

spend·thrift (spĕnd′thrĭft′) *n.* A person who squanders money; a prodigal spender. —*adj.* Wasteful or extravagant. [SPEND + THRIFT (accumulated wealth).]

Spen·se·ri·an sonnet (spĕn-sîr′ē-ən). A sonnet form comprising three interlocking quatrains and a couplet with the rhyme pattern *abab bcbc cdcd ee.* [After Edmund *Spenser* (1552–99), English poet.]

Spenserian stanza. A stanza consisting of eight lines of iambic pentameter and a final Alexandrine, rhymed *ababbcbcc*, used by Edmund Spenser.

spent (spĕnt) *v.* Past tense and past participle of **spend.**

—*adj.* **1.** Consumed; used up. **2.** Passed; come to an end. **3.** Depleted of energy, force, or strength; exhausted.

sperm¹ (spûrm) *n.* **1.** Also **sperm cell.** A **spermatozoon.** **2.** Semen. [Middle English *sperme,* from Old French *esperme,* from Late Latin *sperma,* seed, sperm, from Greek *sperma.*]

sperm² (spûrm) *n.* The sperm whale or a substance associated with it, such as spermaceti. [Short for SPERMACETI.]

-sperm. A suffix meaning a seed: **endosperm.** [From Greek *sperma,* seed.]

sper·ma·ce·ti (spûr′mə-sē′tē, -sĕt′ē) *n.* A white, waxy substance obtained from the head of the sperm whale and used for making candles, ointments, and cosmetics. [Middle English, from Medieval Latin *spermacētī,* "sperm of the whale" : Late Latin *sperma,* sperm + Latin *cētus,* whale.]

sper·ma·ry (spûr′mə-rē) *n., pl.* **-ries.** An organ in which male gametes are formed, esp. in invertebrate animals.

spermat-. Var. of spermato-.

sper·mat·ic (spər-măt′ĭk) *adj.* **1.** Of or resembling sperm. **2.** Of a spermary.

spermato- or **spermat-.** A prefix meaning: **1.** Seed: **spermatophyte.** **2.** Sperm: **spermatic.** [From Greek *sperma,* seed.]

sper·mat·o·phyte (spər-măt′ə-fīt′, spûr′mə-tə-) *n.* Any plant of the division Spermatophyta, which includes all seed-bearing plants. —**sper·mat′o·phyt′ic** (-fĭt′ĭk) *adj.*

sper·mat·o·zo·on (spər-măt′ə-zō′ŏn′, spûr′mə-tə-, -ən)*n., pl.* **-zo·a** (-zō′ə). The fertilizing gamete of a male animal that is usu. a long nucleated cell with a thin, motile tail. Also called **sperm, sperm cell.** —**sper′ma·to·zo′al** or **sper′ma·to·zo′ic** *adj.*

sperm oil. A yellow, waxy oil, obtained chiefly from the head of the sperm whale and used as a lubricant.

sperm whale. A whale, *Physeter catodon,* that has a large head, with cavities containing sperm oil and spermaceti and a long, narrow, lower jaw. Also called **cachalot.**

spew (spyōō) *tr.v.* **1.** To vomit or cast out through the mouth. **2.** To force out in a stream; eject. —*intr.v.* To vomit. —*n.* Vomit. [Middle English *spewen,* from Old English *spīwan* and *spīowan.*]

sphag·num (sfăg′nəm) *n.* Any of various pale or ashy mosses of the genus *Sphagnum,* the decomposed remains of which form peat. [From Latin *sphagnos,* a kind of moss, from Greek.] —**sphag′nous** *adj.*

sphal·er·ite (sfăl′ə-rīt′) *n.* A zinc ore, essentially ZnS with some cadmium, iron, and manganese. Also called **blende, zinc blende.** [German *Sphalerit,* from Greek *sphaleros,* slippery, from *sphallein,* to trip.]

sphe·no·don (sfē′nə-dŏn′, sfĕn′ə-) *n.* The tuatara. [Greek *sphēn,* wedge + *odōn,* tooth.]

sphe·noid (sfē′noid′) *n.* The sphenoid bone. —*adj.* Also **sphe·noid·al** (sfē-noi′dl). **1.** Wedge-shaped. **2.** Of the sphenoid bone. [From Greek *sphēnoeidēs.*]

sphenoid bone. A compound bone with winglike processes, situated at the base of the skull.

sphere (sfîr) *n.* **1.** *Geom.* A three-dimensional surface all points of which are equidistant from a fixed point. **2.** An object or figure having this shape. **3.** A planet, star, or other heavenly body. **4.** The sky, appearing as a hemisphere to an observer. **5.** In ancient astronomy, any of a series of concentric, transparent, revolving globes that together were thought to contain the moon, sun, planets, and stars. **6.** The extent of a person's knowledge, interests, or social position. **7.** An area of power, control, or influence; domain. —See Syns at **range.** [Middle English, from Old French *espere,* from Latin *sphaera,* ball, globe, from Greek *sphaira.*] —**sphe·ric′i·ty** (sfī-rĭs′ī-tē) *n.*

-sphere. A suffix meaning sphere: **bathysphere.** [From SPHERE.]

spher·i·cal (sfîr′ĭ-kəl, sfĕr′-) or **spher·ic** (-ĭk) *adj.* Of, relating to, or having the shape of a sphere. —**spher′i·cal·ly** *adv.* —**spher′i·cal·ness** *n.*

sphe·roid (sfîr′oid′, sfĕr′-) *n.* **1.** A three-dimensional geometric surface generated by rotating an ellipse on or about one of its axes. **2.** A figure or object having such a shape. —**sphe·roid′al** *adj.* —**sphe·roid′al·ly** *adv.* —**sphe·roi·dic′i·ty** (sfîr′oi-dĭs′ī-tē, sfĕr′-) *n.*

spher·ule (sfîr′ōōl, -yōōl, sfĕr′-) *n.* A small sphere.

sphinc·ter (sfĭngk′tər) *n.* A ringlike muscle that normally maintains constriction of a bodily passage or orifice and that relaxes as required by normal physiological functioning. [Late Latin, from Greek *sphinktēr,* that which binds tight, from *sphingein,* to bind tight.] —**sphinc′ter·al** *adj.*

sphinx (sfĭngks) *n., pl.* **sphinx·es** or **sphin·ges** (sfĭn′jēz′). **1.** *Egypt. Myth.* A figure having the body of a lion and the head of a man, ram, or hawk. **2.** *Gk. Myth.* A winged monster having the head of a woman and the body of a lion. **3.** An enigmatic person.

sphyg·mo·ma·nom·e·ter (sfĭg′mō-mə-nŏm′ī-tər) *n.* Also **sphyg·mom·e·ter** (-mŏm′ī-tər). An instrument for measuring blood pressure in the arteries. [Greek *sphygmos,* pulsation + *manos,* rare, sparse + -METER.]

spi·ca (spī′kə) *n.* **1.** A bandage applied in overlapping opposite spirals to immobilize a digit or limb. **2. Spica.** The brightest star in the constellation Virgo, 212 light-years distant from Earth. [Latin *spīca,* point, ear of grain.]

spic-and-span (spĭk′ən-spăn′) *adj.* Var. of **spick-and-span.**

spi·cate (spī′kāt′) *adj. Bot.* Forming a spike: *spicate flowers.* [Latin *spīcātus,* from *spīcāre,* to provide with spikes, from *spīca,* ear of grain, spike.]

spice (spīs) *n.* **1. a.** Any of various pungent vegetable substances, such as cinnamon or nutmeg, used to flavor foods or beverages. **b.** These substances as a group. **3.** A pungent aroma; perfume. —*tr.v.* **spiced, spic·ing. 1.** To season with spices. **2.** To add zest or flavor to. [Middle English, from Old French *espice,* from Late Latin *speciēs,* goods, spices, from Latin, kind, species.]

spice·bush (spīs′bŏŏsh′) *n.* An aromatic shrub, *Lindera benzoin,* of eastern North America, with clusters of small, early-blooming yellow flowers. Also called **benjamin bush.**

spick-and-span (spĭk′ən-spăn′) *adj.* Also **spic-and-span.** Neat and clean; spotless. [Short for obs. *spick and span-new,* "brand-new".]

spic·ule (spĭk′yōōl) *n.* Also **spic·u·la** (-yə-lə) *pl.* **-lae** (-lē′). A small needlelike structure or part, such as one of the processes supporting the soft tissue of sponges. [Latin *spīculum,* thorn, point, dim. of *spica,* spike, point.] —**spic′u·lar** or **spic′u·late** (-lĭt, -lāt′) *adj.*

spic·y (spī′sē) *adj.* **-i·er, -i·est. 1.** Having the characteristics of spice, such as flavor and aroma. **2.** Piquant; zesty: *spicy conversation.* **3.** Slightly scandalous; risqué: *spicy stories.* —**spic′i·ly** *adv.* —**spic′i·ness** *n.*

spi·der (spī′dər) *n.* **1.** Any of numerous arachnids of the

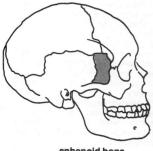

sphenoid bone

sphinx

sphygmomanometer

spider

ă pat	ā pay	â care	ä father	ĕ pet	ē be	hw which	ĭ pit	ī tie	î pier	ŏ pot	ō toe	ô paw, for	oi noise
ŏŏ took	ōō boot	ou out	th thin	*th* this	ŭ cut	û urge	zh vision	ə about, item, edible, gallop, circus

order Araneae, which have eight legs, a body divided into a cephalothorax and an abdomen, and spinnerets that produce silk to make nests, cocoons, or webs for trapping insects. **2.** A frying pan equipped with a long handle and short legs. **3.** A trivet. —*modifier: a spider web.* [Middle English *spither,* from Old English *spīthra.*]

spider crab. Any of various crabs, such as those of the genera *Libinia* and *Macrocheira,* with long legs.

spider monkey. Any of several tropical American monkeys of the genus *Ateles,* with long legs and a long, prehensile tail.

spi·der·wort (spī'dər-wûrt', -wôrt') *n.* Any of various New World plants of the genus *Tradescantia,* esp. *T. virginiana,* with three-petaled blue or purple flowers.

spi·der·y (spī'də-rē) *adj.* **1.** Like or suggesting a spider. **2.** Long and slender: *spidery fingers.*

spied (spīd) *v.* Past tense and past participle of **spy.**

spiel (spēl) *n. Slang.* A lengthy, usu. tedious speech or argument intended to be persuasive. [German *Spiel,* play, from Old High German *spil.*] —**spiel'er** *n.*

spies (spīz) *n.* Plural of **spy.**

spif·fy (spīf'ē) *adj.* **-fi·er, -fi·est.** *Slang.* Smart in appearance or dress; stylish. [Orig. unknown.] —**spif'fi·ness** *n.*

spig·ot (spīg'ət) *n.* **1.** A faucet. **2.** A plug or peg used to stop up the opening of a barrel. [Middle English.]

spike¹ (spīk) *n.* **1. a.** A long, thick, sharp-pointed piece of wood or metal. **b.** A heavy nail. **2. a.** A sharp-pointed projection along the top of a fence or wall. **b.** A sharp metal projection set in the sole of an athletic shoe for grip. **3. a.** Also **spike heel.** A very high thin heel, used on a woman's shoe. **b. spikes.** A pair of shoes having such heels. **4.** A long, pointed, projecting part. —*tr.v.* **spiked, spik·ing.** **1.** To secure or provide with a spike. **2.** To impale, pierce, or injure with a spike. **3.** To render (a muzzleloading gun) useless by driving a spike into the vent. **4.** To put an end to; thwart; block: *spike a plot.* **5.** *Slang.* To add alcoholic liquor to. [Middle English *spyk,* from either Old Norse *spīk,* nail, or Old English *spīcing.*]

spike² (spīk) *n.* **1.** An ear of grain. **2.** *Bot.* A usu. elongated inflorescence with stalkless or nearly stalkless flowers arranged along an axis. [Middle English *spik,* from Latin *spīca,* point, ear of grain.]

spike·let (spīk'lĭt) *n. Bot.* A small or secondary spike.

spike·nard (spīk'närd') *n.* **1. a.** An aromatic plant, *Nardostachys jatamansi,* of India, with rose-purple flowers. Also called **nard. b.** A costly ointment of antiquity, probably prepared from the spikenard. Also called **nard. 3.** A North American plant, *Aralia racemosa,* with small, greenish flowers and an aromatic root. [Middle English, from Medieval Latin *spīca nardi,* spike of a nard (a kind of plant).]

spik·y (spī'kē) *adj.* **-i·er, -i·est.** Having a projecting sharp point or points: *a spiky tail.* —**spik'i·ness** *n.*

spile (spīl) *n.* **1.** A post used as a foundation; a pile. **2.** A wooden plug; a bung. **3.** A spigot used in taking sap from a tree. —*tr.v.* **spiled, spil·ing.** To support, plug, or tap with a spile. [Perh. from Middle Dutch *spile,* bar.]

spill¹ (spĭl) *v.* **spilled** or **spilt** (spĭlt), **spill·ing.** —*tr.v.* **1.** To cause or allow (a substance) to run or fall out of a container. **2.** To shed (blood). **3.** To let the wind out of (a sail). **4.** To cause to fall. **5.** *Informal.* To divulge. —*intr.v.* **1.** To run out of a container. **2.** To come to the ground suddenly and involuntarily. —See Syns at **fall.** —*n.* **1.** An act of spilling. **2.** The amount spilled. [Middle English *spillen,* to shed (blood), spill, from Old English *spillan.*] —**spill'er** *n.*

spill² (spĭl) *n.* **1.** A piece of wood or rolled paper used to light a fire. **2.** A small peg used as a plug; a spile. [Prob. from Middle Dutch *spile.*]

spill·age (spĭl'ĭj) *n.* **1.** An act of spilling. **2.** An amount spilled.

spill·way (spĭl'wā') *n.* A channel for reservoir overflow.

spilt (spĭlt) *v.* A past tense and past participle of **spill** (to shed).

spin (spĭn) *v.* **spun** (spŭn), **spin·ning.** —*tr.v.* **1. a.** To draw out and twist (fibers) into thread. **b.** To make (thread or yarn) by drawing out and twisting fibers. **2.** To form (a thread, web, cocoon, etc.) from a fluid emitted from the body. **3.** To relate; tell. **4.** To cause to rotate swiftly; twirl: *spin the top.* —*intr.v.* **1.** To make thread or yarn by the drawing out and twisting of fibers. **2.** To rotate rapidly;

whirl. **3.** To seem to be whirling, as from dizziness; to reel. **4.** To ride or drive rapidly. —*n.* **1.** The act of spinning. **2.** A swift whirling motion. **3.** *Informal.* A short drive in a vehicle. **4.** A nose-down, spiraling, stalled descent. [Middle English *spinnen,* from Old English *spinnan.*] —**spin'ner** *n.*

spin·ach (spĭn'ĭch) *n.* A widely cultivated plant, *Spinacia oleracea,* native to Asia, with succulent, edible leaves. —*modifier: spinach pie.* [Old French *espinache,* from Old Spanish *espinaca,* from Arabic *isfānākh.*]

spi·nal (spī'nəl) *adj.* **1.** Of, to, or near the spine or spinal cord; vertebral. **2.** Resembling a spine. —*n.* An anesthetic injected injected into the spinal canal. —**spi'nal·ly** *adv.*

spinal canal. The passage formed by the successive openings in the vertebrae through which the spinal cord and its membranes pass. Also called **vertebral canal.**

spinal column. In vertebrate animals, the series of jointed bones, or vertebrae, enclosing the spinal cord and forming the main support of the body; the backbone.

spinal cord. The part of the central nervous system that extends from the brain and through the spinal canal, branching to form smaller nerves.

spin·dle (spĭn'dl) *n.* **1. a.** A slender, rounded rod on which fibers drawn from a distaff are twisted into thread and on which the spun thread is wound when spinning by hand or at a spinning wheel. **b.** A pin or rod holding a bobbin or spool upon which thread is wound on a spinning wheel or spinning machine. **2.** Any of various slender revolving mechanical parts. **3.** *Biol.* The axis between cytoplasm centers, along which the chromosomes are distributed in mitosis. —*v.* **-dled, -dling.** —*tr.v.* To impale or perforate on the spike of a spindle. —*intr.v.* To grow into a thin, elongated, or weakly form. [Middle English *spindel,* rod of a spinning wheel, from Old English *spinel.*]

spin·dle·legs (spĭn'dl-lĕgz') *pl.n.* Long, thin legs. —**spin'dle-leg'ged** *adj.*.

spin·dly (spĭn'dlē) *adj.* **-dli·er, -dli·est.** Thin and weak.

spin·drift (spĭn'drĭft') *n.* Wind-blown sea spray. Also called **spoondrift.** [Var. of SPOONDRIFT.]

spine (spīn) *n.* **1.** The spinal column of a vertebrate. **2.** A sharp-pointed, projecting plant or animal part, such as a thorn or quill. **3.** The supporting part at the back of a book, to which the covers are hinged. [Middle English, from Old French *espine,* from Latin *spīna,* thorn, prickle, spine.]

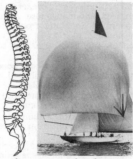

spine   spinnaker

spi·nel (spĭ-nĕl') *n.* Any of several hard minerals with composition $MgAl_2O_4$, the red variety being valued as a gem. [Italian *spinella,* dim. of *spina,* thorn (from its sharply pointed crystals), from Latin *spīna.*]

spine·less (spīn'lĭs) *adj.* **1.** Lacking a vertebral column. **2.** Having no stiff, sharp, projecting plant or animal part. **3.** Lacking in courage or will power. —**spine'less·ness** *n.*

spin·et (spĭn'ĭt) *n.* **1.** A small, compact upright piano. **2.** A small harpsichord with a single keyboard. [Obs. French *espinette,* from Italian *spinetta.*]

spin·na·ker (spĭn'ə-kər) *n.* A large triangular sail set on a spar that swings out opposite the mainsail, used on racing yachts when running before the wind. [Orig. unknown.]

spin·ner·et (spĭn'ə-rĕt') *n.* **1.** In spiders or insect larvae that spin silk, one of the small openings in the back part of the body through which a sticky fluid flows to form a fine

ă pat   ā pay   â care   ä father   ĕ pet   ē be   hw which
ŏŏ took   ōō boot   ou out   th thin   *th* this   ŭ cut
ĭ pit   ī tie   î pier   ŏ pot   ō toe   ô paw, for   oi noise
û urge   zh vision   ə about, item, edible, gallop, circus

thread. **2.** A device for making synthetic fibers, consisting of a plate pierced with holes through which plastic material is forced out.

spinning jenny. An early machine with several spindles used to spin fibers into thread or yarn.

spinning wheel. A device for making yarn or thread, consisting of a foot- or hand-driven wheel and a single spindle.

    spinning wheel   **spiral**

spin-off (spĭn'ôf', -ŏf') n. A product or enterprise derived from a larger or more complex one.

spi·nose (spī'nōs') adj. Bearing spines. —**spi·nose'ly** adv.

spi·nous (spī'nəs) adj. Having spines or similar projections; spiny.

spin·ster (spĭn'stər) n. **1.** A woman who has remained single. **2.** A woman whose occupation is spinning. [Middle English spinnester : spinnen, to spin + -ster, ster (noun suffix).] —**spin'ster·hood'** n.

spi·nule (spī'yōōl) n. A small spine or thorn.

spin·y (spī'nē) adj. **-i·er, -i·est.** Like or covered with spines or thorns. —**spin'i·ness** n.

spiny anteater. An echidna.

spiny lobster. Any of various edible marine decapod crustaceans of the family Palinuridae, having a spiny carapace and lacking large pincers. Also called **rock lobster.**

spi·ra·cle (spī'rə-kəl, spĭr'ə-) n. A respiratory opening, such as a tracheal opening in the exoskeleton of an insect or the blowhole of a whale. [Latin spīrāculum, a breathing hole, from spīrāre, to breathe.]

spi·rae·a (spī-rē'ə) n. Var. of **spirea.**

spi·ral (spī'rəl) n. **1.** The two-dimensional path formed by a point moving around a fixed center at a distance that is always increasing or decreasing. **2. a.** A three-dimensional curve moving about a central axis; a helix. **b.** Something having the form of such a curve: spirals of smoke. **3.** A continuously accelerating increase or decrease: the wage-price spiral. —adj. **1.** Of or resembling a spiral. **2.** Helical. —v. **-raled** or **-ralled, -ral·ing** or **-ral·ling.** —intr.v. **1.** To take a spiral form or course. **2.** To rise or fall with steady acceleration. **3.** To cause to take a spiral form or course. —See Syns at **wind².** [Medieval Latin spīrālis, from Latin spīra, coil.] —**spi'ral·ly** adv.

spi·rant (spī'rənt) n. A fricative. —adj. Fricative. [Latin spīrāns, pres. part. of Latin spīrāre, to breathe.]

spire¹ (spīr) n. **1.** The top part or point of something that tapers upward; a pinnacle. **2.** A formation or structure that tapers to a point at the top, as a steeple. —intr.v. **spired, spir·ing.** To rise taperingly like a spire. [Middle English, slender stalk, from Old English spīr.]

spire² (spīr) n. **1.** A spiral, esp. a single turn of a spiral. **2.** The area nearest the top on a coiled gastropod shell. [French, from Latin spīra, a coil, from Greek speira.]

spi·re·a (spī-rē'ə) n. Also **spi·rae·a.** Any of various plants or shrubs of the genus Spiraea, which have clusters of small white or pink flowers. [Latin spīraea, meadowsweet, from Greek speiraia, from speira, coil.]

spi·ril·lum (spī-rĭl'əm) n., pl. **-ril·la** (-rĭl'ə). Any of various flagellated aerobic bacteria of the genus Spirillum, with an elongated spiral form. [Dim. of Latin spīra, spiral.]

spir·it (spĭr'ĭt) n. **1.** The animating or life-giving principle within a living being. **2.** The soul, considered as departing from the body of a person at death. **3.** The part of a human being associated with the mind and feelings as distin-

guished from the physical body: still with us in spirit. **4.** One's essential nature. **5.** The will. **6.** A person: aided by loyal spirits. **7.** A prevailing mood or attitude: a spirit of rebellion. **8. the Spirit.** The Holy Ghost. **9.** A supernatural being; a ghost. **10. spirits.** One's mood or emotional state: in low spirits. **11. a.** Eagerness to act, try, or take risks. **b.** A lively character or manner. **12.** Strong loyalty or dedication. **13.** The real meaning, sense, or intent of something: the spirit of the law. **14. spirits.** An alcohol solution of an essence derived from a perfume, spice, etc. **15. spirits.** An alcoholic beverage. —tr.v. **1.** To carry off mysteriously or secretly: spirit away the prisoner. **2.** To stimulate; encourage. [Middle English, from Norman French, from Latin spīritus, breath, inspiration, from spīrāre, to breathe.]

    Syns: spirit, brio, dash, élan, esprit, liveliness, pep (Informal) n. Core meaning: A lively, emphatic, eager quality or manner (danced with great spirit).

spir·it·ed (spĭr'ĭ-tĭd) adj. Characterized by vigor or courage. —**spir'it·ed·ly** adv. —**spir'it·ed·ness** n.

spir·it·ism (spĭr'ĭ-tĭz'əm) n. Spiritualism.

spir·it·less (spĭr'ĭt-lĭs) adj. Lacking energy or enthusiasm; listless. —**spir'it·less·ly** adv. —**spir'it·less·ness** n.

spirit level. A leveling device; a level.

spir·i·tu·al (spĭr'ĭ-chōō-əl) adj. **1.** Of, relating to, consisting of, or having the nature of spirit. **2.** Of, concerned with, or affecting the soul. **3.** Of God; deific. **4.** Ecclesiastical; sacred: a spiritual leader. **5.** Supernatural. —n. A religious folk song of black American origin or a song imitating this. —**spir'i·tu·al·ly** adv. —**spir'i·tu·al·ness** n.

spir·i·tu·al·ism (spĭr'ĭ-chōō-ə-lĭz'əm) n. **1. a.** The belief that the dead communicate with the living, usu. through a medium. **b.** The practices of those holding such a belief. **2.** A doctrine or religion emphasizing the spiritual. —**spir'i·tu·al·ist** n. —**spir'i·tu·al·is'tic** adj.

spir·i·tu·al·i·ty (spĭr'ĭ-chōō-ăl'ĭ-tē) n., pl. **-ties.** The condition, quality, or fact of being spiritual.

spir·i·tu·al·ize (spĭr'ĭ-chōō-ə-līz') tr.v. **-ized, -iz·ing.** To impart a spiritual nature to; refine; purify. —**spir'i·tu·al·i·za'tion** n. —**spir'i·tu·al·iz'er** n.

spir·i·tu·ous (spĭr'ĭt-ū-əs) adj. Of or containing alcohol. —**spir'it·u·os'i·ty** (-ŏs'ə-tē) or **spir'i·tu·ous·ness** n.

spiro-. A prefix meaning spiral: spirochete. [Latin spīra, coil.]

spi·ro·chete (spī'rə-kēt') n. Also **spi·ro·chaete.** Any of various slender, flexible, twisted microorganisms of the order Spirochaetales, many of which are pathogenic. [SPIRO- + Greek khaitē, long hair.] —**spi'ro·che'tal** adj.

spi·ro·gy·ra (spī'rə-jī'rə) n. Any of various green, threadlike freshwater algae of the genus Spirogyra, which have chloroplasts. [SPIRO- + Greek guros, ring.]

spi·rom·e·ter (spī-rŏm'ĭ-tər) n. An instrument for measuring the volume of air entering and leaving the lungs. [Latin spīr(āre), to breathe + -METER.]

spirt (spûrt) n. & v. Brit. Var. of **spurt.**

spit¹ (spĭt) v. **spat** (spăt) or **spit, spit·ting.** —tr.v. **1.** To eject from the mouth. **2. a.** To eject as if by spitting: presses spitting out newspapers. **b.** To utter in a violent manner. —intr.v. **1.** To expectorate. **2.** To express contempt by or as if by spitting. **3.** To make a hissing or sputtering noise. —n. **1.** Saliva, esp. when expectorated; spittle. **2.** The act of spitting. **3.** Frothy secretion of certain insects. [Middle English spitten, from Old English spittan.]

spit² (spĭt) n. **1.** A slender, pointed rod on which meat is impaled for broiling. **2.** A narrow, low-lying point of land extending into a body of water. —tr.v. **spit·ted, spit·ting.** To impale on or as if on a spit. [Middle English, from Old English spitu.]

spit·ball (spĭt'bôl') n. **1.** A piece of paper chewed and shaped into a lump for use as a projectile. **2.** An illegal baseball pitch in which the ball is moistened on one side.

spite (spīt) n. Malice or ill will prompting an urge to hurt or thwart. —tr.v. **spit·ed, spit·ing.** To irritate; annoy. —idiom. **in spite of.** Regardless of; despite. [Middle English, insult, ill will, short for Old French despit.]

spite·ful (spīt'fəl) adj. Filled with, prompted by, or showing spite; malicious. —**spite'ful·ly** adv. —**spite'ful·ness** n.

spit·fire (spĭt'fīr') n. A quick-tempered person.

spitting image. An exact copy or likeness.

spit·tle (spĭt'l) n. Spit; saliva. [Middle English *spetil,* from Old English *spætl.*]

spit·tle·bug (spĭt'l-bŭg') n. Any of various insects of the family Cercopidae, the nymphs of which form frothy masses of liquid on plant stems.

spit·toon (spĭ-tōon') n. A bowl-shaped, usu. metal vessel for spitting into. Also called **cuspidor.** [SPIT + -oon (as in such words as BALLOON and DOUBLOON).]

spitz (spĭts) n. A dog of a breed with a long, thick, usu. white coat and a tail curled over the back. [German *Spitz,* from *spitz,* pointed (from its pointed muzzle).]

splash (splăsh) tr.v. **1.** To dash or scatter (a liquid) about in flying masses. **2.** To dash liquid upon. **3.** To mark with bold scattered stripes. —intr.v. **1.** To cause a liquid to fly in scattered masses. **2.** To fall into or move through liquid with this effect. **3.** To move, spill, or fly about in scattered masses. —n. **1.** The act or sound of splashing. **2.** A flying mass of liquid. **3.** A marking produced by or as if by scattered liquid: *a splash of color.* **4.** A great though often short-lived impression; a stir. [Var. of PLASH.] —**splash'er** n.

splash·down (splăsh'doun') n. The landing of a missile or spacecraft on water or its moment of impact.

splash·y (splăsh'ē) adj. **-i·er, -i·est. 1.** Making splashes. **2.** Covered with splashes of color. **3.** Showy; ostentatious. —**splash'i·ly** adv. —**splash'i·ness** n.

splat[1] (splăt) n. A slat of wood. [Orig. unknown.]

splat[2] (splăt) n. A slapping noise. [Imit.]

splat·ter (splăt'ər) tr.v. To spatter, esp. to soil with splashes of liquid. —intr.v. To spatter, esp. to move or fall so as to cause heavy splashes. —n. A splash of liquid. [Perh. a blend of SPLASH and SPATTER.]

splay (splā) adj. **1.** Spread or turned out. **2.** Clumsy; awkward. —n. **1.** Expansion; spread. **2.** *Archit.* An oblique slope given to the sides of a door or a window. —tr.v. **1.** To spread out or apart, esp. clumsily. **2.** To make slanting or sloping; to bevel. —intr.v. **1.** To be spread out or apart. **2.** To slant or slope. [From Middle English *splayen,* to spread out, short for *displayen,* to display.]

splay·foot (splā'fŏot') n., pl. **-feet** (-fēt'). **1.** A physical deformity characterized by abnormally flat and turned-out feet. **2.** A foot of this kind. —**splay'foot'ed** adj.

spleen (splēn) n. **1.** One of the largest lymphoid structures, an organ on the left side below the diaphragm, functioning as a blood filter and to store blood. **2.** Ill temper: *vent his spleen.* [Middle English *splene,* from Old French *esplen,* from Latin *splēn,* from Greek.] —**spleen'y** adj.

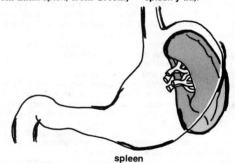

spleen

splen·dent (splĕn'dənt) adj. **1.** Shining or lustrous; brilliant. **2.** Celebrated; illustrious. [Middle English, from Latin *splendēns,* pres. part. of *splendēre,* to shine.]

splen·did (splĕn'dĭd) adj. **1.** Brilliant with light or color; radiant. **2.** Imposing because of showiness or grandeur; magnificent: *a splendid palace.* **3.** Glorious; illustrious: *a splendid career.* **4.** Excellent. —See Syns at **excellent.** [French *splendide,* from Latin *splendidus,* from *splendēre,* to shine.] —**splen'did·ly** adv. —**splen'did·ness** n.

splen·dif·er·ous (splĕn-dĭf'ər-əs) adj. Splendid. [Middle English, from Medieval Latin *splendiferus.*]

splen·dor (splĕn'dər) n. Also *Brit.* **splen·dour. 1.** Brilliance. **2.** Magnificent appearance or display; grandeur. **3.** Illustriousness. [Middle English *splendure,* from Old French *splendeur,* from Latin *splendor,* from *splendēre,* to shine.]

—splen'dor·ous or **splen'drous** (splĕn'drəs) adj.

sple·net·ic (splĭ-nĕt'ĭk) or **sple·net·i·cal** (-ĭ-kəl) adj. **1.** Of the spleen. **2.** Ill-humored; irritable. [Late Latin *splēnēticus,* from Latin *splēn,* spleen.] —**sple·net'i·cal·ly** adv.

splen·ic (splĕn'ĭk) adj. Of or near the spleen. [Latin *splēnicus,* from Greek *splēnikos,* from *splēn,* spleen.]

splice (splīs) tr.v. **spliced, splic·ing. 1. a.** To join (lengths of wire, film, etc.) at the ends. **b.** To join (rope) by weaving together the end strands. **2.** To join by overlapping and binding. —n. A joint made by splicing. [Prob. from Middle Dutch *splissen.*] —**splic'er** n.

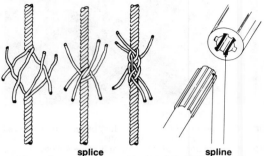

splice   **spline**

spline (splīn) n. **1. a.** Any of a series of projections on a shaft that fit into slots on a corresponding shaft, enabling both to rotate together. **b.** The groove or slot for such a projection. **2.** A flexible piece of wood, hard rubber, or metal used in drawing curves. **3.** A slat. [Orig. unknown.]

splint (splĭnt) n. **1.** A splinter. **2.** A rigid device used to prevent motion of a joint or the ends of a fractured bone. **3.** A thin, flexible wooden strip, such as one used in the making of baskets and chair bottoms. **4.** A bony enlargement of the cannon bone or splint bone of a horse. —tr.v. To support or restrict with or as if with a splint. [Middle English, small strip of metal, splint, from Middle Low German or Middle Dutch *splinte.*]

splint bone. Either of two small metacarpal or metatarsal bones in horses or related animals.

splin·ter (splĭn'tər) n. **1.** A sharp, slender piece, as of wood, bone, or glass, split or broken off from a main body. **2.** A group that has broken away from a parent group, as a church or political party. —intr.v. To form splinters. —tr.v. To cause to splinter. [Middle English, from Middle Dutch.]

split (splĭt) v. **split, split·ting.** —tr.v. **1.** To divide sharply or cleanly, esp. into lengthwise sections. **2.** To break, burst, or rip apart with force; rend. **3.** To separate (persons or groups); disunite. **4.** To divide and share: *split a meal.* **5.** To separate into layers. **6.** To mark (a vote or ballot) in favor of candidates from different parties. **7.** *Sports.* To win half the games of (a series or double-header). —intr.v. **1.** To divide into parts, esp. lengthwise. **2.** To become broken or ripped apart. **3.** To become divided or part company. **4.** To share something with others. **5.** *Slang.* To leave, esp. abruptly. —See Syns at **separate.** —n. **1.** The act or result of splitting. **2.** A breach or rupture in a group. **3.** A splinter. **4. a.** A division. **b.** Something divided; a share. **5.** A dessert of sliced fruit, ice cream, and toppings: *a banana split.* **6.** Often **splits.** An acrobatic feat in which the legs are stretched out in opposite directions at right angles to the trunk. **7.** *Bowling.* A widely spaced arrangement of pins left standing after the first bowl. —adj. **1.** Divided or separated. **2.** Fissured longitudinally; cleft. —*idiom.* **split hairs.** To quibble. [Dutch *splitten.*] —**split'ter** n.

split infinitive. An infinitive verb form with an element, usu. an adverb, interposed between *to* and the verb.

Usage: **split infinitive.** Split infinitives occur and have occurred for hundreds of years in English on all levels. Whether to use or to avoid this construction is really a matter of personal style. In some cases use of a split infinitive may be desirable to prevent awkwardness or ambiguity: *to thoroughly examine the patient* (smoother than *thoroughly to examine the patient*) or *to examine the pa-*

tient thoroughly; arrived in Detroit to unexpectedly find his wife sick (but the meaning is changed if the adverb is transposed to *arrived in Detroit unexpectedly to find his wife sick* or *arrived in Detroit to find his wife unexpectedly sick*). If a writer wants to stress the verbal element of an infinitive or to express an idea that is more precisely and smoothly shown with *to* + adverb + infinitive, such a construction is entirely acceptable. What should be avoided is a long adverbial construction setting *to* and the infinitive very far apart: *wanted to examine the patient completely and thoroughly* (not *wanted to completely and thoroughly examine the patient*).

split-lev·el (splĭt′lĕv′əl) *adj.* Having the floor levels of adjoining rooms separated by about a half story.

split personality. A form of hysteria in which a person exhibits two or more relatively distinct identities.

split second. An instant; a flash.

split ticket. A ballot cast for candidates of two or more political parties.

split·ting (splĭt′ĭng) *adj.* Very severe: *a splitting headache.*

splotch (splŏch) *n.* An irregularly shaped stain. —*tr.v.* To mark with a splotch or splotches. [Perh. a blend of SPOT and BLOTCH.] —**splotch′y** *adj.*

splurge (splûrj) *intr.v.* **splurged, splurg·ing.** 1. To indulge in an extravagant expense or luxury. 2. To be showy or ostentatious. —*n.* 1. An extravagant display. 2. An expensive indulgence; a spree. [Orig. unknown.]

splut·ter (splŭt′ər) *intr.v.* 1. To make a spitting sound. 2. To speak rapidly and unclearly, as when angry. —*tr.v.* To utter hastily and unclearly. —*n.* A spluttering noise. [Perh. alteration of SPUTTER.] —**splut′ter·er** *n.*

spoil (spoil) *v.* **spoiled** or **spoilt** (spoilt), **spoil·ing.** —*tr.v.* 1. To impair the value or quality of; to damage. 2. To impair the completeness, perfection, or unity of. 3. To disrupt; disturb. 4. To overindulge or overpraise so as to do harm to the character. 5. *Archaic.* To plunder; despoil. —*intr.v.* 1. To become tainted, rotten, or otherwise unfit for use; to decay. 2. *Archaic.* To engage in plundering; pillage. —See Syns at **baby** and **botch.** —*phrasal verb.* **spoil for.** To be eager for; crave: *spoiling for a fight.* —*n.* 1. **spoils.** Goods or property seized from a victim after a conflict. 2. **spoils.** Benefits gained by a victor, esp. political appointments or jobs at the disposal of a winning candidate or party in an election. 3. *Archaic.* The act of plundering. [Middle English *spoilen,* to plunder, from Old French *espoillier,* from Latin *spoliāre,* from *spolium,* booty.]

spoil·age (spoi′lĭj) *n.* 1. The condition or process of becoming spoiled; damage. 2. Material that has been spoiled. 3. The degree to which something has been spoiled.

spoil·sport (spoil′spôrt′) *n.* A person whose prudence or sobriety mars the pleasure of others.

spoils system. The practice after an election of rewarding loyal supporters of the winning candidates and party with political jobs or appointments.

spoilt (spoilt) *v.* A past tense and past participle of **spoil.**

spoke[1] (spōk) *n.* 1. One of the rods or braces that connect the hub and the rim of a wheel. 2. A rung of a ladder. —*tr.v.* **spoked, spok·ing.** To equip with spokes. [Middle English, from Old English *spāca.*]

spoke

spoke[2] (spōk) *v.* Past tense and archaic past participle of **speak.** [P. t. formed on the model of such verbs as *break,*

broke; past part. from the p. t.]

spo·ken (spō′kən) *v.* Past participle of **speak.** —*adj.* 1. Uttered; expressed orally. 2. Speaking or using speech in a specified manner or voice. [From SPEAK, on the model of such verbs as *break, broken.*]

spoke·shave (spōk′shāv′) *n.* A drawknife.

spokes·man (spōks′mən) *n.* A person who speaks on behalf of another or others. [From *spoke,* archaic past part. of SPEAK + MAN.]

spokes·wom·an (spōks′wŏom′ən) *n.* A woman who speaks on behalf of another or others.

spo·li·a·tion (spō′lē-ā′shən) *n.* The act of despoiling or plundering or the condition of being plundered. [Middle English *spoliacioun,* from Latin *spoliātiō,* from *spolium,* booty.] —**spo′li·a·tor** *n.*

spon·dee (spŏn′dē) *n.* A metrical foot consisting of two long or stressed syllables. [Middle English *sponde,* from Old French *spondee,* from Latin *spondeum,* from Greek *spondeios (pous),* "(meter) used at a libation," from *spondē,* libation.] —**spon·da·ic** (spŏn-dā′ĭk) *adj.*

sponge (spŭnj) *n.* 1. **a.** Any of numerous primitive, chiefly saltwater animals of the phylum Porifera, often forming irregularly shaped colonies attached to an underwater surface. **b.** The light, porous, absorbent skeleton of certain of these organisms, used for bathing, cleaning, etc. **c.** A similarly used piece of porous, absorbent material, as of rubber or cellulose. 2. A gauze pad used to absorb blood and other fluids, as in surgery. 3. Leavened dough. 4. Any of various light cakes, such as sponge cake. 5. *Slang.* A person who habitually lives off the generosity of others; parasite. —*v.* **sponged, spong·ing.** —*tr.v.* 1. To moisten, wipe, or clean with a sponge. 2. To wipe out; erase. 3. *Slang.* To obtain free: *sponge a meal.* —*intr.v.* 1. To fish for sponges. 2. *Slang.* To live by relying on the generosity of others. [Middle English, from Old English, from Latin *spongia,* from Greek *sphongos,* sponge.]

sponge cake. A very light, porous cake containing no shortening.

sponge rubber. A soft, porous rubber used in toys, cushions, gaskets, and weather stripping.

spong·y (spŭn′jē) *adj.* **-i·er, -i·est.** Like a sponge in elasticity, absorbency, or porousness. —**spong′i·ness** *n.*

spon·son (spŏn′sən) *n.* 1. Any of several structures that project from the side of a boat or ship, esp. a gun platform. 2. A short, curved, air-filled projection on the hull of a seaplane, imparting stability in the water. [Orig. unknown.]

spon·sor (spŏn′sər) *n.* 1. A person who assumes responsibility for another or others, as during a period of instruction. 2. A person who vouches for the suitability of a candidate for admission. 3. A legislator who proposes and urges the adoption of a bill. 4. A godparent. 5. A business enterprise that pays for a radio or television program, usu. in return for advertising time. —*tr.v.* To act as a sponsor for. [Latin, from *spondēre,* to make a solemn pledge.] —**spon·so·ri·al** (-sôr′ē-əl, -sōr′-) *adj.* —**spon′sor·ship′** *n.*

spon·ta·ne·i·ty (spŏn′tə-nē′ĭ-tē, -nā′-) *n.,* pl. **-ties.** 1. The condition or quality of being spontaneous. 2. Spontaneous behavior, impulse, or movement.

spon·ta·ne·ous (spŏn-tā′nē-əs) *adj.* 1. Happening without apparent external cause; self-generated. 2. Voluntary and impulsive; unpremeditated: *spontaneous applause.* [Late Latin *spontāneus,* from Latin *sponte,* of one's own accord.] —**spon·ta′ne·ous·ly** *adv.* —**spon·ta′ne·ous·ness** *n.*

spontaneous combustion. The breaking into flame of a mass of material, such as oily rags or damp hay, as a result of heat generated within the material by slow oxidation.

spontaneous generation. The hypothetical development of living organisms from nonliving matter.

spoof (spoof) *n.* 1. A joke or hoax. 2. A gentle satirical imitation; light parody. —*tr.v.* 1. To deceive. 2. To do a spoof of; satirize gently. [From *spoof,* a card game characterized by nonsense and hoaxing, invented by Arthur Roberts (1852–1933), British comedian.]

spook (spook). *Informal.* —*n.* 1. A ghost. 2. A secret agent. —*tr.v.* 1. To haunt. 2. To frighten. [Dutch.]

spook·y (spoo′kē) *adj.* **-i·er, -i·est.** *Informal.* 1. Ghostly; eerie; unnatural. 2. Easily startled; skittish; nervous. —**spook′i·ly** *adv.* —**spook′i·ness** *n.*

spool (spool) *n.* 1. A small cylinder upon which thread, yarn, wire, tape, ribbon, or film is wound, having a hole through the middle. **2. a.** A spool with something wound on it. **b.** The amount a spool holds. —*tr.v.* To wind on a spool. [Middle English *spole,* from Old French *espole,* from Middle Dutch *spoele.*]

spoon (spo͞on) *n.* **1.** A utensil consisting of a small, shallow bowl on a handle, used in preparing, serving, or eating food. **2.** Something similar to a spoon or its bowl, such as an oar with a curved blade. —*tr.v.* To lift, scoop up, or carry with or as if with a spoon. —*intr.v. Informal.* To make love by kissing or caressing. [Middle English, from Old English *spōn,* chip of wood.]

spoon·bill (spo͞on′bĭl′) *n.* **1.** Any of several long-legged wading birds of the subfamily Plataleinae, which have a long, flat bill with a broad tip. **2.** Any of various broad-billed ducks, such as the shoveler. **3.** The paddlefish.

      spoonbill   **sporran**

spoon·drift (spo͞on′drĭft′) *n.* Spindrift. [Obs. *spoon,* to drive back and forth + DRIFT.]

spoon·er·ism (spo͞o′nə-rĭz′əm) *n.* An unintentional transposition of usu. initial sounds of words, as *Let me sew you to your sheet* for *Let me show you to your seat.* [After William A. *Spooner* (1844–1930), English clergyman, noted for such slips.]

spoon-fed (spo͞on′fĕd′) *adj.* **1.** Fed with a spoon. **2.** Given no chance to think or act independently.

spoon·ful (spo͞on′fo͝ol′) *n., pl.* **-fuls.** The amount a spoon holds.

spoor (spo͝or) *n.* The track or trail of an animal. —*tr.v.* To track by following a spoor. —*intr.v.* To track an animal by its spoor. [Afrikaans, from Middle Dutch.]

spo·rad·ic (spə-răd′ĭk) or **spo·rad·i·cal** (-ĭ-kəl) *adj.* **1.** Occurring at irregular intervals: *sporadic applause.* **2.** Appearing singly or at widely scattered localities: *a sporadic plant.* **3.** Not widespread; isolated: *a sporadic disease.* [Medieval Latin *sporadicus,* from Greek *sporadikos,* scattered, from *sporas,* scattered.] —**spo·rad′i·cal·ly** *adv.* —**spo·rad′i·cal·ness** *n.*

spo·ran·gi·um (spə-răn′jē-əm) *n., pl.* **-gi·a** (-jē-ə). A spore-bearing structure in certain plants, such as fungi, mosses, and ferns; a spore case. [SPOR(E) + Greek *angeion,* vessel, container.] —**spo·ran′gi·al** *adj.*

spore (spôr, spōr) *n.* **1.** An asexual, usu. single-celled reproductive organ characteristic of nonflowering plants such as fungi, mosses, and ferns. **2.** A microorganism, as a bacterium, in a dormant or resting state. [From Greek *spora,* seed.] —**spo·ra′ceous** (spə-rā′shəs) *adj.*

spore case. A structure containing spores; a sporangium.

spo·ro·phyll (spôr′ə-fĭl′, spōr′-) *n.* A leaf or leaflike organ that bears spores.

spo·ro·phyte (spôr′ə-fīt′, spōr′-) *n.* The spore-producing phase in plants that reproduce by metagenesis. —**spo′ro·phyt′ic** (-fĭt′ĭk) *adj.*

spo·ro·zo·an (spôr′ə-zō′ən, spōr′-) *n.* Any of numerous parasitic protozoans of the class Sporozoa, many of which have complex reproductive processes. —**spo′ro·zo′an** *adj.*

spor·ran (spôr′ən, spōr′-) *n.* A pouch worn at the front of the kilt by Scottish Highlanders. [Scottish Gaelic *sporan,* from Late Latin *bursa,* bag, from Greek, hide.]

sport (spôrt, spōrt) *n.* **1.** An active pastime; recreation. **2.** A specific diversion, usu. involving physical exercise and having a set form and body of rules; a game. **3.** Light mockery; jest; fun. **4.** A person known for the manner of his acceptance of defeat or criticism: *a good sport.* **5.** *Informal.* A person who lives a gay, extravagant life. **6.** *Genetics.* A mutation. **7.** *Archaic.* Amorous dalliance; lovemaking. —*intr.v.* **1.** To play; to frolic. **2.** To joke or trifle. **3.** To mutate. —*tr.v.* To display or show off: *"His shoes sported elevated heels"* (Truman Capote). —*adj.* Suitable for active outdoor use or informal wear: *r. sport shirt.* [From Middle English *sporten,* to amuse, short for *disporten,* to disport.]

sport·ing (spôr′tĭng, spōr′-) *adj.* **1.** Used in or appropriate for sports. **2.** Characterized by sportsmanship. **3.** Of or associated with gambling. **4.** Offering a fair hope of success: *a sporting chance.* —**sport′ing·ly** *adv.*

sport·ive (spôr′tĭv, spōr′-) *adj.* Playful; frolicsome. —**sport′ive·ly** *adv.* —**sport′ive·ness** *n.*

sports car. A low, usu. two-passenger high-speed automobile equipped for racing.

sports·man (spôrts′mən, spōrts′-) *n.* **1.** A person who is enthusiastic about and participates in sports. **2.** A person who abides by the rules and accepts victory or defeat graciously. —**sports′man·like′** *adj.* —**sports′man·ly** *adj.*

sports·man·ship (spôrts′mən-shĭp′, spōrts′-) *n.* The qualities and conduct befitting a sportsman.

sports·wear (spôrts′wâr′, spōrts′-) *n.* Clothes designed for active outdoor use or casual wear.

sports·wom·an (spôrts′wo͝om′ən, spōrts′-) *n.* A woman who is active in sports.

sports·writ·er (spôrts′rī′tər) *n.* A person who writes about sports, esp. for a newspaper or magazine.

sport·y (spôr′tē, spōr′-) *adj.* **-i·er, -i·est.** *Informal.* **1.** Appropriate to participation in sports. **2.** Casual; carefree.

spor·u·late (spôr′yə-lāt′, spōr′-) *intr.v.* **-lat·ed, -lat·ing.** To produce or release spores. [From New Latin *sporula,* small spore, from *spora,* spore.] —**spor′u·la′tion** *n.*

spot (spŏt) *n.* **1.** A particular place of relatively small and definite limits. **2.** A mark on a surface, esp. a stain or blot. **3.** A position; location. **4.** *Informal.* A set of circumstances; a situation, esp. a troublesome one. **5.** A personal defect or injury, as in one's reputation. **6.** *Informal.* A small amount; a bit: *a spot of tea.* **7.** *Informal.* A spotlight. —*v.* **spot·ted, spot·ting.** —*tr.v.* **1.** To cause a spot or spots to appear upon. **2.** To decorate with spots; to dot. **3.** To locate precisely. **4.** To detect. **5.** *Sports.* To yield as a handicap: *spotted their opponents 11 points.* —*intr.v.* **1.** To become marked with spots. **2.** To make a stain. — See Syns at **find.** —*adj.* Made, paid, or delivered immediately: *spot cash.* **2.** Presented between major programs: *a spot announcement.* —*idiom.* **on the spot. 1.** At once. **2.** At the scene of action. **3.** Under pressure or attention. [Middle English, perh. of Low German orig.] —**spot′ta·ble** *adj.*

spot check. A random and hasty inspection.

spot-check (spŏt′chĕk′) *tr.v.* To subject to a spot check.

spot·less (spŏt′lĭs) *adj.* **1.** Perfectly clean. **2.** Free from blemish; impeccable. —See Syns at **clean.** —**spot′less·ly** *adv.* —**spot′less·ness** *n.*

spot·light (spŏt′līt′) *n.* **1.** A strong beam of light that illuminates only a small area, as on a stage. **2.** A lamp that produces a spotlight. **3.** Public attention or prominence. —*tr.v.* To illuminate with or as if with a spotlight.

spot·ted (spŏt′ĭd) *adj.* Marked or stained with spots.

spotted fever. 1. Any of various often fatal infectious diseases, such as typhus and Rocky Mountain spotted fever, that are characterized by skin eruptions. **2.** An epidemic form of cerebrospinal meningitis.

spot·ter (spŏt′ər) *n.* **1.** Someone or something that applies spots. **2.** A person who looks for and reports something.

spot·ty (spŏt′ē) *adj.* **-ti·er, -ti·est. 1.** Spotted. **2.** Lacking consistency; uneven. —**spot′ti·ly** *adv.* —**spot′ti·ness** *n.*

spou·sal (spou′zəl, -səl) *adj.* Of or relating to marriage; nuptial. —*n.* Often **spousals.** Marriage; nuptials.

spouse (spous, spouz) *n.* A person's marriage partner; a husband or wife. [Middle English, from Old French *(e)spous,* from Latin *spōnsus,* betrothed (person), from *spondēre,* to make a solemn pledge.]

spout (spout) *intr.v.* **1.** To gush forth in a rapid stream. **2.** To discharge a liquid continuously. **3.** *Informal.* To speak in a pompous or long-winded manner. —*tr.v.* **1.** To cause to flow or spurt out. **2.** To utter pompously. —*n.*

1. A tube, mouth, or pipe through which liquid is discharged. **2.** A continuous stream of liquid. [Middle English *spouten*.] —**spout'er** *n.*

sprain (sprān) *n.* A painful injury caused by a wrenching or laceration of the ligaments of a joint. —*tr.v.* To cause a sprain of (a muscle or joint). [Perh. from Old French *espraindre*, to strain, from Latin *exprimere*, to press out.]

sprang (sprăng) *v.* A past tense of **spring**. [Middle English *sprange*, from Old English *sprang.*]

sprat (sprăt) *n.* **1.** A small saltwater food fish, *Clupea sprattus*, of northeastern Atlantic waters. Also called **brisling**. **2.** Broadly, any similar fish, such as a young herring. [Middle English *sprotte*, from Old English *sprott.*]

sprawl (sprôl) *intr.v.* **1.** To sit or lie with the body and limbs spread out awkwardly. **2.** To spread out in a disordered fashion. **3.** To come to the ground suddenly and involuntarily. —*tr.v.* To cause to spread out in a straggling or disordered fashion. —See Syns at **fall**. —*n.* **1.** A sprawling position or posture. **2.** Haphazard growth or extension outward: *urban sprawl*. [Middle English *spraulen*, from Old English *sprēawlian*.] —**sprawl'er** *n.*

spray¹ (sprā) *n.* **1.** Water or other liquid moving as a mass of dispersed droplets or mist. **2.** A jet of such droplets discharged from a pressurized container. **3.** Such a pressurized container; an atomizer. **4.** Any of numerous commercial products dispensed from containers in this manner. —*modifier: a spray can; a spray paint.* —*tr.v.* **1.** To disperse (a liquid) in a mass or jet of droplets. **2.** To apply a spray to (a surface). —*intr.v.* **1.** To discharge sprays of liquid. **2.** To move in a spray. [From obs. *spray*, to sprinkle, from Middle Dutch *spraeyen*.] —**spray'er** *n.*

spray² (sprā) *n.* **1.** A small branch bearing buds, flowers, or berries. **2.** Any similar design. [Middle English.]

spray gun. A device used to apply a liquid as a spray.

spread (sprĕd) *v.* **spread**, **spread·ing.** —*tr.v.* **1.** To open to a fuller extent; stretch: *spread the tablecloth.* **2.** To make wider the gap between: *spread her fingers.* **3. a.** To distribute over a surface; apply. **b.** To cover with a thin layer: *spread the cracker with butter.* **4.** To distribute widely: *The tornado spread destruction.* **5.** To disseminate: *spread the news.* **6. a.** To prepare (a table) for eating; to set. **b.** To arrange (food or a meal) on a table. —*intr.v.* **1.** To be extended or enlarged. **2.** To become distributed or widely dispersed. **3.** To become known or prevalent over a wide area: *The news spread fast.* **4.** To become distributed in a thin layer. **5.** To be forced farther apart. —*n.* **1.** The act of spreading. **2. a.** An open area of land; expanse. **b.** A ranch. **3.** The extent or limit to which something is or can be spread; a range. **4.** A cloth covering for a bed, table, or other piece of furniture. **5.** *Informal.* An abundant meal laid out on a table. **6.** A food to be spread on bread or crackers. **7.** Printed material that extends across facing pages or adjacent columns. **8.** The difference, as between two figures or totals. [Middle English *spredden*, from Old English *sprædan*.] —**spread'er** *n.*

> **Syns:** **1. spread, expand, extend, open, outstretch, unfold** *v. Core meaning:* To move or arrange so as to cover a larger area *(spread the blanket on the grass; a bird spreading its wings in flight).* **2. spread, diffuse, disperse, radiate, scatter** *v. Core meaning:* To extend over a wide area *(a poisonous gas that spreads quickly).*

spread eagle. 1. The figure of an eagle with wings and legs spread. **2.** A posture or design resembling this.

spread-ea·gle (sprĕd'ē'gəl) *adj.* **1.** With the arms and legs stretched out. **2.** Full of boastful or patriotic rhetoric. —*v.* -**gled**, -**gling.** —*tr.v.* To place in a spread-eagle position. —*intr.v.* To stretch out the arms and legs.

spree (sprē) *n.* **1.** A gay, lively outing. **2.** An overindulgence; binge. [Perh. from Scottish *spreath*, cattle taken as booty, raid, plunder.]

spri·er (sprī'ər) *adj.* A comparative of **spry**.

spri·est (sprī'ĭst) *adj.* A superlative of **spry**.

sprig (sprĭg) *n.* **1. a.** A small shoot or twig of a plant. **b.** An ornament in this shape. **2.** A small brad without a head. **3.** A young, immature person. —*tr.v.* **sprigged, sprig·ging. 1.** To decorate with sprigs. **2.** To fasten with a small headless brad. [Middle English *sprigge*.] —**sprig'ger** *n.*

spright·ly (sprīt'lē) *adj.* -**li·er**, -**li·est.** Lively and brisk; animated. —See Syns at **vigorous**. —*adv.* With briskness,

spring (sprĭng) *v.* **sprang** (sprăng) or **sprung** (sprŭng), **sprung, spring·ing.** —*intr.v.* **1.** To move upward or forward in a single quick motion; leap. **2.** To appear or emerge suddenly. **3.** To shift position suddenly: *The door sprang shut.* **4.** To arise from a source; develop. **5.** To become warped, bent, or cracked. **6.** To move out of place. —*tr.v.* **1.** To cause to leap, dart, or come forth suddenly. **2.** To jump over; to vault. **3.** To release from a checked or held position; actuate: *Motion will spring the trap.* **4.** To cause to warp, bend, or crack. **5.** To present unexpectedly: *spring a surprise.* **6.** *Slang.* To cause to be released from prison. —*n.* **1.** An elastic device, esp. a coil of wire, that regains its original shape after being compressed or extended. **2.** The quality of being elastic; resilience. **3. a.** The act of springing. **b.** The distance covered by a leap. **4.** The return to normal shape after removal of stress; recoil. **5.** A natural fountain or flow of water. **6.** A source, origin, or beginning. **7.** The season of the year, occurring between winter and summer, during which the weather becomes warmer and plants revive. **8.** A warping, bending, or cracking. —*modifier: a spring lock; spring water; a spring outfit.* [Middle English *springen*, from Old English *springan*.] —**spring'er** *n.*

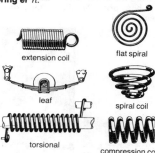

extension coil
flat spiral
leaf
spiral coil
torsional
compression coil

spring

spring beauty. Any of several plants of the genus *Claytonia*, esp. *C. virginica*, of eastern North America, with narrow leaves and white or pinkish flowers.

spring·board (sprĭng'bôrd', -bōrd') *n.* **1.** A flexible board mounted on a fulcrum with one end secured, used by gymnasts to gain momentum in leaping or tumbling. **2.** A **diving board. 3.** Something that provides a start in the attainment of a goal.

spring·bok (sprĭng'bŏk') *n.* Also **spring·buck** (-bŭk'). A small brown and white gazelle, *Antidorcas marsupialis*, of southern Africa, that is capable of leaping high into the air. [Afrikaans : *spring*, to leap up + *bok*, male deer.]

spring-clean·ing (sprĭng-klē'nĭng) *n.* An extensive cleaning, usu. of a home after winter.

springe (sprĭnj) *n.* A device for snaring small game, made by attaching a noose to a branch under tension. —*tr.v.* **springed, spring·ing.** To trap with a springe; ensnare. [Middle English.]

spring·er spaniel (sprĭng'ər). A dog of a breed originating in England or Wales, with drooping ears and a silky brown and white or black and white coat.

springer spaniel

spring fever. The feelings of laziness, rejuvenation, or yearning that may affect people at the advent of spring.

spring peeper. A small, brownish tree frog, *Hyla crucifer*, of eastern North America, with a shrill call.

spring·tail (sprĭng'tāl') *n.* Any of various small wingless insects of the order Collembola, which have appendages that act as springs to catapult them through the air.

spring tide. The tide gen. having the greatest rise and fall, occurring at the new moon and the full moon.

spring·time (sprĭng'tīm') *n.* The season of spring.

spring·y (sprĭng'ē) *adj.* **-i·er, -i·est.** Resilient; elastic. —See Syns at **flexible.** —**spring'i·ly** *adv.* —**spring'i·ness** *n.*

sprin·kle (sprĭng'kəl) *v.* **-kled, -kling.** —*tr.v.* **1.** To scatter in drops or small particles. **2.** To scatter drops or particles upon. —*intr.v.* **1.** To scatter small drops or particles. **2.** To fall or rain in small or infrequent drops. —*n.* **1.** The act of sprinkling. **2.** A light, sparse rainfall. **3.** A small amount. [Middle English *sprenklen*, prob. from Middle Dutch *sprenkelen*.] —**sprin'kler** *n.*

sprin·kling (sprĭng'klĭng) *n.* A small amount.

sprint (sprĭnt) *n.* A short race run at top speed. —*intr.v.* To run at top speed. [Of Scandinavian orig.] —**sprint'er** *n.*

sprit (sprĭt) *n.* **1.** A pole extending diagonally across a fore-and-aft sail from the lower part of the mast to the peak of the sail. **2.** A bowsprit. [Middle English *sprytt*, from Old English *sprēot*, pole.]

sprit   sprocket

sprite (sprīt) *n.* An elf or pixie. [Middle English *spreit*, from Old French *espirit*, from Latin *spīritus*, spirit.]

sprit·sail (sprĭt'sāl', -səl) *n.* A sail extended by a sprit.

sprock·et (sprŏk'ĭt) *n.* **1.** Any of various toothlike projections arranged on a wheel rim to engage the links of a chain. **2.** A wheel with sprockets. [Orig. unknown.]

sprout (sprout) *intr.v.* **1.** To begin to grow; give off shoots or buds. **2.** To grow or develop quickly. —*tr.v.* **1.** To cause to sprout. **2.** To put forth like new growths: *The prairies sprouted oil wells.* —*n.* **1.** A young plant growth, such as a bud or shoot. **2.** Something suggestive of a sprout. **3. sprouts. Brussels sprouts.** [Middle English *spruten*, from Old English *sprūtan*.]

spruce[1] (sproos) *n.* **1.** Any of various coniferous evergreen trees of the genus *Picea*, with needlelike foliage, drooping cones, and soft wood often used for paper pulp. **2.** The wood of any of these trees. —*modifier: a spruce forest.* [Short for *Spruce fir*, "Prussian fir," from obs. *Spruce*, Prussia, Middle English *Sprewse*, alteration of *Pruce*, from Old French, from Medieval Latin *Prussia*.]

spruce[2] (sproos) *adj.* **spruc·er, spruc·est.** Having a neat, trim, or dapper appearance. —*v.* **spruced, spruc·ing.** —*tr.v.* To make spruce; dress neatly. —*intr.v.* To make oneself spruce: *He spruced up for the dance.* [Perh. from obs. *Spruce*, Prussia, Prussian leather (from the fineness of the leather).] —**spruce'ly** *adv.* —**spruce'ness** *n.*

sprung (sprŭng) *v.* The past tense and a past participle of **spring.** [Middle English *sprungen*, from Old English *sprungon* (pl.), *(ge)sprungen*.]

spry (sprī) *adj.* **spri·er** or **spry·er, spri·est** or **spry·est.** Active; nimble; lively; brisk. —See Syns at **vigorous.** [Perh. of Scandinavian orig.] —**spry'ly** *adv.* —**spry'ness** *n.*

spud (spŭd) *n.* **1.** A sharp tool resembling a spade. **2.** *Informal.* A potato. —*tr.v.* **spud·ded, spud·ding.** To remove with a spud. [Middle English *spudde*, short knife.]

spume (spyoom) *n.* Foam or froth on a liquid. —*intr.v.* **spumed, spum·ing.** To foam. [Middle English, from Old French *(e)spume*, from Latin *spūma*.] —**spum'y** *adj.*

spu·mo·ne (spoo-mō'nē) *n.* Also **spu·mo·ni.** An Italian multiflavored ice cream. [Italian, from *spuma*, foam, from Latin *spūma*.]

spun (spŭn) *v.* Past tense and past participle of **spin.** [Middle English *spunnun* (pl.), *spunnen*, from Old English *spunnon* (pl.), *(ge)spunnen*.]

spun glass. Fiber glass.

spunk (spŭngk) *n. Informal.* Spirit; pluck. [Scottish Gaelic *spong*, tinder, sponge, from Latin *spongia*, sponge.]

spunk·y (spŭng'kē) *adj.* **-i·er, -i·est.** Having spunk; spirited; plucky. —**spunk'i·ly** *adv.* —**spunk'i·ness** *n.*

spun silk. A yarn made from short-fibered silk.

spun sugar. Sugar threaded into a confectionary fluff. Also called **cotton candy.**

spur (spûr) *n.* **1.** One of a pair of spikes or spiked wheels attached to a rider's heels and used to urge the horse forward. **2.** An incentive; stimulus. **3.** A narrow, pointed attachment or projection, as: **a.** A spinelike process on the leg of some birds. **b.** A climbing iron; crampon. **c.** The gaff attached to the leg of a gamecock. **4.** A ridge projecting from the side of a mountain. **5.** *Bot.* A tubular extension of the corolla or calyx of a flower, as in a columbine or larkspur. **6.** A **spur track.** —See Syns at **stimulus.** —*v.* **spurred, spur·ring.** —*tr.v.* **1.** To urge (a horse) on by the use of spurs. **2.** To incite; stimulate. —*intr.v.* To ride quickly on horseback. —See Syns at **provoke.** —*idiom.* **on the spur of the moment.** On a sudden impulse. [Middle English *spore*, from Old English *spora*.]

spurge (spûrj) *n.* Any of various chiefly tropical plants of the genus *Euphorbia*, characteristically with milky juice and small flowers. [Middle English, from Old French *espurge*, purge (from the use of certain species as purgatives), from *espurgier*, to purge, from Latin *expurgāre*: *ex-*, away + *purgāre*, to purge, purify.]

spur gear. A gear with radial teeth parallel to its axis.

spu·ri·ous (spyoor'ē-əs) *adj.* Lacking authenticity or validity; counterfeit. [Late Latin *spurius*, false, from Latin, illegitimate.] —**spu'ri·ous·ly** *adv.* —**spu'ri·ous·ness** *n.*

spurn (spûrn) *tr.v.* **1.** To reject or refuse disdainfully; scorn. **2.** *Archaic.* To kick or tread on. —*intr.v.* To show disdain: *spurn at offers of help.* —See Syns at **reject.** —*n.* A contemptuous rejection. [Middle English *spurnen*, from Old English *spurnan*.] —**spurn'er** *n.*

spurt (spûrt) Also *Brit.* **spirt.** —*n.* **1.** A sudden and forcible gush, as of water. **2.** Any sudden outbreak or short burst of energy or activity. —*intr.v.* To burst or gush out suddenly and forcibly. —*tr.v.* To force out in a burst; to squirt. [Orig. unknown.]

spur track. A short side track that connects with the main track of a railroad system. Also called **spur.**

spu·ta (spyoo'tə) *n.* Plural of **sputum.**

sput·nik (spŭt'nĭk, spoot'-) *n.* Any of the artificial earth satellites launched by the U.S.S.R., esp. the first. [Russian *sputnik (zemlyi)*, "fellow traveler (of Earth).")

sput·ter (spŭt'ər) *intr.v.* **1.** To spit out small particles of saliva or food in short bursts, often with corresponding sounds. **2.** To make a sporadic coughing noise. **3.** To stammer. —*tr.v.* **1.** To spit out in short bursts. **2.** To utter in a hasty or confused fashion. —*n.* **1.** The act of sputtering. **2.** The sound of sputtering. **3.** Hasty or confused speech. [From Dutch *sputteren*.] —**sput'ter·er** *n.*

spu·tum (spyoo'təm) *n., pl.* **-ta** (-tə). **1.** Saliva that is spit out; spit; spittle. **2.** Any matter that is spit out. [Latin *spūtum*, from *spuere*, to spit.]

spy (spī) *n., pl.* **spies. 1.** A secret agent employed by a state to obtain intelligence relating to enemies at home or abroad. **2.** A person who secretly watches another or others. —*modifier: a spy organization.* —*v.* **spied, spy·ing.** —*tr.v.* **1.** To keep under surveillance. **2.** To catch sight of; see. —*intr.v.* **1.** To observe secretly and closely: *spied on his fellow workers.* **2.** To investigate; pry: *spying into their activities.* [Middle English *spie*, from Old French *espie*, from *espier*, to spy, watch.]

spy·glass (spī'glăs') *n.* **1.** A small telescope. **2. spyglasses.** Binoculars.

squab (skwŏb) *n.* A young, unfledged pigeon. —*adj.* Newly hatched or unfledged. [Prob. of Scandinavian orig.]

squab·ble (skwŏb'əl) *intr.v.* **-bled, -bling.** To engage in a

---

ă pat	ā pay	â care	ä father	ĕ pet	ē be	hw which	ĭ pit	ī tie	î pier	ŏ pot	ō toe	ô paw, for	oi noise
ŏŏ took	ōō boot	ou out	th thin	th this	ŭ cut		û urge	zh vision	ə about, item, edible, gallop, circus				

minor quarrel; bicker. —*n.* A minor quarrel. —See Syns at **argue**. [Prob. of Scandinavian orig.] —**squab′bler** *n.*

squad (skwŏd) *n.* **1.** A small group of persons organized for a specific purpose. **2.** *Mil.* The smallest unit of personnel, usu. composed of about ten persons. **3.** An athletic team. —*modifier: a squad leader.* [Old French *esquadre*, from Old Spanish *escuadra*, "square formation (of troops)," ult. from Latin *quadrus*, a square.]

squad car. A police patrol car connected by radiotelephone with headquarters. Also called **cruiser**.

squad·ron (skwŏd′rən) *n.* **1.** A group of naval vessels constituting two or more divisions of a fleet. **2.** *U.S. Air Force.* The basic tactical unit, subordinate to a group and consisting of two or more flights. **3.** Any organized multitude; a legion. [Italian *squadrone*, "square formation (of troops)," ult. from Latin *quadrus*, square.]

squal·id (skwŏl′ĭd) *adj.* **1.** Having a dirty, cluttered, or wretched appearance. **2.** Morally repulsive; sordid. [Latin *squālidus*, from *squālus*, scabby, filthy.] —**squal′id·ly** *adv.* —**squal′id·ness** *n.*

squall¹ (skwôl) *n.* A loud, harsh outcry. —*intr.v.* To cry loudly and harshly. [Prob. of Scandinavian orig.]

squall² (skwôl) *n.* **1.** A brief, sudden, and violent windstorm, often accompanied by rain or snow. **2.** *Informal.* A disturbance or commotion. —*intr.v.* To blow strongly for a brief period; blow a squall. [Prob. of Scandinavian orig.]

squal·or (skwŏl′ər) *n.* The condition or quality of being squalid. [Latin, from *squālēre*, to be filthy.]

squa·mous (skwā′məs) *adj.* Also **squa·mose** (-mōs′). **1.** Covered with or formed of scales; scaly. **2.** Resembling a scale or scales; scalelike. —**squa′mous·ly** *adv.* —**squa′mous·ness** *n.*

squan·der (skwŏn′dər) *tr.v.* To use or spend wastefully or extravagantly; dissipate: *squandered his fortune.* —See Syns at **waste**. [Orig. unknown.] —**squan′der·er** *n.*

square (skwâr) *n.* Abbr. **sq. 1.** A rectangle with four equal sides. **2.** Anything characterized by this form. **3.** A T-shaped or L-shaped instrument or tool for drawing or testing right angles. **4.** The product of a number or quantity multiplied by itself: *The square of 4 is 16.* **5.** Any of the quadrilateral spaces dividing a checkerboard. **6.** An open area at the intersection of two or more streets. **7.** *Slang.* A person characterized by rigid conventionality or lack of sophistication. —*adj.* **squar·er, squar·est. 1.** Having four equal sides and four right angles. **2.** Forming a right angle: *square corners.* **3. a.** Of, being, or using units that express the measure of areas: *square feet.* **b.** Having a specified length in each of two equal dimensions: *a lot 200 yards square.* **4.** Set at right angles to the mast and keel, as the yards of a square-rigged ship. **5.** Like a square in form: *a square jaw.* **6.** Honest; direct: *a square answer.* **7.** Just; equitable: *a square deal.* **8.** Paid-up; settled. **9.** Even; tied. **10.** *Slang.* Rigidly conventional; unsophisticated. —*v.* **squared, squar·ing.** —*tr.v.* **1.** To cut to a square or rectangular shape. **2.** To test for conformity to a desired plane, straight line, or right angle. **3.** To bring into conformity or agreement. **4.** To set straight or at right angles. **5.** To bring into balance; settle: *square a debt.* **6.** To even (a score); tie. **7.** To multiply (a number, quantity, or expression) by itself. **8.** To find a square equal in area to (the area of a given figure). —*intr.v.* **1.** To be at right angles. **2.** To agree or conform; balance. —*phrasal verbs.* **square away. 1.** To square the yards of a sailing vessel. **2.** To put away or in order. **square off.** To assume a fighting stance. —*adv.* **1.** At right angles. **2.** In a square shape. **3.** Directly; straight. **4.** Straightforwardly. —*idioms.* **on the square. 1.** At right angles. **2.** Honestly and openly. **out of square.** Not at a precise right angle. [Middle English, from Old French *esquare* : Latin *ex-* (intensive) + *quadrāre*, to square.] —**square′ly** *adv.* —**square′ness** *n.* —**squar′er** *n.*

square dance. 1. A dance in which sets of four couples form squares. **2.** Any of various similar group dances.

square-dance (skwâr′dăns′) *intr.v.* **-danced, -danc·ing.** To perform a square dance.

square knot. A common double knot with the loose ends parallel to the standing parts. Also called **reef knot**.

square rig. A sailing-ship rig with sails of rectangular cut set approx. at right angles to the keel line from horizontal yards. —**square′-rigged′** *adj.*

square-rig·ger (skwâr′rĭg′ər) *n.* A square-rigged vessel.

square root. A number that when multiplied by itself results in a given number: *The square root of 16 is 4.*

square sail. A four-sided sail for a square-rigged ship.

squash¹ (skwŏsh, skwôsh) *n.* **1.** Any of several types of fleshy fruit related to the pumpkins and the gourds, eaten as a vegetable. **2.** A vine that bears such fruit. [Short for *isquoutersquash*, of Algonquian orig.]

squash² (skwŏsh, skwôsh) *tr.v.* **1.** To press, squeeze, or flatten to a pulp; crush. **2.** To put down or suppress; quash. **3.** To silence (a person), as with crushing words. —*intr.v.* **1.** To be crushed or flattened. **2.** To move with a squelching sound. —*n.* **1.** The act or sound of squashing. **2.** A crush or press, esp. of people. **3.** *Brit.* A citrus-base soft drink. **4. a.** A game played in a walled court with a racket and a hard rubber ball. Also called **squash rackets. b.** A similar game played with an inflated rubber ball. In this sense, also called **squash tennis.** —*adv.* With a squashing sound. [Old French *esquasser*: Latin *ex-* (intensive) + *quassāre*, to shatter, freq. of *quatere*, to shake.] —**squash′er** *n.*

squash bug. A blackish North American insect, *Anasa tristis*, destructive to squash and other crops.

squash·y (skwŏ′shē, skwôsh′ē) *adj.* **-i·er, -i·est. 1.** Easily squashed. **2.** Overripe and soft; pulpy. **3.** Boggy; squishy. —**squash′i·ly** *adv.* —**squash′i·ness** *n.*

squat (skwŏt) *v.* **squat·ted** or **squat, squat·ting.** —*intr.v.* **1.** To sit on one's heels. **2.** To settle on unoccupied land without legal claim. **3.** To occupy a given piece of public land in order to acquire title to it. —*tr.v.* To put in a squatting posture. —*adj.* **squat·ter, squat·test. 1.** Seated in a squatting position. **2.** Short and thick. —*n.* The act or posture of squatting. [Middle English *squatten*, to flatten, from Old French *esquatir* : *es-*, from Latin *ex-* (intensive) + *quatir*, to press flat, from Latin *cogere*, to drive together.] —**squat′ter** *n.*

squaw (skwô) *n.* A North American Indian woman. [Massachuset *squa*.]

squawk (skwôk) *intr.v.* **1.** To utter a harsh scream; screech. **2.** *Slang.* To make a loud or angry protest. —*n.* **1.** A loud screech; squall. **2.** *Slang.* A loud or insistent protest. [Perh. blend of SQUALL and SQUEAK.] —**squawk′er** *n.*

squeak (skwēk) *intr.v.* **1.** To utter or make a thin, high-pitched cry or sound. **2.** To pass or win by a slight margin: *squeaked by his opponent in the election.* —*tr.v.* To utter in a squeaky voice. —*n.* A thin, high-pitched cry or sound. [Middle English *squeken*, prob. of Scandinavian orig.] —**squeak′er** *n.*

squeak·y (skwē′kē) *adj.* **-i·er, -i·est.** Making a thin, high-pitched sound. —**squeak′i·ly** *adv.* —**squeak′i·ness** *n.*

squeal (skwēl) *intr.v.* **1.** To utter or produce a high, loud, drawn-out cry or sound. **2.** *Slang.* To turn informer. —*tr.v.* To utter or produce with a squeal. —*n.* A high, loud, drawn-out cry or sound. [Middle English *squelen*, prob. of Scandinavian orig.] —**squeal′er** *n.*

squea·mish (skwē′mĭsh) *adj.* **1. a.** Easily nauseated. **b.** Nauseated. **2.** Easily offended or disgusted. [Middle English *squaymissh*, from Old English *swīma*, dizziness.] —**squea′mish·ly** *adv.* —**squea′mish·ness** *n.*

squee·gee (skwē′jē) *n.* **1.** A tool with a rubber blade set across a handle, used to remove excess water from windows and other smooth surfaces. **2.** A similar tool or a

square rig

rubber roller used in printing and photography. —*tr.v.* **-geed, -gee·ing.** To wipe or smooth with a squeegee. [Prob. from *squeege*, perh. var. of SQUEEZE.]

squeeze (skwēz) *v.* **squeezed, squeez·ing.** —*tr.v.* **1.** To press hard upon or together; to compress. **2.** To exert pressure on, as when extracting liquid: *squeeze an orange.* **3.** To extract by pressure: *squeeze juice from a lemon.* **4.** To extort: *squeezed a confession out of him.* **5.** To obtain room or passage for by pressure; cram. **6.** To oppress. —*intr.v.* **1.** To exert pressure. **2.** To force one's way by pressure. —*n.* **1.** An act of compressing; compression. **2.** A handclasp or brief embrace. **3.** A group crowded together. **4.** An amount squeezed out: *a squeeze of lemon.* **5.** Pressure exerted to obtain some goal. **6.** A pressure-ridden situation: *He's in a tight squeeze.* [Middle English *queysen,* from Old English *cwȳsan.*] —**squeez′er** *n.*

squeeze play. A baseball play in which the batter attempts to bunt while a runner on third base races home.

squelch (skwĕlch) *tr.v.* **1.** To crush by or as if by trampling; suppress. **2.** To put down or silence, as with a crushing remark. —*intr.v.* To make or move with a splashing, squashing, or sucking sound. —*n.* **1.** A squishing sound. **2.** A crushing reply. [Imit.] —**squelch′er** *n.*

squib (skwĭb) *n.* **1.** A firecracker, esp. a broken one that burns but does not explode. **2.** A brief, sometimes witty literary effort, such as a lampoon. [Prob. imit.]

squid (skwĭd) *n., pl.* **squids** or **squid.** Any of various saltwater cephalopod mollusks of the genera *Loligo, Rossia,* and related genera, with a long body, ten arms and a pair of triangular or rounded fins. [Orig. unknown.]

squid

squig·gle (skwĭg′əl) *n.* A small wiggly mark or scrawl. —*intr.v.* **-gled, -gling.** To squirm and wriggle. [Blend of SQUIRM and WRIGGLE.] —**squig′gly** *adj.*

squill (skwĭl) *n.* **1.** Any of several bulbous Eurasian plants of the genus *Scilla,* with narrow leaves and bell-shaped flowers. **2.** A related plant, the **sea onion.** [Middle English, from Latin *squilla,* from Greek *skilla.*]

squint (skwĭnt) *intr.v.* **1.** To look with the eyes partly open. **2.** To look or glance to the side. **3.** To be cross-eyed. —*tr.v.* To close (the eyes) partly. —*n.* **1.** The act of squinting. **2.** The condition of being cross-eyed. —*adj.* Looking obliquely. [Short for *asquint,* with a sidelong glance, from Middle English.] —**squint′er** *n.*

squire (skwīr) *n.* **1.** A young nobleman attendant upon a knight and ranked next below a knight in the feudal hierarchy. **2.** An English country gentleman. **3.** A judge or other local dignitary. **4.** A lady's escort. —*tr.v.* **squired, squir·ing.** To attend as a squire. [Middle English *squier,* from Old French *esquier,* shield-bearer, from Late Latin *scūtārius,* from Latin *scūtum,* a shield.]

squirm (skwûrm) *intr.v.* **1.** To twist about in a wriggling, snakelike motion; writhe. **2.** To feel or exhibit signs of humiliation or embarrassment. —*n.* The act of squirming or a squirming movement. [Perh. imit.] —**squirm′er** *n.* —**squirm′y** *adj.*

squir·rel (skwûr′əl, skwŭr′-) *n.* **1.** Any of various tree-climbing rodents of the family Sciuridae, usu. with gray or reddish-brown fur and a long, flexible, bushy tail. **2.** The fur of a squirrel. —*modifier: a squirrel coat.* —*tr.v.* **squirrel away.** To save or hoard, as a squirrel does nuts. [Middle English *squyrel,* from Norman French *esquirel,* from *sciūrus,* from Greek *skiouros* : *skia,* shadow + *oura,* tail.]

squirrel monkey. Either of two tropical monkeys, *Saimiri sciureus* or *S. örstedii,* with short, thick fur and a long tail.

squirt (skwûrt) *intr.v.* **1.** To be ejected in a thin swift

stream. **2.** To eject a thin swift stream. —*tr.v.* **1.** To eject (liquid) in a thin swift stream. **2.** To wet with liquid so ejected. —*n.* **1.** The act of squirting. **2.** A device used to squirt. **3.** The stream squirted. **4.** *Informal.* An insignificant person, esp. someone young or small. [Middle English *squirten,* of Low German orig.] —**squirt′er** *n.*

squish (skwĭsh) *tr.v. Informal.* To squash noisily. —*intr.v. Informal.* To emit a sound like that of soft mud being compressed. [Var. of SQUASH.] —**squish′y** *adj.*

Sr The symbol for the element strontium.

-st. Var. of **-est** (verb suffix).

stab (stăb) *v.* **stabbed, stab·bing.** —*tr.v.* **1.** To pierce or wound with or as if with a pointed weapon. **2.** To plunge (a weapon) into a body. —*intr.v.* **1.** To lunge with or as if with a pointed weapon: *stabbed at the bull's neck.* —*n.* **1.** A thrust made with a pointed instrument or weapon. **2.** A wound inflicted by stabbing. **3.** An attempt; an effort. [Middle English *stabbe.*] —**stab′ber** *n.*

sta·bil·i·ty (stə-bĭl′ĭ-tē) *n., pl.* **-ties. 1.** Resistance to sudden change, dislodgment, or overthrow. **2.** Constancy of character or purpose; steadfastness.

sta·bi·lize (stā′bə-līz′) *v.* **-lized, -liz·ing.** —*tr.v.* To make stable. —*intr.v.* To become stable. —**sta′bi·li·za′tion** *n.*

sta·bi·liz·er (stā′bə-lī′zər) *n.* Someone or something that stabilizes, esp. a device in a ship or aircraft to prevent excessive rolling.

sta·ble¹ (stā′bəl) *adj.* **-bler, -blest. 1. a.** Resistant to sudden change of position or condition. **b.** Maintaining equilibrium; self-restoring. **2.** *Physics.* Not known to decay; indefinitely long-lived: *a stable isotope.* **3.** Long-lasting; enduring. **4.** Not easily decomposed or otherwise modified chemically. **5.** Consistently dependable. [Middle English, from Old French *estable,* from Latin *stabilis,* standing firm.] —**sta′ble·ness** *n.* —**sta′bly** *adv.*

sta·ble² (stā′bəl) *n.* **1.** A building for the shelter and feeding of domestic animals, esp. horses and cattle. **2.** The animals lodged in such a building. **3.** The racehorses of a single owner. **4.** Any group that serves under a single authority. —*tr.v.* **-bled, -bling.** To put or keep (an animal) in a stable. —*intr.v.* To live or be kept in a stable. [Middle English, from Old French *estable,* from Latin *stabulum.*]

stac·ca·to (stə-kä′tō) *adj.* **1.** *Mus.* Performed with a crisp, sharp attack to simulate rests between successive tones. Used as a direction to the performer. **2.** Composed of abrupt, distinct parts or sounds: *staccato applause.* —*n., pl.* **-tos** or **-ti** (-tē). An abrupt, emphatic manner or sound. [Italian, past part. of *staccare,* to detach, from Old French *destachier.*] —**stac·ca′to** *adv.*

stack (stăk) *n.* **1.** A large, usu. conical pile, as of straw or fodder. **2.** Any orderly pile, esp. one arranged in layers. **3. a.** A chimney or flue. **b.** A group of chimneys. **4.** A vertical exhaust pipe. **5.** A bookcase. **6. stacks.** The area of a library in which most of the books are shelved. **7.** An English measure of coal or cut wood, equal to 108 cubic feet. **8.** Often **stacks.** *Informal.* A large quantity. —*tr.v.* **1.** To arrange in a stack; to pile. **2.** To load with stacks of some material. **3.** To prearrange the order of (playing cards) so as to cheat. —*phrasal verb.* **stack up. 1.** To add up or total. **2.** To measure up; compare. [Middle English *stak,* from Old Norse *stakkr.*] —**stack′er** *n.*

sta·di·a (stā′dē-ə) *n.* **1.** A method of surveying distances using a calibrated rod sighted through a telescope, the fraction of the rod visible being proportional to the intervening distance. **2.** Plural of **stadium** (course and distance). [Italian, prob. from Latin, pl. of *stadium,* measure of length.]

squirrel

sta·di·um (stā′dē-əm) *n.* **1.** *pl.* **-di·a** (dē-ə). In ancient Greece, a course on which foot races were held, usu. semicircular and having tiers of seats for spectators. **2.** *pl.* **-di·a.** An ancient Greek measure of distance equal to about 607 feet. **3.** *pl.* **-di·ums.** A large, often unroofed structure in which athletic events are held. [Middle English, measure of distance, from Latin, from Greek *stadion,* alteration of *spadion,* racetrack, from *span,* to draw, pull.]

staff (stăf) *n.* **1.** *pl.* **staffs** or **staves** (stāvz). A pole, rod, or stick carried for various purposes, specif.: **a.** A stick or cane carried as an aid in walking or climbing. **b.** A cudgel. **c.** A pole upon which a flag is displayed. **d.** A rod, baton, etc., carried as a symbol of authority. **2.** *pl.* **staffs. a.** A group of assistants who aid an executive or other person of authority. **b.** A group of military or naval officers who serve a commanding officer but have no authority to command. **c.** The personnel who carry out a specific enterprise. **3.** *pl.* **staffs** or **staves.** *Mus.* The set of horizontal lines and their intermediate spaces upon which notes are written or printed. In this sense, also called **stave.** —*tr.v.* To provide with a staff of employees. [Middle English *staf,* from Old English *stæf.*]

staff of life. A staple or necessary food, esp. bread.

stag (stăg) *n.* **1.** The adult male of various deer, esp. the red deer. **2.** An animal, esp. a pig, castrated after reaching sexual maturity. **3.** A man who attends a social affair without escorting a woman. **4.** A social affair for men only. —*adj.* For or attended by men only: *a stag party.* —*adv.* As a single male; alone: *go stag.* [Middle English, from Old English *stagga.*]

stage (stāj) *n.* **1.** Any raised and level floor or platform. **2.** A platform on a microscope on which slides to be viewed are mounted. **3.** A workmen's scaffold. **4. a.** The raised platform, as in a theater, on which actors and other entertainers perform. **b.** The acting profession. **c.** Dramatic literature or performance; the theater. **5.** The scene or setting of an event. **6.** A resting place on a journey, esp. one providing overnight accommodations. **7.** The distance between stopping places on a journey. **8.** A stagecoach. **9.** A level or story of a building. **10.** The level of the surface of a river or other fluctuating body of water: *at flood stage.* **11.** A level or period in the course of a process. **12.** *Aerospace.* One of two or more successive propulsion units of a rocket vehicle. —*tr.v.* **staged, stag·ing. 1.** To exhibit, present, or perform on or as if on a stage: *stage a boxing match.* **2.** To produce or direct (a theatrical performance). **3.** To arrange and carry out. [Middle English, from Old French *estage,* ult. from Latin *stāre,* to stand.]

stage·coach (stāj′kōch′) *n.* A four-wheeled horse-drawn vehicle formerly used to transport mail and passengers.

stage·craft (stāj′krăft′) *n.* The practice of or skill in theatrical techniques.

stage fright. The fear or nervousness some people feel when speaking or performing before an audience.

stage·hand (stāj′hănd′) *n.* A person who works backstage in a theater.

stage-struck (stāj′strŭk′) *adj.* Enthralled with the theater or with hopes of becoming an actor.

stage whisper. The conventional whisper of an actor, intended to be heard by the audience.

stag·fla·tion (stăg-flā′shən) *n.* An economic condition in which a high rate of inflation is coupled with stagnant consumer demand and high unemployment. [STAG(NATION) + (IN)FLATION.] —**stag·fla′tion·ar′y** (-shə-něr′ē) *adj.*

stag·ger (stăg′ər) *intr.v.* **1.** To move or stand unsteadily, as if under a great weight; totter. **2.** To lose strength or confidence; begin to yield. —*tr.v.* **1.** To cause to totter or reel: *The blow staggered him.* **2.** To overwhelm with emotion or surprise. **3.** To set in a zigzag row or rows: *theater seats staggered for clear viewing.* **4.** To arrange in alternating or overlapping time periods: *stagger the class schedules.* —*n.* **1.** The act of staggering. **2. staggers** (*used with a sing. verb*). A disease of horses, cattle, etc., in which the animal staggers and often falls. [Middle English *stakeren,* from Old Norse *stakra,* freq. of *staka,* to push, cause to stumble.] —**stag′ger·er** *n.* —**stag′ger·ing·ly** *adv.*

stag·ing (stā′jĭng) *n.* **1.** A temporary platform; scaffold. **2.** The process of producing and directing a stage play.

staging area. A place where armed forces or military supplies are gathered before departure for another locale.

stag·nant (stăg′nənt) *adj.* **1.** Not moving or flowing; motionless. **2.** Foul from standing still; stale. **3.** Lacking liveliness or briskness; sluggish. [Latin *stagnāns,* pres. part. of *stagnāre,* to be stagnant, from *stagnum,* pond, swamp.] —**stag′nan·cy** *n.* —**stag′nant·ly** *adv.*

stag·nate (stăg′nāt′) *intr.v.* **-nat·ed, -nat·ing. 1.** To be or become stagnant. **2.** To lie inactive; fail to change or develop. —**stag·na′tion** *n.*

stag·y (stā′jē) *adj.* **-i·er, -i·est.** Having a theatrical quality. —**stag′i·ly** *adv.* —**stag′i·ness** *n.*

staid (stād) *adj.* **-er, -est.** Prudently reserved and colorless in manner or behavior; sedate. [From *staid,* obs. past part. of STAY.] —**staid′ly** *adv.* —**staid′ness** *n.*

stain (stān) *tr.v.* **1.** To discolor, soil, or spot. **2.** To taint; tarnish. **3.** To color with a coat of penetrating liquid dye or tint. **4.** To treat (specimens for the microscope) with a dye that makes visible certain parts. —*intr.v.* To produce or receive discolorations. —*n.* **1.** A spot or smudge of foreign matter. **2.** A blemish; stigma. **3.** A liquid substance applied esp. to wood that penetrates the surface and imparts a rich color. **4.** A colored solution used for staining microscopic specimens. [Middle English *steynen,* short for *disteynen,* to deprive of color, stain, from Old French *desteindre* : Latin *dis-* (reversal) + *tingere,* to dye.] —**stain′er** *n.*

stained glass. Glass colored by mixing pigments inherently in the glass, by fusing colored metallic oxides onto the glass, or by painting, widely used in church windows. —*modifier* (**stained-glass**): *stained-glass windows.*

stained glass **stalactite**

stain·less (stān′lĭs) *adj.* **1.** Without stain or blemish. **2.** Resistant to stain or corrosion. —See Syns at **clean.** —**stain′less·ly** *adv.*

stainless steel. Any of various steels alloyed with enough chromium to be resistant to rusting and corrosion. —*modifier* (**stainless-steel**): *a stainless-steel knife.*

stair (stâr) *n.* **1. stairs.** A series or flight of steps; a staircase. **2.** One of a flight of steps. [Middle English, from Old English *stæger.*]

stair·case (stâr′kās′) *n.* A flight or series of flights of steps and its supporting structure.

stair·way (stâr′wā′) *n.* A flight of stairs; a staircase.

stair·well (stâr′wĕl′) *n.* A vertical shaft around which a staircase has been built.

stake (stāk) *n.* **1.** A stick or post driven upright into the ground and used as a marker, barrier, support, etc. **2.** A post to which a condemned person is bound for execution by burning. **3.** Often **stakes.** The amount of money or the prize awarded to the winner of a bet, gambling game, contest, or race. **4.** Often **stakes.** A race, esp. a horse race, offering a prize to the winner. **5.** A share or interest in an enterprise. —*tr.v.* **staked, stak·ing. 1.** To mark the location or boundaries of with stakes or other markers: *stake out a piece of land.* **2.** To fasten to a stake for support or safekeeping. **3.** To gamble; risk. **4.** To provide with needed capital or provisions. —*idioms:* **at stake.** In jeopardy. **pull up stakes.** To move on. [Middle English, from Old English *staca.*]

sta·lac·tite (stə-lăk′tīt′) *n.* A deposit, usu. of calcite or aragonite, that projects downward from the roof of a cavern. [From Greek *stalaktos,* dripping, from *stalassein,* to drip.] —**sta·lac·tit′ic** (stăl′ăk-tĭt′ĭk) *adj.*

sta·lag·mite (stə-lăg′mīt′) *n.* A deposit, usu. of calcite or aragonite, that projects upward from the floor of a cavern. [From Greek *stalagma,* a drop, from *stalagmos,* dripping, from *stalassein,* to drip.] —**stal′ag·mit′ic** (stăl′ăg-mĭt′ĭk) *adj.*

stale (stāl) *adj.* **stal·er, stal·est.** **1.** Having lost freshness or flavor: *stale beer.* **2.** Too old or overused to be effective: *stale jokes.* **3.** Weakened by a lack of recent practice. —*v.* **staled, stal·ing.** —*tr.v.* To make stale. —*intr.v.* To become stale. [Middle English, well-aged (liquor).] —**stale′ly** *adv.* —**stale′ness** *n.*

    Syns: stale, flat, tired *adj. Core meaning:* Lacking freshness or effectiveness through age or overuse *(stale ideas; stale soda).* STALE has broad literal and figurative application *(stale crackers; a stale play).* FLAT suggests a lack or loss of sparkle, either literal or metaphorical *(flat champagne; flat jokes).* TIRED refers to what is worn out *(tired outfits)* or hackneyed *(tired comments).*

stale·mate (stāl′māt′) *n.* **1.** A drawing position in chess in which only the king can move and although not in check can move only into check. **2.** A situation in which further progress is impossible; a deadlock. —*tr.v.* **-mat·ed, -mat·ing.** To bring to a stalemate. [Obs. *stale,* stalemate, from Middle English, from Norman French *estale,* fixed position, from Old French *estal* + MATE (checkmate).]

stalk¹ (stôk) *n.* **1.** A stem that supports a herbaceous plant or a plant part such as a flower or leaf. **2.** Any slender or elongated support or structure. [Middle English, prob. of Scandinavian orig.] —**stalk′y** *adj.*

stalk² (stôk) *intr.v.* **1.** To walk with a stiff, haughty, or angry gait. **2.** To move in a stealthy way, as in hunting for prey. —*tr.v.* **1.** To pursue by tracking. **2.** To go through (an area) in pursuit of game or other quarry. **3.** To move threateningly through. —*n.* **1.** A stalking stride. **2.** The act of stalking. [Middle English *stalken,* from Old English *(be)stealcian,* to walk cautiously.] —**stalk′er** *n.*

stalk·ing-horse (stô′kĭng-hôrs′) *n.* **1.** A horse or horselike figure used to conceal a stalking hunter. **2.** Anything used to cover one's true purpose; a decoy.

stall (stôl) *n.* **1.** A space enclosed by walls or barriers for one animal in a barn or stable. **2.** Any small compartment or booth, as one for selling wares at a fair. **3. a.** A large seat with arms, set apart near the altar of a church for a clergyman or dignitary. **b.** A pew in a church. **4.** A designated parking space provided for an automobile. **5.** A protective covering for a finger or thumb. **6.** A sudden, unintended loss of power or effectiveness in an engine. **7.** A delaying tactic. —*tr.v.* **1.** To put or lodge (an animal) in a stall. **2.** To check the motion or progress of. **3.** To employ delaying tactics against: *stall off creditors.* **4.** To cause (an engine) accidentally to stop running. —*intr.v.* **1.** To live or be lodged in a stall. **2.** To come to a standstill. **3.** To employ delaying tactics. **4.** To stop running from mechanical failure. [Middle English, from Old English *steall,* standing place, stable.]

stal·lion (stăl′yən) *n.* An uncastrated adult male horse. [Middle English *staloun,* from Old French *estalon.*]

stal·wart (stôl′wərt) *adj.* **1.** Physically strong; sturdy. **2.** Resolute; uncompromising. —*n.* **1.** A physically and morally strong person. **2.** A loyal supporter. [Middle English, from Old English *stælwierthe,* serviceable.] —**stal′wart·ly** *adv.* —**stal′wart·ness** *n.*

sta·men (stā′mən) *n.* The pollen-producing reproductive organ of a flower, usu. consisting of a filament and an anther. [Latin *stāmen,* thread.]

stam·i·na (stăm′ə-nə) *n.* The physical or moral strength required to resist or withstand disease, fatigue, or hardship; endurance. [Latin, pl. of *stāmen,* thread.]

stam·i·nate (stăm′ə-nət, -nāt′) *adj.* **1.** Having a stamen or stamens. **2.** Bearing stamens but lacking pistils.

stam·mer (stăm′ər) *intr.v.* To speak with involuntary pauses and repetitions of sounds. —*tr.v.* To say with a stammer. —*n.* An occurrence or habit of stammering. [Middle English *stameren,* from Old English *stamerian.*] —**stam′mer·er** *n.*

stamp (stămp) *tr.v.* **1.** To bring down (the foot) forcibly. **2.** To bring the foot down upon (an object or surface) forcibly. **3.** To destroy or put out by or as if by pounding with the foot: *stamped the fire out.* **4.** To form or cut out by application of a mold, form, or die. **5.** To imprint or impress with a mark, design, or seal: *The border guard stamped our passports.* **6.** To impress forcibly or permanently. **7.** To affix an adhesive stamp to. **8.** To identify, characterize, or reveal: *Her accent stamped her as a foreigner.* —*intr.v.* **1.** To thrust the foot forcibly downward. **2.** To walk with forcible, heavy steps. —*n.* **1.** The act of stamping. **2. a.** An implement or device used to impress, cut out, or shape something to which it is applied. **b.** The impression or shape thus formed. **3.** A mark, design, or seal, the impression of which indicates ownership, approval, completion, etc. **4. a.** A small piece of gummed paper sold by a government for attachment to an article to be mailed; postage stamp. **b.** Any similar piece of paper issued for a specific purpose: *trading stamp.* **5.** Any identifying or characterizing mark or impression. **6.** Characteristic nature or quality; class; kind. —*modifier:* *a stamp collection.* [Middle English *stampen.*]

stam·pede (stăm-pēd′) *n.* **1.** A sudden headlong rush of startled animals, esp. cattle or horses. **2.** A sudden headlong rush or mass movement of people. —*v.* **-ped·ed, -ped·ing.** —*intr.v.* To participate in a stampede. —*tr.v.* To cause to stampede. [Mexican Spanish *estampida,* from Spanish, uproar, from *estampar,* to pound, stamp.] —**stam·ped′er** *n.*

stamping ground. A favorite gathering place.

stance (stăns) *n.* **1.** The position or manner in which a person or animal stands; posture. **2.** An attitude regarding some issue: *a judge with a tough stance toward repeated offenders.* [Old French *estance,* position, from Italian *stanza,* from Latin *stāre,* to stand.]

stanch (stônch, stănch) *tr.v.* Also **staunch. 1.** To stop or check the flow of (a bodily fluid, esp. blood). **2.** To check the flow of blood from (a wound). —*adj.* Var. of **staunch** (firm). [Middle English *staunchen,* from Old French *estanchier,* from Latin *stāns,* pres. part. of *stāre,* to stand.]

stan·chion (stăn′chən) *n.* **1.** An upright post. **2.** One of the vertical posts used to secure cattle in a stall. —*tr.v.* **1.** To equip with stanchions. **2.** To confine (cattle) in stanchions. [Middle English *stanchon,* from Norman French, from Old French *estanchon,* from *estanche,* a prop, from *ester,* to stand, from Latin *stāre.*]

stand (stănd) *v.* **stood** (stŏŏd), **stand·ing.** —*intr.v.* **1. a.** To take or maintain an upright position on the feet. **b.** To be placed in or maintain an erect position. **c.** To grow in a vertical direction. **2.** *Hunting.* To point or range. **3.** To measure a specified height in an upright position: *stand five feet tall.* **4.** To remain stable, valid, intact, or unchanged: *The law still stands.* **5.** To have a specified expectation or opportunity: *stand to gain.* **6.** To be situated or placed. **7.** To rank: *stand 12th in line.* **8.** To remain stationary. **9. a.** To remain without flowing or being disturbed. **b.** To stagnate. **10.** To assume or maintain an attitude, conviction, or course: *He stands on his earlier offer.* **11.** *Brit.* To be a candidate for public office. —*tr.v.* **1.** To cause to stand; place upright. **2.** To encounter; engage in: *stand battle.* **3. a.** To resist; withstand. **b.** To tolerate; endure; bear. **4.** To be subjected to; undergo: *stand trial.* **5.** *Informal.* To treat: *stand someone to a drink.* —*phrasal verbs.* **stand by. 1.** To be loyal to. **2.** To keep; fulfill: *stand by a promise.* **3.** To wait until one is needed or called. **stand down.** To leave the witness stand at a trial. **stand for. 1.** To represent in a shortened or symbolic form. **2.** To put up with; accept. **stand in.** To substitute. **stand off.** To withstand; repel. **stand on.** To demand fulfillment or observance of; insist on: *standing on ceremony.* **stand out. 1.** To extend outward; protrude. **2.** To be prominent. **3.** To be outstanding; excel. **stand up. 1.** To remain unweakened or unchanged. **2.** *Informal.* To fail to keep an appointment with. —*n.* **1.** The act of standing. **2.** A ceasing of work or activity; standstill. **3.** A stop on a performance tour. **4.** The place where a person stands. **5.** A booth, stall, or counter for the display of goods for sale. **6.** A parking space reserved for taxis. **7.** A halt for defense or resistance, as in a battle. **8.** A position or opinion one is prepared to defend: *take a stand.* **9. stands.** The bleachers at a playing field or stadium. **10.** A **witness stand.** **11.** A small rack, prop, or table for holding various articles. **12.** A group or growth of tall plants or trees: *a stand of pine.* —*idioms.* **stand a chance.** To have a hope of succeeding. **stand (one's) ground.** To hold out against attack. **stand pat. 1.** In poker, to keep one's original hand without drawing new cards. **2.** To remain unchanged. **3.** To oppose all change. **stand to reason.** To be consistent with reason. **stand up for.** To side with; defend. **stand up to.** To face up to. [Middle English *standen,* from Old English *standan.*] —**stand'er** *n.*

stan·dard (stăn'dərd) *n.* **1.** A flag, banner, or ensign. **2.** An acknowledged measure of comparison; criterion. **3.** A widely known and accepted measure used as a basis for a system of measures. **4.** The commodity used to back a monetary system. **5. a.** A degree or level of requirement, excellence, or attainment. **b.** Often **standards.** A requirement of moral conduct. **6.** A pedestal, stand, or base. **7. a.** The large upper petal of the flower of a pea or related plant. **b.** One of the narrow, upright petals of an iris. —See Syns at **ideal.** —*adj.* **1. a.** Serving as a standard of measurement or value: *The standard barrel of oil contains 42 gallons.* **b.** Commonly used and accepted as an authority: *a standard atlas.* **c.** Of average but acceptable quality. **d.** Of normal or prescribed size or quantity: *bolts of standard length.* **2.** Conforming to established educated usage in speech or writing: *standard English.* [Middle English, from Old French *estandard,* flag marking a place for rallying.]

stan·dard-bear·er (stăn'dərd-bâr'ər) *n.* **1.** A person who bears the colors of a military unit. **2.** A person who is in the vanguard of a political or religious movement.

stan·dard·bred (stăn'dərd-brĕd') *n.* One of an American breed of horses developed for harness racing.

standard gauge. 1. A railroad track that has a width of 56¹/₂ inches. **2.** A railroad or railroad car built to this specification.

stan·dard·ize (stăn'dər-dīz') *tr.v.* **-ized, -iz·ing.** To make or adapt to fit a standard. —**stan'dard·i·za'tion** *n.*

standard of living. A measure of the goods and services affordable by and available to a person or a country.

standard time. The time in any of 24 time zones into which the earth is divided. In the continental United States, there are four standard time zones: Eastern, Central, Mountain, and Pacific.

stand·by (stănd'bī') *n.* **1.** Someone or something kept ready and available for service. **2.** Someone or something that can always be depended on.

stand·ee (stăn-dē') *n.* A person who stands for lack of a seat, as on a bus or in a theater.

stand·in (stănd'ĭn') *n.* **1.** A person who takes the place of an actor during lights and camera adjustments. **2.** A substitute.

stand·ing (stăn'dĭng) *adj.* **1.** Upright on the feet or in place. **2.** Performed from an upright, stationary position. **3.** Remaining in effect or existence; permanent: *a standing army.* —*n.* **1.** A relative position in a group; rank. **2.** Status; reputation. **3.** Persistence in time; duration.

stand·off (stănd'ôf', -ŏf') *n.* A tie, as in a contest; a draw.

stand·off·ish (stănd-ô'fĭsh, -ŏf'ĭsh) *adj.* Unfriendly; aloof.

stand·out (stănd'out') *n.* Someone or something that is outstanding or excellent.

stand·pipe (stănd'pīp') *n.* A large vertical pipe into which water is pumped in order to produce a desired pressure.

stand·point (stănd'point') *n.* A position from which things are considered or judged; point of view.

stand·still (stănd'stĭl') *n.* A halt.

stand·up (stănd'ŭp') *adj.* **1.** Erect; upright. **2.** Taken or performed while standing. **3.** Performing without costume, stage properties, or assisting performers.

stank (stăngk) *v.* A past tense of **stink.** [Middle English, from Old English *stanc.*]

stan·nic (stăn'ĭk) *adj.* Of or containing tin, esp. with valence 4. [From French *stannique,* from Late Latin *stannum,* tin, from Latin, alloy of silver and lead.]

stan·nous (stăn'əs) *adj.* Of or containing tin, esp. with valence 2. [From Late Latin *stannum,* tin.]

stan·za (stăn'zə) *n.* One of the divisions of a poem, composed of two or more lines. [Italian, from Latin *stāns,* pres. part. of *stāre,* to stand.]

sta·pes (stā'pēz') *n., pl.* **stapes** or **sta·pe·des** (stə-pē'dēz'). A small bone of the inner ear, shaped somewhat like a

stirrup. [From Medieval Latin *stapēs,* stirrup.] —**sta·pe'di·al** (stā-pē'dē-əl, stə-) *adj.*

staph (stăf) *n.* Staphylococcus.

staph·y·lo·coc·cus (stăf'ə-lō-kŏk'əs) *n., pl.* **-coc·ci** (-kŏk'sī'). Any of various Gram-positive, spherical parasitic bacteria of the genus *Staphylococcus,* occurring in grapelike clusters and causing boils, septicemia, and other infections. [Greek *staphulē,* bunch of grapes + -coccus.] —**staph'y·lo·coc'cal** (-kŏk'əl) or **staph'y·lo·coc'cic** (-kŏk'sĭk) *adj.*

sta·ple¹ (stā'pəl) *n.* **1.** A major product grown or produced in a region. **2.** A major item of trade in steady demand, as salt, flour, or coffee. **3.** A major part, element, or feature: *The classics are staples of every good library.* **4.** Raw material. **5.** The fiber of cotton, wool, or flax, graded as to length and fineness. —*modifier: a staple food; long-staple cotton.* —*adj.* **1.** Being in constant supply and demand: *staple commodities.* **2.** Regularly grown or produced in large quantities. **3.** Principal; leading: *staple exports.* —*tr.v.* **-pled, -pling.** To grade (fibers) according to length and fineness. [Middle English, market town, from Old French *estaple,* from Middle Dutch *stapel,* pillar, emporium.]

sta·ple² (stā'pəl) *n.* **1.** A U-shaped metal loop with pointed ends, driven into a surface to hold something in place, as a bolt, hook, hasp, or wiring. **2.** A thin piece of wire having the shape of a square bracket, used as a fastening for papers, cloth, and similar materials. —*tr.v.* **-pled, -pling.** To fasten by means of a staple or staples. [Middle English *stapel,* from Old English *stapol,* post, pillar.]

sta·pler (stā'plər) *n.* A device for stapling.

star (stär) *n.* **1.** A celestial object that consists of extremely hot gases and emits radiation and light. **2.** A luminous, relatively stationary celestial body visible from the earth, esp. at night. **3. stars. a.** The celestial bodies, regarded as determining and influencing human events. **b.** Fate; fortune. **4.** A design or emblem representing a star, having several points radiating from a center. **5.** An asterisk. **6. a.** An actor who plays a leading role. **b.** Any outstanding and widely admired performer. —*modifier: a star cluster; a star quarterback.* —*v.* **starred, star·ring.** —*tr.v.* **1. a.** To ornament with stars. **b.** To mark with a star for excellence. **2.** To mark with an asterisk. **3.** To present or feature (a performer) in a leading role. —*intr.v.* **1.** To play the leading role in a theatrical production. **2.** To perform excellently. [Middle English *sterre,* from Old English *steorra.*]

star·board (stär'bərd) *n.* The right-hand side of a ship or aircraft as one faces forward. —*adj.* On the right-hand side. —*adv.* To the right-hand side. [Middle English *sterbord,* from Old English *stēorbord,* "rudder side."]

starch (stärch) *n.* **1.** A naturally abundant nutrient carbohydrate, $(C_6H_{10}O_5)_n$, found notably in corn, potatoes, wheat, and rice, and commonly prepared as a white, tasteless powder. **2.** Any of various substances, including natural starch, used to stiffen fabrics. **3.** Any food having a high content of starch. **4.** Stiff behavior. **5.** Vigor; mettle. —*tr.v.* To stiffen with starch. [Middle English *sterche,* from *sterchen,* to stiffen (with starch).]

Star Chamber. 1. A former English court (abolished in 1641) consisting of judges who were appointed by the Crown and sat in closed session. **2. star chamber.** Any court or group characterized by secret, harsh, or arbitrary procedures. [So called because the ceiling of the original courthouse was decorated with gilded stars.]

starch·y (stär'chē) *adj.* **-i·er, -i·est. 1.** Of, containing, or like starch. **2.** Stiffened with starch: *starchy cotton.* **3.** *Informal.* Stiff; formal. —**starch'i·ly** *adv.* —**starch'i·ness** *n.*

star·dom (stär'dəm) *n.* The celebrated position of an actor or performer acknowledged as a star.

stare (stâr) *v.* **stared, star·ing.** —*intr.v.* To look with a steady, often wide-eyed gaze. —*tr.v.* **1.** To look at insistently: *stare her up and down.* **2.** To affect by staring at: *stared the boy into submission.* —See Syns at **gaze.** —*n.* The act of staring; an intent or fixed gaze. [Middle English *staren,* from Old English *starian.*] —**star'er** *n.*

star·fish (stär'fĭsh') *n., pl.* **starfish** or **-fish·es.** Any of various marine echinoderms of the class Asteroidea, characteristically star-shaped with five arms.

star·gaze (stär'gāz') *intr.v.* **-gazed, -gaz·ing. 1.** To gaze at the stars. **2.** To daydream. **—star'gaz·er** *n.*

stark (stärk) *adj.* **-er, -est. 1.** Bare; blunt: *stark truth.* **2.** Complete or utter; extreme: *stark poverty.* **3.** Harsh in appearance; barren; grim: *stark cliffs.* **—adv.** Utterly. [Middle English, from Old English *stearc,* severe, cruel.] **—stark'ly** *adv.* **—stark'ness** *n.*

star·let (stär'lĭt) *n.* **1.** A small star. **2.** A young motion-picture actress publicized as a future star.

star·light (stär'līt') *n.* The light given by the stars. **—adj. 1.** Of or like starlight. **2.** Illuminated by starlight; starlit.

star·ling (stär'lĭng) *n.* Any of various Old World birds with dark, often iridescent plumage, esp. *Sturnus vulgaris,* widely naturalized in North America. [Middle English, from Old English *stærlinc.*]

starling
George Miksch Sutton

star·lit (stär'lĭt') *adj.* Illuminated by starlight.

star-of-Beth·le·hem (stär'əv-bĕth'lə-hĕm', -həm) *n.* A plant, *Ornithogalum umbellatum,* native to Europe, with narrow leaves and a cluster of star-shaped white flowers.

Star of Da·vid (dā'vĭd). A six-pointed star used as a symbol of Judaism and of Israel. Also called **Magen David.**

star·ry (stär'ē) *adj.* **-ri·er, -ri·est. 1.** Shining like stars: *starry eyes.* **2.** Having many stars visible. **3.** Of or from the stars; stellar. **—star'ri·ness** *n.*

star·ry-eyed (stär'ē-īd') *adj.* Naively enthusiastic.

Stars and Bars. The first official Confederate flag.

Stars and Stripes. The flag of the United States.

Star-Span·gled Banner (stär'spăng'gəld). **1.** The flag of the United States. **2.** The national anthem of the United States, written by Francis Scott Key in 1814.

start (stärt) *intr.v.* **1.** To begin an activity or movement. **2.** To have a beginning; commence. **3.** To move suddenly or involuntarily: *She started at the loud noise.* **4.** To come quickly into view, life, or activity; spring forth. **5.** To be in the line-up for a race. **6.** To protrude or bulge. **7.** To become loosened or disengaged. **—tr.v. 1.** To commence; begin. **2.** To set into motion, operation, or activity. **3.** To introduce; originate. **4.** To enter in a race. **5.** To help in beginning an activity or venture. **6.** To found; establish. **7.** To tend in an early stage of development: *start seedlings.* **8.** To rouse (game) from its hiding place or lair; flush. **9.** To displace; warp. **—See Syns at begin. —n. 1.** A beginning; commencement. **2.** A startled reaction or movement. **3. starts.** Quick, brief spurts of effort or activity: *by fits and starts.* **4.** A starting line or starting point. **5.** A position of advantage over others; an edge; lead. [Middle English *sterten.*]

start·er (stär'tər) *n.* **1.** Someone or something that starts. **2.** A worker who dispatches vehicles. **3.** An attachment for starting an internal-combustion engine without hand cranking. **4.** A person who signals the start of a race. **5.** Material used to begin a process of fermentation, as in making cheese or wine.

star·tle (stär'tl) *v.* **-tled, -tling. —tr.v. 1.** To cause to make a quick involuntary movement through fear or surprise. **2.** To frighten or surprise. **—intr.v.** To become startled. **—** See Syns at **frighten. —n.** A sudden movement of surprise. [Middle English *stertlen,* from Old English *steartlian,* to struggle.] **—star'tling·ly** *adv.*

star·va·tion (stär-vā'shən) *n.* **1.** The act or process of starving. **2.** The condition of being starved.

starve (stärv) *v.* **starved, starv·ing. —intr.v. 1.** To suffer or

die from prolonged lack of food. **2.** To suffer from deprivation: *starving for affection.* **3.** *Informal.* To be hungry. **—tr.v. 1.** To cause to starve. **2.** To force by denying food: *starved the town into submission.* [Middle English *sterven,* from Old English *steorfan,* to die.]

starve·ling (stärv'lĭng) *n.* A starving person or animal.

sta·ses (stā'sēz') *n.* Plural of **stasis.**

stash (stăsh) *tr.v.* To hide or store away in a secret place. **—See Syns at hide. —n. 1.** A hiding place for valuables. **2.** An amount hidden away. [Orig. unknown.]

sta·sis (stā'sĭs) *n.,* pl. **-ses** (-sēz'). **1.** *Pathol.* Stagnation of a bodily fluid, esp. of blood. **2.** Equilibrium; motionlessness. [From Greek, a standing, standstill.]

–stasis. A suffix meaning a stable state or a balance: **homeostasis.** [From Greek *stasis,* a standing, standstill.]

–stat. A suffix meaning stationary: **thermostat.** [From Greek *-statēs,* one that causes to stand.]

state (stāt) *n.* **1.** A set of circumstances in which something exists or is operating; a condition: *a radio in a state of disrepair.* **2.** One of the three principal conditions, solid, liquid, or gaseous, in which material substances occur. **3.** A mental or emotional disposition; mood. **4.** *Informal.* A condition of excitement, confusion, or disorder. **5. a.** A body of people living under a single independent government; a nation. **b.** The territory of such a government. **6.** The means, procedure, or power of governing and representing an independent nation: *matters of state.* **7.** Often **State.** One of the political and geographic subdivisions of a federated country such as the United States. **8.** A social position; rank. **9.** High ceremony: *a queen riding in state.* **—See Syns at nation. —modifier:** *a state law; a state occasion.* **—tr.v. stat·ed, stat·ing.** To set forth in words; declare. **—idiom. lie in state.** To be placed in public view for honors prior to burial. [Middle English, from Old French *estat,* from Latin *status,* manner of standing, condition.]

state·craft (stāt'krăft') *n.* The art of leading a country.

state·hood (stāt'hood') *n.* The status of being a state of the United States.

state house. Also **State House.** A building in which a state legislature holds sessions; state capitol.

state·ly (stāt'lē) *adj.* **-li·er, -li·est. 1.** Dignified; formal: *stately music.* **2.** Majestic; lofty: *a stately oak.* **—See Syns at grand. —adv.** In a ceremonious or imposing manner. [Middle English *statly,* suitable to a person of rank, from *stat,* person of rank, state.] **—state'li·ness** *n.*

state·ment (stāt'mənt) *n.* **1.** The act of stating. **2.** Something stated; a declaration. **3.** *Law.* A formal pleading. **4.** A written summary of a financial account. **5.** A bill.

state·room (stāt'room', -room') *n.* A private compartment with sleeping accommodations on a ship or train.

state's evidence. Also **State's evidence.** Evidence for the prosecution in U.S. state or Federal trials. **—idiom. turn state's evidence.** To give evidence for the state in criminal proceedings usu. in return for immunity from prosecution.

States-Gen·er·al (stāts'jĕn'ər-əl) *n.* **1.** The legislative assembly in France before the Revolution. **2.** The parliament of the Netherlands.

state·side or **State·side** (stāt'sīd') *adj.* Of or in the continental United States. **—adv.** To, toward, or in the continental United States.

states·man (stāts'mən) *n.* **1.** A leader in national or international affairs. **2.** A political leader regarded as a disinterested promoter of the public good. **—states'man·like'** or **states'man·ship'** *n.*

States' rights. Also **State rights. 1.** All rights not delegated to the Federal government by the Constitution nor denied by it to the states. **2.** A political belief in limiting the powers of the Federal government. **—States' righter.**

state·wide (stāt'wīd') *adj.* Occurring throughout a state.

states·wom·an (stāts'woom'ən) *n.* A woman who is a leader in national or international affairs.

stat·ic (stăt'ĭk) *adj.* **1.** Not moving or in motion; at rest. **2.** Of or determined with respect to something stationary. **3.** Electrostatic. **4.** Of or produced by noise that appears at the output of a radio receiver. **—n. 1.** Random noise that appears at the output of a radio receiver. **2.** *Slang.* Interference. [From Greek *statikos,* causing to stand, from *statos,* placed, standing.] **—stat'i·cal·ly** *adv.*

stat·ics (stăt'ĭks) *n.* (used with a sing. verb). A branch of physics that deals with balanced forces on and within stationary physical systems. [From Greek *statikē (tekhnē),* (science) of weighing.]

sta·tion (stā′shən) *n.* **1.** The place where a person or thing stands or is assigned to stand; a post. **2.** The place, building, or establishment from which a service is provided or operations are directed. **3.** A stopping place along a route. **4.** Social position; status; rank. **5.** An establishment equipped for observation and study: *a radar station.* **6.** An establishment equipped for radio or television transmission. —*tr.v.* To assign to a position; to post. [Middle English *stacioun,* a standing place, from Old French *(e)station,* from Latin *statiō.*]

sta·tion·ar·y (stā′shə-nĕr′ē) *adj.* **1. a.** Not moving. **b.** Not capable of being moved; fixed. **2.** Unchanging: *a stationary sound.*

station break. An intermission in a radio or television program for identification of the network or station.

sta·tion·er (stā′shə-nər) *n.* A person who sells stationery. [Middle English *stacioner,* from Medieval Latin *stationārius,* shopkeeper, from *statiō,* shop, from Latin, station.]

sta·tion·er·y (stā′shə-nĕr′ē) *n.* **1.** Writing paper and envelopes. **2.** Writing materials and office supplies. —*modifier: a stationery store.*

station house. **1.** A police station. **2.** A fire station.

sta·tion·mas·ter (stā′shən-măs′tər) *n.* A person in charge of a railroad or bus station.

Stations of the Cross. **1.** A religious devotion consisting of meditating before each of 14 crosses set up in a church or along a path commemorating 14 events in the Passion of Jesus. **2.** The 14 crosses, often accompanied by images.

station wagon. An automobile that has an extended interior with a third seat or luggage platform and a tailgate.

sta·tis·tic (stə-tĭs′tĭk) *n.* Any numerical datum. [Back-formation from STATISTICS.] —**sta·tis′ti·cal** (-tĭ-kəl) *adj.* —**sta·tis′ti·cal·ly** *adv.*

sta·tis·ti·cian (stăt′ĭ-stĭsh′ən) *n.* **1.** A mathematician specializing in statistics. **2.** A compiler of statistical data.

sta·tis·tics (stə-tĭs′tĭks) *n.* **1.** *(used with a sing. verb).* The mathematics of the collection, organization, and interpretation of numerical data. **2.** *(used with a pl. verb).* A collection of numerical data. [German *Statistik,* orig. "political science dealing with state affairs," from Latin *status,* manner of standing, position, state.]

sta·tor (stā′tər) *n.* The stationary part of a machine about which a rotor turns. [From Latin, one that stands, from *status,* past part. of *stāre,* to stand.]

stat·u·ar·y (stăch′oō-ĕr′ē) *n., pl.* **-ies.** **1.** Statues. **2.** A sculptor. **3.** The art of sculpting. —*adj.* Of a statue or statues: *statuary art.*

stat·ue (stăch′oō) *n.* A form representing a person or thing, made by an artist from stone, metal, or another solid substance. [Middle English, from Old French, from Latin *statua,* from *statuere,* to set up, erect.]

stat·u·esque (stăch′oō-ĕsk′) *adj.* Suggestive of a statue, as in proportion or dignity; stately. —**stat′u·esque′ly** *adv.*

stat·u·ette (stăch′oō-ĕt′) *n.* A small statue.

stat·ure (stăch′ər) *n.* **1.** The natural height of a person or animal when upright. **2.** A level of achievement. **3.** Reputation; status. [Middle English, from Old French *estature,* from Latin *statūra.*]

sta·tus (stā′təs, stăt′əs) *n.* **1.** The legal character or condition of a person or thing: *the status of a minor.* **2.** A stage of progress or development. **3. a.** A relative position in a ranked group or in a social system: *the high status of professional people.* **b.** A high relative position. —See Syns at **honor.** —*modifier: a status symbol.* [Latin, manner of standing, condition.]

status quo (stā′təs kwō′, stăt′əs). The existing condition or state of affairs. [Latin, "state in which."]

stat·ute (stăch′oōt) *n.* **1.** A law enacted by a legislature. **2.** An established law or rule, as of a corporation. [Middle English, from Old French *estatut,* from Late Latin *statūtum,* past part. of *statuere,* to set up, decree.]

statute law. A law established by legislative enactment.

statute mile. The standard mile, 5,280 feet.

statute of limitations. A statute setting a time limit on legal action in certain cases.

stat·u·to·ry (stăch′ə-tôr′ē, -tōr′ē) *adj.* **1.** Of or relating to a statute. **2.** Enacted, regulated, or authorized by statute.

staunch[1] (stônch, stänch) *adj.* **-er, -est.** Also **stanch** (stônch, stänch). **1.** Firm and steadfast; true: *a staunch friend.* **2.** Well-built; strong. —See Syns at **faithful.** [Middle English *staunche,* watertight, firm, strong, from Old French *estanchier,* to stanch.] —**staunch′ly** *adv.* —**staunch′ness** *n.*

staunch[2] (stônch, stänch) *v.* Var. of **stanch.**

stave (stāv) *n.* **1.** A narrow strip of wood forming part of the sides of a barrel, tub, etc. **2.** A rung of a ladder. **3.** A staff or cudgel. **4.** A musical staff. **5.** A stanza. —*v.* **staved** or **stove** (stōv), **stav·ing.** —*tr.v.* **1.** To break in or puncture the staves of. **2.** To break or smash a hole in. **3.** To crush or smash inward. —*intr.v.* To become crushed in. —*phrasal verb.* **stave off.** To keep or hold off; repel. [Back-formation from STAVES.]

staves (stāvz) *n.* A plural of **staff.**

stay[1] (stā) *intr.v.* **1.** To remain or continue in a given place or condition: *stay awake.* **2.** To remain as a guest or lodger. **3.** To stop moving; cease; halt. **4.** To wait; pause. **5.** To hold on; endure. —*tr.v.* **1.** To stop or halt; check: *stay his tongue.* **2.** To postpone; delay. **3.** To satisfy or appease temporarily: *stay his anger.* **4.** To wait for; await. —See Syns at **stop.** —*n.* **1.** The action of halting; a check. **2.** A stop or pause. **3.** A brief period of residence or visiting. [Middle English *steyen,* to stop moving, from Old French *ester,* to stand, from Latin *stāre.*]

stay[2] (stā) *tr.v.* **1.** To brace, support, or prop up: *stay an overhanging roof.* **2.** To strengthen or sustain. —*n.* **1.** A support or brace. **2.** A strip of bone, plastic, or metal, used to stiffen a garment or part. **3. stays.** A corset. [Old French *estayer,* to support, from *estaie,* support, from Middle Dutch *stæye,* rope used to support a mast.]

stay[3] (stā) *n.* A heavy rope or cable used as a brace or support, as for a mast or spar. —*tr.v.* **1.** To brace or support with a stay or stays. **2.** To put (a ship) on the opposite tack. —*intr.v.* To come about. [Middle English, from Old English *stæg.*]

staying power. The ability to endure or last.

stay·sail (stā′sāl′, -səl) *n.* A triangular sail hoisted on a stay.

stead (stĕd) *n.* The place of another: *Zeus overthrew his father and ruled in his stead.* —*tr.v.* To benefit; to help. —*idiom.* **stand in good stead.** To be of advantage to. [Middle English *stede,* from Old English.]

stead·fast (stĕd′făst′, -fəst) *adj.* **1.** Fixed or unchanging; steady. **2.** Firmly loyal. —See Syns at **faithful.** [Middle English *stedefast,* from Old English *stedefæst,* fixed.] —**stead′fast′ly** *adv.* —**stead′fast′ness** *n.*

stead·y (stĕd′ē) *adj.* **-i·er, -i·est.** **1.** Firm in position or place; stable; fixed. **2.** Direct and unfaltering; sure. **3.** Having a continuous movement, quality, or pace: *a steady wind.* **4.** Not easily excited or upset; controlled: *steady nerves.* **5.** Temperate; sober. —See Syns at **faithful.** —*v.* **-ied, -y·ing.** —*tr.v.* To make steady; stabilize. —*intr.v.* To become steady. —*interj.* **1.** A word used to urge self-control. **2.** *Naut.* A word used to direct the helmsman to keep the ship's head in the same direction: *Steady as she goes!* —*n., pl.* **-ies.** *Slang.* The boy or girl whom one dates regularly and exclusively. —*idiom.* **go steady.** To date regularly and exclusively. [From STEAD.] —**stead′i·er** *n.* —**stead′i·ly** *adv.* —**stead′i·ness** *n.*

stead·y-state theory (stĕd′ē-stāt′). A cosmological theory that assumes that the expansion of the universe is compensated for by the continuous creation of matter.

steak (stāk) *n.* **1.** A slice of meat, usu. beef, typically cut thick and across the muscle grain. **2.** A thick slice of a large fish cut across the body. **3.** A patty of ground meat broiled or fried. —*modifier: a steak knife.* [Middle English *steyke,* from Old Norse *steik,* piece of meat roasted on a spit, from *steikja,* to roast on a spit.]

steal (stēl) *v.* **stole** (stōl), **sto·len** (stō′lən), **steal·ing.** —*tr.v.* **1.** To take (someone else's property) without right or permission. **2.** To get or effect secretly or artfully: *steal a march on his opponents.* **3.** To move, carry, or place surreptitiously. **4.** *Baseball.* To advance (another base) without the ball being batted, by running during the delivery of a pitch. —*intr.v.* **1.** To commit theft. **2.** To move, happen,

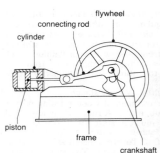

steam engine

steamship

steeplechase

or elapse stealthily or unobtrusively. **3.** *Baseball.* To steal a base. —See Syns at **sneak.** —*n.* **1.** The act of stealing; theft. **2.** *Slang.* A bargain. [Middle English *stelen,* from Old English *stelan.*] —**steal′er** *n.*

stealth (stĕlth) *n.* **1.** The act of moving, proceeding, or acting in a quiet, secret way so as to avoid notice. **2.** Furtiveness; covertness. [Middle English *stelth.*]

stealth·y (stĕl′thē) *adj.* **-i·er, -i·est.** Quiet and cautious so as to avoid notice. —**stealth′i·ly** *adv.* —**stealth′i·ness** *n.*

steam (stēm) *n.* **1. a.** The vapor phase of water. **b.** The mist of cooling water vapor. **2. Steam heating. 3.** Power; energy. —*modifier:* *steam power.* —*intr.v.* **1.** To produce or emit steam. **2.** To become or rise up as steam. **3.** To become misted or covered with steam. **4.** To move by means of steam power. **5.** *Informal.* To become very angry; fume. —*tr.v.* To expose to steam, as in cooking: *steam vegetables.* —*idiom.* **let** (or **blow**) **off steam.** To release pent-up emotions or energy. [Middle English *steme,* vapor, exhalation, from Old English *stēam.*]

steam bath. 1. The act of bathing through exposure to steam, which induces perspiration. **2.** A room or building equipped to provide bathing with steam.

steam·boat (stēm′bōt′) *n.* A steamship.

steam engine. An engine that converts the heat energy of pressurized steam into mechanical energy, esp. one in which steam expands in a closed cylinder to drive a piston.

steam·er (stē′mər) *n.* **1.** A steamship. **2.** A container in which something is steamed. **3.** A soft-shell clam.

steamer trunk. A small trunk orig. designed to fit under the bunk of a steamship cabin.

steam·fit·ter (stēm′fĭt′ər) *n.* A person whose occupation is the installation and repair of steam heating systems.

steam heating. A heating system by which steam is generated in a boiler and piped to radiators.

steam iron. A pressing iron that holds and heats water to be emitted as steam on the cloth being pressed.

steam·roll·er (stēm′rō′lər) *n.* Also **steam roller. 1.** A vehicle equipped with a heavy roller for smoothing road surfaces. **2.** A force that crushes opposition as it advances. —*tr.v.* **1.** To smooth or level (a road) with a steamroller. **2.** To defeat or silence ruthlessly; crush. —*intr.v.* To move or proceed with overwhelming force.

steam·ship (stēm′shĭp′) *n.* A large ship propelled by one or more steam-driven screws or propellers.

steam shovel. A steam-driven machine for digging having a large bucket that scoops up dirt.

steam table. A table equipped to hold containers of food kept warm by hot water or steam circulating below.

steam turbine. A turbine operated by highly pressurized steam directed against or through vanes on a rotor.

steam·y (stē′mē) *adj.* **-i·er, -i·est. 1.** Filled with or emitting steam. **2.** Hot and humid: *a steamy jungle.* —**steam′i·ly** *adv.* —**steam′i·ness** *n.*

ste·ap·sin (stē-ăp′sĭn) *n.* An enzyme of pancreatic juice that promotes the digestion of fats. [Greek *stear,* solid fat + (PE)PSIN.]

ste·a·rate (stē′ə-rāt′) *n.* A salt or ester of stearic acid. [STEAR(IC) + -ATE.]

ste·ar·ic acid (stē-ăr′ĭk) *n.* A colorless, odorless, waxlike fatty acid, $CH_3(CH_2)_{16}COOH$, occurring in natural animal and vegetable fats.

ste·a·rin (stē′ə-rĭn) *n.* **1.** A colorless, odorless ester of glyc-

erol and stearic acid, $C_3H_5(C_{18}H_{35}O_2)_3$, used in the manufacture of soap and candles and for textile sizing. **2.** Stearic acid, esp. as used commercially. **3.** The solid form of fat. [French *stéarine,* from Greek *stear,* solid fat.]

ste·a·tite (stē′ə-tīt′) *n.* A massive, white-to-green talc used in paints, ceramics, and insulation. Also called **soapstone.** [Latin *steatītēs,* from Greek *steatītēs,* "tallow stone."]

steed (stēd) *n.* A horse, esp. a spirited one. [Middle English *stede,* from Old English *stēda,* stallion.]

steel (stēl) *n.* **1.** Any of various hard, strong, durable, malleable alloys of iron and carbon, usu. containing between 0.2 and 1.5 per cent carbon, widely used as a structural material. **2.** A hard, unflinching character: *nerves of steel.* **3.** Something made of steel, as a sword. —*modifier: a steel tower; a steel mill.* —*tr.v.* **1.** To cover, edge, or point with steel. **2.** To make hard or strong; brace; strengthen: *steel oneself against disappointment.* [Middle English *stiel,* from Old English *stēli.*]

steel wool. Fine fibers of steel woven or matted together to form an abrasive for cleaning, smoothing, or polishing.

steel·work (stēl′wûrk′) *n.* **1.** Something made of steel. **2. steelworks.** A plant where steel is made.

steel·work·er (stēl′wûr′kər) *n.* A person who works in the manufacture of steel.

steel·y (stē′lē) *adj.* **-i·er, -i·est. 1.** Made of steel. **2.** Like steel, as in hardness: *steely eyes.* —**steel′i·ness** *n.*

steel·yard (stēl′yärd′) *n.* A portable weighing device made of a horizontal bar marked off in units of weight, with a hook at the shorter end for holding the object to be weighed and a sliding counterweight at the other end that indicates the correct weight when the bar is balanced. [STEEL + YARD (rod).]

steen·bok (stēn′bŏk′, stän′-) *n.* Also **stein·bok** (stīn′-). An African antelope, *Raphicerus campestris,* with a brownish coat and short, pointed horns in the male. [Afrikaans, from Middle Dutch *steenboc,* "stone buck," : *steen,* stone + *boc,* buck.]

steep¹ (stēp) *adj.* **-er, -est. 1.** Sharply sloped: *a steep hill.* **2.** Rising or falling rapidly: *a steep decline in prices.* **3.** Very high: *a steep price.* —*n.* A steep slope. [Middle English *stepe,* from Old English *stēap,* lofty, deep, projecting.] —**steep′ly** *adv.* —**steep′ness** *n.*

steep² (stēp) *v.* **1.** To soak in liquid: *We steeped the cake in rum.* **2.** To infuse or subject thoroughly. **3.** To make thoroughly wet; saturate. —*intr.v.* To undergo a soaking in liquid. —*n.* The process of steeping or the condition of being steeped. [Middle English *stepen,* perh. from Old Norse *steypa,* to pour out.] —**steep′er** *n.*

steep·en (stē′pən) *tr.v.* To make steeper. —*intr.v.* To become steeper.

stee·ple (stē′pəl) *n.* **1.** A tall tower rising from the roof of a building, such as a church or temple. **2.** A spire. [Middle English *stepel,* from Old English *stīpel.*]

stee·ple·chase (stē′pəl-chās′) *n.* A horse race across open country or over an obstacle course. [From the former use of church steeples as goals.] —**stee′ple·chas′er** *n.*

stee·ple·jack (stē′pəl-jăk′) *n.* A worker on steeples or other very high structures. [STEEPLE + JACK (laborer).]

steer¹ (stîr) *tr.v.* **1.** To guide (a vessel or vehicle) by means of a device such as a rudder, paddle, or wheel. **2.** To direct the course of. —*intr.v.* **1.** To guide a vessel or vehicle. **2.** To follow a set course: *steer homeward.* **3.** To be capable of being steered: *a craft that steers easily.* —*n. Informal.* A piece of advice. [Middle English *steren,* from Old English *stīeran.*] —**steer′er** *n.*

steer² (stîr) *n.* A young male of domestic cattle, esp. one castrated before sexual maturity and raised for beef. [Middle English, from Old English *stēor.*]

steer·age (stîr′ĭj) *n.* **1.** The action or practice of steering. **2.** The section of a passenger ship, orig. near the rudder, providing the cheapest accommodations.

steer·age·way (stîr′ĭj-wā′) *n.* The minimum rate of motion required for the helm of a ship or boat to have effect.

steering committee. A committee that sets agenda and schedules business, as for a legislative body.

steering wheel. A wheel that controls steering.

steers·man (stîrz′mən) *n.* A helmsman.

steg·o·saur (stĕg′ə-sôr′) *n.* Also **steg·o·sau·rus** (stĕg′ə-sôr′əs). Any of several herbivorous dinosaurs of the genus *Stegosaurus* and related genera, of the Triassic to the Cretaceous period, with dorsal rows of upright bony plates. [Greek *stegos,* roof + -SAUR.]

stein (stīn) *n.* An earthenware mug. [German *Stein,* prob. short for *Steingut,* stoneware, earthenware.]

stein·bok (stīn′bŏk′) *n.* Var. of **steenbok.**

ste·le (stē′lē) *n., pl.* **-les** or **-lae** (-lē). **1.** An upright stone or slab with an inscribed or sculptured surface, used as a monument or as a commemorative tablet. **2.** *Bot.* The central core of vascular tissue in a plant stem. [Latin *stēla,* from Greek *stēlē,* pillar.] —**ste′lar** (-lər) *adj.*

stel·lar (stĕl′ər) *adj.* **1.** Of, relating to, or consisting of stars. **2. a.** Of or relating to a star performer. **b.** Outstanding. [Late Latin *stellāris,* from *stella,* star.]

stel·late (stĕl′āt′) *adj.* Also **stel·lat·ed** (-ā′tĭd). Star-shaped. [Latin *stellātus,* from *stella,* star.] —**stel′late·ly** *adv.*

stem¹ (stĕm) *n.* **1. a.** The main supporting part of a plant; a stalk or trunk. **b.** A slender stalk supporting another plant part, such as a leaf or flower. **2.** A connecting or supporting part, esp.: **a.** The tube of a tobacco pipe. **b.** The slender upright support of a wine glass or goblet. **c.** The small projecting shaft by which a watch is wound. **d.** The shaft of a feather or hair. **e.** The vertical line extending from the head of a musical note. **3.** A main line of descent; stock. **4.** The main part of a word to which affixes are added. **5.** The curved upright beam at the fore of a vessel. —*v.* **stemmed, stem·ming.** —*tr.v.* **1.** To remove the stem or stems of: *stemming cherries.* **2.** To provide with a stem or stems. **3.** To make headway against: *"The gale increases as we stem the main"* (Philip Freneau). —*intr.v.* **1.** To extend like a stem; branch out: *The spinal cord stems from the brain.* **2.** To derive or originate; spring. [Middle English, from Old English *stemn,* stem, tree trunk.]

stem² (stĕm) *v.* **stemmed, stem·ming.** —*tr.v.* **1.** To stop or hold back; stanch. **2.** To plug up. —*intr.v.* To point skis inward in order to slow down or turn. [Middle English *stemmen,* from Old Norse *stemma.*]

stem·ware (stĕm′wâr′) *n.* Glassware mounted on a stem.

stem-wind·ing (stĕm′wīn′dĭng) *adj.* Wound by turning an expanded crown on the stem: *a stem-winding watch.*

stench (stĕnch) *n.* A strong and foul odor; stink. [Middle English, from Old English *stenc.*]

sten·cil (stĕn′səl) *n.* **1.** A sheet of cardboard or other material in which lettering or a design has been cut so that ink or paint applied to the sheet will reproduce the pattern on the surface beneath. **2.** The lettering or design so produced. —*tr.v.* **-ciled** or **-cilled, -cil·ing** or **-cil·ling.** **1.** To mark with a stencil. **2.** To produce by stencil. [Middle English *stencel,* to adorn with brilliant colors, from Old French *estenceler,* to cause to sparkle, from *estencele,* spark, from Latin *scintilla.*] —**sten′cil·er** or **sten′cil·ler** *n.*

ste·nog·ra·pher (stə-nŏg′rə-fər) *n.* A person skilled in shorthand, esp. one employed to take dictation.

ste·nog·ra·phy (stə-nŏg′rə-fē) *n.* **1.** The art or process of writing in shorthand. **2.** Material written down in shorthand. [Greek *stenos,* narrow + -GRAPHY.] —**sten′o·graph′ic** (stĕn′ə-grăf′ĭk) *adj.* —**sten′o·graph′i·cal·ly** *adv.*

sten·o·type (stĕn′ə-tīp′) *n.* **1.** A symbol or combination of symbols representing a sound, word, or phrase, esp. in shorthand. **2.** A Stenotype.

Sten·o·type (stĕn′ə-tīp′) *n.* A trademark for a keyboard

machine used to record dictation by a phonetic system.

sten·to·ri·an (stĕn-tôr′ē-ən, -tōr′-) *adj.* Extremely loud: *a stentorian voice.* [From Greek *Stentōr,* name of a loud-voiced herald in the *Iliad,* from *stenein,* to groan, moan.]

step (stĕp) *n.* **1.** A single movement made by lifting and putting down one foot, as in walking. **2. a.** The distance covered by such a movement. **b.** A short walking distance. **3.** The sound of someone walking. **4.** A footprint. **5. a.** A manner of walking; a gait. **b.** A manner or pattern of moving the feet in dancing. **6.** A fixed rhythm or pace, as in marching: *keep step.* **7.** Conformity with the rhythm, pace, views, or attitudes of others: *in step with the band leader; out of step with the times.* **8. a.** A small platform or rung placed as a rest for the foot in climbing up or down. **b. steps.** Stairs. **9.** Any of a series of actions or measures taken to achieve some goal. **10.** Any of the stages of a process. **11.** A degree of progress. **12.** A degree, as in a scale of value. **13.** *Mus.* The interval that separates two successive tones of a scale. **14.** *Naut.* The block in which the base of a ship's mast is held. —*v.* **stepped, step·ping.** —*intr.v.* **1.** To put or press the foot: *step on the gas.* **2.** To shift or move by or as if by taking a step or two: *step back.* **3.** To walk, esp. a short distance. —*tr.v.* **1.** To put or set (the foot) down. **2.** To measure by pacing: *step off ten yards.* **3.** To furnish with steps: *step a slope.* **4.** *Naut.* To place (a mast) in its step. —*phrasal verbs.* **step down. 1.** To resign from a high post. **2.** To reduce, esp. in stages: *stepping down the electric power.* **step in. 1.** To enter an activity or situation. **2.** To intervene. **step out. 1.** To walk briskly. **2.** To go outside for a short time. **3.** *Informal.* To go out for a special evening of entertainment. **step up.** To increase, esp. in stages: *step up production.* —See Syns at **expedite.** —*idioms.* **step on it.** *Informal.* To go faster; hurry. **watch (one's) step.** To move or proceed cautiously. [Middle English, from Old English *stæpe, stepe.*] —**step′per** *n.*

step-. A prefix meaning related through remarriage rather than by blood: **stepbrother.** [Middle English, from Old English *stēop-.*]

step·broth·er (stĕp′brŭth′ər) *n.* The son of a person's stepparent by a previous marriage.

step·child (stĕp′chīld′) *n.* The child of a person's spouse by a former marriage.

step·daugh·ter (stĕp′dô′tər) *n.* The daughter of a person's spouse by a former marriage.

step·father (stĕp′fä′thər) *n.* The husband of a person's mother by a later marriage.

step-in (stĕp′ĭn′) *adj.* Put on by being stepped into: *step-in slippers.* —*n.* **1. step-ins.** Panties. **2.** A step-in garment.

step·lad·der (stĕp′lăd′ər) *n.* A portable ladder with a hinged supporting frame.

step·moth·er (stĕp′mŭth′ər) *n.* The wife of a person's father by a later marriage.

step·par·ent (stĕp′pâr′ənt, -păr′-) *n.* A stepfather or a stepmother.

steppe (stĕp) *n.* A vast semiarid grass-covered plain, as in southeastern Europe and Siberia. [Russian *step′.*]

step·ping·stone (stĕp′ĭng-stōn′) *n.* **1.** A stone that provides a place to step, as in crossing a stream. **2.** A step or means toward achievement of a goal.

step·sis·ter (stĕp′sĭs′tər) *n.* The daughter of a person's stepparent by a previous marriage.

step·son (stĕp′sŭn′) *n.* The son of a person's spouse by a former marriage.

step-up (stĕp′ŭp′) *n.* An increase in size, amount, or activity.

step·wise (stĕp′wīz′) *adj.* Step by step; gradual.

-ster. A suffix meaning: **1.** Someone who does, operates, or is engaged in: **teamster. 2.** Someone who takes part in or is associated with: **gangster. 3.** Someone who makes: **prankster. 4.** Someone who is: **youngster.** [Middle English -*ster(e),* -*estere,* from Old English -*estre,* -*ister.*]

stere (stîr) *n. Abbr.* **s** A unit of volume equal to one cubic meter. [French *stère,* from Greek *stereos,* solid, hard.]

stereo-. Var. of **stereo-.**

ste·re·o (stĕr′ē-ō′, stîr′-) *n., pl.* **-os. 1.** A stereophonic sound-reproduction system. **2.** Stereophonic sound. —*adj.* Stereophonic.

stereo– or **stere–.** A prefix meaning solid, firm, or three-dimensional: **stereophonic, stereoscope.** [From Greek *stereos,* solid, hard.]

ster·e·o·phon·ic (stĕr′ē-ə-fŏn′ĭk, -fō′nĭk, stîr′-) *adj.* Of or used in a sound-reproduction system that uses two or more separate channels to give a more natural effect of the distribution of sound. **—ster′e·o·phon′i·cal·ly** *adv.*

ster·e·op·ti·con (stĕr′ē-ŏp′tĭ-kŏn′, stîr′-) *n.* A magic lantern, esp. one made double so as to produce dissolving views. [STEREO- + Greek *optikon,* optic.]

ster·e·o·scope (stĕr′ē-ə-skōp′, stîr′-) *n.* An optical instrument through which two slightly different views of a scene are presented, one to each eye, giving a three-dimensional illusion.

ster·e·o·scop·ic (stĕr′ē-ə-skŏp′ĭk, stîr′-) or **ster·e·o·scop·i·cal** (-ĭ-kəl) *adj.* **1.** Of or relating to stereoscopy. **2.** Of, for, or produced by a stereoscope. **—ster′e·o·scop′i·cal·ly** *adv.*

ster·e·os·co·py (stĕr′ē-ŏs′kə-pē, stîr′-) *n.* The viewing of objects as three-dimensional.

ster·e·o·type (stĕr′ē-ə-tīp′, stîr′-) *n.* **1.** A metal printing plate cast from a matrix that is molded from a raised printing surface, such as type. **2.** A conventional and usu. oversimplified conception or belief that is not checked against particular cases or facts. **3.** Someone or something considered typical of a kind and without individuality. **—modifier:** *a stereotype plate; a stereotype villain.* **—tr.v. -typed, -typ·ing. 1.** To make a stereotype from. **2.** To form a fixed, unvarying idea of. **3.** To represent or treat in a generalized, conventional way. **—ster′e·o·typ′er** *n.* **—ster′e·o·typ′ic** (-tĭp′ĭk) or **ster′e·o·typ′i·cal** *adj.*

ster·e·o·typ·y (stĕr′ē-ə-tī′pē, stîr′-) *n.* The process or art of making stereotype plates.

ster·ile (stĕr′əl, -īl′) *adj.* **1.** Incapable of reproducing sexually; infertile. **2.** Capable of producing little or no vegetation; unfruitful. **3.** Free from bacteria or other microorganisms: *a sterile bandage.* **4.** Lacking in imagination or vitality. **5.** Not productive or effective. [Old French, from Latin *sterilis,* unfruitful.] **—ster′ile·ly** *adv.* **—ste·ril′i·ty** (stə-rĭl′ĭ-tē) or **ster′ile·ness** *n.*

ster·il·ize (stĕr′ə-līz′) *tr.v.* **-ized, -iz·ing.** To make sterile. **—ster′il·i·za′tion** *n.* **—ster′il·iz′er** *n.*

ster·ling (stûr′lĭng) *n.* **1.** British money. **2.** British coinage of silver or gold. **3. a.** Sterling silver. **b.** Articles made of sterling silver. **—adj. 1.** Consisting of or expressed in British money: *the pound sterling.* **2.** Made of sterling silver. **3.** Of the highest quality; superlative. [Middle English, "small star" (from the small star stamped on the silver pennies).]

sterling silver. 1. An alloy of 92.5 per cent silver with copper or another metal. **2.** Objects made of this alloy. **—modifier:** *a sterling silver tray.*

stern¹ (stûrn) *adj.* **-er, -est. 1.** Firm or unyielding; inflexible: *stern discipline.* **2.** Grave or severe in manner or appearance; austere: *"She was silent, cold, and stern, and yet in an odd way very close to her pupils"* (Sherwood Anderson). **3.** Grim or gloomy. **4.** Inexorable; relentless. [Middle English *sterne,* from Old English *stierne.*] **—stern′ly** *adv.* **—stern′ness** *n.*

stern² (stûrn) *n.* The rear part of a ship or boat. [Middle English *sterne,* prob. from Old Norse *stjōrn,* rudder.]

ster·na (stûr′nə) *n.* A plural of **sternum.**

stern·most (stûrn′mōst′, -məst) *adj.* Farthest astern.

ster·num (stûr′nəm) *n., pl.* **-na** (-nə) or **-nums.** A long, flat bone located in the center of the chest, serving as a support for the collarbone and ribs; the breastbone. [From Greek *sternon,* breast, breastbone.]

stern·ward (stûrn′wərd) *adv.* Also **stern·wards** (-wərdz). Toward the stern; astern. **—adj.** In or at the stern.

stern-wheel·er (stûrn′hwē′lər, -wē′-) *n.* A steamboat propelled by a paddle wheel at the stern.

ste·roid (stĭr′oid′, stĕr′-) *n.* Any of a large class of naturally occurring, fat-soluble organic compounds based on a structure having 17 carbon atoms bound in a ring, including many hormones and sterols. [STER(OL) + -OID.]

ste·rol (stĭr′ōl′, stĕr′-) *n.* Any of a group of predominantly unsaturated solid alcohols of the steroid group, as cholesterol and ergosterol, occurring in the fatty tissues of plants and animals. [Short for CHOLESTEROL.]

ster·tor·ous (stûr′tər-əs) *adj.* Marked by a snoring sound.

[From Latin *stertere,* to snore.] **—ster′tor·ous·ly** *adv.*

stet (stĕt) *n.* A printer's term directing that matter marked for omission or correction is to be retained. **—tr.v. stet·ted, stet·ting.** To cancel a correction or omission previously made in (printed matter) by marking with the word *stet* and underlining with dots. [Latin, "let it stand," from *stāre,* to stand.]

steth·o·scope (stĕth′ə-skōp′) *n.* An instrument used to listen to sounds produced within the body. [Greek *stēthos,* chest, breast + –SCOPE.] **—steth′o·scop′ic** (-skŏp′ĭk) or **steth′o·scop′i·cal** *adj.*

Stet·son (stĕt′sən) *n.* A trademark for a felt hat with a high crown and wide brim, popular in the Southwest.

ste·ve·dore (stē′və-dôr′, -dōr′) *n.* A person employed in the loading and unloading of ships. **—v. -dored, -dor·ing. —tr.v.** To load or unload the cargo of (a ship). **—intr.v.** To load or unload a ship. [Spanish *estibador,* from *estivar,* to pack, from Latin *stipāre.*]

stew (stōō, styōō) *tr.v.* To cook (food) by simmering or boiling slowly. **—intr.v. 1.** To be stewed. **2.** *Informal.* To suffer with heat or confinement. **3.** *Informal.* To worry; fret. **—n. 1.** A dish cooked by stewing, esp. a mixture of meat or fish and vegetables with stock. **2.** *Informal.* Mental agitation. [Middle English *stewen,* to bathe in hot water or steam, from Old French *estuver.*]

stew·ard (stōō′ərd, styōō′-) *n.* **1.** A person who manages another's property, finances, or other affairs. **2.** A manager of a large household. **3.** An officer on a ship in charge of food. **4.** An attendant, esp. a male, on a ship or airplane. **5.** A **shop steward. —tr.v.** To serve as steward of. **—intr.v.** To serve as a steward. [Middle English *stywarde,* from Old English *stigweard : stig,* hall + *weard,* keeper.]

stew·ard·ess (stōō′ər-dĭs, styōō′-) *n.* A female steward, esp. a woman who assists airline passengers in flight.

stew·ard·ship (stōō′ərd-shĭp′, styōō′-) *n.* **1.** The job or duties of a steward. **2.** Care; supervision.

stib·nite (stĭb′nīt′) *n.* A lead-gray mineral, Sb_2S_3, that is the chief source of antimony. [French *stibine,* stibnite, from Latin *stibium,* antimony + -ITE.]

stick (stĭk) *n.* **1.** A long, slender piece of wood, such as a branch cut or fallen from a tree. **2.** A narrow length of wood shaped for a certain purpose: *a walking stick; a hockey stick.* **3.** Anything cut into or having the shape of a stick. **4.** A long rod used as a control lever for a machine. **5. the sticks.** *Informal.* Rural, remote country. **6.** *Slang.* A stiff, listless, or boring person. **7.** A poke or thrust with a pointed object. **—v. stuck** (stŭk), **stick·ing. —tr.v. 1.** To pierce, puncture, or penetrate with a pointed instrument, such as a knife or pin. **2.** To kill by piercing. **3.** To thrust or push (a knife, pin, or other pointed instrument) into or through another object. **4.** To fasten or attach with or as if with pins or nails. **5.** To fasten or attach with an adhesive material. **6.** To cover or decorate with objects piercing the surface. **7.** To put or thrust. **8.** To detain or delay: *stuck in heavy traffic.* **9.** *Informal.* To baffle or puzzle. **10.** To put blame or responsibility on; burden: *stuck with paying the bill.* **11.** *Slang.* To defraud or cheat. **—intr.v. 1.** To be fixed in place by having the point thrust in. **2.** To become or remain attached or in close association; cling. **3.** To remain loyal or faithful: *stick by a friend; stick to a promise.* **4.** To persevere. **5.** *Informal.* To remain; linger: *Stick around here until I get back.* **6.** To scruple or hesitate: *She*

stern-wheeler

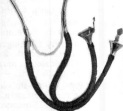

stethoscope

sticks at nothing. **7.** To become fixed, checked, or obstructed. **8.** To project or protrude. —*phrasal verbs.* **stick out.** To be prominent. **stick up.** To rob, esp. at gunpoint. —*idioms.* **be stuck on.** *Informal.* **1.** To reach an impasse concerning. **2.** To be very fond of. **stick up for.** To defend or support. [Middle English *stykke*, from Old English *sticca*.]

stick·ball (stĭk′bôl′) *n.* A form of baseball played with a rubber ball and a stick or broom handle for a bat.

stick·er (stĭk′ər) *n.* **1.** Someone or something that sticks. **2.** An adhesive label. **3.** A thorn or prickle.

sticking plaster. Adhesive tape.

stick-in-the-mud (stĭk′ĭn-thə-mŭd′) *n.* *Informal.* A person who lacks initiative or enthusiasm; an old fogy.

stick·le (stĭk′əl) *intr.v.* **-led, -ling. 1.** To argue stubbornly. **2.** To have or raise objections; scruple. [Middle English *stightlen*, to contend, freq. of *stighten*, to arrange, from Old English *stihtan*.]

stick·le·back (stĭk′əl-băk′) *n.* Any of various small freshwater and marine fishes of the family Gasterosteidae, with erectile spines along the back. [Middle English *stykylbak*, "prickly back."]

stick·ler (stĭk′lər) *n.* **1.** A person who insists on something unyieldingly. **2.** Anything puzzling or difficult.

stick·pin (stĭk′pĭn′) *n.* A decorative pin worn on a necktie.

stick-to-it-ive·ness (stĭk-tōō′ĭ-tĭv-nĭs) *n.* *Informal.* Unwavering tenacity; perseverance.

stick·up (stĭk′ŭp′) *n.* *Slang.* A robbery, esp. at gunpoint.

stick·y (stĭk′ē) *adj.* **-i·er, -i·est. 1.** Tending to stick to a surface. **2.** Covered with an adhesive agent: *a sticky floor.* **3.** Warm and humid. **4.** *Informal.* Painful or difficult: *a sticky situation.* —**stick′i·ly** *adv.* —**stick′i·ness** *n.*

sties (stīz) *n.* **1.** Plural of **sty** (pen). **2.** A plural of **sty** (inflammation).

stiff (stĭf) *adj.* **-er, -est. 1.** Difficult to bend or stretch; rigid: *a stiff fabric.* **2.** Not moving easily; not limber: *a stiff joint.* **3.** Drawn tightly; taut. **4.** Rigidly or excessively formal: *stiff manners.* **5.** Not loose or fluid; firm; thick: *a stiff mixture.* **6.** Firm in purpose or resistance. **7.** Having a strong, steady force. **8.** Potent or strong: *a stiff drink.* **9.** Difficult, laborious, or arduous. **10.** Harsh; severe. **11.** Excessively high: *a stiff price.* —See Syns at **inflexible.** —*adv.* **1.** In a stiff manner. **2.** Completely; totally: *bored stiff.* —*n.* *Slang.* **1.** A corpse. **2.** A dull, lifeless, or haughty person. **3.** A fellow; man: *working stiffs.* [Middle English *stiffe*, from Old English *stīf.*] —**stiff′ly** *adv.* —**stiff′ness** *n.*

stiff·en (stĭf′ən) *tr.v.* To make stiff or stiffer. —*intr.v.* To become stiff or stiffer. —**stiff′en·er** *n.*

stiff-necked (stĭf′nĕkt′) *adj.* Stubborn; unyielding.

sti·fle (stī′fəl) *v.* **-fled, -fling.** —*tr.v.* **1.** To kill by depriving of air or oxygen; smother. **2.** To interrupt or cut off. **3.** To keep or hold back; suppress. —*intr.v.* **1.** To die of suffocation. **2.** To feel smothered by or as if by close confinement. [Middle English *stufflen*, prob. from Old French *estouffer*, to choke, smother.] —**sti′fler** *n.* —**sti′fling·ly** *adv.*

stig·ma (stĭg′mə) *n.* **1.** *pl.* **-mas** or **stig·ma·ta** (stĭg-mä′tə, stĭg′mə-tə). **a.** A mark or reputation of shame or disgrace. **b.** Any small mark or scar. **2.** *pl.* **-mas.** *Bot.* The sticky tip of a flower pistil, on which pollen is deposited. **3. stigmata.** Marks or sores similar to the crucifixion wounds of Christ, sometimes appearing on the bodies of persons in a state of religious ecstasy. [Latin, from Greek, tattoo mark, from *stizein*, to prick, tattoo.]

stig·mat·ic (stĭg-măt′ĭk) or **stig·mat·i·cal** (-ĭ-kəl) *adj.* Relating to, resembling, or having a stigma or stigmata.

stig·ma·tize (stĭg′mə-tīz′) *tr.v.* **-tized, -tiz·ing. 1.** To characterize or brand as disgraceful or ignominious. **2.** To brand or mark with a stigma or stigmata. **3.** To cause stigmata to appear on. —**stig′ma·ti·za′tion** *n.* —**stig′ma·tiz′er** *n.*

stile[1] (stīl) *n.* **1.** A set or series of steps for getting over a fence or wall. **2.** A turnstile. [Middle English, from Old English *stigel.*]

stile[2] (stīl) *n.* A vertical member of a panel or frame, as in a door or window sash. [Prob. from Dutch *stijl*, doorpost, from Middle Dutch, prob. from Latin *stilus*, pole, post.]

sti·let·to (stĭ-lĕt′ō) *n.,* *pl.* **-tos** or **-toes. 1.** A small dagger with a slender, tapering blade. **2.** A sharp-pointed instrument for making eyelet holes. [Italian, dim. of *stilo*, dag-

ger, from Latin *stilus*, pole, stake.]

still[1] (stĭl) *adj.* **-er, -est. 1.** Free from sound; silent; quiet. **2.** Low in sound. **3.** Without movement; at rest. **4.** Free from disturbance; tranquil. **5.** Not carbonated: *a still wine.* **6.** Of or indicating a photograph that shows a single image with no motion, as distinguished from a motion picture. —*n.* **1.** Silence; calm. **2.** A still photograph. —*adv.* **1.** Without movement; motionlessly: *stand still.* **2.** Now as before; yet: *still awake.* **3.** In increasing amount or degree: *still further complaints.* **4.** Nevertheless. —*conj.* Nevertheless; but yet. —*tr.v.* **1.** To make still or tranquil. **2.** To make quiet. **3.** To allay; calm. —*intr.v.* To become still. [Middle English, from Old English *stille.*] —**still′ness** *n.*

still[2] (stĭl) *n.* **1.** An apparatus for distilling liquids, esp. alcohols, by vaporizing and condensing. **2.** A distillery. [From *still*, to distill, from Middle English *stillen*, short for *distillen*, to distill.]

still·birth (stĭl′bûrth′) *n.* **1.** The birth of a dead fetus. **2.** A fetus dead at birth.

still·born (stĭl′bôrn′) *adj.* Born dead.

still life *pl.* **still lifes.** A painting or picture of inanimate objects.

still·y (stĭl′ē) *adj.* **-li·er, -li·est.** *Poet.* Quiet; calm.

stilt (stĭlt) *n.* **1.** Either of a pair of long, slender poles, each equipped with a raised footrest, enabling the person gripping them to walk elevated above the ground. **2.** Any of various tall posts or pillars used as support, as for a dock or an elevated house. **3.** A long-legged wading bird, *Himantopus mexicanus* (or *H. himantopus*), with black and white plumage and a long slender bill. [Middle English *stilte*, stilt, crutch, perh. of Low German orig.]

stilt·ed (stĭl′tĭd) *adj.* **1.** Raised above the ground or water on stilts. **2.** Stiffly or artificially dignified or formal; pompous: *stilted prose.* —**stilt′ed·ly** *adv.* —**stilt′ed·ness** *n.*

stim·u·lant (stĭm′yə-lənt) *n.* **1.** An agent, such as a drug, that temporarily excites or accelerates the function of the body or one of its systems or parts. **2.** A stimulus or incentive. **3.** An alcoholic beverage. —See Syns at **stimulus.** —*adj.* Serving as a stimulant.

stim·u·late (stĭm′yə-lāt′) *v.* **-lat·ed, -lat·ing.** —*tr.v.* To rouse to activity or to increased action or interest; to stir. —*intr.v.* To act or serve as a stimulant or stimulus. —See Syns at **provoke.** —**stim′u·lat′er** or **stim′u·la′tor** *n.* —**stim′u·la′tion** *n.* —**stim′u·la′tive** *adj.*

stim·u·lus (stĭm′yə-ləs) *n.,* *pl.* **-li** (-lī′, -lē′). **1.** Something that incites or rouses to action; an incentive. **2.** An agent, action, or condition that elicits or accelerates a physiological or psychological activity. [Latin, a goad.]

Syns: stimulus, catalyst, impetus, impulse, incentive, motivation, spur, stimulant *n.* *Core meaning:* Something that causes and encourages a given response *(free enterprise as a stimulus to the economy).*

sting (stĭng) *v.* **stung** (stŭng), **sting·ing.** —*tr.v.* **1.** To pierce or wound painfully with a sharp-pointed structure or organ, such as that of certain insects. **2.** To cause to feel a sharp, smarting pain. **3.** To cause to suffer keenly in the mind or feelings. **4.** To spur on by or as if by sharp irritation. **5.** *Slang.* To cheat or overcharge. —*intr.v.* **1.** To have or use a stinger. **2.** To cause or feel a sharp, smarting pain. —*n.* **1.** The act of stinging. **2.** The wound or pain caused by or as if by stinging. **3.** A stinger. **4.** A stinging power, quality, or capacity. [Middle English *stingen*, from Old English *stingan.*]

sting·a·ree (stĭng′ə-rē) *n.* A stingray.

sting·er (stĭng′ər) *n.* **1.** Someone or something that stings. **2.** A sharp, piercing organ, as of certain insects.

sting·ray (stĭng′rā′) *n.* Any of various rays of the family Dasyatidae, with a whiplike tail armed with a venomous spine. Also called **stingaree.**

stin·gy (stĭn′jē) *adj.* **-gi·er, -gi·est. 1.** Giving or spending reluctantly or unwillingly; not generous. **2.** Scanty or meager. [From dial. *stinge*, act of stinging, from Middle English *stingen*, from Old English, from *stingan*, to sting.] —**stin′gi·ly** *adv.* —**stin′gi·ness** *n.*

Syns: stingy, cheap, close, mean, miserly, niggardly, parsimonious, penurious, tight, tightfisted *adj.* *Core meaning:* Reluctant to give or spend *(too stingy to pay the employees well).*

stink (stĭngk) *v.* **stank** (stăngk) or **stunk** (stŭngk), **stunk,**

stink·ing. —*intr.v.* **1.** To give off a strong, offensive odor. **2.** To be highly offensive or abhorrent. **3.** To have something to an extreme or offensive degree: *The deed stinks of treachery.* **4.** *Slang.* To be extremely bad: *This movie stinks.* —*tr.v.* To cause to stink: *The garbage stinks up the yard.* —*n.* A strong offensive odor; a stench. [Middle English *stinken*, from Old English *stincan.*]

stink·bug (stĭngk′bŭg′) *n.* Any of numerous insects of the family Pentatomidae that emit a foul odor.

stink·er (stĭng′kər) *n.* **1.** Someone or something that stinks. **2.** *Slang.* A contemptible or disgusting person.

stink·weed (stĭngk′wēd′) *n.* Any of various plants that have flowers or foliage with an unpleasant odor.

stint (stĭnt) *tr.v.* To be sparing with. —*intr.v.* To be frugal or sparing. —*n.* **1.** A fixed amount or share of work or duty. **2.** A limitation or restriction. [Middle English *stinten*, to cut short, from Old English *styntan*, to blunt.] —**stint′er** *n.*

stipe (stīp) *n.* A plant stalk, such as the stemlike support of a mushroom. [French, from Latin *stīpes*, post, tree trunk.]

sti·pend (stī′pĕnd′, -pənd) *n.* A fixed or regular payment or allowance. [Middle English *stipendie*, from Old French, from Latin *stīpendium*, tax, tribute.]

stip·ple (stĭp′əl) *tr.v.* **-pled, -pling.** **1.** To draw, engrave, or paint in dots or short touches. **2.** To dot, fleck, or speckle. —*n.* The act, technique, or effect of stippling. [Dutch *stippelen*, freq. of *stippen*, to speckle, from *stip*, dot.] —**stip′pler** *n.*

stip·u·lar (stĭp′yə-lər) *adj.* Of or resembling a stipule.

stip·u·late¹ (stĭp′yə-lāt′) *v.* **-lat·ed, -lat·ing.** —*tr.v.* **1.** To specify or demand as a condition of an agreement. **2.** To guarantee in an agreement. —*intr.v.* **1.** To make an express demand or provision in an agreement. **2.** To form an agreement. [From Latin *stipulārī*, to bargain, demand.] —**stip′u·la′tor** *n.*

stip·u·late² (stĭp′yə-lĭt) *adj.* Having stipules.

stip·u·la·tion (stĭp′yə-lā′shən) *n.* **1.** The act of stipulating. **2.** Something stipulated; a term or condition.

stip·ule (stĭp′yōōl′) *n.* One of the usu. small, paired leaflike appendages at the base of a leaf or leafstalk in certain plants. [Latin, stalk, stem.]

stir¹ (stûr) *v.* **stirred, stir·ring.** —*tr.v.* **1.** To pass an implement through (a liquid) in circular motions, so as to mix or cool. **2.** To cause to change position slightly. **3.** To rouse. **4.** To call forth; evoke. **5.** To provoke or instigate: *stir up trouble.* **6.** To move or affect strongly. —*intr.v.* **1.** To change position slightly: *stir in one's sleep.* **2.** To move about actively; to venture. —*n.* **1.** An act of stirring. **2.** A slight or temporary movement. **3.** A disturbance or commotion: *cause a stir.* [Middle English *stiren*, from Old English *styrian*, to move, agitate, excite.] —**stir′rer** *n.*

stir² (stûr) *n.* *Slang.* Prison. [Orig. unknown.]

stir·ring (stûr′ĭng) *adj.* **1. a.** Rousing; exciting; thrilling. **b.** Moving. **2.** Active; lively. —See Syns at **moving.** —**stir′ring·ly** *adv.*

stir·rup (stûr′əp, stĭr′-) *n.* **1.** A flat-based loop or ring hung from either side of a horse's saddle to support the rider's foot in mounting and riding. **2.** Any of various similarly shaped supporting devices. [Middle English *stirope*, from Old English *stigrāp.*]

stirrup

stitch (stĭch) *n.* **1.** A single complete movement of a threaded needle in sewing or surgical suturing. **2.** A single loop of yarn around a knitting needle or similar implement. **3.** The link, loop, or knot made in this way. **4.** A mode of arranging the threads in sewing, knitting, or crocheting: *a purl stitch.* **5.** A sudden sharp pain. **6.** *Informal.* An article of clothing. **7.** *Informal.* The least part; a bit. —*tr.v.* **1.** To fasten or join with stitches. **2.** To fasten with staples. —*intr.v.* To sew. —*idiom.* **in stitches.** *Informal.* Laughing uncontrollably. [Middle English *stiche*, from Old English *stice*, a sting, prick.] —**stitch′er** *n.*

stith·y (stĭth′ē, stĭth′ē) *n., pl.* **-ies.** **1.** An anvil. **2.** A forge or smithy. [Middle English *stethy*, from Old Norse *stedhi*.]

sto·a (stō′ə) *n., pl.* **sto·ae** (stō′ē′) or **-as.** An ancient Greek covered walk or colonnade. [Greek, porch.]

stoat (stōt) *n.* The ermine, esp. when in its brown summer coat. [Middle English *stote.*]

stock (stŏk) *n.* **1.** A supply accumulated for future use; a store. **2.** The total merchandise kept on hand by a commercial establishment. **3.** All the animals kept or raised on a farm; livestock. **4.** *Econ.* **a.** The capital or fund that a corporation raises through the sale of shares. **b.** The number of shares that each stockholder possesses. **c.** A stock certificate. **5.** The trunk or main stem of a tree or other plant. **6. a.** A plant or stem onto which a graft is made. **b.** A plant or tree from which cuttings are taken. **7. a.** The original progenitor of a family line. **b.** Ancestry or lineage. **8. a.** The type from which a group of animals or plants has descended. **b.** A race, family, or other related group. **9.** A group of related languages. **10.** The raw material out of which something is made. **11.** The broth from boiled meat or fish, used in preparing soup, gravy, or sauces. **12. stocks.** The timber frame that supports a ship during construction. **13. stocks.** A former instrument of punishment, consisting of a heavy timber frame with holes for confining the ankles and, sometimes, the wrists; a pillory. **14.** *Naut.* A crosspiece at the end of an anchor's shank. **15.** The wooden or metal handle or part of a rifle, pistol, or automatic weapon, to which the barrel and mechanism are attached. **16.** Any handle, as of a tool. **17.** The frame of a plow, to which the share, handles, and other parts are fastened. **18. a.** *Theater.* A stock company. **b.** The repertoire of such a company. **19.** Any of several plants of the genus *Mathiola*, native to the Old World, esp. one widely cultivated for its clusters of showy flowers. **20.** Personal reputation or status: *His stock with the students is falling.* —*modifier:* *a stock clerk; a stock mare; stock prices.* —*tr.v.* **1.** To provide with merchandise or livestock. **2.** To keep for future sale or use. **3.** To provide with fish or game. **4.** To provide (as a rifle or plow) with a stock. —*intr.v.* **1.** To gather and store a supply: *stock up on canned goods.* **2.** To put forth or sprout new shoots. —*adj.* **1.** Kept regularly in stock: *a stock item.* **2.** Commonplace; ordinary: *a stock answer.* —*adv.* Utterly; completely. Used in combination: *stock-still.* —*idioms.* **in (or out of) stock.** Available (or unavailable) for sale or use. **stock in trade. 1.** Merchandise kept on hand. **2.** A person's resources: *Flattery is his stock in trade.* **take stock. 1.** To take an inventory. **2.** To make an estimate or appraisal. **take (or put) stock in.** *Informal.* To trust or attach importance to. [Middle English *stokke*, from Old English *stocc*, tree trunk.]

stock·ade (stŏ-kād′) *n.* **1.** A defensive barrier made of strong posts or timbers driven upright in the ground. **2.** Any similarly fenced or enclosed area, esp. one used for protection or imprisonment. —*tr.v.* **-ad·ed, -ad·ing.** To protect or surround with a stockade. [Obs. French *estocade*, from Spanish *estacada*, from *estaca*, stake.]

stock·bro·ker (stŏk′brō′kər) *n.* A person who buys and sells stocks or other securities. —**stock′bro′ker·age** *n.*

stock car. 1. An automobile of a standard make, modified for racing. **2.** A railroad car used for carrying livestock.

stock company. 1. A company or corporation whose capital is divided into shares. **2.** A permanent theater company of actors and technicians performing in repertory.

stock exchange. 1. A place where stocks, bonds, or other securities are bought and sold. **2.** An association of stockbrokers who meet to buy and sell securities.

stock·fish (stŏk′fĭsh′) *n.* A fish, such as cod or haddock, cured by being split and air-dried without salt.

stock·hold·er (stŏk′hōl′dər) *n.* A person who owns a share or shares of stock in a company.

stock·i·net (stŏk′ə-nĕt′) *n.* Also **stock·i·nette.** An elastic knitted fabric used in making undergarments, bandages, etc. [Perh. var. of earlier *stocking-net*.]

stock·ing (stŏk′ĭng) *n.* A close-fitting, usu. knitted covering for the foot and leg. [From dial. *stock*, stocking, from Middle English *stokkes*.]

stocking cap. A usu. knitted cap with a long conical part that hangs to one side.

stock market. 1. A stock exchange. 2. The business transacted or the prices offered at a stock exchange.

stock·pile (stŏk′pīl′) *n.* A supply stored for future use. —*v.* **-piled, -pil·ing.** —*tr.v.* To accumulate a stockpile of. —*intr.v.* To accumulate a stockpile.

stock·room (stŏk′rōom′, -rŏom′) *n.* A room in which a store of goods or materials is kept.

stock·y (stŏk′ē) *adj.* **-i·er, -i·est.** Compact and solidly built; sturdy; thickset. —**stock′i·ly** *adv.* —**stock′i·ness** *n.*

stock·yard (stŏk′yärd′) *n.* A large enclosed yard in which livestock is temporarily kept, as for slaughter.

stodg·y (stŏj′ē) *adj.* **-i·er, -i·est.** 1. Lacking excitement or interest; dull. 2. Old-fashioned; prim. 3. Heavy; indigestible. 4. Solidly built; thickset; stocky. [From *stodge*, thick food or mud, from *stodge*, to cram, gorge.] —**stodg′i·ly** *adv.* —**stodg′i·ness** *n.*

sto·gy (stō′gē) *n., pl.* **-gies.** Also **sto·gie** or **sto·gey** *pl.* **-geys.** A cigar. [After *Conestoga*, Pennsylvania.]

sto·ic (stō′ĭk) *n.* 1. **Stoic.** A member of a Greek school of philosophy founded by Zeno about 308 B.C., holding that men should be free from passion and calmly accept all occurrences as unavoidable. 2. A person seemingly indifferent to or unaffected by pleasure or pain. —*adj.* 1. **Stoic.** Of the Stoics or their beliefs. 2. Also **sto·i·cal** (-ĭ-kəl). Indifferent to pleasure or pain. [Latin *Stōicus*, from Greek *Stōikos*, from *stoa*, portico, the porch where Zeno taught.] —**sto′i·cal·ly** *adv.*

sto·i·cism (stō′ĭ-sĭz′əm) *n.* 1. **Stoicism.** The philosophy or doctrines of the Stoics. 2. Indifference to pleasure or pain.

stoke (stōk) *v.* **stoked, stok·ing.** —*tr.v.* 1. To stir up and feed (a fire or furnace). 2. To tend (a furnace). —*intr.v.* To tend a furnace. [Back-formation from STOKER.]

stoke·hold (stōk′hōld′) *n.* The area or compartment into which the ship's furnaces or boilers open.

stoke·hole (stōk′hōl′) *n.* 1. The opening in a furnace. 2. A stokehold.

stok·er (stō′kər) *n.* 1. A person who feeds fuel to and tends a furnace. 2. A mechanical device for feeding coal to a furnace. [Dutch, from *stoken*, to poke, thrust.]

stole[1] (stōl) *n.* 1. A long scarf, usu. of silk or linen, worn over the left shoulder by deacons and over both shoulders by priests and bishops while officiating. 2. A women's long scarf of cloth or fur, worn about the shoulders. [Middle English, long robe, from Old English *stol*, from Latin *stola*, from Greek *stolē*, garment.]

stole[2] (stōl) *v.* Past tense of **steal.** [Back-formation from STOLEN.]

sto·len (stō′lən) *v.* Past participle of **steal.** [Middle English *stollen*, from Old English *(ge)stolen*.]

stol·id (stŏl′ĭd) *adj.* Unemotional; impassive. [Latin *stolidus*.] —**sto·lid′i·ty** (stə-lĭd′ĭ-tē) *n.* —**stol′id·ly** *adv.*

sto·lon (stō′lŏn′, -lən) *n.* 1. *Bot.* A stem growing along or under the ground and taking root at the nodes or apex to form new plants. 2. *Zool.* A stemlike structure of certain colonial organisms, from which new individuals develop by budding. [Latin *stolō*, branch, shoot.]

sto·ma (stō′mə) *n., pl.* **-ma·ta** (-mə-tə) or **-mas.** One of the minute pores in the epidermis of a leaf or stem, through which gases and water vapor pass. [Greek, mouth.]

stom·ach (stŭm′ək) *n.* 1. a. The enlarged, saclike portion of the alimentary canal, one of the principal organs of digestion, located in vertebrates between the esophagus and the small intestine. b. A similar digestive structure of many invertebrates. 2. *Informal.* The abdomen or belly. 3. An appetite for food. 4. Any desire or inclination; liking. —*tr.v.* 1. To bear; tolerate. 2. To digest. [Middle English *stomak*, from Old French *stomaque*, from Latin *stomachus*, from Greek *stomakhos*, throat, gullet, from *stoma*, mouth.]

stom·ach·ache (stŭm′ə-kāk′) *n.* Pain in the abdomen.

stom·ach·er (stŭm′ə-kər) *n.* A decorative garment formerly worn over the chest and stomach, esp. by women.

sto·mach·ic (stə-măk′ĭk) or **sto·mach·i·cal** (-kəl) *adj.* Also **stom·ach·al** (stŭm′ə-kəl). 1. Of the stomach; gastric. 2. Beneficial to or stimulating digestion in the stomach. —*n.* A medicine or agent that aids digestion.

sto·ma·ta (stō′mə-tə) *n.* A plural of **stoma.**

stomp (stômp, stŏmp) *tr.v.* To tread heavily on. —*intr.v.* To tread heavily. —*n.* A jazz dance involving a heavy step. [Var. of STAMP (to pound).]

stone (stōn) *n.* 1. A naturally hardened mass of earthy or mineral matter; rock. 2. Such material used for construction. 3. A small piece of rock. 4. Rock or a piece of rock shaped or finished for a particular purpose, as a gravestone. 5. A gem. 6. *Bot.* The hard covering enclosing the kernel in certain fruits, such as the cherry. 7. *Pathol.* A mineral concretion in a hollow organ, as in the kidney. 8. *pl.* **stone.** A unit of weight in Britain, 14 pounds avoirdupois. —*modifier: a stone wall.* —*tr.v.* **stoned, ston·ing.** 1. To pelt or kill with stones. 2. To remove the stones or pits from. 3. To furnish, fit, or line with stones. [Middle English, from Old English *stān*.]

Stone Age. The earliest known period of human culture, characterized by the use of stone tools.

stone-blind (stōn′blīnd′) *adj.* Completely blind.

stone-broke (stōn′brōk′) *adj.* Completely broke; penniless.

stone·crop (stōn′krŏp′) *n.* Any of various plants of the genus *Sedum*, with fleshy leaves. [Middle English *stoncrop*, from Old English *stāncropp* : *stān*, stone + *cropp*, cluster.]

stone·cut·ter (stōn′kŭt′ər) *n.* Someone or something that cuts or carves stone. —**stone′cut′ting** *n.*

stoned (stōnd) *adj. Slang.* Intoxicated, as from a drug.

stone-deaf (stōn′dĕf′) *adj.* Completely deaf.

stone·fly (stōn′flī′) *n.* Any of numerous winged insects of the order Plecoptera, used as fishing bait.

stone·ma·son (stōn′mā′sən) *n.* A person who prepares and lays stones in building. —**stone′ma′son·ry** *n.*

stone·ware (stōn′wâr′) *n.* A heavy, nonporous pottery.

stone·work (stōn′wûrk′) *n.* 1. The process of working in stone. 2. Work made of stone. —**stone′work′er** *n.*

ston·y (stō′nē) *adj.* **-i·er, -i·est.** Also **ston·ey.** 1. Covered with or full of stones. 2. Hard or rigid as a stone. 3. Hardhearted. 4. Rigid; impassive: *a stony face.* —**ston′i·ly** *adv.* —**ston′i·ness** *n.*

stood (stŏod) *v.* Past tense and past participle of **stand.**

stooge (stōōj) *n.* 1. The straight man to a comedian. 2. Anyone who allows himself to be used by another. 3. A planted spy. [Orig. unknown.]

stool (stōōl) *n.* 1. A backless and armless single seat supported on legs or a pedestal. 2. A low bench or support for the feet or knees. 3. A toilet seat; privy. 4. Waste matter expelled in a bowel movement. 5. *Hort.* a. A stump that produces shoots. b. A shoot from such a stump. —*intr.v.* To send up shoots or suckers. [Middle English *stol*, from Old English *stōl*.]

stool pigeon. 1. A pigeon used as a decoy. 2. *Slang.* An informer or decoy, esp. a spy for the police.

stoop[1] (stōōp) *intr.v.* 1. To bend forward and down. 2. To walk or stand with the head and upper back bent forward. 3. To lower or debase oneself; condescend. 4. To swoop down, as a bird in pursuing its prey. —*tr.v.* To bend (one's

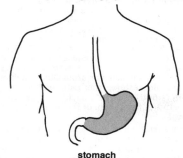

stomach

head or body) forward and down. —*n.* **1.** The act or habit of stooping. **2.** A swooping down, as of a bird of prey. [Middle English *stupen,* from Old English *stūpian.*]

stoop² (sto͞op) *n.* A small porch, platform, or staircase leading to the entrance of a house or building. [Dutch *stoep,* front verandah, from Middle Dutch.]

stop (stŏp) *v.* **stopped, stop·ping.** —*tr.v.* **1.** To close (an opening) by covering, filling in, or plugging. **2.** To cease or halt the movement, progress, action, or operation of. **3.** To prevent the flow or passage of: *stop traffic.* **4.** To restrain; prevent. **5.** To cease doing: *stop running.* **6.** To instruct one's bank not to pay: *stop a check.* **7. a.** To press (a string of a stringed instrument) to produce a tone of a desired pitch. **b.** To close (a hole of a woodwind instrument) to produce a tone of a desired pitch. —*intr.v.* **1.** To cease or halt moving, progressing, acting, or operating. **2.** To come to an end. **3.** To interrupt one's course or journey: *stopped at the store on the way home.* —*n.* **1.** The act of stopping or the condition of being stopped. **2.** A finish; an end. **3.** A stay or visit, as during a trip. **4.** Any place stopped at: *a truck stop.* **5.** Anything that obstructs, blocks, or plugs up. **6.** A part in a machine that stops or regulates movement. **7.** A mark of punctuation, esp. a period. **8.** A hole on a wind instrument or a fret on a stringed instrument. **9.** A tuned set of pipes, as in an organ. **10.** *Phonet.* A consonant articulated with a complete obstruction of the passage of breath, as *p, b, t, d, k,* or *g.* [Middle English *stoppen,* from Old English *stoppian.*]

Syns: 1. stop, arrest, cease, check, discontinue, halt, stay *v. Core meaning:* To prevent the occurrence or continuation of *(stopped the execution of the prisoner; told us to stop the noise).* **2. stop, cease, desist, discontinue, halt, lay off** *(Slang),* **leave off, quit** *v. Core meaning:* To come to a cessation *(snow that finally stopped; a guard who yelled for us to stop).* See also Syns at **abandon.**

stop·cock (stŏp′kŏk′) *n.* A valve that regulates flow.

stope (stōp) *n.* An excavation in the form of steps, made by the mining of ore from steeply inclined or vertical veins. [Perh. from Low German *stope,* a step.]

stop·gap (stŏp′găp′) *n.* A temporary substitute.

stop·light (stŏp′līt′) *n.* **1.** A traffic signal. **2.** A light on the rear of a vehicle, lighted when the brakes are applied.

stop·o·ver (stŏp′ō′vər) *n.* A stop or stopping place in the course of a journey.

stop·page (stŏp′ĭj) *n.* The act of stopping or the condition of being stopped; a halt.

stop·per (stŏp′ər) *n.* **1.** Any device, as a cork or plug, inserted to close an opening. **2.** Someone or something that causes something to stop. —*tr.v.* To close with a stopper.

stop·ple (stŏp′əl) *n.* A stopper; a plug. —*tr.v.* **-pled, -pling.** To close with a stopple. [Middle English *stoppell,* from *stoppen,* to stop.]

stop·watch (stŏp′wŏch′) *n.* A timepiece that can be instantly started and stopped by pushing a button.

stor·age (stôr′ĭj, stōr′-) *n.* **1.** The act of storing or the condition of being stored. **2.** A space for storing. **3.** The price charged for keeping goods stored.

storage battery. A group of reversible or rechargeable electric cells acting as a unit.

sto·rax (stôr′ăks′, stōr′-) *n.* An aromatic resin obtained from any of various trees of the genus *Styrax.* [Middle English, from Latin, from Greek *sturax.*]

store (stôr, stōr) *n.* **1.** A place where merchandise is offered for sale; a shop. **2.** A stock or supply reserved for future use. **3. stores.** Supplies, esp. of food, clothing, or arms. —*tr.v.* **stored, stor·ing. 1.** To reserve or put away for future use. **2.** To fill, supply, or stock. **3.** To deposit or receive in a storehouse or warehouse for safekeeping. —*idioms.* **in store.** Forthcoming. **set store by.** To regard with esteem. [Middle English *stor,* from Old French *estor,* from *estorer,* to build, restore, from Latin *instaurāre.*]

store·front (stôr′frŭnt′, stōr′-) *n.* **1.** The side of a store facing a street. **2.** A front room or rooms in a store building at street level.

store·house (stôr′hous′, stōr′-) *n.* **1.** A building in which goods are stored; a warehouse. **2.** An abundant supply.

store·keep·er (stôr′kē′pər, stōr′-) *n.* **1.** A person who keeps a retail store or shop; a shopkeeper. **2.** A person in charge

of receiving or distributing stores or supplies.

store·room (stôr′ro͞om′, -ro͝om′, stōr′-) *n.* A room in which things are stored.

sto·rey (stôr′ē, stōr′ē) *n. Brit.* Var. of **story** (level).

sto·ried¹ (stôr′ēd, stōr′-) *adj.* **1.** Celebrated or famous in history or story: *a storied valley.* **2.** Ornamented with designs representing scenes from legend or story.

sto·ried² (stôr′ēd, stōr′-) *adj.* Having a specified number of stories: *a three-storied house.*

stork (stôrk) *n.* Any of various large wading birds of the family Ciconiidae, with long legs and a long straight bill. [Middle English, from Old English *storc.*]

stork
George Miksch Sutton

storm (stôrm) *n.* **1.** An atmospheric disturbance accompanied by winds and usu. by rain or snow and often by thunder and lightning. **2.** *Meteorol.* A wind ranging from 64 to 72 miles per hour. **3.** A heavy shower of objects, such as bullets or missiles. **4.** A strong or violent outburst or disturbance. **5.** *Mil.* A violent, sudden attack on a fortified place. —*intr.v.* **1.** To blow with great force; to rain, snow, or otherwise precipitate violently. **2.** To be extremely angry. **3.** To rush or move violently or angrily. —*tr.v.* To try to capture by a violent, sudden attack: *storm the castle.* [Middle English, from Old English.]

storm petrel. Any of various small sea birds of the family Hydrobatidae, esp. one of the North Atlantic and the Mediterranean. Also called **stormy petrel** and **Mother Carey's chicken.**

storm troopers. A Nazi militia noted for brutality.

storm window. An outer or additional window added for protection against cold and inclement weather.

storm·y (stôr′mē) *adj.* **-i·er, -i·est. 1.** Subject to, characterized by, or affected by storms: *stormy weather.* **2.** Characterized by violent emotions, passions, speech, or actions: *a stormy argument.* —**storm′i·ly** *adv.* —**storm′i·ness** *n.*

stormy petrel. A storm petrel.

sto·ry¹ (stôr′ē, stōr′ē) *n., pl.* **-ries. 1.** An account of an event or series of events, either true or fictitious. **2.** A prose or verse narrative, usu. fictional; a tale. **3.** A short story. **4.** The plot of a novel, play, etc. **5.** An explanation. **6.** A news article or broadcast. **7.** A lie. **8.** Romantic legend or tradition. —See Syns at **lie** and **plot.** [Middle English *storie,* from Norman French *estorie,* from Latin *historia,* from Greek, from *histōr,* wisdom.]

sto·ry² (stôr′ē, stōr′ē) *n., pl.* **-ries.** Also *Brit.* **sto·rey** *pl.* **-reys. 1.** A horizontal division of a building. **2.** The set of rooms on the same level of a building. [Middle English *storye,* from Medieval Latin *historia,* a row of windows with pictures on them, from Latin *historia,* story, tale.]

sto·ry·book (stôr′ē-bo͝ok′, stōr′-) *n.* A book of stories.

sto·ry·tell·er (stôr′ē-těl′ər, stōr′-) *n.* **1.** A person who tells or writes stories. **2.** *Informal.* A liar. —**sto′ry·tell′ing** *n.*

stoup (sto͞op) *n.* **1.** A basin for holy water at the entrance of a church. **2.** A cup or other drinking vessel. [Middle English *stowp,* vessel, from Old Norse *staup.*]

stout (stout) *adj.* **-er, -est. 1.** Resolute or bold in character; valiant. **2.** Physically strong and vigorous; robust. **3.** Substantial; solid. **4.** Thickset; fat. —See Syns at **fat.** —*n.* A strong, very dark beer or ale. [Middle English, from Old French *estout.*] —**stout′ly** *adv.* —**stout′ness** *n.*

stout·heart·ed (stout′här′tĭd) *adj.* Bold and courageous; dauntless. —See Syns at **brave.** —**stout′heart′ed·ly** *adv.* —**stout′heart′ed·ness** *n.*

ă pat	ā pay	â care	ä father	ĕ pet	ē be	hw which	ĭ pit	ī tie	î pier	ŏ pot	ō toe	ô paw, for	oi noise
o͝o took	o͞o boot	ou out	th thin	*th* this	ŭ cut		û urge	zh vision	ə about, item, edible, gallop, circus				

stove¹ (stōv) *n.* **1.** An apparatus that uses electricity or burns fuel to furnish heat, as for cooking. **2.** A kiln. [Middle English, heated chamber, of Low German orig.]

stove² (stōv) *v.* A past tense and past participle of **stave.** [From STAVE, formed on the model of such verbs as *break, broke.*]

stove·pipe (stōv′pīp′) *n.* **1.** A pipe used to conduct smoke from a stove into a chimney flue. **2.** A tall silk hat.

stovepipe
A stovepipe hat

stow (stō) *tr.v.* **1.** To put or store away compactly. **2.** To fill by packing tightly. **3.** To have room or space for; to hold. **4.** *Slang.* To cease; stop. *—phrasal verb.* **stow away.** To be a stowaway. [Middle English *stowen,* to place, put, from *stowe,* a place, from Old English *stōw.*]

stow·age (stō′ĭj) *n.* The act or process of stowing or the condition of being stowed; storage.

stow·a·way (stō′ə-wā′) *n.* A person who hides aboard a ship to obtain free passage.

stra·bis·mus (strə-bĭz′məs) *n.* A visual defect in which both eyes cannot be simultaneously focused on an objective because of imbalance of the eye muscles. [Greek *strabismos,* from *strabizein,* to squint, from *strabos,* squinting.] *—stra·bis′mal* or *stra·bis′mic adj.*

strad·dle (străd′l) *v.* **-dled, -dling.** *—tr.v.* **1.** To sit, stand, or move astride of; bestride. **2.** To spread (the legs) wide. **3.** To appear to favor both sides of (an issue). *—intr.v.* **1.** To sit, stand, or move astride. **2.** To appear to favor both sides of an issue. **3.** To sprawl. *—n.* **1.** The act or posture of sitting astride. **2.** An equivocal position. [From *strad,* obs. p. t. of STRIDE.] *—strad′dler n.*

Strad·i·var·i·us (străd′ə-vâr′ē-əs, -vâr′-) *n.* A violin made in the workshop of Antonio Stradivari (1644–1737).

strafe (strāf, sträf) *tr.v.* **strafed, straf·ing.** To attack with machine-gun fire from low-flying aircraft. [From German *(Gott) strafe (England),* "(God) punish (England)."]

strag·gle (străg′əl) *intr.v.* **-gled, -gling. 1.** To stray or fall behind. **2.** To proceed or spread out in a scattered group. [Middle English *straglen.*] *—strag′gler n.*

strag·gly (străg′lē) *adj.* **-gli·er, -gli·est.** Spread out or proceeding irregularly: *straggly troops; a straggly tail.*

straight (strāt) *adj.* **-er, -est. 1.** Extending continuously in the same direction without curving: *a straight line.* **2.** Having no waves or bends: *straight hair.* **3.** Erect; upright. **4.** Direct and candid: *a straight answer.* **5.** Without a break; uninterrupted. **6.** Giving complete support to a political party: *always votes a straight ticket.* **7.** Correct or accurate. **8.** Honest; fair. **9.** Neatly arranged; orderly. **10.** Not deviating from the normal or strict form: *straight Freudian analysis.* **11.** Undiluted or unmixed: *straight whiskey.* **12.** *Slang.* Conventional or conservative. —See Syns at **direct** and **level.** *—adv.* **1.** In a straight line; directly. **2.** In an erect posture; upright. **3.** Continuously. **4.** Without detour or delay. **6.** Honestly or candidly. *—n.* **1.** Something that is straight. **2.** A straightaway. **3.** A numerical sequence of five cards in a poker hand. **4.** *Slang.* **a.** A heterosexual person. **b.** A conventional person. *—idioms.* **go straight.** To reform after having been a criminal. **straight away** (or **off**). Immediately. [Middle English *streit,* from the past part. of *strecchen,* to stretch.] *—straight′ly adv.* *—straight′ness n.*

straight angle. An angle of 180 degrees.

straight·a·way (strāt′ə-wā′) *adj.* **1.** Extending in a straight line or course. **2.** Unhesitating; immediate. *—n.* (strāt′-ə-wā′). A straight course or stretch of road or track, esp.

the stretch of a race course between the last turn and the finish. *—adv.* **1.** At once; immediately.

straight·edge (strāt′ĕj′) *n.* A rigid object with a straight edge for testing or drawing straight lines.

straight·en (strāt′n) *tr.v.* To make straight. *—intr.v.* To become straight. *—phrasal verb.* **straighten out.** To reform or correct. *—straight′en·er n.*

straight face. A face that betrays no sign of emotion. *—straight′-faced′* (strāt′fāst′) *adj.*

straight flush. A straight in poker in which all five cards are of the same suit.

straight·for·ward (strāt-fôr′wərd) *adj.* **1.** Direct. **2.** Honest; frank. —See Syns at **plain.** *—adv.* Also **straight·for·wards** (-wərdz). In a straightforward course or manner. *—straight·for′ward·ly adv.* *—straight·for′ward·ness n.*

straight jacket. Var. of **strait jacket.**

straight-line (strāt′līn′) *adj.* Lying in a straight line.

straight man. An actor who serves as a foil for a comedian.

straight razor. A razor consisting of a blade hinged to a handle into which it slips when not in use.

straight·way (strāt′wā′, -wā′) *adv.* Without delay; at once.

strain¹ (strān) *tr.v.* **1.** To pull, draw, or stretch tight. **2.** To exert or tax to the utmost. **3.** To injure or impair by overexertion. **4.** To stretch or force beyond the proper or legitimate limit. **5.** To deform by applying pressure. **6.** To pass (a substance) through a strainer or other filtering agent. **7.** To draw off or remove by filtration. *—intr.v.* **1.** To strive hard. **2.** To become wrenched or twisted. **3.** To be subjected to great stress. **4.** To pull forcibly or violently. **5.** To filter, trickle, or ooze. *—n.* **1.** The act of straining or the condition of being strained. **2.** A great or extreme effort, force, or tension. **3.** A wrench or other injury resulting from excessive effort or use. **4.** A deformation produced by stress. —See Syns at **effort.** [Middle English *streynen,* from Old French *estreindre,* from Latin *stringere,* to draw tight, tie.]

strain² (strān) *n.* **1.** The collective descendants of a common ancestor. **2.** A line of ancestry; lineage. **3.** *Biol.* A group of organisms of the same species, having distinctive characteristics but not usu. considered a separate breed or variety: *a strain of corn.* **4.** A characteristic tendency. **5.** Often **strains.** A musical passage or tune. **6.** A trace; suggestion. [Middle English *strene,* from Old English *strēon,* acquisition, offspring.]

strain·er (strā′nər) *n.* **1.** A filter, sieve, colander, or similar device used to separate liquids from solids. **2.** Someone or something that strains.

strait (strāt) *n.* **1.** Often **straits.** A narrow passage of water joining two larger bodies of water. **2.** Often **straits.** A difficult or perplexing position. *—adj.* **-er, -est.** *Archaic.* **1.** Narrow. **2.** Strict, rigid, or righteous. [Middle English *streit,* from Old French *estreit,* tight, narrow, from Latin *strictus,* from *stringere,* to draw tight.]

strait·en (strāt′n) *tr.v.* **1.** To make narrow or restricted. **2.** To put into difficulties or distress, esp. financially.

strait·jack·et (strāt′jăk′ĭt) *n.* Also **straight jacket. 1.** A long-sleeved jacketlike garment used to bind down the arms of a violent patient or prisoner. **2.** Any tight restriction.

strait-laced (strāt-lāst′) *adj.* Excessively strict in behavior, morality, or opinions; prudish.

strake (strāk) *n.* A continuous line of planking or plating extending on a vessel's hull. [Middle English.]

stra·mo·ni·um (strə-mō′nē-əm) *n.* The dried leaves of the jimsonweed, used in treating asthma. [New Latin.]

strand¹ (strănd) *n.* Land bordering a body of water; a beach. *—tr.v.* **1.** To drive or run aground. **2.** To bring into or leave in a difficult or helpless position. *—intr.v.* To be stranded. [Middle English, from Old English, shore.]

strand² (strănd) *n.* **1.** Each of the fibers or filaments that are twisted together to form a rope, cable, etc. **2.** Any single fiber, thread, or other filament. **3.** A string of beads, pearls, etc. [Middle English *strond.*]

strange (strānj) *adj.* **strang·er, strang·est. 1.** Not previously known or experienced; unfamiliar. **2.** Differing from the usual; striking or odd. **3.** Uncomfortable or peculiar. **4.** Not of one's own or a particular locality or kind.

ă pat   ā pay   â care   ä father   ĕ pet   ē be   hw which
ŏŏ took   ōō boot   ou out   th thin   *th* this   ŭ cut
ĭ pit   ī tie   î pier   ŏ pot   ō toe   ô paw, for   oi noise
û urge   zh vision   ə about, item, edible, gallop, circus

5. Lacking experience; unaccustomed: *strange to her new duties.* [Middle English *straunge*, from Old French *estrange*, from Latin *extrāneus*, foreign, strange, from *extrā*, outside, beyond.] —**strange′ly** *adv.* —**strange′ness** *n.*
Syns: 1. strange, new, unaccustomed, unfamiliar *adj.* *Core meaning:* Previously unknown *(strange faces).* **2. strange, eccentric, odd, peculiar, quaint, queer, unusual** *adj. Core meaning:* Notably out of the ordinary *(strange behavior; a strange animal).*

strang·er (strān′jər) *n.* **1.** A person with whom one is not acquainted. **2.** A foreigner, newcomer, or outsider. **3.** A person unacquainted with something specified: *no stranger to fine wines.*

stran·gle (străng′gəl) *v.* **-gled, -gling.** —*tr.v.* **1. a.** To kill by squeezing the throat so as to choke or suffocate. **b.** To smother. **2.** To hold back or repress; stifle: *strangle a scream.* **3.** To inhibit; suppress. —*intr.v.* To die or suffer from suffocation or strangulation. [Middle English *stranglen*, from Old French *estrangler*, from Latin *strangulāre*, to strangulate.] —**stran′gler** *n.*

strangle hold. 1. An illegal wrestling hold used to choke an opponent. **2.** A severe restriction.

stran·gu·late (străng′gyə-lāt′) *tr.v.* **-lat·ed, -lat·ing. 1.** To strangle. **2.** *Pathol.* To compress, constrict, or obstruct (a tube, duct, etc.) so as to cut off the flow of blood or other fluid. [From Latin *strangulāre*, from Greek *strangalan*, from *strangalē*, halter.] —**stran′gu·la′tion** *n.*

strap (străp) *n.* **1.** A long, narrow strip of leather or other material, often with a fastener for binding or securing objects or clothing. **2.** A flat, thin metal band used for fastening or clamping. **3.** A narrow band formed into a loop for grasping with the hand. **4.** A razor strop. —*tr.v.* **strapped, strap·ping. 1.** To fasten or secure with a strap. **3.** To beat with a strap. **3.** To strop. [Var. of STROP.]

strapped (străpt) *adj. Informal.* Lacking money; broke. — See Syns at **poor.**

strap·ping (străp′ĭng) *adj.* Tall and sturdy; robust.

stra·ta (strā′tə, străt′ə) *n.* A plural of **stratum.**

strat·a·gem (străt′ə-jəm) *n.* **1.** A maneuver designed to deceive or surprise an enemy. **2.** A scheme designed to obtain a goal. [French *stratagème*, from Latin *stratēgēma*, from Greek, from *stratēgos*, general.]

stra·te·gic (strə-tē′jĭk) or **stra·te·gi·cal** (-jĭ-kəl) *adj.* **1.** Of, pertaining to, or in accordance with strategy. **2.** Designed to destroy the military potential of an enemy: *strategic bombing.* **3.** Important within a planned or step-by-step effort. —**stra·te′gi·cal·ly** *adv.*

strat·e·gist (străt′ə-jĭst) *n.* A person skilled in strategy.

strat·e·gy (străt′ə-jē) *n., pl.* **-gies. 1.** The overall planning and conduct of large-scale military operations. **2.** The art or skill of using stratagems in politics, business, etc. **3.** A plan of action.

strat·i (strā′tī′, străt′ī′) *n.* Plural of **stratus.**

strat·i·fy (străt′ə-fī′) *v.* **-fied, -fy·ing.** —*tr.v.* To form, arrange, or deposit in layers or strata. —*intr.v.* To become stratified. [French *stratifier*, from New Latin *stratificare* : *stratum*, stratum + Latin *facere*, to make, do.] —**strat′i·fi·ca′tion** *n.*

stra·tig·ra·phy (strə-tĭg′rə-fē) *n.* The study of rock strata. —**strat′i·graph′ic** (străt′ĭ-grăf′ĭk) or **strat′·i·graph′i·cal** *adj.*

stra·to·cu·mu·lus (strā′tō-kyōōm′yə-ləs, străt′ō-) *n., pl.* **-li** (-lī′). A low-lying, multilayered cloud in the form of extensive, large, puffy rolls. [STRAT(US) + CUMULUS.]

strat·o·sphere (străt′ə-sfîr′) *n.* The part of the atmosphere above the troposphere and below the mesosphere.[STRAT-(UM) + (ATM)OSPHERE.] —**strat′o·spher′ic** (-sfîr′ĭk, -sfĕr′-) *adj.*

stra·tum (strā′təm, străt′əm) *n., pl.* **-ta** (-tə) or **-tums. 1.** A horizontal layer of any material, esp. one of several parallel layers arranged one on top of another. **2.** *Geol.* A formation containing a number of layers of rock of the same kind of material. **3.** A level of society composed of people with similar social, cultural, or economic status. [Latin *strātum*, stretched out.]

stra·tus (strā′təs, străt′əs) *n., pl.* **-ti** (strā′tī′, străt′ī′). A low-altitude cloud resembling a horizontal layer of fog. [Latin *strātus*, past part. of *sternere*, to stretch out, extend.]

straw (strô) *n.* **1. a.** Stalks of grain after threshing, used as bedding and food for animals and for weaving or braiding.

b. A single stalk of such grain. **2.** A narrow tube of paper, plastic, etc., used to drink or suck up liquids. **3.** Something of little value or substance. —*modifier: a straw hat.* —*adj.* Yellowish in color. [Middle English *strawe*, from Old English *strēaw.*]

straw·ber·ry (strô′bĕr′ē) *n.* **1.** Any of various low-growing plants of the genus *Fragaria*, with white flowers and red, fleshy, edible fruit. **2.** The fruit of any of these plants. —*modifier: strawberry jam.*

strawberry

straw boss. *Informal.* A temporary boss or foreman.

straw man. 1. A person set up as a front for a questionable enterprise. **2.** An argument or opponent set up so as to be easily defeated or refuted.

straw vote. An unofficial vote or poll indicating a trend.

stray (strā) *intr.v.* **1.** To wander from a given place or group or beyond established limits; roam. **2.** To wander about. **3.** To deviate from the right course. **4.** To digress. —*n.* A person or an animal that has strayed, esp. a domestic animal at large or lost. —*adj.* **1.** Straying or having strayed. **2.** Scattered or random: *stray hairs.* [Middle English *straien*, from Old French *estraier* : Latin *extrā-*, outside of + *vagārī*, to wander, roam, from *vagus*, wandering.]

streak (strēk) *n.* **1.** A line, mark, smear, or band differentiated by color or texture from its surroundings. **2.** A slight trace or tendency: *a mean streak.* **3.** *Informal.* An unbroken stretch; a run. —*tr.v.* To mark with a streak. —*intr.v.* **1.** To form a streak. **2.** To become streaked. **3.** To move at high speed; rush. [Middle English *stricke*, from Old English *strica.*]

streak·y (strē′kē) *adj.* **-i·er, -i·est. 1.** Marked with, characterized by, or occurring in streaks. **2.** Variable or uneven. —**streak′i·ly** *adv.* —**streak′i·ness** *n.*

stream (strēm) *n.* **1.** A small body of running water flowing in a regular course over the earth's surface. **2.** A steady current in such a body of water. **3.** A steady current of any fluid. **4.** A steady flow or succession: *a stream of insults.* **5.** A beam or ray of light. —*intr.v.* **1.** To flow in or as if in a stream. **2.** To pour forth or give off a stream. **3.** To move or proceed in large numbers: *a mob streaming through the streets.* **4.** To extend, wave, or float outward. **5.** To hang or trail loosely. **6.** To leave a continuous trail of light. —*tr.v.* To emit, discharge, or exude. [Middle English *streme*, from Old English *strēam.*]

stream·er (strē′mər) *n.* **1.** A long, narrow flag, banner, or pennant. **2.** Any long, narrow pendant strip of material. **3.** A newspaper headline that runs across a full page.

stream·line (strēm′līn′) *tr.v.* **-lined, -lin·ing. 1.** To construct or design so as to offer the least resistance to the flow of a fluid. **2.** To improve efficiency of; modernize. —**stream′lined′** *adj.*

street (strēt) *n.* **1.** A public thoroughfare in a city or town. **2.** The part of such a roadway used by vehicles. **3.** The people who live or work along such a roadway. [Middle English *strete*, from Old English *strǣt*, from Late Latin *strāta*, from Latin *strātus*, past part. of *sternere*, to extend, stretch out.]

street·car (strēt′kär′) *n.* A public passenger car operated on rails along a regular route, usu. through the streets of a city. Also called **trolley** and **trolley car.**

strength (strĕngkth, strĕngth) *n.* **1.** The quality of being strong; physical force. **2.** The power to resist force, strain,

---

å pat   ā pay   â care   ä father   ĕ pet   ē be   hw which   ĭ pit   ī tie   î pier   ŏ pot   ō toe   ô paw, for   oi noise
ōō took   ōō boot   ou out   th thin   th this   ŭ cut   û urge   zh vision   ə about, item, edible, gallop, circus

or stress; toughness; solidity. **3.** The power to sustain or resist an attack; impregnability. **4.** Legal, intellectual, or moral force. **5.** Moral courage or power. **6.** Firmness of will, character, or purpose. **7.** A source of power or force. **8.** Intensity or vehemence. **9.** Intensity of color, light, smell, or sound. **10.** Degree of concentration or potency, as of a drug. **11.** A concentration of numerical force or support. **12.** Military or organizational force in terms of numbers: *at half strength.* [Middle English *strengthe,* from Old English *strengthu.*]

strength·en (strĕngk'thən, strĕng'-) *tr.v.* To make strong or stronger. —*intr.v.* To become strong or stronger. —**strength'en·er** *n.*

stren·u·ous (strĕn'yōō-əs) *adj.* **1.** Requiring or characterized by great effort, energy, or exertion: *a strenuous task.* **2.** Vigorously active. [Latin *strēnuus,* brisk, nimble, quick.] —**stren'u·ous·ly** *adv.* —**stren'u·ous·ness** *n.*

strep throat (strĕp). A throat infection caused by the presence of certain streptococci, and characterized by fever and inflamed tonsils. [*Strep,* short for STREPTOCOCCAL.]

strep·to·coc·cus (strĕp'tə-kŏk'əs) *n., pl.* **-coc·ci** (-kŏk'sī'). Any of various round to ovoid bacteria of the genus *Streptococcus* that occur in pairs or chains and are often a cause of disease. [Greek *streptos,* twisted + -COCCUS.] —**strep'to·coc'cal** or **strep'to·coc'cic** *adj.*

strep·to·my·cin (strĕp'tə-mī'sĭn) *n.* An antibiotic, $C_{21}H_{39}N_7O_{12}$, produced from mold cultures of certain bacteria and used esp. to combat tuberculosis. [Greek *streptos,* twisted + *mukēs,* fungus + -IN.]

stress (strĕs) *n.* **1.** Importance, significance, or emphasis placed upon something. **2.** *Physics.* An applied force or system of forces that tends to strain or deform a body. **3.** Mental or emotional pressure. **4.** *Phonet.* The relative force with which a sound is spoken. **5.** The relative emphasis given a syllable or word in a metrical pattern. **6.** *Mus.* An accent. —*tr.v.* **1.** To place emphasis on. **2.** To subject to mechanical stress. **3.** To subject to pressure or strain. **4.** To pronounce with a stress. [Middle English *stresse,* hardship, distress, from Old French *estresse,* narrowness, from Latin *strictus,* tight, narrow.]

stres·sor (strĕs'ər) *n.* An agent that causes stress.

stretch (strĕch) *tr.v.* **1.** To lengthen, widen, or distend by pulling. **2.** To cause to extend: *Stretch the banner across the front of the building.* **3.** To make taut; tighten. **4.** To reach or put forth: *He stretched out his hand.* **5.** To extend (oneself or a body part) at full length. **6.** To exert (oneself) to the utmost; strain. **7.** To wrench or strain. **8.** To cause to suffice. **9.** To extend the limits of. **10.** To prolong. —*intr.v.* **1.** To become lengthened, widened, or distended. **2.** To reach over a given distance or area or in a given direction. **3.** To lie down at full length: *We stretched out on the beach.* **4.** To extend one's muscles or limbs. **5.** To extend over a given period of time. —*n.* **1.** The act of stretching or the condition of being stretched. **2.** The extent to which something can be stretched. **3.** A continuous length, area, or expanse. **4.** A straight section of a racecourse or track, esp. that leading to the finish line. **5. a.** A continuous period of time. **b.** *Informal.* A final stage. **6.** *Slang.* A term of imprisonment. —*adj.* Elastic: *a stretch sock.* [Middle English *strecchen,* from Old English *streccan,* to spread out, extend.] —**stretch'a·ble** *adj.* —**stretch'y** *adj.*

stretch·er (strĕch'ər) *n.* **1.** Someone or something that stretches. **2.** A litter, usu. of canvas stretched over a frame, used to transport the disabled.

strew (strōō) *tr.v.* **strewed, strewed** or **strewn** (strōōn) **strew·ing. 1.** To spread here and there; scatter. **2.** To cover (a surface) with things scattered or sprinkled. **3.** To be dispersed over: *Litter strewed the campsite.* [Middle English *strewen,* from Old English *strēowian.*]

stri·a (strī'ə) *n., pl.* **stri·ae** (strī'ē'). **1.** A thin, narrow groove or channel. **2.** A thin line or band, esp. one of several that are parallel or close together. [Latin, furrow, channel.]

stri·at·ed (strī'ā'tĭd) *adj.* Also **stri·ate** (strī'-āt'). Marked with striae; striped, grooved, or ridged.

striated muscle. Skeletal, voluntary, and cardiac muscle, made up of fibers with alternate light and dark transverse striations.

stri·a·tion (strī-ā'shən) *n.* **1.** The condition of being striated.

2. The form taken by striae. **3.** A stria.

strick·en (strĭk'ən) *v.* A past participle of **strike.** —*adj.* **1.** Struck or wounded, as by a projectile: *a stricken bird.* **2.** Afflicted, as with emotion or disease. [Middle English, from Old English *(ge)stricen.*]

strict (strĭkt) *adj.* **-er, -est. 1.** Precise; exact: *a strict definition.* **2.** Complete; absolute: *strict loyalty.* **3.** Kept within narrow limits: *a strict application of a law.* **4.** Imposing an exacting discipline: *a strict teacher.* **5.** Rigorous; stringent: *strict standards.* [Latin *strictus,* tight, narrow, from *stringere,* to tighten.] —**strict'ly** *adv.* —**strict'ness** *n.*

stric·ture (strĭk'chər) *n.* **1.** Something that restrains or restricts. **2.** An adverse criticism. **3.** *Pathol.* An abnormal narrowing of a duct or passage. [Middle English, from Latin *strictūra,* contraction, from *strictus,* tight, narrow.]

stride (strīd) *v.* **strode** (strōd), **strid·den** (strĭd'n), **strid·ing.** —*intr.v.* **1.** To walk with long steps. **2.** To take a single long step. —*tr.v.* **1.** To move on, along, or through with long steps. **2.** To straddle. —*n.* **1.** The act or manner of striding. **2. a.** A single long step. **b.** A single coordinated movement of the four legs of a horse or other animal, completed when the legs are returned to their initial relative position. **c.** The distance traveled in a human or animal stride. **3.** Often **strides.** An advance. —*idiom.* **take in (one's) stride.** To handle or accept without disruption of the normal routine. [Middle English *striden,* from Old English *strīdan.*] —**strid'er** *n.*

stri·dent (strīd'nt) *adj.* Having a shrill, harsh, and grating sound or effect: *a strident voice.* —See Syns at **harsh.** [Latin *strīdēns,* pres. part. of *strīdēre,* to make a harsh sound.] —**stri'dence** or **stri'den·cy** *n.* —**stri'dent·ly** *adv.*

strid·u·late (strĭj'ə-lāt') *intr.v.* **-lat·ed, -lat·ing.** To produce a shrill creaking sound by rubbing body parts together, as crickets do. [From Latin *strīdulus,* creaking.] —**strid'u·la'tion** *n.* —**strid'u·la·to'ry** (-lə-tôr'ē, -tōr'ē) *adj.*

strife (strīf) *n.* **1.** Bitter, often violent dissension or conflict. **2.** A contention or struggle between rivals. —See Syns at **conflict.** [Middle English *strif,* from Old French *estrif.*]

strike (strīk) *v.* **struck** (strŭk), **struck** or **strick·en** (strĭk'ən), **strik·ing.** —*tr.v.* **1.** To hit sharply, as with the hand, fist, or a weapon. **b.** To inflict (a blow). **2. a.** To collide with or crash into: *struck the desk with her knee.* **b.** To move into violent contact; dash: *struck her knee against the desk.* **3.** To attack; assault. **4.** To afflict suddenly with a disease or impairment. **5.** To hook (a fish) that has taken the bait. **6.** To form by stamping or printing. **7.** To produce by hitting: *strike a B flat.* **8.** To indicate by a percussive sound: *The clock struck nine.* **9.** To produce by friction. **10.** To eliminate or expunge. **11.** To come upon; discover: *struck gold.* **12.** To fall upon. **13.** To reach; come to. **14.** To occur or appear to: *The thought struck me from out of the blue.* **15.** To make a strong or immediate impression on. **16.** To cause (an emotion) to penetrate deeply. **17. a.** To make or conclude (a bargain). **b.** To achieve by careful weighing or reckoning: *strike a balance.* **18.** To fall into or assume: *strike a pose.* **19.** To lower or haul down, as a flag or sail. **20.** To remove or pack up: *strike camp.* **21.** To engage in a work stoppage against. **22.** To level. —*intr.v.* **1.** To deal or aim a blow or blows. **2.** To make contact suddenly or violently; collide. **3.** To begin an attack. **4.** To take the bait. **5. a.** To make a percussive sound: *The clock strikes.* **b.** To be indicated by sounds: *The hour has struck.* **6.** To come suddenly or unexpectedly. **7.** To proceed or set out. **8.** To engage in a work stoppage against an employer. —See Syns at **affect, attack,** and **hit.** —*phrasal verbs.* **strike out.** *Baseball.* **1.** To pitch three strikes to (a batter), putting him out. **2.** To be put out in such a way. **strike up. 1.** To start to play vigorously. **2.** To initiate or begin: *strike up a conversation.* —*n.* **1.** An act of striking; hit or thrust. **2.** An attack, esp. a military air attack. **3. a.** A work stoppage by employees in support of demands made upon their employer. **b.** A temporary stoppage of normal activity undertaken as a protest. **4.** A sudden achievement or discovery. **5.** A quantity of coins or medals struck at the same time. **6.** *Baseball.* A pitched ball counted against the batter, typically one swung at and missed or one judged to have passed through the strike zone. **7.** *Bowling.* The knocking down of all the pins with the first bowl of a frame. [Middle English *striken,* from Old English *strīcan,* to stroke, rub.]

Old English *strīcan*, to stroke, rub.]

strike·break·er (strīk'brā'kər) *n.* A worker hired to help break a strike. **—strike'break'ing** *n.*

strike·out (strīk'out') *n. Baseball.* An act of striking out.

strik·er (strī'kər) *n.* **1.** Someone or something that strikes. **2.** An employee who is on strike against his employer.

strike zone. *Baseball.* The area over home plate through which a pitch must pass to be called a strike, defined as being between the batter's armpits and knees.

strik·ing (strī'kĭng) *adj.* Immediately or vividly impressive: *a striking similarity; a striking view.* **—strik'ing·ly** *adv.*

string (strĭng) *n.* **1.** A cord usu. made of fiber, thicker than thread, used for fastening, tying, or lacing. **2.** Anything shaped into a long, thin line: *strings of spaghetti.* **3.** A set of objects threaded together: *a string of beads.* **4.** A series; sequence: *a string of victories.* **5.** *Sports.* A group of players constituting a ranked team within a team. **6.** *Mus.* **a.** A cord stretched across the sounding board of an instrument, struck, plucked, or bowed to produce tones. **b. strings.** Instruments having such strings. **7.** *Informal.* Often **strings.** A limiting or hidden condition: *a gift with no strings attached.* **—v. strung** (strŭng), **string·ing.** **—tr.v.** **1.** To fit or furnish with a string or strings: *string a guitar.* **2.** To thread on a string. **3.** To arrange in a series. **4.** To fasten, tie, or hang with a string or strings. **5.** To extend; stretch out. **6.** To strip (vegetables) of stringy fibers. **—intr.v.** **1.** To form strings or become stringlike. **2.** To extend in a line or succession: *cars strung out behind us.* **—phrasal verbs. string along.** To keep (someone) waiting or dangling. **string up.** *Informal.* To hang (someone). [Middle English *stringe*, from Old English *streng*.]

string bean. **1.** A bushy or climbing plant, *Phaseolus vulgaris*, widely cultivated for its narrow, green, edible pods. **2.** The green pod of any bean eaten as a vegetable. Also called **green bean** and **snap bean.** [From the stringy fibers on the pod.]

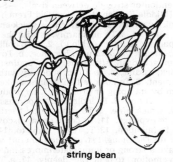

string bean

string·course (strĭng'kôrs', -kōrs') *n.* A horizontal band or molding set in the face of a building as a design element.

stringed instrument. A musical instrument played by plucking, striking, or bowing taut strings, as a violin.

strin·gent (strĭn'jənt) *adj.* **1.** Imposing rigorous standards; severe: *stringent safety measures.* **2.** Constricted; tight. **3.** Characterized by scarcity of money or credit. [Latin *stringēns*, pres. part. of *stringere*, to tighten.] **—strin'gen·cy** *n.* **—strin'gent·ly** *adv.*

string·er (strĭng'ər) *n.* **1.** A person or thing that strings. **2.** A heavy horizontal timber used for any of several connective or supportive purposes. **3.** A member of a specified string or squad on a team: *a second-stringer.* **4.** A part-time or free-lance correspondent for a news publication.

string·halt (strĭng'hôlt') *n.* Lameness accompanied by spasmodic movements in the hind legs of a horse. Also called **springhalt.**

string quartet. **1.** A quartet of musicians playing stringed instruments. **2.** A composition for a quartet of strings.

string tie. A narrow necktie, usu. tied in a bow.

string·y (strĭng'ē) *adj.* **-i·er, -i·est.** **1.** Resembling, forming, or consisting of strings: *stringy hair; stringy beef.* **2.** Slender and sinewy; wiry. **—string'i·ly** *adv.* **—string'i·ness** *n.*

strip¹ (strĭp) *v.* **stripped** or **stript** (strĭpt), **strip·ping.** **—tr.v.** **1. a.** To remove the clothing or other covering from. **b.** To

remove (clothing or other covering). **2.** To deprive as of honors or rank; divest. **3.** To remove all excess details or accessories from. **4.** To dismantle piece by piece. **5.** To damage or break the threads or teeth of (a nut, bolt, screw, or gear). **6.** To rob or plunder. **—intr.v.** To undress completely. **—See Syns at undress.** [Middle English *stripen*, from Old English *(be)strīepan*, to plunder.]

strip² (strĭp) *n.* **1.** A long, narrow piece. **2.** A comic strip. **3.** An airstrip. [Perh. var. of STRIPE (line).]

stripe¹ (strīp) *n.* **1.** A long, narrow band that is different, as in color or texture, from the surrounding material or surface. **2.** A strip of cloth or braid worn on a uniform to indicate rank, awards given, or length of service. **3.** Sort; kind. **—See Syns at kind.** **—tr.v.** **striped, strip·ing.** To mark with a stripe. [From Middle Dutch *strīpe*.]

stripe² (strīp) *n.* A stroke or blow, as with a whip. [Middle English *strype*.]

strip·ling (strĭp'lĭng) *n.* An adolescent youth. [Middle English.]

stript (strĭpt) *v.* A past tense and past participle of **strip** (to remove).

strive (strīv) *intr.v.* **strove** (strōv) or **strived, striv·en** (strĭv'ən) or **strived, striv·ing.** **1.** To exert much effort or energy. **2.** To struggle; contend. [Middle English *striven*, from Old French *estriver*.] **—striv'er** *n.*

strobe light (strōb). A flash lamp used in photography that produces very short, intense flashes of light by means of an electric discharge in a gas. [From STROBOSCOPE.]

strob·ile (strō'bĭl', -bəl) *n.* Also **stro·bi·lus** (strō-bī'ləs, strō'bə-) *pl.* **-li** (-lī'). A fruiting structure characterized by rows of overlapping scales, such as a pine cone. [New Latin *strobilus*, from Late Latin, pine cone, from Greek *strobilos*, round ball, from *strobos*, a whirling around, whirlwind.]

stro·bo·scope (strō'bə-skōp') *n.* An instrument used to view or calculate the speeds of rotating or vibrating objects by making them appear stationary, esp. by intermittently illuminating them with a rapidly flashing electric light. [Greek *strobos*, a whirling round + -SCOPE.] **—stro'bo·scop'ic** (-skŏp'ĭk) *adj.* **—stro'bo·scop'i·cal·ly** *adv.*

strode (strōd) *v.* Past tense of **stride.** [Middle English, from Old English *strād*.]

stroke (strōk) *n.* **1.** An impact; blow. **2.** A single complete movement, as in swimming or rowing. **3.** The act or time of striking. **4.** A single movement or mark made as by a pen, brush, or pencil. **5.** A movement of a piston or similar machine part from one end of its travel to the other. **6.** An effective or inspired idea or act. **7.** A light caressing movement. **8. a.** A sudden, severe onset of a disease or disorder, such as apoplexy or sunstroke. **b.** Apoplexy. **—tr.v.** **stroked, strok·ing.** To rub lightly, as with the hand; caress. [Middle English.]

stroll (strōl) *intr.v.* To go for a leisurely walk. **—tr.v.** To walk at a leisurely pace. **—n.** A leisurely walk. [Perh. from German dial. *strollen*.] **—stroll'er** *n.*

strong (strông) *adj.* **-er, -est.** **1.** Physically powerful; muscular. **2.** In good or sound health; robust: *when the patient gets stronger.* **3.** Capable of enduring stress or strain; not easily broken. **4.** Intense in degree or quality: *strong feelings; a strong wind.* **5.** Concentrated: *a strong salt solution.* **6.** Highly active chemically: *a strong acid.* **7.** Having great mental or spiritual force. **8.** Forceful or persuasive. **9.** Extreme; drastic: *strong measures.* **10.** Having a specified number of units or members: *Five hundred strong, they marched forward.* **11.** Of high saturation; vivid: *a strong color.* **12. a.** Having an intense effect on the senses: *a strong odor; strong cheese.* **b.** High in alcohol content: *strong punch.* **13.** *Ling.* Forming a past tense by means of a vowel change within the word stem; for example, *fly, flew.* **—adv.** In a strong manner. [Middle English, from Old English *strang*.] **—strong'ly** *adv.*

strong-arm (strông'ärm') *adj. Informal.* Coercive: *strong-arm tactics.* **—tr.v.** To use coercion against.

strong·box (strông'bŏks') *n.* A stoutly made safe.

strong·hold (strông'hōld') *n.* **1.** A fortress. **2.** Any area dominated or occupied by a special group.

strong-mind·ed (strông'mīn'dĭd) *adj.* Having a determined will; independent. **—strong'-mind'ed·ly** *adv.* **—strong'-mind'ed·ness** *n.*

stron·ti·um (strŏn′chē-əm, -tē-əm) *n. Symbol* **Sr** A soft, silvery, easily oxidized metallic element that ignites spontaneously in air when finely divided and is used in fireworks and various alloys. Atomic number 38; atomic weight 87.62; melting point 769°C; boiling point 1,384°C; specific gravity 2.54; valence 2. [After *Strontian*, a village in Argyllshire, Scotland.] —**stron′tic** (-tĭk) *adj.*

strontium 90. A radioactive isotope of strontium with a mass number of 90 and a half-life of 28 years, found in hazardous amounts in the fallout from nuclear bombs.

strop (strŏp) *n.* A flexible strip of leather or canvas used for sharpening a razor. —*tr.v.* **stropped, strop·ping.** To sharpen (a razor) on a strop. [Middle English *stroppe*, band of leather, from Middle Low German or Middle Dutch *strop*, from Latin *stroppus*, from Greek *strophos*, twisted cord, from *strephein*, to turn.]

strop

stro·phe (strō′fē) *n.* A stanza of a poem. [Greek *strophē*, a turning, from *strephein*, to turn.] —**stro′phic** (strō′fĭk, strŏf′ĭk) *adj.*

strove (strōv) *v.* A past tense of **strive.** [Middle English *stroove*, from *strive*, to strive, formed on the model of such verbs as *drive, drove.*]

struck (strŭk) *v.* Past tense and a past participle of **strike.** —*adj.* Shut down by a labor strike. [Middle English *strok*, from Old English *strāc*; past part. from p. t.]

struc·tur·al (strŭk′chər-əl) *adj.* **1.** Of, relating to, or having structure. **2.** Used in construction: *structural steel.* **3.** *Biol.* Morphological. —**struc′tur·al·ly** *adv.*

structural formula. A chemical formula that indicates the arrangement of atoms within a molecule.

struc·ture (strŭk′chər) *n.* **1.** Anything made up of a number of parts that are held together or put together in a particular way. **2.** The way in which parts are arranged or put together to form a whole. **3.** Something constructed, as a building or bridge. —*tr.v.* **-tured, -tur·ing.** To give form or arrangement to. [Middle English, from Old French, from Latin *structūra*, from *structus*, past part. of *struere*, to construct.]

stru·del (strōōd′l) *n.* A pastry made with a filling rolled up in a thin sheet of dough and baked. [German *Strudel*, from Middle High German *strudel*, whirlpool.]

strug·gle (strŭg′əl) *intr.v.* **-gled, -gling.** **1.** To make a strenuous effort; strive. **2.** To compete or contend against. **3.** To progress with great difficulty. —*n.* **1.** Strenuous effort or striving. **2.** A contest; battle. —See Syns at **effort.** [Middle English *struglen.*] —**strug′gler** *n.*

strum (strŭm) *v.* **strummed, strum·ming.** —*tr.v.* To play idly on (a stringed musical instrument) by plucking the strings with the fingers. —*intr.v.* To play an instrument in this manner. —*n.* The act or sound of strumming. [Perh. blend of STRING and THRUM.] —**strum′mer** *n.*

strum·pet (strŭm′pĭt) *n.* A whore; prostitute. [Middle English *strompet.*]

strung (strŭng) *v.* Past tense and past participle of **string.** [From STRING, formed after such verbs as *wring, wrung.*]

strut (strŭt) *intr.v.* **strut·ted, strut·ting.** To walk in a stiff, pompous manner; to swagger. —*n.* **1.** A stiff, self-important gait. **2.** A bar or rod used to brace a structure against forces applied from the side. [Middle English *strouten*, to swell, from Old English *strūtian*, to stand out stiffly.] —**strut′ter** *n.*

strych·nine (strĭk′nīn′, -nĭn, -nēn′) *n.* A poisonous white crystalline substance, $C_{21}H_{22}N_2O_2$, derived from nux vom-

ica and related plants and used as a poison and medicinally as a stimulant. [French, from New Latin *Strychnos*, from Latin *strychnos*, nightshade, from Greek *strukhnos.*]

stub (stŭb) *n.* **1.** A short blunt remaining end: *a pencil stub; a cigar stub.* **2. a.** The part of a check or receipt retained as a record. **b.** The part of a ticket returned as a voucher of payment. —*tr.v.* **stubbed, stub·bing.** **1.** To snuff out (a cigarette) by crushing. **2.** To strike (one's toe or foot) against something. [Middle English *stubbe*, from Old English *stubb.*]

stub·ble (stŭb′əl) *n.* **1.** The short, stiff stalks of a grain or hay crop that remain on a field after harvesting. **2.** Something resembling stubble, esp. a short, stiff growth of beard. [Middle English *stuble*, from Old French, from Latin *stipula*, straw.] —**stub′bly** *adj.*

stub·born (stŭb′ərn) *adj.* **1.** Unreasonably determined to exert one's will; obstinate. **2.** Persistent. **3.** Difficult to handle or work with; resistant: *stubborn soil.* —See Syns at **obstinate.** [Middle English *stoborne.*] —**stub′born·ly** *adv.* —**stub′born·ness** *n.*

stub·by (stŭb′ē) *adj.* **-bi·er, -bi·est.** **1.** Short and stocky. **2.** Covered with or consisting of stubs: *stubby grass.* **3.** Short and bristly. —**stub′bi·ly** *adv.* —**stub′bi·ness** *n.*

stuc·co (stŭk′ō) *n., pl.* **-coes** or **-cos.** A durable plaster finish, usu. composed of cement, sand, and lime, used to cover exterior walls or for interior wall ornamentation. —*tr.v.* To finish or decorate with stucco. [Italian, from Old High German *stukki*, fragment, crust, covering.]

stuck (stŭk) *v.* Past tense and past participle of **stick.** [From STICK, formed after such verbs as *wring, wrung.*]

stuck-up (stŭk′ŭp′) *adj. Informal.* Snobbish; conceited.

stud¹ (stŭd) *n.* **1.** An upright post in the framework of a wall for supporting lath or sheathing. **2.** A small knob, nail head, rivet, etc. fixed in and slightly projecting from a surface, used for protection or ornamentation. **3.** A small ornamental button mounted on a short post for insertion through an eyelet, as on a dress shirt. **4.** Any of various protruding pins or pegs in machinery. —*tr.v.* **stud·ded, stud·ding.** **1.** To construct with a stud or studs. **2.** To set with a stud or studs: *stud a bracelet with rubies.* **3.** To strew: *Daisies studded the meadow.* [Middle English *stode*, post, prop, from Old English *studu.*]

stud² (stŭd) *n.* **1.** A group of animals, esp. horses, kept for breeding. **2.** A male animal, esp. a stallion, kept for breeding. —*modifier: a stud farm.* —*idiom.* **at stud.** Available for breeding, as a horse, bull, or dog. [Middle English *stod*, from Old English *stōd*, stable for breeding.]

stud·book (stŭd′bŏŏk′) *n.* A book registering the pedigrees of thoroughbred animals, esp. of horses.

stu·dent (stōōd′nt, styōōd′-) *n.* **1.** A person who attends a school, college, or university. **2.** A person who makes a study of something: *a student of languages.* —*modifier: student leaders.* [Middle English, from Latin *studēns*, pres. part. of *studēre*, to study; be diligent.]

stud·ied (stŭd′ēd) *adj.* Carefully contrived; calculated: *a studied pose.* —**stud′ied·ly** *adv.* —**stud′ied·ness** *n.*

stu·di·o (stōō′dē-ō′, styōō′-) *n., pl.* **-os.** **1.** An artist's or photographer's workroom. **2.** A place where an art is taught or studied: *a dance studio.* **3.** A room or building for motion-picture, television, or radio productions. [Italian, from Latin *studium*, study.]

studio couch. A couch that can serve as a bed.

stu·di·ous (stōō′dē-əs, styōō′-) *adj.* **1.** Devoted to study. **2.** Earnest; purposeful; diligent: *a studious effort.* —**stu′di·ous·ly** *adv.* —**stu′di·ous·ness** *n.*

stud·y (stŭd′ē) *n., pl.* **-ies.** **1.** The act or process of studying. **2. a.** A detailed, attentive examination. **b.** An often published report of such an examination. **3.** A branch of knowledge. **4.** A preliminary sketch, as for a work of art. **5.** A musical composition designed as a technical exercise; étude. **6.** A state of mental absorption; contemplation: *He's in a deep study.* **7.** A room intended or equipped for studying. **8.** A person with reference to his ability to memorize a part: *a quick study.* —*modifier: a study hall.* —*v.* **-ied, -y·ing.** —*tr.v.* **1.** To apply one's mind purposefully in order to gain knowledge or understanding of (a subject). **2.** To memorize. **3.** To inquire into; investigate. **4.** To examine closely; scrutinize. **5.** To give careful thought to; contemplate. —*intr.v.* **1.** To apply oneself to learning, esp. by reading. **2.** To pursue a course of study. [Middle English *studie,* from Old French *estudie,* from Latin *studium,* from *studēre,* to be eager, study.]

stuff (stŭf) *n.* **1.** The material out of which something is made or formed; substance. **2.** Things not specifically identified. **3.** Worthless objects; refuse or junk. **4.** Foolish or empty words or ideas. **5.** *Brit.* Cloth, esp. woolens, of which clothing may be made. —See Syns at **heart.** —*tr.v.* **1. a.** To pack tightly; fill up; cram. **b.** To block or stop up (a passage); to plug: *stuff a leak with plaster.* **2.** To fill with an appropriate stuffing: *stuff a pillow; stuff a cabbage.* **3.** To cram with food. **4.** To fill (the mind): *His head is stuffed with nonsense.* —*intr.v.* To overeat; gorge. [Middle English, from Old French *estoffe,* provisions, from *estoffer,* to cram, pad, from Late Latin *stuppāre,* to plug up, from Latin *stuppa,* plug, cork, from Greek *stuppē.*] —**stuff'er** *n.*

stuffed shirt. *Informal.* A stiff, pompous person.

stuff·ing (stŭf'ĭng) *n.* **1.** Soft material used to stuff, fill, line, or pad things made of or covered with cloth. **2.** A seasoned mixture of food put inside meat or vegetables.

stuff·y (stŭf'ē) *adj.* **-i·er, -i·est. 1.** Lacking sufficient ventilation. **2.** Having the respiratory passages blocked: *a stuffy nose.* **3.** *Informal.* Formal; strait-laced: *a stuffy dinner party.* —**stuff'i·ly** *adv.* —**stuff'i·ness** *n.*

stul·ti·fy (stŭl'tə-fī') *tr.v.* **-fied, -fy·ing. 1.** To stifle; cripple: *stultify free thought.* **2.** To cause to appear stupid or inconsistent. [Late Latin *stultificāre* : Latin *stultus,* foolish + *facere,* to make.] —**stul'ti·fi·ca'tion** *n.* —**stul'ti·fi'er** *n.*

stum·ble (stŭm'bəl) *v.* **-bled, -bling.** —*intr.v.* **1. a.** To trip and almost fall. **b.** To move unsteadily; falter. **c.** To act or speak falteringly or clumsily: *stumble through a speech.* **2.** To make a mistake; to blunder. **3.** To come accidentally: *stumbled on the answer.* —*tr.v.* To cause to stumble. —*n.* **1.** The act of stumbling; a fall. **2.** A mistake or blunder. [Middle English *stumblen.*] —**stum'bler** *n.*

stumbling block. An obstacle or impediment.

stump (stŭmp) *n.* **1.** The part of a tree trunk left in the ground after the tree has fallen or been cut down. **2.** Any part, as of a branch, limb, tooth, pencil, etc., that remains after the main part has been cut off or worn away. **3.** A heavy footfall. **4.** A platform or other place used for political speeches. —*tr.v.* **1.** To reduce to a stump. **2.** To clear stumps from (land). **3.** To stub (a toe or foot). **4.** To travel about (an area) making political speeches. **5.** To walk in a stiff, heavy manner. **6.** *Informal.* To puzzle; perplex; baffle. [Middle English *stumpe,* from Middle Low German *stump.*] —**stump'er** *n.*

stump·y (stŭm'pē) *adj.* **-i·er, -i·est.** Short and stocky.

stun (stŭn) *tr.v.* **stunned, stun·ning. 1.** To daze or render senseless, as by a blow. **2.** To overwhelm with surprise or disbelief; shock. [Middle English *stonen,* from Old French *estoner.*] —**stun'ner** *n.*

stung (stŭng) *v.* Past tense and past participle of **sting.** [Middle English *stonge, stungen,* from Old English *stungon* (pl.), *(ge)stungen.*]

stunk (stŭngk) *v.* A past tense and past participle of **stink.** [Middle English *stonke, stunken,* from Old English *stuncon* (pl.), *(ge)stuncen.*]

stun·ning (stŭn'ĭng) *adj.* **1.** Surprising or astonishing: *a stunning victory.* **2.** *Informal.* Strikingly attractive: *a stunning suit.* —**stun'ning·ly** *adv.*

stunt[1] (stŭnt) *tr.v.* To stop or interfere with the growth or development of. —*n.* A plant disease that causes dwarfing. [Perh. of Scandinavian orig.] —**stunt'ed·ness** *n.*

stunt[2] (stŭnt) *n.* **1.** A feat displaying unusual strength, skill, or daring. **2.** Something unusual done for publicity. —*intr.v.* To perform stunts. [Orig. unknown.]

stunt man. A person who substitutes for an actor in scenes requiring physical prowess or involving physical risk.

stupe (stoop, styoop) *n.* A hot medicated compress. [Middle English, from Latin *stuppa,* plug, from Greek *stuppē.*]

stu·pe·fy (stoo'pə-fī', styoo'-) *tr.v.* **-fied, -fy·ing. 1.** To dull the senses or consciousness of; put into a stupor. **2.** To amaze; astonish. [Old French *stupefier,* from Latin *stupefacere* : *stupēre,* to be stunned + *facere,* to make.] —**stu'pe·fac'tion** (-făk'shən) *n.* —**stu'pe·fi'er** *n.*

stu·pen·dous (stoo-pĕn'dəs, styoo-) *adj.* **1.** Of astounding

force, volume, degree, etc.: *stupendous risks.* **2.** Of tremendous size; huge; immense. —See Syns at **fabulous** and **giant.** [Latin *stupendus,* from *stupēre,* to be stunned.] —**stu·pen'dous·ly** *adv.* —**stu·pen'dous·ness** *n.*

stu·pid (stoo'pĭd, styoo'-) *adj.* **-er, -est. 1.** Slow to apprehend; dumb. **2.** Showing a lack of intelligence. **3.** Dazed or stunned. **4.** *Informal.* Uninteresting; dull: *a stupid job.* —*n. Informal.* A stupid person. [French *stupide,* from Latin *stupidus,* from *stupēre,* to be stunned.] —**stu'pid·ly** *adv.* —**stu'pid·ness** *n.*

 Syns: stupid, dense, dumb (*Informal*), **obtuse, thick** *adj.* *Core meaning:* Lacking intelligence (*a stupid child*).

stu·pid·i·ty (stoo-pĭd'ĭ-tē, styoo-) *n., pl.* **-ties. 1.** The quality or fact of being stupid. **2.** A stupid act or idea.

stu·por (stoo'pər, styoo'-) *n.* **1.** A condition of reduced sensibility or consciousness; daze. **2.** A condition of mental or moral apathy. [Middle English, from Latin, from *stupēre,* to be stunned.] —**stu'por·ous** *adj.*

stur·dy (stûr'dē) *adj.* **-di·er, -di·est. 1.** Substantially built; durable; strong. **2.** Physically healthy and vigorous. **3.** Firm, unyielding. [Middle English, giddy, rash, from Old French *estourdi,* past part. of *estourir,* to stun, daze.] —**stur'di·ly** *adv.* —**stur'di·ness** *n.*

stur·geon (stûr'jən) *n.* Any of various large fishes of the family Acipenseridae, with rows of bony plates instead of true scales, and edible flesh and roe that is a source of caviar. [Middle English, from Norman French.]

stut·ter (stŭt'ər) *intr.v.* To speak with involuntary hesitations and repetitions of sounds. —*tr.v.* To say with a stutter. —*n.* The act or habit of stuttering. [Freq. of obs. *stut,* from Middle English *stutten,* perh. of Low German orig.] —**stut'ter·er** *n.* —**stut'ter·ing·ly** *adv.*

sty[1] (stī) *n., pl.* **sties. 1.** A pen or fenced-in place where pigs are kept. **2.** Any very dirty or untidy place. [Middle English, from Old English *stig.*]

sty[2] (stī) *n., pl.* **sties** or **styes.** Inflammation of one or more of the oil-producing glands of an eyelid. [From obs. *styany,* from Middle English *styanye.*]

styg·i·an or **Styg·i·an** (stĭj'ē-ən) *adj.* **1.** *Gk. Myth.* Of or pertaining to the river Styx. **2.** Gloomy and dark. [Latin *Stygius,* from Greek *Stugios,* from *Stux,* Styx.]

style (stīl) *n.* **1.** The way or manner in which something is said, done, expressed, performed, etc.: *a style of speech.* **2.** Sort; kind; type: *a style of furniture.* **3.** Individuality expressed in one's actions and tastes. **4.** Elegance. **5. a.** The current fashion: *a dress that's in style.* **b.** A particular fashion: *the style of the 1920's.* **6.** A customary manner of presenting printed material, including usage, punctuation, spelling, typography, and arrangement. **7.** A slender, pointed writing instrument used by the ancients; stylus. **8.** *Bot.* The slender stalk of a flower pistil. —See Syns at **fashion.** —*tr.v.* **styled, styl·ing. 1.** To call or name; designate. **2.** To make consistent with rules of style. **3.** To arrange, design, or fashion in a special way. [Middle English, from Old French, from Latin *stilus,* writing instrument.] —**styl'er** *n.*

style book. A book giving rules and examples of usage, punctuation, and typography, used in copy editing.

sty·li (stī'lī') *n.* A plural of **stylus.**

styl·ish (stī'lĭsh) *adj.* Conforming to the current style; fashionable. —**styl'ish·ly** *adv.* —**styl'ish·ness** *n.*

styl·ist (stī'lĭst) *n.* **1.** A writer or speaker who cultivates an artful literary style. **2.** A designer or expert on styles.

sty·lis·tic (stī-lĭs'tĭk) *adj.* Of or relating to style, esp. literary style. —**sty·lis'ti·cal·ly** *adv.*

styl·ize (stī'līz') *tr.v.* **-ized, -iz·ing.** To conform or restrict to a particular style. —**styl'i·za'tion** *n.* —**styl'iz'er** *n.*

sty·lo·bate (stī'lə-bāt') *n. Archit.* The continuous foundation of a row of columns. [Latin *stylobata,* from Greek *stulobatēs,* column base.]

sty·lus (stī'ləs) *n., pl.* **-lus·es** or **-li** (-lī'). **1.** A sharp, pointed instrument used for writing, marking, or engraving. **2.** A needle that transmits vibrations from the grooves of a phonograph record. **3.** The sharp, pointed tool used for cutting record grooves. [Latin *stilus.*]

sty·mie (stī'mē). Also **sty·my.** —*tr.v.* **-mied, -mie·ing** or **-my·ing.** To block; thwart: *stymied their hopes.* —*n.* An obstacle or obstruction. [Orig. unknown.]

styp·tic (stĭp'tĭk) *adj.* Contracting the blood vessels so as

---

â pat	ā pay	â care	ä father	ĕ pet	ē be	hw which	ĭ pit	ī tie	î pier	ŏ pot	ō toe	ô paw, for	oi noise
ŏŏ took	ōō boot	ou out	th thin	*th* this	ŭ cut		û urge	zh vision	ə about, item, edible, gallop, circus				

to check bleeding; astringent. —*n.* A styptic drug or substance. [Middle English *stiptik,* from Late Latin *stypticus,* from Greek *stuptikos,* from *stuphein,* to contract.]

styptic pencil. A short medicated stick, often of alum, applied to a cut to check bleeding.

sty·rene (stī′rēn′) *n.* A colorless oily liquid, C_8H_8, from which polystyrene is made. [Latin *styrax,* storax + -ENE.]

Sty·ro·foam (stī′rə-fōm′) *n.* A trademark for a light, resilient polystyrene plastic.

Styx (stĭks) *n. Gk. Myth.* One of the rivers of Hades, across which Charon ferried the souls of the dead.

sua·sion (swā′zhən) *n.* Persuasion. [Middle English, from Latin *suāsiō,* from *suāsus,* past part. of *suādēre,* to persuade.] **—sua′sive** (-sĭv, -zĭv) *adj.*

suave (swäv) *adj.* **suav·er, suav·est.** Smoothly gracious in social manner. [Old French, from Latin *suāvis,* delightful.] **—suave′ly** *adv.* **—suav′i·ty** or **suave′ness** *n.*

sub (sŭb) *n. Informal.* 1. A submarine. 2. A substitute. **—***intr.v.* **subbed, sub·bing.** To act as a substitute.

sub-. A prefix indicating: 1. Under or beneath: **submarine.** 2. Subordinate: **subprincipal.** 3. Short of or less than: **subhuman, subtropical.** 4. Subordinate part: **subset.** [Latin *sub-,* from *sub,* under.]

sub·al·tern (sŭb′-ôl′tərn; *Brit.* sŭb′əl-tərn) *adj.* 1. Lower in position or rank; secondary. 2. *Brit.* Holding a military rank just below that of captain. —*n.* 1. A subordinate. 2. *Brit.* A subaltern officer. —See Syns at **subordinate.** [Late Latin *subalternus* : Latin *sub-,* below + *alternus,* alternate, from *alter,* other.]

sub·a·que·ous (sŭb′-ā′kwē-əs, -ăk′wē-) *adj.* Formed, existing, or occurring underwater.

sub·arc·tic (sŭb′-ärk′tĭk, -är′tĭk) *adj.* Of or like regions just south of the Arctic Circle.

sub·a·tom·ic (sŭb′ə-tŏm′ĭk) *adj.* Of particles smaller than an atom or physical occurrences within an atom.

sub·class (sŭb′klăs′) *n.* A subdivision of a class.

sub·cla·vi·an (sŭb′-klā′vē-ən) *adj.* Located beneath the clavicle or collarbone. —*n.* A subclavian structure, such as a vein, nerve, or muscle. [SUB- + Latin *clāvis,* key.]

sub·com·mit·tee (sŭb′kə-mĭt′ē) *n.* A subordinate committee made up of members from the main committee.

sub·com·pact (sŭb-kŏm′păkt′) *n.* An automobile smaller than a compact.

sub·con·scious (sŭb′-kŏn′shəs) *adj.* Beneath the threshold of consciousness. **—sub·con′scious** *n.* **—sub·con′scious·ly** *adv.* **—sub·con′scious·ness** *n.*

sub·con·ti·nent (sŭb′-kŏn′tə-nənt) *n.* A large land mass, such as India or southern Africa, that is separate to some degree but is still part of a continent.

sub·con·tract (sŭb′-kŏn′trăkt′) *n.* A contract that assigns some of the obligations of an original contract to another party. —*v.* (sŭb′-kŏn′trăkt′, -kŏn-trăkt′) —*tr.v.* To make a subcontract for. —*intr.v.* To make a subcontract.

sub·con·trac·tor (sŭb′-kən-trăk′tər, sŭb′-kŏn′trăk′tər) *n.* A person who enters into a subcontract and assumes some of the obligations of the primary contractor.

sub·cul·ture (sŭb′kŭl′chər) *n.* 1. A culture of microorganisms that has been derived from another. 2. A cultural subgroup distinguished from the larger culture by factors such as race, religion, or economic status, etc.

sub·cu·ta·ne·ous (sŭb′kyōō-tā′nē-əs) *adj.* Located or found just beneath the skin. **—sub′cu·ta′ne·ous·ly** *adv.*

sub·dea·con (sŭb′dē′kən) *n.* A clergyman with rank just below that of deacon.

sub·deb·u·tante (sŭb′dĕb′yə-tänt′) *n.* 1. A young girl approaching her social debut. 2. A girl in her middle teens.

sub·di·vide (sŭb′də-vīd′) *v.* **-vid·ed, -vid·ing.** —*tr.v.* 1. To divide (something already divided) into smaller parts. 2. To divide into many parts, esp. to divide (land) into lots. —*intr.v.* To form into subdivisions. **—sub′di·vid′er** *n.*

sub·di·vi·sion (sŭb′də-vĭzh′ən) *n.* 1. The act or process of subdividing. 2. A subdivided part.

sub·dom·i·nant (sŭb′-dŏm′ə-nənt) *n. Mus.* The fourth tone of a diatonic scale, next below the dominant.

sub·due (səb-dōō′, -dyōō′) *tr.v.* **-dued, -du·ing.** 1. To conquer and subjugate; put down. 2. To bring under control by force or persuasion. 3. To make less intense. —See Syns at **defeat.** [Middle English *subduen,* from Latin *sub-*

dūcere, to lead away, withdraw : *sub-,* away + *dūcere,* to lead.] **—sub·du′er** *n.*

su·ber·in (sōō′bər-ĭn) *n.* A waxy waterproof substance present in the cell walls of cork tissue in plants. [French *subérine,* from Latin *sūber,* cork.]

sub·fam·i·ly (sŭb′făm′ə-lē) *n., pl.* **-lies.** A subdivision of a family, as in taxonomy.

sub·freez·ing (sŭb-frē′zĭng) *adj.* Below freezing.

sub·group (sŭb′grōōp′) *n.* A group within a group.

sub·head (sŭb′hĕd′) *n.* 1. Also **sub·head·ing** (-hĕd′ĭng). The title of a subdivision. 2. A subordinate heading or title.

sub·hu·man (sŭb′-hyōō′mən) *adj.* 1. Below the human race in evolutionary development. 2. Not fully human.

sub·ja·cent (sŭb′-jā′sənt) *adj.* 1. Located beneath; underlying. 2. Lying lower but not directly beneath. [Latin *subjacēns,* pres. part. of *subjacēre,* to lie under : *sub-,* under + *jacēre,* to lie, from *jacere,* to throw.] **—sub′ja′cen·cy** *n.*

sub·ject (sŭb′jĭkt) *adj.* 1. Under the power or authority of another: *subject to the law.* 2. Prone; disposed: *subject to colds.* 3. Liable to incur or receive; exposed: *subject to misinterpretation.* 4. Contingent or dependent: *subject to approval.* —*n.* 1. A person under the rule of another. 2. **a.** A person or thing about which something is said or done; topic. **b.** The main theme of a work of art. 3. A course or area of study. 4. A theme of a musical composition, esp. a fugue. 5. **a.** An individual that experiences or is subjected to something: *a subject of ridicule.* **b.** An object of clinical study or experimentation. 6. *Gram.* A word, phrase, or clause in a sentence that names who or what does the action, receives the action in passive constructions, or undergoes existence. —*tr.v.* (səb-jĕkt′). 1. To bring under control; subjugate. 2. To render liable; expose: *subjected to infection.* 3. To cause to experience or undergo. [Middle English, from Old French *subget,* from Latin *subjectus,* past part. of *subicere,* to bring under : *sub-,* under + *jacere,* to throw.] **—sub·jec′tion** (-jĕk′shən) *n.*

sub·jec·tive (səb-jĕk′tĭv) *adj.* 1. **a.** Proceeding from or taking place within an individual's mind rather than the external environment. **b.** Particular to a given individual; personal: *subjective experience.* 2. *Gram.* Of or designating the subject of a verb: *subjective case.* **—sub·jec′tive·ly** *adv.* **—sub·jec′tive·ness** or **sub′jec·tiv′i·ty** (sŭb′jĕk-tĭv′ĭ-tē) *n.*

subject matter. Matter under consideration in a written work or speech; theme.

sub·join (sŭb′-join′) *tr.v.* To add at the end; append. [Old French *subjoindre,* from Latin *subjungere* : *sub-,* in addition + *jungere,* to join.]

sub·ju·gate (sŭb′jə-gāt′) *tr.v.* **-gat·ed, -gat·ing.** To bring under dominion; conquer. [Middle English *subjugaten,* from Latin *subjugāre* : *sub-,* under + *jugum,* yoke.] **—sub′ju·ga′tion** *n.* **—sub′ju·ga′tor** *n.*

sub·junc·tive (sŭb-jŭngk′tĭv) *adj.* Of a grammatical mood used to express an uncertainty, a wish, or an unlikely condition. In the sentence *If I were you, I would go,* the word *were* is a subjunctive form. —*n.* 1. The subjunctive mood. 2. A subjunctive form. [Late Latin *subjunctīvus,* from Latin *subjungere,* to subjoin.]

sub·king·dom (sŭb′kĭng′dəm) *n.* A former taxonomic category constituting a major division of a kingdom.

sub·lease (sŭb′lēs′) *n.* A lease of property by a tenant granting all or part of his rights and premises to another person. —*tr.v.* **-leased, -leas·ing.** 1. To sublet (property). 2. To rent (property) under a sublease.

sub·let (sŭb-lĕt′) *tr.v.* 1. To rent (property one holds by lease) to another. 2. To subcontract (work).

sub·li·mate (sŭb′lə-māt′) *v.* **-mat·ed, -mat·ing.** —*tr.v.* 1. *Chem.* To change from a solid to a gas or from a gas to a solid without becoming a liquid. 2. *Psychol.* To express potentially violent or socially unacceptable impulses in a modified, socially acceptable manner. —*intr.v.* To pass between the solid and gaseous states without becoming a liquid. —*n.* A product obtained by sublimating. [From Latin *sublīmāre,* to raise, from *sublīmis,* uplifted, sublime.] **—sub′li·ma′tion** *n.*

sub·lime (sə-blīm′) *adj.* 1. Exalted; lofty: *sublime poetry.* 2. Of high spiritual, moral, or intellectual worth. 3. Inspiring awe; moving. —*v.* **-limed, -lim·ing.** —*tr.v.* 1. To make sublime; elevate; ennoble. 2. *Chem.* To cause to sublimate.

ă pat	ā pay	â care	ä father	ĕ pet	ē be	hw which	ĭ pit ī tie î pier ŏ pot ō toe ô paw, for oi noise
ōō took	ōō boot	ou out	th thin	*th* this	ŭ cut		û urge zh vision ə about, item, edible, gallop, circus

—*intr.v.* *Chem.* To sublimate. [Latin *sublīmis*.] —**sub·lime'ly** *adv.*

sub·lim·i·nal (sŭb-lĭm'ə-nəl) *adj.* **1.** Below the threshold of conscious perception or awareness. **2.** Inadequate to produce conscious perception: *subliminal stimulation.* [SUB- + Latin *līmen,* threshold.] —**sub·lim'i·nal·ly** *adv.*

sub·lim·i·ty (sə-blĭm'ĭ-tē) *n., pl.* **-ties. 1.** The condition or quality of being sublime. **2.** Something that is sublime.

sub·lu·nar·y (sŭb'-loo'nə-rē) *adj.* Also **sub·lu·nar** (-nər). **1.** Situated beneath the moon. **2.** Of this world; earthly. [Late Latin *sublūnāris* : Latin *sub-,* beneath + *lūna,* moon.]

sub·ma·chine gun (sŭb'mə-shēn'). A lightweight automatic or semiautomatic gun fired from the shoulder or hip.

sub·ma·rine (sŭb'mə-rēn', sŭb'mə-rēn') *adj.* Beneath the surface of the water; undersea. —*n.* A ship that can operate underwater.

submarine

sub·max·il·lar·y (sŭb'-măk'sə-lĕr'ē, sŭb'-) *adj.* Of, relating to, or located below the lower jaw. —*n., pl.* **-ries.** A submaxillary part, as a gland or nerve.

sub·merge (səb-mûrj') *v.* **-merged, -merg·ing.** —*tr.v.* **1.** To place or plunge under water or other liquid. **2.** To cover with water; inundate. **3.** To hide from view; obscure. —*intr.v.* To go under or as if under water. [Latin *submergere* : *sub-,* under + *mergere,* to immerse, plunge.] —**sub·mer'gence** *n.* —**sub·mer'gi·ble** *adj.*

sub·merse (səb-mûrs') *tr.v.* **-mersed, -mers·ing.** To submerge. [Latin *submersus,* part part. of *submergere,* to submerge.] —**sub·mers'i·ble** *adj.* —**sub·mer'sion** *n.*

sub·mi·cro·scop·ic (sŭb'mī'krə-skŏp'ĭk) *adj.* Too small to be seen using an optical microscope.

sub·mis·sion (səb-mĭsh'ən) *n.* **1.** The act of submitting to the power of another or the condition of having submitted. **2.** The condition of being submissive. **3.** The act of submitting something for consideration.

sub·mis·sive (səb-mĭs'ĭv) *adj.* Tending to submit; compliant; docile. —**sub·mis'sive·ly** *adv.* —**sub·mis'sive·ness** *n.*

sub·mit (səb-mĭt') *v.* **-mit·ted, -mit·ting.** —*tr.v.* **1.** To yield (oneself) to the will or authority of another. **2.** To commit (something) to the consideration or judgment of another. **3.** To offer as a proposition or contention. —*intr.v.* **1.** To yield to the opinion or authority of another; give in. **2.** To allow oneself to be subjected; acquiesce. —See Syns at **yield.** [Middle English *submitten,* from Latin *submittere,* to place under : *sub-,* under + *mittere,* to throw.] —**sub·mit'tal** *n.* —**sub·mit'ter** *n.*

sub·nor·mal (sŭb'-nôr'məl) *adj.* Less than normal; below the average. —*n.* A person who is subnormal, esp. in intelligence. —**sub·nor'mal·i·ty** (-măl'ĭ-tē) *n.*

sub·or·bit·al (sŭb'-ôr'bĭ-tl) *adj.* **1.** Of or for less than one orbit of the earth: *a suborbital space flight.* **2.** Located below the eye or its orbit.

sub·or·der (sŭb'ôr'dər) *n.* A subdivision of an order.

sub·or·di·nate (sə-bôr'dn-ĭt) *adj.* **1.** Belonging to a lower or inferior class or rank; secondary: *a subordinate position.* **2.** Subject to the authority or control of another. —*n.* Someone or something that is subordinate. —*tr.v.* (-āt') **-nat·ed, -nat·ing.** To put in a lower or inferior rank or class. [Medieval Latin *subōrdinātus,* past part. of *subōrdināre,* to put in a lower rank : Latin *sub-,* below + *ōrdināre,* to arrange in order, from *ōrdō,* order.] —**sub·or'di·nate·ly** *adv.* —**sub·or'di·nate·ness** or **sub·or'di·na'tion** *n.* —**sub·or'di·na'tive** *adj.*

Syns: **subordinate, inferior, junior, subaltern, underling** *n.* Core meaning: One of a lower class or rank than another

(*supervisors who kept a tight rein on their subordinates*).

subordinate clause. A dependent clause.

sub·orn (sə-bôrn') *tr.v.* To induce to commit an unlawful act, esp. perjury. [Latin *subōrnāre* : *sub-,* secretly + *ōrnāre,* to equip.] —**sub·or·na'tion** *n.* —**sub·orn'er** *n.*

sub·phy·lum (sŭb'fī'ləm) *n., pl.* **-la** (-lə). A taxonomic category ranking between a phylum and a class.

sub·plot (sŭb'plŏt') *n.* A subordinate literary plot.

sub·poe·na (sə-pē'nə) *n.* A legal writ requiring a person to appear in court and give testimony. —*tr.v.* To serve or summon with such a writ. [From Latin *sub poenā,* "under penalty" (first words in the writ).]

sub ro·sa (sŭb rō'zə). In secret; privately; confidentially. [Latin, "under the rose," from the practice of hanging a rose over a meeting as a symbol of secrecy.]

sub·scribe (səb-skrīb') *v.* **-scribed, -scrib·ing.** —*tr.v.* **1.** To sign (one's name) at the end of a document. **2.** To sign one's name to in testimony or consent: *subscribe a will.* **3.** To pledge or contribute (a sum of money). —*intr.v.* **1.** To sign one's name to a document. **2.** To express agreement or approval: *subscribe to a belief.* **3.** To promise to pay or contribute money: *subscribe to a charity.* **4.** To contract to receive and pay for a periodical. [Middle English *subscriben,* from Latin *subscrībere* : *sub-,* under + *scrībere,* to write.] —**sub·scrib'er** *n.*

sub·script (sŭb'skrĭpt') *n.* A distinguishing character or symbol written directly beneath or next to and slightly below another letter or number. [Latin *subscriptus,* past part. of *subscrībere,* to subscribe.]

sub·scrip·tion (səb-skrĭp'shən) *n.* **1.** The signing of one's name, as to a document. **2.** Something subscribed. **3.** A purchase of issues of a periodical or a series of performances.

sub·se·quent (sŭb'sĭ-kwənt) *adj.* Following in time or order; succeeding. [Middle English, from Old French, from Latin *subsequēns,* pres. part. of *subsequī,* to follow close after : *sub-,* close to, after + *sequī,* to follow.] —**sub'se·quence** *n.* —**sub'se·quent·ly** *adv.*

sub·serve (səb-sûrv') *tr.v.* **-served, -serv·ing.** To promote; further. [Latin *subservīre,* to serve : *sub-,* under + *servīre,* to serve.]

sub·ser·vi·ent (səb-sûr'vē-ənt) *adj.* **1.** Subordinate. **2.** Obsequious; servile. [Latin *subserviēns,* pres. part. of *subservīre,* to subserve.] —**sub·ser'vi·ent·ly** *adv.* —**sub·ser'vi·ence** or **sub·ser'vi·en·cy** *n.*

sub·set (sŭb'sĕt') *n.* A mathematical set contained within another set.

sub·side (səb-sīd') *intr.v.* **-sid·ed, -sid·ing. 1.** To sink to a lower level: *The flood waters subsided.* **2.** To sink to the bottom; settle. **3.** To become less; abate: *His sorrow subsided.* [Latin *subsīdere,* to sink down : *sub-,* down + *sīdere,* to settle.] —**sub·sid'ence** *n.*

sub·sid·i·ar·y (səb-sĭd'ē-ĕr'ē) *adj.* **1.** Serving to assist or supplement; auxiliary: *subsidiary roads.* **2.** Secondary in importance; subordinate. **3.** Of or like a subsidy. —*n., pl.* **-ries.** Someone or something that is subsidiary, esp. a company owned or controlled by another company. —**sub·sid'i·ar'i·ly** (-âr'ə-lē) *adv.*

sub·si·dize (sŭb'sĭ-dīz') *tr.v.* **-dized, -diz·ing.** To aid or supply with a subsidy. —**sub'si·di·za'tion** *n.* —**sub'si·diz'er** *n.*

sub·si·dy (sŭb'sĭ-dē) *n., pl.* **-dies.** Financial assistance, as that granted by a government to a private enterprise. [Middle English *subsidie,* aid, from Norman French, from Latin *subsidium,* aid, from *subsidēre,* to be placed in reserve : *sub-,* down + *sedēre,* to sit.]

sub·sist (səb-sĭst') *intr.v.* **1.** To exist or continue to exist. **2.** To maintain life: *subsist on one meal a day.* [Latin *subsistere,* to remain standing : *sub-,* from below + *sistere,* to cause to stand.] —**sub·sist'er** *n.*

sub·sis·tence (səb-sĭs'təns) *n.* **1.** The act, condition, or means of subsisting. **2.** Existence. —See Syns at **living.** —*modifier:* *subsistence rations.* —**sub·sis'tent** *adj.*

sub·soil (sŭb'soil') *n.* The layer of earth beneath the surface soil.

sub·son·ic (sŭb'-sŏn'ĭk) *adj.* **1.** Of less than audible frequency. **2.** Of a speed less than that of sound.

sub·spe·cies (sŭb'spē'shēz, -sēz) *n., pl.* **subspecies.** A subdivision of a taxonomic species, usu. based on geographical distribution. —**sub'spe·cif'ic** (-spĭ-sĭf'ĭk) *adj.*

---

sub·stance (sŭb′stəns) *n.* **1. a.** That which has mass and occupies space; matter. **b.** A material of a particular kind or constitution. **2.** The essence; gist. **3.** Reality; actuality: *a dream without substance.* **4.** Density; body: *Air has little substance.* **5.** Material possessions: *a person of substance.* —See Syns at **heart.** [Middle English, essence, from Old French, from Latin *substantia,* from *substāns,* pres. part. of *substāre,* to be present : *sub-,* from below, up + *stāre,* to stand.]

sub·stan·dard (sŭb′-stăn′dərd) *adj.* **1.** Failing to meet a standard; below standard. **2.** Considered unacceptable usage by the educated members of a speech community.

sub·stan·tial (səb-stăn′shəl) *adj.* **1.** Of or having substance; material. **2.** Not imaginary; true; real. **3.** Solidly built; strong. **4.** Ample; sustaining: *a substantial breakfast.* **5.** Considerable; large: *won by a substantial margin.* **6.** Possessing wealth or property; well-to-do. —See Syns at **real.** [Middle English *substancial,* from Late Latin *substantiālis,* from Latin *substantia,* substance.] —**sub·stan′ti·al′i·ty** or **sub·stan′tial·ness** *n.* —**sub·stan′tial·ly** *adv.*

sub·stan·ti·ate (səb-stăn′shē-āt′) *tr.v.* **-at·ed, -at·ing. 1.** To support with proof or evidence. **2.** To give material form to; embody. —See Syns at **prove.** [From Latin *substantia,* substance.] —**sub·stan′ti·a′tion** *n.*

sub·stan·tive (sŭb′stən-tĭv) *adj.* **1.** Substantial; considerable. **2.** Existing by itself; independent. **3.** Not imaginary; real. **4.** Of the essence of something; essential: *substantive changes.* **5.** Expressing or denoting existence. **6.** Functioning as a noun. —See Syns at **real.** —*n.* A word or group of words functioning as a noun. —**sub·stan·tive·ly** *adv.* —**sub′stan·tive·ness** *n.*

sub·sti·tute (sŭb′stĭ-tōōt′, -tyōōt′) *n.* Someone or something that takes the place of another; replacement. —*modifier: a substitute teacher.* —*v.* **-tut·ed, -tut·ing.** —*tr.v.* To put or use in place of another. —*intr.v.* To take the place of another. [Latin *substitūtus,* a replacement, from *substituere,* to substitute : *sub-,* in place of + *statuere,* to cause to stand.] —**sub′sti·tut′a·bil′i·ty** *n.* —**sub′sti·tut′a·ble** *adj.*

sub·sti·tu·tion (sŭb′stĭ-tōō′shən, -tyōō′-) *n.* **1.** The act of substituting or the condition of being substituted. **2.** That which is substituted. —**sub′sti·tu′tion·al** *adj.*

sub·sti·tu·tive (sŭb′stĭ-tōō′tĭv, -tyōō′-) *adj.* Serving or capable of serving as a substitute.

sub·strate (sŭb′strāt′) *n.* **1.** The material on which an enzyme acts. **2.** A surface on which an organism lives or moves. **3.** A substratum. [From SUBSTRATUM.]

sub·stra·tum (sŭb′strā′təm, -străt′əm) *n., pl.* **-ta** (-tə) or **-tums. 1.** An underlying layer, esp. of earth beneath the surface; subsoil. **2.** A foundation or groundwork. —**sub·stra′tive** *adj.*

sub·struc·ture (sŭb′strŭk′chər) *n.* The supporting part of a structure; a foundation. —**sub·struc′tur·al** *adj.*

sub·sume (səb-sōōm′, -syōōm′) *tr.v.* **-sumed, -sum·ing.** To place in a more comprehensive category or under a general principle. [SUB- + Latin *sūmere,* to take up.] —**sub·sum′a·ble** *adj.*

sub·ten·ant (sŭb-těn′ənt) *n.* A person who rents from a tenant. —**sub·ten′an·cy** *n.*

sub·tend (səb-těnd′) *tr.v.* **1.** *Geom.* To be opposite to and delimit: *The side of a triangle subtends the opposite angle.* **2.** *Bot.* To underlie so as to enclose. [Latin *subtendere,* to extend beneath : *sub-,* beneath + *tendere,* to extend.]

sub·ter·fuge (sŭb′tər-fyōōj′) *n.* An evasive plan or tactic used to avoid capture or confrontation. [French, from Late Latin *subterfugium,* from Latin *subterfugere,* to flee secretly : *subter,* secretly + *fugere,* to flee.]

sub·ter·ra·ne·an (sŭb′tə-rā′nē-ən) *adj.* **1.** Situated or operating beneath the earth's surface; underground. **2.** Hidden; secret. [From Latin *subterrāneus* : *sub-,* under + *terra,* earth.] —**sub′ter·ra′ne·an·ly** *adv.*

sub·tile (sŭt′l) *adj.* **-til·er, -til·est.** Subtle. —**sub′tile·ly** *adv.*

sub·ti·tle (sŭb′tīt′l) *n.* **1.** A secondary and usu. explanatory title, as of a literary work. **2.** A printed translation of the dialogue of a foreign-language film shown at the bottom of the screen.

sub·tle (sŭt′l) *adj.* **-tler, -tlest. 1. a.** So slight as to be difficult to detect. **b.** Not obvious; abstruse: *a subtle problem.* **2.** Able to make fine distinctions; keen: *a subtle mind.*

3. a. Skillful; clever. **b.** Sly; devious. [Middle English *subtil,* thin, fine, clever, from Old French, from Latin *subtīlis,* thin, fine.] —**sub′tle·ness** *n.* —**sub′tly** *adv.*

sub·tle·ty (sŭt′l-tē) *n., pl.* **-ties. 1.** The quality of being subtle. **2.** Something subtle, esp. a fine distinction.

sub·ton·ic (sŭb-tŏn′ĭk) *n. Mus.* The seventh tone of a diatonic scale, immediately below the tonic.

sub·top·ic (sŭb′tŏp′ĭk) *n.* A subdivision of a main topic.

sub·to·tal (sŭb′tōt′l) *n.* The total of part of a series of numbers being added. —*tr.v.* **-taled** or **-talled, -tal·ing** or **-tal·ling.** To total part of (a series of numbers). —*intr.v.* To arrive at a subtotal.

sub·tract (səb-trăkt′) *tr.v.* To take away; deduct. —*intr.v.* To perform subtraction. [Latin *subtractus,* past part. of *subtrahere,* to draw away : *sub-,* away + *trahere,* to draw.] —**sub·tract′er** *n.*

sub·trac·tion (səb-trăk′shən) *n.* **1.** The act or process of subtracting. **2.** The mathematical operation of deducting or taking away one quantity from another.

sub·trac·tive (səb-trăk′tĭv) *adj.* Involving subtraction.

sub·tra·hend (sŭb′trə-hěnd′) *n.* A quantity or number to be subtracted from another. [Latin *subtrahendum,* from *subtrahere,* to subtract.]

sub·trop·i·cal (sŭb-trŏp′ĭ-kəl) *adj.* Of, relating to, or being the regions that border the tropics.

sub·trop·ics (sŭb-trŏp′ĭks) *pl.n.* Subtropical regions.

sub·urb (sŭb′ûrb′) *n.* **1.** A usu. residential area near a city. **2. the suburbs.** The usu. residential region surrounding a major city. [Middle English, from Old French *suburbe,* from Latin *suburbium* : *sub-,* near + *urbs,* city.] —**sub·ur′ban** *adj.*

sub·ur·ban·ite (sə-bûr′bə-nīt′) *n.* A person who lives in a suburb.

sub·ur·bi·a (sə-bûr′bē-ə) *n.* **1.** Suburbs. **2.** Suburbanites.

sub·ven·tion (səb-věn′shən) *n.* Financial aid, esp. a subsidy. [Middle English *subvencioun,* from Old French *subvention,* from Late Latin *subventiō,* from Latin *subventus,* past part. of *subvenire,* to come to help : *sub-,* from below + *venīre,* to come.] —**sub·ven′tion·ar′y** (-shə-něr′ē) *adj.*

sub·ver·sion (səb-vûr′zhən, -shən) *n.* The act of subverting or the condition of being subverted. —**sub·ver′sion·ar′y** (-zhə-něr′ē) *adj.*

sub·ver·sive (səb-vûr′sĭv, -zĭv) *adj.* Acting to subvert, esp. intended to undermine an established government. —*n.* A person who advocates subversive means or policies. —**sub·ver′sive·ly** *adv.* —**sub·ver′sive·ness** *n.*

sub·vert (səb-vûrt′) *tr.v.* **1.** To destroy or overthrow completely; ruin. **2.** To undermine the character, morals, or allegiance of; corrupt. [Middle English *subverten,* from Old French *subvertir,* from Latin *subvertere* : *sub-,* from below, up + *vertere,* to turn.] —**sub·vert′er** *n.*

sub·way (sŭb′wā′) *n.* **1.** An underground railroad. **2.** An underground tunnel or passage. —*modifier: a subway train.*

subway

suc·ceed (sək-sēd′) *intr.v.* **1.** To come next in time or order, esp. to replace another in a position: *She succeeded to the throne.* **2.** To accomplish something attempted: *succeeded in repairing the watch.* —*tr.v.* **1.** To follow in time or order. **2.** To replace (another) in office or position. [Middle English *succeden,* from Old French *succeder,* from Latin *succēdere* : *sub-,* under, next to + *cēdere,* to go.] —**suc·ceed′er** *n.*

suc·cess (sək-sĕs′) n. **1.** The achievement of something attempted. **2.** The gaining of fame or prosperity. **3.** Someone or something that is successful. [Latin *successus*, from *succēdere*, to succeed.]

suc·cess·ful (sək-sĕs′fəl) adj. **1.** Having a desired or favorable result. **2.** Having achieved fame or prosperity. **—suc·cess′ful·ly** adv.

suc·ces·sion (sək-sĕsh′ən) n. **1.** The act or process of following in order. **2.** A group of persons or things arranged or following in order; sequence. **3.** The sequence, right, or act of succeeding to a title, throne, or estate. **—suc·ces′sion·al** adj. **—suc·ces′sion·al·ly** adv.

suc·ces·sive (sək-sĕs′ĭv) adj. Following in uninterrupted order. **—suc·ces′sive·ly** adv. **—suc·ces′sive·ness** n.

suc·ces·sor (sək-sĕs′ər) n. Someone or something that succeeds another.

suc·cinct (sək-sĭngkt′) adj. Marked by briefness and clarity of expression; concise: *a succinct explanation.* —See Syns at **concise.** [Latin *succinctus*, girded, concise, from the past part. of *succingere*, to surround : *sub-*, below + *cingere*, to gird.] **—suc·cinct′ly** adv. **—suc·cinct′ness** n.

suc·cor (sŭk′ər) n. Also *Brit.* **suc·cour.** Assistance or help in time of distress; relief. **—tr.v.** To relieve; aid. [Middle English *sucurs*, from Old French, from Medieval Latin *succursus*, from Latin, past part. of *succurrere*, to run to the aid of : *sub-*, under + *currere*, to run.]

suc·co·tash (sŭk′ə-tăsh′) n. Kernels of corn and lima beans cooked together. [Narraganset *msíckquatash*, boiled whole-grain corn (off the cob).]

Suc·coth (sōōk′əs, -ōt′, -ōs′) n. Also **Suk·koth.** A Jewish harvest festival celebrated in the autumn. [Hebrew *sukkōth*, (feast of) booths.]

suc·cour (sŭk′ər) n. & v. *Brit.* Var. of **succor.**

suc·cu·bus (sŭk′yə-bəs) n., pl. **-bus·es** or **-bi** (-bī′, -bē′). A female demon supposed to engage in sexual intercourse with a man while he sleeps. [Medieval Latin, from Late Latin *succuba*, prostitute, from Latin *succubāre*, to lie under : Latin *sub-*, under + *cubāre*, to lie.]

suc·cu·lent (sŭk′yə-lənt) adj. **1.** Full of juice or sap; juicy. **2.** Having thick, fleshy leaves or stems that conserve moisture. **3.** Rich or tasty. **—n.** A succulent plant, as a cactus. [Latin *succulentus*, from *succus*, juice.] **—suc′cu·lence** n. **—suc′cu·lent·ly** adv.

suc·cumb (sə-kŭm′) intr.v. **1.** To yield to something overpowering. **2.** To die. —See Syns at **die** and **yield.** [Middle English *succomben*, from Old French *succomber*, from Latin *succumbere*, to lie down under.]

such (sŭch) adj. **1.** Of this or that kind or extent: *We never dreamed she could do such work.* **2.** Similar. **—adv. 1.** To such a degree: *such good work; such a good job.* **2.** Very; especially. **—pron. 1.** Such a person or persons or thing or things. **2.** Someone or something implied or indicated: *Such are the fortunes of war.* **3.** The like: *pins, needles, and such.* **—idioms. as such.** In itself: *As such the job pays very little.* **such as. 1.** For example. **2.** Of the same kind: *nice ordinary people, such as we always invite.* [Middle English *such*, from Old English *swylc*.]

such·like (sŭch′līk′) adj. Of a similar kind; like. **—pron.** Persons or things of such a kind.

suck (sŭk) tr.v. **1. a.** To draw (liquid) into the mouth by inhaling or pulling in the cheeks. **b.** To draw from in this manner: *suck a lemon.* **2.** To draw in by or as if by suction. **3.** To hold or maneuver in the mouth: *suck a candy.* **—intr.v. 1.** To draw in by or as if by suction. **2.** To suckle. **—n. 1.** The act of sucking. **2.** A sucking sound or movement. [Middle English *souken*, from Old English *sūcan*.]

suck·er (sŭk′ər) n. **1.** Someone or something that sucks. **2.** *Slang.* A person who is easily deceived; dupe. **3.** A lollipop. **4.** Any of numerous chiefly North American freshwater fishes of the family Catostomidae, with a thick-lipped mouth adapted for feeding by suction. **5.** An organ or part adapted for clinging by suction. **6.** *Bot.* A secondary shoot arising from the base of a plant. **—tr.v. 1.** To strip suckers or shoots from. **2.** *Informal.* To trick; dupe. **—intr.v.** To send out suckers or shoots.

suck·le (sŭk′əl) v. **-led, -ling. 1.** To give milk at the breast or udder. **2.** To bring up; rear; nourish. **—intr.v.** To suck at the breast. [Prob. back-formation from SUCKLING.]

suck·ling (sŭk′lĭng) n. A young mammal that has not been weaned. [Middle English *sokelyng.*]

su·crose (sōō′krōs′) n. A crystalline disaccharide carbohydrate sugar, $C_{12}H_{22}O_{11}$, found in many plants, mainly sugar cane and sugar beet. [French *sucre*, sugar + *-OSE*.]

suc·tion (sŭk′shən) n. **1.** The act or process of sucking. **2.** A force that causes something to be drawn into a space because of the difference between the external and internal pressures. [Late Latin *sūctiō*, from Latin *sūctus*, past part. of *sūgere*, to suck.]

Su·dan grass (sōō-dăn′). A hardy variety of sorghum, native to the Sudan, widely cultivated for hay and fodder.

sud·den (sŭd′n) adj. **1.** Happening quickly and without warning: *a sudden storm.* **2.** Abrupt; hasty: *a sudden departure.* [Middle English *sodane*, from Norman French *sodein*, from Late Latin *subitānus*, from Latin *subitus*, past part. of *subīre*, to approach secretly : *sub-*, secretly + *īre*, to go.] **—sud′den·ly** adv. **—sud′den·ness** n.

sudden death. *Sports.* Extra minutes of play added to a tied game, the winner being the first team to score.

su·do·rif·ic (sōō′də-rĭf′ĭk) adj. Causing or increasing sweat. [New Latin *sūdōrificus*, from Latin *sūdor*, sweat.]

suds (sŭdz) pl.n. **1.** Soapy water. **2.** Foam. [Prob. from Middle Dutch *sudse*, marsh, swamp.] **—suds′y** adj.

sue (sōō) v. **sued, su·ing. —tr.v. 1.** To pay court to. **2.** *Law.* To institute legal proceedings against (a person) for redress of grievances. **—intr.v. 1.** To make an appeal or entreaty: *sue for peace.* **2.** To institute legal proceedings; bring suit. **3.** *Archaic.* To woo. [Middle English *sewen*, to pursue, prepare, from Norman French *suer*, from Latin *sequī*, to follow.] **—su′er** n.

suede or **suède** (swād) n. **1.** Leather with a soft napped surface. **2.** Fabric made to resemble suede. [French *(gants de) suède*, "(gloves of) Sweden."]

su·et (sōō′ĭt) n. The hard fat around the kidneys of cattle and sheep, used in cooking and making tallow. [Middle English *sewet*, ult. from Latin *sēbum*.]

suf·fer (sŭf′ər) intr.v. **1.** To feel or endure pain or distress. **2.** To tolerate or undergo damage or loss. **3.** To appear at a disadvantage: *suffers by comparison.* **—tr.v. 1.** To undergo; experience. **2.** To endure or bear. **3.** To permit; allow. [Middle English *sufferen*, to undergo, endure, allow, from Norman French *suffrir*, from Latin *sufferre*, to sustain, : *sub-*, under + *ferre*, to bear.] **—suf′fer·a·ble** adj. **—suf′fer·a·bly** adv. **—suf′fer·er** n.

suf·fer·ance (sŭf′ər-əns, sŭf′rəns) n. **1.** The capacity to tolerate pain or distress. **2.** Sanction or permission implied by failure to prohibit; tolerance.

suf·fer·ing (sŭf′ər-ĭng, sŭf′rĭng) n. **1.** The act or condition of one who suffers. **2.** Physical or mental pain or distress.

suf·fice (sə-fīs′) v. **-ficed, -fic·ing. —intr.v. 1.** To be sufficient. **2.** To be capable or competent. **—tr.v.** To be sufficient for. [Middle English *suffisen*, from Old French *suffire*, from Latin *sufficere* : *sub-*, under + *facere*, to make.]

suf·fi·cien·cy (sə-fĭsh′ən-sē) n. **1.** The quality or condition of being sufficient. **2.** An adequate amount or quantity.

suf·fi·cient (sə-fĭsh′ənt) adj. As much as is needed; enough. [Middle English, from Old French, from Latin *sufficiēns*, pres. part. of *sufficere*, to suffice.] **—suf·fi′cient·ly** adv.

suf·fix (sŭf′ĭks′) n. An affix added to the end of a word or stem. **—tr.v.** To add as a suffix. [From Latin *suffīxus*, past part. of *suffīgere*, to affix : *sub-*, beneath + *fīgere*, to fix.] **—suf′fix′al** adj.

suf·fo·cate (sŭf′ə-kāt′) v. **-cat·ed, -cat·ing. —tr.v. 1.** To kill or destroy by preventing access to oxygen. **2.** To stop the breathing of; asphyxiate. **3.** To cause discomfort to by or as if by cutting off the supply of air. **4.** To suppress; stifle. **—intr.v. 1.** To die from suffocation. **2.** To be stifled. [From Latin *suffocāre* : *sub-*, under, down + *faucēs*, throat.] **—suf′fo·ca′tion** n. **—suf′fo·ca′tive** adj.

suf·fra·gan (sŭf′rə-gən) n. **1.** A bishop acting as an assistant to the bishop or ordinary of a diocese but having no jurisdictional functions. **2.** A bishop subordinate to an archbishop or metropolitan. [Middle English, from Old French, from Medieval Latin *suffrāgāneus*, from *suffrāgium*, suffrage.] **—suf′fra·gan** adj.

suf·frage (sŭf′rĭj) n. **1.** A vote cast in deciding a disputed question or in electing a person to office. **2.** The right, privilege, or act of voting; franchise. [Middle English, intercessory prayer, from Old French, from Medieval Latin *suffrāgium,* vote, prayer, from Latin, ballot, right of voting.]

suf·fra·gette (sŭf'rə-jĕt') *n.* A female advocate of suffrage for women.

suffragette
Demonstrating outside the White House

suf·fra·gist (sŭf'rə-jĭst) *n.* An advocate of the extension of political voting rights, esp. to women.

suf·fuse (sə-fyōōz') *tr.v.* **-fused, -fus·ing.** To spread through or over: *a room suffused with candlelight.* [Latin *suffūsus,* past part. of *suffundere,* to suffuse : *sub-,* underneath + *fundere,* to pour.] **—suf·fu'sion** *n.* **—suf·fu'sive** (sə-fyōō'sĭv, -zĭv) *adj.*

Su·fi (sōō'fē) *n.* A member of a Moslem mystic sect. [Arabic *sūfiy,* "(man) of wool," from *sūf,* wool.] **—Su'fic** (-fĭk) *adj.* **—Su'fism** (-fĭz'əm) *n.*

sug·ar (shŏŏg'ər) *n.* **1.** A sweet crystalline carbohydrate, sucrose. **2.** Any of a class of water-soluble crystalline carbohydrates, including sucrose and lactose, with a characteristically sweet taste. *—tr.v.* **1.** To coat, cover, or sweeten with sugar. **2.** To make less distasteful or more appealing. *—intr.v.* To form sugar. [Middle English *sugre,* from Old French *sukere,* from Old Italian *zucchero,* from Medieval Latin *succarum,* from Arabic *sukkar,* from Persian *shakar,* from Prakrit *sakkara,* from Sanskrit *śarkarā.*]

sugar beet. A beet with white roots from which sugar is obtained.

sugar beet

sugar bush. A grove of sugar maples.

sugar cane. A tall grass, *Saccharum officinarum,* native to the East Indies, with thick stems that yield sugar.

sug·ar-coat (shŏŏg'ər-kōt') *tr.v.* **1.** To coat with sugar. **2.** To cause to seem more appealing or palatable.

sugar loaf. **1.** A large conical loaf of pure concentrated sugar. **2.** Something resembling this, esp. a mountain.

sugar maple. A maple tree, *Acer saccharum,* of eastern North America, with sap that is the source of maple syrup.

sugar pine. A tall evergreen timber tree, *Pinus lambertiana,* of the Pacific coast of North America.

sug·ar-plum (shŏŏg'ər-plŭm') *n.* A small ball of candy.

sug·ar·y (shŏŏg'ə-rē) *adj.* **-i·er, -i·est.** **1.** Tasting of or resembling sugar. **2.** Deceitfully or cloyingly sweet.

sug·gest (səg-jĕst', sə-jĕst') *tr.v.* **1.** To offer for consideration or action; propose. **2.** To bring or call to mind by association: *a cavern that suggests a cathedral.* **3.** To imply. [Latin *suggestus,* past part. of *suggerere,* to suggest :

sub-, underneath + *gerere,* to carry.]

Syns: suggest, hint, imply, insinuate, intimate *v. Core meaning:* To convey thoughts or ideas indirectly (*actions that suggested jealousy*). SUGGEST in this context usually refers to a process in which something is called to mind by an association of ideas (*a cavern that suggests a cathedral*). IMPLY refers to something suggested by logical necessity (*life implying growth and death*). HINT refers to expression that is indirect but contains pointed clues (*hinted that it was time to leave*). INTIMATE applies to veiled expression that may be the result of discretion or reserve (*intimated that there was trouble ahead*). INSINUATE refers to conveying something, usu. unpleasant, in a covert manner (*insinuated that I was dishonest*).

sug·gest·i·ble (səg-jĕs'tə-bəl, sə-jĕs'-) *adj.* Easily influenced or led by suggestion.

sug·ges·tion (səg-jĕs'chən, sə-jĕs'-) *n.* **1.** The act of suggesting. **2.** Something suggested. **3.** The thought process by which one idea leads to another or brings another to mind. **4.** A hint or trace.

sug·ges·tive (səg-jĕs'tĭv, sə-jĕs'-) *adj.* **1.** Tending to suggest thoughts or ideas; provocative. **2.** Conveying a hint or suggestion. **3.** Tending to suggest something improper or indecent; risqué. **—sug·ges'tive·ly** *adv.* **—sug·ges'tive·ness** *n.*

su·i·ci·dal (sōō'ĭ-sīd'l) *adj.* **1.** Of, involving, or related to suicide. **2.** Dangerous to oneself or to one's interests; ruinous. **—su'i·ci'dal·ly** *adv.*

su·i·cide (sōō'ĭ-sīd') *n.* **1.** The act or an instance of intentionally killing oneself. **2.** The destruction or ruin of one's own interests. **3.** A person who commits suicide. [Latin *suī,* of oneself + -CIDE.]

su·i gen·e·ris (sōō'ī jĕn'ər-ĭs, sōō'ē). Unique; individual. [Latin, "of one's own kind."]

suit (sōōt) *n.* **1.** A set of outer garments consisting of a coat and matching trousers or skirt. **2.** Any group of related things; a set. **3.** Any of the four sets of playing cards, each with similar marks, that constitute a deck. **4.** *Law.* A proceeding in court to recover a right or claim. **5.** The act or an instance of petitioning, esp. courtship. *—tr.v.* **1.** To meet the requirements of; accommodate. **2.** To make appropriate or suitable; adapt. **3.** To be proper for or becoming to. **4.** To provide with clothing; dress. *—intr.v.* To be suitable or acceptable. —See Syns at **please.** **—idiom. follow suit. 1.** To play a card of the same suit as the one led. **2.** To do as another has done; follow an example. [Middle English *suite,* attendance at a sheriff's court, litigation, uniform, from Old French.]

suit·a·ble (sōō'tə-bəl) *adj.* Appropriate to a given purpose or occasion. **—suit'a·bil'i·ty** or **suit'a·ble·ness** *n.* **—suit'a·bly** *adv.*

Syns: suitable, due, just, right *adj. Core meaning:* Consistent with prevailing standards or circumstances (*a suitable punishment for the crime*). See also Syns at **convenient.**

suit·case (sōōt'kās') *n.* A usu. rectangular and flat piece of luggage for carrying clothing.

suite (swēt) *n.* **1.** A group of attendants or followers; retinue. **2.** Any group or set of related things. **3.** A series of connected rooms used as a unit, as in a hotel. **4.** (*also* sōōt.) A set of matching furniture. **5.** *Mus.* An instrumental composition consisting of a succession of dances. [French, from Old French *sieute,* following, retinue.]

suit·or (sōō'tər) *n.* **1.** A person who makes a petition or request. **2.** A person who sues in a court of law; plaintiff. **3.** A man who is courting a woman. [Middle English *suitor,* from Norman French, follower, from Latin *secūtor,* from *sequī,* to follow.]

su·ki·ya·ki (sōō'kē-yä'kē, skē-) *n.* A Japanese dish of sliced meat and vegetables fried together. [Japanese.]

Suk·koth (sōōk'əs, -ōt', -ōs') *n.* Var. of **Succoth.**

sul·fa drug (sŭl'fə). Any of a group of synthetic organic compounds, used to inhibit bacterial growth and activity. [SULFA(NILAMIDE) + DRUG.]

sul·fa·nil·a·mide (sŭl'fə-nĭl'ə-mīd') *n.* A white, odorless crystalline sulfonamide, used in treating various bacterial infections. [SULF(UR) + ANIL(INE) + AMIDE.]

sul·fate (sŭl'fāt') *n.* A salt or ester of sulfuric acid SO₄. [SULF(UR) + -ATE.]

sul·fide (sŭl′fīd′) *n.* A compound of sulfur with an electropositive element or group. [SULF(UR) + -IDE.]

sul·fite (sŭl′fīt′) *n.* A salt or ester of sulfurous acid. [SULF(UR) + -ITE.]

sul·fon·a·mide (sŭl-fŏn′ə-mīd′, -mĭd) *n.* Any of the group of sulfa drugs. [*Sulfo-*, sulfonic acid (a derivative of sulfuric acid) + AMIDE.]

sul·fur (sŭl′fər) *n.* Also **sul·phur.** *Symbol* **S** A pale-yellow nonmetallic element occurring widely in nature both free and in combined forms, used esp. in rubber vulcanization and in the manufacture of chemicals. Atomic number 16; atomic weight 32.064; melting point (rhombic) 112.8°C; (monoclinic) 119.0°C; boiling point 444.6°C; specific gravity (rhombic) 2.07; (monoclinic) 1.957; valences 2, 4, 6. [Middle English, from Norman French *sulfere,* from Latin *sulfur.*]

sulfur dioxide. A colorless, extremely irritating gas or liquid, SO_2, used esp. in the manufacture of sulfuric acid.

sul·fu·ric (sŭl-fyŏŏr′ĭk) *adj.* Of, relating to, or containing sulfur, esp. with valence 6.

sulfuric acid. A highly corrosive, dense oily liquid, H_2SO_4, colorless when pure, used to manufacture a wide variety of chemicals and materials. Also called **oil of vitriol.**

sul·fur·ous (sŭl′fər-əs, sŭl-fyŏŏr′əs) *adj.* Also **sul·phur·ous.** **1.** Of, relating to, or containing sulfur, esp. in its lower valence. **2.** Characteristic of burning sulfur, as in odor.

sulfurous acid. A colorless solution of sulfur dioxide in water, H_2SO_3, characterized by a suffocating sulfurous odor, used as a bleach, preservative, and disinfectant.

sulk (sŭlk) *intr.v.* To be sullenly aloof or withdrawn, as in silent resentment or protest. —*n.* A mood or display of sulking. [Back-formation from SULKY.]

sulk·y[1] (sŭl′kē) *adj.* **-i·er, -i·est. 1.** Sullenly aloof or withdrawn. **2.** Gloomy; dismal. [Perh. from obs. *sulke,* sluggish.] —**sulk′i·ly** *adv.* —**sulk′i·ness** *n.*

sulk·y[2] (sŭl′kē) *n., pl.* **-ies.** A light two-wheeled vehicle accommodating one person and drawn by one horse. [From SULKY.]

sulky[2]

sul·len (sŭl′ən) *adj.* **1.** Showing a brooding ill humor; morose; sulky. **2.** Gloomy or somber. [Middle English *solein,* from Old French *sol,* alone, from Latin *sōlus.*] —**sul′len·ly** *adv.* —**sul′len·ness** *n.*

sul·ly (sŭl′ē) *tr.v.* **-lied, -ly·ing. 1.** To soil the cleanness or luster of. **2.** To tarnish the honor or purity of; taint. [Prob. from Old French *souiller,* to soil.]

sul·phur (sŭl′fər) *n.* Var. of **sulfur.**

sul·phur·ous (sŭl′fər-əs, sŭl-fyŏŏr′əs) *adj.* Var. of **sulfurous.**

sul·tan (sŭl′tən) *n.* The ruler esp. of a Moslem country. [Old French, from Medieval Latin *sultānus,* from Arabic *sultān,* ruler, from Aramaic *shultānā,* power, from *shəlēt,* to have power.]

sul·tan·a (sŭl-tăn′ə, -tä′nə) *n.* **1.** The wife, mother, sister, or daughter of a sultan. **2.** A seedless, pale yellow grape.

sul·tan·ate (sŭl′tə-nāt′, -nĭt) *n.* **1.** The office, power, or reign of a sultan. **2.** The domain of a sultan.

sul·try (sŭl′trē) *adj.* **-tri·er, -tri·est. 1.** Very hot and humid. **2.** Hot; torrid. **3.** Sensual; voluptuous. —See Syns at **hot.** [From obs. *sulter,* var. of SWELTER.] —**sul′tri·ness** *n.*

sum (sŭm) *n.* **1.** The result obtained by addition. **2.** The whole quantity; aggregate. **3.** An amount of money. **4.** An arithmetic problem. **5.** A summary. —*tr.v.* **summed, sum·ming.** To add. —*phrasal verb.* **sum up.** To summarize.

[Middle English *summe,* from Old French, from Latin *(res) summa,* "the highest thing," sum, total, from *summus,* highest.]

su·mac (sōō′măk′, shōō′-) *n.* Also **su·mach. 1.** Any of various shrubs or small trees of the genus *Rhus,* with compound leaves and greenish flowers followed by usu. red, hairy fruits. **2.** The dried leaves of some sumac species yielding a material used in tanning. [Middle English, from Old French, from Arabic *summaq,* sumac tree.]

Su·me·ri·an (sōō-mîr′ē-ən, -mĕr′-) *adj.* Of ancient Sumer, its people, culture, or language. —*n.* **1.** A member of a people native to Sumer. **2.** The language of the Sumerians.

sum·ma cum lau·de (sōōm′ə kōōm lou′də, sŭm′ə kŭm lô′dē). *Latin.* With the highest academic honors.

sum·ma·rize (sŭm′ə-rīz′) *tr.v.* **-rized, -riz·ing.** To make a summary of; restate briefly. —**sum′ma·ri·za′tion** *n.*

sum·ma·ry (sŭm′ə-rē) *n., pl.* **-ries.** A condensed statement of the substance or principal points of a larger work. —*adj.* **1.** Presented in condensed form; concise. **2.** Performed speedily and without ceremony: *summary justice.* [Middle English, from Medieval Latin *summārius,* comprising the principal parts, from Latin *summa,* sum.] —**sum·mar′i·ly** *adv.*

sum·ma·tion (sə-mā′shən) *n.* **1.** Addition. **2.** A total or aggregate. **3.** A concluding statement containing a summary of principal points, esp. of a case before a court of law.

sum·mer (sŭm′ər) *n.* **1.** The usu. warmest season of the year, occurring between spring and autumn. **2.** Any period of fruition or fulfillment. —*modifier: summer flowers.* —*tr.v.* To lodge or maintain during the summer. —*intr.v.* To pass the summer. [Middle English *sumer,* from Old English *sumor.*]

sum·mer·house (sŭm′ər-hous′) *n.* A small, roofed structure in a park or garden affording shade and rest.

sum·mer·sault (sŭm′ər-sôlt′) *n. & v.* Var. of **somersault.**

summer squash. Any of several varieties of squash that are eaten shortly after being picked rather than stored.

sum·mer·time (sŭm′ər-tīm′) *n.* The summer season.

sum·mer·y (sŭm′ə-rē) *adj.* Of, for, or suggesting summer.

sum·mit (sŭm′ĭt) *n.* **1.** The highest point, as of a mountain. **2.** The highest degree of achievement or status. **3.** The highest level, as of government. [Middle English *somette,* from Old French *sommette,* dim. of *som,* top, from Latin *summus,* highest, topmost.]

sum·mon (sŭm′ən) *tr.v.* **1.** To call together; convene. **2.** To send for; request to appear. **3.** To order to appear in court by the issuance of a summons. **4.** To call forth; rouse. —See Syns at **gather.** [Middle English *somounen,* from Old French *somondre,* from Latin *summonēre,* to remind secretly : *sub-,* secretly + *monēre,* to remind, warn.]

sum·mons (sŭm′ənz) *n., pl.* **sum·mons·es. 1.** A call to appear or do something. **2.** *Law.* A notice summoning a person to appear in court.

sump (sŭmp) *n.* Any low area which receives drainage, esp. a cesspool. [Middle English *sompe,* a swamp, morass, from Middle Low German or Middle Dutch *sump.*]

sump·ter (sŭmp′tər) *n.* A pack animal, such as a horse or mule. [Middle English, driver of a pack animal, from Old French *sommetier,* from Late Latin *sagma,* packsaddle, from Greek *sattein,* to pack.]

sump·tu·ar·y (sŭmp′chōō-ĕr′ē) *adj.* **1.** Regulating or limiting expenses. **2.** Regulating personal behavior on moral grounds. [Latin *sumptuārius,* from *sumptus,* expense, from *sūmere,* to spend, take.]

sump·tu·ous (sŭmp′chōō-əs) *adj.* Of a size suggesting great expense; lavish. —**sump′tu·ous·ly** *adv.* —**sump′tu·ous·ness** *n.*

sun (sŭn) *n.* **1.** A star that is the center of the solar system, that sustains life on Earth with its heat and light, and has a mean distance from Earth of about 93 million miles and a diameter of approx. 864,000 miles. **2.** Any star like the sun. **3.** The radiant energy, esp. heat and visible light, emitted by the sun; sunshine. —*v.* **sunned, sun·ning.** —*tr.v.* To expose to the sun's rays. —*intr.v.* To bask in the sun. [Middle English *sunne,* from Old English.] —**sun′less** *adj.*

sun-bathe (sŭn′bāth′) *intr.v.* **-bathed, -bath·ing.** To expose the body to the direct rays of the sun. —**sun′-bath′er** *n.*

sunbird
George Miksch Sutton

sunburst

sunflower

sun·beam (sŭn′bēm′) n. A ray of sunlight.

sun·bird (sŭn′bûrd′) n. Any of various small, tropical Old World birds of the family Nectariniidae, with a downward-curving bill and often brightly colored plumage.

sun·bon·net (sŭn′bŏn′ĭt) n. A woman's wide-brimmed bonnet with a flap at the back for shading the neck.

sun·burn (sŭn′bûrn′) n. An inflammation or blistering of the skin caused by overexposure to direct sunlight. —v. **-burned** or **-burnt** (-bûrnt′), **-burn·ing.** —tr.v. To afflict with sunburn. —intr.v. To be afflicted with sunburn.

sun·burst (sŭn′bûrst′) n. **1.** A sudden burst of sunlight, as through broken clouds. **2.** A pattern or design consisting of a central sunlike disk with radiating spires.

sun·dae (sŭn′dē, -dā′) n. A dish of ice cream with toppings such as syrup, fruits, nuts, and whipped cream. [Prob. alteration of SUNDAY.]

Sun·day (sŭn′dē, -dā′) n. The first day of the week, after Saturday and before Monday, and the Christian Sabbath. [Middle English *sunenday,* from Old English *sunnandæg,* "day of the sun."]

Sunday school. A school, gen. affiliated with a church, that offers religious instruction for children on Sundays.

sun·der (sŭn′dər) tr.v. To break apart; divide; sever. —intr.v. To break into parts. [Middle English *sunderen,* from Old English *sundrian.*]

sun·dew (sŭn′dōō, -dyōō) n. Any of several hairy-leaved, insectivorous plants of the genus *Drosera.*

sun·di·al (sŭn′dī′əl) n. An instrument that indicates the time of day by measuring the angle of the sun with a pointer that casts a shadow on a calibrated dial.

sun·dog (sŭn′dôg′, -dŏg′) n. A parhelion.

sun·down (sŭn′doun′) n. Sunset.

sun·dries (sŭn′drēz) pl.n. Small miscellaneous items or articles. [From SUNDRY.]

sun·dry (sŭn′drē) adj. Various; several; miscellaneous: *sundry items of clothing.* [Middle English *sundri,* from Old English *syndrig,* apart, separate.]

sun·fast (sŭn′făst′) adj. Resistant to fading by sunlight.

sun·fish (sŭn′fĭsh′) n., pl. **sunfish** or **-fish·es. 1.** Any of various small North American freshwater fishes of the family Centrarchidae, with laterally compressed, often brightly colored bodies. **2.** Any of several large saltwater fishes of the family Molidae, esp. the ocean sunfish.

sun·flow·er (sŭn′flou′ər) n. Any of several plants of the genus *Helianthus,* esp. *H. annuus,* with large yellow-rayed flowers that produce edible seeds rich in oil.

sung (sŭng) v. A past tense and the past participle of **sing.** [Middle English *sunge, sungen,* from Old English *sungon* (pl.), *(ge)sungen.*]

sun·glass·es (sŭn′glăs′ĭz) pl.n. Eyeglasses with tinted lenses to protect the eyes from the sun's glare.

sunk (sŭngk) v. A past tense and past participle of **sink.** — See Usage note at **sink.** [Middle English *sonke, sunke,* from Old English *suncon* (pl.) *(ge)suncen.*]

sunk·en (sŭng′kən) v. A past participle of **sink.** —See Usage note at **sink.** —adj. **1.** Depressed, fallen in, or hollowed: *sunken cheeks.* **2.** Submerged: *sunken treasure.* **3.** Below the surrounding level: *a sunken bathtub.* [Middle English *sunken,* from Old English *(ge)suncen.*]

sun lamp. A lamp that emits a wide range of radiation, used in therapeutic and cosmetic treatments.

sun·light (sŭn′līt′) n. The light of the sun.

sun·lit (sŭn′lĭt′) adj. Illuminated by the sun.

sun·ny (sŭn′ē) adj. **-ni·er, -ni·est. 1.** Exposed to or abounding in sunshine. **2.** Cheerful; genial: *a sunny smile.* —See Syns at **cheerful.** —**sun′ni·ly** adv. —**sun′ni·ness** n.

sun·rise (sŭn′rīz′) n. **1.** The first appearance of the sun above the horizon. **2.** The time at which this occurs.

sun·set (sŭn′sĕt′) n. **1.** The disappearance of the sun below the horizon. **2.** The time at which this occurs.

sun·shade (sŭn′shād′) n. Something, as a parasol, used as a protection from the sun's rays.

sun·shine (sŭn′shīn′) n. **1.** The direct rays from the sun. **2.** Happiness or cheerfulness. —**sun′shin′y** adj.

sun·spot (sŭn′spŏt′) n. Any of the relatively dark spots that appear in groups on the surface of the sun.

sun·stroke (sŭn′strōk′) n. Heat stroke caused by exposure to the sun.

sun·up (sŭn′ŭp′) n. Sunrise.

sup¹ (sŭp) v. **supped, sup·ping.** —tr.v. To sip (a liquid). —intr.v. To take sips. —n. A mouthful or taste of liquid. [Middle English *soupen,* from Old English *sūpan.*]

sup² (sŭp) intr.v. **supped, sup·ping.** To have supper; dine. [Middle English *soupen,* from Old French *souper,* from *soup,* piece of bread dipped in broth.]

su·per (sōō′pər) n. Informal. **1.** A superintendent in an apartment or office building. **2.** A supernumerary, as in a play. —adj. Slang. Excellent. —See Syns at **excellent.**

super-. A prefix indicating: **1.** Placement above, over, or outside: **superimpose. 2.** Superiority in size, quality, number, or degree: **superfine, supermarket. 3.** A degree exceeding a norm: **supersonic. 4.** Extra; additional: **superphosphate.** [From Latin *super,* above, over.]

su·per·a·ble (sōō′pər-ə-bəl) adj. Capable of being overcome. [Latin *superābilis,* from *superāre,* to overcome, from *super,* above, over.] —**su′per·a·bly** adv.

su·per·a·bound (sōō′pər-ə-bound′) intr.v. To be unusually or excessively abundant.

su·per·a·bun·dant (sōō′pər-ə-bŭn′dənt) adj. Abundant to excess; more than ample. —**su′per·a·bun′dance** n.

su·per·an·nu·ate (sōō′pər-ăn′yōō-āt′) tr.v. **-at·ed, -at·ing. 1.** To retire and pension because of age or infirmity. **2.** To set aside or discard as old-fashioned or obsolete. [Back-formation from SUPERANNUATED.]

su·per·an·nu·at·ed (sōō′pər-ăn′yōō-ā′tĭd) adj. **1.** Retired or discharged with a pension because of age or infirmity. **2.** Antiquated; obsolete. [Medieval Latin *superannuātus,* past part. of *superannuārī,* to be too old : Latin *super,* above + *annus,* year, time of life.]

su·perb (sōō-pûrb′, sə-) adj. **1.** Of unusually high quality; first-rate. **2.** Majestic; imposing. —See Syns at **excellent.** [Old French *superbe,* from Latin *superbus,* superior, proud, arrogant.] —**su·perb′ly** adv. —**su·perb′ness** n.

su·per·car·go (sōō′pər-kär′gō) n., pl. **-goes** or **-gos.** An officer on board a merchant ship who has charge of the cargo. [Spanish *sobrecargo* : *sobre-,* over, from Latin *super-* + *cargo,* cargo.]

su·per·charge (sōō′pər-chärj′) tr.v. **-charged, -charg·ing.** To increase the power of (an engine), as by fitting with a supercharger.

su·per·charg·er (sōō′pər-chär′jər) n. A blower or compressor, usu. driven by the engine, for supplying air under high pressure to the cylinders of an internal-combustion engine.

su·per·cil·i·ous (sōō′pər-sĭl′ē-əs) *adj.* Characterized by haughty scorn; disdainful. —See Syns at **arrogant.** [Latin *superciliōsus,* from Latin *supercilium,* upper eyelid, eyebrow, pride : *super-,* above + *cilium,* eyelid.] —**su′per·cil′i·ous·ly** *adv.* —**su′per·cil′i·ous·ness** *n.*

su·per·con·duc·tiv·i·ty (sōō′pər-kŏn′dŭk-tĭv′ĭ-tē) *n.* The complete loss of electrical resistance in certain metals and alloys at temperatures near absolute zero. —**su′per·con·duc′tive** (-kən-dŭk′tĭv) *adj.* —**su′per·con·duc′tor** *n.*

su·per·cool (sōō′pər-kōōl′) *tr.v.* To cool (a liquid) below the freezing point without causing solidification.

su·per·e·go (sōō′pər-ē′gō, -ĕg′ō) *n.* The consciencelike part of the psyche that develops by the incorporation of the moral standards of the community.

su·per·e·ro·ga·tion (sōō′pər-ĕr′ə-gā′shən) *n.* The performance of more than is required, demanded, or expected. [Late Latin *superērogātiō,* from *superērogāre,* to spend more : *super-,* above + *ērogare,* to spend.]

su·per·e·rog·a·to·ry (sōō′pər-ə-rŏg′ə-tôr′ē, -tōr′ē) *adj.* **1.** Performed or observed beyond the degree required or expected. **2.** Superfluous; unnecessary.

su·per·fam·i·ly (sōō′pər-făm′ə-lē) *n. Biol.* A taxonomic category ranking between an order and a family.

su·per·fi·cial (sōō′pər-fĭsh′əl) *adj.* **1.** Of, affecting, or located on or near the surface: *a superficial wound.* **2.** Concerned with or comprehending only what is apparent or obvious; shallow. —**su′per·fi′ci·al′i·ty** (-fĭsh′ē-ăl′ĭ-tē) or **su′per·fi′cial·ness** *n.* —**su′per·fi′cial·ly** *adv.*

su·per·fi·ci·es (sōō′pər-fĭsh′ē-ēz′, -fĭsh′ēz) *n., pl.* **superficies. 1.** The surface of an area or body. **2.** The external appearance or aspect of a thing. [Latin *superficiēs* : *super-,* above, over + *faciēs,* face.]

su·per·fine (sōō′pər-fīn′) *adj.* **1.** Of exceptional quality. **2.** Overdelicate or refined. **3.** Of extra fine texture.

su·per·flu·i·ty (sōō′pər-flōō′ĭ-tē) *n., pl.* **-ties. 1.** The quality or condition of being superfluous. **2.** Something that is superfluous. **3.** Overabundance. —See Syns at **excess.**

su·per·flu·ous (sōō-pûr′flōō-əs) *adj.* Beyond what is required or sufficient; extra. [Middle English, from Latin *superfluus,* overflowing, from *superfluere,* to overflow : *super-,* over + *fluere,* to flow.] —**su′per′flu·ous·ly** *adv.* —**su·per′flu·ous·ness** *n.*

su·per·heat (sōō′pər-hēt′) *tr.v.* **1.** To heat excessively; overheat. **2.** To heat (steam or other vapor) beyond its saturation point. **3.** To heat (a liquid) above its boiling point without causing vaporization. —**su′per·heat′er** *n.*

su·per·high frequency (sōō′pər-hī′). Any radio frequency between 3,000 and 30,000 megahertz.

su·per·high·way (sōō′pər-hī′wā′) *n.* A broad highway for high-speed traffic, usu. with six or more traffic lanes.

su·per·hu·man (sōō′pər-hyōō′mən) *adj.* **1.** Above or beyond the human; divine; supernatural. **2.** Beyond ordinary or normal human ability. —**su′per·hu′man·ly** *adv.*

su·per·im·pose (sōō′pər-ĭm-pōz′) *tr.v.* **-posed, -pos·ing.** To place on or over something else. —**su′per·im′po·si′tion** *n.*

su·per·in·cum·bent (sōō′pər-ĭn-kŭm′bənt) *adj.* Lying or resting, and often exerting pressure on, something else. [Latin *superincumbēns,* pres. part. of *superincumbere,* to lie down on : *super-,* above + *incumbere,* to lie down.] —**su′per·in·cum′bence** or **su′per·in·cum′ben·cy** *n.*

su·per·in·duce (sōō′pər-ĭn-dōōs′, -dyōōs′) *tr.v.* **-duced, -duc·ing.** To introduce as an addition. —**su′per·in·duc′tion** (-dŭk′shən) *n.*

su·per·in·tend (sōō′pər-ĭn-tĕnd′) *tr.v.* To have charge of; oversee; manage. [Late Latin *superintendere* : *super-,* over + *intendere,* to direct one's attention to.] —**su′per·in·ten′dence** or **su′per·in·ten′den·cy** *n.*

su·per·in·ten·dent (sōō′pər-ĭn-tĕn′dənt) *n.* A person who supervises or manages.

su·pe·ri·or (sōō-pîr′ē-ər, sə-) *adj.* **1.** Higher in rank, station, or authority. **2.** Of a higher nature or kind; far above others. **3.** Greater in number or amount. **4.** Arrogant; haughty. **5.** Indifferent or immune. **6.** Located higher, as an organ or part. —See Syns at **arrogant.** —*n.* **1.** A person who surpasses another in rank or quality. **2.** The head of a religious order or house. [Middle English, from Old French, from Latin, compar. of *superus,* situated above, upper, from *super,* above, over.] —**su·pe′ri·or′i·ty** (-pîr′-

ē-ôr′ĭ-tē, -ŏr′) *n.* —**su·pe′ri·or·ly** *adv.*

Usage: **superior.** A person or thing is said to be *superior to* (not *superior than*) another.

su·per·la·tive (sōō-pûr′lə-tĭv) *adj.* **1.** Of the highest order, quality, or degree. **2.** Excessive or exaggerated. **3.** *Gram.* Expressing or involving the extreme degree of comparison of an adjective or adverb. —*n.* **1.** Something superlative. **2.** *Gram.* **a.** The superlative degree. **b.** An adjective or adverb expressing the superlative degree. [Middle English *superlatyf,* from Old French *superlative,* from Late Latin *superlātīvus,* from *superlātus,* past part. of *superferre,* to carry over.] —**su·per′la·tive·ly** *adv.*

su·per·man (sōō′pər-măn′) *n.* A person with more than human powers.

su·per·mar·ket (sōō′pər-mär′kĭt) *n.* A large self-service retail store selling food and household goods.

su·per·nal (sōō-pûr′nəl) *adj.* **1.** Celestial; heavenly. **2.** Of, coming from, or in the sky. [Middle English, from Old French, from Latin *supernus.*] —**su·per′nal·ly** *adv.*

su·per·na·tant (sōō′pər-nāt′nt) *adj.* Floating on the surface. [Latin *supernatāns,* pres. part. of *supernatāre,* to swim above, float : *super-,* above + *natāre,* to swim.]

su·per·nat·u·ral (sōō′pər-năch′ər-əl) *adj.* **1.** Of an order of existence outside the natural world. **2.** Attributed to the immediate exercise of divine power; miraculous. —**su′per·nat′u·ral·ly** *adv.* —**su′per·nat′u·ral·ness** *n.*

su·per·nat·u·ral·ism (sōō′pər-năch′ər-ə-lĭz′əm) *n.* **1.** The quality of being supernatural. **2.** Belief in a supernatural force that intervenes in the course of natural laws. —**su′per·nat′u·ral·ist** *n.* —**su′per·nat′u·ral·is′tic** *adj.*

su·per·no·va (sōō′pər-nō′və) *n., pl.* **-vae** (-vē′). A rare celestial phenomenon in which a star explodes, resulting in an extremely bright, short-lived object.

su·per·nu·mer·ar·y (sōō′pər-nōō′mə-rĕr′ē, -nyōō′-) *adj.* **1.** Exceeding a fixed or prescribed number; extra. **2.** Superfluous. —*n., pl.* **-ies. 1.** Someone or something in excess of the regular, necessary, or usual number. **2.** A theatrical or cinematic performer without a speaking part. [Late Latin *supernumerārius,* (a soldier) added to a legion in excess of its fixed number, from Latin *super numerum,* "over the number."]

su·per·phos·phate (sōō′pər-fŏs′fāt′) *n.* A fertilizer made by the action of sulfuric acid on phosphate rock.

su·per·pose (sōō′pər-pōz′) *tr.v.* **-posed, -pos·ing.** To set or place over or above something else, esp. so that like parts coincide. —**su′per·po·si′tion** *n.*

su·per·pow·er (sōō′pər-pou′ər) *n.* A powerful and influential nation.

su·per·sat·u·rate (sōō′pər-săch′ə-rāt′) *tr.v.* **-rat·ed, -rat·ing.** To cause (a chemical solution) to be more highly concentrated than is normally possible under given conditions of temperature and pressure. —**su′per·sat′u·ra′tion** *n.*

su·per·scribe (sōō′pər-skrīb′) *tr.v.* **-scribed, -scrib·ing. 1.** To write on the outside or upper part of. **2.** To write (as a name or address) on the top or outside. [Latin *superscrībere,* to write over : *super-,* over + *scrībere,* to write.]

su·per·script (sōō′pər-skrĭpt′) *n.* A character placed above and immediately to one side of another. [Latin *superscriptus,* past part. of *superscrībere,* to superscribe.]

su·per·scrip·tion (sōō′pər-skrĭp′shən) *n.* Something written above or outside something, esp. an address.

su·per·sede (sōō′pər-sēd′) *tr.v.* **-sed·ed, -sed·ing. 1.** To replace or succeed. **2.** To displace; supplant. [Middle English *superceden,* to postpone, from Old French *superseder,* from Latin *supersedēre,* to desist from : *super-,* above + *sedēre,* to sit.] —**su′per·sed′er** *n.*

su·per·sen·si·tive (sōō′pər-sen′sĭ-tĭv) *adj.* Extremely or acutely sensitive. —**su′per·sen′si·tive·ly** *adv.* —**su′per·sen′si·tive·ness** or **su′per·sen′si·tiv′i·ty** (-tĭv′ĭ-tē) *n.*

su·per·son·ic (sōō′pər-sŏn′ĭk) *adj.* Of, caused by, or moving at a speed greater than the speed of sound.

su·per·sti·tion (sōō′pər-stĭsh′ən) *n.* **1.** A belief that some action not logically related to a course of events influences its outcome. **2.** Any belief, practice, or rite unreasoningly upheld by faith in magic, chance, or dogma. [Middle English *supersticion,* from Old French *superstition,* from Latin *superstitiō,* from *superstāre,* to stand over : *super-,* over + *stāre,* to stand.]

su·per·sti·tious (sōō′pər-stĭsh′əs) *adj.* Of, marked by, or believing in superstitions. **—su′per·sti′tious·ly** *adv.* **—su′·per·sti′tious·ness** *n.*

su·per·struc·ture (soo̅′pər-strŭk′chər) *n.* Any structure literally or figuratively built on top of something else, esp. a part of a ship's structure above the main deck.

su·per·ton·ic (soo̅′pər-tŏn′ĭk) *n. Mus.* The second tone of the diatonic scale.

su·per·vene (soo̅′pər-vēn′) *intr.v.* **-vened, -ven·ing.** To come or occur as something extraneous, additional, or unexpected. [Latin *supervenīre* : *super-,* in addition + *venīre,* to come.] **—su′per·ven′tion** (-vĕn′shən) *n.*

su·per·vise (soo̅′pər-vīz′) *tr.v.* **-vised, -vis·ing.** To direct and inspect the work or performance of. [From Medieval Latin *supervīsus,* past part. of *supervidēre,* to look over : Latin *super-,* over + *vidēre,* to see.] **—su′per·vi′sion** (-vĭzh′ən) *n.* **—su′per·vi′sor** *n.* **—su′per·vi′so·ry** (-vī′zə-rē) *adj.*

su·pine (soo̅-pīn′, soo̅′pīn′) *adj.* **1.** Lying on the back or having the face upward. **2.** Lethargic; passive. [Latin *supīnus.*] **—su·pine′ly** *adv.* **—su·pine′ness** *n.*

sup·per (sŭp′ər) *n.* An evening meal, esp. a light meal when dinner is taken at midday. [Middle English *suppere,* from Old French *souper,* from *souper,* to sup.]

sup·plant (sə-plănt′) *tr.v.* **1.** To take the place of; supersede. **2.** To take the place of by treachery, deceit, or force. [Middle English *supplanten,* from Old French *supplanter,* from Latin *supplantāre,* to overthrow: *sub-,* up from under + *planta,* sole of the foot.]

sup·ple (sŭp′əl) *adj.* **-pler, -plest. 1.** Easily bent; pliant: *supple leather.* **2.** Agile; limber. **3.** Yielding or changing readily; adaptable. **4.** Compliant; submissive: *a supple colleague.* —See Syns at **flexible.** [Middle English *souple,* from Old French, from Latin *supplex,* beseeching, submissive.] **—sup′ple·ly** *adv.* **—sup′ple·ness** *n.*

sup·ple·ment (sŭp′lə-mənt) *n.* **1.** Something added to extend or complete a thing or to make up for a deficiency. **2.** *Geom.* The angle or arc that when added to a given angle or arc makes 180 degrees. *—tr.v.* (sŭp′lə-mĕnt′). To provide or form a supplement to. [Middle English, from Latin *supplēmentum,* from *supplēre,* to complete, supply.] **—sup′ple·men′tal** *adj.*

sup·ple·men·ta·ry (sŭp′lə-mĕn′tə-rē, -mĕn′trē) *adj.* Added or serving as a supplement.

supplementary angles. A pair of angles whose sum is 180 degrees.

sup·pli·ant (sŭp′lē-ənt) *adj.* Asking humbly and earnestly; beseeching. *—n.* A person who supplicates. [Middle English, from Old French, pres. part. of *supplier,* to entreat, from Latin *supplicāre,* to supplicate.] **—sup′pli·ant·ly** *adv.*

sup·pli·cant (sŭp′lĭ-kənt) *n.* A person who entreats or supplicates; a suppliant. *—adj.* Supplicating.

sup·pli·cate (sŭp′lĭ-kāt′) *v.* **-cat·ed, -cat·ing.** *—tr.v.* **1.** To ask for humbly or earnestly, as by praying. **2.** To beseech: *supplicate the judge for mercy. —intr.v.* To make a humble and earnest petition; beg. [Middle English *supplicaten,* from Latin *supplicāre,* to kneel down, beg humbly : *sub-,* down + *plicāre,* to fold up.] **—sup′pli·ca′tion** *n.* **—sup′pli·ca·to·ry** (-kə-tôr′ē, -tōr′ē) *adj.*

sup·ply (sə-plī′) *tr.v.* **-plied, -ply·ing. 1.** To make (something needed, desired, or lacking) available for use; provide. **2.** To furnish or equip with what is needed or lacking. **3.** To fill sufficiently; satisfy: *supply a need.* **4.** To make up for; compensate for. *—n., pl.* **-plies. 1.** The act of supplying. **2.** An amount available; stock. **3.** Often **supplies.** Materials or provisions stored and dispensed when needed. **4.** *Econ.* The amount of a commodity available for meeting a demand or for purchase at a given price. [Middle English *supplyen,* from Old French *soupleer,* from Latin *supplēre,* to fill up, complete : *sub-,* from below, up + *plēre,* to fill.] **—sup·pli′er** *n.*

sup·port (sə-pôrt′, -pōrt′) *tr.v.* **1.** To hold up or maintain in position; prevent from falling. **2.** To be capable of bearing; withstand. **3.** To keep from failing during stress. **4.** To provide for or maintain by supplying with money or other necessities. **5.** To furnish evidence for; substantiate. **6.** To aid or promote the cause of. **7.** To act in a secondary or subordinate role to (a leading actor). *—n.* **1.** The act of supporting or the condition of being supported. **2.** Someone or something that supports. **3.** Maintenance or subsistence. —See Syns at **living.** [Middle English *supporten,*

from Old French *supporter,* from Latin *supportāre,* to carry, convey : *sub-,* up, toward + *portāre,* to carry.] **—sup·port′a·ble** *adj.*

sup·port·er (sə-pôr′tər, -pōr′-) *n.* A person that supports.

sup·por·tive (sə-pôr′tĭv, -pōr′-) *adj.* Providing support.

sup·pose (sə-pōz′) *v.* **-posed, -pos·ing.** *—tr.v.* **1.** To assume to be true or real for the sake of an argument or explanation. **2.** To be inclined to think. **3.** To imply as a necessary condition; presuppose. [Middle English *supposen,* to believe, assume, from Old French *supposer,* from Latin *suppositus,* past part. of *suppōnere,* to substitute : *sub-,* under + *ponere,* to place.]

sup·posed (sə-pōzd′, -pō′zĭd) *adj.* **1.** Considered to be so, often mistakenly. **2.** (sə-pōzd′). Required: *was supposed to go the store.* **—sup·pos′ed·ly** (-pō′zĭd-lē) *adv.*

sup·po·si·tion (sŭp′ə-zĭsh′ən) *n.* **1.** The act of supposing. **2.** An assumption. **—sup′po·si′tion·al** *adj.*

sup·pos·i·ti·tious (sə-pŏz′ĭ-tĭsh′əs) *adj.* **1.** Substituted with fraudulent intent. **2.** Hypothetical. **—sup·pos′i·ti′tious·ly** *adv.*

sup·pos·i·to·ry (sə-pŏz′ĭ-tôr′ē, -tōr′ē) *n., pl.* **-ries.** A solid medication designed to melt within a body cavity other than the mouth.

sup·press (sə-prĕs′) *tr.v.* **1.** To put an end to forcibly; subdue. **2.** To keep from being revealed, published, or circulated. **3.** To hold back; restrain: *suppress a smile.* [Middle English *suppressen,* from Latin *suppressus,* past part. of *supprimere,* to press down : *sub-,* down + *premere,* to press.] **—sup·pres′er** or **sup·pres′sor** *n.*

sup·pres·sion (sə-prĕsh′ən) *n.* **1.** The act of suppressing or the condition of being suppressed. **2.** The conscious exclusion of painful desires or thoughts from awareness.

sup·pres·sive (sə-prĕs′ĭv) *adj.* Tending to suppress.

sup·pu·rate (sŭp′yə-rāt′) *intr.v.* **-rat·ed, -rat·ing.** To form or discharge pus. [From Latin *suppūrāre* : *sub-,* under + *pūs,* pus.] **—sup′pu·ra′tion** *n.*

supra-. A prefix meaning: **1.** Above or over: **suprarenal. 2.** Greater than: **supranational.** [Latin, from *suprā,* above, beyond.]

su·pra·na·tion·al (soo̅′prə-năsh′ə-nəl) *adj.* Of or extending beyond the boundaries or authority of a nation.

su·pra·re·nal (soo̅′prə-rē′nəl) *adj.* Located on or above the kidney. *—n.* An adrenal gland or other bodily part. [SU-PRA- + Latin *rēnēs,* kidneys.]

su·prem·a·cist (soo̅-prĕm′ə-sĭst) *n.* A person who believes that a certain group is or should be supreme.

su·prem·a·cy (soo̅-prĕm′ə-sē) *n., pl.* **-cies. 1.** The condition or quality of being supreme. **2.** Supreme power.

su·preme (sə-prēm′) *adj.* **1.** Greatest in power, authority, or rank; paramount; dominant. **2.** Greatest in importance or quality. **3.** Ultimate; final: *the supreme sacrifice.* [Latin *suprēmus,* superl. of *superus,* situated above, upper, from *super,* above.] **—su·preme′ly** *adv.*

Supreme Being. God.

Supreme Court. 1. The highest Federal court in the United States, consisting of nine justices. **2.** The highest court in most states within the United States.

sur-. A prefix meaning over, beyond, or above: **surtax.** [Middle English, from Old French, from Latin *super-,* from *super,* above, over.]

sur·cease (sûr-sēs′, sər-sēs′) *n. Archaic.* Cessation; end. [Middle English *sursesen,* from Old French *surseoir,* to refrain, delay, from Latin *supersedēre,* to desist from.]

sur·charge (sûr′chärj′) *n.* **1.** An additional sum added to the usual amount or cost. **2.** A new value or denomination overprinted on a stamp. *—tr.v.* **-charged, -charg·ing. 1.** To charge an additional amount. **2.** To overcharge. **3.** To overload. **4.** To print a surcharge on.

sur·cin·gle (sûr′sĭng′gəl) *n.* A girth that binds a saddle, pack, or blanket to the body of a horse. [Middle English *sursengle,* from Old French *sourcengle* : *sur-,* over + *cengle,* belt, from Latin *cingula,* from *cingere,* to gird.]

sur·coat (sûr′kōt′) *n.* **1.** A loose outer coat. **2.** A tunic worn over armor. [Middle English *surcote,* from Old French.]

surd (sûrd) *n.* **1.** A sum, as $2 + 3$, containing one or more irrational roots of numbers. **2.** A voiceless speech sound. *—adj.* Voiceless, as a sound. [Latin *surdus,* deaf, mute.]

sure (shoor) *adj.* **sur·er, sur·est. 1.** Incapable of being doubted; certain. **2.** Steady; firm: *a sure grip.* **3.** Confident: *sure of victory.* **4. a.** Bound to happen; inevitable: *sure defeat.* **b.** Destined; bound: *sure to succeed.* **5.** Reliable: *a sure friend.* **—idioms. for sure.** Certainly; without a doubt. **to be sure.** Certainly; indeed. [Middle English, from Old French *sur,* from Latin *sēcūrus,* free from care, safe : *sē,* without + *cūra,* care.] **—sure′ness** *n.*

sure-fire (shŏŏr′fīr′) *adj.* Informal. Bound to be successful.

sure-foot·ed (shŏŏr′fŏŏt′ĭd) *adj.* Not liable to stumble.

sure·ly (shŏŏr′lē) *adv.* **1.** Certainly; without doubt. **2.** With confidence or assurance. **3.** Steadily.

sure·ty (shŏŏr′ĭ-tē) *n., pl.* **-ties. 1.** The condition of being sure. **2.** Something beyond doubt; a certainty. **3.** A guarantee or security. **4.** A person who has contracted to be responsible for another. —See Syns at **certainty.**

surf (sûrf) *n.* The offshore waters or waves between the shoreline and the outermost boundaries of the breakers. *—intr.v.* To engage in surfing. [Orig. unknown.]

sur·face (sûr′fəs) *n.* **1.** The outer or the topmost boundary of an object. **2.** *Geom.* A continuous set of points in a space, having the property that every one of its intersections with a plane forms a line, curve, or in special cases a point. **3.** A superficial or outward appearance: *On the surface, he was a mild-mannered man.* *—adj.* **1.** Of or on a surface. **2.** Superficial. *—v.* **-faced, -fac·ing.** *—tr.v.* To form the surface of. *—intr.v.* To rise or come to the surface. [French : *sur-,* above + *face,* face.]

surface tension. A property of liquids that causes the surface to resemble a stretched elastic membrane, arising from unbalanced molecular cohesive forces at the surface.

surf·board (sûrf′bôrd′, -bōrd′) *n.* A narrow, somewhat rounded board used for surfing.

surf·boat (sûrf′bōt′) *n.* A strong boat used in heavy surf.

surf·cast·ing (sûrf′kăs′tĭng) *n.* The sport of fishing from shore, casting one's line into the surf.

sur·feit (sûr′fĭt) *tr.v.* To feed or supply to excess; to satiate. *—intr.v.* To overindulge. *—n.* **1.** The act or an instance of overindulging in food or drink. **2.** The disgust caused by such overindulgence. **3.** An excessive amount. [Middle English, from Old French.]

surf·ing (sûr′fĭng) *n.* The sport of riding the crests of waves into shore, esp. on a surfboard.

surge (sûrj) *intr.v.* **surged, surg·ing. 1.** To move in a billowing or swelling manner, in or as if in waves. **2.** To increase suddenly. *—n.* **1.** A billowing or swelling motion like that of great waves. **2.** A sudden onrush: *a surge of joy.* [Old French *sourgir,* from Old Spanish *surgir,* from Latin *surgere,* to rise : *sub-,* up from below + *regere,* to lead.]

sur·geon (sûr′jən) *n.* A physician specializing in surgery. [Middle English *surgien,* from Norman French, from Old French *serurgien,* from *serurgie,* surgery.]

sur·ger·y (sûr′jə-rē) *n., pl.* **-ies. 1.** The medical diagnosis and treatment of injury, deformity, and disease by the cutting and removal or repair of bodily parts. **2.** An operating room or laboratory of a surgeon. **3.** The skill or work of a surgeon. [Middle English *surgerie,* from Old French, *serurgerie,* from *serurgie,* from Latin *chirurgia,* from Greek *kheirurgia* : *kheir,* hand + *ergon,* work.]

sur·gi·cal (sûr′jĭ-kəl) *adj.* Of, pertaining to or associated with surgeons or surgery. [From SURGEON.]

sur·ly (sûr′lē) *adj.* **-li·er, -li·est.** Sullenly rude and bad-tempered; gruff. —See Syns at **irritable.** [Earlier *sirly,* lordly, masterful, imperious, from SIR.] **—sur′li·ness** *n.*

sur·mise (sər-mīz′) *v.* **-mised, -mis·ing.** *—tr.v.* To infer with little evidence; guess. *—intr.v.* To make a guess. *—n.* An idea or opinion based upon little evidence; conjecture. [Middle English *surmysen,* to accuse, from Old French *surmettre,* from Medieval Latin *supermittere,* from Late Latin *super-,* upon + *mittere,* to throw.]

sur·mount (sər-mount′) *tr.v.* **1.** To overcome; conquer. **2.** To ascend and cross to the other side of. **3.** To be above or on top of: *the church dome surmounts the square.* [Middle English *surmonten,* from Old French *surmonter* : *sur-,* above + *monter,* to mount.] **—sur·mount′a·ble** *adj.*

sur·name (sûr′nām′) *n.* A person's last or family name. *—tr.v.* **-named, -nam·ing.** To give a surname to.

sur·pass (sər-păs′) *tr.v.* **1.** To go beyond the limit of; tran-

scend. **2.** To be or go beyond; exceed.

Syns: surpass, exceed, excel, outdo, outshine, outstrip, pass, top, transcend *v. Core meaning:* To be/be greater or better than (*a wheat crop that surpassed last year's by two million bushels*).

sur·pass·ing (sər-păs′ĭng) *adj.* Exceptional; superlative: *of surpassing splendor.* **—sur·pass′ing·ly** *adv.*

sur·plice (sûr′plĭs) *n.* A loose-fitting white gown with wide sleeves, worn over a cassock by some clergymen. [Middle English *surplis,* from Old French *sourpeliz,* from Medieval Latin *superpellicium* : *super-,* over + *pellicium,* fur coat, from Latin *pellis,* skin.]

surplice
Anglican surplice

surrey

sur·plus (sûr′pləs) *n.* An amount or quantity in excess of what is needed or used. —See Syns at **excess.** *—adj.* Being a surplus. [Middle English, from Old French, from Medieval Latin *superplūs* : Latin *super-,* in addition + *plūs,* more.]

sur·plus·age (sûr′plŭs′ĭj) *n.* Surplus; excess.

sur·prise (sər-prīz′) *tr.v.* **-prised, -pris·ing. 1.** To encounter suddenly or unexpectedly. **2.** To attack or capture suddenly and without warning. **3.** To astonish by the unexpected. *—n.* **1.** The act of surprising. **2.** The condition of being surprised; a feeling of amazement or wonder. **3.** Something that surprises. [Middle English *surprysen,* to be seized with, from Old French *surprendre,* to overtake : *sur-,* over + *prendre,* to take, from Latin *prehendere,* to seize.] **—sur·pris′er** *n.*

sur·pris·ing (sər-prī′zĭng) *adj.* Causing surprise; unexpected. **—sur·pris′ing·ly** *adv.*

sur·re·al·ism (sə-rē′ə-lĭz′əm) *n.* A 20th-cent. literary and artistic movement that attempts to express the workings of the subconscious by fantastic imagery and incongruous juxtaposition of subject matter. **—sur·re′al** or **sur·re′al·is′tic** *adj.* **—sur·re′al·ist** *n.* **—sur·re′al·is′ti·cal·ly** *adv.*

sur·ren·der (sə-rĕn′dər) *tr.v.* **1.** To relinquish possession or control of to another because of demand or force. **2.** To give up in favor of another. **3.** To give up or give back: *surrender a contractual right.* **4.** To abandon: *surrender all hope.* **5.** To give (oneself) up, as to an emotion: *surrendered himself to grief.* *—intr.v.* To give oneself up to another. —See Syns at **yield.** *—n.* The act of surrendering. [Middle English *sorendren,* from Old French *surrendre* : *sur-,* over + *rendre,* to deliver.]

sur·rep·ti·tious (sûr′əp-tĭsh′əs) *adj.* Secret and stealthy: *a surreptitious glance.* [Latin *surreptīcius,* from *surreptus,* past part. of *surripere,* to take away secretly : *sub-,* secretly + *rapere,* to seize.] **—sur′rep·ti′tious·ly** *adv.* **—sur′rep·ti′tious·ness** *n.*

sur·rey (sûr′ē, sŭr′ē) *n., pl.* **-reys.** A horse-drawn four-wheeled carriage vehicle having two seats. [Short for *Surrey cart,* after *Surrey,* England.]

sur·ro·gate (sûr′ə-gĭt, -gāt′, sŭr′-) *n.* **1.** A substitute. **2.** A judge in some U.S. states having jurisdiction over the settlement of estates. [From Latin *surrogāre, subrogāre,* to subrogate.]

sur·round (sə-round′) *tr.v.* **1.** To extend on all sides of simultaneously; encircle. **2.** To enclose or confine on all sides. [Middle English *sourrounden,* to overflow, from Old French *souronder,* from Late Latin *superundāre* : Latin *super-,* over + *unda,* wave.]

Syns: surround, circle, compass, encircle, enclose, gird,

hem in, ring *v.* *Core meaning:* To shut in on all sides (*a city surrounded by suburbs*).

sur·round·ings (sə-roun'dĭngz) *pl.n.* The external circumstances of something; environment.

sur·tax (sûr'tăks') *n.* **1.** An additional tax. **2.** A graduated income tax added to the normal income tax.

sur·veil·lance (sər-vā'ləns) *n.* Close observation of a person or group, esp. of one under suspicion. [French, from *surveiller*, to oversee : *sur-*, over + *veiller*, to watch, from Latin *vigilare*, from *vigil*, awake.]

sur·vey (sər-vā', sûr'vā') *tr.v.* **1.** To examine or look over comprehensively. **2.** To inspect carefully; scrutinize. **3.** To determine the boundaries, the area, or the elevations of part of the earth's surface by means of measuring angles and distances. —*intr.v.* To make a survey. —*n.* (sûr'vā'). **1.** A detailed inspection or investigation. **2.** A comprehensive view. **3. a.** The process of surveying land. **b.** A plan or map of surveyed land. [Middle English *surveyen*, from Old French *surveeir*, from Medieval Latin *supervidēre*, to look over : Latin *super-*, over + *vidēre*, to see.] —**sur·vey'or** *n.*

sur·vey·ing (sər-vā'ĭng) *n.* The measurement of dimensional relationships on the earth's surface, esp. for use in locating property boundaries and mapmaking.

sur·viv·al (sər-vī'vəl) *n.* **1.** The act of surviving or the fact of having survived. **2.** Something that survives, as an ancient custom or belief. —*modifier:* survival techniques.

sur·vive (sər-vīv') *v.* **-vived, -viv·ing.** —*intr.v.* To remain alive or in existence; endure. —*tr.v.* **1.** To live longer than; outlive: *survived his wife by 5 years.* **2.** To live or persist through: *plants surviving a frost.* [Middle English *surviven*, from Old French *sourvivre*, from Late Latin *supervīvere* : *super-*, over + *vīvere*, to live.] —**sur·vi'vor** *n.*

sus·cep·ti·bil·i·ty (sə-sĕp'tə-bĭl'ĭ-tē) *n., pl.* **-ties. 1.** The condition or quality of being susceptible. **2.** The capacity to be affected by deep emotions or strong feelings; sensitivity. **3. susceptibilities.** Sensibilities; sensitive feelings.

sus·cep·ti·ble (sə-sĕp'tə-bəl) *adj.* **1.** Easily influenced or affected: *not susceptible to persuasion.* **2.** Liable; subject: *susceptible to colds.* **3.** Capable of accepting or permitting: *susceptible of proof.* [Late Latin *susceptibilis*, capable of receiving, from Latin *susceptus*, past part. of *suscipere*, to receive : *sub-*, up from under + *capere*, to take.] —**sus·cep'ti·ble·ness** *n.* —**sus·cep'ti·bly** *adv.*

sus·pect (sə-spĕkt') *tr.v.* **1.** To regard as probable; surmise. **2.** To distrust: *suspect someone's motives.* **3.** To think guilty without proof: *suspect her of murder.* —*intr.v.* To have suspicion. —*n.* (sŭs'pĕkt'). Someone who is suspected, esp. of having committed a crime. —*adj.* (sŭs'pĕkt'). Open to or viewed with suspicion: *His intentions are suspect.* [Latin *suspectāre*, from *suspectus*, past part. of *suspicere*, to watch : *sub-*, under + *specere*, to look at.]

sus·pend (sə-spĕnd') *tr.v.* **1.** To bar for a period from a privilege, office, or position, usu. as a punishment. **2.** To cause to stop for a period; interrupt: *suspend a trial.* **3. a.** To hold in abeyance; defer: *suspend judgment.* **b.** To render ineffective temporarily: *suspend parking regulations.* **4.** To hang so as to allow free movement. **5.** To support or keep from falling without apparent attachment, as by buoyancy: *suspend oneself in the water.* —*intr.v.* To cease for a period. [Middle English *suspenden*, from Old French *suspendre*, from Latin *suspendere*, to hang up : *sub-*, up from under + *pendere*, to hang.]

suspended animation. A dormant or unconscious condition resembling death.

sus·pend·ers (sə-spĕn'dərz) *pl.n.* A pair of straps worn over the shoulders to support trousers or a skirt.

sus·pense (sə-spĕns') *n.* **1.** The condition or quality of being undecided. **2.** Anxiety or apprehension resulting from uncertainty. [Middle English, from Old French, from *suspens*, suspended, from Latin *suspensus*, past part. of *suspendēre*, to suspend.] —**sus·pense'ful** *adj.*

sus·pen·sion (sə-spĕn'shən) *n.* **1.** The act of suspending or the condition of being suspended, esp.: **a.** A temporary deferment. **b.** A debarment. **c.** A postponement of judgment, opinion, or decision. **2.** A device from which a mechanical part is suspended. **3.** The system of springs and other devices that insulates the chassis of a vehicle from shocks. **4.** *Chem.* A relatively coarse, noncolloidal dispersion of solid particles in a liquid.

suspension bridge. A bridge having the roadway suspended from cables usu. supported by towers.

suspension bridge

sus·pen·sive (sə-spĕn'sĭv) *adj.* **1.** Serving or tending to suspend or temporarily stop something. **2.** Of, characterized by, or causing suspense. —**sus·pen'sive·ly** *adv.*

sus·pen·so·ry (sə-spĕn'sə-rē) *adj.* **1.** Supporting or suspending. **2.** Delaying the completion of something.

sus·pi·cion (sə-spĭsh'ən) *n.* **1.** The act of suspecting the existence of something, esp. of something wrong, with little evidence or proof. **2.** The condition of being suspected, esp. of wrongdoing. **3.** Doubt; distrust. **4.** A faint trace; a hint. —See Syns at **distrust.** [Middle English, from Old French, from Latin *suspīciō*, from *suspicere*, to suspect.]

sus·pi·cious (sə-spĭsh'əs) *adj.* **1.** Arousing or apt to arouse suspicion. **2.** Tending to suspect; distrustful: *a suspicious nature.* **3.** Expressing suspicion: *a suspicious look.* —**sus·pi'cious·ly** *adv.* —**sus·pi'cious·ness** *n.*

sus·pire (sə-spīr') *intr.v.* **-pired, -pir·ing. 1.** To breathe. **2.** To sigh. [Middle English *suspiren*, from Latin *suspīrāre* : *sub-*, up from below + *spīrāre*, to breathe.] —**sus·pi·ra'·tion** (sŭs'pə-rā'shən) *n.*

sus·tain (sə-stān') *tr.v.* **1.** To keep in existence or effect; maintain. **2.** To supply with necessities or nourishment; provide for. **3.** To keep from falling or sinking. **4.** To support the spirits or resolution of. **5.** To endure or withstand; bear up under: *sustain hardships.* **6.** To experience or suffer (loss or injury). **7.** To affirm the validity or justice of: *sustain an objection.* **8.** To prove or corroborate; confirm. [Middle English *susteynen*, from Old French *sustenir*, from Latin *sustinēre* : *sub-*, up from under + *tenēre*, to hold.] —**sus·tain'a·ble** *adj.* —**sus·tain'er** *n.*

sus·te·nance (sŭs'tə-nəns) *n.* **1.** The act of sustaining or the condition of being sustained. **2.** That which sustains life or health, esp. food. **3.** Means of livelihood. —See Syns at **living.** [Middle English, from Old French *soustenance*, from *soustenir*, *sustenir*, to sustain.]

sut·tee (sə-tē', sŭt'ē') *n.* The act or practice of a Hindu widow permitting herself to be cremated on her husband's funeral pyre. [Sanskrit *satī*, good woman, faithful wife, from *sat*, virtuous.]

su·ture (soo'chər) *n.* **1. a.** The act of joining together living body tissue by or as if by sewing. **b.** The material used in this procedure, as thread, gut, or wire. **2.** A seamlike joint or line of juction, as between two bones of the skull. —*tr.v.* **-tured, -tur·ing.** To join by means of sutures; sew up. [Old French, from Latin *sūtūra*, from *sūtus*, past part. of *suere*, to sew.] —**su'tur·al** *adj.*

su·ze·rain (soo'zər-ən, -zə-rān') *n.* **1.** A feudal lord. **2.** A nation that controls another nation in international affairs but allows it domestic sovereignty. [French : *sus*, up, above, + (*souv*)*erain*, from Old French *souverain*, sovereign.] —**su'ze·rain·ty** *n.*

svelte (sfĕlt) *adj.* **svelt·er, svelt·est.** Slender or graceful in figure or outline; willowy. [French, from Italian *svelto*, from *svellere*, to stretch, from Latin *evellere* : *ex-*, out + *vellere*, to pull.]

swab (swŏb). Also **swob.** —*n.* **1.** A small piece of cotton or other absorbent material attached to the end of a stick or wire and used for cleansing or applying medicine. **2.** A mop used for cleaning floors or decks. **3.** *Slang.* A sailor. —*tr.v.* **swabbed, swab·bing.** To clean or treat with a swab. [Prob. from Middle Dutch *swabbe*, mop.]

swad·dle (swŏd'l) *tr.v.* **-dled, -dling. 1.** To wrap or bind closely; swathe. **2.** To wrap (a baby) in swaddling clothes. —*n.* A cloth used for swaddling. [Middle English *swadlen,* from *swethel,* swaddling clothes, from Old English *swæthel,* prob. from *swathian,* to swathe.]

swaddling clothes. 1. Strips of cloth formerly wrapped around a newborn infant to hold its legs and arms still. **2.** Restrictions imposed upon the immature.

swag (swăg) *n.* **1.** An ornamental hanging draped in a curve between two points. **2.** *Slang.* Stolen property; loot. [Prob. of Scandinavian orig.]

swage (swāj) *n.* A tool used in bending or shaping cold metal. —*tr.v.* **swaged, swag·ing.** To bend or shape with a swage. [Middle English, from Old French *souaige.*]

swag·ger (swăg'ər) *intr.v.* **1.** To walk or behave with an insolent air; strut. **2.** To brag; bluster. —*n.* A swaggering movement, gait, or expression. [Prob. from SWAG.] —**swag'ger·er** *n.*

swagger stick. A short metal-tipped cane carried esp. by military officers.

Swa·hi·li (swä-hē'lē) *n., pl.* **Swahili** or **-lis. 1.** A Bantu language of eastern and central Africa, widely used as a lingua franca. **2.** A member of a Bantu people of Zanzibar and the neighboring mainland.

swain (swān) *n.* **1.** A country youth. **2.** A lover. [Middle English *swein,* from Old Norse *sveinn,* herdsman.]

swale (swāl) *n.* A low tract of usu. marshy land. [Middle English, shady place, perh. of Scandinavian orig.]

swal·low¹ (swŏl'ō) *tr.v.* **1.** To cause to pass through the mouth and throat into the stomach. **2.** To consume or destroy as if by ingestion; devour. **3.** To bear humbly; tolerate: *swallow an insult.* **4.** *Slang.* To believe without question. **5.** To refrain from expressing; suppress. **6.** To take back; retract: *swallow one's words.* —*intr.v.* To perform the act of swallowing. —See Syns at **believe.** —*n.* **1.** The act of swallowing; a gulp. **2.** The amount swallowed at one time. [Middle English *swalowen,* from Old English *swelgan.*] —**swal'low·er** *n.*

swallow²
George Miksch Sutton

swan

swal·low² (swŏl'ō) *n.* Any of various birds of the family Hirundinidae, with long, pointed wings and a usu. notched or forked tail. [Middle English *swalowe,* from Old English *swealewe.*]

swal·low·tail (swŏl'ō-tāl') *n.* **1.** A deeply forked tail, as of a swallow. **2.** Any of various butterflies of the family Papilionidae, with a taillike extension at the end of each hind wing. —**swal'low·tailed'** *adj.*

swam (swăm) *v.* Past tense of **swim.** [Middle English, from Old English.]

swa·mi (swä'mē) *n.* **-mis.** A Hindu mystic or religious teacher. [Hindi *svāmī,* master, from Sanskrit *svāmin,* owner, prince.]

swamp (swŏmp, swômp) *n.* A lowland region saturated with water; marsh. —*tr.v.* **1.** To drench in or cover with liquid. **2.** To overwhelm: *swamped with work.* **3.** To fill or sink (a ship) with water. —*intr.v.* To become full of water. [Perh. of Low German orig.]

swamp fever. Malaria.

swamp·land (swŏmp'lănd', swômp'-) *n.* Land covered with swamps.

swamp·y (swäm'pē, swôm'-) *adj.* **-i·er, -i·est.** Of or characterized by swamps; boggy; marshy. —**swamp'i·ness** *n.*

swan (swŏn) *n.* Any of various large aquatic birds, chiefly of the genera *Cygnus* and *Olor,* with webbed feet, a long slender neck, and usu. white plumage. [Middle English, from Old English.]

swan dive. A dive performed with the legs together, the back arched, and the arms stretched out to the sides.

swank (swăngk) *adj.* **-er, -est.** Also **swank·y** (swăng'kē) **-i·er, -i·est. 1.** Imposingly luxurious. **2.** Ostentatious. [Perh. from Middle High German *swanken,* to swing, from *swank,* a turn.] —**swank'i·ly** *adv.* —**swank'i·ness** *n.*

swan's-down (swŏnz'doun') *n.* Also **swans·down. 1.** The soft down of a swan. **2.** A soft woolen fabric.

swan song. 1. The legendary last utterance of a dying swan. **2.** A farewell or final appearance, declaration, or action, as by a retiring actor, writer, or athlete.

swap (swŏp) Also **swop.** *Informal.* —*v.* **swapped, swap·ping.** —*intr.v.* To exchange one thing for another; to trade. —*tr.v.* To exchange. —*n.* An exchange; trade. [Middle English *swappen,* to strike, hit (from the practice of striking hands in closing a bargain).] —**swap'per** *n.*

sward (swôrd) *n.* Land covered with grassy turf. [Middle English *swerd,* from Old English *sweard,* skin, rind of bacon.]

swarm¹ (swôrm) *n.* **1.** A large number of insects or other small organisms, esp. when in motion. **2. a.** A group of bees, with a queen bee, in migration to establish a new colony. **b.** Such a group of bees settled in a new hive. **3.** A large group of persons or animals, esp. when in motion. —*intr.v.* **1. a.** To move or emerge in a swarm. **b.** To leave a hive as a swarm. **2.** To move in a mass; to throng. **3.** To be overrun; teem: *a river bank swarming with insects.* —*tr.v.* To fill with a crowd. [Middle English, from Old English *swearm.*]

swarm² (swôrm) *tr.v.* To climb (as a tree or pole) by gripping with the arms and legs. —*intr.v.* To climb something in this way. [Orig. unknown.]

swar·thy (swôr'thē) *adj.* **-thi·er, -thi·est.** Having a dark or sunburned complexion. [Var. of obs. *swarty,* from *swart,* dusky, black.] —**swar'thi·ly** *adv.* —**swar'thi·ness** *n.*

swash (swŏsh, swôsh) *n.* **1.** A splash of liquid. **2.** A narrow channel through which tides flow. **3.** Swagger or bluster. —*intr.v.* **1.** To move or wash with a splashing sound. **2.** To swagger. —*tr.v.* To splash. [Prob. imit.]

swash·buck·ler (swŏsh'bŭk'lər, swôsh'-) *n.* A flamboyant or boastful soldier or adventurer. —**swash'buck'ling** *adj.*

swas·ti·ka (swŏs'tĭ-kə) *n.* **1.** An ancient cosmic or religious symbol, formed by a Greek cross with the ends of the arms bent at right angles. **2.** The emblem of Nazi Germany, officially adopted in 1935. [Sanskrit *svastika,* a sign of good luck, from *svasti,* good luck.]

swastika

swat (swŏt) *tr.v.* **swat·ted, swat·ting.** To deal a sharp blow to. —See Syns at **hit.** —*n.* A quick, sharp blow. [Var. of obs. *squat,* to lay flat with a blow.] —**swat'ter** *n.*

swatch (swŏch) *n.* A sample strip cut from a piece of cloth or other material. [Origin unknown.]

swath (swŏth, swôth) *n.* **1.** The width of a scythe stroke or a mowing-machine blade. **2.** A path of this width made in mowing. **3.** A long strip or width. [Middle English *swathe,* from Old English *swæth,* track, trace.]

swathe (swŏth, swôth) *tr.v.* **swathed, swath·ing. 1.** To wrap or bind with bindings or bandages. **2.** To enfold or surround. —*n.* A wrapping, binding, or bandage. [Middle

ă pat ā pay â care ä father ĕ pet ē be hw which ĭ pit ī tie î pier ŏ pot ō toe ô paw, for oi noise
ōō took ōō boot ou out th thin *th* this ŭ cut û urge zh vision ə about, item, edible, gallop, circus

English *swathen,* from Old English *swathian,* to wrap up.]

sway (swā) *intr.v.* **1.** To move back and forth with a swinging motion. **2.** To lean or bend to one side. **3.** To vacillate. —*tr.v.* **1.** To cause to swing from side to side. **2.** To cause to lean or bend toward one side. **3. a.** To deter dissuade. **b.** To exert influence on or control over. —See Syns at **affect.** —*n.* **1.** The act of swaying. **2.** Power; dominion: *when the Romans held sway.* **3.** Influence; pressure. [Middle English *sweyen,* to move, prob. from Old Norse *sveigja,* to bend.]

sway·back (swā'băk') *n.* An excessive inward or downward curvature of the spine. —**sway'backed'** *adj.*

swear (swâr) *v.* **swore** (swôr, swōr), **sworn** (swôrn, swōrn), **swear·ing.** —*intr.v.* **1.** To make a solemn declaration: *I swear to you I spoke the truth.* **2.** To promise; vow. **3.** To use profane language; to curse. **4.** *Law.* To give evidence or testimony under oath. —*tr.v.* **1.** To declare or affirm solemnly. **2.** To promise or pledge with a solemn oath; vow: *swear his loyalty.* **3.** To utter or bind oneself to. **4.** *Law.* To administer a legal oath to. —*phrasal verbs.* **swear by.** To have great reliance upon or confidence in. **swear in.** To administer an oath of office to. **swear off.** To pledge to renounce; to give up. —See Syns at **abandon. swear out.** To obtain (a warrant for someone's arrest) by making a charge under oath. [Middle English *swerien,* from Old English *swerian.*]

swear·word (swâr'wûrd') *n.* An obscene or blasphemous word.

sweat (swĕt) *v.* **sweat·ed** or **sweat, sweat·ing.** —*intr.v.* **1.** To excrete perspiration through the pores in the skin; perspire. **2.** To exude moisture or sap in droplets. **3.** To collect moisture from the air. **4.** *Informal.* To work long and hard. **6.** *Informal.* To fret or worry. —*tr.v.* **1.** To excrete (moisture) through a porous surface. **2.** To gather and condense (moisture) on a surface. **3.** To cause to perspire. **4.** To make damp or wet with perspiration. **5.** To overwork esp. at low pay. —*phrasal verb.* **sweat out.** *Slang.* **1.** To await or endure anxiously. **2.** To attempt to cure by sweating: *sweat out a cold.* —*n.* **1.** The product of the sweat glands of the skin. **2.** Any condensation of moisture in the form of droplets on a surface. **3.** The process of sweating or the condition of being sweated. **4.** *Informal.* An anxious, fretful condition. [Middle English *sweten,* from Old English *swǣtan.*]

sweat·band (swĕt'bănd') *n.* **1.** A band of fabric or leather sewn inside the crown of a hat as protection against sweat. **2.** A cloth tied around the forehead to absorb sweat.

sweat·er (swĕt'ər) *n.* A garment made of knit, crocheted, or woven wool, worn on the upper part of the body.

sweat gland. Any of the numerous small, tubular glands in the skin that excrete perspiration externally through pores.

sweat shirt. A usu. long-sleeved cotton-jersey pullover.

sweat·shop (swĕt'shŏp') *n.* A shop or factory where employees work long hours for low wages.

sweat·y (swĕt'ē) *adj.* **-i·er, i·est.** **1.** Covered with or smelling of sweat. **2.** Causing sweat. —**sweat'i·ness** *n.*

Swede (swēd) *n.* **1.** A native or inhabitant of Sweden. **2.** A person of Swedish descent.

Swed·ish (swē'dĭsh) *adj.* Of or pertaining to Sweden, the Swedes, or their culture or language. —*n.* The Germanic language of Sweden.

sweep (swēp) *v.* **swept** (swĕpt), **sweep·ing.** —*tr.v.* **1.** To clean or clear the surface of with or as if with a broom or brush. **2.** To clean or clear away (as dust or dirt) with or as if with a broom or brush. **3.** To clear (a space) with or as if with a broom. **4.** To touch or brush lightly with or as if with a trailing garment. **5.** To move, remove, or convey with a flowing motion. **6.** To traverse with speed or intensity range throughout: *Plague swept Europe.* **7.** To drag the bottom of (a body of water). **8. a.** To win all the stages of (a game or contest). **b.** To win overwhelmingly. —*intr.v.* **1.** To clear or clean a surface with or as if with a broom or brush. **2.** To move, surge, or flow with smooth and steady force. **3.** To move swiftly or majestically: *She swept by in silence.* **4.** To trail, as a garment. **5.** To extend gracefully or majestically. —*n.* **1.** The act or motion of sweeping. **2.** The range or scope encompassed by sweeping. **3.** A reach or extent. **4.** A surging or flowing move-

ment, force, or process. **5.** Any curve, bend, or contour. **6.** A person who sweeps, esp. a chimney sweep. **7. a.** The winning of all stages of a game or contest. **b.** A total victory or success. —See Syns at **range.** [Middle English *sweepen.*] —**sweep'er** *n.*

sweep·ing (swē'pĭng) *adj.* **1.** Moving, influencing, or extending over a great area; wide-ranging: *sweeping changes.* **2.** Curving in form or motion. —*n.* Often **sweepings.** That which is swept up; debris; litter. —**sweep'ing·ly** *adv.*

sweep·stakes (swēp'stāks') *n., pl.* **sweepstakes.** Also **sweep·stake** (-stāk'). **1.** A lottery in which the participants' contributions form a fund to be awarded as a prize to the winner or winners. **2.** Any event or contest, esp. a horse race, whose result determines the winner of such a lottery.

sweet (swēt) *adj.* **-er, -est. 1.** Having a sugary or pleasing taste. **2.** Pleasing to the senses, feelings, or the mind; gratifying. **3.** Having an agreeable or pleasing disposition. **4.** Dear; beloved. **5.** Not salty or salted: *sweet water.* **6.** Not spoiled, sour, or decaying; fresh: *sweet soil.* **7.** Free of acid. —*n.* **1.** Something that is sweet or contains sugar. **2.** Often **sweets.** Candy, preserves, or confections. **3.** *Brit.* Dessert. [Middle English *sweete,* from Old English *swēte.*] —**sweet'ly** *adv.* —**sweet'ness** *n.*

sweet a·lys·sum (ə-lĭs'əm). A widely cultivated Mediterranean plant, *Lobularia maritima,* with clusters of small, fragrant white or purplish flowers.

sweet·bread (swēt'brĕd') *n.* The thymus or pancreas of an animal, used for food.

sweet·bri·er (swēt'brī'ər) *n.* Also **sweet·bri·ar.** A rose, *Rosa eglanteria,* native to Europe, with prickly stems, fragrant leaves, and pink flowers. Also called **eglantine.**

sweet corn. The common edible variety of corn, *Zea mays rugosa,* with kernels that are sweet when young.

sweet·en (swēt'n) *tr.v.* **1.** To make sweet or sweeter. **2.** To make more valuable or attractive. —*intr.v.* To become sweet. —**sweet'en·er** *n.*

sweet·en·ing (swēt'n-ĭng) *n.* A sweetener.

sweet fern. An aromatic shrub, *Myrica asplenifolia* (or *Comptonia peregrina*), of eastern North America.

sweet flag. A marsh plant, *Acorus calamus,* with blade-like leaves, minute greenish flowers, and aromatic roots. Also called **calamus.**

sweet gum. **1.** A New World tree, *Liquidambar styraciflua,* with sharply lobed leaves and prickly, ball-like fruit clusters. **2.** The aromatic resin obtained from this tree.

sweet·heart (swēt'härt') *n.* **1.** A person who loves and is loved by another. **2.** A lovable or generous person.

sweet·ing (swē'tĭng) *n.* A sweet apple.

sweet·meat (swēt'mēt') *n.* **1.** Candy. **2.** Crystallized fruit. [SWEET + MEAT (food).]

sweet pea. A climbing plant, *Lathyrus odoratus,* cultivated for its variously colored, fragrant flowers.

sweet pea

sweet pepper. The bell pepper.

sweet potato. **1.** A tropical American vine, *Ipomoea batatas,* cultivated for its thick, orange-colored, edible root. **2.** The root of this plant, eaten cooked as a vegetable.

sweet tooth. *Informal.* A fondness or craving for sweets.

sweet Wil·liam (wĭl'yəm). A widely cultivated plant, *Dianthus barbatus,* with flat, dense clusters of varicolored flowers.

ă pat　ā pay　â care　ä father　ĕ pet　ē be　hw which　ĭ pit　ī tie　î pier　ŏ pot　ō toe　ô paw, for　oi noise
ŏŏ took　ōō boot　ou out　th thin　*th* this　ŭ cut　û urge　zh vision　ə about, item, edible, gallop, circus

swell (swĕl) *v.* **swelled, swelled** or **swol·len** (swō′lən), **swell·ing.** —*intr.v.* **1.** To increase in size or volume as a result of internal pressure; expand. **2. a.** To increase in force, size, number, or degree: *Membership swelled.* **b.** To grow in loudness or intensity, as a sound. **3.** To bulge out; protrude. **4.** To rise in billows. **5.** To be or become filled or puffed up with an emotion: *swelled with pride.* —*tr.v.* **1.** To cause to increase in force, size, number, degree, or intensity: *swell our ranks.* **2.** To cause to protrude or bulge. **3.** To inflate with emotion. —See Syns at **increase.** —*n.* **1.** The act of swelling or the condition of being swollen. **2.** A swollen part. **3.** A long wave that moves continuously without breaking. **4.** A rounded hill. **5.** *Informal.* A person who is fashionably dressed or prominent in fashionable society. **6.** *Mus.* **a.** A crescendo followed by a gradual diminuendo. **b.** The sign indicating this. **c.** A device on an organ or harpsichord for regulating volume. —*adj.* **-er, -est.** *Informal.* **1.** Fashionably elegant; smart; stylish. **2.** *Slang.* Fine; excellent. —See Syns at **excellent.** [Middle English *swellen,* from Old English *swellan.*]
swell·ing (swĕl′ĭng) *n.* Something that is swollen, esp. an abnormally swollen or protuberant bodily part.
swel·ter (swĕl′tər) *intr.v.* To suffer from heat. —*tr.v.* To affect with oppressive heat. —*n.* Oppressive heat and humidity. [Middle English *swelteren,* freq. of *swelten,* to die, faint from heat, from Old English *sweltan,* to die.]
swept (swĕpt) *v.* Past tense and past participle of **sweep.**
swept·back (swĕpt′băk′) *adj.* Angled rearward from the points of attachment.
swerve (swûrv) *v.* **swerved, swerv·ing.** —*intr.v.* To turn aside from a straight course; veer. —*tr.v.* To cause to veer; deflect. —*n.* An act of swerving. [Middle English *swerven,* from Old English *sweorfan,* to file away, scour.]
swift (swĭft) *adj.* **-er, -est. 1.** Moving with great speed; fast; fleet. **2.** Occurring or accomplished quickly: *a swift retort.* **3.** Prompt: *swift to take steps.* —*adv.* Quickly; fast. —See Syns at **fast.** —*n.* Any of various dark-colored birds of the family Apodidae, with long, narrow wings and a relatively short tail. [Middle English, from Old English.] —**swift′ly** *adv.* —**swift′ness** *n.*
swig (swĭg). *Informal.* —*n.* A large swallow or draft, as of a liquid; a gulp. —*v.* **swigged, swig·ging.** —*tr.v.* To drink with great gulps. —*intr.v.* To take a large swallow. [Orig. unknown.] —**swig′ger** *n.*
swill (swĭl) *tr.v.* **1.** To drink eagerly, greedily, or to excess. **2.** To feed (animals) with slop. —*intr.v.* To drink greedily. —*n.* **1.** A mixture of liquid and solid food fed to animals. **2.** Garbage; refuse. **3.** A large swallow. [Middle English *swilen,* from Old English *swilian,* to wash out.]
swim (swĭm) *v.* **swam** (swăm), **swum, swim·ming.** —*intr.v.* **1.** To propel oneself through water by means of movements of the body. **2.** To move as though gliding through water. **3.** To float on water or other liquid. **4.** To be immersed: *chicken swimming in gravy.* **5.** To have a dizzy feeling; to reel. —*tr.v.* To cross (a body of water) by swimming. —*n.* **1.** The act or a period of swimming. **2.** A condition of dizziness. —*idiom.* **in the swim.** *Informal.* Participating in what is current or fashionable. [Middle English *swimmen,* from Old English *swimman.*] —**swim′mer** *n.*
swim bladder. An organ of fishes, the air bladder.
swim·mer·et (swĭm′ə-rĕt′) *n.* One of the paired abdominal appendages of certain aquatic crustaceans that function as organs of respiration or locomotion. [Dim. of *swimmer,* appendage used in swimming, from SWIM.]
swim·ming·ly (swĭm′ĭng-lē) *adv.* Splendidly.
swimming pool. A pool constructed for swimming.
swim·suit (swĭm′sōōt′) *n.* A garment worn while swimming.
swin·dle (swĭn′dl) *v.* **-dled, -dling.** —*tr.v.* **1.** To cheat or defraud of money or property. **2.** To obtain (as money or property) by fraudulent means. —*intr.v.* To practice fraud. —*n.* An act of swindling; a fraud. [Back-formation from *swindler,* from German *Schwindler,* from *schwindeln,* to be dizzy, cheat, from Old High German *swintilōn,* freq. of *swintan,* to vanish, languish, become unconscious.] —**swin′dler** *n.*
swine (swīn) *n., pl.* **swine. 1.** Any of the hoofed mammals of the family Suidae, which includes pigs, hogs, and boars.

2. A contemptible, vicious, or greedy person. [Middle English, from Old English *swin.*]
swine·herd (swīn′hûrd′) *n.* A keeper or tender of swine.
swing (swĭng) *v.* **swung** (swŭng), **swing·ing.** —*intr.v.* **1.** To move rhythmically back and forth suspended from above. **2.** *Sports.* To attempt to strike a ball with a sweeping motion of the arm. **3.** To move smoothly and vigorously: *swing over to the curb.* **4.** To turn in place, as on a pivot. **5.** *Slang.* To be executed by hanging. **6.** To have or play with a compelling or infectious rhythm. **7.** *Slang.* To be lively or active. —*tr.v.* **1.** To cause to move backward and forward. **2.** To cause to move in a broad arc: *swing a bat.* **3.** To move with a sweeping motion: *swung his arms.* **4.** To hang or suspend freely. **5.** To cause to change direction or position. **6.** *Slang.* To manipulate or manage successfully: *Can you swing this deal?* —*n.* **1.** The act of swinging, esp.: **a.** A rhythmic back-and-forth movement. **b.** A single movement of or as if of a suspended object. **2.** The space traveled while swinging. **3.** Freedom of movement or action; license. **4.** A swaying, graceful motion. **5.** A seat suspended from above, on which one may ride back and forth in an arc for recreation. **6.** A form of popular dance music developed about 1935 and based on jazz but employing a larger band and simpler harmonic and rhythmic patterns. —*idiom.* **in full swing.** At full speed or intensity. [Middle English *swingen,* from Old English *swingan,* to whip, strike, fling oneself.]
swin·gle·tree (swĭng′gəl-trē) *n.* A whiffletree. [From *swingle,* wooden instrument for beating hemp, from Middle English, from Middle Dutch *swinghel.*]
swing shift. *Informal.* A factory work shift between the day and night shifts, lasting from about 4 P.M. to midnight.
swin·ish (swī′nĭsh) *adj.* Resembling or befitting swine.
swipe (swīp) *n.* A heavy, sweeping blow. —*tr.v.* **swiped, swip·ing. 1.** To hit with a sweeping blow. **2.** *Slang.* To steal; filch. [Prob. alteration of SWEEP.]
swirl (swûrl) *intr.v.* **1.** To rotate or spin in or as if in a whirlpool or eddy. **2.** To be dizzy or faint. —*tr.v.* To cause to swirl. —*n.* **1.** The motion of whirling or spinning. **2.** Something that is swirled. [Middle English *swyrl,* eddy, whirlpool, prob. of Low German orig.]
swish (swĭsh) *intr.v.* **1.** To move with a whistle or hiss. **2.** To rustle. —*tr.v.* To cause to swish. —*n.* A sharp whistling or rustling sound or movement. [Imit.]
Swiss (swĭs) *adj.* Of or characteristic of Switzerland or its inhabitants. —*n., pl.* **Swiss. 1.** A native or inhabitant of Switzerland. **2.** A person of Swiss descent.
Swiss chard. A vegetable, chard.
Swiss cheese. A firm white or pale-yellow cheese with many large holes, orig. produced in Switzerland.
switch (swĭch) *n.* **1.** A slender flexible rod, stick, or twig. **2.** The bushy tip of the tail of certain animals, as cows. **3.** A thick bunch of real or synthetic hair used in a coiffure. **4.** A flailing or lashing, as with a slender rod. **5.** A device used to break or open an electrical circuit or to divert current from one conductor to another. **6.** A device consisting of two sections of railroad track and the accompanying apparatus, used to transfer rolling stock from one track to another. **7.** A change or shift, as of opinion or attention. —*tr.v.* **1.** To whip or lash with or as if with a switch. **2.** To jerk or move abruptly or sharply. **3.** To change or divert. **4.** To exchange: *switch sides.* **5.** To connect, disconnect, or divert (an electric current) by operating a switch. **6.** To move (rolling stock) from one track to another; shunt. —*intr.v.* To shift or change. [Perh. from Middle Dutch *swijch,* bough, twig.] —**switch′er** *n.*
switch·back (swĭch′băk′) *n.* A road, roadbed, or trail that ascends a steep incline in a winding course.
switch·blade knife (swĭch′blād′). A pocket knife with a spring-operated blade.
switch·board (swĭch′bôrd′, -bōrd′) *n.* One or more panels accommodating apparatus for operating electric circuits.
switch hitter. *Baseball.* A batter who can hit both right-handed and left-handed.
switch·man (swĭch′mən) *n.* A person who operates railroad switches.
switch·yard (swĭch′yärd′) *n.* An area where railroad cars are switched and trains are assembled.

| ă pat | ā pay | â care | ä father | ĕ pet | ē be | hw which | ĭ pit | ī tie | î pier | ŏ pot | ō toe | ô paw, for | oi noise |
| ŏŏ took | ōō boot | ou out | th thin | th this | ŭ cut | | û urge | zh vision | ə about, item, edible, gallop, circus |

swiv·el (swĭv′əl) n. **1.** A link, pivot, or other fastening that permits free turning of attached parts. **2.** A pivoted support that allows an attached object, such as a chair or gun, to turn in a horizontal plane. —v. **-eled** or **-elled, -el·ing** or **-el·ling.** —tr.v. To turn or rotate on or as on a swivel. —intr.v. To turn on a swivel. [Middle English swyvel.]

swivel chair. A chair that swivels on its base.

swiz·zle stick (swĭz′əl). A rod for stirring drinks. [Orig. unknown.]

swob (swŏb) n. & v. Var. of **swab.**

swol·len (swō′lən) v. A past participle of **swell.** [Middle English, from Old English (ge)swollen.]

swoon (swoon) intr.v. To faint. —n. A fainting spell. [Middle English swounen, prob. from Old English swōgan, to suffocate.]

swoop (swoop) intr.v. To make a sudden sweeping movement, as a bird descending upon its prey. —tr.v. To take or snatch suddenly. —n. The act of swooping; a swift, sudden descent. [Middle English swopen, to sweep along, from Old English swāpan, to sweep.]

swop (swŏp) v. & n. Var. of **swap.**

sword (sôrd) n. **1.** A weapon having a long blade for cutting or thrusting. **2.** An instrument of death, combat, or destruction. **3.** Often **the sword.** The use of force, as in war. —idioms. **at swords' points.** Antagonistic. **cross swords. 1.** To fight. **2.** To quarrel violently. [Middle English, from Old English sword.]

sword·fish (sôrd′fĭsh′) n., pl. **swordfish** or **-fish·es.** A large saltwater game and food fish, Xiphias gladius, with a long, swordlike extension of the upper jaw.

sword·knot (sôrd′nŏt′) n. A decorative loop or tassle attached to the hilt of a sword.

sword·play (sôrd′plā′) n. The action of using a sword.

swords·man (sôrdz′mən) n. A person armed with or skilled in the use of the sword. —swords′man·ship′ n.

swore (swôr, swōr) v. Past tense of **swear.** [Middle English, from Old English swor.]

sworn (swôrn, swōrn) v. Past participle of **swear.** [Middle English, from Old English (ge)sworen.]

swounds (zwoundz, zoundz) interj. Var. of **zounds.**

swum (swŭm) v. Past participle and archaic past tense of **swim.** [Middle English swommen, swumme, from Old English (ge)swummen, swummon (pl.).]

swung (swŭng) v. Past tense and past participle of **swing.** [Middle English swong, (i)swungen, from Old English swungon (pl.), (ge)swungen.]

syb·a·rite (sĭb′ər-īt′) n. A person totally devoted to pleasure and luxury. [Latin Sybarita, native of Sybaris, from Greek Subaritēs.] —syb′a·rit′ic (-ə-rĭt′ĭk) or syb′a·rit′i·cal adj.

syc·a·more (sĭk′ə-môr′, -mōr′) n. **1.** A deciduous tree, Platanus occidentalis, of eastern North America, with lobed leaves and ball-like seed clusters. Also called **buttonwood. 2.** A fig tree, Ficus sycomorus, of the Middle East. [Middle English sicamour, from Old French sicamor, from Latin sycomorus, from Greek sukamoros.]

syc·o·phant (sĭk′ə-fənt, -fănt′) n. A flatterer of important persons; a servile self-seeker. [Latin sycophanta, from Greek sukophantēs, informer, flatterer.] —syc′o·phan·cy n. —syc′o·phan′tic (-făn′tĭk) or syc′o·phan′ti·cal adj.

sy·e·nite (sī′ə-nīt′) n. An igneous rock composed primarily of alkali feldspar. [Latin Syēnītēs (lapis), "(stone) of Syene," from Syēnē, Syene, an ancient name for Aswan.]

syl·lab·ic (sĭ-lăb′ĭk) adj. **1.** Of or consisting of syllables. **2.** Forming a syllable without a vowel, as the l in riddle (rĭd′l). **3.** Pronouncing every syllable distinctly. —n. A syllabic sound. —syl·lab′i·cal·ly adv.

syl·lab·i·cate (sĭ-lăb′ĭ-kāt′) tr.v. **-cat·ed, -cat·ing.** To form or divide into syllables. —syl·lab′i·ca′tion n.

syl·lab·i·fy (sĭ-lăb′ə-fī′) tr.v. **-fied, -fy·ing.** To syllabicate.

syl·la·ble (sĭl′ə-bəl) n. **1.** A unit of spoken language consisting of a single uninterrupted sound formed by a vowel or diphthong alone, or a syllabic consonant alone, or of either with one or more consonants. **2.** One or more letters or phonetic symbols written or printed to approximate a spoken syllable. **3.** The slightest bit or expression. —tr.v. **-bled, -bling.** To pronounce in syllables. [Middle English sillable, from Old French sillabe, from Latin syllaba, from

Greek sullabē, a gathering (of letters), from sullambanein, to gather together : sun-, together + lambanein, to take.]

syl·la·bub (sĭl′ə-bŭb′) n. Also **sil·la·bub.** A drink or dessert consisting of wine or liquor mixed with sweetened milk or cream. [Orig. unknown.]

syl·la·bus (sĭl′ə-bəs) n., pl. **-bus·es** or **-bi** (-bī′). An outline or brief statement of the main points of a text, lecture, or course of study. [Medieval Latin, list, from Greek sullabus, book title, label, table of contents.]

syl·lo·gism (sĭl′ə-jĭz′əm) n. **1.** Logic. A form of deductive reasoning consisting of a major premise, a minor premise, and a conclusion; for example, All men are foolish (major premise); Smith is a man (minor premise); therefore, Smith is foolish (conclusion). **2.** Logical deduction. [Middle English silogisme, from Old French, from Latin syllogismus, from Greek sullogismos, from sullogizesthai, to infer : sun-, together + logizesthai, to reason, from logos, word, computation.] —syl′lo·gis′tic adj. —syl′lo·gis′ti·cal·ly adv.

sylph (sĭlf) n. **1.** An imaginary being believed to inhabit the air. **2.** A slim, graceful woman. [New Latin sylphus, prob. from Latin sylvestris nympha, "nymph of the woods."]

syl·van (sĭl′vən) adj. Also **sil·van. 1.** Of or characteristic of woods or forest regions. **2.** Wooded. [Medieval Latin silvānus, from Latin silva, forest.]

sym-. Var. of **syn-.**

sym·bi·ont (sĭm′bī-ŏnt′, -bē′-) n. One of the organisms in a symbiotic relationship. [From Greek sumbiōn, pres. part. of sumbioun, to live together.]

sym·bi·o·sis (sĭm′bī-ō′sĭs, -bē-) n. Biol. The living together of two or more different organisms in a close association, esp. when mutually beneficial. [Greek sumbiōsis, a living together, from sumbioun, to live together : sun-, together + bios, life.] —sym′bi·ot′ic (-ŏt′ĭk) or sym′bi·ot′i·cal adj. —sym′bi·ot′i·cal·ly adv.

sym·bol (sĭm′bəl) n. **1.** Something that represents something else by association, resemblance, or convention. **2.** A printed or written sign used to represent an operation, element, quantity, quality, or relation, as in mathematics or music. —tr.v. To symbolize. [Latin symbolum, token, from Greek sumbolon, token for identification, from sumballein, to compare : sun-, together + ballein, to throw.]

sym·bol·ic (sĭm-bŏl′ĭk) or **sym·bol·i·cal** (-ĭ-kəl) adj. **1.** Of, serving as, or expressed by a symbol. **2.** Characterized by the use of symbols. —sym·bol′i·cal·ly adv.

sym·bol·ism (sĭm′bə-lĭz′əm) n. **1.** The practice of using symbols. **2.** A system of symbols or representations.

sym·bol·ist (sĭm′bə-lĭst) n. **1.** A person who uses symbols or symbolism. **2.** A person who interprets symbols. —sym·bol·is′tic or sym·bol·is′ti·cal adj.

sym·bol·ize (sĭm′bə-līz′) v. **-ized, -iz·ing.** —tr.v. **1.** To be or serve as a symbol of: The dove symbolizes peace. **2.** To represent by a symbol. —intr.v. To use symbols. —See Syns at **represent.** —sym′bol·i·za′tion n.

sym·bol·o·gy (sĭm-bŏl′ə-jē) n. The study of symbols.

sym·met·ric (sĭ-mĕt′rĭk) or **sym·met·ri·cal** (-rĭ-kəl) adj. Of or showing symmetry. —sym·met′ri·cal·ly adv.

sym·me·try (sĭm′ĭ-trē) n., pl. **-tries. 1.** Correspondence of form and arrangement of parts on opposite sides of a boundary, such as a plane or line, or around a point or axis. **2.** Balanced proportions or harmonious arrangement. [Obs. French symmetrie, from Latin symmetria, from Greek summetria : sun-, like, same + metron, measure.]

sym·pa·thet·ic (sĭm′pə-thĕt′ĭk) adj. **1.** Of, expressing, feeling, or resulting from sympathy. **2.** In agreement; favorable: They were sympathetic to our proposal. **3.** In accord with one's disposition or mood; congenial: a sympathetic relationship. [From Greek sumpathetikos, from sumpatheia, sympathy.] —sym′pa·thet′i·cal·ly adv.

sympathetic nervous system. A portion of the autonomic nervous system.

sym·pa·thize (sĭm′pə-thīz′) intr.v. **-thized, -thiz·ing. 1.** To feel or express compassion. **2.** To share or understand another's feelings or ideas. —sym′pa·thiz′er n.

sym·pa·thy (sĭm′pə-thē) n., pl. **-thies. 1. a.** A relationship between persons or things in which whatever affects one correspondingly affects the other. **b.** Mutual understanding or affection. **2.** The act of or capacity for sharing or understanding the feelings of another. **b.** A feeling or expression of sorrow for the distress of another; compassion. **3.** Favor; agreement; accord. [Latin *sympathīa,* from Greek *sumpatheia* : *sun-,* like + *pathos,* emotion, feelings.]

sym·phon·ic (sĭm-fŏn′ĭk) *adj.* **1.** Of or having the character or form of a symphony. **2.** Harmonious in sound.

sym·pho·ny (sĭm′fə-nē) *n., pl.* **-nies. 1.** A usu. long orchestral composition, often consisting of four movements. **2. a.** A symphony orchestra. **b.** An orchestral concert. **3.** Harmony, esp. of sound or color. [Middle English *symphonie,* harmony of sound, from Old French, from Latin *symphōnia,* from Greek *sumphōnia* : *sun-,* together + *phōnē,* voice, sound.]

symphony orchestra

symphony orchestra. A large orchestra of string, wind, and percussion sections, for playing symphonic works.

sym·po·si·um (sĭm-pō′zē-əm) *n., pl.* **-si·ums** or **-si·a** (-zē-ə). **1.** A conference for discussion of some topic. **2.** A collection of writings on a topic. [Latin, from Greek *sumposion,* drinking party : *sun-,* together + *posis,* drink.]

symp·tom (sĭmp′təm) *n.* **1.** A change in normal bodily function, sensation, or appearance, indicating disorder or disease. **2.** An indication. —See Syns at **sign.** [Late Latin *symptōma,* from Greek *sumptōma,* occurrence, phenomenon, from *sumpiptein,* to happen : *sun-,* together + *piptein,* to fall.]

symp·to·mat·ic (sĭmp′tə-măt′ĭk) *adj.* **1.** Indicating or accompanying a disorder or disease: *symptomatic of the flu.* **2.** Indicative; characteristic. —**symp′to·mat′i·cal·ly** *adv.*

syn- or **sym-.** A prefix meaning together or with: **syncline.** [Greek *sun-,* from *sun,* together, with.]

syn·a·gogue (sĭn′ə-gŏg′) *n.* **1.** A building or place of meeting for Jewish worship and religious instruction. **2.** A congregation of Jews for worship or religious study. [Middle English *synagoge,* from Old French, from Latin *synagōga,* from Greek *sunagōgē,* assembly : *sun-,* together + *agein,* to lead.]

syn·apse (sĭn′ăps′) *n.* The point at which a nerve impulse passes between nerve cells. [From Greek *sunapsis,* point of contact, from *sunaptein,* to join together : *sun-,* together + *haptein,* to connect.]

sync (sĭngk). *Informal. n.* Synchronization. —*intr.v.* To synchronize. —*tr.v.* To synchronize with another.

synchro-. A prefix meaning synchronization: **synchromesh.** [From SYNCHRONIZE.]

syn·chro·mesh (sĭn′krō-mĕsh′, sĭn′-) *n.* **1.** An automotive gear-shifting system in which the gears are synchronized at the same speeds before engaging to effect a smooth change. **2.** A gear in such a system. —**syn′chro·mesh′** *adj.*

syn·chro·nism (sĭng′krə-nĭz′əm, sĭn′-) *n.* **1.** The quality or condition of being synchronous. **2.** A chronological listing of historical events so as to indicate simultaneity.

syn·chro·nize (sĭng′krə-nīz′, sĭn′-) *v.* **-nized, -niz·ing.** —*intr.v.* **1.** To occur at the same time; be simultaneous. **2.** To operate in unison. —*tr.v.* **1.** To cause to operate with exact coincidence in time or rate: *synchronize watches.* **2.** To arrange (historical events) so as to indicate parallel existence or occurrence. [From SYNCHRONOUS.] —**syn′chro·ni·za′tion** *n.* —**syn′chro·niz′er** *n.*

syn·chro·nous (sĭng′krə-nəs, sĭn′-) *adj.* **1.** Occurring at the same time. **2.** Moving or operating at the same rate or in phase: *synchronous vibrations.* [Late Latin *synchronos,*

from Greek *sunkhronos* : *sun-,* same + *khronos,* time.] —**syn′chro·nous·ly** *adv.* —**syn′chro·nous·ness** *n.*

syn·chro·tron (sĭng′krə-trŏn′, sĭn′-) *n.* An accelerator in which charged particles are accelerated around a fixed circular path. [SYNCHRO- + (ELEC)TRON.]

syn·cline (sĭng′klīn′, sĭn′-) *n.* A low, troughlike area in bedrock, in which rocks incline together from opposite sides. [SYN- + Greek *klinein,* to lean.] —**syn·clin′al** (sĭn-klī′nəl) *adj.*

syn·co·pate (sĭng′kə-pāt′, sĭn′-) *tr.v.* **-pat·ed, -pat·ing. 1.** To shorten (a word) by means of syncope. **2.** *Mus.* To modify (rhythm) by syncopation.

syn·co·pa·tion (sĭng′kə-pā′shən, sĭn′-) *n.* **1.** The act of syncopating or the condition of being syncopated. **2.** Something syncopated. **3.** *Mus.* A shift of accent that occurs when a normally weak beat is stressed. **4.** Syncope.

syn·co·pe (sĭng′kə-pē, sĭn′-) *n.* **1.** The shortening of a word by the omission of a sound, letter, or syllable from the middle of the word; for example, *bos'n* for *boatswain.* **2.** A fainting spell; a swoon. [Late Latin *syncopē,* from Greek *sunkopē,* from *sunkoptein,* to chop up, cut off : *sun-,* thoroughly + *koptein,* to cut off.]

syn·dic (sĭn′dĭk) *n.* **1.** A business representative, esp. of a university. **2.** A civil magistrate. [French, from Late Latin *syndicus,* from Greek *sundikos,* assistant in a court of justice, public advocate : *sun-,* with + *dike,* judgment.]

syn·di·cal·ism (sĭn′dĭ-kə-lĭz′əm) *n.* A radical political movement that advocates bringing industry and government under the control of labor unions by the use of direct action, such as general strikes and sabotage. [French *syndicalisme,* from *(chambre) syndicale,* trade union, from *syndic,* syndic.] —**syn′di·cal·ist** *n.*

syn·di·cate (sĭn′dĭ-kĭt) *n.* **1.** An association of people authorized to undertake some duty or transact some business. **2.** An agency that sells articles for publication in a number of newspapers or periodicals simultaneously. **3.** *Informal.* A loose group or association of racketeers in control of organized crime. —*v.* (-kāt′) **-cat·ed, -cat·ing.** —*tr.v.* **1.** To organize into a syndicate. **2.** To sell (as an article) through a syndicate for publication. —*intr.v.* To organize a syndicate. [French *syndicat,* from *syndic,* syndic.]

syn·drome (sĭn′drōm′) *n.* A group of symptoms that characterize a disease or disorder. [From Greek *sundromē,* a running together, concurrence (of symptoms) : *sun-,* together + *dromos,* race, racecourse.]

syn·ec·do·che (sĭ-nĕk′də-kē) *n.* A figure of speech by which a more inclusive term is used for a less inclusive term or vice versa; for example, *head* for *cattle* or *the law* for *a policeman.* [Latin, from Greek *sunekdokhē,* from *sunekdekhesthai,* to understand with another : *sun-,* with + *ekdekhesthai,* to understand in a certain sense.]

syn·er·gism (sĭn′ər-jĭz′əm) *n.* The action of two or more substances, organs, or organisms to achieve an effect of which each is individually incapable. [From Greek *sunergos,* working together : *sun-,* together + *ergon,* work.] —**syn′er·gis′tic** *adj.*

syn·od (sĭn′əd) *n.* **1.** A council of churches or church officials. **2.** Any council. [Middle English, from Late Latin *synodus,* from Greek *sunodos,* meeting : *sun-,* together + *hodos,* road, way, journey.] —**syn′od·al** *adj.*

sy·nod·i·cal (sĭ-nŏd′ĭ-kəl) or **sy·nod·ic** (-nŏd′ĭk) *adj.* **1.** Of or like a synod. **2.** Of the conjunction of celestial bodies, esp. the interval between two successive conjunctions of a planet or the moon with the sun.

syn·o·nym (sĭn′ə-nĭm′) *n.* **1.** A word that has a meaning similar to that of another word in the same language. **2.** An expression accepted as a figurative or symbolic substitute: *The White House is a synonym for the executive branch.* **3.** *Biol.* A taxonomic name that has been superseded by another designation. [Middle English *sinonyme,* from Latin *synonymum,* from Greek *sunōnumon,* from *sunōnumos,* synonymous.] —**syn′o·nym′i·ty** *n.*

syn·on·y·mize (sĭ-nŏn′ə-mīz′) *tr.v.* **-mized, -miz·ing.** To provide or analyze the synonyms of (a word).

syn·on·y·mous (sĭ-nŏn′ə-məs) *adj.* Expressing a similar meaning or significance. [Medieval Latin *synonymus,* from Greek *sunōnumos* : *sun-,* same + *onoma,* name.] —**syn·on′y·mous·ly** *adv.*

syn·on·y·my (sĭ-nŏn′ə-mē) *n.*, *pl.* **-mies. 1.** The condition or quality of being synonymous. **2.** The study and classification of synonyms. **3.** A list, book, or system of synonyms.

syn·op·sis (sĭ-nŏp′sĭs) *n.*, *pl.* **-ses** (-sēz′). A brief statement or outline of a subject; abstract. [Late Latin, from Greek *sunopsis*, a general view : *sun-*, together + *opsis*, view.]

syn·op·tic (sĭ-nŏp′tĭk) or **syn·op·ti·cal** (-tĭ-kəl) *adj.* **1.** Of or constituting a synopsis. **2.** Presenting an account from the same point of view. **3.** Often **Synoptic.** Of or designating the first three Gospels of the New Testament, which correspond closely. —**syn·op′ti·cal·ly** *adv.*

sy·no·vi·a (sĭ-nō′vē-ə) *n.* A clear, viscid lubricating fluid secreted by membranes in joint cavities and tendon sheaths. [New Latin.] —**sy·no′vi·al** *adj.*

syn·tac·tic (sĭn-tăk′tĭk) or **syn·tac·ti·cal** (-tĭ-kəl) *adj.* Of or according to the rules of syntax. —**syn·tac′ti·cal·ly** *adv.*

syn·tax (sĭn′tăks) *n.* **1. a.** The way in which words are put together to form phrases and sentences. **b.** The branch of grammar dealing with this. **2.** An orderly arrangement. [French *syntaxe*, from Late Latin *syntaxis*, from Greek *suntaxis*, from *suntassein*, to arrange in order : *sun-*, together + *tassein*, to arrange.]

syn·the·sis (sĭn′thĭ-sĭs) *n.*, *pl.* **-ses** (-sēz′). **1.** The combining of separate elements or substances to form a coherent whole. **2.** The whole formed in this manner. **3.** *Chem.* Formation of a compound from its constituents. **4.** *Philos.* The combination of thesis and antithesis in the dialectical process, producing a new and higher form of being. [Latin, from Greek, combination, from *suntithenai*, to put together : *sun-*, together + *tithenai*, to put.]

syn·the·size (sĭn′thĭ-sīz′) *tr.v.* **-sized, -siz·ing. 1.** To combine so as to form a new, complex product. **2.** To produce by combining separate elements: *synthesize a drug.*

syn·the·siz·er (sĭn′thĭ-sī′zər) *n.* **1.** Someone or something that synthesizes. **2.** A machine that has a simple keyboard using solid-state circuitry to duplicate the sounds of musical instruments.

syn·thet·ic (sĭn-thĕt′ĭk) *adj.* **1.** Involving or of the nature of synthesis. **2.** *Chem.* Produced by synthesis, esp. when not of natural origin; man-made. **3.** Not genuine; artificial. —See Syns at **artificial.** —*n.* A synthetic chemical compound or material. [Greek *sunthetikos*, component, from *sunthetos*, compounded, from *suntithenai*, to put together.] —**syn·thet′i·cal·ly** *adv.*

syph·i·lis (sĭf′ə-lĭs) *n.* A chronic infectious venereal disease caused by a spirochete, transmitted usu. in sexual intercourse, and progressing through three stages of increasing severity. [After *Syphilis*, title character of a Latin poem (1530) by Girolamo Fracastoro (1483–1553), Italian physician and poet.]

syph·i·lit·ic (sĭf′ə-lĭt′ĭk) *adj.* Of, pertaining to, or afflicted with syphilis. —**syph′i·lit′ic** *n.*

sy·phon (sĭ′fən) *n.* Var. of **siphon.**

Syr·i·ac (sĭr′ē-ăk′) *n.* An ancient Aramaic language surviving as the liturgical language of several eastern Christian churches.

sy·rin·ga (sĭ-rĭng′gə) *n.* A shrub, the mock orange. [From Greek *surinx*, pipe.]

syr·inge (sə-rĭnj′, sĭr′ĭnj) *n.* **1.** A medical instrument used to inject fluids into the body or draw them from it. **2.** A hypodermic syringe. [Middle English *syring*, from Medieval Latin *syringa*, from Greek *surinx*, pipe.]

syr·inx (sĭr′ĭngks) *n.*, *pl.* **sy·rin·ges** (sə-rĭng′gēz′, -rĭn′jēz′) or **-inx·es. 1.** A panpipe. **2.** *Zool.* The vocal organ of a bird, consisting of thin, vibrating muscles at or close to the division of the trachea. [Latin, from Greek *surinx, pipe.*]

syr·up (sĭr′əp, sûr′-) *n.* Also **sir·up.** A thick, sweet, sticky liquid, esp. the juice of a fruit or plant boiled with sugar until thick and sticky. [Middle English *sirop*, from Old French, from Medieval Latin *siropus*, from Arabic *sharāb*, beverage, syrup, from *shariba*, to drink.] —**syr′up·y** *adj.*

sys·tem (sĭs′təm) *n.* **1.** A group of interacting, interrelated, or interdependent elements forming a complex whole. **2.** A functionally related group of elements, esp.: **a.** The human body. **b.** A group of physiologically complementary organs or parts: *the nervous system.* **c.** A group of interacting mechanical or electrical components. **d.** A network of structures and channels, as for communications. **3.** A set of interrelated ideas or principles. **4.** A social, economic, or political organizational form. **5.** A naturally occurring group of objects or phenomena: *the solar system.* **6.** *Geol.* A major division of rocks. **7.** A method; procedure. **8.** Orderliness. **9.** A way of doing something. —See Syns at **method.** [Late Latin *systēma*, from Greek *sustēma*, a composite whole, from *sunistanai*, combine : *sun-*, together + *histanai*, to cause to stand.]

sys·tem·at·ic (sĭs′tə-măt′ĭk) or **sys·tem·at·i·cal** (-ĭ-kəl) *adj.* **1.** Of, based upon, or constituting a system: *systematic thought.* **2.** Methodical. —**sys′tem·at′i·cal·ly** *adv.*

sys·tem·a·tize (sĭs′tə-mə-tīz′) *tr.v.* **-tized, -tiz·ing.** To formulate into or reduce to a system. —**sys′tem·a·ti·za′tion** *n.* —**sys′tem·a·tiz′er** *n.*

sys·tem·ic (sĭ-stĕm′ĭk) *adj.* **1.** Of a system. **2.** Of or affecting the entire body. —**sys·tem′i·cal·ly** *adv.*

sys·tem·ize (sĭs′tə-mīz′) *tr.v.* **-ized, -iz·ing.** To systematize.

sys·to·le (sĭs′tə-lē) *n.* The rhythmic contraction of the heart by which blood is driven outward after each dilation or diastole. [Greek *sustolē*, contraction, from *sustellein*, to contract.] —**sys·tol′ic** (sĭ-stŏl′ĭk) *adj.*

Tt

+	⊤	T	τ	Tt
Phoenician	Greek	Roman	Medieval	Modern

t, T (tē) *n., pl.* **t's** or **T's. 1.** The 20th letter of the English alphabet. **2.** Anything shaped like the letter **T. —idiom. to a T.** Perfectly; precisely.

Ta The symbol for the element tantalum.

tab (tăb) *n.* **1.** A projection, flap, or short strip attached to an object to aid in opening, handling, or identifying it. **2.** A small hanging or projecting flap, strap, tongue, or loop on a garment. **3.** *Informal.* A bill or a check, as for a meal in a restaurant. **4.** A tabulator on a typewriter. **5.** A small auxiliary control surface attached to a larger one to help stabilize an airplane. —*tr.v.* **tabbed, tab·bing. 1.** To supply or decorate with a tab or tabs. **2.** To pick or single out: *tabbed her for the leading role.* **—idiom. keep tabs on.** To watch. [Orig. unknown.]

tab·ard (tăb'ərd) *n.* **1.** A tunic worn by a knight over his armor and embroidered with his coat of arms. **2.** A herald's garment that bears his lord's coat of arms. [Middle English, from Old French *tabart.*]

tabard	tabernacle

Ta·bas·co (tə-băs'kō) *n.* A trademark for a spicy-hot sauce made from a strong-flavored red pepper.

tab·by (tăb'ē) *n., pl.* **-bies. 1. a.** A domestic cat with a striped coat of a gray or tawny color. **b.** Any domestic cat, esp. a female. **2.** A rich watered silk fabric. **3.** A plain weave fabric. —*adj.* Having light and dark striped markings, as a cat. [French *tabis,* watered silk, from Old French *atabis,* from Arabic *'attābī.*]

tab·er·na·cle (tăb'ər-năk'əl) *n.* **1. a.** The portable sanctuary in which the Jews carried the Ark of the Covenant from the time of their post-Exodus wandering in the desert until the building of Solomon's Temple in Jerusalem. **b.** The Jewish temple. **2.** Often **Tabernacle.** A case or box that contains the consecrated host and wine of the Eucharist. **3.** A place of worship for a large gathering of worshipers. **4.** A niche for a statue or relic. [Middle English, from Old French, from Late Latin *tabernaculum,* from Latin, tent, dim. of *taberna,* hut.]

ta·ble (tā'bəl) *n.* **1.** An article of furniture that is supported by one or more vertical legs and has a flat horizontal surface. **2.** The food and drink served at a meal. **3.** A company of people assembled around or as if around a table. **4.** A gaming table, as for faro, roulette, or dice. **5.** A plateau or tableland. **6.** *Geol.* A horizontal layer of rock; stratum. **7.** An orderly arrangement of data, esp. one in which the data are arranged in columns and rows in an essentially rectangular form. **8.** An abbreviated list, as of contents; a synopsis. —*tr.v.* **-bled, -bling. 1.** To postpone consideration of; shelve: *table a piece of legislation.* **2.** To put or place on a table. **3.** To enter in a list or table; tabulate. **—idioms. turn the tables.** To reverse a situation and gain the upper hand. **under the table.** In secret. [Middle English, from Old French, from Latin *tabula,* board, list, table.]

tab·leau (tă-blō', tăb'lō') *n., pl.* **-leaux** (-blōz', -lōz') or **leaus. 1.** A vivid or striking description or picture: *The book is a tableau of a soldier's life.* **2.** A representation of a scene, painting, incident, etc., by appropriately costumed actors who remain still and silent. **3.** Any picturesque grouping or striking scene of people. [French, picture, from Old French *tablel,* dim. of *table,* board, table.]

ta·ble·cloth (tā'bəl-klôth', -klŏth') *n.* A cloth to cover a table, esp. during a meal.

ta·ble d'hôte (tä'bəl dōt') *pl.* **ta·bles d'hôte** (tä'bəl dōt'). **1.** A communal table for all guests at a hotel or restaurant. **2.** A full-course meal served at a fixed price in a restaurant or hotel. [French, "table of the host."]

ta·ble·land (tā'bəl-lănd') *n.* A flat, elevated region; plateau.

table linen. Tablecloths and napkins.

ta·ble·spoon (tā'bəl-spoon') *n.* **1.** A large spoon used for eating soups and serving food. **2.** The amount a tablespoon holds. **3.** A household cooking measure equal to three teaspoons or ½ fluid ounce.

ta·ble·spoon·ful (tā'bəl-spoon'fool') *n., pl.* **-fuls.** The amount a tablespoon holds.

tab·let (tăb'lĭt) *n.* **1.** A slab or plaque, as of stone, ivory, metal, etc., suitable for or bearing an inscription. **2.** A thin sheet, as of clay, used as a writing surface. **3.** A pad of writing paper glued together along one edge. **4.** A small, flat cake of a molded substance, esp a small flat pellet of medication to be taken orally. [Middle English *tablette,* from Old French *tablete,* dim. of *table,* board, table.]

table talk. Casual mealtime conversation.

table tennis. A game similar to tennis but played on a table with wooden paddles and a small Celluloid ball.

ta·ble·ware (tā′bəl-wâr′) n. The dishes, glassware, and silverware used in setting a table for a meal.

table wine. Wine with an alcohol content of less than 14%, intended to be served with a meal.

tab·loid (tăb′loid′) n. A newspaper of small format presenting the news in condensed form and often concentrating on sensational material. [From *Tabloid*, trademark for a tablet of condensed medicine.]

ta·boo (tə-bōō′, tă-) Also **ta·bu.** —n., pl. **-boos. 1.** A prohibition against certain objects, words, acts, or people because of their sacred or forbidden nature. **2.** A ban or prohibition imposed on something by social custom or aversion. —adj. Excluded or forbidden from use, approach, or mention: *a taboo subject of conversation.* —tr.v. To place under a taboo; prohibit. [Tongan *tabu.*]

ta·bor (tā′bər) n. A small drum used by a fife player to accompany his fife. [Middle English *tabour,* from Old French, perh. from Persian *ṭabīr,* drum.]

tab·o·ret (tăb′ə-rĕt′, -rā′) n. Also **tab·ou·ret. 1.** A low stool without a back or arms. **2.** A low stand or cabinet. [French *tabouret,* dim. of Old French *ṭabour,* tabor.]

ta·bu (tə-bōō′, tă-) n., adj., & v. Var. of **taboo.**

tab·u·lar (tăb′yə-lər) adj. **1.** Organized or presented in the form of a table or list. **2.** Calculated from information given in a mathematical table. **3.** Having a flat surface. [Latin *tabulāris,* from *tabula,* table.] —**tab′u·lar·ly** adv.

tab·u·la ra·sa (tăb′yə-lə rä′sə, rā′zə). The mind before it receives the impressions gained from experience, esp. in the philosophy of John Locke, the unformed, featureless mind. [Latin, "erased tablet."]

tab·u·late (tăb′yə-lāt′) tr.v. **-lat·ed, -lat·ing.** To put or arrange in a listed form, as in a table: *tabulate the results of a survey.* [From Latin *tabula,* table.] —**tab′u·la′tion** n.

tab·u·la·tor (tăb′yə-lā′tər) n. **1.** Someone or something that makes tabulations, esp. a machine that processes data. **2.** A mechanism on a typewriter for setting automatic stops or margins for columns.

tac·a·ma·hac (tăk′ə-mə-hăk′) n. **1.** Any of several aromatic resinous substances used in ointments and incenses. **2.** The balsam. [Spanish *tacamahaca,* from Nahuatl *tecamaca.*]

ta·chom·e·ter (tə-kŏm′ĭ-tər) n. An instrument used to measure or determine speed, esp. the rotational speed of a shaft. [Greek *takhos,* speed + -METER.] —**tach′o·met′ric** (tăk′ə-mĕt′rĭk) adj. —**ta·chom′e·try** n.

tac·it (tăs′ĭt) adj. **1.** Not spoken; silent: *Her glance was a tacit invitation.* **2.** Inferred or understood without being stated openly; implied: *gave tacit approval to the plan.* —See Syns at **implicit.** [Latin *tacitus,* silent, the past part. of *tacēre,* to be silent.] —**tac′it·ly** adv. —**tac′it·ness** n.

tac·i·turn (tăs′ĭ-tûrn′) adj. Habitually silent or uncommunicative; not talkative. [French *taciturne,* from Latin *taciturnus,* from *tacitus,* silent.] —**tac′i·tur′ni·ty** (-tûr′nĭ-tē) n. —**tac′i·turn′ly** adv.

tack (tăk) n. **1.** A small nail with a sharp point and a flat head. **2.** A large, loose stitch made in sewing either as a temporary binding or as a mark. **3.** A course of action or an approach: *try a new tack.* **4.** A zigzag course or a leg of such a course. **5.** *Naut.* **a.** A rope used to hold down the outer lower corner of a rectangular sail on a square-rigged ship. **b.** The lower forward corner of a fore-and-aft sail. **c.** The direction of a ship in relation to the trim of its sails: *on the starboard tack.* **d.** A change of direction made by a ship in the zigzag course it sails when proceeding to windward. **e.** The straight distance or leg sailed between changes of direction in the zigzag course of a ship sailing to windward. —v. **tacked, tack·ing.** —tr.v. **1.** To fasten or attach with or as if with a tack. **2.** To sew (cloth, a seam, etc.) with a loose basting stitch in order to temporarily fasten or mark. **3.** To put together loosely and arbitrarily: *He tacked some stories together into a novel.* **4.** To add as an extra item; append: *tack two dollars onto the bill.* **5.** *Naut.* To change the course of (a sailing ship) by turning to the opposite direction or tack. —intr.v. **1.** *Naut.* **a.** To change the direction or course of a vessel: *ready to tack on the captain's signal.* **b.** To change tack: *The ship tacked to*

starboard. **2.** To take or follow a zigzag course. **3.** To take or make an abrupt change in action, thought, attitude, etc.: *He tacked in mid-sentence and tried another approach.* [Middle English *takke,* prob. from Old North French *taque,* var. of Old French *tache,* nail, fastening.] —**tack′er** n.

tack·le (tăk′əl) n. **1.** The equipment used in a sport, esp. in fishing; gear. **2.** *(also* tā′kəl*). Naut.* **a.** A ship's running rigging. **b.** A rope and its pulley. **3.** *Football.* **a.** Either of two line players positioned between the guard and the end. **b.** The position of this player. **c.** The act of stopping another player by seizing and bringing him down. —v. **-led, -ling.** —tr.v. **1.** To take on and wrestle with (an opponent, problem, difficulty, etc.) in order to overcome. **2.** *Football.* To seize and throw down (another player). **3.** To harness (a horse): *tackled his mount; tackled up the team.* —intr.v. *Football.* To seize and throw down another player. [Middle English *takel,* of Low German orig.] —**tack′ler** n.

tack·y[1] (tăk′ē) adj. **-i·er, -i·est.** Slightly gummy to the touch; sticky: *paint that is still tacky.* [From TACK (to attach).] —**tack′i·ness** n.

tack·y[2] (tăk′ē) adj. **-i·er, -i·est.** *Informal.* **1.** Marked by neglect and disrepair; run-down; shabby. **2.** Lacking style or good taste; cheap and tasteless: *tacky clothes; a tacky remark.* [From dial. *tacky,* an inferior horse.] —**tack′i·ness** n.

ta·co (tä′kō) n., pl. **-cos.** A tortilla folded around a filling, as of ground meat or cheese. [Mexican Spanish, from Spanish, wad, roll, plug.]

tac·o·nite (tăk′ə-nīt′) n. A fine-grained sedimentary rock that contains magnetite, hematite, and quartz, used as a low-grade iron ore. [After the *Taconic* Mountains in New England and New York.]

tact (tăkt) n. The ability to appreciate a delicate situation and to do or say the kindest or most fitting thing; diplomacy. [French, from Latin *tactus,* sense of touch, from *tangere,* to touch.]

tact·ful (tăkt′fəl) adj. Having or showing tact; considerate; discreet: *a tactful person; a tactful remark.* —**tact′ful·ly** adv. —**tact′ful·ness** n.

tac·tic (tăk′tĭk) n. **1.** A device or expedient for achieving a goal. **2. tactics** *(used with a sing. verb).* The technique or science of gaining objectives, esp. military objectives, by using strategy.

tac·ti·cal (tăk′tĭ-kəl) adj. **1.** Of tactics: *a tactical maneuver.* **2.** Done or made strategically: *a tactical decision.*

tac·ti·cian (tăk-tĭsh′ən) n. **1.** A person skilled in the planning and execution of military tactics. **2.** A clever maneuverer. [New Latin *tactica,* from Greek *taktike* (techne), the art of arrangement, from *taktikos,* of order or arrangement, concerning tactics, from *taktos,* arranged, in order, from *tassein, tattein,* to arrange (in battle formation).]

tac·tile (tăk′təl, -tīl′) adj. **1.** Of, perceptible to, or proceeding from the sense of touch: *tactile sensations; a tactile response.* **2.** Used for feeling: *tactile organs.* [Latin *tactilis,* from *tactus,* sense of touch.] —**tac·til′i·ty** (-tĭl′ĭ-tē) n.

tact·less (tăkt′lĭs) adj. Lacking in tact; brutally blunt; inconsiderate: *a tackless remark.* —**tact′less·ly** adv. —**tact′less·ness** n.

tac·tu·al (tăk′chōō-əl) adj. Of, producing, derived from, or pertaining to the sense of touch; tactile. [From Latin *tactus,* sense of touch.] —**tac′tu·al·ly** adv.

tad·pole (tăd′pōl′) n. The aquatic larval stage of a frog or toad, with a tail and external gills that disappear as the limbs develop and the adult stage is reached. Also called **polliwog.** [Middle English *taddepol* : *tadde,* toad + *pol,* head.]

tael (tāl) n. **1.** Any of various units of weight used in eastern Asia, roughly equivalent to 1¹/₃ ounces. **2.** A Chinese monetary unit formerly in use, equivalent in value to a teal of standard silver. [Portuguese, from Malay *tahil.*]

tae·ni·a (tē′nē-ə) n., pl. **-ni·ae** (-nē-ē′). Also **te·ni·a. 1.** A narrow band or ribbon for the hair worn in ancient Greece. **2.** *Archit.* A band in the Doric order separating the frieze from the architrave. **3.** Any flatworm of the genus *Taenia,* which includes many tapeworms. [Latin, band, ribbon, from Greek *tainia.*]

taf·fe·ta (tăf′ĭ-tə) n. A crisp, smooth fabric with a slight sheen, made of various fibers and used for dresses, blouses, slips, etc. [Middle English, from Old French *taffetas*, from Old Italian *taffettà*, from Turkish *tafta*, from Persian *tāftah*, woven, from *tāftan*, to weave.]

taff·rail (tǎf'rāl', -rəl) *n. Naut.* **1.** The rail around the stern of a vessel. **2.** The flat upper part of the stern of a vessel. [Dutch *taffereel*, carved panel, from *tafel*, panel, table, from Middle Dutch *tāvele*, from Latin *tabula*, table.]

taf·fy (tǎf'ē) *n., pl.* **-fies.** A chewy candy made from molasses or brown sugar boiled until very thick and then pulled until the candy is glossy and holds its shape. [Var. of TOFFEE.]

tag¹ (tǎg) *n.* **1.** A strip, as of paper, metal, or plastic, attached to something or worn by someone for the purpose of identification, classification, or labeling: *a name tag; a price tag.* **2.** The plastic or metal tips at the end of shoelaces. **3.** A small, loose or hanging piece or part; tatter. **4.** A brief quotation used in speaking for added effect. **5.** The final or closing line or lines of a speech, play, poem, story, etc.; tag line. **6.** A descriptive word or phrase applied to a person, group, movement, etc. —*v.* **tagged, tag·ging.** —*tr.v.* **1.** To label or identify with or as with a tag. **2.** To put a traffic violation ticket on (an automobile). **3.** To assign responsibility to. **4.** To add or attach as an appendage to: *He tagged $10.00 onto the bill for waiting time.* **5.** To follow closely. —*intr.v.* To follow along after; accompany: *His little sister always tags along.* [Middle English *tagge*, prob. of Scandinavian orig.]

tag² (tǎg) *n.* **1.** A children's game in which one player pursues the others until he touches one of them, who in turn becomes the pursuer. **2.** *Baseball.* The act of putting another player out by touching him. —*tr.v.* **tagged, tag·ging.** **1.** To touch (another player) as in a game of tag. **2.** *Baseball.* To touch (a base-runner) with the ball in order to put him out. —*phrasal verbs.* **tag out.** *Baseball.* To put (another player) out by touching him with the ball. **tag up.** *Baseball.* To advance on a cleanly fielded fly ball returning to and touching a base after the fielder has caught the ball and then going on to the next base. [Orig. unknown.]

Ta·ga·log (tə-gä'lŏg, -lôg') *n., pl.* **Tagalog** or **-logs. 1.** A member of a people native to the Philippines and inhabiting Manila and its provinces. **2.** The language of the Tagalog.

tag line. The final line of a speech, joke, play, etc.

tai·ga (tī'gə) *n.* The subarctic evergreen forest of Siberia and similar regions elsewhere in Eurasia and North America. [Russian *taïga.*]

tail (tāl) *n.* **1.** The posterior part of an animal, esp. when elongated and extending beyond the trunk or main part of the body. **2.** The bottom, rear, or hindmost part of anything. **3.** Anything that looks, hangs, or trails like an animal's tail: *the tails of a shirt.* **4. a.** The rear portion of the fuselage of an airplane. **b.** An assembly of stabilizing planes and control surfaces in this region. **5. tails.** The reverse side of a coin. **6.** *Informal.* The trail of a person or animal in flight: *on the criminal's tail.* **7.** *Informal.* An agent assigned to follow and report on someone's movements and actions. **9. tails.** Men's full formal evening clothes, including a swallow-tailed coat and a white bow tie. —*modifier: tail feathers; the tail section.* —*tr.v.* **1.** To provide with a tail: *tail a kite.* **2.** To deprive of a tail; to dock. **3.** To serve as the tail of: *The Santa Claus float tailed the parade.* **4.** To attach end to end: *tailed the two cars for easier hauling.* **5.** *Archit.* To set one end of (a beam, board, etc.) into a wall. **6.** *Informal.* To follow and keep under surveillance. —*intr.v.* **1.** To become spaced or lengthened out when moving in a line: *The patrol tailed out in pairs.* **2.** *Archit.* To be inserted at one end, as a floor timber or beam. **3.** *Informal.* To follow. —*phrasal verb.* **tail off** (or **away**). To disappear gradually; dwindle: *The fireworks tailed off into darkness.* [Middle English *tayle*, from Old English *tægel.*]

tail·back (tāl'bǎk') *n. Football.* The back on the offensive team lining up farthest from the line of scrimmage.

tail·board (tāl'bôrd', -bōrd') *n.* The tailgate of a vehicle.

tail end. The very end; conclusion: *the tail end of the day.*

tail·gate (tāl'gāt') *n.* A hinged board or closure at the rear of a truck, wagon, station wagon, etc., that can be lowered during loading and unloading. —*v.* **-gat·ed, -gat·ing.** —*tr.v.* To drive so closely behind (another vehicle) that one cannot stop or swerve in an emergency. —*intr.v.* To follow another car at too close a distance.

tail·ing (tā'lĭng) *n.* **1. tailings.** Refuse or dross remaining after such processes as milling, distilling, or mining. **2.** *Archit.* The portion of a tailed beam, brick, or board inside a wall.

tail·light (tāl'līt') *n.* A red lamp mounted on the rear of a vehicle to make it visible from behind in the dark.

tai·lor (tā'lər) *n.* A person whose trade is to make, repair, and alter garments such as suits, coats, and dresses. —*tr.v.* **1.** To produce (a garment) by tailor's work. **2.** To outfit (someone) with clothes; to dress: *a man who was tailored with faultless taste.* **3.** To make, alter, or adapt for a particular end: *tailor a speech to a special audience.* —*intr.v.* To exercise the trade of a tailor. [Middle English *taillour*, from Anglo-French, ult. from Latin *tālea*, twig, cutting.]

tai·lor·bird (tā'lər-bûrd') *n.* Any of several Old World tropical birds of the genus *Orthotomus*, that use plant fibers to stitch leaves together in making a nest.

tai·lored (tā'lərd) *adj.* **1.** Made by a tailor; custom-made. **2.** Simple, trim, or severe in line or design: *a neat, tailored dress; tailored drapes.*

tai·lor-made (tā'lər-mād') *adj.* **1.** Made by a tailor; tailored. **2.** Perfectly suited to a condition, preference, or purpose; made or as if made to order: *a tailor-made job.*

tail·piece (tāl'pēs') *n.* **1.** Any piece that forms an end to something; appendage. **2.** An engraving or design placed as an ornament at the end of a chapter or at the bottom of a page. **3.** *Archit.* A beam tailed into a wall. **4.** A triangular piece of ebony to which the lower ends of the strings of a violin or cello are attached.

tail pipe. The pipe through which the exhaust gases from an engine are discharged, as in an automobile.

tail·race (tāl'rās') *n.* **1.** The part of a millrace below the water wheel through which the spent water flows. **2.** A channel for floating away mine tailings and refuse.

tail·spin (tāl'spĭn') *n.* **1.** The descent of an aircraft in a spin, characterized by the rapid spiral movement of the tail section. **2.** Any sudden collapse into confusion, esp. a loss of emotional control.

tail wind. A wind blowing in the same direction as that of the course of a vehicle.

Tai·no (tī'nō) *n., pl.* **Taino** or **-nos. 1.** An extinct aboriginal Arawakan Indian people of the West Indies. **2.** The language of the Taino.

taint (tānt) *tr.v.* **1.** To touch or affect with a trace of something undesirable, offensive, or bad; to blemish. **2.** To infect, spoil or contaminate. **3.** To infect with moral corruption. —*intr.v.* To become contaminated or blemished. —*n.* A trace of something undesirable or corrupting; a stain or blemish. [Middle English *taynten*, from Anglo-French *teinter*, from Old French *teint*, color, tint, from Latin *tinctus*, from *tingere*, to dye.]

take (tāk) *v.* **took** (tŏŏk), **tak·en** (tā'kən), **tak·ing.** —*tr.v.* **1.** To get possession of; to capture or seize: *take first prize; take the ship.* **2.** To grasp with the hands; to hold: *take her arm.* **3.** To have room for; accommodate: *The tank takes 10 gallons.* **4.** To carry along or cause to go with one to another place: *take the book to the library.* **5.** To convey to another place: *The train takes you to New York.* **6.** To remove from a place: *Take the cup from the shelf.* **7.** To obtain from a source; derive: *The book takes its title from the Bible.* **8.** To inhale, swallow, eat, drink, or consume: *take a breath; take medicine.* **9.** To expose one's body to (some process or treatment): *take a bath.* **10. a.** To assume for oneself: *take credit.* **b.** To commit oneself to; undertake: *take the initiative.* **c.** To bind oneself by (an oath or vow): *take an oath.* **11.** To perform; do: *take a step; take precautions.* **12.** To come upon: *take her by surprise.* **13.** To charm; captivate: *The child was taken with the little pup.* **14.** To study or commit oneself to studying: *take biology; take courses.* **15.** To require or need: *It takes a thief to know a thief.* **16.** To use as a means of conveyance or transportation: *take a train.* **17.** To assume occupancy of: *take a seat.* **18.** To use, as in operating: *This camera takes 35mm film.* **19.** To select; pick out: *take any card.* **10.** In grammar, to govern: *A transitive verb takes a direct object.* **21.** To make by photography: *take a picture.* **22.** To accept or endure (something given or offered): *take criticism; take a beating.* **23.** To interpret or react to in a certain manner: *take his comments seriously.* **24.** To subtract. **25.** To obtain through certain procedures, as through measurement: *take someone's temperature.* **26.** To write down: *take a letter.* **27.** To buy or subscribe to: *take a magazine.* **28.** *Informal.* To swindle; cheat. —*intr.v.* **1.** To gain possession; acquire. **2.** To have an intend effect; work: *The dye took and turn the fabric red.* **3.** To start growing; root: *Most of the new plants took.* **4.** To gain favor or popularity: *His new TV series didn't take and is being cancelled.* **5.** To detract or lessen: *The mustache takes away from his handsomeness.* **6.** To become: *She took sick.* —See Usage note **1** at **bring.** —*phrasal verbs.* **take after.** To resemble. **take back.** To retract (something stated or written). **take down. 1.** To dismantle. **2.** To lower the status or pride of; to humble. **3.** To put down in writing. **take for.** To suppose to be, often mistakenly. **take in. 1.** To grant admittance to. **2.** To view: *His eyes took in the whole scene.* **3.** To include or comprise. **4.** To understand. —See Syns at **understand. take off. 1.** To remove, as clothing. **2.** To rise up in flight, as an airplane. **3.** *Informal.* To depart. **take on. 1.** To hire. **2.** To undertake. **3.** To oppose in competition. **take out. 1.** To remove; extract. **2.** *Informal.* To escort, as on a date. **take over.** To assume the control or management of. **take to. 1.** To go to, as for safety: *take to the woods.* **2.** To become fond of. **3.** To begin to do habitually; resort to. **take up. 1.** To shorten: *take up a hem.* **2.** To use up, consume, or occupy: *take up space and time.* **3.** To begin again. **4.** To develop an interest in. **take up with.** *Informal.* To develop a friendship with. —*n.* **1. a.** The act or process of taking. **b.** The amount taken, esp. at one time. **2.** *Slang.* The money collected as admission to an event, esp. in sports. **3.** The uninterrupted running of a camera or other equipment, as in filming a movie or making a record. **4.** *Slang.* Any attempt or try. [Middle English *taken,* from Old Norse *taka.*] —**tak'er** *n.*

take·down (tāk'doun') *n.* **1.** The act of taking apart. **2.** *Wrestling.* The act of throwing one's opponent to the mat from a standing position. **3.** *Informal.* The act or an instance of humiliating a person.

take-home pay (tāk'hōm'). The amount of a worker's salary remaining after all deductions, as government taxes, pension contributions, etc., have been withheld.

tak·en (tā'kən) *v.* Past participle of **take.** [Middle English *taken,* from Old Norse *tekinn.*]

take·off (tāk'ôf', -ŏf') *n.* **1.** The act or process of rising in flight, as an airplane, rocket, jumper, etc. **2.** The point or place from which something takes off. **3.** *Informal.* An amusing imitation or burlesque of another person; caricature.

take·o·ver or **take-o·ver** (tāk'ō'vər) *n.* The act or process of seizing or assuming control or management of.

tak·ing (tā'kĭng) *n.* **1.** The act or process of gaining possession. **2. takings.** Receipts, esp. of money. —*adj.* Capturing the interest; attractive: *a taking smile.*

talc (tălk) *n.* A fine-grained white, greenish, or gray mineral, essentially a silicate of magnesium that has a soft soapy texture and is used in talcum powder and face powder, as a coating for paper, and as a filler for paint and plastics. [French, from Medieval Latin *talcum,* from Arabic *talq,* from Persian *talk.*]

tal·cum powder (tăl'kəm). A fine, often perfumed powder made from purified talc, for use on the skin. Also called **talcum.**

tale (tāl) *n.* **1.** A report or recital of events or happenings: *told us a tale of misery and ruin.* **2.** A narrative of imaginary events; story. **3. a.** A piece of gossip, usu. malicious or untrue. **b.** A lie or falsehood. —See Syns at **lie.** [Middle English, from Old English *talu,* discourse, narrative.]

tale·bear·er (tāl'bâr'ər) *n.* Someone who spreads malicious stories or gossip. —**tale'bear'ing** *n.*

tal·ent (tăl'ənt) *n.* **1. a.** A natural or acquired ability, esp. a creative or artistic ability. **b.** A person with such ability: *a great literary talent.* **2.** An ancient coin or weight in the Middle East, Greece, and Rome. [Middle English, unit of weight, ability (from the parable of the talents in Matt. 25:14-13), from Old English *talente,* unit of weight or money, from Latin *talentum,* unit of weight or money, from Greek *talanton.*]

tal·ent·ed (tăl'ən-tĭd) *adj.* Having special ability; gifted.

talent scout. An agent sent on tour to search out and recruit gifted people for acting, sports, etc.

tales·man (tālz'mən, tā'lĕz-) *n. Law.* A person summoned from among the bystanders in a court to serve as a juror.

tale·tell·er (tāl'tĕl'ər) *n.* **1.** An oral narrator. **2.** A talebearer. —**tale'tell'ing** *n.*

ta·li (tā'lī') *n.* Plural of **talus** (bone).

tal·is·man (tăl'ĭs-mən, -ĭz-) *n.* An object marked with magical signs or words and believed to give supernatural powers or protection to its bearer. [French and Spanish *talisman,* from Arabic *tilsamān,* pl. of *tilsām,* from Late Greek *telesma,* completion, consecrated object, from *telein,* to fulfill, consecrate, from *telos,* fulfillment, result.] —**tal'is·man'ic** (-măn'ĭk) or **tal'is·man'i·cal** *adj.*

talk (tôk) *intr.v.* **1.** To use human speech; articulate words. **2.** To imitate human speech: *Parrots can talk.* **3.** To communicate by means of a form of speech replacement: *people talking in sign language.* **4. a.** To express, communicate, or convey ideas, thoughts, etc., by means of speech; converse: *talk seriously.* **b.** To speak of or discuss: *talk business.* **5. a.** To chatter incessantly: *He did nothing but talk.* **b.** To gossip: *People will talk.* **6.** To consult or confer: *talk with a psychiatrist.* **7.** *Informal.* To yield information, usu. under stress: *The prisoner wouldn't talk.* —*tr.v.* **1.** To put into words; speak; express: *They talked treason.* **2.** To use in speaking: *They talked French with the Indonesian refugees.* **3.** To speak of or discuss: *talk music; talk business.* **4.** To bring, put, or influence into specified condition by speaking: *talked the frightened child down from the ledge.* —*phrasal verbs.* **talk back.** To reply rudely. **talk down. 1.** To depreciate. **2.** To silence (a person): *His boss could talk him down with one word.* **3.** To address someone with insulting condescension. **talk out.** To discuss thoroughly. **talk over.** To discuss (something) in depth. **talk up. 1.** *Informal.* To propagandize favorably about something: *talk up his new novel.* **2.** To speak up impertinently or defiantly, esp. to a superior. —*n.* **1. a.** The faculty or act of speaking. **b.** A particular manner of speech or conversation: *baby talk; plain talk.* **2. a.** An informal speech. **b.** A conference or negotiation: *peace talks.* **3.** Any subject of conversation: *the talk of the neighborhood.* **4.** Any hearsay or rumor about something: *talk of trouble.* **5.** Empty or meaningless speech: *all talk and no action.* —See Syns at **speech.** —*idioms.* **talk (someone) into.** To persuade. **talk (someone) out of.** To dissuade. [Middle English *talken,* prob. from Old English *talian,* to reckon, tell, relate.]

talk·a·tive (tô'kə-tĭv) *adj.* Inclined to talk a great deal. —**talk'a·tive·ly** *adv.* —**talk'a·tive·ness** *n.*

talk·ie (tô'kē) *n. Informal.* A motion-picture film with a sound track.

talking picture. An early name for a motion picture with a sound track.

talk·ing-to (tô'kĭng-tōō') *n., pl.* **-tos.** *Informal.* A scolding.

talk·y (tô'kē) *adj.* **-i·er, -i·est. 1.** Talkative; loquacious. **2.** Containing too much talk: *a talky, boring play.*

tall (tôl) *adj.* **-er, -est. 1.** Having greater than ordinary height. **2.** Having a stated height: *a plant three feet tall.* **3.** Fanciful or boastful: *a tall tale.* **4.** Unusual in length, size, or difficulty: *a tall order to fill.* —*adv.* Straight; proudly: *stand tall.* [Middle English, seemly, handsome, valiant, prob. from Old English *getæl,* swift, ready.] —**tall'ness** *n.*

Syns: tall, high, lofty, towering *adj. Core meaning:* Extending to a great height *(tall mountains).*

tal·lith (tä'lĭs, lĭth) *n., pl.* **tal·lith·im** (tä'lĭ-sēm', thēm'). A fringed shawl worn by Jewish men when they say their prayers. [Hebrew *tallīth,* cover, from *tillēl,* he covered.]

tal·low (tăl'ō) *n.* A mixture of fats obtained from animals, as cattle or sheep, and used to make candles, soaps, lubricants, etc. [Middle English *talow.*] —**tal'low·y** *adj.*

tal·ly (tăl'ē) *n., pl.* **-lies. 1.** A stick or rod on which notches are made to keep a count or score. **2.** A reckoning or score, as of business receipts, points in a game, etc.; recorded account or total. **3.** A mark used in recording a number of acts or objects. **4.** Anything that is very similar to something else; a counterpart or double. —*v.* **-lied, -ly·ing.** —*tr.v.* **1.** To record by making a mark; to register.

2. To calculate or reckon; add. **3.** To cause to correspond or agree: *tally his figures with mine.* —*intr.v.* To be alike; agree. [Middle English *taly,* from Anglo-French *tallie,* from Medieval Latin *tallia,* from Latin *tālea,* twig, stick.]

tal·ly·ho (tăl′ē-hō′) *interj.* A word used to urge hounds in fox hunting. —*n., pl.* **-hos. 1.** The act of crying of "tallyho." **2.** A pleasure coach drawn by four horses.

Tal·mud (täl′mo͝od′, tăl′məd) *n.* A collection of ancient Rabbinical writings that constitute the basis of religious authority for orthodox Judaism. [Hebrew *talmūd,* learning, instruction, from *lāmadh,* he learned.] —**Tal·mu′dic** (täl-mo͞o′dĭk, -myo͞o′-, -mŭd′ĭk, -mo͞od′ĭk, tăl-) or **Tal·mu′di·cal** *adj.* —**Tal′mud·ist** (täl′mə-dĭst, tăl′-) *n.*

tal·on (tăl′ən) *n.* **1.** The claw of a bird of prey or other predatory animal. **2.** Anything similar to or suggestive of such a claw. [Middle English, from Old French, heel, spur, from Latin *tālus,* ankle.]

ta·lus[1] (tā′ləs) *n., pl.* **-li** (-lī′). **1.** A tarsal bone that joins with the tibia and fibula to form the anklebone. Also called **anklebone** and **astragalus. 2.** The ankle. [Latin *tālus,* ankle.]

ta·lus[2] (tā′ləs) *n., pl.* **-lus·es. 1.** A slope formed by the accumulation of debris. **2.** A sloping mass of debris at the base of a cliff. [French, from Old French, prob. from Latin *talū-tium,* a technical mining term, "outcrop indicating the presence of gold-bearing topsoil."]

tam (tăm) *n.* A tam-o′-shanter.

ta·ma·le (tə-mä′lē) *n.* A Mexican dish of corn meal dough packed with seasoned chopped meat or other savory fillings, wrapped in corn husks and steamed. [Mexican Spanish *tamales,* pl. of *tamal,* from Nahuatl *tamalli.*]

tam·a·rack (tăm′ə-răk′) *n.* Any of several North American larch trees, esp. *Larix laricina,* valued for its wood. [Of Algonquian orig.]

tam·a·rind (tăm′ə-rĭnd′) *n.* **1.** A tropical Old World tree, *Tamarindus indica,* with compound leaves and red-striped yellow flowers. **2.** The fruit of this tree, consisting of a long pod with an edible acid pulp. [Medieval Latin *tamarindus,* from Arabic *tamr hindī,* "date of India."]

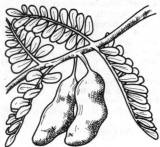

tamarind

tam·a·risk (tăm′ə-rĭsk′) *n.* Any of numerous shrubs or small trees of the genus *Tamarix,* native to Eurasia, with small, scalelike leaves and clusters of pink flowers. [Middle English *tamarisc,* from Late Latin *tamariscus,* from Latin *tamarix.*]

tam·bour (tăm′bo͝or′, tăm-bo͝or′) *n.* **1.** A drum. **2. a.** A small wooden embroidery frame that consists of two hoops set one inside the other between which fabric is stretched for embroidering. **b.** Embroidery made on such a frame. **3.** A rolling front or top for a desk that is made of narrow strips of wood glued to canvas. —*tr.v.* To embroider (cloth) on a tambour. —*intr.v.* To embroider at a tambour frame. [Middle English, from Old French, from Arabic *ṭanbūr,* prob. from Persian *ṭabīr,* drum, tabor.]

tam·bou·rine (tăm′bə-rēn′) *n.* A percussion instrument that consists of a small drumhead stretched over a narrow rim that is fitted with small metal disks that jingle when the drumhead is struck or when the instrument is shaken. [French *tambourin,* dim. of *tambour,* drum.]

tame (tām) *adj.* **tam·er, tam·est. 1.** Changed from natural wildness to a manageable state; domesticated. **2.** Not fierce, dangerous, or timid; gentle and unafraid: *The dodo was so tame that it was easily killed in great numbers and*

soon became extinct. **3.** Made submissive and docile; manageable. **4.** Unexciting or uninteresting; dull: *a tame existence.* —See Syns at **gentle.** —*tr.v.* **tamed, tam·ing. 1.** To train to live with or be useful to human beings: *tame a skunk; tame a bucking bronco.* **2.** To cause to become manageable; subdue: *pioneers who tamed the wilderness.* [Middle English, from Old English *tam.*] —**tame′ly** *adv.* —**tame′ness** *n.* —**tam′er** *n.*

Tam·il (tăm′əl) *n.* **1.** A member of a Dravidian race of southern India and Ceylon. **2.** The language of the Tamils. —*adj.* Of or relating to the Tamils or their language.

Tam·ma·ny (tăm′ə-nē) *n.* A politically powerful organization of the Democratic Party in New York City, founded in 1789 and often associated with corruption in government. Also called **Tammany Hall.** [From *Tammany* Hall, the meeting place of the Tammany Society.]

tam-o′-shan·ter (tăm′ə-shăn′tər) *n.* A tight-fitting Scottish cap that has a soft, full, flat top, often with a pompon or tassel in the center. Also called **tam.** [After the hero of Burns's poem *Tam o′Shanter.*]

tamp (tămp) *tr.v.* **1.** To pack down tightly by a succession of blows or taps: *tamp the tobacco in a pipe.* **2.** To pack clay, sand, or dirt into (a drill hole) above an explosive. [Prob. back-formation from TAMPION.]

tam·per[1] (tăm′pər) *intr.v.* **1.** To interfere in a harmful manner; meddle. **2.** To bring about an improper situation by secret or underhanded means: *tamper with a contract.* —See Syns at **interfere.** [Obs. *tamper,* to prepare (clay) by mixing, var. of TEMPER.] —**tam′per·er** *n.*

tam·pi·on (tăm′pē-ən) *n.* A plug or cover for the muzzle of a cannon or gun to keep out dust and moisture. [Middle English *tampyon,* from Old French *tampon,* cotton plug.]

tam·pon (tăm′pŏn′) *n.* A plug of absorbent material inserted into a bodily cavity or wound to check a flow of blood or to absorb secretions. —*tr.v.* To plug or stop with a tampon. [French, from Old French.]

tam-tam (tăm′tăm′, tŏm′tŏm′) *n.* **1.** A type of saucer-shaped gong used in Indonesian music. **2.** A type of drum; a tom-tom. [Hindi *ṭamṭam.*]

tan (tăn) *v.* **tanned, tan·ning.** —*tr.v.* **1.** To convert (animal hide) into leather, esp. by treating with tannin. **2.** To make brown by exposure to the sun. **3.** *Informal.* To thrash or beat. —*intr.v.* To become brown or tawny from exposure to sun. —*n.* **1.** A light yellowish brown. **2.** The brownish skin color that results from exposure to the sun's rays. **3.** Tanbark. **4.** Tannin or a solution made from it. —*adj.* **tan·ner, tan·nest. 1.** Of a light, yellowish brown color: *a tan jacket.* **2.** Having a sun tan. [Middle English *tannen,* ult. from Medieval Latin *tannāre,* from *tannum,* oak bark.]

tan·a·ger (tăn′ə-jər) *n.* Any of various small New World birds of the family Thraupidae, often with brightly colored plumage in the males. [Portuguese *tangará,* from Tupi : *atá,* to walk + *carä,* around.]

tan·bark (tăn′bärk′) *n.* The bark of certain oaks and other trees, used as a source of tannin for tanning leather and then shredded and used as a ground covering for circus rings, racetracks, etc.

tan·dem (tăn′dəm) *n.* **1.** A bicycle built for two. **2.** An arrangement of two or more persons or objects placed one behind the other and working or acting in conjunction with one another. **3. a.** A two-wheeled carriage drawn by horses harnessed one before the other. **b.** A team of carriage horses harnessed in single file. —*adv.* One behind

tambourine

tam-o′-shanter

the other: *children riding a sled tandem.* [Latin *tandem,* exactly then, at length.]

tang¹ (tăng) *n.* **1.** A sharp, distinctive flavor, taste, or odor. **2.** A trace or hint of something. **3.** A projection by which a tool, such as a file, knife, sword, etc., is attached to its handle. [Middle English *tange,* serpent's tongue, insect's sting, prob. from Old Norse *tangi,* a sting, point.]

tang² (tăng) *n.* A loud ringing sound; a twang. —*tr.v.* To cause to make a loud ringing sound. —*intr.v.* To make a loud ringing sound. [Imit.]

tan·ge·lo (tăn′jə-lō′) *n., pl.* **-los. 1.** A hybrid citrus tree that is a cross between certain varieties of grapefruit and tangerine. **2.** The fruit of this tree, with an acid orange pulp. [Blend of TANGE(RINE) and *(pome)lo,* grapefruit.]

tan·gent (tăn′jənt) *adj.* **1.** Making contact at a single point or along a line but not intersecting; touching. **2.** Touching upon but not germane; divergent; digressive: *ideas that are tangent to the topic.* —*n.* **1.** A line, curve, or surface touching but not intersecting another line, curve, or surface. **2.** *Trig.* The function of an acute angle in a right triangle that is the ratio of the length of the side opposite the angle to the length of the side adjacent to the angle. **3.** A sudden digression or change from one course of action or thought to another; divergence: *go off on a tangent.* [From Latin *tangēns,* pres. part. of *tangere,* to touch.] —**tan′gen·cy** (tăn′jən-sē) *n.*

tan·gen·tial (tăn-jĕn′shəl) *adj.* **1.** Of, along, or in the direction of a tangent. **2.** Barely touching or connected; divergent: *a tangential remark.* —**tan·gen′tial·ly** *adv.*

tan·ger·ine (tăn′jə-rēn′) *n.* **1.** A widely cultivated citrus tree, *Citrus nobilis deliciosa,* that bears edible fruit with an easily peeled deep-orange skin and sweet, juicy pulp. **2.** The fruit of this tree. [Short for *tangerine orange,* "orange of Tangier," after *Tangier,* Morocco.]

tan·gi·ble (tăn′jə-bəl) *adj.* **1.** Capable of being touched; material. **2.** Capable of being understood or realized: *a tangible benefit.* **3.** Real; concrete; substantive: *tangible evidence.* **4.** *Law.* Having physical existence and hence capable of being valued monetarily, as land, securities, etc.: *tangible property.* —See Syns at **real.** —*n.* **1.** Something palpable, concrete, or substantive. **2. tangibles.** Material assets. [Old French, from Late Latin *tangibilis,* from Latin *tangere,* to touch.] —**tan′gi·bil′i·ty** or **tan′gi·ble·ness** *n.* —**tan′gi·bly** *adv.*

tan·gle (tăng′gəl) *v.* **-gled, -gling.** —*tr.v.* **1.** To mix together or intertwine in a confused mass; to snarl. **2.** To involve in hampering or awkward complications; entangle: *tangled herself in a web of deceit.* —*intr.v.* **1.** To be or become snarled or entangled. **1.** *Informal.* To come to grips or blows with: *tangle with a problem.* —*n.* **1.** A confused, snarled mass: *a tangle of vines.* **2.** A jumbled or confused condition: *a tangle of emotions.* **3.** *Informal.* A fight or dispute; altercation. [Middle English *tanglen.*] —**tang′ler** *n.* —**tang′ly** *adj.*

tan·go (tăng′gō) *n., pl.* **-gos. 1.** A ballroom dance of Latin American origin, using various posturing positions and gliding steps. **2.** Music written to accompany this dance. —*intr.v.* To dance the tango. [American Spanish.]

tan·gram (tăng′grəm, tän′-) *n.* A Chinese puzzle that consists of a square cut into five triangles, a square, and a rhomboid, to be reassembled into different figures. [Poss. Mandarin *t'ang²,* Tang, a Chinese dynasty + -GRAM.]

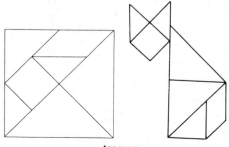

tangram

tang·y (tăng′ē) *adj.* **-i·er, -i·est.** Having a sharp, distinctive taste or odor: *a tangy cheese; a tangy citrus flavor.*

tank (tăngk) *n.* **1.** A large container for holding or storing fluids or gases. **2.** The amount a tank holds: *buy a tank of gas.* **3.** *Mil.* A heavily armored combat vehicle mounted with a cannon and guns and moving on caterpillar treads. **4.** A pool, pond, or reservoir. **5.** *Slang.* A large jail cell for holding several prisoners. —*tr.v.* To place, store, or process in a tank. [Portuguese *tanque,* pond, ult. from Latin *stagnum.*]

tank·age (tăng′kĭj) *n.* **1.** The capacity or contents of a tank. **2.** The act or process of putting or storing in a tank. **3.** The fee or charge for such storage.

tan·kard (tăng′kərd) *n.* A large drinking cup, usu. with a handle and a hinged cover. [Middle English.]

tankard   tansy

tank·er (tăng′kər) *n.* A ship, truck, or plane constructed or equipped to transport oil or other liquids in bulk.

tan·nate (tăn′āt′) *n. Chem.* A salt of tannic acid.

tan·ner (tăn′ər) *n.* Someone who tans hides.

tan·ner·y (tăn′ə-rē) *n., pl.* **-ies.** A place where hides are tanned.

tan·nic (tăn′ĭk) *adj.* Of or derived from tannin.

tannic acid. A yellowish to light-brown substance obtained from the fruit and bark of certain plants and used in tanning hides in dyeing and as a medicine.

tan·nin (tăn′ĭn) *n.* **1.** Tannic acid. **2.** Any of various other chemical substances capable of promoting tanning; tan. [French *tanin,* from *tanner,* to tan.]

tan·ning (tăn′ĭng) *n.* **1.** The art or process of making leather from animal hides. **2.** The browning of the skin by exposure to sun. **3.** *Informal.* A beating or whipping.

tan·sy (tăn′zē) *n., pl.* **-sies.** Any of several plants of the genus *Tanacetum,* esp. one with clusters of buttonlike yellow flowers and pungent, aromatic juice sometimes used medicinally and as a flavoring. [Middle English, from Old French *tanesie,* perh. from Medieval Latin *athanasia,* an elixir of life, from Greek, immortality.]

tan·ta·lize (tăn′tl-īz′) *tr.v.* **-lized, -liz·ing.** To tease or torment by or as if by allowing to see but keeping out of reach something much desired. [From TANTALUS.] —**tan′ta·li·za′tion** *n.* —**tan′ta·liz′er** *n.* —**tan′ta·liz′ing·ly** *adv.*

tan·ta·lum (tăn′til-əm) *n. Symbol* **Ta** A hard, heavy metallic element that is very resistant to corrosion at temperatures below 150°C. Atomic number 73; atomic weight 180.948; valences +2, +3, +4, +5; melting point 2,996°C; boiling point 5,425°C. [After TANTALUS.]

Tan·ta·lus (tăn′tl-əs) *n. Gk. Myth.* A king who was punished in Hades for his crimes by being condemned to remain forever standing in a pool of water that receded when he tried to drink with fruit hanging above his head that receded when he reached for it.

tan·ta·mount (tăn′tə-mount′) *adj.* Equivalent in effect or value: *a request tantamount to a command.* [Orig., to be equal to, from Anglo-French *tant amunter,* to amount to so much.]

tan·ta·ra (tăn-tăr′ə, -tär′ə) *n.* A fanfare blown on a trumpet or horn. [From Latin *taratantara* (imit.).]

tan·trum (tăn′trəm) *n.* A fit of bad temper. [Orig. unknown.]

Tao·ism (tou′ĭz′əm, dou′-) *n.* A principal philosophy and system of religion of China based upon the teachings of Lao-tse in the 6th cent. B.C., emphasizing freedom from desire, effortless action, and simplicity. [From Mandarin *tao⁴*, "the Way."] —**Tao′ist** *n.* —**Tao·is′tic** *adj.*

tap¹ (tăp) *v.* **tapped, tap·ping.** —*tr.v.* **1.** To strike gently with a light blow or blows: *tap him on the shoulder; tap the drum softly.* **2.** To give a light rap with: *tap a pencil.* **3.** To produce with a succession of light blows: *tap out a rhythm.* **4.** To repair or reinforce (shoe heels or toes) by applying a tap. —*intr.v.* **1.** To strike a light blow or blows: *typewriter keys tapping rapidly all afternoon.* **2.** To walk making light clicks. —*n.* **1. a.** A gentle blow. **b.** The sound made by such a blow. **2. a.** A layer of leather or other material used to repair and reinforce the worn heel or toe of a shoe. **b.** A metal plate attached to the toe or heel of a shoe, as for tap-dancing. [Middle English *tappen,* from Old French *taper.*]

tap² (tăp) *n.* **1.** A valve and spout used to regulate the flow of a fluid at the end of a pipe; faucet; spigot. **2. a.** Liquor drawn from a tap or spigot, as in a cask of wine. **b.** Liquor of a particular brew, cask, or quality. **3.** The process or procedure of surgically removing fluid from the human body: *a spinal tap.* **4.** A tool for cutting a screw thread into the inner wall of a drilled hole. **5.** A point at which a connection is made in an electric circuit to add another element in parallel with an existing load. —*tr.v.* **tapped, tap·ping. 1.** To pierce in order to draw off liquid: *tap a maple tree.* **2.** To draw (liquid) from a vessel or container. **3.** To surgically withdraw fluid from (a bodily cavity). **4.** To make a connection with or into, so as to draw from secretly: *tap an electrical power line; tap a telephone.* **5.** To draw upon the resources of: *tap someone's brain.* **6.** To cut screw threads in (a female fitting). **7.** *Informal.* To ask (a person) for money: *tried to tap me for a loan.* —*idiom.* **on tap. 1.** Ready to be drawn, as from a cask: *beer on tap.* **2.** Available for immediate use; ready. [Middle English *tappe,* from Old English *tæppa.*]

ta·pa (tä′pə, tăp′ə) *n.* **1.** The fibrous inner bark of the paper mulberry. **2.** A paperlike cloth made in the Pacific islands by pounding this or similar bark. [Polynesian.]

tap dance. A dance in which the rhythm is sounded out by the clicking heels and toes of the dancer's shoes. —**tap dancer.**

tap-dance (tăp′dăns′) *intr.v.* **-danced, -danc·ing.** To perform a tap dance.

tape (tāp) *n.* **1.** A narrow strip of strong, woven fabric. **2.** Any long, narrow, flexible strip of material, such as cloth, plastic, paper, or metal, esp.: **a. Adhesive tape. b.** A **tape measure. 3.** A tape recording. **4.** A string stretched across the finish line of a race. —*tr.v.* **taped, tap·ing. 1.** To fasten, wrap, or bind with tape: *tape a bow on a package; tape up a sprained wrist.* **2.** To measure with a tape measure. **3.** To tape-record. [Middle English, from Old English *tæppa.*]

tape deck. A tape recorder and player that does not have built-in amplifiers or speakers and is used as part of a high-fidelity sound system.

tape measure. A tape of cloth, paper, or metal marked off in a scale, used for taking measurements.

ta·per (tā′pər) *n.* **1.** A gradual decrease in thickness or width of an elongated object. **2.** A small or slender candle. **3.** A long wax-coated wick used to light candles, fires, pipes, etc. **4.** Something that gives off a feeble light. **5.** Any gradual decrease. —*intr.v.* **1.** To become gradually narrower or thinner toward one end. **2.** To become slowly smaller or less; diminish: *The rain tapered off.* —*tr.v.* **1.** To make thinner or narrower at one end. **2.** To diminish or make smaller gradually. [Middle English, from Old English *tapor.*]

tape-re·cord (tāp′rĭ-kôrd′) *tr.v.* To record on magnetic tape.

tape recorder. An instrument capable of recording sound or electrical signals on magnetic tape and usu. of playing back the recording.

tape recording. 1. a. A magnetic tape on which sound has been recorded. **b.** The sound recorded on a magnetic tape. **2.** The act or procedure of recording on magnetic tape.

tap·es·try (tăp′ĭ-strē) *n., pl.* **-tries.** A heavy cloth woven with rich, often varicolored designs or scenes, hung on walls for decoration and sometimes used to cover furniture. —*tr.v.* **-tried, -try·ing. 1.** To cover or decorate with

tapestry. **2.** To make, weave, or depict in a tapestry. [Middle English *tapstery,* from Old French *tapisserie,* from *tapisser,* to cover with carpet, from *tapis,* carpet, from Greek *tapētion,* dim. of *tapēs,* carpet.]

tape·worm (tāp′wûrm′) *n.* Any of various ribbonlike, often very long flatworms of the class Cestoda, that are parasitic in the intestines of vertebrates, including man.

tap·i·o·ca (tăp′ē-ō′kə) *n.* A beady or grainy starch obtained from the root of the cassava, used for puddings and as a thickening agent in cooking. [Portuguese and Spanish, from Tupi *tipioca.*]

ta·pir (tā′pər, tə-pîr′) *n.* Any of several hoofed mammals of the genus *Tapirus,* of tropical America or southern Asia, with a heavy body and a flexible snout. [Tupi *tapira.*]

tap·pet (tăp′ĭt) *n.* A lever or projecting arm that moves or is moved by contact with another part, usu. to communicate a certain motion, as between a driving mechanism and a valve. [From TAP (to strike lightly).]

tap·room (tăp′rōōm′, -rōōm′) *n.* A bar or barroom.

tap·root (tăp′rōōt′, -rōōt′) *n.* The main root of a plant, growing straight downward from the stem and giving off thinner lateral roots.

taps (tăps) *n.* *(used with a sing. verb).* A military bugle call sounded at night as an order to put out lights or at funerals and memorial services. [From TAP (light blow).]

tap·ster (tăp′stər) *n.* A person who draws and serves liquor for customers in a bar or tavern; bartender.

tar¹ (tär) *n.* **1.** A thick, dark, oily mixture consisting mainly of hydrocarbons and produced by the destructive distillation of wood, coal, peat, or other organic matter. **2. Coal tar.** —*tr.v.* **tarred, tar·ring.** To coat or cover with tar. [Middle English *taar,* from Old English *teoru.*]

tar² (tär) *n.* *Informal.* A sailor. [Short for TARPAULIN.]

tar·an·tel·la (tăr′ən-tĕl′ə) *n.* **1.** A lively, whirling dance of southern Italy done in 6/8 tempo. **2.** The music for this dance. [Italian, dim. of *Taranto,* a city in southern Italy.]

ta·ran·tu·la (tə-răn′chə-lə) *n., pl.* **-las** or **-lae** (-lē′). **1.** Any of various large, hairy, chiefly tropical spiders of the family Theraphosidae, capable of inflicting a painful but not seriously poisonous bite. **2.** A similar spider, *Lycosa tarentula,* of southern Europe. [Medieval Latin, from Italian *tarantola,* after *Taranto,* Italy.]

tar·boosh (tär-bōōsh′, tär′bōōsh′) *n.* Also **tar·bush.** A brimless, usu. red, felt cap with a silk tassel, worn by Moslem men, either by itself or as the base of a turban. [Arabic *tarbush,* "sweating cap."]

tar·dy (tär′dē) *adj.* **-di·er, -di·est. 1.** Occurring or arriving later than expected or scheduled; delayed; late. **2.** Moving or acting slowly; sluggish: *tardy acceptance of new ideas.* —See Syns at **late** and **slow.** [Middle English *tardif,* slow, from Old French, from Latin *tardus,* slow.] —**tar′di·ly** *adv.* —**tar′di·ness** *n.*

tare¹ (târ) *n.* **1.** The common vetch, *Vicia sativa.* **2.** Any of several weedy plants that grow in grain fields. **3. tares.** Noxious elements, likened to the harmful weeds growing among the wheat in the New Testament. [Middle English, seed of the vetch.]

tare² (târ) *n.* A deduction from gross weight made to allow for the weight of a container or wrapper. [Middle English, from Old French, waste, deficiency, from Medieval Latin *tara,* from Arabic *tarhah,* thing thrown away, from *taraha,* to reject, throw.]

targe (tärj) *n. Archaic.* A light shield or buckler. [Middle English, from Old French.]

tar·get (tär′gĭt) *n.* **1. a.** An object with a marked surface that is shot at to test accuracy, esp. a padded disk with colored concentric circles for use in riflery or archery. **b.** Anything aimed or fired at. **2.** An object of criticism, ridicule, or attack: *the target of her satire.* **3.** A desired goal. **4.** A metal part in an x-ray tube on which a beam of electrons is focused and from which x rays are emitted. —*tr.v.* To make a target of; aim at or for. [Middle English, from Old French *targette,* dim. of *targe,* light shield.]

tar·iff (tăr′ĭf) *n.* **1.** A list or system of duties or customs rates imposed by a government on imported or exported goods. **2.** A duty or customs rate imposed in such a way: *a tariff on liquor.* **3.** Any schedule of prices or fees. [French *tarif,* ult. from Arabic *ta′rīf,* information, from *'arafa,* to notify.]

ă pat	ā pay	â care	ä father	ĕ pet	ē be	hw which	ĭ pit	ī tie	î pier	ŏ pot	ō toe	ô paw, for	oi noise
ōō took	ōō boot	ou out	th thin	th this	ŭ cut		û urge	zh vision	ə about, item, edible, gallop, circus				

tar·la·tan (tär′lə-tən) *n.* A thin, stiffly starched open-weave muslin. [French *tarlatane.*]

Tar·mac (tär′măk′) *n.* A trademark for a bituminous substance used as a binder in paving. [Short for TARMACADAM.]

tar·mac·ad·am (tär′mə-kăd′əm) *n.* A pavement that consists of layers of crushed stone with a tar binder pressed to a smooth surface. [TAR + MACADAM.]

tarn (tärn) *n.* A small mountain lake. [Middle English *tarne,* from Old Norse *tjarn.*]

tar·na·tion (tär-nā′shən) *n.* Euphemism for damnation.

tar·nish (tär′nĭsh) *tr.v.* **1.** To dull or discolor, esp. by exposure to air or dirt, as many metals do. **2.** To detract from or spoil; to taint or stain: *tarnish one's reputation.* *—intr.v.* **1.** To lose luster; become discolored: *Silver tarnishes quickly.* **2.** To become tainted or sullied: *His reputation as a scholar tarnished in time.* *—n.* **1.** The condition of being tarnished. **2.** A dullness or discoloration, as on silverware. [From Old French *ternir.*] *—tar′nish·a·ble adj.*

ta·ro (tär′ō, tăr′ō) *n., pl.* **-ros. 1.** A widely cultivated tropical plant, *Colocasia esculenta,* with broad leaves and a large, starchy, edible rootstock. **2.** The rootstock of this plant. [Polynesian.]

tar·ot (tăr′ō) *n.* Any of a set of 22 playing cards consisting of a joker plus 21 cards depicting vices, virtues, and elemental forces, used in fortunetelling. [French, from Italian *tarocco.*]

tarot

tartan

tar·pa·per (tär′pā′pər) *n.* Heavy paper impregnated or coated with tar, used as a waterproof building material.

tar·pau·lin (tär-pô′lĭn, tär′pə-) *n.* Waterproof canvas used to cover and protect things from moisture. [Perh. TAR + PALL (cover).]

tar·pon (tär′pən) *n., pl.* **tarpon** or **-pons.** A large, silvery game fish, *Megalops atlantica,* of Atlantic coastal waters. [Orig. unknown.]

tar·ra·gon (tăr′ə-gŏn′, -gən) *n.* **1.** An aromatic herb, *Artemisia dracunculus,* native to Eurasia. **2.** The leaves of this plant, used as seasoning. [Medieval Latin *tragonia,* from Medieval Greek *tarkhōn,* from Arabic *ṭarkhūn.*]

tar·ry¹ (tăr′ē) *intr.v.* **-ried, -ry·ing. 1.** To delay or be late in going or coming; linger. **2.** To remain or stay temporarily; to sojourn: *We tarried in London for two weeks.* *—See* Syns at **delay.** [Middle English *tarien.*] *—tar′ri·er n.*

tar·ry² (tär′ē) *adj.* **-ri·er, -ri·est.** Of, like, or covered with tar.

tar·sal (tär′səl) *adj.* **1.** Of, pertaining to, or situated near the tarsus of the foot. **2.** Of or pertaining to the tarsus of the eyelid.

tar·si (tär′sī′) *n.* Plural of **tarsus.**

tar·si·er (tär′sē-ər, -sē-ā′) *n.* Any of several small tree-dwelling nocturnal primates of the genus *Tarsius,* of the East Indies, with large, round eyes and a long tail. [French, from *tarse,* ankle (from its elongated ankles), from New Latin *tarsus,* tarsus.]

tar·sus (tär′səs) *n., pl.* **-si** (-sī′). **1. a.** The section of the vertebrate foot between the leg and the metatarsus. **b.** The seven bones making up this section. **2.** A fibrous plate that supports and shapes the edge of the eyelid. **3.** *Zool.* The distal segmented structure on the leg of an insect or an arachnid. [From Greek *tarsos,* flat surface, sole of the foot, ankle.]

tart¹ (tärt) *adj.* **-er, -est. 1.** Having a sharp, pungent taste; sour: *tart apples.* **2.** Sharp or bitter in tone or meaning; cutting: *a tart answer.* [Middle English, from Old English *teart,* sharp, severe.] *—tart′ly adv. —tart′ness n.*

tart² (tärt) *n.* **1.** A small, usu. open pastry shell filled with sweet custard, fruit, or jam. **2.** A prostitute. [Middle English *tarte,* from Old French, var. of *torte,* from Latin *torta,* round bread, from *torquēre,* to turn, twist.]

tar·tan (tär′tn) *n.* **1.** Any of a number of plaid fabric patterns that consist of stripes of varying widths and colors crossed at right angles against a solid background, esp. as worn by the Scottish Highland clans, each clan having its distinctive pattern. **2.** A wool fabric or garment having such a pattern. **3.** Any fabric having a similar pattern; a plaid. *—modifier: a tartan shawl; tartan slacks.* [Prob. from Old French *tiretaine,* linsey-woolsey.]

tar·tar (tär′tər) *n.* **1.** A reddish acid substance, chiefly a potassium salt of tartaric acid, found in the juice of grapes and deposited on the sides of casks during winemaking. **2.** A hard yellowish deposit that collects on the teeth, consisting of food particles and secretions held together by insoluble salts such as calcium carbonate. [Middle English, from Old French *tartre,* from Medieval Latin *tartarum,* from Medieval Greek *tartaron.*]

Tar·tar (tär′tər) *n.* Also **Ta·tar** (tä′tər). **1.** A member of any of the Mongolian peoples of central Asia who invaded western Asia and eastern Europe in the 13th cent. **2.** A descendant of these peoples.

tartar emetic. A poisonous salt in the form of a sweet-tasting powder, used medicinally to cause vomiting and as a fixative for colors in dyeing.

tar·tar·ic acid (tär-tär′ĭk). Any of four organic acids with the composition $C_4H_6O_6$, used in tanning, to make cream of tartar, and in various foods, beverages, and chemicals.

tar·tar·ous (tär′tər-əs) *adj.* Of, derived from, or containing tartar: *tartarous salts.*

tartar sauce. Also **tar·tare sauce.** Mayonnaise mixed with chopped onion, olives, pickles, and capers and served as a sauce with fish.

Tar·ta·rus (tär′tər-əs) *n.* *Gk. Myth.* The dark abyss below Hades where the Titans were confined by Zeus.

tar·trate (tär′trāt′) *n.* A salt or ester of tartaric acid.

task (tăsk) *n.* **1.** A piece of work assigned or done as part of one's duties. **2.** A difficult or tedious undertaking. *—idiom.* **take to task.** To reprimand or censure. [Middle English *taske,* from Norman French *tasque,* from Medieval Latin *taxa,* from *taxāre,* to tax.]

task force. A temporary grouping of forces and resources for a specific goal: *a military task force.*

task·mas·ter (tăsk′măs′tər) *n.* A person who assigns tasks, esp. difficult or burdensome ones.

Tas·ma·ni·an devil (tăz-mā′nē-ən, -mān′yən). A burrowing carnivorous marsupial, *Sarcophilus harrisii,* of Tasmania, with a predominantly blackish coat.

tas·sel (tăs′əl) *n.* **1.** A bunch of loose threads or cords bound at one end and hanging free at the other, used an an ornament on curtains, clothing. etc. **2.** Something resembling this, such as a tuft of hairs on an animal's tail or the pollen-bearing flower cluster of a corn plant. *—v.* **-seled** or **-selled, -sel·ing** or **-sel·ling.** *—tr.v.* **1.** To fringe, trim, or decorate with tassels. *—intr.v.* To put forth a tassellike blossom. [Middle English, from Old French, clasp.]

taste (tāst) *v.* **tast·ed, tast·ing.** *—tr.v.* **1.** To distinguish the flavor of by taking into the mouth. **2.** To eat or drink a small quantity of: *barely tasted his food.* **3.** To experience or partake of, as for the first time. *—intr.v.* **1.** To distinguish flavors in the mouth. **2.** To have a distinct flavor: *The milk tastes sour.* **3.** To eat or drink a small amount. **4.** To have an experience; partake. *—n.* **1.** The sense that distinguishes between the sweet, sour, salty, and bitter qualities of something placed in the mouth. **2.** The sensation produced by or as if by something placed in the mouth; the flavor. **3.** A small quantity eaten or tasted: *Take a taste of this.* **4.** A limited experience; a sample: *a taste of success.* **5.** A personal preference or liking for something. **6.** The ability to perceive what is proper or good for certain situations and in certain fields: *a room furnished with great taste.* [Middle English *tasten,* to examine by touch, from Old French *taster,* from Latin *taxāre,* to touch, freq. of *tangere.*] *—tast′a·ble adj.*

| ă pat | ā pay | â care | ä father | ĕ pet | ē be | hw which | ĭ pit | ī tie | î pier | ŏ pot | ō toe | ô paw, for | oi noise |
| oo took | oo boot | ou out | th thin | th this | ŭ cut | | û urge | | zh vision | ə about, item, edible, gallop, circus | | | |

taste bud. Any of numerous nests of cells embedded in the epithelium of the tongue which constitute the sensory organs of taste.

taste·ful (tāst'fəl) *adj.* Having or showing good taste: *a tasteful dress.* **—taste'ful·ly** *adv.* **—taste'ful·ness** *n.*

tast·er (tā'stər) *n.* **1.** Someone who tastes, esp. a person employed to sample a food or beverage for quality. **2.** Any of several implements used in tasting.

taste·less (tāst'lĭs) *adj.* **1.** Lacking in flavor. **2.** Showing poor taste. **—taste'less·ly** *adv.* **—taste'less·ness** *n.*

tast·y (tā'stē) *adj.* **-i·er, -i·est. 1.** Having a pleasing flavor. **2.** Tasteful. **—See** Syns at **delicious. —tast'i·ly** *adv.* **—tast'i·ness** *n.*

tat (tăt) *tat·ted, tat·ting.* **—***intr.v.* To make lace by looping and knotting a single strand of heavy thread on a small shuttle. **—***tr.v.* To produce by tatting. [Prob. back-formation from TATTING.] **—tat'ter** *n.*

Ta·tar (tä'tər) *n.* Var. of **Tartar.**

tat·ter (tăt'ər) *n.* **1.** A torn and hanging piece, as of cloth; a shred. **2. tatters.** Torn and ragged clothing; rags. **—***tr.v.* To make ragged; reduce to shreds. **—***intr.v.* To become ragged. [Middle English.]

tat·ter·de·ma·lion (tăt'ər-də-māl'yən, -măl'-) *n.* A person wearing ragged or tattered clothing; ragamuffin. [From TATTER.]

tat·tered (tăt'ərd) *adj.* **1.** Torn into shreds; ragged: *tattered clothes.* **2.** Wearing ragged clothes: *a tattered beggar.*

tat·ter·sall (tăt'ər-sôl', -səl) *n.* **1.** A pattern of lines forming squares on a solid background. **2.** Cloth woven in this pattern: *a shirt of navy tattersall.* [After *Tattersall's* horse market, London, England.]

tat·ting (tăt'ĭng) *n.* **1.** Handmade lace produced by looping and knotting a single strand of heavy thread on a small hand shuttle. **2.** The act or art of making such lace. [Orig. unknown.]

tat·tle (tăt'l) *v.* **-tled, -tling. —***intr.v.* **1.** To reveal the plans or activities of another; to gossip. **2.** To chatter idly; prate: *tattled endlessly about nothing in particular.* **—***tr.v.* To reveal through gossiping. **—***n.* **1.** A bearer of tales; tattletail. **2.** Idle chatter; prattle. **3.** Gossip; talebearing. [Flemish *tatelen*, to babble.] **—tat'tling·ly** *adv.*

tat·tler (tăt'lər) *n.* **1.** A person who tattles. **2.** Any of several shore birds related to the sandpipers, esp. one of the genus *Heteroscelus,* of coastal areas of the Pacific.

tat·tle·tale (tăt'l-tāl') *n.* A person who tattles on others; a talebearer.

tat·too¹ (tă-tōo') *n.* **1.** A signal sounded on a drum or bugle to summon soldiers to their quarters in the evening. **2.** A display of military exercises. **3.** Any continuous, even drumming or rapping. [Earlier *tap-too,* from Dutch *taptoe,* "the shutting off of the taps (at taverns at the end of the day)."]

tat·too² (tă-tōo') *n.* A permanent mark or design made on the skin by a process of pricking and ingraining an indelible pigment or by raising scars. **—***tr.v.* **1.** To mark (the skin) with a tattoo or tattoos. **2.** To form (a mark or design) on the skin. [Of Polynesian orig.] **—tat·too'er** *n.*

tau (tou, tô) *n.* The 19th letter of the Greek alphabet, written T, τ. In English it is represented as *T, t.* [Greek.]

taught (tôt) *v.* Past tense and past participle of **teach.**

taunt (tônt) *tr.v.* To challenge, insult, or reproach in a contemptuous or jeering manner. **—See** Syns at **ridicule. —***n.* A scornful or jeering remark intended to challenge or insult. [Perh. from Old French *tanter,* to test, tempt, from Latin *temptāre.*] **—taunt'er** *n.* **—taunt'ing·ly** *adv.*

taupe (tōp) *n.* A brownish gray or dark yellowish brown. **—***adj.* Brownish gray or dark yellowish brown. [French, mole, from Latin *talpa.*]

Tau·rus (tôr'əs) *n.* **1.** A constellation in the Northern Hemisphere near Orion and Aries. **2.** The second sign of the zodiac.

taut (tôt) *adj.* **-er, -est. 1.** Pulled or drawn tight: *sails taut with the wind.* **2.** Strained; tense: *his taut and angry face.* **3.** Kept in trim shape; efficient; tidy: *He runs a taut business operation.* **—See** Syns at **tight.** [Middle English *toght.*] **—taut'ly** *adv.* **—taut'ness** *n.*

tau·tog (tô'tôg', -tŏg', tô-tôg', -tŏg') *n.* Also **tau·taug.** A dark-colored, edible saltwater fish, *Tautoga onitis,* of the North American Atlantic coast; blackfish. [Of Algonquian orig.]

tau·tol·o·gy (tô-tŏl'ə-jē) *n., pl.* **-gies. 1. a.** Needless repetition of the same information or idea in different words; redundancy. **b.** An instance of such repetition. **2.** *Logic.* A statement that includes all logical possibilities and is therefore always true. [Late Latin *tautologia,* from Greek, from *tautologos,* repeating the same ideas.] **—tau'to·log'i·cal** (tô'tə-lŏj'ĭ-kəl) or **tau'to·log'ic** *adj.* **—tau'to·log'i·cal·ly** *adv.*

tav·ern (tăv'ərn) *n.* **1.** An establishment licensed to sell alcoholic beverages to be drunk on the premises; a bar. **2.** An inn for travelers. [Middle English *taverne,* from Old French, from Latin *taberna,* hut, inn.]

taw (tô) *n.* **1.** A large, fancy marble used for shooting. **2.** The line from which a player shoots in marbles. [Orig. unknown.]

taw·dry (tô'drē) *adj.* **-dri·er, -dri·est.** Cheap and gaudy: *a tawdry red dress with spangles.* [From *tawdry lace,* short for *Seynt Audries lace,* cheap and gaudy lace neckties sold at fairs in honor of St. Audrey (d. 679), queen of Northumbria.] **—taw'dri·ly** *adv.* **—taw'dri·ness** *n.*

taw·ny (tô'nē) *adj.* **-ni·er, -ni·est.** Light golden brown. [Middle English from Norman French *taune,* var. of Old French *tane,* tanned, from *taner,* to tan.]

tax (tăks) *n.* **1.** A charge or contribution required of persons or groups within the domain of a government for the support of that government. **2.** An excessive demand; a strain. **—***tr.v.* **1.** To place a tax on income, property, goods, etc. **2.** To exact a tax or taxes from. **3.** To make difficult or excessive demands upon: *Overpopulation taxes a nation's resources.* [Middle English *taxen,* to assess, tax, from Old French *taxer,* from Medieval Latin *taxāre,* from Latin, freq. of *tangere,* to touch.] **—tax'a·ble** *adj.* **—tax'er** *n.*

tax-. Var. of **taxo-.**

tax·a (tăk'sə) *n.* Plural of **taxon.**

tax·a·tion (tăk-sā'shən) *n.* **1.** The practice of imposing taxes. **2.** An assessed amount of tax. **3.** The revenue raised through taxes.

tax·es (tăk'sēz) *n.* Plural of **taxis.**

tax-ex·empt (tăks'ĭg-zĕmpt') *adj.* Not subject to taxation: *tax-exempt interest from municipal bonds.*

tax·i (tăk'sē) *n., pl.* **-is** or **-ies.** A taxicab. **—***v.* **tax·ied, tax·i·ing** or **tax·y·ing. —***intr.v.* **1.** To be transported by taxi. **2.** To move slowly over the surface of ground or water before takeoff or after landing, as an aircraft. **—***tr.v.* To cause (an airplane) to taxi. [Short for TAXICAB.]

taxi-. Var. of **taxo-.**

tax·i·cab (tăk'sē-kăb') *n.* An automobile that carries passengers for a fare, usu. registered on a meter. [TAXI (METER) + CAB.]

tax·i·der·my (tăk'sĭ-dûr'mē) *n.* The art or process of preparing, stuffing, and mounting the skins of dead animals for exhibition in lifelike form. [TAXI- + -DERM + -Y.] **—tax'i·der'mal** or **tax'i·der'mic** *adj.* **—tax'i·derm'ist** *n.*

tax·i·me·ter (tăk'sē-mē'tər) *n.* An instrument installed in a taxicab to automatically compute and indicate the fare. [French *taximètre* : *taxe,* tax, charge, from Old French *taxer,* to tax + *-metre,* meter.]

tax·ing (tăk'sĭng) *adj.* Imposing a severe test of physical or spiritual strength. **—See** Syns at **burdensome.**

tax·is (tăk'sĭs) *n., pl.* **tax·es** (tăk'sēz'). The responsive movement of an organism toward or away from an external stimulus. [Greek, arrangement, order, from *tattein,* to arrange.]

-taxis or **-taxy.** A suffix meaning order or arrangement: *phyllotaxy.* [From Greek *taxis,* arrangement, order.]

taxo- or **tax-** or **taxi-.** A prefix meaning arrangement or order: *taxidermy.* [From Greek *taxis,* arrangement, order.]

tax·on (tăk'sŏn') *n., pl.* **tax·a** (tăk'sə). *Biol.* A group of organisms constituting one of the categories or formal units in taxonomic classification. [Back-formation from TAXONOMY.]

tax·on·o·my (tăk-sŏn'ə-mē) *n.* **1.** The science, laws, or principles of classification. **2.** *Biol.* The theory, principles, and process of classifying organisms in established categories. **—tax'o·nom'ic** (-sə-nŏm'ĭk) or **tax'o·nom'i·cal** *adj.* **—tax'o·**

nom′i·cal·ly *adv.* —tax·on′o·mist *n.*

tax·pay·er (tăks′pā′ər) *n.* Someone who pays or is required to pay taxes.

–taxy. Var. of **-taxis.**

tax·y·ing (tăk′sē-ĭng) *v.* A present participle of **taxi.**

Tb The symbol for the element terbium.

T-bone (tē′bōn′) *n.* A thick porterhouse steak taken from the small end of the loin and containing a T-shaped bone.

Tc The symbol for the element technetium.

Te The symbol for the element tellurium.

tea (tē) *n.* **1.** A shrub, *Thea sinensis* (or *Camellia sinensis*), of eastern Asia, with fragrant white flowers and evergreen leaves. **2.** The dried leaves of this plant, prepared by various processes and in various stages of growth, and used to make a hot beverage. **3.** An aromatic, slightly bitter beverage made by steeping tea leaves in boiling water. **4.** Any of various beverages prepared from the leaves, flowers, etc. of various other plants, or from beef or other extracts. **5. a.** An afternoon refreshment usu. of cakes, small sandwiches, or other light foods served with tea. **b.** A social gathering or party at which tea is served, usu. held in the afternoon. **7.** *Slang.* Marijuana. [Chinese *te.*]

tea bag. A small sack of thin, porous paper or cloth holding a measured amount of crushed tea leaves, usu. enough to make an individual serving of tea.

tea·cart (tē′kärt′) *n.* A tea wagon.

teach (tēch) *v.* **taught** (tôt), **teach·ing.** —*tr.v.* **1.** To impart knowledge or skill to; give instruction to. **2.** To provide knowledge of; instruct in: *He teaches biology.* **3.** To cause to learn by example or experience. —*intr.v.* To give instruction, esp. as an occupation. —See Usage note at **learn.** [Middle English *techen,* from Old English *tǣcan.*]

Syns: teach, instruct, train, tutor *v. Core meaning:* To impart knowledge or skill to *(teach school children).* TEACH is the most widely applicable. INSTRUCT usu. suggests methodical direction in a specific subject or area *(instructing students in English literature).* TUTOR usu. refers to private instruction of one student or a small group *(tutoring children in mathematics after school).* TRAIN gen. implies concentration on particular skills intended to fit one for a desired role *(training young people to be good citizens; a school that trains truck drivers).*

teach·a·ble (tē′chə-bəl) *adj.* Capable of or receptive to being taught. —**teach′a·bil′i·ty** or **teach′a·ble·ness** *n.* —**teach′a·bly** *adv.*

teach·er (tē′chər) *n.* Someone who teaches, esp. a person hired by a school to teach.

teachers college. Also **teachers' college.** A college with a special curriculum for training teachers.

teach-in (tēch′ĭn′) *n.* An extended critical discussion of a public issue held on a college or university campus, with the participation of students, faculty, and guest speakers.

teach·ing (tē′chĭng) *n.* **1.** The work or occupation of teachers. **2.** Often **teachings.** A precept or doctrine: *the teachings of Confucius.*

tea·cup (tē′kŭp′) *n.* A small cup for serving tea.

tea dance. A late-afternoon dance.

tea·cup·ful (tē′kŭp′fŏŏl′) *n., pl.* **-fuls.** The amount that a teacup will hold.

tea·house (tē′hous′) *n.* A public establishment, esp. in Oriental countries, serving tea and other refreshments.

teak (tēk) *n.* **1.** A tall evergreen tree, *Tectona grandis,* of southeastern Asia, with hard, heavy, durable wood. **2.** The hard, strong yellowish-brown wood of this tree, used for furniture, shipbuilding, etc. Also called **teakwood.** [Portuguese *teca,* from Malayalam *tēkka.*] —**teak** *adj.*

tea·ket·tle (tē′kĕt′l) *n.* A covered kettle, with a handle and a spout for pouring, used to boil water, as for tea.

teak·wood (tēk′wŏŏd′) *n.* Teak.

teal (tēl) *n., pl.* **teal** or **teals.** **1.** Any of several small, widely distributed river ducks of the genus *Anas,* many of which have brightly marked plumage. **2.** Moderate or dark bluish green to greenish blue. [Middle English *tele.*] —**teal** *adj.*

team (tēm) *n.* **1.** Two or more animals harnessed to a vehicle or farm implement: *a team of horses.* **2.** A group of players on the same side in a game. **3.** Two or more people organized to work together. —*tr.v.* To join together in a team. —*intr.v.* To form a team: *team up to play baseball.*

[Middle English *teme,* from Old English *tēam,* offspring, brood, team of animals.]

team·mate (tēm′māt′) *n.* A fellow member of a team.

team·ster (tēm′stər) *n.* **1.** A person who drives a team. **2.** A truck driver.

team·work (tēm′wûrk′) *n.* Cooperative effort by the members of a team or group to achieve a common goal.

tea·pot (tē′pŏt′) *n.* A covered pot with a handle and a spout, used for, making and serving tea.

tear[1] (târ) *v.* **tore** (tôr, tōr), **torn** (tôrn, tōrn), **tear·ing.** —*tr.v.* **1.** To pull apart or into pieces forcefully; to rend: *tear a letter to shreds.* **2.** To make (an opening or wound) by or as by ripping: *tore a hole in his trousers; tore the skin on his elbow.* **3.** To separate or remove forcefully; to wrench: *tore his arm from its socket.* **4.** To divide or disrupt emotionally: *Guilt tore her apart.* **5.** To disrupt, destroy, or wreck havoc upon: *tore the house apart in their search; a nation torn by war.* —*intr.v.* **1.** To become torn. **2.** To move with great speed; rush headlong: *He tore down the road.* —See Syns at **rush.** —*phrasal verbs.* **tear down.** To demolish. —See Syns at **destroy. tear into.** *Informal.* To attack violently or with anger. **tear up.** To destroy by or as if by rending. —*n.* **1.** The act of tearing. **2.** A rip, hole, or rent. **3.** A furious or headlong rush. —*idiom.* **wear and tear.** The damage sustained by an object from continual use. [Middle English *teren,* from Old English *teran.*]

Usage: tear. The past participle of *tear* is *torn: He has torn the paper. The paper is torn. Tore* is the past tense: *I tore the paper.* Use of *tore* as a past participle is incorrect.

tear[2] (tîr) *n.* **1.** A drop of the clear salty liquid that is secreted by the lachrymal gland of the eye and lubricates the surface between the eyeball and the eyelid. **2.** A drop of any liquid or hardened fluid. **3. tears.** The act of weeping. —*intr.v.* To fill with tears. [Middle English, from Old English *tēar.*] —**tear′i·ly** *adv.* —**tear′i·ness** *n.* —**tear′y** *adj.*

tear·drop (tîr′drŏp′) *n.* **1.** A single tear. **2.** An object that has the shape of a tear: *a diamond teardrop.*

tear·ful (tîr′fəl) *adj.* Filled with or causing tears; piteous: a tearful tale. —**tear′ful·ly** *adv.* —**tear′ful·ness** *n.*

tear gas (tîr). Any of various chemicals that when dispersed as a gas or mist irritate the eyes and breathing passages severely, causing choking and heavy tears.

tear-jerk·er (tîr′jûr′kər) *n. Slang.* A pathetic story, drama, or performance apt to produce sentimental tears.

tea·room (tē′rōōm′, -rŏŏm′) *n.* A restaurant or shop serving tea and other refreshments.

tea rose. Any of several cultivated roses derived from *Rosa odorata,* with fragrant yellowish or pink flowers.

tease (tēz) *v.* **teased, teas·ing.** —*tr.v.* **1.** To annoy or pester by making fun of or taunting. **2.** To get or try to get by begging or coaxing: *tried to tease the secret out of her.* **3.** To disentangle the fibers of: *tease wool.* **4.** To raise a nap on (cloth), as with a tease: *tease yardgoods to give them a soft, fuzzy nap.* **5.** To brush or comb (the hair) toward the scalp for a full, airy effect. —*intr. v.* To annoy or make fun of someone persistently. —*n.* **1.** Someone who teases. **2.** A remark or taunt used to tease. **3.** The act of teasing. [Middle English *tesen,* to card (wool), tear apart, from Old English *tǣsan.*] —**teas′ing·ly** *adv.*

tea·sel (tē′zəl) *n.* Also **tea·zel** or **tea·zle.** **1.** Any of several plants of the genus *Dipsacus,* native to the Old World, with thistlelike flowers surrounded by prickly bracts. **2. a.** The bristly flower head of such a plant, used to brush the surface of fabrics so as to form a nap. **b.** A mechanical object used for the same purpose. [Middle English *tesel,* from Old English *tǣsel.*]

team

teas·er (tē'zər) n. 1. Someone or something that teases. 2. A device used for teasing wool.

tea service. A matched set of fine chinaware or silverware used in serving tea. Also called **tea set.**

tea·spoon (tē'spōon') n. 1. A small spoon used for stirring liquids and for eating soft foods, esp. desserts. 2. The amount that a teaspoon holds. 3. A household measure equal to 1/3 tablespoon.

tea·spoon·ful (tē'spōon'fŏol') n., pl. **-fuls.** The amount that a teaspoon holds.

teat (tēt, tĭt) n. The part of an udder or breast through which milk is taken; a nipple. [Middle English *tette*, from Old French.]

tea wagon. A small table on wheels for serving tea or holding dishes. Also called **teacart.**

tea·zel or **tea·zle** (tē'zəl) n. Vars. of teasel.

tech·ne·ti·um (tĕk-nē'shē-əm) n. *Symbol* **Tc** A silvery-gray metallic element that has 14 isotopes with mass numbers ranging from 92 to 105 and half-lives up to 2.6 million years. Atomic number 43; valences 3, 4, 6, 7; melting point 2,200°C. [From Greek *tekhnētos*, artificial, from *tekhnasthai*, to make by art, from *tekhnē*, art, skill.]

tech·nic (tĕk'nĭk) n. Var. of technique.

tech·ni·cal (tĕk'nĭ-kəl) adj. 1. Of or derived from technique: *technical ability.* 2. Of a particular subject; specialized: *a technical school.* 3. Of or using scientific knowledge; theoretical: *a technical analysis.* 4. According to principle, esp. formal rather than practical: *a technical advantage.* 5. Industrial and mechanical; technological: *technical assistance overseas.* [Latin *technicus*, from Greek *tekhnikos*, of art or skill, from *tekhnē*, art, skill.] —**tech'ni·cal·ly** adv. —**tech'ni·cal·ness** n.

tech·ni·cal·i·ty (tĕk'nĭ-kăl'ĭ-tē) n., pl. **-ties.** 1. The condition or quality of being technical. 2. Something meaningful or relevant in principle only; a detail or point that is specialized and theoretical: *a legal technicality.*

technical knockout. *Boxing.* A victory won by a fighter when the referee ends the match because it appears that the opponent is too badly beaten to continue without suffering serious injury.

technical sergeant. A noncommissioned officer in the U.S. Airforce, and formerly in the U.S. Army, ranking below a master sergeant and above a staff sergeant.

tech·ni·cian (tĕk-nĭsh'ən) n. A person who is skilled in a certain technical field or process: *a dental technician.* [TECHN(IC) + -ICIAN.]

Tech·ni·col·or (tĕk'nĭ-kŭl'ər) n. A trademark for a process used to make pictures in color.

tech·nique (tĕk-nēk') n. Also **tech·nic** (tĕk'nĭk). 1. A systematic procedure or method by which a complicated task is accomplished, as in a science or art. 2. The degree to which basic skills of procedure have been mastered, esp. as exhibited by performance: *a surgeon with remarkable technique.* [French, "technical," from Greek *tekhnikos*, from *tekhnē*, art, skill.]

tech·noc·ra·cy (tĕk-nŏk'rə-sē) n., pl. **-cies.** 1. A theory of government that advocates that the entire socio-economic system should be controlled by technical scientists and engineers. 2. A government so run. [Greek *tekhnē*, art, skill + -CRACY.] —**tech'no·crat'** (-nə-krăt') n. —**tech'no·crat'ic** adj.

tech·no·log·i·cal (tĕk'nə-lŏj'ĭ-kəl) or **tech·no·log·ic** (-ĭk). adj. Of, involving, or resulting from technology: *technological developments.* —**tech'no·log'i·cal·ly** adv.

tech·nol·o·gy (tĕk-nŏl'ə-jē) n., pl. **-gies.** 1. a. The application of scientific knowledge, esp. in industry and commerce. b. The methods and materials used in applying scientific knowledge in this way. 2. The knowledge that a civilization has available for adapting and using its environment to its needs. [Greek *tekhnē*, skill, art + -LOGY.] —**tech·nol'o·gist** n.

tech·y (tĕch'ē) adj. Var. of tetchy.

tec·ton·ic (tĕk-tŏn'ĭk) adj. 1. Of construction or building. 2. *Geol.* Of, causing, or resulting from structural deformation in the earth's crust. [Late Latin *tectonicus*, from Greek *tektonikos*, from *tektōn*, carpenter, builder.]

ted (tĕd) tr.v. **ted·ded, ted·ding.** To spread (newly mown grass, hay, etc.) for drying. [Ult. from Old Norse *tedhja*, to spread dung, from *tadh*, spread dung.] —**ted'der** n.

ted·dy bear (tĕd'ē). A child's toy bear, esp. one stuffed with soft material and covered with furlike plush. [After President *Theodore* Roosevelt, from his reportedly having spared the life of a bear cub on a hunting trip.]

Te De·um (tā dā'əm, tē dē'əm). 1. A Latin hymn, probably from the early 5th cent. A.D., beginning with the words *Te Deum laudamus,* "We praise Thee, O God." 2. A musical setting of this hymn.

te·di·ous (tē'dē-əs) adj. Tiresome and dull because of length or slowness; boring. [Middle English, from Old French *tedieus*, from Late Latin *taediōsus*, from Latin *taedium*, tedium.] —**te'di·ous·ly** adv. —**te'di·ous·ness** n.

te·di·um (tē'dē-əm) n. The quality or condition of being tedious; boredom. [Latin *taedium*, from *taedēre*, to bore, weary.]

tee¹ (tē) n. 1. A small peg with a concave top for holding a golf ball for an initial drive. 2. The designated area from which a player makes his first stroke in golf. —tr.v. **teed, tee·ing.** To place (a golf ball) on a tee. —*phrasal verbs.* **tee off.** 1. To drive a golf ball from the tee. 2. *Slang.* To start or begin: *teed off the fund-raising campaign with a dinner.* **tee up.** To place or set up a ball for driving. [Orig. unknown.]

tee² (tē) n. A mark aimed at in certain games, such as curling or quoits. —*idiom.* **to a tee.** Perfectly; exactly. [Orig. unknown.]

teem¹ (tēm) intr.v. To be full of; abound or swarm: *The pond teemed with fish.* [Middle English *temen*, to give birth to, breed, from Old English *tīeman.*]

teem² (tēm) intr.v. To fall heavily; pour: *Confetti teemed down on the parading soldiers.* [Middle English *temen*, from Old Norse *tōma*, to empty.]

teen (tēn) n. A teen-ager. —adj. Teen-age.

teen-age (tēn'āj') adj. Also **teen-aged** (-ājd'). Of, for, or involving a person or persons aged 13 through 19.

teen-ag·er (tēn'ā'jər) n. A person between the ages of 13 and 19.

teens (tēnz) pl.n. 1. The numbers that end in -teen. 2. The years of one's life between ages 13 and 19. 3. People in their teens.

tee·ny (tē'nē) adj. **-ni·er, -ni·est.** Also **teen·sy** (tēn'sē), **-si·er, -si·est.** *Informal.* Tiny. [Alteration of TINY.]

tee·pee (tē'pē) n. Var. of tepee.

tee shirt (tē'shûrt') n. Var. of T-shirt.

tee·ter (tē'tər) intr.v. 1. To walk or move unsteadily or unsurely; to totter. 2. To seesaw; vacillate: *teetered on the edge of decision.* —tr.v. To cause to teeter or seesaw. —n. 1. A seesaw. 2. A teetering motion. [Earlier *titter*, prob. ult. from Old Norse *titra*, to tremble.]

tee·ter-tot·ter (tē'tər-tŏt'ər) n. A seesaw.

teeth (tēth) n. Plural of tooth.

teethe (tēth) intr.v. **teethed, teeth·ing.** To have teeth develop and come through the gums; cut one's teeth. [Middle English *tethen*, from *tethe*, teeth.]

teething ring. A ring of hard rubber or plastic upon which a teething baby can bite.

tee·to·tal·er (tē-tōt'l-ər) n. Also *Brit.* **tee·to·tal·ler.** A person who does not drink any alcoholic beverages. [*Tee,* first letter in TOTAL + TOTAL (ABSTINENCE).] —**tee·to'tal·ism** n.

Tef·lon (tĕf'lŏn') n. A trademark for a durable plastic based on compounds of carbon and fluorine, used to coat certain cooking utensils and to prevent sticking of machine parts.

teg·u·ment (tĕg'yə-mənt) n. An outer covering, as a shell or husks; integument. [Middle English, from Latin *tegumentum*, from *tegere*, to cover.]

tek·tite (tĕk'tīt') n. Any of numerous dark brown to green glass objects of unknown origin, usu. small and rounded, found in several parts of the world. [From Greek *tēktos*, molten, from *tēkein*, to melt.]

tele- or **tel-.** A prefix meaning: 1. Distance: **telecommunication.** 2. Television: **telecast.** [From Greek *tēle*, at a distance, far off.]

tel·e·cast (tĕl'ĭ-kăst') v. **-cast** or **-cast·ed, -cast·ing.** —intr.v. To broadcast by television. —tr.v. To broadcast (a program) by television. —n. A television broadcast.

tel·e·com·mu·ni·ca·tion (tĕl'ĭ-kə-myōo'nĭ-kā'shən) n. Often **telecommunications** (*used with a sing. verb*). The science and technology of sending messages over long distances, esp. by electrical or electronic means.

tel·e·gen·ic (tĕl′ə-jĕn′ĭk, -jē′nĭk) *adj.* Presenting an attractive appearance on television. [TELE- + (PHOTO)GENIC.]

tel·e·gram (tĕl′ĭ-grăm′) *n.* A message or communication sent by telegraph; a wire.

tel·e·graph (tĕl′ĭ-grăf) *n.* **1.** Any communications system that sends and receives messages by means of electric impulses transmitted either by wire or through space. **2.** A message sent by such a system. —*tr.v.* **1.** To send (a message) by telegraph. **2.** To send a message to (someone) by telegraph. **3.** To disclose or reveal, esp. unintentionally; broadcast: *The expression on his face telegraphed his disappointment.* —*intr.v.* To send a telegram: *We decided to telegraph rather than telephone.* —**te·leg′ra·pher** (tə-lĕg′rə-fər) or **te·leg′ra·phist** *n.*

tel·e·graph·ic (tĕl′ĭ-grăf′ĭk) or **tel·e·graph·i·cal** (-ĭ-kəl) *adj.* **1.** Of or sent by telegraphy. **2.** Brief; concise: *a telegraphic style of writing.* —**tel′e·graph′i·cal·ly** *adv.*

te·leg·ra·phy (tə-lĕg′rə-fē) *n.* **1.** Communication by means of telegraph. **2.** The science and technology used in accomplishing this.

Tel·e·gu (tĕl′ĭ-gōō′) *n., pl.* **Telegu** or **-gus.** **1.** A Dravidian language spoken in southeastern India. **2.** A member of a Dravidian people who speak Telegu. —*adj.* Of or pertaining to this language or this people.

tel·e·ki·ne·sis (tĕl′ĭ-kĭ-nē′sĭs, -kī-) *n.* **1.** The movement of objects by means other than the application of material or mechanical force, as by the exercise of mental powers. **2.** The ability to produce such movement. [TELE- + Greek *kinēsis,* motion.] —**tel′e·ki·net′ic** (-nĕt′ĭk) *adj.*

Te·lem·a·chus (tə-lĕm′ə-kəs) *n. Gk. Myth.* The son of Odysseus and Penelope who helped his father kill Penelope's suitors.

tel·e·me·ter (tĕl′ə-mē′tər) *n.* Any of various devices used in telemetry. —*tr.v.* To measure and transmit (data) automatically from a distant source, such as spacecraft or remote control aircraft, to a receiving station. —**tel′e·met′ric** (tĕl′ə-mĕt′rĭk) or **tel′e·met′ri·cal** *adj.* —**tel′e·met′ri·cal·ly** *adv.*

te·lem·e·try (tə-lĕm′ĭ-trē) *n.* **1.** The automatic measurement and transmission of data from a distant source to a receiving station. **2.** The science and technology used in doing this.

te·le·ol·o·gy (tē′lē-ŏl′ə-jē, tĕl′ē-) *n., pl.* **-gies.** **1.** The philosophical doctrine that natural phenomena are not determined by mechanical causes but instead are directed toward a definite end in the overall scheme of nature. **2.** Such ultimate purpose or design. [Greek *teleos,* complete, final, from *telos,* completion, end + -LOGY.] —**te′le·o·log′i·cal** (-ə-lŏj′ĭ-kəl) or **te′le·o·log′ic** *adj.* —**te′le·o·log′i·cal·ly** *adv.* —**te′le·ol′o·gist** *n.*

te·lep·a·thy (tə-lĕp′ə-thē) *n.* **1.** Communication between minds without the use of speech, signs, etc., as by the exercise of mystical or mental powers. **2.** The ability to produce or engage in such communication. —**tel′e·path′ic** (tĕl′ə-păth′ĭk) *adj.* —**tel′e·path′i·cal·ly** *adv.* —**te·lep′a·thist** *n.*

tel·e·phone (tĕl′ə-fōn′) *n.* An instrument that reproduces or receives sound, esp. speech, at a distance. —*v.* **-phoned, -phon·ing.** —*tr.v.* **1.** To call or communicate with (someone) by telephone. **2.** To transmit (a message or information) by telephone. —*intr.v.* To communicate by telephone. —**tel′e·phon′er** *n.*

tel·e·phon·ic (tĕl′ə-fŏn′ĭk) *adj.* **1.** Of or pertaining to telephones. **2.** Transmitted or conveyed by a telephone. —**tel′e·phon′i·cal·ly** *adv.*

te·leph·o·ny (tə-lĕf′ə-nē) *n.* **1.** The transmission of sound between distant points, esp. by electronic or electrical means. **2.** The science and technology used in accomplishing this.

tel·e·pho·to (tĕl′ə-fō′tō) *adj.* Of, concerning, or denoting a photographic lens or lens system used to produce a large image of a distant object or to obtain a clear picture of a near object against a blurred background. —*n.* A telephoto lens.

tel·e·pho·to·graph (tĕl′ə-fō′tə-grăf′) *n.* **1.** A photograph transmitted and reproduced by telephotography. **2.** A photograph taken with a telephoto lens. —*tr.v.* To transmit by telephotography.

tel·e·pho·tog·ra·phy (tĕl′ə-fə-tŏg′rə-fē) *n.* **1.** The photographing of distant objects, as with a telephoto lens or telescope on a camera. **2.** The transmission of photographs, charts, pictures, etc., over a long distance by means of telegraph wire or radio channel. —**tel′e·pho′to·graph′ic** (-fō′tə-grăf′ĭk) *adj.*

tel·e·play (tĕl′ə-plā′) *n.* A play written or adapted for television.

tel·e·print·er (tĕl′ə-prĭn′tər) *n.* A teletypewriter.

tel·e·scope (tĕl′ĭ-skōp′) *n.* **1.** A device that uses an arrangement of lenses, mirrors, or both to collect visible light, allowing observation or photographic recording of distant objects. **2.** Any of various devices, such as a radio telescope, used to collect and analyze electromagnetic radiation other than light coming from distant sources. —*tr.v.* **-scoped, -scop·ing.** **1.** To cause to slide inward or outward in overlapping sections, as the tube sections of a small hand telescope. **2.** To crush or compress (an object) inward: *Hitting the wall at high speed telescoped the racing car.* **3.** To make shorter or more precise; condense. [From Greek *teleskopos,* farseeing: *tele,* far off + *skopos,* watcher.]

telescope

tel·e·scop·ic (tĕl′ĭ-skŏp′ĭk) *adj.* **1.** Of a telescope. **2.** Seen or obtained by means of a telescope: *telescopic data.* **3.** Visible only by means of a telescope: *a telescopic binary star.* **4.** Capable of seeing or discerning distant objects: *telescopic vision.* **5.** Capable of telescoping or being telescoped: *a telescopic antenna.* —**tel′e·scop′i·cal·ly** *adv.*

tel·e·thon (tĕl′ə-thŏn′) *n.* A long television program, usu. to raise funds for charity. [TELE- + (MARA)THON.]

Tel·e·type (tĕl′ĭ-tīp′) *n.* **1.** A trademark for a brand of teletypewriter. **2.** A message transmitted by Teletype. —*v.* **-typed, -typ·ing.** —*intr.v.* To send a message by Teletype. —*tr.v.* To send (a message) by Teletype.

tel·e·type·writ·er (tĕl′ĭ-tīp′rī′tər) *n.* An electromechanical typewriter that either transmits or receives messages coded in electrical signals carried by telegraph or telephone wires. Also called **teleprinter.**

tel·e·view (tĕl′ə-vyōō′) *intr.v.* To watch by means of television receiving equipment. —**tel′e·view′er** *n.*

tel·e·vise (tĕl′ə-vīz′) *v.* **-vised, -vis·ing.** —*tr.v.* To broadcast (a program) by television. —*intr.v.* To broadcast by television. [Back-formation from TELEVISION.]

tel·e·vi·sion (tĕl′ə-vĭzh′ən) *n.* **1.** The transmission and reception of visual images of moving or stationary objects, usu. with accompanying sound, as electrical signals or by means of radio. **2.** A device that receives such electrical signals or radio waves and reproduces the transmitted images on a screen. **3.** The industry of broadcasting programs in this medium.

tell (tĕl) *v.* **told** (tōld), **tell·ing.** —*tr.v.* **1.** To give an account of; relate; recount: *tell a story.* **2.** To express in spoken or written words; to say: *tell a lie; a letter telling when he will arrive.* **3.** To make known to; notify; inform: *Tell me what happened.* **4.** To broadcast or announce. **5.** To indicate; reveal; disclose: *a scowl that told his annoyance.* **6.** To command; order: *Do as you are told.* **7.** To discover by observation; discern; identify: *hard to tell what he thinks of the project.* **8.** *Informal.* To assure emphatically: *You will succeed, I tell you.* **9.** To count or name; enumerate. —*intr.v.* **1.** To give an account, enumeration, or description: *Tell about your new job.* **2.** To give evidence or indication: *glum looks telling of disappointment.* **3.** To reveal or disclose something hidden or secret: *Promise you'll never tell!* **4.** To have an effect or impact: *The strain is beginning to tell on his work.* —See Syns at **command.** —*phrasal verb.* **tell off.** *Informal.* To criticize or scold sharply. [Middle English *tellen,* from Old English *tellan.*] —**tell′a·ble** *adj.*

tell·er (tĕl′ər) *n.* **1.** A person who tells something, such as a story, tale, etc. **2.** A bank employee who receives and pays out money. **3.** A person appointed to count votes in a legislative assembly.

tell·ing (tĕl′ĭng) *adj.* **1.** Having force or effect; striking: *a telling victory.* **2.** Full of meaning; revealing: *a telling remark.* —**tell′ing·ly** *adv.*

tell·tale (tĕl′tāl′) *n.* **1.** Someone who informs on another person; tattler; talebearer. **2.** Something that discloses or reveals information about something. **3.** Any of various devices that indicate or register information, such as a time clock, a railroad warning device, etc. —*adj.* **1.** Serving to indicate or reveal: *a telltale odor.* **2.** Serving to disclose what is intended to be kept secret: *a telltale blush.*

tel·lu·ride (tĕl′yə-rīd′) *n.* A chemical compound of tellurium and one other element. [TELLUR(IUM) + -IDE.]

tel·lu·ri·um (tĕ-lŏŏr′ē-əm, tə-) *n. Symbol* **Te** A brittle, silvery metallic element that occurs in nature combined with gold and other metals. Atomic number 52; atomic weight 127.60; valences -2, 2, 4, 6; melting point 449.5°C; boiling point 989.8°C. [From Latin *tellūs,* earth.]

tel·ly (tĕl′ē) *n., pl.* **-lies.** *Brit. Informal.* Television.

te·lo·phase (tē′lə-fāz′, tĕl′ə-) *n.* The final phase of mitosis, in which the chromosomes of the daughter cells are grouped in new nuclei. [Greek *telos,* end + PHASE.]

tem·blor (tĕm′blər, -blôr′) *n. Regional.* An earthquake. [Spanish, from *temblar,* to shake.]

te·mer·i·ty (tə-mĕr′ĭ-tē) *n.* Foolish boldness; recklessness; rashness. [Middle English *temeryte,* from Latin *temeritās,* from *temere,* blindly, rashly.]

> **Syns: temerity, gall, presumption** *n.* **Core meaning:** Excessive, arrogant self-confidence *(had the temerity to accept the invitation for me).*

tem·per (tĕm′pər) *tr.v.* **1.** To soften or moderate: *tempering justice with mercy.* **2.** To harden, strengthen, or toughen (a material, esp. a metal) by heating, alternate heating and cooling, or other special treatment. **3.** To tune or adjust (a keyboard instrument) so that no intervals or chords sound noticeably false although all but the octave are slightly out of tune: *He must temper his harpsichord before every concert.* —*intr. v.* To be or become tempered. —*n.* **1.** A habitual condition of the mind or emotions; mood; disposition: *an even temper.* **2.** Calmness of the mind or emotions; composure: *Don't lose your temper.* **3. a.** A tendency to become angry or irritable: *a bad temper.* **b.** An outburst of rage: *an unusual fit of temper.* **4.** The degree to which a material, esp. a metal, has been hardened, strengthened, or toughened by tempering. —See Syns at **disposition.** [Middle English *temperen,* from Old English *temprian,* to mingle, moderate, from Latin *temperāre,* to mingle in due proportion, prob. from *tempus,* time, due season.] —**tem′per·a·bil′i·ty** *n.* —**tem′per·a·ble** *adj.* —**tem′per·er** *n.*

tem·per·a (tĕm′pər-ə) *n.* **1.** A painting medium in which pigment is mixed with water-soluble glutinous materials such as size or egg yolk. **2.** Painting done with this medium. [Italian, from *temperare,* to mingle, temper, from Latin *temperāre.*]

tem·per·a·ment (tĕm′pər-ə-mənt, -prə-mənt) *n.* **1.** The manner of thinking, behaving, or reacting characteristic of a specific individual; disposition: *a nervous temperament.* **2.** Excessive irritability or sensitiveness; temper. **3.** *Mus.* The way in which a keyboard instrument is tuned as a result of tempering. —See Syns at **disposition.** [Middle English *temperament,* from Latin *temperāmentum,* a mixing (of the humors), from *temperāre,* to mingle, temper.]

tem·per·a·men·tal (tĕm′prə-mĕn′tl, -pər-ə-) *adj.* **1.** Of, caused by, or endowed with temperament: *a tempermental quirk.* **2.** Excessively sensitive, irritable, or changeable; moody. —See Syns at **capricious.** —**tem′per·a·men′tal·ly** *adv.*

tem·per·ance (tĕm′pər-əns, -prəns) *n.* **1.** The condition of being temperate; restraint; moderation. **2.** Total abstinence from alcoholic beverages.

tem·per·ate (tĕm′pər-ĭt, -prĭt) *adj.* **1.** Exercising moderation and self-restraint: *a temperate drinker.* **2.** Moderate in degree or quality; not extreme: *a man of temperate politics.* **3.** Of or having a mild or variable climate that is not subject to prolonged or extreme hot or cold weather.

Temperate Zone. Either of two zones on the earth's surface which enjoy moderate and variable weather, one lies between the Antarctic Circle and the tropic of Capricorn and the other between the Arctic Circle and the tropic of Cancer.

tem·per·a·ture (tĕm′pər-ə-chŏŏr′, -chər, tĕm′prə-) *n.* **1. a.** The relative hotness or coldness of a body or environment. **b.** A numerical measure of hotness or coldness referred to a standard scale. **2.** A body temperature that is raised above normal as a result of some disease or disorder; a fever.

tem·pered (tĕm′pərd) *adj.* **1.** Having a specified type of temper or disposition: *mild-tempered.* **2.** Moderated, qualified, or diminished by the introduction of another element or factor: *courage tempered with wisdom.* **3.** Strengthened, hardened, or toughened by tempering: *a tempered steel blade.* **4.** *Mus.* Tuned to a temperament, as a musical tone, interval, instrument, etc.

tem·pest (tĕm′pĭst) *n.* **1.** A violent windstorm, often accompanied by rain, snow, or hail. **2.** Any violent agitation, commotion, or tumult; uproar. [Middle English *tempeste,* from Old French, from Latin *tempestās,* storm, weather, season, from *tempus,* time, season.]

tem·pes·tu·ous (tĕm-pĕs′chŏŏ-əs) *adj.* Tumultuous; stormy; turbulent. —**tem·pes′tu·ous·ly** *adv.* —**tem·pes′tu·ous·ness** *n.*

tem·pi (tĕm′pē) *n.* A plural of **tempo.**

Tem·plar (tĕm′plər) *n.* **1.** A knight of a religious military order founded in the 12th cent. at Jerusalem by the Crusaders. **2.** A **Knight Templar.** [Middle English *templer,* ult. from Medieval Latin *(mīles) templārius,* "(soldier) of the temple."]

tem·plate (tĕm′plĭt) *n.* A pattern or gauge, such as a thin plate cut to a definite pattern, used in making something accurately or in duplicating something, as in carpentry. [French *templet,* dim. of Old French *temple,* a device in a loom.]

tem·ple¹ (tĕm′pəl) *n.* **1.** A building or place dedicated to the worship or the presence of a deity. **2. Temple.** Any of three successive buildings in ancient Jerusalem dedicated to the worship of Jehovah. **3.** A synagogue. **4.** A building in which the Mormon sacred ordinances are administered. **5.** Anything considered to contain a divine presence, as the body of a Christian. **6.** The headquarters of any of several fraternal orders. **7.** Any place or person serving as the focus of a special activity or of something esp. valued: *a temple of learning.* **8. Temple.** Either of the two Inns of Court in London that house England's major law societies, formerly occupied by the Knights Templar. [Middle English, from Old English *tempel* and Old French *temple,* from Latin *templum,* sanctuary.]

temple¹

tem·ple² (tĕm′pəl) *n.* The flat region on either side of the forehead. [Middle English, from Old French, from Latin *tempora,* pl. of *tempus,* temple of the head.]

tem·po (tĕm′pō) *n., pl.* **-pos** or **-pi** (-pē). **1.** *Mus.* The relative speed at which a composition is to be played, as indicated by a descriptive direction to the performer. **2.** A characteristic rate or rhythm of activity; pace: *the tempo of life in the city.* [Italian, time, from Latin *tempus.*]

tem·po·ral¹ (tĕm′pər-əl, -prəl) *adj.* **1.** Of or limited by time: *temporal and spacial experimentation.* **2.** Of or concerned with the affairs of this world; worldly: *temporal pleasures.* **3.** Enduring for a short time; transitory: *the temporal beauty of youth.* **4.** Civil, secular, or lay, as distinguished from ecclesiastical: *the temporal powers of the church.* **5.** *Gram.* Expressing time: *a temporal conjunction.* [Middle English, from Latin *temporālis,* from *tempus,* time.] —**tem′po·ral·ly** *adv.*

tem·po·ral² (tĕm′pər-əl, -prəl) *adj.* Of or near the temples of the skull. [Late Latin *temporālis,* from Latin *tempus,* temple of the head.]

temporal bone. Either of two complex, three-part bones that form the sides and base of the skull.

tem·po·ral·i·ty (tĕm′pə-răl′ĭ-tē) *n., pl.* **-ties. 1.** The condition of being temporal or temporary. **2. temporalities.** Worldly possessions, esp. of the church or clergy.

tem·po·rar·y (tĕm′pə-rĕr′ē) *adj.* Lasting or used for a limited time only; not permanent. —See Syns at **transitory.** —*n., pl.* **-ies.** A worker, esp. an office worker, hired for a limited time only. —**tem′po·rar′i·ly** (-râr′ə-lē) *adv.* —**tem′po·rar′i·ness** *n.*

tem·po·rize (tĕm′pə-rīz′) *intr.v.* **-rized, -riz·ing. 1.** To compromise or act evasively in order to gain time, avoid argument, or postpone a decision. **2.** To yield or suit one's actions to the circumstances, situation, or conditions, esp. without thought to principles. —**tem′po·ri·za′tion** *n.*

tempt (tĕmpt) *tr.v.* **1.** To entice (someone) to commit an unwise or immoral act. **2.** To provoke or to risk provoking: *Don't tempt fate.* **3.** To incline or dispose strongly; be attractive to: *She was tempted to take his advice.* [Middle English *tempten,* from Old French *tempter,* from Latin *temptāre,* to test.] —**tempt′a·ble** *adj.* —**tempt′er** *n.* —**tempt′ress** (tĕmp′trĭs) *n.*

temp·ta·tion (tĕmp-tā′shən) *n.* **1.** The act of tempting. **2.** The condition of being tempted: *yielding to temptation.* **3.** Something that tempts or entices.

tempt·ing (tĕmp′tĭng) *adj.* Alluring; enticing; seductive: *a tempting offer.* —**tempt′ing·ly** *adv.* —**tempt′ing·ness** *n.*

tem·pu·ra (tĕm′poor-ə, tĕm-poor′ə) *n.* A Japanese dish of vegetables and shrimp or other seafood dipped in batter and fried in deep fat. [Japanese, "fried food."]

ten (tĕn) *n.* **1.** The cardinal number written 10 or in Roman numerals X, equal to the sum of 9 + 1. **2.** The tenth in a series. **3.** A playing card marked with ten pips. **3.** A ten-dollar bill. [Middle English, from Old English *tīen.*]

ten·a·ble (tĕn′ə-bəl) *adj.* Capable of being defended or sustained; logical; defensible: *a tenable theory; a tenable position.* [Old French, from *tenir,* to hold, from Latin *tenēre.*] —**ten′a·bil′i·ty** or **ten′a·ble·ness** *n.* —**ten′a·bly** *adv.*

te·na·cious (tə-nā′shəs) *adj.* **1.** Holding or tending to hold firmly; persistent; stubborn: *a man tenacious of his opinions and averse to new ideas.* **2.** Clinging to another object or surface. **3.** Tending to retain; retentive: *a tenacious memory.* [From Latin *tenāx,* from *tenēre,* to hold.] —**te·na′cious·ly** *adv.* —**te·na′cious·ness** *n.*

te·nac·i·ty (tə-năs′ĭ-tē) *n.* The condition or quality of being tenacious.

ten·an·cy (tĕn′ən-sē) *n., pl.* **-cies. 1.** The possession or occupancy of lands, buildings, etc., by title, lease, or rent. **2.** The period of a tenant's occupancy or possession. **3.** A habitation or other property held or occupied by a tenant.

ten·ant (tĕn′ənt) *n.* **1.** A person who pays rent to use or occupy land, a building, or other property owned by another. **2.** An occupant or dweller in any place. **3.** *Law.* One who holds or possesses property, either real or personal, by any kind of right or title. —*tr.v.* To hold as a tenant; occupy; inhabit. [Middle English, from Old French, from *tenir,* to hold, from Latin *tenēre.*]

tenant farmer. A person who farms land owned by another and pays rent in cash or in a share of the produce.

ten·ant·ry (tĕn′ən-trē) *n., pl.* **-ries. 1.** Tenants in general. **2.** The condition of being a tenant; tenancy.

Ten Commandments. In the Old Testament, the ten laws given by God to Moses on Mount Sinai. Also called **Decalogue.**

tend¹ (tĕnd) *intr.v.* **1.** To move or extend in a certain direc-

tion: *Our course tended toward the north.* **2.** To be likely: *Pressure at the office tends to make her irritable.* **3.** To be disposed or inclined: *He tends toward laziness.* [Middle English *tenden,* from Old French *tendre,* from Latin *tendere,* to stretch, be inclined.]

tend² (tĕnd) *tr.v.* **1.** To look after: *tend a child.* **2.** To serve at: *tend bar.* —*intr.v.* **1.** To serve: *tend on the customers.* **2.** *Informal.* To apply one's attention; attend: *tended to his duties.* [Middle English *tenden,* short for *attenden,* to attend.]

ten·den·cy (tĕn′dən-sē) *n., pl.* **-cies. 1.** A demonstrated inclination to think, act, or behave in a certain way. **2.** A natural bent or drift: *a girl with artistic tendencies.* **3.** The drift or purport of a written work.

ten·den·tious (tĕn-dĕn′shəs) *adj.* Written or said to promote a particular point of view; not impartial; biased: *a tendentious editorial.* [From TENDENCY.]

ten·der¹ (tĕn′dər) *adj.* **1. a.** Easily crushed or bruised; delicate; fragile. **b.** Easily chewed or cut. **2.** Having a soft, subdued quality or tone: *a tender song.* **3.** Young and vulnerable: *a girl of tender age.* **4.** *Hort.* Sensitive to frost or severe cold; not hardy: *tender plants.* **5. a.** Easily hurt; sensitive: *a tender skin.* **b.** Painful; sore. **6. a.** Gentle and loving. **b.** Given to sympathy or sentimentality; easily moved: *a tender heart.* **7.** Requiring tactful treatment; touchy: *a tender subject.* —See Syns at **gentle.** [Middle English, from Old French *tendre,* from Latin *tener,* tender, delicate.] —**ten′der·ly** *adv.* —**ten′der·ness** *n.*

ten·der² (tĕn′dər) *n.* **1.** A formal offer or proffer of something made with the intention of acceptance. **2.** *Law.* An offer of money, services, goods, etc., in payment of an obligation, as an avoidance of legal action, etc. **3.** *Comm.* A written offer to contract goods or services at a specified cost or rate; bid. **4.** Something offered in payment: *The debtor presented a deed to land as tender.* —*tr.v.* To offer formally: *tender a letter of resignation.* —See Syns at **offer.** [From Old French *tendre,* to offer, stretch out, from Latin *tendere,* to stretch.] —**ten′der·er** *n.*

tend·er³ (tĕn′dər) *n.* **1.** Someone who tends or is in charge of something. **2.** *Naut.* A ship that services one or more larger ships, esp. one that ferries supplies or passengers between ship and shore. **3.** A railroad car attached to the rear of a locomotive and designed to carry fuel and water.

ten·der·foot (tĕn′dər-foot′) *n., pl.* **-foots** or **-feet. 1.** An inexperienced person; a novice. **2.** A newcomer to outdoor life who is not yet hardened to its rigors.

ten·der·heart·ed (tĕn′dər-här′tĭd) *adj.* Easily moved by another's distress; compassionate. —See Syns at **gentle.** —**ten′der·heart′ed·ly** *adv.* —**ten′der·heart′ed·ness** *n.*

ten·der·ize (tĕn′də-rīz′) *tr.v.* **-ized, -iz·ing.** To make (meat) tender. —**ten′der·i·za′tion** *n.*

ten·der·iz·er (tĕn′də-rī′zər) *n.* A substance applied to meat to make it tender.

ten·der·loin (tĕn′dər-loin′) *n.* **1.** The tenderest part of a loin of beef or pork. **2.** A city district notorious for its vice and graft.

ten·di·nous (tĕn′də-nəs) *adj.* **1.** Of, having, or resembling a tendon. **2.** Sinewy.

ten·don (tĕn′dən) *n.* A band of tough, fibrous tissue that forms a connection between a muscle, bone, and a sinew. [From Medieval Latin *tendō,* from Latin *tendere,* to stretch.]

ten·dril (tĕn′drəl) *n.* **1.** *Bot.* One of the slender, coiling stemlike parts by means of which a climbing plant clings to something. **2.** Something resembling a tendril: *curls forming tendrils over her ears.* [Prob. from obs. French *tendrillon,* dim. of Old French *tendron,* cartilage, young shoot, from Latin *tener,* tender, delicate.]

ten·e·brous (tĕn′ə-brəs) *adj.* Dark and gloomy. [From Latin *tenebrae,* darkness.]

ten·e·ment (tĕn′ə-mənt) *n.* **1.** A building to live in, esp. one intended for rent. **2.** A cheap run-down apartment building whose facilities and maintenance barely meet minimum standards. **3.** *Brit.* An apartment or room leased to a tenant. **4.** *Law.* Any property of a permanent nature that may be held by one person for another, as land, rents, franchises, etc. [Middle English, from Old French, from Medieval Latin *tenementum,* feudal holding, house, from Latin *tenēre,* to hold.]

ten·et (tĕn'ĭt) *n.* An opinion, doctrine or principle held as being true by a person or an organization. [Latin, "he holds", from *tenēre,* to hold.]

ten·fold (tĕn'fōld') *adj.* **1.** Comprised of ten parts or members. **2.** Ten times as great or as many. —*adv.* Ten times (in extent or number): *Their numbers increased tenfold in a single generation.*

ten-gal·lon hat (tĕn'găl'ən) *n.* A wide-brimmed felt hat with a high crown, popular esp. in the southwestern U.S.

ten-gallon hat

te·ni·a (tē'nē-ə) *n.* Var. of **taenia.**

ten·nis (tĕn'ĭs) *n.* **1.** A game played with rackets and a light ball by two players *(singles)* or two pairs of players *(doubles)* on a flat, rectangular court of grass, clay, or other material that is divided by a net. Also called **lawn tennis.** **2. Court tennis.** [Middle English *tennys.*]

tennis shoes. Sneakers.

ten·on (tĕn'ən) *n.* A projection on the end of a piece of wood or other material, designed to fit into a mortise. —*tr.v.* **1.** To provide with a tenon. **2.** To join with a tenon. [Middle English, from Old French, from *tenir,* to hold, from Latin *tenēre.*]

ten·or (tĕn'ər) *n.* **1.** General sense of something written or spoken; purport. **2.** *Mus.* **a.** The voice of an adult male singer, higher than a baritone and lower than a male alto or counter tenor. **b.** A part for this voice. **c.** A person who sings this part. —*modifier: a tenor solo; a tenor aria; a tenor sax.* [Middle English, from Old French, from Latin, uninterrupted course, a holding on, from *tenēre,* to hold.]

ten·pence (tĕn'pəns) *n. Brit.* A sum of money equal to ten pennies.

ten·pen·ny (tĕn'pĕn'ē) *adj. Brit.* Valued at or costing tenpence.

tenpenny nail. A nail three inches long.

ten·pin (tĕn'pĭn') *n.* **1.** A bowling pin used in playing tenpins. **2. tenpins** *(used with a sing. verb).* A game, bowling.

tense¹ (tĕns) *adj.* **tens·er, tens·est. 1.** Tightly stretched; taut; strained: *tense muscles; a tense fishing line.* **2.** In a condition of or exhibiting mental or nervous tension. **3.** Nerve-racking; suspenseful: *a tense situation.* **4.** *Phonet.* Spoken with taut muscles, as the consonant *t.* —See Syns at **edgy** and **tight.** —*v.* **tensed, tens·ing.** —*tr.v.* To make tense: *He tensed his muscles.* —*intr.v.* To become tense: *His jaw tensed with anger.* [Latin *tensus,* past part. of *tendere,* to stretch out.]

tense² (tĕns) *n.* **1.** Any of the inflected forms of a verb that indicate the time and continuance or completion of the action or state. **2.** A set of such forms indicating a particular time: *the future tense.* [Middle English *tens,* tense, time, from Old French, from Latin *tempus,* time.]

ten·sile (tĕn'səl, -sīl') *adj.* **1.** Of or having to do with tension. **2.** Capable of being stretched or extended; ductile: *the tensile properties of a metal.* [From Latin *tensus,* stretched, tense.] —**ten·sil'i·ty** (tĕn-sĭl'ĭ-tē) *n.*

tensile strength. The resistance of a material to a force that tends to pull it apart, usu. expressed as the measure of the largest force that can be applied in this way before the material ruptures.

ten·sion (tĕn'shən) *n.* **1. a.** The act or process of stretching. **b.** The condition of being stretched. **2. a.** A force that tends to stretch or elongate something. **b.** The measure of such a force: *a tension of 50 pounds.* **3.** Strain or stress that affects the mind, nerves, or emotions. **4.** A strained relation between persons or groups. **5.** A balancing of opposing elements in an artistic work. **6.** Voltage; electromotive force. [Old French, from Latin *tensiō,* from *tensus,* tense.] —**ten'sion·al** *adj.*

ten·si·ty (tĕn'sĭ-tē) *n.* The condition of being tense; tenseness.

ten·sive (tĕn'sĭv) *adj.* Of or causing tension.

ten·sor (tĕn'sər, -sôr') *n. Anat.* Any muscle that tenses a part, making it firm.

ten·strike (tĕn'strīk') *n. Informal.* **1.** A strike in the game of tenpins. **2.** A remarkably successful stroke or action.

tent (tĕnt) *n.* **1.** A portable shelter usu. of canvas or other weather-resistant material stretched over a supporting framework of poles, ropes, and pegs. **2.** Something resembling this in construction or shape. —*intr.v.* To encamp in a tent. —*tr.v.* To cover over or provide with or as with a tent. [Middle English *tente,* from Old French, from Latin *tendere,* to stretch.]

ten·ta·cle (tĕn'tə-kəl) *n.* **1.** *Zool.* One of the narrow, flexible, unjointed parts that extend from the body of certain animals, as an octopus, used for grasping, moving, etc. **2.** *Bot.* One of the hairs on the leaves of insectivorous plants, as the sundew. **3.** Something resembling a tentacle, esp. in the ability to grasp or hold. [From Latin *tentāre,* var. of *temptāre,* to touch, feel, tempt.] —**ten·tac'u·lar** (-tăk'yə-lər) *adj.*

tentacle
Of an octopus

ten·ta·tive (tĕn'tə-tĭv) *adj.* **1.** Of an experimental or trial nature; not definite; provisional: *a tentative schedule of events.* **2.** Not positive or sure; hesitant; uncertain: *a tentative smile.* [Medieval Latin *tentātīvus,* from Latin *tentātus,* past part. of *tentāre,* var. of *temptāre,* to try, tempt.] —**ten'ta·tive·ly** *adv.* —**ten'ta·tive·ness** *n.*

tent caterpillar. Any of several destructive caterpillars, esp. the hairy larva of a North American moth, *Malacosoma americanum,* that live in colonies in tentlike webs constructed in deciduous trees.

ten·ter (tĕn'tər) *n.* A framework upon which milled cloth is stretched for drying without shrinkage. [Middle English *teyntur,* from Medieval Latin *tentōrium,* from Latin *tentus,* past part. of *tendere,* to stretch.]

ten·ter·hook (tĕn'tər-hŏŏk') *n.* A hooked nail for securing cloth on a tenter. —*idiom.* **on tenterhooks.** In a state of uneasiness, suspense, or anxiety.

tenth (tĕnth) *n.* **1.** The ordinal number that matches the number ten in a series. Also written 10th. **2.** One of ten equal parts, written ¹/₁₀. —**tenth** *adj. & adv.*

te·nu·i·ty (tə-nōō'ĭ-tē, -nyōō'-) *n.* The condition of being tenuous; lack of substance or strength.

ten·u·ous (tĕn'yōō-əs) *adj.* **1.** Having a thin or slender form: *a tenuous rope.* **2.** Having a thin consistency; dilute; rarefied: *a tenuous liquid.* **3.** Of little significance or substance; flimsy: *a tenuous argument; tenuous political theories.* [Earlier *tenuious,* from Latin *tenuis,* thin, rare, fine.] —**ten'u·ous·ly** *adv.* —**ten'u·ous·ness** *n.*

ten·ure (tĕn'yər, -yŏŏr') *n.* **1.** The holding of something, as real estate, an office, etc.; occupation. **2.** The terms under which something is held. **3. a.** The period of holding something. **b.** Permanence of position, often granted an employee after a specified number of years. [Middle English, from Old French, from *tenir,* to hold, from Latin *tenēre.*]

te·o·sin·te (tā'ō-sĭn'tē) *n.* A tall Central American grass, *Euchlaena mexicana,* related to corn and cultivated for fodder. [Mexican Spanish, from Nahuatl *teocentli* : *teotl*, god + *centli*, dried ear of corn.]

te·pee (tē′pē) *n.* Also **tee·pee** or **ti·pi.** A cone-shaped tent of skins or bark used by North American Indians, esp. the Plains Indians. [Dakota *tipi*, dwelling.]

tepee

tep·id (tĕp′ĭd) *adj.* Moderately warm; lukewarm: *tepid water.* [Latin *tepidus*, from *tepēre*, to be lukewarm.] —**te·pid′i·ty** (tĕ-pĭd′ĭ-tē) or **tep′id·ness** *n.* —**tep′id·ly** *adv.*

te·qui·la (tə-kē′lə) *n.* An alcoholic liquor distilled from the fermented mash of a Central American century plant. [Mexican Spanish, after *Tequila*, a district in Mexico.]

ter·bi·um (tûr′bē-əm) *n. Symbol* **Tb** A soft, silvery-gray rare-earth element. Atomic number 65; atomic weight 158.924; melting point 1,356°C; boiling point 2,800°C; specific gravity 8.272; valences 3, 4. [After *Ytterby*, a village in Sweden, where it was discovered.]

ter·cel (tûr′səl) *n.* A male hawk used in falconry. [Middle English, from Old French, from Latin *tertius*, third (from the belief that the third egg of a brood was a male).]

ter·cen·ten·a·ry (tûr′sĕn-tĕn′ə-rē, tər-sĕn′tə-nĕr′ē) *n., pl.* **-ries.** Also **ter·cen·ten·ni·al** (tûr′sĕn-tĕn′ē-əl). A 300th anniversary or its celebration. —*adj.* Of or pertaining to a span of 300 years or a 300th anniversary. [Latin *ter*, three times + CENTENARY.]

ter·cet (tûr′sĭt) *n.* 1. *Pros.* A unit of three lines that rhyme together or that are interlocked by rhyme with an adjacent three-line unit. 2. *Mus.* A triplet. [Italian *terzetto*, dim. of *terzo*, third, from Latin *tertius*.]

te·re·do (tə-rē′dō, -rā′-) *n., pl.* **-dos.** Any saltwater mollusk of the genus *Teredo.* [Latin *terēdō*, a kind of worm, from Greek *terēdōn.*]

ter·ga (tûr′gə) *n.* Plural of **tergum.**

ter·giv·er·sate (tər-jĭv′ər-sāt′) *intr.v.* **-sat·ed, -sat·ing.** 1. To use evasions or ambiguities; equivocate. 2. To change sides; defect. [From Latin *tergiversārī*, to shift : *tergum*, back, + *versus*, past part. of *vertere*, to turn.] —**ter·giv′er·sa′tion** *n.* —**ter·giv′er·sa′tor** *n.*

ter·gum (tûr′gəm) *n., pl.* **-ga** (-gə). The upper or dorsal surface, esp. of a body segment of an insect or other arthropod. [Latin, the back.] —**ter′gal** (-gəl) *adj.*

term (tûrm) *n.* 1. a. A period of time during which something lasts: *a school term.* b. A fixed period of service: *a six-year term as senator.* 2. A point of time that begins or ends a period: *a lease approaching its term.* 3. a. A word that has a precise meaning in the special vocabulary of a particular group or activity: *a medical term.* b. **terms.** Language or manner of expression used: *He spoke in no uncertain terms.* 4. **terms.** a. Conditions or stipulations that define the nature and limits of an agreement. b. The relation between persons or groups: *on speaking terms.* 5. a. Each of the quantities or expressions that form the parts of a ratio or the numerator and denominator of a fraction. b. Any of the quantities in an equation that are connected to other quantities by a plus sign or minus sign. 6. *Law.* A period during which a court is in session. —*tr.v.* To designate; call. —*idiom.* **in terms of.** With regard to; respecting. [Middle English *terme*, from Old French, from Latin *terminus*, boundary, limit.]

ter·ma·gant (tûr′mə-gənt) *n.* A quarrelsome or scolding woman; a shrew. —*adj.* Abusive; shrewish. [Middle English *Termagaunt*, a character in Medieval mystery plays.]

ter·mi·na·ble (tûr′mə-nə-bəl) *adj.* 1. Capable of being ter-

minated. 2. Terminating after a designated date: *a terminable annuity.* —**ter′mi·na·bil′i·ty** or **ter′mi·na·ble·ness** *n.* —**ter′mi·na·bly** *adv.*

ter·mi·nal (tûr′mə-nəl) *adj.* 1. Of, pertaining to, or forming the end or boundary of something. 2. *Biol.* Growing at the end of a stem, branch, or similar part. 3. Occurring at the end of a section or series; final; closing: *the terminal stanza of a poem.* 4. Of or occurring in a term or each term; appearing regularly or periodically: *terminal payments over a period of ten years.* 5. Ending in death; fatal: *a terminal disease.* —See Syns at **last.** —*n.* 1. A terminating point, limit, or part. 2. Any ornamental object situated at the end of something, as a finial of a lamp. 3. *Elect.* a. A point in an electric circuit at which an electric connection is made. b. A passive conductor used to make the connection. 4. a. Either end of a railroad, bus line, or air line. b. A station at either end of or at a major junction on such a line. [Latin *terminālis*, from *terminus*, boundary.] —**ter′mi·nal·ly** *adv.*

terminal leave. Final leave equal to accumulated unused leave granted to members of the armed forces immediately prior to their separation or discharge from service.

ter·mi·nate (tûr′mə-nāt′) *v.* **-nat·ed, -nat·ing.** —*tr.v.* 1. To bring to an end: *terminate a contract.* 2. To occur at or form the end of; conclude; finish. —*intr.v.* 1. To come to an end. 2. To have as an end or result. —See Syns at **end.**

ter·mi·na·tion (tûr′mə-nā′shən) *n.* 1. The act of terminating or the condition of being terminated. 2. The spatial or temporal end of something; conclusion or cessation: *the termination of a life.* 3. A result or outcome. 4. The end of a word, as an inflectional ending, suffix, or final morpheme. —**ter′mi·na′tion·al** *adj.*

ter·mi·na·tive (tûr′mə-nā′tĭv) *adj.* Serving, designed, or tending to terminate; conclusive.

ter·mi·na·tor (tûr′mə-nā′tər) *n.* 1. Someone or something that terminates. 2. The line dividing the bright and shaded regions of the disk of the moon or a planet.

ter·mi·nol·o·gy (tûr′mə-nŏl′ə-jē) *n., pl.* **-gies.** The technical terms and usages of a particular trade, science, or art; nomenclature. —See Syns at **language.** [Medieval Latin *terminus*, expression, from Latin, limit + -LOGY.] —**ter′mi·no·log′i·cal** (-nə-lŏj′ĭ-kəl) *adj.* —**ter′mi·no·log′i·cal·ly** *adv.*

term insurance. Insurance for a specified period that only provides coverage for losses incurred during that period.

ter·mi·nus (tûr′mə-nəs) *n., pl.* **-nus·es** or **-ni** (-nī′). 1. The end of something; final point or goal. 2. a. The final stop at either end of a transportation line. b. A terminal on a transportation line or the town in which it is located. 3. a. A boundary or border. b. A stone or post marking such a border. [Latin, boundary, limit.]

ter·mite (tûr′mīt′) *n.* Any of numerous superficially antlike social insects of the order Isoptera, many species of which feed on wood and are highly destructive. Also called **white ant.** [Latin *termes*, wood-eating worm.]

term paper. A lengthy report or essay required of a student on a topic drawn from the subject matter of a course of study.

tern (tûrn) *n.* Any of various sea birds of the genus *Sterna* and related genera, related to but smaller than the gulls and having a deeply forked tail. [Of Scandinavian orig.]

ter·na·ry (tûr′nə-rē) *adj.* 1. Composed of three or arranged in threes. 2. Third in order or rank. 3. *Math.* a. Having the base three. b. Involving three variables. [Middle English, from Latin *ternārius*, from *ternī*, three each.]

ter·nate (tûr′nāt′, -nĭt) *adj.* Arranged in or consisting of sets or groups of three, as a compound leaf with three leaflets. [Medieval Latin *ternātus*, past part. of *ternāre*, to multiply by three, from *ternī*, three each.] —**ter′nate·ly** *adv.*

ter·pene (tûr′pēn′) *n.* Any of various unsaturated hydrocarbons, $C_{10}H_{16}$, found in essential oils and oleoresins of plants such as conifers and used in organic syntheses. [*Terp(entine)*, obs. var. of TURPENTINE + -ENE.]

Terp·sich·o·re (tûrp-sĭk′ə-rē) *n. Gk. Myth.* The Muse of dancing and choral singing.

terp·si·cho·re·an (tûrp′sĭ-kə-rē′ən, sĭ-kôr′ē-ən, -kōr′-) *adj.* Of or pertaining to dancing. —*n.* A dancer. [From TERPSICHORE.]

---

ter·race (tĕr′əs) *n.* **1.** A flat, open, galleried platform or deck; a porch or balcony. **2.** An open area adjacent to a house, used as an outdoor living area; a patio. **3.** A raised bank of earth with vertical or sloping sides and a flat top. **4.** A flat, narrow stretch of ground, often with a steep slope that faces a river or sea. **5.** A row of buildings erected on raised ground or on a sloping site. —*tr.v.* **-raced, -rac·ing.** To form into or supply with a terrace. [Old French *terrasse,* terrace, pile of earth, from Old Provençal *terrassa,* from *terra,* earth, from Latin.]

ter·ra cot·ta (tĕr′ə kŏt′ə). **1.** A hard, waterproof ceramic clay used in pottery and building construction. **2.** Pottery or ceramic ware made of this material. **3.** A brownish orange. [Italian, "cooked earth."]

ter·ra fir·ma (tĕr′ə fûr′mə). Solid ground; dry land: *"For a ship is a bit of terra firma cut off from the main"* (Herman Melville). [Latin, "firm land."]

ter·rain (tə-rān′, tĕ-) *n.* **1.** A tract of land, esp. when considered with respect to its physical features: *hilly terrain; rugged terrain.* **2.** *Var. of* **terrane.** [French, from Latin *terrēnum,* from *terra,* earth.]

ter·rane (tə-rān′, tĕ-) *n. Also* **ter·rain.** *Geol.* A rock formation or series of related rock formations. [*Var.* of TERRAIN.]

ter·ra·pin (tĕr′ə-pĭn) *n.* Any of various aquatic North American turtles of the genus *Malaclemys* and related genera, esp. the diamondback. [Of Algonquian orig.]

ter·rar·i·um (tə-râr′ē-əm, -răr′-) *n.* A small enclosure or closed container in which small plants are grown or small animals, as turtles or lizards, are kept. [Latin *terra,* earth + -ARIUM.]

ter·raz·zo (tə-răz′ō, -rät′sō) *n.* A mozaic flooring made of marble or other stone chips set in mortar. [Italian, terrace.]

ter·res·tri·al (tə-rĕs′trē-əl) *adj.* **1. a.** Of, relating to, or on the earth: *terrestrial magnetism.* **b.** Having a mundane character or quality; prosaic. **2.** Of or consisting of land as distinguished from water or air. **3.** Living or growing on land. —*n.* An inhabitant of the earth. [Middle English, from Latin *terrestris,* from *terra,* earth.] —**ter·res′tri·al·ly** *adv.*

ter·ret (tĕr′ĭt) *n.* **1.** One of the metal rings on a harness through which the reins pass. **2.** A similar ring on an animal's collar, used for attaching a leash. [Middle English *tyret,* from Old French *touret,* dim. of *tour,* circular movement, from *tourner,* to turn.]

ter·ri·ble (tĕr′ə-bəl) *adj.* **1.** Causing terror, fear or awe; dreadful: *a terrible accident; a terrible storm.* **2.** Severe; intense: *the terrible summer heat of the tropics.* **3.** Unpleasant; disagreeable: *made a terrible scene.* **4.** Very bad: *a terrible movie.* —See Syns at **intense.** [Middle English, from Old French, from Latin *terribilis,* from *terrēre,* to frighten.] —**ter′ri·ble·ness** *n.* —**ter′ri·bly** *adv.*

ter·ri·er (tĕr′ē-ər) *n.* Any of various usu. small, active dogs orig. bred to hunt animals that live in burrows. [French *(chien) terrier,* from *terrier,* burrow, from *terre,* earth, from Latin *terra.*]

ter·rif·ic (tə-rĭf′ĭk) *adj.* **1.** Terrifying or frightful: *a terrific hurricane.* **2.** *Informal.* Very good: *a terrific party.* **3.** Awesome; astounding: *a terrific speed.* **4.** Very great; intense: *under terrific pressure.* —See Syns at **excellent.** [Latin *terrificus.*] —**ter·rif′i·cal·ly** *adv.*

ter·ri·fy (tĕr′ə-fī′) *tr.v.* **-fied, -fy·ing.** To fill with terror; make deeply afraid. —See Syns at **frighten.** [Latin *terrificāre,* from *terrificus,* terrific.]

ter·ri·to·ri·al (tĕr′ĭ-tôr′ē-əl, -tōr′-) *adj.* **1.** Of or pertaining to a territory or to its powers of jurisdiction: *territorial claims against the state.* **2.** Pertaining or restricted to a particular territory; regional; local. **3.** Organized for national or home defense. —*n.* A member of a territorial army. —**ter′ri·to′ri·al·ly** *adv.*

ter·ri·to·ri·al·ism (tĕr′ĭ-tôr′ē-ə-lĭz′əm, -tōr′-) *n.* A social system that gives authority and influence in a state to the landowners. —**ter′ri·to′ri·al·ist** *n.*

ter·ri·to·ri·al·i·ty (tĕr′ĭ-tôr′ē-ăl′ĭ-tē, -tōr′-) *n.* **1.** The status of a territory. **2.** The behavior of a male animal in defending its territory.

ter·ri·to·ri·al·ize (tĕr′ĭ-tôr′ē-ə-līz′, -tōr′-) *tr.v.* **-ized, -iz·ing.**

To establish as or give the status of a territory. —**ter′ri·to′ri·al·i·za′tion** *n.*

territorial waters. Inland and coastal waters under the jurisdiction of a country.

ter·ri·to·ry (tĕr′ĭ-tôr′ē, -tōr′ē) *n., pl.* **-ries. 1.** An area of land; a region. **2.** The land and waters under the jurisdiction of a state, nation, or government. **3. Territory.** A part of the United States not admitted as a state, administered by an appointed governor and with its own legislature. **4.** The area for which a person is responsible as a salesman, agent, etc. **5.** An area that is regarded by an individual or group as its own and that is often defended vigorously against outsiders. **6.** A sphere of action or interest; province; domain. [Middle English, from Latin *territōrium,* from *terra,* land.]

ter·ror (tĕr′ər) *n.* **1.** Intense, overpowering fear. **2.** Someone or something that causes such fear. **3.** Violence toward private citizens, public property, or political enemies, esp. when promoted by a political group to achieve or maintain supremacy. **4.** *Informal.* An annoying or intolerable person or thing. [Middle English *terrour,* from Old French *terror,* from Latin *terror,* from *terrēre,* to frighten.]

ter·ror·ism (tĕr′ə-rĭz′əm) *n.* **1.** The use of terror, violence, and intimidation to subjugate people or to achieve an end or purpose. **2.** Fear and subjugation produced by this. —**ter′ror·ist** *n.* —**ter′ror·is′tic** *adj.*

ter·ror·ize (tĕr′ə-rīz′) *tr.v.* **-ized, -iz·ing. 1.** To fill with terror; terrify. **2.** To coerce or control by intimidation or fear. —See Syns at **frighten.** —**ter′ror·i·za′tion** *n.* —**ter′ror·iz′er** *n.*

ter·ry cloth (tĕr′ē). An absorbent cotton fabric with uncut loops forming a pile. [Orig. unknown.]

terse (tûrs) *adj.* **ters·er, ters·est.** Brief and to the point; concise: *a terse reply.* —See Syns at **concise.** [Orig. polished, refined, from Latin *tersus,* past part. of *tergēre,* to wipe off, polish.] —**terse′ly** *adv.* —**terse′ness** *n.*

ter·tian (tûr′shən) *adj.* Recurring in approx. 48-hour cycles, esp. symptoms of disease such as high fever, seizure, paroxysm, etc. —*n.* A form of malaria that recurs every 48 hours. [Latin *tertiānus,* of the third, from *tertius,* third.]

ter·ti·ar·y (tûr′shē-ĕr′ē, -shə-rē) *adj.* **1.** Third in place, order, degree, or rank. **2.** *Chem.* **a.** Pertaining to salts of acids that contain three replaceable hydrogen atoms. **b.** Pertaining to organic compounds in which a group, such as an alcohol or amine, is bound to three nonelementary radicals. **3.** *Eccles.* Of or pertaining to the third order of a monastic system. **4.** *Ornithol.* Of, pertaining to, or designating the short flight feathers nearest the body on the inner edge of a bird's wing. —*n., pl.* **-ies. 1. Tertiary.** Also **Tertiary period.** The geologic period that began about 63 million years ago and ended about 500,000 to 2 million years ago, characterized by the appearance of modern plant life, apes, and other large mammals. **2.** *Eccles.* A member of a tertiary order. **3.** *Ornithol.* A tertiary feather. —*modifier: Tertiary fossils; Tertiary rock strata.* [Latin *tertiārius,* from *tertius,* third.]

ter·za ri·ma (tûrt′sə rē′mə). A verse form that consists of a series of interlocking iambic tercets that have 10-syllable or 11-syllable lines with the second line of each tercet rhyming with the first and third lines of the succeeding one. [Italian, "third rhyme."]

tes·sel·late (tĕs′ə-lāt′) *tr.v.* **-lat·ed, -lat·ing.** To form or cover in a mosaic pattern, esp. to make small squares of stone or glass. [Latin *tessellātus,* from *tessella,* a small cube, dim. of *tessera,* a square piece of stone.] —**tes′sel·la′tion** *n.*

test¹ (tĕst) *n.* **1. a.** A way of examining something to determine its characteristics or properties or to determine whether or not it is working correctly. **b.** Any specific procedure used in this way. **2. a.** A physical or chemical reaction to determine the presence of a particular substance or class of substances, such as disease germs of a particular type. **b.** The procedure, reagents, stains, etc., used in producing this reaction. **3.** A series of questions, problems, tasks, etc., designed to measure someone's intelligence, knowledge, psychological stability, etc. **4.** Something used as a reference in measuring or examining; a standard: *the test of time.* —*tr.v.* **1.** To subject to a test; examine. **2.** To analyze, esp. chemically, in order to determine the presence of a specified property, quality, substance, etc.: *test food for purity; test blood for sugar.* —*intr.v.* **1.** To

ă pat ā pay â care ä father ĕ pet ē be hw which ĭ pit ī tie î pier ŏ pot ō toe ô paw, for oi noise
ōō took ōō boot ou out th thin th this ŭ cut û urge zh vision ə about, item, edible, gallop, circus

undergo a test, esp. with an indicated result. **2.** To achieve as a score or rating through testing. **3.** To administer a test in order to diagnose: *test for acid content.* [Middle English, a vessel for treating ores, from Old French, pot, from Latin *testum,* earthen vessel.]

test² (tĕst) *n.* A hard external covering, such as that of certain insects and other invertebrates. [Latin *testa,* shell.]

tes·ta (tĕs′tə) *n., pl.* **-tae** (-tē′). The often thick or hard outer coat of a seed. [Latin, brick, shell.]

tes·ta·ceous (tĕ-stā′shəs) *adj.* **1.** *Biol.* Of or having a shell or shell-like outer covering. **2.** Having the reddish-brown or brownish-yellow color of bricks.

tes·ta·cy (tĕs′tə-sē) *n.* The condition of being testate.

tes·tae (tĕs′tē′) *n.* Plural of **testa.**

tes·ta·ment (tĕs′tə-mənt) *n.* **1.** *Law.* **1.** A legal document providing for the disposition of a person's property, esp. personal property, after death; a will. **2. Testament.** Either of the two main divisions of the Bible, the Old Testament and the New Testament. **3.** A statement of belief or conviction; credo. [Middle English, from Late Latin *testāmentum,* from Latin, will, from *testārī,* to be a witness, make a will, from *testis,* witness.]

tes·ta·men·tar·y (tĕs′tə-mĕn′tə-rē, -mĕn′trē) *adj.* Of, derived from, or appointed by a will or testament.

tes·tate (tĕs′tāt′) *adj.* Having made a legally valid will before death. [Middle English, from Latin *testātus,* past part. of *testārī,* to make a will.]

tes·ta·tor (tĕs′tā′tər, tĕ-stā′tər) *n.* Someone who has made a legally valid will before death.

tes·ta·trix (tĕ-stā′trĭks) *n.* A woman who has made a legally valid will before death.

test case. A legal action undertaken, often with consent of the parties, to determine the position of the law on a particular matter for which no precedent has been established, esp. on questions involving the constitutionality of a statute, administrative ruling, etc.

tes·ter¹ (tĕs′tər) *n.* A canopy over a bed. [Middle English, from Medieval Latin *testerium,* headpiece, from Late Latin *testa,* skull, head, from Latin, shell.]

test·er² (tĕs′tər) *n.* Someone or something that tests.

tes·tes (tĕs′tēz′) *n.* Plural of **testis.**

tes·ti·cle (tĕs′tĭ-kəl) *n.* A testis. [Middle English *testicule,* from Latin *testiculus,* dim. of *testis,* testis.]

tes·ti·fy (tĕs′tə-fī′) *v.* **-fied, -fy·ing.** —*intr.v.* **1.** To bear witness or make a solemn declaration or affirmation, esp. under oath in a court of law: *testified at the trial.* **3.** To serve as witness or evidence: *results that testify to her ability.* —*tr.v.* **1.** To solemnly state or affirm, esp. under oath in a court of law: *testified he saw the defendant commit the crime.* **2.** To provide evidence for; affirm as true. [Middle English *testifien,* from Latin *testificārī* : *testis,* witness + *facere,* to make.] —**tes′ti·fi′er** *n.*

tes·ti·mo·ni·al (tĕs′tə-mō′nē-əl, -mōn′yəl) *n.* **1.** A formal statement testifying to a particular fact. **2.** A written affirmation of another's character or worth. **3.** Something given as a tribute for a person's service or achievement. —*modifier: a testimonial dinner.*

tes·ti·mo·ny (tĕs′tə-mō′nē) *n., pl.* **-nies.** **1.** *Law.* A declaration or affirmation made under oath, esp. in a court of law. **2.** Any evidence in support of a fact or assertion; proof. **3.** The collective written and spoken testimony offered in a legal case. **4.** A public declaration regarding a religious experience. **5.** In the Old Testament, the original Ten Commandments, inscribed on the tablets of stone. [Middle English, from Latin *testimōnium,* from *testis,* witness.]

tes·tis (tĕs′tĭs) *n., pl.* **-tes** (-tēz′). The male reproductive gland, the source of spermatozoa and of the androgens, normally occurring paired in an external scrotum in man and certain other mammals. [Latin.]

tes·tos·ter·one (tĕ-stŏs′tə-rōn′) *n.* A male sex hormone, $C_{19}H_{28}O_2$, that is produced in the testes and functions to control secondary sex characteristics. [TEST(IS) + STER(OL) + -ONE.]

test paper. A paper saturated with a reagent, such as litmus, used in making chemical tests.

test pilot. A pilot who flies aircraft of new or experimental design to test them for conformity to planned standards.

test tube. A cylindrical tube of clear glass, usu. open at one end and rounded at the other, used in laboratory tests and experiments.

tes·tu·do (tĕ-stōo′dō, -styōo′-) *n., pl.* **-di·nes** (-də-nēz′). A device used by the Romans, consisting of a movable arched screen that protected the besiegers' approach to a wall. [Latin *testūdo,* tortoise, a covering, from *testa,* shell.]

tes·ty (tĕs′tē) *adj.* **-ti·er, -ti·est. 1.** Irritable; touchy. **2.** Marked by irritability or impatience: *a testy remark.* — See Syns at **irritable.** [Middle English *testif,* headstrong, from Norman French, from Old French *teste,* head.] —**tes′ti·ly** *adv.* —**tes′ti·ness** *n.*

Tet (tĕt) *n.* The lunar New Year as celebrated in Southeast Asia. [Vietnamese *tết,* from Chinese *tsiet,* festival.]

te·tan·ic (tə-tăn′ĭk) *adj.* **1.** Of or pertaining to tetanus. **2.** Of or pertaining to tetany.

tet·a·nus (tĕt′n-əs) *n.* **1.** An acute, often fatal infectious disease caused by a bacillus, *Clostridium tetani,* that gen. enters the body through wounds, and is characterized by rigidity and spasmodic contraction of the voluntary muscles. Also called **lockjaw. 2.** A continuous muscular contraction caused by reaction to rapidly repeated stimuli. [Middle English *tetane,* from Latin *tetanus,* from Greek *tetanos,* from *teinein,* to stretch.]

tet·a·ny (tĕt′n-ē) *n.* An abnormal condition characterized by periodic painful muscular spasms caused by faulty calcium metabolism. [From TETANUS.]

tetch·y (tĕch′ē) *adj.* **-i·er, -i·est.** Also **tech·y.** Peevish; testy. [Prob. from obs. *tecche,* blemish, fault (of character), from OldFrench *teche,* blemish.] —**tetch′i·ly** *adv.* —**tetch′i·ness** *n.*

tête-à-tête (tāt′ə-tāt′) *adv.* Together without the intrusion of a third person. —*n.* **1.** A private conversation between two people. **2.** A sofa for two, esp. an S-shaped one that allows the occupants to face each other. —*adj.* For or between two only. [French, "head to head."]

teth·er (tĕth′ər) *n.* **1.** A rope or chain for an animal, that allows it a short radius to move about in. **2.** The range or scope of one's resources or abilities. —*tr.v.* To restrict or bind with or as with a tether. —*idiom.* **at the end of (one's) tether.** At the limit of one's endurance. [Middle English *tethir,* from Old Norse *tjothir.*]

teth·er·ball (tĕth′ər-bôl′) *n.* A game played by two people with paddles and a ball hung by a cord from an upright post, the objective being to wind the cord around the post.

tetr-. Var. of **tetra-.**

tet·ra (tĕt′rə) *n.* Any of various small, colorful tropical freshwater fishes of the family Characidae, popular in home aquariums. [Short for New Latin *Tetragonopterus* : Late Latin *tetragonum,* quadrangle + Greek *pteron,* wing (from its squared-off dorsal fins).]

tetra- or **tetr-.** A prefix meaning four: **tetrachloride.** [Greek.]

tet·ra·chlo·ride (tĕt′rə-klôr′īd′, -klōr′-) *n.* A chemical compound that contains fourth chlorine atoms per molecule.

tet·ra·chord (tĕt′rə-kôrd′) *n. Mus.* A series of four diatonic tones that encompass the interval of a perfect fourth. [Greek *tetrakhordon* : *tetra-,* four + *khordē,* string.] —**tet′ra·chord′al** *adj.*

tet·ra·cy·cline (tĕt′rə-sī′klēn′) *n.* A yellow crystalline compound, $C_{22}H_{24}N_2O_8$, synthesized or derived from certain microorganisms of the genus *Streptomyces* and used as an antibiotic. [TETRA- + CYCL(IC) + -INE.]

tet·rad (tĕt′răd′) *n.* **1.** A group or set of four. **2.** *Biol.* **a.** A group of four chromatids formed at meiosis by synapsis of two chromatids from each of a pair of homologous chromosomes. **b.** A body formed of four cells, as pollen grains from one mother cell. [Greek *tetras.*]

tet·ra·eth·yl lead (tĕt′rə-ĕth′əl). Also **tet·ra·eth·yl·lead** (tĕt′rə-ĕth′əl-lĕd′). A colorless, poisonous, oily liquid, $Pb(C_2H_5)_4$, used in gasoline for internal combustion engines as an antiknock agent.

tet·ra·he·dron (tĕt′rə-hē′drən) *n., pl.* **-drons** or **-dra** (-drə). A solid geometric figure bounded by four triangular faces. —**tet′ra·he′dral** *adj.*

te·tral·o·gy (tĕ-trăl′ə-jē, -trōl-) *n., pl.* **-gies.** Any series of four related dramatic, operatic, or literary works.

te·tram·e·ter (tĕ-trăm′ĭ-tər) *n.* A line of verse consisting of four metrical feet.

tet·ra·pod (tĕt′rə-pŏd′) *adj.* Having four feet, legs, or leg-like appendages.

ă pat	ā pay	â care	ä father	ĕ pet	ē be	hw which	ĭ pit	ī tie	î pier	ŏ pot	ō toe	ô paw, for	oi noise
ōō took	ōō boot	ou out	th thin	th this	ŭ cut		û urge	zh vision	ə about, item, edible, gallop, circus				

tet·rarch (tĕt'rärk', tē'trärk') *n.* **1.** A governor of one of the four divisions of a country or province, esp. under the ancient Roman Empire. **2.** A subordinate ruler. —**te·trar'chic** (tĕ-trär'kĭk, tē-) *adj.* —**tet'rar'chy** *n.*

tet·ra·va·lent (tĕt'rə-vā'lənt) *adj.* Having valence 4.

tet·rode (tĕt'rōd') *n.* An electron tube that contains four electrodes. [TETR(A)- + -ODE (path).]

te·trox·ide (tĕ-trŏk'sīd') *n.* A chemical compound that contains four oxygen atoms per molecule.

tet·ter (tĕt'ər) *n.* Any of various skin diseases characterized by eruptions and itching. [Middle English *teter,* from Old English.]

Teu·ton (tōōt'n, tyōōt'n) *n.* **1.** A member of an ancient people, probably of Germanic or Celtic origin, who lived in northern Europe until about 100 B.C. **2.** A German.

Teu·ton·ic (tōō-tŏn'ĭk, tyōō-) *adj.* Of, relating to, or characteristic of the Teutons or to the Germanic languages. —*n.* The Germanic languages.

tex·as (tĕk'səs) *n.* The structure on a river steamboat containing the pilothouse and the officers' quarters. [From TEXAS.]

Texas fever. An infectious disease of cattle and related animals, caused by a parasitic microorganism, *Babesia bigemina,* and transmitted by ticks.

Texas leaguer. *Baseball.* A fly ball that drops between an infielder and an outfielder for a hit. [From *Texas League,* a minor baseball league.]

Texas Ranger. **1.** A member of the Texas mounted police force. **2.** A member of a band of men orig. organized in Texas to fight Indians and maintain order.

Texas tower. A radar tower built offshore. [So named for its resemblance to the oil derricks off the Texas coast.]

text (tĕkst) *n.* **1. a.** The wording or words of something written or printed. **b.** The words of a speech appearing in print. **2.** The main body of a printed work as distinct from a preface, footnote, or illustration. **3.** A passage from the Bible to be read and expounded upon in a sermon. **4.** The subject matter of a discourse; theme: *the text of a lecture.* **5.** A textbook. [Middle English *texte,* from Old French, from Medieval Latin *textus,* (Scriptural) text, from Latin, literary composition, something woven, from *texere,* to weave.]

text·book (tĕkst'bŏŏk') *n.* A book used as a standard work for the formal study of a particular subject.

tex·tile (tĕk'stīl', -stəl) *n.* **1.** Cloth or fabric, esp. when woven or knitted. **2.** Fiber or yarn for weaving cloth. —*modifier: a textile mill; textile fibers.* [French, from Latin *textilis,* from *texere,* to weave.]

tex·tu·al (tĕks'chōō-əl) *adj.* Of, relating to, or conforming to a text. —**tex'tu·al·ly** *adv.*

tex·ture (tĕks'chər) *n.* **1.** The surface appearance of a fabric that results from the woven arrangement of its yarns or fibers. **2.** The composition or structure of a substance dependent upon the size, type, proportions, and arrangment of its components: *the smooth texture of ivory; a stone of rough texture.* **3.** A grainy, fibrous, woven, or dimensional quality as opposed to a uniformly flat, smooth aspect; surface interest: *Brick walls give a room texture.* **4.** Distinctive or identifying character: *the texture of suburban life.* [Latin *textūra,* structure, web, from *texere,* to weave.] —**tex'tur·al** *adj.* —**tex'tur·al·ly** *adv.*

-th[1]. Var. of -eth (verb suffix).

-th[2] or **-eth.** A suffix used to form ordinal numbers: thousandth, sixtieth. [Middle English *-the,* from Old English *-tha.*]

Th The symbol for the element thorium.

thal·a·mus (thăl'ə-məs) *n., pl.* **-mi** (-mī') **1.** *Anat.* A large ovoid mass of gray matter that relays sensory stimuli to the cerebral cortex and acts in integrative and nonspecific functions. **2.** *Bot.* The receptacle of a flower. [Greek *thalamos,* inner chamber.] —**thal·am'ic** (thə-lăm'ĭk) *adj.*

tha·las·sic (thə-lăs'ĭk) *adj.* **1.** Of or pertaining to seas or oceans. **2.** Of or pertaining to seas and gulfs as distinguished from the oceans. [French *thalassique,* from Greek *thalassa,* sea.]

Tha·li·a (thə-lī'ə) *n. Gk. Myth.* **1.** The Muse of comedy and pastoral poetry. **2.** One of the three Graces.

tha·lid·o·mide (thə-lĭd'ə-mīd') *n.* A sedative drug,

$C_{13}H_{10}N_2O_4$, withdrawn from sale because of association with fetal abnormalities. [Ult. from NAPHTHALENE + AMIDE.]

thal·li (thăl'ī') *n.* A plural of **thallus.**

thal·li·um (thăl'ē-əm) *n. Symbol* **Tl** A soft, malleable, highly toxic metallic element, used in rodent and ant poisons, in photocells, infrared detectors, and low-melting glass. Atomic number 81; atomic weight 204.37; melting point 303.5°C; boiling point 1,457°C; specific gravity 11.85; valences 1, 3. [Latin *thallus,* green shoot, (from its green spectral line) + -IUM.]

thal·lo·phyte (thăl'ə-fīt') *n.* Any plant or plantlike organism of the division or subkingdom Thallophyta, which includes the algae, fungi, and bacteria. [THALL(US) + -PHYTE.] —**thal'lo·phy'tic** (-fĭt'ĭk) *adj.*

thal·lus (thăl'əs) *n., pl.* **thal·li** (thăl'ī') or **-lus·es.** The undifferentiated stemless, rootless, leafless plant body characteristic of thallophytes. [Latin, young shoot, from Greek *thallos,* from *thallein,* to sprout.]

than (thăn; *thən when unstressed) conj.* **1.** —Used to introduce the second element or clause of a comparison of inequality: *Pound cake is richer than angel food cake. She's a better skier than I.* **2.** —Used to introduce the rejected alternative in statements of preference: *I'd much rather play than work.* [Middle English *thanne,* from Old English *thænne.*]
Usage: **than.** The word *than* can be construed as a conjunction or as a preposition. The inflected word that follows it can therefore be in either the nominative or the objective case, depending on the grammatical function of *than* in the particular sentence: *She dances better than I do. They were both somewhat taller than me.* The same principle applies to elliptical clauses introduced by *than,* in which unexpressed words are plainly understood: *She dances better than I* (subject of unexpressed verb do). *She is a better dancer than I* (subject of unexpressed verb am). *The children liked no one more than her* (object of the preposition *than*). In some examples, either the nominative or the objective case can be used: *They had no more devoted follower than he* and *They had no more devoted follower than him.* The objective case always occurs in the expression *than whom: Lee, than whom no more admired general ever lived.*

thane (thān) *n.* Also **thegn. 1.** In Anglo-Saxon England, a freeman granted land by the king in return for military service. **2.** A feudal lord, usu. a clan chief, in Scotland. [Middle English *thayn,* from Old English *thegen.*]

thank (thăngk) *tr.v.* **1.** To express gratitude to. **2.** To hold responsible; credit; blame. [Middle English *thanken,* from Old English *thancian.*]

thank·ful (thăngk'fəl) *adj.* Showing or feeling gratitude; grateful. —**thank'ful·ly** *adv.* —**thank'ful·ness** *n.*

thank·less (thăngk'lĭs) *adj.* **1.** Not feeling or showing gratitude; ungrateful. **2.** Not apt to be appreciated: *a thankless task.* —**thank'less·ly** *adv.* —**thank'less·ness** *n.*

thanks (thăngks) *pl.n.* An acknowledgment of a favor, gift, etc. —*idiom.* **thanks to.** On account of; because of.

thanks·giv·ing (thăngks-gĭv'ĭng) *n.* An act of giving thanks; an expression of gratitude, esp. to God.

Thanksgiving. A national holiday set apart for giving thanks to God, celebrated in the United States on the fourth Thursday of November and in Canada on the second Monday of October. Also called **Thanksgiving Day.**

that (thăt; *thət when unstressed) adj., pl.* **those** (thōz). **1.** Being the one or ones singled out, indicated, or understood: *that place; one of those things.* **2.** Being the one or ones farther away or more remote from consideration: *This room is warm and that one's cold.* —*pron., pl.* **those. 1.** The person or thing specified or implied: *That is my desk.* **2.** Who, whom, or which: *people that I have known; things that have to be done.* **3.** In, on, by, or with which: *I stayed busy the whole time that you were out. She called the day that she arrived.* —*adv.* To that extent: *Is it that difficult to do your homework?* —*conj.* **1.** —Used to introduce a subordinate clause: *I think that he is coming tonight.* **2.** —Used to introduce an exclamatory clause expressing a wish: *Oh, that I might live forever!* [Middle English, from Old English *thæt.*]
Usage: **that, which, who (whom).** These are relative pro-

nouns that introduce subordinate clauses. **1.** *That* may refer to persons, animals, or things. *Which* refers only to animals and things. *Who* and *whom* refer to persons and occasionally to animals. **2.** The choice of a relative pronoun is determined by the nature of the clause introduced by the pronoun. *That* is used to introduce restrictive clauses—clauses that define and limit the antecedent by providing essential information: *The book that you ordered has just arrived.* Such clauses are never set off by commas. A good test of a restrictive clause is that the relative pronoun can be unexpressed: *The book you ordered has just arrived. Who* and *whom* can also be used in restrictive clauses: *I met the person of whom you spoke. Who, whom,* and esp. *which* are also used to introduce nonrestrictive clauses—those that provide nonessential or incidental information not needed for an understanding of the sentence: *The book, which received excellent reviews, is selling well. Later, I spoke to my teacher, who has a German accent.* Such nontrestrictive causes are set off by commas; in theory, they could appear in parentheses. **3.** *Which* is always used for clauses of both types when the relative pronoun is preceded by *that* used as a demonstrative pronoun: *We often long for that which is impossible.* See also Usage note at **there** 2 and **this.**

thatch (thăch) *n.* **1.** Plant stalks or foliage, such as straw, reeds, or palm fronds, used for roofing. **2.** Something that resembles this, such as a thick growth of hair on the head. —*tr.v.* To cover with or as if with thatch: *thatch a hut.* [Middle English *thacche,* from *thacchen,* to thatch, cover, from Old English *theccan.*] —**thatch'er** *n.* —**thatch'y** *adj.*

thatch

thau·ma·tur·gy (thô′mə-tûr′jē) *n.* The working of miracles or wonders; magic. [Greek *thaumaturgia : thauma,* marvel + *ergon,* work.] —**thau'ma·turge'** or **thau'ma·tur'gist** *n.* —**thau'ma·tur'gic** or **thau'ma·tur'gi·cal** *adj.*

thaw (thô) *intr.v.* **1.** To change from a frozen solid to a liquid by gradual warming; melt. **2.** To lose the effects of extreme cold, such as stiffness, numbness, etc. **3.** To become warm enough for snow and ice to melt. **4.** To become less reserved; relax. —*tr.v.* **1.** To melt (a frozen solid) by gradual warming. **2.** To free from the effects of extreme cold by warming; restore to normal or room temperature. —*n.* **1.** The process of thawing. **2.** A period of warm weather during which ice and snow melt. **3.** A lessening or easing of restraint or tension. [Middle English *thawen,* from Old English *thāwian.*]

the (thē *before a vowel;* thə *before a consonant*). *definite article.* **1.** —Used as a determiner to indicate the one or ones previously specified or understood: *The pencil has disappeared.* **2.** —Used before a singular noun to designate a class: *The horse is a quadruped.* **3.** —Used before a noun to indicate one that is the best or most important of its kind: *Last night's party was hardly the event of the season.* **4.** —Used before a noun to indicate one that is unique: *the Pope.* **5.** —Used before an adjective functioning as a noun to signify a class: *the rich and the beautiful.* —*adv.* To that extent; by that much: *the sooner the better.* —*prep.* Per; each: *cost a dollar the box.* [Middle English, from Old English *the* (the masc. demonstrative adj.)]

the-. Var. of **theo-.**

the·a·ter or **the·a·tre** (thē′ə-tər) *n.* **1.** A building, room, or open-air structure for the presentation of plays, motion pictures, or other dramatic performances. **2.** Any room with tiers of seats used for lectures or demonstrations: *an operating theater.* **3.** Dramatic literature or its perform-

ance: *the theater of Shakespeare and Marlowe.* **4.** The work or activity of persons who write or act in or are engaged in the production of plays. **5.** The quality or effectiveness of a theatrical production: *This play is good theater.* **6.** The audience assembled for a dramatic performance. **7. a.** A place or area that is the setting for dramatic events, esp. a geographical area where military action occurs. [Middle English *theatre,* from Old French, from Latin *theātrum,* from Greek *theatron,* from *theasthai,* to watch, look at, from *thea,* a viewing.]

the·a·ter·go·er (thē′ə-tər-gō′ər) *n.* A person who often attends the theater.

the·a·ter-in-the-round (thē′ə-tər-ĭn-thə-round′) *n., pl.* **the·a·ters-in-the-round.** An **arena theater.**

the·a·tre (thē′ə-tər) *n.* Var. of **theater.**

the·at·ri·cal (thē-ăt′rĭ-kəl) or **the·at·ric** (-ăt′rĭk) *adj.* **1.** Of or suitable for the theater or dramatic performance. **2.** Marked by self-display or exaggerated and unnatural behavior: *her theatrical temper tantrums.* —*n.* **theatricals.** Stage performances, esp. by amateurs. —**the·at'ri·cal'i·ty** (-kăl′ĭ-tē) or **the·at'ri·cal·ness** *n.* —**the·at'ri·cal·ly** *adv.*

the·at·rics (thē-ăt′rĭks) *pl.n.* **1.** *(used with a sing. verb).* The art of the theater. **2.** Theatrical effects or mannerisms.

the·ca (thē′kə) *n., pl.* **-cae** (-kē′, -kī′). *Biol.* A case, covering, or sheath, such as the spore case of a moss capsule or the outer covering of the pupa of certain insects. [Latin *thēca,* a case, a sheath, from Greek *thēkē.*] —**the'cal** *adj.*

thee (thē) *pron. Archaic & Poet.* The objective case of **thou.**

theft (thĕft) *n.* The act or an example of stealing; larceny. [Middle English, from Old English *thēofth.*]

thegn (thān) *n.* Var. of **thane.**

their (thâr; thər *when unstressed*) *pron.* The possessive case of **they,** used as a modifier before a noun: *their house; their assignment; their revenge.* [Middle English, from Old Norse *theirra.*]

theirs (thârz) *pron.* Used to indicate the one or ones belonging to them: *The large packages are theirs. If your car isn't working, use theirs.*

the·ism (thē′ĭz′əm) *n.* Belief in the existence of a god or gods, esp. belief in a single God as creator and ruler of the world. [THE(O)- + -ISM.] —**the'ist** *n.* —**the·is'tic** or **the·is'ti·cal** *adj.* —**the·is'ti·cal·ly** *adv.*

them (thĕm; thəm *when unstressed*) *pron.* The objective case of **they,** used: **1.** As the direct object of a verb: *Her appeal touched them deeply.* **2.** As the indirect object of a verb: *Give them what they asked for.* **3.** As the object of a preposition: *He did it for them.* [Middle English, partly from Old Norse *theim,* partly from Old English *thæm.*]

the·mat·ic (thĭ-măt′ĭk) *adj.* Of or relating to a theme or themes. [Greek *thematikos,* from *thema,* proposition, theme.] —**the·mat'i·cal·ly** *adv.*

theme (thēm) *n.* **1.** A subject or topic of discourse or artistic representation. **2.** A short composition assigned to a student as a writing exercise. **3.** *Mus.* A principal melody in a musical composition. [Middle English, theme (of a discussion), from Old French *teme,* from Latin *thema,* from Greek, *prŏposition.*]

theme song. **1.** A melody or song played throughout a dramatic performance and often intended to convey a mood. **2.** A song that is identified with a performer, group, or radio or television program.

them·selves (thĕm-sĕlvz′, thəm-) *pron.* **1.** The ones identical to them. Used: **a.** Reflexively as the direct or indirect object of a verb or as the object of a preposition. **b.** For emphasis: *They themselves were unaware of his presence.* **2.** Their normal or healthy condition or state. —*idiom.* **by themselves. 1.** Alone: *went to the party by themselves.* **2.** Without help: *did all the work by themselves.*

then (thĕn) *adv.* **1.** At that time: *We did a lot of silly things, but after all, we were younger then.* **2.** Next in time, space, or order; after that: *We'll take one more swim, and then we'll go home.* **3. a.** In that case: *If you want to go, then go.* **b.** Consequently: *If x equals 11 and y equals 3, then xy equals 33.* **4.** Moreover; besides: *He wasn't feeling well and then he was in a bad mood anyway.* —*n.* That time or moment: *From then on, I behaved myself.* —*adj.* Being so at the time: *the then President.* —*idioms.* **and then**

ă **pat**   ā **pay**   â **care**   ä **father**   ĕ **pet**   ē **be**   hw **which**
ŏŏ **took**   ōō **boot**   ou **out**   th **thin**   *th* **this**   ŭ **cut**
ĭ **pit**   ī **tie**   î **pier**   ŏ **pot**   ō **toe**   ô **paw, for**   oi **noise**
û **urge**   zh **vision**   ə **about, item, edible, gallop, circus**

some. And considerably more. **now and then.** From time to time; once in a while. **then and there.** At once: *I think we should confront him with the evidence and be done with it then and there.* [Middle English *thenne,* from Old English *thænne.*]

thence (thĕns, thĕns) *adv.* **1.** From that place; from there. **2.** From that circumstance or source. **3.** *Archaic.* From that time; thenceforth. [Middle English *thannes,* from *thanne,* from there, from Old English *thanon.*]

thence·forth (thĕns-fôrth′, thĕns-) *adv.* From then on.

thence·for·ward (thĕns-fôr′wərd, thĕns-) *adv.* Also **thence·for·wards** (-wərdz). From that time on; thenceforth.

theo- or **the-.** A prefix meaning god or gods: **theism.** [From Greek *theos,* god.]

the·oc·ra·cy (thē-ŏk′rə-sē) *n., pl.* **-cies.** **1. a.** Government in which God or a deity is regarded as the ruling power. **b.** Government by religious authorities. **2.** A state so governed. [Greek *theokratia* : *theos,* god + *-kratia,* rule.]

the·o·crat (thē′ə-krăt′) *n.* **1.** A person who rules or is a member of the ruling group in a theocracy. **2.** A person who believes in or advocates theocracy. **—the′o·crat′ic** or **the′o·crat′i·cal** *adj.* **—the′o·crat′i·cal·ly** *adv.*

the·od·o·lite (thē-ŏd′l-īt′) *n.* A surveying instrument used to measure horizontal and vertical angles. [New Latin *theodelitus.*]

the·o·lo·gian (thē′ə-lō′jən) *n.* A specialist in theology.

the·o·log·i·cal (thē′ə-lŏj′ĭ-kəl) or **the·o·log·ic** (-lŏj′ĭk) *adj.* Of or relating to theology. **—the′o·log′i·cal·ly** *adv.*

the·ol·o·gize (thē-ŏl′ə-jīz′) *v.* **-gized, -giz·ing. —tr.v.** To make theological; treat or consider theologically. **—intr.v.** To speculate about theology. **—the·ol′o·giz′er** *n.*

the·ol·o·gy (thē-ŏl′ə-jē) *n., pl.* **-gies.** **1.** The systematic study, through reason based on faith, of the nature of God and of man's relation to God. **2.** An organized theory, system, or body of opinion concerning this study, esp. one belonging to a particular religion.

the·o·rem (thē′ə-rəm) *n.* **1.** An idea or proposition that is demonstrably true or is assumed to be so. **2.** *Math.* A proposition that is provable on the basis of explicit assumptions. [Late Latin *theōrēma,* from Greek, spectacle, intuition, theorem, from *theōrein,* to observe, from *theōros,* spectator, from *thea,* a looking at.]

the·o·ret·i·cal (thē′ə-rĕt′ĭ-kəl) or **the·o·ret·ic** (-rĕt′ĭk) *adj.* **1.** Of, based on, or concerning theory: *a theoretical question.* **2.** Restricted to theory; lacking practical application; hypothetical: *theoretical physics.* **3.** Given to theorizing; speculative. [Late Latin *theōrēticus,* from Greek *theōrētikos,* able to perceive, from *theōretos,* observable, from *theōrein,* to observe.] **—the′o·ret′i·cal·ly** *adv.*

the·o·re·ti·cian (thē′ər-ĭ-tĭsh′ən) *n.* Someone who formulates, studies, or is expert in the theory of a science or art.

the·o·rist (thē′ər-ĭst) *n.* A person who theorizes.

the·o·rize (thē′ə-rīz′) *intr.v.* **-rized, -riz·ing.** To formulate or analyze a theory or theories; speculate. **—the′o·ri·za′tion** *n.* **—the′o·riz′er** *n.*

the·o·ry (thē′ə-rē) *n., pl.* **-ries.** **1.** A statement or set of statements designed to explain a phenomenon or class of phenomena, usu. comprised of conclusions derived through mathematical or logical reasoning. **2.** A set of rules or principles designed for the study or practice of an art or discipline: *the theory of harmony.* **3.** A collection of mathematical theorems and proofs that present and explain a subject in detail: *set theory.* **4.** An assumption or guess based on limited information or knowledge. [Late Latin *theōria,* from Greek, contemplation, theory, from *theōros,* spectator, from *theasthai,* to observe, from *thea,* a viewing.]

the·os·o·phy (thē-ŏs′ə-fē) *n., pl.* **-phies.** **1.** Religious philosophy or speculation based on a claim of mystical insight into the nature of God and of divine teachings. **2. Theosophy.** The doctrines and beliefs of a modern religious sect, the Theosophical Society, that incorporate aspects of Buddhism and Brahmanism. [Medieval Latin *theosophia,* from Late Greek *theosophia* : *theos,* god + *sophia,* knowledge.] **—the′o·soph′ic** (-sŏf′ĭk) or **the′o·soph′i·cal** *adj.* **—the′o·soph′i·cal·ly** *adv.* **—the·os′o·phist** *n.*

ther·a·peu·tic (thĕr′ə-pyōō′tĭk) *adj.* **1.** Having healing or curative powers. **2.** Of or pertaining to therapeutics.

[Greek *therapeutikos,* from *therapeuein,* to treat medically.] **—ther′a·peu′ti·cal·ly** *adv.*

ther·a·peu·tics (thĕr′ə-pyōō′tĭks) *n.* (used with a sing. verb). The medical treatment of disease. **—ther′a·peu′tist** *n.*

ther·a·pist (thĕr′ə-pĭst) *n.* A person trained to conduct some type of rehabilitative or corrective therapy, as physical therapy or speech therapy.

ther·a·py (thĕr′ə-pē) *n., pl.* **-pies.** **1.** Any procedure designed to heal or cure an illness, disability, etc. **2.** Psychotherapy. [From Greek *therapeia,* service, from *theraps,* attendant.]

there (thâr) *adv.* **1.** At or in that place: *Sit over there.* **2.** To or toward that place: *How long did it take to get there?* **3.** At a point of action or time: *The violins come in there.* **4.** In that matter: *I can't go along with you there.* **—pron.** **1.** —Used to introduce a clause or sentence: *There are several different kinds of pepper. There came a loud clap, and then silence.* **2.** Used as an intensive: *Hello there.* **—n.** That place or point: *I stopped and he went on from there.* **—adj.** **1.** Used as an intensive: *That guard there can tell us the way out.* **2.** Present: *She's always there when the trouble begins.* **—interj.** A word used to express satisfaction, sympathy, etc.: *There, it can't hurt that much!* [Middle English, from Old English *thær.*]

Usage: **1. there is/are.** When a sentence is introduced by *there,* often called a "dummy word," the number of the verb is gen. governed by the number of the true, or meaningful subject that follows the verb: *There are* (plural verb) *various objections* (plural subject) *to your proposal. There is* (singular verb) *powerful and effective opposition* (singular subject) *to your proposal.* But several exceptions to this general rule occur in modern English, and the following examples of them are acceptable. First, if the same subject is repeated, a singular verb may be used: *There is a time to love, a time to die, a time to speak, and a time to keep silent.* Secondly, if a compound subject involves two or more nouns whose modifiers are repeated, *there* is often used with a singular verb: *There was no money and no fuel.* Finally, if a singular element of a compound subject appears closest to the verb, the verb can be singular: *There was a man and three women at the bus stop.* But: *There were three women and a man at the bus stop.* **2. that there.** The adverb *there* cannot stand before a noun and the demonstrative adjective *that* cannot modify *there.* This is correct: *That man there is the thief* (not "that there man is the thief").

there·a·bouts (thâr′ə-bouts′) *adv.* Also **there·a·bout** (-bout′). **1.** Near that number, time, or age: *Jim was 10, or thereabouts.* **2.** In that neighborhood.

there·af·ter (thâr-ăf′tər) *adv.* After that; from then on.

there·at (thâr-ăt′) *adv.* **1.** At such time or place; there. **2.** At or because of that; upon that.

there·by (thâr-bī′) *adv.* By that means; as a result.

there·fore (thâr′fôr′, -fōr′) *adv.* For that reason; consequently.

there·from (thâr-frŏm′, -frŭm′) *adv.* From that, this, or it: *Children observe grownups and learn therefrom.*

there·in (thâr-ĭn′) *adv.* **1.** In that place. **2.** In that circumstance or respect: *Money was the problem; therein they could not agree.*

there·in·af·ter (thâr′ĭn-ăf′tər) *adv.* In a later or subsequent portion, as of a speech, book, etc.

there·in·to (thâr-ĭn′tōō) *adv. Archaic.* Into that place, thing, or matter.

there·of (thâr-ŏv′, -ŭv′) *adv.* **1.** Of that or it. **2.** From a given cause or origin; therefrom.

there·on (thâr-ŏn′, -ôn′) *adv.* **1.** On or upon that or it. **2.** Following that immediately; thereupon.

there·to (thâr-tōō′) *adv.* To that or it; thereunto: *affixed his seal thereto.*

there·to·fore (thâr′tə-fôr′, -fōr′) *adv.* Up to that time.

there·un·der (thâr-ŭn′dər) *adv.* Under that or it: *the Constitution and all the laws enacted thereunder.*

there·un·to (thâr′ŭn-tōō′) *adv.* To that or it; thereto.

there·up·on (thâr′ə-pŏn′, -pôn′) *adv.* **1.** Immediately following that. **2.** In consequence of that; therefore.

there·with (thâr-wĭth′, -wĭth′) *adv.* With that: *The murderer confessed and therewith the case was closed.*

there·with·al (thâr-wĭth-ôl′) adv. **1.** Archaic. In addition to that; besides. **2.** Obs. Therewith.

therm-. Var. of thermo-.

-therm. A suffix meaning heat: **poikilotherm.** [From Greek thermē, heat.]

ther·mal (thûr′məl) adj. **1.** Of, using, producing, or caused by heat. **2.** Warm or hot: thermal springs. —n. A current of warm air that rises because it is less dense than the air around it. —**ther′mal·ly** adv.

therm·i·on (thûr′mĭ′ən) n. An electrically charged particle or ion emitted by a conducting material at high temperatures. [THERM(O)- + ION.] —**therm′i·on′ic** (-mĭ-ŏn′ĭk) adj.

therm·is·tor (thər-mĭs′tər) n. A resistor made of semiconductors with resistance that varies rapidly and predictably with temperature. [THERM(AL) + (RES)ISTOR.]

Ther·mit (thûr′mĭt, -mĭt′) n. A trademark for a mixture of fine aluminum powder and iron or chromium oxide, that yields an intense heat when ignited, used in welding and the manufacture of incendiary bombs.

thermo- or **therm-.** A prefix meaning heat: **thermion.** [From Greek thermē, heat, from thermos, hot.]

ther·mo·chem·is·try (thûr′mō-kĕm′ĭ-strē) n. The chemistry of heat and associated chemical phenomena. —**ther′mo·chem′i·cal** (-kĕm′ĭ-kəl) adj. —**ther′mo·chem′ist** n.

ther·mo·cou·ple (thûr′mə-kŭp′əl) n. A thermoelectric device used to accurately measure temperatures, esp. high temperatures, esp. one consisting of two dissimilar metals joined so that a potential difference generated between the points of contact is a measure of the temperature difference between the points. Also called **thermoelectric couple.**

ther·mo·dy·nam·ics (thûr′mō-dī-năm′ĭks) n. (used with a sing. verb). The branch of physics that deals with the relationships between heat and other forms of energy. —**ther′mo·dy·nam′ic** adj. —**ther′mo·dy·nam′i·cal·ly** adv.

ther·mo·e·lec·tric (thûr′mō-ĭ-lĕk′trĭk) adj. Of or having to do with electricity that is generated by the action of heat. —**ther′mo·e·lec′tri·cal·ly** adv.

thermoelectric couple. A thermocouple.

ther·mo·e·lec·tric·i·ty (thûr′mō-ĭ-lĕk-trĭs′ĭ-tē, -ē′lĕk-) n. Electricity generated by a flow of heat, as in a thermocouple.

ther·mo·graph (thûr′mə-grăf′) n. A thermometer that records the temperature it measures, usu. indicating the time at which each measurement was made.

ther·mom·e·ter (thər-mŏm′ə-tər) n. An instrument for measuring temperature, esp. one that consists of a calibrated, sealed glass tube containing a column of liquid, usu. mercury or alcohol, that rises or falls to a level as it expands or contracts with changes in temperature.

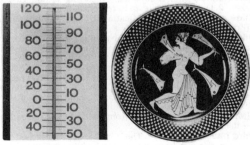

thermometer   Thetis

ther·mom·e·try (thər-mŏm′ĭ-trē) n. **1.** The measurement of temperature. **2.** The technology of temperature measurement. —**ther′mo·met′ric** (thûr′mə-mĕt′rĭk) adj.

ther·mo·nu·cle·ar (thûr′mō-nōō′klē-ər, -nyōō′-) adj. **1.** Of or derived from the fusion of atomic nuclei at high temperatures. **2.** Of atomic weapons based on nuclear fusion, esp. as distinguished from those based on nuclear fission.

ther·mo·plas·tic (thûr′mə-plăs′tĭk) adj. Soft and pliable when heated but hard when cooled. —n. A thermoplastic material.

Ther·mos bottle (thûr′məs). A trademark for a container that has double walls and an evacuated space between the walls, used to prevent the contents from gaining or losing heat. Also called **Thermos.**

ther·mo·set·ting (thûr′mō-sĕt′ĭng) adj. Becoming permanently hardened or rigid when treated with heat: a thermosetting plastic.

ther·mo·stat (thûr′mə-stăt′) n. A device that automatically regulates temperature-controlling equipment, such as furnaces and air conditioners. —**ther′mo·stat′ic** adj. —**ther′mo·stat′i·cal·ly** adv.

the·sau·rus (thĭ-sôr′əs) n., pl. **-sau·ri** (-sôr′ī) or **-rus·es. 1.** A book of words or information about a specific field, as music, medicine, etc. **2.** A book of synonyms. [Latin thēsaurus, treasure, from Greek thēsauros.]

these (thēz) pron. Plural of **this.**

the·ses (thē′sēz′) n. Plural of **thesis.**

The·se·us (thē′sē-əs, -sōōs) n. Gk. Myth. A hero and king of Athens who slew the Minotaur and conquered the Amazons and married their queen, Phaedra.

the·sis (thē′sĭs) n., pl. **-ses** (-sēz′). **1.** A proposition advanced, usu. without proof, and then defended or maintained by argument. **2.** A lengthy essay or treatise that advances an original point of view, esp. as a requirement for an academic degree. [Late Latin, from Greek, position, affirmation, from tithenai, to put, place.]

thes·pi·an (thĕs′pē-ən) adj. Of or pertaining to drama; dramatic. —n. An actor or actress. [After Thespis, Greek poet of the 6th cent. B.C.]

the·ta (thā′tə, thē′-) n. The eighth letter of the Greek alphabet, written Θ, θ, or in English as th. [Greek thēta.]

The·tis (thē′tĭs) n. Gk. Myth. One of the Nereids and the mother of Achilles.

thews (thōōz, thyōōz) pl.n. Well-developed sinews or muscles. [Middle English, habit, characteristic, good physical quality, from Old English thēaw, custom, characteristic.]

they (thā) pron. **1.** Those ones. Used as the plural of **he, she,** and **it:** We used to have a dog and a cat, but they fought constantly. He and she met in April and they were married in July. **2.** People in general: He's as tough as they come. [Middle English thei, partly from Old Norse their, partly from Old English thā.]

they'd (thād). Contraction of: **1.** They had. **2.** They would.

they'll (thāl). Contraction of they will.

they're (thâr). Contraction of they are.

they've (thāv). Contraction of they have.

thi-. Var. of thio-.

thi·a·mine (thī′ə-mĭn, -mēn′) n. Also **thi·a·min** (-mĭn). A B-complex vitamin, necessary for carbohydrate metabolism and maintenance of normal neural activity, produced synthetically and occurring naturally in grains, yeast, and meat. Also called **vitamin B₁.** [THI(O)- + (VIT)AMIN.]

thick (thĭk) adj. **-er, -est. 1.** Relatively great in depth or in extent from one surface to the opposite: a thick board. **2.** Measuring in this dimension: a board two inches thick. **3.** Heavy in build or stature; thickset: a thick neck. **4.** Having a large number of units in a close, compact arrangement; dense; concentrated: a thick forest. **5.** Having a heavy or viscous consistency: a thick tomato sauce. **6.** Having a great number of; abounding: a room thick with flies. **7.** Impenetrable by the eyes; deep; dense: a thick fog. **8.** Not easy to hear or understand; indistinctly articulated: the thick speech of a drunkard. **9.** Lacking mental agility; slow; stupid: Get that through your thick head. **10.** Informal. Very friendly; intimate. —See Syns at **stupid.** —adv. So as to be thick; thickly: Slice it thick. —n. **1.** The thickest part of something. **2.** The most active or intense part: in the thick of the battle. —**idiom. through thick and thin.** Through both good and bad times; faithfully. [Middle English thikke, from Old English thicce.] —**thick′ly** adv.

thick·en (thĭk′ən) tr.v. **1.** To make thick or thicker. **2.** To make more intense, intricate, or complex. —intr.v. **1.** To become thickened. **2.** To become more intricate or complex. The plot thickens. —**thick′en·er** n.

thick·en·ing (thĭk′ə-nĭng) n. **1.** The act or process of making or becoming thick. **2.** Any substance used to thicken a liquid. **3.** A thickened part of something.

thick·et (thĭk′ĭt) n. A dense growth of shrubs or underbrush. [Ult. from Old English thiccet, from thicce, thick.]

thick·head·ed (thĭk'hĕd'ĭd) adj. Slow to learn; dull.

thick·ness (thĭk'nĭs) n. 1. The quality or condition of being thick. 2. The dimension between two of an object's surfaces, usu. the dimension of smallest measure. 3. A layer, sheet, stratum, or ply: *a single thickness of thread.*

thick·set (thĭk'sĕt') adj. 1. Having a solid, stout build; stocky: *a thickset young wrestler.* 2. Placed, planted, or growing closely together: *thickset rose bushes.*

thick·skinned (thĭk'skĭnd') adj. 1. Having a thick skin: *a thick-skinned citrus fruit.* 2. Not easily offended or hurt by insult, criticism, etc.: *thick-skinned politicians.*

thick·wit·ted (thĭk'wĭt'ĭd) adj. Stupid; dull.

thief (thēf) n., pl. **thieves** (thēvz). A person who steals. [Middle English *thefe,* from Old English *thēof.*]

thieve (thēv) v. **thieved, thiev·ing.** —*tr.v.* To take by theft; to steal. —*intr.v.* To engage in or commit theft. [From THIEF.]

thiev·er·y (thē'və-rē) n., pl. **-ies.** The act or practice of thieving.

thieves (thēvz) n. Plural of **thief.**

thiev·ish (thē'vĭsh) adj. 1. Given to thieving or stealing. 2. Of or like a thief; stealthy; furtive.

thigh (thī) n. 1. a. The portion of the human leg between the hip and the knee. b. A similar structure in animals. 2. The femur of an insect's leg. [Middle English *thih,* from Old English *thēoh.*]

thigh·bone (thī'bōn') n. The femur.

thig·mo·tax·is (thĭg'mə-tăk'sĭs) n. Movement of an organism in response to a direct tactile stimulus. [Greek *thigma,* touch + -TAXIS.]

thig·mot·ro·pism (thĭg-mŏt'rə-pĭz'əm) n. The response or motion of an organism to direct contact with a surface or object. Also called **stereotropism.** [Greek *thigma,* touch + -TROPISM.]

thill (thĭl) n. Either of the two long shafts between which an animal is harnessed when pulling a wagon. [Middle English *thille.*]

thim·ble (thĭm'bəl) n. 1. A small metal or plastic cup worn to protect the finger that pushes the needle in sewing. 2. Any of various tubular sockets or sleeves in machinery. 3. *Naut.* a. A metal ring fitted into a sail's ropehole to prevent rubbing and wear. b. A metal ring around which a rope splice is passed. [Middle English *thymbyl,* from Old English *thȳmel,* from *thūma,* thumb.]

thim·ble·ber·ry (thĭm'bəl-bĕr'ē) n. Any of several raspberries with thimble-shaped fruit, esp. *Rubus parviflora,* of western and central North America.

thim·ble·ful (thĭm'bəl-fəl) n., pl. **-fuls.** A very small quantity.

thim·ble·rig (thĭm'bəl-rĭg') n. A sleight-of-hand gambling swindle, in which the operator palms a marker while presumably placing it under one of three inverted shells or thimbles and then, moving the shells or thimbles about, invites spectators to bet on the location of the marker. —*tr.v.* **-rigged, -rig·ging.** To swindle with or as if with a thimblerig. —**thim'ble·rig'ger** n.

thin (thĭn) adj. **thin·ner, thin·nest.** 1. a. Having a relatively small distance between opposite sides or surfaces: *a thin board.* b. Not great in diameter or cross section; fine: *thin wire.* 2. Lean or slender of figure. 3. a. Flowing with relative ease; not viscous: *a thin oil.* b. Watery: *thin soup.* 4. Made of or having a few units widely separated: *His hair is getting thin on top.* 5. Not dense: *a thin mist.* 6. Lacking in strength or resonance, as a sound or tone: *a singer having thin high notes.* 7. Lacking substance, force, etc.; flimsy; poor: *a thin excuse.* —*adv.* So as to be thin; thinly: *Slice it thin.* —*v.* **thinned, thin·ning.** —*intr.v.* To become thin or thinner. —*tr.v.* To make thin or thinner. [Middle English *thinne,* from Old English *thynne.*] —**thin'ly** adv. —**thin'ness** n.

Syns: *thin, bony, lanky, lean, scrawny, skinny, spare, slender, twiggy* adj. *Core meaning:* Having little flesh or fat on the body *(thin refugees).*

thine (thīn) pron. *Archaic & Poet.* 1. A possessive form of **thou.** 2. —Used instead of **thy** before an initial vowel or *h: thine enemy.* [Middle English *thin,* from Old English *thīn.*]

thing (thĭng) n. 1. Whatever can be perceived, known, or thought to have a separate existence; an entity. 2. The subject of thought, action, emotion, discussion, etc.: *I have so many things on my mind today.* 3. An object or creature that cannot or need not be precisely named or described: *What's that thing on the table?* 4. An inanimate object as distinguished from a living being. 5. A creature: *the poor thing.* 6. a. An act or deed: *a mean thing to do.* b. A thought, notion, or utterance: *a terrible thing to say!* c. A piece of information: *Our informant can't tell us a thing.* d. A means; device; recourse: *just the thing to launch our new product line.* e. A matter to be dealt with: *We have to put a lid on this thing.* 7. **things. a.** Personal possessions; belongings. b. The equipment needed for an activity or purpose: *Where are my sewing things?* c. The general state of affairs; conditions: *Things are getting worse and worse.* 8. **the thing.** The latest fashion; the rage. 9. *Slang.* An activity very suitable or satisfying to one: *doing his thing.* —See Syns at **fashion.** [Middle English, from Old English, creature, thing, deed, assembly.]

thing·a·ma·bob (thĭng'ə-mə-bŏb') n. Also **thing·u·ma·bob.** *Informal.* Something for which the exact name has been forgotten or is not known. [From THING.]

thing·a·ma·jig (thĭng'ə-mə-jĭg) n. Also **thing·um·a·jig.** *Informal.* A thingamabob. [From THING.]

think (thĭngk) v. **thought** (thôt), **think·ing.** —*tr.v.* 1. To have as a thought: *He thought he would win.* 2. To reason about; reflect on: *thinking the situation through.* 3. To judge or regard as being; look upon as: *I think it only fair.* 4. To believe; suppose: *I think that she is wrong.* 5. To remember; call to mind: *I can't think now what his name was.* —*intr.v.* 1. To exercise the power of reason: *Think before making a decision.* 2. To believe; suppose: *Does he know the truth, do you think?* —See Syns at **believe.** —*phrasal verbs.* **think about.** 1. To examine; consider. 2. To reflect upon; recall: *thinking about his school days.* **think of.** 1. To weigh the idea: *They are thinking of moving.* 2. To call to mind; recall. 3. To imagine: *Just think of the possibilities.* 4. To suggest: *Can you think of a good hotel for the weekend?* 5. To have an opinion concerning: *She thinks highly of his ability.* **think up.** To devise; invent. —*idioms.* **think better of.** To decide against (something) after reconsidering. **think nothing of.** To regard as routine or usual. **think twice.** To weigh something carefully. [Middle English *thenken,* from Old English *thencan.*] —**think'a·ble** adj. —**think'a·bly** adv. —**think'er** n.

think·ing (thĭng'kĭng) n. 1. Thought: *Their thinking is not in tune with the times.* 2. A way of reasoning; judgment: *not a good idea to my thinking.* —adj. Characterized by thoughtfulness; rational: *Man is a thinking animal.*

thin·ner (thĭn'ər) n. A liquid, such as turpentine, mixed with paint or varnish to make it flow easily as it is applied.

thin-skinned (thĭn'skĭnd') adj. 1. Having a thin rind or skin. 2. Oversensitive, esp. to reproach or insult.

thio- or **thi-.** A prefix indicating divalent sulfur: **thiamin.** [From Greek *theion,* sulfur.]

third (thûrd) n. 1. The ordinal number that matches the number three in a series. 2. One of three equal parts, written ⅓. 3. The musical interval formed by two tones of a diatonic scale that are separated by a tone of the scale lying between them. 4. The next higher gear after second in an automotive transmission. —adj. 1. Being number three in a series; next after second. 2. Being one of three equal parts. —adv. In the third place, rank, or order. [Middle English *thirde,* from Old English *thridda.*] —**third'ly** adv.

third base. *Baseball.* 1. The third base to be reached by a runner, the last base before home plate. 2. The position played by a third baseman.

third baseman. *Baseball.* The player stationed near third base.

third class. 1. The class of accommodations on a train, ship, plane, etc., that is usu. of the lowest order of luxury or price. 2. A class of mail that includes all printed matter, except newspapers and magazines, that weighs less than 16 ounces and is unsealed. —**third'-class'** adj. & adv.

third degree. Intensive questioning and brutal handling of a prisoner in order to obtain information or a confession.

third-degree burn (thûrd'dĭ-grē'). A severe burn in which the outer layer of skin is destroyed and sensitive nerve endings are exposed.

---

third person. A set of grammatical forms used in referring to a person or thing other than the speaker or the one spoken to.

third rail. The rail through which the current runs to power the train on an electric railway. **—third′-rail′** *adj.*

Third World. Also **third world.** The developing countries of Africa, Asia, and Latin America, esp. those not allied with the Communist or non-Communist blocs.

thirst (thûrst) *n.* **1. a.** A sensation of dryness in the mouth related to a desire to drink. **b.** The desire to drink. **2.** An insistent desire or craving. **—intr.v. 1.** To feel a need to drink; be thirsty. **2.** To have a strong desire; crave; yearn. [Middle English, from Old English *thurst.*]

thirst·y (thûr′stē) *adj.* **-i·er, -i·est. 1.** Desiring to drink. **2.** Arid; parched: *rode across the thirsty plains.* **3.** Craving; yearning: *a mind thirsty for knowledge.* **—thirst′i·ly** *adv.* **—thirst′i·ness** *n.*

thir·teen (thûr·tēn′) *n.* The cardinal number written 13, or in Roman numerals XIII, that is equal to the sum of 12 + 1. [Middle English *thrittene,* from Old English *thrēotīne.*]

thir·teenth (thûr′tēnth′) *n.* **1.** The ordinal number that matches the number thirteen in a series. Also written 13th. **2.** One of thirteen equal parts, written 1/13. **—thir′teenth′** *adj. & adv.*

thir·ti·eth (thûr′tē-ĭth) *n.* **1.** The ordinal number that matches the number thirty in a series. Also written 30th. **2.** One of thirty equal parts, written 1/30. **—thir′ti·eth** *adj. & adv.*

thir·ty (thûr′tē) *n., pl.* **thir·ties.** The cardinal number written 30, or in Roman numerals XXX, that is equal to the product of 3 × 10. [Middle English *thritty,* from Old English *thrītig.*]

thir·ty-sec·ond note (thûr′tē-sĕk′ənd). A musical note with a time value equivalent to 1/32 of a whole note.

this (thĭs) *pron., pl.* **these** (thēz). **1.** The person or thing present, nearby, or just mentioned: *This is my friend Judy. This is my house right here.* Also used adjectively: *Take a look at this book.* **2.** What is about to be said: *This will really make you laugh.* Also used adjectively: *Wait till you hear this version of what happened.* **3.** The one that is nearer than another or the one contrasted with the other: *That little scene was nothing compared to this.* Also used adjectively: *Stay on this side of the street; that side is dangerous. This car is smaller but much faster than that one.* **4.** The present occasion or time: *Jim's been out later than this.* **—adv.** To this extent; so: *I never knew Jim to stay out this late.* **—idiom. this and that.** One thing and another. [Middle English, from Old English *thes.*]

> *Usage:* **this, that.** Both of these demonstrative pronouns represent thoughts expressed earlier: *They had good intentions, but that* (or *this*) *cannot excuse the wrong they did.* Either *that* or *this* is acceptable in most such examples. In formal writing, however, many authorities consider *that* the better choice in referring to what has gone before in time, and *this* the better choice in referring to what is about to be stated: *That is what we intended, but this is what we did.* (*This* tends to be overworked in such sentences without regard to consideration of time.) Avoid using *that* and *this* when they are so far removed from the thoughts they represent that the references are unclear. In such cases, restate what is meant. The use of the pronoun *this* should also be avoided when the reference is to a person: *He* (or *she*) *is a public official of integrity* (not *This is a public official of integrity*).

this·tle (thĭs′əl) *n.* Any of numerous weedy plants, chiefly of the genera *Cirsium, Carduus,* or *Onopordum,* with prickly leaves and usu. purplish flowers that are surrounded by prickly bracts. [Middle English *thistel,* from Old English.]

this·tle·down (thĭs′əl-doun′) *n.* The silky down attached to the seeds of a thistle.

thith·er (thĭth′ər, thĭth′-) *adv.* To or toward that place; in that direction. **—adj.** Located or being on the more distant side; farther. [Middle English *thider,* from Old English *thider.*]

thith·er·ward (thĭth′ər-wərd, thĭth′-) *adv.* In that direction; thither.

tho (thō). *adv. & conj. Informal.* Though.**—**See Usage note at *although.*

Thompson submachine gun. A type of .45-caliber submachine gun designed to be fired from the shoulder. Also called **Tommy gun.** [After its co-inventor, John *Thompson* (d. 1940), American army officer.]

thong (thông, thŏng) *n.* **1.** A narrow strip of leather or other material used to fasten something. **2.** The lash of a whip. [Middle English, from Old English *thwong.*]

Thor (thôr) *n. Norse Myth.* The god of thunder.

tho·rac·ic (thə-răs′ĭk) *adj.* Of, in, or near the thorax.

tho·rax (thôr′ăks′, thōr′-) *n., pl.* **-rax·es** or **tho·ra·ces** (thôr′-ə-sēz′, thōr′-, thô-rā′-). **1.** *Anat.* The part of the human body between the neck and the diaphragm, partially encased by the ribs; the chest. **2.** A similar part in other animals. **3.** The second or middle region of the body of an arthropod. [Latin *thōrāx,* from Greek *thōrax,* breastplate, coat of mail.]

tho·rite (thôr′īt′, thōr′-) *n.* A rare brownish-yellow to black mineral ore from which thorium can be extracted. [THOR-(IUM) + -ITE.]

tho·ri·um (thôr′ē-əm, thōr′-) *n. Symbol* **Th** A silvery-white metallic element with 13 radioactive isotopes, used in magnesium alloys; isotope 232 is a source of nuclear energy. Atomic number 90; atomic weight 232.038; valence +4; approx. melting point 1,700°C; approx. boiling point 4,000°C. [After THOR.]

thorn (thôrn) *n.* **1.** A modified branch in the form of a sharp, woody spine. **2.** Any of various shrubs, trees, or woody plants that bear such spines. **3.** Any of various sharp, spiny protuberances; a prickle. **4.** Someone or something that causes physical or emotional distress, annoyance, or irritation. [Middle English, from Old English.]

thorn apple. Any of various plants of the genus *Datura.*

thorn·y (thôr′nē) *adj.* **-i·er, -i·est. 1.** Full of or covered with thorns. **2.** Troublesome; difficult: *a thorny situation.* **—thorn′i·ness** *n.*

tho·ron (thôr′ŏn′, thōr′-) *n.* A radioactive isotope of radon with a half-life of 54.5 seconds. [THOR(IUM) + -ON.]

thor·ough (thûr′ō) *adj.* **1.** Complete in all respects: *a thorough success.* **2.** Painstakingly careful: *a thorough search; a thorough worker.* **—**See Syns at **utter.** [Middle English *thorow,* from *thorugh* through, from Old English *thuruh.*] **—thor′ough·ly** *adv.* **—thor′ough·ness** *n.*

thor·ough·bred (thûr′ō-brĕd′, thûr′ə-) *adj.* **1.** Bred of pure blood or stock; purebred. **2.** Thoroughbred. Pertaining or belonging to the Thoroughbred breed of horses. **3.** Thoroughly trained or educated; well-bred. **—n. 1.** A purebred or pedigreed animal. **2.** Thoroughbred. One of a breed of horse resulting from the mating in the 18th cent. of Arabian stallions with English mares and whose bloodlines have been kept pure. **3.** A person who displays the qualities of good breeding.

thor·ough·fare (thûr′ō-fâr′, thûr′ə-) *n.* **1.** A main or heavily traveled road or highway. **2.** Any way, such as a street, waterway, etc., that is open at both ends and affords passage from one place to another. [Middle English *thurgh-fare : thurgh,* through + *fare,* passage.]

thor·ough·go·ing (thûr′ō-gō′ĭng, thûr′ə-) *adj.* **1.** Complete in all respects: *a thoroughgoing examination.* **2.** Unmitigated; unqualified: *a thoroughgoing scoundrel.*

those (thōz) *adj. & pron.* Plural of **that.**

thou (thou) *pron. Archaic.* The second person singular in

thistle

the nominative case, equivalent to you. [Middle English *thu,* from Old English.]

though (thō) *adv.* However; nevertheless: *We can expect some economic improvement, not right away though.* —*conj.* **1.** Although; while: *The paper, though well conceived, was badly written.* **2.** Even if: *Though our chances of winning are slim, I think we should go ahead.* [Middle English, from Old Norse *thō.*]

thought (thôt) *v.* Past tense and past participle of **think.** —*n.* **1.** The act or process of thinking. **2.** A product of thinking; an idea. **3.** The intellectual product or ideas of a particular period of social history, group, social class, etc: *ancient Greek thought.* **4.** Consideration; attention; concern: *giving thought to the matter.* **5.** Intention; expectation; design: *We have no thought of taking a vacation now.* **6.** A small amount; a bit: *He should be a thought more considerate.* [Middle English *thought,* a thought, from Old English *(ge)thōht.*]

thought·ful (thôt′fəl) *adj.* **1.** Contemplative; meditative. **2.** Well thought-out: *a thoughtful essay.* **3.** Showing regard for others; considerate. —**thought′ful·ly** *adv.* —**thought′ful·ness** *n.*

thought·less (thôt′lĭs) *adj.* **1.** Careless; unthinking. **2.** Reckless; rash. **3.** Inconsiderate; inattentive. —See Syns at **careless.** —**thought′less·ly** *adv.* —**thought′less·ness** *n.*

thou·sand (thou′zənd) *n.* **1.** The cardinal number written 1,000, or in Roman numerals M, that is equal to the sum of 999 + 1. **2.** Often **thousands.** A very great or indeterminate number: *thousands of things to do today.* [Middle English *thousande,* from Old English *thūsend.*]

thou·sandth (thou′zəndth, -zənth) *n.* **1.** The ordinal number that matches the number one thousand in a series. Also written 1,000th. **2.** One of a thousand equal parts, written ¹⁄₁₀₀₀. —**thou′sandth** *adj. & adv.*

thrall (thrôl) *n.* **1.** Someone who is in bondage, as a slave or serf. **2.** A condition of servitude; slavery; bondage. [Middle English, from Old English *thrǣl,* from Old Norse *thrǣll.*] —**thrall′dom** (-dəm) or **thral′dom** *n.*

thrash (thrăsh) *tr.v.* **1.** To beat or flog with or as if with a whip. **2.** To swing or move about wildly; to flail: *The crocodile thrashed his tail.* **3.** To defeat utterly. **4.** To thresh. —*intr.v.* **1.** To move wildly or violently: *thrashed and tossed about all night.* **2.** To thresh. —See Syns at **defeat.** —**thrash out.** To go over or work out fully. —*n.* The act of thrashing. [Var. of THRESH.] —**thrash′er** *n.*

thrash·er (thrăsh′ər) *n.* Any of various New World songbirds of the genus *Toxostoma,* with a long tail, a long, curved beak, and, in several species, a spotted breast. [Perh. dial. from *thrusher,* thrush.]

thrash·ing (thrăsh′ĭng) *n.* A severe beating; a whipping.

thread (thrĕd) *n.* **1.** A length of fine, thin textile cord made of two or more strands of fiber twisted together. **2.** Anything that resembles a thread in thinness, fineness, etc.: *a thread of smoke.* **3.** Something that runs through something else bringing the parts of it together: *He lost the thread of his argument.* **4.** A ridge cut in a spiral or helical path on a screw, nut, bolt, etc. —*tr.v.* **1.** To place or fit thread on or through. **2.** To connect or join (beads or other objects) by passing thread through; to string: *thread pearls.* **3.** To pass or move cautiously through. **4.** To cut a thread onto (a screw, nut, bolt, etc.). —*intr.v.* **1.** To wind cautiously through obstacles or a slender path: *threaded through the heavy underbrush.* **2.** To proceed by a winding course. **3.** To form a thin filament when dropped from a spoon, as boiling sugar syrup. [Middle English *thred,* from Old English *thrǣd.*] —**thread′er** *n.*

thread·bare (thrĕd′bâr′) *adj.* **1.** Having the nap so worn that the threads show through. **2.** Wearing old, shabby clothing. **3.** Hackneyed; stale: *threadbare jokes.*

thread·worm (thrĕd′wûrm′) *n.* Any of various threadlike nematode worms.

thread·y (thrĕd′ē) *adj.* **-i·er, -i·est. 1.** Consisting of or resembling thread; fibrous; stringy. **2.** *Med.* Weak and shallow, as a pulse. **3.** Lacking fullness of tone; thin; weak: *a thready voice.* —**thread′i·ness** *n.*

threat (thrĕt) *n.* **1.** An expression of an intention to inflict pain, injury, evil, punishment, etc. **2.** An indication of impending danger or harm: *The air held a threat of snow.* **3.** A person, thing, idea, etc., regarded as a possible danger; a menace. [Middle English *thret,* from Old English *thrēat,* oppression, use of force, threat.]

threat·en (thrĕt′n) *tr.v.* **1.** To utter a threat against. **2.** To serve as a threat to; endanger; to menace. **3.** To give signs or warning of; portend: *skies threatening rain.* **4.** To announce as possible: *He's always threatening to quit.* —*intr.v.* **1.** To utter or use threats. **2.** To indicate danger or other harm. —**threat′en·er** *n.* —**threat′en·ing·ly** *adv.*

three (thrē) *n.* **1.** The cardinal number written 3, or in Roman numerals III, equal to the sum of 2 + 1. **2.** A playing card marked with three pips. [Middle English, from Old English *thrēo.*]

three-base hit (thrē′bās′). *Baseball.* A hit that allows the batter to reach third base; a triple.

three-D or **3-D** (thrē′dē′) *adj.* Three-dimensional. —*n.* A three-dimensional medium, display, or performance, esp. a cinematic or graphic display in three dimensions.

three-deck·er (thrē′dĕk′ər) *n.* **1.** A ship with three decks, esp. a warship with guns on three decks. **2.** Anything with three layers, esp. a sandwich.

three-di·men·sion·al (thrē′dĭ-mĕn′shən-əl) *adj.* **1.** Of, having, or existing in three dimensions. **2.** Having or appearing to have extension in depth as well as height and width, esp. flat visual images in which there is an illusion of depth and perspective.

three·fold (thrē′fōld′) *adj.* **1.** Having or consisting of three parts. **2.** Three times as many or as much; treble. —*adv.* Three times as much or as great; trebly. —*n.* An amount or number three times more than a specified unit.

three-gait·ed (thrē′gā′tĭd) *adj.* Trained in three gaits, the walk, trot, and canter, as a saddle horse.

Three Graces. The Graces.

three-mile limit (thrē′mīl′). *International Law.* The outer limit of the marine belt extending along the shoreline of a coastal state that constitutes that state's territorial waters.

three·pence (thrĭp′əns, thrŭp′-, threp′-) *n., pl.* **threepence** or **-pences.** *Brit.* **1.** A coin worth three pennies. **2.** The sum of three pennies.

three·pen·ny (thrĭp′ə-nē, thrŭp′-, threp′-) *adj. Brit.* **1.** Worth or priced at threepence. **2.** Very small; trifling.

three-point landing (thrē′point′). **1.** An airplane landing in which the tailskid or tail wheel and the two forward wheels all touch the ground simultaneously. **2.** *Informal.* Anything done perfectly or successfully.

three-ring circus (thrē′rĭng′). **1.** A circus with simultaneous performances in three separate rings. **2.** A situation full of bewildering activity.

three R's. Reading, writing, and arithmetic, considered as the fundamentals of elementary education. [From the phrase *reading, 'riting, and 'rithmetic.*]

three·score (thrē′skôr′, -skōr′) *adj.* Sixty; three times twenty. —**three′score′** *n.*

three·some (thrē′səm) *adj.* Consisting of or performed by three. —*n.* **1.** A group of three persons. **2.** Any activity involving three persons.

thren·o·dy (thrĕn′ə-dē) *n., pl.* **-dies.** A poem or song of lamentation. [Greek *thrēnōidia* : *thrēnos,* lament + *ōidē,* song.] —**thre·no′di·al** (thrĭ-nō′dē-əl) or **thre·nod′ic** (thrĭ-nŏd′ĭk) *adj.* —**thren′o·dist** *n.*

thre·o·nine (thrē′ə-nēn′) *n.* A colorless crystalline amino acid, $C_4H_9NO_3$, an essential component of human nutrition. [Orig. unknown.]

thresh (thrĕsh) *tr.v.* **1.** To separate grain or seed from (a cereal plant) with a machine, flail, or other mechanical means. **2.** To wave or lash about vigorously; *threshed his arms in the air.* —*intr.v.* **1.** To thresh grain. **2.** To thrash or toss about. —*phrasal verb.* **thresh out** (or **over**). To discuss intensively and thoroughly in order to arrive at a conclusion or resolution. [Middle English *threshen,* from Old English *therscan.*]

thresh·er (thrĕsh′ər) *n.* **1.** Someone or something that threshes. **2.** A threshing machine. **3.** Any of various sharks of the genus *Alopias,* that have a tail with a long, whiplike upper lobe.

threshing machine. A farm machine used in threshing grain or seed plants.

thresh·old (thrĕsh′ōld′, thrĕsh′hōld′) *n.* **1.** The piece of wood or stone placed beneath a door. **2.** An entrance to a house, building, room, etc. **3.** The place or point of beginning: the outset: *on the threshold of a new age of scientific space research.* **4.** The lowest level or intensity at which a stimulus can be perceived or can produce a given effect: *the threshold of pain.* [Middle English *thresshold,* from Old English *therscold.*]

threw (thrōō) *v.* Past tense of **throw.** [Middle English, from Old English *thrēow.*]

thrice (thrīs) *adv.* **1.** Three times; on three occasions. **2.** In a threefold quantity or degree. [Middle English *thries,* from *thrie,* from Old English *thriwa.*]

thrift (thrĭft) *n.* **1.** Wise economy in the management of money and other resources; frugality. **2.** Any of several densely tufted, chiefly European plants of the genus *Armeria,* usu. with rounded clusters of pink flowers. [Middle English, prosperity, from Old Norse, from *thrīfask,* to thrive.]

thrift·y (thrĭf′tē) *adj.* **-i·er, -i·est. 1.** Wisely economical; frugal. **2.** Industrious and thriving; prosperous. **3.** Growing and thriving, as a plant. **—thrift′i·ly** *adv.* **—thrift′i·ness** *n.*

thrill (thrĭl) *tr.v.* To cause to feel a sudden intense sensation, as of joy, pleasure, excitement, etc. *—intr.v.* To feel a sudden quiver of intense emotion. *—n.* **1.** A sudden feeling of intense emotion or excitement, often manifesting itself as a trembling sensation passing through the body. **2.** Anything that produces such a feeling of excitement. [Middle English *thrillen,* to pierce, from Old English *thyrlian,* from *thyrel,* hole.] **—thrill′ing·ly** *adv.*

thrill·er (thrĭl′ər) *n.* **1.** Someone or something that thrills. **2.** *Informal.* A sensational or suspenseful story, motion picture, etc., esp. a mystery novel.

thrips (thrĭps) *n., pl.* **thrips.** Any of various small, often wingless insects of the order Thysanoptera, many of which are destructive to plants. [Latin, woodworm, from Greek.]

thrive (thrīv) *intr.v.* **throve** (thrōv) or **thrived,thrived** or **thriv·en** (thrĭv′ən), **thriv·ing. 1.** To grow or do well; flourish. **2.** To be successful; prosper. —See Syns at **prosper.** [Middle English *thrīven,* to increase, flourish, from Old Norse *thrīfask,* reflexive of *thrīfa,* to seize.] **—thriv′er** *n.*

throat (thrōt) *n.* **1.** *Anat.* **a.** The portion of the digestive tract that lies between the rear of the mouth and the esophagus. **b.** The anterior portion of the neck. **2.** Any narrow passage or part suggestive of or resembling the human throat: *the throat of a bottle.* [Middle English *throte,* from Old English.] **—throat′ed** *adj.*

throat·y (thrō′tē) *adj.* **-i·er, -i·est.** Sounded or seemingly sounded deep in the throat; guttural, hoarse, or husky: *a throaty growl.* **—throat′i·ly** *adv.* **—throat′i·ness** *n.*

throb (thrŏb) *intr.v.* **throbbed, throb·bing. 1.** To beat rapidly or violently; to pound. **2.** To vibrate, pulsate, or sound with a steady, pronounced rhythm: *jungle drums throbbing in the night.* *—n.* **1.** The act of throbbing, esp. a beat of the heart or an artery. **2.** A repetitive or pulsating sound. [Middle English *throbben.*] **—throb′bing·ly** *adv.*

throe (thrō) *n.* **1.** Often **throes.** A severe pang or spasm of pain, as in childbirth. **2. throes.** A condition of great struggle or effort: *a country in the throes of war.* [Middle English *throwe,* from Old English *thrawe,* paroxysm.]

throm·bi (thrŏm′bī) *n.* Plural of **thrombus.**

thromb-. Var. of **thrombo-.**

throm·bin (thrŏm′bən) *n.* An enzyme in blood that facilitates blood clotting by reacting with fibrinogen to form fibrin. [THROMB(O)- + -IN.]

thrombo– or **thromb–.** A prefix meaning a blood clot: **thrombin.** [From Greek *thrombos,* lump, clot.]

throm·bo·cyte (thrŏm′bə-sīt′) *n. Anat.* A blood platelet.

throm·bo·sis (thrŏm-bō′sĭs) *n., pl.* **-ses** (-sēz′). *Pathol.* The formation or presence of a blood clot in a blood vessel or a chamber of the heart.

throm·bus (thrŏm′bəs) *n., pl.* **-bi** (-bī′). *Pathol.* A blood clot that obstructs a blood vessel or is formed in a chamber of the heart. [Greek *thrombos,* lump, clot.]

throne (thrōn) *n.* **1.** The chair occupied by a sovereign, pope, bishop, etc., on state or ceremonial occasions. **2.** A person who occupies a throne; sovereign. **3.** The power, rank, or authority of a sovereign: *a plot to usurp the throne.* **throned, thron·ing.** *—tr.v.* To set on a throne; enthrone. [Middle English, from *trone,* from Old French,

from Latin *thronus,* from Greek *thronos.*]

throng (thrông) *n.* A large group of people or things crowded together; a multitude. *—tr.v.* **1.** To crowd into; fill completely. **2.** To press in upon; surround with large numbers: *Fans thronged the singer.* *—intr.v.* To gather or move in a throng; to crowd. [Middle English, from Old English *thrang.*]

throt·tle (thrŏt′l) *n.* **1.** A valve in an internal-combustion engine that controls the flow of fuel to the combustion chamber. **2.** In a steam engine or similar engine, a valve that regulates the flow of hot fluid to the cylinders, turbine, etc. **3.** A pedal or lever that controls a valve of this type. *—tr.v.* **throt·tled, throt·tling. 1.** To control with or as if with a throttle. **2.** To strangle; choke. **3.** To suppress: *throttling all political opposition in the country.* [From Middle English *throtelen,* to choke, from *throte,* throat.] **—throt′tler** *n.*

through (thrōō) *prep.* Also *informal* **thru. 1.** In one side and out the opposite or another side of: *going through the door.* Also used adverbially: *The door opened, and we went through.* **2.** Among or between; in the midst of: *a walk through the flowers.* **3.** By means of: *getting an apartment through an agency.* **4.** As a result of: *The war was lost through lack of money.* **5.** Here and there in; around: *a tour through France.* **6.** From the beginning to the end of: *staying up through the night.* Also used adverbially: *if you'll just hear me through.* **7.** At or to the end or conclusion of: *We are through our testing period.* Also used adverbially: *Let's see this thing through.* **8.** Without stopping for: *driving through a red light.* Also used adverbially: *It's possible but very tiring to drive through from coast to coast.* *—adj.* **1.** Passing from one end or side to another: *a through beam.* **2.** Allowing continuous passage without obstruction: *a through street.* **3.** Going all the way to the end without stopping: *This is a through flight.* **4.** Finished; done: *Tell me you're through.* **5.** *Informal.* **a.** Finished; no longer effective or capable: *If he injures that knee again, he's through.* **b.** Having no further relationship: *She and I are through.* —See Syns at **direct.** *—idiom.* **through and through. 1.** All the way through: *soaked through and through.* **2.** Completely; thoroughly: *She's a staunch Republican through and through.* [Middle English *thrugh,* from Old English *thuruh.*]

through·out (thrōō-out′) *prep.* In, to, through, or during every part of: *throughout the night.* Also used adverbially: *I found this book interesting throughout.*

through·way (thrōō′wā′) *n.* Var. of **thruway.**

throve (thrōv) *v.* A past tense of **thrive.** [Middle English *throf.*]

throw (thrō) *v.* **threw** (thrōō), **thrown** (thrōn), **throw·ing.** *—tr.v.* **1.** To propel through the air with a swift motion of the arm; to fling. **2.** To hurl with great force, as in anger: *He threw himself at his opponent.* **3.** To cast: *throw a shadow.* **4.** To put on or off casually: *threw a sweater over her shoulders.* **5.** To hurl to the ground or floor. **6.** *Informal.* To arrange or give: *throw a party.* **7.** *Informal.* To lose (a fight, race, etc.) purposely. **8.** To put into a specified condition, state, etc.: *That question threw me. He was thrown into jail.* **9.** To actuate (a switch or control lever). **10. a.** To roll (dice). **b.** To roll (a particular number) with dice. **11.** *Card Games.* To discard or play (a card). *—intr.v.* To cast, fling, or hurl something. —See Syns at **confuse.** *—phrasal verbs.* **throw away. 1.** To discard as useless. **2.** To squander or waste: *throw away an opportunity.* **throw back. 1.** To revert to an earlier type of stage in one's ancestry, development, etc. **2.** To hinder or check the progress of. **throw in. 1.** To engage (a clutch, gears, etc.). **2.** To add (something) with no additional charge. **throw in with.** To join company with. **throw off. 1.** To cast out; to reject. **2.** To give off; emit. **3.** To rid oneself of; evade. **throw out. 1.** To give off; emit. **2.** To reject or discard. **3.** To offer, as a suggestion or plan. **4.** To disengage (a clutch or gears). **5.** *Baseball.* To put out (a base runner) by throwing the ball to the player guarding the base to which he is running. **throw over. 1.** To overturn. **2.** To desert or abandon. —See Syns at **abandon. throw up. 1.** To construct hurriedly. **2.** To vomit. *—n.* **1.** The act of throwing; a cast. **2.** The distance, height, or direction of something thrown. **3. a.** A roll or cast of dice. **b.** The number obtained with a cast of dice. **4.** In wrestling or judo, the

ă pat	ā pay	â care	ä father	ĕ pet	ē be	hw which	ĭ pit	ī tie	î pier	ŏ pot	ō toe	ô paw, for	oi noise
ōō took	ōō boot	ou out	th thin	*th* this	ŭ cut		û urge	zh vision	ə about, item, edible, gallop, circus				

act or method of throwing an opponent. **5. a.** A scarf or shawl. **b.** A light coverlet or blanket. **6. a.** The length of the radius of a circle described by a crank, cam, or similar part in machinery. **b.** The maximum displacement of a machine part moved by a crank, cam, etc. [Middle English *thrown*, to turn, twist, hurl, from Old English *thrāwan*, to turn, twist.] —**throw'er** *n.*

throw·a·way (thrō'ə-wā') *n.* Something that is or may be thrown away, esp. a handbill distributed on the street.

throw·back (thrō'băk') *n.* **1.** A reversion to an earlier type, characteristic, or stage in one's ancestry, development, etc.; atavism. **2.** An instance of this.

thrown (thrōn) *v.* Past participle of **throw.** [Middle English *throwen*, from Old English *(ge)thrawen.*]

throw rug. A scatter rug.

thru (thrōō) *prep. & adj. Informal.* Var. of **through.**

thrum[1] (thrŭm) *v.* **thrummed, thrum·ming.** —*tr.v.* **1.** To play (a stringed instrument) in an idle or monotonous way. **2.** To repeat or recite in a monotonous tone of voice. **3.** To strike or tap (an object) monotonously with the fingers. —*intr.v.* **1.** To strum idly on a stringed instrument. **2.** To speak in a dull, monotonous voice; to drone. **3.** To drum or tap idly on something. —*n.* The sound made by thrumming. [Imit.]

thrum[2] (thrŭm) *n.* **1. a.** The fringe of warp threads left on a loom after the cloth has been cut off. **b.** One of these threads. **2.** Any loose end, fringe, or tuft of thread. [Middle English, from Old English *(tunge)thrum*, ligament (of the tongue).]

thrush (thrŭsh) *n.* **1.** Any of various songbirds of the family Turdidae, characteristically with brownish upper plumage and a spotted breast. **2.** Any of various similar or related birds. [Middle English *thrusche*, from Old English *thrysce.*]

thrust (thrŭst) *v.* **thrust, thrust·ing.** —*tr.v.* **1.** To push or drive forcibly: *thrusting our way through the crowd. He thrust his hands in his pockets.* **2.** To stab; pierce: *thrust a dagger into his back.* **3.** To force into a specified condition or situation: *thrust herself into a highpaid job.* —*intr.v.* **1.** To shove or push against or into something. **2.** To make a lunge or stab as with a pointed weapon. **3.** To force one's way: *They thrust past the barricades.* —*n.* **1.** A forceful shove or push. **2.** A force that tends to move an object, esp. an object such as an airplane or rocket. **3.** A stab. **4.** The general direction or tendency: *the thrust of the governor's proposal.* [Middle English *thrusten*, from Old Norse *thrÿsta.*]

thru·way (thrōō'wā') *n.* Also **through·way.** A highway for highspeed traffic, usu. with four or more lanes.

thud (thŭd) *n.* **1.** A dull sound. **2.** A blow or fall causing such a sound. —*intr.v.* **thud·ded, thud·ding.** To make such a sound. [Middle English *thudden*, from Old English *thyddan* (imit.).]

thug (thŭg) *n.* A brutal ruffian or hoodlum. [Hindi *thag*, cheat, thief, from Sanskrit *sthaga*, robber, from *sthagati*, to cover, hide.] —**thug'ger·y** *n.* —**thug'gish** *adj.*

Thu·le (thōō'lē) *n.* **Ultima Thule.** [Latin *Thūlē*, the northernmost region of the world, from Greek.]

thu·li·um (thōō'lē-əm) *n. Symbol* **Tm** A bright silvery rareearth element that has 16 known isotopes with mass numbers ranging from 161 to 176; isotope Tm 170 is used in small portable medical x-ray units. Atomic number 69; atomic weight 168.934; melting point 1,545°C; boiling point 1,727°C; specific gravity 9.332; valences 2, 3. [From THULE.]

thumb (thŭm) *n.* **1.** The short first digit of the human hand, opposable to the other four fingers. **2.** A corresponding digit of other animals, esp. primates. **3.** The part of a glove or mitten that covers the thumb. —*tr.v.* **1.** To soil or wear by careless or frequent handling. **2.** To glance through or turn (the pages of a book, magazine, etc.) casually or quickly. **3.** *Informal.* To solicit (a ride) from a passing automobile by pointing one's thumb in the direction one is traveling; hitchhike. —*intr.v.* To hitchhike. —**idioms. all thumbs.** Clumsy; awkward. **thumbs down.** *Informal.* A sign of refusal or disapproval. **thumbs up.** A sign of hope or success. **under the thumb of.** Under the influence or power of. [Middle English *thombe*, from Old English *thūma.*]

thumb index. A series of rounded indentations cut into the front edge of a reference book, each labeled, as with a letter, to indicate a section of the book.

thumb·nail (thŭm'nāl') *n.* The nail of the thumb. —*adj.* **1.** Of the size of a thumbnail. **2.** Brief: *a thumbnail sketch.*

thumb·screw (thŭm'skrōō') *n.* **1.** A screw made so that it can be turned with the thumb and fingers. **2.** An instrument of torture formerly used to slowly crush the thumb.

thumb·tack (thŭm'tăk') *n.* A tack with a smooth, rounded head that can be pressed into place with the thumb.

thump (thŭmp) *n.* **1.** A blow with a blunt or heavy instrument. **2.** The muffled sound produced by such a blow. —*tr.v.* **1.** To beat with or as if with a heavy, blunt instrument so as to produce a muffled sound. **2.** To beat soundly or thoroughly. —*intr.v.* **1.** To hit or fall in such a way as to produce a thump. **2.** To walk with heavy steps. [Imit.] —**thump'er** *n.*

thump·ing (thŭm'pĭng) *adj.* Outstandingly large, exciting, or satisfying: *a thumping victory; a thumping good time.* —**thump'ing·ly** *adv.*

thun·der (thŭn'dər) *n.* **1.** The explosive noise that accompanies a stroke of lightning, produced by rapid expansion of gases along the path of the electrical charge. **2.** Any similar noise: *thunders of applause.* —*intr.v.* **1.** To produce thunder. **2.** To produce sounds like thunder: *guns thundering in the distance.* **3.** To utter loud or angry remarks. —*tr.v.* To utter loudly or angrily; to roar: *The captain thundered orders to the sailors.* [Middle English, from Old English *thunor.*] —**thun'der·er** *n.*

thun·der·bolt (thŭn'dər-bōlt') *n.* **1.** A discharge or flash of lightning that is accompanied by thunder. **2.** Someone or something that acts with sudden and destructive fury.

thun·der·clap (thŭn'dər-klăp') *n.* **1.** A single sharp crash of thunder. **2.** Anything of similar violence or suddenness, as a startling or shocking piece of news, occurrence, etc.

thun·der·cloud (thŭn'dər-kloud') *n.* A large, dark cloud that produces thunder and lightning.

thun·der·head (thŭn'dər-hĕd') *n.* The rounded upper portion of a thundercloud.

thun·der·ous (thŭn'dər-əs) *adj.* Producing thunder or a similar sound. —**thun'der·ous·ly** *adv.*

thun·der·show·er (thŭn'dər-shou'ər) *n.* A brief rainstorm accompanied by thunder and lightning.

thun·der·storm (thŭn'dər-stôrm') *n.* An·electrical storm accompanied by heavy rain.

thun·der·struck (thŭn'dər-strŭk') *adj.* Also **thun·der·strick·en** (-strĭk'ən). Astonished; stunned.

thu·ri·ble (thōōr'ə-bəl) *n.* A censer. [Middle English *thory·ble*, from Old French *thurible*, from Latin *thūribulum*, from *thūs*, incense, from Greek *thuos.*]

Thurs·day (thûrz'dē, -dā') *n.* The fifth day of the week, after Wednesday and before Friday. [Middle English *thur(e)sday*, from Old English *thūr(e)s dæg*, from earlier *thunresdæg*, "Thor's day."]

thus (thŭs) *adv.* **1.** In this manner. **2.** To a stated degree or extent; so: *I haven't looked at your work thus far.* **3.** Consequently; thereby. [Middle English, from Old English.]

thwack (thwăk) *tr.v.* To strike or hit with something flat. —*n.* A hard blow with something flat; a whack. [Imit.]

thwart (thwôrt) *tr.v.* To prevent from taking place; frustrate; block. —*n.* A seat across a boat, on which the oarsman sits. —*adj.* Extending, lying, or passing across something; transverse. —*adv. & prep. Archaic.* Athwart; across. [From Middle English *thwert*, athwart, across, perverse, from Old Norse *thvert*, transverse.] —**thwart'er** *n.*

thy (thī) *pron. Archaic.* The possessive form of thee. [Middle English *thīn*, thine.]

thyme (tīm) *n.* **1.** Any of several mint herbs or low shrubs of the genus *Thymus*, with small purplish flowers. **2.** The leaves of this plant, used as seasoning. [Middle English, from Old French *thym*, from Latin *thymum*, from Greek *thumon.*]

thy·mine (thī'mēn') *n.* A pyrimidine, $C_5H_6N_2O_2$, that is one of four genetic coding bases of DNA. [THYM(US) + -INE.]

thy·mol (thī'môl', -mōl') *n.* A crystalline, aromatic compound, $C_{10}H_{14}O$, derived from thyme oil and other oils and used as an antiseptic and as a preservative. [THYM(E) + -OL.]

---

thy·mus (thī′məs) *n.* A ductless glandlike structure, situated just behind the top of the sternum, that plays some part in building resistance to disease but is usu. vestigial in adults after reaching its maximum development during early childhood. [Greek *thumos.*]

thy·roid (thī′roid′) *adj.* Of or relating to the thyroid gland or the thyroid cartilage. —*n.* **1.** The thyroid gland. **2.** The thyroid cartilage. **3.** A dried and powdered preparation made from the thyroid gland of certain domestic animals, used in the treatment of hypothyroid conditions, as cretinism. [Obs. French *thyroide,* from Greek *thuroidēs,* shaped like a door, from *thura,* door.]

thyroid cartilage. The largest cartilage of the larynx, that covers the thyroid gland and forms the Adam's apple.

thyroid gland. A two-lobed endocrine gland that produces the hormone thyroxin, located in front of and on either side of the trachea in humans, and producing the hormone thyroxin.

thy·rox·in (thī-rŏk′sĭn) *n.* Also **thy·rox·ine** (thī-rŏk′sēn′, -sĭn). An iodine-containing hormone, $C_{15}H_{11}I_4NO_4$, produced by the thyroid gland to regulate metabolism and made synthetically for treatment of thyroid disorders. [THYR(OID) + OX(Y)- + -IN.]

thy·self (thī-sĕlf′) *pron. Archaic.* Yourself.

ti (tē) *n.* A syllable used in music to represent the seventh tone of a diatonic major scale. [Var. of SI.]

Ti The symbol for the element titanium.

ti·ar·a (tē-ăr′ə, -âr′ə, -är′ə) *n.* **1.** A bejeweled crownlike ornament, worn on the head by women on formal occasions. **2.** The tall, three-tiered crown worn by the pope. [Latin *tiāra,* Persian headdress, from Greek *tiaras.*]

Ti·bet·an (tĭ-bĕt′n) *adj.* Of or pertaining to Tibet, its people, or their language or culture. —*n.* **1.** One of the Mongoloid people of Tibet. **2.** The language of Tibet.

tib·i·a (tĭb′ē-ə) *n., pl.* **-i·ae** (-ē-ē′) *or* **-as. 1.** The inner and larger of the two bones of the lower human leg from the knee to the ankle. Also called **shin** and **shinbone. 2.** A corresponding bone in animals. **3.** The fourth division of an insect's leg, between the femur and the tarsi. **4.** A kind of ancient flute orig. made from an animal's leg bone. [Latin *tībia.*] —**tib′i·al** *adj.*

tic (tĭk) *n.* An involuntary, recurring muscle spasm or twitch, usu. localized in the facial area. [French.]

tick[1] (tĭk) *n.* **1.** Any of the light, sharp taps or clicking noises made by machine parts striking against one another, as in a clock. **2.** A light mark used to check off or call attention to an item. —*intr.v.* **1.** To produce recurring clicking sounds, as a clock. **2.** To function in a particular way, as if by means of a driving mechanism: *What makes him tick?* —*tr.v.* To sound out; announce: *The clock ticked the passing seconds.* —**phrasal verbs. tick away** (or **by**). To pass as time. **tick off. 1.** To count or record by means of ticks. **2.** To mark or check off with a tick. **3.** *Slang.* To make angry or annoyed: *His remark really ticked me off.* [Middle English *tek.*]

tick[2] (tĭk) *n.* **1.** Any of numerous bloodsucking parasitic arachnids of the family Ixodidae within the order Acarina, many of which transmit infectious diseases. **2.** Any of various usu. wingless, louselike insects of the family Hippoboscidae, that are parasitic on sheep, goats, and other animals. [Middle English *tyke,* from Old English *ticia.*]

tick[3] (tĭk) *n.* **1.** The cloth case of a mattress or pillow, enclosing the filler. **2.** Ticking. [Middle English *tikke,* prob. from Middle Dutch *tike,* from Latin *thēca,* cover, case, from Greek *thēkē.*]

tick·er (tĭk′ər) *n.* **1.** A telegraphic receiving instrument, no longer in use, that prints out stock-market quotations and news items on a narrow paper tape. **2.** *Slang.* The heart. **3.** *Slang.* A watch.

ticker tape. The narrow paper strip on which a ticker prints.

tick·et (tĭk′ĭt) *n.* **1.** A paper slip or card indicating that its holder has paid for or is entitled to a specified service, right, or consideration. **2.** A tag or label attached to merchandise and carrying identifying or descriptive information about the item. **3.** A legal summons issued for a traffic violation. **4.** A list of election candidates proposed or endorsed by a particular group or political party. **5.** A certifying document, esp. a captain's or pilot's license.

6. *Slang.* The proper thing: *A change of scene would be just the ticket for her.* —*tr.v.* **1.** To attach a tag to; to label. **2.** To mark for a specified use or end: *His superiors have ticketed him for rapid advancement.* **3.** To give a legal summons to. [Obs. French *etiquet,* ticket, label, from Old French *estiquet,* from *estiquier,* to stick, from Middle Dutch *steken.*]

tick·ing (tĭk′ĭng) *n.* A strong, tightly woven fabric, used to make pillow and mattress coverings.

tick·le (tĭk′əl) *v.* **-led, -ling.** —*tr.v.* **1.** To touch (the body) lightly with a tingling sensation, causing laughter or twitching movements. **2. a.** To tease or excite pleasurably; titillate: *The anecdote tickled the writer's imagination.* **b.** To fill with mirth or pleasure; to delight: *His crazy sense of humor tickles me.* —*intr.v.* To feel or cause a tingling sensation on the skin. —**idiom. tickle pink.** *Informal.* To please; delight. —*n.* **1.** The act of tickling. **2.** A tickling sensation. [Middle English *tikelen.*]

tick·ler (tĭk′lər) *n.* **1.** Someone or something that tickles. **2.** A memorandum book or file to aid the memory.

tick·lish (tĭk′lĭsh) *adj.* **1.** Sensitive to tickling. **2.** Easily offended or upset; touchy: *ticklish about his height.* **3.** Requiring skillful or tactful handling; delicate: *a ticklish problem.* —**tick′lish·ly** *adv.* —**tick′lish·ness** *n.*

tick·seed (tĭk′sēd′) *n.* A plant, the coreopsis. [So called from its shape.]

tick-tack-toe (tĭk′tăk-tō′) *n.* Also **tic-tac-toe.** A game played by two persons each trying to make a line of three X's or three O's in a boxlike figure with nine spaces. [Prob. from *ticktack* (from the sounds made on slates on which an earlier form of the game was played).]

tick·tock (tĭk′tŏk′) *n.* The ticking sound made by a clock. —*intr.v.* To make this sound. [Imit.]

tick trefoil. Any of various plants of the genus *Desmodium,* that have compound leaves with three leaflets, clusters of small purplish or white flowers, and jointed seed pods with easily separable, sticky segments. [From the fact that its seed pods adhere like ticks to animals.]

tic-tac-toe (tĭk′tăk-tō′) *n.* Var. of **tick-tack-toe.**

tid·al (tīd′l) *adj.* **1.** Of, having, or affected by tides: *tidal marshes.* **2.** Dependent upon or scheduled by the time of high tide: *a tidal ship.*

tidal wave. 1. An unusual rise in the level of water along a seacoast, as from a storm or a combination of wind and tide. **2.** A tsunami. **3.** Any overwhelming manifestation of sentiment, desire, or opinion: *swept into office by an electoral tidal wave.*

tid·bit (tĭd′bĭt′) *n.* Also **tit·bit** (tĭt′-). A choice morsel, as of food or gossip. [Perh. from dial. *tid,* tender + BIT.]

tid·dly·winks (tĭd′lē-wĭngks′) *n.* Also **tid·dle·dy·winks** (tĭd′-l-dē-). (*used with a sing. verb*). A game in which players try to pop small disks into a cup by pressing them on the edge with a larger disk. [Earlier *tiddlywink.*]

tide[1] (tīd) *n.* **1. a.** The periodic variation in the surface level of the oceans, seas, and other tidal waters of the earth, caused by the gravitational attraction of the moon and sun. **b.** A specific occurrence of such a variation. **c.** The water that moves when such a variation occurs. **2.** A tendency regarded as alternating and driving forward: *the rising tide of public discontent.* **3.** Anything that rises and falls like the waters of the tide: *a tide of immigrants.* **4.** *Archaic.* A time or season. —*v.* **tid·ed, tid·ing.** —*intr.v.* **1.** To rise and fall like the tide. **2.** To drift or ride with the

tide[1]
Low tide

tide[1]
High tide

tide. —*tr.v.* To carry or support with or as if with the tide. —*phrasal verb.* **tide over.** To support through a difficult period. [Middle English, season, time, tide, from Old English *tīd,* season, time.]

tide² (tīd) *intr.v.* **tid·ed, tid·ing.** *Archaic.* To betide; befall. [Middle English *tiden,* from Old English *tīdan,* to fall as one's lot.]

tide·land (tīd'lănd') *n.* Coastal land that is under water at high tide.

tide·mark (tīd'märk') *n.* A line or artificial indicator marking the high-water or low-water limit of the tides.

tide·wa·ter (tīd'wô'tər, -wŏt'ər) *n.* **1.** Water that flows onto the land when the tide is very high. **2.** Water that is affected by tides, esp. in streams or rivers. **3.** Low coastal land drained by streams that are affected by tides.

tid·ings (tī'dĭngz) *pl.n.* Information; news: *glad tidings.* [Pl. of *tiding,* an event, from Middle English, perh. from Old Norse *tidhendi,* events, from *tidhr,* occurring.]

ti·dy (tī'dē) *adj.* **-di·er, -di·est. 1.** Orderly and neat. **2.** Adequate; satisfactory: *a tidy plan of action.* **3.** *Informal.* Substantial; considerable: *a tidy sum of money.* —See Syns at **big** and **neat.** —*v.* **-died, -dy·ing.** —*tr.v.* To make neat; put in order. —*intr.v.* To put things in order. —*n., pl.* **-dies.** A fancy protective covering for the arms or headrest of a chair. [Middle English, timely, excellent, from *tid,* season, tide.] —**ti'di·ly** *adv.* —**ti'di·ness** *n.*

tie (tī) *v.* **tied, ty·ing.** —*tr.v.* **1.** To fasten or secure with a cord, rope, strap, etc. **2.** To fasten by drawing together with strings or laces and knotting them: *tie shoes.* **3. a.** To make (a knot or bow). **b.** To put a knot or bow in: *tie a necktie.* **4.** To confine or restrict as if with cord. **5.** To bring together closely; bind; unite. **6.** To equal (an opponent or his score) in a contest. **7.** *Mus.* To join (notes) by a tie. —*intr.v.* **1.** To be fastened with strings, laces, etc.: *Her dress ties at the back.* **2.** To achieve equal scores in a contest. —*phrasal verbs.* **tie down.** To restrict the freedom of; limit; confine. **tie in.** To have a connection with. **tie up. 1.** To halt or stop: *an accident that tied up traffic.* **2.** To be busy, in use, etc. **3.** To place or invest (money) so that it cannot be used freely. —*n.* **1.** A cord, string, rope, etc., by which something is tied. **2.** Something that unites; a bond. **3.** A necktie. **4. a.** An equality of scores, votes, or performance in a contest. **b.** A contest resulting in this; a draw. **5.** A beam, rod, fastening, etc., that joins parts of a structure and gives support. **6.** One of the timbers laid across a railroad bed to support the tracks. **7.** *Mus.* A curved line put either above or below two notes of the same pitch, indicating that the tone is to be sustained for their combined duration. [Middle English *tyen,* from Old English *tīgan.*]

    Syns: tie, bind, knot, secure *v. Core meaning:* To make fast by means of a cord, rope, or the like *(tied the package with twine; tied my shoes).*

tie-in (tī'ĭn') *n.* Something that serves as a connection or relation; a link.

tier¹ (tîr) *n.* One of a series of rows placed one above another. —*tr.v.* To arrange in tiers. —*intr.v.* To rise in tiers. [Old French *tire,* sequence, rank, from *tirer,* to draw out.]

ti·er² (tī'ər) *n.* Someone or something that ties.

tierce (tîrs) *n.* **1. a.** A former measure of liquid capacity, equal to 42 gallons. **b.** A vessel that holds this amount. **2.** In card games, a sequence of three cards of the same suit. **3.** *Fencing.* The third position from which a parry or thrust can be made. [Middle English, the third canonical hour, from Old French *tiers,* third, from Latin *tertius.*]

tie-up (tī'ŭp') *n.* **1.** A temporary stoppage or delay of work, traffic, service, etc., due to a strike, accident, mechanical breakdown, etc. **2.** A connection or involvement; association: *looking for a tie-up with a banker.*

tiff (tĭf) *n.* **1.** A fit of irritation. **2.** A petty quarrel. —*intr.v.* To have a petty quarrel. —See Syns at **argue.** [Orig. unknown.]

tif·fin (tĭf'ĭn) *n. Brit.* Luncheon. [From obs. *tiffing,* from *tiff,* to sip.]

ti·ger (tī'gər) *n.* **1. a.** A large carnivorous feline mammal, *Panthera tigris,* of Asia, that has a tawny coat with transverse black stripes. **b.** Any of various other similar felines. **2.** A fierce, aggressive, or audacious person. [Middle Eng-

lish *tigre,* from Old French, from Latin *tigris,* from Greek.] —**ti'ger·ish** *adj.*

tiger beetle. Any of numerous active, often varicolored beetles of the family Cicindelidae.

tiger cat. Any of various small felines resembling the tiger in either appearance or behavior.

tiger lily. A plant, *Lilium tigrinum,* native to Asia, that has large, black-spotted reddish-orange flowers.

tiger lily

tiger moth. Any of numerous often brightly colored moths of the family Arctiidae, characteristically having wings marked with spots or lines.

tight (tīt) *adj.* **-er, -est. 1.** Of such close construction or texture as to be impermeable, esp. by water or air: *a tight roof.* **2.** Fastened, held, or closed securely. **3.** Set closely together; compact: *a tight formation.* **4.** Drawn out to the fullest extent; taut: *a tight rope.* **5.** Fitting close to some part of the body, usu. too close; uncomfortably snug. **6.** Leaving no room or time to spare; very close: *a tight schedule.* **7.** Constricted: *a tight feeling in the chest.* **8.** *Informal.* Close-fisted; stingy. **9. a.** Difficult to obtain: *tight money.* **b.** Affected by scarcity: *a tight money market.* **10.** Difficult to deal with or get out of: *a tight spot.* **11.** Closely contested: *a tight race.* **12.** *Slang.* Drunk. —*adv.* **1.** Firmly; securely. **2.** Soundly: *sleep tight.* —*idiom.* **sit tight.** To make no further move. [Middle English, prob. var. of *thyght,* thickset, dense, from Old Norse *thēttr,* watertight, dense.] —**tight'ly** *adv.* —**tight'ness** *n.*

    Syns: tight, taut, tense *adj. Core meaning:* Stretched to the fullest extent *(a tight anchor line).* See also Syns at **stingy.**

tight·en (tīt'n) *tr.v.* To make tight or tighter. —*intr.v.* To become tight or tighter. —**tight'en·er** *n.*

tight·fist·ed (tīt'fĭs'tĭd) *adj.* Excessively frugal; stingy. —See Syns at **stingy.**

tight-lipped (tīt'lĭpt') *adj.* **1.** Having the lips pressed together. **2.** Not talkative; close-mouthed.

tight·rope (tīt'rōp') *n.* A tightly stretched rope, usu. of wire, raised high above the ground, upon which acrobats perform balancing tricks.

tights (tīts) *pl.n.* A snug stretchable garment covering the body from the waist or neck down.

tight·wad (tīt'wŏd') *n. Slang.* A stingy person; a miser. [TIGHT + WAD (money).]

ti·gress (tī'grĭs) *n.* A female tiger.

tike (tīk) *n.* Var. of **tyke.**

til·bur·y (tĭl'bĕr'ē, -bə-rē) *n., pl.* **-ies.** A light open carriage with two wheels and seating for two persons. [Invented by *Tilbury,* a 19th-cent. London coach maker.]

til·de (tĭl'də) *n.* The diacritical mark (˜) placed over the letter *n* in Spanish to indicate the palatal nasal sound (ny) as in *cañon,* or over a vowel in Portuguese to indicate nasalization as in *lã, pão.* [Spanish, from Latin *titulus,* superscription, title.]

tile (tīl) *n.* **1.** A thin slab of baked clay, plastic, concrete, or other material, laid in rows to cover walls, floors, or roofs. **2.** A short length of clay or concrete pipe, used in sewers, drains, chimneys, etc. **3.** A hollow fired clay or concrete block used for building walls. **4.** Tiling. **5.** One of the marked playing pieces used in mahjong. —*tr.v.* **tiled, til·ing.** To cover or provide with tiles. [Middle English, from Old English *tigele,* from Latin *tēgula,* from *tegere,* to cover.] —**til'er** *n.*

til·ing (tī′lĭng) *n.* **1.** The act or process of laying tiles. **2.** Tiles in general. **3.** A tiled surface.

till¹ (tĭl) *tr.v.* To prepare (land) for the raising of crops by plowing, harrowing, and fertilizing. [Middle English *tilien,* from Old English *tilian,* to work at, labor, cultivate.] —**till′a·ble** *adj.*

till² (tĭl) *prep.* Until: *I won't see you till tomorrow.* —*conj.* **1.** Until: *Wait till I call you.* **2.** Before or unless: *I can't help you till you give me a written request for help.* [Middle English, from Old English *til.*]

   Usage: **till, until.** These are interchangeable. The shortened form " 'til" is a third possibility but hardly a necessary one. Avoid the nonstandard form " 'till".

till³ (tĭl) *n.* A drawer or compartment for money, esp. in a store. [Middle English *tylle.*]

till·age (tĭl′ĭj) *n.* **1.** The cultivation of land. **2.** Tilled land.

till·er¹ (tĭl′ər) *n.* A person who tills land.

till·er² (tĭl′ər) *n.* A lever used to turn a boat's rudder. [Middle English *tiler,* beam of a crossbow, from Norman French *telier,* weaver's beam, from Medieval Latin *tēlārium,* from Latin *tēla.*]

tiller²

tilt¹ (tĭlt) *tr.v.* **1.** To cause to slope, as by raising one end; incline. **2. a.** To thrust (a lance) in a joust. **b.** To charge (an opponent). —*intr.v.* **1.** To slope or incline. **2.** To joust. **3.** To quarrel. —*n.* **1. a.** A slope or slant. **b.** A sloping surface, as of the ground. **2.** A joust. **3.** A verbal duel. —*idiom.* **at full tilt.** At full speed. [Middle English *tilten,* to cause to fall, overthrow.]

tilth (tĭlth) *n.* **1.** The cultivation of land; tillage. **2.** Tilled earth. [Middle English, from Old English, from *tilian,* to till, cultivate.]

tim·bal (tĭm′bəl) *n.* A kettledrum. [French *timbale,* from obs. *tamballe,* from Old Spanish *atabal,* from Arabic *aṭ-ṭabl,* the drum.]

tim·bale (tĭm′bəl) *n.* **1.** A rich, custardlike dish of cheese, chicken, fish, or vegetables baked in a drum-shaped mold. **2.** A pastry shell filled with cooked timbale. [French, timbal (from its shape).]

tim·ber (tĭm′bər) *n.* **1.** Trees or wooded land, esp. when considered as a source of wood. **2.** Wood for building; lumber. **3.** A beam or similarly shaped piece of wood, as one used in building a house or forming a ship's frame. **4.** Character; material: *a man of heroic timber.* —*interj.* A word called out as a warning that a tree being cut down is about to fall. —*tr.v.* To cover, support, or shore up with timbers. [Middle English, building, building material, from Old English.]

tim·bered (tĭm′bərd) *adj.* **1. a.** Constructed of or covered with timber. **b.** Built with exposed timbers. **2.** Covered with trees; wooded.

timber hitch. *Naut.* A knot used for fastening a rope around a spar, log, etc., that is to be hoisted or towed.

tim·ber·ing (tĭm′bər-ĭng) *n.* Timber or work made of it.

tim·ber·land (tĭm′bər-lănd′) *n.* Land wooded with trees of commercial value as timber.

tim·ber·line (tĭm′bər-līn′) *n.* Also **timber line.** In mountainous or artic regions, the altitude or limit beyond which trees do not grow.

timber wolf. A grayish or whitish wolf, *Canis lupus,* of forested northern regions. Also called **gray wolf.**

tim·ber·work (tĭm′bər-wûrk′) *n.* The part of a structure made with timbers, as the framework of a boat.

tim·bre (tĭm′bər, tăm′-) *n.* **1.** The quality or characteristic of musical tones which allows two different tones of the same pitch and loudness to be distinguished. **2.** The tone or quality that is characteristic of an instrument or voice. [French, from Old French, a bell struck with a hammer, ult. from Greek *tumpanon,* drum.]

tim·brel (tĭm′brəl) *n.* An ancient percussion instrument similar to a tambourine. [From Middle English *timbre,* from Old French, a drum.]

time (tīm) *n.* **1.** A continuous measurable quantity, ordinarily distinct from space, in which events occur in apparently irreversible succession. **2. a.** An interval bounded by two points of this quantity, as by the beginning and end of an event; duration: *the time it takes to go from one place to another.* **b.** The numerical measure of such an interval. **c.** A similar number representing a given point, such as the present, as reckoned from a given point in the past. **d.** A system of numerical measure for this quantity: *standard time; solar time.* **3.** A musical meter: *three-quarter time; six-eighth time.* **4.** A moment or period designated for a given activity. **5.** A suitable or opportune moment. **6.** Often **times. a.** A period associated with similar events, conditions, or certain historical figures; era. **b.** The present: *a sign of the times.* **7.** The period during which something is expected to last: *He died before his time.* **8.** *Sports.* **a.** The amount of playing time in a game. **b.** A time-out. **9.** An instance or occasion: *He played the piece five times.* **10. a.** The regular period of work of an employee: *working full time.* **b.** The pay received: *double time.* **11.** A period or occasion associated with a certain experience: *having a good time at the party.* **11.** *Informal.* A prison sentence: *doing time in the county jail.* —*tr.v.* **timed, tim·ing. 1.** To choose or set the time for. **2.** To adjust (a clock, watch, etc.) so that it indicates time accurately. **3.** To regulate or adjust so that each of a sequence of events happens at the correct time: *time a leap; time an automobile engine.* **4.** To record or register the speed or duration of. **5.** To set or maintain the tempo, speed, or duration of. —*adj.* **1.** Of or relating to time. **2.** Constructed so as to operate at a particular moment. **3.** Payable on a future date or dates: *time loan.* **4.** Of or relating to installment buying: *time sale.* —*idioms.* **against time.** With a quickly approaching time limit. **at one time. 1.** At once; at the same time: *girls talking at one time.* **2.** At a period or moment in the past: *At one time they were friends.* **behind the times.** Out-of-date; old-fashioned. **for the time being.** Temporarily. **from time to time.** Once in a while. **in no time.** Almost instantly; immediately: *Take this pill; you will feel better in no time.* **in time. 1.** Before it is too late; early enough. **2.** In the end; eventually. **3.** In tempo; keeping the rhythm. **on time. 1.** According to schedule; promptly. **2.** By paying in installments. **take (one's) time.** To take as much time as is needed to do something. **time after time** or **time and again.** Again and again; repeatedly. [Middle English, from Old English *tīma.*]

time and a half. A rate of pay that is one and a half times the regular rate, as for overtime work.

time bomb. A bomb that can be set to go off at a particular time.

time capsule. A sealed container that preserves articles and records of contemporary culture for discovery and study by scholars in the distant future.

time·card (tīm′kärd′) *n.* A card, usu. stamped by a time clock, that records an employee's arrival and departure time each workday.

time clock. A device that records the arrival and departure times of employees.

time deposit. A bank deposit that cannot be withdrawn before a date specified at the time of deposit.

time draft. A draft payable at or after a future date specified.

time exposure. 1. A photographic exposure in which light strikes the film or plate for a relatively long time. **2.** A photograph made by such an exposure.

time-hon·ored (tīm′ŏn′ərd) *adj.* Respected or adhered to because of age or age-old observance.

time-keep·er (tīm′kē′pər) *n.* **1.** A timepiece. **2.** The person who keeps track of time, as in a sports event.

time-lapse (tīm′lăps′) *adj.* Of or using a motion-picture technique for filming a normally slow process, as the unfolding of a leaf, by photographing it at intervals so that

---

the continuous projection of the frames gives an accelerated view of it.

time·less (tīm'lĭs) *adj.* **1.** Independent of time; eternal. **2.** Unaffected by time; ageless: *timeless beauty.* **3.** Existing or happening without interruption or end. —See Syns at **continuous.** —**time'less·ly** *adv.* —**time'less·ness** *n.*

time lock. A lock set to open at a specific time.

time·ly (tīm'lē) *adj.* **-li·er, -li·est. 1.** Occurring at a suitable or opportune moment; well-timed. **2.** Appropriate for the occasion or circumstances; seasonable: *some timely comments.* —**time'li·ness** *n.*

time-out (tīm'out') *n.* Also **time out. 1.** *Sports.* A brief period during which play is suspended for rest, consultation, player substitutions, etc. **2.** Any short break.

time·piece (tīm'pēs') *n.* An instrument that measures, registers, or records time.

tim·er (tī'mər) *n.* **1.** A timepiece, esp. one used to measure intervals of time. **2.** A timing device that operates a switch or other control at certain times or at fixed intervals.

times (tīmz) *prep.* Multiplied by: *Two times four equals eight.*

time·sav·ing (tīm'sā'vĭng) *adj.* Curtailing or reducing the time spent to accomplish some end or result: *a time-saving recipe for making tomato sauce.* —**time'sav'er** *n.*

time·serv·er (tīm'sûr'vər) *n.* A person who for personal advantage conforms to the prevailing customs and opinions of his time, surroundings, superiors, etc.; an opportunist. —**time'serv'ing** *adj. & n.*

time sharing. In computer technology, a system whereby individual subscribers at different locations are tied into a single master computer, the fee paid entitling each to use the computer for a given number of hours during a specified period to solve individual problems.

time signature. *Mus.* A symbol, commonly in the form of a numerical fraction, placed on a staff to indicate the meter.

time·worn (tīm'wôrn', -wōrn') *adj.* **1.** Showing the effects of long use or wear. **2.** Used too often; trite.

time zone. Any of the 24 parts, each 15 degrees of longitude wide, into which the earth is divided for purposes of keeping time from the primary meridian that passes through Greenwich, England.

tim·id (tĭm'ĭd) *adj.* **1.** Lacking courage and self-confidence; fearful. **2.** Shrinking from notice or attention; shy. [Latin *timidus,* from *timēre,* to fear.] —**ti·mid'i·ty,** or **tim'id·ness** *n.* —**tim'id·ly** *adv.*

tim·ing (tī'mĭng) *n.* **1.** The regulation of occurrence, pace, or coordination to achieve the most desirable effects. **2. a.** A record or measurement of speed or duration. **b.** The act or process of making such a record or measurement. **3.** The regulation or adjustment of the times at which each of a series of events occurs, as in a machine.

tim·or·ous (tĭm'ər-əs) *adj.* Full of fear and apprehension; timid. [Middle English, from Old French *timoureus,* from Medieval Latin *timorōsus,* from Latin *timor,* fear, from *timēre,* to fear.] —**tim'or·ous·ly** *adv.* —**tim'or·ous·ness** *n.*

tim·o·thy (tĭm'ə-thē) *n.* A grass, *Phleum pratense,* native to Eurasia, that has narrow, cylindrical flower spikes, and is widely cultivated for hay. [Perh. after *Timothy Hanson,* 18th cent. American farmer, who was said to have taken it to the Carolinas from New York.]

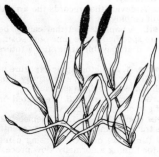

timothy

tim·pa·ni (tĭm'pə-nē) *pl.n.* Also **tym·pa·ni.** A set of kettledrums. [Italian, pl. of *timpano,* kettledrum, from Latin *tympanum,* a drum.] —**tim'pa·nist** *n.*

tim·pa·num (tĭm'pə-nəm) *n.* Var. of **tympanum.**

tin (tĭn) *n.* **1.** *Symbol* **Sn** A malleable, silvery metallic element obtained chiefly from cassiterite, used to coat other metals to prevent corrosion, and to form part of numerous alloys, such as soft solder, pewter, type metal, and bronze. Atomic number 50; atomic weight 118.69; melting point 231.89°C; boiling point 2,270°C; specific gravity 7.31; valences 2, 4. **2.** Tin plate. **3.** A tin container or box. **4.** *Brit.* A container for preserved food; a can. —*tr.v.* **tinned, tin·ning. 1.** To plate or coat with tin or solder. **2.** *Brit.* To preserve or pack in tins. [Middle English, from Old English.]

tin·a·mou (tĭn'ə-mōō') *n.* Any of various chickenlike or quaillike birds of the family Tinamidae, of Central and South America. [French, from Galibi *tinamu.*]

tinct (tĭngkt) *Archaic.* —*n.* A color or tint. —*adj.* Tinged. [Latin *tinctus,* past part. of *tingere,* to tinge.]

tinc·ture (tĭngk'chər) *n.* **1.** An alcohol solution of a medicine. **2.** A dyeing substance; pigment. **3.** An imparted color; tint. **4.** A quality or element that pervades or characterizes something. **5.** A trace; vestige. —*tr.v.* **-tured, -tur·ing. 1.** To stain or tint with a color. **2.** To infuse, as with some quality or element: *Selfishness tinctures everything he does.* [Middle English, from Latin *tinctūra,* a dyeing, from *tinctus,* past part. of *tingere,* to tinge.]

tin·der (tĭn'dər) *n.* Any material that catches fire easily. [Middle English, from Old English *tynder.*]

tin·der·box (tĭn'dər-bŏks') *n.* **1.** A metal box for holding tinder. **2.** A potentially explosive place or situation.

tine (tīn) *n.* A prong or similar narrow, pointed projection, as of a fork or of a deer's antlers. [Middle English *tind,* from Old English.]

tin·e·a (tĭn'ē-ə) *n.* Any of several fungous skin diseases, such as ringworm. [Latin, a gnawing worm, moth.]

tin·foil (tĭn'foil') *n.* Also **tin foil.** A thin, pliable sheet of tin or of an alloy of tin, used as a protective wrapping.

ting (tĭng) *n.* A single light metallic sound, as of a small bell. —*intr.v.* To make such a sound. —*tr.v.* To cause to make such a sound. [From Middle English *tyngen,* to produce a ringing sound.]

tinge (tĭnj) *tr.v.* **tinged** (tĭnjd), **tinge·ing** or **ting·ing. 1.** To give a trace of color to; to tint. **2.** To qualify or affect slightly, as by admixture: *admiration tinged with envy.* —*n.* **1.** A faint trace or small amount of coloring. **2.** A slight admixture: *a tinge of sadness in her smile.* [Middle English *tyngen,* from Latin *tingere,* to moisten, dye.]

tin·gle (tĭng'gəl) *v.* **-gled, -gling.** —*intr.v.* **1.** To have a prickling, stinging sensation as from cold or excitement: *tingle with joy.* **2.** To cause such a sensation. —*tr.v.* To cause to tingle. —*n.* A prickling or stinging sensation. [Middle English *tinglen,* to be affected with a ringing sound in the ears, perh. var. of *tynclen,* to tinkle.] —**tin'gler** *n.* —**tin'gly** *adj.*

tin·horn (tĭn'hôrn') *n. Slang.* A person, esp. a gambler, who pretends to be wealthier and more influential than he is.

tink·er (tĭng'kər) *n.* **1.** A traveling mender of metal household utensils. **3.** A person who is clumsy at his work; bungler. —*intr.v.* **1.** To work as a tinker. **2.** To toy or experiment with repairing or adjusting machinery. **3.** To busy oneself in a casual or aimless way: *tinkering around the garden.* [Middle English *tynekere.*]

tinker's damn. Also **tinker's dam.** *Slang.* Something of little or no value: *not worth a tinker's damn.*

tin·kle (tĭng'kəl) *v.* **-kled, -kling.** —*intr.v.* To make light metallic sounds. —*tr.v.* **1.** To cause to tinkle. **2.** To signal, call, or express by tinkling: *Christmas bells tinkling a message of joy.* —*n.* A light, clear metallic sound or a sound suggestive of it. [Middle English *tynclen.*] —**tin'kly** *adj.*

tin·ny (tĭn'ē) *adj.* **-ni·er, -ni·est. 1.** Of or containing tin. **2.** Thin and cheaply made; not durable; flimsy. **3.** Having a thin metallic sound. —**tin'ni·ly** *adv.* —**tin'ni·ness** *n.*

Tin Pan Alley. Also **tin-pan alley. 1.** A district associated with musicians, composers, and publishers of popular music. **2.** The publishers and composers of popular music as a group. [From earlier *tin-pan,* noisy, tinny.]

tin plate. Thin sheet iron or steel coated with tin.

tin-plate (tĭn′plăt′) *tr.v.* **-plat·ed, -plat·ing.** To coat with tin. **—tin′·plat′er** *n.*

tin·sel (tĭn′səl) *n.* **1.** Very thin sheets, strips, or threads of a glittering material used as a decoration. **2.** Anything superficially sparkling or showy but basically valueless. **—adj.** **1.** Made of or decorated with tinsel. **2.** Gaudy and showy but basically valueless. **—tr.v.** **-seled** or **-selled, -sel·ing** or **-sel·ling. 1.** To decorate with or as if with tinsel. **2.** To give a false sparkle to. [Earlier *tinselle*, adorned with metallic threads, prob. from Old French *estincelle*, past part. of *e(s)tinceller*, to sparkle, from *estincelle*, a spark, from Latin *scintilla.*]

tin·smith (tĭn′smĭth′) *n.* A person who makes and repairs things made of light metal, such as tin.

tint (tĭnt) *n.* **1.** A shade or gradation of a color, esp. a pale or delicate variation; a hue. **2.** A slight coloration; a tinge: *a tint of red in the sky.* **3.** A barely detectable degree of something; a trace. **4.** A dye for the hair. **—tr.v.** To give a tint to. [Var. of earlier *tinct*, from Latin *tinctus*, a dipping or dyeing, from the past part. of *tingere*, to wet, dip, dye.]

tin·tin·nab·u·la·tion (tĭn′tĭ-năb′yə-lā′shən) *n.* The ringing or sounding of bells. [From *tintinnabulum*, a bell, from Latin, from *tinnīre*, to ring.]

tin·type (tĭn′tīp′) *n.* **1.** A positive photograph made directly on an iron plate varnished with a thin sensitized film. **2.** The process by which such photographs are made.

tintype   tippet

tin·ware *n.* Objects made of tin plate.

ti·ny (tī′nē) *adj.* **-ni·er, -ni·est.** Extremely small; minute. [From Middle English *tine.*]

–tion. A suffix indicating action or process: **adsorption.** [Middle English *-cioun*, from Old French *-tion*, from Latin *-tiō.*]

tip¹ (tĭp) *n.* **1.** The end or extremity of something. **2.** A piece meant to be fitted to the end of something. **—tr.v.** **tipped, tip·ping. 1.** To furnish with a tip: *tip cigarettes with filters.* **2.** To cover, decorate, or remove the tip of. [Middle English, prob. from Old Norse *typpi.*]

tip² (tĭp) *v.* **tipped, tip·ping. —tr.v. 1.** To knock over or upset; topple. **2.** To move to a slanting position; to tilt. **3.** To touch or raise (one's hat) in greeting. **—intr.v. 1.** To topple over. **2.** To become tilted; to slant. **—n.** A tilt or slant; an incline. [Middle English *tipen.*]

tip³ (tĭp) *tr.v.* **tipped, tip·ping. 1.** To strike gently; to tap. **2.** *Baseball.* To hit (the ball) with the side of the bat so that it glances off. **—n.** A light blow. [Middle English *tippen.*]

tip⁴ (tĭp) *n.* **1.** A small sum of money given for services rendered; gratuity. **2.** Advance or inside information given as a guide to action. **3.** A helpful hint. **—v.** **tipped, tip·ping. —tr.v. 1.** To give a tip or gratuity to. **2.** To provide advance or inside information to. **—intr.v.** To give a gratuity: *He is known to tip well.* **—phrasal verb. tip off.** To provide advance or inside information to. [Perh. from TIP (to tap).] **—tip′per** *n.*

ti·pi (tē′pē) *n.* Var. of **tepee.**

tip-off (tĭp′ôf′, -ŏf′) *n. Informal.* An item of advance or inside information; a hint or warning.

tip·pet (tĭp′ĭt) *n.* **1.** A stole or cape worn around the shoulders with long ends that hang in front. **2.** A long stole worn by Anglican clergymen. **3.** A long, hanging part, as of a sleeve, hood, or cape. [Middle English *tipet.*]

tip·ple¹ (tĭp′əl) *v.* **-pled, -pling. —intr.v.** To drink alcoholic liquor, esp. habitually or to excess. **—tr.v.** To drink (alcoholic liquor), esp. habitually. **—n.** Alcoholic liquor. [Back-formation from *tippler*, a tapster, bartender, from Middle English *tipler.*] **—tip′pler** *n.*

tip·ple² (tĭp′əl) *n.* **1.** An apparatus for unloading freight cars by tipping them. **2.** A place where this is done. [From dial. *tipple*, to tip, overturn, freq. of TIP.]

tip·ster (tĭp′stər) *n. Informal.* A person who sells tips or information to bettors or speculators.

tip·sy (tĭp′sē) *adj.* **-si·er, -si·est. 1.** Slightly drunk. **2.** Likely to tip over; unsteady. **—tip′si·ly** *adv.* **—tip′si·ness** *n.*

tip·toe (tĭp′tō′) *intr.v.* **-toed, -toe·ing.** To walk or move on or as if on the tips of one's toes. **—n.** The tip of a toe. **—adj. 1.** Standing or walking on or as if on the tips of one's toes: *little tip-toe steps.* **2.** Stealthy; wary: *tip-toe negotiations.* **—adv.** On tiptoe.

tip·top (tĭp′tŏp′) *n.* **1.** The highest point; the summit. **2.** The highest degree of quality or excellence. **—adj.** Excellent; first-rate. **—adv.** Excellently; very well.

ti·rade (tī′rād′, tī-rād′) *n.* A long, very angry or violent speech, usu. denouncing or criticizing something or someone; a diatribe. [French, from Italian *tirata*, act of drawing, from *tirare*, to draw.]

tire¹ (tīr) *v.* **tired, tir·ing. —intr.v. 1.** To become weary or fatigued. **2.** To grow bored or impatient; lose interest. **—tr.v. 1.** To make weary; fatigue. **2.** To exhaust the interest or patience of; bore. **—See Syns at bore. —phrasal verb. tire out.** To fatigue; exhaust. [Middle English *tyren*, to stop, from Old English *tēorian.*]

tire² (tīr) *n.* Also *Brit.* **tyre. 1.** A covering for a wheel, usu. made of rubber reinforced with cords of nylon, fiber glass, etc., and filled with compressed air. **2.** A hoop of metal or rubber fitted around a wheel. [Prob. from earlier *tire*, outfit, from *attire*, attire.]

tired (tīrd) *adj.* **1. a.** Worn-out; fatigued. **b.** Impatient; bored. **2.** Trite; hackneyed. **—See Syns at stale.**

tire·less (tīr′lĭs) *adj.* Untiring; indefatigable: *a tireless worker.* **—tire′less·ly** *adv.* **—tire′less·ness** *n.*

tire·some (tīr′səm) *adj.* **1.** Causing fatigue; wearisome: *a tiresome job.* **2.** Causing boredom; tedious: *a long, tiresome speech.* **3.** Causing annoyance; bothersome. **—tire′some·ly** *adv.* **—tire′some·ness** *n.*

'tis (tĭz). *Archaic Poet.* It is.

tis·sue (tĭsh′ōō) *n.* **1.** *Biol.* **a.** An aggregation of similar cells that perform the same function. **b.** Cellular matter regarded as a collective entity. **2. tissue paper.** Light, thin paper used for wrapping, packing, etc. **3.** A piece of soft, absorbent paper, used esp. as a handkerchief. **4.** A light, thin, sheer cloth. **5.** Something formed as if by interweaving parts: *a tissue of fantastic dreams.* [Middle English *tissu*, a rich cloth, fine gauze, from Old French, from *tistre*, to weave, from Latin *texere.*]

tit¹ (tĭt) *n.* **1.** Any of various small Old World birds of the family Paridae, related to and resembling the New World chickadees. Also called **titmouse. 2.** Any of various similar or related birds. [Short for TITMOUSE.]

tit² (tĭt) *n.* A teat or nipple. [Middle English *titte*, from Old English *titt.*]

Ti·tan (tīt′n). *n.* **1.** *Gk. Myth.* One of a family of giants, the children of Uranus and Gaea, who sought to rule heaven and were overthrown and supplanted by the family of Zeus. **2. titan.** A person of colossal size, strength, achievement, etc.: *a titan of American literature.* **—adj.** Gigantic; titanic. **—See Syns at giant.**

Ti·tan·ess (tīt′n-ĭs) *n. Gk. Myth.* A female Titan.

ti·tan·ic (tī-tăn′ĭk) *adj.* **1.** Of enormous size, strength, influence, etc. **2. Titanic.** Of or concerning the Titans. **—See Syns at giant.** [From TITAN.] **—ti·tan′i·cal·ly** *adv.*

ti·ta·ni·um (tī-tā′nē-əm, tī-) *n. Symbol* **Ti** A strong, low-density, highly corrosion-resistant, lustrous white metallic element that occurs widely in igneous rocks and is used to alloy aircraft metals for low weight, strength, and high-temperature stability. Atomic number 22; atomic weight 47.90; melting point 1,675°C; boiling point 3,260°C; specific gravity 4.54; valences 2, 3, 4. [From TITAN.]

titanium dioxide. A white powder, TiO_2, used as an exceptionally opaque white pigment.

tit·bit (tĭt′bĭt′) *n.* Var. of **tidbit.**

tit for tat. Repayment in kind, as for an injury; retaliation. [Var. of earlier *tip for tap.*]

tithe (tīth) *n.* **1.** A tenth part of one's annual income, either in kind or money, paid over to a church either as a charitable contribution or as a tax levied for the support of its clergy. **2.** Any tax or assessment of one tenth. **3. a.** The tenth part of something. **b.** Any very small part. —*v.* **tithed, tith·ing.** —*tr.v.* **1.** To contribute or pay a tenth part of (one's annual income). **2.** To levy a tithe upon. —*intr.v.* To pay a tithe. [Middle English, from Old English *tēotha, teogetha,* tenth.] —**tith′a·ble** (tī′thə-bəl) *adj.*

ti·tian (tĭsh′ən) *n.* A brownish orange. [After *Titian* (1477–1576), Italian painter.] —**ti′tian** *adj.*

tit·il·late (tĭt′ə-lāt′) *tr.v.* **-lat·ed, -lat·ing. 1.** To stimulate by tickling or touching lightly. **2.** To excite agreeably. [From Latin *tītillāre.*] —**tit′il·lat′ing·ly** *adv.* —**tit′il·la′tion** *n.*

tit·i·vate (tĭt′ə-vāt′) *tr.v.* **-vat·ed, -vat·ing.** To make decorative additions to; spruce up. [Earlier *tidivate* : perh. TIDY + (CULTI)VATE.] —**tit′i·va′tion** *n.*

tit·lark (tĭt′lärk′) *n.* A bird, the pipit. [TIT(MOUSE) + LARK.]

ti·tle (tīt′l) *n.* **1.** An identifying name given to literary work, motion picture, musical composition, work of art, etc. **2. a.** A general or descriptive heading, as of a book chapter. **b.** The heading or caption that names or describes a legal document. **3.** A word or name given to a person as a mark of distinction showing rank, office, or vocation. **4.** A division of a law book, declaration, or bill, generally larger than a section or article. **5.** *Law.* **a.** The aggregate evidence that gives rise to a legal right of possession or control. **b.** The instrument constituting this evidence, such as a deed. **6.** Anything that provides ground for or justifies a claim or entitlement; a right. **7.** A championship in sports. —*tr.v.* **-tled, -tling.** To give a title to. [Middle English, from Old French, from Latin *titulus,* label, title.]

ti·tled (tīt′əld) *adj.* Having a title, esp. of nobility.

title deed. A document evidencing legal right of ownership.

title·hold·er *n.* **1.** Someone who possesses a title. **2.** *Sports.* A current champion.

title page. A page at the front of a book giving the complete title, the names of the author and publisher, and the place of publication.

title role. The character or part from which the name of a play, motion picture, etc., derives.

tit·mouse (tĭt′mous′) *n.* **1.** Any of several small North American birds of the genus *Parus,* with grayish plumage and a pointed crest. **2.** A related Old World bird, a tit. [Perh. dial. *tit,* a small object + MOUSE.]

ti·trate (tī′trāt′) *v.* **-trat·ed, -trat·ing.** —*tr.v.* To determine the concentration of (a solution) by titration. —*intr.v.* To perform the operation of titration. [From French *titrer,* from *titre,* title, fineness of gold or silver in an alloy.]

ti·tra·tion (tī-trā′shən) *n.* The process or method of determining the concentration of a substance in solution by adding to it a standard reagent of known concentration in carefully measured amounts until a reaction of definite and known proportion is completed, and then calculating the unknown concentration.

tit·ter (tĭt′ər) *intr.v.* To utter a restrained, nervous giggle. —*n.* A restrained, nervous giggle. [Imit.]

tit·tle (tĭt′l) *n.* **1.** A small diacritical mark, such as an accent, vowel mark, or dot over an *i.* **2.** The tiniest bit; an iota. [Middle English *titel,* a diacritical mark, from Medieval Latin *titulus,* from Latin, title.]

tit·tle-tat·tle (tĭt′l-tăt′l) *n.* Petty gossip. —*intr.v.* **-tled, -tling.** To gossip. [From TATTLE.]

tit·u·lar (tĭch′ōo-lər) *adj.* **1.** Of or related to a title. **2.** Existing as such in name only; nominal. **3.** Bearing a title. [From Latin *titulus,* title.] —**tit′u·lar·ly** *adv.*

tiz·zy (tĭz′ē) *n., pl.* **-zies.** *Slang.* A state of nervous confusion; dither. [Orig. unknown.]

Tl The symbol for the element thallium.

Tm The symbol for the element thulium.

TNT (tē′ĕn-tē′) *n.* Trinitrotoluene.

to (tōō; *unstressed* tə) *prep.* **1.** In a direction toward: *going to town.* **2.** In the direction of; so as to reach: *a trip to Paris.* **3.** Reaching as far as: *rotten to the core.* **4.** Toward or reaching the state of: *the Nazi rise to power.* **5.** To the extent of: *starving to death.* **6.** In contact with: *back to back.* **7.** In front of: *face to face.* **8.** Through and including; until: *from three to five.* **9.** For the attention, benefit, or possession of: *Tell it to me.* **10.** For the purpose of; for: *working to the same end.* **11.** For or of: *Do you have the belt to this dress?* **12.** Concerning or regarding: *She was deaf to my pleas.* **13.** In relation with: *parallel to the road.* **14.** With the resulting condition of: *torn to shreds.* **15.** As an accompaniment of: *singing to an old tune.* **16.** With regard to: *the secret to his success.* **17.** Composing or constituting; in: *two pints to the quart.* **18.** In accord with: *not to my liking.* **19.** As compared with: *a score of four to three.* **20.** Before: *The time is now ten to five.* **21.** In honor of: *a toast to our visitors.* **22.** —Used before a verb to indicate the infinitive: *I'd like to go.* Also used alone when the infinitive is understood: *Go if you want to.* —*adv.* **1.** Into a shut position: *slammed the door to.* **2.** Into consciousness: *It was a few minutes before I came to.* **3.** Into a state of working at something: *We sat down for lunch and everybody fell to.* [Middle English, from Old English *tō.*]

toad (tōd) *n.* **1.** Any of numerous tailless amphibians chiefly of the family Bufonidae, related to and resembling the frogs but who are more terrestrial and have rougher, drier skin. **2.** A lizard, the **horned toad. 3.** A repulsive person. [Middle English *tode,* from Old English *tādige.*]

toad

toad·fish (tōd′fĭsh′) *n., pl.* **toadfish** or **-fish·es.** Any of various saltwater fishes of the family Batrachoididae, with a broad, flattened head and a wide mouth.

toad·stool (tōd′stōōl′) *n.* An inedible fungus with an umbrella-shaped fruiting body, as distinguished from an edible mushroom.

toad·y (tō′dē) *n., pl.* **-ies.** A person who obsequiously flatters or pays deference to others for the sake of personal gain; a servile parasite; a sycophant. —*v.* **-ied, -y·ing.** —*tr.v.* To be a toady to. —*intr.v.* To be a toady.

to and fro. Back and forth.

toast¹ (tōst) *tr.v.* **1.** To heat and brown (as bread) by placing close to a fire or in a toaster. **2.** To warm thoroughly. —*intr.v.* To become toasted. —*n.* Sliced bread heated and browned. [Middle English *tosten,* from Old French *toster,* from Latin *tostus,* past part. of *torrēre,* to dry, parch.]

toast² (tōst) *n.* **1.** The act of drinking in honor of or to the health of a person, institution, etc. **2.** The person, institution, etc., who is honored in this way. **3.** Any person receiving much attention or acclaim: *the toast of Broadway.* —*tr.v.* To drink in honor of or to the health of. —*intr.v.* To propose or drink a toast. [From the use of pieces of spiced toast to flavor drinks.]

toast·er (tō′stər) *n.* An electrical appliance used to toast bread.

toast·mas·ter (tōst′măs′tər, -mäs′tər) *n.* A person who proposes the toasts and introduces the speakers at a banquet.

to·bac·co (tə-băk′ō) *n., pl.* **-cos** or **-coes. 1.** Any of various plants of the genus *Nicotiana,* esp. *N. tabacum,* native to tropical America, widely cultivated for its leaves, which are used primarily for smoking. **2.** The leaves of such plants, processed for use in smoking, chewing, etc. **3.** Products, as cigarettes, cigars, or snuff, made from tobacco. **4.** The use of such products. [Spanish *tabaco,* prob. from Arabic *ṭabāq,* euphoria-causing herb.]

to·bac·co·nist (tə-băk′ə-nĭst) *n.* A person who sells cigarettes, cigars, pipe tobacco, etc.

to·bog·gan (tə-bŏg′ən) *n.* A long, narrow, runnerless sled constructed of thin boards curved upward at the front.

—*intr.v.* **1.** To coast or ride on a toboggan. **2.** To decline or fall rapidly: *The price of the company's stock tobogganed.* [Canadian French *tobagan*, of Algonquian orig.] —**to·bog'gan·er** or **to·bog'gan·ist** *n.*

to·by (tō'bē) *n., pl.* **-bies.** Also **To·by.** A drinking mug usu. in the shape of a stout man wearing a large three-cornered hat. Also called **Toby jug.** [From the name *Toby.*]

toc·ca·ta (tə-kä'tə) *n.* A musical composition, usu. for the organ or another keyboard instrument, in a free style with elaborate passages that show the player's technique. [Italian, from *toccare*, to touch.]

to·coph·er·ol (tō-kŏf'ə-rôl', -rōl') *n.* Any of a group of four chemically related compounds, differing slightly in structure, that together constitute vitamin E. [Greek *tokos*, childbirth + Greek *pherein*, to carry + -OL.]

toc·sin (tŏk'sĭn) *n.* **1.** An alarm sounded on a bell. **2.** A warning; omen. [French, from Old French *toquesain*, from Old Provençal *tocasenh* : *tocar*, to touch + *senh*, bell, from Latin *signum*, token, sign.]

to·day (tə-dā') Also **to·day.** —*adv.* **1.** During or on the present day: *He arrives today.* **2.** During or at the present time. —*n.* The present day, time, or age. [Middle English *to day*, from Old English *tōdæg(e)*, on this day.]

tod·dle (tŏd'l) *intr.v.* **-dled, -dling.** To walk with short, unsteady steps, as a small child does. —*n.* A slow, unsteady gait. [Orig. unknown.] —**tod'dler** *n.*

tod·dy (tŏd'ē) *n., pl.* **-dies. 1.** An alcoholic beverage made of brandy or other liquor mixed with hot water, sugar, and spices. Also called **hot toddy. 2. a.** The sweet sap of several tropical Asian palm trees, esp. *Caryota urens,* used as a beverage. **b.** A liquor fermented from this sap. [Earlier *tarry*, from Hindi *tāṛī*, sap of a palm, from *tāṛ*, palm yielding toddy, from Sanskrit *tāla, tāra.*]

to·do (tə-dōō') *n., pl.* **-dos** (-dōōz'). *Informal.* Commotion or bustle; a stir.

toe (tō) *n.* **1.** One of the digits of the foot, esp. of a vertebrate animal. **2.** The part of a sock, shoe, boot, etc., that covers the toes. **3.** Anything that resembles a toe in form, function, or location. —*v.* **toed, toe·ing.** —*tr.v.* **1.** To touch or reach with the toes. **2. a.** To drive (a nail or spike) at an oblique angle. **b.** To fasten or secure with nails or spikes driven in this way. —*intr.v.* To walk with the toes pointed in a specified direction: *He toes out.* —**idiom. on (one's) toes.** Ready to act; alert. [Middle English *to*, from Old English *tā.*]

toed (tōd) *adj.* **1.** Having a specified number or kind of toes. **2. a.** Driven obliquely: *a toed nail.* **b.** Secured by obliquely driven nails: *a toed beam.*

toe dance. A dance performed on the toes. —**toe dancer.**

toe·hold (tō'hōld') *n.* **1.** An indentation or ledge which can support the toe in climbing. **2.** Any slight or initial advantage useful for future progress. **3.** *Wrestling.* A hold in which one competitor wrenches the other's foot.

toe·nail (tō'nāl') *n.* **1.** The nail on a toe. **2.** A nail driven at an oblique angle, as in joining a vertical beam to a horizontal beam. —*tr.v.* To join or secure (beams) with nails driven at an oblique angle.

tof·fee (tôf'ē, tŏf'ē) *n.* Also **tof·fy** *pl.* **-fies.** A hard or chewy candy of brown sugar and butter. [Var. of TAFFY.]

tog (tŏg) *n. Informal.* **1.** A coat or cloak. **2. togs.** Clothes: *work togs.* —*tr.v.* **togged, tog·ging.** *Informal.* To dress or clothe: *togged himself out in cowboy boots.* [Short for slang *togeman*, from obs. *toge*, cloak, from Middle English, from Old French *togue*, from Latin *toga*, toga.]

to·ga (tō'gə) *n., pl.* **-gas** or **-gae** (-jē). **1.** A loose one-piece outer garment worn in public by citizens of ancient Rome. **2.** A loose robe or gown characteristic of a profession. [Latin, from *tegere*, to cover.] —**to'gaed** (tō'gəd) *adj.*

to·geth·er (tə-gĕth'ər) *adv.* **1.** In or into a single group or place: *people crowded together.* **2.** Against or in relationship to one another: *getting along together.* **3.** Regarded collectively: *He's done more than all of us together.* **4.** Simultaneously: *The guns all went off together.* **5.** In agreement or cooperation: *stand together.* **6.** *Informal.* In proper condition to do something: *Get yourself together.* —**to·geth'er·ness** *n.* [Middle English *togedere*, from Old English *tōgædere.*]

tog·ger·y (tŏg'ə-rē) *n., pl.* **-ies.** *Informal.* Clothing; togs.

tog·gle (tŏg'əl) *n.* **1.** A pin, rod, or crosspiece fitted or inserted transversely into a loop in a rope, chain, or strap to prevent slipping, to tighten, or to hold an attached object. **2.** An ornamental crosspiece or button of wood, bone, etc., inserted into a loop of rope or other material as a closure or fastening, as on sports clothes. **3.** Any device or apparatus with a toggle joint. —*tr.v.* **-gled, -gling.** To furnish or fasten with a toggle. [Orig. unknown.]

toggle joint. An elbowlike joint consisting of two arms pivoted together so that force applied to the pivot point to straighten the joint produces a corresponding outward force at the end of each arm.

toggle switch. A switch in which a projecting lever employing a toggle joint with a spring is used to open or close an electric circuit.

toil¹ (toil) *intr.v.* **1.** To labor continuously and untiringly. **2.** To proceed with difficulty: *toiling up a hill.* —*n.* Exhausting labor or effort. —See Syns at **labor.** [Middle English *toilen*, to struggle, from Norman French *toiler*, from Old French *tooillier*, to stir, agitate, from Latin *tudiculāre*, to stir about, from *tudicula*, a mill for crushing olives, dim. of *tudes*, a hammer.] —**toil'er** *n.*

toil² (toil) *n.* Often **toils.** Anything that binds, snares, or entangles one; an entrapment: *in the toils of despair.* [Old French *toile*, a net, from Latin *tēla.*]

toi·let (toi'lĭt) *n.* **1.** A disposal apparatus consisting of a porcelain bowl that has a hinged seat and is fitted with a flushing device, used for urination and defecation. **2.** A room or booth containing such an apparatus. **3.** The act or process of grooming and dressing oneself. [French *toilette*, dressing table, from Old French, cloth cover for a dressing table, a dressing table, dim. of *toile*, cloth, net.]

toilet paper. Thin, absorbent paper, usu. in rolls, used for cleansing oneself after defecation or urination.

toi·let·ry (toi'lĭ-trē) *n., pl.* **-ries.** Any article or cosmetic used in dressing or grooming oneself.

toi·lette (twä-lĕt') *n.* **1.** The act or process of dressing or grooming oneself; toilet. **2.** A person's dress or style of dress. **3.** A gown or costume. [French.]

toilet water. A scented liquid, weaker than perfume and stronger than cologne.

toil·some (toil'səm) *adj.* Done with difficulty; laborious. —**toil'some·ly** *adv.* —**toil'some·ness** *n.*

To·kay (tō-kā') *n.* **1.** A variety of grape orig. grown near Tokay, Hungary. **2.** A wine made from these grapes.

to·ken (tō'kən) *n.* **1.** Something that serves as an indication or representation of some fact, event, emotion, etc.; a sign; symbol. **2.** Something that signifies or evidences authority, validity, identity, etc.: *A judge's robes are a token of his office.* **3.** A keepsake or souvenir. **4.** A piece of stamped metal used as a substitute for currency. —See Syns at **sign.** —*adj.* Done as an indication or pledge: *a token payment.* [Middle English, from Old English *tācen.*]

to·ken·ism (tō'kə-nĭz'əm) *n.* The policy of making only a superficial effort toward the accomplishment of a goal, such as racial integration.

told (tōld) *v.* Past tense and past participle of **tell.**

tol·er·a·ble (tŏl'ər-ə-bəl) *adj.* **1.** Able to be tolerated; endurable. **2.** Fair or adequate; passable. —**tol'er·a·bil'i·ty** or **tol'er·a·ble·ness** *n.* —**tol'er·a·bly** *adv.*

tol·er·ance (tŏl'ər-əns) *n.* **1.** The capacity for or practice of recognizing and respecting the opinions, practices, or behavior of others. **2.** The capacity to endure hardship, pain, etc. **3.** In building and engineering, the amount by which the measure of a part or component can be allowed to vary from the value intended: *The bolt was made to a tolerance of .001 inch.* **4.** The degree to which an organism resists the effect of a poison or other drug.

tol·er·ant (tŏl'ər-ənt) *adj.* **1.** Inclined to tolerate the beliefs, practices, or behavior of others. **2.** Able to withstand or endure an adverse environmental condition: *plants tolerant of extreme heat.* —**tol'er·ant·ly** *adv.*

tol·er·ate (tŏl'ə-rāt') *tr.v.* **-at·ed, -at·ing. 1.** To allow without prohibiting or opposing; permit. **2.** To recognize and respect, as the opinions or practices of others. **3.** To put up with; endure. **4.** *Med.* To have tolerance for (a drug or poison). —See Syns at **permit.** [From Latin *tolerāre*, to bear, tolerate.] —**tol'er·a'tion** *n.* —**tol'er·a'tor** *n.*

toll¹ (tōl) *n.* **1.** A fixed tax for a privilege, esp. for passage across a bridge or along a road. **2.** A charge for a service, such as a long-distance telephone call. **3.** The amount or extent of loss or destruction, as of life, health, property, etc., caused by a disaster. [Middle English *tolle,* from Old English *toll,* from Late Latin *telōnium,* customhouse, from Greek *telōnion,* from *telōnēs,* a tax collector, from *telos,* tax.]

toll² (tōl) *tr.v.* **1.** To sound (a bell) slowly at regular intervals. **2.** To announce or summon by tolling. —*intr.v.* To sound in slowly repeated single tones. —*n.* The sound of a tolling bell. [Middle English *tollen.*]

toll·booth (tōl′bōōth′) *n.* A booth at a tollgate, where a toll is collected.

toll call. Any telephone call for which a higher rate is charged than that fixed for a local call.

toll·gate (tōl′gāt′) *n.* A gate barring passage to a road, tunnel, or bridge until a toll is collected.

toll·house (tōl′hous′) *n.* A tollbooth.

tol·u·ene (tŏl′yōō-ēn′) *n.* A colorless flammable liquid, $CH_3C_6H_5$, obtained from coal tar or petroleum and used in aviation and other high-octane fuels and as a solvent. [TOLU (from which it was orig. obtained) + -ENE.]

tom (tŏm) *n.* **1.** A male cat. **2.** A male turkey. [From the name *Tom,* pet form of *Thomas.*]

tom·a·hawk (tŏm′ə-hôk′) *n.* A light ax formerly used as a tool or weapon by North American Indians. —*tr.v.* To strike with a tomahawk. [Of Algonquian orig.]

tomahawk

to·ma·to (tə-mā′tō or -mä′-) *n., pl.* **-toes. 1.** A plant, *Lycopersicon esculentum,* native to South America, widely cultivated for its edible fruit. **2.** The fleshy, usu. reddish fruit of this plant, eaten raw or cooked as a vegetable. **3.** A plant that bears such fruit. [Spanish *tomate,* from Nahuatl *tomatl.*]

tomb (tōōm) *n.* **1.** A vault or chamber for the burial of the dead. **2.** Any grave or place of burial. [Middle English *toumbe,* from Norman French *tumbe,* from Late Latin *tumba,* sepulchral mound, from Greek *tumbos.*]

tom·boy (tŏm′boi′) *n.* A young girl who behaves like a boy. [*Tom,* pet form of the name *Thomas* + BOY.] —**tom′boy′ish** *adj.*

tomb·stone (tōōm′stōn′) *n.* A gravestone.

tom·cat (tŏm′kăt′) *n.* A male cat.

tom·cod (tŏm′kŏd′) *n., pl.* **tomcod** or **-cods.** Either of two edible saltwater fishes, *Microgadus tomcod,* of North American Atlantic waters, or *M. proximus,* of northern Pacific waters, related to and resembling the cod.

Tom, Dick, and Harry. Anybody at all; everyone.

tome (tōm) *n.* A book, esp. a large or scholarly one. [Old French, from Latin *tomus,* from Greek *tomos,* section of a book, from *temnein,* to cut, slice.]

to·men·tose (tō-měn′tōs′, tō′mən-tōs′) *adj. Biol.* Covered with dense, short, matted hairs. [From Latin *tōmentum,* cushion stuffing.]

tom·fool (tŏm′fōōl′) *n.* A fool; blockhead. —*adj.* Extremely foolish or stupid. [Middle English *Thome Fole,* name given to half-witted persons : *Thome,* pet form of the name *Thomas* + *fole,* fool.] —**tom′fool′er·y** (tŏm′fōō′lə-rē) *n.*

Tommy gun. *Informal.* A Thompson submachine gun.

to·mor·row (tə-môr′ō, -mŏr′ō) *n.* Also **to·mor·row. 1.** The day following today. **2.** The near future: *the world of tomorrow.* —*adv.* On or for the day following today. [Middle English *to morowe,* from Old English *tō morgenne* : *to,* on + *morgen,* morrow.]

Tom Thumb. 1. The hero of many English folk tales who was no larger than his father's thumb. **2.** A tiny person.

tom·tit (tŏm′tĭt′) *n. Brit.* A small bird, such as a titmouse. [Perh. TOM + TIT(MOUSE).]

tom-tom (tŏm′tŏm′) Also **tam-tam.** *n.* Any of various small-headed drums that are beaten with the hands. [Hindi *ṭamṭam* (imit.).]

-tomy. A suffix meaning a cutting of (a specified part or tissue): *tracheotomy.* [From Greek *-tomia,* from *tomos,* slice, from *temnein,* to cut.]

ton (tŭn) *n.* **1. a.** A unit of weight equal to 2,240 pounds or 1016.06 kilograms. Also called **long ton. b.** A unit of weight equal to 2,000 pounds or 907.20 kilograms. Also called **short ton. c.** A **metric ton. 2.** A unit of capacity for cargo in maritime shipping, normally estimated at 40 cubic feet. **3.** A unit of inside capacity of a ship equal to 100 cubic feet. **4.** *Informal.* A very large quantity of anything. [Middle English *tonne,* a measure of wine, from Old English *tunne,* tun.]

to·nal (tō′nəl) *adj.* Of or having tonality, a tone, or tones. —**to′nal·ly** *adv.*

to·nal·i·ty (tō-năl′ə-tē) *n., pl.* **-ties. 1.** *Mus.* **a.** A system or arrangement of seven tones built on a tonic; a key. **b.** The arrangement or relationship of all the tones and chords of a musical composition in respect to a tonic. **2.** The scheme or interrelation of the tones in a painting.

tone (tōn) *n.* **1. a.** A sound of distinct pitch, strength, duration, etc.; a musical note. **b.** The quality or character of sound: *the sweet, sad tones of a violin.* **2.** *Mus.* **a.** The interval of a major second; a whole step. **b.** The characteristic quality or timbre of a particular instrument or voice. **3.** The particular or relative pitch of a word, phrase, or sentence: *spoke in high, shrill tones.* **4.** Manner of expression in speech or writing: *an angry tone of voice.* **5.** A general quality, effect, or atmosphere: *a room with a subdued tone of elegance.* **6. a.** A color or shade of color. **b.** Quality of color. **7.** *Physiol.* **a.** The normal tension that remains in healthy muscles when at rest. **b.** Normal firmness of tissue. —*v.* **toned, ton·ing.** —*tr.v.* **1.** To give a particular tone or inflection to. **2.** To soften or change the color of, as a painting or photographic negative. —*intr.v.* To harmonize in color: *These curtains tone in well with your rugs.* —*phrasal verbs.* **tone down.** To make less vivid, harsh, violent, etc.; moderate. **tone up.** To make or become brighter, more vigorous, etc. [Middle English *ton,* from Old French, from Latin *tonus,* tone, sound, from Greek *tonos.*]

tone arm. The pivoted arm of a phonograph that holds the cartridge and stylus.

tone poem. Program music based on an extramusical theme in a single, extended movement for symphony orchestra and typical chiefly of the late 19th century.

tong¹ (tông, tŏng) *tr.v.* **tonged, tong·ing.** To seize, hold, or manipulate with tongs. [Back-formation from TONGS.]

tong² (tông, tŏng) *n.* **1.** A Chinese association, clan, or fraternity. **2.** A secret society of Chinese in the United States, at one time believed to control criminal activity among Chinese Americans. [Cantonese *t'ong,* assembly hall.]

Ton·gan (tŏng′gən) *n.* A Polynesian language spoken in Tonga.

tongs (tôngz, tŏngz) *n.* (*used with a pl. verb*). An implement consisting of two arms joined at one end by a pivot or hinge, used for holding or lifting something. [Middle English *tanges,* from Old English *tange.*]

tongue (tŭng) *n.* **1.** *Anat.* The fleshy muscular organ, attached in most vertebrates to the floor of the mouth, that is the principal organ of taste, an important organ of speech, and moves to aid chewing and swallowing. **2.** A similar invertebrate structure, as in insects or certain mollusks. **3.** The tongue of an animal, such as a cow, used as food. **4. a.** A spoken language. **b.** The power of speech. **c.** A manner of speech: *He has a sarcastic tongue.* **5.** The flap of material under the laces or buckles of a shoe. **6.** A bell clapper. **7.** A narrow spit of land projecting into a body of water; promontory. **8.** A jet of flame. **9.** A protruding strip along the edge of a board that fits into a matching groove on the edge of another board. —See Syns at **language.** —*v.* **tongued, tongu·ing.** —*tr.v.* **1.** To articulate (musical tones played on a wind instrument) by shutting off the stream of air with the tongue. **2.** To touch or lick with the tongue. **3. a.** To provide (a board) with a tongue. **b.** To join by means of a tongue and groove.

—*intr.v.* To articulate musical tones on a wind instrument. —*idioms.* **hold (one's) tongue.** To be or keep silent. **on the tip of (one's) tongue.** On the verge of being remembered or said. [Middle English *tounge*, from Old English *tunge*.]

tongue and groove. A joint in carpentry made by fitting a projection on the edge of one board into a matching groove on the edge of another board.

tongue and groove

tongue-in-cheek (tŭng′ən-chĕk′) *adj.* Meant or expressed ironically or facetiously.

tongue-lash-ing (tŭng′lăsh′ĭng) *n. Informal.* A scolding.

tongue-tied (tŭng′tīd′) *adj.* **1.** Speechless or confused in expression, as from shyness or surprise. **2.** Unable to move the tongue freely because of abnormal shortness of the connective membrane on the bottom of the mouth.

ton-ic (tŏn′ĭk) *n.* **1.** A medicine or natural agent that restores or has an invigorating effect on the body. **2.** Anything that invigorates, refreshes, or restores. **3.** *Mus.* The first note of a scale; a keynote. **4.** Quinine water. **5.** A **tonic accent.** —*adj.* **1.** Stimulating physical, mental, or emotional vigor. **2.** *Physiol.* **a.** Of or concerning the normal tension of healthy muscles. **b.** Producing healthy muscle tone. **c.** Characterized by abnormal or prolonged muscular tension: *tonic spasms.* **3.** *Mus.* Of or based on the tonic. **4.** Stressed, as a syllable; accented. [New Latin *tonicus*, of tension or tone, from Greek *tonikos*, from *tonos*, tone, tension.]

tonic accent. A vocal stress given to a spoken syllable, produced by rising pitch as distinguished from increased volume. Also called **tonic.**

to-nic-i-ty (tō-nĭs′ə-tē) *n.* Normal functional readiness or tone in muscles and other bodily tissues.

to-night (tə-nīt′). Also **to-night.** —*adv.* On or during the present or coming night. —*n.* This night or the night of this day. [Middle English *to night*, from Old English *tōniht* : *to*, at + *niht*, night.]

ton-nage (tŭn′ĭj) *n.* **1.** The number of tons of water a ship displaces afloat. **2.** The capacity of a merchant ship in units of 100 cubic feet. **3.** A charge per ton on cargo. **4.** The total shipping of a country or port, figured in tons. **5.** Weight as measured in tons.

ton-neau (tŭn-ō′) *n.* The rear seating compartment of an early automobile. [French, barrel, from Old French *tonnel.*]

ton-sil (tŏn′səl) *n.* A mass of lymphoid tissue, esp. either of two such masses embedded in the lateral walls of the aperture between the mouth and the pharynx. [Latin *tonsillae*, tonsils.] —**ton′sil-ar** *adj.*

ton-sil-lec-to-my (tŏn′sə-lĕk′tə-mē) *n., pl.* **-mies.** The surgical removal of one or both tonsils. [TONSIL + -ECTOMY.]

ton-sil-li-tis (tŏn′sə-lī′tĭs) *n.* Inflammation of one or both tonsils. [TONSIL + -ITIS.] —**ton′sil-lit′ic** (-lĭt′ĭk) *adj.*

ton-so-ri-al (tŏn-sôr′ē-əl, -sōr′ē-əl) *adj.* Of or pertaining to a barber or to barbering. [From Latin *tonsōrius*, from *tonsor*, a barber, from *tonsus*, past part. of *tondēre*, to shear.]

ton-sure (tŏn′shər) *n.* **1.** The act of shaving the head or a part of the head, as the crown, esp. as a preliminary to entering the priesthood or a monastic order. **2.** The part of a cleric's head so shaven. —*tr.v.* **-sured, -sur-ing.** To shave the head of. [Middle English, from Old French, from Medieval Latin *tonsūra*, from Latin, a shearing, from *tonsus*, past part. of *tondēre*, to shear.]

to-nus (tō′nəs) *n.* Tonicity. [Latin, tension, tone.]

too (too) *adv.* **1.** Also; as well: *I can play the piano too.* **2.** More than enough; excessively: *It's possible to study too hard.* **3.** Very; extremely: *He's not too smart.* **4.** *Informal.* Indeed; so: *I won't do it. You will too!* [Middle English *to*, in addition to, to.]

took (took) *v.* Past tense of **take.** [Middle English, from Old Norse *tōk.*]

tool (tool) *n.* **1.** Any hand-held implement, as a hammer, saw, or drill, used to accomplish or aid in mechanical work. **2.** A machine, such as a lathe, used to cut and shape machinery parts or other objects. **3.** Anything used in the performance of an endeavor; an instrument. **4.** Anything regarded as necessary to the carrying out of one's occupation or profession: *Words are the tools of his trade.* **5.** A person utilized to carry out the designs of another; a dupe. —*tr.v.* **1.** To form, work, or decorate with a tool or tools: *tooled the leather for a handbag.* **2.** To furnish tools or machinery for (a factory, industry, or shop). **3.** *Informal.* To drive (a vehicle). —*intr.v. Informal.* To travel in a vehicle. —*phrasal verb.* **tool up.** To prepare (a factory, shop, etc.) for production by providing machinery and tools suitable for a particular job. [Middle English, from Old English *tōl.*]

tool-box (tool′bŏks′) *n.* A case for hand tools.

tool-ing (too′lĭng) *n.* Work or ornamentation done with tools, esp. stamped or gilded designs on leather.

toot (toot) *intr.v.* **1.** To sound a horn or whistle in short blasts. **2.** To make this sound or a sound resembling this. —*tr.v.* **1.** To blow or sound (a horn or whistle). **2.** To sound (a blast or series of blasts) on a horn or whistle. —*n.* The act or sound of tooting. [Prob. imit.] —**toot′er** *n.*

tooth (tooth) *n., pl.* **teeth** (tēth). **1.** *Anat.* In most vertebrates, one of a set of hard, bonelike structures rooted in sockets in the jaws, typically composed of a core of soft pulp surrounded by a layer of hard dentine that is coated with cement or enamel at the crown, and used to seize, hold, or masticate. **2.** A similar structure in invertebrates, such as one of the pointed denticles or ridges on the exoskeleton of an arthropod or the shell of a mollusk. **3.** Any projecting part resembling a tooth, as on a gearwheel, comb, saw, etc. **4.** Taste, appetite, or liking: *a sweet tooth.* —*idioms.* **get (one's) teeth into.** To be actively involved in; get a firm grasp of. **in the teeth of.** Directly and forcefully against or confronting. **put teeth into.** To make effective or forceful. **to the teeth.** Completely; lacking nothing: *dressed to the teeth.* [Middle English, from Old English *tōth.*]

tooth-ache (tooth′āk′) *n.* An aching pain in or near a tooth.

tooth and nail. With great ferocity; as hard as possible: *He fought tooth and nail to win the nomination.*

tooth-brush (tooth′brŭsh′) *n.* A brush for cleaning teeth.

tooth-less (tooth′lĭs) *adj.* **1.** Lacking teeth. **2.** Lacking force; ineffectual. —**tooth′less-ly** *adv.* —**tooth′less-ness** *n.*

tooth-paste (tooth′pāst′) *n.* A paste for cleaning teeth.

tooth-pick (tooth′pĭk′) *n.* A small slender implement for removing food particles from between the teeth.

tooth-pow-der (tooth′pou′dər) *n.* Also **tooth powder.** A powder for cleaning teeth.

tooth shell. Any of various burrowing saltwater mollusks of the class Scaphopoda, with a long, tapering, slightly curved tubular shell.

tooth-some (tooth′səm) *adj.* **1.** Delicious; luscious. **2.** Pleasant; attractive. —**tooth′some-ly** *adv.* —**tooth′some-ness** *n.*

tooth-y (too′thē) *adj.* **-i-er, -i-est.** Having or showing prominent teeth. —**tooth′i-ly** *adv.*

top¹ (tŏp) *n.* **1.** The uppermost part, point, surface, or end of something: *the top of the hill; the top of the page.* **2.** Something that forms or covers the upper part of something: *a bottle top; women's cotton jersey tops.* **3.** The part of a plant that is above the ground, esp. a plant with an edible root: *turnip tops.* **4.** *Sports.* **a.** A stroke that lands above the center of the ball. **b.** A forward spin on a ball resulting from such a stroke. **5.** The highest degree, pitch, or point; peak: *shouting at the top of his voice.* **6.** The highest position or rank: *at the top of his profession.* **7.** The earliest part or beginning: *the top of the first inning.* —*modifier:* *at top speed; the top shelf; the top pop singers in the country.* —See Syns at **excellent** and **primary.** —*v.* **topped, top-ping.** —*tr.v.* **1.** To furnish with, form, or serve as a top. **2.** To reach the top of: *We topped the hill and started to climb down.* **3.** To exceed or surpass: *topped all previous records.* **4.** To be at the head of: *He tops the list of candidates for the job.* **5.** To remove the top or uppermost part from: *topped all the fruit trees.* **6.** *Sports.* **a.** To strike the upper part of (a ball), giving it forward spin. **b.** To make (a stroke) in this way. —See Syns at **surpass.** —*idioms.* **blow one's top.** *Slang.* To lose one's temper. **on top.** In a dominant, controlling, or successful position. **on top of. 1.** *Informal.* **a.** In control of. **b.** Fully informed about. **2.** Besides; in addition to. **3.** Following closely upon. [Middle English, from Old English *topp.*]

top² (tŏp) *n.* A child's toy made to spin on a pointed end either by releasing a spring or by quickly unwinding a string. [Middle English, from Old English *topp.*]

top–. Var. of **topo–.**

to·paz (tō′păz′) *n.* **1.** A hard mineral consisting largely of aluminum silicate and occurring in many colors, valued as a gem. **2.** Any of various yellow gemstones, esp. a yellow variety of sapphire or corundum. [Middle English *topace,* from Old French, from Latin *topazus,* from Greek *topazos.*]

top boot. A high boot usu. having its upper part trimmed with a contrasting color or texture of leather.

top·coat (tŏp′kōt′) *n.* A lightweight overcoat.

top dog. *Informal.* A person or group considered to have the greatest authority, power, etc.

top-drawer (tŏp′drôr′) *adj. Informal.* Of the highest importance, rank, privilege, or merit.

tope (tōp) *n.* Any of several small sharks, esp. one of the genus *Galeorhinus.* [Orig. unknown.]

top·er (tō′pər) *n.* A chronic drinker; drunkard.

top·flight (tŏp′flīt′) *adj.* First-rate; superior. —See Syns at **excellent.**

top·gal·lant (tə-găl′ənt, tŏp-) *adj. Naut.* Designating the mast above the topmast, its sails, or rigging.

top hat. A man's formal hat with a narrow brim and a tall cylindrical crown.

| top hat | topiary |

top-heav·y (tŏp′hĕv′ē) *adj.* **-i·er, -i·est.** Likely to topple because overloaded at the top. —**top′-heav′i·ness** *n.*

to·pi·ar·y (tō′pē-ĕr′ē) *adj.* Of or characterized by the clipping or trimming of live shrubs or trees into decorative shapes. —*n., pl.* **-ies. 1.** Topiary work or art. **2.** A topiary garden. [Latin *topiārius,* of gardening, from *topia,* landscape gardening, from Greek *topia,* pl. of *topion,* a field, dim. of *topos,* a place.]

top·ic (tŏp′ĭk) *n.* **1.** A subject treated in a speech, essay, thesis, or portion of a discourse; a theme. **2.** A subject of discussion or conversation. **3.** A subdivision or heading in a theme, thesis, or outline. [From Latin *Topica,* a work by Aristotle on kinds of reasoning, from Greek *(Ta) Topika,* from *topikos,* commonplace, from *topos,* a place.]

top·i·cal (tŏp′ĭ-kəl) *adj.* **1.** Of or belonging to a particular location or place; local. **2.** Currently of interest; contemporary: *topical issues.* **3.** *Med.* Of or on an isolated part of the body. [From Greek *topikos,* from *topos,* place.] —**top′i·cal′i·ty** (-kăl′ə-tē) *n.* —**top′i·cal·ly** *adv.*

top·knot (tŏp′nŏt′) *n.* **1.** A crest or tuft, as of hair or feathers, on the top of the head. **2.** Any decorative ribbon, bow, etc., worn as a headdress.

top·less (tŏp′lĭs) *adj.* **1.** Having no top. **2.** Wearing a topless garment. **3.** So high as to appear out of sight.

top·loft·y (tŏp′lôf′tē, -lŏf′tē) *adj.* **-i·er, -i·est.** *Informal.* Condescending in manner or attitude; haughty.

top·mast (tŏp′məst, -măst′, -mäst′) *n.* The mast that is below the topgallant mast in a square-rigged ship and next above the lower mast in a fore-and-aft-rigged ship.

top·min·now (tŏp′mĭn′ō) *n.* Any of various small, viviparous New World fishes of the family Poeciliidae, of fresh or brackish waters. [So called because it swims near the surface of water.]

top·most (tŏp′mōst′) *adj.* Highest; uppermost.

top·notch (tŏp′nŏch′) *adj. Informal.* First-rate; excellent. —See Syns at **excellent.**

topo– or **top–.** A prefix meaning place or region: *topology.* [From Greek *topos,* place.]

to·pog·ra·phy (tə-pŏg′rə-fē) *n., pl.* **-phies. 1.** Detailed and precise description of a place or region. **2.** The technique of representing the exact physical features of a place or region on a map. **3.** The physical features of a place or region. —**to·pog′ra·pher** *n.* —**top′o·graph′ic** (tŏp′ə-grăf′ĭk) or **top′o·graph′i·cal** *adj.* —**top′o·graph′i·cal·ly** *adv.*

to·pol·o·gy (tə-pŏl′ə-jē) *n.* **1.** The topographical study of a given place in relation to its history. **2.** The detailed anatomy of specific areas of the body. **3.** *Math.* The study of the properties of geometric configurations that do not change under transformation by continuous mappings. —**top′o·log′ic** (tŏp′ə-lŏj′ĭk) or **top′o·log′i·cal** *adj.* —**to·pol′o·gist** *n.*

top·per (tŏp′ər) *n.* **1.** Someone or something that tops. **2.** A short, lightweight topcoat for a woman. **3.** *Informal.* A top hat. **4.** *Slang.* Something that outdoes or climaxes that which has gone before, esp. a joke or anecdote.

top·ping (tŏp′ĭng) *n.* A sauce, frosting, or garnish for food.

top·ple (tŏp′əl) *v.* **-pled, -pling.** —*tr.v.* **1.** To push over; overturn. **2.** To overthrow, as a government. —*intr.v.* **1.** To totter and fall. **2.** To lean over as if about to fall; teeter. —See Syns at **fall.** [Freq. of TOP (to remove the top of).]

tops (tŏps) *adj. Slang.* First-rate; excellent; topmost.

top·sail (tŏp′səl, -sāl′) *n.* **1.** A square sail set above the lowest sail on the mast of a square-rigged ship. **2.** A sail set above the gaff of a lower sail on a fore-and-aft-rigged ship.

top-se·cret (tŏp′sē′krĭt) *adj.* Designating information of the highest level of security classification.

top sergeant. *Informal.* A first sergeant.

top·side (tŏp′sīd′) *n.* Often **topsides.** The upper parts of a ship that are above the main deck. —*adv.* On or to the upper parts of a ship; on deck.

top·soil (tŏp′soil′) *n.* The surface layer of soil.

top·sy·tur·vy (tŏp′sē-tûr′vē) *adv.* **1.** With the top downward and the bottom up; upside-down. **2.** In a condition of utter disorder or confusion. —*adj.* Confused; disordered. —*n.* Confusion; chaos. [Prob. from TOP + obs. *tervy,* to turn.] —**top′sy-tur′vi·ly** *adv.* —**top′sy-tur′vi·ness** *n.*

toque (tōk) *n.* **1.** A small, brimless, close-fitting hat worn by women. **2.** A plumed velvet cap with a full crown and small rolled brim, worn by men and women in the 16th cent. [French, from Spanish *toca.*]

tor (tôr) *n.* A high rock or craggy pinnacle on the top of a hill. [Middle English *torre,* from Old English *torr.*]

To·rah (tôr′ə, tōr′ə) *n.* **1.** Also **torah.** The entire body of Jewish religious law and learning including both sacred literature and oral tradition. **2.** A scroll or scrolls of parchment on which the Pentateuch is written, used in a synagogue during services. [Hebrew *tōrāh,* a law, instruction, from *yārāh,* to teach.]

torch (tôrch) *n.* **1.** A portable light produced by the flame of an inflammable material wound about the end of a stick of wood and ignited. **2.** A portable device that burns a fuel, usu. a gas, often with a supply of pure oxygen, to produce a flame hot enough for welding, soldering, brazing, or cutting metals. **3.** Anything that serves to enlighten, guide, inspire, etc. **4.** *Brit.* A flashlight. —*tr.v. Slang.* To cause to burn or undergo combustion. —See Syns at **ignite.** —*idiom.* **carry a torch for.** To be consumed with unrequited love for (someone). [Middle English *torche,* from Old French, a torch (orig. made of twisted straw dipped in wax), ult. from Latin *torquēre,* to twist.]

torch·bear·er (tôrch′bâr′ər) *n.* **1.** A person who carries a torch. **2.** A person who leads or inspires a movement or campaign, as for knowledge, freedom, truth, etc.

torch song. A sentimental popular song, typically one in which the singer laments a lost love. —**torch singer.**

tore (tôr, tōr) *v.* Past tense of **tear** (to rend). —See Usage note at **tear.** [From *tear,* on the model of such verbs as *swear, swore.*]

tor·e·a·dor (tôr'ē-ə-dôr') *n.* A bullfighter. [Spanish, from *torear,* to fight bulls, from *toro,* a bull, from Latin *taurus.*]

to·re·ro (tə-râr'ō, tō-rā'rō) *n., pl.* **-ros** (-ōz; *Sp* -rōs). A bullfighter, esp. a matador. [Spanish, from Late Latin *taurārius,* from Latin *taurus,* a bull.]

to·ri (tôr'ī, tōr'ī) *n.* Plural of **torus.**

to·ri·i (tôr'ē-ē', tōr'-) *n., pl.* **torii.** The gateway of a Shinto temple, made of two uprights with a straight crosspiece at the top and a concave lintel above the crosspiece. [Japanese, "bird residence."]

torii

tor·ment (tôr'mĕnt') *n.* **1.** Great physical pain or mental anguish; agony. **2.** A source of harassment or pain. **3.** Torture or suffering inflicted on prisoners, as in the proceedings of the Inquisition. —*tr.v.* (tôr-mĕnt', tôr'mĕnt') **1.** To cause to undergo great physical or mental anguish. **2.** To annoy, pester, or harass; worry. [Middle English, from Old French, from Latin *tormentum,* a twisted rope, instrument of torture, from *torquēre,* to twist.] —**tor·ment'ing·ly** *adv.* —**tor·men'tor** *n.*

torn (tôrn, tōrn) *v.* Past participle of **tear** (to rend). [Middle English *toren,* from Old English *(ge)toren.*]

tor·na·do (tôr-nā'dō) *n., pl.* **-does** or **-dos. 1.** A violent atmospheric disturbance in the form of a column of air several hundred yards wide spinning at speeds of 300 miles per hour and faster, usu. accompanied by a funnel-shaped downward extension of a thundercloud. **2.** Any violent whirlwind or hurricane. [From Spanish *tronada,* thunderstorm, from *tronar,* to thunder, from Latin *tonāre.*]

tor·pe·do (tôr-pē'dō) *n., pl.* **-does. 1.** A cigar-shaped, self-propelled underwater projectile, designed to detonate on contact with or in the vicinity of a target. **2.** A small explosive charge placed on a railroad track and detonated by the weight of a passing train, thereby warning the engineer of an approaching hazard. **3.** A small firework that explodes when thrown against a hard surface. **4.** Any of several cartilaginous fishes of the genus *Torpedo,* related to the skates and rays. —*tr.v.* To attack or destroy with or as if with a torpedo. —See Syns at **destroy.** [Latin *torpēdō,* stiffness, numbness, the torpedo fish, from *torpēre,* to be stiff.]

torpedo boat. A fast, thinly plated boat equipped with heavy machine guns and torpedo tubes.

tor·pid (tôr'pĭd) *adj.* **1.** Not active; sluggish; slow. **2.** Deprived of the power of motion or feeling; dormant: *a torpid bear at peace in his winter resting place.* **3.** Lethargic; apathetic; dull: *a mind grown torpid and weak.* [Latin *torpidus,* from *torpēre,* to be stiff.] —**tor·pid'i·ty** *n.* —**tor'pid·ly** *adv.*

tor·por (tôr'pər) *n.* **1.** A condition of mental or physical inactivity or insensibility; inertia. **2.** Lethargy; apathy; indifference. [Latin, from *torpēre,* to be stiff.] —**tor'po·rif'ic** (-pə-rĭf'ĭk) *adj.*

torque (tôrk) *n.* The measured ability or tendency of a force to produce rotation about an axis. [From Latin *torquēre,* to twist.]

tor·rent (tôr'ənt, tŏr'-) *n.* **1.** A turbulent, swift-flowing stream. **2.** A deluge: *Rain fell in torrents.* **3.** Any turbulent or overwhelming flow: *a torrent of insults; torrents of mail.* [French, from Italian *torrente,* from Latin *torrēns,* a burning, a torrent, from *torrēre,* to burn.]

tor·ren·tial (tô-rĕn'shəl, tə-) *adj.* **1.** Of or like a torrent: *torrential rainfall.* **2.** Resembling a torrent in turbulence or abundance: *torrential applause.* **3.** Resulting from the action of a torrent: *torrential erosion.* —**tor·ren'tial·ly** *adv.*

tor·rid (tôr'ĭd, tŏr'-) *adj.* **1.** Very dry and hot. **2.** Passionate; ardent: *a torrid romance.* —See Syns at **hot.** [Latin *torridus,* from *torrēre,* to dry, parch.] —**tor·rid'i·ty** or **tor'rid·ness** *n.* —**tor'rid·ly** *adv.*

Torrid Zone. The region of the earth's surface between the tropics, marked in general by a hot, tropical climate.

tor·sion (tôr'shən) *n.* **1. a.** The act of twisting or turning. **b.** The condition of being twisted or turned. **2.** The stress that an object undergoes when one of its ends is twisted out of line with the other end. [Late Latin *torsiō,* from *torsus,* twisted, past part. of Latin *torquēre,* to twist.] —**tor'sion·al** *adj.* —**tor'sion·al·ly** *adv.*

tor·so (tôr'sō) *n., pl.* **-sos. 1.** The portion of the human body from the neck to the hip; trunk. **2.** A statue of the trunk of the human body, esp. in the nude. [Italian, a stalk, trunk of a statue, from Latin *thyrsus,* thyrsus.]

tort (tôrt) *n. Law.* Any wrongful act that does not involve a breach of contract and for which a civil suit can be brought. [Middle English, from Old French, from Medieval Latin *tortum,* from Latin, twisted, distorted, from *torquēre,* to twist.]

torte (tôrt; *German* tôr'tə) *n.* A rich, round layer cake, usu. made with many eggs and very little flour. [German *Torte.*]

tor·til·la (tôr-tē'yə) *n.* A thin, round, unleavened Mexican bread, usu. made from cornmeal and water, and cooked on a flat griddle. [American Spanish, dim. of Spanish *torta,* a round cake, from Late Latin *tōrta.*]

tor·toise (tôr'təs) *n.* Any of various terrestrial turtles, esp. one of the family Testudinidae, with thick, scaly limbs and a high, rounded carapace. [Middle English *tortuce,* from Old French *tortue.*]

tor·toise·shell (tôr'təs-shĕl') *n.* Also **tor·toise-shell** or **tortoise shell. 1.** The mottled, horny, translucent brownish covering of the shell of certain of the sea turtles, used in inlaying and making combs and other articles. **2.** Any of several butterflies, chiefly of the genus *Nymphalis,* that have wings with orange, black, and brown markings. —*modifier: a tortoiseshell comb; tortoiseshell plastic.*

tor·tu·ous (tôr'chōō-əs) *adj.* **1.** Having repeated turns or bends; winding; twisting: *a tortuous road.* **2.** Deceitful; devious: *an insidious tortuous plot.* **3.** Highly involved; circuitous: *a tortuous procedure.* [Middle English, from Old French, from Latin *tortuōsus,* from *tortus,* a twist, from *torquēre,* to twist.] —**tor'tu·ous·ly** *adv.* —**tor'tu·ous·ness** *n.*

tor·ture (tôr'chər) *n.* **1.** The infliction of severe physical pain as a means of punishment or coercion. **2.** The experience of this. **3.** Mental anguish or suffering. **4.** Any method or thing that causes such pain or anguish. —*tr.v.* **-tured, -tur·ing. 1.** To subject to torture. **2.** To afflict with great physical or mental pain. **3.** To twist or turn abnormally; distort: *tortured the models' hair into fantastic shapes.* [French, from Late Latin *tortūra,* torment, from Latin *tortus,* twisted, past part. of *torquēre,* to twist.] —**tor'tur·er** *n.* —**tor'tur·ous·ly** *adv.*

to·rus (tôr'əs, tōr'-) *n., pl.* **to·ri** (tôr'ī, tōr'ī). **1.** *Archit.* A large convex molding, semicircular in cross section, located at the base of a classical column. **2.** *Anat.* A bulging or rounded projection or swelling. **3.** *Biol.* A rounded structure, as the receptacle of a flower. **4.** *Geom.* A surface that has the shape of a doughnut. [From Latin *torus,* a protuberance, round swelling.]

To·ry (tôr'ē, tōr'ē) *n., pl.* **-ries. 1.** A member of a British political party, founded in 1689, that was the rival of the Whigs, has been known as the Conservative Party since 1832, and today is the rival of the Labour Party. **2.** Any American siding with the British during the American Revolution. **3.** Often **tory.** Someone holding to highly conservative political or economic principles. [From Irish *tōraidhe,* runaway, robber, orig. an Irishman who, dispossessed by the English in the mid-17th cent., became a bandit.] —**To'ry** *adj.* —**To'ry·ism** *n.*

---

toss (tôs, tŏs) *tr.v.* **1.** To throw or fling about; pitch to and fro: *Heavy seas tossed the ship.* **2.** To throw lightly with the hand: *tossed the ball to a teammate.* **3.** To move or lift (the head) with a sudden, jerking motion. **4.** To flip a coin to decide something. **5.** To mix (a salad) gently so as to cover with dressing. —*intr.v.* **1.** To be thrown or flung to and fro. **2.** To move or throw oneself about vigorously: *The infant tossed and turned in its mother's arms.* **3.** To flip a coin to decide something. —*phrasal verb.* **toss off.** To do, finish, perform, etc. in a casual, easy manner. —*n.* **1.** The act of tossing. **2.** A throw or pitch. **3.** A rapid lift, as of the head. [Orig. unknown.] —**toss′er** *n.*

toss·up (tôs′ŭp′, tŏs′-) *n. Informal.* **1.** The flipping of a coin to decide an issue. **2.** An even chance or choice.

tot¹ (tŏt) *n.* **1.** A small child. **2.** A small amount of something, as of liquor. [Orig. unknown.]

tot² (tŏt) *tr.v.* **tot·ted, tot·ting.** To total. [Short for TOTAL.]

to·tal (tōt′l) *n.* **1.** A number or quantity obtained by addition; a sum. **2.** A whole quantity; an entirety. —*adj.* **1.** Constituting the whole; entire: *the total population.* **2.** Of, concerning, or utilizing the whole of something; full: *a total eclipse; a total effort.* **3.** Complete; utter; absolute: *a total failure.* —See Syns at **utter** and **whole.** —*v.* **-taled** or **-talled, -taling** or **-tal·ling.** —*tr.v.* **1.** To determine the sum of: *totaling expenses.* **2.** To equal a total of; amount to. **3.** To destroy: *totaled the car.* —*intr.v.* To add up; amount: *The vote count totals to 110 for and 56 against the proposal.* —See Syns at **destroy.** [Middle English, of the whole, from Old French, from Medieval Latin *tōtālis,* from Latin *tōtus,* whole.] —**to′tal·ly** *adv.*

to·tal·i·tar·i·an (tō-tăl′ə-târ′ē-ən) *adj.* Designating a form of government in which one part exercises absolute control over all spheres of human life and opposing parties are not permitted to exist. —See Syns at **absolute.** —*n.* A person who supports or favors such a form of government. [TOTAL + (AUTHOR)ITARIAN.] —**to·tal′i·tar′i·an·ism′** *n.*

to·tal·i·ty (tō-tăl′ə-tē) *n., pl.* **-ties.** **1.** The condition or property of being total. **2.** The aggregate amount; a sum.

tote (tōt) *tr.v.* **tot·ed, tot·ing.** *Informal.* To haul; carry. [Orig. unknown.] —**tot′er** *n.*

tote bag. *Informal.* A large handbag or shopping bag.

to·tem (tō′təm) *n.* **1.** An animal, plant, or natural object that serves as a symbol of a clan or family and is claimed by the members as an ancestor. **2.** A representation of this being or object. [Ojibwa *nintōtēm,* "my family mark."] —**to·tem′ic** (tō-tĕm′ĭk) *adj.*

totem pole. A post carved and painted with a series of totemic symbols and erected before a dwelling, as among certain North American Indian peoples.

toth·er or **t′oth·er** (tŭth′ər) *pron. Informal.* The other. [Middle English *the tother,* from *thet other,* "that other."]

tot·ter (tŏt′ər) *intr.v.* **1. a.** To sway as if about to fall. **b.** To appear about to collapse. **2.** To walk unsteadily. —*n.* An unsteady or wavering movement. [Middle English *toteren,* from Middle Dutch *touteren,* to stagger.] —**tot′ter·ing·ly** *adv.* —**tot′ter·y** *adj.*

tou·can (tōō′kăn′, -kän′) *n.* Any of various tropical American birds of the family Ramphastidae, with brightly colored plumage and a very large bill. [French, from Portuguese *tucano,* from Tupi *tucana.*]

touch (tŭch) *tr.v.* **1.** To come or bring into physical contact with: *touched the pencil to the paper.* **2.** To feel with a part of the body, esp. with the hand or fingers. **3.** To tap, press, or strike lightly. **4.** *Informal.* To harm or injure, as by hitting: *I never touched him.* **5.** To eat or drink; taste: *They wouldn't touch the soup.* **6.** To reach: *touch land; touch base.* **7.** To come up to; equal: *His work couldn't touch his master's.* **8.** To affect, involve, or concern: *a problem that touches many different people.* **9.** To affect or move emotionally: *The plea touched my heart.* **10.** *Slang.* To wheedle a loan from. —*intr.v.* **1.** To touch someone or something. **2.** To be or come in contact. —*phrasal verbs.* **touch down.** To land or make contact with a landing surface, as an airplane or spacecraft. **touch off.** **1.** To cause to explode. **2.** To cause or start; incite. **touch up.** To improve by making minor changes or additions. —*n.* **1.** An act or way of touching. **2.** The sense by which things in contact with the body are felt as hard, soft, rough, smooth, etc.; feeling. **3.** The physical sensation experienced in feeling something; feel: *the touch of velvet.* **4.** Contact or communication: *Stay in touch.* **5.** A light stroke or tap. **6.** A little bit; a hint or trace: *a touch of salt.* **7.** A mild attack: *a touch of the flu.* **8. a.** An addition or detail that improves, completes, or perfects something. **b.** An effect or quality resulting from such an addition or detail: *Fresh flowers give a homey touch to the whole room.* **9.** A characteristic way or style of doing things: *the author's personal touch.* **10.** A special ability to do something demanding skill; a facility or knack. **11.** *Slang.* **a.** The act of approaching someone to wheedle a loan. **b.** A sum of money borrowed. **c.** A person likely to be approached for a loan: *an easy touch.* [Middle English *touchen,* from Old French *tochier.*] —**touch′a·ble** *adj.* —**touch′a·ble·ness** *n.* —**touch′er** *n.*

touch and go. A precarious state of affairs. —*modifier* (**touch-and-go**): *a touch-and-go situation.*

touch·back (tŭch′băk′) *n. Football.* A play in which a player recovers and touches the ball to the ground behind his own goal line after it has been propelled into or beyond the end zone by a player on the opposing team.

touch·down (tŭch′doun′) *n.* **1.** *Football.* A score of six points, made by moving the ball across or gaining possession in the opposing team's end zone. **2.** The contact or moment of contact of an aircraft or spacecraft with the surface on which it lands.

tou·ché (tōō-shā′) *interj.* A word used to concede a hit in fencing or a point well made by an opponent in an argument, discussion, etc. [French, touched (by the opponent's foil in fencing).]

touched (tŭcht) *adj.* **1.** Emotionally affected or moved. **2.** Mentally unbalanced; demented. —See Syns at **insane.**

touch football. A variety of football played without protective equipment and in which players tag rather than tackle each other to put the ball out of play.

touch·ing (tŭch′ĭng) *adj.* Eliciting an emotional reaction. —See Syns at **moving.** —*prep.* Concerning; about: *I have heard nothing touching his plans.* —**touch′ing·ly** *adv.*

touch-me-not (tŭch′mē-nŏt′) *n.* Any of several plants of the genus *Impatiens,* esp. the jewelweed.

touch·stone (tŭch′stōn′) *n.* **1.** A hard black stone, such as jasper or basalt, used to test the purity of gold or silver by comparing the streak left on the stone by the sample with a streak left by a standard alloy. **2.** Anything against which the quality of something may be tested; criterion.

touch-type (tŭch′tīp′) *intr.v.* **-typed, -typ·ing.** To type on a typewriter without having to look at the keyboard.

touch-up (tŭch′ŭp′) *n.* The act or process of finishing or improving by small alterations and additions.

touch·wood (tŭch′wōōd′) *n.* Decayed wood or similar material used as tinder.

touch·y (tŭch′ē) *adj.* **-i·er, -i·est.** **1.** Apt to take offense with very slight cause. **2.** Requiring tact or skill; delicate: *a touchy situation.* **3.** Sensitive to touch: *Her back is touchy from sunburn.* —**touch′i·ly** *adv.* —**touch′i·ness** *n.*

tough (tŭf) *adj.* **-er, -est.** **1.** Strong and resilient; able to withstand great strain without tearing or breaking. **2.** Hard to cut or chew. **3.** Able to endure hardships; physically rugged. **4.** Fraught with hardship; severe; harsh: *a tough winter.* **5.** Difficult to do or accomplish; not easy; demanding: *a tough job; a tough test.* **6.** Unyielding; stubborn: *a tough negotiation.* **7.** Strong-minded; resolute: *a tough man to convince.* **8.** Vicious; rough: *tough criminals.* **9.** *Informal.* Too bad; unfortunate. —See Syns at **burdensome, difficult,** and **obstinate.** —*n.* A thug; hoodlum. [Middle English *togh,* from Old English *tōh.*] —**tough′ly** *adv.* —**tough′ness** *n.*

tough·en (tŭf′ən) *tr.v.* To make tough. —*intr.v.* To become tough. —**tough′en·er** *n.*

tough-mind·ed (tŭf′mīn′dĭd) *adj.* Not sentimental; practical and strong-willed. —**tough′-mind′ed·ly** *adv.* —**tough′-mind′ed·ness** *n.*

tou·pee (tōō-pā′) *n.* A small wig or hair piece worn to cover a bald spot. [French *toupet,* a tuft of hair, forelock, from Old French, from *top,* top, summit.]

tour (tōōr) *n.* **1.** A trip during which various places of interest are visited: *a tour of Europe.* **2.** A brief trip to or through a place for the purpose of seeing it: *a tour of the printing plant.* **3.** A journey to fulfill a round of engagements in several places: *a concert tour.* **4.** A period of duty at a single place or job: *a tour of duty abroad.* —*intr.v.* To go on a tour. —*tr.v.* **1.** To make a tour of. **2.** To present (a theatrical performance) on a tour. [Middle English, a turning, from Old French, turn, circuit, from Latin *tornus,* lathe.]

tour de force (tŏŏr′ də fôrs′). *French.* A feat of exceptional strength, virtuosity, or ingenuity.

touring car. A large open automobile for five or more persons, popular in the 1920's.

tour·ism (tŏŏr′ĭz′əm) *n.* **1.** The practice of traveling for pleasure. **2.** The business of providing tours and services for travelers.

tour·ist (tŏŏr′ĭst) *n.* A person who is traveling for pleasure.

tourist class. A grade of travel accommodations less luxurious than first class.

tour·ma·line (tŏŏr′mə-lĭn, -lēn′) *n.* A complex crystalline silicate containing aluminum, boron, and other elements, used as a gemstone. [French, from Singhalese *toramalli,* carnelian.]

tour·na·ment (tŏŏr′nə-mənt, tûr′-) *n.* **1.** A contest composed of a series of elimination games or trials. **2.** A medieval martial sport in which two groups of mounted and armored contestants fought against each other with blunted weapons. [Middle English *tornement,* from Old French *torneiement,* from *torneier,* to compete in a tournament.]

tour·ney (tŏŏr′nē, tûr′-) *n., pl.* **-neys.** A tournament. [Middle English *torneyen,* from Old French *torneier,* to turn around, ult. from Latin *tornus,* a lathe.]

tour·ni·quet (tŏŏr′nĭ-kĭt, -kā′, tûr′-) *n.* Any device, such as a tight band with a pad under it to concentrate the pressure, used to stop temporarily the flow of blood in a large artery in one of the limbs. [French, from *tourner,* to turn.]

tou·sle (tou′zəl) *tr.v.* **-sled, -sling.** To disarrange or rumple; dishevel. —*n.* A disheveled mass; a tangle. [Middle English *touselen.*]

tout (tout). *Informal.* —*intr.v.* **1.** To solicit customers, votes, patronage, etc., esp. in a brazen way. **2.** To obtain and deal in horseracing information. —*tr.v.* **1.** To solicit or importune. **2.** To obtain or sell information on (a racing horse or stable) for the guidance of bettors. **3.** To publicize or recommend as being of great worth: *a rookie highly touted by the press.* —*n.* **1.** A person who obtains information on racehorses and their prospects and sells it to bettors. **2.** A person who solicits customers. [Middle English *tuten,* to watch.] —**tout′er** *n.*

tow¹ (tō) *tr.v.* To draw or pull along behind by a chain or line: *tow a car.* —*n.* **1.** An act of towing. **2.** The condition of being towed. **3.** Something that tows or is towed, as a boat, car, etc. **4.** A rope or cable used in towing. —*idiom.* **in tow.** Under one's control; in one's charge: *a tour guide with fifty sightseers in tow.* [Middle English *towen,* from Old English *togian.*]

tow² (tō) *n.* Short, coarse flax or hemp fibers that are ready for spinning. [Middle English *towe,* prob. from Old English *tow-,* suitable for spinning.]

tow·age (tō′ĭj) *n.* **1.** The act or service of towing. **2.** A charge for towing.

to·ward (tôrd, tōrd, tə-wôrd′) *prep.* Also **to·wards** (tôrdz, tōrdz, tə-wôrdz′). **1.** In the direction of: *moving toward the frontier.* **2.** In a position facing: *a window toward the square.* **3.** Somewhat before in time; approaching: *It started raining toward dawn.* **4.** With relation to; regarding: *a poor attitude toward his superiors.* **5.** In furtherance or partial fulfillment of: *a payment toward the house.* **6.** With a view to: *efforts toward peace.* —*adj.* (tôrd or tōrd). **1.** Happening; going on or being done: *Nothing's toward.* **2.** Tractable: *a toward child.* [Middle English, from Old English *tōweard,* favorable, future.]

tow·boat (tō′bōt′) *n.* A tugboat.

tow·el (tou′əl) *n.* A piece of absorbent cloth or paper used for wiping or drying. —*v.* **-eled** or **-elled, -el·ing** or **-el·ling.** —*tr.v.* To wipe or rub dry with a towel. —*intr.v.* To dry oneself with a towel. —*idiom.* **throw in the towel.** To give up; quit in defeat. [Middle English *towelle,* from Old French *toaille.*]

tow·el·ing (tou′əl-ĭng) *n.* Any of various fabrics of cotton, linen, or synthetic fiber used for making towels.

tow·er¹ (tou′ər) *n.* **1.** A building or part of a building that is

of unusually great height in proportion to its width and depth. **2.** A tall framework or structure used for observation, signaling, etc. —*intr.v.* To rise to a conspicuous height; to loom: *The son towers over his father.* [Middle English *tour,* from Old English *torr* and Old French *tor,* both from Latin *turris,* from Greek.]

tow·er² (tō′ər) *n.* Someone or something that tows.

tow·er·ing (tou′ər-ĭng) *adj.* **1.** Of imposing height. **2.** Outstanding; pre-eminent: *a towering success.* **3.** Awesomely intense or violent; boundless: *a towering rage.* —See Syns at **tall.**

tow·head (tō′hĕd′) *n.* A person with white-blond hair. [From TOW (flax).] —**tow′head′ed** *adj.*

tow·hee (tō′hē, tō-hē′) *n.* Any of several North American birds of the genera *Pipilo* or *Chlorura,* esp. one with black, white, and rust-colored plumage in the male. [Imit.]

tow·line (tō′līn′) *n.* A line, cable, or chain used in towing a vessel or vehicle. Also called **towrope.**

town (toun) *n.* **1.** A population center larger than a village and smaller than a city. **2.** *Informal.* A city. **3.** The commercial district or center of an area. **4.** The residents of a town. **5.** Urban life as opposed to life in the country. —*idioms.* **go to town.** *Slang.* To do something with no inhibitions or restrictions; go all out. **on the town.** *Slang.* On a spree. [Middle English, from Old English *tūn,* an enclosed place, homestead, village.]

town clerk. A public official in charge of keeping the records of a town.

town crier. In former times, a person employed by a town to walk the streets proclaiming announcements.

town hall. The building that contains the offices of the public officials of a town, houses the town council, and is often a site of meetings on public issues.

town house. **1.** A house or other residence in the city as distinguished from one in the country. **2.** A house sharing one or more side walls with another house.

town meeting. A legislative assembly of townspeople.

towns·folk *pl.n.* Townspeople.

town·ship (toun′shĭp′) *n.* **1.** A subdivision of a county in most Northeastern and Midwestern states, that has the status of a unit of local government with varying governmental powers. **2.** A public land-surveying unit of 36 sections or 36 square miles.

towns·man (tounz′mən) *n.* **1.** An inhabitant of a town. **2.** A fellow inhabitant of one's town.

towns·peo·ple (tounz′pē′pəl) *pl,n.* The inhabitants or citizens of a town or city.

towns·wom·an (tounz′wŏŏm′ən) *n.* A female inhabitant of a town.

tow·path (tō′păth′, -päth′) *n.* A path along a canal or river used by animals towing boats.

tow·rope (tō′rōp′) *n.* A towline.

tox-. A prefix meaning poison: **toxemia.** [From Latin *toxicum,* poison.]

tox·e·mi·a (tŏk-sē′mē-ə) *n.* A condition in which toxins produced by body cells at a local source of infection or derived from the growth of microorganisms are contained in the blood. [TOX- + -EMIA.] —**tox·e′mic** *adj.*

tox·ic (tŏk′sĭk) *adj.* **1.** Of the nature of poison; poisonous; deadly: *toxic fumes.* **2.** Of or caused by a poison or toxin. [Late Latin *toxicus,* from Latin *toxicum,* poison for arrows, from Greek *toxikon,* from *toxon,* a bow.]

tox·ic·i·ty (tŏk-sĭs′ĭ-tē) *n.* The quality, property, or degree of being toxic or poisonous.

tox·i·col·o·gy (tŏk′sĭ-kŏl′ə-jē) *n.* The scientific study of the nature, effects, detection, and antidotes of poisons and the medical treatment of poisoning. —**tox′i·co·log′i·cal** (-kə-lŏj′ĭ-kəl) *adj.* —**tox′i·co·log′i·cal·ly** *adv.* —**tox′i·col′o·gist** *n.*

tox·in (tŏk′sĭn) *n.* A poisonous substance produced by a plant, animal, or microorganism, that has a protein structure and is capable of causing poisoning when introduced into the body but is also capable of stimulating production of an antitoxin. [TOX- + -IN.]

tox·in-an·ti·tox·in (tŏk′sĭn-ăn′tĭ-tŏk′sĭn) *n.* A mixture of a toxin and its antitoxin, formerly used to immunize against various contagious diseases, esp. diphtheria.

tox·oid (tŏk′soid′) *n.* A toxin that has lost toxicity but has

---

ă pat	ā pay	â care	ä father	ĕ pet	ē be	hw which
ŏŏ took	ōō boot	ou out	th thin	th this	ŭ cut	

ĭ pit   ī tie   î pier   ŏ pot   ō toe   ô paw, for   oi noise
û urge   zh vision   ə about, item, edible, gallop, circus

retained the capacity to stimulate the production of or combine with antitoxins, used in immunization.

toy (toi) *n.* **1.** An object for children to play with. **2.** Something of little importance or value; a trinket or trifle. **3.** A breed or variety of dog that is very small. *—intr.v.* To amuse oneself idly; trifle: *toyed with plans for a world cruise.* *—modifier: toy soldiers; a toy store; a toy poodle.* [Middle English *toye,* dallying, amorous sport.]

trace¹ (trās) *n.* **1.** A visible mark or sign of the former presence or passage of some person, thing, or event. **2.** A barely perceivable indication of something; a touch. **3. a.** An extremely small amount. **b.** Something, such as an element or chemical compound, that is present in a substance or mixture in very small amounts. **4.** A line drawn on a graph to represent a continuous set of values of a variable. **5.** A path or trail through a wilderness that has been beaten out by the passage of animals or people. *—v.* **traced, trac·ing.** *—tr.v.* **1.** To follow the course or trail of. **2.** To ascertain the successive stages in the development or progress of. **3.** To locate or discover, as a cause. **4.** To delineate or sketch (a figure). **5.** To imprint (a design) on something. **6.** To form (letters) with special care. **7.** To make a trace that represents a variable, as on a graph. **8.** To make a design or series of markings on (a surface). *—intr.v.* **1.** To have origins; be traceable: *His lineage traces back to William the Conqueror.* **2.** To make one's way; follow a trail, line of development, etc.: *traced through volumes of material before finding the answer.* [Middle English, path, course, from Old French, from *tracier,* to make one's way, from Latin *tractus,* a dragging.] *—trace'a·bil'i·ty* or *trace'a·ble·ness* *n.* *—trace'a·ble* *adj.* *—trace'a·bly* *adv.*

trace² (trās) *n.* One of two side straps or chains connecting a harnessed draft animal to a vehicle. [Middle English *trais,* a pair of traces, from Old French, pl. of *trait,* a pulling, a strap, from Latin *tractus,* a dragging.]

trace element. A chemical substance found in minute amounts in plants and animals, considered essential for their physical well-being.

trac·er (trā'sər) *n.* **1.** Any readily identifiable substance, such as a dye or radioactive isotope, that can be followed through the course of a mechanical, chemical, or biological process, providing information about details of the process and the distribution of the substances involved in it. **2.** A person employed to locate missing persons or goods. **3.** A search instituted to locate missing persons or goods. **4.** A bullet that leaves a luminous or smoky trail.

trac·er·y (trā'sə·rē) *n., pl.* **-ies.** Ornamental work of interlaced and branching lines. [From TRACE (to sketch).]

tracery   tractor

trache-. Var. of **tracheo-.**

tra·che·a (trā'kē-ə) *n., pl.* **-che·ae** (-kē-ē') or **-as.** **1.** *Anat.* A thin-walled tube of cartilaginous and membranous tissue descending from the larynx to the bronchi and carrying air to the lungs. Also called **windpipe.** **2.** *Zool.* One of the internal respiratory tubes of insects and some other terrestrial arthropods. [Middle English *trache,* from Medieval Latin *trāchēa,* from Late Latin *trāchīa,* from Greek (*artēria*) *trakheia,* "rough (artery)," from *trakhus,* rough.] *—tra'che·al* *adj.*

tracheo- or **trache-.** A prefix meaning trachea: **tracheotomy.** [From Medieval Latin *trāchēa,* trachea.]

tra·che·ot·o·my (trā'kē-ŏt'ə-mē) *n., pl.* **-mies.** A surgical procedure in which a small cut is made into the trachea at the base of the throat and a hollow tube inserted in order to faciliate breathing.

tra·cho·ma (trə-kō'mə) *n.* A contagious viral disease of the conjunctiva of the eye characterized by inflammation, hypertrophy, and granules of adenoid tissue. [From Greek *trakhōma,* from *trakhus,* rough.] *—tra·cho'ma·tous* *adj.*

trac·ing (trā'sĭng) *n.* **1.** The act of someone or something that traces. **2.** Something produced by tracing: *a crystal goblet with beautiful tracing.* **3.** A reproduction made by superimposing a transparent sheet and tracing the original upon it. **4.** A graphic record made by a recording instrument, such as a cardiograph, seismograph, etc.

track (trăk) *n.* **1. a.** A mark or trail of marks left behind as evidence that a person, animal, or thing has passed; a trace. **b.** A path or trail marked out or made by the passage of men, animals, or machines: *an old wagon track through the mountains.* **2.** A course or route over or along which something travels or may travel: *a bicycle track in the park.* **3.** A course of action; way of proceeding: *on the right track.* **4.** *Sports.* **a.** A road or course, as of cinder or dirt, laid out for running or racing. **b.** Athletic competition on such a course; track events. **c. Track and field. 5.** A rail or set of parallel rails upon which a train or trolley runs. *—tr.v.* **1.** To follow the footprints or trail of. **2.** To move over or along; traverse: *skiers tracking the face of the mountain.* **3.** To carry on the shoes and deposit as footprints: *track dirt into the house.* **4.** To observe or monitor the course of. *—intr.v.* **1.** To keep a constant distance apart, as the wheels of a vehicle. **2.** To be in alignment, as the front and rear wheels of a vehicle. **3.** To follow a track. *—phrasal verb.* **track down.** To locate by trailing or searching diligently. *—idioms.* **keep track of.** To remain informed about or keep a record of. **lose track of.** To fail to keep up with or stay in touch with. **make tracks.** *Informal.* To move with great haste or speed. [Middle English *trak,* from Old French *trac.*] *—track'a·ble* *adj.* *—track'er* *n.*

track·age (trăk'ĭj) *n.* **1.** Railway tracks. **2. a.** The right of one railroad company to use the track system of another. **b.** The charge for this.

track and field. Athletic events performed on a running track and the field associated with it.

tracking station. A facility containing instruments for tracking an artificial satellite or spacecraft by radar and equipment for receiving radio signals from it.

track·less (trăk'lĭs) *adj.* **1.** Unmarked by trails or paths. **2.** Not running on tracks or rails.

track meet. An athletic competition of track and field events.

tract¹ (trăkt) *n.* **1.** An expanse of land. **2.** *Anat.* **a.** A system of organs and tissues that together perform one specialized function. **b.** A bundle of nerve fibers that have a common origin, termination, and function. [Latin *tractus,* from *trahere,* to draw.]

tract² (trăkt) *n.* A distributed paper or pamphlet containing a declaration or appeal, esp. one put out by a religious or political group. [Middle English *tracte,* from Latin *tractātus,* a discussion, treatise, from *tractāre,* to pull violently, discuss.]

trac·ta·ble (trăk'tə-bəl) *adj.* **1.** Easily managed or controlled; governable: *a tractable child.* **2.** Easily handled or worked; malleable: *tractable metals.* [Latin *tractābilis,* from *tractāre,* to pull violently, manage, freq. of *trahere,* to draw, pull.] *—trac'ta·bil'i·ty* or *trac'ta·ble·ness* *n.* *—trac'ta·bly* *adv.*

trac·tile (trăk'tĭl, -tīl') *adj.* Capable of being drawn out in length, as certain metals; ductile. [From Latin *tractus,* past part. of *trahere,* to pull.] *—trac·til'i·ty* *n.*

trac·tion (trăk'shən) *n.* **1.** The act or process of drawing or pulling, as a load over a surface. **2.** The condition of being drawn or pulled. **3.** The ability of a device, such as a railroad engine, to pull loads. **4.** The friction that prevents a wheel from slipping or skidding over the surface on which it runs. [Medieval Latin *tractiō,* from Latin *tractus,* past part. of *trahere,* to pull.] *—trac'tion·al* *adj.*

trac·tive (trăk'tĭv) *adj.* Serving to pull or draw.

trac·tor (trăk'tər) *n.* **1.** A small engine-powered vehicle equipped with large tires that have deep treads, and used for pulling farm machinery, as plows, harvesters, etc. **2.** A truck with a cab and no body, used for pulling trailers, vans, etc. [From Latin *tractus*, past part. of *trahere*, to pull.]

trade (trād) *n.* **1.** The business of buying and selling goods; commerce. **2.** An exchange of one thing for another, as by bartering. **3.** An occupation, esp. one requiring special skill with the hands; a craft: *the tailor's trade.* **4.** The people who work in a particular business or industry: *the building and construction trades.* **5.** Customers or patrons; clientele. —See Syns at **business.** —*modifier:* trade *routes; a trade center.* —*v.* **trad·ed, trad·ing.** —*intr.v.* **1.** To engage in buying and selling for profit: *He trades in diamonds and gold.* **2.** To make an exchange of one thing for another; barter. **3.** To shop or buy regularly at a given store. —*tr.v.* **1.** To exchange (one thing) for something else. **2.** To buy and sell (stock, commodities, etc.): *He traded his shares in that company.* **3.** To pass back and forth: *We traded anecdotes.* —*phrasal verbs.* **trade in.** To give (an old or used item) as partial payment on a new purchase. **trade on.** To use to the greatest possible advantage; exploit: *traded on his family name to win the election.* [Middle English, a course, way, track, from Middle Low German.]

trade-in (trād′ĭn′) *n.* **1.** A piece of used merchandise accepted as partial payment for a new purchase. **2.** A transaction involving such an item.

trade·mark (trād′märk′) *n.* A name, symbol, or other device identifying a product, legally restricted to the use of the owner or manufacturer. —*tr.v.* **1.** To label (a product) with a trademark. **2.** To register as a trademark.

trade name. 1. The name by which a commodity, service, process, etc., is known to the trade. **2.** The name under which a business firm operates.

trade·off or **trade-off** (trād′ôf′, -ŏf′) *n.* An exchange of one thing in return for another, esp. a giving up of something desirable for another regarded as more desirable.

trad·er (trā′dər) *n.* **1.** A person who trades; dealer. **2.** A ship employed in foreign trade.

trade school. A secondary school that offers instruction in skilled trades; vocational school.

trades·man (trādz′mən) *n.* **1.** A person engaged in the retail trade, esp. a shopkeeper. **2.** A skilled worker.

trade union. A labor union, esp. one limited in membership to people in the same trade, as distinguished from people in the same company or industry. —**trade unionism.** —**trade unionist.**

trade winds. An extremely regular and predictable system of winds blowing over most of the Torrid Zone, with a northeasterly course in the Northern Hemisphere and a southeasterly course in the Southern Hemisphere. [From the phrase *to blow trade*, "to blow in a regular course."]

trading post. A station or store in a sparsely settled area established by traders to barter supplies for local products.

trading stamp. A stamp given by a retailer to a buyer for a purchase of a specified amount and intended to be redeemed in quantity for merchandise.

tra·di·tion (trə-dĭsh′ən) *n.* **1.** The passing down of elements of a culture from generation to generation. **2.** A custom handed down. [Middle English *tradicion*, a handing down, a surrender, from Old French, from Latin *trāditiō*, from *trādere*, to hand over : *trāns-*, over + *dare*, to give.] —**tra·di·tion·al** (trə-dĭsh′ə-nəl) *adj.* —**tra·di·tion·al·ly** *adv.*

tra·di·tion·al·ism (trə-dĭsh′ən-əl-ĭz′əm) *n.* Adherence to traditional beliefs, ideas, or practices, esp. in religious matters. —**tra·di·tion·al·ist** *n. & adj.* —**tra·di·tion·al·is·tic** *adj.*

tra·duce (trə-dōōs′, -dyōōs′) *tr.v.* **-duced, -duc·ing.** To speak falsely or maliciously of; slander; defame. [Latin *trādūcere*, to expose to ridicule : *trāns-*, across + *dūcere*, to lead.] —**tra·duce′ment** *n.* —**tra·duc′er** *n.* —**tra·duc′i·ble** *adj.* —**tra·duc′ing·ly** *adv.*

traf·fic (trăf′ĭk) *n.* **1.** The movement of vehicles and people along roads and streets, of ships on the seas, aircraft in the sky, etc. **2.** The amount of such movement: *Vehicular traffic is heavy during rush hour.* **3.** The commercial exchange of goods; trade: *illegal traffic in drugs.* —See Syns at **business.** —*intr.v.* **-ficked, -fick·ing.** To carry on trade; have dealings: *traffic in spices.* [Old French *traffique*, from Old Italian *traffico*, from *trafficare*, to trade.] —**traf′fick·er** *n.*

traffic circle. A circular one-way road located at a point where several roads come together so that vehicles may pass from one to another without interruption of movement. Also called **rotary.**

traffic island. A raised area over which cars may not pass, placed esp. between opposing traffic lanes.

traffic light. A device that beams red, amber, or green lights, sometimes flashing, to control the flow of traffic along a street, highway, etc. Also called **traffic signal.**

trag·a·canth (trăg′ə-kănth′, trăj′-) *n.* **1.** Any of various thorny shrubs of the genus *Astragalus* that yields a gum used in pharmacy, adhesives, and textile printing. **2.** The gum of such a shrub. [Latin *tragacantha*, from Greek *tragakantha* : *tragos*, goat + *akantha*, thorn.]

tra·ge·di·an (trə-jē′dē-ən) *n.* **1.** A writer of tragedies. **2.** An actor of tragic roles. [Middle English *tragedien*, from Old French, from *tragedie*, tragedy.]

tra·ge·di·enne (trə-jē′dē-ĕn′) *n.* An actress of tragic roles. [French, from Old French, fem. of *tragedien*, tragedian.]

trag·e·dy (trăj′ə-dē) *n., pl.* **-dies. 1.** A dramatic or literary work that deals with a serious theme in which the main character or characters come to a ruinous end as a result of circumstance or esp. of some basic character flaw. **2.** The branch of drama including such plays. **3.** A disastrous event; a calamity. **4.** The tragic aspect or element of something. —See Syns at **disaster.** [Middle English *tragedie*, from Old French, from Latin *tragoedia*, from Greek *tragōidia* : *tragos*, goat + *ōidē*, song, from *aeidein*, to sing.]

trag·ic (trăj′ĭk) or **trag·i·cal** (trăj′ĭ-kəl) *adj.* **1.** Of or having the character of tragedy. **2.** Very sorrowful or sad; mournful: *a tragic tale.* **3.** Bringing or involving disaster or death; calamitous: *a tragic accident.* [French *tragique*, from Latin *tragicus*, from Greek *tragikos*, from *tragos*, goat.] —**trag′i·cal·ly** *adv.* —**trag′i·cal·ness** *n.*

trag·i·com·e·dy (trăj′ĭ-kŏm′ə-dē) *n., pl.* **-dies.** A dramatic or literary work in which elements of both tragedy and comedy are comingled. —**trag′i·com′ic** or **trag′i·com′i·cal** *adj.* —**trag′i·com′i·cal·ly** *adv.*

trail (trāl) *tr.v.* **1.** To drag or allow to drag or stream behind, as along the ground. **2.** To follow the traces or scent of, as in hunting; track. **3.** To lag or follow behind (a competitor or competitors). —*intr.v.* **1.** To be dragged along, brushing the ground: *The train of her gown trailed along behind her.* **2.** To extend or grow along the ground or over a surface, as a vine, plant, etc.: *ivy trailing over the walls of the cottages.* **3.** To drift in a tenuous stream, as smoke. **4.** To become gradually fainter: *Her voice trailed off.* **5.** To walk with dragging steps; to trudge. **6.** To fall behind in competition. —*n.* **1.** Something that streams, follows, or is drawn along behind. **2.** A mark, trace, or path left by a moving body. **3.** The scent of a person or animal: *The bloodhounds followed the man's trail.* **4.** A blazed path or beaten track. [Middle English *trailen*, prob. from Old North French *trailler*, to tow (a boat), from Latin *trāgula*, dragnet, from *trahere*, to pull.]

trail·blaz·er (trāl′blā′zər) *n.* **1.** Someone who marks out a path or route for others. **2.** A leader in any field; pioneer. —**trail′blaz′ing** *adj.*

trail·er (trā′lər) *n.* **1.** A large transport vehicle hauled by a truck or tractor. **2.** A large van that can be hauled by an automobile or truck, designed for use as a home, office, etc., when parked. **3.** Someone or something that trails.

trailer camp. A campsite for house trailers.

trailing arbutus. A low-growing plant, *Epigaea repens,* of eastern North America, with evergreen leaves and clusters of fragrant pink or white flowers. Also called **mayflower.**

trailing edge. The rearmost edge of an airfoil.

train (trān) *n.* **1.** A string of connected railroad cars drawn by a locomotive or powered by electricity. **2.** A long line of moving persons, animals, or vehicles. **3.** The part of a gown that trails behind the wearer. **4.** A staff of followers; a retinue: *persons in the king's train.* **5.** An orderly succession or series, as of events, thoughts, etc. **6.** A set or series of linked mechanical parts: *a train of gears.* —*tr.v.* **1.** To coach or accustom to some mode of behavior or performance: *training a child to be polite.* **2. a.** To instruct (a person) systematically in some art, profession, etc. **b.** To instruct (an animal) to perform in a specified way. **3.** To make fit for an athletic performance. **4.** To cause (a plant or one's hair) to take a desired course or shape. —*intr.v.* To undergo a course of training: *constantly training to stay in peak form.* —See Syns at **teach.** [Middle English *trayne,* from Old French *train,* from *trahiner,* to drag, from Latin *trahere.*] —**train'a·ble** *adj.*

train·ee (trā-nē') *n.* A person who is being trained.

train·er (trā'nər) *n.* A person who trains, esp. one who coaches athletes, racehorses, or show animals.

train·ing (trā'nĭng) *n.* The act, process, or routine of training or being trained; instruction.

train·load (trān'lōd') *n.* The full capacity of a freight or passenger train.

train·man (trān'mən) *n.* A member of the operating crew on a railroad train.

traipse (trāps) *intr.v.* **traipsed, traips·ing.** *Informal.* To walk about idly. [Orig. unknown.]

trait (trāt) *n.* A distinctive feature or characteristic, as of personality, physiognomy, etc. [French, from Old French, pencil mark, stroke, from Latin *tractus,* a pulling, from *trahere,* to pull.]

trai·tor (trā'tər) *n.* A person who betrays his country, a cause, or a trust, esp. one who has committed treason. [Middle English *traitour,* from Old French, from Latin *trāditor,* from *trādere,* to hand over, betray.]

trai·tor·ous (trā'tər-əs) *adj.* **1.** Of or like a traitor; disloyal; treacherous: *a traitorous remark.* **2.** Constituting treason: *a traitorous act.* —See Syns at **faithless.** —**trai'tor·ous·ly** *adv.* —**trai'tor·ous·ness** *n.*

tra·jec·to·ry (trə-jĕk'tə-rē) *n., pl.* **-ries.** The path of a moving particle or body, esp. the flight path of a missile or other projectile. [Medieval Latin *trājectōrius,* from Latin *trājectus,* a passage, from *trājicere,* to throw across : *trans-,* across + *jacere,* to throw.]

tram¹ (trăm) *n.* **1.** *Brit.* A streetcar. **2.** An open wagon or car run on tracks in a coal mine. [Perh. from dial. *tram,* shaft of a cart or wheelbarrow.]

tram·car (trăm'kär') *n.* **1.** *Brit.* A streetcar. **2.** A coal car.

tram·mel (trăm'əl) Also **tram·el** or **tram·ell.** —*n.* **1.** Often **trammels.** Something that restricts activity or free movement; a hindrance. **2.** A shackle used to teach a horse to amble. **3.** A vertically set fishing net of three layers. **4.** An arrangement of links and a hook in a fireplace for raising or lowering a pot or kettle. —*tr.v.* **-meled** or **-melled, -meling** or **-mel·ling. 1.** To hinder; hamper. **2.** To catch or entrap in or as in a net. [Middle English *tramale, trammel* net, from Old French *tramail,* from Late Latin *tremaculum* : *trēs,* three + *macula,* mesh, spot.] —**tram'mel·er** *n.*

tramp (trămp) *intr.v.* **1. a.** To walk with a firm, heavy step; trudge. **b.** To step or tread on heavily: *tramping on someone's toes.* **2.** To go or travel on foot; hike. **3.** To wander about aimlessly, as a tramp. —*tr.v.* **1.** To traverse on foot. **2.** To tread down; trample underfoot: *children tramping the flowers.* —*n.* **1.** The sound of heavy walking or marching. **2.** A walking trip; a hike. **3.** A person who travels aimlessly about on foot; a vagrant. **4.** A cargo vessel that has no regular schedule but takes on freight wherever it may be found. **5.** A metal plate attached to the sole of a shoe. [Middle English *trampen,* prob. of Low German orig.] —**tramp'er** *n.*

tram·ple (trăm'pəl) *v.* **-pled, -pling.** —*tr.v.* **1.** To beat down with the feet so as to crush, bruise, or destroy. **2.** To treat harshly or ruthlessly, as if tramping upon. —*intr.v.* To tread heavily, roughly, or destructively. —*n.* The act or sound of trampling. [Middle English *trampelen,* freq. of *trampen,* to tramp.] —**tram'pler** *n.*

tram·po·line (trăm'pə-lēn') *n.* A sheet of strong, taut canvas attached with springs to a metal frame and used for acrobatic tumbling. [Spanish *trampolin,* springboard, from Italian *trampolino,* from *trampoli,* stilts.] —**tram'po·lin'ist** *n.*

trance (trăns) *n.* **1.** A condition of semiconsciousness in which voluntary physical action may be suspended, usu. induced by drugs, hypnotism, catalepsy, etc. **2.** A condition of complete mental detachment from physical surroundings, as in daydreaming or deep thought. **3.** A dazed condition, as between sleeping and waking; stupor. [Middle English *traunce,* from Old French *transe,* from *transir,* to die, depart, from Latin *transīre,* to go across.]

tran·quil (trăn'kwəl) *adj.* **-quil·er** or **-quil·ler, -quil·est** or **-quil·lest. 1.** Free from agitation, anxiety, or commotion: calm; serene. **2.** Steady; even: *a tranquil temperament.* —See Syns at **calm.** [Latin *tranquillus.*] —**tran'quil·ly** *adv.* —**tran'quil·ness** *n.*

tran·quil·ize (trăn'kwə-līz') *v.* **-ized, -iz·ing.** Also *Brit.* **tran·quil·lize, -lized, -liz·ing.** —*tr.v.* To make tranquil; quiet. —*intr.v.* To become tranquil. —**tran'quil·i·za'tion** *n.*

tran·quil·iz·er (trăn'kwə-līz'ər) *n.* **1.** Any of various drugs that are used to relieve or relax tension, anxiety, etc.; relaxant. **2.** Something that has a calming or relaxing effect.

tran·quil·li·ty or **tran·quil·i·ty** (trăn-kwĭl'ə-tē) *n.* The quality or condition of being tranquil; serenity.

> *Syns:* **tranquillity, calm, placidity, quiet** *n.* Core meaning: Absence of motion or disturbance *(the tranquillity of the moonlit lake).*

trans-. A prefix meaning: **1.** Across or beyond: **transatlantic. 2.** Transferring: **translocate. 3.** Changing: **transliterate.** [From Latin *trāns,* across, over, beyond, through.]

trans·act (trăn-săkt', -zăkt') *tr.v.* To carry out or conduct (business or affairs). [Latin *transactus,* past part. of *transigere,* to complete : *trans-,* through + *agere,* to do.] —**trans·ac'tor** (trăn-săk'tər, -zăk'tər) *n.*

trans·ac·tion (trăn-săk'shən, -zăk'shən) *n.* **1.** The act or process of transacting. **2.** Something transacted; a business deal or operation. —**trans·ac'tion·al** *adj.*

trans·at·lan·tic (trăns'ət-lăn'tĭk, trănz'ət-) *adj.* **1.** On the other side of the Atlantic: *transatlantic military bases.* **2.** Spanning or crossing the Atlantic: *a transatlantic flight.*

trans·ceiv·er (trăn-sē'vər) *n.* A module consisting of a radio receiver and transmitter. [TRANS(MITTER) + (RE)CEIVER.]

tran·scend (trăn-sĕnd') —*tr.v.* **1. a.** To pass beyond or rise above: *generosity that transcends moral duty.* **2.** To overshadow or outdo; surpass; exceed: *a scientific achievement that transcends all others in the field.* **3.** *Theol.* To exist above and independent of (material experience or the universe). —*intr.v.* To be superior; surpass. —See Syns at **surpass.** [Middle English *transcenden,* from Old French *transcendre,* from Latin *transcendere* : *trāns-,* over + *scandere,* to climb.]

tran·scen·dent (trăn-sĕn'dənt) *adj.* **1.** Surpassing others of the same kind; pre-eminent. **2.** Beyond the usual or ordinary limits of experience or nature. **3.** *Theol.* Above and independent of the material universe. —**tran·scen'dence** or **tran·scen'den·cy,** *n.* —**tran·scen'dent·ly** *adv.*

tran·scen·den·tal (trăn'sĕn-dĕnt'l) *adj.* **1.** Not able to be discovered or understood by practical experience; going beyond human knowledge. **2.** Rising above common thought or ideas; exalted; mystical. **3.** Of a philosophy or philosophers that deal with matters outside the world of ordinary experience. —**tran'scen·den'tal·ly** *adv.*

transcendental number. An irrational number that cannot occur as a root or solution of any algebraic equation whose coefficients are all rational numbers.

tran·scen·den·tal·ism (trăn'sən-dĕnt'l-ĭz'əm) *n.* **1.** *Philos.* **a.** The belief that knowledge of reality is derived from intuitive sources rather than from objective experience. **b.** Any doctrine based on this belief, as the philosophy of Kant. **2.** A 19th cent. American intellectual movement, led by Emerson and Thoreau, that asserted that God was manifested in nature and valued the moral and transcendental above the material and empirical. **3.** The quality or condition of being transcendental. —**tran'scen·den'tal·ist** *n.*

trans·con·ti·nen·tal (trăns'kŏn'tə-nĕn'təl, trănz'-) *adj.* Spanning or crossing a continent.

tran·scribe (trăn-skrīb') *tr.v.* **-scribed, -scrib·ing. 1. a.** To write or type a copy of. **b.** To write out fully, as from shorthand notes. **2.** To transfer (information) from one recording and storing system to another. **3.** To adapt or arrange (a musical composition) for a voice or instrument other than the original. **4.** To record for broadcasting at a later date. **5.** To represent (speech sounds) by phonetic symbols. [Latin *transcrībere,* to copy : *trāns-,* across + *scrībere,* to write.] —**tran·scrib'a·ble** *adj.* —**tran·scrib'er** *n.*

tran·script (trăn'skrĭpt') *n.* **1.** Something transcribed; a written or printed copy: *a transcript of a trial.* **2.** An official report of a student's record at school. [Middle English, from Old French *transcrit,* from Latin *transcriptum,* past part. of *transcrībere,* to transcribe.]

tran·scrip·tion (trăn-skrĭp'shən) *n.* **1.** The act or process of transcribing. **2.** Something that has been transcribed; a transcript. **3.** An adaptation of a musical composition. **4.** A recorded radio or television program. **—tran·scrip'tion·al** *adj.* **—tran·scrip'tion·al·ly** *adv.*

trans·duc·er (trăns-dōō'sər, -dyōō'sər, trănz-) *n.* A device that converts input energy of one form into output energy of another. [Latin *transdūcere,* to transfer : *trāns-,* across + *dūcere,* to lead.]

tran·sept (trăn'sĕpt') *n. Archit.* Either of the two lateral arms of a church built in the shape of a cross. [TRANS- + SEPTUM (partition).]

trans·fer (trăns-fûr', trăns'fər) *v.* **-ferred, -fer·ring.** *—tr.v.* **1.** To move or shift from one place, person, or thing to another. **2.** To move or change from one carrier or means of transportation to another. **3.** To move from one job, school, or location to another. **4.** To move (a pattern, design, or set of markings or measurements) from one surface to another. **5.** *Law.* To convey legal ownership of (property) to another. *—intr.v.* **1.** To move, as from one location, job, or school to another. **2.** To change from one carrier or means of transportation to another. *—n.* (trăns'-fər). **1.** Also **transferal.** An act or example of transferring or being transferred. **2.** Also **transferal.** Someone or something that transfers or is transferred, esp. a student who changes schools or a design that is moved from one surface and applied to another. **3. a.** A ticket entitling a passenger to change from one bus, train, etc., to another without paying any or all of the extra fare. **b.** A place where someone or something changes from one carrier or means of transportation to another. **4.** Also **transferal.** *Law.* The conveyance of legal ownership of property from one person to another. [Middle English *transferren,* from Old French *transferer,* from Latin *trānsferre : trāns-,* across + *ferre,* to carry.] **—trans·fer'a·bil'i·ty** *n.* **—trans·fer'a·ble** *adj.* **—trans·fer'er** *n.*

trans·fer·al (trăns-fûr'əl) *n.* Also **transferral.** **1.** A transfer. **2.** *Psychoanal.* Transference.

trans·fer·ee (trăns'fər-ē') *n.* **1.** *Law.* A person to whom a transfer of ownership is made. **2.** Someone who is transferred.

trans·fer·ence (trăns-fûr'əns, trăns'fər-əns) *n.* **1. a.** An act or process of transferring. **b.** The condition of being transferred. **2.** Also **transferal.** *Psychoanal.* The process by which a person's feelings, wishes, thoughts, etc., are attached to a new person. **—trans'fer·en'tial** (trăns'fə-rĕn'-shəl) *adj.*

trans·fer·or (trăns-fûr'ər) *n. Law.* A person who makes a transfer of ownership.

trans·fer·ral (trăns-fûr'əl) *n.* Var. of **transferal.**

trans·fig·u·ra·tion (trăns-fĭg-yə-rā'shən) *n.* **1.** A radical transformation of shape or appearance; metamorphosis. **2. Transfiguration. a.** The sudden emanation of radiance from Jesus' person that occurred on the mountain. **b.** The Christian commemoration of this, observed on August 6.

trans·fig·ure (trăns-fĭg'yər) *tr.v.* **-ured, -ur·ing.** **1.** To change the appearance or shape of. **2.** To change so as to glorify; exalt: *The religious ceremony transfigured the participants who shared its mystery and beauty.* [Middle English, from Latin *trānsfigūrāre : trāns-,* change + *figūra,* figure.] **—trans·fig'ure·ment** *n.*

trans·fix (trăns-fĭks') *tr.v.* **1.** To pierce through with or as if with a pointed weapon; impale. **2.** To render motionless, as with terror, amazement, or awe. [Latin *trānsfīxus,* past part. of *transfīgere : trāns-,* through + *fīgere,* to pierce.] **—trans·fix'ion** (-fĭk'shən) *adj.*

trans·form (trăns-fôrm') *tr.v.* **1.** To change markedly in form or appearance. **2.** To change the nature, function, or condition of; convert. **3.** To perform a mathematical transformation on. **4.** To subject (electricity) to the action of a transformer. **5.** To change (energy) from one form to another. **—trans·form'a·ble** *adj.*

trans·for·ma·tion (trăns'fər-mā'shən) *n.* **1.** The act of transforming or the condition of being transformed. **2.** An example of being transformed. **3. a.** The conversion of an algebraic expression to another expression of a different form. **b.** The replacement of the variables in an algebraic

expression or equation by their values in terms of another set of variables. **—trans·for'ma·tive** (-fôr'mə-tĭv) *adj.*

trans·form·er (trăns-fôr'mər) *n.* **1.** Someone or something that transforms. **2.** A device used to transfer electric energy from one circuit to another.

trans·fuse (trăns-fyōōz') *tr.v.* **-fused, -fus·ing.** **1.** To transfer (liquid) by pouring from one vessel into another. **2.** To permeate; instill. **3.** *Med.* To administer a transfusion of or to. [Middle English *transfusen,* from Latin *trānsfūsus,* past part. of *transfundere : trāns-,* from one place to another + *fundere,* to pour.] **—trans·fus'er** *n.* **—trans·fus'i·ble** *adj.* **—trans·fu'sive** (-fyōō'sĭv, -zĭv) *adj.*

trans·fu·sion (trăns-fyōō'zhən) *n.* **1.** The act or process of transfusing. **2.** *Med.* The direct injection of whole blood, plasma, saline solution, etc., into the bloodstream.

trans·gress (trăns-grĕs', trănz-) *tr.v.* **1.** To go beyond or over (a limit or boundary): *behavior that transgressed court decorum.* **2.** To act in violation of, as a law, commandment, etc.; break: *transgressed the law of man and God alike.* *—intr.v.* To break a law, commandment, moral precept, etc., sin. [Latin *trānsgressus,* past part. of *transgredī : trāns-,* across + *gradī,* to step.] **—trans·gress'i·ble** *adj.* **—trans·gres'sive** *adj.* **—trans·gres'sive·ly** *adv.* **—trans·gres'sor** *n.*

trans·gres·sion (trăns-grĕsh'ən, trănz-) *n.* The act of transgressing; the violation of a law, rule, command.

tran·ship. (trăn-shĭp') *v.* Var. of **transship.**

tran·sient (trăn'shənt, -zhənt, -zē-ənt) *adj.* **1.** Passing away with time; transitory; fleeting: *transient happiness.* **2.** Passing through from one place to another; stopping only briefly: *transient workers.* **—See Syns at transitory.** *—n.* Someone or something that is transient, esp. a person making a brief stay at a hotel. [Latin *transiēns,* pres. part. of *transīre,* to go over : *trāns-,* across + *īre,* to go.] **—tran'sient·ly** *adv.* **—tran'sient·ness** *n.*

tran·sis·tor (trăn-zĭs'tər, trăn-sĭs'-) *n.* **1.** A three-terminal semiconductor device used for amplification, switching, etc. **2.** A radio equipped with transistors. [From a trademark.]

tran·sis·tor·ize (trăn-zĭs'tə-rīz', trăn-sĭs'-) *tr.v.* **-ized, -iz·ing.** To equip (an electronic circuit or device) with transistors.

tran·sit (trăn'sĭt, -zĭt) *n.* **1.** The act of passing over, across, or through; passage. **2.** The conveyance of persons, goods, etc., from one place to another: *apples spoiled in transit.* **3.** The transportation of people, esp. on a local public transportation system: *mass transit.* **4.** *Astron.* **a.** The passage of a celestial body across the observer's meridian. **b.** The passage of a smaller celestial body across the disk of a larger celestial body. **5.** A surveying instrument consisting of a telescope provided with scales for measuring horizontal and vertical angles of objects sighted through it, together with means for setting the entire instrument level. *—tr.v.* **1.** To pass over, across, or through. **2.** *Astron.* To cross (a celestial body, meridian, etc.). **3.** To revolve (the telescope of a surveying transit) about its horizontal transverse axis in order to reverse its direction. *—intr.v. Astron.* To make a transit. [Latin *transitus,* from *transīre,* to go across.]

transit

tran·si·tion (trăn-zĭsh'ən, -sĭsh'ən) *n.* **1.** The process or an example of changing from one form, state, subject, or place to another. **2.** *Mus.* **a.** A change of key, esp. a brief one; modulation. **b.** A short passage connecting two major themes or sections of a musical composition. **—tran·si'-**

tion·al *adj.* —**tran·si'tion·al·ly** *adv.*

tran·si·tive (trăn'sə-tĭv, trăn'zə-) *adj.* Being or using a verb that requires a direct object to complete its meaning. —*n.* A transitive verb. —**tran'si·tive·ly** *adv.* —**tran'si·tive·ness** or **tran'si·tiv'i·ty** *n.*

tran·si·to·ry (trăn'sə-tôr'ē, -tōr'ē, trăn'zə-) *adj.* Existing only briefly. —**tran'si·to'ri·ly** *adv.* —**tran'si·to'ri·ness** *n.*
  Syns: transitory, momentary, passing, short-lived, temporary, transient *adj.* Core meaning: Lasting or existing only for a short time (*the transitory Arctic summer; enjoyed only transitory fame*).

trans·late (trăns-lāt', trănz-, trăns'lāt', trănz'-) *v.* **-lat·ed, -lat·ing.** —*tr.v.* **1.** To express in another language, while retaining the original sense. **2.** To clarify or explain in terms that can be readily understood; interpret: *translating legal jargon for laymen.* **3.** To charge or carry forward from one form to another; convert: *translate ideas into reality.* **4.** *Physics.* To subject (a body) to translation. —*intr.v.* **1. a.** To make a translation. **b.** To work as a translator. **2.** To be capable of translation: *His novels translate well.* [Middle English *translaten,* to transport, to translate, from Latin *trānslātus* past part. of *trānsferre* : *trāns-,* across + *ferre,* to carry.] —**trans·lat'a·bil'i·ty** *n.* —**trans·lat'a·ble** *adj.*

trans·la·tion (trăns-lā'shən, trănz-) *n.* **1. a.** The act or process of translating. **b.** The condition of being translated. **2.** A version of a text in a different language. **3.** Rendition of something into another form; transformation: *the translation of theory into fact.* **4.** *Physics.* Motion of a body in which each of its points moves parallel to, and the same distance as, every other point; motion in a straight line without rotation. —**trans·la'tion·al** *adj.* —**trans·la·tor** *n.*

trans·lit·er·ate (trăns-lĭt'ə-rāt', trănz-) *tr.v.* **-at·ed, -at·ing.** To represent (letters or words) in the corresponding characters of another alphabet. [TRANS- + Latin *littera,* letter + -ATE.] —**trans·lit'er·a'tion** *n.*

trans·lo·cate (trăns'lō-kāt', trănz'-) *tr.v.* **-cat·ed, -cat·ing.** To cause to change from one position to another; displace.

trans·lo·ca·tion (trăns'lō-kā'shən, trănz'-) *n.* **1.** A change in location. **2.** *Genetics.* A chromosomal aberration in which different nonhomologous genes are interchanged.

trans·lu·cent (trăns-lōō'sənt, trănz-) *adj.* Transmitting light but diffusing it sufficiently to cause images to become blurred or indistinct. [Latin *trānslūcēns,* pres. part. of *trānslūcēre,* to shine through : *trāns-,* through + *lūcēre,* to shine.] —**trans·lu'cence** or **trans·lu'cen·cy** *n.* —**trans·lu'cent·ly** *adv.*

trans·mi·grate (trăns-mī'grāt', trănz-) *intr.v.* **-grat·ed, -grat·ing.** **1.** To migrate. **2.** To pass into another body after death, as the soul. —**trans·mi'gra'tor** (-grā'tər) *n.* —**trans·mi'gra·to'ry** (-mī'grə-tôr'ē, -tōr'ē) *adj.*

trans·mi·gra·tion (trăns'mī-grā'shən, trănz'-) *n.* **1.** The act or process of transmigrating. **2.** The passing of a soul at death into another body. —**trans'mi·gra'tion·ism** *n.*

trans·mis·si·ble (trăns-mĭs'ə-bəl, trănz-) *adj.* Capable of being transmitted. —**trans'mis·si·bil'i·ty** *n.*

trans·mis·sion (trăns-mĭsh'ən, trănz-) *n.* **1.** The act or process of transmitting. **2.** The sending of a modulated carrier wave, as in radio, television, telegraphy, etc. **3.** Something transmitted, as by radio, television, etc. **4.** An assembly of gears and associated parts by which power is carried from an engine or motor to a load, as in an automobile, machine tool, etc. [Latin *trānsmissiō,* from *trānsmissus,* past part. of *trānsmittere,* to transmit.] —**trans·mis'sive** (-mĭs'ĭv) *adj.*

trans·mit (trăns-mĭt', trănz-) *v.* **-mit·ted, -mit·ting.** —*tr.v.* **1.** To send from one person, place, or thing to another; convey: *transmit a message.* **2.** To spread or communicate (disease, infection, contagion, etc.) to others; pass. **3.** To pass on or impart (a trait or traits) by biological inheritance. **4.** *Electronics.* To send (an electrical or electromagnetic wave signal), as by wire or radio. **5.** *Physics.* To cause or allow (energy or a disturbance) to travel or spread, as through a medium: *Glass transmits light.* **6.** To carry (power, force, or energy) from one part of a mechanism to another. —*intr.v.* To send out a signal. —See Syns at **send.** [Middle English *transmitten,* from Latin *trānsmittere* : *trāns-,* across + *mittere,* to send.] —**trans·mit'ta·ble** or **trans·mit'ti·ble** *adj.*

trans·mit·tal (trăns-mĭt'l, trănz-) *n.* The act or process of transmitting; a transmission.

trans·mit·ter (trăns-mĭt'ər, trănz-) *n.* **1.** Someone or something that transmits. **2.** A switching device that opens and closes a telegraph circuit; a telegraphic sending device. **3.** The part of a telephone that changes sounds into electrical impulses that are sent over wires to a receiver located elsewhere. **4.** A device capable of generating a radio signal, modulating it with information (as a voice or music signal), and radiating it by means of an antenna.

trans·mog·ri·fy (trăns-mŏg'rə-fī', trănz-) *tr.v.* **-fied, -fy·ing.** To change into a different shape or form, esp. one that is fantastic or bizarre. [Orig. unknown.] —**trans·mog'ri·fi·ca'tion** *n.*

trans·mu·ta·tion (trăns'myōō-tā'shən, trănz'-) *n.* **1. a.** The act or process of transmuting. **b.** An example of transmuting or being transmuted. **2.** *Physics.* The transformation of one element into another by one or a series of nuclear reactions. **3.** In alchemy, the attempted conversion of base metals into gold or silver. —**trans'mu·ta'tion·al** *adj.*

trans·mute (trăns-myōōt', trănz-) *tr.v.* **-mut·ed, -mut·ing.** **1.** To change from one form, nature, condition, etc., into another; transform. **2.** To subject (an element) to transmutation. [Middle English *transmuten,* from Latin *trānsmūtāre* : *trāns-,* from one to another + *mūtāre,* to change.] —**trans·mut'a·bil'i·ty** *n.* —**trans·mut'a·ble** *adj.* —**trans·mut'a·bly** *adv.*

trans·na·tion·al (trăns-nă'shə-nəl) *adj.* Cutting across or going beyond national boarders or interests.

trans·o·ce·an·ic (trăns'ō-shē-ăn'ĭk, trănz'-) *adj.* **1.** Situated beyond or on the other side of the ocean. **2.** Spanning or crossing the ocean: *a transoceanic flight.*

tran·som (trăn'səm) *n.* **1.** A small hinged window above a door or another window. **2. a.** The horizontal crosspiece to which such a window is hinged. **b.** A horizontal dividing piece in a window. [Middle English *traunson,* crossbeam, lintel, perh. from Latin *trānstrum,* from *trāns,* across.] —**tran'somed** *adj.*

tran·son·ic (trăn-sŏn'ĭk) *adj.* Of flight or airflow conditions at speeds close to the speed of sound. [TRANS- + (SUPER)SONIC.]

trans·pa·cif·ic (trăns'pə-sĭf'ĭk) *adj.* **1.** Crossing the Pacific Ocean. **2.** Situated across or beyond the Pacific Ocean.

trans·par·en·cy (trăns-pâr'ən-sē, -păr'ən-sē) *n., pl.* **-cies.** **1.** Also **trans·par·ence.** The condition or property of being transparent. **2.** A transparent object, esp. a photographic slide.

trans·par·ent (trăns-pâr'ənt, -păr'ənt) *adj.* **1.** Capable of transmitting light so that objects or images can be seen as if there were nothing between the viewer and the thing being viewed. **2.** Allowing electromagnetic radiation of a specified frequency, as x-rays or radio waves, to pass with little or no interference. **3.** Of such fine or open texture that objects on the other side can be seen easily; sheer: *a transparent fabric.* **4.** Easily understood or detected; obvious: *transparent motives.* **5.** Guileless; candid; open. [Middle English, from Old French, from Medieval Latin *trānspārēns,* pres. part. of *trānspārēre,* to appear through : Latin *trāns-,* through + *pārēre,* to show.] —**trans·par'ent·ly** *adv.* —**trans·par'ent·ness** *n.*

tran·spire (trăn-spīr') *v.* **-spired, -spir·ing.** —*tr.v.* To give off (vapor containing waste products) through the pores of the skin or the stomata of plant tissue. —*intr.v.* **1.** To give off vapor containing waste products through animal or plant pores. **2.** To become known; come to light. **3.** To happen; occur. [French *transpirer,* from Old French : Latin *trāns-,* out + *spīrāre,* to breathe.] —**tran'spi·ra'tion** (trăn'spə-rā'shən) *n.*

trans·plant (trăns-plănt', -plänt') *tr.v.* **1.** To remove (a living plant) from the place where it is growing and plant it in another place. **2.** To transfer (tissue or an organ) from one body or body part to another. **3.** To transfer to and establish in a new place. —*intr.v.* To withstand transplantation. —*n.* (trăns'plănt', -plänt'). **1.** Something transplanted. **2.** The act or process of transplanting. **3.** *Med.* **a.** An organ or piece of tissue transplanted by surgery. **b.** The surgical method or operation of transplanting tissue or an organ. —**trans'plan·ta'tion** *n.* —**trans·plant'er** *n.*

trans·po·lar (trăns-pō'lər) *adj.* Extending across or passing

---

over either of the geographic polar regions.

trans·port (trăns-pôrt′, -pōrt′) *tr.v.* **1.** To carry from one place to another. **2.** To move to strong emotion; enrapture: *transported with joy.* **3.** To send abroad to a penal colony. —*n.* (trăns′pôrt, -pōrt). **1.** The act or process of transporting; conveyance. **2.** *Mil.* A ship used to transport troops or equipment. **3.** A vehicle, as an aircraft, used to transport passengers or freight. **4.** The condition of being carried away by emotion; rapture: *a transport of rage.* [Middle English *transporten,* from Old French *transporter,* from Latin *trānsportāre* : *trāns-,* from one place to another + *portāre,* to carry.] —**trans·port′a·bil′i·ty** *n.* —**trans·port′a·ble** *adj.* —**trans·port′er** *n.*

trans·por·ta·tion (trăns′pər-tā′shən) *n.* **1.** The act or process of transporting. **2.** A means of transport; a conveyance. **3.** The business of transporting passengers, goods, etc. **4.** A charge for transporting; a fare.

trans·pose (trăns-pōz′) *v.* **-posed, -pos·ing.** —*tr.v.* **1.** To reverse or change the order or placement of. **2.** *Math.* To move (an algebraic term) from one side of an equation to the other side, by adding or subtracting that term to or from both sides. **3.** *Mus.* To write or perform (a composition) in a key other than that in which it is written. —*intr.v. Mus.* To write or perform music in a key other than that in which it is written. —See Syns at **reverse.** [Middle English *transposen,* from Old French *transposer* : *trans-,* from one place to another, from Latin + *poser,* to place.] —**trans·pos′a·ble** *adj.* —**trans·pos′er** *n.* —**trans′po·si′tion** *n.* —**trans′po·si′tion·al** *adj.*

trans·ship (trăns-shĭp′) *v.* **-shipped, -ship·ping.** Also **tran·ship.** —*tr.v.* To transfer from one vessel or vehicle to another for reshipment. —*intr.v.* To transfer cargo from one vessel or conveyance to another. —**trans·ship′ment** *n.*

tran·sub·stan·ti·ate (trăn′səb-stăn′shē-āt′) *tr.v.* **-ated, -at·ing.** **1.** To change (one substance) into another; transmute; transform. **2.** *Theol.* To change the substance of (the Eucharistic bread and wine) into the true presence of Christ. [From Medieval Latin *transubstantiāre* : Latin *trāns-,* change + *substantia,* substance.]

tran·sub·stan·ti·a·tion (trăn′səb-stăn′shē-ā′shən) *n.* **1.** *Theol.* The doctrine that the bread and wine of the Eucharist are transformed into the true presence of Christ, although their appearance remains the same. **2.** The conversion of one substance into another; transformation.

trans·u·ran·ic (trăns′yŏŏ-răn′ĭk, trănz′-) *adj.* Also **trans·u·ra·ni·um** (-nē-əm). Having an atomic number greater than 92. [TRANS- + URAN(IUM) + -IC.]

trans·ver·sal (trăns-vûr′səl, trănz′-) *adj.* Transverse. —*n. Geom.* A line that intersects a system of lines. —**trans·ver′sal·ly** *adv.*

trans·verse (trăns-vûrs′, trănz′-, trăns′vûrs′, trănz′-) *adj.* Situated or lying across; crosswise. —*n.* Something transverse, such as a muscle or beam. [Latin *trānsversus,* from *trānsvertere,* to direct across : *trāns-,* across + *vertere,* to turn.] —**trans·verse′ly** *adv.* —**trans·verse′ness** *n.*

trap¹ (trăp) *n.* **1.** A device for catching and holding animals. **2.** Any stratagem for betraying, tricking, or exposing an unsuspecting person or group. **3. a.** A device for separating solids or other materials from the liquid that flows through a drain. **b.** A device for keeping a drain sealed against a backward flow of foul gases, esp. a U-shaped or S-shaped bend in the pipe that remains full of liquid. **4.** A device used in skeet and trapshooting to hurl disk-shaped, clay targets into the air. **5.** *Golf.* A **sand trap. 6.** Often **traps.** Musical percussion instruments, such as snare drums, cymbals, or bells. **7.** A light two-wheeled carriage with springs. **8.** A trap door. **9.** *Slang.* The mouth. —*v.* **trapped, trap·ping.** —*tr.v.* **1.** To catch in or as if in a trap; ensnare: *trapped a mouse. The police trapped the thief.* **2.** To confine, hold, or block, with or as if with a trap: *gravel and sand trapping water in the sluice.* **3.** To furnish (a drain) with a trap. —*intr.v.* To trap fur-bearing animals, esp. as a business. [Middle English *trappe,* from Old English *træppe.*]

trap² (trăp) *tr.v.* **trapped, trap·ping.** To furnish or deck with trappings. [Middle English *trappe,* a saddle cloth, from Old French *drap,* cloth.]

trap³ (trăp) *n.* Any of several dark, fine-grained igneous rocks, used esp. in building roads. Also called **traprock.**

[Swedish *trapp,* from *trappa,* step, stair, from Middle Low German *trappe.*]

trap door. A hinged or sliding door in a floor, roof, or ceiling.

trap-door spider (trăp′dôr′, -dōr′). Any of various spiders of the family Ctenizidae, that construct a silk-lined burrow concealed by a hinged lid.

tra·peze (tră-pēz′) *n.* A short horizontal bar hung at the ends of two parallel ropes, used for exercises or for acrobatic stunts. [French *trapéze,* from Late Latin *trapezium,* trapezium.]

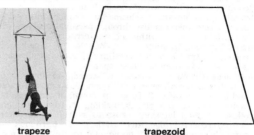

trapeze   trapezoid

tra·pe·zi·um (trə-pē′zē-əm) *n., pl.* **-ums** or **-zi·a** (-zē-ə). **1.** A quadrilateral with no parallel sides. **2.** *Brit.* A trapezoid. [Late Latin, from Greek *trapezion,* dim. of *trapeza,* table : *tra-,* four + *peza,* foot.]

tra·pe·zi·us (trə-pē′zē-əs) *n.* Either of two large, flat muscles that run from the base of the occiput to the middle of the back. [New Latin *(musculus) trapezius,* "trapezium-shaped (pair of muscles)."]

trap·e·zoid (trăp′ə-zoid′) *n.* A quadrilateral with two parallel sides. Also *Brit.* **trapezium.** —**trap′e·zoid′** or **trap′e·zoi′dal** *adj.*

trap·per (trăp′ər) *n.* A person whose occupation is trapping animals for their furs.

trap·pings (trăp′ĭngz) *pl.n.* **1.** An ornamental covering or harness for a horse; caparison. **2.** Articles of dress or ornamentation.

Trap·pist (trăp′ĭst) *n.* A member of a branch of the Cistercian order of monks, known for austerity and absolute silence, established in 1664 in La Trappe, Normandy.

trap·rock (trăp′rŏk′) *n.* Trap (igneous rock).

trap·shoot·ing (trăp′shŏŏ′tĭng) *n.* The sport of shooting at clay targets hurled into the air from a trap.

trash (trăsh) *n.* **1.** Worthless or discarded material or objects; refuse. **2.** Cheap, empty, or worthless expressions, ideas, artwork, etc. **3.** Anything in a broken or torn condition, esp. trimmings or husks from plants. **4.** An ignorant or contemptible person. [Orig. unknown.]

trash·y (trăsh′ē) *adj.* **-i·er, -i·est.** Of or like trash; worthless. —**trash′i·ly** *adv.* —**trash′i·ness** *n.*

trau·ma (trou′mə, trô′-) *n.* **1.** *Pathol.* A bodily wound or injury, esp. one caused by sudden external violence. **2.** *Psychiat.* An emotional shock that has profound and lasting effect on the psychological functioning of an individual. [Greek, wound, hurt.] —**trau·mat′ic** (-măt′ĭk) *adj.* —**trau·mat′i·cal·ly** *adv.*

trau·ma·tize (trou′mə-tīz′, trô′-) *tr.v.* **-tized, -tiz·ing.** To subject to physical or emotional trauma; shock.

tra·vail (trə-vāl′, trăv′āl′) *n.* **1.** Strenuous or laborious exertion; toil. **2.** Tribulation or agony; anguish. **3.** The labor of childbirth. —See Syns at **labor.** —*intr.v.* **1.** To toil painfully or strenuously; labor. **2.** To be in the labor of childbirth. [Middle English, from Old French, from *travailler,* to work hard, from Late Latin *tripālium,* an instrument of torture : *tri-,* three + *pālus,* stake.]

trav·el (trăv′əl) *v.* **-eled** or **-elled, -el·ing** or **-el·ling.** —*intr.v.* **1.** To go from one place to another; journey. **2.** To journey from one place to another as a salesman. **3.** To be transmitted; move, as light. **4.** To keep or be in company: *travel in wealthy circles.* **5.** To be capable of being transported. —*tr.v.* To journey over or through; traverse. —*n.* **1.** The act or process of traveling. **2. travels. a.** A series of journeys. **b.** A written account of these. **3.** Activity or traffic along a route or through a given point. [Middle English *travailen,* from old French *travailler,* to travail.]

travel agency. A business that makes various arrangements, as transportation tickets and accommodations, for private travel. Also called **travel bureau.** —**travel agent.**

trav·eled (trăv′əld) *adj.* **1.** Having traveled widely. **2.** Used by people traveling: *a rarely traveled byway.*

trav·el·er (trăv′əl-ər, trăv′lər) *n.* **1.** Something that travels. **2.** A person who travels or has traveled extensively.

traveler's check. An internationally used and accepted form of draft purchased from a bank, express company, etc., that the holder must sign at the time of purchase and countersign at the time of redemption.

traveling salesman. A salesman who solicits business orders or sells merchandise through personal dealings with potential customers within a given territory.

trav·e·logue or **travelog** (trăv′ə-lôg′, -lŏg′) *n.* A lecture on travel, illustrated by slides or films. [TRAVEL + Greek *logos,* discourse, from *legein,* to speak.]

trav·erse (trăv′ərs, trə-vûrs′) *v.* **-ersed, -ers·ing.** —*tr.v.* **1.** To travel across, over, or through. **2.** To move forward and backward over. **3.** To go up, down, or across (a hill, incline, etc.) at an angle, as in skiing. **4.** To move (a gun, telescope, etc.) laterally; cause to swivel. **5.** To extend across; cross: *A bridge traversed the gorge.* **6.** To look over carefully; examine. **7.** To go counter to; thwart. —*intr.v.* **1.** To move or go along, across, or back and forth. **2.** To turn laterally; swivel. **3.** To descend a slope in a zigzag manner. —*n.* **1. a.** The act of traversing; passage across, over, or through. **2.** A route or path over or across, esp. a zigzag route, as of a skier, sailing ship, etc. **3.** Something lying across something else, as a beam or crosspiece. **4.** *Geom.* A transversal. **5.** *Archit.* A gallery, deck, or loft crossing from one side of a building to the other. **6.** A defensive barrier across a rampart or trench. **7.** The horizontal swivel of a mounted gun. **8.** *Surveying.* A line established by sighting in the measurement of a tract of land. **9.** Something that obstructs and thwarts; an obstacle. —*adj.* Lying or extending across. [Middle English *traversen,* from Old French *traverser,* from Late Latin *trānsversāre,* from Latin *trānsversus,* transverse.] —**trav′ers·a·ble** *adj.* —**tra·vers′al** (trə-vûr′səl) *n.* —**trav′ers·er** *n.*

trav·er·tine (trăv′ər-tēn′, -tĭn) *n.* A light-colored, porous calcite, CaCO₃, deposited from solution in ground or surface waters and forming, among other deposits, the stalactites and stalagmites of caverns. [Italian *travertino,* from Latin *(lapis) Tīburtīnus,* "(stone) of Tibur (Tivoli).")]

trav·es·ty (trăv′ĭ-stē) *n., pl.* **-ties. 1.** A grotesque and debasing imitation; a mockery: *a travesty of justice.* **2.** A broad and grotesque literary parody on a lofty work or theme. —*tr.v.* **-tied, -tying.** To make a travesty on or of: *The show travesties grand opera.* [French *travesti,* from *travestir,* to ridicule, from Italian *travestire,* to disguise : *tra-,* across, from Latin *trāns-* + *vestire,* to dress, from Latin *vestis,* garment.]

tra·vois (trə-voi′, trăv′oi′) *n., pl.* **tra·vois** (trə-voiz′, trăv′oiz′) or **tra·vois·es** (trə-voi′zĭz, trăv′oi′zĭz). Also **tra·voise** (trə-voiz′, trăv′oiz′). A primitive vehicle formerly used by Plains Indians, consisting of a platform or netting supported by two long trailing poles, the forward ends of which are fastened to a dog or horse. [Canadian French.]

trawl (trôl) *n.* A large, tapered fishing net, towed along the sea bottom. —*tr.v.* To catch (fish) with a trawl. —*intr.v.* To fish with a trawl. [Perh. from Dutch *tragel,* dragnet.]

trawl·er (trô′lər) *n.* A boat used for trawling.

tray (trā) *n.* A flat, shallow receptacle with a raised edge or rim, used for carrying, holding, or displaying small articles. [Middle English, from Old English *trēg.*]

treach·er·ous (trĕch′ər-əs) *adj.* **1.** Betraying a trust; disloyal. **2. a.** Not dependable: *He has a treacherous memory.* **b.** Not to be trusted; dangerous: *a beach with a treacherous surf.* —See Syns at **faithless.** —**treach′er·ous·ly** *adv.* —**treach′er·ous·ness** *n.*

treach·er·y (trĕch′ə-rē) *n., pl.* **-ies. 1.** Willful betrayal of loyalty, confidence, or trust; perfidy; treason. **2.** A disloyal or treasonous act. [Middle English *trecherie,* from Old French, from *trichier,* to trick.]

trea·cle (trē′kəl) *n.* **1.** *Brit.* Molasses. **2.** Cloying flattery or sentiment. [Middle English *triacle,* antidote for poison, from Old French, from Latin *thēriaca,* from Greek *thē-*

riakē, from *thērion,* poisonous beast, dim. of *thēr,* beast.] —**trea′cly** (-klē) *adj.*

tread (trĕd) *v.* **trod** (trŏd), **trod·den** (trŏd′n) or **trod, treading.** —*tr.v.* **1.** To walk on, over, or along. **2.** To crush or stamp beneath the foot; trample. **3.** To treat or put down harshly or cruelly; oppress; subdue. **4.** To execute by walking or dancing: *tread a few measures of a waltz.* —*intr.v.* **1.** To walk or step: *treading softly up the stairs.* **2.** To trample so as to crush. —*n.* **1. a.** The act, manner, or sound of treading: *the swift tread of a horse.* **b.** A footstep or footsteps: *a familiar tread.* **2.** The horizontal part of a step in a staircase. **3.** The part of a wheel or shoe sole that touches the ground. **4.** The pattern of grooves or raised ridges on a tire that makes it grip the road better. [Middle English *treden,* from Old English *tredan.*] —**tread′er** *n.*

trea·dle (trĕd′l) *n.* A pedal or lever pushed up and down or back and forth with the foot to drive a wheel, as in a sewing machine. —*intr.v.* **-led, -ling.** To work a treadle. [Middle English *tredel,* from Old English, step of a stair, from *tredan,* to tread.] —**tread′ler** (trĕd′lər) *n.*

tread·mill (trĕd′mĭl′) *n.* **1.** A device operated by one or more persons or animals walking on an endless belt or on a set of moving steps attached to a wheel. **2.** Any monotonous work or routine.

treadmill
An exercise machine

trea·son (trē′zən) *n.* **1.** The betrayal of one's country, esp. by giving aid to an enemy in wartime or by plotting to overthrow the government. **2.** Any betrayal of a trust. [Middle English *treison,* from Norman French *treisoun,* from Medieval Latin *trāditiō,* from Latin, a handing over.]

trea·son·a·ble (trē′zən-ə-bəl) *adj.* Of or involving treason. —**trea′son·a·ble·ness** *n.* —**trea′son·a·bly** *adv.*

trea·son·ous (trē′zən-əs) *adj.* Treasonable. —**trea′son·ous·ly** *adv.*

treas·ure (trĕzh′ər) *n.* **1.** Accumulated, stored, or cached wealth in the form of valuables, such as money or jewels. **2.** A person or thing considered esp. precious or valuable. —*tr.v.* **-ured, -ur·ing. 1.** To accumulate and save for future use; hoard. **2.** To value highly. —See Syns at **appreciate.** [Middle English *tresor,* from Old French, from Latin *thēsaurus,* from Greek *thēsauros.*] —**treas′ur·a·ble** *adj.*

treas·ur·er (trĕzh′ər-ər) *n.* A person with charge of funds or revenues of a government, corporation, club, etc. —**treas′ur·er·ship′** *n.*

treas·ure-trove (trĕzh′ər-trōv′) *n.* **1.** *Law.* Any treasure found hidden and not claimed by its owner. **2.** A discovery of great value. [Norman French *tresor trove,* "discovered treasure."]

treas·ur·y (trĕzh′ə-rē) *n., pl.* **-ies. 1.** A place where treasure is kept or stored. **2.** A place where private or public funds are received, kept, managed, and disbursed. **3.** Such funds or revenues. **4. Treasury.** The department of a government in charge of the public revenue.

treasury note. A note or bill issued by the U.S. Treasury as legal tender for all debts.

treat (trēt) *tr.v.* **1.** To act or behave toward: *treated her fairly.* **2.** To deal with, handle, or cover: *treated his subject in depth. Treat all requests on a first-come, first-served basis.* **3.** To regard or consider in a certain way. **4.** To try or help to cure by administering some remedy or therapy: *treat a patient.* **5.** To subject to a physical or chemical process or action in order to change in some way. **6.** To provide food or entertainment for (another or others) at one's own expense. —*intr.v.* To pay for another's entertainment, food, etc. —*n.* **1. a.** Something, such as refreshments or entertainment, paid for or provided by someone else. **b.** An act of treating or turn to treat. **2.** Anything considered a special delight or pleasure. [Middle English *treten,* from Old French *traitier,* from Latin *tractāre,* freq. of *trahere,* to pull.] —**treat·a·ble** *adj.* —**treat'er** *n.*

trea·tise (trē′tĭs) *n.* A formal, systematic account in writing of some subject. [Middle English *tretis,* from Norman French, from Old French *traitier,* to treat.]

treat·ment (trēt′mənt) *n.* **1.** The act or manner of treating something. **2. a.** The use or application of something meant to relieve or cure a disease or disorder. **b.** An instance of this.

trea·ty (trē′tē) *n., pl.* **-ties. 1. a.** A formal agreement between two or more states containing terms of trade, peace, alliance, etc.; a pact. **b.** A document embodying this. **2.** Any contract or agreement. [Middle English *tretee,* from Old French *traite,* from Medieval Latin *tractātus,* from Latin *tractāre,* to treat.]

treb·le (trĕb′əl) *adj.* **1.** Triple; threefold. **2.** *Mus.* Of, having, or performing the highest part, voice, or range. **3.** High-pitched; shrill. —*n.* **1.** *Mus.* **a.** The highest part, voice, instrument, or range; soprano. **b.** A singer or player that performs this part. **2.** A high, shrill sound or voice. —*v.* **-led, -ling.** —*tr.v.* To increase threefold: *trebled his wager.* —*intr.v.* To become three times as great. [Middle English, from Old French, from Latin *triplus.*] —**treb′le·ness** *n.* —**treb′ly** (trĕb′lē) *adv.*

treble clef. *Mus.* A symbol centered on the second line of the staff to indicate the position of G above middle C.

tree (trē) *n.* **1.** A usu. tall woody plant, distinguished from a shrub by its comparatively greater height and a single trunk rather than several stems. **2.** A plant or shrub that resembles a tree in form or size. **3.** A wooden beam, post, etc., used as a part of a framework or structure. **4.** Something that resembles a tree, such as a pole with pegs or hooks for hanging clothes. **5.** A diagram with a branching configuration, esp. a geneological chart. —*tr.v.* **treed, tree·ing. 1.** To chase and force to climb a tree. **2.** *Informal.* To force into a difficult position; corner. —*idiom.* **up a tree.** In an embarrassing or difficult situation that offers little or no escape. [Middle English, from Old English *treow.*]

tree fern. Any of various treelike tropical ferns, esp. of the family Cyatheaceae, with a woody, trunklike stem and a terminal crown of large, divided fronds.

tree frog. Any of various small, arboreal frogs of the genus *Hyla* and related genera, with long toes terminating in adhesive disks. Also called **tree toad.**

tree of heaven. A tree, the ailanthus.

tree toad. A tree frog.

tree·top (trē′tŏp′) *n.* The uppermost part of a tree.

tref (trāf) *adj.* Unclean and unfit to eat according to Jewish dietary law. [Yiddish *treyf,* from Hebrew *terēphāh,* flesh of an animal torn by wild beasts, from *tāraf,* to tear.]

tre·foil (trē′foil′, trĕf′oil′) *n.* **1.** Any of various plants of the genera *Trifolium, Lotus,* and related genera, with compound leaves that have three leaflets. **2.** Any ornamental or architectural form that has three divisions like a clover leaf. [Middle English, from Norman French *trifoil,* from Latin *trifolium,* three-leaved grass : *tri-,* three + *folium,* leaf.]

trefoil

trek (trĕk) *intr.v.* **trekked, trek·king.** To make a slow or arduous journey. —*n.* A journey, esp. a long and difficult one. [Afrikaans, from Middle Dutch *trekken,* to pull, travel.] —**trek′ker** *n.*

trel·lis (trĕl′ĭs) *n.* An open framework or lattice used for training vines and climbing plants. —*tr.v.* **1.** To provide

with a trellis. **2.** To train (a plant) on a trellis. **3.** To form or interlace like a trellis; lattice. [Middle English *trelis,* from Old French *treliz,* a coarse fabric, trellis, from Latin *trilīx,* triple-twilled.]

trel·lis·work (trĕl′ĭs-wûrk′) *n.* Latticework.

trem·a·tode (trĕm′ə-tōd′) *n.* Any of numerous parasitic flatworms of the class Trematoda, with a thick outer cuticle and one or more suckers for attaching to host tissue. Also called **fluke.** [From Greek *trēmatōdēs,* having a vent to the intestinal canal, from *trēma,* perforation.]

trem·ble (trĕm′bəl) *intr.v.* **-bled, -bling. 1.** To shake involuntarily, as from fear, cold, etc.; to shiver. **2.** To feel or express fear or anxiety: *I tremble to think of it.* —See Syns at **shake.** —*n.* **1.** The act of trembling. **2.** An example of trembling; tremor. [Middle English *tremblen,* from Old French *trembler,* from Latin *tremulus,* tremulous.] —**trem′bler** *n.* —**trem′bling·ly** *adv.* —**trem′bly** *adj.*

tre·men·dous (trĭ-mĕn′dəs) *adj.* **1.** Capable of making one tremble, as with fear, rage, dread, etc. **2. a.** Extremely large in amount, degree, or size; enormous. **b.** *Informal.* Marvelous; wonderful. —See Syns at **giant.** [Latin *tremendus,* from *tremere,* to tremble.] —**tre·men′dous·ly** *adv.* —**tre·men′dous·ness** *n.*

trem·o·lo (trĕm′ə-lō′) *n., pl.* **-los.** *Mus.* **1.** A vibrating effect produced either by the rapid repetition of a single tone or by the rapid alternation of two tones. **2.** A device on an organ for producing this tone. [Italian, "tremulous."]

trem·or (trĕm′ər) *n.* **1.** A quick shaking or vibrating movement: *an earth tremor.* **2.** An involuntary trembling motion of the body: *a nervous tremor.* **3.** A nervous or trembling sensation; a thrill. **4.** A tremulous sound; a quaver. — *intr.v.* To shake or tremble. —See Syns at **shake.** [Middle English *tremour,* from Old French, from Latin *tremor,* from *tremere,* to tremble.]

trem·u·lous (trĕm′yə-ləs) *adj.* **1.** Vibrating or quivering; trembling: *a tremulous voice.* **2.** Timid; fearful; timorous. [Latin *tremulus,* from *tremere,* to tremble.] —**trem′u·lous·ly** *adv.* —**trem′u·lous·ness** *n.*

trench (trĕnch) *n.* **1.** A deep furrow. **2.** A ditch. **3.** A long, narrow, crooked ditch embanked with its own soil and used for concealment and protection in warfare. —*tr.v.* **1.** To cut or dig a trench in. **2.** To fortify with a trench. —*intr.v.* To dig a trench or ditch. —*phrasal verb.* **trench on** (or **upon**). To verge or encroach: *remarks trenching on slander.* [Middle English *trenche,* from Old French, from *trenchier,* to cut, dig.]

trench·ant (trĕn′chənt) *adj.* **1.** Keen; incisive; penetrating: *a trenchant comment.* **2.** Forceful; effective: *a trenchant argument.* **3.** Distinct; sharply defined; clear-cut: *no trenchant limits to progress.* [Middle English, cutting, from Old French, pres. part. of *trenchier,* to cut.] —**trench′an·cy** *n.* —**trench′ant·ly** *adv.*

trench coat. A loose-fitting, belted raincoat with many pockets and flaps that suggest a military style.

trench·er (trĕn′chər) *n.* A wooden board on which food is cut or served. [Middle English *trenchour,* cutting board, from Norman French, from Old French *trenchier,* to cut.]

trench·er·man (trĕn′chər-mən) *n.* A hearty eater.

trench fever. An acute infectious fever caused by a microorganism and transmitted by a louse.

trench foot. A disorder of the foot that resembles frostbite and often afflicts soldiers who must stand in cold water for long periods of time.

trench knife. A knife with a short, heavy double-edged blade, used in hand-to-hand combat.

trench mouth. A form of gingivitis characterized by pain, foul odor, and the formation of a gray film over the diseased area.

trend (trĕnd) *n.* **1.** A general tendency or course; drift: *the upward trend of prices.* **2.** A direction or movement; a flow: *a trend of thought.* —*intr.v.* **1.** To have a certain direction: *The road trends westward.* **2.** To have a certain tendency; tend: *new fashions trending to bold colors.* [From Middle English *trenden,* to turn, roll, from Old English *trendan.*]

trend·y (trĕn′dē) *adj.* **-i·er, -i·est.** *Informal.* Of or in accordance with the latest fad or fashion; modish: *trendy ideas; trendy clothes.* —**trend′i·ly** *adv.* —**trend′i·ness** *n.*

tre·pan (trĭ-păn′) *n.* A trephine. —*tr.v.* **-panned, -pan·ning.**

To trephine. [Middle English *trepane*, from Medieval Latin *trepanum*, from Greek *trupanon*, auger, borer, from *trupan*, to pierce, from *trupē*, hole.] —**trep′a·na′tion** (trĕp′-ə-nā′shən, trĭ-păn′ā′shən) *n.*

tre·pang (trĭ-păng′) *n.* **1.** Any of several sea cucumbers of the genus *Holothuria*, of the southern Pacific and Indian oceans. **2.** The dried flesh of any of these animals, used as food in the Orient. [Malay *tĕripang*.]

tre·phine (trĭ-fīn′, -fēn′) *n.* A surgical instrument that has circular, sawlike edges, used to cut out disks of bone, esp. from the skull. —*tr.v.* **-phined, -phin·ing.** To operate on with a trephine. [Obs. *trafine*, from Latin *trēs fīnes*, "three ends."]

trep·i·da·tion (trĕp′ə-dā′shən) *n.* A condition of alarm or dread; apprehension. [Latin *trepidātiō*, from *trepidāre*, to hurry with alarm, tremble at, from *trepidus*, alarmed.]

tres·pass (trĕs′pəs, -păs′) *n.* **1.** An offense committed against the laws of man, nature, or God; a sin; transgression. **2.** An infringement upon the privacy, time, attention, etc., of another; intrusion. **3.** *Law.* **a.** An unlawful injury committed with violence, either actual or implied, upon the person, property, or rights of another; a tort. **b.** A legal action brought to recover money damages for such an injury. —*intr.v.* **1.** To commit an offense or sin; err; transgress. **2.** To infringe upon; intrude. **3.** *Law.* To make an illegal entry onto the land of another. [Middle English *trespassen*, from Old French *trespasser*, from Medieval Latin *transpassāre* : Latin *trāns-*, across + Medieval Latin *passāre*, to cross, pass, from Latin *passus*, step, pace.] —**tres′pass·er** *n.*

tress (trĕs) *n.* **1.** A lock of hair. **2. tresses.** Long loose hair. [Middle English *tresse*, from Old French.]

tres·tle (trĕs′əl) *n.* **1.** A structure that consists of a horizontal beam or bar held up by two pairs of divergent legs, used as a support for a horizontally placed load, such as a table top. **2.** A framework that consists of vertical, slanted supports and horizontal crosspieces supporting a bridge. [Middle English *trestel*, from Old French, from Latin *transtrum*, crossbeam.]

tres·tle·work (trĕs′əl-wûrk′) *n.* A trestle or system of trestles, as that supporting a bridge.

trews (trōoz) *pl.n.* (used with a sing. verb). Close-fitting trousers, usu. of tartan. [Scottish Gaelic *triubhas*, trousers.]

trey (trā) *n.* A card or die with three pips. [Middle English *treye*, from Old French *treis*, from Latin *trēs*, three.]

tri-. A prefix meaning: **1.** Three: **trioxide. 2. a.** Occurring every three or every third: **trimonthly. b.** Occurring at intervals of three: **triweekly.** [Latin and Greek, three.]

tri·a·ble (trī′ə-bəl) *adj.* **1.** Capable of being tried or tested. **2.** *Law.* Subject to judicial examination. —**tri′a·ble·ness** *n.*

tri·ad (trī′ăd′, -əd) *n.* **1.** A group of three closely related persons or things. **2.** *Mus.* A chord containing three tones, esp. a chord that consists of tones that are separated by thirds. [Late Latin *trias*, from Greek.] —**tri·ad′ic** *adj.*

tri·al (trī′əl, trīl) *n.* **1.** *Law.* The examination and determination by a law court of competent jurisdiction of the legal and factual issues upon which a criminal charge or civil claim is based. **2. a.** The act or process of testing or trying by use and experience. **b.** An example of such testing. **3.** An effort or attempt. **4.** Anything, as a person, thing, or event, that tries one's belief, patience, or endurance. [Norman French, from Old French *trier*, to try.]

trial balance. A statement of all the open debit and credit items in a double-entry ledger made to test their equality.

tri·an·gle (trī′ăng′gəl) *n.* **1.** *Geom.* A closed plane figure formed by three points not in a straight line connected by three line segments; a polygon with three sides. **2.** Something shaped like this figure. **3.** Any of various flat objects having the outline of a triangle and used as guides in drawing or drafting. **4.** A musical percussion instrument with a clear bell-like tone, formed of a bar of metal bent into a triangle that is left open at one vertex.

tri·an·gu·lar (trī-ăng′gyə-lər) *adj.* **1.** Of or shaped like a triangle; three-sided. **2.** Having a base or cross section that is a triangle: *a triangular prism.* **3.** Of, involving, or consisting of three interrelated entities, as three persons, objects, or ideas. —**tri·an′gu·lar′i·ty** (-lăr′ə-tē) *n.* —**tri·an′gu·lar·ly** *adv.*

tri·an·gu·late (trī-ăng′gyə-lāt′) *tr.v.* **-lat·ed, -lat·ing. 1.** To divide into triangles. **2.** To survey by triangulation. —*adj.* (trī-ăng′gyə-lĭt). Made up of or marked with triangles.

tri·an·gu·la·tion (trī-ăng′gyə-lā′shən) *n.* **1.** A surveying technique in which a region is divided into a series of triangular elements based on a line of known length so that accurate measurements of distances and directions may be made by using trigonometry. **2.** A system of triangles laid out for this purpose. **3.** The locating of an unknown point, as in navigation, by forming a triangle with the unknown point and two known points as the vertices.

Tri·as·sic (trī-ăs′ĭk) *n.* Also **Triassic period.** The first period of the Mesozoic era, beginning about 230 million years ago, ending about 180 million years ago, and characterized by the existence of giant tree ferns and similar plants and the development of dinosaurs and other reptiles. —*modifier:* Triassic *fossils.* [From Late Latin *trias*, triad (from the subdivision of the geologic strata beneath the Jurassic into three groups).]

tri·a·tom·ic (trī′ə-tŏm′ĭk) *adj.* Containing three atoms per molecule.

trib·al (trī′bəl) *adj.* Of or characteristic of a tribe: *tribal legends; tribal history.* —**trib′al·ly** *adv.*

tribe (trīb) *n.* **1.** Any of various usu. primitive systems of social organization that unite a group of people in a given area who have a common ancestry, language, and culture. **2.** A group of persons with a common occupation, interest, or habit: *a tribe of beggars.* **3.** *Biol.* A taxonomic category sometimes placed between a family and a genus. [Middle English, from Old French *tribu*, from Latin *tribus*, division of the Roman people.]

tribes·man (trībz′mən) *n.* A member of a tribe.

trib·u·la·tion (trĭb′yə-lā′shən) *n.* **1.** Great affliction or distress; suffering. **2.** That which causes such distress. [Middle English *tribulacioun*, from Old French *tribulation*, from Late Latin *trībulātiō*, from *trībulāre*, to oppress, from Latin, to press, from *trībulum*, threshing sledge.]

tri·bu·nal (trī-byōō′nəl, trĭ-) *n.* **1.** A seat or court of justice. **2.** A board of officials appointed to decide upon or arbitrate a solution to a specific problem or class of problems: *a medical tribunal.* **3.** Anything that has the power of determining or judging: *the tribunal of public opinion.* [Latin *tribūnāle*, from *tribūnus*, tribune.]

trib·u·nate (trĭb′yə-nāt′, trī-byōō′nĭt) *n.* The rank or office of tribune.

trib·une¹ (trĭb′yōōn′, trī-byōōn′) *n.* **1. a.** An official of ancient Rome chosen by the common people to protect their rights from infringement by the ruling patrician class. **b.** One of six military officers who rotated command of a Roman legion. **2.** Any protector or champion of the people. [Middle English, from Latin *tribūnus*, from *tribus*, tribe.] —**trib′u·nar′y** (trĭb′yə-nĕr′ē) *adj.*

trib·une² (trĭb′yōōn′, trī-byōōn′) *n.* A raised platform or dais from which a speaker addresses an assembly. [French, from Italian *tribuna*, from Medieval Latin *tribūna*, from Latin *tribūnal*, tribunal.]

trib·u·tar·y (trĭb′yə-tĕr′ē) *n., pl.* **-ies. 1.** A river or stream that flows into a larger river or stream. **2.** A person, nation, etc., that pays tribute to another. —*adj.* **1.** Flowing into another. **2.** Paying tribute.

trib·ute (trĭb′yōōt) *n.* **1.** A gift or other acknowledgment of

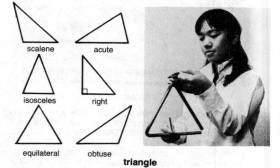

scalene   acute

isosceles   right

equilateral   obtuse

triangle

gratitude, respect, or admiration. **2. a.** A sum of money paid by one ruler or nation to another as acknowledgment of submission or as the price for protection by that nation. **b.** A rent, tax, etc., exacted from a subject by his sovereign to collect funds for such a payment. **c.** Any enforced payment. [Middle English *tribut,* from Latin *tribūtum,* from *tribuere,* to give, distribute, from *tribus,* tribe.]

trice (trīs) *n.* A very short period of time; an instant. *He came in a trice.* —See Syns at **moment.** [Middle English *trisen,* to hoist, from Middle Dutch.]

tri·ceps (trī'sĕps') *n.* A large three-headed muscle that runs along the back of the upper arm and serves to extend the forearm. [Latin, three-headed : *tri-,* three + *caput,* head.]

tri·cer·a·tops (trī-sĕr'ə-tŏps') *n.* A horned herbivorous dinosaur of the genus *Triceratops,* of the Cretaceous period, with a bony plate covering the neck. [TRI- + Greek *keras,* horn + *ōps,* eye, face.]

tri·chi·na (trī-kī'nə) *n., pl.* **-nae** (-nē) or **-nas.** A parasitic nematode worm, *Trichinella spiralis,* that infests the intestines of various mammals, and has larvae that move through the blood vessels and become encysted in the muscles. [From Greek *trikhinos,* hairy, from *thrix,* hair.]

trich·i·no·sis (trĭk'ə-nō'sĭs) *n.* A disease caused by eating inadequately cooked pork that contains trichinae, characterized by intestinal disorders, fever, muscular swelling, pain, and insomnia. [TRICHIN(A) + -OSIS.]

tri·chi·nous (trī-kī'nəs, trĭk'ə-nəs) *adj.* **1.** Containing trichinae. **2.** Of or relating to trichinae or trichinosis.

tricho-. A prefix meaning hair or hairlike part: *trichomonad.* [Greek *trikho-,* from *thrix,* hair.]

trich·ome (trĭk'ōm', trī'kōm') *n.* A hairlike or bristlelike outgrowth, as from the epidermis of a plant. [German *Trichom,* from Greek *trikhōma,* hair growth, from *thrix,* hair.] —**tri·chom'ic** (trī-kōm'ĭk, -kō'mĭk, trī-) *adj.*

trich·o·mon·ad (trĭk'ə-mŏn'ăd', -mō'năd') *n.* Any of various flagellate protozoans of the genus *Trichomonas,* occurring in the digestive and urogenital tracts of vertebrates. [TRICHO- + MONAD.]

tri·chot·o·my (trī-kŏt'ə-mē) *n., pl.* **-mies. 1.** Division into three parts, classifications, groups, etc. **2.** The theological division of man into body, soul, and spirit. [Greek *trikha,* in three parts + -TOMY.]

trick (trĭk) *n.* **1.** An impressive feat or stunt requiring a special skill, talent, or technique: *a juggling trick; magic tricks.* **2.** A special skill or knack. **3. a.** A clever and effective method or technique used by an expert: *the tricks of the trade.* **b.** A crafty and deceptive method or scheme used to fool or outwit someone. **4.** A deception or optical illusion. **5.** A prank or practical joke. **6.** A mean, stupid, or childish act: *That was a low-down dirty trick.* **7.** A certain habit or mannerism: *He has a trick of looking right through you.* **8.** All of the cards played in a single round of a card game. —*adj.* **1.** Involving tricks, stunts, or trickery: *trick photography.* **2.** Tricky; deceptive: *trick arithmetic problems.* **3.** Used to play tricks: *trick spoons that melt in hot coffee.* **4.** Weak and liable to give way: *a trick knee.* —*tr.v.* **1.** To deceive, fool, cheat, or mislead. **2.** To get or persuade by trickery. —*intr.v.* To practice trickery; deceive. —**idioms. do the trick.** To accomplish the desired result. **not miss a trick.** To be aware of everything that is going on. [Middle English *trik,* from Old North French *trique,* from *trikier,* to deceive.] —**trick'er** *n.*

trick·er·y (trĭk'ə-rē) *n., pl.* **-ies.** The practice or use of tricks; deception by stratagem.

trick·le (trĭk'əl) *v.* **-led, -ling.** —*intr.v.* **1.** To flow or fall in drops or in a thin, intermittent stream. **2.** To move or proceed slowly or bit by bit. —*tr.v.* To cause to trickle: *trickled syrup over his pancakes.* —*n.* **1.** The act or condition of trickling. **2.** Any slow, small, or irregular quantity of something that moves, proceeds, or occurs intermittently. [Middle English *triklen.*]

trick·ster (trĭk'stər) *n.* **1.** A person who deceives; a cheater. **2.** A person who plays tricks; prankster.

trick·y (trĭk'ē) *adj.* **-i·er, -i·est. 1.** Crafty; sly; wily: *a tricky ballplayer.* **2.** Requiring caution or skill: *a tricky situation.* —**trick'i·ly** *adv.* —**trick'i·ness** *n.*

tri·clin·ic (trī-klĭn'ĭk) *adj.* Having three unequal axes that intersect at oblique angles, as certain crystals. [TRI- + Greek *klinein,* to lean.]

tri·col·or (trī'kŭl'ər) *adj.* Also **tri·col·ored** (-ərd). Having three colors. —*n.* A tricolor flag.

tri·corn or **tri·corne** (trī'kôrn') *n.* A hat with the brim turned up on three sides. —*adj.* Having three projections, horns, or corners. [French *tricorne,* from Latin *tricornis,* three-horned : *tri-,* three + *cornū,* horn.]

tricorn   tricycle

tri·cot (trē'kō) *n.* **1.** A plain, warp-knitted cloth of any of various yarns. **2.** A soft ribbed cloth of wool or wool blend, usu. used for dresses. [French, from *tricoter,* to knit, from *tricot,* short stick.]

tri·cus·pid (trī-kŭs'pĭd) *adj.* Also **tri·cus·pi·date** (-pə-dāt'). **1.** Having three points or cusps, as a molar tooth. **2.** Concerning the tricuspid valve of the heart. —*n.* A tricuspid organ or part, esp. a tooth.

tricuspid valve. The three-segmented valve of the heart that keeps the blood from flowing back from the right ventricle into the right atrium.

tri·cy·cle (trī'sĭk'əl, -sĭ-kəl) *n.* A vehicle with three wheels usu. propelled by pedals.

tri·dent (trīd'ənt) *n.* A long, three-pronged spear, esp. that carried by the Roman sea god, Neptune. —*adj.* Also **tri·den·tate** (trī-dĕn'tāt'). Having three teeth, prongs, or similar protrusions. [Latin *tridēns : tri-,* three + *dēns,* tooth.]

tried (trīd) *v.* Past tense and past participle of **try.** —*adj.* Tested and proved to be good or trustworthy: *a tried recipe.*

tri·en·ni·al (trī-ĕn'ē-əl) *adj.* **1.** Lasting or living for three years. **2.** Happening every third year. —*n.* **1.** A third anniversary. **2.** An event that occurs once every three years. [From Latin *triennium,* three years : *tri-,* three + *annus,* year.] —**tri·en'ni·al·ly** *adv.*

tri·fid (trī'fĭd) *adj.* Divided or cleft into three narrow parts or lobes. [Latin *trifidus : tri-,* three + *findere,* to split.]

tri·fle (trī'fəl) *n.* **1.** Something of slight importance or very little value. **2.** A small amount; a little. **3.** A dessert of cake soaked in wine or brandy and topped with jam, custard, and whipped cream. —*v.* **-fled, -fling.** —*intr.v.* **1.** To deal with as being of little significance or value: *You are trifling with her future.* **2.** To play or toy with something; handle idly. —*tr.v.* To waste (time, money, etc.). [Middle English, from Old French *truffle,* trickery.] —**tri'fler** (trī'flər) *n.*

tri·fling (trī'flĭng) *adj.* **1.** Of slight importance; insignificant: *"He had come to know every trifling feature that bordered the great river"* (Mark Twain). **2. a.** Characterized by frivolity. **b.** Lazy; idle. —See Syns at **lazy.** —**tri'fling·ly** *adv.*

tri·fo·li·ate (trī-fō'lē-ĭt) *adj.* Having three leaves, leaflets, or leaflike parts.

tri·fur·cate (trī-fûr'kĭt, -kāt', trī'fər-kāt') *adj.* Having three forks or branches.

trig¹ (trĭg) *adj.* Trim; neat; tidy. [Middle English, true, active, from Old Norse *tryggr.*]

trig² (trĭg) *n.* Trigonometry.

trig·ger (trĭg'ər) *n.* **1.** The small lever pressed by the finger to discharge a firearm. **2.** Any similar device used to release or activate a mechanism. **3.** An event that precipitates others; a stimulus. —*tr.v.* **1.** To discharge or detonate by pulling or releasing a trigger. **2.** To start; set in motion; set off: *His remarks triggered the argument.* [Dutch *trekker,* something pulled, from Middle Dutch *trecker,* from *trecken,* to pull.]

trig·ger-hap·py (trĭg'ər-hăp'ē) *adj. Informal.* **1.** Likely to fire

---

ă pat   ā pay   â care   ä father   ĕ pet   ē be   hw which   ĭ pit   ī tie   î pier   ŏ pot   ō toe   ô paw, for   oi noise
ŏŏ took   ōō boot   ou out   th thin   th this   ŭ cut   û urge   zh vision   ə about, item, edible, gallop, circus

a gun at the slightest provocation or excuse. **2.** Prone to react irresponsibly or impetuously without thought of consequences.

tri·glyph (trī′glĭf′) *adj. Archit.* An ornament in a Doric frieze, consisting of a projecting block with three parallel vertical channels on its face. **—tri·glyph′ic** *adj.*

trigonometric function. A function of an angle expressed as the ratio of two of the sides of a right triangle that contains the angle.

trig·o·nom·e·try (trĭg′ə-nŏm′ə-trē) *n.* The study of the properties and applications of trigonometric functions. [Greek *trigōnon,* triangle + -METRY.] **—trig′o·no·met′ric** (-nə-mĕt′rĭk) or **trig′o·no·met′ri·cal** *adj.* **—trig′o·no·met′ri·cal·ly** *adv.*

tri·graph (trī′grăf′) *n.* Three consecutive letters that are pronounced as a single sound, as the "eau" in "beau."

tri·he·dral (trī-hē′drəl) *adj.* Formed or described by three planes meeting in a point. **—n.** A trihedral figure.

trill (trĭl) *n.* **1.** A fluttering or tremulous sound, a warble. **2.** *Mus.* **a.** The rapid alternation of two tones either a whole or a half tone apart. **b.** A vibrato. **3.** *Ling.* **a.** A rapid vibration of one speech organ against another, as of the tongue against the ridge behind the upper front teeth. **b.** A speech sound pronounced with such a vibration. **—tr.v.** **1.** To sound, sing, or play with a trill. **2.** *Phonet.* To articulate with a trill. **—intr.v.** To sing, play, or produce a trill. [Italian *trillo,* from *trillare,* to trill.]

tril·lion (trĭl′yən) *n.* **1.** The cardinal number represented by 1 followed by 12 zeros, usu. written 10^{12}. **2.** *Brit.* The cardinal number represented by 1 followed by 18 zeros, usu. written 10^{18}. **3.** An indefinitely large number. [TRI- + (M)ILLION.]

tril·lionth (trĭl′yənth) *n.* **1.** The ordinal number one billion in a series. **2.** One of one trillion equal parts. **—tril′lionth** *adj. & adv.*

tril·li·um (trĭl′ē-əm) *n.* Any of various plants of the genus *Trillium,* of the lilly family, usu. with a single whorl of three leaves and a variously colored, three-petaled flower. [TRI- + Latin (*vertic*)*ill*(*us*), whorl + -IUM.]

tri·lo·bite (trī′lə-bīt′) *n.* Any of numerous extinct saltwater arthropods of the class Trilobita, of the Paleozoic era, with a segmented exoskeleton divided by grooves into three longitudinal lobes. **—tri′lo·bit′ic** (-bĭt′ĭk) *adj.*

tril·o·gy (trĭl′ə-jē) *n., pl.* **-gies.** A group of three literary, dramatic, musical, or balletic works related in subject or theme.

trim (trĭm) *v.* **trimmed, trim·ming.** **—tr.v.** **1.** To make neat, even, or tidy, esp. by clipping, cutting, or smoothing. **2.** To remove or reduce by cutting: *trimmed operating costs.* **3.** To decorate, ornament, or embellish: *trim a Christmas tree.* **4.** *Informal.* To beat or defeat soundly. **5.** *Naut.* **a.** To adjust (sails and yards) so that they receive the wind properly. **b.** To balance (a ship) by shifting its cargo or contents. **6.** To balance (an airplane) in flight by regulating the control surfaces and tabs. **—intr.v.** **1.** *Naut.* **a.** To be in or take a certain position in the water: *The ship trims to the stern.* **b.** To make sails and yards ready for sailing. **2. a.** To maintain a position or course of cautious neutrality. **b.** To fashion one's views for momentary popularity or advantage. **—See Syns at defeat. —n.** **1.** Ornamentation on the surface of something, such as braid on clothing or moldings around doors and windows. **2.** The act of cutting or clipping: *Your beard needs a trim.* **3.** Proper shape, order, or condition: *in good trim for the game.* **4. a.** The readiness of a ship for sailing. **b.** The balance or position of a ship or aircraft. **—adj.** **trim·mer, trim·mest.** **1.** Neat; tidy; orderly; smart. **2.** Well designed or proportioned, with simple or slim lines: *a trim schooner.* **—See Syns at neat. —adv.** In a trim manner. [Ult. from Old English *trymman, trymian,* to strengthen, arrange.] **—trim′ly** *adv.* **—trim′mer** *n.* **—trim′ness** *n.*

tri·mes·ter (trī-mĕs′tər) *n.* **1.** A period or term of three months. **2.** One of three academic terms of equal length into which the academic year is divided in some educational institutions. [French *trimestre,* from Latin *trimestris,* "of three months" : *tri-,* three + *mēnsis,* month.] **—tri·mes′tral** (-trəl) or **tri·mes′tri·al** (-trē-əl) *adj.*

trim·e·ter (trĭm′ə-tər) *n.* A verse line of three metrical feet.

trim·ming (trĭm′ĭng) *n.* **1.** Anything added as decoration;

an ornament. **2. trimmings.** Accessories; extras. **3. trimmings.** Pieces that are removed in cutting, finishing, or pruning something.

tri·month·ly (trī-mŭnth′lē) *adj.* **1.** Happening every three months. **2.** Happening three times a month. **—adv.** **1.** Once every three months. **2.** Three times a month.

trine (trīn) *adj.* Threefold; triple. [Middle English, from Old French, from Latin *trīnus,* from *trīnī,* three each.]

Trin·i·tar·i·an (trĭn′ə-târ′ē-ən) *adj.* **1.** Of or relating to the Trinity. **2.** Believing or professing belief in the Trinity or the doctrine of the Trinity. **—n.** A person who believes in the doctrine of the Trinity. **—Trin′i·tar′i·an·ism** *n.*

tri·ni·tro·tol·u·ene (trī′nī′trō-tŏl′yōō-ēn′) *n.* A yellow crystalline compound, $C_7H_5N_3O_6$, used mainly as a high explosive. Also called **TNT.** [TRI- + NITRO- + TOLUENE.]

trin·i·ty (trĭn′ə-tē) *n., pl.* **-ties. 1. the Trinity.** *Theol.* The union of the Father, the Son, and the Holy Ghost in a single Godhead. **2.** Any three parts in union; a triad. **3.** The condition of being three. [Middle English *trinite,* from Old French, from Latin *trīnitās,* from *trīnus,* trine.]

trin·ket (trĭng′kĭt) *n.* **1.** A small ornament or piece of jewelry. **2.** A trifle. [Orig. unknown.]

tri·no·mi·al (trī-nō′mē-əl) *adj.* **1.** Consisting of three names or terms, as a taxonomic designation. **2.** *Math.* Consisting of three algebraic terms connected by plus or minus signs. **—n.** **1.** *Math.* A trinomial algebraic expression. **2.** A three-part taxonomic designation indicating genus, species, and subspecies or variety. [TRI- + (BI)NOMIAL.]

tri·o (trē′ō) *n., pl.* **-os. 1.** A group of three. **2.** *Mus.* **a.** A composition for three performers. **b.** The group of musicians who perform such a composition. **c.** The middle section of a scherzo, a march, and various dance forms, as the minuet. [Italian, from Latin *trēs,* three.]

tri·ode (trī′ōd′) *n.* An electron tube with three electrodes, usu. an anode and a cathode and a grid whose voltage with respect to the cathode controls the flow of current between the anode and cathode. [TRI- + -ODE (path).]

tri·o·let (trē′ə-lā′, trī′ə-lĭt) *n.* A poem or stanza of eight lines constructed on two rhymes, the scheme being *abaaabab.* [French, dim. of *trio,* trio, from Italian.]

tri·ox·ide (trī-ŏk′sīd′) *n.* (-ŏk′sĭd). A chemical compound that contains three atoms of oxygen per molecule.

trip (trĭp) *n.* **1.** A journey, voyage, flight, or other passage from one place to another. **2.** An outing or excursion: *a camping trip.* **3.** The distance traveled on a trip or the time required for such a journey. **4.** A stumble or fall. **5.** A mistake or blunder. **6.** A device, as a catch or trigger, for activating a mechanism. **7.** *Slang.* A highly intensive visionary and emotional experience, esp. one brought on by an hallucenogenic drug: *a bad trip.* **—v.** **tripped, tripping.** **—intr.v.** **1.** To lose one's balance, as by catching one's toe on an obstacle; stumble. **2.** To make a mistake: *Do you trip over the use of "lay" and "lie"?* **3.** To move nimbly with light, rapid steps; skip. **4.** To be released, as a catch, switch, tooth on an escapement wheel in a watch, etc.: *The circuit breaker tripped.* **5.** Also **trip out.** *Slang.* To have a drug-induced hallucination. **—tr.v.** **1.** To cause to stumble or fall. **2.** To trap or catch in an error or inconsistency: *The lawyer tripped the witness with a clever question.* **3.** To release (a catch, trigger, switch, etc.) setting something in operation: *trip a circuit breaker.* **4.** *Archaic.* To perform (a dance) nimbly: *trip a waltz.* [Middle English, from *trippen,* to move nimbly, cause to stumble, from Old French *tripper,* from Middle Dutch *trippen,* to hop.] **—trip′per** *n.*

tri·par·tite (trī-pär′tīt′) *adj.* **1.** Composed of or divided into three parts. **2.** Involving or done by three parties.

tripe (trīp) *n.* **1.** The light-colored, rubbery lining of the stomach of cattle or other ruminants, used as food. **2.** *Informal.* Anything with no value; rubbish. [Middle English, from Old French.]

trip hammer. Also **trip·ham·mer** (trĭp′hăm′ər) or **trip-hammer.** A heavy, power-operated hammer that is lifted by a cam or lever and then dropped.

triph·thong (trĭf′thông′, -thŏng′, trĭp′-) *n.* A compound vowel sound resulting from the combination of three simple ones and functioning as a unit. [TRI- + (DI)PHTHONG.]

tri·ple (trĭp′əl) *adj.* **1.** Of or having three parts; threefold. **2.** Three times as many or as much. **—n.** **1.** A number or

tripod

triptych

Triton

amount three times as great as another. **2.** A group or set of three. **3.** *Baseball.* A hit that enables the batter to reach third base safely. —*v.* **-pled, -pling.** —*tr.v.* To make three times as great in number or amount. —*intr.v.* **1.** To be or become three times as great in number or amount. **2.** *Baseball.* To make a three-base hit. [Middle English, from Old French, from Latin *triplus.*] —**tri′ply** *adv.*

triple play. *Baseball.* A rare defensive play in which three players are put out during one turn at bat.

tri·ple-space (trĭp′əl-spās′) *v.* **-spaced, -spac·ing.** —*tr.v.* To type (lines of copy) leaving two blank lines between each. —*intr.v.* To type leaving two blank lines between each line of copy.

trip·let (trĭp′lĭt) *n.* **1.** A group or set of three. **2.** One of three children born at one birth. **3.** *Pros.* A group of three rhyming lines. **4.** *Mus.* A group of three notes allowed the same playing time as that normally given to two notes of the same value. [TRIPL(E) + (DOUBL)ET.]

triple time. A musical meter or rhythm that has three beats to the measure, with the accent on the first beat.

tri·plex (trĭp′lĕks′, trī′plĕks′) *adj.* Composed of three parts; threefold; triple. —*n.* Something composed of three parts, esp. an apartment with three floors. [Latin.]

trip·li·cate (trĭp′lĭ-kĭt) *adj.* Made with three identical copies. —*n.* One of a set of three identical objects or copies. —*tr.v.* (trĭp′lĭ-kāt′) **-cat·ed, -cat·ing. 1.** To triple. **2.** To make three identical copies of. [Middle English, from Latin *triplicātus,* past part. of *triplicāre,* to triple, from *triplex,* triplex.] —**trip′li·cate·ly** *adv.* —**trip′li·ca′tion** *n.*

tri·pod (trī′pŏd′) *n.* **1.** Something that has three legs, as a stool. **2.** An adjustable three-legged stand, esp. one for a camera. —**trip′o·dal** (trĭp′ə-dəl, trī′pŏd′l) *adj.*

trip·tych (trĭp′tĭk) *n.* **1.** An ancient writing tablet consisting of three leaves, hinged together. **2.** A picture, carving, etc., made of three side-by-side, hinged or folding panels. [Greek *triptukhos,* threefold : *tri-,* three + *ptukhē,* fold.]

tri·reme (trī′rēm′) *n.* An ancient Greek or Roman galley or warship, with three tiers of oars on each side. [Latin *trirēmis : tri-,* three + *rēmus,* oar.]

tri·sect (trī′sĕkt′, trī-sĕkt′) *tr.v.* To divide into three equal parts. —**tri′sec′tion** (-sĕk′shən) *n.* —**tri′sec′tor** *n.*

Tris·tan (trĭs′tən, -tän′, -tăn′) *n.* Also **Tris·tram** (trĭs′trəm). *Arthurian Legend.* A prince who fell in love with the Irish princess Iseult and died with her.

tri·syl·la·ble (trī′sĭl′ə-bəl) *n.* A three-syllable word. —**tri′syl·lab′ic** (-sĭ-lăb′ĭk) or **tri′syl·lab′i·cal** *adj.* —**tri′syl·lab′i·cal·ly** *adv.*

trite (trīt) *adj.* **trit·er, trit·est.** Overused and commonplace; hackneyed: *a trite expression.* [Latin *trītus,* past part. of *terere,* to rub, wear out.] —**trite′ly** *adv.* —**trite′ness** *n.*

trit·i·um (trĭt′ē-əm, trĭsh′ē-əm) *n.* A rare radioactive hydrogen isotope, with atomic mass 3 and half-life 12.5 years, prepared artificially for use as a tracer and as a constituent of hydrogen bombs. [From Greek *tritos,* third.]

tri·ton (trīt′n) *n.* **1.** Any of various chiefly tropical saltwater gastropod mollusks of the genus *Cymatium* and related genera, with a spirally twisted, often colorful shell. **2. Triton.** *Gk. Myth.* A god of the sea, son of Poseidon and Amphitrite, portrayed as half man and half fish.

trit·u·rate (trĭch′ə-rāt′) *tr.v.* **-rat·ed, -rat·ing.** To rub, crush, grind, or pound into fine particles or powder; pulverize. —*n.* (trĭch′ər-ĭt). A triturated substance, esp. a powdered drug. [From Late Latin *trītūrāre,* to pulverize corn, from

Latin *trītūra,* a rubbing, from *trītus,* past part. of *terere,* to rub.] —**trit′u·ra·ble** (trĭch′ər-ə-bəl) *adj.* —**trit′u·ra′tion** *n.* —**trit′u·ra′tor** *n.*

tri·umph (trī′əmf) *intr.v.* **1.** To be victorious; win; prevail. **2.** To rejoice over a success or victory; exult. —See Syns at **defeat.** —*n.* **1.** The fact or an example of being victorious; victory; success. **2.** Exultation derived from victory: *a cry of triumph.* **3.** A public celebration in ancient Rome to welcome a returning victorious commander and his army. —See Syns at **victory.** [Latin *triumphāre,* from *triumphus,* a triumph.] —**tri′umph·er** *n.*

tri·um·phal (trī-ŭm′fəl) *adj.* Of, celebrating, or commemorating a victory or triumph: *a triumphal arch.*

tri·um·phant (trī-ŭm′fənt) *adj.* **1.** Victorious; successful. **2.** Rejoicing over having been successful or victorious, *a triumphant return.* —**tri·um′phant·ly** *adv.*

tri·um·vir (trī-ŭm′vər) *n.,* pl. **-virs** or **-vi·ri** (-və-rī′). One of three men sharing civil authority, as in ancient Rome. [Latin, sing. of *triumvirī,* a triumvirate : *trēs,* three + *vir,* man.] —**tri·um′vi·ral** *adj.*

tri·um·vi·rate (trī-ŭm′vər-ĭt) *n.* **1.** A group of three persons governing jointly. **2. a.** The office or term of a triumvir. **b.** Government by triumvirs. **3.** Any association or group of three: *a triumvirate of composers.*

tri·une (trī′yoon′) *adj.* Being three in one, esp. of or concerning the single Godhead of the Trinity. [TRI- + Latin *ūnus,* one.]

tri·va·lent (trī-vā′lənt) *adj. Chem.* Having valence 3. —**tri·va′lence** or **tri·va′len·cy** *n.*

triv·et (trĭv′ĭt) *n.* **1.** A three-legged stand for holding a kettle or pot over or near an open fire. **2.** A stand or thick plate placed under a hot dish or platter on a table. [Middle English *trevet,* prob. from Old English *trefet,* from Latin *tripēs,* three-footed : *tri-,* three + *pēs,* foot.]

triv·i·a¹ (trĭv′ē-ə) *pl.n. (used with a sing. or pl. verb).* Insignificant or inessential matters; trivialities; trifles.

triv·i·a² (trĭv′ē-ə) *n.* Plural of **trivium.**

triv·i·al (trĭv′ē-əl) *adj.* **1.** Not of great importance or significance; trifling: *trivial matters.* **2.** Ordinary; commonplace: *a trivial occurrence.* —See Syns at **little.** [Latin *triviālis,* commonplace, ordinary, from *trivium,* crossroads, public street.] —**triv′i·al′i·ty** *n.* —**triv′i·al·ly** *adv.*

triv·i·um (trĭv′ē-əm) *n.,* pl. **-i·a** (-ē-ə). The elementary division of the seven liberal arts in medieval schools, consisting of grammar, logic, and rhetoric. [Medieval Latin, from Latin, crossroads : *tri-,* three + *via,* way.]

tri·week·ly (trī-wēk′lē) *adj.* **1.** Happening every three weeks. **2.** Happening three times a week. —*adv.* **1.** Once every three weeks. **2.** Three times a week.

-trix. A suffix meaning: **1.** A female that performs a (specified) action: **executrix. 2.** A geometric point, line, or surface: **directrix.** [Latin.]

tro·che (trō′kē) *n.* A small circular medicinal lozenge. [Middle English *trociske,* from Late Latin *trochiscus,* from Greek *trokhiskos,* dim. of *trokhos,* wheel.]

tro·chee (trō′kē) *n.* A metrical foot of two syllables, one long or stressed followed by one short or unstressed. [French *trochée,* from Latin *trochaeus,* from Greek *trokhaios (pous),* "running (foot)," from *trekhein,* to run.]

trod (trŏd) *v.* The past tense and a past participle of **tread.** [Middle English *trad,* from Old English *træd* (p.t.); past part. from TRODDEN.]

trod·den (trŏd′n) *n..* A past participle of **tread.** [From

TREAD, formed on the model of *break, broken.*]

trog·lo·dyte (trŏg′lə-dīt′) *n.* **1.** A prehistoric cave dweller. **2.** A primitive, brutish, or reclusive person. [Latin *Trōglodyta,* from Greek *Trōglodutēs : troglē,* hole + *duein,* to go into.] —**trog′lo·dyt′ic** (-dĭt′ĭk) or **trog′lo·dyt′i·cal** *adj.*

troi·ka (troi′kə) *n.* **1.** A kind of small Russian carriage drawn by a team of three horses abreast. **2.** A triumvirate. [Russian *troyka,* from *troje,* three.]

Troi·lus (troi′ləs, trō′ə-ləs) *n. Gk. Myth.* A son of Priam of Troy, killed by Achilles, and depicted in medieval romance as Cressida's lover.

Tro·jan (trō′jən) *n.* **1.** A native or inhabitant of ancient Troy. **2.** A person of courage, determination, or energy. —*adj.* Of ancient Troy or its residents.

Trojan horse. **1.** The hollow wooden horse in which, according to Virgil, Greeks hid and gained entrance to Troy, later opening the gates to their army. **2.** Any subversive group or device insinuated within enemy ranks.

troll¹ (trōl) *tr.v.* **1.** To fish for by trailing a baited line from behind a slowly moving boat. **2.** To trail or move (a baited line) through the water in fishing. **3.** To sing in succession the parts of (a round). **4.** To sing heartily: *troll a carol.* —*intr.v.* **1.** To fish by trailing a line from a moving boat. **2.** To sing heartily or gaily. **3.** To be sung or uttered in a lusty, rolling voice. —*n.* **1.** A lure used for trolling, as a spoon or spinner. **2.** A vocal composition in successive parts; a round. [Middle English *trollen,* to ramble, roll.] —**troll′er** *n.*

troll² (trōl) *n. Teutonic Folklore.* A supernatural creature variously described as friendly or evil, as a dwarf or a giant, and as living in caves or under bridges. [Norwegian, from Old Norse, monster, demon.]

trol·ley (trŏl′ē) *n., pl.* **-leys.** Also **trol·ly** *pl.* **-lies.** **1.** An electrically operated car that runs on a track; a streetcar. **2.** A carriage, basket, etc., that hangs from wheels that run on an overhead track. **3.** A device, such as a grooved wheel at the end of a metal pole, that makes contact with an overhead wire, third rail, underground conductor, etc., and supplies current to an electrically powered vehicle. [Prob. from obs. *troll,* to move about.]

trolley bus. An electrically powered bus that does not run on tracks and receives current from an overhead wire.

trolley car. A streetcar.

trol·lop (trŏl′əp) *n.* **1.** A slovenly, untidy woman. **2.** A loose woman; strumpet. [Perh. from obs. *troll,* to move about.]

trom·bone (trŏm-bōn′, trəm-, trŏm′bōn′) *n.* A musical wind instrument of the brass family that consists of a long cylindrical tube bent upon itself twice and ending in a bell-shaped mouth, equipped either with valves or a sliding extension to control pitch. [French, from Italian, from *tromba,* trumpet, from Old High German *trumpa.*] —**trom·bon′ist** *n.*

trombone

-tron. A suffix meaning a device for manipulating subatomic particles: *cyclotron.* [Greek, suffix indicating an instrument.]

troop (trōōp) *n.* **1.** A group or company of people, animals, or things. **2.** A group of soldiers. **3. troops.** Military units; soldiers. **4.** A unit of Boy Scouts or Girl Scouts. —*intr.v.* **1.** To move or go as a throng. **2.** To proceed; move along: *children trooping home.* **3.** To consort; associate: *They troop with a lot of artists.* [French *troupe,* back-formation from *troupeau,* herd, from Medieval Latin *troppus.*]

troop·er (trōō′pər) *n.* **1. a.** A cavalryman. **b.** A cavalry horse. **2.** A mounted policeman. **3.** A state policeman.

troop·ship (trōōp′shĭp′) *n.* A transport ship designed for carrying troops.

trope (trōp) *n.* The figurative use of a word or expression; a figure of speech. [Latin *tropus,* from Greek *tropos,* a turn, way, manner.]

tro·phy (trō′fē) *n., pl.* **-phies.** **1.** A prize or memento received as a symbol of victory. **2.** An accumulation of captured arms or other spoils kept as a memorial of victory. **3.** A coin, medal, etc. memorializing a victory. **4.** Any memento, as of one's personal achievements. **5.** In ancient times, a monument of an enemy's defeat raised on the battlefield or in a public place and displaying captured arms and spoils. [Old French *trophee,* from Latin *trophaeum,* from Greek *tropaion,* from *tropē,* a turn, defeat.]

trop·ic (trŏp′ĭk) *n.* **1.** Either of the two parallels of latitude on the earth at 23 degrees 27 minutes north and south that constitute the boundaries of the Torrid Zone. **2.** *Astron.* The projection of either of these parallels onto the celestial sphere marking the limits of the northerly and southerly passages of the sun. **3. tropics.** The region of the earth's surface bounded by these latitudes; the Torrid Zone. —*adj.* Of or concerning the tropics; tropical. [Middle English *tropik,* solstice point, from Late Latin *tropicus,* from Greek *tropikos,* from *tropē,* a turn.]

-tropic. A suffix meaning turning in a (specified) manner or in response to a (specified) stimulus: **isotropic.** [From Greek *tropos,* a turn.]

trop·i·cal (trŏp′ĭ-kəl) *adj.* **1.** Of or characteristic of the tropics. **2.** Hot and humid; torrid. —**trop′i·cal·ly** *adv.*

tropical fish. Any of various small or brightly colored fishes often kept in tropical aquariums.

tropical year. The interval of time between two successive passages of the sun through the vernal equinox; a period of about 365.24 mean solar days.

trop·ic·bird (trŏp′ĭk-bûrd′) *n.* Any of several predominantly white sea birds of the genus *Phaethon,* of warm regions, with a pair of long, projecting tail feathers.

tropic of Cancer. The parallel of latitude 23 degrees 27 minutes north of the equator, forming the boundary between the North Temperate Zone and the Torrid Zone.

tropic of Capricorn. The parallel of latitude 23 degrees 27 minutes south of the equator, forming the boundary between the South Temperate Zone and the Torrid Zone.

tro·pism (trō′pĭz′əm) *n. Biol.* The responsive growth or movement of an organism toward or away from an external stimulus. [From -TROPISM.]

-tropism. A suffix meaning the growth or movement of an organism or part in response to a (specified) stimulus: **phototropism.** [From Greek *tropos,* turn.]

tro·po·sphere (trō′pə-sfîr′, trŏp′ə-) *n.* The lowest region of the atmosphere varying between 5 and 11 miles above the earth's surface and characterized by temperatures that decrease with increasing altitude. [Greek *tropos,* turn, change + SPHERE.]

-tropy. A suffix meaning the condition of turning: **allotropy.** [Greek *-tropia,* from *-tropos,* from *trepein,* to turn.]

trot (trŏt) *n.* **1.** A gait of a horse or other four-footed animal, between a walk and a run, in which diagonal pairs of legs move forward together. **2.** A jogging run or quick walk of a person. **3.** *Informal.* A word-for-word translation of a work in a foreign language, sometimes used secretly in preparing a class assignment; a pony. —*v.* **trot·ted, trot·ting.** —*intr.v.* **1.** To go or move at a trot. **2.** To proceed rapidly; to hurry. —*tr.v.* To ride or cause to move at a trot. —*phrasal verb.* **trot out.** *Informal.* To bring out and show for others to look at or admire. [Middle English, from Old French, from *troter,* to trot.]

troth (trôth, trŏth, trōth) *n.* **1.** Fidelity. **2.** One's pledged fidelity; betrothal. —*tr.v. Archaic.* To pledge or betroth. [Middle English *trouthe,* from Old English *trēowth.*]

trot·ter (trŏt′ər) *n.* A person or animal that trots, esp. a horse trained for harness racing.

trou·ba·dour (trōō′bə-dôr′, -dōr′, -dōōr′) *n.* **1.** One of a class of lyric poet-musicians of the 12th and 13th cent. in Provence and northern Italy. **2.** A strolling minstrel. [French, from Old French, from Old Provençal *trobador,* from *trobar,* to invent, compose poetry.]

trou·ble (trŭb′əl) *n.* **1.** Difficulty: *having trouble getting this door open.* **2.** Danger or distress. **3.** A source of difficulty, annoyance, or distress; a problem or worry. **4.** Extra work or effort; bother; inconvenience. **5.** Conflict, disturbance, or unrest, esp. civil disorder: *labor trouble.* **6. a.** Failure to perform properly; malfunction: *engine trouble.* **b.** A diseased or disordered condition: *stomach trouble.* —*v.* **-bled, -bling.** —*tr.v.* **1.** To make anxious or uneasy; disturb; worry, or upset: *Dark thoughts troubled me.* **2.** To afflict with pain or discomfort. **3.** To inconvenience or bother: *May I trouble you to close the window.* **4.** To agitate or stir up, as water. —*intr.v.* To take pains: *trouble over every detail.* [Middle English, from Old French, from *troubler,* to trouble, ult. from Latin *turbidus,* turbid.] —**troub′ler** *n.* —**troub′ling·ly** *adv.*

troub·le·mak·er (trŭb′əl-mā′kər) *n.* A person who habitually stirs up trouble or strife.

troub·le·shoot·er (trŭb′əl-shoo′tər) *n.* A person who locates and eliminates sources of trouble.

troub·le·some (trŭb′əl-səm) *adj.* **1.** Causing trouble, esp. repeatedly. **2.** Difficult; trying: *a troublesome situation.* —**troub′le·some·ly** *adv.* —**troub′le·some·ness** *n.*

troub·lous (trŭb′ləs) *adj. Archaic.* **1.** Full of trouble; uneasy; troubled. **2.** Causing trouble; troublesome.

trough (trôf, trŏf) *n.* **1.** A long, narrow, gen. shallow receptacle, esp. one for holding water or feed for animals. **2.** A gutter under the eaves of a roof. **3.** A long, narrow depression, as between waves or ridges. **4.** A low point in a business cycle or on a statistical graph. **5.** An extended region of low atmospheric pressure, often associated with a front. [Middle English, from Old English *trog.*]

trounce (trouns) *tr.v.* **trounced, trounc·ing.** **1.** To thrash; beat. **2.** To defeat decisively. —See Syns at **defeat.** [Orig. unknown.]

troupe (troop) *n.* A company or group, esp. of touring actors, singers, or dancers. —*intr.v.* **trouped, troup·ing.** To tour with a theatrical company. [French, troop.]

troup·er (troo′pər) *n.* **1.** A member of a theatrical company. **2.** A veteran actor or performer. **3.** *Informal.* A faithful and good-natured worker.

trou·sers (trou′zərz) *pl.n.* An outer garment worn to cover the lower half of the body, consisting of a pair of leg coverings sewn together from the crotch to the waist. [From earlier *trouse,* from Scottish Gaelic *triubhas.*]

trous·seau (troo′sō, troo-sō′) *n., pl.* **-seaux** (-sōz, -sōz′) or **-seaus.** The special possessions and wardrobe that a bride assembles for her marriage. [French, from Old French, dim. of *trusse,* a bundle.]

trout (trout) *n., pl.* **trout** or **trouts.** **1.** Any of various freshwater or anadromous food and game fishes of the genera *Salvelinus* and *Salmo,* usu. with a speckled body. **2.** Any of various similar fishes. [Middle English *troute,* from Old English *trūht,* from Late Latin *tructa.*]

trove (trōv) *n.* Something of value discovered or found; a find. [Short for TREASURE-TROVE.]

trow (trō) *intr.v. Archaic.* To think; suppose. [Middle English *trowen,* from Old English *trēowian.*]

trow·el (trou′əl) *n.* **1.** A hand tool with a flat blade for spreading and working substances such as cement. **2.** A small spoonlike implement used for digging or scooping earth, as in setting plants. —*tr.v.* **-eled** or **-elled, -el·ing** or **-el·ling.** To work or scoop with a trowel. [Middle English *trowell,* from Old French *truelle,* from Late Latin *truella,* from Latin *trulla,* dim. of *trua,* ladle.] —**trow′el·er** *n.*

troy (troi) *adj.* Of, measured in, or expressed in troy weight. [Middle English *troye,* from Norman French, prob. after *Troyes,* France.]

troy weight. A system of units of weight in which the grain is the same as in the avoirdupois system and the pound contains 12 ounces, 240 pennyweights, or 5,760 grains.

tru·ant (troo′ənt) *n.* **1.** A student who is absent from school without permission. **2.** A person who shirks his work or duty. —*adj.* **1.** Absent without permission: *a truant pupil.* **2.** Idle, lazy, or neglectful: *a truant worker.* [Middle English, beggar, idle rogue, from Old French.] —**tru′an·cy** *n.*

truce (troos) *n.* A temporary cessation of hostilities by agreement of the contending forces; an armistice. [Middle English *trewes,* pl. of *trewe,* truce, peace, from Old English *trēow,* faith, pledge.]

truck¹ (trŭk) *n.* **1.** Any of various automotive vehicles, made in a wide range of sizes and types for carrying loads of freight, materials, etc. **2.** A swiveling frame under each end of a railroad car, streetcar, etc., on which the wheels

are mounted. **2.** A two-wheeled barrow for moving heavy objects by hand; a hand truck. —*tr.v.* To transport by truck. —*intr.v.* **1.** To carry goods by truck. **2.** To drive a truck. [Perh. from Latin *trochus,* a wheel, from Greek *trokhos,* from *trekhein,* to run.]

truck² (trŭk) *tr.v.* To exchange; barter. —*intr.v.* To exchange or trade goods; barter. —*n.* **1.** Garden produce raised for the market. **2.** *Informal.* Worthless articles; rubbish. **3.** *Informal.* Dealings; business. **4.** Barter; exchange. **5.** The **truck system.** [Middle English *trukken,* from Old French *troquer.*]

truck·age (trŭk′ĭj) *n.* **1.** Transportation of goods by truck. **2.** A charge for this.

truck·er (trŭk′ər) *n.* **1.** A truck driver. **2.** A person or company engaged in trucking goods.

truck farm. A farm producing vegetables for the market. —**truck farmer.** —**truck farming.**

truck·le (trŭk′əl) *n.* **1.** A small wheel or roller; caster. **2.** A trundle bed. —*intr.v.* **-led, -ling.** To be servile or submissive; yield weakly. [Middle English *trocle,* pulley, from Norman French, from Latin *trochlea,* system of pulleys.] —**truck′ler** *n.*

truck system. The practice of paying wages in goods instead of money.

truc·u·lent (trŭk′yə-lənt) *adj.* **1.** Savage and cruel; fierce. **2.** Vitriolic; scathing. **3.** Disposed to fight; pugnacious; defiant. [Latin *truculentus,* from *trux,* fierce.] —**truc′u·lence** or **truc′u·len·cy** *n.* —**truc′u·lent·ly** *adv.*

trudge (trŭj) *intr.v.* **trudged, trudg·ing.** To walk in a laborious, heavy-footed way; to plod. —*n.* A long, tedious walk. [Orig. unknown.] —**trudg′er** *n.*

trudg·en (trŭj′ən) *n.* A swimming stroke in which a double overarm movement is combined with a scissors kick. Also called **trudgen stroke.** [After John *Trudgen,* 19th-cent. English swimmer.]

true (troo) *adj.* **tru·er, tru·est.** **1.** Consistent with fact or reality; right; accurate. **2.** Not imitation or counterfeit; real or genuine: *true gold.* **3.** Faithful; loyal: *"This above all, to thine own self be true"* (Shakespeare). **4.** Rightful; legitimate. **5.** Sincerely felt or expressed: *speaking with true emotion.* **6. a.** Rightfully bearing the name; properly so called: *The true vampire bat can be found only in the New World.* **b.** Having the characteristics associated with a certain group or type; typical: *He was lusty and thickset, a true Dutchman.* **c.** Exactly conforming to an original or standard: *a true copy of the birth certificate.* —*adv.* **1.** Rightly; truthfully: *She speaks true.* **2.** Without swerving from a course; accurately: *I'll sail the ship straight and true.* —*tr.v.* **trued, tru·ing** or **true·ing.** To adjust or fit so as to conform with a standard: *true the edges of a seam.* —*n.* **1. the true.** That which is real or genuine; truth. **2.** Proper alignment or adjustment: *in or out of true.* [Middle English *trewe,* from Old English *trēowe,* loyal, trustworthy.] —**true′ness** *n.*

   Syns: 1. true, rightful *adj.* Core meaning: Being so legitimately *(the true heir to the throne).* **2. true, genuine, real, sincere** *adj.* Core meaning: Devoid of any hypocrisy or pretense *(true grief at the loss of a friend).* See also Syns at **faithful.**

true bill. A bill of indictment endorsed by a grand jury.

true-blue (troo′bloo′) *adj.* Of or marked by unswerving loyalty.

true-love (troo′lŭv′) *n.* One's beloved; a sweetheart.

true lovers' knot. Also **true-love knot.** A stylized knot, gen. a form of bowknot, used as an emblem of love.

true rib. One of the ribs, in man any of the upper seven pairs, attached to the sternum by a costal cartilage.

truf·fle (trŭf′əl) *n.* Any of various fleshy subterranean fungi, chiefly of the genus *Tuber,* often valued as food. [French *truffe,* from Old French, from Old Provençal *trufa,* from Latin *tūber,* tuber, truffle.]

tru·ism (troo′ĭz′əm) *n.* An obvious truth. —**tru·is′tic** (-ĭs′tĭk) *adj.*

tru·ly (troo′lē) *adv.* **1.** Sincerely; genuinely: *truly sorry.* **2.** Truthfully; accurately. **3.** Indeed.

trump¹ (trŭmp) *n.* **1. a.** In card games, any card of a suit declared to outrank all other cards during the play of a hand. **b.** The suit of cards declared to outrank the other suits. **2.** *Informal.* A reliable or admirable person. —*tr.v.*

1. To take (a card or trick) with a trump. **2.** To go one better than; outdo. —*intr.v.* To play a trump card. —*phrasal verb.* **trump up.** To devise fraudulently; concoct: *trump up charges.* [Var. of TRIUMPH.]

trump² (trŭmp) *n. Archaic.* A trumpet. [Middle English *trompe,* from Old French, from Old High German *trumpa,*]

trump·er·y (trŭm′pə-rē) *n., pl.* **-ies. 1.** Showy but worthless finery. **2.** Nonsense; rubbish. —*adj.* Showy but valueless. [Middle English *trompery,* from Old French *tromperie,* from *tromper,* to cheat.]

trum·pet (trŭm′pĭt) *n.* **1.** A soprano brass wind instrument that consists of a long metal tube looped once and ending in a flared bell, the modern type being equipped with three valves for producing variations in pitch. **2.** Something shaped like or sounding like a trumpet. **3.** An organ stop that produces a tone like that of the trumpet. **4.** A resounding call, as that of the elephant. —*intr.v.* **1.** To play a trumpet. **2.** To give forth a resounding call. —*tr.v.* **1.** To sound on a trumpet. **2.** To utter or proclaim loudly: *trumpeted words of rage.* [Middle English *trompette,* from Old French, dim. of *trompe,* trump.]

trumpet

trumpet creeper. A woody vine, *Campsis radicans,* with compound leaves and red trumpet-shaped flowers.

trum·pet·er (trŭm′pĭt-ər) *n.* **1.** A trumpet player. **2.** A person who announces something; a herald. **3.** Any of several large birds of the genus *Psophia,* of tropical South America, with a loud, resonant call. **4.** The **trumpeter swan.**

trumpeter swan. A large white swan, *Olor buccinator,* of western North America, with a loud, buglelike call.

trun·cate (trŭng′kāt′) *tr.v.* **-cat·ed, -cat·ing.** To shorten by or as if by cutting off the end or top. —*adj. Biol.* Appearing to terminate abruptly, as certain leaves. [From Latin *truncāre,* from *truncus,* torso, trunk.] —**trun′ca′tion** *n.*

trun·cheon (trŭn′chən) *n.* **1.** A staff carried as a symbol of office or authority. **2.** A short stick carried by policemen. **3.** *Obs.* A cudgel. **4.** *Obs.* A fragment of a spear shaft. —*tr.v. Archaic.* To beat with a club; to bludgeon. [Middle English *tronchon,* fragment, club, from Old French, from Latin *truncus,* torso, trunk.]

trun·dle (trŭn′dl) *n.* **1.** A small wheel or roller. **2.** A trundle bed. **3.** A low-wheeled cart; dolly. —*v.* **-dled, -dling.** —*tr.v.* **1.** To push or propel on wheels or rollers: *trundling a wheelbarrow.* **2.** To cause to spin or rotate; twirl: *a glassblower trundling a ball of glass over heat.* —*intr.v.* To move along by or as if by rolling. [Middle English *trendil,* from Old English *trendel,* circle.] —**trun′dler** *n.*

trundle bed. A low bed on casters that can be rolled under another bed when not in use. Also called **truckle.**

trunk (trŭngk) *n.* **1.** The main woody axis of a tree. **2. a.** The human body excluding the head and limbs; torso. **b.** A similar part of an organism, as the thorax of an insect. **3.** A main body or part of anything, as a blood vessel or river. **4.** A **trunk line. 5.** A large packing case or box that clasps shut. **6.** A covered compartment of an automobile for luggage and storage. **7.** A proboscis, esp. the long, prehensile proboscis of an elephant. **8. trunks.** Men's shorts worn for swimming or athletics. —*modifier: the trunk muscles; a trunk road.* [Middle English *trunke,* from Old French *tronc,* a tree trunk, from Latin *truncus.*]

trunk·fish (trŭngk′fĭsh′) *n., pl.* **trunkfish** or **-fish·es.** Any of various tropical saltwater fishes of the family Ostraciidae, with boxlike armor enclosing the body.

trunk hose. Short, ballooning breeches, extending to midthigh, worn in the 16th and 17th cents. [Prob. from obs. *trunk,* to cut short, from Latin *truncāre,* to truncate.]

trunk line. 1. A direct line between two telephone switchboards. **2.** The main line of a communication or transpor-

tation system. Also called **trunk.**

trun·nion (trŭn′yən) *n.* A pin, esp. either of two small cylindrical projections on a cannon that form an axis on which it pivots. [French *trognon,* core of fruit, tree trunk, from Old French, from *estronchier,* to cut off the branches : *es-,* off, from Latin *ex-* + *tronchier,* to cut, from Latin *truncāre,* to truncate.]

truss (trŭs) *n.* **1.** *Med.* A device worn to support and prevent enlargement of a hernia. **2.** A framework of wooden beams or metal bars, often arranged in triangles, to support a roof, bridge, or other structure. **3.** A bundle; a pack. **4.** *Brit.* A bundle of straw or hay of a set weight. **5.** A compact cluster of flowers at the end of a stalk. —*tr.v.* **1.** To tie up or bind securely. **2.** To bind or skewer the wings or legs of (a fowl) before cooking. **3.** To support or brace with a truss. [Middle English *trusse,* a bundle, from Old French, from *trusser,* to tie in a bundle.]

trust (trŭst) *tr.v.* **1.** To have or place confidence in as being dependable or reliable: *Trust my judgment.* **2.** To depend, rely, or count on: *Can we trust you to pay back what we lend you?* **3.** To place in the care or keeping of another; entrust. **4.** To allow to have money or goods on credit. **5.** To believe: *If you don't trust me, see for yourself.* —*intr.v.* **1.** To hope, expect, or assume: *All went well, I trust.* **2.** To sell on credit. —*phrasal verb.* **trust in** (or **to**). To rely or depend on. —*n.* **1.** Confidence or firm belief in the honesty, dependability, or power of someone or something. **2.** Trustfulness; faith: *The child was all innocence and trust.* **3.** A solemn responsibility or duty placed upon someone; a charge: *Government office is a public trust.* **4.** Custody; care. **5.** Confidence in a buyer's intention and ability to pay at some future time; credit. **6. a.** *Law.* A fiduciary arrangement in which property is held and managed by one party for the benefit of another. **b.** The property so held. **7.** A group of firms or corporations that have combined for the purpose of reducing competition and controlling prices throughout a business or industry. —See Syns at **confidence.** [Middle English *trusten,* prob. from Old Norse *treysta,* to have confidence.] —**trust′er** *n.*

trust·bust·er (trŭst′bŭs′tər) *n. Informal.* A government official who works to dissolve illegal business combines.

trust company. A commercial bank or other corporation that manages trusts.

trus·tee (trŭs′tē′) *n.* **1.** *Law.* A person, either an individual or a corporation such as a bank, required either by appointment or by law to hold title to and administer property, an interest, or a power for the benefit or to the use of another. **2.** A member of a board elected or appointed to direct the affairs of an institution, foundation, etc.

trus·tee·ship (trŭs′tē′shĭp′) *n.* **1.** The position or function of a trustee. **2. a.** The administration of a territory or countries so commissioned by the United Nations. **b.** A territory so administered, a trust territory.

trust·ful (trŭst′fəl) *adj.* Inclined to believe or confide readily; full of trust. —**trust′ful·ly** *adv.* —**trust′ful·ness** *n.*

trust fund. Money, securities, real estate, etc., held and administered by one person for the benefit of another.

trust·ing (trŭs′tĭng) *adj.* Tending to believe; trustful.

trust territory. A territory placed under the administration of a country or countries by commission of the United Nations.

trust·wor·thy (trŭst′wûr′thē) *adj.* Warranting trust; dependable. —**trust′wor′thi·ly** *adv.* —**trust′wor′thi·ness** *n.*

trust·y (trŭs′tē) *adj.* **-i·er, -i·est.** Dependable; reliable. —*n., pl.* **-ies.** A trusted person, esp. a convict granted special privileges. —**trust′i·ly** *adv.* —**trust′i·ness** *n.*

truth (trōōth) *n., pl.* **truths** (trōōthz, trōōths). **1.** Conformity to knowledge, fact, or actuality; veracity. **2.** Something that is the case; the real state of affairs: *tell the truth.* **3.** Reality; actuality: *Even before Appomattox the Civil War was in truth over.* **4.** A statement proven to be or accepted as true: *scientific truths.* **5.** Sincerity; honesty: *There was no truth in his speech or character.* [Middle English *trewthe,* from Old English *trēowth.*]

truth·ful (trōōth′fəl) *adj.* **1.** Consistently telling the truth; honest. **2.** Corresponding to reality; true. —**truth′ful·ly** *adv.* —**truth′ful·ness** *n.*

truth serum. A drug, such as sodium pentothal or scopalomine, which, when injected into the bloodstream, induces in the subject a willingness to answer honestly questions about hidden or repressed information.

truth-val·ue (trōōth′văl′yōō) *n. Logic.* Either the truth or the falsehood of a proposition.

try (trī) *v.* **tried, try·ing.** —*tr.v.* **1.** To taste, sample, or otherwise test in order to determine quality, worth, desirability, or effect. **2.** *Law.* **a.** To examine a controversy or case in a court of law. **b.** To put (a person accused of crime or other wrong) on trial in a court. **3.** To cause to undergo great strain or hardship; tax. **4.** To attempt; make an effort; strive. **5. a.** To melt (fat or lard) so as to separate oil from impurities; render. **b.** To extract or refine (metal) by heating. —*intr.v.* To make an effort; strive. —*phrasal verbs.* **try on.** To put on (a garment) so as to test fit or appearance. **try out. 1.** To take or undergo a competitive test in an attempt to qualify. **2.** To use experimentally. —*n., pl.* **tries.** An attempt; an effort. [Middle English *trien,* to separate, pick out, sift, from Old French *trier.*] —**tri′er** *n.*

try·ing (trī′ĭng) *adj.* Causing severe strain, hardship, or distress. —See Syns at **burdensome.**

try·out (trī′out′) *n. Informal.* A competitive test to ascertain or evaluate the qualifications of applicants, as for an athletic team, a theatrical role, etc.

tryp·sin (trĭp′sĭn) *n.* One of the proteolytic enzymes of the pancreatic juice, important in the digestive processes. [Greek *tripsis,* a rubbing, from *tribein,* to rub + (PEPS)IN.] —**tryp′tic** (-tĭk) *adj.*

try·sail (trī′səl, -sāl′) *n. Naut.* A small fore-and-aft sail hoisted abaft either the foremast or the mainmast in a storm to keep a ship's bow to the wind. [From obs. *try,* the act of lying to in a storm.]

try square. A carpenter's tool consisting of a ruled metal straightedge set at right angles to a wooden straight piece, used for measuring and marking square work.

tryst (trĭst) *n.* **1.** An agreement between lovers to meet at a certain time and place. **2.** The meeting or meeting place so arranged. [Middle English, from Old French *triste,* an appointed station in hunting.]

tsar (zär) *n.* Var. of **czar.**

tsar·e·vitch (zär′ə-vĭch) *n.* Var. of **czarevitch.**

tsa·rev·na (zär-rĕv′nə) *n.* Var. of **czarevna.**

tsa·ri·na (zä-rē′nə) *n.* Var. of **czarina.**

tset·se fly (tsĕt′sē, tsĕt′sē). Also **tzet·ze fly.** Any of several bloodsucking African flies of the genus *Glossina,* often transmitting disease-causing, parasitic protozoans to human beings and livestock. [Afrikaans, of Bantu orig.]

T-shirt (tē′shûrt′) *n.* Also **tee shirt. 1.** A short-sleeved, collarless undershirt worn by men. **2.** An outer shirt of similar design worn with sportswear by men and women. [So called from its shape.]

T-square (tē′skwâr′) *n.* A rule with a short crosspiece at one end, used for drawing parallel lines.

tsu·na·mi (tsōō-nä′mē) *n.* A very large ocean wave caused by an underwater earthquake or volcanic eruption. [Japanese : *tsu,* harbor + *nami,* wave.]

tu·a·ta·ra (tōō′ə-tär′ə) *n.* A lizardlike reptile, *Sphenodon punctatus,* of New Zealand, the only surviving representative of the order Rhynchocephalia that flourished during the Mesozoic era. [Maori *tuatàra.*]

tub (tŭb) *n.* **1. a.** A broad, round, open container with a flat bottom and often handles, used for packing, storing, or washing. **b.** The amount held by such a vessel. **2.** A bathtub. **3.** *Brit. Informal.* A bath taken in a bathtub. **4.** *Informal.* Something resembling a tub, esp. a wide, slow-moving boat. [Middle English *tubbe,* from Middle Dutch and Middle Low German.]

tu·ba (tōō′bə, tyōō′-) *n.* A large brass wind instrument that has a full, mellow tone and a bass range, using several valves to change its pitch. [Italian, from Latin, trumpet.]

tu·bal (tōō′bəl, tyōō′-) *adj.* Of, relating to, or concerning a tube.

tub·by (tŭb′ē) *adj.* **-bi·er, -bi·est.** Short and fat.

tube (tōōb, tyōōb) *n.* **1. a.** A hollow cylinder of metal, glass, rubber, or other material, used to carry liquids. **2.** A cylindrical structure in an animal or plant that functions as a duct. **3.** A small, flexible container that is sealed at one end and has a screw cap at the other from which toothpaste or other similarly thick substances can be squeezed.

4. *Mus.* The part of a wind instrument that extends from the mouthpiece to the end that is open to the air. **5.** *Brit.* The subway. **6.** Often **the tube.** *Informal.* Television or a television set. [French, from Latin *tubus.*] —**tube′less** *adj.*

tube foot. One of the numerous external, fluid-filled muscular tubes of echinoderms, such as the starfish, that serve primarily as organs of locomotion.

tu·ber (tōō′bər, tyōō′-) *n.* **1.** *Bot.* A swollen, usu. underground stem, such as the potato, bearing buds from which new plant shoots arise. **2.** *Pathol.* A swelling; tubercle. [Latin *tūber,* a lump, swelling, tumor.]

tu·ber·cle (tōō′bər-kəl, tyōō′-) *n.* **1.** A small, knobby prominence or excrescence on the roots of some plants or in the skin or on a bone. **2.** *Pathol.* **a.** A nodule or swelling. **b.** The characteristic lesion of tuberculosis. [Latin *tūberculum,* dim. of *tūber,* a lump.]

tubercle bacillus. A rod-shaped bacterium, *Mycobacterium tuberculosis,* that causes tuberculosis.

tu·ber·cu·lar (tōō-bûr′kyə-lər, tyōō-) *adj.* **1.** Of, relating to, or covered with tubercles. **2.** Of, relating to, or afflicted with tuberculosis. —*n.* A person having tuberculosis.

tu·ber·cu·lin (tōō-bûr′kyə-lĭn, tyōō-) *n.* A substance derived from cultures of tubercle bacilli, used in the diagnosis and treatment of tuberculosis. [Latin *tūberculum,* tubercle + -IN.]

tu·ber·cu·lo·sis (tōō-bûr′kyə-lō′sĭs, tyōō-) *n.* **1.** A communicable disease of man and animals, caused by the tubercle bacillus and manifesting itself in lesions of the lung, bone, and other parts of the body. **2.** Tuberculosis of the lungs. Also **consumption** and **pulmonary tuberculosis.** [Latin *tūberculum,* tubercle + -OSIS.]

tu·ber·cu·lous (tōō-bûr′kyə-ləs, tyōō-) *adj.* **1.** Of, relating to, or having tuberculosis. **2.** Of, affected with, or caused by tubercles.

tube·rose (tōōb′rōz′, tōōb′-, tōō′bə-rōz′, tyōō′-, -rōs′) *n.* A tuberous plant, *Polianthes tuberosa,* native to Mexico, cultivated for its fragrant white flowers.

tu·ber·os·i·ty (tōō′bə-rŏs′ə-tē, tyōō-) *n., pl.* **-ties.** A projection or protuberance, esp. one at the end of a bone for the attachment of a muscle or tendon.

tu·ber·ous (tōō′bər-əs, tyōō′-) *adj.* **1.** Producing or bearing tubers. **2.** Resembling a tuber: *a tuberous root.*

tub·ing (tōō′bĭng, tyōō′-) *n.* **1.** Tubes in general. **2.** A system of tubes. **3.** A piece or length of tube.

tu·bu·lar (tōō′byə-lər, tyōō′-) *adj.* **1.** Of or pertaining to a tube or tubes. **2.** Having the form of a tube. **3.** Constituting or consisting of a tube or tubes.

tu·bule (tōō′byōōl, tyōō′-) *n.* A very small tube or tubular structure.

tuck (tŭk) *n.* **1.** A narrow pleat or fold stitched in a garment. **2.** A folded position or stance, as of the body in preparation for making a dive in swimming. —*tr.v.* **1.** To make tucks in. **2.** To gather up and fold; turn under in order to secure or confine: *tucked the shirt into his trousers.* **3.** To cover or wrap snugly. **4. a.** To put in an out-of-the-way and snug place: *a cabin tucked among the pines.* **b.** To store in a safe spot; save. **5.** To draw in; contract. —*intr.v.* To make tucks. —*phrasal verb.* **tuck in.** To put to bed and cover snugly. [From Middle English *tucken,* to punish, tug at, pull, from Old English *tūcian,* to punish, torment.]

tuck·er[1] (tŭk′ər) *n.* **1.** A piece of linen, lace, or other mate-

tuba

rial formerly worn over or tucked into a low-cut bodice. **2.** Someone or something that tucks.

tuck·er² (tŭk'ər) *tr.v. Informal.* To weary; exhaust: *The climb up the hill tuckered him out.* [Freq. of TUCK.]

–tude. A suffix meaning a condition or state of being: **quietude.** [Old French, from Latin *-tūdō.*]

Tues·day (tōōz'dē, tyōōz'-, -dā') *n.* The third day of the week, following Monday and preceding Wednesday. [Middle English *tuesdai,* from Old English *tīwesdæg,* "day of Tiu" (the Anglo-Saxon god of war).]

tu·fa (tōō'fə, tyōō'-) *n.* The calcareous and siliceous rock deposits of springs, lakes, or ground water. [Obs. Italian, from Latin *tōfus.*] —**tu·fa'ceous** (-fā'shəs) *adj.*

tuff (tŭf) *n.* A rock composed of compacted volcanic ash varying in size from fine sand to coarse gravel. Also called **tufa.** [French *tuf,* from obs. Italian *tufa,* tufa.] —**tuff·a'ceous** (tŭ-fā'shəs) *adj.*

tuf·fet (tŭf'ĭt) *n.* **1.** A clump or tuft of grass. **2.** A stool or other low seat. [Perh. var. of TUFT.]

tuft (tŭft) *n.* **1.** A short cluster of hair, feathers, grass, etc., attached at the base or growing close together. **2.** A button or clump of threads drawn through a mattress or cushion to make depressions in it. —*tr.v.* To decorate or supply with a tuft or tufts. —*intr.v.* To separate or form into tufts; grow in a tuft. [Middle English, from Old French *toffe.*] —**tuft'er** *n.* —**tuft'y** *adj.*

tug (tŭg) *v.* **tugged, tug·ging.** —*tr.v.* **1.** To pull at vigorously. **2.** To move by pulling with great effort or exertion. **3.** To tow with a tugboat. —*intr.v.* **1.** To pull hard: *She tugged at her boots.* **2.** To toil or struggle. —See Syns at **jerk.** —*n.* **1.** A strong pull or pulling force. **2.** A contest; struggle: *a tug between loyalty and desire.* **3.** A tugboat. **4.** A rope, chain, or strap used in hauling, esp. a harness trace. [Middle English *tuggen,* from Old English *tēon.*] —**tug'ger** *n.*

tug·boat (tŭg'bōt') *n.* A powerful small boat designed for towing larger vessels. Also called **towboat** and **tug.**

tug of war. **1.** A contest of strength in which two teams tug on opposite ends of a rope, each trying to pull the other across a dividing line. **2.** A struggle for supremacy.

tu·i·tion (tōō-ĭsh'ən, tyōō-) *n.* **1.** A fee for instruction, esp. at a college or private school. **2.** Instruction; teaching. [Middle English, protection, tutelage, from Old French, from Latin *tuitiō,* protection, from *tuērī,* to watch, protect.] —**tu·i'tion·al** *adj.*

tu·la·re·mi·a (tōō'lə-rē'mē-ə, tyōō-) *n.* An infectious disease caused by the bacterium *Pasteurella tularensis,* transmitted from infected rodents to man through carrier insects, characterized by fever and swelling of the lymph nodes. Also called **rabbit fever.** [From *Tulare,* a county in California where it was discovered + -EMIA.]

tu·le (tōō'lē) *n.* Any of several bulrushes of the genus *Scirpus* that grow in marshy lowlands of the southwestern United States. [Spanish, from Nahuatl *tullin.*]

tu·lip (tōō'lĭp, tyōō'-) *n.* Any of several bulbous plants of the genus *Tulipa,* native to Asia, widely cultivated for their showy, variously colored flowers. [From Turkish *tülibend,* turban (from its turban-shaped flower).]

tulip tree. A tall deciduous tree, *Liriodendron tulipifera,* with large, tuliplike green and orange flowers and yellowish, easily worked wood.

tu·lip·wood (tōō'lĭp-wōōd', tyōō'-) *n.* The soft white wood of the tulip tree.

tulle (tōōl) *n.* A fine starched net of silk, rayon, or nylon, used for veils, evening gowns, etc. [French, after *Tulle,* a city in central France.]

tum·ble (tŭm'bəl) *v.* **-bled, -bling.** —*intr.v.* **1.** To perform acrobatic feats, such as somersaults. **2.** To fall or roll end over end. **3.** To spill or roll out in confusion or disorder: *Schoolchildren tumbled out of the bus.* **4.** To pitch headlong; stumble; fall. **5.** To decline or collapse suddenly; topple. **6.** *Slang.* To come to a sudden understanding; catch on. —*tr.v.* **1.** To cause to fall; bring down. **2.** To put, spill, or toss haphazardly. —See Syns at **fall.** —*n.* **1.** An act of tumbling; a fall. **2.** A condition of confusion or disorder. [Middle English *tumblen,* freq. of *tumben,* to tumble, leap, dance, from Old English *tumbian.*]

tum·ble·bug (tŭm'bəl-bŭg') *n.* A **dung beetle.**

tum·ble·down (tŭm'bəl-doun') *adj.* Dilapidated; rickety.

tum·bler (tŭm'blər) *n.* **1.** An acrobat or gymnast. **2.** A drinking glass without a handle, foot, or stem. **3.** The part in a lock that releases the bolt when moved by a key. **4.** A barrel-shaped tumbling device that revolves, esp. the drum of a clothes dryer. **5.** One of a breed of domestic pigeons that characteristically tumble or somersault in flight.

tum·ble·weed (tŭm'bəl-wēd') *n.* Any of various densely branched New World plants, chiefly of the genus *Amaranthus,* that when withered break off and are rolled about by the wind, esp. *A. albus,* of western prairies.

tum·bling (tŭm'blĭng) *n.* The skill or practice of gymnastic falling, rolling, or somersaulting.

tum·brel or **tum·bril** (tŭm'brəl) *n.* **1.** A two-wheeled farmer's cart that can be tilted to dump a load. **2.** A crude cart used to carry condemned prisoners to their place of execution during the French Revolution. [Middle English *tomberel,* a dung cart, from Old French, a dumpcart, from *tomber,* to leap, overturn.]

tu·me·fac·tion (tōō'mə-fāk'shən, tyōō'-) *n.* **1. a.** The action of swelling. **b.** A swollen condition. **2.** A puffy or swollen part. [Old French, from Latin *tumefactus,* past part. of *tumefacere,* to cause to swell.] —**tu'me·fac'tive** *adj.*

tu·mes·cence (tōō-mĕs'əns) *n.* **1. a.** A swelling or enlarging. **b.** A swollen condition. **2.** A swollen part or organ. [From Latin *tumēscēns,* pres. part. of *tumēscere,* to begin to swell, from *tumēre,* to swell.] —**tu·mes'cent** *adj.*

tu·mid (tōō'mĭd, tyōō'-) *adj.* **1.** Swollen; distended; bulging. **2.** Overblown; bombastic. [Latin *tumidus,* from *tumēre,* to swell.] —**tu·mid'i·ty** *n.* —**tu'mid·ly** *adv.*

tum·my (tŭm'ē) *n., pl.* **-mies.** *Informal.* The stomach. [Baby-talk var. of STOMACH.]

tu·mor (tōō'mər, tyōō'-) *n.* **1.** A confined mass of tissue that develops without inflammation from normal tissue, but has an abnormal structure and rate of growth and serves no function within the body. **2.** Any abnormal swelling within the body. —**tu'mor·ous** *adj.* [Latin, from *tumēre,* to swell.]

tump·line (tŭmp'lĭn') *n.* A strap slung across the forehead or the chest to support a load carried on the back. [*Tump,* of Algonquian orig. + LINE.]

tu·mult (tōō'məlt, tyōō'-) *n.* **1.** The din and commotion of a great crowd. **2.** A disorderly or noisy disturbance. **3.** Agitation of the mind or emotions. [Middle English *tumulte,* from Old French, from Latin *tumultus.*]

tu·mul·tu·ous (tə-mŭl'chōō-əs) *adj.* **1.** Noisy and disorderly; riotous: *a tumultuous convention.* **2.** Tending to incite, esp. by violent upheaval. —**tu·mul'tu·ous·ly** *adv.* —**tu·mul'tu·ous·ness** *n.*

tu·mu·lus (tōō'myə-ləs, tyōō'-) *n., pl.* **-li** (-lī'). An ancient grave mound; barrow. [Latin.]

tun (tŭn) *n.* **1.** A large cask for liquids, esp. wine. **2.** A unit of liquid measure, esp. one equivalent to 252 gallons. [Middle English *tunne,* a measure of wine, from Old English, cask, vat.]

tu·na¹ (tōō'nə, tyōō'-) *n., pl.* **tuna** or **-nas. 1.** Any of various, often large saltwater food fishes of the genus *Thunnus* and related genera, many of which are commercially important sources of canned fish. Also called **tunny. 2.** Also **tuna fish.** The canned or commercially processed flesh of any of these fishes. [American Spanish, ult. from Latin *thunnus,* tunny.]

tu·na² (tōō'nə, tyōō'-) *n.* **1.** Any of several tropical American cacti of the genus *Opuntia,* which includes the prickly pears, esp. *O. tuna* that bears edible red fruit. **2.** The fruit of such a plant. [Spanish, from Taino.]

tun·dra (tŭn'drə) *n.* A treeless area between the ice cap and the tree line of arctic regions, with a permanently frozen subsoil and supporting low-growing vegetation. [Russian, of Finno-Ugric orig.]

tune (tōōn, tyōōn) *n.* **1.** A melody, esp. a simple and easily remembered one. **2.** Correct musical pitch: *a piano out of tune.* **3.** Agreement in musical pitch or key: *a piano soloist and orchestra not in tune.* **4.** Agreement or harmony: *ideas in tune with the times.* —*tr.v.* **tuned, tun·ing. 1.** To put in proper musical pitch: *tune a violin.* **2.** To adjust (an engine) for top performance. **3.** To adjust or adapt (oneself) to surroundings or a manner of living or thinking. —*phrasal verbs.* **tune in.** To adjust a radio or television receiver so as to get (a particular broadcast). **tune out.** To

---

adjust a radio or television receiver so as to no longer get (a particular broadcast). **tune up. 1.** To adjust (a musical instrument) to a desired pitch or key. **2.** To adjust (a machine or machinery) so as to put it into proper condition. **3.** To prepare oneself for a specified activity. —*idiom.* **to the tune of.** To the sum or extent of: *awarded back salary to the tune of $40,000.* [Middle English, variant of *tone, tone.*]

tune·ful (tōōn′fəl, tyōōn′-) *adj.* Full of melody; melodious; musical. —**tune′ful·ly** *adv.* —**tune′ful·ness** *n.*

tun·er (tōō′nər, tyōō′-) *n.* **1.** Someone or something that tunes: *a piano tuner.* **2. a.** The part of a radio or television receiver that selects the signal that is to be amplified and demodulated. **b.** A device for use with high-fidelity sound systems, consisting of a radio receiver that lacks only loudspeakers and the amplifiers that drive them.

tune-up (tōōn′ŭp′, tyōōn′-) *n.* **1.** An adjustment of a motor or engine to put it in the most efficient working order. **2.** A preliminary or practice trial.

tung oil (tŭng). A yellow or brownish oil extracted from the seeds of an Asian tree, the tung tree, and used as a drying agent in varnishes and paints and for waterproofing. [Mandarin *t′ung²*, tung tree.]

tung·sten (tŭng′stən) *n. Symbol* **W** A hard, brittle, corrosion-resistant gray to white metallic element extracted from wolframite, and other minerals, with the highest melting point of any metal, used in high-temperature structural materials, electrical elements, notably lamp filaments, and instruments requiring thermally compatible glass-to-metal seals. Atomic number 74; atomic weight 183.85; melting point 3,410°C; boiling point 5,927°C; specific gravity 19.3 (20°C); valences 2, 3, 4, 5, 6. [Swedish : *tung,* heavy, from Old Norse *thungr* + *sten,* stone, from Old Norse *steinn.*]

Tun·gus (tōōng-gōōz′) *n., pl.* **Tungus** or **-es. 1.** A Mongoloid people inhabiting eastern Siberia. **2.** The language of the Tunguses.

tu·nic (tōō′nĭk, tyōō′-) *n.* **1.** A loose-fitting, knee-length garment worn in ancient Greece and Rome. **2.** A fitted outer garment usu. hip-length and often part of a uniform. **3.** A woman's hip-length top worn over a skirt or slacks. **4.** *Anat.* A coat or layer enveloping an organ or part; tunica. [Latin *tunica.*]

tu·ni·ca (tōō′nĭ-kə, tyōō′-) *n., pl.* **-cae** (-kē′, -kī′, -sē′). *Anat.* An integument; a tunic. [Latin, tunic.]

tu·ni·cate (tōō′nĭ-kĭt, -nĭ-kāt′, tyōō′-) *n.* Any of various chordate saltwater animals of the subphylum Urochordata (or Tunicata), that have a cylindrical or globular body enclosed in a tough outer covering and include the sea squirts and salps. —*adj.* **1.** Of or concerning the tunicates. **2.** *Anat.* Having a tunic. **3.** *Bot.* Having concentric layers, as the bulb of an onion.

tuning fork. A small two-pronged instrument that when struck produces a sound of fixed pitch, used as a reference, as in tuning musical instruments.

tuning fork   tureen

tun·nel (tŭn′əl) *n.* An underground passage, esp. a passage through an extended barrier or obstruction. —*v.* **-neled** or **-nelled, -nel·ing** or **-nel·ling.** —*tr.v.* **1.** To make a tunnel under or through. **2.** To shape or dig in the form of a tunnel: *tunnel a passage.* —*intr.v.* To make a tunnel. [Middle English *tonel,* a pipelike net for catching birds, from Old French *tonne,* a cask, from *tonne,* a tun, from Medieval Latin

tonna.] —**tun′nel·er** or **tun′nel·ler** *n.*

tun·ny (tŭn′ē) *n., pl.* **tunny** or **-nies.** A fish, the tuna. [Old French *thon,* from Old Provençal *ton,* from Latin *thunnus,* from Greek *thunnos.*]

tu·pe·lo (tōō′pə-lō′, tyōō′-) *n., pl.* **-los. 1.** Any of several trees of the genus *Nyssa,* of the southeastern United States, with soft, light wood. **2.** The wood of any of these trees. [Creek *ito opilwa* : *ito,* tree + *opilwa,* swamp.]

Tu·pi (tōō′pē, tōō-pē′) *n., pl.* **Tupi** or **-pis. 1.** A member of any of a group of peoples living along the coast of Brazil, in the Amazon River valley, and in Paraguay. **2.** The language of the Tupi.

tup·pence. *Brit. Informal.* Var. of **twopence.**

tuque (tōōk, tyōōk) *n.* A knitted woolen cap with two long ends, worn with one end tucked into the other. [Canadian French, from French *toque,* toque.]

tur·ban (tûr′bən) *n.* **1.** An eastern headdress consisting of a long scarf wound around the head. **2.** Any similar headdress. [Old French *turbant,* from Old Italian *turbante,* from Turkish *tülibend,* from Persian *dulband.*]

tur·bel·lar·i·an (tûr′bə-lâr′ē-ən) *n.* Any of various chiefly aquatic ciliate flatworms of the class Turbellaria. —*adj.* Of or belonging to the Turbellaria. [From Latin *turbellae* (pl.), bustle, stir from *turba,* turmoil, uproar.]

tur·bid (tûr′bĭd) *adj.* **1.** Having sediment or foreign particles stirred up or suspended: *turbid water.* **2.** Heavy, dark, or dense, as smoke or fog. **3.** In turmoil; muddled: *turbid emotions.* [Latin *turbidus,* confused, muddy, from *turba,* turmoil, uproar, from Greek *turbē,* disorder.] —**tur′bid·ly** *adv.* —**tur′bid·ness** or **tur′bid′i·ty** *n.*

tur·bi·nate (tûr′bə-nĭt, -nāt′) *adj.* **1.** Shaped or twirling like a top. **2.** *Zool.* Spiral and decreasing sharply in diameter from base to apex, as certain shells. **3.** *Anat.* Designating a small curved bone located on the wall of the nasal passage. [Latin *turbinātus,* from *turbo,* a top.]

tur·bine (tûr′bĭn, -bīn′) *n.* Any of various machines in which the kinetic energy of a liquid or gas, often at a high temperature, is converted to rotary motion as the fluid reacts with a series of vanes, paddles, etc., arranged about the circumference of one or more wheels. [French, from Latin *turbo,* a spinning thing, top, whirlwind, perh. from Greek *turbē,* disorder.]

turbo-. A prefix meaning: **1.** A turbine: **turbocharger. 2.** Driven by a turbine: **turbojet.** [From **TURBINE.**]

tur·bo·charg·er (tûr′bō-chär′jər) *n.* A device that uses the exhaust gas of an internal-combustion engine to drive a turbine that in turn drives a supercharger attached to the engine.

tur·bo·jet (tûr′bō-jĕt′) *n.* **1.** A jet engine, with a turbine-driven compressor, that develops thrust from the exhaust of hot gases. **2.** An aircraft powered by such an engine.

tur·bo·prop (tûr′bō-prŏp′) *n.* **1.** A turbojet engine used to drive an external propeller. **2.** An aircraft in which such an engine is used. [Short for *turbopropeller.*]

tur·bo·su·per·charg·er (tûr′bō-sōō′pər-chär′jər) *n.* A supercharger that uses an exhaust-driven turbine to maintain air-intake pressure in high-altitude aircraft.

tur·bot (tûr′bət) *n., pl.* **turbot** or **-bots. 1.** A European flatfish, *Psetta maxima* (or *Scophthalmus maximus*), esteemed as food. **2.** Any of various similar or related flatfishes. [Middle English, from Old French.]

tur·bu·lence (tûr′byə-ləns) *n.* Also **tur·bu·len·cy** (-lən-sē). The condition or quality of being agitated, violently disturbed, or in commotion.

tur·bu·lent (tûr′byə-lənt) *adj.* **1.** Violently agitated or disturbed; stormy. **2.** Having a chaotic or restless character or tendency: *a turbulent period of history.* **3.** Causing unrest or disturbance; unruly. [Latin *turbulentus,* from *turba,* confusion.] —**tur′bu·lent·ly** *adv.*

tu·reen (tōō-rēn′, tyōō-) *n.* A broad, deep dish with a cover, used for serving soups, stews, etc. [French *terrine,* earthen vessel, from Old French *terrin,* earthen, from Latin *terra,* earth.]

turf (tûrf) *n.* **1.** A surface layer of earth containing a dense growth of grass and its matted roots; sod. **2.** A piece cut from such a layer of sod. **3.** A piece of peat that is burned as fuel. **4.** *Slang.* The area claimed by a neighborhood gang as its territory. **5. the turf. a.** A track over which horses are raced. **b.** The sport or business of racing horses.

[Middle English, from Old English.] —**turf′y** adj.

turf·man (tûrf′mən) n. Someone devoted to the sport of horse racing, esp. an owner of racehorses.

tur·ges·cence (tûr·jĕs′əns) n. The process of swelling or the condition of being swollen. [Latin turgēscere, to begin to swell, from turgēre, to be swollen.] —**tur′ges′cent** adj.

tur·gid (tûr′jĭd) adj. 1. Swollen or distended. 2. Excessively grand in style or language; bombastic. [Latin turgidus, from turgēre, to be swollen.] —**tur·gid′i·ty** or **tur′gid·ness** n. —**tur′gid·ly** adv.

tur·gor (tûr′gôr, -gər) n. Biol. The normal fullness or tension of plant or animal cells. [Late Latin, from Latin turgēre, to be swollen.]

tur·key (tûr′kē) n., pl. **-keys.** 1. A large North American bird, Meleagris gallopavo, that has brownish plumage and a bare, wattled head and neck and is widely domesticated for food. 2. The meat of this bird used as food. 3. Slang. A stage play or other production that fails. —**idiom. talk turkey.** To discuss something in a straightforward, direct manner. [Short for TURKEY COCK.]

turkey buzzard. Also **turkey vulture.** A New World vulture, Cathartes aura, with dark plumage and a bare red head and neck similar to that of the turkey.

turkey cock. 1. A male turkey. 2. A strutting, conceited person. [After Turkey, from which the guinea fowl, (once confused with the turkey cock) was imported to the New World.]

Tur·kic (tûr′kĭk) n. A group of related languages including Turkish that are spoken in the eastern part of central Asia. —adj. Of or relating to the Turks or the Turkic languages.

Turk·ish (tûr′kĭsh) adj. Of or relating to Turkey, the Turks, or their language. —n. The Turkic language of Turkey.

Turkish bath. 1. A steam bath inducing heavy perspiration, followed by a massage and a cold shower. 2. An establishment where such bathing facilities are available.

Turkish coffee. Very strong, sweet, black coffee made by triple-boiling powdered coffee beans in a thin syrup of sugar and water.

Turkish delight. A candy of Turkish origin, usu. consisting of jellylike cubes covered with powdered sugar.

Turkish towel. Also **turkish towel.** A thick rough towel with a nap of uncut pile.

tur·mer·ic (tûr′mər-ĭk) n. 1. A plant, Curcuma longa, of India, with yellow flowers and an aromatic rootstock. 2. The powdered rootstock of this plant, used as a condiment and as a yellow dye. 3. Any of several other plants with similar roots. [Old French terre mérite, from Medieval Latin terra merita, "meritorious earth."]

tur·moil (tûr′moil) n. A condition of great confusion or disturbance. [Orig. unknown.]

turn (tûrn) tr.v. 1. To cause to move around an axis or center; rotate; revolve. 2. To perform or accomplish by rotating or revolving: turn handsprings. 3. To cause to change direction or course. 4. a. To cause to move in an opposite direction or course; reverse: The strategy turned the tide of battle. b. To make a course or way around or about: They turned the corner. 5. To set or direct in a specified way; point; focus. 6. To direct (one's attention, interest, or mind) toward or away from something: turned his thoughts to home. 7. To change the position of so that the underside becomes the upper side: turn the pancakes; turning the page. 8. To transform; change: Make-up turned her into a beauty. 9. To exchange; convert: turning spare time into earnings. 10. To change the color of or change to a specified color. 11. To make sour; ferment. 12. To shape or form: turned wood in a lathe; turned a phrase neatly. 13. To injure by twisting: turn an ankle. 14. To upset or make nauseated. 15. To change the disposition of: success that turned his head. 16. To make hostile or antagonistic: turned brother against brother. 17. To adopt a new religion, political party, belief, etc. 18. To become, reach, or surpass (a certain age, time, or amount). 19. To get by buying or selling; gain: turn a modest profit. —intr.v. 1. To move around an axis or center; rotate; revolve: a car wheel turning. 2. To appear to revolve or whirl, as in dizziness: as the room turned wildly. 3. To roll from side to side or back and forth: a ship pitching and turning. 4. To direct one's way or course in a specified

manner. 5. To change or reverse one's way, course, or direction. 6. To move in an opposite direction or course: The patient's condition turned for the worse. 7. To change in terms of attitude, action, policy, etc.: The tide of popular opinion turned in his favor. 8. To become suddenly hostile or antagonistic. 9. To direct or withdraw attention, interest, or thought. 10. To switch or convert from one religion, loyalty, side, etc., to another. 11. To change; become transformed: caterpillars turning into butterflies. 12. To turn sour or rancid; spoil. 13. To change color. 14. To become bent or curved; bend. —See Syns at change. —phrasal verbs. **turn away.** To send away; reject. **turn down.** 1. To reduce the volume, degree, speed, or flow of. 2. To reject or refuse (a person or a request, suggestion, etc.). 3. To change the position of by folding, twisting, or bending: turn down the blankets. —See Syns at reject. **turn in.** 1. To turn or go into; enter. 2. To hand in; give over; return or exchange. 3. To deliver or give information about (a fugitive, wrongdoer, etc.) to persons in authority. 4. Informal. To go to bed. **turn loose.** To send or let go; release. **turn off.** 1. To cause to stop the operation, activity, or flow of. 2. To leave by making a turn. **turn on.** 1. To begin or cause to begin the operation, activity, or flow of. 2. To depend on for success, failure, or other result; hinge: A chess match can turn on a single move. **turn out.** 1. To shut off, as a light. 2. To come out or assemble, as for a public event. 3. To produce or create: turned out a large amount of work. 4. To be found to be: a rumor that turned out to be false. 5. To result; end up: plans turning out perfectly. **turn over.** 1. To bring the bottom to the top, or vice versa; reverse in position. 2. To shift position, as by going over on a side surface. 3. To go through at least one cycle of operation: The engine finally turned over. 4. To think about; consider: turned the idea over in his mind. 5. To transfer to another; give over. **turn to.** 1. To apply, appeal, or resort to (someone or something) for aid, support, information, etc. 2. To begin work. **turn up.** 1. To find or be found. 2. To make an appearance; arrive. 3. To occur; happen. 4. To increase the volume, degree, speed, or flow of. —n. 1. The act of turning or the condition of being turned; a rotation or revolution. 2. A change of direction, motion, or position, or the point of such a change. 3. A point of change in time: the turn of the century. 4. A movement or development in the direction of: an unusual turn of events. 5. A chance or opportunity to do something: my turn to deal the cards. 6. A characteristic mood, style, or habit; an inclination; tendency: a scientific turn of mind. 7. A deed or action with a specified effect on another: did him a good turn. 8. A short tour or excursion. 9. A twist or other distortion in shape. 10. Informal. A momentary shock or scare: The noise gave me quite a turn. —idioms. **at every turn.** In every place; at every moment. **by turns.** Alternately; one after another. **to a turn.** With precision and exactness; perfectly. [Middle English turnen, from Old English tyrnan and Old French tourner, both from Latin tornāre, to turn in a lathe, from tornus, a lathe, from Greek tornos.]

turn·a·bout (tûrn′ə-bout′) n. A shift or change to an opposite direction, position, opinion, allegiance, etc.

turn·buck·le (tûrn′bŭk′əl) n. A device for adjusting the tension of a rope or cable, consisting of an oblong center section with threaded holes at the ends that receive threaded rods to which the ends of the rope or cable are fastened.

turn·coat (tûrn′kōt′) n. Someone who traitorously switches allegiance; a traitor.

turn·er (tûr′nər) n. Someone or something that turns, esp. a person who works a lathe.

turn·er·y (tûr′nə-rē) n., pl. **-ies.** The work or workshop of a lathe operator.

turning point. A point at which a crucial decision must be made; decisive moment.

tur·nip (tûr′nĭp) n. 1. A widely cultivated plant, Brassica rapa, native to the Old World, with a large, edible yellow or white root. 2. The root of this plant eaten as a vegetable. 3. The rutabaga. [Perh. TURN (from its shape) + nepe, turnip, from Middle English, from Old English næp, from Latin nāpus.]

turn·key (tûrn′kē′) n. The keeper of the keys in a prison; a jailer.

ă pat   ā pay   â care   ä father   ĕ pet   ē be   hw which   ĭ pit   ī tie   î pier   ŏ pot   ō toe   ô paw, for   oi noise
ōō took   ōō boot   ou out   th thin   th this   ŭ cut   û urge   zh vision   ə about, item, edible, gallop, circus

turn·o·ver (tûrn′ō′vər) *n.* **1.** The act of turning over; an upset. **2.** An abrupt change; reversal. **3.** A small pastry made by spreading a filling on half of a piece of dough and turning the other half over on top. **4.** The number of times a particular stock of goods is sold and restocked during a given period of time. **5.** The amount of business transacted during a given period of time. **6.** The number of workers hired by a given establishment to replace those who have left. **7.** *Sports. Informal.* A giving over or loss of possession of the ball to the opposing team through an error or miscue. —*adj.* Capable of being turned or folded down or over: *a blouse with turnover cuffs.*

turn·pike (tûrn′pīk′) *n.* **1.** A road, esp. a wide highway with tollgates. **2.** A tollgate. [Middle English *turnepike,* a revolving barrier furnished with spikes used to block a road : *turnen,* to turn + *pike,* pike.]

turn·stile (tûrn′stīl′) *n.* A device for controlling or counting the number of persons entering a public area by admitting them one at a time between horizontal bars revolving on a central vertical post.

turn·stone (tûrn′stōn′) *n.* Either of two wading birds, genus *Arenaria,* with predominantly reddish and white or black and white plumage. [From its habit of turning over stones in search of food.]

turn·ta·ble (tûrn′tā′bəl) *n.* **1.** A circular rotating platform equipped with a railway track, used for turning locomotives, esp. in a roundhouse. **2. a.** The rotating circular platform of a phonograph on which the record is placed. **b.** A mechanical device for use with high-fidelity sound systems, consisting of a phonograph without amplifiers or loudspeakers. **3.** Any similar rotating platform or part.

turn·up (tûrn′ŭp′) *n.* Something that is turned up or turns up. —*adj.* Turned up or capable of being turned up.

tur·pen·tine (tûr′pən-tīn′) *n.* **1.** A thin volatile essential oil, $C_{10}H_{16}$, obtained by steam distillation or other means from the wood or the exudate of certain pine trees, and used as a paint thinner, solvent, and medicinally as a liniment. **2.** The sticky mixture of resin and volatile oil from which this oil is distilled. [Middle English *turpentyne,* resin of the terebinth (a kind of tree), from Old French *terebentine,* from Latin *terebinthina,* from *terebinthus,* a kind of tree, from Greek *terebinthos.*]

tur·pi·tude (tûr′pə-tōōd′, -tyōōd′) *n.* Baseness; depravity. [Latin *turpitūdō,* from *turpis,* ugly, vile.]

turps (tûrps) *n. (used with a sing. verb). Informal.* Turpentine. [Short for TURPENTINE.]

tur·quoise (tûr′kwoiz′, -koiz′) *n.* **1.** A blue to blue-green mineral of aluminum and copper, valued in certain of its forms as a gemstone. **2.** A light bluish green. —*modifier: a turquoise necklace.* —*adj.* Light bluish green. [Middle English *turkeis,* from Old French *(pierre) turqueise,* "Turkish (stone)."]

tur·ret (tûr′ĭt) *n.* **1.** A small tower-shaped projection on a building. **2.** *Mil.* **a.** A low, heavily armored, rotating structure, containing mounted guns, as on a warship or tank. **b.** A domelike gunner's enclosure projecting from the fuselage of a military aircraft. **3.** An attachment for a lathe consisting of a rotating, cylindrical block holding various cutting tools. [Middle English *touret,* from Old French *tourete,* dim. of *tour,* a tower.]

tur·ret·ed (tûr′ĭt-ĭd) *adj.* **1.** Furnished with a turret. **2.** Having the shape or form of a turret, as certain long-spired gastropod shells.

tur·tle[1] (tûrt′l) *n.* Any of various reptiles of the order Chelo-

nia, with horny, toothless jaws and the body enclosed in a bony or leathery shell into which the head, limbs, and tail can be withdrawn. —*intr.v.* **-tled, -tling.** To hunt turtles, esp. as an occupation. [Perh. from French *tortue,* tortoise.]

tur·tle[2] (tûrt′l) *n. Archaic.* A turtledove. [Middle English, from Old English *turtla,* from Latin *turtur.*]

tur·tle·dove (tûrt′l-dŭv′) *n.* A slender European dove, *Streptopelia turtur,* with a white-edged tail and a soft, purring voice. [TURTLE (dove) + DOVE.]

tur·tle·neck (tûrt′l-nĕk′) *n.* **1.** A high, turned-down collar that fits closely about the neck. **2.** A garment with such a collar.

tush[1] (tŭsh) *interj.* A word used to express mild reproof, disapproval, or admonition.

tush[2] (tŭsh) *n.* A tusk. —*tr.v.* To tusk. [Middle English *tusche,* from Old English *tūsc.*]

tusk (tŭsk) *n.* **1.** An elongated, pointed tooth, usu. one of a pair, projecting outside of the mouth of certain animals. **2.** Any long, projecting tooth or toothlike part. —*tr.v.* To dig or gore with the tusks or a tusk. [Middle English *tuske,* from Old English *tūsc.*]

tusk·er (tŭs′kər) *n.* An animal that has tusks, as a wild boar.

tus·sle (tŭs′əl) *intr.v.* **-sled, -sling.** To fight roughly; to scuffle. —*n.* A rough-and-tumble fight; a scuffle. [Middle English *tussillen.*]

tus·sock (tŭs′ək) *n.* A clump or tuft, as of grass. [From dial. *tusk,* a tuft of hair.] —**tus′sock·y** *adj.*

tussock moth. Any of various moths of the family Lymantriidae that have hairy caterpillars.

tut (tŭt) *interj.* Also **tut tut.** A word used to express annoyance, impatience, or mild reproof.

tu·te·lage (tōō′tə-lĭj, tyōō′-) *n.* **1.** The function or capacity of a guardian; guardianship. **2.** The act or capacity of a tutor; instruction; teaching. **3.** The state of being under a guardian or tutor. [From Latin *tūtēla,* a watching, from *tūtor,* tutor.] **tu′te·lar′y** (-lĕr′ē) *adj.*

tu·tor (tōō′tər, tyōō′-) *n.* **1. a.** A private instructor. **b.** An instructor, esp. one not affiliated with a formal institution of learning, who gives additional or remedial instruction. **2.** In some American universities and colleges, a teacher with a rank lower than that of an instructor. **3.** In certain British universities, a graduate responsible for the special supervision of an undergraduate. —*tr.v.* **1.** To instruct or teach privately. **2.** To coach, esp. underhandedly. —*intr.v.* **1.** To work as or function as a private instructor. —See Syns at **teach.** [Middle English *tutour,* from Old French, from Latin *tūtor,* a guardian, tutor, from *tūtus,* past part. of *tuērī,* to watch, protect.] —**tu·to′ri·al** (tōō-tôr′ē-əl, -tōr′ē-əl, tyōō-) *adj.* —**tu′tor·ship′** *n.*

tut·ti-frut·ti (tōō′tē-frōō′tē) *n.* **1.** A confection, esp. ice cream, that contains a variety of chopped candied fruits. **2.** A flavoring simulating the combined flavor of many fruits. [Italian, "all fruits."]

tu·tu (tōō′tōō) *n.* A very short ballet skirt that consists of many layers of gathered sheer fabric. [French.]

tux·e·do (tŭk-sē′dō) *n., pl.* **-dos.** Also **Tux·e·do.** A man's formal or semiformal suit, usu. black, that includes a tailless dinner jacket, trousers, and a black bow tie. [After *Tuxedo* Park, New York, where it became popular.]

tu·yère (twē-yâr′) *n.* The pipe, nozzle, or other opening through which air is forced into a blast furnace or forge. [French, from Old French *tuyere,* from *tuyau,* a pipe.]

TV (tē-vē′) *n.* Television.

twad·dle (twŏd′l) *n.* Foolish, trivial, or idle talk. —*intr.v.* **-dled, -dling.** To talk foolishly; prate. [Prob. of Scandinavian orig.] —**twad′dler** *n.*

twain (twān) *adj. & n. Archaic & Poet.* Two. [Middle English *tweien,* from Old English *twēgen.*]

twang (twăng) *intr.v.* **1.** To emit a sharp, vibrating sound, as the string of a musical instrument when plucked. **2.** To speak in a sharply nasal tone of voice. —*tr.v.* **1.** To cause to make a sharp, vibrating sound. **2.** To utter with a twang. —*n.* **1.** A sharp, vibrating sound. **2.** An excessively nasal tone of voice. [Imit.] —**twang′y** *adj.*

'twas (twŭz) *Poet.* It was.

tweak (twēk) *tr.v.* To pinch, pluck, or twist sharply. —*n.* A sharp, twisting pinch. [Dial. *twick,* from Middle English

turtle[1]

twikken, from Old English *twiccian.*] —**tweak'y** *adj.*

tweed (twēd) *n.* **1.** A coarse woolen fabric usu. woven of several colors. **2. tweeds.** Clothes made of tweed. [From a trademark.] —**tweed'i·ness** *n.* —**tweed'y** *adj.*

twee·dle·dum and twee·dle·dee (twēd'l-dŭm'; twēd'-l-dē'). Two persons or groups resembling each other so closely that they are practically indistinguishable. [Imit. of high and low musical notes.]

'tween (twēn) *prep. Poet.* Between.

tweet (twēt) *n.* A high, chirping sound, as of a small bird. —*intr.v.* To make such a sound. [Imit.]

tweet·er (twē'tər) *n.* A loudspeaker designed to reproduce high-pitched sounds in a high-fidelity audio system. [From TWEET.]

tweeze (twēz) *tr.v.* **tweezed, tweez·ing.** To pluck or extract with tweezers. [Back-formation from TWEEZERS.]

tweez·ers (twē'zərz) *pl.n.* A small, usu. metal, pincerlike tool composed of two legs tapered at one end and joined together at the other, used for plucking or handling small objects. [Obs. *tweezes,* a set or case of small instruments, from French *étui.*]

twelfth (twělfth) *n.* **1.** The ordinal number 12 in a series. **2.** One of 12 equal parts. [Middle English *twelfthe,* from Old English *twelfta.*] —**twelfth** *adj. & adv.*

Twelfth-day (twělfth'dā') *n.* The day of Epiphany, January 6, 12 days after Christmas.

Twelfth-night (twělfth'nīt') *n.* The evening of January 5, before Twelfth-day.

twelve (twělv) *n.* The cardinal number written 12 or in Roman numerals XII. [Middle English, from Old English *twelf.*]

twelve·month (twělv'mŭnth') *n.* A year.

twelve-tone (twělv'tōn') *adj. Mus.* Of, consisting of, or based on an atonal arrangement of the traditional 12 chromatic tones.

twen·ti·eth (twěn'tē-ĭth) *n.* **1.** The ordinal number 20 in a series. **2.** One of 20 equal parts. —**twen'ti·eth** *adj. & adv.*

twen·ty (twěn'tē) *n.* The cardinal number written 20 or in Roman numerals XX. [Middle English, from Old English *twēntig.*]

twen·ty-one (twěn'tē-wŭn') *n.* A card game in which the object is to accumulate cards with a total count nearer to 21 than that of the dealer; blackjack.

twen·ty-twen·ty (twěn'tē-twěn'tē) *adj.* Having normal vision.

twerp (twûrp) *n. Slang.* A short or contemptible individual. [Orig. unknown.]

twice (twīs) *adv.* **1.** In two cases or on two occasions; two times. **2.** In doubled degree or amount. [Middle English, from Old English *twiges,* from *twiga,* twice.]

twice·told (twīs'tōld') *adj.* **1.** Having been related before. **2.** Having been repeated so often as to be hackneyed.

twid·dle (twĭd'l) *v.* **-dled, -dling.** —*tr.v.* To turn over or around idly or lightly; fiddle with. —*intr.v.* **1.** To trifle or fiddle with something. **2.** To rotate lightly and purposelessly; twirl. —*n.* The act of twiddling. —*idiom.* **twiddle (one's) thumbs.** To do little or nothing; be idle. [Prob. a blend of TWIRL and FIDDLE.] —**twid'dler** *n.*

twig (twĭg) *n.* A small branch or slender shoot, as of a tree or shrub. [Middle English, from Old English *twigge.*]

twig·gy (twĭg'ē) *adj.* **-gi·er, -gi·est. 1.** Resembling a twig or twigs; skinny; thin. **2.** Full of twigs. —See Syns at **thin.**

twi·light (twī'līt') *n.* **1.** The time interval during which the sun is below the horizon but casts diffuse light through the atmosphere. **2.** The soft, indistinct light from the sky during this interval, esp. after a sunset. **3.** A period or condition of decline following growth, power, or success. —*modifier:* a *twilight sky;* the *twilight years.* [Middle English, half-light : *twi-,* half, two + *light,* light.]

twilight sleep. A semiconscious condition induced by an injection of morphine and scopolamine and characterized by insensibility to pain.

twill (twĭl) *n.* **1.** A weave that produces diagonal ribs on the surface of a fabric. **2.** A fabric with such a weave. —*tr.v.* To weave (cloth) so as to produce diagonal ribs on the surface. [Middle English *twyll,* from Old English *twilic,* two-threaded : *twi-,* two + Latin *līcium,* a thread.]

'twill (twĭl) *Poet.* It will.

twin (twĭn) *n.* **1. a.** Either of a pair of offspring born at the same birth. **b.** Either of such a pair having identical genetic characteristics. **2.** One of two persons, animals, or things that are identical or much alike. —*v.* **twinned, twin·ning.** —*intr.v.* To give birth to twins. —*tr.v.* To provide a match or counterpart to; pair. —*adj.* **1.** Being one or two of two offspring from the same birth. **2.** Being one or two of two identical or similar persons, animals, or things: *twin beds.* [Middle English, from Old English *twinn.*]

twin bill. 1. A doubleheader in sports. **2.** Any combination of two of the same event presented at one time.

twine (twīn) *n.* **1.** A strong string or cord formed of two or more threads twisted together. **2.** Any thing or part formed by twining. —*v.* **twined, twin·ing.** —*tr.v.* **1.** To twist together; intertwine, as threads. **2.** To form by twisting, intertwining, or interlacing. **3.** To wrap or coil about. **4.** To fold or encircle around something: *twined her arms about his neck.* —*intr.v.* **1.** To become twisted, interlaced, or interwoven. **2.** To go in a winding course; twist about. —See Syns at **wind.** [Middle English *twin,* a rope of two strands, from Old English *twīn.*] —**twin'er** *n.*

twinge (twĭnj) *n.* **1.** A sharp, sudden physical pain. **2.** A sudden, brief moment of mental or emotional distress; pang. —*v.* **twinged, twing·ing.** —*tr.v.* To cause to feel a sharp pain. —*intr.v.* To feel a twinge or twinges. [Middle English *twengen,* to pinch, wring, from Old English *twengan.*]

twin·kle (twĭng'kəl) *intr.v.* **-kled, -kling. 1.** To shine with slight, intermittent gleams. **2.** To be bright or sparkling, as with merriment or delight: *Her eyes twinkled.* —*n.* **1.** An intermittent gleam of light. **2.** A sparkle of merriment in the eye. **3.** A brief interval. A wink. [Middle English *twynklen,* from Old English *twinclian.*] —**twin'kler** *n.*

twin·kling (twĭng'klĭng) *n.* **1.** A brief interval; an instant. **2.** An act or example of shining intermittently. **3.** *Archaic.* An act of blinking; a wink.

twin-screw (twĭn'skrōō') *adj. Naut.* Having two propellers, one on either side of the keel, that usu. revolve in opposite directions.

twirl (twûrl) *tr.v.* **1.** To rotate or revolve briskly; spin. **2.** To twist or wind around. **3.** *Baseball. Slang.* To pitch. —*intr.v.* **1.** To whirl or spin around rapidly or repeatedly. **2.** To turn suddenly; make an about-face. —*n.* **1.** A quick spinning or twisting action or movement; a rapid whirl. **2.** Something twirled; a twist: *a twirl of cotton candy.* [Poss. a blend of TWIST and WHIRL.]

twist (twĭst) *tr.v.* **1. a.** To wind together (two or more threads) so as to form a single strand. **b.** To produce (something) in this manner. **2.** To wind or coil (vines, rope, etc.) about something. **3.** To entwine or interlace (something) with another thing: *twist flowers in one's hair.* **4.** To impart a coiling or spiral shape to. **5. a.** To turn or open by turning. **b.** To pull, break, or snap by turning. **6.** To rotate or revolve: *twisted her hips sensuously.* **7.** To wrench or sprain. **8.** To alter the normal shape or aspect of; contort. **9.** To alter or distort the intended meaning of: *twisted the facts to suit his purpose.* —*intr.v.* **1.** To be or become twisted; have or take a bending or coiling shape, position, etc.: *a staircase that twists at the top.* **2.** To move or progress in a winding course; meander. **3.** To squirm; writhe: *twist with pain.* **4.** To move by rotating or revolving with a squirming or writhing motion. —See Syns at **wind.** —*n.* **1.** Something twisted or formed by winding, as a length of yarn or a roll of tobacco leaves. **2.** The act of twisting; a spin or rotation. **3.** The condition of being twisted; a deviation or departure from a straight course, normal position, etc. **4.** A change or development, esp. a sudden or unexpected departure from a pattern. **5.** A sprain or wrench. **6.** A contortion or distortion, as of the face. **7.** A personal inclination or eccentricity. **8.** A spinning motion given to a ball when thrown or struck in a specific way. [Middle English *twysten,* from Old English *-twist,* a rope.]

twist·er (twĭs'tər) *n.* **1.** Someone or something that twists, esp. a ball thrown or batted with a twist. **2.** A storm that consists of a rotating mass of air, esp. a tornado.

twit (twĭt) *tr.v.* **twit·ted, twit·ting.** To taunt or tease, esp. for embarrassing mistakes or faults. —See Syns at **ridicule.** [Middle English *atwiten,* from Old English *ætwitan,* to reproach with.]

ă pat	ā pay	â care	ä father	ě pet	ē be	hw which	ǐ pit	ī tie	î pier	ŏ pot	ō toe	ô paw, for	oi noise
ōō took	ōō boot	ou out	th thin	th this	ŭ cut		û urge	zh vision	ə about, item, edible, gallop, circus				

twitch (twĭch) *tr.v.* **1.** To draw or pull suddenly and sharply; jerk. **2.** To cause to move jerkily or spasmodically. —*intr.v.* To move jerkily or spasmodically, often without conscious control. —*n.* **1.** A sudden involuntary or spasmodic movement, as of a muscle. **2.** A sudden jerk or tug. [Middle English *twicchen*, perh. of Low German orig.] —**twitch′ing·ly** *adv.*

twit·ter (twĭt′ər) *intr.v.* **1.** To utter a succession of light chirping or tremulous sounds, as a bird does; chirrup. **2.** To titter. **3.** To tremble with nervous agitation, excitement, etc. —*tr.v.* To speak or say with a twitter. —*n.* **1.** The light chirping sounds made by certain birds. **2.** Light, tremulous speech or laughter. **3.** A condition of agitation or excitement; a flutter. [Middle English *twiteren.*] —**twit′ter·y** *adj.*

twixt (twĭkst) *prep. & adv.* Also **′twixt** (twĭkst). *Archaic & Poet.* Betwixt.

two (tōō) *n.* **1.** The cardinal number written 2 or in Roman numerals II, equal to the sum of 1 + 1. **2.** A playing card marked with two pips. **3.** A two-dollar bill. [Middle English, from Old English *twā.*]

two-base hit (tōō′bās′). *Baseball.* A hit enabling the batter to reach second base; a double. Also called **two-bagger.**

two-bit (tōō′bĭt′) *adj. Slang.* Worth very little; cheap; insignificant. [From TWO BITS.]

two bits. *Informal.* **1.** Twenty-five cents. **2.** A petty sum.

two-by-four (tōō′bī-fôr′, -fōr′, tōō′bə-) *adj.* **1.** Measuring two by four inches. **2.** *Informal.* Small in size; cramped. —*n.* Any length of lumber measuring 1⅝ inches in thickness and 3⅜ inches in width.

two-di·men·sion·al (tōō′dĭ-měn′shə-nəl) *adj.* **1.** Having only two dimensions, esp. length and width; flat. **2.** Lacking range or depth; superficial: *a two-dimensional characterization.*

two-faced (tōō′fāst′) *adj.* **1.** Having two faces or surfaces. **2.** Hypocritical or double-dealing; deceitful. —**two′-fac′ed·ly** (tōō′fā′sĭd-lē, -fāst′lē) *adv.* —**two′-fac′ed·ness** *n.*

two-fisted (tōō′fĭs′tĭd) *adj. Informal.* Aggressive; virile.

two·fold (tōō′fōld′, -fōld′) *adj.* **1.** Having two components. **2.** Having twice as much or as many; double. —*adv.* Two times as much or as many; doubly.

two-hand·ed (tōō′hăn′dĭd) *adj.* **1.** Requiring the use of two hands at once. **2.** Requiring or involving two people. **3.** Able to use both hands with equal facility.

two·pence (tŭp′əns) *n.* Also *informal* **tup·pence.** *Brit.* **1.** Two pennies regarded as a monetary unit. **2.** A coin worth two pennies. **3.** A very small amount; a whit.

two·pen·ny (tōō′pĕn′ē; British tŭp′ə-nē) *adj.* **1.** Worth or costing twopence. **2.** Cheap; worthless.

two-ply (tōō′plī′) *adj.* **1.** Made of two interwoven layers. **2.** Consisting of two thicknesses or strands: *two-ply yarn.*

two·some (tōō′səm) *n.* **1.** Two people together; a pair. **2.** A game played by two people, as a round of golf.

two-step (tōō′stĕp′) *n.* **1.** A ballroom dance in ²/₄ time and characterized by long, sliding steps. **2.** The music to which such a dance is performed.

two-time (tōō′tīm′) *tr.v.* **-timed, -tim·ing.** *Slang.* To be unfaithful or deceitful to. —**two′-tim′er** *n.*

two-way (tōō′wā′) *adj.* **1.** Affording passage in two directions. **2.** Permitting communication in two directions, as a radio. **3.** Expressive of or involving mutual action, relationship, or responsibility: *a two-way compromise.*

-ty¹. A suffix meaning a condition or quality: **novelty.** [Middle English *-te, -tie,* from Old French *-te, -tet,* from Latin *-tās.*]

-ty². A suffix meaning a multiple of ten: **eighty.** [Middle English, from Old English *-tig.*]

ty·coon (tī-kōōn′) *n. Informal.* A wealthy and powerful businessman or industrialist; magnate. [Japanese *taikun,* title of a shogun.]

tyke (tīk) *n.* Also **tike.** **1.** *Informal.* A small child, esp. a mischievous one. **2.** A mongrel or cur. [Middle English, from Old Norse *tīk,* a bitch.]

tym·bal (tĭm′bəl) *n.* Var. of **timbal.**

tym·pa·na (tĭm′pə-nə) *n.* A plural of **tympanum.**

tym·pa·ni (tĭm′pə-nē) *n.* Var. of **timpani.**

tym·pan·ic (tĭm-păn′ĭk) *adj.* **1.** Of or like a drum. **2.** *Anat.* Of the tympanum.

tympanic membrane. The eardrum.

tym·pa·nist (tĭm′pə-nĭst) *n.* The member of an orchestra who plays the timpani and other percussion instruments.

tym·pa·num (tĭm′pə-nəm) *n., pl.* **-na** (-nə) or **-nums.** Also **tim·pa·num.** **1. a.** The middle ear. **b.** The tympanic membrane; eardrum. **2.** *Zool.* A membranous external auditory structure, as in certain insects. **3.** *Archit.* **a.** The recessed, ornamental space or panel enclosed by the cornices of a triangular pediment. **b.** A similar space between an arch and the lintel of a portal. [Medieval Latin, the eardrum, from Latin, a drum, from Greek *tumpanon.*]

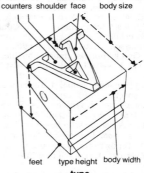

counters   shoulder   face   body size

feet   type height   body width

type
The letter A

type (tīp) *n.* **1.** A group of persons or things sharing common traits or characteristics that distinguish them as an identifiable group or class; a kind; category. **2.** A person or thing having the characteristics of a group or class: *a type of cactus.* **3.** *Printing.* **a.** A small block of metal or wood with a raised letter or character on the upper end that, when inked and pressed upon paper, leaves a printed impression. **b.** A collection of such blocks or metal pieces. **4.** Printed or typewritten characters; print. **5.** *Informal.* A person regarded as exemplifying a certain profession, rank, social group, etc. **6.** An example or model; embodiment. **7.** A figure, representation, or symbol of something to come. —See Syns at **kind.** —*v.* **typed, typ·ing.** —*tr.v.* **1.** To classify according to a particular type or class. **2.** To write with a typewriter. **3.** To determine the type of (a blood sample). **4.** To represent or typify. —*intr.v.* To write with a typewriter. [Late Latin *typus,* a form, from Latin, figure, image, from Greek *tupos,* a blow, impression.]

–type. A suffix meaning: **1.** Type or representative form: **monotype.** **2.** Stamping or printing type, or photographic process: **stereotype.** [French, from Latin *-typus,* from Greek *-tupos,* from *tupos,* type.]

type·cast (tīp′kăst′, -kăst′) *tr.v.* **1.** To cast (an actor) in a role that seems to fit his own personality or physical appearance. **2.** To assign (an actor) so repeatedly in the same kind of part that no other kind is ever offered.

type·face (tīp′fās′) *n. Printing.* The size and style of the characters on type.

type metal. An alloy used for making metal printing type, consisting mainly of tin, lead, and antimony.

type·script (tīp′skrĭpt′) *n.* **1.** A typewritten copy, as of a book. **2.** Typewritten matter.

type·set·ter (tīp′sĕt′ər) *n.* **1.** A person who sets type. **2.** A machine used for setting type. —**type′set′ting** *n.*

type·write (tīp′rīt′) *v.* **-wrote** (-rōt′), **-writ·ten** (-rĭt′n), **-writ·ing.** —*tr.v.* To write (something) with a typewriter; to type. —*intr.v.* To write with a typewriter; to type.

type·writ·er (tīp′rī′tər) *n.* A machine that prints letters and characters on paper by means of keys that, when pressed by hand, strike the paper through an inked ribbon.

type·writ·ing (tīp′rī′tĭng) *n.* **1.** The act, process, or skill of using a typewriter. **2.** Copy produced by typewriting.

typhoid fever. An acute, highly infectious disease caused by the typhoid bacillus, *Salmonella typhosa,* transmitted by contaminated food or water and characterized by red rashes, high fever, bronchitis, and intestinal hemorrhaging. Also called **enteric fever.** [TYPH(US) + -OID.]

ty·phoon (tī-fōōn′) *n.* A severe tropical hurricane that occurs in the western Pacific or the China Sea. [Cantonese *tai fung,* "great wind."]

ty·phus (tī′fəs) *n.* Any of several forms of an infectious disease caused by microorganisms of the genus *Rickettsia,* transmitted esp. by fleas, lice, and mites, and characterized by severe headache, sustained high fever, depression, delirium, and red rashes. Also called **typhus fever.** [From Greek *tuphos,* (fever-causing) delusion, from *tuphein,* to make smoke.] **—ty′phous** (-fəs) *adj.*

typ·i·cal (tĭp′ĭ-kəl) *adj.* **1.** Exhibiting the traits or characteristics peculiar to its kind, class, group, or category; representative. **2.** Of a representative specimen; characteristic: *responded with his typical bluntness.* **3.** Conforming to a type: *a typical criminal mentality.* —See Syns at **characteristic** and **ordinary.** [Late Latin *typicālis,* from *typicus,* typical, from Greek *tupikos,* impressionable, from *tupos,* impression, type.] **—typ′i·cal·ly** *adv.* **—typ′i·cal·ness** or **typ′i·cal′i·ty** *n.*

typ·i·fy (tĭp′ə-fī′) *tr.v.* **-fied, -fy·ing. 1.** To serve as a typical or characteristic specimen of; exemplify. **2.** To represent by an image, form, or model; symbolize. —See Syns at **represent.** [From TYP(E) + -FY.] **—typ′i·fi·ca′tion** *n.* **—typ′i·fi′er** *n.*

typ·ist (tī′pĭst) *n.* A person who operates a typewriter.

ty·po (tī′pō) *n., pl.* **-os.** *Informal.* A typographical error.

ty·pog·ra·pher (tī-pŏg′rə-fər) *n.* A printer or compositor.

typographical error. A mistake in printed or typewritten copy.

ty·pog·ra·phy (tī-pŏg′rə-fē) *n., pl.* **-phies. 1. a.** The composition of printed material from movable type. **b.** The technique of printing in this manner. **2.** The arrangement and appearance of printed matter. **—ty′po·graph′i·cal** (tī′pə-grăf′ĭ-kəl) or **ty′po·graph′ic** *adj.* **—ty′po·graph′i·cal·ly** *adv.*

ty·ran·ni·cal (tĭ-răn′ĭ-kəl, tī-) or **ty·ran·nic** (-răn′ĭk) *adj.* Of or characteristic of a tyrant; despotic. —See Syns at **absolute. —ty·ran′ni·cal·ly** *adv.* **—ty·ran′ni·cal·ness** *n.*

tyr·an·nize (tĭr′ə-nīz′) *v.* **-nized, -niz·ing.** *—intr.v.* **1.** To exercise absolute power, esp. arbitrarily. **2.** To govern as a tyrant, esp. cruelly or oppressively. *—tr.v.* To treat tyrannically; oppress. **—tyr′an·niz′er** *n.* **—tyr′an·niz′ing·ly** *adv.*

ty·ran·no·saur (tĭ-răn′ə-sôr′, tī-) *n.* Also **ty·ran·no·saur·us** (tĭ-răn′ə-sôr′əs, tī-). A large carnivorous dinosaur of the genus *Tyrannosaurus,* of the Cretaceous period, that had small forelimbs and a large head. [Greek *turannos,* tyrant + -SAUR.]

tyr·an·nous (tĭr′ə-nəs) *adj.* Characterized by tyranny; despotic; tyrannical. **—tyr′an·nous·ly** *adv.*

tyr·an·ny (tĭr′ə-nē) *n., pl.* **-nies. 1.** A government in which a single ruler is vested with absolute power. **2.** The office, authority, or jurisdiction of such a ruler. **3.** Absolute power, esp. when exercised unjustly or cruelly. **4.** The arbitrary use of such power; a tyrannical act. **5.** Extreme harshness or severity; rigor. [Middle English *tyrannye,* from Old French *tyrannie,* from Late Latin *tyrannia,* from Greek *turannia,* from *turannos,* tyrant.]

ty·rant (tī′rənt) *n.* **1.** An absolute ruler who governs arbitrarily without constitutional or other restrictions. **2.** A ruler who exercises power in a harsh, cruel manner; an oppressor. **3.** Any tyrannical or despotic person, esp. one who demands total obedience. [Middle English, from Old French, from Latin *tyrannus,* from Greek *turannos.*]

tyre (tīr) *n. Brit.* Var. of **tire** (wheel part).

Tyrian purple. A reddish dyestuff obtained from the bodies of certain mollusks of the genus *Murex,* highly prized in ancient times. [After *Tyre,* a city of ancient Phoenicia.]

ty·ro (tī′rō) *n., pl.* **-ros.** An inexperienced person; a beginner; neophyte. [Medieval Latin *tȳrō,* from Latin *tīrō,* a young soldier, recruit.]

ty·ro·sine (tī′rə-sēn′) *n.* A white crystalline amino acid, $C_9H_{11}NO_3$, derived from the hydrolysis of protein, used as a growth factor in nutrition and as a dietary supplement. [Greek *turos,* cheese + -INE.]

tzar (zär) *n.* Var. of **czar.**

tzet·ze fly (tsĕt′sē, tsĕt′sē). Var. of **tsetse fly.**

ă pat ā pay â care ä father ĕ pet ē be hw which ĭ pit ī tie î pier ŏ pot ō toe ô paw, for oi noise
ōō took ōō boot ou out th thin th this ŭ cut û urge zh vision ə about, item, edible, gallop, circus

Y	Y	V	u	Uu
Phoenician	Greek	Roman	Medieval	Modern

Phoenician – About 3,000 years ago the Phoenicians and other Semitic peoples began to use graphic signs to represent individual speech sounds instead of syllables or whole words. They used this symbol, which is the ancestor of the letters F, V, W, and Y as well as U, to represent the sound of the semivowel "w" and gave it the name wāw, the Phoenician word for "hook."

Greek – The Greeks borrowed the Phoenician alphabet with some modifications. They changed the shape of wāw slightly and altered its name to upsilon. They used upsilon to represent the sound of the vowel "u."

Roman – The Romans borrowed the alphabet from the Greeks via the Etruscans, who used a tailless variant of upsilon. The Romans used upsilon to represent both the vowel "u" and the semivowel "w," which later developed into the consonant "v."

Medieval – By medieval times – around 1,200 years ago – the Roman monumental capitals had become adapted to being relatively quickly written on paper, parchment, or vellum. Like the Roman letter V, medieval U was still used to represent both the vowel "u" and the consonant "v." The cursive minuscule alphabet became the basis of modern printed lower-case letters.

Modern – Even after the invention of printing about 500 years ago U and V were not distinguished by phonetic value but by position: V was used at the beginning of a word and U in the middle or at the end. During the 17th century the distinction between U and V became complete. They were assigned the phonetic values that they have today and the rounded shape of capital U was developed, but it was not until the early 19th century that their position in the alphabet was fixed.

---

u or **U** (yōō) n., pl. **u's** or **U's.** The 21st letter of the English alphabet.

U The symbol for the element uranium.

u·biq·ui·tous (yōō-bĭk'wĭ-təs) adj. Being or seeming to be everywhere at the same time; omnipresent: "He plodded through the shadows fruitlessly like an ubiquitous spook" (Joseph Heller). **—u·biq'ui·tous·ly** adv.

u·biq·ui·ty (yōō-bĭk'wĭ-tē) n. Existence everywhere at the same time; omnipresence. [From Latin ubīque, everywhere.]

U-boat (yōō'bōt') n. A German submarine. [German U-boot, short for Unterseeboot, "undersea boat."]

U-bolt (yōō'bōlt') n. A bolt shaped like the letter U, fitted with threads and a nut at each end.

ud·der (ŭd'ər) n. The baglike mammary organ of a cow, female sheep or goat, etc., in which milk is formed and held and from which it is taken in suckling or milking. [Middle English, from Old English ūder.]

u·do (ōō'dō) n. A Japanese plant, Aralia cordata, of which the young shoots are cooked and eaten as a vegetable. [Japanese.]

UFO n., pl. **UFOs** or **UFO's.** An **unidentified flying object.**

ugh (ŭg, ŭk) interj. Used to express horror, disgust, or repugnance.

ug·ly (ŭg'lē) adj. **-li·er, -li·est. 1.** Not pleasing to the eye; unsightly. **2.** Repulsive or offensive in any way; objectionable; unpleasant. **3.** Morally reprehensible; bad: an ugly character. **4.** Threatening; ominous: ugly weather. **5.** Cross; disagreeable: an ugly temper. [Middle English uglic, frightful, repulsive, from Old Norse uggligr, from uggr, fear.] **—ug'li·ness** n.

    Syns: ugly, hideous, unsightly adj. Core meaning: Displeasing to the eye (an ugly face; a hideous gash; an unsightly scar). UGLY and HIDEOUS, the stronger term, can also describe what is emotionally, morally, or otherwise offensive (the ugly details of the argument; a hideous murder; a hideous accident).

ugly duckling. A child considered ugly or unpromising at first but having the potential of becoming beautiful or admirable in maturity. [From The Ugly Duckling, a story by Hans Christian Andersen.]

uh. interj. A word used to express hesitation, uncertainty, etc.

uh-huh. interj. Informal. Yes.

uh·lan (ōō'län', yōō'lən, ōō'lən) n. One of a body of cavalry armed with lances that formed part of the former Polish and, later, German armies. [German uhlan, from Polish u⫽an, from Turkish oğlan, youth, from oğul, son.]

u·kase (yōō-kās', -kāz', yōō'kās', -kāz') n. **1.** A proclamation of the czar that had the force of law in imperial Russia. **2.** Any authoritative order or decree; an edict. [French, from Russian ukaz, decree, from ukazat', to order, direct.]

uke (yōōk) n. Informal. A ukulele.

U·krain·i·an (yōō-krā'nē-ən) n. **1.** An inhabitant or native of the Ukraine. **2.** A Slavic language spoken by most natives of the Ukraine. **—adj.** Of or relating to the Ukraine, its people, culture, or language.

u·ku·le·le (yōō'kə-lā'lē, ōō'kə-) n. A small four-stringed guitar popularized in Hawaii. [Hawaiian 'ukulele, "jumping little flea."]

ukulele

ul·cer (ŭl'sər) n. **1.** An inflamed, often pus-filled sore or lesion on the skin, or on the stomach or duodenum, resulting in necrosis of the tissue. **2.** Any corrupting condition or influence. [Middle English, from Old French ulcere, from Latin ulcus.]

ul·cer·ate (ŭl'sə-rāt') v. **-at·ed, -at·ing. —intr.v.** To become affected with an ulcer. **—tr.v.** To affect with ulcers. **—ul'cer·a'tion** n.

ul·cer·ous (ŭl'sər-əs) adj. Of or affected with ulcers.

-ule. A suffix meaning small: **valvule.** [French, from Latin -ulus, -ula, -ulum, dim. suffixes.]

ă pat   ā pay   â care   ä father   ĕ pet   ē be   hw which   ĭ pit   ī tie   î pier   ŏ pot   ō toe   ô paw, for   oi noise
ōō took   ōō boot   ou out   th thin   th this   ŭ cut   û urge   zh vision   ə about, item, edible, gallop, circus

ul·na (ŭl′nə) *n., pl.* **-nae** (-nē′) or **-nas.** **1.** The bone extending from the elbow to the wrist on the side of the arm opposite to the thumb. **2.** A similar bone in the vertebrate foreleg. [Latin, elbow, arm.] **—ul′nar** *adj.*

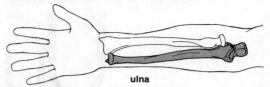

ulna

ul·ster (ŭl′stər) *n.* A loose, long overcoat made of heavy, rugged fabric. [After *Ulster*, Ireland.]

ul·te·ri·or (ŭl-tîr′ē-ər) *adj.* **1.** Beyond or outside what is evident or admitted: *an ulterior motive.* **2.** Beyond or outside a certain area or region; remoter. [Latin, farther, comp. of *ulter*, on the other side, from *uls*, beyond.]

ul·ti·ma (ŭl′tə-mə) *n.* The last syllable of a word. [Latin, farthest, last.]

ul·ti·ma·ta (ŭl′tə-mā′tə, -mä′-) *n.* A plural of **ultimatum.**

ul·ti·mate (ŭl′tə-mĭt) *adj.* **1.** Completing a series or process; final; conclusive: *his ultimate defeat.* **2.** Highest possible; greatest; extreme. **3.** Representing the farthest possible extent of analysis or division into parts: *ultimate particle.* **4.** Fundamental; basic; elemental: *ultimate truths.* **5.** Farthest; most remote: *the ultimate limits of the Galaxy.* —See Syns at **last.** —*n.* **1.** The basic or fundamental fact. **2.** The final point; conclusive result; conclusion. **3.** The maximum; greatest extreme. [Medieval Latin *ultimātus,* past participle of *ultimāre,* to come to an end, from Latin *ultimus,* farthest, last, superl. of *ulter,* on the other side, from *uls,* beyond.] **—ul′ti·mate·ly** *adv.* **—ul′ti·mate·ness** *n.*

ultima Thu·le (thōō′lē, thyōō′-). **1.** The region ancient geographers thought of as the northernmost part of the habitable world. **2.** A remote goal or ideal. [Latin, "farthest Thule."]

ul·ti·ma·tum (ŭl′tə-mā′təm, -mä′-) *n., pl.* **-tums** or **-ta** (-tə). A statement of terms that expresses or implies the threat of serious penalties if the terms are not accepted; a final demand or offer. [New Latin, from Medieval Latin, neut. of *ultimātus,* last, ultimate.]

ul·ti·mo (ŭl′tə-mō′) *adv.* In or of the month before the present one. [Latin *ultimo (mense),* "in (the) last (month)," from *ultimus,* last, ultimate.]

ul·tra (ŭl′trə) *adj.* Going beyond the normal limit. —*n.* An extremist. [From ULTRA-.]

ultra-. A prefix meaning: **1.** Surpassing a specified limit, range, or scope; beyond: **ultrasonic. 2.** Exceeding what is common, moderate, or proper; extreme: **ultraconservative.** [Latin, from *ultrā,* beyond, from *uls,* beyond.]

ul·tra·con·ser·va·tive (ŭl′trə-kən-sûr′və-tĭv) *adj.* Conservative to an extreme, esp. in political beliefs; reactionary. —*n.* A person who is extremely conservative.

ul·tra·high frequency (ŭl′trə-hī′). A band of radio frequencies from 300 to 3,000 megahertz.

ul·tra·ma·rine (ŭl′trə-mə-rēn′) *n.* **1.** A blue pigment made from powdered lapis lazuli. **2.** A bright deep blue. —*adj.* **1.** Bright deep blue. **2.** Of or from some place beyond the sea. [Medieval Latin *ultramarīnus,* "(coming from) beyond the sea" (from the fact that lapis lazuli was imported into Europe from Asia by sea).]

ul·tra·mi·cro·scope (ŭl′trə-mī′krə-skōp′) *n.* A microscope with high-intensity illumination used to study very minute objects, such as colloidal particles, by means of their diffraction system, which appears as a bright spot against a black background.

ul·tra·mi·cro·scop·ic (ŭl′trə-mī′krə-skŏp′ĭk) *adj.* **1.** Too small to be seen with an ordinary microscope. **2.** Of or relating to an ultramicroscope.

ul·tra·mon·tane (ŭl′trə-mŏn-tān′, -mŏn-tān′) *adj.* **1.** Lying or situated beyond the mountains. **2.** Of or pertaining to peoples or regions lying south of the Alps. **3.** Supporting the supreme authority of the pope in ecclesiastical and political matters. —*n.* **1.** A person living beyond the mountains, esp. south of the Alps. **2.** A Roman Catholic who advocates support of papal policy in ecclesiastical and po-

litical matters. [Medieval Latin *ultrāmontānus* : Latin *ultrā-,* beyond + *mōns,* mountain.]

ul·tra·mun·dane (ŭl′trə-mŭn′dān′, -mŭn-dān′) *adj.* Extending or being beyond the world or the limits of the known universe. [Latin *ultrāmundānus* : *ultrā-,* beyond + *mundus,* the world.]

ul·tra·son·ic (ŭl′trə-sŏn′ĭk) *adj.* Pertaining to acoustic frequencies above the range the human ear can hear or above approx. 20,000 cycles per second.

ul·tra·son·ics (ŭl′trə-sŏn′ĭks) *n. (used with a sing. verb.)* The scientific study of ultrasonic sound.

ul·tra·vi·o·let (ŭl′trə-vī′ə-lĭt) *adj.* Of electromagnetic radiation with wavelengths between 4,000 angstroms, just shorter than those of visible light, and 40 angstroms, just longer than those of x-rays. —*n.* Ultraviolet light or the ultraviolet part of the spectrum.

ul·u·late (ŭl′yə-lāt′) *intr.v.* **-lat·ed, -lat·ing.** To howl, hoot, wail, or lament loudly. [From Latin *ululāre,* to howl.] **—ul′u·la′tion** *n.*

U·lys·ses (yōō-lĭs′ēz) *n.* The Latin name for Odysseus.

um·bel (ŭm′bəl) *n. Bot.* A flat-topped or rounded flower cluster in which the individual flower stalks arise from about the same point on the stem, as in the carrot and related plants. [From Latin *umbella,* an umbrella, dim. of *umbra,* shadow.]

um·bel·late (ŭm′bə-lāt′, ŭm-bĕl′ĭt) *adj. Bot.* Having, forming, or of the nature of an umbel.

um·bel·lif·er·ous (ŭm′bə-lĭf′ər-əs) *adj. Bot.* Bearing umbels.

um·ber (ŭm′bər) *n.* **1.** A natural brown earth composed of oxides of iron, silicon, aluminum, calcium, and manganese, used as pigment. **2. a.** A yellowish brown of raw umber. **b.** A dark reddish brown of burnt umber. —*adj.* **1.** Of or related to umber. **2.** Dark reddish brown. **b.** Yellowish brown. —*tr.v.* To cover with or as with umber. [Old French *umbre,* short for *terre d'Umbre,* "earth of Umbria."]

um·bil·i·cal (ŭm-bĭl′ĭ-kəl) *adj.* Of, pertaining to, or located near the umbilical cord or navel. —*n.* An umbilical cord.

umbilical cord. **1.** *Anat.* The flexible cordlike structure that extends from the navel of a fetus to the placenta, containing blood vessels that supply nourishment to the fetus and remove its wastes. **2.** *Aerospace.* **a.** Any of the supply tubes, wires, cables, etc., that are connected to a rocket and removed shortly before launching. **b.** The line that supplies an astronaut with oxygen and communications while he is outside the spacecraft.

um·bil·i·cus (ŭm-bĭl′ĭ-kəs, ŭm′bə-lī′kəs) *n., pl.* **-ci** (-sī′). **1.** The navel. **2.** *Biol.* Any similar small opening or depression, such as the hollow at the base of the shell of some gastropod mollusks or one of the openings in the shaft of a feather. [Latin *umbilīcus.*]

um·bra (ŭm′brə) *n., pl.* **-brae** (-brē). **1.** A dark area, esp. the darkest part of a shadow from which all light is cut off. **2.** *Astron.* **a.** The shadow of the moon that falls on a part of the earth where a solar eclipse is total. **b.** The darkest region of a sunspot. [Latin, shadow.]

um·brage (ŭm′brĭj) *n.* **1.** A feeling aroused by a perceived injury or insult to oneself; offense; resentment: *took umbrage at their rudeness.* **2.** *Archaic.* Shadow or shade. [Middle English, shade, from Old French, from Latin *umbrāticus,* of a shadow, from *umbra,* shadow.]

um·bra·geous (ŭm-brā′jəs) *adj.* **1.** Affording or forming shade; shady or shading. **2.** Easily offended; irritable. **—um·bra′geous·ly** *adv.* **—um·bra′geous·ness** *n.*

um·brel·la (ŭm-brĕl′ə) *n.* **1.** A device for protection from the rain or sun, consisting of a usu. cloth cover on a collapsible frame mounted on a handle. **2.** Anything that covers or protects, esp. a military air cover. **3.** *Zool.* The jellylike rounded mass constituting the major part of the body of most jellyfishes. [Italian *ombrella,* dim. of *ombra,* shade, from Latin *umbra.*]

umbrella tree. **1.** Any of several trees of the genus *Magnolia,* of the southeastern United States, esp. one that has large leaves clustered in an umbrellalike form at the ends of the branches. **2.** A tree, *Schefflera actinophylla,* native to Australia, that has compound leaves and is widely cultivated in its smaller forms as a house plant.

u·mi·ak (ōō′mē-ăk′) *n.* A large open Eskimo boat made of skins stretched on a wooden frame, usu. propelled by paddles. [Eskimo.]

um·laut (ōōm′lout′) *n.* **1. a.** A change in a vowel sound caused by partial assimilation to a sound that has been lost in the following syllable. **b.** A vowel sound changed in this manner. **2.** The diacritical mark (ë) placed over a vowel to indicate an umlaut, esp. in German. —*tr.v.* **1.** To modify a vowel sound by umlaut. **2.** To write or print a vowel with an umlaut. [German *Umlaut* : *um-*, around + *Laut*, sound.]

um·pire (ŭm′pīr′) *n.* **1.** A person appointed to rule on plays in various sports, esp. baseball. **2.** A person selected or empowered to settle a dispute between other persons or groups. —*v.* **-pired, -pir·ing.** —*tr.v.* To act as umpire in or of. —*intr.v.* To be or act as an umpire. —See Syns at **judge.** [Middle English *(an) oumpere*, orig. *(a) noumpere*, (an) umpire, from Old French *nomper*, "not one of a pair (of contestants)."]

ump·teen (ŭmp′tēn′, ŭm′-) *adj. Informal.* Large but indefinite in number. [*umpty*, a great number, from a Morse code term for "dash" + *-teen*, as in *thirteen*.] —**ump·teenth′** *adj.*

un–¹. A prefix meaning not: *unhappy.* [Middle English, from Old English.]

un–². A prefix indicating: **1.** Reversal of an action: *unlock, unmake.* **2.** Deprivation: *unnerve, unfrock.* **3.** Release or removal from: *unearth, unyoke, unhorse.* **4.** Intensified action: *unloose.* [Middle English, from Old English, var. of *ond-, and-,* against.]

un·a·bashed (ŭn′ə-băsht′) *adj.* Not embarrassed or disconcerted. —**un′a·bash′ed·ly** (-băsh′ĭd-lē) *adv.*

un·a·bat·ed (ŭn′ə-bā′tĭd) *adj.* At original full force.

un·a·ble (ŭn-ā′bəl) *adj.* **1.** Lacking the necessary power, authority, or means. **2.** Lacking mental capability or efficiency; incompetent.

un·a·bridged (ŭn′ə-brĭjd′) *adj.* Having the original contents; not condensed: *an unabridged book.*

un·ac·com·pa·nied (ŭn′ə-kŭm′pə-nēd) *adj.* **1.** Going or acting without a companion. **2.** *Mus.* Performed or scored without accompaniment.

un·ac·count·a·ble (ŭn′ə-koun′tə-bəl) *adj.* **1.** Not capable of being explained; inexplicable. **2.** Free from being held to account; not responsible: *unaccountable for his actions.* —**un′ac·count′a·bly** *adv.*

un·ac·count·ed (ŭn′ə-koun′tĭd) *adj.* **1.** Not explained or understood. **2.** Absent with whereabouts unknown: *After the riot, three prisoners were unaccounted for.*

un·ac·cus·tomed (ŭn′ə-kŭs′təmd) *adj.* **1.** Not customary; unusual: *his unaccustomed politeness.* **2.** Unfamiliar. —See Syns at **strange.**

un·a·dorned (ŭn′ə-dôrnd′) *adj.* Without embellishment or artificiality; simple; plain. —See Syns at **plain.**

un·a·dul·ter·at·ed (ŭn′ə-dŭl′tə-rā′tĭd) *adj.* Not mingled or diluted with extraneous matter; pure; natural: *"They had real courage: the unadulterated liking of danger"* (Isak Dinesen). —See Syns at **plain.**

un·ad·vised (ŭn′əd-vīzd′) *adj.* **1.** Not informed. **2.** Ill-advised; rash; imprudent. —**un′ad·vis′ed·ly** (-vī′zĭd-lē) *adv.*

un·af·fect·ed (ŭn′ə-fĕk′tĭd) *adj.* Natural or sincere, as in appearance, manner, etc. —**un′af·fect′ed·ly** *adv.* —**un′af·fect′ed·ness** *n.*

un·a·fraid (ŭn′ə-frād′) *adj.* Not feeling or showing fear. —See Syns at **brave.**

un·al·loyed (ŭn′ə-loid′) *adj.* **1.** Not in mixture with other metals; pure. **2.** Complete; unqualified.

u·na·nim·i·ty (yōō′nə-nĭm′ĭ-tē) *n.* The condition of being unanimous; complete agreement.

u·nan·i·mous (yōō-năn′ə-məs) *adj.* **1.** Sharing the same opinions or views; being in complete harmony or accord. **2.** Based on complete assent or agreement: *a unanimous vote.* [Latin *ūnanimus*, of one mind : *ūnus*, one + *animus*, soul, mind.] —**u·nan′i·mous·ly** *adv.*

un·ap·proach·a·ble (ŭn′ə-prō′chə-bəl) *adj.* **1.** Not friendly; aloof. **2.** Not accessible; inapproachable. —**un′ap·proach′-a·ble·ness** *n.* —**un′ap·proach′a·bly** *adv.*

un·arm (ŭn′-ärm′) *tr.v. Archaic.* To divest of armor or arms; disarm.

un·armed (ŭn-ärmd′) *adj.* **1.** Lacking weapons; defense-

less. **2.** *Biol.* Having no thorns or spines.

un·as·sail·a·ble (ŭn′ə-sā′lə-bəl) *adj.* **1.** Not capable of being disputed or disproven; undeniable; unquestionable. **2.** Not capable of being attacked or seized successfully; impregnable. —**un′as·sail′a·bly** *adv.*

un·as·sist·ed (ŭn′ə-sĭs′tĭd) *adj.* **1.** Not assisted; unaided. **2.** *Baseball.* Designating a play handled by only one fielder. —*adv. Baseball.* Without the help of another player: *He made the play unassisted.*

un·as·sum·ing (ŭn′ə-sōō′mĭng) *adj.* Not boastful or pretentious; modest. —**un′as·sum′ing·ly** *adv.*

un·at·tached (ŭn′ə-tăcht′) *adj.* **1.** Not attached or joined. **2. a.** Not committed to or dependent upon a person, group, organization, etc.. **b.** Not engaged or married. **3.** *Law.* Not possessed or seized as security.

un·at·test·ed (ŭn′ə-tĕs′tĭd) *adj.* Not found in written documents.

un·a·vail·ing (ŭn′ə-vā′lĭng) *adj.* Useless; unsuccessful.

un·a·void·a·ble (ŭn′ə-voi′də-bəl) *adj.* Not capable of being avoided; inevitable. —**un′a·void′a·bly** *adv.*

un·a·ware (ŭn′ə-wâr′) *adj.* Not aware or cognizant. —See Syns at **ignorant.**

un·a·wares (ŭn′ə-wârz′) *adv.* **1.** By surprise; unexpectedly: *"Sorrow comes to all, and to the young it comes with bittered agony because it takes them unawares"* (Lincoln). **2.** Without intention of forethought: *We neglected him unawares.*

un·backed (ŭn-băkt′) *adj.* **1.** Lacking backing or support: *an unbacked candidate for office.* **2.** Not having a back, as a bench.

un·bal·ance (ŭn-băl′əns) *tr.v.* **-anced, -anc·ing.** **1.** To upset the balance, stability, or equilibrium of. **2.** To derange (the mind). —*n.* The condition of being unbalanced. —See Syns at **insanity.**

un·bal·anced (ŭn-băl′ənst) *adj.* **1.** Not in balance or in proper balance: *an unbalanced budget; an unbalanced scale.* **2.** Not mentally sound. **3.** *Bookkeeping.* Not adjusted so that debit and credit correspond.—See Syns at **insane.**

un·bar (ŭn-bär′) *tr.v.* **-barred, -bar·ring.** To remove the bar or bars from; open.

un·bear·a·ble (ŭn-bâr′ə-bəl) *adj.* Unendurable; intolerable. —**un·bear′a·bly** *adv.*

un·beat·a·ble (ŭn-bē′tə-bəl) *adj.* Impossible to surpass or defeat. —**un·beat′a·bly** *adv.*

un·beat·en (ŭn-bēt′n) *adj.* **1.** Never defeated or beaten. **2.** Not walked over or traveled; untrod: *an unbeaten path.* **3.** Not beaten or pounded: *an unbeaten egg.*

un·be·com·ing (ŭn-bĭ-kŭm′ĭng) *adj.* **1.** Not appropriate, attractive, or flattering. **2.** Not seemly; indecorous; improper. —See Syns at **unsuitable.** —**un·be·com′ing·ly** *adv.*

un·be·known (ŭn′bĭ-nōn′) *or* **un·be·knownst** (-nōnst′) *adj.* Occurring or existing without one's knowledge. [UN- + obs. *beknown*, known.]

un·be·lief (ŭn′bĭ-lēf′) *n.* Lack of belief or faith, esp. in religious matters.

un·be·liev·a·ble (ŭn′bĭ-lē′və-bəl) *adj.* Not to be believed. —See Syns at **fabulous.** —**un′be·liev′a·bly** *adv.*

un·be·liev·er (ŭn′bĭ-lē′vər) *n.* **1.** A person who does not believe; a doubter. **2.** A person who does not believe in a particular religion.

un·be·liev·ing (ŭn′bĭ-lē′vĭng) *adj.* Not believing; doubting: *right before our unbelieving eyes.*

un·bend (ŭn-bĕnd′) *v.* **-bent** (-bĕnt′), **-bend·ing.** —*tr.v.* **1.** To make or cause to be straight. **2.** To make less tense; relax: *soothing music to unbend us.* —*intr.v.* **1.** To become less tense; unwind. **2.** To become straight.

un·bend·ing (ŭn-bĕn′dĭng) *adj.* Not flexible; uncompromising. —See Syns at **rigid.**

un·bi·ased (ŭn-bī′əst) *adj.* Without bias or prejudice; impartial. —**un·bi′ased·ly** *adv.*

un·bid·den (ŭn-bĭd′n) *adj. Also* **un·bid** (-bĭd′). Not invited. —*adv.* Without being asked.

un·bind (ŭn-bīnd′) *tr.v.* **-bound** (-bound′), **-bind·ing.** **1.** To untie or unfasten, as wrappings or bindings. **2.** To release from restraints or bonds; set free.

un·blink·ing (ŭn-blĭng′kĭng) *adj.* **1.** Without blinking. **2.** Without visible emotion. **3.** Fearless in facing reality.

---

un·blush·ing (ŭn-blŭsh'ĭng) adj. 1. Without shame or remorse. 2. Not blushing. —**un·blush'ing·ly** adv.

un·bolt (ŭn-bōlt') tr.v. To release the bolts of (a door or gate); unlock.

un·bolt·ed (ŭn-bōl'tĭd) adj. Not sifted: unbolted flour.

un·born (ŭn-bôrn') adj. Not yet in existence; not born.

un·bos·om (ŭn-bŏōz'əm, -bōō'zəm) tr.v. 1. To confide; reveal. 2. **unbosom oneself.** To relieve (oneself) of troublesome thoughts or feelings.

un·bound (ŭn-bound') adj. 1. Not having a binding: a unbound book. 2. Freed from bonds or shackles; released.

un·bound·ed (ŭn-boun'dĭd) adj. 1. Having no boundaries or limits: unbounded space. 2. Not kept within bounds; unrestrained: unbounded enthusiasm.

un·bowed (ŭn-boud') adj. 1. Not bowed; unbent. 2. Not subdued; unyielding: "My head is bloody but unbowed" (W.E. Henley).

un·bri·dled (ŭn-brīd'ld) adj. 1. Not fitted with a bridle. 2. Unrestrained; uncontrolled: unbridled joy.

un·bro·ken (ŭn-brō'kən) adj. 1. Not broken; whole; intact. 2. Not violated or breached. 3. Uninterrupted; continuous. 4. Not tamed or broken. 5. Not bettered or surpassed: his unbroken record of stolen bases. —**un·bro'ken·ly** adv. —**un·bro'ken·ness** n.

un·buck·le (ŭn-bŭk'əl) tr.v. -**led**, -**ling**. To loosen or undo the buckle or buckles of.

un·bur·den (ŭn-bûr'dn) tr.v. To free or relieve from a burden or trouble: unburden one's mind.

un·but·ton (ŭn-bŭt'n) tr.v. 1. To unfasten the button or buttons of. 2. To free or remove (a button) from a buttonhole. 3. To open as if by unbuttoning: unbutton the hatches. 4. To expose or air: unbutton one's secret thoughts. —intr.v. To undo a button or buttons.

un·called-for (ŭn-kôld'fôr') adj. 1. Not required or requested: an uncalled-for appearance. 2. Out of place; impertinent; unnecessary: an uncalled-for insult.

un·can·ny (ŭn-kăn'ē) adj. -**ni·er**, -**ni·est.** 1. Exciting wonder and fear; inexplicable; strange: an uncanny light from the cave. 2. So keen and perceptive as to seem supernatural: uncanny insight. —See Syns at **weird.** —**un·can'ni·ly** adv. —**un·can'ni·ness** n.

un·cap (ŭn-kăp') tr.v. -**capped**, -**cap·ping.** To remove the cap or covering of.

un·ceas·ing (ŭn-sē'sĭng) adj. Not ceasing or letting up; incessant. —**un·ceas'ing·ly** adv.

un·cer·e·mo·ni·ous (ŭn-sĕr'ə-mō'nē-əs) adj. 1. Not ceremonious; informal: an unceremonious dinner. 2. Without the due formalities; abrupt: an unceremonious dismissal. —**un·cer'e·mo'ni·ous·ly** adv.

un·cer·tain (ŭn-sûr'tn) adj. 1. Not having sure knowledge; doubtful. 2. Not capable of being predicted; questionable: an uncertain outcome. 3. Not determined; indefinite; vague; undecided: uncertain plans. 4. Subject to change; variable: uncertain weather. —See Syns at **capricious.** —**un·cer'tain·ly** adv.

un·cer·tain·ty (ŭn-sûr'tn-tē) n., pl. -**ties.** 1. The condition of being in doubt; lack of certainty. 2. Something that is uncertain. —See Syns at **doubt.**

uncertainty principle. The quantum mechanical principle that the product of the uncertainties in the values of certain related variables, as of the position and momentum of a particle, is greater than or equal to Planck's constant.

un·change·a·ble (ŭn-chān'jə-bəl) adj. Not capable of being altered. —See Syns at **inflexible.**

un·char·i·ta·ble (ŭn-chăr'ĭ-tə-bəl) adj. Not charitable or generous; harsh and unforgiving with regard to others. —**un·char'i·ta·ble·ness** n. —**un·char'i·ta·bly** adv.

un·chart·ed (ŭn-chär'tĭd) adj. Not charted or recorded on a map or plan; unexplored; unknown.

un·chaste (ŭn-chāst') adj. Not chaste or modest. —**un·chaste'ly** adv. —**un·chaste'ness** n.

un·chris·tian (ŭn-krĭs'chən) adj. 1. Not Christian in religion. 2. Not in accordance with the Christian spirit.

un·church (ŭn-chûrch') tr.v. 1. To expel from a church or from church membership. 2. To deprive (a congregation or sect) of the status of a church.

un·cial (ŭn'shəl, -shē-əl) adj. Of or pertaining to a style of writing characterized by somewhat rounded capital letters and found esp. in Greek and Latin manuscripts of the 4th to the 8th cent. A.D. —n. 1. The uncial style or hand. 2. An uncial letter. [Late Latin unciāles (litterae), "(letters) of an inch long" from Latin uncia, a 12th part, ounce, inch, from ūnus, one.]

un·ci·form (ŭn'sə-fôrm') adj. Hook-shaped. [Latin uncus, hook + -FORM.]

un·cir·cum·cised (ŭn-sûr'kəm-sīzd') adj. Not circumcised.

un·civ·il (ŭn-sĭv'əl) adj. Impolite; discourteous; rude.

un·civ·i·lized (ŭn-sĭv'ə-līzd') adj. Not civilized; barbarous; savage.

un·clad (ŭn-klăd') v. A past tense and past participle of **unclothe.** —adj. Not wearing clothes; naked.

un·clasp (ŭn-klăsp') tr.v. 1. To release or loosen the clasp of. 2. To release or loosen from a grip or embrace. —intr.v. 1. To become unfastened. 2. To release or relax a grip or grasp; let go.

un·cle (ŭng'kəl) n. 1. The brother of one's mother or father. 2. The husband of one's aunt. —interj. Slang. A word used to express surrender: They beat him until he cried uncle. [Middle English, from Old French oncle, from Late Latin aunculus, from Latin avunculus, maternal uncle.]

un·clean (ŭn-klēn') adj. -**er**, -**est.** 1. Foul or dirty. 2. Morally impure; sinful. 3. Ceremonially impure. —See Syns at **dirty.** —**un·clean'ness** n.

un·clean·ly (ŭn-klĕn'lē) adj. -**li·er**, -**li·est.** Habitually unclean; foul or dirty. —adv. (ŭn'klĕn'lē). In an unclean manner. —**un·clean'li·ness** n.

un·clear (ŭn-klîr') adj. Not clear; not explicit. —See Syns at **vague.**

un·clench (ŭn-klĕnch') tr.v. To loosen from a clenched position; open. —intr.v. To become unclenched.

Uncle Sam (săm) 1. A personification of the U.S. Government. 2. Informal. The United States government.

Uncle Tom (tŏm) A black who is held to be too humble or deferential to whites. [After Uncle Tom a slave in the novel Uncle Tom's Cabin (1851–52), by Harriet Beecher Stowe.]

un·cloak (ŭn-klōk') tr.v. 1. To remove a cloak or cover from. 2. To expose; reveal. —intr.v. To take off one's cloak.

un·close (ŭn-klōz') v. -**closed**, -**clos·ing.** —tr.v. To open. —intr.v. To become opened.

un·clothe (ŭn-klōth') tr.v. -**clothed** or -**clad** (-klăd'), -**clothing.** To remove the clothing or cover from; to strip. —See Syns at **undress.**

un·coil (ŭn-koil') tr.v. To unwind; untwist: uncoil a towline. —intr.v. To become unwound or untwisted.

un·com·fort·a·ble (ŭn-kŭmf'tə-bəl, -kŭm'fər-tə-) adj. 1. Experiencing discomfort. 2. Causing discomfort. 3. Unpleasant; disquieting: an uncomfortable situation. —**un·com'fort·a·bly** adv.

un·com·mit·ted (ŭn'kə-mĭt'ĭd) adj. Not pledged to a specific cause or course of action.

un·com·mon (ŭn-kŏm'ən) adj. 1. Not commonly encountered; rare. 2. Wonderful; remarkable: an uncommon beauty. —**un·com'mon·ly** adv. —**un·com'mon·ness** n.

   Syns: uncommon, exceptional, extraordinary, rare, remarkable, singular, unusual adj. Core meaning: Far beyond what is usual, normal, or customary (uncommon intelligence; an uncommon problem).

un·com·mu·ni·ca·tive (ŭn'kə-myōō'nĭ-kā'tĭv, -kə-tĭv) adj. Not tending or willing to talk or to give out information; reserved. —**un'com·mu'ni·ca'tive·ly** adv. —**un'com·mu'ni·ca'tive·ness** n.

un·com·pli·men·ta·ry (ŭn'kŏm-plə-mĕn'trē, -mĕn'tə-rē) adj. Rather insulting; derogatory.

un·com·pro·mis·ing (ŭn-kŏm'prə-mī'zĭng) adj. Not making compromises; allowing no concession; inflexible; rigid. —**un·com'pro·mis'ing·ly** adv.

un·con·cern (ŭn'kən-sûrn') n. 1. Lack of interest; indifference; apathy. 2. Lack of worry or apprehensiveness. —See Syns at **disinterest.**

un·con·cerned (ŭn'kən-sûrnd') adj. 1. Not interested; indifferent. 2. Not anxious or apprehensive; unworried. —See Syns at **uninterested.** —**un'con·cern'ed·ly** (-sûr'nĭd-lē) adv.

un·con·di·tion·al (ŭn'kən-dĭsh'ə-nəl) adj. 1. Without condi-

ă pat   ā pay   â care   ä father   ĕ pet   ē be   hw which
ōō took   ōō boot   ou out   th thin   th this   ŭ cut
ĭ pit   ī tie   î pier   ŏ pot   ō toe   ô paw, for   oi noise
û urge   zh vision   ə about, item, edible, gallop, circus

tions; absolute. **2.** With no reservations. —See Syns at **im-plicit.** —**un′con·di′tion·al·ly** *adv.*

un·con·di·tioned (ŭn′kən-dĭsh′ənd) *adj.* **1.** Unconditional; unrestricted. **2.** *Psychol.* Not the result of learning or conditioning: *an unconditioned reaction.*

un·con·nect·ed (ŭn′kə-nĕk′tĭd) *adj.* **1.** Not joined or connected. **2.** Not having any clear links; incoherent; disconnected.

un·con·quer·a·ble (ŭn-kŏng′kər-ə-bəl) *adj.* Incapable of being overcome or defeated.

un·con·scion·a·ble (ŭn-kŏn′shə-nə-bəl) *adj.* **1.** Not controlled or guided by conscience. **2.** Beyond what is reasonable; excessive: *an unconscionable price.* —**un-con′scion·a·bly** *adv.*

un·con·scious (ŭn-kŏn′shəs) *adj.* **1.** Not accessible to the conscious part of the mind; not aware: *unconscious rage.* **2. a.** Temporarily lacking awareness. **b.** Not informed. **3.** Without conscious control; involuntary. —See Syns at **ignorant.** —*n.* The part of the mind that operates without conscious awareness and that cannot be directly observed. —**un·con′scious·ly** *adv.* —**un·con′scious·ness** *n.*

un·con·sti·tu·tion·al (ŭn′kŏn-stĭ-tōō′shə-nəl, -tyōō-′) *adj.* Not in accord with the constitution of a country or organization. —**un′con·sti·tu′tion·al′i·ty** *n.* —**un′con·sti·tu′-tion·al·ly** *adv.*

un·con·trol·la·ble (ŭn′kən-trō′lə-bəl) *adj.* Not able to be controlled or governed. —**un′con·trol′la·bil′i·ty** *n.*

un·con·ven·tion·al (ŭn′kən-vĕn′shə-nəl) *adj.* Not adhering to convention; out of the ordinary. —**un′con·ven′tion·al′i·ty** (-nǎl′ĭ-tē) *n.* —**un′con·ven′tion·al·ly** *adv.*

un·cork (ŭn-kôrk′) *tr.v.* **1.** To draw the cork from. **2.** To free from a sealed or constrained state: *uncork a secret.* **3.** *Informal.* To let loose: *The pitcher uncorked his fast ball.*

un·count·ed (ŭn-koun′tĭd) *adj.* **1.** Not counted. **2.** Unable to be counted; innumerable.

un·cou·ple (ŭn-kŭp′əl) *v.* **-led, -ling.** —*tr.v.* **1.** To disconnect (something coupled): *uncouple railroad cars.* **2.** To set loose; release; unleash. —*intr.v.* To come or break loose. —See Syns at **detach.**

un·couth (ŭn-kōōth′) *adj.* **1.** Crude; unrefined; rude: *uncouth behavior.* **2.** Awkward or clumsy; ungraceful: *an uncouth gait.* —See Syns at **coarse.** [Middle English, unknown, strange, from Old English *uncūth* : *un-,* not + *cūth,* known.] —**un·couth′ly** *adv.*

un·cov·er (ŭn-kŭv′ər) *tr.v.* **1.** To remove the cover from. **2.** To manifest or disclose; reveal: *uncovering an ancient secret.* **3.** To remove the hat from (one's head) in respect. —*intr.v.* To bare the head in respect.

un·cross (ŭn-krôs′, -krŏs′) *tr.v.* To move (one's limbs) from a crossed position.

unc·tion (ŭngk′shən) *n.* **1.** The act of anointing as part of a religious, ceremonial, or healing ritual. **2.** An ointment, salve, or oil. **3.** Something that serves to soothe or restore; a balm. **4.** Affected or exaggerated earnestness, esp. in language. [Middle English, from Latin *unctiō,* from *unguere,* to anoint.]

unc·tu·ous (ŭngk′chōō-əs) *adj.* **1.** Containing or resembling oil or ointment; greasy; oily. **2.** Marked by or showing affected, exaggerated, or insincere earnestness or courtesy: *unctuous flattery.* [Middle English, from Medieval Latin *unctuōsus,* from Latin *unctum,* ointment, from *unguere,* to anoint.] —**unc′tu·ous·ly** *adv.* —**unc′tu·ous·ness** *n.*

un·cut (ŭn-kŭt′) *adj.* **1.** Not cut. **2.** Not sliced, carved, etc.: *uncut bread.* **3.** Not abridged or shortened. **4.** Not ground or polished: *an uncut gem.* **5.** Having the page edge not slit or trimmed: *uncut pages.*

un·daunt·ed (ŭn-dôn′tĭd, -dän′-) *adj.* **1.** Not discouraged or disheartened; resolute. **2.** Fearless. —See Syns at **brave.** —**un·daunt′ed·ly** *adv.*

un·de·ceive (ŭn′dĭ-sēv′) *tr.v.* **-ceived, -ceiv·ing.** To free from illusion, error, or deception; disabuse.

un·de·cid·ed (ŭn′dĭ-sī′dĭd) *adj.* **1.** Not yet determined or settled; open. **2.** Not having reached a decision; uncommitted. —**un′de·cid′ed·ly** *adv.*

un·de·mon·stra·tive (ŭn′dĭ-mŏn′strə-tĭv) *adj.* Not given to expressions of feeling; reserved. —**un′de·mon′stra·tive·ly**

adv. —**un′de·mon′stra·tive·ness** *n.*

un·de·ni·a·ble (ŭn′dĭ-nī′ə-bəl) *adj.* **1.** Obviously true; irrefutable. **2.** Unquestionably good; outstanding. —**un′de·ni′-a·bly** *adv.*

un·de·pend·a·ble (ŭn′dĭ-pĕn′də-bəl) *adj.* Incapable of being relied upon. —See Syns at **unreliable.**

un·der (ŭn′dər) *prep.* **1.** In a lower position or place than: *under the table.* **2.** Beneath the surface of: *under the ground.* **3.** Beneath the guise of: *under a false name.* **4.** Less than; smaller than: *under 20 years of age.* **5.** Less than the required amount or degree of: *under voting age.* **6.** Inferior to, as in status: *the complaints of those who were under them.* **7.** Subject to the authority of: *living under a dictatorship.* **8.** Undergoing or receiving the effects of: *under intensive care.* **9.** Subject to the obligation of: *under contract.* **10.** Within the group or classification of: *listed under biology.* **11.** In the process of: *under discussion.* **12.** Because of: *under these conditions.* —*adv.* **1.** In or into a place below or beneath: *Lift the rug and put your hand under.* **2.** Into ruin or defeat: *forced under by bombings.* **3.** So as to be covered, enveloped, or immersed: *You can't swim until you learn how to put your head under.* **4.** Below a quantity, amount, or age: *children of 12 and under.* —*adj.* **1.** Lower: *the under parts of a machine.* **2.** Subordinate; inferior: *all the under folk rushing to and fro.* **3.** Lower in amount or degree: *keeps his prices under.* [Middle English, from Old English.]

under-. A prefix meaning: **1.** Placed below or under: **underground, underclothes. 2.** Inferior in rank or importance: **undersecretary, underclassman. 3.** Lower or less than normal or proper in degree, rate, or quantity: **underestimate.** [Middle English, from Old English *under,* under.]

un·der·a·chieve (ŭn′dər-ə-chēv′) *intr.v.* **-chieved, -chiev·ing.** To perform below an expected level of ability or capacity. —**un′der·a·chiev′er** *n.*

un·der·age (ŭn′dər-āj′) *adj.* Below the customary or required age, esp. below legal age.

un·der·arm[1] (ŭn′dər-ärm′) *adj.* Located, placed, or used under the arm. —*n.* The armpit.

un·der·arm[2] (ŭn′dər ärm′) *adj. & adv.* Underhand.

un·der·bel·ly (ŭn′dər-bĕl′ē) *n.* **1.** The lowest part of an animal's body. **2.** The vulnerable or weak part of something.

un·der·bid (ŭn′dər-bĭd′) *v.* **-bid, -bid·ding.** —*tr.v.* **1.** To bid lower than (a competitor). **2.** To bid less than the full value; bid too low. —*intr.v.* To make an unnecessarily low bid. —*n.* A bid that is very low or too low.

un·der·brush (ŭn′dər-brŭsh′) *n.* Small trees, shrubs, etc., that grow beneath the taller trees in a forest.

un·der·car·riage (ŭn′dər-kăr′ĭj) *n.* **1.** A supporting framework or structure, as for the body of an automobile. **2.** The landing gear of an aircraft.

un·der·charge (ŭn′dər-chärj′) *tr.v.* **-charged, -charg·ing. 1.** To charge (someone) less than is customary or required. **2.** To load (a firearm) with an insufficient charge. —*n.* (ŭn′dər-chärj′). An insufficient or improper charge.

un·der·class·man (ŭn′dər-klăs′mən) *n.* A student in the freshman or sophomore class at a secondary school or college.

un·der·clothes (ŭn′dər-klōz′, -klōthz′) *pl.n.* Also **un·der·cloth·ing** (-klō′thĭng). Clothes worn next to the skin, beneath one's outer clothing; underwear.

un·der·coat (ŭn′dər-kōt′) *n.* **1.** A coat worn beneath another coat. **2.** A covering of short hairs or fur concealed by the longer outer hairs of an animal's coat. **3. a.** Also **under·coat·ing** (-kō′tĭng). A coat of sealing material applied to a surface before the topcoat is applied. **b.** A tarlike substance sprayed on the underside of an automobile to prevent rusting. —*tr.v.* To apply an undercoat.

un·der·cov·er (ŭn′dər-kŭv′ər) *adj.* Performed or carried on in secret. —See Syns at **secret.**

un·der·cur·rent (ŭn′dər-kûr′ənt, -kŭr′-) *n.* **1.** A current, as of air or water, below another current or beneath a surface. **2.** A partly hidden tendency, force, or influence that is often contrary to what is on the surface.

un·der·cut (ŭn′dər-kŭt′) *tr.v.* **-cut, -cut·ting. 1.** To make a cut under or below. **2.** To create an overhang by cutting material away from, as in carving. **3.** To sell at a lower price than or to work for lower wages or fees than (a competitor). **4.** To ruin the effectiveness of; undermine.

5. *Sports.* **a.** To give backspin to (a ball) by striking downward as well as forward, as in golf and baseball. **b.** To cut or slice (a ball) with an underarm stroke, as in tennis. —*n.* **1. a.** A cut made in the under part to remove material. **b.** The material so removed. **2.** A notch cut in a tree to direct its fall and insure a clean break. **3.** *Sports.* **a.** A spin given to a ball opposite to its direction of flight; backspin. **b.** A cut or slice made with an underarm motion. —*adj.* Having undercuts in, as a sculpture or a relief.

un·der·de·vel·oped (ŭn′dər-dĭ-vĕl′əpt) *adj.* **1.** Not adequately or normally developed; immature; deficient. **2.** *Photog.* Left in a developing solution for too short a time to produce a normal degree of contrast. **3.** Industrially or economically backward.

un·der·dog (ŭn′dər-dôg′, -dŏg′) *n.* **1.** Someone who is expected to lose a contest or struggle, as in sports or politics. **2.** Someone who is at a disadvantage.

un·der·done (ŭn′dər-dŭn′) *adj.* Not sufficiently cooked or prepared: *an underdone roast.*

un·der·dressed (ŭn′dər-drĕst′) *adj.* **1.** Too informally dressed. **2.** Wearing insufficient clothing.

un·der·es·ti·mate (ŭn′dər-ĕs′tə-māt′) *tr.v.* **-mat·ed, -mat·ing.** To judge or estimate too low the value, amount, quality, or capacity of. —*n.* (ŭn′dər-ĕs′tə-mĭt). An estimate that is or proves to be too low. —**un′der·es′ti·ma′tion** *n.*

un·der·ex·pose (ŭn′dər-ĭk-spōz′) *tr.v.* **-posed, -pos·ing.** To expose (film) to light for too short a time to produce normal image contrast. —**un′der·ex·po′sure** *n.*

un·der·feed (ŭn′dər-fēd′) *tr.v.* **-fed** (-fĕd′), **-feed·ing.** **1.** To feed insufficiently. **2.** To supply (an engine) with or channel fuel from below.

un·der·foot (ŭn′dər-fŏot′) *adv.* **1.** Below or under the feet. **2.** In the way. —*adj.* Under the feet.

un·der·fur (ŭn′dər-fûr′) *n.* The dense, soft, fine fur beneath the coarse outer hairs of certain mammals.

un·der·gar·ment (ŭn′dər-gär′mənt) *n.* A garment that is worn under outer garments.

un·der·go (ŭn′dər-gō′) *tr.v.* **-went** (-wĕnt′), **-gone** (-gôn′, -gŏn′), **-go·ing.** **1.** To experience; be subjected to: *undergo development.* **2.** To endure; suffer; sustain: *undergo hardships.* [Middle English *undergon,* to submit to : *under,* under + *gon,* go.]

un·der·grad·u·ate (ŭn′dər-grăj′ōō-ĭt) *n.* A college or university student who has not yet received a degree.

un·der·ground (ŭn′dər-ground′) *adj.* **1.** Occurring, operating, or situated below the surface of the earth: *underground oil deposits.* **2.** Acting or done in secret: *an underground black market.* **3.** Of or describing an avant-garde or experimental movement or its films, publications, and art. —*n.* **1.** A secret, often nationalist, organization working against a government in power. **2.** *Brit.* A subway system. —*adv.* (ŭn′dər-ground′). **1.** Below the surface of the earth: *miners digging underground.* **2.** In secret; stealthily.

Underground Railroad. Before 1861 in the United States, a secret network of cooperation helping fugitive slaves reach the free states or Canada.

un·der·growth (ŭn′dər-grōth′) *n.* **1. a.** Low-growing plants, saplings, shrubs, etc., beneath trees in a forest. **b.** Something resembling this, as a growth of short, fine hairs beneath longer ones. **2.** The condition of not being fully grown.

un·der·hand (ŭn′dər-hănd′) *adj.* **1.** Done slyly and secretly; sneaky. **2.** *Sports.* Performed with the hand kept below the level of the shoulder; underarm: *an underhand throw.* —*adv.* **1.** With an underhand movement: *She always throws underhand.* **2.** Slyly and secretly; clandestinely; underhandedly.

un·der·hand·ed (ŭn′dər-hăn′dĭd) *adj.* Underhand. —**un′·der·hand′ed·ly** *adv.* —**un′der·hand′ed·ness** *n.*

un·der·lay (ŭn′dər-lā′) *tr.v.* **-laid** (-lād′), **-lay·ing.** **1.** To put (one thing) under another: *underlay a felt pad beneath the carpet.* **2.** To provide with a base, backing, or lining. **3.** To raise or support with underlays. —*n.* (ŭn′dər-lā′). Something that is laid under.

un·der·lie (ŭn′dər-lī′) *tr.v.* **-lay** (-lā′), **-lain** (-lān′), **-ly·ing.** **1.** To be located under or below. **2.** To be the support or basis for; account for.

un·der·line (ŭn′dər-līn′, ŭn′dər-līn′) *tr.v.* **-lined, -lin·ing.** **1.** To draw a line under; underscore. **2.** To emphasize or stress. —*n.* (ŭn′dər-līn′). A line drawn under writing to indicate emphasis or italic type.

un·der·ling (ŭn′dər-lĭng) *n.* A person in a subordinate position. —See Syns at **subordinate.**

un·der·ly·ing (ŭn′dər-lī′ĭng) *adj.* **1.** Lying under or beneath: *the underlying bedrock of Manhattan.* **2.** Basic; fundamental: *the underlying assumptions.* **3.** Hidden but implied: *an underlying meaning.*

un·der·mine (ŭn′dər-mīn′) *tr.v.* **-mined, -min·ing.** **1.** To dig a mine or tunnel beneath. **2.** To weaken by wearing away, often by degrees or imperceptibly: *Late hours undermine one's health.*

un·der·most (ŭn′dər-mōst′) *adj.* Lowest in position, rank, or place; bottom. —*adv.* Lowest.

un·der·neath (ŭn′dər-nēth′) *prep.* Beneath; below; under: *put newspapers underneath the leaky pail.* Also used adverbially: *I kicked over the stone and found a worm underneath.* —*n.* The bottom surface of something; the underside. [Middle English *undernethe,* from Old English *underneothan* : *under* + *neothan,* below.]

un·der·nour·ish (ŭn′dər-nûr′ĭsh, -nûr′-) *tr.v.* To provide with insufficient nourishment to sustain proper health and growth. —**un′der·nour′ish·ment** *n.*

un·der·pants (ŭn′dər-pănts′) *pl.n.* Pants, shorts, or drawers worn as underwear.

un·der·pass (ŭn′dər-păs′) *n.* A passage underneath something, esp. a section of road that passes under another road or railroad.

un·der·pay (ŭn′dər-pā′) *tr.v.* **-paid** (-pād′), **-pay·ing.** To pay too little or less than deserved.

un·der·pin (ŭn′dər-pĭn′) *tr.v.* **-pinned, -pin·ning.** **1.** To support from below, as with props, girders, masonry, etc. **2.** To corroborate or substantiate: *new facts to underpin her argument.*

un·der·pin·ning (ŭn′dər-pĭn′ĭng) *n.* **1.** A supporting part or structure, as for a wall. **2.** Any prop or support. **3.** Often **underpinnings.** *Informal.* The legs.

un·der·play (ŭn′dər-plā′, ŭn′dər-plā′) *tr.v.* **1.** To minimize the importance of; play down: *The newspaper underplayed the mayor's role in settling the strike.* **2.** To act (a role) subtly or with restraint. —*intr.v.* To act a role subtly or with restraint.

un·der·price (ŭn′dər-prīs′) *tr.v.* **-priced, -pric·ing.** **1.** To price lower than the value. **2.** To undercut in price.

un·der·priv·i·leged (ŭn′dər-prĭv′ə-lĭjd) *adj.* Not having opportunities or advantages enjoyed by other members of society; deprived. —See Syns at **depressed.**

un·der·pro·duc·tion (ŭn′dər-prə-dŭk′shən) *n.* Production below full capacity or demand.

un·der·rate (ŭn′dər-rāt′) *tr.v.* **-rat·ed, -rat·ing.** To judge or rate too low; to underestimate.

un·der·score (ŭn′dər-skôr′, -skōr′) *tr.v.* **-scored, -scor·ing.** **1.** To draw a line under; underline. **2.** To emphasize or stress. —*n.* An underline.

un·der·sea (ŭn′dər-sē′) *adj.* Of, done, existing, or created for use beneath the surface of the sea: *undersea life; undersea exploration.* —*adv.* (ŭn′dər-sē′). Also **un·der·seas** (-sēz′). Beneath the surface of the sea.

un·der·sec·re·tar·y (ŭn′dər-sĕk′rĭ-tĕr′ē) *n., pl.* **-ies.** An official directly subordinate to a Cabinet member.

un·der·sell (ŭn′dər-sĕl′) *tr.v.* **-sold** (-sōld′), **-sell·ing.** **1.** To sell for a lower price than. **2.** To sell at a price less than the actual value. **3.** To present in a way that minimizes the assets or value: *always undersells his own abilities.*

un·der·shirt (ŭn′dər-shûrt′) *n.* A collarless upper undergarment worn under a shirt, blouse, etc.

un·der·shoot (ŭn′dər-shōōt′) *tr.v.* **-shot** (-shŏt′), **-shoot·ing.** **1.** To shoot a missile short of (a target). **2.** To land an aircraft short of (a landing area).

un·der·shot (ŭn′dər-shŏt′) *adj.* **1.** Driven by water passing from below: *an undershot water wheel.* **2.** Projecting from below: *an undershot jaw.*

un·der·side (ŭn′dər-sīd′) *n.* The side or surface that is underneath; bottom side.

un·der·signed (ŭn′dər-sīnd′) *adj.* Having a signature or signatures at the bottom of a document. —*n.* The person or persons who have signed at the bottom of a document.

un·der·sized (ŭn'dər-sīzd') *adj.* Also **un·der·size** (-sīz'). Smaller than the usual, normal, or required size.

un·der·skirt (ŭn'dər-skûrt') *n.* A skirt worn under another; a petticoat.

un·der·sleeve (ŭn'dər-slēv') *n.* A sleeve worn under another, esp. an ornamental sleeve designed to show through slashes in the outer sleeve.

un·der·slung (ŭn'dər-slŭng') *adj.* Having springs attached to the axles from below, as an auto chassis.

un·der·stand (ŭn'dər-stănd') *v.* **-stood** (-stŏŏd'), **-stand·ing.** *—tr.v.* **1.** To comprehend the meaning and significance of; know: *"I don't pretend to understand the Universe—it's a great deal bigger than I am"* (Thomas Carlyle). **2.** To know thoroughly through long acquaintance with: *She understands horses.* **3.** To comprehend the language, sounds, form, or symbols of (any kind of expression): *understands five languages.* **4.** To know and be tolerant or sympathetic toward: *A good teacher understands children.* **5.** To learn indirectly, as by hearsay; gather: *We understand he is moving away.* **6.** To conclude; infer: *Am I to understand that you are quitting?* **7.** To accept as an agreed fact: *It is understood that the fee will be five dollars. —intr.v.* **1.** To have understanding, knowledge, or comprehension: *"Hear and understand"* (Matthew 15:10). **2.** To learn indirectly; gather: *They were just married, or so I understand.* [Middle English *understanden,* from Old English *understandan.*] **—un'der·stand'a·ble** *adj.* **—un'der·stand'a·bly** *adv.*

Syns: understand, apprehend, comprehend, fathom, follow, grasp, take in *v.* **Core meaning:** To perceive and recognize the meaning of *(understood the text).*

un·der·stand·ing (ŭn'dər-stăn'dĭng) *n.* **1.** A grasp of what is intended, expressed, meant, etc.; comprehension; knowledge: *has a limited understanding of quantum mechanics.* **2.** The condition of having reached a stage of full comprehension: *a book beyond a child's understanding.* **3.** The ability to understand: *a person of great understanding.* **4. a.** A friendly relationship, as between nations. **b.** A reconciliation of differences; an agreement: *they finally reached an understanding.* **5.** An agreement reached between two or more persons or groups: *an understanding on how to handle the problem. —adj.* **1.** Having or showing comprehension, wisdom, or good sense. **2.** Tolerant or sympathetic. **—un'der·stand'ing·ly** *adv.*

un·der·state (ŭn'dər-stāt') *tr.v.* **-stat·ed, -stat·ing.** **1.** To state with less completeness or truth than seems warranted by the facts: *understate the problems involved.* **2.** To express with restraint or lack of emphasis, esp. for dramatic impact. **3.** To state (a number, quantity, etc.) that is too low: *understate one's age.*

un·der·state·ment (ŭn'dər-stāt'mənt) *n.* **1.** A disclosure or statement that is less than complete. **2.** Intentional lack of emphasis in expression, as in irony.

un·der·stood (ŭn'dər-stŏŏd') *v.* The past tense and past participle of **understand** *—adj.* **1.** Agreed upon; assumed. **2.** Not expressed in writing.—See Syns at **implicit.**

un·der·stud·y (ŭn'dər-stŭd'ē) *tr.v.* **-ied, -y·ing.** **1.** To study or know (a role) so as to be able to replace the regular actor or actress when required. **2.** To act as an understudy to: *He understudied the star for a year in that play. —n., pl.* **-ies.** An actor or actress who understudies.

un·der·take (ŭn'dər-tāk') *tr.v.* **-took** (-tŏŏk'), **-tak·en, -tak·ing.** **1.** To take upon oneself, as a task. **2.** To pledge or commit oneself to: *"What I had undertaken was the whole care of her"* (Henry James). [Middle English *undertaken,* to accept, take in hand.]

un·der·tak·er *n.* **1.** (ŭn'dər-tā'kər). A person whose business it is to prepare the dead for burial or cremation and to make funeral arrangements. **2.** (ŭn'dər-tā'kər). Someone who undertakes a task or job, esp. an entrepreneur.

un·der·tak·ing (ŭn'dər-tā'kĭng) *n.* **1.** A task or assignment undertaken; an enterprise or venture. **2.** The occupation of an undertaker.

un·der-the-count·er (ŭn'dər-thə-koun'tər) *adj.* Transacted, given, or sold secretly, and often illegally.

un·der·tone (ŭn'dər-tōn') *n.* **1.** A tone of low pitch or volume. **2.** A pale or subdued color, esp. a modifying color seen through another color. **3.** A subdued or partly concealed emotional quality.

un·der·tow (ŭn'dər-tō') *n.* A current beneath the surface of a body of water running in a direction opposite to that of the current at the surface.

un·der·val·ue (ŭn'dər-văl'yŏŏ) *tr.v.* **-ued, -u·ing.** **1.** To assign too low a value to; underestimate. **2.** To have too little regard or esteem for. **—un'der·val'u·a'tion** *n.*

un·der·wa·ter (ŭn'dər-wô'tər, -wŏt'ər) *adj.* Used, done, or existing under the surface of water. **—un'der·wa'ter** *adv.*

un·der·wear (ŭn'dər-wâr') *n.* Clothing worn under the outer clothes and next to the skin; underclothes.

un·der·weight (ŭn'dər-wāt') *adj.* Weighing less than is normal, healthy, or required. *—n.* Weight that is below normal or usual.

un·der·went (ŭn'dər-wĕnt') *v.* Past tense of **undergo.**

un·der·world (ŭn'dər-wûrld') *n.* **1.** Any region, realm, or dwelling place conceived to be below the surface of the earth. **2.** *Gk. & Rom. Myth.* The world of the dead; Hades. **3.** The part of society that is engaged in organized crime. **4.** *Archaic.* The earth.

un·der·write (ŭn'dər-rīt') *v.* **-wrote** (-rōt'), **-writ·ten** (-rĭt'n), **-writ·ing.** *—tr.v.* **1.** To write under, esp. to sign or endorse (a document). **2.** To assume financial responsibility for; guarantee (an enterprise) against failure: *underwrite a theatrical production.* **3.** To sign an insurance policy, thus guaranteeing payment. **4.** *Finance.* To guarantee the purchase of (a full issue of stock or bonds), esp. to agree to buy (the stock in a new enterprise not yet sold publicly) at a fixed time and price. *—intr.v.* To act as an underwriter, esp. to issue an insurance policy. **—un'der·writ'er** *n.*

un·de·sir·a·ble (ŭn'dĭ-zīr'ə-bəl) *adj.* Not desirable; objectionable. *—n.* A person who is considered objectionable. **—un'de·sir·a·bil'i·ty** *n.* **—un'de·sir'a·bly** *adv.*

un·de·ter·mined (ŭn'dĭ-tûr'mĭnd) *adj.* **1.** Not yet determined; undecided. **2.** Not known or ascertained.

un·did (ŭn-dĭd') *v.* Past tense of **undo.**

un·dies (ŭn'dēz) *pl.n. Informal.* Underwear.

un·dig·ni·fied (ŭn-dĭg'nə-fīd') *adj.* Not dignified; lacking in or damaging to dignity.

un·dine (ŭn-dēn', ŭn'dēn') *n.* A female water spirit who could earn a soul by marrying a mortal and bearing his child. [From Latin *unda,* wave.]

un·dis·crim·i·nat·ing (ŭn'dĭ-skrĭm'ə-nā'tĭng) *adj.* **1.** Indiscriminate. **2.** Lacking taste or judgment.

un·dis·posed (ŭn'dĭ-spōzd') *adj.* **1.** Not settled, removed, or resolved: *undisposed wastes; undisposed issues.* **2.** Disinclined; unwilling.

un·dis·tin·guished (ŭn'dĭ-stĭng'gwĭsht) *adj.* Not distinguished; ordinary.

un·dis·turbed (ŭn'dĭ-stûrbd') *adj.* Not disturbed; calm.

un·do (ŭn-dŏŏ') *tr.v.* **-did** (-dĭd'), **-done** (-dŭn'), **-do·ing.** **1.** To reverse or erase; cancel; annul: *tried to undo the injury to his feelings.* **2.** To untie, disassemble, or loosen. **3.** To open (a parcel, package, etc.); unwrap. **4. a.** To cause the ruin or downfall of; destroy. **b.** To throw into confusion; unsettle. [Middle English *undon,* from Old English *undōn,* to unfasten, annul, destroy.] **—un·do'er** *n.*

un·do·ing (ŭn-dŏŏ'ĭng) *n.* **1.** The act of reversing or annulling something accomplished; cancellation. **2.** The act of unfastening or loosening. **3. a.** The act of bringing to ruin. **b.** The cause or source of ruin; downfall.

un·done (ŭn-dŭn') *adj.* Not completed or performed.

un·doubt·ed (ŭn-dou'tĭd) *adj.* Accepted as beyond question; undisputed: *undoubted talent; an undoubted masterpiece.* **—un·doubt'ed·ly** *adv.*

un·draw (ŭn-drô') *tr.v.* **-drew** (-drŏŏ'), **-drawn** (-drôn'), **-draw·ing.** To draw to one side, as a curtain; to open.

un·dress (ŭn-drĕs') *v.* *—tr.v.* **1.** To remove the clothing of; disrobe; to strip. **2.** To remove the bandages from (a wound, burn, etc.). *—intr.v.* To take off one's clothing. *—n.* **1.** Informal attire as distinguished from formal attire. **2.** Nakedness.

Syns: undress, disrobe, strip, unclothe *v.* **Core meaning:** To remove all the clothing from *(undressed the children for their baths).*

un·dressed (ŭn-drĕst') *adj.* **1. a.** Naked. **b.** Not fully dressed. **2.** Not specially treated or processed: *undressed leather.*

un·due (ŭn-dŏŏ', -dyŏŏ') *adj.* **1.** Exceeding what is normal

ă pat	ā pay	â care	ä father	ĕ pet	ē be	hw which	ĭ pit	ī tie	î pier	ŏ pot	ō toe	ô paw, for	oi noise
ŏŏ took	ŏŏ boot	ou out	th thin	*th* this	ŭ cut		û urge	zh vision	ə about, item, edible, gallop, circus				

or appropriate; excessive: *an undue amount of criticism.* **2.** Not proper or legal: *undue powers.* **3.** Not yet payable or due.

un·du·lant (ŭn′jə-lənt, ŭn′dyə-, ŭn′də-) *adj.* Resembling waves in occurrence, appearance, or motion.

undulant fever. A disease characterized by a long-lasting and recurring fever caused by bacteria that are transmitted through meat and milk from infected animals and marked by weakness and pains in the joints.

un·du·late (ŭn′jə-lāt′, ŭn′dyə-, ŭn′də-) *v.* **-lat·ed, -lat·ing.** *—tr.v.* **1.** To cause to move in a smooth wavelike motion. **2.** To give a wavelike appearance or form to. *—intr.v.* **1.** To move in waves or with a wavelike motion; to ripple. **2.** To have a wavelike appearance or form. *—adj.* (-lĭt, -lāt′). Also **un·du·la·ted** (-lāt′ĭd). Having a wavy outline or appearance: *leaves with undulate margins.* [From Late Latin *undulāre,* from *undula,* dim. of Latin *unda,* wave.]

un·du·la·tion (ŭn′jə-lā′shən, ŭn′dyə-, ŭn′də-) *n.* **1.** A regular rising and falling or movement to alternating sides; movement in waves. **2.** A wavelike form, outline, or appearance. **3.** One of a series of waves or wavelike segments; a pulsation.

un·du·ly (ŭn-dōō′lē, -dyōō′-) *adv.* Excessively; immoderately: *unduly fearful.*

un·du·ti·ful (ŭn-dōō′tĭ-fəl, -dyōō′-) *adj.* Lacking a sense of duty; unreliable; disobedient.

un·dy·ing (ŭn′dī′ĭng) *adj.* Endless; everlasting.

un·earned (ŭn-ûrnd′) *adj.* **1.** Not deserved: *unearned praise.* **2.** Not gained by work or service: *unearned income.* **3.** Not yet earned: *unearned interest.*

un·earth (ŭn-ûrth′) *tr.v.* **1.** To bring up out of the earth; dig up. **2.** To bring to public notice; uncover.

un·earth·ly (ŭn-ûrth′lē) *adj.* **-li·er, -li·est. 1.** Not of the earth; supernatural. **2.** Frighteningly unaccountable; unnatural: *"a shriek so unearthly . . . that the blood seemed to freeze in my veins"* (W.H. Hudson). **3.** Ridiculously unreasonable; absurd: *an unearthly hour.* —See Syns at **weird.** **—un·earth′li·ness** *n.*

un·eas·y (ŭn-ē′zē) *adj.* **-i·er, -i·est. 1.** Lacking ease, comfort, or a sense of security. **2.** Affording no ease or reassurance; difficult: *an uneasy calm.* **3.** Awkward or unsure in manner: *uneasy with strangers.* —See Syns at **edgy. —un·eas′i·ly** *adv.* **—un·eas′i·ness** *n.*

un·ed·u·cat·ed (ŭn-ĕj′ə-kā′tĭd) *adj.* Not educated, esp. lacking in literacy. —See Syns at **ignorant.**

un·em·ploy·a·ble (ŭn′ĕm-ploi′ə-bəl) *adj.* Not able to find or hold a job. *—n.* A person who cannot be employed.

un·em·ployed (ŭn′ĕm-ploid′) *adj.* **1.** Out of work; jobless. **2.** Not being used; idle.

un·em·ploy·ment (ŭn′ĕm-ploi′mənt) *n.* **1.** The condition of being unemployed. **2.** The total number or the percentage of people who are not working at regular jobs. *—modifier: unemployment insurance.*

un·e·qual (ŭn-ē′kwəl) *adj.* **1.** Not the same in any measurable aspect, as extent or quantity. **2.** Not the same as another in rank or social position. **3.** Consisting of ill-matched opponents. **4.** Having unbalanced sides or parts; asymmetric. **5.** Not even or consistent; variable; irregular. **6.** Not having the required abilities; inadequate: *unequal to the challenge.* **7.** Not fair. —See Syns at **unfair.** *—n.* Someone or something that is unequal. **—un·e′qual·ly** *adv.*

un·e·qualed (ŭn-ē′kwəld) *adj.* Not matched or paralleled by others of its kind; unrivaled. —See Syns at **unique.**

un·e·quiv·o·cal (ŭn′ĭ-kwĭv′ə-kəl) *adj.* Not open to doubt, disguise, or misunderstanding; perfectly clear. —See Syns at **explicit. —un′e·quiv′o·cal·ly** *adv.*

un·err·ing (ŭn-ûr′ĭng, -ĕr′-) *adj.* Committing no mistakes; consistently accurate. **—un′err′ing·ly** *adv.*

un·es·sen·tial (ŭn′ĭ-sĕn′shəl) *adj.* Not necessary; not of importance; dispensable. *—n.* A nonessential.

un·e·ven (ŭn-ē′vən) *adj.* **-er, -est. 1.** Not level or smooth. **2.** Not straight or parallel. **3.** Not uniform or consistent; varying, as in quality, form, appearance, etc.: *an uneven performance.* **4.** Not balanced; not fair: *an uneven fight.* **5.** Of or indicating an odd number. **—un·e′ven·ly** *adv.* **—un·e′ven·ness** *n.*

un·e·vent·ful (ŭn′ĭ-vĕnt′fəl) *adj.* Lacking in significant events; without incident. **—un′e·vent′ful·ly** *adv.*

un·ex·am·pled (ŭn′ĭg-zăm′pəld) *adj.* Without precedent; unparalleled.

un·ex·cep·tion·a·ble (ŭn′ĭk-sĕp′shə-nə-bəl) *adj.* Beyond the least reasonable objection. **—un′ex·cep′tion·a·ble·ness** *n.* **—un′ex·cep′tion·a·bly** *adv.*

Usage: **unexceptionable, unexceptional.** These are not interchangeable. *Unexceptionable* means not open to objections or above reproach. *Unexceptional* means either not exceptional (and therefore usual or ordinary) or not permitting exceptions to a rule.

un·ex·cep·tion·al (ŭn′ĭk-sĕp′shə-nəl) *adj.* **1.** Not varying from a norm; not unusual. **2.** Not subject to exceptions; absolute. —See Syns at **ordinary** and Usage note at **unexceptionable. —un′ex·cep′tion·al·ly** *adv.*

un·ex·pect·ed (ŭn′ĭk-spĕk′tĭd) *adj.* Coming without warning; unforeseen. **—un′ex·pect′ed·ly** *adv.*

un·fail·ing (ŭn-fā′lĭng) *adj.* **1.** Not failing or running out; inexhaustible. **2.** Constant; reliable. **3.** Incapable of error; infallible. **—un·fail′ing·ly** *adv.*

un·fair (ŭn-fâr′) *adj.* **-er, -est. 1.** Not just or evenhanded; biased. **2.** Contrary to laws or conventions, esp. in commerce; unethical. **—un·fair′ly** *adv.* **—un·fair′ness** *n.*

Syns: **unfair, inequitable, unequal, unjust** *adj.* Core meaning: Not right, or just *(unfair housing laws).*

un·faith·ful (ŭn-fāth′fəl) *adj.* **1.** Not faithful; disloyal. **2. a.** Not true or constant to a spouse or sweetheart. **b.** Guilty of adultery. **3.** Not justly representing or reflecting the original; inaccurate. —See Syns at **faithless. —un·faith′ful·ly** *adv.* **—un·faith′ful·ness** *n.*

un·fa·mil·iar (ŭn′fə-mĭl′yər) *adj.* **1.** Not within one's knowledge; strange. **2.** Not acquainted; not conversant.—See Syns at **ignorant** and **strange. —un′fa·mil′i·ar′i·ty** (-mĭl′ē-ăr′ĭ-tē) *n.* **—un′fa·mil′iar·ly** *adv.*

un·fas·ten (ŭn-făs′ən) *tr.v.* To separate the connected parts of. *—intr.v.* To become loosened or separated. —See Syns at **detach.**

un·fa·vor·a·ble (ŭn-fā′vər-ə-bəl, -fā′vrə-) *adj.* **1.** Not favorable or helpful. **2.** Negative; adverse; opposed. **3.** Undesirable; unpleasing; disadvantageous: *an unfavorable impression.* **—un·fa′vor·a·ble·ness** *n.* **—un·fa′vor·a·bly** *adv.*

un·feel·ing (ŭn-fē′lĭng) *adj.* **1.** Not sympathetic; callous: *an unfeeling remark.* **2.** Having no feeling or sensation; numb; insentient. **—un·feel′ing·ly** *adv.*

un·feigned (ŭn-fānd′) *adj.* Not pretended or simulated; genuine. **—un·feign′ed·ly** (-fā′nĭd-lē) *adv.*

un·fet·ter (ŭn-fĕt′ər) *tr.v.* To free from chains, bonds, or restraints.

un·fin·ished (ŭn-fĭn′ĭsht) *adj.* **1.** Not brought to an end; incomplete: *unfinished business.* **2.** Not having received special processing; natural: *unfinished wood.*

un·fit (ŭn-fĭt′) *adj.* **1.** Not suitable or adapted for a given purpose; inappropriate. **2.** Below the required standard; unqualified: *unfit for the job.* **3.** Not in good physical or mental health. —See Syns at **unsuitable.** *—tr.v.* **-fit·ted, -fit·ting.** To make unfit; disqualify. **—un·fit′ly** *adv.* **—un·fit′ness** *n.*

un·flap·pa·ble (ŭn-flăp′ə-bəl) *adj. Slang.* Not easily upset or excited, even in a crisis; calm. [UN- + FLAP (excited condition) + -ABLE.] **—un·flap′pa·bil′i·ty** *n.*

un·fledged (ŭn-flĕjd′) *adj.* **1.** Having incompletely developed feathers and still unable to fly, as a young bird. **2.** Inexperienced, immature, or untried.

un·flinch·ing (ŭn-flĭn′chĭng) *adj.* Not showing fear or indecision; unwavering. **—un·flinch′ing·ly** *adv.*

un·fold (ŭn-fōld′) *tr.v.* **1.** To open and spread out: *unfold a napkin.* **2.** To remove the coverings from. **3.** To reveal gradually by written or spoken explanation. *—intr.v.* **1.** To become spread out; open out. **2.** To be revealed gradually to the understanding. —See Syns at **spread.**

un·fore·seen (ŭn′fər-sēn′) *adj.* Not anticipated in advance; unexpected: *unforseen difficulties.*

un·for·get·ta·ble (ŭn′fər-gĕt′ə-bəl) *adj.* Permanently impressed on one's memory; memorable. **—un′for·get′ta·bly** *adv.*

un·formed (ŭn-fôrmd′) *adj.* **1.** Having no definite shape or structure; unorganized. **2.** Immature; undeveloped. **3.** Not yet given a physical existence; uncreated.

un·for·tu·nate (ŭn-fôr′chə-nĭt) *adj.* **1.** Characterized by un-

deserved lack of good fortune; unlucky. **2.** Causing misfortune; disastrous. **3.** Regrettable; inappropriate. —*n.* A victim of bad luck, disaster, poverty, etc. —**un·for'tu·nate·ly** *adv.* —**un·for'tu·nate·ness** *n.*
    Syns: 1. unfortunate, hapless, ill-fated, luckless, unhappy, unlucky *adj. Core meaning:* Involving or undergoing chance misfortune *(an unfortunate turn of events; an unfortunate marriage).* **2. unfortunate, awkward, inappropriate, unhappy** *adj. Core meaning:* marked by inappropriateness, esp. in expression *(an unfortunate remark).*

un·found·ed (ŭn-foun'dĭd) *adj.* Not based on fact or sound observation; groundless.

un·fre·quent·ed (ŭn'frĭ-kwĕn'tĭd, ŭn-frē'kwən-) *adj.* Receiving few or no visitors; unpatronized.

un·friend·ly (ŭn-frĕnd'lē) *adj.* **-li·er, -li·est. 1.** Not disposed to friendship; disagreeable. **2.** Unfavorable. —**un·friend'li·ness** *n.*
    Syns: unfriendly, hostile *adj. Core meaning:* Lacking friendliness *(an unfriendly look; unfriendly nations).*

un·frock (ŭn-frŏk') *tr.v.* To strip of priestly privileges and functions; defrock.

un·fruit·ful (ŭn-frōōt'fəl) *adj.* **1.** Not bearing fruit or offspring. **2.** Not productive of good results; unprofitable or unsuccessful. —See Syns at **barren.** —**un·fruit'ful·ly** *adv.* —**un·fruit'ful·ness** *n.*

un·furl (ŭn-fûrl') *tr.v.* To spread or open out; unroll. —*intr.v.* To become spread or opened out.

un·gain·ly (ŭn-gān'lē) *adj.* **-li·er, -li·est. 1.** Without grace or ease of movement; clumsy. **2.** Difficult to move or use; unwieldy. —See Syns at **awkward.** [UN- + obs. *gain,* handy + -LY.] —**un·gain'li·ness** *n.*

un·god·ly (ŭn-gŏd'lē) *adj.* **-li·er, -li·est. 1.** Not revering God; impious. **2.** Sinful; wicked. **3.** *Informal.* Beyond reasonable limits; outrageous. —**un·god'li·ness** *n.*

un·gov·ern·a·ble (ŭn-gŭv'ər-nə-bəl) *adj.* Not capable of being governed or controlled. —**un·gov'ern·a·bly** *adv.*

un·gra·cious (ŭn-grā'shəs) *adj.* **1.** Lacking courtesy or graciousness; rude. **2.** Not welcome; unpleasant. —**un·gra'cious·ly** *adv.* —**un·gra'cious·ness** *n.*

un·grate·ful (ŭn-grāt'fəl) *adj.* **1.** Without feeling or expressing gratitude, thanks, or appreciation. **2.** Not agreeable or pleasant; repellent. —**un·grate'ful·ly** *adv.* —**un·grate'ful·ness** *n.*

un·guard·ed (ŭn-gär'dĭd) *adj.* **1.** Without guard or protection; vulnerable. **2.** Without caution or thought; careless; imprudent. —**un·guard'ed·ness** *n.*

un·guent (ŭng'gwənt) *n.* A salve for soothing or healing; ointment. [Middle English, from Latin *unguentum,* from *unguere,* to anoint.]

un·guis (ŭng'gwĭs) *n., pl.* **-gues** (-gwēz'). Also **un·gu·la** (ŭng'gyə-lə) *pl.* **-lae** (lē'). A nail, claw, hoof, or clawlike structure. [Latin, claw, nail.]

un·gu·late (ŭng'gyə-lĭt, -lāt') *adj.* **1.** Having hoofs. **2.** Of or belonging to the former order Ungulata, now divided into the orders Perissodactyla and Artiodactyla, and including hoofed mammals. —*n.* A hoofed mammal. [Late Latin *ungulātus,* from Latin *ungula,* dim. of *unguis,* claw, nail.]

un·hal·lowed (ŭn-hăl'ōd) *adj.* **1.** Not hallowed or consecrated. **2.** Impious; profane; immoral; wicked.

un·hand (ŭn-hănd') *tr.v.* To remove one's hand or hands from; let go: *"Unhand me, you villain."*

un·hand·y (ŭn-hăn'dē) *adj.* **-i·er, -i·est. 1.** Difficult to handle or manage; unwieldy; cumbersome. **2.** Lacking manual skill or dexterity. —**un·hand'i·ly** *adv.* —**un·hand'i·ness** *n.*

un·hap·py (ŭn-hăp'ē) *adj.* **-pi·er, -pi·est. 1.** Not happy or joyful; sad. **2.** Not bringing good fortune; unlucky: *an unhappy day.* **3.** Not suitable or tactful; inappropriate: *an unhappy choice of words.* **4.** Dissatisfied; disturbed. —See Syns at **gloomy** and **unfortunate.** —**un·hap'pi·ly** (-hăp'ə-lē) *adv.* —**un·hap'pi·ness** *n.*

un·har·ness (ŭn-här'nĭs) *tr.v.* **1.** To remove the harness from. **2.** To release or liberate, as energy or emotions.

un·health·y (ŭn-hĕl'thē) *adj.* **-i·er, -i·est. 1.** In a poor condition of physical or mental health; ill; sick. **2.** Being a sign or symptom of poor health. **3.** Causing or tending to cause poor physical or mental health. **4.** Harmful to character or moral health; corruptive. **b.** Risky; dangerous. —**un·health'i·ly** (-hĕl'thə-lē) *adv.* —**un·health'i·ness** *n.*

un·heard (ŭn-hûrd') *adj.* **1.** Not sensed by the ear. **2.** Not given a hearing; not listened to.

un·heard-of (ŭn-hûrd'ŭv', -ŏv') *adj.* **1.** Not previously known; unknown. **2.** Extreme and outrageous; unprecedented.

un·hes·i·tat·ing (ŭn-hĕz'ĭ-tā'tĭng) *adj.* **1.** Without pause or delay; prompt; ready. **2.** Unfaltering; steadfast. —**un·hes'i·tat·ing·ly** *adv.*

un·hinge (ŭn-hĭnj') *tr.v.* **-hinged, -hing·ing. 1.** To remove from hinges. **2.** To remove the hinges from. **3.** To unbalance (the mind); confuse; upset.

un·hitch (ŭn-hĭch') *tr.v.* To release from or as if from a hitch; unfasten.

un·ho·ly (ŭn-hō'lē) *adj.* **-li·er, -li·est. 1.** Wicked; immoral. **2.** *Informal.* Outrageous; dreadful. —**un·ho'li·ly** (-hō'lə-lē) *adv.* —**un·ho'li·ness** *n.*

un·hook (ŭn-hōōk') *tr.v.* **1.** To release or remove from a hook. **2.** To unfasten the hooks of.

un·hoped-for (ŭn-hōpt'fôr') *adj.* Not expected; unanticipated: *an unhoped-for spell of fine weather.*

un·horse (ŭn-hôrs') *tr.v.* **-horsed, -hors·ing. 1.** To cause to fall from a horse. **2.** To overthrow or dislodge.

uni-. A prefix meaning one: *unicellular.* [Latin, from *ūnus,* one.]

U·ni·ate (yōō'nē-ĭt, -āt') *adj.* Also **U·ni·at** (yōō'nē-ăt'). Of or pertaining to the Uniate Church or its members, practices, or doctrines. —*n.* A member of a Uniate Church. [Russian *uniyat,* from Polish *uniat,* from *unja,* "church-union" (of the Greek and the Roman Catholic Churches), from Late Latin *ūniō,* union.]

Uniate Church. Also **Uniat Church.** Any Eastern Christian church that acknowledges the supremacy of the pope but retains its own distinctive liturgy.

u·ni·cam·er·al (yōō'nĭ-kăm'ər-əl) *adj.* Having or consisting of a single legislative chamber. [UNI- + CAMERA (chamber).]

u·ni·cel·lu·lar (yōō'nĭ-sĕl'yə-lər) *adj.* Consisting of one cell; one-celled: *unicellular microorganisms.*

u·ni·corn (yōō'nĭ-kôrn') *n.* A fabled creature usu. represented as a horse with a single spiraled horn projecting from its forehead and often with a goat's beard and a lion's tail. [Middle English, from Old French, from Latin *ūnicornis* : *uni-,* one + *cornū,* horn.]

    unicorn   **unicycle**

u·ni·cy·cle (yōō'nĭ-sī'kəl) *n.* A vehicle consisting of a frame mounted over a single wheel and usu. propelled by pedals.

un·i·den·ti·fied flying object (ŭn'ī-dĕn'tə-fīd') A flying or apparently flying object that cannot be identified as a known aircraft or object or explained as a natural phenomenon. Also called **UFO.**

u·ni·form (yōō'nə-fôrm') *adj.* **1.** Always the same; unchanging; unvarying. **2.** Being the same as another or others; identical; consonant. **3.** Consistent in appearance; having an unvaried texture, color, or design. —See Syns at **like.** —*n.* **1.** A distinctive outfit intended to identify those who wear it as members of a specific group. **2.** A single outfit of such apparel. —*tr.v.* To provide or dress with a uniform. [Old French *uniforme,* from Latin *ūniformis,* of one form.] —**u'ni·form'ness** *n.* —**u'ni·form'ly** *adv.*

u·ni·for·mi·ty (yōō'nə-fôr'mĭ-tē) *n.* The condition of being the same throughout, sameness.

u·ni·fy (yōō'nə-fī') *v.* **-fied, -fy·ing.** —*tr.v.* To make several into one; consolidate. —*intr.v.* To become one; unite.

[Old French *unifier*, from Late Latin *ūnificāre* : uni-, one + Latin *facere*, to make.] —**u'ni·fi·ca'tion** *n.* —**u'ni·fi'er** *n.*

u·ni·lat·er·al (yōō'nĭ-lăt'ər-əl) *adj.* **1.** Of, on, pertaining to, involving, or affecting only one side: *a unilateral decision to disarm.* **2.** Obligating only one of two or more parties, nations, or persons, as a contract or agreement. —**u'ni·lat'er·al·ly** *adv.*

un·i·mag·in·a·ble (ŭn'ĭ-măj'ə-nə-bəl) *adj.* Difficult or impossible to imagine.

un·im·peach·a·ble (ŭn'ĭm-pē'chə-bəl) *adj.* Beyond doubt or question. —**un'im·peach'a·bly** *adv.*

un·im·por·tant (ŭn'ĭm-pôr'tnt) *adj.* Not important; petty. —See Syns at **little.** —**un'im·por'tance** *n.*

un·in·hab·it·ed (ŭn'ĭn-hăb'ĭ-tĭd) *adj.* Not inhabited; having no residents.

un·in·hib·it·ed (ŭn'ĭn-hĭb'ĭ-tĭd) *adj.* **1.** Not inhibited; unrestrained; open: *uninhibited laughter.* **2.** Free from the expected social or moral constraints. —**un'in·hib'it·ed·ly** *adv.*

un·in·spired (ŭn'ĭn-spīrd') *adj.* Having no intellectual or spiritual excitement; dull.

un·in·tel·li·gent (ŭn'ĭn-tĕl'ə-jənt) *adj.* Lacking in intelligence; stupid; ignorant. —**un'in·tel'li·gent·ly** *adv.*

un·in·tel·li·gi·ble (ŭn'ĭn-tĕl'ə-jə-bəl) *adj.* Not capable of being comprehended. —**un'in·tel'li·gi·bil'i·ty** *n.* —**un'in·tel'li·gi·bly** *adv.*

un·in·ter·est·ed (ŭn-ĭn'trĭs-tĭd, -ĭn'tə-rĕs'tĭd) *adj.* **1.** Without an interest, esp. not having a financial interest. **2.** Not paying attention; unconcerned.

   Syns: *uninterested, incurious, indifferent, unconcerned adj.* Core meaning: Lacking interest in one's surroundings (*a totally uninterested observer*).

un·ion (yōōn'yən) *n.* **1. a.** The act of uniting. **b.** A combination thus formed, esp. an alliance or confederation of persons, parties, or political entities for mutual interest or benefit. **c.** The condition of being united: *a fine union of spirit and reason.* **2. a.** A partnership in matrimony; a marriage. **b.** Sexual congress; intercourse. **3.** An organization of wage earners formed for the purpose of serving their class interest with respect to wages and working conditions; labor union. **4.** Agreement resulting from an alliance; concord; harmony. **5.** *Math.* A set having the property that each of its elements is also an element of two or more given sets. **6. a.** A former combination of parishes for joint administration of relief for the poor in Britain. **b.** A workhouse maintained by such a union. **7.** A coupling device for connecting pipes, rods, etc. **8.** A design on or part of a flag that symbolizes the union of two or more independent states, regions, etc. **9. Union. a.** An organization at a college or university that provides facilities for recreation. **b.** A building that houses such facilities. **10. The Union.** The United States of America, esp. during the Civil War. —*modifier:* union leaders; Union troops. [Middle English, from Old French, from Late Latin *ūniō*, unity, from Latin *ūnus*, one.]

un·ion·ism (yōōn'yə-nĭz'əm) *n.* **1.** The principle or theory of forming a union. **2.** The principles, theory, or system of a union, esp. a trade union. **3. Unionism.** Loyalty to the Federal Government during the Civil War. —**un'ion·ist** *n.*

un·ion·ize (yōōn'yə-nīz') *tr.v.* **-ized, -iz·ing. 1.** To organize into a labor union. **2.** To cause to join such a union. —**un'ion·i·za'tion** *n.*

union jack. 1. Any flag consisting entirely of a union. **2. Union Jack.** The flag of the United Kingdom.

union shop. A business or industrial establishment whose employees are required to be union members or agree to join the union within a specified time after being hired. Also called **closed shop.**

union suit. A one-piece undergarment that combines both shirt and pants.

u·nique (yōō-nēk') *adj.* **1.** Being the only one of its kind. **2.** Being without an equal or equivalent. [French, from Latin *ūnicus*, only, sole.] —**u·nique'ly** *adv.* —**u·nique'ness** *n.*

   Syns: *unique, incomparable, matchless, peerless, unequaled, unparalleled, unrivaled adj.* Core meaning: Being without equal or rival (*an artist with unique creativity*).

u·ni·sex (yōō'nĭ-sĕks') *adj.* Suitable for, common to, or available for both males and females.

u·ni·sex·u·al (yōō'nĭ-sĕk'shōō-əl) *adj.* **1.** Of only one sex.

2. Having only one type of sexual organ. **3.** *Bot.* Having either stamens or pistils but not both. —**u'ni·sex'u·al'i·ty** (-ăl'ĭ-tē) *n.* —**u'ni·sex'u·al·ly** *adv.*

u·ni·son (yōō'nĭ-sən, -zən) *n.* **1. a.** Identity of musical pitch; the interval of a perfect prime. **b.** The combination of musical parts at the same pitch or in octaves. **2.** Any speaking of the same words simultaneously by two or more speakers. **3.** Any instance of agreement; concord; harmony. [Old French, from Medieval Latin *ūnisonus*, of the same sound : uni-, one + Latin *sonus*, sound.]

u·nit (yōō'nĭt) *n.* **1.** A thing, group, person, etc., regarded as a constituent part of a whole. **2.** A single group regarded as a distinct part within a larger group. **3.** A precisely defined quantity in terms of which measurement of quantities of the same kind can be expressed. **4.** The digit located just to the left of the decimal point in the Arabic system of numeration. **5.** A part, device, or module that performs a particular function, as in a machine, electronic device, or system. **6.** A fixed amount of scholastic study used as a basis for calculating academic credits. [Backformation from UNITY.]

U·ni·tar·i·an (yōō'nĭ-târ'ē-ən) *n.* **1.** A monotheist who rejects the doctrine of the Trinity. **2.** A member of a Christian denomination that rejects the doctrine of the Trinity and emphasizes freedom and tolerance in religious belief and the autonomy of each congregation. [From Latin *ūnitās*, unity.] —**U'ni·tar'i·an·ism** *n.*

u·ni·tar·y (yōō'nĭ-tĕr'ē) *adj.* **1.** Of or pertaining to a unit or units. **2.** Having the nature of a unit; whole. **3.** Based on or characterized by one or more units.

u·nite (yōō-nīt') *v.* **-nit·ed, -nit·ing.** —*tr.v.* **1.** To bring together or join so as to form a whole. **2.** To combine (people) in interest, attitude, or action. **3.** To join (a couple) in marriage. **4.** To cause to adhere; to bond. **5.** To have or demonstrate in combination: *He unites common sense with vision.* —*intr.v.* **1.** To become or seem to become joined, formed, or combined into a unit: *Two streams unite to form the river.* **2.** To join and act together in a common purpose or endeavor. **3.** To be or become bound together by adhesion. —See Syns at **join.** [Middle English *uniten*, from Late Latin *ūnītus*, past part. of *ūnīre*, from Latin *ūnus*, one.]

United Nations. An international organization comprising most of the countries of the world, formed in 1945 to promote peace, security, and economic development.

unit pricing. The pricing of goods on the basis of cost per unit of measure.

u·ni·ty (yōō'nĭ-tē) *n., pl.* **-ties. 1.** The condition of being united into a single whole. **2.** The condition of accord or agreement; concord; harmony. **3.** The combination or arrangement of parts into a whole; unification. **4.** An ordering of all elements in a work of art or literature so that each contributes to a unified aesthetic effect. **5.** *Math.* **a.** The number 1. **b.** An element *I* in a set satisfying $x \cdot I = x = I \cdot x$ for each *x* in the set. Also called "identity." **6. the unities.** Three principles of dramatic composition, derived from Aristotle's *Poetics*, based upon unity of time, action, and place. They state that a drama should have but one plot, the action of which should be contained within one day and confined to one locality. —See Syns at **harmony.** [Middle English *unite*, from Old French, from Latin *ūnitās*, from *ūnus*, one.]

u·ni·va·lent (yōō'nĭ-vā'lənt) *adj. Chem.* **1.** Having valence 1. **2.** Having only one valence. —*n.* An unpaired chromosome. —**u'ni·va'lence** or **u'ni·va'len·cy** *n.*

u·ni·valve (yōō'nĭ-vălv') *n.* **1.** A mollusk, esp. a gastropod, that has a single shell. **2.** The shell of such a mollusk. —*adj.* Consisting of a single part rather than paired.

u·ni·ver·sal (yōō'nə-vûr'səl) *adj.* **1.** Of, extending to, or affecting the entire world; worldwide. **2.** Including, pertaining to, or affecting all members of the class or group under consideration: *the universal skepticism of philosophers.* **3.** Applicable or common to all purposes, conditions, or situations. **4.** Of or pertaining to the universe or cosmos; cosmic. **5.** Comprising all or many subjects; comprehensively broad: *a universal genius.* **6.** *Mechanics.* Adapted or adjustable to many sizes or uses. **7.** *Logic.* Predicable of all the members of a class or genus denoted by the subject: *a universal proposition.* —*n.* **1.** *Logic.* **a.** A universal proposition. **b.** A general or abstract concept or term considered absolute or axiomatic. **2.** Any general or widely held principle, concept, or notion. **3.** A trait or pattern of behavior characteristic of all the members of a particular culture or of all human beings. —**u'ni·ver'sal·ly** adv. —**u'ni·ver'sal·ness** n.

u·ni·ver·sal·ism (yōō'nə-vûr'sə-lĭz'əm) n. **1. Universalism.** Theol. The doctrine that all people will ultimately be saved. **2.** Universality.

U·ni·ver·sal·ist (yōō'nə-vûr'sə-lĭst) n. Someone who believes in Universalism.

u·ni·ver·sal·i·ty (yōō'nə-vər-săl'ĭ-tē) n., pl. **-ties. 1.** The quality, fact, or condition of being universal. **2.** Great or unbounded versatility of the mind.

universal joint. A joint that couples a pair of shafts not in the same line so that a rotating motion can be transferred from one to the other.

u·ni·verse (yōō'nə-vûrs') n. **1.** All the matter and space that exists regarded as a whole, including the earth, the heavens, and the galaxies; the cosmos. **2. a.** The earth together with all its inhabitants and created things. **b.** All human beings. **3.** The sphere or realm in which something exists or takes place. **4.** Math. A set that contains all the objects and sets under discussion as elements or subsets. [Middle English, from Old French univers, from Latin ūniversum, the whole world, from ūniversus, whole, entire, : uni-, one + versus, past part. of vertere, to turn.]

u·ni·ver·si·ty (yōō'nə-vûr'sĭ-tē) n., pl. **-ties. 1.** An institution for higher learning with teaching and research facilities comprising a graduate school and professional schools that award master's degrees and doctorates and an undergraduate division that awards bachelor's degrees. **2.** The buildings and grounds of a university. **3.** The students and faculty of a university, regarded as a body. [Middle English universite, from Old French, from Medieval Latin ūniversitās (magistrorum et scholarium), "society (of masters and students)," from Late Latin ūniversitās, a society, guild, from Latin, the whole, from ūniversus, whole.]

un·just (ŭn-jŭst') adj. Violating principles of justice. —See Syns at **unfair.** —**un·just'ly** adv. —**un·just'ness** n.

un·kempt (ŭn-kĕmpt') adj. **1.** Not combed: unkempt hair. **2.** Not neat or tidy; messy. [UN- (not) + kempt, past part. of dial. kemb, to comb, from Middle English kemben, from Old English cemban.]

un·kind (ŭn-kīnd') adj. **-er, -est.** Not kind; harsh; unsympathetic. —**un·kind'ness** n.

un·kind·ly (ŭn-kīnd'lē) adv. In an unkind manner. —adj. **-li·er, -li·est.** Unkind. —**un·kind'li·ness** n.

un·knit (ŭn-nĭt') tr.v. **-knit** or **-knit·ted, -knit·ting.** To unravel or undo (something knit or tied).

un·know·ing (ŭn-nō'ĭng) adj. Not knowing; uninformed. —See Syns at **ignorant.** —**un·know'ing·ly** adv.

un·known (ŭn-nōn') adj. **1.** Not known; unfamiliar; strange. **2.** Not yet discovered. **3. a.** Not identified or ascertained: an unknown quantity. **b.** Not established or verified. **4.** Not heard of before; not publicly known: an unknown artist. —n. **1.** Someone or something that is unknown. **2.** Math. **a.** A quantity of unknown numerical value. **b.** The symbol for this quantity.

un·lace (ŭn-lās') tr.v. **-laced, -lac·ing. 1.** To loosen or undo the lace or laces of. **2.** To remove or loosen the clothing of.

un·latch (ŭn-lăch') tr.v. To unfasten or open by releasing the latch. —intr.v. To become unfastened.

un·law·ful (ŭn-lô'fəl) adj. **1.** Not lawful; in violation of law; illegal. **2.** In violation of moral codes; immoral. **3.** Produced without benefit of marriage; illegitimate: an unlawful child. —See Syns at **criminal** and **illegal.** —**un·law'ful·ly** adv. —**un·law'ful·ness** n.

un·lead·ed (ŭn-lĕd'ĭd) adj. **1.** Not containing lead: unleaded gasoline. **2.** Printing. Not spaced or separated with lead spacers; set solid.

un·learn (ŭn-lûrn') tr.v. **-learned** or **-learnt** (-lûrnt'), **-learn·ing.** To put (something learned) out of the mind.

un·learn·ed (ŭn-lûr'nĭd) adj. **1.** Not educated; ignorant or illiterate. **2.** (ŭn-lûrnd') Not acquired by training or studying: an unlearned response. **3.** Not skilled or versed in a specified discipline.

un·leash (ŭn-lēsh') tr.v. To release from or as if from a leash: unleashed the dog. The enemy unleashed its power against the border cities.

un·leav·ened (ŭn-lĕv'ənd) adj. Made without leaven.

un·less (ŭn-lĕs') conj. Except on the condition that: You can't go out unless you comb your hair. [Middle English unlesse, alteration of onlesse (than), "on a less condition than," except.]

un·let·tered (ŭn-lĕt'ərd) adj. **1. a.** Not educated. **b.** Illiterate. **2.** Having no lettering: an unlettered poster.

un·li·censed (ŭn-lī'sənst) adj. **1.** Having no license: an unlicensed truck. **2.** Without permission or authority; unauthorized: an unlicensed use of a trademark. **3.** Without curbs or checks; unrestrained.

un·like (ŭn-līk') adj. **1.** Not alike; different; dissimilar: unlike poles of a magnet. **2.** Not equal. —See Syns at **different.** —prep. **1.** Different from; not like: a sound unlike any other. **2.** Not typical of: It's unlike him not to thank us. —**un·like'ness** n.

un·like·li·hood (ŭn-līk'lē-hŏŏd') n. The condition of being unlikely or improbable; improbability.

un·like·ly (ŭn-līk'lē) adj. **-li·er, -li·est. 1.** Not likely; improbable. **2.** Likely to fail; unpromising: an unlikely candidate. —**un·like'li·ness** n.

Syns: unlikely, doubtful, improbable adj. Core meaning: Showing little or no likelihood of happening or being true (an unlikely story; an unlikely alibi).

un·lim·ber (ŭn-lĭm'bər) tr.v. To make ready for action. —intr.v. To prepare for action.

un·lim·it·ed (ŭn-lĭm'ĭ-tĭd) adj. Having no limits, bounds, or qualifications: unlimited possibilities.

un·list·ed (ŭn-lĭs'tĭd) adj. **1.** Not appearing on a list: an unlisted telephone number. **2.** Designating stock or securities not listed on a stock exchange.

un·load (ŭn-lōd') tr.v. **1. a.** To remove the load or cargo from. **b.** To remove (cargo): unload furniture from a van. **2. a.** To relieve (oneself) of something oppressive; unburden. **b.** To pour forth (one's troubles). **3. a.** To remove the charge from (a firearm). **b.** To discharge (a firearm); fire. **4.** To dispose of, esp. by selling in great quantity; dump. —intr.v. To discharge a cargo or other burden. —**un·load'er** n.

un·lock (ŭn-lŏk') tr.v. **1. a.** To undo (a lock) by turning a key or a corresponding part. **b.** To undo the lock of. **2.** To cause to become open; permit access to: unlocked her heart. **3.** To set free; release. **4.** To provide a key to; open to solution: unlock a mystery. —intr.v. To become unfastened, loosened, or freed from.

un·looked-for (ŭn-lŏŏkt'fôr') adj. Not looked for or expected; unforeseen.

un·loose (ŭn-lōōs') tr.v. **-loosed, -loos·ing.** Also **un·loos·en** (-lōō'sən). **1.** To let loose or unfasten; release; set free. **2.** To relax or ease: unloose a grip.

un·luck·y (ŭn-lŭk'ē) adj. **-i·er, -i·est. 1.** Subjected to or marked by misfortune. **2.** Forecasting bad luck; inauspicious. **3.** Not producing the desired outcome; disappointing: an unlucky choice. —See Syns at **unfortunate.** —**un·luck'i·ly** adv. —**un·luck'i·ness** n.

un·make (ŭn-māk') tr.v. **-made** (-mād'), **-mak·ing. 1.** To undo the making of: unmake the bed. **2.** To deprive of position, rank, or authority; depose. **3.** To ruin; destroy. **4.** To alter the characteristics of.

un·man (ŭn-măn') tr.v. **-manned, -man·ning. 1.** To cause to lose courage. **2.** To deprive of virility.

un·man·ly (ŭn-măn'lē) adj. **-li·er, -li·est. 1.** Dishonorable; cowardly. **2.** Effeminate. —**un·man'li·ness** n.

un·manned (ŭn-mănd') adj. Without crew: an unmanned ship; an unmanned spacecraft.

un·man·nered (ŭn-măn'ərd) adj. **1.** Without manners; rude. **2.** Without affectations.

un·man·ner·ly (ŭn-măn'ər-lē) adj. Rude; impolite. —See Syns at **rude.** —**un·man'ner·li·ness** n.

un·marked (ŭn-märkt') adj. **1.** Not bearing a mark: unmarked silver. **2.** Not observed or noticed. **3.** Not noticeably affected: unmarked by the tragedy. **4.** Not marked with a grade, corrections, price, etc.

un·mar·ried (ŭn-măr'ēd) adj. Not married. —See Syns at **single.**

un·mask (ŭn-măsk') tr.v. **1.** To remove a mask from. **2.** To disclose the true character of; expose; reveal: *unmasked their true motives.* —*intr.v.* To remove one's mask.

un·mean·ing (ŭn-mē'nĭng) *adj.* **1.** Meaningless; senseless. **2.** Expressionless; vacant. —**un·mean'ing·ly** *adv.*

un·meet (ŭn-mēt') *adj.* Improper; unseemly.

un·men·tion·a·ble (ŭn-měn'shə-nə-bəl) *adj.* Not fit to be mentioned. —See Syns at **unspeakable.** —**un·men'tion·a·ble·ness** *n.*

un·men·tion·a·bles (ŭn-měn'shə-nə-bəlz) *pl.n.* Underwear.

un·mer·ci·ful (ŭn-mûr'sĭ-fəl) *adj.* **1.** Having no mercy; merciless. **2.** Excessive; extreme: *unmerciful heat.* —**un·mer'ci·ful·ly** *adv.* —**un·mer'ci·ful·ness** *n.*

un·mind·ful (ŭn-mīnd'fəl) *adj.* Careless; forgetful; oblivious: *unmindful of the time.* —See Syns at **careless.** —**un·mind'ful·ly** *adv.* —**un·mind'ful·ness** *n.*

un·mis·tak·a·ble (ŭn'mĭ-stā'kə-bəl) *adj.* Obvious; evident. —See Syns at **clear.** —**un'mis·tak'a·bly** *adv.*

un·mit·i·gat·ed (ŭn-mĭt'ĭ-gā'tĭd) *adj.* **1.** Not diminished or moderated in intensity or severity; unrelieved. **2.** Absolute; unqualified. —See Syns at **utter.** —**un·mit'i·gat·ed·ly** *adv.*

un·mor·al (ŭn-môr'əl, -mŏr'-) *adj.* Having no moral quality; amoral. —**un·mor'al·ly** *adv.*

un·nat·u·ral (ŭn-năch'ər-əl, -năch'rəl) *adj.* **1.** Not in accordance with what usu. occurs in nature; abnormal or unusual. **2.** Strained, stiff, or affected; artificial: *an unnatural manner.* **3.** Against natural feelings or normal or accepted standards: *unnatural practices such as slavery.* **4.** Outrageously violating natural feelings; inhuman; shocking: *unnatural cruelty.* —**un·nat'u·ral·ly** *adv.* —**un·nat'u·ral·ness** *n.*

un·nec·es·sar·y (ŭn-něs'ĭ-sěr'ē) *adj.* Not necessary; needless. —**un·nec'es·sar'i·ly** (-sâr'ə-lē) *adv.*

un·nerve (ŭn-nûrv') *tr.v.* **-nerved, -nerv·ing.** To cause to lose courage, composure, etc.

un·no·tice·a·ble (ŭn-nō'tĭ-sə-bəl) *adj.* Not readily noticeable. —See Syns at **imperceptible.**

un·num·bered (ŭn-nŭm'bərd) *adj.* **1.** Not numbered; countless. **2.** Not marked with an identifying number.

un·ob·tru·sive (ŭn'əb-trōō'sĭv, -zĭv) *adj.* Not readily noticed; inconspicuous: *an unobtrusive style of dressing.* —**un'ob·tru'sive·ly** *adv.* —**un'ob·tru'sive·ness** *n.*

un·oc·cu·pied (ŭn-ŏk'yə-pīd') *adj.* **1.** Not occupied; vacant. **2.** Not busy; idle.

un·of·fi·cial (ŭn'ə-fĭsh'əl) *adj.* Not official. —**un'of·fi'cial·ly** *adv.*

un·or·gan·ized (ŭn-ôr'gə-nīzd') *adj.* **1.** Lacking order, system, or unity. **2.** Not unionized.

un·o·rig·i·nal (ŭn'ə-rĭj'ə-nəl) *adj.* Lacking originality; trite.

un·or·tho·dox (ŭn-ôr'thə-dŏks') *adj.* Not orthodox; breaking with convention or tradition: *an unorthodox approach to a problem.* —**un·or'tho·dox'ly** *adv.*

un·pack (ŭn-păk') *tr.v.* **1.** To remove the contents of (a suitcase, trunk, etc.). **2.** To remove from a container or from packaging: *unpacked the vase.* **3.** To remove a pack from (a pack animal). —*intr.v.* To unpack goods, a trunk, etc.

un·paid (ŭn-pād') *adj.* **1.** Not yet paid. **2.** Serving without pay; unsalaried: *an unpaid volunteer.*

un·par·al·leled (ŭn-păr'ə-lĕld') *adj.* Without parallel; unequaled. —See Syns at **unique.**

un·par·lia·men·ta·ry (ŭn'pär-lə-měn'tə-rē, -měn'trē) *adj.* Not in accordance with parliamentary rules or procedures.

un·peo·ple (ŭn-pē'pəl) *tr.v.* **-pled, -pling.** To depopulate (an area).

un·pin (ŭn-pĭn') *tr.v.* **-pinned, -pin·ning. 1.** To remove a pin or pins from. **2.** To open or unfasten by removing pins. **3.** To free from an immobilized condition.

un·pleas·ant (ŭn-plĕz'ənt) *adj.* **-er, -est.** Not pleasing. —**un·pleas'ant·ly** *adv.* —**un·pleas'ant·ness** *n.*

　　Syns: unpleasant, disagreeable, offensive *adj.* Core meaning: Not pleasant *(an unpleasant confrontation; an unpleasant odor; a vain, unpleasant executive).*

un·plug (ŭn-plŭg') *tr.v.* **-plugged, -plug·ging. 1.** To remove a plug, stopper, etc. from. **2.** To disconnect (an electric appliance) by removing its plug from an outlet.

un·plumbed (ŭn-plŭmd') *adj.* **1.** Not measured for depth with a plumb line: *unplumbed waters.* **2.** Not fully ex-

plored or understood: *an unplumbed theory.*

un·pop·u·lar (ŭn-pŏp'yə-lər) *adj.* Not popular; not liked or approved of. —**un·pop'u·lar'i·ty** (-lăr'ĭ-tē) *n.*

un·prac·ticed (ŭn-prăk'tĭst) *adj.* Without benefit of practice or experience; unskilled.

un·prec·e·dent·ed (ŭn-prĕs'ĭ-dĕn'tĭd) *adj.* Without precedent; novel. —**un·prec'e·dent'ed·ly** *adv.*

un·pre·dict·a·ble (ŭn'prĭ-dĭk'tə-bəl) *adj.* Not predictable; not capable of being known in advance. —See Syns at **capricious.** —**un'pre·dict'a·bly** *adv.*

un·pre·med·i·tat·ed (ŭn'prē-mĕd'ĭ-tā'tĭd) *adj.* Not thought out or planned beforehand. —**un'pre·med'i·tat'ed·ly** *adv.* —**un'pre·med'i·ta'tion** *n.*

un·pre·pared (ŭn'prĭ-pârd') *adj.* **1.** Not prepared or ready; not equipped. **2.** Done without preparation; impromptu. —**un'pre·par'ed·ly** (-pâr'ĭd-lē) *adv.* —**un'pre·par'ed·ness** *n.*

un·pre·pos·sess·ing (ŭn-prē'pə-zĕs'ĭng) *adj.* Failing to impress favorably; nondescript: *a small, unprepossessing entrance.* —**un'pre·pos·sess'ing·ly** *adv.*

un·pre·ten·tious (ŭn'prĭ-tĕn'shəs) *adj.* Lacking pretention; modest. —**un'pre·ten'tious·ness** *n.*

un·prin·ci·pled (ŭn-prĭn'sə-pəld) *adj.* Lacking principles or moral scruples; unscrupulous.

un·print·a·ble (ŭn-prĭn'tə-bəl) *adj.* Not proper for publication.

un·pro·fes·sion·al (ŭn'prə-fĕsh'ə-nəl) *adj.* **1.** Not from a member of a qualified profession: *Take my unprofessional advice.* **2.** Not a qualified member of a professional group. **3.** Not conforming to the standards of a profession: *unprofessional behavior for a lawyer.* **4.** Without professional skill; amateurish: *a very unprofessional paint job.* —**un'pro·fes'sion·al·ly** *adv.*

un·prof·it·a·ble (ŭn-prŏf'ĭ-tə-bəl) *adj.* **1.** Not producing a profit or gain. **2.** Not producing a useful result; serving no purpose; useless.

un·qual·i·fied (ŭn-kwŏl'ə-fīd') *adj.* **1.** Lacking the proper or necessary qualifications. **2.** Without reservations; complete; unconditioned: *an unqualified success.* —See Syns at **utter.**

un·ques·tion·a·ble (ŭn-kwĕs'chə-nə-bəl) *adj.* Beyond question or doubt; indisputable; certain. —**un·ques'tion·a·bly** *adv.*

un·ques·tioned (ŭn-kwĕs'chənd) *adj.* **1.** Not subjected to questioning; not interrogated. **2.** Not to be questioned or doubted; indisputable.

un·qui·et (ŭn-kwī'ĭt) *adj.* **-er, -est. 1.** Emotionally or mentally uneasy; distraught. **2.** Characterized by unrest or disorder; turbulent. —**un·qui'et·ly** *adv.* —**un·qui'et·ness** *n.*

un·quote (ŭn'kwōt') *n.* A word used to indicate the end of a quotation.

un·rav·el (ŭn-răv'əl) *v.* **-eled** or **-elled, -el·ing** or **-el·ling.** —*tr.v.* **1. a.** To undo or ravel the knitted fabric of. **b.** To separate (entangled threads) into single loose threads. **2.** To separate and clarify the elements of (something mysterious or baffling); solve; clear up. —*intr.v.* To become unraveled.

un·read (ŭn-rĕd') *adj.* **1.** Not read, studied, or perused: *leaving the book unread.* **2.** Having read little; ignorant.

un·read·a·ble (ŭn-rē'də-bəl) *adj.* **1.** Illegible: *an unreadable handwriting.* **2.** Not interesting; dull.

un·re·al (ŭn-rē'əl, -rēl') *adj.* **1.** Not real or substantial; imaginary; artificial; illusory. **2.** *Slang.* Too good to be true; fantastic.

un·re·al·is·tic (ŭn'rē-ə-lĭs'tĭk) *adj.* Not realistic; unreasonable. —**un're·al·is'ti·cal·ly** *adv.*

un·re·al·i·ty (ŭn'rē-ăl'ĭ-tē) *n.* **1.** The condition of not being real, likely, or true: *the unreality of her plans.* **2.** Something that cannot be real, likely, or true.

un·rea·son·a·ble (ŭn-rē'zə-nə-bəl) *adj.* **1.** Not governed by or acting upon reason. **2.** Exceeding reasonable limits; exorbitant. —See Syns at **outrageous.** —**un·rea'son·a·ble·ness** *n.* —**un·rea'son·a·bly** *adv.*

un·rea·son·ing (ŭn-rē'zə-nĭng) *adj.* Not governed by reason: *an unreasoning temper.* —**un·rea'son·ing·ly** *adv.*

un·reel (ŭn-rēl') *tr.v.* To unwind from or as if from a reel. —*intr.v.* To unwind.

un·re·flec·tive (ŭn'rĭ-flĕk'tĭv) *adj.* Not thoughtful or pensive. —**un're·flec'tive·ly** *adv.*

ă pat	ā pay	â care	ä father	ĕ pet	ē be	hw which	ĭ pit	ī tie	î pier	ŏ pot	ō toe	ô paw, for	oi noise
ōō took	ōō boot	ou out	th thin	th this	ŭ cut		û urge	zh vision	ə about, item, edible, gallop, circus				

un·re·gen·er·ate (ŭn'rĭ-jĕn'ər-ĭt) *adj.* **1.** Not spiritually or morally regenerated; unrepentant. **2.** Not likely to change; stubborn in one's ways: *an unregenerate atheist.*

un·re·lent·ing (ŭn'rĭ-lĕn'tĭng) *adj.* **1.** Not to be altered or stopped; relentless; inexorable. **2.** Not diminishing in intensity, speed, or effort.

un·re·li·a·ble (ŭn'rĭ-lī'ə-bəl) *adj.* Not reliable or trustworthy. —**un're·li·a·bil'i·ty** or **un're·li'a·ble·ness** *n.* —**un're·li'a·bly** *adv.*
> *Syns:* **unreliable, undependable, untrustworthy** *adj.* Core meaning: Not to be depended on (*unreliable workers; an old, unreliable car*).

un·re·mit·ting (ŭn'rĭ-mĭt'ĭng) *adj.* Never slackening; incessant; persistent: *an unremitting struggle for survival.* —**un're·mit'ting·ly** *adv.* —**un're·mit'ting·ness** *n.*

un·re·served (ŭn'rĭ-zûrvd') *adj.* **1.** Not reserved for a particular person. **2.** Given without reservation; unqualified: *unreserved praise.* **3.** Frank; candid. —**un're·serv'ed·ly** (-zûr'vĭd-lē) *adv.*

un·rest (ŭn-rĕst') *n.* Uneasiness; disquiet: *social unrest.*

un·re·strained (ŭn'rĭ-strānd') *adj.* **1. a.** Not controlled; unchecked: *unrestrained hilarity.* **b.** Not given to restraint: *spending in her unrestrained manner.* **2.** Not constrained; natural: *an unrestrained, informal meeting.* —**un're·strain'ed·ly** (-strā'nĭd-lē) *adv.*

un·ripe (ŭn-rīp') *adj.* **-rip·er, -rip·est.** **1.** Not fully ripened. **2.** Not fully formed; immature: *a man of unripe judgment.* **3.** Not ready; unprepared. —**un·ripe'ness** *n.*

un·ri·valed (ŭn-rī'vəld) *adj.* Unequaled; peerless; supreme: *unrivaled skill.* —See Syns at **unique.**

un·roll (ŭn-rōl') *tr.v.* **1.** To unwind and open out (something rolled up). **2.** To unfold; reveal. —*intr.v.* To become unrolled.

un·ruf·fled (ŭn-rŭf'əld) *adj.* Not agitated; calm.

un·ru·ly (ŭn-rōō'lē) *adj.* **-li·er, -li·est.** Difficult or impossible to discipline or control: *an unruly mob.* —See Syns at **disorderly.** [Middle English *unreuly* : *un-* + *reuly,* easy to govern, from *reule,* rule.]

un·sad·dle (ŭn-săd'l) *v.* **-dled, -dling.** —*tr.v.* **1.** To remove the saddle from. **2.** To unhorse. —*intr.v.* To remove the saddle from a horse.

un·said (ŭn-sĕd') *adj.* Not expressed in words. —See Syns at **implicit.**

un·safe (ŭn-sāf') *adj.* Not safe; dangerous.

un·san·i·tar·y (ŭn-săn'ĭ-tĕr'ē) *adj.* Not sanitary.

un·sat·is·fac·to·ry (ŭn-săt'ĭs-făk'tə-rē) *adj.* Not satisfactory; inadequate: *unsatisfactory living conditions.*

un·sat·u·rat·ed (ŭn-săch'ə-rā'tĭd) *adj.* **1.** Of or indicating a chemical compound, esp. of carbon, in which two atoms are joined by more than a single bond. **2.** Capable of dissolving more of a solute at a given temperature.

un·sa·vor·y (ŭn-sā'və-rē) *adj.* **1.** Having a bad or dull taste; insipid. **2.** Distasteful or disagreeable: *an unsavory task.* **3.** Morally offensive: *an unsavory scandal.* —**un·sa'vor·i·ly** *adv.* —**un·sa'vor·i·ness** *n.*

un·scathed (ŭn-skāthd') *adj.* Unharmed; uninjured.

un·schooled (ŭn-skōōld') *adj.* **1.** Not schooled; uninstructed. **2.** Not the result of training; natural.

un·sci·en·tif·ic (ŭn-sī'ən-tĭf'ĭk) *adj.* **1.** Not according to or following the principles of science. **2.** Not knowledgeable of science. —**un·sci'en·tif'i·cal·ly** *adv.*

un·scram·ble (ŭn-skrăm'bəl) *tr.v.* **-bled, -bling.** **1.** To disentangle; straighten out; resolve. **2.** To restore to a form that can be understood.

un·screw (ŭn-skrōō') *tr.v.* **1.** To loosen, adjust, or remove (a screw, nut, etc.) by or as if by turning. **2. a.** To remove the screws from. **b.** To detach or dismount by removing the screws from. **3.** To loosen by rotating. —*intr.v.* To become or be capable of being unscrewed.

un·scru·pu·lous (ŭn-skrōō'pyə-ləs) *adj.* Without scruples or principles; not honorable. —**un·scru'pu·lous·ly** *adv.* —**un·scru'pu·lous·ness** *n.*

un·seal (ŭn-sēl') *tr.v.* To break or remove the seal of; to open.

un·search·a·ble (ŭn-sûr'chə-bəl) *adj.* Beyond research; inscrutable; imponderable.

un·sea·son·a·ble (ŭn-sē'zə-nə-bəl) *adj.* **1.** Not suitable to or appropriate for the season. **2.** Not characteristic of the time of year. **3.** Poorly timed; inopportune. —**un·sea'son·a·ble·ness** *n.* —**un·sea'son·a·bly** *adv.*

un·seat (ŭn-sēt') *tr.v.* **1.** To remove from a seat, esp. from a saddle. **2.** To force out of a position or office.

un·seem·ly (ŭn-sēm'lē) *adj.* **-li·er, -li·est.** Not in good taste; improper; unbecoming. —See Syns at **unsuitable.** —*adv.* In an unseemly manner. —**un·seem'li·ness** *n.*

un·seen (ŭn-sēn') *adj.* **1.** Not noticed; unobtrusive. **2.** Not seen; invisible.

un·sel·fish (ŭn-sĕl'fĭsh) *adj.* Not selfish. —See Syns at **generous.**

un·set·tle (ŭn-sĕt'l) *tr.v.* **-tled, -tling.** **1.** To move from a settled condition; make unstable. **2.** To make uneasy; disturb; discompose.

un·set·tled (ŭn-sĕt'əld) *adj.* **1.** Disordered; disturbed: *unsettled times.* **2.** Variable; uncertain: *unsettled weather.* **3.** Not determined or resolved: *an unsettled issue.* **4.** Not paid or adjusted: *an unsettled bill.* **5.** Not populated; uninhabited: *an unsettled wilderness.* **6.** Not fixed or established, as in a residence or routine.

un·sex (ŭn-sĕks') *tr.v.* **1.** To deprive of sexual capacity or sexual attributes. **2.** To castrate.

un·shack·le (ŭn-shăk'əl) *tr.v.* **-led, -ling.** To release from or as if from prison or shackles; set free.

un·shak·a·ble (ŭn-shā'kə-bəl) *adj.* Not capable of being shaken; firm. —**un·shak'a·bly** *adv.*

un·shak·en (ŭn-shā'kən) *adj.* Not shaken; firm: *His faith remained forever unshaken.*

un·shap·en (ŭn-shā'pən) *adj.* **1.** Also **un·shaped** (-shāpt'). Not shaped or formed. **2.** Misshapen; deformed.

un·sheathe (ŭn-shēth') *tr.v.* **-sheathed, -sheath·ing.** To draw from or as if from a sheath or scabbard.

un·sight·ly (ŭn-sīt'lē) *adj.* **-li·er, -li·est.** Unpleasant or offensive to look at; unattractive. —See Syns at **ugly.** —**un·sight'li·ness** *n.*

un·skilled (ŭn-skĭld') *adj.* **1.** Lacking skill or technical training: *unskilled workers.* **2.** Requiring no training or skill: *unskilled work.* **3.** Showing no skill; crude.

un·skill·ful (ŭn-skĭl'fəl) *adj.* Without skill or proficiency. —**un·skill'ful·ly** *adv.* —**un·skill'ful·ness** *n.*

un·snap (ŭn-snăp') *tr.v.* **-snapped, -snap·ping.** To undo the snaps of; unfasten.

un·snarl (ŭn-snärl') *tr.v.* To free of snarls; disentangle. —*intr.v.* To become free of snarls or entanglements.

un·so·cia·ble (ŭn-sō'shə-bəl) *adj.* **1.** Not inclined to seek the company of others; not friendly or companionable. **2.** Not conducive to social exchange: *an unsociable atmosphere.* —**un·so'cia·bil'i·ty** or **un·so'cia·ble·ness** *n.* —**un·so'cia·bly** *adv.*

un·so·phis·ti·cat·ed (ŭn'sə-fĭs'tĭ-kā'tĭd) *adj.* Not sophisticated; naive; simple. —**un'so·phis'ti·cat·ed·ly** *adv.* —**un'so·phis'ti·cat·ed·ness** *n.*

un·sound (ŭn-sound') *adj.* **-er, -est.** **1.** Not dependably strong or solid: *an unsound structure; an unsound investment.* **2.** Not physically healthy; diseased: *unsound limbs.* **3.** Not logically founded; fallacious; invalid: *an unsound argument.* —**un·sound'ly** *adv.* —**un·sound'ness** *n.*

un·spar·ing (ŭn-spâr'ĭng) *adj.* **1.** Not frugal; not subject to thrift: *unsparing expenses in her behalf.* **2.** Unmerciful; severe; harsh: *unsparing criticism of his work.* —**un·spar'ing·ly** *adv.*

un·speak·a·ble (ŭn-spē'kə-bəl) *adj.* **1.** Beyond description; inexpressible. **2.** Bad beyond description; objectionable. **3.** Unfit to be discussed or spoken aloud. —**un·speak'a·bly** *adv.*
> *Syns:* **1. unspeakable, indescribable, unutterable** *adj.* Core meaning: That cannot be described (*unspeakable happiness*). **2. unspeakable, abominable, frightful, revolting, shocking, sickening** *adj.* Core meaning: Too awful to be described (*unspeakable acts of genocide*). **3. unspeakable, unmentionable, unutterable** *adj.* Core meaning: Unfit to be spoken or mentioned (*unspeakable words of abuse*).

un·spo·ken (ŭn-spō'kən) *adj.* Not expressed; unsaid: *an unspoken wish.* —See Syns at **implicit.**

un·spot·ted (ŭn-spŏt'ĭd) *adj.* **1.** Not marked with spots. **2.** Morally unblemished. **3.** Not having been detected: *an unspotted theft.* —**un·spot'ted·ness** *n.*

un·sta·ble (ŭn-stā'bəl) *adj.* **-bler, -blest.** **1.** Not steady, firm, etc.: *an unstable chair.* **2.** Having a strong tendency to change or fluctuate: *unstable prices.* **3. a.** Of fickle temperament; irresponsible; flighty. **b.** Mentally or psychologically unbalanced. **4.** Tending to decompose easily, as a chemical compound. **5. a.** Decaying after a relatively short time, as an atomic particle. **b.** Radioactive, as an element, isotope, or atomic nucleus. —See Syns at **capricious.** —**un·sta'ble·ness** *n.* —**un·sta'bly** *adv.*

un·stead·y (ŭn-stĕd'ē) *adj.* **-i·er, -i·est. 1.** Not securely in place. **2.** Fluctuating; inconstant. **3.** Wavering; uneven: *an unsteady voice.* **4.** Not reliable or regular. —See Syns at **capricious.** —**un·stead'i·ly** *adv.* —**un·stead'i·ness** *n.*

un·step (ŭn-stĕp') *tr.v.* **-stepped, -step·ping.** *Naut.* To remove (a mast) from a step or supporting framework.

un·stick (ŭn-stĭk') *tr.v.* **-stuck** (-stŭk'), **-stick·ing.** To free from being stuck.

un·stop (ŭn-stŏp') *tr.v.* **-stopped, -stop·ping. 1.** To remove a stopper or stop from. **2.** To remove an obstruction from; open.

un·strap (ŭn-străp') *tr.v.* **-strapped, -strap·ping.** To remove or loosen the strap or straps of.

un·stressed (ŭn-strĕst') *adj.* **1.** Not accented or stressed: *an unstressed syllable.* **2.** Not emphasized.

un·string (ŭn-strĭng') *tr.v.* **-strung** (-strŭng'), **-string·ing. 1.** To remove from a string. **2.** To loosen or remove the strings of. **3.** To weaken the nerves of; unnerve.

un·struc·tured (ŭn-strŭk'chərd) *adj.* **1.** Lacking structure. **2.** *Psychol.* **a.** Having no intrinsic or objective meaning; meaningful by subjective interpretation only: *unstructured inkblot tests.* **b.** Not regulated or regimented: *an unstructured environment.*

un·stud·ied (ŭn-stŭd'ēd) *adj.* **1.** Not contrived for effect; natural: *an unstudied manner.* **2.** Not having been instructed; unversed.

un·sub·stan·tial (ŭn'səb-stăn'shəl) *adj.* **1.** Lacking material substance; not real; imaginary. **2.** Lacking firmness or strength; flimsy. **3.** Lacking basis in fact; insubstantial. —**un'sub·stan'ti·al'i·ty** (-shē-ăl'ĭ-tē) *n.* —**un'sub·stan'tial·ly** *adv.*

un·suc·cess·ful (ŭn'sək-sĕs'fəl) *adj.* Not succeeding; without success. —**un'suc·cess'ful·ly** *adv.*

un·suit·a·ble (ŭn-sōō'tə-bəl) *adj.* Not suitable or proper; not appropriate. —**un·suit'a·bly** *adv.*

> **Syns: unsuitable, improper, inappropriate, inapt, malapropos, unbecoming, unfit, unseemly** *adj.* Core meaning: Not suited to the circumstances (*attire unsuitable for church; behavior unsuitable for polite society*).

un·sung (ŭn-sŭng') *adj.* **1.** Not sung. **2.** Not honored or praised; uncelebrated: *unsung heroes of battle.*

un·sus·pect·ed (ŭn'sə-spĕk'tĭd) *adj.* **1.** Not under suspicion. **2.** Not known or likely to exist.

un·sus·pect·ing (ŭn'sə-spĕk'tĭng) *adj.* Not suspicious; trusting. —**un'sus·pect'ing·ly** *adv.*

un·sym·met·ri·cal (ŭn'sĭ-mĕt'rĭ-kəl) *adj.* Asymmetric. —**un'sym·met'ri·cal·ly** *adv.*

un·tan·gle (ŭn-tăng'gəl) *tr.v.* **-gled, -gling. 1.** To free from tangles or snarls; disentangle. **2.** To settle; clarify; resolve: *untangle a problem.*

un·tapped (ŭn-tăpt') *adj.* **1.** Not tapped: *an untapped keg.* **2.** Not utilized: *untapped resources.*

un·taught (ŭn-tôt') *adj.* **1.** Not instructed. **2.** Not acquired by instruction. —See Syns at **ignorant.**

un·ten·a·ble (ŭn-tĕn'ə-bəl) *adj.* Not capable of being defended or maintained: *an untenable position.*

un·thank·ful (ŭn-thăngk'fəl) *adj.* **1.** Not thankful; ungrateful. **2.** Not drawing thanks; unwelcome; thankless. —**un·thank'ful·ly** *adv.* —**un·thank'ful·ness** *n.*

un·think·a·ble (ŭn-thĭng'kə-bəl) *adj.* Impossible to imagine or consider; inconceivable; out of the question. —**un·think'a·bly** *adv.*

un·think·ing (ŭn-thĭng'kĭng) *adj.* **1.** Inconsiderate or thoughtless; inattentive. **2.** Not deliberate; inadvertent. **3.** Not capable of thought. —**un·think'ing·ly** *adv.*

un·thread (ŭn-thrĕd') *tr.v.* **1.** To remove the thread from. **2.** To find one's way out of (a labyrinth, mystery, etc.).

un·ti·dy (ŭn-tī'dē) *adj.* **-di·er, -di·est. 1.** Not neat and tidy; slovenly; sloppy. **2.** Lacking order or organization. —See Syns at **careless.** —**un·ti'di·ly** *adv.* —**un·ti'di·ness** *n.*

un·tie (ŭn-tī') *v.* **-tied, -ty·ing.** —*tr.v.* **1.** To undo or loosen (a knot or something knotted). **2.** To free from something that binds or restrains. **3.** To straighten out (as difficulties). —*intr.v.* To become untied.

un·til (ŭn-tĭl') *prep.* **1.** Up to the time of: *danced until dawn.* Also used as a conjunction: *danced until it was dawn.* **2.** Before a specified time: *You can't have the car until tomorrow.* Also used as a conjunction: *And tomorrow you can't have it until you pay me.* —*conj.* To the point or extent that: *He talked until he was worn out.* —See Usage note at **till.** [Middle English, to, toward, up to : *un-*, from Old Norse *und*, as far as + *til*, till, to.]

un·time·ly (ŭn-tīm'lē) *adj.* **-li·er, -li·est. 1.** Occurring or done at an inappropriate or unsuitable time; inopportune. **2.** Occurring too soon; premature. —See Syns at **early.** —*adv.* **1.** Inopportunely. **2.** Prematurely. —**un·time'li·ness** *n.*

un·tir·ing (ŭn-tīr'ĭng) *adj.* **1.** Not tiring. **2.** Not ceasing despite fatigue or frustration; indefatigable: *untiring efforts.* —**un·tir'ing·ly** *adv.*

un·to (ŭn'tōō) *prep.* Archaic. To. [Middle English.]

un·told (ŭn-tōld') *adj.* **1.** Not told or revealed: *untold secrets.* **2.** Without limit: *untold suffering.*

un·touch·a·ble (ŭn-tŭch'ə-bəl) *adj.* **1.** Not to be touched. **2.** Out of reach; unobtainable. **3.** Beyond the reach of criticism, impeachment, or attack. **4.** Loathsome or unpleasant to the touch. —*n.* Often **Untouchable.** A member of the lowest Hindu caste, whose touch was considered unclean and with whom physical contact was considered defiling by Hindus of higher castes. —**un·touch'a·bil'i·ty** *n.*

un·to·ward (ŭn-tôrd', -tōrd', ŭn'tə-wôrd') *adj.* **1.** Unfavorable; unpropitious. **2.** Hard to control; refractory: *his untoward behavior.* —See Syns at **unfavorable.** —**un·to'ward·ly** *adv.* —**un·to'ward·ness** *n.*

un·tried (ŭn-trīd') *adj.* **1.** Not tried, tested, or proved. **2.** Not tried in court; without a trial.

un·trod·den (ŭn-trŏd'n) *adj.* Not having been trod upon; unexplored: *untrodden paths.*

un·true (ŭn-trōō') *adj.* **-tru·er, -tru·est. 1.** Not true; false. **2.** Deviating from a standard; not straight, even, level, or exact. **3.** Disloyal; unfaithful. —See Syns at **faithless.** —**un·tru'ly** *adv.*

un·trust·wor·thy (ŭn-trŭst'wôr'thȳ) *adj.* Not to be trusted. —See Syns at **unreliable.**

un·truth (ŭn-trōōth') *n.* **1.** Something untrue; a lie. **2.** Lack of truth. —See Syns at **lie.**

un·truth·ful (ŭn-trōōth'fəl) *adj.* **1.** Contrary to truth: *an untruthful account.* **2.** Given to falsehood; lying; mendacious: *an untruthful child.* —See Syns at **false.** —**un·truth'ful·ly** *adv.* —**un·truth'ful·ness** *n.*

un·tu·tored (ŭn-tōō'tərd, -tyōō'-) *adj.* **1.** Having had no formal education or instruction. **2.** Unsophisticated; unrefined.

un·twine (ŭn-twīn') *v.* **-twined, -twin·ing.** —*tr.v.* **1.** To loosen or separate, as strands of twisted fiber. **2.** To disentangle. —*intr.v.* To become untwined.

un·twist (ŭn-twĭst') *tr.v.* To loosen or separate (that which is twisted together) by turning in the opposite direction; unwind. —*intr.v.* To become untwisted.

un·used (ŭn-yōōzd') *adj.* **1.** Not in use or put to use. **2.** Never having been used. **3.** (ŭn-yōōst'). Not accustomed: *unused to city traffic.*

un·u·su·al (ŭn-yōō'zhōō-əl) *adj.* Not usual, common, or ordinary. —See Syns at **strange** and **uncommon.** —**un·u'su·al·ly** *adv.*

un·ut·ter·a·ble (ŭn-ŭt'ər-ə-bəl) *adj.* **1.** Not capable of being expressed; too profound for expression. **2.** Not capable of being pronounced: *an absolutely unutterable word.* —See Syns at **unspeakable.** —**un·ut'ter·a·ble·ness** *n.* —**un·ut'ter·a·bly** *adv.*

un·var·nished (ŭn-vär'nĭsht) *adj.* **1.** Not varnished. **2.** Presented without any effort to soften or disguise: *the unvarnished truth.*

un·veil (ŭn-vāl') *tr.v.* **1.** To remove a veil or other covering from. **2.** To disclose; reveal: *unveiled his plans.* —*intr.v.* To take off one's veil; reveal oneself.

un·voiced (ŭn-voist') *adj.* **1.** Not expressed or uttered. **2.** *Phonet.* Uttered without vibrating the vocal chords; voiceless.

ă pat   ā pay   â care   ä father   ĕ pet   ē be   hw which   ĭ pit   ī tie   î pier   ŏ pot   ō toe   ô paw, for   oi noise
ōō took   ōō boot   ou out   th thin   th this   ŭ cut   û urge   zh vision   ə about, item, edible, gallop, circus

un·war·rant·ed (ŭn-wôr′ən-tĭd, -wŏr′-) *adj.* Having no justification; groundless.

un·war·y (ŭn-wâr′ē) *adj.* **-i·er, -i·est.** Not alert to danger or deception. **—un·war′i·ly** *adv.* **—un·war′i·ness** *n.*

un·wed (ŭn-wĕd′) *adj.* Not married. —See Syns at **single.**

un·wel·come (ŭn-wĕl′kəm) *adj.* Not welcome or wanted: *an unwelcome visitor.*

un·well (ŭn-wĕl′) *adj.* Not well; ill. —See Syns at **sick.**

un·wept (ŭn-wĕpt′) *adj.* **1.** Not mourned or wept for: *the unwept dead.* **2.** Not shed: *unwept tears.*

un·whole·some (ŭn-hōl′səm) *adj.* **1.** Not healthful or healthy. **2.** Morally decadent or corrupt. **—un·whole′some·ly** *adv.* **—un·whole′some·ness** *n.*

un·wield·y (ŭn-wēl′dē) *adj.* **-i·er, -i·est. 1.** Difficult to carry or handle because of shape or size: *an unwieldy bundle.* **2.** Clumsy; ungainly. **—un·wield′i·ness** *n.*

un·will·ing (ŭn-wĭl′ĭng) *adj.* **1.** Hesitant; reluctant. **2.** Done, given, or said reluctantly: *unwilling consent.* **—un·will′ing·ly** *adv.* **—un·will′ing·ness** *n.*

un·wind (ŭn-wīnd′) *v.* **-wound** (-wound′), **-wind·ing.** —*tr.v.* **1.** To reverse the winding direction of; uncoil: *unwind a cable.* **2.** To separate the tangled parts of; disentangle. —*intr.v.* **1.** To become unwound. **2.** To become free of anxiety, worry, tension, etc.; relax.

un·wise (ŭn-wīz′) *adj.* **-wis·er, -wis·est.** Lacking wisdom; foolish or imprudent. **—un·wise′ly** *adv.*

un·wit·ting (ŭn-wĭt′ĭng) *adj.* **1.** Not intended; unintentional: *an unwitting remark.* **2.** Not knowing; unaware. —See Syns at **ignorant.** [Middle English *un-*, not + *witting,* pres. part. of *witten,* to know, from Old English *witan.*] **—un·wit′ting·ly** *adv.*

un·wont·ed (ŭn-wôn′tĭd, -wōn′-, -wŭn′-) *adj.* **1.** Not habitual or customary; unusual: *His unwonted rudeness surprised everyone.* **2.** *Obs.* Not accustomed. **—un·wont′ed·ly** *adv.* **—un·wont′ed·ness** *n.*

un·world·ly (ŭn-wûrld′lē) *adj.* **-li·er, -li·est. 1.** Not of this world; extraterrestrial; spiritual. **2.** Concerned with matters of the spirit or soul. **3.** Not worldly-wise; naive: *an unworldly scholar.* **—un·world′li·ness** *n.*

un·wor·thy (ŭn-wûr′thē) *adj.* **-thi·er, -thi·est. 1.** Insufficient in worth; undeserving. **2.** Not suiting or befitting. **3.** Vile; despicable: *unworthy behavior.* **—un·wor′thi·ly** *adv.* **—un·wor′thi·ness** *n.*

un·wrap (ŭn-răp′) *v.* **-wrapped, -wrap·ping.** —*tr.v.* To remove the wrappings from; to open. —*intr.v.* To become unwrapped.

un·writ·ten (ŭn-rĭt′n) *adj.* **1.** Not written or recorded: *unwritten myths.* **2.** Forceful or effective through custom; traditional: *unwritten rules of behavior.*

un·yield·ing (ŭn-yēl′dĭng) *adj.* **1.** Not bending; inflexible. **2.** Determined; resolute; persistent. —See Syns at **rigid.**

un·yoke (ŭn-yōk′) *tr.v.* **-yoked, -yok·ing. 1.** To release (a draft animal) from a yoke. **2.** To separate or disjoin.

up (ŭp) *adv.* **1.** From a lower to a higher position: *moving up.* Also used prepositionally: *going up a mountain.* **2.** In or toward a higher position: *looking up.* Also used prepositionally: *looking up the side of a mountain.* **3.** From a reclining to an upright position: *He helped me up.* **4. a.** Above a surface: *come up for air.* **b.** Above the horizon: *The sun came up.* **5.** Into view or consideration: *You never brought this up before.* **6.** In or toward a position conventionally regarded as higher, as on a map: *going up to Canada.* **7.** To or at a higher price: *Fares are going up again.* **8.** So as to advance, increase, or improve: *His hopes keep going up.* **9.** With or to a greater pitch or volume: *Turn the radio up.* **10.** Into a state of excitement or turbulence: *A great wind came up.* **11.** So as to detach or unearth: *pulling up weeds.* **12.** Apart; into pieces: *tore up the paper.* **13.** —Used as an intensive with certain verbs: *cleaning up.* —*adj.* **1.** Moving or directed upward: *an up elevator.* **2.** Being out of bed: *Are you up yet?* **3.** Actively functioning: *He's been up and around for a week.* **4.** *Informal.* Going on; happening: *What's up?* **5.** Being considered: *a contract up for renewal.* **6.** Finished; over: *Time's up!* **7.** *Informal.* Informed, esp. well-informed: *I'm not up on fashions.* **8.** Being ahead of an opponent: *up two games.* **9.** *Baseball.* At bat: *You're up!* —*prep.* **1.** Toward or at a point farther along: *up the road.* **2.** In a direction toward the source of: *up the Hudson.* —*v.* **upped, up·ping.** *Informal.* —*tr.v.* **1.** To increase and so improve or promote:·*he upped his chances for admission with a good interview.* **2.** To increase in amount: *up prices; up production.* **3.** To raise or lift. —*intr.v.* **1.** To get up; rise. **2.** *Informal.* To act suddenly or unexpectedly: *She just upped and left.* —*idioms.* **on the up and up.** Open and honest. **up against.** Confronted with; facing. **up to. 1.** Occupied with, esp. scheming or devising. **2.** *Informal.* Primed or prepared for: *Are you up to a game of tennis?* **3.** Dependent upon: *It's up to us.* [Middle English *up,* upward, and *uppe,* on high, from Old English *ūp* and *uppe.*]

up-. A prefix meaning: **1.** Up: *uplift.* **2.** Upper: *upmost.* **3.** Upward: *upsweep.* [Middle English, from Old English *ūp-, upp-,* upward, on high.]

up-and-com·ing (ŭp′ən-kŭm′ĭng) *adj.* Marked for future success; promising and enterprising.

up-and-down (ŭp′ən-doun′) *adj.* **1.** Consisting of alternating upward and downward movement; fluctuating. **2.** Vertical: *up-and-down stripes.*

U·pan·i·shad (ōō-păn′ĭ-shăd′) *n.* Any of a group of philosophical treatises contributing to the theology of ancient Hinduism, elaborating upon the earlier Vedas. [Sanskrit *upaniṣad,* "a sitting down near to," "secret session."]

u·pas (yōō′pəs) *n.* **1.** A tree, *Antiaris toxicaria,* of tropical Asia, that yields a juice used as an arrow poison. **2.** The poison obtained from this tree or similar trees or plants. [Javanese, poison, dart poison.]

up·beat (ŭp′bēt′) *n. Mus.* An unaccented beat, esp. the last beat of a measure. —*adj. Informal.* Optimistic; happy; cheerful.

up·braid (ŭp-brād′) *tr.v.* To reprove sharply; scold. —See Syns at **scold.** [Middle English *upbreyden,* from Old English *ūpbrēdan,* to throw up against, reproach : *ūp-,* up + *bregdan,* to move quickly, throw.] **—up·braid′er** *n.*

up·bring·ing (ŭp′brĭng′ĭng) *n.* The rearing and training received during childhood.

up·com·ing (ŭp′kŭm′ĭng) *adj.* Happening in the near future; anticipated; forthcoming.

up·coun·try (ŭp′kŭn′trē) *n.* The interior region of a country. —*adj.* (ŭp′kŭn′trē). Of, located, or coming from the upcountry. —*adv.* (ŭp-kŭn′trē). In, to, or toward the upcountry: *traveling upcountry.*

up·date (ŭp-dāt′) *tr.v.* **-dat·ed, -dat·ing.** To bring up to date: *update a textbook.* —*n.* (ŭp′dāt′). Information that brings facts up to date.

up·draft (ŭp′drăft′) *n.* A current of air that flows upward.

up·end (ŭp-ĕnd′) *tr.v.* **1.** To stand, set, or turn on one end. **2.** To overturn or overthrow. —*intr.v.* To be upended.

up·grade (ŭp′grād′, ŭp-grād′) *tr.v.* **-grad·ed, -grad·ing. 1.** To raise to a higher rank, position, grade, or standard. **2.** To improve the quality of (livestock) by selective breeding. —*n.* (ŭp′grād′). An upward incline. **—*idiom.* on the upgrade. 1.** Rising. **2.** Improving or progressing. **—up′grade′** *adv.*

up·growth (ŭp′grōth′) *n.* **1.** The process of growing upward. **2.** Upward growth or development.

up·heav·al (ŭp-hē′vəl) *n.* **1.** The process or an example of being heaved upward. **2.** A sudden and violent disturbance or change. **3.** *Geol.* A lifting up of the earth's crust.

up·heave (ŭp-hēv′) *v.* **-heaved, -heav·ing.** —*tr.v.* To heave upward; lift forcefully from beneath. —*intr.v.* To be lifted or thrust upward.

up·hill (ŭp′hĭl′) *adj.* **1.** Going up a hill or slope. **2.** Long, tedious, or difficult: *an uphill struggle to finish on time.* —*n.* (ŭp′hĭl′). An upward slope or incline. —*adv.* (ŭp′hĭl′). **1.** To or toward higher ground; upward. **2.** Against adversity; with difficulty.

up·hold (ŭp-hōld′) *tr.v.* **-held** (-hĕld′), **-hold·ing. 1.** To hold aloft; to raise. **2.** To prevent from falling or sinking; to support. **3.** To maintain in the face of a challenge. **—up·hold′er** *n.*

up·hol·ster (ŭp-hōl′stər) *tr.v.* To supply (furniture) with stuffing, springs, cushions, and a fabric covering. [Back-formation from UPHOLSTERER.]

up·hol·ster·er (ŭp-hōl′stər-ər) *n.* A person who upholsters furniture as an occupation. [From obs. *upholster,* a dealer in or repairer of small wares, from Middle English *upholdester,* one who upholds or repairs, from *upholden,* to uphold.]

up·hol·ster·y (ŭp-hōl′stər-ē, -hōl′strē) *n., pl.* **-ies. 1.** The fabrics and other materials used in upholstering. **2.** The craft or business of upholstering.

upholstery

up·keep (ŭp′kēp′) *n.* **1.** Maintenance in proper operation and repair. **2.** The cost of such maintenance.

up·land (ŭp′lənd, -lănd′) *n.* Often **uplands.** The higher parts of a region, country, etc. —*adj.* Of or located in an upland: *a little upland town.*

up·lift (ŭp-lĭft′) *tr.v.* **1.** To raise up or aloft; elevate. **2.** To raise to a higher social, moral, or intellectual level. **3.** To raise to spiritual or emotional heights; exalt. —See Syns at **raise.** —*n.* (ŭp′lĭft′). **1.** The act, process, or result of raising or lifting up. **2.** The process of raising to a higher social, moral, or intellectual level. **3.** Any agent or influence causing upward movement or lifting. **4.** *Geol.* An upheaval.

up·most (ŭp′mōst′) *adj.* Uppermost.

up·on (ə-pŏn′, ə-pôn′) *prep.* On. [Middle English.]
Usage: **upon, up on, on.** Both *upon* and *on* can indicate a position of rest or movement in a given position or toward a specified object. *On* primarily implies rest: *The pillow lies on* (or *upon*) *the bed. Upon* is stronger in indicating movement toward: *He jumped upon the platform.* When *up* functions adverbially and *on* as a preposition, the words are not joined: *climbed up on the roof.* Here *up* is, in effect, part of the verb, stressing elevation whereas *upon* would indicate only contact.

up·per (ŭp′ər) *adj.* **1.** Higher in place, position, or rank. **2. a.** Situated on higher ground. **b.** Lying farther inland. **c.** Northern. **3. Upper.** *Geol & Archaeol.* Being a later division of the period named. —*n.* **1.** That part of a shoe or boot above the sole. **2.** *Informal.* An upper berth. **3. uppers.** *Informal.* The upper teeth or a set of upper dentures. **4.** *Slang.* A drug, often an amphetamine, used as a stimulant.

upper case. Capital letters.

up·per-class (ŭp′ər-klăs) *adj.* **1.** Of or belonging to an upper social class. **2.** Of or belonging to the junior and senior classes in a school or college.

up·per·class·man (ŭp′ər-klăs′mən) *n.* A student in the junior or senior class of a secondary school or college.

upper crust. The highest social class or group.

up·per·cut (ŭp′ər-kŭt′) *n. Boxing.* A short swinging blow directed upward, as to the opponent's chin. —*tr.v.* **-cut, -cut·ting.** To punch with an uppercut.

upper hand. A position of control or advantage.

Upper House or **upper house.** The branch of a bicameral legislature that is smaller and less broadly representative of the population.

up·per·most (ŭp′ər-mōst′) *adj.* Highest in position, place, rank, etc.; topmost; foremost. —*adv.* In the first or highest place, position, or rank; first.

up·pi·ty (ŭp′ĭ-tē) *adj. Informal.* Snobbish or arrogant.

up·raise (ŭp-rāz′) *tr.v.* **-raised, -rais·ing.** To raise or lift up; elevate.

up·right (ŭp′rīt′) *adj.* **1.** In a vertical position, direction, or stance. **2.** Morally respectable; honorable. —See Syns at **vertical.** —*adv.* Vertically: *walk upright.* —*n.* **1.** A perpendicular position, place, or thing. **2.** Something standing upright, as a beam. **3.** An upright piano. [Middle English, from Old English *ūpriht.*] —**up′right′ly** *adv.* —**up′right′ness** *n.*

upright piano. A piano having the strings mounted vertically in a rectangular case with the keyboard at a right angle to the case. Also called **upright.**

up·rise (ŭp-rīz′) *intr.v.* **-rose** (-rōz′), **-ris·en** (-rĭz′ən), **-ris·ing. 1.** To get up or stand up; rise. **2.** To go, move, or incline upward; ascend. **3.** To rise into view, esp. from below the horizon. **4.** To increase in size; to swell. —*n.* (ŭp′rīz′). **1.** The act or process of rising up. **2.** An upward slope; ascent.

up·ris·ing (ŭp′rī′zĭng) *n.* A revolt; insurrection. —See Syns at **rebellion.**

up·roar (ŭp′rôr′, -rōr′) *n.* **1.** A condition of noisy excitement and confusion; a tumult. **2.** A heated controversy. [Alteration of Dutch *oproer*, from Middle Dutch : *op*, up + *roer*, motion.]

up·roar·i·ous (ŭp-rôr′ē-əs, -rōr′-) *adj.* **1.** Causing or accompanied by an uproar. **2.** Loud and full; boisterous. **3.** Causing hearty laughter; hilarious. —**up·roar′i·ous·ly** *adv.* —**up·roar′i·ous·ness** *n.*

up·root (ŭp-rōōt′, -rōot′) *tr.v.* **1.** To tear or remove from the ground. **2.** To destroy or remove completely; eradicate. **3.** To force to leave an accustomed or native location. —**up·root′er** *n.*

up·set (ŭp-sĕt′) *v.* **-set, -set·ting.** —*tr.v.* **1.** To overturn or capsize; tip over. **2.** To disturb the usual or normal functioning, order, or course of: *Nothing will upset our plans.* **3. a.** To distress or perturb mentally or emotionally. **b.** To distress physically. **4.** To defeat unexpectedly. **5.** To make shorter and thicker by hammering on the end; to swage. —*intr.v.* **1.** To become overturned; tip over. **2.** To become disturbed. —*n.* (ŭp′sĕt′). **1. a.** An act of upsetting. **b.** The condition of being upset. **2.** A disturbance, disorder, or agitation. **3.** A game or contest in which the favorite is defeated. **4.** A tool used for upsetting; a swage. —*adj.* (ŭp-sĕt′). **1.** Overturned; capsized. **2.** Mentally or emotionally disturbed. **3.** Thrown out of order, arrangement, etc. [Middle English *upsetten*, to set up, erect.] —**up·set′ter** *n.*

upset price. The lowest price at which merchandise or property will be auctioned or sold at public sale.

up·shot (ŭp′shŏt′) *n.* The final result; outcome.

up·side-down (ŭp′sīd-doun′) *adj.* **1.** Overturned completely so that the upper side is down. **2.** In great disorder or confusion. —*adv.* Also **upside down. 1.** With the upper and lower parts reversed in position. **2.** In or into great disorder. [Alteration of earlier *upsedown*, from Middle English *up so doun*, "up as if down."]

upside-down cake. A cake baked with fruit at the bottom, then served with the fruit side up.

up·si·lon (ŭp′sə-lŏn′, yōōp′sə-) *n.* The 20th letter in the Greek alphabet, written Υ, υ. [Medieval Greek *u psilon*, "simple upsilon."]

up·stage (ŭp′stāj′) *adj.* **1.** Of the rear of a stage. **2.** *Informal.* Haughty; aloof. —*adv.* Toward, to, on, or at the back part of the stage. —*tr.v.* (ŭp-stāj′) **-staged, -stag·ing. 1.** To distract audience attention from (another actor). **2.** *Informal.* To force out of the center of attention. **3.** *Informal.* To treat haughtily.

up·stairs (ŭp′stârz′) *adv.* **1.** Up the stairs: *ran upstairs.* **2.** To or on an upper floor: *Look upstairs for your coat.* —*adj.* (ŭp′stârz′). Of an upper floor or floors. —*n.* (ŭp′stârz′). *(used with a sing. verb).* The upper floor or story of a building.

up·stand·ing (ŭp-stăn′dĭng, ŭp′stăn′-) *adj.* **1.** Standing erect or upright. **2.** Morally upright; honest.

up·start (ŭp′stärt′) *n.* **1.** A person of humble origin who has suddenly risen to wealth or high position, esp. one who becomes snobbish or arrogant because of success. **2.** A person who has an exaggerated sense of his own importance or ability. —*adj.* **1.** Suddenly raised to a position of consequence. **2.** Self-important; presumptuous. —*intr.v.* (ŭp-stärt′). To spring or start up suddenly.

up·state (ŭp′stāt′) *adj.* At, toward, or to that part of a state lying inland or farther north of a large city. —*adj.* Of, located in, or designating that part of a state lying inland or farther north of a large city. —*n.* The upstate region. —**up′stat′er** *n.*

up·stream (ŭp′strēm′) *adv.* In, at, or toward the source of a stream or current. —**up′stream′** *adj.*

up·surge (ŭp′sûrj′) *n.* A rapid upward swell or rise.

up·sweep (ŭp'swēp') *n.* A curve or sweep upward. —*tr.v.* **-swept** (-swĕpt'), **-sweep·ing.** To brush, curve, or sweep upward.

up·swing (ŭp'swĭng') *n.* **1.** An upward swing. **2.** An upward trend; an increase as in movement or activity.

up·take (ŭp'tāk') *n.* **1.** A passage for drawing up smoke or air; a flue or ventilating shaft. **2.** *Informal.* Understanding; comprehension: *very quick on the uptake.*

up·tight (ŭp'tīt') *adj.* Also **up tight.** *Slang.* **1.** Very tense or nervous: *an uptight person.* **2.** Conforming rigidly to convention. —See Syns at **edgy.**

up-to-date (ŭp'tə-dāt') *adj.* Reflecting or informed of the latest improvements, facts, style, etc.; modern.

up·town (ŭp'toun') *adv.* In or toward the upper part of a town or city. —*adj.* Of or located in the upper part of a town or city: *an uptown store.* —*n.* The upper part of a town or city.

up·turn (ŭp'tûrn') *n.* An upward movement, curve, or trend: *an upturn in business.* —*tr.v.* (*also* ŭp-tûrn'). **1.** To turn up or over, as soil. **2.** To upset; overturn. **3.** To direct upward. —*intr.v.* To turn over or up.

up·ward (ŭp'wərd) *adv.* Also **up·wards** (-wərdz). **1.** In, to, or toward a higher place, level, or position. **2.** To or toward the source, origin, or interior. **3.** Toward the head or upper parts. **4.** Toward a higher amount, degree, or rank: *Prices soared upward.* **5.** Toward a later time or greater age. **6.** Toward something greater or better. —*adj.* Moving to a higher place, level, or position. —*idiom.* **upward (or upwards) of.** More than; in excess of. [Middle English, Old English *ūpweard.*] —**up'ward·ly** *adv.*

up·wind (ŭp'wĭnd') *adv.* In or toward the direction from which the wind blows. —**up'wind'** *adj.*

ur-. Var. of **uro-.**

u·ra·cil (yoŏr'ə-sĭl) *n.* A nitrogenous pyrimidine base, $C_4H_4N_2O_2$, that is one of four bases constituting ribonucleic acids. [UR(O)- + AC(ETIC) + -IL(E).]

U·ral·ic (yoŏ-răl'ĭk) *n.* Also **U·ra·li·an** (-rā'lē-ən, -răl'ē-ən). A family of languages including the Finno-Ugric and Samoyed languages. —*adj.* Of or designating this language family.

U·ra·ni·a (yoŏ-rā'nē-ə, -rān'yə) *n. Gk. Myth.* The Muse of astronomy.

Urania
Holding a sphere

u·ra·ni·nite (yoŏ-rā'nə-nīt') *n.* A complex brownish-black mineral, chiefly UO_2 partially oxidized to UO_3 and containing variable amounts of radium, lead, thorium, rare-earth metals, helium, argon, and nitrogen. [From German *Uranin,* uraninite.]

u·ra·ni·um (yoŏ-rā'nē-əm) *n. Symbol* **U** A heavy silvery-white metallic element, radioactive, easily oxidized, that has 14 known isotopes of which U 238 is the most abundant in nature, and occurs in several minerals, including pitchblende and carnotite, from which it is extracted and processed for use in research, nuclear fuels, and nuclear weapons. Atomic number 92; atomic weight 238.03; melting point 1,132°C; boiling point 3,818°C; specific gravity 18.95; valences 3, 4, 5, 6. See **element.** [After the planet URANUS.]

uranium 235. The isotope of uranium that has a mass number of 235 and a half-life of 713 million years, is fissionable with slow neutrons, and is capable in a critical mass of sustaining a chain reaction that can proceed explosively with appropriate mechanical arrangements.

uranium 238. The most common isotope of uranium, with a mass number of 238 and a half-life of 4.51 billion years, that is nonfissionable but can be irradiated with neutrons to produce fissionable plutonium 239.

U·ra·nus (yoŏr'ə-nəs, yoŏ-rā'nəs) *n. Gk. Myth.* **1.** The earliest supreme god, a personification of the sky, who was the son and consort of Gaea and the father of the Cyclopes and Titans. **2.** The seventh planet of the solar system in order of increasing distance from the sun. Its diameter is about 29,000 miles, its average distance from the sun is about 1,790 million miles, and it takes about 84 years to complete an orbit of the sun.

u·rate (yoŏr'āt') *n.* A salt of uric acid. [UR(IC ACID) + -ATE.]

ur·ban (ûr'bən) *adj.* **1.** Of, located in, or constituting a city. **2.** Characteristic of the city or city life: *urban problems.* [Latin *urbānus,* from *urbs,* city.]

ur·bane (ûr·bān') *adj.* Having or showing the refined manners of polite society; suave. —See Syns at **refined.** [French *urbaine,* from Latin *urbānus,* urban.] —**ur'bane'ly** *adv.*

ur·ban·ite (ûr'bə-nīt') *n.* A city dweller.

ur·ban·i·ty (ûr-băn'ĭ-tē) *n., pl.* **-ties. 1.** Refinement and elegance of manner; polished courtesy. **2. urbanities.** Courtesies; civilities.

ur·ban·ize (ûr'bə-nīz') *tr.v.* **-ized, -iz·ing.** To make urban in nature or character. —**ur'ban·i·za'tion** *n.*

urban renewal. The state-sponsored reconstruction of slum neighborhoods.

ur·chin (ûr'chĭn) *n.* **1.** A small, mischievous child. **2.** A sea urchin. **3.** *Archaic.* A hedgehog. [Middle English *hirchon,* hedgehog, from Norman French *herichon,* from Latin *ērīcius,* from *ēr,* hedgehog.]

Ur·du (oŏr'doŏ, ûr'-) *n.* An Indic language that is the principal language of Pakistan and is widely used in India.

-ure. A suffix meaning: **1.** An act or process: *erasure.* **2.** A function, office, or a body performing a function: **legislature.** [Middle English, from Old French, from Latin *-ūra.*]

u·re·a (yoŏ-rē'ə) *n.* A white crystalline or powdery compound, $CO(NH_2)_2$, found in mammalian urine and other body fluids, synthesized from ammonia and carbon dioxide, and used as fertilizer, in animal feed, and in resins. [From French *urée,* from *urine,* urine.]

u·re·mi·a (yoŏ-rē'mē-ə) *n.* A condition usu. accompanying kidney disease and characterized by retention of nitrogenous urinary waste products and headache, nausea, vomiting, and coma. [UR(O)- + -EMIA.]

u·re·ter (yoŏ-rē'tər, yoŏr'ĭ-tər) *n.* Either of the long, narrow ducts that carry urine from the kidneys to the urinary bladder. [Greek *ourētēr,* from *ourein,* to urinate, from *ouron,* urine.]

u·re·thra (yoŏ-rē'thrə) *n., pl.* **-thras** or **thrae** (-thrē). The duct through which urine is discharged in most mammals and that serves as the male genital duct. [Late Latin *ūrēthra,* from Greek *ourēthra,* from *ourein,* to urinate, from *ouron,* urine.] —**u·re'thral** *adj.*

urge (ûrj) *tr.v.* **urged, urg·ing. 1.** To push, force, or drive forward or onward; impel; spur. **2.** To entreat earnestly and repeatedly; plead with; exhort. **3.** To advocate strongly the doing, consideration, or approval of; press emphatically: *urge passage of the bill.* **4.** To stimulate; excite: *"It urged him to an intensity like madness"* (D.H. Lawrence). —*n.* An irresistible or impelling force, influence, or desire. [Latin *urgēre,* to push, press.]

    Syns: urge, exhort, press, prod, prompt *v. Core meaning:* To impel to action (*urged the President to act with decisiveness*).

ur·gen·cy (ûr'jən-sē) *n., pl.* **-cies. 1.** The condition of being urgent; pressing importance. **2.** A pressing necessity: *dealing with the urgencies of daily life.*

ur·gent (ûr'jənt) *adj.* **1.** Requiring immediate action: *a crisis of an urgent nature.* **2.** Insistent or importunate; earnest: *urgent pleas for help.* **3.** Conveying a sense of pressing importance: *an urgent message.*

-urgy. A suffix meaning a technology: **metallurgy, zymurgy.** [From Greek *-ourgos,* worker, from *ergon,* work.]

u·ric (yoŏr'ĭk) *adj.* Pertaining to, contained in, or obtained from urine. [UR(O)- + -IC.]

uric acid. A white crystalline compound, $C_5H_4N_4O_3$, that is the end product of purine metabolism in man and other primates, birds, terrestrial reptiles, and most insects.

urin-. Var. of urino-.

u·ri·nal (yŏŏr'ə-nəl) *n.* **1. a.** An upright wall or floor fixture designed for men and boys to urinate into. **b.** A room or other place containing such a fixture. **2.** A receptacle for urine used by a bedridden patient. [Middle English, chamber pot, from Old French, from Late Latin *ūrīnal*, from *ūrīna*, urine.]

u·ri·nal·y·sis (yŏŏr'ə-năl'ĭ-sĭs) *n.* The chemical analysis of urine. [URIN(O)- + (AN)ALYSIS.]

u·ri·nar·y (yŏŏr'ə-něr'ē) *adj.* Of urine or its production, function, or excretion.

urinary bladder. A muscular membrane-lined sac located in the forward part of the lower abdomen and in which urine is stored until excreted.

u·ri·nate (yŏŏr'ə-nāt') *intr.v.* **-nat·ed, -nat·ing.** To discharge urine.

u·rine (yŏŏr'ĭn) *n.* A solution containing body wastes extracted from the blood by the kidneys, stored in the urinary bladder, and discharged from the body through the urethra. [Middle English, from Old French, from Latin *ūrīna*.]

urino- or **urin-.** A prefix meaning urine: **urinalysis, urinogenital.** [From Latin *ūrīna*, urine.]

urn (ûrn) *n.* **1.** A vase used to hold the ashes of a cremated body. **2.** A closed metal container with a spigot, used for making and serving tea or coffee; a samovar. [Middle English *urne*, burial urn, from Latin *urna*.]

urn

uro- or **ur-.** A prefix meaning urine or the urinary tract: **urogenital.** [From Greek *ouro-*, from *ouron*, urine.]

u·ro·gen·i·tal (yŏŏr'ō-jĕn'ĭ-tl) *adj.* Of or involving both the urinary and genital functions and organs.

u·rol·o·gy (yŏŏ-rŏl'ə-jē) *n.* The medical study of the physiology and pathology of the urogenital tract. **—u·rol'o·gist** *n.*

Ur·sa Major (ûr'sə). A constellation that contains the seven stars that comprise the Big Dipper. [Latin, "the greater bear."]

Ursa Minor. A constellation that contains the star Polaris and the stars that comprise the Little Dipper. [Latin, "the lesser bear."]

ur·sine (ûr'sīn') *adj.* Of or characteristic of a bear. [Latin *ursīnus*, from *ursus*, bear.]

us (ŭs) *pron.* The objective case of **we,** used: **1.** As the direct object of a verb: *The movie impressed us greatly.* **2.** As the indirect object of a verb: *His father gave us money.* **3.** As the object of a preposition: *Tom sent his regards to us.* —See Usage note at **we.** [Middle English, from Old English *ūs.*]

us·a·ble (yŏŏ'zə-bəl) *adj.* Also **use·a·ble.** **1.** Capable of being used: *usable waste.* **2.** In a fit condition for use; intact or operative. **—us'a·bil'i·ty** *n.* **—us'a·bly** *adv.*

us·age (yŏŏ'sĭj, -zĭj) *n.* **1.** The act or manner of using something; use or employment. **2.** The customary practice or usual way of doing something. **3. a.** The actual way in which language or its elements, such as words, phrases, grammatical constructions, etc., are used. **b.** A particular example of such use. [Middle English, from Old French, from *user*, to use.]

us·ance (yŏŏ'zəns) *n.* The length of time, established by custom, that is allowed for payment of a foreign bill of exchange. [Middle English *usaunce*, custom, usage, from Old French *usance.*]

use (yŏŏz) *v.* **used, us·ing.** *—tr.v.* **1.** To bring or put into service; employ. **2.** To make a habit of employing. **3.** To conduct oneself toward in treating or handling: *a peace-offering from someone who once used you unkindly.* **4.** *Informal.* To exploit for one's own advantage or gain: *He gave nothing to his friends; he merely used them.* **5.** To take or partake of, as tobacco or alcohol. *—intr.v.* —Used as an auxiliary verb in the past tense to express former practice, fact, or condition: *I used to go there often. He used to be very fat.* **—phrasal verb. use up.** To consume completely; finish all of. *—n.* (yŏŏs). **1.** The act of using; the application or employment of something for some purpose. **2.** The condition or fact of being used: *The telephone is in use now.* **3.** The manner of using; usage: *the proper use of power tools.* **4. a.** The permission to use or the privilege of using something: *have use of the car on Sundays.* **b.** The power or ability of using something: *lose the use of one arm.* **5.** The need or occasion to use or employ: *Do you have any use for this book?* **6.** The quality of being suitable or adaptable to an end; usefulness: *old equipment of no practical use.* **7.** The goal, object, or purpose for which something is used: *a tool with five different uses.* **8.** Accustomed or usual procedure; habitual practice; custom. **9.** *Law.* **a.** The enjoyment of property, as by occupying or exercising it. **b.** The benefit or profit of lands and tenements of which the legal title and possession are vested in another who holds them in trust for the beneficiary. **c.** The arrangement establishing the equitable right to such benefits and profits. **—idiom. used to.** Accustomed to: *We are not used to the cold.* [Middle English *usen,* from Old French *user,* ult. from Latin *ūtī,* to use.]

Usage: **use(d) to.** To express the meaning of regular practice or custom in past time, the verb *use* occurs in the inflected form *used,* or as *use* when coupled with *did.* For example: *He used to walk to work. He used not to ride* (or *did not use to ride*).

use·a·ble (yŏŏ'zə-bəl) *adj.* Var. of **usable.**

used (yŏŏzd) *adj.* Not new; secondhand: *a used car.*

use·ful (yŏŏs'fəl) *adj.* Capable of being used for some beneficial purpose. —See Syns at **convenient** and **practical.** **—use'ful·ly** *adv.* **—use'ful·ness** *n.*

use·less (yŏŏs'lĭs) *adj.* **1.** Of little or no worth. **2.** Producing no result or effect; vain. **—use'less·ly** *adv.* **—use'less·ness** *n.*

us·er (yŏŏ'zər) *n.* **1.** Someone or something that uses. **2.** *Slang.* A drug addict.

ush·er (ŭsh'ər) *n.* **1.** A person employed to escort people to their seats in a theater, stadium, etc. **2.** A member of a wedding party who escorts guests to their seats and accompanies the bridesmaids in the procession. **3.** A person who serves as official doorkeeper, as in a courtroom or legislative chamber. **4.** An official whose duty is to precede persons of rank in a procession, parade, etc. *—tr.v.* **1.** To serve as an usher to; to escort. **2.** To lead or conduct; cause to enter. **3.** To precede and introduce; serve as the beginning of: *a party to usher in the new year.* [Middle English, from Old French *ussier,* from Medieval Latin *ūstiārius,* var. of Latin *ōstiārius,* doorkeeper, from *ōstium,* entrance, from *ōs,* mouth.]

u·su·al (yŏŏ'zhŏŏ-əl) *adj.* **1.** Common; ordinary; normal: *the usual five o'clock traffic jams.* **2.** Habitual or customary: *It is usual for him to walk to work.* —See Syns at **ordinary.** [Middle English, from Old French, from Late Latin *ūsuālis,* ordinary, from Latin *ūsus,* use, custom, from *ūtī,* to use.] **—u'su·al·ly** *adv.* **—u'su·al·ness** *n.*

u·su·fruct (yŏŏ'zə-frŭkt', -sə-) *n. Law.* The right to utilize and enjoy the profits and advantages of something belonging to another so long as the property is not damaged or altered in any way. [From Latin *ūsusfrūctus,* use (and) enjoyment : *ūsus,* use + *frūctus,* enjoyment.]

u·su·rer (yŏŏ'zhər-ər) *n.* A person who lends money at an exorbitant or unlawful rate of interest. [Middle English, from Norman French, from Medieval Latin *ūsūrārius,* from Latin *ūsūra,* interest, usury.]

u·su·ri·ous (yŏŏ-zhŏŏr'ē-əs) *adj.* **1.** Practicing usury. **2.** Of, pertaining to, or constituting usury. **—u·su'ri·ous·ly** *adv.* **—u·su'ri·ous·ness** *n.*

u·surp (yōo-sûrp′, -zûrp′) *tr.v.* To seize and hold, as the possessions, power, position, or rights of another, by force and without legal right or authority. [Middle English *usurpen*, from Old French *usurper*, from Latin *ūsūrpāre*, to take into use.] —**u′sur·pa′tion** *n.* —**u·surp′er** *n.*

u·su·ry (yōo′zhə-rē) *n., pl.* **-ries. 1.** The act or practice of lending money at an exorbitant or illegal rate of interest. **2.** Such an excessive rate of interest. [Middle English, from Medieval Latin *ūsūria*, from Latin *ūsūra*, use of money lent, interest, from *ūsus*, use..]

Ute (yōot) *n., pl.* **Ute** or **Utes. 1.** A tribe of Uto-Aztecan-speaking North American Indians formerly inhabiting Utah, Colorado, and New Mexico. **2.** A member of this tribe. **3.** The language of the Utes.

u·ten·sil (yōo-tĕn′səl) *n.* **1.** Any instrument or container, esp. one used in a household. **2.** Any instrument or tool; implement. [Middle English *utensele*, from Old French *utensile*, from Latin *ūtēnsilia*, things for use, from *ūtēnsilis*, fit for use, from *ūtī*, to use.]

u·ter·ine (yōo′tər-ĭn, -tə-rīn′) *adj.* **1.** Of or pertaining to the uterus. **2.** Having the same mother but different fathers: *uterine brothers.*

u·ter·us (yōo′tər-əs) *n.* **1.** A hollow, muscular organ of female mammals, in which a fertilized egg develops and from which the fully formed young emerges during the process of birth; the womb. **2.** A similar part of the female reproductive tract in many invertebrates, serving as a repository for the storage or development of eggs or embryos. [Latin.]

U·ther Pen·drag·on (yōo′thər pĕn-drăg′ən). A legendary king of Britain and father of King Arthur.

u·tile (yōo′tl, yōo′tīl′) *adj.* Useful. [Middle English *utyle*, from Old French *utile*, from Latin *ūtilis*.]

u·til·i·tar·i·an (yōo-tĭl′ĭ-târ′ē-ən) *adj.* **1.** Of or associated with utility. **2.** Stressing the value of practical over aesthetic qualities. **3.** Intended or made for the purposes of utility: *a utilitarian pair of shoes.* **4.** Believing in or advocating utility. —See Syns at **practical.** —*n.* A person who advocates utilitarianism.

u·til·i·tar·i·an·ism (yōo-tĭl′ĭ-târ′ē-ə-nĭz′əm) *n.* **1.** The philosophical doctrine that considers utility as the criterion of action and the useful as good or worthwhile. **2.** The ethical theory proposed by Jeremy Bentham and John Stuart Mill that all moral, social, or political action should be directed toward achieving the greatest good for the greatest number of people.

u·til·i·ty (yōo-tĭl′ĭ-tē) *n., pl.* **-ties. 1.** The condition or quality of being useful; usefulness. **2.** A useful article or device. **3.** A public service, such as gas, electricity, water, etc. **4. utilities.** Shares of stock in a public service company. **5.** In utilitarianism, the principle of the greatest good for the greatest number. —*modifier: a utility knife; a utility ball player; a utility kitchen.* [Middle English *utilite*, usefulness, from Old French, from Latin *ūtilitās*, from *ūtilis*, useful, from *ūtī*, to use.]

u·til·ize (yōot′l-īz′) *tr.v.* **-ized, -iz·ing.** To put to use for a certain purpose: *utililizing the stream for water power.* [French *utiliser*, from Italian *utilizzare*, from *utile*, useful, from Latin *ūtilis*.] —**u′til·iz′a·ble** *adj.* —**u′til·iz′er** *n.*

ut·most (ŭt′mōst′) *adj.* **1.** Being or situated at the farthest limit or point; most extreme: *the utmost borders of the kingdom.* **2.** Of the highest or greatest degree, amount, intensity, etc.: *a matter of the utmost importance.* —*n.* The greatest possible degree, amount, or extent; maximum: *They worked to their utmost.* [Middle English, from Old English *ūt(e)mest*, outermost.]

U·to-Az·tec·an (yōo′tō-ăz′tĕk′ən) *n.* **1.** A large language family of North and Central America that includes Ute, Shoshone, Nahuatl, and other languages. **2. a.** A tribe speaking a Uto-Aztecan language. **b.** A member of such a tribe. —**U′to-Az′tec′an** *adj.*

u·to·pi·a (yōo-tō′pē-ə) *n.* **1.** Often **Utopia.** Any condition, place, or situation of social or political perfection. **2.** Any idealistic goal. [From *Utopia,* an imaginary ideal land in *Utopia* (1516), by Sir Thomas More : Greek *ou,* no + *topos,* place.] —**u·to′pi·an** *adj. & n.*

u·to·pi·an·ism (yōo-tō′pē-ə-nĭz′əm) *n.* Often **Utopianism. 1.** The ideals or principles of a utopian; idealistic and impractical social theory. **2.** The 19th cent. attempts to establish societies based on utopian ideas.

u·tri·cle (yōo′trĭ-kəl) *n.* Also **u·tric·u·lus** (yōo-trĭk′yə-ləs) *pl.* **-li** (-lī′). A small, delicate membranous sac that connects with the semicircular canals of the inner ear and functions in the maintenance of bodily equilibrium and coordination. [French *utricule,* from Latin *ūtriculus,* dim. of *uter,* leather bag.]

ut·ter¹ (ŭt′ər) *tr.v.* **1.** To pronounce; speak. **2.** To give forth as sound: *utter a sigh.* **3. a.** To put (counterfeit money or a forgery) into circulation. **b.** To deliver (something counterfeit) to another. [Middle English *utteren,* from Middle Dutch *ūteren,* to drive away, announce, speak.] —**ut′ter·a·ble** *adj.* —**ut′ter·er** *n.*

ut·ter² (ŭt′ər) *adj.* Complete; absolute: *utter nonsense.* [Middle English, from Old English *ūtera,* outer, external.]

Syns: utter, all-out, arrant, complete, consummate, flat, out-and-out, outright, positive (*Informal*), **pure, sheer, thorough, total, unmitigated, unqualified** *adj. Core meaning:* Completely such, without qualification or exception (*an utter fool; utter chaos; had utter confidence in them*).

ut·ter·ance (ŭt′ər-əns) *n.* **1. a.** The act of uttering or expressing vocally. **b.** The power of speaking. **2.** Something that is uttered. —See Syns at **speech.**

ut·ter·ly (ŭt′ər-lē) *adv.* Completely; absolutely; entirely.

ut·ter·most (ŭt′ər-mōst′) *adj.* **1.** Utmost. **2.** Outermost. —*n.* Utmost.

U-turn (yōo′tûrn′) *n.* A turn, as by a vehicle, completely reversing the direction of travel.

u·vu·la (yōo′vyə-lə) *n.* The small, conical, fleshy mass of tissue suspended from the center of the soft palate above the back of the tongue. [Middle English, from Late Latin *ūvula,* small grape (from its shape), dim. of Latin *ūva,* a grape.]

u·vu·lar (yōo′vyə-lər) *adj.* **1.** Of or associated with the uvula. **2.** *Phonet.* Articulated by vibration of the uvula or with the back of the tongue near the uvula.

ux·o·ri·al (ŭk-sôr′ē-əl, -sōr′-, ŭg-zôr′-, -zōr′-) *adj.* Pertaining to, characteristic of, or befitting a wife. [From Latin *uxōrius,* of a wife, uxorious.]

ux·o·ri·ous (ŭk-sôr′ē-əs, -sōr′-, ŭg-zôr′-, -zōr′-) *adj.* Excessively or irrationally submissive or devoted to one's wife. [Latin *uxōrius,* from *uxor,* wife.] —**ux·o′ri·ous·ly** *adv.* —**ux·o′ri·ous·ness** *n.*

Phoenician – *About 3,000 years ago the Phoenicians and other Semitic peoples began to use graphic signs to represent individual speech sounds instead of syllables or whole words. They used this symbol, which is the ancestor of the letters F, U, W, and Y as well as V, to represent the sound of the semivowel "w" and gave it the name wāw, the Phoenician word for "hook."*

Greek – *The Greeks borrowed the Phoenician alphabet with some modifications. They changed the shape of wāw slightly and altered its name to upsilon. They used upsilon to represent the sound of the vowel "u."*

Roman – *The Romans borrowed the alphabet from the Greeks via the Etruscans, who used a tailless variant of upsilon. The Romans used upsilon to represent both the vowel "u" and the semivowel "w," which later developed into the consonant "v," and they adapted the shape for carving*

Latin in stone. This monumental script, as it is called, became the basis for both the lower- and upper-case modern printed letter V.

Medieval – *By medieval times – around 1,200 years ago – the Roman monumental capitals had become adapted to being relatively quickly written on paper, parchment, or vellum. Although the cursive alphabet had both tailless and tailed variants of V, they were distinguished not by phonetic value but by position within a word.*

Modern – *Even after the invention of printing about 500 years ago, V and U were considered different forms of the same letter. It was only during the 17th century that the distinction between them became complete and they were assigned the phonetic values that they have today. It was not until the early 19th century, however, that their position in the alphabet was fixed.*

---

v, V (vē) *n., pl.* **v's** or **vs, V's** or **Vs.** The 22nd letter of the English alphabet.

va·can·cy (vā′kən-sē) *n., pl.* **-cies. 1.** The condition of being vacant; emptiness. **2.** An empty or unoccupied space; a gap. **3.** A position, office, or living space that is unfilled or unoccupied. **4.** Emptiness of mind; blankness.

va·cant (vā′kənt) *adj.* **1.** Containing nothing; unoccupied; empty. **2.** Lacking intelligence or knowledge: *a vacant mind.* **3.** Unfilled by activity; idle: *vacant hours.* —See Syns at **empty.** [Middle English, from Old French, from Latin *vacāns,* pres. part. of *vacāre,* to be empty.] —**va′cant·ly** *adv.* —**va′cant·ness** *n.*

va·cate (vā′kāt′) *tr.v.* **-cat·ed, -cat·ing. 1.** To make vacant: *vacate a house.* **2.** *Law.* To make void; annul. [From Latin *vacāre,* to be empty.]

va·ca·tion (vā-kā′shən) *n.* **1.** A period of time devoted to rest or relaxation, as from work or study. **2.** An act or instance of vacating. —*intr.v.* To take or spend a vacation: *We vacationed in Florida.* —**va·ca′tion·er** *n.*

vac·ci·nate (văk′sə-nāt′) *tr.v.* **-nat·ed, -nat·ing.** To inoculate with a vaccine in order to give immunity against an infectious disease.

vac·ci·na·tion (văk′sə-nā′shən) *n.* **1.** The act of vaccinating. **2.** A scar left on the skin by vaccinating.

vac·cine (văk-sēn′) *n.* A suspension of weakened or killed viruses or bacteria used to vaccinate. [French *(virus) vaccine,* (virus) of cowpox, from Latin *vaccīnus,* pertaining to cows, from *vacca,* cow.]

vac·il·late (văs′ə-lāt′) *intr.v.* **-lat·ed, -lat·ing. 1.** To sway from one side to the other; fluctuate. **2.** To waver indecisively between one course of action or opinion and another. —See Syns at **hesitate.** [From Latin *vacillāre,* to waver.] —**vac′il·la′tion** *n.* —**vac′il·la′tor** (-lā′tər) *n.*

va·cu·i·ty (va-kyōō′ĭ-tē) *n.* **1.** The condition of being vacuous. **2.** An empty space. **3.** Emptiness of mind. **4.** Something, as a remark, that is vacuous.

vac·u·ole (văk′yōō-ōl′) *n.* Any small, usu. fluid-filled cavity in the protoplasm of a cell. [French, "little vacuum."]

vac·u·ous (văk′yōō-əs) *adj.* **1.** Empty. **2.** Showing a lack of intelligence; stupid. **3.** Not meaningfully occupied or employed; idle. [Latin *vacuus.*] —**vac′u·ous·ly** *adv.* —**vac′u·ous·ness** *n.*

vac·u·um (văk′yōō-əm, -yōōm) *n., pl.* **-ums** or **-u·a** (văk′-yōō-ə). **1. a.** A space totally empty of matter. **b.** A space relatively empty of matter, esp. one in which matter has been artificially removed. **2.** A condition or feeling of emptiness; a void. **3.** A condition of isolation from external influences. **4.** *Pl.* **-ums.** A vacuum cleaner. —*tr.v.* To clean with a vacuum cleaner. [Latin, neut. of *vacuus,* empty, from *vacāre,* to be empty.]

vacuum cleaner. An electrical appliance that cleans surfaces by means of suction.

vac·u·um-packed (văk′yōō-əm-păkt′, -yōōm-) *adj.* Packed in a container with little or no air.

vacuum tube. An electron tube that has an internal vacuum sufficiently high to permit electrons to move with little likelihood of striking any remaining gas molecules.

va·de me·cum (vā′dē mē′kəm) *pl.* **vade mecums. 1.** A useful thing that is usu. carried about by a person. **2.** A ready reference book, such as a manual. [Latin, "go with me."]

vag·a·bond (văg′ə-bŏnd′) *n.* **1.** A person without a permanent home who moves from place to place; wanderer. **2.** A tramp. —*adj.* Of, relating to, or characteristic of a vagabond. [Middle English *vagabound,* from Old French *vagabond,* from Latin *vagābundus,* wandering, from *vagārī,* to wander, from *vagus,* wandering.] —**vag′a·bond′age** *n.*

va·gar·y (vā′gə-rē, və-gâr′ē) *n., pl.* **-ies.** A capricious or erratic notion or action. [From Latin *vagārī,* to wander, from *vagus,* wandering.]

va·gi·na (və-jī′nə) *n., pl.* **-nas** or **-nae** (-nē). **1.** *Anat.* The passage leading from the external genital orifice to the uterus in female mammals. **2.** *Biol.* A sheathlike structure or part, esp. one formed by the base of a leaf. [Latin *vāgīna,* sheath.] —**vag′i·nal** *adj.*

va·gran·cy (vā′grən-sē) *n., pl.* **-cies. 1.** The condition, quality, or offense of being a vagrant. **2.** A wandering in mind or thought.

va·grant (vā′grənt) *n.* **1.** A person who wanders from place to place without a permanent home or livelihood; a tramp; vagabond. **2.** A wanderer; rover. **3.** *Law.* A person, such as a drunkard, who constitutes a public nuisance. —*adj.* **1.** Wandering from place to place. **2.** Wayward; random: *vagrant thoughts.* [Middle English *vagaraunt,* from Norman French, prob. from Latin *vagārī,* to wander, from *vagus,* wandering.] —**va′grant·ly** *adv.*

vague (vāg) *adj.* **vagu·er, vagu·est. 1.** Not clearly expressed

or stated: *vague instructions.* **2.** Not thinking or expressing oneself clearly: *She was vague about her future.* **3.** Lacking definite shape, form, or character: *the vague outline of a ship on the horizon.* **4.** Imprecise in meaning. **5.** Indistinctly perceived, understood, or recalled: *a vague uneasiness: a vague memory.* [Old French, from Latin *vagus*, wandering, undecided, vague.] **—vague′ly** *adv.* **—vague′ness** *n.*
   Syns: **vague, cloudy, foggy, fuzzy, hazy, indefinite, indistinct, misty, unclear** *adj. Core meaning:* Not clearly perceived or perceptible (*a vague reflection of headlights in the smog; a vague recollection of the incident*).

va·gus (vā′gəs) *n., pl.* **-gi** (-gī′). The longest of the cranial nerves, passing through the neck and thorax into the abdomen and supplying motor and secretory impulses to the abdominal and thoracic viscera. Also called **vagus nerve.** [New Latin *vagus (nervus),* "wandering (nerve)," from Latin *vagus,* wandering.]

vain (vān) *adj.* **-er, -est. 1.** Not successful; futile: *a vain attempt.* **2.** Lacking substance or worth; hollow: *vain talk.* **3.** Overly proud of one's appearance or accomplishments; conceited. **—idiom. in vain. 1.** To no avail; without success. **2.** In an irreverent or disrespectful manner: *take the name of the Lord in vain.* [Middle English, from Old French, from Latin *vānus,* empty.] **—vain′ly** *adv.* **—vain′ness** *n.*

vain·glo·ri·ous (vān-glôr′ē-əs, -glōr′ē-əs) *adj.* Characterized by or showing vainglory. **—vain·glo′ri·ous·ly** *adv.* **—vain·glo′ri·ous·ness** *n.*

vain·glo·ry (vān′glôr′ē, -glōr′ē) *n., pl.* **-ries. 1.** Excessive pride and vanity. **2.** Vain and ostentatious display. [Middle English *vein glory,* from Old French *vaine glorie,* from Latin *vānus glōria,* "empty pride."]

val·ance (văl′əns) *n.* **1.** A short ornamental drapery hung along the top edge, as of a window, shelf, or canopy. **2.** A decorative board or metal strip mounted esp. across the top of a window to conceal structural fixtures. [Middle English *valaunce,* perh. after *Valence,* town in France.]

valance

vale (vāl) *n.* A valley; dale. [Middle English, from Old French *val,* from Latin *vallēs.*]

val·e·dic·tion (văl′ə-dĭk′shən) *n.* An act or expression of leave-taking. [From Latin *valedīcere,* to say farewell : *valē,* farewell + *dīcere,* to say.]

val·e·dic·to·ri·an (văl′ə-dĭk-tôr′ē-ən, -tōr′ē-ən) *n.* A student, usu. ranking highest in the graduating class, who delivers the farewell address at commencement.

val·e·dic·to·ry (văl′ə-dĭk′tə-rē) *n.* A farewell address esp. at a commencement exercise. **—adj.** Having to do with or expressing a farewell: *a valedictory oration.*

va·lence (vā′ləns) *n.* **1.** *Chem.* The capacity of an atom or group of atoms to combine in specific proportions with other atoms or groups of atoms. **2.** An integer used to represent the combinatorial capacity of an atom or group in terms of an arbitrary assignment of 1 to an atom or group capable of forming a single bond with chlorine and of -1 to an atom or group capable of forming a single bond with hydrogen. [Late Latin *valentia,* strength, capacity, from Latin *valēns,* pres. part. of *valēre,* to be strong.]

-valent. A suffix meaning having a specified valence or valences: **polyvalent.** [From VALENCE.]

val·en·tine (văl′ən-tīn′) *n.* **1.** A usu. sentimental card sent to a lover or friend on Saint Valentine's Day. **2.** A person singled out as one's sweetheart on Saint Valentine's Day. **Valentine's Day** or **Valentines Day.** *Saint Valentine's Day.*

va·le·ri·an (və-lîr′ē-ən) *n.* **1.** Any of various plants of the genus *Valeriana,* esp. *V. officinalis,* with dense clusters of small white or pinkish flowers. **2.** The dried roots of *V. officinalis,* used medicinally as a sedative. [Middle English, from Old French *valeriane,* from Medieval Latin *valeriāna,* from Latin *Valeriānus,* of Valeria, a Roman province.]

val·et (văl′ĭt, vă-lā′) *n.* A male attendant who cares for a man's clothing and performs personal services. [French, from Old French *vaslet, varlet,* young nobleman, squire.]

val·e·tu·di·nar·i·an (văl′ə-tōōd′n-âr′ē-ən, văl′ə-tyōōd′-) *n.* A sickly person, esp. one constantly concerned with his health. [Latin *valētūdinārius,* in poor health, from *valētūdō,* state of health, from *valēre,* to be strong.]

Val·hal·la (văl-hăl′ə) *n. Norse Myth.* The great hall of immortality to which the Valkyries conduct warriors slain heroically in battle.

val·iant (văl′yənt) *adj.* Possessing, showing, or acting with valor; courageous. **—See Syns at brave.** [Middle English *valiaunt,* from Norman French, from Latin *valēns,* pres. part. of *valēre,* to be strong.] **—val′iant·ly** *adv.* **—val′iant·ness** *n.*

val·id (văl′ĭd) *adj.* **1.** Well-grounded on evidence or fact; sound: *a valid objection.* **2.** Legally sound: *a valid passport.* [French *valide,* from Old French, from Latin *validus,* strong, effective, from *valēre,* to be strong.] **—va·lid′i·ty** (və-lĭd′ə-tē) or **va·lid·ness** *n.* **—val′id·ly** *adv.*
   Syns: **valid, cogent, solid, sound** *adj. Core meaning:* Based on good judgment, reasoning, or evidence (*a valid argument*).

val·i·date (văl′ə-dāt′) *tr.v.* **-dat·ed, -dat·ing. 1.** To make valid. **2.** To substantiate; verify: *Experiments validated her theory.* **—See Syns at prove.** **—val′i·da′tion** *n.*

Val·kyr·ie (văl-kîr′ē, -kī′rē, văl′kîr′ē, -kī′rē) *n. Norse Myth.* One of the handmaidens of Odin who conduct the souls of slain heroes to Valhalla.

val·ley (văl′ē) *n., pl.* **-leys. 1.** A long, narrow lowland between ranges of mountains or hills. **2.** A depression or hollow. **3.** A place where two slopes of a roof meet and form a drainage channel. [Middle English *valey,* from Norman French, from Latin *vallēs.*]

val·or (văl′ər) *n.* Also *Brit.* **val·our.** Courage and boldness in battle. [Middle English *valour,* worth, from Old French, from Latin *valor,* from *valēre,* to be strong.]

val·or·ous (văl′ər-əs) *adj.* Having or marked by valor. **—See Syns at brave.** **—val′or·ous·ly** *adv.* **—val′or·ous·ness** *n.*

val·our (văl′ər) *n. Brit.* Var. of **valor.**

val·u·a·ble (văl′yōō-ə-bəl, văl′yə-) *adj.* **1.** Having high monetary or material value. **2.** Of great importance, use, or service: *valuable information.* **—n.** Often **valuables.** A valuable personal possession, such as a piece of jewelry. **—val′u·a·ble·ness** *n.* **—val′u·a·bly** *adv.*
   Syns: **valuable, invaluable, precious, priceless,** *adj. Core meaning:* Of great value (*a valuable antique*).

val·u·ate (văl′yōō-āt′) *tr.v.* **-at·ed, -at·ing.** To put a value on; appraise. **—val′u·a′tor** *n.*

val·u·a·tion (văl′yōō-ā′shən) *n.* **1.** The act or process of assessing the value or price of something; appraisal. **2.** The assessed or estimated value. **3.** An estimation of the worth, merit, or character of something.

val·ue (văl′yōō) *n.* **1.** A fair equivalent or return for something, as goods or services. **2.** Monetary or material worth: *the rising value of gold.* **3.** Worth as measured in usefulness or importance: *the value of an education.* **4.** A principle, standard, or quality considered inherently worthwhile or desirable: *traditional values.* **5.** Precise meaning, as of a word. **6.** *Math.* An assigned or calculated numerical quantity. **7.** *Mus.* The relative duration of a tone or rest. **8.** The relative darkness or lightness of a color. **9.** *Phonet.* The sound quality of a graphic unit, as a letter. **—tr.v.** **-ued, -u·ing. 1.** To determine or estimate the monetary worth or value of; appraise: *value an antique.* **2.** To regard highly; to esteem: *value someone's opinion.* **3.** To rate according to relative worth or desirability; evaluate: *valued love above money.* **—See Syns at appreciate.** [Middle English, from Old French, from *valoir,* to be worth, from Latin *valēre,* to be strong, be of value.] **—val′u·er** *n.*

val·ued (văl′yōōd) *adj.* Highly regarded; much esteemed.

val·ue·less (văl′yōō-lĭs) *adj.* Having no value; worthless.

valve (vălv) *n.* **1.** *Anat.* A membranous structure in a hollow organ or passage, such as an artery or vein, that slows or prevents the backward flow of a bodily fluid. **2. a.** A mechanical device that regulates the flow of gases, liquids, or loose materials through a channel by blocking and uncovering openings. **b.** The movable control element of such a device. **c.** *Mus.* A device in a brass wind instrument that permits change in pitch by a rapid varying of the air column in a tube. **3.** *Biol.* One of the paired, hinged shells of many mollusks and of brachiopods. **4.** *Bot.* One of the sections into which a seed pod splits. [Middle English, leaf of a door, from Latin *valva*.] —**valved** *adj.*

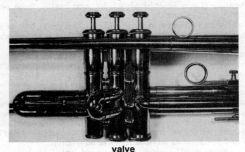

valve

val·vu·lar (văl′vyə-lər) *adj.* Of, pertaining to, having, or operating by means of valves or valvelike parts.

va·moose (vă-mōōs′, və-) *intr.v.* **-moosed, -moos·ing.** *Slang.* To leave hastily. [Spanish *vamos*, "let's go," from Latin *vādāmus*, from *vādere*, to go.]

vamp[1] (vămp) *n.* The upper front part of a boot or shoe covering the instep and often the toes. —*tr.v.* **1.** To provide (a shoe) with a new vamp. **2.** To patch up. **3.** To fabricate; improvise: *vamp up an alibi.* [Middle English *vampe*, from Old French *avantpie* : *avant*, before + *pie(d)*, foot, from Latin *pēs*.]

vamp[2] (vămp) *n.* *Informal.* A usu. unscrupulous woman who seduces and exploits men. —*intr.v.* *Informal.* To seduce or exploit (a man) in the manner of a vamp. [Short for VAMPIRE.]

vam·pire (văm′pīr′) *n.* **1.** In folklore, a corpse that rises from the grave at night to suck the blood of sleeping persons. **2.** A person who preys on others. **3.** Any of various tropical American bats of the family Desmodontidae, that feed on the blood of living mammals. Also called **vampire bat.** [French, from German *Vampir*, from Hungarian *vampir*.] —**vam′pir·ism** *n.*

van[1] (văn) *n.* **1.** A large covered truck or wagon for transporting goods or livestock. **2.** *Brit.* A closed railroad car for carrying baggage or freight. [Short for CARAVAN.]

van[2] (văn) *n.* The vanguard. [Short for VANGUARD.]

va·na·di·um (və-nā′dē-əm) *n.* *Symbol* **V** A ductile metallic element found in several minerals, notably vanadinite and carnotite, used as a carbon stabilizer in some steels, as a titanium-steel bonding agent, and as a catalyst. Atomic number 23; atomic weight 50.942; melting point 1,890°C; boiling point 3,000°C; specific gravity 6.11; valences 2, 3, 4, 5. [From Old Norse *Vanadís*, a name of the goddess Freya.]

Van Allen belt. Either of two zones of high-intensity particulate radiation trapped in the earth's magnetic field and surrounding the planet at various high altitudes. [After James A. *Van Allen* (b. 1914), American physicist.]

van·dal (vănd′l) *n.* **1.** A person who willfully or maliciously defaces or destroys public or private property. **2. Vandal.** A member of a Germanic people who overran Gaul, Spain, Northern Africa, and Rome in the fourth and fifth cent. A.D. —*adj.* Willfully or maliciously destructive.

van·dal·ism (vănd′l-ĭz′əm) *n.* The willful or malicious destruction of public or private property.

van·dal·ize (vănd′l-īz′) *tr.v.* **-ized, -iz·ing.** To destroy or deface (property) willfully or maliciously. [From VANDAL.]

Van de Graaff generator (văn′ də grăf′). An electrostatic generator in which electric charge is either removed from or transferred to a large hollow spherical electrode by a rapidly moving belt used with an acceleration tube as an

electron or ion accelerator. [After Robert J. *Van de Graaff* (1901–67), American physicist.]

Vandyke beard. A short, pointed beard. [After Sir Anthony *Vandyke* (1599–1641), Flemish painter.]

vane (vān) *n.* **1.** A device that turns on a vertical pivot to indicate the direction of the wind. **2.** A thin, rigid blade mounted around or as if around the circumference of a wheel and turned by or used to turn a fluid. **3.** The thin, flat, weblike part of a feather, extending from each side of the main shaft or quill. **4.** One of the metal guidance or stabilizing fins attached to the tail of a bomb or other missile. [Middle English, from Old English *fana*, banner.]

van·guard (văn′gärd′) *n.* **1.** The foremost or leading position in an army. **2. a.** The foremost or leading position in a trend or movement. **b.** Those occupying such a position. [Middle English *vantgard*, short for *avaunt garde*, from Old French *avant-garde* : *avant*, before + *garde*, guard, from *garder*, to guard.]

va·nil·la (və-nĭl′ə) *n.* **1.** Any of various tropical American orchids of the genus *Vanilla*, esp. *V. planifolia*, cultivated for its long, narrow seed pods from which a flavoring agent is obtained. **2.** Also **vanilla bean.** The long, beanlike seed pod of this plant. **3.** A flavoring extract prepared from the vanilla bean. [Spanish *vainilla*, "little sheath" (from its elongated fruit), from *vaina*, sheath, from Latin *vāgīna*.]

van·ish (văn′ĭsh) *intr.v.* **-ished, -ish·ing. 1.** To disappear or become invisible, esp. quickly or in an unexplained manner. **2.** To pass out of existence. [Middle English *vanisshen*, from Old French *esvanir*, from Latin *ēvānēscere* : *ex-*, away from + *vānēscere*, to disappear, from *vānus*, empty.]

vanishing point. 1. A point at which receding parallel lines seem to converge. **2.** A point at which a thing disappears or ceases to exist.

van·i·ty (văn′ə-tē) *n., pl.* **-ties. 1.** Excessive pride in one's appearance or accomplishments; conceit. **2.** Lack of usefulness, worth, or effect; worthlessness. **3.** Something that is vain, futile, or worthless. **4.** A small case for a woman's cosmetics. **5.** A dressing table. [Middle English *vanite*, from Old French, from Latin *vānitās*, from *vānus*, empty, vain.]

Vanity Fair. Also **vanity fair.** A place or scene of ostentation or empty, idle amusement and frivolity. [From the fair in John Bunyan's *Pilgrim's Progress*.]

van·quish (văng′kwĭsh, văn′-) *tr.v.* **1.** To defeat, as in a battle or contest. **2.** To overcome; subdue. —See Syns at **defeat.** [Middle English *vaynquysshen*, from Old French *vainquir*, from Latin *vincere*.] —**van′quish·er** *n.*

van·tage (văn′tĭj) *n.* **1.** An advantage in a competition or conflict; superiority. **2.** Something, as a strategic position, that provides superiority or an advantage. [Middle English, from Norman French, short for Old French *avantage*, advantage.]

vantage point. A position from which a person has a commanding view or outlook.

vap·id (văp′ĭd) *adj.* Lacking liveliness, zest, or interest; dull; flat: *vapid beer; vapid conversation.* [Latin *vapidus*.] —**va·pid′i·ty** or **vap′id·ness** *n.* —**vap′id·ly** *adv.*

va·por (vā′pər) *n.* Also *Brit.* **va·pour. 1.** Fine particles of matter, such as fog, suspended in the air. **2. a.** A substance that is in gaseous form but at a low enough temperature to be liquefied by the application of pressure. **b.** The gaseous state of a substance that is solid or liquid at normal temperatures. **c.** A mixture of a vapor and air, as the fuel mixture of an internal-combustion engine. **3.** Something unsubstantial, worthless, or fleeting. —*intr.v.* **1.** To give off vapor. **2.** To evaporate. **3.** To engage in boastful talk. [Middle English *vapour*, from Old French, from Latin *vapor*, steam.] —**va′por·ish** (-ĭsh) *adj.*

va·por·ize (vā′pə-rīz′) *v.* **-ized, -iz·ing.** —*tr.v.* To convert to vapor, esp. by heating. —*intr.v.* To be converted into vapor. —**va′por·iz′a·ble** *adj.* —**va′por·i·za′tion** (-pər-ə-zā′shən) *n.*

va·por·iz·er (vā′pə-rī′zər) *n.* A device that vaporizes medicine for inhalation.

vapor lock. A pocket of vaporized gasoline in the fuel line of an internal-combustion engine that blocks normal flow of fuel.

va·por·ous (vă′pər-əs) *adj.* **1.** Pertaining to or resembling vapor. **2.** Producing vapors; volatile. **3.** Giving off or obscured by vapors; misty. **4.** Insubstantial, vague, or ethereal: *"The vaporous illusions of twilight"* (John C. Powys). **—va′por·ous·ly** *adv.*

va·por·y (vă′pə-rē) *adj.* Vaporous.

va·pour (vă′pər) *n. Brit.* Var. of *vapor*.

var·i·a·ble (vâr′ē-ə-bəl) *adj.* **1. a.** Liable or likely to change; changeable. **b.** Inconstant; fickle. **2.** *Biol.* Tending to deviate from an established type; aberrant. **3.** *Math.* Having no fixed quantitative value. —See Syns at **capricious**. *—n.* **1.** Something that is variable. **2.** *Math.* **a.** A quantity capable of assuming any of a set of values. **b.** A symbol representing such a quantity. **—var′i·a·bil′i·ty** or **var′i·a·ble·ness** *n.* **—var′i·a·bly** *adv.*

var·i·ance (vâr′ē-əns) *n.* **1.** The act or fact of varying or the condition or quality of being variant or variable; variation; difference: *a variance in product quality.* **2.** A difference of opinion; dissension; a dispute. *—idiom.* **at variance with.** Differing; conflicting.

var·i·ant (vâr′ē-ənt) *adj.* **1.** Exhibiting variation; differing: *words with variant spellings.* **2.** Liable to vary; variable; changeable. *—n.* Something exhibiting slight variation in form from another, as a different spelling of the same word.

var·i·a·tion (vâr′ē-ā′shən) *n.* **1.** The act, process, or result of varying. **2.** An example of varying. **3.** The extent or degree to which a thing varies. **4. Magnetic declination. 5.** *Biol.* Marked difference or deviation from characteristic form, function, or structure. **6.** *Mus.* An altered version of a given theme, diverging from it by melodic ornamentation and by changes in harmony, rhythm, or key. **7.** *Ballet.* A solo dance.

var·i·col·ored (vâr′ī-kŭl′ərd) *adj.* Having a variety of colors; variegated.

var·i·cose (vâr′ə-kōs′) *adj.* Abnormally dilated and knotted. [Latin *varicōsus*, from *varix*, swollen vein.]

var·i·cos·i·ty (vâr′ə-kŏs′ə-tē) *n., pl.* **-ties. 1.** A part esp. of a vein that is varicose. **2.** The condition of being varicose.

var·ied (vâr′ēd) *adj.* **1.** Having various kinds or forms; diverse. **2.** Having a variety of colors.

var·i·e·gate (vâr′ē-ə-gāt′) *tr.v.* **-gat·ed, -gat·ing. 1.** To change the appearance of, esp. by marking with different colors. **2.** To give variety to. [From Late Latin *variēgāre*, from Latin *varius*, various.]

var·i·e·gat·ed (vâr′ē-ə-gā′tĭd) *adj.* **1.** Having streaks, marks, or patches of different colors. **2.** Characterized by variety; diverse.

va·ri·e·ty (və-rī′ə-tē) *n., pl.* **-ties. 1.** The condition or quality of being various or varied; diversity. **2.** A number or collection of different things; assortment: *a variety of outdoor activities.* **3.** A group that is distinguished from other groups by a specific characteristic or set of characteristics. **4.** *Biol.* A taxonomic category forming a subdivision of a species. —See Syns at **kind**. [Old French *variete*, from Latin *varietās*, from *varius*, various.]

var·i·form (vâr′ə-fôrm′) *adj.* Having a variety of forms.

va·ri·o·la (və-rī′ə-lə) *n.* Smallpox. [Medieval Latin, pustule, from Latin *varius*, speckled, various.]

var·i·o·rum (vâr′ē-ôr′əm, -ōr′əm) *n.* An edition or text esp. of a classical author, with notes by various scholars or editors and often including various versions of a text. *—modifier:* the variorum *Keats.* [From Latin *editiō cum notīs variōrium*, "edition with the notes of various (commentators)."]

var·i·ous (vâr′ē-əs) *adj.* **1.** Of different kinds: *can't go for various reasons.* **2.** More than one; several: *discussed the problem with various people.* **3.** Individual and separate: *The various reports all agreed.* **4.** Many-sided; varying; versatile: *a woman of various skills.* **5.** *Archaic.* Changeable; variable. [Latin *varius*, speckled, variegated, changeable.] **—var′i·ous·ly** *adv.* **—var′i·ous·ness** *n.*

var·let (vär′lĭt) *n. Archaic.* **1.** An attendant or servant. **2.** A rascal; knave. [Middle English, from Old French, young nobleman, squire.]

var·mint (vär′mənt) *n. Informal.* A person or animal considered undesirable, obnoxious, or troublesome. [Var. of VERMIN.]

var·nish (vär′nĭsh) *n.* **1.** An oil-based paint that dries to leave a surface coated with a thin, hard, glossy film that is relatively transparent and almost colorless. **2. a.** The smooth coating or finish that results from the application of varnish. **b.** A substance or coating that resembles varnish; gloss. **3.** A deceptive external appearance; show or pretense. *—tr.v.* **1.** To cover with varnish. **2.** To give a deceptively fair appearance to: *varnish the truth.* [Middle English *vernisch*, from Old French *vernis*, from Medieval Latin *veronix*, a kind of resin.] **—var′nish·er** *n.*

var·si·ty (vär′sə-tē) *n., pl.* **-ties.** The principal team representing a university, college, or school in sports or other competitions. *—modifier:* varsity *sports.* [Shortened and altered from UNIVERSITY.]

var·y (vâr′ē) *v.* **-ied, -y·ing.** *—tr.v.* **1.** To make or cause changes in; modify or alter: *vary prices according to the supply.* **2.** To give variety to; diversify: *Vary the sauce by adding spices or wine.* *—intr.v.* **1.** To undergo or show change: *The temperature varies from day to day.* **2.** To be different; deviate or depart: *vary from established patterns of behavior.* **3.** *Math.* To be variable, as a quantity or function. —See Syns at **change.** [Middle English *varien*, from Old French *varier*, from Latin *variāre*, from *varius*, speckled, changeable.]

vas-. Var. of **vaso-.**

vas·cu·lar (văs′kyə-lər) *adj. Biol.* Of, characterized by, or containing vessels that carry circulating blood, lymph, sap, or other plant or animal fluids. [From Latin *vāsculum*, dim. of *vās*, vessel.]

vas def·er·ens (văs′ dĕf′ər-ənz, -ə-rĕnz′). The duct in male vertebrate animals that carries sperm from a testis to the ejaculatory duct. [New Latin, "carrying-off vessel."]

vase (vās, vāz, vȧz) *n.* An open container, as of glass or porcelain, used for holding flowers or for ornamentation. [French, from Latin *vās*, vessel.]

vase   **vat**

va·sec·to·my (vă-sĕk′tə-mē) *n., pl.* **-mies.** Surgical removal of a part of the vas deferens, used as a means of sterilization.

Vas·e·line (văs′ə-lēn′, -lĭn) *n.* A trademark for a petroleum jelly used primarily as a base for medicinal ointments.

vaso- or **vas-.** A prefix meaning: **1.** A blood vessel: *vasomotor.* **2.** The vas deferens: *vasectomy.* [From Latin *vās*, vessel.]

vas·o·con·stric·tion (văs′ō-kən-strĭk′shən) *n.* Constriction of a blood vessel. **—văs′o·con·stric′tor** (-tər) *n.*

vas·o·dil·a·ta·tion (văs′ō-dĭl′ə-tā′shən, -dī′lə-tā′shən) *n.* Dilatation of a blood vessel. **—vas′o·di·la′tor** (-dī-lā′tər, dĭ-lā′tər) *n.*

vas·o·mo·tor (văs′ō-mō′tər, vā′sō-) *adj.* Causing or regulating constriction or dilation of blood vessels.

vas·sal (văs′əl) *n.* **1.** A person who holds land from a feudal lord and receives protection in return for homage and allegiance. **2.** A subordinate or dependent. *—adj.* Of, being, or pertaining to a vassal. [Middle English, from Old French, from Medieval Latin *vassallus*, servant.]

vas·sal·age (văs′ə-lĭj) *n.* **1.** The condition of being a vassal. **2.** The service, homage, and fealty required of a vassal. **3.** A position of subordination or subjection; servitude.

vast (văst, väst) *adj.* **-er, -est.** Very great in size, amount, intensity, degree, or extent: *a vast expanse of desert; a vast difference.* —See Syns at **giant.** [Latin *vastus*.] **—vast′ly** *adv.* **—vast′ness** *n.*

vat (văt) *n.* A large container, used to store or hold liquids.

[Middle English, from Old English *fæt*.]

vat·ic (văt′ĭk) *adj.* Of or characteristic of a prophet. [From Latin *vātēs*, prophet.]

Vat·i·can (văt′ĭ-kən) *n.* **1.** The official residence of the pope in Vatican City, Italy. **2.** The papal government or authority. [French, from Latin *Vāticānus (mōns)*, the Vatican (Hill).]

vaude·ville (vôd′vĭl, vōd′-, vô′də-vĭl′) *n.* Stage entertainment offering a variety of short acts such as slapstick turns, song-and-dance routines, and juggling performances. [French, from Old French *vaudevire*, from *chanson du Vau de Vire*, type of satirical song popularized in the Valley of Vire, a region in Normandy, from *vau, val, vale*.]

vaude·vil·lian (vôd′vĭl′yən, vōd′-, vô′də-vĭl′-) *n.* Someone who performs or works in vaudeville.

vault¹ (vôlt) *n.* **1.** An arched structure, usu. of stone, brick, or concrete, forming a ceiling or roof. **2.** An arched covering resembling a vault. **3.** A room with arched walls and ceiling, esp. when underground, as a storeroom. **4.** A room or compartment, often built of steel, for the safekeeping of valuables: *a bank vault.* **5.** A burial chamber, esp. when underground. —*tr.v.* **1.** To construct, supply, or cover with a vault or arched ceiling. **2.** To build in the shape of a vault; to arch. [Middle English *vaute*, from Old French, from Latin *volūta*, past part. of *volvere*, to turn.]

barrel vault   intersecting vault

vault¹

vault² (vôlt) *tr.v.* To jump or leap over, esp. with the aid of the hands or a pole: *vault a low gate.* —*intr.v.* **1.** To jump or leap, esp. with the aid of the hands or a pole. **2.** To achieve or surmount something, as if by bounding vigorously: *vault into a position of prominence.* —See Syns at **jump.** —*n.* The act of vaulting; jump. [Old French *volter*, from Italian *voltare*, to turn (a horse), leap, gambol, from *volvere*, to turn.] —**vault′er** *n.*

vault·ing (vôl′tĭng) *adj.* **1.** Leaping upward or over. **2.** Reaching too far; exaggerated: *vaulting ambition.*

vaunt (vônt, vänt) *tr.v.* To boast of; brag about. —*intr.v.* To boast; brag. —See Syns at **boast.** —*n.* A boastful remark or speech. [Middle English *vaunten*, from Old French *vanter*, from Late Latin *vānitāre*, to be vain, from Latin *vānus*, empty, vain.] —**vaunt′er** *n.*

veal (vēl) *n.* The meat of a calf, used for food. [Middle English *veel*, from Old French, from Latin *vitellus*, dim. of *vitulus*, calf.]

vec·tor (věk′tər) *n.* **1.** *Math.* A quantity that has magnitude and direction, often represented by an arrow drawn on a system of coordinates. **2.** *Pathol.* An organism that carries pathogens from one host to another. [Latin *vector*, carrier, from *vectus*, past part. of *vehere*, to carry.] —**vec·to·ri·al** (věk-tôr′ē-əl, -tōr′ē-əl) *adj.*

Ve·da (vā′də, vē′-) *n.* Any of the oldest sacred writings of Hinduism, including the psalms, incantations, hymns, and formulas of worship incorporated in four collections. [Sanskrit *veda*, knowledge.]

Ve·dan·ta (vĭ-dän′tə, -dăn′tə) *n.* The system of Hindu philosophy that further develops the implications in the Upanishads that all reality is a single principle. [Sanskrit *vedanta*.]

ve·dette (vĭ-dĕt′) *n.* Also **vi·dette.** **1.** A mounted sentinel stationed in advance of an outpost. **2.** A small naval reconnaissance boat. Also called **vedette boat.** [French, from Italian *vedetta*, from Spanish *vela*, a watch, from *velar*, to watch, from Latin *vigilāre*, from *vigil*, awake.]

Ve·dic (vā′dĭk, vē′-) *adj.* Of or pertaining to the Veda or Vedas, the language in which they are written, or to the early Indian culture that produced them.

veep (vēp) *n. Slang.* Vice president. [From the abbreviation V.P.]

veer (vîr) *intr.v.* To change in course, direction, or purpose; shift; swerve: *The wind veered..* —*tr.v.* To alter the direction of; turn. —*n.* A change in direction; a swerve. [Old French *virer*.]

Ve·ga (vē′gə, vā′-) *n.* The brightest star in the constellation Lyra.

veg·e·ta·ble (věj′tə-bəl, věj′ə-tə-) *n.* **1. a.** A usu. herbaceous plant grown for an edible part or parts, as roots, stems, leaves, or flowers. **b.** The edible part of such a plant. **2.** An organism classified as a plant. **3.** A person who leads a monotonous, passive, or merely physical existence. [Middle English, living, growing, from Old French, from Medieval Latin *vegetābilis*, from Late Latin, enlivening, from Latin *vegetāre*, to enliven, from *vegetus*, lively, from *vegēre*, to be lively.]

veg·e·tar·i·an (věj′ə-târ′ē-ən) *n.* Someone whose diet consists of grains, plants, and plant products and who eats no meat. —*adj.* **1.** Eating only plants and plant products rather than meat. **2.** Consisting only of plants and plant products: *a vegetarian diet.* [From VEGETABLE.] —**veg′e·tar′i·an·ism** *n.*

veg·e·tate (věj′ə-tāt′) *intr.v.* **-tat·ed, -tat·ing.** **1.** To grow, sprout, or exist as a plant does. **2.** To lead a monotonous, passive, or merely physical existence. [Late Latin *vegetāre*, to grow, from Latin, to enliven.]

veg·e·ta·tion (věj′ə-tā′shən) *n.* **1.** The act or process of vegetating. **2.** Plant life in general, esp. the plants of an area or region.

veg·e·ta·tive (věj′ə-tā′tĭv) *adj.* Also **veg·e·tive** (věj′ə-tĭv). **1.** Of, pertaining to, or characteristic of plants or plant growth. **2.** *Biol.* **a.** Of, pertaining to, or characterized by growth or physical change rather than sexual processes, as in the propagation of plants from tubers, cuttings, etc. **b.** Of or pertaining to asexual reproduction, as fission or budding.

ve·he·ment (vē′ə-mənt) *adj.* **1.** Characterized by forcefulness of expression or intensity of emotion; passionate; ardent: *vehement denial.* **2.** Marked by vigor or energy; violent: *a vehement storm.* [Old French, from Latin *vehemēns.*] —**ve′he·mence** *n.* —**ve′he·ment·ly** *adv.*

ve·hi·cle (vē′ĭ-kəl) *n.* **1.** Any device for carrying passengers, goods, or equipment, usu. one that moves on wheels or runners. **2.** A medium through which something is conveyed, transmitted, expressed, or achieved: *used his newspaper column as a vehicle for his conservative views.* **3.** A play, role, or piece of music used to display the special talents of one performer or company. **4.** A substance, such as oil, in which pigments are mixed for application. [French *véhicule*, from Latin *vehiculum*, from *vehere*, to carry.]

ve·hic·u·lar (vē-hĭk′yə-lər) *adj.* Of, pertaining to, or being a vehicle or vehicles: *vehicular traffic.*

veil (vāl) *n.* **1.** A piece of fine, sheer cloth, such as net or lace, worn by women over the head, shoulders, and often part of the face. **2. the veil.** The vows or life of a nun. **3.** A piece of light fabric hung to separate or conceal. **4.** Anything that conceals or obscures: *a veil of secrecy.* —*tr.v.* To cover, conceal, or disguise with or as if with a veil. —See Syns at **wrap.** [Middle English *veile*, from Norman French, from Latin *vēla*, pl. of *vēlum*, covering, veil.]

veil·ing (vā′lĭng) *n.* **1.** A veil. **2.** Material used for veils.

vein (vān) *n.* **1.** *Anat.* A blood vessel through which blood returns to the heart. **2.** *Bot.* One of the vascular bundles that form the branching framework and support of a leaf. **3.** *Zool.* One of the narrow, usu. longitudinal ribs that stiffen and support the wing of an insect. **4.** *Geol.* A long, regularly shaped deposit of an ore, mineral, etc.; a lode. **5.** A long, wavy strip of color, as in wood or marble. **6.** Inherent character, quality, or tendency; a strain or streak: *a pronounced vein of humor in an otherwise gloomy novel.* **7.** A temporary attitude or mood: *a talk in a serious vein.* —*tr.v.* **1.** To supply or fill with veins. **2.** To mark or decorate with veins. [Middle English *veine*, from Old French, from Latin *vēna.*] —**vein′ed** *adj.*

ve·lar (vē′lər) *adj.* **1.** Of or pertaining to a velum, esp. the soft palate. **2.** *Phonet.* Formed with the back of the tongue on or near the soft palate. —*n.* A velar sound.

veldt (fĕlt, vĕlt) *n.* Also **veld.** Any of the open grazing areas of southern Africa. [Afrikaans *veld*, from Middle Dutch, field.]

ă pat   ā pay   â care   ä father   ĕ pet   ē be   hw which   ĭ pit   ī tie   î pier   ŏ pot   ō toe   ô paw, for   oi noise
ŏŏ took   ōō boot   ou out   th thin   th this   ŭ cut   û urge   zh vision   ə about, item, edible, gallop, circus

vel·lum (vĕl′əm) *n*. **1.** A fine parchment made from the skins of calf, lamb, or kid and used for the pages and binding of fine books. **2.** A heavy off-white fine-quality paper resembling vellum. [Middle English *velim*, from Old French *velin*, from *veel*, calf, veal.]

ve·loc·i·ty (və-lŏs′ə-tē) *n., pl.* **-ties. 1.** Rapidity or speed. **2.** *Physics.* A vector quantity, the rate per unit of time at which an object moves in a specified direction. **3.** Distance traveled in a specified time. [French *vélocité*, from Latin *vēlōcitās*, from *vēlōx*, fast.]

ve·lours or **ve·lour** (və-lŏŏr′) *n., pl.* **-lours** (-lŏŏr′). A closely napped, velvetlike fabric, used for clothing and upholstery. [French, from Old French *velous*, from Latin *villōsus*, hairy, from *villus*, shaggy hair, wool.]

vel·vet (vĕl′vĭt) *n*. **1.** A fabric made usu. of silk, rayon, or nylon, that has a smooth, dense pile and a plain back. **2.** Something resembling the surface of this fabric, esp. in smoothness or softness. **3.** The soft covering on the newly developing antlers of deer and related animals. [Middle English *veluet*, from Old French *veluotte*, from *velu*, shaggy, from Medieval Latin *villūtus*, from Latin *villus*, shaggy hair, wool.]

vel·vet·een (vĕl′və-tēn′) *n*. A velvetlike fabric made of cotton that has a short, dense pile. [From VELVET.]

vel·vet·y (vĕl′vĭ-tē) *adj.* **-i·er, -i·est. 1.** Having the softness of velvet. **2.** Having a smooth taste, as some liquors.

ve·na ca·va (vē′nə kā′və, vā′nə kä′və) *pl.* **ve·nae ca·vae** (vē′nē′ kā′vē′, vā′nī′ kä′vī′). Either of the two large veins in air-breathing vertebrates that return blood to the right atrium of the heart. [Latin, "hollow vein."]

ve·nal (vē′nəl) *adj.* **1.** Open or susceptible to bribery; corruptible. **2.** Marked by corruption: *a venal administration.* **3.** Obtainable by purchase or bribery rather than by merit, as a position, contract, etc. [Latin *vēnālis*, for sale, from *vēnum*, sale.] **—ve·nal′i·ty** *n*. **—ve′nal·ly** *adv.*

ve·na·tion (vē-nā′shən, vā-) *n*. The distribution, arrangement, or system of veins. [From Latin *vēna*, vein.]

vend (vĕnd) *tr.v.* To sell (goods). *—intr.v.* To sell goods. —See Syns at **sell.** [French *vendre*, from Latin *vēndere* : *vēnum*, sale + *dare*, to give.] **—vend·er** or **ven·dor** *n*. **—vend′i·ble** *adj. & n.*

ven·det·ta (vĕn-dĕt′ə) *n*. **1.** A bitter blood feud between two families, motivated by the desire for revenge. **2.** Any act or attitude motivated by vengeance. [Italian, revenge, from Latin *vindicta*, from *vindicāre*, to revenge.]

vending machine. A machine that dispenses small goods upon the deposit of a coin or coins in a slot.

ve·neer (və-nîr′) *n*. **1.** A thin layer of fine wood or other material, as laminated plastic, formica, etc., bonded to and used to cover an inferior material underneath. **2.** Any of the thin layers glued together in making plywood. **3.** A deceptive or superficial outward show or pretense. *—tr.v.* **1.** To overlay (a surface) with a decorative or fine material. **2.** To glue together (layers of wood) in making plywood. **3.** To conceal with an attractive but superficial appearance; gloss over. [German *Furnier*, from *furnieren*, to furnish, veneer, from Old French *furnir*.]

ven·er·a·ble (vĕn′ər-ə-bəl) *adj.* **1.** Worthy of reverence or respect by virtue of dignity, position, or age: *a venerable lawyer and scholar.* **2.** Commanding respect or reverence by association: *venerable relics.* **3.** Honored above others. Used in titles of respect in the Roman Catholic and Anglican churches. **4.** Old. —See Syns at **old.** **—ven′er·a·ble·ness** or **ven′er·a·bil′i·ty** *n*. **—ven′er·a·bly** *adv.*

ven·er·ate (vĕn′ə-rāt′) *tr.v.* **-at·ed, -at·ing.** To regard with respect, reverence, or heartfelt deference. [From Latin *venerārī*, from *venus*, love.]

ven·er·a·tion (vĕn′ə-rā′shən) *n*. **1.** The act of venerating or the condition of being venerated. **2.** Profound respect or reverence.

ve·ne·re·al (və-nîr′ē-əl) *adj.* **1.** Of, pertaining to, or transmitted by sexual intercourse. **2.** Of or pertaining to venereal disease. [Middle English *venerealle*, from Latin *venereus*, from *venus*, love, lust.]

venereal disease. Any of several contagious diseases transmitted by sexual intercourse, as syphilis and gonorrhea.

ven·er·y (vĕn′ər-ē) *n. Archaic.* The act, art, or sport of hunting; the chase. [Middle English *venerie*, from Old French, from *vener*, to hunt, from Latin *vēnārī.*]

Venetian blind. A window blind consisting of thin horizontal slats that may be raised and lowered with one cord and set at a desired angle with another cord to regulate the amount of light admitted.

venge·ance (vĕn′jəns) *n*. **1.** The act or motive of punishing another in return for a wrong or injury; retribution. **2. with a vengeance. a.** With great violence or fury. **b.** To an extreme extent; excessively. [Middle English, from Old French, from *venger*, to revenge, from Latin *vindicāre*, to revenge.]

venge·ful (vĕnj′fəl) *adj.* **1.** Desiring vengeance; vindictive: *vengeful thoughts.* **2.** Showing or stemming from a desire for revenge: *vengeful malice.* **3.** Inflicting or serving to inflict vengeance. **—venge′ful·ly** *adv.* **—venge′ful·ness** *n*.

ve·ni·al (vē′nē-əl, vēn′yəl) *adj.* **1.** Easily excused or forgiven; pardonable: *a venial offense.* **2.** *Rom. Cath. Ch.* Minor in nature: *a venial sin.* [Middle English, from Old French, from Late Latin *veniālis*, from *venia*, forgiveness.] **—ve′ni·al′i·ty** (vē′nē-ăl′ə-tē, vēn′yăl′-) *n*. **—ve′ni·al·ly** *adv.*

ve·ni·re (vĭ-nī′rē) *n. Law.* **1.** A writ ordering a sheriff to summon prospective jurors. Also called **venire facias. 2.** The panel of prospective jurors from which a jury is selected. [Medieval Latin *venīre (facias)*, "(you are to cause) to come" (words used in the writ), from Latin *venīre*, to come.]

ve·ni·re·man (və-nī′rē-mən) *n*. A person summoned to jury duty under a venire.

ven·i·son (vĕn′ə-sən, -zən) *n*. The flesh of a deer, used for food. [Middle English *veneso(u)n*, from Old French, from Latin *vēnātiō*, hunting, game, from *vēnārī*, to hunt.]

Venn diagram (vĕn) A diagram in which an area is divided by closed curves into regions that represent sets. Relations and operations on sets can be shown as overlapping, included, and excluded regions. [After John Venn (1834–1923), English logician.]

ven·om (vĕn′əm) *n*. **1.** A poisonous secretion of some animals, such as certain snakes, spiders, scorpions, or insects, usu. transmitted by a bite or sting. **2.** Deep hatred or malice; spite. [Middle English *venim*, from Old French, from Latin *venēnum*.]

ven·om·ous (vĕn′ə-məs) *adj.* **1.** Secreting or able to poison with venom. **2.** Full of or containing venom: *a venomous substance.* **3.** Malicious; spiteful: *a venomous look.* —See Syns at **malevolent.** **—ven′om·ous·ly** *adv.* **—ven′om·ous·ness** *n*.

ve·nous (vē′nəs) *adj.* **1.** Of or pertaining to a vein or veins. **2.** *Physiol.* Returning to the heart through the great veins. [Latin *vēnōsus*, from *vēna*, vein.] **—ve′nous·ly** *adv.*

vent (vĕnt) *n*. **1.** A means of escape; an exit; outlet. **2.** An opening permitting the passage or escape of a liquid, gas, vapor, etc. **3.** *Zool.* The cloacal or anal excretory opening in animals such as birds, reptiles, amphibians, and fish. *—tr.v.* **1.** To discharge through a vent. **2.** To provide with a vent. **3.** To give forceful expression to; to express: *vent one's grief.* **—idiom. give vent to.** To express; give utterance to. [Middle English *venten*, to provide with an outlet, from Old French *esventer*, to let out air : Latin *ex-*, out + *ventus*, wind.]

ven·ti·late (vĕnt′l-āt′) *tr.v.* **-lat·ed, -lat·ing. 1.** To admit fresh air into in order to replace stale air. **2.** To circulate (air) within in order to freshen. **3.** To provide with a vent or a similar means of airing. **4.** To expose (a subject) to public discussion or examination. **5.** To aerate or oxygenate (blood). [Middle English *ventilaten*, to blow away, from Latin *ventilāre*, to fan, from *ventus*, wind.]

ven·ti·la·tion (vĕn′tl-ā′shən) *n*. **1.** The act or process of ventilating. **2.** A means or system used to circulate air indoors in order to freshen.

ven·ti·la·tor (vĕnt′l-ā′tər) *n*. Someone or something that ventilates, as an exhaust fan.

ven·tral (vĕn′trəl) *adj.* **1.** *Anat.* Of or pertaining to the belly; abdominal. **2.** Of, pertaining to, or situated on or near the back section of the human body or the lower surface of the body of an animal. [French, from Latin *ventrālis*, from *venter*, belly.]

ven·tri·cle (vĕn′trĭ-kəl) *n*. A cavity or chamber in an organ, esp. either of the chambers of the heart which contract to pump blood into arteries. [Middle English, from Old

French, from Latin *ventriculus*, dim. of *venter*, belly.]
—**ven·tric′u·lar** (věn-trĭk′yə-lər) *adj.*

ven·tri·cose (věn′trĭ-kōs′) *adj.* Inflated; swollen; distended. [From Latin *venter*, belly.] —**ven′tri·cos′i·ty** (-kŏs′ə-tē) *n.*

ven·tril·o·quism (věn-trĭl′ə-kwĭz′əm) *n.* Also **ven·tril·o·quy** (-kwē) *pl.* **-quies.** The art or practice of producing vocal sounds so that they seem to come from a source other than the speaker, as from a dummy. [From Late Latin *ventriloquus*, "speaking from the belly" : Latin *venter*, belly + *loquī*, to speak.] —**ven·tril′o·quist** (-ə-kwĭst) *n.* —**ven·tril′o·quis′tic** *adj.*

ven·tril·o·quy (věn-trĭl′ə-kwē) *n.* Var. of **ventriloquism**.

ven·ture (věn′chər) *n.* **1.** An undertaking, course of action, etc., that involves risk or uncertainty. **2.** Something at risk in such an undertaking; a stake. —*v.* **-tured, -tur·ing.** —*tr.v.* **1.** To expose to danger or risk; to stake: *ventured his life savings on the scheme.* **2.** To brave the dangers of: *ventured the high seas in a light boat.* **3.** To express at the risk of denial, criticism, or censure: *"Ernest ventured a little mild dissent"* (Samuel Butler). —*intr.v.* To take a risk or dare: *ventured out into unchartered territory.* [Middle English *venturen*, short for *aventuren*, from *aventure*, adventure.] —**ven′tur·er** *n.*

ven·ture·some (věn′chər-səm) *adj.* **1.** Inclined to take risks; daring; bold. **2.** Involving risk or danger; hazardous. —**ven′ture·some·ly** *adv.*

ven·tur·ous (věn′chər-əs) *adj.* **1.** Daring, adventurous, or bold. **2.** Hazardous, dangerous, or risky. —**ven′tur·ous·ly** *adv.* —**ven′tur·ous·ness** *n.*

ven·ue (věn′yōō) *n. Law.* **1.** The locality where a crime or other cause of legal action occurs. **2.** The locality or district from which a jury must be called and in which a trial must be held. [Middle English, arrival, assault, from Old French, from *venir*, to come, from Latin *venīre*.]

ven·ule (věn′yōōl) *n.* A minute vein, esp. one joining with a capillary. [Latin *vēnula*, dim. of *vēna*, vein.]

Ve·nus (vē′nəs) *n.* **1.** *Rom. Myth.* The goddess of love and beauty, identified with the Greek goddess Aphrodite. **2.** The second planet from the sun, having an average radius of 3,800 miles, a mass 0.816 times that of the earth, and a sidereal period of revolution about the sun of 224.7 days at a mean distance of approximately 67.2 million miles.

Ve·nu·sian (vĭ-nōō′zhən, -nyōō′zhən) *adj.* Of, pertaining to, or characteristic of the planet Venus. —*n.* A hypothetical inhabitant of the planet Venus.

Ve·nus's-fly·trap (vē′nə-sĭz-flī′trăp′) *n.* A plant, *Dionaea muscipula*, of boggy areas of the southeastern United States, that has hinged leaf blades edged with needlelike bristles that close and entrap insects.

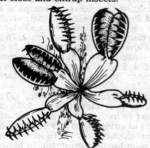

Venus's-flytrap

ve·ra·cious (və-rā′shəs) *adj.* **1.** Honest; truthful. **2.** Accurate; precise. —See Syns at **accurate**. [From Latin *vērāx*, truth.] —**ve·ra′cious·ly** *adv.* —**ve·ra′cious·ness** *n.*

ve·rac·i·ty (və-răs′ə-tē) *n., pl.* **-ties.** **1.** Adherence to the truth; truthfulness. **2.** Conformity to truth or fact; accuracy. **3.** Something that is true. [Medieval Latin *vērācitās*, from Latin *vērāx*, truth.]

ve·ran·dah or **ve·ran·da** (və-răn′də) *n.* An open porch, usu. roofed, extending along the outside of a building. [Hindi, from Portuguese, from *vara*, pole, from Latin *vāra*, forked pole, from *vārus*, bent inward.]

verb (vûrb) *n.* In most languages, that part of speech that expresses existence, action, or occurrence. [Middle English *verbe*, from Old French, from Latin *verbum*, word.]

ver·bal (vûr′bəl) *adj.* **1.** Of, pertaining to, or associated with words: *a verbal symbol.* **2.** Concerned with words rather than with the facts or ideas they represent. **3.** Expressed in speech; unwritten: *a verbal contract.* **4.** Literal; word for word: *a verbal translation.* **5.** *Gram.* **a.** Pertaining to, having the nature or function of, or derived from a verb. **b.** Used to form verbs: *a verbal suffix.* —See Usage note at **oral.** —*n. Gram.* A verbal noun, adjective, or other word derived from a verb and preserving some of the verb's characteristics. [Old French, from Late Latin *verbālis*, from Latin *verbum*, word.] —**ver′bal·ly** *adv.*

ver·bal·ism (vûr′bə-lĭz′əm) *n.* **1.** An expression in words; a word or phrase. **2.** A meaningless phrase or sentence. **3.** An expression, sentence, or other construction emphasizing words over content or idea.

ver·bal·ist (vûr′bə-lĭst) *n.* **1.** A person skilled in the use of words. **2.** A person concerned more with words than ideas or facts.

ver·bal·ize (vûr′bə-līz′) *v.* **-ized, -iz·ing.** —*tr.v.* **1.** To express in words: *couldn't verbalize his feelings.* **2.** To convert (as a noun) to verbal use. —*intr.v.* To express oneself in words. —**ver′bal·i·za′tion** *n.*

ver·ba·tim (vûr-bā′tĭm) *adv.* Word for word; in the same words: *He repeated the speech verbatim.* [Middle English, from Medieval Latin, from Latin *verbum*, word.] —**ver·ba′tim** *adj.*

ver·be·na (vər-bē′nə) *n.* Any of various New World plants of the genus *Verbena*, cultivated for their showy clusters of variously colored flowers. [From Latin *verbēna*, sacred bough of olive or myrtle.]

ver·bi·age (vûr′bē-ĭj) *n.* Words in excess of those needed for clarity or precision; wordiness. [French, from Latin *verbum*, word.]

ver·bose (vər-bōs′) *adj.* Using or containing an excessive number of words; wordy. —**ver·bose′ly** *adv.* —**ver·bose′ness** or **ver·bos′i·ty** (-bŏs′ə-tē) *n.*

ver·bo·ten (fĕr-bōt′n) *adj.* Strictly forbidden. [German, forbidden.]

ver·dant (vûr′dənt) *adj.* **1.** Green with vegetation: *fertile, verdant countryside.* **2.** Green in color. **3.** Inexperienced or unsophisticated. [Old French *verdeant*, pres. part. of *verdier*, to become green, from *verd*, green, from Latin *viridis*, from *virēre*, to be green.] —**ver′dan·cy** *n.*

ver·dict (vûr′dĭkt) *n.* **1.** The decision reached by a jury at the conclusion of a trial. **2.** A conclusion or judgment: *await the verdict of history.* [Middle English *verdit*, Old French *verdit* : *ver*, true, from Latin *vērus* + *dit*, saying, from Latin *dictum*, from *dīcere*, to speak, say.]

ver·di·gris (vûr′də-grēs, -grĭs) *n.* **1.** A blue or green basic copper acetate, used as a paint pigment, fungicide, and insecticide. **2.** A green coating or crust of copper sulfate or copper chloride formed on copper, brass, and bronze exposed to air or sea water for long periods of time. [Middle English *vertegres*, from Old French *vert-de-Grice*, "green of Greece."]

ver·dure (vûr′jər) *n.* **1.** The fresh, vibrant greenness of flourishing vegetation. **2.** Such vegetation itself. **3.** Any fresh or flourishing condition: *the verdure of childhood.* [Middle English, from Old French, from *verd*, green.]

verge[1] (vûrj) *n.* **1.** The edge, rim, or margin of something; brink. **2.** The point beyond which an action or condition is likely to begin or occur: *on the verge of tears.* **3.** An enclosing boundary. **4.** A rod or staff carried as an emblem of authority or office. —*intr.v.* **verged, verg·ing.** To border on; approach: *enthusiasm verging on fanaticism.* [Middle English, margin, from Old French, from Latin *virga*, rod, strip.]

verge[2] (vûrj) *intr.v.* **-ed, -ing.** **1.** To slope or incline. **2.** To be in the process of becoming something else: *dusk verging into night.* [Latin *vergere*, to tend toward.]

verg·er (vûr′jər) *n.* **1.** A person who carries the verge or staff of office before a scholastic, legal, or religious dignitary in a procession. **2.** *Brit.* A person who has charge of the interior of a church.

ver·i·fi·ca·tion (věr′ə-fə-kā′shən) *n.* **1.** The act of verifying or condition of being verified. **2.** A confirmation of the truth of a theory or fact.

ver·i·fy (věr′ə-fī′) *tr.v.* **-fied, -fy·ing. 1.** To prove the truth of by the presentation of evidence; confirm; substantiate: *Two witnesses verified his story.* **2.** To determine or test the truth or accuracy of: *conduct experiments to verify a hypothesis.* —See Syns at **prove.** [Middle English *verifien,* from Old French *verifier,* from Medieval Latin *vērificāre* : Latin *vērus,* true + *facere,* to make.] —**ver′i·fi′a·ble** *adj.* —**ver′i·fi′er** *n.*

ver·i·ly (věr′ə-lē) *adv. Archaic.* In truth; in fact. [Middle English *verraily,* from *verray,* true.]

ver·i·sim·i·lar (věr′ə-sĭm′ə-lər) *adj.* Appearing to be true or real; probable. [From Latin *vērisimilis* : *vērus,* true + *similis,* similar.] —**ver′i·sim′i·lar·ly** *adv.*

ver·i·si·mil·i·tude (věr′ə-sĭm-ĭl′ə-tōōd′, -tyōōd′) *n.* **1.** The quality of appearing to be true or real; likelihood. **2.** Something that has the appearance of being true or real.

ver·i·ta·ble (věr′ə-tə-bəl) *adj.* Unquestionable; actual; genuine: *a veritable success.* [Middle English, from Old French, from *verite,* verity.] —**ver′i·ta·ble·ness** *n.* —**ver′i·ta·bly** *adv.*

ver·i·ty (věr′ə-tē) *n., pl.* **-ties. 1.** The condition or quality of being real, accurate, or true. **2.** A statement, principle, or belief considered to be a proven fact or established truth: *religious verities.* [Middle English *verite,* from Old French, from Latin *vēritās,* from *vērus,* true.]

ver·meil (vûr′mĭl) *n.* **1.** *Poet.* Vermilion or a similar bright-red color. **2.** Gilded metal, such as silver, bronze, or copper. —*adj.* Bright red in color. [Middle English *vermayl,* from Old French *vermeil,* from Late Latin *vermiculus,* from Latin, small worm, cochineal (which yields a red dye), from *vermis,* worm.]

vermi-. A prefix meaning worm: **vermicide.** [From Latin *vermis,* worm.]

ver·mi·cel·li (vûr′mə-chěl′ē, -sěl′ē) *n.* Pasta made into long threads, thinner than spaghetti. [Italian, pl. dim. of *verme,* worm, from Latin *vermis.*]

ver·mi·cide (vûr′mə-sīd′) *n.* Anything used to kill worms.

ver·mic·u·lite (vər-mĭk′yə-līt′) *n.* Any of a group of minerals of varying composition, related to the chlorites and used as heat insulation and for starting plant seeds and cuttings. [Latin *vermiculus,* small worm + -ITE.]

ver·mi·form (vûr′mə-fôrm′) *adj.* Resembling or having the shape of a worm.

vermiform appendix. *Anat.* The appendix.

ver·mi·fuge (vûr′mə-fyōōj′) *n.* Any agent that expels or destroys intestinal worms. [VERMI- + Latin *fuga,* flight.]

ver·mil·ion (vər-mĭl′yən) *n.* Also **ver·mil·lion. 1.** A bright red mercuric sulfide, used as a pigment. **2.** Vivid red to reddish orange. [Middle English *vermelyon,* from Old French *vermeillon,* from *vermeil,* vermeil.]

ver·min (vûr′mĭn) *n., pl.* **vermin. 1.** Any of various small animals or insects that are destructive, annoying, or injurious to health, such as cockroaches or rats. **2. a.** A contemptible or offensive person. **b.** Such persons collectively: *"The most pernicious race of little odious vermin that nature ever suffered to crawl upon the surface of the earth"* (Swift). [Middle English, from Old French, from Latin *vermis,* worm.] —**ver′min·ous** *adj.*

ver·mouth (vər-mōōth′) *n.* A white wine flavored with aromatic herbs and spices, used chiefly in cocktails. [French *vermout,* from German *Wermut,* wormwood, from Middle High German *wermuot,* from Old High German *wermuōta.*]

ver·nac·u·lar (vər-năk′yə-lər) *n.* **1.** The native language of a country or region, esp. as distinct from literary language. **2.** The idiom of a particular trade or profession: *in the legal vernacular.* —See Syns at **language.** —*adj.* **1.** Native to or commonly spoken by the members of a particular country or region. **2.** Of or using the native language of a region, esp. as distinct from literary language: *a vernacular poet.* [From Latin *vernāculus,* domestic, from *verna,* native slave.] —**ver·nac′u·lar·ly** *adv.*

ver·nal (vûr′nəl) *adj.* **1.** Of, pertaining to, or occurring in the spring. **2.** Characteristic of or resembling spring, as in freshness. [Latin *vernālis,* from *vernus,* of spring, from *vēr,* spring.] —**ver′nal·ly** *adv.*

vernal equinox. 1. The point at which the ecliptic intersects the celestial equator, the sun having a northerly motion. **2.** The moment at which the sun passes through this

point, about March 21, marking the beginning of spring.

ver·ni·er (vûr′nē-ər) *n.* **1.** A small auxiliary scale attached parallel to a main scale and arranged to indicate fractional parts of the smallest divisions of the main scale. **2.** An auxiliary device that allows fine adjustments or measurements to be made on or with an instrument or device. [After Pierre *Vernier* (1580–1637), French mathematician, its inventor.]

vernier caliper. A measuring instrument consisting of an L-shaped frame with a linear scale along its longer arm and an L-shaped sliding attachment with a vernier scale.

ve·ron·i·ca (və-rŏn′ĭ-kə) *n.* A plant, the speedwell. [Perh. from the name *Veronica.*]

ver·sa·tile (vûr′sə-təl; *Brit.* vûr′sə-tīl′) *adj.* **1.** Capable of doing many things competently: *a versatile athlete.* **2.** Having varied uses or functions. **3.** Variable; changeable. **4.** *Biol.* Capable of moving freely in all directions, as the antenna of an insect. [French, from Latin *versātilis,* from *versārī,* freq. of *vertere,* to turn.] —**ver′sa·tile·ly** *adv.* —**ver′sa·til′i·ty** *n.*

verse (vûrs) *n.* **1.** Writing arranged according to a metrical pattern; poetry. **2. a.** One line of poetry. **b.** A section or subdivision of a metrical composition, as a stanza. **3.** Light, often whimsical poetry, as distinct from serious poetry. **4.** A specific type of metrical composition, such as blank or free verse. **5.** One of the numbered subdivisions of a chapter in the Bible. [Middle English *vers,* from Latin *versus,* from *vertere,* to turn.]

versed (vûrst) *adj.* Practiced or skilled; knowledgeable: *versed in foreign languages.* [From *versed,* acquainted with, from Latin *versātus,* past part. of *versārī,* to turn, occupy oneself with.]

ver·si·cle (vûr′sĭ-kəl) *n.* **1.** A short verse. **2.** A short sentence spoken or chanted by a priest and followed by a response from the congregation. [Middle English, from Old French *versicule,* from Latin *versiculus,* dim. of *versus,* verse.]

ver·si·fi·ca·tion (vûr′sə-fi-kā′shən) *n.* **1.** The writing or composing of verses. **2.** Poetic meter.

ver·si·fy (vûr′sə-fī′) *v.* **-fied, -fy·ing.** —*tr.v.* **1.** To change from prose into metrical form. **2.** To tell or describe in verse. —*intr.v.* To write verses. [Middle English *versifien,* from Old French *versifier,* from Latin *versificāre* : *versus,* verse + *facere,* to make.] —**ver′si·fi·er** *n.*

ver·sion (vûr′zhən, -shən) *n.* **1.** A description, narration, or account related from a specific point of view: *Her version of the accident differed from his.* **2. a.** A translation from another language. **b.** Often **Version.** A translation of the Bible or of a part of it. **3.** A form or variation of an earlier or original model: *a mildly reworked version of the Ford Model T.* **4.** An adaptation of a work of art or literature into another medium or style: *saw a stage version of a famous novel.* [Old French, from Medieval Latin *versiō,* conversion, translation, from Latin *vertere,* to turn, change.]

ver·so (vûr′sō) *n., pl.* **-sos.** *Printing.* The left-hand page of a book or the reverse side of a leaf. [Latin *versō (folio),* "(the page) being turned," the page one sees when the leaf is turned over.]

verst (vûrst) *n.* A Russian measure of distance, equivalent to about two-thirds of a mile. [French *verste,* from Russian *versta,* "line."]

ver·sus (vûr′səs) *prep.* **1.** Against: *the plaintiff versus the defendant.* **2.** In contrast with: *death versus dishonor.* [Medieval Latin, from Latin, turned toward, from *vertere,* to turn.]

ver·te·bra (vûr′tə-brə) *n., pl.* **-brae** (-brē) or **-bras.** Any of the bones or cartilaginous segments forming the spinal column. [Latin, joint, vertebra, from *vertere,* to turn.]

ver·te·bral (vûr′tə-brəl) *adj.* **1.** Of, pertaining to, or of the nature of a vertebra. **2.** Having or consisting of vertebrae.

vertebral column. *Anat.* The **spinal column.**

ver·te·brate (vûr′tə-brāt′, -brĭt) *adj.* **1.** Having a backbone or spinal column. **2.** Of or characteristic of a vertebrate or vertebrates. —*n.* Any member of the subphylum Vertebrata, a primary division of the phylum Chordata that includes the fishes, amphibians, reptiles, birds, and mammals, all of which are characterized by a segmented bony or cartilaginous spinal column.

ă pat ā pay â care ä father ě pet ē be hw which   ĭ pit ī tie î pier ŏ pot ō toe ô paw, for oi noise
ōō took ōō boot ou out th thin *th* this ŭ cut   û urge zh vision ə about, item, edible, gallop, circus

ver·tex (vûr′tĕks′) *n., pl.* **-tex·es** or **-ti·ces** (-tə-sēz′). **1.** The highest point of anything; apex; summit. **2.** The top of the head. **3.** *Geom.* **a.** The point at which the sides of an angle intersect. **b.** The point on a triangle opposite to and farthest away from its base. **c.** A point on a polyhedron common to three or more sides. **d.** The fixed point that is one of the three generating characteristics of a conic section. [Latin, whirl, crown of the head, highest point, from *vertere,* to turn.]

ver·ti·cal (vûr′tĭ-kəl) *adj.* **1.** Perpendicular to the plane of the horizon; directly upright. **2.** Of, pertaining to, or situated at the vertex or highest point; directly overhead. **3.** *Econ.* Of, pertaining to, or controlling all the grades or levels in the manufacture and sale of a product. —*n.* **1.** A vertical line, plane, circle, etc. **2.** A vertical position. [French, from Late Latin *verticālis,* from Latin *vertex,* vertex.] —**ver′ti·cal′i·ty** or **ver′ti·cal·ness** *n.* —**ver′ti·cal·ly** *adv.*
Syns: **vertical, perpendicular, plumb, upright** *adj.* Core meaning: At right angles to the horizon or to level ground (*careful to make the doorposts vertical*).

vertical union. A labor union in which workers are organized according to the industry for which they work instead of by their particular skill or craft.

ver·ti·ces (vûr′tĭ-sēz′) *n.* A plural of **vertex.**

ver·ti·cil (vûr′tĭ-səl) *n. Biol.* A circular arrangement, as of flowers or leaves, about a point on an axis. [Latin *verticillus,* the whirl of a spindle, dim. of *vertex,* whirl, vertex.]

ver·tig·i·nous (vər-tĭj′ə-nəs) *adj.* **1.** Revolving; whirling; rotary. **2.** Affected by vertigo; dizzy. **3.** Tending to produce vertigo: *vertiginous speed.* [Latin *vertīginōsus,* from *vertīgō,* vertigo.] —**ver·tig′i·nous·ly** *adv.*

ver·ti·go (vûr′tĭ-gō′) *n., pl.* **-goes.** The sensation of dizziness and the feeling that oneself or one's environment is whirling about. [Latin *vertīgō,* from *vertere,* to turn.]

ver·tu (vər-tōō′, vûr′tōō) *n.* Var. of **virtu.**

ver·vain (vûr′vān′) *n.* Any of several plants of the genus *Verbena,* with slender spikes of small blue, purplish, or white flowers. [Middle English *verveine,* from Old French, from Latin *verbēna,* sacred twig of olive, myrtle, or laurel.]

verve (vûrv) *n.* **1.** Energy and enthusiasm in the expression of ideas and esp. in artistic performance or composition. **2.** Liveliness or vivacity; animation. **3.** *Rare.* Aptitude; talent. —See Syns at **spirit.** [French, from Old French, fancy, fanciful expression, from Latin *verba,* pl. of *verbum,* word.]

ver·y (vĕr′ē) *adv.* **1.** In a high degree; extremely: *very happy.* **2.** Truly; absolutely: *the very best way to proceed.* —*adj.* **-i·er, -i·est. 1.** Absolute; utter: *at the very end.* **2.** Identical; selfsame: *the very questions he asked last time.* **3.** Used as an intensive to emphasize the importance of the thing described: *The very mountains crumbled.* **4.** Particular; precise: *the very center of town.* **5.** Mere: *The very mention of the name was frightening.* **6.** Actual: *caught in the very act.* **7.** *Archaic.* Genuine; real; true: *"Like very sanctity she did approach"* (Shakespeare). —See Syns at **same.** [Middle English *verray,* from Old French *verrai,* true, real, from Latin *vērus,* true.]

very high frequency. A band of radio frequencies falling between 30 and 300 megahertz.

very low frequency. A band of radio frequencies falling between 3 and 30 kilohertz.

ves·i·cate *v.* **-cated, -cat·ing.** —*tr.v.* To blister. —*intr.v.* To be or become blistered. [From Late Latin *vēsīcāre,* from Latin *vēsīca,* bladder, blister.]

ves·i·cle (vĕs′ĭ-kəl) *n.* **1.** A small bladderlike cell or cavity. **2.** *Anat.* A small bladder or sac, esp. one containing fluid. [French *vésicule,* from Latin *vēsīcula,* dim. of *vēsīca,* bladder, blister.]

ve·sic·u·lar (və-sĭk′yə-lər) *adj.* **1.** Of or pertaining to vesicles. **2.** Composed of or containing vesicles. **3.** Having the form of a vesicle. —**ve·sic′u·lar·ly** *adv.*

ves·per (vĕs′pər) *n.* **1. vespers** or **Vespers.** Any worship service held in the late afternoon or evening. **2.** A bell used to summon persons to vespers. Also called **vesper bell.** **3.** *Poet. & Archaic.* Evening. [From *Vesper,* the evening star, from Latin, evening, evening star.]

ves·per·tine (vĕs′pər-tīn, -tīn′) *adj.* Also **ves·per·ti·nal** (vĕs′pər-tī′nəl). **1.** Pertaining to or appearing in the evening. **2.** *Bot.* Opening or blooming in the evening. **3.** *Zool.* Becoming active in the evening. [Latin *vespertīnus,* from *vesper,* evening.]

ves·sel (vĕs′əl) *n.* **1.** A ship, large boat, or similar craft. **2.** A hollow container, as a bowl, pitcher, jar, or tank, esp. one for holding liquids. **3.** A person considered as a receptacle or agent of some quality: *a vessel of mercy.* **4.** An airship. **5.** *Anat.* A duct or other narrow tube for containing or circulating a bodily fluid. **6.** *Bot.* One of the tubular structures of woody tissue through which liquid flows or circulates. [Middle English, from Old French, from Late Latin *vascellum,* dim. of Latin *vās,* vessel.]

vest (vĕst) *n.* **1.** A short, sleeveless, collarless garment, either open or fastening in front, worn over a shirt or blouse and often under a suit coat or jacket. **2.** *Brit.* An undershirt. —*tr.v.* **1.** To clothe or dress, esp. with ecclesiastical robes or vestments. **2.** To place (authority, ownership, etc.) in the control of: *He vested his estate in his son.* **3.** To place (authority, power, etc.): *vesting the President with executive powers.* —*intr.v.* **1.** To dress oneself, esp. in ecclesiastical vestments. **2.** To be or become legally vested in or possessed by a person or persons. [French *veste,* from Italian, from Latin *vestis,* garment.]

Ves·ta (vĕs′tə) *n.* **1.** *Rom. Myth.* The goddess of the hearth, identified with the Greek goddess Hestia and worshiped in a temple that contained the sacred fire tended by the vestal virgins. **2.** The third-largest asteroid in the solar system, with a diameter of approx. 240 miles.

ves·tal (vĕs′təl) *adj.* **1.** Often **Vestal.** Pertaining to or sacred to Vesta. **2.** Chaste; pure. —*n.* Also **vestal virgin.** One of the six virgin priestesses who tended the sacred fire in the temple of Vesta in ancient Rome.

vest·ed (vĕs′tĭd) *adj.* **1.** *Law.* Settled, complete, or absolute; without contingency. **2.** Dressed or clothed, esp. in ecclesiastical vestments.

vested interest. 1. A strong concern for something, such as an institution, from which one expects private benefit. **2.** A group that has a vested interest.

ves·ti·bule (vĕs′tə-byōōl′) *n.* **1.** A small entrance hall or lobby. **2.** An enclosed area at the end of a railroad passenger car. **3.** Any chamber, opening, or channel of the body that serves as an entrance to another chamber or cavity. [French, from Latin *vestibulum.*] —**ves·tib′u·lar** (vĕ-stĭb′yə-lər) *adj.*

ves·tige (vĕs′tĭj) *n.* **1.** A visible trace, evidence, or sign of something that has once existed but exists or appears no more. **2.** *Biol.* A small, degenerate, or rudimentary organ or part that exists in an organism as a usu. nonfunctioning remnant of an organ or part fully developed and functional in a preceding generation or earlier developmental stage. [French, from Latin *vestīgium,* footprint, trace.]

ves·tig·i·al (vĕ-stĭj′ē-əl, -stĭj′əl) *adj.* Of, relating to, or constituting a vestige. —**ves·tig′i·al·ly** *adv.*

vest·ment (vĕst′mənt) *n.* **1.** A garment, esp. a robe or gown worn as an indication of office. **2.** *Eccles.* Any of the ritual robes worn by clergymen, altar boys, or other assistants at services or rites. [Middle English *vestiment,* from Old French, from Latin *vestimentum,* from *vestīre,* to dress, from *vestis,* garment.]

vest-pock·et (vĕst′pŏk′ĭt) *adj.* **1.** Designed to fit into a vest pocket: *a vest-pocket book.* **2.** Relatively small.

ves·try (vĕs′trē) *n., pl.* **-tries. 1.** A room in a church where clergymen put on their vestments and where these robes and sacred objects are stored; a sacristy. **2.** A meeting room in a church. **3.** In the Anglican and Episcopal churches, a committee of members of the parish or congregation that administers the affairs of the parish or congregation. [Middle English *vestrie,* var. of *vestiarie,* a dressing room, from Old French, from Medieval Latin *vestiarium,* wardrobe, from *vestis,* garment.]

ves·try·man (vĕs′trē-mən) *n.* A member of a vestry.

ves·ture (vĕs′chər) *n. Archaic.* **1.** Clothing; apparel. **2.** Anything that covers or cloaks: *hills in a vesture of mist.* [Middle English, clothes, from Old French, from Late Latin *vestītūra,* from Latin *vestīre,* to clothe.]

vet·er·an (vĕt′ər-ən, vĕt′rən) *n.* **1.** A person who has a long record of service in a given activity or capacity. **2.** A former member of the armed forces. —*modifier: a veteran actor; veteran benefits.* [French *vétéran,* from Latin *veterānus,* from *vetus,* old.]

ă pat	ā pay	â care	ä father	ĕ pet	ē be	hw which
ōō took	ōō boot	ou out	th thin	*th* this	ŭ cut	

ĭ pit	ī tie	î pier	ŏ pot	ō toe	ô paw, for	oi noise
û urge	zh vision	ə about, item, edible, gallop, circus				

Veterans Day. November 11, a holiday celebrated in memory of the armistice ending World War I in 1918 and in honor of veterans of the armed services.

vet·er·i·nar·i·an (vĕt′ər-ə-nâr′ē-ən, vĕt′rə-) *n.* A person trained and authorized to treat animals medically.

vet·er·i·nar·y (vĕt′ər-ə-nĕr′ē, vĕt′rə-) *adj.* Of or relating to the medical treatment of diseases or injuries of animals. —*n.*, *pl.* **-ies.** A veterinarian. [Latin *veterīnārius*, from *veterīnus*, of cattle.]

ve·to (vē′tō) *n.*, *pl.* **-toes. 1. a.** The vested power or constitutional right of one branch or department of government, esp. the right of a chief executive, to reject a bill passed by a legislative body and thus prevent or delay its enactment into law. **b.** The exercise of this right. **2.** Any authoritative prohibition or rejection of a proposed or intended act. —*tr.v.* **-toed, -to·ing. 1.** To prevent (a legislative bill) from becoming law by exercising the power of veto. **2.** To refuse to consent to; prohibit. [Latin *vetō*, "I forbid," from *vetāre*, to forbid.] —**ve′to·er** *n.*

vex (vĕks) *tr.v.* **1.** To irritate or annoy; bother; pester. **2.** To confuse; baffle; puzzle. —See Syns at **annoy.** [Middle English *vexen*, from Old French *vexer*, from Latin *vexāre*.]

vex·a·tion (vĕk-sā′shən) *n.* **1.** The condition of being vexed; annoyance: *a look of vexation on her face.* **2.** Someone or something that vexes; a source of irritation or annoyance.

vex·a·tious (vĕk-sā′shəs) *adj.* **1.** Causing or creating vexation; annoying; irksome. **2.** Full of vexation; disturbed; annoyed. —**vex·a′tious·ly** *adv.* —**vex·a′tious·ness** *n.*

vexed (vĕkst) *adj.* **1.** Irritated; annoyed. **2.** Much discussed or debated; brought up repeatedly.

vi·a (vī′ə, vē′ə) *prep.* By way of: *going to Montreal via Boston.* [Latin *viā*, ablative of *via*, road, way.]

vi·a·ble (vī′ə-bəl) *adj.* **1.** Capable of living, as a newborn infant or fetus able to survive and develop under normal conditions. **2.** Capable of growing or developing under favorable conditions, as seeds, spores, or eggs. **3.** Capable of success or continuing effectiveness; practicable; workable: *a viable national economy.* [French, from Old French, from *vie*, life, from Latin *vīta*.] —**vi′a·bil′i·ty** *n.*

vi·a·duct (vī′ə-dŭkt′) *n.* A series of spans or arches used to carry a road, railroad, etc., over a wide valley or over other roads or railroads. [Latin *via*, road, way + (AQUA)DUCT.]

vi·al (vī′əl) *n.* Also **phi·al** (fī′əl). A small glass container for liquids. [Middle English *viole*, var. of *fiole*, phial.]

vi·and (vī′ənd) *n.* **1.** An article of food. **2. viands.** Provisions; victuals. [Middle English *viaunde*, from Old French *viande*, from Latin *vīvenda*, from *vīvere*, to live.]

vibes (vībz) *n. (used with a sing. verb).* **1.** *Informal.* A vibraphone. **2.** *Slang.* A distinctive emotional reaction; vibrations.

vi·brant (vī′brənt) *adj.* **1.** Showing, marked by, or resulting from vibration; vibrating. **2.** Full of vigor, energy, etc.: *a vibrant personality.* —**vi′brant·ly** *adv.*

vi·bra·phone (vī′brə-fōn′) *n.* A musical instrument similar to a marimba but with metal bars and rotating disks in the resonators to produce a vibrato. [VIBRA(TE) + -PHONE.]

vibraphone

vi·brate (vī′brāt′) *v.* **-brat·ed, -brat·ing.** —*intr.v.* **1.** To move back and forth rapidly. **2.** To produce a sound; resonate. **3.** To be moved emotionally; thrill: *vibrate with excitement.* —*tr.v.* **1.** To cause to move back and forth rapidly. **2.** To cause to tremble or quiver. [From Latin *vibrāre*.]

vi·bra·tile (vī′brə-tĭl, -tīl′) *adj.* **1.** Characterized by vibra-

tion. **2.** Capable of or adapted to vibratory motion. —**vi′bra·til′i·ty** (-tĭl′ī-tē) *n.*

vi·bra·tion (vī-brā′shən) *n.* **1.** The act of vibrating. **2.** The condition of being vibrated. **3.** *Physics.* A rapid linear motion of a particle or of an elastic solid about an equilibrium position. **4.** A single complete vibrating motion; a quiver; tremor. **5.** Often **vibrations.** *Slang.* A distinctive emotional reaction by a person to another person or thing capable of being instinctively sensed or experienced; vibes. —**vi·bra′tion·al** *adj.*

vi·bra·to (vī-brä′tō, vē-) *n.*, *pl.* **-tos.** *Mus.* A small, moderately rapid back-and-forth variation in the pitch of a musical tone that produces a tremulous or pulsating effect. [Italian, from Latin *vibrātus*, past part. of *vibrāre*, to vibrate.]

vi·bra·tor (vī′brā′tər) *n.* **1.** Something that vibrates. **2.** An electrically operated device used for massage. **3.** An electrical device consisting basically of a vibrating conductor interrupting a current.

vi·bra·to·ry (vī′brə-tôr′ē, -tōr′ē) *adj.* **1.** Of, characterized by, or consisting of vibration. **2.** Capable of vibration.

vi·bur·num (vī-bûr′nəm) *n.* Any of various shrubs or trees of the genus *Viburnum* that characteristically have clusters of small white flowers and berrylike red or black fruit. [Latin *viburnum.*]

vic·ar (vĭk′ər) *n.* **1.** A salaried clergyman in charge of a parish. **2.** *Rom. Cath. Ch.* **a.** A clergyman who acts for or represents another, often higher-ranking member of the clergy. **b. Vicar.** The pope as the earthly deputy of Christ. **3.** Someone who acts for or represents another; deputy. [Middle English, from Old French *vicaire*, from Latin *vicārius*, a substitute, from *vicārius*, substituting, acting for, from *vicis*, change, turn, office.]

vic·ar·age (vĭk′ər-ĭj) *n.* **1.** The residence of a vicar. **2.** The benefice of a vicar. **3.** The position or duties of a vicar.

vicar apostolic *pl.* **vicars apostolic.** *Rom. Cath. Ch.* **1.** A titular bishop who administers a region that is not yet a diocese as a representative of the Holy See. **2.** A titular bishop appointed to administer to a vacant see in which the succession of bishops has been interrupted.

vicar general *.pl.* **vicars general. 1.** *Rom. Cath. Ch.* A priest acting as deputy to a bishop to assist him in the administration of his diocese. **2.** An ecclesiastical official, usu. a layman, in the Church of England who assists an archbishop or bishop in administrative and judicial duties.

vi·car·i·ous (vī-kâr′ē-əs, vĭ-) *adj.* **1.** Felt or undergone as if one were taking part in the experience or feelings of another: *the vicarious thrills provided by reading a rousing adventure story.* **2.** Endured or done by one person substituting for another: *vicarious punishment.* **3.** Acting in place of someone or something else. [Latin *vicārius*, substituting, from *vicis*, change, turn, office.] —**vi·car′i·ous·ly** *adv.* —**vi·car′i·ous·ness** *n.*

vice[1] (vīs) *n.* **1.** Evil, wickedness, or great immorality. **2.** An evil or immoral practice or habit. **3.** A personal failing or shortcoming: *We know his virtues and his vices.* [Middle English, from Old French, from Latin *vitium*, blemish, offense.]

vice[2] (vīs) *adj.* Acting as or having the authority to act as a deputy or substitute for another: *the vice chairman of the committee; the vice dean of the college.* —*prep.* **vi·ce** (vī′sē). In place of; replacing. [Latin, ablative of *vicis*, change.]

vice[3] (vīs) *n.* Var. of **vise.**

vice admiral. A naval officer ranking next below an admiral.

vice-. A prefix meaning one substituting for another: **vice-regal.** [Middle English *vis-*, from Old French, from Late Latin *vice-*, from Latin *vice*, in place of.]

vi·cen·ni·al (vī-sĕn′ē-əl) *adj.* **1.** Happening once every 20 years. **2.** Existing or lasting for 20 years. [From Late Latin *vīcennium*, period of 20 years : Latin *vīciēs*, 20 times, from *vīgintī*, 20 + *annus*, year.]

vice president. 1. An officer ranking next below a president, usu. empowered to assume the president's duties under such conditions as absence, illness, or death. **2.** A deputy of a president, esp. in a corporation, in charge of a separate department or location: *vice president of sales.* —**vice-pres′i·den·cy** *n.*

ă pat   ā pay   â care   ä father   ĕ pet   ē be   hw which
ōō took   ōō boot   ou out   th thin   th this   ŭ cut
ĭ pit   ī tie   î pier   ŏ pot   ō toe   ô paw, for   oi noise
û urge   zh vision   ə about, item, edible, gallop, circus

vice·re·gal (vīs-rē′gəl) *adj.* Of or relating to a viceroy. —**vice·re′gal·ly** *adv.*

vice regent. One who acts as a regent's deputy. —**vice-re′gen·cy** *n.* —**vice-re′gent** *adj.*

vice·roy (vīs′roi′) *n.* **1.** A governor of a country, province, or colony, ruling as the representative of a sovereign or king. **2.** An orange and black North American butterfly, *Limenitis archippus,* that resembles but is somewhat smaller than the monarch butterfly. [French : *vice-,* in place of + *roi,* king, from Latin *rēx.*]

vice·roy·al·ty (vīs′roi′əl-tē, vīs-roi′-) *n., pl.* **-ties. 1.** The office, authority, or term of service of a viceroy. **2.** A district or province governed by a viceroy.

vi·ce ver·sa (vī′sə vûr′sə, vīs vûr′sə). The reverse case being so; the other way around: *Some parents have completely adapted themselves to the desires of the children, rather than vice versa.* [Latin, "the position being changed."]

vi·chys·soise (vĭsh′ē-swäz′, vē′shē-) *n.* A thick, creamy potato soup flavored with leeks or onions and usu. served cold. [French, "(cream) of Vichy."]

vic·i·nage (vĭs′ə-nĭj) *n.* **1.** A limited region around a particular area; neighborhood; vicinity. **2.** A number of places situated near each other considered as a group. [Middle English *vesinage,* from Old French *visenage,* from Latin *vīcīnus,* neighbor.]

vi·cin·i·ty (vĭ-sĭn′ĭ-tē) *n., pl.* **-ties. 1.** The condition of being near in space or relationship; proximity. **2.** A nearby, surrounding, or adjoining region or place; neighborhood; locality. [Latin *vīcīnitās,* from *vīcīnus,* neighbor, from *vīcus,* village.]

vi·cious (vĭsh′əs) *adj.* **1.** Cruel; mean; malicious: *vicious lies.* **2.** Marked by evil or vice; wicked: *a vicious crime.* **3.** Savage and dangerous: *a vicious shark.* **4.** Violent; intense: *sought shelter from the vicious wind.* —See Syns at **fierce** and **malevolent.** [Middle English, from Old French, from Latin *vitiōsus,* from *vitium,* vice.] —**vi′cious·ly** *adv.* —**vi′cious·ness** *n.*

vicious circle. 1. A situation in which the solution of one problem in a chain of circumstances creates a new problem and increases the difficulty of solving the original problem. **2.** *Logic.* A fallacy in reasoning in which the premise is used to prove the conclusion and the conclusion used to prove the premise.

vi·cis·si·tude (vĭ-sĭs′ĭ-tōōd′, -tyōōd′) *n.* **1.** Often **vicissitudes.** Any change or variation in something; mutability. **2.** One of the sudden or unexpected changes or shifts often encountered in one's life, activities, or surroundings. [Old French, from Latin *vicissitūdō,* from *vicissim,* in turn, from *vicis,* change, turn.]

vic·tim (vĭk′tĭm) *n.* **1.** Someone who is harmed or killed by another or by accident, disease, etc.: *the victim of a hungry lion; the victims of an epidemic.* **2.** Someone made to suffer or undergo difficulty, as by trickery, unfair practices, or misunderstanding: *the victim of a hoax.* **3.** A living creature chosen to be killed as a religious sacrifice. [Latin *victima,* sacrifice, victim.]

vic·tim·ize (vĭk′tə-mīz′) *tr.v.* **-ized, -iz·ing. 1.** To subject to swindle or fraud. **2.** To make a victim of by causing discomfort or suffering. —**vic′tim·i·za′tion** *n.* —**vic′tim·iz′er** *n.*

vic·tor (vĭk′tər) *n.* The winner in a fight, battle, contest, or struggle. [Middle English, from Latin, from *victus,* past part. of *vincere,* to conquer.]

vic·to·ri·a (vĭk-tôr′ē-ə, -tōr′-) *n.* **1.** A low, light four-wheeled carriage for two with a folding top and an elevated driver's seat in front. **2.** A touring car with a folding top usu. covering only the rear seat. [After Queen *Victoria* (1819–1901), British sovereign.]

Victoria Cross. A bronze Maltese cross, Britain's highest military award for conspicuous valor.

Vic·to·ri·an (vĭk-tôr′ē-ən, -tōr′-) *adj.* **1.** Pertaining or belonging to the period of the reign of Queen Victoria of Great Britain: *a Victorian novel.* **2.** Exhibiting qualities usu. associated with the time of Queen Victoria, as moral severity or hypocrisy and pompous conservatism. **3.** Being in the highly ornamented, massive style of architecture, decor, and furnishings popular in 19th-cent. England. —*n.* A person belonging to or having qualities typical of the period of Queen Victoria. —**Vic·to′ri·an·ism** *n.*

vic·to·ri·ous (vĭk-tôr′ē-əs, -tōr′-) *adj.* **1.** Being the winner in a contest or struggle: *the victorious team.* **2.** Of, resulting in, or expressing victory: *the army's victorious advance; a victorious cheer.* —**vic·to′ri·ous·ly** *adv.* —**vic·to′ri·ous·ness** *n.*

vic·to·ry (vĭk′tə-rē) *n., pl.* **-ries. 1.** The act or fact of winning in a contest or struggle, as with an opponent or a difficulty; a triumph. **2.** Final and complete defeat of the enemy in a military engagement. [Middle English, from Old French *victorie,* from Latin *victōria,* from *victor,* victor.]

Syns: **victory, conquest, triumph, win** *n.* Core meaning: The act of winning (*the victory of the partisans over the invading army; our team's victory over our rival*).

vict·uals (vĭt′lz) *pl.n.* Food supplies; provisions. [Middle English *vitaille,* from Old French, from Late Latin *vīctuālia,* provisions, from Latin *vīctus,* sustenance, from *vīvere,* to live.]

vi·cu·ña or **vi·cu·na** (vĭ-kōōn′yə, -kōō′nə, -kyōō′nə, və-) *n.* **1.** A llamalike ruminant mammal, *Vicugna vicugna,* of the central Andes, with fine, silky fleece. **2.** Fabric made from the fleece of the vicuña. —*modifier: a vicuña coat.* [Spanish, from Quechua *wikuña.*]

vi·de (vī′dē, vē′dā′) *tr.v.* See. Used to direct a reader's attention: *vide page 64.* [Latin *vidē,* imp. of *vidēre,* to see.]

vi·del·i·cet (vĭ-dĕl′ĭ-sĕt′, vī-) *adv.* That is; namely. Used to introduce examples, lists, or items. [Latin : *vidēre,* to see + *licet,* it is permitted.]

vid·e·o (vĭd′ē-ō′) *adj.* Of or pertaining to television, esp. to televised images. —*n.* **1.** The visual portion of a televised broadcast as distinguished from the audio portion. **2.** Television: *a star of stage, screen, and video.* [From Latin *vidēre,* to see.]

video tape. A relatively wide magnetic tape used to record television images, usu. together with the associated sound, for subsequent playback and broadcasting.

vi·dette (vĭ-dĕt′) *n.* Var. of **vedette.**

vie (vī) *intr.v.* **vied, vy·ing.** To strive for superiority; contend; compete: *The runners vied for first place.* [From Middle English *envien,* from Old French *envier,* to challenge, bid, from Latin *invītāre,* to invite.]

Vi·et·nam·ese (vē-ĕt′nə-mēz′, -mēs′, vyĕt′-) *n.* **1.** A native or inhabitant of Vietnam. **2.** The language of Vietnam. —*adj.* Of or relating to the Vietnamese, their culture, or their language.

view (vyōō) *n.* **1.** The act or an example of seeing something; sight: *The explorer had his first view of the newly discovered land from the deck of his ship.* **2.** Examination; inspection: *picked up the rock specimen for a closer view.* **3.** A scene; vista: *the view from the top of the mountain.* **4.** A picture of a landscape. **5.** Range or field of sight: *The airplane disappeared from view.* **6.** A way of showing or seeing something, as from a particular position or angle: *a side view of the house.* **7.** An opinion; idea: *her views on education.* **8.** An aim; intention: *These laws were made with the view of providing equal rights for all.* —See Syns at **belief.** —*tr.v.* **1.** To be present at a showing of; see; look at. **2.** To regard; consider: *The President viewed the new uprisings with alarm.* —*idioms.* **in view of.** Taking into account; considering: *In view of your past performance I'm sure you will succeed.* **on view.** Displayed for others to see; on exhibit. **with a view to.** With the hope or intention of: *looked around with a view to speedy escape if the wildcat attacked.* [Middle English *vewe,* from Old French *veue,* from *veoir,* to see, from Latin *vidēre.*]

view·er (vyōō′ər) *n.* **1.** Someone who views something, esp. an onlooker or spectator. **2.** Any of various devices used to magnify photographic images so that they are easily visible.

view·point (vyōō′point′) *n.* A way of thinking about or regarding something.

vi·ges·i·mal (vī-jĕs′ə-məl) *adj.* **1.** Twentieth. **2.** Based on or pertaining to 20. [From Latin *vigēsimus,* twentieth, from *vīcēnī,* twenty each, from *vīgintī,* twenty.]

vig·il (vĭj′əl) *n.* **1.** A period of alert watchfulness during normal sleeping hours: *a vigil at an invalid's bedside.* **2. a.** The eve of a religious festival as observed by remaining awake for religious devotions. **b.** Ritual devotions observed on the eve of a holy day. [Middle English *vigile,* from Old French, from Latin *vigilia,* from *vigil,* alert.]

vig·i·lance (vĭj′ə-ləns) *n.* Alert watchfulness.

vig·i·lant (vĭj′ə-lənt) *adj.* On the alert; watchful. —See Syns at **alert.** [Middle English, from Old French, from Latin *vigilāns,* pres. part. of *vigilāre,* to be alert, from *vigil,* alert.] —**vig′i·lant·ly** *adv.*

vig·i·lan·te (vĭj′ə-lăn′tē) *n.* A member of a group that without authority takes on itself such powers as pursuing and punishing those suspected of being criminals or offenders. [Spanish, from Latin *vigilāns,* vigilant.]

vi·gnette (vĭn-yĕt′, vēn-) *n.* **1.** A decorative design placed at the beginning or end of a book or a chapter of a book or along the border of a page. **2.** An unbordered portrait that shades off into the surrounding color at the edges. **3.** A literary sketch having intimate charm and subtlety. [French, from Old French, young vine, dim. of *vigne,* vine.]

vig·or (vĭg′ər) *n.* Also *Brit.* **vig·our.** **1.** Physical energy or strength: *a rosy-cheeked, bright-eyed lass full of health and vigor.* **2.** Strong feeling; enthusiasm or intensity: *The opposing party, with great vigor, claimed the disputed votes for their candidate.* **3.** Effectiveness; force: *the vigor of his literary style.* **4.** Ability to grow, develop, or maintain health and energy. —See Syns at **spirit.** [Middle English *vigour,* from Old French *vigor,* from *vigēre,* to be lively.]

vig·or·ous (vĭg′ər-əs) *adj.* **1.** Robust; hardy. **2.** Energetic; lively. —**vig′or·ous·ly** *adv.* —**vig′or·ous·ness** *n.*
　　　Syns: **vigorous, active, brisk, dynamic, energetic, lively, sprightly, spry** *adj.* Core meaning: Disposed to action (*a vigorous farmer who worked twelve hours a day*).

vig·our (vĭg′ər) *n. Brit.* Var. of **vigor.**

Vi·king or **vi·king** (vī′kĭng) *n.* One of a seafaring Scandinavian people who plundered the coasts of northern and western Europe from the 9th to the 11th cent. and who made early voyages to the New World. —*modifier: Viking raiders; a Viking ship.* [Old Norse *vīkingr.*]

vile (vīl) *adj.* **vil·er, vil·est.** **1.** Hateful; disgusting. **2.** Miserable; base; wretched: *vile slavery.* **3.** Very bad or unpleasant: *a vile temper; vile weather.* **4.** Morally low or base. [Middle English *vyle,* from Old French *vil,* from Latin *vīlis,* cheap, poor, worthless.] —**vile′ly** *adv.* —**vile′ness** *n.*

vil·i·fy (vĭl′ə-fī′) *tr.v.* **-fied, -fy·ing.** To speak evil of; defame; denigrate. [Middle English *vilifien,* from Late Latin *vīlificāre* : Latin *vīlis,* vile + *facere,* to make.] —**vil′i·fi·ca′tion** *n.* —**vil′i·fi′er** *n.*

vil·la (vĭl′ə) *n.* **1.** A sometimes large and luxurious country house, often used as a resort. **2.** *Brit.* A middle-class house in the suburbs. [Italian, from Latin *vīlla,* country home.]

vil·lage (vĭl′ĭj) *n.* **1.** A group of homes and other buildings forming a community smaller than a town. **2.** The inhabitants of a village; villagers. —*modifier: a village square; the village water supply.* [Middle English, from Old French, from *ville,* village, farm, from Latin *vīlla,* country home.]

vil·lag·er (vĭl′ĭ-jər) *n.* An inhabitant of a village.

vil·lain (vĭl′ən) *n.* **1.** A wicked or evil person; scoundrel. **2.** A main character who harms or threatens the good or heroic characters in a story, play, etc. [Middle English *vilain,* from Old French, serf, from Medieval Latin *vīllānus,* from Latin *vīlla,* country house.]

vil·lain·ous (vĭl′ə-nəs) *adj.* **1.** Viciously wicked or criminal. **2.** Obnoxious. —**vil′lain·ous·ly** *adv.* —**vil′lain·ous·ness** *n.*

vil·lain·y (vĭl′ə-nē) *n., pl.* **-ies.** **1.** Wickedness; evil. **2.** A wicked or evil act.

vil·la·nelle (vĭl′ə-nĕl′) *n.* A 19-line poem of fixed form that consists of five tercets and a final quatrain on two rhymes, with the first and third lines of the first tercet repeated alternately as a refrain closing the succeeding stanzas and joined as the final couplet of the quatrain. [French, from Italian *villanella,* an old rustic Italian song, from *villanello,* rustic, from *villano,* peasant, from Medieval Latin *vīllānus.*]

vil·lein (vĭl′ən) *n.* One of a class of feudal serfs who held the legal status of freemen in their dealings with all persons except their lord. [Middle English, var. of *vilain,* a serf.]

vil·lein·age (vĭl′ə-nĭj) *n.* **1.** The legal status or condition of a villein. **2.** The legal tenure by which a villein held his land.

vim (vĭm) *n.* Liveliness and energy; enthusiasm. —See Syns at **spirit.** [Latin, accusative of *vīs,* power.]

vin-. Var. of **vini-.**

vin·ai·grette (vĭn′ə-grĕt′) *n.* **1.** A small decorative bottle or container with a perforated top, used for holding an aromatic restorative such as smelling salts. **2.** Vinaigrette sauce. [French, from Old French *vinaigre,* vinegar.]

vinaigrette sauce. A cold sauce or dressing made of vinegar and oil flavored with finely chopped onions, herbs, and other seasonings.

vin·ci·ble (vĭn′sə-bəl) *adj.* Capable of being overcome or defeated. [Latin *vincibilis,* from *vincere,* to conquer.] —**vin′ci·bil′i·ty** *n.*

vin·cu·lum (vĭng′kyə-ləm) *n., pl.* **-la** (-lə). **1.** *Math.* A bar drawn over two or more algebraic terms to indicate that they are to be treated as a single term. **2.** A bond or tie. [Latin, band, cord, from *vincīre,* to tie.]

vin·di·cate (vĭn′dĭ-kāt′) *tr.v.* **-cat·ed, -cat·ing.** **1.** To clear of accusation, blame, suspicion, or doubt with supporting proof: *vindicated himself from the charges.* **2.** To support, as against criticism. **3.** To justify or prove the worth of, esp. in light of later developments. [From Latin *vindicāre,* to claim, defend, revenge, from *vindex,* claimant, defender, avenger.] —**vin′di·ca′tion** *n.* —**vin′di·ca′tor** *n.*
　　　Syns: **vindicate, absolve, acquit, clear, exonerate** *v.* Core meaning: To free from a charge of guilt (*a defendant who was vindicated by all the evidence*). See also Syns at **defend.**

vin·dic·tive (vĭn-dĭk′tĭv) *adj.* Having or showing a desire for revenge; vengeful. [From Latin *vindicta,* vengeance, from *vindicāre,* to revenge.] —**vin·dic′tive·ly** *adv.* —**vin·dic′tive·ness** *n.*

vine (vīn) *n.* **1. a.** Any plant with a flexible stem that climbs, twines around, clings to, or creeps along a surface for support. **b.** The stem of such a plant. **2.** A grapevine. —*modifier: vine leaves.* [Middle English, from Old French, from Latin *vīnea,* vine.]

vin·e·gar (vĭn′ĭ-gər) *n.* An acid liquid that is basically a dilute solution of acetic acid, obtained by fermenting beyond the alcohol stage, and used in flavoring and preserving food. [Middle English *vinegre,* from Old French *vinaigre* : *vin,* wine, from Latin *vīnum* + *aigre,* sour, from Latin *acer,* sharp.]

vin·e·gar·y (vĭn′ĭ-gə-rē) *adj.* Also **vin·e·gar·ish** (-gər-ĭsh). **1.** Having the nature of vinegar; sour; acid. **2.** Sour in disposition or speech.

vine·yard (vĭn′yərd) *n.* **1.** A piece of ground on which grapevines are grown and tended. **2.** *Informal.* A sphere of spiritual, mental, or physical endeavor.

vini- or **vino-** or **vin-.** A prefix meaning wine: *viniculture.* [From Latin *vīnum,* wine.]

vin·i·cul·ture (vĭn′ĭ-kŭl′chər, vī′nĭ-) *n.* The cultivation of grapes; viticulture.

vino-. Var. of **vini-.**

vi·nous (vī′nəs) *adj.* **1.** Of or relating to wine or its consumption: *"It was good to have a large vinous night"* (Anthony Burgess). **2.** Affected or caused by the consumption of wine: *vinous laughter.*

vin·tage (vĭn′tĭj) *n.* **1. a.** The grapes produced by a particular vineyard or district in a single season. **b.** Wine made from these grapes. **2.** The year or place in which a particular wine was bottled. **3.** The harvesting of a grape crop or the initial stages of winemaking. **4.** A year or time of origin: *a spiked German military helmet, vintage 1914.* —*adj.* **1.** Of or resulting from a vintage of unusually high quality: *vintage wines.* **2.** Of very high quality. **3.** Serving to identify; distinctive. —See Syns at **characteristic.** [Middle English *vyntage,* var. of *vendage,* from Old French, from Latin *vindēmia,* grape gathering : *vīnum,* wine + *dēmere,* to take off.]

vint·ner (vĭnt′nər) *n.* A wine merchant. [Middle English *vineter,* from Old French *vinetier,* from Medieval Latin *vīnātārius,* from Latin *vīnētum,* vineyard, from *vīnum,* wine.]

vi·nyl (vī′nəl) *n.* **1. a.** The univalent chemical radical CH_2CH, derived from ethylene. **b.** Any of various compounds that contains this group, typically highly reactive, easily polymerized, and used as basic materials for plastics. **2.** Any of various plastics, typically tough, flexible, and shiny, often used for coverings and clothing. —*modifier: vinyl floor covering; a vinyl raincoat.* [VIN(I)- + -YL.]

vi·ol (vī′əl) *n.* Any of a family of stringed instruments, chiefly of the 16th and 17th cent., with a fretted fingerboard, usu. six strings, a flat back, and played with a

viola¹   violin   virginal ²

curved bow. [Old French *viole,* from Old Provençal *viola.*]

vi·o·la¹ (vē-ō′lə) *n.* A stringed instrument of the violin family, slightly larger than a violin, tuned a fifth lower, and a deeper, more somber and mellow tone. [Italian, from Old Provençal.]

vi·o·la² (vī-ō′lə, vē-, vī′ə-lə) *n.* Any plant of the genus *Viola,* which includes the violets and pansies, esp. a variety with flowers that resemble violets in size and shape and pansies in coloration. [Latin *viola,* violet.]

vi·o·la·ble (vī′ə-lə-bəl) *adj.* Capable of being violated. —**vi′o·la·bil′i·ty** or **vi′o·la·ble·ness** *n.* —**vi′o·la·bly** *adv.*

vi·o·la da gam·ba (vē-ō′lə də gäm′bə, găm′-). A stringed instrument, the bass of the viol family, with approx. the range of the cello. [Italian, "viola of the leg."]

vi·o·la d'a·mo·re (vē-ō′lə də-môr′ā, -mōr′ā). A stringed instrument, the tenor of the viol family, with six or seven stopped strings and an equal number of sympathetic strings that produce a characteristic silvery tone. [Italian, "viola of love."]

vi·o·late (vī′ə-lāt′) *tr.v.* **-lat·ed, -lat·ing.** **1.** To break (a law, regulation, etc.); transgress; disregard: *violate a promise.* **2.** To do harm to (property or qualities considered sacred); to profane; desecrate. **3.** To disturb rudely or improperly; break in upon: *violated our privacy.* **4.** To rape. [Middle English *violaten,* from Latin *violāre,* from *vīs,* force.] —**vi′o·la·tive** (-lā′tĭv) *adj.* —**vi′o·la·tor** *n.*

vi·o·la·tion (vī′ə-lā′shən) *n.* **1.** The act of violating or the condition of being violated: *the violation of a truce; acting in violation of the law.* **2.** An example of violating: *a traffic violation.*

vi·o·lence (vī′ə-ləns) *n.* **1.** Physical force exerted, as for causing damage or injury: *crimes of violence.* **2.** An act or example of violent action or behavior. **3.** Great force or intensity: *the violence of a hurricane; the violence of a reaction to a drug.* **4.** Damage; injury: *No violence has been done to his sensibilities.* **5.** Vehemence of feeling or expression; fervor.

vi·o·lent (vī′ə-lənt) *adj.* **1.** Marked by or resulting from great physical force or rough action: *a violent attack; violent blows.* **2.** Showing or having great emotional force: *a violent outburst of fury; a man with a violent temper.* **3.** Having great force or effect; severe; harsh: *a violent hurricane; a play marked by violent contrasts between good and evil.* **4.** Caused by unexpected force or injury rather than by natural causes: *a violent death.* —See Syns at **intense.** [Middle English, from Old French, from Latin *violentus.*] —**vi′o·lent·ly** *adv.*

vi·o·let (vī′ə-lĭt) *n.* **1.** Any of various low-growing plants of the genus *Viola,* with spurred, irregular flowers that are characteristically purplish-blue but sometimes yellow or white. **2.** Any of several similar plants, such as the African violet. **3.** A bluish purple. —*adj.* Bluish purple. [Middle English, from Old French *violete,* dim. of *viole,* from Latin *viola.*]

vi·o·lin (vī′ə-lĭn′) *n.* A stringed instrument, played with a bow, that has four strings tuned at intervals of a fifth, an unfretted fingerboard, and a shallower body than the viol and is capable of great flexibility in range, tone, and dynamics. [Italian *violino,* dim. of *viola.*]

vi·o·lin·ist (vī′ə-lĭn′ĭst) *n.* A person who plays the violin.

vi·o·list (vē-ō′lĭst) *n.* **1.** A person who plays the viola. **2.** A person who plays a viol.

vi·o·lon·cel·lo (vē′ə-lən-chĕl′ō) *n., pl.* **-los.** A cello. [Italian,

dim. of *violone,* a double bass.]

vi·os·ter·ol (vī-ŏs′tə-rōl′) *n.* **Vitamin D₂.** [(ULTRA)VIO(LET) + STEROL.]

VIP *Informal.* A very important person.

vi·per (vī′pər) *n.* **1.** Any of various poisonous Old World snakes of the family Viperidae, esp. a common Eurasian species, *Vipera berus,* the adder. **2.** Any poisonous or supposedly poisonous snake. **3.** A treacherous or malicious person. [Old French *vipere,* from Latin *vīpera,* snake.]

vi·per·ous (vī′pər-əs) *adj.* **1.** Suggestive of a viper or poisonous snake. **2.** Venomous; spiteful; malicious.

vi·ra·go (vĭ-rä′gō) *n., pl.* **-goes** or **-gos. 1.** A noisy, domineering woman; a scold. **2.** *Archaic.* A large, strong, or courageous woman. [Latin *virāgō,* from *vir,* man.]

vi·ral (vī′rəl) *adj.* Of, relating to, or caused by a virus.

vi·res·cence (vĭ-rĕs′əns) *n.* The process of becoming green, esp. the abnormal development of green coloration in plant parts normally not green.

vi·res·cent (vĭ-rĕs′ənt) *adj.* Becoming green; greenish. [Latin *virēscēns,* pres. part. of *virēscere,* to become green, from *virēre,* to be green.]

vir·gin (vûr′jĭn) *n.* **1.** A person who has not experienced sexual intercourse. **2.** A chaste or unmarried woman; a maiden. **3.** An unmarried woman who has taken religious vows of chastity. —*adj.* **1.** Of, characteristic of, or suitable to a virgin; chaste; modest: *robes of virgin white.* **2.** Pure and untouched: *virgin snow.* **3.** In the original or natural state; unused, untouched, or unexplored: *virgin forests; virgin territory; the virgin resources of the new continent.* [Middle English, from Old French *virgine,* from Latin *virgō.*]

vir·gin·al¹ (vûr′jə-nəl) *adj.* **1.** Of, relating to, or appropriate to a virgin; chaste; pure. **2.** Untouched or unsullied; fresh.

vir·gin·al² (vûr′jə-nəl) *n.* A small, rectangular harpsichord popular in the 16th and 17th cent. [From VIRGIN (because it was played by young girls).]

virgin birth. *Theol.* The doctrine that Jesus was miraculously begotten by God and born of Mary, who was a virgin.

Virginia creeper. A North American climbing vine, *Parthenocissus quinquefolia,* that has compound leaves with five leaflets and bluish-black, berrylike fruit. Also called **woodbine.**

Virginia deer. The white-tailed deer.

Virginia reel. A country dance in which couples perform various steps together to the instructions of a caller.

vir·gin·i·ty (vər-jĭn′ĭ-tē) *n., pl.* **-ties.** The condition of being a virgin; chastity.

Vir·go (vûr′gō) *n.* **1.** A constellation in the region of the celestial equator near Leo and Libra. **2.** The sixth sign of the zodiac.

vir·gule (vûr′gyōōl) *n.* A diagonal mark (/) used esp. to separate alternatives, as in *and/or,* to represent the word *per,* as in *miles/hour,* and to indicate the ends of verse lines printed continuously, as in *Candy/Is dandy.* Also called **slash.** [French, comma, from Latin *virgula,* small rod, from *virga,* rod, twig.]

vir·i·des·cent (vîr′ĭ-dĕs′ənt) *adj.* Green or slightly green. [Latin *viridis,* green + -ESCENT.] —**vir′i·des′cence** *n.*

vir·ile (vîr′əl) *adj.* **1.** Of, characteristic of, or befitting a man: *the virile tone quality of men's voices.* **2.** Having or showing strength, vigor, energy, and other manly qualities:

ă pat   ā pay   â care   ä father   ĕ pet   ē be   hw which   ĭ pit   ī tie   î pier   ŏ pot   ō toe   ô paw, for   oi noise
ŏŏ took   ōō boot   ou out   th thin   *th* this   ŭ cut   û urge   zh vision   ə about, item, edible, gallop, circus

a virile man; a virile race. **3.** Able to perform sexually as a male; potent. —See Syns at **male.** [Old French *viril,* from Latin *virīlis,* from *vir,* man.] **—vi·ril′i·ty** (-rĭl′ĭ-tē) *n.*

vi·rol·o·gy (vī-rŏl′ə-jē) *n.* The study of viruses and viral diseases. [VIR(US) + -LOGY.] **—vi·rol′o·gist** *n.*

vir·tu (vər-tyōō′, vûr′tyōō) *n.* Also **ver·tu. 1.** A knowledge of or taste for the fine arts. **2.** The quality of being beautiful, rare, or otherwise interesting to a collector. **3.** Beautiful, rare, or otherwise interesting articles or objects of art in general. [Italian, taste, virtue, from Latin *virtūs,* worth, value, power.]

vir·tu·al (vûr′chōō-əl) *adj.* Existing in effect or for practical purposes though not real in actual fact or form: *the virtual extinction of the buffalo; living years in virtual exile.* [Middle English *virtuall,* effective, powerful, from Medieval Latin *virtuālis,* from Latin *virtūs,* capacity, power.] **—vir′tu·al′i·ty** (-ăl′ĭ-tē) *n.*

virtual focus. The point from which divergent rays of reflected or refracted light seem to have emanated, as from the image of a point in a plane mirror.

virtual image. An image from which rays of reflected or refracted light appear to diverge, as from an image seen in a plane mirror.

vir·tu·al·ly (vûr′chōō-ə-lē) *adv.* In fact or to all purposes; essentially; practically: *The mountain lion is now virtually extinct in the East.*

vir·tue (vûr′chōō) *n.* **1. a.** Moral excellence and righteousness; goodness: *Virtue is its own reward.* **b.** Any particular example or kind of moral excellence: *the virtues of patience and kindness.* **2.** Chastity, esp. of a girl or woman. **3.** A particularly efficacious, good, or beneficial quality; an advantage: *a plan with the virtue of being practical; a climate with the virtue of never being too hot or too cold.* **4.** Effective force or power; ability to produce a definite result: *believing in the virtue of herbs to cure diseases.* **—idioms. by virtue of.** On the basis of: *winning a reputation as a great mountain climber by virtue of many spectacular ascents in the Alps.* **make a virtue of necessity.** To appear to do freely or by inclination what one must do necessarily. [Middle English *vertu,* from Old French, from Latin *virtūs,* manliness, strength, from *vir,* man.]

Syns: virtue, goodness, morality *n. Core meaning:* Morally excellent (*a person of great virtue*). VIRTUE and MORALITY suggest a conforming to standards of what is right and just and to approved codes of behavior; all imply uprightness (*virtue as its own reward; questioned the morality of arms sales to warring countries*). GOODNESS often implies inherent qualities of kindness, benevolence, and generosity (*goodness and honesty that showed in his every action*).

vir·tu·o·si (vûr′chōō-ō′sē) *n.* A plural of **virtuoso.**

vir·tu·os·i·ty (vûr′chōō-ŏs′ĭ-tē) *n., pl.* **-ties.** The technical skill, fluency, or style exhibited by a virtuoso.

vir·tu·o·so (vûr′chōō-ō′sō) *n., pl.* **-sos** or **-si** (-sē). **1.** A musician with exceptional ability, technique, or personal style; a brilliant performer. **2.** A person with exceptional skill or technique in any field, esp. in the arts. [Italian, from Late Latin *virtuōsus,* virtuous, skillful, from Latin *virtūs,* worth, power.] **—vir′tu·os′ic** (-ŏs′ĭk) *adj.*

vir·tu·ous (vûr′chōō-əs) *adj.* **1.** Having or showing virtue; morally good; righteous: *a virtuous life; virtuous conduct.* **2.** Chaste; pure: *a virtuous woman.* **—vir′tu·ous·ly** *adv.* **—vir′tu·ous·ness** *n.*

vir·u·lent (vîr′yə-lənt, vîr′ə-) *adj.* **1.** Having a very strong tendency to cause or capability for causing harm, as a disease, toxin, or microorganism. **2.** Bitterly hostile or antagonistic; full of hate: *virulent criticism.* [Middle English, from Latin *vīrulentus,* from *vīrus,* venom.] **—vir′u·lence** *n.* **—vir′u·lent·ly** *adv.*

vi·rus (vī′rəs) *n.* **1.** Any of various submicroscopic pathogens that consist essentially of a core of a single nucleic acid surrounded by a protein coat and are capable of invading living cells and destroying them and causing the release of a large number of new particles identical to thé original one, thus producing a disease. **2.** Any specific pathogen: *a flu virus.* —See Usage note at **germ.** [Latin *vīrus,* poison, slime.]

vi·sa (vē′zə) *n.* An official authorization stamped on a passport that permits entry into and travel within a particular country or region. **—tr.v. 1.** To endorse or ratify (a passport). **2.** To give a visa to. [French, from Latin *vīsa,* " from *vidēre,* to see.]

vis·age (vĭz′ĭj) *n.* **1.** The face or facial expression of a person; countenance. **2.** Appearance; aspect. [Middle English, from Old French, from *vis,* face, from Latin *vīsus,* from *vidēre,* to see.]

vis-à-vis (vē′zə-vē′, -zä-) *n., pl.* **vis-à-vis.** One of two persons or things opposite or corresponding to each other. **—adv.** Face to face. **—prep.** Compared with; in relation to. [French, "face to face."] **—vis′-à-vis′** *adj.*

Vi·sa·yan (vĭ-sī′ən) *n.* **1.** A member of the largest native group of the Philippines, found in the Visayan Islands. **2.** The Malay language of the Visayans. **—adj.** Of or relating to the Visayans, their culture, or their language.

vis·cer·a (vĭs′ər-ə) *pl.n.* The internal organs of the body, esp. those contained within the abdomen and thorax. [Latin *vīscera,* pl. of *vīscus,* body organ.]

vis·cer·al (vĭs′ər-əl) *adj.* **1.** Of, situated in, or affecting the viscera. **2.** Intensely emotional.

vis·cid (vĭs′ĭd) *adj.* Thick and sticky, as a liquid; resembling glue. [Late Latin *viscidus,* from Latin *viscum,* mistletoe, birdlime.] **—vis·cid′i·ty** *n.* **—vis′cid·ly** *adv.*

vis·cose (vĭs′kōs′) *n.* **1.** A thick, golden-brown, viscous solution of cellulose xanthate, used in the manufacture of rayon and cellophane. **2.** Rayon made from viscose. [Middle English, sticky, viscid, from Late Latin *viscōsus.*]

vis·cos·i·ty (vĭ-skŏs′ĭ-tē) *n., pl.* **-ties. 1.** The condition or property of being viscous. **2.** *Physics.* The degree to which a fluid resists flow when pressure is applied to it.

vis·count (vī′kount′) *n.* **1.** A member of the British peerage holding a title and rank below that of an earl and above that of a baron. **2.** In certain European countries, the son or brother of a count. [Middle English, from Old French *visconte,* from Medieval Latin *vicecomes : vice,* substitute + *comes,* count.]

vis·count·cy (vī′kount′sē) *n., pl.* **-cies.** The rank, title, or dignity of a viscount. Also called **viscounty.**

vis·count·ess (vī′koun′tĭs) *n.* **1.** The wife of a viscount. **2.** A woman holding a rank equal to that of viscount in her own right.

vis·count·y (vī′kount′ē) *n.* Viscountcy.

vis·cous (vĭs′kəs) *adj.* **1.** Tending to resist flow when pressure is applied, as a fluid; having a high viscosity. **2.** Viscid. [Middle English *viscouse,* from Norman French *viscous,* from Late Latin *viscōsus,* from Latin *viscum,* mistletoe, birdlime.] **—vis′cous·ly** *adv.* **—vis′cous·ness** *n.*

vise (vīs) *n.* Also **vice.** A clamping device of metal or wood, usu. consisting of two jaws closed or opened by a screw or lever, used in carpentry or metalworking to hold a piece in position. [Middle English *vis,* winding staircase, screw, from Latin *vītis,* vine.]

Vish·nu (vĭsh′nōō) *n. Hinduism.* The chief deity worshiped by the Vaishnava and the second member of the trinity, which includes also Brahma and Shiva.

vis·i·bil·i·ty (vĭz′ə-bĭl′ĭ-tē) *n., pl.* **-ties. 1.** The fact, condition, or degree of being visible. **2.** The greatest distance over which it is possible to see without the aid from instruments under given weather conditions.

vis·i·ble (vĭz′ə-bəl) *adj.* **1.** Capable of being seen; perceptible to the eye: *a visible object. Only one ninth of an iceberg is visible above water.* **2.** Easily noticed; clear; apparent: *no visible solution; visible signs of impatience.* **—vis′i·bly** *adv.*

Vis·i·goth (vĭz′ĭ-gŏth′) *n.* A member of the western Goths, a Teutonic people who invaded the Roman Empire in the 4th cent. A.D. and settled in France and Spain, establishing a monarchy that lasted until the early 8th cent. **—Vis′i·goth′ic** *adj.*

vi·sion (vĭzh′ən) *n.* **1.** The ability to sense light that enters the eye and make fine judgments about the color of the light and the directions from which the rays come; the sense of sight. **2.** Unusual foresight: *With vision and vigor and the help of modern science they are transforming a desert into a fertile land.* **3.** A mental image produced by the imagination: *having visions of future wealth and power.* **4.** Something perceived through unusual means, as a supernatural sight. **5.** A person or thing of extraordinary beauty. —*tr.v.* To see in or as if in a vision. [Middle English, from Old French, from Latin *vīsiō*, from *vīsus*, sight, from *vidēre*, to see.] —**vi'sion·al·ly** *adv.*

vi·sion·ar·y (vĭzh'ə-nĕr'ē) *adj.* **1.** Given to impractical or fanciful ideas: *a visionary explorer in search of fabulous treasures.* **2.** Not practicable at the moment; existing only in the imagination: *visionary schemes. The submarine had been around as a visionary craft for nearly 150 years before it finally became a reality.* —*n., pl.* **-ies. 1.** A person who has visions; a seer; prophet. **2.** A person who is given to impractical or speculative ideas; a dreamer.

vis·it (vĭz'ĭt) *tr.v.* **1.** To go or come to see (a person), as by way of friendship or duty; call on: *visit one's family.* **2.** To go or come to see (a place), as on a tour: *visit a museum.* **3.** To stay with as a guest: *visited his former classmate in California.* **4.** To go or come to see in an official or professional capacity. **5.** To go or come to generally: *I visit the bank on Fridays.* **6.** To go or come to in order to aid: *visit the wounded.* **7.** To afflict; assail: *A plague visited the village.* **8.** To inflict punishment upon or for; avenge: *"I shall visit their sin upon them"* (Exodus 32:34). —*intr.v.* **1.** To pay a call or calls. **2.** *Informal.* To converse or chat: *Stay and visit with me for a while.* —*n.* **1.** An act or an example of visiting a person, place, or thing. **2.** A stay or sojourn as a guest. **3.** An act of visiting in an official capacity, as an inspection or examination. [Middle English *visiten*, from Old French *visiter*, from Latin *visitāre*, to go to see, from *vīsāre*, to view, from *vīsus*, sight, vision.]

vis·i·tant (vĭz'ĭ-tənt) *n.* **1.** A visitor; guest. **2.** A supernatural being; a ghost or specter. **3.** A migratory animal or bird that stops in a particular place for a limited period of time.

vis·i·ta·tion (vĭz'ĭ-tā'shən) *n.* **1.** A visit, esp. for the purpose of making an official inspection or examination. **2.** A visit of affliction or blessing, regarded as being ordained by God. **3. Visitation. a.** In the New Testament, the visit of the Virgin Mary to her cousin Elizabeth. **b.** The church festival held July 2 in commemoration of this visit. —**vis'i·ta'tion·al** *adj.*

vis·i·tor (vĭz'ĭ-tər) *n.* A person who pays a visit.

vi·sor (vī'zər) *n.* Also **vi·zor. 1.** A projecting part, as on a cap or the windshield of a car, that protects the eyes from sun, wind, or rain. **2.** The movable front piece of a helmet of a suit of armor that protects the face. [Middle English *viser*, from Norman French, from Old French *vis*, face, from Latin *vīsus*, sight, vision.]

visor
On a military cap

visor
On a suit of armor

vis·ta (vĭs'tə) *n.* **1.** A distant view, esp. one seen through a passage or opening. **2.** A mental view of a series of events: *a scientific discovery that opens up new vistas of human improvement.* [Italian, from *visto*, past part. of *vedere*, to see, from Latin *vidēre*.]

vi·su·al (vĭzh'ōō-əl) *adj.* **1.** Of, serving, or resulting from the sense of sight. **2.** Capable of being seen by the eye; visible. **3.** Done or performed by means of the unaided vision: *visual navigation.* **4.** Designed to communicate by means of vision: *visual instruction; visual aids.* [Middle English, from Late Latin *visuālis*, from Latin *vīsus*, vision.] —**vi'su·al·ly** *adv.*

visual aid. Graphic material used in education to impart instruction by visual means.

vi·su·al·ize (vĭzh'ōō-ə-līz') *v.* **-ized, -iz·ing.** —*tr.v.* To form a mental image or vision of; envisage. —*intr.v.* To form a mental image or images. —**vi'su·al·i·za'tion** *n.*

vi·tal (vīt'l) *adj.* **1.** Of or characteristic of life: *vital processes; vital signs.* **2.** Essential for the continuation of life:

vital organs; vital functions. **3.** Full of life; energetic. **4.** Having great importance; essential: *Irrigation was vital to early civilization.* See Syns at **necessary.** —*n.* **vitals. 1.** Those organs or parts of the body whose functioning is essential to life. **2.** Elements essential to continued functioning, as of a system. [Middle English, from Old French, from Latin *vītālis*, from *vīta*, life.] —**vi'tal·ly** *adv.* —**vi'tal·ness** *n.*

vi·tal·ism (vīt'l-ĭz'əm) *n.* The philosophical doctrine that life processes possess a unique character radically different from physiochemical phenomena. —**vi'tal·ist** *n.* —**vi'tal·is'tic** *adj.*

vi·tal·i·ty (vī-tăl'ĭ-tē) *n., pl.* **-ties. 1.** An energy, force, or principle characteristic of life that distinguishes the living from the nonliving. **2.** The capacity to live, grow, or develop. **3.** Vigor; energy; exuberance.

vi·tal·ize (vīt'l-īz') *tr.v.* **-ized, -iz·ing.** To fill with life, vigor, energy, etc. —**vi'tal·i·za'tion** *n.* —**vi'tal·iz'er** *n.*

vital statistics. Data that record significant events and dates in human life, as births, deaths, and marriages.

vi·ta·min (vī'tə-mən) *n.* Any of various relatively complex organic substances that occur naturally in plant and animal tissue and are essential in small amounts for the control of metabolic processes. [German *Vitamine* : Latin *vīta*, life + *amine*, amine (so called because it was once thought to be an amine).]

vitamin A. A vitamin or a mixture of vitamins, esp. vitamin A_1, occurring principally in fish-liver oils and some yellow and dark-green vegetables, functioning in normal cell growth and development, and responsible in deficiency for hardening and roughening of the skin, night blindness, and degeneration of mucous membranes.

vitamin A_1. A yellow crystalline compound, $C_{20}H_{30}O$, extracted from fish-liver oils.

vitamin B. 1. Vitamin B complex. 2. A member of the vitamin B complex, esp. thiamine.

vitamin B_1. Thiamine.

vitamin B_2. Riboflavin.

vitamin B_6. Pyridoxine.

vitamin B_{12}. A complex, cobalt-containing coordination compound produced in the normal growth of certain microorganisms, found in liver, and widely used to treat pernicious anemia.

vitamin B complex. A group of vitamins gen. regarded as including thiamine, riboflavin, niacin, pantothenic acid, biotin, pyridoxine, folic acid, inositol, and vitamin B_{12}, and occurring chiefly in yeast, liver, eggs, and some vegetables.

vitamin C. Ascorbic acid.

vitamin D. Any of several chemically similar activated sterols, esp. vitamin D_2 or vitamin D_3, produced in general by ultraviolet irradiation of sterols, obtained from milk, fish, and eggs, required for normal bone growth, and used to treat rickets.

vitamin D_2. A white crystalline compound, $C_{28}H_{44}O$, produced by ultraviolet irradiation of the sterol ergosterol. Also called **calciferol** and **viosterol.**

vitamin D_3. A colorless crystalline compound, $C_{27}H_{44}O$, with essentially the same biological activity as vitamin D_2 but significantly more potent in poultry.

vitamin E. Any of several chemically related viscous oils, esp. $C_{29}H_{50}O_2$, found in grains and vegetable oils and used to treat sterility and various abnormalities of the muscles, red blood cells, liver, and brain.

vitamin G. Riboflavin.

vitamin H. Biotin.

vitamin K. Any of several natural and synthetic substances essential for the promotion of blood clotting and prevention of hemorrhage, occurring naturally in leafy green vegetables, tomatoes, and vegetable oils.

vi·tel·line (vĭ-tĕl'ĭn, -ī') *adj.* **1.** Of, pertaining to, or associated with the yolk of an egg: *the vitelline membrane.* **2.** Having the yellow color of an egg yolk; dull-yellow. —*n.* The yolk of an egg. [Latin *vitellus*, egg yolk + -INE.]

vi·ti·ate (vĭsh'ē-āt') *tr.v.* **-at·ed, -at·ing. 1.** To make ineffective or worthless: *Your objections vitiate my argument.* **2.** To corrupt morally; debase. **3.** To invalidate or make legally ineffective, as a contract. [From Latin *vitiāre*, from

ă pat   ā pay   â care   ä father   ĕ pet   ē be   hw which
ōō took   ōō boot   ou out   th thin   th this   ŭ cut
ĭ pit   ī tie   î pier   ŏ pot   ō toe   ô paw, for   oi noise
û urge   zh vision   ə about, item, edible, gallop, circus

vitium, defect, fault.] **—vi′ti·a·ble** (-ē-ə-bəl) *adj.* **—vi′ti·a′-tion** *n.* **—vi′ti·a′tor** *n.*

vit·i·cul·ture (vĭt′ĭ-kŭl′chər, vī′tĭ-) *n.* The cultivation of grapes. [Latin *vītis,* vine + CULTURE.] **—vit′i·cul′tur·al** *adj.* **—vit′i·cul′tur·ist** *n.*

vit·re·ous (vĭt′rē-əs) *adj.* **1.** Of, resembling, or of the nature of glass; glassy. **2.** Of or pertaining to the vitreous humor. [Latin *vitreus,* from *vitrum,* glass.] **—vit′re·os′i·ty** (-ŏs′ĭ-tē) or **vit′re·ous·ness** *n.*

vitreous body. A transparent, jellylike material composed mainly of vitreous humor that fills the part of the eyeball between the lens and the retina.

vitreous humor. A watery fluid that is a major component of a vitreous body.

vit·ri·fi·ca·tion (vĭt′rə-fĭ-kā′shən) *n.* **1.** The act or process of vitrifying or the condition of being vitrified. **2.** Something vitrified.

vit·ri·fy (vĭt′rə-fī′) *v.* **-fied, -fy·ing.** *—tr.v.* To change into glass or a similar substance, esp. through heat fusion. *—intr.v.* To become vitreous. [French *vitrifier,* from Old French, from Latin *vitrum,* glass.] **—vit′ri·fi′a·bil′i·ty** *n.* **—vit′ri·fi′a·ble** *adj.*

vit·ri·ol (vĭt′rē-ōl′) *n.* **1.** *Chem.* **a. Sulfuric acid. b.** Any of various sulfates of metals, such as ferrous sulfate (green vitriol), zinc sulfate (white vitriol), or copper sulfate (blue vitriol). **2. a.** Vituperative feeling. **b.** Harsh or scathing utterances. [Middle English, from Old French, from Medieval Latin *vitriolum,* from Latin *vitrum,* glass (from the glassy appearance of vitriol's sulfates).]

vit·ri·ol·ic (vĭt′rē-ōl′ĭk) *adj.* **1.** Of, like, or derived from a vitriol. **2.** Bitterly scathing; caustic.

vit·tles (vĭt′lz) *pl.n.* Nonstandard. Victuals.

vi·tu·per·ate (vī-tōō′pə-rāt′, -tyōō′-, vĭ-) *tr.v.* **-at·ed, -at·ing.** To rail against severely or abusively; revile; berate. [From Latin *vituperāre.*] **—vi·tu′per·a′tor** *n.*

vi·tu·per·a·tion (vī-tōō′pə-rā′shən, -tyōō′-, vĭ-) *n.* **1.** Censure; blame. **2.** Invective; railing.

vi·tu·per·a·tive (vī-tōō′pər-ə-tĭv, -tyōō′-, -pə-rā′-, vĭ-) *adj.* Harshly abusive: *"Five minutes won't be ample time for a vituperative phone call"* (Kingsley Amis). **—vi·tu′per·a·tive·ly** *adv.*

vi·va (vē′və) *interj.* A word used to express acclamation, applause, etc. [Italian, from *vivere,* to live, from Latin *vīvere.*]

vi·va·ce (vē-vä′chā) *adv. Mus.* Lively; vivaciously; briskly. Used as direction. [Italian, from Latin *vīvāx,* vivacious.]

vi·va·cious (vĭ-vā′shəs, vī-) *adj.* Animated; lively; spirited. [Latin *vīvāx,* lively, from *vīvere,* to live.] **—vi·va′cious·ly** *adv.* **—vi·va′cious·ness** *n.*

vi·vac·i·ty (vĭ-văs′ĭ-tē, vī-) *n.* The condition or quality of being vivacious. —See Syns at **spirit.**

viv·id (vĭv′ĭd) *adj.* **1.** Perceived as bright and distinct; brilliant: *the vivid evening star.* **2.** Having intensely bright colors: *a vivid tapestry.* **3.** Full of the freshness of immediate experience; distinct and clear: *vivid memories.* **4.** Evoking lifelike images within the mind: *a vivid description.* **5.** Active in forming lifelike images: *a vivid imagination.* [Latin *vīvidus,* full of life, lifelike, from *vīvere,* to live.] **—viv′id·ly** *adv.* **—viv′id·ness** *n.*

viv·i·fy (vĭv′ə-fī′) *tr.v.* **-fied, -fy·ing. 1.** To give or bring life to; to animate. **2.** To make more lively, intense, or striking; enliven. [Old French *vivifier,* from Late Latin *vīvificāre* : Latin *vīvus,* alive + *facere,* to do.] **—viv′i·fi·ca′tion** *n.* **—viv′i·fi′er** *n.*

vi·vip·a·rous (vī-vĭp′ər-əs, vĭ-) *adj.* Giving birth to living young that develop within the mother's body, as most mammals do. [Latin *vīviparus.*] **—vi′vi·par′i·ty** (vī′və-păr′ĭ-tē, vĭv′ə-) *n.* **—vi·vip′a·rous·ly** *adv.*

viv·i·sect (vĭv′ĭ-sĕkt′) *tr.v.* To perform vivisection on (a living animal or animals). *—intr.v.* To practice vivisection. [Back-formation from VIVISECTION.] **—viv′i·sec′tor** *n.*

viv·i·sec·tion (vĭv′ĭ-sĕk′shən) *n.* The act of cutting into or dissecting a living animal, esp. for scientific research. [Latin *vīvus,* alive + SECTION.] **—viv′i·sec′tion·al** *adj.* **—viv′i·sec′tion·ist** *n.*

vix·en (vĭk′sən) *n.* **1.** A female fox. **2.** A quarrelsome, sharp-tempered, or malicious woman. [Middle English *fixene,* Old English *fyxe,* she-fox.] **—vix′en·ish** *adj.*

viz·ard (vĭz′ərd) *n.* A mask. [Var. of VISOR.]

vi·zier (vĭ-zîr′) *n.* Also **vi·zir.** In former times, a high officer in a Moslem government, esp. in the old Turkish Empire. [French *vizir,* from Turkish *vezîr,* from Arabic *wazîr,* porter, from *wazara,* to carry.] **—vi·zier′i·al** (-zîr′ē-əl) *adj.*

vi·zir (vĭ-zîr′) *n.* Var. of **vizier.**

vi·zor (vī′zər) *n.* Var. of **visor.**

vo·ca·ble (vō′kə-bəl) *n.* A word considered only as a sequence of sounds or letters rather than as a unit of meaning. *—adj.* Capable of being voiced or spoken. [French, from Old French, from Latin *vocābulum,* a name, from *vocāre,* to call.]

vo·cab·u·lar·y (vō-kăb′yə-lĕr′ē) *n., pl.* **-ies. 1.** All the words of a language. **2.** The sum of words used by a particular person, profession, etc. **3.** A list of words and phrases, usu. arranged alphabetically and defined or translated; a lexicon. —See Syns at **language.**

vo·cal (vō′kəl) *adj.* **1.** Of or pertaining to the voice: *vocal range; vocal quality.* **2.** Uttered or produced by the voice. **3.** Having a voice; capable of emitting sound or speech. **4.** Full of voices; resounding with speech. **5.** Speaking freely and quickly; outspoken. **6.** *Phonet.* **a.** Vocalic. **b.** Voiced. *—n.* **1.** *Phonet.* A vocal sound. **2.** A popular piece of music that features a singer. [Middle English, from Latin *vōcālis,* speaking, talking, from *vōx,* voice.] **—vo′cal·ly** *adv.* **—vo′cal·ness** *n.*

vocal cords. A pair of muscular bands or folds in the larynx that vibrate when pulled together and when air from the lungs is forced between them, thereby producing the sound of the voice.

vo·cal·ic (vō-kăl′ĭk) *adj.* **1.** Containing many vowel sounds. **2.** Pertaining to or having the nature of a vowel or vowels.

vo·cal·ist (vō′kə-lĭst) *n.* A singer.

vo·cal·ize (vō′kə-līz′) *v.* **-ized, -iz·ing.** *—tr.v.* **1.** To make vocal; produce with the voice. **2.** To give voice to; to articulate. **3.** *Phonet.* **a.** To change (a consonant) into a vowel. **b.** To voice. *—intr.v.* **1.** To use the voice, esp. to sing. **2.** *Phonet.* To be changed into a vowel. **—vo′cal·i·za′tion** *n.* **—vo′cal·iz′er** *n.*

vo·ca·tion (vō-kā′shən) *n.* **1.** A profession, esp. one for which one is specially suited or trained. **2.** A strong desire to do a particular type of work, esp. religious work. [Middle English *vocacioun,* divine call to a religious life, from Old French *vocation,* from Latin *vocātiō,* a calling, from *vocāre,* to call.]

vo·ca·tion·al (vō-kā′shə-nəl) *adj.* **1.** Of or pertaining to vocations or one's vocation. **2.** Pertaining to, providing, or undergoing training in a special skill to be pursued as a trade or occupation. **—vo·ca′tion·al·ly** *adv.*

vocational school. A school that offers special training in specific trades or occupations, such as mechanics; a trade school.

voc·a·tive (vŏk′ə-tĭv) *adj.* Pertaining to or designating a grammatical case used in Latin and certain other languages to indicate the person or thing being addressed. *—n.* **1.** The vocative case. **2.** A word in this case. [Middle English *vocatif,* from Old French, from Latin *vocātīvus,* from *vocāre,* to call.] **—voc′a·tive·ly** *adv.*

vo·cif·er·ate (vō-sĭf′ə-rāt′) *v.* **-at·ed, -at·ing.** *—intr.v.* To cry out loudly; to clamor. *—tr.v.* To exclaim loudly and insistently. [Latin *vōciferārī* : *vōx,* voice + *ferre,* to bear.] **—vo·cif′er·a′tion** *n.* **—vo·cif′er·a′tor** *n.*

vo·cif·er·ous (vō-sĭf′ər-əs) *adj.* Making an outcry; clamorous; noisy: *a vociferous crowd; vociferous protests.* **—vo·cif′er·ous·ly** *adv.* **—vo·cif′er·ous·ness** *n.*

vod·ka (vŏd′kə) *n.* An alcoholic liquor distilled from fermented wheat or rye mash, corn, or potatoes. [Russian, dim. of *voda,* water.]

vogue (vōg) *n.* **1.** The current fashion, practice, or style. **2.** Popular acceptance or favor; popularity: *His novels enjoyed a great vogue in the 1930's.* —See Syns at **fashion.** [French, fashion, from *voguer,* to row, go along smoothly, from Old French.]

voice (vois) *n.* **1. a.** The sound or sounds produced by specialized organs in the respiratory tract of a vertebrate, esp. the sounds made by a human being. **b.** Sound of this kind used for music, as in singing. **c.** The ability to produce such sound: *lost his voice.* **2.** The organs that produce the voice: *Her voice reached the high notes with ease.* **3.** The condition or quality of a person's singing or vocal organs:

a baritone in excellent voice. **4.** A singer: *a chorus of 200 voices.* **5.** Any of the melodic parts in a musical composition. **6.** The expression of feelings, thoughts, etc.: *give voice to one's anger.* **7.** The right or opportunity to express a choice or opinion. **8.** A will, desire, or opinion openly expressed: *the voice of the people.* **9.** Something resembling or likened to human sound or speech in being a medium of expression: *the voice of the wind; heeding the voice of his conscience.* **10.** *Gram.* A verb form indicating the relation between the subject and the action expressed by the verb. **11.** *Phonet.* The expiration of air through vibrating vocal cords, used in the production of the vowels and voiced consonants. —See Syns at **speech.** —*tr.v.* **voiced, voic·ing. 1.** To express or utter; give voice to. **2.** *Phonet.* To produce (a speech sound) with vibration of the vocal cords. **3.** *Mus.* To regulate the tone of (the strings of a piano or pipes of an organ). [Middle English, from Old French *vois,* from Latin *vōx.*]

voice box. The larynx.

voiced (voist) *adj.* **1.** Having a voice or having a specified kind of voice: *a soft-voiced person.* **2.** Expressed by means of the voice: *a voiced opinion.* **3.** *Phonet.* Uttered with vibration of the vocal cords, as the consonant *g*.

voice·less (vois′lĭs) *adj.* **1.** Having no voice; mute; silent. **2.** *Phonet.* Uttered without vibration of the vocal cords, as the consonants *t* and *p*. —**voice′less·ly** *adv.* —**voice′less·ness** *n.*

voice-o·ver (vois′ō′vər) *n.* In motion pictures and television, the voice of an off-camera narrator.

void (void) *adj.* **1.** Having no legal force or effect: *declare a marriage null and void.* **2.** Devoid; lacking: *void of all fear; void of understanding.* **3.** Containing no matter; empty. **4.** Unoccupied; unfilled, as a position. **5.** Ineffective; useless. —*n.* **1.** An empty space; a vacuum: *the void of outer space.* **2.** An open space or break in continuity; a gap. **3.** A feeling or condition of emptiness, loneliness, or loss. —*tr.v.* **1.** To make void or of no effect; invalidate; cancel. **2. a.** To take out (the contents of something); to empty. **b.** To evacuate (body wastes). **3.** *Archaic.* To leave; vacate. [Middle English, from Old French *voide.*] —**void′er** *n.*

void·a·ble (voi′də-bəl) *adj.* Capable of being voided, esp. of being annulled. —**void′a·ble·ness** *n.*

voi·là (vwä-lä′) *interj. French.* There it is! There you are!

voile (voil, vwäl) *n.* A sheer fabric of cotton, rayon, wool, or silk, used in making lightweight curtains, dresses, etc. [French, from Latin *vēla,* pl. of *vēlum,* cloth, veil.]

vo·lant (vō′lənt) *adj.* **1.** Flying or capable of flying. **2.** Quick or nimble; agile. **3.** *Heraldry.* Depicted with the wings extended as in flying. [Latin *volāns,* pres. part. of *volāre,* to fly.]

volant

volcano
Mount St. Helens

vol·a·tile (vŏl′ə-təl, -tīl′) *adj.* **1.** Changing to vapor easily or readily at normal temperatures and pressures. **2.** Changeable, esp.: **a.** Inconstant; fickle: *catering to the volatile preferences of the public.* **b.** Tending to erupt into violent action; explosive: *a volatile political situation.* **c.** Fleeting; ephemeral. —See Syns at **capricious.** [Middle English *volatil,* flying, fleeting, from Old French, from Latin *volātilis,* from *volāre,* to fly.] —**vol·a·til·i·ty** (-tĭl′ĭ-tē) *n.*

vol·a·til·ize (vŏl′ə-tə-līz′) *v.* **-ized, -iz·ing.** —*intr.v.* **1.** To become volatile. **2.** To pass off in vapor; evaporate. —*tr.v.* **1.** To make volatile. **2.** To cause to evaporate. —**vol′a·til·**

iz·a·ble *adj.* —**vol′a·til·i·za′tion** *n.*

vol·can·ic (vŏl-kăn′ĭk) *adj.* **1.** Of, like, or characteristic of an erupting volcano. **2.** Produced or thrown forth by a volcano. **3.** Powerfully explosive: *a volcanic temper.*

volcanic glass. A volcanic igneous rock of vitreous or glassy texture, as obsidian.

vol·can·ism (vŏl′kə-nĭz′əm) *n.* Also **vul·can·ism** (vŭl′-). Volcanic force or activity.

vol·ca·no (vŏl-kā′nō) *n., pl.* **-noes** or **-nos. 1.** An opening in the crust of the earth through which molten rock, dust, ash, and hot gases are thrown forth. **2.** A mountain or other elevation formed by the material thrown forth in this way. [Italian, from Latin *Volcānus,* Vulcan.]

vole (vōl) *n.* Any of various rodents of the genus *Microtus* and related genera, related to and resembling rats or mice but with a relatively short tail. [Earlier *volemouse,* field mouse, from Norwegian *voll,* field, from Old Norse *vǫllr.*]

vo·li·tion (və-lĭsh′ən) *n.* **1.** An act of willing, choosing, or deciding. **2.** The power or capability of choosing; will: *He left of his own volition.* [French, from Medieval Latin *volitiō,* from Latin *velle,* to wish.] —**vo·li′tion·al** *adj.* —**vo·li′tion·al·ly** *adv.*

vol·ley (vŏl′ē) *n., pl.* **-leys. 1. a.** The simultaneous discharge of a number of missiles. **b.** The missiles discharged. **2.** Any burst or outburst of many things at once: *a volley of questions.* **3. a.** A shot, esp. in tennis, made by striking the ball before it touches the ground. **b.** A continuous series of such shots between opponents. —*tr.v.* **1.** To discharge in or as if in a volley. **2.** To strike (a ball) before it touches the ground. —*intr.v.* **1.** To be discharged in or as if in a volley. **2.** To hit a ball back and forth. [Old French *volee,* from Latin *volātus,* past part. of *volāre,* to fly.]

vol·ley·ball (vŏl′ē-bôl′) *n.* **1.** A game played between two teams who hit a ball back and forth over a net with the hands while attempting to score by grounding a ball on the opposing team's court. **2.** The large inflated ball used in this game.

volt (vōlt) *n.* **1.** The International System unit of electric potential and electromotive force, equal to the difference of electric potential between two points on a conducting wire carrying a constant current of one ampere when the power dissipated between the points is one watt. **2.** A unit of electric potential and electromotive force equal to 1.00034 times the International System unit. [After Count Alessandro *Volta* (1745–1827), Italian physicist.]

volt·age (vōl′tĭj) *n.* Electromotive force or potential difference, usu. expressed in volts.

vol·ta·ic (vŏl-tā′ĭk, vōl-, vôl-) *adj.* **1.** Of or indicating electricity that is produced as a result of chemical action; galvanic. **2.** Producing electricity by chemical action.

voltaic battery. An electric battery composed of a primary cell or cells.

voltaic cell. *Elect.* A cell in which an irreversible chemical reaction generates electricity.

voltaic pile. A source of electricity consisting of a number of alternating disks of two different metals separated by acid-moistened pads, forming primary cells connected in series.

vol·tam·e·ter (vŏl-tăm′ĭ-tər, vōl′tə-mē′tər) *n.* An instrument that indirectly measures an electric current by registering the chemical change resulting from producing or conducting the current.

volt·am·me·ter (vōlt′ăm′mē′tər) *n.* An instrument designed to measure current or potential. [VOLT-AM(PERE) + -METER.]

volt·am·pere (vōlt′ăm′pîr′) *n.* A unit of electric power equal to the product of one volt and one ampere, equivalent to one watt.

volt·me·ter (vōlt′mē′tər) *n.* An instrument, such as a galvanometer, that measures and indicates differences of electric potential.

vol·u·ble (vŏl′yə-bəl) *adj.* Talking very quickly and easily; fluent; loquacious. [Old French, from Latin *volūbilis,* from *volūtus,* past part. of *volvere,* to turn.] —**vol′u·bil′i·ty** *n.* —**vol′u·bly** *adv.*

vol·ume (vŏl′yōōm, -yəm) *n.* **1.** A collection of written or printed sheets bound together; a book. **2.** One book of a set. **3.** Any written material in a library, as the issues of a magazine or journal published in one year, that has been

ă pat   ā pay   â care   ä father   ĕ pet   ē be   hw which
ŏŏ took   ōō boot   ou out   th thin   *th* this   ŭ cut
ĭ pit   ī tie   î pier   ŏ pot   ō toe   ô paw, for   oi noise
û urge   zh vision   ə about, item, edible, gallop, circus

assembled and catalogued as an individual unit. **4. a.** The size or extent of a three-dimensional object or region of space. **b.** The capacity of such a region or of a specified container. **5.** A large amount: *volumes of praise.* **6. a.** The force or intensity of a sound; loudness. **b.** A control for adjusting loudness. —See Syns at **bulk.** —**idiom. speak volumes.** To be informative or deeply significant. [Middle English, roll of parchment, from Old French, from Latin *volūmen,* from *volvere,* to roll, turn.]

vol·u·met·ric (vŏl′yə-mĕt′rĭk) *adj.* Of or pertaining to measurement of volume. [VOLU(ME) + METRIC.] —**vol′u·met′ri·cal·ly** *adv.*

vo·lu·mi·nous (və-lōō′mə-nəs) *adj.* **1.** Having great volume, fullness, size, or number: *a voluminous skirt.* **2. a.** Filling or capable of filling many volumes: *voluminous transcripts from the trial.* **b.** Prolific in speech or writing. [Late Latin *volūminōsus,* having many folds, from Latin *volūmen,* roll of writing, volume.] —**vo·lu′mi·nous·ly** *adv.*

vol·un·tar·y (vŏl′ən-tĕr′ē) *adj.* **1.** Made, done, given, etc., of one's own free will. **2.** Acting or serving in a specified capacity without being compelled by another or guaranteed of reward: *voluntary workers at a hospital.* **3.** Arising from an act of choice: *living in voluntary exile in Canada.* **4.** Not accidental; intentional: *voluntary manslaughter.* **5.** Normally controlled by or subject to individual will: *a voluntary muscle.* —*n., pl.* **-ies.** *Mus.* A short solo organ piece, often improvised, usu. played before and sometimes during or after a church service. [Middle English, from Latin *voluntārius,* from *voluntās,* will, free will, from *velle,* to wish.] —**vol′un·tar′i·ly** (-târ′ə-lē) *adv.*

    Syns: voluntary, deliberate, intentional, willful *adj. Core meaning:* Subject to control of the will by an individual (*voluntary enlistment in the army*). VOLUNTARY is the most general; it implies the exercise of free will (*a voluntary contribution*) or of choice (*living in voluntary exile*). DELIBERATE suggests what is done or said on purpose (*a deliberate lie*). INTENTIONAL also implies action undertaken for a specific purpose (*intentional insolence*). What is WILLFUL is done in accordance with one's own will and often suggests obstinacy (*willful disobedience*).

voluntary muscle. Muscle normally controlled by individual volition.

vol·un·teer (vŏl′ən-tîr′) *n.* **1.** Someone who performs or gives services of his own free will. **2.** A person who enlists in the armed forces. —**modifier:** *volunteer campaigners; a volunteer fire brigade.* —*tr.v.* To give or offer of one's own accord. —*intr.v.* To enter into or offer to enter into any undertaking of one's own free will. —See Syns at **offer.** [French *volontaire,* from Latin *voluntārius,* voluntary.]

vo·lup·tu·ar·y (və-lŭp′chōō-ĕr′ē) *n., pl.* **-ies.** A person whose life is given over to luxury and sensual pleasures. [Late Latin *voluptuārius,* from Latin *voluptārius,* from *voluptās,* pleasure.] —**vo·lup′tu·ar′y** *adj.*

vo·lup·tu·ous (və-lŭp′chōō-əs) *adj.* **1.** Of, marked by, or giving sensual pleasure, luxury, etc.: *lead a voluptuous life.* **2.** Devoted to or frequently indulging in sensual gratifications. **3.** Full and appealing in form: *a voluptuous mouth.* —**vo·lup′tu·ous·ly** *adv.* —**vo·lup′tu·ous·ness** *n.*

vo·lute (və-lōōt′) *n.* **1.** A spiral, scroll-like ornament such as that used on an Ionic capital. **2.** A twisted or spiral formation. **3.** Any of various saltwater gastropod mollusks of the family Volutidae, with a spiral, often colorfully marked shell. —*adj.* Also **vo·lut·ed** (və-lōō′tĭd). Having a spiral

volute

voting machine

form; spirally twisted or rolled. [French, from Latin *volūta,* scroll, from *volvere,* to turn.]

vo·mer (vō′mər) *n.* The flat bone forming the inferior and posterior part of the nasal septum. [Latin *vōmer,* plowshare.] —**vo′mer·ine** (vō′mər-ĭn, vŏm′-) *adj.*

vom·it (vŏm′ĭt) *intr.v.* **1.** To eject or discharge part or all of the contents of the stomach through the mouth, usu. in a series of involuntary spasms. **2.** To be discharged forcefully and abundantly; spew forth. —*tr.v.* **1.** To eject from the stomach through the mouth. **2.** To eject or discharge in a gush; spew out: *The volcano vomited lava.* —*n.* Matter discharged from the stomach by vomiting. [Middle English *vomiten,* from Latin *vomere.*] —**vom′it·er** *n.*

voo·doo (vōō′dōō) *n.* **1.** A religious cult of African origin characterized by a belief in sorcery, fetishes, and primitive deities. **2.** A charm, fetish, spell, or curse believed by followers of voodoo to hold magic power. **3.** A person who performs rites at a meeting of followers of voodoo. —*tr.v.* To place under the influence of a voodoo spell; put a hex on. [Louisiana French *voudou,* of African orig.]

vo·ra·cious (vô-rā′shəs, və-) *adj.* **1.** Consuming or greedy for great amounts of food; ravenous: *a voracious appetite.* **2.** Having an insatiable appetite for some activity or pursuit; greedy: *"I continued to spend many hours of each day in rapid voracious reading"* (Susan Sontag). [Latin *vorax,* from *vorāre,* to devour.] —**vo·ra′cious·ly** *adv.* —**vo·rac′i·ty** (vô-răs′ĭ-tē, və-) or **vo·ra′cious·ness** *n.*

-vorous. A suffix meaning eating or feeding on: **herbivorous.** [Latin *-vorus,* from *vorāre,* to devour.]

vor·tex (vôr′tĕks) *n., pl.* **-tex·es** or **-ti·ces** (-tĭ-sēz′). **1.** Fluid flow, as of water or air, involving rotation about an axis; a whirlwind or whirlpool. **2.** Something regarded as drawing into its center all that surrounds it: *"As happened with so many theater actors, he was swept up in the vortex of Hollywood."* (New York Times). [Latin, from *vertere,* to turn.]

vor·ti·cel·la (vôr′tĭ-sĕl′ə) *n., pl.* **-cel·lae** (-sĕl′ē) or **-las.** Any of various bell-shaped, ciliated, stalked protozoans of the genus *Vorticella.* [From Latin *vortex,* vortex.]

vor·ti·ces (vôr′tĭ-sēz′) *n.* A plural of **vortex.**

vo·ta·ry (vō′tə-rē) *n., pl.* **-ries. 1. a.** A person, such as a monk or nun, bound by vows to live a life of religious worship or service. **b.** A devout worshipper. **2.** A person fervently devoted to an activity, leader, or ideal. [From Latin *vōtus,* past part. of *vovēre,* to vow.]

vote (vōt) *n.* **1. a.** A formal expression of one's preference or choice, made in or as if in an election. **b.** The means by which such choice is made known, as a raised hand or a ballot. **2.** The number of votes cast in an election or to resolve an issue: *a heavy vote in his favor.* **3.** A group of voters: *the labor vote.* **4.** The result of an election. **5.** The right to express one's choice in or as if in an election; suffrage: *Women fought to gain the vote.* —*v.* **vot·ed, vot·ing.** —*intr.v.* To express one's choice by a vote; cast a vote: *voted early.* —*tr.v.* **1.** To express one's preference for; endorse by a vote. **2.** To declare by general consent: *voted the play a success.* —**phrasal verbs. vote down.** To defeat in an election. **vote in.** To elect. **vote out.** To remove (an official) by means of an election. [Latin *vōtum,* vow, from *vovēre,* to vow.] —**vot′er** *n.*

voting machine. A machine used in polling places to record and count votes mechanically.

vo·tive (vō′tĭv) *adj.* Given or dedicated in fulfillment of a vow or pledge: *a votive offering; a votive statue.* [Latin *vōtīvus,* from *vōtum,* vow.]

vouch (vouch) *tr.v.* **1.** To substantiate by supplying evidence; verify. **2.** *Obs.* To assert; declare. —*intr.v.* **1.** To furnish a personal guarantee or assurance: *I'll vouch for her integrity.* **2.** To function or serve as a guarantee; furnish supporting evidence: *a deed that vouched for his courage.* [Middle English *vouchen,* to summon (as a witness), from Old French *voucher,* from Latin *vōcāre,* to call.]

vouch·er (vou′chər) *n.* **1.** A person who vouches, as a supporter, sponsor, or witness. **2.** A record, as a receipt, of a business transaction.

vouch·safe (vouch′-sāf′, vouch′sāf′) *tr.v.* **-safed, -saf·ing.** To grant or give, often as if doing a favor. [Middle English *vouchen sauf,* "to warrant as safe."]

vous·soir (vōō-swär′) *n.* Any of the wedge-shaped stones that form the curved parts of an arch or vaulted ceiling. [French, from Old French *vossoir*, ult. from Latin *volutus*, past part. of *volvere*, to roll, turn.]

vow (vou) *n.* **1.** An earnest promise or pledge that binds one to perform a specified act or behave in a certain manner. **2.** A solemn promise to live and act in accordance with the prescriptions of a religious body: *a nun's vows.* **3.** A formal declaration or assertion. —*tr.v.* **1.** To promise or pledge solemnly. **2.** To declare or assert formally. —*intr.v.* To express a promise or pledge; make a vow. —*idiom.* **take vows.** To enter a religious order. [Middle English *vowe*, from Old French, from Latin *vōtum*, from *vovēre*, to pledge, promise.] —**vow′er** *n.*

vow·el (vou′əl) *n.* **1.** *Phonet.* A voiced speech sound produced by relatively free passage of the breath through the larynx and mouth, usu. forming the most prominent and central sound of a syllable. **2.** A letter that represents such a sound, as, in the English alphabet, *a, e, i, o, u,* and sometimes *y.* —*modifier: vowel sounds.* [Middle English *vowelle*, from Old French *vouel*, from Latin *(littera) vōcālis,* "sounding (letter)," from *vōx,* voice.]

vox pop·u·li (vŏks pŏp′yə-lī′, -lē) Popular opinion or sentiment. [Latin, "voice of the people."]

voy·age (voi′ĭj) *n.* **1.** A long journey, made usu. on a ship, but sometimes times on an aircraft or spacecraft: *a voyage around Cape Horn; a voyage to the moon.* **2.** A record or account of a journey of exploration or discovery. —*v.* **-aged, -ag·ing.** —*intr.v.* To make a voyage. —*tr.v.* To travel over in a journey; sail across. [Middle English, from Old French *veiyage,* from Latin *viāticum,* provisions for a journey, from *viāticus,* of a journey, from *via,* road, way.] —**voy′ag·er** *n.*

vo·ya·geur (vwä′yä-zhœr′) *n., pl.* **-geurs** (-zhœr′). A woodsman, boatman, or guide, esp. one employed by fur companies to transport furs and supplies between remote stations in the U.S. and Canadian northwest. [French, "voyager."]

Vul·can (vŭl′kən) *n. Rom. Myth.* The god of fire and craftsmanship, esp. metalworking, identified with the Greek god Hephaestus.

vul·can·ism (vŭl′kə-nĭz′əm) *n.* Var. of **volcanism.**

vul·can·ite (vŭl′kə-nīt′) *n.* A hard rubber produced by treatment with sulfur.

vul·can·ize (vŭl′kə-nīz′) *tr.v.* **-ized, -iz·ing.** To give (rubber or similar materials) greater strength, resistance, or elasticity by combining with sulfur or other additives in the presence of heat and pressure. [From VULCAN.] —**vul′can·i·za′tion** *n.* —**vul′can·iz′er** *n.*

vul·gar (vŭl′gər) *adj.* **1.** Lacking good taste, refinement, or cultivation; crude; coarse: *vulgar jokes; a vulgar display of wealth.* **2.** Of or associated with the great masses of people as distinguished from the educated or cultivated classes; common. **3.** Spoken by or expressed in language spoken by the common people; vernacular: *Vulgar Latin.* —See Syns at **coarse.** [Middle English, from Latin *vulgāris,* from *vulgus,* the common people.] —**vul′gar·ly** *adv.*

vul·gar·i·an (vŭl-gâr′ē-ən) *n.* A vulgar person, esp. one who makes a conspicuous display of his money: *"Curse the whole pack of money-grubbing vulgarians"* (William M. Thackeray).

vul·gar·ism (vŭl′gə-rĭz′əm) *n.* **1.** A word, phrase, or manner of expression used mainly in vernacular speech. **2.** Vulgarity.

vul·gar·i·ty (vŭl-găr′ĭ-tē) *n., pl.* **-ties. 1.** The condition or quality of being vulgar; crudeness; coarseness. **2.** Something vulgar, as an act or expression that offends good taste or propriety.

vul·gar·ize (vŭl′gə-rīz′) *tr.v.* **-ized, -iz·ing. 1.** To make vulgar; cheapen. **2.** To popularize. —**vul′gar·i·za′tion** *n.* —**vul′gar·iz′er** *n.*

Vulgar Latin. The common speech of ancient Rome, differing from the literary or standard Latin.

Vul·gate (vŭl′gāt′, -gĭt) *n.* The Latin version of the Bible, used in the Roman Catholic Church. [Late Latin *vulgāta (ēditiō),* "the popular (edition)," from Latin *vulgātus,* common, popular, from *vulgus,* the common people.]

vul·ner·a·ble (vŭl′nər-ə-bəl) *adj.* **1.** Capable of being physically harmed or injured: *helpless, vulnerable baby birds.* **2.** Open to danger or attack; unprotected: *The retreat of the army had left the outlying territories vulnerable.* **3.** Easily affected or hurt, as by criticism or sarcasm. **4.** *Bridge.* In a position to receive greater penalties or bonuses after winning one game of a rubber. [Late Latin *vulnerābilis,* from Latin *vulnerāre,* to wound, from *vulnus,* wound.] —**vul′ner·a·bil′i·ty** or **vul′ner·a·ble·ness** *n.* —**vul′ner·a·bly** *adv.*

vul·pine (vŭl′pīn′) *adj.* **1.** Of, resembling, or characteristic of a fox. **2.** Clever; devious; cunning. [Latin *vulpīnus,* from *vulpēs,* fox.]

vul·ture (vŭl′chər) *n.* **1.** Any of various large birds of the family Cathartidae, of the New World, or the family Accipitridae, of the Old World, that characteristically have dark plumage and a naked head and neck and that feed on carrion. **2.** A greedy, grasping, ruthless person. [Middle English, from Old French *voltour,* from Latin *vultur.*]

vulture

vul·va (vŭl′və) *n., pl.* **-vae** (-vē). The external parts of the female genital organs. [Latin, womb, covering.] —**vul′val** or **vul′var** *adj.* —**vul′vi·form′** *adj.*

Y	Y	W	ω	Ww
Phoenician	Greek	Roman	Medieval	Modern

Phoenician – About 3,000 years ago the Phoenicians and other Semitic peoples began to use graphic signs to represent individual speech sounds instead of syllables or whole words. They used this symbol, which is the ancestor of the letters F, U, V, and Y as well as W, to represent the sound of the semivowel "w" and gave it the name wāw, the Phoenician word for "hook."

Greek – The Greeks borrowed the Phoenician alphabet with some modifications. They changed the shape of wāw slightly and altered its name to upsilon. They used upsilon to represent the sound of the vowel "u."

Roman – The Romans borrowed the alphabet from the Greeks via the Etruscans, who used a tailless variant of upsilon. The Romans used upsilon to represent both the vowel

"u" and the semivowel "w," which later developed into the consonant "v."

Medieval – The symbol we now know as W was developed in England during the 7th century to represent the semivowel "w," which had been lost in Latin but which was an important sound in Old English. The name "double-u" indicates its origin: it was formed first by writing two cursive U's next to each other. Later the two letters were joined by a ligature.

Modern – Since the invention of printing about 500 years ago the shape of W, based on the medieval letter, has become standardized. Although both the upper- and lower-case printed letters are based on the letter V, the original name has persisted in English.

---

w, W (dŭb′əl-yōō, -yōō) n., pl. **w's** or **W's**. The 23rd letter of the modern English alphabet.

W The symbol for the element tungsten.

wab·ble (wŏb′əl) v. & n. Var. of **wobble**.

Wac (wăk) n. A member of the Women's Army Corps of the U.S. Army, organized during World War II. [W(OM-EN'S) A(RMY) C(ORPS).]

wack·y (wăk′ē) adj. **-i·er, -i·est**. Also **whack·y** (hwăk′ē, wăk′-ē). Slang. Crazy or silly; nutty. —See Syns at **foolish**.

wad (wŏd) n. **1.** A small, soft piece of material, such as cotton, paper, or chewing gum, pressed together in a mass. **2. a.** A plug, as of cloth or paper, used to hold in a powder charge in a muzzleloading gun or cannon. **b.** A disk, as of felt or paper, to keep the powder and shot in place in a shotgun cartridge. **3.** Informal. **a.** A sizable roll of paper money. **b.** A considerable amount of money. —tr.v. **wad·ded, wad·ding. 1.** To compress into a wad: wadded paper into a ball. **2.** To pad, pack, line, or plug with wadding. **3.** To hold (shot or powder) in place with a wad. [Orig. unknown.]

wad·ding (wŏd′ĭng) n. **1.** Wads in general. **2.** A soft layer of fibrous cotton or wool used for padding or stuffing. **3.** Material for gun wads.

wad·dle (wŏd′l) intr.v. **-dled, -dling**. To walk with short steps that tilt or sway the body from side to side, as a duck does. —n. A rocking or swaying walk. [Prob. freq. of WADE.]

wade (wād) v. **wad·ed, wad·ing**. —intr.v. **1.** To walk in or through water, mud or another substance that hinders free or normal movement. **2.** To make one's way slowly and with difficulty: We had to wade through stacks of files. —tr.v. To cross by wading: waded the river. —phrasal verb. **wade in** (or **into**). To plunge into, begin, or attack resolutely and energetically. —n. The act of wading. [Middle English waden, to go, walk through (water), from Old English wadan.]

wad·er (wā′dər) n. **1.** Someone or something that wades. **2.** A long-legged bird that frequents shallow water. **3. waders.** Waterproof hip boots or trousers worn esp. by fishermen or hunters.

wa·di (wä′dē) n., pl. **-dis.** Also **wa·dy** pl. **-dies. 1.** In northern Africa and southwestern Asia, a valley, gully, or riverbed that remains dry except during the rainy season. **2.** A stream that flows through such a channel. [Arabic wādī.]

wa·fer (wā′fər) n. **1.** A small, thin, crisp cookie, cracker, or

candy. **2.** Eccles. A small, thin disk of unleavened bread used in Communion. **3.** A small disk of adhesive material used as a seal for papers. [Middle English wafre, from Norman French, from Middle Low German wāfel.]

waf·fle[1] (wŏf′əl) n. A light, crisp batter cake baked in a waffle iron. [Dutch wafel.]

waf·fle[2] (wŏf′əl) intr.v. **-fled, -fling.** Informal. To speak or write evasively; be willfully misleading: He waffled on the issue of tax reform. [Orig. unknown.]

waffle iron. An appliance with hinged, indented metal plates that impress a grid pattern into waffle batter as it bakes.

waft (wäft, wăft) tr.v. To carry or cause to drift gently and smoothly through the air or over water. —intr.v. To float or drift easily and gently, as on the air. —n. **1.** Something, as a scent or sound, carried through the air. **2.** A light breeze or rush as of air. [Back-formation from obs. wafter, a convoy, from Middle English waughter.]

wag[1] (wăg) v. **wagged, wag·ging.** —intr.v. To move briskly and repeatedly from side to side, to and fro, or up and down. —tr.v. To wag (a part of the body), as in playfulness, agreement, admonition, or chatter. —n. The act or motion of wagging. [Middle English waggen, from Old English wagian, to totter.]

wag[2] (wăg) n. A playful or mischievous person; joker. [Orig. unknown.]

wage (wāj) n. **1.** Often **wages.** A payment made to a worker for work done or services rendered; salary or earnings. **2.** Often **wages** (used with a sing. or pl. verb). A suitable return or reward. —tr.v. **waged, wag·ing.** To engage in or carry on (a war, campaign, etc.): wage war on pov-

wader

---

erty. [Middle English, a pledge, wage, soldier's pay, from Old North French.]

wa·ger (wā′jər) n. **1.** A gambling agreement under which each bettor pledges a certain amount to the other depending upon the outcome of an unsettled matter. **2.** The matter betted on; a gamble. **3.** Something staked on an uncertain outcome; a bet. —tr.v. To risk or stake (an amount or possession) on an uncertain outcome; to bet: I wagered fifty dollars on the race. —intr.v. To make a wager; to bet. [Middle English, a pledge, from Norman French wageure, from wager, to pledge, from wage, a pledge.] —**wa′ger·er** n.

wag·ger·y (wăg′ə-rē) n., pl. **-ies. 1.** Waggish behavior or spirit; mischievousness; playfulness. **2.** A playful remark or act. [From WAG (joker).]

wag·gish (wăg′ĭsh) adj. Characteristic of a wag; playfully humorous. —**wag′gish·ly** adv.

wag·gle (wăg′əl) v. **-gled, -gling.** —tr.v. To move (an attached part) with short, quick motions; wiggle or wag. —intr.v. To move with short, quick motions. —n. A waggling motion. [Freq. of WAG.] —**wag′gly** adj.

wag·on (wăg′ən). Also Brit. **wag·gon.** —n. **1.** A four-wheeled horse-drawn vehicle having a large rectangular body for transporting loads or carrying passengers. **2. a.** A light, roomy motor vehicle used for automotive transport or delivery. **b.** A **station wagon. c.** A police patrol wagon. **3.** A child's low four-wheeled cart hauled by a long handle that controls the direction of the front wheels. **4.** A small table or tray on wheels for serving drinks or food: a dessert wagon. **5.** Brit. An open railway freight car. —**idiom. on the wagon.** Slang. Abstaining from liquor. [Dutch wagen.]

wa·gon-lit (vä-gôN-lē′) n., pl. **wagons-lits** or **wagon-lits** (vä-gôN-lē′). A railroad sleeping car. [French: wagon, railway car + lit, bed.]

wagon train. A line or group of wagons traveling cross-country.

wahoo¹

wa·hoo¹ (wä-hōō′, wä′hōō) n., pl. **-hoos.** A shrub or small tree, Euonymus atropurpureus, of eastern North America, with small purplish flowers and red fruit. [Dakota wáhu.]

wa·hoo² (wä-hōō′, wä′hōō) n., pl. **wahoo** or **-hoos.** A tropical saltwater game fish, Acanthocybium solanderi. [Orig. unknown.]

waif (wāf) n. **1.** A lost or homeless person, esp. a forsaken child. **2.** An abandoned young animal; a stray. [Middle English waife, ownerless property, from Norman French waif, unclaimed.]

wail (wāl) intr.v. **1.** To cry loudly and mournfully, as in grief, dismay, or distress: The injured man wailed in pain. **2.** To make a prolonged, high-pitched sound suggestive of a cry: The wind wailed through the trees. —tr.v. To cry out plaintively; to lament: a widow wailing her grief. —n. **1.** A long, high-pitched, mournful cry, as of grief or pain. **2.** Any similar sound: the wail of the wind. [Middle English wailen.] —**wail′er** n. —**wail′ing·ly** adv.

wain (wān) n. A large open farm wagon. [Middle English wain, from Old English wæg(e)n.]

wain·scot (wān′skət, -skŏt′, -skōt′) n. **1.** A facing or paneling, usu. of wood, applied to the walls of a room. **2.** The lower part of an interior wall when finished in a material different from the upper part. —tr.v. **-scot·ed** or **-scot·ted, -scot·ing** or **-scot·ting.** To line or panel with wainscot. [Middle English waynscotte, from Middle Dutch wagenschot.]

wain·scot·ing (wān′skə-tĭng, -skŏt′ĭng, -skō′tĭng) n. Also **wain·scot·ting. 1.** A wainscoted wall or walls; paneling. **2.** Wood or other material for such paneling.

wain·wright (wān′rīt′) n. A builder and repairer of wagons.

waist (wāst) n. **1.** The part of the human trunk between the bottom of the rib cage and the pelvis. **2. a.** The part of a garment that encircles the waist of the body. **b.** A garment or a part of a garment that extends from the shoulders to the waistline, esp. a woman's dress. **3.** The middle section or part of an object, esp. when narrower than the rest. **4.** Naut. The middle part of the deck of a ship between the forecastle and the quarter-deck. [Middle English waast.]

waist·band (wāst′bănd′) n. **1.** A garment band encircling the waist, as on trousers. **2.** A sash.

waist·coat (wĕs′kĭt, wāst′kōt′) n. Brit. A vest.

waist·line (wāst′līn′) n. **1. a.** The place at which the circumference of the waist is smallest. **b.** The measurement of this circumference. **2.** The point or line at which the skirt and bodice of a dress join.

wait (wāt) intr.v. **1.** To stay somewhere or postpone further action until someone or something comes: Wait for me here. Wait until dark. **2.** To stop, pause, hesitate, or delay: "Wait! I forgot something." **3.** To remain temporarily neglected, unattended to, or postponed: The trip will have to wait. **4.** To work as a waiter or waitress. —tr.v. **1.** To remain or stay in expectation of; await: wait one's turn. **2.** Informal. To delay (an event); postpone: They waited lunch. **3.** To be a waiter at: wait table. —**phrasal verbs. wait on** (or **upon**). **1.** To serve the needs of. **2.** To make a formal call upon; visit. **wait out.** To delay until an end or conclusion is reached. —n. A period of time spent in waiting: a long wait. —**idiom. lie in wait.** To stay in hiding, awaiting a chance to attack. [Middle English waiten, to watch, lie in wait, from Old North French waitier.]

wait·er (wā′tər) n. **1.** A man who serves food and drink to diners, as in a restaurant. **2.** A tray or salver.

wait·ing (wā′tĭng) n. **1.** The act of a person who waits. **2.** The period of time spent waiting. —**idiom. in waiting.** In attendance.

waiting game. The stratagem of allowing the passage of time to work in one's favor by deferring action.

waiting list. A list of persons waiting, as for an appointment.

waiting room. A room, as in a railroad station or doctor's office, for the use of persons waiting.

wait·ress (wā′trĭs) n. A woman who serves food and drink to diners, as in a restaurant.

waive (wāv) tr.v. **waived, waiv·ing. 1.** To give up (a claim or right) voluntarily: The defendant decided to waive a jury trial. **2.** To set aside, dispense with, or postpone: Let's waive the formalities. [Middle English weiven, to outlaw, abandon, from Norman French weyver, from waif, ownerless property.]

waiv·er (wā′vər) n. **1.** The relinquishment of a right, claim, or privilege by choise or consent. **2.** A written agreement to give up a right or claim.

wake¹ (wāk) v. **woke** (wōk) or **waked** (wākt), **waked** or **wo·ken** (wō′kən), **wak·ing.** —intr.v. **1.** To cease to sleep; become awake; awaken. **2.** To be brought into a state of awareness or alertness. —tr.v. **1.** To rouse from sleep; awaken. **2.** To stir, as from a dormant or inactive condition; rouse: wake old animosities. **3.** To make aware of; alert. —See Usage note at **awake.** —n. A watch or vigil kept over the body of a dead person before burial. [Middle English wakien and waken.]

wake² (wāk) n. **1.** The visible track of waves, ripples, or foam left by something moving through water: the wake of a ship. **2.** The track or course left behind anything that has passed: He leaves a wake of broken hearts wherever he goes. The hurricane left destruction in its wake. —**idiom. in the wake of. 1.** Following directly upon: in the wake of the storm. **2.** In the aftermath of; as a consequence of: In the wake of the battle there was pain and suffering. [Of Scandinavian orig.]

wake·ful (wāk′fəl) adj. **1. a.** Not sleeping or able to sleep. **b.** Without sleep; sleepless: a wakeful night of worry. **2.** Watchful. —See Syns at **alert.** —**wake′ful·ly** adv. —**wake′ful·ness** n.

wak·en (wā′kən) tr.v. **1.** To rouse from sleep; awake. **2.** To rouse to a state of awareness; stir: *waken him to the realities of modern life.* —*intr.v.* To become awake; wake up: *He wakens at an early hour.* —See Usage note at **awake.** [Middle English *wakenen,* from Old English *wæcnian.*] —**wak'en·er** *n.*

wake-rob·in (wāk'rŏb'ĭn) *n.* A plant, the trillium. [Orig. unknown.]

wale (wāl) *n.* **1.** One of a series of raised ridges in the texture of some materials, such as corduroy. **2.** A ridge raised on the skin by a lash or blow; a welt. **3.** *Naut.* One of the heavy planks or strakes extending along the sides of a wooden ship. [Middle English, a ridge, gunwale, from Old English *walu,* a ridge of earth or stone, weal.]

walk (wôk) *intr.v.* **1.** To move over a surface by taking steps with the feet at a pace slower than a run. **2.** To go or travel on foot. **3.** To go on foot for pleasure or exercise; stroll: *walking in the park.* **4.** To move in a manner suggestive of walking. **5.** To conduct oneself or behave in a particular manner; live: *He walks in peace and joy among his parishioners.* **6.** To roam about in visible form, as a ghost; appear: *The specter walks the castle grounds each night.* **7. a.** *Baseball.* To go to first base after the pitcher has thrown four balls. **b.** *Basketball.* To travel with the ball in one's possession. —*tr.v.* **1.** To go or pass over, on, or through by walking: *walk the streets.* **2.** To bring to a specified condition by walking: *walk someone to exhaustion.* **3.** To cause to walk or proceed at a walk: *walk a horse around the riding ring.* **4.** To accompany in walking; escort on foot. **5.** To traverse on foot in order to survey or measure; pace off: *walked the bounds of his property.* **6.** To move (a heavy or cumbersome object) in a manner suggestive of walking: *walked the chest from the hall into the den.* **8.** *Baseball.* To allow (a batter) to go to first base by pitching four balls. —*phrasal verbs.* **walk away from. 1.** To outdo, outrun, or defeat with little difficulty: *He just walked away from the competition.* **2.** To survive (an accident) with very little injury. **walk off with. 1.** To win easily or unexpectedly: *walked off with first place in the contest.* **2.** To steal. **walk out.** To go or on strike. **walk out on.** *Informal.* To desert; abandon. **walk over. 1.** *Informal.* To treat badly or ignore the feelings of. **2.** To gain an easy victory. **walk through.** To perform (a play, acting role, dance, etc.) in a perfunctory fashion, as at a first rehearsal. —*n.* **1.** An outing, excursion, or journey on foot. **2.** A distance covered or to be covered in walking, esp. in relation to time required: *a ten-minute walk to town.* **3.** A pathway or sidewalk on which to walk. **4.** An act, way, or speed of walking: *a waddling walk; a brisk walk.* **5. a.** A relatively slow gait in which the feet touch the ground one after another. **b.** The gait of a horse in which at least two feet are always touching the ground. **6.** *Baseball.* The automatic advance of a batter to first base by pitching four balls. **7.** An enclosed area designed for the pasture or exercise of livestock. —*idiom.* **walk of life.** Social class or occupation: *people from all walks of life.* [From both Middle English *walken,* from Old English *wealcan,* to roll, toss, and Middle English *walkien,* from Old English *wealcian,* to roll up, muffle up.]

walk·er (wô'kər) *n.* **1.** Someone or something that walks. **2.** A device, esp. a metal framework, that aids in walking.

walk·a·way (wôk'ə-wā') *n.* A contest or victory easily won; walkover.

walk-ie-talk·ie (wô'kē-tô'kē) *n.* Also **walk-y-talk-y** *pl.* **-ies.** A battery-powered portable sending and receiving radio set.

walk-in (wôk'ĭn') *adj.* **1.** Large enough to admit entrance, as a closet. **2.** Located so as to be entered directly from the street, as an apartment. —**walk'-in'** *n.*

walking papers. *Informal.* Notice of discharge or dismissal.

walking stick. 1. A cane or staff used as an aid in walking. **2.** Any of various insects of the family Phasmidae, that have the appearance of twigs or sticks.

walk-on (wôk'ŏn', -ôn') *n.* A minor role in a theatrical production, usu. without speaking lines.

walk·out (wôk'out') *n.* **1.** A strike of workers. **2.** The act of leaving or quitting a meeting, company, or organization, esp. as a sign of protest.

walk·o·ver (wôk'ō'vər) *n.* **1.** A horse race with only one horse entered, won by the mere formality of walking the length of the track. **2.** A walkaway.

walk·up (wôk'ŭp') *n.* Also **walk-up. 1.** An apartment house or office building with no elevator. **2.** An apartment or office in such a building.

walk·way (wôk'wā') *n.* A passage for walking.

wall (wôl) *n.* **1.** A solid structure or partition that extends upward to enclose an area or to separate two areas from each other. **2.** Anything that encloses or forms the side, surface, or outer boundary of something: *the walls of a canyon; the wall of the stomach.* **3.** Anything that rises, separates, surrounds, or protects like a wall: *a white wall of fog; a wall of silence.* —*tr.v.* To enclose, surround, protect, or separate with or as with a wall. [Middle English *walle,* Old English *weall,* from Latin *vallum,* from *vallus,* stake.]

wal·la·by (wŏl'ə-bē) *n., pl.* **-bies.** Any of various marsupials of the genus *Wallabia* and related genera, of Australia and adjacent islands, that are related to and resemble the kangaroos but are gen. smaller. [From *wolabā,* an Australian native name.]

wallaby

wal·la·roo (wŏl'ə-rōō') *n., pl.* **-roos.** A kangaroo, *Macropus robustus,* of hilly regions of Australia. [From *wolaru,* an Australian native name.]

wall·board (wôl'bôrd', -bōrd') *n.* Any of several rigid sheets of various materials, such as gypsum plaster encased in paper, compressed wood fibers, or plastic, used in construction as a substitute for plaster or wood panels on the interior walls of a building.

wal·let (wŏl'ĭt) *n.* A small, flat folding case, usu. made of leather, for holding paper money, cards, photographs, etc.; billfold. [Middle English *walet,* a pilgrim's knapsack or provisions bag.]

wall·eye (wôl'ī') *n.* **1. a.** An eye that turns out to one side rather than being aligned with the other eye. **b.** An eye in which the cornea is white or opaque. **c.** An eye in which the iris has no color. **2.** A freshwater food and game fish, *Stizostedium vitreum,* of North America, with large, conspicuous eyes. Also called **walleyed pike.** [Back-formation from WALLEYED.]

wall·eyed (wôl'īd') *adj.* **1.** Having a walleye or walleyes. **2.** Having large bulging or staring eyes. [Var. of Middle English *wawil-eghed,* from Old Norse *vagl-eygr.*]

walleyed pike. The **walleye.**

wall·flow·er (wôl'flou'ər) *n.* **1.** A widely cultivated plant, *Cheiranthus cheiri,* native to Europe, with fragrant yellow, orange, or brownish flowers. **2.** *Informal.* A person who does not participate in the activity at a social event because of shyness or unpopularity.

wal·lop (wŏl'əp) *Informal.* —*tr.v.* **1.** To beat soundly; thrash: *walloped the man senseless.* **2.** To strike with a hard blow; hit. **3.** To defeat thoroughly. —See Syns at **hit.** —*n.* **1.** A hard or severe blow: *a wallop to his oponent's midriff.* **2. a.** The force to strike such a blow: *a punch that packs a wallop.* **b.** The capacity to create a forceful effect; impact: *That ad really carries a wallop.* [From Middle English *walopen,* to gallop, from Old North French *waloper.*] —**wal'lop·er** *n.*

wal·lop·ing (wŏl'ə-pĭng). *Informal.* —*adj.* Very large; huge. —*n.* A sound thrashing or defeat.

wal·low (wŏl'ō) *intr.v.* **1.** To roll or flounder about clumsily, as in water, snow, or mud. **2.** To indulge oneself shamelessly; luxuriate; revel: *wallow in luxury.* **3.** To be or become abundantly supplied with something: *wallowing in* money. —*n.* **1.** An act of wallowing. **2.** A place, as a mud hole, where animals go to wallow. [Middle English *walo-wen,* from Old English *wealwian.*]

wall·pa·per (wôl′pā′pər) *n.* Heavy paper printed with designs or colors for use as a pasted-on wall covering inside a house. —*tr.v.* To cover with wallpaper. —*intr.v.* To decorate a wall or room with wallpaper.

Wall Street. The controlling financial interests of the United States. [After *Wall Street* in New York City, the main street of the financial district.]

wall-to-wall (wôl′tə-wôl′) *adj.* Covering a floor completely: *wall-to-wall carpeting.*

wal·nut (wôl′nŭt′, -nət) *n.* **1.** Any of several trees of the genus *Juglans,* with round, sticky fruit that encloses an edible nut. **2.** The ridged or corrugated nut of such a tree. **3.** The hard, dark-brown wood of such a tree. [Middle English *walnot,* from Old English *wealh-hnutu,* "foreign nut."]

walnut   war bonnet

wal·rus (wôl′rəs, wŏl′-) *n., pl.* **-rus·es** or **walrus.** A large saltwater mammal, *Odobenus rosmarus,* of Arctic regions, with tough, wrinkled skin and large tusks. [Dutch, of Scandinavian orig.]

waltz (wôlts) *n.* **1.** A dance in triple time with a strong accent on the first beat of each measure. **2.** The music for this dance. —*intr.v.* **1.** To dance the waltz. **2.** To move lightly and easily, as if dancing: *waltzed out of the room as if carried on air.* **3.** To accomplish a task, chore, or assignment with little effort. —*tr.v.* **1.** To dance the waltz with: *He waltzed her around the ballroom.* **2.** To lead or force to move briskly and purposefully: *waltzed him into the principal's office.* [German *Walzer,* from Middle High German *walzen,* to roll, turn, dance, from Old High German *walzan,* to roll.] —**waltz′er** *n.*

wam·pum (wŏm′pəm, wôm′-) *n.* **1.** Small beads made from pieces of polished shells and strung together into strands or belts, formerly used by North American Indians as money or jewelry. **2.** *Informal.* Money. [From Algonquian *wampumpeage,* "white strings."]

wan (wŏn) *adj.* **wan·ner, wan·nest. 1.** Unnaturally pale, as from physical or emotional distress: *a wan face.* **2.** Weak or faint: *a wan smile.* —See Syns at **haggard.** [Middle English, gloomy, wan, from Old English *wann,* dusky, dark, livid.] —**wan′ly** *adv.* —**wan′ness** *n.*

wand (wŏnd) *n.* A slender rod or stick carried in the hand, esp. one used in working magic. [Middle English, from Old Norse *vöndr.*]

wan·der (wŏn′dər) *intr.v.* **1.** To move or travel about freely or aimlessly with no destination or purpose; roam: *wandered from town to town.* **2.** To go by an indirect route or at no set pace; amble; stroll: *wander towards town.* **3.** To proceed in an irregular course or action; meander. **4.** To stray from a given place, path, group, or subject. **5.** To think or express oneself unclearly or incoherently: *His speech began to wander until he fell silent altogether.* —*tr.v.* To move or travel across or through without a fixed purpose or destination: *wander the forests and fields.* —*n.* The act or an instance of wandering. [Middle English *wanderen,* from Old English *wandrian.*] —**wan′der·er** *n.* —**wan′der·ing·ly** *adv.*

wandering jew. Either of two trailing plants, *Tradescantia fluminensis* or *Zebrina pendula,* native to tropical America, with usu. variegated foliage, popular as house plants.

wan·der·lust (wŏn′dər-lŭst′) *n.* A strong or irresistible impulse to travel. [German *Wanderlust.*]

wane (wān) *intr.v.* **waned, wan·ing. 1.** To show a progressively smaller lighted surface, as the moon does when passing from full to new. **2.** To decrease, as in size, strength, importance, etc. **3.** To draw to a close: *The old year was waning.* —*n.* **1.** The time, phase, or stage during which the moon wanes. **2.** A gradual decrease or decline. —*idiom.* **on the wane.** In a period of decline; waning. [Middle English *wanien,* from Old English *wanian,* to lessen.]

wan·gle (wăng′gəl) *v.* **-gled, -gling.** —*tr.v.* **1.** To make, achieve, or get by clever, tricky, or devious means: *He wangled extra vacation time.* **2.** To manipulate, contrive, or juggle, esp. fraudulently: *wangled them into thinking he's innocent.* **3.** To extricate (oneself) from difficulty: *wangled his way out of debt.* —*intr.v.* To extricate oneself by subtle or indirect means, as from difficulty; wriggle: *wangled out of a bad situation.* [Orig. unknown.] —**wan′gler** *n.*

Wan·kel engine (văng′kəl, wäng′-). A rotary internal-combustion engine in which a single triangular rotor that turns in a specially shaped housing performs the functions allotted to the several pistons of a conventional engine. [After Felix *Wankel* (b. 1902), German engineer.]

want (wŏnt, wônt) *tr.v.* **1.** To desire greatly; wish for. **2.** To fail to have; be without; lack. **3.** To need or require. **4.** To seek with intent to capture or arrest, as a lawbreaker. —*intr.v.* **1.** To have need; be without: *He wants for nothing in life.* **2.** To be destitute or needy: *There are millions of people in the world who want.* **3.** To be disposed; like; wish. —See Syns at **choose.** —**phrasal verb. want in (or out).** *Informal.* To wish to join (or leave) a project, business, or other undertaking. —*n.* **1.** The condition or quality of lacking what's usual or necessary; deficiency; lack: *There was no want of respect in his manner.* **2.** Pressing need; destitution: *live in want; in want of food and shelter.* **3.** Something needed or desired; a need or wish: *moderate wants.* **4.** A defect of character; a fault. [Middle English *wanten,* from Old Norse *vanta,* to be lacking.]

Usage: **want.** The phrase *want for* is standard when expressing need: *She did not want for funds.* Avoid the phrase when expressing a wish or desire: *She wants him to leave* (not *wants for him to leave*).

want ad. A classified advertisement.

want·ing (wŏn′tĭng, wôn′-) *adj.* **1.** Absent; lacking. **2.** Not up to standards or expectations. —*prep.* **1.** Without. **2.** Minus; less.

wan·ton (wŏn′tən) *adj.* **1.** Shameless or immoral: *wanton treachery; wanton lawlessness.* **2.** Maliciously cruel and unjust; merciless: *wanton killing.* **3.** Lewd or openly sensual. **4.** Freely extravagant; excessive: *wanton spending.* **5.** Unrestrained; frolicsome. —*intr.v.* To act in a wanton manner; be wanton. —*tr.v.* To waste or squander wantonly. —*n.* An immoral, shameless, or uncontrolled person. [Middle English *wantowen,* lacking discipline, lewd.] —**wan′ton·ly** *adv.* —**wan′ton·ness** *n.*

wap·i·ti (wŏp′ĭ-tē) *n., pl.* **-tis** or **wapiti.** A large North American deer, *Cervus canadensis,* with many-branched antlers. Also called **elk.** [Shawnee *wapiti,* "white rump."]

war (wôr) *n.* **1.** Armed conflict in which two or more nations, states, factions, or peoples fight each other. **2.** A serious, intense, determined struggle or attack: *a war on poverty.* **3.** The techniques or procedures of war; military science. —See Syns at **conflict.** —*intr.v.* **warred, war·ring. 1.** To carry on or engage in war. **2.** To struggle, contend, or fight. [Middle English *werre,* from Old North French, from Old High German *werra,* confusion, strife.]

war·ble (wôr′bəl) *v.* **-bled, -bling.** —*tr.v.* To sing with trills, runs, or other melodic embellishments, as certain birds do. —*intr.v.* **1.** To sing with trills, runs, or quavers. **2.** To be sounded in a trilling or quavering manner. —*n.* A sound made or a song sung by warbling like a bird. [Old North French *werbler,* from *werble,* a warbling, melody.]

war·bler (wôr′blər) *n.* **1.** Any of various small New World birds of the family Parulidae, many of which have yellowish plumage or markings. **2.** Any of various small, brownish or grayish Old World birds of the subfamily Silviinae.

war bonnet. A ceremonial headdress used by some North American Plains Indians that consists of a band and a trailing extension decorated with feathers.

war crime. Often **war crimes.** Any of various crimes committed during a war and considered to be in violation of the customs of warfare, as mistreatment of prisoners of war or genocide. **—war criminal.**

ward (wôrd) n. **1. a.** A section of a hospital devoted to the care of a particular group of patients. **b.** A large hospital room shared by a number of patients. **c.** One of the divisions of a jail or other penal institution. **2.** An administrative division of a city or town, esp. an election district. **3.** Someone, esp. a child or young person, placed under the care or protection of a guardian or a court. **4. a.** The condition of being under guard; custody. **b.** The act of guarding or protecting someone; guardianship. **5. a.** The projecting ridge of a lock or keyhole that prevents the turning of any key other than the proper one. **b.** The notch cut into a key that corresponds to such a ridge. **—phrasal verb. ward off.** To keep from striking; fend off; avert. **—See Syns at repel.** [Middle English *warde*, a guarding, place for guarding, person or thing in one's care, from Old English *weard*, a watching over.]

-ward or **-wards.** A suffix meaning direction toward: **skyward, westwards.** [Middle English *-ward*, from Old English *-weard*.]

war dance. A tribal dance performed by certain primitive peoples before a battle or as a celebration after a victory.

war·den (wôr'dn) n. **1.** The chief administrative official of a prison. **2.** An official charged with the enforcement of certain laws and regulations: *a game warden; a fire warden.* **3.** In the Anglican and Episcopal churches, a lay officer chosen to handle the secular affairs of the parish. [Middle English *wardein*, from Old North French, from *warder*, to guard, of Germanic orig.]

ward·er (wôr'dər) n. **1.** A guard, porter, or watchman of a gate or tower. **2.** *Brit.* A prison guard. [Middle English, from Norman French *wardere*, from Old North French *warder*, to guard, of Germanic orig.]

ward heel·er (hē'lər). *Slang.* A worker for the ward organization of a political machine.

ward·robe (wôr'drōb') n. **1.** A tall cabinet, closet, or small room designed to hold clothes. **2.** Garments collectively, esp. all the clothing belonging to one person. **3.** The costumes belonging to a theater or theatrical troupe. [Middle English *warderobe*, from Old North French : *warder*, to guard + *robe*, robe.]

ward·room (wôrd'rōōm', -rŏŏm') n. **1.** The common recreation area and dining room for the commissioned officers on a warship. **2.** These officers in general.

-wards. Var. of **-ward.**

ward·ship (wôrd'shĭp') n. **1.** The condition of being a ward. **2.** Guardianship; custody.

ware[1] (wâr) n. **1.** Manufactured articles or goods of the same general kind, such as glassware or hardware. **2.** Pottery or ceramics, such as earthenware or stoneware. **3. wares.** Goods for sale. [Middle English *ware*, from Old English *waru*.]

ware[2] (wâr) tr.v. **wared, war·ing.** *Archaic.* To beware of. **—adj.** *Obs.* Watchful; wary. [Middle English *waren*, from Old English *warian.*]

ware·house (wâr'hous') n. A building in which goods or merchandise are stored. **—tr.v. -housed, -hous·ing.** To place or store in a warehouse.

war·fare (wôr'fâr') n. **1.** The act of waging war; armed conflict. **2.** Conflict of any kind; struggle; strife. **—See Syns at conflict.** [Middle English *werrefare*, a going to war : *werre*, war + *fare*, a journey, from Old English *faru*.]

war·head (wôr'hĕd') n. A section in the forward part of a bomb, guided missile, torpedo, etc., that contains the explosive charge.

war·horse (wôr'hôrs') n. Also **war horse. 1.** A horse used in combat; a charger. **2.** *Informal.* A person who has been through many battles, struggles, or fights.

war·like (wôr'līk') adj. **1.** Liking or easily encouraged to make war; hostile: *a warlike people.* **2.** Threatening or indicating war: *a warlike speech.*

war·lock (wôr'lŏk') n. A male witch; wizard. [Middle English *warloghe*, from Old English *wærloga*, "oath-breaker."]

war·lord (wôr'lôrd') n. **1.** A military leader, esp. of a warlike nation. **2.** A military commander exercising civil

power in a given region, usu. by force of arms.

warm (wôrm) adj. **-er, -est. 1.** Moderately hot; neither cold nor very hot: *warm weather; warm water.* **2.** Giving off or keeping in a moderate amount of heat: *the warm sun; a warm sweater.* **3.** Having a sensation of unusually high bodily heat, as from exercise or hard work; overheated. **4.** Enthusiastic, friendly, kindly, or affectionate: *a warm smile; warm support.* **5.** Excited, animated, or emotional: *a warm debate.* **6. a.** Suggesting the heat or glow of fire, as red, orange, and yellow colors do. **b.** Pleasingly rich and mellow: *The violoncello has a warm sound.* **7.** Recently made; fresh: *a warm trail.* **8.** Close to discovering, guessing, or finding something, as in certain games. **9.** *Informal.* Uncomfortable because of danger or annoyance: *Things are getting warm for the bookies.* **—tr.v. 1.** To heat or raise slightly in temperature. **2.** To inspire with vitality, enthusiasm, or ardor. **3.** To fill with pleasant emotions: *Her smile warmed me.* **—intr.v. 1.** To become warm. **2.** To become ardent, enthusiastic, or animated: *warming to his subject.* **3.** To become kindly disposed or friendly: *I warmed to your friend immediately.* **—phrasal verb. warm up. 1.** To make or become warm or warmer. **2.** To make or become ready for action, as by exercising, practicing beforehand, etc. [Middle English, from Old English *wearm.*] **—warm'er** n. **—warm'ish** adj. **—warm'ly** adv. **—warm'ness** n.

warm-blood·ed (wôrm'blŭd'ĭd) adj. **1.** *Zool.* Maintaining a relatively constant and warm body temperature independent of environmental temperature. **2.** Full of feeling; enthusiastic. **—warm'-blood'ed·ness** n.

warm-heart·ed (wôrm'här'tĭd) adj. Kind; friendly. **—See Syns at friendly. —warm'-heart'ed·ly** adv. **—warm'-heart'ed·ness** n.

war·mon·ger (wôr'mŭng'gər, -mŏng'-) n. Someone who advocates or attempts to stir up war. **—war'mon'ger·ing** n.

warmth (wôrmth) n. **1.** The quality or condition of being, feeling, or seeming warm; warmness. **2.** Friendliness and generosity: *a person of great warmth and charm.* **3.** Excitement or intensity: *warmth of feeling.* **4.** The glowing effect produced by using predominantly red or yellow colors. [Middle English.]

warm-up (wôrm'ŭp') n. The act, procedure, or period of warming up before an event, performance, etc.

warn (wôrn) tr.v. **1.** To make aware of present or approaching harm, danger, or evil; to alert. **2.** To advise, caution, or counsel: *warned them to be careful.* **3.** To notify (a person) to go or stay away: *A sign warned people away.* **4.** To notify or inform in advance. **—intr.v.** To give a warning: *We have warned against taking such action.* [Middle English *warnen*, from Old English *wearnian*, to take heed, warn.] **—warn'er** n.

warn·ing (wôr'nĭng) n. **1.** Advance notice, as of coming danger. **2.** A sign, indication, notice, or threat of coming danger. **3.** The act of giving such a sign or notice. **—warn'ing·ly** adv.

warp (wôrp) tr.v. **1.** To bend, turn, or twist out of shape: *Heat and sun warped the slats of the fence.* **2.** To turn aside from a correct, healthy, or true course; to pervert; to corrupt: *Prejudice warped his mind.* **3.** *Naut.* To move (a ship) by hauling on a line that is fastened to or around a piling, anchor, or pier. **—intr.v. 1.** To become bent or twisted out of shape: *Wood warps when exposed to heat and water.* **2.** To turn aside from a true, correct, or natural course; go astray; deviate. **3.** *Naut.* To move a ship by hauling on a line that is fastened to or around a piling, anchor, or pier. **—n. 1. a.** A distortion or twist, esp. in a piece of wood. **b.** A mental or moral twist, quirk, or deviation. **2.** The threads that run lengthwise in a fabric, crossed at right angles by the woof. **3.** *Naut.* A towline used in warping a vessel. [Middle English *werpen*, to warp, throw, from Old English *weorpan*, to throw.] **—warp'er** n.

war paint. 1. Colored paints applied to the face or body by certain tribes, as the Indians of North America, before going to war. **2.** *Informal.* Cosmetics such as lipstick, rouge, or mascara.

war·path (wôr'păth', -päth') n. The route taken by a party of North American Indians on the attack. **—idiom. on the warpath. 1.** Starting or engaged in hostilities. **2.** In a hostile or belligerent mood; ready to fight.

war·plane (wôr′plān′) n. A combat aircraft.

war·rant (wôr′ənt, wŏr′-) n. **1.** Authorization, sanction, or justification for some action: *without warrant to speak such ill of him.* **2.** A guarantee, as of a result: *His word is sufficient warrant that our contract is good.* **3.** A writing, writ, or other order that serves as authorization for something. **4.** A voucher authorizing payment or receipt of money: *stock warrants entitling the holder to buy shares at a fixed price.* **5.** *Law.* A judicial writ authorizing an officer to make a search, seizure, or arrest or to execute a judgment. **6.** *Mil.* A certificate of appointment given to warrant officers. —*tr.v.* **1.** To guarantee or attest to the quality, accuracy, or condition of: *The seller warrants the painting to be an original Picasso.* **2.** To guarantee (a product). **3.** To attest to with assurance; reliability of; vouch for. **4.** To justify or call for; deserve: *enough evidence to warrant a trial.* **5.** To grant authorization or sanction to (someone); authorize or empower: *The law warrants your right to act as your own lawyer.* **6.** *Law.* To guarantee clear title to an estate, real property, etc. [Middle English *warrant,* protector, protection, authorization, from Old North French *warant,* of Germanic orig.] —**war′rant·a·ble** *adj.* —**war′rant·a·ble·ness** n. —**war′rant·a·bly** *adv.*

war·ran·tee (wôr′ən-tē′, wŏr′-) n. A person to whom a warranty is made.

warrant officer. *Mil.* An officer intermediate in rank between a noncommissioned officer and a commissioned officer, having authority by virtue of a warrant.

war·ran·tor (wôr′ən-tər, -tôr′, wŏr′-) n. A person who makes a warrant or gives a warranty to another.

war·ran·ty (wôr′ən-tē, wŏr′-) n., pl. **-ties. 1.** Official authorization, sanction, or warrant. **2.** Justification or valid grounds for an act or course of action. **3.** *Law.* **a.** An assurance by the seller of property that the goods or property are as represented or will be as promised. **b.** A covenant by which the seller of land binds himself and his heirs to defend the security of the estate conveyed.

war·ren (wôr′ən, wŏr′-) n. **1.** A place where rabbits live and breed. **2.** An enclosure for small game animals. **3.** Any overcrowded place where people live. [Middle English *warenne,* from Old North French, of Germanic orig.]

war·ri·or (wôr′ē-ər, wŏr′-) n. A person who is engaged or experienced in battle. [Middle English *werreour,* from Old North French *werreieor,* from *werreier,* to make war, from *werre,* war.]

war·ship (wôr′shĭp′) n. Any ship constructed or equipped for use in battle.

wart (wôrt) n. **1.** A small, usu. hard outgrowth of the underlying layer of skin, caused by a virus, and occurring typically on the hands or feet. **2.** Any similar protuberance, as on a plant. [Middle English, from Old English *wearte.*]

wart hog. A wild African hog, *Phacochoerus aethiopicus,* with two pairs of tusks and wartlike protuberances on the face.

war·time (wôr′tīm′) n. A period or time of war.

war·y (wâr′ē) adj. **-i·er, -i·est. 1.** Alert to danger; watchful: *wary of the risks involved in the operation.* **2.** Distrustful; cautious: *a wary glance; wary of the weather.* —See Syns at **alert.** [From obs. *ware,* wary, from Middle English, from Old English *wær.*] —**war′i·ly** *adv.* —**war′i·ness** n.

was (wŏz, wŭz; wəz *when unstressed*) v. First and third person singular past tense of **be.** —See Usage note at **were.** [Middle English, from Old English *wæs.*]

wash (wŏsh, wôsh) tr.v. **1.** To clean with water or other liquid and often with soap, detergent, etc., by immersing, dipping, rubbing, or scrubbing: *wash windows; wash one's hands.* **2.** To soak, rinse out, and remove (dirt or stain) with or as with water: *wash grease out of overalls.* **3.** To make moist or wet; dampen; drench: *Tears washed her cheeks.* **4.** To flow or beat over, against, or past: *waves washing the sandy shores.* **5.** To carry, erode, remove, or destroy by the action of moving water: *Heavy rains washed the topsoil away from the fields.* **6.** To rid of corruption or guilt; cleanse or purify: *wash sins away.* **7.** To cover or coat (a painting, drawing, etc.) with a thin layer of paint or other coloring substance. —*intr.v.* **1.** To wash oneself, clothes, dishes, etc., in or by means of water or other liquid. **2.** To undergo washing without fading or

other damage. **3.** To be carried away, removed, or drawn by the action of water: *washed out to sea; washed overboard by a great wave.* **4.** To flow, sweep, or beat with a characteristic lapping sound: *The waves washed against the pilings.* **5.** *Informal.* To hold up under examination; be convincing: *Your excuse won't wash.* —*phrasal verbs.* **wash down. 1.** To clean by washing with water from top to bottom, as a wall, a car, etc. **2.** To follow the eating of (food) with the drinking of a liquid. **wash out. 1.** To remove or be removed by washing. **2.** To carry or wear away or be carried or worn away by the action of moving water: *The river rose and washed out the dam. The road washed out.* **wash up.** To wash one's hands. —n. **1. a.** An act, process, or period of washing: *a wash followed by a rinse.* **b.** A bath. **2.** A batch of clothes or linens that are to be or that have just been washed. **3. a.** A liquid preparation used in cleansing or coating something, as mouthwash, eyewash, or whitewash. **b.** A thin coating, as of water color or whitewash. **4.** A turbulent flow of air or water caused by the passage or action of a boat, aircraft, oar, propeller, etc. **5.** Waste liquid; swill. **6.** Soil, subsoil, debris, and other surface material carried along and deposited by the action of moving water. **7. a.** Low or marshy ground washed by tidal waters. **b.** A stretch of shallow water. **8.** *Western U.S.* The dry bed of a stream. —*idiom.* **wash one's hands of. 1.** To refuse to accept responsibility for. **2.** To abandon or renounce. [Middle English *waschen,* from Old English *wacsan.*]

wash·a·ble (wŏsh′ə-bəl, wô′shə-bəl) adj. Capable of being washed without fading, shrinking, or other injury.

wash-and-wear (wŏsh′ən-wâr′, wôsh′-) adj. Treated so as to be easily washed and to require little or no ironing: *a wash-and-wear shirt.*

wash·ba·sin (wŏsh′bā′sən) n. A washbowl.

wash·board (wŏsh′bôrd′, -bōrd′, wôsh′-) n. A board with a corrugated surface of metal, wood, etc., on which clothes can be rubbed during laundering.

wash·bowl (wŏsh′bōl′, wôsh′-) n. A basin that can be filled with water for use in washing oneself.

wash·cloth (wŏsh′klôth′, -klŏth′, wôsh′-) n. A small cloth of absorbent material used for washing the face or body. Also called **face cloth.**

washed-out (wŏsht′out′, wôsht′-) adj. **1.** Lacking color or intensity; pale; faded. **2.** *Informal.* Exhausted; tired-looking.

washed-up (wŏsht′ŭp′, wôsht′-) adj. **1.** No longer successful; finished. **2.** Ready to give up in disgust.

wash·er (wŏsh′ər, wô′shər) n. **1.** Someone or something that washes, esp. a machine designed to wash clothes or dishes. **2.** A small disk, as of metal, rubber, etc., placed under a nut or at an axle bearing to relieve friction, prevent leakage, etc.

wash·er·wom·an (wŏsh′ər-wōōm′ən, wô′shər-) n. Also **wash·wom·an** (wŏsh′wōōm′ən, wôsh′-). A woman who washes clothes as a means of livelihood; laundress.

wash·ing (wŏsh′ĭng, wô′shĭng) n. **1.** The act or work of someone or something that washes. **2.** A batch of clothes, linens, etc., that are to be or that have just been washed.

washing soda. A hydrated **sodium carbonate,** used as a general cleanser.

wash·out (wŏsh′out′, wôsh′-) n. **1.** The erosion or carrying away of the whole or a part of something, such as a roadbed, bridge, etc., by the action of water. **2.** A total failure or disappointment.

wash·room (wŏsh′rōōm′, -rŏŏm′, wôsh′-) n. A bathroom, rest room, or lavatory, esp. one in a public place.

wash·stand (wŏsh′stănd′, wôsh′-) n. **1.** A stand designed to hold a basin and a pitcher of water for washing. **2.** A stationary bathroom sink.

wash·tub (wŏsh′tŭb′, wôsh′-) n. A tub used for washing clothes.

wash·y (wŏsh′ē, wô′shē) adj. **-i·er, -i·est. 1.** Watery; diluted: *washy tea.* **2.** Lacking intensity or strength: *a washy pink color.* —**wash′i·ness** n.

was·n't (wŏz′ənt, wŭz′-). Contraction of was not.

wasp (wŏsp, wôsp) n. Any of numerous social or solitary insects, chiefly of the superfamilies Vespoidea and Sphecoidea, that have a slender body with a constricted abdomen, membranous wings, and in the females an ovipositor

---

ă pat	ā pay	â care	ä father	ĕ pet	ē be	hw which	ĭ pit	ī tie	î pier	ŏ pot	ō toe	ô paw, for	oi noise
ōō took	ōō boot	ou out	th thin	th this	ŭ cut		û urge	zh vision	ə about, item, edible, gallop, circus

often modified as a sting. [Middle English *waspe*, from Old English *wæsp*.]

Wasp or **WASP** (wŏsp, wôsp) *n.* A white Protestant of Anglo-Saxon ancestry. [W(HITE) A(NGLO)-S(AXON) P(ROTESTANT).]

wasp·ish (wŏs′pĭsh, wô′spĭsh) *adj.* **1.** Of or suggestive of a wasp. **2.** Easily irritated or annoyed; irascible; snappish. **—wasp′ish·ly** *adv.* **—wasp′ish·ness** *n.*

wasp waist. A very slender or tightly corseted waist. **—wasp′waist′ed** (wŏsp′wās′tĭd, wôsp′-) *adj.*

was·sail (wŏs′əl, wŏ-sāl′) *n.* **1.** A toast formerly given when drinking to a person's health or as an expression of good will on festive occasions. **2.** The drink used in such toasting, traditionally ale or wine spiced with roasted apples and sugar. **3.** A festive party or celebration with much drinking. **—tr.v.** To drink to the health of; to toast. **—intr.v.** To engage in or drink a wassail. [Middle English *wassayl*, from *wæs hæil*, from Old Norse *ves heill*, "be in good health."] **—was′sail·er** *n.*

wast (wŏst, wŭst) *v.* Archaic. Second person singular past tense of **be.**

wast·age (wā′stĭj) *n.* **1.** Loss by deterioration, wear, destruction, etc. **2.** That which is wasted or lost by wear or decay.

waste (wāst) *v.* **wast·ed, wast·ing.** **—tr.v.** **1.** To use, consume, or expend thoughtlessly, carelessly, or needlessly; squander. **2.** To cause to lose energy, strength, or vigor; exhaust, tire, or enfeeble: *Disease wasted his body.* **3.** To fail to take advantage of or use for profit; lose: *waste an opportunity.* **4. a.** To destroy completely. **b.** *Slang.* To kill; murder. **—intr.v.** **1.** To lose energy, strength, or vigor; become weak or enfeebled. **2.** To pass without being put to use: *Time is wasting.* **—See Syns at murder. —phrasal verb. waste away.** To grow gradually weaker, thinner, or more feeble. **—n.** **1. a.** The act or an instance of wasting, esp. thoughtless or careless expenditure, consumption, or use. **b.** Loss through careless or needless use, action, or practice; wastefulness. **2.** Worthless or useless material that is produced as a by-product or discarded as refuse: *industrial wastes.* **3.** The material that remains after food has been digested and that is eliminated from the body. **4.** A barren or wild area, region, or expanse. **—idiom. lay waste.** To destroy; ravage. [Middle English *wasten*, from Old North French *waster*, from Latin *vāstāre*, to make empty, from *vāstus*, empty.] **—wast′er** *n.*

Syns: waste, consume, devour, expend, squander *v. Core meaning:* To use up foolishly or needlessly (*a car that wastes gas; wasted their money on junk food*).

waste·bas·ket (wāst′bǎs′kĭt, -bäs′kĭt) *n.* An open container for waste paper and small items of rubbish.

waste·ful (wāst′fəl) *adj.* Characterized by or tending to waste. **—waste′ful·ly** *adv.* **—waste′ful·ness** *n.*

waste·land (wāst′lǎnd′) *n.* **1.** A lonely, usu. barren place. **2.** Any place, era, or aspect of life considered humanistically, spiritually, or culturally barren.

wast·ing (wā′stĭng) *adj.* **1.** Gradually deteriorating or desolating: *the wasting wars that plagued Europe for centuries.* **2.** Sapping the strength, energy, or substance of the body; emaciating: *a wasting disease.*

wast·rel (wā′strəl) *n.* **1.** A person who wastes, esp. one who wastes money. **2.** An idler or loafer; a good-for-nothing. [WAST(E + SCOUND)REL.]

watch (wŏch) *intr.v.* **1.** To look or observe attentively or carefully; be closely observant. **2.** To act as a spectator; look on. **3.** To look and wait expectantly or in anticipation: *watch for an opportunity.* **4.** To be on the lookout or alert: *Remember to watch the time.* **5.** To stay awake and vigilant while serving as a guard, sentinel, watchman, etc.; keep a vigil. **—tr.v.** **1.** To look at steadily; observe carefully or continuously: *watch a parade; watched five hours of tennis.* **2.** To guard; keep a watchful eye on: *Watch the children while I'm gone.* **3.** To observe the course of mentally; keep up on or informed about: *watch the election returns; watched her progress in college.* **4.** To tend, as flocks: *a shepherd watching his sheep.* **—phrasal verb. watch out.** To be careful or on the alert; take care. **—n.** **1.** The act of watching or observing closely: *keeping a watch on how much we're spending.* **2.** The action of guarding or protecting. **3.** A person or group of persons

serving to guard or protect, esp. at night. **4.** The period of duty of a guard, sentinel, or watchman: *a two-hour watch.* **5.** A small, portable timepiece, esp. one worn on the wrist or carried in the pocket. **6.** *Naut.* **a.** Any of the periods of time into which the day aboard ship is divided and during which a part of the crew is assigned to duty. **b.** The members of a ship's crew on duty during a specific watch. **—modifier:** *a watch dial.* **—idiom. on the watch.** On the lookout; waiting for something or someone expectantly: *He's on the watch for a good investment opportunity.* [Middle English *wacchen*, from Old English *wæccan*, to be or stay awake, keep vigil.]

Syns: watch, eye, observe, scrutinize *v. Core meaning:* To look at attentively or watchfully (*guards watching the prisoner closely*).

watch·dog (wŏch′dôg′, -dŏg′) *n.* **1.** A dog trained to guard property. **2.** A person who serves as a guardian or protector for someone or something: *the watchdog of consumer rights.*

watch·ful (wŏch′fəl) *adj.* Closely observant or alert; vigilant. **—See Syns at alert. —watch′ful·ly** *adv.* **—watch′ful·ness** *n.*

watch·mak·er (wŏch′mā′kər) *n.* A person who makes or repairs watches. **—watch′mak′ing** *n.*

watch·man (wŏch′mən) *n.* A man employed to stand guard or keep watch.

watch night. **1.** New Year's Eve. **2.** Also **watch meeting.** A religious service held on New Year's Eve.

watch·tow·er (wŏch′tou′ər) *n.* An observation tower upon which a guard or lookout is stationed.

watch·word (wŏch′wûrd′) *n.* **1.** A prearranged reply to a challenge, as from a guard or sentry; password; countersign. **2.** A rallying cry.

wa·ter (wô′tər, wŏt′ər) *n.* **1.** A clear, colorless, odorless, and tasteless compound of hydrogen and oxygen with the formula H_2O, occurring as a liquid that covers about three-quarters of the earth's surface and also in solid form as ice and in gaseous form as steam. Water freezes at 0°C (32°F) and boils at 100°C (212°F). **2.** A body of this substance, such as an ocean, lake, river, or stream. **3.** Often **waters.** A quantity or area of water, esp. when forming such a body: *the warm waters of the Caribbean Sea.* **4. a.** Any of the liquids passed out of the body, such as urine, perspiration, tears, etc. **b.** The fluid surrounding the fetus in the uterus; amniotic fluid. **5.** Any of various solutions that contain and somewhat resemble water: *soda water; rose water; ammonia water.* **6.** The level reached at a particular stage of the tide: *high water.* **7.** A wavy finish or sheen, as of a fabric. **8.** *Finance.* Shares of stock in a company issued in excess of paid-in capital. **9. a.** Clarity and luster of a gem. **b.** Degree; quality: *of the first water.* **—tr.v.** **1.** To sprinkle, moisten, or supply with water. **2.** To give drinking water to: *watered the horses.* **3.** To dilute or weaken by adding water to. **4.** To give a sheen to the surface of (silk, linen, or metal). **5.** To increase (the number of shares of stock) without increasing the value of the assets they represent. **—intr.v.** **1.** To produce or discharge fluid, as from the eyes. **2.** To salivate in anticipation of food: *My mouth waters when I smell your cooking.* **3.** To take on a supply of water, as a ship. **4.** To drink water, as an animal: *Deer watered at the pool.* **—phrasal verb. water down.** To weaken or reduce the force of as if by diluting. **—idioms. above water.** Out of trouble. **by water.** By boat. **hold water.** To be logical or consistent: *Does his story hold water?* **in deep water.** In great difficulty. **make** (or **pass**) **water.** To urinate. [Middle English, from Old English *wæter.*] **—wa′ter** *adj.* **—wa′ter·er** *n.*

water bed. A bed whose mattress is a large water-filled plastic bag.

water beetle. Any of various aquatic beetles, esp. of the family Dytiscidae, that characteristically have a smooth, oval body and flattened hind legs esp. adapted for swimming.

wa·ter·borne (wô′tər-bôrn′, -bōrn′, wŏt′ər-) *adj.* **1.** Floating on or supported by water; afloat. **2.** Transported by water, as freight.

water buffalo. A large buffalo, *Bubalus bubalis*, of Asia and Africa, that has large, spreading horns and often is domesticated, esp. as a draft animal.

water bug. Any of various insects of wet places, esp. a large aquatic insect of the family Belostomatidae.

water chestnut. **1.** A floating aquatic plant, *Trapa natans,* native to Asia, that bears four-pronged, nutlike fruit. **2.** A Chinese sedge, *Eleocharis tuberosa,* with an edible corm. **3.** The succulent corm of this plant, used in Oriental cookery.

water clock. A device for keeping or measuring time based on the flow of water.

water closet. A bathroom or toilet.

water color. Also **wa·ter·col·or** (wô′tər-kŭl′ər, wŏt′ər-) *n.* **1.** A paint in which water instead of oil is mixed with the coloring material before use. **2.** A painting done in water colors. **3.** The art or process of painting with water colors. **—water colorist** or **wa′ter·col′or·ist** *n.*

wa·ter-cool (wô′tər-kōōl′, wŏt′ər-) *tr.v.* To cool (an engine) with water, esp. with circulating water.

water cooler. A container, device, or apparatus for cooling, storing, and dispensing drinking water.

wa·ter·course (wô′tər-kôrs′, -kōrs′, wŏt′ər-) *n.* **1.** A waterway. **2.** The bed or channel of a waterway.

wa·ter·cress (wô′tər-krĕs′, wŏt′ər-) *n.* **1.** A freshwater plant, *Nasturtium officinale,* native to Eurasia, with pungent leaves that are used in salads as a garnish. **2.** Any of several similar, related plants.

water cure. *Med.* Hydrotherapy.

wa·ter·fall (wô′tər-fôl′, wŏt′ər-) *n.* A natural stream of water descending from a height.

waterfall   **water lily**

wa·ter·fowl (wô′tər-foul′, wŏt′ər-) *n., pl.* **waterfowl** or **-fowls.** **1.** A swimming bird, as a duck or goose, usu. frequenting freshwater areas. **2.** Such birds in general.

wa·ter·front (wô′tər-frŭnt′, wŏt′ər-) *n.* **1.** Land that borders a body of water, such as a harbor or lake. **2.** The district of a town or city that borders the water, esp. a wharf district where ships dock.

water gap. A cleft in a mountain ridge through which a stream flows.

water glass. **1.** A drinking glass or goblet. **2.** A tube or similar structure that has a glass bottom so that observations below the surface of the water can be made.

water hole. A small natural depression in which water collects, esp. such a pool used by animals as a watering place.

water ice. A dessert made from sweetened, flavored, finely crushed ice.

wa·ter·ish (wô′tər-ĭsh, wŏt′ər-) *adj.* Watery.

wa·ter·less (wô′tər-lĭs, wŏt′ər-) *adj.* **1.** Without water; dry. **2.** Not requiring water, as a cooling system.

water level. **1.** The height of the surface of a body of water. **2.** A **water table.** **3.** The water line of a ship.

water lily. **1.** Any of various aquatic plants of the genus *Nymphaea,* with floating leaves and showy, variously colored flowers, esp. *N. odorata* that has fragrant, many-petaled white or pinkish flowers. **2.** Any of various similar or related plants. Also called **pond lily.**

water line. **1.** *Naut.* **a.** The line on the hull of a ship to which the water surface rises when the ship is floating on an even keel. **b.** Any of several parallel lines on the hull of a ship that indicate the depth to which the ship sinks under various loads. **2.** A line or stain, such as that left on a sea wall, indicating the height to which water has risen or may rise; watermark.

wa·ter·logged (wô′tər-lôgd′, -lŏgd′, wŏt′ər-) *adj.* **1.** Heavy, sluggish, and unwieldy in the water because of flooding, as a ship or boat. **2.** Soaked or saturated with water: *waterlogged fields.* [WATER + -logged, prob. "made (unmanageable) like a log in water."]

Wa·ter·loo (wô′tər-lōō′, wŏt′ər-) *n.* A disastrous or crushing defeat: *finally met his Waterloo.*

water main. A principal pipe in a system for conveying water, esp. one installed underground.

wa·ter·man (wô′tər-mən, wŏt′ər-) *n.* A boatman. **—wa′ter·man·ship′** *n.*

wa·ter·mark (wô′tər-märk′, wŏt′ər-) *n.* **1.** A mark showing the height to which water has risen, esp. a line indicating the heights of high and low tide. **2.** A translucent design impressed on paper during manufacture and visible when the finished paper is held to the light. **3.** The metal pattern that produces this design. **—tr.v.** **1.** To mark (paper) with a watermark. **2.** To impress (a pattern or design) as a watermark.

wa·ter·mel·on (wô′tər-mĕl′ən, wŏt′ər-) *n.* **1.** A vine, *Citrullus vulgaris,* native to Africa, cultivated for its large, edible fruit. **2.** The fruit of this plant, with a hard green rind and sweet, watery reddish flesh.

water mill. A mill with machinery driven by water.

water moccasin. A poisonous snake, *Agkistrodon piscivorus* (or *Ancistrodon piscivorus*), of lowlands and swampy regions of the southern United States. Also called **cottonmouth.**

water of crystallization. Water in chemical combination with a crystal and necessary for the maintenance of crystalline properties but capable of being removed by sufficient heat.

water of hydration. Water chemically combined with a substance so that it can be removed, as by heating, without substantially changing the chemical composition of the substance.

water ouzel. Any of several small birds of the genus *Cinclus,* that dive into swift-moving streams and feed along the bottom. Also called **dipper.**

water polo. A water sport with two teams, each of which tries to pass a ball into the other's goal.

wa·ter·pow·er (wô′tər-pou′ər, wŏt′ər-) *n.* **1.** The energy of falling or running water used for driving machinery, esp. for generating electricity. **2.** A source of such power, such as a waterfall, river, etc.

wa·ter·proof (wô′tər-prōōf′, wŏt′ər-) *adj.* **1.** Impenetrable to or unaffected by water. **2.** Made of or treated with rubber, plastic, or a sealing agent to resist water penetration. **—n.** **1.** A waterproof material or fabric. **2.** *Brit.* A raincoat or other waterproof garment. **—tr.v.** To make waterproof.

water rat. **1.** Any of various semiaquatic rodents, as one of the genus *Hydromis,* of Australia and adjacent islands, or *Neofiber alleni,* of Florida and southern Georgia, that resemble the muskrat. **2.** *Slang.* A waterfront thief, ruffian, or habitué.

wa·ter·re·pel·lent (wô′tər-rĭ-pĕl′ənt, wŏt′ər-) *adj.* Resistant to water but not entirely waterproof.

wa·ter·re·sis·tant (wô′tər-rĭ-zĭs′tənt, wŏt′ər-) *adj.* Water-repellent.

water right. **1.** The right to draw water from a particular source, such as a lake, irrigation canal, or stream. **2.** The right to navigate on particular waters.

water scorpion. Any of various aquatic insects of the family Nepidae that have a respiratory tube projecting from the posterior part of the abdomen and are capable of inflicting a painful sting.

wa·ter·shed (wô′tər-shĕd′, wŏt′ər-) *n.* **1.** A ridge of high land that forms the boundary between regions whose water drains into two different systems of rivers. **2.** The region or area that drains water into a lake, river, river system, etc. **3.** A crucially important or divisive factor, time, or event: *reached a watershed in the negotiations.* [WATER + -shed, division.]

wa·ter·side (wô′tər-sīd′, wŏt′ər-) *n.* Land bordering any body of water; a shore.

wa·ter·ski (wô′tər-skē′, wŏt′ər-) *n., pl.* **-skis** or **-ski.** Also **water ski.** Either of a pair of short, broad, skilike runners used for gliding or skimming over water while grasping a

water spaniel

water wheel

wattle

towline from a motorboat. —v. **-skied, -ski·ing.** To glide over water on water-skis. —**wa'ter-ski'er** n.

water snake. 1. Any of various nonpoisonous snakes of the genus *Natrix* that frequent freshwater streams and ponds. **2.** Any of various other aquatic or semiaquatic snakes.

water spaniel. A spaniel of a breed with a curly, water-resistant coat, often used to retrieve waterfowl.

wa·ter·spout (wô'tər-spout', wŏt'ər-) n. **1.** A hole or pipe from which water is discharged, esp. rainwater. **2.** A tornado or whirlwind occurring over water and resulting in a whirling column of spray and mist.

water table. The depth or level below which the ground is saturated with water. Also called **water level.**

wa·ter·tight (wô'tər-tīt', wŏt'ər-) adj. **1.** Assembled or constructed so that water cannot enter or escape. **2.** Having no flaws or loopholes: *a watertight alibi.*

water tower. 1. A standpipe or elevated tank used to store a supply of water or to maintain equal pressure on a water system. **2.** A towerlike fire-fighting apparatus to lift hoses to the upper levels of a tall structure.

water vapor. Water diffused as a vapor in the atmosphere, esp. at a temperature below the boiling point.

wa·ter·way (wô'tər-wā', wŏt'ər-) n. A river, channel, canal, or other navigable body of water used for travel or transport. Also called **watercourse.**

water wheel. A wheel driven by falling or running water, used to power machinery.

water wings. An inflatable device used to support the body while learning to swim.

wa·ter·works (wô'tər-wûrks', wŏt'ər-) pl.n. The water system of a city or town, including reservoirs, tanks, buildings, pumps, pipes, and other apparatus.

wa·ter·y (wô'tə-rē, wŏt'ə-) adj. **-i·er, -i·est. 1.** Filled with, consisting of, or containing water; moist; wet: *watery eyes.* **2.** Resembling or suggestive of water: *a watery blue sky.* **3.** Made weak, thin, or soggy by too much water: *watery soup.* **4.** Without force; insipid; pale: *watery prose; watery colors.* —**wa'ter·i·ness** n.

watt (wŏt) n. A unit of power equal to one joule per second or about ¹/₇₄₆ horsepower. [After James *Watt* (1736–1819), Scottish engineer and inventor.]

watt·age (wŏt'ĭj) n. Power measured or expressed in watts.

watt-hour (wŏt'our') n. *Abbr.* **W-hr** A unit of electrical energy or work equal to the power of one watt acting for one hour and equivalent to 3,600 joules.

wat·tle (wŏt'l) n. **1.** Twigs, branches, plant stalks, and similar materials woven together to form a framework, used for building walls, roofs, fences, etc. **2.** A fleshy, often brightly colored fold of skin hanging from the neck or throat of certain birds. —*tr.v.* **-tled, -tling. 1.** To construct from wattle. **2.** To weave into wattle. [Middle English *wattel,* from Old English *watel.*]

watt·me·ter (wŏt'mē'tər) n. An instrument for measuring in watts the power flowing in a circuit.

wave (wāv) v. **waved, wav·ing.** —*intr.v.* **1.** To move back and forth or up and down in the air: *branches waving in the wind.* **2.** To make a signal with an up-and-down or back-and-forth movement of the hand. **3.** To curve or curl: *Her hair waves.* —*tr.v.* **1.** To move back and forth or up and down; flutter: *She waved her fan.* **2. a.** To move or swing as in giving a signal: *wave one's hand.* **b.** To signal

or express by such movement: *He waved good-by.* **3.** To arrange into curves, curls, or swirls: *wave one's hair.* —n. **1.** A ridge or swell moving along the surface of a body of water. **2.** Often **waves.** The sea or seas: *The British ruled the waves for three centuries.* **3.** A moving curve or a succession of curves in or upon a surface; an undulation: *waves of wheat in the wind.* **4.** A curve or curl, or a succession of curves, curls, or swirls, as in the hair. **5.** A movement up and down or back and forth: *a wave of the hand.* **6.** Something that resembles a wave or waves; a surge: *a wave of indignation.* **7.** A widespread period of unusually hot or cold weather: *a heat wave.* **8.** A group of people, animals, or events that advance in a body: *a wave of pioneers heading west.* **9.** *Physics.* **a.** A disturbance or oscillation that passes from point to point in a medium or in space, described in general by a mathematical function that gives it amplitude, velocity, frequency, and phase at any particular time and place. **b.** A graphic representation of the variation of such a disturbance with time. [Middle English *waven,* from Old English *wafian,* to move back and forth.]

wave·band (wāv'bănd') n. A range of frequencies, esp. of radio frequencies such as those assigned to communication transmissions.

wave·length (wāv'lĕngth') n. Also **wave length. 1.** The distance betrween two points of identical phase in successive cycles of a wave. **2.** *Informal.* A spontaneous understanding of another person's situation, thoughts, motivations, etc.

wave·let (wāv'lĭt) n. A small wave or ripple.

wa·ver (wā'vər) *intr.v.* **1.** To move or swing one way and then another in an uncertain or unsteady way. **2.** To hold back in uncertainty or act in a hesitant way. **3.** To falter or yield: *His resolve began to waver.* **4.** To tremble or flicker, as sound or light. —See Syns at **hesitate.** —n. An act or instance of wavering. [Middle English *waveren,* to wander, stray, fluctuate.] —**wa'ver·er** n. —**wa'ver·ing·ly** adv.

wav·y (wā'vē) adj. **-i·er, -i·est. 1.** Full of waves: *a wavy sea.* **2.** Marked by wavelike curves; sinuous: *a wavy line.* **3.** Having curls, curves, or undulations: *wavy hair.* —**wav'i·ly** adv. —**wav'i·ness** n.

wax¹ (wăks) n. **1.** Any of various solid or soft, sticky substances that melt or soften easily when heated and are insoluble in water but soluble in most organic liquids. **2.** A waxlike substance produced by bees; beeswax. **3.** A waxlike substance found in the ears. **4.** A solid plastic or very thick liquid material, such as paraffin. **5.** A preparation containing wax, used to polish floors, cars, furniture, etc. —*tr.v.* To cover, coat, treat, or polish with wax. [Middle English, from Old English *weax,* beeswax.]

wax² (wăks) *intr.v.* **1.** To show a progressively larger light surface, as the moon does in passing from new to full. **2.** To increase gradually in quantity, extent, strength, importance, etc.: *Discontent waxed among the people.* **3.** To grow or become as specified: *The seas wax calm; a speaker waxing eloquent.* [Middle English *waxen,* from Old English *weaxan.*]

wax bean. A variety of string bean with yellow pods.

wax·ber·ry (wăks'bĕr'ē) n. The waxy fruit of the wax myrtle or the snowberry.

wax·en (wăk'sən) adj. **1.** Made of or covered with wax. **2.** Like wax, as in being pale or smooth: *waxen skin.*

wax myrtle. A shrub, *Myrica cerifera,* of the southeastern

United States, that has evergreen leaves and small, berry-like fruit with a waxy coating.

wax paper. Also **waxed paper.** Paper that has been made moistureproof by being coated with wax.

wax·wing (wăks'wĭng') n. Any of several birds of the genus *Bombycilla*, with crested heads, predominantly brown plumage, and waxy red tips on the secondary wing feathers.

wax·work (wăks'wûrk') n. **1. a.** Figures or ornaments made of wax, esp. life-size wax representations of famous persons. **b.** One such work. **2. waxworks.** An exhibition of or a museum for exhibiting waxwork.

wax·y (wăk'sē) adj. **-i·er, -i·est. 1.** Resembling wax in appearance, texture, or consistency: *waxy petals; a waxy complexion.* **2.** Consisting of, full of, or covered with wax.

way (wā) n. **1.** A manner or fashion: *He walks in a very stiff way.* **2.** A method, means, or technique: *a better way of working math problems.* **3.** A respect, particular, or feature: *They are improving their city in many ways.* **4.** A habit, characteristic, or tendency: *Things have a way of happening when you least expect them.* **5.** A customary manner of acting, living, behaving, or doing things: *a new way of life.* **6.** A road, route, path, or passage that leads from one place to another: *Find your way home.* **7.** A means of passage or advancement accomplished by a particular method: *worked her way up to a higher position.* **8.** Room enough to pass or proceed: *Make way for the fire truck.* **9.** The path taken by something that is moving or going to move: *A farmer once got in the way of a bolt of lightning.* **10.** Distance: *Jump a short way off the ground.* **11.** A specific direction: *Which way did he go?* **12.** Talent; skill; facility: *has a way with words.* **13.** Wish or will: *if I had my way.* **14.** A course of action: *the easy way out.* **15.** *Informal.* A condition: *They are in a bad way financially.* **16.** *Informal.* A neighborhood or district: *I don't know anyone out your way.* —See Syns at **method.** —adv. **1.** Far: *way up high.* **2.** All the distance: *The sweater goes way down to her knees.* —idioms. **by the way.** Incidentally. **by way of. 1.** Through; via: *The road runs by way of the desert.* **2.** As a means of: *What did they do by way of celebration?* **give way.** To fall in; collapse. **go out of one's (or the) way.** To inconvenience oneself by doing more than is required. **in the way.** Of such a nature as to be an obstruction or impediment. **lead the way.** To go first while others follow. **on the (or one's) way. 1.** In the process of coming, going, or traveling: *Snow is on the way. I'm on my way home.* **2.** On the route of one's journey. **out of the way. 1.** Of a nature or position that does not obstruct or impede. **2.** In an inconvenient or unusual location; remote. **3.** Strange or wrong; peculiar: *Her remark was certainly out of the way.* **under way.** In progress. [Middle English, from Old English *weg,* a road, path.]

Usage: **1. way.** The adverb *way* meaning far occurs on all usage levels: *was way ahead in the voting; way behind the other contestants; way over my head; car sales were way down/up.* **2. way, ways.** Usage studies show that the singular form *way* meaning distance is the choice in modern English writing: *a long way* (not *ways*) *to go.* The adverbial genitive *ways* often occurs in speech, however: *a long ways to go.*

way·bill (wā'bĭl') n. A document that contains a list of goods and shipping instructions relative to a shipment.

way·far·er (wā'fâr'ər) n. A person who travels from place to place, esp. one who goes by foot. [Middle English *weyfarere : wey,* way + *fare,* a journey, from Old English *faru.*]

way·far·ing (wā'fâr'ĭng) n. Traveling, esp. on foot.

way·lay (wā'lā') tr.v. **-laid** (-lād'), **-lay·ing. 1.** To lie in wait for and attack from ambush: *Gunmen waylaid the guard.* **2.** To accost unexpectedly. —**way'lay'er** n.

–ways. A suffix meaning manner, direction, or position: **sideways.** [Middle English, from *wayes,* in (such) a way, from Old English *weg,* way.]

ways and means. The financial resources or methods for increasing the financial resources available to a person or group for accomplishing a specific end.

way·side (wā'sĭd') n. The side or edge of a road. —*modifier: a wayside inn.*

way station. A station between major stops on a route.

way·ward (wā'wərd) adj. **1.** Stubborn or disobedient; willful: *a wayward boy.* **2.** Irregular or unpredictable: *a wayward star.* —See Syns at **contrary.** [Middle English, from *awayward,* turned away.] —**way'ward·ly** adv. —**way'ward·ness** n.

we (wē) pron. **1.** The speaker or writer together with one or more others. **2.** Used instead of *I,* as by a ruler or by a writer. [Middle English, from Old English *wē.*]

Usage: **we, us.** The choice between the nominative pronoun *we* and the objective *us* is governed by the grammatical function of the pronoun: *We officers* (subject) *were not consulted. They gave us officers* (indirect object) *no hearing.*

weak (wēk) adj. **-er, -est. 1.** Lacking in physical strength, force, or energy; feeble or frail. **2.** Likely to fail or break if placed under pressure, stress, or strain; lacking strength: *a weak timber in a bridge.* **3.** Lacking effectiveness, firmness, or force of will, purpose, etc.: *a weak leader.* **4.** Lacking the usual, proper, or full strength of some component or ingredient: *weak coffee.* **5.** Lacking the capacity to function well or in a normal manner; unsound: *weak eyes.* **6.** Lacking capacity or capability: *a weak student.* **7.** Resulting from a lack of intelligence; not persuasive or convincing; inadequate: *a weak defense.* **8.** Lacking power or intensity; faint; dim: *a weak voice; weak light.* **9.** Lacking or deficient in a specified thing: *weak in math.* **10.** *Phonet.* Unstressed or unaccented. [Middle English *weike,* from Old Norse *veikr.*] —**weak'ly** adv. —**weak'ness** n.

weak·en (wē'kən) tr.v. To make weak or weaker. —intr.v. To become weak or weaker.

weak·fish (wēk'fĭsh') n., pl. **weakfish** or **-fish·es.** Any of several saltwater food and game fishes of the genus *Cynoscion,* esp. *C. regalis,* of North American Atlantic waters. Also called **sea trout.** [Obs. Dutch *weekvische : week,* soft + *visch,* fish.]

weak-kneed (wēk'nēd') adj. Irresolute; timid.

weak·ling (wēk'lĭng) n. Someone who is weak in body, character, or mind. —adj. Weak; feeble.

weak·ly (wēk'lē) adj. **-li·er, -li·est.** Feeble or sickly; weak. —adv. With little strength or force.

weak-mind·ed (wēk'mīn'dĭd) adj. **1.** Lack of strength of will or purpose; irresolute; indecisive. **2.** Feeble-minded. —**weak'-mind'ed·ness** n.

weak·ness (wēk'nĭs) n. **1.** The condition or feeling of being weak: *physical weakness.* **2.** A weak point; a defect, fault, or failing. **3.** A special fondness or liking: *a weakness for chocolate.*

weal¹ (wēl) n. **1.** Prosperity; happiness: *in weal and woe.* **2.** The welfare of the community; the general good. [Middle English *weole,* from Old English *weola,* wealth, well-being.]

weal² (wēl) n. A ridge on the flesh raised by a blow; welt. [Var. of WALE (ridge).]

wealth (wĕlth) n. **1.** A great quantity of money or valuable possessions; riches. **2.** The condition of being rich; affluence. **3.** A profusion or abundance: *a wealth of information.* [Middle English *welthe,* well-being, riches, from *wele,* welfare.]

wealth·y (wĕl'thē) adj. **-i·er, -i·est. 1.** Having wealth; rich; prosperous; affluent: *wealthy people; a wealthy part of town.* **2.** Richly supplied; abundant: *a region wealthy in wildlife.* —See Syns at **rich.** —**wealth'i·ly** adv. —**wealth'i·ness** n.

wean (wēn) tr.v. **1.** To cause (a young child or young animal) to become accustomed to food other than its mother's milk. **2.** To cause to give up a habit, interest, etc.: *wean him from his addiction to cigarettes.* [Middle English *wenen,* from Old English *wenian,* to accustom, train, wean.]

weap·on (wĕp'ən) n. **1. a.** Any instrument or device used to attack another or to defend oneself from attack. **b.** Any part of the body used in attack or defense, such as an animal's horns, teeth, or claws. **2.** Any means employed to overcome, persuade, or get the better of another: *Her smile was her most effective weapon.* [Middle English *wepen,* from Old English *wǣp(e)n.*]

weap·on·ry (wĕp'ən-rē) n. Weapons in general.

wear (wâr) v. **wore** (wôr, wōr), **worn** (wôrn, wōrn), **wear·ing.**

ă pat	ā pay	â care	ä father	ĕ pet	ē be	hw which	ĭ pit	ī tie	î pier	ŏ pot	ō toe	ô paw, for	oi noise
ŏŏ took	ōō boot	ou out	th thin	th this	ŭ cut		û urge	zh vision	ə about, item, edible, gallop, circus				

—*tr.v.* **1.** To have on or put on, as clothes, make-up, or accessories: *wear a dress; wear a wristwatch.* **2.** To have or carry habitually on one's person: *wear a beard; wear a gun.* **3.** To affect or exhibit; to display: *wear a smile.* **4.** To bear or maintain in a certain way: *He wears his honors well. She wears her hair long.* **5.** To fit into or find suitable: *A brunette can wear that color.* **6.** To damage, diminish, erode, or use up by long or hard use, constant rubbing, exposure to elements, etc.: *wears the knees in trousers.* **7.** To produce or cause by constant use, rubbing, or exposure: *They eventually wore hollows in the steps.* **8.** To bring to a specific condition by use or exposure: *wear clothes to rags; wear one's hands raw washing floors.* **9.** To fatigue, weary, or exhaust: *His incessant criticism wore her patience.* —*intr.v.* **1.** To stand continual or hard use; to last: *That fabric wears well.* **2.** To react to use, strain, etc., in a specified way: *The gold band wore thin.* **3.** To pass slowly or gradually: *The hours wore on endlessly.* —*phrasal verbs.* **wear down. 1.** To reduce in size or substance as the result of friction or use: *Erosion wears down the mountain.* **2.** To break down the resistance of by relentless pressure: *wear down the opposition.* **wear off. 1.** To disappear gradually and cease having any effect: *The headache wore off.* **2.** To become removed; rub off: *The paint soon wore off the fence.* **wear out. 1.** To make or become unusable through heavy use. **2.** To exhaust or tire: *She wore out her welcome.* —*n.* **1.** The act of wearing or condition of being worn; use: *The coat has had heavy wear.* **2.** Clothing, esp. of a particular kind or for a particular use: *men's wear; evening wear.* **3.** Gradual damage or diminution resulting from use, age, etc.: *The rug is beginning to show wear.* **4.** The capacity to withstand use; durability. —*idiom.* **wear and tear.** Loss, damage, or depreciation resulting from ordinary use or exposure. [Middle English *werien,* from Old English *werian,* wear, carry.] —**wear′er** *n.*

wear·ing (wâr′ĭng) *adj.* **1.** Of or made for wear: *wearing apparel.* **2.** Causing wear; tiring; exhausting: *a wearing experience.* —**wear′ing·ly** *adv.*

wea·ri·some (wîr′ē-səm) *adj.* Causing mental or physical fatigue; tedious; tiring. —**wea′ri·some·ly** *adv.* —**wea′ri·some·ness** *n.*

wea·ry (wîr′ē) *adj.* **-ri·er, -ri·est. 1.** Tired; fatigued. **2.** Causing or showing tiredness or fatigue: *a weary task; a weary sigh.* **3.** Exhausted of tolerance; impatient; bored: *weary of constant complaints.* —*v.* **-ried, -ry·ing.** —*tr.v.* To make weary; to fatigue: *Don't weary me with your silly chatter.* —*intr.v.* To become weary; grow tired: *She soon wearied of the social whirl.* [Middle English *wery,* from Old English *wērig.*] —**wea′ri·ly** *adv.* —**wea′ri·ness** *n.*

wea·sel (wē′zəl) *n.* **1.** Any of various carnivorous mammals of the genus *Mustela,* with a long, slender body, a long tail, and brownish fur that in many species turns white in winter. **2.** A sneaky, deceitful person. —*phrasal verb.* **weasel out.** *Informal.* To back out of a situation or commitment in a sneaky or cowardly manner. [Middle English *wesele,* from Old English *wesle.*]

weasel

weath·er (wĕth′ər) *n.* **1.** The condition or activity of the atmosphere at a given time and place, esp. as described by variables such as temperature, humidity, wind velocity, and barometric pressure. **2.** Bad, rough, or stormy atmospheric conditions. —*tr.v.* **1.** To expose to the action of the weather, as for drying, seasoning, or coloring: *weather wood.* **2.** To discolor, roughen, wear, or otherwise affect or alter adversely by exposure. **3.** To pass through safely;

survive; outride: *weather a storm; weathered the loss of his business.* —*intr.v.* **1.** To become discolored, conditioned, worn, or otherwise show the effects of exposure to the weather. **2.** To resist or withstand the effects of weather or adverse conditions: *Some house paints weather better than others.* —**idiom. under the weather.** *Informal.* Not feeling well; slightly ill. [Middle English *weder,* from Old English.] —**weather′ered** *adj.*

weath·er·beat·en (wĕth′ər-bēt′n) *adj.* **1.** Worn by exposure to the weather: *a weather-beaten house.* **2.** Tanned and leathery from being outdoors: *weather-beaten hands.*

weath·er·board (wĕth′ər-bôrd′, -bōrd′) *n.* Clapboard.

weath·er·bound (wĕth′ər-bound′) *adj.* Delayed, halted, or kept indoors by bad weather.

weath·er·cock (wĕth′ər-kŏk′) *n.* **1.** A weather vane in the form of a rooster. **2.** Someone or something that is very changeable or fickle.

weath·er·ing (wĕth′ər-ĭng) *n.* Any of the chemical or mechanical processes by which rocks exposed to the weather are broken up.

weath·er·man (wĕth′ər-măn′) *n.* A person who forecasts or reports weather conditions.

weather map. A map or chart depicting the meteorological conditions over a specific geographical area at a specific time.

weath·er·proof (wĕth′ər-prōōf′) *adj.* Able to withstand exposure to weather without damage. —*tr.v.* To make weatherproof.

weather station. A station at which meteorological data are gathered, recorded, and released.

weath·er·strip (wĕth′ər-strĭp′) *tr.v.* **-stripped, -strip·ping.** To fit or equip with weather stripping.

weather stripping. 1. A narrow piece of material, such as rubber, felt, or metal, installed around doors and windows to protect an interior from external extremes of temperature. **2.** Such pieces in general.

weather vane. A pointer or indicator that turns with the wind to show in which direction the wind is blowing.

weave (wēv) *v.* **wove** (wōv) or **weaved, wo·ven,** (wō′vən), **weav·ing.** —*tr.v.* **1. a.** To make cloth or a cloth article on a loom by interlacing crosswise woof threads and lengthwise warp threads: *weave silk brocade; weave a rug.* **b.** To interlace yarns, threads, strands, strips, etc. to make a fabric. **2.** To construct by interlacing or interweaving the materials or components of: *weave a basket.* **3.** To interweave or combine (elements) into a whole: *He wove the incidents into a story.* **4.** To run (something) in and out through some material or composition: *The composer wove a love theme throughout the final act of the opera.* **5.** To spin (a web) as a spider does. **6.** *past tense* **weaved.** To move or progress by going from side to side or in and out; wind: *carefully weaved the canoe through the reeds.* —*intr.v.* **1.** To engage in weaving; make fabric. **2.** *past tense* **weaved.** To sway or move from side to side: *The dancers weaved about the stage in rhythmic motion.* —See Syns at **wind².** —*n.* The pattern or method of weaving: *a twill weave; a loose weave.* [Middle English *weven,* from Old English *wefan.*] —**weav·er** *n.*

weav·er·bird (wē′vər-bûrd′) *n.* Any of various chiefly tropical Old World birds of the family Ploceidae, many of which build complex communal nests of intricately woven vegetation.

web (wĕb) *n.* **1. a.** A textile fabric, esp. one being woven on a loom or in the process of being removed from it. **b.** The structural part of cloth as distinguished from its pile or pattern. **2.** A latticed or woven structure; an interlacing of materials: *A web of palm branches formed the roof of the hut.* **3.** A structure of threadlike filaments spun by a spider. **4.** Something intricately constructed, esp. something that ensnares or entangles: *a web of lies.* **5.** A complex network: *a web of telephone and electrical wires.* **6.** A fold of skin or membranous tissue, esp. the membrane connecting the toes of certain water birds. **7.** The vane of a feather. **8.** A large continuous roll of paper, such as newsprint, either in the process of manufacture or as it is fed into a rotary printing press. —*tr.v.* **webbed, web·bing. 1.** To provide or cover with a web. **2.** To catch or ensnare in a web. [Middle English, from Old English *webb.*] —**webbed** *adj.*

web·bing (wĕb′ĭng) *n.* **1.** Sturdy cotton or nylon fabric woven in widths gen. of from 1 to 6 in., used where strength is required, as for seat belts, brake lining, or upholstering. **2.** Anything that forms a web.

web-foot·ed (wĕb′fŏŏt′ĭd) *adj.* Having feet with webbed toes.

wed (wĕd) *v.* **wed·ded, wed** or **wed·ded, wed·ding.** —*tr.v.* **1.** To take as husband or wife; marry. **2.** To perform the marriage ceremony for; join in matrimony. **3.** To bind or join; unite. —*intr.v.* To take a husband or wife; marry. [Middle English *wedden,* from Old English *weddian,* to engage (to do something), marry.]

wed·ding (wĕd′ĭng) *n.* **1.** The ceremony or celebration of a marriage. **2.** The anniversary of a marriage: *a silver wedding.* **3.** A close association or union: *the wedding of ideas.* —See Syns at **marriage.** —*modifier: a wedding ring.*

wedge (wĕj) *n.* **1.** A piece of triangularly shaped metal or wood designed to be inserted in a narrow crevice and used for splitting, tightening, levering, etc. **2.** Anything that has the triangular shape of a wedge: *a wedge of pie.* **3.** Something, as a tactic, event, policy, or idea that serves to divide or split or to push a way in like a wedge: *The issue drove a wedge between the party leaders.* —*v.* **wedged, wedg·ing.** —*tr.v.* **1.** To split, force apart, or fix in place with or as with a wedge: *wedged a rock under the tire to keep the car from rolling.* **2.** To crowd, push, force, or squeeze into a limited space: *wedged eight people into the car.* —*intr.v.* To push or be forced into like a wedge: *A piece of food wedged between his teeth. They all wedged into the compact car.* [Middle English *wegge,* from Old English *wecg,* a wedge, ingot of metal.]

wed·lock (wĕd′lŏk′) *n.* The condition of being married; matrimony. [Middle English *wedlocke,* from Old English *wedlāc,* pledge-giving, marriage vow, from *wedd,* a pledge.]

Wednes·day (wĕnz′dē, -dā′) *n.* The fourth day of the week, after Tuesday and before Thursday. [Middle English, from Old English *Wōdnesdæg,* "Woden's day."]

wee (wē) *adj.* **we·er, we·est. 1.** Very little; tiny: *a wee lad; a wee bit afraid.* **2.** Very early: *the wee hours.* [Middle English *we,* from *wei,* a small amount, from Old English *wæge,* a weight.]

weed[1] (wēd) *n.* **1.** A plant that is considered troublesome, useless, or unattractive, esp. one growing freely where it is not wanted, as in a garden or other cultivated area. **2.** *Informal.* **a.** Tobacco. **b.** A cigarette. **3.** *Slang.* Marijuana. —*tr.v.* To remove weeds from; clear of weeds: *weed a flower bed.* —*intr.v.* To remove weeds from a plot: *I weeded for two days before I could plant my garden.* —*phrasal verb.* **weed out.** To remove or get rid of as unsuitable or unwanted: *weed out unqualified applicants.* [Middle English, from Old English *wēod.*]

weed[2] (wēd) *n.* **1.** A token of mourning, as a black band worn usu. on the sleeve. **2. weeds.** A widow's mourning clothes. [Middle English *wede,* a garment, armor, from Old English *wæde,* a garment.]

weed·er (wē′dər) *n.* **1.** A person who weeds. **2.** A device for removing weeds.

week (wēk) *n.* **1.** A period of time equal to seven days, esp. a period that begins on a Sunday and continues through the next Saturday. **2.** A period consisting of the hours or days in a week during which one works or goes to school. [Middle English *weke,* from Old English *wicu.*]

week·day (wēk′dā′) *n.* **1.** Any day of the week except Sunday. **2.** Any day that is not part of the weekend.

week·end (wēk′ĕnd′) *n.* The end of the week, esp. the period from Friday evening through Sunday evening. —*intr.v.* To spend the weekend: *We are going to weekend at the lake.* —*modifier: weekend activities.*

week·ly (wēk′lē) *adv.* **1.** Once a week or every week: *She visits us weekly.* **2.** Per week: *How much does she earn weekly?* —*adj.* **1.** Done, happening, or coming once a week or every week: *a weekly trip.* **2.** Made or figured by the week: *weekly earnings.* —*n., pl.* **-lies.** A newspaper or magazine issued once a week.

weep (wēp) *v.* **wept** (wĕpt), **weep·ing.** —*tr.v.* **1.** To shed (tears) as an expression of emotion. **2.** To grieve or mourn. **3.** To bring to a specified condition by weeping: *She wept herself into a state of exhaustion.* **4.** To ooze, exude, or let fall drops of liquid. —*intr.v.* **1.** To express emotion by shedding tears; cry. **2.** To grieve or feel sorry for. **3.** To emit or run with drops of moisture. [Middle English *wepen,* from Old English *wēpan.*]

weep·er (wē′pər) *n.* **1.** Someone who weeps. **2.** A hired mourner.

weeping willow. A widely cultivated tree, *Salix babylonica,* native to China, with long, slender, drooping branches and narrow leaves.

wee·vil (wē′vəl) *n.* Any of numerous beetles, chiefly of the family Curculionidae, that characteristically have a downward-curving snout and are destructive to plants and stored plant products. [Middle English *wevel,* from Old English *wifel,* a beetle.]

weft (wĕft) *n.* In weaving, the woof. [Middle English, from Old English.]

weigh (wā) *tr.v.* **1.** To determine or measure the weight of by or as if by using a scale or similar instrument. **2.** To measure off an amount equal in weight to: *weigh out a pound of cheese.* **3.** To consider or balance in the mind; ponder; evaluate: *weigh the possible alternatives.* **4.** *Naut.* To raise (anchor). —*intr.v.* **1.** To have or be of a specific weight. **2.** To be considered important; have influence: *That factor weighed heavily in the decision.* **3.** *Naut.* To raise anchor and begin to sail. —*phrasal verbs.* **weigh down.** To burden or oppress. **weigh in.** To be weighed before participating in a contest or sports event, as a fight or race. **weigh on** (or **upon**). To be a burden on; oppress: *The misdeed was weighing on her conscience.* [Middle English *weghen,* from Old English *wegan,* to carry, weigh.]

weight (wāt) *n.* **1. a.** The force with which an object near the earth or another celestial body is attracted toward the center of the body by gravity. **b.** The measure of this force: *The car has a weight of 2,800 pounds.* **c.** A unit used as a measure of this force: *a table of weights and measures.* **d.** A system of such units: *avoirdupois weight; troy weight.* **e.** A material object designed so that its weight is a reference for such a unit: *Place a two-pound weight on the scale.* **f.** Any object whose principal function is to exert a downward force by means of the action of gravity upon it, as a paperweight, dumbbell, etc. **2.** Mass, esp. body mass; load: *dieting to lose weight.* **3.** Something heavy; a heavy object or load. **4.** Any load, burden, or source of pressure: *a heavy weight of worry.* **5.** The greatest part; preponderance: *the weight of evidence.* **6.** Authoritative influence or effect; importance; consequence: *His opinion had weight with her.* —*tr.v.* **1.** To make heavy or heavier with a weight or weights. **2.** To load down; burden or oppress. —*idioms.* **by weight.** According to weight rather than volume or other measure. **carry weight.** To have influence or authority: *Her opinions carry weight.* **pull (one's) weight.** To do one's job or share. **throw (one's) weight around.** *Informal.* To make a show of one's importance. [Middle English *wighte,* from Old English *wiht.*]

weight·less (wāt′lĭs) *adj.* **1.** Having little or no weight. **2.** Experiencing a gravitational force that is zero or very nearly zero. —**weight′less·ly** *adv.* —**weight′less·ness** *n.*

weight lifter. A person who lifts heavy weights as an exercise or in an athletic competition.

weight·lift·ing (wāt′lĭf′tĭng) *n.* The lifting of heavy weights in a prescribed manner as an exercise or in athletic competition.

weight·y (wā′tē) *adj.* **-i·er, -i·est. 1.** Having great weight. **2.** Very serious or important: *a weighty matter.* **3.** Burdensome: *weighty responsibilities.* **4.** Carrying weight; efficacious: *a weighty argument.* **5.** Fat. —See Syns at **burdensome, fat, heavy,** and **important.** —**weight′i·ly** *adv.* —**weight′i·ness** *n.*

weir (wîr) *n.* **1.** A dam placed across a river or canal. **2.** A fence or barrier, as of stakes, branches, or net, placed in a stream to catch or retain fish. [Middle English *were,* from Old English *wer.*]

weird (wîrd) *adj.* **-er, -est. 1.** Suggestive of or concerned with the supernatural; mysterious; unearthly; eerie; uncanny. **2.** Of an odd, peculiar or bizarre character; unusual; strange; fantastic: *all manner of weird machines.* [Middle English *wirde,* having power to control fate, from *wird,* fate, destiny, from Old English *wyrd.*] —**weird′ly** *adv.* —**weird′ness** *n.*

ă pat	ā pay	â care	ä father	ĕ pet	ē be	hw which	ĭ pit	ī tie	î pier	ŏ pot	ō toe	ô paw, for	oi noise
ōō took	ōō boot	ou out	th thin	th this	ŭ cut		û urge	zh vision	ə about, item, edible, gallop, circus

Syns: weird, eerie, uncanny, unearthly *adj. Core meaning:* Of a mysteriously strange and usu. frightening nature (*a weird premonition of disaster*).

weird·o (wûr′dō) *n., pl.* **-os.** *Slang.* An odd or strange person; a nut.

welch (wělch) *v.* Var. of **welsh.**

wel·come (wěl′kəm) *tr.v.* **-comed, -com·ing. 1.** To greet or receive with pleasure, hospitality, or special ceremony: *welcome newcomers.* **2.** To accept willingly or gratefully: *I welcome this opportunity.* —*n.* A warm greeting or hospitable reception. —*adj.* **1.** Greeted, received, or accepted with pleasure. **2.** Freely permitted or gladly invited to have, use, etc. **3.** Under no obligation for a courtesy or kindness: *"Thank you." "You're welcome!"* [Middle English *welcome,* from Old English *wilcuma,* a welcome guest, and *wilcume,* the greeting of welcome.] —**wel′com·er** *n.*

weld (wěld) *tr.v.* **1.** To join (metal pieces or parts) by subjecting them to heat and pressure. **2.** To bring into close association; unite. —*intr.v.* To undergo welding or be capable of being welded. —*n.* **1.** The union of two metal parts by welding. **2.** The joint formed when metal parts are united by welding. [Var. of obs. *well,* to weld, from Middle English *wellen,* to boil, well up, from Old English *wiellan,* to boil.]

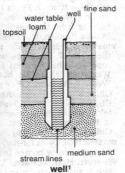

water table   well   fine sand
topsoil   loam
weld   well¹
stream lines   medium sand

wel·fare (wěl′fâr′) *n.* **1.** Health, happiness, or prosperity; well-being. **2.** The provision of economic or social benefits to a certain group of people, esp. aid furnished by the government or by private agencies to the needy or disabled. —*idiom.* **on welfare.** Receiving assistance from the government because of need or poverty. [Middle English *welfare,* well-being, good cheer, from the phrase *wel faren,* to fare well.]

welfare state. A social system whereby the state assumes responsibility for the welfare of citizens.

welfare work. Organized efforts by a community or an organization for the betterment of the poor.

wel·kin (wěl′kĭn) *n. Archaic.* The sky. —*idiom.* **make the welkin ring.** To make a great, reverberating sound. [Middle English *welken,* a cloud, the sky, from Old English *wolcen.*]

well¹ (wěl) *n.* **1.** A deep hole or shaft dug or drilled into the earth to obtain water, oil, gas, sulfur, or brine. **2.** A spring or fountain serving as a natural source of water. **3.** Any source to be drawn upon: *The dictionary is a well of information.* **4.** A container or reservoir used to hold a liquid, as an inkwell. **5.** A vertical opening that passes through the floors of a building, as for stairs or to allow ventilation. **6.** An enclosure in a ship's hold for the pumps. —*intr.v.* To rise or spring: *Tears welled in his eyes. Joy welled up in the old woman.* —*tr.v.* To pour forth: *a wound welling blood.* [Middle English *welle,* from Old English *wielle.*]

well² (wěl) *adv.* **bet·ter** (bět′ər), **best** (běst). **1.** In a good or proper manner; correctly: *carries himself well.* **2.** Skillfully or proficiently: *She plays the piano well.* **3.** Satisfactorily or sufficiently: *Did you sleep well?* **4.** Successfully or effectively: *How well do you get along with others?* **5.** Suitably; appropriately: *The two teams were well matched.* **6.** Favorably: *They spoke well of you.* **7.** Thoroughly: *Blend the ingredients well.* **8.** Perfectly; clearly: *How well do you remember the trip?* **9.** To a considerable

degree or extent; extensively: *It was well after sunset.* **10.** Widely; generally: *He is well known.* **11.** Closely: *Listen well to what I say.* **12.** With reason or justification; reasonably: *Their customs might well seem strange to an outsider.* —*adj.* **1. a.** In good health; not sick. **b.** Cured or healed. **2.** All right: *All is well.* —See Syns at **healthy.** —*interj.* **1.** A word used to express surprise, relief, etc., or as a question prompting someone to proceed or explain. **2.** A word used to introduce a remark or simply to gain time when one is undecided or uncertain. —*idioms.* **as well.** Also; in addition; too. **as well as.** And also; and in addition. **leave** (or **let**) **well enough alone.** To be content with things as they are. [Middle English, from Old English *wel.*]

Usage: well. The adverb *well* appears as an element of many hyphenated compound modifiers: *a well-known actress; an actress who was well-known.* If, however, the adverb *well* merely modifies a verb, an adjective, or another adverb and does not form an integral part of a set compound, it is not used with a hyphen: *a well thought-out plan; a plan that was well thought out.* See also Usage note at **good.**

we'll (wěl). Contraction of: **1.** We will. **2.** We shall.

well-bal·anced (wěl′băl′ənst) *adj.* **1.** Evenly proportioned or regulated. **2.** Mentally stable; sensible.

well-be·ing (wěl′bē′ĭng) *n.* Health, happiness, or prosperity; welfare.

well-bred (wěl′brěd′) *adj.* Having had a good upbringing; well-mannered. —See Syns at **refined.**

well-dis·posed (wěl′dĭ-spōzd′) *adj.* Having a disposition that tends to be kindly, friendly, or sympathetic.

well-done (wěl′dŭn′) *adj.* **1.** Satisfactorily or properly accomplished. **2.** Cooked all the way through.

well-fed (wěl′fěd′) *adj.* **1.** Adequately or properly nourished. **2.** Overfed; fat.

well-fixed (wěl′fĭkst′) *adj. Informal.* Financially secure; well-to-do.

well-found·ed (wěl′foun′dĭd) *adj.* Well-substantiated; based on sound judgment, reasoning, or evidence.

well-groomed (wěl′grōomd′) *adj.* **1.** Neat and clean in dress and personal appearance. **2.** Carefully combed and cared for: *a well-groomed horse.*

well-ground·ed (wěl′groun′dĭd) *adj.* **1.** Totally familiar with the basic principles of a subject. **2.** Having a sound basis; well-founded.

well-han·dled (wěl′hăn′dld) *adj.* **1.** Managed well. **2.** Showing the signs of much handling.

well-heeled (wěl′hēld′) *adj. Slang.* Well-fixed.

well-in·ten·tioned (wěl′ĭn-těn′shənd) *adj.* Having or showing good intentions; meant to be helpful.

well-known (wěl′nōn′) *adj.* **1.** Widely known; familiar or famous. **2.** Fully known.

well-man·nered (wěl′măn′ərd) *adj.* Polite; courteous.

well-mean·ing (wěl′mē′nĭng) *adj.* Having or prompted by good intentions.

well-meant (wěl′měnt′) *adj.* Arising from good intentions; intended to be helpful: *well-meant advice.*

well-nigh (wěl′nī′) *adv.* Nearly; almost.

well-off (wěl′ôf′, -ŏf′) *adj.* **1.** In fortunate circumstances. **2.** Wealthy; prosperous.

well-read (wěl′rěd′) *adj.* Knowledgeable through having read extensively.

well-spo·ken (wěl′spō′kən) *adj.* **1.** Chosen or expressed with aptness or propriety. **2.** Courteous in speech.

well·spring (wěl′sprĭng′) *n.* **1.** The source of a stream or spring; a fountainhead. **2.** A source of supply: *a wellspring of ideas.*

well-thought-of (wěl-thôt′ŭv′, -ŏv′) *adj.* Respected; esteemed.

well-timed (wěl′tīmd′) *adj.* Occurring or done at an opportune moment: *a well-timed remark.*

well-to-do (wěl′tə-dōo′) *adj.* Prosperous; affluent; well-off. [From the phrase *to do well.*]

well-turned (wěl′tûrnd′) *adj.* **1.** Gracefully formed; shapely: *a well-turned ankle.* **2.** Concisely or aptly expressed: *a well-turned phrase.*

well-wish·er (wěl′wĭsh′ər) *n.* A person who wishes another well; one who extends good wishes.

ă pat   ā pay   â care   ä father   ě pet   ē be   hw which
ŏŏ took   ōō boot   ou out   th thin   *th* this   ŭ cut

ī pit   ī tie   î pier   ŏ pot   ō toe   ô paw, for   oi noise
û urge   zh vision   ə about, item, edible, gallop, circus

well-worn (wĕl′wôrn′, -wōrn′) *adj.* **1.** Showing signs of much wear or use. **2.** Trite; hackneyed.

welsh (wĕlsh, wĕlch). *intr.v.* Also **welch** (wĕlch). *Slang.* **1.** To swindle a person by not paying a debt or wager. **2.** To fail to fulfill an obligation: *welshed on his friends.* [Orig. unknown.] —**welsh′er** *n.*

Welsh (wĕlsh) *n.* **1. the Welsh.** The people of Wales. **2.** The Celtic language of Wales. —*adj.* Of Wales, the Welsh, or their language.

Welsh cor·gi (kôr′gē). A dog of a breed originating in Wales, with a long body, short legs, and a foxlike head.

Welsh corgi

Welsh·man (wĕlsh′mən) *n.* **1.** A native or inhabitant of Wales. **2.** A person of Welsh descent.

Welsh rabbit. A dish made of melted cheese, milk or cream, seasonings, and sometimes ale, served hot over toast or crackers. Also called **Welsh rarebit.**

welt (wĕlt) *n.* **1.** A strip of leather or other material stitched into a shoe between the sole and the upper. **2.** A tape or covered cord sewn into a seam as reinforcement or trimming. **3.** A ridge or bump raised on the skin by a lash or blow or sometimes by an allergic reaction. Also called **wale.** —*tr.v.* **1.** To reinforce or trim with a welt. **2.** To beat severely so as to raise a welt or welts; flog. **3.** To raise a welt or welts on by beating or hitting. [Middle English *welte.*]

wel·ter (wĕl′tər) *intr.v.* **1.** To wallow, roll, or toss about, as in mud or high waves. **2.** To lie soaked in a liquid: *welter in blood.* —*n.* **1.** An agitated rolling or tossing: *a welter of waves.* **2. a.** A highly confused condition; turmoil. **b.** A confused mass; a jumble: *a welter of arms and legs.* [Middle English *welteren.*]

wel·ter·weight (wĕl′tər-wāt′) *n.* A boxer or wrestler who weighs between 136 and 147 lbs. or approx. 62 and 67 kilograms. [*Welter,* a heavy weight boxer, from *welt,* to beat + WEIGHT.]

wen (wĕn) *n.* A cyst that contains only secretions from the skin. [Middle English, from Old English *wenn.*]

wench (wĕnch) *n. Archaic.* **1.** A young woman or girl. **2.** A female servant. [Middle English *wenche,* short for *wenchel,* a girl, from Old English *wencel,* a child of either sex.]

wend (wĕnd) *tr.v.* To go or proceed on or along (one's way). —*intr.v.* To go one's way; proceed; travel. [Middle English *wenden,* from Old English *wendan,* to turn.]

went (wĕnt) *v.* Past tense of **go.** [Middle English, from Old English *wende,* p. t. of *wendan,* to turn.]

wept (wĕpt) *v.* Past tense and past participle of **weep.**

were (wûr) *v.* **1.** Second person singular past tense of **be.** **2.** First, second, and third person plural past tense of **be.** **3.** Past subjunctive of **be.** [Middle English *wære, wǣron,* from Old English *wǣre, wǣron.*]
   Usage: **were, was.** As the past subjunctive of *be, were* occurs in statements that are hypothetical or contrary to fact: *If I were you, I'd leave. I wish that the operation were over. She acted as though everything were settled.* In formal writing, *were* is required in such examples; in speech and informal writing, the indicative form *was* often occurs. But more grammatical problems occur through misuse of *were.* Such misuse is esp. common in mere conditional statements and in indirect questions. In each of these, use *was* not *were: They said that if the report was correct, charges would be pressed. I tried to find out whether the crisis was over. They asked if he was agreeable.*

we're (wîr). Contraction of we are.

were·n't (wûrnt, wûr′ənt). Contraction of were not.

were·wolf (wîr′wo͝olf′, wûr′-, wâr′-) *n.* Also **wer·wolf.** In folklore and stories, a person believed to be transformed into a wolf or capable of assuming the form of a wolf at will. [Middle English *werewolf,* from Old English *werewulf : wer,* man + *wulf,* wolf.]

wert (wûrt) *v. Archaic.* A form of the past tense of **be,** used with *thou.* [From WERE.]

wes·kit (wĕs′kĭt) *n.* A waistcoat or vest. [Var. of WAIST-COAT.]

west (wĕst) *n.* **1. a.** The direction opposite to the direction in which the earth rotates on its axis. **b.** One of four cardinal points on the mariner's compass 90° left of north and 180° from east. **2.** Often **West.** A region or part of the earth in this direction. **3. the West. a.** The part of the earth west of Asia and Asia Minor, esp. Europe and the Western Hemisphere; the Occident. **b.** The western part of the United States, esp. the region west of the Mississippi River. —*adj.* **1.** Of, in, or toward the west. **2.** Often **West.** Forming or belonging to a region, country, etc., toward the west: *West Germany.* **3.** From the west: *a west wind.* —*adv.* To or toward the west. [Middle English, from Old English.]

west·bound (wĕst′bound′) *adj.* Going toward the west.

west·er·ly (wĕs′tər-lē) *adj.* **1.** In or toward the west: *a westerly direction.* **2.** From the west: *westerly winds.* —*adv.* To or toward the west. —*n., pl.* **-lies.** A wind or storm coming from the west. [From obs. *wester,* western, from Middle English, from Old English *westra.*]

west·ern (wĕs′tərn) *adj.* **1.** Often **Western.** Of, in, or toward the west. **2.** From the west. **3.** Often **Western. a.** Of Europe and the Western Hemisphere: *western technology; Western civilization.* **b.** Of, like, or used in the American West. **7. Western.** Of or pertaining to the Roman Catholic Church as distinguished from the Eastern Orthodox Church. —*n.* Often **Western.** A book, motion picture, or television or radio program about cowboys or frontier life in the American West. [Middle English *westeren,* from Old English *westerne.*]

west·ern·er (wĕs′tər-nər) *n.* Often **Westerner.** A person who lives in or comes from the west.

Western Hemisphere. The half of the earth that includes North and South America.

west·ern·ize (wĕs′tər-nīz′) *tr.v.* **-ized, -iz·ing.** To convert to the ways of Western civilization. —**west′ern·i·za′tion** *n.*

west·ern·most (wĕs′tərn-mōst′) *adj.* Farthest west.

western omelet. An omelet cooked with diced ham, chopped green pepper, and onion.

west-north·west (wĕst′nôrth-wĕst′; *Naut.* -nôr-wĕst′) *n.* The direction on the mariner's compass halfway between west and northwest; 67° 30 minutes west of due north. —*adj.* Situated toward, facing, or in this direction. —*adv.* In, from, or toward this direction.

west-south·west (wĕst′south-wĕst′; *Naut.* -sou-wĕst′) *n.* The direction on the mariner's compass halfway between west and southwest; 112° 30′ west of due north. —*adj.* Situated toward, facing, or in this direction. —*adv.* In, from, or toward this direction.

west·ward (wĕst′wərd) *adv.* Also **west·wards** (-wərdz). To or toward the west. —*adj.* Situated toward, facing, or in the west. —*n.* A direction or point toward the west.

wet (wĕt) *adj.* **wet·ter, wet·test. 1.** Covered, moistened, soaked, or saturated with a liquid, esp. water. **2.** Containing a relatively large amount of water or water vapor: *wet snow; heavy, wet air.* **3.** Rainy: *a wet day.* **4.** Not yet dry or hardened: *wet paint; wet plaster.* **5.** *Informal.* Allowing the sale of alcoholic beverages: *a wet county.* —*n.* **1.** Water; liquid; moisture. **2.** Rainy or snowy weather. —*tr.v.* **wet** or **wet·ted, wet·ting. 1.** To make wet; moisten or dampen: *wet a sponge.* **2.** To make (a bed or one's clothes) wet by urinating. —*intr.v.* To become wet. —*idioms.* **all wet.** *Slang.* Entirely mistaken. **wet behind the ears.** Inexperienced; green. **wet one's whistle.** To take a drink. [Middle English, from Old English *wæt.*]

wet·back (wĕt′băk′) *n.* A Mexican, esp. a laborer, who crosses the U.S. border illegally.

wet blanket. *Informal.* Someone or something that discourages enjoyment or enthusiasm, etc.

wet cell. A primary electric cell having its electrolyte in the form of a liquid rather than in the form of a paste as in a dry cell.

weth·er (wĕth′ər) n. A castrated male sheep. [Middle English, from Old English *wether*, ram.]

wet·land (wĕt′lănd′) n. Often **wetlands**. A lowland area, as a marsh, that is saturated with moisture.

wet nurse. **1.** A woman who suckles another woman's child. **2.** A person who treats another with excessive care or solicitude.

wet suit. A close-fitting garment of rubber that covers the entire body and is worn for warmth by scuba divers and skin divers.

we've (wēv). Contraction of we have.

whack (hwăk, wăk) tr.v. To strike, hit, or slap with a sharp, resounding blow. —intr.v. To deal a sharp, hard blow. —See Syns at **hit**. —n. **1.** A sharp, hard blow. **2.** The sound made by such a blow. —idioms. **have** (or **take**) **a whack at.** Informal. To attempt; try. **out of whack.** Informal. Improperly ordered or balanced; not working correctly. [Imit.]

whack·y (hwăk′ē, wăk′ē) adj. Var. of **wacky**.

whale[1] (hwāl, wāl) n. **1.** Any of various sea mammals of the order Cetacea, that gen. have a fishlike form with forelimbs modified to form flippers and a tail with horizontal flukes, esp. one of the very large species as distinguished from the smaller dolphins, porpoises, etc. **2.** Informal. An unusually fine, big, or impressive example of something specified: *a whale of a game.* —intr.v. **whaled, whal·ing.** To engage in whaling or the hunting of whales. [Middle English *whale*, from Old English *hwæl.*]

whale[2] (hwāl, wāl) tr.v. **whaled, whal·ing.** To strike repeatedly with a whip, stick, etc.; thrash; flog. —intr.v. To attack vehemently: *The poet whaled away at his critics.* [Orig. unknown.]

whale·back (hwāl′băk′, wāl′-) n. A steamship with the bow and upper deck rounded in order to shed water.

whale·boat (hwāl′bōt′, wāl′-) n. **1.** A long rowboat, pointed at both ends and designed to move and turn swiftly, formerly used in the pursuit and harpooning of whales. **2.** Any boat of similar size and shape. Also called **whaler.**

whaleboat

whale·bone (hwāl′bōn′, wāl′-) n. **1.** The durable, elastic, hornlike material that forms the plates or strips in the upper jaw of certain whales. **2.** A strip of this material, such as one used to stiffen a corset.

whal·er (hwā′lər, wā′-) n. **1.** A person who hunts for whales or works on a whaling ship. **2.** A boat or ship used in whaling. **3.** A whaleboat.

whal·ing (hwā′lĭng, wā′-) n. The business or practice of hunting, killing, and processing whales for their valuable products.

wham (hwăm, wăm) n. **1.** A forceful, resounding blow. **2.** The sound of such a blow; a thud. —v. **whammed, wham·ming.** —tr.v. To strike or smash into with resounding impact; hit: *The car whammed a telephone pole.* —intr.v. To smash with great force: *The bullet whammed into the target.* —See Syns at **hit.** [Imit.]

wham·my (hwăm′ē, wăm′ē) n., pl. **-mies.** Slang. A supernatural spell; the evil eye; a hex: *put the whammy on someone.* [Perh. from WHAM.]

whang (hwăng, wăng). Informal. —tr.v. To strike so as to produce a loud, reverberating noise. —intr.v. To produce a loud, reverberating noise. —n. Informal. A loud, reverberating noise. [Imit.]

wharf (hwôrf, wôrf) n., pl. **wharves** (hwôrvz, wôrvz) or **wharfs.** A landing place or pier at which vessels may tie up

and load or unload. [Middle English *wharfe*, from Old English *hwearf.*]

wharf·age (hwôr′fĭj, wôr′-) n. **1.** The use of a wharf or wharves. **2.** A charge or fee for the use of a wharf. **3.** Wharves in general.

wharves (hwôrz, wôrvz) n. Plural of **wharf.**

what (hwŏt, hwŭt, wŏt, wŭt; hwət, wət *when unstressed*) pron. **1.** Which thing or which particular one of many: *What are we having for supper?* **2.** Which kind, character, or designation: *What are these things?* **3.** Of how much value or significance: *What are possessions to a dying man?* **4. a.** That which or the thing that: *Listen to what I have to say.* **b.** Whatever thing that: *Come what may, I'm staying.* **5.** Informal. Something: *I'll tell you what.* —adj. **1.** Which one or ones of several or many: *What train do I take?* **2.** Whatever: *We repaired what damage had been done.* **3.** How great: *What fools we have been!* —adv. How: *What does it matter, after all?* —interj. A word used to express surprise, disbelief, etc. —idioms. **what for.** Informal. A scolding or strong reprimand: *I really got what for for coming home late.* **what if.** What would happen if; suppose that. **what's what.** Informal The true state of affairs: *I'll tell you what's what.* **what with.** Because of: *What with the heat and humidity, we really suffered.* [Middle English, from Old English *hwæt.*]

what·ev·er (hwŏt-ĕv′ər, hwŭt-, wŏt-, wŭt-) pron. **1.** Everything or anything that: *Please do whatever you can to help.* **2.** No matter what; regardless of what: *Whatever happens, we'll meet here tonight.* **3.** Informal. What; which thing or things: *Whatever does he mean?* —adj. **1.** Of any number or kind; any: *Whatever needs you have, feel free to call on us.* **2.** Of any kind at all: *He was left with nothing whatever.*

what·not (hwŏt′nŏt′, hwŭt′-, wŏt′-, wŭt′-) n. **1.** A set of open shelves to hold small ornaments. **2.** A small or trivial article or item, usu. of a decorative or ornamental nature.

what·so·ev·er (hwŏt′sō-ĕv′ər, hwŭt′-, wŏt′-, wŭt′-) adj. Of any kind at all.

wheal (hwēl, wēl) n. A small acute swelling on the skin. [Var. of WALE (ridge).]

wheat (hwēt, wēt) n. **1.** Any of various cereal grasses of the genus *Triticum*, esp. *T. aestivum*, that is widely cultivated in many varieties for its commercially important edible grain. **2.** The seeds of this plant, usu. ground to produce flour. [Middle English *whete*, from Old English *hwǣte.*]

wheat·en (hwēt′n, wēt′n) adj. Of, made from, or resembling wheat.

wheat germ. The embryo of the wheat kernel, rich in vitamins, used as a cereal or food supplement.

whee·dle (hwēd′l, wēd′l) tr.v. **-dled, -dling.** **1.** To persuade or attempt to persuade by flattering, pleading, or beguiling; cajole. **2.** To obtain through the use of flattery or cajolery: *He wheedled a promise out of me.* —intr.v. To use flattery or cajolery to achieve one's ends; coax: *Don't wheedle; just ask if you need something.* [Orig. unknown.] —whee′dler n. —whee′dling·ly adv.

wheel (hwēl, wēl) n. **1. a.** A solid disk or a rigid circular ring attached to a hub by spokes, designed to turn around an axle or shaft that passes through its center. **b.** Anything resembling such a device in form, appearance, function, or movement or having such a device as its principal part: *a steering wheel; a ferris wheel.* **2.** Informal. A bicycle. **3. wheels.** Forces that provide energy, movement, or direction: *the wheels of commerce.* **4.** A turn, revolution, or rotation around an axis, esp. a military maneuver to change the direction of movement of a formation of troops, ships, etc., in which the formation is maintained while the outer unit describes an arc and the inner unit remains stationary as a pivot. **5. wheels.** Slang. An automobile. **6.** Slang. A very powerful or influential person: *He's a big wheel at the bank.* —tr.v. **1.** To roll, move, or transport on a wheel or wheels: *Put the books on the cart and wheel them to the library.* **2.** To cause to turn around or as if around a central axis; revolve; rotate: *The platoon leader wheeled his troops and marched them in front of the reviewing stand.* —intr.v. **1.** To turn around or as if around a central axis; revolve; rotate: *The carousel wheeled round and round.* **2.** To roll or move on or as if on a wheel or wheels: *Children wheeled down the street on bicycles.* **3.** To fly in a curving or circular course: *A flock of birds wheeled above the trees.* **4.** To turn, spin, or whirl suddenly, changing direction; to pivot: *When his mother called, the boy wheeled and ran toward her.* **—phrasal verb. wheel and deal.** To aggressively promote numerous business or political deals in order to achieve personal fortune or advancement. **—idiom. at** (or **behind**) **the wheel. 1.** Operating the steering mechanism of a vehicle; driving. **2.** In charge; directing or controlling. [Middle English, from Old English *hwēol*.]

wheel·bar·row (hwēl′băr′ō, wēl′-) *n.* An open vehicle used to carry small loads by hand, with a wheel at the front and pushed by two horizontal handles at the back.

wheel·chair (hwēl′châr′, wēl′-) *n.* Also **wheel chair.** A chair mounted on large wheels for the use of sick or disabled persons.

wheel·er (hwē′lər, wē′-) *n.* **1.** Someone or something that wheels. **2.** A thing that moves on or is equipped with a wheel or wheels: *a three-wheeler.* **3.** A **wheel horse.**

wheel·er-deal·er (hwē′lər-dē′lər, wē′-) *n. Informal.* A person who wheels and deals; a sharp operator.

wheel horse. 1. In a team, the horse that follows the leader and is harnessed nearest to the front wheels. **2.** Any diligent, dependable worker, esp. in a political organization.

wheel house. A pilothouse.

wheel·wright (hwēl′rīt′, wēl′-) *n.* A person whose trade is the building and repairing of wheels.

wheeze (hwēz, wēz) *v.* **wheezed, wheez·ing.** *—intr.v.* **1.** To breathe with difficulty, producing a hoarse whistling or hissing sound. **2.** To make a sound suggestive of laborious breathing: *He wheezes when he speaks.* *—tr.v.* To produce or utter with a hoarse whistling sound: *"A tugboat, wheezing wreathes of steam, / Lunged past"* (Hart Crane). *—n.* A wheezing sound: *He talks with a wheeze.* [Middle English *whesen,* prob. from Old Norse *hvæsa,* to hiss.] **—wheez′er** *n.* **—wheez′ing·ly** *adv.*

wheez·y (hwē′zē, wē′-) *adj.* **-i·er, -i·est. 1.** Given to or afflicted with wheezing: *a wheezy horse.* **2.** Having or producing a wheezing sound: *spoken in a wheezy voice.* **—wheez′i·ly** *adv.* **—wheez′i·ness** *n.*

whelk (hwĕlk, wĕlk) *n.* Any of various large, sometimes edible saltwater snails of the family Buccinidae, with pointed, turreted shells. [Middle English *whelke,* from Old English *weoloc.*]

whelk

whelm (hwĕlm, wĕlm) *tr.v.* **1.** To cover with water; submerge: *The flood waters whelmed the village.* **2.** To overwhelm: *A tide of emotion whelmed him.* [Middle English *whelmen,* to turn over.]

whelp (hwĕlp, wĕlp) *n.* **1.** A young offspring of a dog, wolf, or similar animal. **2.** A young and inexperienced or impudent person. *—tr.v.* To give birth to (a whelp or whelps). *—intr.v.* To give birth to a whelp or whelps. [Middle English *whelpe,* from Old English *hwelp.*]

when (hwĕn, wĕn) *adv.* **1.** At what time: *When did you leave?* **2.** At which time: *I know when to leave.* *—conj.* **1.** At the time that: *in April, when the snow melts.* **2.** As soon as: *I'll call you when I get there.* **3.** Whenever: *He always arrives late when he goes to the barber.* **4.** Whereas; although: *He's reading comic books when he should be doing his homework.* **5.** Considering that; since: *How are you going to make the team when you won't stop smoking?* *—pron.* What or which time: *Since when have*

you been giving the orders around here? *—n.* The time or date: *We knew the when but not the where of it.* [Middle English, from Old English *hwanne.*]

whence (hwĕns, wĕns) *adv.* **1.** From where; from what place: *Whence came this man?* **2.** From what origin or source: *Whence comes this splendid feast?* *—conj.* **1.** Out of which place; from or out of which: *His rooms overlooked a garden, whence a cobbled path led down to a small brook.* **2.** By reason of which; from which: *The dog was coal black from nose to tail, whence the name Shadow.* [Middle English *whennes,* from *whenne,* whence, from Old English *hwanon.*]

whence·so·ev·er (hwĕns′sō-ĕv′ər, wĕns′-) *adv.* From whatever place or source. *—conj.* From any place or source that.

when·ev·er (hwĕn-ĕv′ər, wĕn-) *adv.* **1.** At whatever time: *The tools are available to you whenever needed.* **2.** When. Used as an intensive: *Whenever is she coming?* *—conj.* **1.** At whatever time that: *We can leave whenever you're ready.* **2.** Every time that: *I smile whenever I think back on that day.*

when·so·ev·er (hwĕn′sō-ĕv′ər, wĕn′-) *adv. & conj.* Whenever.

where (hwâr, wâr) *adv.* **1.** At or in what place, point, or position: *Where is the telephone?* **2.** To what place or end: *Where does this road lead?* **3.** From what place or source: *Where did you get that crazy idea?* *—conj.* **1.** At or in what or which place: *I am going to my room where I can study.* **2.** In or to a place in which or to which: *She lives where the climate is mild. I will go where you go.* **3.** Wherever: *Where there's smoke, there's fire.* **4.** Whereas: *Mars has two satellites, where Earth has only one.* *—pron.* **1.** What or which place: *Where did they come from?* **2.** The place in, at, or to which: *This is where I found the puppy.* *—n.* The place or occasion: *We know the when but not the where of it.* [Middle English, from Old English *hwǣr.*]

Usage: **where. 1.** Use the adverb *where + from* to indicate motion from a place: *Where did she come from?* **2.** Use *where* alone to indicate motion to a place: *Where did she go* (not *go to*)? and to indicate location or place of rest: *Where is she now* (not *where is she at now*)? **3.** Avoid use of the conjunction *where* to supplant *that* in examples such as this: *I see that* (not *where*) *he has resigned.*

where·a·bouts (hwâr′ə-bouts′, wâr′-) *adv.* Where or about where; in, at, or near what location: *Whereabouts do you live? —n. (used with a sing. or pl. verb).* The approximate location of someone or something: *I don't know his whereabouts now.*

where·as (hwâr-ăz′, wâr′-) *conj.* **1.** It being the fact that; inasmuch as; since. **2.** While on the contrary: *Human beings have speech, whereas animals do not.*

where·at (hwâr-ăt′, wâr-) *adv. Archaic.* **1.** At which place. **2.** Whereupon.

where·by (hwâr-bī′, wâr-) *adv.* By which or by means of which.

where·fore (hwâr′fôr′, -fōr′, wâr′-) *—conj. Archaic.* For which reason; because of which; therefore: *"And the thing which he did displeased the Lord: wherefore he slew him also"* (The Bible, Genesis 38:10). *—adv. Archaic.* Why: *Wherefore should we fear? —n.* A purpose, cause, or reason: *I don't know all the whys and wherefores of the decision.* [Middle English *wherfor.*]

where·from (hwâr′frŏm′, -frŭm′, wâr′-) *adv. Archaic.* From what or where; whence.

where·in (hwâr-ĭn′, wâr-) *adv.* **1.** In what; how: *Wherein have I offended?* **2.** In which thing, place, or situation: *the bed wherein he slept.*

where·in·to (hwâr-ĭn′tōō, wâr-) *adv. Archaic.* Into what or which.

where·of (hwâr-ŏv′, -ŭv′, wâr-) *adv.* Of what, which, or whom: *He made me a long speech, whereof I understood not one syllable.*

where·on (hwâr-ŏn′, -ôn′, wâr-) *adv. Archaic.* On which.

where·so·ev·er (hwâr′sō-ĕv′ər, wâr′-) *conj. Archaic.* Wherever.

where·to (hwâr-tōō′, wâr-) *adv. Archaic.* **1.** To which. **2.** To what place or toward what end.

where·up·on (hwâr′ə-pŏn′, -pôn′, wâr′-) *conj.* **1.** Upon which. **2.** Following which.

wher·ev·er (hwâr-ĕv'ər, wâr-) *adv.* **1.** In or to whatever place or situation: *Use capital letters wherever needed.* **2.** Where. Used as an intensive: *Wherever have you been so long?* —*conj.* In or to whatever place or situation: *My blessing is with you wherever you may go.*

where·with (hwâr'wĭth', -wĭth', wâr-) *conj.* With which: *the supplies wherewith every pharmacy is stocked.*

where·with·al (hwâr'wĭth-ôl', -wĭth-, wâr-) *n.* The necessary means, esp. financial means: *have the wherewithal to buy a new car.*

wher·ry (hwĕr'ē, wĕr'ē) *n., pl.* **-ries. 1.** A light, swift rowboat built for one person and often used in racing. **2.** A large sailing barge used in England, usu. to move freight. [Middle English *whery.*]

wherry

whet (hwĕt, wĕt) *tr.v.* **whet·ted, whet·ting. 1.** To sharpen (a knife or other tool); hone: *whetting a razor against a strap.* **2.** To make more keen; stimulate; heighten: *Cooking odors always whet my appetite.* —*n.* **1.** The act or process of whetting. **2.** Something that whets; an appetizer or aperitif. [Middle English *whetten*, from Old English *hwettan.*]

wheth·er (hwĕth'ər, wĕth'-) *conj.* **1.** —Used in indirect questions involving alternatives: *Have you ever wondered whether animals feel love and grief?* **2.** —Used to introduce alternative possibilities: *whether in victory or defeat; whether they realize it or not.* **3.** Either: *He won the fight, whether by skill or dumb luck.* —See Usage note **1** at **if.** [Middle English, from Old English *hwæther.*]

whet·stone (hwĕt'stōn', wĕt'-) *n.* A stone used for sharpening knives and other cutting tools.

whew (hwōō, hwyōō) *interj.* A word used to express relief, surprise, distress, fatigue, etc.

whey (hwā, wā) *n.* The watery part of milk that separates from the curds, as in the process of making cheese. [Middle English, from Old English *hwæg.*] —**whey'ey** *adj.*

which (hwĭch, wĭch) *pron.* **1.** What particular one or ones: *Which is your house?* Also used adjectivally: *Which coat is yours?* **2.** The particular one or ones that: *Take those which are yours.* **3.** The thing, animal, group of people, or event previously named or implied: *the movie, which was shown later.* Also used adjectivally: *It started raining, at which point we left the park.* **4.** Whichever: *Choose which one of these you like best.* Also used adjectivally: *Do it which way you like.* **5.** A thing or circumstance that: *She ignored us, which was a shame.* [Middle English, from Old English *hwilc.*]

Usage: **which.** In sentences such as the following, *which* means a thing or circumstances that: *He seemed unhappy, which was understandable. Which* refers to an entire preceding clause rather than to a single word. This usage is acceptable provided that the reference is clear. Ambiguity occurs most often when *which* follows a noun that could be construed as the antecedent: *She refused our offer, which caused much surprise.* If the surprise stemmed from the refusal rather than from the nature of the offer, rephrasing is desirable: *She refused our offer, and that caused much surprise.* See also Usage note at **that.**

which·ev·er (hwĭch-ĕv'ər, wĭch-) *pron.* Whatever one or ones which: *The dogs were there, waiting to fall upon whichever was beaten.* Also used adjectivally: *whichever one of you succeeds in catching the thief.*

which·so·ev·er (hwĭch'sō-ĕv'ər, wĭch'-) *pron.* Whichever.

whiff (hwĭf, wĭf) *n.* **1.** A breath or puff, as of air or smoke. **2.** A slight smell carried in the air: *a whiff of buttered popcorn.* **3.** An inhalation: *Take a whiff of this perfume.* —*intr.v.* **1.** To be carried in brief gusts; waft: *puffs of smoke whiffing from the chimney.* **2.** To draw in or breathe out air, smoke, etc.: *There he sat whiffing away at his pipe.* —*tr.v.* **1.** To blow or convey in whiffs: *A light breeze whiffed the clouds through the sky.* **2.** To inhale through the nose; smell; sniff: *Whiffing the air, I smelled smoke.* **3.** To draw in or breathe out (air, tobacco smoke, etc.): *I whiffed some fumes from the solvent and began to choke.* [Imit.]

whif·fle·tree (hwĭf'əl-trē, wĭf'-) *n.* The pivoted horizontal crossbar to which the harness traces of a draft animal are hitched and which is then attached to a carriage, cart, plow, etc. Also called **singletree** and **swingletree.** [Var. of *whippletree*, prob. from WHIP.]

Whig (hwĭg, wĭg) *n.* **1.** In England, a member of a political party of the 18th and 19th cent. opposed to the Tories. **2.** During the American Revolution, a colonist who supported the war against England. **3.** In the United States, a member of a political party (1834–55) formed to oppose the Democratic Party, ultimately succeeded by the Republican Party. [Prob. short for *Whiggamore*, one of a body of 17th-cent. Scottish insurgents.] —**Whig'gish** *adj.*

while (hwīl, wīl) *n.* **1.** A period of time. Used mainly in adverbial phrases: *stay for a while; singing (all) the while.* **2.** The time, effort, or trouble taken in doing something: *I don't think it's worth my while.* —See Syns at **effort.** —*conj.* **1.** As long as; during the time that: *It was great while it lasted.* **2.** Although. **3.** Whereas; and: *The soles of the shoes are leather, while the uppers are canvas.* —*tr.v.* **whiled, whil·ing.** To pass (time) in a pleasant, relaxed way. [Middle English, from Old English *hwīl.*]

Usage: **while. 1.** The conjunction *while* is used to indicate a time period: *He slept while I worked.* It is also acceptably used to mean although: *While the work is difficult, it is nevertheless rewarding.* It is acceptable too in the sense of whereas, so long as the locution is not ambiguous: *The main figure is red, while the background is blue.* But *whereas* is needed for clarity in this example: *He spent his youth in Ohio, whereas* (not *while*) *his brother grew up in England.* **2.** *While* has been used so often in the last 100 years as a substitute for *and* that it can only be regarded as standard: *They took steak, my brother had veal, while I ordered fish.* See also Usage note at **awhile.**

whiles (hwīlz, wīlz) *conj.* While. *Obs.* While.

whi·lom (hwī'ləm, wī'-) *adj.* Former; having once been: *She is the whilom Miss Smith.* —*adv. Archaic.* Formerly. [Middle English, from Old English *hwīlum*, at times.]

whilst (hwīlst, wīlst) *conj.* While. [Middle English *whylst.*]

whim (hwĭm, wĭm) *n.* **1.** A sudden or capricious idea or desire; a passing fancy. **2.** Arbitrary thought or impulse: *governed by whim.* [Short for earlier *whim-wham.*]

whim·per (hwĭm'pər, wĭm'-) *intr.v.* **1.** To cry or sob with soft, intermittent, whining sounds. **2.** To complain: *The child just whimpers and whines about everything.* —*tr.v.* To utter in a whimper: *The little boy whimpered frightened replies.* —*n.* A low, broken, whining sound: *speak in a whimper.* [Imit.] —**whim'per·er** *n.* —**whim'per·ing·ly** *adv.*

whim·sey (hwĭm'zē, wĭm'-) *n.* Var. of **whimsy.**

whim·si·cal (hwĭm'zĭ-kəl, wĭm'-) *adj.* **1.** Playful, fanciful, or capricious: *a whimsical smile; a whimsical painting; a whimsical prank.* **2.** Quaint; fantastic; odd: *Middle English spelling seems whimsical to us now.* —See Syns at **capricious.** [From WHIMSY.] —**whim'si·cal'i·ty** (-kăl'ĭ-tē) *n.* —**whim'si·cal·ly** *adv.*

whim·sy (hwĭm'zē, wĭm'-) *n., pl.* **-sies.** Also **whim·sey** *pl.* **-seys. 1.** An odd or playful idea; an idle fancy. **2.** An amusingly odd and fanciful style of humor: *His stories are full of whimsy and laughter.* **3.** Anything quaint, fanciful, or odd: *The shop window was full of little china whimsies.* [Prob. from WHIM.]

whin (hwĭn, wĭn) *n.* A spiny shrub; gorse. [Middle English *whynne.*]

whine (hwīn, wīn) *v.* **whined, whin·ing.** —*intr.v.* **1.** To utter a plaintive, high-pitched, nasal sound, as in pain, fear, complaint, or protest: *The child began to whine when his mother scolded him.* **2.** To complain in a childish, annoy-

---

ă pat   ā pay   â care   ä father   ĕ pet   ē be   hw which
ŏŏ took   ōō boot   ou out   th thin   *th* this   ŭ cut

ĭ pit   ī tie   î pier   ŏ pot   ō toe   ô paw, for   oi noise
û urge   zh vision   ə about, item, edible, gallop, circus

ing way: *His wife constantly whines that he neglects her.* **3.** To produce a sustained noise of relatively high pitch, as a machine does: *The gears started to whine because they need to be oiled.* —*tr.v.* To utter with a whine. —*n.* **1.** A whining sound or complaint. **2.** The act of whining. [Middle English *whinen,* from Old English *hwīnan.*] —**whin'er** *n.* —**whin'ing·ly** *adv.* —**whin'y** *adj.*

whin·ny (hwĭn'ē, wĭn'ē) *v.* **-nied, -ny·ing.** —*intr.v.* To utter the high-pitched or gentle sound characteristic of a horse; to neigh. —*tr.v.* To express in a whinny: *The pony whinnied his pleasure at being set free.* —*n., pl.* **-nies.** The gentle or high-pitched sound made by a horse; a neigh. [Prob. from WHINE.]

whip (hwĭp, wĭp) *v.* **whipped** or **whipt, whip·ping.** —*tr.v.* **1.** To strike with repeated strokes, as of a strap, rod, etc.; to lash; beat: *The jockey whipped his horse, urging him to run faster.* **2.** To punish, chastise, or reprove by or as if by beating or lashing. **3.** To drive, force, or compel by flogging, lashing, or other means of coercion: *His speech whipped the mob into a frenzy.* **4.** To strike in a manner similar to whipping or lashing: *Icy winds whipped his face.* **5.** To beat (cream, eggs, etc.) into a froth or foam. **6.** To snatch, pull, or remove in a sudden, rapid manner: *He whipped his hat off.* **7.** To sew with a loose overcast or overhand stitch. **8.** To wrap or bind (a rope, wire, rod, etc.) with twine, thread, wire, or other wrapping to strengthen or prevent fraying: *whipped the electrical cord with plastic tape.* **9.** *Informal.* To defeat; outdo; beat. —*intr.v.* **1.** To move in a sudden, quick manner: *She whipped around when I called her name.* **2.** To move in a manner similar to a whip; thrash about: *Branches whipped against the windows.* —See Syns at **defeat.** —*phrasal verb.* **whip up. 1.** To arouse; excite: *whip up a crowd; whip up enthusiasm.* **2.** *Informal.* To prepare quickly, as a meal. —*n.* **1.** A flexible rod or a flexible thong or lash attached to a handle, used for urging animals on or for striking or beating someone. **2.** A whipping or lashing blow, motion or stroke. **3.** Something that looks, bends, or lashes about like a whip. **4.** Flexibility, as in the shaft of a golf club, fishing rod, etc. **5.** A member of a legislature selected by his political party to enforce party discipline: *the majority whip in the Senate.* **6.** A dessert made of sugar, whipped cream or stiffly beaten egg whites, and often fruit or fruit flavoring. [Middle English *wippen.*] —**whip'per** *n.*

whip·cord (hwĭp'kôrd', wĭp'-) *n.* **1.** A worsted fabric with a distinct diagonal rib. **2.** A strong twisted or braided cord sometimes used in making whiplashes. **3.** Catgut.

whip·lash (hwĭp'lăsh', wĭp'-) *n.* **1.** The lash of a whip. **2.** An injury to the neck or spine caused by a sudden forward or backward jerk of the head. —*tr.v.* To beat, drive, or urge on with a whip.

whip·per·snap·per (hwĭp'ər-snăp'ər, wĭp'-) *n.* An insignificant and pretentious person, esp. an impudent youth.

whip·pet (hwĭp'ĭt, wĭp'-) *n.* A short-haired, swift-running dog of a breed developed in England, that resembles the greyhound but is smaller. [Orig. unknown.]

whippet

whip·ping (hwĭp'ĭng, wĭp'-) *n.* **1.** The act of someone or something that whips. **2.** A thrashing administered esp. as punishment. **3.** Material, as cord or thread, used to bind or lash parts.

whipping boy. Someone who is punished for the mistakes or wrongdoing of another; scapegoat.

whip·poor·will (hwĭp'ər-wĭl', wĭp'-, hwĭp'ər-wĭl', wĭp'-) *n.*

Also **whip-poor-will.** A brownish nocturnal North American bird, *Caprimulgus vociferus,* with a distinctive call that sounds like its name. [Imit.]

whip·saw (hwĭp'sô', wĭp'-) *n.* A narrow two-man crosscut saw. —*tr.v.* **-sawed** or **-sawn** (-sôn'), **-saw·ing. 1.** To cut with a whipsaw. **2.** To defeat or best in two ways at once: *We whipsawed the enemy when we got our agent out and took down their top agent in the bargain.*

whip·stock (hwĭp'stŏk', wĭp'-) *n.* The handle of a whip.

whipt (hwĭpt, wĭpt) *v.* Past tense and past participle of **whip.**

whir (hwûr, wûr) *v.* **whirred, whir·ring.** —*intr.v.* To move swiftly so as to make a buzzing or humming sound. —*tr.v.* To cause to make a buzzing sound: *He whirred the wheels of his bicycle.* —*n.* **1.** A buzzing or humming sound: *the whir of turning wheels.* **2.** A bustle or hurry: *a whir of eager shoppers.* [Middle English *whirren,* of Scandinavian orig.]

whirl (hwûrl, wûrl) *intr.v.* **1.** To spin, revolve, or rotate rapidly; to twirl: *The dancer whirled across the stage.* **2.** To turn rapidly, changing direction; to wheel: *Suddenly he whirled and ran back the way he had come.* **3.** To have the sensation of spinning; reel: *My head began to whirl.* **4.** To move or drive rapidly: *The wind whirled across the plain.* —*tr.v.* **1.** To cause to spin, rotate, or turn rapidly: *whirl a baton; whirled himself round like a top.* **2.** To move or drive in a circular or curving course: *The pilot whirled the plane in a slow spiral.* **3.** To drive at high speed: *The racer whirled his car around the track.* —*n.* **1.** The act of whirling. **2.** A whirling or spinning motion. **3.** Something that whirls, as a cloud of dust. **4.** A rapid, dizzying round of events; a bustle or rush: *the social whirl.* **5.** A confused condition: *in a whirl of excitement.* **6.** *Informal.* A short trip or ride: *took a whirl in the car.* **7.** *Informal.* A brief try: *I've never skied before, but I'll give it a whirl.* [Middle English *whirlen,* from Old Norse *hvirfla.*] —**whirl'er** *n.*

whirl·i·gig (hwûr'lĭ-gĭg', wûr'-) *n.* **1.** A child's toy that whirls, such as a pinwheel. **2.** A merry-go-round. **3.** Something that is always turning or whirling. [Middle English *whirlegigge.*]

whirl·pool (hwûrl'pōōl', wûrl'-) *n.* **1.** A rapidly rotating current of water or other liquid, as one produced by the meeting of two tides; an eddy or vortex. **2.** Anything suggesting the rapid motion of whirling water: *caught in a whirlpool of conflicting emotions.*

whirl·wind (hwûrl'wĭnd', wûrl'-) *n.* **1.** A mass of air that rotates, often violently, about a region of low atmospheric pressure, as a tornado. **2.** Anything that moves forward or whirls with violence and force: *A whirlwind of Christmas shoppers descended on the store.* —*adj.* Very fast-moving or hard-driving: *a whirlwind courtship; a whirlwind campaign.*

whirl·y·bird (hwûr'lē-bûrd', wûr'-) *n. Slang.* A helicopter.

whisk (hwĭsk, wĭsk) *tr.v.* **1.** To move or cause to move with quick light sweeping motions: *whisked crumbs off the table; whisked the children from the room.* **2.** To whip (eggs or cream). —*intr.v.* To move lightly, nimbly, and rapidly: *The kitten whisked out of my arms and ran under the bed.* —*n.* **1.** A quick, light, sweeping motion: *the whisk of a cow's tail.* **2.** A whiskbroom. **3.** A kitchen utensil used to whip eggs, cream, potatoes, etc.: *a wire whisk.* [Middle English *wisken,* of Scandinavian orig.]

whisk·broom (hwĭsk'brōōm', -brŏŏm', wĭsk'-) *n.* Also **whisk broom.** A small short-handled broom used esp. to brush clothes.

whisk·er (hwĭs'kər, wĭs'-) *n.* **1. a. whiskers.** The unshaven hair on a man's face that form the beard and mustache. **b.** A single hair of the beard or mustache. **2.** One of the long bristles or hairs that grow near the mouth of certain animals, as cats, rats, and rabbits. **3.** *Informal.* A very narrow margin: *He lost by a whisker.* [From WHISK.] —**whisk'ered** or **whisk'er·y** *adj.*

whis·key (hwĭs'kē, wĭs'-) *n., pl.* **-keys.** Also **whis·ky** *pl.* **-kies. 1.** An alcoholic beverage distilled from fermented grain, such as corn, rye, or barley. **2.** A drink of whiskey. [Short for earlier *whiskybae,* from Gaelic *uisgebeatha,* "water of life."]

whis·per (hwĭs'pər, wĭs'-) *intr.v.* **1.** To speak softly, without full voice: *She whispered in my ear.* **2.** To speak quietly or privately, as when gossiping, plotting, or spreading slander or secrets: *They whispered and intrigued about the government's overthrow.* **3.** To make a soft, low, rustling or hissing sound, as surf or leaves: *waves whispering on the shore.* —*tr.v.* **1.** To utter very softly: *whispered words of endearment.* **2.** To say or tell privately or secretly, as a rumor, gossip, intrigue, etc. —*n.* **1.** An act of whispering. **2.** A soft, low sound or tone of voice. **3.** A low, rustling or hissing sound: *the faintest whisper of rustling leaves.* **4.** A hint or rumor, as of scandal. [Middle English *whisperen*, from Old English *hwisprian.*] —**whis'per·er** *n.*

whist (hwĭst, wĭst) *n.* A card game played by two teams of two players each. [Var. of earlier *whisk.*]

whis·tle (hwĭs'əl, wĭs'-) *v.* **-tled, -tling.** —*intr.v.* **1.** To produce a clear musical, high-pitched sound or series of sounds by forcing air through the teeth or through an aperture formed by pursing the lips. **2.** To produce a clear, shrill, sharp musical sound or series of sounds by some other method, as by blowing on or through a device: *He whistled on his tin pipe.* **3.** To produce a high-pitched sound when moving swiftly through the air: *wind whistling through the trees.* **4.** To emit a shrill, sharp, high-pitched cry, as some birds and animals. **5.** To summon by whistling: *whistle for a cab.* —*tr.v.* **1.** To produce by whistling: *whistle a tune.* **2.** To summon, signal, or direct by whistling: *whistled the boys to come in from play.* **3.** To cause to move with a whistling noise: *whistled the ball through the air.* —*n.* **1.** A device or instrument for making whistling sounds by means of the breath, air, or steam. **2.** A sound produced by such a device or by whistling through the lips. **3.** Any whistling sound, as of an animal or projectile. **4.** The act of whistling. [Middle English *whistelen*, from Old English *hwistlian.*]

whis·tler (hwĭs'lər, wĭs'-) *n.* **1.** Someone or something that whistles. **2.** A marmot, *Marmota caligata,* of the mountains of northwestern North America, with a grayish coat and a shrill, whistling cry. **3.** Any of various birds that produce a whistling sound.

whistle stop. **1.** A town at which a train stops only if signaled. **2.** A brief appearance of a political candidate in a small town, traditionally on the observation platform of a train.

whis·tle-stop (hwĭs'əl-stŏp', wĭs'-) *intr.v.* **-stopped, -stopping.** To conduct a political campaign by making brief appearances in a series of small towns.

whit (hwĭt, wĭt) *n.* The least or smallest bit: *not a whit afraid.* [Var. of Middle English *wight*, thing, creature, from Old English *wiht.*]

white (hwīt, wīt) *n.* **1.** The lightest or brightest of the series of colors that pass from black as the darkest through a series of lighter and lighter grays; the opposite of black. **2.** The white or nearly white part of something, such as an egg or the eyeball. **3.** Often **whites.** White clothes or a white outfit: *tennis whites.* **4.** Any member of a Caucasoid people; a Caucasian. —*adj.* **whit·er, whit·est.** **1.** Of or nearly the color white. **2.** Light-colored: *the white meat of the chicken.* **3.** Pale or bloodless: *turned as white as if he had seen a ghost.* **4.** Belonging to an ethnic group having a comparatively pale skin, esp. Caucasoid. **5.** Pale gray or silvery, as from age: *white hair.* **6.** Snowy: *a white Christmas.* **7.** Incandescent: *white heat.* **8.** Pure; innocent. —*tr.v.* **whit·ed, whit·ing.** To make white; whiten, whitewash, or bleach. [Middle English, from Old English *hwīt.*] —**white'ness** *n.*

white ant. A termite.

white·bait (hwīt'bāt', wīt'-) *n.* **1.** The young of various fishes, such as the herring, considered a delicacy when fried. **2.** Any of various other small edible fishes.

white birch. Any of several birch trees that have white bark, such as *Betula pendula*, of Europe.

white blood cell. Any of the white or colorless cells that have nuclei and appear in the blood, many of them functioning as a defense against infections; a leukocyte.

white·cap (hwīt'kăp', wīt'-) *n.* A wave with a crest of foam.

white cedar. Any of several North American evergreen trees, chiefly of the genus *Chamaecyparis,* with light-colored wood.

white coal. Water regarded as a source of power; hydroelectric power.

white-col·lar (hwīt'kŏl'ər, wīt'-) *adj.* Of or pertaining to workers whose work does not involve manual labor.

white elephant. **1.** A rare whitish or light-gray form of the Asian elephant, often regarded with special veneration in regions of southeastern Asia. **2.** A rare and expensive possession that is of limited usefulness and is financially a burden to maintain. **3.** An article, ornament, or household utensil no longer wanted by its owner.

white-faced (hwīt'fāst', wīt'-) *adj.* **1.** Pale; pallid. **2.** Having a white patch extending from the muzzle to the forehead, as certain animals: *a white-faced horse.*

white feather. A sign of cowardice. —*idiom.* **show the white feather.** To act like a coward.

white·fish (hwīt'fĭsh', wīt'-) *n., pl.* **whitefish** or **-fishes.** **1.** Any of various chiefly North American freshwater food fishes of the genus *Coregonus,* that have a gen. silvery color. **2.** Any of various similar or related fishes.

white flag. A white cloth or flag signaling surrender or truce.

white gold. An alloy of gold and nickel, and sometimes palladium or zinc, that has a platinumlike color.

white-head·ed (hwīt'hĕd'ĭd, wīt'-) *adj.* **1.** Having white hair or plumage on the head, as a bird or animal. **2.** Having white or pale flaxen hair. **3.** *Irish.* Favorite; darling: *the white-headed boy.*

white heat. **1. a.** The temperature of a white-hot substance. **b.** The physical condition of a white-hot substance. **2.** A state of intense emotion or excitement.

white-hot (hwīt'hŏt', wīt'-) *adj.* So hot as to glow with a bright white light; hotter than red-hot.

White House. **1.** The executive mansion of the President of the United States in Washington, D.C. **2.** The supreme executive authority of the U.S. Government.

white lead. A heavy white poisonous compound of basic lead carbonate, lead silicate, or lead sulfate, used in paint pigments.

white lie. A diplomatic or well-intentioned untruth.

white magic. Magic or incantation that is practiced for good purposes or as a counter to evil.

white meat. Light-colored meat, esp. of poultry.

whit·en (hwīt'n, wīt'n) *tr.v.* To make (something) white or whiter, esp. by bleaching. —*intr.v.* To become white. —**whit'en·er** *n.*

white oak. **1.** A large oak, *Quercus alba,* of eastern North America, that has heavy, hard, light-colored wood. **2.** Any of various other oaks.

white·out (hwīt'out', wīt'-) *n.* A polar weather condition caused by a heavy cloud cover over the snow in which the light coming from above is approximately equal to the light reflected from below, characterized by the absence of shadow, the invisibility of the horizon, and the discernibility of only dark objects.

white pepper. A spicy, hot condiment made from the husked, dried berries of a vine grown in the East Indies.

white pine. **1.** A timber tree, *Pinus strobus,* of eastern North America, that has needles in clusters of five and durable, easily worked wood. **2.** Any of several other pines that have needles in clusters of five. **3.** The wood of any of these trees.

white poplar. A tree, *Populus alba,* native to Eurasia, that has leaves with whitish undersides.

white·print (hwīt'prĭnt', wīt'-) *n.* A photomechanical copy, usu. of line drawings, in which black or colored lines appear on a white background.

white sauce. A sauce made with butter, flour, and milk, cream, or stock and used as a base for other sauces.

white slave. A woman held unwillingly for purposes of prostitution. —**white slavery.**

white-tailed deer (hwīt'tāld', wīt'-). A North American deer, *Odocoileus virginianus,* with a grayish coat that turns reddish brown in summer and a tail that is white on the underside. Also called **white tail** and **Virginia deer.**

white tie. **1.** A white bow tie worn as a part of men's formal evening dress. **2.** Also **white tie and tails.** Men's formal evening dress.

white·wall tire (hwīt'wôl', wīt'-). Also **whitewall.** A tire that has a white band on the outer side.

white·wash (hwīt'wŏsh', -wôsh', wīt'-) *n.* **1.** A mixture of lime and water, often with whiting, size, or glue added, that is used to whiten walls, concrete, fences, etc. **2.** A concealing or glossing over of flaws or failures. **3.** *Informal.* A defeat in a game in which the loser scores no points; a shut-out. —*tr.v.* **1.** To paint or coat with or as if with whitewash. **2.** To gloss over (a flaw, failure, etc.): *The scandal was whitewashed by the administration.* —**white'wash'er** *n.*

white water. Turbulent or frothy water, as in rapids.

white whale. A small whale, *Delphinapterus leucas*, chiefly of northern waters, that is white when full-grown. Also called **beluga.**

whith·er (hwĭth'ər, wĭth'-) *adv.* **1.** To what place, result, or condition: *Whither are we wandering?* **2.** To which specified place or position: *the castle whither we had ridden.* **3.** Wherever: *"Whither thou goest, I will go"* (Ruth 1:16). [Middle English, from Old English *hwider*.]

whit·ing[1] (hwī'tĭng, wī'-) *n.* A pure white grade of chalk that has been ground and washed for use in paints, ink, and putty. [Middle English *whityng*, from *whiten*, to make white, from *whit*, white.]

whit·ing[2] (hwī'tĭng, wī'-) *n.* **1.** A food fish, *Gadus merlangus*, of European Atlantic waters, related to the cod. **2.** Any of several saltwater fishes of the genera *Menticirrhus* and *Merluccius*, of North American coastal waters. [Middle English *whitynge*, from Middle Dutch *wijting.*]

whit·ish (hwī'tĭsh, wī'-) *adj.* Somewhat white.

whit·low (hwĭt'lō, wĭt'-) *n. Pathol.* Any inflammation of the area of a finger or toe around the nail. [Middle English *whitflawe* : white + *flawe*, fissure, flaw.]

Whit·sun (hwĭt'sən, wĭt'-) *adj.* Of or observed on Whitsunday or at Whitsuntide. [Middle English *whitsone*, short for *whitsonday*, Whitsunday.]

Whit·sun·day (hwĭt'sŭn'dē, -sən-dā', wĭt'-) *n.* Pentecost. [Middle English *whitsonday*, from Old English *hwīta sunnandæg*, "white Sunday."]

Whit·sun·tide (hwĭt'sən-tīd', wĭt'-) *n.* The week following Whitsunday or Pentecost, esp. the first three days of this week.

whit·tle (hwĭt'l, wĭt'l) *v.* **-tled, -tling.** —*tr.v.* **1.** To cut small bits or pare shavings from (a piece of wood). **2.** To fashion or shape in this way: *whittled a wooden doll.* **3.** To reduce or eliminate gradually by or as if by whittling: *whittled down his expenditures by $60.* —*intr.v.* To whittle wood with a knife. [From Middle English *whyttel*, knife, var. of *thwitel*, from *thwiten*, to whittle down, from Old English *thwītan.*] —**whit'tler** *n.*

whiz (hwĭz, wĭz) *v.* **whizzed, whiz·zing.** Also **whizz.** —*intr.v.* **1.** To make a whirring, buzzing, or hissing sound, as of something rushing through air. **2.** To rush past: *The train whizzed by without stopping.* —*tr.v.* To cause to whiz: *The pitcher whizzed the ball to first.* —See Syns at **rush.** —*n., pl.* **whiz·zes.** Also **whizz. 1.** The sound or passage of something that whizzes. **2.** *Slang.* Someone who has remarkable skill: *a whiz at math.* [Imit.]

who (hōō) *pron.* The interrogative pronoun in the nominative case. **1.** What or which person or persons: *Who was that on the telephone?* **2.** That. —Used as a relative pronoun to introduce a clause when the antecedent is a human: *The boy who came yesterday is now gone.* [Middle English, from Old English *hwa.*]

Usage: who, whom. 1. In modern English usage, *who* is acceptable as the object of a following verb or preposition: *Who did you refer to? Who did you see in the hall?* **2.** *Whom* is required when the preposition is in the immediately preceding position: *To whom it may concern. To whom are you referring? Whom* may also occur as the form of the direct object after a verb, but it is not required in all instances: *You heard whom? You heard who?* **3.** The use of *whom* for *who* is an error that occurs most often when the pronoun is misconstrued as the object of a verb when in fact it is the subject of its own clause: *Who shall I say is calling? They found out who had been promoted.* These same rules apply to the indefinite pronoun *whoever*: *We should give our support to whoever is elected. We should give our support to whomever the delegates prefer.* See also Usage note at **that.**

whoa (hwō, wō) *interj.* A word used in commanding a horse to stop.

who'd (hōōd). Contraction of who would or who had.

who·dun·it (hōō-dŭn'ĭt) *n. Informal.* A mystery story. [WHO + DONE + IT.]

who·ev·er (hōō-ĕv'ər) *pron.* **1.** No matter who: *Whoever comes to our gate should be welcomed into the house.* **2.** Who: *Whoever could have dreamed of such a thing?* —See Usage note at **who.**

whole (hōl) *adj.* **1.** Containing all component parts; complete: *a whole formal wardrobe.* **2.** Not divided or disjoined; in one unit: *He bought a whole acre of land near the beach.* **3.** Sound; healthy: *a whole organism.* **4.** Constituting the full amount, extent, or duration: *The baby cried the whole trip home.* —*n.* **1.** All of the component parts or elements of a thing. **2.** A complete entity or system. —*idiom.* on the whole. Considering everything; in general. [Middle English *hool*, sound, unharmed, from Old English *hāl.*] —**whole'ness** *n.*

Syns: whole, all, complete, entire, gross, total *adj. Core meaning:* Including every constituent or individual (*the whole town talking about the scandal*).

whole blood. Blood that is drawn directly from a living human being and from which no element has been removed, used in transfusion.

whole·heart·ed (hōl'här'tĭd) *adj.* Without reservation: *wholehearted cooperation.* —**whole'heart'ed·ly** *adv.* —**whole'heart'ed·ness** *n.*

whole hog. *Slang.* The whole way or the fullest extent.

whole milk. Milk from which no element has been removed.

whole note. *Mus.* A note having a time value equal to two half notes or four quarter notes.

whole number. An integer.

whole·sale (hōl'sāl') *n.* The sale of goods in large quantities, as for resale by a retailer. —*adj.* **1.** Of or engaged in the sale of goods at wholesale: *a wholesale dealer; wholesale prices.* **2.** Sold in large bulk or quantity, usu. at a lower cost: *wholesale merchandise.* **3.** Made or accomplished extensively and indiscriminately; blanket: *wholesale destruction.* —*adv.* In large bulk or quantity: *sell wholesale.* —*tr.v.* **-saled, -sal·ing.** To sell at wholesale. —*intr.v.* **1.** To engage in wholesale selling. **2.** To be sold wholesale: *That coat wholesales for $175.* —**whole'sal'er** *n.*

whole·some (hōl'səm) *adj.* **1.** Conducive to mental or physical well-being; healthy: *a wholesome diet.* **2.** Having or indicating a healthy physical or mental condition: *a wholesome, rosy complexion; a wholesome attitude toward work.* —**whole'some·ly** *adv.* —**whole'some·ness** *n.*

whole·wheat (hōl'hwēt', -wēt') *adj.* Made from wheat kernels from which the outer covering and the wheat germ have not been removed: *whole-wheat flour; whole-wheat bread.*

who'll (hōōl). Contraction of: **1.** Who will. **2.** Who shall.

whol·ly (hō'lē, hōl'lē) *adv.* Entirely; completely.

whom (hōōm) *pron.* The objective case of **who.** —See Usage note at **that** and **who.**

whom·ev·er (hōōm-ĕv'ər) *pron.* The objective case of **whoever.** —See Usage note at **who.**

whom·so·ev·er (hōōm'sō-ĕv'ər) *pron.* The objective case of **whosoever.**

whoop (hōōp, hwōōp, wōōp) *n.* **1.** A loud cry of exultation or excitement. **2.** A hooting cry, as of a bird. **3.** The gasp characteristic of whooping cough. —*intr.v.* **1.** To utter a loud shout or cry. **2.** To utter a hooting cry. **3.** To gasp, as in whooping cough. —*tr.v.* **1.** To utter with a whoop. **2.** To chase, call, urge on, or drive with a whoop or whoops: *whooping the home team on to victory.* —*phrasal verb.* whoop it up. *Slang.* **1.** To have a jolly time. **2.** To arouse interest or enthusiasm. [Middle English *whope* (interjection).]

whoop·ee (hwōō'pē, wōō'-, hwōō'pē, wōō'-) *interj. Slang.* A word used to express jubilation. —*n.* A jubilant celebration. —*idiom.* make whoopee. **1.** To celebrate noisily. **2.** To make love. [From WHOOP.]

whoop·ing cough (hōō'pĭng, hōōp'ĭng). A bacterial infection of the lungs and respiratory passages that causes spasms of coughing alternating with gasps.

whooping crane. A large, long-legged North American bird, *Grus americana*, with black and white plumage and a shrill, trumpeting cry. It is now very rare and in danger of becoming extinct.

whoops (hwo̅o̅ps, wo̅o̅ps, hwŏŏps, wŏŏps) *interj.* Used to express surprise, excitement, apology, etc.

whoosh (hwo̅o̅sh, wo̅o̅sh, hwŏŏsh, wŏŏsh) *intr.v.* **1.** To hurtle or gush rapidly: *The race cars whooshed past.* **2.** To make a gushing or rushing sound: *We listened to the water whoosh over the rocks.* —*n.* A whooshing sound. [Imit.]

whop (hwŏp, wŏp) *tr.v.* **whopped, whop·ping.** To thrash; defeat: *The little fellow really whopped that big bully.* —*n.* A heavy thud or blow: *The old lady gave the thief a great whop on the head with her umbrella.* [Middle English *whappen.*]

whop·per (hwŏp'ər, wŏp'-) *n.* **1.** Something exceptionally big or remarkable. **2.** A gross untruth; an outrageous lie.

whop·ping (hwŏp'ĭng, wŏp'-) *adj.* Exceptionally big or remarkable. —*adv.* Thoroughly; resoundingly: *a whopping good joke.*

whore (hôr, hōr) *n.* A prostitute. —*intr.v.* **whored, whor·ing.** To have sexual intercourse as or with a prostitute. [Middle English *hoore,* from Old English *hōre.*]

whorl (hwôrl, wôrl, hwûrl, wûrl) *n.* **1.** A coiled, curved, or rounded form, as one of the turns of a spiral shell or one of the ridges of a fingerprint. **2.** An arrangement of three or more parts, as of leaves or petals, radiating from a single point or part. **3.** Anything shaped like a coil, curl, or convolution: *Her hair curled in wild, unruly whorls.* [Middle English *whorle,* perh. var. of *whirle,* a whirl.]

who's (hoōz). Contraction of: **1.** Who is. **2.** Who has.

whose (hoōz) *pron.* **1.** The possessive form of *who: Did you see the poor kid whose arm was broken?* **2.** The possessive form of *which: an old oak in whose branches I sat.* [Middle English *whos,* from Old English *hwæs.*]

Usage: **whose.** *Whose* occurs on all levels as the possessive form of *who* and *which: He is the only one whose ability has been questioned. It is the only work whose authorship is in doubt.* Thus, *whose* can refer to persons and things. The alternative expression *of which* (in reference to things) is also possible, but it is often awkward.

who·so (hoō'sō) *pron.* Who; whoever; whatever person.

who·so·ev·er (hoō'sō-ĕv'ər) *pron.* Whoever.

why (hwī, wī) *adv.* **1.** For what purpose, reason, or cause: *Why did you have to leave?* **2.** For which; on account of which: *The reason why I'm working is I have to live.* —See Usage note at **reason.** —*n. pl.* **whys.** A cause or reason concerning something: *some questions on the hows and whys of food.* —*interj.* A word used to mark a pause indicating surprise, pleasure, etc.: *Why, I'm delighted to help!* [Middle English, from Old English *hwȳ.*]

whyd·ah (hwĭd'ə, wĭd'ə) *n.* Also **whid·ah.** Any of several African birds of the genus *Vidua,* with predominantly black plumage and long tail feathers. Also called **widow bird.** [Perh. var. of WIDOW (BIRD).]

whydah **wickiup**
George Miksch Sutton

wick (wĭk) *n.* A cord or strand of loosely woven, twisted or braided fibers, as on a candle or oil lamp, that draws up fuel to the flame by capillary action. [Middle English *wike,* from Old English *wēoce.*]

wick·ed (wĭk'ĭd) *adj.* **-er, -est. 1.** Morally bad; vicious; depraved: *wicked habits.* **2.** Playfully mischievous or malicious: *a wicked joke.* **3.** Capable of causing harm or injury; harmful; pernicious: *a wicked cough.* **4.** Very skilled or

masterly; formidable; excellent: *a wicked set of tennis.* —See Syns at **malevolent.** [Middle English, from *wicke, wicked,* from Old English *wicca,* wizard.] —**wick'ed·ly** *adv.* —**wick'ed·ness** *n.*

wick·er (wĭk'ər) *n.* **1.** A slender, flexible shoot or twig, as of a willow tree, used in weaving baskets, making furniture, etc. **2.** Wickerwork. —*modifier: a wicker basket.* [Middle English *wiker,* of Scandinavian orig.]

wick·er·work (wĭk'ər-wûrk') *n.* Articles, furniture, etc. made of wicker.

wick·et (wĭk'ĭt) *n.* **1.** *Cricket.* Either of the two sets of three stakes, topped by a crossbar, that forms the target of the bowler. **2.** *Croquet.* Any of the wire arches through which a player tries to hit his ball. **3.** A small door or gate, esp. one built into or near a larger one. **4.** A small window or opening, often fitted with glass or a grating, as a ticket window at a theater, train station, etc. [Middle English, from Old North French *wiket.*]

wick·i·up (wĭk'ē-ŭp') *n.* Also **wik·i·up.** A frame hut covered with matting, bark, brush, etc., used by the nomadic Indians of North America. [Of Algonquian orig.]

wide (wīd) *adj.* **wid·er, wid·est. 1.** Extending over a large area from side to side; broad: *a wide street.* **2.** Having a specified extent from side to side; in width: *a ribbon two inches wide.* **3.** Having wide range or scope: *a wide selection of dresses.* **4.** Full or ample, as clothing: *The legs on the jeans are too wide.* **5.** Fully open or extended: *look with wide eyes.* **6.** Far, apart, or away from the desired goal, point, or issue: *wide of the mark; wide of the truth.* —See Syns at **broad.** —*adv.* **1.** Over a large area; extensively: *traveling far and wide.* **2.** To the full extent; completely: *The door was open wide.* **3.** So as to miss the target; astray: *shoot wide.* [Middle English, from Old English *wīd.*] —**wide'ly** *adv.* —**wide'ness** *n.*

wide-an·gle lens (wīd'ăng'gəl). A lens that has a relatively short focal length and permits an angle of view approx. 70° or more.

wide-a·wake (wīd'ə-wāk') *adj.* **1.** Completely awake. **2.** Alert; watchful. —See Syns at **alert.**

wide-eyed (wīd'īd') *adj.* **1.** With the eyes completely opened, as in wonder: *a look of wide-eyed surprise.* **2.** Believing or accepting with childlike simplicity; ingenuous; credulous; naive: *charmed by her wide-eyed innocence.*

wid·en (wīd'n) *tr.v.* To make wider. —*intr.v.* To be or become wide or wider. —**wid'en·er** *n.*

wide-o·pen (wīd'ō'pən) *adj.* **1.** Opened completely: *a wide-open door.* **2.** Without laws or law enforcement: *a wide-open town.*

wide·spread (wīd'sprĕd') *adj.* **1.** Spread out wide; fully opened: *with widespread arms in a gesture of welcome.* **2.** Spread, scattered, or occurring over a considerable extent or area; common: *widespread disagreement on the question of school integration.* —See Syns at **common** and **general.**

wid·geon (wĭj'ən) *n., pl.* **widgeon** or **-geons.** Also *Brit.* **wig·eon.** Either of two ducks, *Mareca americana,* of North America, or *M. penelope,* of Europe, with brownish plumage. [Orig. unknown.]

wid·ow (wĭd'ō) *n.* A woman whose husband has died and who has not remarried. —*tr.v.* To make a widow of: *She was widowed by the mine explosion.* [Middle English *widewe,* from Old English *widuwe.*]

widow bird. Another name for the **whydah.**

wid·ow·er (wĭd'ō-ər) *n.* A man whose wife has died and who has not remarried. [Middle English *widewer,* from *widewe,* widow.]

widow's mite. A small contribution made by one who has little. [By allusion to Mark 12:42.]

widow's peak. A hairline having a V-shaped point at the middle of the forehead. [WIDOW + *peak,* a widow's hood.]

widow's walk. A railed, rooftop gallery or platform on a dwelling, designed to observe vessels at sea.

width (wĭdth, wĭth) *n.* **1.** The condition, quality, or fact of being wide. **2.** The measurement of the extent of something from side to side: *a room ten feet in width.* **3.** Something that has a specified width, esp. in sewing, a piece of fabric measured from selvage to selvage: *a skirt having three widths.* [From WIDE.]

wield (wēld) *tr.v.* **1.** To handle (a weapon, tool, etc.): *a*

ă pat   ā pay   â care   ä father   ĕ pet   ē be   hw which
oō took   oō boot   ou out   th thin   th this   ŭ cut
ĭ pit   ī tie   î pier   ŏ pot   ō toe   ô paw, for   oi noise
û urge   zh vision   ə about, item, edible, gallop, circus

woodsman *wielding an ax.* **2.** To exercise or exert (power or influence). —See Syns at **handle.** [Middle English *welden,* from Old English *wealdan* and *wieldan*.] **—wield'er** *n.*

wield·y (wēl'dē) *adj.* **-i·er, -i·est.** Easily handled or managed: *a wieldy hammer; wieldy diplomacy.*

wie·ner (wē'nər) *n.* A wienerwurst.

wie·ner·wurst (wē'nər-wûrst', -wŏorst') *n.* A type of smoked pork or beef sausage, similar to a frankfurter. Also called **wiener.** [German *Wienerwurst,* "Vienna sausage."]

wife (wīf) *n., pl.* **wives** (wīvz). **1.** A woman to whom a man is married. **2.** *Archaic.* A woman. Now used chiefly in combination: *housewife; midwife; fishwife.* [Middle English, from Old English *wīf,* woman.] **—wife'hood'** *n.* **—wife'ly** *adj.*

wig (wĭg) *n.* A covering of artificial or human hair worn on the head for adornment, to conceal baldness, or as a part of a costume. [Short for PERIWIG.]

wi·geon (wĭj'ən) *n. Brit.* Var. of **widgeon.**

wig·gle (wĭg'əl) *v.* **-gled, -gling.** —*intr.v.* To move with short irregular motions from side to side: *The dog's ears wiggled.* —*tr.v.* To cause to move in such a fashion: *She wiggled her toes.* —*n.* The act of wiggling; a wiggling movement: *She walks with a wiggle.* **—idiom. get a wiggle on.** *Slang.* To hurry or hurry up. [Middle English *wiglen,* perh. from Middle Dutch or Middle Low, German *wiggelen.*] **—wig'gly** *adj.*

wig·gler (wĭg'lər) *n.* **1.** Someone or something that wiggles. **2.** The larva or pupa of a mosquito.

wig·wag (wĭg'wăg') *v.* **-wagged, -wag·ging.** —*tr.v.* **1.** To move back and forth, esp. as a means of signaling: *wigwag a flag.* **2.** To signal by such motions. —*intr.v.* **1.** To move back and forth; to wag. **2.** To wave the hand or a device in signaling: *wigwagged a call for help.* —*n.* **1.** The act of giving signals by wigwagging. **2.** A message sent in this way. [Dial. *wig,* wiggle + WAG.] **—wig'wag'ger** *n.*

wig·wam (wĭg'wŏm') *n.* A North American Indian dwelling, commonly having an arched or conical framework covered with bark or hides. [Abnaki *wĭkəwam.*]

wigwam

wik·i·up (wĭk'ē-ŭp') *n.* Var. of **wickiup.**

wild (wīld) *adj.* **-er, -est. 1.** Growing, living or found in a natural state; not grown, kept, or cared for by human beings: *wild plants; wild honey.* **2.** Untamed: *a wild pony.* **3.** Lacking discipline or control; unruly: *a wild, fearless tomboy.* **4.** Full of or suggestive of strong, uncontrolled feeling: *wild with joy; wild laughter.* **5.** Stormy: *wild seas.* **6.** Uncivilized; savage: *wild tribes from the mountains.* **7.** Not lived in, cultivated, or used by people: *wild, unsettled country.* **8.** Very strange or unlikely; outlandish: *a wild idea.* **9.** Far from the intended mark, target, etc.: *a wild pitch; a wild bullet.* **10.** In card games, representing any card desired rather than the actual one held or played: *playing poker with deuces wild.* —*adv.* In an unruly or uncontrolled manner: *The weeds in our yard have run wild.* —*n.* Often **wilds.** A region not lived in or cultivated by human beings: *the wilds of northern Canada.* [Middle English *wilde,* from Old English.] **—wild'ly** *adv.* **—wild'ness** *n.*

wild boar. A boar.

wild carrot. A plant, **Queen Anne's lace.**

wild·cat (wīld'kăt') *n.* **1.** Any of various wild felines of small to medium size; esp., one of the genus *Lynx.* **2.** A quick-tempered or fierce person, esp. a woman. **3.** An oil well drilled in an area not known to yield oil. —*adj.* **1.** Risky or unsound, esp. financially. **2.** Accomplished or

operating without official sanction or authority: *a wildcat strike.* —*v.* **-cat·ted, -cat·ting.** —*tr.v.* To prospect for (oil, minerals, etc.) in an area not known to be productive. —*intr.v.* To prospect in an untapped or questionable area.

wild·cat·ter (wīld'kăt'ər) *n.* **1.** A person engaged in mining or oil-drilling in untapped or doubtful areas. **2.** A promoter of speculative or fraudulent enterprises.

wil·de·beest (wĭl'də-bēst', vĭl'-) *n.* An antelope, the gnu. [Obs. Afrikaans : Dutch *wild,* wild + *beest,* beast.]

wil·der·ness (wĭl'dər-nĭs) *n.* **1.** An unsettled, uncultivated, or desolate region left in its natural condition. **2.** Something likened to a wild region in bewildering vastness or profusion: *a wilderness of tall buildings and winding streets; a wilderness of voices.* [Middle English *wildernesse,* from Old English *wildēornes,* from *wildēor,* wild beast.]

wild-eyed (wīld'īd') *adj.* Glaring in or as if in anger, terror, or madness.

wild·fire (wīld'fīr') *n.* A raging fire that travels and spreads rapidly. **—idiom. like wildfire.** Over or through an area, distance, group, etc., in a short time; very rapidly: *He drove like wildfire. The news spread like wildfire.*

wild-goose chase (wīld'gōōs'). A hopeless pursuit of an unattainable or imaginary object.

wild·ing (wīl'dĭng) *n.* **1.** A plant that grows wild or has escaped from cultivation, esp. a wild apple tree or its fruit. **2.** A wild animal. [From WILD.]

wild·life (wīld'līf') *n.* Wild plants and animals, esp. wild animals living in their natural surroundings. **—modifier:** *a wildlife sanctuary.*

wild oat. Often **wild oats.** A grass, *Avena fatua,* native to Eurasia, related to the cultivated oat. **—idiom. sow (one's) wild oats.** To indulge in the indiscretions of youth.

wild pitch. *Baseball.* An erratic pitch that the catcher cannot be expected to catch and that enables a runner to advance.

wild rice. 1. A tall water grass, *Zizania aquatica,* of northern North America, that bears edible brownish seeds. **2.** The seeds of this plant.

Wild West. The western United States during the period of its settlement, esp. with reference to its lawlessness.

wild·wood (wīld'wŏod') *n.* A forest or wooded area in its natural state.

wile (wīl) *n.* **1.** A deceitful stratagem or trick. **2.** A disarming or seductive manner, device, or procedure. —*tr.v.* **wiled, wil·ing.** To influence or lead by seduction or trickery; entice; lure: *wiled him to betray his friends.* **—phrasal verb. wile away.** To pass or spend (time) agreeably: *wiled away the afternoon.* [Middle English *wil.*]

wil·ful (wĭl'fəl) *adj.* Var. of **willful.**

will¹ (wĭl) *n.* **1.** The mental faculty by which one deliberately chooses or decides upon a course of action; volition: *the freedom of the will.* **2.** An example of the exercising of this faculty; a deliberate decision; a choice. **3.** Control exercised over oneself, one's impulses, etc.: *a strong will.* **4.** Something desired or decided upon: *God's will be done.* **5.** Deliberate intention or wish: *going against his will.* **6.** Strong purpose; determination: *the will to win.* **7.** Bearing or attitude toward others; disposition: *a man of good will.* **8.** A legal declaration of how a person wishes his possessions to be disposed of after his death. **—idiom. at will.** At one's discretion or pleasure; freely: *wandered about at will.* —*tr.v.* **1.** To bring about, attempt to effect, or decide upon by use of one's mental powers; choose: *You cannot achieve your goal just by willing success.* **2.** To decree; dictate; order: *The powers that be will common men to live, die, and pay taxes.* **3.** To influence, control, or compel by exercising force of will: *He willed himself to stay awake.* **4.** To grant in a legal will; bequeath. —*intr.v.* **1.** To exercise the will; use the power of the will. **2.** To decree or make a firm choice. —See Syns at **choose.** [Middle English, from Old English *willa.*]

will² (wĭl) *v. past* **would** (wŏod) **1.** Used as an auxiliary followed by a simple infinitive to indicate: **a.** Future action, condition, or state: *They will come later.* **b.** Likelihood or certainty: *You will live to regret what you did today.* **c.** Willingness: *Will you help me with this?* **d.** Intention: *I will too if I feel like it.* **e.** Requirement or command: *You will report to the principal's office.* **f.** Customary or habit-

ual action: *She would spend hours in the kitchen.*
g. *Informal.* Probability or expectation: *Three rings! That will be little Jamie at the door.* **2.** To wish: *Do what you will.* —*intr.v.* To have a desire: *Sit here, if you will.* —*tr.v.* To desire; wish: *Do what you will.* —See Usage note at **shall.** [Middle English *willen,* from Old English *wyllan.*]

willed (wĭld) *adj.* Having a will of a specified kind: *weak-willed.*

will·ful (wĭl'fəl) *adj.* Also **wil·ful.** **1.** Said or done in accordance with one's will; deliberate: *a willful waste of money; his willful disobedience.* **2.** Inclined to impose one's will; obstinate: *a willful child.* —See Syns at **obstinate** and **voluntary.** —**will'ful·ly** *adv.* —**will'ful·ness** *n.*

wil·lies (wĭl'ēz) *pl.n. Slang.* Feelings of uneasiness: *This place gives me the willies.* [Orig. unknown.]

will·ing (wĭl'ĭng) *adj.* **1.** Done, given, etc., readily, without hesitation: *giving willing assistance.* **2.** Disposed to accept or tolerate: *willing to pay the price they're asking.* **3.** Acting or ready to act gladly: *a willing worker.* —**will'ing·ly** *adv.* —**will'ing·ness** *n.*

wil·li·waw (wĭl'ē-wô') *n.* **1.** A violent gust of cold wind blowing seaward from a mountainous coast. **2.** Any sudden gust of wind; a squall. [Orig. unknown.]

will-o'-the-wisp (wĭl'ə-thə-wĭsp') *n.* **1.** A phosphorescent light, **ignis fatuus.** **2.** A misleading goal. [Orig. unknown.]

wil·low (wĭl'ō) *n.* **1.** Any of various deciduous trees or shrubs of the genus *Salix,* having usually narrow leaves, flowers borne in catkins, and strong, lightweight wood. **2.** The wood of a willow tree. [Middle English *wilowe,* from Old English *welig.*]

wil·low·y (wĭl'ō-ē) *adj.* **-i·er, -i·est.** **1.** Of or abounding in willows: *a willowy grove.* **2.** Suggestive of the slender, flexible branches of a willow: *a tall, willowy girl.*

will power. The ability to carry out one's decisions, wishes, or plans; strength of mind.

wil·ly-nil·ly (wĭl'ē-nĭl'ē) *adv.* Whether desired or not; willingly or not: *He must do what we ask, willy-nilly.* —*adj.* Undecided: *She's such a willy-nilly person.* [From *will I nill I,* "whether I am willing or unwilling."]

wilt¹ (wĭlt) *intr.v.* **1.** To lose freshness; wither; droop: *The roses wilted overnight. My organdy dress wilted from the humidity.* **2.** To lose vigor or force; weaken: *His courage began to wilt.* —*tr.v.* **1.** To cause to droop or lose freshness: *The drought wilted all the plants and flowers.* **2.** To deprive of energy or courage; enervate: *Fear wilted his courage.* —*n.* **1.** The act of wilting or the condition of being wilted. **2.** Any of various plant diseases characterized by slow or rapid collapse of terminal shoots, branches, or entire plants. [Var. of dial. *wilk,* from Middle English *welken.*]

wilt² (wĭlt) *v. Archaic.* Second person singular present tense of **will.**

wi·ly (wī'lē) *adj.* **-li·er, -li·est.** Full of wiles; guileful; calculating: *a wily old fox.* —**wi'li·ly** *adv.* —**wi'li·ness** *n.*

wim·ple (wĭm'pəl) *n.* A cloth wound around the head, framing the face, and drawn into folds beneath the chin, worn by women in medieval times and as part of the habit of certain orders of nuns. —*v.* **-pled, -pling.** —*tr.v.* **1.** To cover or furnish with a wimple. **2.** To cause to form folds, pleats, or ripples. —*intr.v.* To form or lie in folds; ripple. [Middle English *wimpel,* from Old English *wimpel.*]

win (wĭn) *v.* **won** (wŭn), **win·ning.** —*intr.v.* **1.** To achieve victory over others in a competition, battle, contest, etc.: *Do you know which team won?* **2.** To achieve success in an effort or venture by means of hard work, perseverance, or force of character. **3.** To struggle through to a desired place or condition. —*tr.v.* **1.** To achieve victory in (a game, battle, competition, etc.): *Our troops won the battle.* **2.** To receive as a prize or reward for performance: *win a scholarship.* **3.** To achieve by effort; earn: *win fame.* **4.** To reach with difficulty: *The ship won a safe port.* **5. a.** To succeed in gaining the favor or support of; prevail upon: *His eloquence won his audience.* **b.** To appeal successfully to (someone's loyalty, sympathy, or other emotion): *He won the respect of his schoolmates.* **c.** To persuade (someone) to marry one. —*phrasal verbs.* **win out.** To succeed or prevail. **win over.** To persuade: *His efforts won them over to our views.* —*n.* A victory, as in sports. —See Syns at

victory. [Middle English *winnen,* to win, strive, from Old English *winnan,* to strive.]

wince (wĭns) *intr.v.* **winced, winc·ing.** To shrink or start involuntarily, as in pain or distress; to flinch. —*n.* A wincing movement or gesture. [Middle English *wincen,* to kick, wince.]

winch (wĭnch) *n.* A stationary motor-driven or hand-powered machine for pulling or hoisting heavy objects, consisting of a drum around which a rope or cable that is attached to the load is wound. [Middle English *winche,* a pulley, from Old English *wince.*]

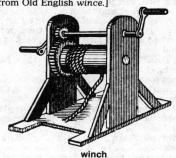

winch

wind¹ (wĭnd) *n.* **1.** A current of air, esp. a natural one that moves along or parallel to the ground. **2.** A current or stream of air produced artificially, as by a blower or fan. **3.** A blast of air that disrupts or destroys; a gale. **4.** A strong or prevailing influence or trend: *The wind of public opinion has shifted.* **5.** A current of air carrying an odor, scent, or sound. **6. winds. a.** The wind instruments of an orchestra or band. **b.** Players of wind instruments. **7.** Gas produced in the body during digestion; flatulence. **8.** The ability to breathe in a normal or adequate way; respiration: *Running took away his wind.* **9.** Meaningless or boastful talk. —*tr.v.* **1.** To cause to be out of or short of breath: *The long race winded the runners.* **2.** To catch a scent or trace of: *The dogs winded a rabbit and gave chase.* **3.** To allow to rest in order to recover breath: *We stopped to wind our horses after such a long gallop.* —*idioms.* **get (or have) wind of.** To receive hints or intimations of. **have the wind of.** To hold an advantage over (an opponent). **in the wind.** Likely to occur; in the offing. **on (or into or down) the wind.** In the same direction as the wind. **sail close to the wind.** **1.** To sail or travel as directly against the wind as possible. **2.** To approach near to a limit; verge on danger or disaster. **up the wind.** In a direction opposite or nearly opposite to the wind. [Middle English, from Old English.]

wind² (wīnd) *v.* **wound** (wound), **wind·ing.** —*tr.v.* **1. a.** To wrap or coil (something) around or over an object or center once or repeatedly: *The caterpillar winds the long silk thread around itself.* **b.** To wrap or encircle (an object) in a series of coils; entwine: *She wound her waist with brightly colored ribbons.* **2.** To proceed on (one's way) with a curving or twisting course: *We wound our way through the forest.* **3.** To present or introduce in a devious or indirect manner; insinuate: *He wound a plea for money into his letter.* **4.** To turn in a series of circular motions, as a crank or handle. **5.** To coil the spring of (a clock or other mechanism) by turning a stem, cord, etc.: *wind the toy to make it work.* **6.** To lift or haul by means of a windlass, winch, etc.: *Wind the pail to the top of the well.* —*intr.v.* **1.** To move in or take a bending or curving course: *The river winds through the valley.* **2. a.** To move in or have a spiral or circular course: *a column of smoke winding into the sky; a windmill winding slowly in the wind.* **b.** To be coiled or spiraled about something: *Vines wound up and along the limbs of the ancient oak.* **3.** To proceed indirectly or circuitously, as in discourse or conduct. **4.** To become wound: *This old clock winds with difficulty.* —*phrasal verb.* **wind up.** **1.** *Informal.* To come or bring to an end; finish: *The book winds up with a happy ending.* **2.** *Baseball.* To swing back the arm and raise the foot in preparation for pitching the ball. —See Syns at **end.** —*n.* A single turn, twist, or curve. [Middle English *winden,* from Old English *windan.*] —**wind'er** *n.*

ă pat   ā pay   â care   ä father   ĕ pet   ē be   hw which   ĭ pit   ī tie   î pier   ŏ pot   ō toe   ô paw, for   oi noise
ŏŏ took   ōō boot   ou out   th thin   th this   ŭ cut   û urge   zh vision   ə about, item, edible, gallop, circus

Syns: wind, coil, curl, entwine, snake, spiral, twine, twist, weave *v. Core meaning:* To move on a repeatedly curving course (*a staircase winding up the tower; a river that wound through the valleys*).

wind³ (wĭnd, wīnd) *tr.v.* **wind·ed** (wīn'dĭd, wĭn'-) or **wound** (wound), **wind·ing. 1.** To blow (a wind instrument). **2.** To sound by blowing. [From WIND (air).]

wind·age (wĭn'dĭj) *n.* **1. a.** The effect of wind on the course of a projectile. **b.** The degree to which the sight on a gun must be adjusted to compensate for the effect of the wind. **2.** The difference, in a given firearm, between the diameter of the projectile fired and the diameter of the bore of the firearm. **3.** The disturbance of air caused by the passage of a fast-moving object, as a railway train, missile, etc. **4.** The part of a ship's surface that is exposed to the action of the wind.

wind·bag (wĭnd'băg') *n. Slang.* A talkative person who says nothing of importance or interest.

wind-blown (wĭnd'blōn') *adj.* **1.** Blown or dispersed by the wind: *a yard full of wind-blown leaves.* **2.** Growing or shaped in a manner governed by the prevailing winds. **3.** Having the appearance of having been tossed or tousled by the wind; loose and natural: *a wind-blown hair style; a fresh, wind-blown look.*

wind-borne (wĭnd'bôrn', -bōrn') *adj.* Carried by the wind.

wind·break (wĭnd'brāk') *n.* A hedge, row of trees, or fence serving to lessen or break the force of the wind.

Wind·break·er (wĭnd'brā'kər) *n.* A trademark for a warm jacket with close-fitting bands at the waist and cuffs.

wind-bro·ken (wĭnd'brō'kən) *adj.* Suffering from the heaves or other breathing impairment, as a horse.

wind-chill factor (wĭnd'chĭl'). *Meteorol.* The temperature of windless air that would have the same effect on the exposed human skin as a given combination of wind speed and air temperature.

wind cone (wĭnd). A windsock.

wind·ed (wĭn'dĭd) *adj.* Out of breath.

wind·fall (wĭnd'fôl') *n.* **1.** Something that has been blown down by the wind, as a ripened fruit. **2.** A sudden and unexpected piece of good fortune.

wind·flow·er (wĭnd'flou'ər) *n.* An anemone.

wind·ing (wīn'dĭng) *adj.* Turning or twisting: *a winding stream.* —*n.* **1.** The act of someone or something that winds. **2.** A curve or bend, as of a stream or road. **3.** Wire wound into a coil. —**wind'ing·ly** *adv.*

wind instrument (wĭnd). Any musical instrument sounded by a current of air, esp. the player's breath, as a clarinet, trumpet, or flute.

wind·jam·mer (wĭnd'jăm'ər) *n.* **1.** *Informal.* A large sailing ship. **2.** A crew member of such a ship. —*modifier:* a *windjammer cruise.* [From WIND + JAM (verb).]

wind·lass (wĭnd'ləs) *n.* Any of various hauling or lifting machines similar to a winch, used esp. on ships. [Middle English *wyndlas,* var. of *windas,* from Norman French, from Old Norse *vindāss* : *vinda,* to wind + *āss,* pole.]

windlass

wind·mill (wĭnd'mĭl') *n.* A mill or other machine that is powered by a wheel of adjustable blades or vanes that are rotated by the wind.

win·dow (wĭn'dō) *n.* **1.** An opening constructed in a wall in order to admit light or air to an enclosure, usu. framed and spanned with glass. **2. a.** A framework enclosing a pane of glass; a sash. **b.** A pane of glass, clear plastic, etc.; windowpane. **3.** Any opening that resembles a window in function or appearance: *envelopes with return address windows.* —*tr.v.* To provide with or as if with a window.

[Middle English *windowe,* from Old Norse *vindauga* : *vindr,* wind + *auga,* eye.]

window box. A long, narrow box for growing plants, placed on a windowsill or ledge.

win·dow-dress·ing (wĭn'dō-drĕs'ĭng) *n.* Also **window dressing. 1. a.** The decorative showing of retail merchandise in store windows. **b.** Goods and trimmings used in such displays. **2.** Anything, as a statement, display, etc., used to improve appearances or create an impression of things being better than they are. —**win'dow-dress'er** *n.*

win·dow·pane (wĭn'dō-pān') *n.* A plate of glass, transparent plastic, etc., in a window.

window shade. An opaque fabric mounted on a roller and used as a cover or blind for a window.

win·dow-shop (wĭn'dō-shŏp') *intr.v.* **-shopped, -shop·ping.** To look at merchandise in store windows or showcases without making purchases. —**win'dow-shop'per** *n.*

win·dow·sill (wĭn'dō-sĭl') *n.* The horizontal ledge at the base of a window opening.

wind·pipe (wĭnd'pīp') *n. Anat.* The trachea.

wind·row (wĭnd'rō') *n.* **1.** A long row of cut hay or grain left to dry in a field before being bundled. **2.** A row, as of leaves or snow, heaped up by the wind. —*tr.v.* To shape or arrange into a windrow.

wind·shield (wĭnd'shēld') *n.* **1.** A framed sheet of glass or other transparent material located at the front of an automobile or other vehicle in order to protect the occupants from the wind. **2.** Any shield placed to protect an object from the wind.

wind·sock (wĭnd'sŏk') *n.* A large, roughly conical device open at both ends and attached to a stand by a pivot so that it points in the direction of the wind that blows through it. Also called **drogue, wind cone,** and **wind sleeve.**

Windsor chair. A wooden chair widely used in 18th-cent. England and America, typically with a high spoked back and outward-slanting legs connected by a crossbar.

wind·storm (wĭnd'stôrm') *n.* A storm with high winds or violent gusts but little or no rain.

wind-swept (wĭnd'swĕpt') *adj.* Exposed to or moved by the force of wind.

wind tee (wĭnd). A large weather vane with a horizontal T-shaped wind indicator, commonly found at airfields.

wind tunnel (wĭnd). A chamber through which air is forced at controlled speeds so its effect on an aircraft, airfoil, scale model, etc., can be studied.

wind-up (wĭnd'ŭp') *n.* **1. a.** The act of bringing something to a conclusion. **b.** The concluding part of an action, presentation, speech, etc. **2.** *Baseball.* The coordinated movements of a pitcher's arm, body, and legs preparatory to pitching the ball.

wind·ward (wĭnd'wərd) *adj.* Facing or moving into or against the wind: *a windward tide; the windward side of the ship.* —*adv.:* sailed *windward of shore.* —*n.* The direction or quarter from which the wind blows.

wind·y (wĭn'dē) *adj.* **-i·er, -i·est. 1.** Characterized by or having much wind: *March is a windy month.* **2.** Open or exposed to the prevailing wind; unsheltered: *The windy side of the apartment.* **3. a.** Given to prolonged or empty talk: *a windy speaker.* **b.** Wordy, boastful, or bombastic: *a windy speech.* —**wind'i·ly** *adv.* —**wind'i·ness** *n.*

wine (wīn) *n.* **1.** The fermented juice of grapes. **2.** The fermented juice of various other fruits or plants: *dandelion wine.* **3.** Something that intoxicates or exhilarates: *tasted the wine of fame.* **4.** A dark purplish red. —*modifier: a wine bottle; a wine merchant.* —*adj.* Dark purplish red. —*v.* **wined, win·ing.** —*tr.v.* To provide or entertain with wines: *The guests were wined and dined.* —*intr.v.* To drink wine: *We wined and dined like kings.* [Middle English, from Old English *wīn,* ult. from Latin *vīnum.*]

wine·glass (wīn'glăs') *n.* A glass, usu. with a stem, from which wine is drunk.

wine-grow·er (wīn'grō'ər) *n.* A person who owns a vineyard and produces wine. —**wine'grow'ing** *adj. & n.*

wine·press (wīn'prĕs') *n.* A vat in which the juice is pressed from grapes.

win·er·y (wī'nə-rē) *n., pl.* **-ies.** An establishment where wine is made.

wine·skin (wīn'skĭn') *n.* A bag for holding and dispensing wine, made from goatskin or other animal skin.

wing (wĭng) n. **1.** One of a pair of specialized parts used for flying, as in birds, bats, and insects. **2.** The enlarged pectoral fin of a flying fish. **3.** Bot. **a.** One of the thin or membranous projections on certain seeds, as of the maple or ash or along a twig or stem. **b.** One of the lateral petals of the flower of a pea or related plant. **4.** Informal. An arm of a human being. **5.** A surface of an aircraft whose principal purpose is to act on the air passing around it so as to provide a force that holds the craft aloft, esp. one of a pair of such surfaces extending from the sides of an airplane. **6.** Anything that resembles a wing in appearance, function, or position relative to a main body; an extending part: One of the wings of the sofa is worn. **7.** A part of a building extending from or attached to the main structure: the West Wing of the White House; the children's wing of the hospital. **8.** A section or faction: the Democratic Party's southern wing. **9. a.** Often **wings.** One of the areas that extend on either side of the stage and are concealed from the audience: The next performer was waiting in the wings. **b.** A flat of scenery projecting onto the stage from the side. **10.** A unit of military aircraft or aviators. **11.** Either the left or right flank of an army or navy unit. **12.** Hockey & Soccer. Either of the forward positions played near the sideline. —intr.v. To fly or soar with or as if with wings: birds winging southward. —tr.v. **1.** To furnish with wings. **2.** To perform or accomplish by flight: We winged our way back to the airbase. **3.** To carry or transport by or as if by flying; speed along: winging the mail overseas. **4.** To wound superficially, as in the wing or arm: The policeman only winged the escaping robber. —idioms. **on the wing.** In the act of flying; in flight. **take wing.** To fly or soar away. **under (one's) wing.** In one's care. **wing it.** To perform without study or preparation; improvise; ad-lib. [From Middle English wenge(n), from Old Norse vængr, bird's wing.] —wing'less adj.

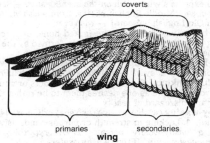

coverts

primaries   secondaries
wing

wing chair. An armchair with a high back from which project large, enclosing sidepieces or wings.

wing·ding (wĭng'dĭng') n. Slang. A lavish or lively party or celebration. [Orig. unknown.]

winged adj. **1.** (wĭngd). Having wings or winglike parts: winged insects; the winged seeds of the maple. **2.** (wĭng'-ĭd). Seeming to move on or as if on wings: the winged words of the poet; his winged rise to power.

wing-foot·ed (wĭng'fŏot'ĭd) adj. Fleet of foot; swift.

wing·let (wĭng'lĭt) n. A small or rudimentary wing.

wing·span (wĭng'spăn') n. Wingspread.

wing·spread (wĭng'sprĕd') n. The distance between the tips of the extended wings, as of a bird, insect, or airplane.

wing tip. **1.** A shoe part, often with a perforated pattern, that covers the toe of the shoe and extends backward along the sides from a point at the center. **2.** A style of shoe having such a toe.

wink (wĭngk) intr.v. **1.** To close and open the eyelid of one eye deliberately, as to convey a message, signal, or suggestion. **2.** To shine fitfully; twinkle: A lighthouse winked in the far distance. —tr.v. **1.** To close and open (an eye or the eyes) rapidly. **2.** To signal or express by winking: He winked his delight at her success. —n. **1. a.** The act of winking. **b.** The time required for a wink; a very short time: I'll be there in a wink. **2.** A gleam; a twinkle. **3.** Informal. A brief moment of sleep: catch a few winks before going out. —idiom. **wink at.** To pretend not to see; ignore intentionally: winked at corruption in the government.

[Middle English winken, from Old English wincian, to close one's eyes.]

win·kle (wĭng'kəl) n. A mollusk, the periwinkle.

win·ner (wĭn'ər) n. Someone or something that wins, esp. a successful person or a victor in sports.

win·ning (wĭn'ĭng) adj. **1.** Successful; victorious: the winning team. **2.** Charming: a winning personality. —n. **1.** The act of someone or something that wins; victory. **2. winnings.** Something that has been won, esp. money. —win'ning·ly adv.

win·now (wĭn'ō) tr.v. **1.** To separate the chaff from (grain) by means of a current of air. **2.** To blow (chaff) off or away. **3.** To examine (something) closely in order to sort; analyze; sift: winnowing through pages of testimony for the answer to his question. **4.** To separate (a desirable or undesirable part); eliminate: winnow out the underqualified applicants. —intr.v. To separate grain from chaff. [Middle English windowen, from Old English windwian, from wind, wind.] —win'now·er n.

win·some (wĭn'səm) adj. Pleasant; charming; engaging: a winsome personality; a winsome girl. [Middle English winsum, from Old English wynsum.] —win'some·ly adv. —win'some·ness n.

win·ter (wĭn'tər) n. **1.** The season of the year between autumn and spring, lasting in the Northern Hemisphere from the Dec. solstice to the next equinox and in the Southern Hemisphere from the June solstice to the next equinox. —modifier: winter sports. —adj. **1.** Planted in the autumn and harvested in the spring or summer: winter wheat; winter crops. **2.** Capable of being stored for use during the winter, as a fruit or vegetable: winter squash. —intr.v. To pass or spend the winter: My aunt winters in Florida. —tr.v. To keep, feed, or care for during the winter: We wintered our cattle on the south range. [Middle English, from Old English.] —win'ter·er n. —win'ter·ish adj. —win'ter·less adj.

win·ter·green (wĭn'tər-grēn') n. **1. a.** A low-growing plant, Gaultheria procumbens, of eastern North America, with white or pinkish flowers, aromatic evergreen leaves, and spicy, edible red berries. Also called **checkerberry. b.** An oil or flavoring obtained from this plant. **2.** Any of several similar or related plants, as the pipsissewa.

win·ter·ize (wĭn'tə-rīz') tr.v. **-ized, -iz·ing.** To prepare or equip for winter weather, as an automobile, house, etc.

winter solstice. The solstice that occurs on or about Dec. 22nd and marks the beginning of the winter season in the Northern Hemisphere.

win·ter·time (wĭn'tər-tīm') n. The winter season. —modifier: wintertime sports.

winter wheat. Wheat planted in the autumn and harvested the following spring or early summer.

win·try (wĭn'trē) adj. **-tri·er, -tri·est.** Also **win·ter·y** (wĭn'tə-rē) **-i·er, -i·est. 1.** Of or like winter; cold: wintry weather. **2.** Suggestive of winter; cheerless; unfriendly: a wintry tone of voice. —win'tri·ly adv. —win'tri·ness n.

win·y (wĭ'nē) adj. **-i·er, -i·est.** Having the qualities of wine, as in color, taste, smell, or effect.

wipe (wīp) tr.v. **wiped, wip·ing. 1.** To rub, as with cloth or paper, in order to clean or dry: I wiped the dishes with paper towels. **2.** To remove by or as if by rubbing; brush: wiped the lint off the coat. **3.** To rub, move, or pass over something for or as if for cleaning, polishing, etc.: wiping a soft cloth over the silver box. —phrasal verb. **wipe out. 1.** To destroy completely; annihilate: a hurricane that wiped out an entire island. **2.** Informal. To murder. **3.** Surfing. To lose balance and fall or jump off a surfboard. —n. **1.** The act of wiping: I gave the table a wipe with a clean cloth. [Middle English wipen, from Old English wīpian.]

wip·er (wī'pər) n. Someone or something that wipes, esp. a device designed for clearing the windshield of a motor vehicle.

wire (wīr) n. **1.** A usu. flexible metallic strand or rod made in many lengths and diameters, often covered with an electrical insulator, used chiefly for structural support or to conduct electricity. **2.** A group of such strands bundled or twisted together as a functional unit; a cable. **3.** Something that resembles a wire, as in slenderness or stiffness. **4. a.** A telegraph service. **b.** A telegram. **5.** An open telephone connection. **6.** The finish line of a racetrack. **—modifier:** *a wire basket; a wire brush.* **—v. wired, wir·ing.** **—tr.v. 1.** To join, connect, or attach with a wire or wires: *wired the fenceposts to the supporting rails.* **2.** To equip with a system of electrical wires: *wire a house; wire a lamp.* **3.** To send a (message, information, etc.) by telegraph: *wire congratulations.* **4.** To send a telegram to: *wire him to meet us at the airport.* **—intr.v.** To send a telegram; telegraph: *I wired early yesterday.* **—idiom. get (in) under the wire.** To arrive somewhere or finish something just in the nick of time. [Middle English, from Old English *wīr.*]

wire-draw (wīr′drô′) *tr.v.* **-drew** (-drōō′), **-drawn** (-drôn′), **-draw·ing. 1.** To draw (metal) into wire: *wiredraw copper sheet.* **2.** To treat at great length or with excessive detail; prolong; draw out.

wire gauge. A tool for measuring the diameter of wire or the thickness of sheet metal, usu. in the form of a disk with slots of various sizes along its edge.

wire-haired (wīr′hârd′) *adj.* Having a coat of stiff, wiry hair: *a wire-haired fox terrier.*

wire·less (wīr′lĭs) *n. Brit.* Radio or radio communications. **—modifier:** *a wireless set; a wireless system.* **—adj.** Having no wire or wires. **—tr.v.** To communicate with by telegraph or telephone. **—intr.v.** To communicate by telegraph or telephone.

wireless telegraphy. Telegraphy by radio rather than by long-distance transmission lines. Also called **wireless telegraph.**

wireless telephone. The **radiotelephone.**

wire·pull·er (wīr′pŏŏl′ər) *n.* Someone who uses private influence or personal contacts in order to further his own or another's interests; manipulator.

wire·tap (wīr′tăp′) *n.* **1.** A concealed listening or recording device connected to a communications circuit that allows messages to be secretly intercepted or overheard: *placed a wiretap on his phone.* **2.** The installation of such a device: *a court order for a wiretap.* **—modifier:** *wiretap evidence.* **—v. -tapped, -tap·ping. —tr.v. 1.** To connect a wiretap to. **2.** To monitor (a telephone line) by means of a wiretap. **—intr.v.** To install or monitor by a wiretap. **—wire′tap′per** *n.*

wire·work (wīr′wûrk′) *n.* **1.** Wire fabric, such as mesh, netting, etc. **2.** Articles made of wire or wire fabric.

wire·worm (wīr′wûrm′) *n.* **1.** The wirelike larva of various click beetles that cause severe damage by boring into the roots of many kinds of plants. **2.** Any of various millipedes.

wir·ing (wīr′ĭng) *n.* **1.** The act or process of attaching, connecting, or installing electric wires. **2.** A system of electric wires.

wir·y (wīr′ē) *adj.* **-i·er, -i·est. 1.** Of or like wire: *a wiry pad of steel wool; wiry hair.* **2.** Sinewy and lean; slender but strong: *a wiry physique.* **—wir′i·ly** *adv.* **—wir′i·ness** *n.*

wis·dom (wĭz′dəm) *n.* **1.** Understanding of what is true, right, or lasting. **2.** Common sense; good judgment. **3.** Scholarly learning; knowledge. **—See Syns at knowledge.** [Middle English *wisedom*, from Old English *wīsdōm.*]

wisdom tooth. One of four molars, the last on each side of both jaws, in human beings, usu. erupting much later than the others.

wise¹ (wīz) *adj.* **wis·er, wis·est. 1.** Having wisdom; judicious: *a wise statesman.* **2.** Showing common sense; prudent: *a wise decision.* **3.** Having great learning; highly educated; learned: *a teacher wise in the subject of European political history.* **4.** Shrewd; crafty; cunning: *a wise move.* **5.** Having knowledge or information; informed; aware of: *a secretary wise in her employer's ways.* **6.** Bold and disrespectful; fresh: *a wise kid.* **—idioms. put (someone) wise.** *Slang.* To inform a person, esp. of something known to others: *Let me put you wise to some of the school rules.* **wise up.** *Slang.* To become or make aware or sophisticated: *Wise up to the fact that success takes hard work. Three years in the big city wises up a country boy.* [Middle English, from Old English *wīs.*] **—wise′ly** *adv.*
Syns: **wise, discerning, knowing, sagacious, sage, sapient** *adj.* **Core meaning:** Having or showing sound judgment and sharp perception (*a wise elder statesman*). See also Syns at **aware** and **impudent.**

wise² (wīz) *n.* Method or manner of doing; way: *in no wise.* [Middle English, from Old English *wīse*, manner, condition.]

-wise. 1. A suffix meaning manner, direction, or position: **clockwise. 2.** *Informal.* With reference to: **taxwise.** [Middle English *-wise*, in a certain manner, from Old English *-wīsan*, from *wīse*, manner.]
Usage: **-wise.** In certain combinations such as *taxwise* and *timewise*, *-wise* means with reference to. While such combinations are appropriate to business writing where conciseness is an asset, they are often considered objectionable in general contexts, particularly if they are overused and seem indiscriminately for such use gives the effect of commercial jargon.

wise·a·cre (wīz′ā′kər) *n. Informal.* An arrogantly fresh or disrespectful person; a wise guy. [Middle Dutch *wijsseg-gher*, soothsayer.]

wise·crack (wīz′krăk′) *Slang. n.* A clever or witty remark, often disrespectful, arrogant, or insulting. **—intr.v.** To make wisecracks. **—wise′crack′er** *n.*

wise guy. *Slang.* An offensively self-assured, arrogant, and often insolent person.

wi·sent (vē′zĕnt′) *n.* The European bison, *Bison bonasus.* [German *Wisent*, from Old High German *wisunt.*]

wish (wĭsh) *n.* **1.** A desire or longing for some specific thing. **2.** An expression of such desire or longing: *She made a wish and blew out the candles.* **3.** Something desired or longed for: *He got his wish.* **—tr.v. 1.** To desire or long for; want: *I wish a long, restful vacation.* **2.** To desire (a person or thing) to be in a specified state or condition: *I wish you were here.* **3.** To entertain or express wishes for; to bid: *He wished her good night.* **4.** To call or invoke upon: *I wish him luck.* **5.** To request, order, or command: *I wish you to go. The President wishes your presence.* **6.** To impose or force; foist: *They wished a hard job on him.* **—intr.v. 1.** To have or feel a desire: *He wishes for a rest.* **2.** To express a wish: *wish on the evening star.* **—See Syns at choose.** [Middle English *wisshe*, from *wisshen*, to wish, from Old English *wȳscan.*] **—wish′er** *n.*

wish·bone (wĭsh′bōn′) *n.* The forked bone, or furcula, in front of the breastbone of most birds, formed by the fusion of the clavicles. [From its use as a wish token.]

wish·ful (wĭsh′fəl) *adj.* Having or expressing a wish or longing: *wishful eyes.* **—wish′ful·ly** *adv.* **—wish′ful·ness** *n.*

wishful thinking. The interpretation of facts or situations confronted in life as one desires them to be rather than as they are; disregard of reality.

wish·y-wash·y (wĭsh′ē-wŏsh′ē, -wô′shē) *adj.* **-i·er, -i·est.** *Informal.* **1.** Lacking in strength or purpose; indecisive; feeble: *a wishy-washy person.* **2.** Watery; thin; weak: *wishy-washy soup.* [From *washy*, watery.]

wisp (wĭsp) *n.* **1.** A small bunch or bundle, as of hair, straw, etc. **2.** Someone or something thin, frail, or slight: *a small wisp of a child.* **3.** A faint streak, as of smoke or clouds. **4.** A fleeting trace or indication; a hint or suggestion: *a wisp of a smile.* [Middle English.] **—wisp′y** *adj.*

wist (wĭst) *v. Archaic.* Past tense and past participle of **wit².** [Middle English *wist, wist*, from Old English *wiste, witen.*]

wis·ter·i·a (wĭ-stîr′ē-ə) *n.* Also **wis·tar·i·a** (wĭ-stâr′ē-ə). Any of several climbing woody vines of the genus *Wisteria*, that have compound leaves and drooping clusters of

wisteria

showy purplish or white flowers. [After Caspar *Wistar* (1761–1818), American anatomist.]

wist·ful (wĭst'fəl) *adj.* Full of a melancholy yearning; longing; wishful: *wistful eyes; a wistful smile.* [From obs. *wistly,* intently.] —**wist'ful·ly** *adv.* —**wist'ful·ness** *n.*

wit¹ (wĭt) *n.* **1. a.** The ability to see and describe humorously those elements of a situation that are amusing or odd. **b.** A person having this ability. **2.** Often **wits. a.** Understanding; intelligence: *using one's wits.* **b.** Sound mental faculties; sanity: *scared out of one's wits.* —**idioms. at (one's) wits' ends.** At the limit of one's mental resources; utterly at a loss. **have (or keep) (one's) wits about (one).** To remain alert or calm, esp. in a crisis. [Middle English, from Old English.]

wit² (wĭt) *v.* **wist** (wĭst), **wit·ting.** *Archaic.* To know. —**idiom. to wit.** That is to say; namely. [Middle English *witen,* from Old English *witan.*]

witch (wĭch) *n.* **1.** A woman who practices black magic; sorceress. **2.** An ugly, nasty old woman; a hag. **3.** *Informal.* A bewitching young woman or girl. —*tr.v.* **1.** To work or cast a spell upon; bewitch. **2.** To cause, bring, or effect by or as if by witchcraft. [Middle English *wicche,* from Old English *wicce.*]

witch·craft (wĭch'krăft') *n.* **1.** Black magic; sorcery. **2.** A magical or irresistible influence, attraction, or charm. — See Syns at **magic.**

witch doctor. A medicine man or shaman among primitive peoples or tribes.

witch·er·y (wĭch'ə-rē) *n., pl.* **-ies. 1.** Sorcery; witchcraft. **2.** Power to charm or fascinate. —See Syns at **magic.**

witch hazel. 1. Any of several shrubs of the genus *Hamamelis,* esp. *H. virginiana,* of eastern North America, that has yellow flowers that bloom in late autumn or winter. **2.** An alcoholic solution that contains an extract of the bark and leaves of this shrub, and is applied externally as a mild astringent. [From Middle English *wyche,* elm + HAZEL.]

witch hunt. An intensive, often politically motivated campaign to search out disloyalty, dishonesty, subversion, etc., usu. founded on slight or unreliable evidence. —**witch'-hunt'er** *n.* —**witch'-hunt'ing** *n.*

witch·ing (wĭch'ĭng) *adj.* **1.** Relating to or appropriate for witchcraft: *the witching hour.* **2.** Having power to charm or enchant; bewitching. —*n.* Witchcraft.

with (wĭth, wĭth) *prep.* **1.** Accompanying: *Come with me.* **2.** Next to: *Walk with him and follow me.* **3.** Having as a possession, attribute, or characteristic: *a clown with a red nose.* **4.** In a manner characterized by: *We were greeted with great friendliness.* **5.** In the charge or keeping of: *You can leave your things with me.* **6.** In the opinion of: *if it's all right with you.* **7.** In support or on the side of: *I'm with you all the way on this.* **8.** Of the same opinion or belief as: *Are you with me in wanting to go swimming?* **9.** In the same group or mixture as: *Plant mint with the other herbs.* **10.** In the membership or employment of: *How long have you been with the Yankees?* **11.** By means of: *our vain efforts to kindle a fire with flint and steel.* **12.** In spite of: *With all that talent, he's getting nowhere.* **13.** In the same direction as: *bending with the wind.* **14.** At the same time as: *rising with the sun.* **15.** In regard to: *I'm pleased with her.* **16.** In comparison or contrast to: *a dress identical with the one I saw you wearing.* **17.** Upon receiving: *With your permission, I think I'll leave.* **18.** And; plus: *Jim, with several of his friends, is arriving tomorrow.* **19.** In opposition to; against: *looking for a fight with somebody all the time.* **20.** As a result of: *trembling with fear.* **21.** To; onto: *Couple the first car with the second.* **22.** So as to be separated from: *parting with a friend.* **23.** In the course of: *With each passing moment he got more scared.* **24.** In proportion to: *improving with age.* **25.** In relationship to: *at ease with his peers.* **26.** As well as: *She can sing with the best of them.* [Middle English *with,* with, against, by means of, from Old English *with,* against or in opposition to, together with.]

with·al (wĭth-ôl', wĭth-) *adv.* **1.** Besides; in addition: *gentle and dangerous withal.* **2.** Despite that; nevertheless. —*prep. Archaic.* With. [Middle English *with alle.*]

with·draw (wĭth-drô', wĭth-) *v.* **-drew** (-drōō'), **-drawn** (-drôn'), **-draw·ing.** —*tr.v.* **1.** To take back or away; re-

move: *withdraw funds from a bank.* **2.** To recall or retract: *withdraw troops from the area; withdrew his objections.* —*intr.v.* **1.** To move or draw back; to retreat; retire: *gave the order for our troops to withdraw.* **2.** To remove oneself from activity, participation, or social or emotional involvement: *withdraw from a political campaign; withdrew into himself.* [Middle English *withdrawen* : *with,* away from + *drawen,* to pull.]

with·draw·al (wĭth-drô'əl, wĭth-) *n.* **1.** The act or process of withdrawing; a retreat or retirement: *a troop withdrawal; a withdrawal from active participation in politics.* **2.** A removal of something that has been deposited: *a withdrawal from a bank account.* **2. a.** The process by which a person, addicted to a habit-forming drug, is deprived of its use, either suddenly or gradually. **b.** The physiological and psychological reactions that take place upon such discontinuation.

with·drawn (wĭth-drôn', wĭth-) *v.* Past participle of **withdraw.** —*adj.* **1.** Not readily accessible; remote; isolated: *a quiet, withdrawn village.* **2.** Socially retiring; shy: *a cold, withdrawn person.* **3.** Emotionally unresponsive: *mental illness in which the patient is depressed and withdrawn.*

with·drew (wĭth-drōō', wĭth-) *v.* Past tense of **withdraw.**

withe (wĭth, wĭth, wĭth) *n.* A tough, supple twig, esp. a willow twig, used for binding things together; withy. [Middle English, from Old English *withthe.*]

with·er (wĭth'ər) *intr.v.* **1.** To dry up or shrivel from lack of moisture: *Flowers and plants withered during the drought.* **2.** To lose freshness, strength, or vitality; become wasted; fade: *old people withering in strange new surroundings.* —*tr.v.* **1.** To cause to dry up from lack of moisture; shrivel: *The hot weather withered the grass.* **2.** To deprive of freshness, strength, or vitality; weaken: *Illness withered his body.* **3.** To cause to feel belittled; cut down; abash: *withered her with a glance.* [Middle English *widderen.*]

with·ers (wĭth'ərz) *pl.n.* The high part of the back of a horse or similar animal, between the shoulder blades. [Ult. from Old English *wither,* against.]

with·hold (wĭth-hōld', wĭth-) *v.* **-held** (-hĕld'), **-hold·ing.** —*tr.v.* **1.** To keep in check; restrain: *withhold the applause until the end of the act.* **2.** To refrain from giving, granting, or permitting: *withhold authorization.* —*intr.v.* To refrain; forbear: *I shall withhold from further comment.* —**with·hold'ing** *adj.: withholding tax.* [Middle English *withholden* : *with,* back, away from + *holden,* to hold.] —**with·hold'er** *n.*

with·in (wĭth-ĭn', wĭth-) *prep.* **1.** Inside of: *within the body.* Also used adverbially: *people outwardly noisy but calm within.* **2.** Inside the limits or extent of in time, degree or distance: *within ten miles of home.* **3.** Not exceeding or transgressing: *within the laws of the land.* —*adv.* Indoors: *We stayed within.*

with·it (wĭth'ĭt) *adj. Slang.* Up-to-date; hip.

with·out (wĭth-out', wĭth-) *adv.* On the outside or outdoors: *The structure is sturdy within and without.* Also used prepositionally: *standing without the door.* —*prep.* **1.** Not having; lacking: *without carfare to get home.* **2. a.** With no or none of: *build up industry without foreign aid.* **b.** Not accompanied by: *no smoke without fire.* [Middle English *withouten,* from Old English *withūtan* : *with,* not together with, separated + *ūtan,* outside of.]

with·stand (wĭth-stănd', wĭth-) *v.* **-stood** (-stōōd'), **-stand·ing.** —*tr.v.* To oppose (something) with force; resist or endure successfully: *a building that can withstand earthquakes.* —*intr.v.* To resist successfully. —See Syns at **resist.** [Middle English *withstanden,* from Old English *withstandan* : *with,* against + *standan,* to stand.]

with·y (wĭth'ē, wĭth'ē) *n., pl.* **-ies. 1.** A long, flexible twig, as that of an osier; withe. **2.** A binding or band made of withes. —*adj.* **-i·er, -i·est.** Flexible and tough; wiry: *a lean, withy body.* [Middle English *wythy,* flexible twig, willow wand, from Old English *wīthig.*]

wit·less (wĭt'lĭs) *adj.* Lacking intelligence or wit; stupid or dull. —**wit'less·ly** *adv.* —**wit'less·ness** *n.*

wit·ness (wĭt'nĭs) *n.* **1.** Someone who has seen or heard something: *a witness to an accident.* **2.** Anything that serves as evidence; a sign. **3. a.** Someone who is called to testify before a court of law. **b.** Someone who is called upon to be present at a transaction or event in order to attest to what took place: *witnesses at a wedding.* **4.** An attestation to a fact, statement, or event: *bore witness to the legitimacy of their claim.* —*tr.v.* **1.** To be present at or have personal knowledge of: *witness a volcanic eruption; witness a conversation.* **2.** To serve as or furnish evidence of: *His tears witnessed the depth of his sorrow.* **3.** To be the setting or site of: *This auditorium witnesses many ceremonies.* **4.** To attest to the legality or authenticity of by signing one's name: *witness a will.* **5.** To testify to: *He witnessed his guilt before the whole congregation.* —*intr.v.* To furnish evidence; bear witness; testify: *He has sworn to witness truthfully.* [Middle English *witnesse,* from Old English *witnes,* witness, knowledge, from *wit,* knowledge, wit.] —**wit′ness·er** *n.*

witness stand. Also *Brit.* **witness box.** The place in a courtroom from which a witness gives testimony.

wit·ti·cism (wĭt′ĭ-sĭz′əm) *n.* A cleverly worded, amusing remark. —See Syns at **joke.** [From WITTY + (CRIT)ICISM.]

wit·ty (wĭt′ē) *adj.* **-ti·er, -ti·est.** Having or showing wit; clever and amusing: *a witty person; a witty remark.* —**wit′ti·ly** *adv.* —**wit′ti·ness** *n.*

wive (wīv) *v.* **wived, wiv·ing.** *Archaic.* —*tr.v.* **1.** To marry (a woman); take as a wife. **2.** To provide a wife for. —*intr.v.* To marry a woman. [Middle English *wiven,* from Old English *wīfian,* from *wīf,* woman, wife.]

wi·vern or **wy·vern** (wī′vərn) *n.* Also **wi·ver** (wī′vər). *Heraldry.* A two-legged dragon with wings and a barbed and knotted tail. [Middle English *wiver,* viper, from Old French *wivre,* from Latin *vīpera,* viper.]

wives (wīvz) *n.* Plural of **wife.**

wiz (wĭz) *n. Informal.* A person considered exceptionally gifted or skilled. [Short for WIZARD.]

wiz·ard (wĭz′ərd) *n.* **1.** A sorcerer or magician. **2.** *Informal.* A person of amazing skill or talent: *a wizard at mathematics.* [Middle English *wysard,* from *wys,* wise.]

wiz·ard·ry (wĭz′ər-drē) *n.* The practice of magic or sorcery. —See Syns at **magic.**

wiz·en[1] (wĭz′ən) *intr.v.* To wither or dry up; shrivel. —*tr.v.* To cause to wither or dry up. —*adj.* Shriveled or dried up; withered: *wrinkled and wizen skin.* [Middle English *wisenen,* from Old English *wisnian.*]

wi·zen[2] (wē′zən) *n.* Another name for **weasand.**

wiz·ened (wĭz′ənd) *adj.* Shriveled; wizen.

woad (wōd) *n.* **1.** An Old World plant, *Isatis tinctoria,* formerly cultivated for its leaves that yield a blue dye. **2.** The dye obtained from this plant. [Middle English *wode,* from Old English *wād.*]

wob·ble (wŏb′əl). —*v.* **-bled, -bling.** Also **wab·ble.** —*intr.v.* **1.** To move erratically from side to side: *The old table wobbles.* **2.** To tremble or quaver, as a voice or sound; shake: *The child's voice wobbled during his recitation.* **3.** To waver or vacillate in one's opinions, feelings, etc.: *This politician wobbles about on every issue until he sees which way his brethren are going to vote.* —*tr.v.* To cause to move unsteadily: *He wobbled the table when he sat down.* —*n.* **1.** An erratic unsteady motion. **2.** A tremulous and uncertain tone or sound: *a vocal wobble.* [Perh. from Low German *wabbeln.*] —**wob′bler** *n.*

wob·bly (wŏb′lē) *adj.* **-bli·er, -bli·est.** Tending to wobble; unsteady; shaky. —**wob′bli·ness** *n.*

Wo·den (wōd′n) *n.* Also **Wo·dan.** The chief Germanic god, identified with the Norse god Odin.

woe (wō) *n.* **1.** Deep sorrow; grief. **2.** Misfortune; calamity: *financial woes.* **3.** Suffering. —See Syns at **distress** and **sorrow.** —*interj.* A word used to express sorrow or dismay. [Middle English *woe,* from Old English *wā* (interjection).]

woe·be·gone (wō′bĭ-gôn′, -gŏn′) *adj.* Mournful or sorrowful in appearance; wretched; dismal: *a woebegone little figure; a woebegone expression.* [Middle English *wo begon* : *wo,* woe + *begon,* beset.]

woe·ful (wō′fəl) *adj.* Also **wo·ful.** **1.** Afflicted with woe; mournful. **2.** Pitiful or deplorable. —**woe′ful·ly** *adv.*

wok (wŏk) *n.* In Chinese cooking, a large, deep metal pan with a convex bottom and flared sides that is used as a general-purpose utensil. [Cantonese.]

woke (wōk) *v.* A past tense of **wake.** [Middle English *wok,* from Old English *wōc.*]

wo·ken (wō′kən) *v.* A past participle of **wake.** [From WOKE (on the model of such verbs as *broke, broken*).]

wold (wōld) *n.* An unforested rolling plain; a moor. [Middle English, a forest, hill, plain, from Old English *weald.*]

wolf (wŏolf) *n., pl.* **wolves** (wŏolvz). **1. a.** Either of two carnivorous mammals, *Canis lupus,* of northern regions, or *C. rufus* (or *C. niger*), of southwestern North America, related to and resembling the dogs. **b.** The fur of such an animal. **2.** A fierce, cruel, predatory person. **3.** *Slang.* A man who pursues women and considers himself a great success as a lover. —*modifier: wolf skins.* —*tr.v.* To eat quickly and greedily: *wolfed down the hamburger.* —*idiom.* **cry wolf.** To raise an alarm about a danger that does not really exist. [Middle English, from Old English *wulf.*] —**wolf′ish** *adj.* —**wolf′ish·ly** *adv.*

wolf   wolverine

wolf·hound (wŏolf′hound′) *n.* Any of various large dogs trained to hunt wolves or other large game, as the borzoi and Irish wolfhound.

wolfs·bane (wŏolfs′bān′) *n.* A plant, the monkshood.

wol·ver·ine (wŏol′və-rēn′) *n.* A carnivorous mammal, *Gulo gulo* (or *G. luscus*), of northern regions, that has dark fur and a bushy tail. Also called **glutton.** [From WOLF.]

wolves (wŏolvz) *n.* Plural of **wolf.**

wom·an (wŏom′ən) *n., pl.* **wom·en** (wĭm′ĭn). **1.** An adult female human being. **2.** Women in general; womankind: *Woman is wise.* **3.** Often **the woman.** Feminine quality or aspect; womanliness: *brought out the woman in her.* **4.** A mistress; paramour. **5.** *Informal.* A wife. —*modifier: a woman athlete; women's suffrage.* [Middle English *wumman,* from Old English *wīfmann* : *wīf,* woman + *man(n),* person.]

wom·an·hood (wŏom′ən-hŏod′) *n.* **1.** The condition of being a woman. **2.** The qualities, feelings, etc., considered typical of women. **3.** Womankind.

wom·an·ish (wŏom′ə-nĭsh) *adj.* **1.** Characteristic of a woman; womanlike. **2.** Considered appropriate in women but undesirable in men; effeminate: *a man who has an affected and womanish manner of speech.* —See Syns at **female.** —**wom′an·ish·ly** *adv.* —**wom′an·ish·ness** *n.*

wom·an·ize (wŏom′ə-nīz′) *v.* **-ized, -iz·ing.** —*tr.v.* To feminize or make effeminate: *an overbearing woman who tried to womanize her son.* —*intr.v.* To pursue women habitually or excessively. —**wom′an·iz′er** *n.*

wom·an·kind (wŏom′ən-kīnd′) *n.* Female human beings in general; women.

wom·an·ly (wŏom′ən-lē) *adj.* **-li·er, -li·est.** Having or showing qualities or characteristics considered typical of, suitable for, or admirable in women: *womanly grace; womanly sympathy.* —See Syns at **female.** —**wom′an·li·ness** *n.*

womb (wŏom) *n.* **1.** *Anat.* The organ of female mammals in which the young develop from a fertilized egg before birth; the uterus. **2.** A place where something has its earliest stages of development. [Middle English, from Old English *wamb,* belly, stomach.]

wom·bat (wŏm′băt′) *n.* Either of two Australian marsupials, *Phascolomis ursinus* or *Lasiorhinus latifrons,* that somewhat resemble small bears. [Native Australian name.]

wom·en (wĭm′ĭn) *n.* Plural of **woman.**

wom·en·folk (wĭm′ĭn-fōk′) *pl.n.* Women in general, esp. the women of a family, community, or group.

won (wŭn) *v.* Past tense and past participle of **win**. [Middle English *wunnen, wunnen,* from Old English *wunnon* (pl.), *(ge)wunnen.*]

won·der (wŭn'dər) *n.* **1.** Someone or something that arouses awe, surprise, or admiration; a marvel. **2.** The feeling or emotion aroused by such awe or admiration. **3.** A feeling of confusion or doubt. —*intr.v.* **1.** To have a feeling of awe or admiration; to marvel: *They wondered at the majestic sight of the canyon.* **2.** To be filled with curiosity or doubt: *She wondered about the future.* **3.** To have doubts or curiosity about: *I wonder what she is doing.* —*idiom.* **no wonder.** Not surprisingly: *No wonder they were impressed when they saw the statue.* [Middle English, from Old English *wundor.*] —**won'der·er** *n.*

won·der·ful (wŭn'dər-fəl) *adj.* **1.** Capable of exciting wonder; astonishing; marvelous: *An eagle in flight is truly wonderful.* **2.** Admirable; excellent; extraordinary: *a wonderful idea; a wonderful performance.* —See Syns at **fabulous.** —**won'der·ful·ly** *adv.* —**won'der·ful·ness** *n.*

won·der·land (wŭn'dər-lănd') *n.* **1.** A marvelous imaginary realm. **2.** A real place or scene that arouses wonder.

won·der·ment (wŭn'dər-mənt) *n.* **1.** A condition or feeling of wonder; astonishment, awe; surprise. **2.** Something or someone that produces wonder; a marvel. **3.** Puzzlement or curiosity.

won·drous (wŭn'drəs) *adj.* Wonderful. —See Syns at **fabulous.** —*adv.* Archaic. To a wonderful or remarkable extent. —**won'drous·ly** *adv.*

wont (wônt, wŏnt, wŭnt) *adj.* Accustomed, apt, or used to: *He was wont to lend money for charitable use.* —*n.* Habit; custom: *He joked playfully as was his wont.* [Middle English, from the past part. of *wonen,* to be accustomed, dwell.]

won't (wŏnt). Contraction of will not.

wont·ed (wôn'tĭd, wŏn'-, wŭn'-) *adj.* Accustomed; usual: *He took his wonted position.*

woo (wōō) *tr.v.* **1.** To seek the affection of, esp. with hopes of marrying. **2.** To solicit or seek the favor of; try to persuade: *Advertisers often woo teen-agers.* **3.** To seek to get or achieve: *woo money from the public.* —*intr.v.* To court a woman. [Middle English *wowen,* from Old English *wōgian.*] —**woo'er** *n.*

wood (wōōd) *n.* **1. a.** The tough, fibrous substance beneath the bark of trees and shrubs and forming the stems of certain other plants. It consists largely of cellulose and lignin. **b.** This substance, often cut and dried, used for building material, as fuel, and for many other purposes. **2.** Often **woods.** A dense growth of trees; a forest. **3.** Something made from wood, as a golf club with a wooden head. —*modifier: wood carvings; a wood bowl.* —*tr.v.* **1.** To cover with trees; to forest. **2.** To fuel with wood. —*intr.v.* To gather or be supplied with wood. —*idiom.* **out of the woods.** Informal. Free of difficulties. [Middle English *wode,* from Old English *wudu.*]

wood alcohol. Methyl alcohol.

wood·bin (wōōd'bĭn') *n.* A box for holding firewood.

wood·bine (wōōd'bīn') *n.* Any of various climbing vines, esp.: **a.** An Old World honeysuckle, *Lonicera periclymenum,* with yellowish flowers. **b.** The **Virginia creeper.** [Middle English *wodebinde,* Old English *wudubinde : wudu,* wood + *bindan,* to bind.]

wood·block (wōōd'blŏk') *n.* A woodcut.

wood·carv·ing (wōōd'kär'vĭng) *n.* **1.** The art of carving in wood. **2.** An object carved from wood. —**wood'carv'er** *n.*

wood·chuck (wōōd'chŭk') *n.* A common rodent, *Marmota monax,* of northern and eastern North America, with a short-legged, heavy-set body and grizzled brownish fur. Also called **ground hog.** [By folk ety. from Cree *ocĕk.*]

wood·cock (wōōd'kŏk') *n.,* pl. **woodcock** or **-cocks.** Either of two related game birds, *Scolopax rusticola,* of the Old World, or *Philohela minor,* of North America, with brownish plumage, short legs, and a long bill.

wood·craft (wōōd'krăft') *n.* **1.** The art or skill of working with wood. **2.** Skill and experience in things pertaining to the woods, as hunting, fishing, or camping.

wood·cut (wōōd'kŭt') *n.* **1.** A piece of wood on which a design for printing has been cut plankwise along the length of the grain with a knife. **2.** A print made from such a piece of wood. Also called **woodblock.**

wood·cut·ter (wōōd'kŭt'ər) *n.* A person who cuts wood or trees. —**wood'cut'ting** *n.*

wood·ed (wōōd'ĭd) *adj.* Having trees or woods.

wood·en (wōōd'n) *adj.* **1.** Made of wood: *a wooden bridge.* **2.** Stiff and unnatural; without spirit: *a wooden smile; an actor who gave a wooden performance.* **3.** Clumsy and awkward; ungainly: *She danced with the wooden motions of a mechanical doll.* —**wood'en·ly** *adv.* —**wood'en·ness** *n.*

wood engraving. **1.** The art or process of cutting a design for printing into the end-grain of a wood block using a burin. **2.** A piece of wood upon which such a design has been cut. **3.** A print made from such a piece of wood.

wooden Indian. A wooden statue of an American Indian brave standing and holding a cluster of cigars, used formerly as an advertisement outside a tobacconist's shop.

wood·land (wōōd'lənd, -lănd') *n.* Land covered with trees and woody shrubs. —*modifier: woodland flowers.*

wood louse. A terrestrial crustacean, the **sow bug.**

wood·man (wōōd'mən) *n.* A woodsman.

wood·peck·er (wōōd'pĕk'ər) *n.* Any of various birds of the family Picidae, that have strong claws and a stiff tail adapted for clinging to and climbing trees, and a chisellike bill for drilling through bark and wood.

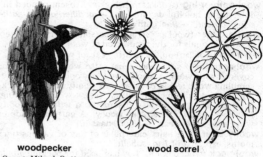

woodpecker   **wood sorrel**
George Miksch Sutton

wood·pile (wōōd'pīl') *n.* A pile of wood, esp. when stacked for use as fuel.

wood pulp. Any of various cellulose pulps ground from wood, treated chemically, and used to make paper, cellophane, rayon, etc.

wood·ruff (wōōd'rəf, -rŭf') *n.* Any of several plants of the genus *Asperula,* esp. *A. odorata,* native to Eurasia, that has small white flowers and narrow, fragrant leaves that are used as flavoring and in sachets. [Middle English *woderofe,* Old English *wudurofe.*]

wood·shed (wōōd'shĕd') *n.* A shed in which firewood is stored.

woods·man (wōōdz'mən) *n.* Also **wood·man** (wōōd'mən). A person who works or lives in the woods or is skilled in woodcraft.

wood sorrel. Any of various plants of the genus *Oxalis,* with compound leaves with three leaflets and yellow, white, or pinkish flowers.

woods·y (wōōd'zē) *adj.* **-i·er, -i·est.** Of, relating to, or suggestive of the woods: *a woodsy scent; a woodsy landscape.*

wood tar. A black, syruplike fluid that is a by-product of the destructive distillation of wood and is used in pitch, medicines, etc.

wood·turn·ing (wōōd'tûr'nĭng) *n.* The art or process of shaping wood into various forms on a lathe. —**wood'turn'er** *n.*

wood·wind (wōōd'wĭnd') *n.* **1.** Any of a group of musical instruments whose tone is started by the vibration of a reed, as a clarinet, oboe, or bassoon, or by the action of a whistlelike device, as a flute. **2. woodwinds.** The section of an orchestra or band composed of such instruments.

wood·work (wōōd'wûrk') *n.* Objects made of or work done in wood, esp. wooden interior fittings in a house, as moldings, doors, windowsills, etc.

wood·worm (wōōd'wûrm') *n.* A worm or insect larva that bores into wood.

wood·y (wōōd'ē) *adj.* **-i·er, -i·est.** **1.** Consisting of or con-

taining wood: *woody plants; woody stems; woody tissue.*
2. Of or suggestive of wood: *a woody smell.* **3.** Covered with trees; wooded: *a woody hill.*

woof¹ (wŏŏf, wŏŏf) *n.* **1.** The threads that run crosswise in a woven fabric, at right angles to the lengthwise warp threads; weft. **2.** The texture of a fabric. [Var. of Middle English *oof,* from Old English *ōwef : ō-,* from *on,* on + *wefan,* to weave.]

woof² (wŏŏf) *n.* A deep, gruff bark or a similar sound. —*intr.v.* To make such a sound. [Imit.]

woof·er (wŏŏf'ər) *n.* A loudspeaker designed to reproduce sounds of low frequency. [From WOOF (sound).]

wool (wŏŏl) *n.* **1.** The dense, soft, often curly hair of sheep and some other animals, used to make yarn, cloth, and clothing. **2.** Yarn, cloth, or clothing made of wool. **3.** Something having the look or feel of wool, as a mass of fine, curled metal strands. —*modifier: wool socks.* —*idiom.* **pull the wool over (someone's) eyes.** To deceive by tricking, misleading, etc. [Middle English *wolle,* from Old English *wull.*]

wool·en (wŏŏl'ən). Also *Brit.* **wool·len.** *adj.* **1.** Made of wool: *a woolen fabric; woolen underwear.* **2.** Making or dealing in wool cloth or clothing: *a woolen mill; a woolen merchant.* —*n.* Often **woolens.** Wool cloth or clothing.

wool·gath·er·ing (wŏŏl'găth'ər-ĭng) *n.* Absent-minded indulgence in fanciful daydreams. —*modifier: a wool-gathering student.* —**wool'gath'er·er** *n.*]

wool·grow·er (wŏŏl'grō'ər) *n.* A person who raises sheep or other animals for the production of wool.

wool·len (wŏŏl'ən) *adj. & n. Brit.* Var. of **woolen.**

wool·ly (wŏŏl'ē) *adj.* **-li·er, -li·est.** Also **wool·y.** **1. a.** Of or covered with wool: *a woolly coat; a woolly lamb.* **b.** Resembling wool: *leaves covered with woolly down.* **2.** Lacking sharp detail; unclear; blurry; fuzzy: *woolly thinking.* **3.** Rough and gen. lawless; disorderly: *a wild and woolly frontier.* —*n., pl.* **-lies.** Also **wool·y.** A garment made of wool, esp. underwear. —**wool'li·ness** *n.*

woolly bear. The hairy caterpillar of any of various tiger moths, esp. that of *Isia isabella.*

wool·pack (wŏŏl'păk') *n.* **1.** A bag used for packing a bale of wool for shipment. **2.** A cumulus cloud.

wool·y (wŏŏl'ē) *adj. & n.* Var. of **woolly.**

wooz·y (wŏŏ'zē, wŏŏz'ē) *adj.* **-i·er, -i·est.** **1.** Confused; muddled: *I'm a little woozy on the facts.* **2.** Dizzy or queasy: *Two drinks make her woozy. He felt woozy from the flu.* [Perh. var. of OOZY.] —**wooz'i·ly** *adv.* —**wooz'i·ness** *n.*

Worces·ter·shire sauce (wŏŏs'tər-shîr', -shər). A sharptasting sauce of soy, vinegar, and spices, orig. made in Worcester, England.

word (wûrd) *n.* **1.** A spoken sound or group of sounds that communicates a meaning and can be represented by letters written or printed in an unbroken series. **2. words.** Spoken or written expression; speech or writing: *learning to put your feelings into words.* **3.** A remark or comment: *a word of advice.* **4.** A short conversation: *May I have a word with you?* **5. words.** Hostile or angry remarks made back and forth; quarrel. **6.** A promise; assurance: *keeping her word to be on time.* **7.** A direction to do something; order: *Just say the word, and we'll send up reinforcements.* **8.** News; information: *sent word of her safe arrival.* **9. Word.** The Scriptures; the Bible. —*modifier: a word puzzle.* —*tr.v.* To express in words: *word a letter carefully.* —*idioms.* **eat (one's) words.** To admit having said or predicted something wrong. **take (someone) at his word.** To trust the word of (someone) and act accordingly. **word for word.** Entirely and without changing or forgetting any word. [Middle English, from Old English.]

word·age (wûr'dĭj) *n.* **1.** Words in general. **2.** The use of an excessive number of words; verbiage. **3.** The number of words used, as in a novel or magazine article. **4.** Choice of language or phraseology; wording.

word blindness. Alexia. —**word'-blind'** *adj.*

word·book (wûrd'bŏŏk') *n.* A lexicon; vocabulary; dictionary.

word deafness. A type of aphasia in which information in the form of speech is incomprehensible.

word·ing (wûr'dĭng) *n.* The way in which something is expressed; choice of words; phraseology.

word·less (wûrd'lĭs) *adj.* **1.** Not expressed in words; unspoken: *a look that served as a wordless reproach.* **2.** Speechless; mute; silent: *wordless with gratitude.* —**word'less·ly** *adv.* —**word'less·ness** *n.*

word order. The sequence or arrangement of words in a sentence, clause, or phrase.

word play. **1.** A witty or clever exchange of words; repartee. **2.** A play on words; pun.

word square. A group of words arranged in a square that read the same vertically and horizontally. Also called **acrostic.**

word·y (wûr'dē) *adj.* **-i·er, -i·est.** Containing or using too many words; verbose. —**word'i·ly** *adv.* —**word'i·ness** *n.*

wore (wôr, wōr). Past tense of **wear.** [From WEAR (on the model of such verbs as *tear, tore.*)]

work (wûrk) *n.* **1.** Physical or mental effort to make or do something; labor: *taking a nap after a morning of work; hard at work on a new scheme.* **2.** Employment; a job: *looking for work.* **3.** The activity by which one makes one's living; one's occupation. **4.** The place, such as an office or factory, where one pursues one's occupation. **5.** A task or a number of tasks: *There's enough work here to last us all day.* **6.** The way in which someone performs a task; workmanship: *The window washer unwisely leaned back to admire his work.* **7. a.** Something that has been done, made, or brought about; the result of an effort: *This mistake is your work, not mine.* **b.** An act; deed: *charitable works.* **c. works.** The total of the material produced by a creative artist: *the works of Bach.* **d. works.** Large structures designed by engineers, as bridges, roads, and dams. **8.** An object or item being made, shaped, studied, or processed: *a carpenter's table with a large vise for holding the work.* **9. works** (used with a sing. verb). A factory, plant, or similar site where industry of some kind is carried on: *a steel works.* **10. works.** The essential or operating parts of a device: *the works of a watch.* **11. the works.** *Slang.* Everything in a whole group or range; the whole lot: *We ordered the works, from soup to nuts.* **12. a.** The transfer of energy from one physical body or system to another. **b.** The measure of the energy transferred from one body or system to another. —*modifier: work shoes.* —*v.* **worked** or *archaic* **wrought** (rôt), **work·ing.** —*intr.v.* **1.** To exert oneself for the purpose of doing or making something; to labor: *work for a better future.* **2.** To be employed; have a job: *She works at a bank.* **3.** To operate or perform a function effectively or successfully: *a mousetrap that really works; a sales promotion that worked.* **4.** To have a steadily increasing influence or effect, as on the mind or the feelings: *The memory worked on her conscience.* **5.** To try to influence or persuade: *Dad hasn't agreed to let us use the car, but we're working on him.* **6.** To change or become through gradual or repeated stress, pressure, or movement: *The stitches worked loose.* **7.** To force a passage or make way with effort: *They worked through the snow to the street.* **8.** To move or contort from emotion or pain: *Her mouth worked with fear.* **9.** To be formed, shaped, or manipulated: *Copper works easily.* —*tr.v.* **1.** To cause or bring about; accomplish: *work wonders.* **2.** To cause to operate or function; handle or use: *work a power mower.* **3.** To make or force to do work: *He works his laborers hard.* **4.** To function or operate in; cover: *a salesman who works the north side of town.* **5.** To form or shape; mold: *They work glass.* **6.** To handle or manipulate for the purpose of preparing: *work clay with the hands; work dough; working the soil with a hoe.* **7.** To move, progress, or achieve by gradual or repeated effort: *He worked his way out of the crowd. She worked herself into a top position with the company.* **8.** To make productive: *work a farm; work a vein of ore.* **9.** To excite, rouse, or provoke: *a speaker who can work a crowd into a frenzy.* **10.** To influence or use to advantage; exploit: *worked his contacts.* —*phrasal verbs.* **work in (or into).** **1.** To put in or introduce; insert: *work a joke into a speech.* **2.** To rub or press in: *work oil into leather.* **work off.** To get rid of; eliminate: *work off excess weight.* **work on (or upon).** **1.** To persuade, influence, or affect. **2.** To attempt to persuade or influence. **work out.** **1.** To devise; develop: *work out a solution.* **2.** To solve or resolve: *worked out his problems.* **3.** To prove successful or suitable: *The cake didn't work out very well.* **4.** To perform athletic exercises. **work over.** **1.** To do again; revise: *The play's second act needs to be worked over.* **2.** *Slang.* To beat severely; thrash: *Two hoodlums grabbed him and worked him over.* **work up. 1.** To arouse the emotions of; excite: *Those rumors only worked him up.* **2.** To develop or prepare; formulate; elaborate: *worked up a financial report; work up an idea.* [Middle English, *worke,* from Old English *weorc,* act, deed, work.]

Syns: work, business, employment, job, occupation *n.* *Core meaning:* What one does to earn a living (*found work in the city*). WORK, the most general of these terms, can refer to the mere fact of employment or to a specific activity (*his work as a lawyer*). A BUSINESS is the activity in which a person engages for a livelihood (*went into the shoe business*). EMPLOYMENT and JOB suggest activity in which a person is hired and paid by another (*regular employment as a baggage handler; a job in a bookstore*). But an OCCUPATION does not necessarily imply being employed by others (*Madame Curie's occupation as a chemist*). See also Syns at **labor.**

work·a·ble (wûr′kə-bəl) *adj.* **1.** Capable of being used or put into effect successfully; practicable: *a workable plan of action.* **2.** Capable of being shaped, molded, or dealt with: *workable metals.* **—work′a·bil′i·ty** or **work′a·ble·ness** *n.*

work·a·day (wûr′kə-dā′) *adj.* **1.** Of or appropriate to working days or occupations; everyday: *the workaday chores of a housekeeper; the workaday responsibilities of running a business.* **2.** Commonplace; ordinary: *the workaday world; the workaday concerns of the average American.* [From Middle English *werkeday,* a workday.]

work·bench (wûrk′bĕnch′) *n.* A sturdy table or bench on which manual work is done, as by a machinist, carpenter, or jeweler.

work·book (wûrk′bŏŏk′) *n.* **1.** A teaching booklet that contains problems and exercises to be worked by students directly on its pages. **2.** A manual of operating instructions, as for an appliance or a machine. **3.** A book for keeping a record of work proposed or completed.

work·day (wûrk′dā′) *n.* **1.** Any day on which work is done: *Sunday is not a workday.* **2.** The part of the day during which one works: *an eight-hour workday.* *—modifier: workday clothes; a workday lunch of sandwiches.*

work·er (wûr′kər) *n.* **1.** Someone or something that works. **2.** Someone who belongs to the working class; a laborer or employee. **3.** One of the sterile females of certain social insects, as the ant or bee, that performs specialized work.

work force. 1. Those workers employed in a specific project; staff. **2.** All workers potentially available for a particular purpose.

work·horse (wûrk′hôrs′) *n.* **1.** A horse that is used for labor rather than for racing or riding. **2.** *Informal.* A person who works tirelessly.

work·ing (wûr′kĭng) *adj.* **1.** Of someone or something that works; employed: *a working person.* **2.** Of, used for, or spent in work: *working clothes; working hours.* **3.** Capable of working; functioning: *a machine in working condition.* **4.** Sufficient or adequate for using: *a working knowledge of a language.* **5.** Capable of being used as a guide or as the basis of further work: *a working script; a working layout for a publicity campaign.*

working capital. 1. The assets of a business enterprise that can be applied to its operation. **2.** The current assets of an individual or business enterprise as opposed to the current liabilities.

working class. The part of society whose income is from wages. *—modifier* (**working-class**): *a working-class neighborhood.*

work·ing·man (wûr′kĭng-măn′) *n.* A man who works for wages.

work·less (wûrk′lĭs) *adj.* Unemployed.

work·load (wûrk′lōd′) *n.* The amount of work assigned to or done by a worker or unit of workers in a given time period.

work·man (wûrk′mən) *n.* A man who performs some form of labor, esp. skilled manual labor.

work·man·like (wûrk′mən-līk′) *adj.* Also **work·man·ly** (-lē). Of or befitting a skilled worker or craftsman; well-done: *workmanlike pottery; a workmanlike piece of carpentry.*

work·man·ship (wûrk′mən-shĭp′) *n.* **1. a.** The art, skill, or technique of a worker. **b.** The quality of such art, skill, or technique: *silver of poor workmanship.* **2.** Something that has been made or produced.

workmen's compensation. Payments required by law to be made to an employee who is injured in the course of his work.

work of art. A piece of creative work that possesses originality of thought and aesthetic merit aside from any utilitarian considerations.

work·out (wûrk′out′) *n.* A period of exercise or practice, esp. in athletics.

work·room (wûrk′rōōm′, -rŏŏm′) *n.* A room where work is done, esp. manual work.

work·shop (wûrk′shŏp′) *n.* **1.** An area, room, or establishment in which manual or industrial work is done. **2.** A group of people who meet regularly for a seminar in some specialized field: *a workshop for creative writing.*

work·ta·ble (wûrk′tā′bəl) *n.* A table designed for use in performing specific manual tasks, esp. such a table having drawers or hooks for tools and materials.

work·week (wûrk′wēk′) *n.* The number of hours worked or required to be worked in one week.

world (wûrld) *n.* **1.** The earth. **2.** The universe. **3.** The earth and its inhabitants. **4.** The human race; mankind: *The world must eliminate poverty and waste if it is to survive.* **5.** Man considered as a social creature; the public: *the world's response to the first flight across the Atlantic.* **6.** A particular part of the earth: *the Western World.* **7.** A particular period in history, including its people, culture, and social order: *the Victorian world.* **8.** A sphere, realm, or domain including all things pertaining to or associated with it: *the animal world; a child's world.* **9.** A field or sphere of human endeavor: *the world of the arts.* **10.** A specified way of life or state of being: *the world of the rich; the world of the deaf.* **11.** Secular life and its concerns as distinguished from religious or spiritual matters: *a man of the world; forsook the world for a hermit's life.* **12.** Often **worlds.** A large amount; much: *spent worlds of time. College did him a world of good.* **13.** A planet or other celestial body: *the possibility of life on another world.* *—idioms.* **for all the world. 1.** For anything; for any reason: *I wouldn't go for all the world.* **2.** Precisely; exactly: *He looked for all the world like a movie star.* **out of this world.** *Informal.* Excellent; very fine: *a dinner that was out of this world.* [Middle English, from Old English, *weorold.*]

world·ling (wûrld′lĭng) *n.* A person absorbed in or devoted to this world; a worldly person.

world·ly (wûrld′lē) *adj.* **-li·er, -li·est. 1.** Of or devoted to the concerns of this world; not spiritual or religious; secular: *worldly concerns.* **2.** Sophisticated or cosmopolitan; worldly-wise: *an experienced, worldly diplomat.* **—world′li·ness** *n.*

world·ly-wise (wûrld′lē-wīz′) *adj.* Experienced in the ways of the world; sophisticated.

world-wea·ry (wûrld′wîr′ē) *adj.* **-ri·er, -ri·est.** Tired of the world and its pleasures. **—world′-wea′ri·ness** *n.*

world·wide (wûrld′wīd′) *adj.* Reaching or extending throughout the world; universal. **—world′wide′** *adv.*

worm (wûrm) *n.* **1.** Any of various invertebrates, as those of the phyla Annelida, Nematoda, or Platyhelminthes, that have a long, flexible rounded or flattened body, often without obvious appendages. **2.** Any of various insect larvae that have a soft, elongated body. **3.** Any of various unrelated animals that resemble a worm in habit or appearance, as the shipworm or the slowworm. **4.** An object or device, as a screw thread, that is like a worm in appearance or action. **5.** An insidiously tormenting or devouring force: *the worm of guilt.* **6.** A scorned, despised, or weak-willed person. **7. worms.** *Pathol.* Intestinal infestation with worms or wormlike parasites. *—tr.v.* **1.** To make (one's way) with or as if with the twisting, crawling motion of a worm: *We wormed our way through the crowd of onlookers.* **2.** To elicit by sly or devious means: *wormed the truth out of the boys.* **3.** To cure of intestinal worms. *—intr.v.* To move in a twisting, devious manner: *He can't worm out of this situation.* [Middle English, from Old English *wyrm,* worm, serpent.]

worm-eat·en (wûrm′ēt′n) *adj.* **1.** Bored through or gnawed by worms: *worm-eaten wood.* **2.** Decayed; rotten. **3.** Antiquated; decrepit; out-dated.

worm gear. **1.** A gear that consists of a threaded shaft and a wheel with teeth that mesh into it. **2.** A **worm wheel.**

worm gear

worm·hole (wûrm′hōl′) *n.* A hole made by a burrowing worm.

worm wheel. A wheel with teeth that mesh with the thread of a worm.

worm·wood (wûrm′wŏŏd′) *n.* **1.** Any of several aromatic plants of the genus *Artemisia,* esp. *A. absinthium,* native to Europe, that yields a bitter extract used in making absinthe and in flavoring certain wines. Also called **absinthe.** **2.** Something harsh or bitter. [Middle English *wormwode,* var. of *wermode,* from Old English *wermōd.*]

worm·y (wûr′mē) *adj.* **-i·er, -i·est. 1.** Infested with or damaged by worms. **2.** Like a worm; groveling.

worn (wôrn, wōrn) *v.* Past participle of **wear.** —*adj.* **1.** Damaged by wear or use: *worn, faded trousers.* **2.** Having a tired, exhausted look, as from worry, sickness, or strain: *a pale, worn face.* **3.** Trite; hackneyed; over-used: *a worn idea; a worn joke.* —See Syns at **haggard.** [From WEAR (on the model of such verbs as *tear, torn*).]

worn-out (wôrn′out′, wōrn′-) *adj.* **1.** Used or worn until no longer usable: *worn-out shoes.* **2.** Thoroughly exhausted; spent: *a runner worn-out after the marathon.*

wor·ri·ment (wûr′ē-mənt, wŭr′-) *n. Informal.* The act or a cause of worrying; worry.

wor·ri·some (wûr′ē-səm, wŭr′-) *adj.* **1.** Causing worry or anxiety. **2.** Tending to worry; anxious. —**wor′ri·some·ly** *adv.*

wor·ry (wûr′ē, wŭr′ē) *v.* **-ried, -ry·ing.** —*intr.v.* **1.** To feel uneasy or troubled about something: *He worries about his health.* **2.** To pull, bite, or tear at something: *a puppy worrying at a bone.* **3.** To work under difficulty or hardship; struggle: *worried away at a problem.* —*tr.v.* **1.** To cause to feel anxious, distressed, or troubled: *a medical report that worried him.* **2.** To bother; annoy: *Don't worry me with your complaints.* **3. a.** To grasp and tug or tear at: *a kitten worrying a ball of yarn.* **b.** To touch, press, or handle: *worrying the sore tooth with his tongue.* —*n., pl.* **-ries. 1.** Mental uneasiness or anxiety. **2.** A source of anxiety or uneasiness. —See Syns at **anxiety.** [Middle English *worien,* to seize by the throat, harass, from Old English *wyrgan,* to strangle.] —**wor′ri·er** *n.*

wor·ry·wart (wûr′ē-wôrt′, wŭr′-) *n. Informal.* Someone who tends to worry excessively and needlessly.

worse (wûrs) *adj.* **1.** Comparative of **bad:** *He's worse than I'd ever imagined a vicious person could be.* **2.** Comparative of **ill:** *Grandpa is worse, and I think you should come home.* **3.** More inferior, as in quality, condition, or effect: *These oranges are worse than those.* —*adv.* In a worse way. —*n.* Something worse: *taking a turn for the worse.* [Middle English, from Old English *wyrsa.*]

wors·en (wûr′sən) —*intr.v.* To be or become worse: *His eyesight has worsened with age.* —*tr.v.* To make worse: *Medical expenses worsened his financial problems.*

wor·ship (wûr′shĭp) *n.* **1.** The reverent love, respect, and allegiance felt, as for a deity or sacred object. **2.** A set of ceremonies, prayers, or other religious forms by which this devotion is expressed: *attends worship every Sunday.* **3.** Love of or devotion to a person or thing: *her worship of her children; the worship of money.* **4.** Often **Worship.** *Brit.* A title of honor used in addressing magistrates, mayors, and certain other officials: *Your Worship.* —*v.* **-shiped** or **-shipped, -ship·ing** or **-ship·ping.** —*tr.v.* **1.** To honor and love as a deity; venerate: *each worshiping God in his own*

way. **2.** To love or pursue devotedly: *worshiped his wife; worships wealth and prestige.* —*intr.v.* To participate in religious rites of worship: *We worship at the oldest church in town.* [Middle English *worschipe,* from Old English *weorthscipe,* honor, dignity, reverence.] —**wor′ship·er** *n.*

wor·ship·ful (wûr′shĭp-fəl) *adj.* **1.** Showing or given to worship: *a worshipful fan of a movie star; a worshipful servant of God.* **2.** *Brit.* Worthy of honor and respect by virtue of position or rank. Used in titles of respect. —**wor′ship·ful·ly** *adv.* —**wor′ship·ful·ness** *n.*

worst (wûrst) *adj.* **1.** Superlative of **bad:** *He was the worst president we ever had.* **2.** Superlative of **ill:** *the worst turn he has ever done anyone.* **3.** Most inferior, as in quality, condition, or effect: *the worst eggs I ever saw.* **4.** Most severe or unfavorable: *the worst winter in years.* **5.** Least desirable or satisfactory: *the worst piece of land.* —*n.* Something or someone that is worst. —*adv.* In the worst manner or degree: *He performs worst in math and science.* —*tr.v.* To gain the advantage over; defeat: *worsted his opponent in a boxing match.* —*idioms.* **at worst.** Under the worst foreseeable circumstances; if the worst should happen. **get the worst of it.** To suffer a defeat or disadvantage. **if (the) worst comes to (the) worst.** At the very worst. [Middle English *worste,* from Old English *wyrsta.*]

wor·sted (wŏŏs′tĭd, wûr′stĭd) *n.* **1.** Smooth, firmly twisted yarn made from combed wool fibers of the same length. **2.** Fabric made from such yarn. —*modifier: a worsted suit.* [Middle English after *Worstead,* England.]

wort (wûrt, wôrt) *n.* **1.** A plant. Used chiefly in combination: *liverwort; milkwort.* **2.** An infusion of malt that is fermented to make beer. [Middle English, from Old English *wyrt,* plant, herb.]

worth (wûrth) *n.* **1.** The quality or condition of excellence that makes someone or something desirable, useful, or valuable: *the worth of a good reputation; a man of worth to his nation's foreign policy.* **2.** The value of something in terms of money: *have a worth of ten million dollars; a jewel of considerable worth.* **3.** The amount of something that a specific sum of money will buy: *two dollars' worth of gasoline.* **4.** Wealth; riches. —*adj.* **1.** Equal in value to something specified: *a pen worth five dollars.* **2.** Having wealth amounting to: *a woman worth $2,000,000.* **3.** Deserving of; meriting: *a proposal worth consideration.* —*idiom.* **for all (one) is worth.** To the utmost of one's powers or ability. [Middle English, from Old English *weorth.*]

worth·less (wûrth′lĭs) *adj.* **1.** Without worth, use, or value: *a worthless promise.* **2.** Without dignity or honor; low and despicable. —**worth′less·ly** *adv.* —**worth′less·ness** *n.*

worth·while (wûrth′hwīl′, -wīl′) *adj.* Sufficiently valuable or important to justify the expenditure of time or effort.

wor·thy (wûr′thē) *adj.* **-thi·er, -thi·est. 1.** Having worth, merit, or value; useful or valuable. **2.** Honorable; admirable: *a worthy fellow.* **3.** Having sufficient worth; deserving: *worthy to be revered; worthy of acclaim.* —*n., pl.* **-thies.** A person esteemed for his worth, dignity, or importance. —**wor′thi·ly** *adv.* —**wor′thi·ness** *n.*

wot (wŏt) *v. Archaic.* First and third person singular present tense of **wit** (to know). [Middle English, from Old English *wāt.*]

Wo·tan (vō′tän′) *n.* A Germanic god, identified with the Norse god Odin.

would (wŏŏd) *v.* Past tense of **will.** [Middle English *wolde,* from Old English.]

   Usage: **would.** *Would have* is frequently misused for *had* in conditional clauses introduced by *if:* The following illustrate correct forms: *They could have come if they had wanted to* (not *if they would have wanted to). If they had come, this would not have occurred* (not *if they would have come). Had* is also the proper auxiliary in clauses following *wish: I wish that she had called* (not *that she would have called).* See also Usage note at **should.**

would-be (wŏŏd′bē′) *adj.* Desiring or pretending to be: *a would-be actor; a would-be millionaire.*

would·n't (wŏŏd′nt). Contraction of would not.

wouldst (wŏŏdst) or **would·est** (wŏŏd′ĭst) *v. Archaic.* Second person singular past tense of **will.**

wound¹ (wŏŏnd) *n.* **1.** An injury, esp. one in which the skin or other outer surface that covers a living thing is torn, cut, broken, or otherwise damaged. **2.** An injury to the feelings: *an emotional wound.* —*tr.v.* To inflict a wound or wounds on: *The hunter wounded the lion but failed to kill him.* —*intr.v.* To inflict a wound or wounds: *Words can often wound more than a slap.* [Middle English, from Old English *wund.*]

wound² (wound) *v.* Past tense and past participle of **wind** (to wrap). [Middle English *wounde, wounden,* from Old English *wond, wunden.*]

wove (wōv) *v.* Past tense of **weave.** [Middle English *wof,* from Old English *wæf.*]

wo·ven (wō′vən) *v.* Past participle of **weave.** [Middle English *woven* (formed on the model of such verbs as *steal, stolen*).]

wow (wou) *interj.* A word used to express wonder, amazement, excitement, enthusiasm, etc. —*n. Informal.* An outstanding success. —*tr.v. Informal.* To be or have a great success with: *wowed the audience.*

wrack (răk) *n.* **1.** Complete destruction; irreparable damage: *bring to wrack and ruin.* **2.** Wreckage or a remnant of something destroyed, esp. of a ship cast ashore: *The storm swept the island, leaving not even a wrack behind.* **3.** A tangled mass of seaweed or other marine vegetation, cast ashore or floating. —*tr.v.* **1.** To cause the ruin of; wreck: *Hurricane-force winds wracked the coastal areas.* **2.** To have a violent or shattering effect on: *Sobs wracked her body.* —*intr.v.* To be wrecked. [Middle English, from Old English *wræc,* punishment, vengeance, and Middle Dutch *wrak,* wreckage, wrecked ship.]

wraith (rāth) *n.* **1.** An apparition of a living person, considered to be a sign or portent of coming death. **2.** The ghost of a dead person. [Orig. unknown.]

wran·gle (răng′gəl) *v.* **-gled, -gling.** —*intr.v.* To dispute noisily or angrily; to quarrel; bicker: *They wrangled for hours over nothing.* —*tr.v.* **1.** To win or obtain by argument: *We wrangled the truth out of him.* **2.** *Regional.* To herd (horses or other livestock). —See Syns at **argue.** —*n.* An angry, noisy dispute. [Middle English *wranglen.*] —**wran′gler** *n.*

wrap (răp) *v.* **wrapped** or **wrapt, wrap·ping.** —*tr.v.* **1.** To draw, fold, or wind about in order to cover or protect something: *She wrapped her stole about her.* **2.** To enclose within a covering: *wrap a baby in a blanket.* **3.** To encase and secure (an object), esp. with paper; to package: *wrapping the Christmas presents.* **4.** To clasp, fold, or wind about something: *Vines wrapped the trunk of the tree. She wrapped her arms about his neck.* **5.** To envelop or surround so as to obscure or conceal: *Fog wrapped the countryside.* **6.** To be or cause to be totally involved or absorbed; immerse; engross: *wraps himself in his studies.* —*intr.v.* To coil, wind, or twist about or around something: *The flag wrapped around the pole. Climbing roses wrapped along the fence.* —*phrasal verb.* **wrap up. 1.** To put on warm clothes: *Wrap up before you go out.* **2.** To finish; conclude: *wrap up a sports event.* **3.** *Informal.* To give a brief, comprehensive statement; summarize: *wrapped up the annual report in a few sentences.* —See Syns at **end.** —*n.* **1.** Often **wraps.** An outer garment worn for warmth, as a coat. **2.** Paper or other material used for wrapping something. —*idiom.* **under wraps.** Secret or concealed. [Middle English *wrappen.*]

Syns: **wrap, cloak, clothe, enfold, enshroud, envelop, enwrap, shroud, veil** *v. Core meaning:* To surround and cover completely so as to hide from view (*fog wrapping the lonely moors*).

wrap·a·round (răp′ə-round′) *adj.* **1.** Designating a garment open to the hem and wrapped around the body before being fastened: *a wraparound skirt; a wraparound dress.* **2.** Having ends that curve back or that overlap the sides: *wraparound shelves.* —*n.* A wraparound garment: *The skirt department is sold out of wraparounds.*

wrap·per (răp′ər) *n.* **1.** Someone who wraps. **2.** A cover, as of paper, in which something is wrapped: *a candy wrapper.* **3.** The tobacco leaf covering a cigar. **4.** A loose robe or negligee.

wrap·ping (răp′ĭng) *n.* Often **wrap·pings.** The material in which something is wrapped.

wrapt. (răpt) *v.* A past tense and past participle of **wrap.**

wrap-up (răp′ŭp′) *n.* A brief summary of something: *the nightly news wrap-up on television.*

wrasse (răs) *n.* Any of numerous chiefly tropical, often brightly colored saltwater fishes of the family Labridae. [Cornish *wrach.*]

wrath (răth, räth) *n.* **1.** Violent, resentful anger; rage. **2.** An action motivated by anger and carried out for punishment or revenge, esp. divine retribution for sin. [Middle English *wrathe,* from Old English *wrǣththu,* from *wrāth,* angry.]

wrath·ful (răth′fəl, räth′-) *adj.* **1.** Full of wrath; angry: *a wrathful mood; a wrathful woman.* **2.** Motivated by or expressing wrath: *wrathful vengeance; wrathful words.* —See Syns at **angry.** —**wrath′ful·ly** *adv.* —**wrath′ful·ness** *n.*

wreak (rēk) *tr.v.* **1.** To inflict (vengeance, harm, or punishment): *wreaked revenge for the death of his son; warriors wreaking havoc on an enemy camp.* **2.** To express or gratify (anger, malevolence, or resentment); to vent. [Middle English *wreken,* from Old English *wrecan,* to drive, expel, vent.]

wreath (rēth) *n., pl.* **wreaths** (rēthz, rēths). **1.** A ring or circular band of flowers, leaves, etc., used as an honor, decoration, adornment, memorial, etc. **2.** A ring or similar curving form: *a wreath of smoke.* [Middle English *wrethe,* from Old English *writha.*]

wreathe (rēth) *v.* **wreathed, wreath·ing.** —*tr.v.* **1.** To twist, entwine, or curl into a wreath or wreathlike shape: *wreathing flowers to form crowns for our hair.* **2.** To crown, adorn, or decorate with or as with a wreath: *Her head was wreathed with roses.* **3.** To coil or curl: *A plant had wreathed itself around the pole.* **4. a.** To form a wreath around; encircle; surround: *Clouds wreathed the top of the mountain. Her face was wreathed with curls.* **b.** To envelop: *a village wreathed in fog.* —*intr.v.* **1.** To assume the form of a wreath: *The smoke from the pipe wreathed above his head.* **2.** To move in or follow a curling path; to spiral: *The fog wreathed through the streets.* [From WREATH.]

wreck (rĕk) *tr.v.* **1.** To destroy accidentally, as by collision: *He wrecked his car.* **2.** To tear down or dismantle: *The crew wrecked the building in five days.* **3.** To bring to a state of ruin: *Inflation is wrecking the economy.* —*intr.v.* **1.** To suffer destruction, ruin, or shipwreck. **2.** To engage in dismantling or tearing down. —*n.* **1.** The action of wrecking or the condition of being wrecked. **2.** The accidental destruction of a ship; shipwreck. **3.** The remains of something that has been wrecked. **4.** Fragments of a ship or goods cast ashore by the sea after a shipwreck; wreckage. **5.** A person, animal, or thing in a shattered, brokendown, or worn-out state: *This hat is a wreck.* [Middle English *wrek,* from Norman French *wrec,* of Old Norse orig.]

wreck·age (rĕk′ĭj) *n.* **1.** The act of wrecking or the condition of being wrecked. **2.** The debris of anything wrecked.

wreck·er (rĕk′ər) *n.* **1.** Someone who wrecks or destroys. **2.** A member of a wrecking or demolition crew. **3. a.** An individual, piece of equipment, vehicle, ship, etc., employed in recovering or removing a wreck. **b.** Someone who salvages wrecked cargo.

wren (rĕn) *n.* **1.** Any of various small, brownish birds of the family Troglodytidae that usu. hold the tail pointing upward. **2.** Any of various birds similar to the wren. [Middle English *wrenne,* from Old English *wrenna.*]

wrench (rĕnch) *n.* **1.** A sudden, forcible twist or turn. **2.** An injury, as to a muscle, joint, etc., produced by twisting or straining. **3.** A sudden tug at one's emotions; a surge of compassion, sorrow, anguish, etc. **4.** Any of various tools with a long handle and adjustable jaws for gripping and holding or turning a nut, bolt, pipe, etc. —*tr.v.* **1. a.** To pull or turn suddenly and forcibly: *He wrenched the gun from the thief's hand.* **b.** To injure and sprain a part of the body: *wrenched his back lifting a box of books.* **2.** To force free by or as if by pulling; wrest. **3.** To pull at the feelings or emotions of; give pain to. **4.** To distort or

wrench

twist the original character or import of: *His idea had been wrenched out of all semblance to the original.* —*intr.v.* To give a wrench, twist, or turn: *Her back wrenched while she was pulling weeds.* —See Syns at **jerk.** [From Middle English *wrenchen,* to twist, wrench, from Old English *wrencan,* to twist.]

wrest (rĕst) *tr.v.* **1.** To obtain by or as by pulling with violent twisting movements: *wrested the book out of his hands.* **2.** To gain or take by force: *The barons wrested power from the king.* **3.** To gain or obtain by persistent effort; wring: *wrest the meaning from an obscure poem; farmers wresting a living from the land.* **4.** To distort or divert to an unnatural or inappropriate use or meaning: *wrested the laws and made mockery of justice.* —*n.* The action of wresting; a twist or wrench. [Middle English *wresten,* from Old English *wræstan,* to twist.] —**wrest′er** *n.*

wres·tle (rĕs′əl) *intr.v.* **-tled, -tling. 1.** To fight by grappling and attempting to throw one's opponent to the ground. **2.** To struggle to solve or master: *wrestle with a problem.* —*tr.v.* **1.** To contend against (an opponent) in the sport of wrestling: *He wrestles his strongest competition in tonight's match.* **2.** To fight with by grappling and throwing down: *He wrestled a bear.* —*n.* **1.** An act of wrestling, esp. a wrestling match. **2.** A struggle: *a little wrestle with his conscience.* [Middle English *wrestelen,* from Old English *wræstlian.*] —**wres′tler** *n.*

wres·tling (rĕs′lĭng) *n.* The sport of fighting by grappling and trying to bring one's opponent to the ground. —*modifier: a wrestling match.*

wrestling

wretch (rĕch) *n.* **1.** A miserable, unfortunate, or unhappy person. **2.** A wicked or despicable person. [Middle English *wrecche,* from Old English *wrecca,* wretch, exile.]

wretch·ed (rĕch′ĭd) *adj.* **-er, -est. 1.** Full of or attended by misery or woe: *I'm lonely and wretched.* **2.** Shabby; mean: *a wretched shack.* **3.** Hateful or contemptible: *a wretched person.* **4.** Inferior in quality: *a wretched performance.* **5.** Very unpleasant; deplorable: *a wretched cold; wretched weather.* [Middle English *wrecched,* from *wrecche,* wretch.] —**wretch′ed·ly** *adv.* —**wretch′ed·ness** *n.*

wrig·gle (rĭg′əl) *v.* **-gled, -gling.** —*intr.v.* **1.** To turn or twist the body with winding, writhing motions; squirm: *The puppy wriggled and fought to be put down.* **2.** To proceed with turning or thrashing motions: *They wriggled through the crowd.* **3.** To insinuate or extricate oneself by sly or subtle means: *wriggled out of a tight spot with his boss.* —*tr.v.* **1.** To move with a wriggling motion: *wriggle a toe.* **2.** To make (one's way) by indirection or devious means: *He wriggled his way through traffic.* —*n.* The action or movement of wriggling. [Middle English *wrigglen,* from Middle Low German *wriggeln.*] —**wrig′gly** *adj.*

wrig·gler (rĭg′lər) *n.* **1.** Someone or something that wriggles. **2.** The larva of a mosquito; wiggler.

wright (rīt) *n.* A person who creates or constructs something. Used chiefly in combination: *playwright; shipwright.* [Middle English, from Old English *wryhta, wyrhta,* workman.]

wring (rĭng) *v.* **wrung** (rŭng), **wring·ing.** —*tr.v.* **1.** To twist and squeeze, esp. to extract liquid: *Wring the wet towels before hanging them up to dry.* **2.** To force or extract by or as if by twisting or compressing: *wring water from a sponge; wring the truth out of a witness.* **3.** To wrench or twist forcibly or painfully: *I'd like to wring his neck.* **4.** To twist or squeeze, as in distress: *wringing her hands.* **5.** To

cause distress or pain; torment. —*intr.v.* To writhe or squirm, as in pain: *His soul wrings with anguish and guilt.* —*n.* A forceful squeeze or twist. [Middle English *wringen,* from Old English *wringan.*]

wring·er (rĭng′ər) *n.* Someone or something that wrings, esp. a device or machine in which laundry is squeezed or spun to extract water.

wrin·kle (rĭng′kəl) *n.* **1.** A small furrow, ridge, or crease on a normally smooth surface such as cloth or skin. **2.** *Informal.* An ingenious new trick or method; a clever innovation. —*v.* **-kled, -kling.** —*tr.v.* **1.** To make a wrinkle or wrinkles in: *Don't wrinkle the suit.* **2.** To draw up or pucker: *wrinkled her nose.* —*intr.v.* To form wrinkles: *Linen wrinkles easily.* [Middle English, back-formation from *wrinkled,* wrinkled, prob. from Old English *gewrinclod,* serrated, winding, past part. of *gewrinclian,* to wind.] —**wrin′kly** *adj.*

wrist (rĭst) *n.* **1. a.** The joint between the hand and forearm. **b.** The system of bones forming this joint; the carpus. **2.** The part of a garment that encircles the wrist. [Middle English, from Old English.]

wrist·band (rĭst′bănd′) *n.* A band of cloth, leather, metal, etc., that encircles the wrist, esp. such a band on a long-sleeved shirt or a wrist watch.

wrist·let (rĭst′lĭt) *n.* **1.** A band of material worn round the wrist for warmth or additional strength. **2.** A bracelet.

wrist·lock (rĭst′lŏk′) *n.* A wrestling hold in which an opponent's wrist is gripped and twisted to immobilize him.

wrist watch. A watch worn on a band that fastens about the wrist.

writ¹ (rĭt) *n.* **1.** *Law.* A written command or formal order issued under seal by a court in the name of the sovereign, state, or other legal authority, directing the person to whom it is addressed to perform or refrain from a specified act. **2.** Something written; a writing: *an ancient writ; a sacred writ.* [Middle English, from Old English.]

writ² (rĭt) *v. Archaic.* Past tense and past participle of **write.** [Middle English *writ, wryte,* from Old English *writon* (pl.), *(ge)writen.*]

write (rīt) *v.* **wrote** (rōt), **writ·ten** (rĭt′n), **writ·ing.** —*tr.v.* **1.** To form (letters, symbols, or characters) on a surface with a pen, pencil, etc.: *wrote his address and telephone number on a card.* **2.** To form (words, sentences, etc.) by inscribing the correct letters or symbols: *wrote his answers on a separate sheet of paper.* **3.** To compose: *writes poetry; write music; write a love letter.* **4.** To draw up in legal form; draft: *write a lease.* **5.** To relate or communicate by writing: *wrote the good news to his friend; wrote his thoughts on the subject in a letter.* **6.** *Informal.* To send a letter or note to: *wrote her niece.* **7.** To underwrite, as an insurance policy. **8.** To show clearly; to mark: *"Utter dejection was written on every face"* (Winston Churchill). —*intr.v.* **1.** To trace or form letters, words, or symbols on paper or another surface: *He writes very legibly. Some pens write better than others.* **2.** To produce articles, books, etc., to be read: *He writes for a living.* **3.** To compose and send a letter or letters; communicate by letter; correspond: *write every week.* —*phrasal verbs.* **write down.** To put into writing: *write down a telephone number.* **write in. 1.** To apply or request by mail: *wrote in for a free sample.* **2.** To cast a vote for (a candidate not listed on a ballot), as by inserting his name: *Write in the senator's name when you cast your ballot.* **write off. 1.** To cancel from accounts, as a loss. **2.** To reduce the book value of; depreciate: *He can write off the cost of that building in 10 years.* **3.** To consider as a loss or failure: *We wrote him off long ago.* **write up.** To write a report or description of: *write up the results of the experiment.* [Middle English *writen,* from Old English *wrītan.*]

write-in (rīt′ĭn′) *n.* A vote for a candidate not listed on a ballot, usu. cast by the insertion of his name in a space provided. —*adj.* Of or concerning such a candidate or such votes: *a write-in ballot.*

write-off (rīt′ôf′, -ŏf′) *n.* **1. a.** A cancellation from account books as a loss: *a business write-off.* **b.** An amount so canceled: *a write-off of $10,000.* **2.** A depreciation.

writ·er (rī′tər) *n.* **1.** A person who has written (something specified): *the writer of the letter.* **2.** A person who writes as an occupation; an author.

writer's cramp. A cramp chiefly affecting the muscles of the thumb and two adjacent fingers after prolonged writing.

write-up (rīt′ŭp′) n. A published account, review, notice, etc.

writhe (rīth) v. **writhed, writh·ing.** —intr.v. **1.** To twist or squirm, as in pain, struggle, distress, etc.: *writhed in agony; writhing with shame.* **2.** To move with a twisting or contorted motion: *Snakes were writhing in the pit.* —tr.v. To cause to twist or squirm; contort: *writhed himself off the chair.* —n. A twisting movement or motion. [Middle English *writhen,* from Old English *writhan.*] —**writh′er** n.

writ·ing (rī′tǐng) n. **1.** Written form: *Make your request in writing.* **2.** Language symbols or characters written or imprinted on a surface. **3. a.** Any written work, esp. a literary composition: *A single writing, a novel, brought him immortality.* **b. writings.** A collection of written works: *the writings of Aristotle.* **4.** The activity, art, or occupation of a writer. —**modifier:** *a writing course.*

writing paper. Stationery specially prepared to receive ink.

wrong (rông, rŏng) adj. **1.** Not correct; erroneous: *a wrong answer.* **2. a.** Contrary to conscience, morality, law, or custom: *Cheating is wrong. You have the wrong idea of how to get ahead.* **b.** Unfair or unjust: *Such severe punishment for so minor an offense is wrong.* **3.** Not intended or wanted: *a wrong telephone number; the wrong person.* **4.** Not fitting or suitable; inappropriate; improper: *the wrong moment.* **5.** Not in accordance with an established usage, method, or procedure: *the wrong way to hit a tennis ball.* **6.** Not functioning properly; amiss: *What's wrong with the car?* —See Syns at **false.** —adv. **1.** Mistakenly; erroneously: *told the story wrong.* **2.** Immorally or unjustly: *behave wrong.* —n. **1.** An unjust, injurious, or immoral act or circumstance: *right a wrong.* **2.** *Law.* A violation of another's legal rights to his damage; a tort. **3.** The condition of being mistaken or to blame: *in the wrong.* —tr.v. **1.** To treat unjustly, injuriously, or dishonorably: *He has dishonored himself and wronged the na-*

tion. **2.** To discredit unjustly; malign: *You wrong this man that you call a thief.* —**idiom. go wrong. 1.** To take a wrong turn or course. **2.** To go astray morally. **3.** To happen or turn out badly. [Middle English, of Old Norse orig.] —**wrong′er** n. —**wrong′ly** adv.

wrong·do·er (rông′dōō′ər, rŏng′-) n. Someone who does wrong. —**wrong′do′ing** n.

wrong·ful (rông′fəl, rŏng′-) adj. **1.** Wrong; injurious; unjust. **2.** Contrary to law; unlawful; illegal. —See Syns at **criminal** and **illegal.** —**wrong′ful·ly** adv. —**wrong′ful·ness** n.

wrong-head·ed (rông′hĕd′ĭd, rŏng′-) adj. Persistently misguided in judgment or opinion; stubbornly wrong. —**wrong′-head′ed·ly** adv. —**wrong′-head′ed·ness** n.

wrote (rōt) v. Past tense of **write.** [Middle English, from Old English *wrāt.*]

wroth (rôth, rŏth) adj. *Archaic.* Wrathful; angry. [Middle English, from Old English *wrāth.*]

wrought (rôt) v. *Archaic.* A past tense and past participle of **work.** —adj. **1.** Made, formed, or fashioned: *a well-wrought cabinet.* **2.** Shaped by hammering with tools, as metal is. —**idiom. wrought up.** Agitated; excited. [Middle English *wrought(e), wroght,* from Old English *worhte, (ge)worht.*]

wrought iron. A highly purified form of iron that is easily shaped, forged, or welded. —**modifier** (**wrought-iron**): *wrought-iron furniture.*

wrung (rŭng) v. Past tense and past participle of **wring.** [Middle English *wrung, wrungen,* from Old English *wrungon* (pl.), *(ge)wrungen.*]

wry (rī) adj. **wri·er** or **wry·er, wri·est** or **wry·est. 1.** Twisted or bent to one side; crooked: *a wry smile.* **2.** Temporarily twisted in an expression of distaste or displeasure: *made a wry face.* **3.** Dryly humorous, often with a touch of irony: *a wry comment.* [From Middle English *wrien,* to bend, twist, turn aside, from Old English *wrīgian,* to proceed, turn.] —**wry′ly** adv. —**wry′ness** n.

wurst (wûrst, wŏōrst) n. Sausage. [German *Wurst,* from Old High German *wurst.*]

wy·vern (wī′vərn) n. Var. of **wivern.**

Xx

Phoenician	Greek	Roman	Medieval	Modern

Phoenician – *About 3,000 years ago the Phoenicians and other Semitic peoples began to use graphic signs to represent individual speech sounds instead of syllables or whole words. They used this symbol to represent the sound of the consonant "s" and gave it the name* sāmekh, *the Phoenician word for "fish."*
Greek – *The Greeks borrowed the Phoenician alphabet with some modifications. They simplified the shape of* sāmekh *and changed its orientation. Some dialects of Greek used* sāmekh *to represent the sound "kh" (as in Scottish* loch) *and gave it the name* chi, *but others used it for the sound "ks" and gave it the name* xi.
Roman – *The Romans borrowed the alphabet from the*

Greeks via the Etruscans, who used X to represent "ks" rather than "kh." The Romans also adapted the alphabet for carving Latin in stone, and this monumental script, as it is called, became the basis for modern printed capital letters.
Medieval – *By medieval times – around 1,200 years ago – the Roman monumental capitals had become adapted to being relatively quickly written on paper, parchment, or vellum. The cursive minuscule alphabet became the basis of modern printed lower-case letters.*
Modern – *Since the invention of printing about 500 years ago the basic form and the phonetic value of the letter X has remained unchanged.*

---

x or **X** (ĕks) *n., pl.* **x's** or **X's. 1.** The 24th letter of the English alphabet. **2.** Any of the speech sounds represented by this letter. **3.** Anything shaped like the letter **X. 4.** The mark X inscribed to represent the signature of an illiterate person. **5.** The Roman numeral for ten. **6.** An unknown quantity, factor, thing, or person. **7.** A symbol for an algebraic variable. —*tr.v.* **x'd** or **xed, x-ing** or **x'ing. 1.** To mark or sign with an x. **2.** To delete or cancel with a series of *x's: x'd out the error.*

xan·thic acid (zăn'thĭk). Any of various unstable acids of the form ROC(S)SH, in which R is usu. an alkyl radical. [From Greek *xanthos,* yellow (from to the color of its salts).]

xan·thine (zăn'thēn', -thĭn) *n.* A yellowish-white purine base, $C_5H_4N_4O_2$, found in blood, urine, and some plants. [From Greek *xanthos,* yellow.]

xan·thous (zăn'thəs) *adj.* Yellow. [From Greek *xanthos,* yellow.]

x-ax·is (ĕks'ăk'sĭs) *n., pl.* **x-ax·es** (-sēz). The horizontal axis of a plane Cartesian coordinate system.

X-chro·mo·some (ĕks'krō'mə-sōm') *n.* The sex chromosome associated with female characteristics, occurring paired in the female and single in the male sex-chromosome pair.

Xe The symbol for the element xenon.

xe·bec (zē'bĕk') *n.* Also **ze·bec, ze·beck.** A small three-masted sailing ship with both square and triangular sails, once used by pirates in the Mediterranean Sea. [Earlier *chebec,* from French, from Italian *sciabecco,* from Arabic *shabbāk.*]

xe·non (zē'nŏn') *n. Symbol* **Xe** A colorless, odorless, highly unreactive gaseous element found in minute quantities in the atmosphere, extracted commercially from liquefied air, and used in stroboscopic, bactericidal, and laser-pumping lamps. Atomic number 54; atomic weight 131.30; melting point –111.9°C; boiling point –107.1°C; density 5.887 grams per liter; specific gravity (liquid) 3.52 (–109°C). [From Greek *xenos,* stranger.]

xen·o·phobe (zĕn'ə-fōb', zē'nəp) *n.* A person unduly fearful or contemptuous of strangers or foreigners, esp. as reflected in his political or cultural views. [Greek *xenos,* stranger + *phobos,* fear.] —**xen'o·pho'bi·a** *n.* —**xen'o·pho'bic** *adj.*

xe·roph·i·lous (zĭ-rŏf'ə-ləs) *adj.* Flourishing in or able to withstand a dry, hot environment. [Greek *xēros,* dry + -PHILOUS.]

xe·ro·graph·ic (zĭr'ə-grăf'ĭk) *adj.* Of, used in, or produced by xerography.

xe·rog·ra·phy (zĭ-rŏg'rə-fē) *n.* A process for producing photographs or photocopies without the use of solutions or wet materials, by causing an image made up of particles of pigment held in place by electric charges on a plate to be transferred to a sheet of paper and fixed to the paper by heat. [Greek *xeros,* dry + -GRAPHY.] —**xe·rog'ra·pher** *n.*

xe·ro·phyte (zĭr'ə-fīt') *n.* A plant that grows in and is adapted to an environment deficient in moisture. [Greek *xēros,* dry + -PHYTE.] —**xe'ro·phyt'ic** (zĭr'ə-fĭt'ĭk) *adj.* —**xe'ro·phyt'i·cal·ly** *adv.*

Xe·rox (zĭr'ŏks') *n.* **1.** A trademark for a machine or process that produces photocopies by xerography. **2.** A copy made on a Xerox machine. —*tr.v.* To copy or print with a Xerox machine.

xi (zī, sī) *n.* **1.** The 14th letter in the Greek alphabet, written Ξ, ξ. Transliterated in English as *X, x.* **2.** *Symbol* Ξ *Physics.* Either of two subatomic particles in the baryon family. [Greek.]

X·mas (krĭs'məs, ĕks'məs) *n. Informal.* Christmas. [From the Greek *X,* chi, initial letter of *Khristos,* Christ.]
   ***Usage:* Xmas.** Although this word dates to the 12th cent., it is now largely confined to commercial and informal writing.

X-rat·ed (ĕks'rā'tĭd) *adj. Informal.* Having the rating X: *an X-rated movie.*

x ray. Also **X ray. 1. a.** A relatively high-energy photon with wavelength in the approximate range from 0.05 angstroms to 100 angstroms. **b.** Often **x rays.** A stream of such photons, used for their penetrating power in radiography, radiology, radiotherapy, and research. Also called **Roentgen ray. 2.** A photograph taken with x rays: *a chest x ray.*

x-ray (ĕks'rā') *tr.v.* **1.** To treat with or subject to x rays. **2.** To photograph with x rays: *x-ray a fracture.*

xy·lem (zī'ləm) *n.* The supporting and water-conducting tissue of vascular plants, consisting primarily of woody tissue. [German *Xylem,* from Greek *xulon,* wood.]

xylo-. A prefix meaning wood or derived from wood: **xylose.** [Greek *xulon,* wood.]

xy·lo·phone (zī'lə-fōn') *n.* A musical percussion instrument consisting of a mounted row of wooden bars graduated in length to sound a chromatic scale, played with two small mallets. —**xy'lo·phon'ist** *n.*

xy·lose (zī'lōs') *n.* A white crystalline aldose sugar, $C_5H_{10}O_5$, used in dyeing, tanning, and in diabetic diets.

ă pat   ā pay   â care   ä father   ĕ pet   ē be   hw which   ĭ pit   ī tie   î pier   ŏ pot   ō toe   ô paw, for   oi noise
ŏŏ took   ōō boot   ou out   th thin   *th* this   ŭ cut   û urge   zh vision   ə about, item, edible, gallop, circus

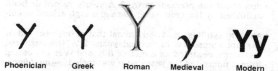

| Phoenician | Greek | Roman | Medieval | Modern |

Phoenician – *About 3,000 years ago the Phoenicians and other Semitic peoples began to use graphic signs to represent individual speech sounds instead of syllables or whole words. They used this symbol, which is the ancestor of F, U, V, and W as well as Y, to represent the sound of the semivowel "w" and gave it name wāw, the Phoenician word for "hook."*

Greek – *The Greeks borrowed the Phoenician alphabet with some modifications. They changed the shape of wāw slightly and altered its name to upsilon. They used upsilon to represent the sound of the vowel "u."*

Roman – *The Romans borrowed the alphabet from the Greeks via the Etruscans, who used a tailless variant of upsilon that ultimately developed into the letter V. After the Romans became acquainted with Greek learning and literature, they re-borrowed upsilon in order to transliterate Greek words in Latin orthography. They also adapted Y, like the other letters of the alphabet, for carving Latin in stone. This monumental script, as it is called, became the basis for modern printed capital letters.*

Medieval – *By medieval times – around 1,200 years ago – the Roman monumental capitals had become adapted to being relatively quickly written on paper, parchment, or vellum. The shape became more curved and could be written with fewer pen strokes. The phonetic value of Y also changed. Because the Greek "u" was different from the Latin, the sounds represented by U and Y diverged until Y acquired the value of I. Like I, Y was then used to represent both the vowel "i" and the semivowel "y." The cursive minuscule alphabet became the basis of modern printed lower-case letters.*

Modern – *Since the invention of printing about 500 years ago the shape of the letter Y has remained unchanged, but its use in English orthography has varied. At first Y was merely a variant of I, but gradually Y alone was used for the semivowel "y," which I and J had formerly also represented. Y also has come to represent several different vowel sounds, as the pronunciation of English has changed and new words have been borrowed.*

---

y or **Y** (wī) *n., pl.* **y's** or **Y's. 1.** The 25th letter of the English alphabet. **2.** Any of the speech sounds represented by this letter. **3.** Anything shaped like the letter **Y**.

Y The symbol for the element yttrium.

–y¹ or **–ey.** A suffix meaning: **1.** Characterized by: **curly, rainy, cloudy. 2.** Like: **clayey, glassy, watery.** [Middle English *-ie, -y, -ey,* from Old English *-ig, -æg.*]

–y². A suffix indicating a condition or quality: **jealousy, beggary.** [Middle English *-ie,* from Old French, from Latin *-ia.*]

–y³ or **–ie.** A suffix indicating: **1.** Smallness: **kiddy, doggy. 2.** Familiarity or endearment: **sweetie, daddy.** [Middle English *-ie.*]

yacht (yät) *n.* A relatively small sailing or motor-driven vessel, gen. with smart, graceful lines, used for pleasure cruises or racing. —*intr.v.* To race, sail, or cruise in a yacht. [From obs. Dutch *jaght(schip),* "chasing (ship)," from *jagen,* to chase, hunt.]

yacht·ing (yät'tĭng) *n.* The sport of sailing in yachts.

yachts·man (yäts'mən) *n.* A person who owns or sails a yacht. —**yachts'man·ship'** *n.*

ya·hoo (yä'hōō, yä'-) *n., pl.* **-hoos.** A crude or brutish person. [After the *Yahoos,* a savage race in *Gulliver's Travels* (1726), by Jonathan Swift.]

Yah·weh (yä'wā) *n.* Also **Yah·veh** (-vā). A name for God used by the ancient Hebrews.

yak¹ (yăk) *n.* A long-haired bovine mammal, *Bos grunniens,* of the mountains of central Asia, where it is often domesticated. [Tibetan *gyag.*]

yak² (yăk) *intr.v.* **yakked, yak·king.** *Slang.* To talk or chatter persistently and meaninglessly. —*n. Slang.* Idle, prolonged chatter. [Imit.]

yam (yăm) *n.* **1.** Any of various chiefly tropical vines of the genus *Dioscorea,* many of which have edible tuberous roots. **2.** The starchy root of such a vine, used in the tropics as food. **3.** A sweet potato with reddish flesh. [Portuguese *inhame,* "edible."]

yang (yăng) *n.* The active, masculine cosmic principle in Chinese dualistic philosophy. [Mandarin *yang²,* the sun.]

yank (yăngk) *tr.v. Informal.* To pull or extract with or as if with a sudden, forceful movement; to jerk. —*intr.v. Informal.* To pull on something suddenly. —See Syns at **jerk.** —*n.* A sudden vigorous pull; a jerk. [Orig. unknown.]

Yank (yăngk) *n. Informal.* A Yankee.

Yan·kee (yăng'kē) *n.* **1.** A native or inhabitant of New England. **2.** A native or inhabitant of a Northern state, esp. a Union soldier during the Civil War. **3.** A native or inhabitant of the United States. [Orig. unknown.]

Yan·kee·ism (yăng'kē-ĭz'əm) *n.* **1.** A Yankee custom or characteristic. **2.** A Yankee peculiarity, as of language or pronunciation.

yap (yăp) *intr.v.* **yapped, yap·ping. 1.** To bark sharply or shrilly; yelp. **2.** *Slang.* To talk noisily or stupidly; jabber. —*n.* **1.** A sharp, shrill bark; yelp. **2.** *Slang.* Noisy, stupid talk; jabbering. **3.** *Slang.* The mouth. [Imit.]

yard¹ (yärd) *n.* **1.** *Abbr.* **yd** The fundamental unit of length in both the U.S. Customary System and the British Imperial System, equal to 0.9144 meter. **2.** *Naut.* A long, tapering pole attached crosswise to a mast to support a sail. [Middle English *yarde,* from Old English *gierd,* staff, twig, measuring rod.]

yard² (yärd) *n.* **1.** A tract of ground next to, surrounding, or surrounded by a building or group of buildings. **2.** A tract of ground, often enclosed, used for a specific work, business, or other activity: *a lumber yard.* **3.** An area provided with a system of tracks where railroad trains are made up and cars are switched, stored, or serviced. **4.** An enclosed tract of ground for livestock. —*tr.v.* To enclose, collect, or put in a yard. [Middle English, from Old English *geard,* enclosure, residence.]

yard·age (yär'dĭj) *n.* **1.** The amount or length of something measured in yards. **2.** Cloth sold by the yard.

yard·arm (yärd'ärm') *n. Naut.* Either end of a yard of a square sail.

yard goods. Cloth sold by the yard.

yard·stick (yärd'stĭk') *n.* **1.** A graduated measuring stick one yard in length. **2.** Any test or standard used in measurement, comparison, or judgment.

ă pat	ā pay	â care	ä father	ĕ pet	ē be	hw which
ōō took	ōō boot	ou out	th thin	*th* this	ŭ cut	

ĭ pit	ī tie	î pier	ŏ pot	ō toe	ô paw, for	oi noise
û urge	zh vision	ə about, item, edible, gallop, circus		

yar·mul·ke (yär′məl-kə, yä′məl-) *n.* A skullcap worn by male Jews, esp. during religious services. [Yiddish, from Polish and Ukrainian *yarmulka.*]

yarmulke

yarrow

yarn (yärn) *n.* **1.** A continuous strand of twisted fibers, as of wool, cotton, or flax used in weaving or knitting. **2.** *Informal.* A long, complicated story. —*intr.v. Informal.* To tell a long, complicated story. [Middle English, from Old English *gearn.*]

yar·row (yăr′ō) *n.* Any of several plants of the genus *Achillea,* esp. *A. millefolium,* native to Eurasia, with finely dissected foliage and flat clusters of usu. white flowers. Also called **milfoil.** [Middle English *yarrowe,* from Old English *gearwe.*]

yaw (yô) *intr.v.* **1.** To turn abruptly or erratically from the intended course; veer: *The ship yawed as the great wave struck it.* **2.** To turn about the vertical axis: *The plane yawed sharply.* —*tr.v.* To cause to yaw. —*n.* **1.** The action of yawing. **2.** The extent of this movement, measured in degrees. [Orig. unknown.]

yawl (yôl) *n.* **1.** A two-masted fore-and-aft-rigged sailing vessel with the shorter mast far to the stern, aft of the tiller. **2.** A ship's small boat, manned by oarsmen. [Middle Low German *jolle.*]

yawn (yôn) *intr.v.* **1.** To open the mouth wide with a deep inward breath, as when sleepy or bored. **2.** To open wide; to gape: *The chasm yawned at our feet.* —*tr.v.* To utter wearily, as if in yawning. —*n.* An act or instance of yawning. [Middle English *yonen,* from Old English *geonian.*] —**yawn′er** *n.*

yaws (yôz) *n.* (used with a sing. or pl. verb). An infectious tropical skin disease, caused by a spirochete, *Treponema pertenue,* and characterized by multiple red pimples. [Cariban.]

y-ax·is (wī′ăk′sĭs) *n., pl.* **y-ax·es** (-sēz). **1.** The vertical axis of a two-dimensional Cartesian coordinate system. **2.** One of three axes in a three-dimensional Cartesian coordinate system.

Yb The symbol for the element ytterbium.

Y-chro·mo·some (wī′krō′mə-sōm′) *n.* The sex chromosome associated with male characteristics, occurring with one X-chromosome in the male sex-chromosome pair.

y-clept (ĭ-klĕpt′) *adj. Archaic.* Known as; named; called. [Middle English *ycleped,* from Old English *gecleopod,* past part. of *cleopian,* to speak, call.]

ye¹ (thē) *adj. Archaic.* The. [Spelling var. of Old English *the,* from the substitution of Y for þ by early printers to represent the sound (th).]

ye² (yē) *pron.* **1.** *Archaic.* You (plural). **2.** *Regional.* You (singular). [Middle English, from Old English *gē.*]

yea (yā) *adv. Archaic.* **1.** Yes; aye. **2.** Indeed; truly. —*n.* **1.** An affirmative statement or vote. **2.** Someone who votes affirmatively. [Middle English *ye,* from Old English *gēa,* yes.]

yeah (yĕ′ə, yă′ə, yă′ə) *adv. Informal.* Yes. [Var. of YEA.]

year (yîr) *n.* **1.** The period of time as measured by the Gregorian calendar in which the earth completes a single revolution around the sun, consisting of 365 days, 5 hours, 49 minutes, and 12 seconds of mean solar time divided into 12 months, 52 weeks, and 365 or 366 days. **2.** A *sidereal year.* **3.** A *tropical year.* **4.** A period of about equal length in other calendars. **5.** Any period of approximately this dura-

tion: *We were married a year ago.* **6.** A period equal to the calendar year but beginning on a different date: *a fiscal year.* **7.** A specific period of time, usu. shorter than 12 months, devoted to some special activity: *the academic year.* **8. years.** Age, esp. old age: *feeling his years.* **9. years.** A long time: *I haven't seen him in years.* [Middle English, from Old English *gēar.*]

year·book (yîr′bŏŏk′) *n.* **1.** A documentary, memorial, or historical book published every year, containing information about the previous year. **2.** A yearly record or book published by the graduating class of a high school or college.

year·ling (yîr′lĭng) *n.* **1.** An animal that is one year old or has not completed its second year. **2.** A thoroughbred racehorse, regarded as a colt or filly one year old dating from January 1 of the year that it was foaled. —*modifier: a yearling calf.*

year·long (yîr′lông′, -lŏng′) *adj.* Lasting one year.

year·ly (yîr′lē) *adv.* Once a year; annually. —*adj.* Happening once a year. —*n., pl.* **-lies.** A publication issued once a year.

yearn (yûrn) *intr.v.* **1.** To have a strong or deep desire; be filled with longing. **2.** To feel deep pity, sympathy, or tenderness: *"he yearns after/you protectively/hopelessly wanting nothing"* (William Carlos Williams). [Middle English *yernen,* from Old English *giernan,* to strive.]

yearn·ing (yûr′nĭng) *n.* A deep longing.

year-round (yîr′round′) *adj.* Existing, active, or continuous throughout the year; during all seasons.

yeast (yēst) *n.* **1.** Any of various unicellular fungi of the genus *Saccharomyces* and related genera, reproducing by budding and capable of fermenting carbohydrates. **2.** Froth consisting of yeast cells together with the carbon dioxide they produce in the process of fermentation, present in or added to fruit juices and other substances in the production of alcoholic beverages. **3.** A commercial preparation containing yeast cells and inert material such as meal, and used esp. as a leavening agent or as a dietary supplement. **4.** An agent of ferment or activity. [Middle English *yest,* from Old English *gist.*]

yeast·y (yē′stē) *adj.* **-i·er, -i·est.** **1.** Of, similar to, or containing yeast. **2.** Causing or characterized by a ferment. **3.** Restless; turbulent. **4.** Frothy; frivolous. —**yeast′i·ness** *n.*

yell (yĕl) *intr.v.* **1.** To cry out loudly, as in pain, fright, surprise, or enthusiasm. —*tr.v.* To utter loudly; to shout. —*n.* **1.** A loud cry; a shriek; shout. **2.** A rhythmic cheer uttered or chanted in unison by a group: *a college yell.* [Middle English *yellen,* from Old English *giellan,* to sound, shout.] —**yell′er** *n.*

yel·low (yĕl′ō) *n.* **1.** The color of ripe lemons or of dandelions. **2.** Something having this color, as the yolk of an egg. **3. yellows.** Any of various plant diseases usu. caused by fungi of the genus *Fusarium* or viruses of the genus *Chlorogenus* and characterized by yellow or yellowish discoloration. —*adj.* **-er, -est.** **1.** Of the color yellow. **2.** *Slang.* Cowardly. —See Syns at **cowardly.** —*tr.v.* To make or render yellow: *Time had yellowed the cloth.* —*intr.v.* To become yellow. [Middle English *yelow,* from Old English *geolu.*] —**yel′low·ly** *adv.* —**yel′low·ness** *n.*

yel·low-bel·lied (yĕl′ō-bĕl′ēd) *adj.* **1.** Having a yellowish belly, as certain birds. **2.** *Slang.* Cowardly.

yellow fever. An acute infectious disease of subtropical and tropical New World areas, caused by a virus transmitted by a mosquito of the genus *Aedes* and characterized by jaundice and dark-colored vomit resulting from hemorrhages.

yel·low·ham·mer (yĕl′ō-hăm′ər) *n.* **1.** A bird, a species of flicker. **2.** A Eurasian bird, *Emberiza citrinella,* with brown and yellow plumage. [By folk ety. from earlier *yelambre.*]

yel·low·ish (yĕl′ō-ĭsh) *adj.* Somewhat yellow.

yellow jack. **1.** Yellow fever. **2.** A yellow flag hoisted by a ship to warn of disease on board. **3.** A silvery and yellowish food fish, *Caranx bartholomaei,* of western Atlantic and Caribbean waters.

yellow jacket. Any of several small wasps of the family *Vespidae,* that have yellow and black markings and usu. nest in the ground.

yellow journalism. Journalism that exploits, distorts, or exaggerates the news to create sensations and attract readers.

yel·low·legs (yĕl'ō-lĕgz') *n., pl.* **yellowlegs.** Either of two North American wading birds, *Totanus melanoleucus* or *T. flavipes,* with yellow legs and a long, narrow bill.

yellow ocher. A yellow pigment, usu. containing limonite.

yellow pine. 1. Any of several North American evergreen trees with yellowish wood, such as *Pinus echinata,* of the southeastern United States, or the ponderosa pine. 2. The wood of any of these trees.

yellow warbler. A small New World bird, *Dendroica petechia,* with predominantly yellow plumage.

yel·low·wood (yĕl'ō-wŏŏd') *n.* 1. A tree, *Cladrastis lutea,* of the southeastern United States, with compound leaves, drooping clusters of white flowers, and yellow wood that yields a yellow dye. 2. Any of various other trees with yellow wood. 3. The wood of any of these trees.

yel·low·y (yĕl'ō-ē) *adj.* Somewhat yellow.

yelp (yĕlp) *intr.v.* 1. To utter a sharp, short bark or cry: *The coyotes yelped in the distance.* 2. To cry out sharply, as in pain or surprise. —*tr.v.* To utter by yelping. —*n.* A sharp, short cry or bark. [Middle English *yelpen,* to cry aloud, from Old English *gielpan,* to boast, exult.] —**yelp'er** *n.*

yen¹ (yĕn) *intr.v.* **yenned, yen·ning.** *Informal.* To yearn; to long. —*n. Informal.* A yearning; a longing. [Cantonese *yan,* addiction.]

yen² (yĕn) *n., pl.* **yen.** The basic monetary unit of Japan.

yen·ta (yĕn'tə) *n. Slang.* A gossipy woman, esp. one who pries into the affairs of others. [Yiddish.]

yeo·man (yō'mən) *n.* 1. An independent farmer, esp. a member of a former class of small freeholding farmers in England. 2. **A yeoman of the guard.** 3. An attendant, servant, or lesser official in a royal or noble household. 4. A petty officer performing chiefly clerical duties in the U.S. Navy. 5. A diligent and dependable worker. —*adj.* Also **yeo·man·ly** (-lē). 1. Relating to or ranking as a yeoman. 2. Befitting a yeoman; sturdy, staunch, or workmanlike. [Middle English *yoman.*]

yeoman of the guard. A member of a ceremonial guard attending the British sovereign and royal family, consisting of 100 yeomen with their officers.

yeo·man·ry (yō'mən-rē) *n.* 1. The class of yeomen; small farmers. 2. A British volunteer cavalry force organized in 1761 to serve as a home guard and later incorporated into the Territorial Army.

yep (yĕp) *adv. Slang.* Yes. [Alteration of YES.]

yes (yĕs) *adv.* It is so; as you say or ask. Used to express affirmation, agreement, positive confirmation, or consent. —*n., pl.* **yes·es.** 1. An affirmative or consenting reply. 2. An affirmative vote or voter. —*tr.v.* **yessed, yes·sing.** To give an affirmative reply to. [Middle English, from Old English *gese.*]

ye·shi·va or **ye·shi·vah** (yə-shē'və) *n.* 1. A Jewish institute of learning where students study the Talmud. 2. An elementary or secondary school with a curriculum that includes Jewish religion and culture as well as general education. [Hebrew *yeshībhāh.*]

yes man. *Informal.* A person who slavishly agrees with his superior; a sycophant.

yes·ter·day (yĕs'tər-dā', -dē) *n.* 1. The day before the present day. 2. Time in the immediate past: *The science fiction of yesterday is the reality of today.* —*adv.* 1. On the day before the present day: *arrived yesterday.* 2. A short while ago. [Middle English *yesterdai,* from Old English *geostran dæg.*]

yes·ter·year (yĕs'tər-yîr') *n.* 1. The year before this one. 2. Time past; years gone by: *the heroes of yesteryear.* [YESTER(DAY) + YEAR.]

yet (yĕt) *adv.* 1. At this time; now: *Don't sing yet.* 2. Up to a specified time; thus far: *The end had not yet come.* 3. In the time remaining; still: *There is yet a solution to be found.* 4. Besides; in addition: *Pay the tape yet another time.* 5. Even; still more: *a yet sadder tale.* 6. Nevertheless: *young yet wise.* 7. At some future time; eventually: *We'll get it right yet.* —*conj.* Nevertheless; and despite this: *He said he would be late, yet he arrived on time.* [Middle English, from Old English *gīet.*]

yet·i (yĕt'ē) *n.* The **abominable snowman.** [Tibetan.]

yew (yōō) *n.* 1. Any of several evergreen trees or shrubs of the genus *Taxus,* of which the flat, dark-green needles and often the scarlet berries are poisonous. 2. The wood of a yew, esp. the durable, fine-grained wood of an Old World species, *T. baccata,* used in cabinetmaking and for archery bows. [Middle English *ew,* from Old English *īw.*]

Ygg·dra·sil (ĭg'drə-sĭl) *n.* Also **Yg·dra·sil.** *Norse Myth.* The great ash tree that holds together earth, heaven, and hell by its roots and branches.

Yid·dish (yĭd'ĭsh) *n.* A High German language with many words borrowed from Hebrew and Slavic that is written in Hebrew characters and spoken chiefly as a vernacular in eastern European Jewish communities and by emigrants from these communities throughout the world. —*adj.* Of or in Yiddish.

yield (yēld) *tr.v.* 1. To give forth; produce; provide. 2. To furnish or give in return; be productive of: *an investment that yields six per cent.* 3. To give up possession of; relinquish. 4. To grant or concede: *yield right of way.* —*intr.v.* 1. To furnish or give a return; be productive. 2. To give up; surrender; submit. 3. To give way to pressure, force, or persuasion: *yielded to her pleas.* 4. To give way to what is stronger or better; be overcome. —*n.* 1. An amount yielded or produced, as of a crop or product. 2. The profit obtained from investment; a return. [Middle English *yieldan,* from Old English *gieldan,* to yield, pay.] —**yield'er** *n.*

Syns: yield, bow, capitulate, fold (Informal), **submit, succumb, surrender** *v. Core Meaning:* To give in from or as if from gradual loss of strength (*yield to a disease; yield to a superior argument*)

yield·ing (yēl'dĭng) *adj.* 1. Giving way readily to pressure: *a soft, yielding substance.* 2. Giving in readily to others; submissive. —**yield'ing·ly** *adv.*

yin (yĭn) *n.* The passive, female cosmic element, force, or principle in Chinese dualistic philosophy. [Mandarin *yin¹,* the moon, shade, femininity.]

yip (yĭp) *n.* A sharp, high-pitched bark; a yelp. —*intr.v.* **yipped, yip·ping.** To make such sounds; to yelp. [Imit.]

yipe (yīp) *interj.* Also **yipes** (yīps). A word used to express surprise, fear, or dismay.

yip·pee (yĭp'ē) *interj.* A word used to express joy.

-yl. A suffix indicating a chemical radical: **carbonyl, ethyl.** [French *-yle,* from Greek *hulē,* wood, matter.]

yo·del (yōd'l) *v.* **-deled** or **-delled, -del·ing** or **-del·ling.** Also **yo·dle, -dled, -dling.** —*intr.v.* To sing so that the voice fluctuates between the normal chest voice and a falsetto. —*tr.v.* To sing (a song) in this fashion. —*n.* A song or cry that is yodeled. [German *jodeln.*] —**yo·del·er** *n.*

yo·ga (yō'gə) *n.* 1. Often **Yoga.** A Hindu discipline aimed at training the consciousness for a condition of perfect spiritual insight and tranquillity. 2. A system of exercises practiced as part of this discipline to promote control of the body and mind. [Sanskrit, union, yoking.]

yo·gi (yō'gē) *n., pl.* **-gis.** A person who practices yoga. [Hindi, from Sanskrit *yogī.*]

yo·gurt (yō'gərt) *n.* Also **yo·ghurt.** A creamy or custardlike food made from milk curdled by certain bacteria and often sweetened or flavored. [Turkish *yogurt.*]

yoke (yōk) *n.* 1. A crossbar with two U-shaped pieces that encircle the necks of a pair of draft animals working in a team. 2. *pl.* **yoke** or **yokes.** A pair of draft animals joined by such a device or trained to work together. 3. A frame or crossbar designed to be carried across a person's shoulders with equal loads suspended from each end. 4. A bar used with a double harness to connect the collar of each horse to the tongue of a wagon or carriage. 5. A clamp or vise that holds a machine part in place or controls its movement or that holds two parts together. 6. A piece of a garment that is closely fitted, either around the neck and shoulders or at the hips, and from which an unfitted or gathered part of the garment is hung. 7. Something that connects or joins together; a bond: *the yoke of matrimony.* 8. Any form or symbol of subjugation or bondage: *the yoke of tyranny.* —*tr.v.* **yoked, yok·ing.** 1. To fit or join with a yoke. 2. **a.** To harness a draft animal to. **b.** To harness (a draft animal) to something: *yoked the oxen to the cart.* 3. To connect, join, or bind together. [Middle English *yok,* from Old English *geoc.*]

yo·kel (yō′kəl) *n.* A simple country person; bumpkin. [Perh. from English dial. *yokel,* green woodpecker.]

yolk (yōk) *n.* **1.** The inner mass of nutritive material in an egg, esp. the yellow, rounded part of a hen's egg, surrounded by the albumen, or white. **2.** A greasy substance found in unprocessed sheep's wool. [Middle English *yolke,* from Old English *geolca,* from *geolu,* yellow.]

yolk sac. A membranous sac attached to the embryo and providing early nourishment in the form of yolk in bony fishes, sharks, reptiles, birds, and primitive mammals, and functioning as the circulatory system of the human embryo prior to the initiation of internal circulation by the pumping of the heart.

Yom Kip·pur (yŏm kĭp′ər, yŏm′ kĭ-pŏŏr′). The holiest Jewish holiday, celebrated on the tenth day after Rosh Hashanah in Sept. or Oct. and observed by fasting, prayer, and atonement for sins or wrongdoing. Also called **Day of Atonement.** [Hebrew *yōm kippūr* : *yōm,* day + *kippūr,* atonement.]

yon (yŏn) *adj. & adv. Archaic.* Yonder. [Middle English, from Old English *geon.*]

yond (yŏnd) *adj. & adv. Archaic.* Yonder. [Middle English, from Old English *geond.*]

yon·der (yŏn′dər) *adj.* Being at an indicated distance, usu. within sight. —*adv.* In or at that indicated place; over there. [Middle English, from *yond,* yon.]

yoo-hoo (yōō′hōō) *interj.* A word used to hail persons.

yore (yôr, yōr) *n.* Time long past: *days of yore.* [Middle English, from Old English *gēara,* formerly, once.]

York·shire pudding (yôrk′shĭr′, -shər). An unsweetened puddinglike preparation made of popover batter baked in meat drippings. [After *Yorkshire,* England.]

Yo·ru·ba (yō′rōō-bä) *n., pl.* **Yoruba** or **-bas. 1.** A member of a West African Negro people living chiefly in southwestern Nigeria. **2.** The language of the Yoruba. —**Yo′ru·ban** *adj.*

you (yōō) *pron.* The second person singular or plural pronoun in the nominative or objective case. **1.** The person or persons addressed by the speaker: *When can I see you?* **2.** One; anyone: *You can't win them all.* —*n.* The individuality of the person being addressed: *Such is the real you.* [Middle English, from Old English *ēow,* dative and accusative of *gē,* ye.]

you-all (yōō-ôl′, yōō′ôl′) *pl. pron. Southeastern U.S.* You. Used in addressing two or more persons or referring to two or more persons, one of whom is addressed.

you'd (yōōd). **1.** You had. **2.** You would.

you'll (yōōl). **1.** You will. **2.** You shall.

young (yŭng) *adj.* **-er, -est. 1.** Being in the early or undeveloped period of life or growth; not old. **2.** Newly begun or formed; not advanced: *The evening is young.* **3.** Having the qualities associated with youth or early life. **4.** Vigorous or fresh; youthful. **5.** Lacking experience; green: *a young hand at plowing.* **6.** Designating the junior of two people having the same name. —*n.* **1.** *(used with a sing. or pl. verb).* Young persons as a group; youth. **2.** Offspring; brood: *a lioness with her young.* —**idiom. with young.** Pregnant. [Middle English *yong,* from Old English *geong.*]

> *Syns:* **young, adolescent, immature, juvenile, youthful** *adj. Core meaning:* Being between childhood and adulthood. Young and youthful are the most general *(the young—or youthful—hero);* both can also suggest the freshness and vigor associated with youth *(young for her age; a youthful face).* Adolescent, juvenile, and immature usu. stress immaturity *(adolescent attitudes; juvenile behavior; immature jokes).*

young·ber·ry (yŭng′bĕr′ē) *n.* **1.** A trailing, prickly hybrid between a blackberry and a dewberry, cultivated in the western United States. **2.** The edible, dark-red berry of this plant. [After B. M. *Young,* 20th-cent. American fruit grower.]

young·ish (yŭng′ĭsh) *adj.* Somewhat young.

young·ling (yŭng′lĭng) *n.* A young person, animal, or plant. —*adj.* Young; immature.

young·ster (yŭng′stər) *n.* **1.** A young person; a child or youth. **2.** A young animal.

Young Turk. A progressive or insurgent member of a political party or other group. [After *Young Turks,* a revolutionary party in 20th cent. Turkey.]

your (yōōr, yôr, yōr; yər *when unstressed*). The possessive form of **you,** used as a modifier before a noun: *your wallet; pursuing your tasks; suffered your first rebuff.* [Middle English, from Old English *ēower,* genitive of *gē,* ye.]

you're (yōōr; yər *when unstressed*). You are.

yours (yōōrz, yôrz, yōrz). **1.** Used to indicate the one or ones belonging to you: *If I can't find my hat, I'll take yours.* **2.** Used in the complimentary closing of letters: *Yours; Very truly yours.* [Middle English *youres,* genitive of *your,* your.]

your·self (yōōr-sĕlf′, yôr-, yōr-, yər-) *pron., pl.* **-selves** (-sĕlvz′). **1.** That one or ones identical to you. Used: **a.** Reflexively as the direct or indirect object of a verb or the object of a preposition: *hurt yourself; give yourself time; talk to yourself.* **b.** For emphasis: *Do it yourself.* **2.** Your normal, healthy condition: *You have not been yourself since your illness.* —*idiom.* **by yourself. 1.** Alone: *You may have to go by yourself.* **2.** Without help: *Don't try to do the job by yourself.*

youth (yōōth) *n., pl.* **youths** (yōōths, yōōthz). **1.** The condition or quality of being young. **2.** An early period of development or existence, esp. the time of life before adulthood. **3.** A young person. **4.** *(used with a sing. or pl. verb).* Young people as a group: *the youth of our city.* [Middle English *youthe,* from Old English *geoguth.*]

youth·ful (yōōth′fəl) *adj.* **1.** Possessing youth; still young: *a youthful hero.* **2.** Of, belonging to, or characteristic of youth: *her youthful face; his youthful impatience.* **3.** In an early stage of development; new. **4.** *Geol.* Having undergone or brought about little erosion: *youthful rivers.* —See Syns at **young.** —**youth′ful·ly** *adv.* —**youth′ful·ness** *n.*

you've (yōōv). You have.

yow (you) *interj.* A word used to express alarm, pain, or surprise.

yowl (youl) *intr.v.* To utter a loud, long, mournful cry; to howl; wail. —*tr.v.* To say or utter with such a cry. —*n.* A loud, mournful cry; a wail. [Middle English *youlen.*]

yo-yo (yō′yō) *n., pl.* **-yos.** A toy in the shape of a spool, around which a string is wound, with the string attached to a finger, the yo-yo being spun down and reeled up by moving the hand. [From a trademark.]

yt·ter·bi·um (ĭ-tûr′bē-əm) *n. Symbol* **Yb** A soft bright silvery rare-earth element occurring in two allotropic forms and used as an x-ray source for portable irradiation devices, in some laser materials, and in some special alloys. Atomic number 70; atomic weight 173.04; melting point 824°C; boiling point 1,427°C; specific gravity 6.977 or 6.54 depending on allotropic form; valences 2, 3. [After *Ytterby,* Sweden, where it was discovered.] —**yt·ter′bic** (ĭ-tûr′bĭk) *adj.*

yt·tri·um (ĭt′rē-əm) *n. Symbol* **Y** A silvery metallic element, not a rare earth but occurring in nearly all rare-earth minerals, used in various metallurgical applications, notably to increase the strength of magnesium and aluminum alloys. Atomic number 39; atomic weight 88.905; melting point 1,495°C; boiling point 2,927°C; specific gravity 4.45; valence 3. [After *Ytterby,* Sweden.] —**yt′tric** (ĭt′rĭk) *adj.*

yu·an (yü-än′) *n., pl.* **yuan** or **yuans.** The basic monetary unit of China. [Mandarin *yüan²,* round (thing), dollar.]

yuc·ca (yŭk′ə) *n.* Any of various chiefly tropical New World plants of the genus *Yucca,* often tall and stout-stemmed, and with a terminal cluster of white flowers. [Spanish *yuca.*]

Yule or **yule** (yōōl) *n.* Christmas or the season or feast celebrating Christmas. [Middle English, from Old English *gēol.*]

Yule log or **yule log.** A large log traditionally burned in the fireplace at Christmas.

Yule·tide or **yuletide** (yōōl′tīd′) *n.* The Christmas season.

yum·my (yŭm′ē) *adj.* **-mi·er, -mi·est.** *Slang.* Delicious. —See Syns at **delicious.** [From *yum,* imit. of the sound made by the lips while eating.]

yurt (yŭrt) *n.* A circular, domed, portable tent used by the nomadic Mongols of Siberia. [Russian *yurta.*]

y·wis (ĭ-wĭs′) *adv. Archaic.* Var. of **iwis.**

| ă pat | ā pay | â care | ä father | ĕ pet | ē be | hw which | ĭ pit | ī tie | î pier | ŏ pot | ō toe | ô paw, for | oi noise |
| ōō took | ōō boot | ou out | th thin | *th* this | ŭ cut | | û urge | zh vision | ə about, item, edible, gallop, circus |

Zz

z	z	Z	z	Zz
Phoenician	Greek	Roman	Medieval	Modern

Phoenician – *About 3,000 years ago the Phoenicians and other Semitic peoples began to use graphic signs to represent individual speech sounds instead of syllables or whole words. They used this symbol to represent the sound of the consonant "z" and gave it the name zayin.*

Greek – *The Greeks borrowed the Phoenician alphabet with some modifications. They kept the shape of zayin but changed its name to zēta. They used zēta to represent the sound of the consonant "z" as zayin did in Phoenician.*

Roman – *The Romans borrowed the alphabet from the Greeks via the Etruscans. Since Latin had no "z" sound, the Romans at first omitted Z from their alphabet, but after they had become acquainted with Greek learning and literature*

they borrowed it directly from Greek in order to transliterate Greek words in Latin orthography. They adapted Z, like the other letters of the alphabet, for carving Latin in stone. This monumental script, as it is called, became the basis for modern printed capital letters.

Medieval – *By medieval times – around 1,200 years ago – the Roman monumental capitals had become adapted to being relatively quickly written on paper, parchment, or vellum. The cursive minuscule alphabet became the basis of modern printed lower-case letters.*

Modern – *Since the invention of printing about 500 years ago the shape and the phonetic value of the letter Z have remained unchanged.*

---

z or **Z** (zē; *Brit.* zĕd) *n., pl.* **z's** or **Z's.** The 26th letter of the English alphabet.

za·ny (zā′nē) *n., pl.* **-nies. 1.** A clown; buffoon. **2.** A comical person given to extravagant or outlandish behavior. —*adj.* **-ni·er, -ni·est. 1.** Ludicrously comical; clownish; droll. **2.** Comical in an outlandish or extravagant way; absurd. —See Syns at **foolish.** [Italian *zanni,* buffoon, from *Zanni,* nickname for *Giovanni,* John.]

zap (zăp) *tr.v.* **zapped, zap·ping.** *Slang.* **1.** To destroy or kill with or as if with a burst of gunfire, flame, or electric current. **2.** To attack (an enemy in warfare) with heavy firepower; strafe or bombard. —See Syns at **kill** and **murder.** [Imit.]

zeal (zēl) *n.* Enthusiastic and diligent devotion in pursuit of a cause, ideal, or goal; ardor; fervor. —See Syns at **passion.** [Middle English *zele,* from Late Latin *zēlus,* from Greek *zēlos.*]

zeal·ot (zĕl′ət) *n.* A person who is intensely or fanatically devoted to a cause. [Late Latin *zēlōtēs,* from Greek, from *zēlos,* zeal.]

zeal·ous (zĕl′əs) *adj.* Filled with or motivated by zeal; ardent; fervent. —**zeal′ous·ly** *adv.* —**zeal′ous·ness** *n.*

ze·bec or **ze·beck** (zē′bĕk′) *n.* Vars. of **xebec.**

ze·bra (zē′brə) *n.* Any of several horselike African mammals of the genus *Equus,* with characteristic overall markings of conspicuous dark and whitish stripes. [Portuguese, from Spanish, wild ass.]

ze·bu (zē′byōō) *n.* A domesticated bovine mammal, *Bos indicus,* of Asia and Africa, with a prominent hump on the back and a large dewlap. [French *zébu.*]

zed (zĕd) *n. Brit.* The letter z. [Middle English, from

Old French *zede,* from Late Latin *zēta,* zeta.]

Zeit·geist (tsīt′gīst′) *n. German.* The spirit of the time; the taste and outlook characteristic of a period.

Zen Buddhism (zĕn). A Chinese and Japanese school of Mahayana Buddhism that asserts that enlightenment can be attained through meditation, self-contemplation, and intuition rather than through the scriptures. Also called **Zen.** [Japanese *zen,* ult. from Sanskrit *dhyāna,* meditation, from *dhyāti,* he meditates.] —**Zen Buddhist.**

Zend-A·ves·ta (zĕn′də-vĕs′tə) *n.* The entire body of sacred writings of the Zoroastrian religion. Also called **Zend.** [Persian *zandavastā.*]

ze·nith (zē′nĭth) *n.* **1.** The point on the celestial sphere that is directly above the observer. **2. a.** The highest part of the sky, directly overhead. **b.** The highest point above the horizon to which a celestial body, as seen by an observer, rises. **3.** The highest point; peak; acme: *the zenith of success.* [Middle English, from Old French *cenith,* from Old Spanish *zenit,* from Arabic *samt ar-ra's,* road (over) the head.]

zeph·yr (zĕf′ər) *n.* **1. a.** The west wind. **b.** A gentle breeze. **2.** Any of various light, soft fabrics, yarns, or garments. **3.** Any airy, insubstantial, or passing thing. [Middle English *zephirus,* from Latin *zephyrus,* from Greek *zephuros.*]

zep·pe·lin (zĕp′ə-lĭn) *n.* Also **Zep·pe·lin.** A rigid airship with a long, cylindrical body supported by internal gas cells. [After Count Ferdinand von *Zeppelin* (1838–1917), German aeronautic designer.]

ze·ro (zîr′ō, zē′rō) *n., pl.* **-ros** or **-roes. 1.** The numerical symbol "0"; a cipher; nought. **2.** *Math.* **a.** An element of a set that when added to any other element in the set pro-

zebra   zeppelin

---

duces a sum identical with the element to which it is added. **b.** A cardinal number indicating the absence of any or all units under consideration. **c.** An ordinal number indicating an initial point or origin. **d.** An argument at which the value of a function vanishes. **3.** The temperature indicated by the numeral 0 on a thermometer. **4.** Someone or something having no influence or importance; nonentity. **5.** The lowest point: *His prospects were set at zero.* **6.** Nothing; nil. —*adj.* **1.** Of or being zero: *a zero growth rate.* **2. a.** Having no measurable or otherwise determinable value. **b.** Absent, inoperative, or irrelevant in specified circumstances: *zero gravity; zero visibility.* —*tr.v.* **-roed, -ro·ing.** To adjust (an instrument or device) to zero value. —*phrasal verb.* **zero in. 1.** To aim or concentrate firepower on an exact target location. **2.** To adjust the aim or sight of by repeated firings: *zero in a new rifle.* **3.** To converge intently; close in: *zero in on the cause of a problem.* [French *zéro,* from Italian *zero,* from Medieval Latin *zephirum,* from Arabic *sifr,* zero, cipher.]

zero hour. The scheduled time for the start of an operation or action, esp. a concerted military attack.

zero population growth. The limiting of population increase to the number of live births needed to replace the existing population.

zest (zěst) *n.* **1.** Added flavor or interest; piquancy; charm: *Spices give zest to simple foods.* **2.** Spirited enjoyment; wholehearted interest; gusto: *"At fifty-three he retains all the heady zest of adolescence"* (Kenneth Tynan). **3.** The outermost part of the rind of an orange or lemon, used as flavoring. [French, orange or lemon peel.] —**zest'y** *adj.*

      Syns: *zest, gusto, relish n. Core meaning:* Spirited enjoyment *(ate with zest).*

zest·ful (zěst'fəl) *adj.* Full of or showing zest. —**zest'ful·ly** *adv.*

ze·ta (zā'tə, zē'-) *n.* The sixth letter in the Greek alphabet, written Z, ζ. [Late Latin *zēta,* from Greek.]

Zeus (zoos) *n.* The presiding god of the Greek pantheon, ruler of the heavens and father of other gods and mortal heroes.

zig·gu·rat (zĭg'ə-rāt') *n.* A temple tower of the ancient Assyrians and Babylonians, that has the form of a terraced pyramid of successively receding stories. [Assyrian *ziqquratu,* summit, mountain top.]

zig·zag (zĭg'zǎg') *n.* **1.** A line or course that proceeds by sharp turns in alternating directions. **2.** One of a series of such sharp turns. **3.** Something exhibiting one or a series of sharp turns, such as a road or design. —*adj.* Having a zigzag: *a zigzag path.* —*adv.* In a zigzag manner or pattern. —*v.* **-zagged, -zag·ging.** —*intr.v.* To move in or form a zigzag: *The trail zigzagged up the mountain.* —*tr.v.* To cause to move in or form a zigzag. [French, from German *Zickzack.*] —**zig'zag'ger** *n.*

zilch (zĭlch) *n. Slang.* Zero; nothing. [Alteration of ZERO.]

zil·lion (zĭl'yən) *n. Informal.* An extremely large indefinite number. [Z + (M)ILLION.]

zinc (zĭngk) *n. Symbol* **Zn** A bluish-white, lustrous metallic element that is brittle at room temperatures but malleable with heating, used to form a wide variety of alloys including brass, bronze, German silver, various solders, and nickel silver, in galvanizing iron and other metals, for electric fuses, anodes, and meter cases, and in roofing, gutters, and various household objects. Atomic number 30; atomic weight 65.37; melting point 419.4°C; boiling point 907°C; specific gravity 7.133 (25°C); valence 2. —*tr.v.* **zinced** or **zincked, zinc·ing** or **zinck·ing.** To coat or treat with zinc; galvanize. [German *Zink.*]

zinc blende. A mineral, sphalerite.

zinc ointment. *Medicine.* A salve consisting of about 20 per cent zinc oxide with beeswax or paraffin and petrolatum, used in the treatment of skin diseases.

zinc oxide. An amorphous white or yellowish powder, ZnO, used as a pigment, in compounding rubber, and in pharmaceuticals and cosmetics.

zinc sulfide. A yellowish-white, flourescent compound, ZnS, used as a pigment and in television screens and other luminous objects.

zin·fan·del (zĭn'fən-děl') *n.* Also **Zin·fan·del.** A dry red table wine from California. [Orig. unknown.]

zing (zĭng) *n.* A brief high-pitched humming or buzzing

sound, such as that made by a swiftly passing object or a taut vibrating string. —*intr.v.* To make or move with such a sound. [Imit.]

zin·ni·a (zĭn'ē-ə) *n.* Any of various plants of the genus *Zinnia,* native to tropical America; esp., *Z. elegans,* widely cultivated for its showy, variously colored flowers. [After Johann Gottfried *Zinn* (1727–59), German botanist and physician.]

Zi·on (zī'ən) *n.* Also **Si·on** (sī'ən). **1. a.** The Jewish people; Israel. **b.** The Jewish homeland as a symbol of Judaism. **2.** A place or religious community regarded as sacredly devoted to God; a city of God. **3.** Heaven. **4.** An idealized harmonious community; a utopia.

Zi·on·ism (zī'ə-nĭz'əm) *n.* **1.** A plan or movement of the Jewish people to return from the Diaspora to Palestine. **2.** A movement orig. aimed at the re-establishment of a Jewish national homeland and state in Palestine and now concerned with development of Israel. —**Zi'on·ist** *adj. & n.* —**Zi'on·is'tic** *adj.*

zip (zĭp) *n.* **1.** A brief, sharp, hissing sound, such as that made by a flying arrow. **2.** *Informal.* Energetic activity; alacrity; vim. —See Syns at **spirit.** —*v.* **zipped, zip·ping.** —*intr.v.* **1.** To move with a sharp, hissing sound. **2.** To move or act with a speed that suggests such a sound. **3.** To become fastened or unfastened by a zipper. —*tr.v.* **1.** To give speed and force to. **2.** To impart life or zest to. **3.** To fasten or unfasten with a zipper. —See Syns at **rush.** [Imit.]

Zip Code. Also **zip code. 1.** A system for speeding and simplifying the delivery of mail by assigning a number to each delivery area in the United States. **2.** One of the set of code numbers used in this system. [Z(ONE) I(MPROVEMENT) P(ROGRAM).]

zip·per (zĭp'ər) *n.* A fastening device consisting of parallel rows of metal or nylon teeth on adjacent edges of an opening which are interlocked by a sliding tab. [From a trademark.]

zip·py (zĭp'ē) *adj.* **-pi·er, -pi·est.** Full of energy; brisk; lively; snappy.

zir·con (zûr'kŏn') *n.* A brown to colorless mineral, essentially $ZrSiO_4$, which is heated, cut, and polished to form a brilliant blue-white gem. [German *Zirkon,* from French *jargon,* from Italian *giargone,* from Arabic *zarqūn,* from Persian *zargūn,* gold-colored.]

zir·co·ni·um (zûr-kō'nē-əm) *n. Symbol* **Zr** A lustrous, grayish-white, strong, ductile metallic element obtained primarily from zircon and used chiefly in ceramic and refractory compounds, as an alloying agent, in nuclear reactors, and in medical prostheses. Atomic number 40; atomic weight 91.22; melting point 1,852°C; boiling point 3,578°C; specific gravity 6.53 (calculated), principal valence 4.

zith·er (zĭth'ər, zĭth'-) *n.* A musical instrument consisting of a flat sounding box with about 30 to 40 strings stretched over it and played horizontally with the fingertips or a plectrum. [German *Zither,* from Old High German *zithera,* from Latin *cithara,* from Greek *kithara,* cithara.] —**zith'er·ist** *n.*

zither

Zn The symbol for the element zinc.

-zoan. *Zool.* A suffix meaning individual (within a taxonomic group): **protozoan.** [From New Latin *-zoa,* animals (in taxonomic groups), ult. from Greek *zōion,* animal.]

zo·di·ac (zō'dē-ăk') *n.* **1. a.** *Astron.* A band of the celestial sphere, extending about eight degrees to either side of the ecliptic, that represents the path of the principal planets, the moon, and the sun. **b.** *Astrol.* This band divided into 12 equal parts called signs, each 30 degrees wide, bearing the name of a constellation for which it was orig. named but with which it no longer coincides owing to the precession of the equinoxes. **2.** A diagram or figure representing the zodiac. [Middle English, from Old French *zodiaque*, from Latin *zōdiacus*, from Greek *zōidiakos (kuklos)*, (circle) of the zodiac, from *zōion*, animal.] **—zo·di'a·cal** (zō-dī'ə-kəl) *adj.*

–zoic. A suffix meaning: **1.** A specific kind of animal existence: **epizoic. 2.** A specific geological division: **Mesozoic.** [From Greek *zōikos*, of animals, from *zōion*, animal.]

zom·bie (zŏm'bē) *n.* Also **zom·bi** *pl.* **-bis. 1.** In voodoo belief or folklore, a corpse revived by sorcery to be the slave of the sorcerer. **2.** A person who looks or behaves like a reanimated corpse. [From a native African word.]

zon·al (zō'nəl) *adj.* **1.** Of or associated with a zone or zones. **2.** Divided into zones. **—zon'al·ly** *adv.*

zone (zōn) *n.* **1.** An area, region, or division distinguished from adjacent parts by some distinctive feature or character: *a time zone; a postal zone.* **2. a.** Any of the five regions of the surface of the earth that are loosely divided according to prevailing climate and latitude, including the Torrid Zone, the North and South Temperate Zones, and the North and South Frigid Zones. **b.** A similar division on any planet. **c.** *Geom.* A portion of a sphere bounded by the intersections of two parallel planes with the sphere. **3.** *Ecol.* An area characterized by distinct physical conditions and populated by communities of certain kinds of organisms. **4.** *Geol.* A region or stratum distinguished by composition or content. **5.** An area in a city designated for a particular type of building, enterprise, or activity: *residential zone.* **6.** *Archaic.* A belt or girdle. **—tr.v. zoned, zon·ing. 1.** To divide into zones. **2.** To designate or mark off into zones. **3.** To surround or encircle with or as if with a belt or girdle. [Latin *zōna*, girdle, zone, from Greek *zōnē*.]

zonked (zŏngkt) *adj.* *Slang.* Intoxicated by alcohol or a narcotic; high. [Orig. unknown.]

zoo (zōō) *n., pl.* **zoos.** A park or institution in which living animals are kept and exhibited to the public. Also called **zoological garden.** [Short for ZOOLOGICAL GARDEN.]

zoo–. A prefix meaning animal: **zoology.** [From Greek *zōon*, living being, animal.]

zo·o·ge·og·ra·phy (zō'ə-jē-ŏg'rə-fē) *n.* The biological study of the geographical distribution of animals. **—zo'o·ge·og'·ra·pher** *n.* **—zo'o·ge'o·graph'ic** (-ə-grăf'ĭk) or **zo'o·ge'o·graph'i·cal** (-ĭ-kəl) *adj.* **—zo'o·ge'o·graph'i·cal·ly** *adv.*

zo·og·ra·phy (zō-ŏg'rə-fē) *n.* The biological description of animals. **—zo'o·graph'ic** (zō'ə-grăf'ĭk) or **zo'o·graph'ic·al** *adj.*

zo·o·log·i·cal (zō'ə-lŏj'ĭ-kəl) or **zo·o·log·ic** (-lŏj'ĭk) *adj.* **1.** Of animals or animal life. **2.** Of the science of zoology. **—zo'o·log'i·cal·ly** *adv.*

zoological garden. A zoo.

zo·ol·o·gy (zō-ŏl'ə-jē) *n., pl.* **-gies. 1.** The biological science of animals. **2.** The animal life of a particular area. **3.** The characteristics of an animal group or category. [ZOO- + -LOGY.] **—zo·ol'o·gist** *n.*

zoom (zōōm) *intr.v.* **1.** To make a continuous low-pitched buzzing or humming sound. **2.** To move while making such a sound: *The jets zoomed low over the airfield.* **3.** To climb suddenly and sharply, as in an airplane. **4. a.** To move very quickly. **b.** To move rapidly up or down: *Expenses zoomed as prices rose. The skiers zoomed down the slopes.* **5. a.** To move rapidly toward or away from a photographic subject: *The camera zoomed in for a close-up.* **b.** To simulate such a movement, as by means of a zoom lens. **—tr.v.** To cause to zoom. **—n.** The act or sound of zooming. —See Syns at **rush.** [Imit.]

zoom lens. A camera lens whose focal length can be rapidly changed, allowing rapid change in the size of an image.

-zoon. A suffix meaning an individual animal or independently moving organic unit: **spermatozoon.** [From Greek *zōion*, animal.

zo·o·spore (zō'ə-spôr', -spōr') *n.* A motile, flagellated asexual spore, as of certain algae and fungi. **—zo'o·spor'ic** or **zo'o·spor'ous** *adj.*

Zo·ro·as·tri·an·ism (zôr'ō-ăs'trē-ə-nĭz'əm) *n.* The ancient Persian religion, founded by the prophet Zoroaster in the sixth cent. B.C. and set forth in the Zend-Avesta, teaching the worship of Ormazd in the context of a universal struggle between the forces of light and of darkness. **—Zo'ro·as'tri·an** *adj. & n.*

zounds (zoundz) *interj.* Also **swounds** (zwoundz, zoundz). A word used to express anger, surprise, or indignation. [Euphemism for *God's wounds.*]

zoy·si·a (zoi'sē-ə, -zē-ə) *n.* Any of several creeping grasses of the genus *Zoysia,* native to Asia and Australia, and widely cultivated as a lawn grass. [After Karl von Zois (d. 1800), German botanist.]

Zr The symbol for the element zirconium.

zuc·chet·to (zōō-kĕt'ō, tsōō-) *n., pl.* **-tos.** A small skullcap worn by Roman Catholic clergymen, varying in color with the rank of the wearer. [Italian, from *zucca,* gourd, head, from Late Latin *cucutia,* gourd.]

zuc·chi·ni (zōō-kē'nē) *n., pl.* **zucchini.** A variety of squash with a long, narrow shape and a dark-green rind. [Italian, pl. of *zuchino,* dim. of *zucca,* gourd.]

Zu·lu (zōō'lōō) *n., pl.* **Zulu** or **-lus. 1.** A member of a large Bantu nation of southeastern Africa. **2.** The Bantu language of the Zulus. **—adj.** Of or relating to the Zulus, their culture, or their language.

zwie·back (zwī'băk', -bäk', zwē'-, swī'-) *n.* A type of biscuit first baked in the form of a slightly sweetened loaf of bread and then sliced and oven-toasted. [German *Zwieback,* "twice-baked (bread)."]

Zwing·li·an (zwĭng'lē-ən, tsfĭng'-) *adj.* Of the 16th-cent. Swiss religious reformer Zwingli or his theological system, esp. his doctrine that the physical body of Christ is not present in the Eucharist and that the ceremony is merely a symbolic commemoration of Christ's death. **—Zwing'li·an** *n.* **—Zwing'li·an·ism** *n.*

zy·go·ma (zī-gō'mə) *n., pl.* **-ma·ta** (-mə-tə) or **-mas. 1.** The zygomatic bone. **2.** The zygomatic arch. **3.** The zygomatic process. [From Greek *zugōma,* bolt, bar, yoke, from *zugoun,* to yoke, connect.] **—zy'go·mat'ic** (zī'gə-măt'ĭk) *adj.*

zygomatic arch. The bony arch in vertebrates that extends along the side of the skull beneath the orbit.

zygomatic bone. The cheekbone.

zygomatic process. Any of the three processes that articulate to make up the zygomatic arch.

zy·go·spore (zī'gə-spôr', -spōr') *n.* A thick-walled resting spore formed by conjugation of similar gametes, as in algae or fungi. [Greek *zygon,* yoke + SPORE.]

zy·gote (zī'gōt') *n.* **1.** The cell formed by the union of two gametes. **2.** The organism that develops from such a cell as characterized by its genetic constitution and subsequent development. [Greek *zugōtos,* joined, yoked, from *zugoun,* to join, yoke.] **—zy·got'ic** (zī-gŏt'ĭk) *adj.* **—zy·got'i·cal·ly** *adv.*

zym–. Var. of **zymo–.**

zy·mase (zī'mās', -māz') *n.* The enzyme complex found in yeasts, bacteria, and higher plants and animals that acts in glycolysis. [ZYM(O)- + -ASE.]

–zyme. A suffix meaning enzyme: **lysozyme.** [From Greek *zumē,* leaven.]

zymo– or **zym–.** A prefix meaning fermentation: **zymase.** [From Greek *zumē,* leaven.]

zy·mo·gen (zī'mə-jən) *n.* The inactive protein precursor of an enzyme.

zy·mo·gen·ic (zī'mə-jĕn'ĭk) *adj.* Also **zy·mog·e·nous** (zī-mŏj'ə-nəs). **1.** Of a zymogen. **2.** Capable of causing fermentation. **3.** Enzyme-producing.

zy·mol·o·gy (zī-mŏl'ə-jē) *n.* The chemistry of fermentation. **—zy'mo·log'ic** (-mə-lŏj'ĭk) or **zy'mo·log'i·cal** *adj.* **—zy·mol'·o·gist** *n.*

zy·mur·gy (zī'mûr-jē) *n.* The manufacturing chemistry of fermentation processes in brewing.

zyz·zy·va (zĭz'ə-və) *n.* Any of various tropical American weevils of the genus *Zyzzyva,* often destructive to plants. [New Latin *Zyzzyva.*]

| ă pat | ā pay | â care | ä father | ĕ pet | ē be | hw which | ĭ pit | ī tie | î pier | ŏ pot | ō toe | ô paw, for | oi noise |
| ōō took | ōō boot | ou out | th thin | th this | ŭ cut | | û urge | zh vision | ə about, item, edible, gallop, circus |

GUIDE TO THE METRIC SYSTEM

Length

Unit	Number of Meters	Approximate U.S. Equivalent
myriameter	10,000	6.2 miles
kilometer	1,000	0.62 mile
hectometer	100	109.36 yards
dekameter	10	32.81 feet
meter	1	39.37 inches
decimeter	0.1	3.94 inches
centimeter	0.01	0.39 inch
millimeter	0.001	0.04 inch

Area

Unit	Number of Square Meters	Approximate U.S. Equivalent
square kilometer	1,000,000	0.3861 square mile
hectare	10,000	2.47 acres
are	100	119.60 square yards
centare	1	10.76 square feet
square centimeter	0.0001	0.115 square inch

Volume

Unit	Number of Cubic Meters	Approximate U.S. Equivalent
dekastere	10	13.10 cubic yards
stere	1	1.31 cubic yards
decistere	0.10	3.53 cubic feet
cubic centimeter	0.000001	0.061 cubic inch

Mass and Weight

Unit	Number of Grams	Approximate U.S. Equivalent
metric ton	1,000,000	1.1 tons
quintal	100,000	220.46 pounds
kilogram	1,000	2.2046 pounds
hectogram	100	3.527 ounces
dekagram	10	0.353 ounce
gram	1	0.035 ounce
decigram	0.10	1.543 grains
centigram	0.01	0.154 grain
milligram	0.001	0.015 grain

METRIC CONVERSION CHART — APPROXIMATIONS

When You Know	Multiply By	To Find
Length		
millimeters	0.04	inches
centimeters	0.4	inches
meters	3.3	feet
meters	1.1	yards
kilometers	0.6	miles
inches	25	millimeters
inches	2.5	centimeters
feet	30·	centimeters
yards	0.9	meters
miles	1.6	kilometers
Area		
square centimeters	0.16	square inches
square meters	1.2	square yards
square kilometers	0.4	square miles
hectares (10,000m²)	2.5	acres
square inches	6.5	square centimeters
square feet	0.09	square meters
Area		
square yards	0.8	square meters
square miles	2.6	square kilometers
acres	0.4	hectares
Mass and Weight		
grams	0.035	ounce
kilograms	2.2	pounds
tons (100kg)	1.1	short tons
ounces	28	grams
pounds	0.45	kilograms
short tons (2000 lb)	0.9	tons
Volume		
milliliters	0.2	teaspoons
milliliters	0.06	tablespoons
milliliters	0.03	fluid ounces
liters	4.2	cups
liters	2.1	pints

Capacity

Unit	Number of Liters	Cubic	Approximate U.S. Equivalents Dry	Liquid
kiloliter	1,000	1.31 cubic yards		
hectoliter	100	3.53 cubic feet	2.84 bushels	
dekaliter	10	0.35 cubic foot	1.14 pecks	2.64 gallons
liter	1	61.02 cubic inches	0.908 quart	1.057 quarts
deciliter	0.10	6.1 cubic inches	0.18 pint	0.21 pint
centiliter	0.01	0.6 cubic inch		0.338 fluid ounce
milliliter	0.001	0.06 cubic inch		0.27 fluid dram

METRIC CONVERSION CHART — APPROXIMATIONS

When You Know	Multiply By	To Find	When You Know	Multiply By	To Find
Volume				**Volume**	
liters	1.06	quarts	cubic feet	0.03	cubic meters
liters	0.26	gallons	cubic yards	0.76	cubic meters
cubic meters	35	cubic feet			
cubic meters	1.3	cubic yards		**Speed**	
teaspoons	5	milliliters	miles per hour	1.6	kilometers per hour
tablespoons	15	milliliters	kilometers per hour	0.6	miles per hour
fluid ounces	30	milliliters			
cups	0.24	liters		**Temperature** (exact)	
pints	0.47	liters	Celsius temp.	9/5, +32	Fahrenheit temp.
quarts	0.95	liters	Fahrenheit temp.	−32, 5/9 x	
gallons	3.8	liters		remainder	Celsius temp.

PERIODIC TABLE OF THE ELEMENTS

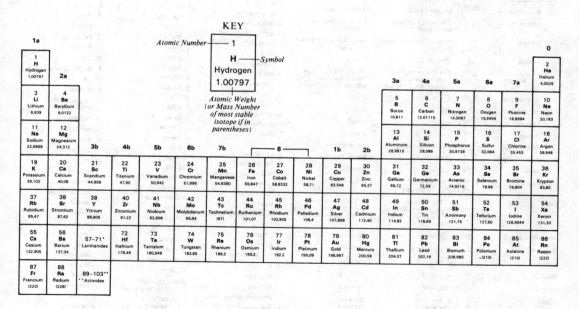

PROOFREADERS' MARKS

Instruction	Mark in Margin	Mark in Type	Corrected Type
Delete	ℯ	the ~~good~~ word	the word
Insert indicated material	good	the‸word	the good word
Let it stand	(stet)	the ~~good~~ word (dotted underline)	the good word
Make capital	(cap)	the word (triple underline)	the Word
Make lower case	(lc)	/The Word	the Word
Set in small capitals	(SC)	See word. (double underline)	See WORD.
Set in italic type	(ital)	The word is word. (underline)	The word is *word.*
Set in roman type	(rom)	the (word)	the word
Set in boldface type	(bf)	the entry word (wavy underline)	the entry **word**
Set in lightface type	(lf)	the entry (**word**)	the entry word
Transpose	(tr)	the word good (transposed)	the good word
Close up space	⁀	the wo‿rd	the word
Delete and close up space	ℯ with close-up	the woord	the word
Spell out	(sp)	(2) words	two words
Insert: space	#	the/word	the word
period	⊙	This is the word‸	This is the word.
comma	‸,	words‸ words, words	words, words, words
hyphen	=/=/	word‸for‸word test	word-for-word test
colon	(:)	The following words‸	The following words:
semicolon	;	Scan the words‸ skim the words.	Scan the words; skim the words.
apostrophe	’	Johns words	John's words
quotation marks	“/”/	the word word	the word "word"
parentheses	(/)/	The word‸word‸is in parentheses.	The word (word) is in parentheses.
brackets	[/]/	He read from the Word ‸the Bible‸	He read from the Word [the Bible].
en dash	1/N	1964‸1972	1964–1972
em dash	1/M / 1/M /	The dictionary‸how often it is needed‸ belongs in every home.	The dictionary—how often it is needed—belongs in every home.
superior type	2	2 = 4	$2^2 = 4$
inferior type	2	HO	H_2O
asterisk	*	word	word*
dagger	†	a word‸	a word†
double dagger	‡	words and words‸	words and words‡
section symbol	§	‸Book Reviews	§Book Reviews
virgule	/	either‸or	either/or
Start paragraph	¶	"Where is it?" ‸"It's on the shelf."	"Where is it?" "It's on the shelf."
Run in	(run in)	The entry word is printed in boldface. The pronunciation follows.	The entry word is printed in boldface. The pronunciation follows.
Turn right side up	↻	the word	the word
Move left	⊏	⊏ the word	the word
Move right	⊐	the word	the word
Move up	⊓	the word	the word
Move down	⊔	the word	the word
Align	‖	the word / the word / the word	the word / the word / the word
Straighten line	=	the word	the word
Wrong font	(wf)	the word	the word
Broken type	×	the word	the word

SYMBOLS AND SIGNS

+ plus
− minus
± plus or minus
∓ minus or plus
× multiplied by
÷ divided by
= equal to
≠ or ≠ not equal to
≈ or ≒ nearly equal to
≡ identical with
≢ not identical with
⇔ equivalent
∼ difference
≅ congruent to
> greater than
≯ not greater than
< less than
≮ not less than
≧ or ≥ greater than or equal to
≦ or ≤ less than or equal to
| | absolute value
∪ logical sum or union
∩ logical product or intersection
⊂ is contained in
∈ is a member of; permittivity; mean error
: is to; ratio
:: as; proportion
≐ approaches
→ approaches limit of
∝ varies as
∥ parallel
⊥ perpendicular
∠ angle
∟ right angle
△ triangle
□ square
▭ rectangle
▱ parallelogram
○ circle
⌒ arc of circle
≟ equilateral
≙ equiangular
√ radical; root; square root
∛ cube root
∜ fourth root
Σ sum
! or ⌊ factorial product
∞ infinity
∫ integral
ƒ function
∂ or δ differential; variation
π pi
∴ therefore
∵ because
‾ vinculum (above letter)
( ) parentheses
[ ] brackets
{ } braces
° degree
′ minute
″ second
Δ increment
ω angular frequency; solid angle
Ω ohm
μΩ microhm
MΩ megohm
Φ magnetic flux
Ψ dielectric flux; electrostatic flux
ρ resistivity
Λ equivalent conductivity
ℛ reluctance
→ direction of flow
⇄ electric current
⬭ benzene ring
→ yields
⇄ reversible reaction
↓ precipitate
↑ gas
‰ salinity
⊙ or ☼ sun
● or ● new moon
☽ first quarter
○ or ⊛ full moon
☾ last quarter
☿ Mercury
♀ Venus
⊖ or ⊕ Earth
♂ Mars
♃ Jupiter
♄ Saturn
♅ Uranus
♆ Neptune
♇ Pluto
♈ Aries
♉ Taurus
♊ Gemini
♋ Cancer
♌ Leo
♍ Virgo
♎ Libra
♏ Scorpius
♐ Sagittarius
♑ Capricornus
♒ Aquarius
♓ Pisces
☌ conjunction
☍ opposition
△ trine
□ quadrature
✶ sextile
☊ dragon's head, ascending node
☋ dragon's tail, descending node
◉ rain
✱ snow
⊠ snow on ground
⟵ floating ice crystals
▲ hail
△ sleet
∨ frostwork
⊔ hoarfrost
≡ fog
∞ haze; dust haze
T thunder
⟨ sheet lightning
⦶ solar corona
⊕ solar halo
⌜ thunderstorm
╲ direction
○ or ⊙ or ① annual
⊙⊙ or ② biennial
♃ perennial
♂ or ♂ male
♀ female
□ male (in charts)
○ female (in charts)
℞ take (from Latin *Recipe*)
ĀĀ or Ā or āā of each (doctor's prescription)
℔ pound
℥ ounce
ʒ dram
℈ scruple
f℥ fluid ounce
fʒ fluid dram
♏ minim
& or & and; ampersand
℘ per
number
/ virgule; slash; solidus; shilling
© copyright
% per cent
℅ care of
℀ account of
@ at
* asterisk
† dagger
‡ double dagger
§ section
☞ index
´ acute
` grave
˜ tilde
ˆ circumflex
¯ macron
˘ breve
¨ dieresis
¸ cedilla
‸ caret

TABLE OF ALPHABETS

HEBREW

Forms	Name	Sound
א	'aleph	'
ב	bēth	b (bh)
ג	gimel	g (gh)
ד	dāleth	d (dh)
ה	hē	h
ו	waw	w
ז	zayin	z
ח	ḥeth	ḥ
ט	ṭeth	ṭ
י	yodh	y
כ ך	kāph	k (kh)
ל	lāmedh	l
מ ם	mēm	m
נ ן	nūn	n
ס	samekh	s
ע	'ayin	'
פ ף	pē	p (ph)
צ ץ	ṣadhe	ṣ
ק	qōph	q
ר	rēsh	r
שׂ	sin	s
שׁ	shin	sh
ת	tāw	t (th)

Vowels are not represented in normal Hebrew writing, but for educational purposes they are indicated by a system of subscript and superscript dots. The transliterations shown in parentheses are used when the letter falls at the end of a word. The transliterations with subscript dots are pharyngeal consonants as in Arabic. The second forms shown are used when the letter falls at the end of a word.

ARABIC

Forms 1	2	3	4	Name	Sound
ا	ا			'alif	'
ب	ب	ـبـ	ـب	bā	b
ت	ت	ـتـ	ـت	tā	t
ث	ث	ـثـ	ـث	thā	th
ج	ج	ـجـ	ـج	jīm	j
ح	ح	ـحـ	ـح	ḥā	ḥ
خ	خ	ـخـ	ـخ	khā	kh
د	د			dāl	d
ذ	ذ			dhāl	dh
ر	ر			rā	r
ز	ز			zāy	z
س	س	ـسـ		sīn	s
ش	ش	ـشـ	ـش	shīn	sh
ص	ص	ـصـ	ـص	ṣād	ṣ
ض	ض	ـضـ	ـض	ḍād	ḍ
ط	ط	ـطـ	ـط	ṭā	ṭ
ظ	ظ	ـظـ	ـظ	ẓā	ẓ
ع	ع	ـعـ	ـع	'ayn	'
غ	غ	ـغـ	ـغ	ghayn	gh
ف	ف	ـفـ	ـف	fā	f
ق	ق	ـقـ	ـق	qāf	q
ك	ك	ـكـ	ـك	kāf	k
ل	ل	ـلـ	ـل	lām	l
م	م	ـمـ	ـم	mīm	m
ن	ن	ـنـ	ـن	nūn	n
ه	ه	ـهـ	ـه	hā	h
و	و			wāw	w
ي	ي	ـيـ	ـي	yā	y

The different forms in the four numbered columns are used when the letters are in: (1) isolation; (2) juncture with a previous letter; (3) juncture with the letters on both sides; (4) juncture with a following letter.

Long vowels are represented by the consonants 'alif (for ā), wāw (for ū), and yā (for ī). Short vowels are not usually written; they can, however, be indicated by the following signs: *l fatha* (for a), */ kesra* (for i), and *' ḍamma* (for u).

Transliterations with subscript dots represent "emphatic" or pharyngeal consonants, which are pronounced in the usual way except that the pharynx is tightly narrowed during articulation. When two dots are placed over the *hā*, the new letter thus formed is called *tā marbūta*, and is pronounced (t).

There are several other diacritical marks indicating such situations as the doubling of a consonant or the elision of a vowel.

GREEK

Forms	Name	Sound
A α	alpha	a,
B β	beta	b
Γ γ	gamma	g (n)
Δ δ	delta	d·
E ε	epsilon	e
Z ζ	zēta	z
H η	ēta	ē
Θ θ	thēta	th
I ι	iota	i
K κ	kappa	k
Λ λ	lambda	l
M μ	mu	m
N ν	nu	n
Ξ ξ	xi	x
O o	omicron	o
Π π	pi	p
P ρ	rhō	r (rh)
Σ σ ς	sigma	s
T τ	tau	t
Υ υ	upsilon	u
Φ φ	phi	ph
X χ	khi	kh
Ψ ψ	psi	ps
Ω ω	ōmega	ō

The superscript ' on an initial vowel or rhō, called the rough breathing, represents an aspirate. Lack of aspiration on an initial vowel is indicated by the superscript ', called the smooth breathing. When gamma precedes kappa, xi, khi, or another gamma, it has the value n and is so transliterated. The second lower-case form of sigma is used only in final position.

RUSSIAN

Forms	Sound
А а	a
Б б	b
В в	v
Г г	g
Д д	d
Е е	e
Ж ж	zh
З з	z
И и Й й	i, ĭ
К к	k
Л л	l
М м	m
Н н	n
О о	o
П п	p
Р р	r
С с	s
Т т	t
У у	u
Ф ф	f
Х х	kh
Ц ц	ts
Ч ч	ch
Ш ш	sh
Щ щ	shch
Ъ ъ	''1
Ы ы	y
Ь ь	'2
Э э	e
Ю ю	yu
Я я	ya

[1] This letter, called the "hard sign," is very rare in modern Russian. It indicates that the previous consonant remains hard even when followed by a front vowel.

[2] This letter, called the "soft sign," indicates that the previous consonant is palatalized even when a front vowel does not follow.

BIOGRAPHICAL ENTRIES

A

Aar·on (âr′ən, ăr′-). The 1st Hebrew high priest. **—Aar·on′ic, Aar·on′·i·cal** *adj.*

A·bel (ā′bəl). A son of Adam and Eve, killed by his brother, Cain.

Ab·e·lard (ăb′ə-lärd′), **Peter.** 1079–1142. French theologian.

A·bra·ham (ā′brə-hăm′). A patriarch and progenitor of the Hebrew people.

Ad·am (ăd′əm). In the Old Testament, the 1st man.

Ad·ams (ăd′əmz). **1. Samuel.** 1722–1803. American Revolutionary leader. **2. John.** 1735–1826. Second U.S. President (1797–1801). **3. John Quincy.** 1767–1848. Sixth U.S. President (1825–29).

Ad·dams (ăd′əmz), **Jane.** 1860–1935. American social worker.

Ad·di·son (ăd′ə-sən), **Joseph.** 1672–1719. English essayist.

A·den·au·er (äd′n-ou′ər, ăd′n-), **Konrad.** 1876–1967. West German statesman; chancellor (1949–63).

Ad·ler (äd′lər), **Alfred.** 1870–1937. Austrian psychiatrist.

Aes·chy·lus (ĕs′kə-ləs, ēs′-). 525–456 B.C. Greek dramatist.

Ae·sop (ē′sŏp′, ē′səp). 620?–560 B.C. Greek fabulist. **—Ae·so′pi·an** *adj.*

Ag·as·siz (ăg′ə-sē), **(Jean) Louis (Rodolphe).** 1807–1873. Swiss-born American naturalist.

Ag·new (ăg′nōō), **Spiro Theodore.** Born 1918. U.S. Vice President under Richard Nixon (1969–73); resigned.

A·gric·o·la (ə-grĭk′ə-lə), **Gnaeus Julius.** A.D. 40–93. Roman general; legate of Britain.

A·grip·pa (ə-grĭp′ə), **Marcus Vipsanius.** 63–12 B.C. Roman general and statesman.

Ag·rip·pi·na (ăg′rĭ-pī′nə). 13 B.C.?–A.D. 33. Mother of Caligula.

A·gui·nal·do (ä′gē-näl′dō), **Emilio.** 1869–1964. Philippine revolutionary leader.

Ai·ken (ā′kĭn), **Conrad (Potter).** 1889–1973. American poet.

A·khe·na·ton or **A·khe·na·ten** (ä′kə-nä′tən). King of Egypt (1375–1358 B.C.).

Al·a·ric (ăl′ə-rĭk). 370?–410. Visigoth king; conqueror of Rome (410).

Al·bert (ăl′bərt). 1819–1861. Prince consort of Queen Victoria.

Al·ber·tus Mag·nus (ăl-bûr′təs măg′nəs), **Saint.** 1206?–1280. German theologian.

Al·ci·bi·a·des (ăl′sĭ-bī′ə-dēz′). 450?–404 B.C. Athenian general.

Al·cott (ôl′kət, -kŏt′), **Louisa May.** 1832–1888. American author.

Al·den (ôl′dən), **John.** 1599?–1687. American Puritan colonist.

A·lem·bert (dä-läN-bâr′), **Jean Le Rond d'.** 1717–1783. French philosopher.

Al·ex·an·der I (ăl′ĭg-zăn′dər, -zän′dər). 1777–1825. Czar of Russia (1801–25).

Alexander II. 1818–1881. Czar of Russia (1855–81).

Alexander III. 1845–1894. Czar of Russia (1881–94).

Alexander VI. 1431?–1503. Pope (1492–1503).

Alexander the Great. 356–323 B.C. King of Macedonia (336–323 B.C.). **—Al′ex·an′dri·an** *adj.*

Al·fon·so XIII (ăl-fŏn′sō, -zō). 1886–1941. King of Spain (1886–1931); deposed.

Al·fred (ăl′frĭd). Called the Great. 849–899. King of the West Saxons (871–899).

A·li, Muhammad. Original name, Cassius Clay. Born 1942. American heavyweight boxer.

Al·len (ăl′ən), **Ethan.** 1738–1789. American Revolutionary soldier.

Al·va·rez (ăl′və-rĕz), **Luis Walter.** Born 1911. American physicist; Nobel Prize winner (1968).

A·ma·ti (ä-mä′tē), **Nicolò.** 1596–1684. Italian violin maker.

A·men·ho·tep III (ä′mən-hō′tĕp). King of Egypt (1411?–1375? B.C.).

Am·herst (ăm′ərst), **Baron Jeffrey.** 1717–1797. British general in America.

A·mos (ā′məs). A Hebrew prophet of the 8th cent. B.C.

A·mund·sen (ä′mən-sən), **Roald.** 1872–1928. Norwegian explorer.

A·nac·re·on (ə-năk′rē-ən, -ŏn′). 572?–488? B.C. Greek poet.

An·ax·ag·o·ras (ăn′ăk-săg′ə-rəs). 500?–428 B.C. Greek philosopher.

An·der·sen (ăn′dər-sən), **Hans Christian.** 1805–1875. Danish author.

An·der·son (ăn′dər-sən). **1. Sherwood.** 1876–1941. American author. **2. Maxwell.** 1888–1959. American dramatist. **3. Marian.** Born 1902. American contralto. **4. Carl David.** Born 1905. American physicist; Nobel Prize winner (1936).

An·dre·a del Sar·to (än-drā′ä dĕl sär′tō). 1486–1531. Italian painter.

An·drew (ăn′drōō). One of the 12 Apostles.

An·gel·i·co (ăn-jĕl′ĭ-kō), **Fra.** 1387–1455. Italian painter.

Anne (ăn). 1665–1714. Queen of Great Britain (1702–14).

A·nou·ilh (à-nōō-ē′), **Jean.** Born 1910. French dramatist.

An·tho·ny (ăn′thə-nē, ăn′tə-nē), **Saint.** A.D. 250?–350? Egyptian monk.

An·tho·ny (ăn′thə-nē), **Susan B(rownell).** 1820–1906. American suffragist.

An·tho·ny of Padua (ăn′thə-nē, ăn′tə-nē′), **Saint.** 1195–1231. Portuguese Franciscan monk.

An·to·ni·nus Pi·us (ăn′tə-nī′nəs pī′əs). A.D. 86–161. Roman emperor (138–161).

An·to·ni·us (ăn-tō′nē-əs), **Marcus.** English name, Mark or Marc Antony. 83?–30 B.C. Roman general.

Ap·u·lei·us (ăp′yə-lē′əs), **Lucius.** Roman satirist of the 2nd cent.

A·qui·nas (ə-kwī′nəs), **Saint Thomas.** 1225–1274. Italian theologian.

Ar·chi·me·des (är′kə-mē′dēz). 287?–212 B.C. Greek mathematician.

A·ri·o·sto (ä′rē-ô′stō), **Lodovico.** 1474–1533. Italian poet.

Ar·is·ti·des (ăr′ĭs-tī′dēz). Called the Just. Athenian 5th cent. B.C. general and statesman.

Ar·is·toph·a·nes (ăr′ĭs-tŏf′ə-nēz′). 448?–380? B.C. Athenian dramatist.

Ar·is·tot·le (ăr′ĭs-tŏt′l). 384–322 B.C. Greek philosopher. **—Ar′is·to·te′li·an** (ăr′ĭs-tə-tē′lē-ən, -tēl′yən) *adj. & n.*

A·ri·us (ə-rī′əs, âr′ē-əs). Died 336. Greek theologian.

Ark·wright (ärk′rīt′), **Sir Richard.** 1732–1792. British inventor.

Ar·min·i·us (är-mĭn′ē-əs), **Jacobus.** 1560–1609. Dutch Protestant theologian.

Arm·strong (ärm′strông′). **1. (Daniel) Louis ("Satchmo").** 1900–1971. American jazz musician. **2. Neil.** Born 1930. U.S. astronaut; first man to walk on the moon.

Ar·nold (är′nəld). **1. Benedict.** 1741–1801. American Revolutionary general and traitor. **2. Matthew.** 1822–1888. English poet and critic.

Ar·thur (är′thər), **Chester Alan.** 1830–1886. Twenty-first U.S. President (1881–85).

As·quith (ăs′kwĭth), **Herbert Henry.** 1852–1928. British prime minister (1908–16).

As·tor (ăs′tər), **John Jacob.** 1763–1848. German-born American fur trader and capitalist.

At·ti·la (ăt′ə-lə, ə-tĭl′ə). 406?–453. King of the Huns (434–53).

Att·lee (ăt′lē), **Clement Richard.** 1883–1967. Prime minister of the United Kingdom (1945–51).

At·tucks (ăt′əks), **Crispus.** 1723?–1770. American patriot.

Au·den (ôd′n), **W(ystan) H(ugh).** 1907–1973. English-born American poet.

Au·du·bon (ô′də-bŏn′, -bən), **John James.** 1785–1851. French-born American naturalist and painter.

Au·gus·tine (ô′gə-stēn′, ô-gŭs′tĭn), **Saint.** 354–430. Early Christian church father. **—Au′gus·tin′i·an** (ô′gə-stĭn′ē-ən) *adj. & n.*

Au·gus·tus (ô-gŭs′təs). Original name, Gaius Octavius. Known as Octavian. 63 B.C.–A.D. 14. Founder of the imperial Roman government.

Aus·ten (ôs′tən), **Jane.** 1775–1817. English novelist.

B

Bach (bäкн), **Johann Sebastian.** 1685–1750. German composer.

Ba·con (bā′kən). **1. Roger.** 1214?–1294. English scientist and philosopher. **2. Francis.** 1561–1626. English philosopher and essayist. **—Ba·co′ni·an** (bā-kō′nē-ən) *adj. &. n.*

Ba·den-Pow·ell (bād′n-pō′əl), **Robert Stephenson Smyth.** 1857–1941. British soldier; founder of the Boy Scouts.

Bae·de·ker (bā′dĭ-kər), **Karl.** 1801–1859. German publisher of travel books.

Baf·fin (băf′ĭn), **William.** 1584–1622. English navigator and explorer.

Ba·ku·nin (bä-kōō′nĭn), **Mikhail.** 1814–1876. Russian anarchist.

Bal·bo·a (băl-bō′ə), **Vasco Núñez de.** 1475–1517. Spanish explorer; discovered the Pacific Ocean (1513).

Bald·win (bôld′wĭn), **Stanley.** 1867–1947. British prime minister (1923–24, 1924–29, and 1935–37).

Bal·four (băl′fŏŏr′), **Arthur James.** 1848–1930. British prime minister (1902–5).

Bal·ti·more, Lord. See George Calvert.

Bal·zac (bôl′zăk′, băl′-), **Honoré de.** 1799–1850. French author.

Ban·ting (băn′tĭng), **Sir Frederick Grant.** 1891–1941. Canadian physiologist; Nobel Prize winner (1923).

Ba·rab·bas (bə-răb′əs). In the New Testament, prisoner released instead of Jesus at the insistence of the multitude.

Bar·deen (bär-dēn′), **John.** Born 1908. American physicist; Nobel Prize winner (1956, 1972).

Bark·ley (bär′klē), **Alben William.** 1877–1956. U.S. Vice President under Harry S Truman (1949–53).

Bar·nard (bär′nərd), **Christiaan Neethling.** Born 1923. South African surgeon; performed first human heart transplant (1967).

Bar·num (bär′nəm), **P(hineas) T(aylor).** 1810–1891. American circus producer.

Bar·rie (băr′ē), **Sir James M(atthew).**

1860–1937. British playwright.

Bar·ry·more (băr′ĭ-môr′, -mōr′), **Lionel.** 1878–1954. American actor; brother of actress **Ethel** (1879–1959) and actor **John** (1882–1942).

Bar·thol·di (bär-thŏl′dē), **Frédéric Auguste.** 1834–1904. French sculptor of the Statue of Liberty.

Bar·thol·o·mew (bär-thŏl′ə-myōō′), Saint. One of the 12 apostles.

Bart·lett (bärt′lĭt), **John.** 1820–1905. American compiler of *Familiar Quotations.*

Bar·tók (bär′tôk), **Béla.** 1881–1945. Hungarian composer.

Bar·ton (bärt′n), **Clara.** 1821–1912. Founder of the American Red Cross (1881).

Bas·il (băz′əl, băz′-), **Saint.** 330?–379. Bishop of Caesarea; founded monastic institutions.

Bath·she·ba (băth-shē′bə, băth′shĭ-bə). In the Old Testament, 2nd wife of David; mother of Solomon.

Bau·de·laire (bōd-lâr′), **Charles.** 1821–1867. French poet.

Bau·douin I (bō-dwăN′). Born 1930. King of Belgium (since 1951).

Bea·dle (bēd′l), **George Wells.** Born 1903. American geneticist; Nobel Prize winner (1958).

Beards·ley (bîrdz′lē), **Aubrey Vincent.** 1872–1898. British illustrator.

Be·a·trix (be′ə-trĭks). Born 1938. Queen of the Netherlands (since 1980).

Beau·mar·chais (bō-mär-shā′), **Pierre Augustin Caron de.** 1732–1799. French dramatist.

Beau·re·gard (bō′rə-gärd), **Pierre Gustave Toutant de.** 1818–1893. American Confederate general.

Beau·voir (bō-vwär′), **Simone de.** Born 1908. French writer.

Beck·et (bĕk′ĭt), **Saint Thomas à.** 1118?–1170. English Roman Catholic martyr.

Bede (bēd), **Saint.** 673–735. English theologian and historian.

Bee·cher (bē′chər), **Henry Ward.** 1813–1887. American Protestant clergyman and abolitionist.

Bee·tho·ven (bā′tō-vən), **Ludwig van.** 1770–1827. German composer.

Be·gin (bā′gĭn), **Menachem.** Born 1913. Premier of Israel (since 1977).

Bé·ké·sy (bā′kā-shē), **Georg von.** Born 1899. Hungarian-born American physicist; Nobel Prize winner (1961).

Bell (bĕl), **Alexander Graham.** 1847–1922. Scottish-born American inventor.

Bel·li·ni (bə-lē′nē). **1. Giovanni.** 1430–1516. Italian painter. **2. Vincenzo.** 1801–1835. Italian composer.

Bel·shaz·zar (bĕl-shăz′ər). In the Old Testament, the last king of Babylon.

Be·na·cer·raf (bā′nə-sĕr′əf), **Baruj.** Born 1920. Venezuelan-born American biochemist; Nobel Prize winner (1980).

Ben·e·dict XIV (bĕn′ə-dĭkt′). 1675–1758. Pope (1740–58).

Benedict XV. 1854–1922. Pope (1914–22).

Benedict of Nur·sia (nûr′shē-ə, -shə), Saint. 480?–543? Founder of the Benedictine order of monks.

Be·nét (bĭ-nā′), **Stephen Vincent.** 1898–1943. American poet.

Ben-Gur·i·on (bĕn-gŏŏr′ē-ən), **David.** 1886–1973. Polish-born Israeli statesman.

Ben·ja·min (bĕn′jə-mən). In the Old Testament, ancestor of one of the 12 tribes of Israel.

Ben·nett (bĕn′ĭt), **Richard Bedford.** 1870–1947. Prime minister of Canada (1930–35).

Ben·tham (bĕn′thəm), **Jeremy.** 1748–1832. English philosopher.

Ben·ton (bĕnt′n), **Thomas Hart.** 1889–1975. American painter.

Berg (bûrg), **Paul.** Born 1926. American microbiologist; Nobel Prize winner (1980).

Be·ring (bîr′ĭng, bâr′-), **Vitus.** 1680–1741. Danish navigator and explorer.

Ber·lin (bĕr-lĭn′), **Irving.** Born 1888. American composer.

Ber·li·oz (bĕr′lē-ōz′), **(Louis) Hector.** 1803–1869. French composer.

Bern·hardt (bûrn′härt′, bĕrn′-), **Sarah.** 1844–1923. French actress.

Ber·ni·ni (bĕr-nē′nē), **Giovanni Lorenzo.** 1598–1680. Italian sculptor, architect, and painter.

Be·the (bā′tə), **Hans Albrecht.** Born 1906. German-born American physicist; Nobel Prize winner (1967).

Be·thune (bĭ-thōōn′), **Mary McLeod.** 1875–1955. American educator.

Bierce (bîrs), **Ambrose (Gwinett).** 1842–1914? American writer.

Bis·marck (bĭz′märk), **Prince Otto Eduard Leopold von.** 1815–1898. First chancellor of the German Empire.

Bi·zet (bē-zā′), **Georges.** 1838–1875. French composer.

Black Hawk (blăk′ hôk′). 1767–1838. American Indian leader.

Black·stone (blăk′stən, -stōn′), **Sir William.** 1723–1780. British jurist.

Black·well (blăk′wĕl, -wəl), **Elizabeth.** 1821–1910. British-born American physician.

Blake (blāk), **William.** 1757–1827. English poet and engraver.

Bloch (blŏk). **1. Felix.** Born 1905. Swiss-born American physicist; Nobel Prize winner (1952). **2. Konrad Emil.** Born 1912. German-born American biochemist; Nobel Prize winner (1964).

Bloom·er (blōō′mər), **Amelia (Jenks).** 1818–1894. American feminist and social reformer.

Boc·cac·cio (bə-kä′chē-ō′), **Giovanni.** 1313–1375. Italian writer.

Bohr (bōr), **Niels Henrik David.** 1885–1962. Danish physicist.

Bol·eyn (bŏŏl′ĭn, bō-lĭn′), **Anne.** 1507–1536. Second wife of Henry VIII; beheaded.

Bo·li·var (bō-lē′vär), **Simón.** 1783–1830. South American independence leader.

Bo·na·parte (bō′nə-pärt′), A Corsican family, including: **1.** See **Napoleon. 2. Joseph.** 1768–1844. King of Naples (1806–8) and of Spain (1808–13). **3. Lucien.** 1775–1840. Prince of Canino. **4. Louis.** 1778–1846. King of Holland (1806–10). **5. Jerome.** 1784–1860. King of Westphalia (1807–13).

Boone (bōōn), **Daniel.** 1734–1820.

American pioneer.

Booth (bōōth). **1. William.** 1829–1912. British founder of Salvation Army. **2. John Wilkes.** 1838–1865. American actor; assassin of Abraham Lincoln.

Bor·don (bôrd'n), Sir **Robert Laird.** 1854–1937. Prime minister of Canada (1911–20).

Bor·gia (bôr'jä, -jə). **1. Cesare.** 1475?–1507. Italian cardinal and political and military leader. **2. Lucrezia.** 1480–1519. Italian noblewoman; patron of the arts.

Bo·ro·din (bôr'ə-dēn'), **Aleksandr Porfirievich.** 1834–1887. Russian composer.

Bosch (bôs, bôs), **Hieronymus.** 1450?–1516. Dutch painter.

Bos·well (bŏz'wĕl', -wəl), **James.** 1740–1795. Scottish lawyer and writer.

Bot·ti·cel·li (bŏt'ĭ-chĕl'ē), **Sandro.** 1444?–1510. Italian painter.

Bour·bon (bōōr'bən). A French royal family including rulers of France, Spain, and Naples.

Bourke-White (bûrk'hwīt'), **Margaret.** 1906–1971. American photographer.

Bow·ell (bou'l), Sir **Mackenzie.** 1823–1917. Prime minister of Canada (1894–96).

Boyle (boil), **Robert.** 1627–1691. English chemist and physicist.

Brad·bur·y (brăd'bĕr'ē), **Ray (Douglas).** Born 1920. American author.

Brad·dock (brăd'ək), **Edward.** 1695–1755. British military leader.

Brad·ford (brăd'fərd), **William.** 1590–1657. English Puritan colonist; governor of Plymouth colony.

Brad·street (brăd'strēt'), **Anne (Dudley).** 1612–1672. American colonial poet.

Brahms (brämz), **Johannes.** 1833–1897. German composer.

Bran·deis (brăn'dīs), **Louis Dembitz.** 1856–1941. American jurist.

Brandt (brănt), **Willy.** Born 1913. West German political leader.

Braque (bräk), **Georges.** 1882–1963. French cubist painter.

Brat·tain (brăt'n), **Walter Houser.** Born 1902. American physicist; Nobel Prize winner (1956).

Braun (broun), **Wernher Magnus Maximilian von.** 1912–1977. German-born American rocket engineer.

Brecht (brĕKHт), **Bertolt.** 1898–1956. German playwright.

Breck·in·ridge (brĕk'ĭn-rĭj), **John Cabell.** 1821–1875. U.S. Vice President under James Buchanan (1857–61).

Breu·ghel (brœ'gəl). See **Brueghel.**

Brezh·nev (brĕzh'nĕf), **Leonid Ilyich.** Born 1906. Soviet statesman; first secretary of the Communist Party (since 1964).

Bri·an Bo·ru (brī'ən bô-rōō'). 926–1014. King of Ireland (1002–14).

Bridg·man (brĭj'mən), **Percy Williams.** 1882–1961. American physicist; Nobel Prize winner (1946).

Brit·ten (brĭt'n), **(Edward) Benjamin.** 1913–1976. British composer.

Bron·të (brŏn'tē). English family of novelists, including: **1. Charlotte.** 1816–1855. **2. Emily Jane.** 1818–1848. **3. Anne.** 1820–1849.

Brooks (brōōks), **Gwendolyn.** Born 1917. Poet and novelist; 1st black to win Pulitzer Prize (1950).

Brown (broun). **1. John.** 1800–1859. American abolitionist. **2. Herbert.** Born 1912. American chemist; Nobel Prize winner (1979).

Browne (broun), Sir **Thomas.** 1605–1682. English physician and author.

Brown·ing (brou'nĭng). **1. Elizabeth Barrett.** 1806–1861. English poet. **2. Robert.** 1812–1889. English poet.

Bruck·ner (brōōk'nər), **Anton.** 1824–1896. Austrian composer.

Brue·ghel (brœ'gəl), **Pieter.** Also **Bruegel, Breu·ghel.** 1520?–1569. Flemish painter.

Bru·nel·le·schi (brōō'nə-lĕs'kē), **Filippo.** 1377?–1446. Florentine architect and engineer.

Bru·tus (brōō'təs), **Marcus Junius.** 85?–42 B.C. Roman political and military leader; participated in assassination of Julius Caesar.

Bry·an (brī'ən), **William Jennings.** 1860–1925. American statesman and lawyer.

Bry·ant (brī'ənt), **William Cullen.** 1794–1878. American poet.

Bu·ber (bōō'bər), **Martin.** 1878–1965. Austrian philosopher and Judaic scholar.

Bu·chan·an (byōō-kăn'ən, bə-), **James.** 1791–1868. Fifteenth U.S. President (1857–61).

Buck (bŭk), **Pearl (Sydenstricker).** 1892–1973. American novelist; Nobel Prize winner (1938).

Bud·dha (bōō'də, bŏod'ə). Title of Gautama Siddhartha. 563?–483? B.C. Indian philosopher; founder of Buddhism.

Buf·fa·lo Bill (bŭf'ə-lō' bĭl'). See William Frederick **Cody.**

Bu·kha·rin (bōō-KHä'rĭn), **Nikolai Ivanovich.** 1888–1938. Russian revolutionary.

Bul·finch (bŏol'fĭnch'), **Thomas.** 1796–1867. American mythologist.

Bul·ga·nin (bŏol-gä'nĭn, -gän'ĭn), **Nikolai Aleksandrovich.** 1895–1975. Soviet statesman; premier (1955–58).

Bunche (bŭnch), **Ralph Johnson.** 1904–1971. American diplomat; 1st black to win Nobel Peace Prize (1950).

Bun·yan (bŭn'yən), **John.** 1628–1688. English preacher and author.

Bur·bank (bûr'băngk'), **Luther.** 1849–1926. American horticulturist.

Bur·goyne (bər-goin'), **John.** 1722–1792. British general in the American Revolution.

Burke (bûrk), **Edmund.** 1729–1797. British statesman and philosopher.

Burns (bûrnz), **Robert.** 1759–1796. Scottish poet.

Burn·side (bûrn'sīd'), **Ambrose E(verett).** 1824–1881. American military and political leader.

Burr (bûr), **Aaron.** 1756–1836. U.S. Vice President under Thomas Jefferson (1801–5).

Bur·roughs (bûr'ōz), **Edgar Rice.** 1875–1950. American writer.

Bur·ton (bûrt'n), Sir **Richard Francis.** 1821–1890. British Orientalist and adventurer.

Bush (bŏosh), **George Herbert Walker.** Born 1924. U.S. Vice President under Ronald Reagan (since 1981).

But·ler (bŭt'lər), **Samuel.** 1835–1902. English novelist.

Byrd (bûrd), **Richard Evelyn.** 1888–1957. American polar explorer.

By·ron (bī'rən), **George Gordon.** 1788–1824. English poet. —**By·ron'ic** (bī-rŏn'ĭk) *adj. & n.*

C

Cab·ot (kăb'ət). **1. John.** 1450–1498. Italian explorer in English service; discovered mainland of North America (1497). **2. Sebastian.** 1476?–1557. English explorer and cartographer.

Ca·bri·ni (kə-brē'nē), Saint **Frances Xavier.** 1850–1917. Italian-born nun; first American canonized (1946).

Cad·il·lac (kăd'l-ăk'), **Antoine de la Mothe.** 1658–1730. French colonial administrator in America.

Caed·mon (kăd'mən). 7th cent. English poet.

Cae·sar (sē'zər), **Gaius Julius.** 100–44 B.C. Roman statesman, general, and historian. —**Cae·sar'e·an** or **Cae·sar'i·an** *adj.*

Cal·houn (kăl-hōōn'), **John Caldwell.** 1782–1850. U.S. Vice President under John Quincy Adams and Andrew Jackson (1825–32).

Ca·lig·u·la (kə-lĭg'yə-lə). Original name, Gaius Caesar. A.D. 12–41. Emperor of Rome (37–41).

Cal·vert (kăl'vərt). English family of colonists in America, including: **1. George.** 1580?–1632. First Baron Baltimore. **2. Cecilius.** 1605–1675. Second Baron and recipient of Maryland charter. **3. Leonard.** 1606–1647. First governor of Maryland (1634–47). **4. Charles.** 1637–1715. Third Baron and governor (1661–75) and proprietor (1675–1715) of Maryland.

Cal·vin (kăl'vĭn). **1. John.** 1509–1564. French religious reformer. **2. Melvin.** Born 1911. American chemist; Nobel Prize winner (1961).

Cam·o·ëns (kăm'ō-ənz', kə-mō'ənz), **Luiz Vaz de.** 1524–1580. Portuguese poet.

Ca·mus (kə-myōō'). **Albert.** 1913–1960. French novelist.

Ca·nute (kə-nōōt', -nyōōt'). 994?–1035. King of England (1016?–35), of Denmark (1018–35), and of Norway (1028–35).

Ca·pet (kā'pĭt, kăp'ĭt), **Hugh.** 940?–996. King of France (987–996). —**Ca·pe'tian** (kə-pē'shən) *adj. & n.*

Car·a·cal·la (kăr'ə-kăl'ə). 188–217. Emperor of Rome (211–17).

Car·lyle (kär-līl'), **Thomas.** 1795–1881. English historian.

Car·ne·gie (kär'nə-gē, kär-nĕg'ē), **Andrew.** 1835–1919. Scottish-born American industrialist.

Car·roll (kăr'əl), **Lewis.** Pen name of Charles Lutwidge Dodgson. 1832–1898. English author and mathematician.

Car·son (kär'sən), **Christopher ("Kit").** 1809–1868. American frontiersman.

Car·ter (kär'tər), **James Earl, Jr.** Born

1924. Thirty-ninth U.S. President (1977–81).

Car·tier (kär-tyā'), **Jacques.** 1491–1557. French explorer.

Cart·wright (kärt'rīt'), **Edmund.** 1743–1823. British inventor of the power loom.

Ca·ru·so (kə-rōō'sō), **Enrico.** 1873–1921. Italian operatic tenor.

Car·ver (kär'vər), **George Washington.** 1864–1943. American botanist and educator.

Ca·sals (kə-sälz'), **Pablo.** 1876–1973. Spanish cellist.

Ca·sa·no·va (kăz'ə-nō'və, kăs'-), **Giovanni Jacopo.** 1725–1798. Italian adventurer.

Cas·satt (kə-săt'), **Mary.** 1845–1926. American painter.

Cas·tro (kăs'trō), **Fidel.** Born 1927. Cuban revolutionary; premier (since 1959).

Cath·er (kăth'ər), **Willa Sibert.** 1873–1947. American author.

Cath·e·rine I (kăth'rĭn, -ər-ĭn). 1684?–1727. Empress of Russia (1725–27).

Catherine II. Called the Great. 1729–1796. Empress of Russia (1762–96).

Catherine de Mé·di·cis (də mĕd'ə-chē, mā'də-sēs'). 1519–1589. Queen of France (1547–59).

Catherine of Ar·a·gon (ăr'ə-gŏn'). 1485–1536. Queen of England; first wife of Henry VIII.

Cat·i·line (kăt'l-īn). 108?–62 B.C. Roman politician and conspirator.

Ca·to (kā'tō). **1. Marcus Porcius.** Called the Elder. 234–149 B.C. Roman consul and censor. **2. Marcus Porcius.** Called the Younger. 95–46 B.C. Roman statesman.

Catt (kăt), **Carrie Chapman Lane.** 1859–1947. American suffragist.

Ca·tul·lus (kə-tŭl'əs), **Gaius Valerius.** Roman poet of the 1st cent. B.C.

Cax·ton (kăk'stən), **William.** 1422?–1491. First English printer.

Ce·cil·ia (sĭ-sēl'yə), **Saint.** Roman martyr of the 3rd cent.

Cel·li·ni (chə-lē'nē), **Benvenuto.** 1500–1571. Italian sculptor.

Cer·van·tes Sa·a·ve·dra (sər-văn'tēz sä'ä-vē'drä), **Miguel de.** 1547–1616. Spanish author.

Cé·zanne (sā-zän'), **Paul.** 1839–1906. French painter.

Cha·gall (shə-gäl'), **Marc.** Born 1887. Russian painter.

Cham·ber·lain (chăm'bər-lĭn). **1. (Arthur) Neville.** 1869–1940. British prime minister (1937–40). **2. Owen.** Born 1920. American physicist; Nobel Prize winner (1959).

Cham·plain (shăm-plān'), **Samuel de.** 1567?–1635. French explorer; governor of New France (1633–35).

Chap·lin (chăp'lĭn), **Sir Charles Spencer ("Charlie").** 1889–1977. British actor, producer, director, writer, and composer.

Chap·man (chăp'mən), **Frank Michler.** 1864–1945. American ornithologist and author.

Char·le·magne (shär'lə-mān'). Known as Charles the Great, Charles I. 742–814. King of the Franks (768–814); crowned emperor of the Romans (800).

Charles (chärlz). Born 1948. Prince of Wales.

Charles I. Title of Charles Stuart. 1600–1649. King of England (1625–49); beheaded.

Charles II. Called the Bald. 823–877. Holy Roman Emperor (875–877); king of France as Charles I (840–877).

Charles II. 1630–1685. King of England following the Restoration (1660–85).

Charles V. 1500–1558. Holy Roman Emperor (1519–56); king of Spain as Charles I (1516–56).

Charles VII. 1403–1461. King of France (1422–61); defeated the English at Orléans (1429).

Charles IX. 1550–1574. King of France (1560–74).

Charles X. 1757–1836. King of France (1824–30); abdicated.

Charles Mar·tel (mär-tĕl'). 689?–741. Frankish ruler (715–741).

Châ·teau·bri·and (shä-tō-brē-äN'), Vicomte **François René de.** 1768–1848. French author and diplomat.

Chat·ter·ton (chăt'ər-tən), **Thomas.** 1752–1770. English poet.

Chau·cer (chô'sər), **Geoffrey.** 1340?–1400. English poet. **—Chau·ce'ri·an** (-sîr'ē-ən) adj. & n.

Chee·ver (chē'vər), **John.** Born 1912. American author.

Che·khov (chĕk'ôf'), **Anton Pavlovich.** 1860–1904. Russian author.

Che·ops (kē'ŏps). King of Egypt of the 4th dynasty (2900?–2877 B.C.); erected the Great Pyramid.

Ches·ter·field (chĕs'tər-fēld'), **Fourth Earl of.** Title of Philip Dormer Stanhope. 1694–1773. English statesman and author.

Ches·ter·ton (chĕs'tər-tən), **G(ilbert) K(eith).** 1874–1936. English author.

Chiang Kai-shek (jyäng' kī'shĕk', chyäng', chăng'). 1887–1975. Chinese military leader and president of Republic of China (1928–31, 1948–75); removed government to Taiwan (1949).

Chis·holm (chĭz'əm), **Shirley.** Born 1924. American political leader.

Cho·pin (shō'păn'), **Frédéric François.** 1810–1849. Polish pianist and composer.

Chou En-lai (jō' ĕn'lī'). 1898–1976. Chinese communist leader; premier (1949–76).

Chris·tie (krĭs'tē), **Agatha (Mary Clarissa).** 1891–1976. English author.

Chris·ti·na (krĭs-tē'nə). 1626–1689. Queen of Sweden (1632–54); abdicated.

Chris·to·pher (krĭs'tə-fər), **Saint.** Legendary Christian martyr of the 3rd cent.

Chrys·os·tom (krĭs'əs-təm, krĭ-sŏs'təm), **Saint John.** 345?–407. Patriarch of Constantinople (398–404).

Church·ill (chûr'chĭl), **Sir Winston (Leonard Spencer).** 1874–1965. Prime minister of the United Kingdom (1940–5 and 1951–5).

Cic·e·ro (sĭs'ə-rō'), **Marcus Tullius.** 106–43 B.C. Roman statesman and orator.

Cid (sĭd), **the.** Real name, Rodrigo Díaz de Bivar. 1040?–1099. Spanish

soldier and epic hero.

Clar·en·don (klăr'ən-dən), **Earl of.** Title of Edward Hyde. 1609–1674. English statesman and historian.

Clark (klärk). **1. George Rogers.** 1752–1818. American frontiersman and Revolutionary military leader. **2. William.** 1770–1838. American military officer and explorer. **3. Charles Joseph ("Joe").** Born 1939. Prime minister of Canada (1979–80).

Clau·di·us I (klô'dē-əs). 10 B.C.–A.D. 54. Roman emperor (A.D. 41–54).

Clay (klā). **1. Henry.** 1777–1852. American statesman. **2. Cassius Marcellus.** See Muhammed Ali.

Cle·men·ceau (klĕm'ən-sō'), **Georges.** 1841–1929. French statesman.

Clem·ens (klĕm'ənz), **Samuel Langhorne.** Pen name, Mark Twain. 1835–1910. American author and humorist.

Cle·o·pat·ra (klē'ə-păt'rə, -pā'trə, -pä'trə). 69–30 B.C. Queen of Egypt (51–49 and 48–30).

Cleve·land (klēv'lənd), **(Stephen) Grover.** 1837–1908. Twenty-second and twenty-fourth U.S. President (1885–89 and 1893–97).

Clin·ton (klĭn'tən). **1. George.** 1739–1812. U.S. Vice President under Thomas Jefferson and James Madison (1805–12). **2. De Witt.** 1769–1828. American political leader.

Clive (klīv), **Robert.** 1725–1774. British military leader; founder of the British Indian empire.

Clo·vis I (klō'vĭs). 466?–511. King of the Franks (481–511) and of most of Gaul.

Co·chise (kō'chēs', -chēz'). 1815?–1874. American Apache Indian leader.

Co·dy (kō'dē), **William Frederick.** Called Buffalo Bill. 1846–1917. American frontiersman, scout, and showman.

Co·han (kō'hăn'), **George M(ichael).** 1878–1942. American singer, playwright, and songwriter.

Coke (kōōk), **Sir Edward.** 1552–1634. English jurist.

Col·bert (kôl-bâr'), **Jean Baptiste.** 1619–1683. French statesman.

Cole·ridge (kōl'rĭj), **Samuel Taylor.** 1772–1834. English poet and critic.

Co·lette (kô-lĕt'). Pen name of Sidonie Gabrielle Claudine Colette. 1873–1954. French novelist.

Col·fax (kōl'făks'), **Schuyler.** 1823–1885. U.S. Vice President under Ulysses S. Grant (1869–73).

Co·lum·bus (kə-lŭm'bəs), **Christopher.** 1451–1506. Italian navigator in the service of Spain; opened the New World to exploration.

Comp·ton (kŏmp'tən), **Arthur Holly.** 1892–1962. American physicist; Nobel Prize winner (1927).

Con·fu·cius (kən-fyōō'shəs). 551–479 B.C. Chinese philosopher and teacher. **—Con·fu'cian** adj. & n.

Con·rad (kŏn'răd), **Joseph.** 1857–1924. Polish-born English author.

Con·stan·tine I (kŏn'stən-tēn). Called The Great. 280?–337. Roman Emperor (306–37).

Cook (kōōk), **James.** 1728–1779. British explorer of the Pacific.

Coo·lidge (koo′lĭj), **(John) Calvin.** 1872–1933. Thirtieth U.S. President (1923–29).

Coop·er (koo′pər), **James Fenimore.** 1789–1851. American novelist.

Co·per·ni·cus (kō-pûr′nə-kəs), **Nicolaus.** 1473–1543. Polish astronomer.

Cop·land (kōp′lənd), **Aaron.** Born 1900. American composer.

Cop·ley (kōp′lē), **John Singleton.** 1738–1815. American painter.

Cor·mack (kôr′măk′), **Allan MacLeod.** South African-born American physician; Nobel Prize winner (1979).

Cor·neille (kôr-nā′y′), **Pierre.** 1606–1684. French dramatist.

Corn·wal·lis (kôrn-wŏl′ĭs), **Charles.** First Marquis Cornwallis. 1738–1805. British general.

Co·ro·na·do (kôr′ə-nä′dō), **Francisco Vásquez de.** 1510–1554. Spanish explorer.

Co·rot (kô-rō′), **Jean Baptiste Camille.** 1796–1875. French painter.

Cor·tés (kôr-tĕz′), **Hernando.** Also **Cortez.** 1485–1547. Spanish explorer; conquered Aztecs.

Cou·pe·rin (koo-prăn′), **François.** 1668–1733. French composer.

Cour·bet (koor-bĕ′), **Gustave.** 1819–1877. French painter.

Cous·teau (koos-tō′), **Jacques Yves.** Born 1910. French underwater explorer and author.

Cow·ley (kou′lē), **Abraham.** 1618–1667. English poet.

Cow·per (koo′pər), **William.** 1731–1800. English poet.

Crabbe (krăb), **George.** 1754–1832. English poet.

Crane (krān). **1. Stephen.** 1871–1900. American writer. **2. (Harold) Hart.** 1899–1932. American poet.

Cra·zy Horse (krā′zē hôrs, hôrs). 1849?–1877. American Sioux Indian leader.

Cro·ce (krō′chā), **Benedetto.** 1866–1952. Italian philosopher and historian.

Crock·ett (krŏk′ĭt), **David ("Davy").** 1786–1836. American frontiersman; died at the Alamo.

Croe·sus (krē′səs). Died 546 B.C. Last King of Lydia (560–546).

Crom·well (krŏm′wĕl′, -wəl, krŭm′-), **Oliver.** 1599–1658. English military and religious leader; Lord Protector of the Commonwealth (1653–58).

Cro·nin (krō′nĭn), **James.** Born 1931. American chemist; Nobel Prize winner (1980).

Crookes (krooks), **Sir William.** 1832–1919. British physicist.

Cruik·shank (krook′shăngk′), **George.** 1792–1878. British illustrator.

Cul·len (kŭl′ən), **Countee.** 1903–1946. American poet.

Cum·mings (kŭm′ĭngz), **Edward Estlin.** Known as e e cummings. 1894–1962. American poet and playwright.

Cu·rie (kyoor′ē, kyoo-rē′). **1. Pierre.** 1859–1906. French chemist; shared Nobel Prize (1903) with his wife, Marie. **2. Marie.** 1867–1934. Polish-born French chemist; Nobel Prize winner (1903 and 1911).

Cur·ri·er and Ives (kûr′ē-ər; īvz).

American lithographers **Nathaniel Currier** (1813–1888) and **James Merritt Ives** (1824–1895).

Cur·tis (kûr′tĭs), **Charles.** 1860–1936. U.S. Vice President under Herbert Hoover (1929–33).

Cus·ter (kŭs′tər), **George Armstrong.** 1839–1876. American army officer; killed at Battle of the Little Bighorn.

Cu·vi·er (koo′vē-ā, kyoo′-), **Baron Georges Léopold.** 1769–1832. French naturalist.

Cyr·a·no de Ber·ge·rac (sîr′ə-nō də bûr′zhə-răk), **Savinien de.** 1619–1655. French author and duelist.

Cyril (sîr′əl), **Saint.** 827–869. Greek Christian theologian.

Cy·rus (sīr′əs). 600?–529 B.C. King of Persia (550–529); founder of the Persian Empire.

D

Da·li (dä′lē), **Salvador.** Born 1904. Spanish artist.

Dal·las (dăl′əs), **George Mifflin.** 1792–1864. U.S. Vice President under James K. Polk (1845–49).

Dal·ton (dôlt′n), **John.** 1766–1844. British physicist and chemist.

Da·na (dā′nə), **Richard Henry.** 1815–1882. American author and sailor.

Dan·te A·li·ghie·ri (dän′tā ä′lē-gyä′rē). 1265–1321. Italian poet.

Dan·ton (däɴ-tôɴ′), **Georges Jacques.** 1759–1794. French revolutionary leader.

Dare (dâr), **Virginia.** 1587–? First child born in America of English parents.

Da·ri·us I (də-rī′əs). Called the Great. 558?–486 B.C. King of Persia (521–486).

Dar·row (dăr′ō), **Clarence Seward.** 1857–1938. American lawyer.

Dar·win (där′wĭn), **Charles Robert.** 1809–1882. British naturalist.

Dau·mier (dō-myā′), **Honoré.** 1808–1879. French painter and cartoonist.

Da·vid (dā′vĭd). Second king of Judah and Israel (1010?–970? B.C.); father of King Solomon.

Da·vid (dä-vēd′), **Jacques Louis.** 1748–1825. French painter.

Da·vis (dā′vĭs), **Jefferson.** 1808–1889. President of the Confederate States of America (1861–65).

Da·vis·son (dā′vĭ-sən), **Clinton Joseph.** 1881–1958. American physicist; Nobel Prize winner (1937).

Da·vy (dā′vē), **Sir Humphry.** 1778–1829. British chemist.

Dawes (dôz), **Charles Gates.** 1865–1951. U.S. Vice President under Calvin Coolidge (1925–29).

Debs (dĕbz), **Eugene Victor.** 1855–1926. American labor leader.

De·bus·sy (də-byoo′sē), **Claude Achille.** 1862–1918. French composer.

De·ca·tur (dĭ-kā′tər), **Stephen.** 1779–1820. American naval officer.

De·foe (dĭ-fō′), **Daniel.** 1660?–1731. English novelist.

De·gas (də-gä′), **(Hilaire Germain) Edgar.** 1834–1917. French painter and sculptor.

De Gaulle (də gōl′), **Charles.** 1890–1970. French general and statesman;

president (1945–46, 1959–69).

De·la·croix (də-lá-krwä′), **Ferdinand Victor Eugène.** 1799–1863. French painter.

De la Mare (də lə mâr′, dĕl′ə mâr′), **Walter (John).** 1873–1956. English poet and novelist.

De La Warr (dĕl′ə wâr′), **Baron.** Known as Lord Delaware. 1577–1618. First governor of Virginia (1610–11).

De·li·us (dē′lē-əs), **Frederick.** 1862–1934. British composer.

De Mille (də mĭl′). **1. Cecil B(lount).** 1881–1959. American motion-picture producer and director. **2. Agnes.** Born 1909. American choreographer.

De·moc·ri·tus (dĭ-mŏk′rə-təs). Greek philosopher of the late 5th cent. B.C.

De·mos·the·nes (dĭ-mŏs′thə-nēz′). 384?–322 B.C. Greek orator and political leader.

Deng Xiao·ping (dŭng′ shou-pĭng′). Born 1904. Chinese head of state (since 1977).

Den·is (dĕn′ĭs, də-nē′), **Saint.** First Bishop of Paris.

De Quin·cey (dĭ kwĭn′sē), **Thomas.** 1785–1859. English essayist.

Des·cartes (dā-kärt′), **René.** 1596–1650. French philosopher and mathematician.

de So·to (dē sō′tō), **Hernando.** 1500?–1542. Spanish explorer; discoverer of the Mississippi River (1541).

de Va·le·ra (dĕv′ə-lâr′ə, -lîr′ə), **Eamon.** 1882–1975. American-born prime minister and president of Ireland (1959–75).

De Vries (də vrēs′), **Hugo.** 1848–1935. Dutch botanist.

Dew·ey (doo′ē, dyoo′ē). **1. George.** 1837–1917. American naval officer. **2. John.** 1859–1952. American philosopher and educator.

Di·as (dē′əs), **Bartholomeu.** Also **Di·az.** 1450?–1500. Portuguese navigator; discovered Cape of Good Hope.

Dick·ens (dĭk′ənz), **Charles (John Huffam).** 1812–1870. English novelist.

Dick·in·son (dĭk′ən-sən), **Emily (Elizabeth).** 1830–1886. American poet.

Di·de·rot (dēd-rō′), **Denis.** 1713–1784. French philosopher and author.

Dief·en·bak·er (dēf′ən-bā′kər), **John George.** 1895–1979. Prime minister of Canada (1957–63).

Di·o·cle·tian (dī′ə-klē′shən). 245–313. Roman emperor (284–305).

Di·og·e·nes (dī-ŏj′ə-nēz′). 412?–323 B.C. Greek philosopher.

Dis·rae·li (dĭz-rā′lē), **Benjamin.** First Earl of Beaconsfield. 1804–1881. British statesman; prime minister (1868, 1874–80).

Dix (dĭks), **Dorothea Lynde.** 1802–1887. American social reformer.

Dom·i·nic (dŏm′ə-nĭk), **Saint.** 1170–1221. Spanish-born founder of the Dominican order of friars.

Do·mi·tian (də-mĭsh′ən). A.D. 51–96. Roman emperor (81–96).

Don·i·zet·ti (dŏn′ə-zĕt′ē), **Gaetano.** 1797–1848. Italian composer.

Donne (dŭn), **John.** 1573–1631. English poet and theologian.

Dos Pas·sos (dəs păs′əs), **John (Roderigo).** 1896–1970. American novelist.

Dos·to·yev·sky (dôs′tô-yĕf′skē), **Fyodor Mikhailovich.** 1821–1881. Russian novelist.

Doug·las (dŭg′ləs), **Stephen Arnold.** 1813–1861. American political leader.

Doug·lass (dŭg′ləs), **Frederick.** 1817?–1895. American abolitionist.

Doyle (doil), Sir **Arthur Conan.** 1859–1930. English physician and novelist.

Dra·co (drā′kō). Athenian lawgiver of the late 7th cent. B.C.

Drake (drāk), Sir **Francis.** 1540?–1596. English navigator.

Drei·ser (drī′sər), **Theodore (Herman Albert).** 1871–1945. American novelist.

Drey·fus (drā′fəs, drī′-), **Alfred.** 1859–1935. French army officer.

Dry·den (drīd′n), **John.** 1631–1700. English poet, dramatist, and critic.

Du Bar·ry (doo bär′ē, dyoo), Comtesse **Jeanne-Marie.** 1746?–1793. French courtesan.

Du Bois (doo bois′), **W(illiam) E(dward) B(urghardt).** 1868–1963. American educator; a founder (1910) of the NAACP.

Du·mas (dü-mä′). **1. Alexandre** Known as Dumas père. 1802–1870. French playwright and novelist. **2. Alexandre** Known as Dumas fils. 1824–1895. French author.

Du·nant (dü-näN′), **Jean Henri.** 1828–1910. Swiss philanthropist; founder of the Red Cross.

Dun·bar (dŭn′bär), **Paul.** 1872–1906. American poet.

Dun·can (dŭng′kən), **Isadora.** 1878–1927. American dancer.

Dun·can I (dŭn′kən). Died 1040. King of Scotland (1034–40).

Dü·rer (dü′rər), **Albrecht.** 1471–1528. German painter and engraver.

Du·se (doo′zā), **Eleonora.** 1859–1924. Italian actress.

Dvoř·ák (dvôr′zhäk), **Anton.** 1841–1904. Czech composer.

E

Ea·kins (ā′kĭnz), **Thomas.** 1844–1916. American painter.

Ear·hart (âr′härt′), **Amelia.** 1898–1937? American aviator.

East·man (ēst′mən), **George.** 1854–1932. American inventor.

Ed·dy (ĕd′ē), **Mary Baker.** 1821–1910. American founder of the Church of Christ, Scientist.

E·den (ēd′n), Sir **(Robert) Anthony.** Earl of Avon. 1897–1977. Prime minister of the United Kingdom (1955–57).

Ed·i·son (ĕd′ə-sən), **Thomas Alva.** 1847–1931. American inventor.

Ed·ward (ĕd′wərd). Called the Confessor. 1004?–1066. Last Anglo-Saxon king of the English (1043–66).

Edward. Called the Black Prince. 1330–1376. Prince of Wales.

Edward I. 1239–1307. King of England (1272–1307).

Edward II. 1284–1327. King of England (1307–27); murdered.

Edward III. 1312–1377. King of England (1327–77).

Edward IV. 1442–1483. King of England (1461–83).

Edward V. 1470–1483. King of England (1483); murdered.

Edward VI. 1537–1553. King of England (1547–53).

Edward VII. 1841–1910. King of the United Kingdom and Emperor of India (1901–10).

Edward VIII. 1894–1972. King of England (1936); abdicated and was created Duke of Windsor.

Ed·wards (ĕd′wərdz), **Jonathan.** 1703–1758. American Puritan theologian.

Ein·stein (īn′stīn′), **Albert.** 1879–1955. German-born American physicist; Nobel Prize winner (1921).

Ei·sen·how·er (ī′zən-hou′ər), **Dwight David.** 1890–1969. Thirty-fourth U.S. President (1953–61).

El·ea·nor of Aquitaine (ĕl′ə-nər, -nôr′). 1122?–1204. Queen of France; later, wife of Henry II of England.

El·gar (ĕl′gär), Sir **Edward William.** 1857–1934. British composer.

E·li·jah (ĭ-lī′jə). Also **E·li·as** (ĭ-lī′əs). Hebrew prophet of the 9th cent. B.C.

El·i·ot (ĕl′ē-ət). **1. George.** Pen name of Mary Ann Evans. 1819–1880. English novelist. **2. T(homas) S(tearns).** 1888–1965. American-born English poet and playwright.

E·li·sha (ĭ-lī′shə). Hebrew prophet of the 9th cent. B.C.

E·liz·a·beth (ĭ-lĭz′ə-bəth), Saint. Also **E·lis·a·beth.** In the New Testament, the mother of John the Baptist.

Elizabeth I. 1533–1603. Queen of England and Ireland (1558–1603).

Elizabeth II. Born 1926. Queen of Great Britain and Northern Ireland (since 1952).

Ell·ing·ton (ĕl′ĭng-tən), **Edward Kennedy ("Duke").** 1899–1974. American jazz musician.

El·lis (ĕl′ĭs), **(Henry) Havelock.** 1859–1939. British psychologist.

Em·er·son (ĕm′ər-sən), **Ralph Waldo.** 1803–1882. American essayist and poet.

Eng·els (ĕng′əls), **Friedrich.** 1820–1895. German socialist leader and writer.

Ep·ic·te·tus (ĕp′ĭk-tē′təs). Greek philosopher of the 1st cent. A.D.

Ep·i·cu·rus (ĕp′ĭ-kyōōr′əs). 342?–270 B.C. Greek philosopher. —**Ep′i·cu′re·an** adj. & n.

E·ras·mus (ĭ-răz′məs), **Desiderius.** 1466?–1536. Dutch theologian and scholar.

Er·ic·son (ĕr′ĭk-sən), **Leif.** Norwegian navigator; discovered Vinland (c. A.D. 1000).

Er·ic the Red (ĕr′ĭk). Norwegian navigator of the 10th cent.

Ernst (ĕrnst), **Max.** 1891–1976. German-born American painter.

Eu·clid (yōō′klĭd). Greek mathematician of the 3rd cent. B.C. —**Eu·clid′e·an** or **Eu·clid′i·an** adj.

Eu·gé·nie (œ-zhä-nē′). 1826–1920. Empress of France (1853–71) as wife of Napoleon III.

Eu·rip·i·des (yōō-rĭp′ə-dēz′). 480?–406 B.C. Greek dramatist.

Eve (ēv). In the Old Testament, the wife of Adam.

E·ze·ki·el (ĭ-zē′kē-əl). A major Hebrew prophet of the 6th cent. B.C.

Ez·ra (ĕz′rə). Hebrew high priest of the 5th cent. B.C.

F

Fahd (fäd), **Fahd ibn Abdel Aziz al-Saud al-.** Born 1922. Crown prince of Saudi Arabia (since 1975).

Fair·banks (fâr′băngks), **Charles Warren.** 1852–1918. U.S. Vice President under Theodore Roosevelt (1905–9).

Far·ra·gut (făr′ə-gət), **David Glasgow.** 1801–1870. American naval commander.

Far·rell (făr′əl), **James T(homas).** 1904–1979. American novelist.

Faulk·ner (fôk′nər), **William Harrison.** Also **Falk·ner.** 1897–1962. American author.

Fawkes (fôks), **Guy.** 1570–1606. English Gunpowder Plot conspirator.

Fer·ber (fûr′bər), **Edna.** 1885–1968. American author.

Fer·di·nand I (fûrd′n-ănd′). 1503–1564. King of Bohemia and Hungary (1526–64); Holy Roman Emperor (1558–64).

Ferdinand V. 1452–1516. Spanish King of Aragon, Castile, Sicily, and Naples; aided Columbus.

Fer·mi (fĕr′mē), **Enrico.** 1901–1954. Italian-born American physicist; Nobel Prize winner (1938).

Feyn·man (fīn′mən), **Richard Phillips.** Born 1918. American theoretical physicist; Nobel Prize winner (1965).

Fitch (fĭtch), **Val.** American physicist; Nobel Prize winner (1980).

Fich·te (fĭKH′tə), **Johann Gottlieb.** 1762–1814. German philosopher.

Field·ing (fēl′dĭng), **Henry.** 1707–1754. English novelist.

Fill·more (fĭl′môr′, -mōr′), **Millard.** 1800–1874. Thirteenth U.S. President (1850–53).

Fitz·Ger·ald (fĭts-jĕr′əld), **Edward.** 1809–1883. English poet and translator.

Fitz·ger·ald (fĭts-jĕr′əld), **F(rancis) Scott (Key).** 1896–1940. American author.

Flau·bert (flō-bâr′), **Gustave.** 1821–1880. French novelist.

Flem·ing (flĕm′ĭng), Sir **Alexander.** 1881–1955. British bacteriologist.

Fletch·er (flĕch′ər), **John.** 1579–1625. English dramatist.

Flo·rey (flō′rē), **Paul John.** Born 1910. American chemist; Nobel Prize winner (1974).

Foch (fôsh, fôsh), **Ferdinand.** 1851–1929. French commander in chief during World War I.

Ford (fôrd, fōrd). **1. Henry.** 1863–1947. American automobile designer and manufacturer. **2. Gerald Rudolph.** Born 1913. Thirty-eighth U.S. President (1974–77).

For·ster (fôr′stər), **E(dward) M(organ).** 1879–1970. English novelist.

Fos·ter (fôs′tər, fŏs′-), **Stephen (Collins).** 1826–1864. American composer.

Fou·cault (foo-kō′), **Jean Bernard Léon.** 1819–1868. French physicist.

Fou·rier (foo-ryā′). **1. (François Marie)**

ă pat ā pay â care ä father ĕ pet ē be hw which ĭ pit ī tie î pier ŏ pot ō toe ô paw, for oi noise
ōō took ōō boot ou out th thin th this ŭ cut û urge zh vision ə about, item, edible, gallop, circus

Charles. 1772–1837. French utopian socialist. **2. Baron Jean Baptiste Joseph.** 1768–1830. French physicist and mathematician.

Fox (fŏks). **1. George.** 1624–1691. English founder of the Society of Friends. **2. Charles James.** 1749–1806. British political leader.

Fra·go·nard (frá-gō-nár′), **Jean Honoré.** 1732–1806. French painter.

Fran·cis I (frăn′sĭs, frän′-). 1494–1547. King of France (1515–47).

Francis II. 1768–1835. Last Holy Roman Emperor (1792–1806); abdicated; as Francis I, emperor of Austria (1804–35).

Francis Fer·di·nand (fûr′dn-ănd′). 1863–1914. Archduke of Austria.

Francis of As·si·si (ə-sē′zē), Saint. 1182?–1226. Italian monk; founder of the Franciscan order.

Franck (frängk), **César Auguste.** 1822–1890. Belgian-born French composer.

Fran·co (fräng′kō, frăng′-), **Francisco.** 1892–1975. Spanish general and chief of state (1939–75).

Frank·furt·er (frăngk′fər-tər), **Felix.** 1882–1965. Austrian-born American jurist.

Frank·lin (frăngk′lĭn). **1. Benjamin.** 1706–1790. American statesman, author, and scientist. **2. Sir John.** 1786–1847. British explorer of the Arctic.

Franz Jo·sef (fränts′ yō′zĕf). 1830–1916. Emperor of Austria (1848–1916) and king of Hungary (1867–1916).

Fra·ser (frā′zər), **(John) Malcolm.** Born 1930. Australian prime minister (since 1975).

Fred·er·ick I (frĕd′rĭk). Called Barbarossa. 1123?–1190. Holy Roman Emperor (1152–90); king of Germany (1152–90); king of Italy (1155–90).

Frederick II[1]. 1194–1250. Holy Roman Emperor (1215–50).

Frederick II[2]. Called the Great. 1712–1786. King of Prussia (1740–86).

Frederick IX. 1899–1972. King of Denmark (1947–1972).

Fré·mont (frē′mŏnt), **John Charles.** 1813–1890. American military leader and explorer.

Freud (froid), **Sigmund.** 1856–1939. Austrian neurologist; founder of psychoanalysis.

Fried·man (frēd′mən), **Milton.** Born 1912. American economist; Nobel Prize winner (1976).

Fro·bish·er (frō′bĭ-shər), **Sir Martin.** 1535?–1594. English navigator and explorer.

Frois·sart (frwä-sär′, froi′särt), **Jean.** 1333?–1400? French historian.

Fron·te·nac (frŏn′tə-năk′), **Comte de.** 1620–1698. French colonial governor of Canada.

Frost (frôst, frŏst), **Robert (Lee).** 1874–1963. American poet.

Ful·ler (fŏŏl′ər), **(Sarah) Margaret.** 1810–1850. American editor and feminist leader.

Ful·ton (fŏŏl′tən), **Robert.** 1765–1815. American inventor.

G

Ga·bri·el (gā′brē-əl). One of the archangels.

Ga·ga·rin (gä-gä′rĭn), **Yuri Alekseyevich.** 1934–1968. Soviet cosmonaut; first man in space (1961).

Gage (gāj), **Thomas.** 1721–1787. British general.

Gains·bor·ough (gānz′bûr′ō, -bər-ə), **Thomas.** 1727–1788. English painter.

Ga·len (gā′lən). 130?–201? Greek anatomist and physician.

Gal·i·le·o (găl′ə-lā′ō). 1564–1642. Italian astronomer and philosopher.

Gals·wor·thy (gôlz′wûr′thē), **John.** 1867–1933. English novelist.

Gal·va·ni (gäl-vä′nē), **Luigi.** 1737–1798. Italian physiologist.

Ga·ma (găm′ə), **Vasco da.** 1469?–1524. Portuguese explorer.

Gan·dhi (gän′dē, gän′-). **1. Mohandas Karamchand.** Called Mahatma. 1869–1948. Hindu nationalist and spiritual leader; assassinated. **2. Indira Nehru.** Born 1917. Prime minister of India (1966–77 and since 1980).

Gar·field (gär′fēld′), **James Abram.** 1831–1881. Twentieth U.S. President (1881); assassinated.

Gar·i·bal·di (gär′ə-bôl′dē), **Giuseppe.** 1807–1882. Italian general and patriot.

Gar·ner (gär′nər), **John Nance.** 1868–1967. U.S. Vice President under Franklin D. Roosevelt (1933–41).

Gar·rick (găr′ĭk), **David.** 1717–1779. British actor and theater manager.

Gar·ri·son (găr′ĭ-sən), **William Lloyd.** 1805–1879. American abolitionist editor.

Gas·ser (găs′ər), **Herbert Spencer.** 1888–1963. American physiologist; Nobel Prize winner (1944).

Gates (gāts), **Horatio.** 1728?–1806. American Revolutionary general.

Gau·guin (gō-găɴ′), **(Eugène Henri) Paul.** 1848–1903. French painter.

Gauss (gous), **Karl Friedrich.** 1777–1855. German mathematician, astronomer, and physicist.

Gau·tier (gō-tyā′), **Théophile.** 1811–1872. French poet.

Gay (gā), **John.** 1685–1732. English poet and playwright.

Gell-Mann (gĕl′män′), **Murray.** Born 1929. American physicist; Nobel Prize winner (1969).

Gen·ghis Khan (jĕn′gĭz kän′, jĕng′gĭs, gĕng′gĭs). 1162?–1227. Mongol conqueror.

Geof·frey of Mon·mouth (jĕf′rē; mŏn′məth). 1100?–1154. Welsh bishop and historian.

George I (jôrj). 1660–1727. King of Great Britain (1714–27).

George II. 1683–1760. King of Great Britain (1727–60).

George III. 1738–1820. King of Great Britain (1760–1820).

George IV. 1762–1830. King of Great Britain (1820–30).

George V. 1865–1936. King of Great Britain (1910–36).

George VI. 1895–1952. King of Great Britain (1936–52).

Ge·ron·i·mo (jə-rŏn′ə-mō′). 1829–1909. American Apache Indian leader.

Ger·ry (gĕr′ē), **Elbridge.** 1744–1814. U.S. Vice President under James Madison (1813–14).

Gersh·win (gûrsh′wĭn), **George.** 1898–1937. American composer.

Gia·co·met·ti (jä′kō-mĕt′tē), **Alberto.** 1901–1966. Swiss sculptor and painter.

Gi·auque (jē-ōk′), **William Francis.** Born 1895. American physical chemist; Nobel Prize winner (1949).

Gib·bon (gĭb′ən), **Edward.** 1737–1794. English historian.

Gide (zhēd), **André.** 1869–1951. French novelist.

Gid·e·on (gĭd′ē-ən). Hebrew hero in the Old Testament.

Gil·bert (gĭl′bərt) **1. Sir William S(chwenck).** 1836–1911. English playwright. **2. Walter.** Born 1932. American microbiologist; Nobel Prize winner (1980).

Gior·gio·ne (jôr-jō′nā). 1478?–1511. Venetian painter.

Giot·to (jôt′tō). 1266?–1337? Florentine painter and sculptor.

Gi·rau·doux (zhē-rō-dōō′), **Jean.** 1882–1944. French playwright and novelist.

Gis·card d'Es·taing (zhē-skär′ dĕ-stăɴ′), **Valéry.** Born 1926. French political leader; president of France (1974–81).

Glad·stone (glăd′stōn′, -stən), **William Ewart.** 1809–1898. British statesman; prime minister (1868–94).

Gla·ser (glā′zər), **Donald Arthur.** Born 1926. American nuclear physicist; Nobel Prize winner (1960).

Glenn (glĕn), **John H(erschel), Jr.** Born 1921. American astronaut and political leader.

God·dard (gŏd′ərd), **Robert Hutchings.** 1882–1945. American physicist.

Goeb·bels (gœb′əls), **Joseph Paul.** 1897–1945. German Nazi propaganda minister.

Goep·pert-May·er (gĕp′ərt-mā′ər), **Marie.** Born 1906. German-born American nuclear physicist; Nobel Prize winner (1963).

Goe·thals (gō′thəlz), **George Washington.** 1858–1928. American army officer and engineer.

Goe·the (gœ′tə), **Johann Wolfgang von.** 1749–1832. German author.

Go·gol (gō′gəl), **Nikolai Vasilievich.** 1809–1852. Russian novelist.

Gold·man (gōld′mən), **Emma.** 1869–1940. Russian-born American anarchist.

Gold·smith (gōld′smĭth′), **Oliver.** 1728–1774. English author.

Go·li·ath (gə-lī′əth). In the Old Testament, Philistine giant killed by David.

Gom·pers (gŏm′pərz), **Samuel.** 1850–1924. British-born American labor leader.

Good·year (gŏŏd′yîr′), **Charles.** 1800–1860. American inventor.

Gor·gas (gôr′gəs), **William Crawford.** 1854–1920. American army surgeon.

Gor·ki (gôr′kē), **Maksim.** 1868–1936. Russian author.

Gou·nod (gōō-nō′), **Charles François.**

ă pat   ā pay   â care   ä father   ĕ pet   ē be   hw which   ĭ pit   ī tie   î pier   ŏ pot   ō toe   ô paw, for   oi noise
ŏŏ took   ōō boot   ou out   th thin   th this   ŭ cut   û urge   zh vision   ə about, item, edible, gallop, circus

1818-1893. French composer.

Go·ya (gō′yä), **Francisco José de.** 1746-1828. Spanish artist.

Grac·chus (grăk′əs). Roman family of statesmen, including: **1. Gaius Sempronius.** 153-121 B.C. **2. Tiberius Sempronius.** 163-133 B.C.

Gra·ham (grā′əm), **Martha.** Born 1894? American choreographer.

Grandma Mo·ses (mō′zĭz, -zĭs). In full, Anna Mary Robertson Moses. 1860-1961. American painter.

Grant (grănt), **Ulysses S(impson).** 1822-1885. Eighteenth U.S. President (1869-77).

Graves (grāvz), **Robert (Ranke).** Born 1895. English poet, novelist, and critic.

Gray (grā), **Thomas.** 1716-1771. English poet.

Gree·ley (grē′lē), **Horace.** 1811-1872. American journalist and politician.

Greene (grēn). **1. Nathanael.** 1742-1786. American Revolutionary general. **2. Graham.** Born 1904. English author.

Greg·o·ry I (grĕg′ə-rē), **Saint.** 540?-604. Pope (590-604).

Gregory VII, Saint. 1020?-1085. Pope (1073-85).

Gregory XIII. 1502-1585. Pope (1572-85).

Grey (grā). **1. Lady Jane.** 1537-1554. Queen of England (July 9-19, 1553); executed. **2. Charles.** 1764-1845. Prime Minister of Great Britain (1830-34). **3. sir Edward.** 1862-1933. English statesman. **4. Zane.** 1875-1939. American author.

Grieg (grēg), **Edvard Hagerup.** 1843-1907. Norwegian composer.

Grif·fith (grĭf′ĭth), **D(avid Lewelyn) W(ark).** 1875-1948. American movie director and producer.

Grimm (grĭm). **1. Jakob.** 1785-1863. German philologist and folklorist. **2. Wilhelm** (1786-1859). German philologist and folklorist; brother of Jakob.

Gris (grēs), **Juan.** 1887-1927. Spanish painter.

Gro·my·ko (grō-mē′kō), **Andrei Andreyevich.** Born 1909. Soviet diplomat.

Gro·pi·us (grō′pē-əs), **Walter.** 1883-1969. German-born American architect.

Grosz (grōs), **George.** 1893-1959. German-born American artist.

Gro·ti·us (grō′shē-əs), **Hugo.** 1583-1645. Dutch jurist and statesman.

Guar·nie·ri (gwär-nyâr′ē). Family of Italian violin makers, including: **1. Andrea** 1626-1698. **2. Giuseppe** 1666-1739. **3. Pietro** 1655-1728.

Gui·do d'A·rez·zo (gwē′dō dä-rät′tsō). 995?-1050? Italian musical theorist.

Gui·zot (gē-zō′), **François.** 1787-1874. French statesman.

Gus·ta·vus I (gŭ-stā′vəs). 1496-1560. King of Sweden (1523-60).

Gustavus II. Known as Gustavus Adolphus. 1594-1632. King of Sweden (1611-32).

Gustavus IV. 1778-1837. King of Sweden (1792-1809).

Gustavus V. 1858-1950. King of Sweden (1907-50).

Gustavus VI. 1882-1973. King of Sweden (1950-73).

Gu·ten·berg (gōōt′n-bûrg′), **Johann.** 1400?-1468? German inventor of movable type.

Guth·rie (gŭth′rē), **Woodrow Wilson ("Woody").** 1912-1967. American composer and folk singer.

H

Ha·bak·kuk (hə-băk′ək, hăb′ə-kŭk′). Hebrew prophet of the late 7th cent. B.C.

Ha·dri·an (hā′drē-ən). A.D. 76-138. Roman emperor (117-138).

Ha·gar (hā′gər). In the Old Testament, Abraham's concubine and mother of Ishmael.

Hag·ga·i (hăg′ē-ī′, hăg′ī′). A Hebrew prophet of the 6th cent. B.C.

Hai·le Se·las·sie (hī′lē sə-lăs′ē, sə-lä′sē). 1892-1975. Emperor of Ethiopia (1930-36, 1941-74); deposed.

Hak·luyt (hăk′lōōt′), **Richard.** 1552?-1616. English geographer.

Hale (hāl). **1. Nathan.** 1755-1776. American army officer; hanged by the British for spying. **2. Edward Everett.** 1822-1909. American minister and author.

Hal·ley (hăl′ē), **Edmund.** 1656-1742. British astronomer.

Hals (häls), **Frans.** 1580?-1666. Dutch painter.

Hal·sey (hôl′zē), **William Frederick.** 1882-1959. American Admiral of the Fleet.

Ham (hăm). In the Old Testament, son of Noah.

Ha·man (hā′mən). In the Old Testament, Persian official executed for plotting to massacre the Jews.

Ha·mil·car Bar·ca (hə-mĭl′kär bär′kə). 270?-228 B.C. Carthaginian general.

Ham·il·ton (hăm′əl-tən). **1. Alexander.** 1755-1804. American Revolutionary statesman. **2. Edith.** 1867-1963. American scholar and author.

Ham·lin (hăm′lən), **Hannibal.** 1809-1891. U.S. Vice President under Abraham Lincoln (1861-65).

Ham·mar·skjöld (hăm′är-shœld′), **Dag Hjalmar Agne Carl.** 1905-1961. Swedish diplomat; secretary-general of the United Nations (1953-61).

Ham·mu·ra·bi (hä′mōō-rä′bē, hăm′ə-). Babylonian king and lawgiver of the 18th cent. B.C.

Han·cock (hăn′kŏk′), **John.** 1737-1793. American statesman; first signer of Declaration of Independence.

Han·del (hăn′dl), **George Frederick.** 1685-1759. German-born British composer.

Han·dy (hăn′dē), **W(illiam) C(hristopher).** 1873-1958. American musician.

Han·na (hăn′ə), **Mark.** 1837-1904. American politician.

Han·ni·bal (hăn′ə-bəl). 247-183 B.C. Carthaginian general.

Han·o·ver (hăn′ō′vər). A royal family of England (1714-1901).

Haps·burg (hăps′bûrg′). A princely German family including sovereigns

of Austria (1278-1918) and Spain (1516-1700).

Har·ding (här′dĭng), **Warren Gamaliel.** 1865-1923. Twenty-ninth U.S. President (1921-23); died in office.

Har·dy (här′dē), **Thomas.** 1840-1928. English novelist.

Har·greaves (här′grēvz′), **James.** Died 1778. British inventor.

Har·old I (hăr′əld). Died 1040. English king (1035-40).

Harold II. 1022?-1066. English king (1066).

Har·ris (hăr′ĭs, hâr′-), **Joel Chandler.** 1848-1908. American author.

Har·ri·son (hăr′ĭ-sən). American political family, including: **1. Benjamin** 1726?-1791. Revolutionary leader. **2. William Henry.** 1773-1841. Ninth President (1841); died in office. **3. Benjamin.** 1833-1901. Twenty-third President (1889-93).

Harte (härt), **(Francis) Bret(t).** 1836-1902. American author.

Hart·line (härt′līnlp), **Haldin.** Born 1903. American physiologist; Nobel Prize winner (1967).

Har·vey (här′vē), **William.** 1578-1657. English physician and anatomist.

Haupt·mann (houpt′män′), **Gerhart.** 1862-1946. German author.

Haw·thorne (hô′thôrn′), **Nathaniel.** 1804-1864. American author.

Hay·dn (hīd′n), **Franz Joseph.** 1732-1809. Austrian composer.

Hayes (hāz), **Rutherford B(irchard).** 1822-1893. Nineteenth U.S. President (1877-81).

Haz·litt (hăz′lĭt), **William.** 1778-1830. English essayist.

Hearst (hûrst), **William Randolph.** 1863-1951. American newspaper publisher.

Heath (hēth), **Edward R(ichard) G(eorge).** Born 1916. Prime minister of the United Kingdom (1970-74).

He·gel (hā′gəl), **Georg Wilhelm Friedrich.** 1770-1831. German philosopher. **—He·ge′li·an** (hā-gā′lē-ən) adj. & n.

Hei·deg·ger (hīdĭg′ər), **Martin.** 1889-1976. German philosopher.

Hei·fetz (hī′fĭts), **Jascha.** Born 1901. Russian-born American violinist.

Hei·ne (hī′nə), **Heinrich.** 1797-1856. German poet and critic.

Helm·holtz (hĕlm′hōlts′), **Baron Hermann Ludwig Ferdinand von.** 1821-1894. German physician, physicist, and mathematician.

Hé·lo·ise (ā-lō-ēz′). 1101?-1164? The beloved of Abelard.

Hel·vé·tius (ĕl-vā′shəs), **Claude Adrian.** 1715-1771. French philosopher.

Hem·ing·way (hĕm′ĭng-wā′), **Ernest (Miller).** 1899-1961. American novelist.

Hench (hĕnch), **Philip.** 1896-1965. American physician; Nobel Prize winner (1950).

Hen·dricks (hĕn′drĭks), **Thomas Andrews.** 1819-1885. U.S. Vice President under Grover Cleveland (1885); died in office.

Hen·ley (hĕn′lē), **William Ernest.** 1849-1903. British author.

Hen·ry I (hĕn′rē). 1068-1135. King of

England (1100–35).

Henry II. 1133–1189. King of England (1154–89).

Henry III. 1207–1272. King of England (1216–72).

Henry III. 1551–1589. King of France (1574–89).

Henry IV. 1050–1106. Holy Roman Emperor and King of Germany (1056–1106).

Henry IV. 1367–1413. King of England (1399–1413).

Henry IV. 1553–1610. King of France (1589–1610).

Henry V. 1387–1422. King of England (1413–22).

Henry VI. 1421–1471. King of England (1422–61; 1470–71).

Henry VII. Known as Henry Tudor. 1457–1509. King of England (1485–1509).

Henry VIII. 1491–1547. King of England (1509–47); created Church of England.

Henry, Patrick. 1736–1799. American Revolutionary leader.

Her·a·cli·tus (hĕr'ə-klī'təs). Greek philosopher of the 6th cent. B.C.

Her·bart (hĕr-bärt), **Johann Friedrich.** 1776–1841. German psychologist and philosopher.

Her·bert (hûr'bərt). **1. George.** 1593–1633. English poet. **2. Victor.** 1859–1924. Irishborn American composer.

Her·der (hûr'dər), **Johann von.** 1744–1803. German philosopher.

Her·od (hĕr'əd). Called the Great. 73?–4 B.C. King of Judea (37–4).

Herod An·ti·pas (ăn'tĭ-păs'). Roman tetrarch of Galilee (4 B.C.–A.D. 40).

He·rod·o·tus (hĭ-rŏd'ə-təs). Greek historian of the 5th cent. B.C.

Her·rick (hĕr'ĭk), **Robert.** 1591–1674. English poet.

Her·schel (hûr'shəl). Family of British astronomers, including: **1. Sir William.** 1738–1822. **2. Caroline Lucretia.** 1750–1848. **3. Sir John Frederick William** 1792–1871.

Her·shey (hûr'shē), **Alfred.** Born 1908. American biologist; Nobel Prize winner (1969).

Her·zl (hĕr'tsəl), **Theodor.** 1860–1904. Hungarian-born Austrian founder of Zionism.

He·si·od (hē'sē-əd, hĕs'ē-). Greek poet of the 8th cent. B.C.

Hes·se (hĕs'ə), **Hermann.** 1877–1962. German author.

Hey·er·dahl (hī'ər-däl'), **Thor.** Born 1914. Norwegian explorer.

Heywood (hā'wŏod), **Thomas.** 1574–1641. English playwright.

Hez·e·ki·ah (hĕz'ĭ-kī'ə). 740?–692? B.C. King of Judah (720?–692?).

Hi·a·wath·a (hī'ə-wŏth'ə, -wô'thə). Sixteenth-cent. Mohawk chief; organized the Five Nations.

Hick·ok (hĭk'ŏk'), **James Butler.** Known as Wild Bill Hickok. 1837–1876. American frontier lawman.

Hil·lar·y (hĭl'ə-rē), **Sir Edmund.** Born 1919. New Zealand-born British explorer; 1st to reach summit of Mount Everest (1953).

Hil·ton (hĭl'tn), **James.** 1900–1954. British novelist.

Himm·ler (hĭm'lər), **Heinrich.** 1900–1945. Nazi head of Gestapo.

Hin·de·mith (hĭn'də-mĭth), **Paul.** 1895–1963. German composer.

Hin·den·burg (hĭn'dən-bûrg'), **Paul von.** 1847–1934. German general; president of Germany (1925–34).

Hip·poc·ra·tes (hĭ-pŏk'rə-tēz'). 460?–377? B.C. Greek physician.

Hi·ro·hi·to (hĭr'ō-hē'tō). Born 1901. Emperor of Japan (since 1926).

Hit·ler (hĭt'lər), **Adolf.** 1889–1945. Austrian-born Nazi leader; dictator of German Reich (1933–45).

Ho·bart (hō'bärt, -bärt), **Garret Augustus.** 1844–1899. U.S. Vice President under William McKinley (1897–99); died in office.

Hobbes (hŏbz), **Thomas.** 1588–1679. English philosopher.

Ho Chi Minh (hō' chē' mĭn'). 1890–1969. President of Vietnam (1945–54) and of North Vietnam (1954–69).

Hof·stadt·er (hŏf'städ'ər), **Robert.** Born 1915. American nuclear physicist; Nobel Prize winner (1961).

Ho·garth (hō'gärth), **William.** 1697–1764. British painter and engraver.

Ho·hen·lo·he (hō'ən-lō'ə). A German princely family; ruled from the 12th to the 19th cent.

Ho·hen·stau·fen (hō'ən-shtou'fən). A German princely family, including rulers of Sicily and the Holy Roman Empire in the 12th and 13th cent.

Ho·hen·zol·lern (hō'ən-tsŏl'ərn). A German royal family, including rulers of Brandenburg (1415–1918), Prussia (1701–1918), and Germany (1871–1918).

Hol·bein (hōl'bīn'). **1. Hans.** 1465?–1524. German painter. **2. Hans.** Called the Younger. 1497?–1543. German painter.

Hol·ley (hŏl'ē), **Robert.** Born 1922; American biochemist; Nobel Prize winner (1968).

Holmes (hōmz, hōlmz). **1. Oliver Wendell.** 1809–1894. American author. **2. Oliver Wendell.** 1841–1935. American jurist.

Ho·mer (hō'mər). Greek epic poet.

Homer, Winslow. 1836–1910. American painter.

Hook·er (hŏok'ər), **Thomas.** 1586?–1647. English Puritan clergyman.

Hoo·ver (hōo'vər). **1. Herbert Clark.** 1874–1964. Thirty-first U.S. President (1929–33). **2. J(ohn) Edgar.** 1895–1972. American director of the F.B.I. (1924–72).

Hop·kins (hŏp'kĭnz). **1. Mark.** 1813–1878. American educator. **2. Gerard Manley.** 1844–1889. English poet.

Hor·ace (hôr'ĭs, hŏr'-). 65–8 B.C. Latin poet.

Ho·se·a (hō-zē'ə, -zā'ə). Hebrew prophet of the 8th cent. B.C.

Hou·di·ni (hōo-dē'nē), **Harry.** 1874–1926. American magician.

Hous·man (hous'mən), **A(lfred) E(dward).** 1859–1936. English poet.

Hous·ton (hyōo'stən), **Sam(uel).** 1793–1863. American general; president of the Republic of Texas (1836–38 and 1841–44).

Howe (hou). **1. Elias.** 1819–1867. American inventor. **2. Julia Ward.** 1819–1910. American feminist and author.

How·ells (hou'əlz), **William Dean.** 1837–1920. American author and editor.

Hua Kuo-feng (hwä' kwō'fŭng'). Born 1920. Chinese statesman; first deputy chairman (1976–79).

Hud·son (hŭd'sən). **1. Henry.** Died 1611. English navigator; explored Arctic waters. **2. William Henry.** 1841–1922. English naturalist and author.

Hug·gins (hŭg'ĭnz), **Charles Brenton.** Born 1901. Canadian-born American surgeon; Nobel Prize winner (1966).

Hughes (hyōoz). **1. Charles Evans.** 1862–1948. American jurist. **2. (James) Langston.** 1902–1967. American novelist and poet.

Hu·go (hyōo'gō), **Victor Marie.** 1802–1885. French author.

Hull (hŭl), **Cordell.** 1871–1955. American political leader.

Hume (hyōom), **David.** 1711–1776. Scottish philosopher and historian.

Hum·phrey (hŭm'frē), **Hubert Horatio.** 1911–1979. U.S. Vice President under Lyndon B. Johnson (1965–69).

Huss (hŭs), **John.** Also **Jan Hus** (yän'hōos'). 1369?–1415. Bohemian religious reformer.

Hus·sein I (hōo-sīn', -sān'). Born 1935. King of Jordan (since 1953).

Hux·ley (hŭk'slē). British family, including: **1. Thomas Henry.** 1825–1895. Biologist. **2. Sir Julian Sorell.** 1887–1975. Biologist and author. **3. Aldous Leonard.** 1894–1963. Novelist and critic.

I

Ib·sen (ĭb'sən), **Henrik.** 1828–1906. Norwegian dramatist.

Ig·na·tius Loy·o·la (ĭg-nā'shəs loi-ō'lə), Saint. 1491–1556. Spanish soldier and founder of the Society of Jesus (1534).

In·gres (ăN'gr'), **Jean Auguste Dominique.** 1780–1867. French painter.

In·no·cent III (ĭn'ə-sənt). 1161–1216. Pope (1198–1216).

Ir·ving (ûr'vĭng), **Washington.** 1783–1859. American author.

Isaac (ī'zək). Hebrew patriarch.

Is·a·bel·la I (ĭz'ə-bĕl'ə). 1451–1501. Queen of Castile and Aragon as wife of Ferdinand V.

I·sa·iah (ī-zā'ə, ī-zī'ə). Hebrew prophet of the 8th cent. B.C.

Ish·ma·el (ĭsh'mē-əl). In the Old Testament, son of Abraham and Hagar.

I·van III Va·sil·ie·vich (ī'vən vä-sēl'yə-vĭch). Called the Great. 1440–1505. Grand Duke of Muscovy (1462–1505).

Ivan IV Vasilievich. Called the Terrible. 1530–1584. Grand Duke of Muscovy (1533–84); first czar (1547–84).

Ives (īvz), **Charles Edward.** 1874–1954. American composer.

J

Jack·son (jăk'sən). **1. Andrew.** 1767–1845. Seventh U.S. President (1829–37). **2. Thomas Jonathan.** Called

Stonewall. 1824-1863. American military leader.

Ja·cob (jā'kəb). Hebrew patriarch.

James I (jāmz). 1566-1625. First Stuart king of England (1603-25); as James VI, king of Scotland (1567-1625).

James II. 1633-1701. King of England, Scotland, and Ireland (1685-88).

James. 1. William. 1842-1910. American philosopher and psychologist. **2. Henry.** 1843-1916. American novelist and critic.

James, Saint. **1.** Called the Less. Traditionally regarded as the brother of Jesus. **2.** Called the Greater. One of the 12 Apostles. **3.** One of the 12 Apostles.

Jay (jā), **John.** 1745-1829. American statesman and jurist.

Jef·fer·son (jĕf'ər-sən), **Thomas.** 1743-1826. Third U.S. President (1801-9).

Je·hosh·a·phat (jə-hŏsh'ə-făt'). In the Old Testament, a king of Judah.

Jen·ner (jĕn'ər), **Edward.** 1749-1823. British physician.

Jeph·thah (jĕf'thə). In the Old Testament, a judge of Israel.

Jer·e·mi·ah (jĕr'ə-mī'ə). A Hebrew prophet of the 7th and 6th cent. B.C.

Jes·se (jĕs'ē). In the Old Testament, father of King David.

Je·sus (jē'zəs) 4? B.C.-A.D. 29? Founder of Christianity.

Jez·e·bel (jĕz'ə-bĕl', -bəl). Queen of Israel as wife of Ahab.

Joan of Arc (jōn'; ärk'), Saint. Also **Jeanne d'Arc** (zhän därk'). Called the Maid of Orléans. 1412-1431. French heroine and military leader.

Job (jōb). Hebrew patriarch.

Jo·el (jō'əl). A Hebrew prophet of the 9th cent. B.C.

John (jŏn). 1167?-1216. King of England (1199-1216).

John XXIII. 1881-1963. Pope (1958-63).

John Paul I (pôl). 1912-1978. Pope (1978).

John Paul II. Born 1920. Pope (since 1978).

John, Saint. One of the 12 Apostles.

John of Gaunt (gônt, gänt). 1340-1399. Duke of Lancaster.

John·son (jŏn'sən). **1. Samuel.** Known as Dr. Johnson. 1709-1784. English lexicographer and author. **2. Richard Mentor.** 1780-1850. U.S. Vice President under Martin Van Buren (1837-41). **3. Andrew.** 1808-1875. Seventeenth U.S. President (1865-69). **4. Lyndon Baines.** 1908-1973. Thirty-sixth U.S. President (1963-69).

John the Baptist, Saint. Cousin of Jesus.

Jo·li·et (jō'lē-ĕt'), **Louis.** 1645-1700. French-Canadian explorer.

Jo·nah (jō'nə). Hebrew prophet.

Jon·a·than (jŏn'ə-thən). In the Old Testament, eldest son of King Saul.

Jones (jōnz). **1. John Paul.** 1747-1792. Scottish-born American naval officer in the Revolutionary War. **2. James.** Born 1921. American novelist.

Jon·son (jŏn'sən), **Ben(jamin).** 1573-1637. English poet and dramatist.

Joseph. 1840-1904. Nez Percé Indian chief.

Joseph. Husband of Mary, the mother of Jesus.

Jo·sé·phine de Beau·har·nais (zhō-zā-fēn' də bō-är-ně'). 1763-1814. Empress of the French as wife of Napoleon I (1804-9).

Joseph of Ar·i·ma·the·a (âr'ə-mə-thē'ə, är'-). In the New Testament, a rich Jew who provided a tomb for Jesus.

Jo·se·phus (jō-sē'fəs), **Flavius.** A.D. 37-100? Jewish historian.

Josh·ua (jŏsh'ōō-ə). Old Testament Hebrew leader.

Joyce (jois), **James.** 1882-1941. Irish novelist.

Juan Car·los I (hwän kär'lōs). Born 1938. King of Spain (since 1975).

Juá·rez (hwä'rās), **Benito Pablo.** 1806-1872. Mexican revolutionary statesman.

Ju·bal (jōō'bəl). In the Old Testament, a descendant of Cain.

Ju·dah (jōō'də). In the Old Testament, a son of Jacob.

Ju·das (jōō'dəs). Called Judas Iscariot. One of the 12 Apostles; betrayer of Jesus.

Jude (jōōd), Saint. One of the 12 Apostles.

Ju·dith (jōō'dĭth). In the Old Testament, a Jewish heroine.

Jul·ian (jōōl'yən). A.D. 331-363. Roman emperor (361-363).

Ju·li·an·a (jōō'lē-än'ə). Born 1909. Queen of the Netherlands (1948-80); abdicated.

Jung (yŏŏng), **Carl Gustav.** 1875-1961. Swiss psychologist.

Jus·tin·i·an I (jŭ-stĭn'ē-ən). 483-565. Roman emperor of the East (527-565).

Ju·ve·nal (jōō'və-nəl). A.D. 60?-140? Roman satirist.

K

Kaf·ka (käf'kä), **Franz.** 1883-1924. Austrian novelist.

Kan·din·sky (kăn-dĭn'skē), **Vasili.** 1866-1944. Russian painter.

Kant (känt, känt), **Immanuel.** 1724-1804. German philosopher. **—Kant'i·an** adj.

Keats (kēts), **John.** 1795-1821. English poet.

Kel·ler (kĕl'ər), **Helen Adams.** 1880-1968. American deaf and blind author and lecturer.

Kel·logg (kĕl'ôg', -ŏg), **Frank Billings.** 1856-1937. American lawyer and diplomat; Nobel Peace Prize winner (1929).

Kel·vin (kĕl'vĭn), **First Baron.** Title of William Thomson. 1824-1907. British physicist and mathematician.

Kem·pis (kĕm'pĭs), **Thomas à.** 1380-1471. German ecclesiastic and writer.

Ken·dall (kĕnd'l), **Edward.** 1886-1792. American biochemist; Nobel Prize winner (1950).

Ken·ne·dy (kĕn'ə-dē), **1. John Fitzgerald.** 1917-1963. Thirty-fifth U.S. President (1961-63); assassinated. **2. Robert Francis.** 1925-1968. American politician; assassinated.

Ken·yat·ta (kĕn-yä'tə), **Jomo.** 1893?-1978. President of Kenya (1963-78).

Kep·ler (kĕp'lər), **Johannes.** 1571-1630. German astronomer.

Ke·ren·sky (kə-rĕn'skē), **Aleksandr Fyodorovich.** 1881-1970. Russian revolutionary leader.

Key (kē), **Francis Scott.** 1779-1843. American lawyer; author of "The Star-Spangled Banner."

Keynes (kānz), **John Maynard.** 1883-1946. British economist.

Kha·lid (кнä-lēd'), **Khalid Abdul Aziz al-Saud al-.** Born 1913. King of Saudi Arabia (since 1975).

Kho·mei·ni (kō-mä'nē, кнō-), **Ayatollah Ruholla.** Born 1900. Iranian leader.

Kho·ra·na (kō-rä'nə), **Har Hobind.** Born 1922. Indian-born American biochemist; Nobel Prize winner (1968).

Khru·shchev (krōōsh-chôf', krōōsh'-cěf'), **Nikita Sergeyevich.** 1894-1971. Premier of the Soviet Union (1958-64).

Kier·ke·gaard (kîr'kə-gärd'), **Sören Aabye.** 1813-1855. Danish philosopher and theologian.

King (kĭng). **1. William Rufus DeVane.** 1786-1853. U.S. Vice President under Franklin Pierce (1853). **2. William Lyon Mackenzie.** 1874-1950. Prime minister of Canada (1921-26, 1926-30, and 1935-48). **3. Martin Luther, Jr.** 1929-1968. American civil-rights leader; Nobel Peace Prize winner (1964); assassinated.

Kip·ling (kĭp'lĭng), **Rudyard.** 1865-1936. English author.

Kis·sin·ger (kĭs'ĭn-jər'), **Henry Alfred.** Born 1923. German-born American statesman; Nobel Peace Prize winner (1973).

Klee (klā, klē), **Paul.** 1879-1940. Swiss painter.

Klein (klīn), **Lawrence.** Born 1920. American economist; Nobel Prize winner (1980).

Knox (nŏks), **John.** 1505-1572. Scottish Protestant religious reformer.

Koch (kōкн), **Robert.** 1843-1910. German bacteriologist.

Korn·berg (kôrn'bûrg'), **Arthur.** Born 1918. American biochemist; Nobel Prize winner (1959).

Kos·ci·us·ko (kŏs'ē-ŭs'kō), **Thaddeus.** 1746-1817. Polish commander in the Revolutionary War.

Kos·suth (kŏs'ōōth), **Louis.** 1802-1894. Hungarian statesman.

Ko·sy·gin (kə-sē'gĭn), **Aleksei Nikolayevich.** 1904-1980. Premier of the Soviet Union (1964-1980).

Ku·blai Khan (kōō'blī kän'). Also **Ku·bla Khan** (kōō'blə). 1216-1294. Founder of the Mongol dynasty.

Kusch (kŏŏsh), **Polycarp.** Born 1911. German-born American physicist; Nobel Prize winner (1955).

Kuz·nets (kōōz'nĕts), **Simon.** Born 1901. Russian-born American economist; Nobel Prize winner (1971).

L

La·fay·ette (lä'fē-ĕt', läf'ē-), **Marquis de.** 1757-1834. French military and political leader.

La Fon·taine (lä fôn-tĕn'), **Jean de.** 1621–1695. French poet and fabulist.

La·marck (lə-märk'), Chevalier **Jean de.** 1744–1829. French naturalist.

Lamb (lăm). **1. Charles.** Pen name, Elia. (ē'lē-ə). 1775–1834. English essayist. **2. Willis Eugene.** Born 1913. American physicist; Nobel Prize winner (1955).

Lan·cas·ter (lăng'kə-stər). Family name of rulers of England (1399–1461). —**Lan·cas'tri·an** adj. & n.

Land·stei·ner (länd'stī'nər), **Karl.** 1868–1943. Austrian-born American pathologist; Nobel Prize winner (1930).

Lang·land (lăng'lənd), **William.** 1332?–1400? English poet.

Lang·ley (lăng'lē), **Samuel Pierpont.** 1834–1906. American astronomer and aeronautical pioneer.

Lang·muir (lăng'myōōr'), **Irving.** 1881–1957. American chemist; Nobel Prize winner (1932).

Lao-tse (lou'dzŭ'). Also **Lao-tsze, Lao-tsu.** 604?–531 B.C. Chinese philosopher; founder of Taoism.

La·place (lä-pläs'), Marquis **Pierre Simon de.** 1749–1827. French mathematician and astronomer.

La Roche·fou·cauld (lä rôsh-fōō-kō'), Duc **François de.** 1613–1680. French author.

La Salle (lə säl'), Sieur de. 1643–1687. French explorer.

Laud (lôd), **William.** 1573–1645. Archbishop of Canterbury; executed for treason.

La·voi·sier (lä-vwä-zyā'), **Antoine Laurent.** 1743–1794. French chemist.

Law·rence (lôr'əns, lŏr'-). **1.** Sir **Thomas.** 1769–1830. British portraitist. **2. D(avid) H(erbert).** 1885–1930. English author. **3. T(homas) E(dward).** Known as Lawrence of Arabia. 1888–1935. British soldier and writer. **4. Ernest Orlando.** 1901–1958. American physicist; Nobel Prize winner (1939).

Laz·a·rus (lăz'ə-rəs). In the New Testament, brother of Mary and Martha, believed to have been raised from the dead.

Laz·a·rus (lăz'ər-əs), **Emma.** 1849–1887. American poet and philanthropist.

Led·er·berg (lĕd'ər-bûrg), **Joshua.** Born 1925. American geneticist; Nobel Prize winner (1958).

Lee (lē). **1. Ann.** 1736–1784. British religious leader; founded first Shaker colony in America (1776). **2. Henry.** Known as Light-Horse Harry. 1756–1818. American statesman and Revolutionary War commander. **3. Robert E(dward).** 1807–1870. Commander in chief of Confederate armies. **4. T(sung) D(ao).** Born 1926. Chinese-born American physicist; Nobel Prize winner (1957).

Leib·nitz (līb'nĭts'), Baron **Gottfried Wilhelm von.** 1646–1716. German philosopher and mathematician.

Le·nin (lĕn'ĭn, -ēn'), **V(ladimir) I(lyich).** 1870–1924. Russian statesman; 1st premier of U.S.S.R. (1918–24).

Le·o I (lē'ō), Saint. A.D. 390?–461. Pope (440–461).

Leo III. Saint. A.D. 750?–816. Pope (795–816).

Leo X. 1475–1521. Pope (1513–21); son of Lorenzo de' Medici.

Le·o XIII. 1810–1903. Pope (1878–1903).

Le·o·nar·do da Vin·ci (lē'ə-när'dō də vĭn'chē). 1452–1519. Florentine artist and engineer.

Le·on·i·das I (lē-ŏn'ə-dəs). King of Sparta (490?–480 B.C.); killed at Thermopylae.

Lep·i·dus (lĕp'ə-dəs), **Marcus Aemilius.** Died 13 B.C. Roman triumvir (43–36 B.C.?).

Les·seps (lĕs'əps), Vicomte **Ferdinand Marie de.** 1805–1894. French diplomat; promoted Suez Canal.

Le·vi (lē'vī). In the Old Testament, son of Jacob.

Lew·is (lōō'ĭs). **1. Meriwether.** 1774–1809. American explorer. **2. John L(lewellyn).** 1880–1969. American labor leader. **3. (Harry) Sinclair.** 1885–1951. American novelist; Nobel Prize winner (1930). **4. C(live) S(taples).** 1898–1963. English novelist.

Lib·by (lĭb'ē), **Willard Frank.** Born 1908. American chemist; Nobel Prize winner (1960).

Lie (lē), **Trygve Halvdan.** 1896–1968. Norwegian statesman; 1st secretary-general of the United Nations (1946–53).

Lin·coln (lĭng'kən), **Abraham.** 1809–1865. Sixteenth U.S. President (1861–65); assassinated.

Lind·bergh (lĭnd'bûrg', lĭn'-), **Charles Augustus.** 1902–1974. American aviator.

Lin·nae·us (lĭ-nē'əs), **Carolus.** 1707–1778. Swedish botanist.

Lip·pi (lĭp'ē). **1. Fra Filippo** or **Lippo.** 1406?–1469. Florentine painter. **2. Filippino.** 1457–1504. Florentine painter, son of Fra Filippo.

Lips·comb (lĭp'skəm), **William.** Born 1919. American physical chemist; Nobel Prize winner (1976).

Lis·ter (lĭs'tər), **Joseph.** First Baron Lister. 1827–1912. British surgeon.

Liszt (lĭst), **Franz.** 1811–1886. Hungarian composer and pianist.

Liv·ing·stone (lĭv'ĭng-stən), **David.** 1813–1873. Scottish medical missionary and explorer in Central Africa.

Liv·y (lĭv'ē). 59 B.C.–A.D. 17. Roman historian.

Lloyd George (loid' jôrj'), **David.** 1863–1945. Prime minister of Great Britain (1916–22).

Locke (lŏk), **John.** 1632–1704. English philosopher.

Loe·wi (lō'ē), **Otto.** 1873–1961. German-born American pharmacologist; Nobel Prize winner (1936).

Lon·don (lŭn'dən), **Jack.** 1876–1916. American author and adventurer.

Long·fel·low (lông'fĕl'ō, lŏng'-), **Henry Wadsworth.** 1807–1882. American poet.

Lo·renz (lō'rĕnts'), **Konrad Zacharias.** Born 1903. Austrian psychologist.

Lou·is IX (lōō'ē). Known as Saint Louis. 1214–1270. King of France (1226–70).

Louis XI. 1423–1483. King of France (1461–83).

Louis XIII. 1601–1643. King of France (1610–43).

Louis XIV. Called the Sun King. 1638–1715. King of France (1643–1715).

Louis XV. 1710–1774. King of France (1715–74).

Louis XVI. 1754–1793. King of France (1774–92).

Louis XVIII. 1755–1824. King of France (1814–24).

Louis Phi·lippe (fĭ-lēp'). Called the Citizen King. 1773–1850. King of France (1830–48).

Low·ell (lō'əl). **1. James Russell.** 1819–1891. American poet, essayist, and diplomat. **2. Amy.** 1874–1925. American poet.

Lu·cre·tius (lōō-krē'shəs). 96?–55 B.C. Roman poet and philosopher.

Luke (lōōk), Saint. A companion of the Apostle Paul; traditionally regarded as author of the 3rd Gospel.

Lu·ria (lōō'ruä), **Salvatore.** Born 1912. American biologist; Nobel Prize winner (1969).

Lu·ther (lōō'thər), **Martin.** 1483–1546. German monk; a founder of Protestantism.

Lyl·y (lĭl'ē), **John.** 1554?–1606. English novelist and dramatist.

Ly·on (lī'ən), **Mary.** 1797–1849. American educator.

M

Mac·Ar·thur (mək-är'thər), **Douglas.** 1880–1964. American General of the Army.

Ma·cau·lay (mə-kô'lē), **Thomas Babington.** 1800–1859. English historian and statesman.

Mac·ca·be·us (măk'ə-bē'əs), **Judas.** Died 160 B.C. Jewish patriot.

Mac·don·ald (mək-dŏn'əld), Sir **John Alexander.** 1815–1891. Prime minister of Canada (1867–73 and 1878–91).

Mac·Don·ald (mək-dŏn'əld), **(James) Ramsay.** 1866–1937. Prime minister of Great Britain (1924 and 1929–35).

Mach (mäкн), **Ernst.** 1836–1916. Austrian physicist.

Mach·i·a·vel·li (măk'ē-ə-vĕl'ē), **Nicco·lò.** 1469–1527. Italian statesman and political theorist.

Mac·ken·zie (mə-kĕn'zē). **1.** Sir **Alexander.** 1764–1820. Scottish explorer of the Canadian NW. **2. Alexander.** 1822–1892. Prime minister of Canada (1873–78).

Mac·Leish (mə-klēsh'), **Archibald.** Born 1892. American poet and dramatist.

Mac·mil·lan (mək-mĭl'ən), **(Maurice) Harold.** Born 1894. Prime minister of Great Britain (1957–63).

Mad·i·son (măd'ĭ-sən), **James.** 1751–1836. Fourth U.S. President (1809–17).

Mae·ter·linck (mä'tər-lĭngk'), Count **Maurice.** 1862–1949. Belgian poet and naturalist.

Ma·gel·lan (mə-jĕl'ən), **Ferdinand.** 1480?–1521. Portuguese navigator and explorer.

Mag·say·say (mäg-sī'sī'), **Ramón.** 1907–1957. President of the Philippines (1953–57).

Mah·ler (mä′lĕr), **Gustav.** 1860–1911. Austrian composer.

Mail·lol (mä-yôl′), **Aristide.** 1861–1944. French sculptor.

Mai·mon·i·des (mī-mŏn′ə-dēz′), **Moses.** 1135–1204. Spanish-born Jewish philosopher and physician.

Ma·kar·i·os III (mä-kä′rē-ōs). 1913–1977. Cypriot statesman and prelate; president (1960–74).

Mal·a·chi (măl′ə-kī′). Hebrew prophet of the 5th cent. B.C.

Mal·lar·mé (má-lár-mā′), **Stéphane.** 1842–1898. French poet.

Mal·o·ry (măl′ə-rē), Sir **Thomas.** English author of the 15th cent.

Mal·raux (mál-rō′), **André.** 1901–1976. French statesman and author.

Mal·thus (măl′thəs), **Thomas Robert.** 1766–1834. English economist.

Ma·nas·seh (mə-năs′ə). A king of Judah in the 7th cent. B.C.

Ma·net (má-nā′), **Edouard.** 1832–1883. French painter.

Mann (măn). **1. Horace.** 1796–1859. American educator. **2. Thomas.** 1875–1955. German-born American author; Nobel Prize winner (1929).

Man·te·gna (män-tā′nyä), **Andrea.** 1431–1506. Italian painter.

Mao Tse-tung (mou′ tsĭ-tŏong′, mou′ dzŭ′dŏong′). 1893–1976. Chinese head of state (1949–59).

Ma·rat (má-rá′), **Jean Paul.** 1743–1793. Swiss-born French revolutionary; assassinated.

Mar·co·ni (mär-kō′nē), Marchese **Guglielmo.** 1874–1937. Italian electrical engineer; Nobel Prize winner (1909).

Mar·cos (mär′kōs), **Ferdinand Edralin.** Born 1917. President of the Philippines (since 1965).

Mar·cus Au·re·li·us An·to·ni·nus (mär′kəs ô-rē′lē-əs). 121–180 Roman emperor and Stoic philosopher.

Mar·gar·et of Na·varre (mär′gə-rət; nə-vär′). 1430–1482. Queen of Henry VI of England.

Margaret of Val·ois (văl-wä′). 1553–1615. Queen of Henry IV of France.

Mar·gre·the II (mär-grā′tə). Born 1940. Queen of Denmark (since 1972).

Ma·ri·a The·re·sa (mə-rē′ə tə-rā′zə, tə-rā′sə). 1717–1780. Queen of Hungary and Bohemia and Archduchess of Austria.

Ma·rie An·toi·nette (mə-rē′ ăn′twə-nĕt′). 1755–1793. Queen of Louis XVI of France (1774–93); executed.

Ma·rie-Lou·ise (mə-rē′lōō-ēz′). 1791–1847. Second wife of Napoleon I Empress of France (1810–14).

Mar·in (măr′ĭn), **John.** 1872–1953. American painter.

Mar·i·on (măr′ē-ən, măr′-), **Francis.** Called the Swamp Fox. 1732?–1795. American general.

Ma·ri·tain (má-rē-tăN′), **Jacques.** 1882–1973. French philosopher and critic.

Mar·i·us (mâr′ē-əs), **Gaius.** 155?–86 B.C. Roman general.

Mark (märk), Saint. Author of the 2nd Gospel.

Mark An·to·ny (märk ăn′tə-nē). See Marcus **Antonius.**

Mark·ham (mär′kəm), **(Charles) Ed-**

win. 1852–1940. American poet.

Marl·bor·ough (märl′bər-ə, môl′-), **First Duke of.** Title of John Churchill. 1650–1722. English general and statesman.

Mar·lowe (mär′lō), **Christopher.** 1564–1593. English dramatist and poet.

Mar·quette (mär-kĕt′), **Jacques.** 1637–1675. French explorer.

Mar·shall (mär′shəl). **1. John.** 1755–1835. American statesman and jurist. **2. Thomas Riley.** 1854–1925. U.S. Vice President under Woodrow Wilson (1913–21). **3. George Catlett.** 1880–1959. American General of the Army, statesman, and diplomat. **4. Thurgood.** Born 1908. American jurist.

Mar·tha (mär′thə). A sister of Lazarus and Mary, and friend of Jesus.

Mar·tial (mär′shəl). Roman poet and epigrammatist of the 1st cent. A.D.

Mar·vell (mär′vəl), **Andrew.** 1621–1678. English poet.

Marx (märks), **Karl.** 1818–1883. German philosopher and political economist.

Mar·y (mâr′ē). The mother of Jesus.

Mary I. Title of Mary Tudor. Called Bloody Mary. 1516–1558. Queen of England and Ireland (1553–58).

Mary II. 1662–1694. Queen of England, Scotland, and Ireland (1689–94); with her husband William III.

Mary Mag·da·lene (măg′də-lēn′,-lən). A woman cured of evil spirits by Jesus; identified with the repentant prostitute who anointed Jesus' feet.

Mar·y Queen of Scots (mâr′ē). Title of Mary Stuart. 1542–1587. Queen of Scotland; abdicated (1567); beheaded.

Ma·sa·ryk (măs′ə-rĭk), **Tomáš Garrigue.** 1850–1937. First president of Czechoslovakia (1918–35).

Mas·ca·gni (mäs-kä′nyē), **Pietro.** 1863–1945. Italian composer.

Mase·field (mās′fēld′), **John.** 1878–1967. English author.

Mas·sa·soit (măs′ə-soit′, măs′ə-soit′). 1580?–1661. Wampanoag Indian chief; aided the Pilgrims.

Mas·se·net (măs′ə-nā′), **Jules Émile Frédéric.** 1842–1912. French composer.

Mas·ters (măs′tərz, mäs′-), **Edgar Lee.** 1869–1950. American poet.

Math·er (măth′ər, măth′ər). **1. Increase.** 1639–1723. American clergyman and author. **2. Cotton.** 1663–1728. American Congregational clergyman and author.

Ma·tisse (mä-tēs′), **Henri.** 1869–1954. French painter.

Mat·thew (măth′yōō), Saint. Apostle and author of the 1st Gospel.

Mat·thi·as (mə-thī′əs), Saint. Apostle chosen by lot to take the place of Judas Iscariot.

Maugham (môm), **W(illiam) Somerset.** 1874–1965. English author.

Mau·pas·sant (mō-pä-säN′), **Guy de.** 1850–1893. French author.

Mau·riac (mô-ryäk′), **François.** 1885–1970. French novelist.

Mau·rois (mô-rwä′), **André.** Pen name of Émile Herzog. 1885–1967. French historian and author.

Max·i·mil·ian (măk′sə-mĭl′yən). 1832–

1867. Austrian archduke; emperor of Mexico (1864); executed.

Maximilian I. 1459–1519. Holy Roman Emperor (1493–1519).

Max·well (măks′wĕl′, -wəl), **James Clerk.** 1831–1879. Scottish physicist.

Maz·a·rin (măz′ə-rĭn), **Jules.** 1602–1661. Italian-born French cardinal and statesman.

Maz·zi·ni (mät-tsē′nē), **Giuseppe.** 1805–1872. Italian patriot and revolutionary.

Mc·Clel·lan (mə-klĕl′ən), **George Brinton.** 1826–1885. Union general in the Civil War.

Mc·Cor·mick (mə-kôr′mĭk), **Cyrus Hall.** 1809–1884. American inventor.

Mc·Kin·ley (mə-kĭn′lē), **William.** 1843–1901. Twenty-fifth U.S. President (1897–1901); assassinated.

Mc·Mil·lan (mək-mĭl′ən), **Edwin Mattison.** Born 1907. American physicist; Nobel Prize winner (1951).

Mead (mēd), **Margaret.** 1901–1978. American anthropologist.

Meade (mēd), **George Gordon.** 1815–1872. Union general in the Civil War.

Med·i·ci (mĕ′dē-chē′). **1. Cosimo de'.** 1389–1464. Florentine banker, statesman, and art patron. **2. Lorenzo de'.** 1449–1492. Florentine statesman, art patron, and author.

Meig·hen (mē′ən), **Arthur.** 1874–1960. Prime Minister of Canada (1920–21 and 1926).

Me·ir (mī′ər, mä-ēr′), **Golda.** 1898–1978. Russian-born premier of Israel (1969–74).

Mel·ville (mĕl′vĭl), **Herman.** 1819–1891. American novelist.

Mem·ling (mĕm′lĭng), **Hans.** 1430?–1495. Flemish painter.

Me·nan·der (mə-năn′dər). Athenian author of the 4th cent. B.C.

Men·del (mĕn′dəl), **Gregor Johann.** 1822–1884. Austrian monk scientist.

Men·de·le·ev (mĕn′də-lā′əf), **Dmitri Ivanovich.** 1834–1907. Russian chemist; devised the periodic table of the elements (1869).

Men·dels·sohn (mĕn′dəl-sən), **Felix.** 1809–1847. German composer, pianist, and conductor.

Me·nes (mē′nēz). Egyptian king; founder (c. 3000 B.C.) of the 1st dynasty.

Me·not·ti (mə-nŏt′ē), **Gian Carlo.** Born 1911. Italian-born American composer and librettist.

Mer·ca·tor (mər-kā′tər), **Gerhardus.** 1512–1594. Flemish geographer and cartographer.

Mer·e·dith (mĕr′ə-dĭth), **George.** 1828–1859. English author.

Met·ter·nich (mĕt′ər-nĭkH), Prince **Klemens Wenzel Nepomuk Lothar von.** 1773–1859. Austrian statesman.

Mey·er·beer (mī′ər-bîr′, -bâr′), **Giacomo.** 1791–1864. German composer.

Mi·cah (mī′kə). A Hebrew prophet of the 8th cent. B.C.

Mi·chel·an·ge·lo (mī′kəl-ăn′jə-lō′, mĭk′əl-). Full name, Michelangelo Buonarroti. 1475–1564. Italian sculptor, painter, architect, and poet.

Mi·chel·son (mī′kəl-sən), **Albert Abraham.** 1852–1931. German-born American physicist; Nobel Prize win-

---

ă pat ā pay â care ä father ĕ pet ē be hw which ĭ pit ī tie î pier ŏ pot ō toe ô paw, for oi noise
ōō took ōō boot ou out th thin *th* this ŭ cut û urge zh vision ə about, item, edible, gallop, circus

Mill (mĭl), **John Stuart.** 1806–1873. English economist and political theorist.

Mil·lay (mĭ-lā′), **Edna St. Vincent.** 1892–1950. American poet.

Mil·ler (mĭl′ər), **Arthur.** Born 1915. American playwright.

Mil·let (mĭ-lā′), **Jean François.** 1814–1875. French painter.

Mil·li·kan (mĭl′ĭ-kən), **Robert Andrews.** 1868–1953. American nuclear physicist; Nobel Prize winner (1923).

Milne (mĭln), **A(lan) A(lexander).** 1882–1956. English author.

Mil·ti·a·des (mĭl-tī′ə-dēz′). 540?–489 B.C. Athenian general; defeated the Persians at the Battle of Marathon (490 B.C.).

Mil·ton (mĭl′tən), **John.** 1608–1674. English poet.

Mi·not (mī′nət), **George Richards.** 1885–1950. American physician; Nobel Prize winner (1934).

Min·u·it (mĭn′yŏŏ-ĭt), **Peter.** 1580–1638. Dutch colonial official in America.

Mi·ra·beau (mĭr′ə-bō′), **Comte de.** 1749–1791. French revolutionary.

Mi·ró (mē-rō′), **Joan.** Born 1893. Spanish artist.

Mith·ri·da·tes VI (mĭth′rə-dā′tēz). 132?–63 B.C. King of Pontus; defeated by Pompey (67 B.C.).

Mit·ter·and (mē′tə-rän′, -ränd′), **François Maurice.** Born 1916. French political leader; president (since 1981).

Mo·di·glia·ni (mō′dē-lyä′nē), **Amedeo.** 1884–1920. Italian painter and sculptor.

Mo·ham·med (mō-hăm′ĭd, -hä′mĭd). Also **Mu·ham·mad** (mŏŏ-hăm′ĭd, -hä′-mĭd). 570?–632. Prophet and founder of Islam.

Mo·lière (mōl-yâr′). Pen name of Jean Baptiste Poquelin. 1622–1673. French playwright and actor.

Mol·nár (mōl′när′), **Ferenc.** 1878–1952. Hungarian author.

Mon·dri·an (mŏn′drē-än′), **Piet.** 1872–1944. Dutch painter.

Mo·net (mō-nā′), **Claude.** 1840–1926. French painter.

Mon·dale (mŏn′dāl′), **Walter Frederic.** Born 1928. U.S. Vice President under Jimmy Carter (1977–1981).

Mon·mouth (mŏn′məth, mŭn′-), **Duke of.** Title of James Scott. 1649–1685. English pretender to the throne.

Mon·roe (mən-rō′), **James.** 1758–1831. Fifth U.S. President (1817–25).

Mon·taigne (mŏn-tān′), **Michel Eyquem de.** 1533–1592. French essayist.

Mont·calm (mŏnt-käm′), **Louis Joseph, Marquis de.** 1712–1759. French commander in chief in Canada.

Mon·tes·quieu (mŏn′təs-kyŏŏ′, mŏn-tĕs′kyŏŏ), **Baron de la Brède et de.** Title of Charles de Secondat. 1689–1755. French political philosopher.

Mon·tes·so·ri (mŏn′tə-sôr′ē, -sōr′ē), **Maria.** 1870–1952. Italian physician and educator.

Mon·te·zu·ma II (mŏn′tə-zŏŏ′mə). 1480?–1520. Last Aztec emperor in Mexico.

Mont·gom·er·y (mənt-gŭm′rē), Sir **Bernard Law.** 1887–1976. British army officer.

Moore (mŏŏr). **1. Marianne Craig.** 1887–1972. American poet. **2. Henry.** Born 1898. English sculptor and artist. **3. Stanford.** Born 1913. American biochemist; Nobel Prize winner (1972).

More (môr, mōr), **Saint** (Sir) **Thomas.** 1478–1535. English statesman and author; beheaded.

Mor·gan (môr′gən). **1. J(ohn) P(ierpont).** 1837–1913. American financier and philanthropist. **2. Thomas Hunt.** 1866–1945. American biologist; Nobel Prize winner (1933).

Mor·ris (môr′ĭs, mŏr′-). **1. Robert.** 1734–1806. American Revolutionary War financier and political leader. **2. Gouverneur.** 1752–1816. American diplomat and political leader. **3. William.** 1834–1896. English poet, artist, and utopian socialist.

Morse (môrs), **Samuel F(inley) B(reese).** 1791–1872. American artist; promoter of the telegraph.

Mor·ton (môrt′n). **Levi Parsons.** 1824–1920. U.S. Vice President under Benjamin Harrison (1889–93).

Mose·ley (mōz′lē), **Henry Gwyn-Jeffreys.** 1887–1915. British physicist.

Mott (mŏt), **Lucretia Coffin.** 1793–1880. American Quaker advocate of abolitionism, women's rights, and temperance.

Mount·bat·ten (mount-băt′n), **Louis.** First Earl Mountbatten of Burma. 1900–1979. British naval officer; assassinated.

Mous·sorg·sky (mə-zôrg′skē), **Modest Petrovich.** 1835–1881. Russian composer.

Mo·zart (mōt′särt′), **Wolfgang Amadeus.** 1756–1791. Austrian composer.

Mu·ham·mad (mŏŏ-hăm′ĭd, -hä′-mĭd). See **Mohammed.**

Muir (myŏŏr), **John.** 1838–1914. Scottish-born American naturalist, explorer, conservationist, and writer.

Mul·ler (mŭl′ər), **Hermann Joseph.** 1890–1967. American geneticist; Nobel Prize winner (1946).

Mul·li·ken (mŭl′ĭ-kən), **Robert Sanderson.** Born 1896. American nuclear physicist; Nobel Prize winner (1966).

Mun·ro (mən-rō′), **H(ector) H(ugh).** Pen name Saki. 1870–1916. English author.

Mu·rat (myŏŏ-rä′), **Joachim.** 1767?–1815. French marshal; king of Naples (1808–15).

Mu·ril·lo (mŏŏ-rē′lyō), **Bartolomé Esteban.** 1617–1682. Spanish painter.

Mur·phy (mûr′fē), **William Parry.** Born 1892. American physician; Nobel Prize winner (1934).

Mus·so·li·ni (mŏŏs′sō-lē′nē), **Benito.** Called Il Duce. 1883–1945. Fascist dictator of Italy (1922–43).

My·ron (mī′rən). Greek sculptor of the 5th cent. B.C..

N

Na·bo·kov (nä-bô′kôf), **Vladimir Vladimirovich.** 1899–1977. Russian-born American novelist and poet.

Na·hum (nā′həm, nā′əm). A Hebrew prophet of the 7th cent. B.C.

Nan·sen (nän′sən, nän′-), **Fridt·jof.** 1861–1930. Norwegian Arctic explorer, statesman, and scientist.

Na·o·mi (nā-ō′mē). In the Old Testament, the mother-in-law of Ruth.

Naph·ta·li (năf′tə-lī′). In the Old Testament, one of Jacob's sons.

Na·pi·er (nā′pē-ər), **John.** 1550–1617. Scottish mathematician.

Na·po·le·on I (nə-pō′lē-ən, -pōl′yən). Surname, Bonaparte. 1769–1821. Emperor of the French (1804–15). **—Na·po′le·on′ic** adj.

Napoleon III. Known as Louis Napoleon. 1808–1873. President of the Second Republic of France (1848–52); emperor of France (1852–70).

Nash (năsh), **Ogden.** 1902–1971. American poet.

Nas·ser (nä′sər, năs′ər), **Gamal Abdel.** 1918–1970. Prime minister of Egypt (1954–58); president of the United Arab Republic (1958–1970).

Na·than·ael (nə-thăn′yəl). One of the disciples of Jesus.

Na·thans (nā′thənz), **Daniel.** Born 1928. American physiologist; Nobel Prize winner (1978).

Na·tion (nā′shən), **Carry Amelia Moore.** 1846–1911. American reformer; temperance leader.

Neb·u·chad·nez·zar II (nĕb′ə-kəd-nĕz′ər, nĕb′yŏŏ-). King of Babylon (605–562 B.C.); destroyed Jerusalem.

Nef·er·ti·ti (nĕf′ər-tē′tē). Queen of Egypt in the early 14th cent. B.C.

Ne·he·mi·ah (nē′hə-mī′əh). Hebrew leader of the 5th cent. B.C.

Neh·ru (nā′rŏŏ), **Jawaharlal.** 1889–1964. First prime minister of India (1947–64).

Nel·son (nĕl′sən), **Viscount Horatio.** 1758–1805. British admiral.

Ne·ro (nîr′ō). A.D. 37–68. Roman emperor (54–68).

New·man (nŏŏ′mən, nyŏŏ′-), **John Henry.** 1801–1890. English theologian.

New·ton (nŏŏt′n, nyŏŏt′n), Sir **Isaac.** 1642–1727. English mathematician, scientist, and philosopher. **—New·ton′i·an** adj.

Nich·o·las II (nĭk′ə-ləs). 1868–1918. Czar of Russia (1894–1917); executed.

Nicholas, Saint. Often identified with Santa Claus. Fourth-cent. bishop.

Nicholas of Cu·sa (kyŏŏ′zə). 1401–1464. German cardinal, philosopher, and mathematician.

Nie·tzsche (nē′chə, -chē), **Friedrich Wilhelm.** 1844–1900. German philosopher.

Night·in·gale (nīt′n-gāl′, nī′tĭng-), **Florence.** 1820–1910. British nursing pioneer.

Ni·jin·sky (nə-jĭn′skē, -zhĭn′skē), **Vas·lav.** 1890–1950. Russian ballet dancer.

Nim·itz (nĭm′ĭts), **Chester William.** 1885–1966. American admiral.

Nir·en·berg (nîr′ən-bûrg′), **Marshall.** Born 1927. American biochemist; Nobel Prize winner (1968).

ă pat   ā pay   â care   ä father   ĕ pet   ē be   hw which   ĭ pit   ī tie   î pier   ŏ pot   ō toe   ô paw, for   oi noise
ŏŏ took   ŏŏ boot   ou out   th thin   th this   ŭ cut   û urge   zh vision   ə about, item, edible, gallop, circus

Nix·on (nĭk'sən), **Richard Milhous.** Born 1913. Thirty-seventh U.S. President (1969–74); resigned.

No·ah (nō'ə). In the Old Testament, patriarch chosen by God to build the Ark.

No·bel (nō-bĕl'), **Alfred Bernhard.** 1833–1896. Swedish chemist and inventor; his will provided for the Nobel Prizes

Nor·throp (nôr'thrəp), **John Howard.** Born 1891. American biochemist; Nobel Prize winner (1946).

Nos·tra·da·mus (nŏs'trə-dä'məs, nŏs'-trə-dā'məs). 1503–1566. French astrologer and physician.

Noyes (noiz), **Alfred.** 1880–1958. English poet and critic.

O

Oak·ley (ōk'lē), **Annie.** 1860–1926. American sharpshooter.

O·ba·di·ah (ō'bə-dī'ə). Hebrew prophet of the 6th cent. B.C.

O'Ca·sey (ō-kā'sē), **Sean.** 1880–1964. Irish dramatist.

O·cho·a (ō-chō'ä), **Severo.** Born 1905. Spanish-born American biochemist; Nobel Prize winner (1959).

Of·fen·bach (ŏf'ən-bäk', ôf'ən-), **Jacques.** 1819–1880. German-born French composer.

O·gle·thorpe (ō'gəl-thôrp'), **James Edward.** 1696–1785. English philanthropist and army officer.

O'Keeffe (ō-kēf'), **Georgia.** Born 1887. American painter.

O·laf I (ō'ləf). Also **O·lav** (ō'läv, ō'läf). 969?–1000. King of Norway (995–1000).

Olaf II. Known as Saint Olaf. 995?–1030. King of Norway (1016–28).

Olaf V. Born 1903. King of Norway (since 1957).

O·mar Khay·yám (ō'mär' kī-yäm', kī-yäm', ō'mər). 1050?–1123? Persian poet, mathematician, and astronomer.

O'Neill (ō-nēl'), **Eugene (Gladstone).** 1888–1953. American dramatist; Nobel Prize winner (1936).

On·sag·er (ŏn'sä'gər), **Lars.** Born 1903. Norwegian-born American chemist; Nobel Prize winner (1968).

Op·pen·heim·er (ŏp'ən-hī'mər), **J(ulius) Robert.** 1904–1967. American theoretical physicist.

Or·ange (ôr'ĭnj). Name of a princely European family ruling the Netherlands since 1815.

Or·te·ga y Gas·set (ôr-tā'gä ē gä-sĕt'), **Jose.** 1883–1955. Spanish author and philosopher.

Or·well (ôr'wĕl', -wəl), **George.** Pen name of Eric Blair. 1903–1950. English author.

O·tis (ō'tĭs), **James.** 1725–1783. American revolutionary leader.

Ot·to I (ŏt'ō). Called Otto the Great. 912–973. King of Germany (936–73); first Holy Roman Emperor (962–73).

Ov·id (ŏv'ĭd). 43 B.C.–A.D. 17? Roman poet.

Ow·en (ō'ĭn), **Robert.** 1771–1858. Welsh industrialist and reformer.

Ow·ens (ō'ĭnz), **Jesse.** 1913–1980. American athlete.

P

Pa·de·rew·ski (păd'ə-rĕf'skē, pä'də-), **Ignace Jan.** 1860–1941. Polish concert pianist and statesman.

Pa·ga·ni·ni (păg'ə-nē'nē, pä'gə-), **Nicolò.** 1782–1840. Italian violinist and composer.

Pah·la·vi (pä'lə-vē'), **Mohammed Riza.** Also **Pah·le·vi.** 1919–1979. Shah of Iran (1941–1978); deposed.

Paine (pān), **Thomas.** 1737–1809. British-born American patriot; active in the American and French Revolutions.

Pa·le·stri·na (păl'ĭ-strē'nə), **Giovanni Pierluigi da.** 1526?–1594. Italian composer.

Palm·er·ston (pä'mər-stən), **Viscount.** 1784–1865. Prime minister of Great Britain (1855–58, 1859–65).

Pank·hurst (păngk'hûrst'), **Emmeline Goulden.** 1858–1928. British feminist leader.

Par·a·cel·sus (păr'ə-sĕl'səs), **Philippus Aureolus.** 1493–1541. Swiss alchemist and physician.

Park (pärk), **Mungo.** 1771–1806. Scottish explorer in Africa.

Par·ker (pär'kər), **Dorothy (Rothschild).** 1893–1967. American writer.

Park·man (pärk'mən), **Francis.** 1823–1893. American historian.

Par·nell (pär-nĕl', pär'nəl), **Charles Stewart.** 1846–1891. Irish nationalist hero.

Parr (pär), **Catherine.** 1512–1548. Queen of England as 6th wife of Henry VIII.

Pas·cal (păs-kăl'), **Blaise.** 1623–1662. French philosopher and mathematician.

Pas·ter·nak (păs'tər-näk'), **Boris Leonidovich.** 1890–1960. Soviet author; declined Nobel Prize (1958).

Pas·teur (pă-stûr'), **Louis.** 1822–1895. French chemist.

Pat·rick (păt'rĭk), **Saint.** 389?–461? Traditionally, patron saint of Ireland.

Pat·ton (păt'n), **George Smith.** 1885–1945. American general.

Paul III (pôl). 1468–1549. Pope (1534–49).

Paul VI. 1897–1978. Pope (1963–1978)

Paul, Saint. A.D. 5?–67? Apostle to the Gentiles; author of several epistles. —**Paul'ine** adj.

Pau·li (pou'lē), **Wolfgang.** 1900–1958. Austrian-born American physicist; Nobel Prize winner (1945).

Paul·ing (pô'lĭng), **Linus Carl.** Born 1901. American chemist; awarded Nobel Prize (1954) and Nobel Peace Prize (1962).

Pav·lov (păv'lôf', păv'lŏv'), **Ivan Petrovich.** 1849–1936. Russian physiologist; Nobel Prize winner (1904).

Pav·lo·va (päv-lō'və, päv-), **Anna.** 1885–1931. Russian ballerina.

Pear·son (pîr'sən), **Lester Bowles.** 1897–1972. Prime minister of Canada (1963–68).

Pea·ry (pîr'ē), **Robert Edwin.** 1856–1920. American naval officer and Arctic explorer.

Peel (pēl), **Sir Robert.** 1788–1850. Prime minister of Great Britain (1834–35 and 1841–46).

Penn (pĕn), **William.** 1644–1718. English Quaker leader; founder of Pennsylvania (1681).

Pepys (pēps), **Samuel.** 1633–1703. English diarist.

Per·i·cles (pĕr'ə-klēz'). 495?–429 B.C. Athenian statesman.

Per·kins (pûr'kənz), **Frances.** 1882–1965. First U.S. woman cabinet member (1933–45).

Per·ry (pĕr'ē). **1. Oliver Hazard.** 1785–1819. American naval officer. **2. Matthew Calbraith.** 1794–1858. American naval officer; brother of O.H. Perry.

Per·shing (pûr'shĭng), **John Joseph.** 1860–1948. American general.

Pé·tain (pā-tăN'), **Henri Philippe.** 1856–1951. Marshal of France and premier of unoccupied (Vichy) France (1940–44).

Pe·ter I (pē'tər). Called Peter the Great. 1672–1725. Czar of Russia (1682–1725).

Peter, Saint. Called Simon Peter. Died A.D. 67? One of the 12 Apostles.

Pe·trarch (pē'trärk'). 1304–1374. Italian poet.

Phid·i·as (fĭd'ē-əs). Athenian sculptor of the 5th cent. B.C.

Phil·ip (fĭl'ĭp). Duke of Edinburgh. Born 1921. Husband of Elizabeth II of Great Britain.

Philip II¹. 382–336 B.C. King of Macedonia (359–336).

Philip II². 1165–1223. King of France (1180–1223).

Philip II³. 1527–1598. King of Spain (1556–98).

Philip IV. 1268–1314. King of France (1285–1314).

Philip, Saint. One of the 12 Apostles.

Pi·cas·so (pĭ-kä'sō, pē-), **Pablo.** 1881–1973. Spanish-born painter and sculptor.

Pick·ett (pĭk'ĭt), **George Edward.** 1825–1875. American Confederate general.

Pierce (pîrs), **Franklin.** 1804–1869. Fourteenth U.S. President (1853–57).

Pi·late (pī'lĭt), **Pontius.** Roman procurator of Judea (A.D. 26?–36?); assumed to have authorized the execution of Jesus.

Pin·dar (pĭn'dər). 522?–443 B.C. Greek lyric poet. —**Pin·dar'ic** (pĭn-dăr'ĭk) adj.

Pi·ran·del·lo (pîr'ən-dĕl'ō), **Luigi.** 1867–1936. Italian author.

Pi·sis·tra·tus (pĭ-sĭs'trə-təs, pī-). 605?–527 B.C. Ruler of Athens (560–527).

Pis·sar·o (pĭ-sär'ō), **Camille.** 1830–1903. French painter.

Pitt (pĭt). **1. William** First Earl of Chatham. Called the Elder. 1708–1778. British statesman. **2. William.** 1759–1806. Called the Younger. British prime minister (1783–1801 and 1804–6).

Pi·us V (pī'əs). 1504–1572. Pope (1566–72).

Pius IX. 1792–1878. Pope (1846–78).

Pius X. 1835–1914. Pope (1903–14).

Pius XI. 1857–1939. Pope (1922–39).

Pius XII. 1876–1958. Pope (1939–58).

Pi·zar·ro (pĭ-zär'ō), **Francisco.** 1470?–1541. Spanish explorer.

Planck (plängk), **Max (Karl Ernst Ludwig).** 1858–1947. German physicist.

Plan·tag·e·net (plăn-tăj'ə-nĭt). Family name of the Angevin line of English sovereigns from Henry II (1154) through Richard III (1485).

Pla·to (plā'tō). 427?–347 B.C. Greek philosopher. **—Pla·ton'ic** plə-tŏn'ĭk) adj.

Plau·tus (plô'təs), **Titus Maccius.** 254?–184 B.C. Roman playwright.

Plin·y (plĭn'ē). **1.** Called the Elder. A.D. 23–79. Roman scholar; uncle of Pliny the Younger. **2. Plin·y** Called the Younger. A.D. 62–113. Roman consul and orator.

Plu·tarch (plōō'tärk'). A.D. 46?–120? Greek biographer and philosopher.

Po·ca·hon·tas (pō'kə-hŏn'təs). 1595?–1617. American Indian princess; allegedly saved the life of Captain John Smith.

Poe (pō), **Edgar Allan.** 1809–1849. American author.

Polk (pōk), **James Knox.** 1795–1849. Eleventh U.S. President (1845–49).

Pol·lock (pŏl'ək), **Jackson.** 1912–1956. American artist.

Po·lo (pō'lō), **Marco.** 1254?–1324? Venetian traveler to the court of Kublai Khan.

Pom·pa·dour (pŏm'pə-dôr', -dōr'), **Marquise de.** 1721–1764. Mistress of Louis XV of France.

Pom·pey (pŏm'pē). 106–48 B.C. Roman statesman and general.

Ponce de Le·ón (pŏns' də lē'ən), **Juan.** 1460?–1521. Spanish explorer; discovered Florida (1513).

Pon·ti·ac (pŏn'tē-ăk'). Died 1769. American Ottawa Indian chief.

Pope (pōp), **Alexander.** 1688–1744. English poet and satirist.

Por·ter (pôr'tər, pōr'-). **1. William Sydney.** Pen name, O. Henry. 1862–1910. American short story author. **2. Katherine Anne.** 1890–1980. American author. **3. Cole.** 1893–1964. American composer and lyricist.

Pot·ter (pŏt'ər), **Beatrix.** 1866–1943. English author and illustrator.

Pound (pound), **Ezra (Loomis).** 1885–1972. American poet and critic.

Pow·ha·tan (pou'ə-tăn'). 1550?–1618. American Indian chief.

Prax·it·e·les (prăk-sĭt'l-ēz'). Greek sculptor of the 4th cent. B.C.

Pres·cott (prĕs'kət), **William Hickling.** 1796–1859. American historian.

Priest·ley (prēst'lē), **Joseph.** 1733–1804. British chemist.

Pro·kof·iev (prə-kôf'yəf, -yĕf'), **Sergei Sergeyevich.** 1891–1953. Soviet composer.

Pro·tag·o·ras (prō-tăg'ər-əs). 481?–411 B.C. Greek philosopher.

Proust (prōōst), **Marcel.** 1871–1922. French novelist and critic.

Ptol·e·my (tŏl'ə-mē). Greek astronomer, mathematician, and geographer of the 2nd cent. **—Ptol'e·ma'ic** adj.

Ptolemy I. 367?–283 B.C. King of Egypt 323–285 B.C.

Puc·ci·ni (pōōt-chē'nē), **Giacomo.**

1858–1924. Italian composer.

Pu·las·ki (pōō-lăs'kē), **Casimir.** 1748?–1779. Polish general in the American Revolutionary War.

Pul·it·zer (pōōl'ĭt-sər, pyōō'lĭt-), **Joseph.** 1847–1911. Hungarian-born American newspaper publisher.

Pur·cell (pûr-sĕl'). **1. Henry.** 1659–1695. English composer. **2. Edward Mills.** Born 1912. American physicist; Nobel Prize winner (1952).

Push·kin (pōōsh'kĭn), **Aleksandr Sergeyevich.** 1799–1837. Russian poet.

Pym (pĭm), **John.** 1584–1643. English statesman.

Py·thag·o·ras (pĭ-thăg'ər-əs). Greek philosopher of the 6th cent. B.C. **—Py·thag'o·re'an** adj. & n.

Q

Que·zon (kā'sôn'), **Manuel Luis.** 1878–1944. First president of the Philippines (1935–44).

Quin·til·ian (kwĭn-tĭl'yən). Roman rhetorician of the 1st cent. A.D.

R

Rab·e·lais (răb'ə-lā), **François.** 1494?–1553. French author.

Rach·ma·ni·noff (răKH-mä'nĭ-nôf'), **Sergei Vasilievich.** 1873–1943. Russian composer and pianist.

Ra·cine (rá-sēn'), **Jean Baptiste.** 1639–1699. French playwright.

Rai·nier III (rĕ-nyā', rā-nyä'). Born 1923. Prince of Monaco (since 1949).

Ra·leigh (rô'lē), **Sir Walter.** 1552?–1618. English navigator, colonizer, and historian.

Ram·e·ses (răm'ə-sēz'). Also **Ram·ses** (răm'sēz). The name of 12 kings of Egypt, reigning from 1315? to 1090 B.C.

Ram·say (răm'zē), **Sir William.** 1852–1916. British chemist.

Raph·a·el (răf'ē-əl, rā'fē-). 1483–1520. Italian painter and architect.

Ras·pu·tin (răs-pyōō'tĭn), **Grigori Efimovich.** 1871?–1916. Russian monk; assassinated.

Ra·vel (rə-vĕl', ră-), **Maurice Joseph.** 1875–1937. French composer.

Rea·gan (rā'gən, rē'-), **Ronald Wilson.** Born 1911. Fortieth U.S. President (since 1981).

Reed (rēd), **Walter.** 1851–1902. American physician.

Re·marque (rə-märk'), **Erich Maria.** 1898–1970. German-born American novelist.

Rem·brandt (rĕm'brănt). 1606–1669. Dutch painter.

Re·noir (rĕn'wär'), **Pierre Auguste.** 1841–1919. French painter.

Reu·ther (rōō'thər), **Walter Philip.** 1907–1970. American labor leader.

Re·vere (rĭ-vîr'), **Paul.** 1735–1818. American silversmith, engraver, and Revolutionary patriot.

Reyn·olds (rĕn'əldz), **Sir Joshua.** 1723–1792. English painter.

Rhodes (rōdz), **Cecil (John).** 1853–

1902. British financier and colonialist.

Rich·ard I (rĭch'ərd). Called the Lionhearted. 1157–1199. King of England (1189–99).

Richard II. 1367–1400. King of England (1377–99).

Richard III. 1452–1485. King of England (1483–85).

Rich·ards (rĭch'ərdz). **1. Theodore.** 1868–1928. American chemist; Nobel Prize winner (1914). **2. Dickinson Woodruff.** Born 1895. American physician; Nobel Prize winner (1956).

Rich·ard·son (rĭch'ərd-sən), **Samuel.** 1689–1761. English author.

Ri·che·lieu (rē-shə-lyœ'), **Duc de.** 1585–1642. French cardinal and statesman.

Rick·o·ver (rĭk'ō-vər), **Hyman George.** Born 1900. Polish-born American naval officer.

Rim·sky-Kor·sa·kov (rĭm'skē-kôr'sə-kôf), **Nikolai Andreyevich.** 1844–1908. Russian composer.

Ri·ve·ra (rē-vĕ'rä), **Diego.** 1886–1957. Mexican artist.

Rob·bins (rŏb'ĭnz), **Frederick Chapman.** Born 1916. American microbiologist; Nobel Prize winner (1954).

Rob·ert I (rŏb'ərt). Called the Bruce. 1274–1329. King of Scotland (1306–29).

Robes·pierre (rōbz'pē-âr), **Maximilien Francois Marie Isidore de.** 1758–1794. French revolutionary leader; guillotined.

Rob·in·son (rŏb'ĭn-sən). **1. Edwin Arlington.** 1869–1935. American poet. **2. Jack Roosevelt ("Jackie").** 1919–1972. American baseball player.

Ro·cham·beau (rō-shän-bō'), **Comte de.** 1725–1807. French army officer in the American Revolution.

Rock·e·fel·ler (rŏk'ə-fĕl'ər). Family of American businessmen and philanthropists, including: **1. John D(avison).** 1839–1937. **2. John Davidson, Jr.** 1874–1960. **3. Nelson Aldrich.** 1908–1979. U.S. Vice President under Gerald Ford (1974–77).

Ro·din (rō-dăn'), **(François) Auguste (René).** 1840–1917. French sculptor.

Roent·gen (rĕnt'gən, rŭnt'-), **Wilhelm Konrad.** 1845–1923. German physicist.

Röl·vaag (rōl'väg), **Ole Edvart.** 1876–1931. Norwegian-born American author.

Ro·ma·nov (rō-mä'nəf, rō'mə-nôf). Also **Ro·ma·noff.** Family name of a Russian ruling dynasty (1613–1917).

Rom·mel (rŏm'əl), **Erwin.** 1891–1944. German army officer.

Rom·ney (rŏm'nē, rŭm'-), **George.** 1734–1802. English painter.

Roo·se·velt (rō'zə-vĕlt, rōz'vĕlt, -vəlt). **1. Theodore.** 1858–1919. Twenty-sixth U.S. President (1901–9); Nobel Peace Prize winner (1906). **2. Franklin Delano.** 1882–1945. Thirty-second U.S. President (1933–45). **3. (Anna) Eleanor.** 1884–1962. American diplomat, writer, and humanitarian.

Root (rōōt), **Elihu.** 1845–1937. American statesman; Nobel Peace Prize winner (1912).

Rose·crans (rōz'krănz), **William**

Starke. 1819–1898. Union general in the Civil War.

Ross (rôs). **1. Betsy (Griscom).** 1752–1836. American Revolutionary patriot. **2. Sir James Clark.** 1800–1862. British explorer.

Ros·set·ti (rō-zĕt′ē). **1. Dante Gabriel.** 1828–1882. English poet and painter. **2. Christina Georgina.** 1830–1894. English poet.

Ros·si·ni (rō-sē′nē), **Gioacchino Antonio.** 1792–1868. Italian composer.

Ros·tand (rō-stän′), **Edmond.** 1868–1918. French author.

Roth·schild (rôth′chīld, rôs-). Family of German bankers, including: **1. Meyer Amschel.** 1743–1812. **2. Nathan Meyer.** 1777–1836.

Rou·ault (rōō-ō′), **Georges.** 1871–1958. French painter.

Rous·seau (rōō-sō′). **1. Jean Jacques.** 1712–1778. French author. **2. Henri.** Called Le Douanier. 1844–1910. French painter.

Ru·bens (rōō′bənz), **Peter Paul.** 1577–1640. Flemish painter.

Ru·bin·stein (rōō′bən-stīn). **1. Anton Gregor.** 1829–1894. Russian pianist and composer. **2. Artur.** Born 1886. Polish-born American pianist.

Ru·dolf I (rōō′dôlf). 1218–1291. Holy Roman Emperor (1273–91).

Ru·pert (rōō′pərt), **Prince.** 1619–1682. German-born English military and political leader.

Rus·kin (rŭs′kĭn), **John.** 1819–1900. English writer.

Rus·sell (rŭs′əl). **1. George.** Pen name Æ. 1867–1935. Irish author. **2. Lord Bertrand (Arthur William).** 1872–1970. English philosopher and mathematician.

Ruth (rōōth), **George Herman ("Babe").** Called the Bambino. 1895–1948. American baseball player.

Ruth·er·ford (rŭth′ər-fərd), **Ernest.** 1871–1937. British physicist.

S

Sa·bin (sā′bĭn), **Albert Bruce.** Born 1906. Polish-born American physician and microbiologist.

Sac·a·ja·we·a (săk′ə-jə-wē′ə). 1788?–1812. American Indian guide and interpreter for Lewis and Clark.

Sa·dat (sə-dăt′, -dät′), **Anwar el-.** Born 1918. President of Egypt (since 1970).

Saint-Gau·dens (sānt-gô′dənz), **Augustus.** 1848–1907. Irish-born American sculptor.

Saint-Saëns (săn-säns′), **(Charles) Camille.** 1835–1921. French composer.

Sal·a·din (săl′ə-dĭn). 1138?–1193. Sultan of Egypt and Syria.

Sal·in·ger (săl′ən-jər), **J(erome) D(avid).** Born 1919. American author.

Salk (sôlk), **Jonas Edward.** Born 1914. American microbiologist.

Sal·lust (săl′əst). 86–34 B.C. Roman historian and politician.

Sa·lo·me (sə-lō′mē). In the New Testament, the daughter of Herodias.

Sam·o·set (săm′ə-sĕt′, sə-mŏs′ĭt). American Indian chief of the early 17th cent.

Sam·son (săm′sən). In the Old Testament, Hebrew hero of extraordinary strength.

Sam·u·el (săm′yōō-əl). Hebrew prophet of the 11th cent. B.C.

Sand (sănd), **George.** Pen name of Amandine Aurore Lucie Dupin. 1804–1876. French novelist.

Sand·burg (sănd′bûrg′, săn′-), **Carl.** 1878–1967. American poet and biographer.

Sang·er (săng′ər). **1. Margaret (Higgins).** 1883–1966. American social reformer. **2. Frederick.** Born 1918. English chemist; Nobel Prize winner (1958 and 1980).

Sap·pho (săf′ō). Greek poet of the 7th cent. B.C.

Sar·ah (sâr′ə). In the Old Testament, the wife of Abraham.

Sar·gent (sär′jənt), **John Singer.** 1856–1925. American painter.

Sar·gon II (sär′gən). Died 705 B.C. King of Assyria (722–705).

Sar·tre (sär′tr′), **Jean Paul.** 1905–1980. French philosopher and author.

Saul (sôl). First king of Israel during the 11th cent. B.C.

Sav·o·na·ro·la (săv′ə-nə-rō′lə), **Girolamo.** 1452–1498. Italian monk and social reformer; burned as a heretic.

Scar·lat·ti (skär-lät′ē). **1. Alessandro.** 1659–1725. Italian composer. **2.(Giuseppe) Domenico.** 1683–1757. Italian harpsichordist and composer.

Schil·ler (shĭl′ər), **Johann Christoph Friedrich von.** 1759–1805. German poet and dramatist.

Schlie·mann (shlē′män′), **Heinrich.** 1822–1890. German archaeologist.

Schmidt (shmĭt), **Helmut.** Born 1918. Chancellor of West Germany (since 1974).

Scho·pen·hau·er (shō′pən-hou′ər), **Arthur.** 1788–1860. German philosopher.

Schrief·fer (shrē′fər), **John.** Born 1931. American physicist; Nobel Prize winner (1972).

Schu·bert (shōō′bərt), **Franz.** 1797–1828. Austrian composer.

Schultz (shōōltz), **Theodore.** Born 1902. American economist; Nobel Prize winner (1979).

Schu·mann (shōō′män), **Robert.** 1810–1856. German composer.

Schweit·zer (shwīt′sər, shvīt′sər), **Albert.** 1875–1965. French philosopher, missionary physician, and musicologist; Nobel Peace Prize winner (1952).

Schwin·ger (shwĭng′ər), **Julian Seymour.** Born 1918. American physicist; Nobel Prize winner (1965).

Scip·i·o (skĭp′ē-ō′). **1. Publius Cornelius.** Known as Scipio the Elder. 237–183 B.C. Roman general. **2. Publius Cornelius.** Known as Scipio the Younger. 185–129 B.C. Roman consul and general.

Scopes (skōps), **John Thomas.** 1901–1970. American teacher; convicted (1925) for teaching evolution.

Scott (skŏt). **1. Sir Walter.** 1771–1832. Scottish author. **2. Winfield.** 1786–1866. American military officer. **3. Dred.** 1795?–1858. American slave; subject of a proslavery decision by Supreme Court (1857). **4. Robert Fal-**

con. 1868–1912. British explorer of the Antarctic.

Sea·borg (sē′bôrg′), **Glenn Theodore.** Born 1912. American chemist; Nobel Prize winner (1951).

Se·grè (sĕ-grä′), **Emilio.** Born 1905. Italian-born American physicist; Nobel Prize winner (1959).

Se·leu·cids (sĭ-lōō′sĭdz). Six dynastic leaders in Asia Minor from 312 B.C. to 64 B.C., esp.: **Se·leu·cus I.** 358?–280 B.C. Ruled in Syria (306–280).

Sel·juk (sĕl′jōōk′, sĕl-jōōk′). A member of one of several Turkish dynasties ruling over central and western Asia from the 11th to the 13th cent.

Sen·e·ca (sĕn′ə-kə), **Lucius Annaeus.** 4? B.C.–A.D. 65. Roman philosopher and author.

Sen·nach·er·ib (sĭ-năk′ər-ĭb′). King of Assyria (705–681 B.C.).

Se·quoy·a (sĭ-kwoi′ə). 1770?–1843. American Indian leader.

Seth (sĕth). A son of Adam and Eve.

Se·ton (sē′tən), **Saint Elizabeth Ann Bayley.** Called Mother Seton. 1774–1821. American religious leader.

Seu·rat (sœ-rä′), **Georges Pierre.** 1859–1891. French painter.

Se·ve·rus (sə-vîr′əs), **Lucius Septimius.** 146–211. Roman emperor (193–211).

Sew·ard (sōō′ərd), **William Henry.** 1801–1872. American statesman.

Shack·le·ton (shăk′əl-tən), **Sir Ernest Henry.** 1874–1922. British explorer of the Antarctic.

Shake·speare (shāk′spîr), **William.** 1564–1616. English dramatist and poet. **—Shake·spear′e·an** or **Shake·spear′i·an** adj. & n.

Shaw (shô), **George Bernard.** 1856–1950. Irish-born English author.

Shel·ley (shĕl′ē). **1. Percy Bysshe.** 1792–1822. English poet. **2. Mary Wollstonecraft (Godwin).** 1797–1851. English novelist.

Shep·ard (shĕp′ərd), **Alan Bartlett, Jr.** Born 1923. First American astronaut in space (1961).

Sher·i·dan (shĕr′ə-dən). **1. Richard Brinsley.** 1751–1816. English dramatist. **2. Philip Henry.** 1831–1888. American commander of Union cavalry.

Sher·man (shûr′mən). **1. Roger.** 1721–1793. American statesman and patriot. **2. William Tecumseh.** 1820–1891. Union commander in the Civil War. **3. John.** 1823–1900. American statesman. **4. James Schoolcraft.** 1855–1912. U.S. Vice President under William Howard Taft (1909–12).

Shock·ley (shŏk′lē), **William Bradford.** Born 1910. British-born American physicist; Nobel Prize winner (1956).

Shos·ta·ko·vich (shŏs′tə-kō′vĭch), **Dmitri.** 1906–1975. Soviet composer.

Si·be·li·us (sĭ-bā′lē-əs, -bäl′yəs), **Jean.** 1865–1957. Finnish composer.

Sid·ney (sĭd′nē), **Sir Philip.** 1554–1586. English poet and essayist.

Si·kor·sky (sĭ-kôr′skē), **Igor Ivanovich.** 1889–1972. Russian-born American aeronautical engineer.

Si·mon (sī′mən), **Herbert.** Born 1916. American economist; Nobel Prize winner (1978).

ă pat   ā pay   â care   ä father   ĕ pet   ē be   hw which   ĭ pit   ī tie   î pier   ŏ pot   ō toe   ô paw, for   oi noise
ōō took   ōō boot   ou out   th thin   th this   ŭ cut   û urge   zh vision   ə about, item, edible, gallop, circus

Simon Ze·lo·tes (zē-lŏ'tēz). One of the 12 Apostles.

Sin·clair (sĭn-klâr'), **Upton (Beall).** 1878–1968. American novelist.

Sit·ting Bull (sĭt'ĭng bŏol). 1834?–1890. American Indian leader.

Smith (smĭth). **1. John.** 1580–1631. English adventurer, colonist in Virginia, and author. **2. Adam.** 1723–1790. Scottish political economist. **3. Joseph.** 1805–1844. American founder of the Church of Jesus Christ of the Latter-day Saints. **4. Alfred Emanuel.** 1873–1944. American political leader. **5. Margaret Chase.** Born 1897. American political leader. **6. Hamilton.** Born 1931. American physiologist; Nobel Prize winner (1978).

Smol·lett (smŏl'ĭt), **Tobias George.** 1721–1771. British novelist.

Smuts (smŭts), **Jan Christiaan.** 1870–1950. A founder and prime minister of the Union of South Africa (1919–24 and 1939–48).

Snell (snĕl), **George.** Born 1903. American biochemist; Nobel Prize winner (1980).

Soc·ra·tes (sŏk'rə-tēz'). 470?–399 B.C. Greek philosopher and teacher. **—So·crat'ic** (sə-krăt'ĭk) *adj.*

Sol·o·mon (sŏl'ə-mən). King of Israel in the 10th cent. B.C..

Soph·o·cles (sŏf'ə-klēz'). 496?–406 B.C. Greek dramatist.

Sou·sa (sōō'zə, -sə), **John Philip.** 1854–1932. American bandmaster and composer.

South·ey (sŭth'ē), **Robert.** 1774–1843. British poet.

Spaatz (spätz), **Carl.** 1891–1974. American general.

Spar·ta·cus (spär'tə-kəs). Died 71 B.C. Thracian leader of a slave revolt against Rome (73–71).

Spen·cer (spĕn'sər), **Herbert.** 1820–1903. British philosopher.

Spen·ser (spĕn'sər), **Edmund.** 1552?–1599. English poet.

Spi·no·za (spĭ-nō'zə), **Baruch.** 1632–1677. Dutch philosopher.

Squan·to (skwän'tō). Died 1622. Indian who befriended Pilgrims at Plymouth Colony.

Staël (stäl), **Madame de.** 1766–1817. French author and literary patron.

Sta·lin (stä'lĭn), **Joseph.** 1879–1953. General secretary of the Communist Party of the Soviet Union (1922–53); premier (1941–53).

Stan·dish (stăn'dĭsh'), **Myles.** 1584?–1656. English colonial settler in America.

Stan·is·lav·sky (stăn'ə-släv'skē, -släf'skē), **Konstantin.** 1863–1938. Russian actor and director.

Stan·ley (stăn'lē). **1. Sir Henry Morton.** 1841–1904. Welsh-born journalist and explorer. **2. Wendell Meredith.** 1904–1971. American biochemist; Nobel Prize winner (1946).

Stan·ton (stăn'tən), **Elizabeth Cady.** 1815–1902. American feminist and social reformer.

Steele (stēl), **Sir Richard.** 1672–1729. English essayist.

Stein (stīn). **1. Gertrude.** 1874–1946. American author; resident in France.

2. William. Born 1911. American biochemist; Nobel Prize winner (1972).

Stein·beck (stīn'bĕk), **John Ernst.** 1902–1968. American novelist; Nobel Prize winner (1962).

Stein·metz (stīn'mĕts), **Charles Proteus.** 1865–1923. German-born American engineer and inventor.

Sten·dhal (stäN-däl'). Pen name of Marie Henri Beyle. 1783–1842. French novelist and biographer.

Ste·phen (stē'vən), **Saint.** First Christian martyr.

Ste·phen of Blois (stē'vən; blwä). 1097?–1154. King of England (1135–54).

Stern (stûrn), **Otto.** 1888–1969. German-born American physicist; Nobel Prize winner (1943).

Sterne (stûrn), **Laurence.** 1713–1768. English novelist.

Steu·ben (stōō'bən, styōō'-), **Baron Friedrich Wilhelm Ludolf Gerhard Augustin von.** 1730–1794. Prussian-born American military leader.

Ste·vens (stē'vənz), **Wallace.** 1879–1955. American poet.

Ste·ven·son (stē'vən-sən). **1. Adlai Ewing.** 1835–1914. U.S. Vice President under Grover Cleveland (1893–97). **2. Robert Louis (Balfour).** 1850–1894. Scottish poet and novelist. **3. Adlai Ewing.** 1900–1965. American statesman.

Stone (stōn), **Lucy.** 1818–1893. American feminist leader.

Stowe (stō), **Harriet (Elizabeth) Beecher.** 1811–1896. American novelist.

Strauss (strous). Family of Austrian composers, including: **1. Johann.** Known as the Elder. 1804–1849. **2. Johann.** Known as the Younger. 1825–1899. **3. Josef.** 1827–1870.

Strauss, Richard. 1864–1949. German composer.

Stra·vin·sky (strə-vĭn'skē), **Igor Fyodorovich.** 1882–1971. Russian-born American composer.

Strind·berg (strĭnd'bûrg'), **(Johan) August.** 1849–1912. Swedish playwright and novelist.

Stu·art (stōō'ərt, styōō'-). Family name of rulers of Scotland (1371–1707), England (1603–1707), and Great Britain (1707–14).

Stuart. 1. Gilbert Charles. 1755–1828. American painter. **2. James Ewell Brown ("Jeb").** 1833–1864. American Confederate general.

Stuy·ve·sant (stī'və-sənt), **Peter.** 1592–1672. Dutch colonial administrator in America.

Sue·to·ni·us (swĭ-tō'nē-əs). Roman historian of the 2nd cent.

Su·lei·man I (sōō'lā-män). 1490?–1566. Sultan of Turkey (1520–66).

Sul·la (sŭl'ə), **Lucius Cornelius.** 138?–78 B.C. Roman general; dictator of Rome (82–79).

Sul·li·van (sŭl'ə-vən). **1. Sir Arthur (Seymour).** 1842–1900. British composer of comic operas. **2. Louis Henri.** 1856–1924. American architect.

Sum·ner (sŭm'nər). **1. Charles.** 1811–1874. American political leader. **2. James Batcheller.** 1887–1955. American biochemist; Nobel Prize

winner (1946).

Sung (sŭng). Dynastic leaders who ruled China (960–1279).

Sun Yat-sen (sōōn' yät'sĕn'). 1866–1925. Chinese revolutionary leader; founder of the Republic of China (1911).

Sur·rey (sûr'ē), **Earl of.** Courtesy title of Henry Howard. 1517?–1547. English poet.

Suth·er·land (sŭth'ər-lənd), **Earl Wilbur.** 1915–1974. American biochemist; Nobel Prize winner (1971).

Swe·den·borg (swēd'n-bôrg'), **Emanuel.** 1688–1772. Swedish scientist and theologian.

Swift (swĭft), **Jonathan.** 1667–1745. English satirist.

Swin·burne (swĭn'bərn), **Algernon Charles.** 1837–1909. English poet and critic.

T

Tac·i·tus (tăs'ə-təs), **Publius Cornelius.** Roman historian and orator of the late 1st and early 2nd cent.

Taft (tăft), **William Howard.** 1857–1930. Twenty-seventh U.S. President. (1909–13).

Ta·gore (tə-gôr', -gōr'), **Sir Rabindranath.** 1861–1941. Indian poet.

Taine (tān), **Hippolyte Adolphe.** 1828–1893. French philosopher and literary historian.

Tal·ley·rand-Pé·ri·gord (tăl'ē-rănd'-pĕr'ə-gôr'), **Charles Maurice de.** 1754–1838. French statesman and diplomat.

Tam·er·lane (tăm'ər-lān'). 1336?–1405. Mongol warrior.

Tan·cred (tăng'krĕd). 1078?–1112. Norman crusader.

Ta·ney (tô'nē), **Roger Brooke.** 1774–1864. American jurist.

Tar·king·ton (tär'kĭng-tən), **(Newton) Booth.** 1869–1946. American novelist and playwright.

Ta·tum (tā'təm), **Edward Lawrie.** 1909–1975. American biochemist; Nobel Prize winner (1958).

Tay·lor (tā'lər), **Zachary.** 1784–1850. Twelfth U.S. President (1849–50).

Tchai·kov·sky (chī-kôf'skē, -kŏf'skē), **Peter Ilyich.** 1840–1893. Russian composer.

Te·cum·seh (tĕ-kŭm'sə, -sē). 1768?–1813. American Shawnee Indian leader.

Ten·ny·son (tĕn'ə-sən), **Alfred, Lord.** 1809–1892. English poet.

Ter·ence (tĕr'əns). 185–159 B.C. Roman author.

Te·resh·ko·va (tĕ-rĕsh-kô'və), **Valentina Vladimirovna.** Born 1937. Soviet cosmonaut; first woman in space (1963).

Tes·la (tĕs'lə), **Nikola.** 1857–1943. Croatian-born American electrical engineer.

Thack·er·ay (thăk'ə-rē, thăk'rē), **William Makepeace.** 1811–1863. English novelist.

Tha·les (thā'lēz'). 640?–546? B.C. Greek philosopher and geometrician.

Thant (thänt), **U** 1909–1974. Burmese diplomat; secretary-general of the

---

ă pat	ā pay	â care	ä father	ĕ pet	ē be	hw which	ĭ pit	ī tie	î pier	ŏ pot	ō toe	ô paw, for	oi noise
ōō took	ōō boot	ou out	th thin	*th* this	ŭ cut	û urge	zh vision	ə about, item, edible, gallop, circus					

United Nations (1961–71).

Thatch·er (thăch′ər), **Margaret.** Born 1925. British prime minister (since 1975).

Thei·ler (tī′lər), **Max.** 1899–1972. South African-born American microbiologist; Nobel Prize winner (1951).

The·mis·to·cles (thə-mĭs′tə-klēz′). 527?–460? B.C. Athenian military and political leader.

The·oc·ri·tus (thē-ŏk′rə-təs). Greek poet of the 3rd cent. B.C.

The·o·do·ra (thē′ə-dôr′ə). 508?–548. Empress of the Eastern Roman Empire.

The·o·do·sius I (thē′ə-dō′shəs). 346?–395. Roman Emperor (379–395).

The·re·sa (tə-rē′sə, -rĕs′ə), **Saint.** Known as Theresa of Ávila. 1515–1582. Spanish Carmelite nun and mystic.

Thes·pis (thĕs′pĭs). Greek poet of the 6th cent. B.C.. —**Thes′pi·an** adj. & n.

Thom·as (tŏm′əs), **Dylan (Marlais).** 1914–1953. Welsh poet.

Thomas, **Saint.** One of the 12 Apostles.

Thomas à Kem·pis (kĕm′pĭs). See Kempis.

Thomas A·qui·nas (ə-kwī′nəs), **Saint.** See Aquinas.

Thomp·son (tŏmp′sən), **Benjamin.** Count Rumford. 1753–1814. American physicist and philanthropist.

Tho·reau (thôr′ō, thə-rō′), **Henry David.** 1817–1862. American essayist.

Thu·cyd·i·des (thōō-sĭd′ə-dēz′). Greek historian of the 5th cent. B.C..

Thur·ber (thûr′bər), **James (Grover).** 1894–1961. American artist and writer.

Ti·be·ri·us (tī-bîr′ī-əs). 42 B.C.–A.D. 37. Roman Emperor (A.D. 14–37).

Tim·o·thy (tĭm′ə-thē), **Saint.** Christian leader of 1st cent. A.D.

Ting (tĭng), **Samuel.** Born 1936. American physicist; Nobel Prize winner (1976).

Tin·to·ret·to (tĭn′tə-rĕt′ō), **Il.** 1518–1594. Italian painter.

Ti·tian (tĭsh′ən). 1477–1576. Italian painter.

Ti·to (tē′tō). Original name, Josip Broz. Known as Marshal Tito. 1892–1980. Yugoslav prime minister (1945–53); president (1953–80).

Ti·tus (tī′təs). A.D. 40?–81. Emperor of Rome (79–81).

Titus, **Saint.** Christian leader of the 1st cent. A.D.

Tocque·ville (tōk′vĭl), **Alexis Charles Henri Maurice Clérel de.** 1805–1859. French statesman and historian.

Tol·kien (tōl′kēn′), **J(ohn) R(onald) R(euel).** 1892–1973. English author.

Tol·stoy (tōl′stoi′, tŏl′-), **Count Leo.** 1828–1910. Russian novelist.

Tomp·kins (tŏm′kənz), **Daniel D.** 1774–1825. U.S. Vice President (1817–25) under James Monroe.

Tor·ri·cel·li (tôr′rē-chĕl′lē), **Evangelista.** 1608–1647. Italian physicist.

Tos·ca·ni·ni (tŏs′kə-nē′nē), **Arturo.** 1867–1957. Italian conductor.

Tou·louse-Lau·trec (tōō-lōōz′lō-trĕk′), **Henri.** 1864–1901. French painter and lithographer.

Townes (tounz), **Charles.** Born 1915. American physicist; Nobel Prize winner (1964).

Tra·jan (trā′jən). A.D. 52–117. Roman Emperor (98–117).

Trol·lope (trŏl′əp), **Anthony.** 1815–1882. English novelist.

Trots·ky (trŏt′skē), **Leon.** 1879–1940. Russian revolutionary; assassinated in Mexico.

Tru·deau (trōō-dō′), **Pierre Elliott.** Born 1919. Prime Minister of Canada (1968–79 and since 1980).

Tru·man (trōō′mən), **Harry S** 1884–1972. Thirty-third U.S. President (1945–53).

Tub·man (tŭb′mən), **Harriet.** 1820?–1913. American abolitionist leader.

Tu·dor (tōō′dər, tyōō′-). Surname of the English royal family from Henry VII (1485) through Elizabeth I (1603).

Tur·ge·nev (tŏŏr-gā′nyəf), **Ivan Sergeyevich.** 1818–1883. Russian novelist.

Tur·ner (tûr′nər), **Joseph Mallord William.** 1775–1851. British painter.

Tut·ankh·a·men (tōō′täng-kä′mən). Also **Tut·ankh·a·mon.** King of Egypt during the late 14th cent. B.C.

Twain (twān), **Mark.** Pen name of Samuel Langhorne Clemens.

Tweed (twēd), **William Marcy.** 1823–1878. American political boss.

Ty·ler (tī′lər), **John.** 1790–1862. Tenth U.S. President (1841–45).

Tyn·dale (tĭn′dəl), **William.** 1492?–1536. English religious reformer and martyr.

U

Up·dike (ŭp′dĭk), **John (Hoyer).** Born 1932. American author.

Ur·ban II (ûr′bən). 1042?–1099. Pope (1088–99).

U·rey (yŏŏr′ē), **Harold Clayton.** 1893–1981. American chemist; Nobel Prize winner (1934).

U·ri·ah (yōō-rī′ə). In the Old Testament, the husband of Bathsheba.

U·tril·lo (ü-trē-yō′), **Maurice.** 1883–1955. French painter.

V

Val·en·tine (văl′ən-tīn′), **Saint.** Roman Christian martyr of the 3rd cent.

Va·lois (vȧ-lwä′). A royal house that held the French throne from 1328 to 1589.

Va·le·ri·an (və-lîr′ē-ən). Died 269? A.D. Emperor of Rome (253–260).

Van Bu·ren (văn byŏŏr′ən), **Martin.** 1782–1862. Eighth U.S. President (1837–41).

Van·der·bilt (văn′dər-bĭlt′), **Cornelius.** 1794–1877. American financier and philanthropist.

Van·dyke (văn-dīk′), **Sir Anthony.** Also **Van Dyck.** 1599–1641. Flemish painter.

van Eyck (văn īk′), **Jan.** 1370?–1440? Flemish painter.

van Gogh (văn gō′, gŏKH′), **Vincent.** 1853–1890. Dutch painter.

Veb·len (vĕb′lən), **Thorstein Bunde.**

1857–1929. American economist.

Ve·ga (vā′gə), **Lope de.** 1562–1635. Spanish dramatist.

Ve·láz·quez (və-läs′kĭs, -käs, və-läs′-), **Diego Rodriguez de Silva y.** Also **Ve·lás·quez.** 1599–1660. Spanish painter.

Ver·di (vâr′dē), **Giuseppe.** 1813–1901. Italian composer.

Ver·gil (vûr′jəl). See Virgil.

Ver·meer (vər-mâr′, -mîr′), **Jan.** 1632–1675. Dutch painter.

Verne (vûrn), **Jules.** 1828–1905. French author.

Ve·ro·ne·se (vā′rō-nā′zā), **Paolo.** 1528–1588. Italian painter.

Ves·pa·sian (vĕs-pā′zhən). A.D. 9–79. Emperor of Rome (69–79).

Ves·puc·ci (vĕs-pōōt′chē), **Amerigo.** 1451–1512. Italian navigator.

Vic·tor Em·man·u·el I (vĭk′tər ĭ-măn′yōō-əl). 1759–1824. King of Sardinia (1802–21).

Victor Emmanuel II. 1820–1878. First king of Italy (1861–78).

Vic·to·ri·a (vĭk-tôr′ē-ə, -tôr′ē-ə). 1819–1901. Queen of the United Kingdom of Great Britain and Ireland (1837–1901); Empress of India (1876–1901). —**Vic·to′ri·an** adj. & n.

Vil·lon (vē-yôn′), **François.** 1431–1463? French poet.

Vin·cent de Paul (vĭn′sənt də pôl′), **Saint.** 1581?–1660. French priest and author.

Vir·gil (vûr′jəl). Also **Ver·gil.** 70–19 B.C. Roman poet. —**Vir·gil′i·an** adj.

Vi·val·di (vē-väl′dē), **Antonio.** 1680?–1743. Italian composer.

Vol·ta (vōl′tä), **Count Alessandro.** 1745–1827. Italian physicist.

Vol·taire (vŏl-târ′, vōl-). Pen name of François Marie Arouet. 1694–1778. French author.

W

Wag·ner (väg′nər), **(Wilhelm) Richard.** 1813–1883. German composer. —**Wag·ne′ri·an** adj. & n.

Waks·man (wăks′mən), **Selman Abraham.** 1888–1973. Russian-born American microbiologist; Nobel Prize winner (1952).

Wald (wôld), **George.** Born 1906. American biologist; Nobel Prize winner (1967).

Wald·heim (wŏld′hīm), **Kurt.** Born 1918. Austrian diplomat; secretary-general of the United Nations (since 1972).

Wal·lace (wŏl′ĭs), **Henry Agard.** 1888–1965. U.S. Vice President under Franklin D. Roosevelt (1941-45).

Wal·pole (wôl′pōl′, wŏl′-), **Horace.** Fourth Earl of Orford (1717–1797). English author.

Wal·ton (wôl′tən), **Izaak.** 1593–1683. English author.

War·ren (wôr′ən, wŏr′-), **Earl.** 1891–1974. American jurist.

Wash·ing·ton (wŏsh′ĭng-tən, wôsh′-). **1. George.** 1732–1799. First U.S. President (1789–97). **2. Booker T(aliaferro).** 1856–1915. American educator.

Wat·son (wŏt′sən), **James Dewey.**

Born 1928. American biologist; Nobel Prize winner (1962).

Watt (wŏt), **James**. 1736–1819. Scottish engineer and inventor.

Wat·teau (wä-tō′, vä-), **Jean Antoine**. 1684–1721. French painter.

Wayne (wān), **Anthony**. Known as Mad Anthony. 1745–1796. American general.

We·ber (vā′bər). **1.** Baron **Carl Maria Friedrich Ernst von**. 1786–1826. German composer and conductor. **2. Max**. 1864–1920. German sociologist.

Web·ster (wĕb′stər). **1. John**. 1580?–1625? English dramatist. **2. Noah**. 1758–1843. American lexicographer. **3. Daniel**. 1782–1852. American statesman.

Wein·berg (wīn′bûrg′), **Steven**. Born 1933. American physicist; Nobel Prize winner (1979).

Wel·ler (wĕl′ər), **Thomas Huckle**. Born 1915. American microbiologist; Nobel Prize winner (1954).

Wel·ling·ton (wĕl′ĭng-tən), **First Duke of**. Title of Arthur Wellesley. Known as the Iron Duke. 1769–1852. British soldier and statesman.

Wells (wĕlz), **H(erbert) G(eorge)**. 1866–1946. English author.

Wes·ley (wĕs′lē, wĕz′-). **1. John**. 1703–1791. British founder of Methodism. **2. Charles**. 1707–1788. British Methodist preacher and hymn writer.

West (wĕst), **Benjamin**. 1738–1820. American painter.

West·ing·house (wĕs′tĭng-hous′), **George**. 1846–1914. American engineer and manufacturer.

Wey·den (vīd′n), **Rogier van der**. 1400–1464. Flemish painter.

Whar·ton (hwôrt′n), **Edith (Newbold Jones)**. 1862–1937. American author.

Wheel·er (hwē′lər), **William Almon**. 1819–1887. U.S. Vice President under Rutherford B. Hayes (1877–81).

Whis·tler (hwĭs′lər), **James Abbott McNeill**. 1834–1903. American artist.

White·field (hwĭt′fēld′, hwĭt′-), **George**. 1714–1770. English evangelist.

White·head (hwĭt′hĕd′), **Alfred North**. 1861–1947. British mathematician and philosopher.

Whit·man (hwĭt′mən), **Walt**. 1819–1892. American poet.

Whit·ney (hwĭt′nē), **Eli**. 1765–1825. American inventor.

Whit·ti·er (hwĭt′ē-ər), **John Greenleaf**. 1807–1892. American poet.

Wig·ner (wĭg′nər), **Eugene Paul**. Born 1902. Hungarian-born American physicist; Nobel Prize winner (1963).

Wil·ber·force (wĭl′bər-fôrs′, -fōrs′), **William**. 1759–1833. English philanthropist and abolitionist.

Wilde (wīld), **Oscar**. 1854–1900. Irish author.

Wil·der (wīl′dər), **Thornton (Niven)**. 1897–1975. American author.

Wil·hel·mi·na (wĭl′hĕl-mē′nə). 1880–1962. Queen of the Netherlands (1890–1948); abdicated.

Wil·liam I (wĭl′yəm). Known as the Conqueror. 1027–1087. King of England (1066–87).

William I. Known as the Silent. 1533–1584. Prince of Orange; founder of the Dutch Republic.

William I. 1797–1888. King of Prussia (1861–88) and emperor of Germany (1871–88).

William II¹. 1056?–1100. King of England (1087–1100).

Wil·liam II². 1859–1941. Emperor of Germany and king of Prussia (1888–1918); abdicated.

William III. 1650–1702. Stadholder of Holland (1672–1702); King of England (1689–1702).

William IV. 1765–1837. King of Great Britain and Ireland and king of Hanover (1830–37).

Wil·liams (wĭl′yəmz). **1. Roger**. 1603?–1683. English clergyman in America; founder of Rhode Island. **2. William Carlos**. 1883–1963. American poet and physician. **3. Tennessee**. Born 1914. American dramatist.

Wil·son (wĭl′sən). **1. Henry**. 1812–1875. U.S. Vice President under Ulysses S. Grant (1873–75). **2. (Thomas) Woodrow**. 1856–1924. Twenty-eighth U.S. President (1913–21); Nobel Peace Prize winner (1919). **3. (James) Harold**. Born 1916. Prime minister of the United Kingdom (1964–1970 and 1974–1979).

Wind·sor (wĭn′zər). Family name of rulers of Great Britain since 1917.

Windsor, Duke of. See Edward VIII.

Win·throp (wĭn′thrəp). Family of English colonial administrators in America, including **1. John**. 1588–1649. Governor of Massachusetts Bay colony (1629–49). **2. John**. 1606–1676. Governor of Connecticut (1636, 1657, and 1659–76). **3. John**. 1638–1707. Governor of Connecticut (1698–1707).

Wolfe (wŏŏlf). **1. James**. 1727–1759. British general. **2. Thomas (Clayton)**. 1900–1938. American novelist.

Wol·sey (wŏŏl′zē), **Thomas**. 1475?–1530. English cardinal and statesman.

Wood (wŏŏd), **Grant**. 1892–1942. American painter.

Wood·ward (wŏŏd′wərd), **Robert**. Born 1917. American chemist; Nobel Prize winner (1965).

Woolf (wŏŏlf), **(Adeline) Virginia (Stephen)**. 1882–1941. English author.

Words·worth (wûrdz′wûrth′), **William**. 1770–1850. English poet.

Wren (rĕn), Sir **Christopher**. 1632–1723. English architect.

Wright (rīt). **1. Wilbur**. 1867–1912. American aviation pioneer. **2. Frank Lloyd**. 1869–1959. American architect. **3. Orville**. 1871–1948. American

aviation pioneer; brother of Wilbur.

Wy·att (wī′ət), **Somas**. 1503–1542. English poet.

Wych·er·ley (′ər-lē), **William**. 1640?–1716. English playwright.

Wyc·liffe (wĭk′lī), **John**. 1320?–1384. English religious reformer.

Wy·eth (wī′ĭth). Family of American painters, includes **1. Newell Convers**. 1882–1945. **Andrew Newell**. Born 1917.

Xan·thip·pe (zăn-tĭp′ē). The wife of Socrates.

Xa·vi·er (zā′vē-ər,′ē-), Saint **Francis**. 1506–1552 Spanish Jesuit missionary.

Xen·o·phon (zĕn′ən). 430?–355? B.C. Greek general and writer.

Xerx·es I (zûrk′sēz). 519?–465 B.C. King of Persia (485?–465? B.C.).

Ya·low (yā′lō), **Rn**. Born 1921. American physicist; Nobel Prize winner (1977).

Yang (yäng), **Chenng**. Born 1922. Chinese-born American physicist; Nobel Prize winner (1957).

Yeats (yāts), **William Butler**. 1865–1939. Irish poet and playwright.

Yev·tu·shen·ko (′tŏŏ-shĕng′kō), **Yevgeny Aleksandrch**. Born 1933. Soviet poet.

York (yôrk), **Alvin Cum**. 1887–1964. Known as Sergeant York. American hero of World War I

Young (yŭng). **1. Brigm**. 1801–1877. American Mormon leader and territorial governor of Utah. **2. Edward**. 1683–1765. English poet and playwright.

Z

Zeb·e·dee (zĕb′ə-dē) In the new Testament, the father of the Apostles James and John.

Zech·a·ri·ah (zĕk′ə-ə). Hebrew prophet of the 6th cen. B.C.

Zed·e·ki·ah (zĕd′ə-kī′). The last king of Judah (597–586 B.C.).

Zeng·er (zĕng′ər), **John Peter**. 1697–1746. German-born printer in America.

Ze·no (zē′nō). 342?–270? B.C. Greek philosopher; founder of Stoicism.

Zeph·a·ni·ah (zĕf′ə-nī). A Hebrew prophet of the 7th cen. B.C.

Zo·la (zō-lä′), **Émil**. 1840–1902. French novelist.

Zo·ro·as·ter (zōr′ō-ă:ər). Persian prophet of the 6th cen. B.C.; founder of Zoroastrianism.

Zwing·li (tsvĭng′lē), **Ulrch**. 1484–1531. Swiss religious reformer.

A

Aa·chen (ä′кнən) city of W West Germany; capital Charlemagne's empire. Pop. 242.

A·ba·dan (ä′bə-däb′ə-dăn′). A port of SW Iran, on Persian Gulf. Pop. 302,000.

A·be·o·ku·ta (ä′bkōō′ta, äb′ē-). A trade city in / Nigeria. Pop. 217,000.

Ab·er·deen (ăb′ən′). A city of NE Scotland. Pop. 2300.

Ab·i·djan (ăb′ī-jä. The capital of the Ivory Coa on the Gulf of Guinea. Pop. 6800.

Ab·i·lene (ăb′ə-lē. **1.** A city in central Kansas; birlace of Dwight D. Eisenhower. Poô,600. **2.** A city in central Texas. F 90,000.

Ab·ing·ton (ăb′īṫən). A city of SE Pennsylvania. F 63,600.

A·bruz·zi e M·se (ä-brōōt′tsē ā mô′lē-zä). A matainous region of S central Italy.

A·bu Dha·bi (ä′dä′bə). A sheikdom in E Arabia anapital of the United Arab Emirates.op. 55,000.

A·ca·di·a Natiol Park (ə-kā′dē-ə). A scenic area cMount Desert Island off the S coast Maine.

A·ca·pul·co (ä′pōōl′kô). A port on the Pacific coa of S Mexico. Pop. 235,000.

Ac·cra (ə-krä′, :′rə). The capital of Ghana, on the ulf of Guinea. Pop. 717,000.

A·con·ca·gua ä′kōn-kä′gwä). The highest mounin (22,835 ft/6,964.7 m) in the Westn Hemisphere, in the Andes of Argeina.

Ac·ti·um (ăk′tēəm, ăk′shē-əm). A promontory ai town of ancient NW Greece; site cAgrippa's naval victory over MarAntony and Cleopatra (31 B.C.).

Ad·dis Ab·a·b (ăd′īs äb′ə-bə). The capital of Ethpia, in the center of the country. Pp. 1,161,300.

Ad·e·laide (ăl-ād′). An industrial city of S Austlia. Pop. 900,400.

A·den (äd′n, d′n). The capital of Southern Yeṁen, in the SE. Pop. 264,000.

Aden, Gulf of. The W arm of the Arabian Sea, htween Somalia and Southern Yeṁen.

A·di·ge (ä′dē-j). A river of N Italy, flowing 225 i (362 km) SE to the Adriatic.

Ad·i·ron·dack Mountains (ăd′ə-rŏn′dăk′). A section of the Appalachian system in NE New York State; highest elevation, Mount Marcy (5,344 ft/ 1,630 m).

Ad·mi·ral·ty Island (ăd′mər-əl-tē). An island in the Alexander Archipelago of SE Alaska.

Admiralty Islands. A group of small volcanic islands in the SW Pacific Ocean, part of the Bismarck Archipelago.

A·dri·a·tic Sea (ā′drē-ăt′īk). An arm of the Mediterranean between Italy and the Balkan Peninsula.

Ae·ge·an Sea (ī-jē′ən). An arm of the Mediterranean between Greece and Turkey, bounded in the S by Crete.

Ae·o·lis (ē′ə-līs). An ancient region on the W coast of Asia Minor. —**Ae·o′li·an** adj. & n.

Af·ghan·i·stan (ăf-găn′ə-stăn′). A landlocked country of SW Asia. Pop. 20,340,000. Cap. Kabul.

Af·ri·ca (ăf′rī-kə). A continent in the Eastern Hemisphere, S of Europe and between the Atlantic and Indian oceans. —**Af′ri·can** adj. & n.

A·ga·na (ä-gä′nyä). The capital of Guam, on the island's W coast. Pop. 2,000.

Ag·as·siz, Lake (ăg′ə-sē). A prehistoric lake in North America, in present-day North Dakota, Minnesota, and Saskatchewan.

Ag·in·court (ăj′īn-kôrt′). A village of N France where Henry V of England defeated the French in 1415.

A·gra (ä′grə). A city of N central India; site of the Taj Mahal. Pop. 594,900.

A·gul·has, Cape (ə-gŭl′əs). A group of rugged cliffs marking the divide between the Atlantic and Indian oceans at the S point of Africa.

A·hag·gar Mountains (ə-hăg′ər, ä′hə-gär′). A mountainous upland region in S Algeria; highest elevation, Tahat (9,573 ft/2,920 m).

Ah·mad·na·gar (ä′məd-nŭg′ər). A city of W central India. Pop. l17,200.

Ah·mad·a·bad (ä′məd-ə-bäd′). A city of NW India. Pop. 1,585,500.

Aisne (ān). A river of NE France, rising in the Argonne Forest and flowing c. 175 mi (282 km) W to the Oise.

Aix-en-Pro·vence (ĕks′äṅ-prô-väṅs′). A city of S France. Pop. 110,700.

A·jac·cio (ä-yät′chō). The capital of Corsica, on the W coast; birthplace of Napoleon. Pop. 42,300.

Aj·mer (ŭj-mîr′). A city of NW India. Pop. 262,500.

A·ka·shi (ä-kä′shē). A city of Japan, on SW Honshu. Pop. 239,400.

A·ki·ta (ä-kē-tä). A city of NW Honshu, Japan. Pop. 266,800.

Ak·kad (ăk′ăd′, ä′kăd′). A region and city of ancient Mesopotamia. —**Ak·kad′i·an** adj. & n.

Ak·ron (ăk′rən). An industrial city of S Ohio. Pop. 242,600.

Al·a·bam·a (ăl′ə-băm′ə). A state of the S United States, bordering on the Gulf of Mexico. Pop. 3,870,200. Cap. Montgomery. —**Al′a·bam′i·an** (-ē-ən), or **Al′a·bam′an** adj. & n.

Alabama River. A river rising in central Alabama and flowing 315 mi (506.8 km) S to the Gulf of Mexico.

Al·a·me·da (ăl′ə-mē′də). A city of W California. Pop. 71,000.

A·la·mein, El (ĕl ăl′ə-mān′). A village in N Egypt; site of a major British victory over the Axis forces (1942) in World War II.

Al·a·mo·gor·do (ăl′ə-mə-gôr′dō). A city in S New Mexico; site of the first atomic bomb explosion (1945). Pop. 24,018.

Å·land Islands (ō′län). An island group of Finland, at the entrance to the Gulf of Bothnia.

A·las·ka (ə-lăs′kə). The largest state of the United States, in extreme NW North America. Pop. 400,100. Cap. Juneau. —**A·las′kan** adj. & n.

Alaska, Gulf of. The N inlet of the Pacific between the Alaska Peninsula and the Alexander Archipelago.

Alaska Peninsula. A continuation of the Aleutian Range of S central Alaska, between the Bering Sea and the Pacific Ocean.

Alaska Range. A mountain range in S central Alaska; highest elevation, Mount McKinley (20,320 ft/6,197.6 m).

Al·ba Lon·ga (ăl′bə lông′gə). A city of ancient Latium, SE of Rome.

Al·ba·ni·a (ăl-bā′nē-ə, -bān′yə, ôl-). A country on the Adriatic coast of the Balkan Peninsula. Pop. 2,690,000. Cap. Tirana. —**Al·ba′ni·an** adj. & n.

Al·ba·ny (ôl′bə-nē). The capital of New York State, on the W bank of the Hudson. Pop. 106,600.

Al·be·marle Sound (ăl′bə-märl′). An arm of the Atlantic, in NE North Carolina.

Al·bert, Lake (ăl′bərt). A lake in the central African Rift Valley, on the Zaire-Uganda border.

Al·ber·ta (ăl-bûr′tə). A Prairie Province of Canada. Pop. 1,948,000. Cap.

Edmonton. —**Al·ber'tan** *adj. & n.*

Al·bu·quer·que (ăl'bə-kûr'kē). A city of central New Mexico. Pop. 328,800.

Al·ca·traz (ăl'kə-trăz'). An island in San Francisco Bay, California, the site of a former Federal prison.

Al·der·ney (ôl'dər-nē). One of the Channel Islands in the English Channel, W of Cherbourg, France.

A·lep·po (ə-lĕp'ō). A city of NW Syria. Pop. 778,500.

A·leu·tian Islands (ə-lōō'shən). A chain of volcanic islands, extending into the N Pacific in a W arc from Alaska.

Al·ex·an·der Archipelago (ăl'ĭg-zăn'dər). A group of more than 1,000 islands off the SE coast of Alaska.

Al·ex·an·dri·a (ăl'ĭg-zăn'drē-ə, -zăn'drē-ə). **1.** A city of Egypt, on the Mediterranean coast W of the Nile delta. Pop. 2,259,000. **2.** A city of N Virginia, on the Potomac River. Pop. 108,700.

Al·ge·ri·a (ăl-jîr'ē-ə). A republic in NW Africa. Pop. 17,910,000. Cap. Algiers. —**Al·ge'ri·an** *adj. & n.*

Al·giers (ăl-jîrz'). The capital of Algeria, on the Mediterranean. Pop. 2,000,000

A·li·can·te (ä'lē-kän'tä). A city of SE Spain. Pop. 943,100.

Al·i·garh (ăl'ĭ-gûr'). A city of N central India. Pop. 252,300.

Al·la·ha·bad (ăl'ə-hə-băd', -bäd'). A city of N central India. Pop. 490,600.

Al·le·ghe·ny Mountains (ăl'ə-gā'nē). A section of the Appalachian mountain system in Virginia, West Virginia, Maryland, and central Pennsylvania.

Allegheny River. A river rising in Pennsylvania and flowing 325 mi (523 km) N to Pittsburgh, where it joins the Monongahela to form the Ohio. .

Al·len·town (ăl'ən-toun'). A city of E Pennsylvania. Pop. 104,900.

Al·ma-A·ta (ăl'mä-ä-tä'). The capital of the Kazakh S.S.R., Central Asian U.S.S.R. Pop. 871,000.

Al Ma·nam·a (ăl mə-năm'ə). The capital of Bahrain, on the Persian Gulf. Pop. 89,100.

Alps (ălps). A major mountain system of S central Europe; highest elevation, Mont Blanc (15,771 ft/4,810.2 m).

Al·sace-Lor·raine (ăl-săs'lô-rān', ăl-säs'-). A region of NE France, annexed by Germany (1871) and recovered by France in 1919.

Al·tai Mountains (ăl'tī'). A mountain system of central Asia, in the Soviet Union, Mongolia, and China; highest elevation, c. 15,157 ft (4,622.9 m).

A·ma·ga·sa·ki (ä-mä'gə-sä'kē). An industrial city of S Honshu, Japan. Pop. 544,300.

Am·a·ril·lo (ăm'ə-rĭl'ō). A commercial center of N Texas. Pop. 140,500.

Am·a·zon (ăm'ə-zŏn', -zən). A river of South America rising in the Peruvian Andes and flowing c. 4,000 mi (6,436 km) N and E through N Brazil to the Atlantic Ocean.

A·mer·i·ca (ə-mĕr'ə-kə). **1.** The United States of America. **2.** North America. **3.** South America. **4.** North America,

Central America, and South America. —**A·mer'i·can** *adj. & n.*

American Sa·mo·a (sə-mō'ə). Seven islands in the South Pacific. Pop. 30,600. Cap. Pago Pago.

Am·herst (ăm'ərst, -hərst). A town of W Massachusetts. Pop. 33,200.

A·miens (à-myăN'). A manufacturing center of N France. Pop. 131,500.

Am·man (ä-män'). The capital of Jordan, in the N. Pop. 691,000.

A·moy (ä-moi', ə-moi'). A city of SE China, on Amoy Island. Pop. 400,000.

Am·rit·sar (ŭm-rĭt'sər). A city of NW India. Pop. 407,600.

Am·ster·dam (ăm'stər-dăm'). The constitutional capital of the Netherlands. Pop. 975,500.

A·mu Dar·ya (ä'mōō där'yə). A river of central Asia, rising in the Pamirs and flowing c. 1,600 mi (2,574.4 km) generally N to the Aral Sea.

A·mund·sen Sea (ä'mən-sən). A part of the South Pacific Ocean, off the Antarctic coast.

A·mur (ä-mōōr'). A river of E Asia, rising in N Mongolia and flowing c. 1,800 mi (2,896.2 km) SE to the Sea of Okhotsk.

An·a·heim (ăn'ə-hīm'). A city in SW California; site of Disneyland. Pop. 203,000.

An·a·to·li·a (ăn'ə-tō'lē-ə). An ancient region of Turkey. —**An'a·to'li·an** *adj. & n.*

An·chor·age (ăng'kər-ĭj). The largest city of Alaska, in the S. Pop. 174,000.

An·co·na (ăng-kō'nə). A city of central Italy. Pop. 107,800.

An·da·lu·sia (ăn'də-lōō'zhə). A region of SW Spain, on the Mediterranean. —**An'da·lu'sian** *adj. & n.*

An·da·man and Nic·o·bar Islands (ăn'də-mən; nĭk'ə-bär'). A territory of India, comprising 2 island groups in the Bay of Bengal.

Andaman Sea. An arm of the Bay of Bengal bounded by the Andaman and Nicobar Islands, Burma, the Malay Peninsula, and Sumatra.

An·der·son·ville (ăn'dər-sən-vĭl'). A village in SW Georgia; site of a Confederate prison during the Civil War.

An·des (ăn'dēz). A 4,000-mi (6,436 km) long mountain system stretching the length of W South America from Venezuela to Tierra del Fuego; highest elevation, Aconcagua (22,835 ft/6,964.7 m).

An·dor·ra (ăn-dôr'ə, -dôr'ə). A republic in the E Pyrenees between France and Spain. Pop. 25,000. Cap. Andorra la Vella.

An·dros (ăn'drəs, -drŏs). An island of Greece in the Aegean Sea.

Andros Island. The largest of the Bahama Islands.

An·gel Fall (ăn'jəl). A waterfall in SE Venezuela, dropping c. 3,212 ft (979.7 m).

An·gers (äN-zhā'). A city of W France. Pop. 137,600.

Ang·kor (ăng'kôr'). A group of ruins in NW Cambodia.

An·gle·sey (ăng'gəl-sē). An island off the NW coast of Wales.

An·go·la (ăng-gō'lə). A country of SW Africa. Pop. 7,205,000. Cap. Luanda.

—**An·go'lan** *adj. & n.*

An·hwei (än'hwā'). A province of E central China. Pop. 35,000,000. Cap. Hofei.

An·jou (äN'jōō'). A region and former province of W France.

An·ka·ra (äng'kə-rə, äng'-). The capital of Turkey. Pop. 1,698,542.

Ann, Cape (ăn). A peninsula in N Massachusetts projecting into the Atlantic Ocean NE of Gloucester.

An·na·ba (ä-nä-bä'). A city of NE Algeria. Pop. 223,000.

An·nam (ä-năm', ăn'ăm'). An administrative region of French Indochina in E central Vietnam.

An·nap·o·lis (ə-năp'ə-lĭs). The capital of Maryland, on Chesapeake Bay. Pop. 31,543.

An·na·pur·na (ăn'ə-pŏŏr'nə, -pûr'nə). A massif of the Himalayas in central Nepal; highest elevation, Annapurna I (26,502 ft/8,083.1 m).

Ann Ar·bor (ăn är'bər). A city of SE Michigan. Pop. 104,500.

An·shan (än'shän'). A city of NE China. Pop. 1,500,000.

Ant·arc·ti·ca (ănt-ärk'tĭ-kə, -är'tĭ-kə). A continent largely contained within the Antarctic Circle and almost entirely covered by a sheet of ice.

Ant·arc·tic Circle (ănt-ärk'tĭk, -är'tĭk). A parallel of latitude, 66 degrees, 33 minutes S, marking the limit of the South Frigid Zone.

Antarctic Ocean. The waters surrounding Antarctica; the S extensions of the Atlantic, Pacific, and Indian oceans, which appear to make up a distinct body of water on most world map projections.

An·tie·tam (ăn-tē'təm). A creek, tributary of the Potomac River, in W Maryland, near the town of Sharpsburg, the site of a Civil War battle (1862).

An·ti·gua (ăn-tē'gwə, -gə). An island in the West Indies. Pop. 69,700. Cap. Saint Johns.

An·ti-Leb·a·non (ăn'tĭ-lĕb'ə-nən). A mountain range running N and S on the border between Syria and Lebanon; highest elevation, Mount Hermon (9,232 ft/2,815.8 m).

An·til·les (ăn-tĭl'ēz). The main island group of the West Indies, with the exception of the Bahamas, forming a chain that separates the Caribbean Sea from the Atlantic Ocean.

An·ti·och (ăn'tē-ŏk'). A city on the Orontes River in S Turkey; capital of ancient Syria. Pop. 66,400.

An·ti·sa·na (än'tē-sä'nä). An active volcano, 18,885 ft (5,760 m) high, in the Andes in N central Ecuador.

An·tung (än'dōōng', -tōōng'). A river port of E China. Pop. 450,000.

Ant·werp (ănt'wûrp). A port city of NW Belgium. Pop. 665,980.

An·yang (än'yäng'). A city of E central China. Pop. 450,000.

An·zi·o (än'zē-ō'). A port on the W coast of Italy; site of an Allied beachhead in World War II (1944).

A·o·mor·i (ä'ō-mō'rē). A city of Japan, a seaport on N Honshu. Pop. 270,000.

Ap·en·nines (ăp'ə-nīnz'). A mountain range of Italy, extending along the length of the peninsula; highest elevation, Mount Corno (9,560 ft/2,915.8 m).

A·pi·a (ä-pē′ä). The capital of Western Samoa, a seaport on Upolu Island. Pop. 30,593.

A·po, Mount (ä′pō). The highest mountain (9,690 ft/2,955.5 m) in the Philippines, an active volcano on SE Mindanao.

Ap·pa·la·chi·an Mountains (ăp′ə-lä′-chē-ən). The major mountain system of E North America, extending from S Quebec to central Alabama; highest elevation, Mount Mitchell (6,684 ft/ 2,038.6 m), in North Carolina.

Appalachian Trail. A system of mountain trails extending c. 2,050 mi (3,298.5 km) along the Appalachian range between Georgia and Maine.

Ap·po·mat·tox (ăp′ə-măt′əks). The town in central Virginia where Gen. Robert E. Lee surrendered to Gen. Ulysses S. Grant on April 9, 1865, bringing the Civil War to a close. Pop. 9,800.

A·pu·lia (ə-pyōōl′yə). A region of SE Italy; formerly a Roman province.

A·qa·ba (ä′kä-bä′). A seaport of Jordan at the N end of the Gulf of Aqaba, an arm of the Red Sea. Pop. 15,000.

Aq·ui·taine (ăk′wə-tān′). A historical region of SW France.

A·ra·bi·a (ə-rā′bē-ə). A peninsula of SW Asia, lying between the Red Sea and the Persian Gulf and including Saudi Arabia, Yemen, and Southern Yemen, as well as a number of sheikdoms. —**A·ra′bi·an** adj. & n.

Arabian Desert. The desert in Egypt between the Nile Valley and the Red Sea.

Arabian Sea. The part of the Indian Ocean bounded by E Africa, Arabia, and W India.

A·ra·ca·jú (ä′rä-kä-zhōō′). A city of NE Brazil. Pop. 183,300.

A·rad (ä-räd′). A city of W Rumania, on the Mureş River. Pop. 171,100.

A·ra·fu·ra Sea (ä′rə-fōō′rə). A part of the W Pacific Ocean between New Guinea and Australia.

Ar·a·gon (ăr′ə-gŏn′). A region of NE Spain, formerly an independent kingdom.

Ar·al Sea (ăr′əl). An inland sea of the Soviet Union, E of the Caspian Sea.

Ar·an Islands (ăr′ən). Three islands at the entrance to Galway Bay, off the SW coast of Ireland.

Ar·a·rat, Mount (ăr′ə-răt′). A mountain, 16,945 ft (5,168.2 m) high, in E Turkey.

Arch·an·gel (ärk′ān′jəl). A seaport of NW European U.S.S.R. Pop. 343,000.

Arc·tic Archipelago (ärk′tĭk, är′tĭk). An extensive group of islands in the Arctic Ocean between North America and Greenland, part of the Northwest Territories, Canada.

Arctic Circle. A parallel of latitude at 66 degrees, 33 minutes N, marking the limit of the North Frigid Zone.

Arctic Ocean. The polar ocean between North America and Eurasia.

Ar·dennes (är-dĕn′). A forested plateau in N France, SE Belgium, and Luxembourg; scene of the Battle of the Bulge in World War II.

A·re·qui·pa (ä′rä-kē′pä). A commercial center in S Peru. Pop. 194,700.

Ar·gen·ti·na (är′jən-tē′nə). A republic of SE South America between Chile and the Atlantic. Pop. 26,060,000. Cap. Buenos Aires. —**Ar′gen·tine′** adj. —**Ar′gen·tin′e·an** (-tĭn′ē-ən). adj. & n.

Ar·go·lis (är′gə-lĭs). A region of ancient Greece, in NE Peloponnesus. —**Ar·go′li·an** adj. & n.

Ar·gonne (är-gŏn′, är′gŏn′). A wooded ridge in NE France; scene of heavy fighting in World Wars I and II.

Ar·gos (är′gŏs, -gəs). A city of S Greece, possibly the country's oldest city.

Ar·hus (ôr′hōōs′). A seaport in E Jutland, Denmark. Pop. 246,300.

Ar·i·zo·na (ăr′ə-zō′nə). A SW state of the United States. Pop. 2,714,000. Cap. Phoenix. —**Ar′i·zo′nan** or **Ar′i·zo′ni·an** adj. & n.

Ar·kan·sas (är′kən-sô′). A state of the S central United States. Pop. 2,284,-000. Cap. Little Rock. —**Ar·kan′san** (-kăn′zən) adj. & n.

Ar·kan·sas River (är′kən-sô′, är-kăn′-zəs). A river of the S central United States, rising in the Rocky Mountains of central Colorado and flowing 1,450 mi (2,335 km) SE to the Mississippi.

Ar·ling·ton (är′lĭng-tən). A county of N Virginia, an urban area across the Potomac from Washington, D.C.; site of Arlington National Cemetery. Pop. 174,300.

Ar·me·ni·a (är-mē′nē-ə, -mēn′yə). An ancient country of W Asia, now constituting a region divided among the Soviet Union, Turkey, and Iran. —**Ar·me′ni·an** adj. & n.

Armenian Soviet Socialist Republic. A constituent republic of SE European U.S.S.R. Pop. 2,834,000. Cap. Yerevan.

Arn·hem Land (är′nəm). A region in extreme N Australia, set aside as a reserve for the Australian aborigines.

Ar·no (är′nō). A river in Tuscany, Italy, rising in the Apennines and flowing c. 150 mi (241.3 km) to the Ligurian Sea near Pisa.

A·ru·ba (ə-rōō′bə). An island of the Netherlands Antilles, N of the coast of Venezuela.

A·sa·hi·ga·wa (ä-sä′hē-gä′wä). Also **A·sa·hi·ka·wa** (-kä′wä). A city in central Hokkaido, Japan. Pop. 320,500.

A·sa·ma, Mount (ä-sä′mä). An active volcano, 8,340 ft (2,543.7 m) high, in central Honshu, Japan.

As·cen·sion Island (ə-sĕn′shən). A British island in the S Atlantic NW of St. Helena.

As·cot (ăs′kət). A village of Berkshire, England, near which a famous horse race is held annually.

A·shan·ti (ə-shăn′tē, ə-shän′-). A former kingdom and British protectorate of W Africa, now a region of central Ghana.

Ashe·ville (ăsh′vĭl′, -vəl). A commercial city and tourist resort in W North Carolina. Pop. 53,700.

Ash·kha·bad (äsh′kə-băd, -bäd′). The capital of the Turkmen S.S.R., S central Asian U.S.S.R. Pop. 302,000.

A·sia (ā′zhə, ā′shə). The largest of the earth's continents, occupying the E part of the Eurasian land mass and adjacent islands and separated from Europe by the Ural Mountains. —**A′sian** or **A′si·at′ic** adj. & n.

Asia Minor. The W peninsula of Asia, lying between the Black Sea and the Mediterranean and including Asian Turkey.

As·ma·ra (ăz-mä′rə). A city of N Ethiopia. Pop. 340,200.

As·pen (ăs′pən). A ski-resort town in W central Colorado. Pop. 3,802.

As·si·si (ə-sē′zē, ə-sē′sē). A religious center in central Italy. Pop. 19,000.

As·syr·i·a (ə-sîr′ē-ə). An ancient empire of W Asia. Cap. Nineveh. —**As·syr′i·an** adj. & n.

As·tra·khan (ăs′trə-kăn′, -kən). A city of SE European U.S.S.R., on the Volga delta. Pop. 458,000.

A·sun·ción (ä′sōōn-syôn′). The capital of Paraguay, a port on the Paraguay River. Pop. 574,000.

As·wan (äs-wän′, -wŏn′, äs-wän′). A city on the E bank of the Nile in S Egypt; site of the Aswan Dam. Pop. 206,000.

As·yut (äs-yōōt′). An industrial city of central Egypt. Pop. 175,700.

A·ta·ca·ma Desert (ä′tə-kä′mə). An arid area of N Chile, possessing major nitrate deposits.

Ath·a·bas·ca or **Ath·a·bas·ka** (ăth′ə-băs′kə). **1.** A lake in N Alberta and Saskatchewan, Canada. **2.** A river of Alberta, Canada, rising in the Rocky Mountains and flowing 765 mi (1,230.9 km) N into Lake Athabasca.

Ath·ens (ăth′ənz). The capital of Greece, in the SE. Pop. 867,023. —**A·the′ni·an** (ə-thē′nē-ən) adj. & n.

Ath·os, Mount (ăth′ŏs, ā′thŏs). A peak, 6,670 ft (620.5 m) high, in NE Greece.

At·lan·ta (ăt-lăn′tə). The capital of Georgia, in the N part of the state. Pop. 406,000.

At·lan·tic City (ăt-lăn′tĭk). A resort and convention city in SE New Jersey. Pop. 43,100.

Atlantic Ocean. The 2nd largest of the earth's oceans, extending from the Arctic in the N to the Antarctic in the S and from the Americas in the W to Europe and Africa in the E.

At·las Mountains (ăt′ləs). A mountain system in NW Africa, between the Sahara and the Mediterranean; highest elevation, Djebel Toubkal (13,665 ft/4,167.8 m).

At·ti·ca (ăt′ĭ-kə). The hinterland of Athens in ancient Greece. —**At′tic** adj. & n.

At·tu (ă′tōō). The westernmost of the Aleutian Islands, in the North Pacific.

Auck·land (ôk′lənd). A city and seaport of New Zealand, on N North Island. Pop. 150,700.

Augs·burg (ouks′bŏŏrk′). A city of S West Germany. Pop. 254,053.

Au·gus·ta (ô-gŭs′tə). **1.** A city of Georgia, in the E on the Savannah; formerly the state capital (1785–95). Pop. 51,200. **2.** The capital of Maine on the Kennebec River. Pop. 21,721.

ă pat ā pay â care ä father ĕ pet ē be hw which ĭ pit ī tie î pier ŏ pot ō toe ô paw, for oi noise
ŏŏ took ōō boot ou out th thin th this ŭ cut û urge zh vision ə about, item, edible, gallop, circus

Aus·ter·litz (ôs′tər-lĭts′, ous′-). A town of S Czechoslovakia, near the site of Napoleon I's victory over the Russian and Austrian armies (1805).

Aus·tin (ôs′tən). The capital of Texas, in the S central part of the state. Pop. 326,000.

Aus·tral·a·sia (ôs′trəl-ā′zhə, -ā′shə). The islands of Oceania in the South Pacific, together with Australia, New Zealand, New Guinea, and associated islands; sometimes, all of Oceania. —**Aus′tral·a′sian** adj. & n.

Aus·tra·lia (ô-strāl′yə). **1.** A continent lying SE of Asia between the Pacific and Indian oceans. **2.** Officially, the Commonwealth of Australia. A country comprising the continent of Australia, Tasmania, 2 external territories, and a number of dependencies. Pop. 12,730,000. Cap. Canberra. —**Aus·tra′lian** adj. & n.

Australian Alps (ălps). A mountain chain in SE Australia; highest elevation, Mt. Kosciusko (7,316 ft/2,231.4 m).

Aus·tri·a (ôs′trē-ə). A landlocked federal republic, formerly an empire, in central Europe. Pop. 7,500,000. Cap. Vienna. —**Aus′tri·an** adj. & n.

Aus·tri·a-Hun·ga·ry (ôs′trē-ə-hŭng′gə-rē). A former dual monarchy of central Europe, formed by the union of Austria, Bohemia, and Hungary and of areas of Poland, Rumania, Yugoslavia, and Italy, and dismembered in 1919.

Aus·tro·ne·sia (ôs′trō-nē′zhə, -shə). The islands in the Pacific including Indonesia, Melanesia, Micronesia, and Polynesia.

Au·vergne (ō-vârn′). A region of central France.

A·ver·no (ä-vĕr′nō). A small crater lake, W of Naples, Italy; regarded by the ancient Romans as the entrance to the underworld.

A·vi·gnon (ȧ-vē-nyôn′). A city on the Rhône in SE France; a seat of the papacy (1309–77). Pop. 90,786.

A·von (ā′vŏn, ā′vən). A river rising in S central England and flowing 96 mi (154.5 km) SW past Stratford to the Severn.

A·zer·bai·jan Soviet Socialist Republic (ä′zər-bī-jän′, ăz′ər-). A constituent republic of SE European U.S.S.R. Pop. 5,111,000. Cap. Baku.

A·zores (ā′zôrz, ə-zôrz′). Three island groups in the North Atlantic 900 mi (1,448 km) W of Portugal, of which they are administrative districts.

Az·ov, Sea of (ăz′ôf′, -ôf′, ä′zôf′.) The N arm of the Black Sea.

B

Baal·bek (bäl′bĕk′, bā′əl-). A town in Lebanon, NE of Beirut; site of a Roman religious center.

Ba·bel·thu·ap (bä′bəl-tōō′äp). The largest island of the Palau group in the SW Pacific Ocean.

Bab·y·lon (băb′ə-lən, -lŏn′). The capital of ancient Babylonia.

Bab·y·lo·ni·a (băb′ə-lō′nē-ə). An ancient empire in the lower Euphrates

Valley of SW Asia. —**Bab′y·lo′ni·an** adj. & n.

Bac·tri·a (băk′trē-ə). An ancient country of SW Asia. —**Bac′tri·an** adj. & n.

Ba·den (bäd′n). A region of SW Germany that was 1st a grand duchy (1809–1918).

Bad·lands (băd′lănz′). An extensive, barren, and deeply eroded region of SW South Dakota and NW Nebraska; includes the Badlands National Monument in South Dakota.

Baf·fin Bay (băf′ĭn). An arm of the Atlantic Ocean off NE Canada, separating Greenland and Baffin Island.

Baffin Island. A Canadian island, lying between Greenland and mainland Canada.

Bagh·dad (băg′dăd′). Also **Bag·dad**. The capital of Iraq, on the Tigris River. Pop. 2,987,000.

Ba·gui·o (bä′gē-ō′). The summer capital of the Philippines, on N Luzon Island. Pop. 100,200.

Ba·ha·ma Islands (bə-hä′mə). Also **Ba·ha·mas** (-məz). A self-governing British colony of more than 700 islands in the Atlantic Ocean between Florida and Hispaniola. Pop. 236,000. Cap. Nassau. —**Ba·ha′mi·an** (bə-hä′mē-ən, -hä′mē-ən) adj. & n.

Bah·rain (bä-rān′). Also **Bah·rein**. An independent sheikdom comprising an archipelago in the Persian Gulf between Qatar and Saudi Arabia. Pop. 370,000. Cap. Al Manama.

Bai·kal (bī-kôl′, -käl′). See **Baykal**.

Ba·ker, Mount (bā′kər). **1.** A peak, 12,406 ft (3,783.8 m) high, in N Colorado. **2.** A peak, 10,750 ft (3,278.7 m) high, of the Cascade Range in Washington.

Ba·kers·field (bā′kərz-fēld′). A city of S central California. Pop. 112,300.

Ba·ku (bä-kōō′). The capital of the Azerbaijan S.S.R., SE European U.S.S.R. Pop. 1,022,000.

Bal·a·ton, Lake (băl′ə-tŏn′). A lake of W central Hungary.

Bal·e·ar·ic Islands (băl′ē-ăr′ĭk, bə-lîr′ĭk). An island group in the Mediterranean, E of Spain. Pop. 564,741. Cap. Palma.

Ba·li (bä′lē). An island of Indonesia, off the E end of Java. —**Ba′li·nese′** (-nēz′, -nēs′) adj. & n.

Bal·kan Mountains (bôl′kən). A range of mountains extending across N Bulgaria from the Black Sea to the border of Yugoslavia; highest elevation, 7,800 ft (2,379 m).

Balkan Peninsula. A peninsula in SE Europe, bounded by the Mediterranean and Aegean seas to the S, the Adriatic and Ionian seas to the W, and the Black Sea to the E.

Balkan States. The countries that occupy the Balkan Peninsula: Albania, Bulgaria, Greece, Rumania, and Yugoslavia.

Bal·khash (bäl-käsh′). A salt lake of Soviet Central Asia.

Bal·tic Sea (bôl′tĭk). A long arm of the Atlantic Ocean in N Europe, bordered by Sweden, Finland, the Soviet Union, Poland, East and West Germany, and Denmark.

Baltic States. The formerly independent states of Estonia, Latvia, and Lithuania, on the E coast of the Baltic Sea.

Bal·ti·more (bôl′tə-môr′, -mōr′). The largest city of Maryland, a seaport on upper Chesapeake Bay. Pop. 784,600. —**Bal′ti·mo′re·an** adj. & n.

Ba·lu·chi·stan (bə-lōō′chĭ-stän′, -stän′). A region in W Pakistan, with a coastline on the Arabian Sea.

Ba·ma·ko (băm′ə-kō′). The capital of Mali, in the S on the Niger River. Pop. 237,000.

Ban·dar Se·ri Be·ga·wan (bän′där sĕr′ē bə-gä′wən). The capital of Brunei, in the N. Pop. 36,500.

Ban·dung (bän′dŏŏng). A city of Indonesia, in W Java. Pop. 1,201,700.

Banff (bămf). A resort town of Alberta, Canada, near Lake Louise in Banff National Park. Pop. 3,500.

Ban·ga·lore (băng′gə-lôr′). A city of S central India. Pop. 1,540,700.

Bang·kok (băng′kŏk′, băng-kŏk′). The capital of Thailand, on the Chao Phraya River near the Gulf of Siam. Pop. 4,178,000.

Ban·gla·desh (băng′glə-dĕsh′). A country of S Asia, bordering on India and Burma. Pop. 88,092,000. Cap. Dacca.

Ban·gor (băng′gôr′, -gər). A river port of E central Maine. Pop. 31,600.

Ban·gui (băng′gə). The capital of the Central African Republic, on the Ubangi River. Pop. 187,000.

Ban·jer·ma·sin (bän′jər-mä′sĭn). A city of Indonesia, on S Borneo. Pop. 281,700.

Ban·jul (bän′jōōl). Formerly **Bath·urst** (băth′ərst). The capital of Gambia, on an island at the mouth of the Gambia River. Pop. 45,600.

Ban·nock·burn (băn′ək-bûrn′, băn′ək-bûrn′). A town in central Scotland, near which Robert the Bruce defeated the English under Edward II (June 1314).

Bar·ba·dos (bär-bā′dōs, -dəs). The easternmost island of the West Indies, independent since 1966. Pop. 279,000. Cap. Bridgetown.

Bar·ba·ry (bär′bə-rē). A region of N Africa stretching from Egypt's W border to the Atlantic Ocean.

Barbary Coast. The Mediterranean coastal area of Barbary and the Barbary States.

Barbary States. Formerly, the collective name for Algeria, Tunisia, Tripoli, and, sometimes, Morocco, where piracy flourished until the early 19th cent.

Bar·bu·da (bär-bōō′də). An island in the Leeward Islands, N of Antigua.

Bar·ce·lo·na (bär′sə-lō′nə). A seaport and industrial center of NE Spain. Pop. 1,809,700.

Ba·reil·ly (bə-rā′lē). A commercial city of N India. Pop. 274,000.

Ba·rents Sea (băr′ənts, bä′rənts). The part of the Arctic Ocean lying N of Norway and the Soviet Union, and S of Spitsbergen and Franz Josef Land.

Ba·ri (bä′rə). An Adriatic seaport of SE Italy. Pop. 384,400.

Bar·na·ul (bər-nŭ-ōōl′). A port city of SW Siberian U.S.S.R., on the Ob

River. Pop. 522,000.

Ba·ro·da (bə-rō′də). A city of W central India. Pop. 467,400.

Bar·qui·si·me·to (bär′kə-sə-mā′tō). A city of Venezuela, W of Caracas. Pop. 430,000.

Bar·ran·quil·la (bär′räng-kē′yä). A city of N Colombia, on the Magdalena. Pop. 661,900.

Bar·ren Grounds (băr′ən). Also **Barren Lands.** A treeless, sparsely inhabited plain in N Canada, extending W from Hudson Bay to Great Slave and Great Bear lakes.

Bar·row, Point (băr′ō). The northernmost point of Alaska, on the Arctic Ocean.

Ba·sel (bä′zəl). A commercial city of NW Switzerland, on the Rhine River. Pop. 185,300.

Ba·si·lan (bə-sē′län). A group of Philippine islands, separated from SE Mindanao by the Basilan Strait.

Basque Provinces (băsk). A region of N Spain, on the Bay of Biscay, with a largely Basque population.

Bas·ra (bŭs′rə, bäs′-). A port city of SE Iraq, on the Shatt-al-Arab. Pop. 313,300.

Bas·sein (bə-sēn′, -sān′). A city of S Burma, on the Bassein River. Pop. 136,000.

Bass Strait (băs). A channel between mainland Australia and Tasmania.

Ba·taan (bə-tăn′, -tän′). A peninsula of W Luzon, the Philippines, surrendered in World War II to the Japanese by U.S. and Philippine forces (1942) and retaken by American forces (Feb., 1945).

Bath (băth, bäth). A city of SW England; site of mineral baths fed by a Roman reservoir. Pop. 83,100.

Bath·urst (băth′ərst). See **Banjul.**

Bat·on Rouge (băt′n rōōzh′). The capital of Louisiana, on the E bank of the Mississippi. Pop. 219,200.

Bat·ter·y, the (băt′ə-rē). A park at the S tip of Manhattan Island on the upper end of New York Bay in New York City.

Ba·tu·mi (bə-tōō′mē). Also **Ba·tum** (bə-tōōm′). A port city of SW Asian U.S.S.R., on the Black Sea. Pop. 117,000.

Ba·var·i·a (bə-vâr′ē-ə). A region of S West Germany. —**Ba·var′i·an** adj. & n.

Bay City (bā). A city of E Michigan. Pop. 41,600.

Bay·kal or **Bai·kal** (bī-kôl′, -käl′). A freshwater lake, the largest in Eurasia and said to be the deepest in the world, located in Soviet Central Asia.

Ba·yonne (bā-yōn′). A seaport of N New Jersey. Pop. 74,100.

Bay·reuth (bī-roit′). A city of S West Germany, noted for its annual Wagnerian festival. Pop. 66,900.

Beard·more Glacier (bîrd′môr′). The largest valley glacier in the world, 260 mi (418.3 km) long, located in Queen Maud Mountains, Antarctica.

Beau·fort Sea (bō′fərt). A part of the Arctic Ocean lying off the coasts of NW Canada and NE Alaska.

Beau·mont (bō′mŏnt). An industrial city of E Texas, on the Gulf of Mex-

ico. Pop. 118,000.

Bei·rut (bā-rōōt′). The capital of Lebanon, on the E Mediterranean. Pop. 702,000.

Be·lém (bə-lĕm′). A city of N Brazil, on the Rio Pará. Pop. 771,600.

Bel·fast (bĕl′făst′, -fäst′, bĕl-făst′, -fäst′). The capital of Northern Ireland, at the head of Belfast Lough on the E coast. Pop. 357,600.

Bel·gian Congo (bĕl′jən). A former Belgian colony in W central Africa.

Bel·gium (bĕl′jəm). A kingdom of NW Europe. Pop. 9,849,000. Cap. Brussels. —**Bel′gian** (bĕl′jən) adj. & n.

Bel·grade (bĕl′grăd′, bĕl-grăd′). The capital of Yugoslavia, in the E on the Danube and Sava rivers. Pop. 793,000.

Be·lize (bə-lēz′). Formerly **Brit·ish Hon·du·ras** (brĭt′ĭsh hŏn-dŏŏr′əs, -dyŏŏr′əs). A British crown colony in Central America, on the Caribbean Sea. Pop.152,000. Cap. Belmopan.

Bel·leau Wood (bĕl′ō). A small forest in N France, where U.S. Marines halted the German drive on Paris (1918).

Bel·mo·pan (bĕl′mə-păn′). The capital of Belize, in the center of the country. Pop. 3,000.

Be·lo Ho·ri·zon·te (bā′lō ô′rē-zōn′tē). An industrial and resort city of E Brazil. Pop. 1,557,500.

Be·lo·rus·sian Soviet Socialist Republic (bĕl′ō-rŭsh′ən). Also **Be·lo·rus·sia** (-rŭsh′ə). A constituent republic of W central European U.S.S.R. Pop. 9,371,000. Cap. Minsk.

Ben·gal (bĕn-gôl′, bĕng-gôl′). A region of NE India and a former province of British India. —**Ben·gal′i** adj. & n.

Bengal, Bay of. That part of the Indian Ocean between India on the W and Burma on the E.

Ben·ga·si (bĕn-gä′zē). A city of NE Libya, on the Mediterranean. Pop. 282,200.

Ben·in (bə-nēn′). Formerly **Da·ho·mey** (də-hō′mē). A republic of W Africa, on the Bight of Benin, the N section of the Gulf of Guinea. Pop. 3,377,000. Cap. Porto Novo.

Ben Ne·vis (bĕn nĕ′vĭs, nĕv′ĭs). The highest elevation, 4,406 ft (1,343.8 m), in Great Britain, in the Grampians, Scotland.

Be·no·ni (bə-nō′nī′). A city in the gold-mining area of S Transvaal, South Africa. Pop. 151,300.

Ber·ga·mo (bĕr′gä-mō). An industrial center of N Italy. Pop. 127,800.

Ber·gen (bûr′gən, bär′-). A seaport of Norway, in the SW. Pop. 212,300.

Be·ring Sea (bîr′ĭng, bâr′-). The part of the North Pacific bounded by Alaska on the E, the Aleutian Islands to the SE, Kamchatka on the W, and Siberia to the NW. It is joined to the Arctic Ocean by the Bering Strait.

Berke·ley (bûrk′lē). A city and educational center of W California. Pop. 103,100.

Berk·shire Hills (bûrk′shîr, -shər). A range of hills in W Massachusetts; highest elevation, Mount Greylock (3,491 ft/1,064.8 m).

Ber·lin (bĕr-lĭn′). The former capital of Germany, now a divided city entirely surrounded by East Germany. **East Berlin,** under Soviet control after 1945, became the capital of East Germany in 1949 (pop. 1,111,400). The sectors under American, British, and French control became **West Berlin,** associated politically and economically with West Germany (pop. 1,926,800). —**Ber·lin′er** n.

Ber·mu·da (bər-myōō′də). An archipelago and British colony in the Atlantic Ocean SE of Cape Hatteras, North Carolina. Pop. 63,000. Cap. Hamilton. —**Ber·mu′di·an** (-dē-ən) adj. & n.

Bern (bûrn, bĕrn). Also **Berne.** The capital of Switzerland, on the Aar River in the NW. Pop. 145,500.

Ber·nese Alps (bûr-nēz′, -nēs′). A range of the Alps in S central Switzerland; highest elevation, Finsteraarhorn (14,032 ft/4,279.7 m).

Ber·wyn (bûr′wĭn). A city in Illinois, W of Chicago. Pop. 46,800.

Bes·kids (bĕs′kĭdz, bĕ-skĕdz′). Two mountain ranges in the W Carpathians along the E border of Czechoslovakia; highest elevation, Babia Góra (5,659 ft/1,725.9 m).

Bes·sa·ra·bi·a (bĕs′ə-rā′bē-ə). A former Rumanian region situated between the Prut and Dniester rivers. —**Bes′sa·ra′bi·an** adj. & n.

Be·thes·da (bə-thĕz′də). An urban center in Maryland; a suburb of Washington, D.C. Pop. 77,700.

Beth·le·hem (bĕth′lĭ-hĕm, bĕth′lē-əm). **1.** A town in W Jordan, S of Jerusalem; traditionally, the birthplace of Jesus. **2.** A city of E central Pennsylvania. Pop. 70,400.

Bev·er·ly Hills (bĕv′ər-lē). A city in S California, W of Los Angeles. Pop. 32,300.

Bhau·na·gar (bou-nŭg′ər). A seaport of W India. Pop. 226,000.

Bho·pal (bō-päl′). A city of central India. Pop. 384,900.

Bhu·tan (bōō-tăn′, -tän′). A kingdom in the Himalaya Mountains between the N border of India and Tibet. Pop. 1,273,000. Cap. Thimphu. —**Bhu·tan·ese′** (-nēz′, -nēs′) adj. & n.

Bi·a·fra, Bight of (bē-ä′frə, bē-ăf′rə). A wide inlet of the Gulf of Guinea, off the coasts of Nigeria and Cameroon.

Bia·ly·stok (bē-ä′lĭ-stôk′). An industrial city of NE Poland. Pop. 195,900.

Bi·ar·ritz (bē′ə-rĭts′). A resort city of SW France. Pop. 27,600.

Big·horn Mountains (bĭg′hôrn′). A range in N central Wyoming, part of the Rocky Mountains; highest elevation, Cloud Peak (13,175 ft/4,018.4 m).

Bi·ki·ni (bĭ-kē′nē). An atoll in the Marshall Islands, in the W Pacific Ocean, the site of atomic bomb tests by the United States in 1946.

Bil·ba·o (bĭl-bä′ō). A port city of N Spain. Pop. 457,700.

Bil·lings (bĭl′ĭngz). A city of S Montana. Pop. 68,400.

Bi·lox·i (bə-lŭk′sē, -lŏk′sē). A city of S Mississippi, on the Gulf of Mexico. Pop. 49,400.

Bim·i·ni (bĭm′ə-nē). Also **Bim·i·nis**

ă pat   ā pay   â care   ä father   ĕ pet   ē be   hw which   ĭ pit   ī tie   î pier   ŏ pot   ō toe   ô paw, for   oi noise
ōō took   ōō boot   ou out   th thin   th this   ŭ cut   û urge   zh vision   ə about, item, edible, gallop, circus

(-nēz). A group of small islands in the Bahamas.

Bing·ham·ton (bĭng′əm-tən). An industrial city of S New York. Pop. 55,700.

Bir·ken·head (bûr′kən-hĕd′). A seaport and industrial city of NW England. Pop. 149,000.

Bir·ming·ham (bûr′mĭng-hăm′, -əm). **1.** The principal city of Alabama, in the N central part of the state. Pop. 282,000. **2.** An industrial city of central England. Pop. 1,058,800.

Bis·cay, Bay of (bĭs′kā). An inlet of the Atlantic Ocean bordered on the S by Spain and on the E and NE by France.

Bis·cayne Bay (bĭs-kān′, bĭs′kān′). An inlet of the Atlantic Ocean along the SE coast of Florida.

Bis·marck (bĭz′märk′). The capital of North Dakota, on the Missouri River in the S central part of the state. Pop. 44,500.

Bismarck Archipelago. A group of over 100 islands in the SW Pacific Ocean, NE of New Guinea.

Bis·sau (bĭ-sou′). The capital of Guinea–Bissau, on an inlet of the North Atlantic Ocean. Pop. 71,200.

Bi·thyn·i·a (bĭ-thĭn′ē-ə). An ancient country of NW Asia Minor.

Black Forest (blăk). A wooded mountain region in SW West Germany.

Black Hills. A mountainous region, rich in mineral deposits, in SW South Dakota and NE Wyoming; highest elevation, Harney Peak (7,242 ft/2,208.8 m).

Black·pool (blăk′pōol′). A seaside resort of NW England, on the Irish Sea. Pop. 150,000.

Black Sea. A large inland sea, between Europe and Asia Minor, connected with the Aegean Sea by the Bosporus, the Sea of Marmara, and the Dardanelles.

Blan·tyre (blăn-tîr′). A city of S Malawi. Pop. 219,000.

Block Island (blŏk). An island and summer resort of Rhode Island.

Bloem·fon·tein (blōōm′fŏn-tān′). A city of E central South Africa. Pop. 149,800.

Bloom·ing·ton (blōō′mĭng-tən). A city of SE Minnesota. Pop. 81,600.

Blue Nile (blōō). A river rising in the highlands of central Ethiopia and flowing c. 1,000 mi (1,610 km) SE and then NW to Khartoum, Sudan, where it joins the White Nile to form the Nile.

Blue Ridge. A range of the Appalachians in the E United States, extending 600 mi (965.4 km) from S Pennsylvania to N Georgia.

Bo·chum (bō′KHŌŌm). A city of W West Germany, in the Ruhr. Pop. 417,300.

Boe·o·tia (bē-ō′shə). An ancient province of SE Greece, between the Gulf of Corinth and the Straits of Euboea. **—Boe·o′tian** adj. & n.

Bo·go·tá (bō′gə-tä′). The capital of Colombia, in the Cordillera Central. Pop. 2,855,000.

Bo·he·mi·a (bō-hē′mē-ə). A region

and former province of W Czechoslovakia. **—Bo·he′mi·an** adj. & n.

Boi·se (boi′zē, -sē). The capital of Idaho, in the Boise River valley in the SW. Pop. 102,100.

Boks·burg (bŏks′bûrg′). A city and mining center of NE South Africa. Pop. 106,100.

Bo·liv·i·a (bə-lĭv′ē-ə). A republic of W central South America. Pop. 5,425,000. Caps. La Paz and Sucre. **—Bo·liv′i·an** adj. & n.

Bo·lo·gna (bō-lō′nyə). An industrial city of N Italy. Pop. 485,600.

Bol·ton (bōl′tən). A textile center of NW England. Pop. 261,000.

Bom·bay (bŏm-bā′). A port city of W India. Pop. 5,970,600.

Bo·nin Islands (bō′nĭn). An archipelago of 15 islands S of Japan.

Bonn (bŏn). The capital of West Germany, on the W bank of the Rhine. Pop. 283,900.

Boo·thi·a Peninsula (bōō′thē-ə). A peninsula of NE Canada, W of Baffin Island.

Bor·deaux (bôr-dō′). A seaport of SW France. Pop. 223,100.

Bor·ne·o (bôr′nē-ō′). An island of the Indonesian Archipelago, lying between the Sulu and Java seas of the W Pacific Ocean.

Bo·ro·di·no (bôr′ə-dē′nō). A village of the Soviet Union, W of Moscow, near which Napoleon defeated the Russians on Sept. 7, 1812.

Bos·ni·a and Her·ze·go·vi·na (bŏz′nē-ə; hĕrt′sə-gō-vē′nə). Two Balkan regions, now constituting an autonomous republic of Yugoslavia.

Bos·po·rus (bŏs′pər-əs). A narrow strait between European and Asian Turkey, linking the Black Sea with the Sea of Marmara.

Bos·ton (bô′stən, bŏs′tən). The capital and chief port of Massachusetts, in the E. Pop. 562,600. **—Bos·to′ni·an** (bô-stō′nē-ən, bŏs-tō′-) adj. & n.

Bot·a·ny Bay (bŏt′n-ē). An inlet of the Tasman Sea on the E coast of New South Wales, Australia.

Both·ni·a, Gulf of (bŏth′nē-ə). A N arm of the Baltic Sea between Sweden and Finland.

Bot·swa·na (bŏt-swä′nə). A republic in S Africa. Pop. 791,000. Cap. Gaborone.

Boul·der (bōl′dər). A city of N Colorado. Pop. 76,200.

Bound·a·ry Peak (bound′drē, -də-rē). The highest elevation (13,145 ft/4,009.2 m) in Nevada, in the SW on the California-Nevada border.

Bourne·mouth (bôrn′məth, bōrn′-, bōōrn′-). A seaside resort in S central England. Pop. 144,100.

Brad·ford (brăd′fərd). An industrial city in N England. Pop. 293,800.

Brah·ma·pu·tra (brä′mə-pōō′trə). A river of Asia, rising in SW Tibet and flowing 1,800 mi (2,896.2 km) to the Bay of Bengal.

Bră·i·la (brə-ē′lə). A city of E central Rumania, on the Danube River. Pop. 194,600.

Bran·den·burg (brăn′dən-bûrg′). **1.** A former German duchy around which the kingdom of Prussia grew during

the 16th and 17th cents. **2.** A city of central East Germany. Pop. 94,100.

Bra·sí·lia (brə-zē′lyə). The capital of Brazil since 1960, in a Federal District within Goiás State. Pop. 763,300.

Bra·ti·sla·va (brä′tĭ-slä′və, brät′ĭ-). A city of S central Czechoslovakia. Pop. 345,500.

Bra·zil (brə-zĭl′). A republic of S South America. Pop. 119,175,000. Cap. Brasília. **—Bra·zil′ian** adj. & n.

Braz·za·ville (brăz′ə-vĭl′). The capital of the Republic of Congo, on the N bank of the Congo. Pop. 289,700.

Bre·men (brĕm′ən). A city of N West Germany, on the Weser River. Pop. 579,400.

Bren·ner Pass (brĕn′ər). A pass through the E Alps between S Austria and NE Italy.

Bre·scia (brā′shä). An industrial city of N central Italy. Pop. 210,100.

Brest (brĕst). **1.** A seaport in extreme W France. Pop. 159,857. **2.** Formerly **Brest Li·tovsk** (lə-tôfsk′, -tôvsk′). A city of W European U.S.S.R., where a treaty was signed in 1918 between the Soviet Union and the Central Powers. Pop. 122,000.

Bridge·port (brĭj′pôrt′, -pōrt′). An industrial city of SW Connecticut. Pop. 142,500.

Bridge·town (brĭj′toun′). The capital of Barbados, on the SW coast of the island. Pop. 8,900.

Brigh·ton (brīt′n). A popular seaside resort of SE England, on the English Channel. Pop. 166,100.

Bris·bane (brĭz′bən, -bān′). A seaport of SE Australia. Pop. 957,000.

Bris·tol (brĭs′təl). A port city in SW England. Pop. 416,300.

Bristol Channel. An inlet of the Atlantic Ocean between Wales and SW England.

Brit·ain (brĭt′n). See **Great Britain.**

Brit·ish Associated State (brĭt′ĭsh). Any of the 6 Caribbean states that are aided by Great Britain but are internally self-governed. They are Antigua, Grenada, St. Christopher-Nevis-Anguilla, St. Lucia, and St. Vincent.

British Co·lum·bi·a (kə-lŭm′bē-ə). The westernmost province of Canada with its W border on the Pacific Ocean and Alaska. Pop. 2,611,700. Cap. Victoria, on Vancouver Island. **—British Columbian.**

British East Af·ri·ca (ăf′rĭ-kə). Collectively, the former British territories in E Africa, including Kenya, Uganda, Tanganyika, and Zanzibar.

British Hon·du·ras (hŏn-dōōr′əs, -dyōōr′əs). See **Belize.**

British Isles. A group of islands off the NW coast of Europe, comprising Great Britain, Ireland, and adjacent smaller islands.

British Vir·gin Islands (vûr′jən). A British colony in the West Indies, E of Puerto Rico, comprising about 30 islands. Pop. 10,000. Cap. Road Town, on Tortola Island.

British West In·dies (ĭn′dēz). The former name for the islands of the West Indies that were colonies or self-governing colonies of the United Kingdom.

ă pat   ā pay   â care   ä father   ĕ pet   ē be   hw which   ĭ pit   ī tie   î pier   ŏ pot   ō toe   ô paw, for   oi noise
ōō took   ōō boot   ou out   th thin   th this   ŭ cut   û urge   zh vision   ə about, item, edible, gallop, circus

Brit·ta·ny (brĭt'n-ē). A region and former province of France on a peninsula extending into the Atlantic between the English Channel and Bay of Biscay. —**Bret'on** (brĕt'n) adj. & n.

Br·no (bûr'nō). A city of central Czechoslovakia. Pop. 361,600.

Brock·ton (brŏk'tən). A manufacturing city of SE Massachusetts. Pop. 95,000.

Bronx, the (brŏngks). The northernmost and only mainland borough of New York City, separated from Manhattan by the Harlem River. Pop. 1,162,600.

Brook·line (brŏok'lĭn'). A residential town of E Massachusetts. Pop. 54,700.

Brook·lyn (brŏok'lĭn). An industrial and residential borough of New York City, at the SW end of Long Island. Pop. 2,218,400.

Brooks Range (brŏoks). A mountain range in Alaska, N of the Arctic Circle; highest elevation, Mt. Michelson (9,239 ft/2,817.8 m).

Browns·ville (brounz'vĭl). A city and port of entry in S Texas. Pop. 83,800.

Bruges (brŏozh). A city of NW Belgium. Pop. 118,000.

Bru·nei (brŏo-nī'). A British-protected sultanate, on the N coast of the island of Borneo. Pop. 213,000. Cap. Bandar Seri Begawan.

Bruns·wick (brŭnz'wĭk). An industrial city E of West Germany. Pop. 289,000.

Brus·sels (brŭs'əlz). The capital of Belgium, in the N central part of the country. Pop. 103,700.

Bry·ansk (brē-änsk'). A city of the W Soviet Union, on the Desna River. Pop. 1,582,000.

Bryce Canyon National Park (brīs). A national park in S Utah, notable for its rock formations and canyons.

Bu·ca·ra·man·ga (bŏo'kä-rä-mäng'gä). A city and transportation center of N central Colombia. Pop. 250,000.

Bu·cha·rest (bŏo'kə-rĕst', byŏo'-). The capital of Rumania, in the SE. Pop. 1,807,000.

Bu·chen·wald (bŏo'kən-wôld', bŏok'-ən-). A village NE of Weimar, East Germany; also the name of a nearby Nazi concentration camp.

Bu·da·pest (bŏo'də-pĕst'). The capital of Hungary, in the N central part of the country. Pop. 2,085,600.

Bue·nos Ai·res (bwā'nəs âr'ēz, ī'rēz, bō'nəs). The capital of Argentina, on the SW shore of the Río de la Plata estuary. Pop. 2,982,000.

Buf·fa·lo (bŭf'ə-lō'). An industrial city of New York State, at the NE end of Lake Erie on the Niagara River. Pop. 357,400.

Bu·jum·bu·ra (bŏo'jəm-bŏor'ə, bŏo-jŏom'bŏor'ə). The capital of Burundi, in the W at the N end of Lake Tanganyika. Pop. 78,800.

Bu·ka·va (bə-kä'vŏo). A city and port on Lake Kivu, E Zaire. Pop. 135,000.

Bu·kha·ra (bŏo-kä'rə, -hä'rə). A city of S Central Asian U.S.S.R., E of the Amu Darya. Pop. 112,000.

Bu·la·wa·yo (bŏo'lə-wä'yō, -wä'ō). A city of SW Zimbabwe. Pop. 358,000.

Bul·gar·i·a (bŭl-gâr'ē-ə, bŏol-). A republic on the Balkan Peninsula, on the Black Sea. Pop. 8,872,000. Cap. Sofia. —**Bul·gar'i·an** adj. & n.

Bull Run (bŏol' rŭn'). A creek in NE Virginia near Manassas, the scene of 2 Civil War battles (July, 1861 and Aug., 1862) in which the Confederates defeated the Union forces.

Bun·ker Hill (bŭng'kər). A hill in Charlestown, Massachusetts, near which the 1st major battle of the American Revolution was fought (June 17, 1775).

Bur·bank (bûr'bangk'). A city of S California. Pop. 83,800.

Bur·gun·dy (bûr'gən-dē). A region, formerly a duchy and province, of SE France. —**Bur·gun'di·an** (bər-gŭn'dē-ən) adj. & n.

Bur·ling·ton (bûr'lĭng-tən). A shipping center of Vermont, on the E shore of Lake Champlain. Pop. 37,700.

Bur·ma (bûr'mə). A republic of SE Asia on the E shore of the Bay of Bengal and the Andaman Sea. Pop. 33,590,000. Cap. Rangoon. —**Burmese'** (bər-mēz', -mēs') adj. & n.

Bur·sa (bŏor-sä', bûr'sə). A city of Turkey, in the NW near the Sea of Marmara. Pop. 276,000.

Bu·run·di (bŏo-rŏon'dē). An independent country of central Africa, NW of Tanzania. Pop. 4,192,000. Cap. Bujumbura.

Bute (byŏot). A small island of Scotland, in the Firth of Clyde.

Butte (byŏot). A city and mining center in SW Montana. Pop. 37,100.

Byd·goszcz (bĭd'gôshch). An industrial city in N Poland. Pop. 280,500.

Byz·an·tine Empire (bĭz'ən-tēn', -tīn'). The E part of the later Roman Empire, founded by Constantine (A.D. 330) and continuing after the Fall of Rome until 1453.

By·zan·ti·um (bĭ-zăn'shē-əm, -tē-əm). An ancient Greek city on the site of Constantinople.

C

Cá·diz (kə-dĭz', kā'dĭz). A city of SE Spain, on the Gulf of Cádiz. Pop. 140,900.

Caen (kän). A city in NW France; a main target of the Allied invasion in World War II (1944). Pop. 119,500.

Cae·sa·re·a (sē'zə-rē'ə, sĕs'ə-, sĕz'ə-). An ancient seaport of Roman Palestine.

Ca·gli·a·ri (kä'lyä-rē). The capital of Sardinia, Italy, on the S shore of the island. Pop. 240,300.

Ca·ho·ki·a Mounds (kə-hō'kĭ-ə). A large group of pre-Columbian Indian mounds in SE Illinois.

Cai·ro (kī'rō). The capital of Egypt, on the Nile in the NE. Pop. 5,084,500.

Ca·la·bri·a (kə-lā'brē-ə). A region of SW Italy. —**Ca·la'bri·an** adj. & n.

Ca·lais (kă-lā', kăl'ā). A seaport and industrial city of NW France, on the Strait of Dover. Pop. 78,900.

Cal·cut·ta (kăl-kŭt'ə). A city of E India, on the Hooghly. Pop. 3,148,700.

Cal·ga·ry (kăl'gə-rē). A city of S Alberta, Canada, in the center of a ranching area. Pop. 470,000.

Ca·li (kä'lē). A city of W central Colombia. Pop. 898,300.

Cal·i·for·nia (kăl'ə-fôrn'yə, -fôr'nē-ə). A state of the SW United States. Pop. 23,545,100. Cap. Sacramento. —**Cal'i·for'nian** adj. & n.

California, Gulf of. An inlet of the Pacific Ocean, between Lower California and NW Mexico.

California Current. A cold ocean current in the Pacific, flowing SE off the W coast of North America.

Cal·la·o (kä-yä'ō). A seaport of W Peru, on the Pacific Ocean. Pop. 196,100.

Ca·ma·güey (kä'mä-gwä'). A city in E central Cuba. Pop. 228,000.

Cam·bay, Gulf of (kăm-bā'). An arm of the Arabian Sea on the NW coast of India.

Cam·bo·di·a (kăm-bō'dē-ə). A republic of SE Asia, bordering on the Gulf of Siam. Pop. 5,200,000. Cap. Phnom Penh. —**Cam·bo'di·an** adj. & n.

Cam·brai (kăm-brā'). A textile center of N France. Pop. 39,000.

Cam·bridge (kām'brĭj). **1.** A city in E England; site of Cambridge University. Pop. 106,400. **2.** A city in E Massachusetts; site of Harvard University and the Massachusetts Institute of Technology. Pop. 95,400.

Cam·den (kăm'dən). A city of SW New Jersey, on the Delaware River. Pop. 84,800.

Cam·e·roon (kăm'ə-rŏon'). Also **Cam·e·roun.** A republic of central Africa, with a coastline on the Bight of Biafra. Pop. 8,058,000. Cap. Yaoundé.

Cam·pa·gna (käm-pä'nyä). A region of Italy, surrounding Rome.

Cam·pa·nia (kăm-păn'yə, -pā'nē-ə). A region of S Italy, on the Tyrrhenian Sea.

Cam·pe·che (kăm-pē'chē). A city of SE Mexico, on the Yucatan Peninsula. Pop. 69,500.

Cam·pi·nas (käNM-pē'näs). A city of S Brazil, N of São Paulo. Pop. 328,700.

Cam·pos (käNM'pŏos). A city of SE Brazil, on the Paraíba River. Pop. 153,300.

Cam·ranh Bay (kăm'răn'). An inlet of the South China Sea on the SE coast of Vietnam.

Ca·naan (kā'nən). In Biblical times, the part of Palestine between the Jordan River and the Mediterranean Sea. —**Ca'naan·ite'** adj. & n.

Can·a·da (kăn'ə-də). A country of N North America, bordering on the United States in the S. Pop. 23,809,-800. Cap. Ottawa. —**Ca·na'di·an** (kə-nā'dē-ən) adj. & n.

Ca·nal Zone (kə-năl'). A strip of territory across the Isthmus of Panama, leased to the United States in 1903 and returned to Panamanian control in 1979.

Ca·nar·y Islands (kə-nâr'ē). A group of Spanish islands in the Atlantic Ocean off the NW coast of Africa.

Ca·nav·er·al, Cape (kə-năv'ər-əl). A low, sandy promontory extending E

ă pat ā pay â care ä father ĕ pet ē be hw which ĭ pit ī tie î pier ŏ pot ō toe ô paw, for oi noise
ŏŏ took ŏŏ boot ou out th thin th this ŭ cut û urge zh vision ə about, item, edible, gallop, circus

into the Atlantic Ocean from a barrier island off E Florida; site of the Kennedy Manned Space Flight Center.

Can·ber·ra (kăn′bĕr′ə, -bər-ə). The capital of Australia, on the Murrumbidgee in SE New South Wales. Pop. 193,000.

Can·nae (kăn′ē). An ancient city in SE Italy where the Romans were defeated by Hannibal (216 B.C.).

Cannes (kăn). A resort city of SE France, on the Mediterranean. Pop. 67,000.

Can·ter·bur·y (kăn′tər-bĕr′ē). A cathedral city of SE England; the ecclesiastical center of England since 597. Pop. 34,500.

Can·ton (kăn′tŏn′, kăn-tŏn′ for sense 1; kăn′tən for sense 2). **1.** The capital of Kwangtung, SE China. Pop. 2,500,000. **2.** A city in NE Ohio. Pop. 94,600.

Can·yon de Chel·ly National Monument (kăn′yən də shā′). An area in NE Arizona, reserved to protect ruins of cliff dwellings.

Cape Bret·on Island (kăp brĕt′n, brĭt′n). An island of NE Nova Scotia, Canada, separated from the mainland by the Strait of Canso.

Ca·per·na·um (kə-pûr′nē-əm). A city of Biblical Palestine, on the NW Shore of the Sea of Galilee.

Cape Town. Also **Cape·town** (kāp′-toun′). The legislative capital of the Republic of South Africa, on the SW tip of Africa. Pop. 697,500.

Cape Verde Islands (vûrd). A republic comprising a group of islands in the Atlantic Ocean c. 400 mi (643.6 km) W of Senegal, Africa. Pop. 314,000. Cap. Praia.

Cape York Peninsula (yôrk). A peninsula of NE Queensland, Australia, between the South Pacific Ocean and the Gulf of Carpentaria.

Capitol Reef National Monument. An area in S central Utah, reserved to protect cliff dwellings, petrified trees, and geologic formations.

Cap·pa·do·ci·a (kăp′ə-dō′shē-ə, -shə). An ancient region of E Asia Minor, now forming the central part of Turkey. —**Cap′pa·do′cian** adj. & n.

Ca·pri (kä′prē). A mountainous island of Italy, S of the Bay of Naples.

Ca·ra·cas (kə-rä′kəs, -răk′əs). The capital of Venezuela, near the Caribbean coast. Pop. 2,576,000.

Car·diff (kär′dĭf). A major port and industrial city of Wales, on Bristol Bay. Pop. 281,500.

Car·ib·be·an Sea (kăr′ə-bē′ən, kə-rĭb′-ē-ən). An extension of the Atlantic Ocean, bounded by the coasts of Central and South America and the West Indies.

Carls·bad Caverns National Park (kärlz′băd′). An area in SE New Mexico, containing the Carlsbad Caverns, a series of huge limestone caves.

Car·mel, Mount (kär′məl). A ridge extending 13 mi (21 km) across NW Israel to the Mediterranean; highest elevation, 1,792 ft (546.6 m).

Car·o·li·na (kär′ə-lī′nə). An English colony, first settled in 1653, divided into what became the present North

and South Carolina in 1729. —**the Carolinas.** North and South Carolina.

Car·o·line Islands (kăr′ə-līn′). An archipelago of some 680 islands and atolls in the Pacific Ocean E of the Philippines.

Car·pa·thi·an Mountains (kär-pā′thē-ən). A mountain system of E Europe, extending in an arc through Czechoslovakia, Hungary, the Soviet Union, and Rumania, and forming a continuation of the Alps; highest elevation, Gerlachovka (8,737 ft /2,664 m).

Car·son City (kär′sən). The capital of Nevada, in the SW. Pop. 32,100.

Car·ta·ge·na (kär′tə-gā′nə). **1.** A seaport of NW Colombia, on the Caribbean coast. Pop. 292,500. **2.** A seaport of SE Spain, on the Mediterranean. Pop. 229,000.

Car·thage (kär′thĭj). An ancient city and state on the N coast of Africa. —**Car′tha·gin′i·an** adj. & n.

Cas·a·blan·ca (kăs′ə-blăng′kə, kä′sə-bläng′kə). A city of Morocco, in the NW on the Atlantic. Pop. 1,753,400.

Cas·cade Range (kăs-kād′). The N section of the Sierra Nevada Mountains, extending from NE California to W Oregon and Washington; highest elevation, Mount Rainier (14,410 ft /4,395.1 m).

Cas·pi·an Sea (kăs′pē-ən). The largest inland body of water in the world, often classified as a salt lake, extending from the Kazakh S.S.R. into N Iran.

Cas·tile (kăs-tēl′). A region and former kingdom of Spain extending from the Bay of Biscay in the N to Andalusia in the S.

Cat·a·lo·ni·a (kăt′l-ō′nē-ə, -nyə). A region and former republic of NE Spain, bordering on France and the Mediterranean Sea. —**Cat′a·lo′ni·an** adj. & n.

Ca·ta·nia (kə-tä′nyə). A port city of E Sicily. Pop. 399,800.

Cats·kill Mountains (kăts′kĭl′). A mountain range in SE New York; highest elevation, Slide Mountain (4,204 ft /1,282.2 m).

Cau·ca·sus (kô′kə-səs). **1.** A region in the Soviet Union between the Black and Caspian seas. **2.** A range of mountains dividing the Caucasus region from NW to SE; highest elevation, Mount Elbrus (18,481 ft /5,636.7 m).

Cay·enne (kī-ĕn′, kā-). The capital of French Guiana, on Cayenne Island. Pop. 25,000.

Cay·man Islands (kā-măn′, kā′mən). A group of 3 islands administered as a British colony, in the Caribbean Sea NW of Jamaica. Pop. 16,000. Cap. Georgetown, on Grand Cayman.

Ce·bu (sā-bōō′). **1.** An island in the Visayan Islands of the Philippines. **2.** The principal city of this island, on the E coast. Pop. 342,100.

Ce·dar Rap·ids (sē′dər răp′ĭdz). An industrial city in E Iowa. Pop. 110,100.

Cel·e·bes (sĕl′ə-bēz, sə-lē′-). An island of E Indonesia, E of Borneo.

Cen·tral Af·ri·can Re·pub·lic (sĕn′trəl ăf′rĭ-kən rē-pŭb′lĭk). A country of central Africa. Pop. 2,284,000. Cap. Bangui.

Central A·mer·i·ca (ə-mĕr′ĭ-kə). The region extending from the S boundary of Mexico to the N boundary of Colombia. —**Central American.**

Ce·ram (sā′răm′). An island of Indonesia, W of New Guinea.

Cey·lon (sĭ-lŏn′). See **Sri Lanka.** —**Cey′lo·nese′** (-nēz′, -nēs′) adj. & n.

Chad (chăd). A republic of N central Africa. Pop. 4,528,000. Cap. Ndjamena.

Chad, Lake. A lake in N central Africa. Its area ranges from 5,000 to 10,000 sq mi (12,950 to 25,900 sq km).

Chaer·o·ne·a (kĕr′ə-nē′ə, kîr′-). An ancient city of E Greece.

Chal·de·a (kăl-dē′ə). An ancient region in S Babylonia along the Euphrates River and the Persian Gulf. —**Chal·de′an** adj. & n.

Cham·pagne (shăm-pān′). A region and former province of NE France, famous for its wines.

Cham·paign (shăm-pān′). A city of E central Illinois. Pop. 57,200.

Cham·plain, Lake (shăm-plān′). A long, narrow lake between E New York State and W Vermont.

Chan·cel·lors·ville (chăn′səl-ərz-vĭl′, -slərz-vĭl′, chăn′-). A town in NE Virginia; site of a Confederate victory in the Civil War (1863).

Chan·di·garh (chŭn′dĭ-gər). A city of NW India. Pop. 218,500.

Chang·chun (chäng′chōōn′). The capital of Kirin, NE China. Pop. 1,500,000.

Chang·sha (chäng′shä′). The capital of Hunan, SE central China. Pop. 850,000.

Chan·nel Islands (chăn′əl). A group of 9 British islands in the English Channel off Normandy, including the islands of Jersey, Guernsey, Alderney, and Sark.

Cha·pa·la (chä-pä′lə). A lake of W Mexico, SE of Guadalajara.

Charles, Cape (chärlz). A cape in Virginia at the N entrance to Chesapeake Bay opposite Cape Henry.

Charles River. A river, c. 60 mi (96.5 km) long, in E Massachusetts.

Charles·ton (chärl′stən). **1.** A seaport of SE South Carolina, on an inlet of the Atlantic Ocean. Pop. 69,300. **2.** The capital of West Virginia, in the W part of the state. Pop. 62,300.

Charles·town (chärlz′toun′). A former city of E Massachusetts, now the oldest part of Boston.

Char·lotte (shär′lət). A city of S North Carolina. Pop. 31,800.

Char·lotte A·ma·lie (shär′lət ə-mäl′yə). The capital of the U.S. Virgin Islands, on the S shore of St. Thomas Island. Pop. 12,400.

Char·lottes·ville (shär′ləts-vĭl′). A city of central Virginia; site of the homes of Thomas Jefferson and James Monroe. Pop. 39,800.

Char·lotte·town (shär′lət-toun′). The capital of Prince Edward Island Province, Canada, on the S coast. Pop. 17,100.

Chartres (shärt, här′trə). A city in N central France, noted for its Gothic cathedral. Pop. 39,000.

Chat·ta·noo·ga (chăt′ə-nōō′gə). An

---

industrial city and port of SE Tennessee, on the Tennessee River. Pop. 165,600.

Che·bok·sa·ry (chĕ'bŏk-sä'rē). A city of NW European U.S.S.R., on the Volga River. Pop. 278,000.

Che·kiang (jŭ'jyäng'). A province of SE China. Pop. 31,000,000. Cap. Hangchow.

Che·lya·binsk (chĭ-lyä'bĭnsk). A city of W Siberian U.S.S.R. Pop. 1,031,000.

Cheng·chou (ŭng'jō'). The capital of Honan, E central China, on the Yellow River. Pop. 1,500,000.

Cheng·tu (chŭng'dōō'). The capital of Szechwan, S China. Pop. 2,000,000.

Cher·bourg (shâr'bŏŏrg'). A seaport of NW France. Pop. 37,000.

Ches·a·peake (chĕs'ə-pēk). A city in SE Virginia. Pop. 113,800.

Chesapeake Bay. An inlet of the Atlantic in Virginia and Maryland.

Ches·ter (chĕs'tər). A city of SE Pennsylvania on the Delaware River. Pop. 45,700.

Chev·i·ot Hills (chĕv'ē-ət, chē'vē-). A range of hills along the boundary between England and Scotland; highest elevation, The Cheviot (2,676 ft/816.1 m).

Chey·enne (shī-ĭn', -ĕn'). The capital of Wyoming, in the SE near the Colorado border. Pop. 47,200.

Chi·ba (chē'bə). A city of E Honshu, Japan. Pop. 68,500.

Chi·ca·go (shə-kä'gō, -kô'gō, -kä'gə). A city of NE Illinois at the S end of Lake Michigan. Pop. 2,986,400. —**Chi·ca·go·an** *n.*

Chi·chén-It·zá (chĭ-chĕn'-ĭt-sä'). A village in NE Yucatán, Mexico; the site of extensive Mayan ruins.

Ch'i-ch'i-ha-erh (chē'chē'här'). A port city in NE China. Pop. 1,500,000.

Chick·a·mau·ga (chĭk'ə-mô'gə). A town in NW Georgia near Chickamauga Creek, the site of a Union defeat (1863).

Chi·co·pee (chĭk'ə-pē). A city of SW Massachusetts. Pop. 55,000.

Chi·hua·hua (chĭ-wä'wä, -wə). An industrial city of N Mexico. Pop. 327,300.

Chil·e (chĭl'ē). A republic of W South America, stretching from Peru to the S tip of the continent. Pop. 10,917,-000. Cap. Santiago de Chile. —**Chil'e·an** *adj. & n.*

Chim·bo·ra·zo (chĭm'bə-rä'zō). A mountain (20,561 ft/6,271.1 m) of Ecuador, in the W range of the Andes.

Chi·na (chī'nə). **1** Officially, People's Republic of China. A republic of E central Asia. Pop. 953,578,000. Cap. Peking. **2.** Officially Republic of China. Also, unofficially Nationalist China. A republic occupying Taiwan and nearby islands. Pop. 16,426,400. Cap. Taipei. —**Chi·nese'** *adj. & n.*

Chi·nan (jē'nän'). Also **Tsi·nan** (tsē'-). The capital of Shantung, E China. Pop. 1,500,000.

China Sea. A W section of the Pacific, extending from S Japan to the Malay Peninsula.

Chin·chow (jĭn'jō'). An industrial city of NE China. Pop. 750,000.

Chi·os (kē'ŏs', kī'-). A Greek island in the Aegean Sea off the W coast of Turkey.

Chis·holm Trail (chĭz'əm). A former cattle trail from San Antonio, Texas, to Abilene, Kansas.

Chit·ta·gong (chĭt'ə-gông', -gŏng'). The principal port of Bangladesh, on the Karnaphuli River. Pop. 416,700.

Chon·ju (chŭn'jōō'). A city of SW South Korea. Pop. 311,400.

Cho·sen (chō'sĕn'). A name traditionally designating Korea since the 2nd millennium B.C.

Christ·church (krīst'chûrch'). The largest city of South Island, New Zealand, near the E coast. Pop. 172,400.

Christ·mas Island (krĭs'məs). The largest of the Line Islands, in the Pacific c. 1,200 mi (1,930.8 km) S of Honolulu; the site of British and American nuclear experiments.

Chu·la Vis·ta (chōō'lə vĭs'tə). A city of S California, on San Diego Bay. Pop. 83,800.

Chung·king (chŏong'kĭng'). A city of S China, on the Yangtze River. Pop. 3,500,000.

Cic·e·ro (sĭs'ə-rō'). A city of NE Illinois, a suburb of Chicago. Pop. 61,200.

Ci·li·cia (sĭ-lĭsh'ə). An ancient country and Roman province in SE Asia Minor. —**Ci·li'cian** *adj. & n.*

Cin·cin·nat·i (sĭn'sə-năt'ē, -năt'ə). An industrial city of SW Ohio, on the Ohio River. Pop. 383,100.

Cis·al·pine Gaul (sĭs-ăl'pīn' gôl). The part of ancient Gaul S of the Alps of N Italy.

Ciu·dad Juá·rez (syōō-*thäth*' hwä'räs). A city of N Mexico, on the Rio Grande opposite El Paso, Texas. Pop. 520,500.

Cleve·land (klēv'lənd). A city of NE Ohio, on Lake Erie. Pop. 572,500.

Cli·chy (klē-shē'). A city of France, NW of Paris. Pop. 47,800.

Clif·ton (klĭf'tən). A city of NE New Jersey. Pop. 74,400.

Clu·ny (klōō'nē, klü-nē'). A former religious and cultural center of E France.

Clyde (klīd). A river rising in S Scotland and flowing N 106 mi (170.5 km) to the Firth of Clyde, an inlet of the Atlantic Ocean.

Coast Mountains (kōst). A continuation of the Cascade Range in W British Columbia; highest elevation, Mount Waddington (13,260 ft/4,044.3 m) in British Columbia.

Coast Ranges. The mountain ranges along the W coast of North America, extending from S California to S Alaska.

Co·chin Chi·na (kō'chĭn chī'nə, kŏch'-ĭn). The former name for the southernmost region of Vietnam, a part of French Indochina.

Cod, Cape (kŏd). A peninsula in SE Massachusetts.

Coeur d'A·lene (kôr də-lān'). A lake in a resort area of N Idaho.

Col·chis (kŏl'kĭs). An ancient region on the Black Sea S of the Caucasus Mountains.

Co·li·ma (kō-lē'mä). A city of SW Mexico. Pop. 58,450.

Co·logne (kə-lōn'). A city of West Germany on the Rhine. Pop. 1,013,771.

Co·lom·bi·a (kə-lŭm'bē-ə). A republic of NW South America. Pop. 26,360,-000. Cap. Bogotá. —**Co·lom'bi·an** *adj. & n.*

Co·lom·bo (kə-lŭm'bō). The capital of Sri Lanka, a seaport on the W coast. Pop. 592,000.

Co·lón (kō-lōn'). A port city of Panama, at the Caribbean entrance to the Panama Canal. Pop. 69,650.

Col·o·ra·do (kŏl'ə-rä'dō, -răd'ə). A state of the W central United States. Pop. 2,882,061. Cap. Denver. —**Col'o·ra'dan** *adj. & n.*

Colorado Desert. A hot, arid region in SE California and NW Mexico.

Colorado River. 1. A river rising in N central Colorado and flowing 1,450 mi (2,333 km) through Utah and Arizona to empty into the N end of the Gulf of California. **2.** A river rising in NW Texas and flowing 894 mi (1,438.5 km) SE to the Gulf of Mexico.

Colorado Springs. A city of central Colorado; the site of the U.S. Air Force Academy. Pop. 207,000.

Co·lum·bi·a (kə-lŭm'bē-ə). The capital of South Carolina, in the central part of the state. Pop. 97,100.

Columbia River. A river rising in SE British Columbia, Canada, and flowing 1,200 mi (1,930.8 km) to the Pacific Ocean, forming most of the Washington-Oregon border along its course.

Co·lum·bus (kə-lŭm'bəs). **1.** The capital of Ohio, an industrial city in the central part of the state. Pop. 562,500. **2.** An industrial city of W Georgia, on the Chattahoochee River. Pop. 168,600.

Com·mon·wealth of Nations (kŏm'-ən-wĕlth'). A political community including the United Kingdom, its dependencies, and former colonies that are now sovereign states.

Co·mo, Lake (kō'mō'). A small lake in N Italy.

Com·o·ro Islands (kŏm'ə-rō'). A group of islands at the N entrance of Mozambique Channel off E Africa.

Con·a·kry (kän'ə-krē). The capital of Guinea, in the SW on the Atlantic. Pop. 198,000.

Con·cep·ción (kôn'sĕp-syôn'). A city of W central Chile. Pop. 178,000.

Con·cord (kŏng'kərd). **1.** A town in E Massachusetts; site of an early battle (Apr. 19, 1775) of the Revolutionary War. Pop. 16,300. **2.** The capital of New Hampshire, on the Merrimack River in the S central part of the state. Pop. 30,400.

Con·fed·er·ate States (kən-fĕd'ər-ĭt). The 11 S states that seceded from the Union in 1860–61. Also called **the Confederacy.**

Con·go (kŏng'gō). The 2nd longest river in Africa (2,900 mi/4,666 km), rising in Zambia and flowing gen. N, W, and then SW to the Atlantic.

Congo, Republic of. A republic in W central Africa. Pop. 1,508,000. Cap. Brazzaville.

ă pat   ā pay   â care   ä father   ĕ pet   be   hw which   ĭ pit   ī tie   î pier   ŏ pot   ō toe   ô paw, for   oi noise
ōō took   ōō boot   ou out   th thin   *h* this   ŭ cut   û urge   zh vision   ə about, item, edible, gallop, circus

Con·nect·i·cut (kə-nĕt′ə-kət). **1.** A state of the NE United States along Long Island Sound. Pop. 3,096,500. Cap. Hartford. **2.** A river of New England, rising in N New Hampshire and flowing 345 mi (555 km) S to Long Island Sound.

Con·stan·ţa (kôn-stän′tsä). A seaport of SE Rumania, on the Black Sea. Pop. 256,900.

Con·stan·tine (kŏn′stən-tēn). A city of NE Algeria. Pop. 335,100.

Con·stan·ti·no·ple (kŏn′stăn-tə-nō′pəl). The capital of the Byzantine Empire; now called Istanbul.

Cook, Mount (kŏok). **1.** The highest mountain (12,349 ft/3,766.5 m) of New Zealand, on South Island in the Southern Alps. **2.** A mountain (13,760 ft/4,196.8 m) in the St. Elias Mountains of SE Alaska.

Cook Inlet. An inlet of the Pacific Ocean in S Alaska.

Cook Islands. A group of islands in the South Pacific SW of the Society Islands.

Cook Strait. The strait between North and South islands, New Zealand.

Co·pen·ha·gen (kō′pən-hā′gən, -hä′gən). The capital of Denmark, on the E coast of Sjaelland. Pop. 699,300.

Cor·al Ga·bles (kôr′əl gā′bəlz, kôr′-). A city of SE Florida. Pop. 42,400.

Coral Sea. A portion of the Pacific Ocean NE of Australia, and SE of New Guinea.

Cor·dil·le·ras (kôr′dĭl-yâr′əz, kôr-dĭl′ər-əz). **1.** The Andes range in W South America. **2.** The complex of ranges in W North America including the Rocky Mountains and the Sierra Nevada, and their extension N into Canada and Alaska. **3.** The entire complex of mountain ranges on the W side of the Americas, extending from Alaska to Cape Horn.

Cór·do·ba (kôr′dō-vä). A city in N central Argentina. Pop. 781,600.

Cor·inth (kôr′ĭnth, kŏr′-). **1.** A city of ancient Greece, in the NE Peloponnesus. **2.** A modern city NE of the site of ancient Corinth. Pop. 20,773.

Corinth, Gulf of. An inlet of the Ionian Sea between the Peloponnesus and central Greece.

Corinth, Isthmus of. A neck of land connecting the Peloponnesus to the rest of Greece.

Cork (kôrk). A city of the Republic of Ireland, in the S at the mouth of the Lee River. Pop. 128,600.

Corn Belt (kôrn). A region in the Midwestern United States where the chief products are corn and corn-fed livestock.

Corn·wall (kôrn′wôl). A peninsula and region of SW England.

Cor·o·man·del Coast (kôr′ə-măn′dĕl, kŏr′-). The SE coast of India.

Cor·pus Chris·ti (kôr′pəs krĭs′tē). An industrial city and seaport of SW Texas. Pop. 230,700.

Cor·reg·i·dor (kə-rĕg′ə-dôr). An island of the Philippines, at the entrance to Manila Bay; site of a World War II battle (1942) after which the Philippines were surrendered to the Japanese.

Cor·si·ca (kôr′sĭ-kə). An island of France in the Mediterranean N of Sardinia. Pop. 289,800. Cap. Ajaccio. **—Cor′si·can** adj. & n.

Cos·ta Me·sa (kŏs′tə mā′sə). A city of S California. Pop. 81,100.

Cos·ta Ri·ca (kŏs′tə rē′kə, kŏ′stə). A republic of Central America between Panama and Nicaragua. Pop. 2,184,000. Cap. San José. **—Costa Rican.**

Côte d'A·zur (kōt′ dà′zr′). The Mediterranean coast of France.

Co·to·nou (kō′tə-nŏo′). A city of S Benin, on the Gulf of Guinea. Pop. 178,000.

Co·to·pax·i (kō′tō-păk′sē). The highest (19,347 ft/5,900.8 m) active volcano in the world, in the Cordillera Real, Ecuador.

Cots·wold Hills (kŏts′wōld′, -wəld). A range in W England; highest elevation, Cleeve Cloud (c. 1,080 ft/330 m).

Cot·ton Belt (kŏt′n). A major agricultural region of the SE United States, on the Atlantic and Gulf coastal plains and the Piedmont upland.

Coun·cil Bluffs (koun′səl blŭfs). A city of SW Iowa, on the Missouri. Pop. 56,300.

Cov·en·try (kŭv′ən-trē). An industrial city of central England. Pop. 336,800.

Cov·ing·ton (kŭv′ĭng-tən). A city of N Kentucky. Pop. 49,000.

Cran·ston (krăn′stən). A city of N Rhode Island. Pop. 72,000.

Cra·ter Lake (krā′tər). A lake in the crater of an extinct volcano at Crater Lake National Park in SW Oregon.

Cré·cy (krā-sē′). A town of NE France; scene of an English victory over the French (1346) during the Hundred Years' War.

Cre·mo·na (krĭ-mō′nə). A city of NW Italy, on the Po River SE of Milan. Pop. 82,500.

Crete (krēt). A Greek island, in the Mediterranean off the SE coast. **—Cre′tan** (krē′tən) adj. & n.

Cri·me·a (krī-mē′ə). A peninsula of extreme S European U.S.S.R., extending into the Black Sea. **—Cri·me′an** adj.

Cro·a·tia (krō-ā′shə). A region of SE Europe, along the NE coast of the Adriatic Sea; an independent kingdom in the Middle Ages, later a crown land of Austria-Hungary, and now part of Yugoslavia. **—Cro·a′tian** adj. & n.

Cu·ba (kyōo′bə). An island republic in the Caribbean off the S coast of Florida. Pop. 9,824,000. Cap. Havana. **—Cu′ban** adj. & n.

Cú·cu·ta (kōo′kōo-tä). A city of NE Colombia, near the border of Venezuela. Pop. 167,400.

Cu·lia·cán (kōo′lyä-kän′). A city of W Mexico. Pop. 228,000.

Cu·ma·ná (kōo′mä-nä′). A city of NE Venezuela on the Caribbean; the oldest permanent Spanish settlement in South America (founded in 1523). Pop. 119,700.

Cum·ber·land Gap (kŭm′bər-lənd). A pass through the Cumberland Mountains at the junction of the borders of Kentucky, Virginia, and Tennessee.

Cumberland Mountains. Also **Cum-**

berland Plateau. The W section of the Appalachian Mountains, extending along the Virginia-Kentucky border and into central Tennessee.

Cum·bri·a (kŭm′brē-ə). The S portion of an ancient Celtic kingdom in NW Britain.

Cum·bri·an Mountains (kŭm′brē-ən). A range of hills in NW England; highest elevation, Scafell Pike (3,210 ft/979 m).

Cu·ra·çao (kyŏor′ə-sou′, -sō′, kŏor′ə-). An island of the Netherlands Antilles, in the Caribbean off the NW coast of Venezuela. Pop. 156,200.

Cu·ri·ti·ba (kŏor′ē-tē′bä). A city of SE Brazil. Pop. 765,700.

Cush (kŭsh, kŏosh). A legendary ancient region of NE Africa, often identified with Ethiopia.

Cyc·la·des (sĭk′lə-dēs). A group of Greek islands in the S Aegean Sea.

Cy·prus (sī′prəs). An island republic in the Mediterranean off S Turkey. Pop. 622,000. Cap. Nicosia. **—Cyp′ri·an** (sĭp′rē-ən) adj. **—Cyp′ri·ot,** also **Cyp′ri·ote** (sĭp′rē-ōt) adj. & n.

Czech·o·slo·va·ki·a (chĕk′ə-slō-vä′kē ə, -väk′ē-ə). A socialist republic of central Europe. Pop. 15,239,000. Cap. Prague. **—Czech′o·slo′vak** or **Czech′o·slo·va′ki·an** adj. & n.

Czę·sto·cho·wa (chĕN′stŏ-KHŌ′vä). A city of S Poland. Pop. 200,300.

D

Dac·ca (dăk′ə, dä′kə). The capital of Bangladesh, in the E central part of the country. Pop. 1,311,000.

Da·chau (dä′KHOU). A city of S West Germany; site of a Nazi concentration camp. Pop. 33,700.

Da·cia (dā′shə). The ancient name for the part of Europe corresponding to modern Rumania. **—Da′cian** adj. & n.

Da·ho·mey (də-hō′mē). See **Benin.**

Da·kar (dä-kär′, də-). The capital of Senegal, on Cape Verde in the W. Pop. 798,800.

Da·ko·ta (də-kō′tə). A former U.S. territory, now consisting of North and South Dakota.

Dal·las (dăl′əs). A city in NE Texas. Pop. 901,500.

Dal·ma·ti·a (dăl-mā′shə). A region of Yugoslavia, along the E coast of the Adriatic Sea. **—Dal·ma′tian** adj. & n.

Da·ly City (dā′lē′). A city in W California. Pop. 76,800.

Da·mas·cus (də-măs′kəs). The capital of Syria, an ancient city in the SW part of the country. Pop. 1,142,000.

Dam·a·vand, Mount (dăm′ə-vănd′). Also **Dem·a·vend** (dĕm′ə-vĕnd′). The highest elevation (18,934 ft/5,774.9 m) of the Elburz Mountains, N Iran.

Da Nang (də näng′, dä näng′). A city of central Vietnam, on the South China Sea. Pop. 438,000.

Dan·ube (dăn′yōob). The major river of SE Europe, rising in the Black Forest of SW West Germany and flowing 1,750 mi (2,815.7 km) E to the Black Sea coast of Rumania. **—Dan·u′bi·an** adj.

Dan·zig (dăn′sĭg, dän′-). See **Gdańsk.**

Dar·da·nelles (därd'n-ĕlz'). A strait linking the Sea of Marmara and the Aegean Sea.

Dar es Sa·laam (där' ĕs sə-läm'). The capital of Tanzania, in the NE. Pop. 870,000.

Dar·ién (dä-ryĕn'). A region of E Panama between the Gulf of Panama and the Gulf of Darién, a wide bay of the Caribbean.

Dar·ling River (där'lĭng). A river of Australia, formed at the Queensland-New South Wales border and flowing 1,702 mi (2,738.5 km) gen. SW through New South Wales to the Murray River.

Dar·win (där'wĭn). A city of N Australia, on the Timor Sea. Pop. 36,900.

Da·vao (dä'vou). A seaport of SE Mindanao, Philippines. Pop. 515,500.

Dav·en·port (dăv'ən-pôrt', -pōrt'). A city of E Iowa, on the Mississippi. Pop. 103,000.

Da·vis Strait (dā'vĭs). An arm of the North Atlantic Ocean between SE Baffin Island and SW Greenland.

Day·ton (dāt'n). A manufacturing center of SW Ohio. Pop. 193,300.

Day·to·na Beach (dā-tō'nə). A city of E central Florida, a winter resort on the Atlantic. Pop. 53,600.

Dead Sea (dĕd). A salt lake between Israel and Jordan, 1,302 ft (397.1 m) below sea level.

Dear·born (dîr'bôrn', -bərn). An automobile-manufacturing center of SE Michigan. Pop. 90,600.

Death Valley (dĕth). A desert basin in E California and W Nevada, containing the lowest point in the Western Hemisphere (280 ft/85.4 m below sea level). Most of it is included in the Death Valley National Monument.

De·bre·cen (dĕb'rĕt-sĕn'). A city of E central Hungary. Pop. 187,100.

De·ca·tur (dĭ-kā'tər). A city of E central Illinois. Pop. 93,500.

Dec·can Plateau (dĕk'ən). A triangular plateau extending over most of peninsular India.

Del·a·ware (dĕl'ə-wâr'). A state of the E United States, on the Atlantic. Pop. 594,800. Cap. Dover.

Delaware Bay. An inlet of the Atlantic between Delaware and New Jersey.

Delaware River. A river flowing 315 mi (506.8 km) gen. SE and S from the Catskill Mountains, New York State, to Delaware Bay, and forming the New York-Pennsylvania, Pennsylvania-New Jersey, and New Jersey-Delaware borders on its course.

Del·hi (dĕl'ē). The capital of India from 1912 to 1931, on the Jumna River adjacent to New Delhi. Pop. 3,287,900.

De·los (dē'lŏs). The smallest island of the Cyclades, Greece.

Del·phi (dĕl'fī'). An ancient town of central Greece, on the S slope of Mount Parnassus; seat of an oracle of Apollo.

Dem·a·vend, Mount (dĕm'ə-vĕnd'). See **Damavand.**

Den·mark (dĕn'märk'). A kingdom of N Europe, consisting of a peninsula and an archipelago between the North and Baltic seas. Pop. 5,118,000.

Cap. Copenhagen. —**Dan'ish** (dā'-nĭsh) adj. & n.

Den·ver (dĕn'vər). The capital of Colorado, in the N central part of the state at an altitude of 5,280 ft (1,610.4 m). Pop. 489,300.

Der·by (där'bē). A mining and manufacturing city in central England. Pop. 213,700.

Des Moines (də moin'). The capital of Iowa, in the S central part on the Des Moines River. Pop. 190,900.

De·troit (dĭ-troit'). A port and automobile-manufacturing center in SE Michigan. Pop. 1,197,300.

Detroit River. A river flowing c. 32 mi (51.5 km) between Lake St. Clair and Lake Erie and forming part of the U.S.-Canadian border.

Dev·il's Island (dĕv'əlz). An islet off the coast of French Guiana; site of a former French penal colony.

Dhau·la·gi·ri (dou'lə-gĭr'ē). A peak rising to 26,810 ft (8,177 m) in the Himalayas of N central Nepal.

Di·jon (dē-zhôN'). A city of E France. Pop. 151,700.

Di·nar·ic Alps (dĭ-nâr'ĭk ălps). The SE range of the Alps, extending along the Adriatic coast of Yugoslavia into N Albania; highest elevation, 8,883 ft (2,709.3 m).

District of Co·lum·bi·a (kə-lŭm'bē-ə). The Federal District of the United States, formerly in Maryland and coextensive with the capital city of Washington. Pop. 635,200.

Dix·ie (dĭk'sē). Those states that joined the Confederacy during the Civil War; the Southern states. Also called **Dixie Land.**

Dja·kar·ta (jə-kär'tə). Also **Ja·kar·ta.** The capital of Indonesia, a seaport on the NW coast of Java. Pop. 5,000,000.

Dji·bou·ti (jĭ-bōō'tē). **1.** A republic of E Africa on the Gulf of Aden. Pop. 250,000. **2.** The capital of Djibouti, near the S entrance to the Red Sea. Pop. 130,000.

Dne·pro·pe·trovsk (nĕp'rō-pə-trôfsk'). A city of S European U.S.S.R., on the Dnieper. Pop. 1,066,000.

Dnie·per (nē'pər). A river of W European U.S.S.R., rising near Smolensk and flowing 1,420 mi (2,284.8 km) gen. SW to the Black Sea.

Dnies·ter (nēs'tər). A river rising in the Carpathian Mountains and flowing 850 mi (1,367.6 km) gen. SE through the Ukrainian S.S.R. to the Black Sea.

Do·dec·a·nese (dō-dĕk'ə-nēs', -nēz'). A group of Greek islands in the Aegean Sea between Turkey and Crete.

Do·ha (dō'hə, -hä). The capital of Qatar, a port on the Persian Gulf. Pop. 130,000.

Do·lo·mites (dŏl'ə-mīts'). A section of the E Alps in N Italy; highest elevation, Marmolada (10,964 ft/3,344 m).

Dom·i·ni·ca (dŏm'ə-nē'kə, də-mĭn'ĭ-kə). An island and former British colony in the West Indies. Pop. 78,000. Cap. Roseau.

Do·min·i·can Republic (də-mĭn'ĭ-kən). A country occupying the E two-thirds of the Caribbean island of His-

paniola. Pop. 5,275,000. Cap. Santo Domingo.

Don (dŏn). A river of the Soviet Union, rising near Tula and flowing 1,222 mi (1,966.2 km) S and then W to the Sea of Azov.

Do·nets Basin (də-nĕts'). A major coal-mining and industrial region of S European U.S.S.R., N of the Sea of Azov.

Do·netsk (də-nĕtsk'). An industrial city of S European U.S.S.R., in the Donets Basin. Pop. 984,000.

Dort·mund (dôrt'mənd). An industrial city of W West Germany. Pop. 650,000.

Dou·ro (dō'rōō). A river rising in N central Spain and flowing 475 mi (764.2 km) gen. W to the Atlantic near Oporto, Portugal.

Do·ver (dō'vər). **1.** A port city of SE England. Pop. 34,700. **2.** The capital of Delaware, in the E central part of the state. Pop. 23,500.

Dover, Strait of. A strait between England and France, connecting the E end of the English Channel with the North Sea.

Downs, The (dounz). **1.** Two parallel hill ranges in S England. **2.** A roadstead in the English Channel, off the SE coast of Kent, England.

Dra·kens·berg (drä'kənz-bûrg'). A mountain range of SE Africa, extending from Swaziland NW through South Africa and Lesotho; highest elevation, Thabantshonyana (11,425 ft/3,484.6 m) in Lesotho.

Dres·den (drĕz'dən). A city of SE East Germany. Pop. 529,300.

Dub·lin (dŭb'lĭn). The capital of the Republic of Ireland, a port on the Irish Sea. Pop. 566,000.

Du·buque (də-byōōk'). A city of E Iowa. Pop. 62,300

Duis·burg (ds'bōōrкн'). An industrial city and river port of W West Germany. Pop. 591,800.

Du·luth (də-lōōth', dōō-). A city of Minnesota, at the W end of Lake Superior. Pop. 92,800.

Dun·dee (dŭn-dē'). A major industrial and commercial city on the Firth of Tay in E Scotland. Pop. 194,400.

Dun·kirk (dŭn'kûrk'). An industrial city of N France, on the North Sea coast; scene of British troop evacuation of May–June, 1940. Pop. 83,200.

Dur·ban (dûr'bən). A port city on the E coast of the Republic of South Africa. Pop. 736,900.

Dur·ham (dûr'əm). A city of N central North Carolina. Pop. 99,700.

Du·shan·be (dōō-shän'bə, dyōō-). The capital of the Tadzhik S.S.R., Central Asian U.S.S.R. Pop. 460,000.

Düs·sel·dorf (d'səl-dôrf'). An industrial city of West Germany, on the Rhine N of Cologne. Pop. 607,600.

E

East An·gli·a (ēst ăng'glē-ə). An Anglo-Saxon kingdom of SE England, in the area now occupied by Norfolk and Suffolk.

East Ber·lin (bûr-lĭn'). See **Berlin.**

ă pat   ā pay   â care   ä father   ĕ pet   ē be   hw which   ĭ pit   ī tie   î pier   ŏ pot   ō toe   ô paw, for   oi noise
ōō took   ōō boot   ou out   th thin   *th* this   ŭ cut   û urge   zh vision   ə about, item, edible, gallop, circus

East·er Island (ē'stər). An island of Chile in the South Pacific Ocean, 2,350 mi (3,781 km) W of the Chilean mainland; site of a number of ancient massive sculptured heads.

East·ern Hemisphere (ē'stərn). The part of the earth including the continents of Europe, Africa, Asia, and Australia.

East Ger·ma·ny (jûr'mə-nē). The unofficial name for the German Democratic Republic. See **Germany.**

East In·dies (ĭn'dēz). 1. The Malay Archipelago. 2. The islands comprising Indonesia.

East Lon·don (lŭn'dən). A seaport and industrial center of SE South Africa. Pop. 119,700.

East Or·ange (ôr'ĭnj, ŏr'-). A city of NE New Jersey. Pop. 76,800.

East Pak·i·stan (pǎ'kĭ-stǎn', pǎk'ĭ-stǎn'). A former name for Bangladesh.

East Prov·i·dence (prŏv'ə-dəns). A suburb of Providence, Rhode Island. Pop. 51,000.

East Prus·sia (prŭsh'ə). A former province of Prussia, divided after 1945 between Poland and the Russian S.F.S.R.

East River. A narrow strait connecting Upper New York Bay with Long Island Sound and separating Manhattan Island from Long Island.

East Saint Lou·is (sānt lōō'ĭs). An industrial city in Illinois, on the Mississippi River opposite St. Louis, Missouri. Pop. 55,000.

Eau Claire (ō klâr'). A city of W central Wisconsin. Pop. 51,500.

E·bro (ē'brō). The longest river of Spain, rising in the Cantabrian Mountains in the N and flowing c. 575 mi (925 km) SE to the Mediterranean Sea.

Ec·ua·dor (ĕk'wə-dôr'). A country of NW South America. Pop. 7,763,000. Cap. Quito. —**Ec·ua·dor'e·an** or **Ec'-ua·dor'i·an** adj. & n.

E·dam (ē'dəm, ē'dǎm'). A town of the NW Netherlands. Pop. 21,500.

Ed·in·burgh (ĕd'n-bûr'ə). The capital of Scotland, in the E on the Firth of Forth. Pop. 464,000.

Ed·mon·ton (ĕd'mən-tən). The capital of Alberta, Canada, on the North Saskatchewan River in the S central part of the province. Pop. 461,400.

E·dom (ē'dəm). An ancient country of SW Asia, S of the Dead Sea. —**E'-dom·ite'** n.

E·gypt (ē'jĭpt). A country of NE Africa, bounded on the N by the Mediterranean Sea and on the E by the Red Sea. Pop. 40,983,000. Cap. Cairo. —**E·gyp'tian** adj. & n.

Eir·e (âr'ə). See **Ireland.**

E·lam (ē'ləm). An ancient kingdom of SW Asia, in what is now SW Iran. —**E'lam·ite'** n.

El·ba (ĕl'bə). The largest island in the Tuscan Archipelago off the W coast of Italy, the place of exile of Napoleon Bonaparte (1814–15).

El·be (ĕl'bə). A major river of central Europe, rising in Bohemia and flowing 725 mi (1,166.5 km) through Czechoslovakia and East and West

Germany to the North Sea.

El·bert, Mount (ĕl'bərt). The highest peak (14,431 ft/4,401.5 m) of the Sawatch Range in central Colorado.

El·brus, Mount (ĕl'brōos). The highest mountain of Europe, in the Caucasus Mountains of the S Soviet Union, rising to 18,481 ft (5,636.7 m).

El·burz (ĕl-bōorz'). A mountain range of N Iran, separating the Caspian Sea from the central Iranian plateau; highest elevation, Mount Damavand (18,934 ft/5,774.9 m).

E·lis (ē'lĭs). A region of the NW Peloponnesus, Greece.

E·lis·a·beth·ville (ĭ-lĭz'ə-bəth-vĭl'). See **Lubumbashi.**

E·liz·a·beth (ĭ-lĭz'ə-bəth). A city in NE New Jersey. Pop. 105,700.

Elles·mere Island (ĕlz'mîr'). The largest of the Queen Elizabeth Islands, Northwest Territories, Canada.

El·lis Island (ĕl'ĭs). An island in Upper New York Bay, a former U.S. immigration center (1892–1943) and now part of the Statue of Liberty National Monument.

El Pas·o (ĕl pǎs'ō). A city of W Texas. Pop. 425,100.

El Sal·va·dor (ĕl sǎl'və-dôr'). A republic of Central America, in the W on the Pacific Coast. Pop. 4,353,000. Cap. San Salvador.

E·mi·lia-Ro·ma·gna (ā-mē'lyä-rō-män'yä). A region in N central Italy.

Eng·land (ĭng'glənd). 1. The largest political division of the United Kingdom of Great Britain and Northern Ireland, in S Great Britain. Pop. 46,102,000. Cap. London. 2. Popularly, Great Britain. 3. Popularly, the United Kingdom of Great Britain and Northern Ireland.

Eng·lish Channel (ĭng'glĭsh). An arm of the Atlantic between England and France, and connected with the North Sea by the Strait of Dover.

E·ni·we·tok (ĕn'ĭ-wē'tŏk', ĕ-nē'wə-tŏk'). An atoll in the Marshall Islands in the W central Pacific Ocean; site of U.S. atomic tests (1948).

Eph·e·sus (ĕf'ə-səs). An ancient Greek city in Asia Minor near the Aegean Sea.

E·phra·im (ē'frē-əm, ē'frəm). 1. A range of low hills in NW Israel. 2. The Kingdom of Israel.

E·pi·rus (ĭ-pī'rəs). An ancient country of NW Greece and S Albania.

Ep·som (ĕp'səm). A town in N central Surrey, England, noted for its nearby racetrack, Epsom Downs.

E·qua·to·ri·al Guin·ea (ĕkwə-tôr'ē-əl gĭn'ē, ĕk'wə-). A country of W Africa, comprising the island of Fernando Po and smaller islands in the Gulf of Guinea and mainland Río Muni. Pop. 346,000. Cap. Malabo.

Er·e·bus, Mount (ĕr'ə-bəs). An active volcano, 12,280 ft (3,745.4 m) high, on Ross Island, Antarctica.

Er·furt (âr'fōort'). An industrial city of S central East Germany. Pop. 203,000.

E·rie (îr'ē). A shipping and industrial center of NW Pennsylvania. Pop. 119,000.

Erie, Lake. One of the Great Lakes, in

E central North America on the boundary between the United States and Canada.

Erie Canal. A historic American waterway, extending 363 mi (584 km) through central New York State, from Albany to Buffalo on Lake Erie.

Er·i·tre·a (ĕr'ĭ-trē'ə). A region of N Ethiopia, along the Red Sea.

Er Rif or **Er Riff** (ĕr rĭf'). See **Rif.**

Erz·ge·bir·ge (ĕrts'gə-bîr'gə). A mountain range, rich in mineral resources, on the border between East Germany and Czechoslovakia.

Er·zu·rum (ĕr'zə-rōōm'). A city in Turkey, E of Ankara; a strategic Armenian fortress in the 19th-cent. Russo-Turkish conflicts. Pop. 134,600.

Es·ki·se·hir (ĕs'kĭ-shē-hîr'). A city in W central Turkey, an early capital of the Ottoman Turks. Pop. 285,300.

Es·sen (ĕs'ən). A steel-producing city in the heart of the Ruhr industrial region of West Germany. Pop. 664,400.

Es·to·ni·a (ĕ-stō'nē-ə, ĕ-stŏn'yə). Officially, **Estonian Soviet Socialist Republic.** A constituent republic of W European U.S.S.R., along the Baltic Sea. Pop. 1,466,000. Cap. Tallinn. —**Es·to'ni·an** adj. & n.

E·thi·o·pi·a (ē'thē-ō'pē-ə). A republic of E Africa. Pop. 31,780,000. Cap. Addis Ababa. —**E·thi·o'pi·an** adj. & n.

Et·na, Mount (ĕt'nə). The highest (11,122 ft/3,392.2 m) active volcano in Europe, in E Sicily.

E·tru·ri·a (ĭ-trōōr'ē-ə). An ancient country of W central Italy, now comprising Tuscany and parts of Umbria.

Eu·boe·a (yōō-bē'ə). The largest Greek island in the Aegean Sea, NE of Attica and Boeotia across the Gulf of Euboea, an arm of the Aegean.

Eu·clid (yōō'klĭd). A city of N Ohio. Pop. 60,000.

Eu·gene (yōō-jēn'). A city and industrial center of W Oregon. Pop. 104,700.

Eu·phra·tes (yōō-frā'tēz). A river of SW Asia, flowing c. 1,700 mi (2,735 km) from E central Turkey, through NE Syria and central Iraq, to the Tigris River.

Eur·a·sia (yōō-rā'zhə). The continents of Europe and Asia, and their offshore islands. —**Eur·a'sian** adj. & n.

Eu·rope (yōor'əp). A continent consisting of the section of the Eurasian land mass that extends W from a line marked unofficially by the Dardanelles, the Black Sea, the Ural River, and the Ural Mountains. —**Eu'ro·pe'-an** adj. & n.

Ev·ans·ton (ĕv'ən-stən). A city of NE Illinois. Pop. 73,300.

Ev·ans·ville (ĕv'ənz-vĭl, -vəl). A city of SW Indiana. Pop. 130,000.

Ev·er·est, Mount (ĕv'ər-ĭst, ĕv'rĭst). A mountain in the Himalayas on the border of Nepal and Tibet, the highest in the world (29,028 ft/8,853.5 m).

Ev·er·ett (ĕv'rĭt, ĕv'ər-ĭt). A port city of NW Washington. Pop. 54,400.

Everglades, The (ĕv'ər-glādz'). A subtropical swamp on a limestone plateau in S Florida, including the Everglades National Park, reserved to protect the abundant wildlife and tropical plants.

ă pat   ā pay   â care   ä father   ĕ pet   ē be   hw which   ĭ pit   ī tie   î pier   ŏ pot   ō toe   ô paw, for   oi noise
ōō took   ōō boot   ou out   th thin   th this   ŭ cut   û urge   zh vision   ə about, item, edible, gallop, circus

F

Eyre, Lake (âr). A shallow salt lake at 39 ft (12 m) below sea level in central South Australia, Australia.

Faer·oe Islands (fâr′ō). A group of Danish islands in the North Atlantic Ocean between the Shetlands and Iceland.

Fair·banks (fâr′băngks′). A city of central Alaska. Pop. 22,500.

Falk·land Islands (fôk′lənd). A group of islands in the South Atlantic Ocean off the SE coast of Argentina.

Fall River (fôl). An industrial city of SE Massachusetts. Pop. 92,200.

Far East. An area traditionally including the countries of China, Japan, and North and South Korea and, sometimes, all Asian lands E of Afghanistan. —**Far Eastern.**

Far·go (fär′gō). A city of North Dakota, in the E on the Red River. Pop. 61,300.

Fay·ette·ville (fā′ĭt-vĭl). A city of S central North Carolina, a former capital of the state. Pop. 59,500.

Fear, Cape (fîr). The S point of Smith Island, off SE North Carolina.

Fer·ra·ra (fə-rär′ə). A city of N central Italy. Pop. 127,200.

Fez (fĕz, fĕs). A city of N central Morocco; the religious center of the country. Pop. 426,000.

Fi·ji (fē′jē). An independent country in the SW Pacific Ocean. Pop. 618,000. Cap. Suva, on Viti Levu.

Fin·ger Lakes (fĭng′gər). A group of elongated glacial lakes in W central New York State.

Fin·land (fĭn′lənd). A republic of N central Europe. Pop. 4,764,000. Cap. Helsinki. —**Finn** (fĭn) n. —**Fin′nish** (fĭn′ĭsh) adj. & n.

Finland, Gulf of. An arm of the Baltic Sea between Finland and the Soviet Union.

Flag·staff (flăg′stăf′, -stäf′). A resort city of N central Arizona. Pop. 34,800.

Flan·ders (flăn′dərz). A region of NW Europe, including part of N France and W Belgium, and bordered by the North Sea. —**Flem′ing** (flĕm′ĭng) n. —**Flem′ish** (flĕm′ĭsh) adj. & n.

Flint (flĭnt). An automobile center of S Michigan. Pop. 159,600.

Flor·ence (flôr′əns, flōr′-). A city and cultural center on the Arno in central Italy. Pop. 465,800. —**Flor′en·tine′** (flôr′ən-tēn′, flōr′-) adj. & n.

Flo·res (flôr′əs, flōr′-). An island of Indonesia separated from Sulawesi to the N by the Flores Sea, a section of the Pacific Ocean.

Flor·i·da (flôr′ə-də, flōr′-). A state of the SE United States. Pop. 9,580,000. Cap. Tallahassee.

Florida, Straits of. The sea passage between the Florida Keys and Cuba, connecting the Atlantic Ocean with the Gulf of Mexico.

Florida Keys. A chain of small islands extending from Miami to Key West.

Fog·gia (fôd′jä). An agricultural center in S Italy. Pop. 153,300.

Fond du Lac (fŏn′ də lăk′, dyə lăk′). A city of E Wisconsin. Pop. 35,800.

Foo·chow (fōō′chou′). See **Fuchou.**

For·a·ker, Mount (fôr′ĭ-kər, fōr′-). A peak rising to 17,280 ft (5,270.4 m) in Mount McKinley National Park, S central Alaska.

For·mo·sa (fôr-mō′sə). The former name for Taiwan.

For·ta·le·za (fôr′tä-lā′zä). A seaport of NE Brazil. Pop. 1,109,800.

Fort-de-France (fôr-də-fräNs′). The capital of Martinique. Pop. 98,600.

Forth, Firth of (fôrth, fôrth). An inlet of the North Sea in SE Scotland.

Fort Knox (nŏks). A military reservation in N Kentucky; site of the U.S. Gold Bullion Depository.

Fort-La·my (fôr′lə-mē′). See **Ndjamena.**

Fort Lau·der·dale (lô′dər-dāl′). A resort of S Florida. Pop. 154,000.

Fort Smith (smĭth). A city of W Arkansas. Pop. 71,500.

Fort Wayne (wān). An industrial center of NE Indiana. Pop. 171,100.

Fort Worth (wûrth). An industrial and commercial center of Texas. Pop. 382,700.

Fra·ming·ham (frā′mĭng-hăm′). A manufacturing center of E Massachusetts. Pop. 65,200.

France (frăns, fräns). A republic of W Europe, with coastlines on both the Atlantic Ocean and the Mediterranean Sea. Pop. 53,478,000. Cap. Paris. —**French** (frĕnch) adj. & n.

Frank·fort (frăngk′fərt). The capital of Kentucky, on the Kentucky River in the N central part of the state. Pop. 25,900.

Frank·furt am Main (frängk′fōōrt′ äm mīn′). An industrial center on the Main River in central West Germany. Pop. 636,200.

Frank·lin (frängk′lĭn). The northernmost district of the Northwest Territories, Canada, comprising Baffin Island, other Arctic islands, and Boothia and Melville peninsulas.

Franz Jo·sef Land (frănts′ jō′səf länd, jō′səf länd′). An archipelago in the Arctic Ocean comprising about 85 islands and claimed by the Soviet Union in 1928.

Fra·ser (frā′zər). A river in British Columbia, Canada, rising in the Rocky Mountains and flowing 850 mi (1,367.6 km) S and then W to the Strait of Georgia, S of Vancouver.

Fred·er·ic·ton (frĕd′rĭk-tən). The capital of New Brunswick, Canada, in the SW. Pop. 45,200.

Free·town (frē′toun′). The capital of Sierra Leone, in the W on the Atlantic Ocean. Pop. 214,400.

French E·qua·to·ri·al Af·ri·ca (ĕ′kwə-tôr′ē-əl ăf′rĭ-kə, ĕk′wə-). A former administrative unit in W and N central Africa, created by France in 1910 and comprising Gabon, Middle Congo, Ubangi-Shari, and Chad until its dissolution in 1958.

French Gui·an·a (gē-ăn′ə, -ä′nə). An Overseas Department of France, on the NE coast of South America between Surinam and Brazil. Pop. 63,000. Cap. Cayenne.

French Pol·y·ne·sia (pŏl′ə-nē′zhə, -shə). An Overseas Territory of France in the South Pacific Ocean, including the Society, Tubuai, Rapa, Tuamotu, and Marquesas islands. Pop. 144,000. Cap. Papeete, on Tahiti.

Fres·no (frĕz′nō). A commercial center of central California. Pop. 215,400.

Fri·sian Islands (frĭzh′ən, frē′zhən). A chain of islands in the North Sea, divided into groups belonging to the Netherlands, West Germany, and Denmark.

Frun·ze (frōōn′zē). The capital of the Kirghiz S.S.R., Central Asian U.S.S.R. Pop. 511,000.

Fu·chou (fōō′chou′). Also **Foo·chow.** The capital of Fukien, SE China. Pop. 900,000.

Fu·ji (fōō′jē). Also **Fu·ji·ya·ma** (fōō′jē-yä′mə). The highest peak (12,389 ft / 3,778.6 m) in Japan, an extinct volcanic cone on S central Honshu.

Fu·kien (fōō′kyĕn′). A province of SE China. Pop. 17,000,000. Cap. Fuchou.

Fu·ku·o·ka (fōō′kōō-ō′kə). A seaport of N Kyushu, Japan. Pop. 1,021,600.

Fu·ku·shi·ma (fōō′kōō-shē′mə). A textile-manufacturing center of NE Honshu, Japan. Pop. 250,400.

Ful·ler·ton (fōōl′ər-tən). An industrial city of SW California. Pop. 101,900.

Fun·dy, Bay of (fŭn′dē). An inlet of the Atlantic Ocean between Maine and New Brunswick on the N and Nova Scotia on the S.

Fu·shun (fōō′shōōn′). A coal-mining center of NE China. Pop. 1,700,000.

G

Ga·bon (gá-bôn′). A republic of W central Africa. Pop. 538,000. Cap. Libreville.

Gab·o·ro·ne (găb′ə-rō′nə). The capital of Botswana, near the the South African border. Pop. 21,000.

Gads·den Purchase (gădz′dən). An area of land in Arizona and New Mexico S of the Gila River, acquired from Mexico in 1853.

Gaines·ville (gānz′vĭl). A city of N central Florida. Pop. 72,300.

Ga·lá·pa·gos Islands (gə-lä′pə-gəs, gə-lăp′ə-). An island group in the Pacific 650 mi (1,045.8 km) W of Ecuador.

Ga·la·tia (gə-lā′shə, -shē-ə). An ancient country forming part of N central Asia Minor. —**Ga·la′tian** adj. & n.

Ga·le·ras Volcano (gä-lā′räs). An active volcano, 13,997 ft (4,269.1 m) high, in the SW Colombian Andes.

Ga·li·ci·a (gə-lĭsh′ē-ə, -lĭsh′ə). **1.** A region of SE Poland and the NW Ukraine. **2.** A region and ancient kingdom of NW Spain. —**Ga·li′cian** adj. & n.

Gal·i·lee (găl′ə-lē′). A hilly region of N Palestine.

Galilee, Sea of. A freshwater lake bordered by Israel, Syria, and Jordan, lying at 696 ft (212.2 m) below sea level.

Gal·lip·o·li (gə-lĭp′ə-lē). A peninsula of European Turkey between the Dardanelles and the Gulf of Saros.

ă pat   ā pay   â care   ä father   ĕ pet   ē be   hw which   ĭ pit   ī tie   î pier   ŏ pot   ō toe   ô paw, for   oi noise
ōō took   ōō boot   ou out   th thin   th this   ŭ cut   û urge   zh vision   ə about, item, edible, gallop, circus

Gal·ves·ton (găl′və-stən). A port city of SE Texas, on Galveston Bay, an inlet of the Gulf of Mexico. Pop. 61,600.

Gam·bi·a (găm′bē-ə). A republic of W Africa. Pop. 585,000. Cap. Banjul. —**Gam′bi·an** adj. & n.

Gan·ges (găn′jēz). A river of N India and East Pakistan, sacred to Hindus, flowing 1,560 mi (2,510 km) SE from the Himalayas to its wide delta and the Bay of Bengal.

Gang·tok (gŭng′tŏk). The capital of Sikkim, in the S central part of the protectorate. Pop. 9,000.

Gar·da, Lake (gär′dä). The largest lake of Italy (143 sq mi/370.3 sq km), in the N.

Gar·den Grove (gärd′n grōv). A city of SW California. Pop. 125,300.

Gar·mo Peak (gär′mō). The highest elevation (24,590 ft/7,499.9 m) in the U.S.S.R., part of the Pamirs in Tadzhik.

Ga·ronne (gȧ-rôn′). A river of SW France, rising in the Spanish Pyrenees and flowing 355 mi (571.1 km) NW to unite with the Dordogne.

Gar·y (gâr′ē). A steel-manufacturing center of NW Indiana. Pop. 151,900.

Gas·co·ny (găs′kə-nē). A region and former province of SW France.

Gas·pé Peninsula (găs-pā′). A peninsula of SE Quebec, Canada, between Chaleur Bay and the mouth of the St. Lawrence River.

Gates·head (gāts′hěd). An industrial center of N England. Pop. 222,000.

Gaul (gôl). The name given in antiquity to the region in Europe S and W of the Rhine, W of the Alps, and N of the Pyrenees, comprising approx. the territory of modern France and Belgium.

Ga·za Strip (gä′zə). An area of S Palestine near the Mediterranean; occupied by Israel in 1967.

Gdańsk (gə-dänsk). Formerly **Dan·zig** (dän′sĭg, dän′-). A port city of N Poland. Pop. 426,800.

Gdy·nia (gə-dĭn′yə). A port city of Poland. Pop. 221,000.

Gel·sen·kir·chen (gěl′zən-kîr′ĸHən). A city of W West Germany. Pop. 327,600.

Ge·ne·va (jə-nē′və). A city of SW Switzerland. Pop. 159,200.

Geneva, Lake of. A lake of SW Switzerland with its S shore in E France.

Gen·o·a (jěn′ō-ə). A port city of NW Italy. Pop. 805,900.

George·town (jôrj′toun′). 1. The capital of Guyana, in the N at the mouth of the Demerara River. Pop. 72,000. 2. The capital of the Caymans, on Grand Cayman Island. Pop. 4,000.

Geor·gia (jôr′jə). 1. See **Georgian S.S.R.** 2. A state of the SE United States. Pop. 5,404,400. Cap. Atlanta. —**Geor′gian** adj. & n.

Georgia, Strait of. A channel bordered on the W by Vancouver Island, on the E and NE by the mainland of British Columbia, and on the SE by Washington State.

Georgian Bay. An inlet of Lake Huron in SE Ontario, Canada.

Georgian Soviet Socialist Republic. Also **Georgia.** A constituent re-public of SE European U.S.S.R. Pop. 4,954,000. Cap. Tbilisi.

Ger·ma·ny (jûr′mə-nē). A former state of central Europe, bordered in the N by the North and Baltic seas and divided in 1949 into the **German Democratic Republic** (East Germany), pop. 16,745,000, cap. East Berlin; and the **German Federal Republic** (West Germany), pop. 61,439,000, cap. Bonn.

Ger·mis·ton (jûr′mĭ-stən). A gold-refining center of South Africa, in S Transvaal. Pop. 222,000.

Get·tys·burg (gět′ĭz-bûrg′). A town in S Pennsylvania; site of a Civil War Union victory (1863).

Gha·na (gä′nə). A republic of W Africa, on the N shore of the Gulf of Guinea. Pop. 10,969,000. Cap. Accra. —**Gha′na·ian** or **Gha′ni·an** adj. & n.

Ghats (gôts, gäts). Two mountain ranges of S India, the Eastern Ghats along the Bay of Bengal coast (highest elevation, Dodabetta, 8,640 ft/2,635.2 m), and the Western Ghats along the Arabian Sea coast (highest elevation, Anai Mudi, 8,841 ft/2,696.5 m).

Ghent (gěnt). A city of NW central Belgium. Pop. 148,200.

Gib·ral·tar (jĭ-brôl′tər). A British crown colony occupying c. 2 sq mi (5.1 sq km) on the Rock of Gibraltar, and comprising a town, seaport, and fortress dominating the Strait of Gibraltar, a waterway between Spain and N Africa, connecting the Mediterranean with the Atlantic. Pop. 29,000.

Gi·la River (hē′lə). A river rising in SW New Mexico and flowing 630 mi (1,013.6 km) gen. W across S Arizona to the Colorado.

Gil·bert Islands (gĭl′bərt). See **Kiribati.**

Gil·e·ad (gĭl′ē-əd, -ăd′). A mountainous region of Jordan, situated E of the Jordan River between the Sea of Galilee and the Dead Sea; highest elevation, Mount Gilead (3,597 ft/1,097 m).

Gi·za (gē′zə). A city of NE Egypt, on the W bank of the Nile. Pop. 1,246,700.

Gla·cier Bay National Monument (glā′shər). An area of mountains and glaciers in SE Alaska on the British Columbia border.

Glacier National Park. A park in NW Montana, including numerous lakes and small glaciers.

Glas·gow (glăs′gō, -kō, glăs′-). A shipbuilding and manufacturing center of SW Scotland, on the Clyde. Pop. 832,100.

Glen·dale (glěn′dāl′). A city of SW California. Pop. 137,500.

Go·a (gō′ə). A district on the W coast of India, formerly under Portuguese rule.

Go·bi Desert (gō′bē). A desert region in E central Asia, mostly in the Mongolian People's Republic.

Godt·haab (gôt′hôp′). The capital of Greenland, on the SW coast of the island. Pop. 8,300.

God·win Aus·ten (gŏd′wĭn ô′stĭn). The 2nd highest mountain in the world (28,250 ft/8,616.2 m), in the Karakoram Range of N Kashmir. Also called **K2.**

Goi·â·ni·a (goi-ä′nē-ə). A city of S central Brazil. Pop. 389,000.

Go·lan Heights (gō′län′, -lən). A hilly area between SW Syria and NE Israel.

Gol·con·da (gŏl-kŏn′də). A ruined city of SE India, the capital (1512–1687) of a former Moslem kingdom.

Gold Coast (gōld). A coast on the Gulf of Guinea in W Africa along the S shore of Ghana, bordering the Ivory Coast on the W.

Gold·en Gate (gōl′dn). A strait in W central California 2 mi (3.2 km) wide and 5 mi (8 km) long connecting the Pacific Ocean and San Francisco Bay.

Go·mel (gō′məl, gô′-). A trade center of W European U.S.S.R. Pop. 349,000.

Go·mor·rah (gə-môr′ə, -mŏr′ə). A city of ancient Palestine.

Good Hope, Cape of (gŏŏd hōp′). A promontory on the SW coast of South Africa.

Go·rakh·pur (gôr′ək-pŏŏr′, gôr′-). A city of N central India. Pop. 230,700.

Gor·ki or **Gor·ky** (gôr′kē). A major industrial center of E European U.S.S.R., on the S bank of the Volga. Pop. 1,344,000.

Gor·lov·ka (gər-lôf′kə). A city of S European U.S.S.R. Pop. 342,000.

Go·shen (gō′shən). A region of ancient Egypt on the E delta of the Nile, inhabited by the Israelites from the time of Joseph until the Exodus.

Gö·te·borg (yœ′tə-bôr′y′). Also **Goth·en·burg** (gŏt′n-bûrg′, gŏth′-). A major seaport and shipbuilding center of SW Sweden. Pop. 442,400.

Got·land (gŏt′lənd). An island of Sweden, in the Baltic Sea off the SE coast.

Gram·pi·ans, The (grăm′pē-ənz). A mountain range of central Scotland, dividing The Highlands from The Lowlands; highest elevation, Ben Nevis (4,406 ft/1,343.8 m).

Gra·na·da (grə-nä′də). 1. An ancient Moorish kingdom in S Spain. 2. A city and manufacturing center of S Spain. Pop. 214,200.

Grand Banks (grănd). Also **Grand Bank.** A shoal and fishing area in the Atlantic off the S and E coasts of Newfoundland.

Grand Canyon. A gorge formed by the Colorado River in NW Arizona, extending W from the mouth of the Little Colorado to Lake Mead, with a width of from 4 to 18 mi (6.4 to 28.9 km) and a maximum depth of 1 mi (1.6 km).

Grand Prairie. A city of N Texas. Pop. 71,346.

Grand Rap·ids (răp′ĭdz). A furniture-manufacturing center of SW central Michigan. Pop. 181,600.

Grand Te·ton National Park (tē′tən). A park in NW Wyoming, including Grand Teton mountain (13,766 ft/4,198.7 m).

Graz (gräts). A city of SE Austria, SW of Vienna. Pop. 248,500.

Great Aus·tra·lian Bight (grăt ô-strāl′yən bīt). A bay of the Indian Ocean on the S coast of Australia.

Great Barrier Reef. The largest coral

formation in the world, off the E coast of Queensland, Australia.

Great Basin. A region of interior drainage, comprising most of Nevada as well as portions of Utah, California, Idaho, Wyoming, and Oregon.

Great Bear Lake. A lake of N central Mackenzie District, Northwest Territories, Canada.

Great Brit·ain (brĭt'n). An island off the W coast of Europe, comprising England, Scotland, and Wales.

Greater An·til·les (grā'tər ăn-tĭl'ēz). An island group forming part of the West Indies and including Cuba, Jamaica, Hispaniola, and Puerto Rico.

Great Falls. An industrial center of W central Montana. Pop. 56,500.

Great Lakes. The largest group of freshwater lakes in the world, in central North America on either side of the U.S.-Canadian boundary and including lakes Superior, Huron, Erie, Ontario, and Michigan.

Great Plains. A region of valley and plateau land in central North America, extending from the Central Plains in the United States and the Laurentian Highlands in Canada to the E base of the Rocky Mountains.

Great Rift Valley (rĭft). A massive depression in SW Asia and E Africa, extending from the valley of the Jordan S to Mozambique.

Great Salt Lake. A highly saline lake N Utah in the Great Basin of the United States.

Great Slave Lake. A lake of S Mackenzie District, Northwest Territories, Canada.

Great Smok·y Mountains (smō'kē). A range forming part of the Appalachians and extending along the North Carolina-Tennessee boundary; highest elevation, Clingmans Dome (6,642 ft/2,025.8 m).

Great Wall of Chi·na (chī'nə). A defensive wall, c. 1,500 mi (2,413.5 km) long, in N China, extending from Kansu in the W to the Yellow Sea in the E, constructed between 246 and 209 B.C.

Greece (grēs). A republic of SE Europe, in the S Balkan Peninsula. Pop. 9,444,000. Cap. Athens. —**Gre'cian** (grē'shən) or **Greek** (grēk) adj. & n.

Green Bay (grēn). A city and port of NE Wisconsin, at the S end of Green Bay, an inlet of Lake Michigan. Pop. 88,000.

Green·land (grēn'lənd, -lănd'). An island in the North Atlantic off the NE coast of Canada. Although part of the Kingdom of Denmark, Greenland has had home rule since 1979. Pop. 49,000. Cap. Gothab.

Green Mountains. A section of the Appalachians, extending from Canada through Vermont to Massachusetts; highest elevation, Mount Mansfield (4,393 ft/1,339.8 m).

Greens·bo·ro (grēnz'bûr'ō). A manufacturing and industrial city of N central North Carolina. Pop. 154,900.

Green·ville (grēn'vĭl). A textile-manufacturing center of NW South Carolina. Pop. 58,200.

Green·wich (grĕn'ĭch). A residential city in SW Connecticut. Pop. 58,700.

Greenwich Village. A section of Manhattan, New York City.

Gre·na·da (grə-nā'də). The southernmost island of the Windward group of the West Indies; with its adjacent island dependencies, the S Grenadines, it is a member of the West Indies Associated States. Pop. 87,300. Cap. St. George's.

Gre·no·ble (grə-nō'bəl). A city of SE central France. Pop. 166,000.

Gret·na Green (grĕt'nə). A village of S Scotland, near the English border; noted as a place where marriages were performed for eloping couples.

Gro·ning·en (grō'nĭng-ən). A city of NE Netherlands. Pop. 161,800.

Groz·ny (grôz'nē). A city and petroleum-producing center of SE European U.S.S.R. Pop. 381,000.

Gua·da·la·ja·ra (gwŏd'l-ə-här'ə). A city of SW Mexico. Pop. 1,560,800.

Gua·dal·ca·nal (gwŏd'l-kə-năl'). An island in the SE Solomon group of the W Pacific.

Gua·dal·qui·vir (gwŏd'l-kwĭv'ər). A river rising in S Spain and flowing c. 350 mi (565 km) W and SW to the Gulf of Cádiz.

Gua·de·loupe (gwŏd'l-ōōp', gŏd'-). Two islands in the West Indies, Basse-Terre (or Guadeloupe proper) and Grande-Terre, and their adjacent island dependencies, constituting an Overseas Department of France. Pop. 319,000. Administrative center, Basse-Terre.

Guam (gwŏm). The largest of the Mariana Islands, in the W Pacific.

Gua·na·ba·ra Bay (gwä'nə-vär'ə). An inlet of the Atlantic in SE Brazil, with Rio de Janeiro on its SW shore.

Guan·tá·na·mo Bay (gwän-tä'nə-mō'). An inlet of the Caribbean in SE Cuba.

Gua·te·ma·la (gwä'tə-mä'lə). 1. A republic in N Central America, with coastlines on the Pacific Ocean and the Caribbean Sea. Pop. 7,046,000. 2. Also **Guatemala City.** The capital of Guatemala, in the S central part of the country. Pop. 700,500. —**Gua'te·ma'lan** adj. & n.

Gua·ya·quil (gwī'ə-kēl'). A seaport of W Ecuador, on the Guayas River. Pop. 814,064.

Guern·sey (gûrn'zē). An island of the Channel group, in the SW central English Channel.

Gui·an·a (gē-ăn'ə, -ä'nə). A region of NE South America bordered by the Orinoco, Negro, and Amazon rivers and the Atlantic Ocean, and including SE Venezuela, part of N Brazil, and French Guiana, Surinam, and Guyana.

Guin·ea (gĭn'ē). A republic of W central Africa, on the Atlantic coast. Pop. 5,275,000. Cap. Conakry.

Guin·ea-Bis·sau (gĭn'ē-bĭ-sou'). A country of W Africa, on the Atlantic N of Guinea. Pop. 535,000. Cap. Bissau.

Guinea, Gulf of. An inlet of the Atlantic on the coast of W central Africa extending E to include the bights of Benin and Biafra.

Guinea Current (gĭn'ē). A warm ocean current in the Atlantic, flowing E off the W coast of Africa and through the Gulf of Guinea.

Gulf States (gŭlf). The 5 southern states of the United States with coastlines on the Gulf of Mexico: Florida, Alabama, Mississippi, Louisiana, and Texas.

Gulf Stream. A warm ocean current of the North Atlantic, issuing from the Gulf of Mexico and flowing E through the Straits of Florida, then NE along the SE coast of the United States, then E to the North Atlantic Current.

Gun·tur (gŏōn-tŏōr'). A city and trading center of SE India. Pop. 270,000.

Guy·a·na (gī-ăn'ə). A republic of NE central South America. Pop. 832,000. Cap. Georgetown.

Gwa·li·or (gwä'lē-ôr'). A city of N central India. Pop. 406,800.

H

Haar·lem (här'ləm). A city of W Netherlands. Pop. 162,800.

Hack·en·sack (hăk'ən-săk'). A manufacturing center of NE New Jersey. Pop. 36,000.

Hague, The (hāg). The de facto capital of the Netherlands, in the W near the North Sea. Pop. 468,000.

Hai·fa (hī'fə). A city and port of NW Israel. Pop. 225,000.

Hai·nan (hī'nän'). An island of China, in the S China Sea.

Hai·k'ou (hī'kō'). A port city on Hainan island, China. Pop. 500,000.

Hai·phong (hī'fŏng'). A port city of NE Vietnam. Pop. 276,000.

Hai·ti (hā'tē). A republic of the West Indies, occupying the W third of Hispaniola. Pop. 4,919,000. Cap. Port-au-Prince. —**Hai'tian** adj. & n.

Ha·ko·da·te (hä'kō-dä'tē). A port city of SW Hokkaido, Japan. Pop. 307,500.

Ha·le·a·ka·la (hä'lä-ä-kä-lä'). A mountain rising to 10,032 ft (3,059.7 m) in Haleakala National Park on E Maui Island, Hawaii, a dormant volcano containing the largest crater in the world.

Hal·i·car·nas·sus (hăl'ə-kär-năs'əs). An ancient Greek city of SW Asia Minor.

Hal·i·fax (hăl'ə-făks'). The capital of Nova Scotia, Canada, an Atlantic port on the S coast. Pop. 235,400.

Hal·le (hä'lə). An industrial center of S central East Germany. Pop. 235,600.

Hal·ma·he·ra (häl-mä-hä'rä). The largest island of the Molucca group, NW central Indonesia.

Ha·mah (hä'mä). Also **Ha·ma.** A city of W central Syria on the Orontes River. Pop. 137,400.

Ha·ma·dan (hä'mä-dän'). A commercial center of W Iran. Pop. 124,200.

Ha·ma·mat·su (hä-mä-mät'sōō). An industrial center of S central Honshu, Japan. Pop. 472,100.

Ham·burg (hăm'bûrg). A port of N central West Germany, on the Elbe. Pop. 1,717,400.

Ham·il·ton (hăm′əl-tən). **1.** A port city and manufacturing center of SE Ontario, Canada. Pop. 536,300. **2.** The capital of Bermuda, a port on Bermuda Island. Pop. 3,000. **3.** An industrial center of SW Ohio. Pop. 62,800.

Ham·mond (hăm′ənd). An industrial center of NW Indiana. Pop. 93,400.

Hamp·ton (hămp′tən). A port and fishing center of SE Virginia. Pop. 122,400.

Hampton Roads. A channel of SE Virginia, connecting the James and Elizabeth rivers with Chesapeake Bay.

Han (hän). A river of SE central China, rising in Shensi and flowing 750 mi (1,206.7 km) SE through Hupeh to the Yangtze.

Hang·chow (hăng′chou′). The capital of Chekiang, E China. Pop. 1,100,000.

Ha·noi (hă-noi′, hä-). The capital of Vietnam, an industrial center in the NE. Pop. 597,000.

Han·o·ver (hăn′ō′vər). **1.** A former independent kingdom and former province of Germany, in N West Germany. **2.** A commercial and industrial center of N West Germany. Pop. 563,000.

Han·tan (hän′dän′). An industrial center of E China. Pop. 500,000.

Har·bin (här′bĭn). The capital of Heilungkiang, NE China. Pop. 1,670,000.

Ha·ri Rud (hä′rē rōōd′). A river of Afghanistan, Iran, and the Turkmen S.S.R., rising in NW Afghanistan and flowing c. 700 mi (1,125 km) W to form part of the Iran-Afghanistan boundary and then N to the Kara Kum desert.

Har·lem (här′ləm). **1.** A river channel in New York City separating the N end of Manhattan Island from the Bronx. **2.** A section of New York City bordering on this river channel and on the East River.

Har·pers Ferry (här′pərz). A town of NE West Virginia; site of John Brown's rebellion (1859). Pop. 360.

Har·ris·burg (här′ĭs-bûrg′, hâr′-). The capital of Pennsylvania, on the Susquehanna in the SE. Pop. 53,100.

Hart·ford (härt′fərd). The capital of Connecticut, on the Connecticut River in the central part of the state. Pop. 136,300.

Harz Mountains (härts). A mountain range of central Germany between the Weser and the Elbe; highest elevation, Brocken (3,747 ft/1,142.8 m).

Has·tings (hā′stĭngz). A resort center of SE England, on the Strait of Dover, near the site of the Saxon defeat by a Norman army under William the Conqueror (1066). Pop. 74,600.

Hat·ter·as, Cape (hăt′ər-əs). A promontory on Hatteras Island, off the coast of North Carolina between Pamlico Sound and the Atlantic Ocean.

Ha·van·a (hə-văn′ə). The capital of Cuba, in the W. Pop. 1,008,500.

Ha·wai·i (hə-wä′ē, -wä′yə). **1.** Also **Ha·wai·ian Islands** (-wä′yən). An island group state of the United States, in the central Pacific. Pop. 964,700. Cap. Honolulu. **2.** The largest island of Hawaii, in the SE. Pop. 92,200.

Hay·ward (hā′wərd). A city of W central California. Pop. 94,300.

Heb·ri·des (hĕb′rə-dēz). An island group in the Atlantic off the W coast of Scotland and divided into the Inner Hebrides and the Outer Hebrides.

Hei·del·berg (hīd′l-bûrg′). A manufacturing center of SW West Germany, on the Neckar. Pop. 129,400.

Hei·lung·kiang (hā′lōong′gyäng′). A province of NE China. Pop. 21,000,-000. Cap. Harbin.

He·jaz (hē-jăz′). A region of NW Saudi Arabia, on the Red Sea.

Hel·e·na (hĕl′ə-nə). The capital of Montana, in the W central part of the state. Pop. 23,810.

Hel·i·con (hĕl′ĭ-kŏn′, -kən). A mountain rising to 5,738 ft (1,750 m) in SW Boeotia, Greece; the home of the Muses in Greek mythology.

He·li·op·o·lis (hē′lē-ŏp′ə-lĭs). An ancient city of N Egypt, in the Nile Delta region near Cairo.

Hel·les·pont (hĕl′ĭs-pŏnt′). The ancient name for the Dardanelles.

Hells Canyon (hĕlz). A gorge of the Snake River, on the Idaho-Oregon boundary and attaining a maximum depth of 7,900 ft (2,409.5 m).

Hel·sin·ki (hĕl′sĭng′kē). The capital of Finland, a Baltic port in the S on the Gulf of Finland. Pop. 496,300.

Heng·yang (hĕng′yäng′). A city of SE central China. Pop. 240,000.

Hen·ry, Cape (hĕn′rē). A promontory of SE Virginia, at the S entrance to Chesapeake Bay.

Her·cu·la·ne·um (hûr′kyə-lā′nē-əm). An ancient city of SW central Italy near Naples; destroyed with Pompeii by a volcanic eruption of Mount Vesuvius (A.D. 79).

Her·mon, Mount (hûr′mən). The highest elevation (9,232 ft/2,815.8 m) of the Anti-Lebanon range, on the Syria-Lebanon boundary.

Her·mo·si·llo (ĕr′mō-sē′yō). A city of NW Mexico. Pop. 232,700.

Her·ze·go·vi·na (hûr′tsə-gō-vē′nə). A region of W central Yugoslavia, now included in Bosnia and Herzegovina.

Hi·a·le·ah (hī′ə-lē′ə). A city of SE Florida. Pop. 143,600.

Hi·ber·ni·a (hī-bûr′nē-ə). The Latin name for Ireland. **—Hi·ber′ni·an** *adj.* & *n.*

High At·las (hī ăt′ləs). A mountain range of central Morocco; part of the Atlas Mountains.

High·lands, The (hī′ləndz). A mountainous region of N and W Scotland, N of and including the Grampians.

High Point. A city of N central North Carolina. Pop. 63,700.

Hi·ma·la·yas (hĭm′ə-lā′əz, hĭ-mäl′yəz). A mountain range of S central Asia, extending through NW Pakistan, Kashmir, N India, S Tibet, Nepal, Sikkim, and Bhutan; highest elevation, Mount Everest (29,028 ft/8,853.5 m).

Hi·me·ji (hē′mĕ′jē′). An industrial center of SW central Honshu, Japan. Pop. 439,700.

Hin·du Kush (hĭn′dōō kōōsh). A mountain range of central Asia, extending from central Afghanistan to the Pakistan boundary; highest elevation, Tirich Mir (25,263 ft/7,705.2 m).

Hin·du·stan (hĭn′dōō-stăn′, -stän′). **1.** The part of N India where Indic languages prevail, roughly the Ganges plain from the Punjab to Assam. **2.** Loosely, the Indian subcontinent.

Hip·po (hĭp′ō). Also **Hippo Re·gi·us** (rē′jē-əs). An ancient Numidian city in Algeria.

Hi·ro·shi·ma (hîr′ə-shē′mə, hĭ-rō′shĭ-mə). A city and port of SW Honshu, Japan; destroyed by the 1st atomic bomb employed in warfare (Aug. 6, 1945). Pop. 863,300.

His·pa·ni·a (hĭs-păn′yə). An ancient name for the Iberian Peninsula.

His·pa·nio·la (hĭs′pən-yō′lə). An island of the West Indies; occupied in the W by the Republic of Haiti and in the center and E by the Dominican Republic.

Ho·bart (hō′bərt, -bärt′). The capital of Tasmania, Australia; a port located in the SE. Pop. 162,000.

Ho·bo·ken (hō′bō′kən). A city of NE New Jersey, on the Hudson River. Pop. 42,400.

Ho Chi Minh City (hō′ chē′ mĭn′). Formerly **Sai·gon** (sī-gŏn′). A port city of Vietnam, on the bank of the Saigon River. Pop. 1,000,000.

Ho·fei (hŭ′fā′). The capital of Anhwei, E central China. Pop. 400,000.

Hok·kai·do (hō-kī′dō). An island of Japan, N of Honshu.

Hol·land (hŏl′ənd). See the **Netherlands.**

Hol·ly·wood (hŏl′ē-wōōd′). A district of Los Angeles, California; center of the American motion-picture industry. Pop. 194,000.

Hol·stein (hōl′stīn). A former duchy of Denmark, annexed by Prussia in 1866, and now part of West Germany.

Hol·yoke (hōl′yōk′). A city of SW central Massachusetts. Pop. 44,810.

Holy Ro·man Empire (hō′lē rō′mən). An empire, consisting largely of Germanic states in central and W Europe, established in A.D. 962 with the crowning of Otto I by the pope, and ending with the renunciation by Francis II in 1806.

Ho·nan (hō′nän′). A province of E central China. Pop. 50,000,000. Cap. Chengchou.

Hon·du·ras (hŏn-dōōr′əs, -dyōōr′əs). A republic of NE Central America. Pop. 3,563,000. Cap. Tegucigalpa. **—Hon·dur′an** or **Hon·dur′e·an** or **Hon·dur′i·an** *adj.* & *n.*

Hong Kong (hŏng′ kŏng′, hŏng′ kŏng′). Also **Hong·kong.** A British Crown Colony on the coast of Kwangtung, China, and including Hong Kong Island, Kowloon Peninsula, and the New Territories. Pop. 4,606,000. Cap. Victoria.

Hon·o·lu·lu (hŏn′ə-lōō′lōō). The capital of Hawaii, a port on the S coast of Oahu. Pop. 365,100.

Hon·shu (hŏn′shōō). The largest island of Japan, located between the Sea of Japan and the Pacific.

Hood, Mount (hōōd). A volcanic peak, 11,235 ft (3,426.7 m) high, of the Cascade Range in NW Oregon.

Hoogh·ly (hōōg′lē). A branch of the

Ganges, rising in West Bengal, India, and flowing 160 mi (260 km) S to the Bay of Bengal.

Ho·peh (hō′pā′). Also **Ho·pei.** A province of NE China. Pop. 47,000,000. Cap. Shih-chia-chuang.

Ho·reb (hôr′ĕb′, hōr′-). A mountain gen. identified in the Old Testament with Mount Sinai.

Hor·muz (hôr′mŭz′, hôr-mōōz′). Also **Or·muz** (ôr′-, ōr-). An island off the SE coast of Iran in the Strait of Hormuz, linking the Persian Gulf with the Gulf of Oman.

Horn, Cape (hôrn). A headland on an island of Tierra del Fuego, Chile; the southernmost point of South America.

Hot Springs. A city and resort center of W central Arkansas within Hot Springs National Park. Pop. 35,800.

Hous·ton (hyōō′stən). A port city of Texas, in the SE. Pop. 1,573,800.

How·rah (hou′rə). A city and industrial center of E central India. Pop. 740,600.

Hsi·an (shē′än′). Also **Si·an** (sē′än, shē′-). The capital of Shensi, N central China. Pop. 1,900,000.

Hsi·ning (shē′nĭng′). The capital of Tsinghai, W China. Pop. 250,000.

Huas·ca·rán (wäs′kä-rän′). An extinct volcano in the Cordillera Occidental; the highest elevation (22,205 ft/6,772.5 m) in Peru.

Hud·ders·field (hŭd′ərz-fēld′). A textile center of N central England. Pop. 130,100.

Hud·son Bay (hŭd′sən). An inland sea in E central Canada.

Hudson River. A river rising in the Adirondacks of E New York State, flowing 315 mi (506.8 km) gen. S to its mouth at New York City.

Hu·he·hot (hōō′hä′hōt′). The capital of the Inner Mongolian Autonomous Region, in the S. Pop. 700,000.

Hull (hŭl). **1.** A port city of NE England. Pop. 276,600. **2.** A city of SW central Quebec, Canada. Pop. 61,000.

Hum·ber (hŭm′bər). An estuary of the Ouse and Trent rivers, rising in NE England, and flowing 40 mi (65 km) gen. E to the North Sea.

Hum·boldt (hŭm′bōlt). A river rising in NE Nevada and flowing c. 300 mi (485 km) W and SW to Rye Patch reservoir.

Humboldt Current. A cold ocean current of the South Pacific, flowing N along the coast of Chile and Peru to S Ecuador.

Hu·nan (hōō′nän′). A province of SE central China. Pop. 38,000,000. Cap. Changsha.

Hun·ga·ry (hŭng′gə-rē). Officially, Hungarian People's Republic. A republic in central Europe. Pop. 10,710,-000. Cap. Budapest. —**Hun·gar′i·an** adj. & n.

Hunt·ing·ton (hŭn′tĭng-tən). A commercial and mining center of W West Virginia, on the Ohio River. Pop. 63,600.

Huntington Beach. A city of S California. Pop. 170,600.

Hunts·ville (hŭnts′vĭl). A city of N Alabama; site of a NASA space-flight

center. Pop. 142,300.

Hu·peh (hōō′pā′). Also **Hu·pei.** A province of E central China. Pop. 33,710,000. Cap. Wuhan.

Hu·ron, Lake (hyōōr′ən, -ŏn′). One of the Great Lakes, between E Michigan and S Ontario, Canada.

Hwai·nan (hwī′nän′). A city of E central China. Pop. 350,000.

Hwang Ho (hwäng′ hō′). See **Yellow River.**

Hyde Park (hīd). **1.** A public park occupying 361 acres (146.2 hectares) in central London, England. **2.** A village of SE New York, on the Hudson River; birthplace of President Franklin D. Roosevelt.

Hy·der·a·bad (hī′dər-ə-băd′, -bäd′). **1.** A city of central India. Pop. 1,607,-400. **2.** A city and handicraft center of S Pakistan. Pop. 628,300.

Hy·met·tus (hī-mĕt′əs). A mountain ridge rising to c. 3,370 ft (1,030 m) in E central Greece, near Athens.

I

Ia·şi (yäsh, yä′shē). A commercial center of NE Rumania. Pop. 265,000.

I·ba·dan (ē-bä′dän). A city of SW Nigeria. Pop. 847,000.

I·be·ri·an Peninsula (ī-bîr′ē-ən). Also **I·be·ri·a** (ī-bîr′ē-ə). The region of SW Europe separated from France by the Pyrenees and consisting of Spain and Portugal.

I·bi·za (ē-vē′thä). An island of the Balearic group, Spain, located in the W Mediterranean.

Ice·land (īs′lənd). An island republic in the North Atlantic. Pop. 224,000. Cap. Reykjavík. —**Ice′land·er** n. —**Ice·land′ic** adj.

I·da, Mount (ī′də). The highest mountain (8,058 ft/2,457.7 km) of Crete, in the central part of the island.

I·da·ho (ī′də-hō′). A state of the NW United States. Pop. 943,600. Cap. Boise. —**I′da·ho′an** adj. & n.

I·da·ho Falls (ī′də-hō). A food-shipping center of SE central Idaho. Pop. 39,600.

If·ni (ĕf′nē). A former Spanish possession of SW Morocco, on the Atlantic Ocean.

I·gua·çu (ē-gwä-sōō′). A waterfall on the Iguaçu River, extending 3 mi (4.8 km) and dropping 210 ft (64 m), near the Argentina-Brazil border.

Ijs·sel (ī′səl). Also **IJs·sel.** A river of the E Netherlands, rising at the N mouth of the Rhine and flowing 72 mi (115.8 km) N to the Ijsselmeer.

Ijs·sel·meer (ī′səl-mâr′). Also **IJs·sel·meer.** A lake of the NW Netherlands, formed by the diking of the Zuyder Zee.

Île-de-France (ēl-də-fräns′). A region and former province of N central France.

Il·i·um (ĭl′ē-əm). The Latin name for Troy.

I·llam·pu (ē-yäm′pōō). A peak rising to 20,873 ft (6,366.3 m) in the Cordillera Oriental of W Bolivia.

Il·li·nois (ĭl′ə-noi′, -noiz′). A Midwestern state of the United States. Pop.

11,355,000. Cap. Springfield. —**Il′li·nois′an** adj. & n.

Il·lyr·i·a (ĭ-lîr′ē-ə). An ancient country of S Europe, on the Adriatic. —**Il·lyr′i·an** adj. & n.

I·lo·i·lo (ē′lō-ē′lō). A port city of SE Panay, Philippines. Pop. 248,000.

I·lo·rin (ē′lôr-ēn′, ĭ-lôr′ēn). A city of SW Nigeria. Pop. 282,000.

Im·pe·ri·al Valley (ĭm-pîr′ē-əl). A valley in SE California and NW Mexico.

In·chon (ĭn′chŏn′). A port of NW South Korea. Pop. 800,000.

In·de·pend·ence (ĭn′dĭ-pĕn′dəns). A residential suburb of Kansas City, Missouri. Pop. 111,800.

In·di·a (ĭn′dē-ə). **1.** A subcontinent in S Asia, comprising the Republic of India, Nepal, Bhutan, Sikkim, Pakistan, and Bangladesh. **2.** A republic of S Asia. Pop. 650,982,000. Cap. New Delhi. —**In′di·an** adj. & n.

In·di·an·a (ĭn′dē-ăn′ə). A Midwestern state of the United States. Pop. 5,461,100. Cap. Indianapolis. —**In′di·an′i·an** n. & adj.

In·di·an·ap·o·lis (ĭn′dē-ə-năp′ə-lĭs). The capital of Indiana, in the central part of the state. Pop. 698,700.

Indian Ocean. An ocean bounded by Asia, Antarctica, Africa, and Australia.

Indian River. A lagoon extending 120 mi (193 km) along the coast of E central Florida.

Indian Territory. A former territory in the S central United States, now part of Oklahoma.

In·dies (ĭn′dēz). See **East Indies, West Indies.**

In·do·chi·na (ĭn′dō-chī′nə). The SE peninsula of Asia, including Vietnam, Laos, Cambodia, Thailand, Burma, and the Malay Peninsula. —**In′do·chi′nese′** adj. & n.

In·do·ne·sia (ĭn′də-nē′zhə, -shə). **1.** A republic of SE Asia, comprising the islands of Sumatra, Java, Sulawesi, and the Moluccas, as well as numerous other islands, and Indonesian Timor, Irian Barat on New Guinea, and Kalimantan on Borneo. Pop. 145,100,-000. Cap. Djakarta on Java. **2.** Loosely, the Malay Archipelago. —**In′do·ne′sian** adj. & n.

In·dore (ĭn-dôr′, -dōr′). A textile-manufacturing center of W central India. Pop. 572,600.

In·dus (ĭn′dəs). A river rising in SW Tibet and flowing 1,900 mi (3,060 km) NW through Tibet, then SW through Pakistan to the Arabian Sea.

In·gle·wood (ĭng′gəl-wōōd′). A SW suburb of Los Angeles, California. Pop. 94,100.

Inland Sea (ĭn′lənd). An inlet of the Pacific in SE Japan, between Honshu on the N and Shikoku and Kyushu on the S.

In·ner Mon·go·li·a (ĭn′ər mŏng-gō′lē-ə). Officially, Inner Mongolian Autonomous Region. An administrative division of N China. Pop. 13,000,000. Cap. Huhehot.

Inns·bruck (ĭnz′brŏŏk′). A resort city of SW Austria. Pop. 120,400.

In·side Passage (ĭn-sīd′, ĭn′sīd′). A protected navigation route extending

950 mi (1,530 km) off the coasts of Alaska and British Columbia, Canada, through the islands of the Alexander Archipelago.

In·ter·la·ken (ĭn'tər-lä'kən, ĭn'tər-lä'kən). A resort town of W central Switzerland. Pop. 4,700.

I·o·ni·a (ī-ō'nē-ə). The Aegean coast of W Asia Minor, settled by the Ionians. —I·o'ni·an *adj. & n.*

Ionian Islands. A group of 7 Greek islands in the Ionian Sea, a section of the Mediterranean between S Italy and W Greece.

I·o·wa (ī'ə-wə). A Midwestern state of the United States. Pop. 2,909,500. Cap. Des Moines. —I'o·wan *adj. & n.*

Iowa City. A city of E Iowa, on both sides of the Iowa River. Pop. 50,500.

I·ran (ĭ-răn', ē-răn'). Formerly **Per·sia** (pûr'zhə, -shə). A Moslem republic of SW Asia. Pop. 35,509,000. Cap. Teheran. —I·ra'ni·an *adj. & n.*

I·raq (ĭ-răk', ē-räk'). A republic of SW Asia. Pop. 12,767,000. Cap. Baghdad. —I·raq'i *adj. & n.*

Ire·land (īr'lənd). **1.** One of the British Isles, in the Atlantic W of Britain, divided into the Republic of Ireland and Northern Ireland. **2.** Also **Eir·e** (âr'ə). A republic occupying most of Ireland. Pop. 3,365,000. Cap. Dublin. —I'rish (ī'rĭsh) *adj. & n.*

Irish Sea. The sea between Britain and Ireland.

Ir·kutsk (ĭr-kōōtsk'). A city of S Siberian U.S.S.R. Pop. 532,000.

Ir·ra·wad·dy (ĭr'ə-wä'dē). A river rising in N Burma and flowing 1,350 mi (2,172.1 km) gen. S to its vast delta on the Andaman Sea.

Ir·tysh (ĭr'tĭsh). A river rising in the Altai Mountains of China and flowing c. 2,650 mi (4,265 km) W and NW to the Ob River.

Is·fa·han (ĭs'fə-hän', -hăn'). A city of W central Iran. Pop. 800,000.

Is·lam·a·bad (ĭs-lä'mə-bäd', ĭz-). The capital of Pakistan, in the NE. Pop. 250,000.

Isle Roy·ale (roi'əl). An island of Michigan in NW Lake Superior.

Is·ma·i·li·a (ĭs'mä-ē'lē-ə). A city of NE Egypt, on the Suez Canal. Pop. 167,500.

Is·ra·el (ĭz'rē-əl). A republic, founded in 1948, in Palestine on the E seaboard of the Mediterranean. Pop. 3,800,000. Cap. Jerusalem. —Is·rae'li (ĭz-rä'lē) *adj. & n.*

Is·tan·bul (ĭs'tăn-bōōl', ĭs'tän-). Formerly **Con·stan·ti·no·ple** (kŏn'stăn-tə-nō'pəl). Originally **By·zan·ti·um** (bĭ-zăn'shē-əm, -tē-əm). A city of Turkey, on the European side of the Bosporus and the Sea of Marmara. Pop. 2,534,800.

Is·tri·a (ĭs'trē-ə). Also **Is·tri·an Penin·sula** (-ən). A peninsula in Italy and Yugoslavia, extending S from Trieste into the Adriatic.

It·a·ly (ĭt'ə-lē). A republic of S Europe, projecting into the Mediterranean Sea. Pop. 56,954,000. Cap. Rome. —I·tal'ian (ĭ-tăl'yən) *adj. & n.*

I·tas·ca (ī-tăs'kə). A lake in NW central Minnesota; a source of the Mississippi.

Ith·a·ca (ĭth'ə-kə). An island of Greece, in the Ionian Sea.

I·va·no·vo (ĭ-vä'nô-vô). An industrial center of central European U.S.S.R. Pop. 458,000.

I·vo·ry Coast (ī'və-rē, ī'vrē). A republic of W Africa on the Gulf of Guinea between Ghana and Liberia. Pop. 7,040,000. Cap. Abidjan.

I·wo (ē'wō). A city of SW Nigeria, near Ibadan. Pop. 192,000.

Iwo Ji·ma (jē'mə). The largest of the Volcano Islands in the W Pacific; captured by the U.S. in World War II; returned to Japan in 1968.

I·zhevsk (ē'zhĭfsk). A city of E European U.S.S.R. Pop. 534,100.

Iz·mir (ĭz-mîr'). Formerly **Smyr·na** (smûr'nə). A port city of W Turkey. Pop. 636,100.

J

Ja·bal·pur (jŭb'əl-pôr'). A city of central India. Pop. 533,700.

Jack·son (jăk'sən). The capital of Mississippi, on the Pearl River. Pop. 200,700.

Jack·son·ville (jăk'sən-vĭl'). A city of N Florida. Pop. 541,300.

Jaf·fa (jăf'ə, yä'fə). A seaport of W central Israel, constituting with Tel Aviv a municipality. Combined pop. 343,300.

Jai·pur (jī'pōōr'). A city of W India. Pop. 613,100.

Ja·kar·ta (jə-kär'tə). See Djakarta.

Ja·la·pa (hä-lä'pä). A city of E central Mexico. Pop. 161,400.

Ja·mai·ca (jə-mā'kə). An independent island in the Caribbean, S of Cuba. Pop. 2,133,000. Cap. Kingston. —Ja·mai'can *n. & adj.*

James Bay (jāmz). An arm of Hudson Bay extending S between Ontario and Quebec, Canada.

James River. A river rising in W Virginia and flowing 340 mi (547 km) gen. E to Hampton Roads.

James·town (jāmz'toun). The 1st permanent English settlement in the New World, founded in 1607 and now a restored village on the James River in Virginia.

Ja·pan (jə-păn'). A country of Asia, occupying an archipelago off the NE coast of the continent and comprising the main islands of Hokkaido, Honshu, Shikoku, and Kyushu, with numerous smaller islands. Pop. 115,870,000. Cap. Tokyo, on Honshu. —Jap'a·nese' (-nēz', -nēs') *adj. & n.*

Japan, Sea of. That part of the Pacific Ocean between Japan and the Asian mainland.

Japan Current. A warm ocean current flowing NE from the Philippine Sea past SE Japan on the North Pacific.

Ja·va (jä'və, jăv'ə). An island of Indonesia between the Indian Ocean and the Java Sea. —Jav'a·nese' (-nēz', -nēs') *adj. & n.*

Java Sea. The part of the Pacific Ocean between the islands of Java and Borneo.

Je·bel Mu·sa (jĕb'əl mōō'sə). A

mountain 2,790 ft (850.9 m) high in N Morocco on the Strait of Gibraltar; 1 of the Pillars of Hercules.

Jef·fer·son City (jĕf'ər-sən). The capital of Missouri, in the center of the state on the Missouri River. Pop. 33,800.

Je·rez (hĕ-rāth'). A city of Spain, in the SW. Pop. 149,900.

Jer·i·cho (jĕr'ĭ-kō'). **1.** An ancient city of Jordan, situated at 800 ft (244 m) below sea level near the N end of the Dead Sea. **2.** A modern village on the site of ancient Jericho.

Jer·sey (jûr'zē). The largest of the Channel Islands in the English Channel.

Jersey City. A city of New Jersey, a river port on the Hudson in the NE. Pop. 222,800.

Je·ru·sa·lem (jə-rōō'sə-ləm, -zə-ləm). The capital of ancient and modern Israel, regarded as holy by Jews, Christians, and Moslems. Pop. 344,200.

Jid·da (jĭd'ə). Also **Jid·dah.** A port city of W central Saudi Arabia. Pop. 561,100.

João Pes·so·a (zhwoun' pĕ-sô'ä). A city of NE Brazil. Pop. 197,400.

Jodh·pur (jŏd'pŏŏr'). A city and former principality in NW India. Pop. 318,900.

Jo·han·nes·burg (jō-hăn'ĭs-bûrg', yō-hä'nĭs-). The largest city of the Republic of South Africa, in S Transvaal. Pop. 654,200.

Johns·town (jŏnz'toun'). A city of SW central Pennsylvania. Pop. 35,400.

Jo·li·et (jō'lē-ĕt', jō'lē-ĕt'). A city of NE Illinois. Pop. 78,100.

Jor·dan (jôrd'n). The principal river of Israel and Jordan, flowing 200 mi (321.8 km) SW from extreme N Israel through the Sea of Galilee to the Dead Sea.

Jordan, Hash·e·mite Kingdom of (hăsh'ə-mīt'). A kingdom in NW Arabia. Pop. 2,984,000. Cap. Amman. —Jor·da'ni·an (jôr-dā'nē-ən) *adj. & n.*

Juan de Fu·ca Strait (hwän' də fōō'kə). An inlet of the Pacific between NW Washington State and Vancouver Island, British Columbia, Canada.

Juan Fer·nán·dez Islands (fər-năn'dēz). A group of 3 volcanic islands of Chile, in the Pacific, 400 mi (643.6 km) W of Valparaiso.

Ju·dah (jōō'də). An ancient kingdom in S Palestine.

Ju·de·a (jōō-dē'ə). Also **Ju·dae·a.** The Greco-Roman name for S Palestine. —Ju·de'an, also Ju·dae'an *adj. & n.*

Juiz de Fo·ra (zhwēzh' də fôr'ə, fôr'ə). A city of SE Brazil. Pop. 238,000.

Ju·neau (jōō'nō). The capital of Alaska, in the SE near the border of British Columbia, Canada. Pop. 19,500.

Jung·frau (yōong'frou'). A mountain rising to 13,653 ft (4,164 m) in the Bernese Alps, in Switzerland.

Ju·ra (jŏŏr'ə, zhŏŏ-rä', yŏŏ'rä). A mountain range, part of the Alpine system, extending through E France and NW Switzerland; highest elevation, Crêt de la Neige (5,652 ft/1,723 m).

ă pat   ā pay   â care   ä father   ĕ pet   ē be   hw which   ĭ pit   ī tie   î pier   ŏ pot   ō toe   ô paw, for   oi noise
ŏŏ took   ōō boot   ou out   th thin   *th* this   ŭ cut   û urge   zh vision   ə about, item, edible, gallop, circus

Jut·land (jŭt′lənd). A peninsula of N Europe, comprising mainland Denmark in the N and Schleswig-Holstein, West Germany, in the S.

K

K2. See **Godwin Austen.**

Ka·bul (kä′bŏŏl). The capital of Afghanistan, on the Kabul River in the E central part of the country. Pop. 604,000.

Kae·song (kā′sŏng). A city of SW North Korea. Pop. 140,000.

Ka·go·shi·ma (kä′gō-shē′mä). A port city in S Kyushu, Japan. Pop. 468,600.

Kai·feng (kī′fŭng′). The capital of Honan, China, in the NE. Pop. 330,000.

Ka·la·ha·ri Desert (kä′lə-här′ē). An arid plateau in S Africa extending over W Botswana and E Namibia.

Kal·a·ma·zoo (kăl′ə-mə-zōō′). A city of SW Michigan. Pop. 79,800.

Ka·li·man·tan (kä′lē-män′tän′). The Indonesian sector of Borneo.

Ka·li·nin (kä-lē′nĭn). A port city in central European U.S.S.R., at the confluence of the Volga and Tver rivers. Pop. 395,000.

Ka·li·nin·grad (kə-lē′nĭn-grăd). Formerly **Kö·nigs·berg** (kŏŏn′ĭgz-bûrg′). A port city of W European U.S.S.R., formerly the capital of East Prussia. Pop. 345,000.

Ka·lu·ga (kä-lōō′gä). A city of central European U.S.S.R. Pop. 255,000.

Kam·chat·ka (kăm-chăt′kə). A peninsula of NE Siberia, between the Sea of Okhotsk and the Bering Sea.

Ka·met (kŭm′ät′). A mountain 25,447 ft (7,761.3 m) high, in the Himalayas on the Indian-Tibetan border.

Kam·pa·la (kăm-pä′lə). The capital of Uganda, in the E on Lake Victoria. Pop. 380,000.

Ka·nan·ga (kə-näng′gə). A city of central Zaire. Pop. 601,200.

Ka·na·za·wa (kä′nə-zä′wə, kə-nä′zə-wə). A port city of W central Honshu, Japan. Pop. 400,400.

Kan·chen·jun·ga (kŭn′chən-jŭng′gə). The 3rd highest mountain in the world (28,146 ft/8,584.5 m), in the Himalayas of Nepal.

Kan·da·har (kăn′də-här′). A city of SE Afghanistan. Pop. 140,000.

Kan·dy (kăn′dē). A city of Sri Lanka, formerly the capital, in the center of the country. Pop. 93,600.

Kan·pur (kän′pŏŏr). A city of N central India. Pop. 1,154,400.

Kan·sas (kăn′zəs). A state of the central United States. Pop. 2,356,000. Cap. Topeka. —**Kan′san** (kăn′zən) *adj & n.*

Kan·sas City (kăn′zəs). **1.** A city of NE Kansas. Pop. 160,000. **2.** A city of NW Missouri, across the Missouri River from Kansas City, Kansas. Pop. 446,900.

Kan·su (kăn′sōō′). A province of N central China. Pop. 13,000,000. Cap. Lanchou.

Kao·hsiung (gou′shyōōng′). A port city of SW Taiwan. Pop. 1,002,000.

Ka·ra·chi (kə-rä′chē). A seaport of SE Pakistan, on the Arabian Sea; formerly the capital (1948–59). Pop. 3,498,600.

Ka·ra·gan·da (kăr′ə-gən-dä′). A city of Central Asian U.S.S.R. Pop. 576,000.

Kar·a·kor·am (kăr′ə-kōr′əm). A mountain range of N Kashmir, along the border with China; highest elevation, Godwin Austen (28,250 ft/8,616.2 m).

Ka·ra Sea (kär′ə). An arm of the Arctic Ocean off the NW coast of the Soviet Union, between the Barents and Laptev seas.

Karl-Marx-Stadt (kärl-märks′shtät′). A city of S East Germany. Pop. 303,800.

Kar·lo·vy Va·ry (kär′lō-vē vä′rē). Also **Karls·bad** (kärls′bät′). A health resort of NW Czechoslovakia. Pop. 50,400.

Karls·ru·he (kärls′rōō′ə). A port of SW West Germany, on the Rhine. Pop. 280,400.

Kar·nak (kär′năk). A village on the Nile in E central Egypt, on part of the site once occupied by Thebes.

Kar·roo (kə-rōō′, kä-). A vast tableland of South Africa.

Kash·gar (kăsh′gär). A trade city of W China. Pop. 175,000.

Kash·mir (kăsh′mîr, kăsh-mîr′). A former princely state in NW India and NE Pakistan; its control has been in dispute since 1949.

Kas·sel (kä′sĕl). An industrial center of E West Germany. Pop. 210,000.

Ka·thi·a·war (kä′tē-ä-wär′). A peninsula of NW India, projecting into the Arabian Sea.

Kat·mai National Monument (kăt′mī). An area on the N end of the Alaska Peninsula, containing the Valley of Ten Thousand Smokes and the active Katmai Volcano (7,000 ft/2,135 m).

Kat·man·du (kăt′män-dōō′). The capital of Nepal, in a valley of the Himalayas SW of Mount Everest. Pop. 105,400.

Ka·to·wi·ce (kä′tō-vēt′sĕ). A city of S Poland. Pop. 343,700.

Kat·te·gat (kăt′ə-gät′). A strait of the North Sea between E Jutland, Denmark, and SW Sweden.

Kau·ai (kou′ī). An island of Hawaii, NW of Oahu.

Kau·nas (kou′näs′). A city of S central Lithuania. Pop. 352,000.

Ka·wa·sa·ki (kä′wə-sä′kē). A city of Japan, on the W shore of Tokyo Bay in central Honshu. Pop. 1,014,900.

Ka·zakh Soviet Socialist Republic (kə-zäk′). Also **Ka·zakh·stan** (kə-zäk′stän′). A constituent republic of S Central Asian U.S.S.R. Pop. 12,850,000. Cap. Alma-Ata.

Ka·zan (kə-zän′). A city of E European U.S.S.R., on the Volga. Pop. 970,000.

Kee·wa·tin (kē-wät′n). A district in the E Northwest Territories, Canada.

Ke·me·ro·vo (kě′mě-rō′vō). A city of central Siberian U.S.S.R. Pop. 446,000.

Ke·nai Peninsula (kē′nī). A peninsula in S central Alaska.

Ke·ni·tra (kə-nē′trə). A port city of NW Morocco. Pop. 139,200.

Ken·ne·saw Mountain (kĕn′ə-sô). A lone peak, 1,809 ft (551.7 m) high, in NW Georgia; site of a Civil War battle during Sherman's drive on Atlanta (1864).

Ke·no·sha (kə-nō′shə). A city of SE Wisconsin. Pop. 77,800.

Ken·tuck·y (kən-tŭk′ē). A state of the E central United States. Pop. 3,642,800. Cap. Frankfort. —**Ken·tuck′i·an** *adj. & n.*

Ken·ya (kĕn′yə, kēn′-). A republic in E central Africa. Pop. 15,322,000. Cap. Nairobi. —**Ken′yan** *adj. & n.*

Kenya, Mount. An extinct volcano (17,040 ft/5,197.2 m) in central Kenya.

Key West (kē wĕst′). A port and resort city of S Florida. Pop. 17,900.

Kha·ba·rovsk (kə-bär′əfsk). A city of Far Eastern U.S.S.R. Pop. 524,000.

Khar·kov (kär′kôf, -kôv′). A city of S European U.S.S.R. Pop. 1,444,000.

Khar·toum (kär-tōōm′). The capital of Sudan, in the E central part of the country at the confluence of the Blue Nile and the White Nile. Pop. 321,700.

Kher·son (кнĕr′sôn′). A city of S European U.S.S.R. Pop. 315,000.

Khul·na (kōōl′nə). A city of SW Bangladesh. Pop. 437,300.

Khy·ber Pass (kī′bər). A pass extending for c. 30 mi (48.2 km) through the mountains between Afghanistan and Pakistan.

Kiang·si (jyäng′sē′). A province of China, in the SE. Pop. 22,000,000. Cap. Nanchang.

Kiang·su (jyäng′sōō′). A province in E central China. Pop. 47,000,000. Cap. Nanking.

Kiel (kēl). A seaport of N West Germany, on the Baltic at the head of the Kiel Canal, an artificial waterway connecting the North Sea with the Baltic. Pop. 264,300.

Kiel·ce (kyĕlt′sĕ). A city of SE Poland. Pop. 151,200.

Ki·ev (kē-ĕv′, kē′ĕf′). The capital of the Ukrainian S.S.R., SW European U.S.S.R. Pop. 2,144,000.

Ki·ga·li (kĭ-gä′lē). The capital of Rwanda, in the central part of the country. Pop. 60,000.

Ki·lau·e·a (kē′lou-ā′ə). A large, active volcanic crater on Mauna Loa, Hawaii.

Kil·i·man·ja·ro (kĭl′ə-mən-jär′ō). The highest mountain (19,565 ft/5,967.3 m) in Africa, in NE Tanzania near the border with Kenya.

Kil·lar·ney (kĭ-lär′nē). A town in SW Republic of Ireland. Pop. 7,200.

Kim·ber·ley (kĭm′bər-lē). A diamond-mining center of central South Africa. Pop. 105,300.

Kings·ton (kĭngz′tən). **1.** The capital of Jamaica, a seaport on the SE coast. Pop. 600,000. **2.** A city of S Ontario, Canada. Pop. 56,000.

Kings·town (kĭngz′toun′). The capital of St. Vincent, West Indies, a seaport on the SW coast. Pop. 17,300.

Kin·sha·sa (kēn-shä′sə). The capital of Zaire, in the W part of the country on the Congo River. Pop. 2,008,300.

Kir·ghiz Soviet Socialist Republic (kîr-gēz′). Also **Kir·giz S.S.R.** A constituent republic of the Soviet Union, in the S on the Chinese border. Pop. 3,368,000. Cap. Frunze.

Ki·ri·ba·ti (kĭr'ĭ-bä'tē). Formerly **Gilbert Islands** (gĭl'bərt). A republic comprising 33 Micronesian islands in the central Pacific Ocean. The equator runs through the center of the group. Pop. 57,000. Cap. Tarawa.

Ki·rin (kē'rĭn'). A province of China, in the NE. Pop. 17,000,000. Cap. Changchun.

Kir·kuk (kĭr-kōōk'). A city of NE Iraq, in an oil-bearing region. Pop. 207,900.

Ki·rov (kē'rəf). A city of central European U.S.S.R. Pop. 376,000.

Ki·ro·va·bad (kĭ-rō'və-băd). A city of SE European U.S.S.R. Pop. 211,000.

Ki·san·ga·ni (kē'säng-gä'nē). Formerly **Stan·ley·ville** (stăn'lē-vĭl'). A city of NE Zaire. Pop. 310,700.

Ki·shi·nev (kĭsh'ĭ-něf', kĭ-shĭ-nyôf'). The capital of the Moldavian S.S.R., SW European U.S.S.R. Pop. 489,000.

Ki·ta·ky·u·shu (kē'tä-kyōō'shōō). A city of N Kyushu, Japan. Pop. 1,068,000.

Kitch·e·ner (kĭch'ə-nər). A city of S Ontario, Canada. Pop. 280,100.

Kit·ty Hawk (kĭt'ē hôk). A village in NE North Carolina; site of the 1st successful flight of a power-driven airplane, made by Orville and Wilbur Wright (1903).

Klon·dike (klŏn'dīk'). A region in the Yukon Territory, NW Canada; the site of abundant gold deposits on both sides of the Klondike River, a tributary of the Yukon.

Knos·sos (nŏs'əs). A city of ancient Crete, metropolis of the Minoan civilization.

Knox·ville (nŏks'vĭl'). A city of E Tennessee. Pop. 182,200.

Ko·be (kō'bē, -bā'). A city of Japan, on Osaka Bay in S Honshu. Pop. 1,360,600.

Ko·chi (kō'chē). A seaport of S central Shikoku, Japan. Pop. 286,600.

Ko·di·ak (kō'dē-ăk). An island in the Gulf of Alaska, SE of the Alaska Peninsula.

Ko·ko·mo (kō'kə-mō'). A city of N central Indiana. Pop. 47,100.

Ko·la Peninsula (kō'lə). A peninsula of the Soviet Union, in the NW between the White and Barents seas.

Ko·lar (kō-lär'). A city and gold-mining center of SW India. Pop. 43,300.

Kol·ha·pur (kō'lə-pōōr). A city of SW India. Pop. 259,100.

Ko·lom·na (kə-lôm'nä). A city of central European U.S.S.R. Pop. 144,000.

Kö·nigs·berg (kœ'nĭgz-bûrg'). See Kaliningrad.

Kon·ya (kôn-yä'). A city of S central Turkey. Pop. 246,400.

Koo·te·nay (kōōt'n-ā'). Also **Koo·te·nai.** A river rising in SE British Columbia, Canada, and flowing c. 450 mi (724 km) S into Montana and then N through Idaho and back into British Columbia, passing through Lake Kootenay to the Columbia River.

Ko·re·a (kə-rē'ə, kō-). A former country occupying a peninsula of E central Asia, opposite Japan, divided since

1948 into 2 political entities: the **People's Democratic Republic of Korea** (unofficially, North Korea), with a pop. of 17,072,000 and its cap. at Pyongyang; and the **Republic of Korea** (unofficially, South Korea), with a pop. of 37,605,000 and its cap. at Seoul. —**Ko·re'an** *adj. & n.*

Korea Bay. An inlet of the Yellow Sea between mainland China and NW North Korea.

Kos·ci·us·ko, Mount (kŏs'ē-ŭs'kō). The highest mountain (7,316 ft/2,231.4 m) of Australia, in SE New South Wales.

Kos·tro·ma (kə-strə-mä', kŏs'trə-). A city of E European U.S.S.R. Pop. 247,000.

Kow·loon (kou'lōōn'). A city of Hong Kong, on Kowloon Peninsula opposite Hong Kong Island. Pop. 729,000.

Kra·ka·to·a (krăk'ə-tō'ə). A small volcanic island of Indonesia between Java and Sumatra, virtually obliterated in 1883 by explosive eruptions.

Kra·ków (krä'kou', krăk'ou', krä'kō'). A city in S Poland. Pop. 693,800.

Kras·no·dar (krăs'nə-där). A port city of SE European U.S.S.R., on the Kuban River. Pop. 552,000.

Kras·no·yarsk (krăs'nə-yärsk'). A city of W Siberian U.S.S.R., on the Yenisei. Pop. 769,000.

Kre·feld (krā'fĕlt). A city of W West Germany, on the Rhine. Pop. 231,600.

Kri·voy Rog (krĭv'oi rôg', rôk'). A city of SW European U.S.S.R., in the Ukraine. Pop. 641,000.

Kru·ger National Park (krōō'gər). An 8,000-sq mi (20,720 sq km) wildlife preserve in NE South Africa.

Kua·la Lum·pur (kwä'lə lōōm'pōōr'). The capital of Malaysia, in the S part of the Malay Peninsula. Pop. 451,800.

Kui·by·shev (kwē'bə-shĕf', -shĕv'). A city of E central European U.S.S.R., on the Volga. Pop. 1,216,000.

Ku·ma·mo·to (kōō'mə-mō'tō). A seaport of W central Kyushu, Japan. Pop. 495,800.

Ku·ma·si (kōō-mä'sē). A city of Ghana, the historic capital of the Ashanti kingdom, NW of Accra. Pop. 260,300.

Kun·lun (kōōn'lōōn'). A mountain system of W China, between Tibet and the Sinkiang-Uigur Autonomous Region; highest elevation, Ulugh Muztagh (25,340 ft/7,728.7 m).

Kun·ming (kōōn'mĭng'). The capital of Yünnan, SW China. Pop. 1,700,000.

Kurd·i·stan (kûr'dĭ-stăn', kōōr'dĭ-stän'). A plateau and mountain region of SW Asia, comprising SE Turkey and parts of Iraq and Iran.

Ku·re (kōō'rĕ). A city of S Honshu, Japan. Pop. 242,000.

Ku·rile Islands (kōōr'īl, kōō-rēl', -rĭl'). Also **Ku·ril Islands.** A chain of islands of the Soviet Union, between Kamchatka and N Hokkaido, Japan. —**Ku·ril'i·an** *adj. & n.*

Kursk (kōōrsk). A city of central European U.S.S.R. Pop. 363,000.

Ku·wait (kōō-wāt', -wĭt'). **1.** A republic on the Arabian Peninsula at the head of the Persian Gulf. Pop. 1,272,-000. **2.** The capital of Kuwait. Pop. 108,200.

Kuz·netsk Basin (kōōz-nĕtsk'). A coal-producing region of the S central Russian S.F.S.R.

Kwang·ju (gwäng'jōō'). A city of SW South Korea. Pop. 607,000.

Kwang·tung (gwäng'dōōng'). A province of SE China. Pop. 40,000,000. Cap. Canton.

Kwei·chow (gwā'jō'). A province of SW China. Pop. 17,000,000. Cap. Kweiyang.

Kwei·yang (gwā'yäng'). The capital of Kweichow, SW China. Pop. 1,500,000.

Kyo·to (kyō'tō, kē-ō'-). An industrial center of Japan, in S Honshu; the capital of Japan until 1868. Pop. 1,461,100.

Kyu·shu (kyōō'shōō). The southernmost of the 4 main islands of Japan.

L

Lab·ra·dor (lăb'rə-dôr). **1.** A peninsula of NE Canada, between Newfoundland and Quebec, where the N section is known as Ungava Peninsula. **2.** The mainland territory of Newfoundland, Canada.

Labrador Current. A cold ocean current flowing S from Baffin Bay along the coast of Labrador and turning E after intersecting with the Gulf Stream.

La·co·ni·a (lə-kō'nē-ə). An ancient region of the Peloponnesus of which Sparta was the metropolis.

La·do·ga (lăd'ə-gə, lä'də-). The largest lake in Europe in the NW European U.S.S.R.

La·gos (lā'gŏs', -gəs). The capital of Nigeria, a seaport on the S on the Gulf of Guinea. Pop. 1,060,900.

La Hague, Cape (lə hāg'). A promontory of NW France.

La·hore (lə-hôr', -hōr'). A city of NE Pakistan. Pop. 2,165,400.

Lake District (lāk). An area in NW England, noted for its scenery and many lakes.

Lake·wood (lāk'wŏŏd'). A city of SW California. Pop. 74,400.

La·na·i (lä-nä'ē). An island of Hawaii, W of Maui.

Lan·chou (län'jō'). The capital of Kansu, N central China. Pop. 1,500,000.

Langue·doc (läng-dôk'). A former province of S France, now a leading wine-producing region.

Lan·sing (lăn'sĭng). The capital of Michigan, in the S central part of the state. Pop. 130,200.

La·nús (lä-nōōs'). A city of E Argentina. Pop. 449,800.

La·os (lā'ŏs, lous, lä'ŏs'). A country of SE Asia. Pop. 3,546,000. Cap. Vientiane.

La Paz (lə päz', päz'). The administrative capital of Bolivia. Pop. 660,700.

Lap·land (lăp'lănd'). A region of N Scandinavia, Finland, and the NW Soviet Union.

La Pla·ta (lä plä'tä). A city of E central Argentina. Pop. 408,300.

Las Pal·mas (läs päl'mäs). A city of the Canary Islands, on the NE coast

---

of Grand Canary Island. Pop. 166,000.

La Spe·zia (lä spä'tsyä). A city of NW Italy. Pop. 128,000.

Las Ve·gas (läs vā'gəs). A city of SE Nevada. Pop. 162,900.

La·ta·ki·a (lăt'ə-kē'ə). A city of Syria, a Mediterranean seaport opposite Cyprus. Pop. 191,300.

Lat·in A·mer·i·ca (lăt'ən ə-měr'ĭ-kə). The countries of the Western Hemisphere S of the United States. **—Lat'·in-A·mer'i·can** adj.

Latin Quarter. A section of Paris on the S bank of the Seine.

La·ti·um (lā'shē-əm). An ancient country in W central Italy.

Lat·vi·a (lăt'vē-ə). Officially, Latvian Soviet Socialist Republic. A constituent republic of NW European U.S.S.R. Pop. 2,497,000. Cap. Riga. **—Lat'vi·an** adj. & n.

Lau·ren·tian Plateau (lə-rĕn'shən). A Precambrian plateau extending over half of Canada from Labrador SW around Hudson Bay and NW to the Arctic Ocean.

La·val (lə-văl'). A city, coextensive with Île-Jésus, S Quebec, Canada. Pop. 246,200.

Leb·a·non (lĕb'ə-nən). A republic between Syria and Israel on the E shore of the Mediterranean. Pop. 3,012,000. Cap. Beirut. **—Leb'a·nese'** (-nēz', -nēs') adj. & n.

Leeds (lēdz). A textile-manufacturing center of N central England. Pop. 744,500.

Leg·horn (lĕg'hôrn). A city of NW Italy, on the Ligurian Sea. Pop. 173,800.

Le Ha·vre (lə hä'vrə). A port city of N France. Pop. 217,000.

Leices·ter (lĕs'tər). A city of central England. Pop. 289,400.

Lei·den (līd'n). Also **Ley·den.** A city of the SW Netherlands. Pop. 100,100.

Leip·zig (līp'sĭg, -sĭk). A city of S central East Germany. Pop. 565,400.

Le Mans (lə mäN'). A city of W central France. Pop. 129,000.

Lem·nos (lĕm'nŏs). An island of Greece, in the Aegean NW of Lesbos.

Le·na (lē'nə, lā'-). A river of the Soviet Union, rising in Lake Baykal in S Siberia, and flowing 2,670 mi (4,295 km) gen. N to the Laptev Sea.

Len·in·grad (lĕn'ĭn-grăd'). Formerly Saint Pe·ters·burg (sānt pē'tərz-bûrg') (1703–1914), Pet·ro·grad (pĕt'rō-grăd') (1914–24). A port city of NW European U.S.S.R. Pop. 4,588,000.

Le·ón (lā-ôn'). **1.** A city of NW Spain, the capital of the ancient kingdom of Leon. Pop. 113,300. **2.** A city of central Mexico. Pop. 496,500. **3.** A city W of Nicaragua, the former capital of Nicaragua (1570–1855). Pop. 54,800.

Les·bos (lĕz'bŏs, -bŏs). An island of Greece in the Aegean off the W coast of Turkey.

Le·so·tho (lə-sō'tō). A kingdom of S Africa within the Republic of South Africa; formerly a British protectorate. Pop. 1,279,000.

Les·ser An·til·les (lĕs'ər ăn-tĭl'ēz). An island group in the West Indies extending in an arc from Curaçao to the Virgin Islands.

Le·vant (lə-vănt'). The countries bordering on the E Mediterranean.

Lev·it·town (lĕv'ĭt-toun'). An urban area on SE Long Island, New York State.

Lew·is·ton (lōō'ĭ-stən). A city of Maine, on the Androscoggin River in the SW. Pop. 40,500.

Lew·is with Har·ris (lōō'ĭs; hăr'ĭs). The largest and northernmost island of the Outer Hebrides, Scotland.

Lex·ing·ton (lĕk'sĭng-tən). **1.** A city of N central Kentucky. Pop. 203,100. **2.** A suburb of Boston, Massachusetts; the site of an armed encounter of Minutemen and British soldiers that started the American Revolution (Apr. 19, 1775). Pop. 29,500.

Ley·den (līd'n). See **Leiden.**

Ley·te (lā'tē, -tā). An island of the Philippines, in the Visayan group N of Mindanao.

Lha·sa (lä'sə, läs'ə). The capital of Tibet, in SW China, in the SE at an altitude of 12,050 ft (3,675 m). Pop. 175,000.

Liao·ning (lyou'nĭng'). A province of NE China. Pop. 28,000,000. Cap. Shenyang.

Li·be·ri·a (lī-bîr'ē-ə). A republic of Africa, on the Gulf of Guinea; founded by freed U.S. slaves in 1847. Pop. 1,742,000. Cap. Monrovia. **—Li·be'ri·an** adj. & n.

Lib·er·ty Island (lĭb'ər-tē). An island in New York Bay; the site of the Statue of Liberty.

Li·bre·ville (lē'brə-vēl'). The capital of Gabon, a seaport in the NW on the Gulf of Guinea. Pop. 57,000.

Lib·y·a (lĭb'ē-ə). A country of N Africa. Pop. 2,580,000. Cap. Tripoli. **—Lib'y·an** adj. & n.

Libyan Desert. The NE part of the Sahara.

Liech·ten·stein (lĭκH'tən-shtīn'). A principality in central Europe between Austria and Switzerland. Pop. 25,000. Cap. Vaduz.

Li·ège (lē-ĕzh', -āzh'). A city of E Belgium, a river port on the Meuse. Pop. 221,400.

Li·gu·ri·a (lī-gyŏor'ē-ə). A region of Italy, along the NW coast. **—Li·gu'ri·an** adj. & n.

Li·kasi (lī-kä'sē). A city of SE Zaire. Pop. 146,400.

Lille (lēl). A major textile-producing center of N France. Pop. 172,300.

Li·long·we (lē-lông'wä'). A city of S central Malawi, the capital since 1966. Pop. 75,000.

Li·ma (lē'mə). **1.** The capital and largest city of Peru, in the W central part of the country. Pop. 2,981,292. **2.** A city of NW Ohio. Pop. 54,000.

Lin·coln (lĭng'kən). The capital of Nebraska, in the SE. Pop. 171,800.

Line Islands (līn). A group of islands in the Pacific Ocean S of Hawaii and on the equator.

Lip·a·ri Islands (lĭp'ə-rē). A group of islands of Italy, in the Tyrrhenian Sea off the NE coast of Sicily.

Lis·bon (lĭz'bən). The capital of Portugal, a port on the Tagus River estuary. Pop. 829,900.

Lith·u·a·ni·a (lĭth'ōō-ā'nē-ə). Offi-cially, Lithuanian Soviet Socialist Republic. A constituent republic of W European U.S.S.R., formerly independent (1918–40). Pop. 3,129,000. Cap. Vilnius. **—Lith'u·a·ni·an** adj. & n.

Lit·tle Big·horn (lĭt'l bĭg'hôrn'). A river rising in N Wyoming and flowing N c. 90 mi (144.8 km) to join the Bighorn in S Montana; on its shores Custer and his men were defeated by Indians (1876).

Little Rock (rŏk). The capital of Arkansas, on the Arkansas River in the center of the state. Pop. 153,800.

Liv·er·pool (lĭv'ər-pōōl). A port city of NW England. Pop. 536,700. **—Liv'er·pud'li·an** (-pŭd'lē-ən) adj. & n.

Li·vo·ni·a (lə-vō'nē-ə). A region of the Soviet Union comprising S Latvia and N Estonia.

Lju·blja·na (lyōō'blyä-nä'). A city of NW Yugoslavia. Pop. 300,000.

Lla·no Es·ta·ca·do (län'ō ĕs'tə-kä'dō, lä'nō). A section of the Great Plains, in SE New Mexico and NW Texas.

Łódź (lōōj). A city of central Poland. Pop. 804,300.

Lo·fo·ten Islands (lō'fōt'n). An island group of Norway, off the NW coast.

Lo·gan, Mount (lō'gən). The highest (19,850 ft/6,054.3 m) of the St. Elias Mountains, in the SW Yukon Territory, Canada.

Loire (lwär). The longest river of France, rising in the SE and flowing 625 mi (1,005.6 km) NW to the Bay of Biscay.

Lom·bar·dy (lŏm'bər-dē, lŭm'-). A region in N Italy.

Lo·mé (lō-mā'). The capital of Togo, in the S on the Gulf of Guinea. Pop. 148,400.

Lo·mond, Loch (lō'mənd). A lake in E central Scotland.

Lon·don (lŭn'dən). **1.** The capital of England and of the United Kingdom, on the Thames in SE England. Pop. 7,028,200. **2.** A city in S Ontario, Canada. Pop. 274,100.

Lon·don·der·ry (lŭn'dən-dĕr'ē). A city of Northern Ireland. Pop. 130,300.

Long Beach (lông). A city of SW California. Pop. 356,900.

Long Island. An island adjacent to and including sections of New York City.

Long Island Sound. An arm of the Atlantic Ocean between Long Island and Connecticut.

Lo·rain (lō-rān', lō-). A port city of N Ohio. Pop. 74,600.

Lor·raine (lō-rān', lō-). A region and former province of E France, ceded to Germany in 1871 and returned to France in 1919.

Los A·la·mos (lôs ăl'ə-mōs', lŏs). A town in N New Mexico; site of a research center where the 1st atomic bomb was developed. Pop. 11,000.

Los An·ge·les (lôs ăn'jə-ləs, -lēz', lŏs). A city of SW California, the largest city in the state and the 3rd largest in the United States. Pop. 2,952,500.

Lou·i·si·an·a (lōō-ē'zē-ăn'ə). A state of the S United States. Pop. 4,199,500. Cap. Baton Rouge.

Louisiana Purchase. The territory extending W from the Mississippi to the Rocky Mountains between the Mexican and Canadian borders, purchased by the United States from France in 1803 for $15,000,000.

Lou·is·ville (lōo'ē-vǐl'). A city of N Kentucky. Pop. 298,300.

Lourdes (lōord). A town at the foot of the Pyrenees in SW France; site of a religious shrine. Pop. 17,900.

Low Countries. The region of W Europe occupied by Belgium, the Netherlands, and Luxembourg.

Low·ell (lō'əl). A city of NE Massachusetts. Pop. 92,200.

Low·lands, The (lō'ləndz). The lowlands of E and S Scotland.

Lo·yang (lō'yäng'). A city of E China. Pop. 750,000.

Lu·an·da (lōo-ǎn'də). The capital of Angola, a seaport in the W on the Atlantic. Pop. 540,000.

Lub·bock (lǔb'ək). A city of NW Texas, in the center of a rich oil-producing region. Pop. 174,200.

Lü·beck (lōo'běk). A city of N West Germany. Pop. 234,500.

Lu·blin (lōo'blǐn, -blēn'). A city in SE Poland. Pop. 272,000.

Lu·bum·ba·shi (lōo'bŏom-bä'shē). Formerly **E·lis·a·beth·ville** (ǐ-lǐz'ə-bəth-vǐl'). A city of Zaire, in the SE near Zambia. Pop. 403,600.

Lu·cerne (lōo-sûrn'). A city of NW Switzerland. Pop. 69,900.

Lucerne, Lake of. A lake in central Switzerland.

Luck·now (lǔk'nou). A city of N central India. Pop. 750,500.

Lud·hi·a·na (lōod'hē-ä'nə). A city of NW India. Pop. 401,100.

Lu·sa·ka (lōo-sä'kə). The capital of Zambia, in the SE central part of the country. Pop. 559,000.

Lux·em·bourg (lǔk'səm-bûrg'). Also **Lux·em·burg.** 1. A constitutional monarchy and grand duchy in W Europe. Pop. 358,000. 2. Also **Luxembourg City.** The capital of Luxembourg. Pop. 78,400.

Lu·zon (lōo-zǒn'). The largest island of the Philippines, at the N end of the archipelago.

Lvov (lə-vôf', -vôv'). A city of SW European U.S.S.R. Pop. 642,000.

Ly·all·pur (lī'əl-pōor'). A city of NE Pakistan. Pop. 822,300.

Lyc·i·a (lǐsh'ē-ə, lǐsh'ə). An ancient country and later a Roman province on the SW coast of Asia Minor.

Lyd·i·a (lǐd'ē-ə). An ancient Aegean country of Asia Minor. **—Lyd'i·an** adj. & n.

Ly·on (lē'ôN'). An industrial center of E central France. Pop. 454,300.

M

Maas (mäs). See **Meuse.**

Maas·tricht (mäs-trǐκнт'). A city of the SE Netherlands. Pop. 110,000.

Ma·cao (mə-kou'). A Portuguese colony of SE China. Pop. 248,000.

Mac·e·do·ni·a (mǎs'ə-dō'nē-ə). 1. Also **Mac·e·don** (mǎs'ə-dǒn'). An ancient kingdom N of Greece, which reached the height of its power under Alex-

ander the Great. 2. A Balkan region consisting of parts of Greece, Bulgaria, and Yugoslavia. **—Mac'e·do'ni·an** adj. & n.

Ma·cei·ó (mä'sä-ô'). A city of E Brazil. Pop. 243,000.

Ma·chu Pic·chu (mä'chōo pēk'chōo). An ancient fortress city in the Peruvian Andes, NW of Cuzco.

Mac·ken·zie (mə-kěn'zē). 1. A district of the Northwest Territories, Canada. 2. A river of NW Canada, flowing c. 1,120 mi (1,800 km) into the Arctic Ocean.

Mack·i·nac, Straits of (mǎk'ǐ-nô'). A channel between Michigan's Upper and Lower peninsulas.

Ma·con (mā'kən). A city of central Georgia. Pop. 121,000.

Mac·quar·ie (mə-kwôr'ē). A river, 590 mi (950 km) long, in New South Wales, Australia.

Mad·a·gas·car (mǎd'ə-gǎs'kər). Formerly **Mal·a·gas·y Republic** (mǎl'ə-gǎs'ē). An island country in the Indian Ocean, off the SE coast of Africa. Pop. 8,520,000. Cap. Tananarive.

Ma·dei·ra (mə-dîr'ə, -děr'ə). 1. A Portuguese-owned archipelago in the Atlantic Ocean W of Morocco. 2. A river of NW Brazil, flowing c. 900 mi (1,450 km) into the Amazon. **—Ma·dei'ran** adj. & n.

Mad·i·son (mǎd'ǐ-sən). The capital of Wisconsin, in the S central part of the state. Pop. 169,000.

Ma·dras (mə-drǎs', -dräs'). A city of SE India. Pop. 2,470,000.

Ma·dre de Di·os (mä'drē dā dē-ôs'). A river, c. 700 mi (1,125 km) long, of S Peru and NW Bolivia.

Ma·drid (mə-drǐd'). The capital of Spain, in the central part of the country. Pop. 3,274,000.

Ma·du·ra (mä-dōor'ä). An Indonesian island near the NE coast of Java.

Ma·du·rai (mǎd'ə-rī'). A city of S India. Pop. 548,000.

Mael·strom, the (māl'strəm). A dangerous whirlpool off the NW coast of Norway.

Mag·da·le·na (mǎg'də-lā'nə). A river rising in SW Colombia, and flowing c. 1,000 mi (1,610 km) gen. N to the Caribbean.

Mag·de·burg (mǎg'də-bûrg'). A city of W East Germany. Pop. 276,000.

Ma·gel·lan, Strait of (mə-jěl'ən). A channel between the S tip of South America and Tierra del Fuego.

Mag·gio·re, La·go (lä'gō mə-jôr'ē). A lake of N Italy and S Switzerland.

Mag·ni·to·gorsk (mǎg-nē'tə-gôrsk'). A city of SW Siberian U.S.S.R. Pop. 393,000.

Mai·kop (mī'kôp). A city of S European U.S.S.R. Pop. 127,000.

Main (mīn, män). A river of E West Germany, flowing c. 310 mi (500 km) to the Rhine.

Maine (mān). A state of the NE United States. Pop. 1,055,000. Cap. Augusta.

Mainz (mīnts). A port city of W central West Germany. Pop. 184,000.

Ma·jor·ca (mə-yôr'kə, -jôr'kə). Also **Mal·lor·ca** (mä-yôr'kä). The largest of the Balearic Islands, in the W Medi-

terranean Sea.

Ma·ka·lu (mǔk'ə-lōo'). A mountain (c. 27,800 ft/8,500 m) in the Himalayas, in NE Nepal.

Ma·kas·sar (mə-kǎs'ər). A city of SW Celebes, Indonesia. Pop. 435,000.

Ma·ke·yev·ka (mə-kā'yəf-kə). A city of S European U.S.S.R. Pop. 437,000.

Ma·khach·ka·la (mə-кнäch'kə-lä'). A city of SE European U.S.S.R. Pop. 231,000.

Mal·a·bar Coast (mǎl'ə-bär'). A region of SW India.

Ma·lac·ca, Strait of (mə-lǎk'ə). A channel between Sumatra and the Malay Peninsula, joining the Andaman and South China seas.

Mál·a·ga (mǎl'ə-gə). A city of S Spain. Pop. 408,000.

Mal·a·gas·y Republic (mǎl'ə-gǎs'ē). See **Madagascar.**

Ma·la·wi (mä-lä'wē). A country of SE Africa. Pop. 5,530,000. Cap. Lilongwe.

Ma·lay Archipelago (mä'lā', mə-lā'). A group of islands in the Indian and Pacific oceans, between Australia and SE Asia.

Malay Peninsula. A narrow extension of SE Asia, composed of parts of Malaysia, Thailand, and Burma.

Ma·lay·sia (mə-lā'zhə, -shə). A country of SE Asia consisting of the S Malay Peninsula and N Borneo. Pop. 12,600,000. Cap. Kuala Lumpur. **—Ma·lay'sian** adj. & n.

Mal·dives (mǎl'dīvz'). An island group and republic in the Indian Ocean, SW of India. Pop. 140,000. Cap. Malé. **—Mal·di·van** (mǎl-dī'vē-ən) or **Mal·di'van** (-dī'vən) adj. & n.

Ma·lé (mä'lā). The capital of the Maldives. Pop. 12,000.

Ma·li (mä'lē). A country of W Africa. Pop. 6,100,000. Cap. Bamako.

Mal·lor·ca. (mä-yôr'kä). See **Majorca.**

Mal·mö (mǎl'mō). A city of S Sweden. Pop. 244,000.

Mal·ta (môl'tə). 1. An island nation in the Mediterranean, S of Sicily. Pop. 330,000. Cap. Valletta. **—Mal·tese'** (-tēz', -tēs') adj. & n.

Mam·moth Cave National Park (mǎm'əth). A park in central Kentucky noted for limestone caverns.

Ma·mo·ré (mä'mō-rā'). A river c. 600 mi (965 km) long, of Bolivia and Brazil.

Man, Isle of (mǎn). A British island in the Irish Sea. **—Manx** (mǎngks) adj. & n.

Ma·na·gua (mä-nä'gwä). The capital of Nicaragua, in the W on the shore of Lake Managua. Pop. 375,000.

Ma·nas·sas (mə-nǎs'əs). A town of N Virginia near the site of the Battles of Bull Run (1861 and 1862), which the Confederates called the Battles of Manassas. Pop. 9,000.

Ma·naus (mə-nous'). A city of NW Brazil. Pop. 284,000.

Man·ches·ter (mǎn'chěs'tər, -chǐs-tər). 1. A city of NW England. Pop. 490,000. 2. A city of SE New Hampshire. Pop. 81,000.

Man·chu·kuo (mǎn'chōo'kwō'). A former state of E Asia (1932–45).

Man·chu·ri·a (mǎn-chōor'ē-ə). A region of NE China. **—Man·chu'ri·an** *adj. & n.*

Man·da·lay (măn'də-lā'). A city of Burma, on the Irrawaddy River. Pop. 402,000.

Man·hat·tan (măn-hăt'n, mən-). An island and borough of New York City, bounded by the Hudson, Harlem, and East rivers. Pop. 1,539,000.

Ma·nil·a (mə-nĭl'ə). A city and former capital of the Philippines, on Luzon Island. Pop. 1,438,000.

Man·i·to·ba (măn'ĭ-tō'bə). A province of SE Canada. Pop. 1,019,000. Cap. Winnipeg. **—Man'i·to'ban** *adj. & n.*

Ma·ni·za·les (mä'nē-sä'lās). A city of W central Colombia. Pop. 231,000.

Mann·heim (măn'hīm'). A city of central West Germany. Pop. 320,000.

Man·tu·a (măn'tōō-ə, -tyōō-ə). A city of N Italy. Pop. 66,000. **—Man'tu·an** *adj. & n.*

Ma·ra·cai·bo (mä'rä-kī'bō). **1.** A seaport of NW Venezuela. Pop. 652,000. **2.** The largest lake in South America, S of the Gulf of Venezuela.

Ma·ra·cay (mär'ə-kī'). A city of N Venezuela. Pop. 255,000.

Ma·ra·ñón (mä'rä-nyōn'). A river rising in Peru and flowing c. 1,000 mi (1,610 km) to the Amazon.

March·es (mär'chĭz). A region of central Italy.

Mar del Pla·ta (mär dĕl plä'tə). A city of E central Argentina. Pop. 302,000.

Mar·i·an·a Islands (mâr'ē-ăn'ə, -ä'nə). A W Pacific island chain, E of the Philippines; a commonwealth of the United States.

Mar·i·an·as Trench (mâr'ē-ăn'əs, -än'əs). A depression in the floor of the Pacific Ocean SE of the Marianas, where depths of 36,200 ft (11,040 m) have been recorded.

Mar·i·time Alps (măr'ə-tīm' ălps). A part of the W Alps between France and Italy.

Maritime Provinces. Nova Scotia, New Brunswick, and Prince Edward Island.

Mark·ham, Mount (mär'kəm). A mountain, 14,200 ft (4,330 m) high, in Victoria Land, Antarctica.

Mar·ma·ra, Sea of (mär'mə-rə). A sea between European and Asiatic Turkey.

Marne (märn). A river in NE France; scene of battles in World War I (1914, 1918) and in World War II (1944).

Ma·ro·ni (mə-rō'nē). A river of N South America, flowing 450 mi (724 km) to the Atlantic Ocean along the border between Surinam and French Guiana.

Mar·que·sas Islands (mär-kā'zəz, -səz). An archipelago of volcanic islands of French Polynesia, in the South Pacific.

Mar·ra·kesh or **Mar·ra·kech** (mə-rä'kĕsh', mär'ə-kĕsh', mär'ə-kĕsh'). A city of W central Morocco. Pop. 333,000.

Mar·seilles (mär-sā', -sālz'). A seaport of SE France. Pop. 909,000. **—Mar'seil·lais'** (mär'sä-yĕ') *adj.*

Mar·shall Islands (mär'shəl). An archipelago of two island chains in the central Pacific N of New Zealand; ad-

ministered by the United States.

Mar·tha's Vineyard (mär'thəz). An island off the SE coast of Massachusetts.

Mar·ti·nique (mär'tĭ-nēk'). An island and overseas department of France, in the West Indies. Pop. 343,000. Cap. Fort-de-France. **—Mar'ti·ni'can** *n.*

Mar·y·land (mâr'ə-lənd). A state of the E central United States. Pop. 4,114,000. Cap. Annapolis. **—Mar'y·land·er** *n.*

Mas·e·ru (măz'ə-rōō'). The capital of Lesotho, in the W near the border of South Africa. Pop. 17,000.

Mash·ar·brum (mŭsh'ər-brōōm'). A mountain peak, 25,660 ft (7,826 m) high, in the Karakoram Mountains in Kashmir.

Mash·had (mäsh-häd'). A city of NE Iran. Pop. 410,000.

Ma·son-Dix·on Line (mā'sən-dĭk'sən). The boundary between Pennsylvania and Maryland, regarded as the division between the free and the slave states before the Civil War.

Mas·sa·chu·setts (măs'ə-chōō'sĭts, -zĭts). A state of the NE United States. Pop. 5,800,000. Cap. Boston.

Massachusetts Bay. An inlet of the Atlantic Ocean extending from Cape Ann to Cape Cod.

Mas·sif Cen·tral (mă-sēf' sĕn-träl'). A plateau region in SE and S France, with an average elevation of 2,500 ft (763 m).

Mas·sive, Mount (măs'ĭv). A mountain (14,418 ft/4,398 m) in W central Colorado.

Mat·a·be·le·land (măt'ə-bē'lē-lănd'). A region of SW Rhodesia inhabited by the Matabele people since 1837.

Ma·ta·di (mə-tä'dē). A city of W Zaire. Pop. 144,000.

Ma·ta·mo·ros (măt'ə-môr'əs). A seaport of NE Mexico. Pop. 165,000.

Mat·a·pan, Cape (măt'ə-păn'). The S tip of mainland Greece.

Ma·thu·ra (mŭt'ə-rə). A pilgrimage city of N central India. Pop. 132,000.

Ma·tsu (mä'tsōō'). An island group of the Republic of China, situated in Formosa Strait off the SE coast of China.

Ma·tsu·mo·to (mä'tsōō-mō'tō). An industrial city of central Honshu, Japan. Pop. 187,000.

Ma·tsu·ya·ma (mä'tsōō-yä'mä). A city of NW Shikoku, Japan. Pop. 374,000.

Mat·ter·horn (măt'ər-hôrn'). A mountain, c. 14,685 ft (4,480 m) high, on the Italian-Swiss border.

Mau·i (mou'ē). An island of Hawaii, between Hawaii and Molokai.

Mau·na Ke·a (mou'nə kā'ə). An inactive volcano, rising to 13,796 ft (4,208 m), on the island of Hawaii.

Mau·na Lo·a (mou'nə lō'ə). A volcanic mountain, 13,680 ft (4,172 m) high, in the S central area of the island of Hawaii.

Mau·re·ta·ni·a (môr'ə-tā'nē-ə). An ancient country of NW Africa including parts of modern Morocco and Algeria.

Mau·ri·ta·ni·a (môr'ĭ-tā'nē-ə). A republic of NW Africa. Pop. 1,500,000.

Cap. Nouakchott. **—Mau'ri·ta'ni·an** *adj. & n.*

Mau·ri·tius (mô-rĭsh'əs). An island nation in the SW Indian Ocean. Pop. 910,000. Cap. Port Louis. **—Mau·ri'tian** *adj. & n.*

May, Cape (mā). A peninsula in S New Jersey, between Delaware Bay and the Atlantic Ocean.

Ma·yon, Mount (mä-yōn'). An active volcano, 8,070 ft (2,461 m) high, in SE Luzon, Philippines.

Ma·zat·lán (mä'sät-län'). A resort city and seaport of W Mexico. Pop. 147,000.

Mba·ba·ne (əm-bä-bä'nā). The capital of Swaziland, in the NW. Pop. 22,000.

Mc·Kin·ley, Mount (mə-kĭn'lē). The highest mountain in North America (20,320 ft/6,197.6 m), in S Alaska.

Mead, Lake (mēd). An artificial lake on the Nevada-Arizona border, formed in the Colorado River by Hoover Dam.

Mec·ca (mĕk'ə). A city of W Saudi Arabia, the birthplace of Mohammed. Pop. 367,000.

Me·dan (mə-dän') A city of NE Sumatra, Indonesia. Pop. 636,000.

Me·de·llín (mĕd'l-ēn', mä'dā-yēn'). A city of W central Colombia. Pop. 1,100,000.

Med·ford (mĕd'fərd). A city of NE Massachusetts. Pop. 59,000.

Me·di·a (mē'dē-ə). An ancient country of SW Asia, now the NW region of Iran. **—Me'di·an** *adj. & n.*

Me·di·na (mə-dē'nə). A city of NW Saudi Arabia; site of Mohammed's tomb. Pop. 198,000.

Med·i·ter·ra·ne·an Sea (mĕd'ə-tə-rā'nē-ən). The world's largest inland sea, bounded by Africa in the S, Asia in the E, and Europe in the N and W. It has access to the Atlantic Ocean through the Strait of Gibraltar.

Mee·rut (mē'rət). A city of N central India. Pop. 271,000.

Mek·nès (mĕk-nĕs'). A city of N central Morocco. Pop. 248,000.

Me·kong (mā'kŏng'). A river of SE Asia, c. 2,600 mi (4,183 km) long, flowing through Tibet, Laos, Burma, Thailand, Cambodia, and Vietnam.

Mel·a·ne·sia (mĕl'ə-nē'zhə, -shə). An island group in the SW Pacific Ocean, extending SE from the Admiralty Islands to the Fiji Islands.

Mel·bourne (mĕl'bərn). A seaport of SE Australia. Pop. 2,603,000.

Me·los (mē'lŏs'). A Greek island of the Cyclades group in the Aegean Sea.

Mel·ville Island (mĕl'vĭl). An island of the Canadian Northwest Territories.

Mem·phis (mĕm'fĭs). **1.** The ruined capital of ancient Egypt, on the Nile S of Cairo. **2.** A city of SW Tennessee. Pop. 655,000.

Men·do·za (mĕn-dō'sä). A city of W central Argentina. Pop. 119,000.

Me·nor·ca (mā-nôr'kä). See **Minorca**.

Mer·ci·a (mûr'shē-ə, -shə). An Anglo-Saxon kingdom extending over most of central England. **—Mer'ci·an** *adj. & n.*

Mé·ri·da (mä'rē-dä). A city of SE

Mexico. Pop. 234,000.

Mer·sey (mûr′zē). A river rising in NW England and flowing c. 70 mi (113 km) NW to Liverpool.

Me·sa·bi Range (mə-sä′bē). A narrow range of low hills in Minnesota, noted for vast deposits of iron ore and taconite.

Me·sa Ver·de National Park (mā′sə vûrd′, vĕr′dē). An area of SW Colorado, noted for its ruins of prehistoric cliff dwellings.

Mes·o·po·ta·mi·a (mĕs′ə-pə-tā′mē-ə). The ancient country between the Tigris and Euphrates rivers. **—Mes′o·po·ta′mi·an** adj. & n.

Mes·si·na (mə-sē′nə). A seaport in NE Sicily. Pop. 265,000.

Messina, Strait of. A narrow channel between Sicily and Italy.

Me·ta (mā′tə). A river rising in W central Colombia, flowing c. 650 mi (1,045 km) gen. NE.

Metz (mĕts, mĕs). A city of NE France. Pop. 112,000.

Meuse (myōoz, mœz). Also **Maas** (mäs). A river rising in E France and flowing c. 560 mi (900 km) through Belgium and the Netherlands to the North Sea.

Mex·i·cal·i (mĕk′sə-kăl′ē, mĕ′hē-kä′lē). A city of NW Mexico. Pop. 317,000.

Mex·i·co (mĕk′sĭ-kō′). A republic of SW North America. Pop. 65,000,000. Cap. Mexico City. **—Mex′i·can** (-kən) adj. & n.

Mexico, Gulf of. An extensive inlet of the Atlantic Ocean S of North America and surrounded by the United States, Mexico, and Cuba.

Mexico City. The capital of Mexico, in the central part of the country. Pop. 8,299,000.

Mi·am·i (mī-ăm′ē, -ăm′ə). A resort city of SE Florida. Pop. 348,000.

Miami Beach. A resort city of SE Florida. Pop. 91,000.

Mich·i·gan (mĭsh′ĭ-gən). A Midwestern state of the United States. Pop. 9,135,000. Cap. Lansing.

Michigan, Lake. One of the Great Lakes, between Michigan and Wisconsin.

Mi·cro·ne·sia (mī′krō-nē′zhə, -shə). The island groups in the Pacific Ocean E of the Philippines and N of the equator. They include the Mariana, Marshall, Caroline, and Gilbert islands. **—Mi′cro·ne′sian** adj. & n.

Mid·dle At·lan·tic States (mĭd′l ăt-lăn′tĭk). Those states of the United States having Atlantic Ocean ports and lying between New England and Virginia. They are New York, Pennsylvania, New Jersey, Delaware, and Maryland.

Middle East. The area in Asia and Africa between and including Libya in the W, Pakistan in the E, Turkey in the N, and the Arabian Peninsula in the S. Also called **Mideast. —Middle Eastern.**

Mid·dles·brough (mĭd′əlz-brə). A borough of NE England. Pop. 154,000.

Mid·dle·sex (mĭd′l-sĕks′). A county of E Massachusetts, where the first engagement of the Revolutionary War (Apr. 19, 1775) was fought.

Middle West. A cultural and historical region of the United States extending roughly from Ohio W through Iowa, and from the Ohio and Missouri rivers N through the Great Lakes. Also called **Midwest. —Middle Western. —Middle Westerner.**

Mid·east (mĭd′ēst′) n. Another name for the **Middle East. —Mid′east′ern** n.

Mi·di (mē-dē′) n. The S of France.

Mid·i·an (mĭd′ē-ən). An ancient region in the NW Arabian Peninsula, E of the Gulf of Aqaba.

Mid·land (mĭd′lənd). A city of W central Texas. Pop. 66,000.

Mid·lands (mĭd′ləndz). A region of central England.

Mid·way Islands (mĭd′wā′). A coral atoll consisting of 2 islets, in the Pacific Ocean NW of Hawaii, near which the U.S. won a decisive naval battle against the Japanese (June, 1942).

Mid·west (mĭd′wĕst′) n. Another name for the **Middle West. —Mid′west′** or **Mid′west′ern** adj. **—Mid′west′ern·er** n.

Mi·lan (mī-lăn′, -län′). A city of N Italy. Pop. 1,724,000. **—Mil′a·nese′** (nĕz′, -nēs′) adj. & n.

Mi·le·tus (mī-lē′təs). An ancient Greek city on the W coast of Asia Minor.

Mil·wau·kee (mĭl-wô′kē). A city of SE Wisconsin. Pop. 641,000.

Min·da·na·o (mĭn′də-nä′ō). An island of the Philippines, at the SE extremity of the archipelago.

Min·do·ro (mĭn-dôr′ō, -dōr′ō). An island of the central Philippines.

Mi·nho (mē′nyōo). A river rising in NW Spain, flowing c. 210 mi (340 km) SW to the Atlantic, and forming part of the Portuguese-Spanish border.

Min·ne·ap·o·lis (mĭn′ē-ăp′ə-lĭs). A city of SE Minnesota. Pop. 359,000.

Min·ne·so·ta (mĭn′ĭ-sō′tə). **1.** A state of the N central United States. Pop. 3,944,000. Cap. St. Paul. **2.** A river rising near the Minnesota-South Dakota border and flowing gen. E 332 mi (534 km) to join the Mississippi River near St. Paul. **—Min′ne·so′tan** n. & adj.

Mi·nor·ca (mĭ-nôr′kə). Also **Me·nor·ca** (mā-nôr′kä). A Spanish island in the Balearics, NE of Majorca. **—Mi·nor′-can** adj. & n.

Minsk (mĭnsk). The capital of the Belorussian S.S.R., W central European U.S.S.R. Pop. 1,215,000.

Miq·ue·lon (mĭk′ə-lŏn′). See **St. Pierre and Miquelon.**

Mis·sis·sip·pi (mĭs′ĭ-sĭp′ē). A state of the S United States. Pop. 2,331,000. Cap. Jackson. **—Mis′sis·sip′pi·an** adj. & n.

Mississippi River. A river of the central United States, rising in NW Minnesota and flowing c. 2,350 mi (3,780 km) SE to the Gulf of Mexico.

Mis·sou·ri (mĭ-zŏor′ē, -zŏor′ə). A Midwestern state of the United States. Pop. 4,786,000. Cap. Jefferson City. **—Mis·sou′ri·an** (mĭ-zŏor′ē-ən) adj. & n.

Missouri River. The longest river of the United States, rising in the Rocky Mountains in W Montana and flowing

c. 2,565 mi (4,130 km) to join the Mississippi River N of St. Louis.

Mis·tas·si·ni Lake (mĭs′tə-sē′nē). A lake in central Quebec, Canada.

Mitch·ell (mĭch′əl), **Mount.** A peak, 6,684 ft (2,038.6 m) high, of the Appalachians , in W North Carolina.

Mo·ab (mō′ăb′). An ancient kingdom E of the Dead Sea, in an area that is now part of Jordan.

Mo·bile (mō′bēl′, mō-bēl′). A port city of SW Alabama. Pop. 208,000.

Mobile Bay. An inlet of the Gulf of Mexico in SW Alabama.

Mo·de·na (mō′dä-nä). A city of N Italy. Pop. 179,000.

Mog·a·dish·o (mŏg′ə-dĭsh′ōo). The capital of Somalia. Pop. 230,000.

Mo·gi·lev (mŏg′ə-lĕf′). A city of W European U.S.S.R. Pop. 264,000.

Mo·hen·jo-Da·ro (mō-hĕn′jō-dä′rō). A ruined ancient city on the Indus River in Pakistan.

Mo·ja·ve Desert (mō-hä′vē). Also **Mo·ha·ve Desert.** A desert region of S California.

Mol·da·vi·a (mŏl-dā′vē-ə). A historic region of E Rumania.

Mol·da·vi·an Soviet Socialist Republic (mŏl-dā′vē-ən). A constituent republic of SW European U.S.S.R. Pop. 3,850,000. Cap. Kishinev.

Mo·lo·kai (mōl′ə-kī′, mō′lō-). One of the islands of Hawaii, between Oahu and Maui.

Mo·luc·ca Islands (mə-lŭk′ə). Formerly **Spice Islands** (spīs). An island group of E Indonesia between Sulawesi and New Guinea.

Mom·ba·sa (mŏm-bä′sä, -bäs′ə). A seaport of SE Kenya. Pop. 301,000.

Mon·a·co (mŏn′ə-kō′, mə-nä′kō). An independent principality on the Mediterranean coast in the S of France. Pop. 25,000. Cap. Monaco-Ville. **—Mon′a·can** adj. & n.

Mön·chen·glad·bach (mŭn′kən-glād′-bäk). A city of W West Germany. Pop. 263,000.

Mon·go·li·a (mŏng-gō′lē-ə, -gōl′yə, mŏn-). A region of E central Asia, extending from Siberia to N China. **—Mon·go′li·an** adj. & n.

Mongolian People's Republic. A country of N central Asia. Pop. 1,530,-000. Cap. Ulan Bator.

Mo·non·ga·he·la (mə-nŏng′gə-hē′lə). A river rising in West Virginia and flowing 128 mi (206 km) N to Pittsburgh, Pennsylvania, where it joins the Allegheny to form the Ohio.

Mon·ro·vi·a (mən-rō′vē-ə). The capital of Liberia, in the NW. Pop. 100,000.

Mon·tan·a (mŏn-tăn′ə). A state of the W United States. Pop. 740,000. Cap. Helena. **—Mon·tan′an** adj. & n.

Mont Blanc (môN blÄN′). A peak, 15,771 ft (4,810.2 m) high, near the French-Italian border.

Mon·te Car·lo (mŏn′tē kär′lō). A resort town of Monaco. Pop. 10,000.

Mon·te·go Bay (mŏn-tē′gō). A seaport of NW Jamaica, in the West Indies. Pop. 44,000.

Mon·te·rey (mŏn′tə-rā′). A city of W California. Pop. 28,000.

Mon·ter·rey (mŏn′tə-rā′). A city of NE Mexico. Pop. 1,006,000.

Mon·te·vi·de·o (mŏn'tə-vĭ-dā'ō). The capital of Uruguay, a seaport in the S. Pop. 1,230,000.

Mont·gom·er·y (mŏnt-gŭm'ər-ē, -gŭm'rē). The capital of Alabama, in the central part of the state. Pop. 161,000.

Mont·mar·tre (môN-már'tr'). A district in N Paris noted for its cafés and nightclubs.

Mont·par·nasse (môN-pár-nás'). A district of S Paris, on the left bank of the Seine, noted as a gathering place for intellectuals and artists.

Mont·pe·lier (mŏnt-pēl'yər). The capital of Vermont, in the center of the state. Pop. 8,200.

Mont·pel·lier (môN-pĕ-lyā'). A city of S France. Pop. 191,000.

Mon·tre·al (mŏn'trē-ôl', mŏN-rā-äl'). Canada's largest city, located in S Quebec. Pop. 2,802,000.

Mont-Saint-Mi·chel (môN-săN-mē-shĕl'). A small island off the coast of Brittany, celebrated for its Benedictine abbey.

Mont·ser·rat (mŏnt'sə-răt'). One of the Leeward Islands, a British dependency in the West Indies. Pop. 12,000.

Mo·ra·da·bad (mŏr'ə-də-băd'). A city of N central India. Pop. 259,000.

Mo·ra·va (mŏr'ä-vä). A river rising on the Polish-Czech border and flowing S c. 240 mi (385 km) to join the Danube.

Mo·ra·vi·a (mə-rā'vē-ə). A historic region of central Czechoslovakia.

Mor·ay Firth (mûr'ē). An inlet of the North Sea extending into NE Scotland.

Mo·re·lia (mō-rā'lyä). A city of W Mexico. Pop. 199,000.

Mo·roc·co (mə-rŏk'ō). A kingdom of NW Africa, on the Mediterranean. Pop. 18,240,000. Cap. Rabat. —**Mo·roc'can** (mə-rŏk'ən) adj. & n.

Mor·ris Jes·up, Cape (mŏr'ĭs jĕs'əp, mŏr'ĭs). The world's northernmost point of land, in N Greenland on the Arctic Ocean.

Mos·cow (mŏs'kou', -kō). The capital of the U.S.S.R., in the W. Pop. 7,061,000.

Mo·selle (mō-zĕl'). A river rising in NE France and flowing 320 mi (515 km) to join the Rhine.

Mo·sul (mō-sōol'). A city of N Iraq. Pop. 293,000.

Moul·mein (mōol-mān', mōl-). A seaport of SE Burma. Pop. 173,000.

Mount Ver·non (vûr'nən). 1. The estate of George and Martha Washington, situated on the banks of the Potomac River near Washington, D.C. 2. A city of SE New York. Pop. 67,000.

Mo·zam·bique (mō'zăm-bēk'). A country of SE Africa. Pop. 9,680,000. Cap. Lourenço Marques.

Mozambique Channel. The strait between Mozambique and Madagascar.

Muir Glacier (myŏor'). A glacier in the St. Elias Mountains of SE Alaska.

Mul·ha·cén (mōo'lä-thān'). The highest mountain (11,424 ft/3,484 m) in Spain, in the Sierra Nevada.

Mül·heim (mül'hīm'). A city of W

West Germany. Pop. 191,000.

Mul·house (mü-lōoz'). A city of NE France. Pop. 117,000.

Mul·tan (mōol-tän'). A city of E central Pakistan. Pop. 542,000.

Mun·cie (mŭn'sē). A city of E Indiana. Pop. 77,000.

Mu·nich (myōo'nĭk). A city of S West Germany. Pop. 1,294,000.

Mün·ster (mün'stər). A city of W West Germany. Pop. 263,000.

Mur·chi·son Falls (mûr'chĭ-sən). A series of cascades in NW Uganda, formed as the Victoria Nile drops 400 ft (122 m) through a narrow cleft to Lake Albert.

Mur·cia (mŏor'shə). 1. A region of SE Spain. 2. A city in this region. Pop. 172,000.

Mur·frees·bor·o (mûr'frēz-bûr'ō). A city of central Tennessee near the site of a Civil War battle (December 31, 1862 to January 2, 1863). Pop. 32,000.

Mur·mansk (mŏor-mänsk'). A city of extreme NW European U.S.S.R. Pop. 369,000.

Mu·ro·ran (mōo'rō-rän'). A city of SW Hokkaido, Japan. Pop. 159,000.

Mur·ray River (mûr'ē). A river of Australia, rising in the Australian Alps and flowing W 1,609 mi (2,589 km) to the Indian Ocean.

Mur·rum·bidg·ee (mûr'əm-bĭj'ē). A river of New South Wales, Australia, rising in the Eastern Highlands and flowing gen. W c. 1,050 mi (1,689 km) to join the Murray River.

Mus·cat (mŭs'kăt'). The capital of Oman. Pop. 10,000.

Mus·co·vy (mŭs'kə-vē). The principality of Moscow (12th–16th cent.)

Mus·sel·shell (mŭs'əl-shĕl'). A river rising in central Montana and flowing c. 292 mi (470 km) to the Missouri.

Muz·tagh (mōos-tä'). A mountain, 24,757 ft (7,550 m) high, in W China.

My·ce·nae (mī-sē'nē). An ancient city of Greece, in the NE Peloponnesus. —**My'ce·nae'an** adj. & n.

N

Nab·a·tae·a (năb'ə-tē'ə). An ancient kingdom of Arabia, S of Edom, in present-day Jordan.

Na·ga·sa·ki (nä'gə-sä'kē). A seaport of Japan, on W Kyushu Island; target of a U.S. atomic bomb dropped on Aug. 9, 1945. Pop. 449,400.

Na·go·ya (nä-goi'ä). A seaport and industrial center of Japan, in S central Honshu. Pop. 2,079,700.

Nai·ro·bi (nī-rō'bē). The capital of Kenya, in the S central part of the country. Pop. 776,000.

Na·mi·bia (nə-mĭb'ē-ə). Formerly **Southwest Af·ri·ca** (ăf'rĭ-kə). A territory in SW Africa. Pop. 1,000,000. Cap. Windhoek. —**Na·mib'i·an** adj. & n.

Nam Tso (näm' tsō'). A saltwater lake in E Tibet, at an altitude of over 15,000 ft (4,575 m).

Nan·chang (nän'chäng'). The capital of Kiangsi, SE China. Pop. 900,000.

Nan·cy (nän'sē). A city of NE France. Pop. 107,900.

Nan·ga Par·bat (nŭng'gə pûr'bət). A Himalayan peak rising to 26,660 ft (8,131.3 m) in NW Kashmir.

Nan·king (năn'kĭng'). The capital of Kiangsu, E central China. Pop. 2,000,000.

Nantes (nănts). An industrial city of W France. Pop. 265,000.

Nan·tuck·et (năn-tŭk'ĭt). An island of Massachusetts in the Atlantic Ocean S of Cape Cod.

Na·ples (nā'pəlz). A seaport of S central Italy. Pop. 1,223,800. —**Na·po'li·an** adj. & n.

Nar·ra·gan·sett Bay (năr'ə-găn'sĭt). An inlet of the Atlantic Ocean extending N from SE Rhode Island.

Na·ra·yan·ganj (nä-rä'yən-gənj). A port city of E central Bangladesh. Pop. 176,400.

Nash·u·a (năsh'ōo-ə). An industrial city in S central New Hampshire. Pop. 67,800.

Nash·ville (năsh'vĭl'). The capital of Tennessee, on the Cumberland River. Pop. 438,900.

Nas·sau (năs'ô'). The capital of the Bahama Islands, on the NE coast of New Providence Island. Pop. 101,500.

Natch·i·toches (năk'ə-tŏsh'). The oldest city in Louisiana, founded in 1714. Pop.16,700.

Na·u·ru (nä-ōo'rōo). An island in the central Pacific Ocean; a U.N. Trust Territory administered by Australia.

Naz·a·reth (năz'ə-rĭth). A town in N Israel. Pop. 25,000.

Ndja·me·na (ən-jä'mä-nä). Formerly **Fort-La·my** (fôr'lə-mē'). The capital of Chad, in the SW on the Chari River. Pop. 179,000.

Neagh, Lough (lŏкн nā'). The largest lake of the United Kingdom, in Northern Ireland.

Near East. A region including the countries of the E Mediterranean, the Arabian Peninsula, and, sometimes, NE Africa. —**Near Eastern.**

Ne·bras·ka (nə-brăs'kə). A Midwestern state of the United States. Pop. 1,564,900. Cap. Lincoln. —**Ne·bras'kan** adj. & n.

Neg·ev (nĕg'ĕv'). A triangular desert region in S Israel.

Ne·gros (nā'grōs). An island of the Philippines, one of the Visayan group S of Panay, in the Sulu Sea.

Ne·pal (nə-pôl', -päl'). A kingdom in the Himalayas between India and Tibet. Pop. 13,713,000. Cap. Katmandu. —**Nep'a·lese'** (-lēz', -lēs') adj. & n.

Ness, Loch (lŏкн nĕs'). A lake in N Scotland, noted for persistent, unconfirmed reports of a monster inhabiting it.

Neth·er·lands, the (nĕth'ər-ləndz). A kingdom of W Europe, N of Belgium, between West Germany and the North Sea. Pop. 14,083,000. Constitutional cap. Amsterdam; de facto cap. The Hague. Also called **Holland.**

Netherlands An·til·les (ăn-tĭl'ēz). An autonomous territory of the Netherlands, consisting of 6 islands, in the West Indies. Pop. 246,000. Cap. Willemstad, on Curaçao.

Ne·va (nē'və). A navigable river of the Soviet Union, flowing c. 40 mi (64.3

ă pat   ā pay   â care   ä father   ĕ pet   ē be   hw which   ĭ pit   ī tie   î pier   ŏ pot   ō toe   ô paw, for   oi noise
ōō took   ōō boot   ou out   th thin   th this   ŭ cut   û urge   zh vision   ə about, item, edible, gallop, circus

km) W from Lake Ladoga to the Gulf of Finland.

Ne·vad·a (nə-văd′ə, -vä′də). A state of the W United States. Pop. 800,300. Cap. Carson City. **—Ne·vad′an** *adj.& n.*

Ne·vis (nē′vĭs). An island in the Caribbean Sea, near St. Christopher.

New Am·ster·dam (ăm′stər-dăm′). The capital of New Netherland, founded on Manhattan Island in 1625, and renamed New York after its capture by the English in 1664.

New·ark (nōō′ərk, nyōō′-). A city of NE New Jersey. Pop. 330,100.

New Bed·ford (bĕd′fərd). A port and industrial city of SE Massachusetts. Pop. 98,400.

New Brit·ain (brĭt′n). A city of central Connecticut. Pop. 73,700.

New Bruns·wick (brŭnz′wĭk). A Maritime Province of Canada. Pop. 705,700. Cap. Fredericton.

New Cal·e·do·ni·a (kăl′ə-dō′nē-ə, -dōn′yə). 1. An island in the SW Pacific Ocean E of Australia. 2. A French Overseas Territory consisting of this island and several smaller island dependencies nearby. Pop. 136,000. Cap. Nouméa.

New·cas·tle (nōō′kăs′əl, -kăs′əl, nyōō′-). A port city of New South Wales, Australia, on the Tasman Sea coast. Pop. 138,696.

New·cas·tle-up·on-Tyne (nōō′kăs′əl-ə-pŏn′tīn′, nōō′kăs′əl-, nyōō′-). Also **New·cas·tle.** A coal-mining center of NE England. Pop. 295,800.

New Del·hi (dĕl′ē). The capital of India, constructed in the early 20th cent. just S of Delhi (or Old Delhi), on the W bank of the Jumna River. Pop. 292,900.

New Eng·land (ĭng′glənd). The NE United States, comprising the states of Maine, New Hampshire, Vermont, Massachusetts, Connecticut, and Rhode Island. **—New Englander.**

New·found·land (nōō′fən-lənd, -lănd′, nyōō′-, nōō-found′lənd, nyōō-). 1. An island off the SE coast of Canada, separated from the mainland by the Strait of Belle Isle, the Gulf of St. Lawrence, and Cabot Strait. 2. A province of Canada, consisting of this island and Labrador. Pop. 577,400. Cap. St. John's. **—New′found·land·er** *n.*

New France. (frăns). The French territory in North America, which developed from 16th cent. settlements on the St. Lawrence River to include much of SE Canada, the Great Lakes region, and the Mississippi valley. All of it except St. Pierre and Miquelon was surrendered to England and Spain by 1763.

New Guin·ea (gĭn′ē). An island in the Pacific Ocean N of Australia; divided politically between Indonesia and Papua New Guinea.

New Hamp·shire (hămp′shər, hăm′shər, -shĭr). A state of the NE United States, with a short coastline on the Atlantic. Pop. 919,100. Cap. Concord.

New Ha·ven (hā′vən). A port and industrial city of S Connecticut; seat of Yale University. Pop. 125,800.

New Heb·ri·des (hĕb′rə-dēz′). A group of islands in the Pacific Ocean

E of Australia, constituting a condominium of the United Kingdom and France. Pop. 114,000. Cap. Vila.

New Jer·sey (jûr′zē). A Middle Atlantic state of the United States. Pop. 7,342,200. Cap. Trenton. **—New Jerseyite.**

New Mex·i·co (měk′sĭ-kō′). A state of the SW United States. Pop. 1,295,500. Cap. Santa Fe. **—New Mexican.**

New Neth·er·land (něth′ər-lənd). The early Dutch colony comprising several settlements along the Hudson and lower Delaware rivers. By 1664 the English had incorporated it into Delaware, New Jersey, and New York.

New Or·le·ans (ôr′lē-ənz, ôr′lənz, ôr-lēnz′). A city and river port of SE Louisiana, on the Mississippi. Pop. 557,800.

New·port (nōō′pôrt, -pōrt′, nyōō′-). A resort city and port in SE Rhode Island, at the entrance to Narragansett Bay. Pop. 29,300.

Newport News (nōōz, nyōōz). A harbor city in SE Virginia. Pop. 144,800.

New Prov·i·dence Island (prŏv′ə-dəns). An island of the British West Indies; site of Nassau, capital of the Bahamas.

New Ro·chelle (rō-shĕl′, rə-). A city of SE New York. Pop. 70,500.

New Spain (spān). The former Spanish possessions governed from Mexico City, including islands in the West Indies, Central America N of Panama, Mexico, the SW United States, and the Philippine Islands.

New Swe·den (swē′dn). An early Swedish colony (1638–55) in North America, extending roughly from the site of present-day Trenton, New Jersey, S to the mouth of the Delaware River.

New·ton (nōōt′n, nyōōt′n). A city and suburb of Boston, in E Massachusetts. Pop. 83,600.

New York (yôrk). 1. A Middle Atlantic state of the United States. Pop. 17,508,000. Cap. Albany. 2. The largest city and leading seaport of the United States, in SE New York State at the mouth of the Hudson River. Pop. 7,035,300. **—New Yorker.**

New York State Barge Canal. A system of inland waterways in New York State totaling 525 mi (845 km). It connects the Hudson River with Lakes Erie and Ontario, and, via Lake Champlain, with the St. Lawrence River.

New Zea·land (zē′lənd). An independent member of the Commonwealth of Nations, in the Pacific Ocean SE of Australia. It comprises North Island, South Island, and several smaller adjacent islands. Pop. 3,069,000. Cap. Wellington. **—New Zealander.**

Ni·ag·a·ra Falls (nī-ăg′rə, -ăg′ər-ə). 1. An industrial and resort city of W New York State. Pop. 71,300. 2. An industrial and resort city of Ontario, Canada. Pop. 306,000.

Niagara Falls. The waterfalls of the Niagara River between the cities of Niagara Falls, consisting of 2 main falls, the Canadian or Horseshoe Falls (c. 160 ft/48.8 m high and 2,500 ft/

762.5 m wide), and the American Falls (c. 167 ft/50.9 m high and 1,000 ft/305 m wide).

Niagara River. A river flowing 34 mi (54.7 km) N from Lake Erie to Lake Ontario, forming part of the boundary between W New York State and Ontario, Canada.

Nia·mey (nyä-mā′). The capital of Niger, on the Niger River in the SW part of the country. Pop. 130,300.

Nic·a·ra·gua (nĭk′ə-rä′gwə). A republic of Central America, S of Honduras. Pop. 2,481,000. Cap. Managua. **—Nic·a·ra′guan** *adj. & n.*

Nicaragua, Lake. The largest lake of Central America, in S Nicaragua.

Nice (nēs). A seaport and resort of the French Riviera. Pop. 344,500.

Nic·o·bar Islands (nĭk′ə-bär′). An island group in the Bay of Bengal.

Nic·o·si·a (nĭk′ə-sē′ə). The capital of Cyprus, in the N central part of the island. Pop. 51,000.

Ni·ger (nī′jər). A republic in W central Africa. Pop. 4,994,000. Cap. Niamey.

Niger River. A major river of Africa, rising near the Sierra Leone-Guinea border and flowing 2,600 mi (4,185 km) NE and then SE to the Gulf of Guinea.

Ni·ge·ri·a (nī-jîr′ē-ə). A republic in Africa on the Gulf of Guinea. Pop. 84,500,000. Cap. Lagos. **—Ni·ge′ri·an** *adj. & n.*

Ni·ko·la·ev (nĭk′ə-lä′yəf). A port of S European U.S.S.R., in the Ukraine. Pop. 436,000.

Nile (nīl). A river in E Africa, the longest in the world (4,160 mi/6,695 km). It flows from its headstream in Burundi, central Africa, to its delta on the Mediterranean Sea, NE Egypt.

Nîmes (nēm). A city of SE France. Pop. 128,000.

Nin·e·veh (nĭn′ə-və). A capital of Assyria, the ruins of which are located on the Tigris River, opposite Mosul.

Ning·po (nĭng′pō′). A port city of SE China. Pop. 350,000.

Nip·i·gon, Lake (nĭp′ĭ-gŏn′). A lake in SW Ontario, Canada.

Ni·shi·no·mi·ya (nē′shē-nō′mē-yä′). A city of SW Honshu, Japan. Pop. 403,800.

Ni·te·rói (nē′tĕ-roi′). A city of SE Brazil, on Guanabara Bay. Pop. 376,000.

Nizh·ni Ta·gil (nĭzh′nē tə-gĭl′). A city of E European U.S.S.R., in the central Urals. Pop. 396,000.

Nome (nōm). The westernmost city of the continental United States, on Seward Peninsula in Alaska. Pop. 2,273.

Nor·folk (nôr′fək). A seaport, naval base, and industrial city of SE Virginia. Pop. 262,800.

Nor·man·dy (nôr′mən-dē). A region of NW France on the English Channel.

North A·mer·i·ca (nôrth ə-měr′ə-kə). The N continent of the Western Hemisphere, extending from the Colombia-Panama border in the S through Central America, the United States (except Hawaii), Canada, and the Arctic Archipelago to the N tip of Greenland. **—North American.**

North·amp·ton (nôr-thămp′tən, nôrth-hămp′-). A city of central England. Pop. 142,000.

North Cape. A point on an island in the Arctic Sea off N Norway, popularly held to be the northernmost part of Europe.

North Car·o·li·na (kăr′ə-lī′nə). A state of the S United States. Pop. 5,847,800. Cap. Raleigh. **—North Car′o·lin′i·an** (-lĭn′ē-ən).

North Da·ko·ta (də-kō′tə). A Middle Western state of the United States, on the Canadian border. Pop. 652,400. Cap. Bismarck. **—North Dakotan.**

North·ern Ire·land (nôr′thərn īr′lənd). A component of the United Kingdom, in the NE part of the island of Ireland. Pop. 1,540,000. Cap. Belfast.

North Island. The smaller of the 2 principal islands of New Zealand.

North River. That part of the Hudson River estuary separating New Jersey and New York City.

North Sea. A part of the Atlantic Ocean bordered by Belgium, the Netherlands, West Germany, Denmark, and Norway on the E and Britain on the W.

North·um·bri·a (nôr-thŭm′brē-ə). An Anglo-Saxon kingdom of Britain, extending N from the Humber to the Forth.

North·west Passage (nôrth′wĕst′). The water route from the Atlantic to the Pacific through the Arctic Archipelago of Canada and N of Alaska; first navigated in 1903–06.

Northwest Territories. A territorial and political division of Canada that includes the Arctic Archipelago, the islands in Hudson Bay, and the mainland N of the Canadian provinces and E of the Yukon Territory. Pop. 43,100. Cap. Yellowknife.

Northwest Territory. A region extending from the Ohio and Mississippi rivers to the Great Lakes, awarded to the United States in 1783 by the Treaty of Paris. It included the present states of Illinois, Indiana, Michigan, Ohio, Wisconsin, and part of Minnesota.

Nor·walk (nôr′wôk′). **1.** A city of S California. Pop. 85,300. **2.** A city of SW Connecticut. Pop. 76,700.

Nor·way (nôr′wā′). A kingdom of N Europe, on the Scandinavian Peninsula. Pop. 4,080,000. Cap. Oslo. **—Nor·we′gian** (nôr-wē′jən) adj. & n.

Norwegian Sea. The part of the Arctic Ocean between Greenland and Norway.

Not·ting·ham (nŏt′ĭng-əm). A city of central England, on the Trent River. Pop. 280,300.

Nouak·chott (nwäk′shŏt′). The capital of Mauritania, in the W. Pop. 135,000.

Nou·mé·a (noō-mā′ə). The capital of New Caledonia, on the SW coast. Pop. 60,200.

No·va Sco·tia (nō′və skō′shə). A Maritime Province and peninsula of SE Canada. Pop. 851,000. Cap. Halifax. **—Nova Scotian.**

No·va·ya Zem·lya (nō′və-yə zĕm-lyä′). A Soviet archipelago between the Barents and Kara seas.

Nov·go·rod (nŏv′gə-rŏd′). An ancient city of NW European U.S.S.R. Pop. 128,000.

No·vi Sad (nō′vē säd′). A city of NE Yugoslavia. Pop. 141,700.

No·vo Kuz·netsk (nō′vō koōz-nĕtsk′). A steel center of S central Siberian U.S.S.R. Pop. 537,000.

No·vo·si·birsk (nō′vō-sĭ-bîrsk′). A city of S central Siberian U.S.S.R., on the Ob River. Pop. 1,312,000.

Nu·bi·a (noō′bē-ə, nyoō′-). A desert region and ancient kingdom in the Nile valley of S Egypt and N Sudan. **—Nu′bi·an** adj. & n.

Nubian Desert. A desert in NE Sudan, extending E of the Nile to the Red Sea.

Nu·ku·a·lo·fa (noō′koō-ə-lō′fə). The capital of Tonga, on Tongatabu Island. Pop. 18,400.

Nu·mid·i·a (noō-mĭd′ē-ə, nyoō-). An ancient kingdom of N Africa. **—Nu·mid′i·an** adj. & n.

Nu·rem·berg (noōr′əm-bûrg′, nyoōr′-), A city of S West Germany. Pop. 509,800.

Ny·as·a, Lake (nī-ăs′ə). A lake in SE Africa, between Tanzania, Mozambique, and Malawi.

O

O·a·hu (ō-ä′hoō). An island of Hawaii; site of the state capital, Honolulu.

Oak·land (ōk′lənd). A city of W California. Pop. 338,700.

Oak Ridge (ōk′ rĭj′). A city in E Tennessee, at the site orig. occupied in 1943 by a unit of the Manhattan District to produce materials for atomic bombs. Pop. 27,600.

Ob (ŏb, ôb). A river of W Siberian U.S.S.R., flowing 2,113 mi (3,399.8 km) NW and then N to the Kara Sea.

O·ber·am·mer·gau (ō′bər-ä′mər-gou′). A town of S West Germany; noted for a Passion play performed every 10 years. Pop. 4,700.

O·ber·hau·sen (ō′bər-hou′zən). A city and steel-producing center of W West Germany. Pop. 239,300.

O·ce·an·i·a (ō′shē-ăn′ē-ə, -ä′nē-ə). The islands of the central, W, and S Pacific Ocean, customarily including Australia and New Zealand. **—O′ce·an′i·an** adj. & n.

O·den·se (ō′thən-sə). An industrial center of S central Denmark. Pop. 168,200.

O·der (ō′dər). A river rising in N central Czechoslovakia and flowing 562 mi (904.3 km) through Poland and East Germany to the Baltic Sea.

O·des·sa (ō-dĕs′ə). **1.** An industrial city of SW European U.S.S.R. Pop. 1,046,000. **2.** A city of W central Texas. Pop. 89,800.

Og·bo·mo·sho (ŏg′bō-mō′shō). A city of W Nigeria. Pop. 432,000.

Og·den (ŏg′dən). An industrial city of N Utah. Pop. 64,400.

O·hi·o (ō-hī′ō). A Middle Western state of the United States. Pop. 10,772,300. Cap. Columbus. **—O·hi′o·an** adj. & n.

Ohio River. A river formed by the Allegheny and Monongahela rivers at Pittsburgh, Pennsylvania, and flowing 980 mi (1,576.8 km) W and SW to the Mississippi River at Cairo, Illinois.

Oise (wäz). A river of France, 186 mi (299.3 km) long, formed in the NE and flowing SW to the Seine.

O·i·ta (ō′ē-tä). A seaport in NE Kyushu, Japan. Pop. 329,500.

O·ka·ya·ma (ō′kä-yä′mä). A seaport of SW Honshu, Japan, on the Inland Sea. Pop. 520,500.

O·kee·cho·bee, Lake (ō′kē-chō′bē). A lake in S central Florida, with access to the Atlantic Ocean via the Okeechobee Waterway.

O·ke·fe·no·kee Swamp (ō′kə-fə-nō′kē). A swamp in NE Florida and SE Georgia.

O·khotsk, Sea of (ō-kŏtsk′). An arm of the Pacific Ocean between the Kamchatka Peninsula and Kurile Islands and Sakhalin Island.

O·ki·na·wa (ō′kĭ-nä′wə). The largest of the Ryukyu Islands, off the S tip of Japan; the scene of heavy combat in World War II.

O·kla·ho·ma (ō′klə-hō′mə). A state of the SW United States. Pop. 3,001,200. Cap. Oklahoma City. **—O′kla·ho′man** adj. & n.

O·kla·ho·ma City (ō′klə-hō′mə). The capital of Oklahoma, in the center of the state. Pop. 401,600.

Old·ham (ōl′dəm). A city of NW England. Pop. 227,500.

Ol·du·vai (ōl′də-wä′, -vä′, -vī′). A gorge in N Tanzania; site of fossil remains.

Ol·ives, Mount of (ŏl′ĭvz). Also **Ol·i·vet** (ŏl′ə-vĕt′). A hill E of Jerusalem, in Jordan.

O·lym·pi·a (ō-lĭm′pē-ə). **1.** A plain of Elis in the NW Peloponnesus, where the Olympic games of antiquity were held. **2.** The capital of the state of Washington, at the S end of Puget Sound. Pop. 27,500.

O·lym·pic Peninsula (ō-lĭm′pĭk). A peninsula of NW Washington, between the Pacific Ocean and Puget Sound.

O·lym·pus (ō-lĭm′pəs). The highest mountain in Greece (9,750 ft/2,920 m), the fabled home of the Olympian gods.

O·ma·ha (ō′mə-hô′, -hä′). An industrial city of E Nebraska. Pop. 312,900.

O·man (ō-män′). An independent nation at the E tip of the Arabian peninsula. Pop. 864,000. Cap. Muscat.

Oman, Gulf of. An inlet of the Arabian Sea between Oman and Iran.

Om·dur·man (ŏm′doōr-män′). A city in NE central Sudan, on the White Nile. Pop. 299,400.

Omsk (ômsk). A city of W Siberian U.S.S.R. Pop. 1,026,000.

On·ta·ke (ōn-tä′kē). A mountain, 10,049 ft (3,064.9 m), of central Honshu, Japan.

On·tar·i·o (ŏn-târ′ē-ō′). A province of Canada between Hudson Bay to the N and the Great Lakes to the S. Pop. 8,543,300. Cap. Toronto. **—On·tar′i·an** adj. & n.

ă pat ā pay â care ä father ĕ pet ē be hw which ĭ pit ī tie î pier ŏ pot ō toe ô paw, for oi noise
oō took ōō boot ou out th thin th this ŭ cut û urge zh vision ə about, item, edible, gallop, circus

Ontario, Lake. The easternmost of the Great Lakes, between SE Ontario, Canada, and NW New York.

O·por·to (ō-pôr′tō, ō-pōr′tō). An industrial city and seaport of NW Portugal. Pop. 335,700.

O·ra·dea (ô-rä′dyä). A city in NW Rumania. Pop. 171,300.

O·ran (ō-rän′, ō-rän′). A seaport in NW Algeria, on the Mediterranean. Pop. 491,900.

Or·ange River (ôr′ĭnj, ŏr′-). A river rising in Lesotho, S Africa, and flowing 1,300 mi (2,090 km) W across South Africa to the Atlantic Ocean.

Or·dos (ôr′dəs). A sandy desert plateau region of N China.

Or·dzho·ni·kid·ze (ôr′jŏn-ə-kĭd′zə). A city of SE European U.S.S.R. Pop. 276,000.

Or·e·gon (ôr′ə-gən, -gŏn′, ôr′-). A state of the NW United States. Pop. 2,618,-100. Cap. Salem. **—Or′e·go′ni·an** (ôr′-ə-gō′nē-ən, ôr′-) adj. & n.

Oregon Trail. The main route to the Oregon Country for settlers in the 1840's. It stretched over 2,000 mi (3,218 km) from Independence, Missouri, to Astoria, Oregon, at the mouth of the Columbia River.

O·rel (ô-rĕl′). A city of central European U.S.S.R. Pop. 282,000.

O·ri·no·co (ôr′ə-nō′kō, ŏr′-). A river rising in SE Venezuela and flowing 1,500 mi (2,416 km) W, then N, and then E to the Atlantic Ocean.

O·ri·za·ba, Pi·co de (pē′kō dä ô′rē-sä′vä). An 18,700 ft (5,703.5 m) volcanic peak in E central Mexico.

Ork·ney Islands (ôrk′nē). A cluster of islands off the NE coast of Scotland.

Or·lan·do (ôr-lăn′dō). A winter resort of central Florida. Pop. 127,800.

Or·lé·ans (ôr-lā-äN′). A city of N central France. Pop. 106,200.

Or·muz (ôr′mŭz′, ôr-mōōz′). See **Hormuz.**

Orsk (ôrsk). A city of E European U.S.S.R., in the Urals. Pop. 243,000.

O·sa·ka (ō-sä′kə). An industrial metropolis and seaport of Japan, on SW Honshu Island. Pop. 2,779,000.

Osh·kosh (ŏsh′kŏsh′). A city of E Wisconsin. Pop. 49,600.

Os·lo (ŏz′lō, ŏs′lō). The capital of Norway, in the SE. Pop. 462,700.

Os·sa (ŏs′ə). A mountain peak (6,489 ft/1,979.1 m) in E central Greece, near the Aegean Sea.

Os·ti·a (ŏs′tē-ə). A town of E central Italy, at the mouth of the Tiber east of ancient Ostia, the port of Rome.

O·stra·va (ô′strə-və). A city of N central Czechoslovakia. Pop. 300,100.

O·ta·ru (ō-tä′rōō). A seaport of Japan on the W coast of Hokkaido. Pop. 184,400.

O·tran·to, Strait of (ō-trän′tō). A strait between Italy and Albania, connecting the Adriatic and Ionian seas.

Ot·ta·wa (ŏt′ə-wə, -wä′, -wô′). The capital of Canada, on the Ottawa River, at the SE tip of Ontario near the U.S. border. Pop. 304,500.

Ot·to·man Empire (ŏt′ō-mən). The Turkish Empire (1299–1919) in SW Asia, NE Africa, and SE Europe.

Oua·ga·dou·gou (wä′gə-dōō′gōō). The capital of Upper Volta, in the center of the country. Pop. 105,000.

O·vie·do (ō-vyā′thō). An industrial city of NW Spain. Pop. 159,600.

Ox·ford (ŏks′fərd). A city of S central England, on the Thames. Pop. 117,400. **—Ox·o′ni·an** (ŏks-ō′nē-ən) adj.

Ox·nard (ŏks′närd). A city of S California. Pop. 115,800.

O·zark Mountains (ō′zärk). A range of low mountains in SW Missouri, NW Arkansas, and E Oklahoma.

P

Pa·cif·ic Islands, Trust Territory of the (pə-sĭf′ĭk). A United Nations strategic trust territory in the Pacific Ocean administered by the United States. It comprises c. 2,000 islands in the Caroline, Mariana, and Marshall islands. Pop. 140,000.

Pacific Ocean. The earth's largest body of water, extending from the Arctic to the Antarctic and the Americas to Asia and Australia.

Pa·dre Island (pä′drä, -drē). A low sandy island of S Texas. The Padre Island National Seashore is located in the central part of the island.

Pad·u·a (păj′ōō-ə, păd′yōō-ə). An industrial city and cultural center of NE Italy. Pop. 242,200.

Paes·tum (pĕs′təm). An ancient city of SW Italy, famous for its temples.

Pa·go Pa·go (päng′gō päng′gō, päng′ō päng′ō). The capital of American Samoa, a port on the S coast of Tutuila Island. Pop. 2,400.

Paint·ed Desert (pān′təd). A colorful, eroded plateau area in E central Arizona.

Pak·i·stan (păk′ĭ-stän′, pä′kĭ-stän′). A republic in S Asia, on the Arabian Sea. Pop. 76,770,000. Cap. Islamabad. **—Pak′i·stan′i** adj. & n.

Pa·lat·i·nate, the (pə-lăt′n-ăt′, -ĭt). A state of the Holy Roman Empire, consisting of the Lower Palatinate (now in the state of Rhineland-Palatinate), and the Upper Palatinate (now in Bavaria).

Pa·la·wan (pä-lä′wän). A long, narrow island in the SW Philippines.

Pa·lem·bang (pä′lĕm-bäng′). A trade center and river port of SE Sumatra, Indonesia. Pop. 583,000.

Pa·ler·mo (pä-lĕr′mō). The capital of Sicily, a seaport on the NW coast. Pop. 662,600.

Pal·es·tine (păl′ĭ-stīn′). A historic region on the E shore of the Mediterranean Sea, comprising parts of modern Israel, Jordan, and Egypt. Also called "the Holy Land." **—Pal′es·tin′i·an** (păl′ĭ-stĭn′ē-ən) n.

Pal·i·sades, the (păl′ə-sādz′). A row of cliffs in NE New Jersey, along the W bank of the Hudson River.

Pal·ma (päl′mä). The capital and principal port of the Balearic Islands, on Majorca. Pop. 263,000.

Palm Beach (päm). A winter resort town of SE Florida. Pop. 9,600.

Pal·o Al·to (păl′ō ăl′tō). A city of W California. Pop. 54,900.

Pa·mirs, the (pə-mîrz′). A mountain region of central Asia, chiefly in Tadzhik S.S.R., bordering on Afghanistan, Kashmir, and China; highest elevation, Mount Communism (24,590 ft/7,480 m).

Pam·li·co Sound (păm′lĭ-kō′). An inlet of the Atlantic Ocean between the E coast of North Carolina and its chain of offshore islands.

Pam·plo·na (päm-plō′nä). A city of N Spain. Pop. 163,200.

Pan·a·ma (păn′ə-mä′). 1. A republic of Central America, on the Isthmus of Panama. Pop. 1,900,000. 2. Also **Panama City.** The capital of Panama, at the Pacific terminus of the Panama Canal. Pop. 438,000. **—Pan′a·ma′ni·an** (păn′ə-mä′nē-ən) adj. & n.

Panama, Isthmus of. A 420-mi (675.7 km) long isthmus connecting North and South America and separating the Pacific Ocean from the Caribbean Sea.

Panama Canal. A ship canal, 51 mi (82 km) long, across the Isthmus of Panama, connecting the Caribbean with the Pacific.

Pa·nay (pə-nī′). An island of the Visayan Islands, Philippines.

Pan·mun·jom (păn′mŏon′jŏm′). A village of W South Korea; site of armistice talks leading to the end of the Korean War.

Pao·ting (bou′dĭng′). A city in NE China. Pop. 350,000.

Pao-t'ou (bou′tō′). A city of Inner Mongolian Autonomous Region, China. Pop. 800,000.

Pa·pal States (pā′pəl). The territories in central Italy ruled by the popes until 1870.

Pa·pe·e·te (pä′pä-ā′tä, pə-pē′tē). A city of NW Tahiti. Pop. 25,300.

Pap·u·a New Guin·ea (păp′yōō-ə; gĭn′ē). An independent nation occupying the E half of the island of New Guinea. Pop. 3,079,000. Cap. Port Moresby.

Par·a·guay (păr′ə-gwī′, -gwä′). A republic of central South America. Pop. 2,973,000. Cap. Asunción. **—Par′a·guay′an** adj. & n.

Par·a·mar·i·bo (păr′ə-măr′ə-bō′). The capital of Surinam, on the Atlantic Ocean. Pop. 150,000.

Pa·ra·ná (păr′ə-nä′). A river rising in E central Brazil and flowing 2,040 mi (3,282.3 km) S to the Río de la Plata in NE Argentina.

Par·is (păr′ĭs, pä-rē′). The capital and principal city of France, in the NW on the Seine. Pop. 2,291,600. **—Pa·ri′sian** (pə-rĭzh′ən, -rē′zhən) adj. & n.

Par·ma (pär′mə). 1. A city in N Italy. Pop. 178,000. 2. A city of NE Ohio. Pop. 92,600.

Par·nas·sus, Mount (pär-năs′əs). A peak, c. 8,060 ft (2,460 m) high, in S Greece; sacred in Greek mythology to Apollo and the Muses.

Par·ra·mat·ta (păr′ə-măt′ə). A city of New South Wales, SE Australia. Pop. 131,700.

Par·thi·a (pär′thē-ə). An ancient country in W Asia, roughly corresponding to NE Iran. **—Par′thi·an** adj. & n.

ă pat ā pay â care ä father ĕ pet ē be hw which ĭ pit ī tie î pier ŏ pot ō toe ô paw, for oi noise
ōō took ōō boot ou out th thin th this ŭ cut û urge zh vision ə about, item, edible, gallop, circus

Pas·a·de·na (păs′ə-dē′nə). **1.** A residential city of SW California. Pop. 117,900. **2.** An industrial city of SE Texas. Pop. 111,900.

Pas·sa·ic (pə-sā′ĭk). An industrial city in NE New Jersey, on the Passaic River. Pop. 52,300.

Pat·a·go·ni·a (păt′ə-gō′nē-ə, -gōn′yə). A region in S South America, extending from the Strait of Magellan N to the Limay and Río Negro rivers, and from the Andes E to the Atlantic Ocean. —**Pat′a·go′ni·an** adj. & n.

Pat·er·son (păt′ər-sən). An industrial city of NE New Jersey. Pop. 138,000.

Pat·na (pŭt′nə). A city of NE India, on the river Ganges. Pop. 474,300.

Paw·tuck·et (pô-tŭk′ĭt). A city of NE Rhode Island. Pop. 71,000.

Pearl Harbor (pûrl). A harbor on the S coast of Oahu island, Hawaii; site of a surprise attack by the Japanese on Dec. 7, 1941, that resulted in the U.S. declaration of war on Japan.

Pe·cos River (pā′kəs). A river rising in the Sangre de Christo Mountains in N central New Mexico and flowing 926 mi (1,490 km) SE to the Rio Grande.

Pe·king (pē′kĭng′). Formerly **Pei·ping** (bā′pĭng′). The capital of China, S of the Great Wall in the NE part of the country. Pop. 8,000,000.

Pe·lée, Mount (pə-lā′). A volcanic mountain peak, 4,428 ft (1,350.5 m) high, on N Martinique.

Pe·li·on (pē′lē-ən). A mountain peak, 5,252 ft (1,601.9 m) high, in NE Greece.

Pel·o·pon·ne·sus (pĕl′ə-pə-nē′səs). A peninsula S of the Gulf of Corinth and forming the S part of Greece. —**Pel′o·pon·ne′sian** adj. & n.

Pem·ba (pĕm′bə). An island of Tanzania in the Indian Ocean.

Pe·nang (pē-năng′). An island off the W coast of the Malay Peninsula.

Pen·chi (bĕn′chē). An industrial center of NE China. Pop. 750,000.

Pen·nine Alps (pĕn′īn′). A mountain range of the Alps, in SW Switzerland on the Italian border; highest elevation, Monte Rosa (15,203 ft/4,637 m).

Pennine Chain. A range of hills extending from S Scotland to the Trent River in central England.

Penn·syl·va·nia (pĕn′səl-vān′yə, -vā′-nē-ə). Officially, the Commonwealth of Pennsylvania. A state of the E United States. Pop. 11,828,100. Cap. Harrisburg. —**Penn′syl·va′nian** adj. & n.

Pen·za (pĕn′zə). A shipping center of S central European U.S.S.R. Pop. 436,000.

Pe·o·ri·a (pē-ôr′ē-ə, -ōr′ē-ə). A city of N central Illinois. Pop. 123,600.

Per·ga·mum (pûr′gə-məm). Also **Per·ga·mon** (-mŏn′). A Greek city in W Asia Minor, on the site of modern Bergama, that became the center of a Hellenistic kingdom.

Perm (pĕrm). A city of NE European U.S.S.R. Pop. 972,000.

Per·sep·o·lis (pər-sĕp′ə-lĭs). A ruined capital of ancient Persia.

Per·sia (pûr′zhə). An ancient country in SW Asia; officially renamed Iran in 1935. —**Per′sian** adj. & n.

Persian Empire. The empire founded by Cyrus the Great (6th cent. B.C.), who expanded the small kingdom of Anshan, at the head of the Persian Gulf, from the Mediterranean Sea to the Indus River and from the Caucasus to the Indian Ocean.

Persian Gulf. An inlet of the Arabian Sea between the Arabian Peninsula and Iran.

Perth (pûrth). A city of SW Australia. Pop. 805,000.

Pe·ru (pə-rōō′). A republic in W South America, with a coastline on the Pacific. Pop. 17,293,000. Cap. Lima. —**Pe·ru′vi·an** (pə-rōō′vē-ən) adj. & n.

Pe·ru·gia (pā-rōō′jä). A city in central Italy. Pop. 137,000.

Pes·ca·do·res (pĕs′kə-dôr′ēz, -dôr′ĭs). A group of islands in Formosa Strait between Taiwan and the Chinese mainland.

Pe·sha·war (pə-shä′wər). A city of N Pakistan, SE of the entrance to the Khyber Pass. Pop. 210,000.

Pe·ters·burg (pē′tərz-bûrg′). A city of SE Virginia. Pop. 40,900.

Pe·tra (pē′trə). The ancient capital of Edom, in SW Jordan, famous for its Hellenistic tombs carved in rock.

Pet·ri·fied Forest National Monument (pĕt′rə-fīd′). An area in the Painted Desert of E Arizona, reserved for the protection of its petrified trees.

Pet·ro·grad (pĕt′rō-grăd′). See Leningrad.

Pet·ro·za·vodsk (pĕt′rə-zä-vôtsk′). A city of NW European U.S.S.R. Pop. 216,000.

Phil·a·del·phi·a (fĭl′ə-dĕl′fē-ə). A city of SE Pennsylvania. Pop. 1,681,200. —**Phil′a·del′phi·an** adj. & n.

Phi·lip·pi (fĭ-lĭp′ī′). An ancient town in N central Macedonia, Greece, near the Aegean Sea; the scene of the defeat of Brutus and Cassius by Antony and Octavian (42 B.C.).

Phil·ip·pine Islands (fĭl′ə-pēn′). A group of about 7,000 islands in the W Pacific Ocean, SE of China.

Phil·ip·pines, Republic of the (fĭl′ə-pēnz′, fĭl′ə-pēnz′). A republic consisting of the Philippine Islands. Pop. 47,719,000. Cap. Manila.

Philippine Sea. A large area of the W Pacific Ocean, E of the Philippine Islands, extending NW to Taiwan.

Phi·lis·ti·a (fĭ-lĭs′tē-ə). An ancient country on the SW coast of Palestine.

Phnom Penh (pə-nôm′ pĕn′). The capital of Cambodia, on the Mekong River in the S central part of the country. Pop. 600,000.

Phoe·ni·cia (fĭ-nĭsh′ə, -nē′shə). An ancient maritime country consisting of a group of city-states of Syria, extending from the Mediterranean Sea E to the Lebanon Mountains. —**Phoe·ni′cian** adj. & n.

Phoe·nix (fē′nĭks). The capital of Arizona, in the S central part of the state. Pop. 772,900.

Phryg·i·a (frĭj′ē-ə). An ancient country of W central Asia Minor, settled in the 13th cent. B.C. —**Phryg′i·an** adj. & n.

Pic·ar·dy (pĭk′ər-dē). A region and former province in N France, extending from the English Channel to the Belgian border.

Pic·ca·dil·ly (pĭk′ə-dĭl′ē). A well-known thoroughfare in London, running from the Haymarket to Hyde Park Corner.

Pied·mont (pēd′mŏnt′). **1.** A region of NW Italy, bordered on the W by France, on the N by Switzerland, and on the E by Lombardy. **2.** The low platform in the E United States extending E from the Appalachian and Blue Ridge mountains to the Fall Line, and N from Alabama to New Jersey.

Pierre (pîr). The capital of South Dakota, in the center of the state on the Missouri River. Pop. 12,000.

Pie·ter·mar·itz·burg (pē′tər-măr′ĭts-bûrg′). A city of E South Africa. Pop. 114,800.

Pikes Peak (pīks′). Also **Pike's Peak.** A mountain peak, 14,110 ft (4,303.6 m) high, in central Colorado in the Rocky Mountains.

Pin·dus Mountains (pĭn′dəs). The chief mountain range of Greece, extending S from the Albanian border through NW Greece.

Pi·rae·us (pī-rē′əs). The chief seaport of Greece, near Athens. Pop. 187,500.

Pi·sa (pē′zə). A city of Tuscany, Italy, on the Arno River; famous for its leaning tower. Pop. 103,500.

Pit·cairn Island (pĭt′kârn′). A small British island in the South Pacific, between Easter Island and Tahiti; settled in 1790 by the mutineers from H.M.S. Bounty.

Pitts·burgh (pĭts′bûrg′). An industrial city of SW Pennsylvania. Pop. 424,200.

Pitts·field (pĭts′fēld′). A city of W Massachusetts, on the Housatonic River. Pop. 51,900.

Platte (plăt). A river formed by the confluence of the North Platte and South Platte rivers in SW Nebraska. It flows 310 mi (498.7 km) E to the Missouri below Omaha, Nebraska.

Plov·div (plôv′dĭf). The principal city of S Bulgaria. Pop. 305,100.

Plym·outh (plĭm′əth). **1.** A city of SW England, on the English Channel. Pop. 259,100. **2.** A town of SE Massachusetts on Plymouth Bay, where the Pilgrims from the Mayflower landed (1620). Pop. 35,800.

Plymouth Colony. A New England settlement established in December 1620 by the Pilgrims. It became part of the Massachusetts Bay Colony in 1691.

Po (pō). A river rising on the slope of Mount Viso in NW Italy and flowing 418 mi (672.5 km) to the Adriatic Sea SW of Venice.

Po Hai, Gulf of (bō′ hī′). An inlet of the Yellow Sea in NE China between Manchuria and Shantung.

Poi·tiers (pwä-tyā′). A city of W central France, S of Tours. Pop. 81,300.

Po·land (pō′lənd). Officially, Polish People's Republic. A country of central Europe, on the Baltic Sea. Pop. 35,409,000. Cap. Warsaw. —**Po′lish** (pō′lĭsh) adj. & n.

ă pat   ā pay   â care   ä father   ĕ pet   ē be   hw which   ĭ pit   ī tie   î pier   ŏ pot   ō toe   ô paw, for   oi noise
ōō took   ōō boot   ou out   th thin   th this   ŭ cut   û urge   zh vision   ə about, item, edible, gallop, circus

Polish Corridor. A strip of territory separating East Prussia from the rest of Germany; awarded to Poland in the Treaty of Versailles.

Pol·ta·va (pəl-tä′və). A city of S European U.S.S.R. Pop. 270,000.

Pol·y·ne·sia (pŏl′ə-nē′zhə, -shə). One of the 3 major divisions of Oceania, a group of islands of the E and SE Pacific Ocean, extending from New Zealand N to Hawaii and E to Easter Island. —**Pol′y·ne′sian** adj. & n.

Pom·er·a·ni·a (pŏm′ə-rā′nē-ə, -rān′yə). A historic region of N central Europe, extending along the S coast of the Baltic Sea from Stralsund to the Vistula River, now divided between Poland and East Germany.

Po·mo·na (pə-mō′nə). A city in California, E of Los Angeles. Pop. 92,600.

Pom·pe·ii (pŏm-pā′, -pā′ē). An ancient city of Campania, destroyed by an eruption of Mount Vesuvius in A.D. 79. —**Pom·pe′ian** adj. & n.

Pon·ce (pôn′sā). A seaport in S Puerto Rico. Pop. 128,200.

Pon·ta Del·ga·da (pŏn′tə dĕl-gä′də). The capital of the Azores, on the SW coast of São Miguel Island. Pop. 20,200.

Pont·char·train, Lake (pŏn′chər-trān′). A shallow lake in SE Louisiana.

Pon·ti·ac (pŏn′tē-ăk′). An automobile-manufacturing city of SE Michigan. Pop. 76,300.

Pon·tus (pŏn′təs). An ancient region in NE Asia Minor along the S shore of the Black Sea.

Poo·na (pōō′nə). A city of W central India. Pop. 853,200.

Po·po·ca·té·petl (pō′pō-kăt′ə-pĕt′l, -kə-tä′pĕt′l). A dormant volcano, 17,887 ft (5,455.5 m) high, of central Mexico.

Port Ar·thur (pôrt är′thər, pōrt). **1.** A port of Ontario, Canada, on Lake Superior. Pop. 45,000. **2.** A city and entry port of SE Texas. Pop. 61,100.

Port-au-Prince (pôrt′ō-prĭns′, pōrt′-). The capital of Haiti. Pop. 493,900.

Port E·liz·a·beth (ĭ-lĭz′ə-bəth, ē-). A seaport of SE South Africa. Pop. 392,200.

Port Har·court (här′kərt, -kôrt). A port city of SE Nigeria, on the Bonny River. Pop. 242,000.

Port·land (pôrt′lənd, pōrt′-). **1.** A seaport city of SW Maine. Pop. 61,600. **2.** An industrial city of NW Oregon on the Willamette River. Pop. 365,100.

Port Lou·is (lōō′ĭs, lōō′ē, lōō-ē′). The capital city and principal seaport of Mauritius. Pop. 138,200.

Port Mores·by (môrz′bē, mōrz′-). The capital of Papua New Guinea, on the SE coast of New Guinea Island. Pop. 117,000.

Pôr·to A·le·gre (pôr′tōō ä-lĕg′rĕ). A city in extreme S Brazil. Pop. 1,044,000.

Port-of-Spain (pôrt′əv-spān′, pōrt′-). Also **Port of Spain.** The capital of Trinidad and Tobago, on the NW coast of Trinidad. Pop. 62,700.

Por·to-No·vo (pôr′tō-nō′vō). The capital of Benin. Pop. 104,000.

Port Sa·id (sä-ēd′). A port city of Egypt, at the Mediterranean end of the Suez Canal. Pop. 262,600.

Ports·mouth (pôrts′məth, pōrts′-). **1.** A port city of S England, on the English Channel. Pop. 198,500. **2.** A city and seaport of SE New Hampshire. Pop. 26,200. **3.** A city of SE Virginia. Pop. 104,100.

Por·tu·gal (pôr′chə-gəl, pōr′-). A republic of Europe, in the W part of the Iberian Peninsula and including Madeira and the Azores. Pop. 9,866,000. Cap. Lisbon. —**Por′tu·guese′** (-gēz′, -gēs′) adj. & n.

Po·to·mac (pə-tō′mək). A river flowing 285 mi (458.6 km) from NW Maryland NE, E, and then SE to Chesapeake Bay.

Pots·dam (pŏts′dăm′). A city of central East Germany, on the Havel River. Pop. 117,200.

Poz·nań (pŏz′năn′y′). An industrial city on the Warta River in W central Poland. Pop. 521,600.

Prague (präg). The capital of Czechoslovakia, on the Vltava River. Pop. 1,173,000.

Prai·rie Provinces (prâr′ē). Manitoba, Saskatchewan, and Alberta.

Pra·to (prä′tō). A textile-making center of central Italy. Pop. 154,400.

Pres·ton (prĕs′tən). A county borough of NW England. Pop. 131,200.

Pre·to·ri·a (prĭ-tôr′ē-ə, -tōr′ē-ə). The administrative capital of the Republic of South Africa, in central Transvaal. Pop. 545,400.

Prib·i·lof Islands (prĭb′ə-lôf′). A group of islands in the Bering Sea, off the SW coast of Alaska. They are the breeding ground for most of the world's fur-bearing seals.

Prince Ed·ward Island (prĭns ĕd′wərd). A Maritime Province of Canada, consisting of an island in the Gulf of St. Lawrence. Pop. 124,000. Cap. Charlottetown.

Prin·ci·pe Island (prĭn′sə-pē′, -pä′). A Portuguese island in the Gulf of Guinea N of the equator.

Pro·ko·pyevsk (prə-kô′pyəfsk). A city of E Siberian U.S.S.R. Pop. 267,000.

Pro·vence (prô-väNs′). A region of SE France, on the Mediterranean between the Rhône and Italy. —**Pro′ven·çal′** (prō′vən-säl′) adj. & n.

Prov·i·dence (prŏv′ə-dəns, -dĕns′). The capital and largest city of Rhode Island. Pop. 156,500.

Prus·sia (prŭsh′ə). A former German state in N and central Germany, formally dissolved (1947) and divided among East and West Germany, Poland, and the Soviet Union. —**Prus′sian** adj. & n.

Pue·bla (pwĕb′lä). A city of S central Mexico, one of the oldest cities in the country, founded c. 1532. Pop. 482,100.

Pueb·lo (pwĕb′lō). An industrial city of S central Colorado. Pop. 101,500.

Puer·to Ri·co (pwĕr′tō rē′kō, pōr′-). An island in the E Greater Antilles. A U.S. territory since 1898, it became a self-governing commonwealth in 1952. Pop. 3,214,000. Cap. San Juan. —**Puerto Rican.**

Pu·get Sound (pyōō′jĭt). An inlet of the Pacific Ocean in NW Washington, extending from Admiralty Inlet and Juan de Fuca Strait to Olympia.

Pun·jab (pŭn-jäb′, -jăb′, pŭn′jäb′, -jăb′). A region and former province of NW India.

Pu·rus (pōō-rōōs′). A navigable river rising in the Andes Mountains in E Peru and flowing 2,000 mi (5,180 km) NE to join the Amazon near Manaus, NW Brazil.

Pu·san (pōō′sän′). A city of South Korea, on Korea Strait at the extreme SE tip of the Korean Peninsula. Pop. 2,454,000.

Pyong·yang (pyŭng′yäng′). The capital of North Korea, on the Taedong River E of Korea Bay. Pop. 1,500,000.

Pyr·e·nees (pĭr′ə-nēz′). The mountain range between France and Spain, extending for 260 mi (418.3 km) between the Bay of Biscay and the Mediterranean; highest elevation, Pico de Aneto (11,168 ft/3,406.2 m).

Q

Qa·tar (kä′tär′). A nation on a peninsula in the Persian Gulf. Pop. 250,000. Cap. Doha.

Que·bec (kwĭ-bĕk′). Also **Qué·bec** (kā-bĕk′). **1.** A province of E Canada. Pop. 6,288,300. **2.** The capital of Quebec province, in the S on the St. Lawrence. Pop. 554,500.

Queens (kwēnz). The largest borough of New York City, on Long Island. Pop. 1,886,500.

Que·moy (kē-moi′). An island off the coast of China, E of Amoy.

Que·zon City (kā′zŏn′). The former capital of the Philippines (1948–76), on Luzon near Manila. Pop. 994,700.

Quin·cy (kwĭn′zē). A city of E Massachusetts; the birthplace of John Adams and John Quincy Adams. Pop. 84,100.

Qui·to (kē′tō). The capital of Ecuador, on the Andean plateau. Pop. 597,100.

R

Ra·bat (rä-bät′). The capital of Morocco, a seaport on the Atlantic coast. Pop. 596,600.

Ra·cine (rə-sēn′). An industrial city of SE Wisconsin. Pop. 85,100.

Ra·dom (rä′dôm). An industrial city of E central Poland. Pop. 175,300.

Rai·nier, Mount (rā-nîr′, rā′nîr). A volcanic peak, 14,410 ft (4,395.1 m) high, of the Cascade Range, in W central Washington.

Ra·jah·mun·dry (rä′jə-mŭn′drē). A city of central India. Pop. 165,900.

Ra·leigh (rô′lē, rä′-). The capital of North Carolina, near the center of the state. Pop. 148,400.

Ran·goon (răng-gōōn′). The capital of Burma, on the Rangoon River estuary. Pop. 2,055,000.

Ra·ven·na (rä-vĕn′nä). A city of N Italy. Pop. 101,400.

Ra·wal·pin·di (rä′wəl-pĭn′dē, rôl-pĭn′dē). A city in the N Punjab of Pakistan. Pop. 615,400.

ă pat　ā pay　â care　ä father　ĕ pet　　ē be　hw which　ĭ pit　ī tie　î pier　　ŏ pot　ō toe　ô paw, for　oi noise
ōō took　ōō boot　ou out　th thin　　th this　ŭ cut　û urge　zh vision　ə about, item, edible, gallop, circus

Read·ing (rĕd'ĭng). **1.** A city of S central England. Pop. 131,200. **2.** A city of SE Pennsylvania. Pop. 78,600.

Re·ci·fe (rə-sē'fē). A seaport of NE Brazil. Pop. 1,249,800.

Red River (rĕd). **1.** A river of the SW United States, rising in the Texas Panhandle and flowing 1,018 mi (1,637.9 km) along the Texas-Oklahoma boundary, through Arkansas, and into Louisiana to join the Mississippi. **2.** A river of the United States and Canada, flowing N 533 mi (857.5 km) along the Minnesota-North Dakota boundary into Lake Winnipeg, Manitoba, Canada.

Red Sea. An elongated body of water separating the Arabian Peninsula from Africa and connected with the Mediterranean by the Suez Canal.

Red·wood National Park (rĕd'-wŏŏd'). A national park along the Pacific coast of NW California.

Reg·gio di Ca·la·bri·a (rãd'jō dē kä-lä'brē-ä). A city in S Italy, on the Strait of Messina. Pop. 177,900.

Re·gi·na (rĭ-jī'nə). The capital of Saskatchewan, Canada. Pop. 160,000.

Reims (rēmz). Also **Rheims.** A city of NE France. Pop. 177,300.

Rennes (rĕn). A city of NW France. Pop. 198,300.

Re·no (rē'nō). A tourist center of W Nevada. Pop. 101,000.

Ré·un·ion (rē-yōōn'yən). An island and overseas department of France, in the Indian Ocean SW of Mauritius. Pop. 489,000. Cap. Saint-Denis.

Rey·kja·vik (rā'kyə-vēk'). The capital of Iceland, in the S on Faxa Bay. Pop. 84,500.

Rheims (rēmz). See **Reims.**

Rhine (rīn). A river of Europe, rising in E Switzerland and flowing c. 820 mi (1,320 km) gen. N through West Germany and the Netherlands to the North Sea.

Rhine·land (rīn'lănd', -lənd). A general term for the regions along the Rhine in West Germany.

Rhode Island (rōd). Officially, The State of Rhode Island and Providence Plantations. A state of the NE United States. Pop. 945,800. Cap. Providence. —**Rhode Islander.**

Rhodes (rōdz). The largest of the Dodecanese Islands in the Aegean Sea, SW of Turkey; ceded by Italy to Greece in 1947. —**Rho'di·an** (rō'dē-ən) adj. & n.

Rho·de·sia (rō-dē'zhə). See **Zimbabwe.** —**Rho·de'sian** adj. & n.

Rhon·dda (rŏn'də, rŏn'thə). A municipal borough of S Wales. Pop. 88,900.

Rhône (rōn). Also **Rhone.** A European river rising in central Switzerland and flowing 505 mi (812.5 km) W and then S to the Mediterranean near Arles, France.

Ri·ad (rē-yäd'). See **Riyadh.**

Rich·mond (rĭch'mənd). **1.** The capital of Virginia and a port on the James River; the capital of the American Confederacy (1861–65). Pop. 219,400. **2.** A city and port of W California. Pop. 74,200. **3.** A borough of New York City, coextensive with Staten Island. Pop. 349,600.

Rif (rĭf). Also **Riff, Er Rif** (ĕr rĭf'), **Er Riff.** A coastal arç of hills in northern Morocco, Africa.

Ri·ga (rē'gə). The capital of Latvia, NW European U.S.S.R. Pop. 733,000.

Ri·je·ka (rē-yĕ'kä). A seaport on the Adriatic in NW Yugoslavia. Pop. 132,900.

Rim·i·ni (rĭm'ĭ-nē). A resort on the Adriatic coast of N central Italy. Pop. 125,800.

Ri·o Bran·co (rē'ō brăng'kō). A river rising in N Brazil and flowing S c. 350 mi (565 km) to the Rio Negro.

Ri·o de Ja·nei·ro (rē'ō dĭ jə-nâr'ō, zhə-nâr'ō). A seaport of SE Brazil; the former capital of the country. Pop. 4,857,700.

Ri·o de O·ro (rē'ō thĕ ō'rō). The S zone of Western Sahara.

Ri·o Grande (rē'ō grănd). A river rising in S Colorado and flowing 1,885 mi (3,035 km) gen. SE to the Gulf of Mexico, forming much of the U.S.-Mexican border on its course.

Ri·o Ne·gro (rē'ō nā'grō). A river rising in E Colombia and flowing c. 1,400 mi (2,252.6 km) to the Amazon in N Brazil.

Riv·er·side (rĭv'ər-sīd'). A city of S California. Pop. 169,900.

Riv·i·er·a (rĭv'ē-âr'ə). A resort area extending along the Mediterranean coast from La Spezia, Italy, to Hyères, France.

Ri·yadh (rē-yäd'). Also **Ri·ad.** The capital of Saudi Arabia, in the E part of the country. Pop. 666,800.

Ro·a·noke (rō'ə-nōk). A city of SW Virginia. Pop. 99,700.

Roanoke Island. An island off the coast of North Carolina, where Sir Walter Raleigh attempted to found a colony (1585–87).

Roch·es·ter (rŏch'ĕs-tər). **1.** A city of W New York State. Pop. 241,500. **2.** A city of SE Minnesota. Pop. 54,300.

Rock·ford (rŏk'fərd). A city and manufacturing center of N Illinois. Pop. 139,200.

Rock·y Mountain National Park (rŏk'ē). A resort region of Colorado, established in 1915 in the Rocky Mountains, 50 mi (80.4 km) NW of Denver.

Rocky Mountains. The major mountain system of North America, extending c. 3,000 mi (4,800 km) from N Mexico to Alaska, and forming the Continental Divide; highest elevation, Mt. McKinley (20,320 ft/6,197.6 m).

Ro·ma·gna (rō-män'yä). A historical region of N central Italy, now part of Emilia-Romagna.

Ro·ma·ni·a (rō-mā'nē-ə, -mān'yə). See **Rumania.**

Ro·man Empire (rō'mən). The empire of ancient Rome that began in 27 B.C., ended in A.D. 395, and reached from Britain to North Africa to the Persian Gulf.

Rome (rōm). The capital of Italy, on the Tiber in the W central part of the country. It is the site of Vatican City and was formerly the capital of the Roman Republic, the Roman Empire, and the Papal States. Pop. 2,868,200.

Ron·ces·valles (rŏn'sə-välz'). A village in Navarre, N Spain, near the Pass of Roncesvalles through the Pyrenees, which has long served as an invasion and pilgrimage route.

Ro·sa·rio (rō-sä'ryō). A trade center of E central Argentina. Pop. 750,400.

Ross Sea (rôs). A large inlet of the Pacific Ocean in Antarctica.

Ros·tock (rŏs'tŏk). A seaport of N East Germany, on the Baltic. Pop. 210,200.

Ros·tov (rŏs'tŏv). Also **Ros·tov-on-Don** (rŏs'tŏv-ŏn-dŏn'). A river port of the E European U.S.S.R. Pop. 921,000.

Rot·ter·dam (rŏt'ər-dăm). A river port of the SW Netherlands. Pop. 614,800.

Rou·en (rōō-än'). A city of N France; the place where Joan of Arc was executed. Pop. 114,900.

Ru·an·da-U·run·di (rōō-än'də-ōō-rōōn'dē). A former United Nations trust territory of E central Africa, divided in 1962 into the independent countries of Burundi and Rwanda.

Ru·dolf, Lake (rōō'dŏlf). A salt lake of E Africa, in the Great Rift Valley in NW Kenya.

Ruhr (rōōr). **1.** A river of West Germany flowing W for 145 mi (233.3 km) through North Rhine-Westphalia to join the Rhine at Duisburg. **2.** The major coal-mining and industrial region of West Germany, bounded on the S by the Ruhr River.

Ru·ma·ni·a (rōō-mā'nē-ə, -nyə). Also **Ro·ma·ni·a** (rō-). Officially, the Rumanian People's Republic. A country of SE Europe. Pop. 21,855,000. Cap. Bucharest. —**Ru·ma'ni·an,** also **Ro·ma'ni·an** adj. & n.

Ru·me·li·a (rōō-mē'lē-ə). The possessions of the former Ottoman Empire in the Balkan Peninsula, including Macedonia, Albania, and Thrace.

Run·ny·mede (rŭn'ĭ-mēd). A meadow on the Thames, W of London, where King John is thought to have signed the Magna Carta in 1215.

Rush·more, Mount (rŭsh'môr). A mountain in the Black Hills of W South Dakota; site of a national memorial with 60-ft (18.3 m) high carved likenesses of Washington, Jefferson, Lincoln, and Theodore Roosevelt.

Rus·sia (rŭsh'ə). **1.** The name commonly applied to the Union of Soviet Socialist Republics. **2.** The Russian Soviet Federated Socialist Republic. **3.** Historically, the Russian Empire under czarist rule until its termination in 1917 by the Russian Revolution. —**Rus'sian** adj. & n.

Russian Soviet Federated Socialist Republic. The largest constituent republic of the U.S.S.R., in Europe and Asia. Pop. 137,552,000. Cap. Moscow.

Ru·the·ni·a (rōō-thē'nē-ə). A historic region of E Europe, in W Ukraine, S of the Carpathian Mountains.

Rwan·da (rōō-än'də). A republic, independent since 1962, of E central Africa. Pop. 4,819,000. Cap. Kigali.

Rya·zan (rē-ä-zän'). A city of E central European U.S.S.R. Pop. 432,000.

Ry·binsk (rē'byĭnsk). A city of NE European U.S.S.R. Pop. 236,000.

ă pat ā pay â care ä father ĕ pet ē be hw which ĭ pit ī tie î pier ŏ pot ō toe ô paw, for oi noise
ōō took ōō boot ou out th thin th this ŭ cut û urge zh vision ə about, item, edible, gallop, circus

Ryu·kyu Islands (ryōō'kyōō'). An archipelago in the Pacific between Kyushu, Japan, and Taiwan.

S

Saar (sär). A river rising in NE France and flowing c. 150 mi (240 km) N to the Moselle in W West Germany.

Saar·brück·en (sär'brŏŏk'ən). An industrial city on the Saar River in W West Germany. Pop. 206,000.

Saar·land (sär'länd'). A region of Europe between France and Germany.

Sa·ba (sä'bä). An island of the N Netherlands Antilles, between St. Martin and St. Eustatius.

Sac·ra·men·to (săk'rə-mĕn'tō). The capital of California, on the Sacramento River in the N central part of the state. Pop. 274,500.

Sag·i·naw (săg'ə-nô'). A city of S Michigan. Pop. 77,400.

Sag·ue·nay (săg'ə-nā'). A river of S central Quebec, Canada, flowing c. 125 mi (200 km) SE from Lake Saint John to the St. Lawrence.

Sa·har·a (sə-hâr'ə, -hăr'ə). A vast arid area of N Africa, extending from the Atlantic coast to the Nile Valley and from the Atlas Mountains S to the Sudan.

Sa·ha·ran·pur (sə-hä'rən-pōōr'). A city of N central India. Pop. 225,700.

Sai·gon (sī-gŏn'). See **Ho Chi Minh City.**

Saint Au·gus·tine (sānt ô'gə-stēn'). A city of NE Florida. Pop. 11,800.

Saint Ber·nard (săn' bĕr-när'). Two Alpine passes connecting Switzerland and France with Italy: The Great Saint Bernard (alt. 8,110 ft/2,473.6 m); and the Little Saint Bernard (alt. 7,178 ft/2,189.3 m).

Saint Croix (kroi). One of the U.S. Virgin Islands, in the West Indies.

Saint Croix. 1. A river, 75 mi (120.7 km) long, rising in the Chiputneticook Lakes and flowing SE, forming part of the U.S.-Canadian border. **2.** A river, 164 mi (263.9 km) long, rising in NW Wisconsin and flowing S to the Mississippi.

Saint E·li·as Mountains (ĭ-lī'əs). A range in SW Yukon Territory and SE Alaska; highest elevation, Mount Logan (19,850 ft/6,054.3 m).

Saint-É·tienne (săn-tā-tyĕn'). An industrial city in a coal-mining area of SE France. Pop. 220,100.

Saint George's Channel (jôr'jĭz). A strait linking the Atlantic Ocean and the Irish Sea.

Saint Gott·hard (gŏt'ərd). A mountain group of the Lepontine Alps, S central Switzerland.

Saint Hel·ens, Mount (hĕl'ənz). An active volcanic peak, 9,671 ft (2,949.7 m) high, in SW Washington.

Saint John (jŏn'). A port city of New Brunswick, Canada, in the S on the Bay of Fundy. Pop. 113,000.

Saint Johns (jŏnz'). The capital of Antigua, on the N coast of the island. Pop. 25,000.

Saint Joseph (jō'zəf, -səf). A port city of NW Missouri, on the Missouri River. Pop. 76,600.

Saint Kitts (kĭts). An island in the British West Indies.

Saint Kitts-Nevis (kĭts'nē'vĭs, -nĕv'ĭs). A self-governing, British-associated island state in the British West Indies. Pop. 60,000. Cap. Basseterre, on Saint Kitts.

Saint Lawrence (lôr'əns). A river, 744 mi (1.197 km) long, rising in Lake Ontario and flowing NE along the U.S.-Canadian border to the Gulf of St. Lawrence.

Saint Lawrence, Gulf of. An arm of the Atlantic Ocean in SE Canada.

Saint Lawrence Sea·way (sē'wā'). An international waterway, 2,342 mi (3,768.3 km) long, consisting of a system of canals, dams, and locks in the St. Lawrence River and connecting channels between the Great Lakes.

Saint Lou·is (lōō'ĭs, lōō'ē). A city of E Missouri, on the Mississippi River. Pop. 450,800.

Saint Lu·ci·a (lōō'shə, lōō-sē'ə). An independent island nation in the E Caribbean. Pop. 112,000. Cap. Castries.

Saint Mo·ritz (mə-rĭtz'). A town and winter-sports center of SE Switzerland. Pop. 7,400.

Saint Pe·ters·burg (pē'tərz-bûrg'). See **Leningrad.**

Saint Thom·as (tŏm'əs). One of the U.S. Virgin Islands in the West Indies.

Saint-Tro·pez (săN-trô-pā'). A resort town of SE France. Pop. 4,500.

Saint Vin·cent and the Gren·a·dines (vĭn'sənt; grĕn'ə-dēnz', grĕn'ə-dēnz'). An independent island nation in the E Caribbean. Pop. 104,000. Cap. Kingstown.

Sai·pan (sī-pän', -păn', sī'păn). The largest of the Mariana Islands in the W Pacific.

Sa·kai (sä'kī'). A city and seaport of Japan, on S Honshu. Pop. 768,700.

Sa·kha·lin (săk'ə-lēn). An island of the Soviet Union, in the Sea of Okhotsk N of Hokkaido, Japan.

Sal·a·man·ca (săl-lä-mäng'kä). A city of W central Spain. Pop. 131,400.

Sal·a·mis (săl'ə-mĭs). An island of Greece, in the Saronic Gulf E of Athens, off which the Greeks defeated the Persians (480 B.C.).

Sa·lem (sā'ləm). **1.** A seaport of NE Massachusetts; the site in the 17th cent. of witch trials and executions. Pop. 38,300. **2.** The capital of Oregon, in the NW on the Willamette River. Pop. 89,200.

Sa·ler·no (sä-lâr'nō). A seaport of SW Italy. Pop. 161,645.

Sal·ford (sôl'fərd). A city of NW England. Pop. 261,000.

Salis·bur·y (sôlz'bĕr'ē, -brē). The capital of Zimbabwe, in the NE part of the country. Pop. 569,000.

Salis·bur·y Plain (sôlz'bĕr'ē, -brē). A plateau in S Wiltshire, England; site of Stonehenge.

Sa·lon·i·ka (sə-lŏn'ĭ-kə, săl'ə-nē'kə). A seaport of NE Greece. Pop. 345,800.

Sal·ta (säl'tä). A commercial center of NW Argentina. Pop. 176,200.

Salt Lake City (sôlt). The capital of Utah, in the N central part of the state. Pop. 163,000.

Sal·va·dor (săl'və-dôr). A seaport of E Brazil. Pop. 1,237,400.

Sal·ween (săl'wēn'). A river of SE Asia, rising in E Tibet and flowing 1,750 mi (2,815 km) SE to the Gulf of Martaban in Burma.

Salz·burg (sôlz'bûrg'). A resort city in W central Austria. Pop. 139,000.

Sa·mar (sä'mär). An island of the Philippines, in the E Visayan Islands.

Sa·mar·i·a (sə-mâr'ē-ə). **1.** A division of ancient Palestine, now in W Jordan. **2.** The ancient N kingdom of Israel. **3.** The capital of this kingdom in the 9th cent. B.C. **—Sa·mar'i·tan** (sə-mâr'ĭ-tən) adj. & n.

Sam·ar·kand (săm'ər-kănd'). A city of central Asian U.S.S.R. Pop. 267,000.

Sa·mo·a (sə-mō'ə). An island group in the South Pacific Ocean, divided into American Samoa and the independent state of Western Samoa.

Sa·mos (sā'mŏs). An island of Greece, off the W coast of Turkey.

Sam·o·thrace (săm'ō-thrās). An island of Greece, in the NE Aegean.

San·a (sä-nä'). Also **Sa·n'a, Sa·naa.** The capital of Yemen, on a central plateau at an altitude of 7,250 ft (2,210 m). Pop. 134,600.

San An·dre·as Fault (săn ăn-drā'əs). A series of cracks in the earth's crust extending from NW California to the Gulf of California.

San An·ge·lo (săn ăn'jə-lō'). A resort city in W Texas. Pop 73,100.

San An·to·ni·o (ăn-tō'nē-ō'). An industrial and commercial center of S central Texas. Pop. 788,000.

San Ber·nar·di·no (bûr'nər-dē'nō, -nə-dē'nō). A city of SE California. Pop. 116,800.

San Cris·tó·bal (krĭs-tō'bəl). A city of Venezuela in the extreme W. Pop. 151,700.

San Di·e·go (dē-ā'gō). A seaport of S California. Pop. 874,800.

San Fer·nan·do Valley (fər-năn'dō). A fertile valley in SW California.

San Fran·cis·co (frən-sĭs'kō). A seaport of W California, on San Francisco Bay, an inlet of the Pacific. Pop. 674,100. **—San Franciscan.**

San Joa·quin (wô-kēn', wä-kēn'). A river of California, rising in the Sierra Nevada and flowing c. 320 mi (515 km) NW to join the Sacramento.

San Jo·se (hō-zā'). A city of W California. Pop. 628,100.

San Jo·sé (sän' hō-zā'). The capital of Costa Rica, on the central plateau. Pop. 228,300.

San Juan (hwän', wän'). The capital of Puerto Rico, on the N coast. Pop. 452,700.

San Le·an·dro (lē-ăn'drō). A city of W California. Pop. 63,400.

San Lu·is Po·to·sí (sän' lōō-ēs' pō'tō-sē'). A city of N central Mexico. Pop. 271,100.

San Ma·ri·no (mə-rē'nō). **1.** An independent republic in the Apennines near the Adriatic coast of Italy. Pop. 21,000. **2.** The capital of this republic. Pop. 4,600.

San Ma·te·o (mə-tā′ō). A city of W California. Pop. 78,600.

San Sal·va·dor (săl′və-dôr′). The capital of El Salvador, in the center of the country. Pop. 368,000.

San Se·bas·tián (sə-băs′chĭn). A city of N Spain, on the Bay of Biscay. Pop. 166,300.

San·ta An·a (săn′tə ăn′ə). **1.** A city of W El Salvador. Pop. 105,300. **2.** A city of SW California. Pop. 205,700.

Santa Bar·ba·ra (bär′bər-ə, bär′brə). A seaside resort of SW California. Pop. 74,800.

Santa Cla·ra (klăr′ə). A city of W California. Pop. 87,300.

Santa Cruz (krōōz′). A city of Bolivia, E of the Andes in the center of the country. Pop. 149,200.

Santa Cruz de Ten·er·ife (krōōz′ də těn′ə-rīf′). A seaport and resort in the Canary Islands, on the NE coast of Tenerife. Pop. 175,600.

Santa Fe (fā′). The capital of New Mexico, in the N central part of the state. Pop. 49,000.

San·ta Fé (săn′tä fā′). A port in E central Argentina, on the Salado River. Pop. 312,400.

Santa Fe Trail. A 19th cent. wagon and trade route between Independence, Missouri, and Santa Fe, New Mexico.

Santa Mar·ta (mär′tə). A port city of N Colombia. Pop. 128,600.

Santa Mon·i·ca (mŏn′ĭ-kə). A city of S California. Pop. 88,100.

San·tan·der (săn′tän-dĕr′). A seaport of N Spain. Pop. 165,000.

San·ti·a·go (săn′tē-ä′gō). The capital of Chile, at the foot of the Andes in the central part of the country. Pop. 3,361,000.

San·ti·a·go de Cu·ba (săn-tyä′gō dĕ kōō′bä). A city and seaport of SE Cuba. Pop. 322,000.

San·to An·dré (săn′tōō än-drā′). A city of S Brazil. Pop. 418,600.

San·to Do·min·go (săn′tō də-mǐng′gō). The capital of the Dominican Republic, a seaport in the SE. Pop. 802,600.

São Lu·is (soun LŌŌ-ēs′). A seaport of NE Brazil. Pop. 167,500.

Saône (sōn). A river of E central France, rising in the Vosges Mountains and flowing 268 mi (431 km) SW to the Rhône.

São Pau·lo (pou′lōō). A major industrial and commercial center of SE Brazil. Pop. 7,198,600.

São To·mé e Prín·ci·pe (TOO-mě′ ě prĕn′sē-pǐ). An island republic in the Gulf of Guinea W of Gabon. Pop. 83,000. Cap. São Tomé, on São Tome Island.

Sap·po·ro (săp-pō′rō). A city of SW Hokkaido, Japan. Pop. 1,240,600.

Sar·a·gos·sa (săr′ə-gŏs′ə). A city of NE Spain. Pop. 542,300.

Sa·ra·je·vo (sä′rä-yě-vō). A city in central Yugoslavia. Pop. 400,000.

Sa·ra·tov (sŭ-rä′təf). An industrial center of E European U.S.S.R. Pop. 856,000.

Sar·din·i·a (sär-dĭn′ē-ə). An island in the Mediterranean, separated from Italy by the Tyrrhenian Sea. Pop.

1,600,000. Cap. Cagliari. **—Sar·din′i·an** adj. & n.

Sar·dis (sär′dĭs). An ancient city in W Asia Minor, the capital of the Lydian Empire.

Sar·gas·so Sea (sär-găs′ō). A section of the North Atlantic between the West Indies and the Azores.

Sark (särk). A small island in the Channel Islands; a feudal manor governed by the Dame of Sark. Pop. 600.

Sar·ma·ti·a (sär-mā′shē-, -shə). An ancient region in E Europe between the Vistula and the Volga Rivers. **—Sar·ma′tian** adj. & n.

Sa·ron·ic Gulf (sə-rŏn′ĭk). An inlet of the Aegean in Greece, between Attica and the Peloponnesus.

Sa·ros, Gulf of (sä′rŏs). An inlet of the Aegean, extending into Turkey N of the Gallipoli Peninsula.

Sa·se·bo (sä′sě-bō′). A seaport of Japan, on the W coast of Kyushu. Pop. 251,600.

Sas·katch·e·wan (săs-kăch′ə-wän′, -wən). A province of Canada, in the S central part of the country. Pop. 967,400. Cap. Regina.

Sas·ka·toon (săs′kə-tōōn′). A city of S central Saskatchewan, Canada. Pop. 139,200.

Sa·u·di A·ra·bi·a (sä-ōō′dē ə-rā′bē-ə, sou′dē, sô′dē). A kingdom on the Arabian peninsula. Pop. 7,866,000. Cap. Riyadh.

Sault Sainte Ma·rie Canals (sōō′ sănt′ mə-rē′). One Canadian and 2 U.S. canals by-passing the rapids of the St. Marys River and providing ship passage between Lake Huron and Lake Superior.

Sa·van·nah (sə-văn′ə). A seaport of Georgia, at the mouth of the Savannah River. Pop. 138,500.

Sa·voy (sə-voi′). A region of SE France, bordering on Switzerland and Italy; a duchy in the Middle Ages and later part of the Kingdom of Sardinia (1720–1860). **—Sa·voy′ard** (sə-voi′ərd) adj. & n.

Sax·o·ny (săk′sə-nē). **1.** A former region with undefined boundaries in NW Germany. **2.** A former duchy, kingdom, and electorate in central Germany. **—Sax′on** adj. & n.

Sca·fell Pike (skô′fěl′). The highest (3,210 ft/979 m) of the Cumbrian Mountains in NW England.

Scan·di·na·vi·a (skăn′də-nā′vē-ə, -năv′yə). **1.** The NW European countries of Norway, Sweden, and Denmark. **2.** Broadly, Norway, Sweden, Denmark, Iceland, Finland, and the Faeroe Islands. **—Scan′di·na′vi·an** adj. & n.

Sche·nec·ta·dy (skə-něk′tə-dē). A city and industrial center of E New York State. Pop. 67,900.

Schles·wig-Hol·stein (shlěs′wĭg-hōl′stīn). A former region, now a state, of N West Germany.

Scil·ly Islands (sĭl′ē). A group of islets at the entrance to the English Channel off Cornwall.

Scot·land (skŏt′lənd). A constituent country of the United Kingdom of Great Britain and Northern Ireland, in N Great Britain. Pop. 5,195,600. Cap. Edinburgh.

Scran·ton (skrăn′tən). A manufacturing center of NE Pennsylvania. Pop. 87,400.

Scyth·i·a (sĭth′ē-ə). An ancient region of Asia and SE Europe. **—Scyth′i·an** adj. & n.

Sea Islands (sē). A chain of islands in the Atlantic off the coasts of South Carolina, Georgia, and N Florida.

Se·at·tle (sē-ăt′l). A seaport in W central Washington. Pop. 491,900.

Se·go·vi·a (sē-gō′vē-ä). A city of central Spain. Pop. 44,200.

Seine (sěn). A river of N France, rising in the E and flowing 482 mi (770 km) gen. NW to its estuary on the English Channel near Le Havre.

Sek·on·di-Ta·ko·ra·di (sěk′ən-dē-tä-kô-rä′dē). A port city of SW Ghana, on the Gulf of Guinea. Pop. 91,900.

Sel·kirk Mountains (sěl′kûrk). A range of the Rocky Mountains in SE British Columbia, Canada.

Se·ma·rang (sə-mä′räng). A port city of Indonesia, in N Java. Pop. 646,600.

Sem·i·pa·la·tinsk (sěm′ĭ-pə-lä′tĭnsk). A city of Central Asian U.S.S.R. Pop. 259,000.

Sen·dai (sěn′dī′). A city of N Honshu, Japan. Pop. 545,100.

Sen·e·gal, Republic of (sěn′ə-gôl′). A republic of W Africa. Pop. 5,381,000. Cap. Dakar. **—Sen′e·ga·lese′** (-lēz′, -lēs′) adj. & n.

Seoul (sōl). The capital of South Korea, in the NW on the Han River. Pop. 7,500,000.

Se·quoi·a National Park (sĭ-kwoi′ə). An area in the Sierra Nevada of central California, noted for its stands of sequoias and its mountain scenery.

Ser·bi·a (sûr′bē-ə). A constituent republic of Yugoslavia, formerly an independent state, in the E part of the country. **—Ser′bi·an** adj. & n.

Se·vas·to·pol (sə-văs′tə-pōl′). A port city of SE European U.S.S.R. Pop. 252,000.

Sev·ern (sěv′ərn). **1.** A river rising in central Wales and flowing 210 mi (338 km) NE, SE, S, and SW through W England to the Bristol Channel. **2.** A river rising in W Ontario, Canada, and flowing 420 mi (675.7 km) NE to Hudson Bay.

Se·ville (sə-vĭl′). A city and inland port of SW Spain. Pop. 588,800.

Sey·chelles (sā-shěl′, -shělz′). An island republic in the Indian Ocean E of Tanzania. Pop. 63,000. Cap. Victoria on Mahé.

Shang·hai (shăng-hī′). A seaport of E China, on the Yangtze estuary. Pop. 10,000,000.

Shan·non (shăn′ən). A river of the Republic of Ireland, rising in the central part of the country and flowing 220 mi (354 km) SW to the Atlantic.

Shan·tung (shăn′tŭng′). A province of NE China. Pop. 57,000,000. Cap. Tsinan.

Shao·hsing (shou′shǐng′). Also **Shao·hing** (-hǐng′). A city of SE China. Pop. 225,000.

Shas·ta, Mount (shăs′tə). An extinct volcano, 14,162 ft (4,319.4 m) high, in the Cascade Range of N California.

Shatt-al-Ar·ab (shăt′ăl-är′əb). A river

formed by the confluence of the Tigris and the Euphrates in SE Iraq and flowing SE c. 120 mi (193.1 km) to the Persian Gulf.

She·ba (shē'bə). The Biblical name for a region of the Arabian peninsula now occupied by Yemen.

Shef·field (shĕf'ēld). A cutlery-manufacturing center of N England. Pop. 558,000.

Shen·an·do·ah (shĕn'ən-dō'ə). A river flowing 55 mi (88.4 km) NE from N Virginia to the Potomac at Harpers Ferry, West Virginia.

Shen·si (shĕn'sē'). A province of N central China. Pop. 21,000,000. Cap. Sian.

Shen·yang (shŭn'yäng'). The capital of Liaoning, NE China. Pop. 3,750,000.

Sher·wood Forest (shûr'wŏŏd'). Formerly an extensive royal forest in central England, traditionally the retreat of Robin Hood.

Shet·land Islands (shĕt'lənd). A group of islands in the North Atlantic NE of Scotland.

Shih·chia·chuang (shĭr'jē-ä'jwäng'). The capital of Hopeh, E central China. Pop. 1,500,000.

Shi·ko·ku (shĭ-kō'kōō). One of the major islands of Japan, between SW Honshu and E Kyushu.

Shi·mi·zu (shē-mē'zōō). A seaport of S central Honshu, Japan. Pop. 235,000.

Shim·o·no·se·ki (shē-mō'nō-sĕk'ē). A seaport of SW Honshu, Japan. Pop. 258,400.

Shi·raz (shĭ-räz'). A city of SW Iran, famous for carpets. Pop. 380,000.

Shi·zu·o·ka (shē-zōō-ō'kä). An industrial city in central Honshu, Japan. Pop. 416,400.

Sho·la·pur (shō'lə-pŏŏr'). A cotton-milling center of W central India. Pop. 398,400.

Shreve·port (shrĕv'pôrt', -pōrt'). A city of NW Louisiana. Pop. 194,800.

Si·am, Gulf of (sī-ăm'). An arm of the South China Sea between the Malay Peninsula and Indochina.

Si·an (syän, shē'-). See **Hsian.**

Si·be·ri·a (sī-bîr'ē-ə). A region of the Soviet Union in Asia, extending from the Ural Mountains to the Pacific Ocean. —**Si·be'ri·an** adj. & n.

Sic·i·ly (sĭs'ə-lē). An island in the Mediterranean, separated from Italy by the Strait of Messina. —**Si·cil'ian** (sĭ-sĭl'yən) adj. & n.

Si·don (sīd'n). An ancient seaport of Phoenicia, on the Mediterranean.

Si·en·a (sē-ĕn'ə). A city and cultural center of central Italy. Pop. 65,700. —**Si·en·ese'** (sē'ə-nēz', -nēs') adj. & n.

Si·er·ra Le·one (sē-ĕr'ə lē-ōn'). A country of NW Africa. Pop. 3,470,000. Cap. Freetown.

Si·er·ra Ma·dre (sē-ĕr'ə mä'drā). The major mountain system of Mexico, comprising 3 ranges: **1.** The **Sierra Madre del Sur,** in the S along the Pacific to the Isthmus of Tehuantepec. **2.** The **Sierra Madre Oriental,** extending S from the Rio Grande, roughly parallel to the Gulf of Mexico. **3.** The **Sierra Madre Occidental,** extending S

from the U.S. border, paralleling the Pacific coast.

Sierra Ne·vad·a (nə-vä'də, -văd'ə). **1.** A mountain range in E California; highest elevation, Mount Whitney (14,495 ft/4,421 m). **2.** A mountain range in S Spain; highest elevation, Mulhacén (11,424 ft/3,484 m).

Sik·kim (sĭk'ĭm). A kingdom between India and Tibet, China. Pop. 250,000. Cap. Gangtok.

Si·le·sia (sī-lē'zhə, -shə, sī-). A region of central Europe, now chiefly within SW Poland. —**Si·le'sian** adj. & n.

Sim·fe·ro·pol (sĭm'fə-rô'pəl). A city of the SE European U.S.S.R., in the Crimea. Pop. 269,000.

Sim·plon Pass (sĭm'plŏn'). A pass between the Lepontine and Pennine Alps, connecting Switzerland and Italy.

Si·nai (sī'nī'). A peninsula between the Gulf of Suez and the Gulf of Aqaba.

Sin·ga·pore (sĭng'gə-pôr', sĭng'ə-). **1.** A republic comprising the island of Singapore and adjacent islands off the S tip of the Malay Peninsula. Pop. 2,363,000. **2.** The capital of this republic, a seaport on the Strait of Singapore. Pop. 2,308,200.

Sioux City (sōō). A meat-packing center of W Iowa. Pop. 81,800.

Sioux Falls. A city of SE South Dakota. Pop. 81,200.

Sjael·land (shĕl'län). An island of E Denmark, site of Copenhagen.

Skag·er·rak (skăg'ə-răk'). An arm of the North Sea between Norway and Jutland.

Skop·lje (skôp'lyĕ, skōp'-). A city of SE Yugoslavia, the capital of ancient Macedonia. Pop. 440,000.

Skye, Isle of (skī). An island of NW Scotland, one of the Inner Hebrides.

Sla·vo·ni·a (slə-vō'nē-ə). A region of N Yugoslavia, between the Drava and Sava rivers. —**Sla·vo'ni·an** adj. & n.

Slo·vak·i·a (slō-vä'kē-ə). The E region of Czechoslovakia. —**Slo·vak'i·an** adj. & n.

Smo·lensk (smō-lĕnsk'). A city of W central European U.S.S.R. Pop. 234,000.

Smyr·na (smûr'nə). See **Izmir.**

Snake River (snāk). A river of the NW U.S., flowing 1,038 mi (1,670 km) W from NW Wyoming to the Columbia in SE Washington.

Snow·don (snōd'n). A massif in NW Wales, rising to 3,560 ft (1,085.8 m).

So·chi (sō'chē). A health resort of S European U.S.S.R., on the Black Sea. Pop. 241,000.

Society Islands. A group of islands in the South Pacific Ocean, part of French Polynesia. Pop. 105,300. Cap. Papeete on Tahiti.

So·co·tra (sō-kō'trə). An island, part of Southern Yemen, in the Indian Ocean, off the Horn of Africa.

Sod·om (sŏd'əm). A city of ancient Palestine.

So·fi·a (sō'fē-ə, sō-fē'ə). The capital of Bulgaria, in the W. Pop. 965,300.

So·ho (sō'hō, sō-hō'). A district of London, England, noted for its night life and foreign restaurants.

So·ling·en (zō'lĭng-ən). A city of W West Germany. Pop. 176,700.

Sol·o·mon Islands (sŏl'ə-mən). An independent group of volcanic islands in the SW Pacific. Pop. 215,000. Cap. Honiara, on Guadalcanal.

Sol·way Firth (sŏl'wā'). An arm of the Irish Sea between England and Scotland.

So·ma·li·a (sō-mä'lē-ə, -mäl'yə). A republic in E Africa, on the Indian Ocean. Pop. 3,443,000. Cap. Mogadishu. —**So·ma'li·an** adj. & n.

So·ma·li·land (sō-mä'lē-lănd'). A region of E Africa, including Somalia and parts of Ethiopia.

So·mer·ville (sŭm'ər-vĭl'). An industrial city of NE Massachusetts. Pop. 77,400.

Somme (sŏm). A river of N France, in the valley of which were fought major battles in World War I (1916 and 1918) and World War II (1940 and 1944).

Soo·chow (sōō'jō', -chou'). A city of E central China. Pop. 1,300,000.

So·ro·ca·ba (sŏr'ō-cä'bä). A commercial center of S Brazil. Pop. 166,000.

South Af·ri·ca (south ăf'rĭ-kə). A republic in S Africa. Pop. 27,700,000. Cap. Pretoria; seat of legislature, Cape Town. —**South African.**

South A·mer·i·ca (ə-mĕr'ĭ-kə). The S continent of the Western Hemisphere, lying mostly S of the equator. —**South American.**

South·amp·ton (south-hămp'tən, sou-thămp'-). A seaport in S England. Pop. 213,700.

South Bend (bĕnd). An educational and industrial center in N Indiana. Pop. 108,200.

South Car·o·li·na (kăr'ə-lī'nə). A state of the SE United States. Pop. 3,069,800. Cap. Columbia. —**South Car'o·lin'i·an** (-lĭn'ē-ən).

South Chi·na Sea (chī'nə). A section of the Pacific bordered by China, Vietnam, Cambodia, Thailand, Malaysia, Indonesia, and the Philippines.

South Da·ko·ta (də-kō'tə). A Middle Western state of the United States. Pop. 688,200. Cap. Pierre. —**South Dakotan.**

South·east A·sia (south-ēst' ā'zhə, ā'shə). A region gen. considered to include the Philippines, Indochina, Malaysia, Singapore, Indonesia, and Brunei.

South·ern Alps (sŭth'ərn ălps). A mountain range in W central South Island, New Zealand; highest elevation, Mount Cook (12,349 ft/3,766.5 m).

South·field (south'fēld'). A city of SE Michigan. Pop. 75,500.

South Island. The larger of the 2 main islands of New Zealand.

South Seas. 1. All seas S of the equator. **2.** The S Pacific.

South·west Af·ri·ca (south-wĕst' ăf'rĭ-kə). See **Namibia.**

Spain (spān). A country of W Europe on the Iberian Peninsula and including the Balearic and Canary islands. Pop. 36,775,000. Cap. Madrid. —**Span'iard** (spăn'yərd) n. —**Span'ish** (spăn'ĭsh) adj. & n.

Spanish A·mer·i·ca (ə-mĕr′ĭ-kə). The parts of the central and S Western Hemisphere inhabited mostly by Spanish-speaking people. —**Spanish American.**

Spanish Main (mān). **1.** The coast of N South America between Panama and the Orinoco. **2.** Those parts of the Caribbean traversed by Spanish ships in colonial times.

Spanish Sa·ha·ra (sə-hăr′ə). See **Western Sahara.**

Spar·ta (spär′tə). A Dorian city-state of ancient Greece, in the SE Peloponnesus. —**Spar′tan** adj. & n.

Spits·ber·gen (spĭts′bûr′gən). A Norwegian archipelago in the Arctic Ocean, between Greenland and Franz Josef Land.

Split (splĭt). A seaport of W Yugoslavia. Pop. 152,000.

Spo·kane (spō-kăn′). A city of NE Washington. Pop. 171,000.

Spor·a·des (spôr′ə-dēz′). All the Greek islands in the Aegean, except the Cyclades.

Spot·syl·va·ni·a (spŏt′səl-vā′nē-ə). A village in NE Virginia; scene of an indecisive Civil War battle (1864).

Spring·field (sprĭng′fēld). **1.** The capital of Illinois, in the center of the state; the home and burial place of Abraham Lincoln. Pop. 99,100. **2.** A city of SW Massachusetts. Pop. 152,200. **3.** A trade center of SW Missouri. Pop. 133,000. **4.** An industrial city of W central Ohio. Pop. 72,300.

Springs (sprĭngz). A city of South Africa, in a gold-mining region of S Transvaal. Pop. 142,800.

Sri Lan·ka (srē läng′kə). Formerly **Cey·lon** (sĭ-lŏn′). An island republic in the Indian Ocean SE of India. Pop. 14,184,000. Cap. Colombo.

Sri·nag·ar (srē′nŭg′ər). The historic capital of Kashmir, on the Jhelum River. Pop. 403,400.

Stam·ford (stăm′fərd). A city of SW Connecticut. Pop. 101,600.

Stat·en Island (stăt′n). An island in New York Bay, coextensive with the County and New York City Borough of Richmond. Pop. 349,600.

Stock·holm (stŏk′hōlm). The capital of Sweden, in the E on the Baltic Sea. Pop. 699,200.

Stock·ton (stŏk′tən). A commercial center of central California. Pop. 149,600.

Stoke-on-Trent (stōk′ŏn-trĕnt′). A ceramics-manufacturing city of W central England. Pop. 262,100.

Stone·henge (stōn′hĕnj′) A prehistoric ceremonial ruin on the Salisbury Plain in S England.

Stone Mountain (stōn). A mountain, 1,686 ft (514.2 m) high, in NW central Georgia.

Stras·bourg (sträs′bûrg, sträz′-). A city of NE France. Pop. 251,500.

Strat·ford-on-A·von (străt′fərd-ŏn-ā′vŏn, -ā′vən). A town on the Avon in central England; the birthplace and burial site of Shakespeare.

Strom·bo·li (strŏm-bō′lē). **1.** An island of Italy, off the NE coast of Sicily. **2.** An active volcano, 3,038 ft (926.5 m) high, on Stromboli.

Stutt·gart (stŭt′gärt). A city of SW West Germany. Pop. 600,400.

Su·cre (sōō′krā). The constitutional capital of Bolivia, in the S central part of the country. Pop. 106,600.

Su·dan (sōō-dăn′). A region lying across Africa, S of the Sahara and N of the equator. —**Su·da·nese′** (-də-nēz′, -nēs′) adj. & n.

Sudan, Republic of the. A country of NE Africa. Pop. 17,376,000. Cap. Khartoum.

Su·de·ten·land (sōō-dāt′n-lănd′). A border region of Bohemia, Moravia, and Silesia, in Czechoslovakia.

Su·ez (sōō-ĕz′, sōō′ĕz′). A port city of Egypt, at the head of the Gulf of Suez. Pop. 381,000.

Suez, Isthmus of. The strip of land in NE Egypt connecting Asia and Africa and traversed by the Suez Canal, a waterway connecting the Mediterranean and the Gulf of Suez.

Su·lu Archipelago (sōō′lōō). A group of islands in the W Pacific Ocean, belonging to the Philippines.

Sulu Sea. The section of the W Pacific Ocean between the central Philippines and Borneo.

Su·ma·tra (sōō-mä′trə). An island of Indonesia, in the Indian Ocean W of Malaysia and Borneo. —**Su·ma′tran** adj. & n.

Su·mer (sōō′mər). An ancient country of Mesopotamia in a region now part of S Iraq. —**Su·me′ri·an** (-mĕr′ē-ən) adj. & n.

Sun·da Islands (sŭn′də, sōōn′də). The W section of the Malay Archipelago, between the South China Sea and the Indian Ocean.

Sunda Strait. A channel between Sumatra and Java, connecting the Java Sea with the Indian Ocean.

Sun·der·land (sŭn′dər-lənd). A shipbuilding center of NE England. Pop. 215,300.

Su·pe·ri·or, Lake (sə-pîr′ē-ər). One of the Great Lakes between the United States and Canada.

Su·ra·ba·ya (sōōr′ə-bī′ə). A seaport of Indonesia, in NE Java. Pop. 2,000,000.

Su·ra·kar·ta (sōōr′ə-kär′tə). A city of Java, Indonesia, in the S central part of the island. Pop. 368,000.

Su·rat (sōōr′ət, sə-rät′). A seaport of W central India. Pop. 471,600.

Su·ri·nam (sōōr′ə-năm). A republic of N South America. Pop. 374,000. Cap. Paramaribo.

Su·sa (sōō′sə, -zə). A ruined city in SW Iran, the capital of ancient Elam.

Sus·que·han·na (sŭs′kwə-hăn′ə). A river of the NE United States, rising in central New York State and flowing 444 mi (715 km) S to Chesapeake Bay.

Su·va (sōō′vä). The capital of Fiji, a seaport on the SE coast of Viti Levu. Pop. 66,600.

Su·wan·nee (sə-wä′nē). Also **Swa·nee** (swä′nē). A river rising in SE Georgia and meandering 250 mi (402 km) across Florida to the Gulf of Mexico.

Sverd·lovsk (sfĕrd′lôfsk′). A city of E European U.S.S.R.; site of the execution of Nicholas II and his family (1918). Pop. 1,211,000.

Swa·bi·a (swä′bē-ə). **1.** A historic region of SW Germany. **2.** A duchy of S Germany from the 10th to the mid-13th cent. —**Swa′bi·an** adj. & n.

Swa·nee (swä′nē). See **Suwannee.**

Swan·sea (swän′sē). A port of S Wales, on the Bristol Channel. Pop. 171,500.

Swa·zi·land (swä′zĭ-lănd′). A kingdom in SE Africa between South Africa and Mozambique. Pop. 544,000. Cap. Mbabane.

Swe·den (swēd′n). A kingdom on the E part of the Scandinavian Peninsula in N Europe. Pop. 8,294,000. Cap. Stockholm. —**Swe′dish** (swē′dĭsh) adj. & n.

Swit·zer·land (swĭt′sər-lənd). A federal republic of central Europe. Pop. 6,298,000. Cap. Bern. —**Swiss** (swĭs) adj. & n.

Syd·ney (sĭd′nē). A city of SE Australia, on the Tasman Sea. Pop. 3,021,300.

Syr·a·cuse (sîr′ə-kyōōz′, -kyōōs′). **1.** A city of Italy on the SE coast of Sicily; in ancient times the leading Greek city of Sicily. Pop. 111,300. **2.** A city and manufacturing center of central New York State. Pop. 170,300.

Syr·i·a (sîr′ē-ə). **1.** A republic of SW Asia on the E Mediterranean coast. Pop. 8,088,000. Cap. Damascus. **2.** An ancient country of W Asia that included present-day Syria, Lebanon, and the Palestine region. —**Syr′i·an** adj. & n.

Syrian Desert. An arid region in the N Arabian Peninsula, including parts of Syria, Iraq, Saudi Arabia, and Jordan.

Szcze·cin (shchĕ′tsēn). A seaport of NW Poland. Pop. 372,900.

Sze·chwan (sŭ′chwän′). A province of China, in the SW. Pop. 70,000,000. Cap. Chengtu.

T

Ta·ble Bay (tā′bəl). An inlet of the Atlantic in SW South Africa.

Ta·briz (tä-brēz′). A city of NW Iran. Pop. 550,000.

Ta·co·ma (tə-kō′mə). A seaport of W Washington, on Puget Sound. Pop. 158,000.

Tae·gu (tī-gōō′). A commercial city of SE South Korea. Pop. 1,311,100.

Tae·jon (tī-jŏn′). A city of SW South Korea. Pop. 414,600.

Ta·gan·rog (tăg′ən-rŏg′). A port city of S European U.S.S.R. Pop. 268,000.

Ta·gus (tā′gəs). A river rising in E central Spain and flowing 600 mi (965.4 km) NW and then gen. SW to the Atlantic at Lisbon, Portugal.

Ta·hi·ti (tə-hē′tē, tä-). One of the Society Islands in French Polynesia. Pop. 84,500. —**Ta·hi′tian** adj. & n.

Ta·hoe, Lake (tä′hō). A large lake in E California and W Nevada.

Tai·chung (tī′chōōng′). A city of W central Taiwan. Pop. 549,000.

Tai·nan (tī′nän′). A major commercial center of SW Taiwan. Pop. 525,000.

Tai·pei (tī′pā′). The capital of the Republic of China, on Taiwan at the N end of the island. Pop. 2,165,500.

Tai·wan (tī′wän′). Formerly **For·mo·sa** (fôr-mō′sə). An island off the SE coast of China, constituting along with the Pescadores and other smaller islands the Republic of China.

Tai·yü·an (tī′yōō′än′). A city of N China. Pop. 2,725,000.

Ta·ka·mat·su (tä′kä-mät′sōō). A major seaport of NE Shikoku, Japan. Pop. 274,400.

Ta·kla·ma·kan Desert (tä′klə-mə-kän′). A vast arid area in NW China.

Ta·lien (dä′lyĕn′). A city of NE China. Pop. 4,000,000.

Tal·la·has·see (tăl′ə-hăs′ē). The capital of Florida, in the NW part of the state. Pop. 80,800.

Tal·linn (tä′lĭn, tăl′ĭn). The capital of Estonia, a seaport on the Gulf of Finland opposite Helsinki. Pop. 392,000.

Tam·bov (täm-bôf′). A city of S Central European U.S.S.R. Pop. 245,000.

Tam·pa (tăm′pə). A seaport of W central Florida, on Tampa Bay, an inlet of the Gulf of Mexico. Pop. 268,700.

Tam·pe·re (täm′pĕ-rĕ). A city of SW Finland. Pop. 166,200.

Tam·pi·co (tăm-pē′kō). A port city and petroleum-producing center of E central Mexico. Pop. 179,600.

Ta·nan·a·rive (tə-năn′ə-rēv′). The capital of Madagascar, in the E central part of the island. Pop. 400,000.

Tan·gan·yi·ka (tăn′gən-yē′kə, tăng′-). A former nation of E central Africa that joined with Zanzibar in 1964 to form Tanzania.

Tanganyika, Lake. The longest (400 mi/643.6 km) lake in Africa, between Tanzania and the Congo.

Tan·gier (tăn-jîr′). A seaport of N Morocco. Pop. 208,000.

Tang·shan (täng′shän′). A city of NE China. Pop. 1,200,000.

Tan·za·ni·a (tăn′zə-nē′ə, tăn-zā′nē-ə). A republic of E Africa, on the Indian Ocean. Pop. 17,048,000. Cap. Dar es Salaam. —**Tan′za·ni′an** adj. & n.

Ta·ran·to (tä′rän-tō). A seaport of S Italy. Pop. 229,200.

Tar·sus (tär′səs). A seaport of S Turkey. Pop.74,500.

Tar·ta·ry (tär′tə-rē). A historical region comprising the areas of E Europe and Asia overrun by Tatars in the 13th and 14th cent. and extending as far E as the Pacific under Genghis Khan. —**Tar·tar′i·an** adj.

Tash·kent (täsh-kĕnt′). The capital of the Uzbek S.S.R., Central Asian U.S.S.R. Pop. 1,780,000.

Tas·ma·ni·a (tăz-mā′nē-ə). An island off the SE coast of Australia. —**Tas·ma′ni·an** adj. & n.

Tas·man Sea (tăz′mən). The part of the South Pacific between Australia and New Zealand.

Ta·tra Mountains (tä′trä). The highest range of the Carpathians, along the border between Poland and Czechoslovakia; highest elevation, Gerlachova (8,737 ft/2,664.7 m).

Ta·tung (tä′tōōng′). A city of NE China. Pop. 300,000.

Tau·rus Mountains (tôr′əs). The major mountain range of S Turkey, extending parallel to the Mediterranean

coast; highest elevation, Kaldi Dag (12,251 ft/3,736.6 m).

Tbi·li·si (tə-bē-lē′sē). The capital of the Georgian S.S.R., on the Kura River. Pop. 1,066,000.

Te·gu·ci·gal·pa (tā-gōō′sē-gäl′pä). The capital of Honduras, in the S central part of the country. Pop. 316,500.

Te·he·ran (tĕ′ə-răn′, -răn′, tā′-). Also **Te·hran** (tĕ-rän′). The capital of Iran, in the N central part of the country. Pop. 4,400,000.

Tel A·viv (tĕl′ ə-vēv′). A seaport of Israel, on the Mediterranean. Pop. 357,600.

Ten·nes·see (tĕn′ĭ-sē′). A state of the S United States. Pop. 4,545,600. Cap. Nashville. —**Ten′nes·se′an** adj. & n.

Tennessee River. A river of the SE United States, flowing c. 652 mi (1,049 km) from E Tennessee to the Ohio River.

Te·noch·ti·tlán (tā-nŏch′tĕt-län′). The ancient capital of the Aztec empire.

Ter·re Haute (tĕr′ə hōt′, hŭt′, hôt′). A city of W Indiana. Pop. 61,000.

Te·ton Range (tē′tŏn). A range of the Rocky Mountains in SE Idaho and NW Wyoming; highest elevation, Grand Teton (13,766 ft/4,198.7 m).

Te·tuán (tĕ-twän′). A port city of NE Morocco. Pop. 308,700.

Tex·ar·kan·a (tĕk′sär-kăn′ə). A city lying on both sides of the border between NE Texas and SW Arkansas, with 2 municipal governments. Pop. 52,000.

Tex·as (tĕk′səs). A state of the S central United States. Pop. 14,173,900. Cap. Austin. —**Tex′an** adj. & n.

Thai·land (tī′lănd′). Formerly **Si·am** (sī-ăm′). A kingdom of SE Asia, with a coastline on the Gulf of Siam. Pop. 46,142,000. Cap. Bangkok.

Thames (tĕmz). **1.** A river of England, rising in Gloucestershire and flowing 210 mi (337.8 km) E past London to its wide estuary on the North Sea. **2.** A river S Ontario, flowing 160 mi (257.4 km) SE to Lake St. Clair.

Thar Desert (tär). A vast sandy region in NW India and E Pakistan.

Thebes (thēbz). **1.** An ancient religious and political capital of Upper Egypt. **2.** An ancient city of E central Greece. —**The′ban** adj. & n.

Ther·mop·y·lae (thər-mŏp′ə-lē). A locality in E Greece, near Lamia, an invasion route since ancient times.

Thes·sa·ly (thĕs′ə-lē). An ancient region of N central Greece, along the Aegean Sea. —**Thes′sa·li·an** adj. & n.

Thim·phu (thĭm′pōō). Also **Thim·bu** (-bōō). The capital of the Himalayan kingdom of Bhutan. Pop. 50,000.

Thou·sand Islands. A group of over 1,500 islands in the St. Lawrence at the outlet of Lake Ontario.

Thrace (thrās). An ancient country in the SE part of the Balkan Peninsula, comprising modern Bulgaria and parts of Greece and Turkey.

Thun·der Bay (thŭn′dər). A city of SW Ontario, Canada. Pop. 120,700.

Thur·rock (thûr′ək). An urban district of SE England. Pop. 127,100.

Ti·ber (tī′bər). A river of central Italy,

rising in the Apennines and flowing 251 mi (404 km) S past Rome to the Tyrrhenian Sea.

Ti·bes·ti Mas·sif (tĭ-bĕs′tĭ mă-sēf′). A Saharan mountain group in N Chad; highest elevation, Emi Koussi (11,204 ft/3,417.2 m).

Ti·bet (tĭ-bĕt′). A former theocratic state in S Asia, constituting the Tibetan Autonomous Region of S China since 1957. Pop. 1,700,000. Cap. Lhasa. —**Ti·bet′an** adj. & n.

Ti·con·der·o·ga (tī′kŏn-də-rō′gə, tī-kŏn′-). A village in NE New York State; site of Fort Ticonderoga.

Tien Shan (tī-ĕn′ shän′). A major mountain system of central Asia; highest elevation, Pobeda Peak (24,406 ft/7,443.8 m).

Ti·er·ra del Fu·e·go (tĭ-ĕr′ə dĕl fōō-ā′gō, fyōō-). **1.** An archipelago at the extreme S tip of South America. **2.** The main island of this archipelago, divided between Chile and Argentina.

Ti·gris (tī′grĭs). A river of SW Asia, rising in the Taurus Mountains of Turkey and flowing c. 1,150 mi (1,850 km) SE to join the Euphrates in S Iraq and form the Shatt-al-Arab.

Ti·jua·na (tē-wä′nə) A city of NW Mexico. Pop. 386,800.

Tim·buk·tu (tĭm′bŭk-tōō′, tĭm-bŭk′-tōō). A town of central Mali, near the Niger River. Pop. 11,900.

Ti·mor (tē′môr, tē-môr′). An island at the E end of the Indonesian Archipelago.

Ti·ra·na (tĭ-rä′nə). The capital of Albania, in the center of the country. Pop. 170,000.

Ti·ti·ca·ca (tē′tē-kä′kä). A lake of South America in the Andes between Peru and Bolivia, at an altitude of 12,507 ft (3,814.6 m).

To·ba·go (tə-bā′gō). An island in the Atlantic Ocean off Venezuela; part of the independent state of Trinidad and Tobago.

To·go (tō′gō). A republic of W Africa, on the Gulf of Guinea. Pop. 2,472,000. Cap. Lomé.

To·go·land (tō′gō-lănd′). A former German protectorate in W Africa, divided after World War I into what is now Togo and part of Ghana.

To·ky·o (tō′kē-ō′). The capital of Japan, a seaport on Honshu on the NW shore of Tokyo Bay. Pop. 8,739,000.

To·le·do (tə-lē′dō). **1.** A city of central Spain, bordered on 3 sides by the Tagus River. Pop. 46,000. **2.** A port city of NW Ohio, on Lake Erie. Pop. 354,600.

Tomsk (tômsk, tŏmsk). A city of W central Siberian U.S.S.R. Pop. 374,000.

Ton·ga (tŏng′gə). An island kingdom in the South Pacific. Pop. 93,000. Cap. Nukualofa, on Tongatabu Island.

Ton·kin, Gulf of (tŏn′kĭn′, tŏng′kĭn′). An arm of the South China Sea between Vietnam and S China.

To·pe·ka (tə-pē′kə). The capital of Kansas, in the NE on the Kansas River. Pop. 116,000.

To·ron·to (tə-rŏn′tō). The capital of Ontario, Canada, on the N shore of Lake Ontario. Pop. 2,856,500.

ă pat   ā pay   â care   ä father   ĕ pet   ē be   hw which   ĭ pit   ī tie   î pier   ŏ pot   ō toe   ô paw, for   oi noise
ōō took   ōō boot   ou out   th thin   th this   ŭ cut   û urge   zh vision   ə about, item, edible, gallop, circus

Tor·rance (tôr′əns, tŏr′-). A manufacturing city of SW California. Pop. 131,300.

Tor·tu·ga (tôr-tōo′gə). An island of Haiti; a base and stronghold of pirates in the 17th cent.

Tou·lon (tōo-lôn′). A seaport of SE France. Pop. 180,500.

Tou·louse (tōo-lōoz′). A city of SW France. Pop. 371,100.

Tou·raine (tōo-rĕn′). A region and former province of W central France.

Tours (tōor). A city of W central France, on the Loire. Pop. 128,100.

Tra·fal·gar, Cape (trə-făl′gər). A cape on the Atlantic coast of S Spain; site of a naval battle in which Nelson defeated the French and Spanish fleets (1805).

Trans·al·pine Gaul (trăns-ăl′pīn gôl). The section of Gaul that lay NW of the Alps.

Trans·cau·ca·sia (trăns′kô-kā′zhə, -shə, trănz′-). A region of the SE U.S.S.R. between the Caucasus Mountains and the borders of Turkey and Iran.

Trans·kei, The (trăns-kā′, -kī′). A semiautonomous Bantu homeland in E Cape Province, South Africa. Pop. 2,200,000. Cap. Umtata.

Trans·vaal (trăns-väl′, trănz′-). A province of NE South Africa.

Tran·syl·va·ni·a (trăn′sĭl-vā′nē-ə, -vān′yə). A historic region and former province of central Rumania. —**Tran·syl·va′ni·an** adj. & n.

Transylvanian Alps. The S section of the Carpathian Mountains, in central and SW Rumania.

Tren·ton (trĕn′tən). The capital of New Jersey, on the Delaware River in the W. Pop. 90,700.

Tri·este (trē-ĕst′). A seaport of N Italy. Pop. 272,400.

Trin·i·dad (trĭn′ə-dăd′). An island in the Atlantic Ocean off Venezuela. —**Trin′i·dad′i·an** adj. & n.

Trinidad and To·ba·go (tə-bā′gō). A state comprising the islands and former British colonies of Trinidad and Tobago. Pop. 1,133,000. Cap. Port-of-Spain.

Trip·o·li (trĭp′ə-lē). **1.** A seaport of NW Lebanon. Pop. 175,000. **2.** The capital of Libya, a seaport in the NW on the Mediterranean. Pop. 281,500.

Trip·o·li·ta·ni·a (trĭp′ə-lĭ-tă′nē-ə). A region of NW Libya; established as a Phoenician colony in the 7th cent. B.C.

Tri·van·drum (trī-văn′drəm). A city of SW India. Pop. 409,600.

Tro·bri·and Islands (trō′brē-änd′). A group of small islands off E New Guinea in the SW Pacific.

Trond·heim (trŏn′hām′, trŏn′-). A seaport of W Norway. Pop. 133,200.

Troy (troi). An ancient city in Troas, NW Asia Minor, the site of the Trojan War.

Truk (trŭk, trŏok). An island group in the Caroline Islands in the W Pacific; site of a major Japanese naval base in World War II.

Tse·lin·o·grad (tsĕ-lĭn′ə-grăd′). A city of Central Asian U.S.S.R. Pop. 201,000.

Tsi·nan (tsē′năn′). See **Chinan.**

Tsing·tao (chĭng′dou′). A port city of E China. Pop. 1,900,000.

Tsi·tsi·har (chē′chē′här′, tsē′tsē′-). A city of NE China. Pop. 1,500,000.

Tsun·i (dzōo′nē). A city of SW China. Pop. 275,000.

Tu·a·mo·tu Archipelago (tōo′ə-mō′tōo). A group of islands in French Polynesia in the South Pacific.

Tu·bu·ai Islands (tōo′bōo-ī′). An island group of S French Polynesia in the South Pacific.

Tuc·son (tōo′sŏn′). A city of Arizona, a noted winter health resort in the S part of the state. Pop. 331,500.

Tu·cu·mán (tōo′kōo-män′). A city of NW Argentina. Pop. 766,000.

Tu·la (tōo′lə). An industrial city of N central European U.S.S.R. Pop. 486,000.

Tul·sa (tŭl′sə). A city of NE Oklahoma. Pop. 355,800.

Tu·nis (tōo′nĭs, tyōo′-). The capital of Tunisia, a seaport in the N on the Mediterranean. Pop. 873,500.

Tu·ni·sia (tōo-nē′zhə, -shə, -nĭzh′ə, -nĭsh′ə, tyōo-). A republic in N Africa. Pop. 6,367,000. —**Tu·ni′sian** adj. & n.

Tu·rin (tōo′rĭn, tyōo′-). An industrial center of NW Italy. Pop. 1,202,200.

Tur·key (tûr′kē). A republic mainly in Asia Minor and partly in SE Europe. Pop. 44,375,000. Cap. Ankara. —**Turk′ish** adj. & n.

Turk·men Soviet Socialist Republic (tûrk′mĕn′, -mən). Also **Turk·men·i·stan** (tûrk′mĕn-ĭ-stăn′, -stän′). A constituent republic of Central Asian U.S.S.R. Pop. 3,031,000. Cap. Ashkhabad.

Turks and Cai·cos Islands (tûrks; kī′kōs). Two British island groups in the West Indies, SE of the Bahamas.

Tur·ku (tōor′kōo′). A seaport of SW Finland. Pop. 164,500.

Tus·ca·loo·sa (tŭs′kə-lōo′sə). A city in W central Alabama; formerly the state capital (1826–46). Pop. 73,300.

Tus·ca·ny (tŭs′kə-nē). A region of NW Italy.

Tyre (tīr). The capital of ancient Phoenicia, a seaport on the Mediterranean, the site of which is in S Lebanon. —**Tyr′i·an** (tîr′ē-ən) adj. & n.

Ty·rol (tĭ-rōl′, tī′rōl′, tīr′ōl′). A region and former Austrian territory in W Austria and N Italy. —**Ty′ro·lese** (-lēz′, -lēs′) or **Ty·ro′le·an** adj. & n.

Tyr·rhe·ni·an Sea (tĭ-rē′nē-ən). The section of the Mediterranean Sea lying between Italy and the islands of Corsica, Sardinia, and Sicily.

U

U·ban·gi (yōo-băng′gē, ōo-băng′gē). A river of central Africa, formed on the Zaire-Central African Republic border and flowing c. 700 mi (1,125 km) gen. SW to the Congo River.

U·fa (ōo-fä′). A city of E European U.S.S.R., in the Urals. Pop. 871,000.

U·gan·da (yōo-găn′də, ōo-gän′dä). A country in E central Africa. Pop. 13,225,000. Cap. Kampala. —**U·gan′dan** adj. & n.

Uj·jain (ōo′jīn′). A city of central In-

dia; sacred to Hindus. Pop. 203,300.

U·krain·i·an Soviet Socialist Republic (yōo-krā′nē-ən). Also **U·kraine** (yōo-krān′, yōo′krān′). A constituent republic of SW European U.S.S.R. Pop. 49,757,000. Cap. Kiev.

U·lan Ba·tor (ōo′län bä′tôr′). The capital of the Mongolian People's Republic, in the N central part of the country. Pop. 400,000.

U·lan-U·de (ōo′län-ōo′də). A city of SE Siberian U.S.S.R., E of Lake Baikal. Pop. 279,000.

Ul·ster (ŭl′stər). A region of Ireland, of which the N part is now officially Northern Ireland.

Ul·ya·novsk (ōol-yä′nəfsk). A river port of W central European U.S.S.R. Pop. 395,000.

Um·bri·a (ŭm′brē-ə). A region of Italy, in the center of the country. Pop. 780,600. Cap. Perugia.

Un·ga·va Bay (ŭng-gä′və, -gä′və). An inlet of Hudson Strait extending into N Quebec, Canada.

Ungava Peninsula. A peninsula of N Quebec, Canada, extending N between Hudson and Ungava bays.

Un·ion City (yōon′yən). A city of NE New Jersey. Pop. 55,400.

Union of Soviet Socialist Republics. A country in N Eurasia, bordered by the Pacific on the E, the Arctic Ocean on the N, and the Black and Caspian seas in the SW. Also called **Soviet Union, Russia.** Pop. 262,400,000. Cap. Moscow.

U·nit·ed Ar·ab E·mir·ates (yōo-nī′təd ăr′əb ē-mîr′ĭts, -äts′). A nation on the E coast of the Arabian Peninsula. Pop. 862,000. Cap. Abu Dhabi.

United Kingdom. 1. In full, United Kingdom of Great Britain and Northern Ireland. A kingdom of W Europe, consisting of England, Scotland, Wales, and Northern Ireland. Pop. 55,883,100. Cap. London. **2.** In full, United Kingdom of Great Britain and Ireland. A former kingdom comprising England, Scotland, Wales, and all of Ireland.

United States of A·mer·i·ca (ə-mĕr′ə-kə). A federal republic composed of 50 states (48 of them in central North America, Alaska in NW North America, and Hawaii, an archipelago in the Pacific Ocean) and the District of Columbia. Pop. 225,478,700. Cap. Washington, coextensive with the District of Columbia.

Up·per Vol·ta (ŭp′ər vŏl′tə). A landlocked republic of W Africa, S of Mali. Pop. 6,554,000. Cap. Ouagadougou.

Ur (ûr, ōor). An ancient city in Sumer, on a site now in SE Iraq.

U·ral (yōor′əl). A river of the Soviet Union, rising in the Ural Mountains and flowing 1,574 mi (2,532.5 km) W and then S to the Caspian Sea.

Ural Mountains. A mountain system of the Soviet Union, extending 1,300 mi (2,091.7 km) across the Russian S.F.S.R. from the Arctic Ocean to the Kazakh S.S.R. and constituting the traditional boundary between Europe and Asia.

U·ra·wa (ōo-rä′wä). A city of central

ă pat ā pay â care ä father ĕ pet ē be hw which ĭ pit ī tie î pier ŏ pot ō toe ô paw, for oi noise
ōō took ōō boot ou out th thin th this ŭ cut û urge zh vision ə about, item, edible, gallop, circus

Honshu, Japan. Pop. 269,400.

U·ru·guay (yŏŏr′ə-gwī′, -gwä′). A republic of South America, in the SE on the Atlantic. Pop. 2,864,000. Cap. Montevideo. —**U′ru·guay′an** adj. & n.

Uruguay River. A river of SE South America, rising in S Brazil and flowing c. 1,000 mi (1,609 km) gen. S to the Río de la Plata.

U·tah (yŏŏ′tô′, -tä′). A state of the W central United States. Pop. 1,459,010. Cap. Salt Lake City.

U·ti·ca (yŏŏ′tĭ-kə). A city on the Mohawk River in central New York State. Pop. 75,400.

U·trecht (yŏŏ′trĕkt′). A city of central Netherlands; site of the signing of the treaty that ended the War of the Spanish Succession (1713). Pop. 250,900.

U·tsu·no·mi·ya (ŏŏ′tsŏŏ-nŏ′mē-yä). A city of Japan, on central Honshu. Pop. 301,200.

Uz·bek Soviet Socialist Republic (ŏŏz′bĕk′, ŭz′-). Also **Uz·bek·i·stan** (ŏŏz-bĕk′ĭ-stän′, -stän′, ŭz-). A constituent republic of Central Asian U.S.S.R. Pop. 15,391,000. Cap. Tashkent.

V

Va·duz (fä-dŏŏts′). The capital of Liechtenstein, on the upper Rhine. Pop. 7,500.

Va·len·ci·a (və-lĕn′shē-ə, -shə). **1.** A region and former kingdom of E Spain. **2.** A seaport of E Spain, on the Mediterranean. Pop. 713,000. **3.** A city of N Venezuela. Pop. 439,000.

Va·lla·do·lid (vä′lyä-thō-lēth′). A city of N central Spain. Pop. 247,200.

Val·le·jo (və-lā′ō, -lā′hō). A city of W California, NE of San Francisco. Pop. 77,000.

Val·let·ta (və-lĕt′ə). The capital of Malta, on the NE coast. Pop. 15,500.

Val·ley Forge (văl′ē fôrj′). A village in SE Pennsylvania; site of George Washington's winter headquarters (1777–78).

Val·pa·rai·so (văl′pə-rī′zō, -rā′zō). A seaport of W central Chile. Pop. 248,400.

Van·cou·ver (văn-kŏŏ′vər). A port city of British Columbia, Canada. Pop. 1,173,300.

Vancouver Island. An island of British Columbia, Canada, off the SW coast of the province.

Var·na (vär′nə). A city of E Bulgaria, on the Black Sea. Pop. 235,200.

Vat·i·can City (văt′ĭ-kən). A sovereign papal state, established in 1929, in an enclave of c. 108 acres (43 hectares) in the city of Rome, Italy. Pop. 700.

Ven·e·zue·la (vĕn′ə-zwā′lə, -zwē′lə). A republic in N South America. Pop. 13,515,000. Cap. Caracas. —**Ven′e·zue′lan** adj. & n.

Ven·ice (vĕn′ĭs). A port city of NE Italy, located on 118 islands in the Lagoon of Venice. Pop. 362,500. —**Ve·ne′tian** (və-nē′shən) adj. & n.

Ve·ra·cruz (vĕr′ə-krŏŏz′). A port city in E central Mexico, on the Gulf

Coast. Pop. 214,100.

Verde, Cape (vûrd). The westernmost point of the African continent, a peninsula on the coast of Senegal.

Ver·dun (vər-dŭn′). A city in NE France; site of a prolonged World War I battle (1916). Pop. 22,000.

Ve·ree·ni·ging (fə-rē′nə-кнĭng). A city of NE South Africa. Pop. 172,500.

Ver·mont (vər-mŏnt′). A state of the NE United States. Pop. 511,300. Cap. Montpelier. —**Ver·mont′er** n.

Ve·ro·na (və-rō′nə). A city of NE Italy. Pop. 271,400.

Ver·sailles (vər-sī′, vĕr-). A city of N central France; site of the palace of Louis XIV and of the signing of the treaty between the Allies and Germany after World War I (1919). Pop. 95,000.

Ve·su·vi·us (və-sŏŏ′vē-əs). An active volcano, 3,891 ft (1,186.7 m) high, in W Italy near Naples.

Vi·cen·za (vē-chĕn′tsä). A city of NE Italy. Pop. 118,000.

Vi·chy (vĭsh′ē, vē-shē′). A city of central France, a health resort since Roman times; seat of the French government during World War II (1940–44). Pop. 33,500.

Vicks·burg (vĭks′bûrg′). A city of W Mississippi, on the bluffs above the Mississippi; captured by Union forces in the Civil War (1863). Pop. 25,600.

Vic·to·ri·a (vĭk-tôr′ē-ə, -tôr′ē-ə). **1.** The capital of British Columbia, a seaport on the S tip of Vancouver Island. Pop. 222,500. **2.** The capital of the British Crown Colony of Hong Kong, a port and commercial center on the island of Hong Kong. Pop. 658,000.

Victoria, Lake. The largest lake in Africa, in the E central part of the continent.

Victoria Falls. A waterfall, c. 1 mi (1.6 km) wide, with a maximum drop of 420 ft (128 m), in the Zambezi River, S central Africa.

Victoria Island. An island in the Northwest Territories, Canada.

Vi·en·na (vē-ĕn′ə). The capital of Austria, in the NE on the Danube. Pop. 1,592,800. —**Vi′en·nese′** (-nēz′, -nēs′) adj. & n.

Vien·tiane (vyĕn-tyän′). The capital of Laos, in the NW on the Mekong River. Pop. 150,000.

Vi·et·nam (vē-ĕt′näm′, -năm′, vyĕt′-). A country on the E coast of the Southeast Asia peninsula. Formerly 2 separate nations (North Vietnam and South Vietnam), the countries were united in 1976. Pop. 47,870,000. Cap. Hanoi. —**Vi·et′na·mese′** (-mēz′, -mēs′) adj. & n.

Vi·ja·ya·va·da (vĭj′ə-yə-wä′də, -vä′də). A city of SE India. Pop. 317,300.

Vil·ni·us (vĭl′nē-əs, vēl′-). Also **Vil·na** (vĭl′nə, vēl′-). The capital of Lithuania, in the SE. Pop. 420,000.

Vi·ña del Mar (vē′nyä thĕl mär′). A seaside resort in W central Chile. Pop. 153,100.

Vin·land (vĭn′lənd). Also **Vine·land** (vīn′lənd). The name given to the area of NE North America, possibly Nova Scotia, visited by early Norse voyagers.

Vin·son Mas·sif (vĭn′sən mə-sēf′). The highest peak (16,860 ft/5,142.3 m) of Antarctica.

Vir·gin·ia (vər-jĭn′yə). A state of the E United States. Pop. 5,323,400. Cap. Richmond. —**Vir·gin′ian** adj. & n.

Virgin Islands (vûr′jĭn). A group of about 100 islands, E of Puerto Rico in the West Indies and divided into the British Virgin Islands; and the Virgin Islands of the United States, including the islands of St. Thomas, St. John, and St. Croix and several islets (pop. 110,000, cap. Charlotte Amalie on St. Thomas).

Vi·sa·yan Islands (vē-sä′yən). An island group of the Philippines, between Luzon and Mindanao.

Vis·tu·la (vĭs′chŏŏ-lə). A river of Poland, rising in the Carpathians in the S and flowing 678 mi (1,091 km) NE, NW, and then N to the Gulf of Danzig.

Vi·ti Le·vu (vē′tē lā′vŏŏ). The principal island of the Fiji Islands; site of Suva, the capital of the colony.

Vi·to·ri·a (vĭ-tôr′ē-ə, -tôr′ē-ə). A city of N central Spain; site of a battle (1813) in which Wellington defeated the French. Pop. 144,000.

Vi·tó·ria (vĭ-tôr′ē-ə, -tôr′ē-ə). A city of E Brazil, a seaport on the Atlantic Coast. Pop. 122,000.

Vlad·i·vos·tok (vlăd′ə-vŏs-tŏk′, -vŏs′-tŏk′). A city of Far Eastern U.S.S.R., on the Sea of Japan. Pop. 481,000.

Vol·ca·no Islands (vŏl-kā′nō). Three small islands in the W Pacific, administered by the United States from 1945 to 1968, when they were restored to Japan.

Vol·ga (vŏl′gə). The longest river of Europe, rising in the Valdai Hills of the NW Russian S.F.S.R. and flowing 2,290 mi (3,684.6 km) in a winding course to the Caspian Sea in the S.

Vol·go·grad (vŏl′gə-grăd′). Formerly **Sta·lin·grad** (stä′lĭn-grăd′, stăl′ĭn-). A city of SE European U.S.S.R. Pop. 885,000.

Vol·ta (vŏl′tə). A river of W Africa, flowing c. 290 mi (465 km) gen. S through Ghana to the Gulf of Guinea.

Vo·ro·nezh (vŏ-rō′nĭsh). An industrial city of E central European U.S.S.R. Pop. 729,000.

Vosges Mountains (vōzh). A range of mountains in E France, along the Rhine opposite the Black Forest of West Germany; highest elevation, Grand Ballon (4,672 ft/1,425 m).

W

Wa·co (wā′kō). A city of central Texas. Pop. 101,300.

Wai·ki·ki (wī′kē-kē′, wĭ′kē-kē′). A resort area of Honolulu, Hawaii, on the S shore of Oahu.

Wa·ka·ya·ma (wä′kä-yä′mä). A seaport of S Honshu, Japan. Pop. 365,300.

Wake Island (wāk). An atoll in the Pacific, between Hawaii and the Marianas; administered by the United States.

Wa·la·chia (wŏ-lā′kē-ə). Also **Wal·la·**

ă pat   ā pay   â care   ä father   ĕ pet   ē be   hw which   ĭ pit   ī tie   î pier   ŏ pot   ō toe   ô paw, for   oi noise
ŏŏ took   ŏŏ boot   ou out   th thin   th this   ŭ cut   û urge   zh vision   ə about, item, edible, gallop, circus

chi·a. A region and former principality of SE Rumania.

Wales (wālz). A principality comprising part of the United Kingdom of Great Britain and Northern Ireland in Great Britain W of England. Pop. 2,723,600. —**Welsh** (wĕlsh) *adj. & n.*

Wal·lis and Fu·tu·na Islands (wŏl'ĭs; fōō-tōō'nä). Two island groups in the SW Pacific, administered by France.

Wal·sall (wŏl'sôl', -səl). An industrial center of W central England. Pop. 183,800.

Wa·ran·gal (wûr'əng-gəl). A city of SE India. Pop. 297,500.

War·ren (wôr'ən, wŏr'-). A city of SE Michigan. Pop. 161,200.

War·saw (wôr'sô). The capital of Poland, a city on the Vistula in the central part of the country. Pop. 1,448,900.

War·wick (wôr'wĭk, wŏr'-). A textile manufacturing city in E central Rhode Island. Pop. 87,100.

Wa·satch Range (wŏ'săch). A range of the Rocky Mountains, extending from SE Idaho into N Utah; highest elevation, Mount Timpanogos (12,008 ft/3,662.4 m).

Wash·ing·ton (wŏsh'ĭng-tən, wôsh'-). A state of the NW United States. Pop. 4,114,700. Cap. Olympia. —**Wash'ing·to'ni·an** (-tō'nē-ən) *adj. & n.*

Washington, Mount. The highest (6,288 ft/1,917.8 m) of the White Mountains in New Hampshire.

Wa·ter·bur·y (wô'tər-bĕr'ē, -bə-rē, wŏt'ər-). A city of W Connecticut. Pop. 102,200.

Wa·ter·loo (wô'tər-lōō'). A town in central Belgium, near the site of a decisive defeat of Napoleon by Wellington and Blücher (1815). Pop. 18,500.

Wau·ke·gan (wô-kē'gən). A resort city of NE Illinois. Pop. 67,100.

Wau·wa·to·sa (wô'wə-tō'sə). A city of SE Wisconsin. Pop. 51,300.

Wed·dell Sea (wĕd'l). An inlet of the South Atlantic in Antarctica.

Wei·mar (vī'mär', wī'-). A city and cultural center of SW East Germany. Pop. 63,300.

Wel·land Ship Canal (wĕl'ənd). A waterway of Canada, connecting Lakes Ontario and Erie in S Ontario.

Wel·ling·ton (wĕl'ĭng-tən). The capital of New Zealand, a port on S North Island. Pop. 327,400.

Wen·chow (wŭn'jō'). A port city of SE China. Pop. 250,000.

We·ser (vā'zər). A river of West Germany, flowing c. 300 mi (480 km) NW to the North Sea.

Wes·sex (wĕs'ĭks). An Anglo-Saxon kingdom established in the 5th cent. in S England.

West Al·lis (wĕst ăl'ĭs). A city of SE Wisconsin. Pop. 63,900.

West Ber·lin (bûr-lĭn'). See **Berlin.**

West Brom·wich (brŭm'ĭj, -ĭch, brŏm'wĭch). A borough of W central England. Pop. 165,400.

West·ern Sa·ha·ra (wĕs'tərn sə-hăr'ə). Formerly **Span·ish Sahara** (spăn'ĭsh). A region of NW Africa; annexed in 1976 by neighboring Morocco and Mauritania.

Western Sa·mo·a (sə-mō'ə). The W

section of the Samoa island group in the Pacific, a state independent since 1962. Pop. 154,000. Cap. Apia.

West Ger·ma·ny (jûr'mə-nē). The unofficial name for the German Federal Republic. See **Germany.**

West In·dies (ĭn'dēz). An island chain extending in an E arc between the SE United States and the N shore of South America, separating the Caribbean Sea from the Atlantic Ocean. —**West Indian.**

West·min·ster (wĕst'mĭn'stər). A borough of Greater London, SE England. Pop. 225,600.

West·pha·lia (wĕst-fāl'yə, -fā'lē-ə). A former Prussian province, incorporated into West Germany in 1945.

West Vir·gin·ia (vûr-jĭn'yə). A state of the E central United States. Pop. 1,930,400. Cap. Charleston. —**West Virginian.**

Wheel·ing (hwē'lĭng). A river port of N West Virginia. Pop. 43,100.

Whid·by Island (hwĭd'bē). An island in Puget Sound, NW Washington.

White·horse (hwīt'hôrs'). The capital of the Yukon Territory, Canada, on the Yukon River. Pop. 11,200.

White Mountains (hwīt, wīt). A range of the Appalachians in N New Hampshire; highest elevation, Mount Washington (6,288 ft/1,917.8 m).

White Nile (nīl). The section of the Nile that flows N from Lake No, in Sudan, to the Blue Nile at Khartoum.

White Sea. An inlet of the Barents Sea in the extreme NW U.S.S.R.

Whit·ney, Mount (hwĭt'nē). The highest elevation (14,495 ft/4,421 m) in the United States, excluding Alaska, in the Sierra Nevada of E California.

Wich·i·ta (wĭch'ə-tô'). A city of S Kansas. Pop. 279,400.

Wichita Falls. A city of N central Texas. Pop. 93,500.

Wies·ba·den (vēs'bäd'n). A city of central West Germany, on the Rhine. Pop. 252,200.

Wight, Isle of (wīt). An island in the English Channel off S central England.

Wilkes-Bar·re (wĭlks'băr'ē, -băr'ə). A city and industrial center of N central Pennsylvania. Pop. 57,100.

Wil·lem·stad (vĭl'əm-stät). The capital of the Netherlands Antilles, on the S coast of Curaçao. Pop. 95,000.

Wil·liams·burg (wĭl'yəmz-bûrg). A town in E central Virginia; the capital of colonial Virginia (1699–1779). Pop. 9,900.

Wil·ming·ton (wĭl'mĭng-tən). A port city of N Delaware. Pop. 72,400.

Wil·son, Mount (wĭl'sən). A mountain, 5,710 ft (1,741.6 km) high, in the San Gabriel Mountains of S California; the site of Mount Wilson Observatory.

Win·ches·ter (wĭn'chĕs'tər, -chə-stər). A city of S central England. Pop. 31,600.

Win·der·mere, Lake (wĭn'dər-mîr). A lake of NW England, in the Lake District.

Wind·hoek (vĭnt'hōōk). The capital of Namibia, located in the center of the territory. Pop. 61,400.

Wind·sor (wĭn'zər). A city of Ontario, Canada, across the Detroit River from Detroit, Michigan. Pop. 203,300.

Wind·ward Islands (wĭnd'wərd). A group of islands in the E Caribbean, comprising the S Lesser Antilles.

Win·ni·peg (wĭn'ə-pĕg). The capital of Manitoba, Canada, in the S. Pop. 578,200.

Winnipeg, Lake. A lake of Canada in S central Manitoba.

Win·ston-Sa·lem (wĭn'stən-sā'ləm). A city of North Carolina, in the N central part of the state. Pop. 132,400.

Wis·con·sin (wĭs-kŏn'sən). A state of the N United States. Pop. 4,693,900. Cap. Madison.

Wit·wa·ters·rand (wĭt-wô'tərz-rănd, wĭt-wŏt'ərz-). A region of South Africa, in S Transvaal, noted for its rich deposits of gold and other minerals.

Wol·lon·gong (wōōl'ən-gäng, -gŏng). A city of SE Australia, on the Tasman Sea. Pop. 205,800.

Wol·ver·hamp·ton (wōōl'vər-hămp'tən). A city of central England. Pop. 269,500.

Won·san (wœn'sän'). A city of SE North Korea. Pop. 215,000.

Worces·ter (wōōs'tər). A city of central Massachusetts. Pop. 161,400.

Worms (wûrmz). A city of S central West Germany, on the Rhine; site of the Diet of Worms (1521), at which Luther was declared to be a heretic. Pop. 76,700.

Wran·gel Island (răng'gəl). An island off the NE coast of Siberia.

Wran·gell Mountains (răng'gəl). A range in SE Alaska, near the Canadian border; highest elevation, Mount Blackmore (16,523 ft/5,039.5 m).

Wro·claw (vrô'tswäf). A city of SW Poland, on the Oder. Pop. 579,600.

Wu·han (wōō'hän'). A city of central China, on the Yangtze. Pop 2,560,000.

Wu·hu (wōō'hōō'). A port city of China, on the Yangtze. Pop. 300,000.

Wup·per·tal (vōōp'ər-täl). A city of W West Germany. Pop. 413,200.

Würz·burg (wûrts'bûrg). A city of S central West Germany. Pop. 114,200.

Wy·o·ming (wī-ō'mĭng). A state of the W central United States. Pop. 468,900. Cap. Cheyenne.

Y

Yal·ta (yäl'tə, yôl'tə). A city of the SW European U.S.S.R.; site of a conference attended by Roosevelt, Stalin, and Churchill (1945). Pop. 66,000.

Ya·lu (yä'lōō). A river rising in N Korea and flowing c. 500 mi (805 km) to the Yellow Sea.

Yang·tze (yăng'tsē'). A river of China, the longest (3,430 mi/5,518.8 km) in Asia, rising in the highlands of Tibet and flowing SE and then NE to the East China Sea.

Ya·oun·dé (yä-ōōn-dā'). The capital of Cameroun, central Africa. Pop. 274,000.

Yap (yäp, yăp). An island group in the Caroline Islands of the W Pacific.

ă pat   ā pay   â care   ä father   ĕ pet   ē be   hw which   ĭ pit   ī tie   î pier   ŏ pot   ō toe   ô paw, for   oi noise
ōō took   ōō boot   ou out   th thin   th this   ŭ cut   û urge   zh vision   ə about, item, edible, gallop, circus

Ya·ro·slavl (yə-rŏ-släv′ly′). A city of E European U.S.S.R. Pop. 558,000.

Yel·low·knife (yĕl′ō-nīf′). The capital since 1967 of the Northwest Territories, Canada, on the N shore of Great Slave Lake. Pop. 6,100.

Yel·low River (yĕl′ō). Also **Huang Ho** (hwäng′ hō′). A river of China, rising in the highlands of Tibet and flowing 2,900 mi (4,666 km) N and NE to the Gulf of Po Hai.

Yellow Sea. An arm of the Pacific between China and Korea.

Yel·low·stone National Park (yĕl′ō-stōn′). A U.S. national park, located mostly in NW Wyoming, noted for its wildlife and geysers.

Yellowstone River. A river rising in NW Wyoming and flowing 671 mi (1,079.6 km) N into Montana and then NE to the Missouri.

Yem·en (yĕm′ən, yä′mən). **1.** Officially, Yemen Arab Republic. Known as North Yemen. A country on the S Arabian Peninsula. Pop. 7,080,000. Cap. Sana. **2.** Officially, People's Democratic Republic of Yemen. Known as Southern Yemen. A country on the S Arabian Peninsula, located on the Gulf of Aqaba. Pop. 1,853,000. Cap. Aden.

Yen·i·sei (yĭ-nyĭ-syā′). A river rising in the highlands of N Mongolia and flowing 2,364 mi (3,803 km) N to the Kara Sea.

Ye·re·van (yĕ-rĕ-vän′). The capital of the Armenian S.S.R., SE European U.S.S.R. Pop. 879,000.

Yo·ko·ha·ma (yō′kə-hä′mə). A city of Japan, a seaport on Tokyo Bay in central Honshu. Pop. 2,621,000.

Yo·ko·su·ka (yō′kə-sōō′kə). A seaport of Japan, in central Honshu on the W shore of Tokyo Bay. Pop. 347,600.

Yon·kers (yŏng′kərz). A city of New York State, on the Hudson just N of New York City. Pop. 194,600.

York (yôrk). **1.** A city of NE England. Pop. 104,800. **2.** A city and industrial center of S Pennsylvania. Pop. 44,500.

York, Cape. The northernmost point of Australia, on Torres Strait at the tip of Cape York Peninsula.

York·town (yôrk′toun). A village in SE Virginia; site of the surrender of Cornwallis in the Revolutionary War (1781).

Yo·sem·i·te National Park (yō-sĕm′ə-tē). An area of E central California, the site of Yosemite Valley, a gorge extending for 7 mi (11.2 km) and containing Yosemite Falls.

Youngs·town (yŭngz′toun′). A steel-producing center of NE Ohio. Pop. 115,400.

Yu·ca·tán Channel (yōō′kə-tän′). The channel between S Mexico and W Cuba, connecting the Gulf of Mexico with the Caribbean Sea.

Yucatán Peninsula. A peninsula mostly in SE Mexico, separating the Caribbean Sea from the Gulf of Mexico.

Yu·go·sla·vi·a (yōō′gō-slä′vē-ə). A republic of SE Europe, with a long shoreline on the Adriatic. Pop. 22,107,000. Cap. Belgrade. —**Yu′go·slav′** or **Yu′go·sla′vi·an** adj. & n.

Yu·kon (yōō′kŏn′). A territory of Canada, in the NW between Alaska and the Northwest Territories. Pop. 21,800. Cap. Whitehorse.

Yukon River. A river flowing 1,979 mi (3,184.2 km) gen. NW from S Yukon Territory, Canada, through Alaska to the Bering Sea.

Yü·men (yōō′mŭn′). A city and petroleum center of N central China. Pop. 325,000.

Z

Zab·rze (zäb′zhĕ). An industrial center of SW Poland. Pop. 201,200.

Za·ca·te·cas (sä′kä-tā′käs). A silver-mining center of N central Mexico. Pop. 50,200.

Za·greb (zä′grĕb′). A city of NW Yugoslavia. Pop. 700,000.

Zaire (zär). A republic in W central Africa. Pop. 27,936,000. Cap. Kinshasa.

Zam·be·zi (zăm-bē′zē). A river of S Africa, rising in E Angola and flowing 1,600 mi (2,574.4 km) S and then gen. E to the Mozambique Channel.

Zam·bi·a (zăm′bē-ə, zäm′-). A republic of S central Africa. Pop. 5,649,000. Cap. Lusaka. —**Zam′bi·an** adj. & n.

Zam·bo·an·ga (säm′bō-äng′gä). A seaport of the Philippines, on SW Mindanao. Pop. 41,700.

Zan·zi·bar (zăn′zə-bär′). A region of Tanzania, consisting of the islands of Zanzibar and Pemba in the Indian Ocean off E central Africa.

Za·po·ro·zhe (zə-pə-rô′zhyĕ). A city of S European U.S.S.R. Pop. 729,000.

Zhda·nov (zhdä′nôf′). A port city of S European U.S.S.R. Pop. 442,000.

Zim·ba·bwe (zĭm-bä′bwä). Formerly **Rho·de·sia** (rō-dē′zhə). A republic of S central Africa. Pop. 7,140,000. Cap. Salisbury. —**Zim·ba′bwe·an** or **Zim·ba′bwan** adj. & n.

Zi·on, Mount (zī′ən). The hill in Jerusalem on which Solomon's temple was built.

Zu·lu·land (zōō′lōō-lănd′). A former kingdom in S Africa, now a district of Natal, South Africa.

Zu·rich (zōōr′ĭk). A city of NE Switzerland. Pop. 401,600.

Zuy·der Zee (zī′dər zä′, zē′, zoi′dər). Also **Zui·der Zee.** A former marshy inlet of the North Sea in the N coast of the Netherlands, now divided by a dike into the Ijsselmeer and the Waddenzee.

Zwick·au (tsvĭk′ou′). A city of S central East Germany. Pop. 123,800.

ABBREVIATIONS

A 1. ammeter. **2.** Also **a, A.** acre.
3. ampere. **4.** area.
a. 1. acceleration. **2.** adjective.
3. answer. **4.** Also **A.** are
(measurement).
A. 1. alto. **2.** America; American.
A.A. Associate in Arts.
A.B. Bachelor of Arts.
abbr., abbrev. abbreviation.
abr. 1. abridge. **2.** abridgment.
acad. 1. academic. **2.** academy.
acct. account.
ack. 1. acknowledge.
2. acknowledgement.
A.D. anno Domini (usually small
capitals A.D.).
add. 1. addition. **2.** additional.
3. address.
adj. 1. adjacent. **2.** adjective.
3. adjourned. **4.** adjunct.
ad loc. to (or at) the place (Latin *ad
locum*).
admin. administration.
adv. 1. adverb. **2.** adverbial.
adv., advt. advertisement.
A.F., AF 1. air force. **2.** Anglo-
French. **3.** audio frequency.
AFL-CIO, A.F.L.-C.I.O. American
Federation of Labor and Congress of
Industrial Organizations.
agr. 1. agriculture. **2.** agricultural.
agt. 1. agent. **2.** agreement.
AK Alaska (with Zip Code).
AL Alabama (with Zip Code).
Alta. Alberta.
a.m. Also **A.M.** ante meridiem
(usually small capitals A.M.).
Am., Amer. 1. America.
2. American.
amt. amount.
anal. 1. analogy. **2.** analysis.
3. analytic.
ans. answer.
appt. 1. appoint. **2.** appointed.
approx. 1. approximate.
2. approximately.
Apr. April.
AR 1. account receivable.
2. Arkansas (with Zip Code).
assoc. 1. associate. **2.** Also **assn.**
association.
asst. assistant.
attn. attention.
atty., at., att. attorney.
Aug. August.
av., ave., avenue.
avg., av. average.
AZ Arizona (with Zip Code).

b., B. 1. base. **2.** bay. **3.** book.
B. 1. bachelor. **2.** Baume scale.
3. British. **4.** Bible.

B.A. Bachelor of Arts.
bal. balance.
bar. 1. barometer. **2.** barometric.
3. barrel.
B.B.A. Bachelor of Business
Administration.
B.C. 1. before Christ (usually small
capitals B.C.) **2.** British Columbia.
bd. 1. board. **2.** bond.
3. bookbinding. **4.** bound.
B.D. 1. bank draft. **2.** bills
discounted.
bdl. bundle.
B/E 1. bill of entry. **2.** bill of
exchange.
bet. between.
bf, bf., b.f. boldface.
B/F *Accounting.* brought forward.
bg. bag.
Bib. 1. Bible. **2.** Biblical.
bibliog. 1. bibliographer.
2. bibliography.
biog. 1. biographer. **2.** biographical.
3. biography.
biol. 1. biological. **2.** biologist.
3. biology.
bk. 1. bank. **2.** book.
bkg. banking.
bkpg. bookkeeping.
bkpt. bankrupt.
bl. 1. barrel. **2.** black. **3.** blue.
B/L bill of lading.
bldg. building.
blk. 1. black. **2.** block. **3.** bulk.
blvd. boulevard.
b.o. 1. box office. **2.** branch office.
3. buyer's option.
B/P bills payable.
br. 1. branch. **2.** brief. **3.** bronze.
4. brother. **5.** brown.
B.S. 1. Bachelor of Science.
2. balance sheet. **3.** bill of sale.
bu. 1. Also **Bur.** bureau. **2.** bushel.
bull. bulletin.
bus. business.
bx. box.

c 1. carat. **2.** centi-. **3.** cubic.
C 1. Celsius. **2.** centigrade.
c., C. 1. cape. **2.** cent. **3.** century.
4. Also **chap.** chapter. **5.** Also **ca**
circa. **6.** copy. **7.** copyright.
CA California (with Zip Code).
cal. 1. calendar. **2.** caliber.
canc. cancel.
C.B.D. cash before delivery.
cc cubic centimeter.
cc. chapters.
c.c., C.C. carbon copy.
c.d. cash discount.
C.D. civil defense.
Cdr., Cmdr., Comdr. commander.

cert. 1. certificate. **2.** certification.
3. certified.
cf., cp. compare.
c.f.i., C.F.I. cost, freight, and
insurance.
char. charter.
chg. charge.
cit. 1. citation. **2.** cited. **3.** citizen.
C.J. 1. chief justice. **2.** corpus juris.
ck. check.
cl. 1. class. **2.** classification.
3. clause. **4.** clearance. **5.** Also **clk.**
clerk.
cm. centimeter.
cml. commercial.
C/N credit note.
CO Colorado (with Zip Code).
co. 1. Also **Co.** company. **2.** county.
c.o. 1. Also **c/o** care of.
2. *Accounting.* carried over. **3.** cash
order.
COD, C.O.D. 1. cash on delivery.
2. collect on delivery.
col. 1. collect. **2.** collected.
3. collector. **4.** college. **5.** collegiate.
6. column.
Com. 1. commission.
2. commissioner.
comm. 1. commission.
2. commissioner. **3.** commerce.
4. communication.
con. 1. *Law.* conclusion.
2. consolidate. **3.** consolidated.
cons. 1. consignment.
2. construction. **3.** constitution.
Const. 1. constable. **2.** constitution.
cont. 1. contents. **2.** continue.
3. continued. **4.** control.
contr. contract.
coop. cooperative.
corp. corporation.
cos, c.o.s. cash on shipment.
C.P.A. certified public accountant.
cpd. compound.
cr. credit.
CST, C.S.T. Central Standard Time.
CT Connecticut (with Zip Code).
C.T. Central Time.
ct. 1. Also **c., C.,** cent. **2.** court.
ctn. carton.
ctr. center.
cu. Also **c** cubic.
cur. currency.
c.w.o. 1. cash with order. **2.** chief
warrant officer.
cwt. hundredweight.
CZ Canal Zone (with Zip Code).

d 1. day. **2.** deci-.
d. 1. date. **2.** daughter. **3.** died.
4. Also **D.** dose.
D. 1. December. **2.** Also **D.** democrat;

democratic. **3.** doctor (in academic degrees).
D.A. district attorney.
dB decibel.
D.B. daybook.
d.b.a doing business as.
dbl. double.
DC District of Columbia (with Zip Code).
D.D.S. Doctor of Dental Science.
DE Delaware (with Zip Code).
deb. debenture.
dec. 1. deceased. **2.** decrease.
Dec. December.
def. 1. definite. **2.** definition.
deg, deg. degree (thermometric).
del. 1. delegate. **2.** delegation. **3.** delete.
Dem. Democrat.
dep. 1. depart. **2.** departure. **3.** deposit. **4.** deputy.
dept. department.
dia. diameter.
dim. dimension.
dir. director.
disc. discount.
div. 1. divided. **2.** division. **3.** dividend.
dlvy. delivery.
do. ditto.
dol. dollar.
doz. dozen.
dr. 1. debit. **2.** debtor.
DST, D.S.T. daylight-saving time.
dup. duplicate.

e 1. electron. **2.** Also **E, e., E.,** east; eastern.
E Earth.
E. 1. Also **e.,** engineer; engineering. **2.** Also **E** English.
ea. each.
econ. 1. economics. **2.** economist. **3.** economy.
ed. 1. edition. **2.** editor.
E.D.T. Eastern Daylight Time.
educ. 1. education. **2.** educational.
e.g. for example (Latin *exempli gratia*).
elec. 1. electric. **2.** electrical. **3.** electricity.
enc., encl. 1. enclosed. **2.** enclosure.
eng., engr. Also **e., E.,** engineer.
esp. especially.
Esq. Esquire (title).
est. 1. established. **2.** *Law.* estate. **3.** estimate.
EST, E.S.T. Eastern Standard Time.
E.T. Eastern Time.
et al. and others (Latin *et alii*).
etc. and so forth (Latin *et cetera*).
Eur. 1. Europe. **2.** European.
ex. 1. example. **2.** Also **exch.** exchange. **3.** Also **exam.** examination.
exec. 1. executive. **2.** executor.
exp. 1. expenses. **2.** export. **3.** express.

f.1. Also, **f, F., F** female. **2.** Also **F.** folio.
F Fahrenheit.
F.B. freight bill.
FBI, F.B.I. Federal Bureau of Investigation.
Feb. February.
fed. 1. federal. **2.** federated. **3.** federation.

FL Florida (with Zip Code).
fl oz fluid ounce.
fm frequency modulation.
F.O.B., f.o.b. free on board.
fol. 1. folio. **2.** following.
fpm, f.p.m. feet per minute.
fr. 1. franc. **2.** from. **3.** Also **freq.** frequently.
Fri. Friday.
frt. freight.
ft foot.
fut. future.
fwd. forward.

g 1. gravity. **2.** gram.
GA Georgia (with Zip Code).
gal. gallon.
GAW guaranteed annual wage.
gds. goods.
gen., genl. general.
geog. 1. geographer. **2.** geographic. **3.** geography.
geol. 1. geologic. **2.** geologist. **3.** geology.
geom. 1. geometric. **2.** geometry.
gm gram.
GNP gross national product.
gov., Gov. governor.
govt. government.
G.P. general practitioner.
gr. 1. grade. **2.** gross. **3.** group.
grad. 1. graduate. **2.** graduated.
GU Guam (with Zip Code).
guar., gtd. guaranteed.

h hour.
h. Also **H.,** height.
ha hectare.
hdqrs. headquarters.
hf high frequency.
HI Hawaii (with Zip Code).
ho. house.
Hon. 1. Honorable (title). **2.** Also **hon.** honorary.
hor. horizontal.
hosp. hospital.
hp horsepower.
hr hour.
h.s., H.S. high school
ht height.
hyp., hypoth. hypothesis.

i., I., 1. island. **2.** isle.
Is., is. island.
IA Iowa (with Zip Code).
ib., ibid. in the same place (Latin *ibidem*).
ID Idaho (with Zip Code).
I.D. 1. identification. **2.** intelligence department.
i.e. that is (Latin *id est*).
IF, i.f. intermediate frequency.
IL Illinois (with Zip Code).
IN Indiana (with Zip Code).
in. inch.
inc. 1. income. **2.** Also **Inc.** incorporated. **3.** increase.
ins. inspector.
inst. 1. instant. **2.** institute. **3.** institution. **4.** instrument.
int. 1. interest. **2.** interior. **3.** interval. **4.** international.
intr. *Grammar.* intransitive.
inv. 1. invention. **2.** invoice.
IQ, I.Q. intelligence quotient.

IRS Internal Revenue Service.
ital. italic.

J joule.
J. 1. journal. **2.** judge. **3.** justice.
J.A. 1. joint account. **2.** judge advocate.
Jan. January.
jct., junc. junction.
J.D. Doctor of Laws.
jour. 1. journal. **2.** journalist. **3.** journeyman.
J.P. justice of the peace.
jr., Jr. junior.

k 1. karat. **2.** kilo.
K 1. kelvin (temperature unit). **2.** Kelvin (temperature scale).
kc kilocycle.
kg kilogram.
km kilometer.
KS Kansas (with Zip Code).
kW kilowatt.
KY Kentucky (with Zip Code).

l liter.
l. 1. Also **L.** lake. **2.** left. **3.** length. **4.** line.
LA Louisiana (with Zip Code).
lab. laboratory.
lat. latitude.
Lat. Also **L.** Latin.
lb pound.
l.c. lower-case.
L/C letter of credit
l.c.d. lowest common denominator.
leg., legis. 1. legislation. **2.** legislative. **3.** legislature.
lf 1. *Printing.* lightface. **2.** low frequency.
lg., lge. large.
lib. 1. liberal. **2.** librarian. **3.** library.
lit. 1. literary. **2.** literature.
LL.B. Bachelor of Laws.
LL.D. Doctor of Laws.
loc. cit. in the place cited (Latin *loco citato*).
log logarithm.
long. longitude.
ltd., Ltd. limited.

m 1. Also **M, m., M.** male; medium. **2.** meter.
m. mile.
MA Massachusetts (with Zip Code).
M.A. Master of Arts.
Man. Manitoba.
Mar. March.
masc. masculine.
math. 1. mathematical. **2.** mathematician. **3.** mathematics.
max. maximum.
M.B.A. Master of Business Administration.
Mc megacycle.
m.c. master of ceremonies.
MD Maryland (with Zip Code).
M.D. Doctor of Medicine.
mdse. merchandise.
ME Maine (with Zip Code).
M.E. 1. mechanical engineer. **2.** mechanical engineering. **3.** Middle English.
meas. 1. measurable. **2.** measure.

mech. 1. mechanical. 2. mechanics. 3. mechanism.
med. 1. medical. 2. medieval. 3. medium.
M. Ed. Master of Education.
mem. 1. member. 2. memoir. 3. memorandum. 4. memorial.
Messrs. 1. Messieurs. 2. Plural of Mr.
mfg. 1. manufacture. 2. manufactured. 3. manufacturing.
mfr. 1. manufacture. 2. manufacturer.
MI Michigan (with Zip Code).
mi. 1. mile. 2. mill (monetary unit).
min minute (unit of time).
min. minimum.
misc. miscellaneous.
mkt. market.
ml milliliter.
mm millimeter.
MN Minnesota (with Zip Code).
MO Missouri (with Zip Code).
mo. month.
m.o., M.O. 1. mail order. 2. medical officer. 3. money order.
mol. 1. molecular. 2. molecule.
mon. monetary.
Mon. Monday.
mpg, m.p.g. miles per gallon.
mph, m.p.h. miles per hour.
Mr. Mister.
Mrs. mistress.
ms 1. manuscript. 2. millisecond.
MS 1. manuscript. 2. Mississippi (with Zip Code). 3. multiple sclerosis.
Ms., Ms Title of courtesy for a woman.
msg. message.
MST, M.S.T. Mountain Standard Time.
MT Montana (with Zip Code).
mt., Mt. 1. mount. 2. mountain.
m.t., M.T. 1. metric ton. 2. Mountain Time.
mtg. 1. meeting. 2. Also **mtge.** mortgage.
mtn. mountain.
mun. 1. municipal. 2. municipality.
mus. 1. museum. 2. music. 3. musical. 4. musician.

N Also **n, n., n.** north; northern.
n. 1. net. 2. noun. 3. number.
N. 1. Norse. 2. November.
N.A. North America.
nat. 1. Also **natl.** national. 2. native. 3. natural.
nav. 1. naval. 2. navigation.
NB Nebraska (with Zip Code).
n.b. note carefully (Latin *nota bene*).
N.B. New Brunswick.
NC North Carolina (with Zip Code).
ND North Dakota (with Zip Code).
NE northeast.
N.E. New England.
neg. negative.
Nfld. Newfoundland.
NH New Hampshire (with Zip Code).
NJ New Jersey (with Zip Code).
NM New Mexico (with Zip Code).
no., No. 1. north. 2. northern. 3. number.
nos., Nos. numbers.
Nov. November.
N.P. notary public.

N.S. Nova Scotia.
NV Nevada (with Zip Code).
NW northwest.
N.W.T. Northwest Territories.
NY New York (with Zip Code).

O 1. Also **O.** ocean. 2. Also **O.** order.
obj. 1. *Grammar.* object; objective. 2. objection.
obs. 1. obscure. 2. observation. 3. Also **Obs.** observatory. 4. obsolete.
Oct. October.
O.D. 1. Doctor of Optometry. 2. overdraft. 3. overdrawn.
OH Ohio (with Zip Code).
OK Oklahoma (with Zip Code).
Ont. Ontario.
OR Oregon (with Zip Code).
org. 1. organic. 2. organization. 3. organized.
o.s., o/s out of stock.
oz ounce.

p. 1. page. 2. participle. 3. per. 4. pint. 5. population. 6. Also **P.** president.
PA 1. Pennsylvania (with Zip Code). 2. public-address system.
P.A. 1. Also **P/A** power of attorney. 2. press agent. 3. prosecuting attorney.
Pac. Pacific.
par. 1. paragraph. 2. parallel. 3. parenthesis. 4. parish.
pat. patent.
P.A.Y.E. 1. pay as you earn. 2. pay as you enter.
payt., p.t. payment.
P.B. 1. passbook. 2. prayer book.
p.c. Also **pct.** per cent.
p/c, P/C. 1. Also **p.c.** petty cash. 2. prices current.
pd. paid.
P.E.I. Prince Edward Island.
pf. preferred.
Pfc, Pfc. private first class.
phar., Phar., pharm., Pharm., 1. pharmaceutical. 2. pharmacist. 3. pharmacy.
phi., philos. 1. philosopher. 2. philosophical. 3. philosophy.
phr. phrase.
pk. 1. pack. 2. park. 3. peak. 4. Also **pk** peck.
pkg., pkge. package.
pl. 1. platform. 2. platoon.
plf. plaintiff.
pm., prem. premium.
p.m. 1. post mortem. 2. Also **P.M.** postmortem examination. 3. Also **P.M.** post meridiem (usually small capitals P.M.).
P.M. 1. past master. 2. Also **PM** postmaster. 3. prime minister. 4. provost marshal.
P.M.G. postmaster general.
p.n., P/N promissory note.
P.O. 1. Personnel Officer. 2. Also **p.o.** petty officer; post office. 3. postal order.
P.O.E. port of entry.
poet. 1. poetic. 2. poetical. 3. poetry.
pol. 1. Also **polit.** political. 2. politician. 3. Also **polit.** politics.
pos. 1. position. 2. positive.
poss. 1. possession. 2. possessive.

3. possible. 4. possibly.
pot. potential.
POW, P.O.W. prisoner of war.
pp. 1. pages. 2. past participle.
p.p., P.P. 1. parcel post. 2. parish priest. 3. past participle. 4. postpaid.
ppd. 1. postpaid. 2. prepaid.
pr. 1. pair. 2. present. 3. price. 4. printing. 5. pronoun.
PR 1. Also **P.R.** public relations. 2. Puerto Rico (with Zip Code).
Pr. 1. priest. 2. prince.
pref. 1. preface. 2. prefatory. 3. preference. 4. preferred. 5. prefix.
prep. 1. preparation. 2. preparatory. 3. prepare. 4. preposition.
pres. 1. present (time). 2. Also **Pres.** president.
prim. 1. primary. 2. primitive.
prin. 1. principal. 2. principle.
prob. 1. probable. 2. probably. 3. problem.
prof., Prof. professor.
pron. 1. pronominal. 2. pronoun. 3. pronounced. 4. pronunciation.
prop. 1. proper. 2. properly. 3. property. 4. proposition. 5. proprietary. 6. proprietor.
pro tem., p.t. for the time being; temporarily (Latin *pro tempore*).
P.S. 1. Police Sergeant. 2. postscript. 3. public school.
PST, P.S.T. Pacific Standard Time.
pt. 1. part. 2. pint. 3. point. 4. port.
P.T. 1. Pacific Time. 2. physical therapy.
PTA, P.T.A. Parent-Teachers Association.
ptg. printing.
pub. 1. public. 2. publication. 3. published. 4. publisher.
pvt. Also **Pvt.** private.

q. 1. Also **qt** quart. 2. Also **qu., ques.** question.
quad. 1. quadrangle. 2. quadrant. 3. quadrilateral.
Que. Quebec.
quot. quotation.
qr. 1. quarter. 2. quarterly.
qt. 1. quantity. 2. Also **qt.** quart.

r 1. Also **R** radius. 2. *Electricity.* Also **R** resistance.
r. 1. Also **R.** railroad; railway. 2. range. 3. rare. 4. retired. 5. Also **R.** right. 6. Also **R.** river. 7. Also **R.** road. 8. rod (unit of length). 9. Also **R.** rouble.
R. 1. rabbi. 2. rector. 3. Republican (party). 4. royal.
rd. 1. road. 2. round.
R.D. rural delivery.
R.E. real estate.
re concerning; in reference to; in the case of.
rec. 1. receipt. 2. recipe. 3. record. 4. recording. 5. recreation.
recd. received.
ref. 1. reference. 2. referred. 3. refining. 4. reformation. 5. reformed. 6. refunding.
reg. 1. Also **Regt.** regent. 2. regiment. 3. region. 4. Also **regd.** register; registered. 5. registrar. 6. registry. 7. regular. 8. regularly. 9. regulation. 10. regulator.
rep. 1. repair. 2. Also **rpt.** report.

3. reporter. **4.** Also **Rep.**
representative. **5.** reprint. **6.** Also
Rep. republic.
Rep. Republican (party).
req. 1. require. **2.** required.
3. requisition.
rev. 1. revenue. **2.** reverse.
3. reversed. **4.** review. **5.** reviewed.
6. revise. **7.** revision. **8.** revolution.
9. revolving.
RF radio frequency.
RFD, R.F.D. rural free delivery.
RI Rhode Island (with Zip Code).
rm. 1. ream. **2.** room.
r.p.m. revolutions per minute.
R.R. 1. Also **RR** railroad. **2.** Also **Rt.**
Rev. Right Reverend (title). **3.** rural
route.
r.s.v.p., R.S.V.P. please reply.

s 1. second. **2.** Also **S, s.,** **S.** south;
southern. **3.** stere.
s 1. son. **2.** substantive. **3.** shilling.
S. 1. Saturday. **2.** school. **3.** sea.
4. September. **5.** Sunday.
S.A. 1. South Africa. **2.** South
America.
S.B. Bachelor of Science.
Sask. Saskatchewan.
Sat. Saturday.
SC 1. Security Council (United
Nations). **2.** South Carolina (with
Zip Code).
sc. 1. scene. **2.** scruple (weight).
3. scilicet.
s.c. *Printing.* small capitals.
S.C. Supreme Court.
sch. school.
sci. 1. science. **2.** scientific.
SD South Dakota (with Zip Code).
S.D. special delivery.
SE 1. southeast. **2.** southeastern.
sec. 1. Also **secy.** secretary.
2. sector. **3.** second.
sen., Sen. 1. senate. **2.** senator.
3. Also **sr.** senior.
Sept. September.
seq. 1. sequel. **2.** the following (Latin
sequens).
ser. 1. serial. **2.** series. **3.** sermon.
serv. service.
sgd. signed.
sgt. sergeant.
sh. 1. Also **shr.** share (capital stock).
2. sheet. **3.** shilling.
shpt. shipment.
shtg. shortage.
ic thus; so.
ig. 1. signal. **2.** signature.
g. singular.
small.
1. socialist. **2.** society.
south. 2. southern.
seller's option. 2. strikeout.
olution.
andard operating procedure.
ophomore.

SOS 1. international distress signal.
2. Any call or signal for help.
sp. 1. special. **2.** species. **3.** spelling.
Sr. 1. senior (after surname). **2.** sister
(religious).
S.R.O. standing room only.
st. 1. stanza. **2.** state. **3.** Also **St.**
statute. **4.** stet. **5.** stitch. **6.** stone.
7. Also **St.** street **8.** strophe.
St. 1. saint. **2.** strait.
sta. 1. station. **2.** stationary.
std. standard.
stk. stock.
sub. 1. Also **subs.** subscription.
2. Also **subst.** substitute. **3.** suburb.
4. suburban.
subj. 1. subject. **2.** subjective.
3. subjunctive.
suff. 1. sufficient. **2.** Also **suf.** suffix.
Sun. Sunday.
sup. 1. above (Latin *supra*). **2.** Also
super. superior. **3.** *Grammar.* Also
superl. superlative. **4.** supplement.
5. supply.
supt., Supt. Also **super.**
superintendent.
surg. 1. surgeon. **2.** surgery.
3. surgical.
SW southwest.
sym. 1. symbol. **2.** symphony.
syn. 1. synonymous. **2.** synonym.
3. synonymy.

t 1. ton. **2.** troy.
T temperature.
t. 1. teaspoon. **2.** *Grammar.* tense.
3. Also **T.** time. **4.** *Grammar.*
transitive.
T. 1. tablespoon. **2.** territory.
3. Testament. **4.** transit.
t.b. trial balance.
tbs., tbsp. tablespoon.
tech. technical.
technol. 1. technological.
2. technology.
tel. 1. telegram. **2.** telegraph.
3. telephone.
temp. 1. in the time of (Latin
tempore). **2.** temperature.
3. temporary.
Thurs. Thursday.
tkt. ticket.
TN Tennessee (with Zip Code).
tn. 1. town. **2.** train.
tnpk. turnpike.
t.o. turnover.
trans. 1. transaction. **2.** *Grammar.*
transitive. **3.** translated.
4. translation. **5.** translator. **6.** Also
transp. transportation.
treas. 1. treasurer. **2.** treasury.
Tues. Tuesday.
TV television.
TX Texas (with Zip Code).

U. 1. university. **2.** upper.

uhf ultra high frequency.
UN United Nations.
univ. 1. universal. **2.** Also **Univ.**
university.
USA, U.S.A. 1. United States Army.
2. United States of America.
UT Utah (with Zip Code).

V 1. *Physics.* velocity. **2.** *Electricity.*
volt. **3.** volume.
v. 1. verb. **2.** verse. **3.** version.
4. Also **vs.** versus. **5.** vide. **6.** voice.
7. volume (book). **8.** vowel.
V. 1. Also **v.** vice (in titles). **2.** village.
VA 1. Also **V.A.** Veterans'
Administration. **2.** Virginia (with Zip
Code).
var. 1. variable. **2.** variant.
3. variation. **4.** variety. **5.** various.
vhf, VHF very high frequency.
VI Virgin Islands (with Zip Code).
VIP *Informal.* very important person.
vol. 1. volume. **2.** volunteer.
V.P. Vice President.
VT Vermont (with Zip Code).
v.v. vice versa.

w 1. width. **2.** Also **W, w., W.** west;
western.
W 1. *Electricity.* **watt. 2.** *Physics.*
Also **w** work.
w. 1. week. **2.** width. **3.** wife. **4.** with.
W. Wednesday.
WA Washington (with Zip Code).
Wed. Wednesday.
whse., whs. warehouse.
whsle. wholesale.
WI Wisconsin (with Zip Code).
w.i. when issued (financial stock).
wk. 1. weak. **2.** week. **3.** work.
wkly. weekly.
w.o.c. without compensation.
wt. weight.
WV West Virginia (with Zip Code).
WY Wyoming (with Zip Code).

x symbol for an unknown or
unnamed factor, thing, or person.
XL extra large.

y ordinate.
y. year.
YMCA Young Men's Christian
Association.
yr. 1. year. **2.** younger. **3.** your.
Y.T. Yukon Territory.
YWCA Young Women's Christian
Association.

Z 1. atomic number. **2.** *Electricity.*
impedance.
z. 1. zero. **2.** zone.
zool. 1. zoological. **2.** zoology.

ANSWERS

Quarters of the alphabet

president 3d; advent 1st; intense 2d; unusual 4th.

Guide words

1. legal age / lemon
2. legal age — lemon

Alphabetical entry order

1. high; highball; highborn; highboy; highbred; highbrow; High-Church; high-class; higher-up; highfalutin.
2. strontium
3. id; I'd; -id; -ide; idea; ideal.

Centered dots: *syllable division*

sa·bra; space·craft; la·bor; jus·ti·fy; que·bra·cho; jus·ti·fi·ca·tion.

Superscript numerals: *homographs*

1. Because they are spelled alike but have different origins. 2. Four (4). 3. Four (4). 4. Four (4). Because they have different origins.

Pronunciation

Stress — be·*gin*; *coun*·ter·feit.

Syllabication — 1; 2; 3; 1; 4; 2.

The Schwa — motivate; pa*r*ent; *a*nemia; para*keet*; fount*ain*; inaugurate; vin*y*l.

The Macron — 1. pane; fade; they; feign; rain; rein; weight; straight; suede; reign; pay. 2. beet; beat; seize; people; aegis; aerial; conceit; key; peace; piece. 3. pie; pine; my; aisle; height; sight; buy; sky. 4. show; foam; sew; shoulder; broach; beau; though; toe; oh. 5. boot; new; soup; do; shoe; fruit; sleuth; blue.

The Breve — a. hăt; b. kŭp; c. bŏŏk; d. hĕd; e. pŏŏl; f. mĭt; g. pŏt.

The Circumflex — â pair; pear; pare. î pier; peer. ô pore; pour. û purr; per; pearl.

The Dieresis — ärk, fär, pärk, sarcastic.

Other Vowel Sounds — 1. loud; now; spout; brown. 2. point; Freudian; joy; loin.

Consonants — 1. s, k, g, j, k, m, f, n, l, g. 2. f, m, m, m, z, f, n, a, l. 3·1. 1, 2, 2, 1, 1, 1, 2, 1, 2. 4. hw, w; h; hw, w; w; w; hw, w; hw, w; w; h; hw, w; hw, w; hw, w. 5. treasure; measure; division; decision.

Part-of-speech labels

1. Because it is an open compound. 2. well[1], two—n. and intr.v.; well[2], three—adv., adj., interj. 3. Verb. 4. Adv. & adj. Because sometimes it is possible to define multiple parts of speech by means of a single sense.

Capitalization of entries

1. Easter—proper; fiddler crab—common; gascon—common; gasconade—common.

2.
Word	Sense Number(s)
galaxy	1.b.
cabala	1.
grace	5., 10.
black	2., 3.
dame	1., 2.

3.
Word	Sense Number(s)
Babel	2.
Bolshevik	2.
Deity	1., 2.
Puritan	n. 1., adj. 2.

Variant spellings of main entries

1.
Entry	Variant Spelling(s)	Type of Variant
hijack	highjack	secondary
cabala	cabbala & kabala	secondary
endoblast	entoblast	secondary
dz	adze	primary
vespertine	vespertinal	secondary

2. highjack, cabbala & kabala, and entoblast are entered at their own alphabetical places because their spellings place them at a distance from their head words. adze and vespertinal have no separate entries because there are no intervening words.

Inflected forms

1. did or archaic didst, done, doing, does. Present tense, first person, do; second person, do or archaic doest, dost; third person singular, does or archaic doeth, doth, third person plural, do. wagged, wagging. dreamed or dreamt, dreaming. proved, proved or proven, proving. rode, ridden, riding. lent, lending. woke or waked, waked or woken, waking. shone or shined, shining. wrung, wringing. got or archaic gat, got or gotten, getting. led, leading. tore, torn, tearing.

2. a. The past tense and an alternate past participle of bite. b. Past tense of take. c. Past tense and past participle of catch. d. Past tense of eat. e. Past tense and past participle of lay (to put). f. 1. A past tense and past participle of light (to illuminate). 2. A past tense and past participle of light (to descend). g. Past participle and archaic past tense of swim. h. Past participle of lie (to rest). i. Past tense and past participle of dig. j. The alternate past participle of bite.

3. teeth; sheep; geese; fathers-in-law; antennae for sense 1, antennas for sense 2; cacti or cactuses; curricula or curriculums; indexes or indices; banjos or banjoes; ferries; syllabuses or syllabi; vertebrae or vertebras; diagnoses; sergeants at arms.

4. good, better, best; hot, hotter, hottest; littler or less, littlest or least; many, more, most.

Labels — Latin; None; Informal; Archaic; Slang; Law; Slang; Slang; Mus.

Phrasal verbs

1. 20—come about, come across, come again, come around (or round), come back, come by, come down, come down on (or upon), come down with, come in for, come into, come off, come out, come out with, come over, come through, come to, come up, come up to, come up with.

2. push; make; face; buy.

Idioms — arm; ease; face; good.

Modifiers — Answers will vary.

Etymologies

1. Middle English *bagge*, from Old Norse *baggio*.
2. French. 3. Russian. 4. Michel Bégon. 5. A compound word formed from *sky* and *hijack*. 6. Origin unknown.

Undefined run-on entries

1. fabulously, fabulousness; oafish, oafishly, oafishnes habitability or habitableness, habitably; kaleidosc or kaleidoscopical, kaleidoscopically.

2. a. RO; b. RO; c. RO; d. ME; e. RO; f. ME.

Synonyms

1. help; awkward; false.
2. a. bulk, mass. b. cheerful, happy. c. complex, la rinthine. d. forbid, proscribe. e. judge, decree. toil. g. name, moniker. h. primary, premier.

Biography

1. the Great; 1729-1796. 2. English; Arctic wat
3. Prime minister of Canada, 1867-73 and 187
4. Arthur Wellesley. 5. American anthropolo
6. The Nobel Prize in 1980.

Geography

1. 12,000; pîr. 2. An ancient empire in the tes Valley, SW Asia. 3. Rhodesia. 4. Defeat by a Norman army led by William the Conc 5. 2,952,500. 6. Toronto. 7. Viennese.